GW00643143

Associated Raceform products

The Form Book, is updated weekly. Subscribers receive a binder, together with all the early racing. Weekly sections and a new index are threaded into the binder to keep it up to date.

The data contained in The Form Book Flat Annual for 2013 is available in paper form or on computer disk. The disk service, Raceform Interactive, contains the same data as Raceform, The Form Book, and operates on any PC within a 'Windows' environment. The database is designed to allow access to the information in a number of different ways, and is extremely quick and easy to use.

Published in 2013 by Raceform Ltd
Compton, Newbury, Berkshire, RG20 6NL

A catalogue record for this book is available from the British Library,

ISBN 978-1-906216-80-9

Printed in the UK by CPI William Clowes Beccles NR34 7TL

Full details of all Raceform services and publications are available from:

Raceform Ltd, Compton, Newbury, Berkshire RG20 6NL
Tel: 01933 304858 • Fax: 01933 270300
Email: rfsubscription@racingpost.co.uk
www.racingpost.com

Cover photo: Frankel and Tom Queally receive applause from the crowd at Ascot after winning the Qipco Champion Stakes to complete an unbeaten 14-race career.
© Edward Whitaker/Racing Post

The Form Book ®

FLAT ANNUAL FOR 2013

THE OFFICIAL FORM BOOK

ALL THE 2012 RETURNS

Complete record of Flat Racing
from 1 January to 31 December 2012

CONTENTS

Weight for Age scale ... iv
Introduction ... v
Abbreviations and their meanings ... vii
Racing Post Ratings ... ix
Course descriptions ... x
Key to Racereaders' initials ... xii
2012 Turf and All-Weather racing ... 1
Index to Horses ... 1531
Index to Meetings ... 1642
Statistics (jockeys/trainers/owners) ... 1643
Racing Post Top Rated ... 1646
Median Times ... 1647
Record Times ... 1649
Speed Figures ... 1653

Editor: Graham Dench

Head of Analysis Team: Ashley Rumney

Race Analysts & Notebook Writers:
Gavin Beech, Dave Bellingham, Matt Boyle, Mark Brown, Marcus Buckland, Steffan Edwards,Walter Glynn, Jeremy Grayson, Joseph Isherwood, David Lawrence, Richard Lowther, Lee McKenzie, Tim Mitchell, David Moon, Graeme North, Sandra Noble, David Orton, David Randall, David Revers, Ashley Rumney, Andrew Sheret, David Toft, Ron Wood, Richard Young.

Production: Ashley Rumney

Key to racereaders' initials

WG ... Walter Glynn	JN ... Jonathan Neesom	JR ... Joe Rowntree
RL ... Richard Lowther	DO ... Darren Owen	AS ... Andrew Sheret
LM ... Lee McKenzie	SP ... Steve Payne	ST ... Steve Taylor
TM ... Tim Mitchell	CR ... Colin Roberts	RY ... Richard Young

The Official Scale of Weight, Age & Distance (Flat)

The following scale should only be used in conjunction with the Official ratings published in this book. Use of any other scale will introduce errors into calculations. The allowances are expressed as the number of pounds that is deemed the average horse in each group falls short of maturity at different dates and distances.

Dist		Jan		Feb		Mar		Apr		May		Jun		Jul		Aug		Sep		Oct		Nov		Dec	
(fur)	Age	1-15	16-31	1-14	15-28	1-15	16-31	1-15	16-30	1-15	16-31	1-15	16-30	1-15	16-31	1-15	16-31	1-15	16-30	1-15	16-31	1-15	16-30	1-15	16-31
5	2	-	-	-	-	-	47	44	41	38	36	34	32	30	28	26	24	22	20	19	18	17	17	16	16
	3	15	15	14	14	13	12	11	10	9	8	7	6	5	4	3	2	1	1	-	-	-	-	-	-
6	2	-	-	-	-	-	-	-	-	44	41	38	36	33	31	28	26	24	22	21	20	19	18	17	17
	3	16	16	15	15	14	13	12	11	10	9	8	7	6	5	4	3	2	2	1	1	-	-	-	-
7	2	-	-	-	-	-	-	-	-	-	-	-	-	38	35	32	30	27	25	23	22	21	20	19	19
	3	18	18	17	17	16	15	14	13	12	11	10	9	8	7	6	5	4	3	2	2	1	1	-	-
8	2	-	-	-	-	-	-	-	-	-	-	-	-	-	-	37	34	31	28	26	24	23	22	21	20
	3	20	20	19	19	18	17	15	14	13	12	11	10	9	8	7	6	5	4	3	3	2	2	1	1
9	3	22	22	21	21	20	19	17	15	14	13	12	11	10	9	8	7	6	5	4	4	3	3	2	2
	4	1	1	-	-	-	-	-	-	-	-	-	-	-	-	-	-	-	-	-	-	-	-	-	-
10	3	23	23	22	22	21	20	19	17	15	14	13	12	11	10	9	8	7	6	5	5	4	4	3	3
	4	2	2	1	1	-	-	-	-	-	-	-	-	-	-	-	-	-	-	-	-	-	-	-	-
11	3	24	24	23	23	22	21	20	19	17	15	14	13	12	11	10	9	8	7	6	6	5	5	4	4
	4	3	3	2	2	1	1	-	-	-	-	-	-	-	-	-	-	-	-	-	-	-	-	-	-
12	3	25	25	24	24	23	22	21	20	19	17	15	14	13	12	11	10	9	8	7	7	6	6	5	5
	4	4	4	3	3	2	2	1	1	-	-	-	-	-	-	-	-	-	-	-	-	-	-	-	-
13	3	26	26	25	25	24	23	22	21	20	19	17	15	14	13	12	11	10	9	8	8	7	7	6	6
	4	5	5	4	4	3	3	2	1	-	-	-	-	-	-	-	-	-	-	-	-	-	-	-	-
14	3	27	27	26	26	25	24	23	22	21	20	19	17	15	14	13	12	11	10	9	9	8	8	7	7
	4	6	6	5	5	4	4	3	2	1	-	-	-	-	-	-	-	-	-	-	-	-	-	-	-
15	3	28	28	27	27	26	25	24	23	22	21	20	19	17	15	14	13	12	11	10	9	8	8	7	7
	4	6	6	5	5	4	4	3	3	2	1	-	-	-	-	-	-	-	-	-	-	-	-	-	-
16	3	29	29	28	28	27	26	25	24	23	22	21	20	19	17	15	14	13	12	11	10	9	9	8	8
	4	7	7	6	6	5	5	4	4	3	2	1	-	-	-	-	-	-	-	-	-	-	-	-	-
18	3	31	31	30	30	29	28	27	26	25	24	23	22	21	20	18	16	14	13	12	11	10	10	9	9
	4	8	8	7	7	6	6	5	5	4	3	2	1	-	-	-	-	-	-	-	-	-	-	-	-
20	3	33	33	32	32	31	30	29	28	27	26	25	24	23	22	20	18	16	14	13	12	11	11	10	10
	4	9	9	8	8	7	7	6	6	5	4	3	2	1	-	-	-	-	-	-	-	-	-	-	-

The Form Book

Welcome to the 2013 edition of *The Form Book,* comprising the complete year's results from 2012.

Race details contain Racing Post Ratings assessing the merit of each individual performance, speed figures for every horse that clocks a worthwhile time, weight-for-age allowances, stall positions for every race and the starting price percentage, in addition to the traditional features.

Race Focus comments are printed below each race along with official explanations and notebook comments for all British races of Class 3 and above, all two-year-old races and foreign races. The comments provide an analysis of the winning performance and, where applicable, explain possible reasons for improvement or attempt to explain why any horse failed to run to its best. More importantly, our team will also indicate the conditions under which horses are likely to be seen to best advantage.

The official record

THE FORM BOOK records comprehensive race details of every domestic race, every major European Group race and every foreign event in which a British-trained runner participated. In the **NOTEBOOK** section, extended interpretation is provided for all runners worthy of a mention, including all placed horses and all favourites. Generally speaking, the higher the class of race, the greater the number of runners noted.

MEETING BACK REFERENCE NUMBER is the Raceform number of the last meeting run at the track and is shown to the left of the course name. Abandoned meetings are signified by a dagger.

THE GOING, The Official going, shown at the head of each meeting, is recorded as follows: Turf: Hard; Firm; Good to firm; Good; Good to soft; Soft; Heavy. All-Weather: Fast; Standard to fast; Standard; Standard to slow; Slow. There may be variations for non-British meetings

Where appropriate, a note is included indicating track bias and any differences to the official going indicated by race times.

THE WEATHER is shown below to th e date for selected meetings.

THE WIND is given as a strength and direction at the Winning Post, classified as follows:
Strength: gale; v.str; str; fresh; mod; slt; almost nil; nil.
Direction: (half) against; (half) bhd; (half) across from or towards stands.

VISIBILITY is good unless otherwise stated.

RACE NUMBERS for foreign races carry the suffix 'a' in the race header and in the index.

RACE TITLE is the name of the race as shown in the Racing Calendar.

COMPETITIVE RACING CLASSIFICATIONS are shown on a scale from Class 1 to Class 7. All Pattern races are Class 1.

THE RACE DISTANCE is given for all races, and is accompanied by (s) for races run on straight courses and (r) for courses where there is a round track of comparable distance. On All-Weather courses (F) for Fibresand or (P) for Polytrack indicates the nature of the artificial surface on which the race is run.

OFFICIAL RACE TIME as published in the Racing Calendar is followed in parentheses by the time when the race actually started. This is followed by the race class, age restrictions, handicap restrictions and the official rating of the top weight.

PRIZE MONEY shows penalty values down to sixth place (where applicable).

THE POSITION OF THE STARTING STALLS is shown against each race, in the form of: High (H), Centre (C) or Low (L). In keeping with all other major racing nations, stalls are now numbered from the inside rail. If the stalls are placed adjacent to the inside rail they are described as low, if against the outside rail they are described as high. Otherwise they are central.

IN THE RACE RESULT, the figures to the far left of each horse (under FORM) show the most recent form figures. The figure in bold is the finishing position in this race as detailed below.

1...40 - finishing positions first to fortieth; **b** - brought down; **c** - carried out; **f** - fell; **p** - pulled up; **r** - refused; **ro** - ran out; **s** - slipped up; **u** - unseated rider; **v** - void race.

THE OFFICIAL DISTANCES between the horses are shown on the left-hand side immediately after their position at the finish.

NUMBER OF DAYS SINCE PREVIOUS RUN is the superscript figure immediately following the horse name and suffix.

PREVIOUS RACEFORM RACE NUMBER is the boxed figure to the right of the horse's name.

THE HORSE'S AGE is shown immediately before the weight carried.

WEIGHTS shown are actual weights carried.

OFFICIAL RATING is the figure in bold type directly after the horse's name in the race result. This figure indicates the Official BHA rating, at entry, after the following adjustments had been made:
(i) Overweight carried by the rider.
(ii) The number of pounds out of the handicap (if applicable).
(iii) Penalties incurred after the publication of the weights.
However, no adjustments have been made for:
(i) Weight-for-age.
(ii) Riders' claims.

HEADGEAR is shown immediately before the jockey's name and in parentheses and expressed as: **b** (blinkers); **v** (visor); **h** (hood); **e** (eyeshield); **c** (eyecover); **p** (sheepskin cheekpieces).

THE JOCKEY is shown for every runner followed, in superscript, by apprentice allowances in parentheses.

APPRENTICE ALLOWANCES The holders of apprentice jockeys' licences under the provisions of Rule 60(iii) are permitted to claim the following allowances in Flat races:
7lb until they have won 20 Flat races run under the Rules of any recognised Turf Authority; thereafter 5lb until they have won 50 such Flat races; thereafter 3lb until they have won 95 such Flat races. These allowances can be claimed in the Flat races set out below, with the exception of races confined to apprentice jockeys:
(a) All handicap handicaps other than those Rated stakes which are classified as listed races.
(b) All selling and claiming races.
(b) All weight-for-age races classified 3, 4, 5, 6 and 7.

THE DRAW for places at the start is shown after each jockey's name.

RACING POST RATINGS, which record the level of performance attained in this race for each horse, appear in the end column after each horse. These are the work of handicappers Simon Turner, Sam Walker and Paul Curtis, who head a dedicated team dealing with Flat races for Raceform and sister publication, the *Racing Post*.

THE TRAINER is shown for every runner.

COMMENT-IN-RUNNING is shown for each horse in an abbreviated form. Details of abbreviations appear later in this section.

STARTING PRICES appear below the jockey in the race result. The favourite indicator appears to the right of the Starting Price; 1 for the favourite, 2 for the second-favourite and 3 for third-favourite. Joint favourites share the same number.

RACE TIMES in Great Britain are official times which are electronically recorded and shown to 100th of a second. Figures in parentheses following the time show the number of seconds faster or slower than the Raceform Median Time for the course and distance.

RACEFORM MEDIAN TIMES are compiled from all races run over the course and distance in the preceding five years. Times equal to the median are shown as (0.00). Times under the median are preceded by minus, for instance, 1.8 seconds under the median would be shown (-1.8). Record times are displayed either referring to the juvenile record (1.2 under 2y best) or to the overall record (1.2 under best).

GOING CORRECTION appears against each race to allow for changing conditions of the ground. It is shown to a hundredth of a second and indicates the adjustment per furlong against the median time. The going based on the going correction is shown in parentheses and is recorded in the following stages:
Turf: HD (Hard); F (Firm); GF (Good to firm); G (Good); GS (Good to soft); S (Soft); HVY (Heavy). All-Weather: FST (Fast); SF (Standard to fast); STD (Standard); SS (Standard to slow); SLW (Slow)

WEIGHT-FOR-AGE allowances are given where applicable for mixed-age races.

STARTING PRICE PERCENTAGE follows the going correction and weight-for-age details, and gives the total SP percentage of all runners that competed. It precedes the number of runners taking part in the race.

SELLING DETAILS (where applicable) and details of any claim are given. Friendly claims are not detailed.

SPEED RATINGS appear below the race time and going correction. They are the work of time expert Dave Bellingham and differ from conventional ratings systems in that they are an expression of a horse's ability in terms of lengths-per-mile, as opposed to pounds in weight. They are not directly comparable with BHA and Racing Post Ratings.

The ratings take no account of the effect of weight, either historically or on the day, and this component is left completely to the user's discretion. What is shown is a speed rating represented in its purest form, rather than one that has been altered for weight using a mathematical formula that treats all types of horses as if they were the same.

A comparison of the rating achieved with the 'par' figure for the grade of race - the rating that should be achievable by an average winner in that class of race - will both provide an at-a-glance indication of whether or not a race was truly run and also highlight the value of the form from a time perspective.

In theory, if a horse has a best speed figure five points superior to another and both run to their best form in a race over a mile, the first horse should beat the second by five lengths. In a race run over two miles, the margin should be ten lengths and so on.

Before the speed figures can be calculated, it is necessary to establish a set of standard or median times for every distance at every track, and this is done by averaging the times of all winners over a particular trip going back several years. No speed ratings are produced when insufficient races have been run over a distance for a reliable median time to be calculated.

Once a meeting has taken place, a raw unadjusted speed rating is calculated for each winner by calculating how many lengths per mile the winning time was faster or slower than the median for the trip. A difference of 0.2 of a second equals one length. The raw speed ratings of all winners on the card are then compared with the 'par' figure for the class of race. The difference between the 'raw' speed rating and the 'par' figure for each race is then noted, and both the fastest and slowest races are discarded before the rest are averaged to produce the going allowance or track variant. This figure gives an idea as to how much the elements, of which the going is one, have affected the final times of each race.

The figure representing the going allowance is then used to adjust the raw speed figures and produce the final ratings, which represent how fast the winners would have run on a perfectly good surface with no external influences, including the weather. The ratings for beaten horses are worked out by taking the number of lengths they were behind the winner, adjusting that to take into account the distance of the race, and deducting that figure from the winner's rating. The reader is left with a rating which provides an instant impression of the value of a time performance.

The speed 'pars' below act as benchmark with which to compare the speed figures earned by each horse in each race. A horse that has already exceeded the 'par' for the class he is about to run in is of special interest, especially if he has done it more than once, as are horses that have consistently earned higher figures than their rivals.

Class 1 Group One	117
Class 1 Group Two	115
Class 1 Group Three	113
Class 1 Listed	111
Class 2	109
Class 3	107
Class 4	105
Class 5	103
Class 6	101
Class 7	97

Allowances need to be made for younger horses and for fillies. These allowances are as follows.

MONTH	2yo	3yo
Jan / Feb	n/a	-6
Mar / Apr	-11	-5
May / Jun	-10	-4
Jul / Aug	-9	-3
Sep / Oct	-8	-2
Nov / Dec	-7	-1
Races contested by fillies only		-3

Allowances are cumulative. For example, using a combination of the above pars and allowances, the par figure for the Epsom Oaks would be 110. The Group One par is 117, then deduct 4 because the race is confined to three year olds and run in June, then subtract another 3 because the race is confined to fillies.

TOTE prices include £1 stake. Exacta dividends are shown in parentheses. The Computer Straight Forecast dividend is preceded by the letters CSF, Computer Tricast is preceded by CT and Trifecta dividend is preceded by the word Trifecta. Jackpot, Placepot and Quadpot details appear at the end of the meeting to which they refer.

OWNER is followed by the breeder's name and the trainer's location.

STEWARDS' ENQUIRIES are included with the result, and any suspensions and/or fines incurred. Objections by jockeys and officials are included, where relevant.

HISTORICAL FOCUS details occasional points of historical significance.

FOCUS The Focus section has been enhanced to help readers distinguish good races from bad races and reliable form from unreliable form, by drawing together the opinions of handicapper, time expert and paddock watcher and interpreting their views in a punter-friendly manner.

NOTEBOOK horses marked with the diamond symbol are those deemed by our racereaders especially worthy of note in future races.

OFFICIAL EXPLANATIONS, where the horse is deemed to have run well above or below expectations

Abbreviations and their meanings

Paddock comments

attr - attractive
gd bodied - good bodied, well put together
gd sort - well made, above average on looks
h.d.w - has done well, improved in looks
wl grwn - well grown, has filled to its frame
lengthy - longer than average for its height
tall - tall
rangy - lengthy and tall but in proportion.
cl cpld - close coupled
scope - scope for physical development
str - strong, powerful looking
w'like - workmanlike, ordinary in looks
lt-f - light-framed, not much substance
cmpt - compact
neat - smallish, well put together
leggy - long legs compared with body
angular - unfurnished behind the saddle, not filled to frame
unf - unfurnished in the midriff, not filled to frame
narrow - not as wide as side appearance would suggest
small - lacks any physical scope
nt grwn - not grown
lw - looked fit and well
bkwd - backward in condition
t - tubed
swtg - sweating
b (off fore or nr fore) - bandaged in front
b.hind (off or nr) - bandaged behind

At the start

stdd s - jockey purposely reins back the horse
dwlt - missed the break and left for a short time
s.s - slow to start, left longer than a horse that dwelt
s.v.s - started very slowly
s.i.s - started on terms but took time to get going
ref to r - does not jump off, or travels a few yards then stops
rel to r - tries to pull itself up in mid-race
w.r.s - whipped round start

Position in the race

led - in lead on its own

disp ld - upsides the leader
w ldr - almost upsides the leader
w ldrs - in a line of three or more disputing the lead
prom - on the heels of the leaders, in front third of the field
trckd ldr(s) - just in behind the leaders giving impression that it could lead if asked
chsd ldr - horse in second place
chsd clr ldrs - horse heads main body of field behind two clear leaders
chsd ldrs - horse is in the first four or five but making more of an effort to stay close to the pace than if it were tracking the leaders.
clsd - closed
in tch - close enough to have a chance
hdwy - making ground on the leader
gd hdwy - making ground quickly on the leader, could be a deliberate move
sme hdwy - making some ground but no real impact on the race
w.w - waited with
stdy hdwy - gradually making ground
ev ch - upsides the leaders when the race starts in earnest
rr - at the back of main group but not detached
bhd - detached from the main body of runners
hld up - restrained as a deliberate tactical move
nt rcvr - lost all chance after interference, mistake etc.
wknd - stride shortened as it began to tire
lost tch - had been in the main body but a gap appeared as it tired
lost pl - remains in main body of runners but lost several positions quickly

Riding

effrt - short-lived effort
pushed along - received urgings with hands only, jockey not using legs
rdn - received urgings from saddle, including use of whip
hrd rdn - received maximum assistance from the saddle including use of whip
drvn - received forceful urgings, jockey putting in a lot of effort and using whip
hrd drvn - jockey very animated, plenty of kicking, pushing and reminders

Finishing comments

jst failed - closing rapidly on the winner and probably would have led a stride after the line
r.o - jockey's efforts usually involved to produce an increase in pace without finding an appreciable turn of speed
r.o wl - jockey's efforts usually involved to produce an obvious increase in pace without finding an appreciable turn of speed
unable qckn - not visibly tiring but does not possess a sufficient change of pace
one pce - not tiring but does not find a turn of speed, from a position further out than unable qckn
nt r.o. - did not consent to respond to pressure
styd on - going on well towards the end, utilising stamina
nvr able to chal - unable to produce sufficient to reach a challenging position
nvr nr to chal - in the opinion of the racereader, the horse was never in a suitable position to challenge.
nrst fin - nearer to the winner in distance beaten than at any time since the race had begun in earnest
nvr nrr - nearer to the winner position-wise than at any time since the race had begun in earnest
rallied - responded to pressure to come back with a chance having lost its place
no ex - unable to sustain its run
bttr for r - likely to improve for the run and experience
rn green - inclined to wander and falter through inexperience
too much to do - left with too much leeway to make up

Winning comments

v.easily - a great deal in hand
easily - plenty in hand
comf - something in hand, always holding the others
pushed out - kept up to its work with hands and heels without jockey resorting to whip or kicking along and wins fairly comfortably
rdn out - pushed and kicked out to the line, with the whip employed
drvn out - pushed and kicked out to the line, with considerable effort and the whip employed
all out - nothing to spare, could not have found any more
jst hld on - holding on to a rapidly diminishing lead, could not have found any more if passed
unchal - must either make all or a majority of the running and not be challenged from an early stage

Complete list of abbreviations

a - always
abt - about
a.p - always prominent
appr - approaching
awrdd - awarded
b.b.v - broke blood-vessel
b.d - brought down
bdly - badly
bef - before
bhd - behind
bk - back
blkd - baulked
blnd - blundered
bmpd - bumped
bnd - bend
btn- beaten
bttr - better
c - came
ch - chance
chal - challenged
chse - chase
chsd - chased
chsng - chasing
circ - circuit
cl - close
clr - clear
clsd - closed
comf - comfortably
cpld - coupled
crse - course
ct - caught
def - definite
dismntd - dismounted
disp - disputed
dist - distance
div - division
drvn - driven
dwlt - dwelt
edgd - edged
effrt - effort

ent - entering
ev ch - every chance
ex - extra
f - furlong
fin - finished
fnd - found
fnl - final
fr - from
gd - good
gng - going
gp - group
grad - gradually
grnd - ground
hd - head
hdd - headed
hdwy - headway
hld - held
hmpd - hampered
imp - impression
ins - inside
j.b - jumped badly
j.w - jumped well
jnd - joined
jst - just
kpt - kept
l - length
ld - lead
ldr - leader
lft - left
mod - moderate
m - mile
m.n.s - made no show
mde - made
mid div - mid division
mstke - mistake
n.d - never dangerous
n.g.t - not go through
n.m.r - not much room
nk - neck
no ex - no extra
nr - near
nrr - nearer
nrst fin - nearest finish
nt - not
nvr - never
one pce - one pace
out - from finish
outpcd - outpaced
p.u - pulled up
pce - pace
pckd - pecked
pl - place
plcd - placed
plld - pulled
press - pressure
prog - progress
prom - prominent
qckly - quickly
qckn - quicken
r - race
racd - raced
rch - reach
rcvr - recover
rdn - ridden
rdr - rider
reard - reared
ref - refused
rn - ran
rnd - round
r.o - ran on
rr - rear
rspnse - response
rt - right
s - start
sddle - saddle
shkn - shaken
slt - slight
sme - some
sn - soon
spd- speed
st - straight
stmbld - stumbled
stdd - steadied
stdy - steady
strly - strongly
styd - stayed
styng - staying
s. u - slipped up
swtchd - switched
swvd - swerved
tk - took
t.k.h - took keen hold
t.o - tailed off
tch - touch
thrght - throughout
trbld - troubled
trckd - tracked
u.p - under pressure
u.str.p- under strong pressure
w - with
w.r.s - whipped round start
wd - wide
whn - when
wknd - weakened
wl - well
wnr - winner
wnt - went
1/2-wy - halfway

Racing Post Ratings

Racing Post Ratings for each horse are shown in the right hand column, headed RPR, and indicate the actual level of performance attained in that race. The figure in the back index represents the BEST public form that Raceform's Handicappers still believe the horse capable of reproducing.

To use the ratings constructively in determining those horses best-in in future events, the following procedure should be followed:

(i) In races where all runners are the same age and are set to carry the same weight, no calculations are necessary. The horse with the highest rating is best-in.

(ii) In races where all runners are the same age but are set to carry different weights, add one point to the Raceform Rating for every pound less than 10 stone to be carried; deduct one point for every pound more than 10 stone.

For example,

Horse	Age & wt	Adjustment from 10st	Base rating	Adjusted rating
Treclare	3-10-1	-1	78	77
Buchan	3-9-13	+1	80	81
Paper Money	3-9-7	+7	71	78
Archaic	3-8-11	+17	60	77

Therefore Buchan is top-rated (best-in)

(iii) In races concerning horses of different ages the procedure in (ii) should again be followed, but reference must also be made to the Official Scale of Weight-For-Age.

For example,

12 furlongs, July 20th

Horse	Age & wt	Adjustment from 10st	Base rating	Adjusted rating	W-F-A deduct	Final rating
Archaic	5-10-0	0	90	90	Nil	90
Orpheus	4-9-9	+5	88	88	Nil	88
Lemonora	3-9-4	+10	85	95	-12	83
Tamar	4-8-7	+21	73	94	Nil	94

Therefore Tamar is top-rated (best-in)

(A 3-y-o is deemed 12lb less mature than a 4-y-o or older horse on 20th July over 12f. Therefore, the deduction of 12 points is necessary.)

The following symbols are used in conjunction with the ratings:

++: almost certain to prove better

+: likely to prove better

d: disappointing (has run well below best recently)

?: form hard to evaluate

t: tentative rating based on race-time rating may prove unreliable

Weight adjusted ratings for every race are published daily in Raceform Private Handicap and our new service Raceform Private handicap ONLINE (www.raceform.co.uk).

For subscription terms please contact the Subscription Department on 01933 304858.

Course descriptions

(R.H.) denotes right-hand and (L.H.) left-hand courses.

ASCOT (R.H)

Right-handed triangular track just under 1m 6f in length. The Round course descends from the 1m 4f start into Swinley Bottom, the lowest part of the track. It then turns right-handed and joins the Old Mile Course, which starts on a separate chute. The course then rises to the right-handed home turn over a new underpass to join the straight mile course. The run-in is about 3f, rising slightly to the winning post. The whole course is of a galloping nature with easy turns.

AYR (L.H)

A left-handed, galloping, flat oval track of 1m 4f with a 4f run-in. The straight 6f is essentially flat.

BATH (L.H)

Galloping, left-handed, level oval of 1m 4f 25y, with long, stiff run-in of about 4f which bends to the left. An extended chute provides for races over 5f 11y and 5f 161y.

BEVERLEY (R.H)

A right-handed oval of 1m 3f, generally galloping, with an uphill run-in of two and a half furlongs. The 5f course is very stiff.

BRIGHTON (L.H)

Left-handed, 1m 4f horseshoe with easy turns and a run-in of three and a half furlongs. Undulating and sharp, the track suits handy types.

CARLISLE (R.H)

Right-handed, 1m 4f pear-shaped track. Galloping and undulating with easy turns and a stiff uphill run-in of three and a half furlongs. 6f course begins on an extended chute.

CATTERICK (L.H)

A sharp, left-handed, undulating oval of 1m 180y with a downhill run-in of 3f.

CHEPSTOW (L.H)

A left-handed, undulating oval of about 2m, with easy turns, and a straight run-in of 5f. There is a straight track of 1m 14y.

CHESTER (L.H)

A level, sharp, left-handed, circular course of 1m 73y, with a short run-in of 230y. Chester is a specialists' track which generally suits the sharp-actioned horse.

DONCASTER (L.H)

A left-handed, flat, galloping course of 1m 7f 110y, with a long run-in which extends to a straight mile.

EPSOM (L.H)

Left-handed and undulating with easy turns, and a run-in of just under 4f. The straight 5f course is also undulating and downhill all the way, making it the fastest 5f in the world.

FFOS LAS (L.H)

The track is a 60m wide, basically flat, 1m4f oval with sweeping bends.

FOLKESTONE (R.H)

Right-handed, undulating, circuit of 1m 3f, with a two and a half furlong run-in. There is a straight 7f course. Due to close at the end of 2012.

GOODWOOD (R.H)

A sharp, undulating, essentially right-handed track with a long run-in. There is also a straight 6f course.

HAMILTON PARK (R.H)

Sharp, undulating, right-handed course of 1m 5f with a five and a half furlong, uphill run-in. There is a straight track of 6f.

HAYDOCK PARK (L.H)

A galloping, almost flat, oval track, 1m 5f round, with a run-in of four and a half furlongs and a straight 6f course.

KEMPTON PARK (R.H)

A floodlit Polytrack circuit opened in March 2006. A 10f outer track accommodates races over 6f, 7f, 1m, 1m 3f, 1m 4f and 2m. The 8f inner track caters for races over 5f and 1m 2f.

LEICESTER (R.H)

Stiff, galloping, right-handed oval of 1m 5f, with a 5f run-in. There is a straight course of 7f.

LINGFIELD PARK (L.H)

Turf Course: A sharp, undulating left-handed circuit, with a 7f 140y straight course.

Polytrack course: left-handed all-weather is 1m2f round, with an extended chute to provide a 1m5f start. It is a sharp, level track with a short run-in.

MUSSELBURGH (R.H)

A sharp, level, right-handed oval of 1m 2f, with a run-in of 4f. There is an additional 5f straight course.

NEWBURY (L.H)

Left-handed, oval track of about 1m 7f, with a slightly undulating straight mile. The round course is level and galloping with a four and a half furlong run-in. Races over the round mile and 7f 60y start on the adjoining chute.

NEWCASTLE (L.H)

Galloping, easy, left-handed oval of 1m 6f, with an uphill 4f run-in. There is a straight course of 1m 8y.

NEWMARKET (R.H)

Rowley Mile Course: There is a straight 1m2f course, which is wide and galloping. Races over 1m4f or more are right-handed. The Rowley course has a long run-in and a stiff finish.

July Course: Races up to a mile are run on the Bunbury course, which is straight. Races over 1m2f or more are right-handed, with a 7f run-in. Like the Rowley course, the July track is stiff.

NOTTINGHAM (L.H)

Left-handed, galloping, oval of about 1m 4f, and a run-in of four and a half furlongs. Flat with easy turns.

PONTEFRACT (L.H)

Left-handed oval, undulating course of 2m 133y, with a short run-in of 2f. It is a particularly stiff track with the last 3f uphill.

REDCAR (L.H)

Left-handed, level, galloping, oval course of 14f with a straight run-in of 5f. There is also a straight 8f.

RIPON (R.H)

A sharp, undulating, right-handed oval of 1m 5f, with a 5f run-in. There is also a 6f straight course.

SALISBURY (R.H)

Right-handed and level, with a run-in of 4f. There is a straight 8f track. The last half mile is uphill, providing a stiff test of stamina.

SANDOWN PARK (R.H)

An easy right-handed oval course of 1m 5f with a stiff straight uphill run-in of 4f. Separate straight 5f track is also uphill. Galloping.

SOUTHWELL (L.H)

Left-handed oval, Fibresand course of 1m 2f with a 3f run-in. There is a straight 5f. Sharp and level, Southwell suits front-runners.

THIRSK (L.H)

Left-handed, oval of 1m 2f with sharp turns and an undulating run-in of 4f. There is a straight 6f track.

WARWICK (L.H)

Left-handed, sharp, level track of 1m 6f 32y in circumference, with a run-in of two and a half furlongs.

WINDSOR (Fig. 8)

Figure eight track of 1m 4f 110y. The course is level and sharp with a long run-in. The 6f course is essentially straight.

WOLVERHAMPTON (L.H)

Left-handed oval of 1m, with a run-in of 380y. A level track with sharp bends, the Polytrack surface, in use since October 2004, generally rides slower than that at Lingfield.

YARMOUTH (L.H)

Left-handed, level circuit of 1m 4f, with a run-in of 5f. The straight course is 8f long.

YORK (L.H)

Left-handed, level, galloping track, with a straight 6f. There is also an adjoining course of 6f 214y.

SOUTHWELL (L-H)

Sunday, January 1

OFFICIAL GOING: Standard

Wind: Cloudy Weather: Moderate across

1 BET AND WATCH AT BLUESQ.COM APPRENTICE MEDIAN AUCTION MAIDEN STKS 1m 3f (F)

12:15 (12:15) (Class 6) 4-6-Y-O **£1,704** (£503; £251) **Stalls** Low

Form RPR

523- **1** **Kishanda**[17] 7774 4-8-8 63 (v[1]) AmyRyan 4 66
(Gay Kelleway) *mde all: pushed clr fnl 2f: comf* **1/7**[1]

220- **2** *7* **Arizona High**[10] 7858 4-8-8 57 DannyBrock(5) 3 50
(Andrew Crook) *chsd wnr: rdn along over 3f out: drvn and one pce fnl 2f* **10/1**[2]

3 *77* **Punta Baluarte**[39] 6-8-11 0 AdamBeschizza 1
(Julie Camacho) *v s.i.s and lost many l s: a wl bhd* **14/1**[3]

5- **U** **Supastarqueen (USA)**[20] 7739 4-8-5 0 RyanPowell(3) 2
(Brian Baugh) *chsd ldng pair: rdn along 4f out: sn outpcd: swvd violently rt on home turn and uns rdr* **33/1**

2m 26.14s (-1.86) **Going Correction** -0.275s/f (Stan)
WFA 4 from 6yo 3lb 4 Ran SP% **106.2**
Speed ratings: **95,89,33,**
CSF £2.06 TOTE £1.10; EX 1.90.
Owner John Farley & Gay Kelleway **Bred** Mrs David Low **Trained** Exning, Suffolk

FOCUS
About as moderate a start to the 2012 Flat season as you are likely to get and made even less competitive (were that possible) when Punta Baluarte virtually refused to come out of the stalls and Supastarqueen dumped her rider on the Fibresand when losing touch over 3f from home.

2 NEW YEAR AT SOUTHWELL GOLF CLUB (S) STKS 1m (F)

12:50 (12:50) (Class 6) 3-Y-O **£1,704** (£503; £251) **Stalls** Low

Form RPR

1 **Miss Cato** 3-8-7 0 WilliamCarson 3 63
(Rae Guest) *dwlt: sn prom: led over 3f out: rdn and hung lft over 1f out: kpt on gamely u.p fnl f* **9/1**

052- **2** *1 1/4* **Samasana (IRE)**[10] 7852 3-8-7 51 (p) LukeMorris 1 60
(Ian Wood) *stdd s and hld up in tch: hdwy 3f out: chal on inner 2f out: rdn and ev ch whn carried lft over 1f out: n.m.r and kpt on same pce ins fnl f* **3/1**[3]

541- **3** *3/4* **Spartilla**[10] 7852 3-9-4 57 JamesSullivan 4 69
(James Given) *trckd ldrs: hdwy to chse wnr over 2f out: rdn wl over 1f out and kpt on same pce* **5/4**[1]

025- **4** *23* **Duke Liam (IRE)**[17] 7769 3-8-12 65 (b[1]) AdrianNicholls 5
(David Nicholls) *t.k.h: cl up on outer: effrt 3f out: sn rdn along and wknd 2f out* **11/4**[2]

430- **5** *14* **The Coulbeck Kid**[187] 3491 3-8-12 50 (b) DavidProbert 2
(Des Donovan) *led: pushed along and hdd over 3f out: sn wknd* **25/1**

1m 42.7s (-1.00) **Going Correction** -0.275s/f (Stan) 5 Ran SP% **110.0**
Speed ratings (Par 95): **94,92,92,69,55**
toteswingers: 1&2 £12.50 CSF £35.08 TOTE £11.90: £5.70, £2.00; EX 39.80.The winner was bought in for 5,750gns.
Owner A H Bennett **Bred** A H Bennett **Trained** Newmarket, Suffolk
■ Stewards' Enquiry : William Carson one-day ban: careless riding (Jan 15)

FOCUS
A poor seller.

3 HAPPY NEW YEAR FROM BLUE SQUARE H'CAP 5f (F)

1:20 (1:21) (Class 3) (0-95,91) 4-Y-O+ **£6,616** (£1,980; £990; £495; £246) **Stalls** High

Form RPR

001- **1** **Even Stevens**[26] 7643 4-9-7 91 GrahamGibbons 9 104
(Scott Dixon) *cl up towards stands' rail: led 2f out: rdn and hung lft over 1f out: drvn and edgd lft ins fnl f: kpt on wl* **11/4**[1]

142- **2** *1 1/4* **Mottley Crewe**[26] 7644 5-8-11 81 (b) MartinHarley 4 89
(Richard Guest) *led: rdn along and hdd 2f out: cl up and carried lft over 1f out: ev ch tl no ex ins fnl f* **5/1**[3]

051- **3** *1 1/2* **Six Wives**[19] 7746 5-8-9 79 RichardKingscote 5 82
(Scott Dixon) *sn cl up: effrt 2f out and ev ch tl rdn and one pce fnl f* **11/2**

535- **4** *3/4* **Captain Scooby**[12] 7832 6-8-0 77 CharlesEddery(7) 6 77
(Richard Guest) *chsd ldrs: rdn along and outpcd 1/2-way: styd on wl fnl f* **14/1**

421- **5** *shd* **Sleepy Blue Ocean**[26] 7644 6-8-8 78 (p) LukeMorris 2 78
(John Balding) *chsd ldrs: rdn along 1/2-way: no imp appr fnl f* **9/2**[2]

032- **6** *hd* **What About You (IRE)**[12] 7833 4-9-1 85 (p) TonyHamilton 1 84
(Richard Fahey) *dwlt: hdwy to chse ldrs on wd outside 1/2-way: rdn along wl over 1f out and sn wknd* **9/1**

012- **7** *3/4* **Monsieur Jamie**[26] 7643 4-8-11 81 JoeFanning 7 77
(J R Jenkins) *dwlt: a towards rr* **8/1**

000- **8** *6* **Falasteen (IRE)**[99] 6332 5-8-12 82 JamieSpencer 3 57
(Kevin Ryan) *sn outpcd and towards rr: swtchd lft 1/2-way: nvr a factor* **9/1**

58.25s (-1.45) **Going Correction** -0.10s/f (Stan) 8 Ran SP% **114.7**
Speed ratings (Par 107): **107,105,102,101,101 100,99,90**
toteswingers: 1&2 £3.00, 1&3 £4.00, 2&3 £4.40 CSF £16.62 CT £70.38 TOTE £2.90: £2.20, £1.70, £2.50; EX 15.60 Trifecta £56.60 Pool £384.61 - 5.02 winning units.
Owner Paul J Dixon **Bred** Mrs Yvette Dixon **Trained** Babworth, Notts
■ Stewards' Enquiry : Graham Gibbons one-day ban: careless riding (Jan 15)

FOCUS
A hot sprint handicap for the track, but the front pair dominated throughout.

NOTEBOOK
Even Stevens came into this 5-6 here and found himself off a career-high mark following his C&D success last month, but that didn't stop the money coming for him. Quickly into stride from the stands'-rail draw, he was in front well over a furlong out and kept on strongly despite persistently hanging away to his left, taking his nearest rivals with him. He was still the best horse on the day, however. (op 7-2)
Mottley Crewe, contesting a race of this class for the first time, has been running consistently well both here and on Polytrack in recent months and was closely matched with Sleepy Blue Ocean and Captain Scooby on last month's C&D running. Soon in front, he was done few favours by the winner carrying him away to his left from over a furlong out, but still looked very much second-best. (op 6-1)
Six Wives, 2-6 over C&D and stable companion of the winner, was bumped up 7lb for last month's win here which looked harsh, but she still had every chance despite being inconvenienced by the favourite carrying the runner-up into her inside the last furlong. It seems unlikely that she will be dropped for this. (op 9-2)
Captain Scooby struggled to go the early pace before running on and, not for the first time, looked badly in need of a return to further. (op 12-1)
Sleepy Blue Ocean had a couple of these behind when winning off 4lb lower over C&D last month, but he was in a better race this time and it proved too much for him. (op 11-2 tchd 6-1)
What About You(IRE) was having his first try on Fibresand, but found himself marooned out in the centre of the track whilst the main action was unfolding closer to the stands' rail. (op 17-2 tchd 7-1)

4 MEMBERSHIP OF SOUTHWELL GOLF CLUB H'CAP 1m 4f (F)

1:55 (1:55) (Class 5) (0-70,70) 4-Y-O+ **£2,264** (£673; £336; £168) **Stalls** Low

Form RPR

613- **1** **First Rock (IRE)**[3] 7914 6-9-1 66 GarryWhillans(5) 4 73+
(Alan Swinbank) *t.k.h early: trckd ldng pair: hdwy to chse ldr 3f out: rdn wl over 1f out: styd on u.p to ld ins fnl f* **6/4**[1]

343- **2** *1/2* **Bow River Arch (USA)**[40] 7503 4-9-6 70 WilliamCarson 1 76
(Peter Hiatt) *set stdy pce: qcknd 3f out: rdn and edgd rt over 1f out: drvn: hdd and no ex ins fnl f* **15/2**

000- **3** *2 3/4* **Brunello**[165] 4208 4-8-7 57 TomEaves 5 59
(David O'Meara) *trckd ldr: pushed along 4f out: rdn 3f out: kpt on same pce appr fnl f* **9/1**

005- **4** *12* **Jasmeno**[34] 7570 5-9-9 69 (t) SteveDrowne 3 58
(Hughie Morrison) *hld up in tch: pushed along over 4f out: rdn wl over 2f out: sn btn* **7/2**[3]

643- **5** *2 3/4* **Irish Jugger (USA)**[23] 7689 5-9-4 64 JamesMillman 2 42
(Rod Millman) *hld up: hdwy to trck ldrs 1/2-way: rdn along 4f out: sn outpcd and bhd* **10/3**[2]

2m 37.65s (-3.35) **Going Correction** -0.275s/f (Stan)
WFA 4 from 5yo+ 4lb 5 Ran SP% **107.1**
Speed ratings (Par 103): **100,99,97,89,88**
CSF £12.12 TOTE £2.50: £1.60, £1.60; EX 8.70.
Owner United Five Racing **Bred** K Molloy **Trained** Melsonby, N Yorks

FOCUS
An ordinary middle-distance handicap, but the pace seemed solid enough which was to the benefit of the winner.
Irish Jugger(USA) Official explanation: vet said gelding lost a front shoe

5 PLAY GOLF BEFORE RACING AT SOUTHWELL H'CAP 1m (F)

2:30 (2:31) (Class 3) (0-95,94) 4-Y-O+ **£6,616** (£1,980; £990; £495; £246) **Stalls** Low

Form RPR

111- **1** **William Haigh (IRE)**[23] 7699 4-9-1 88 JoeFanning 6 101+
(Alan Swinbank) *prom: rdn along and outpcd on inner 3f out: styd on to chse ldr appr fnl f: sn rdn and styd on to ld fnl 100yds: in control whn rdr dropped whip nr fin* **5/2**[1]

1/0- **2** *3/4* **Reve De Nuit (USA)**[337] 353 6-9-7 94 ShaneKelly 8 105
(Alan McCabe) *trckd ldrs on outer: hdwy on bit and cl up 3f out: led 1 1/2f out: rdn and jnd 1f out: sn drvn: hdd and no ex fnl 100yds* **7/2**[3]

200- **3** *4 1/2* **Call To Reason (IRE)**[43] 7486 5-8-8 81 BarryMcHugh 2 82
(Ian Williams) *towards rr: hdwy on inner wl over 2f out: sn rdn: styd on appr fnl f: nrst fin* **14/1**

533- **4** *1 3/4* **Blue Moon**[22] 7719 5-9-6 93 PhillipMakin 7 90
(Kevin Ryan) *led over 3f: prom: ev ch 2f out: sn rdn and kpt on same pce* **11/2**

122- **5** *3/4* **Standpoint**[17] 7771 6-8-3 83 (e) JackDuern(7) 9 78
(Reg Hollinshead) *prom: led over 4f out: rdn along over 2f out: hdd 1 1/2f out and grad wknd* **10/3**[2]

160- **6** *1 3/4* **Toto Skyllachy**[33] 5648 7-8-8 81 TomEaves 1 72
(Ollie Pears) *hld up towards rr: hdwy 3f out: rdn over 2f out: no imp* **25/1**

060- **7** *1* **Justonefortheroad**[22] 7719 6-9-3 90 TonyHamilton 4 79
(Richard Fahey) *chsd ldrs: rdn over 3f out: sn wknd* **14/1**

100- **8** *18* **Tevez**[162] 4310 7-9-0 87 DavidProbert 10 34
(Des Donovan) *dwlt: a in rr* **20/1**

1m 39.78s (-3.92) **Going Correction** -0.275s/f (Stan) 8 Ran SP% **111.2**
Speed ratings (Par 107): **108,107,102,101,100 98,97,79**
toteswingers: 1&2 £3.10, 1&3 £5.30, 2&3 £6.50 CSF £10.66 CT £94.36 TOTE £3.00: £1.10, £2.00, £2.60; EX 11.00 Trifecta £106.50 Pool £275.06 - 1.91 winning units.
Owner Shropshire Wolves II **Bred** Mrs C L Weld **Trained** Melsonby, N Yorks

FOCUS
A decent handicap, but the shape of the race was different to how it may have looked at the declaration stage with the absences of both Benandonner (self certificate) and Trans Sonic (withdrawn after getting under his stall) robbing the contest of two potential front-runners.

NOTEBOOK
William Haigh(IRE), a dual winner over C&D bidding for a four-timer off a 5lb higher mark, won over 1m4f at Wolverhampton last time so a solid pace was imperative and fortunately he got one. Handy from the off, he did come off the bridle briefly on the home bend, but his stamina then kicked in once into the long home straight and, sticking to the inside rail, gradually wore down the runner-up. He has become a credit to his trainer. (op 7-2)
Reve De Nuit(USA) had taken this race for the previous two years, but on neither occasion was he returning from an absence as long as this (337 days). He looked like completing the hat-trick when arriving there swinging off the bridle passing the 2f pole, but couldn't shake off the winner once coming under pressure and was worried out of it. Given the margin back to the third, it's more likely that he just ran into a progressive rival rather than being short of peak fitness. (op 4-1)
Call To Reason(IRE) ♦, making her debut for the yard and on Fibresand for the first time, stayed on to finish third at a respectable distance and there was enough in this performance to make her of interest if returning here. (op 12-1 tchd 11-1)
Blue Moon has been mainly in decent form on Polytrack since the autumn and had every chance, but had nothing more to offer from over a furlong out. She was having her first try here since finishing third on her racecourse debut and this surface doesn't seem to suit her quite so well. (op 4-1)
Standpoint was left as the only recognised pace angle and although he managed to work his way to the front after a couple of furlongs, it was clear soon after turning in that he was going to be overhauled. He has been creeping up the handicap for getting beaten and could do with some respite. (op 7-2 tchd 3-1)
Toto Skyllachy, back on the Flat after a couple of tries over hurdles, was on Fibresand for the first time but never threatened to take a hand. (tchd 22-1)
Justonefortheroad had finished unplaced in four starts since winning off this mark at Thirsk in April, but his sire's record here suggested he might take to the Fibresand at the first time of asking. As it turned out he was just about the first to come off the bridle.

6 PAY AND PLAY SOUTHWELL GOLF CLUB H'CAP 6f (F)

3:05 (3:07) (Class 5) (0-75,73) 3-Y-O **£2,264** (£673; £336; £168) **Stalls** Low

Form RPR

054- **1** **Laffan (IRE)**[158] 4436 3-9-0 66 ow3 PhillipMakin 1 76
(Kevin Ryan) *mde most: rdn 2f out: kpt on wl u.p fnl f* **7/4**[1]

612- **2** *1 3/4* **Point At Issue (IRE)**[23] 7684 3-8-8 60 (b) AdrianNicholls 4 64
(David Nicholls) *trckd ldrs: hdwy on inner over 2f out: rdn to chse wnr appr fnl f: sn ev ch tl drvn and no ex fnl 100yds* **6/1**[3]

241- **3** *2 1/2* **Man Of My Word**[5] 7881 3-9-3 69 6ex (p) GrahamGibbons 2 65
(Scott Dixon) *cl up: rdn 2f out: drvn and ev ch over 1f out: sn wknd* **7/4**[1]

166- **4** *10* **Flying Pickets (IRE)**[5] 7881 3-9-0 **73** SAJackson(7) 3 44+
(Alan McCabe) *v.s.a: a bhd* **4/1**[2]
010- **5** *8* **Laura's Bairn**[121] 5690 3-8-9 **61** JoeFanning 5
(J R Jenkins) *chsd ldrs: effrt on outer wl over 2f out: rdn wl over 1f out: sn wknd* **20/1**

1m 15.56s (-0.94) **Going Correction** -0.275s/f (Stan) **5** Ran SP% **111.8**
Speed ratings (Par 97): **95,92,89,76,65**
CSF £12.94 TOTE £2.30: £1.10, £3.40; EX 11.40.
Owner Mubarak Al Naemi **Bred** Vincent Dunne **Trained** Hambleton, N Yorks
■ Stewards' Enquiry : Phillip Makin three-day ban: weighed in 3lb heavy (Jan 15-16, 18)

FOCUS
A modest sprint handicap for 3yos.
Flying Pickets(IRE) Official explanation: jockey said gelding hung right leaving the stalls

7 BET AT BLUESQ.COM H'CAP 1m (F)
3:35 (3:36) (Class 6) (0-55,56) 4-Y-0+ **£1,704** (£503; £251) **Stalls** Low

Form RPR
011- **1** **Mataajir (USA)**[4] 7899 4-9-3 **56** 6ex GrahamGibbons 8 70+
(Derek Shaw) *chsd ldrs: hdwy on outer 3f out: rdn 2f out: styd on to ld ent fnl f: drvn out* **11/10**[1]
561- **2** *2 ½* **Spacecraft (IRE)**[17] 7775 5-8-11 **50** (b) JoeFanning 1 58
(Christopher Kellett) *trckd ldrs: hdwy over 2f out: rdn wl over 1f out: swtchd rt appr fnl f: styd on to take 2nd nr fin* **6/1**[2]
623- **3** *½* **Billy Cadiz**[16] 7781 7-8-11 **50** BarryMcHugh 5 57
(Julie Camacho) *cl up: led over 2f out: sn rdn: drvn and hdd ent fnl f: kpt on same pce: lost 2nd nr fin* **8/1**
045- **4** *1 ¾* **Phoenix Flame**[10] 7859 4-9-0 **53** (vt) ShaneKelly 3 56
(Alan McCabe) *led: rdn along over 3f out: hdd over 2f out: one pce appr fnl f* **12/1**
510- **5** *½* **Monsieur Pontaven**[22] 7714 5-9-2 **55** (b) DanielTudhope 2 57
(Robin Bastiman) *trckd ldrs on inner: hdwy 3f out: cl up 2f out: sn rdn and ev ch tl wknd appr fnl f* **20/1**
003- **6** *4* **Jay Jays Joy**[5] 7885 4-9-1 **54** (v) RussKennemore 11 46
(Paul Midgley) *n.m.r and in rr s: hdwy 1/2-way: chsd ldrs over 2f out: sn rdn and no imp* **11/1**
300- **7** *2* **Aggbag**[173] 3943 8-8-8 **47** LukeMorris 12 35
(Michael Appleby) *midfield: effrt over 3f out: sn rdn along and n.d* **33/1**
050- **8** *2 ½* **Like A Boy**[3] 7910 4-8-3 **49** JakePayne(7) 13 31
(Bill Turner) *a towards rr* **15/2**[3]
600- **9** *8* **Bentley**[22] 7720 8-9-2 **55** (b) PhillipMakin 10 37
(Brian Baugh) *chsd ldrs on outer: rdn along wl over 2f out: sn wknd* **14/1**
0P0- **10** *14* **Le Reveur**[4] 7787 10-8-0 **46** oh1 (e[1]) CharlesEddery(7) 6
(Richard Guest) *chsd ldrs whn stmbld bdly and rdr lost iron after 1f: bhd after* **66/1**
/00- **11** *6* **Dado Mush**[17] 7775 9-8-4 **46** oh1 (p) AdamBeschizza(3) 7
(Terry Clement) *dwlt: a in rr* **50/1**
046/ **12** *3 ¾* **Roman Sioux (IRE)**[14] 6077 5-8-8 **50** JulieBurke(3) 9
(Robin Bastiman) *a in rr* **50/1**

1m 41.05s (-2.65) **Going Correction** -0.275s/f (Stan) **12** Ran SP% **120.6**
Speed ratings (Par 101): **102,99,99,97,96 92,90,88,80,66 60,56**
toteswingers: 1&2 £2.80, 1&3 £2.60, 2&3 £5.30 CSF £7.50 CT £39.56 TOTE £1.60: £1.10, £2.20, £2.80; EX 8.40 Trifecta £40.00 Pool £676.55 - 12.50 winning units.
Owner Derek Shaw **Bred** Shadwell Australia Ltd **Trained** Sproxton, Leics

FOCUS
A moderate handicap and few ever got into it.
Bentley Official explanation: jockey said gelding hung left-handed
Dado Mush Official explanation: jockey said gelding lost its action
T/Plt: £86.80 to a £1 stake. Pool: £30,601.39 - 257.15 winning tickets T/Qpdt: £11.50 to a £1 stake. Pool: £2,691.60 - 171.80 winning tickets JR

[1]SOUTHWELL (L-H)
Monday, January 2

OFFICIAL GOING: Standard
Wind: Moderate, across Weather: Fine

8 5% WINNERS' BONUS AT BLUESQ.COM H'CAP 5f (F)
12:15 (12:55) (Class 6) (0-60,60) 4-Y-0+ **£1,704** (£503; £251) **Stalls** High

Form RPR
422- **1** **Argentine (IRE)**[11] 7854 8-9-1 **54** (b) TomEaves 5 66
(Ian Semple) *dwlt and squeezed out after s: sn swtchd lft and hdwy to trck ldrs: effrt 2f out: rdn to chal over 1f out: kpt on wl to ld last 100yds* **5/1**[2]
040- **2** *hd* **Fear Nothing**[59] 7266 5-9-4 **57** DanielTudhope 6 68
(David O'Meara) *slt ld: rdn over 1f out: edgd lft and drvn ins fnl f: hdd and no ex last 100yds* **11/4**[1]
202- **3** *1 ¾* **Gorgeous Goblin (IRE)**[6] 7886 5-8-10 **49** (t) JamesSullivan 1 54
(David C Griffiths) *chsd ldrs: hdwy 2f out: rdn and ev ch over 1f out: kpt on same pce* **5/1**[2]
2- **4** *1 ½* **Nafa (IRE)**[11] 7853 4-9-4 **57** RichardKingscote 2 57
(Michael Mullineaux) *prom: rdn along 2f out: wknd appr fnl f* **8/1**
050- **5** *1 ¼* **Divertimenti (IRE)**[12] 7844 8-9-4 **57** (bt) RussKennemore 4 52
(Roy Bowring) *chsd ldrs: rdn along and outpcd after 2f: styd on strly fnl f* **10/1**
600- **6** *shd* **Skylla**[12] 7844 5-9-4 **57** GrahamGibbons 12 52
(Derek Shaw) *racd towards stands' rail: chsd ldrs: rdn wl over 1f out: sn one pce* **10/1**
014- **7** *nse* **Steel City Boy (IRE)**[11] 7854 9-9-0 **60** DannyBrock(7) 8 55
(Garry Woodward) *cl up: rdn along 2f out: grad wknd* **16/1**
663- **8** *¾* **Flow Chart (IRE)**[214] 2655 5-8-7 **46** oh1 (b) JoeFanning 7 38
(Peter Grayson) *a towards rr* **66/1**
643- **9** *1* **Tancred Spirit**[11] 7854 4-8-8 **47** (v) BarryMcHugh 9 35
(Paul Midgley) *in tch: hdwy to chse ldrs 2f out: sn rdn and wknd appr fnl f* **16/1**
005- **10** *1* **Sharp Shoes**[11] 7853 5-9-5 **58** (p) WilliamCarson 3 43
(Ann Duffield) *in tch: rdn along over 2f out: sn wknd* **15/2**[3]
604- **11** *6* **Striking Willow**[13] 7829 4-8-7 **46** oh1 (b) JamesMillman 10
(Rod Millman) *a in rr* **50/1**
050- **12** *12* **Egyptian Lord**[79] 6875 9-8-7 **46** oh1 (b) LukeMorris 11
(Peter Grayson) *a in rr* **100/1**

58.39s (-1.31) **Going Correction** -0.20s/f (Stan) **12** Ran SP% **117.3**
Speed ratings (Par 101): **102,101,98,96,94 94,94,93,91,89 80,61**
toteswingers:1&2:£4.80, 2&3:£4.90, 1&3:£3.10 CSF £18.79 CT £74.15 TOTE £3.70: £1.10, £1.60, £3.50; EX 25.60 Trifecta £120.00 Pool: £366.65 - 2.26 winning units..
Owner Robert Reid **Bred** Tony Hirschfeld & L K Piggott **Trained** Carluke, S Lanarks
■ Stewards' Enquiry : James Sullivan two-day ban; excessive use of whip (16th-18th Jan)

FOCUS
A modest handicap but competitive enough for the grade and the first two are likely to remain of interest at a similar level in the coming weeks. Straightforward form. The action took place centre to far side.
Gorgeous Goblin(IRE) Official explanation: jockey said that the mare hung right throughout

9 PLAY GOLF AND RACING AT SOUTHWELL AMATEUR RIDERS' H'CAP 2m (F)
12:50 (12:51) (Class 6) (0-65,65) 4-Y-0+ **£1,646** (£506; £253) **Stalls** Low

Form RPR
014- **1** **Captain Bellamy (USA)**[139] 5145 4-10-3 **65** MissNDumelow(5) 2 75+
(Hughie Morrison) *a.p: hdwy 3f out: rdn to ld over 1f out: kpt on* **3/1**[1]
305- **2** *3* **Turjuman (USA)**[14] 7817 7-10-3 **60** (p) MissAlexOwen(7) 13 67
(Alan Bailey) *in tch: hdwy to chse ldng pair 4f out: rdn to ld over 2f out: hdd over 1f out and kpt on same pce* **9/1**
360- **3** *1 ½* **Delorain (IRE)**[54] 7331 9-9-7 **50** (p) MissCScott(7) 10 54
(William Stone) *midfield: hdwy 4f out: rdn 3f out: kpt on fnl 2f: nrst fin* **7/1**[3]
040- **4** *4 ½* **Harare**[20] 7426 11-9-10 **51** (v) GemmaTutty(5) 8 50
(Karen Tutty) *hld up towards rr: hdwy 4f out: styd on fnl 2f: nvr gng pce to rch ldrs* **33/1**
503- **5** *½* **Bring It On Home**[27] 7574 8-9-7 **50** (b) MissSKerswell(7) 9 48
(Brendan Powell) *in rr: rdn along and bhd 1/2-way: styd on fnl 3f: nvr a factor* **14/1**
313- **6** *½* **Squad**[25] 7674 6-10-9 **64** (be) MrJCoffill-Brown(5) 11 62
(Simon Dow) *hld up in rr: hdwy 6f out: rdn along to chse ldrs over 3f out: sn one pce* **4/1**[2]
305- **7** *6* **Miereveld**[3] 7920 5-9-8 **49** ow2 (b) MrOGarner(5) 5 39
(Shaun Harris) *cl up: led 1/2-way: rdn along over 3f out: hdd over 2f out and sn wknd* **28/1**
065- **8** *2* **William's Way**[34] 7574 10-10-5 **55** (t) MrSWalker 7 43
(Ian Wood) *hld up in rr: hdwy 7f out: in tch 4f out: sn rdn and btn* **4/1**[2]
044- **9** *4* **Carlton Scroop (FR)**[14] 7816 9-10-0 **55** (b) MissMBryant(5) 3 38
(Paddy Butler) *led to 1/2-way: cl up: rdn along over 3f out: sn wknd* **20/1**
430- **10** *24* **Treacle Tart**[45] 7461 7-10-6 **63** MrDIrving(7) 4 17
(James Ewart) *midfield: rdn along 1/2-way: sn lost pl and bhd* **20/1**
000- **11** *10* **Herrera (IRE)**[12] 7850 7-10-0 **57** (p) MrJHamilton(7) 12
(Richard Fahey) *chsd ldrs: rdn along 6f out: sn wknd* **33/1**
0/0- **12** *18* **Rustic Gold**[193] 3300 8-10-4 **54** MissCarolineHurley 6
(Richard Ford) *prom: rdn along 7f out: sn wknd* **66/1**

3m 43.44s (-2.06) **Going Correction** -0.20s/f (Stan)
WFA 4 from 5yo+ 7lb **12** Ran SP% **114.5**
Speed ratings (Par 101): **97,95,94,92,92 92,89,88,86,74 69,60**
toteswingers: 1&2 £6.20, 1&3 £4.80, 2&3 £10.10 CSF £26.72 CT £173.59 TOTE £3.10: £1.10, £4.20, £2.40; EX 27.90 Trifecta £118.50 Pool: £286.72 - 1.79 winning units..
Owner H Morrison **Bred** Brereton C Jones **Trained** East Ilsley, Berks

FOCUS
Only two of these had finished placed on their most recent Flat start and not form to get carried away with, although it seems sound and the winner is progressive. A fair pace really picked up after halfway when the field quickly got strung out.

10 FOLLOW SOUTHWELL RACECOURSE ON TWITTER MAIDEN STKS 1m 4f (F)
1:20 (1:20) (Class 5) 4-Y-0+ **£2,264** (£673; £336; £168) **Stalls** Low

Form RPR
3- **1** **Chabada (JPN)**[110] 6054 4-8-12 0 JamieSpencer 1 74
(Ian Williams) *trckd ldrs: hdwy over 4f out: cl up 3f out: rdn 2f out: drvn ent fnl f: kpt on to ld last 100yds* **3/1**[2]
205- **2** *½* **White Fusion**[82] 3734 4-9-3 57 ShaneKelly 7 78
(Andrew Crook) *trckd ldrs: hdwy 4f out: cl up 3f out: rdn 2f out: led over 1f out: sn drvn: hdd and no ex last 100yds* **66/1**
230- **3** *6* **Eyedoro (USA)**[60] 7255 4-9-3 75 JoeFanning 2 69
(Mark Johnston) *trckd ldr: led over 4f out: rdn over 2f out: drvn and hdd over 1f out: sn one pce* **5/1**[3]
332- **4** *11* **Bravestofthebrave (USA)**[23] 7712 4-9-3 76 SteveDrowne 6 51
(John Gosden) *dwlt and sn pushed along to chse ldrs: rdn along 1/2-way: drvn along over 4f out: sn outpcd* **8/13**[1]
3- **5** *11* **Vehement**[11] 7856 6-8-13 0 SimonPearce(3) 4 28
(Andy Turnell) *in rr: hdwy over 3f out: sn rdn and nvr a factor* **33/1**
600- **6** *45* **Mrs Medley**[20] 7747 6-9-2 27 (b) GrahamGibbons 5
(Garry Woodward) *led: rdn along and hdd over 4f out: sn wknd* **200/1**

2m 36.72s (-4.28) **Going Correction** -0.20s/f (Stan)
WFA 4 from 5yo+ 4lb **6** Ran SP% **108.5**
Speed ratings (Par 103): **106,105,101,94,87 57**
toteswingers: 1&2 £6.00, 1&3 £1.40, 2&3 £6.10 CSF £99.83 TOTE £3.30: £1.10, £8.80; EX 85.70.
Owner Dr Marwan Koukash **Bred** Flaxman Holdings Limited **Trained** Portway, Worcs

FOCUS
No more than a modest maiden with the 57-rated runner-up having looked a doubtful stayer beforehand and the odds-on favourite running a stinker. The winner and third set a fair standard though. The pace was only fair.
Bravestofthebrave(USA) Official explanation: jockey said that the gelding was never travelling

11 DOWNLOAD THE BLUE SQUARE IPHONE APP H'CAP 7f (F)
1:50 (1:50) (Class 4) (0-85,81) 4-Y-0+ **£4,204** (£1,251; £625; £312) **Stalls** Low

Form RPR
364- **1** **Tewin Wood**[58] 7299 5-8-11 **74** DominicFox(3) 6 82
(Alan Bailey) *cl up: led wl over 2f out: drvn over 1f out: edgd lft ins fnl f: kpt on gamely towards fin* **16/1**
311- **2** *½* **Global Village (IRE)**[20] 7744 7-9-3 **77** BarryMcHugh 1 84
(Brian Ellison) *in rr and rdn along 1/2-way: hdwy on inner 2f out: drvn and styd on ins fnl f: ev ch tl no ex nr fin* **11/8**[1]
301- **3** *½* **Maverik**[94] 6505 4-9-2 **76** RichardKingscote 3 81
(Ralph Beckett) *led: rdn along 3f out: hdd over 2f out: rallied u.p and kpt on fnl f* **13/2**[3]
451- **4** *1* **Tamareen (IRE)**[23] 7716 4-9-3 **77** TonyHamilton 7 80
(Richard Fahey) *trckd ldrs: hdwy and cl up 2f out: sn rdn and ev ch tl drvn and one pce fnl f* **18/1**
321- **5** *1* **Il Battista**[18] 7771 4-9-2 **76** (be) ShaneKelly 5 76
(Alan McCabe) *trckd ldrs: hdwy on outer over 2f out: rdn wl over 1f out: kpt on same pce* **3/1**[2]
030- **6** *shd* **Levitate**[25] 7675 4-9-0 **81** (v) SAJackson(7) 4 81
(Alan McCabe) *dwlt: hdwy over 3f out: rdn over 2f out: kpt on same pce* **12/1**

243- **7** 2¾ **J R Hartley**[41] 7502 4-9-1 **75**....(e) TomEaves 2 67
(Bryan Smart) *cl up: rdn along 3f out: sn wknd* **15/2**

1m 27.44s (-2.86) **Going Correction** -0.20s/f (Stan) 7 Ran SP% **111.0**
Speed ratings (Par 105): **108,107,106,105,104 104,101**
toteswingers: 1&2 £4.80, 1&3 £13.60, 2&3 £3.20 CSF £36.51 TOTE £22.00: £6.00, £1.30; EX 56.20.
Owner North Cheshire Trading & Storage Ltd **Bred** Perle D'Or Partnership **Trained** Newmarket, Suffolk

FOCUS
Only seven runners but four of them had won last time out, albeit all in lower grade, and it was competitive enough for all it wasn't as strong a race as the 0-85 rating band might imply. Straightforward form. The pace was only fair.

12 MEMBERSHIP OF SOUTHWELL GOLF CLUB CLAIMING STKS 1m (F)
2:20 (2:22) (Class 6) 4-Y-0+ **£1,704** (£503; £251) Stalls Low

Form RPR

014- **1** **Mcconnell (USA)**[23] 7710 7-8-11 72....(b) WilliamCarson 1 72
(Richard Guest) *trckd ldng pair: hdwy on outer 3f out: chal over 2f out: sn rdn: styd on u.p to ld ins fnl f* **4/1**[3]

412- **2** ¾ **Sunnyside Tom (IRE)**[72] 6006 8-9-1 80.... TonyHamilton 2 74
(Richard Fahey) *led: rdn along 2f out: drvn over 1f out: hdd and one pce fnl f* **11/10**[1]

064- **3** ½ **Horatio Carter**[11] 7857 7-8-9 63....(p) TomEaves 4 67
(David O'Meara) *trckd ldng pair: hdwy over 2f out: rdn to chal over 1f out and ev ch tl drvn and no ex ins fnl f* **9/4**[2]

020- **4** 23 **Kheskianto (IRE)**[104] 6235 6-8-3 45....(bt) AdamBeschizza(3) 5 11
(Michael Chapman) *dwlt: sn cl up: rdn along 3f out and sn wknd* **40/1**

1m 42.15s (-1.55) **Going Correction** -0.20s/f (Stan) 4 Ran SP% **100.8**
Speed ratings (Par 101): **99,98,97,74**
CSF £7.77 TOTE £3.20; EX 7.90.
Owner Rakebackmypoker.com **Bred** Hall Et Al Farm **Trained** Stainforth, S Yorks

FOCUS
A good finish to an ordinary claimer run run at just a modest pace to the home turn. The form is rated around the winner. William Morgan was withdrawn after unseating his rider at the stalls.

13 GOLF BEFORE RACING AT SOUTHWELL H'CAP 6f (F)
2:55 (2:58) (Class 5) (0-70,70) 4-Y-0+ **£2,264** (£673; £336; £168) Stalls Low

Form RPR

300- **1** **Upper Lambourn (IRE)**[20] 7746 4-9-6 **69**.... PhillipMakin 2 82+
(Jamie Osborne) *towards rr: swtchd lft 2f out: gd hdwy on inner over 1f out: sn rdn and str run ent fnl f to ld last 50yds* **15/2**

053- **2** 1 **Mazovian (USA)**[6] 7887 4-8-8 **60**.... AdamBeschizza(3) 3 70
(Michael Chapman) *towards rr and rdn along after 2f: hdwy over 2f out: chsd ldr ins fnl f: led briefly tl hdd and no ex last 50yds* **12/1**

522- **3** ¾ **Greenhead High**[22] 7728 4-8-11 **60**.... AdrianNicholls 6 67+
(David Nicholls) *sn led: wd st: rdn 2f out: drvn and hdd wl ins fnl f: no ex* **6/1**[2]

303- **4** ¾ **Elhamri**[11] 7857 8-9-2 **65**.... HayleyTurner 1 70
(Conor Dore) *trckd ldrs: hdwy 2f out: sn rdn and kpt on same pce fnl f* **6/1**[2]

502- **5** 1 **El Dececy (USA)**[20] 7744 8-9-7 **70**....(t) WilliamCarson 8 72
(Richard Guest) *prom: chsd ldr 1/2-way: rdn over 2f out: one pce appr fnl f* **10/1**

046- **6** 2¾ **Incomparable**[20] 7744 7-9-1 **64**....(b) GrahamGibbons 5 57
(Scott Dixon) *in tch: hdwy over 2f out: sn rdn and no imp appr fnl f* **7/1**[3]

000- **7** hd **Sir Mozart (IRE)**[46] 7448 9-9-0 **63**.... ShaneKelly 7 55
(Barney Curley) *dwlt: towards rr tl styd on fnl 2f* **33/1**

350- **8** 1 **Ace Of Spies (IRE)**[5] 7897 7-8-13 **62**....(b) JamesSullivan 14 51
(Conor Dore) *cl up on outer: rdn to chal 2f out and ev ch tl wknd over 1f out* **18/1**

344- **9** 1¾ **Spitfire**[20] 7744 7-9-4 **67**....(v) FrederikTylicki 12 51
(J R Jenkins) *hld up: a towards rr* **4/1**[1]

023- **10** 1¾ **Cyflymder (IRE)**[20] 7748 6-8-8 **62**....(p) MarkCoumbe(5) 13 40
(David C Griffiths) *nvr nr ldrs* **8/1**

000- **11** 6 **Forty Proof (IRE)**[5] 7893 4-9-0 **70**....(tp) RobJFitzpatrick(7) 11 29
(Alan McCabe) *chsd ldrs: rdn wl over 2f out: sn wknd* **33/1**

000- **12** 14 **Sir Louis**[20] 7746 5-9-0 **63**.... TonyHamilton 9
(Richard Fahey) *prom: rdn along wl over 2f out: sn wknd* **20/1**

1m 15.09s (-1.41) **Going Correction** -0.20s/f (Stan) 12 Ran SP% **116.6**
Speed ratings (Par 103): **101,99,98,97,96 92,92,91,88,86 78,59**
toteswingers: 1&2 £23.80, 1&3 £10.00, 2&3 £13.70 CSF £90.40 CT £573.47 TOTE £10.20: £2.80, £3.20, £3.00; EX 146.90 Trifecta £515.50 Pool: £696.68 - 0.20 winning units..
Owner L S M Building Contractors **Bred** Messrs Derek Gibbons & Peter Gibbons **Trained** Upper Lambourn, Berks
■ Stewards' Enquiry : Adam Beschizza two-day ban; excessive use of whip (16th-18th Jan)

FOCUS
A fair handicap that was run at a good pace and there seemed no advantage either being held up or prominent. The winner was the least exposed of these and is likely to do a bit better.
Spitfire Official explanation: vet said that the gelding finished distressed
Sir Louis Official explanation: vet said gelding bled from the nose

14 PLAY ROULETTE AT BLUESQ.COM/CASINO H'CAP 7f (F)
3:30 (3:31) (Class 6) (0-55,55) 4-Y-0+ **£1,704** (£503; £251) Stalls Low

Form RPR

125- **1** **Dashing Eddie (IRE)**[17] 7781 4-9-1 **54**....(p) PhillipMakin 9 69+
(Kevin Ryan) *chsd ldrs: rdn along on outer wl over 2f out: styd on to ld over 1f out: kpt on strly* **9/2**[2]

00- **2** 2 **Raise The Rafters (IRE)**[27] 7648 7-8-13 **52**....(t) FrankieMcDonald 7 62+
(Pat Murphy) *towards rr: rdn along 1/2-way: hdwy wl over 1f out: fin wl* **50/1**

402- **3** 2¾ **Fluctuation (IRE)**[4] 7911 4-8-12 **51**....(b) StevieDonohoe 12 53
(Ian Williams) *in tch: hdwy on outer 2f out: sn rdn and kpt on appr fnl f: nrst fin* **9/2**[2]

003- **4** ½ **Pilgrim Dancer (IRE)**[5] 7899 5-8-8 **50**....(b) AmyRyan(3) 4 51
(Tony Coyle) *chse ldrs: hdwy 3f out: rdn to chal 2f out: ev ch tl drvn and wknd ent fnl f* **6/1**[3]

050- **5** 1¼ **Fathey (IRE)**[61] 7230 6-8-7 **46** oh1....(t) MartinLane 5 43
(Charles Smith) *in tch: hdwy to chse ldrs over 2f out: sn rdn and no imp* **40/1**

000- **6** ½ **Crocodile Bay (IRE)**[93] 6541 9-8-7 **46** oh1....(b) WilliamCarson 11 42
(Richard Guest) *cl up: rdn wl over 2f out: ev ch tl wknd over 1f out* **25/1**

061- **7** 1¾ **Seamster**[17] 7781 5-9-2 **55**....(vt) FrederikTylicki 10 46
(Richard Ford) *led: rdn along 2f out: hdd over 1f out: sn wknd* **9/2**[2]

544- **8** 6 **St Ignatius**[5] 7899 5-8-9 **48**....(p) LukeMorris 1 23
(Michael Appleby) *in rr and rdn along 1/2-way: nvr a factor* **7/2**[1]

000- **9** 5 **Bertbrand**[17] 7785 7-8-4 **46** oh1....(b) JulieBurke(3) 6
(Ian McInnes) *chsd ldrs on inner: rdn along 3f out: sn wknd* **100/1**

002- **10** 3½ **Twennyshortkid**[17] 7781 4-8-11 **50**....(b) BarryMcHugh 8
(Paul Midgley) *a in rr* **9/1**

505- **11** 2 **Kwik Time**[145] 4930 4-8-7 **46**.... TomEaves 2
(Robin Bastiman) *a in rr: bhd fr 1/2-way* **20/1**

1m 29.56s (-0.74) **Going Correction** -0.20s/f (Stan) 11 Ran SP% **115.1**
Speed ratings (Par 101): **96,93,90,90,88 88,86,79,73,69 67**
toteswingers: 1&2 £31.50, 1&3 £4.60, 2&3 £41.40 CSF £218.38 CT £1081.48 TOTE £5.70: £2.10, £17.50, £1.80; EX 184.30 Trifecta £689.30 Pool: £931.59 - 0.82 winning units..
Owner T A Rahman **Bred** Scuderia San Pancrazio Sas **Trained** Hambleton, N Yorks
■ Stewards' Enquiry : Amy Ryan seven-day ban; excessive use of whip (16th-23th Jan)

FOCUS
A low-grade finale run at a decent pace. The winner is on the upgrade.
St Ignatius Official explanation: jockey said gelding was unsuited by kickback.
T/Jkpt: £37,138.00 to a £1 stake. Pool: £52,307.12. 1.00 winning ticket. T/Plt: £367.60 to a £1 stake. Pool £69,367.02. 137.75 winning tickets. T/Qpdt: £146.30 to a £1 stake. Pool: £4,310.52. 21.80 winning tickets. JR

DEAUVILLE (R-H)
Monday, January 2

OFFICIAL GOING: Fibresand: standard

15a PRIX DE COLOMBIERES (CLAIMER) (4YO FILLIES) (FIBRESAND) 7f 110y
11:30 (12:00) 4-Y-0 **£6,666** (£2,666; £2,000; £1,333; £666)

RPR

1 **The Turtle (FR)**[16] 4-9-2 0....(p) SylvainRuis 10 73
(A Junk, France) **27/1**

2 snk **Heidikly (FR)**[26] 7667 4-9-6 0.... Francois-XavierBertras 4 77
(B De Montzey, France) **3/1**[1]

3 nk **Fille D'Avril (FR)**[16] 4-8-13 0.... MathieuAndrouin 9 69
(E Leenders, France) **27/1**

4 nk **Finefrenzyrolling (IRE)**[26] 7658 4-8-10 0 ow1....(p) MartinHarley 6 66
(Mrs K Burke) *broke fast: restrained in midfield: racd freely: swtchd towards stands' rail early in st: rdn and picked up wl over 1f out: ev ch 150yds out: wnt 2nd 100yds out: r.o wl: lost 2nd cl home* **9/1**[3]

5 1¼ **Heaven's Gift (GER)**[17] 4-8-13 0....(b[1]) IoritzMendizabal 11 65
(S Smrczek, Germany) **9/2**[2]

6 ½ **Golden Speed (SPA)**[11] 4-8-9 0....(b) MatthieuAutier(4) 2 64
(L A Urbano-Grajales, France) **3/1**[1]

7 3½ **Lamora**[17] 4-8-9 0.... WilliamsSaraiva 7 51
(Mme J Bidgood, France) **37/1**

8 nse **Samantha Glaz (IRE)**[96] 4-8-7 0.... ChristopherGrosbois(6) 14 55
(C Plisson, France) **74/1**

9 nk **A Moment With You (IRE)**[26] 4-8-9 0....(p) AlexisBadel 13 51
(F-X De Chevigny, France) **12/1**

10 ½ **Fatara Froto (FR)**[17] 4-9-2 0.... FabienLefebvre 16 56
(Y-M Porzier, France) **30/1**

0 **Irish Chope (FR)**[80] 4-9-0 0.... TonyPiccone 15
(C Boutin, France) **22/1**

0 **Echappee Belle**[17] 4-8-10 0....(b[1]) CesarPasserat(6) 1
(F Vermeulen, France) **23/1**

0 **Dancing All Night**[445] 6859 4-8-10 0 ow1.... ThomasHuet 8
(Mme J Hendriks, Holland) **30/1**

0 **Star Dust Melody (FR)**[11] 4-9-1 0.... ElliotCanal(5) 12
(N Caullery, France) **27/1**

0 **April Love Song (USA)**[80] 4-9-0 0.... AlexandreRoussel 3
(S Kobayashi, France) **34/1**

1m 30.8s (90.80) 15 Ran SP% **118.4**
WIN (incl. 1 euro stake): 27.50. PLACES: 7.30, 2.10, 7.30. DF: 66.60. SF: 81.00.
Owner A Junk **Bred** Alain Junk **Trained** France

16a PRIX DES RESNIERS (CLAIMER) (4YO COLTS & GELDINGS) (FIBRESAND) 7f 110y
12:00 (12:00) 4-Y-0 **£6,666** (£2,666; £2,000; £1,333; £666)

RPR

1 **Olynthos (IRE)**[25] 4-8-9 0.... JeromeClaudic 10 73
(C Laffon-Parias, France) **27/1**

2 1¾ **Beat The Ground (IRE)**[17] 4-8-4 0.... EddyHardouin(5) 14 69
(Robert Collet, France) **15/1**

3 nk **Bearheart (IRE)**[67] 4-8-13 0....(b) AlexandreRoussel 4 72
(P Monfort, France) **32/1**

4 nk **Aquilifer (IRE)**[28] 7637 4-9-6 0.... MartinHarley 11 79
(Mrs K Burke) *broke wl: prom bhd ldrs on outside: rdn over 1 1/2f out: r.o wl ins fnl f to go 4th cl home* **9/1**[3]

5 nk **Ciel De Jade (FR)**[46] 4-9-0 0....(p) JulienAuge 2 72
(B Goudot, France) **26/1**

6 hd **Lewis De La Vis (FR)**[17] 4-8-9 0....(p) SebastienMaillot 9 66
(D Windrif, France) **15/1**

7 nk **Marpol (ITY)**[17] 4-9-4 0.... ThomasHuet 5 75
(G Botti, Italy) **9/5**[1]

8 shd **Vespa Blue (FR)**[17] 4-8-13 0....(p) MickaelForest 15 69
(P Demercastel, France) **39/1**

9 ¾ **Loch Garry (IRE)**[7] 4-8-9 0.... NicolasGauffenic(8) 6 71
(C Boutin, France) **58/10**[2]

10 ¾ **Venetien (FR)**[125] 4-8-10 0....(b) CesarPasserat(6) 12 69
(F Vermeulen, France) **11/1**

0 **Domino Rock (FR)**[17] 4-8-8 0....(p) SoufyaneMoulin(8) 7
(C Boutin, France) **13/1**

0 **Bolt (FR)**[53] 4-8-6 0.... PierreHouel(8) 8
(M Boutin, France) **30/1**

0 **Perpignon (FR)**[226] 4-8-9 0....(p) FilipMinarik 1
(Mme C Janssen, Belgium) **44/1**

0 **Cash Des Aigles (FR)**[6] 4-8-7 0....(p) ChristopherGrosbois(6) 13
(C Plisson, France) **38/1**

0 **Tobey (IRE)**[75] 4-8-13 0.... APietsch 16
(W Hickst, Germany) **21/1**

0 **Valmerovic (FR)**[25] 4-8-9 0....(p) IoritzMendizabal 3
(J Boisnard, France) **23/1**

1m 30.4s (90.40) 16 Ran SP% **117.9**
WIN (incl. 1 euro stake): 28.10. PLACES: 10.40, 5.70, 9.40. DF: 146.20. SF: 345.70.
Owner Leonidas Marinopoulos **Bred** Fiona Craig & S Couldridge **Trained** Chantilly, France

17a PRIX DE PASSE TEMPS (CLAIMER) (3YO) (FIBRESAND) 6f 110y
1:05 (12:00) 3-Y-O £8,333 (£3,333; £2,500; £1,666; £833)

RPR

1 **Ma Victoryan (FR)**[17] 7814 3-8-8 0.......................... AurelienLemaitre 6 80
(C Baillet, France) **192/10**

2 2 ½ **Class Monitor**[17] 7814 3-8-13 0.......................... MartinHarley 8 78
(Mrs K Burke) *racd midfield on rail: swtchd away fr rail bef st: hrd rdn and swtchd bk towards rail 1 1/2f out: r.o strly ins fnl f to go 2nd: no ch w wnr* **11/2**[2]

3 *nse* **Princess Vati (FR)**[26] 7665 3-8-8 0.......................... JeromeCabre 9 73
(S Wattel, France) **13/1**

4 ¾ **Singapore Sand (FR)**[11] 3-8-11 0.......................... FabriceVeron 3 74
(H-A Pantall, France) **78/10**[3]

5 *hd* **Picante (IRE)**[53] 3-8-8 0..........................(p) JohanVictoire 7 70
(C Boutin, France) **9/1**

6 ½ **Cruel Summer (FR)** 3-8-8 0.......................... SylvainRuis 10 69
(J-F Bernard, France) **22/1**

7 1 ¼ **Sonik (FR)**[11] 3-8-6 0.......................... RomainAuray(5) 4 68
(J Heloury, France) **29/1**

8 *hd* **Caraside (FR)**[11] 3-9-3 0.......................... ThierryThulliez 11 74
(S Wattel, France) **23/10**[1]

9 2 **Anabaa Stone (FR)**[53] 3-9-1 0..........................(b) FlavienPrat 14 66
(T Clout, France) **12/1**

10 1 ½ **Safina Blue (FR)**[17] 3-8-8 0..........................(p) IoritzMendizabal 5 54
(Y Barberot, France) **12/1**

0 **Villerambert (FR)**[12] 3-8-11 0..........................(b) JulienAuge 2
(H-A Pantall, France) **33/1**

0 **Golden Beet (FR)**[80] 3-8-8 0..........................(b[1]) SebastienMaillot 1
(Mlle Valerie Boussin, France) **81/1**

0 **Mossa (IRE)**[171] 3-8-8 0.......................... WilliamsSaraiva 12
(Mme J Bidgood, France) **36/1**

0 **Stronger (FR)**[17] 7814 3-8-6 0.......................... AnthonyCaramanolis(5) 16
(N Clement, France) **13/1**

0 **Miss Mauresque (FR)**[11] 3-8-3 0.......................... MarcLerner(5) 15
(C Lerner, France) **97/1**

1m 18.7s (78.70) **15** Ran SP% **117.2**
WIN (incl. 1 euro stake): 20.20. PLACES: 5.00, 2.60, 4.00. DF: 39.50. SF: 81.30.
Owner Alain Millard **Bred** Comunidad Hereditar Quereda H. **Trained** France

18a PRIX DE LA VALLEE DE LA SEINE (H'CAP) (4YO+) (FIBRESAND) 7f 110y
3:35 (12:00) 4-Y-O+ £11,666 (£4,666; £3,500; £2,333; £1,166)

RPR

1 **Nenzo (GER)**[16] 6-9-6 **0**.......................... IoritzMendizabal 7 87
(Mme N Verheyen, Belgium) **17/5**[1]

2 *hd* **Birthday Sun (GER)**[26] 4-9-6 **0**.......................... APietsch 5 86
(W Hickst, Germany) **15/1**

3 *snk* **Sargasses (FR)**[16] 6-9-5 **0**.......................... Francois-XavierBertras 10 85
(Mlle V Dissaux, France) **11/1**

4 ½ **Stelrock (FR)**[16] 5-9-1 **0**..........................(b) JohanVictoire 11 79
(R Chotard, France) **14/1**

5 *shd* **Rovos (FR)**[26] 4-9-4 **0**.......................... ThierryThulliez 3 82
(S Wattel, France) **7/1**[2]

6 *snk* **Caraziyan (FR)**[25] 6-9-6 **0**.......................... SebastienMaillot 6 84
(M Boutin, France) **20/1**

7 *hd* **Ohne Tadel (GER)**[16] 5-9-0 **0**.......................... FilipMinarik 8 77
(S Smrczek, Germany) **10/1**

8 1 ½ **Lonsome Drive (FR)**[11] 5-9-5 **0**.......................... AlexisBadel 12 79
(Y De Nicolay, France) **24/1**

9 *hd* **Bold Marc (IRE)**[58] 7314 10-8-11 **0**..........................(p) MartinHarley 9 70
(Mrs K Burke) *broke smartly: sn led: chal and u.p over 1f out: hdd ent fnl f: no ex: wknd* **101/1**

10 *nse* **Royally**[25] 6-9-4 **0**..........................(b) AlexandreRoussel 4 77
(Mlle S-V Tarrou, France) **25/1**

0 **Vantage Point (FR)**[16] 9-9-0 **0**..........................(p) AlexisAchard(3) 14
(Mlle C Cardenne, France) **20/1**

0 **Alkmaar**[184] 5-9-6 **0**..........................(p) TonyPiccone 15
(J Reynier, France) **9/1**[3]

0 **Jag War (FR)**[17] 4-9-6 **0**.......................... FabriceVeron 2
(H-A Pantall, France) **7/1**[2]

0 **Jolie Noce (FR)**[26] 4-9-2 **0**.......................... ThomasHuet 1
(F Doumen, France) **17/1**

0 **Inarco (FR)**[16] 4-8-11 **0**.......................... FlavienPrat 13
(Mlle V Dissaux, France) **22/1**

0 **Frenesia**[16] 4-8-8 **0**.......................... MarcLerner(3) 16
(C Lerner, France) **73/1**

1m 29.5s (89.50) **16** Ran SP% **117.7**
WIN (incl. 1 euro stake): 4.40. PLACES: 2.20, 5.90, 3.50. DF: 33.10. SF: 46.00.
Owner Stall Molenhof **Bred** Stal Molenhof **Trained** Belgium

[8]SOUTHWELL (L-H)
Tuesday, January 3

OFFICIAL GOING: Standard
Wind: Fresh behind Weather: Overcast

19 BLUE SQUARE WINTER CARNIVAL IPHONE APP CLAIMING STKS 6f (F)
12:25 (12:25) (Class 6) 4-Y-0+ £1,704 (£503; £251) Stalls Low

Form RPR

056- 1 **Dickie Le Davoir**[3] 7942 8-8-4 63..........................(b) CharlesEddery(7) 6 74
(Richard Guest) *dwlt and in rr: hdwy on inner 1/2-way: rdn to ld over 1f out: kpt on wl* **14/1**

501- 2 1 ¼ **Ingleby Arch (USA)**[23] 7726 9-8-11 78 ow2.............. GrahamGibbons 2 70
(David Barron) *sn pushed along to chse ldng pair: swtchd rt to outer after 2f: wd st and hdwy 2f out: sn drvn and styd on same pce fnl f* **5/6**[1]

230- 3 1 ¼ **Salerosa (IRE)**[12] 7857 7-8-0 67..........................(p) LukeMorris 4 55
(Ann Duffield) *chsd ldrs: pushed along 1/2-way: hdwy 2f out: sn rdn and kpt on fnl f* **4/1**[3]

104- 4 ½ **Punching**[6] 7893 8-9-1 72.......................... HayleyTurner 5 68
(Conor Dore) *cl up: led wl over 2f out: sn rdn: hdd over 1f out and wknd ent fnl f* **11/4**[2]

000- 5 9 **Sophie's Beau (USA)**[28] 7646 5-8-2 43..............(p) AdamBeschizza(3) 3 30
(Michael Chapman) *led: rdn along and hdd wl over 2f out: sn wknd* **100/1**

600- 6 2 ¾ **Bravo King (IRE)**[14] 7832 4-9-7 72..........................(t) MartinHarley 1 37
(Richard Guest) *s.i.s: a bhd* **25/1**

1m 14.25s (-2.25) **Going Correction** -0.15s/f (Stan) **6** Ran SP% **112.7**
Speed ratings (Par 101): **109,107,105,105,93 89**
toteswingers: 1&2 £2.30, 1&3 £4.00, 2&3 £1.40. CSF £26.85 TOTE £15.20: £5.90, £1.30; EX 32.40.
Owner Mick White **Bred** P And Mrs A G Venner **Trained** Stainforth, S Yorks

FOCUS
Fair form in a claimer which was run at a good gallop. Tricky form to pin down, with the winner stepping up on recent efforts.

20 SOUTHWELL-RACECOURSE.CO.UK MAIDEN FILLIES' STKS 6f (F)
12:55 (12:55) (Class 5) 3-Y-O+ £2,264 (£673; £336; £168) Stalls Low

Form RPR

5- 1 **Blaugrana (IRE)**[20] 7757 3-8-8 0.......................... LukeMorris 5 72+
(John Gosden) *trckd ldrs: hdwy to ld over 3f out: shkn up and pushed clr wl over 1f out: kpt on* **4/9**[1]

000- 2 3 ¼ **Arrivaderci**[28] 7641 4-9-3 57..........................(e) CharlesEddery(7) 1 62
(Richard Guest) *towards rr: hdwy on inner over 2f out: sn rdn and styd on to take 2nd ins fnl f* **8/1**[3]

200- 3 1 ½ **Diamond Finesse (IRE)**[13] 7838 3-8-8 66..........................(b) ChrisCatlin 4 53
(Ed Dunlop) *cl up: green and pushed along home turn: sn chsng wnr: rdn 2f out and kpt on same pce* **4/1**[2]

030- 4 13 **Romany Spirit (IRE)**[82] 6821 3-8-8 58.......................... MichaelStainton 7 11
(Jason Ward) *s.i.s and bhd: styd on inner fnl 2f: nvr nr ldrs* **12/1**

5- 5 *nk* **Darcy May**[5] 7913 4-9-10 0.......................... GrahamGibbons 2 14
(Garry Woodward) *led: rdn along and hdd over 3f out: sn wknd* **40/1**

00- 6 3 ¼ **Miss Bloom**[18] 7784 3-8-8 0.......................... KellyHarrison 3
(Garry Woodward) *cl up: rdn along 1/2-way: sn wknd* **100/1**

00- 7 6 **La Danse Champetre**[24] 7710 4-9-10 0.......................... MartinLane 6
(Charles Smith) *a in rr* **100/1**

1m 17.16s (0.66) **Going Correction** -0.15s/f (Stan)
WFA 3 from 4yo 16lb **7** Ran SP% **112.5**
Speed ratings (Par 100): **89,84,82,65,64 60,52**
toteswingers: 1&2 £2.00, 1&3 £1.70, 2&3 £2.10. CSF £4.74 TOTE £1.60: £1.10, £1.70; EX 4.90.
Owner Prince A A Faisal **Bred** Nawara Stud Co Ltd **Trained** Newmarket, Suffolk

FOCUS
A most one-sided maiden.

21 SOUTHWELL-RACECOURSE.CO.UK (S) H'CAP 7f (F)
1:25 (1:25) (Class 6) (0-60,60) 4-Y-O+ £1,704 (£503; £251) Stalls Low

Form RPR

600- 1 **Fibs And Flannel**[28] 7641 5-9-7 **60**..........................(p) AndrewMullen 4 69
(Tony Coyle) *trckd ldrs: hdwy 1/2-way: led wl over 2f out: rdn wl over 1f out: kpt on* **2/1**[1]

600- 2 ½ **Dunmore Boy (IRE)**[23] 7728 4-9-5 **58**.......................... TonyHamilton 5 66
(Richard Fahey) *prom: pushed along and sltly outpcd 3f out: hdwy wl over 1f out: rdn to chse wnr ins fnl f: kpt on* **16/1**

025- 3 2 ¾ **Eastern Gift**[19] 7775 7-9-6 **59**.......................... StevieDonohoe 6 60
(Gay Kelleway) *in rr and sn pushed along: hdwy wl over 2f out: rdn to chse ldng pair appr fnl f: kpt on same pce* **7/2**[3]

406- 4 1 ¾ **Avalon Bay**[16] 7807 4-8-12 **54**..........................(b[1]) RyanClark(3) 2 50
(Pat Eddery) *trckd ldrs on inner: hdwy 2f out and sn cl up: rdn wl over 1f out and kpt on same pce* **4/1**

664- 5 1 ¼ **Jonnie Skull (IRE)**[4] 7924 6-9-0 **53**..........................(vt) HayleyTurner 7 45
(Phil McEntee) *led: pushed along and hdd 1/2-way: sn rdn and wknd 2f out* **5/2**[2]

000- 6 ¾ **Vogarth**[7] 7885 8-8-4 **46** oh1..........................(b) AdamBeschizza(3) 9 36
(Michael Chapman) *dwlt: hdwy and cl up after 2f: rdn to ld 1/2-way: hdd wl over 2f out and grad wknd* **33/1**

1m 28.62s (-1.68) **Going Correction** -0.15s/f (Stan) **6** Ran SP% **113.0**
Speed ratings (Par 101): **103,102,99,97,95 95**
toteswingers: 1&2 £5.40, 1&3 £2.60, 2&3 £4.60. CSF £32.71 CT £105.58 TOTE £2.90: £1.60, £5.30; EX 42.80 Trifecta £288.70 Pool: £639.89 - 1.64 winning units..The winner was sold to Willie Musson for 6,000gns.
Owner Tony Coyle **Bred** J A And Mrs M A Knox **Trained** Norton, N Yorks

FOCUS
Very much run-of-the-mill fare. Ordinary form, rated around the runner-up.

22 EXCLUSIVE LIVE SHOWS AT BLUESQ.COM H'CAP 1m (F)
1:55 (1:55) (Class 5) (0-75,75) 4-Y-O+ £2,264 (£673; £336; £168) Stalls Low

Form RPR

605- 1 **Dubaianswer**[7] 7887 4-9-7 **75**.......................... BarryMcHugh 3 87+
(Tony Coyle) *in tch: smooth hdwy on outer to ld over 3f out: rdn 2f out: drvn and edgd lft ins fnl f: kpt on gamely* **16/1**

002- 2 *nk* **The Lock Master (IRE)**[7] 7884 5-9-5 **73**.......................... LukeMorris 4 84
(Michael Appleby) *chsd ldrs: pushed along and n.m.r over 3f out: hdwy to chse wnr over 2f out and sn rdn: drvn to chal appr fnl f: ev ch tl no ex nr fin* **5/2**[2]

112- 3 15 **Minortransgression (USA)**[7] 7887 5-8-10 **71**.......... LeonnaMayor(7) 5 48
(Paul Rich) *cl up: rdn along wl over 2f out: sn drvn and one pce* **10/3**[3]

311- 4 3 ¾ **On The Cusp (IRE)**[7] 7887 5-9-4 **72** 6ex..........................(p) MartinHarley 6 40
(Richard Guest) *led: rdn along and hdd over 3f out: sn wknd* **11/10**[1]

212- 5 1 ¾ **St Oswald**[18] 7782 4-8-4 **65**..........................(b) JakePayne(7) 1 29
(David O'Meara) *cl up on inner: rdn along 3f out: sn wknd* **12/1**

1m 42.08s (-1.62) **Going Correction** -0.15s/f (Stan) **5** Ran SP% **112.8**
Speed ratings (Par 103): **102,101,86,82,81**
toteswingers: 1&2 £15.30. CSF £56.25 TOTE £17.70: £3.80, £3.30; EX 53.90.
Owner C E Whiteley **Bred** Dave Curran & Eric Cantillon **Trained** Norton, N Yorks

FOCUS
Hard to know what to make of this with three of the quintet clearly well below their best, and the winner posting a big turnaround with the third and fourth on last week's C&D form.
On The Cusp(IRE) Official explanation: jockey said gelding ran flat

23 PLAY GOLF AT SOUTHWELL GOLF CLUB H'CAP 1m 6f (F)
2:25 (2:26) (Class 6) (0-60,55) 4-Y-O+ £1,704 (£503; £251) Stalls Low

Form RPR

000- 1 **Hada Men (USA)**[41] 5790 7-9-0 **45**.......................... BarryMcHugh 4 64+
(Brian Ellison) *hld up in tch: smooth hdwy 4f out: led 3f out: pushed clr 2f out: easily* **4/7**[1]

330- 2 7 **Bold Adventure**[40] 7528 8-9-6 **51**.......................... StevieDonohoe 1 56
(Willie Musson) *hld up and bhd: hdwy 6f out: trckd ldrs 4f out: chsd wnr 3f out: rdn wl over 1f out and sn no imp* **13/2**[2]

214- 3 3 ½ **Six Of Clubs**[238] 1973 6-9-3 **55**......(b) JakePayne(7) 2 55+
(Bill Turner) *hld up: hdwy on inner to trck ldrs 4f out: swtchd rt and effrt 3f out: sn rdn and one pce* **8/1**[3]

610- 4 15 **Spiritonthemount (USA)**[224] 2377 7-9-5 **50**......(b) WilliamCarson 5 29
(Peter Hiatt) *trckd ldrs: led after 3f and sn clr: rdn along 5f out: hdd 3f out and sn wknd* **16/1**

054- 5 5 **Toucan Tango (IRE)**[18] 7779 4-9-1 **52**...... FrannyNorton 6 24
(Michael Quinn) *prom: rdn along over 4f out: wknd 3f out* **17/2**

604- 6 26 **Empyrean (USA)**[12] 7858 4-8-8 **45**......(b1) LukeMorris 7
(Sir Mark Prescott Bt) *chsd ldrs: rdn along after 3f: drvn along over 4f out: sn wknd* **10/1**

7 dict **Drummanmoremaster (IRE)**[431] 7219 5-9-0 **45**...... MartinHarley 3
(Niall Moran, Ire) *led 3f: pushed along over 7f out: sn lost pl and bhd whn virtually p.u 3f out* **40/1**

3m 6.03s (-2.27) **Going Correction** -0.15s/f (Stan)
WFA 4 from 5yo+ 6lb 7 Ran SP% **116.0**
Speed ratings (Par 101): **100,96,94,85,82 67,**
toteswingers: 1&2 £2.20, 1&3 £2.20, 2&3 £3.10. CSF £5.15 TOTE £1.80: £1.30, £1.30; EX 6.20.
Owner Brian Ellison **Bred** Overbrook Farm **Trained** Norton, N Yorks

FOCUS
A handicap which was all about the winner, who is clearly still a grade or two above these. The form is rated around the runner-up.
Drummanmoremaster(IRE) Official explanation: trainer said gelding scoped badly post race

24 HOSPITALITY AT SOUTHWELL RACECOURSE H'CAP 5f (F)
3:00 (3:01) (Class 5) (0-75,75) 4-Y-O+ £2,264 (£673; £336; £168) Stalls High

Form RPR
002- 1 **Ghostwing**[5] 7917 5-9-7 **75**...... FergusSweeney 3 88
(James Evans) *a.p: hdwy to ld over 1f out: sn rdn and styd on strly* **3/1**[1]

613- 2 1 ½ **No Mean Trick (USA)**[6] 7897 6-8-9 **63**...... MickyFenton 4 71
(Paul Midgley) *prom: hdwy and cl up 1/2-way: rdn to ld briefly wl over 1f out: sn hdd and kpt on same pce fnl f* **9/2**[2]

455- 3 1 ¼ **Dancing Freddy (IRE)**[5] 7917 5-9-5 **73**......(tp) MartinHarley 6 77
(Richard Guest) *slt ld: rdn along over 2f out: hdd wl over 1f out: kpt on same pce fnl f* **6/1**[3]

/00- 4 1 **Love You Louis**[206] 2929 6-9-5 **73**...... JoeFanning 8 73
(J R Jenkins) *cl up: effrt 2f out: sn rdn and ev ch tl drvn and one pce ent fnl f* **33/1**

003- 5 1 ½ **Shawkantango**[6] 7896 5-8-11 **65**......(v) GrahamGibbons 2 60
(Derek Shaw) *dwlt: sn swtchd lft and pushed along: sme hdwy 2f out: sn rdn and no imp* **9/2**[2]

430- 6 1 ¼ **Bookiesindex Boy**[6] 7896 8-8-8 **62**......(b) FrannyNorton 1 52
(J R Jenkins) *a midfield* **7/1**

003- 7 2 **Rylee Mooch**[5] 7917 4-8-9 **70**......(e) CharlesEddery(7) 5 53
(Richard Guest) *dwlt: sn chsng ldrs: rdn along over 2f out and sn wknd* **8/1**

000- 8 ½ **Clear Ice (IRE)**[6] 7893 5-9-6 **74**......(b) RobertWinston 9 55
(Gay Kelleway) *a towards rr* **11/1**

263- 9 20 **Grudge**[7] 7883 7-8-12 **66**......(b) HayleyTurner 7
(Conor Dore) *s.i.s: a bhd* **14/1**

56.8s (-2.90) **Going Correction** -0.50s/f (Stan) course record 9 Ran SP% **117.2**
Speed ratings (Par 103): **103,100,98,97,94 92,89,88,56**
toteswingers: 1&2 £2.70, 1&3 £4.10, 2&3 £6.40. CSF £16.68 CT £76.50 TOTE £3.10: £1.50, £2.50, £1.80; EX 19.60 Trifecta £53.90 Pool: £777.52 - 10.66 winning units..
Owner Mark Benton **Bred** D R Botterill **Trained** Broadwas, Worcs

FOCUS
A fair sprint which was run at a good pace (broke track record) and threw up a comfortable winner. He is well treated on old form.
Clear Ice(IRE) Official explanation: jockey said gelding hung left-handed
Grudge Official explanation: jockey said gelding missed the break

25 PLAY DA VINCI DIAMONDS AT BLUESQ.COM/GAMES H'CAP 6f (F)
3:30 (3:30) (Class 6) (0-60,60) 3-Y-O £1,704 (£503; £251) Stalls Low

Form RPR
515- 1 **M J Woodward**[7] 7881 3-9-2 **55**...... LukeMorris 4 58
(Paul Green) *prom: effrt 2f out: rdn to chse ldr ent fnl f: drvn and styd on wl to ld last 50yds* **3/1**[1]

341- 2 ¾ **Heidi's Delight (IRE)**[21] 7742 3-9-2 **55**......(b) WilliamCarson 8 56
(Ann Duffield) *led: clr wl over 2f out: rdn over 1f out: edgd rt ins fnl f: hdd and no ex last 50yds* **4/1**[2]

033- 3 ½ **Burnwynd Spirit (IRE)**[19] 7770 3-8-12 **51**...... BarryMcHugh 2 50
(Ian Semple) *prom: hdwy to chal 2f out: sn rdn and ev ch tl drvn and one pce ins fnl f* **17/2**

03- 4 ½ **Son Of May**[21] 7742 3-9-0 **53**......(b) StevieDonohoe 3 50
(Jo Hughes) *chsd ldrs: hdwy over 2f out: rdn over 1f out: kpt on fnl f* **6/1**[3]

121- 5 1 ¼ **Russian Bullet**[14] 7830 3-9-6 **59**...... FergusSweeney 9 52
(Jamie Osborne) *hld up: hdwy on outer to chse ldrs wl over 2f out: rdn wl over 1f out: no imp appr fnl f* **3/1**[1]

605- 6 ¾ **Littlecote Lady**[21] 7742 3-9-1 **54**......(v1) DavidProbert 10 45
(Mark Usher) *a towards rr* **12/1**

042- 7 3 **Miserere Mei (IRE)**[21] 7742 3-8-12 **58**......(e) CharlesEddery(7) 1 39
(Richard Guest) *in tch on inner: hdwy 1/2-way: rdn 2f out and sn ev ch tl drvn and wknd appr fnl f* **14/1**

503- 8 6 **Well Wishes**[25] 7694 3-8-7 **46** oh1...... TomEaves 5 8
(Bryan Smart) *chsd ldrs: rdn along 1/2-way: sn wknd* **28/1**

441- 9 2 **Lady Nickandy (IRE)**[7] 7882 3-9-3 **56** 6ex......(v) AndrewMullen 6 12
(Alan McCabe) *dwlt: sn chsng ldrs: rdn along wl over 2f out and sn wknd* **14/1**

1m 16.71s (0.21) **Going Correction** -0.15s/f (Stan) 9 Ran SP% **119.3**
Speed ratings (Par 95): **92,91,90,89,88 87,83,75,72**
toteswingers: 1&2 £3.50, 1&3 £4.80, 2&3 £8.50. CSF £15.63 CT £93.95 TOTE £3.20: £1.10, £1.70, £3.00; EX 15.20 Trifecta £118.90 Pool: £937.05 - 5.83 winning units..
Owner E Sciarrillo **Bred** Paul Green **Trained** Lydiate, Merseyside

FOCUS
Modest fare, though no reason why the form won't hold up for the grade as it makes sense at face value. The time was relatively slow but it was one of the few races where the pace held up.
T/Jkpt: £25,000.00 to a £1 stake. Pool: £32,455.53. 0.50 winning tickets. T/Plt: £116.50 to a £1 stake. Pool: £86,653.43. 542.69 winning tickets. T/Qpdt: £54.30 to a £1 stake. Pool: £9,677.40. 131.70 winning tickets. JR

KEMPTON (A.W) (R-H)
Wednesday, January 4

OFFICIAL GOING: Standard
Wind: Brisk behind

26 FREE ENTRY FOR BETDAQ MEMBERS MEDIAN AUCTION MAIDEN STKS 6f (P)
4:00 (4:00) (Class 6) 3-Y-O £1,617 (£481; £240; £120) Stalls Low

Form RPR
442- 1 **By Invitation (USA)**[14] 7838 3-8-12 **69**...... JimCrowley 1 72+
(Ralph Beckett) *trckd ldr: chal 2f out: sn led: pushed clr fnl f* **4/6**[1]

22- 2 4 **Like The Night**[19] 7784 3-8-12 **0**...... AndreaAtzeni 3 59
(Marco Botti) *chsd ldrs 1/2-way: chsd wnr ins fnl f: nvr any ch and eased fnl strides: jst hld on for 2nd* **5/1**[3]

3 nk **Profit Again (IRE)** 3-9-3 **0**...... DavidProbert 4 63+
(Andrew Balding) *in rr and pushed along 1/2-way: styd on fnl f and gaining on eased 2nd fnl strides but no ch w wnr* **15/2**

0- 4 1 ¼ **Prince Gabrial (IRE)**[207] 2907 3-9-3 **0**...... EddieAhern 5 59
(Kevin Ryan) *sn led: hdd ins fnl 2f: wknd ins fnl f* **9/2**[2]

5- 5 6 **Saint Boniface**[23] 7736 3-9-3 **0**...... SteveDrowne 2 40
(Peter Makin) *plld hrd: sn chsng ldrs: rdn 2f out: wknd over 1f out* **33/1**

6 1 ¾ **Gem Of Wizdom (IRE)** 3-8-12 **0**...... StevieDonohoe 6 29
(Paul Cole) *a in rr: rdn over 2f out and no ch after* **33/1**

1m 13.98s (0.88) **Going Correction** +0.075s/f (Slow) 6 Ran SP% **112.5**
Speed ratings (Par 95): **97,91,91,89,81 79**
toteswingers:1&2:£1.50, 1&3:£1.60, 2&3:£3.10 CSF £4.52 TOTE £2.00: £1.60, £1.70; EX 5.10.
Owner Clipper Logistics **Bred** Galleria B'Stock & Summerhill B'Stock **Trained** Kimpton, Hants

FOCUS
There was a strong tailwind in the straight and the going was standard. The 69-rated hot favourite cashed in on a good opportunity in smooth style in this auction maiden.
Saint Boniface Official explanation: jockey said that the gelding ran too free

27 BACK OR LAY AT BETDAQ.COM H'CAP 6f (P)
4:30 (4:30) (Class 5) (0-70,68) 3-Y-O £2,264 (£673; £336; £168) Stalls Low

Form RPR
633- 1 **Oratorian (IRE)**[17] 7809 3-9-7 **68**...... LiamKeniry 6 77
(Sylvester Kirk) *wnt rt s and bmpd: sn rr: hdwy ins fnl 2f: chsd ldr 1f out: drvn to ld fnl 120yds: pushed out clsng stages* **4/1**[3]

152- 2 1 **Dressed In Lace**[79] 6921 3-9-5 **66**...... IanMongan 5 72
(Jo Crowley) *bmpd s: chsd ldrs: led over 2f out: kpt on tl hdd fnl 120yds: one pce* **3/1**[2]

002- 3 2 ½ **Leenavesta (USA)**[46] 7491 3-9-4 **68**...... KieranO'Neill(3) 4 66
(Richard Hannon) *bmpd s: disputed ld tl over 3f out: styd on same pce fnl f* **9/4**[1]

655- 4 1 ¼ **Lady Heartbeat**[20] 7763 3-8-7 **54** oh3...... FrankieMcDonald 2 48
(Michael Blanshard) *led: rdn and hdd over 2f out: wknd fnl f* **10/1**

446- 5 nk **Lana (IRE)**[39] 7555 3-8-11 **58**...... LukeMorris 1 51
(David Evans) *chsd ldrs: rdn 2 out: wknd ins fnl f* **16/1**

504- 6 1 **Princess Alessia**[47] 7452 3-8-11 **58**...... MarcHalford 3 48
(Terry Clement) *chsd ldrs: outpcd over 2f out: styd on again clsoing stages* **8/1**

033- 7 5 **Marie's Fantasy**[15] 7830 3-8-8 **55** ow1...... SamHitchcott 7 29
(Zoe Davison) *s.i.s: in tch and drvn 3f out: wknd over 2f out* **8/1**

1m 13.56s (0.46) **Going Correction** +0.075s/f (Slow) 7 Ran SP% **113.0**
Speed ratings (Par 97): **99,97,94,92,92 90,84**
toteswingers:1&2:£2.00, 1&3:£2.70, 2&3:£1.50 CSF £15.99 TOTE £4.50: £2.10, £2.80; EX 16.70.
Owner Miss J A Challen & T Pearson **Bred** Knockainey Stud **Trained** Upper Lambourn, Berks

FOCUS
A minor handicap. It was run a fair pace and an unexposed type reeled in the clear second who looks a solid marker for the form.
Marie's Fantasy Official explanation: jockey said that the filly ran flat

28 BETDAQ MULTIPLES H'CAP 1m 4f (P)
5:00 (5:00) (Class 6) (0-60,60) 4-Y-O+ £1,617 (£481; £240; £120) Stalls Centre

Form RPR
660- 1 **Now**[28] 7654 6-8-11 **47**......(b1) JamesMillman 3 55
(Rod Millman) *in tch: hdwy on outside over 2f out: drvn to ld appr fnl f: rdn out* **25/1**

525- 2 nk **Laconicos (IRE)**[7] 7891 10-9-0 **55**......(t) RyanPowell(5) 7 62
(William Stone) *chsd ldrs: rdn and kpt on to chse wnr fnl 120yds: gng on clsng stages but a jst hld* **14/1**

/00- 3 2 ¼ **Sumani (FR)**[55] 7346 6-9-10 **60**...... EddieAhern 5 64
(Simon Dow) *chsd ldrs: rdn to go 2nd appr fnl f: no imp and one pce into 3rd fnl 120yds* **5/1**[3]

045- 4 2 **Cantor**[119] 5832 4-8-12 **52**...... JoeFanning 6 52
(Giles Bravery) *prom: chsd ldr over 3f out: ev ch wl over 1f out: wknd ins fnl f* **3/1**[1]

010- 5 hd **Rose Aurora**[21] 7761 5-9-5 **55**......(bt1) HayleyTurner 10 55
(Marcus Tregoning) *s.i.s: in rr: drvn and hdwy over 2f out: styd on fnl f: nt pce to rch ldrs* **15/2**

043- 6 ½ **Spartan King (IRE)**[7] 7903 4-8-13 **53**...... StevieDonohoe 11 52
(Ian Williams) *v.s.a: in rr: hdwy on ins fr over 2f out: styd on fnl f: nt rch ldrs* **4/1**[2]

000- 7 2 ¾ **Lucas Pitt**[28] 7654 5-9-0 **50**......(p) SamHitchcott 9 45
(Michael Scudamore) *chsd ldrs: led 6f out: rdn 3f out: hdd & wknd appr fnl f* **22/1**

140- 8 1 ¼ **Valdan (IRE)**[16] 7817 8-9-5 **55**......(p) JamieSpencer 13 48
(David Evans) *in rr: hdwy over 2f out: kpt on fnl f: nvr a threat* **11/1**

520- 9 ¾ **Rodrigo De Freitas (IRE)**[21] 7761 5-8-13 **56**...... DanielCremin(7) 12 48
(Jim Boyle) *s.i.s: in rr: rdn 3f out: nvr rchd ldrs* **14/1**

030- 10 7 **El Libertador (USA)**[28] 7654 6-9-4 **54**......(b) LukeMorris 1 34
(Eric Wheeler) *in tch: rdn 3f out: wknd 2f out* **20/1**

004- 11 2 **Venir Rouge**[83] 6503 8-9-10 **60**...... RobertWinston 14 37
(Matthew Salaman) *rdn 4f out: a in rr* **20/1**

506- 12 7 **Warrior Nation (FR)**[36] 7574 6-8-10 **46** oh1...... NeilChalmers 4 12
(Adrian Chamberlain) *chsd ldrs: wknd 4f out* **66/1**

005- 13 22 **Missionaire (USA)**[16] 7202 5-9-9 **59**......(p) AdamKirby 8
(Tony Carroll) *led tl hdd 6f out: wknd over 4f out* **16/1**

2m 35.56s (1.06) **Going Correction** +0.075s/f (Slow)
WFA 4 from 5yo+ 4lb 13 Ran SP% **120.2**
Speed ratings (Par 101): **99,98,97,95,95 95,93,92,92,87 86,81,67**
toteswingers:1&2:£55.90, 1&3:£28.20, 2&3:£18.60 CSF £322.43 CT £2047.31 TOTE £34.50: £7.90, £5.30, £1.60; EX 733.10.

Owner Exors of the late Mrs Jenny Willment **Bred** Mrs Jenny Willment **Trained** Kentisbeare, Devon
FOCUS
A low-grade handicap run at a reasonable pace.
Now Official explanation: trainer said, regarding the apparent improvement of form, that the mare had improved with the application of blinkers, and was ridden more prominently
Spartan King(IRE) Official explanation: jockey said that the gelding planted and was slowly away

29 BETDAQ MOBILE APPS CONDITIONS STKS 7f (P)
5:30 (5:30) (Class 4) 4-Y-0+ **£4,075** (£1,212; £606; £303) **Stalls** Low

Form RPR
230- **1** **The Rectifier (USA)**[112] 6061 5-9-2 105 MickyFenton 2 99
(Jim Boyle) *chsd ldrs: led 2f out: drvn fnl f: edgd lft clsng stages: all out* **7/2**[1]
013- **2** *hd* **Clockmaker (IRE)**[18] 7801 6-9-2 96 DuranFentiman 6 98
(Tim Easterby) *led after 1f: hdd 2f out: rallied fnl f: styd on clsng stages: nt quite get up* **9/2**[2]
500- **3** *3/4* **Hazzard County (USA)**[25] 7719 8-8-11 92 LauraPike(5) 5 96
(David Simcock) *in rr: stl plenty to do whn hdwy on outside over 1f out: str run fnl 120yds: gng on cl home* **16/1**
150- **4** *shd* **Nazreef**[19] 7393 5-9-2 97 (bt) HayleyTurner 8 96
(Hughie Morrison) *in rr: drvn and hdwy towards outer over 1f out: styd on fnl 120yds: gng on cl home* **8/1**
000- **5** *3 1/4* **Dozy Joe**[36] 7578 4-9-2 85 (t) LukeMorris 3 87?
(Ian Wood) *in rr but in tch: rdn over 2f out: styd on ins fnl f: nt pce to troble ldrs* **14/1**
205- **6** *3/4* **Kakatosi**[18] 7801 5-9-2 98 DavidProbert 9 85
(Andrew Balding) *chsd ldrs: drvn to dsputed 2nd 2f out: wknd fnl f* **9/2**[2]
312- **7** *2* **Amitola (IRE)**[28] 7660 5-8-11 88 JamieSpencer 7 75
(David Barron) *chsd ldrs: rdn and hung rt ins 3f out: sn outpcd: kpt on again clsng stages* **5/1**[3]
/04- **8** *1* **Treadwell (IRE)**[25] 7721 5-9-2 95 FergusSweeney 1 77
(Jamie Osborne) *outpcd* **8/1**
006- **9** *5* **Quasi Congaree (GER)**[33] 7602 6-9-2 82 (t) JoeFanning 4 63
(Ian Wood) *in rr: rdn and effrt on outside 2f out: nvr rchd ldrs and sn wknd* **40/1**

1m 25.5s (-0.50) **Going Correction** +0.075s/f (Slow) 9 Ran SP% **112.5**
Speed ratings (Par 105): **105,104,103,103,100 99,96,95,90**
toteswingers:1&2:£2.90, 1&3:£8.40, 2&3:£16.30 CSF £18.47 TOTE £5.20: £1.80, £1.70, £5.80; EX 18.80.
Owner Mrs Anne Cowley **Bred** Ceka Ireland Ltd **Trained** Epsom, Surrey
■ Stewards' Enquiry : Duran Fentiman five-day ban: used whip with excessive frequency (18-22 Jan)
FOCUS
A useful conditions event. It was run at a good pace, but the first two filled those positions throughout.
Hazzard County(USA) Official explanation: jockey said that the gelding was denied a clear run

30 BOOK KEMPTON TICKETS ON 0844 579 3008 (S) H'CAP 1m 3f (P)
6:00 (6:00) (Class 6) (0-60,57) 3-Y-0 **£1,617** (£481; £240; £120) **Stalls** Low

Form RPR
41-3 **1** **Spartilla**[3] 2 3-9-7 57 JamesSullivan 1 62+
(James Given) *led tl hdd after 3f: styd chsng ldr: led again wl over 1f out: readily* **11/8**[1]
005- **2** *3* **Cotes Du Rhone (IRE)**[69] 7117 3-8-9 45 LukeMorris 6 45
(David Evans) *in rr: drvn along fr 6f out: styd on fr over 1f out to take 2nd fnl 50yds but no ch* **16/1**
060- **3** *1 1/4* **Skyblue**[49] 7435 3-8-9 45 (bt[1]) StevieDonohoe 5 42
(Tobias B P Coles) *in rr: rdn and hdwy 3f out: styd on for 3rd ins fnl f but nvr any ch w wnr* **20/1**
000- **4** *3/4* **Castalian Spring (IRE)**[15] 7830 3-8-6 45 AdamBeschizza(3) 3 41
(Robert Eddery) *chsd wnr: led after 3f: 5 l clr 4f out: hdd wl over 1f out: wknd and hung lft ins fnl f* **33/1**
030- **5** *10* **Notnowstanley**[25] 7718 3-8-4 45 RyanPowell(5) 7 23
(J S Moore) *chsd ldrs: rdn 3f out: wknd over 2f out* **14/1**
053- **6** *27* **Meet Joe Black (IRE)**[16] 7821 3-9-2 52 TomMcLaughlin 4
(David Evans) *rdn 4f out: a bhd: lost tch fnl 3f* **9/1**[3]
000- **7** *13* **Graylyn Olivaa**[42] 7521 3-8-9 45 AndreaAtzeni 2
(Robert Eddery) *chsd ldrs tl wknd over 3f out* **7/4**[2]

2m 25.1s (3.20) **Going Correction** +0.075s/f (Slow) 7 Ran SP% **108.7**
Speed ratings (Par 95): **91,88,87,87,80 60,51**
toteswingers:1&2:£4.70, 1&3:£4.20, 2&3:£20.70 CSF £21.90 TOTE £2.60: £1.70, £7.30; EX 23.10.The winner was bought in for £5,600.
Owner Bolton Grange **Bred** J Ellis **Trained** Willoughton, Lincs
FOCUS
The favourite ran out a comfortable winner in this selling handicap.
Graylyn Olivaa Official explanation: jockey said that the gelding stopped quickly

31 SKYSPORTS.COM H'CAP 1m (P)
6:30 (6:30) (Class 5) (0-70,70) 4-Y-0+ **£2,264** (£673; £336; £168) **Stalls** Low

Form RPR
600- **1** **Hip Hip Hooray**[74] 7033 6-9-0 63 IanMongan 12 74
(Luke Dace) *s.i.s: in rr: hdwy towards outside 2f out: drvn and str run fnl f out to ld 120yds out: styd on wl* **25/1**
325- **2** *1 3/4* **Grand Theft Equine**[17] 7806 4-9-3 66 StephenCraine 10 73
(Jim Boyle) *in rr: hdwy over 2f out: drvn to ld over 1f out: hdd and outpcd fnl 120yds* **20/1**
523- **3** *3/4* **Woolston Ferry (IRE)**[20] 7764 6-9-4 67 EddieAhern 8 72
(David Pinder) *trckd ldrs: chal wl over 1f out: one pce into 3rd fnl 120yds* **8/1**
234- **4** *1/2* **Having A Ball**[6] 7910 8-8-2 56 oh1 RyanPowell(5) 9 60
(Jonathan Portman) *in rr unrtil hdwy 2f out: drvn and kpt on fnl f: nvr gng pce to rch ldrs* **10/1**
244- **5** *2* **Shared Moment (IRE)**[20] 7764 6-8-12 61 (v) ChrisCatlin 7 61
(John Gallagher) *in tch: hdwy whn hmpd over 2f out: kpt on again fnl f: nt trble ldrs* **16/1**
50- **6** *nk* **Mount Abora (IRE)**[40] 7548 5-9-3 66 JamieSpencer 5 65
(Ian Williams) *s.i.s: in rr: hdwy on ins fr 3f out: nvr rchd ldrs: one pce fnl f* **8/1**
050- **7** *nk* **Silvee**[7] 7895 5-8-8 57 oh1 ow1 SamHitchcott 11 55
(John Bridger) *reae hdwy 2f out: styng on whn hmpd over 1f out: kpt on again clsng stages* **33/1**
001- **8** *2* **Whitechapel**[20] 7764 5-9-7 70 LiamKeniry 2 64
(Andrew Balding) *chsd ldr: led over 2f: hdd & wknd over 1f out* **5/1**[2]
000- **9** *7* **Ibiza Sunset (IRE)**[16] 7817 4-9-3 66 KierenFallon 1 43
(Brendan Powell) *s.i.s: sn rcvrd and in tch: chsd ldrs 2f out: wknd over 1f out* **11/4**[1]
003- **10** *nk* **Bubbly Braveheart (IRE)**[17] 7805 5-8-6 60 JemmaMarshall(5) 14 37
(Pat Phelan) *in tch: rdn on outside 3f out: wknd over 2f out* **25/1**
002- **11** *nk* **Hecton Lad (USA)**[17] 7810 5-9-1 64 (b) LukeMorris 4 40
(John Best) *led: rdn over 3f out: edgd lft: hdd & wknd over 2f out* **6/1**[3]
000- **12** *2 3/4* **Huzzah (IRE)**[13] 7857 7-9-4 67 MichaelStainton 13 37
(Paul Howling) *chsd ldrs: rdn over 2f out: sn wknd* **33/1**
003/ **13** *11* **Red Avalanche (IRE)**[442] 6996 5-9-4 67 FergusSweeney 3 11
(Tony Newcombe) *chsd ldrs: hmpd and wknd over 2f out* **6/1**[3]

1m 39.94s (0.14) **Going Correction** +0.075s/f (Slow) 13 Ran SP% **127.4**
Speed ratings (Par 103): **102,100,99,99,97 96,96,94,87,87 86,84,73**
toteswingers:1&2:£63.00, 1&3:£37.40, 2&3:£25.60 CSF £457.11 CT £4332.30 TOTE £35.80: £5.20, £5.20, £2.80; EX 361.00.
Owner M C S D Racing Partnership **Bred** Mrs R S Evans **Trained** Five Oaks, W Sussex
FOCUS
A competitive handicap. There was a 25-1 winner who came from a long way back.
Hecton Lad(USA) Official explanation: jockey said that the gelding's blinkers had slipped over one of its' eyes

32 SKYSPORTS.COM RACING H'CAP 1m (P)
7:00 (7:00) (Class 5) (0-75,78) 3-Y-0 **£2,264** (£673; £336; £168) **Stalls** Low

Form RPR
111- **1** **Mr Red Clubs (IRE)**[9] 7875 3-9-5 78 6ex RaulDaSilva(5) 3 88
(Tim Pitt) *trckd ldr 3f out: led over 2f out: clr fnl f: easily* **11/4**[2]
010- **2** *5* **Biba Diva (IRE)**[87] 6724 3-9-7 75 JamieSpencer 6 74
(Jeremy Noseda) *stdd s: in rr: hdwy 3f out: pushed along and hung rt fr over 2f out: rdn to chse wnr over 1f out but nvr any ch* **13/8**[1]
332- **3** *3/4* **Haafhd Handsome**[28] 7650 3-9-2 73 KieranO'Neill(3) 5 70
(Richard Hannon) *chsd ldrs: rdn 2f out: styd on same pce fr over 1f out* **7/1**
323- **4** *1 1/2* **Bapak Pintar**[129] 5503 3-9-0 68 PhillipMakin 4 62
(Kevin Ryan) *led: rdn 3f out: hdd over 2f out: sn no ch w wnr: wknd ins fnl f* **5/1**[3]
660- **5** *hd* **Saucy Cat (IRE)**[69] 7125 3-8-5 59 LukeMorris 2 52
(John Best) *in rr but in tch: rdn over 2f out: styd on fnl f: nvr rchd ldrs* **25/1**
223- **6** *8* **Let Your Love Flow (IRE)**[14] 7849 3-8-10 64 LiamKeniry 1 39
(Sylvester Kirk) *chsd ldrs: wkng whn n.m.r on rails ins fnl 3f* **6/1**

1m 41.51s (1.71) **Going Correction** +0.075s/f (Slow) 6 Ran SP% **112.1**
Speed ratings (Par 97): **94,89,88,86,86 78**
toteswingers:1&2:£1.70, 1&3:£2.30, 2&3:£2.10 CSF £7.62 TOTE £3.70: £2.00, £1.50; EX 9.50.
Owner Ferrybank Properties Limited **Bred** Tally-Ho Stud **Trained** Newmarket, Suffolk
FOCUS
A fairly tactical event in which the in-form winner was never in any danger after quickening clear early in the straight.
T/Plt: £263.50 to a £1 stake. Pool:£72,607.60 - 201.10 winning tickets T/Qpdt: £142.70 to a £1 stake. Pool:£7,872.41 - 40.80 winning tickets ST

LINGFIELD (L-H)
Wednesday, January 4

OFFICIAL GOING: Standard
Wind: Fairly Strong, Across Weather: dry, breezy

33 BET AND WATCH AT BLUESQ.COM H'CAP 7f (P)
12:50 (12:50) (Class 5) (0-75,75) 4-Y-0+ **£2,385** (£704; £352) **Stalls** Low

Form RPR
030- **1** **Scottish Glen**[20] 7767 6-9-2 70 JimCrowley 5 80
(Patrick Chamings) *hld up in tch travelling wl: swtchd lft and effrt to press ldr 1f out: drvn ahd ins fnl f: r.o wl* **5/1**[2]
320- **2** *1 1/2* **Choral**[47] 7465 4-9-2 73 KieranO'Neill(3) 8 79
(Richard Hannon) *hmpd over 5f out and dropped to rr: swtchd to outer and hdwy to chse ldrs over 3f out: rdn 2f out: drvn 1f out: kpt on same pce: wnt 2nd cl home* **12/1**
044- **3** *hd* **Satwa Laird**[87] 6727 6-9-5 73 JamieSpencer 10 78
(David Simcock) *led and grad crossed to rail: rdn wl over 1f out: edgd rt u.p jst over 1f out: hdd ins fnl f: styd on same pce and lost 2nd cl home* **9/2**[1]
014- **4** *shd* **City Legend**[17] 7807 4-9-1 69 (v) RobertWinston 3 74+
(Alan McCabe) *rdn along early and reminders sn after s: chsd ldrs: jostling w rival after 1f: hmpd and lost pl over 4f out: swtchd wd bnd 2f out: r.o strly ins fnl f: nt rch wnr* **8/1**[3]
430- **5** *3/4* **Lastkingofscotland (IRE)**[7] 7895 6-8-11 65 (b) HayleyTurner 2 68
(Conor Dore) *chsd ldr tl 4f out: styd chsng ldrs: rdn and unable qck 2f out: rallied to press ldrs 1f out: no ex and one pce ins fnl f* **8/1**[3]
166- **6** *hd* **Mishrif (USA)**[65] 7199 6-9-7 75 (b) JoeFanning 7 78
(J R Jenkins) *dwlt: hld up in last pair: rdn and effrt wl over 1f out: kpt on but nvr gng pce to chal ldrs* **8/1**[3]
201- **7** *nk* **Wigram's Turn (USA)**[26] 7696 7-8-12 66 (t) PaddyAspell 1 68
(Michael Easterby) *hld up in tch in last pair: rdn and effrt on inner over 1f out: no ex and no imp ins fnl f* **8/1**[3]
506- **8** *1/2* **Al Aqabah (IRE)**[20] 7767 7-9-1 72 (b) AdamBeschizza(3) 9 72
(Brian Gubby) *dwlt: hdwy on outer and chsd ldrs over 5f out: pressed ldr 4f out: rdn and ev ch wl over 1f out: wknd jst ins fnl f* **8/1**[3]
013- **9** *9* **Ezra Church (IRE)**[9] 7876 5-9-4 72 GrahamGibbons 6 48
(David Barron) *chsd ldrs: jostling match w rival after 1f out: short of room and rdn over 4f out: dropped to rr over 3f out: lost tch wl over 1f out* **9/2**[1]

1m 23.56s (-1.24) **Going Correction** -0.075s/f (Stan) 9 Ran SP% **116.3**
Speed ratings (Par 103): **104,102,102,101,101 100,100,99,89**
toteswingers:1&2:£19.10, 1&3:£3.50, 2&3:£11.70 CSF £63.17 CT £292.16 TOTE £7.40: £2.80, £3.60, £1.70; EX 90.30 TRIFECTA Not won..
Owner The Foxford House Partnership **Bred** Mrs Ann Jenkins **Trained** Baughurst, Hants
FOCUS
A modest handicap.
City Legend Official explanation: jockey said the gelding had suffered interference in running
Wigram's Turn(USA) Official explanation: jockey said that the gelding had hit its head on the stalls
Ezra Church(IRE) Official explanation: jockey said that the gelding hung left throughout

34 COWDEN MAIDEN STKS 7f (P)
1:20 (1:20) (Class 5) 3-4-Y-0 **£2,385** (£704; £352) **Stalls** Low

Form RPR
52- **1** **Forceful Appeal (USA)**[7] 7894 4-9-13 84 HayleyTurner 5 77+
(Simon Dow) *mde all: pushed clr 2f out: in command after: pushed out: comf* **7/4**[2]

2- **2** *2* **Henry Clay**[76] 6970 3-8-9 0 .... JoeFanning 3 68+
(Mark Johnston) *hld up in tch: pushed along wl over 2f out: hdwy u.p on inner wl over 1f out: chsd clr wnr jst over 1f out: r.o u.p but no threat to wnr* **8/13**[1]

200- **3** *2 1/2* **Princess Willow**[70] 7096 4-9-8 53 .... SamHitchcott 4 60
(John E Long) *chsd ldrs: rdn to chse wnr but outpcd 2f out: lost 2nd jst over 1f out: wl hld and kpt on same pce fnl f* **50/1**

0- **4** *4* **Archina (IRE)**[21] 7751 3-8-4 0 .... DavidProbert 7 45
(Andrew Balding) *hld up in tch: rdn over 2f out: hung rt and lost pl bnd 2f out: n.d after* **15/2**[3]

5 *6* **Sweetest Friend (IRE)** 3-7-13 0 ....(p) RyanPowell(5) 1 29
(J S Moore) *s.i.s: rn green and rdn along thrght: clsd and in tch 1/2-way: wknd jst over 2f out* **20/1**

5- **6** *1 3/4* **Queen Of Heaven (USA)**[28] 7652 4-9-8 0 .... SteveDrowne 8 28
(Peter Makin) *chsd wnr tl 2f out: sn wknd* **33/1**

1m 23.87s (-0.93) **Going Correction** -0.075s/f (Stan)
WFA 3 from 4yo 18lb **6** Ran SP% **119.7**
Speed ratings (Par 103): **102,99,96,92,85 83**
toteswingers:1&2:£1.10, 1&3:£6.60, 2&3:£5.40 CSF £3.41 TOTE £3.10: £1.40, £1.10; EX 4.10 Trifecta £24.60 Pool: £622.15 - 18.66 winning units..
Owner Simon Caunce **Bred** Juddmonte Farms Inc **Trained** Epsom, Surrey

FOCUS
An uncompetitive maiden, run in a time 0.31 second slower than the preceding 61-75 handicap.

35 LINGFIELDPARK.CO.UK (S) STKS 1m 2f (P)
1:50 (1:50) (Class 6) 4-Y-O+ **£1,704** (£503; £251) **Stalls** Low

Form RPR

032- **1** **Wisecraic**[5] 7920 5-9-0 61 .... LiamKeniry 9 67
(J S Moore) *hld up in tch: smooth hdwy on outer to join ldrs over 2f out: ev ch and rdn wl over 1f out: led ins fnl f: kpt on: rdn out* **5/1**[3]

022- **2** *nk* **Marvo**[25] 7710 8-9-0 66 ....(b) EddieAhern 4 66
(Mark H Tompkins) *chsd ldrs: wnt 2nd over 3f out: led gng wl ent fnl 2f: rdn over 1f out: drvn and hdd ins fnl f: one pce* **11/2**

635- **3** *4* **Kidlat**[23] 7734 7-8-7 70 ....(t) NatashaEaton(7) 7 58
(Alan Bailey) *press ldr tl led over 8f out: rdn and hdd ent fnl 2f: 3rd and wknd u.p over 1f out* **11/8**[1]

346- **4** *2 1/4* **Roman Flame**[18] 7800 4-8-4 55 .... KieranO'Neill(3) 5 49
(Michael Quinn) *short of room and lost pl after 1f: pushed along after: rdn and chsd clr ldng trio over 2f out: no imp* **33/1**

000- **5** *2 1/4* **Tous Les Deux**[30] 7640 9-8-9 46 ....(b[1]) MatthewCosham(5) 6 49
(Dr Jeremy Naylor) *t.k.h: hld up in tch: rdn and outpcd over 2f out: 5th and wl hld over 1f out* **100/1**

6 *14* **It's Me And You** 4-8-12 0 .... JamesSullivan 3 21
(Michael Easterby) *s.i.s: rdn along thrght: a in rr: lost tch over 2f out* **9/1**

604- **7** *1 1/2* **Vivre La Secret**[7] 7888 4-8-0 41 .... JakePayne(7) 8 13
(Bill Turner) *chsd ldrs: rdn and wknd over 3f out: wknd over 2f out: fdd wl over 1f and wl bhd 1f out* **100/1**

6/6- **D** *1 1/2* **Peppertree Lane (IRE)**[185] 1188 9-9-0 89 ....(b[1]) KierenFallon 2 15
(Emmet Michael Butterly, Ire) *pressed ldr tl over 3f out: sn rdn and lost pl: bhd fnl 2f* **9/4**[2]

2m 5.38s (-1.22) **Going Correction** -0.075s/f (Stan)
WFA 4 from 5yo+ 2lb **8** Ran SP% **119.8**
Speed ratings (Par 101): **101,100,97,95,93 82,81,80**
toteswingers:1&2:£2.40, 1&3:£2.00, 2&3:£3.20 CSF £33.81 TOTE £5.60: £1.60, £1.40, £1.30; EX 20.80 Trifecta £48.80 Pool: £466.24 - 7.06 winning units..There was no bid for the winner.
Owner Mrs L Mann & N Attenborough **Bred** Darley **Trained** Upper Lambourn, Berks
■ Stewards' Enquiry : Jake PayneM two-day ban: careless riding

FOCUS
The pair that fought out the finish both arrived in decent heart in this sort of company.

36 DOWNLOAD THE BLUE SQUARE BET APP H'CAP 1m 2f (P)
2:20 (2:22) (Class 4) (0-85,81) 4-Y-O+ **£4,528** (£1,347; £673; £336) **Stalls** Low

Form RPR

006- **1** **Thunderstruck**[39] 7558 7-9-7 **81** ....(p) IanMongan 12 90
(Scott Dixon) *chsd ldrs tl led 1/2-way: mde rest: edgd rt u.p jst over 1f out: styd on gamely fnl f* **20/1**

1- **2** *1/2* **Ariyfa (IRE)**[16] 7822 4-9-0 **76** .... AdamKirby 3 84
(Noel Quinlan) *chsd ldr tl over 8f out: chsd ldrs after: rdn and effrt on inner over 1f out: ev ch ins fnl f: kpt on but hld fnl 50yds* **6/1**[3]

121- **3** *1 1/2* **Aerodynamic (IRE)**[16] 7823 5-9-2 **76** .... PaddyAspell 10 81
(Michael Easterby) *led tl 1/2-way: chsd ldrs after: rdn and effrt over 1f out: swtchd lft 1f out: kpt on same pce ins fnl f* **7/2**[1]

303- **4** *1/2* **Focail Maith**[23] 7734 4-8-12 **74** ow1 .... KierenFallon 9 78
(John Ryan) *in tch: rdn and chsd ldrs over 1f out: styd on same pce u.p ins fnl f* **11/1**

500- **5** *3/4* **Big Creek (IRE)**[95] 6528 5-9-6 **80** .... JamieSpencer 7 83+
(Jeremy Noseda) *in tch in midfield: effrt u.p and wd bnd 2f out: kpt on ins fnl f* **4/1**[2]

152- **6** *shd* **Choral Festival**[15] 7831 6-8-8 **71** .... KieranO'Neill(3) 5 73
(John Bridger) *chsd ldrs: rdn and unable qck 2f out: styd on same pce fr over 1f out* **16/1**

166- **7** *1* **Jordaura**[9] 7877 6-9-3 **77** .... RobertWinston 8 77
(Gay Kelleway) *hld up in tch towards rr: rdn and effrt over 1f out: kpt on: nvr trbld ldrs* **25/1**

166- **8** *nk* **Green Wadi**[21] 7759 7-9-3 **77** ....(p) FergusSweeney 1 77
(Gary Moore) *hld up in tch towards rr: rdn and effrt on inner over 1f out: kpt on fnl f: nvr trbld ldrs* **20/1**

261- **9** *1/2* **Opus Maximus (IRE)**[9] 7877 7-9-7 **81** 6ex .... HayleyTurner 6 80
(Conor Dore) *stdd s: hld up in rr: nt clr run over 2f out: rdn and effrt over 1f out: kpt on but nvr trbld ldrs* **8/1**

000- **10** *1 1/4* **Guest Book (IRE)**[26] 7699 5-9-6 **80** .... SamHitchcott 13 76
(Michael Scudamore) *stdd and dropped in bhd after s: hld up in rr: rdn and effrt over 1f out: no real imp: n.d* **40/1**

111- **11** *1/2* **Archie Rice (USA)**[16] 7817 6-8-13 **76** .... RyanClark(3) 11 71
(Tom Keddy) *hld up in tch towards rr: effrt on outer over 1f out: rdn and no imp fnl f: n.d* **9/1**

123- **12** *1 1/4* **Follow The Flag (IRE)**[9] 7877 8-9-6 **80** ....(v) MartinHarley 2 73
(Alan McCabe) *in tch in midfield: rdn and unable qck over 2f out: wknd over 1f out* **25/1**

300- **13** *4 1/2* **Ampleforth**[63] 7227 4-8-12 **74** .... JoeFanning 4 58
(Mark Johnston) *chsd ldr over 8f out: rdn and unable qck over 2f out: wknd wl over 1f out* **14/1**

2m 5.03s (-1.57) **Going Correction** -0.075s/f (Stan)
WFA 4 from 5yo+ 2lb **13** Ran SP% **118.2**
Speed ratings (Par 105): **103,102,101,101,100 100,99,99,98,97 97,96,92**
toteswingers:1&2:£18.90, 1&3:£34.70, 2&3:£4.40 CSF £127.02 CT £531.41 TOTE £31.50: £6.70, £2.40, £1.90; EX 176.60 TRIFECTA Not won..

Owner The Doncaster Racing Club **Bred** Mrs Yvette Dixon **Trained** Babworth, Notts

FOCUS
Despite the topweight racing off 4lb below the race ceiling, this still looked a competitive handicap contested by a number of in-form runners. However, the pace was steady and those attempting to come from the rear could never get involved. The form should therefore be treated with a little caution.
Archie Rice(USA) Official explanation: jockey said that the gelding was slowly away and never travelling

37 TANDRIDGE MAIDEN STKS 5f (P)
2:50 (2:50) (Class 5) 3-Y-O+ **£2,385** (£704; £352) **Stalls** High

Form RPR

22- **1** **Pale Orchid (IRE)**[6] 7906 3-8-6 0 .... LukeMorris 4 78+
(David Evans) *chsd ldrs: swtchd rt and effrt to chal 2f out: sn led and rdn clr: eased towards fin* **2/9**[1]

2- **2** *8* **Magilini (IRE)**[9] 7874 3-8-6 0 .... WilliamCarson 2 49
(David Barron) *led tl over 2f out: chsd clr wnr but wl hld fr over 1f out* **6/1**[2]

560- **3** *3/4* **Miakora**[28] 7652 4-9-4 44 .... KieranO'Neill(3) 6 52
(Michael Quinn) *restless in stalls: in tch in midfield: rdn and struggling 1/2-way: 5th and wl btn over 1f out: swtchd rt over 1f out: styd on to go 3rd ins fnl f: no threat to wnr* **20/1**

000- **4** *4* **Papageno**[77] 6943 5-9-12 46 .... JoeFanning 1 43
(J R Jenkins) *chsd ldr tl 3f out: 4th and drvn 2f out: sn outpcd and wl btn* **16/1**[3]

400- **5** *1* **Lady Royal Oak (IRE)**[13] 7854 5-9-0 47 .... JenniferFerguson(7) 3 34
(Olivia Maylam) *taken down early: v.s.a: racd freely: hdwy to chse ldrs after 2f out: led over 2f out tl wl over 1f out: sn btn: wknd ins fnl f* **20/1**

00- **6** *3 1/2* **Fifth Auntie**[25] 7717 5-9-2 0 .... RaulDaSilva(5) 5 21
(J R Jenkins) *dwlt: sn outpcd in rr: wl bhd fr 1/2-way* **50/1**

00- **7** *1* **Pill Boy**[25] 7717 4-9-12 0 .... SamHitchcott 7 23
(Dai Burchell) *in tch in midfield: lost pl and struggling 1/2-way: sn bhd* **100/1**

57.73s (-1.07) **Going Correction** -0.075s/f (Stan)
WFA 3 from 4yo+ 15lb **7** Ran SP% **114.5**
Speed ratings (Par 103): **105,92,91,84,83 77,75**
toteswingers:1&2:£1.10, 1&3:£3.30, 2&3:£4.00 CSF £1.91 TOTE £1.20: £1.10, £1.50; EX 1.90.
Owner Mrs E Evans **Bred** Mrs A J Donnelly **Trained** Pandy, Monmouths

FOCUS
A weak sprint maiden.

38 DRY HILL H'CAP 7f (P)
3:20 (3:34) (Class 6) (0-65,65) 3-Y-O **£1,704** (£503; £251) **Stalls** Low

Form RPR

006- **1** **Sudden Wish (IRE)**[149] 4848 3-8-3 **50** .... DominicFox(3) 8 54
(Alan Bailey) *towards rr: shkn up 3f out: rdn and effrt whn edgd lft over 1f out: str run ins fnl f to ld last strides* **9/1**

606- **2** *hd* **Illustrious Lad (IRE)**[4] 7937 3-8-12 **56** .... WilliamCarson 4 59
(Jim Boyle) *chsd ldrs: wnt 2nd and qcknd 2 l clr jst over 2f out: pressed fnl 100yds: r.o tl hdd and no ex last strides* **9/2**[2]

116- **3** *3/4* **Masters Club**[20] 7763 3-9-7 **65** .... AdamKirby 2 66
(John Ryan) *chsd ldr tl 3f out: styd chsng ldrs: rdn and unable qck 2f out: rallied u.p 1f out: pressed wnr fnl 100yds: no ex* **8/1**

525- **4** *3/4* **Songbird Blues**[19] 7780 3-8-6 **50** .... JohnFahy 10 49+
(Mark Usher) *stdd and dropped in bhd after s: hld up in rr: rdn and effrt 2f out: swtchd rt over 1f out: styd on strly on outer ins fnl f: nt rch ldrs* **15/2**

433- **5** *nk* **Arabian Flight**[18] 7798 3-8-11 **60** .... RyanPowell(5) 11 58
(John Bridger) *in tch on outer: rdn and effrt 2f out: kpt on u.p fnl f* **20/1**

000- **6** *nk* **Moataz (USA)**[72] 7052 3-8-6 **50** .... JoeFanning 6 47
(Mark Johnston) *chsd ldrs: rdn and chsd clr wnr 2f out: drvn over 1f out: no ex and outpcd fnl 150yds* **9/1**

060- **7** *2 3/4* **J J Leary (IRE)**[230] 2214 3-8-11 **55** .... JamieSpencer 3 45
(Ian Williams) *stdd s: in tch towards rr: rdn over 2f out: swtchd lft and effrt u.p over 1f out: no imp and no threat to ldrs fnl f* **5/2**[1]

046- **8** *1 1/4* **Small Steps (IRE)**[19] 7780 3-8-11 **55** ow2 ....(v[1]) GrahamGibbons 13 42
(Ed McMahon) *led tl jst over 2f out: sn struggling u.p: wknd ent fnl f* **13/2**[3]

000- **9** *2 3/4* **Strategic Action (IRE)**[27] 7672 3-9-0 **58** .... FergusSweeney 12 37
(Linda Jewell) *stdd s: hld up in last pair: swtchd wd over 2f out: no imp: n.d* **100/1**

\- **10** *2 1/2* **Echo Knight (IRE)**[26] 7702 3-9-2 **60** .... KierenFallon 1 32
(A Kinsella, Ire) *in tch: rdn and unable qck wl over 1f out: wknd ent fnl f* **16/1**

040- **11** *3 3/4* **Al Doha**[97] 6480 3-8-13 **57** .... PhillipMakin 7 19
(Kevin Ryan) *in tch in midfield: rdn and lost pl over 3f out: bhd fnl 2f* **12/1**

1m 24.85s (0.05) **Going Correction** -0.075s/f (Stan) **11** Ran SP% **122.3**
Speed ratings (Par 95): **96,95,94,94,93 93,90,88,85,82 78**
toteswingers:1&2:£12.40, 1&3:£14.20, 2&3:£7.10 CSF £51.32 CT £354.57 TOTE £13.40: £2.70, £2.50, £1.70; EX 67.70 Trifecta £406.50 Pool: £681.31 - 1.24 winning units..
Owner M&R Refurbishments Ltd **Bred** Catridge Farm Stud & S Von Schilcher **Trained** Newmarket, Suffolk
■ Stewards' Enquiry : Dominic Fox trainer said, regarding the apparent improvement in form, that this was the filly's first run from his yard and he was unable to give any explanation for her improvement in form.

FOCUS
A moderate event containing a number of handicap debutants. The runners were delayed at the start for a lengthy period after Synfonica unfortunately broke down going to post.

39 PLAY RAINBOW RICHES AT BLUESQ.COM APPRENTICE H'CAP 7f (P)
3:50 (3:52) (Class 6) (0-60,64) 4-Y-O+ **£1,704** (£503; £251) **Stalls** Low

Form RPR

031- **1** **Cut And Thrust (IRE)**[28] 7656 6-9-2 **60** .... NicoleNordblad(5) 5 69
(Mark Wellings) *hld up in tch: rdn and qcknd to ld 1f out: sn in command: pushed out: comf* **5/4**[1]

660- **2** *2* **My Jeanie (IRE)**[35] 7581 8-8-7 **46** oh1 .... LeonnaMayor 7 50
(Jimmy Fox) *stdd s: hld up in rr: rdn and effrt over 1f out: r.o wl ins fnl f: wnt 2nd towards fin: no threat to wnr* **33/1**

400- **3** *1/2* **Pytheas (USA)**[36] 7579 5-8-11 **57** ....(p) AaronChave(7) 4 60
(Michael Attwater) *t.k.h: hld up in last trio: effrt and n.m.r ent fnl f: hdwy and rdr dropped reins jst ins fnl f: styd on wl to snatch 3rd last stride: no ch w wnr* **8/1**

443- **4** *nse* **Polar Auroras**[21] 7754 4-9-2 **58** ....(p) GeorgeDowning(3) 2 61
(Tony Carroll) *in tch: effrt and drvn on inner over 1f out: chsd wnr ins fnl f: no imp and lost 2 pls towards fin* **13/2**[3]

651- **5** *hd* **Efistorm**[4] 7943 11-9-11 **64** 6ex .... LucyKBarry 6 66
(Conor Dore) *in tch on outer: rdn and outpcd 2f out: styd on same pce fr over 1f out* **3/1**[2]

004- 6 3/4 **Gazboolou**[14] 7843 8-9-0 56 .... JakePayne(3) 3 56
(David Pinder) *w ldr: rdn to ld wl over 1f out: hdd 1f out: wknd ins fnl f* 14/1

003- 7 *nse* **Kenswick**[14] 7843 5-8-4 46 .... (b) NoelGarbutt(3) 8 46
(Pat Eddery) *racd in last trio: wd bnd 2f out: rdn over 1f out: styd on same pce and no imp* 12/1

600- 8 4 1/2 **C'Mon You Irons (IRE)**[15] 7834 7-9-4 57 .... (b) RaulDaSilva 1 45
(Mark Hoad) *led tl wl over 1f out: sn rdn: wknd qckly ent fnl f* 25/1

1m 25.51s (0.71) **Going Correction** -0.075s/f (Stan) **8** Ran SP% **115.0**
Speed ratings (Par 101): **92,89,89,89,88 88,87,82**
toteswingers:1&2:£13.40, 1&3:£3.80, 2&3:£25.40 CSF £49.90 CT £248.28 TOTE £2.10: £1.40, £8.60, £2.80; EX 58.50 Trifecta £572.40 Part won. Pool: £773.59 - 0.30 winning units..
Owner Nicholls Family **Bred** Bloomsbury Stud **Trained** Six Ashes, Shropshire

FOCUS
A weak, low-grade handicap for apprentices who have ridden no more than 25 winners.
T/Plt: £39.20 to a £1 stake. Pool:£61,618.07 - 1,146.56 winning tickets T/Qpdt: £18.60 to a £1 stake. Pool:£5,115.71 - 203.16 winning tickets SP

WOLVERHAMPTON (A.W) (L-H)

Thursday, January 5

OFFICIAL GOING: Standard
Wind: Strong, half-behind Weather: Cloudy

40 BLUE SQUARE WISH TAMWORTH GOOD LUCK H'CAP 5f 20y(P)
4:10 (4:11) (Class 6) (0-55,55) 3-Y-O **£1,704** (£503; £251) **Stalls** Low

Form RPR

365- 1 **Lady Caprice**[129] 5535 3-9-1 54 .... (p) AdamKirby 8 62
(Jane Chapple-Hyam) *chsd ldr tl led over 1f out: edgd lft: rdn out* 5/2[2]

503- 2 2 **Villa Reigns**[10] 7874 3-8-13 52 .... (be) LukeMorris 3 53
(John Weymes) *led: rdn and hdd over 1f out: styd on same pce ins fnl f* 9/4[1]

453- 3 1 3/4 **Lord Buffhead**[9] 7882 3-8-11 53 .... RobertLButler(3) 1 48
(Richard Guest) *chsd ldrs: rdn 2f out: styd on same pce fnl f* 16/1

020- 4 3/4 **Auntie Kathryn (IRE)**[50] 7432 3-8-10 49 .... (v) WilliamCarson 2 41
(Stuart Williams) *s.i.s and edgd rt s: sn in tch: rdn 1/2-way: styd on: nt pce to chal* 7/2[3]

440- 5 1 1/2 **Emma Jean (IRE)**[115] 6001 3-8-4 48 .... (tp) RyanPowell(5) 6 34
(Niall Moran, Ire) *s.i.s: outpcd: nvr nrr* 11/1

405- 6 *nk* **Bitter Lemon**[73] 7059 3-9-2 55 .... FergusSweeney 7 40
(Tony Newcombe) *prom: pushed along 1/2-way: rdn over 1f out: no ex fnl f* 7/1

1m 3.21s (0.91) **Going Correction** +0.125s/f (Slow) **6** Ran SP% **108.3**
Speed ratings (Par 95): **97,93,91,89,87 86**
toteswingers:1&2:£1.90, 2&3:£5.00, 1&3:£7.20 CSF £7.89 CT £58.13 TOTE £2.40: £1.10, £2.20; EX 9.80.
Owner Mrs A Cantillon **Bred** Lady Betambeau Partnership **Trained** Dalham, Suffolk

FOCUS
A very weak 3-y-o sprint handicap.
Emma Jean(IRE) Official explanation: jockey said filly was slowly away

41 ENJOY THE PUNTERS PACKAGE GROUP OFFER MEDIAN AUCTION MAIDEN STKS 5f 216y(P)
4:40 (4:41) (Class 6) 3-5-Y-O **£1,704** (£503; £251) **Stalls** Low

Form RPR

6- 1 **Pettochside**[22] 7749 3-8-10 0 .... WilliamCarson 5 72
(Stuart Williams) *chsd ldrs: rdn and hmpd ins fnl f: hung lft and r.o to ld towards fin* 25/1

326- 2 3/4 **Marcus Augustus (IRE)**[104] 6293 3-8-10 72 .... JamieSpencer 9 70
(Jamie Osborne) *chsd ldr: shkn up to ld over 1f out: sn rdn and hung rt: hung lft and hdd towards fin* 4/5[1]

3 3 **Henry Bee** 3-8-10 0 .... PaulHanagan 10 62+
(Richard Fahey) *s.i.s: hld up: hdwy over 1f out: hmpd ins fnl f: styd on same pce* 9/2[3]

4 1 1/2 **Ambitious Boy** 3-8-11 0 ow1 .... RussKennemore 3 56
(Reg Hollinshead) *s.i.s: in rr tl r.o ins fnl f: nrst fin* 25/1

33- 5 3 1/2 **Wild Sauce**[40] 7555 3-8-5 0 .... JamesSullivan 1 39
(Bryan Smart) *plld hrd: trckd ldrs: hmpd wl over 3f out: rdn over 1f out: wknd ins fnl f* 3/1[2]

6 3 **Jolie Etoile** 4-9-7 0 .... DavidProbert 8 33
(Tony Carroll) *s.i.s: rdn over 2f out: n.d* 33/1

550- 7 10 **Take Root**[187] 3635 4-9-5 64 .... JackDuern(7) 7
(Reg Hollinshead) *led: rdn and hdd over 1f out: wknd fnl f* 12/1

0- 8 8 **Fireball Express**[15] 7845 4-9-12 0 .... TomEaves 2
(Brian Baugh) *hld up: rdn and wknd over 2f out* 33/1

1m 15.65s (0.65) **Going Correction** +0.125s/f (Slow)
WFA 3 from 4yo 16lb **8** Ran SP% **120.0**
Speed ratings (Par 101): **100,99,95,93,88 84,71,60**
toteswingers:1&2:£6.90, 2&3:£1.50, 1&3:£12.00 CSF £47.20 TOTE £41.10: £5.10, £1.10, £1.10; EX 76.80.
Owner James Thom **Bred** New Hall Stud **Trained** Newmarket, Suffolk

FOCUS
An ordinary maiden and a tight finish.

42 GREAT OFFERS AT WOLVERHAMPTON-RACECOURSE.CO.UK CLASSIFIED CLAIMING STKS 5f 216y(P)
5:10 (5:10) (Class 5) 3-Y-O **£2,264** (£673; £336; £168) **Stalls** Low

Form RPR

250- 1 **Adranian (IRE)**[9] 7881 3-8-9 70 .... (v) KieranO'Neill(3) 3 81
(David C Griffiths) *chsd ldr tl led over 2f out: rdn clr fr over 1f out* 7/2[3]

141- 2 6 **One More Roman (IRE)**[6] 7927 3-8-3 65 .... (bt) AmyRyan(3) 2 56
(Gay Kelleway) *led: rdn and hdd over 2f out: styd on same pce* 11/4[2]

142- 3 3 1/4 **Faraway**[7] 7907 3-9-0 70 .... (p) LukeMorris 6 53
(Ronald Harris) *chsd ldrs: rdn over 2f out: sn outpcd* 6/5[1]

332- 4 1/2 **The Dancing Lord**[31] 7635 3-8-4 62 ow3 .... RyanWhile(7) 4 49
(Bill Turner) *plld hrd and prom: rdn over 2f out: sn outpcd* 8/1

026- 5 8 **I'm Still The Man (IRE)**[19] 7798 3-7-13 62 .... (p) JakePayne(7) 5 18
(Bill Turner) *s.i.s: sn prom: rdn over 2f out: wknd over 1f out* 33/1

1m 15.46s (0.46) **Going Correction** +0.125s/f (Slow) **5** Ran SP% **108.4**
Speed ratings (Par 97): **101,93,88,88,77**
toteswingers:1&2:£3.40 CSF £12.92 TOTE £2.40: £1.50, £1.80; EX 12.80.
Owner Eros Bloodstock **Bred** Hugh O'Brien **Trained** Bawtry, S Yorks

FOCUS
Above-average form for the class.

43 WOLVERHAMPTON-RACECOURSE.CO.UK H'CAP 1m 4f 50y(P)
5:40 (5:40) (Class 5) (0-75,80) 4-Y-O+ **£2,264** (£673; £336; £168) **Stalls** Low

Form RPR

013- 1 **Shieldmaiden (USA)**[18] 7806 4-9-6 75 .... (b) JoeFanning 2 87
(Mark Johnston) *a.p: chsd ldr 10f out: led over 2f out: shkn up and hdd wl over 1f out: rallied ins fnl f: styd on to ld nr fin* 10/1[3]

211- 2 *nse* **Tornado Force (IRE)**[10] 7878 4-9-11 80 6ex .... JamieSpencer 1 92
(Jeremy Noseda) *hld up in tch: trckd wnr over 2f out: shkn up to ld wl over 1f out: rdn ins fnl f: hdd nr fin* 4/9[1]

034- 3 13 **Trend Line (IRE)**[19] 7803 4-9-4 73 .... EddieAhern 7 64
(Peter Chapple-Hyam) *set stdy pce for 1f: chsd ldrs: rdn over 2f out: sn outpcd* 7/2[2]

600- 4 7 **Jeer (IRE)**[27] 7699 8-9-5 70 .... (bt) PaddyAspell 4 50
(Michael Easterby) *led at stdy pce after 1f: qcknd over 4f out: rdn and hdd over 2f out: wknd over 1f out* 22/1

645- 5 *nk* **Pelham Crescent (IRE)**[10] 7878 9-9-0 70 .... RaulDaSilva(5) 3 49
(Bryn Palling) *hld up: rdn and wknd over 2f out* 33/1

005- 6 1 1/2 **Effervesce (IRE)**[44] 7506 5-8-11 62 .... (p) JimCrowley 6 39
(David Pipe) *s.s: hld up: rdn and wknd over 2f out* 28/1

2m 41.49s (0.39) **Going Correction** +0.125s/f (Slow)
WFA 4 from 5yo+ 4lb **6** Ran SP% **111.3**
Speed ratings (Par 103): **103,102,94,89,89 88**
toteswingers:1&2:£1.10, 2&3:£1.30, 1&3:£2.10 CSF £15.10 TOTE £7.50: £2.80, £1.10; EX 17.70.
Owner Sheikh Hamdan Bin Mohammed Al Maktoum **Bred** W S Farish, Bcwt Ltd And Inwood Stable **Trained** Middleham Moor, N Yorks

FOCUS
A modest handicap, run at a fair pace. The first pair dominated in the home straight in a battling finish and came right away from the remainder.

44 THOUSANDS OF SPORTS EXPERIENCES AT BLUESQ.COM H'CAP 2m 119y(P)
6:10 (6:11) (Class 4) (0-85,89) 4-Y-O+ **£4,204** (£1,251; £625; £312) **Stalls** Low

Form RPR

005- 1 **Rosewood Lad**[22] 7753 5-8-13 70 .... LukeMorris 6 77
(J S Moore) *sn chsng ldr: rdn over 2f out: styd on u.p to ld nr fin* 11/2[3]

002- 2 1/2 **Exemplary**[76] 6988 5-10-0 85 .... FrannyNorton 2 91
(Mark Johnston) *led: rdn and hdd over 1f out: ev ch and edgd lft ins fnl f: styd on* 5/2[2]

012- 3 *nk* **Wild Desert (FR)**[28] 7674 7-9-12 83 .... AdamKirby 3 89
(Charlie Longsdon) *chsd ldrs tl rdn to ld over 1f out: hdd nr fin* 9/4[1]

000- 4 1 1/4 **Nezhenka**[27] 7699 5-9-9 80 .... JoeFanning 8 85
(Mark Johnston) *hld up: hdwy over 3f out: rdn over 2f out: styng on whn hmpd ins fnl f: nvr able to chal* 7/1

411/ 5 2 1/2 **Ascendant**[25] 6313 6-9-11 85 .... (t) KieranO'Neill(3) 5 87
(Andrew Reid) *sn prom: rdn over 3f out: edgd lft and styd on same pce fnl f* 10/1

/13- 6 9 **Bivouac (UAE)**[9] 7884 8-9-2 73 .... JimCrowley 1 64
(Alan Swinbank) *prom: rdn over 2f out: wknd over 1f out* 8/1

7 3/4 **Rock Of Deauville (IRE)**[42] 5-9-11 82 .... BarryMcHugh 7 72?
(Julie Camacho) *hld up: rdn over 2f out: sn wknd* 28/1

3m 42.82s (1.02) **Going Correction** +0.125s/f (Slow) **7** Ran SP% **110.9**
Speed ratings (Par 105): **102,101,101,101,99 95,95**
toteswingers:1&2:£3.80, 2&3:£2.00, 1&3:£2.30 CSF £18.43 CT £37.28 TOTE £6.00: £2.90, £1.50; EX 20.20.
Owner Miss D L Wisbey & R J Viney **Bred** Miss D L Wisbey **Trained** Upper Lambourn, Berks
■ Stewards' Enquiry : Franny Norton caution: careless riding.

FOCUS
This looked competitive enough for the class. It was run at an ordinary pace, though, which didn't help the closers.

45 HORIZONS RESTAURANT, THE PLACE TO DINE H'CAP 1m 141y(P)
6:40 (6:40) (Class 7) (0-50,50) 4-Y-O+ **£1,704** (£503; £251) **Stalls** Low

Form RPR

044- 1 **Brave Decision**[20] 7787 5-8-12 45 .... (p) JimCrowley 4 51
(Robert Cowell) *a.p: rdn over 1f out: styd on u.p to ld post* 11/4[1]

005- 2 *hd* **My Mate Les (IRE)**[83] 6844 4-8-13 47 .... DavidProbert 9 53
(Tony Carroll) *a.p: chsd ldr over 3f out: rdn to ld over 1f out: hdd post* 10/1

/00- 3 3/4 **Kirstys Lad**[8] 7899 10-8-13 46 .... KellyHarrison 13 50
(Michael Mullineaux) *chsd ldrs: led over 6f out: rdn over 2f out: hdd over 1f out: styd on* 40/1

000- 4 1 **Aurora Lights**[18] 7805 5-8-12 45 .... (p) PaulHanagan 11 47
(Richard Fahey) *led: hdd over 6f out: chsd ldr tl over 3f out: sn rdn: styd on* 16/1

003- 5 *nk* **Wing N Prayer (IRE)**[17] 7822 5-9-2 49 .... PaddyAspell 3 50
(John Wainwright) *hld up: hdwy over 2f out: rdn over 1f out: r.o: nt rch ldrs* 25/1

003- 6 1/2 **Cwmni**[27] 7696 6-9-2 49 .... LukeMorris 2 49+
(Bryn Palling) *hld up: rdn over 2f out: hdwy u.p over 1f out: styd on* 15/2

603- 7 1 1/2 **Harvest Mist (IRE)**[20] 7787 4-9-0 48 .... NeilChalmers 6 44+
(Michael Blanshard) *hld up: rdn and swtchd rt over 1f out: r.o ins fnl f: nt rch ldrs* 5/1[3]

343- 8 1 **Baby Driver**[34] 7610 4-9-2 50 .... FergusSweeney 1 44
(Tony Newcombe) *trckd ldrs: plld hrd: rdn over 1f out: no ex fnl f* 9/2[2]

000- 9 6 **Zee Zee Dan (IRE)**[20] 7787 4-9-0 48 ow2 .... AdamKirby 7 28
(Noel Quinlan) *stdd s: hld up: hdwy u.p over 1f out: wknd ins fnl f* 5/1[3]

660- 10 3/4 **Watchmaker**[138] 749 9-8-12 50 .... (p) RyanPowell(5) 10 29
(Dai Williams) *hld up: pushed along and hdwy over 3f out: rdn over 2f out: wknd wl over 1f out* 25/1

006- 11 *hd* **Northern Genes (AUS)**[17] 7822 6-8-10 50 .... (be) JackDuern(7) 8 28
(Michael Appleby) *s.s: hld up: rdn over 2f out: a in rr* 50/1

00/- 12 1 3/4 **Weet In Nerja**[56] 7609 6-8-13 46 .... (t) ChrisCatlin 12 20
(Ken Wingrove) *hld up: rdn and wknd over 2f out* 100/1

1m 53.75s (3.25) **Going Correction** +0.125s/f (Slow)
WFA 4 from 5yo+ 1lb **12** Ran SP% **118.0**
Speed ratings (Par 97): **90,89,89,88,88 87,86,85,80,79 79,77**
toteswingers:1&2:£10.80, 2&3:£53.10, 1&3:£25.40 CSF £30.43 CT £922.25 TOTE £4.30: £1.60, £3.20, £11.80; EX 40.10.
Owner Bottisham Heath Stud **Bred** K A Dasmal **Trained** Six Mile Bottom, Cambs

FOCUS
A bottom-drawer handicap and a typically tight-looking affair.

Zee Zee Dan(IRE) Official explanation: vet said gelding bled from the nose

46 PLAY BINGO FREE AT BLUESQ.COM H'CAP 7f 32y(P)
7:10 (7:11) (Class 7) (0-50,50) 4-Y-0+ **£1,704** (£503; £251) **Stalls** High

Form	Pos	Dist	Horse	RPR
300-	1		**Clerical (USA)**[29] 7655 6-8-12 **45**....(p) JimCrowley 1 (Robert Cowell) *chsd ldrs: rdn over 1f out: hung rt and led wl ins fnl f* **10/1**	56
323-	2	¾	**Blueberry Fizz (IRE)**[6] 7924 4-9-0 **47** ow1....(v) AdamKirby 8 (John Ryan) *trckd ldrs: plld hrd: led over 2f out: rdn over 1f out: edgd rt and hdd wl ins fnl f* **5/2**[2]	56
03-4	3	1 ¾	**Pilgrim Dancer (IRE)**[3] 14 5-9-0 **50**....(p) AmyRyan[(3)] 4 (Tony Coyle) *pushed along in rr early: rdn 1/2-way: hdwy over 2f out: no ex towards fin* **9/4**[1]	54
032-	4	2 ¼	**Royal Acclamation (IRE)**[6] 7923 7-8-12 **45**....(p) SamHitchcott 9 (Michael Scudamore) *chsd ldrs: rdn over 1f out: styd on same pce fnl f* **11/4**[3]	43
636-	5	1	**American Lover (FR)**[20] 7781 5-9-3 **50**.... PaddyAspell 11 (John Wainwright) *s.i.s: hld up: rdn over 2f out: edgd lft over 1f out: styd on: nt trble ldrs* **14/1**	45
203-	6	1	**My Best Man**[23] 7747 6-9-1 **48**.... LukeMorris 7 (Tony Carroll) *hld up: hdwy over 2f out: rdn over 1f out: wknd ins fnl f* **16/1**	41
360-	7	6	**Raimond Ridge (IRE)**[281] 1043 6-8-8 **46**.... MatthewCosham[(5)] 3 (Derek Shaw) *hld up: rdn over 2f out: nvr on terms* **12/1**	22
640-	8	9	**Kyncraighe (IRE)**[21] 7768 4-8-7 **45**....(tp) CharlesBishop[(5)] 5 (Joseph Tuite) *led: hdd over 5f out: chsd ldrs: pushed along whn nt clr run and lost pl over 2f out: nt rcvr* **16/1**	
600-	9	1 ½	**Farmers Dream (IRE)**[70] 7119 5-8-12 **45**.... WilliamCarson 6 (Richard Price) *hld up: rdn over 2f out: sn wknd* **20/1**	
000-	10	10	**Chambers (IRE)**[27] 7696 6-9-1 **48**.... JoeFanning 10 (Bruce Hellier, Germany) *s.i.s: hdwy to ld over 5f out: hdd over 2f out: sn wknd and eased* **66/1**	

1m 30.54s (0.94) **Going Correction** +0.125s/f (Slow) **10** Ran SP% **127.5**
Speed ratings (Par 97): **99,98,96,93,92 91,84,74,72,61**
toteswingers:1&2:£7.10, 2&3:£2.10, 1&3:£6.70 CSF £38.68 CT £83.06 TOTE £11.40: £2.00, £1.30, £1.70; EX 42.50.
Owner J Sargeant **Bred** Walmac Stud Management Llc **Trained** Six Mile Bottom, Cambs

FOCUS
Another bottom-drawer handicap and the first four had it to themselves off the home turn.
Chambers(IRE) Official explanation: jockey said gelding lost its action on the bend
T/Plt: £39.90 to a £1 stake. Pool: £83,478.08. 1,523.63 winning tickets. T/Qpdt: £22.60 to a £1 stake. Pool: £8,902.60. 290.96 winning tickets. CR

MEYDAN (L-H)
Thursday, January 5
OFFICIAL GOING: Tapeta - standard; turf - good
Rail out 4m on Turf course.

47a LONGINES CONQUEST COLLECTION (H'CAP) (TAPETA) 1m 1f 110y
2:30 (2:30) (95-105,105) 3-Y-0+
£42,580 (£14,193; £7,096; £3,548; £2,129; £1,419)

Pos	Dist	Horse	RPR
1		**Sarrsar**[64] 7234 5-9-2 101....(vt) MickaelBarzalona 3 (Saeed Bin Suroor) *mid-div on rail: smooth prog 2 1/2f out: led fnl 110yds* **9/2**[3]	109+
2	1	**Capponi (IRE)**[301] 827 5-9-4 104.... FrankieDettori 2 (Mahmood Al Zarooni) *sn led: kicked clr 2f out: r.o same pce: hdd fnl 110yds* **3/1**[2]	110
3	5 ½	**Marching Time**[18] 7815 6-9-2 101.... RichardHills 6 (Doug Watson, UAE) *trckd ldr: ev ch 2f out: nt qckn fnl f* **17/2**	96
4	1	**Modern History (IRE)**[207] 2978 4-9-3 105.... AhmedAjtebi 5 (Mahmood Al Zarooni) *a mid-div: nvr able to chal* **5/1**	97
5	1	**Secretive**[6] 7934 5-8-9 95....(bt) PatCosgrave 7 (M bin Shafya, UAE) *settled in rr: rdn 3 1/2f out: nvr able to chal* **11/1**	85
6	2 ¼	**Glen Nevis (USA)**[6] 7932 8-8-13 98....(v) RoystonFfrench 1 (A Al Raihe, UAE) *slowly away: settled in rr: rdn 3 1/2f out: nvr nr to chal* **16/1**	84
7	¾	**Kal Barg**[28] 7683 7-9-0 99.... WilliamBuick 4 (D Selvaratnam, UAE) *trckd ldr: ev ch 2 1/2f out: one pce fnl 1 1/2f* **5/2**[1]	83

1m 59.47s (0.47)
WFA 4 from 5yo+ 1lb **7** Ran SP% **113.2**
CSF £17.99..
Owner Godolphin **Bred** Darley **Trained** Newmarket, Suffolk

FOCUS
The opening race of the 2012 Dubai World Cup Carnival was a reasonable contest and the front two finished clear. The pace was slow - they went a half-mile in 54.16 and 1.19.62 at the 6f point. The form is rated around the second and third.

NOTEBOOK
Sarrsar, returning from a two-month break and making his debut in Dubai, improved his record on synthetic tracks to 3-3, adding to a couple of Lingfield victories. Having travelled nicely, he quickened well in the straight and, once switched away from the inside, just needed his mind making up to go past the runner-up. He has also shown smart form on turf, but it's no surprise this surface suited so well considering he's a half-brother to a couple of Polytrack winners and his sire has a good strike-rate on such tracks.
Capponi(IRE) finished a long way clear of the remainder and this was a promising return from 301 days off. (op 11-4)
Marching Time has yet to convince under these conditions but basically wasn't as well handicapped as the front two. (op 8-1)
Modern History(IRE), like the winner, is by Shamardal, but he was seemingly the owner's third string and ran accordingly. He was below his smart French form and, although still lightly raced, can only be watched next time.
Secretive is another by Shamardal, but he's yet to convince on synthetics and looks better at Jebel Ali, where he was successful from 4lb lower last time. (op 10-1)
Kal Barg was heavily punted, surprisingly going off favourite, but he found nothing after being well placed and something was presumably amiss. (op 11-4)

48a LONGINES PRIMA LUNA (H'CAP) (TAPETA) 1m 3f
3:05 (3:05) (95-105,102) 3-Y-0+
£42,580 (£14,193; £7,096; £3,548; £2,129; £1,419)

Pos	Dist	Horse	RPR
1		**Honour System (IRE)**[68] 7170 5-9-0 102.... FrankieDettori 7 (Saeed Bin Suroor) *trckd ldr: led 3f out: rdn clr 2f out: r.o wl: comf* **7/4**[1]	106
2	1 ¼	**Lyssio (GER)**[19] 7802 5-8-10 99.... JamesDoyle 6 (Michael Attwater) *mid-div: r.o wl fnl 1 1/2f: nrest at fin* **10/1**	100+
3	½	**Manjakani**[123] 5771 4-8-8 100.... TadhgO'Shea 4 (Ismail Mohammed) *mid-div on rail: chsd wnr 3f out: ev ch 2f out: one pce fnl f* **4/1**[2]	100
4	1 ¼	**Monte Alto (IRE)**[5] 7945 8-8-11 100....(t) RichardHills 9 (A Al Raihe, UAE) *in rr of mid-div: smooth prog 3f out: ev ch 2f out: r.o same pce fnl 1 1/2f* **7/1**	98
5	4	**Falcativ**[293] 7-7-13 95....(b) SaeedAlMazrooe[(7)] 5 (Ismail Mohammed) *settled in rr: n.d* **20/1**	85
6	4	**Dr Faustus (IRE)**[41] 7552 7-8-11 100....(t) PatDobbs 1 (Doug Watson, UAE) *slowly away: in rr of mid-div: rdn 3 1/2f out: nvr able to chal* **9/1**	83
7	2 ¼	**Ahlaain (USA)**[28] 7683 4-8-7 99.... RoystonFfrench 3 (A Al Raihe, UAE) *s.i.s: trckd ldr tl wknd 2 1/2f out* **6/1**[3]	78
8	5	**Snowmaster (USA)**[329] 499 6-9-0 102....(bt) RichardMullen 2 (S Seemar, UAE) *sn led: hdd 3f out then trckd ldr: rdn and wknd 2 1/2f out* **16/1**	73
9	4	**We'll Come**[333] 8-8-11 100.... AhmedAjtebi 8 (A bin Huzaim, UAE) *mid-div: rdn 4f out: nvr able to chal* **25/1**	63

2m 18.9s (0.50)
WFA 4 from 5yo+ 3lb **9** Ran SP% **116.7**
CSF: £21.16; Tricast: £63.57..
Owner Godolphin **Bred** Darley **Trained** Newmarket, Suffolk

FOCUS
A weak race for a 95-105 and it was run at a slow pace. The first half-mile was run in 52.60, at which point Honour System took over, but he continued to set steady fractions, going 1.18.14 at the 6f point and 1.43.32 for the opening 1m. The winner is rated to his mark.

NOTEBOOK
Honour System(IRE) was still going easily turning into the straight before finding enough when pushed out. He was only 2lb higher than when successful over a shorter trip at last year's carnival and this sort of distance is more suitable. The winning margin might underplay his superiority.
Lyssio(GER) was formerly trained in Germany and this was just his second start for Michael Attwater. He ran well to pick up a nice prize for second.
Manjakani offered encouragement on his first start since leaving Andre Fabre. He stays well so this relative speed test was not in his favour.
Monte Alto(IRE) is a tricky sort and the race did not unfold to suit. He needs the leaders to come back.

50a LONGINES COLUMN WHEEL CHRONOGRAPH (H'CAP) (TURF) 5f
4:20 (4:20) (100-110,110) 3-Y-0+
£46,451 (£15,483; £7,741; £3,870; £2,322; £1,548)

Pos	Dist	Horse	RPR
1		**Addictive Dream (IRE)**[89] 6706 5-8-10 101.... AdrianNicholls 3 (David Nicholls) *trckd ldr: led 2f out: r.o wl: comf* **10/1**	107
2	½	**Nocturnal Affair (SAF)**[76] 7012 6-9-0 105.... CO'Donoghue 11 (David Marnane, Ire) *mid-div: smooth prog 2 1/2f out: ev ch 1f out: one pce fnl 110yds* **5/1**[1]	109+
3	1 ¼	**Humidor (IRE)**[81] 6906 5-9-3 108....(t) FrankieDettori 9 (George Baker) *squeezed at s: settled in rr: r.o fnl 1 1/2f: nrst fin* **15/2**[3]	108+
4	hd	**Invincible Ash (IRE)**[130] 5524 7-9-1 106....(p) TadhgO'Shea 5 (M Halford, Ire) *mid-div: r.o at one pce fnl 1 1/2f* **7/1**[2]	105
5	1 ¼	**Green Beret (IRE)**[301] 825 6-9-1 106.... RoystonFfrench 2 (A Al Raihe, UAE) *chsd ldrs: ev ch 2f out: r.o same pce fnl f* **7/1**[2]	100
6	¾	**Monsieur Joe (IRE)**[96] 6522 5-8-9 100.... MickaelBarzalona 4 (Robert Cowell) *settled in rr: sme prog fnl 2f: nvr threatened* **9/1**	92+
7	¾	**Internationaldebut (IRE)**[89] 6706 7-8-11 102.... FrederikTylicki 8 (Paul Midgley) *nvr bttr than mid-div* **11/1**	91
8	1 ¾	**Happy Dubai (IRE)**[28] 7680 5-9-5 110....(t) ChristopheSoumillon 6 (A Al Raihe, UAE) *chsd ldrs in centre: nt qckn fnl 1 1/2f* **10/1**	93
9	nk	**Russian Rock (IRE)**[13] 7869 5-8-13 104.... WayneSmith 1 (M Al Muhairi, UAE) *racd alone far side: prom tl wknd fnl 2f* **7/1**[2]	86
10	nse	**Zero Money (IRE)**[96] 6522 6-8-9 100....(b) JamesDoyle 10 (Roger Charlton) *nvr bttr than mid-div* **7/1**[2]	81
11	1 ½	**Spin Cycle (IRE)**[34] 7621 6-9-5 110....(t) RichardMullen 7 (S Seemar, UAE) *sn led: hdd & wknd 2f out* **20/1**	86

57.69s (57.69) **11** Ran SP% **119.7**
CSF: £60.52; Tricast: £406.17.
Owner Brian Morton **Bred** Eugene Matthews **Trained** Sessay, N Yorks
■ David Nicholls' first UAE winner.

FOCUS
A quality sprint handicap. Only the fifth race over this C&D and the winning time was just 0.05 outside Happy Dubai's track record. They raced middle to far side, but there was no draw bias.

NOTEBOOK
Addictive Dream(IRE) ◆ deserves a deal of credit. Having his first start since being purchased out of Walter Swinburn's yard for 90,000gns in October, he tanked along for much of the way and kept on much stronger than could have been expected. He was sitting fourth after two furlongs, at which point the next three finishers were ninth, eleventh and eighth respectively. This was only the 19th start of his career (fourth success) and it's not at all out of the question he could progress enough to make it to the Al Quoz Sprint on World Cup night. Before then there's a handicap for horses rated 100 and above over C&D on February 3.
Nocturnal Affair(SAF) had Addictive Dream behind on these terms when winning last year's Portland, but he couldn't confirm form despite the race setting up well. He still ran a good race and there could be more to come. (op 11-2)
Humidor(IRE) was short of room at the start and again when looking to make his bid. Consequently he was left with too much to do by the time he was in the clear and he's capable of better.
Invincible Ash(IRE) had been given a chance by the handicapper but might have needed this first run after a 130-day break
Green Beret(IRE) ◆, much like the winner, tanked along through the early stages and, although not seeing it out as well as that rival, there was still much to like considering he was having his first start for 301 days. The suspicion is he hasn't finished improving and he's one to keep in mind.
Monsieur Joe(IRE), another ex-Swinburn runner, is better than he showed as he was squeezed for room when pointed towards an ambitious gap in the closing stages and again found trouble when switched towards the far side. (op 8-1)
Internationaldebut(IRE) was short of room at the same time as Monsieur Joe and there's no telling where he might have finished.

Zero Money(IRE) disappointed after a three-month break.

51a LONGINES MASTER COLLECTION MOON PHASES (H'CAP) (TAPETA) 1m

5:00 (5:00) (95-105,105) 3-Y-0+

£42,580 (£14,193; £7,096; £3,548; £2,129; £1,419)

RPR
1 **City Style (USA)**[343] 326 6-9-1 102 .... MickaelBarzalona 5 107+
(Mahmood Al Zarooni) *in rr of mid-div: smooth prog 3f out: r.o wl fnl 1 1/2f: led fnl 55yds* **9/1**
2 *1 1/2* **Bridgefield (USA)**[124] 5699 4-8-13 100 .... AhmedAjtebi 11 102
(Mahmood Al Zarooni) *trckd ldrs: led 1f out: hdd fnl 55yds* **16/1**
3 *1* **Start Right**[187] 3645 5-9-1 102 .... FrankieDettori 3 102+
(Saeed Bin Suroor) *mid-div: r.o wl fnl 1 1/2f: nrest at fin* **5/2**[1]
4 *1/4* **Famous Warrior (IRE)**[28] 7682 5-9-1 102 .... TadhgO'Shea 13 101
(Doug Watson, UAE) *sn led: kicked clr 2 1/2f out: hdd 1f out: no ex* **20/1**
5 *1 3/4* **Canwinn (IRE)**[28] 7682 6-9-3 105 .... WilliamBuick 9 99
(D Selvaratnam, UAE) *mid-div: r.o fnl 2f but nvr nr to chal* **6/1**[3]
6 *1 3/4* **Tamaathul**[28] 7682 5-9-1 102 .... (t) RichardHills 12 93
(A Al Raihe, UAE) *mid-div: rn wd: chsd ldrs 3f out: ev ch 1 1/2f out: one pce fnl f* **12/1**
7 *shd* **Banna Boirche (IRE)**[135] 5361 6-9-3 105 .... ShaneFoley 2 95
(M Halford, Ire) *settled in rr: nvr nr to chal* **16/1**
8 *1/4* **Spirit Of Sharjah (IRE)**[19] 7801 7-9-0 101 .... TedDurcan 10 91
(Julia Feilden) *settled in rr: r.o fnl 2f but n.d* **16/1**
9 *5* **Anaerobio (ARG)**[446] 5-9-1 102 .... ChristopheSoumillon 4 81
(M F De Kock, South Africa) *in rr of mid-div: nvr able to chal* **10/3**[2]
10 *1* **Quick Wit**[322] 583 5-8-13 100 .... KierenFallon 8 76
(Saeed Bin Suroor) *squeezed at s: settled in rr: n.d* **9/1**
11 *2* **Bravo Echo**[19] 7801 6-8-10 98 .... JamesDoyle 7 69
(Michael Attwater) *nvr bttr than mid-div* **25/1**
12 *5* **Capital Market (USA)**[126] 5-8-9 102 .... AntiocoMurgia(6) 6 62
(Ismail Mohammed) *trckd ldrs tl 3 1/2f out: sn wknd* **25/1**
13 *13* **Mureb (USA)**[20] 7825 5-8-11 99 .... (t) PatCosgrave 1 28
(M bin Shafya, UAE) *trckd ldr tl 3f out: sn wknd* **20/1**

1m 36.95s (-0.55) **13** Ran SP% **128.5**
CSF: £146.70; Tricast: £476.62..
Owner Sheikh Hamdan Bin Mohammed Al Maktoum **Bred** Stonerside Stable **Trained** Newmarket, Suffolk

FOCUS
A solid Carnival handicap and Famous Warrior took them along for most of the way, going 26.03 for the first quarter, 49.12 for the half and 1.12.29 for 6f.

NOTEBOOK
City Style(USA) had a wide trip into the straight (covered more ground than any other rival) and lugged left under pressure, but he still did enough. He was only 1lb higher than when successful over C&D when last seen in this month last year, so was entitled to take this.
Bridgefield(USA) ran a solid race after a 124-day break. He's not short of speed and might be capable of even better back at 7f.
Start Right ◆ so often finds trouble and that was the case once again. Debuting for Godolphin after a 187-day break, he lost his chance when having to wait for a run around the final bend. The ease with which he had travelled before then running on when eventually in the clear suggests he retains sufficient ability to take one of these handicaps with ease.
Famous Warrior(IRE) gave it a good shot, but an uncontested lead helped his chance considerably.
Canwinn(IRE) had won his last two starts over C&D in non-Carnival handicaps, but this was tougher and he struggled off 8lb higher.
Banna Boirche(IRE) ◆, returning from a 135-day break, ran better than results suggests. He travelled easily under a hold-up ride, but lost his momentum when short of room on the final bend (stuck behind Start Right) before eventually running on quite nicely when the race was as good as over. It's likely he'll be eased in the weights and he can do better.

52a AL RASHIDIYA TRIAL PRESENTED BY LONGINES (CONDITIONS RACE) (TURF) 1m 1f

5:35 (5:35) 3-Y-0+

£48,387 (£16,129; £8,064; £4,032; £2,419; £1,612)

RPR
1 **Mahbooba (AUS)**[81] 6909 5-8-10 110 ow1.......... ChristopheSoumillon 4 112+
(M F De Kock, South Africa) *trckd ldr: led 1 1/2f out: comf* **11/8**[1]
2 *4 1/4* **Laajooj (IRE)**[203] 3068 4-8-13 108 .... MickaelBarzalona 7 107+
(Mahmood Al Zarooni) *settled in rr: r.o wl fnl 2f: nrest at fin* **7/1**[3]
3 *2 1/4* **Derbaas (USA)**[285] 1000 6-9-0 115 .... (t) RichardHills 2 102
(A Al Raihe, UAE) *trckd ldrs: led 2f out: hdd 1 1/2f out: one pce fnl f* **3/1**[2]
4 *2 1/4* **Sea Lord (IRE)**[26] 5-9-0 113 .... FrankieDettori 10 98
(Mahmood Al Zarooni) *sn led: rn wd: hdd 4f out: ev ch 2f out: r.o same pce fnl 1 1/2f* **15/2**
5 *1* **War Monger (USA)**[39] 8-9-0 104 .... TadhgO'Shea 6 96
(Doug Watson, UAE) *trckd ldr: led 4f out: hdd 2f out: one pce fnl f* **18/1**
6 *4* **St Moritz (IRE)**[165] 4368 6-9-0 107 .... AdrianNicholls 1 87+
(David Nicholls) *nvr bttr than mid-div* **7/1**[3]
7 *3* **Trois Rois (FR)**[291] 7-9-0 109 .... (b) RoystonFfrench 9 81+
(Ismail Mohammed) *nvr bttr than mid-div* **16/1**
8 *1 1/4* **Colony (IRE)**[28] 7683 7-9-0 93 .... (b) PatCosgrave 3 78+
(M bin Shafya, UAE) *s.i.s: nvr nr to chal* **66/1**
9 *3/4* **Energia Cosmica (BRZ)**[263] 5-9-1 104 ow1........(tp) ValmirDeAzeredo 5 78+
(Fabricio Borges, Sweden) *a in rr* **33/1**
10 *8 1/4* **Happy Today (USA)**[18] 7815 4-8-13 97 .... (v) WayneSmith 8 59
(M Al Muhairi, UAE) *trckd ldr tl wknd 2 1/2f out* **66/1**

1m 48.74s (108.74)
WFA 4 from 5yo+ 1lb **10** Ran SP% **120.9**
CSF: £12.49.
Owner Sheikh Mohammed Bin Khalifa Al Maktoum **Bred** Sheikh Mohammed Bin Khalifa Al Maktoum **Trained** South Africa

FOCUS
A trial for the Al Rashidiya, a Group 2 to be staged over C&D on January 26. This was the 13th race over 1m1f at Meydan and Mahbooba lowered the track record (set by the same trainer's River Jetez in 2011 Group 2 Balanchine) by 0.05 seconds. They went 26.64 for the first quarter-mile, 49.78 for the half and 1.12.81 to the 6f point.

NOTEBOOK
Mahbooba(AUS) settled better than is often the case and drew clear in the straight to take this impressively. It looked a career-best effort from last year's UAE 1000 Guineas heroine and her victory is all the more meritorious considering her most recent win (Newmarket Listed event in October) came over 1m4f. She has a host of options, obviously including the Al Rashidiya itself, and can be seriously competitive back in Group company provided this big comeback run doesn't leave its mark. (op 6-4)
Laajooj(IRE) was seemingly passed over by Frankie Dettori but made a pleasing return from a 203-day break. He should come on for this.
Derbaas(USA), having his first start since failing to beat a rival in last year's Duty Free, made nothing more than a satisfactory comeback, but he has no real record of going well fresh so there should be better to come. (op 5-2)
Sea Lord(IRE) had Frankie Dettori aboard (trainer also had the runner-up), but he faded noticeably late on. He helped set a pace that was ultimately fair, and he may also have needed what was his first start for 315 days, but he lacks scope. (op 7-1)
War Monger(USA) faced a tough task on these terms. (op 16-1)

53a LONGINES SAINT IMIER COLLECTION (H'CAP) (TURF) 7f

6:15 (6:15) (100-110,108) 3-Y-0+

£46,451 (£15,483; £7,741; £3,870; £2,322; £1,548)

RPR
1 **Time Prisoner (USA)**[130] 5532 5-9-2 108 .... FrankieDettori 14 112
(Mahmood Al Zarooni) *mid-div: smooth prog 2 1/2f out: led 1f out: comf* **7/1**[2]
2 *1 3/4* **Regal Parade**[110] 6147 8-9-0 106 .... AdrianNicholls 3 105+
(David Nicholls) *mid-div: r.o wl fnl 2f but no ch w wnr* **17/2**
3 *2 1/2* **Yaa Wayl (IRE)**[111] 6129 5-8-11 104 .... (vt) TedDurcan 9 95+
(Saeed Bin Suroor) *mid-div: r.o wl fnl 1 1/2f: nrest at fin* **16/1**
4 *shd* **As De Trebol (USA)**[65] 6-9-0 106 .... BFayosMartin 8 98
(M Delcher-Sanchez, Spain) *wl away: sn led: kicked clr 2f out: hdd 1f out: kpt on same pce* **14/1**
5 *nse* **Dandy Boy (ITY)**[60] 7318 6-8-11 104 .... CO'Donoghue 11 95
(David Marnane, Ire) *mid-div: r.o wl fnl 2f: nrst fin* **7/1**[2]
6 *1 3/4* **Mujaazef**[6] 7936 5-9-2 108 .... (t) TadhgO'Shea 10 95
(A Al Raihe, UAE) *mid-div: rdn to chse ldrs 3f out: one pce fnl 2f* **14/1**
7 *nse* **Hujaylea (IRE)**[124] 5746 9-8-13 105 .... (p) ShaneFoley 7 92
(M Halford, Ire) *in rr of mid-div: r.o fnl 2f but n.d* **8/1**[3]
8 *2 3/4* **Hunting Tower (SAF)**[291] 10-9-1 107 .... (t) ChristopheSoumillon 6 87
(M F De Kock, South Africa) *nvr able to chal* **12/1**
9 *3/4* **Mabait**[19] 7801 6-8-13 105 .... WilliamBuick 16 83
(David Simcock) *nvr able to chal* **16/1**
10 *nk* **Iguazu Falls (USA)**[18] 7815 7-8-8 100 .... (t) XZiani 77
(M bin Shafya, UAE) *wl away: trckd ldr: ev ch 2f out: wknd fnl 1 1/2f* **16/1**
11 *nk* **Colonial (IRE)**[96] 6534 5-9-1 107 .... MickaelBarzalona 13 83
(Saeed Bin Suroor) *nvr bttr than mid-div* **12/1**
12 *2 1/4* **Montmorency (IRE)**[39] 6-8-10 102 .... (t) RichardMullen 1 72
(S Seemar, UAE) *trckd ldng duo tl wknd 3f out* **25/1**
13 *2 1/2* **Wonder Lawn (SAF)**[293] 9-8-11 104 .... (t) KShea 15 66
(M F De Kock, South Africa) *nvr able to chal* **16/1**
14 *1 1/4* **Ouqba**[481] 5946 6-9-1 107 .... RichardHills 12 67
(Doug Watson, UAE) *s.i.s: mid-div: n.d* **9/1**
15 *2* **Moran Gra (USA)**[130] 5526 5-8-13 105 .... (p) RyanMoore 5 59
(Ms Joanna Morgan, Ire) *nvr able to chal* **6/1**[1]
16 *8 1/2* **Abjer (FR)**[301] 823 4-8-10 102 .... (b) RoystonFfrench 4 33
(Ismail Mohammed) *nvr bttr than mid-div* **25/1**

1m 23.82s (83.82) **16** Ran SP% **130.9**
CSF: £70.32; Tricast: £949.24. Placepot: £17.20 to a £1 stake. Pool: £7,561.26. 319.32 winning tickets. Quadpot: £7.60 to a £1 stake. Pool: £330.42. 32.10 winning tickets..
Owner Godolphin **Bred** Darley **Trained** Newmarket, Suffolk

FOCUS
The second fastest race to date over 7f on the Meydan turf - the current tack record was set in this race last year. It's no surprise the time was rapid considering As De Trebol and Iguazu Falls duelled for the lead, going 25.25 for the opening quarter-mile and 47.57 for the half.

NOTEBOOK
Time Prisoner(USA) ◆, a Group 3 winner over 6f for Andre Fabre (also successful at up to 1m), produced a really smart performance to readily defy a mark of 108 after a 130-day break. He should be comfortable back in pattern company.
Regal Parade ran well to confirm that David Nicholls (winner earlier on the card) has his Dubai string in good order. The runner-up, whose last success came in the 2010 Prix Maurice de Gheest, has clearly dropped to a workable mark.
Yaa Wayl(IRE) hasn't looked straightforward but he finished well from off the good pace.
As De Trebol(USA) ◆ seemed to confirm the suspicion that he's improved since last year's carnival and he can exploit a mark of 106 when ridden less aggressively and/or allowed an easy lead.
Dandy Boy(ITY) couldn't take advantage of a mark 2lb lower than when winning this last year. He was set a bit to do but it was disappointing how his run flattened out in the closing stages.
Hujaylea(IRE), 3lb higher than when runner-up in this last season, is better than he showed as he was denied a clear run when staying on from a long way back.
Hunting Tower(SAF) ◆, returning from a 291-day break, very much caught the eye running on from a long way back under sympathetic handling. He's at the veteran stage of his career, but was only 2lb higher than when successful (1m3f, Tapeta) at last year's carnival and is likely to be eased.

49 - 53a (Foreign Racing) - See Raceform Interactive

[33]LINGFIELD (L-H)

Friday, January 6

OFFICIAL GOING: Standard

Wind: Moderate, across, towards stands Weather: Sunny

54 PLACE ONLY BETTING AT BLUESQ.COM H'CAP 1m (P)

12:40 (12:40) (Class 5) (0-75,74) 4-Y-0+ **£2,385** (£704; £352) **Stalls** High

Form RPR
600- **1** **Aquarian Spirit**[97] 6533 5-9-7 **74** .... TomEaves 5 80
(Richard Fahey) *trckd ldr: rdn wl over 1f out: lost 2nd ins fnl f but stl cl up: rallied between rivals to ld post* **9/1**
220- **2** *shd* **Hereford Boy**[18] 7823 8-9-6 **73** .... (v[1]) AdamKirby 7 79
(Dean Ivory) *hld up in 5th: cajoled along and prog over 1f out: wl-timed chal to ld last 100yds: fnd little and hdd post* **7/2**[3]
021- **3** *hd* **Perfect Mission**[25] 7739 4-9-3 **70** .... (v) DavidProbert 1 75
(Andrew Balding) *led: set mod pce tl kicked on over 2f out: drvn and hdd last 100yds: styd on but jst hld* **11/4**[1]
000- **4** *2 1/4* **My Kingdom (IRE)**[42] 7542 6-9-7 **74** .... (t) JamieSpencer 4 74
(Ian Williams) *dwlt: hld up in last: effrt against rail over 1f out: nt qckn and wl hld fnl f* **7/2**[3]
500- **5** *nse* **Muhandis (IRE)**[44] 7519 4-9-0 **67** .... (p) ChrisCatlin 2 67
(Nick Littmoden) *t.k.h: trckd ldng pair: drvn over 1f out: fdd ins fnl f* **50/1**
10-4 **6** *8* **Aquilifer (IRE)**[4] 16 4-9-6 **73** .... ShaneKelly 6 55
(Mrs K Burke) *trckd ldng trio: rn wd bnd 2f out and lost grnd: nvr on terms after* **3/1**[2]

1m 37.56s (-0.64) **Going Correction** +0.10s/f (Slow) **6** Ran SP% **108.1**
Speed ratings (Par 103): **107,106,106,104,104 96**
toteswingers:1&2:£6.90, 2&3:£1.40, 1&3:£6.00 CSF £37.02 TOTE £11.20: £3.90, £2.10; EX 50.40.
Owner P S Cresswell & Mrs P A Morrison **Bred** Whitwell Bloodstock **Trained** Musley Bank, N Yorks

FOCUS
A modest handicap and the pace didn't quicken significantly until 3f from home. There was very little to choose between the front three at the line.
Aquilifer(IRE) Official explanation: jockey said gelding hung right

55 LINGFIELDPARK.CO.UK (S) STKS 1m (P)
1:10 (1:10) (Class 6) 4-Y-0+ **£1,704** (£503; £251) **Stalls** High

Form RPR
046- **1** **Divine Rule (IRE)**[8] 7910 4-8-6 53........................(b[1]) CharlotteJenner(7) 1 59
(Laura Mongan) *sn led: gng best 2f out: reminders fnl f: styd on and nvr seriously chal* **25/1**
412- **2** 2 ¼ **Northern Spy (USA)**[18] 7817 8-8-13 65.................... EddieAhern 2 54
(Simon Dow) *cn restrained bhd wnr: pushed along and dropped to 3rd 3f out: struggling after: kpt on to take 2nd again last 150yds: unable to chal* **1/3**[1]
603- **3** ½ **Querido (GER)**[9] 7888 8-8-10 50..............................(tp) RobertLButler(3) 4 53
(Paddy Butler) *trckd ldng pair: chsd wnr 3f out: rdn and nt qckn over 1f out: lost 2nd last 150yds* **15/2**[3]
663- **4** ¾ **Dichoh**[30] 7663 9-9-5 58..(p) ChrisCatlin 3 57
(Michael Madgwick) *hld up in last: pushed along bef 1/2-way and lost tch: drvn 3f out: no imp tl styd on fnl f* **11/2**[2]

1m 38.2s **Going Correction** +0.10s/f (Slow) 4 Ran SP% **106.0**
Speed ratings (Par 101): **104,101,101,100**
CSF £35.02 TOTE £17.80; EX 12.40.There was no bid for the winner.
Owner Mrs L J Mongan **Bred** Car Colston Hall Stud **Trained** Epsom, Surrey
■ Charlotte Jenner's first winner.
FOCUS
A poor seller with a long odds-on favourite, but it became one of those races that will leave many punters jumping up and down on their formbooks. The winning time was 0.64 seconds slower than the opener.

56 COWDEN MEDIAN AUCTION MAIDEN STKS 1m (P)
1:45 (1:46) (Class 6) 3-5-Y-0 **£1,704** (£503; £251) **Stalls** High

Form RPR
0- **1** **Flash Crash**[23] 7751 3-8-8 0.. ShaneKelly 6 68
(Robert Cowell) *nt that wl away but rcvrd to ld: kicked on over 2f out: drvn clr over 1f out: styd on wl* **7/4**[2]
46- **2** 5 **Athletic**[6] 7938 3-8-5 0.. KieranO'Neill(3) 7 57
(Andrew Reid) *hld up in 5th: prog on outer to chse wnr 3f out: rdn 2f out: no imp over 1f out: jst hld on for 2nd* **25/1**
03- **3** nk **Pearl Frost**[23] 7758 3-8-8 0..(b[1]) MartinLane 4 56
(Ralph Beckett) *mostly chsd wnr to 3f out: outpcd over 2f out: kpt on fr over 1f out: nrly snatched 2nd* **8/1**
035- **4** 3 **Fine Resolve**[23] 7752 3-8-8 70..(p) DavidProbert 2 49
(Andrew Balding) *settled in 4th: lost pl on inner over 3f out: sn pushed along and nt qckn: one pce and no hdwy fnl 2f* **5/4**[1]
5 2 ¾ **Friends Of Ama Gi** 3-8-8 0.. ChrisCatlin 1 43
(Mark Hoad) *s.i.s: hld up in last pair: outpcd fr 1/2-way: styd on inner and kpt on fr over 1f out* **25/1**
00- **6** 1 ¼ **Bellinda**[8] 7909 3-8-3 0.. FrankieMcDonald 3 35
(Martin Bosley) *a towards rr: outpcd over 3f out: nvr on terms after* **50/1**
00- **7** 6 **The Young Master**[23] 7751 3-8-8 0................................ SamHitchcott 8 26
(Neil Mulholland) *chsd ldng pair: rdn 1/2-way: wknd rapidly over 2f out* **100/1**
8 1 **Taglietelle** 3-8-5 0.. SimonPearce(3) 5 24
(Andrew Balding) *dwlt: a in last pair: outpcd fr 1/2-way: bhd fnl 2f* **7/1**[3]

1m 38.34s (0.14) **Going Correction** +0.10s/f (Slow) 8 Ran SP% **115.1**
Speed ratings (Par 101): **103,98,97,94,91 90,84,83**
toteswingers:1&2:£7.50, 2&3:£5.70, 1&3:£2.70 CSF £45.55 TOTE £1.90: £1.10, £5.00, £2.10; EX 29.60 Trifecta £92.10 Pool: £866.54 - 6.96 winning units..
Owner Jim Furlong **Bred** J R Furlong **Trained** Six Mile Bottom, Cambs
FOCUS
The winning time was slower than the first two races for older horses, which might have been expected, but still not a maiden to set the pulse racing.
Fine Resolve Official explanation: jockey said gelding had no more to give

57 MARRIOTT HOTEL AT LINGFIELD PARK (S) STKS 1m 4f (P)
2:15 (2:15) (Class 6) 4-Y-0+ **£1,704** (£503; £251) **Stalls** Low

Form RPR
002- **1** **Eagle Nebula**[6] 7939 8-9-3 69... IanMongan 5 67
(Brett Johnson) *trckd ldr: quick move to ld 4f out: drvn clr over 1f out* **4/6**[1]
414- **2** 3 ¾ **Rowan Ridge**[6] 7939 4-9-5 68..(b) EddieAhern 1 67
(Jim Boyle) *led at dawdle: hdd wl over 3f out and outpcd: barging match w rival over 2f out: no imp on wnr after* **9/4**[2]
605- **3** 1 **Herschel (IRE)**[18] 7818 6-9-3 53....................................(be[1]) AmirQuinn 6 59?
(Gary Moore) *stdd s: hld up last: wnt 3rd 4f out: chal for 2nd 3f out and barging match w rival sn after: rdn and fnd nil 2f out* **15/2**[3]
006- **4** 4 ½ **Sunset Boulevard (IRE)**[9] 7891 9-9-0 50..............(v) RobertLButler(3) 3 52
(Paddy Butler) *trckd ldng pair: dropped to last 4f out: shkn up over 2f out: no rspnse* **18/1**

2m 38.83s (5.83) **Going Correction** +0.10s/f (Slow)
WFA 4 from 6yo+ 4lb 4 Ran SP% **107.8**
Speed ratings (Par 101): **84,81,80,77**
CSF £2.38 TOTE £1.70; EX 1.90.There was no bid for the winner.
Owner Tann Racing **Bred** Juddmonte Farms Ltd **Trained** Epsom, Surrey
FOCUS
Another moderate seller, especially with the two non-runners, and although there was some "handbags" between the riders of the second and third over 2f out, it made no difference to the result.

58 FOLLOW US ON TWITTER @BLUESQ H'CAP 1m 5f (P)
2:50 (2:50) (Class 6) (0-65,65) 4-Y-0+ **£1,704** (£503; £251) **Stalls** Low

Form RPR
342- **1** **Maslak (IRE)**[18] 7818 8-8-13 **54**.. ChrisCatlin 6 62
(Peter Hiatt) *mde all: set modest pce tl wound it up fr 4f out: drvn over 1f out: hld on* **9/4**[2]
562- **2** 1 ¼ **Broughtons Paradis (IRE)**[9] 7903 6-9-10 **65**................ JamieMackay 3 71
(Willie Musson) *hld up in tch: clsd on ldrs over 2f out: shkn up to chse wnr over 1f out: nt qckn ins fnl f* **10/3**[3]
320- **3** ½ **Opera Prince**[21] 7789 7-9-6 **61**... DavidProbert 1 66
(Simon Earle) *hld up in tch: clsd on ldrs over 2f out: rdn to dispute 2nd over 1f out: nt qckn fnl f* **8/1**
644- **4** 2 ½ **Guards Chapel**[20] 7800 4-9-0 **60**......................................(v) AdamKirby 2 62
(Gary Moore) *trckd ldng pair: hd to one side whn pce lifted 4f out and sn dropped to last pair: no ch 2f out: snatched 4th post* **15/8**[1]
442- **5** nk **Lucky Diva**[16] 7850 5-8-8 **56**...(p) JakePayne(7) 5 57
(Bill Turner) *trckd wnr: rdn over 2f out: lost 2nd over 1f out: wknd fnl f* **10/1**
000- **6** 5 **Nesnaas (USA)**[9] 7892 11-8-3 **51** oh6.....................(tp) LeonnaMayor(7) 4 45?
(Alastair Lidderdale) *hld up: a in last pair: pushed along and no prog over 3f out: sn btn* **66/1**

2m 52.45s (6.45) **Going Correction** +0.10s/f (Slow)
WFA 4 from 5yo+ 5lb 6 Ran SP% **110.3**
Speed ratings (Par 101): **84,83,82,81,81 78**
toteswingers:1&2:£2.80, 2&3:£4.10, 1&3:£5.90 CSF £9.78 TOTE £3.90: £1.90, £2.50; EX 11.60.
Owner P W Hiatt **Bred** Shadwell Estate Company Limited **Trained** Hook Norton, Oxon
FOCUS
Not much pace on early for this staying handicap and another example of the advantages of being allowed a soft lead.

59 DORMANSLAND H'CAP 5f (P)
3:25 (3:26) (Class 6) (0-65,70) 4-Y-0+ **£1,704** (£503; £251) **Stalls** High

Form RPR
120- **1** **Jimmy Ryan (IRE)**[66] 7201 11-8-9 **60**..........................(t) RaulDaSilva(5) 7 71
(Tim McCarthy) *trckd ldrs: prog gng wl 2f out: led over 1f out: pushed clr: comf* **12/1**
600- **2** 2 ¼ **Sherjawy (IRE)**[6] 7940 8-9-2 **62**.. SamHitchcott 2 65
(Zoe Davison) *unable to hold prom pl after 1f: urged along after 2f and sn in 7th: prog over 1f out: styd on to take 2nd ins fnl f: no ch w wnr* **18/1**
063- **3** 1 **Welsh Inlet (IRE)**[6] 7940 4-9-0 **63**.................................. KieranO'Neill(3) 4 62
(John Bridger) *led 100yds: trapped on inner bhd rival fr 3f out to wl over 1f out: styd on fnl f to take 4th last strides* **11/2**[3]
602- **4** nk **Liberal Lady**[19] 7812 4-9-0 **60**.....................................(e) JamieGoldstein 9 58
(Ralph Smith) *prom on outer: led 3f out: hdd over 1f out: wknd ins fnl f* **16/1**
051- **5** 1 ½ **Jolly Ranch**[102] 6398 6-9-4 **64**.. FergusSweeney 1 57
(Tony Newcombe) *n.m.r on inner after 1f and sn last: detached fr main gp over 2f out: kpt on fr over 1f out: n.d* **20/1**
452- **6** shd **Even Bolder**[6] 7940 9-9-5 **65**.. ShaneKelly 8 57
(Eric Wheeler) *nt that wl away: prog on outer fr last trio to press ldrs 2f out: rdn and hd at awkward angle over 1f out: fnd nil* **6/1**
051- **7** ½ **Royal Bajan (USA)**[6] 7940 4-9-10 **70** 6ex........................... TomEaves 6 61
(James Given) *nt that wl away: racd in last trio: effrt and in tch in 6th 2f out: shkn up and one pce over 1f out: wl btn fnl f* **11/8**[1]
324- **8** 3 ¼ **Novabridge**[16] 7844 4-9-2 **62**..(p) AdamKirby 3 41
(Neil Mulholland) *sn towards rr: detached in last pair 1/2-way: no prog* **5/1**[2]
560- **9** 10 **Miss Polly Plum**[114] 6065 5-9-2 **62**................................(p) AndreaAtzeni 5
(Chris Dwyer) *led after 100yds to 3f out: wknd v rapidly wl over 1f: t.o* **33/1**

58.1s (-0.70) **Going Correction** +0.10s/f (Slow) 9 Ran SP% **115.0**
Speed ratings (Par 101): **109,105,103,103,100 100,99,94,78**
toteswingers:1&2:£15.40, 2&3:£11.00, 1&3:£9.00 CSF £201.29 CT £1333.40 TOTE £14.30: £4.30, £5.20, £1.60; EX 142.00 Trifecta £1003.00 Part won. Pool: £1355.50 - 0.64 winning units..
Owner Mrs D H McCarthy **Bred** Barronstown Stud And Orpendale **Trained** Godstone, Surrey
FOCUS
There was certainly no hiding place in this sprint handicap.

60 PLAY DA VINCI DIAMONDS AT BLUESQ.COM/GAMES APPRENTICE H'CAP 1m 2f (P)
3:55 (3:55) (Class 6) (0-65,66) 4-Y-0+ **£1,704** (£503; £251) **Stalls** Low

Form RPR
031- **1** **Whodunit (UAE)**[19] 7805 8-9-5 **62**...................................(b) LucyKBarry 1 75
(Peter Hiatt) *mde all: at least 2 l ahd fr 1/2-way: drvn clr fr 2f out: unchal* **6/4**[1]
312- **2** 4 **Resplendent Alpha**[7] 7924 8-9-1 **58** 6ex......................... LeonnaMayor 6 63
(Alastair Lidderdale) *s.s and lft 6 l: ct up w rest after 4f: prog over 2f out: styd on to take 2nd ins fnl f: no ch w wnr* **5/1**[3]
035- **3** 1 **Patriotic (IRE)**[16] 7842 4-9-1 **63**..................................... DannyBrock(3) 3 66
(Chris Dwyer) *chsd wnr: rdn and no imp 2f out: one pce and lost 2nd ins fnl f* **11/2**
621- **4** 6 **Beggers Belief**[9] 7902 4-9-7 **66** 6ex...............................(b) RaulDaSilva 5 57
(Eric Wheeler) *hld up in 5th: rdn and struggling 3f out: dropped to last over 2f out: plugged on fnl f* **3/1**[2]
150- **5** ½ **Newby Lodge (IRE)**[93] 6621 4-8-12 **60**....................... NatashaEaton(3) 7 50
(Alan Bailey) *hld up in 4th: gng wl enough 3f out: pushed along and wknd wl over 1f out* **16/1**
045- **6** 1 **Red Yarn**[78] 6969 5-9-7 **64**.. CharlesBishop 2 52
(Joseph Tuite) *chsd ldng pair: rdn over 3f out: wknd 2f out* **10/1**

2m 5.06s (-1.54) **Going Correction** +0.10s/f (Slow)
WFA 4 from 5yo+ 2lb 6 Ran SP% **112.0**
Speed ratings (Par 101): **110,106,106,101,100 100**
toteswingers:1&2:£2.30, 2&3:£3.10, 1&3:£2.70 CSF £9.40 TOTE £2.50: £1.40, £1.20; EX 7.80.
Owner Exors of the Late John Hedges **Bred** Darley **Trained** Hook Norton, Oxon
■ Stewards' Enquiry : Leonna Mayor one-day ban: careless riding (Jan 20)
FOCUS
This was all very straightforward.
T/Plt: £4,337.20 to a £1 stake. Pool of £62,088.03 - 10.45 winning tickets. T/Qpdt: £86.30 to a £1 stake. Pool of £8,031.67 - 68.80 winning tickets. JN

[40]WOLVERHAMPTON (A.W) (L-H)
Friday, January 6

OFFICIAL GOING: Standard
Wind: Light behind Weather: Fine

61 PLACE ONLY BETTING AT BLUESQ.COM MEDIAN AUCTION MAIDEN STKS 7f 32y(P)
4:15 (4:18) (Class 6) 3-5-Y-0 **£1,704** (£503; £251) **Stalls** High

Form RPR
2- **1** **Appealing (IRE)**[23] 7757 3-8-2 0.............................. AdamBeschizza(3) 2 80
(Marco Botti) *mde all: shkn up over 1f out: sn clr: readily* **4/9**[1]
350- **2** 3 ½ **Roedean (IRE)**[97] 6526 3-8-5 74.. FrannyNorton 6 71
(Jamie Osborne) *chsd wnr 6f out: pushed along 3f out: styd on same pce appr fnl f* **3/1**[2]
3 10 **Time To Dance** 3-8-10 0.. LiamKeniry 1 49
(Joseph Tuite) *chsd wnr 1f: remained handy: rdn over 2f out: wknd over 1f out* **12/1**[3]

224- **4** *1 ¾* **Sannibel**[135] 5377 4-9-9 68 SteveDrowne 4 43
(Tony Carroll) *prom: rdn over 2f out: wknd over 1f out* **16/1**

0- **5** *3* **Homeward Strut**[227] 2387 3-8-10 0 RobbieFitzpatrick 3 36
(Frank Sheridan) *dwlt: hld up: rdn over 2f out: sn wknd* **100/1**

6- **6** *14* **Pink Evie**[21] 7784 3-8-5 0 PaulHanagan 5
(Gay Kelleway) *hld up: a in rr: wknd 3f out: t.o* **40/1**

1m 29.6s **Going Correction** +0.05s/f (Slow)
WFA 3 from 4yo 18lb **6** Ran SP% **111.3**
Speed ratings (Par 101): **102,98,86,84,81 65**
toteswingers:1&2:£1.10, 2&3:£1.90, 1&3:£1.90 CSF £1.99 TOTE £1.60: £1.10, £1.50; EX 2.20.
Owner Miss Yvonne Jacques **Bred** Ms Michelle Lyons **Trained** Newmarket, Suffolk

62 STAY AT THE WOLVERHAMPTON HOLIDAY INN CLAIMING STKS 5f 20y(P)

4:45 (4:45) (Class 5) 4-Y-0+ **£2,264** (£673; £336; £168) **Stalls** Low

Form RPR

360- **1** **Desert Strike**[17] 7833 6-8-7 74 (p) NoraLooby(7) 5 81
(Alan McCabe) *s.i.s: plld hrd and sn trcking ldrs: led over 1f out: edgd rt ins fnl f: r.o* **12/1**

503- **2** *1* **Angelo Poliziano**[171] 4174 6-8-7 75 (p) PaulHanagan 3 70
(Ann Duffield) *chsd ldrs: rdn over 1f out: r.o* **10/1**

353- **3** *½* **Drawnfromthepast (IRE)**[38] 7575 7-9-3 89 JamieSpencer 7 79
(Jamie Osborne) *chsd ldrs: rdn over 1f out: styd on* **7/2**[2]

330- **4** *shd* **Riflessione**[18] 7819 6-8-13 68 (b) LukeMorris 1 74?
(Ronald Harris) *disp ld tl rdn over 1f out: styd on u.p* **11/1**

532- **5** *hd* **Hinton Admiral**[34] 7629 8-9-1 79 JoeFanning 8 76
(Keith Dalgleish) *sn pushed along and prom: rdn over 1f out: r.o: nt gng pce to chal* **9/2**[3]

021- **6** *1 ¼* **Red Cape (FR)**[7] 7926 9-9-5 78 (b) JamesSullivan 2 75
(Ruth Carr) *disp ld over 3f: sn rdn: no ex ins fnl f* **5/2**[1]

00-0 **7** *1 ¼* **Forty Proof (IRE)**[4] 13 4-8-2 70 (tp) RobJFitzpatrick(7) 6 61
(Alan McCabe) *s.i.s: outpcd: hdwy over 1f out: no ex ins fnl f* **14/1**

1m 1.74s (-0.56) **Going Correction** +0.05s/f (Slow) **7** Ran SP% **100.8**
Speed ratings (Par 103): **106,104,103,103,103 101,99**
toteswingers:1&2:£8.60, 2&3:£3.80, 1&3:£4.90 CSF £91.67 TOTE £14.80: £4.80, £3.80; EX 83.80.
Owner Mrs M J McCabe **Bred** Mrs Mary Rowlands **Trained** Averham Park, Notts

FOCUS
A decent claimer run at a good pace and it was decided on the turn into the straight when Riflessione, who was in the front rank on the inside up until then, failed to corner as well as his rider would have liked, and carried much of the field wide with him.

63 SPONSOR A RACE BY CALLING 01902 390000 H'CAP 1m 5f 194y(P)

5:15 (5:17) (Class 5) (0-70,70) 4-Y-0+ **£2,264** (£673; £336; £168) **Stalls** Low

Form RPR

112- **1** **Appeal (IRE)**[9] 7900 4-9-6 70 LukeMorris 3 83+
(Sir Mark Prescott Bt) *chsd ldr 1f: remained handy: pushed along over 3f out: led 2f out: sn rdn: hung lft ins fnl f: styd on* **1/1**[1]

604- **2** *2 ¼* **Leyte Gulf (USA)**[16] 7850 9-9-0 58 DaneO'Neill 2 66
(Chris Bealby) *s.i.s: hld up: hdwy over 3f out: rdn to go 2nd over 1f out: no ch w wnr* **12/1**

003- **3** *1* **Dart**[16] 7850 8-9-1 62 MichaelO'Connell(3) 4 69
(John Mackie) *hld up: hdwy over 2f out: rdn over 1f out: styd on* **12/1**

534- **4** *5* **Little Jazz**[50] 7446 4-9-3 67 (b) RobertWinston 6 67
(Paul D'Arcy) *chsd ldr after 1f tl led over 3f out: sn rdn: hdd 2f out: wknd fnl f* **14/1**

343- **5** *1 ¼* **The Winged Assasin (USA)**[9] 7900 6-9-4 67 (t) RyanPowell(5) 5 65
(Shaun Lycett) *prom: rdn over 2f out: sn ev ch: wknd fnl f* **6/1**[3]

000- **6** *5* **Ghufa (IRE)**[23] 7761 8-9-1 62 SimonPearce(3) 1 53
(Lydia Pearce) *chsd ldrs: lost pl over 4f out: wknd wl over 2f out* **28/1**

013- **7** *11* **Cadgers Brig**[27] 7720 4-9-6 70 (v) JoeFanning 7 45
(Keith Dalgleish) *set stdy pce tl qcknd over 4f out: hdd over 3f out: wknd wl over 1f out* **7/2**[2]

3m 10.1s (4.10) **Going Correction** +0.05s/f (Slow)
WFA 4 from 6yo+ 6lb **7** Ran SP% **112.0**
Speed ratings (Par 103): **90,88,88,85,84 81,75**
toteswingers:1&2:£3.10, 2&3:£7.60, 1&3:£3.2 CSF £14.12 TOTE £1.80: £1.20, £3.90; EX 12.20.
Owner Denford Stud **Bred** Norelands Stallions **Trained** Newmarket, Suffolk

FOCUS
They didn't go a great pace early and the race developed into something of a sprint finish.
The Winged Assasin(USA) Official explanation: jockey said gelding hung right

64 FOLLOW US ON TWITTER @BLUESQ H'CAP 5f 216y(P)

5:45 (5:46) (Class 4) (0-85,85) 4-Y-0+ **£4,204** (£1,251; £625; £312) **Stalls** Low

Form RPR

16/- **1** **Alben Star (IRE)**[455] 6719 4-9-7 85 PaulHanagan 11 98+
(Richard Fahey) *s.i.s: hld up: hdwy over 1f out: nt clr run ins fnl f: r.o to ld post* **4/1**[1]

132- **2** *hd* **Earlsmedic**[17] 7832 7-8-7 74 (v) RyanClark(3) 6 83
(Stuart Williams) *hld up: hdwy and nt clr run over 1f out: rdn to ld wl ins fnl f: hdd post* **6/1**[3]

221- **3** *hd* **Woolfall Sovereign (IRE)**[16] 7846 6-9-1 79 IanMongan 2 88
(George Margarson) *chsd ldrs: pushed along over 2f out: led ins fnl f: sn rdn and hdd: r.o* **5/1**[2]

313- **4** *½* **Caldercruix (USA)**[7] 7926 5-8-8 75 (v) SimonPearce(3) 8 82
(James Evans) *chsd ldrs: led over 1f out: sn hung lft: rdn and hdd ins fnl f: styd on* **7/1**

140- **5** *1 ¼* **Pick A Little**[139] 5262 4-9-2 80 DaneO'Neill 9 83
(Hughie Morrison) *prom: pushed along over 2f out: styd on* **10/1**

130- **6** *3 ¼* **Restless Bay (IRE)**[7] 7926 4-8-13 77 (e) FrederikTylicki 12 70
(Reg Hollinshead) *hld up: hdwy over 2f out: rdn over 1f out: no ex fnl f* **9/1**

35-4 **7** *½* **Captain Scooby**[5] 3 6-8-6 77 CharlesEddery(7) 5 68
(Richard Guest) *chsd ldr tl rdn over 1f out: no ex fnl f* **10/1**

304- **8** *hd* **Hotham**[21] 7776 9-8-11 75 BarryMcHugh 3 65
(Noel Wilson) *hld up in tch: plld hrd: rdn over 2f out: styd on same pce fnl f* **33/1**

144- **9** *nk* **Forever's Girl**[16] 7847 6-8-12 79 DaleSwift(3) 1 69
(Geoffrey Oldroyd) *led: rdn and hdd over 1f out: wknd ins fnl f* **16/1**

530- **10** *1* **Street Power (USA)**[254] 1610 7-9-4 82 SteveDrowne 13 68
(Jeremy Gask) *s.i.s: a in rr* **25/1**

303- **11** *1 ¾* **Night Trade (IRE)**[16] 7847 5-8-13 77 (p) LukeMorris 4 58
(Ronald Harris) *s.i.s: hld up: nt clr run over 2f out: rdn over 1f out: eased whn btn fnl f* **20/1**

161- **12** *11* **Frequency**[53] 7416 5-9-1 79 (b) JoeFanning 10 25
(Keith Dalgleish) *hld up: plld hrd: wknd 2f out* **10/1**

104- **13** *21* **Volcanic Dust (IRE)**[17] 7833 4-9-2 80 LiamKeniry 7
(Milton Bradley) *prom tl rdn and wknd over 2f out* **20/1**

1m 14.43s (-0.57) **Going Correction** +0.05s/f (Slow) **13** Ran SP% **122.9**
Speed ratings (Par 105): **105,104,104,103,102 97,97,96,96,95 92,78,50**
toteswingers:1&2:£5.90, 2&3:£6.50, 1&3:£3.50 CSF £26.74 CT £130.77 TOTE £5.50: £1.80, £3.60, £1.50; EX 33.80.
Owner J K Shannon & M A Scaife **Bred** Rathasker Stud **Trained** Musley Bank, N Yorks
■ Stewards' Enquiry : Ian Mongan two-day ban: used whip with excessive frequency (Jan 20-21)

FOCUS
A competitive handicap.
Volcanic Dust(IRE) Official explanation: jockey said filly stopped very quickly

65 HORIZONS RESTAURANT MEDIAN AUCTION MAIDEN STKS 1m 4f 50y(P)

6:15 (6:15) (Class 6) 4-6-Y-O **£1,704** (£503; £251) **Stalls** Low

Form RPR

335- **1** **Rocky Rebel**[88] 6748 4-9-3 67 DaneO'Neill 7 67+
(Chris Bealby) *led 3f: chsd ldr tl over 6f out: wnt 2nd again over 2f out: led over 1f out: styd on wl: comf* **11/8**[1]

000- **2** *2 ¼* **Satwa Ballerina**[37] 7581 4-8-5 45 (b[1]) RachealKneller(7) 1 58?
(Mark Rimmer) *hld up in tch: rdn to chse wnr over 1f out: styd on same pce ins fnl f* **50/1**

224- **3** *4* **Bull Five**[35] 7609 5-9-7 65 (p) SteveDrowne 4 57
(Nick Littmoden) *chsd ldrs: wnt 2nd over 6f out: led 3f out: rdn and hdd over 1f out: no ex* **7/1**[3]

4 *7* **Danaher**[29] 5-9-7 0 IanMongan 3 45
(George Margarson) *s.i.s: hld up: pushed along over 3f out: wknd 2f out* **11/1**

/30- **5** *12* **Praxios**[242] 1947 4-9-3 71 (t) BarryMcHugh 5 26
(Noel Wilson) *prom: rdn over 3f out: wknd wl over 1f out* **2/1**[2]

0- **6** *46* **Hiscano**[7] 7921 4-9-3 0 MarcHalford 6
(Terry Clement) *chsd ldrs: led at set stdy pce 9f out: rdn and hdd 3f out: wknd 2f out: t.o* **8/1**

2m 42.9s (1.80) **Going Correction** +0.05s/f (Slow)
WFA 4 from 5yo+ 4lb **6** Ran SP% **109.3**
Speed ratings: **96,94,91,87,79 48**
toteswingers:1&2:£8.50, 2&3:£5.90, 1&3:£1.60 CSF £52.15 TOTE £3.00: £1.90, £13.50; EX 68.50.
Owner Robert Jenkinson **Bred** Littleton Stud **Trained** Barrowby, Lincs

FOCUS
A weak maiden.
Hiscano Official explanation: vet said colt bled from the nose

66 WOLVERHAMPTON-RACECOURSE.CO.UK H'CAP 1m 1f 103y(P)

6:45 (6:45) (Class 7) (0-50,50) 4-Y-0+ **£1,704** (£503; £251) **Stalls** Low

Form RPR

023- **1** **Vanilla Rum**[21] 7788 5-9-3 50 (b) JoeFanning 4 66
(John Mackie) *hld up: racd keenly: hdwy over 2f out: led over 1f out: sn clr: comf* **2/1**[1]

340- **2** *6* **Love In The Park**[16] 7851 7-8-13 46 (b[1]) PhillipMakin 1 49
(Roy Brotherton) *a.p: chsd ldr over 2f out: rdn and ev ch over 1f out: sn outpcd* **11/2**[3]

664- **3** *3 ¼* **Ballinargh Boy**[9] 7902 4-8-11 45 (v[1]) JamesSullivan 2 41
(Robert Wylie) *led: rdn and hdd over 1f out: wknd fnl f* **11/1**

426- **4** *2* **Rigid**[21] 6494 5-8-13 49 MichaelO'Connell(3) 12 41
(Tony Carroll) *hld up: rdn over 2f out: hdwy over 1f out: nvr on terms* **11/1**

665- **5** *¾* **Our Princess Ellie (USA)**[8] 7910 4-8-12 46 ow1 DaneO'Neill 9 36
(Derek Shaw) *s.i.s: hld up: hdwy and hmpd wl over 1f out: n.d* **8/1**

424- **6** *2 ¾* **Red Flash (IRE)**[9] 7891 5-9-1 48 LukeMorris 13 33
(David Bridgwater) *prom: rdn over 3f out: wknd wl over 1f out* **5/1**[2]

5- **7** *1 ¾* **Sable (IRE)**[63] 7274 6-8-12 45 (bt) LiamKeniry 3 26
(Adrian McGuinness, Ire) *prom: rdn over 2f out: hmpd wl over 1f out: sn wknd* **16/1**

600- **8** *3 ¼* **Yossi (IRE)**[11] 7878 8-8-5 45 (b) CharlesEddery(7) 5 19
(Richard Guest) *s.s and rel to r: drvn along over 2f out: n.d* **33/1**

0/0- **9** *7* **Portrush Storm**[10] 7885 7-8-12 45 BarryMcHugh 10
(Ray Peacock) *hld up: rdn and wknd over 2f out* **50/1**

300- **10** *17* **Beating Harmony**[21] 7787 4-9-0 48 (be[1]) PaulHanagan 6
(Michael Appleby) *chsd ldr tl rdn and wknd over 2f out* **20/1**

36-5 **F** **American Lover (FR)**[1] 46 5-9-3 50 PaddyAspell 11
(John Wainwright) *hld up: hdwy over 3f out: cl 3rd and gng wl whn clipped heels and fell wl over 1f out* **12/1**

2m 1.34s (-0.36) **Going Correction** +0.05s/f (Slow)
WFA 4 from 5yo+ 1lb **11** Ran SP% **116.4**
Speed ratings (Par 97): **103,97,94,93,92 89,88,85,79,64**
toteswingers: 1&2:£3.70, 2&3:£13.90, 1&3:£5.60 CSF £12.12 CT £97.07 TOTE £2.20: £1.10, £2.90, £2.50; EX 13.00.
Owner Derbyshire Racing VI **Bred** Charley Knoll Partnership **Trained** Church Broughton , Derbys

FOCUS
A poor handicap.

67 PLAY DA VINCI DIAMONDS AT BLUESQ.COM/GAMES H'CAP 1m 141y(P)

7:15 (7:18) (Class 6) (0-65,65) 4-Y-0+ **£1,704** (£503; £251) **Stalls** Low

Form RPR

400- **1** **Postscript (IRE)**[53] 7416 4-9-6 65 JamieSpencer 1 73+
(Ian Williams) *hld up in tch: nt clr run and swtchd lft over 1f out: shkn up to ld ins fnl f: r.o* **9/4**[1]

160- **2** *1* **Justcallmehandsome**[7] 7930 10-9-2 65 (v) LucyKBarry(5) 8 71
(Dominic Ffrench Davis) *dwlt: hld up: hdwy over 2f out: rdn and ev ch ins fnl f: styd on same pce* **12/1**

034- **3** *shd* **Beetuna (IRE)**[18] 3251 7-9-2 60 (p) FrankieMcDonald 2 65
(Oliver Sherwood) *hld up in tch: racd keenly: rdn and ev ch ins fnl f: styd on same pce* **33/1**

/33- **4** *2* **Land Hawk (IRE)**[19] 7810 6-8-12 59 SimonPearce(3) 6 60
(Lydia Pearce) *chsd ldrs: led over 1f out: sn rdn: hdd and unable qck ins fnl f* **9/1**

010- **5** *½* **Join Up**[16] 7848 6-8-8 59 RachealKneller(7) 11 59
(Mark Brisbourne) *trckd ldrs: racd keenly: rdn and ev ch 1f out: no ex ins fnl f* **18/1**

440- **6** *nse* **Galloping Minister (IRE)**[45] 7507 4-8-11 56 HayleyTurner 5 56
(Tom Dascombe) *led 1f: chsd ldrs: rdn over 2f out: no ex fnl f* **13/2**[3]

0/0- **7** *2 ¾* **Secret Hero**[98] 6511 6-9-1 59 (b) RobertWinston 13 52
(Adrian McGuinness, Ire) *led over 7f out: hdd over 5f out: led again 2f out: sn rdn and hdd: wknd ins fnl f* **20/1**

0/3- **8** *1* **Mystic Halo**[27] 7717 9-9-3 61 (t) RobbieFitzpatrick 12 52
(Frank Sheridan) *hld up: rdn over 1f out: n.d* **33/1**

100- **9** *1 1/4* **Valley Tiger**[19] 7810 4-8-13 **58** .... PaulHanagan 10 46
(Richard Fahey) *hld up: rdn over 1f out: nvr on terms* **9/1**

061- **10** *1/2* **Fleetwoodsands (IRE)**[18] 7820 5-9-7 **65** .... (t) LiamKeniry 7 52
(Milton Bradley) *stdd s: hld up: effrt over 1f out: n.d* **4/1**[2]

1/0- **11** *1 1/4* **Diamond Fire (IRE)**[200] 3234 8-8-7 **51** oh6 .... (bt) MartinLane 9 35
(Adrian McGuinness, Ire) *hld up: a in rr* **100/1**

12 *hd* **Engai (GER)**[89] 6-9-7 **65** .... LukeMorris 3 49
(David Bridgwater) *prom: led over 5f out tl rdn and hdd 2f out: sn wknd* **13/2**[3]

1m 50.96s (0.46) **Going Correction** +0.05s/f (Slow)
WFA 4 from 5yo+ 1lb **12** Ran SP% **122.0**
Speed ratings (Par 101): **99,98,98,96,95 95,93,92,91,90 89,89**
toteswingers 1&2:£5.50, 2&3:£54.50, 1&3:£10.50 CSF £31.80 CT £742.94 TOTE £3.80: £1.50, £4.20, £8.00; EX 47.60.
Owner Dr Marwan Koukash **Bred** Darley **Trained** Portway, Worcs

FOCUS
A competitive handicap featuring several well-supported horses.
T/Jkpt: £5,555.50 to a £1 stake. Pool of £25,000.00 - 4.50 winning tickets. T/Plt: £187.80 to a £1 stake. Pool of £99,677.38 - 387.31 winning tickets. T/Qpdt: £5.10 to a £1 stake. Pool of £11,653.09 - 1,684.70 winning tickets. CR

68 - 76a (Foreign Racing) - See Raceform Interactive

[47]MEYDAN (L-H)
Friday, January 6

OFFICIAL GOING: Tapeta - standard; turf - good

77a UAE 1000 GUINEAS TRIAL PRESENTED BY LONGINES (FILLIES) (CONDITIONS RACE) (TAPETA) 7f
11:35 (11:35) 3-Y-O
£19,354 (£6,451; £3,225; £1,612; £967; £645)

RPR

1 **Gamilati**[141] 5217 3-8-13 108 .... FrankieDettori 3 111+
(Mahmood Al Zarooni) *mid-div: smooth prog 2 1/2f out: led 1 1/2f out: comf* **4/11**[1]

2 *2 3/4* **Alsindi (IRE)**[90] 6691 3-8-10 102 .... RoystonFfrench 2 98+
(A Al Raihe, UAE) *in rr of mid-div: trckd wnr 2f out: r.o same pce* **3/1**[2]

3 *5* **Mary Fildes (IRE)**[76] 7028 3-8-8 97 .... JamesDoyle 5 82
(J S Moore) *sn led: t.k.h: hdd 1 1/2f out: kpt on same pce* **10/1**[3]

4 *1 1/2* **Queen Of Alba (IRE)**[105] 6314 3-8-8 .... PShanahan 6 78
(E Charpy, UAE) *trckd ldr tl 2f out: kpt on same pce* **40/1**

5 *1* **Ballroom Blitz**[101] 6425 3-8-8 .... TadhgO'Shea 1 75?
(Doug Watson, UAE) *slowly away: settled in last: chsd ldrs 2 1/2f out: one pce fnl f* **66/1**

6 *15* **Princess Ghalya (USA)**[27] 3-8-8 .... MickaelBarzalona 4 35
(M Gharib, UAE) *trckd ldng duo: rdn 3 1/2f out: sn btn* **66/1**

1m 27.45s (2.25) **6** Ran SP% **112.8**
CSF £1.79..
Owner Godolphin **Bred** Darley **Trained** Newmarket, Suffolk

FOCUS
Mike de Kock had won the last two editions with runners bred in the Southern Hemisphere, but he wasn't represented here and this disappointingly small field was made up entirely of fillies from the Northern Hemisphere. An outbreak of African Horse Sickness, which prevented De Kock from travelling his home team, could be partly to blame and this was the first indication that the forthcoming UAE Classics may be weaker than usual. There was still an interesting clash, but it proved one-sided, as the market strongly suggested. The pace was steady (27.65 for the first quarter-mile, 51.94 for the half) and the time was the slowest to date from 35 races over this C&D. Gamilati is rated to her best.

NOTEBOOK
Gamilati last year's Cherry Hinton winner, outsprinted her rivals in the straight to take this with ease, but she was very much the winner on merit and her performance is all the more creditable considering she was conceding upwards of 3lb. From a stable with a cracking bunch of fillies, it was good to see her bounce back from a flop in the Lowther and evidently this surface suited. There's sufficient stamina in her pedigree to believe 1m could be within reach and the UAE 1000 Guineas (February 3) is the target.
Alsindi(IRE), who hadn't been seen since failing to beat a rival in the Rockfel, raced further back than the winner and couldn't match that one's speed. While more of a test may have suited, she's not exactly bred for stamina and it will be a surprise if she reverses form in the Guineas.
Mary Fildes(IRE) didn't offer much on this switch to Tapeta, not finishing that far clear of the others.
Queen Of Alba(IRE) had shown ability (behind subsequent Rockfel winner Wading) on her debut at Dundalk when trained by Dermot Weld, and she did so again.
Ballroom Blitz was taking a step up, having been well beaten at Ayr on her sole outing for Richard Guest.

80a LONGINES ST IMIER COLLECTION (MEYDAN MASTERS INTERNATIONAL JOCKEYS CH'SHIP) (H'CAP) (TURF) 7f
1:30 (1:30) Class F (90-102,102) 3-Y-O+
£11,612 (£3,870; £1,935; £967; £580; £387)

RPR

1 **Firestreak**[14] 7869 7-9-1 **95** .... (t) Christophe-PatriceLemaire 4 96
(M Al Muhairi, UAE) *mid-div: smooth prog 2f out: rdn to ld last 55yds* **5/1**[2]

2 *shd* **Angel's Pursuit (IRE)**[35] 7612 5-9-4 **98** .... CraigAWilliams 2 99
(David Marnane, Ire) *trckd ldr: led 1 1/2f out: hdd 55yds out* **9/2**[1]

3 *hd* **Finjaan**[19] 7815 6-9-8 **102** .... MaximeGuyon 5 102
(Doug Watson, UAE) *mid-div: chsd ldr 2f out: ev ch 100yds out: nt qckn cl home* **7/1**

4 *3/4* **Al Aasifh (IRE)**[88] 6747 4-9-5 **99** .... MircoDemuro 3 97
(Saeed Bin Suroor) *in rr of mid-div: nvr able to chal but r.o fnl 1 1/2f* **7/1**

5 *1/4* **Spirit Of Battle (USA)**[133] 4-9-6 **100** .... MickaelBarzalona 10 97
(A bin Huzaim, UAE) *settled in rr: chsd ldrs 2 1/2f out: kpt on same pce* **12/1**

6 *1 1/4* **Laa Rayb (USA)**[33] 7633 8-9-6 **100** .... (t) KenichiIkezoe 1 94
(D Selvaratnam, UAE) *a mid-div* **12/1**

7 *1/4* **Cartel (IRE)**[120] 6-8-11 **91** .... (b) FrankieDettori 6 84
(M bin Shafya, UAE) *sn led: hdd 1 1/2f out: wknd fnl f* **6/1**[3]

8 *nse* **Les Troyens**[181] 4-9-3 **97** .... TomQueally 7 90
(Saeed Bin Suroor) *in rr of mid-div: nvr able to chal* **6/1**[3]

9 *1 3/4* **Classic Blade (IRE)**[21] 7826 6-9-0 **94** .... RyanMoore 9 83
(Doug Watson, UAE) *settled in rr: nvr nr to chal* **12/1**

10 *4* **Kaiss (USA)**[19] 7815 5-9-2 **96** .... (t) AStarke 11 74
(S Seemar, UAE) *trckd ldr: ev ch 1 1/2f out: wknd fnl 100yds* **12/1**

11 *7 1/2* **Energia Carioca (BRZ)**[99] 5-9-1 **95** .... (t) CO'Donoghue 8 53
(Fabricio Borges, Sweden) *a in rr* **20/1**

1m 25.07s (85.07) **11** Ran SP% **124.0**
CSF £29.47. TRICAST £164.16.
Owner Sheikh Ahmed Bin Mohammed Al Maktoum **Bred** The Queen **Trained** UAE

FOCUS
None of these looked particularly well handicapped. The pace was fair with the first quarter-mile covered in 25.75 and the half in 49.27.

NOTEBOOK
Firestreak was difficult to fancy, but the return to turf and step back up in trip clearly suited and he ended a losing run dating back to 2008, having travelled well throughout. He won't appeal as one to back to follow up.
Angel's Pursuit(IRE) was still travelling easily for much of the straight, but Craig Williams was at pains not to get there too soon and the gelding just kept on at the one pace when finally asked. A recent winner over 6f at Dundalk, he's clearly versatile so will have plenty of options.
Finjaan kept on admirably but this is about as good as he is these days.
Al Aasifh(IRE) hasn't always looked straightforward but shaped as though he'll be better for this first run in 88 days. He started sluggishly and then didn't get the clearest of runs in the straight, but he kept on gradually.
Spirit Of Battle(USA) ran on from a fair way back.
Laa Rayb(USA) hinted that he retains sufficient ability to get competitive in similar company.

81 - 82a (Foreign Racing) - See Raceform Interactive

[15]DEAUVILLE (R-H)
Friday, January 6

OFFICIAL GOING: Fibresand: standard

83a PRIX MISS SATAMIXA (LISTED RACE) (4YO+ FILLIES & MARES) (FIBRESAND) 7f 110y
12:50 (12:00) 4-Y-O+
£21,666 (£8,666; £5,416; £2,166)

RPR

1 **Glory Power (IRE)**[21] 4-8-11 0 .... (b) AlexisBadel 8 98
(J-M Beguigne, France) **124/10**

2 *shd* **Baroness (FR)**[29] 7678 5-8-11 0 .... MathieuAndrouin 7 98
(F Monnier, France) **52/1**

3 *snk* **Night Lily (IRE)**[20] 7801 6-8-11 0 .... IoritzMendizabal 15 98
(Paul D'Arcy) *broke wl to r 2nd: r.o wl in st to chal for ld 1f out: nt qckn ins fnl 100yds: lost 2nd cl home* **10/1**

3 *dht* **Alchimia (FR)**[20] 4-8-11 0 .... FranckBlondel 2 98
(P Bary, France) **9/1**

5 *3/4* **Nicea (GER)**[30] 7668 5-8-11 0 .... SebastienMaillot 5 96
(P Schiergen, Germany) **9/1**

6 *shd* **Amelia's Surprise**[21] 4-8-11 0 .... RonanThomas 13 96?
(M Delzangles, France) **27/1**

7 *hd* **Kya One (FR)**[105] 6321 4-8-11 0 .... Pierre-CharlesBoudot 4 95
(Y De Nicolay, France) **13/2**[3]

8 *3/4* **Faithful One (IRE)**[87] 6783 5-8-11 0 .... ThomasHuet 12 93
(F Doumen, France) **36/1**

9 *nk* **Seeharn (IRE)**[45] 7509 4-8-11 0 .... ChrisHayes 14 92
(Kevin Prendergast, Ire) *racd in midfield on wd outside: qcknd 1 1/2f out and threatened briefly: nt qckn ins fnl f* **11/2**[2]

10 *nk* **Libys Dream (IRE)**[27] 7715 4-8-11 0 .... RichardKingscote 3 92
(Tom Dascombe) *broke wl: sn led: hdd over 1 1/2f out: nt qckn u.p: fdd* **17/1**

0 **Requisite**[16] 7846 7-8-11 0 .... (b) JulienAuge 16
(Ian Wood) *racd towards rr on outside: swtchd towards stands' rail in st: picked up and r.o ent fnl f: no ex fr 100yds out: eased fnl 50yds* **36/1**

0 **Spain Blues (FR)**[85] 6-8-11 0 .... Roberto-CarlosMontenegro 11
(X Thomas-Demeaulte, France) **25/1**

0 **Angel Of Harlem (FR)**[15] 4-8-11 0 .... (b) FabriceVeron 9
(H-A Pantall, France) **24/1**

0 **Lady Meydan (FR)**[45] 7509 4-9-2 0 .... Francois-XavierBertras 1
(F Rohaut, France) **4/1**[1]

0 **Cornucopia (FR)**[106] 6288 4-8-11 0 .... SylvainRuis 6
(E J O'Neill, France) **33/1**

0 **Amandara (USA)**[21] 4-8-11 0 .... FlavienPrat 10
(D Prod'Homme, France) **15/1**

1m 29.5s (89.50) **16** Ran SP% **118.7**
WIN (incl. 1 euro stake): 13.40. PLACES: 4.20, 12.30, 2.30 (Alchimia), 2.50 (Night Lily). DF: 283.50. SF: 666.70.
Owner Salah Mosbah El Mabruk **Bred** Petra Bloodstock Agency **Trained** France

NOTEBOOK
Night Lily(IRE)'s jockey said he didn't have the opportunity to get the mare covered up from that wide draw and that he was surprised there wasn't more pace, which she needs.
Seeharn(IRE) came to win her race but she did not pick up on her first try on the all-weather. She may well be retired now.

[54]LINGFIELD (L-H)
Saturday, January 7

OFFICIAL GOING: Standard
Wind: Strong, across Weather: Dry and breezy

84 FA CUP BETTING AT BLUESQ.COM MAIDEN STKS 1m 2f (P)
12:10 (12:11) (Class 5) 3-Y-O **£2,385** (£704; £352) **Stalls** Low

Form RPR

540- **1** **Ex Oriente (IRE)**[116] 6031 3-9-3 70 .... (b) MarcHalford 8 74
(John Gosden) *t.k.h: hld up in tch in midfield: hdwy to join ldrs over 2f out: ev ch but nt qckning u.p over 1f out: styd on fnl 75yds to ld but veered lft and bmpd rival cl home* **16/1**

05- **2** *1/2* **Key Gold**[88] 6771 3-8-12 0 .... JoeFanning 4 68
(Mark Johnston) *in tch in midfield: n.m.r ent fnl 2f: effrt u.p over 1f out: ev ch ins fnl f: kpt on: wnt 2nd last stride* **5/1**[3]

0- **3** *shd* **Three Bards (IRE)**[74] 7082 3-9-3 0 .... FrannyNorton 2 73
(Mark Johnston) *led at steady gallop: rdn and qcknd ent fnl 2f: hrd pressed and battled on wl ins fnl f: edgd rt hdd and bmpd cl home: lost 2nd last stride* **7/1**

42- **4** *1* **Josam (IRE)**[20] 7809 3-9-3 0 .... DaneO'Neill 5 71
(Richard Hannon) *in tch in midfield: rdn and effrt on outer jst over 2f out: hdwy but hung lft u.p 1f out: styd on same pce fnl 100yds* **3/1**[1]

245- **5** 2 1/4 **Macdonald Mor (IRE)**[118] 5959 3-9-3 78 JamieSpencer 9 66
(David Simcock) *dwlt and pushed along leaving stalls: sn in tch in midfield: rdn swtchd ins ent fnl 2f: hdwy and chsd ldrs 1f out: hung rt and no ex ins fnl f: wknd fnl 75yds* **6/1**

03- **6** 1/2 **Cape Safari (IRE)**[36] 7599 3-8-12 0 JimCrowley 6 60
(James Tate) *chsd ldr: rdn and ev ch wl over 2f out: unable qck over 1f out: wknd ins fnl f* **7/2**[2]

0- **7** 3/4 **Jennifer J**[33] 7634 3-8-12 0 EddieAhern 11 59
(Mark H Tompkins) *t.k.h: hld up in tch in last trio: pushed and outpcd over 2f out: rallied ent fnl f: styd on fnl f: nt pce to rch ldrs* **40/1**

8 shd **Lyrical Gangster (IRE)** 3-9-3 0 LukeMorris 7 64?
(J S Moore) *s.i.s and rdn along leaving stalls: in tch in midfield: rdn and outpcd over 2f out: rallied and styd on ins fnl f: nt pce to rch ldrs* **66/1**

04- **9** 1 1/2 **Frock (IRE)**[36] 7598 3-8-12 0 LiamKeniry 1 56
(Sylvester Kirk) *chsd ldrs: rdn and unable qck ent fnl 2f: wknd over 1f out* **18/1**

030- **10** 1/2 **Masters Blazing**[18] 7835 3-9-0 67 MichaelO'Connell(3) 10 60
(John Ryan) *chsd ldrs: rdn and ev ch over 1f out: struggling and btn over 1f out: wknd fnl f* **40/1**

11 1/2 **Guiletta (IRE)** 3-8-12 0 SteveDrowne 3 54
(Rae Guest) *in tch: dropped to last and pushed along over 4f out: wknd 2f out* **25/1**

12 1 3/4 **Dalmo** 3-9-3 0 ShaneKelly 12 55
(Gary Moore) *s.i.s and pushed along leaving stalls: a in rr: in tch tl outpcd over 2f out: n.d fr wl over 1f out* **80/1**

2m 7.56s (0.96) **Going Correction** -0.025s/f (Stan) 12 Ran SP% **113.3**
Speed ratings (Par 97): **95,94,94,93,91 91,90,90,89,89 88,87**
toteswingers:1&2:£15.70, 1&3:£24.30, 2&3:£8.20 CSF £87.44 TOTE £20.30: £5.60, £1.90, £2.00; EX 103.60 Trifecta £219.70 Part won. Pool: £296.97 - 0.91 winning units..
Owner Nicholas Cooper & Rachel Hood **Bred** Mrs Vanessa Hutch **Trained** Newmarket, Suffolk

FOCUS
A modest maiden and a tight finish.

85 SHARPTHORNE CLASSIFIED CLAIMING STKS 1m 2f (P)
12:40 (12:40) (Class 6) 4-Y-0+ **£1,704** (£503; £251) **Stalls** Low

Form RPR

021- **1** **Irons On Fire (USA)**[7] 7939 4-8-7 69 (p) FrankieMcDonald 4 70
(George Baker) *chsd ldr tl led gng wl jst over 2f out: hrd pressed and rdn over 1f out: hdd ins fnl f: n.m.r and leaned on fnl 100yds: kpt on gamely to ld again last stride* **15/2**

601- **2** shd **King's Colour**[24] 7756 7-8-13 68 AdamKirby 2 74
(Brett Johnson) *chsd ldrs: rdn and effrt over 1f out: ev ch 1f out: led fnl 75yds tl hdd last stride* **11/4**[1]

051- **3** hd **Ajdaad (USA)**[10] 7888 5-8-8 68 ow1 ShaneKelly 1 68
(Alan McCabe) *hld up in tch: rdn and hdwy on inner over 1f out: ev ch and edging rt ins fnl f: no ex cl home* **9/2**[2]

220- **4** hd **Spinning Ridge (IRE)**[19] 7823 7-8-7 70 (v) LukeMorris 5 67
(Ronald Harris) *t.k.h: hld up in tch: rdn and effrt 2f out: ev ch 1f out: led ins fnl f: hdd and no ex fnl 75yds* **13/2**[3]

040- **5** 3/4 **Aviso (GER)**[19] 7817 8-8-3 57 MartinLane 9 62
(David Evans) *stdd after s: t.k.h: hld up in last trio: rdn and no imp jst over 2f out: rallied 1f out: swtchd rt and r.o wl fnl 100yds: nt rch ldrs* **22/1**

066- **6** 1/2 **Cloudy Start**[24] 7756 6-8-5 63 HayleyTurner 3 63
(Jamie Osborne) *hld up in tch in last trio: rdn and no prog over 2f out: rallied and styd on wl ins fnl f: nt rch ldrs* **7/1**

000- **7** 1/2 **Classically (IRE)**[18] 7831 6-8-6 69 (p) ChrisCatlin 8 65
(Peter Hedger) *led: rdn and hdd jst over 2f out: stl ev ch 1f out: one pce whn squeezed out and hmpd fnl 100yds: nt rcvr* **9/2**[2]

005- **8** 2 **The Which Doctor**[24] 7756 7-8-5 65 (p) WilliamCarson 6 58
(Richard Guest) *t.k.h: hld up in last trio: rdn and no prog wl over 2f out: wknd jst over 1f out* **14/1**

2m 6.48s (-0.12) **Going Correction** -0.025s/f (Stan)
WFA 4 from 5yo+ 2lb 8 Ran SP% **111.6**
Speed ratings (Par 101): **99,98,98,98,98 97,97,95**
toteswingers:1&2:£3.20, 1&3:£4.50, 2&3:£4.00 CSF £27.09 TOTE £6.60: £1.90, £1.50, £1.80; EX 13.30 Trifecta £55.40 Pool: £453.53 - 6.05 winning units..
Owner George Baker & Partners **Bred** Woodford Thoroughbreds LLC **Trained** Whitsbury, Hants

FOCUS
A tight claimer at the weights and that was played out in the race itself with a four-way photo.

86 HOLTYE H'CAP 5f (P)
1:10 (1:10) (Class 5) (0-75,71) 3-Y-O **£2,385** (£704; £352) **Stalls** High

Form RPR

612- **1** **Sonko (IRE)**[9] 7905 3-9-7 71 (p) ShaneKelly 4 85
(Tim Pitt) *mde all: edgd rt but pushed clr over 1f out: clr and pushed out ins fnl f: comf* **2/1**[1]

21-5 **2** 2 1/4 **Russian Bullet**[4] 25 3-8-9 59 FergusSweeney 3 64
(Jamie Osborne) *in tch: rdn and effrt but outpcd by wnr over 1f out: styd on to chse clr wnr fnl 75yds: kpt on but no threat to wnr* **9/4**[2]

363- **3** 1 1/2 **Superplex**[22] 7778 3-9-2 66 (v[1]) TomEaves 2 66
(John Quinn) *t.k.h: chsd wnr for 1f: in tch after: rdn and effrt on inner 2f out: chsd clr wnr ent fnl f: no imp and lost 2nd fnl 75yds* **10/1**

223- **4** 1 3/4 **Bookiesindexdotnet**[9] 7905 3-9-6 70 FrederikTylicki 7 64
(J R Jenkins) *chsd wnr on outer after 1f: rdn and outpcd by wnr 2f out: wknd over 1f out* **10/1**

061- **5** 1/2 **Claretintheblood (IRE)**[23] 7770 3-8-8 58 BarryMcHugh 5 50
(Richard Fahey) *restless in stalls: s.i.s: a in rr: rdn and struggling 1/2-way: n.d* **11/1**

365- **6** 1 3/4 **Dawn Lightning**[184] 3776 3-9-0 67 KieranO'Neill(3) 6 53
(Alan McCabe) *chsd ldrs: rdn and outpcd by wnr wl over 1f out: wknd qckly ent fnl f* **6/1**[3]

46-5 **7** 3 **Lana (IRE)**[3] 27 3-8-8 58 (v[1]) LukeMorris 1 33
(David Evans) *in tch: rdn and struggling 1/2-way: wl bhd over 1f out* **12/1**

58.67s (-0.13) **Going Correction** -0.025s/f (Stan) 7 Ran SP% **112.6**
Speed ratings (Par 97): **100,96,94,91,90 87,82**
toteswingers:1&2:£1.90, 1&3:£3.80, 2&3:£5.40 CSF £6.50 TOTE £2.50: £1.10, £2.10; EX 5.90.
Owner Saintly Racing **Bred** Tally-Ho Stud **Trained** Newmarket, Suffolk

FOCUS
Just a modest sprint handicap.

Superplex Official explanation: jockey said colt hung left

87 BLUE SQUARE SPRINT SERIES ROUND 1 H'CAP (QUALIFIER) (DIV I) 6f (P)
1:45 (1:45) (Class 6) (0-65,69) 4-Y-0+ **£2,726** (£805; £402) **Stalls** Low

Form RPR

622- **1** **Speak The Truth (IRE)**[7] 7943 6-8-13 62 (p) NathanAlison(5) 4 71
(Jim Boyle) *in tch in midfield: rdn and hdwy jst over 1f out: ev ch ins fnl f: r.o wl to ld fnl 75yds* **7/1**

51-5 **2** hd **Efistorm**[3] 39 11-9-3 61 HayleyTurner 10 69
(Conor Dore) *chsd ldrs: rdn ent fnl 2f: ev ch 1f out: led fnl 100yds: sn hdd and kpt on same pce* **7/1**

210- **3** 1 1/4 **Glastonberry**[20] 7812 4-9-0 58 JamieSpencer 2 62
(Geoffrey Deacon) *chsd ldrs: rdn and ev ch ent fnl f: led ins fnl f: hdd fnl 100yds and outpcd towards fin* **11/1**

644- **4** nse **Fantasy Fighter (IRE)**[49] 7488 7-8-13 57 DaneO'Neill 12 61
(John E Long) *in tch in midfield on outer: rdn and effrt over 1f out: drvn and kpt on ins fnl f* **14/1**

264- **5** hd **Dvinsky (USA)**[7] 7942 11-9-6 64 (b) LukeMorris 9 68
(Paul Howling) *chsd ldr: ev ch and rdn 2f out: no ex ins fnl f: wknd fnl 75yds* **33/1**

312- **6** 1 1/2 **Rio Royale (IRE)**[49] 7485 6-9-6 64 (b) JimCrowley 5 63
(Amanda Perrett) *led and crossed to r against inner rail: rdn wl over 1f out: hdd ins fnl f: wknd fnl 150yds* **7/2**[1]

301- **7** nk **Steelcut**[10] 7897 8-9-11 69 (p) TomMcLaughlin 8 67
(David Evans) *stdd after s: hld up wl off the pce in last quartet: hdwy towards inner wl over 1f out: swtchd rt ent fnl f: r.o ins fnl f: nvr able to chal* **16/1**

226- **8** 2 1/2 **Amber Heights**[20] 7812 4-9-2 60 FergusSweeney 11 50
(David Pinder) *racd off the pce in last quartet: rdn and effrt over 1f out: kpt on fnl f: nvr trbld ldrs* **14/1**

350- **9** 1/2 **Vitznau (IRE)**[10] 7896 8-8-11 62 LeonnaMayor(7) 3 50
(Alastair Lidderdale) *hld up in rr: wd and rdn bnd 2f out: kpt on but n.d* **25/1**

52- **10** 1 1/2 **Picansort**[21] 7804 5-9-7 65 ShaneKelly 1 48
(Peter Crate) *s.i.s: sn in tch in midfield: hdwy to chse ldrs and rdn over 1f out: fnd little and btn 1f out: fdd and edgd rt ins fnl f* **4/1**[2]

001- **11** hd **Green Earth (IRE)**[20] 7810 5-9-7 65 (e[1]) IanMongan 7 48
(Pat Phelan) *hld up in rr: n.d* **13/2**[3]

140- **12** 1 1/2 **Captainrisk (IRE)**[137] 5355 6-9-3 61 WilliamCarson 6 39
(Christine Dunnett) *a towards rr: rdn over 3f out: nvr on terms* **50/1**

1m 11.49s (-0.41) **Going Correction** -0.025s/f (Stan) 12 Ran SP% **116.9**
Speed ratings (Par 101): **101,100,99,99,98 96,96,93,92,90 90,88**
toteswingers:1&2:£8.00, 1&3:£8.50, 2&3:£11.80 CSF £53.66 CT £545.72 TOTE £9.20: £3.00, £3.00, £2.00; EX 51.70 Trifecta £364.30 Part won. Pool: £492.40 - 0.20 winning units..
Owner Inside Track Racing Club **Bred** Gerard Mulligan **Trained** Epsom, Surrey

FOCUS
The first of the Blue Square Sprint Series qualifiers and a tight finish.

88 BLUE SQUARE SPRINT SERIES ROUND 1 H'CAP (QUALIFIER) (DIV II) 6f (P)
2:15 (2:15) (Class 6) (0-65,65) 4-Y-0+ **£2,726** (£805; £402) **Stalls** Low

Form RPR

660- **1** **Captain Dimitrios**[105] 6343 4-8-12 56 (v) MartinLane 9 67
(David Evans) *chsd ldr: ev ch and rdn over 1f out: led ins fnl f: r.o wl* **33/1**

340- **2** 1 1/2 **Loyal Royal (IRE)**[10] 7893 9-9-7 65 (bt) LiamKeniry 10 71
(Milton Bradley) *stdd s: hld up in rr: hdwy ent fnl f: r.o strly u.p to go 2nd last strides: nvr gng to rch wnr* **16/1**

050- **3** shd **Waabel**[16] 7857 5-9-4 62 MartinHarley 11 68
(Richard Guest) *led: rdn and hrd pressed over 1f out: hdd and styd on same pce ins fnl f: lost 2nd last strides* **16/1**

605- **4** 1/2 **Diamond Vine (IRE)**[38] 7587 4-9-2 60 (p) LukeMorris 12 64
(Ronald Harris) *hld up in last trio: hdwy over 1f out: styd on ins fnl f: no threat to wnr* **14/1**

000- **5** 1/2 **Chjimes (IRE)**[7] 7942 8-9-1 59 (b) HayleyTurner 1 61
(Conor Dore) *in tch: rdn to chse ldng trio wl over 1f out: unable qck ent fnl f: one pce fnl f* **12/1**

403- **6** hd **Paperetto**[7] 7942 4-8-13 57 SteveDrowne 8 59
(Robert Mills) *t.k.h: hld up in tch in midfield: rdn and styd on same pce fr over 1f out* **5/1**[3]

400- **7** 1 **Waterloo Dock**[8] 7919 7-9-4 62 (v) ChrisCatlin 3 61
(Michael Quinn) *chsd ldrs: rdn 1/2-way: unable qck 2f: plugged on same pce and no threat to wnr fr over 1f out* **50/1**

060- **8** 1/2 **Strictly Pink (IRE)**[45] 7519 4-9-4 65 (v) DominicFox(3) 5 62
(Alan Bailey) *hld up in last trio: kpt on ins fnl f: nvr trbld ldrs* **9/2**[2]

424- **9** 1/2 **Silver Wind**[10] 7895 7-9-7 65 (b) ShaneKelly 6 60
(Alan McCabe) *chsd ldrs: rdn and unable qck wl over 1f out: wknd ent fnl f* **7/2**[1]

531- **10** 1 1/4 **Towy Boy (IRE)**[17] 7844 7-9-1 64 (bt) RaulDaSilva(5) 2 55
(Ian Wood) *hld up in midfield: rdn and no prog wl over 1f out: one pce and no threat to ldrs fnl f* **15/2**

/02- **11** 1 **Amosite**[7] 7942 6-9-3 61 (p) FrederikTylicki 7 49
(J R Jenkins) *in tch in midfield on outer: wd and lost pl bnd 2f out: no threat to ldrs after* **5/1**[3]

300- **12** 6 **Custom House (IRE)**[7] 7942 4-9-5 63 (b) DaneO'Neill 4 32
(John E Long) *a towards rr: lost tch over 1f out* **20/1**

1m 10.98s (-0.92) **Going Correction** -0.025s/f (Stan) 12 Ran SP% **121.3**
Speed ratings (Par 101): **105,103,102,102,101 101,99,99,98,96 95,87**
toteswingers:1&2:£44.30, 1&3:£65.20, 2&3:£38.20 CSF £491.29 CT £4874.16 TOTE £51.40: £9.20, £4.90, £6.10; EX 495.00 TRIFECTA Not won..
Owner Wayne Clifford **Bred** W G H Barrons **Trained** Pandy, Monmouths
■ Stewards' Enquiry : Martin Harley one-day ban: failed to ride to draw (Jan 21)

FOCUS
The quicker of the two divisions by 0.51sec.

89 LINGFIELDPARK.CO.UK H'CAP 6f (P)
2:45 (2:45) (Class 2) (0-100,100) 4-Y-0+ **£10,350** (£3,080; £1,539; £769) **Stalls** Low

Form RPR

421- **1** **Oasis Dancer**[28] 7721 5-9-5 98 JimCrowley 7 111+
(Ralph Beckett) *hld up wl in tch: rdn and hdwy to chse ldr ent fnl f: qcknd to ld ins fnl f: sn in command and pushed out: comf* **9/4**[1]

002- **2** 2 **Fratellino**[251] 1720 5-8-12 91 (t) MartinHarley 1 97
(Alan McCabe) *led: rdn and qcknd ent fnl 2f: hdd and nt pce of wnr ins fnl f: kpt on same pce* **14/1**

031- **3** *nse* **Capone (IRE)**[39] 7578 7-9-3 **96** HayleyTurner 3 102+
(Scott Dixon) *hld up in tch towards rr: rdn and hdwy on inner over 1f out: styd on wl ins fnl f and nrly snatched 2nd: no ch w wnr* **7/2**[2]

001- **4** *3/4* **Googlette (IRE)**[50] 7457 4-8-9 **88** LukeMorris 5 91
(Ed Vaughan) *chsd ldr: edgd rt and rdn wl over 1f out: styd on same pce and no threat to wnr ins fnl f* **8/1**[3]

210- **5** *1/2* **Seek The Fair Land**[35] 7628 6-8-11 **90** (b) EddieAhern 4 92
(Jim Boyle) *hld up wl in tch in midfield: swtchd rt and effrt over 1f out: styd on same pce u.p ins fnl f* **9/1**

002- **6** *nk* **Piscean (USA)**[28] 7721 7-8-11 **90** WilliamCarson 12 91
(Tom Keddy) *t.k.h: chsd ldrs: rdn wl over 1f out: drvn and styd on same pce fnl f* **25/1**

021- **7** *3/4* **Novellen Lad (IRE)**[7] 7941 7-8-9 **88** StevieDonohoe 10 86+
(Willie Musson) *jostled sn after s: in tch in midfield: rdn and effrt over 1f out: kpt on same pce and nvr able to chal* **12/1**

606- **8** *3 1/4* **Norville (IRE)**[39] 7578 5-8-10 **94** (b) MatthewCosham(5) 11 82
(David Evans) *t.k.h: in tch in midfield on outer: sltly hmpd 5f out: rdn and effrt wl over 1f out: no prog and wl hld fnl f* **16/1**

140- **9** *nk* **Colonel Mak**[91] 6706 5-9-6 **99** JamieSpencer 6 86
(David Barron) *chsd ldr tl 2f out: unable qck and hmpd wl over 1f out: lost pl and sn btn: wknd fnl f* **8/1**[3]

300- **10** *1 1/4* **Five Star Junior (USA)**[39] 7578 6-9-2 **95** JamesSullivan 2 78
(Linda Stubbs) *in tch: hmpd and lost pl after 1f out: effrt u.p on inner over 1f out: wknd 1f out* **25/1**

100- **11** *2 1/4* **Elna Bright**[21] 7801 7-9-1 **94** ShaneKelly 9 70
(Peter Crate) *stdd and dropped in bhd after s: hld up in rr: n.d* **25/1**

006- **12** *1 1/4* **Malcheek (IRE)**[84] 6867 10-9-7 **100** DuranFentiman 8 72
(Tim Easterby) *jostling match sn after s: hld up in last trio: n.d* **66/1**

1m 10.41s (-1.49) **Going Correction** -0.025s/f (Stan) **12** Ran SP% **118.5**
Speed ratings (Par 109): **108,105,105,104,103 103,102,97,97,95 92,91**
toteswingers:1&2:£8.20, 1&3:£3.30, 2&3:£10.90 CSF £34.84 CT £112.85 TOTE £4.10: £1.90, £4.80, £1.10; EX 37.60 Trifecta £285.40 Pool: £891.21 - 2.31 winning units..

Owner Mrs M E Slade **Bred** Whitsbury Manor Stud And Mrs M E Slade **Trained** Kimpton, Hants

FOCUS

A decent sprint. The early pace wasn't that strong but the form looks pretty solid for the grade.

NOTEBOOK

Oasis Dancer bolted up at Wolverhampton last time and a 6lb rise in the weights didn't look harsh. He travelled well, putting the race to bed when quickening up smartly early in the straight, and his rider only had to push him out to win comfortably. He looks a bit better than a handicapper and could be capable of winning in Listed company on this surface. (tchd 5-2)

Fratellino ◆ didn't go that quick in front and was able to save a bit for the straight. He had no chance with Oasis Dancer but ran a sound race on his return from a long break and clearly retains the ability to win a race off this sort of mark. (tchd 16-1)

Capone(IRE), debuting for an in-form yard, stayed on best of those held up off the pace. He could have done with a stronger all-round gallop and can win again off his current mark when he gets that. (op 9-2)

Googlette(IRE) was never too far away and had her chance. This was a step up in class for her and she shaped well enough considering her relative lack of experience. There should be more to come from her. (op 15-2)

Seek The Fair Land, whose six wins have come over 7f, travelled strongly but lacked the change of gear required in the straight. He'll be suited by a return to the longer trip. (op 14-1 tchd 17-2)

Piscean(USA), who was put in his place by Oasis Dancer at Wolverhampton last time, than had an 8lb pull in the weights, but he raced keenly out wide and only finished marginally closer.

Novellen Lad(IRE) possibly wants 7f these days as he got outpaced running down the hill and was staying on all too late. (op 14-1)

Norville(IRE)'s rider reported that the horse hung right throughout. Official explanation: jockey said horse hung right throughout (op 14-1)

90 FOREST ROW H'CAP 1m (P)

3:20 (3:20) (Class 4) (0-85,84) 4-Y-0+ **£4,431** (£1,308; £654) **Stalls** High

Form RPR

341- **1** **Marajaa (IRE)**[20] 7807 10-9-3 **80** JamieMackay 5 88
(Willie Musson) *hld up in rr: last and nt clr run 2f out: stl plenty to do over 1f out: str run on inner ins fnl f to ld last strides* **17/2**

231- **2** *hd* **Nibani (IRE)**[8] 7920 5-8-4 **74** (p) LeonnaMayor(7) 11 81
(Alastair Lidderdale) *s.i.s: hld up in rr: rdn and effrt on outer 2f out: r.o wl ins fnl f: ev ch wl ins fnl f: wnt 2nd last strides* **8/1**

020- **3** *hd* **Den's Gift (IRE)**[80] 6948 8-8-10 **78** (b) LucyKBarry(5) 3 85
(Clive Cox) *sn led: rdn wl over 1f out: battled on wl u.p tl hdd and lost 2 pls cl home* **17/2**

042- **4** *hd* **Titan Triumph**[8] 7922 8-9-1 **78** (t) JimCrowley 10 84
(William Knight) *hld up in tch towards rr: hdwy into midfield 2f out: rdn and chsd ldrs 1f out: ev ch ins fnl f: no ex cl home* **9/2**[1]

030- **5** *shd* **Chilli Green**[17] 7841 5-9-5 **82** DaneO'Neill 4 88
(John Akehurst) *chsd ldr: rdn 2f out: drvn and ev ch ins fnl f: no ex towards fin* **13/2**[3]

200- **6** *3/4* **Tartan Trip**[182] 3840 5-8-13 **83** ThomasBrown(7) 12 87
(Andrew Balding) *in tch in midfield: rdn and hdwy over 1f out: chsd ldrs and drvn ins fnl f: no ex fnl 75yds: hld whn short of room cl home* **11/2**[2]

322- **7** *nk* **One Way Or Another (AUS)**[8] 7926 9-8-13 **76** (b) LukeMorris 2 80
(David Evans) *chsd ldrs: rdn 2f out: styd on same pce u.p ins fnl f* **15/2**

450- **8** *2* **Focail Eile**[8] 7922 7-9-0 **77** FrederikTylicki 9 76
(John Ryan) *chsd ldrs: rdn wl over 1f out: unable qck ent fnl f: styd on same pce fnl f* **14/1**

041- **9** *1* **Bawaardi (IRE)**[12] 7876 6-9-3 **80** AdamKirby 7 77
(David Evans) *in tch: rdn and unable qck over 1f out: styd on same pce and btn jst ins fnl f* **12/1**

004- **10** *1/2* **Honey Of A Kitten (USA)**[12] 7877 4-9-0 **82** MatthewCosham(5) 8 78
(David Evans) *sn pushed along towards rr: kpt on fr over 1f out: nvr trbld ldrs* **16/1**

/00- **11** *3 3/4* **Spirit Of Xaar (IRE)**[126] 5746 6-9-7 **84** SteveDrowne 1 71
(Linda Jewell) *sn niggled along: in tch towards rr: rdn and effrt on inner wl over 1f out: wknd 1f out* **40/1**

1m 36.83s (-1.37) **Going Correction** -0.025s/f (Stan) **11** Ran SP% **113.5**
Speed ratings (Par 105): **105,104,104,104,104 103,103,101,100,99 96**
toteswingers:1&2:£11.90, 1&3:£12.00, 2&3:£11.70 CSF £72.14 CT £604.75 TOTE £11.10: £3.20, £3.50, £3.30; EX 89.40 Trifecta £168.20 Pool: £454.68 - 2.00 winning units..

Owner W J Musson **Bred** Shadwell Estate Company Limited **Trained** Newmarket, Suffolk

■ Stewards' Enquiry : Dane O'Neill four-day ban: used whip with excessive frequency (Jan 21-24)

FOCUS

They went no pace early here and that resulted in a sprint to the line and a bunch finish.

91 PLAY RAINBOW RICHES AT BLUESQ.COM H'CAP 7f (P)

3:55 (3:55) (Class 5) (0-70,69) 4-Y-0+ **£1,545** (£1,545; £352) **Stalls** Low

Form RPR

442- **1** **Eager To Bow (IRE)**[10] 7895 6-9-2 **64** JimCrowley 1 72
(Patrick Chamings) *chsd ldrs: rdn and effrt on inner to chse ldr over 1f out: kpt on u.p to join ldr on line* **5/2**[1]

14-4 **1** *dht* **City Legend**[3] 33 4-9-4 **69** (vt) KieranO'Neill(3) 10 77
(Alan McCabe) *pressed ldr: rdn to ld 2f out: drvn ent fnl f: kpt on: jnd on line* **4/1**[2]

336- **3** *2* **Sienna Blue**[100] 6490 4-8-7 **62** JakePayne(7) 5 65
(Bill Turner) *hld up in tch towards rr: swtchd lft and hdwy over 1f out: styd on to go 3rd ins fnl f: nt pce to rch ldng pair* **33/1**

50-0 **4** *1 1/4* **Silvee**[3] 31 5-8-7 **55** DavidProbert 4 54
(John Bridger) *in tch in midfield: rdn 3f out: outpcd and drvn over 1f out: styd on same pce fnl f* **5/1**[3]

164- **5** *nk* **Cativo Cavallino**[33] 7637 9-9-6 **68** SamHitchcott 9 66
(John E Long) *led and crossed to r against inner rail: rdn and hdd 2f out: nt pce of ldng pair over 1f out: styd on same pce fnl f* **14/1**

462- **6** *1 1/2* **Pipers Piping (IRE)**[10] 7888 6-9-5 **67** (p) FergusSweeney 8 61
(Alastair Lidderdale) *t.k.h: hld up in tch in midfield: rdn and no prog over 1f out: styd on same pce fnl f* **8/1**

001- **7** *3 1/4* **The Strig**[45] 7512 5-9-4 **66** WilliamCarson 7 52
(Stuart Williams) *t.k.h: hld up in tch towards rr: rdn and effrt over 1f out: sn wknd* **12/1**

000- **8** *1* **High On The Hog (IRE)**[23] 7764 4-9-5 **67** IanMongan 2 50
(Paul Howling) *hld up in tch in rr: rdn and no prog wl over 1f out: wl hld fnl f* **40/1**

31- **9** *3 1/2* **Sketchy Evidence (USA)**[31] 7652 4-9-4 **66** LukeMorris 6 39
(John Best) *dwlt: sn rcvrd to chse ldrs: rdn and unable qck ent fnl f: wknd over 1f out* **4/1**[2]

1m 24.76s (-0.04) **Going Correction** -0.025s/f (Stan) **9** Ran SP% **116.1**
Speed ratings (Par 103): **99,99,96,95,94 93,89,88,84**WIN: Eager To Bow £1.90, City Legend £2.50 PL: ETB £1.40, CL £1.30 , SB £5.20. EX: ETB/CL £6.27, CL/ETB £7.25 CSF: ETB/CL £6.27, CL/ETB £7.25. T/C: ETB/CL/SB £130.94, CL/ETB/SB £143.75. toteswingers:ETB&CL:£3.40, ETB&SB:£11.70, CL&SB:£15.40 TOTE £0.0027: £Owner, £Contango Syndicate, £Bred, £Contango Bloodstock LtdTrained Averham Park, Notts.

Owner Mrs J E L Wright **Bred** Stone Ridge Farm **Trained** Baughurst, Hants

FOCUS

A modest handicap but a ding-dong battle inside the last resulted in a dead-heat.

T/Plt: £318.90 to a £1 stake. Pool: £73,859.81. 169.05 winning tickets. T/Qpdt: £58.70 to a £1 stake. Pool: £5,374.54. 67.70 winning tickets. SP

[83]DEAUVILLE (R-H)

Saturday, January 7

OFFICIAL GOING: Fibresand: standard

92a PRIX DE LA CROIX MESNIL (CONDITIONS) (5YO+) (FIBRESAND) 7f 110y

9:45 (12:00) 5-Y-0+ **£8,750** (£3,500; £2,625; £1,750; £875)

RPR

1 **Blazon (FR)**[17] 5-9-2 0 KarlMartin 10 79
(P Van De Poele, France) **5/2**[2]

2 *3 1/2* **Voussoir (IRE)**[16] 5-8-11 0 (b) NicolasGuilbert 6 65
(T Castanheira, France) **12/1**

3 *1* **Bold Marc (IRE)**[5] 18 10-9-6 0 (p) StephaneLaurent 7 72
(Mrs K Burke) *broke wl: sn led: 3 l clr ent st: r.o wl: rdn 1 1/2f out: hdd 150yds out: styd on* **60/1**

4 *snk* **Amelkis (FR)**[17] 7-8-8 0 AllanBonnefoy 3 59
(J-V Toux, France) **15/1**

5 *1 1/4* **Miss Antonia (IRE)**[72] 5-8-8 0 PJWerning 8 56
(R Werning, Germany) **76/1**

6 *3/4* **Vantage Point (FR)**[5] 18 9-9-0 0 MorganDelalande 2 60
(Mlle C Cardenne, France) **9/1**[3]

7 *1 3/4* **Serpotta (FR)**[17] 6-8-11 0 YannickLetondeur 9 53
(Y De Nicolay, France) **21/1**

8 *1 1/2* **Frozen Ardour (IRE)**[16] 5-8-10 0 LouisBeuzelin 11 48
(P Bary, France) **6/4**[1]

9 *snk* **Mr Jeremy** 5-8-11 0 CesarPasserat 1 49
(F Vermeulen, France) **13/1**

10 *3/4* **Tiger Cliff (FR)**[16] 7-8-8 0 (p) DavidFournier 5 44
(J Bertin, France) **15/1**

0 **Pure Land (FR)**[155] 6-9-8 0 FreddyDiFede 4
(F Vermeulen, France) **19/1**

0 **Sarafy De Monnaie (FR)**[12] 6-8-8 0 FlavienMasse 12
(J Vittori, France) **134/1**

1m 30.1s (90.10) **12** Ran SP% **119.1**
WIN (incl. 1 euro stake): 3.50. PLACES: 1.70, 3.80, 15.20. DF: 18.30. SF: 45.10.

Owner Anthony Baudouin **Bred** Haras Des Sablonnets **Trained** France

93a PRIX DU TAILLIS (CONDITIONS) (5YO+) (FIBRESAND) 1m 4f

11:45 (12:00) 5-Y-0+ **£8,750** (£3,500; £2,625; £1,750; £875)

RPR

1 **Uphold**[31] 7651 5-9-6 0 (b) IoritzMendizabal 6 81
(Gay Kelleway) *broke smartly to ld: set mod pce gng easily: rdn over 1 1/2f out: hdd and bmpd w eventual runner-up over 1f out: rallied u.str.p to regain ld 150yds out: hld on bravely fnl 100yds* **79/10**

2 *nse* **Falun (GER)**[16] 6-9-0 0 (p) FlavienPrat 7 75
(M Nigge, France) **13/2**[2]

3 *1/2* **Street Lair (USA)**[16] 5-9-0 0 KarenBeaumard 9 74
(L Baudron, France) **78/10**

4 *2* **Perspicace (FR)**[8] 7-9-0 0 (p) BenjaminHubert(3) 4 74
(N Leenders, France) **15/1**

5 *hd* **Fellini (GER)**[21] 5-9-2 0 (p) FabriceVeron 3 73
(N Leenders, France) **3/1**[1]

6 *snk* **Nijinsky Blood (FR)**[5] 5-9-8 0 (b) FranckBlondel 14 78
(P Van De Poele, France) **28/1**

7 *1 1/4* **Casta Diva (FR)**[21] 5-8-10 0 (p) AlexisBadel 11 64
(F-X De Chevigny, France) **11/1**

8 *1 1/2* **Country Music (FR)**[21] 5-9-4 0 (b) RonanThomas 2 70
(P Van De Poele, France) **68/10**[3]

9 2 **Belleza (FR)**[31] 5-8-10 0 MaximeFoulon 15 59
(S Smrczek, Germany) **8/1**
10 3 **Melodie D'Aze (FR)**[8] 5-8-10 0 DavidFournier 10 54
(N Leenders, France) **16/1**
0 **Satwa Prince (FR)**[79] 9-8-11 0 Pierre-CharlesBoudot 5
(Y Fouin, France) **27/1**
0 **Secret Agent (FR)**[409] 8-8-7 0 ow3 (p) MlleLaurieFoulard(7) 13
(D Windrif, France) **54/1**
0 **Narjan**[69] 6-8-11 0 MorganDelalande 12
(C Plisson, France) **69/1**
0 **Troc Des Brieres (FR)** 5-8-6 0 StephaneLaurent(5) 1
(L Tassart, France) **101/1**

2m 36.7s (156.70) **14** Ran SP% **116.6**
WIN (incl. 1 euro stake): 8.90. PLACES: 3.50, 2.60, 3.20. DF: 25.90. SF: 73.00.
Owner J Ballamy, G Kelleway & T Hawthorne **Bred** Juddmonte Farms Ltd **Trained** Exning, Suffolk

NOTEBOOK
Uphold got a soft lead and kept finding in the straight to hold on under a fine ride.

94a PRIX DE RUCQUEVILLE (CLAIMER) (5YO+) (FIBRESAND) 1m 1f 110y
1:20 (12:00) 5-Y-0+ **£6,250** (£2,500; £1,875; £1,250; £625)

RPR
1 **Lord Lansing (IRE)**[30] [7671] 5-8-11 0 IoritzMendizabal 12 71
(Mrs K Burke) *settled towards rr: swtchd towards stands' rail ent st: qcknd wl to chal for ld 1f out: led 150yds out: r.o wl: comf* **19/5**[2]
2 1 **New Best (FR)**[12] 7-9-2 0 SylvainRuis 1 74
(Alex Fracas, France) **8/1**
3 1 1/4 **Go Michelangelo (FR)**[12] 5-9-2 0 RonanThomas 15 71
(P Van De Poele, France) **7/2**[1]
4 3/4 **Jasmines Hero (USA)**[56] 7-9-2 0 JulienAuge 5 70
(H Hesse, Germany) **13/1**
5 1/2 **Floribundus (GER)**[12] 7-9-2 0 YannickLetondeur 16 69
(M Munch, Germany) **15/2**
6 1 **Tinera (FR)**[12] 6-8-9 0 (p) MathieuTavaresDaSilva(4) 10 64
(P Demercastel, France) **12/1**
7 nk **Amancaya (GER)**[17] 5-9-2 0 FlavienMasse(5) 11 71
(W Hickst, Germany) **10/1**
8 3/4 **Darabani (FR)**[12] 7-9-6 0 FabriceVeron 2 69
(P Monfort, France) **73/10**[3]
9 2 1/2 **El Bulli (USA)**[289] [1012] 5-8-4 0 AntoineCoutier(7) 6 55
(F Chappet, France) **16/1**
10 6 **Vobois (FR)**[61] 7-9-2 0 (p) NadegeOuakli 7 47
(C Herbline, France) **110/1**
0 **Montauk (FR)**[364] 6-8-8 0 (p) TristanNormand(3) 9
(G Doleuze, France) **38/1**
0 **Roadster**[12] 5-8-11 0 AnthonyClement 3
(C Plisson, France) **27/1**
0 **Blackboard (FR)** 5-9-2 0 (p) CedricSagot 14
(A Sagot, France) **65/1**
0 **Theo Speed (FR)** 5-8-7 0 ow1 YoannBarille(5) 8
(S Gouvaze, France) **139/1**

2m 0.3s (120.30) **14** Ran SP% **117.1**
WIN (incl. 1 euro stake): 4.80. PLACES: 2.00, 2.60, 1.70. DF: 22.20. SF: 50.90.
Owner The Mount Racing Club & Mrs E Burke **Bred** C J Wall **Trained** Middleham Moor, N Yorks

[19]SOUTHWELL (L-H)
Sunday, January 8

OFFICIAL GOING: Standard
Wind: Moderate behind Weather: Cloudy

95 BET AND WATCH AT BLUESQ.COM AW "HANDS & HEELS" APPRENTICE SERIES H'CAP (RACING EXCELLENCE) 5f (F)
12:50 (12:50) (Class 6) (0-55,54) 4-Y-0+ **£1,704** (£503; £251) **Stalls** High

Form RPR
103- 1 **Bird Dog**[10] [7911] 6-8-12 **50** (v) DannyBrock 7 56
(Phil McEntee) *cl up: rdn to chal 2f out: styd on to ld ins fnl f: jst hld on* **9/4**[1]
063- 2 shd **Canadian Danehill (IRE)**[23] [7785] 10-8-12 **50** (e) JakePayne 8 56
(Robert Cowell) *cl up: rdn and sltly outpcd jst over 1f out: styd on wl fnl f: jst failed* **4/1**[3]
005- 3 1 1/4 **The Magic Of Rio**[30] [7691] 6-8-7 **45** JasonHart 6 46
(John Balding) *t.k.h: slt ld: rdn jst over 1f out: hdd ins fnl f: one pce* **5/2**[2]
430- 4 3 3/4 **Slatey Hen (IRE)**[25] [7760] 4-8-13 **51** (p) NoraLooby 2 39
(Richard Guest) *dwlt and in rr: hdwy on stands' rails wl over 1f out: nvr nr ldrs* **8/1**
/00- 5 3/4 **Clanachy**[105] [6386] 6-8-4 **45** (tp) KevinLundie(3) 1 30
(George Foster) *wnt lft s: sn chsng ldrs on outer: rdn along over 2f out: sn wknd* **25/1**
000- 6 9 **Tunza The Lion**[30] [7693] 5-8-7 **45** NoelGarbutt 5
(Bruce Hellier, Germany) *dwlt: a bhd* **40/1**
010- 7 1/2 **Novay Essjay (IRE)**[249] [1818] 5-9-0 **52** GeorgeDowning 4
(Dai Williams) *chsd ldrs: rdn along after 1f: sn lost pl and bhd fr 1/2-way* **6/1**

1m 0.09s (0.39) **Going Correction** -0.10s/f (Stan) **7** Ran SP% **111.0**
Speed ratings (Par 101): **93,92,90,84,83 69,68**
Tote Swingers: 1&2 £1.90, 1&3 £1.80, 2&3 £3.00 CSF £10.91 CT £21.73 TOTE £3.00: £1.30, £1.90; EX 8.20 Trifecta £20.30 Pool: £320.87 - 11.66 winning units..
Owner Steve Shore **Bred** Caroline Shore **Trained** Newmarket, Suffolk

FOCUS
This hands and heels handicap for apprentice riders proved a lively betting heat. There was no hanging about and the lowly form makes sense.
The Magic Of Rio Official explanation: trainer said mare bled from the nose

96 FOLLOW US ON FACEBOOK H'CAP 1m (F)
1:20 (1:21) (Class 6) (0-60,64) 4-Y-0+ **£1,704** (£503; £251) **Stalls** Low

Form RPR
034- 1 **General Tufto**[24] [7775] 7-9-4 **57** (b) RobbieFitzpatrick 2 68
(Charles Smith) *sn outpcd and pushed along in rr: hdwy wl over 2f out: rdn over 1f out: styd on strly ent fnl f to ld last 100yds* **10/1**
142- 2 3/4 **Arkaim**[12] [7885] 4-9-11 **64** (v) MickyFenton 9 73
(Pam Sly) *prom: cl up 3f out: chal over 2f out: rdn to ld over 1f out: drvn ins fnl f: hdd and no ex last 100yds* **3/1**[2]
501- 3 2 1/2 **Ace Master**[12] [7885] 4-9-8 **61** RussKennemore 4 64
(Roy Bowring) *slt ld and set gd pce: jnd 3f out: rdn 2f out: hdd over 1f out: sn drvn and kpt on same pce* **9/4**[1]
00-0 4 2 1/4 **Bentley**[7] [7] 8-8-11 **55** (p) NathanAlison(5) 7 53
(Brian Baugh) *outpcd and towards rr 1/2-way: hdwy on inner 3f out: rdn over 2f out: kpt on same pce appr fnl f* **33/1**
225- 5 1 **Hilbre Court (USA)**[12] [7885] 7-9-3 **56** (e[1]) WilliamCarson 1 52
(Brian Baugh) *chsd ldrs: rdn along over 3f out: drvn 2f out and sn one pce* **13/2**[3]
625- 6 1/2 **So Is She (IRE)**[38] [7333] 4-8-8 **50** (p) DominicFox(3) 6 45
(Alan Bailey) *s.i.s and swtchd rt to r wd: bhd tl sme late hdwy* **13/2**[3]
206- 7 1 1/2 **Exopuntia**[12] [7885] 6-9-1 **54** JoeFanning 8 45
(Julia Feilden) *trckd ldrs: hdwy 3f out: rdn over 2f out: sn drvn and wknd over 1f out* **8/1**
000- 8 15 **Mi Regalo**[8] [7942] 4-8-11 **57** LeonnaMayor(7) 5 14
(Phil McEntee) *chsd ldrs: rdn along 3f out: sn wknd* **20/1**
001/ 9 27 **Jozafeen**[508] [5201] 5-9-7 **60** LeeNewman 3
(Robin Bastiman) *a in rr: bhd fnl 3f* **16/1**

1m 42.92s (-0.78) **Going Correction** -0.10s/f (Stan) **9** Ran SP% **116.2**
Speed ratings (Par 101): **99,98,95,93,92 92,90,75,48**
Tote Swingers: 1&2 £4.60, 1&3 £4.90, 2&3 £2.20 CSF £40.44 CT £93.79 TOTE £11.60: £2.90, £1.10, £1.80; EX 48.80 Trifecta £54.90 Pool: £448.89 - 6.04 winning units..
Owner J R Theaker **Bred** Hascombe And Valiant Studs **Trained** Temple Bruer, Lincs

FOCUS
An ordinary but competitive enough handicap for the class and it saw changing fortunes in the home straight.

97 HOLD YOUR BIRTHDAY PARTY AT SOUTHWELL H'CAP 1m 3f (F)
1:50 (1:50) (Class 6) (0-65,65) 4-Y-0+ **£1,704** (£503; £251) **Stalls** Low

Form RPR
033- 1 **Magic Millie (IRE)**[17] [7859] 5-8-2 **51** oh2 RyanPowell(5) 6 65
(David O'Meara) *trckd ldrs: hdwy over 3f out: rdn to chse ldr wl over 1f out: sn edgd rt: styd on wl u.p fnl f to ld last 50yds* **10/1**
613/ 2 1/2 **Hunters Belt (IRE)**[19] [7541] 8-9-4 **62** BarryMcHugh 9 75
(Noel Wilson) *hld up towards rr: stdy hdwy 5f out: led 3f out: pushed clr over 2f out: rdn over 1f out: edgd lft ins fnl f: hdd and no ex last 50yds* **7/1**[3]
002- 3 1 3/4 **Newport Arch**[17] [7859] 4-8-8 **58** MichaelO'Connell(3) 4 68+
(John Quinn) *chsd ldrs: rdn along and lost pl over 5f out: hdwy over 2f out: sn rdn and kpt on fnl f: nrst fin* **7/4**[1]
503- 4 8 **Kipchak (IRE)**[10] [7912] 7-8-12 **56** (b) HayleyTurner 7 52
(Conor Dore) *cl up: led after 3f: rdn and hdd 3f out: drvn 2f out and grad wknd* **12/1**
044- 5 hd **Corvette**[12] [7885] 4-8-11 **58** LukeMorris 2 53
(Michael Appleby) *prom: rdn along and outpcd over 4f out: plugged on u.p fnl 2f* **10/1**
64-5 6 2 3/4 **Jonnie Skull (IRE)**[5] [21] 6-8-1 **52** (t) DannyBrock(7) 5 42
(Phil McEntee) *led 3f: chsd ldrs on inner: rdn along 4f out: wknd over 3f out* **18/1**
20-2 7 16 **Arizona High**[7] [1] 4-8-10 **57** JoeFanning 3 18
(Andrew Crook) *trckd ldrs: rdn along over 3f out: sn wknd* **25/1**
140- 8 1/2 **Master Of Song**[23] [7789] 5-9-4 **62** (p) RussKennemore 8 23
(Roy Bowring) *dwlt: sn trcking ldrs: cl up 1/2-way: effrt to chal 3f out: ev ch tl rdn and wknd wl over 1f out* **11/4**[2]
000- 9 13 **Bilidn**[19] [7831] 4-9-4 **65** AdamKirby 1
(Noel Quinlan) *racd wd: a in rr: bhd fr 1/2-way* **20/1**

2m 25.05s (-2.95) **Going Correction** -0.10s/f (Stan)
WFA 4 from 5yo+ 3lb **9** Ran SP% **115.3**
Speed ratings (Par 101): **106,105,104,98,98 96,84,84,74**
Tote Swingers: 1&2 £4.80, 1&3 £4.00, 2&3 £6.00 CSF £77.69 CT £181.07 TOTE £8.70: £3.10, £2.30, £1.10; EX 69.30 Trifecta £375.50 Part won. Pool: £507.45 - 0.95 winning units..
Owner C Varley, K Everitt & R Fell **Bred** John C Little **Trained** Nawton, N Yorks

FOCUS
A moderate handicap but not bad form for the class.

98 SOUTHWELL-RACECOURSE.CO.UK (S) STKS 1m 3f (F)
2:20 (2:20) (Class 6) 4-Y-0+ **£1,704** (£503; £251) **Stalls** Low

Form RPR
605- 1 **Overrule (USA)**[28] [7722] 8-9-3 65 (p) BarryMcHugh 1 54
(Brian Ellison) *hld up in tch: swtchd wd 5f out: hdwy 3f out: chal over 2f out: rdn to ld wl over 1f out: drvn ins fnl f: hld on wl* **4/1**[2]
05-0 2 3/4 **Miereveld**[6] [9] 5-9-3 47 (b) RobertWinston 5 53
(Shaun Harris) *dwlt: in tch: hdwy to chse ldrs 5f out: rdn along 3f out: cl up 2f out: drvn and ev ch over 1f out tl no ex wl ins fnl f* **15/2**
240- 3 1/2 **Ay Tay Tate (IRE)**[10] [7914] 6-9-3 66 LukeMorris 6 52
(David C Griffiths) *prom: led 4f out: rdn along 3f out: hdd wl over 1f out: sn drvn: ev ch tl edgd rt and one pce ins fnl f* **1/1**[1]
202- 4 8 **Flying Applause**[10] [7912] 7-9-3 53 (bt) RussKennemore 3 38
(Roy Bowring) *tk keen: chsd ldng pair: led after 3f: pushed along and hdd 4f out: rdn over 3f out and sn wknd* **6/1**[3]
666- 5 nk **Putin (IRE)**[9] [7923] 4-8-13 53 LeonnaMayor(7) 2 45
(Phil McEntee) *led 3f: cl up tl rdn along 3f out and sn wknd: eased and lost poor 4th nr line* **12/1**
004- 6 18 **Marina's Ocean**[10] [7912] 8-8-9 39 (bt) RyanClark(3) 4
(Roy Bowring) *hld up in rr: swtchd wd 1/2-way: rdn along 4f out: sn outpcd* **20/1**

2m 27.52s (-0.48) **Going Correction** -0.10s/f (Stan)
WFA 4 from 5yo+ 3lb **6** Ran SP% **108.5**
Speed ratings (Par 101): **97,96,96,90,90 76**
Tote Swingers: 1&2 £3.30, 1&3 £2.70, 2&3 £1.50 CSF £30.04 TOTE £4.00: £2.60, £3.00; EX 55.20.No bid for the winner.
Owner Steve May **Bred** Avalon Farms Inc **Trained** Norton, N Yorks
■ Stewards' Enquiry : Leonna Mayor two-day ban: failed to take all reasonable and permissable measures to obtain best placing (Jan 22-23)

FOCUS
There was a tight three-way finish in this seller.

99 THOUSANDS OF SPORTS EXPERIENCES AT BLUESQ.COM H'CAP 6f (F)
2:50 (2:50) (Class 4) (0-85,80) 3-Y-0 **£4,204** (£1,251; £625; £312) **Stalls** Low

Form RPR
500- 1 **Verbeeck**[78] [7021] 3-9-7 **80** AdamKirby 5 86
(George Prodromou) *cl up: effrt over 2f out: rdn wl over 1f out: led jst ins fnl f and styd on strly* **8/1**
040- 2 2 1/2 **Key Ambition**[52] [7445] 3-9-3 **79** (t) DaleSwift(3) 3 77
(Deborah Sanderson) *chsd ldrs: rdn along and outpcd 1/2-way: swtchd wd st: hdwy wl over 1f out: styd on wl u.p fnl f* **3/1**[2]

231- **3** *nk* **Ishiamiracle**[10] 7916 3-8-0 **66**......(p) DannyBrock(7) 4 63
(Phil McEntee) *led: rdn along over 2f out: hdd wl over 1f out: kpt on same pce* **15/8**[1]

324- **4** *½* **Wicked Wench**[10] 7905 3-8-11 **70**...... JoeFanning 1 65
(Jo Hughes) *cl up: chal wl over 2f out: rdn to ld wl over 1f out: hdd jst ins fnl f and sn wknd* **3/1**[2]

41-2 **5** *1 ½* **One More Roman (IRE)**[3] 42 3-8-4 **66** oh1......(bt) AmyRyan(3) 2 57
(Gay Kelleway) *in rr and swtchd wd after 1f: hdwy over 2f out: sn rdn and n.d* **11/2**[3]

1m 15.6s (-0.90) **Going Correction** -0.10s/f (Stan) **5 Ran SP% 111.3**
Speed ratings (Par 99): **102,98,98,97,95**
CSF £31.70 TOTE £8.70: £5.10, £2.20; EX 34.10.
Owner Fahed Al Dabbous **Bred** Peter Winkworth **Trained** East Harling, Norfolk

FOCUS
A moderate 3-y-o handicap, the first of three consecutive races over C&D that ended the card. It was run at a strong pace.

100 MIRROR PUNTERS CLUB H'CAP 6f (F)
3:20 (3:21) (Class 5) (0-75,75) 4-Y-0+ **£2,522** (£750; £375; £187) **Stalls Low**

Form RPR

300- **1** **Bandstand**[39] 7586 6-9-2 **75**...... JustinNewman(5) 6 84
(Bryan Smart) *in rr and pushed along 1/2-way: hdwy over 2f out: swtchd rt and rdn wl over 1f out: styd on wl fnl f to ld nr fin* **10/3**[1]

55-3 **2** *nk* **Dancing Freddy (IRE)**[5] 24 5-9-4 **72**......(tp) MartinHarley 9 80
(Richard Guest) *trckd ldrs: hdwy 1/2-way: led wl over 2f out: rdn over 1f out: drvn ins fnl f: hdd and no ex nr fin* **4/1**[2]

50-0 **3** *nk* **Ace Of Spies (IRE)**[6] 13 7-8-7 **61** oh1......(b) JamesSullivan 7 68
(Conor Dore) *towards rr: wd st: hdwy wl over 1f out: sn rdn and styd on strly fnl f* **16/1**

004- **4** *1 ½* **La Capriosa**[26] 7746 6-8-12 **66**...... RobertWinston 2 68
(Scott Dixon) *cl up: rdn 2f out: sn chsng ldr and ev ch tl one pce ent fnl f* **8/1**

14-0 **5** *shd* **Steel City Boy (IRE)**[6] 8 9-8-0 **61** oh1...... DannyBrock(7) 5 63
(Garry Woodward) *chsd ldrs: rdn along over 2f out: one pce appr fnl f* **25/1**

00-0 **6** *½* **Clear Ice (IRE)**[5] 24 5-9-1 **72**......(b) AmyRyan(3) 4 72
(Gay Kelleway) *chsd ldrs: hdwy on inner 1/2-way: rdn and ch 2f out: drvn and one pce appr fnl f* **8/1**

03-4 **7** *shd* **Elhamri**[6] 13 8-8-11 **65**...... HayleyTurner 10 65
(Conor Dore) *in rr tl styd on fnl 2f: nrst fin* **4/1**[2]

500- **8** *1 ¼* **Avonrose**[9] 7928 5-9-1 **72**...... DaleSwift(3) 11 72+
(Derek Shaw) *racd wd: bhd: hdwy over 2f out: hmpd and swtchd lft over 1f out: styd on: nrst fin* **15/2**[3]

120- **9** *2 ¼* **Babich Bay (IRE)**[103] 6426 4-9-0 **68**......(p) StevieDonohoe 1 57
(Jo Hughes) *nvr nr ldrs* **16/1**

600- **10** *1 ½* **Cheery Cat (USA)**[256] 1612 8-8-8 **62** oh3 ow1......(p) LeeNewman 3 46
(Bruce Hellier, Germany) *prom: rdn along wl over 2f out: sn wknd* **100/1**

015- **11** *2* **Mother Jones**[181] 3900 4-9-4 **72**...... JoeFanning 8 50
(Deborah Sanderson) *led: rdn along 1/2-way: hdd wl over 2f out and sn wknd* **20/1**

1m 15.71s (-0.79) **Going Correction** -0.10s/f (Stan) **11 Ran SP% 118.4**
Speed ratings (Par 103): **101,100,100,98,98 97,97,95,92,90 87**
Tote Swingers: 1&2 £4.10, 1&3 £12.60, 2&3 £11.40 CSF £16.29 CT £188.56 TOTE £3.90: £1.70, £2.20, £3.20; EX 20.70 Trifecta £314.20 Pool: £896.17 - 2.11 winning units..
Owner Crossfields Racing **Bred** D J And Mrs Brown **Trained** Hambleton, N Yorks

FOCUS
This competitive sprint handicap was run at a strong pace and it saw a cracking finish. Sound form.

101 PLAY ROULETTE AT BLUESQ.COM/CASINO H'CAP 6f (F)
3:50 (3:54) (Class 6) (0-55,56) 4-Y-0+ **£1,704** (£503; £251) **Stalls Low**

Form RPR

201- **1** **Beachwood Bay**[10] 7911 4-9-3 **56**...... StevieDonohoe 3 67+
(Jo Hughes) *towards rr: pushed along and hdwy 1/2-way: rdn 2f out: str run to ld over 1f out: edgd lft ins fnl f: drvn out* **4/1**[1]

500- **2** *1* **Saktoon (USA)**[87] 6816 4-8-13 **52**......(v[1]) JoeFanning 2 58
(Derek Shaw) *chsd ldrs on inner: hdwy 2f out: rdn over 1f out: kpt on wl fnl f* **16/1**

036- **3** *½* **Prince Of Vasa (IRE)**[17] 7857 5-9-2 **55**...... AndrewMullen 12 59
(Michael Smith) *prom: effrt and cl up 2f out: sn rdn and ev ch tl edgd edgd lft and one pce ins fnl f* **4/1**[1]

02-3 **4** *nk* **Gorgeous Goblin (IRE)**[6] 8 5-8-10 **49**......(t) LukeMorris 11 52
(David C Griffiths) *chsd ldrs: hdwy wl over 2f out: rdn to ld briefly wl over 1f out: sn hdd and one pce fnl f* **6/1**[2]

600- **5** *2* **Silly Billy (IRE)**[25] 7754 4-8-10 **54**...... JemmaMarshall(5) 9 51+
(Sylvester Kirk) *hld up and bhd: stdy hdwy on inner over 2f out: kpt on fnl f: nrst fin* **28/1**

606- **6** *½* **Takajan (IRE)**[28] 7728 5-8-9 **55**...... RachealKneller(7) 10 50
(Mark Brisbourne) *trckd ldrs on outer: wd st: hdwy and ch wl over 1f out: sn rdn and one pce appr fnl f* **8/1**[3]

00-0 **7** *5* **Bertbrand**[6] 14 7-8-7 **46** oh1...... JamesSullivan 4 25
(Ian McInnes) *chsd ldrs: rdn along over 2f out: n.m.r and swtchd rt wl over 1f out: sn wknd* **100/1**

004- **8** *2* **Morermaloke**[10] 7911 4-8-10 **52**...... DaleSwift(3) 1 25
(Ian McInnes) *in rr: sme hdwy 2f out: sn rdn and n.d* **25/1**

051- **9** *¾* **Da'Quonde (IRE)**[12] 7886 4-8-13 **52**...... TomEaves 7 23
(Bryan Smart) *prom: hdwy and cl up 1/2-way: led wl over 2f out and sn rdn: drvn and hdd wl over 1f out: sn wknd* **4/1**[1]

000- **10** *1 ½* **Bachelor Knight (IRE)**[41] 7565 4-9-1 **54**......(t) DuranFentiman 13 20
(Suzzanne France) *a towards rr* **25/1**

066- **11** *1 ¾* **Georgian Silver**[30] 7690 4-8-8 **47** oh1 ow1......(b) LeeNewman 6
(George Foster) *led: rdn along 1/2-way: sn hdd & wknd* **40/1**

255- **12** *1 ½* **Blue Noodles**[67] 7229 6-9-1 **54**......(p) PaddyAspell 8
(John Wainwright) *a in rr* **25/1**

1m 15.92s (-0.58) **Going Correction** -0.10s/f (Stan) **12 Ran SP% 109.7**
Speed ratings (Par 101): **99,97,97,96,93 93,86,83,82,80 78,76**
Tote Swingers: 1&2 £16.50, 1&3 £3.00, 2&3 £18.30 CSF £54.57 CT £206.32 TOTE £4.50: £2.00, £4.70, £1.40; EX 71.70 Trifecta £746.00 Part won. Pool: £1,008.22 - 0.41 winning units..
Owner Mrs Joanna Hughes **Bred** Bumble Bloodstock Ltd **Trained** Lambourn, Berks

FOCUS
A low-grade sprint handicap and another race over the C&D run at a decent pace.
Bertbrand Official explanation: jockey said gelding was denied a clear run
T/Plt: £463.50 to a £1 stake. Pool: £85,182.98 - 134.15 winning tickets. T/Qpdt: £246.20 to a £1 stake. Pool: £5,390.81 - 16.20 winning tickets. JR

[61]WOLVERHAMPTON (A.W) (L-H)
Monday, January 9

OFFICIAL GOING: Standard
Wind: Light behind Weather: Overcast

102 BET AT BLUE SQUARE APPRENTICE H'CAP 7f 32y(P)
2:25 (2:26) (Class 6) (0-65,67) 4-Y-0+ **£1,704** (£503; £251) **Stalls High**

Form RPR

30-5 **1** **Lastkingofscotland (IRE)**[5] 33 6-9-7 **65**......(b) KieranO'Neill 3 74
(Conor Dore) *hld up: rdn over 2f out: swtchd lft and hdwy over 1f out: r.o to ld wl ins fnl f* **4/1**[2]

006- **2** *1* **Needwood Ridge**[10] 7928 5-9-2 **65**......(bt) RaulDaSilva(5) 12 71
(Frank Sheridan) *hld up: hdwy over 2f out: r.o* **10/1**

000- **3** *¾* **Spin Again (IRE)**[21] 7819 7-9-1 **64**...... LucyKBarry(5) 1 68
(Mark Wellings) *chsd ldr tl led over 2f out: rdn and hdd wl ins fnl f* **40/1**

305- **4** *shd* **Trojan Rocket (IRE)**[21] 7819 4-9-4 **67** ow2...... MichaelJMurphy(5) 7 71
(George Prodromou) *hld up in tch: lost pl 1/2-way: hdwy: nt clr run and swtchd rt 1f out: r.o: nt rch ldrs* **3/1**[1]

000- **5** *nk* **Double Carpet (IRE)**[30] 7715 9-9-4 **62**...... JohnFahy 8 65
(Garry Woodward) *chsd ldrs: rdn over 1f out: styd on* **14/1**

005- **6** *¾* **Katmai River (IRE)**[21] 7820 5-8-8 **57**......(v) RachealKneller(5) 2 58
(Mark Usher) *hld up: hdwy over 1f out: sn rdn: styd on same pce ins fnl f* **6/1**[3]

024- **7** *1* **Loves Theme (IRE)**[70] 7198 4-8-10 **59**......(v) NatashaEaton(5) 6 57
(Alan Bailey) *chsd ldrs: rdn and edgd rt ins fnl f: no ex towards fin* **20/1**

250- **8** *1 ¾* **Anjomarba (IRE)**[10] 7930 5-8-12 **59**......(p) RyanPowell(3) 11 52
(Conor Dore) *chsd ldrs: rdn over 2f out: no ex fnl f* **16/1**

600- **9** *1 ¼* **Just Timmy Marcus**[285] 1052 6-8-9 **56**...... JamesRogers(3) 5 46
(Brian Baugh) *dwlt: nvr on terms* **22/1**

606- **10** *½* **Smirfy's Silver**[90] 6773 8-9-4 **65**...... GarryWhillans(3) 4 54
(Michael Mullineaux) *led: rdn and hdd over 2f out: wkng whn hmpd ins fnl f* **33/1**

553- **11** *1 ¾* **Downhill Skier (IRE)**[21] 7819 8-9-2 **65**...... JackDuern(5) 9 49
(Mark Brisbourne) *hld up: a towards rr* **12/1**

50-0 **12** *¾* **Vitznau (IRE)**[2] 87 8-8-13 **62**...... LeonnaMayor(5) 10 44
(Alastair Lidderdale) *dwlt: hld up: hdwy on outer 3f out: wknd wl over 1f out* **13/2**

1m 29.51s (-0.09) **Going Correction** +0.025s/f (Slow) **12 Ran SP% 116.4**
Speed ratings (Par 101): **101,99,99,98,98 97,96,94,93,92 90,89**
toteswingers:1&2:£7.90, 1&3:£29.30, 2&3:£75.10 CSF £40.70 CT £1412.50 TOTE £6.50: £1.70, £3.70, £17.20; EX 54.70 Trifecta £321.00 Part won. Pool: £321.00 - 0.10 winning units..
Owner Mrs Jennifer Marsh **Bred** Baronrath Stud **Trained** Hubbert's Bridge, Lincs

FOCUS
Exposed performers in a modest handicap. The gallop was a reasonable one and the winner raced against the far rail in the closing stages.
Just Timmy Marcus Official explanation: jockey said gelding missed the break

103 PARADE RESTAURANT (S) STKS 1m 141y(P)
2:55 (3:00) (Class 6) 4-Y-0+ **£1,704** (£503; £251) **Stalls Low**

Form RPR

154- **1** **Faithful Ruler (USA)**[14] 7876 8-9-4 74......(p) LukeMorris 1 79
(Ronald Harris) *chsd ldr: rdn over 2f out: led ins fnl f: edgd lft: styd on u.p* **2/1**[2]

126- **2** *shd* **Unlimited**[100] 6541 10-8-13 79...... DavidProbert 6 74
(Tony Carroll) *a.p: led over 1f out: rdn and hdd ins fnl f: styd on* **13/2**

225- **3** *nk* **Autumn Blades (IRE)**[24] 7776 7-8-13 80......(b) JamesSullivan 2 73
(Ruth Carr) *trckd ldrs: plld hrd: rdn and ev ch fr over 1f out: hung lft ins fnl f: styd on* **15/8**[1]

200- **4** *1 ½* **Georgebernardshaw (IRE)**[87] 6831 7-8-13 82......(b[1]) JamieSpencer 5 70
(John Quinn) *set stdy pce tl qcknd over 2f out: rdn: hung lft and hdd over 1f out: styd on same pce ins fnl f: eased nr fin* **5/2**[3]

5- **5** *7* **Ravanchi**[18] 7856 8-8-8 0...... RobbieFitzpatrick 3 49?
(Frank Sheridan) *s.i.s: hld up: outpcd fr over 3f out* **100/1**

1m 52.84s (2.34) **Going Correction** +0.025s/f (Slow)
WFA 4 from 6yo+ 1lb **5 Ran SP% 111.0**
Speed ratings (Par 101): **90,89,89,88,82**
CSF £14.63 TOTE £2.10: £1.10, £2.80; EX 11.70.There was no bid for the winner. Georgebernardshaw was claimed by R. C. Guest for £6,000.
Owner Ridge House Stables Ltd **Bred** WinStar Farm LLC **Trained** Earlswood, Monmouths

FOCUS
Only five runners but not the worst race of its type with four of them rated 74 and above. The first "running" resulted in a false start but one in which all the runners pulled up after a furlong or so. The gallop was a muddling one and the winner raced centre-to-far side in the straight.

104 ENJOY THE PUNTERS PACKAGE GROUP OFFER H'CAP 1m 1f 103y(P)
3:25 (3:26) (Class 6) (0-58,61) 4-Y-0+ **£1,704** (£503; £251) **Stalls Low**

Form RPR

40-5 **1** **Aviso (GER)**[2] 85 8-8-13 **57**...... MatthewCosham(5) 6 65
(David Evans) *hld up: plld hrd: hdwy u.p and edgd lft over 1f out: r.o to ld post* **11/1**

11-1 **2** *hd* **Mataajir (USA)**[8] 7 4-9-7 **61** 6ex...... JoeFanning 3 69+
(Derek Shaw) *led: rdn and hdd over 1f out: r.o* **1/1**[1]

312- **3** *nse* **Idol Deputy (FR)**[12] 7892 6-8-12 **58**...... RachealKneller(7) 2 66
(Mark Usher) *chsd ldrs: led over 1f out: rdn ins fnl f: hdd post* **11/4**[2]

406- **4** *1 ¼* **Petomic (IRE)**[24] 7788 7-8-12 **54**......(p) RobertLButler(3) 4 59
(Richard Guest) *hld up in tch: rdn over 1f out: styd on* **22/1**

036- **5** *1 ½* **Excellent Vision**[19] 7848 5-9-1 **54**......(t) RichardKingscote 11 56
(Milton Bradley) *hld up: hdwy over 1f out: sn rdn: no ex towards fin* **10/1**[3]

/50- **6** *1 ½* **Marksbury**[37] 7632 5-9-5 **58**...... LukeMorris 12 57
(Mark Brisbourne) *chsd ldr tl rdn over 2f out: styd on same pce fnl f* **50/1**

600- **7** *1 ¼* **Ergo (FR)**[34] 7077 8-9-2 **55**......(b) PaulHanagan 10 51
(James Moffatt) *prom: rdn over 1f out: styd on same pce* **25/1**

8 *1 ½* **Tara Fay (IRE)**[24] 7797 5-8-13 **52**...... JamieSpencer 7 45
(Gordon Elliott, Ire) *hld up: hdwy over 2f out: rdn over 1f out: wknd ins fnl f* **10/1**[3]

9 *½* **The Last Straw (IRE)**[80] 7007 7-8-7 **46** oh1...... ChrisCatlin 5 38
(Gordon Elliott, Ire) *hld up: rdn over 1f out: n.d* **33/1**

42- **10** *2* **Pacey Outswinger (IRE)**[72] 7159 5-8-11 **50**...... MartinHarley 1 38
(John C McConnell, Ire) *chsd ldrs: rdn and lost pl over 3f out: wknd over 1f out* **14/1**

240- 11 3/4 **Lytham (IRE)**[175] 4153 11-9-2 55 .... DavidProbert 9 41
(Tony Carroll) *s.i.s: hld up: a in rr* 40/1
2m 2.91s (1.21) **Going Correction** +0.025s/f (Slow)
WFA 4 from 5yo+ 1lb 11 Ran SP% **125.4**
Speed ratings (Par 101): **95,94,94,93,92 91,89,88,88,86 85**
toteswingers:1&2:£6.30, 1&3:£6.70, 2&3:£1.90 CSF £23.07 CT £44.93 TOTE £9.00: £2.30, £1.40, £1.30; EX 35.00 Trifecta £85.60 Pool: £805.13 - 6.96 winning units..
Owner Mrs E Evans **Bred** Gestut Schlenderhan **Trained** Pandy, Monmouths
FOCUS
A modest handicap. The gallop was just an ordinary one and the winner came down the centre.

105 SPONSOR A RACE BY CALLING 01902 390000 H'CAP 1m 4f 50y(P)
3:55 (3:55) (Class 6) (0-52,52) 4-Y-0+ £1,704 (£503; £251) Stalls Low

Form RPR
400- 1 **Sommersturm (GER)**[35] 7639 8-8-13 48 .... MickyFenton 9 64+
(Barney Curley) *chsd ldr tl led over 3f out: rdn over 1f out: styd on u.p* 7/2[1]
530- 2 3 1/4 **Black Iceman**[47] 7515 4-8-8 50 .... SimonPearce(3) 4 61
(Lydia Pearce) *a.p: chsd wnr over 2f out: sn ev ch: no ex ins fnl f* 7/2[1]
/00- 3 2 1/4 **Safwaan**[333] 490 5-9-1 50 .... JamieMackay 11 57+
(Willie Musson) *hld up: plld hrd: hdwy over 1f out: r.o: nt rch ldrs* 8/1
406- 4 3 3/4 **Grecian Goddess (IRE)**[164] 4510 4-8-10 52 .... MichaelO'Connell(3) 8 53
(John Ryan) *hld up: hdwy 5f out: rdn over 2f out: styd on same pce* 50/1
5/0- 5 2 1/4 **Arisea (IRE)**[33] 6137 9-9-1 50 .... PaulHanagan 7 48
(James Moffatt) *hld up: pushed along over 3f out: nvr nr to chal* 6/1[3]
405/ 6 2 1/4 **Golden Flight (IRE)**[24] 7797 6-8-11 46 .... MartinHarley 2 40
(John C McConnell, Ire) *chsd ldrs: rdn over 2f out: wknd over 1f out* 9/1
056- 7 2 **Nha Trang (IRE)**[18] 7859 5-8-11 46 oh1 ....(p) LukeMorris 3 37
(Michael Appleby) *led over 8f: sn rdn: wknd over 1f out* 5/1[2]
002- 8 2 **Hathaway (IRE)**[19] 7851 5-8-6 48 .... RachealKneller(7) 12 36
(Mark Brisbourne) *hld up: pushed along over 2f out: n.d* 8/1
140- 9 10 **Magnitude**[185] 3811 7-8-12 52 ow1 ....(p) LMcNiff(5) 10 24
(Brian Baugh) *hld up: pushed along 1/2-way: a in rr: lost tch fr over 2f out* 16/1
000- 10 10 **Miss Whippy**[28] 7206 5-8-12 47 .... IanMongan 6
(Paul Howling) *chsd ldrs tl rdn and wknd over 2f out: t.o* 25/1
2m 40.22s (-0.88) **Going Correction** +0.025s/f (Slow)
WFA 4 from 5yo+ 4lb 10 Ran SP% **119.3**
Speed ratings (Par 101): **103,100,99,96,95 93,92,91,84,77**
toteswingers:1&2:£4.90, 1&3:£12.10, 2&3:£7.20 CSF £15.67 CT £93.03 TOTE £5.90: £2.10, £2.20, £4.00; EX 29.70 Trifecta £414.30 Pool: £671.91 - 1.20 winning units..
Owner Curley Leisure **Bred** Gestut Schlenderhan **Trained** Newmarket, Suffolk
FOCUS
A low-grade handicap run at an ordinary pace. The winner edged towards the far side in the straight.
Sommersturm(GER) Official explanation: trainer's rep said, regarding apparent improvement in form, that the gelding is an ungenuine sort and may have benefited from a longer trip and weaker contest.

106 EXCLUSIVE LIVE SHOWS AT BLUESQ.COM FILLIES' H'CAP 5f 216y(P)
4:25 (4:26) (Class 5) (0-70,70) 4-Y-0+ £2,264 (£673; £336; £168) Stalls Low

Form RPR
545- 1 **Dancing Welcome**[97] 6610 6-9-2 65 ....(b) RichardKingscote 6 77
(Milton Bradley) *chsd ldr tl led 2f out: clr fnl f: readily* 7/1
011- 2 3 **Chester Deelyte (IRE)**[24] 7785 4-8-8 57 ....(v) TomEaves 1 59
(Lisa Williamson) *prom: lost pl 4f out: hdwy over 1f out: chsd wnr fnl f: no imp* 10/3[1]
400- 3 1 1/4 **Two Turtle Doves (IRE)**[12] 7896 6-8-8 60 .... AmyRyan(3) 3 58
(Michael Mullineaux) *chsd ldrs: rdn over 2f out: styd on same pce appr fnl f* 9/2[3]
06- 4 1 1/4 **Polemica (IRE)**[21] 7819 6-9-1 64 ....(bt) RobbieFitzpatrick 5 58
(Frank Sheridan) *s.s: hld up: r.o ins fnl f: nrst fin* 11/1
030- 5 1 3/4 **Spirit Of Grace**[173] 4210 4-9-4 67 .... MartinHarley 4 56
(Alan McCabe) *led: rdn and hdd 2f out: wknd fnl f* 13/2
/00- 6 3/4 **Wishbone (IRE)**[21] 7819 5-9-4 67 .... StevieDonohoe 9 53
(Jo Hughes) *s.i.s: hld up: pushed along over 2f out: nvr nrr* 12/1
502- 7 hd **Perfect Act**[20] 7834 7-9-7 70 .... DavidProbert 2 56
(Andrew Balding) *plld hrd and prom: rdn over 1f out: sn wknd* 7/2[2]
000- 8 1 1/4 **Athaakeel (IRE)**[19] 7844 6-8-9 58 ....(b) LukeMorris 8 40
(Ronald Harris) *hld up in tch: rdn over 2f out: wknd over 1f out* 8/1
1m 14.4s (-0.60) **Going Correction** +0.025s/f (Slow) 8 Ran SP% **116.5**
Speed ratings (Par 100): **105,101,99,97,95 94,94,92**
toteswingers:1&2:£3.60, 1&3:£5.90, 2&3:£5.90 CSF £31.20 CT £118.89 TOTE £7.50: £1.90, £1.50, £1.20; EX 39.40 Trifecta £223.90 Pool: £968.41 - 3.20 winning units..
Owner J M Bradley **Bred** The Hon Mrs E J Wills **Trained** Sedbury, Gloucs
FOCUS
A modest fillies' handicap run at a reasonable gallop, but it was a race in which very few figured. The winner raced centre-to-far side in the straight.
Perfect Act Official explanation: jockey said mare never travelled

107 HOTEL & CONFERENCING AT WOLVERHAMPTON MAIDEN STKS 7f 32y(P)
4:55 (4:57) (Class 5) 3-Y-0 £2,264 (£673; £336; £168) Stalls High

Form RPR
2-2 1 **Henry Clay**[5] 34 3-9-3 0 .... JoeFanning 6 85
(Mark Johnston) *sn led: shkn up over 1f out: rdn and edgd lft ins fnl f: styd on* 4/5[1]
2 2 1/4 **Dubawi Cheetah (IRE)** 3-8-12 0 .... PaulHanagan 1 74
(Richard Fahey) *led early: stdd to trck ldrs: racd keenly: rdn and edgd lft over 1f out: styd on to go 2nd nr fin: nt trble wnr* 11/4[3]
3 3/4 **Angel Gabrial (IRE)**[107] 6366 3-9-3 0 .... JamieSpencer 4 77
(Ian Williams) *a.p: chsd wnr over 5f out: rdn over 1f out: styd on same pce ins fnl f: lost 2nd nr fin* 2/1[2]
0- 4 10 **Picalily**[131] 5632 3-8-12 0 .... LukeMorris 8 45
(David Evans) *prom: rdn 1/2-way: wknd over 2f out* 28/1
6- 5 5 **Showsinger**[18] 7855 3-8-12 0 .... BarryMcHugh 5 31
(Richard Fahey) *s.i.s: hld up: wknd over 2f out* 50/1
6 1 1/4 **Dear Ben** 3-9-3 0 .... TomEaves 3 33
(Brian Baugh) *hld up: rdn over 2f out: sn wknd* 25/1
06- 7 nk **Danafisiak (IRE)**[10] 7927 3-9-3 0 .... RussKennemore 2 32
(Frank Sheridan) *hld up: rdn and wknd over 2f out* 100/1
8 1 3/4 **Jacasa Too** 3-8-12 0 .... JamesMillman 7 22
(Rod Millman) *sn pushed along and prom: rdn and wknd wl over 2f out* 50/1
1m 29.84s (0.24) **Going Correction** +0.025s/f (Slow) 8 Ran SP% **127.8**
Speed ratings (Par 97): **99,96,95,84,78 77,76,74**
toteswingers:1&2:£1.50, 1&3:£1.10, 2&3:£1.30 CSF £4.02 TOTE £1.90: £1.02, £1.10, £1.10; EX 5.40 Trifecta £12.70 Pool: £1,177.93 - 68.27 winning units..
Owner Sheikh Hamdan Bin Mohammed Al Maktoum **Bred** Rabbah Bloodstock Limited **Trained** Middleham Moor, N Yorks
FOCUS
A fair maiden which, as the betting suggested, only concerned the first three at the head of the market. The gallop was an ordinary one and the winner raced near the inside rail in the straight.

108 PLAY RAINBOW RICHES AT BLUESQ.COM H'CAP 1m 141y(P)
5:25 (5:25) (Class 6) (0-60,59) 3-Y-O £1,704 (£503; £251) Stalls Low

Form RPR
531- 1 **Complex**[21] 7821 3-9-1 53 .... LukeMorris 4 57
(David Evans) *chsd clr ld tl led 2f out: sn rdn: hdd over 1f out: hmpd ins fnl f: sn hdd: rallied to ld nr fin* 7/1[3]
05- 2 nk **Gabrial's King (IRE)**[59] 7368 3-8-12 50 .... JamieSpencer 3 53
(Ian Williams) *hld up: hdwy to ld over 1f out: sn rdn and hung rt: hdd towards fin* 4/9[1]
405- 3 1 3/4 **Clean Bowled (IRE)**[14] 7875 3-9-7 59 .... MartinHarley 7 58
(Alan McCabe) *hld up: rdn over 2f out: hdwy over 1f out: nt clr run and swtchd lft ins fnl f: r.o* 11/2[2]
004- 4 3 1/4 **Ferdy (IRE)**[24] 7780 3-8-7 45 .... JamesSullivan 1 37
(Paul Green) *trckd ldrs: racd keenly: rdn over 1f out: styd on same pce fnl f* 16/1
335- 5 1/2 **Siouxies Dream**[31] 7684 3-9-0 57 .... RyanPowell(5) 6 48
(Michael Appleby) *prom: rdn over 2f out: no ex fr over 1f out* 20/1
041- 6 4 1/2 **Cat Queen**[25] 7769 3-9-3 58 .... AmyRyan(3) 2 38
(Gay Kelleway) *led and sn clr: rdn and hdd 2f out: wknd fnl f* 20/1
044- 7 hd **Gone To Ground**[37] 7626 3-8-2 45 ....(p) RaulDaSilva(5) 5 25
(Jeremy Gask) *chsd ldrs: rdn over 2f out: wknd over 1f out* 40/1
1m 51.83s (1.33) **Going Correction** +0.025s/f (Slow) 7 Ran SP% **115.0**
Speed ratings (Par 95): **95,94,93,90,89 85,85**
toteswingers:1&2:£1.80, 1&3:£4.30, 2&3:£1.60 CSF £10.63 TOTE £10.00: £5.60, £1.02; EX 17.70.
Owner S Michael & A Stennett **Bred** Mickley Stud **Trained** Pandy, Monmouths
■ Stewards' Enquiry : Jamie Spencer three-day ban: careless riding (Jan 23-25)
FOCUS
A moderate handicap notable for the narrow defeat of the gambled-on runner-up. The gallop was an ordinary one (free-going clear leader Cat Queen largely ignored) and the winner was carried from the centre towards the stands side late on.
T/Jkpt: Not won. T/Plt: £46.80 to a £1 stake. Pool:£100,122.65 - 1,561.70 winning tickets T/Qpdt: £6.40 to a £1 stake. Pool:£8,682.10 - 1,002.29 winning tickets CR

[95]SOUTHWELL (L-H)
Tuesday, January 10

OFFICIAL GOING: Standard
Wind: Moderate half behind Weather: Fine and dry

109 BET ON WINNING DISTANCES AT BLUESQ.COM H'CAP 1m (F)
12:55 (12:55) (Class 6) (0-52,50) 4-Y-0+ £1,704 (£503; £251) Stalls Low

Form RPR
44-0 1 **St Ignatius**[8] 14 5-8-6 47 ....(p) JackDuern(7) 2 57
(Michael Appleby) *cl up on inner: slt ld 1/2-way: rdn 2f out: edgd rt over 1f out: kpt on gamely fnl f* 15/2[3]
61-2 2 3/4 **Spacecraft (IRE)**[9] 7 5-9-2 50 ....(b) JoeFanning 4 58+
(Christopher Kellett) *in tch: nt clr run on inner over 3f out: hdwy to chse ldng pair over 2f out: swtchd rt over 1f out: sn rdn and chal ent fnl f: ev ch tl no ex nr fin* 5/4[1]
000- 3 1/2 **Very Well Red**[12] 7910 9-9-2 50 .... WilliamCarson 12 57
(Peter Hiatt) *led to 1/2-way: cl up: rdn wl over 1f out and ev ch tl drvn: n.m.r and no ex wl ins fnl f* 11/1
234- 4 5 **Fearless Poet (IRE)**[25] 7781 4-9-1 49 ....(b[1]) TomEaves 3 44
(Bryan Smart) *chsd ldrs on inner: rdn along over 3f out: kpt on same pce* 4/1[2]
00-0 5 1 1/4 **Dado Mush**[9] 7 9-8-11 45 ....(p) DavidProbert 5 37
(Terry Clement) *s.i.s and bhd: hdwy over 3f out: rdn over 2f out: styd on: nrst fin* 50/1
00-0 6 2 **Aggbag**[9] 7 8-8-13 47 ....(p) LukeMorris 8 35
(Michael Appleby) *chsd ldrs: rdn along over 2f out: sn no hdwy* 12/1
00-6 7 1/2 **Vogarth**[7] 21 8-8-11 45 ....(b) RobbieFitzpatrick 10 32
(Michael Chapman) *chsd ldng pair: rdn along over 2f out: wknd wl over 1f out* 50/1
600- 8 5 **Noble Attitude**[14] 2401 6-8-11 45 .... BarryMcHugh 9 20
(Julie Camacho) *a towards rr* 25/1
000- 9 3 3/4 **Blonde Maite**[111] 6262 6-8-11 45 ....(b) MartinLane 11 12
(Roy Bowring) *s.i.s: a in rr* 16/1
/60- 10 3 **Just Zak**[260] 1567 7-8-9 48 .... RyanPowell(5) 6
(Garry Woodward) *a towards rr* 25/1
065- 11 5 **Hot Tub**[27] 7750 4-9-1 49 ....(t) ChrisCatlin 1
(Christine Dunnett) *chsd ldrs 2f: sn lost pl and bhd fnl 3f* 33/1
1m 43.57s (-0.13) **Going Correction** -0.10s/f (Stan) 11 Ran SP% **112.7**
Speed ratings (Par 101): **96,95,94,89,88 86,86,81,77,74 69**
toteswingers:1&2:£2.70, 2&3:£3.90, 1&3:£5.70 CSF £15.73 CT £103.92 TOTE £5.00: £1.60, £1.10, £4.00; EX 19.80 Trifecta £185.20 Pool: £575.87 - 2.30 winning units..
Owner Cheshire Elite Racing **Bred** Simon And Helen Plumbly **Trained** Danethorpe, Notts
■ Stewards' Enquiry : Jack Duern two-day ban: used whip with excessive frequency (Jan 24-25)
FOCUS
Plenty of these came into this rock-bottom handicap in indifferent form.

110 BOOK TICKETS AT SOUTHWELL-RACECOURSE.CO.UK H'CAP 1m 4f (F)
1:25 (1:26) (Class 6) (0-65,65) 4-Y-0+ £1,704 (£503; £251) Stalls Low

Form RPR
/40- 1 **Unex Picasso**[52] 2930 4-9-6 65 ....(tp) StevieDonohoe 2 73
(Ian Williams) *s.i.s and reminders after 100yds: hdwy on outer over 3f out: wd st and rdn along wl over 2f out: styd on strly fr over 1f out to ld last 100yds* 15/2
00-3 2 1 **Brunello**[9] 4 4-8-13 58 ow1 .... DanielTudhope 1 64
(David O'Meara) *trckd ldng pair: effrt over 3f out: rdn to ld 2f out: drvn clr over 1f out: hdd and no ex last 100yds* 13/8[1]
300- 3 4 **Savaronola (USA)**[104] 6446 7-8-12 53 .... DavidProbert 6 53
(Des Donovan) *trckd ldrs: hdwy over 4f out: rdn along over 2f out: kpt on same pce appr fnl f* 16/1
520- 4 1 1/4 **Magic Haze**[126] 4814 6-8-13 59 .... RyanPowell(5) 5 57
(Sally Hall) *in tch: rdn along and outpcd over 4f out: wd st: kpt on u.p fr over 1f out: nrst fin* 7/2[2]

310/ **5** 3/4 **Extremely So**[36] 6213 6-9-3 **58** MartinLane 8 55
(Philip McBride) *led: rdn along and hdd 4f out: led again 3f out: hdd 2f out and grad wknd* **11/1**

600/ **6** 1 **Myraid**[463] 6623 5-9-0 **55** JamesSullivan 3 50
(Ruth Carr) *hld up in tch: hdwy to chse ldrs over 3f out: swtchd rt and rdn over 2f out: sn drvn and wknd wl over 1f out* **20/1**

303- **7** 11 **Jibouti (IRE)**[20] 7848 4-8-8 **53** (b) HayleyTurner 7 31
(Clive Brittain) *cl up: slt ld 4f out: hdd 3f out: sn rdn and wknd 2f out* **5/1**[3]

000- **8** 9 **Addikt (IRE)**[35] 7647 7-9-7 **62** JamieGoldstein 9 25
(Michael Scudamore) *dwlt: a bhd* **33/1**

2m 39.35s (-1.65) **Going Correction** -0.10s/f (Stan)
WFA 4 from 5yo+ 4lb **8** Ran SP% **110.7**
Speed ratings (Par 101): **101,100,97,96,96 95,88,82**
toteswingers:1&2:£2.80, 2&3:£5.40, 1&3:£7.40 CSF £18.81 CT £179.60 TOTE £10.40: £2.20, £1.10, £3.30; EX 20.60 Trifecta £218.50 Pool: £572.88 - 1.94 winning units..
Owner Mrs A J Forde & D Nicholls **Bred** Norelands, Hugo Lascelles & D Clarke **Trained** Portway, Worcs

FOCUS
The pace was just steady until exiting the back stretch and the overall picture changed dramatically late on.

111 PLAY GOLF BEFORE RACING H'CAP 2m (F)
1:55 (1:55) (Class 6) (0-60,52) 4-Y-O+ **£1,704** (£503; £251) **Stalls** Low

Form RPR

00-1 **1** **Hada Men (USA)**[7] 23 7-9-6 **51** 6ex BarryMcHugh 3 74+
(Brian Ellison) *hld up in rr: stdy hdwy over 5f out: trckd ldng pair 4f out: led 3f out: sn clr: unchal* **1/6**[1]

60-3 **2** 12 **Delorain (IRE)**[8] 9 9-9-0 **50** (v) RyanPowell(5) 4 55
(William Stone) *in rr: pushed along 1/2-way: sn outpcd and bhd: hdwy 3f out: styd on fnl 2f: wnt 2nd appr fnl f: no ch w wnr* **6/1**[2]

10-4 **3** 9 **Spiritonthemount (USA)**[7] 23 7-9-5 **50** (b) WilliamCarson 1 44
(Peter Hiatt) *cl up: led 1/2-way: rdn along over 4f out: hdd 3f out and sn outpcd* **16/1**

054- **4** 8 **Mecox Bay (IRE)**[32] 7688 5-9-7 **52** LukeMorris 2 37
(Michael Appleby) *set str pce: hdd 1/2-way: rdn and cl up over 3f out: sn drvn and wknd* **12/1**[3]

000- **5** 27 **Always Dixie (IRE)**[223] 2618 5-9-0 **45** (p) JoeFanning 5
(Andrew Crook) *chsd ldng pair: rdn along over 4f out: sn wknd and bhd* **80/1**

3m 43.2s (-2.30) **Going Correction** -0.10s/f (Stan) **5** Ran SP% **114.8**
Speed ratings (Par 101): **101,95,90,86,73**
CSF £2.04 TOTE £1.10: £1.02, £1.90; EX 2.30.
Owner Brian Ellison **Bred** Overbrook Farm **Trained** Norton, N Yorks

FOCUS
The leading pair seemed to go off very strong and in the end the first two came from the last two places.

112 THOUSANDS OF SPORTS EXPERIENCES AT BLUESQ.COM H'CAP 6f (F)
2:25 (2:26) (Class 5) (0-70,69) 3-Y-O **£2,264** (£673; £336; £168) **Stalls** Low

Form RPR

54-1 **1** **Laffan (IRE)**[9] 6 3-9-11 **69** 6ex PhillipMakin 8 81
(Kevin Ryan) *chsd ldr: rdn along 1/2-way: drvn over 1f out: styd on u.p fnl f to ld last 50yds* **11/10**[1]

163- **2** 3/4 **Sonsie Lass**[32] 7686 3-9-4 **62** JoeFanning 3 72
(Keith Dalgleish) *led: clr over 2f out: rdn over 1f out: wknd ins fnl f: hdd and no ex last 50yds* **16/1**

612- **3** 7 **Sunny Side Up (IRE)**[14] 7881 3-9-2 **65** ShaneBKelly(5) 7 53
(Richard Fahey) *chsd ldng pair: rdn along over 2f out: kpt on same pce* **15/2**

15-1 **4** 1/2 **M J Woodward**[7] 25 3-9-2 **60** 6ex LukeMorris 2 46
(Paul Green) *chsd ldrs: rdn along over 2f out: sn no imp* **8/1**

104- **5** 7 **Bitaphon (IRE)**[12] 7915 3-9-2 **65** RaulDaSilva(5) 9 29
(Deborah Sanderson) *dwlt: sn in tch: rdn to chse ldrs over 2f out: sn no imp* **11/2**[2]

664- **6** 2 3/4 **Gulf Storm (IRE)**[12] 7916 3-8-13 **57** TomEaves 6 12
(Bryan Smart) *a outpcd in rr* **16/1**

442- **7** 1 3/4 **Abshir Zain (IRE)**[15] 7875 3-9-5 **63** (bt) HayleyTurner 1 12
(Clive Brittain) *a outpcd and bhd* **13/2**[3]

1m 15.03s (-1.47) **Going Correction** -0.10s/f (Stan) **7** Ran SP% **111.0**
Speed ratings (Par 97): **105,104,94,94,84 81,78**
toteswingers:1&2:£5.10, 2&3:£3.70, 1&3:£2.60 CSF £19.57 CT £87.27 TOTE £2.50: £1.60, £5.00; EX 18.00 Trifecta £75.80 Pool: £943.16 - 9.20 winning units..
Owner Mubarak Al Naemi **Bred** Vincent Dunne **Trained** Hambleton, N Yorks

113 SOUTHWELL-RACECOURSE.CO.UK H'CAP 7f (F)
2:55 (2:55) (Class 6) (0-52,52) 4-Y-O+ **£1,704** (£503; £251) **Stalls** Low

Form RPR

015- **1** **Monte Cassino (IRE)**[12] 7911 7-9-1 **51** (e[1]) TomEaves 12 61
(Bryan Smart) *prom: cl up 1/2-way: rdn to ld wl over 1f out: drvn ins fnl f: jst hld on* **6/1**[3]

00-6 **2** nse **Crocodile Bay (IRE)**[8] 14 9-8-10 **46** oh1 (p) FrannyNorton 7 56
(Richard Guest) *trckd ldrs: hdwy whn n.m.r 3f out: effrt to chal wl over 1f out: sn rdn and ev ch tl drvn ins fnl f and no ex nr line* **10/1**

4-56 **3** 4 1/2 **Jonnie Skull (IRE)**[2] 97 6-9-2 **52** (vt) RobertWinston 5 50
(Phil McEntee) *led 2f: cl up: rdn to ld briefly again over 2f out: hdd wl over 1f out: n.m.r and swtchd rt ent fnl f: one pce* **5/2**[1]

63-0 **4** 4 1/2 **Flow Chart (IRE)**[8] 8 5-8-10 **46** oh1 (b) RobbieFitzpatrick 11 32
(Peter Grayson) *in tch on outer: wd st: rdn over 2f out: kpt on appr fnl f: nt rch ldrs* **20/1**

000- **5** nk **Milton Of Campsie**[70] 7216 7-9-2 **52** WilliamCarson 1 37
(Richard Guest) *dwlt: hdwy to chse ldrs after 2f: wd st: rdn and hung rt 2f out: grad wknd* **16/1**

000- **6** 1 3/4 **Norton Girl**[13] 7714 4-8-10 **46** oh1 JoeFanning 10 26
(Tracy Waggott) *towards rr: hdwy 2f out: sn rdn: kpt on: nt rch ldrs* **14/1**

02-0 **7** 1 **Twennyshortkid**[8] 14 4-9-0 **50** (b) FrederikTylicki 3 27
(Paul Midgley) *nvr bttr than midfield* **11/2**[2]

20-4 **8** 3/4 **Kheskianto (IRE)**[8] 12 6-8-3 **46** oh1 (b) JackDuern(7) 6 21
(Michael Chapman) *s.i.s and bhd: sme hdwy over 2f out: nvr a factor* **20/1**

05-0 **9** 6 **Kwik Time**[8] 14 4-8-10 **46** (b) LeeNewman 2
(Robin Bastiman) *rdn along on outer s: nvr a factor* **20/1**

50-5 **10** 1 3/4 **Fathey (IRE)**[8] 14 6-8-10 **46** oh1 (t) MartinLane 13
(Charles Smith) *dwlt: a towards rr* **12/1**

000- **11** 4 1/2 **Blazing Apostle (IRE)**[118] 6070 4-8-10 **46** oh1 (p) ChrisCatlin 4
(Christine Dunnett) *chsd ldrs: rdn along over 3f out: sn wknd* **40/1**

000/ **12** 1 **Michael Collins (IRE)**[624] 1583 6-8-10 **46** oh1 LukeMorris 8
(Michael Appleby) *midfield: lost pl and bhd fr 1/2-way* **8/1**

/00- **13** 3/4 **Bahri Beat (IRE)**[28] 7743 4-8-10 **46** oh1 PaddyAspell 9
(John Norton) *a towards rr* **100/1**

04-0 **14** 10 **Striking Willow**[8] 8 4-8-10 **46** oh1 (b) JamesMillman 14
(Rod Millman) *prom: led after 2f: rdn along 3f out: sn hdd & wknd* **25/1**

1m 29.37s (-0.93) **Going Correction** -0.10s/f (Stan) **14** Ran SP% **120.2**
Speed ratings (Par 101): **101,100,95,90,90 88,87,86,79,77 72,71,70,58**
toteswingers:1&2:£9.70, 2&3:£6.60, 1&3:£4.20 CSF £58.56 CT £195.69 TOTE £4.70: £1.30, £3.70, £1.60; EX 37.80 Trifecta £69.30 Pool: £543.25 - 5.80 winning units..
Owner Woodcock Electrical Limited **Bred** R N Auld **Trained** Hambleton, N Yorks

FOCUS
A rock-bottom handicap with just five of the 14 runners running from their official mark.
Milton Of Campsie Official explanation: jockey said mare hung right

114 VISIT NOTTINGHAMSHIRE MAIDEN STKS 1m (F)
3:25 (3:25) (Class 5) 3-Y-O+ **£2,385** (£704; £352) **Stalls** Low

Form RPR

023- **1** **Ecossaise**[12] 7913 4-9-9 64 (b) JoeFanning 9 65
(Mark Johnston) *prom: rdn to chal over 2f out: drvn over 1f out: kpt on to ld last 100yds* **3/1**[2]

320- **2** 1 1/4 **Maxamillion Bounty**[189] 3706 4-10-0 69 (t) TomEaves 7 67
(Michael Dods) *cl up: led over 3f out: rdn 2f out: drvn and slt ld ent fnl f: hdd last 100yds* **5/1**

/34- **3** 1/2 **Spin Cast**[82] 6980 4-10-0 70 (v) FrannyNorton 5 66
(Joseph Tuite) *towards rr: hdwy over 2f out: rdn to chse ldng pair wl over 1f out: styd on ins fnl f: nrst fin* **2/1**[1]

45- **4** 8 **Minnie Diva (IRE)**[25] 7777 3-8-0 0 JulieBurke(3) 4 38
(Kevin Ryan) *s.i.s and bhd: hdwy over 2f out: styd on appr fnl f: nrst fin* **9/2**[3]

0/ **5** 1 3/4 **Somerset Island (IRE)**[14] 5814 4-10-0 0 AndrewMullen 6 43
(Michael Smith) *chsd ldrs: rdn along wl over 2f out: sn no imp* **66/1**

443- **6** 2 3/4 **Angel Cake (IRE)**[19] 7852 3-7-10 50 (p) DannyBrock(7) 2 28
(Phil McEntee) *led: rdn along and hdd 3f out: wknd fnl 2f* **18/1**

00- **7** 1 1/4 **Luctor Emergo (IRE)**[19] 7855 3-8-8 0 JamesSullivan 8 30
(Keith Dalgleish) *a towards rr* **50/1**

60- **8** 4 **Kuwait Moon**[38] 7626 3-8-1 0 SAJackson(7) 3 21
(Alan McCabe) *a towards rr* **66/1**

0- **9** 3 1/4 **Pivotal Prospect**[115] 6156 4-9-9 0 PJMcDonald 10 13
(Tracy Waggott) *dwlt: sn chsng ldrs: rdn along over 2f out: sn wknd* **16/1**

10 8 **Gold Deal (IRE)** 3-8-9 0 ow1 (t) LiamKeniry 1
(Deborah Sanderson) *chsd ldrs: rdn along over 3f out and sn wknd* **16/1**

1m 44.02s (0.32) **Going Correction** -0.10s/f (Stan)
WFA 3 from 4yo 20lb **10** Ran SP% **115.2**
Speed ratings (Par 103): **94,92,92,84,82 79,78,74,71,63**
toteswingers:1&2:£3.30, 2&3:£3.20, 1&3:£1.80 CSF £18.15 TOTE £3.60: £1.30, £1.10, £1.30; EX 17.30 Trifecta £26.10 Pool: £728.15 - 20.62 winning units..
Owner Miss K Rausing **Bred** Miss K Rausing **Trained** Middleham Moor, N Yorks

FOCUS
Just four to seriously consider in this maiden event.

115 PLAY BINGO FREE AT BLUESQ.COM H'CAP 7f (F)
3:55 (3:56) (Class 5) (0-75,75) 4-Y-O+ **£2,264** (£673; £336; £168) **Stalls** Low

Form RPR

056- **1** **Podgies Boy (IRE)**[11] 7922 4-9-0 **73** ShaneBKelly(5) 6 82
(Richard Fahey) *hld up: hdwy over 2f out: swtchd to inner over 2f out: chsd ldng pair over 1f out: sn rdn and styd on wl to ld last 100yds* **6/1**[3]

342- **2** 1/2 **Bianca De Medici**[28] 7745 5-9-6 **74** (b) RobertWinston 7 82
(Hughie Morrison) *prom: hdwy to ld wl over 2f out: rdn wl over 1f out: hdd and no ex last 100yds* **11/4**[1]

051- **3** 1/2 **Andiamo Via**[19] 7857 5-8-7 **61** oh1 AndrewMullen 10 68
(Michael Smith) *cl up on outer: led after 3f: rdn and hdd over 2f out: ev ch tl drvn and one pce fnl f* **6/1**[3]

64-3 **4** 3 1/2 **Horatio Carter**[8] 12 7-8-9 **63** (p) TomEaves 3 60
(David O'Meara) *trckd ldrs: hdwy to chse ldrs over 2f out: rdn wl over 1f out: no imp fnl f* **8/1**

3-40 **5** hd **Elhamri**[2] 100 8-8-11 **65** HayleyTurner 1 62
(Conor Dore) *chsd ldrs: rdn along over 2f out: drvn and no imp appr fnl f* **10/1**

02-5 **6** 1 1/4 **El Dececy (USA)**[8] 13 8-9-2 **70** (t) WilliamCarson 5 63
(Richard Guest) *prom: rdn along 3f out: sn wknd* **11/1**

23-0 **7** 1 1/4 **Cyflymder (IRE)**[8] 13 6-8-8 **62** FrannyNorton 9 52
(David C Griffiths) *towards rr: effrt and sme hdwy over 2f out: n.d* **7/1**

342- **8** 2 **Chookie Avon**[19] 7857 5-9-2 **70** (p) JoeFanning 2 55
(Keith Dalgleish) *hld up: a in rr* **5/1**[2]

250- **9** 1 **Goal (IRE)**[66] 7299 4-9-5 **73** (t) RobbieFitzpatrick 8 55
(Richard Guest) *a towards rr* **25/1**

303- **10** nk **Catalyze**[113] 6223 4-9-7 **75** (t) LeeNewman 4 56
(Richard Guest) *prom: chsd ldng pair wl over 2f out: sn rdn and wknd* **25/1**

1m 28.67s (-1.63) **Going Correction** -0.10s/f (Stan) **10** Ran SP% **120.6**
Speed ratings (Par 103): **105,104,103,99,99 98,96,94,93,93**
toteswingers:1&2:£2.10, 2&3:£5.40, 1&3:£5.70 CSF £23.71 CT £104.69 TOTE £7.60: £2.70, £1.10, £2.50; EX 28.80 Trifecta £878.40 Part won. Pool: £1187.13 - 0.91 winning units..
Owner Seamus Duffy **Bred** S Duffy **Trained** Musley Bank, N Yorks
■ Stewards' Enquiry : Shane B Kelly two-day ban: used whip with excessive frequency (Jan 24-25)

FOCUS
Easily the strongest handicap on the card, a competitive 61-75 affair.
T/Jkpt: £4,647.90 to a £1 stake. Pool of £58,918.06 - 9.00 winning tickets. T/Plt: £5.80 to a £1 stake. Pool of £86,558.68 - 10,731.31 winning tickets. T/Qpdt: £2.40 to a £1 stake. Pool of £6,739.52 - 2,066.30 winning tickets. JR

92 DEAUVILLE (R-H)
Tuesday, January 10

OFFICIAL GOING: Fibresand: standard

116a PRIX DE LA PEROTIERE (CONDITIONS) (4YO FILLIES) (FIBRESAND) 7f 110y
10:00 (12:00) 4-Y-O **£8,333** (£3,333; £2,500; £1,666; £833)

RPR

1 **Nymfia (IRE)**[34] 4-8-11 0 JeromeClaudic 8 80
(C Laffon-Parias, France) **49/10**[3]

2 1 3/4 **Meisho Olivia (FR)**^{164} 4-8-9 0 AurelienLemaitre 10 74
(S Kobayashi, France) 44/1

3 1 **Saharan (IRE)**^{4} 4-9-2 0 Pierre-CharlesBoudot 9 78
(Y De Nicolay, France) 13/2

4 1 1/2 **La Jiheska (FR)**^{15} 4-8-9 0 FlavienPrat 1 67
(D Windrif, France) 39/1

5 shd **Halesia**^{406} 4-8-3 0 AlexisAchard(6) 2 67
(M Delzangles, France) 5/2^{1}

6 nse **Queen Menantie (FR)**^{25} 4-8-11 0 (p) IoritzMendizabal 5 69
(J Boisnard, France) 7/2^{2}

7 1 **Finefrenzyrolling (IRE)**^{8} [15] 4-8-11 0 (b) MartinHarley 4 66
(Mrs K Burke) *racd in midfield: rdn early in st: nt qckn u.p: r.o one pce fnl f* 73/10

8 1 1/2 **Vauville (IRE)**^{20} 4-9-7 0 (p) AlexandreChampenois(4) 3 77
(Y De Nicolay, France) 63/10

9 1 3/4 **Okaleeski (FR)**^{19} 4-8-11 0 (p) DavidBreux 6 58
(Mlle C Courtade, France) 50/1

10 5 **Hot Heart**^{230} 4-8-9 0 WilliamsSaraiva 7 44
(P Leblanc, France) 32/1

1m 32.9s (92.90) **10** Ran SP% **116.5**
WIN (incl. 1 euro stake): 5.90. PLACES: 2.30, 11.00, 2.90. DF: 109.50. SF: 160.50.
Owner Leonidas Marinopoulos **Bred** Gerrardstown Stud **Trained** Chantilly, France

117a PRIX DE CHAUMES (MAIDEN) (3YO) (FIBRESAND) 6f 110y

10:30 (12:00) 3-Y-O **£10,000** (£4,000; £3,000; £2,000; £1,000)

RPR

1 **Small Frida (FR)**^{34} [7665] 3-8-13 0 (b^{1}) GregoryBenoist 7 86
(Mme Pia Brandt, France) 16/5^{1}

2 1 1/2 **Portovino (FR)**^{14} 3-9-2 0 JulienAuge 11 84
(E J O'Neill, France) 11/1

3 1/2 **Happy Sun Percy**^{14} 3-9-2 0 ThierryThulliez 13 83
(G Doleuze, France) 68/10^{3}

4 1 1/4 **Living Portrait (FR)**^{14} 3-8-9 0 MathieuTavaresDaSilva(4) 15 76
(J E Pease, France) 48/10^{2}

5 1 1/4 **Osiris Emery (FR)**^{34} 3-9-2 0 FabriceVeron 9 75
(E Libaud, France) 20/1

6 1/2 **Boots And Spurs**^{27} [7758] 3-9-2 0 MartinHarley 4 74
(Mrs K Burke) *racd in midfield: rdn bef st: r.o u.p fnl 1 1/2f wout threatening ldrs* 9/1

7 1/2 **Turcoman's (FR)**^{8} 3-9-2 0 MathieuAndrouin 16 73
(A Junk, France) 30/1

8 1/2 **Fauvelinx (FR)**^{15} 3-8-13 0 Pierre-CharlesBoudot 5 68
(Y De Nicolay, France) 45/1

9 3 1/2 **Chahimanga (FR)**^{14} 3-8-13 0 JohanVictoire 2 58
(C Baillet, France) 14/1

10 1 1/4 **Pretty Madd (FR)**^{14} 3-8-13 0 FlavienPrat 3 54
(J-V Toux, France) 49/1

0 **Belle Echappee (FR)**^{20} 3-8-13 0 ThomasHuet 14
(A Lyon, France) 37/1

0 **Perle Rose (FR)**^{19} 3-8-13 0 AlexisBadel 6
(Y De Nicolay, France) 15/1

0 **Lisa Post (FR)**^{34} 3-8-13 0 BriceRaballand 10
(Mme M Bollack-Badel, France) 64/1

0 **Thunderball (FR)**^{34} 3-9-2 0 Roberto-CarlosMontenegro 12
(X Thomas-Demeaulte, France) 10/1

0 **Viking Quest (FR)** 3-9-2 0 AurelienLemaitre 8
(C Baillet, France) 23/1

0 **Toulio (GER)** 3-9-2 0 PVanDeKeere 1
(A Kleinkorres, Germany) 25/1

1m 18.6s (78.60) **16** Ran SP% **118.6**
WIN (incl. 1 euro stake): 4.20. PLACES: 1.70, 3.00, 2.20. DF: 25.20. SF: 37.70.
Owner P-H Lassen & Mme E Vidal **Bred** Investment A B Rustningen **Trained** France

26 KEMPTON (A.W) (R-H)

Wednesday, January 11

OFFICIAL GOING: Standard
Wind: light, across Weather: dry

118 FREE ENTRY FOR BETDAQ MEMBERS H'CAP 5f (P)

4:15 (4:15) (Class 7) (0-50,51) 4-Y-0+ **£1,455** (£433; £216; £108) **Stalls** Low

Form RPR

020- 1 **Deveze (IRE)**^{26} [7785] 4-8-12 45 (b) RichardKingscote 8 54
(Milton Bradley) *awkward leaving stalls: hld up in last trio: rdn and hdwy ent fnl f: led fnl 100yds: r.o wl* 12/1

400- 2 3/4 **Pharoh Jake**^{11} [7943] 4-8-9 45 KieranO'Neill(3) 7 52
(John Bridger) *in tch in midfield: rdn and hdwy over 1f out: ev ch ins fnl f: r.o same pce fnl 100yds* 14/1

550- 3 1 1/4 **Porthgwidden Beach (USA)**^{11} [7942] 4-9-0 47 (t) ChrisCatlin 6 49
(Anthony Middleton) *in tch: rdn and hdwy to chse ldr ent fnl f: led fnl 150yds: sn hdd: outpcd fnl 75yds* 4/1^{3}

206- 4 1 **Brian Sprout**^{26} [7785] 4-8-13 51 ow2 JustinNewman(5) 3 49
(John Weymes) *in tch: effrt on inner to chse ldrs 1f out: hmpd and edgd lft ins fnl f: outpcd fnl 100yds* 3/1^{1}

052- 5 nse **Lisselton Cross**^{22} [7829] 4-9-3 50 (v) LukeMorris 10 48
(Martin Bosley) *hld up in last trio: effrt and nt clr run ent fnl f: swtchd lft 1f out: styd on wl ins fnl f: nt rch ldrs* 7/2^{2}

006- 6 3/4 **Cara Carmela**^{22} [7829] 4-8-9 45 ^{1} RyanClark(3) 5 41
(Stuart Williams) *in tch in midfield: effrt over 1f out: pushed lft and hmpd jst ins fnl f: styd on but nvr able to chal* 14/1

00-4 7 1 1/4 **Papageno**^{7} [37] 5-8-8 46 (p) RaulDaSilva(5) 9 37
(J R Jenkins) *chsd ldrs tl wknd u.p over 1f out* 8/1

3- 8 shd **Avonvalley**^{70} [7230] 5-9-1 48 RobbieFitzpatrick 4 39+
(Peter Grayson) *hld up in last trio: effrt on ins rail over 1f out: nt clr run and unable to make prog ins fnl f: nvr trbld ldrs* 14/1

400- 9 1 3/4 **Pavement Games**^{78} [7086] 5-8-7 45 CharlesEddery(5) 11 29
(Richard Guest) *stdd s and dropped in bhd: a in rr: effrt on outer 2f out: n.d* 25/1

400- 10 1 1/4 **Lois Lane**^{14} [7899] 4-8-7 45 CharlesBishop(5) 2 25
(Ron Hodges) *chsd ldr tl ent fnl f: sn wknd* 33/1

00-5 11 2 3/4 **Lady Royal Oak (IRE)**^{7} [37] 5-8-7 47 JenniferFerguson(7) 1 17
(Olivia Maylam) *sn led: clr over 3f out: rdn and hdd ins fnl 150yds: sn btn and wkng whn pushed lft and hmpd: fdd* 14/1

1m 0.4s (-0.10) **Going Correction** -0.05s/f (Stan) **11** Ran SP% **119.5**
Speed ratings (Par 97): **98,96,94,93,93 91,89,89,86,84 80**
toteswingers:1&2:£30.30, 1&3:£7.70, 2&3:£16.30 CSF £170.85 CT £799.86 TOTE £10.90: £5.10, £5.30, £1.60; EX 180.90 TRIFECTA Not won..
Owner J M Bradley **Bred** Maurice Craig **Trained** Sedbury, Gloucs
■ Stewards' Enquiry : Justin Newman 1st incident, two-day ban: careless riding (Jan 25-26); 2nd, one-day ban: careless riding (Jan 27)

FOCUS
This bottom-drawer sprint handicap was run at a frantic gallop.

119 BETDAQ MULTIPLES H'CAP 1m 2f (P)

4:45 (4:47) (Class 5) (0-75,75) 4-Y-0+ **£2,264** (£673; £336; £168) **Stalls** Low

Form RPR

31-2 1 **Nibani (IRE)**^{4} [90] 5-8-13 74 (p) LeonnaMayor(7) 9 83+
(Alastair Lidderdale) *stdd and dropped in bhd after s: hld up in rr: hdwy 3f out: rdn and chal ins fnl f: led fnl 75yds: r.o wl* 5/2^{1}

03-4 2 1/2 **Focail Maith**^{7} [36] 4-9-3 73 (p) AdamKirby 2 81
(John Ryan) *chsd ldrs: rdn to chse ldr over 2f out: led jst ins fnl f: hdd fnl 75yds: kpt on wl u.p but a jst hld* 9/2^{2}

610- 3 2 1/2 **Megalala (IRE)**^{13} [7908] 11-9-3 74 KieranO'Neill(3) 6 77
(John Bridger) *led: rdn over 2f out: hdd jst ins fnl f: no ex and one pce ins fnl f* 6/1^{3}

402- 4 1/2 **Dazzling Valentine**^{23} [7823] 4-9-2 75 DominicFox(3) 4 77
(Alan Bailey) *in tch in last trio: rdn wl over 2f out: outpcd 2f out: rallied u.p ent fnl f: styd on wl but no threat to ldng pair* 13/2

304- 5 1/2 **Lisahane Bog**^{28} [7759] 5-9-5 73 (b) JohnFahy 5 74
(Peter Hedger) *dwlt and rdn along early: sn in tch in midfield: rdn over 3f out: no imp u.p over 1f out: one pce and wl hld after* 8/1

654- 6 4 1/2 **Sergeant Troy (IRE)**^{140} [5376] 4-8-12 68 (t) LiamKeniry 1 60
(George Baker) *in tch in midfield: rdn and effrt over 2f out: drvn and no prog over 1f out: wknd ent fnl f* 14/1

3- 7 2 1/4 **Rocky Elsom (USA)**^{14} [7894] 5-9-7 75 JimCrowley 8 63
(David Arbuthnot) *in tch: rdn and no prog 2f out: edgd rt and wknd over 1f out* 14/1

012- 8 2 1/2 **Cheylesmore (IRE)**^{21} [7842] 4-9-2 72 (v) WilliamCarson 7 55
(Stuart Williams) *t.k.h: chsd ldr tl over 2f out: wknd u.p over 1f out* 17/2

000- 9 2 **Bengal Tiger**^{22} [7831] 6-8-10 64 DavidProbert 3 43
(Tony Carroll) *hld up in last pair: rdn and no prog over 2f out: wknd wl over 1f out* 40/1

2m 5.65s (-2.35) **Going Correction** -0.05s/f (Stan)
WFA 4 from 5yo+ 2lb **9** Ran SP% **111.8**
Speed ratings (Par 103): **107,106,104,104,103 100,98,96,94**
toteswingers:1&2:£2.60, 1&3:£4.00, 2&3:£5.20 CSF £12.79 CT £58.01 TOTE £3.20: £1.40, £1.70, £1.80; EX 13.30 Trifecta £25.70 Pool: £822.05 - 23.63 winning units..
Owner C S J Beek **Bred** Ballymacoll Stud Farm Ltd **Trained** Lambourn, Berks
■ Stewards' Enquiry : Leonna Mayor one-day ban: careless riding (Jan 25)

FOCUS
This fair handicap was run at a solid pace thanks to the front-running Megalala and the form looks sound.

120 BACK OR LAY AT BETDAQ.COM H'CAP 5f (P)

5:15 (5:15) (Class 4) (0-85,85) 4-Y-0+ **£4,075** (£1,212; £606; £303) **Stalls** Low

Form RPR

001- 1 **Cadeaux Pearl**^{13} [7917] 4-8-10 79 (b) RyanPowell(5) 2 88
(Scott Dixon) *in tch: rdn and hdwy over 1f out: qcknd to chal ins fnl f: led fnl 75yds: r.o wl* 7/1

050- 2 nk **West Coast Dream**^{68} [7262] 5-9-5 83 TomEaves 6 91
(Roy Brotherton) *chsd ldr: rdn to ld over 1f out: drvn and hrd pressed ins fnl f: hdd and styd on same pce fnl 75yds* 12/1

300- 3 hd **Sir Geoffrey (IRE)**^{21} [7846] 6-9-1 79 (b) IanMongan 9 86
(Scott Dixon) *chsd ldrs: rdn over 1f out: drvn and ev ch ins fnl f: unable qck towards fin* 12/1

150- 4 1 **Titus Gent**^{12} [7926] 7-9-3 81 AdamKirby 3 85
(Jeremy Gask) *s.i.s: hld up in last pair: rdn and hdwy over 1f out: r.o wl ins fnl f: nt rch ldrs* 14/1

60-1 5 1 1/2 **Desert Strike**^{5} [62] 6-9-2 80 6ex (p) ShaneKelly 1 78
(Alan McCabe) *s.i.s: outpcd in rr: hdwy 1f out: r.o wl ins fnl f: nt rch ldrs* 8/1

356- 6 1 **Island Legend (IRE)**^{22} [7832] 6-8-13 77 (p) RichardKingscote 4 72
(Milton Bradley) *in tch in midfield: effrt u.p over 1f out: no imp 1f out and styd on same pce fnl f* 4/1^{2}

32-2 7 3/4 **Earlsmedic**^{5} [64] 7-8-7 74 (v) RyanClark(3) 8 66
(Stuart Williams) *in tch towards rr: barging match w rival bnd 4f out: hdwy into midfield 1/2-way: unable qck u.p over 1f out: styd on same pce fnl f* 11/4^{1}

04-0 8 3/4 **Volcanic Dust (IRE)**^{5} [64] 4-9-2 80 LiamKeniry 7 69
(Milton Bradley) *dwlt and short of room s: in tch towards rr: effrt and rdn over 1f out: no imp and styd on same pce after* 13/2^{3}

030- 9 2 **Kylladdie**^{173} [4291] 5-9-1 79 (b) RobertWinston 11 61
(Steve Gollings) *racd on outer: midfield: barging match w rival bnd 4f out: rdn and dropped to rr over 2f out: no threat to ldrs fr wl over 1f out* 25/1

00- 10 1 **Best Trip (IRE)**^{22} [7832] 5-9-0 78 FrannyNorton 10 56
(Richard Guest) *led: rdn and hdd over 1f out: wknd ins fnl f* 12/1

59.54s (-0.96) **Going Correction** -0.05s/f (Stan) **10** Ran SP% **117.2**
Speed ratings (Par 105): **105,104,104,102,100 98,97,96,93,91**
toteswingers:1&2:£18.20, 1&3:£8.20, 2&3:£22.80 CSF £87.87 CT £1016.71 TOTE £5.10: £2.70, £3.10, £2.60; EX 131.90 TRIFECTA Not won..
Owner Paul J Dixon **Bred** Catridge Farm Stud Ltd **Trained** Babworth, Notts

FOCUS
It looked a near certainty that this competitive sprint handicap would be run at a strong pace, but ultimately it proved hard to make up sufficient ground from out the back.

121 BETDAQ MOBILE APPS MEDIAN AUCTION MAIDEN STKS 6f (P)

5:45 (5:46) (Class 6) 3-5-Y-0 **£1,617** (£481; £240; £120) **Stalls** Low

Form RPR

6- 1 **Dark Castle**^{28} [7751] 3-8-12 0 LiamKeniry 6 81+
(Sylvester Kirk) *chsd ldng trio: rdn and qcknd to ld 2f out: clr 1f out: r.o wl: comf* 6/5^{1}

530- 2 2 1/4 **Gabrial's Bounty (IRE)**^{79} [7051] 3-8-12 62 FrannyNorton 10 69
(Mick Channon) *chsd ldrs: rdn and unable qck 2f out: kpt on again ins fnl f: chsd wnr fnl 100yds: no imp* 8/1

334- **3** 3/4 **Mister Mackenzie**[93] [6751] 3-8-12 67 .... LukeMorris 4 67
(John Best) *wnt rt s: chsd ldrs: drvn to chse wnr wl over 1f out: styd on same pce fr over 1f out: lost 2nd fnl 100yds* **4/1**[3]

025- **4** *hd* **Casa Bex**[159] [4760] 3-8-12 66 .... (vt[1]) MartinLane 3 66
(Philip McBride) *bmpd s and slowly away: towards rr: rdn and effrt over 2f out: kpt on wl u.p ins fnl f: nt rch ldrs* **12/1**

5 1/2 **Cats Eyes** 3-8-8 0 ow1 .... ShaneKelly 2 61+
(Robert Cowell) *s.i.s: bhd: swtchd ins and gd hdwy over 2f out: pressing for placings but no threat to ldr over 1f out: no ex fnl 100yds* **7/2**[2]

043- **6** 9 **House Limit (IRE)**[37] [7635] 3-8-12 51 .... (b) JoeFanning 1 36
(Harry Dunlop) *led tl 2f out: wknd u.p over 1f out: fdd fnl f* **33/1**

05- **7** *nk* **Maria Montez**[25] [7798] 3-8-7 0 .... ChrisCatlin 8 30
(J W Hills) *in tch in midfield: rdn and outpcd over 2f out: wknd wl over 1f out* **20/1**

04- **8** 3/4 **Sleepy Lucy**[14] [7898] 3-8-2 0 .... CharlesEddery(5) 9 28
(Richard Guest) *s.i.s: hld up in last trio: edgd rt and sltly hmpd wl over 2f out: stl edging rt and wknd ent fnl 2f* **66/1**

6 **9** 2 1/4 **Gem Of Wizdom (IRE)**[7] [26] 3-8-2 0 .... RyanPowell(5) 5 20
(Paul Cole) *pressed ldr tl over 2f out: sn wknd: wl bhd fnl f* **80/1**

10 3 1/2 **Abi Scarlet (IRE)** 3-8-7 0 .... HayleyTurner 7
(Hughie Morrison) *s.i.s: rdn along in last pair: lost tch over 2f out* **20/1**

1m 12.15s (-0.95) **Going Correction** -0.05s/f (Stan)
WFA 3 from 4yo 16lb — **10** Ran SP% **121.7**
Speed ratings (Par 101): **104,101,100,99,99 87,86,85,82,78**
toteswingers:1&2:£3.30, 1&3:£2.20, 2&3:£5.70 CSF £12.13 TOTE £2.50: £1.10, £2.90, £1.10; EX 10.90 Trifecta £41.40 Pool: £790.70 - 14.13 winning units..
Owner Ms Carol Cleary **Bred** Hedsor Stud **Trained** Upper Lambourn, Berks

122 BOOK NOW FOR SATURDAY H'CAP (DIV I) 6f (P)

6:15 (6:16) (Class 6) (0-65,67) 4-Y-O+ **£1,617** (£481; £240; £120) **Stalls** Low

Form RPR

20P- **1** **Belinsky (IRE)**[42] [7587] 5-9-2 60 .... JimCrowley 1 68
(Julie Camacho) *in tch: rdn and effrt to ld 1f out: kpt on wl: rdn out* **9/2**[1]

000- **2** *nk* **Memphis Man**[30] [7737] 9-8-7 56 .... MatthewCosham(5) 3 63
(David Evans) *taken down early and v free to post: bhd: stl plenty to do and rdn over 1f out: str run ins fnl f: clsng on wnr cl home: nvr quite getting up* **25/1**

64-5 **3** *1* **Dvinsky (USA)**[4] [87] 11-9-6 64 .... (b) TomMcLaughlin 8 68
(Paul Howling) *sn bustled up to ld: rdn 2f out: hdd 1f out: styd on same pce fnl 150yds* **11/1**

302- **4** *nk* **Meia Noite**[21] [7844] 5-8-9 60 .... DannyBrock(7) 5 63
(Chris Wall) *in tch in midfield: rdn and nt qckn over 1f out: kpt on fnl 100yds: unable to rch ldrs* **5/1**[2]

230- **5** 1/2 **Ermyntrude**[104] [6486] 5-8-12 56 .... IanMongan 4 59+
(Pat Phelan) *hld up towards rr: rdn ent fnl 2f: hdwy 1f out: styng on wl tl nt clr run and eased fnl 50yds* **11/1**

03-5 **6** *nk* **Shawkantango**[8] [24] 5-9-7 65 .... (v) JoeFanning 2 65
(Derek Shaw) *stdd s: hld up in rr: rdn over 2f out: hdwy on outer 1f out: r.o fnl f: nt rch ldrs* **15/2**[3]

/00- **7** *nk* **Darwin Star**[20] [7853] 4-8-11 55 .... MartinLane 6 54
(Dean Ivory) *chsd ldrs: rdn and ev ch 2f out: no ex ent fnl f: styd on same pce after* **12/1**

035- **8** 3/4 **Dingaan (IRE)**[11] [7943] 9-8-12 56 ow2 .... DaneO'Neill 10 53
(Peter Grayson) *in tch towards rr: rdn and no imp jst over 2f out: kpt on fnl f: nvr able to chal* **12/1**

56-1 **9** 1/2 **Dickie Le Davoir**[8] [19] 8-9-4 67 6ex .... (b) CharlesEddery(5) 9 62
(Richard Guest) *s.i.s and rdn along in rr: sme hdwy u.p on inner over 1f out: no imp ins fnl f* **8/1**

052- **10** *shd* **Replicator**[34] [7676] 7-8-1 52 .... (e) LukeRowe(7) 11 47
(Patrick Gilligan) *pressed ldrs on outer: rdn and ev ch 2f out: wknd ent fnl f* **9/1**

63-3 **11** 1/2 **Welsh Inlet (IRE)**[5] [59] 4-9-2 63 .... KieranO'Neill(3) 7 56
(John Bridger) *chsd ldrs tl unable qck u.p over 1f out: wknd 1f out* **5/1**[2]

1m 12.73s (-0.37) **Going Correction** -0.05s/f (Stan) — **11** Ran SP% **120.3**
Speed ratings (Par 101): **100,99,98,97,97 96,96,95,94,94 93**
toteswingers:1&2:£38.70, 1&3:£4.90, 2&3:£39.50 CSF £119.57 CT £1205.71 TOTE £4.10: £1.40, £10.00, £3.40; EX 186.90 TRIFECTA Not won..
Owner Wentdale Limited **Bred** Camogue Stud Ltd **Trained** Norton, N Yorks

123 BOOK NOW FOR SATURDAY H'CAP (DIV II) 6f (P)

6:45 (6:45) (Class 6) (0-65,65) 4-Y-O+ **£1,617** (£481; £240; £120) **Stalls** Low

Form RPR

645- **1** **Vhujon (IRE)**[11] [7940] 7-8-11 55 .... RobbieFitzpatrick 10 66
(Peter Grayson) *stdd s: hld up towards rr: swtchd lft over 2f out: str run ent fnl f: led wl ins fnl f and sn in command: eased nr fin* **14/1**

2P0- **2** 1 1/2 **Torres Del Paine**[42] [7588] 5-9-1 62 .... KieranO'Neill(3) 4 68
(Jimmy Fox) *in tch: led gng wl 2f out: rdn over 1f out: kpt on wl tl hdd and nt pce of wnr wl ins fnl f* **4/1**[2]

020- **3** 3/4 **Rapid Water**[11] [7943] 6-9-2 60 .... AdamKirby 5 64
(Gary Moore) *short of room sn after s: in tch in last trio: rdn and hdwy over 2f out: drvn and pressed ldrs 1f out: no ex and outpcd fnl 100yds* **11/2**[3]

645- **4** 3/4 **First In Command (IRE)**[14] [7896] 7-8-12 56 .... (tp) ShaneKelly 1 57
(Daniel Mark Loughnane) *in tch in midfield: rdn and effrt on inner over 1f out: drvn and pressed wnr 1f out: no ex and btn fnl 100yds* **7/2**[1]

000- **5** 1 3/4 **Welcome Approach**[21] [7844] 9-8-13 57 .... TomEaves 11 53
(John Weymes) *racd in last trio: pushed along 1/2-way: styd on ins fnl f: nvr trbld ldrs* **25/1**

061- **6** *hd* **Mack's Sister**[42] [7588] 5-9-5 63 .... LukeMorris 12 58
(Dean Ivory) *in tch in midfield: rdn and n.m.r 2f out: kpt on u.p fnl f but no threat to ldrs* **4/1**[2]

404- **7** 1/2 **Demoiselle Bond**[28] [7754] 4-8-12 56 .... FrannyNorton 2 49
(Lydia Richards) *led tl 2f out: wknd ent fnl f* **10/1**

151- **8** 3 **Microlight**[28] [7760] 4-8-9 53 .... (b) SamHitchcott 8 37
(John E Long) *chsd ldrs on outer: rdn and unable qck ent fnl 2f: wknd jst ins fnl f* **10/1**

506- **9** 6 **White Shift (IRE)**[24] [7811] 6-8-7 51 oh2 .... JoeFanning 7 16
(Paul Howling) *chsd ldrs tl 3f out: wknd 2f out: bhd and eased ins fnl f* **25/1**

000- **10** 1 1/4 **Smoky Cloud (IRE)**[14] [7893] 5-9-7 65 .... MarcHalford 3 26
(Amy Weaver) *pressed ldr tl jst over 2f out: wknd u.p wl over 1f out: bhd fnl f* **12/1**

1m 12.52s (-0.58) **Going Correction** -0.05s/f (Stan) — **10** Ran SP% **117.8**
Speed ratings (Par 101): **101,99,98,97,94 94,93,89,81,80**
toteswingers:1&2:£15.20, 1&3:£14.30, 2&3:£6.10 CSF £70.12 CT £351.17 TOTE £17.00: £4.00, £1.50, £3.30; EX 94.30 Trifecta £320.00 Part won. Pool: £432.49 - 0.64 winning units..
Owner Richard Teatum **Bred** Robert Berns **Trained** Formby, Lancs

FOCUS
The second division of the ordinary 6f handicap and again it is straightforward form.

124 SKYSPORTS.COM FILLIES' H'CAP 7f (P)

7:15 (7:15) (Class 5) (0-70,69) 4-Y-O+ **£2,264** (£673; £336; £168) **Stalls** Low

Form RPR

013- **1** **Fedora (IRE)**[76] [7131] 6-8-9 57 .... (t) ChrisCatlin 7 65
(Olivia Maylam) *stdd s: hld up in last pair: rdn and str run on outer over 1f out: led ins fnl f: r.o wl* **8/1**

530- **2** *nk* **Bold Ring**[14] [7895] 6-8-11 64 .... RyanPowell(5) 3 71
(Eric Wheeler) *in tch towards rr: rdn and hdwy between horses over 1f out: led 1f out: rdr dropped reins and hdd ins fnl f: r.o wl but a hld fnl 75yds* **10/1**

631- **3** 2 1/4 **Gold Tobougg**[21] [7845] 4-9-3 65 .... MartinLane 8 66
(David Simcock) *wnt lft s and slowly away: swtchd rt and hld up in rr: rdn and hdwy on inner over 1f out: drvn and chsd ldng pair ins fnl f: no imp fnl 100yds* **11/4**[2]

102- **4** 2 **Nina Rose**[12] [7930] 5-9-0 62 .... (v[1]) AdamKirby 1 58
(Clive Cox) *led: rdn jst over 2f out: hdd 1f out: wknd ins fnl f* **13/8**[1]

300- **5** 6 **Perfect Ch'I (IRE)**[210] [3045] 5-9-7 69 .... LukeMorris 6 49
(Ian Wood) *chsd ldrs on outer: drvn to chse ldr 2f out tl over 1f out: sn wknd* **5/1**[3]

/00- **6** 2 1/4 **Efisio Princess**[29] [7744] 9-9-0 62 .... SamHitchcott 2 35
(John E Long) *chsd ldrs: rdn and effrt on inner to press wnr over 1f out: wknd ent fnl f: fdd ins fnl f* **66/1**

406- **7** 2 **Casternova**[250] [1865] 4-8-8 56 .... HayleyTurner 5 24
(Hughie Morrison) *t.k.h: hld up wl in tch: rdn and unable qck ent fnl 2f: wknd qckly over 1f out: bhd ins fnl f* **10/1**

400- **8** 8 **Toms River Tess (IRE)**[11] [7942] 4-8-8 56 ow1 .... JamieGoldstein 4
(Zoe Davison) *chsd ldr tl 2f: sn wknd: wl bhd fnl f* **50/1**

1m 26.29s (0.29) **Going Correction** -0.05s/f (Stan) — **8** Ran SP% **114.2**
Speed ratings (Par 100): **96,95,93,90,83 81,79,69**
toteswingers:1&2:£5.40, 1&3:£3.90, 2&3:£2.80 CSF £82.89 CT £276.57 TOTE £14.60: £3.00, £3.70, £1.10; EX 48.10 Trifecta £77.00 Pool: £514.32 - 4.94 winning units..
Owner Mrs V A Ward **Bred** Forenaghts Stud And Dermot Cantillon **Trained** Epsom, Surrey

FOCUS
This moderate fillies' handicap was run to suit the closers.

125 SKYSPORTS.COM RACING H'CAP 7f (P)

7:45 (7:45) (Class 7) (0-50,51) 4-Y-O+ **£1,455** (£433; £216; £108) **Stalls** Low

Form RPR

03-6 **1** **My Best Man**[6] [46] 6-9-1 48 .... (t) DavidProbert 7 55
(Tony Carroll) *in tch in midfield: rdn and effrt over 1f out: drvn to chse ldrs ent fnl f: styd on wl to ld wl ins fnl f: rdn out* **12/1**

23-2 **2** 1/2 **Blueberry Fizz (IRE)**[6] [46] 4-9-1 48 .... (v) AdamKirby 13 54
(John Ryan) *led and crossed towards inner: rdn and forged ahd w rival 2f out: asserted ent fnl f: hdd and no ex wl ins fnl f* **11/4**[1]

046- **3** 1/2 **Ocean Countess (IRE)**[42] [7581] 6-8-12 48 .... (t) MichaelO'Connell(3) 10 52
(Tony Carroll) *stdd s: hld up in rr: rdn and effrt wl over 1f out: styd on wl ins fnl f: nt quite rch ldrs* **10/1**

434- **4** *nk* **Lovat Lane**[15] [7886] 4-8-13 46 .... ChrisCatlin 2 49
(Eve Johnson Houghton) *stdd s: hld up in tch in midfield: rdn and hdwy over 1f out: kpt on wl u.p ins fnl f* **20/1**

003- **5** *hd* **Evening Pinot**[35] [7659] 4-9-3 50 .... HayleyTurner 8 53
(Simon Dow) *chsd ldrs: rdn and unable qck ent fnl 2f: rallied and styd on ins fnl f: nt rch ldrs* **9/1**[3]

60-0 **6** *hd* **Raimond Ridge (IRE)**[6] [46] 6-8-8 46 .... MatthewCosham(5) 5 48
(Derek Shaw) *hld up in tch in last trio: nt clr run wl over 2f out: hdwy u.p on inner over 1f out: styd on same pce ins fnl f* **16/1**

310- **7** *hd* **Jackie Love (IRE)**[14] [7899] 4-8-10 50 .... (b) JenniferFerguson(7) 14 52
(Olivia Maylam) *s.i.s: hld up in rr: hdwy on outer into midfield 1/2-way: rdn and unable qck 2f out: kpt on ins fnl f* **16/1**

340- **8** 3/4 **Royal Envoy (IRE)**[14] [7899] 9-8-12 45 .... MichaelStainton 4 45
(Paul Howling) *chsd ldrs: jnd ldr 1/2-way: rdn over 2f out: edgd rt and no ex jst over 1f out: wknd fnl 100yds* **7/1**[2]

000- **9** *hd* **Heading To First**[14] [7892] 5-8-12 48 ow3 .... (p) RobertLButler(3) 3 47
(Paddy Butler) *chsd ldrs: chsd ldng pair and unable qck 2f out: styd on same pce u.p fnl f* **14/1**

\- **10** *nk* **Noinformation (IRE)**[147] [5188] 5-8-11 47 .... (b) KieranO'Neill(3) 6 45
(Mark Michael McNiff, Ire) *in tch in midfield: rdn and effrt 2f out: kpt on u.p but nvr gng pce to chal* **7/1**[2]

03-0 **11** *nk* **Kenswick**[7] [39] 5-8-13 46 .... (b) DaneO'Neill 12 44
(Pat Eddery) *in tch in midfield: rdn and unable qck jst over 2f out: kpt on fnl f: nt pce to chal* **10/1**

455- **12** 1 3/4 **Welsh Dancer**[15] [7886] 4-9-3 50 .... (p) LukeMorris 9 43
(Ronald Harris) *in tch in midfield: rdn and unable qck 2f out: rallied ent fnl f: keeping on whn nt clr run and eased ins fnl f* **16/1**

003- **13** *1* **Cairanne**[28] [7750] 4-8-9 45 .... RyanClark(3) 1 35
(Tom Keddy) *in tch: rdn and unable qck ent fnl 2f: wknd jst over 1f out: eased wl ins fnl f* **16/1**

1m 26.6s (0.60) **Going Correction** -0.05s/f (Stan) — **13** Ran SP% **122.5**
Speed ratings (Par 97): **94,93,92,92,92 92,91,90,90,90 90,88,86**
toteswingers:1&2:£7.60, 1&3:£22.20, 2&3:£6.30 CSF £46.02 CT £361.10 TOTE £15.40: £3.90, £1.20, £2.70; EX 55.50 Trifecta £309.20 Pool: £417.96 - 1.00 winning units..
Owner D Lowe **Bred** D Lowe **Trained** Cropthorne, Worcs

FOCUS
Another bottom-drawer handicap to end the card. It was run at a solid tempo.
T/Jkpt: Part won. £25,000.00 Pool:£13,659.64 0.50 winning tickets. T/Plt: £392.30 to a £1 stake. Pool:£94,533.44 - 175.90 winning tickets T/Qpdt: £75.40 to a £1 stake. Pool:£9,845.48 - 96.60 winning tickets SP

[118]KEMPTON (A.W) (R-H)

Thursday, January 12

OFFICIAL GOING: Standard

Wind: medium, across Weather: dry

126 32RED H'CAP 6f (P)

4:15 (4:16) (Class 7) (0-50,54) 4-Y-0+ **£1,533** (£452; £226) **Stalls** Low

Form RPR

064- **1** **First Class**[35] 7676 4-8-13 **46** DavidProbert 9 54
(Rae Guest) *in tch: rdn and hdwy 2f out: led 1f out: kpt on wl u.p* **3/1**[1]

3-61 **2** *1* **My Best Man**[1] 125 6-9-2 **54** 6ex (t) RaulDaSilva(5) 6 59
(Tony Carroll) *hld up in tch: swtchd lft and effrt wl over 1f out: kpt on ins fnl f: wnt 2nd towards fin* **4/1**[2]

000- **3** *nk* **Do More Business (IRE)**[15] 7892 5-9-3 **50** IanMongan 3 54
(Pat Phelan) *in tch: rdn and effrt ent fnl 2f: ev ch 1f out: styd on same pce ins fnl f: lost 2nd towards fin* **9/2**[3]

054- **4** *nk* **Suhayl Star (IRE)**[13] 7923 8-8-7 **45** CharlesBishop(5) 10 48
(Paul Burgoyne) *t.k.h: chsd ldrs: rdn and ev ch 2f out: led over 1f out tl hdd 1f out: styd on same pce u.p fnl f* **20/1**

405- **5** *1* **Jemimaville (IRE)**[35] 7676 5-8-12 **45** WilliamCarson 12 45
(Giles Bravery) *stdd and swtchd rt after s: hld up in last quartet: rdn and hdwy on inner ent fnl 2f: chsd ldrs 1f out: kpt on same pce ins fnl f* **12/1**

504- **6** *nk* **Thalia Grace**[57] 7429 5-9-1 **48** (t) DaneO'Neill 2 47
(Les Hall) *in tch in midfield: rdn and effrt 2f out: chsd ldrs and drvn 1f out: no ex and btn ins fnl f* **12/1**

300- **7** *½* **Fayre Bella**[28] 7768 5-8-12 **45** (bt[1]) JohnFahy 7 42
(John Gallagher) *v.s.a: hld up in rr: gd hdwy over 1f out: chsd ldrs and rdn 1f out: no ex and no imp ins fnl f* **11/1**

00-0 **8** *2¾* **Pavement Games**[1] 118 5-8-7 **45** CharlesEddery(5) 1 34
(Richard Guest) *rring and v awkward leaving stalls: bhd: c wd and rdn over 2f out: kpt on but nvr any threat to ldrs* **33/1**

035- **9** *nk* **A Pocketful Of Rye (IRE)**[13] 7923 5-8-12 **45** MichaelStainton 8 33
(Paul Howling) *in tch in midfield: rdn over 2f out: wknd u.p jst over 1f out* **16/1**

00-1 **10** *4½* **Clerical (USA)**[7] 46 6-9-4 **51** 6ex (p) ShaneKelly 4 24
(Robert Cowell) *hld up in rr: rdn over 2f out: no prog: n.d* **6/1**

/00- **11** *1½* **Wee Buns**[13] 7924 7-8-12 **45** LiamKeniry 5 13
(Paul Burgoyne) *t.k.h: led for 1f: chsd ldr: rdn to ld 2f out: sn hdd & wknd* **66/1**

664- **12** *2* **Little Perisher**[21] 7853 5-9-2 **49** TomMcLaughlin 11 11
(Paul Howling) *reminders sn after s: chsd ldrs: hdwy to ld after 1f: hdd 2f out: btn over 1f out: eased ins fnl f* **16/1**

1m 13.28s (0.18) **Going Correction** 0.0s/f (Stan) 12 Ran SP% **122.1**
Speed ratings (Par 97): **98,96,96,95,94 94,93,89,89,83 81,78**
toteswingers:1&2:£4.70, 2&3:£4.80, 1&3:£5.00 CSF £14.81 CT £55.93 TOTE £6.30: £2.80, £1.30, £3.00; EX 20.20.
Owner Brian Cooper And Miss Elaine Reffo **Bred** Amethyst Stud **Trained** Newmarket, Suffolk
■ Stewards' Enquiry : Michael Stainton two-day ban: used whip with excessive frequency (Jan 26-27)

FOCUS
Low-grade stuff. The gallop was sound and the winner came down the centre in the straight.

127 32RED.COM H'CAP 7f (P)

4:45 (4:45) (Class 5) (0-75,75) 3-Y-O **£2,264** (£673; £336; £168) **Stalls** Low

Form RPR

1- **1** **Pearl Rebel**[22] 7837 3-9-7 **75** WilliamCarson 6 86+
(Stuart Williams) *mounted on crse: stdd after s: chsd clr ldng pair: rdn and clsd over 1f out: led ins fnl f: styd on wl and forged clr towards fin* **5/6**[1]

322- **2** *1¾* **Tenbridge**[15] 7898 3-8-11 **65** (p) DaneO'Neill 1 68
(Derek Haydn Jones) *mounted on crse: chsd clr ldr: drvn 2f out: clsd over 1f out: ev ch ins fnl f: styd on same pce fnl 100yds* **16/1**

001- **3** *1* **Chambles**[13] 7925 3-8-10 **64** (t) HayleyTurner 8 65
(Andrew Reid) *stdd s: hld up wl off the pce in last pair: rdn over 2f out: kpt on wl ins fnl f: wnt 3rd cl home* **7/1**[3]

445- **4** *½* **Chapellerie (IRE)**[15] 7889 3-9-1 **69** (b[1]) ShaneKelly 7 68
(Brian Meehan) *sn led and clr: rdn over 1f out: hdd ins fnl f: wknd fnl 100yds* **9/1**

635- **5** *2* **Words Come Easy**[22] 7838 3-8-9 **66** AdamBeschizza(3) 2 60
(Philip McBride) *hld up wl off the pce in last pair: rdn and effrt over 2f out: styd on ins fnl f: nvr trbld ldrs* **20/1**

040- **6** *½* **Bareback (IRE)**[50] 7520 3-9-5 **73** AdamKirby 5 65
(John Best) *racd off the pce towards rr: rdn and effrt over 2f out: kpt on fnl f: nvr trbld ldrs* **14/1**

02-3 **7** *¾* **Leenavesta (USA)**[8] 27 3-8-11 **68** KieranO'Neill(3) 4 58
(Richard Hannon) *chsd clr ldng pair: rdn and no imp jst over 2f out: plugged on fnl f: nvr able to chal* **5/1**[2]

100- **8** *9* **Jawking**[17] 7875 3-8-8 **67** MatthewCosham(5) 3 33
(David Evans) *hld up wl off the pce in last trio: rdn and no hdwy over 2f out: n.d* **50/1**

1m 25.97s (-0.03) **Going Correction** 0.0s/f (Stan) 8 Ran SP% **113.0**
Speed ratings (Par 97): **100,98,96,96,94 93,92,82**
toteswingers:1&2:£3.00, 2&3:£4.90, 1&3:£2.60 CSF £16.39 CT £60.59 TOTE £1.60: £1.02, £4.50, £3.30; EX 14.50.
Owner Pearl Bloodstock Ltd **Bred** Mrs T A Foreman **Trained** Newmarket, Suffolk

FOCUS
A couple of interesting performers in a fair handicap. The gallop was soon reasonable and the progressive winner came down the centre in the straight.

128 32RED CASINO H'CAP 7f (P)

5:15 (5:16) (Class 5) (0-70,69) 4-Y-0+ **£2,264** (£673; £336; £168) **Stalls** Low

Form RPR

650- **1** **April Fool**[100] 6616 8-9-2 **69** (b) RaulDaSilva(5) 3 78
(Ronald Harris) *mde all: rdn and clr wl over 1f out: styd on wl: comf* **10/3**[1]

05-6 **2** *3¼* **Katmai River (IRE)**[3] 102 5-8-9 **57** (v) DavidProbert 8 57
(Mark Usher) *dwlt and rdn along early: bhd: swtchd rt and effrt jst over 2f out: styd on u.p to go 2nd fnl 100yds: no ch w wnr* **13/2**[3]

002- **3** *½* **Moral Issue**[34] 7695 4-9-0 **67** ShaneBKelly(5) 5 66
(Ian McInnes) *chsd wnr: rdn and unable qck 2f out: styd on same pce and no imp after: lost 2nd fnl 100yds* **13/2**[3]

/53- **4** *shd* **Jo Boy**[331] 546 5-9-1 **63** HayleyTurner 6 61
(Michael Bell) *in tch in midfield: rdn and effrt ent fnl 2f: kpt on u.p ins fnl f: no ch w wnr* **15/2**

066- **5** *1* **The Happy Hammer (IRE)**[33] 7716 6-9-6 **68** WilliamCarson 2 64
(Eugene Stanford) *hld up in tch in midfield: rdn and effrt jst over 2f out: drvn and no imp over 1f out: wl hld fnl f* **7/2**[2]

000- **6** *6* **Powerful Pierre**[130] 5760 5-9-5 **67** JamesSullivan 7 46
(Ian McInnes) *hld up towards rr: rdn and struggling wl over 2f out: wknd 2f out* **50/1**

024- **7** *1½* **This Ones For Eddy**[24] 7820 7-9-0 **62** (p) MartinLane 1 37
(John Balding) *hld up in rr: rdn and no rspnse over 2f out: wknd 2f out* **20/1**

601- **8** *nse* **Tourist**[15] 7895 7-9-4 **66** StevieDonohoe 4 41
(Ian Williams) *chsd ldrs: rdn and unable qck jst over 2f out: wknd jst over 1f out: fdd ins fnl f* **10/3**[1]

1m 25.45s (-0.55) **Going Correction** 0.0s/f (Stan) 8 Ran SP% **113.5**
Speed ratings (Par 103): **103,99,98,98,97 90,88,88**
toteswingers:1&2:£4.90, 2&3:£5.70, 1&3:£3.90 CSF £24.94 CT £133.08 TOTE £3.80: £1.40, £3.20, £2.90; EX 27.70.
Owner S & A Mares **Bred** Miss B Swire **Trained** Earlswood, Monmouths

FOCUS
Exposed performers in a modest handicap. The ordinary gallop suited those right up with the pace and the winner raced in the centre in the straight.
Tourist Official explanation: vet said gelding finished distressed

129 £32 FREE AT 32RED.COM H'CAP 2m (P)

5:45 (5:45) (Class 6) (0-65,64) 4-Y-0+ **£1,617** (£481; £240; £120) **Stalls** Low

Form RPR

600- **1** **Prince Charlemagne (IRE)**[119] 6087 9-8-9 **50** (p) MatthewCosham(5) 4 58
(Dr Jeremy Naylor) *t.k.h: hld up in tch in last trio: hdwy over 3f out: rdn and ev ch over 1f out: led 1f out: kpt on wl* **25/1**

30-2 **2** *nk* **Bold Adventure**[9] 23 8-9-1 **51** StevieDonohoe 7 58
(Willie Musson) *hld up in rr: stl plenty to do and rdn 2f out: gd hdwy on inner over 1f out: ev ch and hrd drvn ins fnl f: no ex towards fin* **7/2**[1]

0/5- **3** *1* **Santera (IRE)**[68] 733 8-8-9 **45** (p) WilliamCarson 6 51
(Tony Carroll) *in tch in midfield: rdn and effrt to ld 2f out: drvn and hdd 1f out: styd on same pce ins fnl f* **9/2**[2]

000- **4** *1½* **Vinces**[15] 7891 8-8-4 **45** (p) RaulDaSilva(5) 3 49
(Tim McCarthy) *chsd ldrs: rdn and styd on same pce fnl 2f* **25/1**

331- **5** *3¼* **Galiotto (IRE)**[44] 7574 6-9-11 **61** (v) AdamKirby 1 61
(Gary Moore) *dwlt and rdn along leaving stalls: in tch in midfield: rdn and outpcd over 2f out: wl hld and swtchd lft over 1f out: kpt on but no threat to ldrs fnl f* **11/2**

142- **6** *1* **Henry Holmes**[44] 7574 9-9-0 **50** IanMongan 2 49
(Lydia Richards) *chsd ldrs: rdn and effrt on inner 2f out: wknd ent fnl f* **9/1**

341- **7** *nk* **Dream Catcher (SWE)**[22] 7850 9-10-0 **64** (p) HayleyTurner 5 63
(Jonjo O'Neill) *led: rdn over 2f out: hdd and drvn 2f out: wknd ent fnl f* **6/1**

005- **8** *4½* **Perfect Vision**[22] 7850 5-9-10 **60** (t) LiamKeniry 10 53
(Charlie Longsdon) *chsd ldr: rdn over 2f out: sn struggling: wknd qckly over 1f out* **12/1**

14B- **9** *10* **Blue Cossack (IRE)**[31] 7738 4-9-0 **57** (be) DavidProbert 9 38
(Mark Usher) *s.i.s: hld up in last trio: effrt on outer over 2f out: drvn and wknd 2f out: wl bhd fnl f* **5/1**[3]

14-3 **10** *5* **Six Of Clubs**[9] 23 6-8-12 **55** (b) JakePayne(7) 8 30
(Bill Turner) *in tch: rdn and unable qck wl over 2f out: sn struggling: wknd 2f out: wl bhd fnl f* **14/1**

3m 30.91s (0.81) **Going Correction** 0.0s/f (Stan)
WFA 4 from 5yo+ 7lb 10 Ran SP% **118.8**
Speed ratings (Par 101): **97,96,96,95,93 93,93,91,86,83**
toteswingers:1&2:£40.00, 2&3:£6.00, 1&3:£48.40 CSF £113.11 CT £480.10 TOTE £40.10: £9.40, £2.70, £1.30; EX 133.00.
Owner Cleeve Stables Racing Partnership **Bred** Michael O'Mahony **Trained** Shrewton, Wilts

FOCUS
A couple of recent winners in a very ordinary handicap. The pace was a modest one to the home turn and the winner came down the centre in the straight.

130 32REDBET.COM H'CAP 1m 4f (P)

6:15 (6:18) (Class 6) (0-58,57) 4-Y-0+ **£1,617** (£481; £240; £120) **Stalls** Centre

Form RPR

112- **1** **Shirataki (IRE)**[13] 7931 4-9-3 **56** ChrisCatlin 3 69+
(Peter Hiatt) *t.k.h: chsd ldrs: rdn and qcknd to ld over 1f out: sn clr and r.o wl: comf* **2/1**[1]

053- **2** *3* **Kai Mook**[15] 7891 5-9-6 **55** AdamKirby 8 63
(Roger Ingram) *hld up towards rr: rdn and hdwy 2f out: chsd clr wnr ins fnl f: r.o but no threat to wnr* **11/2**[2]

006- **3** *1¾* **Four Steps Back**[36] 7662 5-9-1 **50** DavidProbert 4 55
(Mark Usher) *in tch in midfield: rdn and effrt on outer jst over 2f out: styd on u.p ins fnl f to go 3rd towards fin: no ch w wnr* **50/1**

44-0 **4** *1* **Carlton Scroop (FR)**[10] 9 9-9-0 **54** (b) NathanAlison(5) 5 58
(Paddy Butler) *led: rdn over 2f out: hdd and nt pce of wnr over 1f out: stl 2nd but wl hld 1f out: lost 2nd ins fnl f: plugged on* **12/1**

25-2 **5** *nk* **Laconicos (IRE)**[8] 28 10-9-0 **54** (t) RyanPowell(5) 1 57
(William Stone) *taken down early: in tch: rdn and effrt on inner 2f out: outpcd by wnr and wl hld 1f out: plugged on fnl f* **6/1**[3]

005- **6** *3¼* **Sondray**[13] 7921 4-9-2 **55** (t) IanMongan 9 53
(Jo Crowley) *chsd ldrs: rdn and hld hd high wl over 1f out: sn unable qck and btn: wknd 1f out* **9/1**

500- **7** *½* **Sawahill**[25] 7805 4-8-13 **52** HayleyTurner 6 49
(Clive Brittain) *chsd ldr tl wl over 1f out: wknd u.p over 1f out* **14/1**

140- **8** *2¾* **Gallantry**[25] 7810 10-9-8 **57** TomMcLaughlin 10 50
(Paul Howling) *stdd and stmbld s: hld up in rr: rdn and effrt over 1f out: nvr trbld ldrs* **20/1**

440- **9** *3¼* **Olimamu (IRE)**[38] 7640 5-8-8 **46** (t) SimonPearce(3) 12 34
(Lydia Pearce) *stdd s: hld up in last pair: c wd and rdn 3f out: no hdwy and sn lost tch* **16/1**

006- **10** *½* **Turbulent Priest**[28] 7766 4-9-2 **55** (b) JamieGoldstein 2 42
(Zoe Davison) *in tch towards rr: rdn and effrt over 2f out: sn struggling and wknd 2f out* **33/1**

106- **11** *3¾* **Thank You Joy**[32] 7723 4-8-11 **55** RaulDaSilva(5) 7 36
(J R Jenkins) *t.k.h: hld up towards rr: rdn and wknd over 2f out: wl bhd over 1f out* **10/1**

2m 37.18s (2.68) **Going Correction** 0.0s/f (Stan)
WFA 4 from 5yo+ 4lb 11 Ran SP% **112.0**
Speed ratings (Par 101): **91,89,87,87,86 84,84,82,80,80 77**
toteswingers:1&2:£1.70, 2&3:£41.40, 1&3:£28.70 CSF £10.95 CT £349.80 TOTE £2.60: £1.20, £1.10, £12.80; EX 13.00.
Owner P W Hiatt **Bred** Deerfield Farm **Trained** Hook Norton, Oxon

FOCUS
A moderate handicap in which the gallop was a steady one to the home turn. The winner raced centre-to-far-side in the in the straight.

131 32REDPOKER.COM H'CAP — 1m (P)
6:45 (6:45) (Class 4) (0-85,85) 4-Y-0+ — **£4,075** (£1,212; £606; £303) **Stalls** Low

Form — RPR

303- **1** **Sunset Kitty (USA)**[22] 7841 5-9-6 **84** ShaneKelly 5 — 92+
(Mike Murphy) *hld up in tch: hdwy to press ldrs ent fnl f: rdn hands and heels ins fnl f and r.o to ld cl home* **11/4**[1]

662- **2** *shd* **Shifting Star (IRE)**[12] 7941 7-9-5 **83** (b) IanMongan 8 — 90
(John Bridger) *in tch: drvn and effrt 2f out: led jst ins fnl f: kpt on wl u.p tl hdd cl home* **9/1**

21-3 **3** *¾* **Perfect Mission**[6] 54 4-8-7 **71** oh1 (v) DavidProbert 10 — 76
(Andrew Balding) *t.k.h: prom: chsd ldr over 5f out: rdn and qcknd to ld 2f out: hdd jst ins fnl f: no ex wl ins fnl f* **11/2**[3]

055- **4** *¾* **Veroon (IRE)**[13] 7922 6-9-2 **80** (p) JamesSullivan 9 — 84+
(James Given) *stdd after s: hld up in last pair: rdn and gd hdwy over 1f out: chsd ldrs and drvn jst ins fnl f: kpt on same pce fnl 100yds* **9/2**[2]

000- **5** *2* **May's Boy**[106] 6457 4-9-0 **78** (p) DaneO'Neill 2 — 77
(Mark Usher) *chsd ldrs: drvn and effrt to press ldrs over 1f out: unable qck 1f out: wknd ins fnl f* **25/1**

514- **6** *hd* **Simayill**[22] 7841 4-9-5 **83** HayleyTurner 4 — 81
(Clive Brittain) *hld up in tch: rdn and effrt towards inner over 1f out: no prog ent fnl f: styd on same pce after* **9/2**[2]

001- **7** *nk* **Ocean Legend (IRE)**[50] 7517 7-8-8 **77** RaulDaSilva(5) 11 — 75
(Tony Carroll) *t.k.h: led for 1f: chsd ldrs: rdn and ev ch 2f out: wknd jst ins fnl f* **10/1**

020- **8** *4 ½* **All Right Now**[13] 7926 5-8-11 **75** ChrisCatlin 1 — 62
(Derek Haydn Jones) *stdd after s: hld up in last pair: rdn and effrt on inner wl over 1f out: wknd ent fnl f* **25/1**

560- **9** *¾* **Calypso Magic (IRE)**[33] 7719 4-9-7 **85** LiamKeniry 3 — 71
(Linda Jewell) *t.k.h: led tl rdn and hdd 2f out: wknd over 1f out* **14/1**

1m 38.88s (-0.92) **Going Correction** 0.0s/f (Stan) — **9** Ran SP% **111.9**
Speed ratings (Par 105): **104,103,103,102,100 100,99,95,94**
toteswingers:1&2:£6.90, 2&3:£6.10, 1&3:£3.20 CSF £27.21 CT £124.30 TOTE £1.80: £1.10, £3.00, £2.20; EX 26.80.
Owner Cool Cats **Bred** Mckee Stables Inc **Trained** Westoning, Beds
■ Stewards' Enquiry : Ian Mongan four-day ban, 2nd offence in 12mths; used whip down shoulder ion the forehand (Jan 26-28,30)

FOCUS
A useful handicap but one in which progressive sorts were thin on the ground. A modest gallop only picked up around the intersection and the winner came down the in the straight.

132 32REDBINGO.COM H'CAP — 1m (P)
7:15 (7:16) (Class 6) (0-60,60) 3-Y-0 — **£1,617** (£481; £240; £120) **Stalls** Low

Form — RPR

304- **1** **Whipcrackaway (IRE)**[25] 7809 3-9-6 **59** JohnFahy 9 — 64
(Peter Hedger) *in tch in midfield: rdn over 3f out: hdwy and drvn to chal over 1f out: led ins fnl f: kpt on* **15/2**

000- **2** *½* **Green Legacy (USA)**[29] 7751 3-9-3 **56** (b[1]) EddieAhern 4 — 60
(Amanda Perrett) *chsd ldrs: rdn to ld ent fnl 2f: hung lft u.p and hdd over 1f out: 4th and looked hld ins fnl f: consented to run on again fnl 100yds: wnt 2nd wl ins fnl f and pressing wnr cl home* **5/1**[1]

350- **3** *1* **First Bid**[16] 7881 3-9-7 **60** JamesSullivan 11 — 62
(James Given) *hld up in rr: rdn and gd hdwy on inner wl over 1f out: pressed ldrs 1f out: no ex and styd on same pce ins fnl f* **25/1**

53-6 **4** *nk* **Meet Joe Black (IRE)**[8] 30 3-8-8 **52** (v) MatthewCosham(5) 8 — 53+
(David Evans) *in tch in midfield on outer: rdn over 3f out: press ldrs 2f out: led over 1f out tl hdd ins fnl f: no ex and lost 2 pls wl ins fnl f* **16/1**

624- **5** *3 ¼* **Moment In The Sun**[12] 7937 3-9-5 **58** WilliamCarson 10 — 51
(William Muir) *hmpd sn after s and bhd: stl plenty to do and rdn over 2f out: styd on fr over 1f out: nvr able to chal* **6/1**[2]

003- **6** *½* **Holy Empress (IRE)**[40] 7626 3-8-8 **47** HayleyTurner 7 — 39
(Michael Bell) *hld up in rr: rdn and rn green over 2f out: hdwy towards inner 2f out: styd on same pce and no imp 1f out* **9/1**

060- **7** *2 ½* **Here Comes Jeanie**[29] 7749 3-9-0 **53** JamieGoldstein 12 — 39
(Michael Madgwick) *in tch in midfield: rdn and n.m.r 2f out: hdwy over 1f out: no prog jst ins fnl f: wknd fnl 100yds* **50/1**

000- **8** *10* **Gabrial The Prince (IRE)**[62] 7369 3-8-11 **50** StevieDonohoe 1 — 13
(David Simcock) *in tch: rdn and unable qck ent fnl 2f: wknd over 1f out: wl btn and eased ins fnl f* **13/2**[3]

364- **9** *hd* **Can Do Les (IRE)**[28] 7763 3-9-1 **54** MartinHarley 13 — 17
(Des Donovan) *chsd ldr tl over 2f out: sn hrd drvn and no ex: wknd over 1f out: bhd fnl f* **10/1**

52-2 **10** *nk* **Samasana (IRE)**[11] 2 3-8-12 **51** (b[1]) TomMcLaughlin 2 — 13
(Ian Wood) *chsd ldrs tl wknd u.p 2f out: wl btn and eased ins fnl f* **13/2**[3]

44-0 **11** *8* **Gone To Ground**[3] 108 3-8-2 **46** oh1 (p) RaulDaSilva(5) 3
(Jeremy Gask) *led: veered lft and reminders 6f out: hdd over 2f out: sn btn and eased: wl bhd fnl f* **16/1**

604- **12** *14* **Deduction (IRE)**[16] 7882 3-8-9 **51** AdamBeschizza(3) 5
(Nigel Tinkler) *hld up in last quartet: rdn and no rspnse over 2f out: bhd w rdr looking down and eased fnl 2f: t.o fnl f* **25/1**

13 *16* **Mallt (IRE)**[125] 5903 3-8-13 **52** (be) MartinLane 6
(Philip McBride) *veered sharply lft and virtually ref to r leaving stalls: eventually got gng and continued t.o* **25/1**

330- **R** **Clarkson (IRE)**[27] 7780 3-9-0 **53** FergusSweeney 14
(Jamie Osborne) *ref to r sn after s and dismntd* **33/1**

1m 40.35s (0.55) **Going Correction** 0.0s/f (Stan) — **14** Ran SP% **116.7**
Speed ratings (Par 95): **97,96,95,95,91 91,88,78,78,78 70,56,40,**
toteswingers:1&2:£10.40, 2&3:£11.20, 1&3:£26.00 CSF £40.71 CT £921.33 TOTE £9.80: £2.40, £1.90, £6.80; EX 59.00.
Owner P R Hedger **Bred** Kilfrush Stud **Trained** Dogmersfield, Hampshire
■ Stewards' Enquiry : John Fahy six-day ban, 3rd offence in 12mths; used whip with excessive ferquency (Jan 26-28,30,31,Feb 1)

FOCUS
A moderate but open handicap run at a reasonable gallop. The winner came down the centre in the straight.
Deduction(IRE) Official explanation: jockey said filly hung right
T/Plt: £19.00 to a £1 stake. Pool of £77,751.33 - 2,974.70 winning tickets. T/Qpdt: £9.50 to a £1 stake.Pool of £8,239.74 - 636.07 winning tickets. SP

[109] SOUTHWELL (L-H)
Thursday, January 12

OFFICIAL GOING: Standard
Wind: Fresh behind Weather: Fine and dry

133 BET AT BLUE SQUARE APPRENTICE CLASSIFIED CLAIMING STKS — 5f (F)
12:55 (12:57) (Class 6) 4-Y-0+ — **£1,704** (£503; £251) **Stalls** High

Form — RPR

00-1 **1** **Upper Lambourn (IRE)**[10] 13 4-8-9 69 LeonnaMayor(5) 4 — 78+
(Jamie Osborne) *sn outpcd and bhd: gd hdwy over 1f out: str run ins fnl f to ld last 40yds* **2/1**[2]

022- **2** *¾* **Soopacal (IRE)**[37] 7646 7-8-9 67 JohnFahy 2 — 70
(Brian Ellison) *trckd ldrs: hdwy and cl up over 2f out: sn led: rdn wl over 1f out: hdd and no ex last 40yds* **11/10**[1]

30-6 **3** *1 ¾* **Bookiesindex Boy**[9] 24 8-8-8 61 (b) RaulDaSilva(5) 5 — 68?
(J R Jenkins) *cl up: rdn and ev ch wl over 1f out: one pce fnl f* **16/1**

006- **4** *2 ¼* **Luscivious**[14] 7917 8-8-13 70 (b) MichaelO'Connell 3 — 60
(Scott Dixon) *led 2f: cl up and ev ch tl rdn wl over 1f out and grad wknd* **11/2**[3]

200- **5** *¾* **Royal Intruder**[32] 7726 7-8-12 68 ow1 (p) MartinHarley 1 — 56
(Richard Guest) *racd wd: chsd ldrs: rdn along 2f out: sn btn* **22/1**

63-0 **6** *3 ¼* **Grudge**[9] 24 7-8-7 65 (b) JulieBurke 7 — 39
(Conor Dore) *cl up: led after 2f: rdn along over 2f out: sn hdd & wknd* **33/1**

57.75s (-1.95) **Going Correction** -0.30s/f (Stan) — **6** Ran SP% **109.5**
Speed ratings (Par 101): **103,101,99,95,94 89**
.Upper Lambourn was claimed by B Ellison for £13,000.\n\x\x
Owner L S M Building Contractors **Bred** Messrs Derek Gibbons & Peter Gibbons **Trained** Upper Lambourn, Berks

FOCUS
A modest claimer but one not without interest and the first two look worth keeping on side in the next few weeks.
Luscivious Official explanation: trainer's rep said gelding had a breathing problem

134 DAVID BELLINGHAM SCRAMBLES TO 50 H'CAP — 7f (F)
1:25 (1:25) (Class 5) (0-75,78) 4-Y-0+ — **£2,522** (£750; £375; £187) **Stalls** Low

Form — RPR

00-0 **1** **Avonrose**[4] 100 5-9-4 **72** PhillipMakin 4 — 79
(Derek Shaw) *cl up: effrt wl over 2f out: rdn to ld over 1f out: drvn and edgd lft ins fnl f: hld on wl* **3/1**[2]

334- **2** *½* **Piceno (IRE)**[28] 7771 4-9-2 **75** (b) RyanPowell(5) 3 — 81
(Scott Dixon) *led: rdn along over 2f out: hdd over 1f out: sn drvn and rallied ins fnl f: ev ch tl no ex nr fin* **13/8**[1]

42-0 **3** *1 ¼* **Chookie Avon**[2] 115 5-9-2 **70** (p) JoeFanning 1 — 72
(Keith Dalgleish) *trckd ldng pair: hdwy on inner and cl up over 2f out: rdn to chal wl over 1f out and ev ch tl one pce wl ins fnl f* **4/1**[3]

14-1 **4** *2 ¾* **Mcconnell (USA)**[10] 12 7-9-10 **78** 6ex (b) MartinHarley 7 — 73
(Richard Guest) *hld up: hdwy 3f out: rdn along 2f out: sn no imp* **8/1**

415/ **5** *24* **Liteup My World (USA)**[573] 3149 6-8-10 **64** BarryMcHugh 8
(Brian Ellison) *dwlt: a in rr: bhd fnl 3f* **9/1**

010- **6** *16* **Prize Point**[327] 612 6-9-0 **68** RobertWinston 2
(Tom Gretton) *dwlt: t.k.h and sn chsng ldrs: rdn along 3f out and sn wknd* **12/1**

1m 28.09s (-2.21) **Going Correction** -0.10s/f (Stan) — **6** Ran SP% **111.9**
Speed ratings (Par 103): **108,107,106,102,75 57**
toteswingers:1&2:£2.20, 2&3:£1.60, 1&3:£3.30 CSF £8.25 CT £17.73 TOTE £2.30: £2.80, £1.70; EX 15.00 Trifecta £35.80 Pool: £312.26 - 6.45 winning units..
Owner Moorland Racing **Bred** Mrs Mary Taylor **Trained** Sproxton, Leics

FOCUS
A fair handicap that provided a good finish but just ordinary form. The pace wasn't particularly strong.

135 GOLF AT SOUTHWELL MEDIAN AUCTION MAIDEN STKS — 5f (F)
1:55 (1:55) (Class 6) 3-5-Y-0 — **£1,704** (£503; £251) **Stalls** High

Form — RPR

00- **1** **Bella Ophelia (IRE)**[48] 7540 3-8-6 0 NickyMackay 9 — 66+
(Hughie Morrison) *mde all: shkn up appr fnl f: sn clr* **4/1**[3]

420- **2** *3* **Ladydolly**[132] 5678 4-9-7 52 (p) PhillipMakin 2 — 58
(Roy Brotherton) *sn cl up: effrt 2f out: sn rdn and kpt on same pce appr fnl f* **7/2**[2]

304- **3** *7* **Art Show**[23] 7830 3-8-6 60 ChrisCatlin 7 — 27
(Ed Dunlop) *dwlt and sn rdn along in rr: hdwy 1/2-way: kpt on appr fnl f* **5/4**[1]

050- **4** *2 ¼* **Bygones For Coins (IRE)**[100] 6602 4-9-0 39 MatthewHopkins(7) 1 — 25
(Alan Berry) *chsd ldrs on outer: rdn along 1/2-way: sn one pce* **80/1**

00-6 **5** *¾* **Miss Bloom**[9] 20 3-8-1 0 RyanPowell(5) 3 — 16
(Garry Woodward) *midfield: hdwy to chse ldrs over 2f out: sn rdn and no imp* **100/1**

355- **6** *1* **Regal Lady**[16] 7882 3-8-0 58 ow1 ClaireMurray(7) 6 — 13
(David Brown) *chsd ldrs: rdn along 1/2-way: sn outpcd* **20/1**

042- **7** *hd* **Italian Ice**[16] 7882 3-8-7 44 ow1 TomEaves 4 — 13
(Bryan Smart) *prom: rdn along 1/2-way: sn wknd* **16/1**

8 *6* **Just Me'Lady** 3-8-6 0 JoeFanning 5
(Bill Turner) *dwlt: a towards rr* **10/1**

5-5 **9** *8* **Darcy May**[9] 20 4-9-2 0 JustinNewman(5) 8
(Garry Woodward) *a in rr: bhd fnl 2f* **22/1**

58.11s (-1.59) **Going Correction** -0.30s/f (Stan)
WFA 3 from 4yo 15lb — **9** Ran SP% **113.0**
Speed ratings (Par 101): **100,95,84,80,79 77,77,67,54**
toteswingers:1&2:£3.10, 2&3:£1.90, 1&3:£2.40 CSF £17.36 TOTE £3.10: £1.50, £1.90, £1.10; EX 17.20 Trifecta £48.90 Pool: £413.67 - 6.25 winning units..
Owner Mrs Belinda Scott & Partners **Bred** Tally-Ho Stud **Trained** East Ilsley, Berks

FOCUS
A very weak maiden dominated by the first two from a long way out.
Art Show Official explanation: jockey said filly suffered interference at start

136 FOLLOW US ON TWITTER @BLUESQ H'CAP — 1m (F)
2:25 (2:25) (Class 5) (0-70,70) 4-Y-0+ — **£2,264** (£673; £336; £168) **Stalls** Low

Form — RPR

25-1 **1** **Dashing Eddie (IRE)**[10] 14 4-8-11 **60** 6ex (p) PhillipMakin 7 — 70
(Kevin Ryan) *trckd ldr: cl up 1/2-way: led over 2f out: rdn over 1f out: drvn ins fnl f: hld on wl* **5/6**[1]

034- **2** *nk* **Zenarinda**[28] 7774 5-8-13 **62** .... RobertWinston 1 71
(Mark H Tompkins) *trckd ldrs: hdwy 3f out: rdn 2f out: drvn to chal over 1f out and ev ch tl no ex last 50yds* **8/1**

011/ **3** *5* **D'Urberville**[391] 7912 5-9-7 **70** .... StephenCraine 2 68
(J R Jenkins) *trckd ldrs on inner: hdwy 3f out: cl up over 2f out: sn rdn and ev ch tl wknd ent fnl f* **14/1**

U51- **4** *nse* **Community (USA)**[21] 7856 4-8-13 **69** .... LeonnaMayor(7) 5 66
(Phil McEntee) *led: rdn along and jnd 3f out: hdd over 2f out: grad wknd* **13/2**[3]

000- **5** *4 1/2* **Twice Red**[21] 7857 4-9-4 **67** .... TomEaves 4 54
(Derek Shaw) *chsd ldrs: hdwy 3f out: rdn wl over 2f out: sn one pce* **14/1**

566- **6** *4 1/2* **Rubi Dia**[16] 7884 5-8-13 **62** .... BarryMcHugh 8 39
(Kevin M Prendergast) *hld up: a in rr* **16/1**

320- **7** *2* **Master Of Dance (IRE)**[40] 7625 5-9-7 **70** .... (p) JoeFanning 6 42
(Keith Dalgleish) *chsd ldrs: rdn along 3f out: wknd over 2f out* **11/2**[2]

000- **8** *19* **Christmas Carnival**[17] 7876 5-8-9 **65** .... DavidSimmonson(7) 3
(Michael Easterby) *a in rr* **80/1**

1m 42.83s (-0.87) **Going Correction** -0.10s/f (Stan) **8** Ran SP% **114.8**
Speed ratings (Par 103): **100,99,94,94,90 85,83,64**
CSF £8.43 CT £56.12 TOTE £2.20: £1.10, £2.00, £2.80; EX 9.60 Trifecta £53.70 Pool: £422.45 - 5.82 winning units..
Owner T A Rahman **Bred** Scuderia San Pancrazio Sas **Trained** Hambleton, N Yorks
■ Stewards' Enquiry : Robert Winston 22-day ban, 2nd offence in 12mths; used whip with excessive frequency down shoulder in the forehand (Jan 26-28,Jan 30-Feb 4,Feb 6-11,Feb 13-18,20)

FOCUS
A fair handicap run at a reasonable gallop.

137 18TH JANUARY COME JUMPING AT SOUTHWELL MAIDEN STKS 1m 3f (F)
2:55 (2:56) (Class 5) 4-Y-O+ **£2,385** (£704; £352) **Stalls** Low

Form RPR

32-4 **1** **Bravestofthebrave (USA)**[10] 10 4-9-3 76 .... (b[1]) NickyMackay 3 76+
(John Gosden) *trckd ldrs on inner: hdwy 3f out: cl up over 2f out: chal wl over 1f out and sn rdn: drvn ins fnl f: kpt on to ld last 75yds* **85/40**[2]

30-3 **2** *shd* **Eyedoro (USA)**[10] 10 4-9-3 75 .... JoeFanning 5 76+
(Mark Johnston) *led: rdn along 2f out: jnd wl over 1f out: hdd and no ex last 75yds* **13/8**[1]

/32- **3** *9* **Frosty Friday**[31] 7739 4-8-12 62 .... RobbieFitzpatrick 7 55
(J R Jenkins) *trckd ldrs: hdwy 4f out: cl up 3f out: rdn wl over 1f out: sn one pce* **11/2**[3]

4 *2 1/4* **Candelita**[42] 5-9-1 0 .... RobertWinston 2 51
(Jo Hughes) *hld up in rr: hdwy on inner 3f out: chsd ldrs 2f out: sn rdn and hung rt over 1f out: kpt on same pce* **15/2**

5 *2 1/4* **Eight Keys**[11] 4-9-3 0 .... JamesMillman 4 52
(Rod Millman) *chsd ldrs: rdn along over 4f out: sn wknd* **14/1**

6 *10* **Las Hilanderas (USA)**[50] 4-8-9 0 .... RyanClark(3) 6 29
(Stuart Williams) *cl up: rdn along over 3f out: sn wknd* **25/1**

7 *2 3/4* **Bellapais Abbey (IRE)**[14] 6-8-13 0 .... (t) PNolan(7) 1 29
(David Brown) *dwlt and in rr: hdwy on outer and in tch 5f out: rdn along 4f out and sn wknd* **33/1**

2m 27.28s (-0.72) **Going Correction** -0.10s/f (Stan)
WFA 4 from 5yo+ 3lb **7** Ran SP% **110.7**
Speed ratings (Par 103): **98,97,91,89,88 80,78**
CSF £5.53 TOTE £2.30: £1.10, £1.40; EX 6.30 Trifecta £14.20 Pool: £586.43 - 30.50 winning units..
Owner A E Oppenheimer **Bred** Hascombe And Valiant Studs **Trained** Newmarket, Suffolk
■ Stewards' Enquiry : Nicky Mackay two-day ban: used whip with excessive frequency (Jan 26-27)

FOCUS
No more than a fair maiden dominated by the pair at the head of the market. The pace was only modest, leading to something of a sprint finish.

138 JETBET.CO.UK FREE BETTING EXCHANGE SOFTWARE H'CAP 5f (F)
3:25 (3:25) (Class 6) (0-60,59) 3-Y-O **£1,704** (£503; £251) **Stalls** Low

Form RPR

1 **Drinmoy Lad (IRE)**[62] 7372 3-8-13 **51** .... MartinHarley 1 60
(Michael McElhone, Ire) *cl up: led after 2f: jnd and rdn 1 1/2f out: drvn and edgd lft ins fnl f: kpt on wl* **2/1**[2]

1-52 **2** *1* **Russian Bullet**[5] 86 3-9-7 **59** .... FergusSweeney 3 64
(Jamie Osborne) *trckd ldng pair: hdwy and cl up 1/2-way: effrt to chal 1 1/2f out: sn rdn and ev ch tl one pce wl ins fnl f* **11/8**[1]

41-0 **3** *3 3/4* **Lady Nickandy (IRE)**[9] 25 3-8-11 **56** .... (b[1]) RobJFitzpatrick(7) 4 48
(Alan McCabe) *in tch: hdwy 1/2-way: chsd ldng pair wl over 1f out: sn rdn and no imp* **14/1**

53-3 **4** *nk* **Lord Buffhead**[7] 40 3-8-13 **51** .... RobbieFitzpatrick 5 42
(Richard Guest) *in rr and swtchd lft after 1f: rdn along 1/2-way: kpt on appr fnl f: n.d* **16/1**

565- **5** *5* **Essexvale (IRE)**[14] 7916 3-9-2 **57** .... JulieBurke(3) 2 30
(Alan Berry) *chsd ldrs: rdn along 1/2-way: sn outpcd* **40/1**

554- **6** *nk* **Lowtherwood**[153] 5017 3-9-6 **58** .... TomEaves 6 30
(Bryan Smart) *led 2f: cl up tl rdn along 2f out and sn wknd* **4/1**[3]

59.0s (-0.70) **Going Correction** -0.30s/f (Stan) **6** Ran SP% **110.4**
Speed ratings (Par 95): **93,91,85,84,76 76**
toteswingers:1&2:£1.40, 2&3:£3.50, 1&3:£3.40 CSF £4.93 TOTE £3.40: £1.60, £1.10; EX 5.60.
Owner Mrs Anne McElhone **Bred** Kevin Bishop **Trained** Strandhill, Co. Sligo

FOCUS
A low-grade handicap once again controlled by the first two from a long way out.

139 PLAY ROULETTE AT BLUESQ.COM/CASINO H'CAP 6f (F)
3:55 (3:55) (Class 6) (0-60,62) 4-Y-O+ **£1,704** (£503; £251) **Stalls** Low

Form RPR

22-3 **1** **Greenhead High**[10] 13 4-9-7 **60** .... AndrewMullen 4 69
(David Nicholls) *mde all: rdn 2f out: drifted rt wl over 1f out: drvn out* **5/1**[3]

034- **2** *1* **Gracie's Gift (IRE)**[32] 7728 10-8-12 **51** .... (v) MartinHarley 3 57
(Richard Guest) *prom: effrt 2f out: rdn to chse wnr ins fnl f and ev ch tl drvn and nt qckn last 75yds* **16/1**

53-2 **3** *1* **Mazovian (USA)**[10] 13 4-9-4 **60** .... JulieBurke(3) 10 63
(Michael Chapman) *in tch: pushed along and lost pl after 2f: sn bhd and rdn along 1/2-way: hdwy towards inner wl over 1f out: styd on strly appr fnl f: nrst fin* **9/1**

0-03 **4** *2* **Ace Of Spies (IRE)**[4] 100 7-9-7 **60** .... (b) TomEaves 7 56
(Conor Dore) *in rr: hdwy on inner wl over 2f out: sn rdn and styd on to chse ldrs fnl f: nrst fin* **8/1**

200- **5** *3/4* **Ridgeway Hawk**[22] 7844 4-8-12 **56** .... (v) LeeNewnes(5) 14 50
(Mark Usher) *chsd ldrs on outer: wd st: racd nr stands' rail: rdn wl over 1f out: no imp fnl f* **50/1**

40-2 **6** *1/2* **Fear Nothing**[10] 8 5-9-4 **57** .... DanielTudhope 12 49
(David O'Meara) *chsd ldrs on outer: wd st: racd nr stands' rail and rdn wl over 1f out: no imp* **9/2**[2]

01-1 **7** *nk* **Beachwood Bay**[4] 101 4-9-6 **62** 6ex .... (p) MichaelO'Connell(3) 1 53
(Jo Hughes) *trckd ldrs on inner: pushed along wl over 2f out: hdwy wl over 1f out: sn rdn and ch tl drvn ent fnl f and sn wknd* **3/1**[1]

4-05 **8** *1 3/4* **Steel City Boy (IRE)**[4] 100 9-9-0 **60** .... DannyBrock(7) 2 46
(Garry Woodward) *cl up on inner: rdn along 2f out: sn wknd* **28/1**

043- **9** *nk* **Caramelita**[32] 7728 5-9-7 **60** .... (v) StephenCraine 6 45
(J R Jenkins) *midfield: hdwy to chse ldrs over 2f out: rdn wl over 1f out and sn one pce* **12/1**

003- **10** *1* **Fantasy Fry**[24] 7820 4-9-5 **58** .... (t) RichardKingscote 11 40
(Tom Dascombe) *in tch: rdn along 1/2-way: sn wknd* **12/1**

030- **11** *4 1/2* **Lindoro**[22] 7844 7-9-5 **58** .... BarryMcHugh 5 25
(Kevin M Prendergast) *hld up: a in rr* **14/1**

50-5 **12** *2 1/4* **Divertimenti (IRE)**[10] 8 8-9-4 **57** .... (bt) RobertWinston 8 17
(Roy Bowring) *cl up: rdn along 1/2-way: sn wknd* **25/1**

004- **13** *4 1/2* **Finn's Rainbow**[16] 7883 4-9-2 **60** .... JustinNewman(5) 13
(John Weymes) *a in rr* **100/1**

1m 15.34s (-1.16) **Going Correction** -0.10s/f (Stan) **13** Ran SP% **119.1**
Speed ratings (Par 101): **103,101,100,97,96 96,95,93,92,91 85,82,76**
toteswingers:1&2:£23.40, 2&3:£27.50, 1&3:£7.50 CSF £79.64 CT £730.65 TOTE £3.60: £1.20, £6.70, £3.70; EX 116.40 TRIFECTA Not won..
Owner Charles Castle **Bred** Wyck Hall Stud Ltd **Trained** Sessay, N Yorks

FOCUS
Quite a well-contested handicap for the grade and one run at a decent pace, so the form promises to be reliable.
Beachwood Bay Official explanation: jockey said gelding ran flat
T/Plt: £4.30 to a £1 stake. Pool of £59,233.00 - 9,916.51 winning tickets. T/Qpdt: £1.80 to a £1 stake. Pool of £3,306.87 - 1,307.97 winning tickets. JR

[76]MEYDAN (L-H)
Thursday, January 12
OFFICIAL GOING: Turf - good; tapeta - standard

140a ETISALAT MY PLAN (H'CAP) (TAPETA) 7f
3:05 (3:05) (95-105,105) 3-Y-O+
£42,580 (£14,193; £7,096; £3,548; £2,129; £1,419)

RPR

1 **Barbecue Eddie (USA)**[35] 7680 8-9-2 105 .... (b) RichardHills 2 110
(Doug Watson, UAE) *trckd ldrs: led 2 1/2f out: kicked clr 1 1/2f out: r.o wl: comf* **6/1**[2]

2 *1 3/4* **Ariete Arrollador**[35] 7678 5-9-0 102 .... MircoDemuro 4 103
(G Arizkorreta Elosegui, Spain) *mid-div: chsd ldrs 2 1/2f out: r.o fnl 1 1/2f but no ch w wnr* **9/1**

3 *3/4* **Russian Rock (IRE)**[7] 50 5-9-0 102 .... WayneSmith 1 101
(M Al Muhairi, UAE) *mid-div: r.o wl fnl 2f: nrst fin* **20/1**

4 *2 1/4* **Tertio Bloom (SWE)**[25] 7815 7-9-2 105 .... (t) ValmirDeAzeredo 13 97
(Fabricio Borges, Sweden) *wl away: trckd ldrs: ev ch 1 1/2f out: one pce fnl 110yds* **20/1**

5 *1 1/4* **Storm Chispazo (ARG)**[179] 6-9-0 102 .... (t) RyanMoore 6 92+
(H J Brown, South Africa) *nvr nr to chal but r.o fnl 2f* **16/1**

6 *hd* **Spirit Of Sharjah (IRE)**[7] 51 7-8-11 100 .... TadhgO'Shea 3 88+
(Julia Feilden) *settled in rr: smooth prog 2 1/2f out: nt qckn fnl 1 1/2f* **16/1**

7 *nse* **Captain Ramius (IRE)**[159] 4802 6-8-11 100 .... JamieSpencer 7 88
(Kevin Ryan) *sn led: hdd 2 1/2f out: kpt on same pce* **13/2**[3]

8 *1 1/4* **Red Gulch**[93] 6783 5-9-0 102 .... FrankieDettori 5 88
(Mahmood Al Zarooni) *trckd ldng gp tl 2 1/2f out: one pce fnl 110yds* **9/4**[1]

9 *1 3/4* **Royal Destination (IRE)**[322] 679 7-9-0 102 .... (v) RoystonFfrench 9 83+
(F Nass, Bahrain) *nvr bttr than mid-div* **33/1**

10 *4 1/4* **Reem (AUS)**[111] 6297 5-9-1 104 .... ChristopheSoumillon 14 73
(M F De Kock, South Africa) *trckd ldr tl 2 1/2f out: sn wknd* **10/1**

11 *3/4* **Lowther**[131] 5699 7-9-0 102 .... (b) AdrianNicholls 11 70+
(David Nicholls) *settled in rr: nvr able to chal* **16/1**

12 *3/4* **Swop (IRE)**[152] 5032 9-8-11 100 .... KierenFallon 12 65+
(Luca Cumani) *nvr bttr than mid-div* **16/1**

13 *1 1/4* **Toolain (IRE)**[121] 6027 4-9-0 102 .... (e) WilliamBuick 8 64+
(D Selvaratnam, UAE) *nvr bttr than mid-div* **14/1**

14 *2* **Nova Step**[35] 7678 4-9-0 101 ow1 .... OlivierPeslier 10 59+
(Stephane Chevalier, UAE) *nvr bttr than mid-div* **14/1**

1m 24.66s (-0.54) **14** Ran SP% **126.8**
CSF: £61.05; Tricast: £1,049.17.
Owner Hamdan Al Maktoum **Bred** Margaret Addis **Trained** United Arab Emirates

FOCUS
No obviously well-handicapped types here and it was a below-par race for a 95-105. It paid to be handy and those drawn low dominated, with nothing making up much ground out wide in the straight. Captain Ramius took the field along at a steady pace, going through the first quarter-mile in 26.13 and the half in 50.11. The winner is rated to the mark he showed when winning here the last two years.

NOTEBOOK
Barbecue Eddie(USA) was 5lb higher than when winning over C&D at last year's Carnival and the fact he was able to score so readily strongly supports the view this wasn't a great race. He did well to overcome a sluggish start, but he won't appeal off a higher mark next time.
Ariete Arrollador, a recent French Listed winner, travelled with enthusiasm into the straight (touched 1.5 in-running) but his rider didn't go for him until late, which allowed the winner a bit of a start, and he was held once off the bridle. It looked as though Mirco Demuro was overconfident, although it's possible he was trying to keep something in reserve considering his mount could have settled better.
Russian Rock(IRE) seemed to appreciate the return to Tapeta and was helped by his draw, but he's not particularly well handicapped. (op 16/1)
Tertio Bloom(SWE) managed to get a handy position from an outside draw without losing significant ground, but he gradually faded in the straight.
Storm Chispazo(ARG) ◆ won the 2009 Argentine Derby over a bit further than 1m4f, so this trip was always likely to be shorter than ideal, especially in a modestly run race, and he'd been absent for 179 days, but he stayed on nicely from a long way back. He struggled when last seen in Dubai in 2010, but could do better now.
Captain Ramius(IRE), racing from a mark 5lb higher than when winning on turf in August, he faded a bit disappointingly in the straight.
Red Gulch, a Listed winner in France in October, had since been sold out of Ed Walker's yard for 250,000gns but made a disappointing debut for Godolphin, finding little after travelling well enough.

Reem(AUS) ◆, returning from a 111-day break, was drawn wide and covered plenty of ground over what's probably an inadequate trip these days. She can do better. (op 12/1)

141a ETISALAT ELIFE (H'CAP) (TURF) 6f
3:45 (3:45) (100-110,106) 3-Y-O+

£46,451 (£15,483; £7,741; £3,870; £2,322; £1,548)

RPR

1 **Addictive Dream (IRE)**[7] [50] 5-9-2 106 AdrianNicholls 3 111+
(David Nicholls) *sn led: kicked clr 1 1/2f out: r.o gamely* **7/2**[2]

2 1 ½ **Internationaldebut (IRE)**[7] [50] 7-8-13 102 FrederikTylicki 5 101
(Paul Midgley) *mid-div: chsd wnr 2f out: r.o wl fnl f: nrst fin* **11/1**

3 1 ¼ **The Reaper (IRE)**[76] [7149] 4-8-10 100 (b) RyanMoore 7 94
(G M Lyons, Ire) *mid-div: r.o fnl 2f: nrst fin* **10/1**

4 1 ¼ **Apache Crown (AUS)**[32] 7-9-0 104 (t) TedDurcan 2 94
(S Burridge, Singapore) *settled towards rr: rdn 3f out: r.o fnl f: nrst fin* **16/1**

5 ¼ **Bohemian Melody**[83] [6987] 5-8-13 102 (b) WilliamBuick 6 92
(Marco Botti) *a mid-div* **5/2**[1]

6 ½ **Forjatt (IRE)**[136] [5563] 4-8-13 102 JamesDoyle 9 91
(D Selvaratnam, UAE) *a mid-div* **10/1**

7 1 ¼ **Terrific Challenge (USA)**[13] [7936] 10-8-11 101 (vt) RichardMullen 1 85
(S Seemar, UAE) *trckd ldrs: ev ch 1 1/2f out: wknd fnl 110yds* **20/1**

8 1 ¾ **Green Beret (IRE)**[7] [50] 6-9-2 106 RoystonFfrench 8 84
(A Al Raihe, UAE) *trckd ldrs: ev ch 3f out: wknd fnl f* **9/1**

9 4 **Sir Reginald**[274] [1317] 4-8-13 102 PaulHanagan 11 68
(Richard Fahey) *trckd ldr tl 2f out: wknd fnl f* **8/1**[3]

10 20 **Winker Watson**[158] [4836] 7-8-10 100 (v) KierenFallon 10
(Mick Channon) *nvr bttr than mid-div* **25/1**

R **Rock Jock (IRE)**[123] [5979] 5-8-13 102 (b) PShanahan 4
(E Charpy, UAE) *ref to r* **14/1**

1m 10.62s (70.62) **11** Ran SP% **119.6**
CSF: £42.87; Tricast: £359.52.
Owner Pinnacle Dream Partnership **Bred** Eugene Matthews **Trained** Sessay, N Yorks

FOCUS
A good sprint handicap, but nothing could live with the progressive Addictive Dream, who looked value for more than double the winning margin. He's rated to the better view of last week's C&D win.

NOTEBOOK
Addictive Dream(IRE) shot around 5l clear when first asked for his effort, quickly sealing the race with over a furlong to run before understandably tiring. It does need pointing out he was allowed a soft lead - in contrast to when successful over 5f from 5lb lower the previous week - and he will have to prove he can cope more competition up front in better company, but there's a good chance he'll be up to the task. Now 2-2 since joining David Nicholls, he's already repaid his 90,000gns purchase price and there are plenty more options for him in Dubai, not least considering his versatility. Indeed, it's interesting to note he's 2-3 on Polytrack and his connections might want to try him on Tapeta. Whatever, at this rate he remains on course for World Cup night.
Internationaldebut(IRE) didn't get a clear run when behind Addictive Dream here the previous week so it was no surprise to see him fare better.
The Reaper(IRE) ◆, returning from 76 days off, was soon further back than ideal and covered more ground than any other rival, including nine meters more than the winner. He's capable of better.
Apache Crown(AUS), representing Singapore, didn't travel at all well through the middle stage of the race but finished most strongly. On this evidence he'll be well suited by a return to 7f.
Bohemian Melody disappointed off 11lb higher than when winning impressively in first-time blinkers at Doncaster in October, but he might be worth another chance. He never looked in the ideal spot after being restrained, having raced keenly early on, and had no chance of building up momentum when denied a clear run at a crucial stage.
Forjatt(IRE) shaped as though he needed the run after a 136-day break and should do better.
Green Beret(IRE) didn't go forward from his reappearance (behind Addictive Dream) but this might have come too soon and he's not one to give up on. (op 8/1)
Sir Reginald was well beaten after a 274-day break and has to prove he's still up to a three-figure mark.
Winker Watson offered little after being reluctant to load.

142a UAE 2000 GUINEAS TRIAL SPONSORED BY ETISALAT (CONDITIONS RACE) (TAPETA) 7f
4:25 (4:25) 3-Y-O

£19,354 (£6,451; £3,225; £1,612; £967; £645)

RPR

1 **Dark Matter (AUS)**[32] 4-9-4 107 TedDurcan 2 103
(S Burridge, Singapore) *trckd ldrs: rdn wf out: led ins fnl f: r.o wl* **16/1**

2 ½ **Kinglet (USA)**[92] [6788] 3-8-8 100 MickaelBarzalona 10 105+
(Mahmood Al Zarooni) *mid-div: r.o wl fnl 2f: nrst fin* **8/1**[3]

3 ¾ **Rassam (IRE)**[64] [7330] 3-8-8 97 FrankieDettori 3 102
(Saeed Bin Suroor) *sn led: rdn 2f out: hdd ins fnl f* **8/11**[1]

4 1 **Mehdi (IRE)**[82] [7026] 3-8-8 101 (t) WilliamBuick 14 99
(Brian Meehan) *trckd ldng gp: ev ch 1 1/2f out: one pce ins fnl f* **20/1**

5 ¼ **Surfer (USA)**[20] [7868] 3-8-8 99 RichardMullen 13 99
(S Seemar, UAE) *mid-div: chsd ldrs 2 1/2f out: one pce fnl f* **25/1**

6 ½ **Mickdaam (IRE)**[96] [6702] 3-8-9 80 ow1 ChristopheSoumillon 9 98+
(M F De Kock, South Africa) *towards rr of mid-div: rdn 3f out: r.o wl fnl 1 1/2f: nrst fin* **7/1**[2]

7 ¼ **Prepared**[139] [5454] 3-8-8 AhmedAjtebi 1 97+
(A Al Raihe, UAE) *s.i.s: nvr nr to chal but r.o fnl 1 1/2f* **50/1**

8 4 **Factory Time (IRE)**[20] [7868] 3-8-8 105 RoystonFfrench 11 86+
(A Al Raihe, UAE) *a mid-div* **16/1**

9 2 ¼ **Strait Of Zanzibar (USA)**[82] [7026] 3-8-8 104 ShaneFoley 12 80
(K J Condon, Ire) *trckd ldr tl 2 1/2f out: wknd fnl f* **20/1**

10 6 ¾ **Enjoy Dubai (ARG)**[195] 4-9-6 97 KShea 7 61+
(M F De Kock, South Africa) *settled towards rr: nvr able to chal* **16/1**

11 ¾ **Mabroor (USA)**[97] [6670] 3-8-8 83 RichardHills 5 59+
(Doug Watson, UAE) *towards rr of mid-div: n.d* **33/1**

12 ½ **That's Plenty (IRE)**[97] [6678] 3-8-8 PShanahan 8 58+
(E Charpy, UAE) *towards rr of mid-div: n.d* **66/1**

13 ¾ **Bible Black (IRE)**[97] [6680] 3-8-8 102 RyanMoore 4 56+
(G M Lyons, Ire) *nvr nr to chal* **7/1**[2]

14 ½ **Right To Dream (IRE)**[167] [4495] 3-8-8 91 MartinDwyer 6 55+
(Brian Meehan) *nvr nr to chal* **22/1**

1m 24.63s (-0.57)
WFA 3 from 4yo 18lb **14** Ran SP% **135.8**
CSF: £145.52.
Owner Hippocrates Stable **Bred** Bellagio Lodge Pty Ltd **Trained** Singapore

FOCUS
Only the third time this race has officially been named as a Guineas trial and it was held a week earlier than in 2011. Last season's one-two, Zanzamar and Splash Point, subsequently finished in the reverse order in the main event, while a year earlier Musir had taken this en-route to landing both the UAE Guineas and Derby. This latest running looked a pretty ordinary contest, but if the UAE 2000 Guineas - to be held over another furlong on February 9 - is of a similar standard then a few of these beaten runners will be worth a second look. The time was almost identical to the earlier 95-105 handicap, but there was a faster early pace thanks to the free-running favourite Rassam. The form is rated around the placed horses.

NOTEBOOK
Dark Matter(AUS) covered less ground than his rivals. This Singapore-trained colt had sweated up beforehand, but he showed a good attitude under pressure. He will not appeal in the Guineas, however. (op 14/1)
Kinglet(USA) ◆ covered 14 meters more than the winner and got going too late. The way he ran on strongly suggests he'll appreciate a return to 1m (winner over that trip at Kempton when last seen in October) and he could go close in the Guineas under a more sensible ride.
Rassam(IRE) got away with being headstrong when heavily punted on his debut in a 7f Kempton maiden in November - he just kept going to win by 6l - but not this time. Once more he was strongly supported and he's presumably well regarded, but he didn't settle in front and again carried his head high. Unless he learns to relax then he's going to struggle to fulfil his potential. (op Evs)
Mehdi(IRE) didn't lose too much ground from the widest draw and threatened to throw down a big challenge in the straight, but he didn't do enough. It was a difficult performance to read, but this was his first start on the surface and maybe he'll be happier back on turf. (op 16/1)
Surfer(USA) ◆ covered more ground than any of his rivals, including 17 metres more than the winner. This run went some way to confirming the promise he showed on his Dubai debut and it won't surprise if he runs well in the Guineas. (op 16/1)
Mickdaam(IRE) was last seen winning a York maiden for Richard Fahey over this trip in October. He shaped as though in need of the run, whilst also giving the impression he now needs further, and he could do better in the Guineas.
Prepared ◆ showed promise in two runs for Mahmood Al Zarooni and this was an eyecatching Dubai debut. He lost several lengths at the start but made up plenty of ground in the straight before his run flattened out near the line. There should be a good deal more to come and he'll be one to have on side if a nice price in the Guineas.

143a ETISALAT MY DATA PLAN (H'CAP) (TURF) 1m 4f 11y
5:00 (5:00) (95-105,105) 3-Y-O+

£42,580 (£14,193; £7,096; £3,548; £2,129; £1,419)

RPR

1 **Naqshabban (USA)**[82] [7029] 4-8-11 102 FrankieDettori 1 109+
(Mahmood Al Zarooni) *trckd ldrs: a gng wl: led 1f out: comf* **2/1**[1]

2 2 **Jedi**[298] 6-8-13 100 CSanchez 5 103
(A bin Huzaim, UAE) *sn led: kicked clr 2f out: hdd1f out: r.o but no ch w wnr* **25/1**

3 3 **Emirates Champion**[131] [5754] 6-9-1 102 (t) MickaelBarzalona 2 100+
(Saeed Bin Suroor) *mid-div on rail: r.o fnl 2 1/2f: nrst fin* **5/1**[3]

4 ½ **Ottoman Empire (FR)**[436] [7287] 6-8-13 100 JamieSpencer 4 97+
(David Simcock) *mid-div: smooth prog 3f out: r.o fnl 1 1/2f* **11/1**

5 2 ¼ **Glen's Diamond**[209] [3105] 4-9-0 105 PaulHanagan 10 99+
(Richard Fahey) *mid-div: t.k.h: kpt on same pce fnl 2f* **11/4**[2]

6 1 **Plantagenet (SPA)**[36] [7668] 5-8-11 99 MircoDemuro 9 90+
(G Arizkorreta Elosegui, Spain) *settled towards rr: nvr nr to chal but r.o fnl 2f* **25/1**

7 shd **Dr Faustus (IRE)**[7] [48] 7-8-13 100 (t) TadhgO'Shea 3 92+
(Doug Watson, UAE) *a mid-div* **25/1**

8 5 ½ **Montaff**[68] [7297] 6-9-1 102 JamesDoyle 12 85+
(Mick Channon) *settled towards rr: nvr able to chal* **20/1**

9 1 ½ **Royaaty (IRE)**[12] [7945] 6-8-13 100 PatCosgrave 11 81+
(M bin Shafya, UAE) *towards rr of mid-div: rdn 3 1/2f out: sn struggling* **20/1**

10 3 ¼ **Too Much Trouble**[298] 6-8-13 100 (t) WayneSmith 7 76+
(M Al Muhairi, UAE) *settled towards rr: n.d* **14/1**

11 3 **Fiery Lad (IRE)**[558] [3672] 7-9-2 104 KierenFallon 6 74
(Luca Cumani) *trckd ldng pair tl 3f out: sn wknd* **14/1**

12 1 ¾ **Goldplated (IRE)**[126] [5850] 4-8-10 101 ShaneFoley 8 69+
(John Joseph Murphy, Ire) *nvr bttr than mid-div* **12/1**

2m 34.39s (154.39)
WFA 4 from 5yo+ 4lb **12** Ran SP% **127.1**
CSF: £68.13; Tricast: £232.12.
Owner Godolphin **Bred** Darley **Trained** Newmarket, Suffolk

FOCUS
The form doesn't look anything special, but the winner is one to keep on side. Jedi took them along at a slow pace (sectionals for each quarter were 28.95, 55.44, 1.21.96, 1.47.90 and 2.11.02) and one of the few jockeys sensible enough to keep the leader within reach was Frankie Dettori. The form is rated around the runner-up.

NOTEBOOK
Naqshabban(USA) had plenty in his favour, but he's not one to underestimate and could prove a good purchase out of Luca Cumani's yard for 200,000gns. This was only his seventh start and a real plus was his straightforward attitude considering he twice refused to enter the stalls last year. He was having his first try at 1m4f, but this was not a severe stamina test and he would probably cope with a drop in trip. It's also quite possible he'll take to the Tapeta considering his sire's fantastic record with runners on an artificial surface (progeny include Street Sense and Zenyatta). Whatever the case, though, Naqshabban is open to plenty of improvement now he's maturing in the desired manner.
Jedi has rarely had conditions to suit since switching to Dubai but he had his chance this time. (op 20/1)
Emirates Champion was one of a few runners set too much to do. His three Carnival wins have been gained on Tapeta.
Ottoman Empire(FR), recently sold for 42,000gns, was a bit keen off the steady pace but plugged on and this was a promising return from a 436-day absence.
Glen's Diamond, having his first start since finishing well beaten in the King Edward VII Stakes at Royal Ascot last June, was plenty keen enough and covered more ground than the four who finished ahead of him. He should be able to build on this.
Plantagenet(SPA) ◆ was set a near impossible task and can be given another chance.

144a AL MAKTOUM CHALLENGE R1 SPONSORED BY ETISALAT (GROUP 3) (TAPETA) 1m
5:35 (5:35) 3-Y-O+

£77,419 (£25,806; £12,903; £6,451; £3,870; £2,580)

RPR

1 **Musir (AUS)**[130] [5777] 6-8-11 117 ChristopheSoumillon 4 122+
(M F De Kock, South Africa) *trckd ldrs: smooth prog 2 1/2f out: led 1f out: comf* **9/4**[2]

2 3 **Master Of Hounds (USA)**[215] [2950] 4-8-11 115 KShea 12 113+
(M F De Kock, South Africa) *settled towards rr: r.o wl fnl 2f: nrst fin* **16/1**

3 1 **Secrecy**[75] 7166 6-8-11 109............(p) KierenFallon 9 111
(Saeed Bin Suroor) *trckd ldrs: led 3f out: hdd 1f out: kpt on wl* **16/1**
4 1/2 **Mendip (USA)**[292] 1000 5-8-11 115............ FrankieDettori 1 110
(Saeed Bin Suroor) *mid-div: n.m.r 2f out: kpt on same pce fnl 1 1/2f* **7/4**[1]
5 3/4 **Derbaas (USA)**[7] 52 6-8-11 115............(t) RichardHills 2 108
(A Al Raihe, UAE) *trckd ldrs: ev ch 3f out: one pce 1 1/2f* **14/1**
6 shd **Dance And Dance (IRE)**[96] 6721 6-8-11 110............ JamieSpencer 3 108
(Ed Vaughan) *settled towards rr: nvr nr to chal but r.o fnl 2f* **12/1**
7 1 1/2 **Kavango (IRE)**[308] 828 5-8-11 106............ PatCosgrave 8 104
(M bin Shafya, UAE) *trckd ldrs tl 2 1/2f out: wknd fnl 1 1/2f* **40/1**
8 1/4 **Escape Route (USA)**[25] 7815 8-8-11 110............(t) RichardMullen 6 104
(S Seemar, UAE) *mid-div: rdn 3 1/2f out: kpt on same pce* **40/1**
9 1 **Le Drakkar (AUS)**[97] 6671 7-8-11 110............(t) AhmedAjtebi 5 101
(A bin Huzaim, UAE) *nvr bttr than mid-div* **40/1**
10 1 1/2 **Fanunalter**[110] 6369 6-8-11 117............ RyanMoore 10 98
(Marco Botti) *slowly away: settled in last: nvr nr to chal* **11/2**[3]
11 3/4 **Snaafy (USA)**[315] 756 8-8-11 110............(v) TadhgO'Shea 11 96
(M Al Muhairi, UAE) *towards rr of mid-div: nvr able to chal* **33/1**
12 15 1/2 **Xin Xu Lin (BRZ)**[292] 998 5-8-11 115............ MickaelBarzalona 7 60
(Mahmood Al Zarooni) *sn led: hdd 3f out: wknd qckly* **11/1**

1m 35.85s (-1.65) **12** Ran SP% **127.2**
CSF: £40.96.
Owner Sheikh Mohammed Bin Khalifa Al Maktoum **Bred** Sh Mohd Bin Khalifa Al Maktoum **Trained** South Africa

FOCUS
Over the years this has been the weakest of the three rounds, but in 2010 - the first running to be held at Meydan - it went to subsequent World Cup winner Gloria De Campeao. This latest edition saw a couple of the fancied runners underperform and it might be unwise to get carried away with the bare form. Xin Xu Lin took the field through the first quarter-mile in 25.86 and the half 48.77, but he weakened before the race got serious. The time at the 6f point was 1.12.35. The form is rated around the third.

NOTEBOOK
Musir(AUS) thrashed his rivals on this return to Dubai, with his jockey able to showboat in the final few yards. However, while he again showed he's capable of high-class form, he does have his limitations (winless in three starts at last season's Carnival) and it's questionable whether he's now improved. It seems he was simply better equipped to cope with this challenge than the runner-up. That's not to say he can't add to this, but he'll probably remain vulnerable back in Group 1 company. There's talk of him returning to turf, with the Duty Free his main goal. (op 5/2)
Master Of Hounds(USA) ◆ looks the one to take from the race. Last seen underperforming in the Belmont Stakes for Aidan O'Brien, he was reappearing over an inadequate trip but made rapid progress in the straight to take second. To put his finishing effort into context it's worth noting he was still 11th with only two furlongs left to run, while the winner, third, fourth and fifth were 2nd, 1st, 4th, and 6th respectively. He also covered nine metres more than the winner. Whether he can progress enough to take the World Cup remains to be seen, but he can surely improve when upped in trip and the second round of this challenge over just short of 1m2f on February 9 is the obvious target.
Secrecy found this tougher than Newmarket Listed race he won when last seen in October.
Mendip(USA), who took this last year, didn't run to his best after a lengthy absence. (op 15/8)
Derbaas(USA) looks to be coming to hand and could do better again next time.
Dance And Dance(IRE) didn't have the race run to suit. He needs the leaders to come back to him, which wasn't the case. (op 14/1)
Fanunalter looked likely to be suited by this track, but a slow start didn't bode well and he didn't travel with his usual enthusiasm. That, combined with the pace horses not coming back, resulted in his dismal showing.
Xin Xu Lin(BRZ) High-class performer in his native Brazil, winning five times between 6-12f, including on four occasions in Grade 1 company; lightly-raced since joining Godolphin, failing to make an impact in two runs at the Dubai Carnival; not seen since finishing last of 12 at Meydan in January 2012 (op 10/1 tchd 12/1)

145a ETISALAT 4G (H'CAP) (TURF) 1m 2f
6:15 (6:15) (100-110,110) 3-Y-0+
£46,451 (£15,483; £7,741; £3,870; £2,322; £1,548)

RPR
1 **Songcraft (IRE)**[121] 4-8-13 105............ SilvestreDeSousa 1 109
(Saeed Bin Suroor) *s.i.s: mid-div: smooth prog 2 1/2f out: led ins fnl f: comf* **13/2**[2]
2 3/4 **Belgian Bill**[131] 5754 4-8-10 102............(t) TedDurcan 2 104
(George Baker) *trckd ldrs: led 2f out: hdd ins fnl f: kpt on same pce* **12/1**
3 2 **Mikhail Glinka (IRE)**[88] 6910 5-9-6 110............(t) RyanMoore 9 108+
(H J Brown, South Africa) *mid-div: r.o wl fnl 1 1/2: nrst fin* **33/1**
4 1/4 **Rostrum (FR)**[198] 3532 5-9-5 109............ MickaelBarzalona 13 107+
(Mahmood Al Zarooni) *settled in rr: nvr nr to chal but r.o fnl 1 1/2f* **12/1**
5 shd **Nationalism**[124] 5934 5-9-2 106............ AhmedAjtebi 6 103+
(Mahmood Al Zarooni) *settled rr: r.o wl fnl 1 1/2f: nrst fin* **16/1**
6 3/4 **Alkimos (IRE)**[210] 3068 4-8-11 104............ FrankieDettori 4 99
(Saeed Bin Suroor) *trckd ldrs: n.m.r 2 1/2f out: r.o one pce fnl 1 1/2f* **10/11**[1]
7 nse **Topclas (FR)**[298] 6-9-3 107............(v) PatCosgrave 3 103
(M bin Shafya, UAE) *settled rr: kpt on same pce fnl 2f* **33/1**
8 2 **Rasmy**[97] 6671 5-8-13 102............ RichardHills 5 95
(M Al Muhairi, UAE) *nvr bttr than mid-div* **25/1**
9 1 **Zain Shamardal (IRE)**[35] 7682 4-8-8 100............ RoystonFfrench 12 90
(A Al Raihe, UAE) *trckd ldrs: ev ch 3f out: one pce fnl 2f* **16/1**
10 nse **Happy Valley (ARG)**[350] 328 6-9-3 107............ KShea 7 97
(M F De Kock, South Africa) *in rr of mid-div: nvr nr to chal* **28/1**
11 2 1/2 **St Moritz (IRE)**[7] 52 6-9-3 107............ AdrianNicholls 8 92
(David Nicholls) *sn led: hdd 2f out: sn struggling* **14/1**
12 12 **Hunting Tower (SAF)**[7] 53 10-9-3 107........(t) ChristopheSoumillon 11 68
(M F De Kock, South Africa) *a in rr* **10/1**[3]
13 2 1/2 **Summit Surge (IRE)**[418] 7523 8-9-4 108............(t) KierenFallon 10 64
(Luca Cumani) *trckd ldrs: ev ch 3 /2f out: sn wknd* **20/1**

2m 2.61s (122.61)
WFA 4 from 5yo+ 2lb **13** Ran SP% **126.6**
CSF: £81.29; Tricast: 2424.78. Placepot: £108.50 to a £1 stake. Pool of £6301.12 - 42.39 winning tickets. Quadpot: £24.40 to a £1 stake. Pool of £575.56 - 17.43 winning tickets..
Owner Godolphin **Bred** Darley **Trained** Newmarket, Suffolk

FOCUS
This looked a decent enough handicap and the fractions, set by St Moritz, were 27.04, 50.48, 1.14.49 and 1.38.73.

NOTEBOOK
Songcraft(IRE) ◆ was 2-2 when trained in France by Andre Fabre but had done his winning in relatively minor company on a soft surface. He sported the red cap here, suggesting he was the owner's third string, but showed he's pretty smart by defying a mark of 105 to extend his unbeaten record. It appeared he idled once he front and he can continue his progression, maybe into Group company in due course.
Belgian Bill, like Musir, who won the Al Maktoum Challenge on the card, was last seen competing in Turkey. This was a fine effort and he looks up to landing a similar race.
Mikhail Glinka(IRE) was continually denied a clear run at a crucial stage in the Canadian International when last seen, but he showed something like his true worth this time. He should do even better when faced with more of a stamina test.
Rostrum(FR) was another having his first start since leaving Andre Fabre, and he shaped nicely enough. (op 11-1)
Nationalism, now trained by Mahmood Al Zarooni but not in the Godolphin colours, didn't show himself to be obviously well handicapped on his first start since leaving John Gosden.
Alkimos(IRE), who had Frankie Dettori aboard, couldn't justify short odds. He hadn't been seen since finishing second in a Group 3 at Royal Ascot when trained by Luca Cumani last June and may have needed the run. (op 11-10)

84 LINGFIELD (L-H)
Friday, January 13

OFFICIAL GOING: Standard
Wind: light, half against Weather: dry and sunny

146 BLUE SQUARE WINTER CARNIVAL IPHONE APP (S) STKS 7f (P)
1:00 (1:00) (Class 6) 4-Y-0+ **£1,704** (£503; £251) **Stalls** Low

Form RPR
32-5 1 **Hinton Admiral**[7] 62 8-8-10 79............ JoeFanning 9 74
(Keith Dalgleish) *taken down early: mde all and grad crossed to inner rail: shkn up and wnt clr wl over 1f out: tiring and drvn fnl 100yds: a jst holding on* **5/4**[1]
265- 2 nk **Alhaban (IRE)**[48] 7557 6-8-10 61............ LiamKeniry 2 73
(Ronald Harris) *hld up in tch: effrt and wd bnd wl over 1f out: chsd clr wnr over 1f out: kpt on wl fnl 100yds: nvr quite getting to wnr* **8/1**[3]
25-3 3 4 **Eastern Gift**[10] 21 7-8-3 59............ PaulHainey(7) 7 62
(Gay Kelleway) *hld up in tch in rr: stl plenty to do and pushed along wl over 1f out: stuck bhd a wall of horses over 1f out tl ins fnl f: pushed along and kpt on to go 3rd towards fin: nvr able to chal* **20/1**
201- 4 nk **Stevie Gee (IRE)**[14] 7919 8-8-12 73............(p) RyanClark(3) 5 66
(Ian Williams) *in tch: chsd ldng pair wl over 2f out: rdn and unable qck jst over 2f out: plugged on same pce and wl hld fr over 1f out* **11/4**[2]
05-0 5 1 **The Which Doctor**[6] 85 7-9-1 65............(e) MartinHarley 8 64
(Richard Guest) *stdd s and dropped in bhd: rdn and effrt on inner over 1f out: kpt on same pce u.p fnl f: nvr trbld ldrs* **12/1**
46-1 6 2 3/4 **Divine Rule (IRE)**[7] 55 4-8-8 52............(b) CharlotteJenner(7) 3 56
(Laura Mongan) *hld up in tch: hdwy on outer to chse ldr wl over 2f out: pushed along and fnd nil over 1f out: wknd 1f out* **16/1**
36-3 7 19 **Sienna Blue**[6] 91 4-7-13 62 ow1............ JakePayne(7) 6
(Bill Turner) *chsd ldrs on outer: wnt 2nd 4f over 4f out tl wl over 2f out: sn struggling: lost tch wl over 1f out* **9/1**
050- 8 1 1/4 **Whats Your Story**[30] 7750 4-8-5 35............(t) RyanPowell(5) 1
(Murty McGrath) *chsd ldr tl over 4f out: lost pl u.p wl over 2f out: wl bhd fr wl over 1f out* **100/1**

1m 25.02s (0.22) **Going Correction** +0.225s/f (Slow) **8** Ran SP% **111.5**
Speed ratings (Par 101): **107,106,102,101,100 97,75,74**
toteswingers:1&2:£2.70, 1&3:£5.30, 2&3:£17.80 CSF £11.60 TOTE £2.20: £1.20, £1.10, £6.40; EX 15.30 Trifecta £149.20 Part won. Pool: £201.72 - 0.84 winning units..There was no bid for the winner.
Owner William Brand & Gordon McDowall **Bred** Gainsborough Stud Management Ltd **Trained** Carluke, S Lanarks

FOCUS
A modest seller.

147 FOREST ROW MAIDEN STKS 7f (P)
1:30 (1:31) (Class 5) 3-Y-0+ **£2,385** (£704; £352) **Stalls** Low

Form RPR
2- 1 **Discoverer (IRE)**[16] 7889 3-8-9 0............ NickyMackay 2 71+
(John Gosden) *mde all: rdn over 1f out: kpt on same pce u.p fnl f: a holding rival: rdn out* **1/7**[1]
0- 2 1/2 **Ashdown Lad**[24] 7835 3-8-9 0............ SteveDrowne 5 69
(William Jarvis) *chsd ldrs: rdn 2f out: chsd wnr over 1f out: kpt on under hands and heels riding and pressing wnr fnl 100yds: a hld* **10/1**[2]
3 2 **Yajber (USA)** 3-8-9 0............ MarcHalford 3 64
(Terry Clement) *chsd wnr tl hung lft u.p over 1f out: swtchd rt and styd on same pce fnl f* **12/1**[3]
4 2 1/4 **Beggar's Banquet (IRE)** 3-8-9 0............ ChrisCatlin 4 58
(George Baker) *in tch: pushed along over 4f out: clsd and chsd ldrs over 2f out: rdn and outpcd over 1f out: one pce and wl hld fnl f* **12/1**[3]
0- 5 19 **Norwood Lane**[16] 7889 3-8-9 0............ JohnFahy 6
(Peter Hedger) *sn outpcd in rr: lost tch over 2f out* **33/1**
6 19 **Lingtren** 4-9-13 0............ WilliamCarson 7
(Roger Ingram) *wnt rt s and v.s.a: clsd and chsd ldrs 4f out: rdn and wknd over 2f out: sn bhd* **66/1**

1m 26.09s (1.29) **Going Correction** +0.225s/f (Slow)
WFA 3 from 4yo 18lb **6** Ran SP% **116.4**
Speed ratings (Par 103): **101,100,98,95,73 52**
toteswingers:1&2:£1.60, 1&3:£2.30, 2&3:£3.40 CSF £3.08 TOTE £1.10: £1.02, £3.70; EX 3.50.Breeze On Bye was withdrawn. Price at time of withdrawal 25/1. Rule 4 does not apply.
Owner H R H Princess Haya Of Jordan **Bred** Darley **Trained** Newmarket, Suffolk

FOCUS
An ordinary maiden.

148 GOLF AT LINGFIELD PARK FILLIES' H'CAP 1m (P)
2:00 (2:01) (Class 5) (0-75,71) 4-Y-0+ **£2,385** (£704; £352) **Stalls** High

Form RPR
44-5 1 **Shared Moment (IRE)**[9] 31 6-8-8 61............(v) AmyRyan(3) 2 69+
(John Gallagher) *in tch: hdwy to chse ldr and swtchd rt jst over 2f out: rdn to ld and wnt clr over 1f out: idling fnl 100yds: a holding on: rdn out* **7/2**[1]
205- 2 3/4 **Abigails Angel**[23] 7843 5-8-7 57 oh1............ WilliamCarson 5 62
(Brett Johnson) *hld up in tch towards rr: rdn and hdwy to chse ldng pair 2f out: chsd clr wnr over 1f out tl ins fnl f: kpt on and chsd wnr again fnl 75yds: kpt on* **8/1**
213- 3 nk **Russian Ice**[23] 7842 4-9-7 71............(b) ShaneKelly 7 75
(Dean Ivory) *stdd after s: hld up in last pair: hdwy on outer over 2f out: drvn and chsd ldrs over 1f out: chsd wnr ins fnl f tl fnl 75yds: kpt on u.p* **4/1**[2]
203- 4 7 **Favorite Girl (GER)**[176] 4241 4-8-12 62............ LiamKeniry 3 50
(Michael Appleby) *dwlt: in tch towards rr: rdn and effrt on inner 2f out: outpcd by ldng trio and btn over 1f out: wnt modest 4th ins fnl f* **14/1**
106- 5 1 **Sweet Secret**[25] 7823 5-9-7 71............(b) FergusSweeney 1 57
(Jeremy Gask) *led: rdn and hdd over 1f out: sn btn: fdd 1f out* **4/1**[2]

111- **6** ¾ **Lucky Royale**14 7924 4-8-4 59 RaulDaSilva(5) 4 43
(Jeremy Gask) *t.k.h: chsd ldrs: rdn and unable qck wl over 1f out: wknd over 1f out and wl btn fnl f* **5/1**3

000- **7** 1 **Renoir's Lady**166 4584 4-8-7 57 DavidProbert 8 38
(Simon Dow) *in tch in midfield: rdn and outpcd wl over 1f out: no ch ent fnl f* **5/1**3

6/5- **8** 8 **Athenian Garden (USA)**31 7745 5-8-12 62 MartinHarley 6 25
(Richard Guest) *stdd s: hld up in rr: short-lived effrt on inner 2f out: sn wknd and wl btn over 1f out* **25/1**

060- **9** 1¼ **Ryedale Dancer (IRE)**49 6450 4-8-12 65 (t) RobertLButler(3) 9 25
(Richard Guest) *chsd ldr tl jst over 2f out: sn dropped out and wl bhd over 1f out* **16/1**

1m 38.04s (-0.16) **Going Correction** +0.225s/f (Slow) **9** Ran SP% **123.1**
Speed ratings (Par 100): **109,108,107,100,99 99,98,90,88**
toteswingers:1&2:£6.10, 1&3:£5.40, 2&3:£6.30 CSF £34.57 CT £121.40 TOTE £3.70: £1.10, £4.00, £2.10; EX 36.40 Trifecta £322.90 Part won. Pool: £436.42 - 0.20 winning units..
Owner Mark Benton **Bred** Mrs E R Cantillon **Trained** Chastleton, Oxon

FOCUS
Just a modest fillies' handicap.
Sweet Secret Official explanation: trainer's rep said mare was in season

149 LINGFIELDPARK.CO.UK MAIDEN STKS 1m 4f (P)
2:30 (2:30) (Class 5) 4-Y-O+ **£2,385** (£704; £352) **Stalls** Low

Form RPR
23- **1** **Bert The Alert**14 7921 4-9-3 0 FergusSweeney 8 67+
(Gary Moore) *sn led and set stdy gallop: pushed and qcknd clr 2f out: clr: pushed along and rdr looking arnd ins fnl f: rapidly being ct nr fin but a gng to hang on* **11/10**1

4- **2** nk **Broughton Sands**14 7921 4-8-12 0 StevieDonohoe 1 60+
(Willie Musson) *t.k.h: hld up in last pair: rdn: swtchd rt and wnt modest 4th wl over 1f out: looked wl hld tl str run u.p fnl 100yds: clsng rapidly nr fin* **7/4**2

3-5 **3** 2 **Vehement**11 10 6-9-2 0 JamieGoldstein 4 56
(Andy Turnell) *chsd ldrs: rdn to chse clr wnr 2f out: kpt on same pce fnl f* **20/1**

235/ **4** 2 **Mutanaker**22 6313 5-9-7 70 (p) JohnFahy 5 58
(Ed de Giles) *in tch: rdn to chse clr wnr jst over 2f out tl 2f out: outpcd and btn over 1f out: plugged on same pce fnl f* **10/1**3

5 6 **Chhota Naa** 4-9-3 0 DavidProbert 6 49
(Harry Dunlop) *s.i.s: rn green and pushed along at times in rr: in tch tl rdn and wknd 3f out: wl btn fnl 2f* **16/1**

405- **6** 4½ **Roanstar**206 2055 5-9-7 64 LiamKeniry 7 41
(Chris Gordon) *chsd ldrs: wnt 2nd 6f out tl jst over 2f out: sn wknd* **14/1**

6 **7** 44 **Las Hilanderas (USA)**1 137 4-8-12 0 WilliamCarson 3
(Stuart Williams) *chsd wnr tl 6f out: sn rdn: wknd wl over 2f out: wl bhd and virtually p.u ins fnl f: t.o* **12/1**

2m 37.03s (4.03) **Going Correction** +0.225s/f (Slow)
WFA 4 from 5yo+ 4lb **7** Ran SP% **118.1**
Speed ratings (Par 103): **95,94,93,92,88 85,55**
toteswingers:1&2:£2.20, 1&3:£5.10, 2&3:£6.90 CSF £3.41 TOTE £2.10: £1.70, £1.50; EX 4.80 Trifecta £20.10 Pool: £362.49 - 13.29 winning units..
Owner Herbert Curwen Hinds & Waddingham **Bred** Pleasure Palace Racing **Trained** Lower Beeding, W Sussex

FOCUS
An ordinary maiden in which the winner set a steady pace, although the time was 0.10 seconds quicker than the following Class 5 handicap.

150 THOUSANDS OF SPORTS EXPERIENCES AT BLUESQ.COM H'CAP 1m 4f (P)
3:00 (3:00) (Class 5) (0-70,70) 4-Y-O+ **£2,385** (£704; £352) **Stalls** Low

Form RPR
030- **1** **The Holyman (IRE)**39 7637 4-9-2 69 LiamKeniry 8 76
(Jo Crowley) *mde all: rdn and qcknd 2f out: kpt on wl fnl f* **7/2**3

163- **2** 1¼ **Sunset Place**199 2312 5-9-4 67 (p) SteveDrowne 3 72
(Jonathan Geake) *hld up in midfield: rdn and effrt over 1f out: drvn and styd on ins fnl f: wnt 2nd towards fin* **12/1**

543- **3** nk **Kames Park (IRE)**13 7939 10-9-1 67 RobertLButler(3) 4 72
(Richard Guest) *stdd s: hld up in last trio: hdwy on outer 3f out: rdn and chsd ldrs over 1f out: chsd wnr and drvn ins fnl f: no imp and lost 2nd towards fin* **7/1**

243- **4** nk **Strike Force**16 7901 8-9-4 70 (t) AdamBeschizza(3) 7 74
(Clifford Lines) *t.k.h: chsd ldr: rdn and unable qck 2f out: styd on same pce u.p fr over 1f out: lost 2 pls ins fnl f* **3/1**2

021- **5** 1¾ **Thundering Home**16 7903 5-8-12 66 (tp) DavidKenny(5) 2 67
(George Baker) *chsd ldrs: n.m.r and jostled jst over 2f out: swtchd ins and rdn wl over 1f out: styd on same pce fr over 1f out* **2/1**1

000- **6** 3½ **Broughtons Swinger**42 7603 5-9-0 63 StevieDonohoe 1 59
(Willie Musson) *chsd ldrs: rdn and unable qck ent fnl 2f: wknd 1f out* **5/1**

0/6- **7** 2 **Perfect Shot (IRE)**13 7939 6-9-5 68 AmirQuinn 6 60
(Jim Best) *hld up in last trio: outpcd over 2f out: rdn and hld hd awkwardly over 1f out: no imp* **16/1**

4/5- **8** 16 **Ayaarah (IRE)**151 5114 4-8-7 67 LukeRowe(7) 5 34
(Les Hall) *slowly away and flashing tail early: a bhd: rdn and lost tch over 3f out: wl bhd fnl 2f* **33/1**

2m 37.13s (4.13) **Going Correction** +0.225s/f (Slow)
WFA 4 from 5yo+ 4lb **8** Ran SP% **126.2**
Speed ratings (Par 103): **95,94,93,93,92 90,88,78**
toteswingers:1&2:£6.70, 1&3:£5.90, 2&3:£5.60 CSF £49.11 CT £293.87 TOTE £5.80: £2.10, £3.00, £3.10; EX 49.30 Trifecta £197.80 Pool: £577.41 - 2.16 winning units..
Owner Kilstone Limited **Bred** Old Carhue Stud **Trained** Whitcombe, Dorset

FOCUS
Another modestly run race and the time was 0.10 seconds slower than the earlier maiden. This was just an ordinary handicap.

151 USE CASH NOT VISA AT "LONDON 2012" H'CAP 1m 2f (P)
3:30 (3:30) (Class 6) (0-55,55) 4-Y-O+ **£1,704** (£503; £251) **Stalls** Low

Form RPR
343- **1** **Daniel Thomas (IRE)**15 7904 10-8-12 51 (tp) MartinHarley 9 60
(Richard Guest) *hld up in last trio: hdwy towards inner jst over 2f out: rdn and qcknd to ld ins fnl f: sn in command: comf* **9/2**2

623- **2** 1¼ **Regal Rave (USA)**16 7892 5-8-11 50 (v) JohnFahy 4 56
(Peter Hedger) *s.i.s: hld up in tch in rr: hdwy on inner over 2f out: switching rt and chsng ldrs 1f out: drvn ins fnl f and r.o to go 2nd towards fin* **3/1**1

054- **3** ½ **Prince Blue**16 7892 5-8-12 51 SamHitchcott 3 56
(John E Long) *led: rdn ent fnl 2f: hdd and nt pce of wnr ins fnl f: lost 2nd towards fin* **6/1**

30-0 **4** 1¼ **El Libertador (USA)**9 28 6-9-1 54 (b) ShaneKelly 7 57
(Eric Wheeler) *hld up in tch: hdwy on outer over 2f out: chsd ldrs and rdn over 1f out: drvn and styd on same pce fnl f* **12/1**

333- **5** ½ **Poppy Golightly**23 7851 5-8-6 52 JasonHart(7) 2 54
(Declan Carroll) *t.k.h: chsd ldrs: rdn and pressed ldr 2f out: stl ev ch 1f out: no ex and wknd fnl 100yds* **15/2**

420- **6** nk **Avon Supreme**16 7891 4-8-13 54 StevieDonohoe 14 55
(Gay Kelleway) *hld up in lst trio: rdn and effrt on outer over 1f out: kpt on fnl f: nvr trbld ldrs* **9/1**

300- **7** 2½ **Forbidden (IRE)**14 7930 9-8-9 51 (bt) AmyRyan(3) 5 47
(Ian McInnes) *hld up in tch in midfield: lost pl and towards rr 2f out: tried to rally u.p over 1f out: no hdwy 1f out and wl hld after* **20/1**

0/6- **8** ¾ **Equine Science**26 7805 5-8-10 49 AWhelan 13 43
(Jane Chapple-Hyam) *t.k.h: hld up in midfield: hdwy to chse ldrs 7f out: rdn jst over 2f out: wknd over 1f out* **11/2**3

004- **9** 2¼ **Ponte Di Rosa**25 7822 4-8-8 54 RaulDaSilva(5) 6 44
(Michael Appleby) *t.k.h: hld up wl in tch: rdn and unable qck 2f out: wknd over 1f out* **20/1**

004- **10** 1¾ **Ossie Ardiles (IRE)**156 4920 4-8-13 54 LiamKeniry 10 40
(Michael Appleby) *t.k.h: chsd ldr tl 2f out: sn rdn: wknd over 1f out* **12/1**

/00- **11** 11 **Confide In Me**15 7910 8-8-8 47 WilliamCarson 11 11
(Mark Hoad) *in tch in midfield: rdn and dropped to rr 2f out: sn wknd: bhd and eased ins fnl f* **40/1**

2m 8.89s (2.29) **Going Correction** +0.225s/f (Slow)
WFA 4 from 5yo+ 2lb **11** Ran SP% **122.0**
Speed ratings (Par 101): **99,98,97,96,96 95,93,93,91,90 81**
toteswingers:1&2:£3.40, 1&3:£7.00, 2&3:£5.10 CSF £18.67 CT £84.62 TOTE £3.60: £1.20, £2.30, £2.30; EX 19.70 Trifecta £64.90 Pool: £349.07 - 3.98 winning units..
Owner Rakebackmypoker.com **Bred** Lawn Stud **Trained** Stainforth, S Yorks

FOCUS
The time was slow, but Daniel Thomas was still able to come from well off the pace and was a cosy winner.

152 PLAY DA VINCI DIAMONDS AT BLUESQ.COM/GAMES H'CAP 5f (P)
4:00 (4:00) (Class 6) (0-65,66) 4-Y-O+ **£1,704** (£503; £251) **Stalls** High

Form RPR
20-1 **1** **Jimmy Ryan (IRE)**7 59 11-9-3 66 6ex (t) RaulDaSilva(5) 7 75
(Tim McCarthy) *taken down early: trckd ldr: pushed rt jst over 2f out: jnd ldrs over 1f out: rdn to ld ins fnl f: r.o wl: pushed out* **7/2**2

224- **2** ¾ **Blown It (USA)**46 7566 6-9-7 65 ShaneKelly 6 71
(Keith Dalgleish) *hld up in tch in last trio: hdwy on inner 2f out: pressed ldrs ins fnl f: styd on but a jst hld fnl 75yds* **3/1**1

241- **3** ½ **Cliffords Reprieve**24 7829 4-9-0 58 (b) WilliamCarson 10 63+
(Eric Wheeler) *in tch towards rr: nt clr run wl over 1f out: hdwy to chse ldrs jst ins fnl f: keeping on same pce and hld whn nt clr run cl home* **4/1**3

00-2 **4** ¾ **Sherjawy (IRE)**7 59 8-9-1 59 SamHitchcott 9 61
(Zoe Davison) *in tch towards rr: rdn and effrt on outer over 1f out: kpt on wl ins fnl f: nt rch ldrs* **8/1**

400- **5** shd **Decider (USA)**16 7897 9-9-4 62 (v1) ChrisCatlin 5 63
(Ronald Harris) *taken down early: led: rdn over 1f out: hdd ins fnl f: no ex* **16/1**

336- **6** 2¼ **Grand Stitch (USA)**16 7897 6-8-10 59 (v) NeilFarley(5) 2 52
(Declan Carroll) *chsd ldrs: rdn and edgd rt jst over 2f out: no ex u.p over 1f out: wknd 1f out* **6/1**

026- **7** ½ **Super Frank (IRE)**13 7943 9-8-9 53 ow1 (b) JamieGoldstein 3 45
(Zoe Davison) *awkward leaving stalls: in tch: rdn and effrt on inner over 1f out: no imp ins fnl f* **16/1**

00-0 **8** 4½ **Darwin Star**2 122 4-8-11 55 (p) StevieDonohoe 4 30
(Dean Ivory) *w ldr tl rdn and wknd over 1f out: bhd and eased wl ins fnl f* **10/1**

59.54s (0.74) **Going Correction** +0.225s/f (Slow) **8** Ran SP% **113.5**
Speed ratings (Par 101): **103,101,101,99,99 96,95,88**
toteswingers:1&2:£2.80, 1&3:£3.30, 2&3:£2.70 CSF £14.21 CT £42.25 TOTE £3.20: £1.10, £2.00, £1.30; EX 11.20 Trifecta £23.50 Pool: £684.56 - 21.53 winning units..
Owner Mrs D H McCarthy **Bred** Barronstown Stud And Orpendale **Trained** Godstone, Surrey

FOCUS
A modest sprint handicap.
T/Plt: £13.80 to a £1 stake. Pool:£57,617.22 - 3,037.52 winning tickets T/Qpdt: £6.30 to a £1 stake. Pool:£5,399.39 - 627.70 winning tickets SP

102WOLVERHAMPTON (A.W) (L-H)
Friday, January 13

OFFICIAL GOING: Standard
Wind: Almost nil Weather: clear

153 BLUE SQUARE WINTER CARNIVAL IPHONE APP H'CAP (DIV I) 7f 32y(P)
4:10 (4:11) (Class 6) (0-60,60) 4-Y-O+ **£1,704** (£503; £251) **Stalls** High

Form RPR
506- **1** **Drive Home (USA)**106 6488 5-9-4 57 (p) BarryMcHugh 3 70
(Noel Wilson) *trckd ldrs: rdn 2f out: swtched lft to ins rail over 1f out: sn chalng: led ins fnl f: styd on* **13/2**

0-62 **2** 1 **Crocodile Bay (IRE)**3 113 9-8-2 46 oh1 (p) CharlesEddery(5) 7 56
(Richard Guest) *a.p: str chal fr over 1f out: styd on: nt quite gng pce of wnr towards fin* **7/1**

500/ **3** ½ **Shaluca**419 7529 5-9-2 55 MartinLane 2 64
(Ed McMahon) *led: rdn whn pressed over 1f out: hdd ins fnl f: kpt on same pce towards fin* **5/1**3

225- **4** 1 **Michael's Nook**33 7728 5-9-0 58 LMcNiff(5) 10 64
(David Barron) *hld up: hdwy on outer 3f out: rdn and wanted to lugg lft whn chsng ldrs over 1f out: styd on towards fin: nt quite gng pce to mount serious chal* **10/3**2

460- **5** 2½ **Desert Hunter (IRE)**135 5622 9-8-7 53 KatieDowson(7) 6 53
(Micky Hammond) *midfield: lost pl 4f out: pushed along over 2f out: kpt on over 1f out: nt pce to trble ldrs* **25/1**

630- **6** 2½ **Piccolo Express**119 6138 6-9-2 55 MickyFenton 8 48
(Brian Baugh) *midfield: effrt to chse ldrs over 3f out: one pce over 1f out* **9/1**

252- **7** 2 **Pulsatilla**15 7913 4-9-6 59 TomEaves 1 46
(Bryan Smart) *wnt lft s and s.i.s: racd in rr div and pushed along: nvr gng pce to get competitive* **11/4**1

000- **8** nk **Born To Be Achamp (BRZ)**106 6490 6-9-4 57 (p) FrannyNorton 9 44
(Geoffrey Harker) *bhd: nvr able to rch ldrs* **20/1**

050- **9** 6 **Fortunelini**25 7822 7-9-7 60 TomMcLaughlin 12 30
(Frank Sheridan) *chsd ldrs tl pushed along and wknd 2f out* **25/1**

0/-0 **10** 5 **Weet In Nerja**[8] 45 6-8-7 **46**...............(b[1]) FrankieMcDonald 4
(Ken Wingrove) *midfield: pushed along 4f out: wknd 3f out* **200/1**
000- **P** **Stoneacre Joe Joe**[24] 7829 4-8-8 **47** oh1 ow1......... RobbieFitzpatrick 5
(Peter Grayson) *dwlt: a outpcd and bhd: t.o whn p.u ins fnl f* **125/1**
1m 30.07s (0.47) **Going Correction** +0.20s/f (Slow) **11** Ran SP% **116.0**
Speed ratings (Par 101): **105,103,103,102,99 96,94,93,86,81**
toteswingers:1&2:£8.40, 1&3:£7.60, 2&3:£4.70 CSF £48.08 CT £250.94 TOTE £14.70: £5.80, £2.00, £3.10; EX 60.90.
Owner Wilson Downes Kennedy Tobin **Bred** Moyglare Stud **Trained** Middleham, N Yorks
■ Stewards' Enquiry : Barry McHugh two-day ban: used whip with excessive frequency (Jan 27-28)
FOCUS
There was a lively market for this minor handicap. The pace was not very strong and the first three were always prominent.
Pulsatilla Official explanation: jockey said filly ducked left leaving stalls
Stoneacre Joe Joe Official explanation: trainer said gelding had a breathing problem

154 BLUE SQUARE WINTER CARNIVAL IPHONE APP H'CAP (DIV II) 7f 32y(P)
4:40 (4:40) (Class 6) (0-60,66) 4-Y-0+ **£1,704** (£503; £251) **Stalls** High

Form RPR
001- **1** **Cheers**[14] 7923 4-9-7 **59**.................... FrankieMcDonald 4 68+
(Oliver Sherwood) *trckd ldrs: rdn 2f out: led jst over 1f out: r.o: a doing enough cl home* **3/1**[1]
360- **2** ¾ **Transmit (IRE)**[14] 7930 5-9-6 **58**...............(b) RobertWinston 9 65
(Tim Easterby) *hld up in midfield: hdwy 2f out: styd on to press wnr wl ins fnl f: a looked hld* **5/1**
40-0 **3** ¾ **Kyncraighe (IRE)**[8] 46 4-8-0 **45**...............(tp) LeonnaMayor(7) 10 50
(Joseph Tuite) *stdd s: hld up: hdwy over 2f out: r.o ins fnl f: jst hld by front 2* **66/1**
5-11 **4** 3 **Dashing Eddie (IRE)**[1] 136 4-9-11 **66** 12ex...............(p) JulieBurke(3) 5 63
(Kevin Ryan) *w ldr: rdn whn stl chalng over 1f out: hung lft ins fnl f: no ex fnl 75yds* **7/2**[2]
50-0 **5** 2 **Anjomarba (IRE)**[4] 102 5-9-7 **59**...............(v[1]) HayleyTurner 1 50
(Conor Dore) *led: hdd 5f out: lost pl and outpcd over 3f out: kpt on same pce and no imp fr over 1f out* **7/1**
/23- **6** 5 **Only Ten Per Cent (IRE)**[17] 7886 4-9-1 **53**............... FrannyNorton 2 31
(J R Jenkins) *racd keenly: prom: led 5f out: rdn and hdd jst over 1f out: wknd fnl 110yds* **9/2**[3]
10-5 **7** 4 **Monsieur Pontaven**[12] 7 5-9-3 **55**...............(b) LeeNewman 11 22
(Robin Bastiman) *chsd ldrs and racd wd: chalng 3 wd 3f out: wknd jst over 1f out: eased whn wl btn ins fnl f* **10/1**
006- **8** hd **Valentino Swing (IRE)**[23] 7843 9-8-2 **45**...............(p) RyanPowell(5) 3 12
(Michael Appleby) *s.s: a bhd* **20/1**
00-3 **9** 3¾ **Pytheas (USA)**[9] 39 5-9-5 **57**...............(p) JoeFanning 6 14
(Michael Attwater) *prom: n.m.r and squeezed out after 1f: chsd ldrs after: pushed along 3f out: wknd 2f out* **8/1**
000- **10** 2 **Odd Ball (IRE)**[15] 7911 5-8-12 **50**...............(v[1]) TomEaves 7
(Lisa Williamson) *s.v.s: a bhd* **100/1**
00-2 **11** 95 **Arrivaderci**[10] 20 4-9-0 **57**...............(p) CharlesEddery(5) 8
(Richard Guest) *s.v.s: a bhd: t.o fnl 3f* **20/1**
1m 30.78s (1.18) **Going Correction** +0.20s/f (Slow) **11** Ran SP% **126.8**
Speed ratings (Par 101): **101,100,99,95,93 87,83,83,78,76**
toteswingers:1&2:£5.30, 1&3:£106.10, 2&3:£59.30 CSF £19.40 CT £877.05 TOTE £7.70: £2.90, £3.50, £27.30; EX 31.50.
Owner John Duddy **Bred** Honeypuddle Stud **Trained** Upper Lambourn, Berks
■ Stewards' Enquiry : Frankie McDonald two-day ban: used whip with excessive frequency (Jan 27-28)
FOCUS
The first three pulled clear in the second division of this handicap.
Valentino Swing(IRE) Official explanation: jockey said gelding missed the break
Pytheas(USA) Official explanation: vet said gelding finished lame behind

155 ENJOY THE PUNTERS PACKAGE GROUP OFFER H'CAP 5f 216y(P)
5:10 (5:10) (Class 6) (0-55,55) 4-Y-0+ **£1,704** (£503; £251) **Stalls** Low

Form RPR
645- **1** **Consistant**[127] 5864 4-9-0 **53**.................... AdamKirby 11 65
(Brian Baugh) *hld up: hdwy and swtchd rt over 1f out: r.o to ld wl ins fnl f: readily* **8/1**
405- **2** 1½ **Rightcar**[13] 7942 5-8-12 **51**.................... RobbieFitzpatrick 10 58
(Peter Grayson) *s.i.s: hld up: hdwy on inner wl over 1f out: led jst over 1f out: hdd wl ins fnl f: hld cl home* **17/2**
533- **3** ¾ **Mr Skipiton (IRE)**[95] 6765 7-9-1 **54**.................... TomMcLaughlin 12 59+
(Terry Clement) *hld up: hdwy over 2f out: ev ch over 1f out: nt qckn fnl 75yds* **13/2**[2]
06-0 **4** ¾ **White Shift (IRE)**[2] 123 6-8-10 **49**.................... JoeFanning 9 51
(Paul Howling) *hld up in rr: hdwy over 1f out: styd on towards fin: nt rch ldrs* **14/1**
034- **5** nk **Young Simon**[16] 7897 5-8-12 **51**...............(v) IanMongan 7 52
(George Margarson) *midfield: effrt to chse ldrs 3f out: styd on same pce ins fnl f* **11/4**[1]
606- **6** 1 **Hambleton**[84] 6999 5-9-0 **53**.................... TomEaves 3 51
(Bryan Smart) *racd keenly in midfield: hdwy to chse ldrs over 2f out: rdn over 1f out: one pce ins fnl f* **7/1**[3]
000- **7** 1 **Simple Rhythm**[33] 7728 6-8-8 **52**...............(p) RyanPowell(5) 4 47
(John Ryan) *trckd ldrs: rdn and outpcd wl over 1f out: kpt on same pce ins fnl f: no imp* **25/1**
00-0 **8** ¾ **Bachelor Knight (IRE)**[5] 101 4-9-1 **54**...............(t) DuranFentiman 6 46
(Suzzanne France) *prom: led jst over 2f out: hdd jst over 1f out: wknd fnl 110yds* **16/1**
06-6 **9** 7 **Takajan (IRE)**[5] 101 5-8-9 **55**...............(p) RachealKneller(7) 13 25
(Mark Brisbourne) *prom: u.p and lost pl 2f out: wknd over 1f out* **13/2**[2]
04-0 **10** 8 **Morermaloke**[5] 101 4-8-13 **52**.................... BarryMcHugh 5
(Ian McInnes) *led: hdd jst over 2f out: wknd wl over 1f out: eased whn wl btn ins fnl f* **8/1**
1m 16.07s (1.07) **Going Correction** +0.20s/f (Slow) **10** Ran SP% **115.0**
Speed ratings (Par 101): **100,98,97,96,95 94,92,91,82,71**
toteswingers:1&2:£10.40, 2&3:£5.40, 1&3:£10.60 CSF £73.02 CT £363.65 TOTE £8.60: £2.50, £2.10, £2.80; EX 98.00.
Owner Miss J A Price **Bred** Bearstone Stud **Trained** Audley, Staffs
FOCUS
They went a decent pace in this modest sprint handicap and the decisive winner came from some way back.
Morermaloke Official explanation: jockey said gelding hung right

156 GREAT OFFERS AT WOLVERHAMPTON-RACECOURSE.CO.UK H'CAP 1m 5f 194y(P)
5:40 (5:40) (Class 6) (0-65,65) 4-Y-0+ **£1,704** (£503; £251) **Stalls** High

Form RPR
115- **1** **Jamarjo (IRE)**[16] 7903 5-9-6 **59**.................... RobertWinston 7 70+
(Steve Gollings) *racd keenly: chsd ldr after 2f: led 2f out: rdn over 1f out: r.o ins fnl f: in command towards fin* **5/2**[1]
/06- **2** 1½ **Maison Brillet (IRE)**[32] 3225 5-9-9 **65**...............(p) RyanClark(3) 2 74
(Clive Drew) *in tch: rdn to chse wnr over 1f out: ev ch ins fnl f: nt qckn towards fin* **33/1**
04-2 **3** 1¾ **Leyte Gulf (USA)**[7] 63 9-9-5 **58**.................... DaneO'Neill 5 65+
(Chris Bealby) *s.i.s: hld up: rdn 2f out: hdwy over 1f out: styd on to take 3rd fnl 150yds: nt rch front 2* **5/2**[1]
524- **4** 2 **Straversjoy**[16] 7903 5-9-12 **65**.................... AdamKirby 8 69
(Reg Hollinshead) *in tch: rdn wl over 1f out: one pce fnl f* **11/2**[2]
103/ **5** 1¾ **Mexican Bob**[32] 7847 9-9-4 **60**.................... SimonPearce(3) 1 61
(James Evans) *led: rdn and hdd 2f out: stl chsng ldrs 1f out: wknd fnl 110yds* **20/1**
500- **6** ¾ **Art Thief**[16] 7903 4-8-4 **54**.................... RyanPowell(5) 4 54
(Michael Appleby) *hld up: rdn 2f out: nvr able to get on terms* **8/1**
43-5 **7** ¾ **Irish Jugger (USA)**[12] 4 5-9-11 **64**.................... JamesMillman 6 63
(Rod Millman) *hld up: rdn 3f out: edgd lft over 1f out: nvr able to get on terms w ldrs* **14/1**
003- **8** shd **Fantino**[49] 6666 6-9-8 **61**...............(t) PaddyAspell 3 60
(Pat Murphy) *prom: rdn and nt qckn 2f out: wknd fnl f* **7/1**[3]
3m 10.8s (4.80) **Going Correction** +0.20s/f (Slow)
WFA 4 from 5yo+ 6lb **8** Ran SP% **110.5**
Speed ratings (Par 101): **94,93,92,91,90 89,89,89**
toteswingers:1&2:£15.60, 2&3:£14.20, 1&3:£1.50 CSF £85.12 CT £211.94 TOTE £4.50: £2.10, £10.70, £1.80; EX 72.00.
Owner Northern Bloodstock Racing **Bred** Frank Dunne **Trained** Scamblesby, Lincs
FOCUS
They went a steady pace in this staying handicap but a progressive type scored with something in hand.

157 THOUSANDS OF SPORTS EXPERIENCES AT BLUESQ.COM H'CAP 5f 216y(P)
6:10 (6:10) (Class 4) (0-85,82) 4-Y-0+ **£4,204** (£1,251; £625; £312) **Stalls** Low

Form RPR
21-3 **1** **Woolfall Sovereign (IRE)**[7] 64 6-9-6 **79**.................... IanMongan 11 89
(George Margarson) *hld up: hdwy 2f out: r.o to ld fnl 150yds: a doing enough cl home* **5/2**[1]
51-4 **2** nk **Tamareen (IRE)**[11] 11 4-8-13 **77**...............(p) ShaneBKelly(5) 6 86
(Richard Fahey) *chsd ldrs: rdn over 1f out: str chal ins fnl f: hld cl home* **8/1**
221- **3** 1¼ **Tislaam (IRE)**[14] 7928 5-9-3 **76**...............(p) RobertWinston 7 81
(Alan McCabe) *chsd ldr: led 2f out: rdn over 1f out: hdd fnl 150yds: no ex fnl strides* **13/2**
40-5 **4** 1½ **Pick A Little**[7] 64 4-9-7 **80**.................... DaneO'Neill 10 80
(Hughie Morrison) *midfield: rdn to chse ldrs 2f out: no imp and one pce over 1f out* **9/2**[2]
30-6 **5** 1 **Restless Bay (IRE)**[7] 64 4-9-4 **77**...............(e) AdamKirby 5 74
(Reg Hollinshead) *hld up: rdn and hdwy ins fnl f: styd on: nt gng pce to rch ldrs* **5/1**[3]
61-0 **6** 3 **Frequency**[7] 64 5-9-6 **79**...............(b) JoeFanning 3 66
(Keith Dalgleish) *s.i.s: in rr: pushed along over 1f out: no imp* **20/1**
04-4 **7** ½ **Punching**[10] 19 8-8-13 **72**.................... HayleyTurner 1 58
(Conor Dore) *led: hdd 2f out: rdn over 1f out: wknd ins fnl f* **22/1**
02-1 **8** 1 **Ghostwing**[10] 24 5-9-9 **82** 6ex.................... FergusSweeney 2 65
(James Evans) *chsd ldrs: pushed along over 2f out: wknd wl over 1f out* **5/1**[3]
1m 14.75s (-0.25) **Going Correction** +0.20s/f (Slow) **8** Ran SP% **113.6**
Speed ratings (Par 105): **109,108,106,104,103 99,98,97**
toteswingers:1&2:£6.30, 2&3:£7.40, 1&3:£1.80 CSF £23.08 CT £115.06 TOTE £4.30: £1.80, £3.30, £2.30; EX 28.80.
Owner Graham Lodge Partnership **Bred** Saud Bin Saad **Trained** Newmarket, Suffolk
FOCUS
A decent handicap. It was run a good tempo and the improving favourite delivered from off the pace.

158 STAY AT THE WOLVERHAMPTON HOLIDAY INN CLAIMING STKS 1m 141y(P)
6:40 (6:40) (Class 5) 4-Y-0+ **£2,264** (£673; £336; £168) **Stalls** Low

Form RPR
334- **1** **Munsarim (IRE)**[49] 7542 5-9-8 78...............(b[1]) JoeFanning 6 88
(Keith Dalgleish) *chsd ldrs: drifted rt and led fr jst over 1f out: styd on and in control ins fnl f* **7/2**[3]
22-5 **2** ¾ **Standpoint**[12] 5 6-9-4 83...............(p) AdamKirby 5 82
(Reg Hollinshead) *chsd ldr: led 2f out: drifted rt fr over 1f out: sn hdd: kpt on ins fnl f but hld* **7/4**[1]
120- **3** 2¾ **Elijah Pepper (USA)**[14] 7922 7-8-9 78.................... LMcNiff(5) 4 72
(David Barron) *hld up: niggled along 3f out: rdn over 2f out: chsd ldrs over 1f out: no imp on front 2 ins fnl f* **3/1**[2]
345- **4** 4 **Saharia (IRE)**[25] 7823 5-9-4 68...............(v) HayleyTurner 1 67
(Michael Attwater) *hld up in tch: outpcd fr over 1f out: no imp fnl f* **10/1**
12-2 **5** nk **Sunnyside Tom (IRE)**[11] 12 8-8-9 80...............(p) ShaneBKelly(5) 3 62
(Richard Fahey) *led: rdn and hdd 2f out: ev ch wl over 1f out: wknd fnl 100yds* **9/2**
5-5 **6** 2¼ **Ravanchi**[4] 103 8-8-3 0.................... AndrewMullen 2 46?
(Frank Sheridan) *fly-jmpd leaving stalls: in rr: pushed along and lft wl bhd fr over 2f out* **200/1**
1m 52.46s (1.96) **Going Correction** +0.20s/f (Slow) **6** Ran SP% **111.4**
Speed ratings (Par 103): **99,98,95,92,92 90**
toteswingers:1&2:£1.10, 2&3:£1.70, 1&3:£2.50 CSF £9.90 TOTE £3.30: £1.10, £1.90; EX 10.40.
Owner Joseph Leckie & Sons Ltd **Bred** Shadwell Estate Company Limited **Trained** Carluke, S Lanarks
FOCUS
Four of the runners had BHA ratings between 78 and 83 in this claimer, but the first two pulled clear in a steadily run race.

159 HOTEL & CONFERENCING MEDIAN AUCTION MAIDEN STKS 1m 141y(P)
7:10 (7:12) (Class 6) 3-4-Y-0 **£1,617** (£481; £240; £120) **Stalls** Low

Form RPR
1 **Frosty Berry** 3-8-1 0.................... NickyMackay 6 65+
(Marco Botti) *trckd ldrs: upsides 4f out: rdn over 1f out: led and hung lft ins fnl f: r.o: hld on wl cl home* **12/1**

5- 2 nk **Somemothersdohavem**143 5353 3 -8-10 RyanPowell(5) 7 69
(John Ryan) *prom after 1f: upsides 4f out: str chal whn hmpd ins fnl f: r.o: jst hld cl home* 50/1

520- 3 3/4 **Cool Hand Luke (IRE)**37 5565 3 -8-671 RichardKingscote 2 68
(Tom Dascombe) *led: pushed along whn pressed 3f out: rdn over 1f out: hdd ins fnl f: stl ev ch after: one pce cl home* 13/8²

50-2 4 1 **Roedean (IRE)**7 61 3 -8-174 FrannyNorton 1 60
(Jamie Osborne) *trckd ldrs: pushed along over 3f out: nt qckn 2f out: swtchd rt over 1f out: styd on ins fnl f: nt pce to chal front trio* 11/10¹

5 3 1/2 **Ma Kellys (IRE)** 3 -8-60 BarryMcHugh 8 57
(Micky Hammond) *s.i.s: racd keenly: hld up: pushed along 3f out: kpt on fnl f: nvr able to chal* 33/1

0 6 hd **Tigresa (IRE)**70 7257 3 -8-10 JoeFanning 5 52
(Mark Johnston) *racd keenly: in tch: effrt to chse ldrs over 2f out: one pce fnl f* 11/1³

000- 7 3 1/2 **Little Red Minx (IRE)**98 7777 3 -8-162 DavidProbert 9 44
(Peter Chapple-Hyam) *prom: lost pl over 4f out: wknd over 2f out* 25/1

05/ 8 2 1/2 **Omega Centauri**406 7682 4 -9-80 MartinLane 3 42
(Ed McMahon) *hld up: pushed along over 2f out: nvr able to get on terms w ldrs* 66/1

0-5 9 2 3/4 **Homeward Strut**7 61 3 -8-80 ow2 RobbieFitzpatrick 4 39
(Frank Sheridan) *racd keenly: trckd ldrs for 1f: stdd after 1f: hld up: toiling fr over 2f out* 100/1

1m 53.51s (3.01) **Going Correction** +0.20s/f (Slow)
WFA 3 from 4yo 22lb 9Ran SP% 113.0
Speed ratings (Par 101): **94,93,93,92,89 88,85,83,81**
toteswingers:1&2:£53.60, 2&3:£31.80, 1&3:£5.20 CSF £430.39 TOTE £15.50 : £2.90 , £11.80 , £1.20; EX 502.00 .
Owner J H Widdows **Bred** J H Widdows **Trained** Newmarket, Suffolk
■ Stewards' Enquiry : Nicky Mackay two-day ban: careless riding (Jan 28,30)

FOCUS
The favourite was laboured and a newcomer beat an outsider in this ordinary maiden. The first four were clear of the rest.

160 PLAY DA VINCI DIAMONDS AT BLUESQ.COM/GAMES H'CAP 1m 4f 50y (P)
7:40 (7:40) (Class 7) (0-50,50) 4-Y-0+ £1,704 (£503; £251) Stalls Low

Form RPR

30-2 1 **Black Iceman**4 105 4 -8-950 SimonPearce(3) 1 63+
(Lydia Pearce) *chse ldrs: wnt 2nd over 1f out: styd on to ld fnl 110yds: in command towards fin* 10/11¹

463- 2 1 3/4 **Mayan Flight (IRE)**24 7836 4 -8-846 DavidProbert 6 56
(Tony Carroll) *prom: led under 4f out: over 3 l clr 2f out: edgd rt ins fnl f: hdd fnl 110yds: hld after* 3/1²

005- 3 7 **Dazzling Begum**45 7573 7 -8-1246 BarryMcHugh 7 45
(Des Donovan) *hld up: hdwy 3f out: rdn over 2f out: styd on to take 3rd towards fin: no imp on front 2* 16/1

00-0 4 1 3/4 **Yossi (IRE)**7 66 8 -8-645 (p) CharlesEddery(5) 9 41
(Richard Guest) *s.s: hdwy after 1f: w ldr over 9f out: led briefly 4f out: u.p and over 3 l down 2f out: lost 2nd over 1f out: no ex fnl f* 20/1

/55- 5 6 **Time To Play**37 7654 7 -8-950 (v¹) LeonnaMayor(7) 5 36
(Gary Brown) *hld up: outpcd 3f out: plugged on at one pce over 1f out: nvr a threat* 7/2³

000- 6 2 **Libre**16 7891 12 -8-1145 (p) JoeFanning 2 28
(Violet M Jordan) *hld up: hdwy 3f out: plugged on at one pce fnl 2f: nvr a threat* 33/1

00-6 7 8 **Nesnaas (USA)**7 58 11 -8-645 (bt) JemmaMarshall(5) 3 15
(Alastair Lidderdale) *s.i.s: rdn along early: hdwy into midfield after 2f: rdn and dropped bhd 6f out: toiling after* 50/1

00- 8 16 **King Of Connacht**111 6357 9 -8-1145 (p) RobbieFitzpatrick 8
(Mark Wellings) *in tch: rdn over 3f out: outpcd over 2f out: wknd wl over 1f out: t.o* 40/1

000- 9 14 **Fitzwarren**23 7851 11 -8-1145 (tp) AndrewMullen 4
(Alan Brown) *led: hdd 4f out: sn rdn and wknd: t.o* 100/1

2m 43.11s (2.01) **Going Correction** +0.20s/f (Slow)
WFA 4 from 7yo+ 4lb 9Ran SP% 118.6
Speed ratings (Par 97): **101,99,95,94,90 88,83,72,63**
toteswingers:1&2:£1.50, 2&3:£9.00, 1&3:£8.40 CSF £3.81 CT £25.18 TOTE £2.10 : £1.10 , £2.00 , £2.90; EX 5.60 .
Owner P J Stephenson **Bred** Graham Wilson **Trained** Newmarket, Suffolk

FOCUS
Five of the runners were on long losing runs and the other four were still maidens in this weak handicap.
T/Jkpt: Not won. T/Plt: £87.20 to a £1 stake. Pool of £95,615.96 - 799.54 winning tickets. T/Qpdt: £11.00 to a £1 stake. Pool of £11,937.56 - 800.05 winning tickets. DO

161 - 174a (Foreign Racing) - See Raceform Interactive

146 LINGFIELD (L-H)
Saturday, January 14

OFFICIAL GOING: Standard
Wind: Nil Weather: Sunny, crisp

175 BET ON TODAY'S FOOTBALL AT BLUESQ.COM CLAIMING STKS 1m 2f (P)
11:55 (11:55) (Class 6) 4-Y-0+ £1,704 (£503; £251) Stalls Low

Form RPR

0-51 1 **Aviso (GER)**5 104 8 -8-257 DominicFox(3) 7 68
(David Evans) *hld up in 4th: pushed along over 4f out: clsd u.p fr 2f out: drvn ahd jst ins fnl f: hung rt but styd on* 17/2

305- 2 1 1/2 **Shabak Hom (IRE)**14 7214 5 -9-174 MartinLane 4 75
(David Simcock) *rrd bdly s: hld up in last and wl off the pce: rdn over 4f out: grad clsd u.p 2f out: c wd in st: styd on to take 2nd nr fin* 15/2

0/0- 3 1/2 **Brunston**28 7803 6 -9-1184 (t) JamieSpencer 3 84
(Roger Charlton) *chsd clr ldng pair: rdn over 3f out: clsd 2f out: chal 1f out: nt qckn* 11/8¹

00- 4 1/2 **Ivory Jazz**172 4404 5 -9-380 MartinHarley 6 75?
(Richard Guest) *led and stretched field out: rdn over 3f out: sn pressed: hdd and fdd jst ins fnl f* 12/1

51-3 5 3 1/2 **Ajdaad (USA)**7 85 5 -8-467 SAJackson(7) 5 62
(Alan McCabe) *rrd s: hld up in 6th and wl off the pce: nudged along 3f out: nvr able to make contact w ldrs* 11/2³

01-2 6 hd **King's Colour**7 85 7 -9-168 KierenFallon 2 66
(Brett Johnson) *trckd ldr and clr of rest: gng best whn chal 3f out: drvn 2f out: hung rt and fnd nil over 1f out: fdd* 7/2²

6- 7 6 **Broughton Place**15 7920 4 -8-20 JamieMackay 1 43
(Willie Musson) *fractious preliminaries: dwlt: hld up in 5th and wl off the pce: pushed along over 3f out: no prog* 100/1

2m 6.26s (-0.34) **Going Correction** +0.075s/f (Slow)
WFA 4 from 5yo+ 2lb 7Ran SP% 110.7
Speed ratings (Par 101): **104,102,102,102,99 99,94**
Tote Swingers: 1&2 £7.30, 2&3 £2.90 CSF £64.12 TOTE £8.90 : £4.40 , £4.00 ; EX 84.00 .
Owner Mrs E Evans **Bred** Gestut Schlenderhan **Trained** Pandy, Monmouths

FOCUS
Form to treat with caution. The pace was unusually strong and the field was soon strung out.

176 LINGFIELDPARK.CO.UK H'CAP 1m 2f (P)
12:25 (12:25) (Class 5) (0-70,70) 4-Y-0+ £2,385 (£704; £352) Stalls Low

Form RPR

453- 1 **Kiss A Prince**26 7816 6 -9-467 (b) ShaneKelly 4 76+
(Dean Ivory) *hld up in last pair: prog on wd outside over 2f out: sweeping run to ld jst ins fnl f: r.o wl* 9/2²

211- 2 2 **Trip Switch**16 7904 6 -9-063 ow1 AdamKirby 8 68+
(George Prodromou) *hld up towards rr on outer: prog over 2f out: hrd rdn to cl on ldrs 1f out: styd on but outpcd by wnr* 7/2¹

014- 3 1 **Yourinthewill (USA)**17 7901 4 -9-469 StephenCraine 7 72
(Daniel Mark Loughnane) *hld up in last quartet: prog over 2f out: on heels of ldrs wl over 1f out gng strly: drvn and r.o to take 3rd nr fin: nt pce to chal* 12/1

536- 4 1/2 **The Mongoose**96 6755 4 -9-570 MartinLane 2 72
(David Evans) *stdd s: hld up in last quartet: stdy prog on inner fr 3f out gng wl: drvn over 1f out: styd on but nt pce to threaten* 10/1

22-2 5 nk **Marvo**10 35 8 -9-063 (b) EddieAhern 3 64
(Mark H Tompkins) *hld up in midfield: smooth prog over 2f out: trckd ldr wl over 1f out gng easily: shkn up and fnd nil* 8/1³

24-3 6 1 1/4 **Bull Five**8 65 5 -9-063 (b¹) SteveDrowne 9 62
(Nick Littmoden) *t.k.h: trckd ldng pair: rdn over 2f out: nt qckn over 1f out: fdd ins fnl f* 50/1

521- 7 1 **Prince Of Thebes (IRE)**17 7892 11 -8-756 (p) JohnFahy 1 53
(Michael Attwater) *trckd ldng pair: rdn on inner over 2f out: tried to chal over 1f out: fdd fnl f* 12/1

200- 8 2 3/4 **Khun John (IRE)**17 7901 9 -8-1059 StevieDonohoe 11 50
(Willie Musson) *hld up in last pair: detached and pushed along 4f out: nvr on terms after: modest late prog* 16/1

31-1 9 3/4 **Whodunit (UAE)**8 60 8 -9-770 (b) ChrisCatlin 6 60
(Peter Hiatt) *led: rdn over 2f out: hdd & wknd jst ins fnl f* 9/2²

10- 10 2 1/2 **Calypso Cay**24 7839 4 -9-570 JoeFanning 10 55
(Mark Johnston) *trckd ldr tl wknd tamely wl over 1f out* 12/1

00-0 11 14 **Ibiza Sunset (IRE)**10 31 4 -8-1364 KierenFallon 5 21
(Brendan Powell) *hld up in midfield: pushed along 4f out: wknd 3f out: eased and t.o* 16/1

106- 12 7 **Abriachan**35 7715 5 -9-467 LiamKeniry 12
(Noel Quinlan) *trckd ldng pair tl wknd rapidly over 3f out: sn t.o* 25/1

2m 6.08s (-0.52) **Going Correction** +0.075s/f (Slow)
WFA 4 from 5yo+ 2lb 12Ran SP% 119.4
Speed ratings (Par 103): **105,103,102,102,101 100,100,97,97,95 84,78**
Tote Swingers: 1&2 £4.10, 1&3 £12.60, 2&3 £9.90 CSF £20.75 CT £180.38 TOTE £6.00 : £1.80 , £1.90, £4.30 ; EX 22.60 Trifecta £217.20 Part won. Pool: £293.59 - 0.41 winning units.
Owner A Pryer **Bred** Baroness, Magnusson, Myriade, Redmyre **Trained** Radlett, Herts

FOCUS
They went a fair enough pace, helping to set the race up for those waited with, but the front two were forced wider than ideal and might be a bit better than result indicates.
Ibiza Sunset (IRE) Official explanation: jockey said gelding had no more to give

177 MARSH GREEN H'CAP 1m 2f (P)
1:00 (1:02) (Class 3) (0-95,95) 4-Y-0+ £6,792 (£2,021; £1,010 ; £505) Stalls Low

Form RPR

221- 1 **Emerald Wilderness (IRE)**31 7759 8 -8-1387 (p) EddieAhern 11 96
(Robert Cowell) *dwlt sltly: sn in midfield: trckd ldrs in 6th over 2f out gng easily: prog on outer to ld jst ins fnl f: sn clr: rdn out* 15/2

23-0 2 1 **Follow The Flag (IRE)**7 36 8 -8-781 oh2 (be) JohnFahy 4 88
(Alan McCabe) *towards rr: rdn and struggling over 4f out: rdr persisted and rspnse fnlly c on outer over 1f out: r.o wl to take 2nd nr fin and cl on wnr* 40/1

126- 3 1 1/2 **Raucous Behaviour (USA)**16 7908 4 -8-283 RaulDaSilva(5) 8 87+
(George Prodromou) *racd on outer: trckd ldrs: over 2f out: rdn to dispute ld jst over 1f out to jst ins fnl f: outpcd* 7/2¹

011- 4 1/2 **Tinshu (IRE)**28 7802 6 -9-391 (p) DaneO'Neill 9 94
(Derek Haydn Jones) *prom on inner: gng strly over 2f out: effrt to dispute ld jst over 1f out: hdd and nt qckn jst ins fnl f* 4/1²

61-0 5 hd **Opus Maximus (IRE)**10 36 7 -8-781 oh2 HayleyTurner 5 84
(Conor Dore) *stdd s: hld up in last pair: stl there over 2f out: pushed along over 1f out: reminder and r.o fnl f: hopeless task* 16/1

/50- 6 nk **Cashelgar (IRE)**149 5218 6 -9-295 CharlesEddery(5) 2 97
(Richard Guest) *dwlt: t.k.h: hld up towards rr: 9th and pushed along over 2f out: no prog tl styd on wl fnl f: nrst fin* 66/1

060- 7 1 3/4 **Layline (IRE)**28 7801 5 -9-189 RobertWinston 7 88
(Gay Kelleway) *hld up in midfield: rdn in 8th over 2f out: effrt on inner over 1f out: one pce fnl f* 12/1

000- 8 nk **Majuro (IRE)**126 5929 8 -8-882 (t) WilliamCarson 10 80
(Richard Guest) *led at gd pce: kicked on over 3f out: hdd jst over 1f out: wknd ins fnl f* 40/1

310- 9 1 1/4 **Fakhuur**19 7877 4 -8-581 oh4 ChrisCatlin 1 76
(Clive Brittain) *hld up in last pair: rdn and struggling over 4f out: effrt on inner over 1f out: sn no prog* 25/1

241- 10 1/2 **Tadabeer**15 7921 4 -8-081 oh3 RyanPowell(5) 6 75
(Ian Williams) *trckd ldr to 2f out: sn wknd* 9/2³

06-1 11 1/2 **Thunderstruck**10 36 7 -8-1286 (p) IanMongan 12 79
(Scott Dixon) *pressed ldng pair: rdn over 3f out: lost pl and wknd wl over 1f out* 10/1

006- 12 3/4 **Mawaakef (IRE)**52 7523 4 -8-1187 (p) KierenFallon 13 79
(J R Jenkins) *trckd ldng trio: drvn over 2f out: wknd over 1f out* 14/1

04-0 13 3 **Honey Of A Kitten (USA)**7 90 4 -8-581 oh1 MartinLane 3 67
(David Evans) *hld up: a wl in rr: rdn and no prog 3f out* 22/1

2m 3.62s (-2.98) **Going Correction** +0.075s/f (Slow)
WFA 4 from 5yo+ 2lb 13Ran SP% 116.1
Speed ratings (Par 107): **114,113,112,111,111 111,109,109,108,108 107,107,104**
Tote Swingers: 1&2 £25.90, 1&3 £4.80, 2&3 £26.70 CSF £286.11 CT £1230.76 TOTE £7.20 : £2.10, £9.10 , £1.70 ; EX 231.80 Trifecta £161.20 Part won. Pool: £196.12 - 0.10 winning units.
Owner Mrs J Morley & Khalifa Dasmal **Bred** Mrs Joan Murphy **Trained** Six Mile Bottom, Cambs

FOCUS
A good handicap and the pace was decent thanks to Majuro. Consequently, the time was significantly quicker than the two lesser races at this trip earlier on the card, and the way events unfolded very much suited Emerald Wilderness, essentially a bridle horse who needs the leaders to come back.

NOTEBOOK
Emerald Wilderness(IRE) had idled in front and only scrambled home when successful over C&D off 4lb lower last time, but this race was set up more favourably and he followed up in good style. He was formerly quite smart and is not far off returning to his best. (op 13-2)
Follow The Flag(IRE), 2lb out of the handicap, was niggled along a fair way out, as is so often the case, but he ran on strongly in the straight. He's difficult to predict. (tchd 50-1)
Raucous Behaviour(USA) was committed a fair way out and was also caught wider than ideal, but it seemed he was struggling to hold his position and needed plenty of use making of him on this drop in trip from 1m4f. He plugged on and, although not matching the late speed of the front two, saw it out better than Tinshu for third. (op 3-1 tchd 11-4)
Tinshu(IRE)'s finishing effort was a bit disappointing after she enjoyed a ground-saving trip into the straight. She had won her last couple of starts over C&D, but the latest came in a Listed race and she was 11lb higher than two starts ago. (op 9-2 tchd 7-2)
Opus Maximus(IRE), another 2lb out of the handicap, was given his usual hold-up ride but didn't pick up well enough. The way the race unfolded shouldn't have been a problem considering the runner-up came from similarly far back. (tchd 18-1)
Cashelgar(IRE), reported to have lost his action when last seen in August, made a respectable debut for new connections. (tchd 80-1)
Tadabeer found this tougher than the maiden won here last time, especially being 3lb out of the handicap, but even so he was a little disappointing. (op 6-1 tchd 13-2)

178 BLUE SQUARE SPRINT SERIES (ROUND 2) H'CAP (QUALIFIER) (DIV I) — 6f (P)
1:35 (1:42) (Class 5) (0-70,70) 4-Y-0+ **£2,726** (£805; £402) **Stalls** Low

Form RPR
01-0 **1** **The Strig**[7] [91] 5-9-3 **66** WilliamCarson 5 75
(Stuart Williams) *pressed ldr at mod pce: rdn to ld over 1f out: hld on as pack clsd nr fin* **10/1**
05-4 **2** ½ **Diamond Vine (IRE)**[7] [88] 4-8-10 **59** (p) JoeFanning 7 66
(Ronald Harris) *trckd ldrs: effrt 2f out: rdn and styd on to take 2nd ins fnl f: a hld* **6/1**[3]
065- **3** nk **Showboating (IRE)**[14] [7941] 4-9-2 **70** (tp) RaulDaSilva(5) 6 76+
(Alan McCabe) *hld up in last quartet off a mod pce: awkward and nt qckn bnd 2f out: r.o fnl f: fin wl* **4/1**[2]
365- **4** nk **Roman Strait**[17] [7893] 4-9-4 **67** DaneO'Neill 2 72
(Michael Blanshard) *trckd ldng pair: rdn 2f out: disp 2nd on inner fnl f: one pce nr fin* **13/2**
44-4 **5** nk **Fantasy Fighter (IRE)**[7] [87] 7-8-8 **57** JohnFahy 4 61
(John E Long) *ref to go to post tl dismntd and dragged along: tk fierce hold early: hld up bhd ldrs: rdn over 1f out: kpt on but nvr chal* **10/1**
1-52 **6** nk **Efistorm**[7] [87] 11-9-1 **64** JimmyFortune 8 67
(Conor Dore) *trckd ldng pair: rdn 2f out: disp 2nd 1f out: nt qckn* **15/2**
140- **7** 1 **Nubar Boy**[227] [2609] 5-9-3 **66** (v) MartinLane 3 66
(David Evans) *dwlt: towards rr off a mod pce: rdn 2f out: kpt on at same pce fr over 1f out* **20/1**
0-51 **8** hd **Lastkingofscotland (IRE)**[5] [102] 6-9-1 **64** (b) HayleyTurner 10 63+
(Conor Dore) *stdd s and sn swtchd to inner: hld up in last quartet: pushed along 2f out: keeping on but no ch whn short of room nr fin* **7/2**[1]
000- **9** nk **Johnstown Lad (IRE)**[17] [7893] 8-9-6 **69** (bt) ShaneKelly 11 67
(Daniel Mark Loughnane) *a in last trio: pushed along and no prog 2f out: reminder fnl f: kpt on* **25/1**
6-10 **10** 1 **Dickie Le Davoir**[3] [122] 8-9-0 **68** (b) CharlesEddery(5) 9 63
(Richard Guest) *nt that wl away: pushed along in last pair bef 1/2-way: nvr a factor* **22/1**
600- **11** 2 **Overwhelm**[63] [7395] 4-8-13 **62** (t) JimCrowley 1 51
(Andrew Reid) *led at mod pce: rdn and hdd over 1f out: wknd v rapidly last 150yds* **50/1**

1m 13.21s (1.31) **Going Correction** +0.075s/f (Slow) **11** Ran SP% **114.7**
Speed ratings (Par 103): **94,93,92,92,92 91,90,90,89,88 85**
Tote Swingers: 1&2 £16.90, 1&3 £10.90, 2&3 £6.10 CSF £63.92 CT £281.96 TOTE £13.70: £4.20, £2.70, £1.20; EX 115.40 TRIFECTA Not won..
Owner Brian Piper & David Cobill **Bred** Old Mill Stud **Trained** Newmarket, Suffolk
FOCUS
They didn't go that quick and the time was the slowest of three races at the trip, including 0.59 second off the other division.

179 BLUE SQUARE SPRINT SERIES (ROUND 2) H'CAP (QUALIFIER) (DIV II) — 6f (P)
2:10 (2:10) (Class 5) (0-70,70) 4-Y-0+ **£2,726** (£805; £402) **Stalls** Low

Form RPR
22-1 **1** **Speak The Truth (IRE)**[7] [87] 6-8-12 **66** (p) NathanAlison(5) 1 76
(Jim Boyle) *wl plcd in 4th in modly run r: chsd wnr on inner 2f out: shkn up to chal 1f out: narrow ld ins fnl f: pushed out* **15/2**
60-1 **2** hd **Captain Dimitrios**[7] [88] 4-8-12 **61** (v) MartinLane 2 70
(David Evans) *led at mod pce: rdn over 1f out: narrowly hdd ins fnl f: styd on but jst hld* **13/2**[3]
060- **3** 1¾ **Aldermoor (USA)**[30] [7767] 6-9-6 **69** WilliamCarson 7 73
(Stuart Williams) *trckd ldrs in 5th off mod pce: effrt 2f out: chsd ldng pair over 1f out: styd on but no imp* **13/2**[3]
50-3 **4** 1½ **Waabel**[7] [88] 5-8-13 **62** MartinHarley 8 61
(Richard Guest) *stdd s: t.k.h and hld up in 6th: effrt 2f out but nvr gng pce to threaten as ldrs qcknd away* **3/1**[1]
00-5 **5** ¾ **Chjimes (IRE)**[7] [88] 8-8-9 **58** (b) HayleyTurner 10 55+
(Conor Dore) *stdd s and swtchd ins: t.k.h and hld up in last pair off mod pce: swtchd rt and effrt over 1f out: styd on but no ch* **17/2**
040- **6** 1½ **Dead Cool**[58] [7448] 4-9-3 **66** EddieAhern 5 58
(Robert Cowell) *rrd s: hld up in rr off mod pce: effrt 2f out: no real prog* **12/1**
30-4 **7** 1 **Riflessione**[8] [62] 6-9-5 **68** (v) JoeFanning 11 57
(Ronald Harris) *pressed ldr tl wknd tamely 2f out* **20/1**
0-00 **8** nk **Forty Proof (IRE)**[8] [62] 4-8-11 **65** (v) RaulDaSilva(5) 6 53
(Alan McCabe) *settled in last trio off mod pce: rdn and no prog 2f out* **14/1**
12-6 **9** nse **Rio Royale (IRE)**[7] [87] 6-9-1 **64** (p) JimCrowley 3 51
(Amanda Perrett) *chsd ldng pair: rdn to dispute 2nd 2f out: wknd over 1f out* **6/1**[2]
00-2 **10** nk **Memphis Man**[3] [122] 9-8-4 **56** DominicFox(3) 4 42
(David Evans) *a in last trio off mod pce: nvr a factor* **14/1**

1m 12.62s (0.72) **Going Correction** +0.075s/f (Slow) **10** Ran SP% **114.0**
Speed ratings (Par 103): **98,97,95,93,92 90,89,88,88,88**
Tote Swingers: 1&2 £4.60, 1&3 £11.00, 2&3 £6.60 CSF £54.29 CT £340.80 TOTE £6.70: £2.40, £2.50, £2.20; EX 34.60 Trifecta £143.80 Pool: £342.14 - 1.76 winning units..
Owner Inside Track Racing Club **Bred** Gerard Mulligan **Trained** Epsom, Surrey
FOCUS
Again, they didn't go a quick early pace, but the time was 0.59 seconds faster than the first leg. Speak The Truth (off 4lb lower) and Captain Dimitrios (off 5lb lower) had each won a division of the first round of the Blue Square Sprint Series over C&D the previous week, and they dominated in what was an intriguing clash.
Riflessione Official explanation: jockey said gelding hung right

180 FOREST ROW H'CAP — 1m (P)
2:40 (2:40) (Class 4) (0-85,88) 3-Y-O **£4,204** (£1,251; £625; £312) **Stalls** High

Form RPR
421- **1** **Bronze Angel (IRE)**[17] [7889] 3-9-5 **83** HayleyTurner 5 89+
(Marcus Tregoning) *trckd ldr's mod pce: shkn up to ld over 1f out: hrd rdn to hold on fnl f* **1/1**[1]
11-1 **2** ½ **Mr Red Clubs (IRE)**[10] [32] 3-9-5 **88** RaulDaSilva(5) 4 93+
(Tim Pitt) *hld up in last pair off mod pce: prog on outer to take 3rd jst over 1f out but ldng pair already gone: hrd rdn and r.o to take 2nd nr fin: too much to do* **7/2**[2]
651- **3** ½ **Shabora (IRE)**[63] [7396] 3-8-12 **79** DominicFox(3) 2 82
(Roger Varian) *led: dictated modest pce tl wound it up over 2f out: narrowly hdd over 1f out: nt qckn and lost 2nd nr fin* **9/2**[3]
454- **4** 3½ **Millibar (IRE)**[17] [7889] 3-8-8 **72** (p) ChrisCatlin 6 67
(Nick Littmoden) *hld up in 4th: rdn whn pce lifted over 2f out: outpcd sn after* **16/1**
251- **5** 2 **King Of Wing (IRE)**[123] [6019] 3-9-0 **78** EddieAhern 3 68
(Jim Boyle) *trckd ldng pair: pushed along whn pce lifted over 2f out: wknd over 1f out* **15/2**
000- **6** hd **Baltic Fizz (IRE)**[29] [7813] 3-8-7 **71** oh3 WilliamCarson 1 61
(Mrs K Burke) *hld up in last pair: drvn whn pce lifted over 2f out: sn btn* **25/1**

1m 39.71s (1.51) **Going Correction** +0.075s/f (Slow) **6** Ran SP% **111.9**
Speed ratings (Par 99): **95,94,94,90,88 88**
Tote Swingers: 1&2 £1.90, 1&3 £2.20, 2&3 £2.50 CSF £4.70 TOTE £1.90: £1.10, £2.30; EX 4.90.
Owner Lady Tennant **Bred** Rihana Partnership **Trained** Lambourn, Berks
FOCUS
A fair handicap in which three progressive types finished well clear, despite the pace being modest.

181 LINGFIELDPARK.CO.UK MAIDEN STKS — 6f (P)
3:15 (3:16) (Class 5) 3-Y-O **£2,385** (£704; £352) **Stalls** Low

Form RPR
64- **1** **Switzerland (IRE)**[85] [6991] 3-9-3 0 JoeFanning 2 82+
(Mark Johnston) *trckd ldng trio: shkn up 2f out: clsd to ld jst ins fnl f: r.o wl* **4/1**[2]
2- **2** 1¾ **Al Freej (IRE)**[50] [7540] 3-8-9 0 DominicFox(3) 1 71+
(Roger Varian) *dwlt: t.k.h and sn rcvrd to trck ldrs: shkn up and rn green wl over 1f out: r.o after to take 2nd nr fin: no ch to chal* **10/11**[1]
342- **3** 1¼ **Sujet Bellagio**[17] [7889] 3-9-3 80 ShaneKelly 3 72
(Brian Meehan) *trckd ldr: led 2f out: hdd and outpcd jst ins fnl f* **4/1**[2]
3- **4** ¾ **Vale Of Lingfield (IRE)**[59] [7435] 3-9-3 0 AdamKirby 10 70
(John Best) *dwlt: sn rcvrd to trck ldrs: shkn up 2f out: styd on same pce after* **12/1**[3]
5 2¼ **Marinus (IRE)** 3-9-3 0 LiamKeniry 6 62
(Sylvester Kirk) *pressed ldng pair to over 1f out: steadily fdd* **80/1**
502- **6** 2 **Reve Du Jour (IRE)**[15] [7925] 3-8-12 60 [1] MartinHarley 8 51
(Alan McCabe) *plld hrd: sn led: hdd 2f out: wknd over 1f out* **20/1**
6- **7** 1 **Cambridge Duchess**[108] [6441] 3-8-9 0 RyanClark(3) 4 48+
(Stuart Williams) *dwlt: hld up and sn in rr: jst pushed along fr 2f out and kpt on steadily at one pce* **33/1**
8 ½ **Strike A Pose (IRE)** 3-8-12 0 HayleyTurner 11 46+
(Jim Boyle) *hld up in rr: nudged along and sme prog on inner fr 2f out: nt disgracd: sddle slipped* **50/1**
05- **9** 1¾ **Rainbow Riches (IRE)**[16] [7906] 3-8-5 0 NedCurtis(7) 5 41
(Roger Curtis) *nvr beyond midfield: dropped to rr and btn over 2f out* **200/1**
00- **10** ½ **Mrs Cash (IRE)**[31] [7749] 3-8-12 0 DavidProbert 9 39
(Sylvester Kirk) *hld up in rr and racd on outer: no prog over 2f out* **66/1**
6- **11** 4 **Nip And Tuck**[17] [7889] 3-9-3 0 JimCrowley 12 31
(William Jarvis) *a in last pair: no ch fnl 2f* **14/1**
60- **12** 19 **Stormin Gordon (IRE)**[249] [1981] 3-8-12 0 EddieAhern 7
(Noel Quinlan) *racd wd in midfield: wknd over 2f out: sn eased and t.o* **80/1**

1m 12.99s (1.09) **Going Correction** +0.075s/f (Slow) **12** Ran SP% **120.9**
Speed ratings (Par 97): **95,92,91,90,87 84,83,82,80,79 74,48**
Tote Swingers: 1&2 £2.10, 1&3 £2.80, 2&3 £1.70 CSF £7.91 TOTE £4.80: £1.80, £1.10, £1.40; EX 10.70 Trifecta £35.00 Pool: £618.94 - 13.06 winning units..
Owner Sheikh Majid Bin Mohammed al Maktoum **Bred** Rabbah Bloodstock Limited **Trained** Middleham Moor, N Yorks
FOCUS
Hard to know the exact worth of this form, but it looked a good sprint maiden, especially for the time of year.
Strike A Pose(IRE) Official explanation: jockey said saddle slipped

182 PLAY RAINBOW RICHES AT BLUESQ.COM MEDIAN AUCTION MAIDEN STKS — 1m (P)
3:45 (3:47) (Class 6) 3-Y-O **£1,704** (£503; £251) **Stalls** High

Form RPR
033- **1** **All Nighter (IRE)**[31] [7752] 3-9-3 70 ShaneKelly 9 73+
(Brian Meehan) *prom: trckd ldr over 4f out: led wl over 2f out: kicked 4 l clr over 1f out: tied up ins fnl f: jst hld on* **2/1**[1]
2 hd **Prussian** 3-8-12 0 JoeFanning 1 68+
(Mark Johnston) *chsd ldrs but rn green: outpcd fr 3f out: styd on again 2f out: tk 2nd 1f out: clsd on wnr rapidly nr fin: jst failed* **5/2**[2]
0- **3** 5 **Bramshill Lass**[96] [6744] 3-8-12 0 JimCrowley 10 56
(Amanda Perrett) *towards rr: outpcd 3f out: styd on fr over 1f out to win bunch fin for 3rd* **14/1**
564- **4** ½ **Fugitive Motel (IRE)**[151] [5142] 3-9-3 70 JamieSpencer 5 59
(Peter Chapple-Hyam) *t.k.h: hld up bhd ldrs tl allowed to ld after 2f: hdd wl over 2f out: wknd over 1f out* **4/1**[3]
6-6 **5** ¾ **Pink Evie**[8] [61] 3-8-12 0 (t) StevieDonohoe 8 53?
(Gay Kelleway) *dwlt: towards rr: outpcd 3f out: drvn and kpt on fr over 1f out* **150/1**
5 **6** nse **Sweetest Friend (IRE)**[10] [34] 3-8-12 0 (p) LiamKeniry 4 52?
(J S Moore) *dwlt: sn in tch: chsd clr ldng pair over 2f out to over 1f out: wknd* **50/1**

02- **7** ½ **Chankillo**[35] 7709 3-9-3 0 .... EddieAhern 2 56
(Mark H Tompkins) *dwlt: settled in rr: outpcd fr 3f out: jst pushed along and kpt on in main bunch nr fin* **11/1**

8 ¾ **Cutting It Fine (IRE)** 3-9-3 0 .... HayleyTurner 3 54+
(Jeremy Noseda) *dwlt: rn v green in last: reminder after 2f: nvr on terms but kpt on fnl f* **7/1**

9 8 **Fleeting Indian (IRE)** 3-8-12 0 .... RyanPowell(5) 6 35
(Linda Jewell) *dwlt: a in rr: rdn over 3f out: wknd 3f out: t.o* **150/1**

000- **10** 3 **Pink Belini**[16] 7915 3-8-12 46 .... (vt1) MartinHarley 7 23
(Alan McCabe) *led 2f: rdn in 3rd over 3f out: wknd over 2f out* **150/1**

1m 39.18s (0.98) **Going Correction** +0.075s/f (Slow) **10** Ran SP% **113.4**
Speed ratings (Par 95): **98,97,92,92,91 91,91,90,82,79**
Tote Swingers: 1&2 £3.30, 1&3 £5.90, 2&3 £6.70 CSF £6.91 TOTE £2.80: £1.70, £1.40, £2.90; EX 8.90 Trifecta £91.00 Pool: £393.86 - 3.20 winning units..
Owner Decadent Racing **Bred** John Malone **Trained** Manton, Wilts

FOCUS
The time was only 0.53 seconds quicker than the earlier modestly run Class 4 handicap and the form looks no better than fair, but the runner-up shaped nicely.
T/Plt: £318.10 to a £1 stake. Pool:£76,967.82 - 176.60 winning tickets T/Qpdt: £23.90 to a £1 stake. Pool:£8,282.56 - 256.28 winning tickets JN

[126]KEMPTON (A.W) (R-H)

Sunday, January 15

OFFICIAL GOING: Standard
Wind: Fresh, behind Weather: Bright, cold

183 32RED APPRENTICE H'CAP 1m (P)
1:40 (1:41) (Class 6) (0-65,65) 4-Y-0+ £1,617 (£481; £240; £120) Stalls Low

Form RPR

500- **1** **Qeethaara (USA)**[43] 7632 8-8-11 **58** .... (p) JackDuern(3) 5 68
(Mark Brisbourne) *slowest away: in tch in rr: prog 3f out: squeezed through to chal 2f out: led over 1f out: hung lft but styd on* **40/1**

415- **2** ½ **Hierarch (IRE)**[16] 7930 5-8-12 **61** .... AliceHaynes(5) 3 70
(David Simcock) *hld up in midfield: prog and nt clr run over 2f out: tried to chal wl over 1f out: chsd wnr jst ins fnl f: styd on but a hld* **4/1**[2]

111- **3** ¾ **Storm Runner (IRE)**[18] 7890 4-9-1 **59** .... RaulDaSilva 10 66
(George Margarson) *hld up and sn last: stil only one bhd 2f out: gd prog over 1f out: tk 3rd ins fnl f and styd on all the way to fin: too much to do* **7/2**[1]

520- **4** 4 **Nolecce**[27] 7817 5-9-6 **64** .... (p) CharlesEddery 7 62
(Richard Guest) *taken down early: prom: rdn to chse ldr 3f out: led 2f out: edgd lft and hdd over 1f out: wknd* **8/1**

10-5 **5** 3 ¼ **Join Up**[9] 67 6-9-0 **58** .... RachealKneller 11 49
(Mark Brisbourne) *towards rr: modest prog and shkn up over 2f out: no imp over 1f out: wknd* **20/1**

321- **6** ½ **Rock Anthem (IRE)**[16] 7930 8-9-6 **64** .... CharlesBishop 9 53
(Mike Murphy) *chsd ldrs: prog 3f out: tried to chal 2f out: nudged by rival sn after and wknd* **5/1**[3]

550- **7** ¾ **Olynard (IRE)**[18] 7897 6-8-10 **57** .... NoelGarbutt(3) 2 45
(Michael Mullineaux) *sn chsd ldrs: drvn over 2f out: wknd over 1f out* **100/1**

210- **8** 6 **Mad Ginger Alice**[52] 7532 4-9-2 **65** .... JenniferFerguson(5) 1 39
(Olivia Maylam) *taken down early and difficult to load into stall: wl in rr: tk evasive action after 2f: brief effrt over 2f out: sn wknd* **33/1**

050- **9** 1 **Scary Movie (IRE)**[34] 7734 7-9-2 **65** .... (p) JoshBaudains(5) 13 37
(Ronald Harris) *racd wd: wl in rr fr 1/2-way: struggling and wl btn over 2f out* **12/1**

360- **10** 3 ¼ **Sky Diamond (IRE)**[18] 7901 4-9-2 **60** .... (b) JustinNewman 4 24
(John Mackie) *chsd ldr to 3f out: wknd qckly 2f out* **6/1**

624- **11** 3 **Ice Cold Bex**[18] 7890 4-8-13 **60** .... (b) DannyBrock(3) 12 17
(Philip McBride) *led to 2f out: wknd rapidly* **16/1**

052- **R** **Indian Violet (IRE)**[64] 7394 6-9-2 **60** .... LukeRowe 8
(Ralph Smith) *in tch in midfield whn crashed through rail after 2f* **12/1**

1m 39.58s (-0.22) **Going Correction** 0.0s/f (Stan) **12** Ran SP% **116.7**
Speed ratings (Par 101): **101,100,99,95,92 92,91,85,84,81 78,**
toteswingers:1&2:£51.20, 2&3:£4.50, 1&3:£32.90 CSF £188.41 CT £737.53 TOTE £51.90: £13.80, £1.20, £1.50; EX 413.60 Trifecta £219.40 Part won. Pool: £296.58 - 0.65 winning units..
Owner Crewe And Nantwich Racing Club **Bred** Shadwell Farm LLC **Trained** Great Ness, Shropshire

FOCUS
An ordinary apprentice handicap run at a sound pace in a time 2.66 seconds outside the standard. The first three finished clear.
Mad Ginger Alice Official explanation: jockey said filly suffered interference and never travelled

184 32RED.COM H'CAP (LONDON MILE QUALIFIER) 1m (P)
2:10 (2:10) (Class 5) (0-70,70) 3-Y-0 £2,264 (£673; £336; £168) Stalls Low

Form RPR

262- **1** **Majestic Zafeen**[15] 7937 3-9-4 **67** .... MartinHarley 3 74
(Alastair Lidderdale) *trckd ldng pair: clsd 2f out gng much bttr than rest: led over 1f out: shkn up and sn clr: decisively* **5/1**[3]

621- **2** 3 ½ **Fistful Of Dollars (IRE)**[37] 7685 3-9-7 **70** .... FergusSweeney 2 68
(Jamie Osborne) *trckd ldr: shkn up to ld over 2f out: rdn and hdd over 1f out: no ch w wnr after: jst hld on for 2nd* **4/1**[2]

444- **3** nk **Availed Speaker (IRE)**[24] 7855 3-8-8 **62** .... ShaneBKelly(5) 1 59
(Richard Fahey) *hld up in 4th: dropped to last 1/2-way and pushed along: struggling over 2f out: kpt on fr over 1f out* **4/1**[2]

12- **4** hd **Speedi Mouse**[163] 4761 3-8-13 **62** .... MartinLane 5 59
(Philip McBride) *stdd s: hld up last: wnt 4th 1/2-way: rdn and nt qckn over 2f out: plugged on* **7/1**

314- **5** 5 **Next Cry (USA)**[39] 7653 3-9-7 **70** .... DaneO'Neill 4 55
(Richard Hannon) *led: set brisk pce into the breeze to 1/2-way: rdn and hdd over 2f out: wknd tamely* **6/4**[1]

1m 40.67s (0.87) **Going Correction** 0.0s/f (Stan) **5** Ran SP% **109.2**
Speed ratings (Par 97): **95,91,91,91,86**
CSF £23.74 TOTE £7.00: £3.40, £3.50; EX 15.30.
Owner Lambourn Valley Racing II **Bred** Mike Channon Bloodstock Ltd **Trained** Lambourn, Berks

FOCUS
A modest handicap in which the favourite flopped. It was run in a time around a second slower than the older horses recorded in the opener.

185 32RED CASINO MEDIAN AUCTION MAIDEN FILLIES' STKS 7f (P)
2:40 (2:40) (Class 5) 3-5-Y-0 £2,264 (£673; £336; £168) Stalls Low

Form RPR

53- **1** **Boudoir (IRE)**[25] 7838 3-8-10 0 .... DaneO'Neill 3 67+
(Richard Hannon) *dwlt: hld up in 5th: prog to chse ldr 2f out: led against rail over 1f out: shkn up and idled ins fnl f: jst hld on* **5/6**[1]

63- **2** shd **Kickingthelilly**[30] 7784 3-8-10 0 .... SteveDrowne 4 67
(Rae Guest) *led: rdn and hdd over 1f out: edgd lft but kpt on fnl f: jst failed* **7/2**[3]

044- **3** ½ **Naughtical**[51] 7540 3-8-10 65 .... HayleyTurner 1 65
(J W Hills) *cl up: chsd ldr 3f out to 2f out: rdn and tried to rally fnl f: nt qckn last 100yds* **3/1**[2]

0- **4** 2 **Play Street**[17] 7909 3-8-10 0 .... LeeNewman 2 60
(Jonathan Portman) *cl up: rdn 3f out: nt qckn over 2f out: kpt on fnl 2f but no imp* **25/1**

630- **5** 12 **Flying Kitty**[137] 5634 3-8-7 52 .... RyanPowell(3) 7 28
(John Bridger) *chsd ldr to 3f out: wknd qckly: t.o* **33/1**

0- **6** 8 **Daphne Joy**[15] 7938 3-8-10 0 .... JohnFahy 6
(Peter Hedger) *outpcd and pushed along after 2f: bhd after: wl t.o* **100/1**

1m 25.9s (-0.10) **Going Correction** 0.0s/f (Stan) **6** Ran SP% **109.6**
Speed ratings (Par 100): **100,99,99,97,83 74**
toteswingers:1&2:£1.20, 2&3:£1.50, 1&3:£1.60 CSF £3.83 TOTE £2.10: £1.30, £1.20; EX 4.10.
Owner Highclere Thoroughbred Racing - Leonie **Bred** Airlie Stud **Trained** East Everleigh, Wilts

FOCUS
Just a modest fillies' maiden.

186 KEMPTON FOR WEDDINGS CLASSIFIED CLAIMING STKS 6f (P)
3:10 (3:10) (Class 6) 4-Y-0+ £1,617 (£481; £240; £120) Stalls Low

Form RPR

01-4 **1** **Stevie Gee (IRE)**[2] 146 8-8-6 73 .... (v) RyanClark(3) 4 79
(Ian Williams) *trckd ldrs: wnt 2nd over 2f out: drvn to ld over 1f out but sn hrd pressed: hld on wl* **9/4**[1]

0-15 **2** 1 **Desert Strike**[4] 120 6-8-13 75 .... (p) ShaneKelly 6 80
(Alan McCabe) *taken down early: dwlt: hld up in 6th: cruised through to trck wnr over 1f out and looked sure to win: chal delayed tl ent fnl f then rdn and fnd nil* **10/3**[2]

156- **3** 4 **Royal Box**[27] 7817 5-8-6 62 .... RyanPowell(3) 5 63
(Dai Burchell) *chsd ldng pair to over 2f out: outpcd u.p: kpt on to take 3rd again fnl f: n.d* **15/2**

553- **4** 1 **Lutine Charlie (IRE)**[16] 7919 5-8-4 69 .... (p) RaulDaSilva(5) 1 60
(Ronald Harris) *t.k.h: hmpd against rail after 1f: detached in last after tl styd on fr over 1f out* **9/2**[3]

000- **5** 1 **Zip Lock (IRE)**[115] 6282 6-8-4 73 .... (t) JenniferFerguson(7) 7 59
(Olivia Maylam) *hld up in 5th: drvn 3f out: struggling after* **16/1**

1/0- **6** 2 ½ **Speedfit Girl (IRE)**[265] 1571 4-9-3 73 .... IanMongan 2 57
(George Margarson) *chsd ldr to over 2f out: tried briefly to rally over 1f out: sn wknd* **9/1**

00-5 **7** 5 **Royal Intruder**[3] 133 7-9-3 68 .... MartinHarley 3 41
(Richard Guest) *led at brisk pce: kicked more than 3 l clr 1/2-way: hdd & wknd rapidly over 1f out* **11/1**

1m 11.29s (-1.81) **Going Correction** 0.0s/f (Stan) **7** Ran SP% **108.0**
Speed ratings (Par 101): **112,110,105,104,102 99,92**
toteswingers:1&2:£2.40, 2&3:£5.00, 1&3:£3.80 CSF £8.62 TOTE £2.40: £1.60, £2.10; EX 7.40.
Owner Steve Gray **Bred** Irish National Stud **Trained** Portway, Worcs

FOCUS
Fair claiming form with the first two pulling clear. The gallop was brisk and the time was just inside the standard, only a length and half off the track record.

187 £32 FREE AT 32RED.COM H'CAP 1m 4f (P)
3:40 (3:41) (Class 4) (0-85,84) 4-Y-0+ £4,528 (£1,347; £673; £336) Stalls Low

Form RPR

443- **1** **Art Scholar (IRE)**[17] 7908 5-9-4 **78** .... LiamKeniry 2 89
(Michael Appleby) *hld up in last quartet: looking for room fr over 3f out: prog on inner over 2f out: led 1f out: shkn up and sn clr* **9/1**

00-5 **2** 3 **Big Creek (IRE)**[11] 36 5-9-5 **79** .... JamieSpencer 3 85
(Jeremy Noseda) *prom: trckd ldr 5f out: rdn to ld over 2f out: hdd 1f out: outpcd but kpt on* **6/1**[3]

2/5- **3** 1 **Switched Off**[17] 6988 7-8-13 **73** .... (p) StevieDonohoe 7 77
(Ian Williams) *trckd ldrs in 6th: prog to chal and upsides 2f out: sn rdn and nt qckn: one pce after* **16/1**

335- **4** hd **Ellemujie**[17] 7908 7-9-10 **84** .... (p) AdamKirby 8 88
(Dean Ivory) *hld up in last quartet: prog over 2f out: chsd ldrs in 5th over 1f out: styd on same pce and nrly snatched 3rd* **9/2**[2]

021- **5** ¾ **Refractor (IRE)**[31] 7766 4-8-12 **76** .... MartinLane 1 79
(James Fanshawe) *hld up bhd ldrs: prog on inner to chal 2f out: stl upsides jst over 1f out: fdd* **5/2**[1]

/01- **6** 2 **All The Winds (GER)**[17] 7908 7-9-6 **83** .... RyanPowell(3) 10 83
(Shaun Lycett) *dwlt: hld up in last pair: brought wdst of all in st: sme prog over 1f out: no ch ins fnl f: eased last 50yds* **13/2**

66-0 **7** ¾ **Jordaura**[11] 36 6-9-1 **75** .... HayleyTurner 4 73
(Gay Kelleway) *stdd s: hld up in last pair: effrt over 2f out: limited prog over 1f out: no hdwy fnl f* **18/1**

050- **8** 3 **Sir Boss (IRE)**[37] 7699 7-9-5 **82** .... AmyRyan(3) 6 76
(Michael Mullineaux) *trckd ldrs: drvn and nt qckn over 2f out: wknd over 1f out* **33/1**

02-2 **9** nk **The Lock Master (IRE)**[12] 22 5-9-3 **77** .... NeilChalmers 5 70
(Michael Appleby) *led 1f: chsd ldr to 5f out: sn pushed along: styd prom tl wknd 2f out* **14/1**

000- **10** 5 **Plattsburgh (USA)**[17] 7908 4-8-11 **75** .... (b1) JoeFanning 9 60
(Mark Johnston) *led after 1f and racd freely in front: hdd & wknd qckly over 2f out* **17/2**

2m 33.07s (-1.43) **Going Correction** 0.0s/f (Stan)
WFA 4 from 5yo+ 4lb **10** Ran SP% **115.7**
Speed ratings (Par 105): **104,102,101,101,100 99,98,96,96,93**
toteswingers:1&2:£8.10, 2&3:£21.70, 1&3:£11.50 CSF £61.61 CT £855.68 TOTE £11.90: £3.60, £3.10, £5.80; EX 71.00 TRIFECTA Not won..
Owner Mrs J Scrivens **Bred** John Ramsbottom **Trained** Danethorpe, Notts

FOCUS
An open handicap run at a sound pace, and reasonable form.

All The Winds(GER) Official explanation: jockey said gelding hung left

188 32REDBET.COM H'CAP 1m 3f (P)
4:10 (4:11) (Class 6) (0-52,52) 4-Y-0+ £1,617 (£481; £240; £120) Stalls Low

Form RPR
660- 1 **Fire In Babylon (IRE)**214 3053 4-9-1 52 JimCrowley 2 60
(Michael Wigham) *hld up in midfield: swtchd lft over 2f out and prog after: clsd to join ldr 1f out: narrow ld wl ins fnl f: hld on* 11/2[3]
02-0 2 shd **Hathaway (IRE)**6 105 5-8-7 48 RachealKneller(7) 3 56
(Mark Brisbourne) *hld up wl in rr: gd prog on wd outside fr over 2f out: narrow ld 1f out: hdd wl ins fnl f: jst failed* 20/1
233- 3 2 1/2 **Warden Bond**41 7639 4-9-1 52 (p) MartinLane 11 56
(William Stone) *wl plcd bhd ldrs: prog 3f out: clsd u.p to chal jst over 1f out: one pce* 10/1
60-1 4 3/4 **Now**11 28 6-9-3 51 (b) JamesMillman 4 56+
(Rod Millman) *hld up wl in rr: gng strly but short of room on inner 4f out tl swtchd lft over 2f out: gd prog after: clsng on ldrs whn rn into trble jst ins fnl f: nt rcvr* 7/1
065- 5 2 **Laser Blazer**18 7892 4-9-1 52 AdamKirby 14 51
(Jeremy Gask) *led and clr: rel to r bnd 8f out: hdd 1/2-way by runaway ldr: clsd to ld again 2f out: hdd and fdd 1f out* 10/1
45-4 6 1/2 **Cantor**11 28 4-9-1 52 JoeFanning 13 50
(Giles Bravery) *hld up in midfield: prog wl over 2f out: tried to cl on ldrs over 1f out: no ex and eased ins fnl f* 9/2[2]
23-2 7 1 1/4 **Regal Rave (USA)**2 151 5-9-2 50 (v) JohnFahy 8 45
(Peter Hedger) *dwlt: hld up wl in rr: rdn and prog over 2f out to chse ldrs over 1f out: sn wknd* 5/2[1]
200- 8 3 3/4 **Pursuing**34 7741 4-8-10 52 ShaneBKelly(5) 5 41
(Nigel Tinkler) *a towards rr: rdn and no prog wl over 2f out: n.d after* 20/1
230/ 9 3 **Highcliffe**472 6500 4-9-1 52 DaneO'Neill 10 35
(Martin Bosley) *nvr bttr than midfield: rdn over 3f out: hmpd on inner over 2f out: sn btn* 50/1
5-02 10 1 **Miereveld**7 98 5-8-13 47 (v) StevieDonohoe 1 28
(Shaun Harris) *rel to r and urged along: mostly in last: struggling over 3f out* 20/1
460- 11 nse **Don't Call Me Tiny (IRE)**170 3742 4-8-9 46 HayleyTurner 9 27
(Don Cantillon) *chsd ldr 3f: styd handy: rdn 4f out: wknd 2f out* 28/1
00-5 12 12 **Tous Les Deux**11 35 9-9-0 48 (b) MichaelStainton 7
(Dr Jeremy Naylor) *t.k.h: hld up in midfield tl plld way through to ld 1/2-way and sn wl clr: hdd & wknd rapidly 2f out: sddle slipped* 50/1
066- 13 dist **Nuba (IRE)**85 7037 4-8-13 50 (b1) IanMongan 6
(Luke Dace) *t.k.h: trckd ldr after 3f to 1/2-way: rdn over 3f out: wknd rapidly over 2f out: virtually p.u over 1f out* 16/1

2m 22.11s (0.21) **Going Correction** 0.0s/f (Stan)
WFA 4 from 5yo+ 3lb 13 Ran SP% 120.4
Speed ratings (Par 101): **99,98,97,96,95 94,93,91,88,88 88,79,**
toteswingers:1&2:£34.20, 2&3:£17.90, 1&3:£12.00 CSF £117.95 CT £1078.88 TOTE £8.20: £2.40, £7.60, £3.10; EX 194.50 TRIFECTA Not won..
Owner Palatinate Thoroughbred Racing Limited **Bred** The Goldsmith Bloodstock Partnership **Trained** Newmarket, Suffolk

FOCUS
A low-grade handicap and a somewhat messy race run at a steady early pace. The picture changed rapidly in the straight and the first two came from some way back.
Fire In Babylon(IRE) ◆ Official explanation: trainer said, regarding apparent improvement in form, that since its last run it had been gelded and was suited by the longer trip.
Now Official explanation: jockey said mare was denied a clear run
Tous Les Deux Official explanation: jockey said saddle slipped

189 RACING UK H'CAP 6f (P)
4:40 (4:41) (Class 5) (0-75,74) 3-Y-0 £2,264 (£673; £336; £168) Stalls Low

Form RPR
33-1 1 **Oratorian (IRE)**11 27 3-9-7 74 LiamKeniry 6 81
(Sylvester Kirk) *pressed ldr: narrow ld 2f out: rdn over 1f out and hrd pressed sn after: asserted and pushed out last 150yds* 10/11[1]
65-6 2 1 1/4 **Dawn Lightning**8 86 3-8-11 64 ShaneKelly 2 66
(Alan McCabe) *dwlt: hld up in last pair: prog against rail 2f out: wnt 2nd jst over 1f out and sn chal: hrd rdn and hld ins fnl f* 25/1
111- 3 1/2 **Le King Beau (USA)**17 7907 3-9-3 70 DaneO'Neill 4 70
(John Bridger) *hld up in last pair: clsd on ldrs over 1f out: rdn to try to chal fnl f: nt qckn* 7/2[2]
41- 4 1/2 **Chester'Slittlegem (IRE)**18 7898 3-8-11 67 AmyRyan(3) 1 65
(Ed de Giles) *dwlt: sn trckd ldrs: effrt 2f out: tried to chal 1f out: one pce* 12/1
424- 5 1 1/4 **Redair (IRE)**92 6863 3-9-4 71 (v) MartinLane 3 65
(David Evans) *led to 2f out: pressed wnr to jst over 1f out: wknd* 15/2[3]
31-3 6 1 1/4 **Ishiamiracle**7 99 3-8-6 66 (p) LeonnaMayor(7) 5 56
(Phil McEntee) *t.k.h: chsd ldrs: awkward bnd over 4f out: dropped to last and struggling 2f out* 9/1

1m 13.32s (0.22) **Going Correction** 0.0s/f (Stan) 6 Ran SP% 107.9
Speed ratings (Par 97): **98,96,95,95,93 91**
toteswingers:1&2:£5.70, 2&3:£5.40, 1&3:£1.10 CSF £23.31 TOTE £1.80: £1.50, £6.00; EX 20.70.
Owner Miss J A Challen & T Pearson **Bred** Knockainey Stud **Trained** Upper Lambourn, Berks

FOCUS
A fair little handicap for 3yos.
T/Plt: £165.40 to a £1 stake. Pool: £126,281.25. 557.26 winning tickets. T/Qpdt: £24.90 to a £1 stake. Pool: £9,045.28. 268.40 winning tickets. JN

153 WOLVERHAMPTON (A.W) (L-H)
Monday, January 16

OFFICIAL GOING: Standard
Wind: Nil Weather: Fine

190 BET AND WATCH AT BLUESQ.COM CLAIMING STKS 7f 32y(P)
2:25 (2:25) (Class 6) 4-Y-0+ £1,704 (£503; £251) Stalls High

Form RPR
41-0 1 **Bawaardi (IRE)**9 90 6-8-13 80 AdamKirby 5 88
(David Evans) *a.p: chsd ldr 1/2-way: led over 1f out: rdn out* 5/2[1]
22-0 2 2 **One Way Or Another (AUS)**9 90 9-8-6 76 (b) RaulDaSilva(5) 7 81
(David Evans) *hld up: racd keenly: hdwy over 2f out: rdn to chse wnr ins fnl f: styd on* 11/4[2]
050- 3 1 1/2 **Khandaq (USA)**175 4380 5-8-13 76 ShaneKelly 6 79
(Keith Dalgleish) *s.i.s: hld up: hdwy over 2f out: rdn over 1f out: styd on* 4/1[3]
13-0 4 1 1/2 **Ezra Church (IRE)**12 33 5-8-8 72 LeeNewman 8 70
(David Barron) *chsd ldr tl led over 5f out: rdn: edgd lft and hdd over 1f out: no ex ins fnl f* 9/2
400- 5 1 **Last Sovereign**114 6327 8-8-13 79 TomEaves 3 72
(Ollie Pears) *led: hdd over 5f out: chsd ldr to 1/2-way: wknd ins fnl f* 10/1
000- 6 7 **Istiqdaam**37 7715 7-8-8 70 HayleyTurner 4 48
(Conor Dore) *sn outpcd: lost tch fr over 2f out* 22/1
6 7 8 **It's Me And You**12 35 4-8-6 0 DavidSimmonson(7) 2 31
(Michael Easterby) *sn pushed along in rr: rdn and wknd over 2f out* 100/1

1m 30.4s (0.80) **Going Correction** +0.15s/f (Slow) 7 Ran SP% 107.8
Speed ratings (Par 101): **101,98,97,95,94 86,77**
toteswingers:1&2:£2.00, 1&3:£1.90, 2&3:£2.80 CSF £8.47 TOTE £3.10: £1.70, £1.60; EX 7.00 Trifecta £24.90 Pool: £17.66 - 595.37 winning units..
Owner Exors of the late Mrs Sally Edwards **Bred** Millsec Limited **Trained** Pandy, Monmouths

FOCUS
Temperatures dipped below -5C overnight and the track was power harrowed and rolled four times before being reinstated with the gallop master before racing began. Jockey Adam Kirby reported: "It's riding a bit deeper than normal." A fair claimer in which the majority were closely matched on official ratings. The gallop was only fair and the winner raced centre-to-far side in the straight. The first three are rated close to their marks.

191 RINGSIDE CONFERENCE SUITE - 700 THEATRE STYLE H'CAP 5f 216y(P)
2:55 (2:55) (Class 6) (0-55,55) 3-Y-0 £1,704 (£503; £251) Stalls Low

Form RPR
466- 1 **Sweet Ovation**17 7925 3-9-2 55 HayleyTurner 10 61
(Mark Usher) *hld up: hdwy over 1f out: edgd lft and r.o to ld towards fin: comf* 8/1
006- 2 3/4 **Gabrial's Princess (IRE)**34 7742 3-8-10 49 (p) JamieSpencer 1 52
(Bryan Smart) *sn pushed along to ld: rdn over 1f out: edgd lft and hdd towards fin* 10/1
004- 3 1/2 **Dicky Mint**17 7925 3-9-2 55 (bt) PaddyAspell 5 57
(Michael Easterby) *chsd ldrs: rdn over 1f out: sn ev ch: no ex towards fin* 7/2[1]
045- 4 2 1/4 **Flaming Ferrari (IRE)**17 7925 3-9-1 54 JimmyFortune 8 49
(Peter Chapple-Hyam) *led early: stdd to chse ldrs: rdn over 1f out: no ex ins fnl f* 5/1[2]
5 1/2 **Ihavetonuff (IRE)**184 4113 3-8-10 49 ShaneKelly 7 42
(Daniel Mark Loughnane) *hld up: hdwy over 2f out: rdn over 1f out: no ex fnl f* 7/1
20-4 6 2 1/2 **Auntie Kathryn (IRE)**11 40 3-8-9 48 (v) WilliamCarson 11 33
(Stuart Williams) *hld up: hdwy and nt clr run over 1f out: sn rdn: nt trble ldrs* 13/2
630- 7 9 **Very First Blade**145 5374 3-9-2 55 FrannyNorton 3 11
(Mark Brisbourne) *sn chsng ldr: rdn over 2f out: wknd fnl f* 6/1[3]
060- 8 1 **Stepharlie**60 7444 3-9-1 54 (p) TomEaves 9
(Bryan Smart) *chsd ldrs: rdn over 2f out: wknd over 1f out* 12/1
050- 9 1 3/4 **Gadreel (IRE)**16 7937 3-8-8 47 LeeNewman 2
(Anthony Middleton) *mid-div: hdwy over 2f out: rdn and wknd over 1f out* 40/1
000- 10 2 **L'Arlesienne**26 7838 3-8-7 46 (b1) ChrisCatlin 4
(Sylvester Kirk) *sn outpcd* 25/1
40-5 11 hd **Emma Jean (IRE)**11 40 3-8-5 47 (tp) RyanPowell(3) 6
(Niall Moran, Ire) *sn pushed along in rr: wknd over 2f out* 22/1

1m 15.9s (0.90) **Going Correction** +0.15s/f (Slow) 11 Ran SP% 117.5
Speed ratings (Par 95): **100,99,98,95,94 91,79,78,75,73 72**
toteswingers:1&2:£9.90, 1&3:£5.80, 2&3:£7.00 CSF £83.26 CT £339.94 TOTE £10.10: £3.10, £3.70, £1.90; EX 73.20 Trifecta £310.60 Part won. Pool: £419.86 - 0.41 winning units..
Owner The Ridgeway Bloodstock Company Ltd **Bred** Ridgeway Bloodstock **Trained** Upper Lambourn, Berks

FOCUS
A moderate handicap run at a decent gallop. The winner came down the centre in the straight and reversed C&D form with the third and fourth.

192 BLUE SQUARE WINTER CARNIVAL IPHONE APP H'CAP 1m 4f 50y(P)
3:25 (3:25) (Class 5) (0-75,75) 4-Y-0+ £2,264 (£673; £336; £168) Stalls Low

Form RPR
50-6 1 **Mount Abora (IRE)**12 31 5-9-0 65 JamieSpencer 7 75
(Ian Williams) *hld up: hdwy over 2f out: rdn ins fnl f: edgd lft and styd on to ld wl ins fnl f* 16/1
036- 2 hd **Boa**21 7878 7-9-3 68 HayleyTurner 6 78
(Reg Hollinshead) *a.p: chsd ldr over 3f out: led over 2f out: rdn and hdd wl ins fnl f* 16/1
00-0 3 1 1/4 **Ampleforth**12 36 4-9-1 70 (b1) FrannyNorton 8 78
(Mark Johnston) *hld up: hdwy over 2f out: rdn over 1f out: styd on* 22/1
000- 4 5 **Jawaab (IRE)**21 7877 8-9-5 70 (e) AdamKirby 3 70
(Richard Guest) *hld up: hdwy 1/2-way: drvn along over 3f out: rallied over 1f out: styd on same pce fnl f* 6/1
600- 5 4 **Lyric Poet (USA)**40 7651 5-9-6 71 (t) WilliamCarson 12 65
(Anthony Carson) *hld up: last and drvn along over 4f out: hung lft over 1f out: kpt on ins fnl f: nvr nrr* 10/1
521- 6 1/2 **Warneford**97 6769 4-9-5 74 (v) KierenFallon 11 67
(George Baker) *prom: chsd ldr over 4f out tl pushed along over 3f out: wknd over 1f out* 3/1[1]
450- 7 shd **Russian George (IRE)**18 7908 6-9-10 75 (tp) RobertWinston 5 68
(Steve Gollings) *hld up: drvn along 1/2-way: nvr nrr* 11/2[3]
225- 8 1/2 **Echos Of Motivator**26 7839 4-8-8 68 (p) RaulDaSilva(5) 10 60
(Ronald Harris) *hld up in rr: rdn over 3f out: sn outpcd* 9/1
00-4 9 1 **Jeer (IRE)**11 43 8-9-4 69 (t) PaddyAspell 4 59
(Michael Easterby) *chsd ldrs: rdn over 3f out: wknd wl over 1f out* 33/1
0-32 10 9 **Eyedoro (USA)**4 137 4-9-0 69 JoeFanning 9 45
(Mark Johnston) *sn chsng ldr: led over 5f out tl hdd over 2f out: wknd fnl f* 7/2[2]
11P- 11 20 **War Of The Roses (IRE)**35 7738 9-9-3 68 TomEaves 1 12
(Roy Brotherton) *mid-div: rdn over 4f out: wknd 3f out: t.o* 28/1
051- 12 6 **With Hindsight (IRE)**87 7004 4-8-13 73 DavidKenny(5) 2
(Michael Scudamore) *led: hdd over 5f out: wknd over 3f out: t.o* 20/1

2m 41.4s (0.30) **Going Correction** +0.15s/f (Slow)
WFA 4 from 5yo+ 4lb 12 Ran SP% 123.2
Speed ratings (Par 103): **105,104,104,100,98 97,97,97,96,90 77,73**
toteswingers:1&2:£4.80, 1&3:£23.60, 2&3:£34.10 CSF £243.99 CT £5555.16 TOTE £17.90: £5.30, £4.60, £8.80; EX 131.50 TRIFECTA Not won..
Owner Dr Marwan Koukash **Bred** Dr M V O'Brien **Trained** Portway, Worcs

FOCUS
A fair handicap run at an ordinary gallop. although four of the first five came from the rear. The winner came down the centre in the straight and the first three pulled clear.

With Hindsight(IRE) Official explanation: jockey said gelding hung left-handed

193 WOLVERHAMPTON-RACECOURSE.CO.UK H'CAP 1m 141y(P)
3:55 (3:55) (Class 5) (0-75,75) 3-Y-O **£2,264** (£673; £336; £168) **Stalls** Low

Form RPR
111- **1** **Karma Chameleon**[18] 7915 3-9-4 **72** ShaneKelly 3 82+
(John Berry) *hld up: hdwy 1/2-way: led over 1f out: shkn up and r.o wl* **1/1**[1]
030- **2** 1 3/4 **New Decade**[68] 7336 3-9-0 **68** JoeFanning 6 72
(Mark Johnston) *prom: chsd ldr 7f out: led over 2f out: rdn and hdd over 1f out: edgd lft and styd on same pce fnl f* **13/2**[3]
136- **3** 3 **Chelsea Mick**[21] 7875 3-8-13 **72** JustinNewman(5) 2 69
(John Mackie) *chsd ldr over 1f: remained handy: rdn over 1f out: no ex fnl f* **9/1**
311- **4** 6 **Maybeagrey**[38] 7697 3-9-2 **70** DuranFentiman 1 53
(Tim Easterby) *prom: rdn over 3f out: wknd over 1f out* **11/4**[2]
052- **5** 1 **Foursquare Funtime**[17] 7929 3-9-2 **70** AdamKirby 5 51
(Reg Hollinshead) *sn led: rdn and hdd over 2f out: wknd fnl f* **14/1**
354- **6** 7 **Nant Saeson (IRE)**[128] 5937 3-9-7 **75** PaddyAspell 4 40
(John Wainwright) *hld up: rdn over 2f out: wknd wl over 1f out* **25/1**

1m 52.18s (1.68) **Going Correction** +0.15s/f (Slow) **6** Ran SP% **110.5**
Speed ratings (Par 97): **98,96,93,88,87 81**
toteswingers:1&2:£2.70, 1&3:£2.40, 2&3:£5.10 CSF £7.90 TOTE £1.80: £1.40, £2.90; EX 7.40.
Owner EERC **Bred** D R Tucker **Trained** Newmarket, Suffolk

FOCUS
A fair handicap in which the second favourite disappointed. The pace was just an ordinary one and the progressive winner came down the centre in the straight. He rates better than the bare form.
Foursquare Funtime Official explanation: jockey said gelding hung right-handed

194 WOLVERHAMPTON HOSPITALITY - A PLEASURE CLAIMING STKS 1m 141y(P)
4:25 (4:25) (Class 6) 3-Y-O **£1,704** (£503; £251) **Stalls** Low

Form RPR
444- **1** **Anginola (IRE)**[47] 7582 3-7-11 65 (v[1]) RyanPowell(3) 6 63+
(Joseph Tuite) *chsd ldr tl led over 1f out: sn edgd lft and rdn clr: eased nr fin* **7/2**[2]
404- **2** 3 1/4 **Orwellian**[26] 7849 3-8-3 61 (b[1]) NickyMackay 3 57
(Brian Meehan) *set stady pce tl wnt clr over 5f out: rdn and hdd over 1f out: no ex fnl f* **4/1**[3]
005- **3** 2 1/4 **Bulldog Beasley (USA)**[31] 7783 3-8-13 62 (bt[1]) ShaneKelly 8 61
(Brian Meehan) *prom: pushed along to go 3rd 3f out: rdn over 2f out: hung lft and no ex fnl f* **14/1**
23-6 **4** 1 1/2 **Let Your Love Flow (IRE)**[12] 32 3-7-12 63 ow3 RaulDaSilva(5) 5 48
(Sylvester Kirk) *chsd ldrs: rdn over 2f out: sn edgd lft and outpcd* **9/4**[1]
6- **5** 1 1/2 **Redclue (IRE)**[28] 7821 3-8-13 0 (b[1]) AdamKirby 2 54
(Marco Botti) *s.i.s: hld up: rdn over 3f out: nvr on terms* **7/2**[2]
3-64 **6** nk **Meet Joe Black (IRE)**[4] 132 3-8-0 52 (v) DominicFox(3) 7 44
(David Evans) *dwlt: hld up: rdn over 3f out: hung lft over 1f out: n.d* **8/1**

1m 53.33s (2.83) **Going Correction** +0.15s/f (Slow) **6** Ran SP% **113.0**
Speed ratings (Par 95): **93,90,88,86,85 85**
toteswingers:1&2:£3.30, 1&3:£6.50, 2&3:£6.50 CSF £17.91 TOTE £2.70: £1.40, £3.00; EX 15.20 Trifecta £82.50 Pool: £820.65 - 7.36 winning units..Anginola was claimed by P. D. Evans for £6,000.
Owner Andrew Liddiard **Bred** T C Clarke **Trained** Great Shefford, Berks

FOCUS
A modest and uncompetitive claimer in which a steady gallop picked up leaving the back straight. The winner drifted to the far rail in the closing stages. With the favourite disappointing she didn't need to match her best.
Bulldog Beasley(USA) Official explanation: jockey said gelding hung left-handed

195 THE BLACK COUNTRY'S ONLY RACECOURSE MAIDEN STKS 1m 1f 103y(P)
4:55 (4:56) (Class 5) 3-Y-O **£2,264** (£673; £336; £168) **Stalls** Low

Form RPR
1 **Canary Wharf (IRE)**[89] 6962 3-9-3 0 (b) AdamKirby 6 81
(Marco Botti) *chsd ldrs: rdn to go 2nd over 2f out: styd on u.p to ld post* **11/4**[2]
332- **2** shd **Cotton Trader (USA)**[40] 7664 3-9-3 0 NickyMackay 4 81
(John Gosden) *led: rdn and edgd rt ins fnl f: hdd post* **1/1**[1]
3 **3** 5 **Angel Gabrial (IRE)**[7] 107 3-9-3 0 JamieSpencer 2 73+
(Ian Williams) *prom: rdn over 2f out: wnt 3rd wl over 1f out: eased whn btn wl ins fnl f* **4/1**[3]
0-4 **4** 4 **Picalily**[7] 107 3-8-9 0 DominicFox(3) 7 57
(David Evans) *mid-div: hung rt and hdwy 5f out: rdn over 2f out: wknd over 1f out* **40/1**
5 3 **Authentication** 3-9-3 0 JoeFanning 9 56
(Mark Johnston) *sn chsng ldr: rdn and ev ch over 2f out: wknd over 1f out* **10/1**
00- **6** hd **Fleeting Fashion**[31] 7777 3-8-5 0 JackDuern(7) 3 50
(Michael Appleby) *sn pushed along in rr: nvr nrr* **100/1**
7 3/4 **Burning Passion** 3-8-10 0 DavidSimmonson(7) 10 54
(Michael Easterby) *s.i.s: hld up: n.d* **50/1**
0- **8** 5 **Corn Maiden**[121] 6168 3-8-12 0 TomMcLaughlin 11 38
(Phil McEntee) *hld up: rdn and wknd over 3f out* **50/1**
0- **9** 3 1/2 **Symphony Of Space**[186] 4021 3-8-12 0 MartinHarley 8 31
(Alan McCabe) *plld hrd and prom: rdn over 3f out: wknd over 2f out* **66/1**
10 3 1/4 **Piper Cherokee** 3-8-12 0 PaddyAspell 5 24
(Michael Easterby) *sn pushed along in rr: lost tch fnl 4f* **80/1**

2m 4.63s (2.93) **Going Correction** +0.15s/f (Slow) **10** Ran SP% **115.8**
Speed ratings (Par 97): **92,91,87,83,81 81,80,75,72,69**
toteswingers:1&2:£1.30, 1&3:£2.00, 2&3:£1.70 CSF £5.76 TOTE £3.40: £1.10, £1.20, £1.10; EX 6.60 Trifecta £19.00 Pool: £1,143.41 - 44.38 winning units..
Owner G Manfredini & J Allison **Bred** Michael Lowry **Trained** Newmarket, Suffolk

FOCUS
The first three are fair sorts but this was a maiden lacking anything in the way of depth. The pace was an ordinary one and the winner came down the centre. The form is rated around the principals.

196 PLAY DA VINCI DIAMONDS AT BLUESQ.COM/GAMES H'CAP 1m 1f 103y(P)
5:25 (5:25) (Class 6) (0-60,60) 3-Y-O **£1,704** (£503; £251) **Stalls** Low

Form RPR
05-2 **1** **Gabrial's King (IRE)**[7] 108 3-8-11 **50** JamieSpencer 8 60+
(Ian Williams) *stdd s: hld up: hdwy over 1f out: r.o to ld wl ins fnl f* **5/6**[1]
622- **2** 1 1/4 **Quixote**[26] 7849 3-9-7 **60** (b) HayleyTurner 4 65
(Clive Brittain) *prom: rdn to ld and hung lft ins fnl f: sn hdd and unable qck* **9/4**[2]
063- **3** 4 1/2 **Rhyme Royal**[31] 7777 3-8-13 **52** FrederikTylicki 7 48
(James Given) *prom: chsd ldr over 5f out: led 3f out: rdn over 1f out: hdd and no ex ins fnl f* **22/1**
05-3 **4** nk **Clean Bowled (IRE)**[7] 108 3-9-6 **59** MartinHarley 1 54
(Alan McCabe) *hld up: nt clr run over 2f out: hdwy over 1f out: no imp fnl f* **7/1**[3]
000- **5** 1 1/2 **Waspy**[132] 5813 3-8-13 **52** TomMcLaughlin 2 44
(Ed Dunlop) *hld up: hdwy over 2f out: rdn over 1f out: wknd fnl f* **16/1**
004- **6** 1 1/2 **Aloysia**[17] 7929 3-8-7 **46** oh1 ChrisCatlin 3 35
(Sylvester Kirk) *hld up: hdwy over 6f out: rdn over 3f out: wknd fnl f* **100/1**
400- **7** 16 **Si Sealy (IRE)**[220] 2889 3-9-0 **56** DominicFox(3) 5
(David Evans) *chsd ldrs tl rdn and wknd over 2f out* **33/1**
00-4 **8** 22 **Castalian Spring (IRE)**[12] 30 3-8-7 **46** oh1 (b[1]) MartinLane 6
(Robert Eddery) *led: rdn and hdd 3f out: sn wknd: t.o* **33/1**

2m 5.61s (3.91) **Going Correction** +0.15s/f (Slow) **8** Ran SP% **114.9**
Speed ratings (Par 95): **88,86,82,82,81 79,65,46**
toteswingers:1&2:£1.20, 1&3:£3.80, 2&3:£6.00 CSF £2.74 CT £18.55 TOTE £1.90: £1.50, £1.10, £2.10; EX 3.40 Trifecta £32.80 Pool: £722.60 - 16.29 winning units..
Owner Dr Marwan Koukash **Bred** Danella Partnership **Trained** Portway, Worcs
■ Stewards' Enquiry : Frederik Tylicki three-day ban: careless riding (Jan 30-31,Feb 1)

FOCUS
A weak handicap run at a fair gallop. The winner came down the centre in the straight. He won with a bit in hand and there is likely more to come.
T/Jkpt: £15,353.30 to a £1 stake. Pool:£237,869.19 - 11.00 winning tickets T/Plt: £126.40 to a £1 stake. Pool:£114,425.06 - 660.72 winning tickets T/Qpdt: £41.50 to a £1 stake. Pool:£8,840.15 - 157.60 winning tickets CR

[183]KEMPTON (A.W) (R-H)
Wednesday, January 18

OFFICIAL GOING: Standard
Wind: Light, across Weather: Very overcast

197 FREE ENTRY FOR BETDAQ MEMBERS H'CAP 1m (P)
4:25 (4:25) (Class 7) (0-50,50) 4-Y-O+ **£1,455** (£433; £216; £108) **Stalls** Low

Form RPR
03-3 **1** **Querido (GER)**[12] 55 8-9-0 **50** (tp) RobertLButler(3) 6 57
(Paddy Butler) *sn hld up in 4th: clsd fr over 2f out: led over 1f out: drvn clr jst ins fnl f: styd on* **8/1**
00-3 **2** 2 1/4 **Very Well Red**[8] 109 9-9-3 **50** WilliamCarson 2 52
(Peter Hiatt) *led: rdn and hdd over 1f out: kpt on one pce after* **2/1**[1]
006- **3** 1 **Tawseef (IRE)**[21] 7902 4-9-3 **50** TomEaves 12 50
(Roy Brotherton) *hld up in last pair: rdn over 2f out: prog u.p to go 3rd 1f out: kpt on same pce* **8/1**
65-0 **4** 1 1/2 **Hot Tub**[8] 109 4-9-2 **49** (t) IanMongan 13 45
(Christine Dunnett) *hld up in last pair: off the bridle sn after 1/2-way: looked reluctant w hd high over 2f out: nt clr run jst ins fnl f: kpt on late to take 4th last stride* **33/1**
025- **5** nse **Lennoxwood (IRE)**[21] 7899 4-8-9 **49** (be) RachealKneller(7) 3 45
(Mark Usher) *hld up in 5th: shkn up and no prog over 2f out: n.d after* **4/1**[3]
05-2 **6** 1 1/4 **My Mate Les (IRE)**[13] 45 4-9-2 **49** DavidProbert 5 42
(Tony Carroll) *chsd ldr: rdn and fnd nil 2f out: sn btn* **7/2**[2]
545- **7** 2 1/2 **Batchworth Blaise**[21] 7888 9-8-10 **48** (b) RaulDaSilva(5) 8 36
(Eric Wheeler) *hld up tl quick move to dispute 2nd after 2f: wknd wl over 1f out* **11/1**

1m 40.91s (1.11) **Going Correction** -0.075s/f (Stan) **7** Ran SP% **109.1**
Speed ratings (Par 97): **91,88,87,86,86 84,82**
toteswingers: 1&2 £4.00, 1&3 £6.30, 2&3 £7.70. CSF £22.18 CT £119.32 TOTE £9.50: £4.10, £1.40; EX 22.90.
Owner Homewoodgate Racing Club **Bred** Gestut Brummerhof **Trained** East Chiltington, E Sussex

FOCUS
A basement-level handicap most notable for gambles on a couple of horses who failed to make the line-up. There were seven non-runners in total, all self-certificated. Two came out the previous day (Noinformation and Harvest Mist), while another three (Kenswick, Gordy Bee and Five Cool Kats) came out between 9am and 11am, during which gambles on both Aegean King and All About You developed. All About You was trading at around the 3-1 mark when taken out at around 2pm, leaving Aegean King an 11-8 favourite, but he too was declared a non-runner in the hour before the race. Both were returning from lengthy absences and have been rated higher in the past. Aegean King hails from the Michael Wigham yard, known for landing gambles, while All About You was supposed to be John Butler's first ever runner. A former jockey, he's now a tenant of Barney Curley's yard. Whatever the story, the bookmakers have now been alerted. Modest form with the winner still a fair way off his best.

198 BETDAQ MULTIPLES CLAIMING STKS 1m (P)
4:55 (4:56) (Class 6) 4-Y-O+ **£1,617** (£481; £240; £120) **Stalls** Low

Form RPR
20-4 **1** **Spinning Ridge (IRE)**[11] 85 7-9-1 68 (v) LukeMorris 7 76
(Ronald Harris) *t.k.h: prom: trckd ldng pair 5f out: cruised up to ld over 1f out: booted clr ent fnl f: jst hld on* **11/1**
41-1 **2** hd **Marajaa (IRE)**[11] 90 10-9-9 82 JamieMackay 1 84+
(Willie Musson) *sn hld up in last and wl off the pce: prog jst over 2f out: wnt 3rd bhd clr ldrs over 1f out: asked for effrt ins fnl f: wnt 2nd last 100yds: clsd rapidly on wnr: too much to do* **5/6**[1]
046- **3** 3 **Red Somerset (USA)**[91] 6948 9-8-10 78 KieranO'Neill(3) 9 67
(Mike Murphy) *v s.i.s: rapid rcvry to chse ldr after 2f: drvn to ld over 2f out: hdd over 1f out: fdd ins fnl f* **4/1**[2]
254- **4** 3 **Inpursuitoffreedom**[133] 5828 5-8-8 68 (v[1]) MartinLane 2 55
(Philip McBride) *towards rr and wl off the pce: rdn 3f out: effrt to dispute 3rd briefly over 1f out but no ch: one pce* **8/1**[3]
030- **5** 1 1/4 **Tuxedo**[121] 6227 7-9-1 65 WilliamCarson 6 59
(Peter Hiatt) *led 1f: dropped to 4th after 3f: urged along over 2f out: disp 3rd briefly over 1f out: fdd* **25/1**
020/ **6** 2 3/4 **Slam**[40] 1986 7-9-5 82 (t) EddieAhern 8 57
(Tom George) *towards rr and wl off the pce: rdn and struggling over 3f out: no real prog* **14/1**
400- **7** 3/4 **Amethyst Dawn (IRE)**[28] 7841 6-8-13 80 (t) DavidKenny(5) 3 54
(Andrew Reid) *towards rr and wl off the pce: rdn 3f out: no prog fnl 2f* **20/1**
6-16 **8** 3 **Divine Rule (IRE)**[5] 146 4-8-4 55 (b) CharlotteJenner(7) 5 40
(Laura Mongan) *led after 1f and set str pce: hdd over 2f out: wknd rapidly over 1f out* **40/1**

060- **9** 3 ½ **Green Pearl (IRE)**[61] 7455 4-9-0 58................................(t) JimCrowley 4 35
(Ralph Beckett) *s.s and blindfold in rdr's lap early: drvn and no prog in last pair 3f out* **25/1**

1m 38.86s (-0.94) **Going Correction** -0.075s/f (Stan) **9** Ran SP% **115.6**
Speed ratings (Par 101): **101,100,97,94,93 90,90,87,83**
toteswingers: 1&2 £3.10, 1&3 £4.00, 2&3 £1.90. CSF £19.97 TOTE £7.10: £1.30, £1.10, £1.80; EX 25.00.
Owner Robert & Nina Bailey **Bred** Eddie O'Leary **Trained** Earlswood, Monmouths

Green Pearl(IRE) Official explanation: jockey said gelding reared on leaving stalls

199 BACK OR LAY AT BETDAQ.COM H'CAP (LONDON MILE QUALIFIER) 1m (P)

5:25 (5:26) (Class 5) (0-75,75) 4-Y-0+ **£2,264** (£673; £336; £168) **Stalls** Low

Form RPR

400- **1** **Prince Of Burma (IRE)**[28] 7841 4-9-7 **75**......................(b[1]) IanMongan 3 89
(Jeremy Gask) *settled in midfield: prog over 3f out: drvn and clsd on outer fr 2f out: led last 150yds: styd on wl* **6/1**[2]

405- **2** 1 **Legal Legacy**[19] 7928 6-9-1 **69**............................ AndrewMullen 5 80
(David C Griffiths) *slowest away: hld up wl in rr: gd prog on inner wl over 2f out: led over 1f out: hdd last 150yds: styd on* **20/1**

000- **3** 2 **Big Bay (USA)**[42] 7651 6-9-4 **72**..............................(b) ChrisCatlin 13 79+
(Jane Chapple-Hyam) *chsd ldr after 1f: rdn and clsd to ld 2f out: hdd over 1f out: kpt on* **16/1**

252- **4** 1 ¼ **Peponi**[30] 7822 6-9-7 **75**...................................... SteveDrowne 4 79
(Peter Makin) *chsd ldr 1f: styd prom: effrt over 2f out: cl enough over 1f out: steadily fdd* **9/1**

50-0 **5** ½ **Focail Eile**[11] 90 7-9-7 **75**.. AdamKirby 1 78
(John Ryan) *wl in tch in midfield: looking for room wl over 2f out: effrt over 1f out: kpt on same pce* **10/1**

066- **6** nk **Menadati (USA)**[70] 7334 4-9-1 **69**.......................... WilliamCarson 8 71
(Peter Hiatt) *hld up wl in rr: jst pushed along fr over 2f out: kpt on steadily after: nvr nr ldrs* **12/1**

44-3 **7** ½ **Satwa Laird**[14] 33 6-9-5 **73**.................................... JamieSpencer 7 74
(David Simcock) *broke wl but sn restrained in last trio and racd wd: cajoled along w hd to one side over 2f out: kpt on fr over 1f out: no ch* **5/1**[1]

443- **8** hd **John Louis**[168] 4663 4-9-0 **68**................................ JimmyFortune 6 70
(Philip McBride) *t.k.h: prom: rdn to dispute 3rd 2f out: losing pl whn squeezed out over 1f out: kpt on again after* **8/1**

2-03 **9** 3 ¼ **Chookie Avon**[6] 134 5-9-2 **70**.................................(p) JoeFanning 10 63
(Keith Dalgleish) *t.k.h: hld up in last trio: brought wdst of all bnd 3f out: urged along and nt qckn over 2f out: limited prog over 1f out: eased whn no ch nr fin* **7/1**[3]

50-1 **10** 1 ¾ **April Fool**[6] 128 8-9-2 **75** 6ex...............................(b) RaulDaSilva[(5)] 14 64
(Ronald Harris) *fast away: led to 2f out: wknd qckly over 1f out* **5/1**[1]

060- **11** 25 **She Ain't A Saint**[35] 7759 4-9-7 **75**.......................(p) LukeMorris 12
(Jane Chapple-Hyam) *prom to 1/2-way: sn wknd rapidly: t.o and eased* **14/1**

51-4 **12** 4 **Community (USA)**[6] 136 4-9-1 **69**............................ JimCrowley 11
(Phil McEntee) *racd wd thrght: prog fr rr to go prom after 2f: wknd over 3f out: eased and t.o* **25/1**

1m 38.28s (-1.52) **Going Correction** -0.075s/f (Stan) **12** Ran SP% **119.2**
Speed ratings (Par 103): **104,103,101,99,99 98,98,98,95,93 68,64**
toteswingers: 1&2 £40.20, 1&3 £23.90, 2&3 £58.60. CSF £120.02 CT £1859.24 TOTE £6.00: £2.20, £12.10, £7.80; EX 237.30.
Owner The Nobles **Bred** P Burns **Trained** Sutton Veny, Wilts

FOCUS
A competitive handicap.

200 BETDAQ MOBILE APPS H'CAP 1m 4f (P)

5:55 (5:56) (Class 7) (0-50,50) 4-Y-0+ **£1,455** (£433; £216; £108) **Stalls** Centre

Form RPR

63-2 **1** **Mayan Flight (IRE)**[5] 160 4-8-9 **46**.......................... DavidProbert 9 54
(Tony Carroll) *hld up in last trio: stdy prog over 3f out: wnt 3rd jst over 2f out and chsd ldr over 1f out: styd on u.p to ld last 120yds: sn clr* **11/4**[1]

00/- **2** 2 ¼ **Celtic Charlie (FR)**[35] 6770 7-8-13 **46** ow1.............. IanMongan 5 50
(Pat Phelan) *restless in stalls: led 2f and again after 4f: drvn over 2f out: hdd and no ex last 120yds* **16/1**

600- **3** 1 ½ **Farmers Hill**[21] 7891 4-8-5 **45**.............................. RyanPowell[(3)] 8 47
(Mark Hoad) *t.k.h: hld up in tch: lost pl 5f out: rdn in rr over 2f out: stl only 7th 1f out: styd on wl to take 3rd nr fin* **33/1**

64- **4** ¾ **The Catenian (IRE)**[44] 7639 4-8-8 **45**...................... ShaneKelly 3 46
(Eoin Doyle, Ire) *towards rr: bmpd over 9f out: prog over 3f out: chsd ldng pair briefly over 2f out: kpt on u.p* **11/4**[1]

00-0 **5** 1 ¾ **Lucas Pitt**[14] 28 5-8-10 **48**..................................(p) DavidKenny[(5)] 6 46
(Michael Scudamore) *racd wd: hld up towards rr: bmpd over 9f out: drvn and no prog wl over 2f out: kpt on fr over 1f out: n.d* **8/1**[2]

00-4 **6** ¾ **Vinces**[6] 129 8-8-7 **45**...(p) RaulDaSilva[(5)] 13 42
(Tim McCarthy) *hld up in last pair: rdn wl over 2f out: kpt on fnl 2f: nt gng pce to threaten* **10/1**[3]

604/ **7** 2 ¾ **Asterales**[434] 7387 5-8-12 **45**.................................... JamieMackay 1 37
(Willie Musson) *hld up in last: stl only one bhd 2f out: nudged along and passed toiling rivals after: nvr nr ldrs* **12/1**

246- **8** 2 ¼ **Dolly Colman (IRE)**[29] 7836 4-8-9 **46**...................... LukeMorris 10 35
(Michael Blake) *trckd ldr 2f: wnt 2nd again over 3f out to over 1f out: wknd qckly* **10/1**[3]

06-4 **9** 8 **Sunset Boulevard (IRE)**[12] 57 9-8-12 **48**...........(v) RobertLButler[(3)] 2 24
(Paddy Butler) *trckd ldrs: rdn to go 3rd 3f out to over 2f out: wknd qckly* **25/1**

000- **10** 7 **Corlough Mountain**[50] 7574 8-8-5 **45**...................... CharlotteJenner[(7)] 4 10
(Paddy Butler) *towards rr: bmpd over 9f out: pushed along 7f out: nvr on terms: t.o* **50/1**

005- **11** 1 ½ **Cragganmore Creek**[36] 7743 9-8-12 **45**......................(v) MartinLane 14
(Dave Morris) *s.i.s: pushed along and rapid prog to ld after 2f: hdd after 4f: pressed ldr tl wknd rapidly over 3f out: t.o* **50/1**

55-5 **12** 6 **Time To Play**[5] 160 7-9-3 **50**.................................... LiamKeniry 11
(Gary Brown) *racd wd: wl in tch tl wknd over 3f out: t.o* **10/1**[3]

2m 34.3s (-0.20) **Going Correction** -0.075s/f (Stan)
WFA 4 from 5yo+ 4lb **12** Ran SP% **116.0**
Speed ratings (Par 97): **97,95,94,94,92 92,90,89,83,79 78,74**
toteswingers: 1&2 £8.70, 1&3 £14.90, 2&3 £79.10. CSF £51.10 CT £1181.17 TOTE £4.40: £1.80, £5.80, £10.50; EX 43.20.
Owner Burns, Carroll, Miles & Ward **Bred** Razza Pallorsi **Trained** Cropthorne, Worcs
■ Stewards' Enquiry : Charlotte Jenner caution: careless riding.

FOCUS
A poor-quality handicap.

201 SKYSPORTS.COM H'CAP 6f (P)

6:25 (6:26) (Class 5) (0-70,70) 3-Y-O **£2,264** (£673; £336; £168) **Stalls** Low

Form RPR

30-2 **1** **Gabrial's Bounty (IRE)**[7] 121 3-8-13 **62**.................. FrannyNorton 1 73
(Mick Channon) *hld up in mdifield: prog on inner over 2f out: hrd rdn to ld jst over 1f out: styd on wl* **2/1**[1]

1- **2** 1 ¾ **Just Breathe (IRE)**[60] 7490 3-8-12 **61**...................... LukeMorris 6 67
(Jane Chapple-Hyam) *trckd ldrs: rdn to ld 2f out: hdd u.p jst over 1f out: one pce* **7/2**[2]

06-2 **3** hd **Illustrious Lad (IRE)**[14] 38 3-8-4 **58**.................. NathanAlison[(5)] 4 64+
(Jim Boyle) *t.k.h: hld up in midfield: nt clr run 2f out: pushed along and styd on wl fnl f: nrly snatched 2nd* **14/1**

134- **4** 1 ½ **Berlusca (IRE)**[32] 7798 3-9-3 **66**.............................. WilliamCarson 2 66
(William Jarvis) *s.i.s: wl in rr: clsd over 2f out: rdn and styd on same pce fr over 1f out* **12/1**

11-3 **5** nse **Le King Beau (USA)**[3] 189 3-9-4 **70**...................... KieranO'Neill[(3)] 3 70
(John Bridger) *cl up: effrt 2f out: rdn to chse ldng pair over 1f out: sn nt qckn: fdd ins fnl f* **7/1**

334- **6** 4 **Monty Fay (IRE)**[34] 7770 3-8-7 **56**........................(p) FrankieMcDonald 8 43
(Derek Haydn Jones) *plld hrd: prom: lost pl and wknd 2f out* **40/1**

52-2 **7** 2 **Dressed In Lace**[14] 27 3-9-6 **69**................................ IanMongan 5 50
(Jo Crowley) *led to 2f out: wknd tamely* **13/2**[3]

63-2 **8** nse **Sonsie Lass**[8] 112 3-8-13 **62**................................ JoeFanning 10 43
(Keith Dalgleish) *pressed ldr to over 2f out: sn btn* **10/1**

000- **9** nk **Chart**[48] 7593 3-8-7 **59**.. RyanPowell[(3)] 7 39
(William Jarvis) *hld up in last: shuffled along over 2f out: nvr remotely involved* **33/1**

1-36 **10** 18 **Ishiamiracle**[3] 189 3-8-10 **66**.................................(p) LeonnaMayor[(7)] 9
(Phil McEntee) *plld hrd: racd extremely wd: lost grnd bef 1/2-way: t.o* **25/1**

1m 12.43s (-0.67) **Going Correction** -0.075s/f (Stan) **10** Ran SP% **114.1**
Speed ratings (Par 97): **101,98,98,96,96 91,88,88,87,63**
toteswingers: 1&2 £3.00, 1&3 £6.70, 2&3 £11.20. CSF £8.29 CT £75.53 TOTE £3.80: £1.30, £1.10, £4.40; EX 11.40.
Owner Dr Marwan Koukash **Bred** D And Mrs D Veitch **Trained** West Ilsley, Berks
■ Stewards' Enquiry : Luke Morris caution: careless riding.

FOCUS
A modest handicap, but it was well run and the form is solid. Further improvement from the winner.
Monty Fay(IRE) Official explanation: jockey said gelding hung left

202 SKYSPORTS.COM RACING H'CAP 2m (P)

6:55 (6:56) (Class 4) (0-85,83) 4-Y-0+ **£4,075** (£1,212; £606; £303) **Stalls** Low

Form RPR

024- **1** **First Avenue**[20] 7908 7-9-7 **76**.................................... IanMongan 4 85
(Laura Mongan) *hld up in rr: gd prog on inner over 2f out: led over 1f out but pressed: drvn and styd on wl* **13/2**[3]

232- **2** 1 **Dark Ranger**[35] 7753 6-9-4 **73**................................ JamieSpencer 3 84+
(Tim Pitt) *hld up in last trio: swtchd ins over 2f out: rn into all sorts of trble and snatched up wl over 1f out: r.o strly fnl f: tk 2nd last 50yds and clsd on wnr: no ch to chal* **3/1**[1]

152- **3** 1 ½ **Where's Susie**[20] 7908 7-9-9 **78**.............................. DaneO'Neill 10 84
(Michael Madgwick) *hld up in last trio: prog on outer over 2f out: c to chal and w wnr 1f out: nt qckn fnl f: lost 2nd last 50yds* **7/1**

00-4 **4** 3 **Nezhenka**[13] 44 5-9-11 **80**.. JoeFanning 9 82
(Mark Johnston) *hld up in 5th: effrt 3f out: rdn to dispute 2nd briefly 2f out: sn readily outpcd* **9/2**[2]

12-3 **5** 1 ½ **Wild Desert (FR)**[13] 44 7-9-11 **83**.......................... RyanPowell[(3)] 6 84
(Charlie Longsdon) *trckd ldr: led 5f out: kicked on over 2f out: hdd & wknd over 1f out* **8/1**

342- **6** 4 ½ **Chookie Hamilton**[81] 7162 8-9-7 **76**........................ JimCrowley 7 71
(Keith Dalgleish) *trckd ldng trio: rdn and cl enough jst over 2f out: steadily wknd wl over 1f out* **14/1**

120- **7** nk **Quinsman**[35] 7753 6-9-3 **72**...................................... LiamKeniry 2 67
(J S Moore) *wl in tch in 6th: rdn over 3f out: no imp 2f out: sn wknd* **16/1**

131- **8** 3 **Epsom Salts**[41] 7674 7-9-2 **76**.............................. JemmaMarshall[(5)] 1 67
(Pat Phelan) *hld up disputing 7th: prog on outer to chse ldr 4f out to 2f out: wknd qckly* **10/1**

311- **9** shd **Kahfre**[60] 718 5-9-3 **72**...(v) DavidProbert 11 63
(Gary Moore) *restless in stalls: prom: rdn in 3rd 3f out: wknd wl over 1f out* **16/1**

/6-0 **10** 13 **Perfect Shot (IRE)**[5] 150 6-8-13 **68**........................(tp) AmirQuinn 8 44
(Jim Best) *a in rr: lost tch over 3f out: t.o* **33/1**

11/5 **11** 8 **Ascendant**[13] 44 6-9-10 **82**....................................(t) KieranO'Neill[(3)] 5 48
(Andrew Reid) *led at gd pce to 5f out: wknd over 3f out: t.o* **16/1**

3m 27.64s (-2.46) **Going Correction** -0.075s/f (Stan) **11** Ran SP% **116.5**
Speed ratings (Par 105): **103,102,101,100,99 97,97,95,95,89 85**
toteswingers: 1&2 £5.70, 1&3 £14.10, 2&3 £5.00. CSF £25.97 CT £142.51 TOTE £4.10: £1.50, £2.00, £2.90; EX 29.10.
Owner Mrs L J Mongan **Bred** The National Stud Never Say Die Club Ltd **Trained** Epsom, Surrey

FOCUS
They went a solid gallop here and the first three came from well off the pace. The winner reversed recent form with the third and the runner-up was unlucky.

203 KEMPTON FOR WEDDINGS H'CAP 7f (P)

7:25 (7:26) (Class 6) (0-55,61) 4-Y-0+ **£1,617** (£481; £240; £120) **Stalls** Low

Form RPR

253- **1** **Shaunas Spirit (IRE)**[20] 7910 4-8-12 **51**.................. ShaneKelly 1 63
(Dean Ivory) *prom: trckd ldr over 3f out: rdn to cl fr 2f out and clr of rest: led jst ins fnl f: styd on* **5/2**[1]

000- **2** 1 ½ **Nacho Libre**[38] 7728 7-9-1 **54**................................(b) PaddyAspell 6 62+
(Michael Easterby) *taken down early: restrained into last sn after s: looking for room over 2f out: gd prog over 1f out: r.o to take 2nd last strides: too much to do* **9/2**[3]

014- **3** ½ **Gala Spirit (IRE)**[75] 7268 5-9-2 **55**........................(p) TomEaves 3 61
(Peter Niven) *led: drew 2 l clr over 2f out: urged along over 1f out: hdd jst ins fnl f: one pce and lost 2nd last strides* **10/1**

065- **4** 2 ¼ **Snow Ridge**[197] 3709 4-9-2 **55**.................................. JimCrowley 5 55
(Ralph Beckett) *dwlt: wl in rr: prog on inner over 2f out: drvn to chse ldng pair over 1f out: no imp: lost 3rd ins fnl f* **7/2**[2]

04-6 **5** 3 **Gazboolou**[14] 39 8-9-2 **55**.. FergusSweeney 8 47
(David Pinder) *hld up in rr: pushed along and no real prog over 2f out: rdn and styd on fnl f: nvr involved* **20/1**

35-0 **6** *nk* **Dingaan (IRE)**[7] 122 9-9-1 **54** DaneO'Neill 7 45
(Peter Grayson) *dwlt: hld up in last pair: nt clr run over 2f out whn looking to be gng wl: late prog: nvr remotely involved* **12/1**

002- **7** *shd* **Warbond**[20] 7910 4-9-0 **53** (p) JamieGoldstein 13 44
(Michael Madgwick) *dwlt: racd wdst of all and hld up wl in rr: pushed along over 2f out: styd on fnl f: nvr involved* **10/1**

006- **8** *1 1/2* **Grand Honour (IRE)**[19] 7924 6-8-7 **46** oh1 LukeMorris 4 33
(Paul Howling) *chsd ldrs: disp 3rd 2f out: wknd over 1f out* **25/1**

430- **9** *3 3/4* **Chandrayaan**[19] 7923 5-8-4 **46** oh1 (v) SimonPearce(3) 14 23
(John E Long) *racd wd: chsd ldrs over 3f: sn btn* **40/1**

00-5 **10** *1* **Silly Billy (IRE)**[10] 101 4-8-10 **54** (t) JemmaMarshall(5) 9 28
(Sylvester Kirk) *chsd ldr to over 3f out: wknd over 2f out* **10/1**

563- **11** *2 1/2* **Hollie**[75] 7260 4-9-0 **53** SteveDrowne 2 20
(Peter Makin) *taken down early: dwlt: prog on inner 1/2-way: chsd ldng pair over 2f out to wl over 1f out: wknd qckly* **25/1**

00-3 **12** *shd* **Princess Willow**[14] 34 4-9-2 **55** SamHitchcott 10 22
(John E Long) *racd wd: prom to 1/2-way: sn wknd* **16/1**

1m 25.33s (-0.67) **Going Correction** -0.075s/f (Stan) **12** Ran SP% **124.7**
Speed ratings (Par 101): **100,98,97,95,91 91,91,89,85,84 81,81**
toteswingers: 1&2 £4.00, 1&3 £5.50, 2&3 £16.30. CSF £13.75 CT £103.52 TOTE £4.10: £1.30, £1.60, £4.20; EX 22.20.
Owner John Connolly & Rahul Bajaj **Bred** Miss Breda Wright **Trained** Radlett, Herts

FOCUS
A low-grade sprint handicap. The early gallop wasn't at all hectic. Modest form but it's probably sound.
Nacho Libre ◆ Official explanation: trainer's rep said gelding had a breathing problem
T/Jkpt: Not won. T/Plt: £130.30 to a £1 stake. Pool of £98,784.18 - 553.16 winning tickets.
T/Qpdt: £53.10 to a £1 stake. Pool of £9,060.12 - 126.07 winning tickets. JN

175 LINGFIELD (L-H)
Wednesday, January 18

OFFICIAL GOING: Standard
Wind: Fresh, half behind Weather: Overcast, breezy

204 PLACE ONLY BETTING AT BLUESQ.COM MEDIAN AUCTION MAIDEN STKS 7f (P)
12:50 (12:50) (Class 6) 3-Y-O **£1,704** (£503; £251) **Stalls** Low

Form RPR

2- **1** **Gaul Wood (IRE)**[163] 4864 3-9-3 0 RichardKingscote 3 68+
(Tom Dascombe) *stdd after s: in tch: effrt and hdwy bnd 2f out: pushed ahd ent fnl f: sn in command: eased wl ins fnl f: v easily* **1/7**[1]

0-4 **2** *1 1/4* **Prince Gabrial (IRE)**[14] 26 3-9-3 0 StevieDonohoe 6 57
(Kevin Ryan) *t.k.h: led after 1f: rdn wl over 1f out: hdd ent fnl f: sn outpcd by wnr and wl hld ins fnl f: kpt on for clr 2nd* **11/2**[2]

43-6 **3** *1 1/2* **Angel Cake (IRE)**[8] 114 3-8-5 50 (be) DannyBrock(7) 5 48
(Phil McEntee) *chsd ldrs: rdn and unable qck wl over 1f out: styd on same pce fr over 1f out* **16/1**[3]

00- **4** *2 1/2* **Nic Nok**[182] 4205 3-9-3 0 JoeFanning 4 46
(Harry Dunlop) *stdd s: in tch in rr: pushed along 3f out: outpcd and rdn 2f out: one pce and wl hld ent fnl f* **16/1**[3]

00- **5** *nk* **Echo Of Thunder (IRE)**[134] 5813 3-8-7 0 ChrisDCogan(5) 1 40
(Nick Littmoden) *t.k.h: led for 1f: chsd ldr after tl wl over 1f out: sn struggling u.p: wknd jst ins fnl f* **25/1**

1m 25.99s (1.19) **Going Correction** +0.05s/f (Slow) **5** Ran SP% **118.5**
Speed ratings (Par 95): **95,93,91,89,88**
toteswinger: 1&2 £1.10. CSF £1.96 TOTE £1.10: £1.02, £2.30; EX 1.70.
Owner Star Sports **Bred** Patrick J Monahan **Trained** Malpas, Cheshire

FOCUS
The hot favourite had no trouble cashing in on a good opportunity in this weak maiden. The third sets the standard.

205 DORMANSLAND CLASSIFIED CLAIMING STKS 7f (P)
1:20 (1:20) (Class 6) 4-Y-O+ **£1,704** (£503; £251) **Stalls** Low

Form RPR

-510 **1** **Lastkingofscotland (IRE)**[4] 178 6-8-6 64 (b) HayleyTurner 7 71
(Conor Dore) *mde all: rdn and edgd rt wl over 1f out: drvn and kpt on wl fnl f* **3/1**[2]

53-4 **2** *3/4* **Lutine Charlie (IRE)**[3] 186 5-8-2 69 (p) LukeMorris 6 65
(Ronald Harris) *t.k.h: chsd ldrs tl wnt 2nd over 4f out: rdn wl over 1f out: kpt on u.p and pressing wnr ins fnl f: no imp and hld fnl 75yds* **11/4**[1]

/40- **3** *1 1/2* **Prince Namid**[247] 2155 10-7-12 55 JamieMackay 2 57+
(Jonathen de Giles) *t.k.h: hld up in rr: stl last wl over 1f out: pushed along and hdwy over 1f out: edgd rt and r.o strly ins fnl f: wnt 3rd last strides* **50/1**

003- **4** *nk* **Cristaliyev**[56] 7518 4-7-9 62 (b) NathanAlison(5) 5 58
(Jim Boyle) *chsd ldrs: rdn and unable qck 2f out: styd on same pce u.p fr over 1f out* **12/1**

115- **5** *nse* **Joe Le Taxi (IRE)**[221] 4-8-8 70 JoeFanning 3 66
(Mark Johnston) *chsd ldrs: rdn wl over 1f out: drvn and no ex ins fnl f: lost 2 pls cl home* **15/2**

006- **6** *nk* **Copperwood**[19] 7097 7-8-7 67 RyanPowell(3) 8 67
(Michael Blanshard) *stdd after s: hld up in last trio: rdn and effrt over 1f out: r.o u.p ins fnl f: nt rch ldrs* **15/2**

00-5 **7** *3/4* **Twice Red**[6] 136 4-8-8 67 TomEaves 1 63
(Derek Shaw) *in tch in midfield: rdn and unble to qckn 2f out: styng on same pce whn carried rt ins fnl f* **16/1**

45-4 **8** *2 1/4* **Saharia (IRE)**[5] 158 5-8-8 68 (v) ShaneKelly 4 57
(Michael Attwater) *reluctant to go to post: dwlt and rdn along early: a towards rr: rdn and effrt on outer wl over 1f out: nvr trbld ldrs* **6/1**[3]

-000 **9** *3* **Forty Proof (IRE)**[4] 179 4-7-11 65 (tp) KieranO'Neill(3) 9 41
(Alan McCabe) *taken down early: t.k.h: hld up in tch: rdn and effrt over 2f out: wknd over 1f out* **12/1**

1m 25.12s (0.32) **Going Correction** +0.05s/f (Slow) **9** Ran SP% **112.7**
Speed ratings (Par 101): **100,99,97,97,97 96,95,93,89**
toteswingers: 1&2 £2.30, 1&3 £17.10, 2&3 £22.60. CSF £11.32 TOTE £2.80: £1.30, £1.60, £12.10; EX 9.20 Trifecta £165.40 Part won. Pool: £223.56 - 0.65 winning units..
Owner Mrs Jennifer Marsh **Bred** Baronrath Stud **Trained** Hubbert's Bridge, Lincs

FOCUS
A competitive claimer. The hold-up runners couldn't get involved in a steadily run race, but the two market leaders filled the first two positions. The winner was a length off his penultimate Wolverhampton form.

206 CROWHURST MAIDEN FILLIES' STKS 1m (P)
1:55 (1:55) (Class 5) 3-Y-O+ **£2,385** (£704; £352) **Stalls** High

Form RPR

0- **1** **Samedi**[84] 7094 3-8-7 0 JoeFanning 6 70+
(Mark Johnston) *mde all: rdn and wnt clr over 1f out: kpt on and a gng to hold on ins fnl f* **9/2**[3]

54-4 **2** *3/4* **Millibar (IRE)**[4] 180 3-8-7 72 (p) LukeMorris 8 68
(Nick Littmoden) *t.k.h: in tch: rdn and effrt jst over 2f out: drvn and chsd clr wnr 1f out: styd on wl and clsng on wnr fnl 75yds* **5/2**[2]

00- **3** *4* **News Desk**[21] 7009 3-8-7 0 NickyMackay 5 59
(John Gosden) *chsd ldrs: rdn and chsd wnr over 2f out: outpcd and no imp over 1f out: lost 2nd 1f out and wl hld after* **8/1**

4 *hd* **Burke's Rock** 3-8-7 0 HayleyTurner 3 66+
(Jeremy Noseda) *dwlt: sn rcvrd and in tch: rdn over 2f out: short of room and bdly hmpd jst over 2f out: no ch w wnr but kpt on fr over 1f out: pressing for 3rd cl home* **7/4**[1]

0- **5** *3 1/4* **Zowaina**[83] 7118 3-8-4 0 DominicFox(3) 7 51
(Roger Varian) *s.i.s and flashed tail leaving stalls: towards rr: rdn and effrt on outer bnd jst over 2f out: no imp and wl hld fr over 1f out* **9/1**

56 **6** *3* **Sweetest Friend (IRE)**[4] 182 3-8-4 0 (p) RyanPowell(3) 4 44
(J S Moore) *t.k.h: sn chsng ldr: lost 2nd over 2f out and edgd lft bnd jst over 2f out: sn wknd* **20/1**

400- **7** *4 1/2* **Aiaam Al Wafa (IRE)**[28] 7849 3-8-7 65 ChrisCatlin 9 34
(James Tate) *a towards rr: rdn and wknd over 2f out: wl bhd and racing awkwardly over 1f out* **40/1**

0- **8** *1 1/2* **Pink Delight (IRE)**[29] 7835 3-8-4 0 KieranO'Neill(3) 2 30
(J S Moore) *chsd ldr early: in tch: rdn 1/2-way: losing pl whn bdly hmpd and dropped to rr jst over 2f out: wl bhd fr over 1f out* **40/1**

9 *1/2* **Tiger Who** 4-9-13 0 StephenCraine 1 34
(David Flood) *s.i.s: a towards rr: lost tch jst over 2f out: wl bhd over 1f out* **100/1**

1m 39.33s (1.13) **Going Correction** +0.05s/f (Slow)
WFA 3 from 4yo 20lb **9** Ran SP% **114.9**
Speed ratings (Par 100): **96,95,91,91,87 84,80,78,78**
toteswingers: 1&2 £2.50, 1&3 £6.70, 2&3 £3.70. CSF £15.68 TOTE £7.70: £2.20, £1.10, £2.40; EX 20.80 Trifecta £163.90 Pool: £412.00 - 1.86 winning units..
Owner Sheikh Hamdan Bin Mohammed Al Maktoum **Bred** Darley **Trained** Middleham Moor, N Yorks
■ Stewards' Enquiry : Ryan Powell three-day ban: careless riding (Feb 1-3)

FOCUS
A steadily run fillies' maiden. The favourite ran into some major traffic problems and the front-running winner held off the 72-rated clear second. The form is rated around the runner-up, with the winner a big improver.
Sweetest Friend(IRE) Official explanation: jockey said filly hung left
Aiaam Al Wafa(IRE) Official explanation: jockey said filly hung left

207 MARRIOTT PLAY & STAY CLAIMING STKS 2m (P)
2:25 (2:25) (Class 6) 4-Y-O+ **£1,704** (£503; £251) **Stalls** Low

Form RPR

02-2 **1** **Exemplary**[13] 44 5-9-12 86 JoeFanning 6 83+
(Mark Johnston) *chsd clr ldr after 3f tl lft in ld 9f out: mde rest: rdn and kpt on fr over 1f out: rdn out* **2/7**[1]

203- **2** *1 3/4* **Crunched**[23] 7878 5-9-12 75 (v[1]) ShaneKelly 3 81
(Tim Pitt) *chsd ldr for 3f: chsd ldrs after: lft 2nd 9f out: rdn ent fnl f: edgd lft and styd on same pce ins fnl f* **6/1**[2]

130- **3** *15* **Kavaloti (IRE)**[189] 3978 8-9-5 72 AmirQuinn 5 56
(Gary Moore) *s.i.s: hld up in last pair: lft handy 9f out: rdn to chse ldng pair wl over 2f out: sn outpcd and wl btn 2f out* **9/1**[3]

/00- **4** *6* **Keep A Welcome**[18] 7939 9-9-0 34 SimonPearce(3) 4 47?
(Gerry Enright) *hld up in last pair: lft handy 9f out: rdn and struggling over 4f out: wl btn fnl 2f: wnt modest 4th ins fnl f* **66/1**

/00- **5** *4 1/2* **No Rules**[64] 7120 7-9-7 60 (b[1]) RobertWinston 2 45
(Mark H Tompkins) *prom in main gp: lft cl 3rd 9f out: rdn and lost tch qckly 3f out: bhd fnl 2f* **16/1**

66-5 **6** *72* **Putin (IRE)**[10] 98 4-8-2 53 (p) LeonnaMayor(7) 1
(Phil McEntee) *led and sn clr: hung bdly rt and hdd bnd 9f out: dropped to last and lost tch 5f out: t.o fnl 3f: eased fr wl over 1f out* **33/1**

3m 22.96s (-2.74) **Going Correction** +0.05s/f (Slow)
WFA 4 from 5yo+ 7lb **6** Ran SP% **112.4**
Speed ratings (Par 101): **108,107,99,96,94 58**
toteswingers: 1&2 £1.80, 1&3 £1.50, 2&3 £1.10. CSF £2.59 TOTE £1.30: £1.10, £1.60; EX 2.90.Exemplary was the subject of a friendly claim.
Owner Dr Marwan Koukash **Bred** Darley **Trained** Middleham Moor, N Yorks

FOCUS
The odds-on favourite scored with a bit in hand in this staying claimer, and did not need to match his reappearance form. The time was slow.
Keep A Welcome Official explanation: jockey said gelding hung left
Putin(IRE) Official explanation: jockey said gelding hung right

208 THOUSANDS OF SPORTS EXPERIENCES AT BLUESQ.COM H'CAP 5f (P)
3:00 (3:00) (Class 5) (0-75,75) 4-Y-O+ **£2,385** (£704; £352) **Stalls** High

Form RPR

-152 **1** **Desert Strike**[3] 186 6-9-0 **75** (p) NoraLooby(7) 5 82
(Alan McCabe) *t.k.h: hld up wl in tch in last pair: swtchd rt and effrt jst over 1f out: r.o wl ins fnl f to ld cl home* **3/1**[2]

03-0 **2** *nk* **Rylee Mooch**[15] 24 4-8-10 **69** (e) CharlesEddery(5) 6 75
(Richard Guest) *led: rdn over 1f out: hrd pressed and drvn ins fnl f: hdd cl home* **9/2**[3]

105- **3** *nse* **Estonia**[29] 7833 5-9-5 **73** LukeMorris 2 79
(Michael Squance) *t.k.h: hld up wl in tch in last pair: rdn and effrt ent fnl f: gd hdwy to chal wl ins fnl f: r.o* **9/2**[3]

030- **4** *3/4* **Black Baccara**[20] 7917 5-8-13 **70** (be) RyanClark(3) 3 73
(Phil McEntee) *in tch: rdn and effrt over 1f out: drvn and ev ch jst ins fnl f: no ex towards fin* **15/2**

414- **5** *hd* **Triple Dream**[20] 7917 7-9-7 **75** (tp) RichardKingscote 1 77
(Milton Bradley) *chsd ldrs: rdn and effrt on inner over 1f out: ev ch 1f out: no ex wl ins fnl f* **5/2**[1]

0-24 **6** *shd* **Sherjawy (IRE)**[5] 152 8-8-8 **62** SamHitchcott 7 64
(Zoe Davison) *restless in stalls: chsd ldr: rdn 2f out: unable qck and outpcd over 1f out: styd on same pce ins fnl f* **8/1**

000- 7 7 **Mandy's Hero**[29] 7832 4-9-1 **69**........................(p) ChrisCatlin 4 46
(Olivia Maylam) *chsd ldrs: rdn 2f out: wknd qckly ent fnl f* **16/1**
58.5s (-0.30) **Going Correction** +0.05s/f (Slow) 7 Ran SP% **118.7**
Speed ratings (Par 103): **104,103,103,102,101 101,90**
toteswingers: 1&2 £4.10, 1&3 £3.40, 2&3 £4.40. CSF £17.89 TOTE £4.70: £1.30, £2.90; EX 21.00.
Owner Mrs M J McCabe **Bred** Mrs Mary Rowlands **Trained** Averham Park, Notts

FOCUS
There was an exciting bunch finish in this sprint handicap which was run at a good pace. Ordinary form.

209 HOLTYE H'CAP — 1m 2f (P)
3:30 (3:30) (Class 5) (0-75,73) 3-Y-O — £2,385 (£704; £352) Stalls Low

Form RPR
450- 1 **Good Morning Star (IRE)**[98] 6792 3-9-1 **67**........................ JoeFanning 1 71+
(Mark Johnston) *in tch: rdn over 2f out: chsd ldr over 1f out: sustained effrt to ld wl ins fnl f: sn in command* **4/1**[3]
46-2 2 1 1/4 **Athletic**[12] 56 3-8-8 **60**........................ HayleyTurner 5 61
(Andrew Reid) *w ldr tl led 8f out and set stdy gallop: rdn and qcknd 2 l clr over 2f out: edgd rt over 1f out: pressed fnl 100yds: hdd wl ins fnl f and no ex towards fin* **7/1**
051- 3 1 **Island Melody (IRE)**[31] 7809 3-9-4 **70**........................ LukeMorris 2 69
(J S Moore) *chsd ldrs: rdn over 2f out: drvn and no imp over 1f out: kpt on ins fnl f: swtchd rt wl ins fnl f* **2/1**[1]
32-3 4 3/4 **Haafhd Handsome**[14] 32 3-9-3 **72**........................ KieranO'Neill(3) 4 70
(Richard Hannon) *led and set stdy gallop for 2f: chsd ldr after: rdn over 2f out: drvn and nt qckn over 1f out: racd awkwardly: no imp and hung bdly rt ins fnl f* **11/4**[2]
21- 5 5 **Final Delivery**[19] 7929 3-9-2 **73**........................ DavidKenny(5) 3 61
(George Baker) *hld up in tch in rr: rdn and effrt whn rdr dropped reins ent fnl 2f: drvn and no prog wl over 1f out* **5/1**
2m 9.71s (3.11) **Going Correction** +0.05s/f (Slow) 5 Ran SP% **109.2**
Speed ratings (Par 97): **89,88,87,86,82**
CSF £28.35 TOTE £4.80: £2.40, £3.10; EX 24.00.
Owner Jaber Abdullah **Bred** Wardstown Stud Ltd **Trained** Middleham Moor, N Yorks

FOCUS
They were tightly bunched for a long way in this very steadily run handicap. It's hard to be positive about the form given the slow pace.

210 PLAY ROULETTE AT BLUESQ.COM/CASINO APPRENTICE H'CAP — 6f (P)
4:05 (4:05) (Class 6) (0-60,60) 4-Y-O+ — £1,704 (£503; £251) Stalls Low

Form RPR
00-0 1 **Waterloo Dock**[11] 88 7-9-4 **60**........................(v) DannyBrock(3) 4 70
(Michael Quinn) *mde all: rdn and wnt clr 2f out: kpt on wl fnl f* **13/2**
00-3 2 2 1/2 **Do More Business (IRE)**[6] 126 5-8-11 **50**........................(v[1]) NathanAlison 1 52+
(Pat Phelan) *bhd: hdwy on inner over 2f out: rdn and chsd clr wnr wl over 1f out: kpt on but no imp fnl f* **10/3**[2]
0-55 3 shd **Chjimes (IRE)**[4] 179 8-9-5 **58**........................(b) JustinNewman 3 60+
(Conor Dore) *hld up in last trio: effrt and wd bnd 2f out: drvn to chse ldng pair jst over 1f out: r.o and pressing for 2nd cl home: no ch w wnr* **11/4**[1]
00-0 4 2 **Athaakeel (IRE)**[9] 106 6-9-2 **58**........................(b) NicoleNordblad(3) 6 53
(Ronald Harris) *t.k.h: stdd bk into last pair after s: hld up: rdn and effrt whn edgd rt over 1f out: kpt on fnl f: no ch w wnr* **15/2**
00-0 5 5 **Mi Regalo**[10] 96 4-9-4 **57**........................ DarylByrne 7 36
(Phil McEntee) *racd wd: chsd ldrs tl rdn and struggling over 2f out: wd and lost pl bnd 2f out: sn bhd* **12/1**
/34- 6 1 **Tamino (IRE)**[259] 1815 9-8-7 **46**........................ LeonnaMayor 2 22
(Alastair Lidderdale) *chsd ldrs: rdn and struggling over 2f out: wknd and towards rr whn short of room jst over 1f out: wl btn fnl f* **8/1**
34-5 7 2 1/4 **Young Simon**[5] 155 5-8-9 **51**........................(v) NatashaEaton(3) 5 20
(George Margarson) *w ldr tl rdn and unable qck over 2f out: 3rd and btn over 1f out: wknd ins fnl f* **9/2**[3]
1m 11.34s (-0.56) **Going Correction** +0.05s/f (Slow) 7 Ran SP% **111.8**
Speed ratings (Par 101): **105,101,101,98,92 90,87**
toteswingers: 1&2 £4.50, 1&3 £3.90, 2&3 £1.70. CSF £27.07 TOTE £8.80: £3.40, £2.50; EX 30.40.
Owner M J Quinn **Bred** Norman Court Stud **Trained** Newmarket, Suffolk
■ Stewards' Enquiry : Danny Brock three-day ban: careless riding (Feb 1-3)

FOCUS
A minor apprentice sprint handicap. The winner is rated back to something like his best.
T/Plt: £36.00 to a £1 stake. Pool of £50,778.36 - 1,027.84 winning tickets. T/Qpdt: £16.70 to a £1 stake. Pool of £3,751.21 - 165.73 winning tickets. SP

CAGNES-SUR-MER
Wednesday, January 18

OFFICIAL GOING: Fibresand: standard

211a PRIX DE FABRON (MAIDEN) (UNRACED 3YO) (FIBRESAND) — 1m (F)
1:20 (12:00) 3-Y-O — £9,583 (£3,833; £2,875; £1,916; £958)

RPR
1 **Studio (USA)** 3-9-2 0........................ IoritzMendizabal 7 78
(J-C Rouget, France) **6/4**[1]
2 hd **Golden Club (FR)** 3-9-2 0........................ JohanVictoire 11 77
(J-C Rouget, France) **48/10**[2]
3 3/4 **Darnetal (IRE)** 3-9-2 0........................ GregoryBenoist 5 75
(F Rohaut, France) **58/10**[3]
4 1 **Maria Crista (IRE)** 3-8-7 0........................ MatthieuAutier(6) 10 70
(J-C Rouget, France) **15/1**
5 2 1/2 **Black Jewel (FR)** 3-9-2 0........................ FranckBlondel 1 67
(Mlle S-V Tarrou, France) **19/1**
6 1 **Hyson** 3-9-2 0........................ Francois-XavierBertras 4 65
(Reg Hollinshead) *chsd ldrs: bdly hmpd by wkng ldr at s of fnl bnd and lost all ch: styd on ins fnl 1 1/2f: tk 6th cl home* **20/1**
7 1 **Majestic Speed (IRE)** 3-9-2 0........................ ThierryThulliez 3 63
(Rod Collet, France) **15/1**
8 1 1/2 **Mister Koala (FR)** 3-8-10 0........................ ASuborics(6) 6 59
(J Heloury, France) **35/1**
9 10 **Athaar (USA)** 3-8-13 0........................(p) TonyPiccone 9 33
(J-C Rouget, France) **83/10**
10 1 3/4 **Rehearse (FR)** 3-8-13 0........................ Pierre-CharlesBoudot 12 29
(D Prod'Homme, France) **13/1**
11 **Sky King (FR)** 3-9-2 0........................ JulienAuge 2 32
(B Goudot, France) **36/1**
1m 39.96s (99.96) 11 Ran SP% **117.6**
WIN (incl. 1 euro stake): 2.50. PLACES: 1.30, 1.50, 1.60. DF: 5.30. SF: 7.90.
Owner Joseph Allen **Bred** J Allen **Trained** Pau, France

190 WOLVERHAMPTON (A.W) (L-H)
Thursday, January 19

OFFICIAL GOING: Standard
Wind: Moderate, behind, turned blustery after race 4 Weather: Fine

212 BET ON WINNING DISTANCES AT BLUESQ.COM FILLIES' H'CAP — 5f 216y(P)
4:30 (4:30) (Class 5) (0-70,71) 4-Y-O+ — £2,264 (£673; £336; £168) Stalls Low

Form RPR
45-1 1 **Dancing Welcome**[10] 106 6-9-12 **71** 6ex........................(b) RichardKingscote 5 79
(Milton Bradley) *chsd ldr: rdn to ld 1f out: r.o and in control ins fnl f* **85/40**[1]
31-3 2 1 **Gold Tobougg**[8] 124 4-9-1 **65**........................ LauraPike(5) 3 70
(David Simcock) *hld up: pushed along over 2f out: hdwy and hung lft over 1f out: swtchd rt ins fnl f: r.o to take 2nd cl home: nt trble wnr* **5/2**[2]
11-2 3 nk **Chester Deelyte (IRE)**[10] 106 4-8-7 **57**........................(v) ShaneBKelly(5) 2 60
(Lisa Williamson) *towards rr: niggled along over 2f out: edgd lft over 1f out: hdwy sn after: r.o towards fin: nt pce to mount serious chal* **5/1**
310- 4 1/2 **Suddenly Susan (IRE)**[37] 7744 4-9-6 **65**........................(b) IanMongan 6 66
(Scott Dixon) *racd keenly: led: rdn and hdd 1f out: no ex fnl 50yds* **4/1**[3]
06-4 5 1 3/4 **Polemica (IRE)**[10] 106 6-9-5 **64**........................(bt) TomMcLaughlin 1 59
(Frank Sheridan) *stdd s: hld up: outpcd 2f out: kpt on ins fnl f: nvr able to trble ldrs* **20/1**
00-3 6 nk **Two Turtle Doves (IRE)**[10] 106 6-8-8 **60**........................ NoelGarbutt(7) 4 54
(Michael Mullineaux) *chsd ldrs: rdn jst over 1f out: kpt on same pce ins fnl f* **22/1**
036- 7 4 1/2 **Basle**[161] 4942 5-9-7 **66**........................(t) RobertWinston 7 46
(Gay Kelleway) *hld up: hdwy to chse ldrs over 3f out: pushed along over 2f out: wknd fnl f* **28/1**
1m 15.36s (0.36) **Going Correction** +0.05s/f (Slow) 7 Ran SP% **109.8**
Speed ratings (Par 100): **99,97,97,96,94 93,87**
toteswingers:1&2:£1.60, 1&3:£2.60, 2&3:£2.40 CSF £6.94 CT £19.64 TOTE £3.00: £1.50, £1.10; EX 10.00 Trifecta £14.10 Pool: £779.47 - 40.63 winning units..
Owner J M Bradley **Bred** The Hon Mrs E J Wills **Trained** Sedbury, Gloucs

FOCUS
An ordinary fillies' handicap run in a time 0.29 seconds slower than the later seller.

213 DINE IN HORIZONS CLAIMING STKS — 1m 5f 194y(P)
5:00 (5:00) (Class 6) 4-Y-O+ — £1,704 (£503; £251) Stalls Low

Form RPR
131- 1 **La Estrella (USA)**[22] 7900 9-9-11 87........................ DaneO'Neill 7 82
(Don Cantillon) *hld up: hdwy 4f out: chsd ldrs 3f out: rdn to ld 1f out: drew clr ins fnl f: eased cl home* **2/7**[1]
61- 2 5 **Country Road (IRE)**[197] 3743 6-9-1 77........................(p) LukeMorris 1 65
(Michael Appleby) *trckd ldrs: wnt 2nd over 3f out: led 2f out: rdn and hung lft over 1f out: sn hdd: no ch w wnr fnl 150yds* **7/1**[3]
015- 3 2 1/4 **Admirable Duque (IRE)**[22] 7900 6-9-4 79........................(be) JoshBaudains(7) 4 72
(Dominic Ffrench Davis) *hld up: gd hdwy over 5f out: led 4f out: hdd 2f out: stl ev ch u.p wl over 1f out: one pce and wl hld fnl f* **11/2**[2]
655- 4 3 **Dot's Delight**[22] 5916 8-8-10 46........................(t) PaulHanagan 8 53
(Mark Rimell) *in tch: pushed along over 3f out: outpcd over 2f out: kpt on wout threatening ins fnl f* **25/1**
5 21 **Kildare Kitten (USA)**[29] 3970 4-8-4 49 ow2........................(tp) ChrisCatlin 5 24
(Matt Sheppard) *chsd ldr: led over 5f out: hdd 4f out: wknd wl over 2f out* **100/1**
6 3/4 **Lady Hannah**[24] 7-8-9 0........................ RyanPowell(3) 6 25
(Shaun Lycett) *hld up: rdn over 3f out: sn outpcd: nvr a threat* **100/1**
0- 7 dist **Exeptional Girl**[28] 7856 6-9-3 0........................(t) TomMcLaughlin 2
(Frank Sheridan) *racd keenly: sn led: hdd over 5f out: sn wknd: lost tch 4f out: t.o* **100/1**
3m 4.13s (-1.87) **Going Correction** +0.05s/f (Slow)
WFA 4 from 6yo+ 6lb 7 Ran SP% **112.5**
Speed ratings (Par 101): **107,104,102,101,89 88,**
toteswingers:1&2:£1.50, 1&3:£1.10, 2&3:£1.40 CSF £2.81 TOTE £1.40: £1.10, £1.90; EX 3.80 Trifecta £6.60 Pool: £1102.35 - 121.91 winning units..Dot's Delight was claimed by Mr J. J. Best for £5,000.
Owner Don Cantillon **Bred** Five Horses Ltd And Theatrical Syndicate **Trained** Newmarket, Suffolk

FOCUS
The pace was steady until the third took over down the back straight on the final circuit. The proximity of the 46-rated fourth limits the form.

214 CALL 01902 390000 TO SPONSOR A RACE MEDIAN AUCTION MAIDEN STKS — 5f 216y(P)
5:30 (5:33) (Class 5) 3-5-Y-O — £2,264 (£673; £336; £168) Stalls Low

Form RPR
052- 1 **Les Verguettes (IRE)**[66] 7411 4-9-7 67........................ ChrisCatlin 3 71
(Chris Wall) *handy: sn stdd: hld up: hdwy 2f out: r.o to ld narrowly wl ins fnl f: jst hld on* **5/1**[3]
3 2 nse **Henry Bee**[14] 41 3-8-10 0........................ PaulHanagan 4 72
(Richard Fahey) *prom: n.m.r and hmpd after nrly 1f: in tch: trckd ldrs 3f out: rdn to ld wl over 1f out: hdd narrowly wl ins fnl f: r.o: jst denied* **9/4**[1]
026- 3 5 **Chorister Sport (IRE)**[29] 7837 3-8-10 71........................ JoeFanning 1 56
(William Jarvis) *prom for 1f: racd in midfield tl hdwy to chse ldrs over 1f out: kpt on: nt gng pce of front pair fnl 100yds* **4/1**[2]
003- 4 1/2 **How Sweet It Is (IRE)**[20] 7925 3-8-5 61........................ WilliamCarson 9 49
(James Bethell) *led: hdd narrowly 3f out: rdn over 2f out: stl ev ch wl over 1f out: kpt on same pce wl ins fnl f* **4/1**[2]
5 3/4 **Demora** 3-8-5 0........................ NeilChalmers 8 47
(Michael Appleby) *towards rr: hdwy over 4f out: led 3f out: rdn and hdd wl over 1f out: fdd wl ins fnl f* **66/1**
00- 6 1/2 **Field Finner**[37] 7747 4-9-7 0........................ IanMongan 5 49
(Scott Dixon) *s.s: bhd: pushed along over 2f out: styd on ins fnl f: nt gng pce to get competitive* **66/1**
50-4 7 2 3/4 **Bygones For Coins (IRE)**[7] 135 4-9-0 39........................ MatthewHopkins(7) 2 40
(Alan Berry) *racd keenly: prom: lost pl over 3f out: n.d after* **100/1**
22-2 8 3/4 **Like The Night**[15] 26 3-8-2 64........................ AdamBeschizza(3) 6 34
(Marco Botti) *towards rr: hdwy into midfield 4f out: rdn over 2f out: no imp over 1f out: wknd ins fnl f* **4/1**[2]

005- 9 2 3/4 **Sailing North (USA)**197 3747 4-9-12 58 LukeMorris 7 34
(Ronald Harris) *prom: rdn over 2f out: wknd over 1f out* **40/1**

1m 15.7s (0.70) **Going Correction** +0.05s/f (Slow)
WFA 3 from 4yo 16lb **9** Ran SP% **113.9**
Speed ratings (Par 103): **97,96,90,89,88 87,84,83,79**
toteswingers:1&2:£3.70, 2&3:£3.70, 1&3:£3.50 CSF £16.37 TOTE £6.30: £1.70, £1.40, £1.10; EX 18.70 Trifecta £48.70 Pool: £709.81 - 10.78 winning units..
Owner David Gilbert **Bred** Camogue Stud Ltd **Trained** Newmarket, Suffolk

FOCUS
Just a modest sprint maiden and the time was the slowest of three races at the trip.
Like The Night Official explanation: jockey said filly had no more to give

215 WOLVERHAMPTON-RACECOURSE.CO.UK (S) STKS 5f 216y(P)
6:00 (6:00) (Class 6) 4-Y-0+ **£1,704** (£503; £251) **Stalls** Low

Form RPR
050- 1 **Cape Of Storms**37 7744 9-8-12 63 (b) TomEaves 9 71
(Roy Brotherton) *mde all: rdn over 1f out: styd on and kpt finding more ins fnl f* **40/1**
054- 2 1 1/4 **Master Of Disguise**20 7926 6-9-3 78 (t) WilliamCarson 8 72
(Brian Baugh) *racd in 2nd pl: rdn over 1f out: kpt on ins fnl f but no real imp on wnr* **9/4**1
010- 3 1 1/4 **Tombi (USA)**20 7926 8-9-3 75 PaulHanagan 4 68
(Ollie Pears) *hld up: rdn and hdwy over 1f out: styd on ins fnl f: nt quite gng pce of front 2* **9/4**1
630- 4 hd **Ebraam (USA)**152 5262 9-8-12 88 LukeMorris 5 62
(Ronald Harris) *racd keenly: hld up: hdwy over 3f out: chsd ldrs over 1f out: nt qckn ins fnl f* **3/1**2
31-0 5 2 **Towy Boy (IRE)**12 88 7-8-12 64 (bt) RaulDaSilva(5) 2 61
(Ian Wood) *hld up: hdwy to chse ldrs over 1f out: one pce fnl 100yds* **11/1**3
/65- 6 3 **Mercers Row**22 7897 5-8-12 62 BarryMcHugh 3 46
(Noel Wilson) *chsd ldrs: rdn over 2f out: stl wl there over 1f out: wknd fnl 150yds* **14/1**
0-20 7 7 **Memphis Man**5 179 9-8-10 56 KevinLundie(7) 1 29
(David Evans) *dwlt: bhd: outpcd 3f out: lft wl bhd over 2f out: nvr on terms* **20/1**
200- 8 1 1/2 **Sofias Number One (USA)**44 7647 4-8-12 63 (b) RobertWinston 6 19
(Roy Bowring) *chsd ldrs: rdn and wknd 2f out: eased whn btn ins fnl f* **25/1**
10-0 9 5 **Novay Essjay (IRE)**11 95 5-8-8 52 ow1 DavidKenny(5) 7
(Dai Williams) *hld up: u.p and outpcd over 3f out: lft wl bhd over 2f out* **100/1**

1m 15.07s (0.07) **Going Correction** +0.05s/f (Slow) **9** Ran SP% **113.6**
Speed ratings (Par 101): **101,99,97,97,94 90,81,79,72**
toteswingers:1&2:£12.90, 2&3:£1.60, 1&3:£19.50 CSF £124.80 TOTE £58.10: £6.80, £1.60, £1.02; EX 174.90 Trifecta £530.30 Pool: £716.65 - 1.00 winning units..There was no bid for the winner.
Owner Arthur Clayton **Bred** R J Turner **Trained** Elmley Castle, Worcs

FOCUS
The time was the quickest of three races at the trip.
Cape Of Storms Official explanation: trainer said, regarding apparent improvement in form, that the gelding appreciated being fitted with a cross nose band.
Novay Essjay(IRE) Official explanation: jockey said gelding hung right

216 FOLLOW US ON TWITTER @BLUESQ H'CAP 1m 1f 103y(P)
6:30 (6:31) (Class 4) (0-80,79) 4-Y-0+ **£4,204** (£1,251; £625; £312) **Stalls** Low

Form RPR
11-0 1 **Archie Rice (USA)**15 36 6-9-1 76 RyanClark(3) 3 85
(Tom Keddy) *trckd ldrs: rdn over 1f out: r.o to ld ins fnl f: in command towards fin* **16/1**
531- 2 1 1/4 **West End Lad**37 7743 9-9-7 79 (b) RussKennemore 9 85
(Roy Bowring) *led for 1f: racd in 2nd pl: regained ld 2f out: hdd ins fnl f: kpt on but hld after* **33/1**
36-4 3 hd **The Mongoose**5 176 4-8-11 70 LukeMorris 11 76
(David Evans) *hld up: pushed along 2f out: rdn and hdwy over 1f out: styd on ins fnl f* **6/1**2
000- 4 3/4 **Hidden Glory**24 7877 5-9-4 76 (b) FrederikTylicki 2 80
(James Given) *midfield: rdn and hdwy over 1f out: chsd ldrs ins fnl f: one pce nr fin* **20/1**
232- 5 nk **Knowe Head (NZ)**22 7901 5-8-9 70 AdamBeschizza(3) 4 73+
(James Unett) *midfield: effrt wl over 1f out: prog ins fnl f: gng on at fin* **7/1**3
00-1 6 1/2 **Postscript (IRE)**13 67 4-8-9 68 StevieDonohoe 8 70
(Ian Williams) *in tch: trckd ldrs 2f out: rdn over 1f out: styd on same pce ins fnl f* **9/2**1
1-05 7 nk **Opus Maximus (IRE)**5 177 7-9-7 79 HayleyTurner 6 81
(Conor Dore) *in rr: u.p 3f out: hdwy over 1f out: styd on ins fnl f: nvr able to trble ldrs* **9/2**1
405- 8 1 **Hawaana (IRE)**18 6631 7-8-13 76 RaulDaSilva(5) 13 76
(Gay Kelleway) *midfield: pushed along 2f out: no imp over 1f out: one pce fnl f* **50/1**
044- 9 1 3/4 **Full Toss**55 7549 6-9-1 73 JohnFahy 10 69
(Jim Goldie) *hld up: pushed along over 2f out: nvr able to trble ldrs* **16/1**
440- 10 1/2 **Snow Dancer (IRE)**24 7877 8-9-6 78 JamesSullivan 12 73
(Hugh McWilliams) *in rr: nvr able to trble ldrs* **22/1**
152- 11 1 1/4 **Chosen Forever**24 7877 7-9-4 79 DaleSwift(3) 5 71
(Geoffrey Oldroyd) *trckd ldrs: rdn over 2f out: edgd rt and nt handle bnd wl ent st: wknd over 1f out* **11/1**
111- 12 5 **Maven**31 7816 4-8-8 72 AdamCarter(5) 7 54
(Tim Easterby) *led after 1f: rdn and hdd 2f out: wknd 1f out* **6/1**2
100- 13 dist **Mountain Cat (IRE)**223 2887 8-9-7 79 RobertWinston 1
(Geoffrey Harker) *midfield: wknd 4f out: sn bhd: t.o over 2f out: virtually p.u ins fnl f* **50/1**

1m 59.88s (-1.82) **Going Correction** +0.05s/f (Slow)
WFA 4 from 5yo+ 1lb **13** Ran SP% **113.5**
Speed ratings (Par 105): **110,108,108,108,107 107,107,106,104,104 103,98,**
toteswingers:1&2:£57.20, 2&3:£32.90, 1&3:£18.60 CSF £463.35 CT £3476.92 TOTE £15.90: £4.90, £7.30, £2.80; EX 235.60 Trifecta £648.00 Pool: £875.69 - 1.00 winning units..
Owner Andrew Duffield **Bred** Baltusrol Thoughbreds Llc Et Al **Trained** Newmarket, Suffolk

FOCUS
A good, competitive-looking handicap, but the early pace was modest and a handy ride proved advantageous.
Snow Dancer(IRE) Official explanation: jockey said mare never travelled
Mountain Cat(IRE) Official explanation: trainer said gelding finished sore

217 GREAT OFFERS AT WOLVERHAMPTON-RACECOURSE.CO.UK H'CAP 1m 4f 50y(P)
7:00 (7:00) (Class 6) (0-65,65) 3-Y-O **£1,704** (£503; £251) **Stalls** Low

Form RPR
002- 1 **Quiet Appeal (IRE)**21 7915 3-8-4 48 JoeFanning 6 58+
(Mark Johnston) *chsd ldr: led over 1 m out: stdd pce over 5f out: slipped field and over 3 l clr 2f out: a in command after: readily* **11/8**1
023- 2 1 3/4 **Astroscarlet**40 7708 3-8-5 49 JohnFahy 4 53
(Mark H Tompkins) *hld up: hdwy 3f out: rdn to take 2nd over 1f out: styd on ins fnl f but no ch w wnr* **6/1**3
05-2 3 1 **Cotes Du Rhone (IRE)**15 30 3-8-2 46 oh1 (v1) LukeMorris 2 49
(David Evans) *chsd ldrs: rdn over 6f out: chsd wnr over 2f out tl over 1f out: kpt on but no ch after* **9/2**2
060- 4 9 **Lady Author**34 7777 3-8-2 46 oh1 PaulHanagan 1 34
(Richard Fahey) *chsd ldrs: rdn and outpcd 3f out: no imp after* **12/1**
005- 5 11 **Lone Star State (IRE)**31 7821 3-9-4 62 (t) TomMcLaughlin 3 33
(Frank Sheridan) *hld up: pushed along and outpcd 4f out: n.d after* **10/1**
034- 6 21 **Our Ivor**40 7709 3-9-5 63 NeilChalmers 8
(Michael Appleby) *in tch: wnt 2nd after 4f: lost 2nd over 2f out: wknd wl over 1f out* **8/1**
000- 7 3 **Silver Native (IRE)**21 7915 3-8-2 46 oh1 FrankieMcDonald 7
(Mike Murphy) *hld up in rr: toiling fr over 3f out* **66/1**
360- 8 1/2 **Jimmy The Lollipop (IRE)**29 7849 3-9-7 65 (b) TomEaves 5
(Neil Mulholland) *led: hdd over 1m out: trckd ldrs after: wkng whn n.m.r and hmpd jst under 3f out: sn bhd* **14/1**

2m 42.81s (1.71) **Going Correction** +0.05s/f (Slow) **8** Ran SP% **110.6**
Speed ratings (Par 95): **96,94,94,88,80 66,64,64**
toteswingers:1&2:£2.50, 2&3:£3.30, 1&3:£2.00 CSF £9.18 CT £26.76 TOTE £2.30: £1.10, £1.10, £1.30; EX 10.50 Trifecta £18.20 Pool: £394.69 - 16.04 winning units..
Owner T T Bloodstocks **Bred** Corduff Stud Ltd & T J Rooney **Trained** Middleham Moor, N Yorks

FOCUS
A long trip for moderate young horses, but the early pace was modest and it wasn't a severe stamina test. The time was over seven seconds above standard.

218 PLAY RAINBOW RICHES AT BLUESQ.COM H'CAP 7f 32y(P)
7:30 (7:31) (Class 7) (0-50,50) 4-Y-0+ **£1,704** (£503; £251) **Stalls** High

Form RPR
256- 1 **Look For Love**22 7899 4-8-8 48 (e) JackDuern(7) 1 56
(Reg Hollinshead) *chsd ldrs: wnt 2nd over 3f out: led wl over 1f out: sn rdn: kpt on ins fnl f: a doing enough cl home* **16/1**
03-0 2 3/4 **Cairanne**8 125 4-8-9 45 RyanClark(3) 4 51
(Tom Keddy) *hld up: hdwy whn nt clr run over 1f out: edgd sltly rt ins fnl f: r.o to snatch 2nd nr fin: could nt quite rch wnr* **16/1**
3/0- 3 nk **Vigano (IRE)**78 7229 7-9-0 47 (b) JFEgan 8 52
(Jaclyn Tyrrell, Ire) *racd keenly in midfield: rdn and hdwy over 1f out: r.o ins fnl f: hld fnl strides* **3/1**2
4 3/4 **Esytopolishadimond (IRE)**13 72 5-8-12 45 HayleyTurner 10 48
(Michael J Browne, Ire) *hld up: hdwy on wd outside over 1f out: styd on ins fnl f: one pce fnl strides* **8/11**1
036- 5 shd **Set To Go**191 3943 5-8-10 46 (b) RossAtkinson(3) 2 49
(Tor Sturgis) *led: rdn 2f out: hdd wl over 1f out: remained in contention tl no ex cl home* **20/1**
626/ 6 2 1/2 **Secret Assassin (IRE)**143 9-8-13 46 JamieGoldstein 3 42
(Mrs J L Le Brocq, Jersey) *in tch: effrt on inner 2f out: chsd ldrs over 1f out: fdd fnl 75yds* **12/1**
00-3 7 2 3/4 **Kirstys Lad**14 45 10-8-7 47 NoelGarbutt(7) 5 36
(Michael Mullineaux) *chsd ldr tl over 3f out: rdn over 2f out: wknd ent fnl f* **7/1**3
05- 8 1 3/4 **Rise To Glory (IRE)**20 7924 4-8-12 45 (t) LiamKeniry 6 29
(Denis P Quinn, Ire) *racd keenly: chsd ldrs: effrt over 2f out: wknd ins fnl f* **20/1**
600- 9 1 3/4 **Sweet Mirasol (IRE)**217 3096 5-8-7 45 (t) NathanAlison(5) 9 24
(Mandy Rowland) *hld up: struggling over 3f out: nvr on terms* **66/1**
55-0 10 10 **Welsh Dancer**8 125 4-9-3 50 (p) LukeMorris 12
(Ronald Harris) *struggling over 3f out: a bhd* **7/1**3

1m 30.96s (1.36) **Going Correction** +0.05s/f (Slow) **10** Ran SP% **138.4**
Speed ratings (Par 97): **94,93,92,91,91 88,85,83,81,70**
toteswingers:1&2:£45.20, 2&3:£33.70, 1&3:£9.30 CSF £275.80 CT £1028.91 TOTE £27.50: £4.80, £8.40, £3.10; EX 442.60 TRIFECTA Not won..
Owner S L Edwards **Bred** S L Edwards & Sarah Hollinshead **Trained** Upper Longdon, Staffs
■ Stewards' Enquiry : J F Egan five-day ban: used whip with excessive frequency (Feb 2-4,6,7)

FOCUS
A really moderate contest.
T/Plt: £28.50 to a £1 stake. Pool of £86,712.03 - 2,217.02 winning tickets. T/Qpdt: £15.60 to a £1 stake. Pool of £10,233.83 - 483.20 winning tickets. DO

204 LINGFIELD (L-H)
Friday, January 20

OFFICIAL GOING: Standard
Wind: Strong, across (towards stands) Weather: Overcast

219 PLACE ONLY BETTING AT BLUESQ.COM MAIDEN STKS 5f (P)
12:50 (12:50) (Class 5) 3-Y-O **£2,385** (£704; £352) **Stalls** High

Form RPR
520- 1 **Pucon**30 7837 3-8-12 68 DaneO'Neill 2 58
(Roger Teal) *mde all: drvn over 1f out: hld on nr fin* **5/2**2
63- 2 nk **Place That Face**37 7749 3-8-12 0 HayleyTurner 5 57
(Hughie Morrison) *trckd ldng pair on outer: hanging and nt qckn over 1f out: rdn and r.o to take 2nd ins fnl f: could nt rch wnr* **7/4**1
5-5 3 3/4 **Saint Boniface**16 26 3-9-3 0 FergusSweeney 4 59
(Peter Makin) *dwlt: hld up in tch in last: pushed along and same pl 1f out: shkn up and r.o to take 3rd nr fin* **25/1**
33-0 4 nk **Marie's Fantasy**16 27 3-8-12 53 JamieGoldstein 3 53
(Zoe Davison) *pressed wnr: rdn and nt qckn over 1f out: one pce and lost 2nd ins fnl f* **12/1**
6-0 5 nk **Cambridge Duchess**6 181 3-8-9 0 RyanClark(3) 1 52
(Stuart Williams) *trckd ldrs on inner: shkn up 1f out: kpt on same pce: nvr chal* **10/3**3

446- **6** *shd* **Thorpe Bay**[36] 7770 3-9-3 58 SteveDrowne 6 57
(Mark Rimmer) *trckd ldrs: cl up over 1f out: shkn up and kpt on same pce: nvr chal* **8/1**

59.37s (0.57) **Going Correction** +0.125s/f (Slow) 6 Ran SP% **110.7**
Speed ratings (Par 97): **100,99,98,97,97 97**
toteswingers:1&2:£1.30, 2&3:£13.00, 1&3:£13.00 CSF £7.07 TOTE £2.60: £1.10, £1.60; EX 6.20.
Owner J A Redmond **Bred** J Redmond **Trained** Ashtead, Surrey

FOCUS
A weak sprint maiden. It was run at an average sort of pace and the entire field was covered by around two lengths at the finish.

220 LINGFIELDPARK.CO.UK CLAIMING STKS 6f (P)
1:25 (1:25) (Class 6) 4-Y-0+ **£1,704** (£503; £251) **Stalls** Low

Form RPR
53-3 **1** **Drawnfromthepast (IRE)**[14] 62 7-8-10 85 StevieDonohoe 3 68
(Jamie Osborne) *trckd ldng pair: gap appeared over 1f out: drvn to ld ins fnl f: hld on* **15/8**[2]

2-51 **2** *nk* **Hinton Admiral**[7] 146 8-8-13 75 JoeFanning 1 70
(Keith Dalgleish) *awkward s: t.k.h and hld up in 4th: effrt and hanging over 1f out: shkn up and carried rt fnl f: r.o to take 2nd nr fin and clsd on wnr* **4/6**[1]

660- **3** *½* **My Lord**[48] 7629 4-8-12 69 LukeMorris 6 68
(Ronald Harris) *pressed ldr: led jst over 2f out: drvn over 1f out: hdd and one pce ins fnl f* **14/1**[3]

26-0 **4** *1 ¾* **Super Frank (IRE)**[7] 152 9-8-7 52 (b) SamHitchcott 2 57
(Zoe Davison) *hld up in last: effrt and hanging wl over 1f out: kpt on ins fnl f to take 4th nr fin* **100/1**

/0-6 **5** *1* **Speedfit Girl (IRE)**[5] 186 4-8-5 73 RyanPowell(3) 5 55
(George Margarson) *led to jst over 2f out: wknd fnl f* **20/1**

1m 12.32s (0.42) **Going Correction** +0.125s/f (Slow) 5 Ran SP% **107.2**
Speed ratings (Par 101): **102,101,100,98,97**
CSF £3.24 TOTE £2.40: £1.60, £1.10; EX 4.50.
Owner Dr Marwan Koukash **Bred** D And Mrs D Veitch **Trained** Upper Lambourn, Berks

FOCUS
Fairly straightforward claiming form.

221 FELBRIDGE H'CAP 2m (P)
2:00 (2:00) (Class 6) (0-65,65) 4-Y-0+ **£1,704** (£503; £251) **Stalls** Low

Form RPR
44-4 **1** **Guards Chapel**[14] 58 4-9-0 59 (be[1]) AdamKirby 7 66
(Gary Moore) *hld up tl wnt prom after 6f: trckd ldr 6f out: rdn to chal over 2f out: pressed new ldr ins fnl f: led post* **7/2**[2]

06-2 **2** *nse* **Maison Brillet (IRE)**[7] 156 5-9-10 65 (p) RyanClark(3) 3 72
(Clive Drew) *trckd ldrs: effrt fr 3f out: chal over 1f out: narrow ld jst ins fnl f: hdd post* **9/2**[3]

42-1 **3** *1 ½* **Maslak (IRE)**[14] 58 8-9-6 58 ChrisCatlin 6 63
(Peter Hiatt) *led: set mod pce but untrbld: kicked on 3f out: sn pressed: worn down jst ins fnl f* **3/1**[1]

035- **4** *¾* **Frederick William**[45] 5420 4-9-6 65 (p) DaneO'Neill 5 69
(Chris Gordon) *hld up and sn in last pair: prog on wd outside 3f out: lost grnd bnd 2f out and hanging sn after: styd on again ins fnl f* **14/1**

252- **5** *1 ¾* **Red Current**[48] 7631 8-9-3 60 DavidKenny(5) 1 62
(Michael Scudamore) *trckd ldrs: cl up bhd ldng quartet over 2f out: rdn and nt qckn over 1f out* **8/1**

20-0 **6** *4 ½* **Rodrigo De Freitas (IRE)**[16] 28 5-9-3 55 (v) JimCrowley 4 52
(Jim Boyle) *hld up in last: pushed along and lost tch w ldrs over 3f out: nvr on terms after* **7/2**[2]

6/6- **7** *4* **Red Lancer**[57] 7527 11-9-3 55 (p) LukeMorris 2 47
(Jonathen de Giles) *trckd ldr 6f: rdn 4f out: sn lost pl and btn* **10/1**

3m 32.6s (6.90) **Going Correction** +0.125s/f (Slow)
WFA 4 from 5yo+ 7lb 7 Ran SP% **114.5**
Speed ratings (Par 101): **87,86,86,85,84 82,80**
toteswingers:1&2:£3.80, 2&3:£1.70, 1&3:£3.60 CSF £19.60 TOTE £4.40: £2.20, £3.60; EX 19.00.
Owner Andrew Bradmore **Bred** Mrs J Chandris **Trained** Lower Beeding, W Sussex

FOCUS
An ordinary staying handicap that turned into something of a sprint from around 3f out.

222 MARSH GREEN (S) STKS 1m 4f (P)
2:30 (2:30) (Class 6) 4-6-Y-0 **£1,704** (£503; £251) **Stalls** Low

Form RPR
40-3 **1** **Ay Tay Tate (IRE)**[12] 98 6-9-3 66 (p) JimmyFortune 4 67
(David C Griffiths) *mde all: shoved along fr 3f out: hrd rdn over 1f out: hld on* **11/2**

14-2 **2** *hd* **Rowan Ridge**[14] 57 4-9-4 67 (b) JimCrowley 1 72
(Jim Boyle) *trckd wnr: rdn and nt qckn wl over 1f out: styd on ins fnl f: jst hld* **4/1**[2]

21-1 **3** *1* **Irons On Fire (USA)**[13] 85 4-9-4 69 (p) DaneO'Neill 3 70
(George Baker) *dwlt: hld up bhd ldng pair: effrt over 2f out: drvn to cl over 1f out: nt qckn and hld fnl f* **5/6**[1]

32-1 **4** *6* **Wisecraic**[16] 35 5-9-8 63 LiamKeniry 2 60
(J S Moore) *hld up bhd ldng pair: pushed along over 2f out: sn outpcd: shkn up over 1f out: wknd* **9/2**[3]

2m 35.83s (2.83) **Going Correction** +0.125s/f (Slow)
WFA 4 from 5yo+ 4lb 4 Ran SP% **108.1**
Speed ratings: **95,94,94,90**
CSF £24.30 TOTE £4.00; EX 17.00.Irons On Fire was subject to a friendly claim.
Owner Andrew Langan **Bred** Kelly's Vintage Partnership **Trained** Bawtry, S Yorks

FOCUS
A tight-looking seller and another race that developed into a sprint nearing the home turn.

223 EXCLUSIVE LIVE SHOWS AT BLUESQ.COM CONDITIONS STKS 1m 4f (P)
3:05 (3:05) (Class 4) 4-Y-0+ **£4,204** (£1,251; £625; £312) **Stalls** Low

Form RPR
112- **1** **Junoob**[34] 7802 4-8-12 95 RichardKingscote 4 95+
(Tom Dascombe) *hld up bhd ldng pair: pushed up to chal on outer 2f out: led over 1f out: sn clr: eased last 75yds* **30/100**[1]

60-0 **2** *3* **Layline (IRE)**[6] 177 5-9-7 89 RobertWinston 2 93
(Gay Kelleway) *t.k.h early: hld up bhd ldng pair: effrt 2f out: n.m.r jst over 1f out: sn chsd wnr but no ch* **14/1**

06-1 **3** *3* **Uphold**[13] 93 5-9-0 82 (vt) RaulDaSilva(5) 1 86
(Gay Kelleway) *led: kicked on over 2f out: hdd over 1f out: sn btn* **10/1**[3]

13-1 **4** *3 ¼* **Shieldmaiden (USA)**[15] 43 4-8-10 81 (b) JoeFanning 3 76
(Mark Johnston) *pressed ldr: chal and upsides 2f out: wknd tamely over 1f out* **11/2**[2]

2m 33.45s (0.45) **Going Correction** +0.125s/f (Slow)
WFA 4 from 5yo 4lb 4 Ran SP% **108.1**
Speed ratings (Par 105): **103,101,99,96**
CSF £5.39 TOTE £1.20; EX 5.20.
Owner Alan Solomon **Bred** Shadwell Estate Company Limited **Trained** Malpas, Cheshire

FOCUS
An easy success for the well-treated winner.

224 HARE LANE H'CAP 1m 2f (P)
3:40 (3:40) (Class 6) (0-65,65) 4-Y-0+ **£1,704** (£503; £251) **Stalls** Low

Form RPR
11-2 **1** **Trip Switch**[6] 176 6-9-4 62 AdamKirby 10 75+
(George Prodromou) *hld up off str pce: stdy prog 4f out: led over 2f out: sn clr: rdn out and in n.d fnl f* **5/2**[1]

404- **2** *3* **Princess Lexi (IRE)**[22] 7904 5-8-12 56 JimCrowley 11 63+
(William Knight) *hld up and in last early: gng strly and prog over 3f out: trbld passage after: r.o to take 2nd ins fnl f: no ch w wnr* **11/1**

33-4 **3** *¾* **Land Hawk (IRE)**[14] 67 6-8-11 58 SimonPearce(3) 6 64
(Lydia Pearce) *hld up off a str pce: prog fr 3f out: rdn to chse wnr wl over 1f out: no imp: lost 2nd ins fnl f: kpt on* **12/1**

644- **4** *3* **Striding Edge (IRE)**[21] 7930 6-8-8 59 NicoleNordblad(7) 7 59+
(Hans Adielsson) *hld up wl in rr: dropped to last 5f out: gng wl enough but trbld passage fr 3f out: styd on fnl f: no ch* **8/1**

12-3 **5** *1 ½* **Idol Deputy (FR)**[11] 104 6-8-7 58 RachealKneller(7) 1 55
(Mark Usher) *hld up off the pce on inner: crept clsr over 2f out: rdn to take 3rd briefly over 1f out: sn wknd* **8/1**

21-0 **6** *1* **Prince Of Thebes (IRE)**[6] 176 11-8-7 56 (p) MarkCoumbe(5) 5 51
(Michael Attwater) *s.i.s: hld up towards rr: prog on outer 3f out: chsd ldrs and in tch 2f out: sn wl outpcd* **16/1**

222- **7** *3* **Edgware Road**[22] 7904 4-9-2 65 (b) RyanPowell(3) 4 54+
(Paul Rich) *hld at decent pce to over 7f out: trckd ldrs after: lost pl and nt clr run over 2f out: nowhere to go wl over 1f out: no prog after* **11/2**[3]

01-0 **8** *shd* **Green Earth (IRE)**[13] 87 5-9-2 65 JemmaMarshall(5) 8 53
(Pat Phelan) *s.s: wl in rr: effrt and sme prog on wd outside 3f out: no imp 2f out: outpcd after* **25/1**

050/ **9** *9* **Mosqueta**[15] 2480 5-8-9 53 LukeMorris 2 23
(Andrew Reid) *prom: drvn 1/2-way: wknd qckly 4f out: sn bhd* **80/1**

000- **10** *2 ½* **Strong Vigilance (IRE)**[49] 7601 5-9-0 63 RaulDaSilva(5) 9 28
(Michael Bell) *prom: drvn 5f out: led jst over 3f out to over 2f out: wknd rapidly* **4/1**[2]

4-36 **11** *8* **Bull Five**[6] 176 5-9-5 63 (b) SteveDrowne 12 12
(Nick Littmoden) *furiously rdn arnd outside of field fr wd draw to ld over 7f out: hdd jst over 3f out: wknd 2f out: heavily eased: t.o* **25/1**

500- **12** *26* **Timpanist (USA)**[44] 7658 5-8-12 56 (b) HayleyTurner 3
(Simon Dow) *pressed ldrs to 1/2-way: wknd rapidly 4f out: wl t.o* **50/1**

2m 4.97s (-1.63) **Going Correction** +0.125s/f (Slow)
WFA 4 from 5yo+ 2lb 12 Ran SP% **119.0**
Speed ratings (Par 101): **111,108,108,105,104 103,101,101,93,91 85,64**
toteswingers:1&2:£5.50, 2&3:£19.60, 1&3:£7.10 CSF £30.98 CT £285.88 TOTE £2.70: £1.10, £3.30, £4.80; EX 25.50 Trifecta £205.40 Pool: £705.27 - 2.54 winning units..
Owner George Prodromou **Bred** A Saccomando **Trained** East Harling, Norfolk

FOCUS
A moderate handicap. It was run at a solid pace and the form makes sense.

225 PLAY BINGO FREE AT BLUESQ.COM H'CAP 1m (P)
4:10 (4:10) (Class 6) (0-65,66) 4-Y-0+ **£1,704** (£503; £251) **Stalls** High

Form RPR
65-2 **1** **Alhaban (IRE)**[7] 146 6-9-4 61 LukeMorris 7 71
(Ronald Harris) *prom: trckd ldr after 3f: drvn to ld over 1f out: styd on wl* **11/4**[1]

42-2 **2** *1 ½* **Arkaim**[12] 96 4-9-7 64 (v) HayleyTurner 4 71
(Pam Sly) *led: drvn and hdd over 1f out: kpt on same pce fnl f* **11/4**[1]

4-51 **3** *½* **Shared Moment (IRE)**[7] 148 6-9-4 66 6ex (v) RaulDaSilva(5) 8 72
(John Gallagher) *prog to trck ldrs after 3f: chal on outer 2f out: nt qckn over 1f out: urged along and styd on* **9/2**[2]

11-3 **4** *hd* **Storm Runner (IRE)**[5] 183 4-8-13 59 RyanPowell(3) 6 64+
(George Margarson) *hld up in last pair: lft w plenty to do after ldrs skipped clr wl over 2f out: effrt and brought v wd in st: r.o wl fnl f: nrst fin* **11/4**[1]

000- **5** *3 ¼* **Sottovoce**[23] 7890 4-9-3 60 JimCrowley 3 58
(Simon Dow) *trckd ldr 3f: styd prom: pushed along 3f out: tried to chal on inner over 1f out: wknd fnl f* **16/1**

02-0 **6** *3 ½* **Hecton Lad (USA)**[16] 31 5-9-7 64 (b) SteveDrowne 2 54
(John Best) *t.k.h: hld up bhd ldrs: outpcd and rdn over 2f out: nvr on terms after* **12/1**[3]

03-0 **7** *1 ¾* **Bubbly Braveheart (IRE)**[16] 31 5-8-12 60 JemmaMarshall(5) 5 46
(Pat Phelan) *hld up in last pair: outpcd fr 3f out: nvr a factor* **33/1**

305- **8** *10* **Chasin' Rainbows**[32] 7822 4-9-0 57 LiamKeniry 1 20
(Sylvester Kirk) *in tch: pushed along fr 1/2-way: wknd over 2f out: t.o* **50/1**

1m 38.3s (0.10) **Going Correction** +0.125s/f (Slow) 8 Ran SP% **116.7**
Speed ratings (Par 101): **104,102,102,101,98 95,93,83**
toteswingers:1&2:£2.30, 2&3:£2.50, 1&3:£2.50 CSF £10.58 CT £32.69 TOTE £3.00: £1.10, £1.10, £1.80; EX 12.50 Trifecta £65.20 Pool: £974.63 - 11.05 winning units..
Owner Robert Bailey **Bred** Eimear Mulhern **Trained** Earlswood, Monmouths

Storm Runner(IRE) Official explanation: jockey said that the gelding was kicked at the start
T/Plt: £55.60 to a £1 stake. Pool of £57,964.60 - 760.78 winning tickets. T/Qpdt: £28.00 to a £ stake. Pool of £3,816.72 - 100.80 winning tickets. JN

[212]WOLVERHAMPTON (A.W) (L-H)
Friday, January 20

OFFICIAL GOING: Standard
Wind: Light, half-behind Weather: Part cloudy

226 PLACE ONLY BETTING AT BLUESQ.COM H'CAP 5f 216y(P)
4:20 (4:21) (Class 7) (0-50,52) 4-Y-0+ **£1,704** (£503; £251) **Stalls** Low

Form RPR
136- **1** **Cheyenne Red (IRE)**[29] 7853 6-9-2 49 PhillipMakin 10 58
(Michael Herrington) *chsd ldr for 2f: pushed along over 2f out: wnt 2nd and swtchd rt over 1f out: led ins fnl f: r.o* **10/1**

3-43 **2** 1 ¼ **Pilgrim Dancer (IRE)**[15] 46 5-9-3 **50**......................(v) BarryMcHugh 6 55+
(Tony Coyle) *s.i.s: in rr: hdwy on outer over 2f out: rdn wl over 1f out: styd on to take 2nd ins fnl f: no imp on wnr cl home* **4/1**[2]

64-1 **3** *nk* **First Class**[8] 126 4-9-5 **52** 6ex... DavidProbert 1 56
(Rae Guest) *midfield: rdn and hdwy over 1f out: chsd ldrs ins fnl f: r.o cl home* **10/11**[1]

660- **4** *hd* **Meydan Style (USA)**[42] 7695 6-8-12 **45**..................(b) WilliamCarson 11 48
(Bruce Hellier, Germany) *racd keenly: led: rdn over 1f out: hdd ins fnl f: styd on same pce towards fin* **16/1**

6-04 **5** *2* **White Shift (IRE)**[7] 155 6-9-2 **49**....................................... ShaneKelly 8 46
(Paul Howling) *hld up: rdn and hdwy over 1f out: kpt on ins fnl f: nt quite pce of ldrs* **16/1**

0-06 **6** 2 ¾ **Raimond Ridge (IRE)**[9] 125 6-8-9 **45**.............................. DaleSwift(3) 7 33
(Derek Shaw) *hld up: pushed along 3f out: outpcd wl over 1f out: nvr able to chal* **8/1**[3]

6/0- **7** ¾ **Cheshire Lady (IRE)**[21] 7924 5-8-12 **45**.......................... LeeNewman 3 31
(David Barron) *racd keenly: chsd ldrs: stmbld over 5f out: wnt 2nd 4f out: rdn and lost 2nd over 1f out: wknd ins fnl f* **16/1**

000- **8** *nse* **Dubonny**[25] 7876 5-9-0 **47**..(t) TomMcLaughlin 5 33
(Frank Sheridan) *hld up: pushed along wl over 1f out: nvr able to trble ldrs* **40/1**

0-00 **9** 2 ¾ **Bertbrand**[12] 101 7-8-12 **45**.. JamesSullivan 2 22
(Ian McInnes) *chsd ldrs: pushed along and wknd over 2f out* **80/1**

1m 15.54s (0.54) **Going Correction** +0.05s/f (Slow) 9 Ran SP% **113.9**
Speed ratings (Par 97): **98,96,95,95,93 89,88,88,84**
Tote Swingers: 1&2 £3.60, 1&3 £2.80, 2&3 £2.20 CSF £49.11 CT £72.32 TOTE £8.50: £2.10, £1.20, £1.10; EX 42.80.
Owner Stuart Herrington **Bred** Crandon Park Stud **Trained** Cold Kirby, N Yorks

FOCUS
A low-grade handicap. They went steady early on but the pace gradually increased.

227 SPONSOR A RACE BY CALLING 01902 390000 H'CAP 5f 20y(P)
4:55 (4:55) (Class 7) (0-50,51) 4-Y-O+ **£1,704** (£503; £251) **Stalls** Low

Form RPR

3-0 **1** **Avonvalley**[9] 118 5-9-1 **48**.. RobbieFitzpatrick 8 59
(Peter Grayson) *dwlt: in rr: hdwy 1f out: str run ins fnl f: led towards fin and won gng away* **8/1**

63-2 **2** 1 ¼ **Canadian Danehill (IRE)**[12] 95 10-8-10 **50**............(e) JakePayne(7) 7 57
(Robert Cowell) *chsd ldrs: wnt 2nd over 2f out: r.o to ld wl ins fnl f: hdd and hld towards fin* **5/1**[3]

52-5 **3** 1 ¾ **Lisselton Cross**[9] 118 4-9-3 **50**...................................(v) MartinLane 11 50
(Martin Bosley) *in tch: effrt to chse ldrs 2f out: styd on same pce ins fnl f* **7/1**

600- **4** *shd* **Rio's Girl**[40] 7728 5-9-2 **49**..(b) BarryMcHugh 3 49
(Tony Coyle) *led: rdn over 1f out: hdd wl ins fnl f: no ex fnl 50yds* **7/2**[2]

430- **5** ¾ **Lizzy's Dream**[159] 5082 4-8-12 **45**.................................... LeeNewman 9 42+
(Robin Bastiman) *dwlt: in rr: hdwy on outer 2f out: styd on ins fnl f: nt pce to trble ldrs* **9/4**[1]

044- **6** *1* **Running Water**[30] 7845 4-8-12 **45**.................................... PaddyAspell 6 39
(Hugh McWilliams) *midfield: outpcd over 2f out: rdn and hdwy over 1f out: kpt on ins fnl f but nt pce of ldrs* **20/1**

20-1 **7** *2* **Deveze (IRE)**[9] 118 4-9-4 **51** 6ex...............................(b) WilliamCarson 10 37
(Milton Bradley) *hld up: rdn over 1f out: no imp fnl f* **7/1**

/00- **8** 4 ½ **Leahness (IRE)**[286] 1247 5-8-12 **45**.............................. RussKennemore 1 15
(Ken Wingrove) *towards rr: toiling fr over 2f out* **100/1**

005- **9** 1 ½ **Una Vita Pius (IRE)**[31] 7829 4-8-9 **45**........................ AdamBeschizza(3) 5
(Patrick Gilligan) *chsd ldr tl over 2f out: rdn and wknd over 1f out* **33/1**

000/ **10** *nk* **Skiddaw View**[430] 7469 4-8-12 **45**.................................. AndrewMullen 2
(Alan Brown) *in tch: rdn and wknd over 1f out* **40/1**

1m 2.17s (-0.13) **Going Correction** +0.05s/f (Slow) 10 Ran SP% **116.9**
Speed ratings (Par 97): **103,101,98,98,96 95,92,84,82,81**
Tote Swingers: 1&2 £6.90, 1&3 £5.90, 2&3 £5.20 CSF £46.42 CT £297.71 TOTE £13.50: £3.70, £1.10, £3.10; EX 37.40.
Owner Richard Teatum **Bred** Ercan Dogan **Trained** Formby, Lancs

FOCUS
A modest sprint handicap.

228 STAY AT THE WOLVERHAMPTON HOLIDAY INN H'CAP 5f 20y(P)
5:25 (5:26) (Class 6) (0-55,54) 3-Y-O **£1,704** (£503; £251) **Stalls** Low

Form RPR

002- **1** **Welease Bwian (IRE)**[93] 6942 3-9-2 **54**......................(t) WilliamCarson 8 67+
(Stuart Williams) *in tch: carried wd over 3f out: sn in 2nd pl: confidently rdn to ld on bit over 1f out: a travelling strly and in command fnl f: cheekily* **1/1**[1]

03-2 **2** ¾ **Villa Reigns**[15] 40 3-9-2 **54**..(be) PhillipMakin 4 57
(John Weymes) *prom: led after 1f: rdn over 1f out: sn hdd: continued to chse easy wnr ins fnl f: a fighting losing battle* **10/3**[2]

3-34 **3** 3 ½ **Lord Buffhead**[8] 138 3-8-9 **50**.................................... RobertLButler(3) 2 40
(Richard Guest) *led for 1f: remained prom: rdn 2f out: sn one pce* **17/2**

402- **4** 4 ½ **Forever Janey**[22] 7916 3-8-12 **50**................................... JamesSullivan 5 24
(Paul Green) *in tch: niggled along 3f out: sn outpcd: carred wd ent st whn no ch* **15/2**[3]

605- **5** 2 ¾ **Misred Melissa (IRE)**[197] 3767 3-9-0 **52**........................ DavidProbert 1 16
(Ronald Harris) *towards rr: outpcd over 3f out: nvr a threat* **12/1**

055- **6** 2 ½ **River Nova**[72] 7338 3-8-0 **45**...................................(b[1]) MatthewHopkins(7) 7
(Alan Berry) *in rr: sn outpcd* **80/1**

000- **7** ¾ **Make A Fuss**[22] 7909 3-9-2 **54**....................................... StephenCraine 6
(Sylvester Kirk) *prom: hung rt fr over 3f out: wknd over 2f out* **14/1**

1m 2.88s (0.58) **Going Correction** +0.05s/f (Slow) 7 Ran SP% **111.0**
Speed ratings (Par 95): **97,95,90,83,78 74,73**
Tote Swingers: 1&2 £1.30, 1&3 £1.50, 2&3 £2.60 CSF £4.12 CT £15.02 TOTE £1.20: £1.10, £3.20; EX 5.00.
Owner W E Enticknap **Bred** Nils Koop **Trained** Newmarket, Suffolk

FOCUS
An ordinary handicap, but it was run at a good pace and an unexposed improver coasted to victory and was value for much more than the winning margin.
Make A Fuss Official explanation: jockey said that the filly hung badly right-handed

229 ENJOY THE PUNTERS PACKAGE GROUP OFFER H'CAP 1m 4f 50y(P)
6:00 (6:00) (Class 6) (0-60,65) 4-Y-O+ **£1,704** (£503; £251) **Stalls** Low

Form RPR

0-11 **1** **Hada Men (USA)**[10] 111 7-9-10 **65** 6ex........................ BrianToomey(5) 5 71+
(Brian Ellison) *hld up in rr: rdn over 3f out: failed to pick-up tl styd on ins fnl f to ld post* **6/5**[1]

0-04 **2** *hd* **Yossi (IRE)**[7] 160 8-8-10 **46** oh1.................................(b) FrannyNorton 1 52
(Richard Guest) *hld up: rdn and hdwy wl over 1f out: r.o to chal fnl strides* **33/1**

02-3 **3** *nse* **Newport Arch**[12] 97 4-9-4 **58**..(p) TomEaves 2 64
(John Quinn) *led for 1f: chsd ldr: chalng 2f out: rdn to ld jst over 1f out: hdd post* **9/4**[2]

355- **4** 1 ½ **Prickles**[43] 7087 7-8-8 **47** ow1.. DaleSwift(3) 7 51
(Derek Shaw) *led after 1f: rdn and hdd jst over 1f out: stl chalng ins fnl f: no ex towards fin* **22/1**

255- **5** *hd* **Rapturous Applause**[84] 6577 4-8-12 **52**...................... FrederikTylicki 6 55
(Micky Hammond) *hld up: pushed along 2f out: styd on ins fnl f to chse ldrs: one pce towards fin* **14/1**

010- **6** *1* **Ahlawy (IRE)**[23] 7903 9-9-10 **60**................................(t) TomMcLaughlin 4 62
(Frank Sheridan) *chsd ldrs: rdn over 2f out: one pce ins fnl f* **12/1**

/00- **7** *5* **Tilos Gem (IRE)**[45] 7645 6-9-4 **54**.................................. BarryMcHugh 3 48
(Brian Ellison) *chsd ldrs: rdn 3f out: outpcd over 2f out: wknd over 1f out* **15/2**[3]

2m 43.42s (2.32) **Going Correction** +0.05s/f (Slow)
WFA 4 from 6yo+ 4lb 7 Ran SP% **109.6**
Speed ratings (Par 101): **94,93,93,92,92 92,88**
Tote Swingers: 1&2 £5.70, 1&3 £1.40, 2&3 £6.40 CSF £39.24 TOTE £1.60: £1.20, £8.40; EX 14.10.
Owner Brian Ellison **Bred** Overbrook Farm **Trained** Norton, N Yorks

FOCUS
There was a very tight three-way finish in this handicap.

230 EXCLUSIVE LIVE SHOWS AT BLUESQ.COM H'CAP 7f 32y(P)
6:30 (6:31) (Class 4) (0-85,80) 3-Y-O **£4,204** (£1,251; £625; £312) **Stalls** High

Form RPR

50-1 **1** **Adranian (IRE)**[15] 42 3-9-2 **75**....................................(v) DavidProbert 8 81
(David C Griffiths) *chsd ldr: led 4f out: kicked clr 2f out: kpt on wl fnl f* **13/2**

3-11 **2** *1* **Oratorian (IRE)**[5] 189 3-9-2 **80** 6ex.......................... BrendanPowell(5) 4 83
(Sylvester Kirk) *chsd ldrs: rdn to take 2nd 1f out: hung lft ins fnl f: kpt on but nt rch wnr* **11/8**[1]

042- **3** *2* **Crowning Star (IRE)**[21] 7927 3-8-5 **64**........................ WilliamCarson 3 62
(J S Moore) *hld up: pushed along over 3f out: edgd rt and stdy prog ent fnl f: styd on towards fin* **7/1**

143- **4** *nk* **Not Bad For A Boy (IRE)**[21] 7927 3-9-0 **76**.............. KieranO'Neill(3) 6 73
(Richard Hannon) *led: hdd 4f out: chsd ldr: rdn over 2f out: sn outpcd by wnr: lost 2nd 1f out: no ex fnl 50yds* **11/2**[3]

060- **5** *2* **Monnoyer**[111] 6535 3-9-7 **80**.. FrederikTylicki 7 72
(Scott Dixon) *plld hrd: hld up: pushed along and outpcd over 2f out: nvr able to trble ldrs* **4/1**[2]

012- **6** *nse* **Worth**[70] 7364 3-9-4 **77**..(b) ShaneKelly 2 69
(Brian Meehan) *racd keenly: chsd ldrs: outpcd over 2f out: n.d after* **11/1**

1m 30.16s (0.56) **Going Correction** +0.05s/f (Slow) 6 Ran SP% **111.7**
Speed ratings (Par 99): **98,96,94,94,91 91**
Tote Swingers: 1&2 £2.20, 1&3 £5.30, 2&3 £3.40 CSF £15.82 CT £62.59 TOTE £8.80: £4.20, £1.10; EX 13.20.
Owner Eros Bloodstock **Bred** Hugh O'Brien **Trained** Bawtry, S Yorks

FOCUS
A decent handicap, but the pace was steady and it became tactical.

231 WOLVERHAMPTON - THE BLACK COUNTRY'S ONLY RACECOURSE MAIDEN STKS 7f 32y(P)
7:00 (7:02) (Class 5) 3-Y-O+ **£2,264** (£673; £336; £168) **Stalls** High

Form RPR

0-24 **1** **Roedean (IRE)**[7] 159 3-8-4 73......................................(p) FrannyNorton 4 71
(Jamie Osborne) *mde all: rdn over 2f out: hld on gamely cl home* **9/2**[3]

2 *hd* **Laugh Out Loud** 3-8-4 0.. ChrisCatlin 3 70+
(Mick Channon) *midfield: hdwy on outer under 2f out: wnt 2nd 1f out: r.o ins fnl f: pressed wnr cl home* **13/2**

3 1 ¾ **Falcon's Reign (FR)** 3-8-9 0.. ShaneKelly 7 71
(Jeremy Noseda) *hld up: hdwy 3f out: chsd ldrs 2f out: kpt on ins fnl f: edgd lft whn hld towards fin* **7/2**[2]

34- **4** *nk* **Burnhope**[78] 7240 3-8-9 0.. FrederikTylicki 9 70
(Scott Dixon) *chsd wnr: rdn over 2f out: lost 2nd 1f out: edgd lft and one pce towards fin* **12/1**

5 *hd* **Baileys Strider** 3-8-9 0.. JoeFanning 1 69+
(Mark Johnston) *chsd ldrs: rdn over 2f out: nt qckn over 1f out: kpt on same pce and no imp ins fnl f* **2/1**[1]

6 4 ½ **Dilizan (IRE)** 3-8-8 0 ow2.. PaulPickard(3) 2 59
(Brian Ellison) *in rr: sn niggled along: kpt on ins fnl f: nvr able to trble ldrs* **40/1**

036- **7** *2* **Cerejeira (IRE)**[32] 7820 4-9-8 56..(bt) TomEaves 5 52
(Eric Alston) *racd keenly: chsd ldrs: rdn over 1f out: wknd ins fnl f* **20/1**

4 **8** ¾ **Ambitious Boy**[15] 41 3-8-10 0 ow1.......................... RussKennemore 6 51
(Reg Hollinshead) *stdd s: hld up: pushed along over 2f out: nvr a threat* **14/1**

9 ½ **Charlcot** 4-9-13 0.. WilliamCarson 8 53
(James Bethell) *hld up: pushed along 3f out: hung lft over 1f out: no imp* **40/1**

1m 29.37s (-0.23) **Going Correction** +0.05s/f (Slow)
WFA 3 from 4yo 18lb 9 Ran SP% **111.1**
Speed ratings (Par 103): **103,102,100,100,100 95,92,91,91**
Tote Swingers: 1&2 £5.50, 1&3 £2.70, 2&3 £3.50 CSF £31.44 TOTE £4.90: £1.40, £2.20, £1.40; EX 23.20.
Owner Dr Marwan Koukash **Bred** C McEvoy **Trained** Upper Lambourn, Berks
■ Stewards' Enquiry : Franny Norton 13 day ban: used whip with excessive frequency (3- 11 Feb & 13-17 Feb)

FOCUS
Two newcomers dominated the betting for this maiden, but it won by an exposed 73-rated filly.

232 PLAY FREE BINGO AT BLUESQ.COM H'CAP 7f 32y(P)
7:30 (7:31) (Class 6) (0-60,60) 4-Y-O+ **£1,704** (£503; £251) **Stalls** High

Form RPR

0-03 **1** **Kyncraighe (IRE)**[7] 154 4-8-0 **46** oh1....................(tp) LeonnaMayor(7) 5 55
(Joseph Tuite) *hld up: hdwy on outer 2f out: str chal ins fnl f: r.o to ld post* **11/1**

30-6 **2** *shd* **Piccolo Express**[7] 153 6-9-2 **55**................................ RussKennemore 6 64
(Brian Baugh) *trckd ldrs: gng wl 2f out: rdn to ld jst over 1f out: hrd pressed ins fnl f: hdd post* **13/2**[2]

60-2 **3** 2 ¼ **Transmit (IRE)**[7] 154 5-9-5 **58**................................(b) RobertWinston 2 61+
(Tim Easterby) *racd keenly: in tch: rdn and nt qckn over 1f out: styd on ins fnl f: edgd rt and no imp on front pair towards fin* **5/4**[1]

/20- **4** 1 1/2 **Kenton Street**[7] 163 7 -9-5**58**..........(p) JohnFahy 9 57
(Michael J Browne, Ire) *trckd ldrs: rdn over 2f out: chalng wl over 1f out: no ex fnl 100yds* **11/1**

000- **5** nk **Monadreen Dancer**[41] 7716 4 -9-2**55**.......... ShaneKelly 8 53+
(Daniel Mark Loughnane) *midfield: nt clr run wl over 1f out: kpt on ins fnl f: nt pce of ldrs* **20/1**

/3-0 **6** 1/2 **Mystic Halo**[14] 67 9 -9-6**59**..........(t) TomMcLaughlin 7 55
(Frank Sheridan) *s.i.s: in rr: rdn over 1f out: styd on ins fnl f: nt pce to trble ldrs* **33/1**

314/ **7** 1 1/4 **High Voltage**[144] 11 -9-5**58**..........(tp) JamieGoldstein 3 51
(Mrs J L Le Brocq, Jersey) *led: hdd after 1f: led over 5f out: rdn and hdd jst over 1f out: wknd wl ins fnl f* **33/1**

425- **8** 1 1/2 **Flaxen Lake**[107] 6626 5 -9-3**56**.......... RichardKingscote 4 45
(Milton Bradley) *in tch tl wknd over 2f out* **11/1**

00-0 **9** 1/2 **Odd Ball (IRE)**[7] 154 5 -8-8**50**.......... JulieBurke(3) 12 38
(Lisa Williamson) *midfld: pushed along and hdwy 3f out: chsd ldrs 2f out: wknd ins fnl f* **50/1**

530- **10** 4 **Yours**[45] 7641 4 -8-12**51**..........(b[1]) PhillipMakin 1 28
(Kevin Ryan) *dwlt: hld up: struggling 3f out: nvr on terms* **16/1**

645- **11** 5 **Ad Vitam (IRE)**[53] 7459 4 -8-11**50**..........(bt[1]) MichaelStainton 10 13
(Micky Hammond) *s.i.s: in rr: pushed along over 4f out: nvr on terms* **8/1**[3]

000- **12** 8 **Regency Art (IRE)**[71] 7930 5 -9-7**60**..........(b) WilliamCarson 11
(Milton Bradley) *racd keenly: led after 1f: hdd over 5f out: rdn 2f out: wknd wl over 1f out: eased whn btn fnl f* **14/1**

1m 30.31s (0.71) **Going Correction** +0.05s/f (Slow) **12**Ran SP% **119.0**
Speed ratings (Par 101): **97,96,94,92,92 91,90,88,87,83 77,68**
Tote Swingers: 1&2 £10.20, 2&3 £3.30 CSF £78.37 CT £153.99 TOTE £12.70 : £3.40 , £2.50, £1.10; EX 95.80 .
Owner Chris Beek Racing **Bred** Giacinto Guglielmi **Trained** Great Shefford, Berks
■ Stewards' Enquiry : Leonna Mayor 18 day ban: used whip with excessive frequency (3-4, 6-11, 13-18 & 20-23 Feb)

FOCUS
The first two pulled clear in this handicap and the winner can be marked up because he came from some way off the steady pace.
T/Plt: £7.50 to a £1 stake. Pool of £98,100.64 - 9,517.77 winning tickets. T/Qpdt: £3.50 to a £1 stake. Pool of £9,192.21 - 1,925.13 winning tickets. DO

233 - 240a (Foreign Racing) - See Raceform Interactive

[140]MEYDAN (L-H)
Friday, January 20

OFFICIAL GOING: Tapeta - standard; turf - good

241a SWAIDAN TRADING COMPANY - VDL (H'CAP) (TAPETA) 1m 3f
11:00 (11:00) (95-105,105) 3-Y-0+

£42,580 (£14,193; £7,096 ; £3,548 ; £2,129 ; £1,419)

RPR

1 **Jamr**[14] 81 4 -8-11**98**..........(v) PatCosgrave 5 103
(M bin Shafya, UAE) *trckd ldng gp: led 2f out: tired fnl 100yds: jst hld on* **11/2**[3]

2 shd **Measuring Time**[132] 5934 4 -9-2**102**.......... MickaelBarzalona 4 108
(Mahmood Al Zarooni) *in rr of mid-div: r.o wl fnl 2f: jst failed* **10/3**[2]

3 3 1/4 **Sirvino**[119] 6301 7 -9-2**100**.......... RyanMoore 6 99
(David Barron) *settled in rr: r.o fnl 3f: nrst fin* **12/1**

4 6 **Rochdale**[56] 7552 9 -9-6**105**..........(t) RoystonFfrench 10 92
(A Al Raihe, UAE) *in rr of mid-div: chsd ldrs 3 1/2f out: one pce fnl 1 1/2f* **11/1**

5 1 1/2 **Club Oceanic**[134] 5853 4 -9-2**102**..........(p) FrankieDettori 3 89
(Saeed Bin Suroor) *nvr bttr than mid-div* **2/1**[1]

6 shd **Royal Revival**[120] 6277 5 -9-2**100**.......... SilvestreDeSousa 9 85
(Saeed Bin Suroor) *sn led: hdd 2f out: kpt on same pce* **20/1**

7 3 1/2 **Lyssio (GER)**[15] 48 5 -9-2**100**.......... JamesDoyle 8 79
(Michael Attwater) *trckd ldr: ev ch 3 1/2f out: one pce fnl 2 1/2f* **9/1**

8 2 1/4 **Royal Destination (IRE)**[7] 140 7 -9-4**102**..........(v) WayneSmith 1 77
(F Nass, Bahrain) *mid-div on rail: nvr able to chal* **33/1**

9 3/4 **Mantoba**[34] 7802 4 -8-8**95**..........(t) WilliamBuick 7 69
(Brian Meehan) *trckd ldr: ev ch 3 1/2f out: wknd fnl 2f* **8/1**

10 13 **Goldplated (IRE)**[8] 143 4 -9-1**101**.......... ShaneFoley 2 52
(John Joseph Murphy, Ire) *a in rr* **25/1**

2m 16.87s (-1.53)
WFA 4 from 5yo+ 3lb **10**Ran SP% **120.5**
CSF £24.50; TRICAST £217.27 .
Owner Sheikh Mansoor bin Mohammed al Maktoum **Bred** J Knight And E Cantillon **Trained** United Arab Emirates

FOCUS
A lack of well-handicapped types, but still a reasonable contest. The pace was modest, Royal Revival taking the field to the 1m point in splits of 27.10, 52.09, 1.16.94 and 1.41.03. However, the final time was not at all bad, being the fifth quickest to date over this C&D.

NOTEBOOK
Jamr made it 3-3 since switching to Dubai, getting first run on the second and just doing enough to defy a 5lb rise. He had nothing in hand, but that's not to say he can't go on progressing.
Measuring Time, a 310,000gns purchase out of Richard Hannon's yard, hasn't won since he was a juvenile but he's faced some tough tasks and this was his first try in a handicap. It's a good indication of his natural talent that he was able to get so close despite racing further back than the winner and covering three meters more than that rival, and that's despite not travelling with much enthusiasm after a sluggish start. He might be sharper next time, but he'll also probably be higher in the weights and it wouldn't surprise to see him tried in headgear at some stage.
Sirvino was having his first try off the turf but is a half-brother to a triple Polytrack winner. Returning from a four-month break, he plugged on from an unpromising position without threatening.
Rochdale had stamina to prove and this was tougher than the two non-Carnival events he won earlier in the UAE season.
Club Oceanic won five of his nine starts for Jeremy Noseda (including a maiden on Polytrack), but he ran disappointingly on his first start since being sold for 155,00gns. He was beaten before the straight.
Lyssio(GER) disappointed off a mark 1lb than when second in a weaker race on his Dubai debut.
Mantoba offered nothing.

242a AL NABOODAH TRAVEL & TOURISM (H'CAP) (TAPETA) 1m 2f
11:35 (11:35) 3-Y-0+

£58,064 (£19,354; £9,677 ; £4,838 ; £2,903 ; £1,935)

RPR

1 **Prince Bishop (IRE)**[79] 7226 5 -9-6**110**..........(v) FrankieDettori 4 118
(Saeed Bin Suroor) *trckd ldr: led 2 1/2f out: r.o wl: comf* **11/8**[1]

2 5 1/4 **Spring Of Fame (USA)**[27] 6088 6 -9-3**107**.......... MickaelBarzalona 10 105
(Saeed Bin Suroor) *settled in rr: rdn 6f out: r.o wl fnl 1 1/2f: nrst fin* **13/2**[3]

3 1/4 **Monte Alto (IRE)**[5] 48 8 -8-9**99**..........(t) RichardHills 7 96
(A Al Raihe, UAE) *in rr of mid-div: r.o fnl 2 1/2f: nrst fin* **16/1**

4 3/4 **Suits Me**[34] 7802 9 -8-8**98**.......... TedDurcan 2 94
(David Barron) *sn led: hdd 2 1/2f out: kpt on same pce* **12/1**

5 1/4 **Mr Brock (SAF)**[306] 9 -9-6**110**.......... KShea 6 105
(M F De Kock, South Africa) *mid-div: chsd wnr 3f out: ev ch 2 1/2f out: nt qckn fnl 1 1/2f* **15/2**

6 1 1/4 **Famusa**[49] 7606 5 -8-7**97**.......... SilvestreDeSousa 1 90
(Marco Botti) *trckd ldng duo: ev ch 3f out: one pce fnl 1 1/2f* **5/1**[2]

7 1 3/4 **Capital Attraction (USA)**[20] 7947 5 -8-6**96**.......... MircoDemuro 9 85
(Ernst Oertel, UAE) *hld up in rr: nvr able to chal* **20/1**

8 1 1/4 **Fanditha (IRE)**[160] 5075 6 -8-9**99**.......... JamesDoyle 5 86
(Mick Channon) *nvr bttr than mid-div* **25/1**

9 hd **Topclas (FR)**[8] 145 6 -9-2**106**..........(v) PatCosgrave 8 92
(M bin Shafya, UAE) *hld up in rr: nvr nr to chal* **20/1**

10 3/4 **Bronze Cannon (USA)**[96] 6910 7 -9-5**109**..........(t) RyanMoore 3 94
(H J Brown, South Africa) *mid-div: rdn 3f out: sn btn* **10/1**

2m 4.32s (-0.38) **10**Ran SP% **119.9**
CSF £10.60; TRICAST £105.60 .
Owner Godolphin **Bred** Thurso Limited **Trained** Newmarket, Suffolk

FOCUS
An uncompetitive handicap, and with Suits Me taking the field through fractions of 27.16, 52.32 and 1.17.43 (all three splits slower than the earlier 1m3f handicap), it paid to be handy.

NOTEBOOK
Prince Bishop (IRE)was ideally placed and found plenty to take his record to 2-2 since being gelded, this easy victory following on from a Listed success at Kempton last November. It's likely he'll return to pattern company next time, possibly in the second round of the Al Maktoum Challenge, and that will provide more of a test, although he did win at up to Group 2 level when with Andre Fabre.
Spring Of Fame (USA)had lost his way when last seen. This was more encouraging, with him running on strongly from much further back than ideal, and having covered eight meters more than the winner, but it was disconcerting that he didn't travel with any enthusiasm. He could benefit from headgear.
Monte Alto (IRE)ran creditably, but he's not a horse to follow in the win market.
Suits Me had the run of the race.
Mr Brock (SAF)might have needed this after a 306-day absence but he doesn't look well handicapped.
Famusa disappointed on this switch to Dubai, finding little despite having been well placed.
Capital Attraction (USA)was 6lb higher than when winning over 7f here last time and it was a surprise to see him stepped up to this trip.

243a SWAIDAN TRADING COMPANY PEUGEOT (H'CAP) (TURF) 1m 1f
12:10 (12:10) 3-Y-0+

£58,064 (£19,354; £9,677 ; £4,838 ; £2,903 ; £1,935)

RPR

1 **Mutahadee (IRE)**[139] 5744 4 -8-10**105**.......... ChristopheSoumillon 6 108+
(M F De Kock, South Africa) *mid-div: smooth prog 2 1/2f out: led 1 1/2f out: r.o wl: comf* **9/4**[1]

2 4 **Viscount Nelson (USA)**[139] 5744 5 -9-6**113**..........(b) KShea 8 109
(M F De Kock, South Africa) *s.i.s: smooth prog 3f out: r.o fnl 1 1/2f: nrst fin* **13/2**

3 shd **Alrasm (IRE)**[54] 5 -8-7**100**.......... TadhgO'Shea 2 95
(E Charpy, UAE) *mid-div on rail: r.o wl fnl 2f: nrst fin* **25/1**

4 1/2 **War Monger (USA)**[5] 52 8 -8-9**102**.......... RichardHills 5 96
(Doug Watson, UAE) *sn led: kicked clr 3f out: hdd 1 1/2f out: wknd fnl 100yds* **14/1**

5 1 3/4 **Banna Boirche (IRE)**[5] 51 6 -8-11**105**.......... ShaneFoley 1 95
(M Halford, Ire) *settled in rr: nvr nr to chal* **11/1**

6 1 1/4 **Moran Gra (USA)**[5] 53 5 -8-10**104**..........(p) TedDurcan 7 91
(Ms Joanna Morgan, Ire) *trckd ldng pair: ev ch 3 1/2f out: nt qckn fnl 2f* **10/1**

7 12 **Emerald Commander (IRE)**[75] 7323 5 -9-5**112**..........(t) FrankieDettori 4 75
(Saeed Bin Suroor) *trckd ldrs: ev ch 3f out: one pce fnl 2f* **5/2**[2]

8 3 1/4 **Sea Lord (IRE)**[5] 52 5 -9-3**110**.......... MickaelBarzalona 3 66
(Mahmood Al Zarooni) *in rr of mid-div: nvr nr to chal* **11/2**[3]

1m 49.99s (109.99)
WFA 4 from 5yo+ 1lb **8**Ran SP% **116.0**
CSF £17.81; TRICAST £288.32 .
Owner Sheikh Mohammed Bin Khalifa Al Maktoum **Bred** Epona Bloodstock Ltd **Trained** South Africa

FOCUS
They covered the first quarter-mile in 27.07, the half in 51.72 and went 1.16.39 at the 6f point, with War Monger taking them along.

NOTEBOOK
Mutahadee(IRE) showed himself to be leniently treated, taking it in the manner of a horse who will be comfortable back in pattern company. He may have had his issues (only made it to the track four times when with Tommy Stack), but he had already shown smart form at up to Group 2 level and produced a career best on his debut for Mike de Kock. There's enough stamina in his pedigree to believe he'll get 1m4f and if keeps progressing he could develop into a Sheema Classic contender.
Viscount Nelson (USA)may have had some issues as well - he never quite fulfilled his potential for Aidan O'Brien - but interestingly he has only been leased by Coolmore and this was an adequate debut for Mike de Kock. For a horse who hasn't always found much for pressure, it was encouraging to see him battle on for second when he could have been expected to recoil, and time may show he faced a mightily tough task conceding 10lb to his promising stablemate.
Alrasm(IRE), returning from a 54-day break, didn't help himself by racing keenly.
War Monger (USA)plugged on but basically wasn't good enough.
Banna Boirche (IRE)shaped okay two weeks earlier, but this was disappointing.
Emerald Commander (IRE)dropped right away after racing a bit freely through the opening stages and something was presumably amiss.
Sea Lord (IRE)was a bit keen and found absolutely nothing.

244a AL NABOODAH CONSTRUCTION GROUP (CONDITIONS RACE) (TAPETA) 6f
12:45 (12:45) 3-Y-0+

£38,709 (£12,903; £6,451 ; £3,225 ; £1,935 ; £1,290)

RPR

1 **Captain Obvious (AUS)**[40] 7 -9-2**116**..........(t) OChavez 6 111
(S Burridge, Singapore) *trckd ldr: led 1 1/2f out: r.o wl: comf* **7/2**[1]

2 3/4 **Hitchens (IRE)**[96] 6908 7 -9-0**113**.......... SilvestreDeSousa 9 107
(David Barron) *in rr of mid-div: r.o wl fnl 2f: nrst fin* **11/2**[3]

3 1/4 **Iver Bridge Lad**[76] 7298 5 -9-2**112**..........(b) MichaelO'Connell 4 108
(John Ryan) *mid-div: r.o wl fnl 2 1/2f: nrst fin* **8/1**

4 *shd* **Reynaldothewizard (USA)**[43] 7680 6-9-0 105..........(t) RichardMullen 1 106
(S Seemar, UAE) *trckd ldng pair: n.m.r 2f out: r.o fnl f* **9/2**[2]

5 *1/4* **Silaah**[69] 7392 8-8-7 100.. ShirleyTeasdale(7) 10 105
(David Nicholls) *chsd ldrs tl 2f out: wknd fnl f* **33/1**

6 *1 1/2* **Alo Pura**[21] 7936 8-8-9 106...(e) WilliamBuick 2 95
(D Selvaratnam, UAE) *mid-div on rail: no room 2f out: nt rcvr* **6/1**

7 *hd* **Inxile (IRE)**[154] 5253 7-9-0 112....................................(p) AdrianNicholls 5 100
(David Nicholls) *sn led: hdd 1 1/2f out: one pce fnl 100yds* **6/1**

8 *3/4* **Alazeyab (USA)**[71] 7382 6-9-0 109................................(vt) RichardHills 3 97
(A Al Raihe, UAE) *settled in rr: nvr nr to chal* **12/1**

9 *1/4* **Seachantach (USA)**[21] 7936 6-9-0 97..........................(t) HarryBentley 7 96
(S Seemar, UAE) *broke awkwardly: nvr nr to chal* **33/1**

10 *1 1/4* **Invincible Ash (IRE)**[15] 50 7-8-9 105........................(p) ShaneFoley 8 87
(M Halford, Ire) *a mid-div* **10/1**

11 *1 1/4* **Murbeh (IRE)**[118] 6347 4-9-0 97.................................... TadhgO'Shea 11 88
(A Al Raihe, UAE) *settled in rr: nvr able to chal* **25/1**

1m 11.0s (-0.60) **11** Ran SP% **122.0**
CSF £23.23.

Owner Milton Stable **Bred** Alwyn Park **Trained** Singapore

FOCUS
This was a really good, competitive conditions sprint. They went 24.44 for the first quarter-mile and 47.76 for the half.

NOTEBOOK
Captain Obvious(AUS), from a stable who made a good impression at Meydan the previous week, confirmed himself a really smart sort. He showed good speed to get a handy position and was always doing enough in the straight, despite conceding weight to all bar one of his rivals. An obvious short-term target is the Group 3 Al Shindagha Sprint over C&D on February 3 and he should be competitive if lining up.

Hitchens(IRE) got shuffled further back than ideal before the straight and conceded too much ground to the winner, although it would be hard to argue he was an unlucky loser.

Iver Bridge Lad was a bit free but kept on well. This was a good effort under his 2lb penalty.

Reynaldothewizard(USA) defeated subsequent Carnival winner Barbecue Eddie when taking C&D conditions event on reappearance, but this was tougher.

Silaah, returning from over two months off, was caught wider than ideal, though he only covered three metres more than the winner.

Alo Pura is better than she showed. She had got away with racing keenly at Jebel Ali on her return, but it compromised her chance in this better company and she then found trouble when trying to deliver a challenge in the straight.

Inxile(IRE) checked out pretty tamely and is better suited by 5f.

Alazeyab(USA), a winner off 105 over C&D on his reappearance, lost his chance with a slow start but was going on at the finish.

245a CAPE VERDI SPONSORED BY THE SAEED & MOHAMMED AL NABOODAH GROUP (GROUP 2) (F&M) (TURF) 1m

1:20 (1:20) 3-Y-0+

£77,419 (£25,806; £12,903; £6,451; £3,870; £2,580)

RPR

1 **First City**[139] 5704 6-9-0 110.. RoystonFfrench 1 110
(A Al Raihe, UAE) *in rr of mid-div: r.o wl fnl 2 1/2f: led last strides* **10/1**[3]

2 *nse* **Mahbooba (AUS)**[15] 52 5-9-0 113.................. ChristopheSoumillon 7 110
(M F De Kock, South Africa) *sn led: kicked clr 2f out: r.o bravely: hdd cl home* **2/5**[1]

3 *4 1/2* **Reem (AUS)**[8] 140 5-9-0 99.. KShea 3 100
(M F De Kock, South Africa) *s.i.s: trckd ldr: ev ch 3f out: kpt on same pce fnl 1 1/2f* **25/1**

4 *nse* **Hurricane Havoc (IRE)**[82] 7187 4-9-0 100................(bt) KevinManning 4 100
(J S Bolger, Ire) *trckd ldrs pair: rdn to chse ldr 3 1/2f out: one pce fnl 1 1/2f* **25/1**

5 *1 1/4* **Al Sharood**[28] 7868 4-9-0 98.. TadhgO'Shea 2 97
(Doug Watson, UAE) *in rr of mid-div: chsd ldrs 2f out: n.m.r 1 1/2f out: wknd fnl 100yds* **25/1**

6 *1/4* **Marvada (IRE)**[111] 6523 4-9-0 102...................................... ShaneFoley 6 96
(K J Condon, Ire) *settled in rr: nvr nr to chal* **25/1**

7 *3/4* **Rhythm Of Light**[139] 5753 4-9-0 107............................... KierenFallon 8 94
(Tom Dascombe) *mid-div: nvr able to chal* **11/2**[2]

8 *1/4* **Sooraah**[85] 7128 5-9-0 97.. RyanMoore 5 94
(William Haggas) *settled in last: n.d* **11/2**[2]

1m 38.33s (98.33) **8** Ran SP% **126.7**
CSF £14.83.

Owner Saeed Hamad Al Ahbabi **Bred** Darley **Trained** UAE

FOCUS
The second straight year this race has held Group 2 status and it was more competitive than the market suggested, although a couple of likely types underperformed. The fractions, set by the runner-up, were 26.96, 51.23 and 1.15.21 (slower than in the following handicap and final time was 0.70 seconds slower than that race), and it proved hard for all bar the winner to make up ground.

NOTEBOOK
First City deserves credit for being the only runner to make up significant ground, but any enthusiasm is tempered by her attitude - it hasn't improved for a switch of stables. Having her first start since leaving David Simcock, she quickened well in the straight but held both her head and her tail high and didn't look keen. Clearly, credit must go to Royston Ffrench, who impressed with how swiftly he changed his whip hand in the closing stages, but the winner is unlikely to add to this at the 2012 Carnival.

Mahbooba(AUS) was able to set fractions to suit and the tactics were spot on. She gave it her all under a noticeably hard ride and virtually the only time she was passed was on the line - she galloped out much stronger than the winner. A return to further should suit and the 1m1f Group 2 Balanchine Stakes on February 17 (trainer has won the race four times, including last year with a runner who was beaten in this) is the obvious target, although she did have a tough race.

Reem(AUS) didn't have a chance to show her best form when caught wide on her reappearance and this was better, but she's not easy to place.

Hurricane Havoc(IRE), returning from 82 days off, had a bit to find at this level but was helped by a forward ride.

Al Sharood was up in class and trip and both factors probably found her out.

Marvada(IRE) wasn't helped by racing off the modest pace.

Rhythm Of Light was a disappointment, although she raced keenly without cover and covered more ground than any of her rivals.

Sooraah had no chance after being held up in last, but it was still disappointing she couldn't make any impression.

246a SMKA - MK BY HONEYWELL (H'CAP) (TURF) 1m

1:55 (1:55) (100-110,109) 3-Y-0+

£46,451 (£15,483; £7,741; £3,870; £2,322; £1,548)

RPR

1 **Blue Panis (FR)**[45] 5-9-6 **109**.. OlivierPeslier 8 113
(X Thomas-Demeaulte, France) *trckd ldrs: rdn 2 1/2f out: led 1f out: comf* **25/1**

2 *2 1/4* **Masteroftherolls (IRE)**[173] 4595 4-9-1 **104**............. MickaelBarzalona 3 103
(Saeed Bin Suroor) *mid-div: smooth prog 3f out: one pce fnl 100yds* **10/3**[2]

3 *1* **Hujaylea (IRE)**[15] 53 9-9-2 **105**....................................(p) ShaneFoley 5 102
(M Halford, Ire) *settled in rr: r.o wl fnl 1 1/2f: nrst fin* **14/1**

4 *1/2* **Start Right**[15] 51 5-9-0 **102**... FrankieDettori 14 99
(Saeed Bin Suroor) *mid-div: chsd ldrs 3f out: one pce fnl 1 1/2f* **3/1**[1]

5 *1/4* **Anaerobio (ARG)**[15] 51 5-9-0 **102**.................(t) ChristopheSoumillon 4 98
(M F De Kock, South Africa) *s.i.s: settled in rr: smooth prog 2 1/2f out: nt qckn fnl f* **7/1**[3]

6 *1/2* **Field Of Dream**[116] 6416 5-8-11 **100**.............................. JamesDoyle 15 94
(Jamie Osborne) *sn led: hdd 1f out: kpt on same pce* **25/1**

7 *5 1/4* **Finjaan**[14] 80 6-9-1 **104**.. RichardHills 1 86
(Doug Watson, UAE) *s.i.s: nvr bttr than mid-div* **12/1**

8 *1/4* **Navajo Chief**[34] 7802 5-9-0 **102**...................................... KierenFallon 13 84
(Alan Jarvis) *trckd ldrs: ev ch 1 1/2f out: one pce fnl f* **14/1**

9 *1* **Disa Leader (SAF)**[188] 7-9-6 **109**...................................... JGeroudis 10 88
(M F De Kock, South Africa) *trckd ldrs tl 2 1/2f out: wknd fnl f* **12/1**

10 *3 1/4* **Mabait**[15] 53 6-9-1 **104**... WilliamBuick 11 75
(David Simcock) *nvr able to chal* **25/1**

11 *1/2* **Balducci**[174] 4554 5-9-2 **105**.. MircoDemuro 2 75
(Ernst Oertel, UAE) *nvr bttr than mid-div* **16/1**

12 *2* **Dubawi Star**[70] 7376 4-8-11 **100**..............................(p) JohnnyMurtagh 6 66
(John M Oxx, Ire) *nvr bttr than mid-div* **14/1**

13 *6* **The Rectifier (USA)**[16] 29 5-9-2 **105**........................... MickyFenton 9 57
(Jim Boyle) *trckd ldrs: nt qckn fnl 1 1/2f* **10/1**

14 *8* **Do It All (USA)**[148] 5-9-4 **107**................................(t) SilvestreDeSousa 7 40
(Saeed Bin Suroor) *trckd ldng gp: one pce fnl 1 1/2f* **20/1**

15 *dist* **Capital Market (USA)**[15] 51 5-8-11 **100**...............(bt) TadhgO'Shea 12
(Ismail Mohammed) *sn rdn in rr: n.d* **33/1**

1m 37.63s (97.63) **15** Ran SP% **130.2**
CSF £108.59; TRICAST £1,292.75. Placepot: £82.30 to a £1 stake. Pool of £2543.03 - 22.55 winning units. Quadpot: £13.60 to a £1 stake. Pool of £206.90 - 11.20 winning units..

Owner Prime Equestrian S.A.R.L. **Bred** Karine Belluteau **Trained** France

FOCUS
The pace was a bit too quick with Field Of Dream hassled up front by Navajo Chief - the sectionals were 25.70, 49.47 and 1.13.32.

NOTEBOOK
Blue Panis(FR) produced a smart performance to readily defy a mark of 109 on his Dubai debut and was ending a losing run dating to his success in a Deauville Listed race in 2010. He'll be worth his place back in Group company.

Masteroftherolls(IRE), an ex-French-trained runner, made a promising debut for his new yard and it wouldn't surprise to see him find a similar race.

Hujaylea(IRE) didn't get a clear run over 7f on his return but this was better. He stayed on from a long way back and was really going on at the finish.

Start Right looked a bit unlucky on the Tapeta on his recent debut for Godolphin, but this time he was faced with better company and paid for chasing the hot pace.

Anaerobio(ARG) showed little on his recent Dubai debut, but he was switched from Tapeta and had a tongue-tie on. This was an improvement and he may be capable of even better.

Field Of Dream, a 75,000gns purchase out of Luca Cumani's yard, may not be straightforward but he did well to last so long considering he was forced to go quicker than ideal and might be worth keeping in mind.

211 CAGNES-SUR-MER

Friday, January 20

OFFICIAL GOING: Fibresand: standard

247a PRIX CHERET (MAIDEN) (3YO) (FIBRESAND) 1m (F)

2:20 (12:00) 3-Y-0 **£9,583** (£3,833; £2,875; £1,916; £958)

RPR

1 **Baby Cross**[112] 3-9-2 0.. IoritzMendizabal 12 77
(J-C Rouget, France) **19/5**[2]

2 *1 3/4* **Faraway Run (IRE)** 3-9-2 0.. SylvainRuis 8 73
(P Khozian, France) **13/1**

3 *1* **Lady Ana (FR)**[18] 3-8-13 0.. GregoryBenoist 4 67
(N Clement, France) **7/2**[1]

4 *1* **Passior (FR)**[13] 3-8-8 0.................................(p) FabriceNicoleau(8) 5 68
(H-A Pantall, France) **54/1**

5 *nk* **Very Bad Trip (FR)**[24] 3-9-2 0.....................................(p) AlexisBadel 16 67
(T Castanheira, France) **29/1**

6 *nk* **Dinnar (FR)**[150] 3-9-2 0... StefanieHofer 15 67
(Mario Hofer, Germany) **18/1**

7 *3/4* **Path Finder (FR)**[105] 6663 3-9-2 0................ Francois-XavierBertras 13 65
(Reg Hollinshead) *broke wl fr outside draw: settled 5th on outside: moved into 4th bef st: sn rdn: u.p over 1 1/2f out: nt qckn: styd on fnl f* **24/1**

8 *1 1/4* **Mouhjim (FR)**[98] 3-9-2 0.. FabienLefebvre 7 62
(Mme P Butel, France) **87/1**

9 *3/4* **Ticinello (GER)**[101] 3-9-2 0....................................(p) GaetanMasure 10 60
(T Doumen, France) **60/1**

10 *2* **Sandakam (FR)**[24] 3-9-2 0....................................(b[1]) JohanVictoire 9 56
(C Baillet, France) **14/1**

0 **Surrey Storm**[103] 6726 3-8-13 0..................................... ThierryThulliez 11
(Mme G Rarick, France) **21/1**

0 **Chez Laurent (IRE)**[18] 3-9-2 0.................................. SebastienMaillot 2
(Robert Collet, France) **9/2**[3]

0 **Anoumane (FR)**[67] 3-9-2 0... FranckBlondel 6
(J-C Rouget, France) **68/10**

0 **Dollar King (GER)** 3-9-2 0... ASuborics 1
(C Sprengel, Germany) **25/1**

0 **Everstone (FR)** 3-9-2 0.. ThomasMessina 14
(D Allard, France) **62/1**

0 **Royale Demeure (FR)** 3-8-13 0........................ Pierre-CharlesBoudot 3
(M Cesandri, France) 77/1
1m 37.75s (97.75) **16** Ran SP% **116.3**
WIN (incl. 1 euro stake): 4.80. PLACES: 1.90, 3.10, 2.00. DF: 25.50. SF: 55.50.
Owner Gerard Laboureau **Bred** Ecurie Skymarc Farm **Trained** Pau, France

219 LINGFIELD (L-H)
Saturday, January 21

OFFICIAL GOING: Standard
Wind: fresh, across Weather: dry and breezy

248 BLUE SQUARE WINTER CARNIVAL IPHONE APP (S) STKS 1m 2f (P)
12:20 (12:20) (Class 6) 4-6-Y-O **£1,704** (£503; £251) **Stalls** Low

Form RPR
030- **1** **Buxfizz (USA)**[33] 7661 4-8-12 75........................(p) JimCrowley 1 71
(Robert Mills) *sn bustled up to ld and mde virtually all: rdn and qcknd 2f out: clr and drvn 1f out: styd on wl* 5/1[3]
324- **2** 3 **Mighty Clarets (IRE)**[25] 7887 5-9-0 70........................ PaulHanagan 7 65
(Richard Fahey) *chsd wnr thrght: rdn and unable qck 2f out: styd on same pce and no imp fr over 1f out* 2/1[2]
1-35 **3** ¾ **Ajdaad (USA)**[7] 175 5-9-6 65........................ ShaneKelly 5 69
(Alan McCabe) *hld up in tch in last pair: effrt and n.m.r wl over 1f out: switching rt and lft ent fnl f: kpt on fnl 100yds to go 3rd nr fin: no ch w wnr* 10/1
2-14 **4** hd **Wisecraic**[1] 222 5-9-6 63........................ LiamKeniry 3 69
(J S Moore) *in tch: rdn and unable qck 2f out: styd on same pce and no threat to wnr fr over 1f out* 8/1
042- **5** nk **Archelao (IRE)**[22] 7921 4-8-12 72........................ HayleyTurner 2 62
(Marcus Tregoning) *chsd ldng pair: rdn and unable qck over 2f out: styd on same pce u.p fr over 1f out: lost 2 pls ins fnl f* 7/4[1]
56- **6** 42 **Debbie Doo**[40] 7739 4-8-7 0........................ WilliamCarson 4
(Anthony Carson) *a in rr: rdn 4f out: lost tch over 2f out: t.o and eased fnl f* 66/1
2m 5.79s (-0.81) **Going Correction** -0.075s/f (Stan)
WFA 4 from 5yo 2lb **6** Ran SP% **108.1**
Speed ratings: **100,97,97,96,96 63**
Tote Swingers: 1&2 £2.50, 1&3 £5.30, 2&3 £3.00 CSF £14.26 TOTE £6.00: £2.30, £2.00; EX 14.90.The winner was sold to George Prodromou for 6,200gns.
Owner Buxted Partnership **Bred** Darley **Trained** Headley, Surrey
FOCUS
A moderate seller and the order didn't change very much during the race.
Ajdaad(USA) Official explanation: jockey said that the gelding was denied a clear run

249 MARSH GREEN MAIDEN STKS 1m (P)
12:50 (12:51) (Class 5) 3-Y-O **£2,385** (£704; £352) **Stalls** High

Form RPR
1 **Basseterre (IRE)** 3-9-3 0........................ MichaelHills 6 77+
(Charles Hills) *dwlt: sn rcvrd and chsd ldrs over 6f out: pushed along and qcknd clr w ldr wl over 1f out: led ent fnl f: pushed along and a holding rival fnl f* 2/1[1]
2 1 **Scatter Dice (IRE)** 3-8-12 0........................ JoeFanning 1 69+
(Mark Johnston) *led tl over 5f out: chsd ldr tl led again 3f out: rdn and qcknd clr w wnr wl over 1f out: hdd ent fnl f: kpt on wl but a hld* 9/1[3]
5- **3** 4 **Cape Savannah**[38] 7751 3-9-3 0........................ MartinLane 5 65
(David Simcock) *in tch: rdn and unable qck over 2f out: no ch w ldng pair and styd on same pce fr over 1f out: wnt 3rd on post* 8/1[2]
4 nse **Attain** 3-9-3 0........................ JimCrowley 4 64
(Julia Feilden) *in tch: rdn and unable qck over 2f out: sme hdwy on inner and chsd clr ldng pair over 1f out: no imp: lost 3rd on post* 22/1
60- **5** hd **Supreme Rock**[88] 7083 3-9-3 0........................ StephenCraine 3 64
(Jim Boyle) *stdd after s: hld up in tch in rr: rdn and struggling 3f out: rallied ent fnl f: kpt on and pressing for 3rd towards fin: no ch w ldng pair* 20/1
5- **6** 6 **First Glance**[49] 7626 3-9-3 0........................ LukeMorris 7 50
(Michael Appleby) *chsd ldr tl led over 5f out: hdd 3f out: 3rd and struggling u.p wl over 1f out: wknd ent fnl f* 100/1
1m 39.35s (1.15) **Going Correction** -0.075s/f (Stan) **6** Ran SP% **64.5**
Speed ratings (Par 97): **91,90,86,85,85 79**
Tote Swingers: 1&2 £1.30, 1&3 £1.30, 2&3 £1.70 CSF £4.86 TOTE £1.60: £1.10, £2.30; EX 6.30.
Owner H R Mould **Bred** D G Hardisty Bloodstock **Trained** Lambourn, Berks
FOCUS
The shape of this maiden changed completely when the favourite Dubawi Cheetah was withdrawn after getting under her stall (6/5F, deduct 45p in the £ under R4). Nevertheless the two newcomers who ultimately dominated this event both have a future.

250 5TH "SHAREN BLAQUIERE - CELEBRATE A LIFE" (S) STKS 6f (P)
1:20 (1:20) (Class 6) 3-Y-O **£1,704** (£503; £251) **Stalls** Low

Form RPR
45-4 **1** **Chapellerie (IRE)**[9] 127 3-8-7 69........................(b) ShaneKelly 1 66
(Brian Meehan) *chsd ldr: hdwy and ev ch 2f out: rdn to ld ent fnl f: r.o wl* 11/10[1]
32-4 **2** 1 ¾ **The Dancing Lord**[16] 42 3-8-10 62........................ RyanWhile(7) 5 70
(Bill Turner) *chsd ldrs: wd on bnd 2f out: chsd wnr jst ins fnl f: kpt on* 12/1
6-50 **3** 2 ¼ **Lana (IRE)**[14] 86 3-8-7 53........................ HayleyTurner 6 53
(David Evans) *hld up in tch: rdn and hdwy over 1f out: wnt 3rd fnl 100yds: kpt on but no threat to wnr* 25/1
42-3 **4** nk **Faraway**[16] 42 3-9-3 69........................ LukeMorris 2 62
(Ronald Harris) *s.i.s: in tch in last trio: effrt u.p jst over 2f out: styd on same pce ins fnl f* 9/2[2]
666- **5** 1 ¼ **Umph (IRE)**[165] 4884 3-8-12 60........................ JimmyFortune 3 53
(David Evans) *w ldr tl 1/2-way: sn rdn: outpcd and struggling 2f out: wknd ent fnl f* 12/1
254- **6** nk **Tiablo (IRE)**[22] 7927 3-8-2 63........................ LauraPike(5) 7 47
(David Simcock) *in tch towards rr: rdn and effrt on outer over 2f out: wknd over 1f out* 8/1
024- **7** shd **Finalist**[38] 7749 3-8-7 60........................(b) ChrisCatlin 4 47
(Dean Ivory) *wnt rt s: bhd: rdn and effrt over 1f out: nvr trbld ldrs* 7/1[3]

1-03 **8** 1 ¼ **Lady Nickandy (IRE)**[9] 138 3-8-9 53........................(b) KieranO'Neill(3) 8 48
(Alan McCabe) *led: rdn 2f out: hdd ent fnl f: wknd qckly fnl f* 33/1
1m 11.75s (-0.15) **Going Correction** -0.075s/f (Stan) **8** Ran SP% **111.6**
Speed ratings (Par 95): **98,95,92,92,90 90,90,88**
Tote Swingers: 1&2 £4.10, 1&3 £8.10, 2&3 £17.30 CSF £15.18 TOTE £2.20: £1.20, £2.00, £4.60; EX 16.70 Trifecta £371.60 Part won. Pool: £502.22 - 0.40 winning units..The winner was sold to Richard Guest for 7,000gns.
Owner Smoke & Mirrors **Bred** Castellane Partnership **Trained** Manton, Wilts
FOCUS
Another modest seller.

251 BLUE SQUARE SPRINT SERIES ROUND 3 H'CAP (QUALIFIER) (DIV I) 6f (P)
1:55 (1:56) (Class 5) (0-75,81) 4-Y-O+ **£2,726** (£805; £402) **Stalls** Low

Form RPR
061- **1** **Sulis Minerva (IRE)**[21] 7942 5-8-12 71........................ RaulDaSilva(5) 8 84+
(Jeremy Gask) *hld up in midfield: clsd and travelling wl 2f out: swtchd rt and effrt over 1f out: pushed along fnl f and r.o wl to ld fnl 75yds: comf* 6/1[2]
1-01 **2** ½ **The Strig**[7] 178 5-9-1 69........................ WilliamCarson 2 78
(Stuart Williams) *chsd ldrs: rdn over 2f out: ev ch ent fnl f: led ins fnl f: sn hdd and styd on same pce after* 9/2[1]
40-0 **3** nk **Nubar Boy**[7] 178 5-8-11 65........................(v) PaulHanagan 1 73
(David Evans) *stdd after s: hld up in rr: c wd and effrt jst over 1f out: r.o strly ins fnl f: nt quite rch ldrs* 14/1
1521 **4** 1 ¼ **Desert Strike**[3] 208 6-9-6 81 6ex........................(p) NoraLooby(7) 3 85
(Alan McCabe) *taken down early: stdd s: t.k.h: hld up in rr: c wd and effrt over 1f out: r.o wl ins fnl f: nt rch ldrs* 12/1
303- **4** dht **Sermons Mount (USA)**[24] 7893 6-9-6 74........................ JohnFahy 11 78
(Paul Howling) *chsd ldrs: rdn and effrt jst over 2f out: pressed ldrs 1f out: styd on same pce fnl 100yds* 7/1[3]
-526 **6** 1 **Efistorm**[7] 178 11-8-10 64........................ HayleyTurner 5 65
(Conor Dore) *in tch in midfield: rdn and effrt over 1f out: drvn and styd on ins fnl f: swtchd lft fnl 50yds: unable to rch ldrs* 11/1
5-32 **7** nk **Dancing Freddy (IRE)**[13] 100 5-9-5 73........................(tp) MartinHarley 9 73
(Richard Guest) *led: rdn ent fnl 2f: hdd ins fnl f: wknd fnl 100yds* 6/1[2]
203- **8** ½ **Hoover**[185] 4206 4-8-11 70........................ NathanAlison(5) 4 69+
(Jim Boyle) *chsd ldrs: rdn and ev ch over 1f out: wknd fnl 100yds* 15/2
40-2 **9** shd **Loyal Royal (IRE)**[14] 88 9-8-11 65........................(bt) LiamKeniry 10 63
(Milton Bradley) *stdd after s: hld up off the pce in last trio: rdn and effrt over 1f out: kpt on fnl f: nvr trbld ldrs* 10/1
01-0 **10** 4 ½ **Steelcut**[14] 87 8-9-1 69........................(p) JimCrowley 6 53
(David Evans) *racd in midfield: rdn and effrt over 2f out: wknd u.p over 1f out* 14/1
000- **11** 4 **Reposer (IRE)**[31] 7846 4-9-7 75........................ RobertWinston 7 46
(Noel Quinlan) *dwlt: sn rdn and rcvrd: in tch on outer: rdn and struggling over 2f out: wknd 2f out* 16/1
1m 10.81s (-1.09) **Going Correction** -0.075s/f (Stan) **11** Ran SP% **115.4**
Speed ratings (Par 103): **104,103,102,101,101 99,99,98,98,92 87**
Tote Swingers: 1&2 £3.80, 1&3 £21.40, 2&3 £13.30 CSF £32.46 CT £368.58 TOTE £6.70: £2.30, £1.80, £4.70; EX 32.90 Trifecta £393.20 Part won. Pool: £425.09 - 0.20 winning units..
Owner Richard L Page **Bred** Kevin Blake **Trained** Sutton Veny, Wilts
FOCUS
The latest competitive qualifier in this series and an interesting race as the first five home all came very wide up the home straight.

252 BLUE SQUARE SPRINT SERIES ROUND 3 H'CAP (QUALIFIER) (DIV II) 6f (P)
2:25 (2:25) (Class 5) (0-75,75) 4-Y-O+ **£2,726** (£805; £402) **Stalls** Low

Form RPR
60-3 **1** **Aldermoor (USA)**[7] 179 6-9-1 69........................ WilliamCarson 4 77
(Stuart Williams) *in tch in midfield: rdn and effrt on outer over 1f out: str run u.p ins fnl f: led last strides* 13/2[3]
061- **2** hd **Hatta Stream (IRE)**[24] 7893 6-9-6 74........................ SteveDrowne 2 81
(Lydia Pearce) *chsd ldrs: rdn to chse clr ldng pair 2f out: drvn and kpt on wl ins fnl f: led towards fin tl hdd and no ex last strides* 9/2[1]
03-0 **3** hd **Night Trade (IRE)**[15] 64 5-9-7 75........................ LukeMorris 1 82
(Ronald Harris) *in tch: rdn and effrt on inner over 1f out: drvn and ev ch ins fnl f: led fnl 100yds tl hdd and lost 2 pls towards fin* 20/1
2-11 **4** ½ **Speak The Truth (IRE)**[7] 179 6-8-11 70........................(p) NathanAlison(5) 10 75
(Jim Boyle) *restless in stalls: pushed along and in tch in midfield: travelling bttr 1/2-way: rdn and effrt over 1f out: styd on wl u.p fnl 150yds: nt quite rch ldrs* 9/1
0-12 **5** hd **Captain Dimitrios**[7] 179 4-8-10 64........................(v) MartinLane 3 68
(David Evans) *led: rdn and forged ahd wl over 1f out: drvn 1f out: hdd and no ex fnl 100yds* 8/1
0-34 **6** 1 ¾ **Waabel**[7] 179 5-8-8 62........................ MartinHarley 8 61
(Richard Guest) *s.i.s: bhd: rdn and hdwy towards inner over 1f out: kpt on fnl f: unable to chal* 6/1[2]
65-3 **7** 1 ¼ **Showboating (IRE)**[7] 178 4-8-9 70........................(tp) NoraLooby(7) 11 65
(Alan McCabe) *s.i.s: bhd: effrt on inner over 1f out: styd on same pce fnl f: nvr able to chal* 7/1
52-0 **8** ½ **Picansort**[14] 87 5-8-11 65........................ ShaneKelly 5 58
(Peter Crate) *stdd and swtchd lft after s: hld up in tch in rr: hdwy towards inner 2f out: drvn and no prog 1f out* 8/1
120- **9** nk **Ice Trooper**[51] 7596 4-9-6 74........................(p) JamesSullivan 7 66
(Linda Stubbs) *racd keenly: w ldr: stl upsides and rdn 2f out: struggling over 1f out: wknd ins fnl f* 20/1
506- **10** ¾ **Baby Dottie**[144] 5578 5-8-7 66........................ JemmaMarshall(5) 6 56
(Pat Phelan) *in tch in midfield: stuck bhd wkng rival and lost pl over 1f out: kpt on same pce fnl f and nvr able to rcvr* 20/1
4-40 **11** hd **Punching**[8] 157 8-9-3 71........................ HayleyTurner 12 60
(Conor Dore) *chsd ldrs: rdn and unable qck 2f out: wknd over 1f out* 22/1
5-40 **12** 1 **Captain Scooby**[15] 64 6-9-2 75........................ CharlesEddery(5) 9 61
(Richard Guest) *sn rdn along towards rr: n.d* 16/1
1m 11.34s (-0.56) **Going Correction** -0.075s/f (Stan) **12** Ran SP% **115.0**
Speed ratings (Par 103): **100,99,99,98,98 96,94,93,93,92 92,90**
Tote Swingers: 1&2 £11.60, 1&3 £34.80, 2&3 £28.10 CSF £32.33 CT £431.10 TOTE £7.80: £2.60, £1.90, £6.10; EX 44.90 TRIFECTA Not won..
Owner Darren Hudson-Wood **Bred** Gulf Coast Farms LLC **Trained** Newmarket, Suffolk

FOCUS
The early pace was good thanks to a contested lead, though the winning time was 0.53 seconds slower than division one. The first four home from another qualifier here seven days earlier took each other on again and the form worked out with the quartet finishing 4-5-1-6. A large horse blanket would have covered the first five at the line.

253 VIEW OUR 2012 FIXTURES AT LINGFIELDPARK.CO.UK H'CAP 6f (P)
3:00 (3:01) (Class 3) (0-95,93) 4-Y-0+ **£6,792** (£2,021; £1,010; £505) **Stalls** Low

Form RPR
10-5 **1** **Seek The Fair Land**14 89 6-8-12 **89**....................(b) NathanAlison(5) 3 100
(Jim Boyle) *racd keenly: chsd ldr after 2f: rdn 2f out: led 1f out: clr ins fnl f: kpt on and a holding on* **16/1**
6/-1 **2** ½ **Alben Star (IRE)**15 64 4-9-3 **89**.................................. PaulHanagan 10 98
(Richard Fahey) *taken down early: stdd s: t.k.h: hld up in midfield: rdn and effrt over 1f out: hdwy u.p 1f out: chsd wnr ins fnl f: r.o wl but nvr quite getting to wnr* **11/8**1
220/ **3** 1 ¼ **Brenin Taran**848 6240 6-8-8 **80**.. MartinLane 12 85
(David Simcock) *stdd and dropped in bhd after s: t.k.h and hld up in rr: hdwy over 1f out: styd on wl ins fnl f: wnt 3rd fnl 75yds* **66/1**
06-0 **4** ½ **Norville (IRE)**14 89 5-9-6 **92**....................................(b) JimmyFortune 7 96
(David Evans) *chsd ldrs: rdn over 2f out: styd on same pce u.p fnl f* **7/1**3
02-6 **5** *hd* **Piscean (USA)**14 89 7-9-2 **88**.................................. WilliamCarson 11 91
(Tom Keddy) *stdd and dropped in bhd after s: hld up in last quartet: rdn and hdwy ent fnl f: r.o: nt rch ldrs* **16/1**
00-0 **6** *1* **Five Star Junior (USA)**14 89 6-9-7 **93**..................... JamesSullivan 2 93
(Linda Stubbs) *t.k.h: hld up in last quartet: rdn and hdwy ent fnl f: styd on but nvr threatened ldrs* **28/1**
02-2 **7** ¾ **Fratellino**14 89 5-9-6 **92**...(t) MartinHarley 1 90
(Alan McCabe) *chsd ldr for 2f: styd chsng ldrs: rdn and unable qck 2f out: no ex and btn jst ins fnl f* **5/1**2
314- **8** *nse* **Lujeanie**31 7846 6-8-13 **85**..(p) ShaneKelly 6 82
(Dean Ivory) *in tch in midfield: lost pl bnd 2f out: rallied u.p ent fnl f: kpt on but nt pce to threaten ldrs* **15/2**
064- **9** 1 ½ **Thunderball**53 7578 6-9-1 **87**...(b) LukeMorris 5 80
(Scott Dixon) *chsd ldrs: rdn and unable qck 2f out: wknd ent fnl f* **12/1**
000- **10** ½ **Arteus**146 5516 6-9-2 **88**...(b) ChrisCatlin 8 79
(Jane Chapple-Hyam) *led: rdn 2f out: hdd 1f out: wknd ins fnl f* **66/1**
0U6- **11** 1 ½ **Little Garcon (USA)**42 7721 5-9-6 **92**............................... AdamKirby 4 78
(Marco Botti) *in tch in midfield: effrt on inner over 1f out: no prog and btn jst ins fnl f: wknd fnl 150yds* **28/1**
30-0 **12** *4* **Street Power (USA)**15 64 7-8-7 **79**........................... HayleyTurner 9 52
(Jeremy Gask) *v.s.a: a bhd: short-lived effrt over 1f out: sn wknd* **33/1**

1m 10.1s (-1.80) **Going Correction** -0.075s/f (Stan) **12** Ran SP% **115.3**
Speed ratings (Par 107): **109,108,106,106,105 104,103,103,101,100 98,93**
Tote Swingers: 1&2 £5.80, 1&3 £50.20, 2&3 £19.70 CSF £36.17 CT £1496.12 TOTE £21.20: £4.90, £1.30, £10.50; EX 59.80 Trifecta £418.80 Part won. Pool: £565.95 - 0.20 winning units..
Owner Chris Watkins And David N Reynolds **Bred** Raimon Bloodstock **Trained** Epsom, Surrey

FOCUS
A competitive sprint handicap run at a strong pace and the winning time was much faster than both divisions of the Class 5 handicap, as would have been expected.

NOTEBOOK
Seek The Fair Land loves Polytrack, but up until now has looked a 7f specialist. However, being ridden handily in a strongly run race over this trip proved ideal and his replacement rider timed it to a tee, hitting the front a furlong out and getting first run on the favourite. He was 3lb above his previous highest winning mark and this opens up more options for him.
Alben Star(IRE) ◆, still completely unexposed, overcame a 455-day absence when winning with much more in hand than the head margin would suggest at Wolverhampton 15 days earlier. Now 4lb higher, he wasn't ideally drawn here but seemed to travel well enough off the pace. Admittedly he had to be pulled out wide over a furlong out, at which point the winner had gone for home, but he can't have too many excuses and he ran well enough to suggest that the 'bounce' was not a factor. He still looks capable of going on the better things. (op 6-4 tchd 13-8)
Brenin Taran ◆ made up plenty of late ground from off the pace and, as he was returning from an 848-day absence, this was a cracking effort. He may need plenty of time to get over this, but the engine is obviously still there.
Norville(IRE) could never get into it from a wide draw over C&D last time, but may have been guilty of racing too keenly here. Even so, he never stopped trying and is becoming better handicapped now. (op 8-1 tchd 13-2)
Piscean(USA), now 5lb below his last winning mark, is another who needs a strong pace to run at and was noted doing all his best work late. (op 14-1)
Five Star Junior(USA) was back down to the mark off which he gained his last victory over C&D 11 months earlier, was another coming home strongly but could never get to the leaders. (op 22-1)
Arteus ◆ had shown nothing in five starts since winning over 7f here in November 2010, but was back with his original trainer on this return from 146 days off. He ended up well beaten, but set the strong pace until appearing to blow up a furlong out and can probably do better. (op 50-1)

254 LINGFIELDPARK.CO.UK H'CAP 1m (P)
3:35 (3:35) (Class 2) (0-100,101) 4-Y-0+ **£10,350** (£3,080; £1,539; £769) **Stalls** High

Form RPR
235- **1** **Mull Of Killough (IRE)**42 7719 6-9-1 **94**........................... ShaneKelly 6 101
(Jane Chapple-Hyam) *in tch in midfield: rdn and effrt towards inner over 1f out: chal ins fnl f: led fnl 100yds: r.o wl: drvn out* **11/4**1
212- **2** *nk* **Tarooq (USA)**31 7841 6-8-8 **87**.. PaulHanagan 3 93
(Richard Fahey) *led for 2f: chsd ldr after: drvn and ev ch over 1f out: led ins fnl f: sn hdd and styd on same pce towards fin* **9/2**2
13-2 **3** ½ **Clockmaker (IRE)**17 29 6-9-3 **96**............................. RobertWinston 7 101
(Tim Easterby) *t.k.h: sn chsng ldr: led 6f out: rdn wl over 1f out: hdd ins fnl f: styd on same pce fnl 100yds* **11/2**
211- **4** *shd* **Lockantanks**22 7922 5-9-0 **93**... LukeMorris 2 98
(Michael Appleby) *broke wl: stdd to chse ldng pair: rdn ent fnl 2f: drvn and kpt on ins fnl f* **5/1**3
141- **5** 1 ¼ **Mia's Boy**42 7719 8-9-5 **101**... RyanClark(3) 5 103
(Chris Dwyer) *s.i.s: hld up in rr: effrt ent fnl f: drvn and kpt on fnl 150yds: nt rch ldrs* **13/2**
150- **6** ½ **Greensward**49 7628 6-8-9 **91**... KieranO'Neill(3) 1 92
(Mike Murphy) *s.i.s: in tch: hdwy on inner to chse ldrs 2f out: wknd ins fnl f* **11/1**
040- **7** *nse* **Zacynthus (IRE)**70 7393 4-8-9 **88**... JohnFahy 4 89
(Alan McCabe) *stdd s: hld up in last pair: rdn and effrt over 1f out: kpt on ins fnl f: nvr quite gng pce to rch ldrs* **22/1**
52-3 **8** ¾ **Night Lily (IRE)**15 83 6-8-8 **92**.................................... RaulDaSilva(5) 8 91
(Paul D'Arcy) *chsd ldrs: rdn and unable qck 2f out: wknd 1f out* **8/1**

1m 35.32s (-2.88) **Going Correction** -0.075s/f (Stan) **8** Ran SP% **114.0**
Speed ratings (Par 109): **111,110,110,110,108 108,108,107**
Tote Swingers: 1&2 £3.10, 1&3 £4.20, 2&3 £5.40 CSF £15.01 CT £62.62 TOTE £3.30: £1.60, £2.20, £1.50; EX 17.10 Trifecta £213.40 Pool: £331.70 - 1.15 winning units..
Owner Invictus **Bred** Owenstown Stud **Trained** Dalham, Suffolk

FOCUS
The feature race on the card, but nothing wanted to go on early and this became a messy contest, with the pace not quickening significantly until over 2f from home.

NOTEBOOK
Mull Of Killough(IRE) had changed stables since doing too much in the first-time blinkers when 3l behind Mia's Boy at Wolverhampton last month, and seemed to appreciate their removal here. Despite being held up in a steadily run race, he put in a sustained effort to lead inside the last furlong and saw it out gamely. He will go up a little bit for this, but is 2lb lower than when third in the 2010 Lincoln and he may have still more to offer with the change of stables obviously not doing him any harm at all. (op 7-2 tchd 5-2)
Tarooq(USA), very consistent on Polytrack, was weighted to comfortably reverse last month's Kempton form with Lockantanks, but had never raced at above Class 4 level before. His rider was probably relieved to get a lead from Clockmaker fairly early on in the contest and he was back in front over a furlong out, but the winner proved too strong in the run to the line. (op 11-2)
Clockmaker(IRE) had twice run well from the front in conditions events since winning a handicap off 6lb lower at Wolverhampton last month, and soon found himself bowling along in the lead again, but he hung right rounding the home bend which allowed the first two to come though on his inside and although he battled on bravely, the damage had been done. (op 5-1)
Lockantanks was bidding for a hat-trick off a 4lb higher mark, but had never competed at Class 2 level before. He may have found himself racing closer to the pace than was ideal due to the steady early tempo, but he still gave it his best shot and had every chance. (tchd 6-1)
Mia's Boy, 3lb higher than when beating a subsequent winner at Wolverhampton last time, wasn't best positioned in a slowly run race and his finishing effort down the wide outside was never getting him there. (op 6-1)
Greensward didn't shine in his one previous try at this trip and again didn't proved his stamina. (op 10-1)
Zacynthus(IRE), ex-Godolphin, reportedly lost his action when last of 12 on his debut for the yard over C&D last time and made little impression from off the pace here. (op 28-1)
Night Lily(IRE), winner of just one of her last 17 starts, needs them to go a decent pace up front so this wasn't run to suit her, but she still folded rather disappointingly. (op 7-1 tchd 13-2)

255 ROULETTE AT BLUESQ.COM/CASINO H'CAP 1m 2f (P)
4:10 (4:11) (Class 6) (0-65,65) 3-Y-0 **£1,704** (£503; £251) **Stalls** Low

Form RPR
00-6 **1** **Moataz (USA)**17 38 3-8-7 **51** oh3.................................... JoeFanning 8 59+
(Mark Johnston) *sn chsng ldr: rdn and qcknd clr w ldr jst over 2f out: led 1f out: clr and in command ins fnl f: eased towards fin* **11/2**3
16-3 **2** 3 ½ **Masters Club**17 38 3-9-7 **65**... AdamKirby 6 66
(John Ryan) *led and set stdy gallop: rdn and qcknd wl over 1f out: clr w wnr jst over 2f out: hdd 1f out: sn btn: wl hld and eased towards fin* **3/1**2
31-1 **3** ¾ **Complex**12 108 3-8-12 **56**... LukeMorris 1 56
(David Evans) *chsd ldng pair: rdn and outpcd wl over 1f out: 3rd and drvn over 1f out: plugged on same pce fnl f* **13/2**
500- **4** ¾ **Foster's Road**37 7763 3-8-13 **62**..........................(v1) CharlesBishop(5) 4 60
(Mick Channon) *t.k.h: hld up wl in tch: rdn and outpcd over 2f out: sme hdwy over 1f out: styd on same pce ins fnl f: no ch w wnr* **10/1**
00-0 **5** ½ **Little Red Minx (IRE)**8 159 3-9-0 **58**........................... JimmyFortune 3 55
(Peter Chapple-Hyam) *stdd after s: hld up wl in tch in rr: rdn and no prog wl over 2f out: no ch but kpt on ins fnl f* **33/1**
24-5 **6** *nk* **Moment In The Sun**9 132 3-8-12 **56**........................... WilliamCarson 5 52
(William Muir) *wl in tch in midfield: rdn and unable qck over 2f out: kpt on same pce u.p and no ch w wnr fnl 2f* **15/2**
00-2 **7** 1 ½ **Green Legacy (USA)**9 132 3-9-0 **58**............................(b) JimCrowley 7 51
(Amanda Perrett) *dwlt and rdn along early: hdwy to chse ldrs on outer after 2f: rdn and unable qck over 2f out: drvn and no rspnse wl over 1f out: wl btn 1f out* **9/4**1
403- **8** 1 ¾ **Canning Vale**23 7909 3-8-13 **57**....................................... MartinHarley 2 47
(Julia Feilden) *wl in tch in midfield: rdn and outpcd over 2f out: bhd and wl hld 1f out* **25/1**

2m 10.08s (3.48) **Going Correction** -0.075s/f (Stan) **8** Ran SP% **112.1**
Speed ratings (Par 95): **83,80,79,79,78 78,77,75**
Tote Swingers: 1&2 £3.80, 1&3 £7.20, 2&3 £2.20 CSF £21.47 CT £107.62 TOTE £6.80: £2.30, £1.10, £2.30; EX 25.50 Trifecta £90.60 Pool: £1,042.56 - 8.51 winning units..
Owner Dr Marwan Koukash **Bred** Stonestreet Thoroughbred Holdings LLC **Trained** Middleham Moor, N Yorks

FOCUS
A moderate handicap and this sort of trip would have been a new experience for the majority of these. The front pair dominated from the start.
Moataz(USA) Official explanation: trainer's representative was unable to provide any explanation for the apparent improvement in form
T/Plt: £40.20 to a £1 stake. Pool: £65,706.26 - 1,191.14 winning tickets. T/Qpdt: £10.10 to a £1 stake. Pool: £4,664.37 - 340.63 winning tickets SP

256 - 259a (Foreign Racing) - See Raceform Interactive

241 MEYDAN (L-H)
Saturday, January 21
OFFICIAL GOING: Tapeta - standard; turf - good

260a AL NABOODAH CONSTRUCTION GROUP (H'CAP) (TURF) 1m
4:40 (4:42) (90-102,102) 3-Y-0+
£11,612 (£3,870; £1,935; £967; £580; £387)

RPR
1 **Iguazu Falls (USA)**16 53 7-8-13 98......................................(t) XZiani 8 101
(M bin Shafya, UAE) *trckd ldrs: led 2f out: r.o gamely* **25/1**
2 1 ¼ **Krypton Factor**317 823 4-9-1 100................................(b) KierenFallon 5 100
(F Nass, Bahrain) *sn led: hdd 2f out: kpt on same pce* **16/1**
3 *shd* **Spirit Of Sharjah (IRE)**9 140 7-8-7 93........................ TadhgO'Shea 9 92+
(Julia Feilden) *settled in rr: r.o fnl 2f: nrst fin* **12/1**
4 ¼ **Prince D'Alienor (IRE)**85 4-9-3 102............................. MircoDemuro 4 101+
(X Nakkachdji, France) *settled in rr: nvr nr to chal but r.o wl fnl 2f: nrst fin* **10/1**3
5 2 ¼ **Wealthy (IRE)**136 5829 5-9-0 99..(t) TedDurcan 7 93
(Saeed Bin Suroor) *mid-div: r.o same pce fnl 2f* **12/1**
6 *shd* **Man Of Action (USA)**119 6339 5-9-2 101...........(v) MickaelBarzalona 12 95+
(Saeed Bin Suroor) *settled in rr: mid-div 4f out: r.o one pce fnl 2f* **4/6**1
7 3 ¼ **Marching Time**16 47 6-9-1 100.. RichardHills 1 86
(Doug Watson, UAE) *mid-div: chsd ldrs 2f out: one pce fnl f* **10/1**3
8 2 ¾ **Firestreak**15 80 7-8-13 98.......................................(t) WayneSmith 10 78
(M Al Muhairi, UAE) *nvr bttr than mid-div* **8/1**2
9 *4* **Concordat**134 5910 4-8-13 98... HarryBentley 6 69
(S Seemar, UAE) *nvr bttr than mid-div* **20/1**
10 1 ¾ **Swinging Sixties (IRE)**50 7623 7-9-2 101.................(e) WilliamBuick 11 68
(D Selvaratnam, UAE) *trckd ldng pair: ev ch 3f out: wknd fnl 1 1/2f* **10/1**3

11 4 1/4 **Abjer (FR)**[16] [53] 4-9-1 100 .... (b) RoystonFfrench 3 57
(Ismail Mohammed) *nvr bttr than mid-div* **25/1**

12 16 1/2 **Burdlaz (IRE)**[331] [677] 7-9-1 100 .... RichardMullen 2 19
(S Seemar, UAE) *sn rdn in rr: n.d* **20/1**

1m 37.66s (97.66) **12** Ran SP% **136.9**
CSF: 408.57; TRICAST: 5,021.66..
Owner Sheikh Mansoor bin Mohammed al Maktoum **Bred** Darley **Trained** United Arab Emirates

FOCUS
No obviously well-handicapped types here and a forward ride proved essential.

NOTEBOOK
Iguazu Falls(USA) was difficult to fancy, although he had chased an overly quick pace in a better race last time and this clearly set up a lot more favourably.
Krypton Factor took them along through fractions of 25.95, 49.04 and 1.12.64, but was picked off by the winner. He is smart when things go his way and this was a respectable showing after a 317-day break. He did, however, cover five metres less than the winner. (op 14-1)
Spirit Of Sharjah(IRE) had been well held in a couple of runs on Tapeta recently, but he was 7lb lower than last time on this switch to turf and ran a noteworthy race. He fared best of those held up, having travelled well, although he didn't look totally comfortable in the closing stages. This trip just stretches him.
Prince D'Alienor(IRE), a winner at Longchamp when last seen in October, was set even more to do than the third and simply got going too late. (op 8-1)
Wealthy(IRE) might have needed this after 136 days off, but otherwise had no excuse. (op 10-1)
Man Of Action(USA) had looked unlucky not to go close in the Cambridgeshire when last seen, but this was a disappointing performance, even though he covered a little bit more ground than most. (op Evens)

261a SAEED & MOHAMMED AL NABOODAH GROUP (H'CAP) (TAPETA) 7f
5:20 (5:20) (95-105,105) 3-Y-0+

£42,580 (£14,193; £7,096; £3,548; £2,129; £1,419)

RPR

1 **Ip Man (NZ)**[43] 4-8-11 105 .... (t) OChavez 3 114
(S Burridge, Singapore) *in rr of mid-div: smooth prog 2 1/2f out: led 1f out: r.o wl* **7/2**[2]

2 2 1/2 **Primaeval**[66] [7433] 6-8-11 99 .... (v) JamieSpencer 11 101+
(James Fanshawe) *settled in rr: r.o wl fnl 2f: nrst fin* **3/1**[1]

3 shd **Tamaathul**[16] [51] 5-8-13 100 .... (t) RichardHills 8 103
(A Al Raihe, UAE) *slowly away: in rr of mid-div: r.o wl fnl 1 1/2f out: nrst fin* **20/1**

4 1/2 **Global City (IRE)**[70] [7392] 6-8-13 100 .... (t) KierenFallon 9 101
(Saeed Bin Suroor) *in rr of mid-div: r.o fnl 2f: nrst fin* **12/1**

5 3/4 **Canwinn (IRE)**[16] [51] 6-9-2 104 .... WilliamBuick 10 102
(D Selvaratnam, UAE) *settled in rr: r.o fnl 2f: nrst fin* **20/1**

6 1/4 **Montmorency (IRE)**[16] [53] 6-8-13 100 .... (vt) RichardMullen 6 99
(S Seemar, UAE) *trckd ldrs: ev ch 2f out: one pce fnl f* **33/1**

7 1/2 **Bridgefield (USA)**[16] [51] 4-8-13 100 .... MickaelBarzalona 7 97
(Mahmood Al Zarooni) *slowly away: nvr bttr than mid-div* **7/2**[2]

8 1 **Bravo Echo**[16] [51] 6-8-10 98 .... JamesDoyle 2 92
(Michael Attwater) *trckd ldrs tl wknd 2f out* **50/1**

9 4 **Al Aasifh (IRE)**[15] [80] 4-8-11 99 .... SilvestreDeSousa 4 82
(Saeed Bin Suroor) *slowly away: n.d* **11/1**

10 1 3/4 **Famous Warrior (IRE)**[16] [51] 5-9-0 101 .... TadhgO'Shea 14 80
(Doug Watson, UAE) *sn led: hdd & wknd 1 1/2f out* **20/1**

11 3/4 **Russian Rock (IRE)**[9] [140] 5-9-1 102 .... WayneSmith 12 79
(M Al Muhairi, UAE) *nvr bttr than mid-div* **20/1**

12 hd **Desuetude (AUS)**[21] [7947] 7-8-8 96 .... HarryBentley 5 72
(S Seemar, UAE) *nvr bttr than mid-div* **40/1**

13 2 1/4 **Zabarajad (IRE)**[36] [7793] 4-8-13 100 .... (b) JohnnyMurtagh 13 70
(John M Oxx, Ire) *settled in rr: nvr nr to chal* **7/1**[3]

14 3 1/2 **Il Grande Maurizio (IRE)**[34] [7815] 8-9-2 104 .... RoystonFfrench 1 64
(A Al Raihe, UAE) *trckd ldrs tl 3f out: sn wknd* **25/1**

1m 22.6s (-2.60) **14** Ran SP% **128.2**
CSF: 13.63; TRICAST: 197.23. Placepot: £2,013.90 to a £1 stake. Pool of £3,724.51 - 1.35 winning units. Quadpot: Not won..
Owner Law Teck Hin **Bred** Assured Assets Pty Ltd **Trained** Singapore

FOCUS
The pace was too fast, with Famous Warrior going 24.21 for the opening quarter-mile and 46.90 for the half. The winner took over in the straight and clocked 1.10.54 at the 6f point. All three sectionals were significantly quicker than the earlier lower-class race and the final time was 1.37 seconds faster. This was also a new track record by 0.29 seconds - the previous best was set in March 2010 by the then 110-rated Sirocco Breeze.

NOTEBOOK
Ip Man(NZ), making his Dubai debut, produced a really smart performance and in the process improved the Carnival record of his Singapore-based trainer to a remarkable 3-4. Clearly, this is an operation that must be afforded the utmost respect. (op 4-1)
Primaeval, the form of whose Kempton conditions race, when he was last seen in November, has worked out nicely, was no match at all for the well-handicapped winner. (op 5-2)
Tamaathul covered five metres more than the winner and eight metres more than the second. This was a promising effort. (op 16-1)
Global City(IRE) travelled well but his run flattened out in the closing stages. He's better suited by 6f. (op 11-1)
Canwinn(IRE) ran on from a long way back and should be suited by a return to 1m.
Montmorency(IRE) ◆ paid for racing too close to the quick pace, and wants upgrading a touch.
Bridgefield(USA) was expected to be suited by this drop in trip after a creditable effort over 1m on his recent reappearance, but he disappointed.
Bravo Echo ◆ was another who raced too close to the pace and can be rated slightly better than the bare form. (op 40-1)

197 KEMPTON (A.W) (R-H)
Sunday, January 22

OFFICIAL GOING: Standard
Wind: Light, across. Weather: overcast

262 32RED H'CAP 7f (P)
2:20 (2:21) (Class 6) (0-65,67) 4-Y-0+ **£1,617** (£481; £240; £120) **Stalls** Low

Form RPR

045- 1 **Garstang**[44] [7696] 9-9-5 63 .... JoeFanning 1 74
(Bruce Hellier, Germany) *mid-div: rdn over 2f out: hdwy over 1f out: r.o wl to ld nring fin: rdn out* **12/1**

5-62 2 nk **Katmai River (IRE)**[10] [128] 5-8-13 57 .... (v) DavidProbert 10 67
(Mark Usher) *chsd ldrs: rdn 2f out: led ins fnl f: kpt on but no ex whn hdd nring fin* **13/2**[2]

05-4 3 3/4 **Trojan Rocket (IRE)**[13] [102] 4-9-3 66 .... RaulDaSilva(5) 14 74+
(George Prodromou) *mid-div: rdn and hdwy over 1f out: styd on same pce fnl f* **9/2**[1]

244- 4 1 **Comadoir (IRE)**[132] [5995] 6-9-4 62 .... IanMongan 11 67
(Jo Crowley) *mid-div: rdn over 2f out: kpt on fnl f: nt pce to chal* **20/1**

31-1 5 nse **Cut And Thrust (IRE)**[18] [39] 6-9-7 65 .... AdamKirby 12 70+
(Mark Wellings) *sn swtchd rt: towards rr: rdn over 2f out: hdwy over 1f out: kpt on ins fnl f* **9/2**[1]

43-4 6 3/4 **Polar Auroras**[18] [39] 4-8-13 57 .... (t) LukeMorris 13 60
(Tony Carroll) *hld up towards rr: rdn and no imp fr over 2f out tl r.o ins fnl f* **12/1**

20-3 7 nk **Rapid Water**[11] [123] 6-9-2 60 .... (p) JimmyFortune 8 62
(Gary Moore) *led: rdn whn hdd ins fnl f: no ex* **10/1**

30-2 8 1/4 **Bold Ring**[11] [124] 6-9-6 67 .... RyanPowell(3) 7 67
(Eric Wheeler) *chsd ldrs: rdn over 2f out: one pce fnl f* **12/1**

00-0 9 nk **Huzzah (IRE)**[18] [31] 7-9-4 62 .... MichaelStainton 6 61
(Paul Howling) *t.k.h: sn prom: rdn to chse ldrs over 2f out: fdd fnl f* **33/1**

00-3 10 9 **Spin Again (IRE)**[13] [102] 7-9-0 63 .... LucyKBarry(5) 5 38
(Mark Wellings) *trckd ldrs: sddle slipped after 3f: sn upsides ldr: fdd fr 2f out: nt rcvr* **9/1**[3]

056- 11 6 **Fleetwoodmaxi (USA)**[131] [6020] 5-9-2 60 .... SteveDrowne 2 19
(Peter Makin) *s.i.s: a towards rr* **14/1**

13-1 12 nk **Fedora (IRE)**[11] [124] 6-9-3 61 .... (t) ChrisCatlin 9 19
(Olivia Maylam) *a towards rr* **9/1**[3]

1m 25.94s (-0.06) **Going Correction** +0.05s/f (Slow) **12** Ran SP% **116.2**
Speed ratings (Par 101): **102,101,100,99,99 98,98,97,97,86 80,79**
Tote Swingers:1&2:£16.10, 2&3:£6.90, 1&3:£11.10 CSF £86.28 CT £415.30 TOTE £14.70: £3.90, £2.30, £2.00; EX 61.90 Trifecta £421.90 Part won. Pool £570.26 - 0.74 winning units..
Owner The Foulrice Twenty **Bred** Mrs S E Barclay **Trained**

FOCUS
A moderate handicap.

263 32RED.COM H'CAP 1m 3f (P)
2:50 (2:50) (Class 5) (0-75,78) 4-Y-0+ **£2,264** (£673; £336; £168) **Stalls** Low

Form RPR

3-42 1 **Focail Maith**[11] [119] 4-9-7 75 .... (p) AdamKirby 6 84
(John Ryan) *trckd ldr: led over 2f out: sn rdn: styd on wl* **7/2**[2]

104- 2 1 **Hurricane Hymnbook (USA)**[33] [7831] 7-9-4 69 .... StevieDonohoe 2 76
(Willie Musson) *trckd ldrs: rdn 2f out: sn chsng wnr: kpt on but a being hld* **3/1**[1]

05-2 3 2 **Shabak Hom (IRE)**[8] [175] 5-9-7 72 .... MartinLane 5 75
(David Simcock) *hld up bhd ldrs: rdn over 2f out: hdwy jst over 1f out: styd on ins fnl f* **12/1**

104- 4 2 1/4 **Bennelong**[39] [7761] 6-9-3 68 .... AmirQuinn 7 67
(Richard Rowe) *trckd ldrs: rdn 2f out: kpt on same pce* **9/1**

/35- 5 1 3/4 **Ostentation**[26] [7884] 5-8-13 67 .... MichaelO'Connell(3) 3 63
(Roger Teal) *trckd ldr: rdn 2f out: sn one pce* **20/1**

1-12 6 nse **Mataajir (USA)**[13] [104] 4-8-9 63 .... JoeFanning 8 59
(Derek Shaw) *led: rdn and hdd over 2f out: one pce after* **7/2**[2]

1-21 7 3/4 **Nibani (IRE)**[11] [119] 5-9-8 78 .... (p) AmyScott(5) 1 73
(Alastair Lidderdale) *slowly away: hld up last tl hdwy on outer over 3f out: outpcd 2f out* **4/1**[3]

2m 21.84s (-0.06) **Going Correction** +0.05s/f (Slow)
WFA 4 from 5yo+ 3lb **7** Ran SP% **111.9**
Speed ratings (Par 103): **102,101,99,98,96 96,96**
Tote Swingers:1&2:£3.00, 2&3:£6.90, 1&3:£7.00 CSF £13.77 CT £108.06 TOTE £5.30: £2.50, £1.70; EX 14.20 Trifecta £143.70 Pool £359.45 - 1.85 winning units..
Owner Cathal Fegan **Bred** D Robb **Trained** Newmarket, Suffolk

FOCUS
An ordinary handicap and the early pace didn't look that strong.

264 32RED CASINO H'CAP 7f (P)
3:25 (3:25) (Class 6) (0-52,57) 4-Y-0+ **£1,617** (£481; £240; £120) **Stalls** Low

Form RPR

000- 1 **Diplomatic (IRE)**[134] [5944] 7-9-3 52 .... LukeMorris 11 62
(Michael Squance) *chsd ldrs: rdn over 2f out: kpt on to ld wl ins fnl f: rdn out* **16/1**

05-2 2 1 **Rightcar**[9] [155] 5-9-3 52 .... RobbieFitzpatrick 5 59
(Peter Grayson) *mid-div: hdwy 2f out: rdn and ev ch ins fnl f: kpt on but hld nring fin* **11/1**

00-5 3 nk **Milton Of Campsie**[12] [113] 7-9-1 50 .... MartinHarley 10 56
(Richard Guest) *sn mid-div: rdn and hdwy over 1f out: styd on ins fnl f* **10/1**

53-1 4 1 1/2 **Shaunas Spirit (IRE)**[4] [203] 4-9-8 57 6ex .... ShaneKelly 4 59
(Dean Ivory) *trckd ldrs: travelling wl whn in ld over 1f out: sn rdn: nt qckn: hdd ins fnl f: no ex* **1/1**[1]

10-0 5 1/2 **Jackie Love (IRE)**[11] [125] 4-8-7 49 .... (b) JenniferFerguson(7) 2 50
(Olivia Maylam) *hld up in rr: pushed along over 4f out: hdwy 2f out: sn rdn: styd on ins fnl f: nt rch ldrs* **14/1**

4-00 6 1/2 **Striking Willow**[12] [113] 4-8-11 46 oh1 .... (t) JamesMillman 8 45
(Rod Millman) *mid-div: rdn 2f out: styd on fnl f* **33/1**

-031 7 2 1/2 **Kyncraighe (IRE)**[2] [232] 4-8-13 51 6ex .... (tp) SophieDoyle(3) 7 44
(Joseph Tuite) *nvr bttr than mid-div* **7/1**[2]

60-2 8 2 1/4 **My Jeanie (IRE)**[18] [39] 8-8-8 46 .... KieranO'Neill(3) 3 33
(Jimmy Fox) *a mid-div* **20/1**

34-6 9 hd **Tamino (IRE)**[4] [210] 9-8-6 46 .... (bt[1]) JemmaMarshall(5) 13 32
(Alastair Lidderdale) *t.k.h: prom: led after 2f: rdn and hdd over 1f out: wknd fnl f* **33/1**

00-6 10 3/4 **Tunza The Lion**[14] [95] 5-8-11 46 oh1 .... NeilChalmers 6 30
(Bruce Hellier, Germany) *a towards rr* **100/1**

-612 11 2 **My Best Man**[10] [126] 6-9-5 54 .... (t) DavidProbert 1 33
(Tony Carroll) *a towards rr* **8/1**[3]

500- 12 hd **Cavalry Guard (USA)**[23] [7923] 8-8-6 46 oh1 .... (b) RaulDaSilva(5) 9 24
(Tim McCarthy) *led for 2f: trckd ldr: rdn over 2f out: wknd fnl f* **40/1**

00-0 13 4 1/2 **Blazing Apostle (IRE)**[12] [113] 4-8-11 46 oh1 .... (p) ChrisCatlin 12 12
(Christine Dunnett) *chsd ldrs: rdn over 2f out: sn wknd* **66/1**

1m 26.52s (0.52) **Going Correction** +0.05s/f (Slow) **13** Ran SP% **119.2**
Speed ratings (Par 101): **99,97,97,95,95 94,91,89,89,88 85,85,80**
Tote Swingers:1&2:£14.10, 2&3:£21.70, 1&3:£19.10 CSF £170.02 CT £1918.15 TOTE £16.10: £4.70, £3.10, £4.00; EX 295.20 TRIFECTA Not won..
Owner K Squance & R Favarulo **Bred** Darley **Trained** Newmarket, Suffolk

FOCUS
The betting for this moderate handicap had a very lopsided look to it.

265 £32 FREE AT 32RED.COM H'CAP 1m 4f (P)
3:55 (3:59) (Class 6) (0-55,58) 4-Y-0+ £1,617 (£481; £240; £120) Stalls Centre

Form RPR
53-2 **1** **Kai Mook**[10] 130 5-9-9 **57** AdamKirby 14 67
(Roger Ingram) *led for 3f: trckd ldr: regained ld over 2f out: rdn clr over 1f out: styd on strly: eased nring fin* **8/1**[3]
60-1 **2** 4 **Fire In Babylon (IRE)**[7] 188 4-9-6 **58** 6ex JimCrowley 5 62
(Michael Wigham) *mid-div: pushed along over 3f out: rdn over 2f out: no imp tl styd on ent fnl f: wnt 2nd fnl 140yds: no ch w wnr* **13/8**[1]
05-0 **3** 3/4 **Missionaire (USA)**[18] 28 5-9-7 **55** LukeMorris 7 57
(Tony Carroll) *trckd ldrs: rdn over 2f out: chsd wnr over 1f out but a being hld: styng on at same pce whn lost 2nd fnl 140yds* **25/1**
06-4 **4** hd **Grecian Goddess (IRE)**[13] 105 4-8-10 **51** MichaelO'Connell(3) 1 53
(John Ryan) *in tch: rdn over 2f out: nt pce to mount chal: styd on fnl f* **25/1**
05-3 **5** 1/2 **Herschel (IRE)**[16] 57 6-9-5 **53** (be) AmirQuinn 9 54
(Gary Moore) *s.i.s: towards rr: rdn over 2f out: no imp tl r.o ins fnl f: nrst fin* **25/1**
20-6 **6** hd **Avon Supreme**[9] 151 4-9-1 **53** StevieDonohoe 10 54
(Gay Kelleway) *mid-div: rdn over 2f out: styd on same pce* **12/1**
10-5 **7** 1/2 **Rose Aurora**[18] 28 5-9-6 **54** (vt) HayleyTurner 6 54+
(Marcus Tregoning) *hld up towards rr: rdn and sme hdwy 2f out: nvr threatened ldrs: one pce fnl f* **10/1**
0-04 **8** 1 **El Libertador (USA)**[9] 151 6-9-5 **53** (b) ShaneKelly 2 51
(Eric Wheeler) *hld up towards rr: hdwy 2f out: sn rdn: no further imp* **25/1**
0-14 **9** 3/4 **Now**[7] 188 6-9-3 **51** (b) JamesMillman 11 48
(Rod Millman) *t.k.h in mid-div: hdwy after 2f: led after 3f: rdn and hdd over 2f out: wknd fnl f* **4/1**[2]
000- **10** 1/2 **Visions Of Johanna (USA)**[80] 7241 7-9-7 **55** (p) MartinHarley 12 51
(Richard Guest) *mid-div: effrt over 2f out: fdd fnl f* **12/1**
/00- **11** nse **Moscow Oznick**[25] 7903 7-9-2 **50** (b) DavidProbert 8 46
(Des Donovan) *in tch: rdn over 2f out: wknd ent fnl f* **66/1**
440- **12** 4 **Raghdaan**[31] 7859 5-9-3 **51** ChrisCatlin 3 41
(Peter Hiatt) *chsd ldrs tl wknd 2f out* **20/1**
40-0 **13** 12 **Lytham (IRE)**[13] 104 11-9-6 **54** FergusSweeney 13 25
(Tony Carroll) *a towards rr* **33/1**
030- **14** 3 **Carr Hall (IRE)**[223] 2991 9-9-0 **55** GeorgeDowning(7) 4 21
(Tony Carroll) *mid-div tl wknd 2f out* **33/1**

2m 37.52s (3.02) **Going Correction** +0.05s/f (Slow) 14 Ran SP% **121.2**
WFA 4 from 5yo+ 4lb
Speed ratings (Par 101): **91,88,87,87,87 87,86,86,85,85 85,82,74,72**
Tote Swingers:1&2:£4.20, 2&3:£19.00, 1&3:£38.80 CSF £19.30 CT £331.05 TOTE £7.00: £2.30, £1.20, £9.20; EX 26.10 Trifecta £470.60 Pool £877.63 - 1.38 winning units..
Owner G E Ley **Bred** Miss Lois McIntosh **Trained** Epsom, Surrey
■ Stewards' Enquiry : Amir Quinn five-day ban: used whip with excessive frequency (6 -10 Feb)
FOCUS
Another modest handicap. There was little pace on early with the result that a few were keen and it paid to race prominently.

266 32REDBET.COM CONDITIONS STKS 7f (P)
4:25 (4:26) (Class 4) 4-Y-0+ £4,075 (£1,212; £606; £303) Stalls Low

Form RPR
0- **1** **Palace Moon**[141] 5699 7-9-2 95 (t) JimCrowley 5 95+
(William Knight) *hld up: smooth hdwy over 2f out: led ent fnl f: drifted lft: r.o: rdn out* **9/2**[3]
00-0 **2** 1 1/2 **Elna Bright**[15] 89 7-9-2 92 ShaneKelly 4 91
(Peter Crate) *trckd ldrs: rdn 2f out: kpt on ins fnl f but a being hld by wnr* **8/1**
50-4 **3** 1/2 **Nazreef**[18] 29 5-9-2 95 (bt) HayleyTurner 1 90
(Hughie Morrison) *pushed along briefly leaving stalls: prom: led after 4f: rdn whn hrd pressed fr over 2f out: hdd ent fnl f: kpt on same pce* **13/8**[1]
00-0 **4** 1/2 **Tevez**[21] 5 7-9-2 85 (p) DavidProbert 7 88
(Des Donovan) *stdd s: hld up: rdn and styd on fr over 1f out but nt gng pce to get on terms* **25/1**
00-3 **5** nk **Hazzard County (USA)**[18] 29 8-8-11 94 LauraPike(5) 3 87
(David Simcock) *in tch: rdn over 2f out: kpt on fnl f but nvr gng pce to get involved* **4/1**[2]
000- **6** 1 1/4 **Reignier**[96] 6958 5-9-7 90 MartinHarley 6 89
(Mrs K Burke) *sn led: narrowly hdd over 4f out: rdn and ev ch fr over 2f out: no ex ent fnl f* **4/1**[2]
330- **7** 1 1/2 **Where's Reiley (USA)**[23] 7926 6-8-13 80 (b) RyanPowell(3) 2 80?
(Alastair Lidderdale) *cl up: rdn over 2f out: one pce fr over 1f out* **33/1**

1m 25.45s (-0.55) **Going Correction** +0.05s/f (Slow) 7 Ran SP% **114.2**
Speed ratings (Par 105): **105,103,102,102,101 100,98**
Tote Swingers:1&2:£8.20, 2&3:£3.80, 1&3:£1.90 CSF £38.99 TOTE £5.40: £2.90, £4.90; EX 34.30.
Owner Canisbay Bloodstock **Bred** Miss B Swire **Trained** Patching, W Sussex
FOCUS
An interesting conditions event, but the pace was ordinary and all seven runners were within a couple of lengths of each other coming to the last furlong.

267 32REDBINGO.COM H'CAP 6f (P)
4:55 (4:55) (Class 5) (0-70,70) 4-Y-0+ £2,264 (£673; £336; £168) Stalls Low

Form RPR
P0-2 **1** **Torres Del Paine**[11] 123 5-8-12 **64** KieranO'Neill(3) 7 78+
(Jimmy Fox) *stdd and squeezed out s: bhd: nt clrest of runs whn swtchd rt over 1f out: str run ins fnl f: led fnl 75yds: comf* **9/2**[2]
014- **2** 1 1/2 **Valmina**[134] 5917 5-8-11 **67** (t) GeorgeDowning(7) 11 74
(Tony Carroll) *hld up towards rr: gd hdwy on outer fr over 2f out: rdn to ld ent fnl f: no ex whn hdd fnl 75yds* **16/1**
4-53 **3** 3/4 **Dvinsky (USA)**[11] 122 11-9-0 **63** (b) TomMcLaughlin 8 68
(Paul Howling) *sn pushed along: chsd ldrs: rdn to ld over 1f out: hdd ent fnl f: kpt on same pce* **20/1**
61-6 **4** 1 3/4 **Mack's Sister**[11] 123 5-9-0 **63** AdamKirby 6 62
(Dean Ivory) *trckd ldrs: rdn over 2f out: ev ch ent fnl f: kpt on same pce* **5/1**[3]
45-1 **5** nk **Vhujon (IRE)**[11] 123 7-8-12 **61** RobbieFitzpatrick 3 61+
(Peter Grayson) *hld up: nt clr run over 1f out: swtchd rt: styd on fnl f: nrest at fin* **7/1**
00-0 **6** shd **Cheery Cat (USA)**[14] 100 8-8-8 **57** (p) JoeFanning 1 55
(Bruce Hellier, Germany) *chsd ldrs: rdn over 2f out: kpt on same pce* **20/1**
0P-1 **7** nk **Belinsky (IRE)**[11] 122 5-9-0 **63** JimCrowley 2 60
(Julie Camacho) *mid-div: rdn over 2f out: styd on same pce* **11/4**[1]
8 1 1/2 **Volcanic Jack (IRE)**[86] 7154 4-9-0 **63** DavidProbert 4 55
(Tony Carroll) *mid-div: struggling in last pair whn sltly hmpd over 1f out: nt a danger after* **7/1**
440- **9** 1 1/4 **Whipphound**[52] 7595 4-9-7 **70** ShaneKelly 5 58
(Mark Brisbourne) *in tch: rdn and short of room whn wkng ent fnl f* **8/1**
0-50 **10** 1/2 **Royal Intruder**[7] 186 7-9-2 **65** MartinHarley 12 52
(Richard Guest) *sn led: rdn and hdd over 1f out: wknd fnl f* **25/1**

1m 12.78s (-0.32) **Going Correction** +0.05s/f (Slow) 10 Ran SP% **116.9**
Speed ratings (Par 103): **104,102,101,98,98 98,97,95,94,93**
Tote Swingers:1&2:£16.80, 2&3:£10.10, 1&3:£8.00 CSF £70.57 CT £941.80 TOTE £6.10: £2.30, £5.80, £2.80; EX 104.30 Trifecta £339.40 Pool £1,179.05 - 2.57 winning units..
Owner Mrs Sarah-Jane Fox **Bred** Deepwood Farm Stud **Trained** Collingbourne Ducis, Wilts
FOCUS
An ordinary sprint handicap, but they went a decent pace and the first two home came from last and last but one. A few met trouble in running.
T/Plt: £1,630.60 to a £1 stake. Pool £69,133.00. 30.95 winning tickets T/Qpdt: £161.10 to a £1 stake. Pool £4,856.14. 22.30 winning tickets TM

226 WOLVERHAMPTON (A.W) (L-H)
Monday, January 23

OFFICIAL GOING: Standard
Wind: dry and windy Weather: behind, half

268 BET & WATCH AT BLUESQ.COM (S) STKS 1m 141y(P)
2:00 (2:00) (Class 6) 4-Y-0+ £1,704 (£503; £251) Stalls Low

Form RPR
50-3 **1** **Khandaq (USA)**[7] 190 5-9-0 76 JoeFanning 5 78
(Keith Dalgleish) *mde virtually all: shkn up over 2f out: drvn to assert fnl f: wl in command fnl 75yds* **9/2**
54-1 **2** 1 3/4 **Faithful Ruler (USA)**[14] 103 8-9-5 75 (p) LukeMorris 4 79
(Ronald Harris) *chsd ldr: drvn along over 2f out: unable to cl on wnr ins fnl f: one pce* **3/1**[2]
24-2 **3** 1 **Mighty Clarets (IRE)**[2] 248 5-8-9 70 ShaneBKelly(5) 3 72
(Richard Fahey) *hld up in last: shkn up over 4f out: drvn along 3f out: plugged on and looking awkward u.p fr over 1f out* **5/4**[1]
26-2 **4** 4 **Unlimited**[14] 103 10-9-0 77 DavidProbert 1 65
(Tony Carroll) *t.k.h in 3rd: pushed along over 2f out: drvn and wknd 1f out and sn btn: eased cl home* **4/1**[3]

1m 51.53s (1.03) **Going Correction** +0.05s/f (Slow) 4 Ran SP% **107.6**
Speed ratings (Par 101): **97,95,94,91**
CSF £16.93 TOTE £5.70; EX 13.90.There was no bid for the winner. Mighty Clarets was claimed by Barry Leavy for £6,000.
Owner Gordon McDowall **Bred** Shadwell Farm LLC **Trained** Carluke, S Lanarks
FOCUS
Khandaq, who had 6lb in hand over the runner-up and third on official figures, was allowed to dominate and took this in a time 1.19 seconds slower than the later Class 6 handicap. The form has been rated around the winner.

269 DINE IN HORIZONS H'CAP 7f 32y(P)
2:30 (2:31) (Class 5) (0-75,75) 4-Y-0+ £2,264 (£673; £336; £168) Stalls High

Form RPR
4-41 **1** **City Legend**[16] 91 4-9-1 72 (bt) KieranO'Neill(3) 6 80
(Alan McCabe) *chsd ldr tl led after 1f: pushed along and qcknd tempo 2f out: kpt on wl u.p: all out* **4/1**[2]
0-01 **2** 3/4 **Avonrose**[11] 134 5-9-7 75 PhillipMakin 2 81
(Derek Shaw) *led tl hdd after 1f: chsd wnr after: shkn up to chal for ld 2f out: kpt on u.p ins fnl f: unable to catch wnr* **8/1**
06-2 **3** 1 **Needwood Ridge**[14] 102 5-8-6 65 (bt) RaulDaSilva(5) 8 68
(Frank Sheridan) *t.k.h bhd ldrs: rdn along and outpcd over 2f out: responded to driving and kpt on wl ins fnl f* **9/2**[3]
004- **4** nk **Viva Ronaldo (IRE)**[24] 7928 6-9-2 75 ShaneBKelly(5) 3 77+
(Richard Fahey) *hld up: drvn along and carried hd high over 2f out: eventually picked up and kpt on wl ins fnl f: nt rch ldrs* **7/4**[1]
000- **5** 1 3/4 **Ivory Silk**[26] 7893 7-9-5 73 AdamKirby 7 71
(Jeremy Gask) *mounted outside paddock: midfield: rdn over 2f out and sme prog: hrd drvn and no ex ins fnl f* **7/1**
400- **6** 2 1/2 **Riverdale (IRE)**[128] 6167 4-9-1 72 DaleSwift(3) 4 63
(Nigel Tinkler) *midfield: lost pl 3f out: sn drvn along and outpcd: btn over 1f out* **22/1**
004- **7** 17 **Dunseverick (IRE)**[40] 7754 4-8-8 62 RobbieFitzpatrick 5
(Jo Hughes) *v keen to post: slow away: pushed along 3f out: sn no imp and btn: eased fnl f* **12/1**

1m 29.94s (0.34) **Going Correction** +0.05s/f (Slow) 7 Ran SP% **110.2**
Speed ratings (Par 103): **100,99,98,97,95 92,73**
toteswingers:1&2:£3.10, 1&3:£3.50, 2&3:£3.70 CSF £32.37 CT £138.42 TOTE £5.80: £2.60, £4.80; EX 19.00 Trifecta £27.40 Pool £848.93 - 22.89 winning units..
Owner Contango Syndicate **Bred** Contango Bloodstock Ltd **Trained** Averham Park, Notts
FOCUS
Form to treat with a bit of caution as City Legend was allowed an uncontested lead after around a furlong.

270 WOLVERHAMPTON-RACECOURSE.CO.UK H'CAP 7f 32y(P)
3:00 (3:01) (Class 6) (0-55,55) 3-Y-O £1,704 (£503; £251) Stalls High

Form RPR
00- **1** **Speedy Yaki (IRE)**[119] 6406 3-9-2 **55** (bt[1]) ShaneKelly 1 68
(Daniel Mark Loughnane) *midfield: short of room briefly on inner 3f out: pushed along and str run to ld over 1f out: surged clr: easy* **13/2**
43-6 **2** 4 1/2 **House Limit (IRE)**[12] 121 3-8-12 **51** LukeMorris 7 52
(Harry Dunlop) *wnt rt s: sn cl up: drvn over 2f out: hdwy over 1f out: kpt on to take 2nd cl home* **6/1**[3]
04-3 **3** nk **Dicky Mint**[7] 191 3-8-9 **55** (b) DavidSimmonson(7) 12 55
(Michael Easterby) *wore no hind shoes: led tl hdd after 1f: remained chsng ldr tl led again 4f out: tried to kick clr 2f out: sn hrd drvn and hdd over 1f out: lost 2nd cl home* **15/2**
03-4 **4** 3/4 **Son Of May**[20] 25 3-9-0 **53** (b) FrannyNorton 10 51
(Jo Hughes) *led after 1f: pushed along and hdd 4f out: remained chsng ldr u.str.p tl no ex fnl f* **9/2**[2]
30-R **5** 2 1/4 **Clarkson (IRE)**[11] 132 3-8-11 **53** SophieDoyle(3) 8 45
(Jamie Osborne) *sltly hmpd s: in rr: drvn along 3f out: kpt on fr wl over 1f out: nvr a threat* **20/1**
000- **6** 3/4 **Pelican Rock (IRE)**[98] 6912 3-8-13 **52** RichardKingscote 11 42
(Tom Dascombe) *t.k.h in midfield: effrt to chse ldrs 3f out: hrd drvn and nt finding much for press over 1f out: sn btn* **9/4**[1]

050- **7** 1¾ **Aglaja**[93] 7035 3-8-10 **49**..(bt[1]) RobbieFitzpatrick 4 34
(Frank Sheridan) *hld up: drvn along 3f out: one pce and no hdwy fnl f* **40/1**

024- **8** 4½ **Johnson's Cat (IRE)**[109] 6645 3-8-13 **55**.................... RobertLButler(3) 5 28
(Richard Guest) *in rr: drvn along 3f out: no hdwy fnl 2f* **14/1**

000- **9** 1¾ **Salaaheb (IRE)**[70] 7414 3-8-6 **50**.............................. JemmaMarshall(5) 3 18
(Alastair Lidderdale) *dwlt: last and drvn 4f out: no imp fnl 3f* **33/1**

026- **10** 1 **Inya House**[110] 6628 3-9-0 **53**.. TomEaves 9 18
(Nigel Tinkler) *in rr: rdn 4f out: no imp fnl 2f* **16/1**

40-0 **11** 1 **Al Doha**[19] 38 3-9-0 **53**...(b[1]) PhillipMakin 6 16
(Kevin Ryan) *midfield: shkn up 4f out: effrt 3f out: drvn and no imp 2f out* **20/1**

1m 29.64s (0.04) **Going Correction** +0.05s/f (Slow) **11** Ran SP% **115.8**
Speed ratings (Par 95): **101,95,95,94,92 91,89,84,82,80 79**
toteswingers:1&2:£7.20, 1&3:£8.00, 2&3:£7.10 CSF £42.31 CT £305.09 TOTE £8.40: £2.20, £2.30, £1.70; EX 47.70 Trifecta £522.20 Part won. Pool £705.74 - 0.51 winning units..
Owner Mrs C Loughnane **Bred** Mrs G P Booth And J Porteous **Trained** Baldwin's Gate, Staffs

FOCUS
A moderate handicap run in a slightly quicker time than the earlier Class 5. The form looks solid enough for the grade.
Speedy Yaki(IRE) Official explanation: trainer said, regarding the apparent improvement in form shown, colt benefitted from the first-time application of blinkers and a tongue-tie and a poor quality race.

271 LES *RANTER* BROOKES 70TH BIRTHDAY CELEBRATION H'CAP 1m 5f 194y(P)
3:30 (3:30) (Class 5) (0-75,73) 4-Y-0+ **£2,264** (£673; £336; £168) **Stalls** Low

Form RPR

3-1 **1** **Chabada (JPN)**[21] 10 4-9-6 **73**.................................... StevieDonohoe 2 83+
(Ian Williams) *prom: urged along 3f out: str run on inner to ld over 1f out: kpt on strly* **7/4**[1]

00-5 **2** 3¼ **Lyric Poet (USA)**[7] 192 5-9-7 **71**...............................(t) KieranO'Neill(3) 6 77
(Anthony Carson) *hld up: rdn 4f out: no immediate rspnse: hdwy 2f out to chse ldrs: kpt on wl to take 2nd ins fnl f: no ch w wnr* **3/1**[2]

13-0 **3** 2½ **Cadgers Brig**[17] 63 4-9-3 **70**..(p) JoeFanning 5 72
(Keith Dalgleish) *chsd ldr: rdn along 5f out: hrd drvn and ev ch 2f out: no ex and wknd fnl f* **8/1**

43-2 **4** nse **Bow River Arch (USA)**[22] 4 4-9-5 **72**...................... WilliamCarson 7 74
(Peter Hiatt) *led: pushed along over 3f out: strly chal 2f out: hdd over 1f out: wknd and lost 2 pls fnl 75yds* **11/2**[3]

43-3 **5** ½ **Kames Park (IRE)**[10] 150 10-9-3 **67**.......................... RobertLButler(3) 3 68
(Richard Guest) *stdd s: last tl passed a rival 3f out: pushed along 2f out: no real imp after: btn fnl f* **16/1**

44-5 **6** 1¼ **Corvette**[15] 97 4-8-3 **56**... LukeMorris 4 56
(Michael Appleby) *in tch: drvn along 3f out: no imp 2f out* **22/1**

03-3 **7** dist **Dart**[17] 63 8-8-12 **62**... MichaelO'Connell(3) 8
(John Mackie) *midfield: drvn along 4f out: dropped last 3f out: eased to a walk and virtually p.u fnl f* **12/1**

3m 3.96s (-2.04) **Going Correction** +0.05s/f (Slow)
WFA 4 from 5yo+ 6lb **7** Ran SP% **105.8**
Speed ratings (Par 103): **107,105,103,103,103 102,**
toteswingers:1&2:£2.10, 1&3:£3.30, 2&3:£3.00 CSF £5.84 CT £22.98 TOTE £3.20: £1.90, £1.50; EX 7.50 Trifecta £67.70 Pool £851.13 - 9.29 winning units..
Owner Dr Marwan Koukash **Bred** Flaxman Holdings Limited **Trained** Portway, Worcs

FOCUS
A modest handicap in which they didn't go that quick.
Dart Official explanation: jockey said mare lost her action; vet subsquently said mare was lame behind

272 THOUSANDS OF SPORTS EXPERIENCES AT BLUESQ.COM H'CAP 5f 20y(P)
4:00 (4:00) (Class 5) (0-75,75) 4-Y-0+ **£2,264** (£673; £336; £168) **Stalls** Low

Form RPR

24-2 **1** **Blown It (USA)**[10] 152 6-8-11 **65**.. JoeFanning 1 76
(Keith Dalgleish) *midfield: 4th and pushed along 2f out: pressed ldrs 1f out: produced under hands and heels riding to ld fnl 75yds: comf* **2/1**[1]

00-0 **2** ¾ **Falasteen (IRE)**[22] 3 5-9-7 **75**..............................(b[1]) StevieDonohoe 3 83
(Kevin Ryan) *taken to post early: prom: urged along on inner 2f out: drvn to press ldr 1f out: kpt on to take 2nd cl home: no ch w wnr* **9/2**[3]

56-6 **3** nk **Island Legend (IRE)**[12] 120 6-9-7 **75**....................(p) RichardKingscote 8 82
(Milton Bradley) *sn led: hrd drvn over 1f out: strly chal 1f out: hdd fnl 75yds: lost 2nd cl home* **5/2**[2]

400- **4** 1¾ **Lucky Dan (IRE)**[35] 7819 6-8-10 **67**............................ RobertLButler(3) 4 68
(Paul Green) *midfield: bhd and rdn along 2f out: kpt on u.p 1f out: sltly hmpd 75yds out: fin wl* **10/1**

030- **5** 1 **Atlantic Beach**[25] 7917 7-9-0 **68**...................................(b) LiamKeniry 9 65
(Milton Bradley) *prom: rdn along 2f out: ev ch tl drvn and wknd fnl f* **10/1**

3-56 **6** 1½ **Shawkantango**[12] 122 5-8-8 **65** ow2..............................(v) DaleSwift(3) 5 57
(Derek Shaw) *nvr on terms: drvn and no imp fnl 2f* **10/1**

400- **7** 2¼ **Absa Lutte (IRE)**[53] 7594 9-8-13 **70**............................ SimonPearce(3) 7 54
(Michael Mullineaux) *taken to post early: missed break and nvr on terms: urged along 3f out: rn v wd off bnd ent st: sn btn* **18/1**

1m 1.88s (-0.42) **Going Correction** +0.05s/f (Slow) **7** Ran SP% **112.6**
Speed ratings (Par 103): **105,103,103,100,98 96,92**
toteswingers:1&2:£2.50, 1&3:£2.10, 2&3:£2.10 CSF £11.03 CT £22.06 TOTE £2.50: £1.60, £3.10; EX 10.90 Trifecta £15.20 Pool £633.95 - 30.67 winning units..
Owner D G Savala **Bred** H & W Thoroughbreds & Adrian Regan **Trained** Carluke, S Lanarks
■ Stewards' Enquiry : Richard Kingscote one-day ban: failed to keep straight from draw (Feb 6)

FOCUS
An ordinary sprint handicap, but truly run.
Absa Lutte(IRE) Official explanation: jockey said mare was slowly away

273 NAME A RACE TO ENHANCE YOUR BRAND MAIDEN STKS 1m 1f 103y(P)
4:30 (4:30) (Class 5) 4-Y-0+ **£2,264** (£673; £336; £168) **Stalls** Low

Form RPR

33- **1** **Alfred Hutchinson**[140] 5792 4-9-0 0.................................... DaleSwift(3) 7 79+
(Geoffrey Oldroyd) *cl up: pushed along to ld 2f out: drvn along and chal fnl f: hld on wl* **7/2**[3]

2 ¾ **Southern State (USA)** 4-9-3 0... JoeFanning 2 77+
(Mark Johnston) *in tch: rdn and outpcd 3f out: pushed up to chse wnr 1f out: kpt on nicely fnl f: rn green: should improve* **15/2**

34-3 **3** 5 **Spin Cast**[13] 114 4-9-3 69..(v) StevieDonohoe 6 66
(Joseph Tuite) *in tch: pushed along over 3f out: hrd rdn and ev ch 2f out: one pce fnl f* **10/3**[2]

65- **4** 1½ **Hubood**[41] 7747 4-8-12 0.. HayleyTurner 1 58
(Clive Brittain) *led: pushed along 3f out: hdd 2f out: drvn along and grad wknd after* **20/1**

602- **5** hd **Musnad (USA)**[54] 6674 4-9-3 70.. BarryMcHugh 5 62
(Brian Ellison) *in tch: lost pl 4f out: short of room briefly 3f out: hrd drvn and no imp fnl 2f* **11/4**[1]

0/ **6** 4 **Red Soles (IRE)**[493] 6150 4-8-12 0................................... RobertWinston 8 49+
(Charles Hills) *nvr on terms: niggled along 5f out: pushed along and no imp fnl 2f* **12/1**

6- **7** ¾ **House Of Mirrors (USA)**[24] 7921 4-9-3 0...............(vt[1]) NickyMackay 3 52
(John Gosden) *in rr: hdwy 4f out: pushed along to chse ldrs on outer 3f out: hrd drvn and no imp over 1f out: eased and btn fnl f* **9/2**

000- **8** 18 **Bowmans Well (IRE)**[26] 7903 7-8-13 24........................(e) NeilChalmers 4 10
(Peter Purdy) *t.k.h chsd ldr tl pushed along 4f out: stopped to nil 3f out: sn t.o* **500/1**

2m 1.6s (-0.10) **Going Correction** +0.05s/f (Slow)
WFA 4 from 7yo 1lb **8** Ran SP% **114.6**
Speed ratings (Par 103): **102,101,96,95,95 91,91,75**
toteswingers:1&2:£5.90, 1&3:£3.30, 2&3:£4.10 CSF £29.79 TOTE £3.80: £1.60, £2.90, £1.30; EX 25.90 Trifecta £60.10 Pool £931.77 - 11.46 winning units..
Owner R C Bond **Bred** R C Bond **Trained** Brawby, N Yorks

FOCUS
An ordinary maiden and disappointing efforts by the two market leaders puts a question mark against the form.

274 ENJOY THE PUNTERS PACKAGE GROUP OFFER H'CAP 1m 141y(P)
5:00 (5:00) (Class 6) (0-55,55) 4-Y-0+ **£1,704** (£503; £251) **Stalls** Low

Form RPR

06-4 **1** **Petomic (IRE)**[14] 104 7-8-12 **54**...............................(p) RobertLButler(3) 10 64
(Richard Guest) *in rr of midfield: hdwy 3f out: drvn to chse ldrs 2f out: swtchd rt and str run to ld ins fnl f: r.o wl* **10/1**

0-04 **2** 2½ **Bentley**[15] 96 8-8-8 **52**...(p) JemmaMarshall(5) 7 56
(Brian Baugh) *hld up: hdwy wl over 2f out: chsng ldrs whn short of room 2f out: rdn and ev ch on inner fnl f: kpt on wl: no ch w wnr* **9/2**[1]

00-0 **3** hd **Just Timmy Marcus**[14] 102 6-9-1 **54**.....................(p) RussKennemore 6 58+
(Brian Baugh) *slow away: in rr: stl plenty to do and nt asked for an effrt 3f out: pushed along and hdwy 2f out: kpt on strly ins fnl f: nrly snatched 2nd* **8/1**

4 1 **Apple Blossom Time (IRE)**[193] 4032 5-9-0 **53**........... RobertWinston 4 54
(Derek Haydn Jones) *t.k.h in rr: pushed along and hdwy over 2f out: kpt on nicely past btn horses fnl f* **8/1**

002- **5** ½ **Penbryn (USA)**[26] 7891 5-9-2 **55**.................................... SteveDrowne 12 55
(Nick Littmoden) *t.k.h: cl up: pushed along to chse ldr over 1f out: drvn along to ld 1f out: carried hd high and hdd ins fnl f: wknd qckly* **8/1**

020- **6** ½ **Stamp Duty (IRE)**[27] 7885 4-9-1 **55**............................ DuranFentiman 2 54
(Suzzanne France) *hld up: pushed along and briefly short of room over 2f out: mod late hdwy* **20/1**

430- **7** nk **Shaws Diamond (USA)**[80] 7270 6-8-12 **54**..................(v) DaleSwift(3) 3 53
(Derek Shaw) *cl up: ev ch whn drvn 2f out: no imp fnl f* **14/1**

000- **8** 1¼ **Misere**[26] 7902 4-9-0 **54**...(p) PhillipMakin 1 50
(Kevin Ryan) *led: drvn along 2f out: hdd 1f out: wknd qckly* **22/1**

500- **9** 1 **Lean Machine**[196] 3926 5-9-2 **55**....................................(p) LukeMorris 5 49
(Ronald Harris) *cl up: lost pl 3f out: drvn and no hdwy fnl 2f* **13/2**[3]

320- **10** 3¾ **Deslaya (IRE)**[25] 7910 4-8-13 **53**.................................... ShaneKelly 11 38
(Linda Stubbs) *cl up: pushed along 3f out: wknd over 2f out* **13/2**[3]

03-0 **11** ½ **Jibouti (IRE)**[13] 110 4-8-13 **53**....................................(b) HayleyTurner 9 37
(Clive Brittain) *nvr on terms: drvn and no hdwy 3f out: struggling after* **6/1**[2]

/00- **12** 2½ **Flotation (USA)**[58] 7556 5-8-13 **52**.................................(p) TomEaves 8 30
(Roy Brotherton) *nvr on terms: rdn and btn over 2f out* **33/1**

/10- **13** 3¾ **Mnarani (IRE)**[94] 7005 5-8-13 **52**............................ FergusSweeney 13 21
(James Evans) *nvr on terms: drvn and no hdwy fnl 3f: eased fnl f* **33/1**

1m 50.34s (-0.16) **Going Correction** +0.05s/f (Slow)
WFA 4 from 5yo+ 1lb **13** Ran SP% **123.2**
Speed ratings (Par 101): **102,99,99,98,98 97,97,96,95,92 91,89,86**
toteswingers:1&2:£13.80, 1&3:£19.80, 2&3:£17.40 CSF £53.94 CT £388.59 TOTE £14.40: £3.90, £1.60, £3.90; EX 61.10 Trifecta £406.70 Part won. Pool £406.70 - 0.90 winning units..
Owner Johnson Racing **Bred** Neil McGrath **Trained** Stainforth, S Yorks

FOCUS
The time was 1.19 seconds faster than the earlier modestly run seller. The race has been rated around the winner.
Penbryn(USA) Official explanation: jockey said gelding hung left-handed
Misere Official explanation: jockey said filly hung right-handed throughout

275 PLAY DA VINCI DIAMONDS AT BLUESQ.COM/GAMES H'CAP 1m 1f 103y(P)
5:30 (5:30) (Class 5) (0-75,75) 4-Y-0+ **£2,264** (£673; £336; £168) **Stalls** Low

Form RPR

000- **1** **Dubai Bounty**[25] 7908 5-9-7 **75**.....................................(p) NickyMackay 7 84
(Gerard Butler) *hld up: stl last 3f out: rdn to ld on outer 2f out: kpt on wl* **14/1**

02-4 **2** 2½ **Dazzling Valentine**[12] 119 4-9-5 **74**................................ PhillipMakin 6 78
(Alan Bailey) *hld up: pushed along and outpcd 2f out: kpt on u.p ins fnl f: nvr a threat* **4/1**[2]

025- **3** nk **John Potts**[26] 7901 7-9-2 **70**.. RussKennemore 4 73
(Brian Baugh) *midfield: hdwy 3f out: pressed for ld 2f out: drvn along and unable qck: no ch w wnr* **12/1**

43-4 **4** shd **Strike Force**[10] 150 8-8-13 **70**...............................(t) AdamBeschizza(3) 1 73
(Clifford Lines) *in tch: drvn and sltly short of room over 2f out: kpt on u.p ins fnl f: nrly grabbed 3rd post* **6/1**[3]

440- **5** 1½ **Pandorica**[106] 6729 4-9-4 **73**.. MartinLane 9 73
(Bernard Llewellyn) *cl up: drvn and pressed for ld over 2f out: wknd u.p fnl f* **33/1**

6-00 **6** shd **Jordaura**[8] 187 6-9-7 **75**.. RobertWinston 8 75
(Gay Kelleway) *hld up: effrt to chse ldrs 2f out: hung lft u.p and wknd fnl f* **12/1**

23-1 **7** shd **Vanilla Rum**[17] 66 5-8-7 **61** oh1..(b) JoeFanning 3 63+
(John Mackie) *hld up: nt clr run and travelling wl enough over 2f out: pushed along and short of room again 1f out: nt rcvr* **4/1**[2]

53-1 **8** 1½ **Kiss A Prince**[9] 176 6-9-5 **73**..(b) ShaneKelly 2 69
(Dean Ivory) *slow away: nvr on terms: rdn and no imp fnl 2f* **7/2**[1]

300- **9** 3 **Dream Lodge (IRE)**[130] 6093 8-9-6 **74**...........................(v) IanMongan 5 64
(Scott Dixon) *drvn to ld: drvn along 3f out: hdd 2f out: wknd qckly after: lame* **7/1**

2m 1.93s (0.23) **Going Correction** +0.05s/f (Slow)
WFA 4 from 5yo+ 1lb **9** Ran SP% **114.0**
Speed ratings (Par 103): **100,97,97,97,96 96,95,94,91**
toteswingers:1&2:£14.90, 1&3:£27.80, 2&3:£10.80 CSF £68.42 CT £701.29 TOTE £18.50: £4.50, £2.20, £4.70; EX 81.00 TRIFECTA Not won..
Owner Mrs F Denniff **Bred** A S Denniff **Trained** Newmarket, Suffolk
■ Stewards' Enquiry : Adam Beschizza caution: careless riding

FOCUS
The time was ordinary, being 0.33 seconds slower than the earlier maiden, and the principals came from off the pace.
Jordaura Official explanation: jockey said gelding hung left in the straight
Kiss A Prince Official explanation: jockey said gelding was unsuited by the slow pace
Dream Lodge(IRE) Official explanation: vet said gelding finished lame on its left-fore
T/Jkpt: £3,571.40 to a £1 stake. Pool:£22,322.86 - 7.00 winning tickets T/Plt: £90.90 to a £1 stake. Pool:£100,683.56 - 807.92 winning tickets T/Qpdt: £6.20 to a £1 stake. Pool:£11,977.34 - 1,415.98 winning tickets CS

262 KEMPTON (A.W) (R-H)
Tuesday, January 24

OFFICIAL GOING: Standard
Wind: Virtually nil Weather: Overcast, damp

276 32RED H'CAP — 1m 2f (P)
2:30 (2:30) (Class 6) (0-60,60) 4-Y-O+ — **£1,617** (£481; £240; £120) **Stalls** Low

Form — RPR
000- **1** **Super Duplex**[55] 7587 5-9-7 **60** IanMongan 3 70
(Pat Phelan) *t.k.h: trckd ldrs: drvn ahd styd on appr fnl f: led fnl 120yds: pushed out* **5/2**[1]
05-2 **2** 1 1/2 **Abigails Angel**[11] 148 5-9-6 **59** AdamKirby 2 66
(Brett Johnson) *trckd ldr: drvn to chal 2f out: slt ld over 1f out: hdd and no ex u.p fnl 120yds* **11/2**[2]
000- **3** 3/4 **Allanit (GER)**[47] 7671 8-9-7 **60** MickyFenton 6 66
(Barney Curley) *led: rdn over 2f out: sn jnd: narrowly hdd over 1f out: kpt on same pce ins fnl f* **16/1**
463- **4** 1 1/2 **Cane Cat (IRE)**[54] 7203 5-9-7 **60** (t) LukeMorris 9 63+
(Tony Carroll) *in rr: pushed along and hdwy over 1f out: kpt on fnl f: nt rch ldrs* **8/1**
33-3 **5** 1 1/4 **Warden Bond**[9] 188 4-8-11 **52** (p) MartinLane 4 52
(William Stone) *mid-div: rdn and one pce over 2f out: styd on ins fnl f: nt rch ldrs* **7/1**
66-6 **6** nk **Cloudy Start**[17] 85 6-9-7 **60** FergusSweeney 8 59+
(Jamie Osborne) *in rr: drvn and hdwy appr fnl f: styd on in clsng stages* **6/1**[3]
3- **7** nk **Kucharova (IRE)**[27] 7890 4-9-1 **56** LiamKeniry 5 55
(Seamus Mullins) *chsd ldrs: rdn over 2f out: styd on same pce* **14/1**
0-50 **8** 1 1/4 **Tous Les Deux**[9] 188 9-8-7 **51** ow3 (be) MatthewCosham(5) 7 47
(Dr Jeremy Naylor) *plld hrd in rr: hdwy 3f out: nvr rchd ldrs and wknd fnl f* **66/1**
12-2 **9** 7 **Resplendent Alpha**[18] 60 8-8-13 **59** LeonnaMayor(7) 10 41
(Alastair Lidderdale) *stdd s and bhd: hdwy on outer over 4f out: wd into st and wknd over 2f out* **10/1**
00- **10** 12 **Indus Valley (IRE)**[27] 7901 5-9-5 **58** JoeFanning 11 16
(Des Donovan) *chsd ldrs over 6f* **16/1**
00-0 **11** 1/2 **Bengal Tiger**[13] 119 6-9-6 **59** DavidProbert 12 16
(Tony Carroll) *in rr: hdwy on outside over 4f out: wknd fr 3f out* **33/1**
2m 7.59s (-0.41) **Going Correction** -0.05s/f (Stan)
WFA 4 from 5yo+ 2lb — 11 Ran SP% **113.8**
Speed ratings (Par 101): **99,97,97,96,95 94,94,93,87,78 77**
toteswingers:1&2:£3.50, 2&3:£21.70, 1&3:£14.80 CSF £14.91 CT £177.68 TOTE £3.00: £1.30, £1.50, £5.70; EX 16.90 Trifecta £228.90 Pool: £451.77 - 1.46 winning units..
Owner Special Piping Materials Ltd **Bred** Ermyn Lodge Stud Limited **Trained** Epsom, Surrey
FOCUS
A moderate contest and they went a muddling gallop. The winner is rated back to soemthing like his old Polytrack best.

277 32RED.COM H'CAP — 5f (P)
3:00 (3:00) (Class 5) (0-70,70) 4-Y-O+ — **£2,264** (£673; £336; £168) **Stalls** Low

Form — RPR
51-0 **1** **Royal Bajan (USA)**[18] 59 4-9-7 **70** FrederikTylicki 5 81
(James Given) *mde all: drvn over 1f out: styd on strly: unchal* **11/8**[1]
02-4 **2** 1 **Liberal Lady**[18] 59 4-8-5 **59** (e) RaulDaSilva(5) 3 66
(Ralph Smith) *trckd ldrs: hdwy to chse wnr over 1f out styd on but no imp ins fnl f* **11/2**[3]
41-3 **3** 1/2 **Cliffords Reprieve**[11] 152 4-8-9 **58** (b) LiamKeniry 7 63+
(Eric Wheeler) *s.i.s: hld up in rr: hdwy over 1f out: drvn and styd on fnl f: tk 3rd fnl 30yds and clsng on 2nd nr fin: nvr any ch w wnr* **4/1**[2]
00-5 **4** 3/4 **Decider (USA)**[11] 152 9-8-11 **60** (v) LukeMorris 2 63
(Ronald Harris) *sn chsng wnr: rdn 2f out: sn no imp: styd on same pce and lost 3rd fnl 30yds* **8/1**
426- **5** 3 1/4 **Griffin Point (IRE)**[24] 7940 5-9-2 **65** (p) DavidProbert 6 56
(William Muir) *sn rdn along and outpcd towards rr: nvr in contention fr 1/2-way* **13/2**
00-0 **6** 1/2 **Mandy's Hero**[6] 208 4-8-13 **69** (b[1]) JenniferFerguson(7) 1 58
(Olivia Maylam) *sn chsng ldrs: rdn 2f out: wknd over 1f out* **25/1**
3-06 **7** 3 3/4 **Grudge**[12] 133 7-8-8 **60** (b) KieranO'Neill(3) 4 36
(Conor Dore) *in rr: sn rdn: hanging lft and wd: a struggling* **14/1**
59.38s (-1.12) **Going Correction** -0.05s/f (Stan) — 7 Ran SP% **112.4**
Speed ratings (Par 103): **106,104,103,102,97 96,90**
toteswingers:1&2:£2.60, 2&3:£3.60, 1&3:£2.10 CSF £9.00 CT £23.60 TOTE £2.30: £1.40, £2.90; EX 8.70 Trifecta £20.50 Pool: £797.50 - 28.73 winning units..
Owner Danethorpe Racing Partnership **Bred** West Wind Farm **Trained** Willoughton, Lincs
■ Stewards' Enquiry : Frederik Tylicki one-day ban: careless riding (Feb 7)
FOCUS
A modest sprint handicap. The winner built on his Lingfield win but may do better. The form is rated around the runner-up.

278 32RED CASINO H'CAP — 2m (P)
3:30 (3:30) (Class 6) (0-55,55) 4-Y-O+ — **£1,617** (£481; £240; £120) **Stalls** Low

Form — RPR
160- **1** **Steady Gaze**[95] 6998 7-9-7 **55** AmirQuinn 5 69
(Richard Rowe) *led tl narrowly hdd after 7f: styd trcking ldr: led again appr fnl 3f: pushed clr over 2f out: in n.d after: easily* **15/2**[2]
40-0 **2** 6 **Valdan (IRE)**[20] 28 8-9-6 **54** LukeMorris 9 61
(David Evans) *mid-div: hdwy and rdn 3f out: chsd wnr jst ins fnl 2f: styd on: nvr any ch but wl clr of 3rd* **14/1**
0-06 **3** 6 **Rodrigo De Freitas (IRE)**[4] 221 5-9-7 **55** (v) JimCrowley 1 55
(Jim Boyle) *in rr tl hdwy on inner fr 3f out: tk 3rd ins fnl 2f: no imp on ldng duo but clr of 4th* **8/1**[3]
0-22 **4** 3 1/2 **Bold Adventure**[12] 129 8-9-6 **54** (p) StevieDonohoe 4 50+
(Willie Musson) *in rr: stl plenty to do over 2f out: rdn and styd on over 1f out: hung rt and styd on for wl hld 4th fnl 120yds* **4/1**[1]
00-1 **5** 1/2 **Prince Charlemagne (IRE)**[12] 129 9-9-1 **54**...(p) MatthewCosham(5) 8 49
(Dr Jeremy Naylor) *in rr: hdwy on outside over 3f out: disp one-pced 2nd 2f out: nvr nr wnr and sn btn* **9/1**
005- **6** 3 3/4 **In The Long Grass (IRE)**[46] 7688 4-8-0 **46** oh1 (b) NathanAlison(5) 10 37
(Jim Boyle) *chsd ldrs: rdn 3f out: wknd 2f out* **40/1**
0-60 **7** 1 1/4 **Nesnaas (USA)**[11] 160 11-8-7 **46** oh1 (bt) JemmaMarshall(5) 6 35
(Alastair Lidderdale) *in rr: c wd into st fr 3f out: nvr in contention* **66/1**
00- **8** 3/4 **Rosenblatt (GER)**[67] 7461 10-8-10 **49** (p) DavidKenny(5) 7 37
(John Spearing) *trckd ldrs: rdn 3f out: btn sn after* **10/1**
/5-3 **9** 7 **Santera (IRE)**[12] 129 8-8-13 **47** (p) DavidProbert 11 27
(Tony Carroll) *chsd ldrs: rdn 3f out: wknd over 2f out* **4/1**[1]
42-6 **10** hd **Henry Holmes**[12] 129 9-9-1 **49** SteveDrowne 2 28
(Lydia Richards) *trckd ldr: led after 7f: hdd appr fnl 3f: styd disputing 2nd tl wknd ins fnl 2f* **9/1**
0-32 **11** 1 3/4 **Delorain (IRE)**[14] 111 9-9-3 **51** (vt) MartinLane 13 28
(William Stone) *s.i.s: sn drvn and in tch: chsd ldrs 5f out: wknd qckly 3f out* **14/1**
0-43 **12** 2 **Spiritonthemount (USA)**[14] 111 7-9-1 **49** (b) ChrisCatlin 3 24
(Peter Hiatt) *nvr beyond mid-div: bhd fnl 5f* **25/1**
00-3 **13** 1 **Savaronola (USA)**[14] 110 7-9-4 **52** (p) JoeFanning 12 26
(Des Donovan) *chsd ldrs: rdn 5f out: wknd over 3f out* **16/1**
3m 29.47s (-0.63) **Going Correction** -0.05s/f (Stan)
WFA 4 from 5yo+ 7lb — 13 Ran SP% **119.0**
Speed ratings (Par 101): **99,96,93,91,91 89,88,88,84,84 83,82,82**
toteswingers:1&2:£30.30, 2&3:£22.50, 1&3:£9.60 CSF £106.08 CT £870.41 TOTE £9.20: £2.10, £4.40, £3.20; EX 156.50 Trifecta £335.20 Part won. Pool: £453.05 - 0.64 winning units..
Owner Miss Victoria Baalham **Bred** Juddmonte Farms Ltd **Trained** Sullington, W Sussex
FOCUS
A moderate staying handicap. They didn't seem to go that quick and the time was over six seconds above standard. A couple disappointed and the form is pretty ordinary.

279 £32 FREE AT 32RED.COM MEDIAN AUCTION MAIDEN STKS — 1m (P)
4:00 (4:00) (Class 5) 3-5-Y-O — **£2,264** (£673; £336; £168) **Stalls** Low

Form — RPR
2 **1** **Prussian**[10] 182 3-8-3 0 JoeFanning 6 80+
(Mark Johnston) *trckd ldr: pushed along 3f out: styd on wl to ld over 1f out: in n.d wh edgd lft fnl 120yds* **1/5**[1]
324- **2** 3 3/4 **Miss Astragal (IRE)**[26] 7909 3-8-0 70 (b[1]) KieranO'Neill(3) 4 70
(Richard Hannon) *led: pushed along over 2f out: hdd over 1f out: sn no ch w wnr but kpt on to hold 2nd in clsng stages* **7/1**[2]
3 1/2 **Bint Alzain (IRE)** 3-8-3 0 LukeMorris 5 69
(Gerard Butler) *s.i.s: in last pl but wl in tch: tk 3rd 4f out: drvn and styd on fnl f to cl on 2nd fnl 120yds but nvr any ch w wnr* **20/1**
4 12 **Klang Valley** 3-8-3 0 ChrisCatlin 2 42
(Marco Botti) *racd in 3rd to 1/2-way and dropped to 4th: drvn over 3f out: sn dropped away* **14/1**[3]
1m 39.89s (0.09) **Going Correction** -0.05s/f (Stan)
WFA 3 from 4yo 20lb — 4 Ran SP% **107.3**
Speed ratings (Par 103): **97,93,92,80**
CSF £2.04 TOTE £1.20; EX 2.20.
Owner Sheikh Hamdan Bin Mohammed Al Maktoum **Bred** Darley **Trained** Middleham Moor, N Yorks
FOCUS
An uncompetitive maiden run in a time 1.98 seconds slower than the following Class 4 handicap for older horses. Weak form, with the winner granted normal improvement from his debut and the second rated 5lb off her best.

280 32REDBET.COM H'CAP (LONDON MILE QUALIFIER) — 1m (P)
4:30 (4:30) (Class 4) (0-85,84) 4-Y-O+ — **£4,075** (£1,212; £606; £303) **Stalls** Low

Form — RPR
01-3 **1** **Maverik**[22] 11 4-8-13 **76** JimCrowley 5 87
(Ralph Beckett) *t.k.h early: trckd ldr: led over 2f out: rdn and jnd 1f out: hrd pressed thrght fnl f: hld on all out* **7/2**[1]
312- **2** nk **George Guru**[83] 7227 5-8-11 **79** MarkCoumbe(5) 3 89
(Michael Attwater) *t.k.h early: trckd ldrs: chsd wnr over 1f out: str and persistant chal thrght fnl f: no ex last strides* **11/2**[3]
100- **3** 1 3/4 **Reachforthebucks**[34] 7841 4-9-0 **77** (p) AdamKirby 9 83+
(Jane Chapple-Hyam) *hld up in rr: hdwy on ins appr fnl 2f: tk 3rd ins fnl f: kpt on but no imp on ldng duo* **4/1**[2]
55-4 **4** 3/4 **Veroon (IRE)**[12] 131 6-9-3 **80** (p) FrederikTylicki 8 84
(James Given) *in rr: hdwy over 2f out: drvn to chse ldrs and take 3rd over 1f out: one pce into 4th fnl f* **15/2**
00-6 **5** 1/2 **Tartan Trip**[17] 90 5-8-13 **83** ThomasBrown(7) 12 86
(Andrew Balding) *chsd ldrs: disp 3rd fr 2f out tl one pce fnl f* **9/1**
-050 **6** 1 1/2 **Opus Maximus (IRE)**[5] 216 7-8-11 **79** DavidKenny(5) 10 79+
(Conor Dore) *s.i.s: in rr: drvn and hdwy over 1f out: styd on in clsng stages* **12/1**
200- **7** 1 **Edgewater (IRE)**[178] 4537 5-9-0 **77** DavidProbert 4 74
(John Akehurst) *chsd ldrs: rdn 2f out: wknd fnl f* **18/1**
64-1 **8** 1/2 **Tewin Wood**[22] 11 5-8-10 **76** DominicFox(3) 7 72
(Alan Bailey) *sn led: hdd over 2f out: wkng whn n.m.r ins fnl f* **10/1**
0-05 **9** 1/2 **Focail Eile**[6] 199 7-8-5 **75** (v[1]) LeonnaMayor(7) 11 70
(John Ryan) *s.i.s: in rr: racd wd: sme hdwy on outside fr 3f out: nvr rchd ldrs: wknd 2f out* **16/1**
035- **10** 2 1/4 **Chevise (IRE)**[48] 7660 4-8-11 **79** RaulDaSilva(5) 2 69
(Steve Woodman) *chsd ldrs: rdn 3f out: wknd over 1f out* **20/1**
030- **11** 1 **Just Bond (IRE)**[90] 7110 10-9-4 **84** DaleSwift(3) 6 72
(Geoffrey Oldroyd) *t.k.h: in tch: rdn 3f out: wknd over 2f out* **25/1**
4-00 **12** 1 1/4 **Honey Of A Kitten (USA)**[10] 177 4-9-1 **78** MartinLane 1 63
(David Evans) *a towards rr* **25/1**
1m 37.91s (-1.89) **Going Correction** -0.05s/f (Stan) — 12 Ran SP% **119.8**
Speed ratings (Par 105): **107,106,104,104,103 102,101,100,100,97 96,95**
toteswingers:1&2:£4.00, 2&3:£4.50, 1&3:£5.00 CSF £22.17 CT £81.01 TOTE £5.70: £2.10, £2.10, £1.40; EX 32.30 Trifecta £131.80 Pool: £493.66 - 2.77 winning units..
Owner Athos, Cooper, Quinn, EPL **Bred** J G Davis & Star Pointe Ltd **Trained** Kimpton, Hants
FOCUS
A fair, competitive handicap, but those ridden handily seemed favoured. There's a chance the form is worth more at face value.

281 CALVERTS CARPETS YORK LTD FILLIES' H'CAP — 1m 3f (P)
5:00 (5:00) (Class 5) (0-70,70) 4-Y-O+ — **£2,264** (£673; £336; £168) **Stalls** Low

Form — RPR
624- **1** **Sail Home**[45] 7713 5-9-0 **63** AdamBeschizza(3) 3 73
(Julia Feilden) *trckd ldrs: drvn over 2f out: sn chsng ldr: rdn to ld over 1f out: styd on wl ins fnl f* **8/1**

200- **2** 2 ¾ **If I Were A Boy (IRE)**[19] 7328 5-9-10 **70**........................(p) LiamKeniry 2 75
(Dominic Ffrench Davis) *led: rdn over 2f out: hdd over 1f out: styd on fnl f but no ch w wnr: jst hld 2nd last strides* **13/2**
62-2 **3** *hd* **Broughtons Paradis (IRE)**[18] 58 6-9-7 **67**............. StevieDonohoe 6 72
(Willie Musson) *in rr: hdwy ins fnl 2f: drvn and styd on wl fnl f: tk 3rd clsng stages and gaining on 2nd last strides but no imp on wnr* **7/2**[1]
34-4 **4** *nse* **Little Jazz**[18] 63 4-8-11 **65**..(b) RaulDaSilva[(5)] 7 70
(Paul D'Arcy) *in rr: hdwy to chse ldrs over 2f out: disp 2nd ins fnl f but no ch w wnr: dropped to 4th in clsng stages* **13/2**
46-4 **5** *8* **Roman Flame**[20] 35 4-8-3 **55**..................................... KieranO'Neill[(3)] 1 45
(Michael Quinn) *chsd ldrs: rdn over 2f out: wknd qckly over 1f out* **14/1**
320- **6** *6* **Lady Elsie**[92] 7070 4-9-7 **70**... AdamKirby 9 49
(George Prodromou) *chsd ldr tl over 2f out: sn btn* **4/1**[2]
3-21 **7** *½* **Kai Mook**[2] 265 5-8-12 **63** 6ex..................................... MarkCoumbe[(5)] 8 42+
(Roger Ingram) *plunged as stalls opened and v.s.a: tried to rcvrd 1/2-way but nvr rchd ldrs: wknd 3f out* **9/2**[3]
00-0 **8** *3* **Bilidn**[16] 97 4-8-13 **62**.. MartinLane 5 35
(Noel Quinlan) *s.i.s: a towards rr* **40/1**
340- **9** *6* **Out Of The Storm**[99] 6923 4-8-8 **57**.................................. LukeMorris 4 19
(Simon Dow) *in tch: rdn 3f out: sn btn* **16/1**

2m 20.28s (-1.62) **Going Correction** -0.05s/f (Stan)
WFA 4 from 5yo+ 3lb 9 Ran SP% **113.2**
Speed ratings (Par 100): **103,101,100,100,95 90,90,88,83**
toteswingers:1&2:£8.40, 2&3:£5.00, 1&3:£6.90 CSF £57.73 CT £214.61 TOTE £10.20: £3.30, £2.50, £1.80; EX 39.30 Trifecta £69.40 Pool: £769.69 - 8.20 winning units..
Owner Hoofbeats Racing Club **Bred** Juddmonte Farms Ltd **Trained** Exning, Suffolk
■ Stewards' Enquiry : Adam Kirby one-day ban: careless riding (Feb 7)

FOCUS
A fillies-only race and not as competitive as it might have been. It's doubtful if it's a race to be positive about.
Kai Mook Official explanation: jockey said mare tried to go under gate prior to opening and was slowly away

282 CALVERTS CARPETS H'CAP 6f (P)
5:30 (5:30) (Class 5) (0-75,75) 4-Y-0+ **£2,264** (£673; £336; £168) **Stalls** Low

Form RPR
0-21 **1** **Torres Del Paine**[2] 267 5-8-13 **70** 6ex........................ KieranO'Neill[(3)] 1 82
(Jimmy Fox) *hld up in rr: hdwy ins fnl 2f: drvn to ld fnl 120yds: kpt on wl* **11/8**[1]
250- **2** *½* **Haadeeth**[42] 7744 5-8-9 **70**.. LauraBarry[(7)] 2 80
(Richard Fahey) *t.k.h: trckd ldrs: wnt 2nd over 2f out: drvn to ld over 1f out: edge lft and hdd fnl 120yds: kpt on same pce* **12/1**
230- **3** *2* **Bond Fastrac**[25] 7926 5-9-4 **75**.. DaleSwift[(3)] 6 79
(Geoffrey Oldroyd) *hld up in rr: hdwy 2f out: swtchd rt and styd on to chse ldng duo fnl f: no imp* **9/1**
02-0 **4** *1 ¾* **Perfect Act**[15] 106 7-8-13 **67**.. DavidProbert 5 65
(Andrew Balding) *hld up towards rr but in tch: hdwy 2f out: rdn over 1f out: styd on same pce* **12/1**
132- **5** *hd* **Rambo Will**[42] 7746 4-9-4 **72**... JoeFanning 3 69
(J R Jenkins) *t.k.h: sn trcking ldr: rdn over 2f out and dropped to 3rd sn after: styd on same pce fnl f* **13/2**[3]
00-0 **6** *2* **Best Trip (IRE)**[13] 120 5-9-6 **74**...................................... AdamKirby 8 65
(Richard Guest) *sn led: hdd over 1f out: wknd qckly fnl f* **5/1**[2]
500- **7** *3 ½* **Tom Sawyer**[87] 7173 4-8-13 **67**.. FrederikTylicki 4 47
(Julie Camacho) *chsd ldrs: rdn over 2f out: wknd over 1f out* **12/1**
060- **8** *3* **Italian Tom (IRE)**[42] 7746 5-9-5 **73**................................... LukeMorris 7 43
(Ronald Harris) *t.k.h: racd on outside: towards rr: effrt over 2f out: nvr rchd ldrs and sn wknd* **7/1**

1m 12.53s (-0.57) **Going Correction** -0.05s/f (Stan) 8 Ran SP% **117.7**
Speed ratings (Par 103): **101,100,97,95,95 92,87,83**
toteswingers:1&2:£4.70, 2&3:£10.00, 1&3:£6.00 CSF £20.72 CT £114.85 TOTE £2.10: £1.10, £4.20, £2.90; EX 21.80 Trifecta £255.20 Pool: £676.19 - 1.96 winning units..
Owner Mrs Sarah-Jane Fox **Bred** Deepwood Farm Stud **Trained** Collingbourne Ducis, Wilts

FOCUS
An ordinary race and the pace was a bit muddling. Another step up from the winner.
T/Jkpt: Not won. T/Plt: £103.30 to a £1 stake. Pool of £67,498.23 - 476.92 winning tickets.
T/Qpdt: £44.90 to a £1 stake. Pool of £5,182.19 - 85.40 winning tickets. ST

[133]SOUTHWELL (L-H)
Tuesday, January 24

OFFICIAL GOING: Standard
Wind: Virtually nil Weather: Heavy cloud

283 BET AT BLUE SQUARE MAIDEN STKS 6f (F)
1:20 (1:21) (Class 5) 3-Y-0+ **£2,385** (£704; £352) **Stalls** Low

Form RPR
0 **1** **Abi Scarlet (IRE)**[13] 121 3-8-6 **0**.. HayleyTurner 3 73
(Hughie Morrison) *prom: hdwy on inner and cl up 1/2-way: rdn to chal wl over 1f out: kpt on ins fnl f to ld nr fin* **25/1**
433- **2** *shd* **Derivatives (IRE)**[26] 7906 3-8-6 **70**................................. NickyMackay 6 72
(John Gosden) *cl up: led over 3f out: jnd and rdn along wl over 1f out: drvn ins fnl f: hdd and no ex nr fin* **4/11**[1]
0- **3** *12* **Coral Sands (IRE)**[28] 7886 4-9-13 **0**............................... PJMcDonald 5 44
(Alan Swinbank) *towards rr and swtchd wd sn after s: hdwy over 2f out: styd on appr fnl f: tk 3rd nr fin* **25/1**
2-2 **4** *nk* **Magilini (IRE)**[20] 37 3-8-6 **0**.. LeeNewman 7 34
(David Barron) *chsd ldrs: rdn along over 3f out: outpcd fnl 2f* **13/2**[2]
5 *¾* **Mayforde Jack** 3-8-11 **0**.. RobbieFitzpatrick 2 36
(Jo Hughes) *dwlt: chsd ldrs 1/2-way: sn rdn and wknd wl over 1f out* **40/1**
00- **6** *7* **Release The Funds (IRE)**[84] 7210 3-8-11 **0**................... AndrewMullen 4 14
(David Nicholls) *led: rdn along and hdd over 3f out: sn wknd* **33/1**
7 *nk* **Adili (IRE)** 3-8-9 **0** ow1.. PaulPickard[(3)] 1 14
(Brian Ellison) *s.i.s: a bhd* **9/1**[3]

1m 15.03s (-1.47) **Going Correction** -0.175s/f (Stan)
WFA 3 from 4yo 16lb 7 Ran SP% **109.7**
Speed ratings (Par 103): **102,101,85,85,84 75,74**
toteswingers:1&2:£3.80, 2&3:£3.00, 1&3:£15.10 CSF £32.97 TOTE £22.40: £7.50, £1.10; EX 50.40.
Owner H Morrison **Bred** Henry O'Callaghan **Trained** East Ilsley, Berks

FOCUS
A moderate maiden with the front pair pulling a very long way clear of the rest.

284 MEMBERSHIP OF SOUTHWELL GOLF CLUB (S) STKS 7f (F)
1:50 (1:53) (Class 6) 4-Y-0+ **£1,704** (£503; £251) **Stalls** Low

Form RPR
01-2 **1** **Ingleby Arch (USA)**[21] 19 9-9-0 **75**.................................... LMcNiff[(5)] 4 73
(David Barron) *mde all: rdn wl over 1f out: kpt on u.p ins fnl f* **7/4**[1]
03-0 **2** *1* **Fantasy Fry**[12] 139 4-9-0 **56**...................................(t) RichardKingscote 6 65
(Tom Dascombe) *cl up: rdn to chal wl over 1f out and ev ch tl edgd lft and one pce fnl f* **14/1**
022- **3** *1 ½* **Fishforcompliments**[37] 7807 8-9-0 **73**..........................(p) PaulHanagan 1 61
(Richard Fahey) *in tch on inner: swtchd rt and hdwy over 2f out: sn rdn and kpt on appr fnl f: nrst fin* **15/8**[2]
-034 **4** *4 ½* **Ace Of Spies (IRE)**[12] 139 7-9-0 **61**..........................(b) HayleyTurner 3 49
(Conor Dore) *trckd ldrs: effrt 3f out: sn rdn and one pce* **6/1**
006- **5** *4* **Imprimis Tagula (IRE)**[151] 5425 8-8-7 **81**...............(v) NatashaEaton[(7)] 2 38
(Alan Bailey) *chsd ldng pair on inner: rdn along 3f out: sn wknd* **5/1**[3]
/00- **6** *7* **Countrycraft**[82] 7246 5-8-11 **35**...................................... RyanPowell[(3)] 5 19
(Sally Hall) *dwlt: sn chsng ldrs: rdn along 3f out: sn wknd* **100/1**
040- **7** *2 ¾* **Apassionforfashion**[45] 7714 4-8-9 **36**............................(e[1]) TomEaves 7
(Bryan Smart) *s.i.s: a in rr* **66/1**

1m 28.34s (-1.96) **Going Correction** -0.175s/f (Stan) 7 Ran SP% **111.2**
Speed ratings (Par 101): **104,102,101,96,91 83,80**
toteswingers:1&2:£4.70, 2&3:£4.80, 1&3:£1.40 CSF £24.99 TOTE £2.90: £1.70, £5.80; EX 27.20.There was no bid for winner.
Owner Dave Scott **Bred** Alexander-Groves Thoroughbreds **Trained** Maunby, N Yorks

FOCUS
A wide range of abilities in this seller and it was important to race handily.

285 GOLF AND RACING AT SOUTHWELL H'CAP 1m 4f (F)
2:20 (2:20) (Class 4) (0-85,81) 4-Y-0+ **£4,204** (£1,251; £625; £312) **Stalls** Low

Form RPR
15-3 **1** **Admirable Duque (IRE)**[5] 213 6-9-0 **79**.............(be) JoshBaudains[(7)] 4 88
(Dominic Ffrench Davis) *hld up in rr: hdwy on inner 4f out: n.m.r 3f out: sn swtchd rt to outer: rdn to chse ldrs wl over 1f out: str run ent fnl f to ld nr fin* **16/1**
2-20 **2** *hd* **The Lock Master (IRE)**[9] 187 5-9-5 **77**......................... HayleyTurner 3 85
(Michael Appleby) *hld up: stdy hdwy 4f out: chsd ldrs 2f out: sn rdn and styd on to ld last 100yds: hdd and no ex nr line* **7/2**[1]
111- **3** *1* **Mazij**[40] 7772 4-9-0 **76**.. WilliamCarson 5 83+
(Peter Hiatt) *chsd clr ldng pair: hdwy to ld wl over 3f out: rdn clr 2f out: drvn ent fnl f: hdd and no ex last 100yds* **7/2**[1]
365- **4** *2 ¼* **Bedouin Bay**[47] 4697 5-9-5 **77**... MartinHarley 2 80
(Alan McCabe) *chsd ldrs: hdwy over 3f out: rdn 2f out: sn drvn and one pce* **12/1**
301- **5** *4 ½* **Union Island (IRE)**[175] 4635 6-9-8 **80**.......................... BarryMcHugh 10 76
(Brian Ellison) *trckd ldrs: hdwy to chse ldr 3f out: rdn 2f out and sn one pce* **8/1**[3]
00-4 **6** *5* **Ivory Jazz**[10] 175 5-8-9 **74**.. NoraLooby[(7)] 6 62
(Richard Guest) *chsd clr ldr: rdn along 4f out: sn wknd* **16/1**
42-6 **7** *4* **Chookie Hamilton**[6] 202 8-9-4 **76**................................... ShaneKelly 8 57
(Keith Dalgleish) *towards rr: rdn along bef 1/2-way: nvr a factor* **13/2**[2]
024- **8** *1* **Tartan Gunna**[94] 7022 6-9-4 **76**...................................... JamesSullivan 7 56
(James Given) *dwlt: a in rr* **8/1**[3]
13-6 **9** *7* **Bivouac (UAE)**[19] 44 8-9-0 **72**...................................... PJMcDonald 1 41
(Alan Swinbank) *midfield: sme hdwy over 4f out: sn rdn and wknd* **12/1**
00-0 **10** *18* **Majuro (IRE)**[10] 177 8-9-9 **81**.....................................(t) LeeNewman 11 21
(Richard Guest) *sn led and set str pce: rdn along and hdd wl over 3f out: sn wknd* **14/1**
0 **11** *2 ¼* **Rock Of Deauville (IRE)**[19] 44 5-9-5 **77**........................ TomEaves 9 13
(Julie Camacho) *a in rr: rdn along and bhd fnl 4f* **33/1**

2m 36.84s (-4.16) **Going Correction** -0.175s/f (Stan)
WFA 4 from 5yo+ 4lb 11 Ran SP% **116.8**
Speed ratings (Par 105): **106,105,105,103,100 97,94,94,89,77 75**
toteswingers:1&2:£15.10, 2&3:£3.90, 1&3:£10.10 CSF £70.92 CT £248.01 TOTE £25.20: £4.50, £1.80, £1.80; EX 108.60.
Owner Exors of the Late Brian W Taylor **Bred** Airlie Stud And R N Clay **Trained** Lambourn, Berks
■ Stewards' Enquiry : William Carson two-day ban: used whip with excessive frequency (Feb 7-8)

FOCUS
A fair handicap and there was no hiding place with the Richard Guest pair Majuro and Ivory Jazz going off at a suicidal pace. Not surprisingly both paid for it.

286 DOWNLOAD THE BLUE SQUARE BET APP H'CAP 5f (F)
2:50 (2:50) (Class 2) (0-100,98) 4-Y-0+ **£10,350** (£3,080; £1,539; £769) **Stalls** High

Form RPR
1-31 **1** **Woolfall Sovereign (IRE)**[11] 157 6-8-7 **84** oh1........... BarryMcHugh 1 93+
(George Margarson) *racd wd: hld up: hdwy 1/2-way: chsd ldrs wl over 1f out: sn rdn and styd on ins fnl f to ld nr fin* **7/1**[3]
42-2 **2** *½* **Mottley Crewe**[23] 3 5-8-7 **84** oh2..............................(b) MartinHarley 5 91
(Richard Guest) *qckly away and swtchd rt towards stands' rail after 100yds: rdn wl over 1f out: clr ent fnl f: sn drvn: edgd lft and hdd nr fin* **6/1**[2]
01-1 **3** *½* **Even Stevens**[23] 3 4-9-2 **96**.. RyanClark[(3)] 4 101
(Scott Dixon) *racd centre: chsd ldr: rdn over 1f out: drvn and one pce ins fnl f* **13/8**[1]
00-3 **4** *2 ¾* **Sir Geoffrey (IRE)**[13] 120 6-8-0 **84** oh4...................(b) DannyBrock[(7)] 6 79
(Scott Dixon) *n.m.r and swtchd lft after 100yds: sn prom: rdn and ev ch over 1f out: wknd fnl f* **11/1**
425- **5** *½* **Close To The Edge (IRE)**[25] 7926 4-8-7 **84** oh2............. ShaneKelly 2 78
(Alan McCabe) *towards rr: pushed along 1/2-way: swtchd lft and rdn wl over 1f out: kpt on appr fnl f: nvr nr ldrs* **20/1**
01-1 **6** *2 ½* **Cadeaux Pearl**[13] 120 4-8-4 **84** oh2..........................(b) RyanPowell[(3)] 3 69
(Scott Dixon) *racd centre: chsd ldrs: rdn along 1/2-way: sn wknd* **8/1**
000- **7** *2 ½* **Alpha Tauri (USA)**[141] 5789 6-8-0 **84** oh10.................(t) NoraLooby[(7)] 9 60
(Richard Guest) *hmpd after 100yds: a bhd after* **100/1**
50-2 **8** *6* **West Coast Dream**[13] 120 5-8-8 **85**..................................... TomEaves 8 39
(Roy Brotherton) *n.m.r and hmpd sn after s: hdwy to chse ldrs after 1f: rdn along over 2f out: sn wknd* **9/1**
40-0 **9** *1 ¾* **Colonel Mak**[17] 89 5-9-7 **98**.. LeeNewman 10 46
(David Barron) *cl up on stands' rail: rdn along bef 1/2-way: sn wknd* **9/1**

58.43s (-1.27) **Going Correction** -0.025s/f (Stan) 9 Ran SP% **110.1**
Speed ratings (Par 109): **109,108,107,103,102 98,94,84,81**
toteswingers:1&2:£3.50, 2&3:£2.80, 1&3:£3.30 CSF £44.91 CT £94.48 TOTE £6.20: £2.00, £1.40, £1.10; EX 45.10.
Owner Graham Lodge Partnership **Bred** Saud Bin Saad **Trained** Newmarket, Suffolk
■ Stewards' Enquiry : Martin Harley three-day ban: careless riding (Feb 7-9)

The Form Book Flat, Raceform Ltd, Compton, RG20 6NL

FOCUS
The first Class 2 race run at Southwell in 13 months. Six of the nine runners were out of the handicap.
NOTEBOOK
Woolfall Sovereign(IRE) put up an extraordinary performance. He came into this having been in fine form at Wolverhampton but was racing over the minimum trip for the first time on this Fibresand debut. He was always travelling well from the outside stall, however, and with stamina on his side, maintained his effort down the centre of the track to hit the front close to the line. This was a nice prize to win and the surface obviously suited, but he will do well to find many more opportunities back here. (op 8-1)
Mottley Crewe loves it here, but was comfortably held by Even Stevens over C&D on New Year's Day and being 2lb wrong meant he was only 2lb better off. However, he still managed to reverse the form, having blazed a trail against the nearside rail, and it looked as though he might see it through, but the winner had the legs of him in the very closing stages. (op 7-1)
Even Stevens, 6-7 at the track and 4-4 over C&D before this, was put up 5lb for his success here on New Year's Day and that might have found him out. Always handy in the centre of the track, he had every chance and ran his race, but he may be awkward to place now until the turf season starts. (op 6-4 tchd 7-4)
Sir Geoffrey(IRE), 4lb wrong, was still 2lb lower than when third in this last year (when it was a 0-95) having slid down the weights in recent months. Off the bridle throughout, he again ran creditably but is at his best when able to dominate. (tchd 12-1)
Close To The Edge(IRE) has gone well here before, but she was always being taken off her feet and her three wins have come over further. (tchd 16-1)
Cadeaux Pearl was bidding for a hat-trick, but being 2lb wrong meant he was 10lb higher than when winning over C&D two starts back and he found this too tough an ask. (op 9-1)
West Coast Dream Official explanation: trainer said gelding bled from the nose
Colonel Mak Official explanation: trainer's rep said gelding finished distressed

287 PLAY GOLF BEFORE RACING H'CAP — 1m (F)
3:20 (3:21) (Class 6) (0-65,65) 4-Y-O+ — £1,704 (£503; £251) — Stalls Low

Form				RPR
02-3	1		**Fluctuation (IRE)**[22] 14 4-8-10 **54**.....(b) FrannyNorton 10 (Ian Williams) *prom: led after 3f: clr 2f out: rdn and styd on strly fnl f* **11/2**[2]	70
62-6	2	2 ¾	**Pipers Piping (IRE)**[17] 91 6-9-7 **65**.....(p) MartinHarley 11 (Alastair Lidderdale) *in tch: hdwy 3f out: rdn to chse wnr wl over 1f out: kpt on* **14/1**	74
53-4	3	3 ½	**Jo Boy**[12] 128 5-9-5 **63**..... HayleyTurner 2 (Michael Bell) *trckd ldrs: hdwy 3f out: chsd wnr 2f out: sn rdn and no imp* **4/1**[1]	64
450-	4	3 ½	**Symphonic Dancer (USA)**[115] 6546 5-8-13 **57**..... RussKennemore 9 (Brian Baugh) *chsd ldrs: rdn and edgd lft wl over 1f out: sn one pce* **14/1**	50
34-1	5	1 ½	**General Tufto**[16] 96 7-9-4 **62**.....(b) RobbieFitzpatrick 14 (Charles Smith) *sn outpcd and bhd: hdwy on inner 2f out: styd on appr fnl f: nrst fin* **8/1**	51
5-05	6	½	**The Which Doctor**[11] 146 7-8-10 **61**.....(e) NoraLooby(7) 8 (Richard Guest) *s.i.s and bhd: rdn along and hdwy over 3f out: chsd ldrs over 2f out: sn no imp* **20/1**	49
00-0	7	3 ¾	**Valley Tiger**[18] 67 4-8-13 **57**..... PaulHanagan 7 (Richard Fahey) *towards rr: rdn along over 3f out: n.d* **16/1**	36
25-5	8	¾	**Hilbre Court (USA)**[16] 96 7-8-11 **55**.....(e) WilliamCarson 13 (Brian Baugh) *midfield: hdwy on outer 3f out: rdn along over 2f out: n.d* **15/2**[3]	33
-405	9	1	**Elhamri**[14] 115 8-9-6 **64**..... PJMcDonald 6 (Conor Dore) *prom: rdn along wl over 2f out: sn wknd* **14/1**	39
0-00	10	nse	**Vitznau (IRE)**[15] 102 8-8-12 **59**..... SophieDoyle(3) 12 (Alastair Lidderdale) *in tch: rdn along 3f out: sn wknd* **10/1**	34
400-	11	½	**Stansonnit**[28] 7887 4-9-2 **65**..... GarryWhillans(5) 1 (Alan Swinbank) *a towards rr* **22/1**	39
000-	12	4	**Master Leon**[28] 7887 5-9-5 **63**.....(p) TomEaves 4 (Bryan Smart) *a in rr* **25/1**	28
60-0	13	5	**Ryedale Dancer (IRE)**[11] 148 4-9-2 **63**..... RobertLButler(3) 5 (Richard Guest) *led 3f: chsd wnr: rdn along over 3f out: sn wknd* **50/1**	16
2-06	14	nk	**Hecton Lad (USA)**[4] 225 5-9-6 **64**..... RobertWinston 3 (John Best) *midfield: rdn along 1/2-way: sn bhd* **9/1**	17

1m 41.25s (-2.45) **Going Correction** -0.175s/f (Stan) — 14 Ran SP% **118.2**
Speed ratings (Par 101): **105,102,98,95,93 93,89,88,87,87 87,83,78,77**
toteswingers:1&2:£17.40, 2&3:£10.60, 1&3:£3.20 CSF £74.75 CT £352.55 TOTE £5.80: £1.60, £2.70, £1.70; EX 68.50.
Owner J Tredwell **Bred** Corduff Stud & T J Rooney **Trained** Portway, Worcs
■ Stewards' Enquiry : Russ Kennemore two-day ban: careless riding (Feb 7-8)
FOCUS
A moderate handicap and the principals all raced handily.

288 FOLLOW SOUTHWELL ON TWITTER H'CAP — 1m (F)
3:50 (3:51) (Class 6) (0-60,60) 3-Y-O — £1,704 (£503; £251) — Stalls Low

Form				RPR
1	1		**Miss Cato**[23] 2 3-9-0 **53**..... WilliamCarson 1 (Rae Guest) *dwlt and sn pushed along: in tch 1/2-way: hdwy to ld 3f out: rdn and edgd rt over 1f out: kpt on wl ins fnl f* **4/1**[2]	66
0-61	2	4	**Moataz (USA)**[3] 255 3-9-1 **54** 6ex..... FrannyNorton 5 (Mark Johnston) *trckd ldr: effrt 3f out: sn rdn along: edgd lft and outpcd: styd on ins fnl f to take 2nd nr fin* **4/7**[1]	58
50-3	3	nk	**First Bid**[12] 132 3-9-7 **60**.....(b[1]) JamesSullivan 2 (James Given) *led: hdd 3f out: rdn 2f out: ch and drvn whn edgd lft appr fnl f: one pce: lost 2nd nr fin* **10/1**	63
41-6	4	3 ¾	**Cat Queen**[15] 108 3-9-0 **56**..... AmyRyan(3) 7 (Gay Kelleway) *in tch: rdn along 1/2-way: hdwy on inner 3f out: sn one pce* **9/1**[3]	50
3-63	5	4 ½	**Angel Cake (IRE)**[6] 204 3-8-2 **48**.....(v) DannyBrock(7) 8 (Phil McEntee) *cl up: rdn along 3f out: sn wknd* **25/1**	32
010-	6	23	**Seven Year Itch (IRE)**[203] 3700 3-8-11 **50**..... JohnFahy 3 (James Bethell) *in tch: rdn along wl over 3f out: sn wknd* **28/1**	

1m 44.31s (0.61) **Going Correction** -0.175s/f (Stan) — 6 Ran SP% **110.0**
Speed ratings (Par 95): **89,85,84,80,76 53**
toteswingers:1&2:£1.70, 2&3:£2.10, 1&3:£1.80 CSF £6.40 CT £16.08 TOTE £2.80: £1.10, £1.30; EX 8.50.
Owner A H Bennett **Bred** A H Bennett **Trained** Newmarket, Suffolk
FOCUS
A moderate 3yo handicap with the favourite disappointing.

289 PLAY RAINBOW RICHES AT BLUESQ.COM H'CAP — 6f (F)
4:20 (4:22) (Class 6) (0-60,60) 4-Y-O+ — £1,704 (£503; £251) — Stalls Low

Form				RPR
00-5	1		**Ridgeway Hawk**[12] 139 4-8-13 **57** ow2.....(v) LeeNewnes(5) 2 (Mark Usher) *prom: effrt and cl up 2f out: rdn over 1f out: kpt on to ld ins fnl f: sn edgd rt and drvn out* **15/2**	66
3-04	2	½	**Flow Chart (IRE)**[14] 113 5-8-8 **47** oh1 ow1.....(b) RobbieFitzpatrick 8 (Peter Grayson) *midfield: hdwy 3f out: chsd ldrs wl over 1f out: rdn to chal ins fnl f and ev ch tl no ex last 50yds* **25/1**	54
34-2	3	1 ¼	**Gracie's Gift (IRE)**[12] 139 10-9-0 **53**.....(v) MartinHarley 12 (Richard Guest) *cl up on outer: chal over 2f out: led wl over 1f out and sn rdn: drvn and hdd ins fnl f: kpt on same pce* **7/1**	56
45-4	4	2 ¼	**First In Command (IRE)**[13] 123 7-9-2 **55**.....(bt[1]) ShaneKelly 5 (Daniel Mark Loughnane) *towards rr: hdwy 1/2-way: chsd ldrs 2f out: sn rdn and kpt on same pce appr fnl f* **9/2**[2]	51
6-60	5	2 ¼	**Takajan (IRE)**[11] 155 5-8-6 **52**..... RachealKneller(7) 9 (Mark Brisbourne) *towards rr: hdwy on outer over 2f out: sn rdn and no imp* **6/1**[3]	41
0-23	6	½	**Transmit (IRE)**[4] 232 5-9-7 **60**.....(b) RobertWinston 6 (Tim Easterby) *in rr: rdn along wl over 2f out: kpt on appr fnl f: nrst fin* **5/2**[1]	47
03-1	7	1	**Bird Dog**[16] 95 6-8-5 **51**.....(v) DannyBrock(7) 1 (Phil McEntee) *led: rdn along and jnd over 2f out: hdd wl over 1f out: sn drvn: edgd rt: wknd* **10/1**	35
00-0	8	3 ½	**Fayre Bella**[12] 126 5-8-7 **46** oh1.....(bt) JohnFahy 3 (John Gallagher) *dwlt: a towards rr* **20/1**	19
046-	9	2 ½	**Musical Leap**[82] 7245 4-8-0 **46** oh1..... NoraLooby(7) 4 (Shaun Harris) *towards rr: sme hdwy on inner over 2f out: sn rdn and nvr a factor* **66/1**	11
/5-0	10	4 ½	**Athenian Garden (USA)**[11] 148 5-9-6 **59**..... WilliamCarson 7 (Richard Guest) *dwlt: a in rr* **20/1**	9
044-	11	½	**Jaldarshaan (IRE)**[122] 6358 5-9-3 **56**..... TomEaves 11 (Colin Teague) *chsd ldrs: rdn along 1/2-way: sn wknd* **25/1**	5
/64-	12	1	**Dancing Wave**[357] 375 6-8-2 **46** oh1..... DanielleMcCreery(5) 10 (Michael Chapman) *chsd ldrs: rdn along over 3f out and sn wknd* **50/1**	

1m 15.96s (-0.54) **Going Correction** -0.175s/f (Stan) — 12 Ran SP% **115.1**
Speed ratings (Par 101): **96,95,93,90,87 87,85,81,77,71 71,69**
toteswingers:1&2:£27.30, 2&3:£14.90, 1&3:£11.50 CSF £183.97 CT £1386.72 TOTE £4.50: £2.60, £6.20, £2.50; EX 197.80.
Owner The Goodracing Partnership **Bred** Ridgeway Bloodstock **Trained** Upper Lambourn, Berks
■ Stewards' Enquiry : Robbie Fitzpatrick 18-day ban (2nd offence in 12mths); used whip with excessive frequency (Feb 7-11,13-18, 20-25,27)
Lee Newnes two-day ban: used whip with excessive frequency (Feb 7-8)
Nora Looby three-day ban: careless riding (Feb 7-9)
FOCUS
A moderate sprint handicap.
T/Plt: £10.50 to a £1 stake. Pool of £65,281.42 - 4,536.83 winning tickets. T/Qpdt: £4.00 to a £1 stake. Pool of £5,645.42 - 1,043.13 winning tickets. JR

247 CAGNES-SUR-MER
Tuesday, January 24
OFFICIAL GOING: Fibresand: standard

290a PRIX DES CITRONNIERS (CLAIMER) (3YO COLTS & GELDINGS) (FIBRESAND) — 1m 2f (D)
1:20 (12:00) 3-Y-O — £6,250 (£2,500; £1,875; £1,250; £625)

			RPR
1		**Man Fieber (FR)** 3-8-9 0.....(b[1]) GaetanMasure 8 (J-M Capitte, France) **47/1**	69
2	1 ¾	**Jack Sparrow (FR)**[14] 3-9-0 0.....(b) FabienLefebvre 2 (S Jesus, France) **7/1**	70
3	nk	**Dylans Verse (IRE)**[57] 7568 3-8-9 0.....(b[1]) Francois-XavierBertras 13 (Reg Hollinshead) *settled in 3rd travelling comf: dropped bk to 6th bef st: rdn and ev ch 1 1/2f out: chal for ld 1f out: nt qckn: rallied fnl 50yds to claim 3rd cl home* **7/2**[1]	64
4	nk	**Flipou (FR)** 3-8-8 0..... MatthieuAutier(6) 11 (J-C Rouget, France) **11/2**[2]	69
5	hd	**Potkol (FR)**[33] 3-8-9 0.....(b) ThomasMessina 6 (C Boutin, France) **37/1**	63
6	1 ¼	**Abrasivo (ITY)** 3-8-9 0..... SUrru 9 (P Caravati, Italy) **79/1**	61
7	nse	**Rock Junior (IRE)**[97] 3-9-0 0..... FranckBlondel 10 (M Pimbonnet, France) **15/1**	66
8	½	**Kentucky Winner (FR)** 3-9-0 0..... Pierre-CharlesBoudot 14 (J-M Capitte, France) **78/10**	65
9	nse	**King Red (FR)**[22] 3-8-8 0..... RomainAuray(6) 7 (J Heloury, France) **25/1**	65
10	shd	**Narkotic (FR)**[34] 3-9-1 0..... AntoineHamelin(3) 3 (J-P Gauvin, France) **63/10**[3]	69
0		**Mille Waki (FR)**[33] 3-8-2 0..... SoufyaneMoulin(7) 4 (C Boutin, France) **78/10**	
0		**Pont A Marcq (FR)**[29] 3-8-9 0..... ThierryThulliez 5 (J Heloury, France) **40/1**	
0		**Walk On The Water (FR)** 3-8-10 0..... MathieuTavaresDaSilva(4) 12 (J-P Roman, France) **44/1**	
0		**Becqualink (FR)** 3-8-9 0.....(b) MickaelForest 1 (M Gentile, France) **9/1**	

2m 3.51s (123.51) — 14 Ran SP% **117.3**
WIN (incl. 1 euro stake): 7.40 (Man Fieber coupled with Kentucky Winner). PLACES: 9.50, 2.70, 2.40. DF: 170.10. SF: 400.10.
Owner Ecurie Haras de Quetieville **Bred** Ecurie Haras De Quetieville **Trained** France

276 KEMPTON (A.W) (R-H)
Wednesday, January 25
OFFICIAL GOING: Standard
Wind: Moderate, half behind Weather: Overcast

291 FREE ENTRY FOR BETDAQ MEMBERS MAIDEN FILLIES' STKS — 7f (P)
4:40 (4:42) (Class 5) 3-Y-O+ — £2,264 (£673; £336; £168) — Stalls Low

Form				RPR
543-	1		**Jellicle (IRE)**[81] 7292 3-8-10 **75**..... NickyMackay 6 (John Gosden) *chsd ldr 2f: racd in 3rd after tl clsd to ld 2f out: rdn clr over 1f out: styd on wl* **11/10**[1]	76
040-	2	3 ¼	**Chatterati (USA)**[92] 7081 3-8-10 **70**..... MartinLane 3 (Mark Johnston) *dwlt: racd in 5th: rdn and prog over 2f out: chsd wnr over 1f out: kpt on but no imp* **4/1**[3]	67

- **3** *1* **Barbarella Blue (IRE)** 3-8-7 0 AdamBeschizza(3) 1 65+
(Marco Botti) *dwlt: rn green in last: shkn up 3f out: prog over 1f out to take 3rd jst ins fnl f: kpt on* **9/4**[2]

5-6 **4** *6* **Queen Of Heaven (USA)**[21] 34 4-10-0 0 SteveDrowne 5 53
(Peter Makin) *chsd ldrs: wnt 3rd over 2f out: no imp after: fdd fnl f* **25/1**

0 **5** *1* **Jacasa Too**[16] 107 3-8-10 0 JamesMillman 2 46
(Rod Millman) *mostly in last pair: pushed along wl over 2f out: sn lft bhd: n.d after* **66/1**

6 **6** *9* **Jolie Etoile**[20] 41 4-10-0 0 DavidProbert 4 26
(Tony Carroll) *led to s and mounted at post: led 2f: led again 3f out to 2f out: wknd rapidly* **50/1**

7 *30* **Roundelay** 3-8-10 0 WilliamCarson 7
(Anthony Carson) *completely missed the break: stormed up on outer to ld after 2f: hdd 3f out: wknd v rapidly and sn t.o* **33/1**

1m 26.69s (0.69) **Going Correction** 0.0s/f (Stan)
WFA 3 from 4yo 18lb 7 Ran SP% **108.6**
Speed ratings (Par 100): **96,92,91,84,83 72,38**
toteswingers:1&2:£1.30, 1&3:£1.60, 2&3:£1.40 CSF £5.16 TOTE £2.00: £1.50, £1.70; EX 3.40.
Owner H R H Princess Haya Of Jordan **Bred** Darley **Trained** Newmarket, Suffolk

FOCUS
Probably a fair fillies' maiden for the time of year. The pace was solid.

292 BETDAQ MULTIPLES MAIDEN STKS 1m 3f (P)
5:10 (5:11) (Class 5) 3-Y-0+ **£2,264** (£673; £336; £168) **Stalls** Low

Form RPR

1 **Queen Of Denmark (USA)** 4-9-6 0 JoeFanning 5 78+
(Mark Johnston) *hld up in 5th: shkn up and prog over 2f out: rdn to ld jst over 1f out: styd on wl* **7/2**[3]

3/4- **2** *2* **Hawawi**[210] 3519 4-9-11 0 JimmyFortune 2 80
(James Tate) *trckd ldr 2f: styd prom: clsd on inner to ld 2f out: rdn and hdd jst over 1f out: hd high and nt qckn* **11/8**[1]

53- **3** *3 ¾* **Stars In Your Eyes**[70] 7440 4-9-6 0 NickyMackay 6 68
(John Gosden) *trckd ldr after 2f: rdn to chal over 2f out: nt qckn w ldng pair over 1f out: jst pushed along whn hld fnl f* **5/2**[2]

4 *9* **Midnight Opera**[36] 6-10-0 0 AdamKirby 4 57
(Neil Mulholland) *led to 2f out: wknd qckly* **20/1**

00- **5** *1 ¼* **Midnight Sequel**[42] 7751 3-7-10 0 DominicFox(3) 3 47
(Michael Blake) *t.k.h early: sn in 4th: urged along 5f out: lost pl and btn over 2f out: wknd* **100/1**

0 **6** *2* **Lyrical Gangster (IRE)**[18] 84 3-8-4 0 ChrisCatlin 1 48
(J S Moore) *s.i.s: pushed along in last after 2f: rdn 4f out: no prog and wl btn 2f out* **15/2**

6- **7** *4* **Finlodex**[28] 7894 5-10-0 0 LiamKeniry 8 44
(Murty McGrath) *hld up in last pair: gng wl enough 3f out: drvn and no rspnse over 2f out: wknd* **100/1**

2m 21.83s (-0.07) **Going Correction** 0.0s/f (Stan)
WFA 3 from 4yo 24lb 4 from 5yo+ 3lb 7 Ran SP% **111.4**
Speed ratings (Par 103): **100,98,95,89,88 86,84**
toteswingers:1&2:£1.70, 1&3:£1.50, 2&3:£1.10 CSF £8.27 TOTE £5.90: £2.90, £1.10; EX 9.90.
Owner Sheikh Hamdan Bin Mohammed Al Maktoum **Bred** Darley **Trained** Middleham Moor, N Yorks

FOCUS
A steady early pace, but the big three in the market were still able to pull clear in what looked quite an interesting older-horse maiden.

293 BACK OR LAY AT BETDAQ.COM H'CAP 1m (P)
5:40 (5:40) (Class 6) (0-55,56) 4-Y-0+ **£1,617** (£481; £240; £120) **Stalls** Low

Form RPR

43-1 **1** **Daniel Thomas (IRE)**[12] 151 10-9-4 55 (tp) MartinHarley 7 74
(Richard Guest) *hld up in last trio: plld out jst over 2f out: shkn up and unleashed to ld on outer over 1f out: sn drew rt away* **9/2**[1]

006- **2** *7* **Emerald Royal**[48] 7676 4-8-6 46 oh1 RyanPowell(3) 10 49
(Eric Wheeler) *hld up in last: gd prog on inner over 2f out to chal over 1f out: no rspnse to wnr after: kpt on to win battle for 2nd* **20/1**

3-31 **3** *nk* **Querido (GER)**[7] 197 8-9-2 56 6ex (tp) RobertLButler(3) 8 58
(Paddy Butler) *racd wd: trckd ldrs: rdn and prog to chal wl over 1f out: sn lft bhd by wnr: lost out in battle for 2nd nr fin* **8/1**

0-32 **4** *4* **Very Well Red**[7] 197 9-9-0 51 WilliamCarson 6 44
(Peter Hiatt) *prom: chsd ldr 3f out: drvn to chal over 2f out: upsides wl over 1f out: sn lft bhd* **15/2**[3]

4-65 **5** *1 ¼* **Gazboolou**[7] 203 8-9-4 55 FergusSweeney 4 45
(David Pinder) *sn settled to trck ldrs: rdn and nt qckn over 2f out: outpcd over 1f out: plugged on* **11/2**[2]

610- **6** *1 ¼* **Monashee Rock (IRE)**[113] 6610 7-9-4 55 LiamKeniry 3 42
(Patrick Chamings) *settled towards rr on inner: effrt over 2f out: shkn up and wl outpcd over 1f out* **8/1**

600- **7** *¾* **Ain't Talkin'**[26] 7924 6-8-5 47 oh1 ow1 (p) MarkCoumbe(5) 2 33
(Michael Attwater) *led: hrd pressed over 2f out: hdd & wknd over 1f out* **33/1**

003- **8** *6* **Sir Ike (IRE)**[26] 7923 7-8-10 47 (tp) LukeMorris 1 19
(Michael Appleby) *prom: drvn to try to chal 2f out: wknd qckly over 1f out* **8/1**

005- **9** *5* **Ragda**[28] 7894 4-9-1 52 (b[1]) AdamKirby 9
(Marco Botti) *racd wd: hld up in last trio: rdn and struggling in last wl over 2f out: sn bhd* **9/2**[1]

00-0 **10** *1 ½* **Renoir's Lady**[12] 148 4-9-4 55 HayleyTurner 5
(Simon Dow) *chsd ldr to 3f out: wknd rapidly* **15/2**[3]

1m 39.74s (-0.06) **Going Correction** 0.0s/f (Stan) 10 Ran SP% **116.3**
Speed ratings (Par 101): **100,93,92,88,87 86,85,79,74,72**
toteswingers:1&2:£13.60, 1&3:£3.70, 2&3:£23.40 CSF £95.64 CT £538.06 TOTE £7.30: £1.50, £5.70, £2.10; EX 118.20.
Owner Rakebackmypoker.com **Bred** Lawn Stud **Trained** Stainforth, S Yorks

FOCUS
What had looked quite a competitive handicap, albeit a moderate one, was turned into a rout by the winner.
Sir Ike(IRE) Official explanation: trainer said gelding bled from the nose

294 BETDAQ MOBILE APPS H'CAP 1m (P)
6:10 (6:10) (Class 6) (0-55,55) 3-Y-0 **£1,617** (£481; £240; £120) **Stalls** Low

Form RPR

400- **1** **Liquid Sunshine**[25] 7937 3-8-6 46 oh1 RyanPowell(3) 6 52
(Sylvester Kirk) *wl plcd bhd ldrs: rdn and prog jst over 2f out: led over 1f out: drvn out* **16/1**

35-5 **2** *2* **Siouxies Dream**[16] 108 3-9-4 55 AdamKirby 2 56
(Michael Appleby) *led 1f: styd cl up bhd ldrs: prog to ld again jst over 2f out: hdd over 1f out: kpt on same pce* **10/1**

-646 **3** *nse* **Meet Joe Black (IRE)**[9] 194 3-9-0 51 (v) LukeMorris 11 52
(David Evans) *s.i.s: rousted along to rch midfield after 2f: nt gng wl fr 1/2-way: rdr persisted and styd on fr 2f out: tk 3rd fnl f: nrly snatched 2nd* **9/1**[3]

045- **4** *1 ¼* **Ice Loch**[25] 7937 3-8-13 50 (b) DaneO'Neill 4 48
(Michael Blanshard) *wl in rr: rdn wl over 2f out: prog wl over 1f out: styd on same pce fnl f* **12/1**

0-46 **5** *½* **Auntie Kathryn (IRE)**[9] 191 3-8-11 48 WilliamCarson 7 45+
(Stuart Williams) *hld up in rr: rdn over 2f out on outer: kpt on same pce fr over 1f out: no threat* **6/1**[2]

001- **6** *¾* **My Scat Daddy (USA)**[25] 7937 3-8-13 50 DavidProbert 8 45
(Brett Johnson) *wl plcd bhd ldrs: rdn on outer over 2f out: nt qckn wl over 1f out: btn after* **11/10**[1]

00-6 **7** *½* **Bellinda**[19] 56 3-8-10 47 FrankieMcDonald 10 41
(Martin Bosley) *trckd ldr after 2f: led 1/2-way: hdd jst over 2f out: steadily wknd* **66/1**

64-0 **8** *8* **Can Do Les (IRE)**[13] 132 3-9-2 53 (p) MartinHarley 9 29
(Des Donovan) *hld up wl in rr: gng wl enough over 3f out: rdn over 2f out: wknd over 1f out: sn bhd* **16/1**

05-0 **9** *2* **Rainbow Riches (IRE)**[11] 181 3-8-8 52 NedCurtis(7) 3 23
(Roger Curtis) *towards rr: effrt wl over 2f out: no prog wl over 1f out: sn wknd* **16/1**

00-0 **10** *¾* **Gabrial The Prince (IRE)**[13] 132 3-8-11 48 StevieDonohoe 1 17
(David Simcock) *led after 1f to 1/2-way: rdn over 2f out: sn wknd qckly* **16/1**

00-0 **11** *7* **L'Arlesienne**[9] 191 3-8-10 47 ow1 LiamKeniry 12
(Sylvester Kirk) *hld up in last: shkn up and no prog over 2f out: sn wknd: t.o* **66/1**

000- **12** *16* **Luna Vale**[27] 7909 3-8-6 46 oh1 (b[1]) AdamBeschizza(3) 13
(Robert Eddery) *pushed along in rr early: prog on wd outside to go prom 1/2-way: wknd rapidly wl over 2f out: wl t.o* **50/1**

1m 41.02s (1.22) **Going Correction** 0.0s/f (Stan) 12 Ran SP% **117.2**
Speed ratings (Par 95): **93,91,90,89,89 88,87,79,77,77 70,54**
toteswingers:1&2:£14.20, 1&3:£27.30, 2&3:£7.30 CSF £164.44 CT £1564.40 TOTE £19.70: £4.60, £2.20, £2.70; EX 250.20.
Owner R Gander, R A Gadd, R Hannon **Bred** Hedsor Stud **Trained** Upper Lambourn, Berks

FOCUS
Although My Scat Daddy was a short price, this handicap looked relatively open, but a slow pace puts a question mark against the form.
My Scat Daddy(USA) Official explanation: trainer said gelding had a breathing problem

295 SKYSPORTS.COM H'CAP 6f (P)
6:40 (6:40) (Class 4) (0-85,82) 3-Y-0 **£4,075** (£1,212; £606; £303) **Stalls** Low

Form RPR

22-1 **1** **Pale Orchid (IRE)**[21] 37 3-8-11 72 LukeMorris 1 86+
(David Evans) *hld up in 5th: pushed along and prog 2f out: drvn to ld between rivals jst ins fnl f: styd on wl* **3/1**[2]

6-1 **2** *2 ¼* **Dark Castle**[14] 121 3-8-13 74 LiamKeniry 6 81+
(Sylvester Kirk) *hld up in 4th: prog to press ldr over 1f out: upsides ent fnl f: sn one pce and btn* **8/13**[1]

625- **3** *1 ¾* **Waseem Faris (IRE)**[26] 7918 3-9-7 82 MartinHarley 3 83
(Mick Channon) *led at decent pce: rdn 2f out: hdd jst ins fnl f: fdd* **12/1**

12-6 **4** *1 ¾* **Worth**[5] 230 3-9-2 77 (b) ShaneKelly 4 72
(Brian Meehan) *awkward s: settled in last: pushed along and no rspnse 2f out: kpt on to take 4th ins fnl f* **25/1**

000- **5** *4 ½* **Roy's Legacy**[81] 7294 3-7-11 65 NoraLooby(7) 2 46
(Shaun Harris) *chsd ldng pair to wl over 1f out: sn wknd* **66/1**

531- **6** *1 ¾* **Taffe**[26] 7918 3-9-7 82 FrederikTylicki 5 57
(James Given) *chsd ldr to wl over 1f out: wknd qckly* **7/1**[3]

1m 11.46s (-1.64) **Going Correction** 0.0s/f (Stan) 6 Ran SP% **112.5**
Speed ratings (Par 99): **110,107,104,102,96 94**
toteswingers:1&2:£1.50, 1&3:£2.40, 2&3:£2.00 CSF £5.22 TOTE £4.60: £1.40, £1.10; EX 5.30.
Owner Mrs E Evans **Bred** Mrs A J Donnelly **Trained** Pandy, Monmouths

FOCUS
A decent and strongly run handicap. The time was good.

296 ELLEN WESTCOTT MEMORIAL H'CAP 1m 4f (P)
7:10 (7:10) (Class 6) (0-65,65) 4-Y-0+ **£1,617** (£481; £240; £120) **Stalls** Centre

Form RPR

135- **1** **Honourable Knight (IRE)**[26] 7931 4-9-4 63 (be) DavidProbert 7 72
(Mark Usher) *racd wd in midfield: prog over 3f out to press ldrs 2f out: drvn to ld narrowly jst ins fnl f: kpt on wl* **4/1**[3]

21-4 **2** *½* **Beggers Belief**[19] 60 4-9-2 61 (b) WilliamCarson 6 69
(Eric Wheeler) *hld up in midfield: prog over 4f out to chse ldr over 3f out: drvn to chal 2f out: w wnr jst ins fnl f: could nt qckn last 75yds* **8/1**

12-1 **3** *2 ¼* **Shirataki (IRE)**[13] 130 4-9-5 64 ChrisCatlin 9 69+
(Peter Hiatt) *t.k.h: trckd ldr tl plld way into ld 7f out: hrd pressed over 2f out: kpt on tl hdd and no ex jst ins fnl f* **11/4**[1]

/12- **4** *1 ¼* **Sovento (GER)**[49] 7654 8-9-8 63 MartinHarley 4 66
(Shaun Harley, Ire) *hld up in 8th: prog over 3f out to trck ldrs over 2f out: rdn to chal wl over 1f out: nt qckn on inner and fdd ins fnl f* **10/3**[2]

000- **5** *½* **Time Square (FR)**[68] 7458 5-9-5 60 (t) LukeMorris 10 62
(Tony Carroll) *t.k.h: hld up in 9th: prog over 3f out to chse ldrs in 5th over 2f out: rdn and kpt on but nvr gng pce to threaten* **10/1**

556/ **6** *2 ¾* **Valmari (IRE)**[579] 3416 9-9-0 58 SimonPearce(3) 8 55
(Tom Symonds) *led 5f: chsd ldr to over 3f out: lost pl and struggling over 2f out: plugged on* **20/1**

030- **7** *10* **The Snorer**[26] 7931 4-9-0 59 RussKennemore 2 40
(John Holt) *prom: rdn over 3f out: sn wknd* **50/1**

3-50 **8** *½* **Irish Jugger (USA)**[12] 156 5-9-7 62 JamesMillman 3 43
(Rod Millman) *stdd s: hld up in last: brought wd bnd 3f out: shkn up briefly sn after: nvr remotely involved* **20/1**

020- **9** *hd* **Bin End**[28] 7121 6-9-3 58 FrankieMcDonald 1 38
(Barry Brennan) *chsd ldrs: rdn over 3f out: wknd over 2f out* **8/1**

/5-0 **10** *35* **Ayaarah (IRE)**[12] 150 4-9-1 60 (b[1]) LiamKeniry 5
(Les Hall) *prom tl rdn and wknd 4f out: wl t.o* **66/1**

2m 33.7s (-0.80) **Going Correction** 0.0s/f (Stan)
WFA 4 from 5yo+ 4lb 10 Ran SP% **114.0**
Speed ratings (Par 101): **102,101,100,99,99 97,90,90,90,66**
toteswingers:1&2:£7.70, 2&3:£3.10, 1&3:£3.30 CSF £33.33 CT £101.16 TOTE £4.30: £1.60, £2.20, £1.80; EX 27.40.
Owner Bryan Fry **Bred** Mohammed Al Sulaim **Trained** Upper Lambourn, Berks
■ Stewards' Enquiry : David Probert six-day ban: used whip with excessive frequency (Feb 8-11,13-14)
William Carson four-day ban: used whip with erxcessive frequency (Feb 9-11,13)

FOCUS
The form of this handicap looks sound.

Honourable Knight(IRE) Official explanation: trainer had no explanation for the apparent improvement in form
The Snorer Official explanation: jockey said gelding hung left in home straight
Bin End Official explanation: jockey said gelding had no more to give

297 SKYSPORTS.COM RACING H'CAP 6f (P)
7:40 (7:40) (Class 7) (0-50,54) 4-Y-0+ **£1,455** (£433; £216; £108) **Stalls** Low

Form RPR
40-0 **1** **Royal Envoy (IRE)**[14] 125 9-8-12 **45**....................(b[1]) MichaelStainton 8 52
(Paul Howling) *dwlt: t.k.h: hld up towards rr: prog jst over 2f out: rdn and styd on fr over 1f out to ld last strides* **8/1**[3]
30-4 **2** *nk* **Slatey Hen (IRE)**[17] 95 4-9-3 **50**.................................(p) MartinHarley 2 56
(Richard Guest) *trckd ldng trio gng wl: prog to ld over 1f out: drvn fnl f: hdd and nt qckn last strides* **10/1**
-01 **3** *3/4* **Avonvalley**[5] 227 5-9-7 **54** 6ex................................. RobbieFitzpatrick 11 58
(Peter Grayson) *t.k.h: hld up in last trio: prog on inner over 2f out: styd on to take 3rd wl ins fnl f: jst unable to chal* **13/2**[2]
-066 **4** *1/2* **Raimond Ridge (IRE)**[5] 226 6-8-12 **45**............................ MartinLane 7 47
(Derek Shaw) *trckd ldrs in 5th: rdn and prog on outer to chse ldr briefly jst over 1f out: nt qckn after* **16/1**
000/ **5** *nk* **All About You (IRE)**[425] 7570 6-9-3 **50**............................. AdamKirby 5 56+
(John Butler) *hld up in 6th: pushed along 2f out: nt clr run briefly 1f out: reminders and r.o wl nr fin: no ch* **7/4**[1]
00-2 **6** *3* **Pharoh Jake**[14] 118 4-8-12 **48**..................................... KieranO'Neill[(3)] 4 39
(John Bridger) *prom: chsd ldr wl over 2f out to over 1f out: wknd fnl f* **8/1**[3]
00-0 **7** *3/4* **Wee Buns**[13] 126 7-8-12 **45**... LiamKeniry 12 34
(Paul Burgoyne) *hld up in last trio: stl there and jst pushed along 2f out: one pce and no ch after* **50/1**
54-4 **8** *1/2* **Suhayl Star (IRE)**[13] 126 8-8-12 **45**................................. LukeMorris 6 32
(Paul Burgoyne) *led after 1f to over 1f out: wknd* **8/1**[3]
06-6 **9** *4* **Cara Carmela**[14] 118 4-8-9 **45**.. RyanClark[(3)] 1 20
(Stuart Williams) *led 1f: chsd ldr to wl over 2f out: wknd qckly* **14/1**
05-5 **10** *1 1/2* **Jemimaville (IRE)**[13] 126 5-8-12 **45**.......................... WilliamCarson 10 15
(Giles Bravery) *a towards rr: wd bnd 3f out: rdn and struggling sn after* **12/1**
000/ **11** *14* **Muktasb (USA)**[616] 2234 11-9-0 **50**..........................(v) RobertLButler[(3)] 9
(Richard Guest) *awkward s: a in last trio: wknd 1/2-way: t.o* **25/1**

1m 12.81s (-0.29) **Going Correction** 0.0s/f (Stan) **11** Ran SP% **118.2**
Speed ratings (Par 97): **101,100,99,98,98 94,93,92,87,85 66**
toteswingers:1&2:£13.30, 2&3:£7.00, 1&3:£15.20 CSF £85.84 CT £565.40 TOTE £10.90: £2.80, £3.50, £2.00; EX 99.90.
Owner James Esau **Bred** Northern Lights Bloodstock **Trained** Lee-On-The-Solent, Hants

FOCUS
Very moderate stuff.
T/Jkpt: £29,611.50 to a £1 stake. Pool of £41,706.45 - 1.00 winning tickets. T/Plt: £76.60 to a £1 stake. Pool of £68,483.97 - 652.22 winning tickets. T/Qpdt: £27.70 to a £1 stake. Pool of £8,366.63 -223.10 winning tickets. JN

[248]LINGFIELD (L-H)
Wednesday, January 25

OFFICIAL GOING: Standard
Wind: medium, half behind Weather: overcast, dry

298 BLUE SQUARE WINTER CARNIVAL IPHONE APP MAIDEN STKS 6f (P)
12:50 (12:53) (Class 5) 3-Y-0 **£2,385** (£704; £352) **Stalls** Low

Form RPR
42-3 **1** **Sujet Bellagio**[11] 181 3-9-3 78.. ShaneKelly 5 77
(Brian Meehan) *mde all: rdn and qcknd ahd wl over 1f out: styd on wl: rdn out* **5/4**[1]
2 *1 1/4* **Piece Of Cake** 3-8-12 0.. MichaelHills 1 68
(Charles Hills) *dwlt: in tch in last pair: pushed along over 2f out: hdwy on inner over 1f out: chsd wnr fnl 100yds: kpt on* **5/1**[3]
64-4 **3** *1/2* **Fugitive Motel (IRE)**[11] 182 3-9-3 69........................... JimmyFortune 4 71
(Peter Chapple-Hyam) *taken down early: in tch: rdn over 2f out: hdwy u.p 1f out: edgd lft but r.o wl ins fnl f* **8/1**
4 *1* **Sugar Prince (IRE)** 3-9-3 0.. MartinLane 2 68
(Tim Pitt) *in tch: rdn 1/2-way: kpt on u.p and chsd wnr briefly ins fnl f: no imp and lost 2 pls fnl 100yds* **66/1**
3-4 **5** *1 1/2* **Vale Of Lingfield (IRE)**[11] 181 3-9-3 0............................ LukeMorris 8 63
(John Best) *w wnr: ev ch and rdn 2f out: drvn and unable qck wl over 1f out: wknd 1f out* **7/2**[2]
6 *1/2* **Ginger Monkey (IRE)** 3-9-3 0... AdamKirby 3 61
(J S Moore) *s.i.s: rn green in last pair: sme hdwy u.p over 1f out: kpt on ins fnl f: nvr threatened ldrs* **20/1**
5 **7** *1* **Marinus (IRE)**[11] 181 3-9-3 0.. LiamKeniry 6 58
(Sylvester Kirk) *t.k.h early: chsd ldng pair: rdn and unable qck wl over 1f out: drvn and wknd ent fnl f* **7/1**

1m 12.08s (0.18) **Going Correction** -0.025s/f (Stan) **7** Ran SP% **113.2**
Speed ratings (Par 97): **97,95,94,93,91 90,89**
toteswingers:1&2:£2.10, 1&3:£2.10, 2&3:£5.10 CSF £7.78 TOTE £2.00: £1.10, £3.50; EX 8.60 Trifecta £55.70 Pool: £428.61 - 5.69 winning units..
Owner Lanesborough **Bred** Howard Barton Stud **Trained** Manton, Wilts

FOCUS
Probably just a fair maiden but one run at a steady gallop initially with experience and a prominent position proving key, so it's likely to be muddling form.

299 TANDRIDGE CLAIMING STKS 1m (P)
1:20 (1:20) (Class 6) 4-Y-0+ **£1,704** (£503; £251) **Stalls** High

Form RPR
34-1 **1** **Munsarim (IRE)**[12] 158 5-9-5 80...................................(b) JoeFanning 1 87
(Keith Dalgleish) *trckd ldrs: shkn up wl over 1f out: rdn to chal jst ins fnl f: edgd rt and led wl ins fnl f: r.o wl* **5/2**[2]
46-3 **2** *1/2* **Red Somerset (USA)**[7] 198 9-8-4 78.......................... KieranO'Neill[(3)] 6 74
(Mike Murphy) *chsd ldr: ev ch and rdn 2f out: drvn over 1f out: led jst ins fnl f: hdd and no ex wl ins fnl f* **7/1**
1-12 **3** *1 1/4* **Marajaa (IRE)**[7] 198 10-9-3 82...................................... JamieMackay 3 81
(Willie Musson) *stdd s: hld up in tch in last trio: rdn and effrt over 1f out: nt clr run and swtchd rt 1f out: r.o fnl 100yds: unable to rch ldrs* **7/4**[1]
0-41 **4** *nk* **Spinning Ridge (IRE)**[7] 198 7-8-13 68.........................(v) LukeMorris 5 76
(Ronald Harris) *in tch: chsd ldrs and rdn 2f out: drvn over 1f out: kpt on same pce ins fnl f* **14/1**
0506 **5** *1/2* **Opus Maximus (IRE)**[1] 280 7-9-5 79............................ HayleyTurner 4 81
(Conor Dore) *stdd s: hld up in tch in last: rdn and effrt over 1f out: kpt on ins fnl f: nvr able to chal* **6/1**[3]
2-25 **6** *2 1/4* **Sunnyside Tom (IRE)**[12] 158 8-8-9 73.......................... PaulHanagan 2 66
(Richard Fahey) *taken down early: led: rdn wl over 1f out: drvn and hdd jst ins fnl f: sn wknd* **12/1**
044- **7** *9* **Wishformore (IRE)**[74] 7399 5-7-13 59.........................(p) RyanPowell[(3)] 7 38
(J S Moore) *in tch in outer: rdn and struggling over 2f out: wknd and bhd over 1f out* **33/1**

1m 36.72s (-1.48) **Going Correction** -0.025s/f (Stan) **7** Ran SP% **109.0**
Speed ratings (Par 101): **106,105,104,103,103 101,92**
toteswingers:1&2:£2.90, 1&3:£1.90, 2&3:£3.10 CSF £18.14 TOTE £2.90: £1.40, £3.40; EX 18.20.
Owner Joseph Leckie & Sons Ltd **Bred** Shadwell Estate Company Limited **Trained** Carluke, S Lanarks

FOCUS
A wide variety of abilities on show in a claimer that turned into something of a tactical affair, with a prominent position an advantage.
Wishformore(IRE) Official explanation: jockey said mare hung right

300 LINGFIELD PARK MEDIAN AUCTION MAIDEN STKS 1m 4f (P)
1:50 (1:50) (Class 6) 4-6-Y-0 **£1,704** (£503; £251) **Stalls** Low

Form RPR
224- **1** **Tappanappa (IRE)**[213] 3428 5-9-7 79.............................. DavidProbert 5 74+
(Andrew Balding) *chsd ldrs: wnt 2nd over 2f out: rdn to ld over 1f out: nt doing much in front and drvn 1f out: kpt on and a holding rival* **2/11**[1]
2 *3/4* **Red Shuttle**[375] 5-9-7 0...(t) AdamKirby 2 73
(Noel Quinlan) *stdd s: hld up in last pair: hdwy to chse ldng pair over 2f out: rdn and chsd wnr 1f out: drvn and styd on same pce ins fnl f* **20/1**
4 **3** *4 1/2* **Candelita**[13] 137 5-8-9 0.. JoshBaudains[(7)] 6 61
(Jo Hughes) *chsd ldr tl led over 3f out: rdn 2f out: hdd over 1f out: outpcd ins fnl f* **5/1**[2]
4 **4** *25* **Danaher**[19] 65 5-9-7 0.. IanMongan 3 26
(George Margarson) *stdd s: hld up in last pair: rdn over 4f out: lost tch over 2f out* **20/1**
043- **5** *4* **Gay Gallivanter**[26] 7920 4-8-12 46.................................. NickyMackay 7 15
(Michael Quinn) *led tl hdd and rdn over 3f out: wknd over 2f out: wl bhd over 1f out* **14/1**[3]

2m 31.84s (-1.16) **Going Correction** -0.025s/f (Stan)
WFA 4 from 5yo 4lb **5** Ran SP% **117.5**
Speed ratings: **102,101,98,81,79**
CSF £7.51 TOTE £1.20: £1.02, £6.40; EX 9.70.
Owner McMahon/Gorell/Pausewang **Bred** P Monaghan, J Collins & G Dillon **Trained** Kingsclere, Hants

FOCUS
A typically uncompetitive older horse maiden for the time of year, though at least it seemed to be well run.

301 LINGFIELDPARK.CO.UK H'CAP (DIV I) 1m (P)
2:20 (2:20) (Class 5) (0-75,81) 4-Y-0+ **£2,385** (£704; £352) **Stalls** High

Form RPR
00-1 **1** **Prince Of Burma (IRE)**[7] 199 4-9-13 **81** 6ex...............(b) IanMongan 8 92
(Jeremy Gask) *dwlt: sn rcvrd and t.k.h in midfield: gd hdwy on inner to ld 2f out: clr whn veered rt u.p 1f out: r.o wl and drew clr again fnl 100yds: readily* **2/1**[1]
20-0 **2** *2 1/2* **Master Of Dance (IRE)**[13] 136 5-9-1 **69**.......................(p) JoeFanning 4 75
(Keith Dalgleish) *hld up in tch: rdn and hdwy over 1f out: chsd ldrs ins fnl f: r.o wl and wnt 2nd wl ins fnl f: no threat to wnr* **12/1**
20-2 **3** *3/4* **Hereford Boy**[19] 54 8-9-5 **73**..(v) AdamKirby 6 77
(Dean Ivory) *stdd after s: hld up in tch towards rr: hdwy on inner over 2f out: chsd wnr 1f out: no ex and outpcd fnl 100yds: lost 2nd wl ins fnl f* **11/2**[3]
23-3 **4** *1/2* **Woolston Ferry (IRE)**[21] 31 6-8-13 **67**.................... FergusSweeney 2 70
(David Pinder) *hld up in tch towards rr: rdn and effrt towards inner over 1f out: r.o ins fnl f: nvr threatened wnr* **14/1**
004- **5** *1/2* **Salient**[25] 7941 8-9-2 **70**.. ShaneKelly 10 72
(Michael Attwater) *chsd ldr tl led over 4f out: hdd and rdn 2f out: 3rd and hld whn sltly hmpd 1f out: wknd fnl 150yds* **12/1**
106- **6** *hd* **Casual Mover (IRE)**[35] 7842 4-9-4 **72**............................... LukeMorris 9 73
(John Best) *t.k.h: hld up in tch in midfield: rdn over 2f out: lost pl bnd 2f out: rallied and kpt on ins fnl f: no threat to wnr* **33/1**
-411 **7** *1 1/2* **City Legend**[2] 269 4-9-7 **78** 6ex...............................(bt) KieranO'Neill[(3)] 1 76
(Alan McCabe) *led tl over 4f out: chsd ldr tl rdn and lost pl jst over 2f out: no threat to wnr and plugged on same pce u.p fr over 1f out* **5/1**[2]
25-2 **8** *3/4* **Grand Theft Equine**[21] 31 4-8-13 **67**........................ StephenCraine 5 63
(Jim Boyle) *hld up in tch towards rr: hdwy and midfield whn rdn 2f out: no ex over 1f out: wknd fnl f* **13/2**
64-5 **9** *nse* **Cativo Cavallino**[18] 91 9-8-12 **66**................................ SamHitchcott 7 62
(John E Long) *chsd ldrs: rdn and unable qck over 2f out: wknd over 1f out* **16/1**
143- **10** *11* **Full Bloom**[43] 7745 4-9-6 **74**...(p) SteveDrowne 3 45
(Gerard Butler) *chsd ldrs tl pushed along and lost pl qckly over 3f out: bhd fr wl over 1f out* **10/1**

1m 37.41s (-0.79) **Going Correction** -0.025s/f (Stan) **10** Ran SP% **118.7**
Speed ratings (Par 103): **102,99,98,98,97 97,96,95,95,84**
toteswingers:1&2:£7.80, 1&3:£1.70, 2&3:£22.80 CSF £29.24 CT £119.24 TOTE £3.40: £1.30, £4.20, £1.40; EX 32.00 Trifecta £149.00 Pool: £670.61 - 3.33 winning units..
Owner The Nobles **Bred** P Burns **Trained** Sutton Veny, Wilts

FOCUS
A fair handicap that only really started to take shape once the pace lifted soon after halfway.
Full Bloom Official explanation: jockey said filly never travelled

302 LINGFIELDPARK.CO.UK H'CAP (DIV II) 1m (P)
2:50 (2:50) (Class 5) (0-75,75) 4-Y-0+ **£2,385** (£704; £352) **Stalls** High

Form RPR
00-1 **1** **Aquarian Spirit**[19] 54 5-9-7 **75**....................................... PaulHanagan 5 81
(Richard Fahey) *led at stdy gallop: rdn 2f out: hdd over 1f out: stl ev ch 1f out: led again ins fnl f: kpt on wl* **4/1**[2]
66-5 **2** *nk* **The Happy Hammer (IRE)**[13] 128 6-8-13 **67**............ WilliamCarson 7 73
(Eugene Stanford) *chsd ldrs: rdn and effrt 2f out: ev ch ins fnl f: kpt on* **3/1**[1]
043- **3** *hd* **Tiradito (USA)**[51] 7636 5-9-0 **73**..............................(p) MarkCoumbe[(5)] 9 78
(Michael Attwater) *t.k.h: hld up in tch: hdwy on outer to chse ldrs 2f out: drvn and led narrowly over 1f out: hdd ins fnl f: no ex u.p fnl 100yds* **8/1**
66-6 **4** *1/2* **Mishrif (USA)**[21] 33 6-9-6 **74**...(b) JoeFanning 8 78
(J R Jenkins) *chsd ldrs: wnt 2nd 5f out: rdn and ev ch wl over 1f out: no ex wl ins fnl f: stl cl up but btn whn short of room and eased nr fin* **4/1**[2]

00-1 5 1 **Hip Hip Hooray**[21] 31 6-9-0 **68** .... IanMongan 3 70
(Luke Dace) *stdd s: hld up in tch in last pair: hdwy on outer into midfield over 3f out: rdn and unable qck wl over 1f out: styd on same pce u.p ins fnl f* **8/1**

406- 6 *shd* **Getcarter**[124] 6303 6-9-2 **70** .... LukeMorris 2 73+
(John Best) *t.k.h: hld up in tch: stdd bk and last but stl wl in tch 3f out: rdn and hdwy to chse ldrs over 1f out: nt clr run 1f out: swtchd rt ins fnl f but stl nt clr run and eased off fnl 50yds* **22/1**

306- 7 1 ¾ **Junket**[81] 7299 5-9-4 **72** .... ShaneKelly 4 69
(Dr Jon Scargill) *hld up in tch in midfield: effrt whn short of room 2f out: rdn over 1f out: styd on ins fnl f but no threat to ldrs: eased towards fin* **11/2**[3]

12-2 8 1 ¼ **Northern Spy (USA)**[19] 55 8-8-11 **65** .... HayleyTurner 1 59
(Simon Dow) *chsd ldr tl 5f out: chsd ldrs after tl rdn and struggling over 2f out: wknd 1f out* **16/1**

1m 38.43s (0.23) **Going Correction** -0.025s/f (Stan) **8** Ran SP% **112.8**
Speed ratings (Par 103): **97,96,96,96,95 94,93,91**
toteswingers:1&2:£2.90, 1&3:£8.20, 2&3:£5.60 CSF £15.97 CT £89.01 TOTE £3.80: £1.70, £1.40, £2.20; EX 13.40 Trifecta £127.40 Pool: £626.91 - 3.64 winning units..
Owner P S Cresswell & Mrs P A Morrison **Bred** Whitwell Bloodstock **Trained** Musley Bank, N Yorks

FOCUS
The weaker of the two divisions but, like the first, another race run at a muddling gallop and probably not form to take too much at face value.
Getcarter Official explanation: jockey said gelding was denied a clear run

303 HOLLOW LANE H'CAP 1m 5f (P)
3:20 (3:21) (Class 6) (0-60,60) 4-Y-O+ **£1,704** (£503; £251) **Stalls** Low

Form RPR

0/-2 1 **Celtic Charlie (FR)**[7] 200 7-8-5 **46** oh1 .... JemmaMarshall(5) 1 53
(Pat Phelan) *chsd ldr tl led over 2f out: sn rdn clr: drvn 1f out: coming bk to rivals but a gng to hold on: eased nr fin* **8/1**

5/4- 2 1 **Broughtons Bandit**[34] 7859 5-8-10 **46** oh1 .... StevieDonohoe 3 52
(Willie Musson) *hld up in last trio: rdn and effrt on outer 3f out: modest 5th and drvn wl over 1f out: styd on wl ins fnl f: wnt 2nd wl ins fnl f: nvr quite getting to wnr* **14/1**

220- 3 ½ **Vertueux (FR)**[30] 6722 7-9-4 **57** .... MichaelO'Connell(3) 4 62
(Tony Carroll) *rrd s and slowly away: sn in tch in midfield: rdn and effrt into modest 4th over 2f out: kpt on u.p ins fnl f: wnt 3rd cl home* **10/1**

54-3 4 ½ **Prince Blue**[12] 151 5-9-2 **52** .... SamHitchcott 2 56
(John E Long) *led tl over 9f out: chsd ldrs after: 3rd and rdn over 2f out: chsd clr wnr 2f out: kpt on: lost 2 pls wl ins fnl f* **7/1**[3]

00-2 5 8 **Satwa Ballerina**[19] 65 4-8-5 **53** ....(b) RachealKneller(7) 8 45
(Mark Rimmer) *in tch: hmpd: stmbld and dropped to rr after 1f: rdn and sme modest hdwy over 2f out: no imp and wl hld fnl 2f* **16/1**

00-3 6 3 ¾ **Sumani (FR)**[21] 28 6-9-10 **60** .... HayleyTurner 6 47
(Simon Dow) *chsd ldr tl led over 9f out: hdd and rdn over 2f out: 3rd and wkng 2f out: sn fdd* **5/2**[1]

00-3 7 1 ¾ **Farmers Hill**[7] 200 4-8-2 **46** oh1 .... RyanPowell(3) 7 30
(Mark Hoad) *hld up in tch: rdn and struggling wl over 3f out: wknd wl over 2f out* **8/1**

30- 8 9 **Manshoor (IRE)**[78] 6546 7-9-9 **59** .... LukeMorris 5 30
(Lucy Wadham) *dwlt: sn rcvrd and in tch: rdn and wknd 3f out: wl bhd fnl 2f* **7/2**[2]

3-53 9 1 **Vehement**[12] 149 6-9-10 **60** .... DaneO'Neill 9 29
(Andy Turnell) *t.k.h: chsd ldrs: edgd lft bnd after 1f: rdn and struggling 4f out: sn wknd: bhd fnl 2f* **10/1**

2m 45.26s (-0.74) **Going Correction** -0.025s/f (Stan)
WFA 4 from 5yo+ 5lb **9** Ran SP% **116.2**
Speed ratings (Par 101): **101,100,100,99,94 92,91,85,85**
toteswingers:1&2:£29.10, 1&3:£8.40, 2&3:£20.20 CSF £112.57 CT £1131.91 TOTE £11.50: £2.80, £3.80, £2.30; EX 177.90 TRIFECTA Not won..
Owner Celtic Contractors Limited **Bred** S N C Regnier & San Gabriel Inv Inc **Trained** Epsom, Surrey
■ Stewards' Enquiry : Dane O'Neill four-day ban: careless riding (Feb 8-11)

FOCUS
A modest handicap run at a steady gallop until the pace increased sharply at the top of the hill, leaving the second and third with plenty to do.

304 EXCLUSIVE LIVE SHOWS AT BLUESQ.COM H'CAP 7f (P)
3:50 (3:50) (Class 4) (0-85,85) 4-Y-O+ **£4,431** (£1,308; £654) **Stalls** Low

Form RPR

62-2 1 **Shifting Star (IRE)**[13] 131 7-9-6 **84** .... IanMongan 7 93
(John Bridger) *hld up in tch: rdn and hdwy 2f out: chsd ldr jst over 1f out: r.o wl to ld cl home* **13/2**[3]

30-5 2 *nk* **Chilli Green**[18] 90 5-9-4 **82** .... DaneO'Neill 6 90
(John Akehurst) *chsd ldrs: hdwy to ld over 2f out: rdn over 1f out: r.o u.p fnl f: hdd and no ex cl home* **9/2**[2]

022- 3 3 ¾ **Arctic Lynx (IRE)**[28] 7893 5-8-12 **76** .... JimCrowley 2 74
(John Best) *hld up in tch in last trio: hdwy on inner over 1f out: drvn and chsd ldng pair ent fnl f: no ex and wknd 100yds out* **9/2**[2]

56-1 4 1 ¼ **Podgies Boy (IRE)**[15] 115 4-8-12 **76** .... PaulHanagan 8 71
(Richard Fahey) *t.k.h: hld up in last pair: rdn and effrt on outer ent fnl 2f: no imp over 1f out tl styd on ins fnl f: nvr trbld ldrs* **9/4**[1]

21-3 5 *nk* **Tislaam (IRE)**[12] 157 5-8-12 **76** ....(p) MartinHarley 1 70
(Alan McCabe) *led: rdn and hdd over 2f out: 4th and btn ent fnl f* **7/1**

34-2 6 ¾ **Piceno (IRE)**[13] 134 4-8-10 **77** ....(b) RyanPowell(3) 4 69
(Scott Dixon) *chsd ldr tl over 2f out: wknd u.p over 1f out* **10/1**

1-06 7 *hd* **Frequency**[12] 157 5-9-0 **78** ....(b) ShaneKelly 3 69
(Keith Dalgleish) *chsd ldrs: rdn and unable qck wl over 1f out: wknd ent fnl f* **12/1**

00-5 8 3 **Dozy Joe**[21] 29 4-9-7 **85** ....(vt¹) LukeMorris 5 68
(Ian Wood) *dwlt: in tch in rr: pushed along wl over 2f out: rdn and wknd over 1f out* **9/1**

1m 23.22s (-1.58) **Going Correction** -0.025s/f (Stan) **8** Ran SP% **119.7**
Speed ratings (Par 105): **108,107,103,101,101 100,100,97**
toteswingers:1&2:£6.20, 1&3:£5.60, 2&3:£4.70 CSF £37.55 CT £149.17 TOTE £8.50: £2.90, £2.20, £1.90; EX 47.60 Trifecta £113.40 Pool: £443.10 - 2.89 winning units..
Owner Night Shadow Syndicate **Bred** Hardys Of Kilkeel Ltd **Trained** Liphook, Hants

FOCUS
Not quite the depth that one expects in a 0-85 handicap, so probably just ordinary form. The pace was just fair.

305 PLAY BINGO FREE AT BLUESQ.COM APPRENTICE H'CAP 7f (P)
4:20 (4:20) (Class 6) (0-60,66) 4-Y-O+ **£1,704** (£503; £251) **Stalls** Low

Form RPR

-622 1 **Crocodile Bay (IRE)**[12] 153 9-8-10 **49** ....(p) NoraLooby 3 55
(Richard Guest) *chsd ldr tl pushed into ld over 1f out: kpt on wl fnl f* **4/1**[3]

00-5 2 ½ **Monadreen Dancer**[5] 232 4-9-2 **55** .... ThomasBrown 5 60
(Daniel Mark Loughnane) *hld up in tch: rdn and effrt 2f out: styd on u.p to chse wnr fnl f: clsng towards fin* **13/2**

34-4 3 ¾ **Lovat Lane**[14] 125 4-8-7 **46** .... NatashaEaton 4 49
(Eve Johnson Houghton) *t.k.h: hld up in last pair: rdn and hdwy over 1f out: wnt 3rd wl ins fnl f: styd on* **9/1**

30-5 4 1 **Ermyntrude**[14] 122 5-9-3 **56** .... JakePayne 2 56
(Pat Phelan) *chsd ldrs: styd on same pce u.p fr over 1f out* **11/4**[2]

0-01 5 *hd* **Waterloo Dock**[7] 210 7-9-13 **66** 6ex ....(v) MichaelJMurphy 1 66
(Michael Quinn) *led tl hdd and drvn over 1f out: no ex and btn jst ins fnl f* **5/2**[1]

-563 6 *hd* **Jonnie Skull (IRE)**[15] 113 6-8-12 **51** ....(vt) DannyBrock 7 50
(Phil McEntee) *stdd and dropped in bhd after s: t.k.h: hld up in tch in rr: rdn over 2f out: kpt on ins fnl f* **6/1**

1m 24.84s (0.04) **Going Correction** -0.025s/f (Stan) **6** Ran SP% **112.9**
Speed ratings (Par 101): **98,97,96,95,95 94**
toteswingers:1&2:£3.70, 1&3:£5.10, 2&3:£7.30 CSF £29.20 TOTE £5.70: £2.90, £3.10; EX 29.90.
Owner Future Racing (Notts) Limited **Bred** James And Joe Brannigan **Trained** Stainforth, S Yorks
■ Stewards' Enquiry : Thomas Brown two-day ban: used whip with excessive frequency (Feb 8-9)

FOCUS
A modest finale for apprentices which was run at just an ordinary gallop.
T/Plt: £121.50 to a £1 stake. Pool:£50,997.06 - 306.34 winning tickets T/Qpdt: £42.90 to a £1 stake. Pool:£4,384.89 - 75.60 winning tickets SP

291 KEMPTON (A.W) (R-H)
Thursday, January 26

OFFICIAL GOING: Standard
Wind: moderate, across Weather: Fine

306 32RED H'CAP 1m (P)
4:35 (4:35) (Class 6) (0-60,59) 4-Y-O+ **£1,617** (£481; £240; £120) **Stalls** Low

Form RPR

066- 1 **Rezwaan**[28] 7904 5-9-6 **58** ....(be) ShaneKelly 12 75+
(Murty McGrath) *hld up in last trio: smooth prog over 2f out: led over 1f out: drew rt away: easily* **7/1**

40-0 2 4 ½ **Gallantry**[14] 130 10-9-4 **56** .... TomMcLaughlin 7 61
(Paul Howling) *hld up in last trio: prog over 2f out following wnr through: rdn and styd on to take 2nd ins fnl f: no ch* **20/1**

00-1 3 1 ½ **Qeethaara (USA)**[11] 183 8-8-13 **58** ....(p) JackDuern(7) 4 60
(Mark Brisbourne) *dwlt: hld up towards rr: prog over 3f out: led jst over 2f out: hung lft and hdd over 1f out: no ch w wnr after: lost 2nd ins fnl f* **11/2**[2]

1-34 4 1 ¾ **Storm Runner (IRE)**[6] 225 4-9-4 **59** .... RyanPowell(3) 10 57+
(George Margarson) *stdd s and sn detached in last: alongside eventual wnr and runner-up in last trio 1/2-way: effrt over 2f out: styd on fr over 1f out: nvr able to land a blow* **9/4**[1]

051- 5 *hd* **Karate (IRE)**[28] 7910 4-9-0 **59** ....(t) NicoleNordblad(7) 6 56
(Hans Adielsson) *w.w in midfield: prog and cl up bhd ldrs 2f out: sn outpcd: fdd ins fnl f* **7/1**

63-4 6 8 **Dichoh**[20] 55 9-9-6 **58** ....(v) ChrisCatlin 8 37
(Michael Madgwick) *prom tl wknd over 2f out* **16/1**

/00- 7 1 **Sabys Gem (IRE)**[115] 6580 4-9-0 **52** .... JimCrowley 13 28
(Michael Wigham) *racd wd: in tch tl wknd over 2f out* **12/1**

000- 8 ½ **Pie Poudre**[154] 5414 5-9-4 **56** .... TomEaves 9 31
(Roy Brotherton) *taken down early: towards rr: brief effrt 2f out but already no ch: sn wknd* **33/1**

6-56 9 1 ¼ **Putin (IRE)**[8] 207 4-8-8 **53** ....(bt) LeonnaMayor(7) 2 25
(Phil McEntee) *mistimed break: rcvrd and sn chsd ldr: led 5f out to over 2f out: wknd* **33/1**

535- 10 7 **Isdaal**[28] 7904 5-9-4 **56** ....(p) JoeFanning 3 12
(Kevin Morgan) *led to 5f out: led again briefly over 2f out: wknd rapidly over 1f out: t.o* **13/2**[3]

306- 11 ½ **Gordy Bee (USA)**[44] 7748 6-8-7 **50** ....(e) CharlesEddery(5) 1
(Richard Guest) *prom: rdn and lost grnd qckly on inner over 3f out: t.o* **33/1**

000- 12 33 **Unbreak My Heart (IRE)**[150] 5538 7-9-1 **53** ....(tp) WilliamCarson 11
(Richard Guest) *chsd ldrs tl wknd v rapidly over 2f out: wl t.o* **16/1**

1m 38.6s (-1.20) **Going Correction** +0.025s/f (Slow) **12** Ran SP% **117.5**
Speed ratings (Par 101): **107,102,101,99,99 91,90,89,88,81 80,47**
toteswingers:1&2:£39.60, 1&3:£5.90, 2&3:£28.80 CSF £142.21 CT £827.35 TOTE £9.90: £2.30, £6.10, £1.80; EX 212.70 TRIFECTA Not won..
Owner Gallagher Equine Ltd **Bred** Shadwell Estate Company Limited **Trained** East Malling, Kent
■ Murty McGrath's first winner since 2009.

FOCUS
An ordinary handicap which looked competitive enough on paper. The pace was good and the principals came from the rear, with the first five a long way clear of the others. The bare form of the winner is still around 8lb off his best.

307 32RED.COM H'CAP 7f (P)
5:05 (5:05) (Class 7) (0-50,51) 4-Y-O+ **£1,455** (£433; £216; £108) **Stalls** Low

Form RPR

34-4 1 **Fearless Poet (IRE)**[16] 109 4-9-1 **48** ....(b) TomEaves 6 58
(Bryan Smart) *trckd ldr: led 2f out: drvn and styd on fr over 1f out* **7/2**[1]

32-4 2 1 ½ **Royal Acclamation (IRE)**[21] 46 7-8-10 **48** ....(p) DavidKenny(5) 2 54
(Michael Scudamore) *trckd ldrs: rdn to chse wnr wl over 1f out: one pce and hld ins fnl f* **4/1**[2]

0-05 3 *hd* **Jackie Love (IRE)**[4] 264 4-8-9 **49** ....(v) JenniferFerguson(7) 7 54
(Olivia Maylam) *dwlt: settled in last trio: prog on inner 2f out: styd on fnl f: nrly snatched 2nd* **15/2**

0310 4 ¾ **Kyncraighe (IRE)**[4] 264 4-8-11 **51** 6ex ....(tp) LeonnaMayor(7) 10 54+
(Joseph Tuite) *stdd s: hld up in detached last: brought wd in st: sme prog 2f out: styd on fnl f: no ch of rching ldrs* **13/2**

36-5 **5** 1 **Set To Go**[7] 218 5-8-10 **46**....(v[1]) RossAtkinson(3) 9 47
(Tor Sturgis) *chsd ldrs: rdn over 2f out: nt qckn and lost pl: styd on again ins fnl f* **13/2**

566- **6** ½ **Bunkered Again**[37] 7834 5-8-7 **45**....(bt) RaulDaSilva(5) 3 44
(Jeremy Gask) *towards rr: prog over 2f out: chsd ldng pair over 1f out tl ins fnl f: fdd* **5/1**[3]

50-0 **7** 1 ¾ **Whats Your Story**[13] 146 4-8-12 **45**....(b[1]) ShaneKelly 12 40
(Murty McGrath) *stdd s: hld up in last trio: sme prog 2f out: shkn up and no hdwy fnl f: eased whn no ch nr fin* **40/1**

505- **8** ¾ **Magical Star**[214] 3431 4-8-5 **45**.... RichardOld(7) 1 38
(Michael Wigham) *towards rr: effrt over 2f out and cl enough wl over 1f out: bmpd along and wknd* **25/1**

0-00 **9** 5 **Blazing Apostle (IRE)**[4] 264 4-8-12 **45**....(v[1]) ChrisCatlin 4 24
(Christine Dunnett) *led to 2f out: wknd qckly* **40/1**

05-0 **10** 6 **Rise To Glory (IRE)**[7] 218 4-8-5 **45**....(t) NoraLooby(7) 14
(Denis P Quinn, Ire) *racd wd: prom tl lost grnd on bnd 3f out: wknd qckly sn after* **12/1**

1m 26.44s (0.44) **Going Correction** +0.025s/f (Slow) **10** Ran SP% **113.7**
Speed ratings (Par 97): **98,96,96,95,94 93,91,90,84,78**
toteswingers:1&2:£2.60, 1&3:£6.20, 2&3:£8.20 CSF £16.65 CT £95.48 TOTE £4.20: £1.70, £1.60, £2.60; EX 14.90 Trifecta £49.40 Pool: £349.19 - 5.23 winning units..
Owner The Smart Fear Not Partnership **Bred** Messrs N McSweeney & Jeff O'Callaghan **Trained** Hambleton, N Yorks

FOCUS
A bottom-drawer handicap and straightforward form. The winner is rated to his Southwell mark.

308 32RED CASINO MEDIAN AUCTION MAIDEN STKS 7f (P)
5:35 (5:35) (Class 6) 3-5-Y-O **£1,617** (£481; £240; £120) **Stalls** Low

Form RPR

1 **Fairway To Heaven (IRE)** 3-8-8 0.... JimCrowley 2 75+
(Michael Wigham) *t.k.h: hld up in last pair: smooth prog and squeezed through 2f out: led over 1f out: rdn and hung bdly lft ent fnl f and bmpd runner-up: styd on* **11/2**

53- **2** ½ **Kalokagathia (IRE)**[49] 7672 3-8-8 0.... FergusSweeney 3 74+
(Jo Crowley) *sn settled bhd ldrs: effrt 2f out: wnt 2nd 1f out: bmpd by wnr sn after: clsd grad nr fin* **16/5**[1]

0-2 **3** 1 ¼ **Ashdown Lad**[13] 147 3-8-8 0.... SteveDrowne 1 70
(William Jarvis) *hld up in last pair: prog to chal 2f out: sn rdn and nt qckn: styd on same pce fnl f* **4/1**[2]

34-3 **4** 1 ¼ **Mister Mackenzie**[15] 121 3-8-8 65.... LukeMorris 8 67
(John Best) *t.k.h: sn trckd ldr: led over 4f out: drvn and hdd over 1f out: one pce* **4/1**[2]

322- **5** 2 ¼ **Remix (IRE)**[41] 7783 3-8-3 69.... ChrisCatlin 5 56
(J W Hills) *in tch: pushed along fr 1/2-way: struggling over 2f out: tried to rally over 1f out: no imp after* **7/1**

6 3 ¼ **Red Trump (IRE)** 3-8-8 0.... WilliamCarson 4 52+
(Charles Hills) *nvr really gng wl: rdn on outer 1/2-way: struggling over 2f out* **9/2**[3]

0 **7** 2 ¼ **Fleeting Indian (IRE)**[12] 182 3-8-8 0.... MartinLane 6 46
(Linda Jewell) *led to over 4f out: chsd ldr to jst over 2f out: wknd* **100/1**

0- **8** 3 ½ **Yalding Dancer**[49] 7672 3-8-3 0.... DavidProbert 7 31
(John Best) *tk fierce hold: prom and rn green: wknd 2f out* **66/1**

1m 26.53s (0.53) **Going Correction** +0.025s/f (Slow) **8** Ran SP% **112.4**
Speed ratings (Par 101): **97,96,95,93,91 87,84,80**
toteswingers:1&2:£6.00, 2&3:£2.60, 1&3:£5.90 CSF £22.60 TOTE £3.50: £1.10, £1.70, £1.90; EX 30.00 Trifecta £93.80 Pool: £252.39 - 1.99 winning units..
Owner Palatinate Thoroughbred Racing Limited **Bred** J Cullinan **Trained** Newmarket, Suffolk

FOCUS
An interesting maiden which was run at a muddling early pace with several pulling for their heads, and in an ordinary time. There was a stewards' enquiry into an incident between the first two but the result stood. Ordinary form but there are positives to take from the first two. The level is set around the fourth.

309 £32 FREE AT 32RED.COM H'CAP 2m (P)
6:05 (6:05) (Class 5) (0-70,70) 4-Y-0+ **£2,264** (£673; £336; £168) **Stalls** Low

Form RPR

60-1 **1** **Steady Gaze**[2] 278 7-9-5 **61** 6ex.... AmirQuinn 1 72+
(Richard Rowe) *trckd ldr to 9f out: styd cl up: effrt gng wl to ld on inner wl over 1f out: edgd lft but pushed clr: readily* **5/2**[1]

442- **2** 3 ½ **Blackmore**[28] 7914 5-9-12 **68**.... LukeMorris 7 75
(Julia Feilden) *led: set stdy pce tl past 1/2-way: drvn and hdd wl over 1f out: one pce and no match for wnr* **7/2**[2]

4-23 **3** 1 **Leyte Gulf (USA)**[13] 156 9-9-3 **59**.... DaneO'Neill 3 65
(Chris Bealby) *s.s: hld up in rr: prog over 2f out: chsd ldng pair over 1f out: one pce* **10/1**

40-1 **4** 1 ½ **Unex Picasso**[16] 110 4-9-6 **69**....(p) StevieDonohoe 6 73
(Ian Williams) *dwlt: hld up tl prog after 3f: trckd ldr 9f out tl drvn and nt qckn over 2f out: one pce after* **9/2**[3]

20-3 **5** 4 ½ **Opera Prince**[20] 58 7-9-6 **62**.... DavidProbert 2 60
(Simon Earle) *hld up and sn in last: rdn and effrt over 2f out: sn no prog and btn* **20/1**

63-2 **6** 4 **Sunset Place**[13] 150 5-9-12 **68**....(p) SteveDrowne 5 62
(Jonathan Geake) *t.k.h: hld up in tch: rdn and no prog wl over 2f out: wknd over 1f out* **15/2**

13-1 **7** 2 **First Rock (IRE)**[25] 4 6-9-9 **70**.... GarryWhillans(5) 4 61
(Alan Swinbank) *t.k.h: trckd ldng pair 4f: in tch after: rdn over 2f out: sn wknd* **9/2**[3]

3m 34.18s (4.08) **Going Correction** +0.025s/f (Slow)
WFA 4 from 5yo+ 7lb **7** Ran SP% **112.8**
Speed ratings (Par 103): **90,88,87,87,84 82,81**
toteswingers:1&2:£1.70, 2&3:£3.30, 1&3:£6.30 CSF £11.06 TOTE £3.10: £1.40, £2.20; EX 10.20.
Owner Miss Victoria Baalham **Bred** Juddmonte Farms Ltd **Trained** Sullington, W Sussex

FOCUS
This staying handicap was run at a steady pace, which inconvenienced those who were held up. The tempo lifted gradually from halfway. The winner confirmed the good impression of his recent C&D win.
Sunset Place Official explanation: jockey said gelding ran too free

310 32REDBET.COM H'CAP 1m 4f (P)
6:35 (6:36) (Class 5) (0-75,75) 4-Y-0+ **£2,264** (£673; £336; £168) **Stalls** Centre

Form RPR

35-1 **1** **Rocky Rebel**[20] 65 4-8-12 **67**.... DaneO'Neill 5 76
(Chris Bealby) *hld up in 6th: prog jst over 2f out: decisive move to ld over 1f out: rdn and in command fnl f* **4/1**[1]

4-22 **2** 1 ¾ **Rowan Ridge**[6] 222 4-8-12 **67**....(b) JimCrowley 6 73
(Jim Boyle) *hld up in 4th: clsd on ldrs over 2f out: brought to chal over 1f out but wnr wnt by: styd on same pce* **8/1**

051- **3** ½ **Rasheed**[36] 7839 4-9-4 **73**....(b) MarcHalford 1 78
(John Gosden) *racd freely: led at stdy pce 2f: settled bttr to trck new ldr after: effrt to ld again briefly wl over 1f out: sn outpcd* **9/2**[2]

/5-3 **4** hd **Switched Off**[11] 187 7-9-8 **73**....(p) StevieDonohoe 9 78
(Ian Williams) *t.k.h: hld up in last trio: coaxed along to cl jst over 2f out: kpt on fr over 1f out but nvr nr enough to chal* **11/2**[3]

320- **5** ½ **Sand Skier**[29] 7900 5-9-2 **74**.... NicoleNordblad(7) 2 78
(Hans Adielsson) *t.k.h: trckd clr ldng pair: clsd 3f out but sn lost pl as r unfolded over 2f out: styd on fnl f: nvr able to chal* **8/1**

04-4 **6** shd **Bennelong**[4] 263 6-9-3 **68**.... AmirQuinn 4 72
(Richard Rowe) *hld up in 5th: prog against ins rail to chal 2f out: upsides over 1f out: sn outpcd* **11/2**[3]

3-35 **7** nk **Kames Park (IRE)**[3] 271 10-8-11 **67**.... CharlesEddery(5) 8 70
(Richard Guest) *stdd s: hld up in last: taken to outer and effrt over 2f out: styd on same pce and nvr gng to rch ldrs* **7/1**

35-3 **8** 4 **Kidlat**[22] 35 7-9-4 **69**....(bt[1]) JoeFanning 3 66
(Alan Bailey) *racd freely: led after 3f and clr w one rival: hdd & wknd qckly wl over 1f out* **8/1**

500- **9** 1 **Magicalmysterytour (IRE)**[90] 7139 9-9-10 **75**.... JamieMackay 7 70
(Willie Musson) *hld up in last trio: urged along whn r unfolded over 2f out: nt qckn and no prog* **16/1**

2m 33.57s (-0.93) **Going Correction** +0.025s/f (Slow)
WFA 4 from 5yo+ 4lb **9** Ran SP% **120.7**
Speed ratings (Par 103): **104,102,102,102,102 101,101,99,98**
toteswingers:1&2:£7.90, 2&3:£5.90, 1&3:£3.10 CSF £38.11 CT £153.16 TOTE £4.60: £1.60, £2.10, £1.70; EX 46.70 Trifecta £92.80 Pool: £894.59 - 7.13 winning units..
Owner Robert Jenkinson **Bred** Littleton Stud **Trained** Barrowby, Lincs

FOCUS
A modest handicap run at a fairly steady gallop. Ordinary from, the winner back to his early maiden best.

311 FLORENCE MOORE BIG BIRTHDAY H'CAP 6f (P)
7:05 (7:05) (Class 4) (0-85,85) 4-Y-0+ **£4,075** (£1,212; £606; £303) **Stalls** Low

Form RPR

026- **1** **Whaileyy (IRE)**[26] 7941 4-9-4 **82**....(b[1]) AdamKirby 8 98
(Marco Botti) *pressed ldr: led 2f out: shkn up and drew clr jst over 1f out: comf* **11/2**[3]

2-20 **2** 3 ¾ **Earlsmedic**[15] 120 7-8-9 **76**....(e) RyanClark(3) 6 80
(Stuart Williams) *chsd ldng pair: rdn 2f out: styd on fnl f: tk 2nd post* **8/1**

166- **3** shd **Dasho**[27] 7926 4-8-13 **82**.... LucyKBarry(5) 12 86
(Olivia Maylam) *led to 2f out: kpt on but no ch w wnr fnl f: lost 2nd last stride* **12/1**

14-0 **4** ½ **Lujeanie**[5] 253 6-9-7 **85**....(p) ShaneKelly 2 87
(Dean Ivory) *chsd ldng trio: effrt 2f out but already outpcd: kpt on fr over 1f out: nvr able to chal* **6/1**

650- **5** ½ **Taajub (IRE)**[26] 7941 5-9-4 **82**.... LiamKeniry 9 82+
(Peter Crate) *t.k.h: hld up towards rr: outpcd 2f out: rdn over 1f out: styd on: no ch to catch ldrs* **9/2**[1]

63-0 **6** ½ **Requisite**[20] 83 7-9-2 **80**....(b) LukeMorris 5 79+
(Ian Wood) *dwlt: racd in last trio: drvn and prog over 2f out: styd on thrght fnl 2f: nrst fin* **10/1**

00-1 **7** 3 ¼ **Bandstand**[18] 100 6-8-13 **77**.... TomEaves 3 65
(Bryan Smart) *t.k.h: hld up disputing 4th: nt qckn over 2f out: sn btn* **10/1**

50-4 **8** 2 **Titus Gent**[15] 120 7-8-12 **81**.... RaulDaSilva(5) 10 63
(Jeremy Gask) *racd wdst of trio disputing 4th: lost grnd wl over 2f out: sn btn* **11/1**

600- **9** nk **Local Singer (IRE)**[26] 7941 4-8-13 **77**.... TomMcLaughlin 1 58
(Paul Howling) *a towards rr: effrt on inner over 2f out: sn no prog and btn* **33/1**

060- **10** 2 **Clear Praise (USA)**[26] 7941 5-9-2 **80**.... JimCrowley 7 55
(Simon Dow) *stdd s: hld up in last trio: shkn up and no prog over 2f out: wl btn after* **5/1**[2]

6/0- **11** ½ **Evelyn May (IRE)**[297] 1140 6-8-13 **77**.... WilliamCarson 4 50
(Charles Hills) *awkward and wnt lft s: a in last trio: wl btn over 2f out* **40/1**

3-02 **12** 16 **Rylee Mooch**[8] 208 4-8-2 **71** oh2....(p) CharlesEddery(5) 11
(Richard Guest) *tried to break out of stalls jst bef they opened and completely missed the s: brief effrt on wd outside after 2f: sn wknd: t.o* **20/1**

1m 11.44s (-1.66) **Going Correction** +0.025s/f (Slow) **12** Ran SP% **120.0**
Speed ratings (Par 105): **112,107,106,106,105 104,100,97,97,94 94,72**
toteswingers:1&2:£9.60, 2&3:£12.20, 1&3:£15.80 CSF £48.76 CT £523.41 TOTE £6.40: £2.40, £2.70, £3.90; EX 55.10 Trifecta £291.30 Part won. Pool: £393.77 - 0.52 winning units..
Owner Saleh Al Homaizi & Imad Al Sagar **Bred** Iona Equine **Trained** Newmarket, Suffolk

FOCUS
A decent sprint handicap. The principals were always prominent and nothing got involved from the rear. A clear personal best for the winner.

312 32REDPOKER.COM H'CAP (DIV I) 6f (P)
7:35 (7:36) (Class 6) (0-55,55) 4-Y-0+ **£1,617** (£481; £240; £120) **Stalls** Low

Form RPR

5-22 **1** **Rightcar**[4] 264 5-9-1 **52**.... RobbieFitzpatrick 2 61
(Peter Grayson) *settled in midfield: prog on inner over 2f out: rdn to chal over 1f out: led ins fnl f: r.o* **3/1**[1]

35- **2** ½ **Cut The Cackle (IRE)**[50] 7655 6-9-3 **54**....(bt) WilliamCarson 9 64+
(Richard Guest) *blindfold off sltly late and dwlt: prog fr last pair wl over 2f out: tried to chal between rivals over 1f out but gap clsd: rdr persisted and had to snatch up ent fnl f: swtchd lft and r.o to take 2nd fin* **3/1**[1]

-045 **3** ¾ **White Shift (IRE)**[6] 226 6-8-11 **48**....(p) ShaneKelly 1 53
(Paul Howling) *trckd ldrs: led jst over 2f out: edgd sltly rt over 1f out: hdd ins fnl f: lost 2nd nr fin* **14/1**

40-3 **4** 2 ½ **Prince Namid**[8] 205 10-9-4 **55**.... LukeMorris 3 52
(Jonathen de Giles) *settled towards rr: urged along over 2f out: nvr on terms: tk 4th fnl f: no imp* **7/1**[3]

52-0 **5** 1 ¼ **Replicator**[15] 122 7-8-11 **51**....(e) RyanClark(3) 5 44
(Patrick Gilligan) *trckd ldrs: tried to chal 2f out: sn rdn and nt qckn: one pce after* **11/2**[2]

04-0 **6** 2 ¾ **Demoiselle Bond**[15] 123 4-9-4 **55**.... SteveDrowne 10 39
(Lydia Richards) *disp ld at str pce to jst over 2f out: steadily wknd* **14/1**

51-0 **7** 1 ½ **Microlight**[15] 123 4-9-2 **53**....(b) SamHitchcott 7 32
(John E Long) *pushed along in last trio after 2f: tried to make prog 2f out: nt gng pce to threaten* **16/1**

00-6 **8** 4 ½ **Fifth Auntie**[22] 37 5-8-2 **46** oh1.... JackDuern(7) 4 11
(J R Jenkins) *dwlt: a wl in rr* **66/1**

0-05 **9** ¾ **Mi Regalo**[8] [210] 4-9-2 **53**..........(v[1]) DavidProbert 8 16
(Phil McEntee) *a towards rr: struggling over 2f out: wknd* **9/1**
00-0 **10** *1* **C'Mon You Irons (IRE)**[22] [39] 7-8-12 **54**..........(vt) RaulDaSilva(5) 11 13
(Mark Hoad) *disp ld at str pce to over 2f out: wknd qckly* **14/1**
00-0 **11** *30* **Simple Rhythm**[13] [155] 6-8-10 **50**..........(p) RyanPowell(3) 6
(John Ryan) *racd wd towards rr: wknd 1/2-way: t.o* **25/1**

1m 12.11s (-0.99) **Going Correction** +0.025s/f (Slow) **11** Ran SP% **119.1**
Speed ratings (Par 101): **107,106,105,102,100 96,94,88,87,86 46**
toteswingers:1&2:£2.00, 2&3:£12.90, 1&3:£9.30 CSF £11.18 CT £111.67 TOTE £4.60: £1.50, £1.60, £2.50; EX 15.90 Trifecta £115.90 Pool: £432.81- 2.76 winning units..
Owner Richard Teatum **Bred** J M Beever **Trained** Formby, Lancs
■ Stewards' Enquiry : Raul Da Silva four-day ban; careless riding (Feb 9, 10-11,13)
Shane Kelly two-day ban; careless riding (9th-10th Feb)

FOCUS
Division one of a low-grade handicap. The pace was brisk and the time was decent for the class, 2.58sec quicker than the falsely run second division. The form is pretty solid.

313 32REDPOKER.COM H'CAP (DIV II) 6f (P)

8:05 (8:05) (Class 6) (0-55,55) 4-Y-0+ **£1,617** (£481; £240; £120) **Stalls** Low

Form RPR
00-5 **1** **Welcome Approach**[15] [123] 9-9-4 **55**.......... LukeMorris 4 62
(John Weymes) *hld up in tch: prog through rivals to ld wl over 1f out: drvn fnl f: jst hld on* **4/1**[2]
5-06 **2** *hd* **Dingaan (IRE)**[8] [203] 9-9-2 **53**.......... RobbieFitzpatrick 10 59
(Peter Grayson) *hld up in last in slowly run event: effrt on outer 2f out: r.o fnl f: tk 2nd last 50yds: jst failed* **11/2**[3]
00-2 **3** *nk* **Nacho Libre**[8] [203] 7-9-3 **54**..........(bt) PaddyAspell 8 59
(Michael Easterby) *dwlt: racd wd and sn in tch: pushed along over 2f out: prog to chse wnr 1f out but hanging rt: clsd fnl f but lost 2nd last 50yds* **10/11**[1]
0-00 **4** *2 ½* **Darwin Star**[13] [152] 4-8-8 **52**..........(p) PaulBooth(7) 6 49
(Dean Ivory) *t.k.h: trckd ldr to 2f out: sn rdn and nt qckn: fdd ins fnl f* **12/1**
234- **5** *½* **Metropolitan Chief**[69] [7459] 8-8-7 **49**.......... CharlesBishop(5) 1 45
(Paul Burgoyne) *t.k.h: led at stdy pce: hdd and nt qckn wl over 1f out: fdd ins fnl f* **10/1**
00-0 **6** *1* **Toms River Tess (IRE)**[15] [124] 4-9-1 **52**.......... JamieGoldstein 5 45
(Zoe Davison) *hld up in tch: nt qckn over 2f out: no prog over 1f out* **25/1**
000- **7** *4 ½* **Green Warrior**[29] [7896] 4-9-1 **55**..........(p) RobertLButler(3) 3 33
(Richard Guest) *plld hrd: hld up bhd ldrs: folded tamely whn pce qcknd jst over 2f out* **10/1**

1m 14.69s (1.59) **Going Correction** +0.025s/f (Slow) **7** Ran SP% **117.5**
Speed ratings (Par 101): **90,89,89,86,85 84,78**
toteswingers:1&2:£2.20, 2&3:£1.80, 1&3:£1.90 CSF £27.11 CT £35.98 TOTE £4.10: £2.10, £2.40; EX 22.30 Trifecta £40.10 Pool: £565.78 - 10.44 winning units..
Owner T A Scothern & Tag Racing **Bred** P Wyatt And Ranby Hall **Trained** Middleham Moor, N Yorks

FOCUS
This was run at a very slow initial pace and in a time no less than 2.58sec slower than the first division. The form is unlikely to prove too reliable, with the winner rated just to his summer best..
T/Jkpt: Not won. T/Plt: £66.70 to a £1 stake. Pool of £84,682.40 - 926.79 winning tickets. T/Qpdt: £11.60 to a £1 stake. Pool of £10,008.44 - 637.82 winning tickets. JN

256 MEYDAN (L-H)

Thursday, January 26

OFFICIAL GOING: Tapeta - standard; turf - good

314a DUBAI DUTY FREE FINEST SURPRISE (H'CAP) (TAPETA) 6f

2:45 (2:45) (95-105,105) 3-Y-0+

£42,580 (£14,193; £7,096; £3,548; £2,129; £1,419)

RPR
1 **Krypton Factor**[5] [260] 4-9-1 100..........(b) KierenFallon 5 112
(F Nass, Bahrain) *sn led: kicked clr 2 1/2f out: r.o wl: comf* **7/1**
2 *3 ½* **Ariete Arrollador**[14] [140] 5-9-3 102.......... MircoDemuro 4 103+
(G Arizkorreta Elosegui, Spain) *chsd ldrs: r.o fnl 2f but no ch w wnr* **5/2**[1]
3 *½* **The Reaper (IRE)**[14] [141] 4-9-1 100..........(b) RyanMoore 8 99
(G M Lyons, Ire) *trckd ldrs: ev ch 2f out: nt qckn fnl f* **9/2**[2]
4 *1 ¾* **Rock Jock (IRE)**[14] [141] 5-9-3 102.......... TedDurcan 9 96
(E Charpy, UAE) *mid-div: r.o fnl 2f: nrst fin* **12/1**
5 *1 ¼* **Sir Reginald**[14] [141] 4-9-3 102.......... JamieSpencer 6 92
(Richard Fahey) *slowly away: settled last: r.o wl fnl 2f: nrst fin* **20/1**
6 *¼* **Silaah**[6] [244] 8-9-5 105.......... AdrianNicholls 3 93
(David Nicholls) *trckd ldrs: ev ch 2 1/2f out: one pce fnl f* **9/1**
7 *1* **Tertio Bloom (SWE)**[14] [140] 7-9-3 102..........(t) ValmirDeAzeredo 13 88
(Fabricio Borges, Sweden) *nvr nr to chal* **20/1**
8 *1 ¾* **Jimmy Styles**[103] [6858] 8-9-4 104..........(p) JamesDoyle 10 83
(Clive Cox) *trckd ldr: ev ch 2 1/2f out: nt qckn fnl f* **16/1**
9 *2 ½* **Signs In The Sand**[34] [7868] 4-8-13 98..........(t) RichardMullen 1 70
(S Seemar, UAE) *s.i.s: in rr of mid-div: n.d* **16/1**
10 *1 ¾* **Spirit Of Battle (USA)**[20] [80] 4-9-1 100.......... CSanchez 12 67
(A bin Huzaim, UAE) *in rr of mid-div: wd: nvr able to chal* **14/1**
11 *¾* **Prinzde Glas (IRE)**[113] [6643] 5-8-13 98..........(b) RoystonFfrench 14 62
(Stephane Chevalier, UAE) *nvr bttr than mid-div* **25/1**
12 *2 ¼* **Internationaldebut (IRE)**[14] [141] 7-9-3 102.......... FrederikTylicki 11 59
(Paul Midgley) *nvr bttr than mid-div* **11/2**[3]
13 *4 ¼* **Comradeship (IRE)**[343] [583] 5-9-1 100..........(bt) YohannBourgois 2 43
(R Bouresly, Kuwait) *nvr bttr than mid-div* **33/1**
14 *2* **Enjoy Dubai (ARG)**[14] [142] 4-8-7 97.......... PatCosgrave 7 29
(M F De Kock, South Africa) *nvr bttr than mid-div* **10/1**

1m 10.51s (-1.09) **14** Ran SP% **136.2**
CSF: 26.93 TRI: 97.64.
Owner Fawzi Abdulla Nass **Bred** Lady Fairhaven **Trained** Bahrain

FOCUS
An ordinary handicap for a 95-105. A personal best from the winner.

NOTEBOOK
Krypton Factor faced competition up front, but setting fractions of 24.82 and 47.42 allowed him to keep plenty in reserve and he drew clear in the straight. He was runner-up over 1m here when reappearing the previous week, but the key to this success was probably the drop back to a sprint trip for the first time since he was trained by Sir Mark Prescott as a juvenile. (op 15-2)
Ariete Arrollador ◆ was tried in a hood. Just as when runner-up over 7f here on his recent Dubai debut, travelled really strongly, but he had little chance considering how the race unfolded. He kept on to fare best of those held up and can win a similar race when getting a strong pace to chase. (op 3-1)
The Reaper(IRE) was always well placed but didn't see it out. He's not well handicapped.
Rock Jock(IRE) refused to race last time, but he showed a lot more enthusiasm on this occasion. (op 25-1)
Sir Reginald ◆ was left with far too much to do after missing the break and having to wait for a clear run in the straight, but this was still a pleasing performance. He hadn't shown much at all on his recent comeback from a lengthy absence, but the way he travelled here, before belatedly keeping on, suggests he retains all of his ability. (op 16-1)
Jimmy Styles ◆, on the face of it, was disappointing, but he might just be worth another chance. It's true to say he was in the right place considering the pace scenario, but he's at his best when held up off a decent gallop and he just looked a bit too fresh from an unhelpful draw on what was his first start for over three months. (op 12-1)

315a DUBAI DUTY FREE FOUNDATION (H'CAP) (TAPETA) 7f

3:20 (3:20) (100-110,110) 3-Y-0+

£46,451 (£15,483; £7,741; £3,870; £2,322; £1,548)

RPR
1 **African Story**[151] [5530] 5-9-5 110.......... FrankieDettori 3 111+
(Saeed Bin Suroor) *trckd ldrs: rdn to ld 110yds out: comf* **6/4**[1]
2 *1* **Barbecue Eddie (USA)**[14] [140] 8-9-3 108..........(b) RichardHills 5 106
(Doug Watson, UAE) *trckd ldrs: led 2f out: hdd fnl 110yds* **7/2**[2]
3 *2* **Silver Ocean (USA)**[124] [6369] 4-9-3 108.......... WilliamBuick 1 101
(Niels Petersen, Norway) *mid-div: r.o wl fnl 1 1/2f: nrst fin* **12/1**
4 *1* **Spectacle Du Mars (FR)**[86] [7221] 5-9-4 109.......... GregoryBenoist 9 99
(X Nakkachdji, France) *trckd ldrs: ev ch 2f out: nt qckn fnl f* **14/1**
5 *¼* **As De Trebol (USA)**[21] [53] 6-9-1 106.......... BFayosMartin 2 95
(M Delcher-Sanchez, Spain) *sn led: hdd 2f out: one pce fnl f* **6/1**[3]
6 *1 ¼* **Escape Route (USA)**[14] [144] 8-9-3 108..........(t) RichardMullen 7 94
(S Seemar, UAE) *in rr of mid-div: nvr able to chal but r.o fnl 1 1/2f* **12/1**
7 *1 ¾* **Sweet Ducky (USA)**[88] 4-9-0 105..........(t) RyanMoore 6 86
(H J Brown, South Africa) *in rr of mid-div: r.o fnl 2f but n.d* **16/1**
8 *½* **Captain Ramius (IRE)**[14] [140] 6-8-9 100.......... JamieSpencer 8 80
(Kevin Ryan) *s.i.s: settled in last: n.d* **10/1**
9 *1 ¼* **Il Grande Maurizio (IRE)**[5] [261] 8-8-11 102.......... RoystonFfrench 4 78
(A Al Raihe, UAE) *nvr bttr than mid-div* **16/1**
10 *dist* **Lowther**[14] [140] 7-8-9 100.......... AdrianNicholls 10
(David Nicholls) *s.i.s: trckd ldrs: ev ch 3f out: sn btn* **16/1**

1m 23.65s (-1.55) **10** Ran SP% **125.3**
CSF: 7.18 TRICAST: 50.11.
Owner Godolphin **Bred** Darley **Trained** Newmarket, Suffolk

FOCUS
More than one confirmed front-runner here, but the jockeys were wary of a potential burn up and consequently the pace was just modest. Lowther recovered from a slow start to lead the field through the quarter-mile spilt in 25.98, then As De Trebol was in front at the half-mile point, going 48.83, and it was Barbecue Eddie who led at 6f, clocking 1.11.77. Frankie Dettori reads pace scenarios better than many of his colleagues and was yet again in more or less the right spot.

NOTEBOOK
African Story was in a prominent position throughout. He was up to Group company when trained in France by Andre Fabre, as he showed when running subsequent Prix Maurice de Gheest winner Moonlight Cloud close, and he was good enough to defy a mark of 110 on his Dubai debut. He'll probably be forced back into pattern company and that will provide more of a test, but this was his first run since August, and just his ninth in total, so there may be more to come. Plus this surface clearly suits - he's a half-brother to a dual Polytrack winner and is now 2-2 off the turf.
Barbecue Eddie(USA) was found out by a 3lb rise for his recent C&D win. (op 4-1)
Silver Ocean(USA)'s form in Europe suggested he wasn't badly treated from a mark of 108, but he was comfortably held despite travelling eight meters less than the winner. This was, however, his first start for four months and he may come on for it.
Spectacle Du Mars(FR) has shown his best form over sprint trips.
As De Trebol(USA) didn't get an uncontested lead, but that's no real excuse as he was still able to save plenty and it was disappointing he failed to see his race out, especially as he'd shaped so well when faced with a much tougher pace scenario on his reappearance. (op 7-1)
Escape Route(USA) ◆ didn't run badly in a hot race last time and on this occasion he covered too much ground out wide. It wouldn't surprise to see him go in at a fair price this Carnival.

316a DUBAI DUTY FREE H'CAP (TURF) 7f

4:00 (4:00) (100-113,113) 3-Y-0+

£67,741 (£22,580; £11,290; £5,645; £3,387; £2,258)

RPR
1 **Dark Matter (AUS)**[14] [142] 4-8-11 110.......... TedDurcan 1 111+
(S Burridge, Singapore) *trckd ldrs: r.o wl fnl f: led last strides* **7/2**[2]
2 *shd* **Albaasil (IRE)**[187] [4313] 4-8-10 104.......... RichardHills 3 104+
(Doug Watson, UAE) *s.i.s: chsd ldrs 3f out: led 110yds out: hdd cl home* **9/2**[3]
3 *¼* **Time Prisoner (USA)**[21] [53] 5-9-5 112.......... FrankieDettori 8 112
(Mahmood Al Zarooni) *trckd ldrs: smooth prog to ld 2f out: hdd ins fnl f: one pce fnl 110yds* **11/8**[1]
4 *2* **Regal Parade**[21] [53] 8-8-13 106.......... AdrianNicholls 4 101
(David Nicholls) *trckd ldrs: ev ch 2f out: one pce fnl 1 1/2f* **6/1**
5 *2 ½* **Otaared**[13] [172] 7-8-13 106..........(t) WilliamBuick 7 94
(D Selvaratnam, UAE) *in rr of mid-div: nvr able to chal* **14/1**
6 *¼* **Swop (IRE)**[14] [140] 9-8-7 100.......... KierenFallon 2 88
(Luca Cumani) *sn led: hdd 2f out: one pce fnl f* **25/1**
7 *4 ¼* **Redemptor**[294] [1206] 4-8-13 106.......... TadhgO'Shea 6 82
(E Charpy, UAE) *s.i.s: settled in last: nvr nr to chal* **14/1**
8 *3 ¼* **Hunting Tower (SAF)**[14] [145] 10-8-11 105.....(t) ChristopheSoumillon 5 71
(M F De Kock, South Africa) *settled in rr: nvr nr to chal* **25/1**

1m 25.51s (85.51) **8** Ran SP% **117.8**
CSF: 20.37 TRICAST 30.54.
Owner Hippocrates Stable **Bred** Bellagio Lodge Pty Ltd **Trained** Singapore

FOCUS
Rail out 4m on turf course. A good handicap, although a handy ride was helpful. This was yet another one for Singapore trainer Steven Burridge, whose 2012 Carnival record now stands out 4-5 (from four individual horses).

NOTEBOOK
Dark Matter(AUS) had plenty go his way when winning the UAE 2000 Guineas Trial on the Tapeta when making his Dubai debut, but this looked a much-improved performance. He was helped by being forwardly place and only won on the nod, but his Guineas credentials look quite a bit stronger now.
Albaasil(IRE) ◆, lightly raced and progressive for Sir Michael Stoute, made a promising debut for his new trainer. He came from further back than those who finished around him and his exertions may have just told late on.
Time Prisoner(USA) led at the 6f point, clocking 1.13.87, and he had every chance but was just run out of it. He was up 4lb for a C&D win on his Dubai debut and that seemingly found him out, but he confirmed form with Regal Parade.
Otaared plugged on from off the modest pace.

Swop(IRE) took them through the opening sectionals in 26.99 and 51.34 before fading.

317a DUBAI DUTY FREE MILLENNIUM MILLIONAIRE (H'CAP) (TAPETA) 1m 1f 110y

4:40 (4:40) (95-105,105) 3-Y-O+

£42,580 (£14,193; £7,096; £3,548; £2,129; £1,419)

RPR

1 *shd* **Sarrsar**[21] [47] 5-9-5 105 (vt) MickaelBarzalona 6 110
(Saeed Bin Suroor) *in rr of mid-div: smooth prog 3f out: chsd ldrs 1 1/2f out: led 110yds out: hdd cl home* **7/2**[1]

2 *6 1/2* **Nationalism**[14] [145] 5-9-5 105 AhmedAjtebi 1 96
(Mahmood Al Zarooni) *trckd ldng gp: ev ch 2f out: r.o same pce fnl f* **10/1**

3 *shd* **Maraheb**[175] [4718] 4-9-2 102 (t) RichardHills 9 95
(A Al Raihe, UAE) *settled in rr: gng wl 2 1/2 out: r.o fnl 1 1/2f: nrst fin* **7/1**

4 *1/2* **Jedi**[14] [143] 6-9-2 101 CSanchez 14 92
(A bin Huzaim, UAE) *sn led: hdd 1 1/2 out: kpt on same pce* **20/1**

5 *2 3/4* **Dr Faustus (IRE)**[5] [257] 7-8-9 95 (t) KierenFallon 11 80
(Doug Watson, UAE) *s.i.s: nvr nr to chal but r.o fnl 2f* **20/1**

6 *2* **Belgian Bill**[14] [145] 4-9-3 104 (t) TedDurcan 4 86
(George Baker) *trckd ldr: ev ch 1 1/2f out: wknd fnl 110yds* **4/1**[2]

7 *1* **Spirit Of Sharjah (IRE)**[5] [260] 7-8-13 98 TadhgO'Shea 12 77
(Julia Feilden) *settled rr: nvr able to chal* **12/1**

8 *1* **Rochdale**[6] [241] 9-9-4 104 (t) RoystonFfrench 3 80
(A Al Raihe, UAE) *a mid-div* **14/1**

9 *2* **Ibn Al Nafis (USA)**[13] [171] 6-8-9 95 (bt) RichardMullen 5 67
(S Seemar, UAE) *nvr bttr than mid-div* **16/1**

10 *1 1/4* **Eddie Jock (IRE)**[27] [7932] 8-8-13 98 (vt) HarryBentley 10 69
(S Seemar, UAE) *in rr of mid-div: rdn 3 1/2f out: n.d* **20/1**

11 *5 1/4* **Canadian (IRE)**[266] 4-8-13 99 PatCosgrave 2 60
(M bin Shafya, UAE) *trckd ldr tl wknd 2 1/2f out* **20/1**

12 *6* **Storm Chispazo (ARG)**[14] [140] 6-9-3 102 (t) RyanMoore 13 50
(H J Brown, South Africa) *in rr of mid-div: n.d* **16/1**

13 *5 1/4* **We'll Come**[21] [48] 8-8-11 97 (p) CSandoval 8 33
(A bin Huzaim, UAE) *a in rr* **33/1**

D **Capponi (IRE)**[21] [47] 5-9-5 105 FrankieDettori 7 110
(Mahmood Al Zarooni) *trckd ldng gp: smooth prog to ld 1 1/2 out: hdd 110yds out: led again on line* **9/2**[3]

1m 56.08s (-2.92)
WFA 4 from 5yo+ 1lb **14** Ran SP% **130.1**
CSF: 20.57 TRICAST: 161.37.
Owner Godolphin **Bred** Darley **Trained** Newmarket, Suffolk

FOCUS
The field were taken along at a reasonable pace, Jedi clocking 26.22, 50.35, 1.14.73 and 1.38.86, and the final time was a new course record.

NOTEBOOK
Sarrsar looked like confirming recent form with Capponi as he edged ahead near the line, despite having covered five meters more than his old rival. However, Mickael Barzalona's mount isn't the most genuine and looked to throw it away in the final strides.
Nationalism covered 12 metres less than the winner and 17 metres less than the runner-up.
Maraheb ◆ caught the eye on his debut for a new trainer. He tended to be ridden positively when with John Dunlop, but he was held up here, presumably in a bid to conserve his stamina on this step up in trip, and was left with far too much to do. The ease with which he travelled was most taking, and although his run seemed to flatten out late on, that's understandable considering he may not have stayed and/or needed the run.
Belgian Bill couldn't confirm recent form with Nationalism, failing to build on a promising Dubai debut. His finishing effort was tame and he may have seen too much daylight.
Spirit Of Sharjah(IRE) was a doubtful stayer and covered more ground than most.
Capponi(IRE) stepped up from his promising return from a long layoff over C&D earlier this month and deserves credit for the way he battled on to reverse the form from that race with Sarrsar.

318a AL RASHIDIYA SPONSORED BY DUBAI DUTY FREE (GROUP 2) (TURF) 1m 1f

5:15 (5:15) 3-Y-O+

£77,419 (£25,806; £12,903; £6,451; £3,870; £2,580)

RPR

1 **Musir (AUS)**[14] [144] 6-9-3 117 ChristopheSoumillon 7 120+
(M F De Kock, South Africa) *trckd ldr: smooth prog to ld 2f out: comf* **4/7**[1]

2 *1* **City Style (USA)**[21] [51] 6-9-0 107 MickaelBarzalona 3 112
(Mahmood Al Zarooni) *mid-div: chsd ldrs 3f out: r.o wl fnl 1 1/2f but no ch w wnr* **14/1**

3 *3 1/2* **Marcret (ITY)**[81] [7323] 5-9-0 110 MircoDemuro 5 105
(Marco Botti) *sn led: hdd 2f out: kpt on same pce* **16/1**

4 *1 1/4* **Trois Rois (FR)**[21] [52] 7-9-0 107 (b) TadhgO'Shea 2 102+
(Ismail Mohammed) *in rr of mid-div: kpt on same pce fnl 2f* **66/1**

5 *3/4* **Presvis**[249] [2340] 8-9-0 120 RyanMoore 6 100+
(Luca Cumani) *settled in rr: nvr nr to chal but r.o fnl 2f* **3/1**[2]

6 *3/4* **Le Drakkar (AUS)**[14] [144] 7-9-0 110 FrankieDettori 1 99+
(A bin Huzaim, UAE) *slowly away: settled in last: n.d* **25/1**

7 *1/4* **Win For Sure (GER)**[329] [758] 7-9-0 113 GregoryBenoist 8 98+
(X Nakkachdji, France) *mid-div: rdn 4f out: one pce fnl 2 1/2f* **16/1**

8 *2* **Rajsaman (FR)**[46] [7731] 5-9-3 119 (b) RoystonFfrench 4 97+
(A Al Raihe, UAE) *mid-div: rdn 2 1/2f out: sn wknd* **6/1**[3]

1m 54.0s (114.00)
WFA 4 from 5yo+ 1lb **8** Ran SP% **126.7**
CSF: 13.85.
Owner Sheikh Mohammed Bin Khalifa Al Maktoum **Bred** Sh Mohd Bin Khalifa Al Maktoum **Trained** South Africa

FOCUS
The second straight year this race has held Group 2 status, but it was a disappointing contest. Only three could be seriously considered and two of them underperformed.

NOTEBOOK
Musir(AUS) took over ahead and clocked 1.42.57 at the mile point. He didn't require a hard ride and did not have to get near the form he showed when winning the first round of the Al Maktoum Challenge two weeks earlier. It's a real bonus he was able to pick up a Group 2 prize without overexerting himself and there are more opportunities for him ahead of World Cup meeting, when his target is said to be the Duty Free.
City Style(USA) had won back-to-back Tapeta handicaps that were separated by almost a year, the latest earlier this month off just 101, but he had been shaping as though the longer straight of the turf course would suit even better. The problem is he doesn't seem to let himself down properly on quick going anymore and he looked uncomfortable under pressure, but he still ran as well as ever. (op 12-1)
Marcret(ITY) led the field through sectionals of 28.95, 54.49, a.1.20.20, before the winner took over. An ex-Italian-trained runner who was debuting for Marco Botti, he could not have been better positioned.
Trois Rois(FR) finished only seventh in the inaugural Al Rashidiya Trial over C&D three weeks earlier, but this was a better effort, especially as he raced keenly off what was a slow pace.
Presvis won this last year before adding the Group 1 Duty Free, but he was nowhere near his best here. He was only around 90% ready according to Luca Cumani, but he's gone well when fresh in previous years (including 12 months ago), so that can't really be used as an excuse, and it would also be hard argue to lack of pace cost him. It's true he was a bit keen and would have preferred an end-to-end gallop, but he wasn't exactly going on strongly at the line. He'll have much to prove next time.
Rajsaman(FR) looked interesting on his debut for leading UAE trainer Ali Al Raihe, even with a 3lb penalty, but something was presumably amiss.

319a DUBAI DUTY FREE TENNIS CHAMPIONSHIPS (H'CAP) (TURF) 1m 2f

5:50 (5:50) (95-113,113) 3-Y-O+

£58,064 (£19,354; £9,677; £4,838; £2,903; £1,935)

RPR

1 **Quick Wit**[21] [51] 5-8-7 100 SilvestreDeSousa 8 107
(Saeed Bin Suroor) *trckd ldrs: rdn to ld 1 1/2f out: r.o wl* **10/1**

2 *2 1/2* **Fallen Idol**[127] [6247] 5-9-1 108 FrankieDettori 11 110
(Saeed Bin Suroor) *mid-div: chsd ldrs 3f out: ev ch 1 1/2f out: one pce fnl f* **5/2**[1]

3 *shd* **Al Shemali**[94] [7053] 8-8-9 102 (t) RoystonFfrench 2 104+
(A Al Raihe, UAE) *in rr of mid-div: nvr nr to chal but r.o wl fnl 1 1/2f: nrst fin* **10/1**

4 *shd* **Manjakani**[21] [48] 4-8-6 100 TadhgO'Shea 5 103
(Ismail Mohammed) *settled in rr: chsd ldrs 2 1/2f out: nt qckn fnl f* **7/1**[3]

5 *1 1/2* **Moran Gra (USA)**[6] [243] 5-8-9 102 (p) ShaneFoley 13 101
(Ms Joanna Morgan, Ire) *sn led: hdd 1 1/2f out: kpt on same pce* **16/1**

6 *1/4* **Rostrum (FR)**[14] [145] 5-9-2 109 MickaelBarzalona 10 107
(Mahmood Al Zarooni) *mid-div: t.k.h: r.o one pce fnl 110yds* **7/2**[2]

7 *1/4* **Summit Surge (IRE)**[14] [145] 8-9-1 108 (t) KierenFallon 3 106
(Luca Cumani) *nvr bttr than mid-div* **16/1**

8 *2 1/4* **Abjer (FR)**[5] [260] 4-8-5 97 MircoDemuro 4 93
(Ismail Mohammed) *trckd ldrs: ev ch 3 1/2f out: one pce fnl f* **33/1**

9 *1 1/4* **Firebet (IRE)**[692] [820] 6-8-11 105 JRosales 6 95
(A bin Huzaim, UAE) *trckd ldrs tl 2 1/2f out: wknd fnl f* **14/1**

10 *1 3/4* **Nanton (USA)**[96] [7029] 10-8-10 104 RyanMoore 1 90
(E Charpy, UAE) *s.i.s: settled in rr: n.d* **14/1**

11 *1 3/4* **Famusa**[6] [242] 5-8-5 97 AndreaAtzeni 9 82
(Marco Botti) *broke awkwardly: mid-div: rdn 4f out: n.d* **10/1**

12 *1 1/4* **Bank Of Burden (USA)**[137] [5984] 5-9-2 109 (t) Per-AndersGraberg 7 90
(Niels Petersen, Norway) *settled in rr: n.d* **12/1**

2m 4.89s (124.89)
WFA 4 from 5yo+ 2lb **12** Ran SP% **126.3**
CSF: 37.48 TRICAST 275.52. Placepot: £5.20 to a £1 stake. Pool of £7034.15 - 976.75 winning units. Quadpot: £6.40 to a £1 stake. Pool of £687.73 - 79.50 winning units..
Owner Godolphin **Bred** Ptarmigan Bloodstock Limited **Trained** Newmarket, Suffolk

FOCUS
The pace was ordinary and consequently a prominent ride proved advantageous.

NOTEBOOK
Quick Wit's connections deserve credit for working out he wanted this trip. He had shown little on his return from a lengthy absence over 1m on the Tapeta three weeks earlier and looked an extremely doubtful stayer at this longer trip, being mainly bred for speed, although one of his siblings did win at 1m2f on the Flat before adding a hurdles victory. Admittedly, the winner was helped by being well placed, but he saw it out well.
Fallen Idol cost 250,000gns out of John Gosden's yard, but he had previously looked a bit soft and he also had something to prove on quick ground. This was an adequate debut for his new yard.
Al Shemali ◆ has been mainly disappointing since a stunning win in the 2010 Duty Free for Ali Al Raihe, but he's now back with that yard after a spell with Mahmood Al Zarooni. With a tongue-tie re-fitted, he fared best of those held up after having to being switched into the clear, and he retains sufficient ability to win a similar race.
Manjakani ◆ raced further back than ideal and covered more ground than the three who finished ahead of him. He can do better.
Moran Gra(USA) took them along in 26.44, 51.38, 1.16.95 and 1.41.07.
Rostrum(FR) travelled well but found disappointingly little for pressure.

298 LINGFIELD (L-H)

Friday, January 27

OFFICIAL GOING: Standard
Wind: Moderate across Weather: Sunny

320 5% WINNERS' BONUS AT BLUESQ.COM H'CAP 5f (P)

1:20 (1:21) (Class 6) (0-62,62) 4-Y-O+ **£1,704** (£503; £251) **Stalls** High

Form RPR

-553 **1** **Chjimes (IRE)**[9] [210] 8-8-13 **57** (b) HayleyTurner 3 65
(Conor Dore) *chsd ldrs: wnt 2nd 2f out: drvn to chal jst ins fnl f: sn led and rdn: jst lasted* **4/1**[2]

1-33 **2** *shd* **Cliffords Reprieve**[3] [277] 4-9-0 **58** (b) WilliamCarson 4 66
(Eric Wheeler) *chsd ldrs: rdn over 1f out: styd on to chse wnr fnl 120yds: r.o strly clsng stages: jst failed* **15/8**[1]

00-0 **3** *1 3/4* **Overwhelm**[13] [178] 4-9-0 **58** (t) JimCrowley 5 60
(Andrew Reid) *in tch: chsd ldrs and rdn over 1f out: styd on fnl f to take 3rd clsng stages: nt rch ldng duo* **16/1**

556- **4** *hd* **Spic 'n Span**[123] [6398] 7-9-4 **62** (v) LukeMorris 1 63
(Ronald Harris) *led: drvn over 1f out: jnd jst ins fnl f: sn hdd: wknd and lost 3rd clsng stages* **20/1**

6-04 **5** *1/2* **Super Frank (IRE)**[7] [220] 9-8-10 **54** ow2 (b) JamieGoldstein 7 53
(Zoe Davison) *in rr: drvn and styd on fnl f: kpt on clsng stages: nt rch ldrs* **33/1**

554- **6** *nse* **Dorothy's Dancing (IRE)**[27] [7940] 4-8-13 **57** FergusSweeney 8 56
(Gary Moore) *t.k.h towards rr: drvn and hdwy fnl f: styd on clsng stages: nt rch ldrs* **6/1**[3]

3-30 **7** *1/2* **Welsh Inlet (IRE)**[16] [122] 4-9-4 **62** KieranO'Neill 2 59
(John Bridger) *chsd ldr to 2f out: wknd fnl f* **13/2**

-246 **8** *3* **Sherjawy (IRE)**[9] [208] 8-9-4 **62** SamHitchcott 9 48
(Zoe Davison) *racd towards outside early: a outpcd* **8/1**

/60- **9** *2 1/4* **Dells Breezer**[27] [7940] 4-8-6 **55** JemmaMarshall(5) 6 33
(Pat Phelan) *s.i.s: a outpcd* **20/1**

58.16s (-0.64) **Going Correction** -0.125s/f (Stan) **9** Ran SP% **111.9**
Speed ratings (Par 101): **100,99,97,96,95 95,95,90,86**
Tote Swingers: 1&2 £1.20, 1&3 £15.20, 2&3 £5.00 CSF £11.12 CT £101.99 TOTE £4.40: £1.90, £1.10, £4.60; EX 11.20 Trifecta £88.50 Pool: £411.43 - 3.44 winning units..
Owner Mrs Louise Marsh **Bred** Morgan O'Flaherty **Trained** Hubbert's Bridge, Lincs

FOCUS
Run-of-the-mill Class 6 fare, but the pace looked sound enough (resulting in a strong time for the grade) thanks to Spic 'N Span and that played into the hands of the winner.

321 MARSH GREEN CLAIMING STKS 5f (P)
1:50 (1:50) (Class 6) 3-Y-O **£1,704** (£503; £251) **Stalls** High

Form RPR
24-5 **1** **Redair (IRE)**[12] 189 3-8-5 71 .... MartinLane 2 64
(David Evans) *trckd ldrs: nt clr run and edgd lft over 1f out: drvn to chal fnl 120yds and sn led: readily* **5/6**[1]
46-6 **2** *1* **Thorpe Bay**[7] 219 3-8-5 58 .... (b) DavidProbert 4 61
(Mark Rimmer) *chsd ldrs: rdn to chal 1f out: slt ld fnl 120yds but sn hdd and outpcd by wnr* **9/2**[3]
45-4 **3** *1 1/4* **Flaming Ferrari (IRE)**[11] 191 3-8-2 54 .... (p) KieranO'Neill 5 53
(Peter Chapple-Hyam) *led: drvn ins fnl 2f: jnd u.p 1f out: hdd and outpcd fnl 120yds* **9/2**[3]
0 **4** *1* **Strike A Pose (IRE)**[13] 181 3-8-3 0 ow1 .... HayleyTurner 1 50
(Jim Boyle) *veered lft s: t.k.h towards rr but in tch: nt clr run and hung lft appr fnl f: styd on clsng stages* **4/1**[2]
42-0 **5** *shd* **Miserere Mei (IRE)**[24] 25 3-8-2 58 .... (p) JamesSullivan 3 49
(Richard Guest) *in rr: racd on outside and wd into st: drvn and styd on fnl f: no imp on ldrs clsng stages* **12/1**
60 **6** *2 1/2* **Gem Of Wizdom (IRE)**[16] 121 3-7-11 0 .... RyanPowell(3) 6 38
(J S Moore) *chsd ldr tl over 2f out: wknd appr fnl f* **80/1**

58.86s (0.06) **Going Correction** -0.125s/f (Stan) 6 Ran SP% **119.8**
Speed ratings (Par 95): **94,92,90,88,88 84**
Tote Swingers: 1&2 £2.00, 1&3 £1.10, 2&3 £3.80 CSF £5.77 TOTE £2.00: £1.10, £3.20; EX 6.20.Strike A Pose was claimed by Mr P. D. Evans £7,000.
Owner J & J Potter & The late Mrs S Edwards **Bred** Noel O'Callaghan **Trained** Pandy, Monmouths

FOCUS
Just a modest claimer.

322 BLACKBERRY LANE H'CAP 7f (P)
2:20 (2:22) (Class 6) (0-65,65) 3-Y-O **£1,704** (£503; £251) **Stalls** Low

Form RPR
-503 **1** **Lana (IRE)**[6] 250 3-8-9 53 .... HayleyTurner 8 56+
(David Evans) *t.k.h towards rr but in tch: drvn over 1f out: styd on strly fnl 120yds: chal fnl 50yds tl led fnl 30yds: kpt on wl* **16/1**
6-23 **2** *hd* **Illustrious Lad (IRE)**[9] 201 3-8-9 58 .... NathanAlison(5) 2 60+
(Jim Boyle) *chsd ldrs: drvn along fr 2f out: r.o strly fnl 120yds and upsides fnl 50yds: nt pce of wnr clsng stages* **4/1**[1]
44-3 **3** *1* **Naughtical**[12] 185 3-9-7 65 .... MichaelHills 1 65
(J W Hills) *chsd ldrs: wnt 2nd ins fnl 2f: chal fr 1f out on ins tl slt ld fnl 120yds: hdd and no ex fnl 30yds* **15/2**
000- **4** *hd* **Miss Purity Pinker (IRE)**[111] 6695 3-8-13 60 .... (v) RyanClark(3) 3 59
(David Evans) *led: rdn and jnd 1f out: hdd fnl 120yds: edgd rt fnl 50yds: outpcd clsng stages* **33/1**
25-4 **5** *nk* **Songbird Blues**[23] 38 3-8-7 51 oh1 .... DavidProbert 12 49
(Mark Usher) *chsd ldr tl ins fnl 2f: drvn to chal again ins fnl f: one pce clsng stages* **6/1**[3]
25-4 **6** *1 1/2* **Casa Bex**[16] 121 3-9-7 65 .... (vt) MartinLane 7 67+
(Philip McBride) *in rr: drvn and hdwy 1f out: styng on whn nt clr run fnl 50yds: nt rcvr* **4/1**[1]
056- **7** *hd* **Princess Maya**[37] 7838 3-9-6 64 .... DaneO'Neill 11 58
(Jo Crowley) *in rr: drvn and stl plenty to do 1f out: swtchd rt and r.o wl: gng on cl home* **6/1**[3]
140- **8** *1 1/2* **Outlaw Torn (IRE)**[106] 6817 3-8-8 57 .... (e[1]) CharlesEddery(5) 9 47
(Richard Guest) *t.k.h: trckd ldrs: drvn along 3f out: styd on fnl f but nvr a threat* **20/1**
01-3 **9** *shd* **Chambles**[15] 127 3-9-6 64 .... (t) JimCrowley 5 53
(Andrew Reid) *s.i.s sn in tch: rdn and outpcd 2f out: kpt on same pce ins fnl f* **5/1**[2]
33-5 **10** *nk* **Arabian Flight**[23] 38 3-9-2 60 .... KieranO'Neill 13 48
(John Bridger) *t.k.h in rr: drvn over 1f out: a struggling for pce* **16/1**

1m 25.11s (0.31) **Going Correction** -0.125s/f (Stan) 10 Ran SP% **116.5**
Speed ratings (Par 95): **93,92,91,91,91 89,89,87,87,86**
Tote Swingers: 1&2 £10.60, 1&3 £10.50, 2&3 £5.50 CSF £79.03 CT £544.92 TOTE £16.50: £3.70, £1.10, £2.40; EX 93.90 Trifecta £231.70 Pool: £344.46 - 1.10 winning units..
Owner Will Dawson **Bred** Mrs Brid Cosgrove **Trained** Pandy, Monmouths

FOCUS
An open handicap in which several came into the race in reasonable form and the pace looked fairly honest, which set things up for the closers.
Casa Bex Official explanation: jockey said gelding was denied a clear run

323 LINGFIELDPARK.CO.UK CLASSIFIED CLAIMING STKS 7f (P)
2:50 (2:50) (Class 6) 4-Y-O+ **£1,704** (£503; £251) **Stalls** Low

Form RPR
4-30 **1** **Satwa Laird**[9] 199 6-8-4 73 .... HayleyTurner 4 74
(David Simcock) *trckd ldr: chal fr 2f out tl drvn to ld jst ins fnl f: kpt on wl cl home* **1/1**[1]
22-3 **2** *1/2* **Fishforcompliments**[3] 284 8-8-2 73 .... (p) JamesSullivan 5 71
(Richard Fahey) *nudged along after s: in rr but wl in tch: drvn: hdwy and hung lft over 1f out: drvn between horses fnl 120yds: chsd wnr fnl 75yds but a hld* **2/1**[2]
60-3 **3** *3/4* **My Lord**[7] 220 4-7-11 69 .... DarrenEgan(7) 2 71
(Ronald Harris) *chsd ldrs: drvn to chal 1f out: stl ev ch ins fnl f: outpcd into 3rd fnl 75yds* **15/2**[3]
0-20 **4** *4 1/2* **Bold Ring**[5] 262 6-8-1 67 .... JackDuern(7) 3 63
(Eric Wheeler) *chsd ldrs: rdn over 1f out: sn wknd* **10/1**
60-0 **5** *3/4* **Strictly Pink (IRE)**[20] 88 4-7-11 63 .... (t) DominicFox(3) 1 53
(Alan Bailey) *sn led: jnd 2f out: sn rdn: hdd jst ins fnl f: sn btn* **15/2**[3]

1m 23.62s (-1.18) **Going Correction** -0.125s/f (Stan) 5 Ran SP% **116.0**
Speed ratings (Par 101): **101,100,99,94,93**
CSF £3.52 TOTE £2.10: £1.40, £1.60; EX 3.40.
Owner Dr Marwan Koukash **Bred** The Policy Setters **Trained** Newmarket, Suffolk

FOCUS
Just an ordinary claimer.

324 LINGFIELDPARK.CO.UK MAIDEN STKS 1m 2f (P)
3:20 (3:21) (Class 5) 3-Y-O **£2,385** (£704; £352) **Stalls** Low

Form RPR
0-3 **1** **Bramshill Lass**[13] 182 3-8-12 0 .... JimCrowley 7 72
(Amanda Perrett) *chsd ldrs in 3rd: rdn and outpcd 2f out: styd on u.p ins fnl f to join 3-way chal fnl 50yds: led last strides* **11/1**[3]
32-2 **2** *nk* **Cotton Trader (USA)**[11] 195 3-9-3 0 .... SteveDrowne 3 76
(John Gosden) *trckd ldr: chal fr 2f out: stl upsides and drvn 1f out tl jnd in 3-way chal and fractional ld fnl 50yds: hdd last strides* **1/2**[1]
0-3 **3** *1/2* **Three Bards (IRE)**[20] 84 3-9-3 0 .... SamHitchcott 1 75
(Mark Johnston) *led: jnd fr 2f out and strly chal fr over 1f out tl jnd in 3-way chal and narrowly hdd fnl 50yds: one pce into 3rd clsng stages* **3/1**[2]
000- **4** *7* **Never Satisfied**[120] 6483 3-9-3 68 .... MichaelHills 6 61
(Charles Hills) *in rr but in tch: drvn and tk 4th over 2f out: no ch w ldng trio and styd same pce fr over 1f out* **12/1**
5 *3 1/2* **Roughlyn** 3-9-3 0 .... TomEaves 4 54
(Kevin Ryan) *in rr: rdn along fr 4f out: wknd 2f out* **33/1**
6 *9* **Cuore (IRE)** 3-9-3 0 .... FergusSweeney 5 36
(Jamie Osborne) *pushed along 4f out: a in rr* **50/1**
000- **7** *1 1/4* **Hearduthefirsttime (IRE)**[38] 7835 3-9-3 30 .... (b[1]) MickyFenton 2 34
(Barney Curley) *chsd ldrs: rdn over 3f out: wknd qckly over 2f out* **100/1**

2m 6.16s (-0.44) **Going Correction** -0.125s/f (Stan) 7 Ran SP% **113.6**
Speed ratings (Par 97): **96,95,95,89,86 79,78**
Tote Swingers: 1&2 £1.90, 2&3 £1.50 CSF £17.07 TOTE £8.60: £2.50, £1.10; EX 27.70.
Owner Mrs Karen Hancock **Bred** Bloomsbury Stud **Trained** Pulborough, W Sussex

FOCUS
The market suggested this was all about Cotton Trader, who was very well backed, but while his form set a useful standard he had achieved nothing spectacular on the clock so far and he lacked the finishing kick to get the job done once again.

325 BLUE SQUARE WINTER CARNIVAL IPHONE APP H'CAP 6f (P)
3:50 (3:51) (Class 5) (0-75,75) 4-Y-O+ **£2,385** (£704; £352) **Stalls** High

Form RPR
65-4 **1** **Roman Strait**[13] 178 4-8-13 67 .... DaneO'Neill 3 76
(Michael Blanshard) *in rr: hdwy on outside wl over 1f out: styd on to chse ldr jst ins fnl f: kpt on strly to ld fnl 100yds: pushed out* **3/1**[2]
0-02 **2** *1* **Falasteen (IRE)**[4] 272 5-9-7 75 .... (b) HayleyTurner 2 81
(Kevin Ryan) *led: rdn 2 l clr appr fnl f: hdd and outpcd fnl 100yds but stl hld on for 2nd* **7/4**[1]
30-0 **3** *nk* **Kylladdie**[16] 120 5-9-7 75 .... (b) JimmyFortune 7 80
(Steve Gollings) *chsd ldrs: rdn over 1f out and tk 3rd ins fnl f: clsng on 2nd nr fin but no imp on wnr* **7/1**
001- **4** *2* **Caledonia Princess**[90] 7173 6-9-7 75 .... WilliamCarson 5 73
(Stuart Williams) *chsd ldrs: rdn to disp 2nd 1f out but no imp on ldr: one pce ins fnl f* **9/2**[3]
0-06 **5** *1/2* **Clear Ice (IRE)**[19] 100 5-9-2 70 .... (bt) ChrisCatlin 6 67
(Gay Kelleway) *chsd ldr tl jst ins fnl f: sn btn* **10/1**
143- **6** *5* **Yankee Storm**[279] 1523 7-9-3 74 .... RyanClark(3) 1 55
(Michael Wigham) *chsd ldrs on ins: drvn to dispute 2nd appr fnl f: wknd sn after* **12/1**
-100 **7** *1* **Dickie Le Davoir**[13] 178 8-8-6 65 .... (p) CharlesEddery(5) 4 43
(Richard Guest) *awkward leaving stalls and slowly away: sn rdn along: nvr travelling and a bhd* **20/1**

1m 10.61s (-1.29) **Going Correction** -0.125s/f (Stan) 7 Ran SP% **113.6**
Speed ratings (Par 103): **103,101,101,98,97 91,89**
Tote Swingers: 1&2 £2.00, 1&3 £3.50, 2&3 £3.70 CSF £8.55 TOTE £3.10: £1.40, £1.60; EX 10.60.
Owner J M Beever **Bred** J M Beever **Trained** Upper Lambourn, Berks

FOCUS
A fair sprint.
Dickie Le Davoir Official explanation: jockey said gelding was slowly away

326 PLAY RAINBOW RICHES AT BLUESQ.COM H'CAP 5f (P)
4:20 (4:20) (Class 6) (0-65,62) 3-Y-O **£1,704** (£503; £251) **Stalls** High

Form RPR
65-1 **1** **Lady Caprice**[22] 40 3-9-7 62 .... (p) ChrisCatlin 1 71
(Jane Chapple-Hyam) *disp ld tl led 1/2-way: drvn over 1f out: jnd fnl120yds: hld on all out* **5/1**[2]
02-1 **2** *nse* **Welease Bwian (IRE)**[7] 228 3-9-5 60 6ex .... (t) WilliamCarson 5 69
(Stuart Williams) *in tch: hdwy whn n.m.r and awkward bnd 2f out: drvn to chse wnr over 1f out: str chal thrght fnl 120yds: no ex last strides* **1/2**[1]
33-5 **3** *2* **Wild Sauce**[22] 41 3-9-5 60 .... TomEaves 3 62
(Bryan Smart) *disp ld tl chsd wnr 1/2-way: rdn and outpcd over 1f out: styd on again to take one-pced 3rd ins fnl f* **7/1**[3]
3-04 **4** *2 1/2* **Marie's Fantasy**[7] 219 3-8-12 53 .... JamieGoldstein 6 46
(Zoe Davison) *in rr early: hdwy on ins to chse wnr ins fnl 2f: wknd ins fnl f* **10/1**
55-6 **5** *3 1/4* **Regal Lady**[15] 135 3-8-5 53 .... ClaireMurray(7) 4 34
(David Brown) *chsd ldrs on outside: rdn 2f out and sn wknd* **33/1**

58.35s (-0.45) **Going Correction** -0.125s/f (Stan) 5 Ran SP% **107.9**
Speed ratings (Par 95): **98,97,94,90,85**
CSF £7.73 TOTE £4.00: £1.80, £1.10; EX 5.90.
Owner Mrs A Cantillon **Bred** Lady Betambeau Partnership **Trained** Dalham, Suffolk

FOCUS
A modest race.
T/Plt: £8.90 to a £1 stake. Pool: £62,490.53 - 3.44 winning tickets. T/Qpdt: £5.50 to a £1 stake. Pool: £4,459.94 - 589.72 winning tickets. ST

268 WOLVERHAMPTON (A.W) (L-H)
Friday, January 27

OFFICIAL GOING: Standard
Wind: Fresh, behind. Weather: Cloudy

327 BET AT BLUE SQUARE CLAIMING STKS 5f 20y(P)
4:40 (4:41) (Class 6) 4-Y-O+ **£1,704** (£503; £251) **Stalls** Low

Form RPR
54-2 **1** **Master Of Disguise**[8] 215 6-8-11 78 .... (t) RussKennemore 6 72
(Brian Baugh) *a.p: edgd lft wl over 3f out: chsd ldr over 1f out: rdn to ld wl ins fnl f: r.o* **5/2**[1]
10-4 **2** *1* **Suddenly Susan (IRE)**[8] 212 4-8-3 65 .... (b) RaulDaSilva(5) 7 66
(Scott Dixon) *chsd ldrs: rdn over 1f out: r.o* **9/1**
1-00 **3** *1/2* **Steelcut**[6] 251 8-8-7 69 .... (p) MatthewCosham(5) 2 68
(David Evans) *hld up: hdwy and nt clr run over 1f out: sn rdn: r.o to go 3rd post: nt rch ldrs* **8/1**[3]
30-4 **4** *shd* **Ebraam (USA)**[8] 215 9-8-11 88 .... LukeMorris 3 67
(Ronald Harris) *hld up: hdwy over 1f out: sn rdn: r.o* **7/2**[2]
36-6 **5** *3/4* **Grand Stitch (USA)**[14] 152 6-8-8 58 .... (v) NeilFarley(5) 8 66?
(Declan Carroll) *sn led: pushed along 1/2-way: rdn over 1f out: hdd and no ex wl ins fnl f* **66/1**

100- **6** 3/4 **Lucky Art (USA)**[69] 7487 6-8-6 77 .... DavidKenny(5) 5 61
(Conor Dore) *chsd ldr: pushed along 1/2-way: rdn over 1f out: styd on same pce ins fnl f* **16/1**

30-0 **7** 3 1/4 **Where's Reiley (USA)**[5] 266 6-9-1 80 ....(b) KierenFallon 4 54
(Alastair Lidderdale) *s.s: outpcd* **5/2**[1]

06-4 **8** 1 1/2 **Luscivious**[15] 133 8-8-9 67 ....(bt) MichaelO'Connell(3) 1 45
(Scott Dixon) *s.i.s: mid-div whn hmpd wl over 3f out: rdn 1/2-way: wknd over 1f out* **28/1**

1m 2.28s (-0.02) **Going Correction** +0.10s/f (Slow) **8** Ran SP% **111.3**
Speed ratings (Par 101): **104,102,101,101,100 99,93,91**
Tote Swingers:1&2:£3.60, 2&3:£6.80, 1&3:£4.10 CSF £24.74 TOTE £3.00: £1.30, £3.20, £2.40; EX 19.60.
Owner 21C Telecom.co.uk **Bred** T R Lock **Trained** Audley, Staffs

FOCUS
The track was worked to nearly full depth to allow for the introduction of some additional "binder", which was completed on Wednesday. The track has since been rolled and reinstated to "standard". Exposed performers in a fair claimer. The gallop was sound and the winner came down the centre in the straight.
Where's Reiley(USA) Official explanation: jockey said gelding started awkwardly and was slowly away

328 WOLVERHAMPTON HOLIDAY INN H'CAP (DIV I) 7f 32y(P)
5:10 (5:11) (Class 6) (0-65,69) 4-Y-O+ **£1,704** (£503; £251) **Stalls** High

Form RPR

61-0 **1** **Fleetwoodsands (IRE)**[21] 67 5-9-7 65 ....(t) LiamKeniry 9 77
(Milton Bradley) *s.s: hld up: hdwy over 2f out: rdn to ld over 1f out: edgd rt: r.o* **4/1**[2]

45-1 **2** shd **Garstang**[5] 262 9-9-11 69 6ex .... JoeFanning 3 80
(Bruce Hellier, Germany) *mid-div: pushed along 1/2-way: hdwy over 2f out: rdn and ev ch fr over 1f out: r.o* **6/1**

00-5 **3** 4 **Double Carpet (IRE)**[18] 102 9-9-2 60 .... AdamKirby 5 61
(Garry Woodward) *chsd ldrs: outpcd over 2f out: edgd lft and r.o ins fnl f* **9/2**[3]

24-0 **4** 2 3/4 **Silver Wind**[20] 88 7-9-7 65 ....(b) ShaneKelly 6 58
(Alan McCabe) *prom: rdn over 1f out: wknd ins fnl f* **7/2**[1]

0-30 **5** 1 **Spin Again (IRE)**[5] 262 7-9-0 63 .... LucyKBarry(5) 4 53
(Mark Wellings) *chsd ldr tl led 4f out: rdn and hdd over 1f out: wknd ins fnl f* **15/2**

20-0 **6** 1 1/4 **Babich Bay (IRE)**[19] 100 4-9-0 65 ....(p) JoshBaudains(7) 10 52
(Jo Hughes) *chsd ldrs: pushed along and ev ch fr over 2f out tl wknd ins fnl f* **14/1**

010- **7** 10 **Ensnare**[74] 7418 7-9-5 63 .... StevieDonohoe 1 23
(John Butler) *s.s: nudged along in rr: nvr nr to chal* **6/1**

50-0 **8** 7 **Fortunelini**[14] 153 7-8-5 54 ....(t) RaulDaSilva(5) 8
(Frank Sheridan) *sn led: hdd 4f out: rdn and wknd over 2f out* **16/1**

10-6 **9** 4 **Prize Point**[15] 134 6-9-7 65 .... PaddyAspell 7
(Tom Gretton) *chsd ldrs tl wknd over 2f out* **33/1**

1m 29.33s (-0.27) **Going Correction** +0.10s/f (Slow) **9** Ran SP% **116.2**
Speed ratings (Par 101): **105,104,100,97,96 94,83,75,70**
Tote Swingers:1&2:£3.60, 2&3:£4.60, 1&3:£4.90 CSF £28.47 CT £113.04 TOTE £5.70: £1.80, £1.90, £1.90; EX 29.80.
Owner E R Griffiths **Bred** Gary O'Reilly **Trained** Sedbury, Gloucs

FOCUS
A modest handicap but a reasonable gallop in which the first two pulled clear in the straight. The winner raced against the inside rail in the straight.
Fleetwoodsands(IRE) Official explanation: trainer's rep said, regarding apparent improvement in form, that the gelding had settled better and been dropped back in trip.

329 WOLVERHAMPTON HOLIDAY INN H'CAP (DIV II) 7f 32y(P)
5:40 (5:41) (Class 6) (0-65,65) 4-Y-O+ **£1,704** (£503; £251) **Stalls** High

Form RPR

6-23 **1** **Needwood Ridge**[4] 269 5-9-2 65 ....(bt) RaulDaSilva(5) 2 73
(Frank Sheridan) *chsd ldrs: rdn to ld ins fnl f: r.o* **5/2**[1]

0-50 **2** 3/4 **Monsieur Pontaven**[14] 154 5-8-9 53 .... LeeNewman 9 59
(Robin Bastiman) *hld up in tch: pushed along 1/2-way: rdn over 1f out: r.o* **20/1**

00-6 **3** 1/2 **Powerful Pierre**[15] 128 5-9-4 65 ....(v) DaleSwift(3) 1 70
(Ian McInnes) *prom: rdn over 2f out: r.o* **40/1**

320- **4** nk **Could It Be Magic**[116] 6586 5-9-6 64 ....(b) LukeMorris 4 68+
(Olivia Maylam) *mid-div: whn hmpd: rdr lost irons and dropped to rr over 6f out: hdwy over 1f out: r.o: nvr able to chal: fin lame* **7/2**[2]

00-2 **5** 1/2 **Dunmore Boy (IRE)**[24] 21 4-9-2 60 .... TonyHamilton 3 62
(Richard Fahey) *plld hrd: led: rdn over 1f out: hdd and unable qck ins fnl f* **10/1**

2-20 **6** 1 1/2 **Resplendent Alpha**[3] 276 8-8-10 59 ....(tp) JemmaMarshall(5) 5 57
(Alastair Lidderdale) *hld up: pushed along over 2f out: rdn and r.o ins fnl f: nvr trbld ldrs* **10/1**

430- **7** 2 3/4 **Boy The Bell**[36] 7857 5-9-2 65 .... ShaneBKelly(5) 6 56
(Ollie Pears) *prom: hmpd over 6f out: pushed along 1/2-way: rdn over 2f out: wknd fnl f* **8/1**

30-5 **8** hd **Spirit Of Grace**[18] 106 4-9-7 65 .... KierenFallon 8 55
(Alan McCabe) *w ldr tl rdn over 1f out: wknd ins fnl f* **8/1**

53/- **9** 11 **Khateer**[454] 7244 5-9-4 62 .... RichardKingscote 10 23
(Milton Bradley) *prom: pushed along over 2f out: sn wknd* **13/2**[3]

00-6 **10** 1/2 **Wishbone (IRE)**[18] 106 5-9-5 63 .... RobbieFitzpatrick 7 22
(Jo Hughes) *s.i.s: hld up: nvr on terms* **33/1**

1m 30.49s (0.89) **Going Correction** +0.10s/f (Slow) **10** Ran SP% **114.7**
Speed ratings (Par 101): **98,97,96,96,95 93,90,90,78,77**
Tote Swingers:1&2:£12.90, 2&3:£83.30, 1&3:£20.10 CSF £56.52 CT £1630.13 TOTE £3.30: £1.60, £6.50, £10.80; EX 54.20.
Owner Frank Sheridan **Bred** Mrs Joy Maund-Powell **Trained** Wolverhampton, W Midlands

FOCUS
The second division of a modest handicap in which several met early trouble. The gallop was fair and the winner raced towards the centre in the straight.
Could It Be Magic Official explanation: vet said gelding finished lame

330 HOTEL & CONFERENCING AT WOLVERHAMPTON CLASSIFIED CLAIMING STKS 1m 141y(P)
6:10 (6:10) (Class 5) 4-Y-O+ **£2,264** (£673; £336; £168) **Stalls** Low

Form RPR

-414 **1** **Spinning Ridge (IRE)**[2] 299 7-8-10 68 ....(v) LukeMorris 5 70
(Ronald Harris) *trckd ldr: racd keenly: led over 1f out: sn rdn and edgd lft: jst hld on* **11/4**[2]

2-25 **2** hd **Marvo**[13] 176 8-8-8 62 ....(b) JoeFanning 8 68
(Mark H Tompkins) *hld up: shkn up over 1f out: r.o to go 2nd wl ins fnl f: jst failed* **10/1**

500- **3** 3/4 **Dream Of Fortune (IRE)**[56] 7605 8-8-5 64 ....(bt) FrannyNorton 1 63
(David Evans) *hld up: hdwy over 2f out: rdn and hung lft ins fnl f: styd on* **16/1**

2-62 **4** 3/4 **Pipers Piping (IRE)**[3] 287 6-8-8 65 ....(p) KierenFallon 2 64
(Alastair Lidderdale) *chsd ldrs: pushed along over 2f out: rdn and edgd lft over 1f out: styd on* **9/4**[1]

-353 **5** 1/2 **Ajdaad (USA)**[6] 248 5-8-0 65 .... NoraLooby(7) 3 63
(Alan McCabe) *hld up: hdwy over 1f out: hmpd ins fnl f: styd on same pce* **7/1**

4-33 **6** nse **Spin Cast**[4] 273 4-8-7 69 ....(v) StevieDonohoe 4 63
(Joseph Tuite) *prom: pushed along over 2f out: rdn over 1f out: styd on* **9/2**[3]

130- **7** hd **Quite A Catch (IRE)**[36] 7857 4-8-10 68 ....(v) LeeNewman 9 65
(Jonathan Portman) *racd keenly: sn led: rdn and hdd over 1f out: styd on same pce fnl f* **16/1**

10-6 **8** 1 **Ahlawy (IRE)**[7] 229 9-8-0 60 ....(t) RaulDaSilva(5) 7 57
(Frank Sheridan) *dwlt: hld up: rdn over 1f out: nvr trbld ldrs* **25/1**

1m 52.56s (2.06) **Going Correction** +0.10s/f (Slow)
WFA 4 from 5yo+ 1lb **8** Ran SP% **112.8**
Speed ratings (Par 103): **94,93,93,92,92 92,91,90**
Tote Swingers:1&2:£6.90, 2&3:£19.30, 1&3:£10.20 CSF £29.23 TOTE £2.70: £1.10, £3.10, £4.00; EX 33.10.
Owner Robert & Nina Bailey **Bred** Eddie O'Leary **Trained** Earlswood, Monmouths

FOCUS
A modest event run at an ordinary gallop. The winner edged towards the far side in the closing stages.

331 WOLVERHAMPTON-RACECOURSE.CO.UK MAIDEN FILLIES' STKS 1m 141y(P)
6:40 (6:41) (Class 5) 3-Y-O+ **£2,264** (£673; £336; £168) **Stalls** Low

Form RPR

6- **1** **Arch Of Colours**[177] 4662 3-8-5 0 .... JoeFanning 5 73+
(Mark Johnston) *mde all: set stdy pce tl qcknd 2f out: edgd lft ins fnl f: readily* **5/1**[2]

34-2 **2** 3 1/4 **Zenarinda**[15] 136 5-9-13 67 .... KierenFallon 1 71
(Mark H Tompkins) *trckd wnr: racd keenly: shkn up over 1f out: sn outpcd* **14/1**

3 nk **Margate** 3-8-5 0 .... FrannyNorton 4 65
(Charles Hills) *chsd ldrs: shkn up over 2f out: styd on same pce* **4/6**[1]

4-42 **4** 6 **Millibar (IRE)**[9] 206 3-8-5 70 ....(p) LukeMorris 2 52
(Nick Littmoden) *hld up: hdwy 5f out: rdn over 2f out: wknd over 1f out* **10/1**

5 3/4 **Strawberrymystique** 4-9-7 0 .... RaulDaSilva(5) 3 55
(Marco Botti) *hld up: rdn and wknd over 1f out* **11/2**[3]

1m 51.12s (0.62) **Going Correction** +0.10s/f (Slow)
WFA 3 from 4yo 22lb 4 from 5yo 1lb **5** Ran SP% **107.8**
Speed ratings (Par 100): **101,98,97,92,91**
CSF £54.00 TOTE £3.60: £1.50, £5.40; EX 36.80.
Owner Sheikh Hamdan Bin Mohammed Al Maktoum **Bred** Darley **Trained** Middleham Moor, N Yorks

FOCUS
An uncompetitive fillies' maiden run at a steady gallop to the home turn but an improved effort from the winner, who came down the centre.

332 BLUE SQUARE WINTER CARNIVAL IPHONE APP H'CAP 2m 119y(P)
7:10 (7:10) (Class 4) (0-85,83) 4-Y-O+ **£4,204** (£1,251; £625; £312) **Stalls** Low

Form RPR

0-44 **1** **Nezhenka**[9] 202 5-9-11 80 .... JoeFanning 8 89
(Mark Johnston) *hld up: hdwy 5f out: led over 1f out: styd on wl* **9/2**[2]

05-1 **2** 2 1/4 **Rosewood Lad**[22] 44 5-9-3 72 .... LukeMorris 10 78
(J S Moore) *chsd ldrs: pushed along 4f out: led 2f out: sn rdn and hdd: styd on same pce ins fnl f* **7/2**[1]

03-2 **3** 3/4 **Crunched**[9] 207 5-9-6 75 ....(v) ShaneKelly 3 80
(Tim Pitt) *trckd ldrs: hmpd wl over 2f out: rdn over 1f out: styd on same pce ins fnl f* **13/2**

214- **4** shd **C P Joe (IRE)**[31] 7884 4-8-6 68 ....(v) FrannyNorton 5 73
(Paul Green) *hld up: hdwy over 2f out: rdn over 1f out: styd on* **11/1**

015/ **5** 1 3/4 **Sam Lord**[7] 4098 8-9-6 75 .... PaddyAspell 6 78
(James Moffatt) *hld up: hdwy 5f out: rdn over 2f out: styd on same pce fr over 1f out* **40/1**

520- **6** 3/4 **Penangdouble O One**[30] 6893 5-9-3 72 ....(t) RichardKingscote 9 74
(Alex Hales) *chsd ldr tl led over 3f out: rdn and hdd 2f out: no ex fnl f* **40/1**

3-02 **7** 1 1/4 **Follow The Flag (IRE)**[13] 177 8-10-0 83 ....(be) AdamKirby 7 83
(Alan McCabe) *hld up: rdn over 2f out: n.d* **11/1**

100- **8** 7 **Not Til Monday (IRE)**[26] 7236 6-9-3 72 ....(v) KierenFallon 4 64
(J R Jenkins) *set stdy pce tl hdd over 3f out: n.m.r over 2f out: sn wknd* **6/1**[3]

024- **9** hd **Westlin' Winds (IRE)**[17] 3450 6-8-4 64 oh2 ....(t) RaulDaSilva(5) 1 56+
(Graeme McPherson) *hld up: leather broke after 2f and rdr rode wout irons thereafter: a in rr* **28/1**

311- **10** 2 1/2 **Three White Socks (IRE)**[239] 2654 5-8-8 66 .... PaulPickard(3) 2 55
(Brian Ellison) *prom: rdn over 3f out: wknd over 2f out* **7/2**[1]

3m 40.99s (-0.81) **Going Correction** +0.10s/f (Slow)
WFA 4 from 5yo+ 7lb **10** Ran SP% **115.2**
Speed ratings (Par 105): **105,103,103,103,102 102,101,98,98,97**
Tote Swingers:1&2:£5.60, 2&3:£6.80, 1&3:£5.30 CSF £20.07 CT £99.90 TOTE £3.90: £1.40, £1.30, £4.10; EX 24.50.
Owner Miss K Rausing **Bred** Miss K Rausing **Trained** Middleham Moor, N Yorks
■ Stewards' Enquiry : Richard Kingscote caution: careless riding.

FOCUS
A reasonable handicap run at an ordinary gallop. The winner came down the centre in the straight.
Westlin' Winds(IRE) Official explanation: jockey said stirrup buckle became unfastened

333 SPONSOR A BY CALLING 01902 390000 H'CAP 1m 1f 103y(P)
7:40 (7:41) (Class 6) (0-55,60) 4-Y-O+ **£1,704** (£503; £251) **Stalls** Low

Form RPR

3-35 **1** **Warden Bond**[3] 276 4-8-12 52 ....(p) MartinLane 11 59
(William Stone) *trckd ldrs: led over 2f out: rdn over 1f out: styd on* **5/1**[2]

02-5 **2** 3/4 **Penbryn (USA)**[4] 274 5-9-2 55 ....(v[1]) SteveDrowne 7 61
(Nick Littmoden) *hld up: hdwy over 1f out: sn rdn and hung lft: styd on: nt rch wnr* **7/1**[3]

000- **3** nk **Beneath**[107] 6784 5-9-2 55 ....(b) AdamKirby 3 60
(Neil Mulholland) *a.p: pushed along to chse wnr 2f out: sn rdn: styd on* **9/2**[1]

00-0 **4** 1 1/4 **Ergo (FR)**[18] 104 8-9-0 53 ....(b) PaddyAspell 4 55+
(James Moffatt) *hld up: hdwy u.p over 1f out: nrst fin* **18/1**

06-0 **5** *hd* **Thank You Joy**[15] [130] 4-8-12 **52**..............................(v[1]) FrannyNorton 9 54
(J R Jenkins) *hld up: hdwy over 1f out: r.o: nt trble ldrs* **33/1**

00-2 **6** *2* **Raise The Rafters (IRE)**[25] [14] 7-9-1 **54**......................(t) LiamKeniry 8 52
(John Butler) *trckd ldrs: rdn over 1f out: styd on same pce fnl f* **9/1**

660- **7** *1 ¾* **Granny Anne (IRE)**[29] [7910] 4-8-8 **53**......................(p) RaulDaSilva[(5)] 6 47
(Paul D'Arcy) *hld up: hdwy over 1f out: nvr nrr* **20/1**

33-5 **8** *½* **Poppy Golightly**[14] [151] 5-8-8 **52**.................................... NeilFarley[(5)] 1 45
(Declan Carroll) *led 2f: chsd ldr tl over 3f out: rdn over 2f out: wknd over 1f out* **11/1**

00-0 **9** *1 ¾* **Pursuing**[12] [188] 4-8-12 **52**..(p) JoeFanning 2 41
(Nigel Tinkler) *hld up: sme hdwy over 1f out: hung lft and wknd fnl f* **22/1**

200- **10** *3 ½* **Final Tune (IRE)**[37] [7848] 9-9-1 **54**............................ TomMcLaughlin 6 36
(Mandy Rowland) *mid-div: rdn over 3f out: wknd over 1f out: eased fnl f* **50/1**

6-41 **11** *4 ½* **Petomic (IRE)**[4] [274] 7-9-4 **60** 6ex........................(p) RobertLButler[(3)] 13 33
(Richard Guest) *dwlt: pushed along in rr early: rdn over 3f out: wknd over 2f out* **9/2[1]**

00-0 **12** *6* **Lean Machine**[4] [274] 5-9-2 **55**.......................................(p) LukeMorris 12 15
(Ronald Harris) *prom tl wknd over 2f out: eased: sddle slipped* **9/1**

00-0 **13** *3 ½* **Flotation (USA)**[4] [274] 5-8-13 **52**..............................(b[1]) PhillipMakin 10
(Roy Brotherton) *prom: led over 7f out: rdn and hdd over 2f out: wknd wl over 1f out* **33/1**

2m 1.9s (0.20) **Going Correction** +0.10s/f (Slow)
WFA 4 from 5yo+ 1lb **13** Ran SP% **116.1**
Speed ratings (Par 101): **103,102,102,100,100 99,97,97,95,92 88,83,79**
Tote Swingers:1&2:£6.60, 2&3:£10.00, 1&3:£6.20 CSF £36.06 CT £169.19 TOTE £8.30: £3.80, £4.80, £1.10; EX 49.00.
Owner J A Ross & Miss C Scott **Bred** Park Farm Racing **Trained** West Wickham, Cambs

FOCUS
A moderate handicap run at an ordinary gallop. The winner raced centre-to-far-side in the straight.
Penbryn(USA) Official explanation: jockey said gelding hung left-handed in home straight
Lean Machine Official explanation: jockey said saddle slipped

334 PLAY RAINBOW RICHES AT BLUESQ.COM H'CAP 1m 141y(P)
8:10 (8:10) (Class 7) (0-50,54) 4-Y-0+ **£1,704** (£503; £251) **Stalls** Low

Form RPR

03-6 **1** **Cwmni**[22] [45] 6-9-3 **49**... LukeMorris 9 57+
(Bryn Palling) *hld up: hdwy over 1f out: rdn to ld wl ins fnl f: r.o* **6/1[2]**

56-1 **2** *1 ¾* **Look For Love**[8] [218] 4-9-0 **54** 6ex...............................(e) JackDuern[(7)] 5 58
(Reg Hollinshead) *a.p: rdn to chse ldr and swtchd rt over 1f out: styd on* **3/1[1]**

40-2 **3** *1* **Love In The Park**[21] [66] 7-9-0 **46**................................(b) PhillipMakin 8 48
(Roy Brotherton) *chsd ldr tl led over 2f out: rdn over 1f out: hdd and no ex wl ins fnl f* **3/1[1]**

606- **4** *shd* **Luv U Noo**[37] [7851] 5-8-8 **45**.. JamesRogers[(5)] 3 47+
(Brian Baugh) *s.i.s: hld up: swtchd rt and r.o wl ins fnl f: nrst fin* **13/2[3]**

P0-0 **5** *2 ¼* **Le Reveur**[17] [7] 10-8-10 **45**.................................(e) RobertLButler[(3)] 10 42
(Richard Guest) *hld up: rdn over 2f out: styd on: nt trble ldrs* **50/1**

03-5 **6** *shd* **Wing N Prayer (IRE)**[22] [45] 5-9-2 **48**.......................(p) PaddyAspell 11 44
(John Wainwright) *chsd ldrs: rdn over 2f out: styd on same pce fnl f* **10/1**

0/0- **7** *¾* **Expensive Legacy**[53] [7639] 5-8-6 **45**.......................... RachealKneller[(7)] 4 40
(Tor Sturgis) *mid-div: lost pl 4f out: n.d after* **33/1**

/0-0 **8** *1 ¼* **Portrush Storm**[21] [66] 7-8-13 **45**.................................. StevieDonohoe 7 37
(Ray Peacock) *hld up: rdn over 1f out: styd on: nt trble ldrs* **33/1**

60-0 **9** *1 ½* **Don't Call Me Tiny (IRE)**[12] [188] 4-8-13 **46**..................... LiamKeniry 2 34
(Don Cantillon) *chsd ldrs: rdn over 3f out: wknd fnl f* **8/1**

0-30 **10** *1 ¼* **Kirstys Lad**[8] [218] 10-8-8 **47**.. NoelGarbutt[(7)] 6 32
(Michael Mullineaux) *led: rdn and hdd over 2f out: wknd fnl f* **12/1**

00-6 **11** *7* **Mrs Medley**[25] [10] 6-8-10 **45**....................................(b) RyanPowell[(3)] 1 14
(Garry Woodward) *hld up in tch: rdn 1/2-way: wknd over 2f out* **150/1**

1m 52.08s (1.58) **Going Correction** +0.10s/f (Slow)
WFA 4 from 5yo+ 1lb **11** Ran SP% **114.0**
Speed ratings (Par 97): **96,94,93,93,91 91,90,89,88,87 80**
Tote Swingers:1&2:£4.30, 2&3:£2.00, 1&3:£3.90 CSF £23.12 CT £64.20 TOTE £6.30: £2.00, £1.20, £1.40; EX 24.30.
Owner Flying Eight Partnership **Bred** Exors Of The Late Mrs M M Palling **Trained** Tredodridge, Vale Of Glamorgan

FOCUS
A moderate handicap run at just an ordinary gallop. The winner came down the centre in the straight.
T/Plt: £157.20 to a £1 stake. Pool £88,095.82. 409.01 winning units. T/Qpdt: £46.40 to a £1 stake. Pool £10,263.49. 163.60 winning units. CR

233 DUNDALK (A.W) (L-H)
Friday, January 27

OFFICIAL GOING: Standard

335a GROUP BOOKINGS AT DUNDALK RATED RACE 6f (P)
5:50 (5:50) 4-Y-0+ **£4,600** (£1,066; £466; £266)

RPR

1 **An Saighdiur (IRE)**[141] [5870] 5-9-0 68.................................... WJLee 12 71
(Andrew Slattery, Ire) *chsd ldrs: 4th 1/2-way: travelled wl 2f out: rdn to chal 1f out: sn led and strly pressed: kpt on wl u.p: all out* **8/1**

2 *hd* **Tsar Paul (IRE)**[7] [237] 7-9-0 68..................................(t) PatSmullen 4 71+
(J A Nash, Ire) *chsd ldrs: 5th 1/2-way: rdn to chal 1f out: pressed wnr fnl f: jst hld (reported to have burst blood vessel)* **10/3[1]**

3 *1 ½* **Almadaa**[14] [162] 5-9-0 65.. JFEgan 11 66
(David Marnane, Ire) *mid-div: 7th 1/2-way: hdwy in 5th 2f out: rdn to ld over 1f out: hdd under 1f out: no ex and kpt on same pce* **9/2[2]**

4 *1 ¼* **Joe Le Taxi (IRE)**[9] [205] 4-8-9 .... DarylByrne[(5)] 8 62
(Mark Johnston) *chsd ldrs: 3rd 1/2-way: rdn to chal over 1f out: no ex ins fnl f: kpt on same pce* **9/2[2]**

5 *1 ¾* **Richelieu**[14] [163] 10-9-0 67..(b) KevinManning 2 56
(Lee Smyth, Ire) *hld up towards rr: hdwy into 7th 2f out: rdn in 5th and no imp 1f out: kpt on same pce* **5/1[3]**

6 *2 ¼* **Romeo's On Fire (IRE)**[7] [236] 8-8-5 68 ow1............. DavidParkes[(10)] 5 50
(Lee Smyth, Ire) *hld up towards rr: sme late hdwy fr over 1f out: nvr a danger* **16/1**

7 *nk* **Alvar (USA)**[163] [5191] 4-8-9 45.. ConorHoban[(5)] 7 48
(M Halford, Ire) *hld up towards rr: sme late hdwy fr over 1f out: nvr a danger* **66/1**

8 *1 ¾* **Mrs Batt (IRE)**[14] [163] 6-8-4 46....................................(b) ShaneGray[(7)] 6 40
(John W Nicholson, Ire) *led and disp: rdn and hdd over 1f out: no ex* **10/1**

9 *nk* **Grigorovitch (IRE)**[14] [163] 10-8-7 61......................... GaryPhillips[(7)] 13 42
(Liam McAteer, Ire) *sn disp: rdn in 2nd 2f out: sn no ex* **33/1**

10 *shd* **Gandolfini (IRE)**[7] [236] 9-9-0 59.....................................(p) WayneLordan 9 41
(H Rogers, Ire) *mid-div: 8th 1/2-way: rdn 2f out: sn no ex* **25/1**

11 *1* **Rum King (USA)**[146] [5734] 5-8-11 66...............(b[1]) AndrewPThornton[(3)] 3 38
(S Donohoe, Ire) *a towards rr* **33/1**

12 *2 ½* **Red Army Blues (IRE)**[7] [237] 4-9-0 66.................(b) JohnnyMurtagh 10 52+
(G M Lyons, Ire) *rrd leaving stalls: trailing for most* **5/1[3]**

13 *1 ½* **The Yellow Bin (IRE)**[14] [165] 4-9-0 .... MichaelHussey 14 25
(S Donohoe, Ire) *chsd ldrs: 6th 1/2-way: rdn and wknd ent st* **50/1**

14 *13* **Hi Kort Lady (IRE)**[193] [4109] 5-8-11 ....(p) RoryCleary 1
(Niall Moran, Ire) *in rr of mid-div: rdn and wknd ent st: eased over 1f out* **66/1**

1m 11.96s (71.96) **14** Ran SP% **133.5**
CSF £37.47 TOTE £12.90: £4.10, £1.10, £2.60; DF 78.70.
Owner Men Of Forty Eight Syndicate **Bred** S Ross **Trained** Thurles, Co Tipperary
■ Stewards' Enquiry : Pat Smullen caution: used whip without giving gelding time to respond
W J Lee caution: used whip other than down the shoulder or on hind quarters

FOCUS
Not a bad handicap for the time of year and for the class of race with a few of them coming into the race in form. The third has been rated close to his previous C&D win.

NOTEBOOK
An Saighdiur(IRE) wasn't necessarily one of them as he hadn't run since Laytown in September but he was a previous course winner and travelled really well here the whole way. He quickened up smartly enough and then showed a bit of mettle to hold off the challenge of the favourite. He looked well in at the weights and the handicappers assessment of him and the runner-up proved spot-on. He should be capable of coming back and winning a handicap. Winning trainer Andy Slattery: "He looked well in at the weights. I think he'll stay 1m 2f if he can be dropped in and maybe even 2 miles over hurdles but he'll stick to these at the moment."
Tsar Paul(IRE) travelled well and was produced with every chance a furlong out. He just couldn't get past the winner although he was getting there inch by inch. He'll get his turn. Official explanation: trainer said gelding was found to have burst a blood vessel post-race which was confirmed by the vet (op 3/1 tchd 7/2)
Almadaa came there with every chance between horses inside the final furlong and a half but just wasn't good enough. According to his mark though he ran as well as his mark entitled him to.
Joe Le Taxi(IRE) helped set much of the pace but couldn't sustain it inside the final quarter. (op 5/1)
Richelieu kept on at one pace inside the last and ran a race more in keeping with his pre-penalty mark than his new one. (op 11/2)
Red Army Blues(IRE) was hopelessly left in the stalls. (op 66/1)

336a FUNDRAISING MADE EASY AT DUNDALK 3YO MAIDEN 7f (P)
6:20 (6:20) 3-Y-O **£5,750** (£1,333; £583; £333)

RPR

1 **Honourable Emperor (IRE)**[56] [7611] 3-9-5 .... JPO'Brien 2 79
(Noel Meade, Ire) *chsd ldrs: 4th 1/2-way: pushed along in 3rd 2f out: rdn into 2nd under 1f out: kpt on wl fnl f to ld on line* **7/1[3]**

2 *shd* **Atticus Finch (IRE)**[14] [161] 3-9-5 74......................... WayneLordan 8 79
(Edward Lynam, Ire) *attempted to make all: rdn to assert over 1f out: kpt on fnl f: hdd on line* **3/1[2]**

3 *2 ¼* **Roman General (IRE)**[119] [6508] 3-9-5 73.................... JohnnyMurtagh 1 73
(Edward Lynam, Ire) *chsd ldr in 2nd: rdn under 2f out: no ex over 1f out: kpt on same pce* **8/13[1]**

4 *4 ¾* **Asteroid Belt (IRE)**[35] [7860] 3-9-5 .... KevinManning 4 60
(J S Bolger, Ire) *chsd ldrs: 3rd 1/2-way: rdn in 4th 2f out: no imp over 1f out: kpt on one pce* **11/1**

5 *2 ¾* **July Revolution (IRE)**[21] [68] 3-9-5 .... FergalLynch 5 53+
(David Marnane, Ire) *hld up towards rr: rdn into 6th 2f out: 5th and no imp 1f out: kpt on one pce* **33/1**

6 *nse* **Buachaill Tapa (IRE)**[21] [68] 3-9-5 .... SeamieHeffernan 7 53
(H Rogers, Ire) *mid-div: 6th 1/2-way: rdn in 5th 2f out: sn no ex and kpt on one pce* **50/1**

7 *2 ¾* **Zaroud (IRE)**[35] [7860] 3-9-2 ....(t) AndrewPThornton[(3)] 3 45
(R McGlinchey, Ire) *a towards rr* **100/1**

8 *20* **Tigresa (IRE)**[14] [159] 3-9-0 .... PatSmullen 6
(Mark Johnston) *chsd ldrs: 5th 1/2-way: rdn and no ex ent st: eased over 1f out: t.o* **16/1**

1m 24.3s (84.30) **8** Ran SP% **119.5**
CSF £29.54 TOTE £7.50: £1.40, £1.20, £1.10; DF 59.40.
Owner A S O'Brien **Bred** Mrs A S O'Brien **Trained** Castletown, Co Meath

FOCUS
Eddie Lynam is normally the man for 3yo maidens here but he was thwarted here by Noel Meade. The first two have been rated to personal bests and the third to his AW mark.

NOTEBOOK
Honourable Emperor(IRE) got up in the last stride. Gradually moving into contention, this colt really started to pick up inside the last and while he was aided by the runner-up getting a bit weary, he ran well to the line. It will be a question now of waiting to see what the handicapper does, but there would seem to be improvement and the ability to stay a mile with this horse.
Atticus Finch(IRE) almost stole the show. He dictated a steady gallop, his rider saved enough for him to quicken into a few lengths lead over a furlong out but he just got a bit tired inside the last hundred yards. It may turn out that six furlongs is his best trip. (op 5/2)
Roman General(IRE) had a good position but appeared to race a little over-keenly and once his stable companion quickened up he was really struggling. He's better than this and may well come on for it. (op 8/11 tchd 4/5)
Asteroid Belt(IRE) came off the bridle before the home turn and was onepaced. It's likely this trip is on the short side but he could be interesting with a handicap mark.
July Revolution(IRE) now qualifies for a handicap mark but looks modest on all known evidence.

337a WWW.DUNDALKSTADIUM.COM H'CAP 1m (P)
6:50 (6:52) 4-Y-0+ **£5,750** (£1,333; £583; £333)

RPR

1 **Iron Major (IRE)**[21] [70] 5-9-9 84.................................... SamJames[(5)] 8 90
(Edward Lynam, Ire) *hld up towards rr: hdwy into 5th 2f out: nt clr run over 1f out: rdn to chal ins fnl f: led ins fnl 100yds: kpt on wl cl home* **12/1**

2 *1* **Joe Eile (IRE)**[14] [166] 4-9-7 77..............................(p) JohnnyMurtagh 10 81
(G M Lyons, Ire) *chsd ldrs: 3rd 1/2-way: rdn to ld and dispute 1 1/2f out: hdd ins fnl 100yds: no ex and kpt on same pce* **4/1[2]**

3 *hd* **Akasaka (IRE)**[21] [69] 5-9-12 82... JPO'Brien 3 86
(Edward Lynam, Ire) *mid-div: 7th 1/2-way: hdwy into 4th 2f out: rdn to ld and dispute 1 1/2f out: hdd ins fnl 100yds: no ex and kpt on same pce* **9/2[3]**

4 *¾* **Aragorn Icon (IRE)**[21] [69] 5-8-10 66............................. FergalLynch 7 68
(David Marnane, Ire) *hld up towards rr: rdn in 9th 2f out: 7th 1f out: kpt on same pce fnl f* **16/1**

5 *nse* **Whipless (IRE)**[56] 7614 4 -10-089..........................(b) RonanWhelan(5) 6 91
(J S Bolger, Ire) *chsd ldrs: 5th 1/2-way: rdn in 8th whn lost pl 2f out: no imp in 5th 1f out: kpt on same pce* **10/1**

6 *1/2* **If Per Chance (IRE)**[9] 7793 7 -9-580......................(p) ConorHoban(5) 5 81
(M Halford, Ire) *mid-div: 8th 1/2-way: 6th 2f out: sn rdn: no ex in 8th 1f out: kpt on one pce* **8/1**

7 *2 1/2* **Toufan Express**[21] 70 10 -9-1181..................................(b) AELynch 1 76
(Adrian McGuinness, Ire) *chsd ldrs: 4th 1/2-way: hdwy to ld 2f out: rdn and hdd 1 1/2f out: no ex* **16/1**

8 *3/4* **Tarrsille (IRE)**[21] 70 6 -9-784..................................(t) GaryPhillips(7) 9 77
(G M Lyons, Ire) *mid-div: 6th 1/2-way: rdn 2f out: no imp in 6th 1f out: kpt on one pce* **3/1**[1]

9 *3 3/4* **King's Bastion (IRE)**[7] 235 8 8 662........ ..... MichaelHussey 11 46
(Luke Comer, Ire) *chsd ldrs early: mid-div 1/2-way: rdn and dropped towards rr 3f out: kpt on one pce st* **33/1**

10 *1 1/4* **Casela Park (IRE)**[21] 70 7 -9-474...................................... JFEgan 12 56
(Jaclyn Tyrrell, Ire) *led: rdn and hdd 2f out: no ex and wknd* **25/1**

11 *4 1/2* **Ecossaise**[17] 114 4 -8-1167..(b) WayneLordan 2 38
(Mark Johnston) *chsd ldr in 2nd: rdn and wknd ent st* **6/1**

1m 37.16s (97.16) **11**Ran SP% **123.9**
CSF £57.26 CT £202.15 TOTE £18.10 : £4.60 , £1.80 , £1.90 ; DF 81.60 .
Owner Edward Lynam **Bred** Millinium Partnership **Trained** Dunshaughlin, Co Meath
■ Stewards' Enquiry : J P O'Brien severe caution: hit gelding in front of the saddle while whip was held in the forehand position
Johnny Murtagh one-day ban: hit gelding in front of the saddle while whip was held in the forehand position (Feb 10)

FOCUS
A good ride here from Sam James. The second and fourth set the standard.

NOTEBOOK
Iron Major (IRE)looked as though he would be denied a clear run in the straight but James sat and suffered in patience and when the prospect of a gap came on his outside he took it. The horse did the rest as he responded well for him inside the last furlong to get up close home. He doesn't have any secrets from the handicapper and is always a likely one to pop up at a price in races like this. (op 10/1)
Joe Eile (IRE)travelled sweetly into the straight and led over a furlong out, even battling on when challenged and eventually headed inside the last. Knowing what this his trip is seems to be as big a puzzle as anything but one would feel sure that his consistency will be rewarded in due course. 7/2)
Akasaka(IRE) has seen his handicap mark yo-yo a bit over the past eight months but this may have been a career-best effort off his highest mark. Settled in mid-division, he threw down his challenge inside the final furlong and kept on at the same pace, running all the way to the line. He's a horse that wouldn't need to go up too much further one suspects.
Aragorn Icon (IRE)ran on to good effect inside the last furlong without managing to get on terms. Taking penalties into account he probably ran more or less the same race with Akasaka as when they met here two weeks ago. (op 16/1 tchd 18/1)
Whipless(IRE) stayed on to reasonable effect and it was a good effort under his big weight. 10/1 tchd 11/1)
If Per Chance (IRE)didn't get any closer to winning a race here as he was quite one-paced inside the last furlong or so. (op 8/1 tchd 15/2)

341a FOLLOW DUNDALK ON FACEBOOK RACE 1m 2f 150y (P)
8:50 (8:51) 4-Y-O+ **£7,187** (£1,666; £729 ; £416)

RPR

1 **Solo Performer (IRE)**[95] 7867 7 -9-1290..........................(b) AELynch 2 89+
(H Rogers, Ire) *s.i.s: hld up in rr: rdn in 5th 2f out: kpt on wl fnl f to ld cl home* **8/1**[3]

2 *1* **King's Trail (JPN)**[41] 7802 10 -9-5.................................... PatSmullen 4 80+
(Takashi Kodama, Ire) *chsd ldrs in 3rd: rdn 2f out: kpt on: disp ins fnl f: hdd cl home and no ex* **11/1**

3 *hd* **Oceanway (USA)**[83] 7297 4 -9-5................................ JohnnyMurtagh 3 83+
(Mark Johnston) *chsd ldr in 2nd: pushed along 4f out: rdn 3f out: kpt on u.p: led 1f out: disp ins fnl f: hdd cl home and no ex* **1/1**[1]

4 *1 1/2* **Baitsileir (IRE)**[14] 166 4 -9-584.........................(bt) RonanWhelan(5) 6 85
(J S Bolger, Ire) *sn led: rdn 2f out: hdd 1f out: no ex ins fnl f: kpt on same pce* **12/1**

5 *nk* **Flavia Tatiana (IRE)**[14] 166 4 -9-585................................. JPO'Brien 1 79+
(A P O'Brien, Ire) *hld up in 5th: 4th 2f out: nt clr run and checked 1f out: no ex ins fnl f* **7/4**[2]

6 *4 3/4* **Syrian**[14] 166 5 -9-1283...(t) GaryCarroll 5 74
(S M Duffy, Ire) *chsd ldrs in 4th: rdn and dropped to rr 2f out: no ex* **25/1**

2m 14.13s (134.13)
WFA 4 from 5yo+ 3lb **6**Ran SP% **117.3**
CSF £86.54 TOTE £7.10 : £1.90 , £4.20 ; DF 85.00 .
Owner Mrs Margot McGuinness **Bred** Peter J McGuinness **Trained** Ardee, Co. Louth
■ Stewards' Enquiry : A E Lynch one-day ban: used whip with excessive frequency (Feb 10)

FOCUS
This was run at a generous pace which suited the winner. The front-running fourth sets the standard.

NOTEBOOK
Solo Performer (IRE)was a rare ride on the Flat for rider Andrew Lynch, who rode him to perfection. Dropping him out off a decent pace, he didn't pick up until inside the two-furlong pole but once getting into gear he built up a lot of momentum and won going away well inside the last. Dropping him out is the best way to ride him now. (op 8/1 tchd 9/1)
King's Trail (JPN)◆ ran a very solid race. He was in a good position to challenge early in the straight and ran on well but just didn't have the same momentum as the winner. He should come on for the run and a small-field conditions race could be ideal for him. (op 10/1)
Oceanway(USA) was content to sit off the lead but was almost the first horse off the bridle. He ran on but didn't really show any change of pace and just wasn't good enough. (op 11/10 tchd 4/5)
Baitsileir(IRE) had a reasonable advantage at one stage. To his credit he kept going well enough when headed. Official explanation: jockey said gelding hung outwards in the straight (op 8/1)
Flavia Tatiana (IRE)◆ closed up with apparently plenty in the tank turning in but she couldn't get a gap in the straight and ended up being badly tightened up. She certainly would have made it interesting with a clear run. Official explanation: jockey said filly was unable to get a clear run at the furlong pole and was eased (op 2/1 tchd 9/4)

342a WINTER RACING AT DUNDALK H'CAP 1m 4f (P)
9:15 (9:19) 4-Y-O+ **£5,750** (£1,333; £583 ; £333)

RPR

1 **Tribes And Banner (IRE)**[14] 168 8 -8-1273...........(t) ConorHoban(5) 1 77
(C F Swan, Ire) *settled bhd ldrs: 4th 1/2-way: hdwy into 3rd 2f out: rdn to chal 1f out: kpt on fnl f to ld last strides* **11/4**[2]

2 *hd* **Mutasareb (USA)**[7] 240 5 -9-979......................................(p) JPO'Brien 6 83+
(A Oliver, Ire) *chsd ldrs: 3rd 1/2-way: rdn to ld 1f out: strly pressed ins fnl f and drifted rt: hdd last strides* **2/1**[1]

3 *3 1/2* **Confidence (USA)**[14] 166 5 -9-080......................(bt) MarkRafferty(10) 5 78
(Luke Comer, Ire) *led: rdn 2f out: hdd 1f out: no ex fnl f: kpt on same pce* **14/1**

4 *2 3/4* **Strandfield Lady (IRE)**[95] 7867 7 -9-979....................(b) NiallPMadden 7 73
(H Rogers, Ire) *hld up: 6th 1/2-way: hdwy into 4th 2f out: sn rdn: no ex 1f out: kpt on same pce* **15/2**

5 *1* **Reggae Rock (IRE)**[14] 166 5 -9-582..........................(p) ColinKeane(7) 2 74
(John C McConnell, Ire) *settled bhd ldrs: 5th 1/2-way: rdn 2f out: no imp over 1f out: kpt on one pce* **12/1**

6 *6* **Paramount (FR)**[14] 168 10 -9-373.................................. MsKWalsh 4 56
(T M Walsh, Ire) *hld up towards rr: trailing 1/2-way: rdn and no imp 3f out: kpt on one pce st* **7/1**

7 *4 3/4* **Shieldmaiden (USA)**[7] 223 4 -9-680......................(b) JohnnyMurtagh 3 55
(Mark Johnston) *chsd ldr in 2nd: rdn 3f out: no ex in 5th 2f out: eased ins fnl f* **4/1**[3]

2m 29.8s (149.80)
WFA 4 from 5yo+ 4lb **7**Ran SP% **118.6**
Daily Double: 387.50 to a 5 euro stake. CSF £9.22 TOTE £3.30 : £2.50 , £1.70 ; DF 11.70 .
Owner Kill Be Canty Syndicate **Bred** Patrick Costello **Trained** Cloughjordan, Co Tipperary

FOCUS
A steady gallop was likely to suit hold-up horses with a change of gear and so it proved. Personal bests from the first two.

NOTEBOOK
Tribes And Banner (IRE)showed a belated liking for this venue and surface. Held up and tucked away on the inside, he had to be switched to the outer well in the straight to make his challenge but once asked he knuckled down well under pressure and had to contend with the runner-up carrying him to the right inside the final furlong. It was a good tough performance. (op 10/3)
Mutasareb(USA) ran a blinder off yet another revised mark. He travelled well in pursuit of the leaders and despite drifting right inside the last he continued to battle all the way to the line. He'll probably go up again but he shows no signs of his improvement stopping or his enthusiasm waning.
Confidence(USA) continued to find plenty. The first two were just too good on the night.
Strandfield Lady (IRE)had the race run to suit her as well and was in a good position to challenge inside the two furlong pole but her effort just flattened out. (op 7/1)
Reggae Rock (IRE)kept on at the same pace but just wasn't able to make an impression.
T/Jkpt: @26,222.20. Pool of @34,963.00 - 1 winning unit. T/Plt: @315.30. Pool of @27,173.44 - 65 winning units. II

(op

338a -339a & 343a -348a (Foreign Racing) - See Raceform Interactive

[320]LINGFIELD (L-H)
Saturday, January 28

OFFICIAL GOING: Standard
Wind: fairly modest, against Weather: dry, chilly

349 FA CUP BETTING AT BLUESQ.COM H'CAP 1m 2f (P)
12:50 (12:50) (Class 5) (0-70,70) 4-Y-O+ **£2,385** (£704; £352) **Stalls** Low

Form RPR

43-0 1 **John Louis**[10] 199 4 -9-267.. JimmyFortune 5 75
(Philip McBride) *chsd ldr: rdn and ev ch 2f out: led 1f: hrd pressed and hld on gamely fnl 100yds* **11/1**

04-2 2 *nk* **Hurricane Hymnbook (USA)**[6] 263 7 -9-669.......... StevieDonohoe 8 76
(Willie Musson) *dwlt: hld up in tch: rdn and effrt on outer 2f out: r.o u.p to press wnr fnl 100yds: r.o wl but a jst hld* **7/2**[2]

233- 3 *1 1/4* **Conducting**[43] 7779 4 -9-368.. ShaneKelly 1 73
(Gay Kelleway) *chsd ldrs: rdn and effrt on inner over 1f out: pressed ldrs jst ins fnl f: no ex fnl 75yds* **16/1**

44-4 4 *shd* **Striding Edge (IRE)**[8] 224 6 -8-258........................ NicoleNordblad(7) 3 62
(Hans Adielsson) *t.k.h: hld up in tch: pushed along 2f out: kpt on wl ins fnl f* **12/1**

1-21 5 *3/4* **Trip Switch**[8] 224 6 -9-770.. AdamKirby 4 73
(George Prodromou) *hld up in tch: effrt on inner over 1f out: drvn and chsd ldrs 1f out: styd on same pce ins fnl f* **5/4**[1]

-511 6 *1/2* **Aviso (GER)**[9] 175 8 -9-063... MartinLane 6 65
(David Evans) *hld up in last pair: clsd wl over 2f out: rdn and hdwy over 1f out: styd on ins fnl f: nt rch ldrs* **16/1**

52-6 7 *hd* **Choral Festival**[24] 36 6 -9-770...................................... KieranO'Neill 7 71
(John Bridger) *in tch: rdn and effrt on outer over 2f out: unable qck over 1f out: styd on same pce fnl f* **10/1**[3]

1-10 8 *1 1/2* **Whodunit (UAE)**[14] 176 8 -9-770..................................(b) ChrisCatlin 2 68
(Peter Hiatt) *led: rdn and qcknd jst over 2f out: hdd 1f out: wknd ins fnl f* **10/1**[3]

00-0 9 *3/4* **Khun John (IRE)**[14] 176 9 -8-958................................ JamieMackay 9 55
(Willie Musson) *stdd and dropped in bhd after s: hld up in last: pushed along over 3f out: kpt on ins fnl f: nvr trbld ldrs* **40/1**

2m 6.16s (-0.44)**Going Correction** +0.025s/f (Slow)
WFA 4 from 6yo+ 2lb **9**Ran SP% **115.1**
Speed ratings (Par 103): **102,101,100,100,100 99,99,98,97**
toteswingers:1&2:£10.30, 2&3:£10.70, 1&3:£12.80 CSF £49.25 CT £623.89 TOTE £11.80 : £3.50, £2.20 , £3.60 ; EX 89.50 Trifecta £366.10 Part won. Pool: £494.85 - 0.52 winning units.
Owner Four Winds Racing **Bred** Wood Farm Stud (Waresley) **Trained** Newmarket, Suffolk

FOCUS
An ordinary handicap run at a modest pace.

350 MIRROR PUNTERS CLUB MAIDEN STKS 1m (P)
1:25 (1:25) (Class 5) 3-Y-O+ **£2,385** (£704; £352) **Stalls** High

Form RPR

5 1 **Baileys Strider**[8] 231 3 -8-70.. JoeFanning 8 71+
(Mark Johnston) *chsd ldr: rdn and sltly outpcd by ldr 2f out: drvn and rallied ins fnl f: kpt on wl to ld fnl 75yds: jst hld on* **7/2**[3]

2 *shd* **Imtithal (IRE)** 3 -8-20... MartinLane 4 66+
(James Tate) *hld up wl in tch in midfield: switching rt bnd 2f out: rdn and hdwy ent fnl f: str run to press wnr fnl 75yds: jst failed* **100/1**

3 3 *1* **Yajber (USA)**[15] 147 3 -8-70... MarcHalford 10 68
(Terry Clement) *led: rdn and qcknd 2f out: hld hd high but kpt on u.p tl hdd and lost 2 pls fnl 75yds* **9/1**

0 4 *1 1/4* **Cutting It Fine (IRE)**[14] 182 3 -8-70................................ ShaneKelly 5 66
(Jeremy Noseda) *chsd ldrs: rdn and effrt over 2f out: drvn and styd on same pce ins fnl f* **10/1**

02-6 5 *1 1/4* **Boots And Spurs**[18] 117 3 -8-70...................................... LukeMorris 3 63
(Mrs K Burke) *chsd ldrs on inner: n.m.r on inner briefly 2f out: drvn and styd on same pce fr over 1f out: edgd rt u.p ins fnl f* **2/1**[1]

6 *1/2* **Chronic Flame (TUR)**3 -8-70.. HayleyTurner 9 62
(Marcus Tregoning) *chsd ldrs: rdn and unable qck wl over 1f out: outpcd over 1f out: one pce and no threat to ldrs fnl f* **20/1**

0-5 **7** 1 ½ **Zowaina**[10] 206 3-7-13 0 .... DominicFox(3) 1 53
(Roger Varian) *s.i.s and flashed tail leaving stalls: in tch in rr: rdn over 2f out: no prog tl styd on fnl f: nvr trbld ldrs* **25/1**

8 2 **Noosa Boy** 3-8-8 0 ow1 .... JimCrowley 2 55+
(Ralph Beckett) *s.i.s: rn green in last trio: effrt and wd bnd 2f out: kpt on same pce and no threat to ldrs after* **11/4**[2]

9 4 **Scripturist** 3-8-7 0 .... WilliamCarson 7 44
(William Jarvis) *s.i.s: rn green and in tch in last pair: wknd wl over 1f out* **66/1**

1m 38.98s (0.78) **Going Correction** +0.025s/f (Slow)
WFA 3 from 4yo 20lb **9** Ran SP% **112.4**
Speed ratings (Par 103): **97,96,95,94,93 92,91,89,85**
toteswingers:1&2:£20.00, 2&3:£47.50, 1&3:£3.90 CSF £307.33 TOTE £2.80: £1.50, £8.40, £2.00; EX 139.90 TRIFECTA Not won..
Owner G R Bailey Ltd (Baileys Horse Feeds) **Bred** P And Mrs A G Venner **Trained** Middleham Moor, N Yorks

FOCUS
Just a modest maiden run in a time 2.16 seconds slower than the following Class 4 handicap for older horses, but it's a race that should produce some winners.

351 FOLLOW US ON TWITTER @LINGFIELDPARK H'CAP 1m (P)
2:00 (2:00) (Class 4) (0-85,85) 4-Y-0+ **£4,204** (£1,251; £625; £312) **Stalls** High

Form RPR

52-1 **1** **Forceful Appeal (USA)**[24] 34 4-9-1 **79** .... HayleyTurner 7 86+
(Simon Dow) *hld up in tch: hdwy to trck ldr over 2f out: rdn to ld 1f out: hld on wl towards fin* **15/8**[1]

42-4 **2** *nk* **Titan Triumph**[21] 90 8-9-0 **78** ....(t) JimCrowley 5 84
(William Knight) *stdd after s: hld up in rr: hdwy 2f out: str run u.p 1f out: ev ch wl ins fnl f: no imp and hld towards fin* **4/1**[2]

0-04 **3** *1* **Tevez**[6] 266 7-9-7 **85** ....(p) DavidProbert 1 89
(Des Donovan) *dwlt: hld up in tch in rr: hdwy 2f out: swtchd rt and drvn ent fnl f: pressing ldrs fnl 100yds: styng on same pce and hld whn short of room towards fin* **12/1**

0-46 **4** 1 ½ **Aquilifer (IRE)**[22] 54 4-8-9 **73** .... ShaneKelly 6 73
(Mrs K Burke) *hld up in tch: hdwy jst over 2f out: pressed ldrs and drvn 1f out: no ex and btn fnl 75yds* **20/1**

016- **5** 1 ¾ **Young Dottie**[52] 7660 6-8-9 **78** .... JemmaMarshall(5) 3 74
(Pat Phelan) *hld up in tch: edgd lft and hdwy on inner jst over 2f out: chsd ldrs and rdn over 1f out: no ex and btn fnl 150yds* **10/1**

0-10 **6** *1* **April Fool**[10] 199 8-8-11 **75** ....(b) LukeMorris 9 69
(Ronald Harris) *dwlt: rcvrd and hdwy on outer to ld over 6f out: rdn ent fnl 2f: hdd 1f out: wknd fnl 100yds* **11/2**[3]

30-1 **7** ½ **Buxfizz (USA)**[7] 248 4-8-6 **75** ....(p) RaulDaSilva(5) 4 72+
(George Prodromou) *led for 2f: chsd ldrs: rdn and struggling over 2f out: squeezed for room and hmpd jst over 2f out: dropped to last pair: swtchd rt and rallied over 1f out: kpt on ins fnl f but no threat to ldrs* **14/1**

21-5 **8** 1 ½ **Il Battista**[26] 11 4-8-11 **75** ....(be) KieranO'Neill 8 64
(Alan McCabe) *rdn along early: chsd ldr 5f out tl over 2f out: wknd u.p over 1f out* **9/1**

20-0 **9** 1 ¼ **All Right Now**[16] 131 5-8-9 **73** .... ChrisCatlin 2 59
(Derek Haydn Jones) *hld up in last pair: rdn over 3f out: no prog and no threat to ldrs fnl 2f* **28/1**

1m 36.82s (-1.38) **Going Correction** +0.025s/f (Slow) **9** Ran SP% **111.8**
Speed ratings (Par 105): **107,106,105,104,102 101,100,99,98**
toteswingers:1&2:£2.40, 2&3:£7.50, 1&3:£6.50 CSF £8.61 CT £65.72 TOTE £2.70: £1.10, £1.30, £3.10; EX 10.00 Trifecta £15.00 Pool: £523.96 - 25.78 winning units..
Owner Simon Caunce **Bred** Juddmonte Farms Inc **Trained** Epsom, Surrey
■ Stewards' Enquiry : Jemma Marshall four-day ban: careless riding (Feb 11,13-15)

FOCUS
A fair handicap run at a reasonable pace thanks to April Fool, who wasn't at his best.

352 FOREST ROW H'CAP 6f (P)
2:30 (2:31) (Class 5) (0-70,65) 3-Y-0 **£2,385** (£704; £352) **Stalls** Low

Form RPR

35-5 **1** **Words Come Easy**[16] 127 3-9-6 **64** .... JimmyFortune 4 67
(Philip McBride) *hld up wl in tch: rdn and effrt over 1f out: hdwy u.p 1f out: r.o wl to ld fnl 50yds* **6/1**

451- **2** ¾ **Hey Fiddle Fiddle (IRE)**[33] 7874 3-9-5 **63** ....(b) WilliamCarson 6 64
(Charles Hills) *t.k.h: pressed ldrs on outer: rdn and ev ch wl over 1f out: led jst ins fnl f: edgd lft u.p: hdd fnl 50yds: wkng cl home* **5/2**[1]

04-3 **3** *nk* **Art Show**[16] 135 3-9-0 **58** .... HayleyTurner 5 58
(Ed Dunlop) *t.k.h: hld up in tch in last pair: rdn and racd awkardly bnd 2f out: rallied and hdwy on outer ent fnl f: r.o wl and pressing for 2nd cl home* **9/2**[3]

00-0 **4** ¾ **Jawking**[16] 127 3-9-4 **62** .... LukeMorris 1 60
(David Evans) *t.k.h: hld up wl in tch: rdn 2f out: drvn and chsd ldrs jst over 1f out: keeping on same pce and nt clr run whn swtchd rt ins fnl f* **8/1**

66-5 **5** *1* **Umph (IRE)**[7] 250 3-9-0 **58** ....(v) MartinLane 3 52
(David Evans) *w ldr: drvn and ev ch over 1f out: wknd ins fnl f* **15/2**

230- **6** 1 ¼ **Ionwy**[29] 7925 3-9-0 **58** .... DaneO'Neill 2 48
(Derek Haydn Jones) *sn led: rdn 2f out: hdd jst ins fnl f: wknd fnl 100yds* **20/1**

5-62 **7** 3 ¼ **Dawn Lightning**[13] 189 3-9-7 **65** .... ShaneKelly 7 48
(Alan McCabe) *awkward leaving stalls and s.i.s: sn swtchd lft and hld up in last pair: effrt on inner over 1f out: nvr quite enough room and no imp: btn whn swtchd rt and eased fnl 100yds* **3/1**[2]

1m 13.18s (1.28) **Going Correction** +0.025s/f (Slow) **7** Ran SP% **113.7**
Speed ratings (Par 97): **92,91,90,89,88 86,82**
toteswingers:1&2:£3.60, 2&3:£2.50, 1&3:£4.50 CSF £21.14 TOTE £8.50: £4.10, £1.30; EX 30.30.
Owner Four Winds Racing **Bred** Wood Farm Stud (Waresley) **Trained** Newmarket, Suffolk

FOCUS
This didn't look much of a race and it rather fell into the lap of the winner.
Dawn Lightning Official explanation: jockey said filly hung left

353 BLUE SQUARE SPRINT SERIES ROUND 4 H'CAP (QUALIFIER) 6f (P)
3:00 (3:00) (Class 6) (0-65,66) 4-Y-0+ **£2,726** (£805; £402) **Stalls** Low

Form RPR

5-42 **1** **Diamond Vine (IRE)**[14] 178 4-9-2 **60** ....(p) LukeMorris 5 70
(Ronald Harris) *hld up in midfield: clsd on ldrs 2f out: drvn to ld 1f out: r.o wl u.p* **9/2**[2]

0-03 **2** *nk* **Nubar Boy**[7] 251 5-9-8 **66** ....(v) MartinLane 7 75
(David Evans) *stdd after s: hld up wl off the pce in rr: clsd 2f out: str run u.p on outer ins fnl f: chsd wnr wl ins fnl f: nvr quite getting to wnr* **9/2**[2]

-346 **3** 1 ¼ **Waabel**[7] 252 5-9-3 **61** .... WilliamCarson 6 66
(Richard Guest) *dwlt: racd off the pce in last trio: hdwy on inner 2f out: drvn and chsd wnr jst ins fnl f: no imp: styd on same pce and lost 2nd wl ins fnl f* **5/2**[1]

40-0 **4** *nk* **Captainrisk (IRE)**[21] 87 6-9-2 **60** ....(v) DavidProbert 8 64
(Christine Dunnett) *racd in midfield: rdn over 2f out: rdr dropped whip 1f out: styd on wl ins fnl f* **33/1**

52-6 **5** *hd* **Even Bolder**[22] 59 9-9-7 **65** .... ShaneKelly 9 70+
(Eric Wheeler) *t.k.h: broke wl: chsd ldrs tl stdd bk into midfield after 1f: clsd on ldrs 2f out: nt clr run and looking to switch rt over 1f out: swtchd lft ins fnl f: kpt on but unable to rcvr* **14/1**

00-0 **6** ½ **Custom House (IRE)**[21] 88 4-9-2 **60** ....(p) DaneO'Neill 2 62
(John E Long) *led tl over 3f out: clsd on ldr 2f out: rdn and led again over 1f out: hdd 1f out: no ex* **28/1**

-200 **7** ½ **Memphis Man**[9] 215 9-9-0 **58** .... AdamKirby 3 58
(David Evans) *taken down early: racd wl off the pce in last pair: rdn wl over 1f out: r.o ins fnl f: nvr trbld ldrs* **33/1**

0-20 **8** 1 ¼ **Loyal Royal (IRE)**[7] 251 9-9-7 **65** ....(bt) LiamKeniry 12 61
(Milton Bradley) *t.k.h: hld up in midfield: clsd on ldrs and travelling wl 2f out: drvn and styd on same pce fr over 1f out* **10/1**

5266 **9** ¾ **Efistorm**[7] 251 11-9-5 **63** .... HayleyTurner 4 60+
(Conor Dore) *chsd ldrs: rdn wl over 1f out: unable qck over 1f out: wknd and btn whn nt clr run ins fnl f: esaed wl ins fnl f* **8/1**

305- **10** *nk* **Beautiful Lando (FR)**[52] 7667 4-9-7 **65** ....(b) KierenFallon 10 58
(Heather Main) *racd freely: chsd ldrs on outer: led over 3f out and sn clr: rdn and hdd over 1f out: wknd fnl f* **13/2**[3]

1m 12.09s (0.19) **Going Correction** +0.025s/f (Slow) **10** Ran SP% **114.5**
Speed ratings (Par 101): **99,98,96,96,96 95,94,93,92,91**
toteswingers:1&2:£2.80, 2&3:£3.50, 1&3:£3.30 CSF £24.11 CT £59.88 TOTE £4.20: £1.60, £2.00, £1.10; EX 14.10 Trifecta £24.00 Pool: £420.84 - 12.94 winning units..
Owner Ridge House Stables Ltd **Bred** Michael O'Mahony **Trained** Earlswood, Monmouths

FOCUS
The latest round of the Blue Square Sprint Series produced another competitive handicap.
Even Bolder ◆ Official explanation: jockey said gelding was denied a clear run

354 LINGFIELDPARK.CO.UK H'CAP 1m 2f (P)
3:35 (3:36) (Class 2) (0-100,95) 4-Y-0+ **£10,350** (£3,080; £1,539; £769) **Stalls** Low

Form RPR

21-1 **1** **Emerald Wilderness (IRE)**[14] 177 8-9-4 **92** ....(p) EddieAhern 7 100
(Robert Cowell) *hld up in tch: chsd ldrs and edgd lft jst over 2f out: pushed along and qcknd to ld jst ins fnl f: rdn fnl 150yds: hld on cl home* **5/1**[2]

11-4 **2** *shd* **Tinshu (IRE)**[14] 177 6-9-3 **91** ....(p) DaneO'Neill 4 99
(Derek Haydn Jones) *hld up in tch in last trio: hdwy on outer and rdn to chse ldng trio 2f out: no imp tl str run ins fnl f: str chal fnl 50yds: hld cl home* **6/1**

011- **3** 1 ¼ **Licence To Till (USA)**[112] 6708 5-9-7 **95** .... JoeFanning 5 100
(Mark Johnston) *w ldr: rdn and ev ch over 1f out: drvn 1f out: styd on same pce fnl f* **11/2**[3]

12-1 **4** ½ **Junoob**[8] 223 4-9-5 **95** .... RichardKingscote 3 99
(Tom Dascombe) *led: rdn over 1f out: hdd and unable qck jst ins fnl f: no ex and outpcd fnl 150yds* **7/4**[1]

116- **5** *4* **Greyfriarschorista**[44] 7771 5-8-10 **84** .... LukeMorris 8 83+
(Brian Ellison) *in tch in last trio: rdn over 3f out: struggling to qckn whn hmpd jst over 2f out: plugged on but no threat to ldrs after* **8/1**

40-0 **6** 2 ¼ **Zacynthus (IRE)**[7] 254 4-8-10 **86** ....(tp) KierenFallon 6 78
(Alan McCabe) *chsd ldrs: rdn and edgd lft and hmpd jst over 2f out: no ch w ldrs after* **14/1**

03-1 **7** *34* **Sunset Kitty (USA)**[16] 131 5-8-13 **87** .... ShaneKelly 1 +
(Mike Murphy) *chsd ldrs: squeezed and bdly hmpd and lost pl jst over 2f out: eased after: t.o* **10/1**

222- **U** **Emma's Gift (IRE)**[41] 7806 4-8-2 **81** oh1 ....(b) AdamBeschizza(3) 2
(Julia Feilden) *hld up in tch in last trio: squeezed for room: bdly hmpd: clipped heels and uns rdr jst over 2f out* **16/1**

2m 3.04s (-3.56) **Going Correction** +0.025s/f (Slow)
WFA 4 from 5yo+ 2lb **8** Ran SP% **115.5**
Speed ratings (Par 109): **115,114,113,113,110 108,81,**
toteswingers:1&2:£5.50, 2&3:£4.80, 1&3:£3.30 CSF £35.21 CT £170.86 TOTE £5.70: £1.40, £2.10, £2.20; EX 39.10 Trifecta £65.10 Pool: £969.59 - 11.02 winning units..
Owner Mrs J Morley & Khalifa Dasmal **Bred** Mrs Joan Murphy **Trained** Six Mile Bottom, Cambs
■ Stewards' Enquiry : Eddie Ahern six-day ban: careless riding (Feb 11,13-17)

FOCUS
A slightly disappointing turnout numerically and the top weight was rated just 95. The race was weakened due to an incident on the final bend, with Emma's Gift unshipping her rider after being badly squeezed for room, and a couple more hampered. The successful rider got the blame, Eddie Ahern picking up a six-day careless riding ban. Despite all of that, the winner deserves plenty of credit as the pace was just modest, which wasn't ideal for him.

NOTEBOOK
Emerald Wilderness(IRE) was still able to complete a hat-trick of C&D victories despite the steady pace, and he looked value for more than the narrow winning margin. Having travelled much the best, he was in front sooner than ideal (doesn't do much off the bridle) and looked vulnerable to the runner-up's late surge, but he pulled out extra in the final strides. He was 5lb higher than last time and 9lb higher than when beginning his winning run, but he could defy another rise. (op 4-1 tchd 11-2)
Tinshu(IRE) didn't see her race out when behind Emerald Wilderness here two weeks earlier, but she was played later this time and just failed. She went wider into the straight than ideal, but looked second best. (tchd 11-2)
Licence To Till(USA) had won his last two starts, but hadn't been seen for 112 days and was 6lb higher than when winning on Polytrack at Dundalk two starts previously. He basically wasn't quite good enough, although perhaps more of a galloping track suits him better these days. (op 13-2)
Junoob was very well backed but he was held by Tinshu on their meeting in a Listed race on December 17 and this was tougher than the 1m4f conditions race he won last time. (op 11-4)
Greyfriarschorista, another short of space in an incident on the final bend, could never get involved. (op 11-1)
Sunset Kitty(USA) lost all chance when seriously hampered on the home turn. (op 7-1)

355 PLAY ROULETTE AT BLUESQ.COM/CASINO MAIDEN STKS 1m 4f (P)
4:05 (4:05) (Class 5) 4-Y-0+ **£2,385** (£704; £352) **Stalls** Low

Form RPR

\- **1** **Kangaroo Court (IRE)**[220] 8-9-7 0 .... MickyFenton 4 77+
(Emma Lavelle) *hld up wl bhd: swtchd wd and sme hdwy 4f out: 8th and rdn along 2f out: stl only 6th 1f out: str run to ld wl ins fnl f: sn in command* **14/1**

4-2 **2** 1 ½ **Broughton Sands**[15] 149 4-8-12 0 .... StevieDonohoe 5 69
(Willie Musson) *chsd ldrs: clsd 3f out: rdn and ev ch 2f out: drvn and unable qck over 1f out: kpt on but nt gng pce of wnr wl ins fnl f* **6/1**[3]

2 **3** *hd* **Southern State (USA)**[5] 273 4-9-3 0 .... JoeFanning 8 74+
(Mark Johnston) *chsd ldng pair: clsd 3f out: led on inner over 1f out and pushed clr 1f out: isolated on rail and rn green whn rdn ins fnl f: fnd little and hdd wl ins fnl f: sn btn: lost 2nd last strides* **10/11**[1]

25-0 **4** *1/2* **Echos Of Motivator**[12] 192 4-9-3 67 ....(p) LukeMorris 2 73
(Ronald Harris) *racd off the pce in midfield: rdn and clsd 3f out: drvn and chsd ldrs 1f out: kpt on u.p* **14/1**

20-6 **5** *7* **Lady Elsie**[4] 281 4-8-7 70 ....(p) RaulDaSilva(5) 11 57
(George Prodromou) *led: rdn 2f out: hdd over 1f out: wknd fnl f* **20/1**

220- **6** *3 3/4* **Oneiric**[124] 6405 4-9-0 71 ow2 .... AdamKirby 3 53
(Brett Johnson) *chsd ldrs: rdn over 4f out: clsd on ldrs over 2f out: drvn and unable qck wl over 1f out: wknd jst over 1f out* **14/1**

7 *nk* **Eurhythmic (IRE)**[18] 6944 5-9-4 76 .... RobertLButler(3) 9 55
(Jim Old) *w.w off the pce in midfield: clsd on outer 3f out: rdn and wknd wl over 1f out* **50/1**

5 **8** *2* **Chhota Naa**[15] 149 4-9-3 0 .... DavidProbert 7 52
(Harry Dunlop) *a in rr: rdn 8f out: struggling 3f out: no ch fnl 2f* **66/1**

3-24 **9** *1* **Bow River Arch (USA)**[5] 271 4-8-12 72 .... WilliamCarson 10 46
(Peter Hiatt) *w ldr: rdn over 2f out: wknd qckly wl over 1f out* **7/2**[2]

10 *10* **Southerness**[87] 8-9-7 0 .... JamesMillman 6 35
(Rod Millman) *s.i.s: a in rr: rdn over 4f out: lost tch over 2f out* **66/1**

6 **11** *33* **Lingtren**[15] 147 4-9-3 0 .... MartinLane 1
(Roger Ingram) *a in rr: dropped to last and rdn 5f out: lost tch and t.o fnl 3f* **100/1**

2m 31.43s (-1.57) **Going Correction** +0.025s/f (Slow)
WFA 4 from 5yo+ 4lb **11** Ran SP% **119.6**
Speed ratings (Par 103): **106,105,104,104,99 97,97,95,95,88 66**
toteswingers:1&2:£7.50, 2&3:£1.10, 1&3:£8.60 CSF £94.55 TOTE £18.80: £3.80, £1.20, £1.10; EX 76.50 Trifecta £80.70 Pool: £441.02 - 4.04 winning units..
Owner N Mustoe **Bred** Brian Wilson **Trained** Hatherden, Hants

FOCUS
An ordinary maiden.
T/Plt: £97.10 to a £1 stake. Pool of £66,160.46 - 497.26 winning tickets. T/Qpdt: £6.90 to a £1 stake. Pool of £5,741.23 - 608.92 winning tickets. SP

[327]WOLVERHAMPTON (A.W) (L-H)
Monday, January 30

OFFICIAL GOING: Standard
Wind: Light across Weather: Fine

356 BLUE SQUARE WINTER CARNIVAL IPHONE APP AMATEUR RIDERS' H'CAP 5f 216y(P)
2:00 (2:00) (Class 6) (0-55,61) 4-Y-0+ **£1,646** (£506; £253) **Stalls** Low

Form RPR

400- **1** **Avoncreek**[114] 6694 8-10-2 48 ....(v) MissCBoxall(5) 7 56
(Brian Baugh) *prom: lost pl 4f out: hdwy over 2f out: led over 1f out: rdn out* **25/1**

64-0 **2** *nk* **Little Perisher**[18] 126 5-10-2 48 ....(p) MrOGarner(5) 10 55
(Paul Howling) *mid-div: sn pushed along: hdwy over 1f out: edgd lft ins fnl f: r.o* **12/1**

55-0 **3** *hd* **Blue Noodles**[22] 101 6-10-4 52 ....(p) MrAFrench(7) 9 58
(John Wainwright) *hld up: hdwy over 1f out: sn rdn: r.o* **16/1**

0-00 **4** *3/4* **Bachelor Knight (IRE)**[17] 155 4-10-4 50 .... MrAaronJames(5) 6 56+
(Suzzanne France) *hood removed late: dwlt: r.o wl ins fnl f: nrst fin* **16/1**

-605 **5** *1 3/4* **Takajan (IRE)**[6] 289 5-10-6 52 .... MrNdeBoinville(5) 4 50
(Mark Brisbourne) *trckd ldrs: racd keenly: rdn and ev ch over 1f out: styd on same pce ins fnl f* **5/1**[2]

406- **6** *3 3/4* **Itsthursdayalready**[136] 6138 5-11-0 55 .... JoshHamer 8 41
(Mark Brisbourne) *broke wl and led early: prom: nt clr run over 2f out: rdn over 1f out: styd on same pce* **7/1**

36-1 **7** *1 1/2* **Cheyenne Red (IRE)**[10] 226 6-10-11 52 .... MrSWalker 11 33
(Michael Herrington) *chsd ldrs: rdn and n.m.r over 1f out: wknd ins fnl f* **7/4**[1]

00- **8** *1/2* **Royal Blade (IRE)**[50] 7728 5-10-6 54 .... MissAChadwick(7) 2 34
(Alan Berry) *chsd ldr: pushed along and ev ch over 1f out: wknd fnl f* **50/1**

500- **9** *nk* **Avonlini**[164] 5244 6-10-12 53 .... MissSBrotherton 12 32
(Brian Baugh) *chsd ldrs: hmpd over 1f out: wknd fnl f* **12/1**

4-50 **10** *2* **Young Simon**[12] 210 5-10-1 49 ....(p) MissKMargarson(7) 3 21
(George Margarson) *racd keenly: sn led: hdd over 1f out: wknd fnl f* **6/1**[3]

0-00 **11** *2 3/4* **Novay Essjay (IRE)**[11] 215 5-10-2 50 .... MrLMichael(7) 1 13
(Dai Williams) *mid-div: sn pushed along: wknd over 2f out* **66/1**

60/- **12** *30* **Louise Sauvage**[847] 6551 6-10-4 52 ....(b[1]) MrDRogerson(7) 5
(Ken Wingrove) *s.s: sn pushed along in rr: wknd wl over 2f out: t.o* **100/1**

1m 17.22s (2.22) **Going Correction** +0.175s/f (Slow) **12** Ran SP% **115.3**
Speed ratings (Par 101): **92,91,91,90,88 83,81,80,79,77 73,33**
toteswingers:1&2:£49.80, 2&3:£21.20, 1&3:£34.60 CSF £287.18 CT £4878.91 TOTE £28.20: £6.40, £2.80, £3.90; EX 347.30 Trifecta £226.10 Part won. Pool: £305.66 - 0.50 winning units..
Owner Messrs Chrimes, Winn & Wilson **Bred** J H Chrimes **Trained** Audley, Staffs
■ Chloe Boxall's first Flat winner.
■ Stewards' Enquiry : Josh Hamer two-day ban: careless riding (TBA)

FOCUS
A modest amateur riders' handicap and they were strung out over the entire width of the track once in line for home.

357 GREAT OFFERS AT WOLVERHAMPTON-RACECOURSE.CO.UK CLAIMING STKS 5f 216y(P)
2:35 (2:35) (Class 6) 3-Y-0 **£1,704** (£503; £251) **Stalls** Low

Form RPR

54-6 **1** **Tiablo (IRE)**[9] 250 3-7-9 60 .... DominicFox(3) 5 61
(David Simcock) *a.p: rdn over 1f out: styd on u.p to ld wl ins fnl f* **15/2**

1-25 **2** *1 1/2* **One More Roman (IRE)**[22] 99 3-8-2 62 ....(bt) AmyRyan(3) 1 63
(Gay Kelleway) *sn led: rdn: hdd and unable qck wl ins fnl f* **3/1**[3]

2-34 **3** *1/2* **Faraway**[9] 250 3-8-5 68 .... LukeMorris 2 62
(Ronald Harris) *chsd ldrs: wnt 2nd 1/2-way: sn rdn: styd on same pce ins fnl f* **6/4**[1]

4-51 **4** *5* **Redair (IRE)**[3] 321 3-8-1 70 .... KevinLundie(7) 4 49
(David Evans) *chsd ldr to 1/2-way: rdn over 2f out: wknd ins fnl f* **5/2**[2]

0-65 **5** *17* **Miss Bloom**[18] 135 3-8-1 35 .... RyanPowell(3) 6
(Garry Woodward) *broke wl: sn lost pl: rdn and wknd over 2f out* **100/1**

1m 15.2s (0.20) **Going Correction** +0.175s/f (Slow) **5** Ran SP% **106.3**
Speed ratings (Par 95): **105,103,102,95,73**
CSF £27.50 TOTE £12.40: £3.30, £1.30; EX 25.70.Tiablo was claimed by P. D. Evans for £5000.
Owner Mamalie Racing **Bred** Hyde Park Stud **Trained** Newmarket, Suffolk

FOCUS
A tight claimer with three of the runners split by only 1lb on official ratings.

358 SPONSOR A RACE BY CALLING 01902 390000 MAIDEN STKS 7f 32y(P)
3:05 (3:06) (Class 5) 3-Y-O **£2,264** (£673; £336; £168) **Stalls** High

Form RPR

5-2 **1** **Somemothersdohavem**[17] 159 3-9-0 0 .... RyanPowell(3) 2 71
(John Ryan) *a.p: pushed along to chse ldr 2f out: sn rdn and edgd rt: styd on u.p to ld towards fin* **4/1**[3]

6 **2** *nk* **Red Trump (IRE)**[4] 308 3-9-3 0 .... WilliamCarson 6 70
(Charles Hills) *led: rdn and edgd rt fr over 1f out: hdd towards fin* **5/1**

0- **3** *1 3/4* **Arte Del Calcio**[157] 5447 3-9-3 0 .... DaneO'Neill 4 65
(David Elsworth) *hld up in tch: shkn up over 1f out: styd on: nt rch ldrs* **7/2**[2]

0- **4** *1/2* **Moorside Magic**[90] 7209 3-8-12 0 .... PaulHanagan 9 59
(Richard Fahey) *chsd ldr 2f: remained handy: pushed along 1/2-way: styd on same pce ins fnl f* **14/1**

6-5 **5** *5* **Showsinger**[21] 107 3-8-5 0 .... LauraBarry(7) 1 45+
(Richard Fahey) *in rr: rdn over 1f out: r.o ins fnl f: nvr nrr* **80/1**

\- **6** *nk* **Gabrial's Lexi (IRE)** 3-8-7 0 .... ShaneBKelly(5) 3 44+
(Richard Fahey) *unruly to post: s.s: hld up: nt clr run over 2f out: styd on fnl f: nvr nrr* **16/1**

6-0 **7** *1/2* **Nip And Tuck**[16] 181 3-9-3 0 .... LiamKeniry 7 48+
(William Jarvis) *pushed along early in rr: rdn over 1f out: n.d* **12/1**

8 *2 1/4* **Brandy Snapping** 3-8-12 0 .... ShaneKelly 5 37
(Mark Brisbourne) *sn pushed along in rr: nvr on terms* **100/1**

56- **9** *3/4* **Dance For Georgie**[131] 6259 3-8-12 0 .... PhillipMakin 8 35
(Ben Haslam) *hld up in tch: rdn whn nt clr run over 2f out: sn wknd* **33/1**

10 *1 1/4* **Lanarkshire (IRE)** 3-9-3 0 .... JoeFanning 10 37
(Mark Johnston) *prom: chsd ldr 5f out tl rdn 2f out: sn wknd* **6/4**[1]

00- **11** *13* **Script**[118] 6598 3-8-9 0 .... JulieBurke(3) 11
(Alan Berry) *s.i.s: a bhd: hdwy over 5f out: hung rt and wknd over 2f out* **200/1**

1m 30.8s (1.20) **Going Correction** +0.175s/f (Slow) **11** Ran SP% **124.8**
Speed ratings (Par 97): **100,99,97,97,91 91,90,87,87,85 70**
toteswingers:1&2:£4.60, 2&3:£4.00, 1&3:£3.30 CSF £26.05 TOTE £3.40: £1.10, £1.70, £1.90; EX 21.40 Trifecta £141.80 Pool: £467.66 - 2.44 winning units..
Owner J Ryan **Bred** John And Susan Davis **Trained** Newmarket, Suffolk

FOCUS
They went a good gallop. Only four were seriously fancied judging by the betting.

359 DOWNLOAD THE BLUE SQUARE BET APP H'CAP 7f 32y(P)
3:40 (3:40) (Class 5) (0-70,70) 4-Y-0+ **£2,264** (£673; £336; £168) **Stalls** High

Form RPR

000- **1** **Hawk Moth (IRE)**[149] 5735 4-9-1 64 .... ChrisCatlin 10 73
(John Spearing) *s.i.s: hld up: hdwy over 1f out: r.o to ld wl ins fnl f* **22/1**

01-0 **2** *3/4* **Wigram's Turn (USA)**[26] 33 7-9-3 66 ....(t) PaddyAspell 11 73+
(Michael Easterby) *hld up: nt clr run over 1f out: swtchd lft and r.o wl ins fnl f: wnt 2nd nr fin: nt rch wnr* **8/1**[3]

5101 **3** *3/4* **Lastkingofscotland (IRE)**[12] 205 6-9-6 69 ....(b) HayleyTurner 3 74
(Conor Dore) *led: rdn and hdd wl ins fnl f: lost 2nd towards fin* **5/1**[2]

052- **4** *nk* **Striker Torres (IRE)**[93] 7176 6-9-3 69 .... DaleSwift(3) 6 73
(Geoffrey Oldroyd) *hld up: hdwy u.p over 1f out: edgd lft ins fnl f: r.o* **8/1**[3]

56-3 **5** *2* **Royal Box**[15] 186 5-8-13 62 ....(p) SamHitchcott 12 61
(Dai Burchell) *chsd ldr: rdn over 1f out: styd on same pce fnl f* **14/1**

0-50 **6** *1 1/4* **Twice Red**[12] 205 4-9-0 63 .... JoeFanning 1 58
(Derek Shaw) *prom: lost pl over 5f out: effrt over 2f out: no imp fnl f* **10/1**

100- **7** *1/2* **Bahamian Lad**[31] 7928 7-9-4 67 ....(p) AdamKirby 5 62
(Reg Hollinshead) *chsd ldrs: drvn along 1/2-way: wknd wl ins fnl f* **8/1**[3]

/34- **8** *nk* **Sole Danser (IRE)**[192] 4286 4-9-5 68 .... RichardKingscote 2 63
(Milton Bradley) *plld hrd and prom: hung rt fr over 2f out: eased ins fnl f* **11/1**

513- **9** *8* **Bavarian Princess (USA)**[77] 7416 4-9-7 70 .... LukeMorris 4 42
(Mrs K Burke) *s.i.s: hld up: rdn and wknd over 1f out: eased* **7/2**[1]

054- **10** *7* **Barista (IRE)**[89] 7235 4-9-3 66 .... DavidProbert 7 19
(Brian Forsey) *prom: hung rt fr 1/2-way: wknd over 2f out* **25/1**

0-53 **11** *9* **Double Carpet (IRE)**[3] 328 9-8-11 60 .... FergusSweeney 9
(Garry Woodward) *hld up in tch: carried wd and wknd over 2f out* **17/2**

1m 29.94s (0.34) **Going Correction** +0.175s/f (Slow) **11** Ran SP% **115.0**
Speed ratings (Par 103): **105,104,103,102,100 99,98,98,89,81 70**
toteswingers:1&2:£33.90, 2&3:£13.40, 1&3:£20.90 CSF £184.42 CT £1047.01 TOTE £28.00: £4.30, £2.80, £1.30; EX 273.30 TRIFECTA Not won..
Owner Kinnersley Partnership **Bred** Dr D Harron **Trained** Kinnersley, Worcs

FOCUS
No hanging about here and the eventual winner came from last to first.

360 HOTEL & CONFERENCING AT WOLVERHAMPTON (S) STKS 1m 141y(P)
4:10 (4:10) (Class 6) 3-Y-O **£1,704** (£503; £251) **Stalls** Low

Form RPR

-241 **1** **Roedean (IRE)**[10] 231 3-8-13 70 ....(p) FrannyNorton 4 72
(Jamie Osborne) *chsd ldr tl led wl over 1f out: sn rdn: edgd rt ins fnl f: styd on u.p* **1/1**[1]

2 *nk* **Devote Myself (IRE)** 3-8-7 0 ....(t) MartinLane 3 65
(Neil Mulholland) *awkward leaving stalls: sn chsng ldrs: rdn and ev ch whn carried rt ins fnl f: styd on* **5/2**[2]

1-13 **3** *9* **Complex**[9] 255 3-8-13 56 .... LukeMorris 2 50
(David Evans) *led tl pushed along and hdd wl over 1f out: wknd ins fnl f* **9/2**[3]

05-3 **4** *2* **Bulldog Beasley (USA)**[14] 194 3-8-12 66 ....(bt) ShaneKelly 1 45
(Brian Meehan) *chsd ldrs: rdn over 2f out: wknd over 1f out* **7/1**

00-0 **5** *7* **Salaaheb (IRE)**[7] 270 3-8-2 50 ....(b[1]) JemmaMarshall(5) 5 24
(Alastair Lidderdale) *s.s: hld up: effrt over 3f out: rdn and wknd 2f out* **100/1**

1m 52.65s (2.15) **Going Correction** +0.175s/f (Slow) **5** Ran SP% **110.2**
Speed ratings (Par 95): **97,96,88,86,80**
CSF £3.77 TOTE £1.40: £1.20, £1.50; EX 4.70.The winner was bought in for 7,500gns. Devote Myself was claimed by P. D. Evans for £6000.
Owner Dr Marwan Koukash **Bred** C McEvoy **Trained** Upper Lambourn, Berks

361 HOTEL & CONFERENCING AT WOLVERHAMPTON H'CAP 1m 141y(P)
4:40 (4:40) (Class 6) (0-65,65) 4-Y-0+ **£1,704** (£503; £251) **Stalls** Low

Form RPR

0-00 **1** **Valley Tiger**[6] 287 4-8-12 57 .... PaulHanagan 6 67
(Richard Fahey) *hld up: hdwy over 2f out: edgd rt and led over 1f out: rdn and edgd lft ins fnl f: styd on* **14/1**

024- **2** *½* **McCool Bannanas**[31] 7931 4-9-5 64 .... HayleyTurner 13 73
(James Unett) *hld up: hdwy: nt clr run and swtchd rt over 1f out: r.o wl ins fnl f: nt quite rch wnr* **8/1**[3]

-126 **3** *1* **Mataajir (USA)**[8] 263 4-9-4 63 .... JoeFanning 3 70
(Derek Shaw) *chsd ldrs: rdn and ev ch over 1f out: styd on same pce ins fnl f* **5/2**[1]

50-6 **4** *1 ¼* **Marksbury**[21] 104 5-8-12 56 .... LukeMorris 2 60
(Mark Brisbourne) *hld up in tch: rdn and swtchd rt over 1f out: edgd lft ins fnl f: styd on same pce* **9/1**

03-4 **5** *1 ¼* **Cristaliyev**[12] 205 4-8-10 60 .... (b) NathanAlison(5) 4 62
(Jim Boyle) *plld hrd and prom: nt clr run over 1f out: n.m.r sn after: styd on same pce ins fnl f* **10/1**

60-2 **6** *shd* **Justcallmehandsome**[24] 67 10-9-0 65 .... (v) JoshBaudains(7) 7 66
(Dominic Ffrench Davis) *s.s: hld up: hdwy over 1f out: r.o* **8/1**[3]

-000 **7** *1 ¼* **Vitznau (IRE)**[6] 287 8-9-1 59 .... (bt[1]) FergusSweeney 12 57
(Alastair Lidderdale) *dwlt: hld up: stl last over 1f out: shkn up and r.o ins fnl f: nvr nrr* **14/1**

06-0 **8** *½* **Smirfy's Silver**[21] 102 8-9-0 63 .... GarryWhillans(5) 5 60
(Michael Mullineaux) *chsd ldr tl led over 2f out: rdn and hdd over 1f out: no ex fnl f* **25/1**

02-4 **9** *hd* **Nina Rose**[19] 124 5-9-4 62 .... AdamKirby 11 58
(Clive Cox) *hld up in tch: rdn 3f out: no ex fnl f* **6/1**[2]

3-06 **10** *1 ¾* **Mystic Halo**[10] 232 9-8-13 57 .... (t) TomMcLaughlin 8 49
(Frank Sheridan) *mid-div: rdn over 2f out: eased whn hld fnl f* **33/1**

514- **11** *2* **Kyle Of Bute**[136] 6134 6-9-7 65 .... RussKennemore 9 52
(Brian Baugh) *chsd ldrs: rdn and ev ch 2f out: hmpd and wknd ent fnl f* **16/1**

010- **12** *hd* **Roman Ruler (IRE)**[149] 5731 4-8-11 56 .... ChrisCatlin 1 43
(Chris Fairhurst) *led: rdn and hdd over 2f out: wknd fnl f* **20/1**

341- **13** *nk* **Reason To Believe (IRE)**[147] 5788 4-9-4 63 .... PhillipMakin 10 49
(Ben Haslam) *hld up: a in rr: rdn over 2f out: sn wknd* **14/1**

1m 51.14s (0.64) **Going Correction** +0.175s/f (Slow)
WFA 4 from 5yo+ 1lb **13** Ran SP% **121.6**
Speed ratings (Par 101): **104,103,102,101,100 100,99,98,98,97 95,95,94**
toteswingers:1&2:£20.40, 2&3:£6.00, 1&3:£7.60 CSF £121.19 CT £391.85 TOTE £19.00: £5.20, £3.30, £1.10; EX 121.10 TRIFECTA Not won..

Owner Dr Marwan Koukash **Bred** Usk Valley Stud **Trained** Musley Bank, N Yorks

FOCUS
A modest handicap run at just a steady pace to past halfway.

362 ENJOY THE PUNTERS PACKAGE GROUP OFFER H'CAP 1m 1f 103y(P)
5:10 (5:11) (Class 5) (0-75,74) 3-Y-O **£2,264** (£673; £336; £168) **Stalls** Low

Form RPR

44-3 **1** **Availed Speaker (IRE)**[15] 184 3-8-8 **61** .... PaulHanagan 7 68
(Richard Fahey) *chsd ldr tl led over 2f out: sn pushed along: rdn and edgd lft ins fnl f: r.o* **5/1**

33 **2** *1 ¼* **Angel Gabrial (IRE)**[14] 195 3-9-7 **74** .... StevieDonohoe 1 77
(Ian Williams) *awkward leaving stalls: sn chsd ldrs: rdn to chse wnr over 1f out: sn ev ch: no ex towards fin* **9/4**[1]

50-1 **3** *¾* **Good Morning Star (IRE)**[12] 209 3-9-5 **72** .... JoeFanning 4 73
(Mark Johnston) *trckd ldrs: chsd wnr over 2f out tl rdn over 1f out: edgd lft: styd on same pce ins fnl f* **4/1**[3]

44-1 **4** *1* **Anginola (IRE)**[14] 194 3-8-13 **66** .... (v) LukeMorris 3 65
(David Evans) *hld up: hdwy u.p over 1f out: sn hung lft: styd on same pce* **7/2**[2]

30-0 **5** *4* **Masters Blazing**[23] 84 3-8-8 **64** .... RyanPowell(3) 2 55
(John Ryan) *hld up: hdwy over 1f out: rdn and wknd ins fnl f* **14/1**

21-2 **6** *1 ¼* **Fistful Of Dollars (IRE)**[15] 184 3-9-3 **70** .... FergusSweeney 5 58
(Jamie Osborne) *hld up: hdwy over 2f out: rdn over 1f out: sn hung lft and wknd* **11/2**

54-6 **7** *11* **Nant Saeson (IRE)**[14] 193 3-9-3 **70** .... PaddyAspell 6 35
(John Wainwright) *racd keenly: set stdy pce tl pushed along: hung rt and hdd over 2f out: wknd over 1f out* **66/1**

2m 4.51s (2.81) **Going Correction** +0.175s/f (Slow) 7 Ran SP% **113.2**
Speed ratings (Par 97): **94,92,92,91,87 86,76**
toteswingers:1&2:£3.50, 2&3:£2.60, 1&3:£3.00 CSF £16.34 TOTE £8.30: £3.70, £2.20; EX 23.40.

Owner R A Fahey **Bred** D Veitch, E McEvoy & P Costigan **Trained** Musley Bank, N Yorks

FOCUS
They set off at a good gallop but it soon steadied until around the final half-mile.

363 PLAY BINGO FREE AT BLUESQ.COM FILLIES' H'CAP 1m 4f 50y(P)
5:40 (5:40) (Class 5) (0-75,79) 4-Y-O+ **£2,264** (£673; £336; £168) **Stalls** Low

Form RPR

36-2 **1** **Boa**[14] 192 7-9-6 **72** .... HayleyTurner 1 77
(Reg Hollinshead) *chsd ldr tl led over 1f out: styd on gamely u.p* **5/2**[3]

24-1 **2** *hd* **Sail Home**[6] 281 5-9-3 **69** 6ex .... PaulHanagan 4 74
(Julia Feilden) *chsd ldrs: pushed along over 2f out: rdn and ev ch ins fnl f: styd on* **15/8**[1]

0-61 **3** *1 ½* **Mount Abora (IRE)**[14] 192 5-9-4 **70** .... StevieDonohoe 5 72
(Ian Williams) *hld up in tch: racd keenly: rdn over 1f out: hung lft and styd on same pce ins fnl f* **9/4**[2]

0-65 **4** *1 ½* **Lady Elsie**[2] 355 4-9-0 **70** .... (p) LukeMorris 3 70
(George Prodromou) *set stdy pce tl qcknd over 2f out: sn rdn: hdd over 1f out: no ex ins fnl f* **7/1**

2m 46.74s (5.64) **Going Correction** +0.175s/f (Slow)
WFA 4 from 5yo+ 4lb 4 Ran SP% **106.6**
Speed ratings (Par 100): **88,87,86,85**
CSF £7.32 TOTE £4.60; EX 6.60.

Owner Geoff Lloyd **Bred** R Hollinshead **Trained** Upper Longdon, Staffs

FOCUS
Only four runners for this fillies' handicap. The gallop was steady before a 3f dash for home.

T/Jkpt: Not won. T/Plt: £1,220.00 to a £1 stake. Pool of £80,475.93 - 48.15 winning tickets. T/Qpdt: £14.50 to a £1 stake. Pool of £11,744.83 - 597.24 winning tickets. CR

290 CAGNES-SUR-MER
Monday, January 30
OFFICIAL GOING: Fibresand: standard

364a PRIX DE VICHY (CONDITIONS) (3YO) (FIBRESAND) 1m 2f (D)
11:30 (12:00) 3-Y-O **£12,083** (£4,833; £3,625; £2,416; £1,208)

RPR

1 **Remus De La Tour (FR)**[55] 3-9-4 0 .... LaurentDoreau 6 95
(K Borgel, France) **161/10**

2 *½* **Spoil The Fun (FR)**[80] 7385 3-9-4 0 .... JulienAuge 5 94
(C Ferland, France) **3/5**[1]

3 *½* **Loverdose (USA)**[35] 3-8-13 0 .... CesarPasserat(5) 4 93
(F Vermeulen, France) **8/1**[3]

4 *2* **Bling King**[40] 3-9-4 0 .... JohanVictoire 8 89
(F Vermeulen, France) **5/1**[2]

5 *2 ½* **Mamoue (IRE)**[14] 3-9-1 0 .... Pierre-CharlesBoudot 7 81
(D Prod'Homme, France) **11/1**

6 *nk* **Pearl Charm (USA)**[103] 6957 3-8-11 0 .... ThierryThulliez 3 76
(D Grilli, Italy) **48/1**

7 *1 ¼* **Path Finder (FR)**[10] 247 3-8-11 0 .... IoritzMendizabal 1 74
(Reg Hollinshead) *broke smartly on ins: sn led: rdn over 2 1/2f out: chal 2f out: hdd over 1 1/2f out: grad wknd* **32/1**

8 *6 ½* **Chattleya (FR)** 3-9-1 0 .... SylvainRuis 2 65
(L A Urbano-Grajales, France) **12/1**

2m 4.49s (124.49) **8** Ran SP% **117.2**
WIN (incl. 1 euro stake): 17.10. PLACES: 2.20, 1.20, 1.60. DF: 12.80. SF: 47.30.
Owner Barthelemy Vives **Bred** Mme A De Clermont Tonnerre **Trained** France

365a PRIX DE GRIMAUD (MAIDEN) (3YO COLTS & GELDINGS) (FIBRESAND) 1m 2f (D)
1:05 (12:00) 3-Y-O **£9,583** (£3,833; £2,875; £1,916; £958)

RPR

1 **Marquis Du Nonan (FR)**[28] 3-8-8 0 .... NicolasLarenaudie(8) 4 82
(G Collet, France) **229/10**

2 *¾* **Welanus (GER)** 3-9-2 0 .... ASuborics 6 81
(H Blume, Germany) **14/5**[1]

3 *1* **Fritz The Cat (FR)** 3-9-2 0 .... TonyPiccone 16 79
(J Rossi, France) **17/1**

4 *snk* **Syndic (FR)** 3-9-2 0 .... IoritzMendizabal 9 78
(J-C Rouget, France) **14/1**

5 *nk* **Brooklyn Thomas (IRE)** 3-9-2 0 .... Francois-XavierBertras 1 78
(F Rohaut, France) **14/5**[1]

6 *nk* **Glamour Star (GER)** 3-9-2 0 .... DavyBonilla 10 77
(Exors Of W Baltromei, Germany) **6/1**[2]

7 *1* **Bramante Di Parma (ITY)** 3-9-2 0 .... ThierryThulliez 13 75
(D Grilli, Italy) **66/1**

8 *½* **Vedremo (FR)** 3-9-2 0 .... ThomasHuet 11 74
(K Borgel, France) **16/1**

9 *½* **Everstone (FR)**[10] 247 3-9-2 0 .... ThomasMessina 2 73
(D Allard, France) **133/1**

10 *1* **Mizzen Reef (USA)** 3-9-2 0 .... (b[1]) JulienAuge 5 71
(C Ferland, France) **78/10**[3]

0 **Ve Solo Tu (FR)**[28] 3-9-2 0 .... FabienLefebvre 15
(G Collet, France) **35/1**

0 **Mister Koala (FR)**[12] 211 3-8-10 0 .... RomainAuray(6) 8
(J Heloury, France) **125/1**

0 **Hyson**[12] 211 3-9-2 0 .... SylvainRuis 7
(Reg Hollinshead) *settled towards rr: swtchd towards outside early in st: u.p 2 1/2f out: nt qckn: nvr a factor fnl 2f* **17/1**

0 **Lightly Chilled (FR)** 3-9-2 0 .... RemiCampos 14
(T Larriviere, France) **76/1**

0 **Moonlight Gambler (FR)** 3-9-2 0 .... FranckBlondel 12
(N Bertran De Balanda, France) **19/1**

2m 7.61s (127.61) **15** Ran SP% **118.2**
WIN (incl. 1 euro stake): 23.90. PLACES: 4.90, 2.20, 4.00. DF: 73.20. SF: 138.50.
Owner Earl Ecurie Viganne **Bred** Earl Ecurie Viganne **Trained** France

283 SOUTHWELL (L-H)
Tuesday, January 31
OFFICIAL GOING: Standard
Wind: Moderate across Weather: Overcast

366 BET AT BLUE SQUARE AMATEUR RIDERS' H'CAP 1m 6f (F)
1:30 (1:32) (Class 6) (0-65,65) 4-Y-O+ **£1,646** (£506; £253) **Stalls** Low

Form RPR

623- **1** **Sistine**[51] 7723 4-9-11 **59** .... MrNdeBoinville(5) 2 75
(Nicky Henderson) *hld up: stdy hdwy 5f out: trckd ldrs over 3f out: rdn to ld 1 1/2f out: edgd rt and kpt on wl fnl f* **7/1**

1/3- **2** *2* **Aaman (IRE)**[260] 2140 6-10-11 **65** .... RobertWilliams(3) 9 78
(Bernard Llewellyn) *trckd ldrs: hdwy to ld wl over 2f out: rdn and hdd 1 1/2f out: kpt on u.p fnl f* **7/1**

0-32 **3** *1* **Brunello**[21] 110 4-9-11 **59** .... MrNSlatter(5) 7 71
(David O'Meara) *trckd ldrs: effrt 3f out: rdn over 2f out: kpt on same pce u.p appr fnl f* **11/2**[1]

2-33 **4** *5* **Newport Arch**[11] 229 4-10-2 **59** .... MrSWalker 12 64
(John Quinn) *in tch: hdwy to trck ldrs 4f out: effrt 3f out: rdn over 2f out and sn one pce* **13/2**[3]

453- **5** *7* **Uncut Stone (IRE)**[40] 7858 4-10-5 **62** .... MissSBrotherton 6 57
(Peter Niven) *in tch on inner: pushed along and outpcd over 4f out: kpt on fnl 2f: n.d* **6/1**[2]

-020 **6** *½* **Miereveld**[5] 188 5-9-8 **50** .... (b) MrOGarner(5) 4 45
(Shaun Harris) *s.i.s and bhd: hdwy after 3f: cl up on outer 1/2-way: rdn along over 3f out: grad wknd fnl 2f* **50/1**

120- **7** *½* **Carnac (IRE)**[33] 7914 6-9-12 **56** .... (p) MissDLenge(7) 8 50
(Alan McCabe) *cl up: led over 4f out: rdn along over 3f out: hdd wl over 2f out: grad wknd* **18/1**

05-2 **8** *10* **Turjuman (USA)**[4] 9 7-10-4 **62** .... (p) MissAlexOwen(7) 1 42
(Alan Bailey) *a in midfield* **10/1**

The Form Book Flat, Raceform Ltd, Compton, RG20 6NL

030/ **9** *4 ½* **Mujamead**[7] 263 8-10-6 **60** MrMJJSmith(3) 10 34
(Tony Carroll) *hld up towards rr: effrt 1/2-way: sn rdn along and n.d* **20/1**

423- **10** *13* **Bandanaman (IRE)**[147] 5079 6-10-3 **61** MissEMelbourn(7) 5 16
(Alan Swinbank) *towards rr: pushed along 1/2-way: sn bhd* **16/1**

0-02 **11** *1 ¾* **Valdan (IRE)**[7] 278 8-10-3 **54** MrsEEvans 11
(David Evans) *in tch: rdn along over 5f out: sn wknd* **14/1**

000- **12** *9* **Flag Of Glory**[64] 7564 5-10-3 **61** MissMEdden(7) 13
(Peter Hiatt) *led: rdn along and hdd over 4f out: sn wknd and bhd* **66/1**

064- **13** *23* **Grand Art (IRE)**[14] 6656 8-10-6 **62** (v) MissKBannon(5) 3
(Noel Wilson) *cl up: rdn along over 5f out: sn wknd* **40/1**

040- **14** *73* **Teutonic Knight (IRE)**[165] 5247 5-9-8 **50** MrJHodson(5) 14
(Ian Williams) *a in rr: rdn along bef 1/2-way: sn bhd: t.o fnl 3f* **17/2**

3m 7.09s (-1.21) **Going Correction** -0.125s/f (Stan)
WFA 4 from 5yo+ 6lb **14** Ran SP% **116.1**
Speed ratings (Par 101): **98,96,96,93,89 89,88,83,80,73 72,67,53,12**
toteswingers:1&2:£5.20, 1&3:£6.40, 2&3:£9.00 CSF £51.75 CT £290.94 TOTE £8.80: £2.50, £1.80, £2.20; EX 56.40 TRIFECTA Not won..
Owner Elite Racing Club **Bred** Sheikh Abdulla Bin Isa Al Khalifa **Trained** Upper Lambourn, Berks

FOCUS
A modest handicap but a race that could throw up a few winners. The gallop was a reasonable one and the winner raced in the centre in the straight.

367 PLAY GOLF BEFORE RACING AT SOUTHWELL (S) STKS 1m 4f (F)
2:00 (2:00) (Class 6) 4-Y-0+ **£1,704** (£503; £251) **Stalls** Low

Form RPR

33-1 **1** **Magic Millie (IRE)**[23] 97 5-9-0 56 DanielTudhope 4 68
(David O'Meara) *trckd ldng pair on inner: hdwy 4f out: led 3f out: jnd 2f out and sn rdn: hdd over 1f out: drvn and rallied ins fnl f to ld nr fin* **85/40**[1]

05-1 **2** *nk* **Overrule (USA)**[23] 98 8-9-5 65 (p) BarryMcHugh 10 73
(Brian Ellison) *hld up in rr: hdwy over 4f out: effrt on outer to join ldrs 3f out: wd st and rdn to chal 2f out: led over 1f out: drvn ins fnl f: hdd and no ex towards fin* **9/2**[2]

0/4- **3** *nk* **Wine 'n Dine**[24] 5417 7-9-0 75 MartinLane 2 67
(Bernard Llewellyn) *chsd ldrs: rdn along 1/2-way: hdwy to chse ldng pair over 2f out: sn drvn: kpt on wl u.p fnl f: gaining towards fin* **10/1**

4-14 **4** *10* **Mcconnell (USA)**[19] 134 7-9-5 72 (b) WilliamCarson 5 56
(Richard Guest) *hld up in tch: hdwy to trck ldrs 4f out: effrt 3f out: sn rdn and no imp* **5/1**[3]

02-4 **5** *½* **Flying Applause**[23] 98 7-9-0 52 (vt[1]) RussKennemore 3 50
(Roy Bowring) *sn led: rdn along 4f out: hdd 3f out and grad wknd* **12/1**

40-0 **6** *7* **Raghdaan**[9] 265 5-9-0 51 (p) ChrisCatlin 7 39
(Peter Hiatt) *chsd ldrs: rdn along 4f out: wknd over 3f out* **20/1**

00-0 **7** *2 ¾* **Blonde Maite**[21] 109 6-9-0 36 (b) JamesSullivan 6 35
(Roy Bowring) *t.k.h: prom: rdn along over 4f out: sn wknd* **80/1**

061- **8** *1 ¼* **Dunaskin (IRE)**[33] 7912 12-9-0 46 (b) CharlesEddery(5) 1 38
(Richard Guest) *dwlt and reminders s: a in rr* **25/1**

0 **9** *13* **Tiger Who**[13] 206 4-8-0 0 RaulDaSilva(5) 8
(David Flood) *a in rr: bhd fnl 3f* **66/1**

/20- **10** *40* **Alaghiraar (IRE)**[41] 7850 8-9-0 61 (b) HayleyTurner 9
(Richard Ford) *a towards rr: bhd 1/2-way: t.o fnl 3f* **5/1**[3]

2m 39.89s (-1.11) **Going Correction** -0.125s/f (Stan)
WFA 4 from 5yo+ 4lb **10** Ran SP% **111.6**
Speed ratings (Par 101): **98,97,97,90,90 85,84,83,74,47**
toteswingers:1&2:£2.30, 1&3:£5.40, 2&3:£6.10 CSF £10.49 TOTE £2.90: £1.20, £2.30, £3.20; EX 12.00 Trifecta £64.50 Pool: £355.16 - 4.07 winning units..There was no bid for the winner.
Owner C Varley, K Everitt & R Fell **Bred** John C Little **Trained** Nawton, N Yorks

■ Stewards' Enquiry : Barry McHugh seven-day ban: used whip with excessive frequency (Feb 14-18,20-21)
Daniel Tudhope four-day ban: used whip with excessive frequency (Feb 14-17)

FOCUS
A wide display of ability on show in just an ordinary seller. The gallop was fair and the winner came down the centre.

368 SOUTHWELL-RACECOURSE.CO.UK CLAIMING STKS 6f (F)
2:30 (2:30) (Class 6) 4-Y-0+ **£1,704** (£503; £251) **Stalls** Low

Form RPR

0-54 **1** **Pick A Little**[18] 157 4-9-1 78 DaneO'Neill 3 75
(Hughie Morrison) *led 1f: cl up tl led again wl over 2f out: rdn wl over 1f out: drvn ins fnl f: hld on wl* **6/5**[1]

06-5 **2** *nk* **Imprimis Tagula (IRE)**[7] 284 8-8-4 81 (v) NatashaEaton(7) 2 70
(Alan Bailey) *cl up: led after 1f: pushed along and hdd wl over 2f out: sn rdn and rallied to have ev ch ins fnl f tl no ex nr fin* **15/2**

-432 **3** *¾* **Pilgrim Dancer (IRE)**[11] 226 5-8-9 50 BarryMcHugh 4 66
(Tony Coyle) *trckd ldrs: hdwy and wd st: chsd ldrs wl over 1f out: sn rdn and kpt on wl fnl f* **16/1**

201- **4** *2 ¾* **Katy's Secret**[46] 7776 5-9-3 70 RyanPowell(3) 1 68
(William Jarvis) *hld up in tch: hdwy on inner 1/2-way: chsd ldrs 2f out: rdn wl over 1f out: one pce ent fnl f* **4/1**[3]

06-0 **5** *1 ½* **Malcheek (IRE)**[24] 89 10-9-11 98 DuranFentiman 6 68
(Tim Easterby) *chsd ldrs: rdn along over 2f out: wknd over 1f out* **10/3**[2]

-000 **6** *10* **Bertbrand**[11] 226 7-8-7 41 JamesSullivan 5 18
(Ian McInnes) *in tch: wd st: rdn over 2f out: sn wknd* **100/1**

1m 14.92s (-1.58) **Going Correction** -0.125s/f (Stan) **6** Ran SP% **107.2**
Speed ratings (Par 101): **105,104,103,99,97 84**
toteswingers:1&2:£2.40, 1&3:£3.40, 2&3:£7.00 CSF £9.91 TOTE £2.20: £1.40, £3.50; EX 11.40.Pick A Little was claimed by Mr C. E. Weare for £9,000.
Owner K B Hodges **Bred** D R Tucker **Trained** East Ilsley, Berks

FOCUS
A fair claimer, though the proximity of the 50-rated third casts a doubt over the worth of this form. The gallop was only fair and the winner came down the centre.

369 BET BLUE SQUARE ON YOUR MOBILE MAIDEN STKS 1m (F)
3:00 (3:00) (Class 5) 3-4-Y-0 **£2,385** (£704; £352) **Stalls** Low

Form RPR

05- **1** **Dubai Sunshine (IRE)**[81] 7367 3-8-6 0 HayleyTurner 9 81+
(Michael Bell) *prom: hdwy to ld over 3f out: pushed clr fr wl over 1f out: easily* **7/2**[1]

03-6 **2** *3* **Cape Safari (IRE)**[24] 84 3-8-1 67 MartinLane 7 66
(James Tate) *trckd ldrs: hdwy 3f out: rdn to chse wnr wl over 1f out: no imp* **9/2**[3]

0/5 **3** *9* **Somerset Island (IRE)**[21] 114 4-9-12 0 AndrewMullen 10 55
(Michael Smith) *chsd ldrs on outer: wd st and sn rdn along: kpt on same pce u.p fnl 2f: tk modest 3rd ins fnl f* **50/1**

4 *½* **Linroyale Boy (USA)** 4-9-12 0 PJMcDonald 3 54+
(Alan Swinbank) *dwlt and bhd: hdwy over 2f out: styd on wl appr fnl f: nrst fin* **4/1**[2]

5 *nk* **Dewala** 3-7-12 0 DominicFox(3) 12 43
(Michael Appleby) *in rr: hdwy over 2f out: swtchd lft and rdn wl over 1f out: styd on fnl f: nrst fin* **100/1**

50- **6** *1 ½* **Swinger**[166] 5212 4-9-7 0 RaulDaSilva(5) 8 50
(Scott Dixon) *cl up: effrt 3f out: sn rdn to chse wnr: wknd wl over 1f out: lost modest 3rd ins fnl f* **22/1**

P4- **7** *hd* **King's Wharf (IRE)**[46] 7783 3-8-6 0 LukeMorris 5 45
(David Evans) *midfield: hdwy to chse ldrs 1/2-way: rdn and edgd lft over 3f out: sn wknd* **7/1**

8 *4* **Zenaad (USA)** 3-8-6 0 ChrisCatlin 4 35
(Seamus Durack) *s.i.s: a towards rr* **6/1**

0 **9** *7* **Burning Passion**[15] 195 3-8-6 0 JamesSullivan 6 19
(Michael Easterby) *a towards rr* **33/1**

10 *12* **Ruby Doo** 4-9-7 0 DaneO'Neill 11
(Alastair Lidderdale) *dwlt: sn outpcd and wl bhd fr 1/2-way* **80/1**

0- **11** *¾* **Henry George**[122] 6532 3-8-6 0 JoeFanning 1
(Mark Johnston) *led: rdn along and hdd over 3f out: sn wknd and bhd whn eased fr wl over 1f out* **6/1**

40-0 **12** *¾* **Apassionforfashion**[7] 284 4-9-7 36 (e) TomEaves 2
(Bryan Smart) *chsd ldrs on inner: wkng whn n.m.r and hmpd over 3f out: sn bhd and eased fnl 2f* **66/1**

1m 41.4s (-2.30) **Going Correction** -0.125s/f (Stan)
WFA 3 from 4yo 20lb **12** Ran SP% **114.4**
Speed ratings (Par 103): **106,103,94,93,93 91,91,87,80,68 67,67**
toteswingers:1&2:£3.00, 1&3:£44.30, 2&3:£21.40 CSF £17.78 TOTE £4.90: £2.00, £2.60, £12.30; EX 14.70 Trifecta £294.20 Pool: £445.35 - 1.12 winning units..
Owner Dr Ali Ridha **Bred** Rabbah Bloodstock Limited **Trained** Newmarket, Suffolk

FOCUS
A most uncompetitive maiden but fair form from the winner, who along with the runner-up, pulled a long way clear. The gallop was reasonable and the winner came down the centre in the straight.

370 MEMBERSHIP OF SOUTHWELL GOLF CLUB H'CAP 7f (F)
3:30 (3:31) (Class 6) (0-60,60) 4-Y-0+ **£1,704** (£503; £251) **Stalls** Low

Form RPR

2-31 **1** **Fluctuation (IRE)**[7] 287 4-9-8 **60** 6ex (b) StevieDonohoe 14 74
(Ian Williams) *chsd ldrs on outer: cl up 1/2-way: wd st: led wl over 2f out: rdn clr over 1f out: drvn ins fnl f: edgd lft and jst hld on* **10/3**[2]

050- **2** *shd* **Caledonia Prince**[110] 6816 4-8-8 **53** (p) JoshBaudains(7) 13 67
(Jo Hughes) *prom: wd st: pushed along and sltly outpcd over 2f out: rdn over 1f out: styd on strly fnl f: jst failed* **33/1**

00-2 **3** *4* **Saktoon (USA)**[23] 101 4-9-1 **53** (v) JoeFanning 7 56+
(Derek Shaw) *in rr and sn pushed along: n.m.r over 3f out: rdn over 2f out: n.m.r and swtchd lft over 1f out: styd on ins fnl f: nrst fin* **12/1**

1-22 **4** *1* **Spacecraft (IRE)**[21] 109 5-9-1 **53** (b) PhillipMakin 9 53+
(Christopher Kellett) *dwlt and bhd: wd st and hdwy wl over 2f out: rdn wl over 1f out: styd on ins fnl f: nrst fin* **13/2**[3]

23-6 **5** *nk* **Only Ten Per Cent (IRE)**[18] 154 4-9-0 **52** LukeMorris 12 51
(J R Jenkins) *in tch on outer: hdwy over 2f out: sn rdn and chsd ldrs whn edgd rt over 1f out: one pce fnl f* **8/1**

3-02 **6** *2* **Fantasy Fry**[7] 284 4-9-4 **56** (bt[1]) RichardKingscote 4 50
(Tom Dascombe) *cl up on inner: led after 3f: rdn along 3f out: sn hdd: prom tl drvn and wknd over 1f out* **11/4**[1]

30-0 **7** *½* **Shaws Diamond (USA)**[8] 274 6-8-13 **54** (v) DaleSwift(3) 1 47
(Derek Shaw) *chsd ldrs on inner: rdn along wl over 2f out: grad wknd* **33/1**

6221 **8** *1 ½* **Crocodile Bay (IRE)**[6] 305 9-8-11 **49** (p) FrannyNorton 6 42
(Richard Guest) *in tch: hdwy to chse ldrs over 2f out: sn rdn and no imp* **10/1**

04-0 **9** *hd* **Ossie Ardiles (IRE)**[18] 151 4-9-0 **52** (p) LiamKeniry 3 40
(Michael Appleby) *chsd ldrs: rdn along wl over 2f out: sn wknd* **66/1**

0-50 **10** *1 ¾* **Divertimenti (IRE)**[19] 139 8-9-2 **54** (vt[1]) RussKennemore 10 37
(Roy Bowring) *led 3f: cl up tl rdn along wl over 2f out and sn wknd* **33/1**

4-01 **11** *nk* **St Ignatius**[21] 109 5-8-6 **51** (p) JackDuern(7) 8 34
(Michael Appleby) *in tch: rdn along 3f out: sn wknd* **16/1**

52-0 **12** *1 ½* **Pulsatilla**[18] 153 4-9-7 **59** TomEaves 2 38
(Bryan Smart) *midfield: rdn along 1/2-way: sn wknd* **11/1**

060/ **13** *2* **Komreyev Star**[604] 2789 10-8-7 **45** BarryMcHugh 11 18
(Ray Peacock) *a in rr: bhd fr 1/2-way* **100/1**

5-00 **14** *4 ½* **Kwik Time**[21] 113 4-8-7 **45** (b) LeeNewman 5 6
(Robin Bastiman) *sn rdn along in rr: bhd fnl 3f* **66/1**

1m 29.72s (-0.58) **Going Correction** -0.125s/f (Stan) **14** Ran SP% **118.0**
Speed ratings (Par 101): **98,97,93,92,91 89,88,87,87,85 84,82,80,75**
toteswingers:1&2:£4.80, 1&3:£10.70, 2&3:£1.80 CSF £122.79 CT £1226.32 TOTE £3.50: £1.20, £9.60, £5.00; EX 124.30 TRIFECTA Not won..
Owner J Tredwell **Bred** Corduff Stud & T J Rooney **Trained** Portway, Worcs

FOCUS
A moderate handicap in which the pace was soon reasonable. The winner continued the usual trend of racing down the centre.

371 DINE IN THE PANTRY H'CAP 6f (F)
4:00 (4:00) (Class 5) (0-75,75) 4-Y-0+ **£2,264** (£673; £336; £168) **Stalls** Low

Form RPR

51-3 **1** **Andiamo Via**[21] 115 5-8-7 **61** JoeFanning 11 72
(Michael Smith) *cl up: wd st: chal 2f out: rdn over 1f out: ev ch whn sltly hmpd ins fnl f: styd on gamely to ld towards fin* **7/2**[1]

2-31 **2** *½* **Greenhead High**[19] 139 4-8-11 **65** AndrewMullen 1 74
(David Nicholls) *sn led: wd st: rdn 2f out: drvn and edgd rt ins fnl f: hdd and no ex towards fin* **11/2**[3]

1-50 **3** *1 ½* **Il Battista**[3] 351 4-9-2 **75** (be) RaulDaSilva(5) 7 79
(Alan McCabe) *midfield: hdwy on inner 2f out: rdn wl over 1f out: styd on fnl f: nrst fin* **11/2**[3]

-012 **4** *1* **Avonrose**[8] 269 5-9-7 **75** PhillipMakin 6 76
(Derek Shaw) *trckd ldrs: hdwy wl over 2f out: rdn wl over 1f out: one pce ent fnl f* **9/1**

-400 **5** *¾* **Punching**[10] 252 8-9-1 **69** HayleyTurner 3 68
(Conor Dore) *prom: effrt to chse ldr wl over 2f out: sn rdn and ev ch tl drvn and one pce appr fnl f* **6/1**

22-2 **6** *2 ¼* **Soopacal (IRE)**[19] 133 7-8-13 **67** BarryMcHugh 9 58
(Brian Ellison) *chsd ldrs: effrt over 2f out: sn rdn and wknd appr fnl f* **4/1**[2]

03-0 **7** *1 ¾* **Catalyze**[21] 115 4-9-2 **70** LeeNewman 4 56
(Richard Guest) *racd wout declared tongue strap: in tch: hdwy to chse ldrs wl over 2f out: sn rdn and kpt on same pce* **33/1**

120- **8** *2 ½* **Rowan Spirit (IRE)**[70] 7500 4-9-7 **75**................................ ShaneKelly 10 53
(Mark Brisbourne) *a towards rr* **14/1**
0-50 **9** *4* **Spirit Of Grace**[4] 329 4-8-4 **65**..............................(p) NoraLooby(7) 12 30
(Alan McCabe) *chsd ldrs: rdn along 1/2-way: wd st and sn wknd* **33/1**
00-6 **10** *2 ½* **Bravo King (IRE)**[28] 19 4-9-0 **68**............................(t) WilliamCarson 2 25
(Richard Guest) *dwlt: a in rr* **50/1**
220- **11** *4 ½* **Legal Eagle (IRE)**[106] 6917 7-9-3 **74**.......................(p) RobertLButler(3) 5 17
(Paul Green) *dwlt: a in rr* **33/1**
400- **12** *7* **Brynfa Boy**[94] 7173 6-8-13 **67** ow1.............................(t) StephenCraine 8
(Daniel Mark Loughnane) *a in rr* **33/1**

1m 15.44s (-1.06) **Going Correction** -0.125s/f (Stan) **12** Ran SP% **117.7**
Speed ratings (Par 103): **102,101,99,98,97 94,91,90,90,79 73,64**
toteswingers:1&2:£4.30, 1&3:£5.20, 2&3:£7.80 CSF £21.57 CT £106.19 TOTE £5.40: £2.50, £2.40, £2.30; EX 26.50 Trifecta £332.90 Part won. Pool: £449.94 - 0.60 winning units..
Owner Mrs H I S Calzini **Bred** Mrs H I S Calzini **Trained** Kirkheaton, Northumberland

FOCUS
Mainly exposed performers in an ordinary handicap. Although the gallop was reasonable those held up never figured and the winner came towards the stands' rail in the straight.
Greenhead High Official explanation: jockey said gelding hung right-handed

372 PLAY ROULETTE AT BLUESQ.COM/CASINO H'CAP 6f (F)
4:30 (4:31) (Class 6) (0-60,60) 4-Y-0+ **£1,704** (£503; £251) **Stalls** Low

Form RPR
36-3 **1** **Prince Of Vasa (IRE)**[23] 101 5-9-2 **55**.....................(v[1]) AndrewMullen 3 69
(Michael Smith) *chsd ldr: hdwy to ld wl over 1f out: sn clr: styd on* **7/2**[1]
4-23 **2** *3 ½* **Gracie's Gift (IRE)**[7] 289 10-9-0 **53**.....................(v) FrannyNorton 12 56
(Richard Guest) *chsd ldrs on outer: wd st and sltly outpcd: hdwy wl over 1f out: kpt on: nrst fin* **11/2**[3]
006- **3** *hd* **Bond Blade**[40] 7854 4-9-2 **58**.................................. DaleSwift(3) 11 60
(Geoffrey Oldroyd) *hld up towards rr: wd st: hdwy over 2f out: rdn wl over 1f out: kpt on same pce fnl f* **17/2**
1-10 **4** *1 ¼* **Beachwood Bay**[19] 139 4-9-7 **60**.............................. StevieDonohoe 8 58
(Jo Hughes) *hld up: hdwy wl over 2f out: rdn to chse ldrs wl over 1f out: sn no imp* **4/1**[2]
00-0 **5** *nk* **Sofias Number One (USA)**[12] 215 4-9-7 **60**................(b) MartinLane 4 57
(Roy Bowring) *bhd: wd st: racd nr stands' rail: hdwy wl over 1f out: sn rdn and styd on fnl f: nrst fin* **20/1**
3-10 **6** *hd* **Bird Dog**[7] 289 6-8-5 **51**......................................(v) DannyBrock(7) 5 48
(Phil McEntee) *led: rdn along over 2f out: hdd wl over 1f out and sn wknd* **10/1**
000- **7** *1 ¾* **Bonnie Prince Blue**[77] 7419 9-9-3 **56**.....................(b) PatrickMathers 10 47
(Ian McInnes) *s.i.s: sn rdn along and bhd tl sme late hdwy* **22/1**
36-0 **8** *¾* **Basle**[12] 212 5-9-4 **60**..(t) AmyRyan(3) 1 49
(Gay Kelleway) *towards rr: sme hdwy on inner over 2f out: sn rdn and n.d* **33/1**
0-30 **9** *1 ¾* **Rapid Water**[9] 262 6-9-7 **60**....................................(be) FergusSweeney 6 43
(Gary Moore) *chsd ldrs: rdn to chse front pair over 2f out: sn drvn and wknd over 1f out* **7/1**
150- **10** *¾* **Invigilator**[247] 2524 4-9-5 **58**................................ JoeFanning 9 39
(Derek Shaw) *towards rr: hdwy and in tch 1/2-way: sn rdn and wknd over 2f out* **16/1**
06-0 **11** *7* **Casternova**[20] 124 4-9-0 **53**.................................... HayleyTurner 7
(Hughie Morrison) *chsd ldrs: rdn along 1/2-way: sn wknd* **16/1**
000- **12** *dist* **Hand Painted**[78] 7412 6-9-4 **57**................................ LeeNewman 2
(Anthony Middleton) *anticipated s and hit front of stalls: j. awkwardly: stmbld and lost many l s: virtually tk no part* **50/1**

1m 15.89s (-0.61) **Going Correction** -0.125s/f (Stan) **12** Ran SP% **115.5**
Speed ratings (Par 101): **99,94,94,92,92 91,89,88,86,85 75,**
toteswingers:1&2:£3.80, 1&3:£8.60, 2&3:£11.00 CSF £20.87 CT £153.60 TOTE £3.90: £1.70, £1.20, £3.00; EX 18.90 Trifecta £527.40 Part won. Pool: £712.75 - 0.52 winning units..
Owner Mrs Sandra Smith **Bred** E O'Gorman **Trained** Kirkheaton, Northumberland

FOCUS
A moderate handicap run at a decent gallop but, as is often the case over this C&D, this was a race in which very few figured. The winner came down the centre.
Hand Painted Official explanation: jockey said gelding became unruly as he tried to remove blindfold and jumped awkwardly causing him to lose his irons
T/Jkpt: £4,166.60 to a £1 stake. Pool:£12,621.96 - 6.00 winning tickets T/Plt: £61.10 to a £1 stake. Pool:£81,965.24 - 978.25 winning tickets T/Qpdt: £26.00 to a £1 stake. Pool:£5,727.45 - 162.40 winning tickets JR

[306]KEMPTON (A.W) (R-H)
Wednesday, February 1

OFFICIAL GOING: Standard
Wind: Fresh, against Weather: Cloudless, bitterly cold

373 FREE ENTRY FOR BETDAQ MEMBERS MEDIAN AUCTION MAIDEN STKS 5f (P)
4:50 (4:51) (Class 5) 3-5-Y-0 **£2,264** (£673; £336; £168) **Stalls** Low

Form RPR
5 **1** **Cats Eyes**[21] 121 3-8-9 0.. ShaneKelly 1 59+
(Robert Cowell) *chsd ldr: clsd to ld 1f out: jst pushed along to maintain narrow but decisive advantage* **1/2**[1]
24-4 **2** *½* **Sannibel**[26] 61 4-9-9 65... DavidProbert 2 63
(Tony Carroll) *led: hung lft and hdd 1f out: styd on but readily hld by wnr* **13/2**[2]
000- **3** *4 ½* **Bobbyow**[208] 3804 4-9-9 49...................................... MarkCoumbe(5) 7 54
(Terry Clement) *outpcd in 6th after 2f: styd on u.p fr over 1f out to take 3rd last stride* **40/1**
60-3 **4** *nse* **Miakora**[28] 37 4-9-9 46.. KieranO'Neill 6 49
(Michael Quinn) *racd in 5th and nt on terms: drvn to chse ldng pair over 1f out: no imp: lost 3rd last stride* **33/1**
05-0 **5** *½* **Sailing North (USA)**[13] 214 4-10-0 55........................ LukeMorris 3 52
(Ronald Harris) *chsd ldng pair but nt on terms: lost 3rd over 1f out: one pce after* **20/1**
366- **6** *8* **Bint Alakaaber (IRE)**[133] 6251 4-9-9 54...................... StephenCraine 5 22
(J R Jenkins) *stdd s: hld up but chsd ldng trio over 3f out: wknd rapidly over 1f out* **16/1**[3]
- **7** *6* **Kiss My Heart** 3-8-9 0.. SteveDrowne 8
(Peter Makin) *s.s: sn outpcd: a wl bhd* **16/1**[3]

59.96s (-0.54) **Going Correction** -0.10s/f (Stan)
WFA 3 from 4yo 14lb **7** Ran SP% **101.9**
Speed ratings (Par 103): **100,99,92,91,91 78,68**
toteswingers:1&2:£1.10, 1&3:£4.30, 2&3:£9.80 CSF £2.79 TOTE £1.20: £1.10, £2.50; EX 2.90 Trifecta £37.70 Pool: £587.85 - 11.52 winning units..
Owner Manor Farm Stud (rutland) **Bred** Manor Farm Stud & Mrs A J Ralli **Trained** Six Mile Bottom, Cambs
■ Stewards' Enquiry : David Probert two-day ban: careless riding (Feb 15-16)

FOCUS
A weak maiden and the winner did not need to improve on her debut promise.

374 BETDAQ MULTIPLES H'CAP 1m 2f (P)
5:20 (5:22) (Class 5) (0-75,81) 4-Y-0+ **£2,264** (£673; £336; £168) **Stalls** Low

Form RPR
10-3 **1** **Megalala (IRE)**[21] 119 11-9-6 **74**.............................. KieranO'Neill 9 92
(John Bridger) *mde all: drew clr after 4f: drvn 2f out: hrd pressed ins fnl f: hld on gamely* **11/1**
-421 **2** *¾* **Focail Maith**[10] 263 4-9-12 **81** 6ex..............................(p) AdamKirby 5 88
(John Ryan) *trckd ldrs: sent off in pursuit of wnr 3f out: drvn and grad clsd fr 2f out: chal last 100yds: nt qckn* **6/1**[3]
66-6 **3** *¾* **Menadati (USA)**[14] 199 4-8-12 **67**.............................. TomMcLaughlin 3 72
(Peter Hiatt) *dwlt: hld up and sn in last trio: stl there 2f out: gd prog to take 3rd 1f out but 6 l bhd ldng pair: clsd rapidly nr fin: far too much to do* **12/1**
04-5 **4** *2 ½* **Lisahane Bog**[21] 119 5-9-3 **71**....................................(v) DaneO'Neill 10 71
(Peter Hedger) *s.v.s: ct up in last pair after 2f but wl off the pce: drvn over 3f out: styd on fr over 1f out to take 4th ins fnl f* **11/1**
500- **5** *½* **Edgeworth (IRE)**[131] 6295 6-8-5 **66**............................ JoshBaudains(7) 4 66
(David Bridgwater) *awkward s: hld up and mostly in 7th: v wd bnd 2f out and lost grnd: pushed along over 1f out: hanging rt but styd on: no ch* **25/1**
6-43 **6** *2 ¼* **The Mongoose**[13] 216 4-9-2 **71**................................. LukeMorris 7 66
(David Evans) *hld up in midfield: rdn and prog over 3f out: chsd clr ldng pair 2f out to 1f out: wknd* **10/3**[2]
003- **7** *½* **King Of Windsor (IRE)**[49] 7759 5-9-7 **75**..................... JimCrowley 6 69
(Keith Dalgleish) *hld up in last pair and wl off the pce: no ch whn shkn up over 1f out: r.o ins fnl f: no ch* **5/1**[1]
0-10 **8** *2* **Buxfizz (USA)**[4] 351 4-9-1 **75**................................(p) RaulDaSilva(5) 11 65
(George Prodromou) *chsd clr wnr to 3f out: wknd over 1f out* **20/1**
005/ **9** *nse* **Consider Yourself (USA)**[255] 5-9-4 **72**........................ WilliamCarson 1 61
(Anthony Carson) *t.k.h: chsd ldng pair for 4f: rdn 3f out: sn btn* **14/1**
52-4 **10** *1 ¾* **Peponi**[14] 199 6-9-5 **73**... SteveDrowne 2 59
(Peter Makin) *chsd ldrs in 5th: rdn and no prog 3f out: wknd 2f out* **12/1**

2m 5.49s (-2.51) **Going Correction** -0.10s/f (Stan)
WFA 4 from 5yo+ 1lb **10** Ran SP% **113.3**
Speed ratings (Par 103): **106,105,104,102,102 100,100,98,98,97**
toteswingers:1&2:£6.20, 1&3:£41.40, 2&3:£16.80 CSF £73.37 CT £806.91 TOTE £14.50: £2.50, £1.90, £3.60; EX 48.70 TRIFECTA Not won..
Owner Tommy Ware **Bred** Joseph Gallagher **Trained** Liphook, Hants

FOCUS
It usually pays to race handily on this inner track and Megalala and Kieran O'Neill stole this. The winner is rated to his C&D win in December.
Lisahane Bog Official explanation: jockey said gelding was slowly away

375 BACK OR LAY AT BETDAQ.COM H'CAP 1m (P)
5:50 (5:55) (Class 7) (0-50,50) 4-Y-0+ **£1,455** (£433; £216; £108) **Stalls** Low

Form RPR
06-2 **1** **Emerald Royal**[7] 293 4-8-12 **45**.................................. ShaneKelly 5 54
(Eric Wheeler) *hld up in midfield: waiting for room and lost pl fr over 2f out: gd prog on outer over 1f out: led jst ins fnl f: styd on wl* **9/2**[2]
3-02 **2** *1* **Cairanne**[13] 218 4-8-9 **45**.. RyanClark(3) 8 52
(Tom Keddy) *hld up bhd ldrs: prog towards outer 2f out: rdn to chal 1f out: chsd wnr after: styd on* **7/1**
03-0 **3** *1 ½* **Harvest Mist (IRE)**[27] 45 4-9-1 **48**.............................. HayleyTurner 2 52
(Michael Blanshard) *hld up in midfield: prog 2f out: drvn to ld for a few strides 1f out: one pce after* **6/1**[3]
000- **4** *nk* **Henry's Hero**[28] 7387 6-9-0 **47**.................................. FrannyNorton 3 50
(Chris Dwyer) *led 2f: styd prom: rdn on inner over 2f out: styd on to chal and one of five in line 1f out: one pce* **66/1**
43-5 **5** *hd* **Gay Gallivanter**[7] 300 4-8-13 **46**...............................(p) NickyMackay 9 48
(Michael Quinn) *led after 2f: drvn over 2f out: hdd and fdd 1f out* **16/1**
166- **6** *1* **Teen Ager (FR)**[76] 7442 8-9-3 **50**................................. LiamKeniry 10 53+
(Paul Burgoyne) *blindfold off late and slowly away: t.k.h: hld up in last trio: smooth prog over 2f out: clsng on ldrs and abt to be asked for effrt whn gap shut 1f out: nt rcvr* **9/1**
30-0 **7** *shd* **Chandrayaan**[14] 203 5-8-9 **45**...................................(v) SimonPearce(3) 6 45
(John E Long) *prom: rdn to press ldr over 3f out: drvn and nt qckn 2f out: sn lost pl and btn* **20/1**
000- **8** *1* **By Implication**[125] 6494 4-9-0 **47**...............................(p) LukeMorris 12 45
(Ed de Giles) *mostly in midfield: rdn on outer and struggling wl over 2f out: plugged on* **6/1**[3]
6-40 **9** *3 ¼* **Sunset Boulevard (IRE)**[14] 200 9-8-9 **47**...............(b) NathanAlison(5) 1 37
(Paddy Butler) *towards rr whn hmpd over 5f out: drvn on inner over 2f out: no real prog* **20/1**
0-05 **10** *1* **Le Reveur**[5] 334 10-8-9 **45**.......................................(e) RobertLButler(3) 11 33
(Richard Guest) *stdd into last trio sn after s: drvn and no real prog 2f out* **25/1**
46-3 **11** *½* **Ocean Countess (IRE)**[21] 125 6-9-2 **49**........................(t) AdamKirby 7 36
(Tony Carroll) *s.s: mostly in last trio: rdn and mod prog into midfield over 1f out: sn wknd* **10/3**[1]
550- **12** *17* **Five Cool Kats (IRE)**[48] 7768 4-8-12 **45**........................ JoeFanning 4
(Bill Turner) *pressed ldr tl wknd rapidly 2f out: t.o* **20/1**

1m 40.13s (0.33) **Going Correction** -0.10s/f (Stan) **12** Ran SP% **117.8**
Speed ratings (Par 97): **94,93,91,91,91 90,89,88,85,84 84,67**
toteswingers:1&2:£5.80, 1&3:£5.70, 2&3:£12.10 CSF £32.81 CT £195.77 TOTE £4.70: £1.70, £2.20, £2.50; EX 33.30 Trifecta £160.30 Pool: £719.57 - 3.32 winning units..
Owner Four Provinces Partnership **Bred** Genesis Green Stud Ltd **Trained** Lambourn, Berks
■ Stewards' Enquiry : Nicky Mackay one-day ban: careless riding (Feb 22)

FOCUS
A modest handicap rated around the second and third.
Teen Ager(FR) Official explanation: jockey said that the gelding became restless as he went to remove blindfold and was denied a clear run
Ocean Countess(IRE) Official explanation: jockey said mare never travelled

376 BETDAQ MOBILE APPS H'CAP 6f (P)
6:20 (6:22) (Class 6) (0-55,55) 3-Y-0 **£1,617** (£481; £240; £120) **Stalls** Low

Form RPR
046- **1** **Clodhopper (IRE)**[183] 4648 3-8-7 **46** oh1........................ ChrisCatlin 4 53+
(Jamie Osborne) *dwlt: t.k.h: hld up in last trio: stl there over 2f out but gng strly: prog over 1f out: wnt 2nd ins fnl f: clsd on tiring ldr to ld nr fin* **20/1**

00-0 **2** 1 1/4 **Chart**[14] [201] 3-9-2 **55** LeeNewman 1 58
(William Jarvis) *disp ld on inner: def advantage 1/2-way: clr 2f out: 3 l up ins fnl f: wknd and hdd last strides* **11/2[3]**

30-5 **3** 1 3/4 **Flying Kitty**[17] [185] 3-8-11 **50** KieranO'Neill 3 47
(John Bridger) *chsd ldrs: pushed along bef 1/2-way: wnt 2nd on inner over 2f out: no imp on ldr over 1f out: lost 2nd ins fnl f: one pce* **16/1**

30-0 **4** 1 1/2 **Very First Blade**[16] [191] 3-9-0 **53** FrannyNorton 12 46
(Mark Brisbourne) *hld up in last trio: awkward bnd over 3f out: prog on inner 2f out: rdn over 1f out: one pce after* **12/1**

000- **5** 2 1/2 **Periwinkle Way**[172] [5047] 3-8-5 **49** RaulDaSilva(5) 10 34
(Tim McCarthy) *trckd ldrs: gng wl 1/2-way: rdn and nt qckn 2f out: no imp after* **14/1**

00-1 **6** nk **Liquid Sunshine**[7] [294] 3-8-12 **51** 6ex JimmyFortune 11 35
(Sylvester Kirk) *in tch: effrt on outer over 2f out: tried to make prog over 1f out: wknd fnl f* **4/1[2]**

-343 **7** 4 1/2 **Lord Buffhead**[12] [228] 3-8-4 **48** CharlesEddery(5) 8 17
(Richard Guest) *moved up on wd outside to dispute ld 4f out to 3f out: sn btn* **10/1**

040- **8** 1 1/2 **Gone By Sunrise**[99] [7072] 3-8-10 **54** ShaneBKelly(5) 5 18
(Richard Fahey) *hld up in last trio: effrt on inner 2f out: no prog over 1f out: wknd* **13/8[1]**

060- **9** 8 **Willow Beauty**[48] [7770] 3-9-1 **54** StephenCraine 7
(J R Jenkins) *disp ld to 1/2-way: sn wknd* **25/1**

05-5 **10** 3 **Misred Melissa (IRE)**[12] [228] 3-8-4 **50** DarrenEgan(7) 2
(Ronald Harris) *disp ld to over 3f out: wknd qckly* **50/1**

1m 13.22s (0.12) **Going Correction** -0.10s/f (Stan) 10 Ran SP% **113.4**
Speed ratings (Par 95): **95,93,91,89,85 85,79,77,66,62**
toteswingers:1&2:£14.60, 1&3:£36.20, 2&3:£15.60 CSF £120.97 CT £1259.08 TOTE £24.90: £5.00, £1.70, £3.80; EX 110.50 TRIFECTA Not won..
Owner A Taylor **Bred** Yeomanstown Stud **Trained** Upper Lambourn, Berks

FOCUS
A couple of these were well supported for this very modest handicap. The winner showed her first real form.
Gone By Sunrise Official explanation: trainer's rep said colt bled from the nose

377 SKYSPORTS.COM H'CAP 7f (P)
6:50 (6:50) (Class 5) (0-75,75) 3-Y-O £2,264 (£673; £336; £168) Stalls Low

Form RPR
150- **1** **Four Better**[99] [7081] 3-9-2 **70** FergusSweeney 6 78
(Jamie Osborne) *sn trckd ldr: led jst over 2f out: drvn over 1f out: edgd rt fnl f: hld on* **8/1**

22-2 **2** 1/2 **Tenbridge**[20] [127] 3-8-13 **67** (p) DaneO'Neill 2 73
(Derek Haydn Jones) *sn trckd ldng pair: rdn to chse wnr over 1f out: styd on but a jst hld* **7/2[2]**

34-4 **3** nk **Berlusca (IRE)**[14] [201] 3-8-12 **66** WilliamCarson 3 72
(William Jarvis) *hld up in 5th: shkn up over 2f out: swtchd lft over 1f out: prog to take 3rd ins fnl f: clsng at fin* **4/1[3]**

0-42 **4** 4 **Prince Gabrial (IRE)**[14] [204] 3-8-8 **62** HayleyTurner 4 57
(Kevin Ryan) *led to jst over 2f out: nt qckn: wknd fnl f* **9/1**

04-1 **5** 1/2 **Whipcrackaway (IRE)**[20] [132] 3-8-8 **62** MartinLane 7 55
(Peter Hedger) *stdd s: hld up in 6th: rdn and detached fr ldrs 2f out: threatened to stay on ins fnl f: no ch* **5/1**

146- **6** 1 1/2 **Darnathean**[121] [6573] 3-9-7 **75** (b) LukeMorris 8 64
(Paul D'Arcy) *t.k.h: hld up in 4th: effrt over 2f out: nt qckn wl over 1f out: fdd* **11/4[1]**

04-0 **7** 2 **Frock (IRE)**[25] [84] 3-8-10 **64** LiamKeniry 5 48
(Sylvester Kirk) *mostly in last: struggling over 2f out* **14/1**

1m 25.21s (-0.79) **Going Correction** -0.10s/f (Stan) 7 Ran SP% **113.3**
Speed ratings (Par 97): **100,99,99,94,93 92,89**
toteswingers:1&2:£8.70, 1&3:£5.10, 2&3:£4.80 CSF £35.32 CT £128.88 TOTE £10.40: £4.70, £2.10; EX 51.80 Trifecta £97.50 Pool: £823.99 - 6.25 winning units..
Owner C Woollett P Hearn & Mr & Mrs J Wilson **Bred** Lordship Stud **Trained** Upper Lambourn, Berks

FOCUS
Confirmation of the good form of Jamie Osborne's stable as he notched a 188-1 double from his two runners on the card. Ordinary form, but it was sound run and a fairly positive view has been taken with the first three clear.

378 SKYSPORTS RACING H'CAP 7f (P)
7:20 (7:20) (Class 4) (0-85,86) 4-Y-0+ £4,075 (£1,212; £606; £303) Stalls Low

Form RPR
01-0 **1** **Ocean Legend (IRE)**[20] [131] 7-9-0 **77** AdamKirby 5 89
(Tony Carroll) *wl plcd bhd ldrs: prog over 2f out to ld jst over 1f out: rdn and styd on wl* **9/1**

365- **2** 1 1/4 **Santefisio**[42] [7841] 6-9-7 **84** (p) JoeFanning 4 93
(Keith Dalgleish) *stdd s: t.k.h: hld up last: gd prog on bit fr 2f out to take 2nd 1f out: sn rdn and nt qckn: hld after* **7/2[1]**

42-2 **3** 2 1/4 **Bianca De Medici**[22] [115] 5-8-12 **75** (b) HayleyTurner 10 78
(Hughie Morrison) *mostly chsd ldr to wl over 1f out: outpcd: kpt on again ins fnl f* **6/1[3]**

05-2 **4** 1 1/2 **Legal Legacy**[14] [199] 6-8-9 **72** AndrewMullen 8 71
(David C Griffiths) *moved up to go prom on outer 4f out: rdn over 2f out: sn lost pl and struggling: kpt on again fnl f* **11/2[2]**

00-5 **5** hd **Last Sovereign**[16] [190] 8-9-0 **77** (b) TomEaves 3 75
(Ollie Pears) *led to jst over 1f out: steadily wknd* **20/1**

1-42 **6** nk **Tamareen (IRE)**[19] [157] 4-8-12 **80** ShaneBKelly(5) 1 78
(Richard Fahey) *prom: rdn and cl up 2f out: sn outpcd: n.d fnl f* **6/1[3]**

1-01 **7** 1/2 **Bawaardi (IRE)**[16] [190] 6-9-0 **82** MatthewCosham(5) 9 78
(David Evans) *prom: shkn up and nt qckn over 2f out: lost pl wl over 1f out: one pce after* **16/1**

430- **8** 2 1/4 **Judd Street**[56] [7660] 10-9-2 **79** (v) DaneO'Neill 7 69
(Eve Johnson Houghton) *dwlt: a towards rr: effrt over 2f out: no real prog* **20/1**

06-0 **9** 2 1/2 **Al Aqabah (IRE)**[28] [33] 7-8-5 **71** (b) AdamBeschizza(3) 12 54
(Brian Gubby) *dwlt: wl in rr on outer: wd bnd 3f out: no real prog after* **12/1**

00-5 **10** 1 **May's Boy**[20] [131] 4-8-13 **76** (p) DavidProbert 2 57
(Mark Usher) *a in rr: rdn and no prog over 2f out* **7/1**

00-0 **11** 6 **Amethyst Dawn (IRE)**[14] [198] 6-8-8 **76** (t) DavidKenny(5) 6 40
(Andrew Reid) *nvr gng wl: dropped to rr 3f out: sn wl bhd* **66/1**

1m 24.47s (-1.53) **Going Correction** -0.10s/f (Stan) 11 Ran SP% **113.3**
Speed ratings (Par 105): **104,102,100,98,98 97,97,94,91,90 83**
toteswingers:1&2:£8.40, 1&3:£11.10, 2&3:£4.90 CSF £38.09 CT £208.35 TOTE £12.80: £3.30, £1.20, £2.10; EX 49.60 Trifecta £557.40 Part won. Pool: £753.31 - 0.10 winning units..
Owner W McLuskey **Bred** Mark Commins **Trained** Cropthorne, Worcs

FOCUS
Quite a competitive heat and probably sound form for the grade. The winner is rated back to his form of this time last year.
May's Boy Official explanation: jockey said colt ran flat
Amethyst Dawn(IRE) Official explanation: jockey said mare never travelled

379 KEMPTON FOR WEDDINGS H'CAP 7f (P)
7:50 (7:50) (Class 7) (0-50,50) 4-Y-0+ £1,455 (£433; £216; £108) Stalls Low

Form RPR
4-43 **1** **Lovat Lane**[7] [305] 4-8-13 **46** ChrisCatlin 1 50
(Eve Johnson Houghton) *prom: effrt over 2f out to chal over 1f out: led ins fnl f: drvn out* **8/1**

0-00 **2** 3/4 **Wee Buns**[7] [297] 7-8-12 **45** LiamKeniry 12 47
(Paul Burgoyne) *t.k.h: hld up bhd ldrs: effrt 2f out: rdn to ld on outer 1f out: hdd and nt qckn ins fnl f* **33/1**

004- **3** hd **Pastoral Jet**[48] [7768] 4-8-9 **49** LukeRowe(7) 5 51+
(Richard Rowe) *hld up in rr: rapid prog on outer to chse ldrs over 3f out: lost pl bnd sn after: styd on again over 1f out: gaining on ldrs at fin* **5/2[2]**

00-0 **4** nk **Cavalry Guard (USA)**[10] [264] 8-8-7 **45** (b) RaulDaSilva(5) 2 46
(Tim McCarthy) *dwlt: hld up in rr: urged along fr over 2f out: prog over 1f out: styd on wl fnl f: nrst fin* **33/1**

-053 **5** 1/2 **Jackie Love (IRE)**[6] [307] 4-8-9 **49** (b) JenniferFerguson(7) 7 49
(Olivia Maylam) *hld up in rr: pushed along over 2f out: limited prog fr over 1f out tl styd on strly last 100yds* **5/1[3]**

3-22 **6** nk **Blueberry Fizz (IRE)**[21] [125] 4-9-3 **50** (v) AdamKirby 4 49
(John Ryan) *trckd ldr: led over 2f out: hdd 1f out: one pce in 3rd after tl lost 3 pls nr fin* **9/4[1]**

-006 **7** 2 1/4 **Striking Willow**[10] [264] 4-8-12 **45** JamesMillman 6 38
(Rod Millman) *mde most to over 2f out: wknd fnl f* **12/1**

06-3 **8** 1 1/2 **Tawseef (IRE)**[14] [197] 4-9-2 **49** TomEaves 11 38
(Roy Brotherton) *hld up in midfield: pushed along and no prog over 2f out: no ch over 1f out* **9/1**

00-0 **9** 1 1/2 **Heading To First**[21] [125] 5-8-10 **46** ow1 (tp) RobertLButler(3) 3 31
(Paddy Butler) *awkward s: t.k.h and sn in midfield: rdn over 2f out: wknd over 1f out* **20/1**

00-0 **10** 3/4 **Ain't Talkin'**[7] [293] 6-8-7 **45** (p) MarkCoumbe(5) 13 28
(Michael Attwater) *a in rr: struggling over 2f out* **25/1**

600- **11** 3 3/4 **Sid**[43] [7829] 4-8-12 **45** JamieGoldstein 8 18
(Zoe Davison) *t.k.h: pressed ldrs tl wknd over 2f out* **66/1**

0-00 **12** 3 1/2 **Pavement Games**[20] [126] 5-8-12 **45** (b[1]) FrannyNorton 9 8
(Richard Guest) *s.s: plld hrd: hld up and a in last* **25/1**

1m 28.05s (2.05) **Going Correction** -0.10s/f (Stan) 12 Ran SP% **124.6**
Speed ratings (Par 97): **84,83,82,82,82 81,79,77,75,74 70,66**
toteswingers:1&2:£19.70, 1&3:£6.10, 2&3:£30.00 CSF £258.26 CT £875.48 TOTE £8.50: £1.90, £7.10, £1.50; EX 270.50 TRIFECTA Not won..
Owner R F Johnson Houghton **Bred** R F Johnson Houghton **Trained** Blewbury, Oxon

FOCUS
A standard low-grade handicap in which the early gallop was not strong and the run of the race proved all important. The time was slow and the form is a bit dubious.
Pavement Games Official explanation: jockey said mare ran too free
T/Jkpt: Not won. T/Plt: £825.50 to a £1 stake. Pool:£98,718.73 - 87.29 winning tickets T/Qpdt: £170.10 to a £1 stake. Pool:£9,681.03 - 42.10 winning tickets JN

366 SOUTHWELL (L-H)
Thursday, February 2

OFFICIAL GOING: Standard
Wind: Almost nil Weather: Fine but cold

380 BLUE SQUARE WINTER CARNIVAL IPHONE APP H'CAP 5f (F)
1:30 (1:30) (Class 6) (0-65,65) 4-Y-0+ £1,704 (£503; £251) Stalls High

Form RPR
13-2 **1** **No Mean Trick (USA)**[30] [24] 6-9-6 **64** MickyFenton 5 74
(Paul Midgley) *mde all: kpt on fnl f: jst hld on* **3/1[1]**

-566 **2** nse **Shawkantango**[10] [272] 5-9-2 **63** (v) DaleSwift(3) 8 73
(Derek Shaw) *s.i.s: hdwy stands' side 2f out: ev ch ins fnl f: jst hld* **8/1**

5-44 **3** 1 1/4 **First In Command (IRE)**[9] [289] 7-8-11 **55** (t) HayleyTurner 4 61
(Daniel Mark Loughnane) *sn chsng ldrs: outpcd 3f out: kpt on to chal appr fnl f: one pce fnl 100yds* **7/1**

0-63 **4** 1 **Bookiesindex Boy**[21] [133] 8-9-2 **60** (b) StephenCraine 6 62
(J R Jenkins) *trckd ldrs travelling strly: pushed along 1f out: fnd little* **10/1**

56-4 **5** 6 **Spic 'n Span**[6] [320] 7-9-4 **62** (v) LukeMorris 3 42
(Ronald Harris) *s.i.s: sn drvn to chse ldrs: wknd over 1f out* **10/1**

0-26 **6** 1 1/2 **Fear Nothing**[21] [139] 5-9-2 **60** (b) DanielTudhope 9 35
(David O'Meara) *chsd ldrs: rdn 2f out: sn btn* **9/2[3]**

20-2 **7** 1 **Ladydolly**[21] [135] 4-8-11 **55** (p) PhillipMakin 7 26
(Roy Brotherton) *chsd ldrs: wknd over 1f out* **14/1**

04-4 **8** 2 1/2 **La Capriosa**[25] [100] 6-9-2 **65** RaulDaSilva(5) 1 27
(Scott Dixon) *sn chsng ldrs: lost pl over 1f out* **4/1[2]**

050- **9** 4 1/2 **Fashion Icon (USA)**[283] [1555] 6-9-2 **60** BarryMcHugh 2
(David O'Meara) *sn outpcd: bhd fnl 3f* **50/1**

1m 0.82s (1.12) **Going Correction** +0.25s/f (Slow) 9 Ran SP% **113.6**
Speed ratings (Par 101): **101,100,98,97,87 85,83,79,72**
toteswingers:1&2:£6.20, 2&3:£9.80, 1&3:£3.50 CSF £27.13 CT £154.24 TOTE £4.00: £1.50, £2.50, £2.60; EX 29.30 Trifecta £394.10 Part won. Pool: £532.67 - 0.63 winning units..
Owner John Allan Milburn **Bred** Larry Byer **Trained** Westow, N Yorks

FOCUS
A moderate sprint handicap, but six of the nine runners were previous C&D winners. There seemed to be no draw bias, but the winning time was 2.82 seconds outside standard, suggesting the Fibresand was riding on the slow side. The form looks solid enough.

381 PLAY GOLF BEFORE RACING AT SOUTHWELL H'CAP 1m 3f (F)
2:00 (2:00) (Class 5) (0-70,70) 4-Y-0+ £2,264 (£673; £336; £168) Stalls Low

Form RPR
011- **1** **Mediterranean Sea (IRE)**[58] [7647] 6-9-6 **69** StephenCraine 3 76
(J R Jenkins) *hld up in rr: smooth hdwy to trck ldrs over 4f out: upsides over 2f out: rdn to ld appr fnl f: kpt on wl* **9/4[1]**

040- **2** 1 1/2 **Absolute Princess**[37] [7887] 4-8-6 **62** RaulDaSilva(5) 4 66
(Scott Dixon) *trckd ldrs: led 3f out: hdd appr fnl f: fdd last 50yds* **11/1**

51-0 **3** 3/4 **With Hindsight (IRE)**[17] [192] 4-9-0 **70** DavidKenny(5) 1 73
(Michael Scudamore) *t.k.h in rr: effrt over 4f out: hdwy ins over 2f out: kpt on to take 3rd last 100yds* **20/1**

P05- **4** 2 1/2 **Kingaroo (IRE)**[35] [7912] 6-8-7 **56** oh6 FrannyNorton 2 55
(Garry Woodward) *led 1f: chsd ldrs: wknd fnl f* **16/1**

5-04 **5** *13* **Echos Of Motivator**[5] 355 4-9-2 **67**..............................(p) LukeMorris 8 42
(Ronald Harris) *in rr and sn drvn along: reminders 7f out: lost pl over 4f out: no ch after: lame* **9/4**[1]

0-00 **6** *2 ¾* **Apassionforfashion**[2] 369 4-8-7 **58** oh11 ow2..............(e) TomEaves 5 28
(Bryan Smart) *led after 1f: hdd 3f out: wknd over 2f out* **50/1**

24-4 **7** *½* **Straversjoy**[20] 156 5-9-1 **64**..(e[1]) ChrisCatlin 7 33
(Reg Hollinshead) *mid-div: chsd ldrs 7f out: drvn and outpcd over 4f out: lost pl 3f out* **6/1**[3]

54-6 **8** *11* **Sergeant Troy (IRE)**[22] 119 4-9-2 **67**.......................... HayleyTurner 6 16
(George Baker) *chsd ldrs: pushed along 6f out: outpcd over 4f out: lost pl 3f out: sn bhd* **9/2**[2]

2m 29.26s (1.26) **Going Correction** +0.05s/f (Slow)
WFA 4 from 5yo+ 2lb **8** Ran SP% **114.9**
Speed ratings (Par 103): **97,95,95,93,84 82,81,73**
toteswingers:1&2:£5.20, 2&3:£20.70, 1&3:£7.30 CSF £29.82 CT £395.18 TOTE £4.50: £1.70, £4.20, £6.20; EX 32.80 Trifecta £61.10 Pool: £615.25 - 7.44 winning units..
Owner Mrs Wendy Jenkins **Bred** D H W Dobson **Trained** Royston, Herts

FOCUS
A race that fell into the lap of the winner, and potentially shaky form. The winner is rated to her recent C&D level.
Echos Of Motivator Official explanation: trainer said colt returned lame

382 FOLLOW SOUTHWELL RACECOURSE ON TWITTER (S) STKS 1m (F)
2:30 (2:30) (Class 6) 3-Y-O **£1,704** (£503; £251) **Stalls** Low

Form RPR

2411 **1** **Roedean (IRE)**[3] 360 3-8-12 70..................................(p) FrannyNorton 3 68
(Jamie Osborne) *w ldrs: effrt and hung lft over 2f out: rdn to ld over 1f out: drvn out* **4/9**[1]

2-20 **2** *1 ¼* **Samasana (IRE)**[21] 132 3-8-6 51.................................... LukeMorris 6 59
(Ian Wood) *led: hdd over 1f out: kpt on same pce* **7/2**[2]

40-0 **3** *7* **Outlaw Torn (IRE)**[6] 322 3-8-12 57.....................(e) CharlesEddery(5) 2 54
(Richard Guest) *trckd ldrs: drvn and 3rd over 3f out: one pce fnl 2f* **20/1**

04-0 **4** *8* **Deduction (IRE)**[21] 132 3-8-6 47................................... AndrewMullen 1 25
(Nigel Tinkler) *swtchd rt after 1f and racd wd: chsd ldrs: drvn over 4f out: hung rt and wknd over 2f out* **50/1**

000- **5** *7* **Classy Lass**[35] 7915 3-8-3 30.................................... DominicFox(3) 4
(Derek Shaw) *rn in snatches in rr: hung bdly rt 3f out: sn lost pl and bhd* **50/1**

6- **6** *2* **Baileys Dutch**[101] 7066 3-8-11 0...................................... PhillipMakin 5
(Mark Johnston) *sn drvn along in rr: early reminders: lost pl over 4f out: sn bhd* **7/1**[3]

1m 44.63s (0.93) **Going Correction** +0.05s/f (Slow) **6** Ran SP% **112.7**
Speed ratings (Par 95): **97,95,88,80,73 71**
toteswingers:1&2:£1.20, 2&3:£2.90, 1&3:£2.10 CSF £2.29 TOTE £1.30: £1.02, £2.50; EX 2.50.The winner was bought in for 8,000gns.
Owner Dr Marwan Koukash **Bred** C McEvoy **Trained** Upper Lambourn, Berks

FOCUS
A weak seller and the winner did not need to match her recent form. The runner-up is the key.
Deduction(IRE) Official explanation: jockey said filly hung right throughout
Classy Lass Official explanation: jockey said filly hung right

383 TICKETS AT SOUTHWELL-RACECOURSE.CO.UK MEDIAN AUCTION MAIDEN STKS 7f (F)
3:00 (3:01) (Class 6) 3-5-Y-O **£1,704** (£503; £251) **Stalls** Low

Form RPR

63-2 **1** **Kickingthelilly**[18] 185 3-8-4 66... ChrisCatlin 3 61
(Rae Guest) *mde virtually all: styd on u.p fnl 2f: hld on* **2/1**[1]

663- **2** *1 ¼* **Bond Style**[53] 7724 3-8-9 60..(p) TomEaves 5 62
(Bryan Smart) *drvn along to r w wnr: chal 3f out: sn rdn: kpt on same pce fnl f* **4/1**[3]

3/0- **3** *nse* **Handsome King**[199] 4163 5-9-12 62.........................(p) StephenCraine 4 67
(J R Jenkins) *trckd ldrs: effrt over 2f out: kpt on same pce* **8/1**

0 **4** *nse* **Adili (IRE)**[9] 283 3-8-9 0 ow3.. PaulPickard(3) 1 66
(Brian Ellison) *s.i.s: sn chsng ldrs: outpcd over 4f out: hdwy over 2f out: edgd rt and kpt on same pce fnl f: eased and lost 2nd nr fin* **20/1**

6 **5** *2* **Dilizan (IRE)**[13] 231 3-8-9 0.. BarryMcHugh 2 56
(Brian Ellison) *chsd ldrs: outpcd over 4f out: hdwy 3f out: one pce* **4/1**[3]

32 **6** *¾* **Henry Bee**[14] 214 3-8-9 0.. TonyHamilton 6 54
(Richard Fahey) *trckd ldrs: effrt over 2f out: wknd fnl f* **10/3**[2]

1m 30.83s (0.53) **Going Correction** +0.05s/f (Slow)
WFA 3 from 5yo 17lb **6** Ran SP% **112.3**
Speed ratings (Par 101): **98,96,96,96,94 93**
toteswingers:1&2:£2.10, 2&3:£4.40, 1&3:£3.10 CSF £10.32 TOTE £2.80: £1.50, £3.00; EX 11.10.
Owner Tony Hirschfeld **Bred** Tony Hirschfeld & L K Piggott **Trained** Newmarket, Suffolk
■ Stewards' Enquiry : Paul Pickard ten-day ban: failed to ride out for second (Feb 16-18,20-25,27)

FOCUS
An interesting if modest maiden. There was a bunch finish and a slow time, and the winner did not need to match his previous efforts.

384 DOWNLOAD BLUE SQUARE IPHONE APP H'CAP 1m (F)
3:30 (3:30) (Class 5) (0-70,70) 4-Y-O+ **£2,264** (£673; £336; £168) **Stalls** Low

Form RPR

-624 **1** **Pipers Piping (IRE)**[6] 330 6-8-9 **65**.........................(p) LeonnaMayor(7) 3 74
(Alastair Lidderdale) *dwlt: t.k.h: sn trcking ldrs: led on ins 2f out: hung lft and drew clr: eased nr fin* **4/1**[3]

50-4 **2** *4* **Symphonic Dancer (USA)**[9] 287 5-8-9 **58** ow1..... RussKennemore 4 58
(Brian Baugh) *trckd ldr: drvn to ld 3f out: hdd 2f out: kpt on same pce* **6/1**

2-22 **3** *3 ¾* **Arkaim**[13] 225 4-9-3 **66**..(v) MickyFenton 2 57
(Pam Sly) *led: hdd 3f out: wknd over 1f out* **11/4**[1]

-114 **4** *6* **Dashing Eddie (IRE)**[20] 154 4-9-4 **67**.........................(p) PhillipMakin 1 44
(Kevin Ryan) *sn drvn along to chse ldrs: reminders over 4f out: lost pl over 2f out* **11/4**[1]

11/3 **5** *3 ¾* **D'Urberville**[21] 136 5-9-7 **70**.. StephenCraine 5 39
(J R Jenkins) *t.k.h: sn trcking ldrs: rdn over 2f out: sn btn* **3/1**[2]

1m 42.75s (-0.95) **Going Correction** +0.05s/f (Slow) **5** Ran SP% **112.6**
Speed ratings (Par 103): **106,102,98,92,88**
CSF £26.48 TOTE £6.20: £2.50, £4.60; EX 34.40.
Owner Chris Beek Racing **Bred** Drumhass Stud **Trained** Lambourn, Berks

FOCUS
With a couple of the fancied horses underperforming, the form of this handicap may be a little suspect. The form is rated around the winner's penultimate C&D run.
Dashing Eddie(IRE) Official explanation: jockey said colt never travelled
D'Urberville Official explanation: jockey said gelding ran flat

385 SOUTHWELL GOLF CLUB LADY MEMBERS H'CAP 6f (F)
4:00 (4:00) (Class 6) (0-65,65) 4-Y-O+ **£1,704** (£503; £251) **Stalls** Low

Form RPR

0-42 **1** **Suddenly Susan (IRE)**[6] 327 4-9-1 **64**.....................(b) RaulDaSilva(5) 7 74
(Scott Dixon) *mde all: edgd lft after 1f: 4 l clr over 2f out: rdn over 1f out: drvn and styd on: eased nr fin: unchal* **6/5**[1]

1000 **2** *2 ¼* **Dickie Le Davoir**[6] 325 8-9-2 **65**...........................(b) CharlesEddery(5) 5 68
(Richard Guest) *s.s: drvn and detached in last: hdwy over 2f out: hung rt and kpt on to take 2nd last 50yds* **8/1**

0344 **3** *nk* **Ace Of Spies (IRE)**[9] 284 7-9-3 **61**.............................(b) HayleyTurner 6 63
(Conor Dore) *trckd ldrs: chsd wnr over 2f out: sn rdn: kpt on same pce* **7/2**[2]

-506 **4** *1 ¾* **Twice Red**[3] 359 4-9-5 **63**... TomEaves 2 59
(Derek Shaw) *chsd wnr: drvn over 3f out: one pce* **7/1**[3]

0-51 **5** *hd* **Ridgeway Hawk**[9] 289 4-8-12 **61** 6ex.......................(v) LeeNewnes(5) 1 57
(Mark Usher) *stmbld s: chsd ldrs: drvn over 4f out: one pce fnl 3f* **7/2**[2]

1m 16.9s (0.40) **Going Correction** +0.05s/f (Slow) **5** Ran SP% **113.5**
Speed ratings (Par 101): **99,96,95,93,93**
CSF £11.83 TOTE £2.00: £1.10, £3.50; EX 9.20.
Owner Paul J Dixon **Bred** L Mulryan **Trained** Babworth, Notts

FOCUS
A moderate sprint handicap. A personal best from the winner, and the form could be rated a little higher.
Ridgeway Hawk Official explanation: jockey said gelding stumbled shortly after start

386 PLAY RAINBOW RICHES AT BLUESQ.COM APPRENTICE H'CAP 7f (F)
4:30 (4:30) (Class 5) (0-70,70) 4-Y-O+ **£2,264** (£673; £336; £168) **Stalls** Low

Form RPR

3-04 **1** **Ezra Church (IRE)**[17] 190 5-9-4 **70**.................................. DeanHeslop(3) 5 84
(David Barron) *w ldr: led 2f out: sn rdn clr: eased nr fin* **7/2**[3]

005- **2** *8* **Arachnophobia (IRE)**[128] 6433 6-8-9 **65**.................(v[1]) KirstenSmith(7) 1 56
(Martin Bosley) *led: hdd 2f out: no ch w wnr* **25/1**

00-1 **3** *1* **Fibs And Flannel**[30] 21 5-8-12 **64**.................................. RaulDaSilva(3) 4 52
(Willie Musson) *hld up: effrt and wnt 3rd 3f out: rdn over 1f out: kpt on one pce* **7/4**[1]

-026 **4** *¾* **Fantasy Fry**[2] 370 4-8-7 **56**...(bt) RossAtkinson 2 42
(Tom Dascombe) *dwlt: sn pushed along in last: swtchd wd after 1f: reminders over 3f out: kpt on fnl 2f: nvr a factor* **5/2**[2]

0-00 **5** *1 ¼* **Shaws Diamond (USA)**[2] 370 6-8-7 **56** oh2..........(v) AdamBeschizza 6 39
(Derek Shaw) *chsd ldrs: drvn and lost pl over 3f out: kpt on one pce fnl 2f* **5/1**

1m 28.77s (-1.53) **Going Correction** +0.05s/f (Slow) **5** Ran SP% **107.7**
Speed ratings (Par 103): **110,100,99,98,97**
CSF £54.96 TOTE £4.80: £1.60, £8.00; EX 30.00.
Owner Clive Washbourn **Bred** Mrs E Byrne **Trained** Maunby, N Yorks
■ Dean Heslop's first winner since taking a year's sabbatical from riding.

FOCUS
A modest apprentice handicap, though the pace was sound and the time was the best on the card. The winner was much improved.
T/Plt: £80.40 to a £1 stake. Pool:£71,902.30. 652.10 winning tickets. T/Qpdt: £15.60 to a £1 stake. Pool:£5,947.89. 281.90 winning tickets. WG

[356]WOLVERHAMPTON (A.W) (L-H)
Thursday, February 2

OFFICIAL GOING: Standard
Wind: Light, half-against Weather: Overcast

387 BLUE SQUARE WINTER CARNIVAL IPHONE APP APPRENTICE H'CAP 5f 216y(P)
1:50 (1:51) (Class 5) (0-75,75) 4-Y-O+ **£2,264** (£673; £336; £168) **Stalls** Low

Form RPR

3-03 **1** **Night Trade (IRE)**[12] 252 5-9-2 **75**.................................. DarrenEgan(5) 2 80
(Ronald Harris) *chsd ldrs: wnt 2nd over 1f out: rdn to ld wl ins fnl f* **9/2**[2]

00-6 **2** *hd* **Riverdale (IRE)**[10] 269 4-9-4 **72**.................................. JustinNewman 1 76
(Nigel Tinkler) *set stdy pce tl qcknd over 2f out: rdn and hdd wl ins fnl f: r.o* **14/1**

5-11 **3** *1* **Dancing Welcome**[14] 212 6-9-4 **75**...........................(b) JackDuern(3) 3 76
(Milton Bradley) *chsd ldr: pushed along over 2f out: rdn and lost 2nd over 1f out: edgd lft: styd on* **5/2**[1]

00-4 **4** *1* **Lucky Dan (IRE)**[10] 272 6-8-13 **67**.. DarylByrne 7 65
(Paul Green) *dwlt: hld up: r.o ins fnl f: nvr nrr* **8/1**

4-21 **5** *shd* **Blown It (USA)**[10] 272 6-8-12 **71** 6ex..................... ShirleyTeasdale(5) 5 69
(Keith Dalgleish) *hld up in tch: effrt over 1f out: hung lft ins fnl f: styd on same pce* **5/2**[1]

40-0 **6** *shd* **Whipphound**[11] 267 4-9-2 **70**...................................... RachealKneller 6 69+
(Mark Brisbourne) *hld up: hdwy and nt clr run over 1f out: swtchd rt ins fnl f: r.o: nvr able to chal* **15/2**[3]

040- **7** *½* **Methaaly (IRE)**[63] 7595 9-8-11 **68**.................................. NoelGarbutt(3) 4 64
(Michael Mullineaux) *prom: pushed along over 2f out: edgd lft over 1f out: no ex ins fnl f* **16/1**

1m 16.99s (1.99) **Going Correction** +0.20s/f (Slow) **7** Ran SP% **110.7**
Speed ratings (Par 103): **94,93,92,91,90 90,90**
toteswingers:1&2:£8.40, 2&3:£6.90, 1&3:£1.50 CSF £57.38 TOTE £5.80: £2.50, £9.70; EX 76.50.
Owner Alan & Adam Darlow, A Darlow Productions **Bred** John Foley **Trained** Earlswood, Monmouths
■ Darren Egan's first winner in Britain, to go with three in Ireland.
■ Stewards' Enquiry : Noel Garbutt three-day ban: careless riding (Feb 16-18)

FOCUS
A fair contest run at a modest gallop, which meant the field finished in a bunch. There is some doubt over the form with the winner rated to her Polytrack best.

388 RINGSIDE SUITE CLASSIFIED CLAIMING STKS 5f 216y(P)
2:20 (2:20) (Class 5) 3-Y-O+ **£2,264** (£673; £336; £168) **Stalls** Low

Form RPR

-512 **1** **Hinton Admiral**[13] 220 8-9-11 72...................................... JoeFanning 1 76
(Keith Dalgleish) *set stdy pce tl qcknd 2f out: sn shkn up: hdd ins fnl f: rallied to ld towards fin* **15/8**[1]

-003 **2** *hd* **Steelcut**[6] 327 8-9-5 68.......................................(p) RichardEvans(3) 4 72
(David Evans) *a.p: rdn to ld and hung lft ins fnl f: hdd towards fin* **8/1**

005- **3** *½* **Dancing Maite**[58] 7643 7-9-12 73......................................(b[1]) DaneO'Neill 7 74
(Roy Bowring) *s.s: hld up: hdwy over 1f out: r.o: nt rch ldrs* **3/1**[3]

50-2 **4** 1 1/4 **Haadeeth**[9] [282] 5-9-1 70 .... LauraBarry(7) 6 67
(Richard Fahey) *chsd wnr tl pushed along over 1f out: hmpd ins fnl f: sn edgd lft: styd on* **9/4**[2]
0-40 **5** 2 **Riflessione**[19] [179] 6-9-2 67 .... (v) DarrenEgan(7) 2 61
(Ronald Harris) *hld up: outpcd 2f out: r.o ins fnl f: nvr nrr* **12/1**
56-0 **6** 5 **Rum King (USA)**[6] [335] 5-9-4 66 .... (b) ShaneKelly 5 40
(S Donohoe, Ire) *s.s: hdwy to go 3rd 5f out tl pushed along over 2f out: wknd over 1f out* **28/1**

1m 15.88s (0.88) **Going Correction** +0.20s/f (Slow) **6** Ran SP% **112.8**
Speed ratings (Par 103): **102,101,101,99,96 90**
toteswingers:1&2:£1.80, 2&3:£2.50, 1&3:£2.40 CSF £17.43 TOTE £2.50: £1.40, £5.00; EX 10.80.Haadeeth was claimed by P D Evans for £6,000.
Owner William Brand & Gordon McDowall **Bred** Gainsborough Stud Management Ltd **Trained** Carluke, S Lanarks

FOCUS
This claimer was run at a routine pace. It's doubtful if it's a race to be positive about.

389 SPONSOR A RACE BY CALLING 01902 390000 H'CAP 1m 4f 50y(P)
2:50 (2:50) (Class 6) (0-55,55) 4-Y-O+ **£1,704** (£503; £251) **Stalls** Low

Form RPR
0-21 **1** **Black Iceman**[20] [160] 4-8-10 **55** .... SimonPearce(3) 10 63+
(Lydia Pearce) *s.s: hld up: hdwy over 3f out: led wl over 1f out: edgd lft ins fnl f: jst hld on* **11/4**[1]
5-46 **2** *shd* **Cantor**[18] [188] 4-8-8 **50** .... (b[1]) JoeFanning 3 58
(Giles Bravery) *hld up: hdwy over 3f out: rdn over 1f out: r.o: jst failed* **7/2**[2]
00-3 **3** *hd* **Beneath**[6] [333] 5-9-2 **55** .... (b) AdamKirby 1 64+
(Neil Mulholland) *broke wl: sn stdd and lost pl: hld up: hmpd and dropped to rr wl over 3f out: hdwy over 1f out: r.o wl u.p: nt quite get there* **4/1**[3]
250- **4** 1 1/2 **Port Hill**[328] [839] 5-9-1 **54** .... ShaneKelly 12 58
(Mark Brisbourne) *a.p: chsd ldr over 6f out: led over 4f out: rdn and hdd over 1f out: styd on same pce ins fnl f* **25/1**
6-44 **5** 1 1/2 **Grecian Goddess (IRE)**[11] [265] 4-8-9 **51** .... MartinLane 2 53
(John Ryan) *hld up: rdn over 2f out: edgd lft and r.o ins fnl f: nt rch ldrs* **14/1**
00-0 **6** 2 3/4 **Moscow Oznick**[11] [265] 7-8-11 **50** .... (p) DavidProbert 11 47
(Des Donovan) *hld up: rdn over 3f out: styd on: nvr trbld ldrs* **22/1**
-042 **7** 1/2 **Yossi (IRE)**[13] [229] 8-8-8 **47** .... (b) WilliamCarson 4 44
(Richard Guest) *prom: rdn over 2f out: wknd ins fnl f* **12/1**
00-6 **8** *nk* **Art Thief**[20] [156] 4-8-11 **53** .... LiamKeniry 6 49
(Michael Appleby) *prom: rdn over 2f out: wknd over 1f out* **11/1**
520- **9** 2 1/2 **Marina Ballerina**[42] [7859] 4-8-4 **51** .... (p) JamesRogers(5) 9 43
(Roy Bowring) *hld up: rdn over 2f out: n.d* **8/1**
00/6 **10** 2 3/4 **Myraid**[23] [110] 5-9-0 **53** .... JamesSullivan 5 41
(Ruth Carr) *chsd ldr over 5f: edgd lft wl over 3f out: wknd 2f out* **14/1**
55-5 **11** 3 1/2 **Rapturous Applause**[13] [229] 4-8-9 **51** .... PJMcDonald 7 33
(Micky Hammond) *mid-div: hdwy 5f out: rdn over 2f out: sn wknd* **16/1**
500/ **12** 80 **During The War (USA)**[29] [283] 5-8-11 **50** .... (b[1]) SteveDrowne 8
(Chris Dwyer) *plld hrd: sn led: hdd over 4f out: hmpd and wknd wl over 3f out: eased: t.o* **100/1**

2m 42.2s (1.10) **Going Correction** +0.20s/f (Slow)
WFA 4 from 5yo+ 3lb **12** Ran SP% **124.4**
Speed ratings (Par 101): **104,103,103,102,101 99,99,99,97,95 93,40**
toteswingers:1&2:£3.80, 2&3:£3.70, 1&3:£3.60 CSF £12.58 CT £40.24 TOTE £2.50: £1.30, £1.50, £1.70; EX 15.40 Trifecta £49.00 Pool: £594.04 - 8.97 winning units..
Owner P J Stephenson **Bred** Graham Wilson **Trained** Newmarket, Suffolk
■ Stewards' Enquiry : Liam Keniry two-day ban: careless riding (Feb 16-17)

FOCUS
Nothing more than a moderate contest, but it was sound run and produced a really close finish. The second and third were both arguably unlucky, and the winner and third are possibly better than the bare form.
During The War(USA) Official explanation: vet said gelding lost a shoe

390 GREAT OFFERS ONLINE AT WOLVERHAMPTON-RACECOURSE.CO.UK H'CAP 1m 1f 103y(P)
3:20 (3:20) (Class 7) (0-50,50) 4-Y-O+ **£1,704** (£503; £251) **Stalls** Low

Form RPR
500- **1** **Harrys Yer Man**[54] [7720] 8-9-3 **50** .... ShaneKelly 4 58+
(Mark Brisbourne) *hld up: hdwy 2f out: led ins fnl f: pushed out* **11/2**[2]
5-26 **2** 1 1/4 **My Mate Les (IRE)**[15] [197] 4-9-2 **49** .... DavidProbert 7 54
(Tony Carroll) *s.s: chsd ldr over 2f out: led over 1f out: rdn and hdd ins fnl f: styd on same pce* **11/2**[2]
55-4 **3** 1 1/4 **Prickles**[13] [229] 7-8-13 **46** .... JoeFanning 11 49
(Derek Shaw) *sn prom: pushed along 3f out: rdn over 1f out: edgd lft ins fnl f: styd on same pce* **9/2**[1]
0-06 **4** 1 **Aggbag**[23] [109] 8-8-5 **45** .... (p) JackDuern(7) 2 46
(Michael Appleby) *led: hdd after 1f: led again 7f out: rdn and hdd over 1f out: no ex ins fnl f* **11/1**
660- **5** 3/4 **Deferto Delphi**[59] [5167] 5-8-10 **46** .... (b[1]) JulieBurke(3) 6 45
(Barry Murtagh) *a.p: rdn over 1f out: no ex ins fnl f* **9/1**
60-0 **6** 6 **Just Zak**[23] [109] 7-8-12 **45** .... (b[1]) FergusSweeney 8 31
(Garry Woodward) *hld up: rdn over 3f out: nvr on terms* **22/1**
606- **7** 3 **Littleportnbrandy (IRE)**[51] [7747] 4-9-1 **48** .... (bt) WilliamCarson 12 28
(Richard Guest) *hld up: racd keenly: hdwy over 2f out: rdn and wknd over 1f out* **40/1**
45-0 **8** 1/2 **Ad Vitam (IRE)**[13] [232] 4-9-1 **48** .... (bt) MichaelStainton 10 27
(Micky Hammond) *hld up: nt clr run over 2f out: shkn up over 1f out: nvr on terms* **13/2**[3]
-300 **9** 3 1/4 **Kirstys Lad**[6] [334] 10-8-7 **47** .... NoelGarbutt(7) 1 19
(Michael Mullineaux) *hld up: pushed along over 3f out: a in rr* **14/1**
26/6 **10** 1 3/4 **Secret Assassin (IRE)**[14] [218] 9-8-13 **46** .... JamieGoldstein 9 15
(Mrs J L Le Brocq, Jersey) *hld up: hdwy 5f out: rdn and wknd over 1f out* **14/1**
05/0 **11** 3 3/4 **Omega Centauri**[20] [159] 4-9-0 **47** .... MartinLane 13
(Ed McMahon) *led after 1f tl 7f out: chsd ldr tl rdn over 2f out: wknd over 1f out* **16/1**
5-56 **12** 8 **Ravanchi**[20] [158] 8-8-13 **46** .... TomMcLaughlin 5
(Frank Sheridan) *s.i.s: drvn along in rr early: hdwy 5f out: rdn and wknd 3f out: t.o* **25/1**
5-04 **13** 18 **Hot Tub**[15] [197] 4-9-0 **47** .... (p) IanMongan 3
(Christine Dunnett) *mid-div: rdn over 3f out: wknd over 2f out: t.o* **7/1**

2m 4.06s (2.36) **Going Correction** +0.20s/f (Slow) **13** Ran SP% **123.0**
Speed ratings (Par 97): **97,95,94,93,93 87,85,84,81,80 77,69,53**
totewingers:1&2:£8.20, 2&3:£3.90, 1&3:£6.50 CSF £36.20 CT £152.34 TOTE £7.50: £2.50, £2.00, £1.70; EX 38.80 Trifecta £139.80 Pool: £483.81 - 2.56 winning units..
Owner D G Blagden **Bred** D G Blagden **Trained** Great Ness, Shropshire

FOCUS
A bottom-drawer handicap, run at a solid pace. The winner rates positively.
Harrys Yer Man Official explanation: trainer's rep said, regarding apparent improvement in form, that they had a virus in the yard and the gelding may also have benefited from a drop in class.

391 DOWNLOAD BLUE SQUARE IPHONE APP H'CAP 1m 141y(P)
3:50 (3:50) (Class 4) (0-85,85) 4-Y-O+ **£4,204** (£1,251; £625; £312) **Stalls** Low

Form RPR
04-4 **1** **Viva Ronaldo (IRE)**[10] [269] 6-8-6 **75** .... ShaneBKelly(5) 6 81
(Richard Fahey) *hld up: pushed along over 2f out: hdwy over 1f out: r.o to ld wl ins fnl f* **6/1**[3]
000- **2** 1/2 **Mullins Way (USA)**[106] [6949] 4-9-6 **84** .... StevieDonohoe 7 89
(Jo Hughes) *hld up: rdn over 2f out: r.o wl ins fnl f: nt quite get there* **20/1**
6-10 **3** *nk* **Thunderstruck**[19] [177] 7-9-7 **85** .... (p) IanMongan 5 89
(Scott Dixon) *led: rdn over 1f out: hdd wl ins fnl f* **9/2**[2]
03- **4** 1/2 **Star Links (USA)**[69] [7542] 6-9-5 **83** .... (b) ShaneKelly 1 86
(S Donohoe, Ire) *chsd ldrs: rdn and ev ch over 1f out tl unable qck wl ins fnl f* **7/2**[1]
20-3 **5** 1 1/2 **Elijah Pepper (USA)**[20] [158] 7-8-7 **76** .... LMcNiff(5) 4 75
(David Barron) *prom: chsd ldr over 2f out: rdn and ev ch over 1f out: styd on same pce ins fnl f* **9/2**[2]
2-52 **6** 1 1/4 **Standpoint**[20] [158] 6-8-10 **81** .... (p) JackDuern(7) 2 78
(Reg Hollinshead) *chsd ldrs: rdn over 2f out: no ex ins fnl f* **7/2**[1]
50-0 **7** 8 **Goal (IRE)**[23] [115] 4-8-7 **71** .... (t) WilliamCarson 3 49
(Richard Guest) *hld up: rdn over 1f out: sn wknd* **25/1**
00-0 **8** 6 **Guest Book (IRE)**[29] [36] 5-8-8 **77** .... JamesRogers(5) 8 41
(Michael Scudamore) *s.i.s: hld up: rdn and bhd fr 1/2-way* **12/1**
4/0- **9** 5 **Photo Opportunity**[319] [925] 5-9-7 **85** .... FergusSweeney 9 38
(Alastair Lidderdale) *chsd ldr: pushed along over 3f out: wknd 2f out* **14/1**

1m 50.24s (-0.26) **Going Correction** +0.20s/f (Slow) **9** Ran SP% **118.1**
Speed ratings (Par 105): **109,108,108,107,106 105,98,92,88**
toteswingers:1&2:£22.70, 2&3:£15.10, 1&3:£6.30 CSF £117.25 CT £594.58 TOTE £7.70: £2.20, £3.60, £1.90; EX 164.60 Trifecta £613.90 Part won. Pool: £829.63 - 0.63 winning units..
Owner Aykroyd And Sons Ltd **Bred** Thomas Foy **Trained** Musley Bank, N Yorks

FOCUS
A modest handicap. It was run at a sound pace and the first five all held every chance. The winner can win again if building on this.

392 ENJOY THE PUNTERS PACKAGE GROUP OFFER H'CAP 2m 119y(P)
4:20 (4:20) (Class 6) (0-60,60) 4-Y-O+ **£1,704** (£503; £251) **Stalls** Low

Form RPR
03-0 **1** **Fantino**[20] [156] 6-9-10 **60** .... (t) SteveDrowne 2 68
(Pat Murphy) *mde all: rdn over 1f out: styd on wl* **8/1**
4B-0 **2** *nse* **Blue Cossack (IRE)**[21] [129] 4-8-13 **55** .... DavidProbert 4 63
(Mark Usher) *a.p: chsd wnr 2f out: rdn and ev ch ins fnl f: styd on* **6/1**[3]
-233 **3** 2 **Leyte Gulf (USA)**[7] [309] 9-9-9 **59** .... DaneO'Neill 9 65
(Chris Bealby) *hld up in tch: rdn over 1f out: styd on* **2/1**[1]
243- **4** 3 **Royal Bonsai**[54] [7495] 4-9-4 **60** .... LiamKeniry 6 62
(John Quinn) *chsd wnr to 1/2-way: remained handy: rdn over 2f out: styd on same pce appr fnl f* **9/4**[2]
42-5 **5** 1/2 **Lucky Diva**[27] [58] 5-8-12 **55** .... (p) JakePayne(7) 3 56
(Bill Turner) *hld up: hdwy over 2f out: sn rdn: styd on same pce fr over 1f out* **9/1**
102- **6** 5 **Imperial Fong**[62] [7608] 4-8-7 **52** .... RyanClark(3) 7 47
(Chris Dwyer) *prom: chsd wnr 1/2-way tl rdn over 2f out: btn whn rdr dropped whip over 1f out* **14/1**
-600 **7** 3/4 **Nesnaas (USA)**[9] [278] 11-8-10 **46** oh1 .... (bt) FergusSweeney 5 41
(Alastair Lidderdale) *s.i.s: hdwy 1/2-way: rdn and wknd over 2f out* **100/1**
315- **8** 2 **Sendali (FR)**[38] [4602] 8-9-3 **60** .... LauraBarry(7) 8 52
(Chris Grant) *s.i.s: hld up: hdwy over 5f out: wknd over 2f out* **11/1**
664- **9** 3/4 **Inside Knowledge (USA)**[108] [6915] 6-9-8 **58** .... TomMcLaughlin 1 49
(Garry Woodward) *hld up: hdwy over 2f out: rdn and wknd over 1f out* **20/1**

3m 48.42s (6.62) **Going Correction** +0.20s/f (Slow)
WFA 4 from 5yo+ 6lb **9** Ran SP% **120.3**
Speed ratings (Par 101): **92,91,91,89,89 87,86,85,85**
toteswingers:1&2:£10.30, 2&3:£4.20, 1&3:£5.60 CSF £57.61 CT £135.25 TOTE £13.90: £4.60, £1.90, £1.10; EX 65.30 Trifecta £662.00 Part won. Pool: £894.64 - 0.92 winning units..
Owner Norman A Blyth **Bred** Norman A Blyth **Trained** East Garston, Berks

FOCUS
This moderate staying handicap was run at an ordinary pace and it paid to race handily. The winner is up marginally on last year's form.

393 PLAY RAINBOW RICHES AT BLUESQ.COM H'CAP 1m 141y(P)
4:50 (4:51) (Class 6) (0-60,60) 3-Y-O **£1,704** (£503; £251) **Stalls** Low

Form RPR
00-0 **1** **Luctor Emergo (IRE)**[23] [114] 3-8-7 **46** .... (b[1]) JoeFanning 7 56
(Keith Dalgleish) *s.i.s: sn prom: led 7f out: rdn ins fnl f: styd on* **8/1**
5-21 **2** 1 **Gabrial's King (IRE)**[17] [196] 3-9-4 **57** .... StevieDonohoe 9 65
(Ian Williams) *hld up: hdwy over 1f out: rdn to chse wnr and hung lft ins fnl f: r.o* **10/11**[1]
11 **3** 2 1/4 **Miss Cato**[9] [288] 3-9-6 **59** 6ex .... WilliamCarson 5 62
(Rae Guest) *led: hdd 7f out: chsd ldr to over 4f out: remained handy: rdn over 1f out: styd on* **9/2**[2]
05-5 **4** 5 **Lone Star State (IRE)**[14] [217] 3-9-7 **60** .... (bt[1]) TomMcLaughlin 4 51
(Frank Sheridan) *prom: rdn over 2f out: wknd over 1f out* **16/1**
005- **5** 1 **My New Angel (IRE)**[35] [7915] 3-8-7 **46** oh1 .... (v[1]) JamieMackay 3 35
(Paul Green) *sn pushed along in rr: rdn over 2f out: n.d* **50/1**
6463 **6** 1 1/4 **Meet Joe Black (IRE)**[8] [294] 3-8-12 **51** .... (v) LukeMorris 1 37
(David Evans) *sn drvn along in rr: hdwy over 4f out: rdn and wknd over 1f out* **15/2**
7 *hd* **Samollie (IRE)**[20] [164] 3-9-0 **53** .... ShaneKelly 8 38
(Garvan Donnelly, Ire) *prom: chsd wnr over 4f out tl rdn over 1f out: wknd fnl f* **7/1**[3]
00-0 **8** 37 **Si Sealy (IRE)**[17] [196] 3-9-0 **56** .... RyanClark(3) 6
(David Evans) *prom tl rdn and wknd 3f out: t.o* **66/1**

1m 52.13s (1.63) **Going Correction** +0.20s/f (Slow) **8** Ran SP% **115.3**
Speed ratings (Par 95): **100,99,97,92,91 90,90,57**
toteswingers:1&2:£2.80, 2&3:£2.00, 1&3:£6.10 CSF £15.87 CT £38.69 TOTE £7.70: £2.30, £1.10, £1.10; EX 23.90 Trifecta £144.60 Pool: £1,247.48 - 6.38 winning units..
Owner Gordon McDowall **Bred** Kilnamoragh Stud **Trained** Carluke, S Lanarks

FOCUS
A weak handicap, run at an uneven pace, but the time compared favourably with the card as a whole. The winner showed his first form and the race has been given a bit of a chance.
Luctor Emergo(IRE) Official explanation: trainer's rep said, regarding apparent improvement in form, that the gelding had benefited from the first-time blinkers.

T/Jkpt: Not won. T/Plt: £117.00 to a £1 stake. Pool: £92,780.10. 578.73 winning units. T/Qpdt: £15.90 to a £1 stake. Pool: £9,320.06. 431.25 winning units. CR

349 LINGFIELD (L-H)
Friday, February 3

OFFICIAL GOING: Standard
Wind: Almost nil Weather: Sunny, cold

394 5% WINNERS' BONUS AT BLUESQ.COM LIVE H'CAP 6f (P)
1:20 (1:21) (Class 6) (0-65,65) 3-Y-O **£1,704** (£503; £251) **Stalls** Low

Form RPR
66-1 1 **Sweet Ovation**[18] [191] 3-9-2 **60** HayleyTurner 7 68
(Mark Usher) *hld up last: brought wd bnd 2f out: swooping run to ld jst ins fnl f: sn clr: pushed out* **4/1**[3]
4-34 2 2 3/4 **Mister Mackenzie**[8] [308] 3-9-7 **65** AdamKirby 3 64
(John Best) *t.k.h: hld up bhd ldrs: effrt 2f out: rdn to chal 1f out: sn outpcd* **11/8**[1]
-252 3 nk **One More Roman (IRE)**[4] [357] 3-9-4 **62** (bt) JimmyFortune 4 60
(Gay Kelleway) *t.k.h early: pressed ldr: drvn to chal jst over 1f out: nt qckn* **9/4**[2]
3-50 4 nk **Arabian Flight**[7] [322] 3-9-2 **60** KieranO'Neill 6 57
(John Bridger) *racd wd: pressed ldng pair: pushed along 1/2-way: nt qckn u.p over 1f out: one pce* **8/1**
-044 5 1 **Marie's Fantasy**[7] [326] 3-8-12 **56** JamieGoldstein 1 50
(Zoe Davison) *trckd ldrs on inner: tried to chal 1f out: sn outpcd and btn* **25/1**
2-05 6 1 1/2 **Miserere Mei (IRE)**[7] [321] 3-8-11 **58** (p) RobertLButler(3) 2 47
(Richard Guest) *led: drvn over 1f out: hdd & wknd jst ins fnl f* **16/1**

1m 11.73s (-0.17) **Going Correction** +0.025s/f (Slow) **6** Ran SP% **113.7**
Speed ratings (Par 95): **102,98,97,97,96 94**
Tote Swingers: 1&2 £1.40, 1&3 £1.80, 2&3 £1.30 CSF £10.19 CT £14.43 TOTE £4.60: £1.80, £1.10; EX 11.10 Trifecta £16.60 Pool: £185.93 - 8.24 winning units..
Owner The Ridgeway Bloodstock Company Ltd **Bred** Ridgeway Bloodstock **Trained** Upper Lambourn, Berks
■ Russian Bullet (4/1) was withdrawn after unseating his rider and bolting. Deduct 20p in the £ under R4.

FOCUS
A low-grade 3yo handicap that produced a clear-cut winner. It was sound run and the runner-up helps with the form.

395 ASHDOWN FOREST (S) H'CAP 2m (P)
1:55 (1:55) (Class 6) (0-60,56) 4-Y-O+ **£1,704** (£503; £251) **Stalls** Low

Form RPR
435- 1 **Dew Reward (IRE)**[34] [7939] 4-8-13 **56** CharlesBishop(5) 7 65
(Bill Turner) *hld up towards rr: stdy prog to chse ldng pair wl over 2f out: clsd to ld jst ins fnl f: styd on wl* **5/1**[3]
04/0 2 2 1/2 **Asterales**[16] [200] 5-8-13 **45** JamieMackay 3 51
(Willie Musson) *hld up in rr: smooth prog 4f out to chal 3f out: pressed ldr after: upsides 1f out: sn outpcd by wnr* **11/2**
/20- 3 nse **Waldsee (GER)**[7] [5916] 7-9-6 **52** AdamKirby 4 58
(Paul Rich) *hld up: in last pair 5f out: pushed along and rapid prog on outer 4f out to ld narrowly 3f out: drvn and hdd jst ins fnl f: one pce* **8/1**
40-0 4 7 **Olimamu (IRE)**[22] [130] 5-8-10 **45** (t) SimonPearce(3) 1 43
(Lydia Pearce) *hld up in last pair: effrt on outer fr 4f out: wnt 4th over 2f out but nt on terms: no imp after* **10/1**
0-50 5 nse **Rose Aurora**[12] [265] 5-9-8 **54** (vt) HayleyTurner 2 52
(Marcus Tregoning) *hld up in rr: stl covered up 3f out: effrt to go 5th over 2f out but nt on terms: no imp after* **3/1**[1]
/25- 6 9 **Mac Federal (IRE)**[25] [1761] 10-9-3 **56** MartinLeonard(7) 9 43
(Sheena West) *led 2f: prom after: lost pl 6f out: trapped bhd wkng rival over 4f out and dropped to last pair: nvr on terms after* **7/2**[2]
000- 7 8 **Diamond Twister (USA)**[15] [7892] 6-9-4 **50** (v[1]) JimmyFortune 6 27
(Lisa Williamson) *trckd ldrs: nudged along and lost grnd qckly fr over 2f out: eased whn no ch* **16/1**
353/ 8 1 **Benozzo Gozzoli**[17] [3760] 6-9-8 **54** IanMongan 8 30
(Seamus Mullins) *t.k.h early: trckd ldrs: prog to ld 4f out to 3f out: wknd rapidly* **11/1**
6000 9 4 **Nesnaas (USA)**[1] [392] 11-8-13 **45** (bt) FergusSweeney 10 16
(Alastair Lidderdale) *trckd ldr after 6f: led 5f out to 4f out: wknd qckly* **66/1**
-430 10 2 1/4 **Spiritonthemount (USA)**[10] [278] 7-9-3 **49** (b) ChrisCatlin 11 17
(Peter Hiatt) *slowly away: rousted along to rcvr and led after 2f: hdd u.p 5f out: wknd qckly* **20/1**

3m 23.51s (-2.19) **Going Correction** +0.025s/f (Slow)
WFA 4 from 5yo+ 6lb **10** Ran SP% **119.9**
Speed ratings (Par 101): **106,104,104,101,101 96,92,92,90,89**
Tote Swingers: 1&2 £5.70, 1&3 £12.80, 2&3 £13.40 CSF £33.74 CT £221.28 TOTE £5.90: £2.20, £2.30, £2.90; EX 46.60 Trifecta £302.70 Part won. Pool: £409.10 - 0.63 winning units..There was no bid for the winner.
Owner Mrs Derien Tucker **Bred** Tim Hyde Jnr **Trained** Sigwells, Somerset
■ Stewards' Enquiry : Jamie Mackay six-day ban: used whip down shoulder in the forehand (Feb 17-18,20-23)

FOCUS
Three drew clear in this weak selling handicap. The winner rates a small personal best.

396 MARRIOTT HOTEL AT LINGFIELD PARK H'CAP 6f (P)
2:25 (2:26) (Class 6) (0-52,52) 4-Y-O+ **£1,704** (£503; £251) **Stalls** Low

Form RPR
0-32 1 **Do More Business (IRE)**[16] [210] 5-9-1 **50** (v) IanMongan 1 56
(Pat Phelan) *trckd ldng pair: chal on outer over 2f out: hrd rdn over 1f out: kpt on to ld last strides: jst hld on* **7/2**[1]
2-34 2 shd **Gorgeous Goblin (IRE)**[26] [101] 5-8-13 **48** (t) JimmyFortune 10 54
(David C Griffiths) *chsd ldng trio: hrd rdn to cl over 1f out: chal ins fnl f: jst failed* **7/2**[1]
-045 3 nk **Super Frank (IRE)**[7] [320] 9-9-3 **52** (b) JamieGoldstein 7 57
(Zoe Davison) *hld up disputing 6th and off the pce: effrt on outer over 1f out: styd on and clsd on ldrs nr fin: nvr quite got there* **7/1**[3]
00-3 4 nse **Bobbyow**[2] [373] 4-8-9 **49** MarkCoumbe(5) 8 54
(Terry Clement) *led: jnd and rdn 2f out: kpt on wl fnl f: hdd last strides* **12/1**
0664 5 3/4 **Raimond Ridge (IRE)**[9] [297] 6-8-8 **46** oh1 DominicFox(3) 5 48+
(Derek Shaw) *s.i.s: hld up in last pair and wl off the pce: stl last whn swtchd out wd ins fnl f: r.o last 100yds: too much to do* **8/1**
34-5 6 nk **Metropolitan Chief**[8] [313] 8-8-9 **49** CharlesBishop(5) 4 52+
(Paul Burgoyne) *trckd ldr: chal and upsides fr 2f out: nt qckn last 75yds: squeezed out and lost pls nr fin* **16/1**
-013 7 nk **Avonvalley**[9] [297] 5-9-3 **52** FergusSweeney 6 58+
(Peter Grayson) *hld up in 5th and off the pce: clsd 2f out: stuck bhd ldrs fr over 1f out and nvr chal: lost pls nr fin* **4/1**[2]
0-26 8 1 1/4 **Pharoh Jake**[9] [297] 4-8-13 **48** KieranO'Neill 9 45
(John Bridger) *fractious bef ent stalls: mostly in last pair: rdn and no imp fnl 2f* **16/1**
4-40 9 1/2 **Suhayl Star (IRE)**[9] [297] 8-8-11 **46** oh1 JohnFahy 3 41
(Paul Burgoyne) *a towards rr: effrt on inner wl over 1f out: no prog* **11/1**

1m 12.4s (0.50) **Going Correction** +0.025s/f (Slow) **9** Ran SP% **115.8**
Speed ratings (Par 101): **97,96,96,96,95 95,94,92,92**
Tote Swingers: 1&2 £2.50, 1&3 £4.80, 2&3 £5.80 CSF £15.77 CT £81.20 TOTE £3.90: £1.60, £1.60, £2.00; EX 15.40 Trifecta £231.00 Pool: £540.05 - 1.73 winning units..
Owner C Fisher **Bred** Hardys Of Kilkeel Ltd **Trained** Epsom, Surrey
■ Stewards' Enquiry : Mark Coumbe two-day ban: careless riding (Feb 17-18)

FOCUS
This looked tight beforehand and the race played out that way also, the front seven being separated by little over a length. The form, as a result, needs treating with caution. The winner is rated to last year's best.
Avonvalley Official explanation: jockey said mare was denied a clear run

397 DORMANS PARK CLAIMING STKS 7f (P)
2:55 (2:55) (Class 6) 3-Y-O **£1,704** (£503; £251) **Stalls** Low

Form RPR
4111 1 **Roedean (IRE)**[1] [382] 3-8-10 70 (p) HayleyTurner 4 72
(Jamie Osborne) *trckd ldr: led 2f out and gng best: shkn up and drew clr fnl f* **4/7**[1]
2-34 2 5 **Haafhd Handsome**[16] [209] 3-9-3 72 (b[1]) JimmyFortune 3 66
(Richard Hannon) *led: drvn and hdd 2f out: one pce and no ch w wnr fnl f* **15/8**[2]
24-0 3 6 **Finalist**[13] [250] 3-8-10 58 (p) KieranO'Neill 1 42
(Dean Ivory) *n.m.r s: cl up in 3rd: rdn 1/2-way: effrt on inner whn no room wl over 1f out: wknd fnl f* **12/1**[3]

1m 24.02s (-0.78) **Going Correction** +0.025s/f (Slow) **3** Ran SP% **106.1**
Speed ratings (Par 95): **105,99,92**
CSF £1.88 TOTE £1.40; EX 1.60.Roedean was claimed by W. Stone for £8,000.
Owner Dr Marwan Koukash **Bred** C McEvoy **Trained** Upper Lambourn, Berks

FOCUS
Not a race that took much winning, but the pace was at least fair. The winner is rated to her recent form.

398 FOLLOW US ON TWITTER @BLUESQ H'CAP 1m 2f (P)
3:30 (3:30) (Class 4) (0-85,80) 3-Y-O **£4,431** (£1,308; £654) **Stalls** Low

Form RPR
51-3 1 **Shabora (IRE)**[20] [180] 3-9-4 80 DominicFox(3) 6 88+
(Roger Varian) *trckd ldng trio: forced wd bnd 2f out: rdn and prog to ld 1f out: r.o wl to maintain narrow but decisive advantage after* **9/2**[3]
110- 2 nk **Come On Blue Chip (IRE)**[107] [6957] 3-9-6 79 (b) AdamKirby 3 84
(Paul D'Arcy) *trckd ldng pair: effrt towards inner 2f out: led briefly jst over 1f out: r.o but a hld by wnr* **2/1**[1]
1- 3 2 3/4 **Moderator**[57] [7672] 3-9-6 79 GeorgeBaker 5 79
(Gary Moore) *hld up last: effrt whn nt clrest of runs over 1f out: kpt on same pce to take 3rd nr fin* **3/1**[2]
160- 4 hd **Rythmic**[121] [6623] 3-9-4 77 SamHitchcott 2 76
(Mark Johnston) *trckd ldr: chal fr 3f out: carried rt bnd 2f out: upsides jst over 1f out: outpcd fnl f: lost 3rd nr fin* **6/1**
10-2 5 4 1/2 **Biba Diva (IRE)**[30] [32] 3-9-3 76 JimmyFortune 1 66
(Jeremy Noseda) *led: jnd 3f out: edgd rt bnd 2f out: hdd jst over 1f out: wknd qckly* **7/1**
240- 6 2 1/4 **Captain Cardington (IRE)**[51] [7752] 3-8-8 67 ChrisCatlin 4 53
(Mick Channon) *hld up in 5th: rdn and struggling over 2f out: sn no ch* **14/1**

2m 9.08s (2.48) **Going Correction** +0.025s/f (Slow) **6** Ran SP% **110.0**
Speed ratings (Par 99): **91,90,88,88,84 83**
Tote Swingers: 1&2 £2.50, 1&3 £2.20, 2&3 £1.60 CSF £13.36 TOTE £5.70: £3.20, £1.10; EX 15.40.
Owner Sheikh Ahmed Al Maktoum **Bred** Darley **Trained** Newmarket, Suffolk

FOCUS
Probably a fair 3yo handicap, but it was slowly run. The form has been given a chance, with the winner and third progressive and the second unexposed.

399 SHARPTHORNE MAIDEN STKS 1m 2f (P)
4:05 (4:06) (Class 5) 3-Y-O+ **£2,385** (£704; £352) **Stalls** Low

Form RPR
1 **Good Of Luck** 3-8-5 0 ChrisCatlin 10 76+
(Mick Channon) *green in preliminaries: trckd ldng trio: wnt 2nd 3f out: urged into ld over 1f out: r.o wl and sn clr* **9/2**[3]
2 3 3/4 **Gabrial The Hero (USA)** 3-8-5 0 HayleyTurner 8 68+
(David Simcock) *green in preliminaries: dwlt: hld up in 8th: prog gng strly over 2f out: wnt 3rd over 1f out: reminder and veered rt last 75yds but r.o to take 2nd nr fin* **11/4**[2]
2 3 1/2 **Scatter Dice (IRE)**[13] [249] 3-7-11 0 DominicFox(3) 5 62
(Mark Johnston) *led and allowed to dictate mod pce: hdd over 1f out: easily outpcd and lost 2nd nr fin* **6/4**[1]
6-0 4 3 1/4 **Broughton Place**[20] [175] 4-9-7 0 NickyMackay 11 60
(Willie Musson) *racd wd: wl in tch: prog to dispute 3rd 2f out: outpcd over 1f out* **25/1**
5 1 3/4 **Marmas** 3-8-5 0 KieranO'Neill 4 57+
(Marcus Tregoning) *rn green in last pair and urged along early: nvr on terms but kpt on fnl 2f* **5/1**
/00- 6 3/4 **Maxiyow (IRE)**[259] [2243] 4-9-2 31 MarkCoumbe(5) 6 55?
(Terry Clement) *wl in tch: rdn over 2f out: outpcd and n.d fr wl over 1f out* **100/1**
0- 7 1 **Buckley Boy**[175] [5011] 3-8-0 0 CharlesEddery(5) 12 54?
(K F Clutterbuck) *dwlt: a towards rr: outpcd fnl 2f* **40/1**
006/ 8 1 **Ngina**[430] [7641] 4-9-0 30 NatashaEaton(7) 7 51?
(Terry Clement) *trckd ldng pair: rdn over 2f out: wknd qckly on inner over 1f out* **100/1**
0- 9 2 1/4 **Estee Will**[37] [7894] 5-9-8 0 SamHitchcott 3 46?
(John E Long) *wl in tch in midfield: trapped bhd wkng rival and lost pl over 2f out: nvr on terms after* **100/1**
10 2 **Miss Tooty Fruiti (IRE)** 4-9-2 0 DavidKenny(5) 1 42?
(Paul Burgoyne) *green in preliminaries: s.v.s: reminder after 1f and swished tail: a in last pair* **66/1**

0/0- **11** 2½ **Mollyow (IRE)**[263] 2155 4-9-7 53 .... AdamKirby 9 37?
(Terry Clement) *chsd ldr to 3f out: wknd rapidly* **40/1**

2m 10.28s (3.68) **Going Correction** +0.025s/f (Slow)
WFA 3 from 4yo 22lb 4 from 5yo 1lb **11** Ran SP% **114.7**
Speed ratings (Par 103): **86,83,82,80,78 78,77,76,74,73 71**
Tote Swingers: 1&2 £2.70, 1&3 £1.80, 2&3 £2.50 CSF £16.41 TOTE £8.40: £1.90, £1.10, £1.70; EX 20.30 Trifecta £43.50 Pool: £1,572.92 - 26.71 winning units..
Owner Jaber Abdullah **Bred** Mrs G Slater **Trained** West Ilsley, Berks

FOCUS
A decent maiden for the time of year, one that should produce winners, but it was slowly run and the bare form is dubious. Several of these should rate higher in time.

400 PLAY BINGO FREE AT BLUESQ.COM AMATEUR RIDERS' H'CAP 1m 4f (P)
4:35 (4:35) (Class 5) (0-70,70) 4-Y-O+ £2,305 (£709; £354) Stalls Low

Form RPR
2-13 **1** **Maslak (IRE)**[14] 221 8-9-10 **59** .... MrMMitchell(7) 12 67
(Peter Hiatt) *mde all: kicked 4 l clr 3f out: urged along fnl 2f: jst hld on* **12/1**

526- **2** *nk* **Sircozy (IRE)**[58] 7661 6-10-9 **70** ....(be) MissHayleyMoore(5) 8 77
(Gary Moore) *trckd ldrs: wnt 2nd over 2f out: rdn and clsd grad on wnr fnl f: jst hld* **4/1**[1]

-350 **3** *nk* **Kames Park (IRE)**[8] 310 10-10-11 **67** .... MissSBrotherton 9 74
(Richard Guest) *hld up wl in rr: stdy prog over 3f out: wnt 3rd over 1f out: threatened to cl on ldng pair ins fnl f: reminder 50yds out and gave up* **11/2**[3]

5-20 **4** 3¼ **Turjuman (USA)**[3] 366 7-9-13 **62** ....(p) MissAlexOwen(7) 11 64
(Alan Bailey) *trckd ldrs: prog to go 2nd over 4f out to over 2f out: one pce after* **20/1**

13-6 **5** 2½ **Squad**[32] 9 6-10-3 **64** ....(be) MrJCoffill-Brown(5) 1 62
(Simon Dow) *s.s: hld up in rr: effrt on inner 3f out: nt pce to threaten ldrs fnl 2f* **6/1**

5-25 **6** ¾ **Laconicos (IRE)**[22] 130 10-9-7 **56** ....(t) MissCScott(7) 7 53
(William Stone) *chsd wnr to over 4f out: sn lost pl and btn* **12/1**

3-44 **7** *nse* **Strike Force**[11] 275 8-10-11 **70** ....(t) MissALHutchinson(3) 6 67
(Clifford Lines) *trckd ldng pair to 3f out: grad wknd* **15/2**

4-44 **8** 1½ **Striding Edge (IRE)**[6] 349 6-10-2 **58** .... MissTinaHenriksson 3 52
(Hans Adielsson) *hld up towards rr: sddle slipped bef 1/2-way: lost tch w main gp 3f out: nvr on terms after* **8/1**

632- **9** ¾ **Merrjanah**[37] 7902 4-9-5 **57** .... MrAFrench(7) 2 50
(John Wainwright) *wl in tch in midfield tl wknd over 2f out* **16/1**

15-1 **10** 2¼ **Jamarjo (IRE)**[21] 156 5-10-2 **65** .... MrMatthewRochford(7) 5 54
(Steve Gollings) *racd wd: wl in tch tl wknd wl over 2f out* **5/1**[2]

-400 **11** *1* **Sunset Boulevard (IRE)**[2] 375 9-9-9 **56** oh9......(b) MissMBryant(5) 10 44
(Paddy Butler) *hld up in last trio: effrt 3f out: sn no prog* **66/1**

060- **12** *7* **Whodathought (IRE)**[46] 7817 4-9-11 **63** .... MissBHampson(7) 4 40
(Paul Rich) *rel to r: mostly in last: lost tch over 3f out* **33/1**

2m 33.11s (0.11) **Going Correction** +0.025s/f (Slow)
WFA 4 from 5yo+ 3lb **12** Ran SP% **119.7**
Speed ratings (Par 103): **100,99,99,97,95 95,95,94,93,92 91,86**
Tote Swingers: 1&2 £10.40, 1&3 £11.30, 2&3 £6.50 CSF £59.20 CT £303.51 TOTE £10.50: £4.70, £2.20, £2.80; EX 47.20 Trifecta £107.60 Pool: £705.71 - 4.85 winning units..
Owner P W Hiatt **Bred** Shadwell Estate Company Limited **Trained** Hook Norton, Oxon
■ Michael Mitchell's first winner.

FOCUS
An ordinary pace on in this amateur riders' handicap. The winner is rated up slightly on his recent form.
Striding Edge(IRE) Official explanation: jockey said saddle slipped
T/Plt: £20.90 to a £1 stake. Pool: £86,240.25 - 3,008.54 winning tickets. T/Qpdt: £4.50 to a £1 stake. Pool: £6,735.62 - 1,102.53 winning tickets. JN

387 WOLVERHAMPTON (A.W) (L-H)
Friday, February 3

OFFICIAL GOING: Standard
Wind: Light behind Weather: Fine

401 BET AT BLUE SQUARE APPRENTICE H'CAP 1m 1f 103y(P)
2:10 (2:10) (Class 6) (0-65,71) 4-Y-O+ £1,704 (£503; £251) Stalls Low

Form RPR
35-3 **1** **Patriotic (IRE)**[28] 60 4-9-1 **64** ow1 .... JoshCrane(5) 5 72
(Chris Dwyer) *a.p: chsd ldr over 2f out: led over 1f out: edgd lft ins fnl f: rdn out* **10/3**[1]

50-0 **2** 1¾ **Scary Movie (IRE)**[19] 183 7-9-0 **63** ....(p) DarrenEgan(5) 9 67
(Ronald Harris) *s.i.s and drvn along in rr early: hdwy over 1f out: sn rdn: r.o to go 2nd nr fin: nt rch wnr* **12/1**

03-4 **3** *nk* **Favorite Girl (GER)**[21] 148 4-9-2 **60** .... JackDuern 4 64
(Michael Appleby) *led: rdn and hdd over 1f out: edgd rt and styd on same pce ins fnl f: lost 2nd nr fin* **15/2**[2]

6241 **4** 1½ **Pipers Piping (IRE)**[1] 384 6-9-13 **71** 6ex........(p) NicoleNordblad 2 72
(Alastair Lidderdale) *hld up in tch: rdn over 1f out: edgd lft: styng on same pce whn nt clr run ins fnl f* **10/3**[1]

302- **5** 1¾ **Potentiale (IRE)**[51] 7756 8-9-0 **65** ....(p) Leah-AnneAvery(7) 10 62
(J W Hills) *hld up: edgd lft and styd on ins fnl f: nvr trbld ldrs* **9/1**[3]

055- **6** ¾ **Philharmonic Hall**[21] 7779 4-8-10 **57** .... LauraBarry(3) 1 52
(Richard Fahey) *chsd ldrs: rdn over 2f out: styd on same pce fr over 1f out* **12/1**

2-02 **7** 1¼ **Hathaway (IRE)**[19] 188 5-8-8 **52** .... NoraLooby 3 45
(Mark Brisbourne) *hld up: pushed along over 3f out: nt clr run over 2f out: styd on same pce appr fnl f* **9/1**[3]

60-5 **8** 3¼ **Desert Hunter (IRE)**[21] 153 9-8-2 **53** .... KatieDowson(7) 8 39
(Micky Hammond) *plld hrd and prom: trckd ldr over 6f out: pushed along over 2f out: rdn and wknd over 1f out* **22/1**

500- **9** *5* **Hackett (IRE)**[127] 6472 4-8-8 **52** .... GeorgeDowning 6 27
(Shaun Lycett) *prom tl rdn and wknd over 2f out* **9/1**[3]

2m 2.4s (0.70) **Going Correction** +0.025s/f (Slow) **9** Ran SP% **107.7**
Speed ratings (Par 101): **97,95,95,93,92 91,90,87,83**
Tote Swingers: 1&2 £10.90, 1&3 £3.60, 2&3 £18.50 CSF £40.42 CT £235.81 TOTE £2.70: £1.10, £6.40, £2.50; EX 51.60 Trifecta £277.30 Part won. Pool: £374.79 - 0.10 winning units..
Owner M M Foulger **Bred** Darley **Trained** Six Mile Bottom, Cambs
■ Stewards' Enquiry : Jack Duern three-day ban: careless riding (Feb 17-18,tbn)

FOCUS
This weak handicap, confined to apprentice riders, was run at just an ordinary pace and it no doubt proved a big advantage racing handily. The winner is rated close to his Southwell best.

402 SPONSOR A RACE BY CALLING 01902 390000 CLAIMING STKS 1m 1f 103y(P)
2:40 (2:40) (Class 5) 4-Y-O+ £2,264 (£673; £336; £168) Stalls Low

Form RPR
4-11 **1** **Munsarim (IRE)**[9] 299 5-9-5 80 ....(b) JoeFanning 5 88
(Keith Dalgleish) *trckd ldr after 1f: a gng wl: led over 5f out: clr whn hung rt fr over 1f out: comf* **40/85**[1]

5-23 **2** 4½ **Shabak Hom (IRE)**[12] 263 5-9-1 72 .... MartinLane 1 75
(David Simcock) *led over 8f out: hdd over 5f out: chsd wnr: rdn over 2f out: hung rt over 1f out: styd on same pce* **8/1**[3]

61-2 **3** 1¼ **Country Road (IRE)**[15] 213 6-8-5 75 ....(p) JackDuern(7) 7 69
(Michael Appleby) *led 1f: chsd ldrs: lost pl over 6f out: rdn over 3f out: styd on to go 3rd ins fnl f* **7/1**[2]

00-3 **4** *6* **Dream Of Fortune (IRE)**[7] 330 8-8-7 64........(bt) MatthewCosham(5) 2 56
(David Evans) *hld up in tch: wnt 3rd over 6f out: rdn over 2f out: wknd over 1f out* **25/1**

4-12 **5** 4½ **Faithful Ruler (USA)**[11] 268 8-8-13 75 ....(p) LukeMorris 6 53
(Ronald Harris) *hld up: hdwy over 3f out: sn drvn along: wknd wl over 1f out: eased fnl f* **7/1**[2]

2m 1.47s (-0.23) **Going Correction** +0.025s/f (Slow) **5** Ran SP% **107.9**
Speed ratings (Par 103): **102,98,96,91,87**
CSF £4.60 TOTE £1.40: £1.20, £2.20; EX 4.50.Shabak Hom was claimed by P.D. Evans for £8,000.
Owner Joseph Leckie & Sons Ltd **Bred** Shadwell Estate Company Limited **Trained** Carluke, S Lanarks

FOCUS
There was a modest pace on in this claimer and it saw a clear-cut success from the heavily backed winner. The form is rated around the second.

403 STAY AT THE WOLVERHAMPTON HOLIDAY INN H'CAP 1m 141y(P)
3:15 (3:17) (Class 5) (0-70,70) 4-Y-O+ £2,264 (£673; £336; £168) Stalls Low

Form RPR
3-11 **1** **Daniel Thomas (IRE)**[9] 293 10-8-11 **60** 6ex........(tp) WilliamCarson 9 76
(Richard Guest) *dwlt: hld up: hdwy to ld over 1f out: shkn up ins fnl f: r.o wl: comf* **3/1**[1]

0-02 **2** *4* **Master Of Dance (IRE)**[9] 301 5-9-6 **69** ....(p) JoeFanning 4 76
(Keith Dalgleish) *hld up: hdwy and hung lft fr over 1f out: styd on to go 2nd wl ins fnl f: no ch w wnr* **9/2**[2]

02-3 **3** *1* **Moral Issue**[22] 128 4-9-1 **67** .... DaleSwift(3) 7 72
(Ian McInnes) *chsd ldr: rdn over 2f out: ev ch over 1f out: styd on same pce ins fnl f* **14/1**

562- **4** ½ **Without Prejudice (USA)**[35] 7928 7-9-5 **68** .... PaddyAspell 3 71
(Michael Easterby) *chsd ldrs: rdn over 1f out: hung lft and styd on same pce ins fnl f* **16/1**

06-5 **5** 1½ **Sweet Secret**[21] 148 5-9-2 **70** ....(b) RaulDaSilva(5) 5 70
(Jeremy Gask) *led: rdn and hdd over 1f out: wknd ins fnl f* **7/1**

5-21 **6** ¾ **Alhaban (IRE)**[14] 225 6-9-2 **65** .... LukeMorris 2 63
(Ronald Harris) *prom: rdn 3f out: hung lft and wknd ins fnl f* **9/2**[2]

25-3 **7** *nk* **John Potts**[11] 275 7-9-7 **70** .... RussKennemore 1 67
(Brian Baugh) *prom: rdn over 2f out: wknd ins fnl f* **7/1**

0-26 **8** 3¾ **Justcallmehandsome**[4] 361 10-8-9 **65** ....(v) JoshBaudains(7) 6 54
(Dominic Ffrench Davis) *dwlt: hld up: hdwy over 5f out: wknd 2f out* **12/1**

050- **9** *1* **Prince Of Sorrento**[147] 5894 5-8-13 **62** .... StevieDonohoe 8 49
(John Akehurst) *prom: racd keenly: rdn and wknd over 1f out* **6/1**[3]

1m 49.55s (-0.95) **Going Correction** +0.025s/f (Slow) **9** Ran SP% **120.9**
Speed ratings (Par 103): **105,101,100,100,98 98,97,94,93**
Tote Swingers: 1&2 £2.90, 1&3 £10.30, 2&3 £11.90 CSF £17.34 CT £169.01 TOTE £2.90: £1.10, £2.10, £5.50; EX 16.40 Trifecta £145.40 Pool: £1,092.54 - 5.56 winning units..
Owner Rakebackmypoker.com **Bred** Lawn Stud **Trained** Stainforth, S Yorks

FOCUS
This modest handicap looked competitive and was run at a fair pace. The winner's best form for years, the race rated around the placed horses.
Sweet Secret Official explanation: trainer said mare was struck into

404 WOLVERHAMPTON-RACECOURSE.CO.UK MEDIAN AUCTION MAIDEN STKS 1m 141y(P)
3:50 (3:52) (Class 5) 3-5-Y-O £2,264 (£673; £336; £168) Stalls Low

Form RPR
03- **1** **Rei D'Oro (USA)**[45] 7835 3-8-7 0 .... MartinLane 7 75+
(David Simcock) *s.i.s: sn prom: pushed along over 3f out: rdn over 1f out: styd on u.p to ld towards fin* **1/1**[1]

020- **2** 1¼ **Captivity**[94] 7205 3-8-7 75 .... JoeFanning 6 72
(Mark Johnston) *chsd ldr: rdn and hung lft over 1f out: styd on to ld wl ins fnl f: hdd towards fin* **7/4**[2]

3 **3** *1* **Time To Dance**[28] 61 3-8-7 0 .... LukeMorris 5 70
(Joseph Tuite) *led: rdn over 1f out: hdd and unable qck wl ins fnl f* **6/1**[3]

4 3¼ **Source Of Light (IRE)**[107] 6963 3-8-2 0 .... FrankieMcDonald 1 57
(Daniel Mark Loughnane) *chsd ldrs: rdn over 3f out: sn outpcd: styd on fr over 1f out* **20/1**

5 **5** 4½ **Ma Kellys (IRE)**[21] 159 3-8-7 0 .... BarryMcHugh 5 52
(Micky Hammond) *hld up: hdwy 2f out: wknd fnl f* **14/1**

0-0 **6** *6* **Symphony Of Space**[18] 195 3-7-9 0 .... NoraLooby(7) 4 33
(Alan McCabe) *chsd ldrs tl wknd wl over 1f out* **150/1**

0 **7** *12* **Piper Cherokee**[18] 195 3-8-2 0 .... JamesSullivan 8
(Michael Easterby) *in rr: drvn along 5f out: lost tch fr over 3f out* **100/1**

60 **8** 2¼ **It's Me And You**[18] 190 4-9-7 0 .... DavidSimmonson(7) 2
(Michael Easterby) *hld up: pushed along 4f out: sn lost tch* **250/1**

1m 50.43s (-0.07) **Going Correction** +0.025s/f (Slow)
WFA 3 from 4yo 21lb **8** Ran SP% **114.1**
Speed ratings (Par 103): **101,99,99,96,92 86,76,74**
Tote Swingers: 1&2 £1.20, 1&3 £2.10, 2&3 £2.00 CSF £2.91 TOTE £2.00: £1.10, £1.10, £2.10; EX 3.50 Trifecta £8.60 Pool: £1,440.32 - 123.31 winning units..
Owner Trillium Place Racing **Bred** B D Gibbs Farm Llc Et Al **Trained** Newmarket, Suffolk

FOCUS
Probably a fair maiden, but there are one or two doubts over the bare form. The winner is getting his act together.

405 FOLLOW US ON TWITTER @BLUESQ CONDITIONS STKS 5f 216y(P)
4:20 (4:20) (Class 4) 4-Y-O+ £4,204 (£1,251; £625; £312) Stalls Low

Form RPR
31-3 **1** **Capone (IRE)**[27] 89 7-9-2 97 .... ShaneKelly 2 92+
(Scott Dixon) *hld up: smooth hdwy on bit to ld wl ins fnl f: readily* **11/8**[2]

/-12 **2** *1 ¼* **Alben Star (IRE)**[13] 253 4-9-2 92 TonyHamilton 5 88
(Richard Fahey) *s.s: hld up: hdwy over 1f out: sn pushed along: rdn and ev ch ins fnl f: sn outpcd* **5/4**[1]

0-00 **3** *1* **Where's Reiley (USA)**[7] 327 6-9-2 80 (b) FrankieMcDonald 3 85
(Alastair Lidderdale) *led: rdn over 1f out: hdd and unable qck wl ins fnl f* **80/1**

101- **4** *½* **Sugar Beet**[45] 7832 4-8-11 87 LukeMorris 1 78
(Ronald Harris) *chsd ldr: rdn over 1f out: ev ch ins fnl f: no ex towards fin* **12/1**

0-02 **5** *3 ½* **Elna Bright**[12] 266 7-9-2 92 LiamKeniry 4 72
(Peter Crate) *chsd ldrs: rdn over 2f out: wknd ins fnl f* **7/1**[3]

1m 13.97s (-1.03) **Going Correction** +0.025s/f (Slow) **5** Ran SP% **108.0**
Speed ratings (Par 105): **107,105,104,103,98**
CSF £3.27 TOTE £2.00: £2.00, £1.10; EX 3.80.
Owner Brooklands Racing **Bred** S J Macdonald **Trained** Babworth, Notts

FOCUS
A decent little conditions sprint. They went a sound pace and the form looks fair enough, though it's doubtful the first pair ran right up to their marks. The third is the key.

406 MIRROR PUNTERS CLUB H'CAP 5f 20y(P)

4:50 (4:51) (Class 5) (0-75,75) 4-Y-O+ **£2,264** (£673; £336; £168) **Stalls** Low

Form RPR

112- **1** **Perlachy**[58] 7649 8-8-12 66 (v) LukeMorris 7 74
(Ronald Harris) *hld up: hdwy over 1f out: r.o u.p to ld post* **11/2**

6-63 **2** *shd* **Island Legend (IRE)**[11] 272 6-9-7 75 (p) DaneO'Neill 2 83
(Milton Bradley) *led: clr over 1f out: rdn ins fnl f: hdd post* **3/1**[2]

-320 **3** *½* **Dancing Freddy (IRE)**[13] 251 5-9-5 73 (tp) WilliamCarson 1 79
(Richard Guest) *a.p: pushed along to chse ldr 1/2-way: rdn over 1f out: r.o* **4/1**[3]

00-0 **4** *nk* **Absa Lutte (IRE)**[11] 272 9-8-9 70 NoelGarbutt(7) 5 75
(Michael Mullineaux) *dwlt: hld up: r.o wl ins fnl f: nt rch ldrs* **28/1**

-215 **5** *2 ½* **Blown It (USA)**[1] 387 6-9-3 71 6ex JoeFanning 3 68
(Keith Dalgleish) *s.i.s: hld up: hdwy 1/2-way: rdn over 1f out: no ex ins fnl f* **11/4**[1]

14-5 **6** *nk* **Triple Dream**[16] 208 7-9-6 74 (tp) LiamKeniry 4 70
(Milton Bradley) *chsd ldrs: rdn 1/2-way: styd on same pce appr fnl f* **13/2**

100- **7** *18* **Ingleby Star (IRE)**[109] 6913 7-9-0 71 (p) PaulPickard(3) 6
(Ian McInnes) *chsd ldr tl rdn and hung lft 1/2-way: sddle slipped sn after: eased* **12/1**

1m 2.11s (-0.19) **Going Correction** +0.025s/f (Slow) 7 Ran SP% **111.5**
Speed ratings (Par 103): **102,101,101,100,96 96,67**
Tote Swingers: 1&2 £2.50, 1&3 £2.40, 2&3 £4.30 CSF £21.20 TOTE £4.30: £2.00, £1.20; EX 21.80.
Owner Mrs N Macauley **Bred** J James **Trained** Earlswood, Monmouths

FOCUS
There was no hanging about in this moderate sprint handicap and it saw a tight finish as the pack closed in on the long-time leader Island Legend, who was cruelly denied. The second and third set the standard.
Ingleby Star(IRE) Official explanation: jockey said saddle slipped

407 PLAY BINGO FREE AT BLUESQ.COM H'CAP 7f 32y(P)

5:20 (5:21) (Class 6) (0-60,61) 3-Y-O **£1,704** (£503; £251) **Stalls** High

Form RPR

0-50 **1** **Homeward Strut**[21] 159 3-8-6 49 (b[1]) RaulDaSilva(5) 9 58
(Frank Sheridan) *chsd ldr tl led over 2f out: rdn out* **50/1**

5-45 **2** *½* **Songbird Blues**[7] 322 3-8-12 50 DavidProbert 5 58
(Mark Usher) *hld up: hdwy over 1f out: rdn to chse wnr ins fnl f: r.o* **8/1**[2]

00-1 **3** *1* **Speedy Yaki (IRE)**[11] 270 3-9-9 61 6ex (bt) ShaneKelly 3 66
(Daniel Mark Loughnane) *a.p: chsd wnr over 1f out: sn rdn: styd on same pce ins fnl f* **4/7**[1]

000- **4** *4 ½* **Martha's Way**[172] 5104 3-9-4 56 JamesSullivan 4 49
(Michael Easterby) *hld up: rdn over 2f out: styd on fr over 1f out: nt trble ldrs* **33/1**

5-14 **5** *½* **M J Woodward**[24] 112 3-9-7 59 LukeMorris 6 50
(Paul Green) *chsd ldrs: rdn over 2f out: styd on same pce appr fnl f* **8/1**[2]

060- **6** *3 ¾* **Angel Warrior (IRE)**[167] 5287 3-9-7 59 PJMcDonald 8 40
(Ben Haslam) *mid-div: rdn 1/2-way: hdwy over 2f out: wknd over 1f out* **17/2**[3]

4-00 **7** *3* **Can Do Les (IRE)**[9] 294 3-9-1 53 (b) JoeFanning 7 26
(Des Donovan) *sn led: rdn and hdd over 2f out: wknd over 1f out* **20/1**

200- **8** *7* **Clone Devil (IRE)**[144] 6001 3-8-10 48 (p) FrankieMcDonald 1
(Alastair Lidderdale) *s.i.s: hld up: pushed along 1/2-way: wknd over 2f out* **28/1**

1m 30.69s (1.09) **Going Correction** +0.025s/f (Slow) 8 Ran SP% **109.5**
Speed ratings (Par 95): **94,93,92,87,86 82,78,70**
Tote Swingers: 1&2 £10.30, 1&3 £8.70, 2&3 £2.20 CSF £365.91 CT £587.69 TOTE £21.10: £8.90, £1.90, £1.10; EX 165.90 Trifecta £542.00 Pool: £922.99 - 1.26 winning units..
Owner Mersey Racing, Bolingbroke Racing **Bred** Mickley Stud **Trained** Wolverhampton, W Midlands

■ Stewards' Enquiry : Raul Da Silva trainer said, regarding apparent improvement in form, that the gelding appreciated the first-time blinkers and first run in a handicap.

FOCUS
A very weak handicap. It was run at a sound pace and the principals came clear. The shock winner showed his first real form but the favourite disappointed.
T/Jkpt: £1,802.00 to a £1 stake. Pool: £118,859.89 - 46.83 winning tickets. T/Plt: £21.10 to a £1 stake. Pool: £99,886.52 - 3,445.02 winning tickets. T/Qpdt: £3.30 to a £1 stake. Pool: £10,463.94 - 2,344.60 winning tickets. CR

408 - 415a (Foreign Racing) - See Raceform Interactive

[314]MEYDAN (L-H)
Friday, February 3

OFFICIAL GOING: Tapeta - standard; turf - good
Rail out 12m on turf track.

416a FREEHOLD TROPHY (H'CAP) (TAPETA) 1m

11:00 (11:00) (100-110,110) 3-Y-O+
£46,451 (£15,483; £7,741; £3,870; £2,322; £1,548)

RPR

1 **Maraheb**[8] 317 4-8-11 102 (t) RoystonFfrench 1 107
(A Al Raihe, UAE) *s.i.s: rdn to trck ldrs: led 2f out: r.o wl* **9/2**[1]

2 *2* **Alazeyab (USA)**[7] 346 6-9-2 107 (vt) TadhgO'Shea 4 107
(A Al Raihe, UAE) *chsd ldrs: ev ch 2f out: kpt on same pce fnl 1 1/2f* **20/1**

3 *hd* **Red Gulch**[22] 140 5-8-11 102 FrankieDettori 3 102
(Mahmood Al Zarooni) *trckd ldrs: ev ch 1f out: one pce fnl 100yds* **5/1**[2]

4 *¾* **Disa Leader (SAF)**[14] 246 7-9-4 109 JGeroudis 5 107
(M F De Kock, South Africa) *mid-div: r.o wl fnl 1 1/2f: nrst fin* **20/1**

5 *hd* **Vagabond Shoes (IRE)**[125] 6558 5-9-5 110 OlivierPeslier 13 107
(Stephane Chevalier, UAE) *in rr of mid-div: r.o wl fnl 1 1/2f but nvr able to chal* **12/1**

6 *2 ¼* **Banna Boirche (IRE)**[14] 243 6-8-11 102 RyanMoore 7 94
(M Halford, Ire) *a mid-div* **9/1**[3]

7 *1* **Reem (AUS)**[14] 245 5-8-13 104 ChristopheSoumillon 6 94
(M F De Kock, South Africa) *nvr bttr than mid-div* **10/1**

8 *¾* **Jardim (BRZ)**[211] 6-8-11 102 KShea 14 90
(M F De Kock, South Africa) *settled in rr: n.d* **14/1**

9 *¾* **Dandy Boy (ITY)**[29] 53 6-8-11 102 CO'Donoghue 10 88
(David Marnane, Ire) *settled in rr: nvr able to chal* **9/1**[3]

10 *1 ¼* **Balducci**[14] 246 5-9-0 105 MircoDemuro 2 89
(Ernst Oertel, UAE) *sn led: hdd & wknd 2f out* **25/1**

11 *2 ¼* **Regal Parade**[8] 316 8-9-0 105 AdrianNicholls 12 83
(David Nicholls) *a in rr* **10/1**

12 *½* **Zanzamar (SAF)**[314] 998 5-9-4 109 (b) RichardHills 8 86
(M F De Kock, South Africa) *in rr of mid-div: rdn 4f out: sn btn* **5/1**[2]

13 *¾* **Hujaylea (IRE)**[14] 246 9-8-13 104 (p) ShaneFoley 9 80
(M Halford, Ire) *settled in rr: n.d* **9/1**[3]

14 *2 ¼* **Bay Knight (IRE)**[117] 6733 6-9-3 108 JamesDoyle 11 78
(J S Moore) *in rr of mid-div: n.d* **25/1**

1m 37.06s (-0.44) **14** Ran SP% **131.3**
CSF: 106.05; TRICAST: 486.10.
Owner Hamdan Al Maktoum **Bred** Shadwell Estate Co Ltd **Trained** UAE

FOCUS
The early pace was cut out by Balducci, who went 25.39 and 48.45, before Maraheb took over ahead of the 6f point, clocking 1.12.91. It proved hard to make up significant ground.

NOTEBOOK
Maraheb may be worthy of extra credit considering he missed the break and had to be rushed into a stalking position. He flashed his tail under pressure, but otherwise there was much to like and he was confirming the promise of his recent Dubai debut when he had been caught wide and left with too much to do over a bit further.
Alazeyab(USA), back up in trip, ran well despite having got warm.
Red Gulch had his chance but again lacked a finishing kick. This was an improvement on the form of his Dubai debut and he may step forward again, but he looks expensive at 250,000gns.
Disa Leader(SAF) ran a bit better for this switch to Tapeta.
Vagabond Shoes(IRE) wants upgrading. He fared best of those held up but had been left with far too much to do.
Reem(AUS) had a wide trip and can do better.
Jardim(BRZ), making his Dubai debut after an absence of 211 days, was another left with too much to do and also covered plenty of ground.
Dandy Boy(ITY) disappointed on this switch to Tapeta, finding nothing after travelling well.
Regal Parade could never get involved having raced in an unpromising position.
Zanzamar(SAF) had reportedly had joint surgery since he was last seen, but he showed nothing on this return.

417a MEYDAN CLASSIC TRIAL SPONSORED BY XPRESS (CONDITIONS RACE) (TURF) 7f

11:35 (11:35) 3-Y-O
£38,709 (£12,903; £6,451; £3,225; £1,935; £1,290)

RPR

1 **Factory Time (IRE)**[22] 142 3-8-9 100 (t) SilvestreDeSousa 5 102
(A Al Raihe, UAE) *sn led: kicked clr 2f out: r.o wl: comf* **11/1**[2]

2 *1 ½* **Kenny Powers**[211] 3773 3-8-9 91 (t) KierenFallon 1 98
(Tom Dascombe) *mid-div: r.o wl fnl 1 1/2f: nrst fin* **14/1**[3]

3 *nse* **Fiscal**[210] 3823 3-8-9 AndreaAtzeni 14 98
(M Al Jahouri, UAE) *racd in rr: r.o wl fnl 2f: nrst fin* **40/1**

4 *shd* **Right To Dream (IRE)**[22] 142 3-8-9 91 (b) FrankieDettori 12 98
(Brian Meehan) *trckd ldng pair: ev ch 100yds out: nt qckn fnl 55yds* **16/1**

5 *shd* **Burano (IRE)**[146] 5931 3-8-9 89 RichardHills 7 97+
(Brian Meehan) *racd in last: r.o wl fnl 2f: nrst fin* **14/1**[3]

6 *½* **Bible Black (IRE)**[22] 142 3-8-9 100 RyanMoore 4 96+
(G M Lyons, Ire) *hld up in rr: r.o same pce fnl 1 1/2f* **11/1**[2]

7 *½* **Energia Dust (BRZ)**[42] 7868 4-9-4 96 ValmirDeAzeredo 10 92
(Fabricio Borges, Sweden) *chsd ldrs: kpt on same pce fnl 1 1/2f* **25/1**

8 *3* **Need To Know (SAF)**[28] 76 4-9-4 RoystonFfrench 3 84
(A Al Raihe, UAE) *trckd ldrs: ev ch 1 1/2f out: one pce fnl f* **14/1**[3]

9 *¼* **Cody Maverick (IRE)**[33] 3-8-9 (bt) JamesDoyle 11 86
(A Al Raihe, UAE) *nvr able to chal* **150/1**

10 *shd* **Sand Stamp (FR)**[28] 76 3-8-9 88 RichardMullen 13 86
(S Seemar, UAE) *trckd ldng gp: ev ch 1 1/2f out: wknd fnl f* **20/1**

11 *hd* **Strait Of Zanzibar (USA)**[22] 142 3-8-9 102 ShaneFoley 8 85
(K J Condon, Ire) *nvr bttr than mid-div* **20/1**

12 *¼* **Old Pal (FR)**[117] 3-8-9 97 (t) WilliamBuick 6 84
(Niels Petersen, Norway) *nvr bttr than mid-div* **25/1**

13 *8 ½* **Ip Man (NZ)**[13] 261 4-9-4 112 (t) OChavez 9 58
(S Burridge, Singapore) *chsd ldrs tl rdn and wknd 2 1/2f out* **2/5**[1]

14 *dist* **Royal Tigre (USA)** 3-8-9 MircoDemuro 2
(M Ramadan, UAE) *nvr nr to chal* **33/1**

1m 25.64s (85.64)
WFA 3 from 4yo 17lb **14** Ran SP% **137.2**
CSF: 164.33.
Owner Jaber Abdullah **Bred** Tally-Ho Stud **Trained** UAE

FOCUS
Only the second running of this trial for the Meydan Classic - a 1m turf Listed event to be staged for just the fourth time on February 23. It's hard to be positive about the form as the red-hot favourite completely flopped, the winner was an allowed an uncontested lead, and there was just over 2l covering the next six finishers.

NOTEBOOK
Factory Time(IRE) was allowed to set fractions of 25.54, 49.12 and 1.12.81. He had failed to get near the form of his Dewhurst sixth on his first two starts since switching to Dubai, but both of those runs came on Tapeta and he had a tough trip last time. The return to turf evidently suited, but it's questionable just what he achieved.
Kenny Powers had been absent since finishing fifth in the July Stakes. This was a promising return.
Fiscal showed ability in two July course maidens for John Gosden ahead of being sold for just 10,000gns. That looks money well spent as he showed himself to be pretty useful, not beaten far despite having used up energy to recover from a slow start.
Right To Dream(IRE) ran better than on the Tapeta last time.
Burano(IRE), returning from 146 days off, was set an impossible task.
Bible Black(IRE) was another set far too much to do.

Ip Man(NZ) ran to a really smart level when winning over this trip on Tapeta two weeks earlier, but something was presumably amiss here.

418a UAE 1000 GUINEAS SPONSORED BY GULF NEWS (LISTED RACE) (FILLIES) (TAPETA) 1m

12:10 (12:10) 3-Y-O

£96,774 (£32,258; £16,129; £8,064; £4,838; £3,225)

RPR

1 **Gamilati**[28] 77 3-8-9 108 FrankieDettori 5 114+
(Mahmood Al Zarooni) *settled in last: smooth prog 2f out: led 1f out: easily* **1/2**[1]

2 *5 1/2* **Pimpernel (IRE)**[104] 7028 3-8-9 106 MickaelBarzalona 6 101+
(Mahmood Al Zarooni) *settled in rr: smooth prog 3f out: n.m.r 2f out: r.o once clr but no ch w wnr* **11/4**[2]

3 *2 1/4* **Alsindi (IRE)**[28] 77 3-8-9 102 RoystonFfrench 1 95
(A Al Raihe, UAE) *mid-div: chsd ldrs 2 1/2f out: led 1 1/2f out: hdd 1f out: r.o same pce fnl f* **10/1**[3]

4 *5 1/2* **Moon Spun (SAF)**[274] 4-9-5 93 RyanMoore 2 80
(H J Brown, South Africa) *s.i.s: sn led: hdd 1 1/2f out: kpt on same pce* **12/1**

5 *1* **Colorful Notion (IRE)**[48] 7799 3-8-9 80 MircoDemuro 3 80
(Marco Botti) *trckd ldrs: ev ch 3f out: one pce fnl 1 1/2f* **28/1**

6 *1/4* **Mary Fildes (IRE)**[28] 77 3-8-9 97 JamesDoyle 4 79
(J S Moore) *mid-div: rdn 3 1/2f out: sn btn* **40/1**

1m 38.84s (1.34)
WFA 3 from 4yo 19lb **6 Ran SP% 116.0**
CSF: 2.31.
Owner Godolphin **Bred** Darley **Trained** Newmarket, Suffolk

FOCUS
The first UAE Classic of the season. In three of the last four years it was won by a filly bred in the southern hemisphere, but that side of the world had just a solitary contender this time. The absence of any Mike de Kock representatives was particularly notable and quite possibly a consequence of the African Horse Sickness outbreak which prevented the trainer from travelling his home team. Last year de Kock had the winner, second and fourth - a trio of runners all bred in the southern hemisphere. The pace was slow (time 1.78 seconds slower than earlier 100-110 handicap), but the winner was impressive. The form is rated around her and the third.

NOTEBOOK
Gamilati ◆ followed up her trial success with ease and is evidently maturing into a really smart 3yo. She was held up in last, but was cruising when the field bunched on the final bend and, once switched wide in the straight, sprinted clear without needing to be seriously asked. She looked a write off for the English 1000 Guineas following her flop in the Lowther, but she has now well and truly restored her reputation, and for all that she's been suited by both the surface and the way her two races have unfolded, she must now re-enter calculations, provided her connections confirm she's being aimed at Newmarket. The bookies make her a general 16-1 shot, although her trainer has two shorter-priced contenders in Discourse (around 8-1) and Lyric Of Light (12-1).
Pimpernel(IRE) was a surprise runner considering her connections already had by far the likeliest winner in Gamilati, and it suggests she's being lined up for a tilt at the UAE Oaks. If that's the case then she'll have to settle better, but she did well to keep on for second, despite having been denied a clear run early in the straight until barging her way through.
Alsindi(IRE) was brushed aside by Gamilati in the trial and was even more comprehensively beaten this time. She has so far failed to match the form she showed when winning the Oh So Sharp Stakes at Newmarket last year, but her Dubai profile is not too dissimilar to stablemate Factory Time, who had also underperformed in two Tapeta starts before coming good on this card when returned to turf. Perhaps Alsindi will be switched back to the grass for the Meydan Classic.
Moon Spun(SAF), the only runner from the southern hemisphere, hadn't been seen for 274 days and offered little.
Colorful Notion(IRE) was outclassed.
Mary Fildes(IRE) ran below the level she showed in the trial.

419a CLASSIFIEDS TROPHY (H'CAP) (TURF) 5f

12:45 (12:45) 3-Y-O+

£67,741 (£22,580; £11,290; £5,645; £3,387; £2,258)

RPR

1 **Monsieur Joe (IRE)**[29] 50 5-8-8 **100** WilliamBuick 6 104
(Robert Cowell) *settled in last: rdn 2 1/2f out: r.o wl fnl 1 1/2f: led fnl 55yds* **8/1**

2 *1/4* **Inxile (IRE)**[14] 244 7-9-6 **112** (p) AdrianNicholls 9 115
(David Nicholls) *sn led in centre: rdn 2f out: r.o wl: hdd fnl 55yds* **10/1**

3 *1/4* **Bohemian Melody**[22] 141 5-8-10 **102** (b) RyanMoore 4 104
(Marco Botti) *in rr of mid-div: r.o fnl 2f: nrst fin* **11/2**[3]

4 *3/4* **Iver Bridge Lad**[14] 244 5-9-1 **112** (b) MichaelO'Connell(5) 1 111
(John Ryan) *mid-div: chsd ldrs 2 1/2f out: nt qckn fnl f* **10/1**

5 *1/4* **Nocturnal Affair (SAF)**[29] 50 6-9-0 **106** CO'Donoghue 12 104
(David Marnane, Ire) *trckd ldr: ev ch 1f out: one pce fnl f* **4/1**[2]

6 *1 1/4* **Mar Adentro (FR)**[94] 7221 6-9-5 **111** (tp) ChristopheSoumillon 3 105
(R Chotard, France) *prom far side: ev ch 2f out: one pce fnl f* **16/1**

7 *3/4* **Green Beret (IRE)**[22] 141 6-8-10 **102** (t) RoystonFfrench 7 93
(A Al Raihe, UAE) *chsd ldrs: r.o same pce fnl 1 1/2f* **20/1**

8 *1/2* **Dafeef**[111] 6858 5-9-3 **109** RichardHills 2 98
(Doug Watson, UAE) *a mid-div* **20/1**

9 *1 1/4* **Internationaldebut (IRE)**[8] 314 7-8-10 **102** KierenFallon 5 87
(Paul Midgley) *nvr bttr than mid-div* **12/1**

10 *1/2* **Invincible Ash (IRE)**[14] 244 7-8-10 **102** (tp) ShaneFoley 14 85
(M Halford, Ire) *nvr bttr than mid-div* **14/1**

11 *9 1/4* **Happy Dubai (IRE)**[29] 50 5-9-4 **110** (t) TadhgO'Shea 11 60
(A Al Raihe, UAE) *trckd ldr tl 2 1/2f out: sn wknd* **22/1**

12 *1* **Humidor (IRE)**[29] 50 5-9-2 **108** (t) FrankieDettori 10 54
(George Baker) *in rr of mid-div: wknd fnl 1 1/2f* **7/2**[1]

13 *1 1/4* **Winker Watson**[22] 141 7-8-8 **100** SilvestreDeSousa 8 42
(Mick Channon) *n.d* **50/1**

14 *dist* **Rock Jock (IRE)**[8] 314 5-8-10 **102** TedDurcan 13
(E Charpy, UAE) *v.s.a: a last* **16/1**

58.51s (58.51) **14 Ran SP% 128.9**
CSF: 87.73; TRICAST: 494.68.
Owner Mrs Helen Checkley **Bred** Nicola And Eleanor Kent **Trained** Six Mile Bottom, Cambs

FOCUS
The usually expansive straight course was narrowed significantly with the rail out 12 metres. While the majority raced up the centre, a trio of runners (Iver Bridge Lad, Mar Adentro and Dafeef) were positioned towards the far rail early on before joining the main bunch.

NOTEBOOK
Monsieur Joe(IRE), whose trainer took this last year with subsequent King's Stand winner Prohibit, stepped up on the form he showed when behind a few of these on his debut for Robert Cowell a month earlier. He probably didn't have to improve on the form he showed when runner-up over C&D last year, but he's only a 5yo and there should be more to come.
Inxile(IRE) might have needed his run over 6f on the Tapeta two weeks earlier. The return to this trip suited and he just failed after showing typically bright speed.
Bohemian Melody didn't get the smoothest of trips. He gave the impression he's not straightforward, but that he's capable of better.
Iver Bridge Lad fared best of those who raced towards the far side early on.
Nocturnal Affair(SAF) had today's winner behind when runner-up over C&D on his Dubai debut, but clearly he failed to build on that effort.
Mar Adentro(FR) might have needed this after three months off.
Dafeef, returning from a 111-day break and debuting for a new trainer, was a bit free and probably could have done with a bit more cover.
Humidor(IRE) ran as though he had a problem.
Rock Jock(IRE) was up to his old tricks, looking reluctant to race.

420a AL SHINDAGHA SPRINT SPONSORED BY GULF NEWS (GROUP 3) (TAPETA) 6f

1:26 (1:25) 3-Y-O+

£77,419 (£25,806; £12,903; £6,451; £3,870; £2,580)

RPR

1 **Hitchens (IRE)**[14] 244 7-9-0 113 SilvestreDeSousa 9 114
(David Barron) *chsd ldrs: rdn 1 1/2f out: r.o to ld fnl 100yds* **4/1**[2]

2 *shd* **Krypton Factor**[8] 314 4-9-0 109 (b) KierenFallon 3 114
(F Nass, Bahrain) *trckd ldrs: led 1 1/2f out: hdd 100yds out: fought bk: jst failed* **5/1**[3]

3 *1 3/4* **Alo Pura**[14] 244 8-8-9 105 (e) WilliamBuick 2 103
(D Selvaratnam, UAE) *mid-div on rail: chsd ldrs 2f out: r.o fnl f: nrst fin* **5/1**[3]

4 *3/4* **Captain Obvious (AUS)**[14] 244 7-9-2 116 (t) OChavez 11 108
(S Burridge, Singapore) *sn led: rdn 2 1/2f out: hdd 1 1/2f out: kpt on same pce* **9/4**[1]

5 *3/4* **Rerouted (USA)**[209] 3852 4-9-0 105 ChristopheSoumillon 12 103+
(M F De Kock, South Africa) *racd in last: r.o wl fnl 2f: nrst fin* **16/1**

6 *2 1/4* **Seachantach (USA)**[14] 244 6-9-0 100 (t) RichardMullen 13 96
(S Seemar, UAE) *mid-div: r.o fnl 2f but n.d* **33/1**

7 *1/4* **Jimmy Styles**[8] 314 8-9-0 104 JamesDoyle 1 95
(Clive Cox) *s.i.s: nvr bttr than mid-div* **20/1**

8 *1 3/4* **Angel's Pursuit (IRE)**[28] 80 5-9-0 100 CO'Donoghue 7 90
(David Marnane, Ire) *nvr bttr than mid-div* **12/1**

9 *hd* **Sir Reginald**[8] 314 4-9-0 102 PaulHanagan 8 89
(Richard Fahey) *nvr nr to chal* **16/1**

10 *2 1/2* **Dohasa (IRE)**[329] 7-9-0 108 AntiocoMurgia 5 81
(Ismail Mohammed) *nvr bttr than mid-div* **25/1**

11 *3* **Mujaazef**[29] 53 5-9-0 108 (t) RichardHills 6 71
(A Al Raihe, UAE) *trckd ldng duo: ev ch 3f out: one pce fnl f* **16/1**

12 *2* **Critical Moment (USA)**[142] 6061 5-9-0 100 TedDurcan 10 65
(F Nass, Bahrain) *sn rdn in rr: n.d* **33/1**

13 *3 1/4* **Hajoum (IRE)**[34] 7946 6-9-0 95 (vt) RoystonFfrench 14 55
(A Al Raihe, UAE) *nvr bttr than mid-div* **33/1**

1m 11.22s (-0.38) **13 Ran SP% 126.9**
CSF: 24.48.
Owner Laurence O'Kane & Paul Murphy **Bred** Curragh Bloodstock Agency Ltd **Trained** Maunby, N Yorks

FOCUS
There was a three-way battle for the lead, with Captain Obvious taken on by Krypton Factor and Mujaazef. The sectionals were 24.34 and 46.78.

NOTEBOOK
Hitchens(IRE) had the run of the race but only scrambled home. He was confirming the promise he showed when a closing second to Captain Obvious over C&D on his reappearance, and this was a nice prize to pick up, but he's unlikely to add to it this Carnival.
Krypton Factor proved suited by the drop to this trip when winning off 100 the previous week and he confirmed himself an improving sprinter with a huge effort in defeat. He readily saw off the other two who were ridden prominently and just failed to a really smart type who benefited from a good trip. Clearly he'll be well worth his place in the Group 3 Mahab Al Shimaal on Super Saturday (March 10).
Alo Pura wasn't in a cooperative mood when placed under pressure, tending to lug to her left and generally looking awkward.
Captain Obvious(AUS) didn't build on the form of his recent conditions race win, simply being unable to sustain his bid having been softened up through the opening stages.
Rerouted(USA) ◆ was detached from the main bunch at the top of the straight but made rapid late headway. While his late kick owes much to sitting well off the hot fractions, there wasn't much else finishing and this was a promising debut for Mike de Kock. He should build on this when back up in trip and could prove a cheap purchase at 55,000gns.

421a TABLOID TROPHY (H'CAP) (TURF) 1m 6f 11y

2:00 (2:00) 3-Y-O+

£58,064 (£19,354; £9,677; £4,838; £2,903; £1,935)

RPR

1 **Fox Hunt (IRE)**[94] 7218 5-9-6 **110** (v) FrankieDettori 11 118+
(Mahmood Al Zarooni) *trckd ldng pair: smooth prog to ld 1 1/2f out: r.o wl: comf* **15/8**[1]

2 *3 1/4* **Averroes (IRE)**[34] 7945 5-9-1 **105** MircoDemuro 2 107
(Ernst Oertel, UAE) *trckd ldr: led 2 1/2f out: hdd 1 1/2f out: nt qckn* **11/2**[3]

3 *1/2* **Manjakani**[8] 319 4-8-6 **100** TadhgO'Shea 13 102
(Ismail Mohammed) *mid-div: r.o fnl 2f: nrst fin* **6/1**

4 *1* **Glen's Diamond**[22] 143 4-8-10 **105** PaulHanagan 6 105
(Richard Fahey) *mid-div: chsd ldrs 3f out: kpt on same pce fnl 1 1/2f* **5/1**[2]

5 *3/4* **Tanfeeth**[13] 257 4-8-6 **100** RichardHills 12 100
(M Al Muhairi, UAE) *settled in rr: r.o fnl 2 1/2f: nrst fin* **8/1**

6 *1 1/2* **Electrolyser (IRE)**[103] 7049 7-9-5 **109** JamesDoyle 7 106
(Clive Cox) *sn led: kicked clr 5f out: hdd 2 1/2f out: one pce fnl 1 1/2f* **18/1**

7 *7 1/4* **Royaaty (IRE)**[22] 143 6-8-8 **98** XZiani 3 85
(M bin Shafya, UAE) *in rr of mid-div: n.d* **25/1**

8 *1 1/4* **Plantagenet (SPA)**[22] 143 5-8-9 **99** WilliamBuick 10 84
(G Arizkorreta Elosegui, Spain) *settled in rr: nvr nr to chal* **14/1**

9 *3 1/2* **Happy Valley (ARG)**[22] 145 6-9-1 **105** (b) ChristopheSoumillon 5 85
(M F De Kock, South Africa) *trckd ldr: rdn 4 1/2f out: sn btn* **14/1**

10 *1/4* **Glen Nevis (USA)**[13] 257 8-8-5 **95** (vt) RoystonFfrench 9 75
(A Al Raihe, UAE) *mid-div on rail: nrst fin* **40/1**

11 *3* **Montaff**[22] 143 6-8-13 **102** TedDurcan 1 78
(Mick Channon) *trckd ldrs tl one pce 3f out* **25/1**

12 *13 1/2* **Nanton (USA)**[8] 319 10-9-0 **104** RyanMoore 8 61
(E Charpy, UAE) *settled in rr: nvr able to chal* **25/1**

13 *14 1/2* **Astral Thunder (ARG)**[69] 5-8-10 **100** KierenFallon 4 36
(Doug Watson, UAE) *s.i.s: bdly hmpd after 1 1/2f: racd in rr: n.d* **16/1**

3m 1.54s (181.54)
WFA 4 from 5yo+ 5lb **13 Ran SP% 130.7**
CSF: 12.68; TRICAST: 59.13; PLACEPOT: £323.60 to a £1 stake. Pool of £5098.30 - 11.50 winning units. QUADPOT: £7.00 to a £1 stake. Pool of £570.43 - 59.50 winning units..

Owner Sheikh Hamdan Bin Mohammed Al Maktoum **Bred** Ballylinch Stud **Trained** Newmarket, Suffolk

FOCUS

A good staying handicap. The pace, set by Electrolyser was just modest, with the sectionals 28.31 at the quarter-mile point, 55.12 for the half and 1.47.70 after a mile.

NOTEBOOK

Fox Hunt(IRE) ◆ had an extremely busy 2011 for Mark Johnston, but he kept improving. When last seen he was a fast-finishing seventh in the Melbourne Cup and that form continues to work out exceptionally well, with the winner and runner-up subsequently finishing first and third in the Hong Kong Vase, and the fourth and fifth going one-two in Group 2 company. The question here was whether he could return from a gruelling campaign in the same form, but he's a tough sort and readily defied a mark of 110. He has been known to hit a flat spot, but was always well placed by Dettori and, despite initially lugging left under pressure, was straightened up and well on top in good time. The Dubai Gold Cup - to be run on World Cup night for the first time this year - is the obvious target and he'll relish the return to 2m. In the longer term, it's not out of the question he could develop into an Ascot Gold Cup contender. He won at the meeting last year and shapes as though he'd get every inch of 2m4f.

Averroes(IRE) was 6lb higher than when easily winning a lesser race on Tapeta when making his Dubai debut, but he's an improving sort and ran a fine race behind the Group-class winner.

Manjakani was better than the bare form of his last run and this was a respectable effort back up in distance.

Glen's Diamond was again a bit keen, but he ran respectably and looks likely to build on this again.

Tanfeeth, up in trip after winning off 6lb lower on Tapeta, kept on having been set plenty to do.

Montaff was badly hampered early on.

Astral Thunder(ARG) lost all chance when badly hampered in the opening stages.

394 LINGFIELD (L-H)

Saturday, February 4

OFFICIAL GOING: Standard

Wind: Light, behind Weather: Cloudy, cold

422 BET ON TODAY'S FOOTBALL AT BLUESQ.COM APPRENTICE H'CAP — 7f (P)

12:55 (12:55) (Class 6) (0-60,60) 4-Y-0+ — **£1,704** (£503; £251) **Stalls** Low

Form — RPR

2210 **1** — **Crocodile Bay (IRE)**[4] 370 9-8-10 **52**..................(p) CharlesEddery(3) 3 — 59
(Richard Guest) *t.k.h: trckd ldr: led over 1f out: urged along and a jst fending off rivals fnl f* **13/2**

3-0 **2** ¾ **Kucharova (IRE)**[11] 276 4-9-2 **55**.................................... DavidKenny 6 — 60
(Seamus Mullins) *chsd ldng trio: rdn over 2f out: styd on fr over 1f out to take 2nd last 100yds: a hld* **12/1**

606- **3** *nk* **Saucy Buck (IRE)**[77] 7484 4-9-2 **60**...........................(b[1]) DarrenEgan(5) 8 — 64
(Jamie Poulton) *hld up disputing 5th: effrt 2f out: r.o between rivals fnl f to take 3rd last 75yds* **6/1**[3]

-160 **4** ¾ **Divine Rule (IRE)**[17] 198 4-8-10 **54**....................... CharlotteJenner(5) 1 — 56
(Laura Mongan) *led: rdn and hdd over 1f out: one pce ins fnl f* **8/1**

3-45 **5** *shd* **Cristaliyev**[5] 361 4-9-4 **60**.................................(b) NathanAlison(3) 7 — 62
(Jim Boyle) *hld up disputing 5th: effrt on inner 2f out: clsd on ldrs 1f out: urged along and nt qckn after* **10/3**[1]

0-52 **6** *nse* **Monadreen Dancer**[10] 305 4-9-4 **57**................................ RaulDaSilva 5 — 59
(Daniel Mark Loughnane) *dwlt: t.k.h and sn trckd ldng pair: cl enough over 1f out: nt qckn fnl f and lost pls* **9/2**[2]

0-20 **7** 3 ¼ **My Jeanie (IRE)**[13] 264 8-8-2 **46** oh1.............................. NoraLooby(5) 2 — 39
(Jimmy Fox) *t.k.h: hld up in last trio: rdn and no prog over 1f out* **33/1**

45-0 **8** ½ **Batchworth Blaise**[17] 197 9-8-5 **47**......................(b) CharlesBishop(3) 4 — 39
(Eric Wheeler) *dwlt: t.k.h: hld up in last trio: rdn and no prog over 1f out* **14/1**

464- **9** 7 **Graceful Spirit**[241] 2828 5-8-7 **46** oh1......................... MatthewCosham 9 — 19
(David Evans) *dwlt: racd wd: hld up in last trio: wknd 2f out* **13/2**

1m 24.52s (-0.28) **Going Correction** -0.025s/f (Stan) — 9 Ran SP% **110.6**

Speed ratings (Par 101): **100,99,98,97,97 97,94,93,85**

toteswingers: 1&2 £10.10, 1&3 £13.30, 2&3 £17.40. CSF £75.47 CT £470.25 TOTE £6.30: £1.90, £2.80, £2.60; EX 62.60 Trifecta £425.60 Pool: £604.00 - 1.05 winning units..

Owner Future Racing (Notts) Limited **Bred** James And Joe Brannigan **Trained** Stainforth, S Yorks

FOCUS

A moderate contest in which the pace was muddling.

423 BLUE SQUARE CARNIVAL IPHONE APP (S) STKS — 1m (P)

1:25 (1:25) (Class 6) 4-Y-0+ — **£1,704** (£503; £251) **Stalls** High

Form — RPR

020- **1** — **Twinkled**[107] 6971 4-8-6 67.. IanBurns(7) 5 — 70
(Michael Bell) *hld up in last: quick prog on outer over 3f out to ld over 2f out: rdn and styd on fnl f* **13/8**[1]

30-5 **2** ¾ **Tuxedo**[17] 198 7-8-13 64.. WilliamCarson 3 — 68
(Peter Hiatt) *trckd ldrs in 4th: rdn over 2f out: styd on u.p over 1f out to take 2nd last 50yds* **7/1**

-252 **3** ¾ **Marvo**[8] 330 8-8-6 65..(b) DannyBrock(7) 1 — 66
(Mark H Tompkins) *dwlt: t.k.h and sn cl up: rdn on inner to chse wnr wl over 1f out: sn chalng: nt qckn fnl f and lost 2nd last 50yds* **5/2**[2]

-060 **4** 4 ½ **Hecton Lad (USA)**[11] 287 5-8-13 62..........................(b) LukeMorris 2 — 56
(John Best) *led 1f: trckd ldr to over 2f out: hanging and fnd nil over 1f out: btn after* **10/1**

6-30 **5** 1 ½ **Sienna Blue**[22] 146 4-8-1 62.. JakePayne(7) 6 — 47
(Bill Turner) *a abt same pl: rdn and no prog 2f out: wl btn after* **20/1**

3-42 **6** 4 **Lutine Charlie (IRE)**[17] 205 5-8-12 65.....................(v[1]) DarrenEgan(7) 4 — 49
(Ronald Harris) *tk fierce hold: led after 1f to over 2f out: wknd qckly over 1f out* **11/2**[3]

1m 37.32s (-0.88) **Going Correction** -0.025s/f (Stan) — 6 Ran SP% **108.4**

Speed ratings (Par 101): **103,102,101,97,95 91**

toteswingers: 1&2 £4.00, 1&3 £1.10, 2&3 £3.80. CSF £12.47 TOTE £2.80: £1.60, £2.30; EX 12.50.There was no bid for the winner.

Owner D W & L Y Payne **Bred** D W And L Y Payne And Barton Stud **Trained** Newmarket, Suffolk

FOCUS

A modest seller. None of these seemed keen to lead.

424 BLUE SQUARE SPRINT SERIES ROUND 5 H'CAP (QUALIFIER) (DIV I) — 6f (P)

2:00 (2:00) (Class 6) (0-65,65) 4-Y-0+ — **£2,726** (£805; £402) **Stalls** Low

Form — RPR

35-2 **1** — **Cut The Cackle (IRE)**[9] 312 6-8-11 **55**...................(bt) WilliamCarson 1 — 65
(Richard Guest) *dwlt: hld up in last: sme prog over 2f out: wl-timed run fr over 1f out to ld last 75yds: won gng away* **3/1**[1]

-015 **2** 1 ¼ **Waterloo Dock**[10] 305 7-9-7 **65**.................................(v) LukeMorris 4 — 71
(Michael Quinn) *chsd ldr: rdn to ld over 1f out: idled in front: hdd and outpcd last 75yds* **7/1**[3]

3463 **3** ½ **Waabel**[7] 353 5-8-12 **61**.. NathanAlison(5) 3 — 65
(Richard Guest) *sn led: rdn and hdd over 1f out: styd on same pce after* **4/1**[2]

-125 **4** ½ **Captain Dimitrios**[14] 252 4-9-1 **64**.....................(v) MatthewCosham(5) 6 — 67
(David Evans) *prom: rdn to dispute 3rd over 1f out: kpt on same pce fnl f: nvr able to chal* **4/1**[2]

0000 **5** ½ **Forty Proof (IRE)**[17] 205 4-8-9 **60**..........................(be[1]) NoraLooby(7) 8 — 61
(Alan McCabe) *hld up in midfield: gng bttr than most over 2f out: disp 3rd over 1f out: pushed along nt qckn after* **25/1**

2660 **6** 1 **Efistorm**[7] 353 11-9-4 **62**... HayleyTurner 5 — 60
(Conor Dore) *trckd ldrs: pushed along and lost pl over 2f out: struggling after: kpt on fnl f* **12/1**

4-45 **7** 1 ½ **Fantasy Fighter (IRE)**[21] 178 7-8-13 **57**.......................... JohnFahy 10 — 50
(John E Long) *a in rr: rdn on outer sn after 1/2-way: no imp after* **9/1**

0-04 **8** *hd* **Captainrisk (IRE)**[7] 353 6-9-1 **59**.................................(v) DavidProbert 7 — 52
(Christine Dunnett) *a towards rr: rdn in last over 2f out: n.d after* **9/1**

0-06 **9** *hd* **Mandy's Hero**[11] 277 4-9-0 **65**.........................(b) JenniferFerguson(7) 2 — 57
(Olivia Maylam) *taken down early: cl up on inner tl steadily wknd fr over 1f out* **66/1**

1-00 **10** 1 ¾ **Microlight**[9] 312 4-8-5 **52**..(b) SimonPearce(3) 9 — 38
(John E Long) *dwlt: in tch in midfield: rdn on outer over 2f out: wknd over 1f out* **28/1**

1m 11.37s (-0.53) **Going Correction** -0.025s/f (Stan) — 10 Ran SP% **114.0**

Speed ratings (Par 101): **102,100,99,99,98 97,95,94,94,92**

toteswingers: 1&2 £3.30, 1&3 £2.70, 2&3 £5.50. CSF £23.41 CT £81.91 TOTE £3.20: £1.80, £2.40, £1.50; EX 19.10 Trifecta £34.30 Pool: £875.33 - 18.87 winning units..

Owner Rakebackmypoker.com **Bred** Mountarmstrong Stud **Trained** Stainforth, S Yorks

FOCUS

The fifth round of the Blue Square Sprint Series. Waabel ensured the pace was good and the winner, representing the same owner/trainer combination, was held up. The time was almost the same as the second leg.

Captainrisk(IRE) Official explanation: jockey said gelding ran flat

425 BLUE SQUARE SPRINT SERIES ROUND 5 H'CAP (QUALIFIER) (DIV II) — 6f (P)

2:30 (2:30) (Class 6) (0-65,65) 4-Y-0+ — **£2,726** (£805; £402) **Stalls** Low

Form — RPR

536- **1** — **The Wee Chief (IRE)**[226] 3322 6-9-7 **65**......................... KieranO'Neill 10 — 75
(Jimmy Fox) *stdd s and dropped in fr wd draw: hld up in last pair: gd prog and clr run through on inner fr wl over 1f out: led last 100yds: pushed out* **7/1**

2-00 **2** ½ **Picansort**[14] 252 5-9-6 **64**.. ShaneKelly 6 — 72
(Peter Crate) *trckd ldng trio: prog on outer to ld over 1f out: hdd and nt qckn last 100yds* **11/2**[3]

-421 **3** *hd* **Diamond Vine (IRE)**[7] 353 4-9-5 **63**................................(p) LukeMorris 1 — 70
(Ronald Harris) *settled in midfield: drvn on outer 2f out: styd on wl fnl f: nrly snatched 2nd* **3/1**[1]

5531 **4** ¾ **Chjimes (IRE)**[8] 320 8-9-2 **60**..................................(b) HayleyTurner 5 — 65
(Conor Dore) *t.k.h: hld up bhd ldrs: stl gng strly over 2f out: nt qckn over 1f out: styd on ins fnl f: unable to chal* **5/1**[2]

0-42 **5** 1 ½ **Slatey Hen (IRE)**[10] 297 4-8-8 **52**..............................(p) WilliamCarson 3 — 55+
(Richard Guest) *hld up in midfield: effrt whn chopped off wl over 1f out: swtchd out wd and styd on: no ch* **7/1**

224- **6** *hd* **Court Applause (IRE)**[35] 7943 4-9-4 **62**......................... GeorgeBaker 8 — 62
(William Muir) *trckd ldr: chal and upsides over 1f out: wknd ins fnl f* **6/1**

14/0 **7** 3 ¼ **High Voltage**[15] 232 11-8-11 **55**.............................(tp) JamieGoldstein 4 — 44
(Mrs J L Le Brocq, Jersey) *cl up bhd ldng pair tl wknd wl over 1f out* **18/1**

2000 **8** *nk* **Memphis Man**[7] 353 9-8-8 **57**................................ MatthewCosham(5) 9 — 45
(David Evans) *taken down early: a in last trio: rdn 1/2-way: no prog* **20/1**

0-06 **9** 2 **Custom House (IRE)**[7] 353 4-8-11 **58**..................(p) SimonPearce(3) 2 — 40
(John E Long) *restless in stalls: awkward s: a wl in rr: nvr a factor* **12/1**

-500 **10** 2 **Royal Intruder**[13] 267 7-8-11 **60**................................ NathanAlison(5) 7 — 35
(Richard Guest) *led at str pce: hdd & wknd rapidly over 1f out* **22/1**

1m 11.36s (-0.54) **Going Correction** -0.025s/f (Stan) — 10 Ran SP% **118.4**

Speed ratings (Par 101): **102,101,101,100,98 97,93,93,90,87**

toteswingers: 1&2 £9.50, 1&3 £6.70, 2&3 £3.80. CSF £46.05 CT £145.69 TOTE £8.10: £2.70, £1.70, £1.70; EX 53.20 Trifecta £979.30 Part won. Pool: £1,323.45 - 0.73 winning units..

Owner R E Kavanagh **Bred** Dermot Kilmartin **Trained** Collingbourne Ducis, Wilts

FOCUS

The time was almost identical to the first division.

426 BET AT BLUE SQUARE H'CAP — 1m (P)

3:00 (3:00) (Class 3) (0-95,93) 4-Y-0+ — **£6,792** (£2,021; £1,010; £505) **Stalls** High

Form — RPR

12-0 **1** — **Amitola (IRE)**[31] 29 5-9-2 **88**... JoeFanning 6 — 95
(David Barron) *mde all: shkn up 2f out: styd on strly and in command ins fnl f* **9/1**

11-4 **2** 1 **Lockantanks**[14] 254 5-9-7 **93**... LukeMorris 3 — 98
(Michael Appleby) *trckd ldrs: gng strly over 2f out: rdn over 1f out: styd on to take 2nd last 100yds: unable to chal* **11/2**[3]

036- **3** *hd* **Mr Willis**[49] 7801 6-9-7 **93**.. MarcHalford 4 — 98+
(Terry Clement) *stdd s: hld up in last pair: stl last 2f out: prog over 1f out: r.o wl to take 3rd nr fin* **18/1**

121- **4** *nk* **Numeral (IRE)**[59] 7660 4-9-0 **86**.................................... KieranO'Neill 7 — 90
(Richard Hannon) *trckd wnr: poised to chal 2f out: rdn over 1f out: nt qckn and hld fnl f: lost 2nd last 100yds* **9/2**[1]

12-2 **5** *nk* **Tarooq (USA)**[14] 254 6-9-2 **88**.. TonyHamilton 1 — 91
(Richard Fahey) *trckd wnr on inner: looking for room 2f out: rdn over 1f out: disp 2nd ins fnl f: one pce* **9/2**[1]

2-21 **6** ¾ **Shifting Star (IRE)**[10] 304 7-9-2 **88**................................(b) LiamKeniry 2 — 89
(John Bridger) *t.k.h: hld up in midfield: lost pl over 3f out: prog on inner 2f out: tried to cl on ldrs 1f out: nt qckn after* **14/1**

0-11 **7** 3 ½ **Prince Of Burma (IRE)**[10] 301 4-9-2 **88**.......................(b) IanMongan 10 — 81
(Jeremy Gask) *tk fierce hold: hld up bhd ldrs: effrt 2f out: stl in tch over 1f out: wknd fnl f* **5/1**[2]

2-42 **8** 1 ¼ **Titan Triumph**[7] 351 8-8-8 **80**...(t) ShaneKelly 5 — 71
(William Knight) *hld up towards rr: gng wl enough 2f out: shkn up and nt qckn over 1f out: wknd fnl f* **8/1**

30-6 **9** 4 ½ **Levitate**[33] 11 4-8-8 **80**...(vt) JohnFahy 9 — 60
(Alan McCabe) *sltly awkward s: racd wd in midfield: drvn over 2f out: wknd over 1f out* **8/1**

0P0/ **10** 1 1/2 **Smokey Oakey (IRE)**[98] 6562 8-8-9 **88**........................ DannyBrock[(7)] 8 65
(Mark H Tompkins) *hld up in last pair: effrt on wd outside 3f out: struggling and lost grnd bnd 2f out: wknd* **40/1**

1m 36.54s (-1.66) **Going Correction** -0.025s/f (Stan) **10** Ran SP% **115.0**
Speed ratings (Par 107): **107,106,105,105,105 104,100,99,95,93**
toteswingers: 1&2 £13.10, 1&3 £12.20, 2&3 £25.00. CSF £57.06 CT £875.48 TOTE £9.90: £4.20, £1.90, £7.90; EX 69.50 Trifecta £1343.00 Pool: £27,950.92 - 15.40 winning units..
Owner J Browne **Bred** Patrick J Monahan **Trained** Maunby, N Yorks

FOCUS
A good race on paper, but the form is misleading as the winner was allowed an uncontested lead.

NOTEBOOK
Amitola(IRE) was allowed an uncontested lead. She was trying 1m for the first time but her stamina wasn't severely tested. (tchd 11-1)
Lockantanks ran well behind a rival who had saved plenty.
Mr Willis ◆ might be the one to take from the race. His rider can't be blamed for waiting for a run on the final bend, rather than conceding ground by going wide, but the gaps came too late, with the gelding flashing home to be in front soon after the line. He hasn't won since December 2009, but he's by no means overraced for his age, this being just his 26th start. (op 16-1 tchd 20-1)
Numeral(IRE) had Amitola behind when winning over 7f here last time (off 5lb lower), but this race didn't set up as kindly. He would have preferred a stronger gallop. (op 5-1 tchd 11-2)
Tarooq(USA) was closest to the inside rail in the straight and didn't see his race out.
Prince Of Burma(IRE), up 7lb on this hat-trick bid, didn't get much cover and was too keen. Ian Mongan unsurprisingly reported the colt ran too free. Official explanation: jockey said colt ran too free (tchd 9-2)

427 BLUE SQUARE BET H'CAP 1m 4f (P)
3:35 (3:36) (Class 3) (0-95,95) 4-Y-0+ **£6,792** (£2,021; £1,010; £505) **Stalls** Low

Form RPR

0-02 **1** **Layline (IRE)**[15] 223 5-8-11 **85**.. ShaneKelly 5 96+
(Gay Kelleway) *trckd ldng pair: wnt 2nd over 2f out gng easily: led over 1f out: r.o wl: comf* **9/2[2]**

550- **2** 2 3/4 **Franco Is My Name**[170] 4432 6-8-10 **84**........................ JohnFahy 6 91
(Peter Hedger) *hld up in 5th: clsd on ldrs and squeezed through to go 3rd over 2f out: rdn to chse wnr jst over 1f out: r.o but no ch* **14/1**

2-21 **3** 4 1/2 **Exemplary**[17] 207 5-8-12 **86**.. JoeFanning 4 85
(Mark Johnston) *pressed ldr: led over 3f out: drvn and hdd over 1f out: wl outpcd after* **9/2[2]**

/0-3 **4** 1/2 **Brunston**[21] 175 6-8-8 **82**.. HayleyTurner 2 81
(Brendan Powell) *trckd ldng pair: n.m.r wl over 2f out and lost pl sn after: rdn and one pce over 1f out* **16/1**

43-1 **5** 1/2 **Art Scholar (IRE)**[20] 187 5-8-10 **84**.............................. LiamKeniry 1 82
(Michael Appleby) *hld up in last trio: effrt on outer over 2f out: lft bhd fr wl over 1f out* **4/1[1]**

24-1 **6** nk **First Avenue**[17] 202 7-8-7 **81** oh1.............................. FergusSweeney 8 78
(Laura Mongan) *hld up in last and wl off the pce: tried to cl fr over 2f out: rdn over 1f out: fnd nil* **8/1**

50-6 **7** 6 **Cashelgar (IRE)**[21] 177 6-9-6 **94**...................................... LukeMorris 7 82
(Richard Guest) *hld up in last trio: drvn over 4f out: effrt on wd outside over 2f out: sn wknd* **9/2[2]**

300- **8** 38 **Status Symbol (IRE)**[25] 7802 7-9-7 **95**........................ WilliamCarson 3 22
(Anthony Carson) *pushed up to ld: set decent pce but pressed thrght: hdd & wknd rapidly over 3f out: t.o* **7/1[3]**

2m 28.63s (-4.37) **Going Correction** -0.025s/f (Stan) **8** Ran SP% **110.7**
Speed ratings (Par 107): **113,111,108,107,107 107,103,77**
toteswingers: 1&2 £11.70, 1&3 £5.60, 2&3 £9.80. CSF £59.35 CT £283.75 TOTE £5.00: £1.30, £4.40, £1.10; EX 70.40 Trifecta £369.20 Pool: £1,247.32 - 2.50 winning units..
Owner Whispering Winds & Bob Smith **Bred** Mrs M E Slade **Trained** Exning, Suffolk

FOCUS
This was the only race on the card run in a time under standard. A modest handicap that set up nicely for those ridden patiently.

NOTEBOOK
Layline(IRE) was on the lowest rating from which has ever competed on Polytrack and he won with ease. (op 11-2)
Franco Is My Name, back on the Flat after a 170-day break, ran a solid race behind the well-handicapped winner. (tchd 16-1)
Exemplary is a one-paced galloper who was successful over 2m here last time, so it's easy to understand why Joe Fanning wanted to be positive, but the rider's decision to take on Status Symbol (reported to have stopped quickly) looked counterproductive as the leader was already setting a brisk enough gallop. (op 11-2)
Brunston didn't get the clearest of runs into the straight and can probably do a bit better. (op 14-1)
Art Scholar(IRE) was nowhere near the form he showed when winning off 6lb lower at Kempton on his previous start. His form figures here now read 74075. (tchd 9-2)
Cashelgar(IRE) failed to confirm the promise he showed when running to a decent level over 1m2f here on his return/debut for this stable, even allowing for a wide trip into the straight.
Status Symbol(IRE) Official explanation: jockey said gelding stopped quickly

428 FOLLOW US ON TWITTER @BLUESQ MEDIAN AUCTION MAIDEN STKS 1m (P)
4:05 (4:05) (Class 6) 3-5-Y-0 **£1,704** (£503; £251) **Stalls** High

Form RPR

6- **1** **Palmyra (IRE)**[37] 7909 3-8-4 0.. MartinLane 6 63+
(David Simcock) *hld up in last: effrt wl over 1f out: drvn on outer and r.o to ld ins fnl f: in command after* **11/2[2]**

3 **2** 1 1/4 **Falcon's Reign (FR)**[15] 231 3-8-9 0................................ ShaneKelly 1 65+
(Jeremy Noseda) *hld up in 6th: nt asked for effrt tl wl over 1f out: swtchd lft jst ins fnl f and shkn up: styd on to take 2nd last strides but lacked wnr's momentum* **4/11[1]**

44- **3** hd **Jumeirah Liberty**[38] 7894 4-10-0 60............................ JamieGoldstein 4 65
(Zoe Davison) *led after 1f: drvn 2f out: hdd and one pce ins fnl f: lost 2nd last strides* **40/1**

6-45 **4** 3/4 **Roman Flame**[11] 281 4-9-9 52.. KieranO'Neill 5 58?
(Michael Quinn) *led 1f: settled bhd ldng pair after 3f: rdn to chse ldr over 2f out tl jst ins fnl f: one pce* **28/1**

000- **5** 6 **Search And Rescue (USA)**[108] 6956 3-8-9 62................ LukeMorris 7 44
(J W Hills) *prom: rdn over 2f out: wknd over 1f out* **18/1**

6 5 **Barristers Brief**[17] 4-10-0 0.. HayleyTurner 3 37
(Eve Johnson Houghton) *hld up in 5th: pushed along whn n.m.r on inner 2f out: hmpd over 1f out: bhd after* **12/1[3]**

305- **7** 7 **Godber (IRE)**[35] 7938 3-8-2 56.................................... PhoebeCruse[(7)] 2 15
(Ralph Smith) *awkward s: t.k.h and moved up fr last to join ldr after 3f: wknd rapidly over 2f out: t.o* **100/1**

1m 40.01s (1.81) **Going Correction** -0.025s/f (Stan)
WFA 3 from 4yo 19lb **7** Ran SP% **108.5**
Speed ratings (Par 101): **89,87,87,86,80 75,68**
toteswingers: 1&2 £1.60, 1&3 £8.80, 2&3 £5.70. CSF £7.11 TOTE £5.70: £2.20, £1.10; EX 8.80.
Owner Sultan Ali **Bred** Thurso & Hyphen Bloodstock **Trained** Newmarket, Suffolk
■ Stewards' Enquiry : Phoebe Cruse one-day ban: careless riding (Feb 18)

FOCUS
There wasn't much pace on and the time was by far the slowest of three races at the trip. This was a modest maiden with the form being limited by the third.

429 PLAY BLACKJACK AT BLUESQ.COM MAIDEN STKS 7f (P)
4:35 (4:36) (Class 5) 3-Y-0+ **£2,385** (£704; £352) **Stalls** Low

Form RPR

34-4 **1** **Burnhope**[15] 231 3-8-10 69.. LukeMorris 7 71
(Scott Dixon) *mde all: kicked clr jst over 2f out: at least 4 l clr over 1f out: in no real danger after: eased last strides* **4/1[3]**

2 1 **Roxelana (IRE)** 3-8-5 0.. HayleyTurner 6 62+
(Jeremy Noseda) *s.i.s: rn green in last: stl there 2f out: prog through rivals jst over 1f out: r.o fnl f to take 2nd last strides* **9/4[2]**

3 nk **Infortual (TUR)** 3-8-5 0.. NickyMackay 1 62+
(Marco Botti) *hld up in last trio: effrt on inner 2f out but wnr already gone: wnt 2nd jst over 1f out: clsd but nvr able to chal: lost 2nd last strides* **6/5[1]**

0-0 **4** hd **Jennifer J**[28] 84 3-8-5 0.. MartinLane 2 61
(Mark H Tompkins) *in tch in last trio: effrt on outer 2f out: drvn and clsd w other plcd horses fnl f: unable to chal* **14/1**

0-5 **5** 3 3/4 **Norwood Lane**[22] 147 3-8-10 0......................................(p) LiamKeniry 5 56?
(Peter Hedger) *mostly chsd wnr: outpcd 2f out: lost 2nd and wknd jst over 1f out* **80/1**

6/ **6** 2 **Josie's Dream (IRE)**[597] 3112 4-9-6 0.......................... JoshBaudains[(7)] 3 55?
(Jo Hughes) *racd wd: prom: rdn 2f out: hanging and wknd over 1f out* **33/1**

60- **7** 4 1/2 **Mandianna (IRE)**[100] 7124 3-8-5 0.................................... JohnFahy 4 33?
(Jo Crowley) *prom tl wknd 2f out* **20/1**

1m 25.47s (0.67) **Going Correction** -0.025s/f (Stan)
WFA 3 from 4yo 17lb **7** Ran SP% **111.8**
Speed ratings (Par 103): **95,93,93,93,89 86,81**
toteswingers: 1&2 £1.80, 1&3 £2.00, 2&3 £1.40. CSF £12.78 TOTE £4.80: £2.30, £1.50; EX 10.50.
Owner Mrs Susan Roy **Bred** Mrs S M Roy **Trained** Babworth, Notts

FOCUS
A modest maiden run in a time around a second slower than the earlier Class 6 handicap.
T/Jkpt: Not won. T/Plt: £313.90 to a £1 stake. Pool: £131,864.14 - 306.60 winning tickets. T/Qpdt: £34.20 to a £1 stake. Pool: £13,214.96 - 285.70 winning tickets. JN

401 WOLVERHAMPTON (A.W) (L-H)
Saturday, February 4

OFFICIAL GOING: Standard changing to standard to slow after race 1 (2.05) (meeting abandoned after race 4 (3.45))
Wind: Fresh behind Weather: Snowing

430 BLUE SQUARE WINTER CARNIVAL IPHONE APP H'CAP 7f 32y(P)
2:05 (2:06) (Class 6) (0-55,55) 4-Y-0+ **£1,704** (£503; £251) **Stalls** High

Form RPR

504- **1** **July Days (IRE)**[128] 6488 6-9-2 55.............................. RussKennemore 4 66
(Brian Baugh) *chsd ldr tl led over 4f out: rdn over 1f out: hung rt ins fnl f: styd on* **15/2**

14-3 **2** 1 1/2 **Gala Spirit (IRE)**[17] 203 5-9-2 55.................................... TomEaves 6 61
(Peter Niven) *a.p: chsd wnr over 2f out: rdn over 1f out: styd on same pce ins fnl f* **7/2[1]**

6-12 **3** 2 1/2 **Look For Love**[8] 334 4-8-8 54......................................(e) JackDuern[(7)] 5 54+
(Reg Hollinshead) *hld up: rdn and nt clr run over 2f out: hdwy over 1f out: nt rch ldrs* **9/2[2]**

00-0 **4** 3/4 **Misere**[12] 274 4-8-12 51.. PhillipMakin 2 49
(Kevin Ryan) *prom: rdn over 1f out: styd on same pce* **10/1**

5-03 **5** 1 **Blue Noodles**[5] 356 6-8-13 52......................................(p) PaddyAspell 8 47+
(John Wainwright) *hld up in tch: pushed along whn hmpd and lost pl wl over 2f out: styd on u.p fnl f* **9/1**

-502 **6** 3/4 **Monsieur Pontaven**[8] 329 5-9-1 54.............................. LeeNewman 3 47
(Robin Bastiman) *mid-div: pushed along 1/2-way: rdn over 2f out: nt trble ldrs* **5/1[3]**

5-00 **7** 1 **Rise To Glory (IRE)**[9] 307 4-8-8 47 oh1 ow1.........(bt[1]) BarryMcHugh 9 37
(Shaun Harris) *hld up in tch: drvn along 3f out: styd on same pce fr over 1f out* **40/1**

-000 **8** 3/4 **Kwik Time**[4] 370 4-8-4 46 oh1.. JulieBurke[(3)] 11 34
(Robin Bastiman) *s.i.s: nvr on terms* **40/1**

3104 **9** 1 3/4 **Kyncraighe (IRE)**[9] 307 4-8-11 50..........................(tp) JamieSpencer 7 34
(Joseph Tuite) *s.i.s: hld up: rdn over 1f out: n.d* **6/1**

30-0 **10** hd **Yours**[15] 232 4-8-7 49..(p) AmyRyan[(3)] 1 32
(Kevin Ryan) *led: hdd over 4f out: chsd wnr tl rdn over 2f out: wknd wl over 1f out* **28/1**

0-00 **11** 8 **Portrush Storm**[8] 334 7-8-7 46 oh1.............................. ChrisCatlin 10
(Ray Peacock) *chsd ldrs tl rdn and wknd over 2f out* **66/1**

1m 31.37s (1.77) **Going Correction** +0.25s/f (Slow) **11** Ran SP% **112.0**
Speed ratings (Par 101): **99,97,94,93,92 91,90,89,87,87 78**
toteswingers: 1&2 £6.50, 1&3 £8.60, 2&3 £3.80. CSF £31.46 CT £131.11 TOTE £10.10: £3.70, £1.10, £2.00; EX 47.80.
Owner S Holmes **Bred** Deer Forest Stud **Trained** Audley, Staffs

FOCUS
The temperature dropped to -9C in the early hours of the morning and the snow began to fall before racing, but the tractors were out on the course soon enough and the meeting got the go-ahead.
Look For Love Official explanation: jockey said gelding hung right-handed on bend

431 GET YOUR BET ON AT BLUESQ.COM H'CAP 7f 32y(P)
2:40 (2:40) (Class 3) (0-95,94) 4-Y-0+ **£6,792** (£2,021; £1,010; £505) **Stalls** High

Form RPR

2-65 **1** **Piscean (USA)**[14] 253 7-9-0 87...................................... JamieSpencer 7 97
(Tom Keddy) *hld up: hdwy over 1f out: shkn up to ld and hung rt ins fnl f: pushed out* **11/2[3]**

-426 **2** 3/4 **Tamareen (IRE)**[3] 378 4-8-7 80................................(p) FrederikTylicki 2 88+
(Richard Fahey) *chsd ldrs: rdn over 1f out: styd on* **9/2[1]**

0-35 **3** 1 1/4 **Hazzard County (USA)**[13] 266 8-9-2 94........................ LauraPike[(5)] 6 99
(David Simcock) *hld up: hdwy and edgd lft fr over 1f out: r.o* **11/1**

-010 **4** 3/4 **Bawaardi (IRE)**[3] 378 6-8-9 82.................................... NeilChalmers 10 85
(David Evans) *hld up: hdwy and nt clr run over 1f out: r.o* **9/1**

U6-0 **5** 1/2 **Little Garcon (USA)**[14] 253 5-9-1 88..........................(b[1]) AdamKirby 1 90
(Marco Botti) *hld up: hdwy 2f out: rdn over 1f out: styd on* **16/1**

6-04 **6** 2 1/4 **Norville (IRE)**[14] 253 5-9-4 91......................................(b) JimmyFortune 3 87
(David Evans) *chsd ldrs: rdn over 2f out: styd on same pce fr over 1f out* **5/1[2]**

110- **7** ½ **Pat's Legacy (USA)**[111] 6150 6-9-1 88 StevieDonohoe 9 82
(Jo Hughes) *chsd ldrs: rdn over 2f out: styd on same pce appr fnl f* **8/1**

524- **8** *hd* **Oil Strike**[129] 6467 5-8-9 89 DavidSimmonson(7) 4 83
(Michael Easterby) *led: rdn over 1f out: hdd & wknd ins fnl f* **10/1**

003- **9** *nk* **Masai Moon**[217] 3634 8-8-10 83 JamesMillman 5 76
(Rod Millman) *s.i.s: hld up: rdn 3f out: nvr trbld ldrs* **14/1**

00-0 **10** 1 ¾ **Arteus**[14] 253 6-8-12 85 (b) ChrisCatlin 8 73
(Jane Chapple-Hyam) *chsd ldr: rdn and ev ch over 1f out: wknd ins fnl f* **9/1**

1m 29.51s (-0.09) **Going Correction** +0.25s/f (Slow) **10** Ran SP% **111.3**
Speed ratings (Par 107): **110,109,107,106,106 103,103,102,102,100**
toteswingers: 1&2 £3.10, 1&3 £7.00, 2&3 £12.80. CSF £28.89 CT £258.76 TOTE £7.50: £2.50, £2.20, £4.40; EX 36.00 Trifecta £166.70 Pool: £468.78 - 2.08 winning units..

Owner Andrew Duffield **Bred** Connie And John Iacuone **Trained** Newmarket, Suffolk

FOCUS
A good quality handicap in which the leaders went off miles too fast and set it up for those that had been settled out the back.

NOTEBOOK
Piscean(USA) was still in last place with 2f to run, but he picked up well once switched inside on straightening up for home and saw the extra furlong out well. He won cosily in the end - he had dropped to a mark he should be competitive off - but the race did set up nicely for him. (tchd 5-1 and 6-1)

Tamareen(IRE) ◆ did best of those that raced handily and can probably have his effort upgraded. The return of the cheekpieces was a plus, as was the return to his favoured track, and he can win something similar. (tchd 4-1 and 5-1)

Hazzard County(USA), along with the winner, was held up out the back and watched the race fall apart in front of him. Forced to challenge widest of all, he didn't help his chances by hanging left under pressure. (op 9-1)

Bawaardi(IRE) made some headway but didn't get a clear run. (op 10-1 tchd 17-2)

Little Garcon(USA) kept on from off the pace. (op 12-1)

Norville(IRE) probably did too much early. (tchd 9-2 and 11-2)

432 BET AT BLUE SQUARE H'CAP 1m 1f 103y(P)
3:15 (3:16) (Class 4) (0-85,84) 4-Y-0+ **£4,204** (£1,251; £625; £312) **Stalls** Low

Form RPR

22-U **1** **Emma's Gift (IRE)**[7] 354 4-9-0 80 (b) AdamBeschizza(3) 3 92
(Julia Feilden) *chsd ldrs: led over 1f out: rdn out* **8/1**

5-44 **2** 2 ½ **Veroon (IRE)**[11] 280 6-9-2 79 (p) FrederikTylicki 6 86
(James Given) *hld up: pushed along over 2f out: hdwy over 1f out: r.o: nt trble wnr* **9/2**[2]

5065 **3** 2 ½ **Opus Maximus (IRE)**[10] 299 7-9-0 77 TomEaves 9 79
(Conor Dore) *hld up: hdwy and nt clr run over 1f out: r.o to go 3rd towards fin: nt rch ldrs* **8/1**

-202 **4** *nk* **The Lock Master (IRE)**[11] 285 5-9-2 79 NeilChalmers 8 80
(Michael Appleby) *sn pushed along in rr: rdn over 2f out: r.o ins fnl f: nrst fin* **10/1**

0-11 **5** *hd* **Aquarian Spirit**[10] 302 5-8-9 77 ShaneBKelly(5) 4 78
(Richard Fahey) *awkward leaving stalls: sn chsng ldrs: rdn and hung lft over 1f out: styd on same pce* **7/1**[3]

1-01 **6** 3 **Archie Rice (USA)**[16] 216 6-9-3 80 JamieSpencer 7 74
(Tom Keddy) *prom: chsd ldr over 7f out tl led over 2f out: rdn and hdd over 1f out: wknd ins fnl f* **11/4**[1]

1- **7** 1 ¼ **Son Vida (IRE)**[389] 121 4-9-5 82 SamHitchcott 2 74
(Mark Johnston) *led: rdn and hdd over 2f out: wknd over 1f out* **7/1**[3]

00-4 **8** 1 **Georgebernardshaw (IRE)**[26] 103 7-9-1 78 AdamKirby 5 68
(Richard Guest) *prom: rdn over 2f out: wknd over 1f out* **28/1**

-000 **9** 3 ¼ **Honey Of A Kitten (USA)**[11] 280 4-8-12 75 (v[1]) JimmyFortune 10 58
(David Evans) *hld up: hdwy over 3f out: wknd wl over 1f out* **12/1**

2m 2.45s (0.75) **Going Correction** +0.25s/f (Slow) **9** Ran SP% **112.3**
Speed ratings (Par 105): **106,103,101,101,101 98,97,96,93**
toteswingers: 1&2 £7.00, 1&3 £8.60, 2&3 £6.70. CSF £42.35 CT £296.40 TOTE £9.30: £3.40, £3.00, £3.00; EX 39.20 Trifecta £263.90 Pool: £938.18 - 2.63 winning units..

Owner Mrs Emma Raffan **Bred** Mark Commins **Trained** Exning, Suffolk

FOCUS
The going was changed to standard to slow before this race. It was just a fair contest.

433 BET AND WATCH AT BLUESQ.COM H'CAP 1m 5f 194y(P)
3:45 (3:47) (Class 5) (0-70,70) 4-Y-0+ **£2,264** (£673; £336; £168) **Stalls** Low

Form RPR

000- **1** **Face Value**[15] 238 4-8-12 61 JimmyFortune 6 73+
(Gordon Elliott, Ire) *chsd ldrs: wnt 2nd over 3f out: led over 1f out: rdn and edgd rt ins fnl f: styd on strly* **7/4**[1]

6-22 **2** 3 ½ **Maison Brillet (IRE)**[15] 221 5-9-7 68 (p) RyanClark(3) 5 75
(Clive Drew) *hld up: hdwy 4f out: rdn and ev ch over 1f out: styd on same pce ins fnl f* **8/1**

-613 **3** 4 ½ **Mount Abora (IRE)**[5] 363 5-9-12 70 JamieSpencer 7 71
(Ian Williams) *hld up: hdwy over 2f out: rdn over 1f out: edgd lft and wknd ins fnl f* **11/2**[3]

21-5 **4** ¾ **Thundering Home**[22] 150 5-9-8 66 (t) DaneO'Neill 1 66
(George Baker) *chsd ldrs: rdn over 2f out: wknd ins fnl f* **9/2**[2]

0-00 **5** ¾ **Bilidn**[11] 281 4-8-8 57 ChrisCatlin 4 56
(Noel Quinlan) *hld up: rdn over 3f out: nvr trbld ldrs* **40/1**

200- **6** *nk* **Prince Freddie**[84] 3364 4-9-4 67 RussKennemore 3 65
(Philip Kirby) *chsd ldr tl led 5f out: rdn and hdd over 1f out: wknd fnl f* **25/1**

062- **7** 14 **Mr Plod**[93] 7254 7-8-13 57 (p) TomEaves 2 36
(Andrew Reid) *prom: lost pl 4f out: nt clr run over 2f out: sn rdn: hung lft and wknd* **15/2**

20-6 **8** 27 **Penangdouble O One**[8] 332 5-9-12 70 (tp) PhillipMakin 8
(Alex Hales) *led 9f: rdn and wknd over 2f out* **7/1**

3m 10.08s (4.08) **Going Correction** +0.25s/f (Slow)
WFA 4 from 5yo+ 5lb **8** Ran SP% **111.6**
Speed ratings (Par 103): **98,96,93,93,92 92,84,68**
toteswingers: 1&2 £3.20, 1&3 £3.60, 2&3 £3.60. CSF £15.79 CT £61.62 TOTE £2.60: £1.40, £2.60, £2.30; EX 20.00 Trifecta £57.00 Pool: £941.38 - 12.22 winning units..

Owner Sean F Gallagher **Bred** Biddestone Stud **Trained** Trim, Co Meath

FOCUS
The meeting was abandoned after this race as conditions were forecast to deteriorate. This was just a modest stayers' event and an easy enough success for the solidly supported Irish raider.

434 BLUE SQUARE BET CLAIMING STKS 1m 4f 50y(P)
() (Class 6) 4-Y-0+ £

435 FOLLOW US ON TWITTER @BLUESQ MEDIAN AUCTION MAIDEN STKS 5f 216y(P)
() (Class 6) 3-Y-0 £

436 PLAY BLACKJACK AT BLUESQ.COM H'CAP 1m 141y(P)
() (Class 6) (0-65,) 4-Y-0+ £

T/Plt: £19.60 to a £1 stake. Pool: £116,966.92 - 4,353.17 winning tickets. T/Qpdt: £5.30 to a £1 stake. Pool: £7,510.70 - 1,040.53 winning tickets. CR

373 KEMPTON (A.W) (R-H)
Sunday, February 5
437 Meeting Abandoned - snow

ST MORITZ (R-H)
Sunday, February 5
OFFICIAL GOING: Snow: frozen

443a GRAND PRIX GUARDAVAL IMMOBILIEN (CONDITIONS) (4YO+) (SNOW) 1m 1f
1:15 (1:30) 4-Y-0+
£5,753 (£2,876; £2,054; £1,369; £684; £410)

RPR

1 **Earl Of Winds (GER)**[469] 7-9-2 0 StephaneLaurent 7 88
(P Schaerer, Switzerland) **18/1**

2 1 ½ **Winterwind (IRE)**[40] 7-9-6 0 GeorgBocskai 11 89
(Carmen Bocskai, Switzerland) **58/10**

3 1 **The Bells O Peover**[128] 6497 4-8-13 0 (b) FrannyNorton 9 80
(Mark Johnston) *midfield on outer: impr to trck ldrs over 2f out: rdn to chal on turn into st: stl ev ch tl wl ins fnl f: hld cl home* **131/10**

4 2 **Pouvoir Absolu**[122] 6661 7-9-2 0 (b) FilipMinarik 2 79
(P Schaerer, Switzerland) **99/10**

5 *nk* **African Art (USA)**[350] 629 6-9-4 0 FreddyDiFede 12 80
(P Schaerer, Switzerland) **149/10**

6 4 **Mascarpone (GER)**[350] 628 8-9-0 0 RobertHavlin 4 68
(M Weiss, Switzerland) **51/10**[3]

7 ½ **Close To Heaven (GER)**[46] 5-9-4 0 EPedroza 3 71
(A Trybuhl, Germany) **145/10**

8 **Pont Des Arts (FR)**[323] 920 8-9-4 0 FredericSpanu 10
(A Schaerer, Switzerland) **47/10**[2]

9 **Letty**[117] 6783 5-8-10 0 NicolPolli 8
(A Klimscha Jr, Hungary) **156/10**

10 **Song Of Victory (GER)**[364] 442 8-9-0 0 (p) SteveDrowne 1
(M Weiss, Switzerland) **171/10**

11 **Licence To Till (USA)**[8] 354 5-9-4 0 JoeFanning 5
(Mark Johnston) *disp ld: hdd over 4f out: rdn over 3f out: wknd: eased whn btn* **11/10**[1]

12 **Calypso Magic (IRE)**[24] 131 4-8-13 0 MiguelLopez 6
(Linda Jewell) *midfield on inner: rdn and wknd over 4f out: t.o* **31/1**

1m 55.7s (115.70) **12** Ran SP% **145.2**
PARI-MUTUEL (all including 1 chf stakes): WIN 19.00; PLACE 3.30, 2.00, 3.80.
Owner Stall Allegra Racing Club **Bred** Hannes K Gutschow **Trained** Switzerland

444a GRAND PRIX AMERICAN AIRLINES (CONDITIONS) (4YO+) (SNOW) 1m
1:45 (2:10) 4-Y-0+
£4,315 (£2,157; £1,541; £1,027; £513; £308)

RPR

1 **Ziking (FR)**[311] 7-9-11 0 FredericSpanu 4 74
(A Schaerer, Switzerland) **18/5**[2]

2 *nk* **Devineur (FR)**[114] 4-9-8 0 MiguelLopez 2 70
(A Schaerer, Switzerland) **117/10**

3 3 **Sweet Venture (FR)**[350] 627 10-9-13 0 RobertHavlin 9 68
(M Weiss, Switzerland) **17/10**[1]

4 2 **Buddhist Monk**[728] 461 7-8-5 0 TimBurgin 3 42
(Dagmar Geissmann, Switzerland) **59/10**

5 2 ½ **Halling River (IRE)**[595] 5-9-4 0 SteveDrowne 5 49
(M Weiss, Switzerland) **47/10**[3]

6 ½ **Newton Circus**[842] 6819 5-9-6 0 StephaneLaurent 8 50
(K Klein, Switzerland) **10/1**

7 3 ½ **Niya (FR)** 5-8-9 0 FilipMinarik 6 31
(P Schaerer, Switzerland) **129/10**

8 **Lignon's Hero (BRZ)**[161] 7-9-0 0 EPedroza 1 36
(J D Hillis, Germany) **96/10**

9 **Spirit Of Xaar (IRE)**[29] 90 6-9-0 0 JoeFanning 7 36
(Linda Jewell) *a bhd: rdn over 2f out: qckly btn: eased ins fnl f* **31/5**

1m 42.5s (102.50) **9** Ran SP% **138.3**
PARI-MUTUEL (all including 1 chf stakes): WIN 3.60; PLACE 1.50, 2.20, 1.30.
Owner A Krauliger & V Krauliger **Bred** J Baud **Trained** Switzerland

[430]WOLVERHAMPTON (A.W) (L-H)

Monday, February 6

OFFICIAL GOING: Standard

Wind: Light behind Weather: Foggy

445 BET AT BLUE SQUARE H'CAP 5f 20y(P)

2:20 (2:20) (Class 6) (0-60,60) 4-Y-0+ **£1,704** (£503; £251) **Stalls** Low

Form RPR

24-0 **1** **Novabridge**[31] 59 4-9-7 **60**....(b) AdamKirby 5 71
(Neil Mulholland) *mde all: clr over 1f out: drvn out* **3/1**[1]

22-1 **2** *2* **Argentine (IRE)**[35] 8 8-9-5 **58**....(b) TomEaves 2 62
(Ian Semple) *s.i.s: hld up: hdwy over 1f out: rdn to go 2nd ins fnl f: r.o: no ch w wnr* **5/1**[2]

54-6 **3** *1 ½* **Dorothy's Dancing (IRE)**[10] 320 4-9-2 **55**.... FergusSweeney 1 54
(Gary Moore) *hld up: hdwy and nt clr run over 1f out: swtchd lft: r.o: nrst fin* **6/1**[3]

3-22 **4** *1 ¼* **Canadian Danehill (IRE)**[17] 227 10-8-4 **50**....(e) JakePayne(7) 8 44
(Robert Cowell) *prom: pushed along to chse wnr 1/2-way: styd on same pce fnl f* **8/1**

00-4 **5** *shd* **Rio's Girl**[17] 227 5-8-9 **48**....(b) BarryMcHugh 6 42
(Tony Coyle) *chsd ldrs: rdn over 1f out: styd on same pce fnl f* **12/1**

006- **6** *shd* **Crimson Queen**[40] 7896 5-9-4 **60**....(b) DaleSwift(3) 3 53
(Roy Brotherton) *mid-div: sn pushed along: nvr trbld ldrs* **9/1**

0-03 **7** *hd* **Overwhelm**[10] 320 4-9-4 **57**....(t) LukeMorris 10 50
(Andrew Reid) *s.i.s: outpcd: swtchd rt and hdwy over 1f out: nt rch ldrs* **8/1**

50-0 **8** *1 ¼* **Take Root**[32] 41 4-9-0 **60**....(p) JackDuern(7) 4 48
(Reg Hollinshead) *s.i.s: hdwy 1/2-way: no ex fnl f* **40/1**

0-54 **9** *8* **Decider (USA)**[13] 277 9-8-13 **59**....(v) DarrenEgan(7) 11 18
(Ronald Harris) *chsd ldrs: rdn 1/2-way: wknd over 1f out* **14/1**

000- **10** *2 ¾* **Lady Brookie**[50] 7812 4-9-2 **55**.... RobbieFitzpatrick 7
(Peter Grayson) *hood removed late and s.s: outpcd* **100/1**

43-0 **11** *20* **Tancred Spirit**[35] 8 4-8-7 **46**....(p) JoeFanning 9
(Paul Midgley) *chsd ldrs: rdn 1/2-way: wknd wl over 1f out: eased* **12/1**

1m 2.67s (0.37) **Going Correction** +0.20s/f (Slow) **11** Ran SP% **113.7**

Speed ratings (Par 101): **105,101,99,97,97 97,96,94,81,77 45**

Tote Swingers: 1&2 £4.30, 1&3 £5.10, 2&3 £3.80 CSF £16.59 CT £82.98 TOTE £4.40: £1.70, £1.50, £2.50; EX 22.30 Trifecta £123.80 Pool: £667.57 - 3.99 winning units..

Owner Dajam Ltd **Bred** Bishopswood Bloodstock & Trickledown Stud **Trained** Limpley Stoke, Wilts

FOCUS

Snow on the track meant there was a morning inspection, but while racing got the go-ahead, viewing was restricted by fog throughout the day. This was just a moderate sprint handicap. The winner's best form since he was a 2yo.

Lady Brookie Official explanation: jockey said he was slow to remove blindfold as it had become trapped in the bridle

446 RACING EXCELLENCE ALL WEATHER "HANDS AND HEELS" APPRENTICE SERIES H'CAP 1m 5f 194y(P)

2:50 (2:50) (Class 6) (0-60,58) 4-Y-0+ **£1,704** (£503; £251) **Stalls** Low

Form RPR

20-3 **1** **Vertueux (FR)**[12] 303 7-9-9 **57**.... GeorgeDowning 5 65
(Tony Carroll) *a.p: pushed along over 4f out: chsd ldr over 2f out: led ins fnl f: styd on* **5/2**[1]

4-56 **2** *1 ¾* **Corvette**[14] 271 4-9-0 **53**.... JackDuern 7 58
(Michael Appleby) *hld up: hdwy 8f out: led wl over 3f out: pushed along over 1f out: hdd and unable qck ins fnl f* **6/1**

6-66 **3** *2 ¼* **Cloudy Start**[13] 276 6-9-7 **58**.... ThomasGarner(3) 6 60
(Jamie Osborne) *hld up: pushed along over 3f out: hdwy and swtchd lft over 1f out: styd on: wnt 3rd post: nt rch ldrs* **11/4**[2]

0000 **4** *hd* **Nesnaas (USA)**[3] 395 11-8-11 **45**.... NicoleNordblad 2 47
(Alastair Lidderdale) *hld up: hdwy over 1f out: pushed along and hung lft ins fnl f: styd on: nt rch ldrs* **66/1**

05-6 **5** *6* **In The Long Grass (IRE)**[13] 278 4-8-1 **45**....(v[1]) DanielCremin(5) 3 39
(Jim Boyle) *chsd ldr 9f: pushed along over 3f out: wknd fnl f* **9/1**

326/ **6** *7* **Bluecrop Boy**[35] 5885 8-8-8 **45**....(be) JoshBaudains(3) 8 29
(Dominic Ffrench Davis) *led: hdd wl over 3f out: sn pushed along: wknd over 1f out* **20/1**

/06- **7** *4 ½* **Pobs Trophy**[19] 4198 5-8-11 **45**....(p) JasonHart 4 23
(Richard Guest) *chsd ldrs: pushed along over 3f out: wknd 2f out* **16/1**

2-55 **8** *8* **Lucky Diva**[4] 392 5-9-7 **55**....(p) JakePayne 1 21
(Bill Turner) *prom: pushed along over 3f out: wknd over 2f out* **4/1**[3]

3m 8.73s (2.73) **Going Correction** +0.20s/f (Slow)

WFA 4 from 5yo+ 5lb **8** Ran SP% **111.7**

Speed ratings (Par 101): **100,99,97,97,94 90,87,83**

Tote Swingers: 1&2 not won, 1&3 not won, 2&3 not won. CSF £17.09 CT £41.74 TOTE £3.90: £1.10, £2.20, £1.30; EX 20.10 Trifecta £54.20 Pool: £581.27 - 7.93 winning units..

Owner John Rutter **Bred** Roger Baudouin **Trained** Cropthorne, Worcs

FOCUS

Again, viewing was limited owing to fog. This was a really moderate race and it isn't hard to have doubts over the form.

Pobs Trophy Official explanation: jockey said gelding lost its action

Lucky Diva Official explanation: trainer's rep said race came too quickly for the mare

447 ENJOY THE PUNTERS PACKAGE GROUP OFFER (S) STKS 7f 32y(P)

3:25 (3:25) (Class 6) 3-Y-0+ **£1,704** (£503; £251) **Stalls** High

Form RPR

-125 **1** **Faithful Ruler (USA)**[3] 402 8-9-7 75....(p) DarrenEgan(7) 6 75
(Ronald Harris) *hld up: hdwy over 1f out: rdn to ld wl ins fnl f: edgd lft nr fin* **12/1**

3-00 **2** *¾* **Cyflymder (IRE)**[27] 115 6-9-10 60.... JimmyFortune 2 69
(David C Griffiths) *chsd ldrs: pushed along over 2f out: rdn and ev ch ins fnl f: r.o* **12/1**

502- **3** *½* **Zomerlust**[128] 6541 10-9-7 82....(v) MichaelO'Connell(3) 4 68
(John Quinn) *chsd ldr: led over 5f out: rdn over 1f out: hdd wl ins fnl f* **11/4**[1]

2-02 **4** *nk* **One Way Or Another (AUS)**[21] 190 9-10-0 76....(b) LukeMorris 5 71
(David Evans) *hld up in tch: carried rt over 1f out: sn rdn: kpt on* **11/4**[1]

52-4 **5** *nse* **Striker Torres (IRE)**[7] 359 6-9-7 69.... DaleSwift(3) 1 67
(Geoffrey Oldroyd) *led: hdd over 5f out: chsd ldr: rdn and ev ch fr over 1f out: unable qck wl ins fnl f* **7/2**[2]

4323 **6** *5* **Pilgrim Dancer (IRE)**[6] 368 5-9-10 50....(p) BarryMcHugh 7 53
(Tony Coyle) *s.i.s: hld up: rdn over 2f out: n.d* **25/1**

6-24 **7** *18* **Unlimited**[14] 268 10-9-10 75.... DavidProbert 3
(Tony Carroll) *hld up in tch: rdn and wknd over 2f out* **7/1**[3]

1m 30.66s (1.06) **Going Correction** +0.20s/f (Slow) **7** Ran SP% **107.3**

Speed ratings (Par 101): **101,100,99,99,99 93,72**

Tote Swingers: 1&2 £8.60, 1&3 £6.20, 2&3 £5.60 CSF £121.86 TOTE £11.60: £4.30, £8.70; EX 83.30.There was no bid for the winner. Striker Torres was claimed by Mr I. W. McInnes for £6,000.

Owner Ridge House Stables Ltd **Bred** WinStar Farm LLC **Trained** Earlswood, Monmouths

FOCUS

The fog hadn't gone anywhere. A modest seller in which a few of the more likely types underperformed, and the time was 0.56sec slower than the following Class 5 handicap. The runner-up is the key to this form.

Faithful Ruler(USA) Official explanation: trainer said, regarding apparent improvement in form, that the gelding was better suited by having the run of the race.

Unlimited Official explanation: jockey said gelding ran flat

448 BET AT BLUE SQUARE ON YOUR MOBILE H'CAP 7f 32y(P)

3:55 (3:56) (Class 5) (0-75,73) 4-Y-0+ **£2,264** (£673; £336; £168) **Stalls** High

Form RPR

5-43 **1** **Trojan Rocket (IRE)**[15] 262 4-8-7 **66**.... DarrenEgan(7) 5 73
(George Prodromou) *hld up: hdwy over 1f out: rdn to ld and edgd lft towards fin* **5/2**[1]

5-24 **2** *½* **Legal Legacy**[5] 378 6-9-7 **73**.... AndrewMullen 7 79
(David C Griffiths) *s.i.s: hld up: hdwy over 1f out: sn rdn: r.o* **4/1**[2]

450- **3** *hd* **Khajaaly (IRE)**[38] 7928 5-9-6 **72**.... LukeMorris 4 77
(Julia Feilden) *trckd ldrs: rdn ins fnl f: r.o* **10/1**

234- **4** *hd* **I Confess**[49] 7823 7-9-7 **73**....(b) JoeFanning 3 78
(Geoffrey Harker) *led: edgd rt over 1f out: sn rdn: hdd towards fin* **6/1**

0-62 **5** *2 ¼* **Riverdale (IRE)**[4] 387 4-9-0 **69**.... DaleSwift(3) 1 67
(Nigel Tinkler) *chsd ldr 1f: remained handy: pushed along to take 2nd again 2f out: rdn over 1f out: no ex ins fnl f* **9/1**

-231 **6** *2* **Needwood Ridge**[10] 329 5-8-11 **68**....(bt) RaulDaSilva(5) 6 61
(Frank Sheridan) *chsd ldrs: rdn over 2f out: no ex fnl f* **4/1**[2]

0-00 **7** *9* **Ryedale Dancer (IRE)**[13] 287 4-8-2 **59** oh1....(t) CharlesEddery(5) 8 28
(Richard Guest) *s.i.s: outpcd: bhd 4f out* **50/1**

62-4 **8** *6* **Without Prejudice (USA)**[3] 403 7-9-2 **68**....(b[1]) PaddyAspell 2 21
(Michael Easterby) *pushed along to chse ldr 6f out tl rdn over 2f out: wknd over 1f out* **5/1**[3]

1m 30.1s (0.50) **Going Correction** +0.20s/f (Slow) **8** Ran SP% **120.6**

Speed ratings (Par 103): **105,104,104,103,101 99,88,81**

Tote Swingers: 1&2 £4.10, 1&3 £8.30, 2&3 £5.70 CSF £13.52 CT £87.69 TOTE £3.60: £1.10, £1.80, £3.50; EX 18.70 Trifecta £230.20 Pool: £858.73 - 2.76 winning units..

Owner G D J Linder **Bred** J G F Fox **Trained** East Harling, Norfolk

FOCUS

Misty conditions continued to restrict viewing, but it was clear that those held up were favoured. The time was 0.56sec quicker than the earlier seller. Straightforward form.

449 SPONSOR A RACE BY CALLING 01902 390000 CLAIMING STKS 1m 141y(P)

4:30 (4:32) (Class 6) 4-Y-0+ **£1,704** (£503; £251) **Stalls** Low

Form RPR

214- **1** **Violent Velocity (IRE)**[101] 7146 9-8-12 70.... MichaelO'Connell(3) 4 73
(John Quinn) *a.p: chsd ldr over 1f out: led ins fnl f: r.o wl* **7/2**[2]

0-60 **2** *1 ½* **Ahlawy (IRE)**[10] 330 9-8-7 59....(t) RaulDaSilva(5) 5 67
(Frank Sheridan) *chsd ldr tl led over 2f out: rdn over 1f out: hdd and unable qck ins fnl f* **12/1**

4141 **3** *3 ¾* **Spinning Ridge (IRE)**[10] 330 7-9-2 72....(v) LukeMorris 3 62
(Ronald Harris) *hld up: hdwy over 1f out: sn rdn: styd on same pce ins fnl f* **10/11**[1]

105- **4** *2 ¾* **Cheers Buddy (IRE)**[58] 7710 4-8-13 75.... JimmyFortune 1 53
(David C Griffiths) *chsd ldrs: rdn over 1f out: wknd fnl f* **16/1**

-410 **5** *6* **Petomic (IRE)**[10] 333 7-8-11 60....(p) HayleyTurner 2 37
(Richard Guest) *led: rdn and hdd over 2f out: wknd over 1f out* **5/1**[3]

054- **6** *2 ¼* **Dazakhee**[55] 7745 5-8-9 62.... RobbieFitzpatrick 6 30
(Jo Hughes) *dwlt: hld up: pushed along and hung lft over 3f out: a in rr* **10/1**

1m 51.91s (1.41) **Going Correction** +0.20s/f (Slow) **6** Ran SP% **113.9**

Speed ratings (Par 101): **101,99,96,93,88 86**

Tote Swingers: 1&2 £5.10, 1&3 £1.20, 2&3 £3.80 CSF £41.53 TOTE £5.40: £3.10, £6.70; EX 36.20.

Owner Mrs S Quinn **Bred** Miss Jill Finegan **Trained** Settrington, N Yorks

FOCUS

Visibility was now poor owing to the persistent fog. Just a modest claimer, although the time was 1.58sec quicker than the following Class 6 handicap. The time was slow and the unpredictable runner-up is the key to the form.

450 GREAT OFFERS AT WOLVERHAMPTON-RACECOURSE.CO.UK H'CAP 1m 141y(P)

5:00 (5:00) (Class 6) (0-55,61) 4-Y-0+ **£1,704** (£503; £251) **Stalls** Low

Form RPR

-351 **1** **Warden Bond**[10] 333 4-9-1 **54**....(p) MartinLane 6 63
(William Stone) *a.p: rdn to ld 1f out: hdd ins fnl f: rallied to ld towards fin* **9/2**[2]

-001 **2** *nk* **Valley Tiger**[7] 361 4-9-8 **61** 6ex.... JamieSpencer 7 69
(Richard Fahey) *hld up: hdwy over 1f out: rdn to ld ins fnl f: edgd lft: hdd towards fin* **5/2**[1]

0-03 **3** *1 ¾* **Just Timmy Marcus**[14] 274 6-9-1 **54**....(v) RussKennemore 3 58
(Brian Baugh) *s.i.s: hld up: hdwy over 1f out: r.o to go 3rd nr fin: nt rch ldrs* **5/1**[3]

-123 **4** *hd* **Look For Love**[2] 430 4-8-8 **54**....(e) JackDuern(7) 11 58
(Reg Hollinshead) *chsd ldr tl led over 2f out: rdn and hdd over 1f out: styd on same pce ins fnl f: lost 3rd nr fin* **8/1**

00-0 **5** *nk* **Dubonny**[17] 226 5-8-2 **46** oh1....(t) RaulDaSilva(5) 5 49
(Frank Sheridan) *chsd ldrs: rdn and swtchd lft over 1f out: styd on* **14/1**

0000 **6** *1* **Vitznau (IRE)**[7] 361 8-9-2 **55**....(bt) FergusSweeney 8 56
(Alastair Lidderdale) *hld up: rdn over 1f out: r.o ins fnl f: nt rch ldrs* **13/2**

30-0 **7** *¾* **Carr Hall (IRE)**[15] 265 9-9-1 **54**.... LukeMorris 9 53
(Tony Carroll) *hld up: rdn over 1f out: r.o ins fnl f: nrst fin* **40/1**

20-6 **8** *½* **Stamp Duty (IRE)**[14] 274 4-9-1 **54**.... DuranFentiman 10 52
(Suzzanne France) *prom: rdn to ld over 1f out: sn hdd: no ex ins fnl f* **16/1**

-042 **9** *4* **Bentley**[14] 274 8-8-8 **52**....(p) JemmaMarshall(5) 1 41
(Brian Baugh) *led: rdn and hdd over 2f out: wknd over 1f out* **10/1**

0-00 **10** *4 ½* **Lytham (IRE)**[15] 265 11-8-10 **52**.... MichaelO'Connell(3) 2 31
(Tony Carroll) *s.i.s: hld up: rdn over 3f out: a in rr* **50/1**

66-6 **11** *1 1/4* **Bunkered Again**[11] [307] 5-8-4 **46** oh1......................(tp) SimonPearce(3) 4 22
(Jeremy Gask) *prom: rdn over 2f out: wknd over 1f out* **28/1**
1m 53.49s (2.99) **Going Correction** +0.20s/f (Slow) **11** Ran SP% **117.4**
Speed ratings (Par 101): **94,93,92,92,91 90,90,89,86,82 81**
Tote Swingers: 1&2 £3.30, 1&3 £3.70, 2&3 £4.60 CSF £15.87 CT £58.71 TOTE £4.90: £1.50, £1.80, £2.70; EX 16.90 Trifecta £39.00 Pool: £773.26 - 14.65 winning units..
Owner J A Ross & Miss C Scott **Bred** Park Farm Racing **Trained** West Wickham, Cambs

FOCUS
Fog again severely limited viewing. The time was 1.58sec slower than the earlier claimer and the first two both improved a little again.

451 THE BLACK COUNTRY'S ONLY RACECOURSE MAIDEN STKS 1m 4f 50y(P)
5:30 (5:30) (Class 5) 4-Y-0+ **£2,264** (£673; £336; £168) **Stalls** Low

Form RPR
1 **Belle Josephine** 4-8-12 0.. JoeFanning 2 69+
(Mark Johnston) *s.i.s: hld ujp: hdwy to chse ldr 8f out: rn green and pushed along over 6f out: led over 3f out: sn rdn: hdd over 1f out: rallied to ld ins fnl f: styd on* **2/1**[2]
2 **2** *3/4* **Red Shuttle**[12] [300] 5-9-6 0..(t) AdamKirby 5 73
(Noel Quinlan) *hld up: hdwy over 4f out: led over 1f out: sn shkn up: rdn and hdd ins fnl f: styd on same pce* **4/7**[1]
3 *3 3/4* **Mister Fizz**[76] 4-8-12 0.. RaulDaSilva(5) 4 67
(Andrew Price) *chsd ldr over 4f: remained handy: rdn over 1f out: styd on same pce fnl f* **40/1**
600 **4** *8* **It's Me And You**[3] [404] 4-9-3 0.. PaddyAspell 1 54?
(Michael Easterby) *chsd ldrs: lost pl over 4f out: rdn over 2f out: wknd wl over 1f out* **100/1**
0/6 **5** *49* **Red Soles (IRE)**[14] [273] 4-8-12 0.. WilliamCarson 6
(Charles Hills) *sn led: rdn and hdd over 3f out: wknd 2f out: t.o* **10/1**[3]
2m 45.44s (4.34) **Going Correction** +0.20s/f (Slow)
WFA 4 from 5yo+ 3lb **5** Ran SP% **109.5**
Speed ratings (Par 103): **93,92,90,84,52**
CSF £3.43 TOTE £3.20: £1.50, £1.10; EX 3.50.
Owner Sheikh Hamdan Bin Mohammed Al Maktoum **Bred** Meon Valley Stud **Trained** Middleham Moor, N Yorks

FOCUS
The runners disappeared into the mist at various stages, but conditions were not as bad as in some earlier races. Not much strength in depth to this maiden, but Red Shuttle had shown ability when runner-up on his Flat debut and helps give the form some substance. The pace was slow until increasing on the final circuit and the final time was 2.74secs slower than the following Class 6 handicap. The bare form is very modest but the winner should do better.

452 PLAY ROULETTE AT BLUESQ.COM/CASINO H'CAP 1m 4f 50y(P)
6:00 (6:00) (Class 6) (0-65,67) 4-Y-0+ **£1,704** (£503; £251) **Stalls** Low

Form RPR
051- **1** **Illustrious Forest**[38] [7931] 4-9-1 **65**........................ MichaelO'Connell(3) 7 78+
(John Mackie) *chsd ldr tl led 4f out: clr whn rdn and hung rt over 1f out: styd on* **3/1**[2]
006- **2** *3/4* **Royal Alcor (IRE)**[40] [7903] 5-9-3 **61**.........................(b) FrankieMcDonald 5 70
(Alastair Lidderdale) *s.i.s: hld up: hdwy over 2f out: rdn to chse wnr ins fnl f: r.o* **20/1**
1P-0 **3** *2 3/4* **War Of The Roses (IRE)**[21] [192] 9-9-7 **65**......................... TomEaves 8 70
(Roy Brotherton) *hld up in tch: rdn over 1f out: styd on same pce ins fnl f* **50/1**
00-1 **4** *nk* **Face Value**[2] [433] 4-9-6 **67** 6ex.. LiamKeniry 11 72
(Gordon Elliott, Ire) *chsd ldrs: rdn over 2f out: styd on same pce fnl f* **6/4**[1]
3-43 **5** *3/4* **Land Hawk (IRE)**[17] [224] 6-8-11 **58**........................... SimonPearce(3) 10 61
(Lydia Pearce) *hld up: hdwy over 1f out: nt rch ldrs* **9/1**
-440 **6** *hd* **Striding Edge (IRE)**[3] [400] 6-8-7 **58**........................ NicoleNordblad(7) 4 61
(Hans Adielsson) *prom: nt clr run and lost pl over 2f out: swtchd lft and styd on ins fnl f* **10/1**
0/6- **7** *3 1/2* **Akula (IRE)**[65] [7107] 5-8-12 **56**.. JoeFanning 2 55+
(Mark H Tompkins) *prom: rdn over 2f out: wknd and eased fnl f* **11/2**[3]
540- **8** *3 1/2* **Blackstone Vegas**[215] [3738] 6-8-13 **60**........................... DaleSwift(3) 9 52
(Derek Shaw) *s.i.s: hld up: rdn and wknd over 2f out* **14/1**
0-31 **9** *8* **Ay Tay Tate (IRE)**[17] [222] 6-9-7 **65**.................................(p) AdamKirby 3 44
(David C Griffiths) *led 8f: rdn and wknd over 2f out* **16/1**
/00- **10** *30* **Joyously**[53] [7775] 4-8-7 **54**.. WilliamCarson 1
(Richard Guest) *hld up: rdn 5f out: wknd over 2f out: t.o* **50/1**
2m 42.7s (1.60) **Going Correction** +0.20s/f (Slow)
WFA 4 from 5yo+ 3lb **10** Ran SP% **120.7**
Speed ratings (Par 101): **102,101,99,99,98 98,96,94,88,68**
Tote Swingers: 1&2 £13.40, 1&3 £31.20, 2&3 £44.00 CSF £64.77 CT £2506.78 TOTE £4.30: £1.30, £4.50, £6.70; EX 60.40 Trifecta £108.80 Pool: £798.45 - 5.43 winning units..
Owner Derbyshire Racing VII **Bred** Norman A Blyth **Trained** Church Broughton , Derbys

FOCUS
The fog had finally lifted and this race went to a horse who looks above average for the level and a bit better than this bare form. The race was sound run and the form is pretty solid.
T/Jkpt: Part won. £25,000.00 to a £1 stake. Pool: £25,000.00 - 0.50 winning tickets. T/Plt: £720.10 to a £1 stake. Pool: £119,997.13 - 115.56 winning tickets. T/Qpdt: £128.00 to a £1 stake. Pool: £8,528.64 - 49.30 winning tickets. CR

380 SOUTHWELL (L-H)
Tuesday, February 7

OFFICIAL GOING: Slow
Wind: Virtually nil Weather: Overcast

453 PLACE ONLY BETTING AT BLUESQ.COM AMATEUR RIDERS' H'CAP (DIV I) 1m 3f (F)
1:15 (1:15) (Class 6) (0-52,56) 4-Y-0+ **£1,646** (£506; £253) **Stalls** Low

Form RPR
000- **1** **Mustajed**[71] [7564] 11-10-7 **50**.....................................(b) MrPMillman(5) 12 62
(Rod Millman) *trckd ldrs: smooth hdwy over 3f out: led 2f out: rdn clr over 1f out: kpt on wl* **12/1**
4-04 **2** *5* **Carlton Scroop (FR)**[26] [130] 9-10-9 **52**.................(b) MissMBryant(5) 14 55
(Paddy Butler) *trckd ldrs on outer: hdwy over 3f out: rdn to chse wnr over 1f out: kpt on same pce fnl f* **12/1**
000- **3** *nk* **Revolving World (IRE)**[159] [5650] 9-10-3 **46** oh1....(t) MrAaronJames(5) 5 48
(Lee James) *s.i.s and bhd: hdwy on outer over 3f out: rdn to chse ldrs wl over 1f out: edgd lft and one pce ent fnl f* **14/1**
05-4 **4** *1 1/4* **Kingaroo (IRE)**[5] [381] 6-10-12 **50**.............................. MissSBrotherton 11 50
(Garry Woodward) *prom: effrt 3f out: rdn 2f out: one pce appr fnl f* **3/1**[1]
00-1 **5** *3/4* **Harrys Yer Man**[5] [390] 8-10-13 **56** 6ex........... MissBeckyBrisbourne(5) 3 55
(Mark Brisbourne) *hld up towards rr: stdy hdwy 5f out: chsd ldrs wl over 2f out: rdn wl over 1f out: sn no imp* **7/2**[2]
60-0 **6** *5* **Granny Anne (IRE)**[11] [333] 4-10-4 **51**........................(p) MrsRWilson(7) 8 41
(Paul D'Arcy) *chsd ldr: effrt and cl up 3f out: rdn and ev ch over 2f out: wknd wl over 1f out* **10/1**
444- **7** *2 1/2* **Sing Alana Sing**[221] [3596] 4-10-3 **48**..............................(t) PhilipPrince(5) 1 33
(Bill Turner) *towards rr: pushed along and bhd 7f out: sme late hdwy* **20/1**
000- **8** *2 1/4* **Tayarat (IRE)**[19] [6235] 7-10-2 **47**..............................(b) MissAliceMills(7) 13 28
(Michael Chapman) *chsd ldrs: rdn along over 4f out: sn outpcd* **33/1**
03-6 **9** *3/4* **Jay Jays Joy**[37] [7] 4-10-5 **52**.....................................(v) MissHDukes(7) 4 32
(Paul Midgley) *t.k.h: sn led: rdn along 3f out: hdd 2f out and wknd qckly* **10/1**
006- **10** *5* **Swords**[80] [7496] 10-10-1 **46** oh1.................................. MissSPeacock(7) 6 17
(Ray Peacock) *a towards rr* **33/1**
0420 **11** *19* **Yossi (IRE)**[5] [389] 8-10-9 **47**..(b) MrSWalker 9
(Richard Guest) *trckd ldrs on inner: hdwy over 4f out: rdn along wl over 3f out and sn wknd* **6/1**[3]
000/ **12** *5* **Lord Of The Wing**[162] 7-10-1 **46** oh1...................... MissKMargarson(7) 7
(Mrs J L Le Brocq, Jersey) *a in rr: bhd fnl 3f* **50/1**
00/ **13** *11* **Aegean Pride**[972] [2812] 7-10-1 **46** oh1................................ MrRHogg(7) 2
(Barry Murtagh) *a towards rr: bhd fnl 4f* **50/1**
005- **14** *24* **Fantastic Storm**[26] [5122] 5-10-3 **46** oh1...................(b[1]) MrSBushby(5) 10
(Robin Bastiman) *sn bhd: t.o fnl 3f* **40/1**
2m 32.58s (4.58) **Going Correction** +0.25s/f (Slow)
WFA 4 from 5yo+ 2lb **14** Ran SP% **118.7**
Speed ratings (Par 101): **93,89,89,88,87 84,82,80,80,76 62,58,50,33**
toteswingers:1&2:£15.50, 2&3:£23.70, 1&3:£35.00 CSF £136.76 CT £2036.25 TOTE £11.60: £5.00, £5.90, £5.80; EX 88.20 TRIFECTA Not won..
Owner Rod Millman Racing Club **Bred** Shadwell Estate Company Limited **Trained** Kentisbeare, Devon
■ Stewards' Enquiry : Philip Prince seven-day ban: used whip with excessive frequency when out of contention (tbn)

FOCUS
The track had been worked on all through the night and as a result the official going description was change to 'slow'. The winning rider in the opener said: "The ground is pretty deep and the kickback is desperate." The winner is rated to his latter 2011 form.

454 PLACE ONLY BETTING AT BLUESQ.COM AMATEUR RIDERS' H'CAP (DIV II) 1m 3f (F)
1:45 (1:45) (Class 6) (0-52,52) 4-Y-0+ **£1,646** (£506; £253) **Stalls** Low

Form RPR
645- **1** **Mister Frosty (IRE)**[75] [7527] 6-10-13 **51**..................... MrDHDunsdon 13 63
(George Prodromou) *hld up in midfield: stdy hdwy on outer 1/2-way: trckd ldrs over 3f out: effrt to ld wl over 1f out: sn rdn clr: styd on* **11/2**[2]
0206 **2** *6* **Miereveld**[7] [366] 5-10-7 **50**...................................(b) MrJohnWilley(5) 10 51
(Shaun Harris) *s.i.s and bhd: hdwy 4f out: rdn over 2f out: styd on strly appr fnl f: tk 2nd towards fin* **6/1**[3]
0-00 **3** *1/2* **Heading To First**[6] [379] 5-10-3 **46** oh1....................(p) MissMBryant(5) 3 46
(Paddy Butler) *towards rr: hdwy over 3f out: rdn to chse ldrs 2f out: kpt on same pce fnl f* **25/1**
40-0 **4** *nk* **Magnitude**[29] [105] 7-10-12 **50**.................................(v) MissSBrotherton 2 50
(Brian Baugh) *midfield: hdwy and in tch over 4f out: sn pushed along and sltly outpcd over 3f out: kpt on u.p fnl 2f: nrst fin* **10/1**
61-0 **5** *shd* **Dunaskin (IRE)**[7] [367] 12-10-8 **46**....................................(b) MrSWalker 8 46
(Richard Guest) *chsd ldrs: led after 1f and sn clr: rdn along and hdd 3f out: grad wknd* **6/1**[3]
45-4 **6** *1 1/4* **Phoenix Flame**[37] [7] 4-10-7 **52**..................................(vt) MrOGarner(5) 12 49
(Alan McCabe) *trckd ldrs: hdwy to chse ldr over 4f out: led 3f out: rdn and edgd lft over 2f out: hdd wl over 1f out and grad wknd* **7/1**
040- **7** *2* **Laura Land**[62] [7654] 6-10-3 **46**............................ MissBeckyBrisbourne(5) 9 40
(Mark Brisbourne) *trckd ldrs: hdwy 4f out: chsd ldng pair 3f out: rdn 2f out and grad wknd* **10/1**
0-06 **8** *2 3/4* **Raghdaan**[7] [367] 5-10-4 **47**.. PhilipPrince(5) 1 36
(Peter Hiatt) *led 1f: prom tl rdn along over 3f out and sn wknd* **12/1**
46-0 **9** *shd* **Dolly Colman (IRE)**[20] [200] 4-10-6 **46** oh1............... MissGAndrews 11 35
(Michael Blake) *hld up towards rr: hdwy 4f out: rdn to chse ldrs over 2f out: sn wknd* **10/1**
60-0 **10** *13* **Watchmaker**[25] [45] 9-10-3 **48**.. MrLMichael(7) 14 13
(Dai Williams) *a towards rr* **50/1**
00-0 **11** *2* **Noble Attitude**[28] [109] 6-10-1 **46** oh1........................(be[1]) MissLWilson(7) 5
(Julie Camacho) *a towards rr* **40/1**
005/ **12** *4 1/2* **Flynn's Island (IRE)**[948] [3614] 6-10-8 **46** oh1........ MissCarolineHurley 4
(Richard Ford) *t.k.h: chsd ldrs: rdn along over 4f out and sn wknd* **50/1**
000/ **13** *2 1/4* **Peak Seasons (IRE)**[300] [3218] 9-10-1 **46** oh1............ MissAliceMills(7) 7
(Michael Chapman) *prom: pushed along 1/2-way: sn wknd* **50/1**
000- **14** *3 3/4* **Apache Warrior**[236] [3088] 5-10-9 **52**.................................. MrNSlatter(5) 6
(David O'Meara) *trckd ldrs on inner: effrt over 3f out: sn rdn along and wknd* **9/2**[1]
2m 33.86s (5.86) **Going Correction** +0.25s/f (Slow)
WFA 4 from 5yo+ 2lb **14** Ran SP% **121.8**
Speed ratings (Par 101): **88,83,83,83,82 82,80,78,78,69 67,64,62,60**
toteswingers:1&2:£6.90, 2&3:£31.50, 1&3:£36.40 CSF £37.65 CT £767.12 TOTE £6.10: £2.40, £2.10, £10.90; EX 40.80 Trifecta £250.80 Part won. Pool: £338.99 - 0.20 winning units..
Owner Matt Bartram **Bred** Thomas McDonogh **Trained** East Harling, Norfolk
■ Stewards' Enquiry : Mr John Willey two-day ban: used whip with excessive frequency (tbn)

FOCUS
Again the pace seemed decent due to Dunaskin soon establishing a clear lead, but the winning time was 1.28 seconds slower than the first division. The wide-margin winner rates back to his best.

455 GOLF AND RACING AT SOUTHWELL H'CAP 5f (F)
2:15 (2:15) (Class 6) (0-60,60) 3-Y-O **£1,704** (£503; £251) **Stalls** High

Form RPR
10-5 **1** **Laura's Bairn**[37] [6] 3-9-5 **58**....................................(v) FrederikTylicki 9 69
(J R Jenkins) *qckly away: mde all: rdn and qckndd clr appr fnl f: kpt on strly* **10/1**
2-24 **2** *2* **Magilini (IRE)**[14] [283] 3-8-11 **50**...................................(b[1]) LeeNewman 1 54
(David Barron) *wnt rt s: chsd ldrs on outer and edgd rt after 1f: hdwy to chse wnr wl over 1f out: sn rdn: edgd rt and no imp fnl f* **9/2**[3]
61-5 **3** *1 3/4* **Claretintheblood (IRE)**[31] [86] 3-9-5 **58**..................... TonyHamilton 4 56
(Richard Fahey) *chsd ldrs: rdn along over 2f out: kpt on fnl f: nrst fin* **3/1**[1]
41-2 **4** *5* **Heidi's Delight (IRE)**[35] [25] 3-9-4 **57**............................(b) TomEaves 3 37
(Ann Duffield) *cl up: rdn 2f out: sn edgd rt and wknd* **3/1**[1]
400- **5** *1 1/4* **Chateau Lola**[39] [7925] 3-8-7 **46** oh1......................................(v) MartinLane 5 21
(Derek Shaw) *chsd ldrs: rdn along over 2f out: sn one pce* **50/1**

240- **6** 1 ¼ **Wish Again (IRE)**[106] 7059 3-8-12 **58**....................... ShirleyTeasdale(7) 6 29
(David Nicholls) *chsd ldrs: rdn along over 2f out: sn wknd* **4/1**[2]
000- **7** 14 **Brian's Best**[76] 7514 3-8-7 **46** oh1.................................. PJMcDonald 10
(Richard Ford) *a in rr: bhd fr 1/2-way* **50/1**
603- **8** 47 **Tuibama (IRE)**[189] 4648 3-9-2 **55**.................................. DanielTudhope 2
(Ben Haslam) *bmpd s: chsd ldrs whn hmpd: stmbld and lost action after 1f: sn eased and t.o* **8/1**

1m 1.7s (2.00) **Going Correction** +0.275s/f (Slow) **8** Ran SP% **112.3**
Speed ratings (Par 95): **95,91,89,81,79 77,54,**
toteswingers:1&2:£5.50, 2&3:£4.10, 1&3:£6.70 CSF £52.45 CT £169.38 TOTE £9.40: £3.20, £1.20, £1.30; EX 55.90 Trifecta £217.50 Pool: £893.62 - 3.04 winning units..
Owner Mark Goldstein **Bred** Greg Parsons **Trained** Royston, Herts
■ Stewards' Enquiry : Lee Newman five-day ban: used whip with excessive frequency (Feb 21-25)

FOCUS
A modest sprint handicap in which there was trouble after a furlong when the winner edged away to his left, causing a concertina effect which caused Tuibama to lose his footing and be effectively knocked out of the race. The form looks a bit above average for the grade.
Laura's Bairn Official explanation: trainer said regarding apparent improvement in form that the colt had been dropped back to a 5f trip and had benefited from a long break
Heidi's Delight(IRE) Official explanation: trainer said filly was struck into
Tuibama(IRE) Official explanation: jockey said gelding suffered interference in running and lost its action

456 SOUTHWELL GOLF CLUB MEMBERS (S) STKS 5f (F)
2:45 (2:45) (Class 6) 4-Y-0+ **£1,704** (£503; £251) **Stalls** High

Form RPR
3-31 **1** **Drawnfromthepast (IRE)**[18] 220 7-9-3 82................. JamieSpencer 5 76+
(Jamie Osborne) *trckd ldrs on bit: swtchd lft and hdwy over 1f out: shkn up to chal ent fnl f: qcknd wl to ld last 110yds* **4/6**[1]
2-12 **2** 1 ¾ **Argentine (IRE)**[1] 445 8-9-3 58.......................................(b) TomEaves 1 70
(Ian Semple) *dwlt and wnt lft s: smooth hdwy and cl up 1/2-way: led over 1f out: rdn and jnd ent fnl f: hdd and one pce last 110yds* **3/1**[2]
520- **3** 1 ½ **Spirit Of Coniston**[105] 7079 9-8-5 62.............................. NedCurtis(7) 3 60
(Paul Midgley) *led: rdn along and hdd over 1f out: sn edgd lft and one pce* **14/1**
26-5 **4** 7 **Griffin Point (IRE)**[14] 277 5-8-7 63.............................(p) DavidProbert 6 29
(William Muir) *cl up: rdn along 1/2-way: sn wknd* **11/2**[3]
300- **5** 5 **Patch Patch**[118] 6802 5-8-12 54.......................................(p) MartinLane 2
(Derek Shaw) *cl up: rdn along over 2f out: sn wknd* **50/1**
300- **6** nk **Tenancy (IRE)**[106] 7071 8-8-5 47............................. NatashaEaton(7) 7
(Shaun Harris) *dwlt: hdwy to chse ldrs after 2f: rdn along 1/2-way: sn edgd lft and wknd* **50/1**

1m 0.87s (1.17) **Going Correction** +0.275s/f (Slow) **6** Ran SP% **111.0**
Speed ratings (Par 101): **101,98,95,84,76 76**
toteswingers:1&2:£1.30, 2&3:£2.20, 1&3:£2.70 CSF £2.83 TOTE £1.60: £1.30, £2.00; EX 2.90.The winner was bought in for 8,500gns.
Owner Dr Marwan Koukash **Bred** D And Mrs D Veitch **Trained** Upper Lambourn, Berks

FOCUS
An uncompetitive seller. The winner stood out at the weights and the level revolves around the runner-up.

457 GOLF BEFORE RACING AT SOUTHWELL MAIDEN STKS 6f (F)
3:15 (3:18) (Class 5) 3-Y-0+ **£2,385** (£704; £352) **Stalls** Low

Form RPR
62- **1** **Aqua Ardens (GER)**[59] 7717 4-9-13 0.......................... StephenCraine 4 73
(George Baker) *cl up: rdn along 2f out: kpt on u.p to ld jst ins fnl f: rn green and kpt on wl* **8/1**[2]
33-2 **2** ½ **Derivatives (IRE)**[14] 283 3-8-7 70................................ NickyMackay 1 62
(John Gosden) *led: rdn along 2f out: jnd and drvn ent fnl f: sn hdd and one pce* **1/8**[1]
0-3 **3** 7 **Coral Sands (IRE)**[14] 283 4-9-13 0.................................. PJMcDonald 3 49
(Alan Swinbank) *chsd ldng pair: pushed along and outpcd 1/2-way: kpt on appr fnl f* **25/1**[3]
4 59 **Madam Joy** 3-8-7 0... ChrisCatlin 2
(Christopher Kellett) *missed break and veered bdly rt s: v green: sn outpcd and wl bhd* **50/1**

1m 17.83s (1.33) **Going Correction** +0.25s/f (Slow)
WFA 3 from 4yo 15lb **4** Ran SP% **105.8**
Speed ratings (Par 103): **101,100,91,12**
CSF £9.67 TOTE £7.40; EX 9.60.
Owner M Khan X2 **Bred** Gestut Karlshof **Trained** Whitsbury, Hants

FOCUS
A shock result in this weak maiden. It's doubtful the favourite ran to form so it's hard to know quite what the winner achieved.

458 THOUSANDS OF SPORTS EXPERIENCES AT BLUESQ.COM H'CAP 6f (F)
3:45 (3:46) (Class 4) (0-85,82) 4-Y-0+ **£4,204** (£1,251; £625; £312) **Stalls** Low

Form RPR
0-10 **1** **Bandstand**[12] 311 6-9-1 **76**.. TomEaves 5 85
(Bryan Smart) *chsd ldrs: hdwy over 2f out: rdn to chal appr fnl f: led last 100yds: hld on wl* **12/1**
0-11 **2** ½ **Upper Lambourn (IRE)**[26] 133 4-8-13 **74**................... TonyHamilton 8 81+
(Brian Ellison) *hld up: wd st: gd hdwy wl over 1f out: sn rdn and str run ent fnl f: jst hld* **6/1**[3]
13-4 **3** ½ **Caldercruix (USA)**[32] 64 5-8-12 **76**......................(v) SimonPearce(3) 6 81
(James Evans) *dwlt: hdwy to chse ldrs after 2f: rdn 2f out and ev ch tl drvn and kpt on same pce fnl f* **5/1**[2]
25-5 **4** nk **Close To The Edge (IRE)**[14] 286 4-9-7 **82**................. DavidProbert 10 86
(Alan McCabe) *sn led: rdn wl over 1f out: drvn ent fnl f: hdd & wknd last 100yds* **16/1**
4005 **5** 1 ½ **Punching**[7] 371 8-8-8 **69**.. HayleyTurner 7 69
(Conor Dore) *hld up in tch: hdwy wl over 1f out: kpt on fnl f: nrst fin* **7/1**
5-54 **6** hd **Joe Le Taxi (IRE)**[11] 335 4-8-4 **65**................................... MartinLane 3 64
(Mark Johnston) *chsd ldrs on inner: rdn along and outpcd bef 1/2-way: kpt on u.p fnl 2f: n.d* **8/1**
11-2 **7** shd **Global Village (IRE)**[36] 11 7-9-3 **78**............................. BarryMcHugh 1 77
(Brian Ellison) *in rr on inner and sn rdn along: swtchd outside and wd st: hdwy 2f out: rdn to chse ldrs appr fnl f: sn drvn and no imp* **4/1**[1]
3203 **8** ½ **Dancing Freddy (IRE)**[4] 406 5-8-11 **72**.....................(tp) LeeNewman 9 69
(Richard Guest) *cl up: rdn along over 2f out: grad wknd over 1f out* **10/1**
2-10 **9** shd **Ghostwing**[25] 157 5-8-13 **81**.. DarrenEgan(7) 4 78
(James Evans) *cl up: effrt over 2f out: sn rdn and ev ch tl drvn and wknd over 1f out* **6/1**[3]
0124 **10** 1 **Avonrose**[7] 371 5-8-11 **77**...(v[1]) NeilFarley(5) 2 71
(Derek Shaw) *racd on inner: a towards rr* **20/1**

1m 16.48s (-0.02) **Going Correction** +0.25s/f (Slow) **10** Ran SP% **116.3**
Speed ratings (Par 105): **110,109,108,108,106 106,105,105,105,103**
toteswingers:1&2:£16.40, 2&3:£7.20, 1&3:£14.40 CSF £82.05 CT £412.84 TOTE £16.10: £4.00, £2.00, £1.60; EX 119.60 Trifecta £493.90 Pool: £687.48 - 1.03 winning units..
Owner Crossfields Racing **Bred** D J And Mrs Brown **Trained** Hambleton, N Yorks

FOCUS
A competitive sprint handicap and the whole field were still within a couple of lengths of each other passing the furlong pole. An unusually bunched finish for the track, and ordinary form.
Global Village(IRE) Official explanation: jockey said gelding hung left

459 BOOK YOUR TICKETS ON-LINE AT SOUTHWELL-RACECOURSE.CO.UK MAIDEN H'CAP 1m (F)
4:15 (4:16) (Class 6) (0-55,55) 3-Y-O **£1,704** (£503; £251) **Stalls** Low

Form RPR
-202 **1** **Samasana (IRE)**[5] 382 3-8-12 **51**................................. TonyHamilton 2 59
(Ian Wood) *cl up: led over 3f out: rdn clr 2f out: kpt on wl u.p fnl f* **9/2**[2]
00-6 **2** 1 ½ **Pelican Rock (IRE)**[15] 270 3-8-11 **50**............................. DavidProbert 7 54
(Tom Dascombe) *hld up in tch: hdwy wl over 2f out: rdn over 1f out: kpt on ins fnl f* **14/1**
60-0 **3** 1 ¼ **J J Leary (IRE)**[34] 38 3-9-0 **53**.................................... JamieSpencer 4 54
(Ian Williams) *trckd ldrs: hdwy 3f out: rdn to chse wnr wl over 1f out: drvn and one pce fnl f* **5/1**[3]
600- **4** 4 ½ **Emirates Jack (IRE)**[89] 7342 3-9-2 **55**.......................... MartinLane 5 46
(David Simcock) *midfield: hdwy and in tch over 3f out: chsd ldrs over 2f out: sn rdn and no imp* **9/4**[1]
0-R5 **5** 7 **Clarkson (IRE)**[15] 270 3-8-11 **50**...................................... ChrisCatlin 1 25
(Jamie Osborne) *chsd ldrs on inner: led over 5f out: rdn along and hdd over 3f out: wkng whn hung rt fnl 2f* **14/1**
6-65 **6** nk **Pink Evie**[24] 182 3-9-2 **55**...(t) StevieDonohoe 8 29
(Gay Kelleway) *dwlt and bhd tl styd on fnl 2f: nvr a factor* **20/1**
33-3 **7** 7 **Burnwynd Spirit (IRE)**[35] 25 3-8-13 **52**........................ TomEaves 9
(Ian Semple) *in tch: rdn along 3f out: sn wknd* **16/1**
63-3 **8** 2 ¼ **Rhyme Royal**[22] 196 3-8-11 **50**................................. FrederikTylicki 6
(James Given) *led 2f: prom: rdn along over 3f out: sn wknd* **8/1**
000- **9** 3 ¾ **King Laertis (IRE)**[245] 2780 3-8-7 **46** oh1................(b[1]) BarryMcHugh 10
(Ben Haslam) *dwlt: a towards rr* **20/1**
03-6 **10** 25 **Holy Empress (IRE)**[26] 132 3-8-8 **47**............................ HayleyTurner 3
(Michael Bell) *towards rr: rdn along 3f out: sn bhd and eased* **7/1**

1m 44.6s (0.90) **Going Correction** +0.25s/f (Slow) **10** Ran SP% **118.0**
Speed ratings (Par 95): **105,103,102,97,90 90,83,81,77,52**
toteswingers:1&2:£1.40, 2&3:£2.20, 1&3:£1.90 CSF £66.35 CT £333.10 TOTE £3.70: £1.20, £5.80, £1.80; EX 76.30 Trifecta £488.00 Part won. Pool: £659.52 - 0.83 winning units..
Owner Paddy Barrett **Bred** Patrick Cassidy **Trained** Upper Lambourn, Berks

FOCUS
This was a poor contest, as both the race title and a ratings band of 46-55 would suggest, but the form is reasonable for the grade. The winner rates a small personal best.
Pink Evie Official explanation: jockey said filly was unsuited by the fibresand surface

460 PLAY RAINBOW RICHES AT BLUESQ.COM H'CAP 1m 4f (F)
4:45 (4:45) (Class 5) (0-70,69) 4-Y-0+ **£2,264** (£673; £336; £168) **Stalls** Low

Form RPR
444- **1** **Tricksofthetrade (IRE)**[105] 7075 6-9-6 **68**...................... PJMcDonald 9 79
(Alan Swinbank) *cl up: led wl over 3f out: rdn wl over 1f out: kpt on strly fnl f* **9/2**[3]
13/2 **2** 1 ¾ **Hunters Belt (IRE)**[13] 97 8-9-3 **65**...........................(p) BarryMcHugh 3 73
(Noel Wilson) *in tch on inner: smooth hdwy 4f out: trckd wnr 2f out: shkn up to chal wl over 1f out and ev ch tl drvn and one pce fnl f* **10/3**[1]
0-14 **3** 2 ¾ **Unex Picasso**[12] 309 4-9-4 **69**.................................(tp) StevieDonohoe 5 73
(Ian Williams) *dwlt and in rr: hdwy on outer 5f out: chsd ldrs 3f out: wd st: rdn 2f out: kpt on same pce appr fnl f* **7/2**[2]
20-4 **4** 2 ½ **Magic Haze**[28] 110 6-8-7 **58**.. RyanPowell(3) 6 58
(Sally Hall) *trckd ldrs: effrt 3f out: rdn 2f out: drvn over 1f out and no imp* **10/1**
00-4 **5** shd **Jawaab (IRE)**[22] 192 8-9-6 **68**...(e) MartinLane 4 67
(Richard Guest) *hld up in rr: hdwy 3f out: rdn 2f out: kpt on: nrst fin* **6/1**
11-0 **6** 1 ¼ **Three White Socks (IRE)**[11] 332 5-9-0 **65**................. PaulPickard(3) 7 62
(Brian Ellison) *led: rdn along over 4f out: hdd wl over 3f out: wknd over 2f out* **5/1**
20-4 **7** 15 **Nolecce**[23] 183 5-8-10 **63**...(p) CharlesEddery(5) 2 36
(Richard Guest) *chsd ldrs: rdn along over 3f out: sn wknd* **16/1**
253- **8** 15 **Trachonitis (IRE)**[253] 2562 8-9-7 **69**............................ StephenCraine 1 18
(J R Jenkins) *hld up: a in rr: bhd fnl 3f* **20/1**
410/ **9** hd **Stop On**[370] 2840 7-8-12 **60**... TonyHamilton 8
(Chris Grant) *cl up: rdn along 4f out: sn wknd* **50/1**

2m 42.41s (1.41) **Going Correction** +0.25s/f (Slow)
WFA 4 from 5yo+ 3lb **9** Ran SP% **116.1**
Speed ratings (Par 103): **105,103,102,100,100 99,89,79,79**
toteswingers:1&2:£4.20, 2&3:£3.70, 1&3:£4.60 CSF £20.03 CT £58.31 TOTE £4.00: £2.10, £2.00, £1.30; EX 28.30 Trifecta £68.90 Pool: £846.17 - 9.08 winning units..
Owner Adrian Butler **Bred** Glencarrig Stud **Trained** Melsonby, N Yorks

FOCUS
An ordinary middle-distance handicap and the pace was modest. A bit muddling but the form is rated at face value.
T/Jkpt: Not won. T/Plt: £949.70 to a £1 stake. Pool of £92,385.84 - 71.01 winning tickets. T/Qpdt: £37.90 to a £1 stake. Pool of £9,873.43 - 192.30 winning tickets. JR

445 WOLVERHAMPTON (A.W) (L-H)
Tuesday, February 7

OFFICIAL GOING: Standard
Wind: virtually nil Weather: dry and cold

461 BLUE SQUARE WINTER CARNIVAL IPHONE APP H'CAP 5f 20y(P)
2:00 (2:00) (Class 5) (0-70,72) 4-Y-0+ **£2,264** (£673; £336; £168) **Stalls** Low

Form RPR
5662 **1** **Shawkantango**[5] 380 5-8-11 62....................................(v) DaleSwift(3) 6 70
(Derek Shaw) *taken down early: chsd ldrs on outer: rdn and effrt to press ldrs over 2f out: drvn to ld ins fnl f: hld on wl fnl 75yds* **11/2**
0032 **2** hd **Steelcut**[5] 388 8-9-6 68...(p) JoeFanning 5 75
(David Evans) *t.k.h: hld up in tch: travelling strly whn nt clr run and swtchd rt ent fnl f: rdn and qcknd to chal fnl 75yds: a jst hld* **5/2**[2]

-421 **3** 3/4 **Suddenly Susan (IRE)**[5] 385 4-9-3 70 6ex..............(b) RaulDaSilva(5) 4 74
(Scott Dixon) *t.k.h: chsd ldr: ev ch over 1f out: drvn and styd on same pce ins fnl f* **9/4**[1]

0-04 **4** 1 **Absa Lutte (IRE)**[4] 406 9-8-13 68................................ NoelGarbutt(7) 7 69
(Michael Mullineaux) *taken down early: awkward leaving stalls and s.i.s: niggled along in last: clsd 1/2-way: effrt on inner and pressed ldrs over 1f out: no ex and btn fnl 100yds* **12/1**

4-40 **5** 3 3/4 **La Capriosa**[5] 380 6-9-2 64..(p) IanMongan 3 51
(Scott Dixon) *sn bustled along to ld: rdn wl over 1f out: hdd ins fnl f: sn wknd* **14/1**

12-1 **6** nk **Perlachy**[4] 406 8-9-10 72 6ex..(v) LukeMorris 1 50
(Ronald Harris) *chsd ldrs: rdn 2f out: drvn and unable qck 1f out: wknd ins fnl f* **3/1**[3]

1m 2.51s (0.21) **Going Correction** +0.325s/f (Slow) **6** Ran SP% **114.1**
Speed ratings (Par 103): **111,110,109,107,101 101**
toteswingers:1&2:£2.00, 2&3:£2.30, 1&3:£1.70 CSF £20.09 TOTE £4.50: £3.90, £2.20; EX 25.70.
Owner Shawthing Racing Partnership **Bred** Derek Shaw **Trained** Sproxton, Leics

FOCUS
An ordinary sprint handicap, rated through the second. The winner did not need to improve much on his previous course form.

462 GET YOUR BET ON AT BLUESQ.COM MAIDEN STKS 7f 32y(P)
2:30 (2:32) (Class 5) 3-Y-O **£2,587** (£770; £384; £192) **Stalls** High

Form RPR

060- **1** **Jericho (IRE)**[82] 7444 3-9-3 63..................................... FergusSweeney 3 61
(Jamie Osborne) *chsd ldrs: rdn to chal 1f out: led fnl 100yds: kpt on wl* **5/1**[3]

63-2 **2** 3/4 **Bond Style**[5] 383 3-9-3 60..(p) PaulHanagan 4 59
(Bryan Smart) *led: rdn wl over 2f out: drvn over 1f out: hdd and one pce fnl 100yds* **8/11**[1]

206- **3** 1 3/4 **Bengaline**[63] 7642 3-9-3 65.. IanMongan 1 54
(Scott Dixon) *in tch in last pair: reminders 5f out: rdn 4f out: styd on u.p to chse ldng pair ins fnl f: no imp fnl 100yds* **7/1**

65-5 **4** 2 1/4 **Essexvale (IRE)**[26] 138 3-8-5 53.......................... MatthewHopkins(7) 5 43
(Alan Berry) *chsd ldrs on outer: pressed ldr over 2f out: rdn and unable qck wl over 1f out: wknd ins fnl f* **80/1**

5 8 **Dancing Ellie Mae** 3-8-10 0 ow1.................................... DaleSwift(3) 2 22
(Derek Shaw) *dwlt and pushed lft s: a in rr: rdn and no prog wl over 1f out: sn wknd* **33/1**

6 13 **Windygoul Lad** 3-9-3 0... JoeFanning 6 29
(Keith Dalgleish) *dwlt: sn rcvrd to chse ldr and t.k.h: lost 2nd and rdn over 2f out: wknd qckly over 1f out: wl btn and eased ins fnl f* **3/1**[2]

1m 32.62s (3.02) **Going Correction** +0.325s/f (Slow) **6** Ran SP% **116.2**
Speed ratings (Par 97): **95,94,92,89,80 65**
toteswingers:1&2:£2.50, 2&3:£1.10, 1&3:£2.30 CSF £9.55 TOTE £5.90: £3.10, £1.10; EX 11.60.
Owner Morsethehorse Syndicate **Bred** Myles And Mrs Joan Doyle **Trained** Upper Lambourn, Berks

FOCUS
The general opinion of the riders after the first two races was that the track was riding slower than usual. A weak 3-y-o maiden, run at a fairly steady pace. The winner only needed to run to his previous maiden form.
Windygoul Lad Official explanation: jockey said gelding lost its action in home straight but returned sound

463 BET AT BLUE SQUARE H'CAP 1m 141y(P)
3:00 (3:00) (Class 5) (0-75,72) 4-Y-O+ **£2,264** (£673; £336; £168) **Stalls** Low

Form RPR

5-31 **1** **Patriotic (IRE)**[4] 401 4-8-6 62.. RaulDaSilva(5) 2 69+
(Chris Dwyer) *chsd ldr tl over 4f out: trcking ldrs and gng wl 2f out: swtchd rt and nt clr run over 1f out tl squeezed between horses ins fnl f: qcknd and r.o wl to ld towards fin* **11/10**[1]

2414 **2** hd **Pipers Piping (IRE)**[4] 401 6-9-1 71 6ex.......................(p) AmyScott(5) 3 76
(Alastair Lidderdale) *stdd after s: hld up in rr: rdn and effrt on outer over 1f out: chal and edgd lft 1f out: led ins fnl f: kpt on wl tl hdd and no ex towards fin* **8/1**

-022 **3** 1 1/4 **Master Of Dance (IRE)**[4] 403 5-9-5 70.........................(p) JoeFanning 5 72
(Keith Dalgleish) *in tch in last pair: rdn and effrt over 2f out: ev ch jst over 1f out: pushed lft and unable qck ins fnl f: one pce fnl 100yds* **3/1**[2]

24-2 **4** 1/2 **McCool Bannanas**[8] 361 4-8-13 64....................... RichardKingscote 4 65
(James Unett) *chsd ldrs tl wnt 2nd over 4f out: led 2f out: drvn over 1f out: hdd ins fnl f: no ex* **7/2**[3]

-144 **5** 7 **Mcconnell (USA)**[7] 367 7-9-7 72..(b) PaulHanagan 1 57
(Richard Guest) *racd keenly: led: jnd and rdn over 2f out: hdd 2f out: wknd 1f out* **16/1**

1m 51.67s (1.17) **Going Correction** +0.325s/f (Slow) **5** Ran SP% **111.8**
Speed ratings (Par 103): **107,106,105,105,99**
CSF £10.77 TOTE £2.30: £1.90, £4.50; EX 11.60.
Owner M M Foulger **Bred** Darley **Trained** Six Mile Bottom, Cambs

FOCUS
This was competitive for the class and, after an uneven pace, it saw another tight finish. Shaky form. The winner was well in and did not quite match his previous best here.
Mcconnell(USA) Official explanation: jockey said gelding hung right-handed throughout

464 BET AND WATCH AT BLUESQ.COM MAIDEN STKS 1m 141y(P)
3:30 (3:31) (Class 5) 3-Y-O+ **£2,587** (£770; £384) **Stalls** Low

Form RPR

20-3 **1** **Cool Hand Luke (IRE)**[25] 159 3-8-7 70................. RichardKingscote 4 68
(Tom Dascombe) *led: rdn over 1f out: drvn and hdd ins fnl f: rallied under hands and heels riding and r.o wl to ld again fnl 50yds* **4/6**[1]

2- **2** 1/2 **Macy Anne (IRE)**[61] 7673 3-8-2 0.. JoeFanning 1 62
(Robert Mills) *stdd after s: hld up in tch: swtchd lft and effrt on inner over 1f out: chal and rn green 1f out: led ins fnl f: hdd and no ex fnl 50yds: eased nr fin* **11/8**[2]

6 **3** 4 **Cuore (IRE)**[11] 324 3-8-8 0 ow1.................................. FergusSweeney 2 59?
(Jamie Osborne) *chsd wnr: rdn over 3f out: drvn and stl pressing ldr 2f out: wknd ins fnl f* **16/1**[3]

1m 55.26s (4.76) **Going Correction** +0.325s/f (Slow)
WFA 3 from 4yo 21lb **3** Ran SP% **108.0**
Speed ratings (Par 103): **91,90,87**
CSF £1.90 TOTE £1.50; EX 1.10.
Owner Phil Mousley **Bred** Nicola And Eleanor Kent **Trained** Malpas, Cheshire

FOCUS
A weak little maiden which was slowly run. The form is rated around the first two.
Macy Anne(IRE) Official explanation: jockey said, regarding riding, that this was the filly's second racecourse appearance, ran green, hung right in home straight and when he eased approaching line, they were a neck down on winner and would not have finished significantly closer for more rigorous riding.

465 BLUE SQUARE BET H'CAP 2m 119y(P)
4:00 (4:00) (Class 6) (0-60,62) 4-Y-O+ **£1,704** (£503; £251) **Stalls** Low

Form RPR

-224 **1** **Bold Adventure**[14] 278 8-9-7 53.................................. JamieMackay 5 59
(Willie Musson) *stdd s: hld up in tch in last: hdwy on outer and gng best over 1f out: rdn to ld ins fnl f: r.o wl* **13/8**[1]

200- **2** 1 1/2 **Sacco D'Oro**[32] 3086 6-9-1 47.. JoeFanning 2 51
(Michael Mullineaux) *chsd ldr: rdn and effrt on inner over 1f out: chsd wnr ins fnl f: styd on* **12/1**[3]

6/5- **3** 2 **Arctic Wings (IRE)**[10] 2272 8-8-11 50.................... GeorgeDowning(7) 1 52
(Tony Carroll) *t.k.h: set stdy gallop: rdn and qcknd 3f out: hdd ins fnl f: styd on same pce after* **11/4**[2]

35-1 **D** shd **Dew Reward (IRE)**[4] 395 4-9-5 62 6ex..................... CharlesBishop(5) 3 63
(Bill Turner) *stdd after s: trckd ldng pair: wnt 2nd over 3f out: rdn to press ldr ent fnl 2f: unable qck over 1f out: one pce fnl f: fin 4th: disqualified: prohibited substance in post r sample* **13/8**[1]

4m 8.68s (26.88) **Going Correction** +0.325s/f (Slow)
WFA 4 from 6yo+ 6lb **4** Ran SP% **110.5**
Speed ratings (Par 101): **49,48,47,47**
CSF £16.99 TOTE £3.70; EX 13.70.
Owner The Adventurers **Bred** Bricklow Ltd **Trained** Newmarket, Suffolk

FOCUS
This ordinary staying handicap was run at a very steady pace and it was hardly a proper test as the sprint for home developed 3f out. Suspect form.

466 FOLLOW US ON TWITTER @BLUESQ H'CAP 1m 1f 103y(P)
4:30 (4:31) (Class 6) (0-65,64) 3-Y-O **£1,704** (£503; £251) **Stalls** Low

Form RPR

-212 **1** **Gabrial's King (IRE)**[5] 393 3-9-3 57.............................. PaulHanagan 6 68
(Ian Williams) *chsd ldng trio: pushed along at times: rdn to chse ldr and racd awkwardly over 1f out: led ins fnl f: r.o wl* **5/6**[1]

0-01 **2** 1 **Luctor Emergo (IRE)**[5] 393 3-8-12 52 6ex..................(b) JoeFanning 5 61
(Keith Dalgleish) *chsd ldrs tl wnt 2nd 6f out: led gng wl 2f out: rdn over 1f out: hdd and styd on same pce ins fnl f* **11/4**[2]

-133 **3** 6 **Complex**[8] 360 3-9-2 56... LukeMorris 2 52
(David Evans) *chsd ldr tl 6f out: sn pushed along: rdn 3f out: hrd drvn and outpcd over 1f out: wl hld fnl f* **8/1**

12-4 **4** 1 1/2 **Speedi Mouse**[23] 184 3-9-4 64............................ MichaelO'Connell(3) 3 54
(Philip McBride) *stdd s: hld up in rr: hdwy 3f out: rdn and no prog over 1f out: wl hld whn hung lft and swtchd lft ins fnl f* **11/2**[3]

50-0 **5** 1 1/2 **Aglaja**[15] 270 3-8-1 46..(b) RaulDaSilva(5) 1 36
(Frank Sheridan) *hld up in last trio: rdn and effrt wl over 1f out: no prog and wknd 1f out* **28/1**

00-0 **6** 7 **Clone Devil (IRE)**[4] 407 3-8-8 48.................................. JamieMackay 7 28
(Alastair Lidderdale) *led tl 2f out: wknd over 1f out: wl btn and eased ins fnl f* **66/1**

0-05 **7** shd **Salaaheb (IRE)**[8] 360 3-8-5 45...............................(p) FrankieMcDonald 4 20
(Alastair Lidderdale) *in tch in last trio: rdn over 6f out: nvr gng wl after: wknd u.p 2f out* **100/1**

2m 3.75s (2.05) **Going Correction** +0.325s/f (Slow) **7** Ran SP% **113.6**
Speed ratings (Par 95): **103,102,96,95,94 87,87**
CSF £3.28 TOTE £2.00: £1.20, £1.70; EX 3.80.
Owner Dr Marwan Koukash **Bred** Danella Partnership **Trained** Portway, Worcs

FOCUS
Not a bad handicap for the lowly grade. There was a sound pace on and the form is straightforward with the first pair clear.
Speedi Mouse Official explanation: jockey said filly hung left in home straight
Clone Devil(IRE) Official explanation: jockey said gelding jumped to the left on leaving stalls
T/Plt: £38.60 to a £1 stake. Pool of £80,188.58 - 1,513.49 winning tickets. T/Qpdt: £13.50 to a £1 stake. Pool of £6,490.13 - 355.11 winning tickets. SP

373 KEMPTON (A.W) (R-H)
Wednesday, February 8

OFFICIAL GOING: Standard
Wind: Moderate ahead Weather: Overcast

467 FREE ENTRY FOR BETDAQ MEMBERS H'CAP 5f (P)
2:20 (2:21) (Class 7) (0-50,50) 4-Y-O+ **£1,455** (£433; £216; £108) **Stalls** Low

Form RPR

600- **1** **Silver Linnet (IRE)**[330] 857 5-9-3 **50**.............................(v1) AdamKirby 5 62+
(John Butler) *mde all: drvn 5 l clr 2f out: rdn out fnl f: unchal* **15/8**[1]

330- **2** 1 **Good Timin'**[48] 7853 4-9-0 **47**.. JamieSpencer 9 53
(David Brown) *chsd wnr thrght but 5 l down 2f out: styd on fnl f but a hld* **17/2**

0-34 **3** 1 **Bobbyow**[5] 396 4-8-11 **49**.. MarkCoumbe(5) 2 51
(Terry Clement) *chsd ldrs: t.k.h and stmbld after 1f: styd on fnl f but nvr gng pce of wnr* **13/2**[2]

-260 **4** shd **Pharoh Jake**[5] 396 4-9-0 **47**.. KieranO'Neill 6 49
(John Bridger) *s.i.s: in rr: hdwy over 1f out: styd in fnl f: kpt on cl home* **12/1**

6645 **5** 1/2 **Raimond Ridge (IRE)**[5] 396 6-8-12 **45**............................ MartinLane 7 45+
(Derek Shaw) *s.i.s: in rr: drvn and hdwy appr fnl f: fin wl* **9/1**

50-3 **6** 1/2 **Porthgwidden Beach (USA)**[28] 118 4-9-0 **47**..............(t) LeeNewman 4 45
(Anthony Middleton) *chsd ldrs: rdn 2f out: styd on same pce fnl f* **8/1**[3]

5-50 **7** 1/2 **Jemimaville (IRE)**[14] 297 5-8-7 **45**................................ RaulDaSilva(5) 1 42
(Giles Bravery) *chsd ldrs: rdn 2f out: outpcd ins fnl f* **20/1**

0453 **8** 1/2 **White Shift (IRE)**[13] 312 6-9-0 **47**...............................(p) JoeFanning 11 42
(Paul Howling) *in rr: hdwy fnl f: nvr gng pce to rch ldrs* **10/1**

0-10 **9** 1 1/2 **Deveze (IRE)**[19] 227 4-9-3 **50**.................................(b) RichardKingscote 3 39
(Milton Bradley) *towards rr: sme prog fnl f* **11/1**

2-05 **10** nse **Replicator**[13] 312 7-9-3 **50**...(e) LukeMorris 12 39
(Patrick Gilligan) *in rr and racd on outer: sme late prog* **14/1**

00-0 **11** 3 1/4 **Green Warrior**[13] 313 4-9-3 **50**......................................(p) GeorgeBaker 10 28
(Richard Guest) *chsd ldrs 3f* **33/1**

59.87s (-0.63) **Going Correction** -0.025s/f (Stan) **11** Ran SP% **119.2**
Speed ratings (Par 97): **104,102,100,100,99 98,98,97,95,94 89**
toteswingers:1&2:£7.40, 1&3:£3.60, 2&3:£12.10 CSF £18.51 CT £91.88 TOTE £2.50: £1.20, £3.10, £2.50; EX 27.30 Trifecta £378.00 Pool: £510.87 - 0.82 winning units..
Owner The Chicken On A Chain Partnership **Bred** L Mulryan **Trained** Newmarket, Suffolk
■ Stewards' Enquiry : Adam Kirby two-day ban: used whip in incorrect place (Feb 22-23)

The Form Book Flat, Raceform Ltd, Compton, RG20 6NL

FOCUS
A bottom-grade sprint in which the winner set a good pace, and the time was respectable for a Class 7 event. The winner was very well in although this bare form is just modest, rated around the third and fourth.

468 BACK OR LAY AT BETDAQ.COM H'CAP 1m 2f (P)
2:50 (2:51) (Class 7) (0-50,50) 4-Y-O+ £1,455 (£433; £216; £108) Stalls Low

Form RPR

000- **1** **Sylas Ings**105 [7096] 4-9-2 **50**....(v) IanMongan 6 60
(Pat Phelan) *s.i.s: in rr: hdwy over 2f out: sn rdn: slt ld 1f out: edgd lft fnl 120yds: drvn out* **15/2**

505- **2** *1* **Trecase**44 [5943] 5-9-2 **49**....(t) LukeMorris 2 56
(Tony Carroll) *slowly away: sn drvn in rr: hdwy over 2f out: rdn to chal appr fnl f: styd on same pce ins fnl f* **8/1**

65-5 **3** *½* **Laser Blazer**24 [188] 4-9-2 **50**....(p) AdamKirby 7 56
(Jeremy Gask) *trckd ldrs: led 2f out: sn rdn hdd 1f out: styng on one pce and disputing 2nd whn carried lft and one pce into 3rd fnl 120yds* **9/4**1

366- **4** *4 ½* **It's Dubai Dolly**54 [7787] 6-9-2 **49**....(b) SteveDrowne 12 46
(Alastair Lidderdale) *in rr: hdwy on outer over 2f out: kpt on to take 4th jst ins fnl f* **9/1**

64-4 **5** *4* **The Catenian (IRE)**21 [200] 4-8-11 **45**....(p) MartinLane 10 34
(John Butler) *chsd ldr: led 3f out: hdd 2f out: wknd appr fnl f* **7/1**3

00-0 **6** *½* **Forbidden (IRE)**26 [151] 9-8-13 **49**....(bt) DaleSwift(3) 1 37
(Ian McInnes) *mid-div: hdwy on inner 2f out: no imp on ldrs fr over 1f out* **25/1**

-050 **7** *hd* **Le Reveur**7 [375] 10-8-7 **45**....(e) CharlesEddery(5) 13 35
(Richard Guest) *stdd s and swtchd lft: hdwy 2f out: one pce fr over 1f out* **66/1**

00-0 **8** *2 ¼* **Miss Whippy**30 [105] 5-8-12 **45**.... HayleyTurner 8 28
(Paul Howling) *chsd ldrs: rdn and continually flashed tail fr 2f out: sn btn* **33/1**

564- **9** *1 ½* **Delagoa Bay (IRE)**204 [4181] 4-8-11 **45**.... LiamKeniry 4 25
(Sylvester Kirk) *chsd ldrs: drvn 1/2-way wknd over 2f out* **20/1**

5-43 **10** *6* **Prickles**6 [390] 7-8-13 **46**.... JoeFanning 5 14
(Derek Shaw) *led tl hdd 3f out: wknd ins fnl 2f: eased whn no ch fnl f* **6/1**2

256- **11** *1 ¾* **Brent Pelham**258 [2419] 5-9-2 **49**....(vt1) StevieDonohoe 3 14
(Tobias B P Coles) *chsd ldrs to 3f out: sn wknd* **20/1**

0-00 **12** *3 ¾* **Flotation (USA)**12 [333] 5-9-0 **47**....(b) TomEaves 9
(Roy Brotherton) *nvr bttr than mid-div: bhd fnl 3f* **50/1**

060- **13** *1 ¾* **Invent**180 [5015] 4-8-11 **48**....(t) AdamBeschizza(3) 14 2
(Robert Eddery) *s.i.s: towards rr for most of way* **10/1**

2m 7.32s (-0.68) **Going Correction** -0.025s/f (Stan)
WFA 4 from 5yo+ 1lb 13 Ran SP% **119.3**
Speed ratings (Par 97): **101,100,99,96,93 92,92,90,89,84 83,80,78**
toteswingers:1&2:£10.90, 1&3:£5.40, 2&3:£5.90 CSF £60.71 CT £181.02 TOTE £8.60: £2.90, £2.70, £1.40; EX 99.30 Trifecta £465.60 Pool: £629.31 - 0.70 winning units..
Owner I W Harfitt **Bred** Wayne And Hilary Thornton **Trained** Epsom, Surrey

FOCUS
A weak handicap run at an ordinary pace. The first three finished clear but it's not form to be too positive about with the winner down a long way in the weights.
Prickles Official explanation: jockey said mare hung left

469 BETDAQ MULTIPLES H'CAP 5f (P)
3:25 (3:26) (Class 5) (0-75,69) 3-Y-O £2,264 (£673; £336; £168) Stalls Low

Form RPR

410- **1** **Gin Twist**55 [7765] 3-9-4 **66**....(b) RichardKingscote 3 68
(Tom Dascombe) *t.k.h: trckd ldrs: drvn to chal between horses fnl 120yds: led clsng stages: pushed out* **4/1**3

353- **2** *hd* **Rooknrasbryripple**39 [7937] 3-8-1 **56**.... PhoebeCruse(7) 4 57
(Ralph Smith) *awkward s and s.i.s: sn t.k.h and trckd ldrs: chal ins fnl f and slt ld fnl 120yds: hdd and outpcd clsng stages* **20/1**

5-11 **3** *1* **Lady Caprice**12 [326] 3-9-5 **67**....(p) ChrisCatlin 5 64
(Jane Chapple-Hyam) *led and modest pce: drvn and qcknd 2f out: hrd pressed ins fnl f: hdd fnl 120yds: styd on same pce* **13/8**1

-514 **4** *½* **Redair (IRE)**9 [357] 3-9-7 **69**.... LukeMorris 2 65
(David Evans) *chsd ldr: rdn over 2f out: ev ch 1f out: outpcd ins fnl f* **13/2**

-620 **5** *nk* **Dawn Lightning**11 [352] 3-9-3 **65**.... KieranO'Neill 7 60
(Alan McCabe) *in rr: drvn and sme hdwy on ins appr fnl f: styd on same pce* **9/1**

354- **6** *¾* **Majestic Rose**144 [6166] 3-9-0 **67**.... CharlesBishop(5) 6 59
(Mick Channon) *s.i.s: in rr: drvn and no imp fnl f* **9/4**2

1m 1.04s (0.54) **Going Correction** -0.025s/f (Stan) 6 Ran SP% **117.0**
Speed ratings (Par 97): **94,93,92,91,90 89**
toteswingers:1&2:£7.30, 1&3:£2.20, 2&3:£4.20 CSF £69.24 TOTE £5.40: £2.50, £5.80; EX 57.10.
Owner Manor House Stables LLP **Bred** Highclere Stud **Trained** Malpas, Cheshire

FOCUS
A modest handicap which was falsely run, and the form may not stand up. The favourite was a bit disappointing and the race has been rated negatively.

470 BETDAQ MOBILE APPS CLASSIFIED CLAIMING STKS 7f (P)
3:55 (3:55) (Class 5) 4-Y-O+ £2,264 (£673; £336; £168) Stalls Low

Form RPR

-301 **1** **Satwa Laird**12 [323] 6-8-10 73.... JamieSpencer 2 73
(David Simcock) *trckd ldr: led 2f out: drvn fnl f and a jst doing enough clsng stages* **11/10**1

13-3 **2** *½* **Russian Ice**26 [148] 4-9-3 72....(b) JimmyFortune 3 79
(Dean Ivory) *s.i.s: racd in 4th tl wnt 3rd 4f out: sn drvn: chsd wnr 1f out: kpt on u.p clsng stages but a hld* **11/4**3

-106 **3** *1 ¼* **April Fool**11 [351] 8-8-10 75....(b) DarrenEgan(7) 4 75
(Ronald Harris) *led: drvn ins fnl 3f: hdd 2f out: lost 2nd 1f out: sn wknd* **9/4**2

00-0 **4** *12* **Hand Painted**8 [372] 6-8-7 57.... LeeNewman 1 33
(Anthony Middleton) *racd in 3rd tl over 3f out: rdn over 3f out: wknd 2f out* **50/1**

1m 25.81s (-0.19) **Going Correction** -0.025s/f (Stan) 4 Ran SP% **107.0**
Speed ratings (Par 103): **100,99,98,84**
CSF £4.35 TOTE £1.80; EX 4.10.Satwa Laird was claimed by Mr C. R. Dore for £6,500.
Owner Dr Marwan Koukash **Bred** The Policy Setters **Trained** Newmarket, Suffolk

FOCUS
Only three really mattered in this classified claimer. Unsurprisingly it was run at a sound pace thanks to the front-running veteran April Fool, and it was another cute tactical ride from the excellent Jamie Spencer. The winner was best in and the second is a decent guide to the form.

471 RACINGPLUS.CO.UK H'CAP 7f (P)
4:30 (4:30) (Class 4) (0-85,84) 3-Y-O £4,075 (£1,212; £606; £303) Stalls Low

Form RPR

2-1 **1** **Discoverer (IRE)**26 [147] 3-9-1 **78**.... NickyMackay 4 91
(John Gosden) *in tch: hdwy into 3rd over 3f out: pushed along to ld 2f out: narrowly hdd 1f out: styd chalng and r.o gamely to ld again last stride* **3/1**2

2-11 **2** *shd* **Pale Orchid (IRE)**14 [295] 3-9-2 **79**.... LukeMorris 6 92
(David Evans) *in tch: stdy hdwy 2f out: tk slt ld travelling wl 1f out: styd hrd pressed and rdn ins fnl f: hdd last stride* **7/4**1

0-11 **3** *8* **Adranian (IRE)**19 [230] 3-9-3 **80**....(v) KieranO'Neill 3 71
(David C Griffiths) *t.k.h: chsd ldr tl over 2f out: wknd into wl-hld 3rd 1f out* **10/1**

010- **4** *1* **Right Divine (IRE)**109 [7026] 3-9-7 **84**.... JimmyFortune 2 73
(Brian Meehan) *chsd ldrs: rdn and outpcd over 2f out: no ch after but styd on fnl f* **5/1**

224- **5** *nk* **Mr Knightley (IRE)**40 [7918] 3-8-13 **76**....(b) StephenCraine 1 64
(Jim Boyle) *led tl hdd 2f out: wknd over 1f out* **20/1**

1 **6** *2 ¼* **Fairway To Heaven (IRE)**13 [308] 3-9-0 **77**.... TomEaves 7 59
(Michael Wigham) *s.i.s: t.k.h in rr: effrt 2f out: nvr rchd ldrs and sn wknd* **9/2**3

1m 24.75s (-1.25) **Going Correction** -0.025s/f (Stan) 6 Ran SP% **110.1**
Speed ratings (Par 99): **106,105,96,95,95 92**
toteswingers: 1&2 £1.50, 2&3 £4.40, 1&3 £3.70 CSF £8.32 TOTE £3.90: £1.50, £1.60; EX 3.90.
Owner H R H Princess Haya Of Jordan **Bred** Darley **Trained** Newmarket, Suffolk

FOCUS
A fair and competitive handicap. There was a generous pace on and the first pair came well clear in a bobbing finish. The form is rated to the best view of the runner-up's recent form.
Right Divine(IRE) ◆ Official explanation: jockey said gelding hung right

472 SKYSPORTS.COM H'CAP 1m 4f (P)
5:00 (5:00) (Class 6) (0-65,63) 3-Y-O £1,617 (£481; £240; £120) Stalls Centre

Form RPR

1-31 **1** **Spartilla**35 [30] 3-9-4 **60**.... JamesSullivan 7 63+
(James Given) *trckd ldrs: drvn to go 2nd ins fnl 2f: led 1f out: comf* **7/4**1

305- **2** *1 ¼* **Ctappers**54 [7786] 3-9-2 **63**.... CharlesBishop(5) 5 64
(Mick Channon) *in rr: hdwy 2f out: kpt on fnl f to take 2nd last strides but no ch w wnr* **16/1**

000- **3** *hd* **Leading Star**56 [7752] 3-8-0 **45**.... RyanPowell(3) 2 46
(Michael Madgwick) *led 4f: styd chsng ldrs: drvn to ld again 2f out: hdd 1f out: nt pce of wnr fnl f and lost 2nd last strides* **25/1**

23-2 **4** *1 ¼* **Astroscarlet**20 [217] 3-8-8 **50**.... NickyMackay 9 49
(Mark H Tompkins) *chsd ldrs: wnt 2nd over 6f out: rdn and hung bdly lft bnd 3f out: sn lost pl: styd on again fnl f but nvr a threat* **4/1**2

005- **5** *hd* **Catchy Tune (IRE)**190 [4632] 3-8-10 **52**.... JamieSpencer 1 50
(David Brown) *in rr: hdwy 3f out: rdn and edgd lft 2f out: styd on same pce fnl f* **9/2**3

0-05 **6** *nk* **Little Red Minx (IRE)**18 [255] 3-8-13 **55**.... JimmyFortune 8 53
(Peter Chapple-Hyam) *in rr: hdwy and wl in tch whn pushed lft 2f out: sn rdn and no prog after* **12/1**

5-23 **7** *shd* **Cotes Du Rhone (IRE)**20 [217] 3-8-3 **45**....(v) LukeMorris 10 43
(David Evans) *trckd ldr: led after 4f: rdn 3f out: sn edgd lft: hdd 2f out: styd on same pce u.p* **5/1**

000- **8** *5* **Imperial Stargazer**55 [7763] 3-9-1 **57**.... ChrisCatlin 4 47
(Mick Channon) *in rr: rdn ins fnl 3f: no ch after* **25/1**

2m 41.7s (7.20) **Going Correction** -0.025s/f (Stan) 8 Ran SP% **112.5**
Speed ratings (Par 95): **75,74,74,73,73 72,72,69**
toteswingers:1&2:£7.70, 1&3:£8.80, 2&3:£22.80 CSF £32.06 CT £510.37 TOTE £2.20: £1.20, £4.70, £5.30; EX 31.90 Trifecta £484.90 Pool: £655.31 - 0.63 winning units..
Owner Bolton Grange **Bred** J Ellis **Trained** Willoughton, Lincs

FOCUS
A weak 3yo handicap, run at an ordinary pace and many took a keen early hold, resulting in a muddling affair. It's doubtful if the winner had to improve on his latest win here.
Astroscarlet Official explanation: jockey said filly hung left
Cotes Du Rhone(IRE) Official explanation: jockey said gelding hung left

473 SKYSPORTS.COM DVINSKY'S 200TH RUN RACING H'CAP (DIV I) 6f (P)
5:30 (5:31) (Class 5) (0-70,70) 4-Y-O+ £2,264 (£673; £336; £168) Stalls Low

Form RPR

00-5 **1** **Zip Lock (IRE)**24 [186] 6-9-7 **70**.... GeorgeBaker 11 77
(Olivia Maylam) *led after 1f: jnd fr 2f out: drvn along fnl f: kpt on strly clsng stages* **16/1**

-221 **2** *nk* **Rightcar**13 [312] 5-8-7 **56** oh1.... LukeMorris 8 62
(Peter Grayson) *chsd ldrs: rdn 2f out: styd on to chse wnr ins fnl f: kpt on wl but a hld* **4/1**2

P-10 **3** *½* **Belinsky (IRE)**17 [267] 5-8-10 **62**.... DaleSwift(3) 3 66
(Julie Camacho) *led 1f: styd chsng wnr: drvn to chal fr 2f out tl ins fnl f: kpt on same pce* **7/1**

2-65 **4** *¾* **Even Bolder**11 [353] 9-9-2 **65**.... JimmyFortune 5 67
(Eric Wheeler) *trckd ldrs: edgd lft ins fnl f and styng on one pce whn n.m.r fnl 120yds* **7/2**1

52-1 **5** *hd* **Les Verguettes (IRE)**20 [214] 4-9-6 **69**.... ChrisCatlin 9 70+
(Chris Wall) *t.k.h: in rr: drvn and hdwy over 1f out: styd on clsng stages: nt rch ldrs* **13/2**3

2460 **6** *1 ½* **Sherjawy (IRE)**12 [320] 8-8-11 **60**.... JamieGoldstein 2 56
(Zoe Davison) *chsd ldrs: rdn 2f out wknd fnl 120yds* **9/1**

000- **7** *shd* **Athwaab**77 [7512] 5-8-10 **62**.... RyanPowell(3) 10 58
(Noel Chance) *in rr: hdwy over 1f out: styd on fnl f but nvr gng pce to rch ldrs* **40/1**

-062 **8** *hd* **Dingaan (IRE)**13 [313] 9-8-7 **56** oh2.... JoeFanning 4 54+
(Peter Grayson) *in rr: hdwy over 1f out: styng on whn hmpd and swtchd lft fnl 120yds: kpt on clsng stages* **7/1**

0-06 **9** *1* **Whipphound**6 [387] 4-9-4 **67**.... TomMcLaughlin 7 59
(Mark Brisbourne) *sn chsng ldrs: rdn 2f out: wknd fnl f: btn whn edgd lft fnl 120yds* **15/2**

0002 **10** *1 ½* **Dickie Le Davoir**6 [385] 8-8-9 **63**....(b) CharlesEddery(5) 1 50
(Richard Guest) *outpcd most of way* **14/1**

1m 13.98s (0.88) **Going Correction** -0.025s/f (Stan) 10 Ran SP% **117.3**
Speed ratings (Par 103): **93,92,91,90,90 88,88,88,86,84**
toteswingers: 1&2 £11.40, 2&3 £4.40, 1&3 £17.00 CSF £79.60 CT £515.40 TOTE £20.10: £5.20, £2.20, £2.30; EX 130.50 Trifecta £544.50 Pool: £735.88 - 0.73 winning units..
Owner B Neaves **Bred** Major K R Thompson **Trained** Epsom, Surrey

FOCUS
The opening division of a moderate 6f handicap in which only two were not previous course winners. It was run at a modest pace and it paid to race handily. The form looks very ordinary.
Dingaan(IRE) Official explanation: jockey said gelding was denied a clear run

474 SKYSPORTS.COM DVINSKY'S 200TH RUN RACING H'CAP (DIV II) 6f (P)
6:00 (6:00) (Class 5) (0-70,72) 4-Y-0+ **£2,264** (£673; £336; £168) **Stalls** Low

Form RPR
34-0 **1** **Sole Danser (IRE)**[9] 359 4-9-6 **68**.......................... RichardKingscote 3 78
(Milton Bradley) *stdd s: hld up in rr: hdwy ins fnl 2f: led 1f out: pushed along fnl f: comf* **13/2**[3]
-622 **2** *1 ¼* **Katmai River (IRE)**[17] 262 5-8-11 **59**.........................(v) SteveDrowne 5 65
(Mark Usher) *chsd ldrs: rdn over 1f out: styd on ins fnl f to take 2nd last strides but no ch w wnr* **4/1**[1]
1013 **3** *shd* **Lastkingofscotland (IRE)**[9] 359 6-9-7 **69**..............(b) HayleyTurner 10 75
(Conor Dore) *in rr: hdwy fr 2f out: styd on fnl f to take 3rd clsng stages but no ch w wnr* **6/1**[2]
-533 **4** *hd* **Dvinsky (USA)**[17] 267 11-9-0 **62**............................(b) TomMcLaughlin 7 67
(Paul Howling) *sn chasig ldr: slt ld 2f out tl hdd 1f out: styd chsng wnr tl no ex and dropped 2 pls last strides* **12/1**
5-15 **5** *1* **Vhujon (IRE)**[17] 267 7-8-13 **61**....................................... LukeMorris 9 63
(Peter Grayson) *in rr: drvn and hdwy over 1f out: styd on fnl f: nt rch ldrs* **4/1**[1]
1-64 **6** *1* **Mack's Sister**[17] 267 5-9-0 **62**.. AdamKirby 1 61
(Dean Ivory) *chsd ldrs: rdn over 1f out: wknd ins fnl f* **6/1**[2]
06-0 **7** *nk* **Baby Dottie**[18] 252 5-9-2 **64**.. IanMongan 6 62
(Pat Phelan) *in rr: pushed along over 2f out: styd on wl clsng stages biut nvr a threat* **7/1**
-405 **8** *1 ¼* **Riflessione**[6] 388 6-8-12 **67**..(v) DarrenEgan[(7)] 2 61
(Ronald Harris) *led tl hdd 2f out: wknd qckly ins fnl f* **16/1**
020- **9** *nk* **Amazing Win (IRE)**[49] 7848 4-8-3 **56** ow1........................ CharlesBishop[(5)] 4 49
(Mick Channon) *chsd ldrs: drvn over 2f out: wknd qckly fnl f* **9/1**

1m 12.04s (-1.06) **Going Correction** -0.025s/f (Stan) **9** Ran SP% **118.0**
Speed ratings (Par 103): **106,104,104,103,102 101,100,99,98**
toteswingers:1&2:£3.00, 1&3:£9.60, 2&3:£2.70 CSF £33.45 CT £167.96 TOTE £10.40: £3.10, £1.80, £2.20; EX 51.60 Trifecta £230.00 Pool: £1,137.67 - 3.66 winning units..
Owner E A Hayward **Bred** Airlie Stud **Trained** Sedbury, Gloucs

FOCUS
The second division of the moderate 6f handicap and it was run at a decent pace. Sound form, set around the runner-up.
Katmai River(IRE) Official explanation: trainer's rep said gelding lost a front shoe
T/Jkpt: £12,979.50 to a £1 stake. Pool:£127,967.85 - 7.00 winning tickets T/Plt: £309.40 to a £1 stake. Pool:£139,829.98 - 329.81 winning tickets T/Qpdt: £120.70 to a £1 stake. Pool:£12,087.32 - 74.10 winning tickets ST

364 CAGNES-SUR-MER
Wednesday, February 8

OFFICIAL GOING: Fibresand: standard

475a PRIX DU BORD DE MER (MAIDEN) (3YO) (FIBRESAND) 1m 2f (D)
12:00 (12:00) 3-Y-O **£9,583** (£3,833; £2,875; £1,916; £958)

RPR
1 **Sorellino (FR)** 3-9-2 0.. JulienAuge 12 81
(J Boisnard, France) **106/10**
2 *½* **Faraway Run (IRE)**[19] 247 3-9-2 0........................... SylvainRuis 3 80
(P Khozian, France) **5/2**[2]
3 *nse* **Saint Loup (FR)**[23] 3-9-2 0..........................(p) IoritzMendizabal 7 79
(J-C Rouget, France) **6/4**[1]
4 *1* **Coeur A Coeur (FR)** 3-9-2 0.................................. MickaelForest 1 77
(W Walton, France) **19/5**[3]
5 *3* **Rabhi Jacob (FR)** 3-8-11 0 ow1.......................... XavierBergeron[(6)] 10 72
(D Rabhi, France) **48/1**
6 *1* **Coolita (FR)**[138] 3-8-13 0.. FabriceVeron 8 66
(D Allard, France) **12/1**
7 *hd* **Macharov (FR)**[29] 3-9-2 0................................ SebastienMaillot 9 69
(J Van Handenhove, France) **57/1**
8 *2* **Orarabit (IRE)**[29] 3-8-7 0..................................... MarcLerner[(6)] 11 62
(C Boutin, France) **77/1**
9 *2* **Hyson**[9] 365 3-9-2 0.........................(p) Francois-XavierBertras 5 61
(Reg Hollinshead) *racd midfield: rdn bef st: no ex: grad fdd* **22/1**
10 *snk* **Surrey Storm**[19] 247 3-8-13 0............................ CarlaO'Halloran 2 58
(Mme G Rarick, France) **62/1**
11 **American Folie (FR)** 3-8-13 0................................ LaurentDoreau 4 58
(K Borgel, France) **98/1**

2m 5.06s (125.06) **11** Ran SP% **117.7**
WIN (incl. 1 euro stake): 11.60. PLACES: 1.80, 1.30, 1.20. DF: 14.40. SF: 48.30.
Owner Michel Chartier **Bred** M Chartier, J Boisnard & G Margogne **Trained** France

476a PRIX DES MIMOSAS (CLAIMER) (3YO) (FIBRESAND) 1m 2f (D)
12:30 (12:00) 3-Y-O **£7,083** (£2,833; £2,125; £1,416; £708)

RPR
1 **Mohica Glaz (FR)**[29] 3-9-2 0..........................(b) AntoineCoutier[(5)] 4 79
(S Cerulis, France) **18/5**[1]
2 *nk* **Dylans Verse (IRE)**[15] 290 3-9-2 0...........(p) Francois-XavierBertras 15 73
(P Monfort, France) **7/1**
3 *1 ½* **Soir D'Ete (FR)**[48] 3-8-8 0................................ BriceRaballand 14 62
(J-P Delaporte, France) **106/1**
4 *1* **Potkol (FR)**[15] 290 3-8-11 0..........................(b) ThomasMessina 5 63
(C Boutin, France) **22/1**
5 *shd* **Verdelet (FR)**[37] 3-8-8 0.. SylvainRuis 1 60
(Mlle M Henry, France) **19/1**
6 *hd* **Path Finder (FR)**[9] 364 3-9-6 0............................ IoritzMendizabal 16 71
(Reg Hollinshead) *settled towards rr: proged to midfield bef st: u.p 2f out: racd w hd hanging on one side: r.o fnl f: no threat to ldrs* **11/2**[2]
7 *snk* **Mille Waki (FR)**[15] 290 3-8-7 0............................ NicolasGauffenic[(4)] 12 62
(C Boutin, France) **45/1**
8 *1 ¼* **Spidermania (FR)**[83] 7449 3-8-6 0.........................(p) EddyHardouin[(5)] 8 60
(Robert Collet, France) **15/2**
9 *1* **Abrasivo (ITY)**[15] 290 3-8-11 0.. SUrru 10 58
(P Caravati, Italy) **44/1**
10 *1* **Baraamej (IRE)**[54] 3-8-8 0..................................(b) JohanVictoire 9 53
(C Boutin, France) **17/2**
0 **Lord Bedarrides (FR)**[29] 3-8-10 0.........................(b) RomainAuray[(6)] 6
(J Heloury, France) **63/10**[3]
0 **Askell Gwen (FR)**[33] 3-8-0 0.........................(p) NicolasLarenaudie[(8)] 11
(G Collet, France) **73/1**
0 **Pasco (BEL)** 3-8-10 0.. CesarPasserat[(6)] 3
(F Vermeulen, France) **31/1**
0 **Pont A Marcq (FR)**[15] 290 3-8-8 0.................................. MatthieuAutier[(3)] 2
(J Heloury, France) **96/1**
0 **Light Opera (FR)** 3-8-13 0...............................(p) StephaneRichardot 13
(D Rabhi, France) **13/1**
0 **Zatkova (ITY)** 3-8-8 0.. ThierryThulliez 7
(L Racco, Italy) **25/1**

2m 3.98s (123.98) **16** Ran SP% **116.8**
WIN (incl. 1 euro stake): 4.60. PLACES: 1.80, 2.60, 15.40. DF: 9.70. SF: 20.30.
Owner Mme Sylvain Aknin **Bred** T Grandsir **Trained** France

461 WOLVERHAMPTON (A.W) (L-H)
Thursday, February 9

OFFICIAL GOING: Standard
Wind: Light, behind Weather: Cloudy and cold

477 BET AT BLUE SQUARE APPRENTICE H'CAP 1m 1f 103y(P)
2:25 (2:25) (Class 6) (0-58,58) 4-Y-0+ **£1,704** (£503; £251) **Stalls** Low

Form RPR
2-45 **1** **Flying Applause**[9] 367 7-8-10 **52**.........................(bt) CharlesEddery[(3)] 9 59
(Roy Bowring) *in tch: nt clr run over 2f out: impr to ld over 1f out: hung lft ins fnl f: r.o towards fin* **6/1**[3]
-206 **2** *1 ¼* **Resplendent Alpha**[13] 329 8-9-5 **58**..............................(p) AmyScott 5 64+
(Alastair Lidderdale) *stdd s: hld up: hdwy 2f out: wnt 2nd over 1f out: ev ch whn n.m.r and hmpd ins fnl f: kpt on towards fin but wl hld* **10/1**
460- **3** *shd* **Cabal**[61] 7714 5-8-3 **47** oh1 ow1..................................(p) JackDuern[(5)] 10 51
(Andrew Crook) *hld up: hdwy on outer wl over 1f out: r.o towards fin: nt quite gng pce to mount serious chal* **10/1**
0-33 **4** *shd* **Beneath**[7] 389 5-9-2 **55**..(b) LMcNiff 8 59+
(Neil Mulholland) *a.p: kicked into ld 2f out: hdd over 1f out: nt qckn: kpt on towards fin* **1/1**[1]
5-50 **5** *1 ¼* **Hilbre Court (USA)**[16] 287 7-9-0 **53**..............................(p) DavidKenny 1 54
(Brian Baugh) *hld up in tch: dropped to midfield over 6f out: rdn 3f out: styd on same pce fr over 1f out* **16/1**
000- **6** *9* **Ashgrove Nell (IRE)**[43] 7902 4-9-1 **57**..................(be[1]) LukeRowe[(3)] 11 39
(Daniel Mark Loughnane) *stdd s: hld up: pushed along and kpt on over 1f out: nvr able to rch ldrs* **25/1**
24-0 **7** *2 ¼* **Ice Cold Bex**[25] 183 4-9-5 **58**..................................(v[1]) MatthewCosham 4 36
(Philip McBride) *led: hdd over 6f out: remained prom: regained ld 3f out: hdd 2f out: wknd over 1f out* **5/1**[2]
3000 **8** *8* **Kirstys Lad**[7] 390 10-8-2 **46**.. NoelGarbutt[(5)] 2
(Michael Mullineaux) *chsd ldr: led over 6f out: hdd over 4f out: remained prom: ev ch over 2f out: wknd over 1f out* **50/1**
0-60 **9** *3 ¼* **Tunza The Lion**[18] 264 5-8-2 **46** oh1.............................. DarrenEgan[(5)] 6
(Richard Ford) *plld hrd: prom: led over 4f out: hdd 3f out: sn rdn: wknd wl over 1f out* **33/1**
0-00 **10** *11* **Blonde Maite**[9] 367 6-8-7 **46** oh1..................................(b) JamesRogers 7
(Roy Bowring) *pushed along early: hdwy 6f out: sn prom: u.p over 3f out: sn wknd* **100/1**

2m 3.23s (1.53) **Going Correction** +0.125s/f (Slow) **10** Ran SP% **114.8**
Speed ratings (Par 101): **98,96,96,96,95 87,85,78,75,65**
toteswingers:1&2:£3.50, 2&3:£8.70, 1&3:£6.40 CSF £60.82 CT £589.06 TOTE £5.70: £2.00, £1.90, £3.30; EX 38.20 Trifecta £541.60 Pool: £768.53 - 1.05 winning units..
Owner K Nicholls **Bred** G H Beeby And Viscount Marchwood **Trained** Edwinstowe, Notts
■ Stewards' Enquiry : Charles Eddery three-day ban: careless riding (Feb 23-25)

FOCUS
A moderate apprentice handicap in which the front five pulled clear. The winner is rated back to November's C&D form.

478 SPONSOR A RACE BY CALLING 01902 390000 H'CAP 7f 32y(P)
3:00 (3:01) (Class 6) (0-65,65) 4-Y-0+ **£1,704** (£503; £251) **Stalls** High

Form RPR
00-5 **1** **Muhandis (IRE)**[34] 54 4-9-6 **64**.................................(v[1]) ChrisCatlin 5 73
(Nick Littmoden) *hld up in rr: swtchd to wd outside and hdwy over 1f out: r.o ins fnl f: led and edgd lft towards fin* **12/1**
06-1 **2** *nk* **Drive Home (USA)**[27] 153 5-9-4 **62**..........................(p) BarryMcHugh 8 70
(Noel Wilson) *dwlt: hld up: hdwy 2f out: str chal wl ins fnl f: nt quite gng pce of wnr fnl strides* **7/2**[2]
53-0 **3** *nk* **Downhill Skier (IRE)**[31] 102 8-8-12 **63**............................ JackDuern[(7)] 3 70
(Mark Brisbourne) *midfield: hdwy 3f out: chalng ins fnl f: led narrowly fnl 110yds: hdd towards fin* **12/1**
0-44 **4** *½* **Lucky Dan (IRE)**[7] 387 6-9-2 **65**..................................... DarylByrne[(5)] 2 71
(Paul Green) *hld up: hdwy on inner over 1f out: r.o ins fnl f: ev ch fnl 110yds: hld fnl strides* **9/1**[3]
1263 **5** *shd* **Mataajir (USA)**[10] 361 4-9-5 **63**.. JoeFanning 10 69
(Derek Shaw) *chsd ldr: rdn wl over 2f out: lost 2nd jst over 1f out: stl ch ins fnl f: styd on same pce fnl 75yds* **7/2**[2]
01-3 **6** *shd* **Ace Master**[32] 96 4-9-3 **61**................................. RussKennemore 1 66
(Roy Bowring) *led: rdn over 1f out: hdd fnl 110yds: no ex cl home* **10/3**[1]
-526 **7** *2 ¾* **Monadreen Dancer**[5] 422 4-8-13 **57**........................ StephenCraine 7 55
(Daniel Mark Loughnane) *prom: rdn and nt qckn over 1f out: sltly short of room ins fnl f: hld after* **14/1**
-305 **8** *¾* **Spin Again (IRE)**[13] 328 7-9-0 **63** ow1........................ LucyKBarry[(5)] 6 59
(Mark Wellings) *trckd ldrs: rdn and outpcd wl over 1f out: no imp ins fnl f* **16/1**
00-6 **9** *1 ¾* **Field Finner**[21] 214 4-8-8 **52**.. LukeMorris 4 43
(Scott Dixon) *dwlt: a bhd: pushed along over 3f out: nvr a threat* **25/1**
0-63 **10** *3* **Powerful Pierre**[13] 329 5-9-4 **65**..............................(b) DaleSwift[(3)] 9 48
(Ian McInnes) *in tch: rdn over 3f out: wknd under 2f out* **22/1**

1m 30.16s (0.56) **Going Correction** +0.125s/f (Slow) **10** Ran SP% **113.7**
Speed ratings (Par 101): **101,100,100,99,99 99,96,95,93,90**
toteswingers:1&2:£7.20, 2&3:£10.80, 1&3:£9.70 CSF £52.44 CT £531.91 TOTE £14.90: £3.40, £1.30, £4.50; EX 58.40 Trifecta £557.30 Part won. Pool: £753.12 - 0.80 winning units..
Owner A A Goodman **Bred** Shadwell Estate Co Ltd **Trained** Newmarket, Suffolk

FOCUS
Another moderate handicap, but a thrilling finish and little separated the front six at the line. Modest form, but straightforward.

479 ENJOY THE PUNTERS PACKAGE GROUP OFFER CLAIMING STKS 1m 141y(P)
3:30 (3:31) (Class 6) 3-Y-O £1,704 (£503; £251) Stalls Low

Form RPR
5-34 **1** **Clean Bowled (IRE)**[24] 196 3-8-13 58 (p) HayleyTurner 4 70
(Alan McCabe) *mde all: kicked over 3 l clr 2f out: edgd lft ent fnl f whn wl in command and drawing clr: r.o wl* **9/4**[2]
42-3 **2** *10* **Crowning Star (IRE)**[20] 230 3-9-0 62 LukeMorris 5 48
(J S Moore) *chsd wnr: rdn over 3f out: hung lft over 1f out: no ch w wnr after* **1/2**[1]
0 **3** *3 1/2* **Mallt (IRE)**[28] 132 3-8-6 52 (be) MartinLane 1 32
(Philip McBride) *s.s: hld up in rr: wnt 3rd over 3f out: rdn over 2f out and sn outpcd: flashed tail u.p: no imp and wl hld after* **25/1**
10-6 **4** *26* **Seven Year Itch (IRE)**[16] 288 3-8-4 46 ow1 AmyRyan(3) 2
(James Bethell) *trckd ldrs: pushed along 4f out: dropped in rr over 3f out: lost tch 2f out: t.o* **20/1**[3]
1m 50.04s (-0.46) **Going Correction** +0.125s/f (Slow) 4 Ran SP% **106.0**
Speed ratings (Par 95): **107,98,95,71**
CSF £3.66 TOTE £3.10; EX 3.50.Clean Bowled was claimed by R Dean for £6000.
Owner Mrs M J McCabe **Bred** Cathal Ennis **Trained** Averham Park, Notts
■ Stewards' Enquiry : Martin Lane Fine: £80. Improper riding, struck filly with blindfold leaving stalls.

FOCUS
A poor race, but something of a surprise result despite this being virtually a match. The runner-up disappointed and it's hard to know quite what the winner achieved.

480 BET AT BLUE SQUARE ON YOUR MOBILE H'CAP 1m 1f 103y(P)
4:05 (4:06) (Class 5) (0-75,75) 4-Y-O+ £2,425 (£721; £360; £180) Stalls Low

Form RPR
24/- **1** **Copper Canyon**[195] 7755 4-8-11 68 RyanPowell(3) 6 77
(J S Moore) *dwlt due to late removal of blindfold: hld up: hdwy over 4f out: sn prom: wnt 2nd over 2f out: led ins fnl f: edgd rt whn pressed: r.o and doing jst enough cl home* **20/1**
32-5 **2** *nk* **Knowe Head (NZ)**[21] 216 5-9-2 70 AdamKirby 10 78
(James Unett) *trckd ldrs: rdn and swtchd rt wl over 1f out: drew upsides wnr wl ins fnl f: sn carried rt: r.o but jst hld* **11/4**[2]
00-4 **3** *1 3/4* **Hidden Glory**[21] 216 5-9-7 75 (b) FrederikTylicki 5 79
(James Given) *midfield: hdwy 2f out: carried rt u.p over 1f out: sn chsd ldrs: styd on same pce towards fin* **11/2**[3]
000- **4** *hd* **Fastnet Storm (IRE)**[45] 7877 6-9-6 74 JoeFanning 9 78
(David Barron) *led: rdn and edgd rt ins fnl f: sn hdd: no ex cl home* **6/1**
000- **5** *1/2* **Black Coffee**[75] 7556 7-9-0 68 (b) TomMcLaughlin 2 71
(Mark Brisbourne) *dwlt: pushed along early: sn in midfield: rdn over 1f out: styd on ins fnl f: nt gng pce to rch ldrs* **20/1**
05-0 **6** *1 3/4* **Hawaana (IRE)**[21] 216 7-9-7 75 StevieDonohoe 1 74
(Gay Kelleway) *trckd ldrs: rdn and outpcd over 1f out: styd on same pce fnl 100yds* **17/2**
356- **7** *nk* **Captain Loui (IRE)**[67] 6409 4-8-8 62 LukeMorris 4 61
(Dai Burchell) *prom: rdn over 1f out: one pce fnl 100yds* **25/1**
-215 **8** *1 3/4* **Trip Switch**[12] 349 6-8-9 70 DarrenEgan(7) 3 65
(George Prodromou) *hld up: rdn and outpcd over 1f out: nvr able to chal* **2/1**[1]
460- **9** *1 3/4* **Peadar Miguel**[180] 1649 5-9-1 69 MartinLane 11 60
(Noel Quinlan) *hld up: rdn and sme hdwy over 1f out: no imp ins fnl f* **12/1**
600- **10** *8* **Angelena Ballerina (IRE)**[186] 4822 5-8-4 63 AmyScott(5) 8 37
(Dai Williams) *stdd s: hld up in rr: pushed along over 2f out: nvr a threat* **50/1**
000- **11** *1 1/4* **Lord Theo**[114] 6938 8-9-6 74 SteveDrowne 7 46
(Nick Littmoden) *prom: pushed along over 2f out: rdn and wknd wl over 1f out* **40/1**
2m 4.19s (2.49) **Going Correction** +0.125s/f (Slow) 11 Ran SP% **125.7**
Speed ratings (Par 103): **93,92,91,91,90 89,88,87,85,78 77**
toteswingers:1&2:£4.20, 2&3:£3.70, 1&3:£9.50 CSF £76.20 CT £368.77 TOTE £18.60: £4.70, £1.70, £1.80; EX 83.20 Trifecta £619.40 Part won. Pool: £837.07 - 0.10 winning units..
Owner Gary B Watts **Bred** Snailwell Stud Co Ltd **Trained** Upper Lambourn, Berks
■ Stewards' Enquiry : Darren Egan two-day ban: used whip with excessive frequency (Feb 23-24)
Ryan Powell two-day ban: careless riding (Feb 23-24)

FOCUS
A modest but open handicap in which the early pace didn't look that strong. A clear personal best from the winner with the third the best guide.

481 RINGSIDE CONFERENCE SUITE MAIDEN STKS 5f 20y(P)
4:35 (4:35) (Class 5) 3-Y-O £2,264 (£673; £336; £168) Stalls Low

Form RPR
2-2 **1** **Al Freej (IRE)**[26] 181 3-8-9 0 DominicFox(3) 5 76+
(Roger Varian) *prom: led after 1f: a travelling strly: effrtlessly asserted ins fnl f: easily* **1/6**[1]
3- **2** *2 1/4* **El McGlynn (IRE)**[43] 7898 3-8-12 62 LukeMorris 2 62
(John O'Shea) *prom: wnt 2nd over 3f out: rdn and ev ch wl over 1f out but a fighting losing battle: no ch w wnr ins fnl f* **10/1**[3]
63-3 **3** *2* **Superplex**[33] 86 3-9-0 64 (p) MichaelO'Connell(3) 3 60
(John Quinn) *led for 1f: chsd ldrs after: rdn over 1f out: one pce fnl f* **6/1**[2]
00-0 **4** *2* **Script**[10] 358 3-8-9 0 JulieBurke(3) 4 48
(Alan Berry) *hld up: pushed along 2f out: sn outpcd: nvr a threat* **100/1**
55 **5** *3/4* **Ma Kellys (IRE)**[6] 404 3-9-3 0 BarryMcHugh 1 50
(Micky Hammond) *hld up in rr: outpcd over 1f out: nvr a threat* **40/1**
1m 3.52s (1.22) **Going Correction** +0.125s/f (Slow) 5 Ran SP% **112.5**
Speed ratings (Par 97): **95,91,88,85,83**
CSF £3.10 TOTE £1.10: £1.02, £3.30; EX 2.90.
Owner Saif Ali **Bred** Mrs Sandra McCarthy **Trained** Newmarket, Suffolk

FOCUS
An uncompetitive maiden with a predictable result. The level is set around the second and third.

482 NAME A RACE TO ENHANCE YOUR BRAND H'CAP 5f 216y(P)
5:10 (5:12) (Class 5) (0-75,75) 3-Y-O £2,425 (£721; £360; £180) Stalls Low

Form RPR
0-21 **1** **Gabrial's Bounty (IRE)**[22] 201 3-9-2 70 StevieDonohoe 4 76
(Mick Channon) *hld up: rdn to cl 1f out: led narrowly wl ins fnl f: jst doing enough cl home* **8/15**[1]
01 **2** *nk* **Abi Scarlet (IRE)**[16] 283 3-9-3 71 HayleyTurner 3 76
(Hughie Morrison) *broke wl: led early: chsd ldr: led over 1f out: rdn and edgd rt ins fnl f: sn hdd narrowly: hld cl home* **4/1**[2]
41-3 **3** *5* **Man Of My Word**[39] 6 3-8-10 69 (p) MarkCoumbe(5) 2 58
(Scott Dixon) *bustled along to sn ld: rdn and hdd over 1f out: one pce and no ch w front duo ins fnl f* **13/2**[3]
150- **4** *1/2* **Pressure Drop (IRE)**[210] 3993 3-9-0 68 JoeFanning 1 55
(Jo Hughes) *racd keenly: trckd ldrs: effrt on inner over 1f out: no ex ins fnl f* **11/1**
1m 15.94s (0.94) **Going Correction** +0.125s/f (Slow) 4 Ran SP% **106.9**
Speed ratings (Par 97): **98,97,90,90**
CSF £2.88 TOTE £1.20; EX 2.80.
Owner Dr Marwan Koukash **Bred** D And Mrs D Veitch **Trained** West Ilsley, Berks
■ Stewards' Enquiry : Mark Coumbe four-day ban: used whip with excessive frequency (Feb 23-25,27)

FOCUS
An uncompetitive handicap, but the pace was honest. The winner may not have needed to improve.

483 PLAY ROULETTE AT BLUESQ.COM/CASINO H'CAP 5f 216y(P)
5:40 (5:41) (Class 7) (0-50,50) 4-Y-O+ £1,704 (£503; £251) Stalls Low

Form RPR
2-53 **1** **Lisselton Cross**[20] 227 4-9-2 49 (v) LukeMorris 5 57
(Martin Bosley) *chsd ldrs: rdn over 2f out: prog to take 2nd wl ins fnl f: r.o ld towards fin* **11/2**[3]
4-60 **2** *nk* **Tamino (IRE)**[18] 264 9-8-12 45 (b) FrankieMcDonald 8 52
(Alastair Lidderdale) *prom: led after 1f: set str pce: abt 3 l clr 2f out: rdn over 1f out: worn down towards fin* **20/1**
-042 **3** *2 1/2* **Flow Chart (IRE)**[16] 289 5-9-1 48 (b) AdamKirby 9 47
(Peter Grayson) *racd in rr div: hdwy on inner 1f out: r.o ins fnl f: nt rch front duo* **9/2**[2]
0-00 **4** *1* **Odd Ball (IRE)**[20] 232 5-8-9 45 AmyRyan(3) 2 41+
(Lisa Williamson) *s.i.s: in rr div: rdn and hdwy over 1f out: running on whn nt clr run towards fin* **14/1**
60-4 **5** *1/2* **Meydan Style (USA)**[20] 226 6-8-12 45 (b) JoeFanning 3 39
(Richard Ford) *led for 1f: chsd ldr tl 2f out: rdn over 1f out: one pce ins fnl f* **4/1**[1]
/0-0 **6** *hd* **Diamond Fire (IRE)**[34] 67 8-8-12 45 (bt) LiamKeniry 13 38
(Adrian McGuinness, Ire) *chsd ldrs: wnt 2nd 2f out: rdn over 1f out: lost 2nd wl ins fnl f: no ex* **20/1**
00-0 **7** *1 3/4* **Farmers Dream (IRE)**[35] 46 5-8-9 45 DaleSwift(3) 4 33
(Richard Price) *midfield: pushed along 3f out: nvr able to chal* **14/1**
00-0 **8** *1/2* **Sweet Mirasol (IRE)**[21] 218 5-8-7 45 (t) JamesRogers(5) 6 31
(Mandy Rowland) *in tch: pushed along 3f out: sn outpcd: no imp after* **22/1**
600- **9** *2 1/4* **Lady Rumba**[145] 6176 4-8-9 45 RyanPowell(3) 10 24
(John O'Shea) *midfield: rdn 2f out: no imp: wknd fnl f* **50/1**
5-00 **10** *1 3/4* **Ad Vitam (IRE)**[7] 390 4-9-1 48 (v) MichaelStainton 11 21
(Micky Hammond) *a bhd: nvr on terms* **12/1**
-004 **11** *nk* **Bachelor Knight (IRE)**[10] 356 4-9-3 50 DuranFentiman 7 22
(Suzzanne France) *midfield: rdn 2f out: wknd fnl f* **4/1**[1]
400- **12** *2* **Passing Moment**[212] 3942 4-8-12 45 RussKennemore 12
(Brian Baugh) *racd on outer in midfield: rdn and wknd over 1f out* **16/1**
-000 **13** *3 1/4* **Novay Essjay (IRE)**[10] 356 5-8-12 50 DavidKenny(5) 1
(Dai Williams) *midfield: rdn 3f out: wknd 2f out* **33/1**
1m 15.77s (0.77) **Going Correction** +0.125s/f (Slow) 13 Ran SP% **119.2**
Speed ratings (Par 97): **99,98,95,93,93 93,90,90,87,84 84,81,77**
toteswingers:1&2:£9.70, 2&3:£16.10, 1&3:£3.70 CSF £117.17 CT £542.23 TOTE £7.10: £2.20, £4.30, £1.50; EX 114.40 Trifecta £397.50 Pool: £967.12 - 1.80 winning units..
Owner Mrs Jean M O'Connor **Bred** Burns Farm Stud **Trained** Chalfont St Giles, Bucks

FOCUS
Basement stuff, but a race run at a scorching gallop although little got involved from the rear. Not form to enthuse over.
Ad Vitam(IRE) Official explanation: jockey said, regarding running and riding, that his orders were to drop the gelding in and ride his race thereafter but from the outset it was outpaced in what was a fast run contest, it was stopped in its run turning into the home straight and he felt it would benefit from a longer trip.
T/Jkpt: £14,292.00 to a £1 stake. Pool of £40,259.43 - 2.00 winning tickets. T/Plt: £150.00 to a £1 stake. Pool of £116,595.80 - 567.35 winning tickets. T/Qpdt: £14.50 to a £1 stake. Pool of £11,151.13 - 567.42 winning tickets. DO

416 MEYDAN (L-H)
Thursday, February 9

OFFICIAL GOING: Tapeta - standard; turf - good
Rail out 12m on turf track.

484a DUBAL CASTHOUSE TROPHY (H'CAP) (TAPETA) 1m 3f
3:05 (3:05) (100-110,109) 3-Y-O+
£46,451 (£15,483; £7,741; £3,870; £2,322; £1,548)

RPR
1 **Spring Of Fame (USA)**[20] 242 6-9-3 107 MickaelBarzalona 11 114
(Saeed Bin Suroor) *settled in rr: smooth prog 2 1/2f out: rdn to ld fnl 55yds* **8/1**
2 *1* **Jamr**[20] 241 4-8-10 102 (v) PatCosgrave 8 107
(M bin Shafya, UAE) *mid-div: smooth prog to chse to ldrs 3f out: led 1 1/2f out: hdd 55yds out* **4/1**[1]
3 *1/4* **Ottoman Empire (FR)**[28] 143 6-8-10 100 JamieSpencer 4 104
(David Simcock) *s.i.s: in rr of mid-div: chsd ldrs 2 1/2f out: ev ch 1 1/2f out: one pce fnl 110yds* **11/2**[2]
4 *2* **Bronze Cannon (USA)**[20] 242 7-9-1 105 (t) RyanMoore 3 106
(H J Brown, South Africa) *in rr of mid-div: nvr nr to chal but r.o wl fnl 2f* **14/1**
5 *3/4* **Once More Dubai (USA)**[364] 498 7-9-1 105 (bt) WilliamBuick 1 104
(Saeed Bin Suroor) *settled in last: n.d but r.o fnl 2f* **16/1**
6 *1 1/4* **Honour System (IRE)**[35] 48 5-9-2 106 SilvestreDeSousa 10 103
(Saeed Bin Suroor) *sn led: hdd 1 1/2f out: kpt on same pce* **6/1**[3]
7 *1 1/4* **Sirvino**[20] 241 7-8-10 100 TedDurcan 9 95
(David Barron) *trckd ldrs: ev ch 3f out: nt qckn fnl 1 1/2f* **9/1**
8 *1 3/4* **Lyssio (GER)**[20] 241 5-8-10 100 JamesDoyle 5 92
(Michael Attwater) *nvr bttr than mid-div* **25/1**
9 *2* **Fiery Lad (IRE)**[28] 143 7-8-13 102 KierenFallon 2 91
(Luca Cumani) *settled in rr: rdn 5f out: n.d* **22/1**
10 *1 1/2* **Trois Rois (FR)**[14] 318 7-9-1 105 (b) TadhgO'Shea 7 90
(Ismail Mohammed) *a in rr* **20/1**

11 ½ **Holberg (UAE)**[238] [3066] 6-9-5 109 .... FrankieDettori 6 94
(Saeed Bin Suroor) *trckd ldng duo: rdn to chal 4f out: wknd fnl 2f* **4/1**[1]

12 6 **Mr Brock (SAF)**[20] [242] 9-9-4 108 .... KShea 12 82
(M F De Kock, South Africa) *trckd ldrs: ev ch 2f out: wknd fnl f* **11/1**

2m 17.65s (-0.75)
WFA 4 from 5yo+ 2lb **12** Ran SP% **124.6**
CSF: 41.06 TRICAST: 199.75.
Owner Godolphin **Bred** Brushwood Stable **Trained** Newmarket, Suffolk

FOCUS
A decent handicap, but the form may be slightly misleading as the winner enjoyed a better trip than the runner-up and third. The field were taken along by Honour System, who went 27.76 for the first quarter mile, 52.00 for the half, 1.17.00 at the 6f point and 1.41.70 at the 1m point.

NOTEBOOK
Spring Of Fame(USA) didn't travel well when behind Prince Bishop on his reappearance, but that run clearly sharpened him up as he moved with much more enthusiasm from the off this time, and the slightly longer trip was also in his favour. He was entitled to win, having been successful from the same mark at last year's Carnival before chasing home Bold Silvano in the second round of the Al Maktoum Challenge on this card, but plenty went his way and he probably won't appeal as one to follow up.
Jamr couldn't sustain his bid after going clear early in the straight, but he would surely have won had he been produced a little later. He had landed his first three starts since switching to Dubai and clearly remains on the up. (op 9-2)
Ottoman Empire(FR) was stuck wider than ideal without much cover and did well to get so close. This run confirmed the promise he showed on the turf on his return from a lengthy absence/debut for this stable a month earlier, and next time might be the time to catch him. (op 11/2, tchd 5-1)
Bronze Cannon(USA) plugged on without mustering the required speed.
Once More Dubai(USA) either didn't go through with his effort or needed the run after a year off, his run flattening out after coming wide into the straight. He's a bit tricky.
Honour System(IRE) was a winner over C&D earlier in the Carnival, but was 4lb higher in better company here, and was deserted by Frankie Dettori.
Holberg(UAE), last seen finishing tailed off in the Ascot Gold Cup, failed to bounce back, despite having plenty going for him on this significant drop in class. Admittedly, the trip was short of his optimum, but he had won first time out in two previous seasons and also has smart synthetic track form. He was soon well placed, sitting in second for much of the way, but he hadn't shown much eagerness to get there, and he was beaten when under pressure before the turn. (op 9-2)

485a UAE 2000 GUINEAS SPONSORED BY DUBAL (GROUP 3) (TAPETA) 1m

3:45 (3:45) 3-Y-O

£96,774 (£32,258; £16,129; £8,064; £4,838; £3,225)

RPR

1 **Kinglet (USA)**[28] [142] 3-8-9 105 .... MickaelBarzalona 5 106
(Mahmood Al Zarooni) *settled in rr: rdn 4f out: chsd ldrs 2 1/2f out: led 55yds out* **2/1**[1]

2 ¼ **Mickdaam (IRE)**[28] [142] 3-8-9 100 .... ChristopheSoumillon 6 106
(M F De Kock, South Africa) *mid-div: chsd ldrs 3f out: ev ch whn n.m.r 1 1/2f out: r.o wl fnl 55yds* **7/1**

3 ¾ **Mehdi (IRE)**[28] [142] 3-8-9 101 ....(t) KierenFallon 7 104
(Brian Meehan) *mid-div: chsd ldrs 2 1/2f out: ev ch ins fnl f: nt qckn fnl 110yds* **14/1**

4 1 ¼ **Surfer (USA)**[28] [142] 3-8-9 100 .... RichardMullen 8 101
(S Seemar, UAE) *in rr of mid-div: kpt on same pce fnl 2f* **25/1**

5 1 **Dark Matter (AUS)**[14] [316] 4-9-5 107 .... TedDurcan 1 97
(S Burridge, Singapore) *trckd ldrs: led briefly 1 1/2f out: hdd 110yds out: one pce fnl 55yds* **7/2**[3]

6 ¼ **Noor Zabeel (USA)**[131] [6527] 3-8-9 88 .... RoystonFfrench 4 98
(A Al Raihe, UAE) *Tracked ldrs: ev ch 3f out: led briefly 2 1/2f out: wknd fnl 1 1/2f* **33/1**

7 1 ½ **Rassam (IRE)**[28] [142] 3-8-9 102 .... FrankieDettori 9 95
(Saeed Bin Suroor) *settled in last: nvr nr to chal* **11/4**[2]

8 4 **Burano (IRE)**[6] [417] 3-8-9 97 .... RichardHills 3 86
(Brian Meehan) *slowly away: nvr bttr than mid-div* **10/1**

9 5 ¼ **Sand Stamp (FR)**[6] [417] 3-8-9 88 .... HarryBentley 2 74
(S Seemar, UAE) *sn led: hdd 2 1/2f out: sn wknd* **66/1**

1m 37.72s (0.22)
WFA 3 from 4yo 19lb **9** Ran SP% **118.8**
CSF: 17.29.
Owner Godolphin **Bred** Darley **Trained** Newmarket, Suffolk

FOCUS
This was more competitive than the fillies' equivalent run the previous week, but still not a strong race, the Classics suffering from a lack of runners who were bred in the southern hemisphere. That side of the world held a 6-43 (14%) record over the 11 previous runnings of the UAE 2000 Guineas, compared to just 5-86 (6%) for the northern hemisphere, but they had only one representative this time. It's been said before, but the African Horse Sickness outbreak is surely to blame. The time was 1.43 seconds slower than the later Group 3 Firebreak Stakes for older horses.

NOTEBOOK
Kinglet(USA) had a dire trip when runner-up in the trial, but this panned out much better and he did enough. His rider once again felt the need to celebrate before the line, but it's becoming a bad habit and a potentially costly one, especially when the margins are so fine - here the runner-up was the horse with all the late momentum. The winner will presumably be considered for both other legs of the Triple Crown, the Al Bastakiya on March 10 and UAE Derby on March 31, but the 1m11/2f trip of those races may see him struggle to confirm form with the strong-staying Mickdaam.
Mickdaam(IRE) ◆ is very much going the right way, building on his sixth-place finish in the 7f trial, and surely has more to offer granted extra yardage. (op 8-1)
Mehdi(IRE) ran well with no obvious excuse.
Surfer(USA) had the opportunity to run a big race judged on his effort in the trial, when beaten under 3l despite covering more ground than any of his rivals, according to Trakus data. Bizarrely, though, he was again taken widest and once more covered most ground.
Dark Matter(AUS) was the sole runner bred in the southern hemisphere and he'd won both his starts since switching to Dubai. However, he had the ideal trip when taking the trial and it was always going to be tough for him to confirm form.
Rassam(IRE) is an extremely headstrong individual and, while he got away with it when winning his maiden, he had faded into third in the trial. In complete contrast to the tactics employed on those first two starts, he was this time held up in last, and it was a fascinating move that could have paid dividends had he relaxed. But he didn't, and that cost him his chance. He's one to leave alone for now, but he's a horse with a deal of raw talent and it won't surprise if this expert team eventually get the best out of him.

486a DUBAL POTLINES TROPHY (H'CAP) (TURF) 1m 4f 38y

4:20 (4:20) (100-113,113) 3-Y-O+

£67,741 (£22,580; £11,290; £5,645; £3,387; £2,258)

RPR

1 **Songcraft (IRE)**[28] [145] 4-9-1 110 .... SilvestreDeSousa 8 113
(Saeed Bin Suroor) *settled in rr: smooth prog 2 1/2f out: r.o wl fnl 1 1/2f: led fnl strides* **3/1**[1]

2 *nse* **Laajooj (IRE)**[35] [52] 4-8-13 108 .... FrankieDettori 4 111
(Mahmood Al Zarooni) *mid-div: chsd ldr 2 1/2f out: led 1 1/2f out: hdd nr line* **7/2**[2]

3 4 ¼ **Alkimos (IRE)**[28] [145] 4-8-8 104 .... KierenFallon 3 99
(Saeed Bin Suroor) *s.i.s: mid-div: chsd ldrs 2 1/2f out: ev ch whn one pce fnl f* **5/1**

4 5 ½ **Mikhail Glinka (IRE)**[28] [145] 5-9-3 110 ....(t) RyanMoore 9 96+
(H J Brown, South Africa) *trckd ldrs: led 2f out: hdd 1 1/2f out* **10/1**

5 ¼ **Irish Flame (SAF)**[91] [7347] 6-9-5 112 .... KShea 5 98
(M F De Kock, South Africa) *settled in last: chsd ldrs 3f out: ev ch 1 1/2f out: one pce fnl 110yds* **6/1**

6 8 ¼ **Jedi**[14] [317] 6-8-8 101 .... CSanchez 7 74
(A bin Huzaim, UAE) *in rr of mid-div: rdn 4f out: n.d* **18/1**

7 ½ **Joshua Tree (IRE)**[116] [6910] 5-9-6 113 .... WilliamBuick 6 85
(Marco Botti) *in rr of mid-div: nvr nr to chal* **4/1**[3]

8 *dist* **Bank Of Burden (USA)**[14] [319] 5-9-2 109 ....(t) Per-AndersGraberg 1
(Niels Petersen, Norway) *trckd ldrs tl 3f out: wknd fnl 1 1/2f* **33/1**

P **Royal Revival**[20] [241] 5-8-7 100 .... MickaelBarzalona 2
(Saeed Bin Suroor) *sn led: rdn and wknd 4f out: p.u* **33/1**

2m 34.77s (154.77)
WFA 4 from 5yo+ 3lb **9** Ran SP% **118.4**
CSF: 14.04 TRICAST: 50.01.
Owner Godolphin **Bred** Darley **Trained** Newmarket, Suffolk

FOCUS
They went just an okay pace - 27.31, 52.47, 1.16.71 and 1.42.69 - and a trio of patiently ridden runners, who were sporting the ever-familiar Godolphin silks, dominated the finish.

NOTEBOOK
Songcraft(IRE) improved his perfect record to four, just defying a 5lb rise for his win over 1m2f on his recent Dubai debut. He needed the extra trip and probably would have preferred a stronger-run race, although he did cover 11 meters more than the runner-up according to Trakus data. There may be more to come, but there will need to be before he can be considered a genuine Sheema Classic contender. Maybe he'll test his credentials in the Group 2 Dubai City Of Gold over C&D on Super Saturday (March 10). (op 100/30 tch 7/2)
Laajooj(IRE) probably found himself in front earlier than ideal. The horse had stamina to prove on this step up in trip (by Azamour but out of smart sprinter), and may also be the type who does little off the bridle, but in fairness he did find a bit extra when joined. Clearly he got this distance, but he won't mind a return to shorter. (op 4/1)
Alkimos(IRE) was beaten at odds-on behind Songcraft on his reappearance and first start since leaving Luca Cumani. This was a bit better, but he still didn't see his race out, even allowing for being committed before the first two. (op 9-2)
Mikhail Glinka(IRE) wasn't good enough.
Irish Flame(SAF) failed to build on the form he showed when breaking the 1m3f track record on the Kempton Polytrack when last seen. He travelled well but just doesn't let himself down on quick turf. (op 5-1)
Joshua Tree(IRE) disappointed on his first start since finishing runner-up in the Canadian International. (op 9-2)

487a FIREBREAK STKS SPONSORED BY DUBAL (GROUP 3) (TAPETA) 1m

4:55 (4:55) 3-Y-O+

£77,419 (£25,806; £12,903; £6,451; £3,870; £2,580)

RPR

1 **Sandagiyr (FR)**[131] [6556] 4-9-0 110 .... SilvestreDeSousa 9 111
(Saeed Bin Suroor) *mid-div: smooth prog 2 1/2f out: led 110yds out: r.o wl* **20/1**

2 ¼ **Tamaathul**[19] [261] 5-9-0 101 ....(t) AhmedAjtebi 8 110
(A Al Raihe, UAE) *settled in rr: chsd ldrs 2 1/2f out: ev ch fnl f out: one pce fnl 110yds* **40/1**

3 *shd* **African Story**[14] [315] 5-9-0 113 .... MickaelBarzalona 3 110+
(Saeed Bin Suroor) *mid-div: rdn to chse ldrs 2f out: r.o wl: nrst fin* **9/2**[2]

4 1 ¼ **Derbaas (USA)**[28] [144] 6-9-0 113 ....(t) RichardHills 6 107
(A Al Raihe, UAE) *trckd ldr: hdd 110yds out: kpt on same pce* **14/1**

5 ¼ **Bold Silvano (SAF)**[371] [416] 6-9-0 118 .... ChristopheSoumillon 7 106
(M F De Kock, South Africa) *in rr of mid-div: rdn 3 1/2f out: r.o same pce fnl 2f: nrst fin* **4/6**[1]

6 1 ¾ **Barbecue Eddie (USA)**[14] [315] 8-9-0 108 ....(b) TadhgO'Shea 5 102
(Doug Watson, UAE) *sn led: hdd 1 1/2f out: kpt on same pce* **16/1**

7 6 ½ **Ecliptic (USA)**[103] [7166] 4-9-0 107 .... FrankieDettori 4 87
(Mahmood Al Zarooni) *settled in last: nvr nr to chal* **13/2**[3]

8 ½ **Shamalgan (FR)**[138] [6369] 5-9-3 115 .... GregoryBenoist 2 89
(X Nakkachdji, France) *settled in rr: nvr nr to chal* **25/1**

9 8 **Alazeyab (USA)**[6] [416] 6-9-0 107 ....(vt) RoystonFfrench 1 68
(A Al Raihe, UAE) *trckd ldr: ev ch 1 1/2f out: wknd fnl f* **28/1**

1m 36.29s (-1.21) **9** Ran SP% **118.5**
CSF: 603.68.
Owner Godolphin **Bred** H H The Aga Khan's Studs Sc **Trained** Newmarket, Suffolk

FOCUS
Last year's running went to Skysurfers, who followed up in the Godolphin Mile, and runner-up was the high-class Musir. However, this season's race, upgraded from a Listed contest, proved an anticlimax and trying to establish the true worth of the form is not easy. The time was 1.43 seconds quicker than the UAE 2000 Guineas, but even so it's probably not a race to be positive about. The form is rated around the runner-up.

NOTEBOOK
Sandagiyr(FR), a 140,000euros purchase out of Alain de Royer-Dupre's yard, had been due to debut for Godolphin in the Al Rashidiya on January 26, but was a non-runner. He struggled when upped to Group company in France, but had only raced six times, so was open to plenty of improvement. It's hard to know exactly what he achieved and his next run will tell us more.
Tamaathul earned an RPR of 110 when trained in Britain, but he had been beaten off official marks of 102 and most recently 100 in a couple of starts here this year. For now at least, he anchors this form.
African Story, who was successful over 7f off 110 on his Dubai debut, didn't get a clear run in the straight until it was too late. He was really going on at the finish and would have won with an untroubled trip, making the form even more muddling.
Derbaas(USA) might do better back on turf.
Bold Silvano(SAF), sidelined since winning the second round of the Al Maktoum Challenge on this card last year, was well backed, but he found little off the bridle and was nowhere near his best. He might come on plenty for the run and will be suited by further, but he cannot be backed with any confidence next time.

Ecliptic(USA) was disappointing. He had Frankie Dettori aboard, but was a major market drifter and ruined his chance by refusing to settle. While he's shown glimpses of real talent, he has presumably had some issues and can only be watched for now. (op 6-1)

488a AL MAKTOUM CHALLENGE R2 SPONSORED BY DUBAL (GROUP 2) (TAPETA) 1m 1f 110y

5:30 (5:30) 3-Y-0+

£96,774 (£32,258; £16,129; £8,064; £4,838; £3,225)

RPR

1 **Mendip (USA)**[28] 144 5-9-0 115 KierenFallon 4 114+
(Saeed Bin Suroor) *settled in rr: smooth prog 3f out: led 1 1/2f out: r.o wl* **10/1**

2 1 1/4 **Haatheq (USA)**[13] 344 5-9-0 107 RichardHills 9 111
(A Al Raihe, UAE) *trckd ldrs: led 2f out: r.o same pce* **25/1**

3 1 **Master Of Hounds (USA)**[28] 144 4-8-13 115 ChristopheSoumillon 5 109
(M F De Kock, South Africa) *mid-div: chsd ldrs 2 1/2 out: kpt on same pce fnl 1 1/2f* **6/4**[1]

4 hd **Biondetti (USA)**[174] 5252 4-8-13 109 (t) MickaelBarzalona 3 109
(Mahmood Al Zarooni) *settled in last: nvr nr to chal but r.o fnl 2f* **14/1**

5 2 **Prince Bishop (IRE)**[20] 242 5-9-0 117 (v) SilvestreDeSousa 1 104
(Saeed Bin Suroor) *trckd ldng pair: ev ch 2 1/2 out: one pce fnl 1 1/2f* **3/1**[2]

6 1/4 **Richard's Kid (USA)**[320] 1002 7-9-0 116 (bt) RichardMullen 7 104
(S Seemar, UAE) *a in mid-div* **33/1**

7 4 **Dubai Prince (IRE)**[117] 6861 4-8-13 113 FrankieDettori 2 96
(Mahmood Al Zarooni) *a in mid-div* **10/3**[3]

8 5 **Submariner (USA)**[63] 7683 6-9-0 105 CSanchez 10 85
(A bin Huzaim, UAE) *mid-div: wd: n.d* **28/1**

9 14 1/2 **Hunting Tower (SAF)**[14] 316 10-9-0 100 (t) KShea 8 56
(M F De Kock, South Africa) *sn led: rdn 4f out: sn wknd* **50/1**

10 1/4 **Firebet (IRE)**[14] 319 6-9-0 105 AhmedAjtebi 6 55
(A bin Huzaim, UAE) *in rr of mid-div: n.d* **40/1**

11 10 1/2 **Pisco Sour (USA)**[200] 4376 4-8-13 115 WilliamBuick 11 34
(Saeed Bin Suroor) *trckd ldr tl 3 1/2 out* **8/1**

1m 56.42s (-2.58) **11 Ran SP% 129.6**
CSF: 244.15.

Owner Sheikh Hamdan Bin Mohammed Al Maktoum **Bred** Jayeff B Stables **Trained** Newmarket, Suffolk

FOCUS
The 2003 winner Moon Ballad remains the only horse to take this round of the Al Maktoum Challenge en-route to Dubai World Cup glory, and that's unlikely to change this year. A few of the interesting types disappointed and the form is limited by runner-up Haatheq. The sectionals were 26.81, 50.56, 1.14.78 and 1.38.46.

NOTEBOOK
Mendip(USA) presumably needed the run when only fourth in the first round of this challenge (behind Master Of Hounds) and this was more like it. His form figures on synthetic tracks now read 11131141 and maybe there will be more to come as he's long looked a slow-maturing type. However, he has hasn't looked top class and this form doesn't suddenly elevate him to that level.
Haatheq(USA) has been competing without success at Jebel Ali this season and was beaten off 109 when last racing on Tapeta. (op 22-1)
Master Of Hounds(USA) didn't get the clearest of runs in the straight but was basically one paced, failing to build on his fast-finishing second over 1m in the first round. He has just a Tipperary maiden win to his name and is probably best avoided. (op 13-8)
Biondetti(USA) was in need of the run according to his trainer, and he was set a lot to do. (op 20-1)
Prince Bishop(IRE) had won both his starts since being gelded, including defying a mark of 110 here last time, but he struggled on this return to Group company. (op 4-1)
Richard's Kid(USA) ran well considering he'd been absent for 320 days and came wide into the straight. (op 25-1)
Dubai Prince(IRE) flopped. He was reported to have a breathing problem when tailed off in the Champion Stakes when last seen and he's a horse with plenty to prove. (op 3-1)
Pisco Sour(USA) was last seen winning the Group 2 Prix Eugene Adam for Hughie Morrison in July 2011. He was beaten before the straight and weakened like a horse with a problem. (op 6-1)

489a DUBAL TROPHY (H'CAP) (TURF) 1m 1f

6:05 (6:05) (100-111,111) 3-Y-0+

£67,741 (£22,580; £11,290; £5,645; £3,387; £2,258)

RPR

1 **Mutahadee (IRE)**[20] 243 4-9-5 111 ChristopheSoumillon 13 117+
(M F De Kock, South Africa) *settled in rr: smooth prog 2 1/2f out: swtchd to stands' side rail: led 1 1/2f out: comf* **13/8**[1]

2 1 1/2 **Anaerobio (ARG)**[20] 246 5-8-9 101 (t) PatCosgrave 4 101
(M F De Kock, South Africa) *settled in rr: r.o fnl 2f but no ch w wnr* **12/1**

3 shd **Masteroftherolls (IRE)**[20] 246 4-8-11 104 MickaelBarzalona 6 103
(Saeed Bin Suroor) *in rr of mid-div: chsd ldrs 2 1/2f out: nt qckn fnl 1 1/2f* **13/2**[3]

4 1 1/2 **Navajo Chief**[20] 246 5-8-10 102 KierenFallon 1 99
(Alan Jarvis) *mid-div: chsd ldrs 2 1/2f out: nt qckn fnl f* **16/1**

5 1 **Club Oceanic**[20] 241 4-8-10 102 (v) SilvestreDeSousa 2 97
(Saeed Bin Suroor) *mid-div: r.o same pce fnl 2f* **8/1**

6 2 1/2 **Dubawi Star**[20] 246 4-8-8 100 (b) JamesDoyle 7 89
(John M Oxx, Ire) *trckd ldng pair: ev ch 1 1/2f out: nt qckn fnl f* **25/1**

7 2 1/4 **Rochdale**[14] 317 9-8-10 102 (t) RoystonFfrench 8 87
(A Al Raihe, UAE) *in ear of mid-div: nvr able to chal but r.o same pce fnl 1 1/2f* **33/1**

8 2 **Iguazu Falls (USA)**[19] 260 7-8-10 102 (t) XZiani 11 82
(M bin Shafya, UAE) *sn led: hdd & wknd 1 1/2f out* **12/1**

9 6 1/2 **Moran Gra (USA)**[14] 319 5-8-10 102 (p) ShaneFoley 5 69
(Ms Joanna Morgan, Ire) *trckd ldr: ev ch 2 1/2f out: wknd fnl f* **20/1**

10 1/4 **Storm Chispazo (ARG)**[14] 317 6-8-8 100 (t) HarryBentley 3 66
(H J Brown, South Africa) *settled in rr: n.d* **40/1**

11 12 **War Monger (USA)**[20] 243 8-8-9 101 RichardHills 12 42
(Doug Watson, UAE) *broke awkwardly: mid-div wd: wknd fnl f* **20/1**

12 16 1/2 **Secrecy**[28] 144 6-9-3 109 (p) FrankieDettori 10 15
(Saeed Bin Suroor) *nvr bttr than mid-div* **10/3**[2]

1m 51.62s (111.62) **12 Ran SP% 125.6**
CSF: 23.47 TRICAST: 113.30 PLACEPOT: £123.80 to a £1 stake. Pool of £13466.01 - 79.38 winning tickets. QUADPOT: £54.50 to a £1 stake. Pool of £781.92 - 10.60 winning tickets..

Owner Sheikh Mohammed Bin Khalifa Al Maktoum **Bred** Epona Bloodstock Ltd **Trained** South Africa

FOCUS
The sectionals were 26.60, 49.96, 1.14.11 and 1.38.06. The improving top-weight confirmed the good impression of his recent Dubai debut (when winning off 106) by totally outclassing a bunch of runners with little in hand of their current ratings.

NOTEBOOK
Mutahadee(IRE) ended up stands' side in the straight, through accident or design, and was eased off from fully a furlong out, looking value for at least treble the winning margin. Things are about to get tougher, but surely he's a Group horse. (op 7-4)
Anaerobio(ARG) was next best, just reversing recent form with Masteroftherolls.
Masteroftherolls(IRE) does not look particularly well handicapped. (op 6-1)
Navajo Chief, racing over a trip that probably stretches him, was a bit keen early and did well to finish so close.
Club Oceanic had a visor replacing cheekpieces but didn't look keen. He is very much one to avoid. (op 10-1)

453 SOUTHWELL (L-H)

Friday, February 10

OFFICIAL GOING: Slow
Wind: Light against Weather: Bright and cold

490 BET ON WINNING DISTANCES AT BLUESQ.COM H'CAP 1m (F)

1:20 (1:20) (Class 6) (0-60,60) 4-Y-0+ £1,704 (£503; £251) Stalls Low

Form RPR

50-2 1 **Caledonia Prince**[10] 370 4-8-7 53 (p) JoshBaudains(7) 6 67
(Jo Hughes) *prom: trckd ldr after 3f: effrt 2f out: rdn to ld appr fnl f: sn clr* **5/2**[1]

-560 2 4 1/2 **Putin (IRE)**[15] 306 4-8-4 48 (bt) LauraPike(5) 8 52
(Phil McEntee) *led: rdn along over 2f out: hdd appr fnl f: kpt on same pce* **28/1**

060- 3 3/4 **Just Five (IRE)**[45] 7887 6-9-4 57 (v) TomEaves 1 59
(John Weymes) *trckd ldrs: hdwy to chse ldng pair 2f out: sn rdn: kpt on same pce* **20/1**

-224 4 nk **Spacecraft (IRE)**[10] 370 5-9-0 53 (b) JoeFanning 9 54
(Christopher Kellett) *in tch: n.m.r over 3f out: hdwy towards inner over 2f out: rdn to chse ldrs over 1f out: one pce fnl f* **4/1**[3]

0-42 5 2 1/4 **Symphonic Dancer (USA)**[8] 384 5-9-2 55 RussKennemore 11 51
(Brian Baugh) *in tch on outer: rdn along over 2f out: kpt on: nt rch ldrs* **7/2**[2]

0-05 6 2 3/4 **Sofias Number One (USA)**[10] 372 4-9-7 60 (b) MartinLane 5 50
(Roy Bowring) *chsd ldrs: rdn over 2f out: sn one pce* **5/1**

-324 7 2 3/4 **Very Well Red**[16] 293 9-8-11 50 ChrisCatlin 10 33
(Peter Hiatt) *prom: rdn along 3f out: grad wknd* **14/1**

60-0 8 nse **Sky Diamond (IRE)**[26] 183 4-9-5 58 FrederikTylicki 3 41
(John Mackie) *a in rr* **16/1**

3-60 9 7 **Jay Jays Joy**[3] 453 4-8-13 52 (b) MickyFenton 2 19
(Paul Midgley) *chsd ldrs on inner: rdn along over 3f out: sn wknd* **14/1**

0-40 10 15 **Kheskianto (IRE)**[31] 113 6-8-3 49 oh1 ow3 (bt) DannyBrock(7) 7
(Michael Chapman) *s.i.s and a in rr* **50/1**

1m 42.97s (-0.73) **Going Correction** +0.075s/f (Slow) **10 Ran SP% 116.8**
Speed ratings (Par 101): **106,101,100,100,98 95,92,92,85,70**
toteswingers:1&2:£10.10, 2&3:£21.00, 1&3:£15.90 CSF £82.23 CT £1192.52 TOTE £3.90: £1.30, £4.30, £7.00; EX 74.20 TRIFECTA Not won..

Owner Isla & Colin Cage **Bred** Mrs I M Cage And C J Cage **Trained** Lambourn, Berks

FOCUS
A moderate contest. The winner was well in and it's doubtful he had to improve on his latest second. The form is not particularly solid.
Spacecraft(IRE) Official explanation: jockey said gelding hung right
Sofias Number One(USA) Official explanation: trainer said gelding had a breathing problem

491 TICKETS AT SOUTHWELL-RACECOURSE.CO.UK H'CAP 6f (F)

1:50 (1:52) (Class 6) (0-65,65) 3-Y-0 £1,704 (£503; £251) Stalls Low

Form RPR

02-6 1 **Reve Du Jour (IRE)**[27] 181 3-9-2 60 JimmyFortune 6 67
(Alan McCabe) *set stdy pce: jnd wl over 2f out: rdn over 1f out: hung rt ins fnl f: kpt on* **10/3**[2]

300- 2 3/4 **Dansili Dutch (IRE)**[71] 7592 3-8-10 59 DeanHeslop(5) 5 64+
(David Barron) *trckd ldrs: n.m.r and swtchd rt to outer over 3f out: sn rdn along and outpcd: hdwy wl over 1f out: kpt on wl u.p fnl f* **8/1**

-360 3 1 1/4 **Ishiamiracle**[23] 201 3-9-0 65 (p) DannyBrock(7) 8 66
(Phil McEntee) *cl up: chal wl over 2f out: sn rdn and ev ch tl one pce ins fnl f* **9/2**[3]

46-1 4 1/2 **Clodhopper (IRE)**[9] 376 3-8-7 51 6ex FergusSweeney 2 50
(Jamie Osborne) *hld up towards rr: hdwy whn n.m.r 3f out: rdn to chse ldrs and edgd lft wl over 1f out: kpt on u.p fnl f* **3/1**[1]

323- 5 1/2 **Ambitious Icarus**[43] 7916 3-9-2 65 CharlesEddery(5) 7 63
(Richard Guest) *dwlt: sn pushed along to chse ldrs after 2f: rdn wl over 2f out: sn one pce* **7/1**

-424 6 6 **Prince Gabrial (IRE)**[9] 377 3-9-4 62 StevieDonohoe 1 41
(Kevin Ryan) *a in rr* **6/1**

463- 7 1 3/4 **Justbookies Dotnet**[51] 7837 3-9-7 65 (v) ChrisCatlin 4 38
(Louise Best) *chsd ldng pair: rdn along wl over 2f out: sn wknd* **12/1**

1m 18.26s (1.76) **Going Correction** +0.075s/f (Slow) **7 Ran SP% 111.8**
Speed ratings (Par 95): **91,90,88,87,87 79,76**
toteswingers:1&2:£6.10, 2&3:£7.50, 1&3:£2.90 CSF £28.09 CT £117.68 TOTE £4.80: £2.20, £4.30; EX 27.20 Trifecta £202.20 Pool £727.12 - 2.66 winning units..

Owner Mrs Z Wentworth **Bred** John Jones **Trained** Averham Park, Notts

■ Stewards' Enquiry : Dean Heslop two-day ban: used whip with excessive frequency (Feb 24-25)

FOCUS
A moderate sprint handicap run at an ordinary pace. The form is rated around the third.

492 GOLF BEFORE RACING AT SOUTHWELL CLAIMING STKS 5f (F)

2:25 (2:25) (Class 6) 4-Y-0+ £1,617 (£481; £240; £120) Stalls High

Form RPR

-003 1 **Where's Reiley (USA)**[7] 405 6-9-2 78 (b) FrankieMcDonald 2 84
(Alastair Lidderdale) *chsd ldrs on outer: rdn along 1/2-way: hdwy wl over 1f out: styd on to ld ins fnl f* **11/10**[1]

0055 2 1 3/4 **Punching**[3] 458 8-9-0 69 HayleyTurner 1 76
(Conor Dore) *cl up: led wl over 1f out: sn rdn: hdd ins fnl f: kpt on same pce* **7/2**[2]

315- 3 1 1/2 **Fair Passion**[167] 5484 5-8-11 77 DaleSwift(3) 5 70+
(Derek Shaw) *dwlt and towards rr: hdwy after 2f: rdn to chse ldng pair and ch ent fnl f: sn edgd lft and one pce* **11/2**

05-3 4 1 **Dancing Maite**[8] 388 7-9-4 73 (b) MartinLane 3 71
(Roy Bowring) *chsd ldrs: rdn along 2f out: wknd over 1f out* **5/1**[3]

6-45 5 3/4 **Spic 'n Span**[8] 380 7-8-11 60 (v) LukeMorris 4 61
(Ronald Harris) *led: rdn along over 2f out: hdd wl over 1f out: grad wknd appr fnl f* **16/1**

00-5 **6** *16* **Clanachy**[33] 95 6-8-4 36..............................(tp) DuranFentiman 6
(George Foster) *chsd ldrs: rdn along bef 1/2-way: sn outpcd and bhd* **50/1**

1m 0.12s (0.42) **Going Correction** +0.125s/f (Slow) 6 Ran SP% **109.7**
Speed ratings (Par 101): **101,98,95,94,93 67**
toteswingers:1&2:£1.40, 2&3:£2.20, 1&3:£2.10 CSF £4.89 TOTE £1.90: £1.10, £2.20; EX 5.30.
Owner C S J Beek **Bred** Overbrook Farm **Trained** Lambourn, Berks

FOCUS
Not a bad claimer. The form is a little shaky with the winner not needing to improve on his recent efforts.

493 TICKETS ON LINE AT SOUTHWELL-RACECOURSE.CO.UK (S) H'CAP 1m 4f (F)

3:00 (3:02) (Class 6) (0-60,62) 4-Y-0+ **£1,704** (£503; £251) **Stalls** Low

Form RPR
-663 **1** **Cloudy Start**[4] 446 6-9-7 58.............................. FergusSweeney 6 66
(Jamie Osborne) *trckd ldrs: cl up 1/2-way: chal 3f out: led 2f out and sn rdn: drvn ins fnl f: hld on wl* **5/2**[1]

/4-2 **2** *nk* **Broughtons Bandit**[16] 303 5-8-10 47.............................. StevieDonohoe 3 54
(Willie Musson) *prom: cl up 1/2-way: led 3f out: rdn and hdd 2f out: drvn and rallied ins fnl f: jst hld* **11/4**[2]

3-11 **3** *nk* **Magic Millie (IRE)**[10] 367 5-9-11 62 6ex.............................. DanielTudhope 5 69
(David O'Meara) *hld up in rr: stdy hdwy 4f out: wd st and sn chsng ldrs: rdn over 1f out: styd on to chal ent fnl f: ev ch tl no ex nr fin* **7/2**[3]

00-0 **4** *3/4* **Final Tune (IRE)**[14] 333 9-8-11 51.............................. RyanClark(3) 9 57
(Mandy Rowland) *in tch on outer: hdwy 4f out: chsd ldrs 3f out: rdn and ev ch over 1f out tl no ex wl ins fnl f* **25/1**

1-05 **5** *2 1/4* **Dunaskin (IRE)**[3] 454 12-8-4 46..............................(b) CharlesEddery(5) 1 48
(Richard Guest) *chsd ldng pair: rdn along 1/2-way and sn lost pl: kpt on u.p fnl 2f* **14/1**

/50- **6** *10* **Antoella (IRE)**[23] 7105 5-8-8 45.............................. ChrisCatlin 8 31
(Philip Kirby) *cl up: led 5f out: rdn along over 3f out: sn hdd & wknd* **20/1**

00-0 **7** *2 1/4* **Tayarat (IRE)**[3] 453 7-8-5 47..............................(bt) MarkCoumbe(5) 4 29
(Michael Chapman) *hld up: a in rr* **40/1**

633- **8** *1* **My Mate Mal**[325] 939 8-9-3 54..............................(p) MartinLane 2 35
(William Stone) *sn led: rdn along and hdd over 4f out: sn wknd* **8/1**

000- **9** *21* **Court Wing (IRE)**[22] 7631 6-8-11 48.............................. JoeFanning 7
(Richard Price) *a in rr: outpcd and bhd fr over 4f out* **14/1**

2m 42.49s (1.49) **Going Correction** +0.075s/f (Slow) 9 Ran SP% **113.0**
Speed ratings (Par 101): **98,97,97,97,95 88,87,86,72**
toteswingers:1&2:£2.20, 2&3:£2.50, 1&3:£2.50 CSF £9.04 CT £22.54 TOTE £3.60: £1.50, £1.10, £1.80; EX 11.10 Trifecta £23.50 Pool: £1104.37 - 34.76 winning units..The winner was bought in for 4,250gns. Magic Millie was claimed by A. J. D. Lidderdale for £5000. Tayarat was subject to a friendly claim.
Owner Martin St Quinton & Giles Wilson **Bred** Juddmonte Farms Ltd **Trained** Upper Lambourn, Berks

■ Stewards' Enquiry : Fergus Sweeney 14-day ban: (2nd offence in 12mths) used whip with excessive frequency (Mar 5-10,13-15)

FOCUS
The first four were covered by less than 2l at the line and this is really moderate form, although it was competitive enough for the grade. The winner did not need to improve.

494 FOLLOW US ON TWITTER @BLUESQ FILLIES' H'CAP 1m (F)

3:35 (3:35) (Class 5) (0-75,72) 4-Y-0+ **£2,264** (£673; £336) **Stalls** Low

Form RPR
54-4 **1** **Inpursuitoffreedom**[23] 198 5-9-0 66..............................(v) JimmyFortune 3 71
(Philip McBride) *trckd ldr: cl up over 2f out: rdn to chal wl over 1f out: ev ch and carried hd high ent fnl f: drvn to ld last 100yds: sn edgd lft and styd on* **11/8**[1]

4-22 **2** *1 1/2* **Zenarinda**[14] 331 5-9-2 68.............................. MartinLane 4 70
(Mark H Tompkins) *trckd ldng pair: hdwy on inner 2f out: rdn to chal ever 1f out: slt ld jst ins fnl f: sn drvn: hdd and no ex last 100yds* **11/8**[1]

1-40 **3** *nk* **Community (USA)**[23] 199 4-9-0 66.............................. JoeFanning 2 67
(Phil McEntee) *led: rdn and jnd 2f out: drvn over 1f out: hdd jst ins fnl f: hld whn n.m.r nr fin* **7/2**[2]

1m 44.12s (0.42) **Going Correction** +0.075s/f (Slow) 3 Ran SP% **106.4**
Speed ratings (Par 100): **100,98,98**
CSF £3.48 TOTE £2.00; EX 3.30.
Owner P J McBride **Bred** Lord Fairhaven **Trained** Newmarket, Suffolk

FOCUS
There wasn't much to recommend this trio pre-race, and the time was 1.15 seconds slower than the earlier Class 6 handicap, so it's doubtful the form is worth much. None of the three looked well treated.

495 MIRROR PUNTERS CLUB MAIDEN STKS 7f (F)

4:10 (4:11) (Class 5) 3-Y-0+ **£2,385** (£704; £352) **Stalls** Low

Form RPR
1 **Colour Guard** 4-9-13 0.............................. JoeFanning 1 76+
(Mark Johnston) *trckd ldrs on inner: hdwy to chse ldr over 3f out: led wl over 1f out: green and wandered ins fnl f: kpt on* **6/4**[1]

054- **2** *1 3/4* **Darsan (IRE)**[88] 7418 4-9-1 64.............................. DannyBrock(7) 2 66
(Phil McEntee) *sn chsng ldrs: led over 4f out: rdn and hdd wl over 1f out: kpt on u.p fnl f* **4/1**[3]

05- **3** *5* **Diva Donkey (IRE)**[63] 7685 3-8-5 0.............................. DuranFentiman 6 48
(Bryan Smart) *dwlt and in rr: hdwy on outer wl over 2f out: sn rdn: chsd ldng pair wl over 1f out: sn no imp* **16/1**

6/6 **4** *5* **Josie's Dream (IRE)**[6] 429 4-9-6 0.............................. JoshBaudains(7) 4 44
(Jo Hughes) *chsd ldrs: rdn along 3f out: sn one pce* **14/1**

5 *1/2* **Profile Storm (IRE)** 3-8-10 0.............................. LeeNewman 5 38
(David Barron) *prom: rdn along 3f out: wknd fnl 2f* **2/1**[2]

00-0 **6** *26* **Aiaam Al Wafa (IRE)**[23] 206 3-8-5 60..............................(be[1]) MartinLane 3
(Phil McEntee) *led: hdd over 4f out: sn wknd: bhd and eased fnl 2f* **20/1**

1m 30.17s (-0.13) **Going Correction** +0.075s/f (Slow)
WFA 3 from 4yo 17lb 6 Ran SP% **110.6**
Speed ratings (Par 103): **103,101,95,89,89 59**
toteswingers:1&2:£1.50, 2&3:£4.70, 1&3:£3.40 CSF £7.69 TOTE £2.30: £1.10, £1.40; EX 6.80.
Owner Sheikh Hamdan Bin Mohammed Al Maktoum **Bred** Meon Valley Stud **Trained** Middleham Moor, N Yorks

FOCUS
A weak maiden, but a winner with potential. The form is rated around the runner-up.

Aiaam Al Wafa(IRE) Official explanation: jockey said filly hung left

496 PLAY ROULETTE AT BLUESQ.COM/CASINO H'CAP 7f (F)

4:40 (4:40) (Class 5) (0-70,70) 4-Y-0+ **£2,264** (£673; £336; £168) **Stalls** Low

Form RPR
041- **1** **Myboyalfie (USA)**[136] 6434 5-9-5 68..............................(v) FrederikTylicki 3 83
(J R Jenkins) *in rr and pushed along 1/2-way: rdn over 2f out: gd hdwy over 1f out: styd on wl to ld ins fnl f: sn clr* **11/4**[2]

3-23 **2** *2 1/4* **Mazovian (USA)**[29] 139 4-8-8 62.............................. MarkCoumbe(5) 5 71
(Michael Chapman) *led: rdn clr wl over 1f out: drvn and hdd ins fnl f: one pce* **10/1**

6-31 **3** *nse* **Prince Of Vasa (IRE)**[10] 372 5-8-12 61 6ex..............................(v) AndrewMullen 6 70
(Michael Smith) *t.k.h: chsd ldrs on outer: hdwy to chse ldr 2f out: rdn over 1f out: kpt on same pce fnl f* **9/2**[3]

-041 **4** *5* **Ezra Church (IRE)**[8] 386 5-9-2 70.............................. DeanHeslop(5) 2 65
(David Barron) *trckd ldr: effrt over 2f out: sn rdn and grad wknd* **4/6**[1]

02-4 **5** *9* **Meia Noite**[30] 122 5-8-4 60..............................(p) DannyBrock(7) 4 31
(Alan McCabe) *chsd ldrs: rdn along 3f out: sn wknd* **25/1**

1m 28.5s (-1.80) **Going Correction** +0.075s/f (Slow) 5 Ran SP% **117.8**
Speed ratings (Par 103): **113,110,110,104,94**
CSF £27.97 TOTE £1.90: £1.50, £3.90; EX 26.80.
Owner D Badham **Bred** Robert Pierz & Robert Brooks **Trained** Royston, Herts

FOCUS
Just an ordinary handicap with the well-in favourite disappointing, but the time was good for the grade. The runner-up sets the standard.
T/Plt: £115.30 to a £1 stake. Pool of £77,783.81 - 492.13 winning tickets. T/Qpdt: £6.30 to a £1 stake. Pool of £8,469.51- 987.76 winning tickets. JR

477 WOLVERHAMPTON (A.W) (L-H)

Friday, February 10

OFFICIAL GOING: Standard
Wind: Fresh behind Weather: Overcast

497 BET ON WINNING DISTANCES AT BLUESQ.COM H'CAP 5f 20y(P)

5:10 (5:11) (Class 6) (0-65,70) 4-Y-0+ **£1,704** (£503; £251) **Stalls** Low

Form RPR
51-0 **1** **Da'Quonde (IRE)**[33] 101 4-8-8 51.............................. TomEaves 4 63
(Bryan Smart) *a.p: rdn to chse ldr over 1f out: r.o u.p to ld wl ins fnl f* **8/1**

24-6 **2** *2 1/4* **Court Applause (IRE)**[6] 425 4-9-5 62.............................. GeorgeBaker 8 66
(William Muir) *hld up: hdwy over 1f out: sn rdn: r.o to go 2nd post: nt trble wnr* **5/1**[3]

4-01 **3** *hd* **Novabridge**[4] 445 4-9-9 66 6ex..............................(b) AdamKirby 3 69
(Neil Mulholland) *sn led: rdn over 1f out: edgd lft and hdd wl ins fnl f: lost 2nd post* **15/8**[1]

-540 **4** *1 1/2* **Decider (USA)**[4] 445 9-8-9 59..............................(b) DarrenEgan(7) 6 57
(Ronald Harris) *prom: chsd ldr 1/2-way tl rdn over 1f out: edgd lft and no ex ins fnl f* **20/1**

3-21 **5** *hd* **No Mean Trick (USA)**[8] 380 6-9-6 70 6ex.............................. NedCurtis(7) 2 67
(Paul Midgley) *dwlt: hdwy over 1f out: nt trble ldrs* **9/2**[2]

-425 **6** *3/4* **Slatey Hen (IRE)**[6] 425 4-8-9 52..............................(p) JohnFahy 5 46
(Richard Guest) *hld up: hdwy over 1f out: rdn and no imp fnl f* **10/1**

00-5 **7** *3 1/2* **Patch Patch**[3] 456 5-8-8 54..............................(v) DaleSwift(3) 1 36
(Derek Shaw) *led early: chsd ldr to 1/2-way: rdn and wknd over 1f out* **40/1**

6-65 **8** *9* **Grand Stitch (USA)**[14] 327 6-8-10 58..............................(v) NeilFarley(5) 7
(Declan Carroll) *sn drvn along and prom: wknd 1/2-way* **15/2**

1m 2.21s (-0.09) **Going Correction** +0.125s/f (Slow) 8 Ran SP% **108.8**
Speed ratings (Par 101): **105,101,101,98,98 97,91,77**
toteswingers:1&2:£6.80, 2&3:£2.00, 1&3:£3.90 CSF £42.90 CT £95.78 TOTE £7.80: £3.20, £1.30, £1.20; EX 53.90.
Owner The Barber Girls **Bred** Gestut Sohrenhof **Trained** Hambleton, N Yorks

FOCUS
The going was given as standard although the winning rider of the first race described it as riding deeper than normal. This was well run although the pace held up. The winner built on her penultimate Southwell win.
Novabridge Official explanation: jockey said, regarding riding, that as the gelding had made the running and tired final furlong, he felt it prudent to ride to the line with hands and heels.

498 GREAT OFFERS AT WOLVERHAMPTON-RACECOURSE.CO.UK H'CAP 5f 216y(P)

5:40 (5:40) (Class 6) (0-60,62) 4-Y-0+ **£1,704** (£503; £251) **Stalls** Low

Form RPR
45-1 **1** **Consistant**[28] 155 4-9-3 58.............................. AdamKirby 10 66+
(Brian Baugh) *hld up: racd keenly: hdwy and edgd lft wl over 1f out: rdn ins fnl f: r.o to ld post* **3/1**[1]

0-25 **2** *shd* **Dunmore Boy (IRE)**[14] 329 4-9-2 60..............................(p) LeeTopliss(3) 6 68
(Richard Fahey) *a.p: chsd ldr over 2f out: rdn to ld ins fnl f: hdd post* **4/1**[2]

0-51 **3** *3 1/4* **Welcome Approach**[15] 313 9-9-2 57.............................. LukeMorris 12 55
(John Weymes) *prom: rdn over 2f out: styd on: wnt 3rd nr fin* **8/1**

003- **4** *1/2* **Almaty Express**[51] 7844 10-9-2 57..............................(b) KieranO'Neill 2 53
(John Weymes) *led 1f: led again over 3f out: clr over 2f out: rdn over 1f out: hdd and no ex ins fnl f: lost 3rd nr fin:* **8/1**

003- **5** *1 3/4* **Indian Arrow**[60] 7739 4-9-5 60.............................. TomEaves 8 50+
(John Quinn) *s.i.s: hld up: rdn over 1f out: r.o ins fnl f: nvr nrr* **14/1**

0-04 **6** *1/2* **Athaakeel (IRE)**[23] 210 6-8-7 55.............................. DarrenEgan(7) 11 44
(Ronald Harris) *hld up: hdwy u.p fr over 1f out: nvr nrr* **14/1**

0005 **7** *1/2* **Forty Proof (IRE)**[6] 424 4-8-12 60..............................(be) NoraLooby(7) 5 47
(Alan McCabe) *hld up: rdn over 1f out: styd on ins fnl f: nrst fin* **10/1**

60-0 **8** *1 1/2* **Miss Polly Plum**[35] 59 5-9-0 62 ow3..............................(p) JoshCrane(7) 1 44
(Chris Dwyer) *trckd ldrs: plld hrd: rdn over 1f out: wknd fnl f* **16/1**

0 **9** *2* **Volcanic Jack (IRE)**[19] 267 4-9-2 60.............................. MichaelO'Connell(3) 9 36
(Tony Carroll) *sn pushed along in rr: nvr on terms* **13/2**[3]

020- **10** *hd* **Namir (IRE)**[60] 7737 10-9-0 55..............................(t) FergusSweeney 3 30
(James Evans) *prom: rdn over 2f out: wkng whn hmpd and clipped heels wl over 1f out* **50/1**

0-60 **11** *8* **Prize Point**[14] 328 6-9-5 60.............................. PaddyAspell 13 10
(Tom Gretton) *chsd ldr tl led 5f out: hdd over 3f out: sn rdn: wknd 2f out* **40/1**

1m 15.27s (0.27) **Going Correction** +0.125s/f (Slow) 11 Ran SP% **113.3**
Speed ratings (Par 101): **103,102,98,97,95 94,94,92,89,89 78**
toteswingers:1&2:£4.10, 2&3:£8.00, 1&3:£3.60 CSF £13.83 CT £86.22 TOTE £4.30: £1.50, £1.10, £2.70; EX 14.70.
Owner Miss J A Price **Bred** Bearstone Stud **Trained** Audley, Staffs
■ Stewards' Enquiry : Paddy Aspell one-day ban: failed to ride to draw (Feb 24)

FOCUS
They went fast early in this sprint handicap and it paid to be ridden patiently. The runner-up sets the standard and the winner can do better.

499 PUNTERS PACKAGE GROUP OFFER MEDIAN AUCTION MAIDEN STKS 5f 216y(P)
6:10 (6:12) (Class 6) 3-5-Y-0 **£1,704** (£503; £251) **Stalls** Low

Form RPR
4-42 **1** **Sannibel**[9] 373 4-9-8 65 LukeMorris 2 69
(Tony Carroll) *pushed along early to chse ldrs: rdn 1/2-way: swtchd rt over 1f out: styd on u.p to ld wl ins fnl f* **2/1**[2]
2 *2* **Lord Paget** 3-8-5 0 JackDuern(7) 1 63+
(Reg Hollinshead) *s.s: outpcd: r.o ins fnl f: wnt 2nd post: nt trble wnr* **16/1**
63-2 **3** *hd* **Place That Face**[21] 219 3-8-7 62 HayleyTurner 3 58
(Hughie Morrison) *sn led: rdn over 1f out: hdd and no ex wl ins fnl f: lost 2nd post* **11/8**[1]
4 *3/4* **Diamondsinhereyes (IRE)** 3-8-7 0 ChrisCatlin 8 55+
(Ed Vaughan) *sn outpcd: hdwy over 1f out: hung lft and r.o ins fnl f: nvr nrr* **5/1**[3]
5 *hd* **The Kicking Lord** 3-8-5 0 JakePayne(7) 5 60
(Bill Turner) *prom: rdn over 2f out: styd on* **33/1**
05-0 **6** *2 1/2* **Maria Montez**[30] 121 3-8-7 59 KieranO'Neill 6 47
(J W Hills) *led early: chsd ldr: rdn and ev ch 2f out: sn hung lft: no ex fnl f* **16/1**
66 **7** *3 1/4* **Jolie Etoile**[16] 291 4-9-8 0 AdamKirby 7 40
(Tony Carroll) *broke wl: sn stdd and lost pl: hld up: shkn up over 1f out: nvr nr to chal* **28/1**
8 *3 1/4* **Aureolin Gulf** 3-8-12 0 LiamKeniry 4 31
(Reg Hollinshead) *prom: pushed along over 3f out: wknd over 1f out* **22/1**

1m 16.53s (1.53) **Going Correction** +0.125s/f (Slow)
WFA 3 from 4yo 15lb **8** Ran SP% **114.6**
Speed ratings (Par 101): **94,91,91,90,89 86,82,77**
CSF £31.73 TOTE £2.60: £1.10, £7.10, £1.50; EX 40.90.
Owner P & Mrs V Williams **Bred** Miss V Woodward **Trained** Cropthorne, Worcs

FOCUS
Modest maiden form with teh favourite again a bit disappointing. The winner is rated to his 3yo best.

500 WOLVERHAMPTON-RACECOURSE.CO.UK H'CAP 1m 5f 194y(P)
6:40 (6:42) (Class 5) (0-75,75) 4-Y-0+ **£2,264** (£673; £336; £168) **Stalls** Low

Form RPR
040- **1** **Accumulate**[140] 6306 9-9-7 70 (p) AdamKirby 9 81
(Bill Moore) *a.p: chsd ldr 4f out: led over 2f out: rdn clr fr over 1f out: eased nr fin* **5/1**[3]
20-0 **2** *3 3/4* **Quinsman**[23] 202 6-9-8 71 LiamKeniry 6 78+
(J S Moore) *hld up: nt clr run over 2f out: hdwy over 1f out: styd on to go 2nd nr fin: no ch w wnr* **7/1**
2-60 **3** *1/2* **Chookie Hamilton**[17] 285 8-9-10 73 TomEaves 11 78
(Keith Dalgleish) *led early: racd keenly and trckd ldr tl over 8f out: remained handy: rdn to chse wnr 2f out: styd on same pce appr fnl f: lost 2nd nr fin* **11/1**
5-11 **4** *1 1/4* **Rocky Rebel**[15] 310 4-9-4 72 PhillipMakin 1 76
(Chris Bealby) *chsd ldrs: pushed along over 3f out: rdn over 1f out: no ex fnl f* **7/2**[1]
3-03 **5** *1/2* **Cadgers Brig**[18] 271 4-9-1 69 (p) JoeFanning 4 72
(Keith Dalgleish) *prom: lost pl over 5f out: hdwy over 2f out: sn rdn: edgd lft over 1f out: no ex fnl f* **9/2**[2]
633/ **6** *2 1/4* **Painted Sky**[116] 361 9-9-1 64 LukeMorris 5 64
(Donald McCain) *hld up: hdwy over 2f out: sn rdn: wknd fnl f* **11/1**
40-0 **7** *3/4* **Blackstone Vegas**[4] 452 6-8-8 60 DaleSwift(3) 12 59
(Derek Shaw) *hld up: rdn over 2f out: nvr on terms* **13/2**
506- **8** *1 1/4* **Redhotdoc**[74] 7564 8-8-8 64 MatthewMcGhee(7) 2 61
(Bill Moore) *s.i.s: hld up: hdwy to ld over 8f out: hdd over 2f out: rdn and wknd over 1f out* **50/1**
9 *3 1/2* **Bocamix (FR)**[23] 6-9-7 75 (t) JustinNewman(5) 8 67
(Andrew Crook) *hld up: hdwy over 5f out: rdn and wknd over 2f out* **20/1**
15/5 **10** *3 1/2* **Sam Lord**[14] 332 8-9-12 75 PaddyAspell 10 62
(James Moffatt) *sn led: hdd over 8f out: rdn over 3f out: wknd over 2f out* **12/1**

3m 6.17s (0.17) **Going Correction** +0.125s/f (Slow)
WFA 4 from 5yo+ 5lb **10** Ran SP% **114.0**
Speed ratings (Par 103): **104,101,101,100,100 99,98,98,96,94**
toteswingers:1&2:£8.30, 2&3:£13.10, 1&3:£11.90 CSF £38.94 CT £365.43 TOTE £7.90: £2.10, £2.90, £3.20; EX 42.00.
Owner C W Moore **Bred** Raymond Cowie **Trained** Ledsham, Cheshire
■ Stewards' Enquiry : Matthew McGhee two-day ban: used whip with excessive frequency (Feb 24-25)

FOCUS
The early pace was quite steady and it only picked up when Redhotdoc went to the front heading out on the final circuit. An ordinary race for the grade, but a 3lb personal best from the winner.

501 FOLLOW US ON TWITTER @BLUESQ H'CAP 1m 4f 50y(P)
7:10 (7:10) (Class 4) (0-85,82) 4-Y-0+ **£4,204** (£1,251; £625; £312) **Stalls** Low

Form RPR
1 **1** **Queen Of Denmark (USA)**[16] 292 4-9-1 79 JoeFanning 3 89+
(Mark Johnston) *a.p: chsd ldr over 6f out: led over 2f out: sn rdn: styd on wl* **1/1**[1]
11-3 **2** *3 1/4* **Mazij**[17] 285 4-8-13 77 ChrisCatlin 6 82
(Peter Hiatt) *chsd ldr over 5f: remained handy: rdn to chse wnr over 1f out: styd on same pce ins fnl f* **9/2**[2]
-020 **3** *1 1/4* **Follow The Flag (IRE)**[14] 332 8-9-7 82 (be) JohnFahy 1 85
(Alan McCabe) *chsd ldrs: rdn over 3f out: styd on u.p* **12/1**
411/ **4** *nse* **City Ground (USA)**[16] 6276 5-8-12 80 DavidSimmonson(7) 2 83?
(Michael Easterby) *led: rdn and hdd over 2f out: no ex ins fnl f* **14/1**
210- **5** *1/2* **Royal Opera**[44] 6601 4-7-11 68 DarrenEgan(7) 7 70
(Brian Ellison) *rrd s: bhd: latched onto the rr of the field whn stmbld wl over 9f out: rdn over 2f out: styd on u.p but nvr trbld ldrs* **7/1**[3]
026- **6** *3/4* **Brouhaha**[63] 7699 8-9-2 80 RossAtkinson(3) 5 81
(Tom Dascombe) *hld up: rdn over 3f out: nt clr run over 1f out: no ex fnl f* **10/1**
031- **7** *6* **Countess Comet (IRE)**[29] 6592 5-9-3 78 PhillipMakin 4 69
(Chris Bealby) *hld up: hdwy over 5f out: rdn over 3f out: wknd over 1f out* **16/1**

2m 42.52s (1.42) **Going Correction** +0.125s/f (Slow)
WFA 4 from 5yo+ 3lb **7** Ran SP% **110.0**
Speed ratings (Par 105): **100,97,97,96,96 96,92**
toteswingers:1&2:£1.20, 2&3:£7.50, 1&3:£4.50 CSF £5.13 TOTE £2.50: £1.30, £2.40; EX 4.00.
Owner Sheikh Hamdan Bin Mohammed Al Maktoum **Bred** Darley **Trained** Middleham Moor, N Yorks
■ Stewards' Enquiry : Phillip Makin two-day ban: careless riding (Feb 24-25)
Darren Egan five-day ban: used whip with excessive frequency (Feb 25,27-29,Mar 1)

FOCUS
An interesting handicap, but it was steadily run and the form is possibly not solid. The winner could prove a fair bit better than this.

502 BLACK COUNTRY MEDIAN AUCTION MAIDEN STKS 1m 1f 103y(P)
7:40 (7:40) (Class 6) 3-5-Y-0 **£1,704** (£503; £251) **Stalls** Low

Form RPR
20-2 **1** **Captivity**[7] 404 3-8-7 75 JoeFanning 3 71
(Mark Johnston) *mde all: rdn and hung lft ins fnl f: styd on* **5/6**[1]
33 **2** *3/4* **Time To Dance**[7] 404 3-8-7 0 LukeMorris 1 69
(Joseph Tuite) *chsd wnr: rdn over 2f out: hung rt ins fnl f: styd on* **11/4**[2]
3 *hd* **Munificence** 3-8-7 0 ChrisCatlin 6 69+
(Marco Botti) *a.p: rdn over 1f out: styd on* **11/2**[3]
4 **4** *7* **Klang Valley**[17] 279 3-8-2 0 NickyMackay 2 49
(Marco Botti) *prom: rdn over 2f out: wknd fnl f* **12/1**
5 *3 3/4* **Halogen** 3-8-7 0 JamesSullivan 7 46
(James Given) *rn green in rr early: pushed along over 3f out: wknd over 1f out* **22/1**
6 *3/4* **By Popular Demand (IRE)**[23] 4-10-0 0 TomEaves 5 50
(Lisa Williamson) *s.s: hld up: hdwy over 1f out: wknd fnl f* **200/1**
7 *44* **Idarose (IRE)** 3-7-13 0 DominicFox(3) 4
(Hugh McWilliams) *dwlt: hld up: rdn and wknd 3f out: t.o* **100/1**

2m 3.32s (1.62) **Going Correction** +0.125s/f (Slow)
WFA 3 from 4yo 21lb **7** Ran SP% **110.1**
Speed ratings (Par 101): **97,96,96,89,86 85,46**
toteswingers:1&2:£1.30, 2&3:£2.00, 1&3:£1.90 CSF £2.98 TOTE £1.40: £1.10, £1.80; EX 2.80.
Owner Sheikh Hamdan Bin Mohammed Al Maktoum **Bred** N Poole And A Franklin **Trained** Middleham Moor, N Yorks

FOCUS
No more than modest form. The winner confirmed recent form with the runner-up.

503 PLAY ROULETTE AT BLUESQ.COM/CASINO H'CAP 7f 32y(P)
8:10 (8:10) (Class 7) (0-50,50) 4-Y-0+ **£1,704** (£503; £251) **Stalls** High

Form RPR
5636 **1** **Jonnie Skull (IRE)**[16] 305 6-8-10 50 (vt) DannyBrock(7) 5 61
(Phil McEntee) *chsd ldrs: led wl over 1f out: sn rdn clr* **13/2**
-022 **2** *3 1/2* **Cairanne**[9] 375 4-8-9 45 RyanClark(3) 10 46+
(Tom Keddy) *s.i.s: hld up: swtchd rt and hdwy over 1f out: r.o: nt rch wnr* **11/2**[2]
06-0 **3** *1 1/4* **Littleportnbrandy (IRE)**[8] 390 4-9-1 48 (bt) JohnFahy 7 46
(Richard Guest) *a.p: nt clr run 2f out: rdn and swtchd rt ent fnl f: r.o* **25/1**
0-06 **4** *1* **Diamond Fire (IRE)**[1] 483 8-8-12 45 (bt) LiamKeniry 6 40
(Adrian McGuinness, Ire) *mid-div: hdwy 3f out: hung lft 2f out: sn rdn: no ex fnl f* **10/1**
3-50 **5** *1* **Poppy Golightly**[14] 333 5-8-12 50 NeilFarley(5) 8 43
(Declan Carroll) *led: rdn over 2f out: hdd wl over 1f out: wknd ins fnl f* **11/2**[2]
6-30 **6** *2 1/4* **Tawseef (IRE)**[9] 379 4-9-2 49 (b[1]) TomEaves 11 36
(Roy Brotherton) *s.i.s: hdwy over 5f out: rdn over 2f out: wknd fnl f* **10/1**
005- **7** *1* **Gambatte**[191] 4681 5-9-1 48 LukeMorris 2 32
(Tony Carroll) *hld up: rdn over 2f out: nvr trbld ldrs* **18/1**
0-10 **8** *3/4* **Clerical (USA)**[29] 126 6-9-3 50 (p) HayleyTurner 9 32
(Robert Cowell) *mid-div: rdn over 2f out: hdwy over 1f out: wknd fnl f* **4/1**[1]
000- **9** *1 3/4* **Ellielusive (IRE)**[155] 5865 5-8-12 45 TomMcLaughlin 4 22
(Mark Brisbourne) *hld up: rdn over 2f out: wknd over 1f out* **40/1**
10-0 **10** *1/2* **Mnarani (IRE)**[18] 274 5-9-2 49 FergusSweeney 12 25
(James Evans) *chsd ldr tl rdn over 2f out: hung lft and wknd over 1f out* **22/1**
406- **11** *nk* **Bint Elnadim (IRE)**[43] 7911 4-9-2 49 JoeFanning 9 24
(Derek Shaw) *hld up: rdn over 2f out: sn wknd* **20/1**
1040 **12** *7* **Kyncraighe (IRE)**[6] 430 4-8-10 50 (tp) NicoleNordblad(7) 1
(Joseph Tuite) *hld up: rdn over 2f out: wknd over 1f out* **6/1**[3]

1m 29.99s (0.39) **Going Correction** +0.125s/f (Slow) **12** Ran SP% **117.2**
Speed ratings (Par 97): **102,98,96,95,94 91,90,89,87,87 86,78**
toteswingers:1&2:£5.00, 2&3:£33.10, 1&3:£48.80 CSF £39.54 CT £857.09 TOTE £10.60: £4.00, £1.80, £11.80; EX 41.30.
Owner Eventmaker Racehorses **Bred** Canice Farrell Jnr **Trained** Newmarket, Suffolk

FOCUS
A regular low-grade handicap.
T/Plt: £31.80 to a £1 stake. Pool of £90,942.04 - 2,085.40 winning tickets. T/Qpdt: £14.70 to a £1 stake. Pool of £8,990.95 - 449.64 winning tickets. CR

504 - 516a (Foreign Racing) - See Raceform Interactive

467 KEMPTON (A.W) (R-H)
Saturday, February 11

OFFICIAL GOING: Standard
Wind: Mild across Weather: Cloudy with sunny periods

517 WILLIAM HILL - THE HOME OF BETTING H'CAP 7f (P)
2:30 (2:30) (Class 5) (0-75,74) 4-Y-0+ **£2,385** (£704; £352) **Stalls** Low

Form RPR
0133 **1** **Lastkingofscotland (IRE)**[3] 474 6-9-2 69 (b) GeorgeBaker 2 78
(Conor Dore) *mde all: travelled wl most of way: rdn over 2f out: kpt on wl and in command fnl f* **9/2**[3]
6-64 **2** *2* **Mishrif (USA)**[17] 302 6-9-7 74 (b) RichardHughes 4 78
(J R Jenkins) *trckd wnr: rdn over 2f out: nt pce to get on terms w wnr: hld on wl for 2nd* **7/2**[1]
-155 **3** *1/2* **Vhujon (IRE)**[3] 474 7-8-5 61 DominicFox(3) 1 63
(Peter Grayson) *hld up in last 3 but wl in tch: rdn over 3f out: styd on steadily to chal for 2nd ent fnl f: drifted rt and no ex nring fin* **7/1**
0-50 **4** *4 1/2* **May's Boy**[10] 378 4-8-13 73 (p) RachealKneller(7) 5 63
(Mark Usher) *rrd leaving stalls: in last 3 but wl in tch: rdn wl over 2f out: wnt 4th ins fnl f: nvr gng pce to threaten ldrs* **9/1**

0-52 **5** *2* **Tuxedo**[7] 423 7-8-12 65 ChrisCatlin 6 50
(Peter Hiatt) *trckd ldrs: rdn over 3f out: sn hld* **7/1**

03-4 **6** *shd* **Sermons Mount (USA)**[21] 251 6-9-6 73 JohnFahy 3 57
(Paul Howling) *trckd wnr: rdn over 2f out: wknd fnl f* **13/2**

00-3 **7** *1 1/2* **Big Bay (USA)**[24] 199 6-9-5 72 (b) LukeMorris 7 52
(Jane Chapple-Hyam) *sn drvn along in last 3 but wl in tch: nvr gng pce to get involved* **4/1**[2]

1m 25.44s (-0.56) **Going Correction** -0.025s/f (Stan) **7** Ran SP% **108.7**
Speed ratings (Par 103): **102,99,99,94,91 91,89**
toteswingers:1&2:£6.50, 1&3:£11.20, 2&3:£20.10 CSF £18.48 TOTE £5.20: £2.00, £2.50; EX 21.10.
Owner Mrs Jennifer Marsh **Bred** Baronrath Stud **Trained** Hubbert's Bridge, Lincs

FOCUS
A modest handicap run at an uneven pace. The winner was allowed an easy lead and is rated up a length on his recent form.
Big Bay(USA) Official explanation: jockey said gelding was slowly away and never travelled

518 DOWNLOAD WILLIAMHILL.COM ON YOUR MOBILE H'CAP 7f (P)
3:00 (3:01) (Class 5) (0-70,70) 3-Y-O **£2,385** (£704; £352) **Stalls** Low

Form RPR

3-21 **1** **Kickingthelilly**[9] 383 3-9-3 66 ChrisCatlin 10 77+
(Rae Guest) *stdd s: bhd: nudged along 4f out: str run fr 2f out to ld ent fnl f: r.o wl* **10/1**

-452 **2** *3* **Songbird Blues**[8] 407 3-8-3 52 FrankieMcDonald 1 56+
(Mark Usher) *s.i.s: towards rr: hmpd over 3f out: hdwy 2f out: running on whn hmpd over 1f out: kpt on fnl f: no ch w wnr* **12/1**

546- **3** *nse* **Purple Affair (IRE)**[185] 4907 3-8-3 59 RachealKneller(7) 9 62+
(J S Moore) *mid-div: outpcd over 2f out: hdwy over 1f out: styd on to go 3rd ins fnl f* **11/2**[3]

5-46 **4** *2 1/2* **Casa Bex**[15] 322 3-9-3 66 (vt) LukeMorris 7 62
(Philip McBride) *bmpd leaving stalls: mid-div: effrt 2f out: styd on same pce fnl f* **11/4**[1]

4-00 **5** *hd* **Frock (IRE)**[10] 377 3-8-11 60 JamieMackay 6 56
(Sylvester Kirk) *bmpd leaving stalls: towards rr: pushed along over 3f out: r.o ins fnl f: nrst fin* **33/1**

60-0 **6** *hd* **Jimmy The Lollipop (IRE)**[23] 217 3-9-1 64 (b) MickyFenton 5 59
(Neil Mulholland) *led: rdn 2f out: hdd ent fnl f: fdd* **33/1**

-504 **7** *2* **Arabian Flight**[8] 394 3-8-10 59 JohnFahy 4 49
(John Bridger) *rdn whn hmpd over 1f out: a towards rr* **25/1**

1-26 **8** *2* **Fistful Of Dollars (IRE)**[12] 362 3-9-7 70 (b1) FergusSweeney 2 54
(Jamie Osborne) *trckd ldr: rdn over 2f out: wkng whn briefly hmpd over 1f out* **9/2**[2]

4-33 **9** *nk* **Naughtical**[15] 322 3-9-2 65 (p) MichaelHills 8 49
(J W Hills) *chsd ldrs: rdn over 2f out: wknd fnl f* **15/2**

-342 **P** **Haafhd Handsome**[8] 397 3-9-7 70 RichardHughes 3
(Richard Hannon) *trcking ldrs whn lost action over 3f out: sn p.u* **6/1**

1m 26.22s (0.22) **Going Correction** -0.025s/f (Stan) **10** Ran SP% **112.8**
Speed ratings (Par 97): **97,93,93,90,90 90,87,85,85,**
toteswingers: 1&2 £15.10, 1&3 £23.60, 2&3 £39.10. CSF £115.87 CT £736.95 TOTE £7.40: £1.70, £3.00, £2.60; EX 38.30.
Owner Tony Hirschfeld **Bred** Tony Hirschfeld & L K Piggott **Trained** Newmarket, Suffolk

FOCUS
This ordinary handicap was run at a sound pace and the form should work out. The winner improved nicely.
Songbird Blues Official explanation: jockey said filly hung right
Frock(IRE) Official explanation: jockey said, regarding running and riding, that his orders were to drop the filly in, as it has been struggling to finish previously, and to finish as close as possible, adding that it ran past beaten horses closing stages.
Arabian Flight Official explanation: jockey said filly had suffered interference in running

519 BET WITH WILLIAMHILL.COM ON YOUR MOBILE H'CAP 1m 3f (P)
3:35 (3:35) (Class 6) (0-55,55) 4-Y-0+ **£1,704** (£503; £251) **Stalls** Low

Form RPR

-462 **1** **Cantor**[9] 389 4-9-2 53 (b) RichardHughes 2 61
(Giles Bravery) *trckd ldrs: nt clrest of runs 2f out: sn rdn: led ins fnl f: rdn out* **4/5**[1]

5-03 **2** *1/2* **Missionaire (USA)**[20] 265 5-9-6 55 LukeMorris 7 62
(Tony Carroll) *led for 2f: trckd ldrs: rdn over 2f out: sn tk narrow advantage: kpt on tl no ex whn hdd ins fnl f* **10/1**

5-35 **3** *2* **Herschel (IRE)**[20] 265 6-9-4 53 (be) AmirQuinn 5 56
(Gary Moore) *trckd ldr: chal jst over 3f out: tk v narrow advantage briefly u.p over 2f out: remained w ev ch tl no ex ins fnl f: hld on for 3rd* **6/1**[3]

2-52 **4** *nk* **Penbryn (USA)**[15] 333 5-9-6 55 (v) SteveDrowne 1 57
(Nick Littmoden) *hld up: hdwy over 2f out whn nt clr run and swtchd lft: sn rdn: styd on fnl f but nt pce to threaten* **9/2**[2]

0-25 **5** *3/4* **Satwa Ballerina**[17] 303 4-8-9 53 (b) NatashaEaton(7) 6 54
(Mark Rimmer) *trckd ldrs: rdn over 2f out: sn one pce* **20/1**

1-06 **6** *2* **Prince Of Thebes (IRE)**[22] 224 11-9-1 55 (p) MarkCoumbe(5) 4 53
(Michael Attwater) *s.i.s: last: rdn 3f out: nvr gng pce to get on terms w ldrs* **9/1**

00-6 **7** *13* **Maxiyow (IRE)**[8] 399 4-8-2 46 oh1 DannyBrock(7) 3 20
(Terry Clement) *hld up: effrt to cl 3f out: nvr threatened: wknd over 1f out:* **33/1**

06-0 **8** *4 1/2* **Turbulent Priest**[30] 130 4-8-13 50 (bt) JamieGoldstein 8 16
(Zoe Davison) *little slowly away: sn trcking ldr: led after 2f: rdn and hdd over 2f out: sn wknd* **33/1**

2m 22.75s (0.85) **Going Correction** -0.025s/f (Stan)
WFA 4 from 5yo+ 2lb **8** Ran SP% **117.8**
Speed ratings (Par 101): **95,94,93,92,92 90,81,78**
toteswingers: 1&2 £3.30, 1&3 £1.70, 2&3 £6.50. CSF £10.38 CT £31.26 TOTE £1.80: £1.10, £1.80, £1.40; EX 7.90.
Owner Jim Tew **Bred** Cheveley Park Stud Ltd **Trained** Newmarket, Suffolk

FOCUS
A weak handicap, run at something of an uneven pace. A small personal best from the winner, but shaky form.

520 WILLIAMHILL.COM H'CAP 1m (P)
4:10 (4:10) (Class 4) (0-85,83) 4-Y-0+ **£4,075** (£1,212; £606; £303) **Stalls** Low

Form RPR

12-2 **1** **George Guru**[18] 280 5-9-1 82 MarkCoumbe(5) 1 93+
(Michael Attwater) *in tch: rdn 2f out: tk narrow ld ent fnl f: r.o wl: rdn out* **11/4**[1]

300- **2** *1 1/4* **Dunhoy (IRE)**[182] 5056 4-9-2 78 FergusSweeney 9 86+
(Tony Newcombe) *hld up: hdwy over 2f out: rdn over 1f out: r.o ins fnl f: snatched 2nd nr fin* **20/1**

60-0 **3** *nk* **She Ain't A Saint**[24] 199 4-8-10 72 (b1) LukeMorris 5 78
(Jane Chapple-Hyam) *trckd ldr: rdn to chal 2f out: ev ch ent fnl f: kpt on but no ex whn lost 2nd nr fin: jst hld on for 3rd* **16/1**

4-41 **4** *shd* **Viva Ronaldo (IRE)**[9] 391 6-8-10 77 ShaneBKelly(5) 8 83
(Richard Fahey) *awkward leaving stalls: sn settled in mid-div: rdn over 2f out: no imp tl r.o ins fnl f: jst failed to snatch 3rd* **6/1**

20-3 **5** *1* **Den's Gift (IRE)**[35] 90 8-8-9 78 (b) RyanTate(7) 2 81
(Clive Cox) *led: rdn over 1f out: hdd ent fnl f: no ex* **5/1**[3]

3-06 **6** *1 1/2* **Requisite**[16] 311 7-9-3 79 (b) GeorgeBaker 3 79
(Ian Wood) *mid-div: rdn over 2f out: nt pce to get on terms: wknd fnl 75yds* **12/1**

0055 **7** *1 1/4* **Opus Maximus (IRE)**[7] 432 7-9-0 76 JimCrowley 6 73
(Conor Dore) *hld up: rdn over 2f out: nvr any imp on ldrs* **15/2**

/4-2 **8** *5* **Hawawi**[17] 292 4-9-1 77 RichardHughes 7 70
(James Tate) *trckd ldrs: rdn over 2f out: btn ent fnl f: eased* **3/1**[2]

/0-0 **9** *1* **Photo Opportunity**[9] 391 5-9-2 83 AmyScott(5) 4 66
(Alastair Lidderdale) *hld up wl off pce: rdn over 2f out: nvr any imp* **33/1**

1m 38.33s (-1.47) **Going Correction** -0.025s/f (Stan) **9** Ran SP% **115.7**
Speed ratings (Par 105): **106,104,104,104,103 101,100,95,94**
toteswingers: 1&2 £8.20, 1&3 £8.30, 2&3 £24.70. CSF £58.12 CT £750.51 TOTE £2.60: £1.10, £4.80, £4.90; EX 49.80.
Owner T M Jones **Bred** T M Jones **Trained** Epsom, Surrey

FOCUS
A competitive handicap, and there was a solid pace. The winner continued his progress.
Hawawi Official explanation: jockey said gelding stopped quickly and hung right throughout

521 BEST ODDS GUARANTEED WITH WILLIAMHILL.COM MOBILE H'CAP 2m (P)
4:45 (4:45) (Class 5) (0-75,73) 4-Y-0+ **£2,385** (£704; £352) **Stalls** Low

Form RPR

51-3 **1** **Rasheed**[16] 310 4-9-6 73 JimCrowley 1 85+
(John Gosden) *mid-div: hdwy over 4f out: rdn over 2f out: led over 1f out: clr ent fnl f: styd on wl* **11/4**[1]

112- **2** *4 1/2* **Dance For Livvy (IRE)**[20] 7839 4-8-11 64 FrederikTylicki 3 70
(Robin Dickin) *mid-div: rdn wl over 2f out: hdwy sn after: styd on to go 2nd ins fnl f: no ch w wnr* **11/2**[3]

3/0- **3** *1 1/4* **American Spin**[63] 1839 8-9-8 69 TomMcLaughlin 8 74
(Luke Dace) *prom: led after 4f tl over 4f out: rdn and ev ch over 2f out tl over 1f out: kpt on same pce fnl f* **13/2**

012- **4** *1/2* **Shalambar (IRE)**[44] 7331 6-9-4 65 (p) LukeMorris 5 69
(Tony Carroll) *trckd ldrs: jnd ldr over 5f out: tk narrow advantage 4f out travelling wl: rdn over 2f out: hdd over 1f out: no ex fnl f* **11/1**

150- **5** *1* **Boston Blue**[14] 6749 5-9-6 72 LucyKBarry(5) 9 75
(Tony Carroll) *hld up: rdn over 2f out: styd on fr over 1f out: nvr trbld ldrs* **12/1**

120- **6** *hd* **Marcus Antonius**[26] 6988 5-9-6 67 MickyFenton 7 70
(Jim Boyle) *hld up: hdwy on outer over 4f out: outpcd over 2f out: styd on fnl f* **8/1**

00-0 **7** *nk* **Not Til Monday (IRE)**[15] 332 6-9-10 71 (v) RichardHughes 2 73
(J R Jenkins) *trckd ldrs: jnd ldr over 8f out tl over 5f out: rdn over 2f out: no ex fnl f* **8/1**

11-0 **8** *hd* **Kahfre**[24] 202 5-9-4 72 (be) ThomasBrown(7) 11 74
(Gary Moore) *hld up: midfield over 5f out: rdn over 2f out: no further imp* **25/1**

30-3 **9** *1* **Kavaloti (IRE)**[24] 207 8-9-11 72 (b) GeorgeBaker 6 73
(Gary Moore) *s.i.s: bhd: rdn over 3f out: styd on but nt gng pce to threaten* **5/1**[2]

/00- **10** *2 1/2* **Promised Wings (GER)**[30] 6121 5-9-1 62 FrankieMcDonald 4 60
(Chris Gordon) *led for 4f: rdn 5f out: sn lost pl: wknd 2f out* **50/1**

500- **11** *12* **Brilliant Barca**[21] 2186 4-8-8 68 MartinLeonard(7) 10 51
(Sheena West) *chsd ldrs tl 4f out: wknd over 2f out* **11/1**

3m 28.86s (-1.24) **Going Correction** -0.025s/f (Stan)
WFA 4 from 5yo+ 6lb **11** Ran SP% **124.4**
Speed ratings (Par 103): **102,99,99,98,98 98,98,98,97,96 90**
toteswingers: 1&2 £2.10, 1&3 £7.10, 2&3 £10.50. CSF £18.80 CT £95.07 TOTE £2.90: £1.90, £2.60, £3.00; EX 21.80.
Owner Ms Rachel D S Hood **Bred** Miss K Rausing And Mrs S M Rogers **Trained** Newmarket, Suffolk

FOCUS
A modest staying handicap, run at an uneven pace. The form seems sound enough, among the principals at least.
Marcus Antonius Official explanation: jockey said gelding hung right
Promised Wings(GER) Official explanation: jockey said gelding hung right

522 WILLIAM HILL H'CAP 6f (P)
5:15 (5:15) (Class 6) (0-65,71) 4-Y-0+ **£1,704** (£503; £251) **Stalls** Low

Form RPR

5334 **1** **Dvinsky (USA)**[3] 474 11-9-4 62 (b) TomMcLaughlin 11 70
(Paul Howling) *mde all: rdn 2f out: hld on v gamely thrght fnl f: drvn out* **25/1**

4-01 **2** *1/2* **Sole Danser (IRE)**[3] 474 4-9-13 71 6ex RussKennemore 4 77
(Milton Bradley) *stdd s: t.k.h in rr: weaved way through field fr 2f out: chsd wnr over 1f out: rdn and 1/2 l down ent fnl f: kpt on but a being jst hld* **9/4**[1]

2212 **3** *1 1/2* **Rightcar**[3] 473 5-8-11 55 RichardHughes 2 57
(Peter Grayson) *mid-div: short of room 4f out: rdn to chse ldng pair over 1f out: kpt on but nt gng pce to get on terms: jst hld on for 3rd* **5/2**[2]

-321 **4** *shd* **Do More Business (IRE)**[8] 396 5-8-3 52 (v) NathanAlison(5) 8 53
(Pat Phelan) *hld up: pushed along over 2f out: gd hdwy over 1f out: r.o wl ins fnl f: nrly snatched 3rd* **14/1**

33-3 **5** *1 1/2* **Mr Skipiton (IRE)**[29] 155 7-8-5 54 LauraPike(5) 6 50
(Terry Clement) *mid-div: hmpd 4f out: rdn over 2f out: no imp tl kpt on ins fnl f* **10/1**

-300 **6** *3/4* **Rapid Water**[11] 372 6-9-0 58 (p) MickyFenton 9 52
(Gary Moore) *mid-div: nt clrest of runs over 1f out: sn rdn: hld but styng on whn short of room and bmpd ins fnl f* **22/1**

4606 **7** *nk* **Sherjawy (IRE)**[3] 473 8-9-2 60 JamieGoldstein 5 53
(Zoe Davison) *trckd ldrs: rdn 2f out: sn one pce* **25/1**

5314 **8** *shd* **Chjimes (IRE)**[7] 425 8-9-2 60 (b) GeorgeBaker 3 53
(Conor Dore) *trckd wnr: rdn 2f out: nt gng pce to chal: wandered and bmpd ins fnl f: fdd* **12/1**

65-4 **9** *1 1/2* **Snow Ridge**[24] 203 4-8-11 55 (b1) JimCrowley 1 43
(Ralph Beckett) *in tch: bmpd on rails whn short of room 4f out: rdn wl over 2f out: wknd over 1f out* **4/1**[3]

-060 **10** *1 ¾* **Mandy's Hero**[7] 424 4-8-11 60.....(b) MarkCoumbe(5) 10 42
(Olivia Maylam) *dwlt: bhd: effrt over 2f out: wknd over 1f out* **50/1**
1m 12.9s (-0.20) **Going Correction** -0.025s/f (Stan) **10** Ran SP% **116.8**
Speed ratings (Par 101): **100,99,97,97,95 94,93,93,91,89**
toteswingers: 1&2 £15.70, 1&3 £7.40, 2&3 £1.80. CSF £79.00 CT £205.54 TOTE £20.80: £3.00, £1.20, £1.60; EX 81.20.
Owner David Hardaker **Bred** Eclipse Bloodstock & Tipperary Bloodstock **Trained** Lee-On-The-Solent, Hants
FOCUS
This was a moderate sprint handicap in which the first pair came nicely clear at the finish. The winner is rated up a length on his recent form, with the second to his C&D latest.
Do More Business(IRE) Official explanation: jockey said gelding hung left
Mandy's Hero Official explanation: jockey said gelding fly-leapt leaving stalls
T/Plt: £26.80 to a £1 stake. Pool of £67,061.89 - 1,820.50 winning tickets. T/Qpdt: £4.40 to a £1 stake. Pool of £5,460.81 - 910.34 winning tickets. TM

422 LINGFIELD (L-H)
Saturday, February 11

OFFICIAL GOING: Standard
Wind: virtually nil Weather: dry and very cold

523 BET ON TODAY'S FOOTBALL AT BLUESQ.COM MAIDEN STKS 1m (P)
12:35 (12:40) (Class 5) 3-Y-O **£2,385** (£704; £352) **Stalls** High

Form RPR
4 **1** **Burke's Rock**[24] 206 3-8-12 0..... JimmyFortune 4 75+
(Jeremy Noseda) *chsd ldrs tl wnt 2nd over 2f out: rdn to ld over 1f out: r.o wl and in command ins fnl f: eased towards fin* **11/4**[1]
4 **2** *2* **Attain**[21] 249 3-9-3 0..... JimCrowley 1 74
(Julia Feilden) *hld up towards rr: gd hdwy on inner over 2f out: chsd ldrs and rdn over 1f out: chsd wnr ins fnl f: kpt on but no threat to wnr* **6/1**[3]
2 **3** *1* **Imtithal (IRE)**[14] 350 3-8-12 0..... KierenFallon 2 67
(James Tate) *chsd ldrs: pushed along 1/2-way: rdn and chsd ldng pair 2f out: chsd wnr 1f out tl ins fnl f: kpt on same pce* **11/2**[2]
2 **4** *1 ¼* **Devote Myself (IRE)**[12] 360 3-8-12 0..... MartinLane 7 64
(David Evans) *chsd ldrs: rdn and unable qck jst over 2f out: drvn over 1f out: kpt on but no threat to wnr fnl f* **11/1**
33 **5** *1 ¾* **Yajber (USA)**[14] 350 3-9-3 0..... MarcHalford 8 65
(Terry Clement) *in tch in midfield: effrt on outer bnd 2f out: drvn and no imp fr over 1f out* **9/1**
P4-0 **6** *hd* **King's Wharf (IRE)**[11] 369 3-8-12 0..... MatthewCosham(5) 9 64
(David Evans) *led tl rdn and hdd over 1f out: lost 2nd 1f out: wknd fnl f* **100/1**
7 *3* **Bordoni (USA)** 3-9-3 0..... JoeFanning 6 57+
(Mark Johnston) *s.i.s: rn green in rr: struggling wl over 2f out: styd on fnl f: nvr trbld ldrs* **13/2**
0 **8** *hd* **Zenaad (USA)**[11] 369 3-9-3 0..... ChrisCatlin 5 57
(Seamus Durack) *s.i.s: t.k.h and rn green in rr: struggling 3f out: no threat to ldrs fnl 2f* **50/1**
6 **9** *2* **Chronic Flame (TUR)**[14] 350 3-9-3 0..... HayleyTurner 3 52
(Marcus Tregoning) *in tch in midfield: rdn and struggling wl over 2f out: wknd 2f out* **10/1**
10 *6* **Eastern Amour (IRE)** 3-9-3 0..... AdamKirby 11 37
(Marco Botti) *awkward leaving stalls and v.s.a: a bhd* **8/1**
00 **11** *1* **Fleeting Indian (IRE)**[16] 308 3-9-3 0..... FergusSweeney 12 35
(Linda Jewell) *chsd ldr tl over 2f out: wknd qckly 2f out: wl bhd fnl f* **250/1**
12 *53* **Payback (GER)**[139] 3-9-3 0..... LiamKeniry 10
(John Butler) *stdd after s: t.k.h: hld up in rr: lost tch rapidly 1/2-way: t.o fnl 2f* **80/1**
1m 36.64s (-1.56) **Going Correction** -0.075s/f (Stan) **12** Ran SP% **112.8**
Speed ratings (Par 97): **104,102,101,99,98 97,94,94,92,86 85,32**
toteswingers:1&2:£4.50, 1&3:£2.80, 2&3:£6.30 CSF £17.81 TOTE £3.30: £1.50, £2.20, £1.20; EX 21.70 Trifecta £121.30 Pool £424.64 - 2.59 winning units..
Owner S E Construction (Kent) Ltd **Bred** Brook Stud Bloodstock Ltd **Trained** Newmarket, Suffolk
FOCUS
Quite an interesting maiden for the time of year.
Eastern Amour(IRE) Official explanation: jockey said gelding ran green

524 BLUE SQUARE WINTER CARNIVAL IPHONE APP MAIDEN STKS 5f (P)
1:05 (1:09) (Class 5) 3-Y-O+ **£2,385** (£704; £352) **Stalls** High

Form RPR
1 **Cut Across (IRE)** 4-9-13 0..... SteveDrowne 8 67+
(Nick Littmoden) *in tch in midfield: pushed along 1/2-way: rdn and hdwy over 1f out: str run to ld fnl 75yds: r.o wl* **6/1**[3]
40- **2** *½* **Absent Amy (IRE)**[217] 3865 3-8-8 0..... JamieMackay 7 54+
(Willie Musson) *s.i.s: detached in last and niggled along: c wd bnd 2f out: stl last ent fnl f: hdwy and swtchd rt ins fnl f: r.o v strly fnl 100yds: wnt 2nd cl home* **9/2**[2]
024- **3** *nk* **Look At Me Now**[47] 7874 3-8-13 60.....(v) StephenCraine 3 58
(Jim Boyle) *pressed ldr: rdn 2f out: drvn ahd over 1f out: hdd and styd on same pce fnl 75yds* **7/1**
5-53 **4** *½* **Saint Boniface**[22] 219 3-8-13 66..... FergusSweeney 5 56
(Peter Makin) *pressed ldrs: rdn wl over 1f out: kpt on ins fnl f: styng on same pce and hld whn n.m.r towards fin* **7/4**[1]
04 **5** *¾* **Strike A Pose (IRE)**[15] 321 3-8-8 0..... MartinLane 4 49
(David Evans) *stdd after s: t.k.h: hld up in rr: hdwy over 1f out: drvn and ev ch ins fnl f: wknd fnl 75yds* **10/1**
5-05 **6** *¾* **Sailing North (USA)**[10] 373 4-9-6 50..... DarrenEgan(7) 9 57?
(Ronald Harris) *in tch towards rr: rdn and hdwy over 1f out: no ex and styd on same pce fnl f* **18/1**
635- **7** *2* **Betty Brook (IRE)**[87] 7435 3-8-8 60..... ChrisCatlin 1 39
(Nick Littmoden) *t.k.h: chsd ldrs: effrt on inner and press ldrs 1f out: wknd qckly fnl 100yds* **13/2**
0-34 **8** *½* **Miakora**[10] 373 4-9-8 46..... KieranO'Neill 2 43
(Michael Quinn) *led: rdn and hdd over 1f out: wknd fnl 150yds* **28/1**
59.68s (0.88) **Going Correction** -0.075s/f (Stan)
WFA 3 from 4yo 14lb **8** Ran SP% **112.5**
Speed ratings (Par 103): **89,88,87,86,85 84,81,80**
toteswingers:1&2:£5.50, 1&3:£8.00, 2&3:£5.80 CSF £31.93 TOTE £6.60: £1.60, £2.40, £2.30; EX 35.60 Trifecta £480.40 Part won. Pool £649.22 - 0.30 winning units..
Owner Nick Littmoden **Bred** D J And Mrs Brown **Trained** Newmarket, Suffolk
■ Stewards' Enquiry : Steve Drowne two-day ban: careless riding (Feb 25,27)

FOCUS
No world-beaters in this sprint maiden and the fact that it was won by a 4yo newcomer rather sums it up.

525 PLAY DA VINCI DIAMONDS AT BLUESQ.COM/GAMES H'CAP 5f (P)
1:40 (1:44) (Class 4) (0-85,86) 4-Y-O+ **£4,204** (£1,251; £625; £312) **Stalls** High

Form RPR
50-5 **1** **Taajub (IRE)**[16] 311 5-9-5 80..... IanMongan 2 91
(Peter Crate) *hld up in midfield: rdn and hdwy over 1f out: nt clr run and swtchd rt jst ins fnl f: r.o wl to ld wl ins fnl f* **11/4**[1]
61-1 **2** *½* **Sulis Minerva (IRE)**[21] 251 5-9-2 77..... KieranO'Neill 1 86
(Jeremy Gask) *taken down early: hld up off the pce in last trio: effrt and n.m.r over 1f out: hdwy 1f out: pressed wnr wl ins fnl f: r.o* **5/1**[2]
60-0 **3** *1* **Clear Praise (USA)**[16] 311 5-9-3 78..... HayleyTurner 6 83
(Simon Dow) *hld up off the pce in last trio: effrt over 1f out: kpt on wl u.p ins fnl f: wnt 3rd on post* **7/1**[3]
-632 **4** *nse* **Island Legend (IRE)**[8] 406 6-9-0 75.....(p) RichardKingscote 10 80+
(Milton Bradley) *led: rdn over 2f out: hdd and lost 3 pls wl ins fnl f* **10/1**
0031 **5** *1 ¼* **Where's Reiley (USA)**[1] 492 6-9-11 86 6ex.....(b) FrankieMcDonald 4 87
(Alastair Lidderdale) *racd in midfield: rdn over 2f out: kpt on ins fnl f: nvr gng pce to chal ldrs* **25/1**
51-3 **6** *nk* **Six Wives**[41] 3 5-8-11 79..... DarrenEgan(7) 9 78
(Scott Dixon) *in tch: n.m.r and swtchd lft over 1f out: drvn and chsd ldrs 1f out: wknd fnl 100yds* **12/1**
0-34 **7** *hd* **Sir Geoffrey (IRE)**[18] 286 6-9-2 80.....(b) RyanPowell(3) 3 79
(Scott Dixon) *in tch: rdn 2f out: unable qck over 1f out: wknd ins fnl f* **12/1**
1-01 **8** *½* **Royal Bajan (USA)**[18] 277 4-9-0 75..... FrederikTylicki 5 72
(James Given) *taken down early: chsd ldr: rdn over 1f out: no ex 1f out: lost 2nd ins fnl f: wknd* **5/1**[2]
-022 **9** *2 ¾* **Falasteen (IRE)**[15] 325 5-9-1 76.....(b) StevieDonohoe 7 63
(Kevin Ryan) *taken down early: s.i.s: sn rdn along: a bhd* **17/2**
340- **10** *2 ¼* **Billy Red**[71] 7602 8-9-2 77.....(b) FergusSweeney 8 56
(J R Jenkins) *chsd ldrs: rdn 2f out: wkng whn sltly hmpd jst ins fnl f: fdd* **50/1**
57.81s (-0.99) **Going Correction** -0.075s/f (Stan) **10** Ran SP% **113.3**
Speed ratings (Par 105): **104,103,101,101,99 99,98,97,93,89**
toteswingers:1&2:£3.00, 1&3:£5.20, 2&3:£8.80 CSF £15.50 CT £87.16 TOTE £2.70: £1.90, £2.00, £2.30; EX 17.70 Trifecta £285.60 Pool £876.09 - 2.27 winning units..
Owner Peter Crate **Bred** Rabbah Bloodstock Limited **Trained** Newdigate, Surrey
■ Stewards' Enquiry : Ian Mongan two-day ban: careless riding (Feb 29-Mar 1)
FOCUS
A furious pace was always likely here, but with so many established trailblazers in the field not all of them could lead and a few can be excused.
Where's Reiley(USA) Official explanation: jockey said gelding hung right
Falasteen(IRE) Official explanation: jockey said gelding was slowly away

526 BLUE SQUARE SPRINT SERIES ROUND 6 H'CAP (QUALIFIER) (DIV I) 6f (P)
2:15 (2:20) (Class 5) (0-75,78) 4-Y-O+ **£2,726** (£805; £402) **Stalls** Low

Form RPR
0-24 **1** **Haadeeth**[9] 388 5-9-0 73..... MatthewCosham(5) 3 81
(David Evans) *chsd ldrs: rdn and chal ent fnl f: led ins fnl f: hld on cl home* **8/1**
5-41 **2** *nk* **Roman Strait**[15] 325 4-9-3 71..... KierenFallon 9 78+
(Michael Blanshard) *hld up in tch towards rr: pushed along and hdwy 1f out: r.o wl ins fnl f: pressing wnr cl home: nvr quite getting there* **5/1**[2]
61-2 **3** *½* **Hatta Stream (IRE)**[21] 252 6-9-7 75..... SteveDrowne 6 80
(Lydia Pearce) *chsd ldrs: rdn and effrt over 1f out: ev ch ins fnl f: kpt on same pce towards fin* **4/1**[1]
14-2 **4** *hd* **Valmina**[20] 267 5-8-7 68.....(t) GeorgeDowning(7) 1 72
(Tony Carroll) *chsd ldrs: rdn over 1f out: ev ch jst ins fnl f: no ex towards fin* **10/1**
-031 **5** *hd* **Night Trade (IRE)**[9] 387 5-9-3 78..... DarrenEgan(7) 7 82
(Ronald Harris) *hld up in tch in rr: swtchd lft and hdwy over 1f out: kpt on u.p ins fnl f* **12/1**
3-00 **6** *¾* **Catalyze**[11] 371 4-9-0 68 ow1.....(t) AdamKirby 10 69
(Richard Guest) *w ldr tl led 2f out: rdn over 1f out: hdd ins fnl f: no ex: btn whn eased nr fin* **15/2**[3]
43-6 **7** *½* **Yankee Storm**[15] 325 7-9-1 72.....(v) RyanClark(3) 8 77+
(Michael Wigham) *hld up in tch in rr: hdwy on inner and chsng ldrs whn nt clr run and snatched up jst ins fnl f: swtchd rt and kpt on ins fnl f: unable to chal* **25/1**
-200 **8** *hd* **Loyal Royal (IRE)**[14] 353 9-8-9 63.....(bt) RichardKingscote 5 62
(Milton Bradley) *stdd after s: t.k.h: hld up in tch: rdn and effrt over 1f out: drvn and styd on same pce ins fnl f* **14/1**
0000 **9** *1* **Memphis Man**[7] 425 9-8-7 61 oh6..... MartinLane 4 57
(David Evans) *pushed along early to chse ldrs: rdn and lost pl 2f out: kpt on again ins fnl f* **66/1**
20-0 **10** *1* **Ice Trooper**[21] 252 4-9-4 72.....(p) JamesSullivan 2 65
(Linda Stubbs) *led: hdd 2f out: rdn over 1f out: wknd ins fnl f* **8/1**
5-21 **11** *nk* **Cut The Cackle (IRE)**[7] 424 6-8-7 61 oh1.....(bt) LeeNewman 11 53
(Richard Guest) *racd on outer: a in rr: edgd lft and no prog over 1f out: no threat to ldrs fnl f* **4/1**[1]
1m 11.42s (-0.48) **Going Correction** -0.075s/f (Stan) **11** Ran SP% **119.4**
Speed ratings (Par 103): **100,99,98,98,98 97,96,96,95,93 93**
toteswingers:1&2:£7.10, 1&3:£7.80, 2&3:£2.60 CSF £48.56 CT £191.07 TOTE £10.80: £4.00, £2.40, £1.20; EX 72.70 Trifecta £147.40 Pool £773.07 - 3.88 winning units..
Owner A Whelan **Bred** Bolton Grange **Trained** Pandy, Monmouths
FOCUS
A modest sprint handicap for the latest qualifier in this series.
Yankee Storm ◆ Official explanation: jockey said gelding was denied a clear run
Cut The Cackle(IRE) Official explanation: trainer's rep said mare had lost a left front shoe

527 GET YOUR BET ON AT BLUESQ.COM H'CAP 6f (P)
2:45 (2:49) (Class 2) (0-100,98) 4-Y-O+ **£10,350** (£3,080; £1,539; £769) **Stalls** Low

Form RPR
0-1 **1** **Palace Moon**[20] 266 7-9-7 98.....(t) JimCrowley 2 107
(William Knight) *in tch in midfield: hdwy to chse ldrs ent fnl f: pushed along and qcknd to ld ins fnl f: pushed out* **7/2**[2]
21-0 **2** *1* **Novellen Lad (IRE)**[35] 89 7-8-11 88..... StevieDonohoe 8 94
(Willie Musson) *in tch in midfield: rdn: hdwy over 1f out: drvn and kpt on to chse wnr fnl 75yds: kpt on but no threat to wnr* **9/1**
0-06 **3** *hd* **Five Star Junior (USA)**[21] 253 6-9-0 91..... JamesSullivan 6 96
(Linda Stubbs) *stdd s: hld up in last trio: clsd 2f out: pressed ldrs on outer 1f out: rdn fnl 75yds: kpt on to go 3rd last strides* **9/1**

-651 **4** *nk* **Piscean (USA)**[7] 431 7-8-11 91.. RyanClark(3) 4 95
(Tom Keddy) *stdd s: hld up in rr: clsd 2f out: rdn 1f out: n.m.r jst ins fnl f: styd on u.p fnl 100yds* **15/2**

65-2 **5** *hd* **Santefisio**[10] 378 6-8-10 87..(p) JoeFanning 3 91
(Keith Dalgleish) *racd in last trio: clsd 2f out: kpt on u.p fnl f* **10/3**[1]

-046 **6** *nk* **Norville (IRE)**[7] 431 5-8-8 90..............................(b) MatthewCosham(5) 1 93
(David Evans) *led: rdn wl over 1f out: hdd and nt pce of wnr ins fnl f: no ex and lost 4 pls nr fin* **6/1**

0-51 **7** *¾* **Seek The Fair Land**[21] 253 6-8-12 94....................(b) NathanAlison(5) 5 94
(Jim Boyle) *chsd ldrs: effrt u.p on inner and pressed ldr jst over 1f out: no ex and btn fnl 75yds* **5/1**[3]

2-22 **8** *2* **Mottley Crewe**[18] 286 5-8-8 85..........(b) LeeNewman 7 75
(Richard Guest) *sn pressing ldr: rdn wl over 1f out: wknd fnl 150yds* **14/1**

1m 10.25s (-1.65) **Going Correction** -0.075s/f (Stan) **8** Ran SP% **114.7**
Speed ratings (Par 109): **108,106,106,106,105 105,104,101**
toteswingers:1&2:£8.10, 1&3:£7.60, 2&3:£11.70 CSF £34.71 CT £262.51 TOTE £4.40: £2.00, £3.90, £3.60; EX 49.70 Trifecta £323.20 Pool £1,139.99 - 2.61 winning units..
Owner Canisbay Bloodstock **Bred** Miss B Swire **Trained** Patching, W Sussex

FOCUS
A decent handicap run at a true pace and a taking winner.

NOTEBOOK
Palace Moon ◆ was back in a handicap after making a successful belated AW debut in a Kempton conditions event last month, for which he was raised 3lb, but he has a touch of class and was officially rated 12lb higher a couple of years back. His class was still there for all to see when he arrived there on the bridle a furlong from home and he quickened up like a good horse when asked to do so. He seems to adore this surface and he has a few options open to him now including Chantilly and Dubai, while he could reappear over this C&D for the Listed Cleves Stakes in a fortnight. (op 10-3 tchd 3-1 and 4-1)
Novellen Lad(IRE) ◆ had looked high enough in the weights and probably needs further now, so it perhaps wasn't a surprise to see him staying on well at the line. He was probably unlucky to bump into one such as the winner and should be winning again on this surface before long. (op 12-1)
Five Star Junior(USA), over 3l behind Seek The Fair Land over C&D last month and 7lb better off, seemed to be travelling every bit as well as the winner on the outside passing the furlong pole, but he took much longer in responding to pressure and by the time he did it was too late. He has plenty of talent, but has only managed to win one of his last 29 starts and is becoming frustrating. (op 10-1)
Piscean(USA) was put up 3lb for his Wolverhampton success over 7f the previous week and his finishing effort was too late this time. He may be worth persevering with over the longer trip. (op 6-1)
Santefisio made a creditable debut for the yard at Kempton ten days earlier, but this was his first try over a trip this short since his second start as a 3yo and his finishing effort fell short. (op 4-1)
Norville(IRE) tried to make all, but the winner was running all over him a furlong out and he proved a sitting duck. (op 7-1 tchd 11-2)
Seek The Fair Land had seemed best over 7f, but proved that he had the necessary speed when winning over C&D off 5lb lower three weeks earlier with three of today's rivals behind him. He had his chance again here but challenged tight against the inside rail and that probably counted against him. (op 6-1)

528 BLUE SQUARE SPRINT SERIES ROUND 6 H'CAP (QUALIFIER) (DIV II) 6f (P)
3:20 (3:24) (Class 5) (0-75,75) 4-Y-0+ **£2,726** (£805; £402) **Stalls** Low

Form RPR

-032 **1** **Nubar Boy**[14] 353 5-9-0 68...(v) MartinLane 2 78
(David Evans) *stdd s: hld up in rr: hdwy over 2f out: swtchd lft and effrt over 1f out: ev ch jst ins fnl f: led fnl 100yds: r.o wl* **4/1**[1]

-002 **2** *½* **Picansort**[7] 425 5-8-11 65.. KierenFallon 10 73
(Peter Crate) *chsd ldrs: wnt 2nd over 2f out: ev ch 1f out: edgd lft u.p ins fnl f: kpt on* **9/2**[2]

1254 **3** *shd* **Captain Dimitrios**[7] 424 4-8-4 63......................(v) MatthewCosham(5) 8 71
(David Evans) *chsd ldr tl over 2f out: drvn and ev ch ent fnl f: led jst ins fnl tl hdd and one pce fnl 100yds* **9/2**[2]

60-0 **4** *1¼* **Italian Tom (IRE)**[18] 282 5-8-9 70................................ DarrenEgan(7) 7 74
(Ronald Harris) *stdd after s: hld up in rr: rdn and hdwy over 1f out: chsd ldng pair ins fnl f: no imp fnl 75yds* **18/1**

1-01 **5** *1½* **Fleetwoodsands (IRE)**[15] 328 5-9-2 70........................(t) LiamKeniry 5 69
(Milton Bradley) *hld up in midfield: rdn and effrt over 1f out: styd on same pce ins fnl f* **11/2**[3]

00-0 **6** *2* **Reposer (IRE)**[21] 251 4-9-4 72... AdamKirby 1 65
(Noel Quinlan) *in tch in midfield: lost pl and dropped to rr 2f out: nudged along and kpt on ins fnl f: no threat to ldrs* **17/2**

5000 **7** *¾* **Royal Intruder**[7] 425 7-8-7 61 oh4.................................. LeeNewman 9 51
(Richard Guest) *led: rdn and hrd pressed over 1f out: hdd jst ins fnl f: wknd fnl 100yds* **50/1**

-400 **8** *½* **Captain Scooby**[21] 252 6-8-13 72............................ CharlesEddery(5) 3 61
(Richard Guest) *sn outpcd in rr: rdn over 2f out: kpt on fnl f: nvr trbld ldr* **20/1**

406- **9** *nk* **Highland Harvest**[45] 7893 8-9-6 74................................. RobertHavlin 4 62
(Jamie Poulton) *in tch in midfield: rdn and unable qck wl over 1f out: wknd over 1f out* **8/1**

01-4 **10** *nk* **Caledonia Princess**[15] 325 6-9-7 75......................... FrederikTylicki 6 62
(Stuart Williams) *in tch in midfield: rdn and struggling whn wd bnd 2f out: wknd over 1f out* **8/1**

1m 11.07s (-0.83) **Going Correction** -0.075s/f (Stan) **10** Ran SP% **116.5**
Speed ratings (Par 103): **102,101,101,99,97 94,93,93,92,92**
toteswingers:1&2:£3.50, 1&3:£3.90, 2&3:£4.10 CSF £21.88 CT £86.18 TOTE £3.50: £1.10, £1.50, £2.40; EX 10.50 Trifecta £29.10 Pool £1,244.16 - 31.63 winning units..
Owner Phil Slater **Bred** Low Ground Stud **Trained** Pandy, Monmouths

FOCUS
With Royal Intruder again tearing off in front at a pace he was never going to maintain, the winning time was 0.35sec faster than the first division.

529 BLUE SQUARE BET H'CAP 1m 2f (P)
3:55 (4:00) (Class 3) (0-95,87) 4-Y-0+ **£6,792** (£2,021; £1,010; £505) **Stalls** Low

Form RPR

2-U1 **1** **Emma's Gift (IRE)**[7] 432 4-9-2 86.......................(b) AdamBeschizza(3) 5 96
(Julia Feilden) *hld up in midfield: dropped to last trio but stl in tch 5f out: pushed along and hdwy 2f out: rdn to chal 1f out: led ins fnl f: edgd rt and styd on wl* **7/2**[2]

11-2 **2** *1* **Tornado Force (IRE)**[37] 43 4-9-4 85......................... JimmyFortune 4 93
(Jeremy Noseda) *chsd ldrs: hdwy to press ldrs 2f out: rdn to ld over 1f out: drvn and hdd ins fnl f: one pce after* **7/4**[1]

0-65 **3** *2* **Tartan Trip**[18] 280 5-8-12 81....................................(v) SimonPearce(3) 3 85
(Andrew Balding) *t.k.h: hld up in tch: chsd ldrs 7f out: clsd and trcking ldrs whn n.m.r wl over 1f out: rdn to chse ldng pair 1f out: one pce after* **6/1**

-043 **4** *1* **Tevez**[14] 351 7-8-12 85...(p) DarrenEgan(7) 2 87
(Des Donovan) *s.i.s: hld up in last pair: effrt u.p over 1f out: kpt on ins fnl f: nt pce to rch ldrs* **18/1**

P0/0 **5** *3¾* **Smokey Oakey (IRE)**[7] 426 8-9-2 82................................ TomEaves 7 77
(Mark H Tompkins) *stdd s: hld up in last pair: rdn over 2f out: drvn and no prog over 1f out: wl hld fnl f* **33/1**

-016 **6** *½* **Archie Rice (USA)**[7] 432 6-8-11 80.............................. RyanClark(3) 6 74
(Tom Keddy) *sn pushed along to ld: hdd 8f out: rdn to ld again over 2f out: drvn and hdd over 1f out: wknd 1f out* **6/1**

310- **7** *2¾* **Sonoran Sands (IRE)**[28] 5483 4-9-6 87............................ KierenFallon 1 78
(Brendan Powell) *racd keenly: chsd ldr tl led 8f out: rdn and hdd over 2f out: wknd over 1f out: wl btn and eased ins fnl f* **9/2**[3]

2m 2.62s (-3.98) **Going Correction** -0.075s/f (Stan)
WFA 4 from 5yo+ 1lb **7** Ran SP% **113.5**
Speed ratings (Par 107): **112,111,109,108,105 105,103**
toteswingers:1&2:£4.90, 1&3:£28.70, 2&3:£17.70 CSF £9.91 TOTE £5.00: £2.20, £1.20; EX 9.90.
Owner Mrs Emma Raffan **Bred** Mark Commins **Trained** Exning, Suffolk

FOCUS
A decent middle-distance handicap, but the pair who vied for the early advantage may have done too much as they ended up finishing last and last-but-one.

NOTEBOOK
Emma's Gift(IRE) was raised 6lb for her Wolverhampton success seven days earlier, but it made little difference. She travelled well off the pace before making her move rounding the home turn and, having been brought with her effort close to the stands' rail (no bad thing here), had more speed in the run to the line than the runner-up. Another rise in the weights beckons, but as a filly in form the hat-trick is definitely on. (tchd 11-4)
Tornado Force(IRE) has been in good form over 1m4f lately, but was up another 5lb despite being narrowly thwarted in his bid for a hat-trick at Wolverhampton last time. He travelled into the race like a winner on the home bend and soon hit the front, but he was done for foot well inside the last furlong and looks in need of a return to further. (op 15-8 tchd 2-1)
Tartan Trip was attempting this trip for the first time, but travelled well behind the leaders and had every chance a furlong from home before his effort flattened out. A record of 1-17 is a slight concern. (op 11-2)
Tevez ran on from the back towards the nearside rail, but never looked like winning and all his best form has come over shorter. (op 14-1)
Smokey Oakey(IRE) never figured. He scored over hurdles last summer but hasn't won on the Flat since taking the Brigadier Gerard Stakes at Sandown in May 2008. (op 40-1)

530 FOLLOW US ON TWITTER @BLUESQ H'CAP 1m 4f (P)
4:30 (4:35) (Class 6) (0-52,57) 4-Y-0+ **£1,103** (£1,103; £251) **Stalls** Low

Form RPR

/-21 **1** **Celtic Charlie (FR)**[17] 303 7-8-13 49................................ IanMongan 7 58+
(Pat Phelan) *rrd s: t.k.h and sn chsng ldrs: led gng wl 3f out: clr 2f out: rdn over 1f out: stl clr and drvn ins fnl f: jnd on post* **2/1**[1]

-040 **1** *dht* **El Libertador (USA)**[20] 265 6-9-1 51......................(b) JimmyFortune 10 58
(Eric Wheeler) *stdd and dropped in bhd s: hld up in last: stl plenty to do and n.m.r wl over 2f out: hdwy jst over 1f out: chsd clr ldr wl ins fnl f: r.o wl to join ldr on post* **20/1**

02-6 **3** *1¾* **Imperial Fong**[9] 392 4-8-8 50... RyanClark(3) 2 54
(Chris Dwyer) *hld up towards rr: rdn and hdwy over 1f out: keeping on whn n.m.r and swtchd lft wl ins fnl f: r.o to snatch 3rd last stride* **33/1**

45-1 **4** *shd* **Mister Frosty (IRE)**[4] 454 6-9-7 57 6ex........................ KierenFallon 5 61
(George Prodromou) *t.k.h: in tch: rdn to chse clr wnr 2f out: kpt on but nvr gng pce to chal wnr: lost 2 pls wl ins fnl f* **4/1**[3]

0-66 **5** *½* **Avon Supreme**[20] 265 4-8-12 51.................................... HayleyTurner 4 54
(Gay Kelleway) *t.k.h: hld up in tch in midfield: rdn and effrt on inner over 1f out: kpt on ins fnl f: nt pce to rch ldrs* **12/1**

00-3 **6** *nk* **Safwaan**[33] 105 5-9-2 52.. StevieDonohoe 13 55
(Willie Musson) *t.k.h: hld up in midfield: rdn to chse ldng trio 2f out: kpt on ins fnl f but nt pce to chal wnr* **3/1**[2]

00-0 **7** *2¾* **Visions Of Johanna (USA)**[20] 265 7-9-2 52...........(tp) LeeNewman 11 50
(Richard Guest) *stdd and swtchd lft s: hld up in midfield: swtchd rt and hdwy over 2f out: drvn and no imp over 1f out: wknd ins fnl f* **12/1**

440- **8** *shd* **Astrolibra**[76] 6613 8-9-1 51.. TomEaves 6 49
(Mark H Tompkins) *hld up in tch towards rr: rdn wl over 2f out: plugged on fr over 1f out: nvr gng pce to threaten ldrs* **33/1**

-445 **9** *½* **Grecian Goddess (IRE)**[9] 389 4-8-8 50.................... RyanPowell(3) 12 47
(John Ryan) *chsd ldrs: chsd clr ldr wl over 2f out tl 2f out: wknd ent fnl f* **20/1**

5-30 **10** *hd* **Santera (IRE)**[18] 278 8-8-5 46 oh1............................ CharlesBishop(5) 1 43
(Tony Carroll) *led for 2f: chsd ldrs after: rdn and struggling over 2f out: no threat to ldrs fr over 1f out* **20/1**

0-06 **11** *5* **Moscow Oznick**[9] 389 7-8-4 47..................................(p) DarrenEgan(7) 8 36
(Des Donovan) *chsd ldr tl led 5f out: hdd 3f out: sn lost pl: bhd fnl f* **14/1**

30/0 **12** *11* **Highcliffe**[27] 188 4-8-11 50.. LiamKeniry 9 21
(Martin Bosley) *chsd ldrs: led 10f out tl 5f out: lost pl qckly 3f out: wl bhd over 1f out* **80/1**

2m 32.29s (-0.71) **Going Correction** -0.075s/f (Stan)
WFA 4 from 5yo+ 3lb **12** Ran SP% **121.8**
Speed ratings (Par 101): **99,99,97,97,97 97,95,95,95,94 91,84**WIN: El Liberator £16.70, Celtic Charlie £1.60 PL: EL £5.60, CC £1.10, IF £10.90, EX: EL/CC £29.10, CC/EL £51.50 CSF: EL/CC £29.10, CC/EL £22.08. T/C: EL/CC/IF £703.20, CC/EL/IF £532.25. toteswingers:EL&CC:£11.50, EL&IF:£71.00, CC&IF:£23.50 TOTE £0.027: £Owner, £Celtic Contractors Limited, £Bred, £S N C Regnier & San Gabriel Inv IncTrained Epsom, Surrey.
Owner J L Day **Bred** Kingswood Farm **Trained** Lambourn, Berks
■ Stewards' Enquiry : Jimmy Fortune one-day ban: careless riding (Feb 25)

FOCUS
A moderate event and, as with so many races over this trip here, the pace was ordinary.
T/Plt: £62.70 to a £1 stake. Pool:£92,074.59 - 1,070.41 winning tickets T/Qpdt: £9.40 to a £1 stake. Pool:£8,655.91 - 676.60 winning tickets SP

497 WOLVERHAMPTON (A.W) (L-H)
Saturday, February 11

OFFICIAL GOING: Standard
Wind: Light behind Weather: Fine

531 BET ON TODAY'S FOOTBALL AT BLUESQ.COM AMATEUR RIDERS' H'CAP (DIV I) 1m 141y(P)
5:50 (5:50) (Class 6) (0-60,60) 4-Y-0+ **£1,646** (£506; £253) **Stalls** Low

Form RPR

-64 **1** **Marksbury**[12] 361 5-10-4 55.......................... MissBeckyBrisbourne(5) 1 63+
(Mark Brisbourne) *hld up: hdwy over 1f out: rdn to chse ldr and hung lft fnl f: r.o to ld nr fin* **2/1**[1]

0-00 **2** ½ **Ibiza Sunset (IRE)**^{28} [176] 4-10-7 **60**........................ MissSKerswell$^{(7)}$ 9 67
(Brendan Powell) *a.p: chsd ldr over 7f out: led 5f out: clr 2f out: rdn ins fnl f: wknd and hdd nr fin* **9/2**^{2}
32-0 **3** 2 **Merrjanah**^{8} [400] 4-10-4 **57**.............................. MrAFrench$^{(7)}$ 10 59
(John Wainwright) *hld up: hdwy over 2f out: rdn over 1f out: r.o* **11/2**^{3}
0-50 **4** 4½ **Desert Hunter (IRE)**^{8} [401] 9-10-1 **52**........................(p) MissRSmith$^{(5)}$ 7 44
(Micky Hammond) *chsd ldrs: rdn over 1f out: wknd fnl f* **6/1**
-064 **5** 1¼ **Aggbag**^{9} [390] 8-10-0 **46** oh1..(p) MrSWalker 3 35
(Michael Appleby) *led: hdd over 7f out: chsd ldrs: rdn over 2f out: wknd over 1f out* **13/2**
0-06 **6** 2½ **Granny Anne (IRE)**^{4} [453] 4-9-12 **51**.......................(p) MrsRWilson$^{(7)}$ 4 34
(Paul D'Arcy) *s.i.s: hdwy to ld over 7f out: hdd 5f out: rdn over 2f out: wknd fnl f* **6/1**
00-0 **7** 11 **Corlough Mountain**^{24} [200] 8-9-9 **46** oh1..............(t) MissMBryant$^{(5)}$ 11
(Paddy Butler) *s.s: hld up: wknd wl over 2f out* **100/1**
0000 **8** 2¼ **Novay Essjay (IRE)**^{2} [483] 5-9-8 **47**.............................. MrLMichael$^{(7)}$ 2
(Dai Williams) *hld up: wknd 3f out* **40/1**

1m 52.69s (2.19) **Going Correction** +0.175s/f (Slow) **8** Ran SP% **112.2**
Speed ratings (Par 101): **97,96,94,90,89 87,77,75**
toteswingers: 1&2 £5.70, 1&3 £5.10, 2&3 £6.50. CSF £10.65 CT £41.10 TOTE £2.90: £1.50, £1.80, £1.60; EX 14.20.
Owner Wayne Hennessey **Bred** Dunchurch Lodge Stud Company **Trained** Great Ness, Shropshire

FOCUS
A well-run handicap for amateur riders but none of the runners had finished in the first three last time out or look well handicapped in the wider scheme of things and it's most likely weak form.

532 BET ON TODAY'S FOOTBALL AT BLUESQ.COM AMATEUR RIDERS' H'CAP (DIV II) 1m 141y(P)
6:20 (6:20) (Class 6) (0-60,58) 4-Y-0+ **£1,646** (£506; £253) **Stalls** Low

Form RPR
0-60 **1** **Stamp Duty (IRE)**^{5} [450] 4-10-5 **54**........................ MrAaronJames$^{(5)}$ 10 63
(Suzzanne France) *hld up: hdwy over 2f out: chsd ldr over 1f out: rdn to ld wl ins fnl f: styd on* **11/2**^{3}
4-00 **2** ¾ **Ossie Ardiles (IRE)**^{11} [370] 4-10-5 **49**...........................(v^{1}) MrSWalker 8 56
(Michael Appleby) *chsd ldrs: led over 2f out: rdn over 1f out: hdd wl ins fnl f* **5/1**^{2}
0-55 **3** 2¾ **Join Up**^{27} [183] 6-10-8 **57**................................ MissBeckyBrisbourne$^{(5)}$ 6 58
(Mark Brisbourne) *plld hrd and prom: rdn over 1f out: styd on same pce fnl f* **9/2**^{1}
0420 **4** 1¾ **Bentley**^{5} [450] 8-10-8 **52**...(v) MissSBrotherton 2 49
(Brian Baugh) *chsd ldrs: nt clr run and lost pl over 2f out: rallied wl over 1f out: sn hung lft: styd on same pce fnl f* **9/2**^{1}
-035 **5** nk **Blue Noodles**^{7} [430] 6-10-1 **52**....................................(p) MrAFrench$^{(7)}$ 5 48
(John Wainwright) *led: plld hrd: hdd over 6f out: led again 3f out: hdd over 2f out: no ex fnl f* **5/1**^{2}
050- **6** nse **Swish Dish (CAN)**^{91} [3953] 5-9-10 **45**........................(p) MissRSmith$^{(5)}$ 3 41
(Micky Hammond) *s.i.s: hld up: r.o towards fin: nvr nrr* **33/1**
-313 **7** nk **Querido (GER)**^{17} [293] 8-10-6 **55**...........................(tp) MissMBryant$^{(5)}$ 1 50
(Paddy Butler) *s.i.s: hdwy over 6f out: rdn over 1f out: styd on same pce* **5/1**^{2}
000/ **8** 22 **Gifted Heir (IRE)**^{792} [7719] 8-9-13 **50**......................... MissSPeacock$^{(7)}$ 7
(Ray Peacock) *chsd ldrs: led over 6f out: hdd 3f out: wknd 2f out* **66/1**
000- **9** 3¼ **Chillianwallah**^{52} [7851] 4-9-10 **45**.............................. MissCHJones$^{(5)}$ 9
(James Unett) *a in rr: wknd wl over 2f out* **16/1**

1m 53.05s (2.55) **Going Correction** +0.175s/f (Slow) **9** Ran SP% **112.1**
Speed ratings (Par 101): **95,94,91,90,90 90,89,70,67**
toteswingers: 1&2 £3.30, 1&3 £3.10, 2&3 £3.70. CSF £31.78 CT £132.86 TOTE £7.00: £2.50, £2.00, £1.40; EX 39.00.
Owner Newstart Partnership **Bred** Windymains Farm Ltd **Trained** Norton, N Yorks
■ The first training success for Suzzanne France, whose riding career was ended by serious injury.

FOCUS
The second division of the amateur handicap and, like the first, another weak race, with nearly all the runners coming into it with something to prove. It wasn't as strongly run, either, with several taking a keen hold.
Bentley Official explanation: trainer said gelding finished lame left-fore

533 SARAH BRAILEY 21ST BIRTHDAY MAIDEN FILLIES' STKS 1m 141y(P)
6:50 (6:50) (Class 5) 3-Y-0+ **£2,264** (£673; £336; £168) **Stalls** Low

Form RPR
43- **1** **Parley (USA)**^{211} [4061] 3-8-5 0.. JoeFanning 9 73
(Mark Johnston) *chsd ldr: pushed along over 2f out: led over 1f out: rdn and edgd rt ins fnl f: styd on* **4/6**^{1}
2- **2** 2½ **Zaina (IRE)**^{71} [7599] 3-8-5 0.. NickyMackay 6 67
(Gerard Butler) *hld up: hdwy over 5f out: rdn over 1f out: sn hung lft: hung rt ins fnl f: styd on same pce* **11/4**^{2}
5 **3** 1½ **Strawberrymystique**^{15} [331] 4-9-12 0.................................. AdamKirby 2 69
(Marco Botti) *chsd ldrs: rdn over 1f out: hung lft and no ex ins fnl f* **8/1**
4 2 **Big Wave (IRE)** 4-9-9 0... MichaelO'Connell$^{(3)}$ 4 64
(Clifford Lines) *led: rdn: hung lft and hdd over 1f out: btn whn carried lft ins fnl f* **33/1**
-6 **5** ¾ **Gabrial's Lexi (IRE)**^{12} [358] 3-8-5 0............................ PatrickMathers 1 59+
(Richard Fahey) *hld up in tch: rdn over 2f out: hung lft and hit rails over 1f out: styng on same pce whn hmpd ins fnl f* **14/1**
0 **6** 8 **Brandy Snapping**^{12} [358] 3-8-5 0...................................... KieranO'Neill 7 39
(Mark Brisbourne) *prom: pushed along 6f out: wknd wl over 2f out* **100/1**
7 2¼ **Morilles** 3-8-5 0.. JohnFahy 5 34
(Clive Cox) *s.i.s: in rr: drvn along over 3f out: wknd over 2f out* **7/1**^{3}
8 48 **Khatella (IRE)** 3-8-2 0.. DominicFox$^{(3)}$ 3
(John Flint) *s.s: outpcd and a t.o* **50/1**

1m 51.12s (0.62) **Going Correction** +0.175s/f (Slow)
WFA 3 from 4yo+ 21lb **8** Ran SP% **122.8**
Speed ratings (Par 100): **104,101,100,98,98 90,88,46**
toteswingers: 1&2 £1.10, 1&3 £3.80, 2&3 £2.50. CSF £3.06 TOTE £1.60: £1.02, £1.10, £2.70; EX 3.40.
Owner Sheikh Hamdan Bin Mohammed Al Maktoum **Bred** Darley **Trained** Middleham Moor, N Yorks

FOCUS
Little strength in depth to a maiden run at an ordinary gallop.

534 INGRAM RACING PARTNERSHIP, SHARES AVAILABLE (S) STKS 1m 1f 103y(P)
7:20 (7:20) (Class 6) 3-Y-0 **£1,704** (£503; £251) **Stalls** Low

Form RPR
00- **1** **Zain Princess (IRE)**^{252} [2709] 3-8-7 0.................................. NickyMackay 5 59
(Gerard Butler) *hld up: hdwy over 4f out: rdn to ld wl ins fnl f: r.o* **15/8**^{1}
5-52 **2** 2½ **Siouxies Dream**^{17} [294] 3-8-7 **56**.. LukeMorris 7 54
(Michael Appleby) *a.p: chsd ldr 4f out: rdn to ld over 1f out: hdd and unable qck wl ins fnl f* **3/1**^{2}
0-03 **3** 2¼ **Outlaw Torn (IRE)**^{9} [382] 3-8-7 **55**........................(e) CharlesEddery$^{(5)}$ 4 54
(Richard Guest) *plld hrd: led: rdn over 3f out: hdd over 1f out: no ex fnl f* **7/1**
6-5 **4** hd **Redclue (IRE)**^{26} [194] 3-8-12 0..(b) ChrisCatlin 2 54
(Marco Botti) *hld up: rdn over 3f out: styd on ins fnl f: nvr nrr* **11/2**^{3}
1-64 **5** 6 **Cat Queen**^{18} [288] 3-8-10 **54**.. AmyRyan$^{(3)}$ 9 42
(Gay Kelleway) *trckd ldrs: rdn over 2f out: wknd fnl f* **11/2**^{3}
00-4 **6** 1¼ **Nic Nok**^{24} [204] 3-8-12 **50**.. JoeFanning 1 39
(Harry Dunlop) *s.i.s: pushed along in rr early: rdn over 3f out: hdwy over 2f out: wknd over 1f out* **14/1**
356- **7** 8 **Brackendale**^{72} [7590] 3-8-12 **45**................................(p) KieranO'Neill 3 22
(John Weymes) *chsd ldr over 5f: sn rdn: wknd over 2f out* **50/1**

2m 3.36s (1.66) **Going Correction** +0.175s/f (Slow) **7** Ran SP% **111.7**
Speed ratings (Par 95): **99,96,94,94,89 88,81**
toteswingers: 1&2 £1.70, 1&3 £6.80, 2&3 £2.40. CSF £7.23 TOTE £2.50: £1.50, £2.00; EX 8.90.There was no bid for the winner.
Owner Darren Hudson-Wood **Bred** Star Pointe Ltd & Miss J Elmes **Trained** Newmarket, Suffolk

FOCUS
An ordinary seller run at something of a muddling gallop, but the winner is at least of some interest.
Brackendale Official explanation: jockey said gelding hung right-handed

535 BET AT BLUE SQUARE H'CAP 1m 4f 50y(P)
7:50 (7:50) (Class 5) (0-75,73) 4-Y-0+ **£2,264** (£673; £336; £168) **Stalls** Low

Form RPR
0-40 **1** **Jeer (IRE)**^{26} [192] 8-9-0 **66**..(t) PaddyAspell 6 72
(Michael Easterby) *a.p: rdn over 1f out: styd on to ld wl ins fnl f* **16/1**
3503 **2** ½ **Kames Park (IRE)**^{8} [400] 10-8-12 **69**...................... CharlesEddery$^{(5)}$ 7 74
(Richard Guest) *s.i.s: hld up: hdwy over 2f out: led over 1f out: rdn and hdd wl ins fnl f* **4/1**
6-21 **3** nk **Boa**^{12} [363] 7-9-4 **73**.. AmyRyan$^{(3)}$ 2 78
(Reg Hollinshead) *chsd ldrs: nt clr run and lost pl over 2f out: hdwy over 1f out: sn rdn and ev ch: styd on* **11/4**^{2}
233- **4** 2 **Minsky Mine (IRE)**^{20} [6546] 5-9-2 **68**.................................. LukeMorris 5 70
(Michael Appleby) *a.p: chsd ldr over 5f out: led 3f out: rdn and hdd over 1f out: hung lft and styd on same pce ins fnl f* **5/2**^{1}
000/ **5** ½ **Novikov**^{505} [3432] 8-8-11 **68**...................................(t) MatthewCosham$^{(5)}$ 1 69
(David Evans) *a.p: rdn over 2f out: no ex ins fnl f* **28/1**
406- **6** 2¾ **If You Whisper (IRE)**^{45} [7901] 4-8-12 **67**......................... MickyFenton 8 64
(Mike Murphy) *s.i.s: hld up: hdwy over 4f out: jnd ldrs over 3f out: rdn over 2f out: edgd lft over 1f out: styd on same pce* **7/2**^{3}
20/6 **7** nk **Slam**^{24} [198] 7-9-6 **72**.. ChrisCatlin 3 68
(Tom George) *led: rdn and hdd 3f out: ev ch over 1f out: wknd ins fnl f* **14/1**

2m 43.05s (1.95) **Going Correction** +0.175s/f (Slow)
WFA 4 from 5yo+ 3lb **7** Ran SP% **113.5**
Speed ratings (Par 103): **100,99,99,98,97 95,95**
toteswingers: 1&2 £13.10, 1&3 £11.90, 2&3 £1.40. CSF £76.98 CT £233.11 TOTE £17.50: £6.70, £1.30; EX 67.20.
Owner Mrs Jean Turpin **Bred** Floors Farming And Side Hill Stud **Trained** Sheriff Hutton, N Yorks

FOCUS
A fair handicap comprised of exposed and none-too-well handicapped sorts and that barely a length covered the field early in the straight off an admittedly steady gallop suggests that this isn't form worth lionising.

536 BRIAN HOUGH 75TH BIRTHDAY CLAIMING STKS 7f 32y(P)
8:20 (8:22) (Class 6) 3-Y-0 **£1,704** (£503; £251) **Stalls** High

Form RPR
0-13 **1** **Speedy Yaki (IRE)**^{8} [407] 3-9-1 65..............................(t) StephenCraine 3 71
(Daniel Mark Loughnane) *hld up: hdwy over 2f out: chsd ldr over 1f out: r.o u.p to ld wl ins fnl f* **10/3**^{2}
5-41 **2** 1½ **Chapellerie (IRE)**^{21} [250] 3-8-9 69.................................... LeeNewman 6 61
(Richard Guest) *chsd ldr tl led over 2f out: rdn and hdd wl ins fnl f* **15/8**^{1}
3-22 **3** 2¾ **Bond Style**^{4} [462] 3-9-1 64...(b^{1}) TomEaves 5 59
(Bryan Smart) *s.s: sn prom: rdn over 2f out: hung lft over 1f out: no ex fnl f* **10/3**^{2}
2523 **4** 2¼ **One More Roman (IRE)**^{8} [394] 3-8-4 62..................(bt) PaulHainey$^{(7)}$ 1 49
(Gay Kelleway) *s.s: hdwy over 5f out: chsd ldr over 2f out tl over 1f out: wknd ins fnl f* **9/2**^{3}
26-0 **5** 3 **Inya House**^{19} [270] 3-8-12 53......................................(p) AndrewMullen 2 42
(Nigel Tinkler) *chsd ldrs: drvn along and lost pl over 4f out: wknd over 1f out* **50/1**
00-4 **6** 7 **Miss Purity Pinker (IRE)**^{15} [322] 3-8-7 60....................(v) LukeMorris 4 18
(David Evans) *led: rdn and hdd over 2f out: wkng whn n.m.r over 1f out* **11/1**

1m 30.56s (0.96) **Going Correction** +0.175s/f (Slow) **6** Ran SP% **109.4**
Speed ratings (Par 95): **101,99,96,93,90 82**
toteswingers: 1&2 £2.70, 1&3 £1.70, 2&3 £1.70. CSF £9.48 TOTE £4.80: £2.10, £1.80; EX 13.00.
Owner Pak Kau Yeung **Bred** Mrs G P Booth And J Porteous **Trained** Baldwin's Gate, Staffs

FOCUS
No more than a modest claimer but it was well run and the first three had been in good form recently, so the form looks solid enough.

537 WOLVERHAMPTON-RACECOURSE.CO.UK FILLIES' H'CAP 7f 32y(P)
8:50 (8:50) (Class 5) (0-75,75) 4-Y-0+ **£2,264** (£673; £336; £168) **Stalls** High

Form RPR
13-0 **1** **Bavarian Princess (USA)**^{12} [359] 4-9-2 **70**....................... LukeMorris 1 77
(Mrs K Burke) *chsd ldrs: rdn over 1f out: r.o to ld wl ins fnl f* **13/8**^{1}
0-13 **2** ¾ **Qeethaara (USA)**^{16} [306] 8-8-1 **62**............................(p) JackDuern$^{(7)}$ 3 67
(Mark Brisbourne) *s.i.s: hld up: hdwy over 1f out: rdn and ev ch ins fnl f: styd on* **5/1**^{3}
-113 **3** nk **Dancing Welcome**^{9} [387] 6-9-7 **75**.......................(b) RichardKingscote 5 79
(Milton Bradley) *chsd ldr tl led over 1f out: rdn and hdd wl ins fnl f* **15/8**^{2}
3-10 **4** 2 **Fedora (IRE)**^{20} [262] 6-8-7 **61** oh2....................................(t) ChrisCatlin 2 60
(Olivia Maylam) *set stdy pce tl qcknd over 2f out: hdd over 1f out: styd on same pce ins fnl f* **5/1**^{3}

1m 32.38s (2.78) **Going Correction** +0.175s/f (Slow) **4** Ran SP% **106.2**
Speed ratings (Par 100): **91,90,89,87**
CSF £9.03 TOTE £2.70; EX 11.10.
Owner Aricabeau Syndicate II & Partners **Bred** Maura Gittens **Trained** Middleham Moor, N Yorks

FOCUS
Little between the runners in what looked a tight-knit handicap even before a steady gallop muddied the waters even further.

Bavarian Princess (USA) Official explanation: trainer's rep said, regarding apparent improvement in form, that the filly, having been off for 77 days, may have benefited from its previous run.

538 PLAY DA VINCI DIAMONDS AT BLUESQ.COM/GAMES H'CAP 1m 141y (P)

9:20 (9:20) (Class 5) (0-75,73) 4-Y-0+ **£2,264** (£673; £336 ; £168) **Stalls** Low

Form RPR
34-4 **1** **I Confess**[5] 448 7 -9-773 (b) JoeFanning 3 85
(Geoffrey Harker) *chsd clr ldr tl led over 1f out: rdn out* **5/1**[3]
0-16 **2** *4 1/2* **Postscript (IRE)**[23] 216 4 -9-268 LukeMorris 5 70
(Ian Williams) *hld up: hdwy 2f out: rdn to chse wnr fnl f: no imp* **7/4**[1]
4-24 **3** *1 3/4* **McCool Bannanas**[4] 463 4 -9-066 RichardKingscote 6 64
(James Unett) *hld up: hdwy over 1f out: sn rdn: no ex fnl f* **6/1**
1-02 **4** *1 3/4* **Wigram's Turn (USA)**[12] 359 7 -9-167 (t) PaddyAspell 4 61
(Michael Easterby) *prom: rdn over 2f out: wknd fnl f* **6/1**
0000 **5** *1 1/4* **Honey Of A Kitten (USA)** 432 4 -9-470 (b) StephenCraine 1 61
(David Evans) *sn led: clr over 6f out: rdn and hdd over 1f out: wknd fnl f* **16/1**
-436 **6** *5* **The Mongoose**[10] 374 4 -9-071 (t) MatthewCosham(5) 2 50
(David Evans) *chsd ldrs: rdn over 2f out: wknd over 1f out* **7/2**[2]

1m 49.16s (-1.34)**Going Correction** +0.175s/f (Slow) **6**Ran SP% **109.7**
Speed ratings (Par 103): **112,108,106,104,103 99**
toteswingers: 1&2 £4.90, 1&3 £1.10, 2&3 £3.80. CSF £13.56 TOTE £7.20 : £1.80 , £1.50 ; EX 17.40.
Owner Brian Harker **Bred** Gestut Sohrenhof **Trained** Thirkleby, N Yorks

FOCUS
A fair handicap to end proceedings seemingly run at a strong gallop but the leader was largely ignored and stamina wasn't tested as much as it might have looked.
T/Plt: £30.90 to a £1 stake. Pool of £85,885.76 - 2,023.78 winning tickets. T/Qpdt: £6.70 to a £1 stake. Pool of £8,914.96 - 979.30 winning tickets. CR

539 - 541a & 543a (Foreign Racing) - See Raceform Interactive

[475]CAGNES-SUR-MER

Sunday, February 12

OFFICIAL GOING: Fibresand: standard

542a PRIX DE LA CALIFORNIE (LISTED RACE) (3YO) (FIBRESAND) 1m (F)

1:30 (12:00) 3-Y-0 **£22,916** (£9,166; £6,875 ; £4,583 ; £2,291)

RPR
1 **Reality (FR)**[47] 3 -8-80 SylvainRuis 3 95
(D Prod'Homme, France) **14/1**
2 *1/2* **Moustache (IRE)**[63] 3 -9-20 ThierryThulliez 6 102
(D Grilli, Italy) **17/1**
3 *1/2* **Final Destination (FR)**[73] 3 -8-110 ASuborics 8 96
(Mario Hofer, Germany) **7/2**[2]
4 *1* **Cashmere Cat (IRE)**[25] 3 -8-80 FabienLefebvre 2 91
(T Lemer, France) **3/1**[2]
5 *1 1/2* **Tribune (FR)**[26] 3 -8-80 IoritzMendizabal 10 87
(J-C Rouget, France) **14/5**[1]
6 *1* **Forces Of Darkness (IRE)** 3 -8-80 GregoryBenoist 1 85
(F Vermeulen, France) **9/1**
7 *1* **Robert Le Diable (FR)**[52] 3 -8-110 Pierre-CharlesBoudot 4 86
(D Prod'Homme, France) **10/1**
8 *nse* **Swing Alone (IRE)**[105] 7192 3 -8-110 Francois-XavierBertras 7 86
(Gay Kelleway) *broke wl: sent to ld: sn clr: set gd pce: led into st: chal and hdd 2f out: no ex u.p: fdd* **25/1**
9 *hd* **Prinz David (FR)**[25] 3 -8-110 XavierBergeron 5 85
(D Rabhi, France) **12/1**
10 *8* **Private Riviera**[161] 5770 3 -8-80 JohanVictoire 9 64
(C Boutin, France) **43/1**

1m 35.53s (95.53) **10**Ran SP% **118.7**
WIN (incl. 1 euro stake): 3.00 (Reality coupled with Tribune). PLACES: 4.20, 5.30, 2.30. DF: 75.70. SF: 227.70 .
Owner Ecurie Des Monceaux **Bred** Ecuie Des Monceaux **Trained** France

[531]WOLVERHAMPTON (A.W) (L-H)

Monday, February 13

OFFICIAL GOING: Standard
Wind: Fresh across Weather: Overcast

544 BET AT BLUE SQUARE H'CAP 5f 20y (P)

2:40 (2:40) (Class 6) (0-52,56) 4-Y-0+ **£1,704** (£503; £251) **Stalls** Low

Form RPR
-224 **1** **Canadian Danehill (IRE)**[7] 445 10 -9-050 (e) JoeFanning 11 61
(Robert Cowell) *chsd ldrs: rdn to ld ins fnl f: r.o* **17/2**
30-2 **2** *1 1/4* **Good Timin'**[5] 467 4 -8-1147 PhillipMakin 5 55+
(David Brown) *hld up in tch: racd keenly: rdn: nt clr and swtchd rt 2f out: r.o* **2/1**[1]
00-1 **3** *1/2* **Silver Linnet (IRE)**[7] 467 5 -9-656 6ex (p) AdamKirby 13 61
(John Butler) *dwlt: hld up: hdwy over 1f out: sn rdn: r.o* **7/2**[2]
614- **4** *1/2* **Cri Na Mara (IRE)**[1] 162 4 -9-252 (t) KierenFallon 6 55
(Mark Michael McNiff, Ire) *prom: pushed along and lost pl over 3f out: hdwy over 1f out: r.o* **9/2**[3]
034- **5** *nk* **Mosa Mine**[63] 7737 5 -9-252 LukeMorris 10 54
(Bryn Palling) *trckd ldrs: racd keenly: rdn over 1f out: ev ch ins fnl f: styd on same pce* **12/1**
06-6 **6** *shd* **Hambleton**[31] 155 5 -9-151 (p) TomEaves 7 52
(Bryan Smart) *s.i.s: sn pushed along in rr: r.o ins fnl f: nvr nrr* **9/1**
060- **7** *1/2* **Love Club**[216] 3939 4 -8-746 oh1 RyanPowell(3) 3 46
(Brian Baugh) *w ldr: rdn and ev ch over 1f out: styd on same pce ins fnl f* **40/1**
-500 **8** *nk* **Divertimenti (IRE)**[13] 370 8 -9-151 (bt) RussKennemore 8 50
(Roy Bowring) *hld up: hdwy over 1f out: no ex ins fnl f* **14/1**
-050 **9** *nse* **Replicator**[5] 467 7 -8-1150 (e) RyanClark(3) 9 48
(Patrick Gilligan) *led: rdn over 1f out: hdd and no ex ins fnl f* **20/1**
616- **10** *3/4* **Sally's Swansong**[329] 934 6 -8-1349 (p) AndrewMullen 4 45
(Eric Alston) *s.i.s: sn prom: rdn and nt clr run over 1f out: no ex ins fnl f* **16/1**
00-0 **11** *10* **Lois Lane**[33] 118 4 -8-546 oh1 CharlesBishop(5) 12
(Ron Hodges) *sn outpcd* **100/1**

1m 2.77s (0.47)**Going Correction** +0.125s/f (Slow) **11**Ran SP% **122.7**
Speed ratings (Par 101): **101,99,98,97,96 96,95,95,95,94 78**
toteswingers:1&2:£3.70, 2&3:£2.70, 1&3:£7.80 CSF £26.67 CT £76.35 TOTE £6.20 : £1.40 , £1.60, £1.90 ; EX 32.60 Trifecta £67.10 Pool: £482.08 - 5.31 winning units.
Owner T W Morley **Bred** Skymarc Farm Inc And Dr A J O'Reilly **Trained** Six Mile Bottom, Cambs

FOCUS
A moderate but competitive sprint handicap. The fourth is the best guide to the level.
Good Timin' Official explanation: trainer said gelding finished distressed
Silver Linnet (IRE)♦ Official explanation: jockey said mare reared as stalls opened

545 WOLVERHAMPTON-RACECOURSE.CO.UK (S) STKS 5f 216y (P)

3:10 (3:10) (Class 6) 3-Y-0+ **£1,704** (£503; £251) **Stalls** Low

Form RPR
5121 **1** **Hinton Admiral**[11] 388 8 -9-1372 JoeFanning 7 79
(Keith Dalgleish) *chsd ldrs: shkn up to ld ins fnl f: edgd lft: r.o: readily* **2/1**[2]
4-21 **2** *1 1/2* **Master Of Disguise**[17] 327 6 -9-1378 (t) RussKennemore 4 74
(Brian Baugh) *hld up: hdwy 1f out: sn rdn: r.o to go 2nd wl ins fnl f: nt rch wnr* **6/4**[1]
10-3 **3** *1/2* **Tombi (USA)**[25] 215 8 -9-1372 PJMcDonald 3 72
(Ollie Pears) *trckd ldrs: rdn and ev ch ins fnl f: styd on same pce* **11/2**[3]
15-0 **4** *2 1/2* **Mother Jones**[36] 100 4 -9-369 PhillipMakin 1 54
(David Brown) *led at stdy pce tl qcknd over 2f out: rdn over 1f out: hdd and no ex ins fnl f* **22/1**
6-52 **5** *nk* **Imprimis Tagula (IRE)**[13] 368 8 -9-173 (v) NatashaEaton(7) 6 58
(Alan Bailey) *chsd ldr: pushed along over 2f out: rdn over 1f out: no ex fnl f* **13/2**

1m 15.41s (0.41)**Going Correction** +0.125s/f (Slow) **5**Ran SP% **106.4**
Speed ratings (Par 101): **102,100,99,96,95**
CSF £4.98 TOTE £2.40 : £1.20 , £1.70 ; EX 4.40 Trifecta £8.40 Pool: £705.27 - 61.95 winning units..The winner was bought in for 4,250gns. Tombi was claimed by K. W. Dalgleish for £6000.
Owner William Brand & Gordon McDowall **Bred** Gainsborough Stud Management Ltd **Trained** Carluke, S Lanarks

FOCUS
A good seller but they didn't seem to go that quick. The runner-up is better over 5f while the third travelled well but didn't find much.

546 ENJOY THE HORIZONS RESTAURANT EXPERIENCE MAIDEN STKS 1m 4f 50y (P)

3:40 (3:40) (Class 5) 4-Y-0+ **£2,264** (£673; £336 ; £168) **Stalls** Low

Form RPR
53-3 **1** **Stars In Your Eyes**[19] 292 4 -8-1270 NickyMackay 6 64+
(John Gosden) *mde all: hung rt 7f out: clr whn rdn and hung rt fr over 1f out: jst hld on* **1/2**[1]
3 **2** *nse* **Mister Fizz**[7] 451 4 -8-100 DarrenEgan(7) 3 69
(Andrew Price) *mid-div: hdwy over 5f out: chsd wnr over 2f out: sn rdn: ev ch ins fnl f: r.o* **20/1**
25/ **3** *12* **Akarshan (IRE)**[39] 3473 7 -9-60 TomEaves 5 50
(Evan Williams) *mid-div: hdwy over 5f out: rdn and outpcd fr over 2f out: wnt 3rd ins fnl f* **15/2**[3]
50- **4** *2 1/2* **Counterparty**[185] 5001 4 -8-120 FergusSweeney 8 41
(Alan King) *chsd ldrs: rdn over 2f out: wknd over 1f out* **10/1**
5 *nk* **Madrilene (USA)** 4 -8-120 JoeFanning 10 40
(Mark Johnston) *sn chsng wnr: rdn and lost 2nd over 2f out: wknd over 1f out* **4/1**[2]
6 *1 1/2* **Icy Quiet** 4 -8-120 MartinLane 1 38
(Tobias B P Coles) *hld up: rdn over 2f out: hdwy over 2f out: wknd over 1f out* **40/1**
50 **7** *7* **Chhota Naa**[16] 355 4 -9-30 LukeMorris 4 32
(Harry Dunlop) *chsd ldrs: drvn along lost pl over 5f out: wknd 3f out* **33/1**
0 **8** *1 3/4* **Miss Tooty Fruiti (IRE)**[10] 399 4 -8-70 DavidKenny(5) 9 24
(Paul Burgoyne) *hld up: drvn along over 3f out: sn wknd* **100/1**
9 *3 1/4* **Bold Duke**[26] 4 -8-120 MatthewCosham(5) 7 24
(Edward Bevan) *hld up: rdn and wknd over 3f out* **100/1**

2m 44.51s (3.41)**Going Correction** +0.125s/f (Slow)
WFA 4 from 7yo 3lb **9**Ran SP% **119.6**
Speed ratings (Par 103): **93,92,84,83,83 82,77,76,74**
CSF £18.74 TOTE £1.70 : £1.02 , £3.00 , £1.90 ; EX 15.40 Trifecta £36.10 Pool: £989.80 - 20.25 winning units. .
Owner Mrs Hugo Morris **Bred** Hascombe & Valiant Studs & Carragh Bstck **Trained** Newmarket, Suffolk

■ Stewards' Enquiry : Nicky Mackay ten-day ban: used whip with excessive frequency (2nd offence in 12mths) (Feb 27-29,Mar1-3,5-8)
Darren Egan four-day ban: used whip with excessive frequency (2nd offence in 12mths) (Mar 2-3,5-6)

FOCUS
A really weak maiden and doubtful the winner matched her previous best in success.

547 SPONSOR A RACE BY CALLING 01902 390000 H'CAP 1m 1f 103y (P)

4:10 (4:10) (Class 5) (0-75,73) 3-Y-0 **£2,264** (£673; £336 ; £168) **Stalls** Low

Form RPR
222- **1** **Enery (IRE)**[95] 7350 3 -9-672 JoeFanning 2 79+
(Mark Johnston) *chsd ldrs: nt clr run and lost pl over 2f out: hdwy over 1f out: shkn up and r.o to ld wl ins fnl f: readily* **5/4**[1]
51-3 **2** *1/2* **Island Melody (IRE)**[26] 209 3 -9-470 LukeMorris 4 73
(J S Moore) *hld up: pushed along over 5f out: hdwy over 2f out: rdn and ev ch ins fnl f: r.o* **6/1**
4-31 **3** *1/2* **Availed Speaker (IRE)**[14] 362 3 -8-1365 TonyHamilton 5 67
(Richard Fahey) *trckd ldrs: plld hrd: led over 2f out: rdn and edgd rt over 1f out: hdd and unable qck wl ins fnl f* **3/1**[2]
1111 **4** *7* **Roedean (IRE)**[10] 397 3 -9-773 (p) HayleyTurner 3 60
(William Stone) *chsd ldr tl rdn over 2f out: wknd ins fnl f* **4/1**[3]
4-14 **5** *17* **Anginola (IRE)**[14] 362 3 -8-865 (b[1]) MatthewCosham(5) 1 17
(David Evans) *sn led: rdn and hdd over 2f out: wknd over 1f out* **14/1**

2m 3.27s (1.57)**Going Correction** +0.125s/f (Slow) **5**Ran SP% **110.4**
Speed ratings (Par 97): **98,97,97,90,75**
CSF £9.23 TOTE £2.40 : £1.40 , £3.40 ; EX 10.90 .
Owner Sheikh Hamdan Bin Mohammed Al Maktoum **Bred** Ceka Ireland Limited **Trained** Middleham Moor, N Yorks

FOCUS
The time was 1.74sec slower than the following Class 4 handicap for older horses. This wasn't a strong race. It has been rated around the third.

548 DOWNLOAD THE BLUE SQUARE BET APP H'CAP 1m 1f 103y(P)
4:40 (4:40) (Class 4) (0-80,80) 4-Y-O+ £4,204 (£1,251; £625; £312) Stalls Low

Form RPR
00-3 1 **Reachforthebucks**[20] 280 4-9-4 77 AdamKirby 10 87+
(Jane Chapple-Hyam) *stdd s: hld up: hdwy 2f out: r.o u.p to ld wl ins fnl f* 9/4[1]
-526 2 ½ **Standpoint**[11] 391 6-8-13 79 (p) JackDuern(7) 5 88
(Reg Hollinshead) *hld up: hdwy over 2f out: led over 1f out: rdn and hdd wl ins fnl f* 8/1
2024 3 4 **The Lock Master (IRE)**[0] 432 5-9-0 70 LukeMorris 8 80
(Michael Appleby) *a.p: rdn over 1f out: styd on same pce fnl f* 8/1
2-42 4 ½ **Dazzling Valentine**[21] 275 4-8-8 74 NatashaEaton(7) 7 74
(Alan Bailey) *chsd ldr tl led 2f out: pushed along and hdd over 1f out: edgd lft and no ex ins fnl f* 11/1
00-1 5 2 **Dubai Bounty**[21] 275 5-9-7 80 (p) NickyMackay 4 75
(Gerard Butler) *hld up: rdn over 2f out: styd on fr over 1f out: nvr trbld ldrs* 5/1[2]
6530 6 ½ **Opus Maximus (IRE)**[2] 520 7-9-3 76 HayleyTurner 9 70
(Conor Dore) *hld up: swtchd rt over 4f out: hdwy over 3f out: rdn over 1f out: styd on same pce* 6/1[3]
0-40 7 2 **Georgebernardshaw (IRE)**[9] 432 7-8-11 75 CharlesEddery(5) 6 65
(Richard Guest) *prom: lost pl 4f out: nt clr run over 2f out: n.d after* 28/1
31-2 8 nk **West End Lad**[25] 216 9-9-7 80 (b) RussKennemore 3 69
(Roy Bowring) *led: rdn and hdd over 2f out: wknd fnl f* 9/1
0-31 9 2 **Khandaq (USA)**[21] 268 5-9-3 76 JoeFanning 2 61
(Keith Dalgleish) *s.s: hdwy 6f out: lost pl 5f out: rdn and edgd lft over 1f out: wknd and eased fnl f* 14/1
10 18 **Sublime Talent (IRE)**[63] 3443 6-8-13 72 (t) TomEaves 1 19
(Evan Williams) *chsd ldrs: rdn over 3f out: wknd over 2f out* 25/1

2m 1.53s (-0.17) **Going Correction** +0.125s/f (Slow) 10 Ran SP% 116.2
Speed ratings (Par 105): **105,104,101,100,98 98,96,96,94,78**
toteswingers:1&2:£5.70, 2&3:£12.80, 1&3:£5.30 CSF £20.74 CT £123.78 TOTE £2.20: £1.10, £2.50, £3.10; EX 21.50 Trifecta £220.90 Pool: £1140.75 - 3.82 winning units..
Owner Reach For The Bucks Racing Partnership **Bred** Miss D Gibbins **Trained** Dalham, Suffolk

FOCUS
A fair handicap rated through the runner-up.
West End Lad Official explanation: jockey said gelding hung right-handed throughout

549 STAY AT THE WOLVERHAMPTON HOLIDAY INN H'CAP 1m 141y(P)
5:10 (5:10) (Class 5) (0-70,70) 3-Y-O £2,264 (£673; £336; £168) Stalls Low

Form RPR
4-43 1 **Berlusca (IRE)**[12] 377 3-9-3 66 KierenFallon 2 73
(Mark Brisbourne) *trckd ldrs: plld hrd: shkn up to ld 1f out: r.o: comf* 10/3[3]
5031 2 1¼ **Lana (IRE)**[17] 322 3-8-7 56 HayleyTurner 3 60
(David Evans) *hld up: hdwy over 1f out: rdn to chse wnr ins fnl f: r.o* 16/1
-012 3 3 **Luctor Emergo (IRE)**[6] 466 3-8-7 56 oh4 (b) TomEaves 4 53
(Keith Dalgleish) *prom: chsd ldr over 6f out: rdn and ev ch over 1f out: edgd rt and styd on same pce fnl f* 2/1[2]
0-1 4 hd **Samedi**[26] 206 3-9-7 70 JoeFanning 6 67
(Mark Johnston) *led: rdn over 2f out: hdd 1f out: no ex ins fnl f* 11/8[1]
52-5 5 1¼ **Foursquare Funtime**[28] 193 3-9-5 68 ChrisCatlin 5 62
(Reg Hollinshead) *hld up: shkn up over 1f out: nvr nr to chal* 22/1
066- 6 2½ **Excellent News (IRE)**[68] 7653 3-9-0 63 MichaelHills 1 51
(J W Hills) *chsd ldr tl over 6f out: remained handy: rdn over 3f out: wknd fnl f* 10/1

1m 51.73s (1.23) **Going Correction** +0.125s/f (Slow) 6 Ran SP% 117.8
Speed ratings (Par 97): **99,97,95,95,93 91**
toteswingers:1&2:£3.90, 2&3:£7.10, 1&3:£1.70 CSF £50.69 TOTE £4.50: £2.20, £4.20; EX 26.70.
Owner Peter R Ball **Bred** Value Bloodstock **Trained** Great Ness, Shropshire

FOCUS
A modest handicap and muddling form to rate. The second is probably the best guide.

550 PLAY BINGO FREE AT BLUESQ.COM H'CAP 7f 32y(P)
5:40 (5:40) (Class 6) (0-60,60) 4-Y-O+ £1,704 (£503; £251) Stalls High

Form RPR
0-62 1 **Piccolo Express**[24] 232 6-9-5 58 RussKennemore 10 68+
(Brian Baugh) *hld up: hdwy over 1f out: rdn to ld ins fnl f: r.o* 11/1
1-23 2 1¾ **Chester Deelyte (IRE)**[25] 212 4-8-11 57 (v) ShirleyTeasdale(7) 4 62
(Lisa Williamson) *hld up in tch: n.m.r and lost pl 4f out: hdwy over 1f out: r.o: nt rch wnr* 12/1
-002 3 nse **Cyflymder (IRE)**[7] 447 6-9-0 60 DarrenEgan(7) 12 65
(David C Griffiths) *sn chsng ldrs: rdn over 1f out: r.o* 3/1[2]
6606 4 hd **Efistorm**[9] 424 11-9-7 60 HayleyTurner 9 64
(Conor Dore) *a.p: chsd ldr over 5f out: rdn to ld over 1f out: hdd and unable qck ins fnl f* 14/1
1234 5 1 **Look For Love**[7] 450 4-8-8 54 (p) JackDuern(7) 6 56
(Reg Hollinshead) *mid-div: hdwy over 2f out: rdn over 1f out: styd on same pce fnl f* 5/1[3]
4-32 6 1 **Gala Spirit (IRE)**[9] 430 5-9-2 55 TomEaves 7 54
(Peter Niven) *chsd ldrs: nt clr run over 1f out: sn rdn: no ex ins fnl f* 11/4[1]
650- 7 1¼ **Sopran Nad (ITY)**[69] 7648 8-8-13 52 (b) RichardKingscote 2 48
(James Unett) *led: rdn and hdd over 1f out: no ex ins fnl f* 14/1
06-0 8 2¼ **Bint Elnadim (IRE)**[3] 503 4-8-10 49 JoeFanning 3 38
(Derek Shaw) *hld up: effrt over 1f out: eased whn btn ins fnl f* 40/1
2101 9 4½ **Crocodile Bay (IRE)**[9] 422 9-8-10 54 (p) CharlesEddery(5) 8 31
(Richard Guest) *prom: rdn over 2f out: wknd over 1f out* 8/1
-305 10 5 **Sienna Blue**[9] 423 4-8-13 59 (v¹) JakePayne(7) 5 23
(Bill Turner) *hld up: racd keenly: rdn over 2f out: sn wknd* 20/1

1m 30.54s (0.94) **Going Correction** +0.125s/f (Slow) 10 Ran SP% 116.0
Speed ratings (Par 101): **99,97,96,96,95 94,93,90,85,79**
toteswingers:1&2:£31.50, 2&3:£11.40, 1&3:£5.40 CSF £134.18 CT £512.92 TOTE £10.80: £3.40, £3.60, £1.80; EX 78.30 Trifecta £734.30 Pool: £1131.23 - 1.14 winning units..
Owner G B Hignett **Bred** G B Hignett **Trained** Audley, Staffs

FOCUS
A moderate contest. The fifth, rated to his C&D form, helps set the level.
Crocodile Bay(IRE) Official explanation: jockey said gelding ran too freely
T/Jkpt: £2,886.80 to a £1 stake. Pool of £65,055.10 - 16.00 winning tickets. T/Plt: £43.60 to a £1 stake. Pool of £155,780.30 - 2,602.59 winning tickets. T/Qpdt: £19.20 to a £1 stake. Pool of £11,175.37 - 429.79 winning tickets. CR

[490] SOUTHWELL (L-H)
Tuesday, February 14

OFFICIAL GOING: Standard to slow
Wind: Moderate behind Weather: Cloudy and dry

551 SHARE THE LOVE WITH BLUESQ.COM H'CAP 6f (F)
1:40 (1:40) (Class 6) (0-55,54) 4-Y-O+ £1,704 (£503; £251) Stalls Low

Form RPR
0-50 1 **Silly Billy (IRE)**[27] 203 4-8-5 50 LukeRowe(7) 4 63
(Sylvester Kirk) *in tch on inner: hdwy over 2f out: rdn to chse ldrs over 1f out: styd on to ld last 100yds: sn edgd rt and kpt on strly* 7/1
06-6 2 1¼ **Itsthursdayalready**[15] 356 5-9-1 53 ShaneKelly 5 62
(Mark Brisbourne) *trckd ldrs: smooth hdwy over 2f out: rdn to ld appr fnl f: drvn: hdd and one pce last 100yds* 6/1[3]
6-10 3 3 **Cheyenne Red (IRE)**[15] 356 6-9-0 52 PhillipMakin 8 51
(Michael Herrington) *led 2f: cl up: rdn to ld 2f out: drvn and hdd appr fnl f: kpt on same pce* 10/1
6055 4 ½ **Takajan (IRE)**[15] 356 5-8-12 50 KierenFallon 6 48
(Mark Brisbourne) *t.k.h: hld up in tch: gd hdwy on outer over 2f out: rdn to chse ldrs over 1f out: sn edgd lft and no imp fnl f* 5/2[1]
-106 5 nk **Bird Dog**[14] 372 6-8-6 51 (v) DannyBrock(7) 11 48
(Phil McEntee) *dwlt: sn cl up: rdn along over 2f out: grad wknd* 12/1
00-0 6 hd **Bonnie Prince Blue**[14] 372 9-9-2 54 (b) PatrickMathers 3 50
(Ian McInnes) *bhd tl styd on fnl 2f: nrst fin* 20/1
-443 7 ½ **First In Command (IRE)**[12] 380 7-9-2 54 (t) HayleyTurner 2 49
(Daniel Mark Loughnane) *bhd tl styd on fnl 2f: nrst fin* 5/1[2]
0-20 8 hd **Ladydolly**[12] 380 4-9-1 53 (p) TomEaves 1 47
(Roy Brotherton) *cl up: led after 2f: rdn over 2f out sn hdd & wknd over 1f out* 25/1
232 9 ½ **Gracie's Gift (IRE)**[14] 372 10-9-1 53 (v) LukeMorris 10 45
(Richard Guest) *chsd ldrs: rdn along wl over 2f out: sn wknd* 6/1[3]
/00- 10 shd **Footstepsofspring (FR)**[70] 7641 5-9-2 54 StevieDonohoe 9 46
(Willie Musson) *a towards rr* 8/1
0-04 11 2¼ **Misere**[10] 430 4-8-8 49 (p) AmyRyan(3) 13 34
(Kevin Ryan) *a towards rr* 16/1
46-0 12 1 **Musical Leap**[21] 289 4-8-0 45 DarrenEgan(7) 12 27
(Shaun Harris) *chsd ldrs: rdn along 1/2-way: sn wknd* 50/1

1m 16.32s (-0.18) **Going Correction** +0.025s/f (Slow) 12 Ran SP% 130.7
Speed ratings (Par 101): **102,100,96,95,95 95,94,94,93,93 90,88**
toteswingers:1&2:£11.70, 2&3:£12.70, 1&3:£16.20 CSF £53.01 CT £441.93 TOTE £12.50: £3.70, £2.50, £4.60; EX 61.40 Trifecta £417.00 Pool: £563.62 - 0.74 winning units..
Owner The Only Pub In The World Too **Bred** Sir E J Loder **Trained** Upper Lambourn, Berks

FOCUS
The Fibresand was officially described as Standard to slow. A moderate 46-55 handicap contested by a bunch of horses that are hard to win with. The form has been rated through the runner-up.
Silly Billy(IRE) Official explanation: trainer's rep said, regarding apparent improvement in form, that the gelding settled better over the strongly run 6f trip and appears to go well for the rider

552 MIRROR PUNTERS CLUB MAIDEN STKS 1m (F)
2:10 (2:11) (Class 5) 3-Y-O+ £2,385 (£704; £352) Stalls Low

Form RPR
0-33 1 **Three Bards (IRE)**[18] 324 3-8-8 77 JoeFanning 4 78+
(Mark Johnston) *mde all: pushed clr over 2f out: idled and edgd lft fnl f: eased towards fin* 5/6[1]
2 1¾ **Za'Lan (USA)** 3-8-8 0 MartinLane 1 70+
(Mark Johnston) *green sn outpcd and wl bhd: swtchd to outer and wd st: gd hdwy 2f out: styd on strly fnl f* 14/1
54-2 3 3¼ **Darsan (IRE)**[4] 495 4-9-1 64 DannyBrock(7) 3 63
(Phil McEntee) *trckd ldrs: hdwy over 3f out: chsd wnr wl over 1f out: sn rdn and no imp* 5/1[2]
4 4 3¾ **Linroyale Boy (USA)**[14] 369 4-9-13 0 PJMcDonald 8 59
(Alan Swinbank) *prom: sltly outpcd on outer 3f out: pushed along 2f out: kpt on same pce* 8/1
/0-3 5 1½ **Handsome King**[12] 383 5-9-13 64 (p) StephenCraine 7 56
(J R Jenkins) *towards rr: hdwy 3f out: rdn 2f out: sn no impression* 14/1
0 6 ¾ **Gold Deal (IRE)**[35] 114 3-8-8 0 (t) LeeNewman 6 49
(Deborah Sanderson) *cl up: rdn along over 3f out: sn wknd* 50/1
7 1½ **Dream Prospector** 3-8-8 0 KierenFallon 10 46+
(James Tate) *trckd ldrs: hdwy to chse wnr over 3f out: rdn and edgd lft 2f out: sn wknd* 11/2[3]
5 8 1 **Dewala**[14] 369 3-8-0 0 DominicFox(3) 2 38
(Michael Appleby) *chsd ldrs on inner: rdn along 3f out: sn wknd* 33/1
0- 9 3¼ **Medlaur**[60] 7777 3-8-3 0 JamesSullivan 9 31
(James Given) *a towards rr* 50/1
24- 10 2½ **Vinniespride (IRE)**[148] 6210 5-9-8 0 (t) LMcNiff(5) 5 35
(Mark Michael McNiff, Ire) *a towards rr* 33/1

1m 44.21s (0.51) **Going Correction** +0.025s/f (Slow)
WFA 3 from 4yo+ 19lb 10 Ran SP% 120.9
Speed ratings (Par 103): **98,96,93,89,87 87,85,84,81,78**
toteswingers:1&2:£4.80, 2&3:£9.20, 1&3:£2.10 CSF £15.64 TOTE £1.80: £1.10, £4.00, £1.30; EX 11.90 Trifecta £55.50 Pool: £425.27 - 5.67 winning units..
Owner Sheikh Hamdan Bin Mohammed Al Maktoum **Bred** Thomas G Cooke **Trained** Middleham Moor, N Yorks

FOCUS
An ordinary maiden and a 1-2 for trainer Mark Johnston. The form has been rated around the third horse.

553 DINE IN THE PANTRY (S) STKS 7f (F)
2:45 (2:45) (Class 6) 4-Y-O+ £1,704 (£503; £251) Stalls Low

Form RPR
-525 1 **Imprimis Tagula (IRE)**[1] 545 8-8-12 73 (v) JoeFanning 3 80
(Alan Bailey) *trckd ldng pair: hdwy to chse ldr 2f out: rdn to ld ent fnl f: kpt on strly* 7/1[3]
1-21 2 2¾ **Ingleby Arch (USA)**[21] 284 9-8-13 75 LMcNiff(5) 8 79
(David Barron) *led: rdn along 2f out: drvn and hdd ent fnl f: kpt on one pce* 9/4[1]
12-5 3 1½ **St Oswald**[42] 22 4-9-4 65 AndrewMullen 5 75
(David Nicholls) *chsd ldrs: pushed along wl over 2f out: rdn wl over 1f out: sn one pce* 7/1[3]
600- 4 1 **Trans Sonic**[60] 7776 9-8-12 85 KierenFallon 6 66
(David O'Meara) *cl up: rdn along wl over 2f out: wknd wl over 1f out* 3/1[2]

1251 **5** *nk* **Faithful Ruler (USA)**[8] 447 8-8-11 75........................(p) DarrenEgan(7) 4 71
(Ronald Harris) *s.i.s and bhd: hdwy 1/2-way: rdn to chse ldrs wl over 1f out: sn rdn and kpt on same pce* **14/1**

02-3 **6** *11* **Zomerlust**[8] 447 10-8-9 82..............................(v) MichaelO'Connell(3) 1 36
(John Quinn) *trckd ldrs on inner: effrt 3f out: sn rdn along and wknd over 2f out* **3/1**[2]

0-60 **7** *27* **Vogarth**[35] 109 8-8-8 40 ow1..................................(b) MarkCoumbe(5) 2
(Michael Chapman) *dwlt: a in rr: bhd fnl 3f* **50/1**

1m 28.61s (-1.69) **Going Correction** +0.025s/f (Slow) **7** Ran SP% **114.4**
Speed ratings (Par 101): **110,106,105,104,103 91,60**
toteswingers:1&2:£3.40, 2&3:£2.80, 1&3:£3.90 CSF £23.20 TOTE £7.50: £4.10, £1.80; EX 23.20 Trifecta £71.90 Pool: £743.31 - 7.64 winning units. The winner was bought in for 6,250gns.
Owner Middleham Park Racing XLI & Alan Bailey **Bred** Glashare House Stud **Trained** Newmarket, Suffolk
■ Stewards' Enquiry : Darren Egan six-day ban: used whip with excessive frequency (Mar 7-10, 13-14)

FOCUS
A routine seller and plenty of experience amongst these horses, with six of the seven runners 8yos or older.
Zomerlust Official explanation: jockey said gelding was unsuited by the standard to slow Fibresand

554 BET AND WATCH AT BLUESQ.COM H'CAP 7f (F)
3:15 (3:15) (Class 3) (0-95,94) 4-Y-O+ **£6,792** (£2,021; £1,010; £505) **Stalls** Low

Form RPR
110- **1** **True To Form (IRE)**[59] 7803 5-9-2 89..............................(p) LukeMorris 4 97
(Ronald Harris) *chsd ldng pair: pushed along 1/2-way: hdwy to chal 2f out and sn rdn: drvn to ld ent fnl f: kpt on wl* **4/1**[3]

314- **2** *1½* **Sound Amigo (IRE)**[131] 6658 4-8-7 80 oh2...................... PJMcDonald 1 84
(Ollie Pears) *cl up on inner: effrt 2f out: rdn to ld briefly over 1f out: hdd ent fnl f: no ex last 100yds* **15/8**[2]

0203 **3** *1¼* **Follow The Flag (IRE)**[4] 501 8-8-9 82..........................(be) JohnFahy 5 83
(Alan McCabe) *sn rdn along and outpcd in rr: hdwy 3f out: sn swtchd wd and styd on wl u.p fnl f: nrst fin* **6/1**

5-54 **4** *2¾* **Close To The Edge (IRE)**[7] 458 4-8-9 82....................... ShaneKelly 7 76
(Alan McCabe) *sn led: rdn and jnd 2f out: drvn and hdd appr fnl f: sn wknd* **6/4**[1]

060- **5** *6* **Phoenix Flight (IRE)**[75] 6690 7-9-0 87....................... FergusSweeney 3 64
(James Evans) *outpcd and bhd fr 1/2-way* **14/1**

1m 29.06s (-1.24) **Going Correction** +0.025s/f (Slow) **5** Ran SP% **115.7**
Speed ratings (Par 107): **108,106,104,101,94**
CSF £12.62 TOTE £5.10: £2.60, £2.20; EX 12.60.
Owner David & Gwyn Joseph **Bred** Sir E J Loder **Trained** Earlswood, Monmouths

FOCUS
This race was weakened by the absence of Nazreef, who would have been sent off a warm favourite, and there were question marks over the suitability of the trip for a few of the remaining quintet.

NOTEBOOK
True To Form(IRE) was taking a significant drop in trip after three wins on Polytrack towards the end of last year and didn't show much in his only previous try here. The omens didn't look good when he was ridden along and had to be given a reminder at halfway, but the way the track was riding made this quite a test and his stamina eventually came to his aid. He was 24lb higher than when winning at Wolverhampton in October, which shows just how much progress he has made this winter. (tchd 7-2)
Sound Amigo(IRE) ◆ was back down to a more suitable trip on this return from 131 days off, but he was 2lb wrong and had never raced on Fibresand before. Always handy, he had every chance until well inside the last furlong and, as his trainer had warned beforehand that he might need it, this was encouraging. (op 5-2 tchd 11-4)
Follow The Flag(IRE) has winning form here, but is usually seen over much further than this so it was little surprise that he was running on strongly at the end after getting outpaced early. (op 5-1)
Close To The Edge(IRE) had the run of the race out in front, but she was collared on either side over a furlong from home and the conclusion must be that she didn't see out the trip on this testing surface. (op 13-8 tchd 7-4)
Phoenix Flight(IRE), last seen winning over hurdles and third over 2m4f in last year's Ascot Stakes at the Royal meeting, was always going to find this far too sharp. (op 16-1)

555 BOOK YOUR TICKETS ON LINE AT SOUTHWELL-RACECOURSE.CO.UK H'CAP 2m (F)
3:50 (3:50) (Class 5) (0-75,73) 4-Y-O+ **£2,264** (£673; £336; £168) **Stalls** Low

Form RPR
14-1 **1** **Captain Bellamy (USA)**[43] 9 4-9-4 71..................... JimmyFortune 7 83+
(Hughie Morrison) *trckd ldrs: hdwy 4f out: led over 2f out: rdn clr over 1f out: kpt on strly* **11/4**[2]

42-2 **2** *2½* **Blackmore**[19] 309 5-9-8 69.. LukeMorris 1 76
(Julia Feilden) *trckd ldrs: hdwy over 3f out: chsd wnr wl over 1f out: sn rdn and no imp ins fnl f* **5/1**[3]

544- **3** *2¾* **Salontyre (GER)**[26] 6405 6-9-4 65...................................(p) MartinLane 5 69
(Bernard Llewellyn) *hld up in tch: hdwy 3f out: swtchd rt and rdn wl over 1f out: kpt on u.p fnl f* **10/1**

/4-3 **4** *2¾* **Wine 'n Dine**[14] 367 7-9-9 70......................................(p) RobertHavlin 8 70
(Bernard Llewellyn) *cl up: effrt 3f out and ev ch tl rdn and one pce fnl 2f* **16/1**

3-10 **5** *½* **First Rock (IRE)**[19] 309 6-9-8 69...................................... PJMcDonald 6 69
(Alan Swinbank) *led: rdn along 3f out: hdd over 2f out and grad wknd* **15/2**

011- **6** *3¼* **Storm Hawk (IRE)**[47] 7914 5-9-9 73...............................(b) RyanClark(3) 3 69
(Pat Eddery) *dwlt and hld up in rr: stdy hdwy 4f out: chsd ldrs on inner 2f out: sn rdn and no imp appr fnl f* **9/4**[1]

20-0 **7** *8* **Carnac (IRE)**[14] 366 6-8-1 55......................................(p) NoraLooby(7) 10 41
(Alan McCabe) *in tch: effrt and sme hdwy 4f out: rdn along 3f out and n.d* **25/1**

155- **8** *2* **Shifting Gold (IRE)**[25] 7914 6-9-3 67...............................(bt) AmyRyan(3) 4 51
(Kevin Ryan) *dwlt and sn rdn along: a in rr* **14/1**

03/5 **9** *hd* **Mexican Bob**[32] 156 9-8-4 58.. DarrenEgan(7) 9 42
(James Evans) *chsd ldrs: rdn along 5f out: sn wknd* **50/1**

0-52 **10** *1¼* **Lyric Poet (USA)**[22] 271 5-9-10 71.............................(t) WilliamCarson 2 53
(Anthony Carson) *hld up in rr: rdn along over 4f out and sn bhd* **10/1**

3m 44.77s (-0.73) **Going Correction** +0.025s/f (Slow)
WFA 4 from 5yo+ 6lb **10** Ran SP% **122.4**
Speed ratings (Par 103): **102,100,99,98,97 96,92,91,91,90**
CSF £18.13 CT £125.00 TOTE £3.00: £1.10, £1.60, £4.30; EX 16.60 Trifecta £181.60 Pool: £910.74 - 3.71 winning units..
Owner H Morrison **Bred** Brereton C Jones **Trained** East Ilsley, Berks

FOCUS
This promised to be a severe test of stamina in the conditions, but the riders seemed aware of that and they went a very sensible pace. As a result those that raced prominently were at a major advantage and several still had a chance straightening up for home. The form has been rated through the second.
Storm Hawk(IRE) Official explanation: trainer had no explanation for the poor form shown

556 SOUTHWELL H'CAP 7f (F)
4:20 (4:20) (Class 6) (0-60,60) 3-Y-O **£1,704** (£503; £251) **Stalls** Low

Form RPR
2021 **1** **Samasana (IRE)**[7] 459 3-9-5 58 6ex.......................... TonyHamilton 7 65
(Ian Wood) *cl up: rdn to chal 2f out: drvn ent fnl f: kpt on gamely to ld nr fin* **5/2**[1]

0-33 **2** *hd* **First Bid**[21] 288 3-9-7 60...(b) FrederikTylicki 2 66
(James Given) *led: rdn 2f out: drvn and edgd lft ins fnl f: hdd and no ex nr fin* **5/1**[3]

0-03 **3** *3¼* **J J Leary (IRE)**[7] 459 3-9-0 53.......................................(v) KierenFallon 6 51
(Ian Williams) *cl up: effrt to chal over 2f out: sn rdn and ev ch tl wknd appr fnl f* **5/2**[1]

3-44 **4** *2* **Son Of May**[22] 270 3-8-13 52..(p) JoeFanning 4 44
(Jo Hughes) *chsd ldrs: rdn along over 2f out: sn one pce* **3/1**[2]

000- **5** *4½* **Bojangle (IRE)**[144] 6293 3-8-8 47...................................... HayleyTurner 3 27
(Dominic Ffrench Davis) *chsd ldrs: rdn along 3f out: sn wknd* **12/1**

0-06 **6** *13* **Aiaam Al Wafa (IRE)**[4] 495 3-9-2 60..........................(bt) LauraPike(5) 8
(Phil McEntee) *chsd ldrs on outer: rdn along over 3f out: sn wknd* **50/1**

0-40 **7** *15* **Castalian Spring (IRE)**[29] 196 3-8-0 46 oh1............. DannyBrock(7) 5
(Phil McEntee) *dwlt: a towards rr: bhd fr over 2f out* **25/1**

30-4 **8** *1½* **Romany Spirit (IRE)**[42] 20 3-9-4 57........................ MichaelStainton 1
(Jason Ward) *chsd ldrs on inner: rdn along bef 1/2-way and sn bhd* **33/1**

1m 30.73s (0.43) **Going Correction** +0.025s/f (Slow) **8** Ran SP% **115.2**
Speed ratings (Par 95): **98,97,94,91,86 71,54,52**
CSF £15.43 CT £33.82 TOTE £3.30: £1.50, £1.30, £1.30; EX 15.40 Trifecta £20.30 Pool: £1007.91 - 36.60 winning units..
Owner Paddy Barrett **Bred** Patrick Cassidy **Trained** Upper Lambourn, Berks
■ Stewards' Enquiry : Frederik Tylicki two-day ban: used whip with excessive frequency (Feb 28-29)

FOCUS
A weak contest and the front three had the race to themselves from the start.

557 PLAY DA VINCI DIAMONDS AT BLUESQ.COM/GAMES H'CAP 1m 4f (F)
4:55 (4:55) (Class 6) (0-65,65) 4-Y-O+ **£1,704** (£503; £251) **Stalls** Low

Form RPR
-323 **1** **Brunello**[14] 366 4-8-13 60......................................(p) KierenFallon 4 68+
(David O'Meara) *prom: hdwy to ld 3f out: jnd and rdn over 2f out: hung rt wl over 1f out: drvn and edgd rt ins fnl f: kpt on* **4/6**[1]

-204 **2** *½* **Turjuman (USA)**[11] 400 7-9-3 61..................................(p) JoeFanning 7 68
(Alan Bailey) *trckd ldrs: hdwy over 3f out: chal whn carried rt wl over 1f out: sn rdn and ev ch whn n.m.r wl ins fnl f: no ex nr fin* **6/1**[3]

205- **3** *2½* **Captain Sharpe**[25] 4642 4-8-8 55.................................(p) MartinLane 1 58
(Bernard Llewellyn) *hld up towards rr: hdwy on outer 3f out: sn rdn to chse ldrs 2f out: kpt on same pce fnl f* **14/1**

00-1 **4** *4* **Mustajed**[7] 453 11-8-12 56 6ex.................................(b) JamesMillman 5 53
(Rod Millman) *hld up in rr: hdwy on inner to trck ldrs 1/2-way: rdn along 3f out: one pce fnl 2f* **11/2**[2]

0/60 **5** *2½* **Myraid**[12] 389 5-8-7 51 oh1.. JamesSullivan 3 44
(Ruth Carr) *led: rdn along 4f out: hdd 3f out: grad wknd fnl 2f* **20/1**

352/ **6** *9* **Budva**[20] 7397 5-9-2 65..(b) CharlesBishop(5) 2 43
(Bernard Llewellyn) *cl up: rdn along over 4f out: wknd over 3f out* **14/1**

4-60 **7** *7* **Sergeant Troy (IRE)**[12] 381 4-9-3 64......................(tp) StephenCraine 6 31
(George Baker) *in tch: rdn along 1/2-way: sn lost pl and bhd fnl 3f* **25/1**

2m 42.16s (1.16) **Going Correction** +0.025s/f (Slow)
WFA 4 from 5yo+ 3lb **7** Ran SP% **111.6**
Speed ratings (Par 101): **97,96,95,92,90 84,80**
toteswingers:1&2:£1.50, 2&3:£4.70, 1&3:£3.30 CSF £4.82 TOTE £1.50: £1.10, £1.50; EX 5.40.
Owner Mrs Lynne Lumley **Bred** Pendley Farm **Trained** Nawton, N Yorks
■ Stewards' Enquiry : Kieren Fallon caution: careless riding

FOCUS
A moderate affair. The winner probably didn't need to improve from recent form.
T/Jkpt: Not won. T/Plt: £50.00 to a £1 stake. Pool of £98,290.34 - 1,433.03 winning tickets. T/Qpdt: £11.00 to a £1 stake. Pool of £9,332.84 - 625.80 winning tickets. JR

517 KEMPTON (A.W) (R-H)
Wednesday, February 15

OFFICIAL GOING: Standard
Wind: Moderate, against Weather: Cloudy

558 FREE ENTRY FOR BETDAQ MEMBERS APPRENTICE H'CAP 1m 2f (P)
5:10 (5:10) (Class 7) (0-50,50) 4-Y-O+ **£1,455** (£433; £216; £108) **Stalls** Low

Form RPR
05-2 **1** **Trecase**[7] 468 5-8-11 49..(t) DarrenEgan(5) 2 58
(Tony Carroll) *hld up: sltly hmpd after 100yds: wl off the pce after 4f: rapid prog on outer 2f out to ld over 1f out: rdn out* **10/11**[1]

00-0 **2** *3¼* **Diamond Twister (USA)**[12] 395 6-8-9 47..........(t) ShirleyTeasdale(5) 3 49
(Lisa Williamson) *cl up bhd ldng pair at str pce: rdn over 2f out: kpt on to take 2nd 1f out but wnr already gone by: no imp* **16/1**

300- **3** *1* **Escape Artist**[95] 7394 5-9-3 50... DavidKenny 7 52+
(John Bridger) *hld up and wl off the pce after 4f: clsd qckly 2f out: nt clr run over 1f out and lost any ch: kpt on to take 3rd ins fnl f* **8/1**

0500 **4** *1½* **Le Reveur**[7] 468 10-8-9 45......................................(e) CharlesEddery(3) 4 42
(Richard Guest) *hld up: wl off the pce in last pair after 4f: nt on terms whn hanging and reminders 2f out: kpt on fr over 1f out* **25/1**

000- **5** *shd* **The Right Time**[26] 7400 4-8-6 45............................ GeorgeDowning(5) 6 42
(Tony Carroll) *chsd ldng trio: clr of rest after 4f but already pushed along: styd cl up tl outpcd over 1f out* **14/1**

600- **6** *2½* **Rosy Dawn**[112] 7092 7-8-12 45.. DeanHeslop 5 37
(Brett Johnson) *racd freely: led: stepped up to a decent clip after 4f but a pressed: hdd & wknd over 1f out* **14/1**

00-0 **7** *4* **Hackett (IRE)**[12] 401 4-9-1 49....................................(bt[1]) LucyKBarry 8 33
(Shaun Lycett) *pressed ldr even whn pce lifted after 4f: upsides jst over 2f out: wknd over 1f out* **7/1**[3]

4/0- **8** 4 ½ **Ray Diamond**[85] 5642 7-8-7 **45**.......... JakePayne[(5)] 1 20
(Michael Madgwick) *bdly hmpd after 100yds and dropped to last: nvr on terms after* **13/2**[2]

2m 9.1s (1.10) **Going Correction** +0.05s/f (Slow)
WFA 4 from 5yo+ 1lb **8** Ran SP% **112.4**
Speed ratings (Par 97): **97,94,93,92,92 90,87,83**
toteswingers:1&2:£6.60, 1&3:£2.90, 2&3:£7.40 CSF £17.22 CT £75.09 TOTE £2.00: £1.10, £4.50, £2.10; EX 11.50.
Owner Serafino Agodino **Bred** T W R Chugg & Overbury Stallions Ltd **Trained** Cropthorne, Worcs
■ Stewards' Enquiry : Dean Heslop seven-day ban: careless riding (Feb 29,Mar 1-3,5-7)

FOCUS
A pretty desperate race in which there was a disputed lead. The third has been rated to his old Polytrack form.

559 BETDAQ MULTIPLES H'CAP 1m 2f (P)
5:40 (5:41) (Class 6) (0-60,60) 4-Y-0+ **£1,617** (£360; £360; £120) **Stalls** Low

Form RPR
5-22 **1** **Abigails Angel**[22] 276 5-9-7 **60**.......... AdamKirby 9 72
(Brett Johnson) *mde all: allowed to set modest pce: wound it up fr 3f out: kicked on 2f out: in n.d after: r.o wl* **9/2**[2]
63-4 **2** 3 ¼ **Cane Cat (IRE)**[22] 276 5-9-7 **60**..........(t) LukeMorris 6 65
(Tony Carroll) *cl up: rdn to chse wnr 2f out but sn outpcd: kpt on same pce after* **5/1**[3]
-344 **2** dht **Storm Runner (IRE)**[20] 306 4-9-5 **59**.......... FrederikTylicki 10 64
(George Margarson) *mostly chsd wnr to 2f out: nt qckn and outpcd: styd on again fnl f to dead-heat for 2nd last stride* **5/1**[3]
0-00 **4** 2 ¼ **Khun John (IRE)**[18] 349 9-9-3 **56**.......... StevieDonohoe 2 57
(Willie Musson) *hld up in last: outpcd whn pce lifted and no ch 2f out: styd on fr over 1f out* **12/1**
40-6 **5** 1 ½ **Galloping Minister (IRE)**[40] 67 4-8-8 **55**..........(v[1]) DarrenEgan[(7)] 7 53+
(Pat Phelan) *tk fierce hold: cl up on outer: lost pl jst over 2f out: outpcd sn after: no ch over 1f out* **11/4**[1]
0012 **6** ½ **Valley Tiger**[9] 450 4-9-1 **60**.......... ShaneBKelly[(5)] 1 57
(Richard Fahey) *t.k.h: cl up: rdn over 2f out: lft bhd wl over 1f out* **5/1**[3]
-020 **7** 2 **Hathaway (IRE)**[12] 401 5-8-6 **52**.......... RachealKneller[(7)] 8 45
(Mark Brisbourne) *stdd s: racd wd thrght: prom: pushed along and struggling over 2f out: sn btn* **20/1**
-056 **8** 2 **The Which Doctor**[22] 287 7-9-6 **59**..........(e) LeeNewman 4 48
(Richard Guest) *dwlt: t.k.h: hld up in last pair: effrt and cl up over 2f out: wknd wl over 1f out* **12/1**

2m 12.46s (4.46) **Going Correction** +0.05s/f (Slow)
WFA 4 from 5yo+ 1lb **8** Ran SP% **115.0**
Speed ratings (Par 101): **84,81,81,79,78 78,76,74**
toteswingers:1&2:£2.80, 1&2:£4.30, 2&2:£5.20 CSF £13.69 CT £58.07 TOTE £4.40: £1.60, £2.40; EX 17.10.
Owner B R Johnson **Bred** P Balding **Trained** Epsom, Surrey

FOCUS
A slowly run handicap in which the winner dominated throughout. The runner-up and third have been rated close to their marks.
Valley Tiger Official explanation: jockey said gelding ran too free

560 BACK OR LAY AT BETDAQ.COM H'CAP 5f (P)
6:10 (6:10) (Class 5) (0-75,75) 4-Y-0+ **£2,264** (£673; £336; £168) **Stalls** Low

Form RPR
4-56 **1** **Triple Dream**[12] 406 7-9-3 **73**..........(tp) RussKennemore 5 82
(Milton Bradley) *chsd ldng trio and racd on outer: lost grnd bnd 2f out: r.o fr over 1f out: rdn to ld last 75yds* **20/1**
6324 **2** ¾ **Island Legend (IRE)**[4] 525 6-9-5 **75**..........(p) RichardKingscote 4 81
(Milton Bradley) *led but had to worko fend off early chalr: hrd pressed fr over 1f out: hdd and no ex last 75yds* **5/2**[1]
4000 **3** ¾ **Captain Scooby**[4] 528 6-8-11 **72**.......... CharlesEddery[(5)] 2 75
(Richard Guest) *outpcd in last: detached fr rest 1/2-way and scrubbed along: gd prog on inner over 1f out: r.o to take 3rd wl ins fnl f* **7/1**
00-4 **4** 1 **Love You Louis**[43] 24 6-9-2 **72**.......... FrederikTylicki 1 72
(J R Jenkins) *trckd ldng pair: chsd wnr 2f out: tried to chal over 1f out: nt qckn and lost 2nd ins fnl f* **5/1**[3]
05-3 **5** 1 ¾ **Estonia**[28] 208 5-9-4 **74**.......... LukeMorris 8 67
(Michael Squance) *s.i.s: off the pce in last pair: gd prog on inner jst over 2f out: disp 2nd over 1f out: nt qckn: fdd fnl f* **11/2**
30-4 **6** 1 ¼ **Black Baccara**[28] 208 5-8-11 **70**..........(be) RyanClark[(3)] 7 59
(Phil McEntee) *in tch towards rr: rdn and effrt 2f out: chsd ldrs over 1f out: no imp and fdd ins fnl f* **16/1**
0-06 **7** 8 **Best Trip (IRE)**[22] 282 5-9-0 **70**..........(t) TomEaves 6 30
(Richard Guest) *w ldr 1f: chsd afterwards to 2f out: wknd rapidly* **9/2**[2]
00-0 **8** 3 ½ **Alpha Tauri (USA)**[22] 286 6-9-4 **74**..........(t) LeeNewman 3 22
(Richard Guest) *in tch towards rr to 2f out: wknd rapidly* **80/1**
0-31 **9** 13 **Aldermoor (USA)**[25] 252 6-9-1 **71**.......... WilliamCarson 9
(Stuart Williams) *racd wd: rdn to stay in tch in midfield: wknd rapidly 2f out: t.o* **15/2**

59.23s (-1.27) **Going Correction** +0.05s/f (Slow) **9** Ran SP% **114.9**
Speed ratings (Par 103): **112,110,109,108,105 103,90,84,64**
toteswingers:1&2:£6.00, 1&3:£17.40, 2&3:£4.70 CSF £69.70 CT £399.64 TOTE £17.30: £5.10, £1.20, £2.20; EX 50.80.
Owner J M Bradley **Bred** Hesmonds Stud Ltd **Trained** Sedbury, Gloucs

FOCUS
This looked like it might be a burn-up on paper and Island Legend and Best Trip took each other on up front and set it up for a closer. The winner has been rated back to his best.
Island Legend(IRE) Official explanation: jockey said gelding hung left
Aldermoor(USA) Official explanation: jockey said gelding never travelled

561 BETDAQ MOBILE APPS H'CAP 1m (P)
6:40 (6:40) (Class 6) (0-55,55) 4-Y-0+ **£1,617** (£481; £240; £120) **Stalls** Low

Form RPR
02-0 **1** **Warbond**[28] 203 4-9-2 **53**.......... JamieGoldstein 6 62
(Michael Madgwick) *awkward s and slowest away: mde up a few pls early to sit abt 10th: sustained prog fr 2f out to ld 1f out: drvn and styd on wl* **7/1**[3]
6-21 **2** 1 **Emerald Royal**[14] 375 4-8-12 **49**.......... ShaneKelly 9 56+
(Eric Wheeler) *hld up in last trio: shkn up over 2f out: gd prog on outer over 1f out: r.o to take 2nd nr fin* **9/2**[1]
650- **3** ½ **Holyfield Warrior (IRE)**[48] 7910 8-8-6 **48** ow2.......... MarkCoumbe[(5)] 1 54
(Michael Attwater) *trckd ldrs disputing 5th: clsd to chal over 1f out: upsides ent fnl f: one pce* **14/1**
00-0 **4** ¾ **By Implication**[14] 375 4-8-9 **46** oh1..........(b[1]) JohnFahy 13 50
(Ed de Giles) *hld up in 7th: rdn over 2f out: styd on fr over 1f out: tk 4th last 100yds: nt pce to chal* **25/1**
66-6 **5** 1 **Teen Ager (FR)**[14] 375 8-8-13 **50**.......... LiamKeniry 11 52
(Paul Burgoyne) *dwlt: hld up in last pair: looking for room over 2f out: stylish prog after to trck ldrs on inner jst over 1f out: shkn up and nt qckn* **11/1**
3-46 **6** hd **Polar Auroras**[24] 262 4-9-4 **55**..........(t) LukeMorris 10 56
(Tony Carroll) *hld up wl in rr: stdy prog fr over 2f out to cl on ldrs over 1f out: one pce fnl f* **15/2**
3-02 **7** 1 ½ **Kucharova (IRE)**[11] 422 4-9-4 **55**.......... IanMongan 14 53
(Seamus Mullins) *pressed ldr: chal 2f out: drvn and stl there jst over 1f out: wknd* **8/1**
4-41 **8** nk **Fearless Poet (IRE)**[20] 307 4-9-1 **52**..........(b) TomEaves 3 49
(Bryan Smart) *led at decent pce: rdn 2f out: hdd & wknd 1f out* **5/1**[2]
0-00 **9** ½ **Lean Machine**[19] 333 5-8-9 **53**..........(p) DarrenEgan[(7)] 12 49
(Ronald Harris) *hld up in 9th and racd on outer: rdn and nt qckn over 2f out: no ch after: kpt on nr fin* **20/1**
0535 **10** shd **Jackie Love (IRE)**[14] 379 4-8-5 **49**..........(v) JenniferFerguson[(7)] 5 48+
(Olivia Maylam) *dwlt: hld up in last trio: nt clr run over 2f out: hmpd wl over 1f out: no ch after: keeping on nr fin* **16/1**
-431 **11** ½ **Lovat Lane**[14] 379 4-8-11 **48**.......... ChrisCatlin 7 42
(Eve Johnson Houghton) *trckd ldrs disputing 5th: rdn over 2f out: wknd over 1f out* **20/1**
520- **12** 3 **Yanbu (USA)**[89] 7463 7-9-3 **54**.......... GeorgeBaker 8 41
(Tobias B P Coles) *trckd ldng trio: rdn over 2f out: wknd wl over 1f out* **8/1**
-040 **13** 1 ¾ **Hot Tub**[13] 390 4-8-9 **46** oh1..........(p) WilliamCarson 4 29
(Christine Dunnett) *chsd ldng pair: rdn wl over 2f out: struggling after: wknd qckly over 1f out* **66/1**
650/ **14** 11 **Pahente**[484] 7004 4-9-1 **55**.......... MichaelO'Connell[(3)] 2 13
(Tony Carroll) *settled in 8th: rdn over 2f out: sn wknd: t.o* **40/1**

1m 40.82s (1.02) **Going Correction** +0.125s/f (Slow) **14** Ran SP% **119.5**
Speed ratings (Par 101): **99,98,97,96,95 95,94,93,93,93 92,89,87,76**
toteswingers:1&2:£9.70, 1&3:£26.80, 2&3:£20.00 CSF £35.75 CT £450.88 TOTE £10.50: £2.90, £2.50, £5.10; EX 57.50.
Owner M Madgwick **Bred** J W Ford **Trained** Denmead, Hants

FOCUS
There was a fair gallop and they were well strung out heading to the turn. The third is the guide to the level.
Teen Ager(FR) Official explanation: jockey said gelding was restless in stalls, and tried to anticipate the start, which resulted in being unable to remove the blindfold immediately as stalls opened.

562 DOWNLOAD THE RACING PLUS APP CLASSIFIED CLAIMING STKS 7f (P)
7:10 (7:10) (Class 5) 4-Y-0+ **£2,264** (£673; £336; £168) **Stalls** Low

Form RPR
1445 **1** **Mcconnell (USA)**[8] 463 7-8-8 **70**..........(b) DuilioDaSilva[(5)] 2 76
(Richard Guest) *hld up last: clsd on ldrs over 2f out: rdn to ld jst over 1f out: styd on wl* **16/1**
20-1 **2** 2 ½ **Twinkled**[11] 423 4-8-4 **67**.......... IanBurns[(7)] 3 67
(Michael Bell) *t.k.h early: trckd ldr: led wl over 1f out gng strly: hdd and shkn up jst over 1f out: one pce* **1/2**[1]
2-56 **3** 4 **El Dececy (USA)**[36] 115 8-9-3 **68**..........(t) LeeNewman 5 62
(Richard Guest) *led at gd pce: rdn and hdd wl over 1f out: readily lft bhd by front pair* **8/1**[3]
0-00 **4** 1 ¼ **Goal (IRE)**[13] 391 4-9-5 **68**..........(t) WilliamCarson 6 61
(Richard Guest) *dwlt: tk fierce hold: hld up in 5th: rdn and brief effrt over 2f out: wl outpcd fr over 1f out* **14/1**
-426 **5** 1 ¾ **Lutine Charlie (IRE)**[11] 423 5-8-13 **64**..........(v) LukeMorris 4 50
(Ronald Harris) *t.k.h: trckd ldng pair: gng wl over 2f out: sn shkn up and fnd nil* **7/2**[2]
603/ **6** nk **Ejeed (USA)**[613] 2964 7-8-13 **56**.......... JamieGoldstein 1 50
(Zoe Davison) *hld up in 4th: shkn up and cl enough 2f out: wknd over 1f out* **40/1**

1m 25.72s (-0.28) **Going Correction** +0.125s/f (Slow) **6** Ran SP% **115.0**
Speed ratings (Par 103): **106,103,98,97,95 94**
toteswingers:1&2:£2.40, 1&3:£3.50, 2&3:£1.40 CSF £25.87 TOTE £14.20: £5.20, £1.10; EX 28.10.Twinkled was subject to a friendly claim.
Owner Rakebackmypoker.com **Bred** Hall Et Al Farm **Trained** Stainforth, S Yorks
■ Stewards' Enquiry : Ian Burns one-day ban: careless riding (Feb 29)

FOCUS
An interesting claimer in which the odds-on favourite Twinkled was turned over by team Guest, who had three in the race and made it a test at the trip. The winner has been rated to his winter best.

563 SKYSPORTS.COM H'CAP 7f (P)
7:40 (7:43) (Class 4) (0-85,85) 4-Y-0+ **£4,075** (£1,212; £606; £303) **Stalls** Low

Form RPR
0-52 **1** **Chilli Green**[21] 304 5-9-2 **85**..........(p) MatthewCosham[(5)] 2 93
(John Akehurst) *t.k.h early: trckd ldrs on inner: taken wdr and rdn over 2f out: styd on to ld narrowly last 150yds: hld on wl* **7/2**[1]
03-0 **2** hd **Masai Moon**[11] 431 8-9-2 **80**.......... JamesMillman 1 87
(Rod Millman) *chsd ldrs: rdn and prog on inner 2f out: chal 1f out: w wnr after: jst hld* **10/1**
-066 **3** 1 ½ **Requisite**[4] 520 7-9-1 **79**..........(b) MartinLane 3 82
(Ian Wood) *settled in last trio: drvn over 2f out: gd prog over 1f out to try to chal jst ins fnl f: nt qckn after* **12/1**
0-50 **4** nk **Dozy Joe**[21] 304 4-9-4 **82**.......... LukeMorris 8 84
(Ian Wood) *chsd ldrs: rdn over 2f out: tried to cl u.p over 1f out: kpt on same pce* **6/1**[3]
0-00 **5** ½ **Arteus**[11] 431 6-9-2 **80**..........(b) GeorgeBaker 5 81
(Jane Chapple-Hyam) *reluctant to enter stalls: led: rdn and hdd 2f out: nt qckn over 1f out: plugged on* **13/2**
0-00 **6** ½ **Majuro (IRE)**[22] 285 8-9-1 **79**..........(t) LiamKeniry 7 78+
(Richard Guest) *heavily restrained s: hld up in last: pushed along over 2f out: couple of reminders and styd on fnl f: nvr nr ldrs* **25/1**
1-01 **7** ½ **Ocean Legend (IRE)**[14] 378 7-9-2 **83**.......... MichaelO'Connell[(3)] 4 81
(Tony Carroll) *trckd ldr 2f: styd prom: led 2f out: drvn and edgd lft after: hdd & wknd last 150yds* **9/2**[2]
0-46 **8** 3 **Ivory Jazz**[22] 285 5-8-8 **72**.......... LeeNewman 10 62
(Richard Guest) *stdd s: hld up in last trio: pushed along 2f out: no real prog* **12/1**
-012 **9** ½ **The Strig**[25] 251 5-8-8 **72**.......... WilliamCarson 6 61
(Stuart Williams) *racd wd: towards rr: shkn up over 2f out: no prog* **14/1**

35-0 **10** *1 ¾* **Chevise (IRE)**[22] [280] 4-9-0 **78**.. HayleyTurner 9 62
(Steve Woodman) *chsd ldr after 2f to over 2f out: nt qckn wl over 1f out: wknd rapidly fnl f* **7/1**

1m 25.5s (-0.50) **Going Correction** +0.125s/f (Slow) **10** Ran SP% **115.5**
Speed ratings (Par 105): **107,106,105,104,104 103,103,99,99,97**
toteswingers:1&2:£7.30, 1&3:£3.60, 2&3:£17.70 CSF £38.88 CT £306.80 TOTE £4.20: £1.40, £3.90, £4.10; EX 52.30.
Owner Peter M Crane **Bred** P M Crane **Trained** Epsom, Surrey

FOCUS
A fair handicap and sound form for the grade.

564 SKYSPORTS.COM RACING H'CAP 6f (P)
8:10 (8:10) (Class 6) (0-55,55) 3-Y-O **£1,617** (£481; £240; £120) **Stalls** Low

Form RPR

6-14 **1** **Clodhopper (IRE)**[5] [491] 3-9-2 **53**.. FergusSweeney 1 64+
(Jamie Osborne) *trckd ldrs: pushed along and prog on inner to ld over 1f out: shkn up and firmly in command fnl f* **2/1**[1]

0445 **2** *2 ½* **Marie's Fantasy**[12] [394] 3-9-2 **53**.. JamieGoldstein 4 56
(Zoe Davison) *bmpd s: chsd ldrs: rdn 2f out: styd on u.p fnl f: tk 2nd last stride* **14/1**

05-6 **3** *nse* **Littlecote Lady**[43] [25] 3-9-2 **53**..(v) HayleyTurner 2 56
(Mark Usher) *swvd lft s but sn prom: rdn over 2f out: chsd wnr 1f out: no imp: lost 2nd last stride* **8/1**

0-53 **4** *1 ½* **Flying Kitty**[14] [376] 3-8-11 **48**.. KieranO'Neill 8 46
(John Bridger) *led: edgd lft and hdd over 1f out: fdd ins fnl f* **10/1**

0- **5** *½* **George Fenton**[121] [6912] 3-8-11 **48**..(tp) MartinLane 7 44
(Richard Guest) *towards rr: rdn over 2f out: styd on fr over 1f out: nvr gng pce to threaten* **4/1**[2]

0-04 **6** *½* **Very First Blade**[14] [376] 3-9-1 **52**.. ShaneKelly 11 47+
(Mark Brisbourne) *stdd s: hld up in last pair: pushed along 2f out: sme prog fr over 1f out: no ch whn rdn ins fnl f* **8/1**

355- **7** *3 ½* **First Rebellion**[104] [7252] 3-8-11 **48**.. LukeMorris 10 32
(Tony Carroll) *t.k.h: hld up towards rr: shkn up and nt qckn over 2f out: n.d to ldrs over 1f out: fdd* **12/1**

566 **8** *2 ¼* **Sweetest Friend (IRE)**[28] [206] 3-9-4 **55**..(p) LiamKeniry 5 31
(J S Moore) *bmpd s: wl in rr: rdn and effrt on inner over 2f out: sn no prog* **12/1**

540- **9** *¾* **Trending (IRE)**[125] [6817] 3-9-4 **55**.. GeorgeBaker 6 29
(Jeremy Gask) *stdd s: t.k.h: hld up in last pair: nudged along 2f out: nvr nr ldrs* **7/1**[3]

00-5 **10** *1 ¼* **Periwinkle Way**[14] [376] 3-8-11 **48**.. WilliamCarson 3 18
(Tim McCarthy) *bmpd s: chsd ldr to wl over 1f out: wknd rapidly* **16/1**

606 **11** *1 ¾* **Gem Of Wizdom (IRE)**[19] [321] 3-8-6 **46** oh1.. RyanPowell(3) 9
(J S Moore) *chsd ldrs on outer tl over 2f out: sn wknd* **66/1**

1m 14.9s (1.80) **Going Correction** +0.125s/f (Slow) **11** Ran SP% **126.6**
Speed ratings (Par 95): **93,89,89,87,86 86,81,78,77,75 73**
toteswingers:1&2:£9.20, 1&3:£4.70, 2&3:£19.80 CSF £36.89 CT £187.23 TOTE £2.40: £1.30, £5.40, £2.80; EX 33.70.
Owner A Taylor **Bred** Yeomanstown Stud **Trained** Upper Lambourn, Berks

FOCUS
An ordinary handicap, but a comfortable win for the lightly raced winner. The exposed runner-up and third to her Septmeber C&D win help set the standard.
Sweetest Friend(IRE) Official explanation: jockey said filly was hampered leaving stalls
T/Plt: £59.40 to a £1 stake. Pool:£68,702.77 - 844.16 winning tickets T/Qpdt: £17.10 to a £1 stake. Pool:£7,380.62 - 317.85 winning tickets JN

[523]LINGFIELD (L-H)
Wednesday, February 15

OFFICIAL GOING: Standard
Wind: medium, half against Weather: overcast

565 BET AND WATCH AT BLUESQ.COM MAIDEN STKS 7f (P)
2:00 (2:00) (Class 5) 3-Y-O **£2,385** (£704; £352) **Stalls** Low

Form RPR

2-65 **1** **Boots And Spurs**[18] [350] 3-9-3 72..(v[1]) LukeMorris 6 77
(Mrs K Burke) *taken down early: chsd ldr: rdn to ld over 1f out: edgd lft but drew clr jst ins fnl f: styd on wl* **5/2**[2]

04- **2** *3 ½* **Lionrock (FR)**[193] [4798] 3-9-3 0.. JoeFanning 8 68
(Mark Johnston) *chsd ldrs tl led 5f out: rdn and hdd over 1f out: btn whn sltly hmpd jst ins fnl f:* **13/8**[1]

4-43 **3** *1 ¾* **Fugitive Motel (IRE)**[21] [298] 3-8-10 73.. NicoleNordblad(7) 7 63
(Hans Adielsson) *taken down early: t.k.h: hld up in midfield: 3rd and outpcd 2f out: plugged on but wl hld after* **4/1**[3]

0- **4** *2 ¼* **Silky Bleu**[77] [7583] 3-8-5 0.. JenniferFerguson(7) 5 52
(Terry Clement) *t.k.h: hld up in midfield: rdn and outpcd over 2f out: 4th and plugged on same pce fr over 1f out* **25/1**

0- **5** *7* **Diamond Marks (IRE)**[229] [3595] 3-9-3 0.. JohnFahy 3 38
(John Gallagher) *hld up in rr: rdn and struggling over 2f out: wl btn fnl 2f* **33/1**

0- **6** *2 ½* **One Cool Dancer (IRE)**[176] [5337] 3-8-12 0.. MartinLane 2 26
(John Gallagher) *in tch in midfield: rdn and struggling 3f out: bhd fnl 2f* **33/1**

7 *2 ½* **Australia Fair** 3-8-12 0.. MichaelHills 1 19
(Charles Hills) *a in rr: wl bhd fnl 2f* **5/1**

50- **8** *2 ½* **Tumbleowtashoes**[251] [2854] 3-9-3 0.. AdamKirby 4 18
(John Ryan) *led for 2f: 4th and wkng jst over 2f out: wl bhd fnl f* **100/1**

1m 25.23s (0.43) **Going Correction** +0.05s/f (Slow) **8** Ran SP% **114.1**
Speed ratings (Par 97): **99,95,93,90,82 79,76,73**
toteswingers:1&2:£1.80, 1&3:£2.20, 2&3:£1.70 CSF £6.77 TOTE £2.50: £1.10, £1.10, £1.80; EX 7.90 Trifecta £24.00 Pool: £478.23 - 14.71 winning units..
Owner Colin Bryce **Bred** Miss G Abbey **Trained** Middleham Moor, N Yorks

FOCUS
This was probably a weak maiden and few got into it. The winner has been rated to his best previous form, which came in France.

566 CROWHURST H'CAP 2m (P)
2:30 (2:30) (Class 6) (0-60,60) 4-Y-O+ **£1,704** (£503; £251) **Stalls** Low

Form RPR

20-3 **1** **Waldsee (GER)**[12] [395] 7-9-3 **53**.. AdamKirby 6 61
(Paul Rich) *chsd ldrs: rdn to ld wl over 1f out: kpt on wl fnl f* **7/1**[2]

4-30 **2** *1 ¾* **Six Of Clubs**[34] [129] 6-8-11 **54**..(b) JakePayne(7) 12 60
(Bill Turner) *stdd and dropped in bhd after s: hld up in rr: hdwy and travelling wl whn nt clr run 2f out: gd hdwy on inner over 1f out: chsd wnr ins fnl f: no imp fnl 100yds* **25/1**

B-02 **3** *2* **Blue Cossack (IRE)**[13] [392] 4-9-1 **57**.. LiamKeniry 7 61
(Mark Usher) *in tch: effrt u.p 2f out: chsd wnr ent fnl f tl jst ins fnl f: styd on same pce after* **9/1**

-020 **4** *¾* **Valdan (IRE)**[15] [366] 8-9-7 **57**.. LukeMorris 8 60
(David Evans) *in tch in midfield: rdn and effrt jst over 2f out: chsd ldrs and styd on same pce u.p fnl f* **22/1**

0-31 **5** *1 ¼* **Vertueux (FR)**[9] [446] 7-9-0 **57**.. GeorgeDowning(7) 3 58
(Tony Carroll) *restless in stalls: in tch in midfield: pushed along 5f out: hmpd and stmbld over 4f out: kpt on same pce fr over 1f out* **4/1**[1]

600- **6** *nk* **Tecktal (FR)**[51] [3946] 9-8-3 **46** oh1.. JenniferFerguson(7) 5 47
(Pat Phelan) *stdd s: hld up in tch towards rr: hdwy on inner 6f out: chsd ldrs and rdn over 1f out: no prog and outpcd fnl f* **10/1**

31-5 **7** *2* **Galiotto (IRE)**[34] [129] 6-9-10 **60**..(v) GeorgeBaker 4 58
(Gary Moore) *hld up in tch towards rr: rdn and effrt over 1f out: no imp 1f out: plugged on same pce and wl hld after* **4/1**[1]

10/5 **8** *4 ½* **Extremely So**[26] [110] 6-9-7 **57**..(t) MartinLane 10 50
(Philip McBride) *chsd ldrs tl led 10f out: rdn and hdd wl over 1f out: wknd fnl f* **15/2**[3]

/00- **9** *¾* **Miss Tenacious**[27] [1625] 5-8-10 **46** oh1.. JimCrowley 2 38
(Ron Hodges) *led tl 10f out: pressed ldr after tl wknd u.p jst over 1f out* **15/2**[3]

-320 **10** *½* **Delorain (IRE)**[22] [278] 9-8-9 **50**.. LauraPike(5) 1 42
(William Stone) *chsd ldrs: pushed along 7f out: struggling in rr 2f out: plugged on but no threat to ldrs after* **14/1**

52-5 **11** *¾* **Red Current**[26] [221] 8-9-4 **59**.. DavidKenny(5) 11 50
(Michael Scudamore) *stdd s: t.k.h: hld up in tch in rr: hdwy on outer over 3f out: chsd ldrs over 2f out: drvn and fnd little over 1f out: wknd fnl f* **25/1**

00-4 **12** *13* **Keep A Welcome**[28] [207] 9-8-9 **48**.. SimonPearce(3) 13 23
(Gerry Enright) *t.k.h: hld up towards rr: hdwy into midfield on outer after 2f: lost pl and rdn 5f out: wl bhd over 2f out* **66/1**

0-15 **13** *7* **Prince Charlemagne (IRE)**[22] [278] 9-8-12 **53**.(p) MatthewCosham(5) 9 20
(Dr Jeremy Naylor) *t.k.h: hld up in tch towards rr: hdwy 1/2-way: chsd ldrs 6f out: rdn and struggling over 2f out: wl bhd over 1f out* **16/1**

3m 27.39s (1.69) **Going Correction** +0.05s/f (Slow)
WFA 4 from 5yo+ 6lb **13** Ran SP% **121.2**
Speed ratings (Par 101): **97,96,95,94,94 93,92,90,90,90 89,83,79**
toteswingers:1&2:£30.30, 1&3:£7.80, 2&3:£39.80 CSF £178.68 CT £1601.63 TOTE £8.80: £3.40, £10.20, £2.50; EX 194.90 TRIFECTA Not won..
Owner L M Power & Global Self Drive **Bred** Gestut Ravensburg **Trained** Newport, Gwent

FOCUS
A moderate handicap rated around the fourth.
Keep A Welcome Official explanation: jockey said gelding hung left

567 LINGFIELD MARRIOTT HOTEL AND COUNTRY CLUB (S) STKS 1m 2f (P)
3:00 (3:00) (Class 6) 4-6-Y-O **£1,704** (£503; £251) **Stalls** Low

Form RPR

-216 **1** *nse* **Alhaban (IRE)**[12] [403] 6-9-5 65.. LukeMorris 1 69
(Ronald Harris) *chsd ldrs: rdn 2f out: effrt between horses to chal 1f out: drvn to ld 1f out: kpt on wl: bmpd cl home: hdd post: fin 2nd: awrdd the r* **9/4**[1]

-144 **2** **Wisecraic**[25] [248] 5-9-5 64.. LiamKeniry 5 69
(J S Moore) *chsd ldr for 2f: hld up in tch in last after tl hdwy to join ldr 3f out: rdn to ld wl over 1f out: hdd fnl 75yds: edgd lft and bmpd rival cl home but styd on wl to ld on post: disqualified and plcd 2nd* **7/2**[3]

35-5 **3** *1 ¾* **Ostentation**[16] [263] 5-8-10 65.. MichaelO'Connell(3) 2 59
(Roger Teal) *led: rdn 2f out: hdd wl over 1f out: ev ch tl no ex ins fnl f* **5/2**[2]

-336 **4** *2 ¼* **Spin Cast**[19] [330] 4-8-12 66..(v) StevieDonohoe 4 55
(Joseph Tuite) *chsd ldr after 2f tl 3f out: sn rdn: wknd ins fnl f* **5/2**[2]

2m 6.86s (0.26) **Going Correction** +0.05s/f (Slow)
WFA 4 from 5yo+ 1lb **4** Ran SP% **110.1**
Speed ratings: **99,100,98,96**
CSF £10.06 TOTE £2.60; EX 7.30.There was no bid for the winner.
Owner Robert Bailey **Bred** Eimear Mulhern **Trained** Earlswood, Monmouths

FOCUS
A poor seller, but an eventful race. It's been rated around the winner and runner-up.

568 EXCLUSIVE LIVE SHOWS AT BLUESQ.COM H'CAP 1m (P)
3:30 (3:30) (Class 5) (0-70,69) 4-Y-O+ **£2,385** (£704; £352) **Stalls** High

Form RPR

52-0 **1** **Indian Violet (IRE)**[31] [183] 6-8-5 **60**.. LukeRowe(7) 6 68
(Ralph Smith) *broke fast: mde all: styd wd tl 1/2-way: rdn over 1f out: kpt on: a jst gng to hold on* **8/1**

04-2 **2** *nk* **Princess Lexi (IRE)**[26] [224] 5-8-10 **58**.. JimCrowley 3 66
(William Knight) *hld up towards rr: hdwy into midfield 5f out: chsd ldrs and rdn wl over 1f out: chsd wnr ins fnl f: styd on wl towards fin: nvr quite getting to wnr* **11/4**[1]

15-2 **3** *¾* **Hierarch (IRE)**[31] [183] 5-9-1 **63**.. HayleyTurner 9 69
(David Simcock) *chsd ldrs: rdn to chse wnr 2f out: kpt on u.p: lost 2nd ins fnl f: kpt on but nvr quite pce to rch wnr* **3/1**[2]

06-6 **4** *nk* **Getcarter**[21] [302] 6-9-6 **68**.. LukeMorris 8 73
(John Best) *stdd s: t.k.h: hld up towards rr: rdn and effrt whn hung lft over 1f out: n.m.r ins fnl f: kpt on fnl 50yds* **8/1**

-513 **5** *½* **Shared Moment (IRE)**[26] [225] 6-9-4 **66**..(v) JoeFanning 1 70
(John Gallagher) *chsd ldng trio: rdn and unable qck wl over 1f out: kpt on ins fnl f: nvr gng pce to threaten wnr* **15/2**[3]

66-1 **6** *hd* **Rezwaan**[20] [306] 5-9-6 **68**..(be) ShaneKelly 2 72
(Murty McGrath) *restrained in rr: effrt delayed tl pushed along ent fnl f: hdwy whn short of room: kpt on towards fin* **12/1**

3-00 **7** *2 ¾* **Bubbly Braveheart (IRE)**[26] [225] 5-8-11 **59**........... FergusSweeney 10 56
(Pat Phelan) *stdd s: hld up in tch in rr: rdn and effrt over 1f out: no imp* **33/1**

04-5 **8** *½* **Salient**[21] [301] 8-9-2 **69**.. MarkCoumbe(5) 5 65
(Michael Attwater) *chsd wnr tl 2f out: drvn and wknd 1f out* **8/1**

01-0 **P** **Tourist**[34] [128] 7-9-1 **66**.. RyanPowell(3) 4
(Ian Williams) *t.k.h: hld up in midfield: rdn and dropped to rr over 2f out: wl bhd whn p.u and dismntd 1f out* **8/1**

1m 37.83s (-0.37) **Going Correction** +0.05s/f (Slow) **9** Ran SP% **118.5**
Speed ratings (Par 103): **103,102,101,101,101 100,98,97,**
toteswingers:1&2:£5.00, 1&3:£6.30, 2&3:£3.10 CSF £31.15 CT £83.72 TOTE £9.30: £2.60, £1.50, £1.60; EX 32.20 Trifecta £296.30 Pool: £708.82 - 1.77 winning units..
Owner H Bulteel **Bred** James F Hanly **Trained** Epsom, Surrey

FOCUS
A fair handicap run at a reasonable pace and the market got it right. The winner has been rated to last year's best, with the third and fourth to their latest form.

Rezwaan ◆ Official explanation: jockey said, regarding running and riding, that his orders were to hold the gelding up and make smooth headway as this is how it has been ridden, it travelled well into the straight but it was not good enough and would be better suited by Kempton which has a longer straight; trainer confirmed and said that it would be suited by Kempton.

569 BREATHE SPA AT MARRIOTT LINGFIELD MAIDEN STKS — 1m 5f (P)
4:00 (4:00) (Class 5) 4-Y-0+ — **£2,385** (£704; £352) **Stalls** Low

Form — RPR

1 — **Kayalar (IRE)**[123] 6885 4-9-3 70 ... ShaneKelly 7 — 76+
(Evan Williams) *stdd s: t.k.h: hld up in last pair: hdwy and gng wl over 2f out: swtchd rt and effrt over 1f out: edging lft after: chsd ldr 1f out: r.o under hands and heels riding to ld fnl 50yds: comf* **13/2**

2 ¾ **Zarzal (IRE)**[117] 7014 4-9-3 66 ... LukeMorris 4 — 73
(Evan Williams) *racd in midfield: clsd on ldrs over 3f out: rdn to ld over 2f out: drvn and clr over 1f out: hdd and nt pce of wnr fnl 50yds* **9/2**[2]

23 3 2 ¼ **Southern State (USA)**[18] 355 4-9-3 0 ... JoeFanning 2 — 70
(Mark Johnston) *t.k.h: led for 1f: chsd ldng pair after: rdn and nt qckn 2f out: 3rd and styd on one pce fnl f* **4/5**[1]

030- 4 2 ¾ **Dynamic Idol (USA)**[15] 6121 5-9-7 67 ... GeorgeBaker 8 — 66
(Gary Moore) *hld up towards rr: hdwy on outer over 4f out: rdn to chse ldr 2f out tl 1f out: wknd ins fnl f* **5/1**[3]

5 ½ **Synthe Davis (FR)**[5] 7-9-2 0 ... IanMongan 5 — 60
(Laura Mongan) *chsd ldr after 1f tl 2f out: unable qck u.p: wknd 1f out* **14/1**

35-4 6 1 ¼ **Frederick William**[26] 221 4-9-3 65 ...(p) HayleyTurner 3 — 63
(Chris Gordon) *racd in midfield: rdn over 5f out: swtchd rt and struggling over 2f out: no prog and no threat to ldrs after* **14/1**

44-0 7 16 **Sing Alana Sing**[8] 453 4-8-7 48 ow2 ...(t) RyanWhile(7) 1 — 36
(Bill Turner) *dwlt: hdwy on inner to ld after 1f: clr 10f out tl rdn and hdd wl over 2f out: sn dropped out and bhd* **50/1**

8 22 **Delightful Sleep** 4-9-3 0 ... RichardThomas 6
(David Evans) *dwlt: hld up in last pair: lost tch wl over 3f out: t.o fnl 2f* **50/1**

2m 46.0s **Going Correction** +0.05s/f (Slow)
WFA 4 from 5yo+ 4lb — **8** Ran SP% **121.0**
Speed ratings (Par 103): **102,101,100,98,98 97,87,74**
toteswingers:1&2:£5.30, 1&3:£2.80, 2&3:£1.60 CSF £37.97 TOTE £7.50: £3.10, £1.40, £1.02; EX 39.40 Trifecta £67.30 Pool: £1,171.40 - 12.88 winning units..
Owner R E R Williams **Bred** His Highness The Aga Khan's Studs S C **Trained** Llancarfan, Vale Of Glamorgan

FOCUS
Not a strong staying maiden, but a triumph for trainer Evan Williams who managed a 1-2 with a couple of ex-John Oxx horses. It's been rated through the second to his Dundalk latest.

570 PLAY GOLF AT LINGFIELD MARRIOTT H'CAP — 1m 2f (P)
4:30 (4:32) (Class 5) (0-70,74) 4-Y-0+ — **£2,385** (£704; £352) **Stalls** Low

Form — RPR

06-6 1 **Casual Mover (IRE)**[21] 301 4-9-6 70 ... SteveDrowne 2 — 81
(John Best) *t.k.h: hld up in tch: rdn to chse ldr 2f out: led over 1f out: on wl fnl f* **7/1**[3]

00-5 2 1 ½ **Edgeworth (IRE)**[14] 374 6-8-9 65 ... JoshBaudains(7) 12 — 73
(David Bridgwater) *hld up towards rr: hdwy 4f out: rdn to chse ldrs over 1f out: pressed ldrs 1f out: chsd wnr and styd on same pce ins fnl f* **6/1**[2]

5116 3 1 **Aviso (GER)**[18] 349 8-8-9 63 ... MatthewCosham(5) 10 — 69
(David Evans) *hld up in midfield: n.m.r 2f out: swtchd rt and effrt wl over 1f out: styd on wl ins fnl f* **11/1**

4/-1 4 1 ¼ **Copper Canyon**[6] 480 4-9-7 74 6ex ... RyanPowell(3) 6 — 78
(J S Moore) *stmbld sn after s: sn detached in last and pushed along early: in rr: clsd on ldrs and n.m.r 2f out: hdwy over 1f out: styd on wl ins fnl f: nvr trbld ldrs* **3/1**[1]

03- 5 1 ½ **Mister Green (FR)**[46] 7943 6-9-0 63 ...(bt) StephenCraine 8 — 64
(David Flood) *stdd and hmpd s: hld up in rr: hdwy over 2f out: sltly hmpd and hung lft over 1f out: kpt on ins fnl f: nvr trbld ldrs* **9/1**

-210 6 nk **Kai Mook**[22] 281 5-9-1 64 ... JoeFanning 14 — 64
(Roger Ingram) *chsd ldrs: wnt 2nd 5f out: rdn to ld over 2f out: drvn and hdd over 1f out: fdd ins fnl f* **14/1**

-100 7 2 ¼ **Buxfizz (USA)**[14] 374 4-9-6 70 ...(p) MartinLane 11 — 65
(George Prodromou) *racd in last pair: rdn along 8f out: rdn and effrt whn wd bnd 2f out: kpt on fnl f: nvr gng pce to threaten ldrs* **16/1**

42-5 8 nse **Archelao (IRE)**[25] 248 4-9-6 70 ... AmirQuinn 4 — 65
(Richard Rowe) *in tch in midfield: shkn up and brief effrt on inner over 1f out: sn outpcd and btn 1f out* **16/1**

330- 9 2 **Timocracy**[97] 5135 7-9-5 68 ... RobertHavlin 13 — 59
(Alastair Lidderdale) *led tl over 7f out: chsd ldrs after tl wknd u.p over 1f out* **16/1**

540- 10 2 **Spiritual Art**[77] 7057 6-9-7 70 ...(b[1]) JimCrowley 1 — 57
(Luke Dace) *chsd ldrs: rdn and unable qck ent fnl 2f: wknd over 1f out* **33/1**

1-00 11 9 **Green Earth (IRE)**[26] 224 5-9-1 64 ...(p) IanMongan 9 — 33
(Pat Phelan) *midfield early: hdwy on outer 9f out: led over 7f out tl over 2f out: wknd wl over 1f out* **15/2**

-100 12 7 **Whodunit (UAE)**[18] 349 8-9-5 68 ...(b) ChrisCatlin 3 — 23
(Peter Hiatt) *midfield tl rdn and lost pl over 4f out: bhd fr over 2f out* **9/1**

2m 3.58s (-3.02) **Going Correction** +0.05s/f (Slow)
WFA 4 from 5yo+ 1lb — **12** Ran SP% **119.1**
Speed ratings (Par 103): **114,112,112,111,109 109,107,107,106,104 97,91**
toteswingers:1&2:£8.70, 1&3:£17.20, 2&3:£11.90 CSF £48.94 CT £465.35 TOTE £7.30: £2.50, £2.00, £4.30; EX 58.00 Trifecta £465.30 Pool: £654.03 - 1.04 winning units..
Owner Brian Goodyear & Rhonda Wilson **Bred** M S And C S Griffiths **Trained** Hucking, Kent

FOCUS
A modest if competitive handicap, run at a fair pace, and it's been rated through the third to his recent claiming form.

Copper Canyon ◆ Official explanation: jockey said gelding stumbled out of stalls
Archelao(IRE) Official explanation: jockey said gelding had a breathing problem

571 PLAY RAINBOW RICHES AT BLUESQ.COM H'CAP — 1m 2f (P)
5:00 (5:00) (Class 6) (0-60,60) 3-Y-0 — **£1,704** (£503; £251) **Stalls** Low

Form — RPR

00-3 1 **News Desk**[28] 206 3-9-7 60 ... RobertHavlin 7 — 68
(John Gosden) *chsd ldrs: rdn and qcknd to ld 2f out: clr over 1f out: r.o wl* **9/2**[3]

4-56 2 2 ¾ **Moment In The Sun**[25] 255 3-9-0 53 ... JimCrowley 4 — 55
(William Muir) *wl in tch: rdn 2f out: drvn to chse clr wnr jst ins fnl f: r.o but no imp* **13/2**

60-5 3 ½ **Saucy Cat (IRE)**[42] 32 3-9-3 56 ... SteveDrowne 9 — 57
(John Best) *t.k.h: in tch in last trio: rdn and hdwy on outer over 1f out: kpt on fnl f: no threat to wnr* **14/1**

333- 4 1 **Stag Hill (IRE)**[51] 7875 3-9-5 58 ... LiamKeniry 5 — 57
(Sylvester Kirk) *t.k.h: hld up wl in tch in midfield: nt clr run and shuffled bk to rr jst over 2f out: rdn and rallied ent fnl f: r.o but no threat to wnr* **11/4**[1]

00-5 5 ½ **Waspy**[30] 196 3-8-9 48 ... ChrisCatlin 8 — 46
(Ed Dunlop) *t.k.h: hld up in tch in rr: rdn and hdwy on outer over 2f out: chsd wnr wl over 1f out: kpt on but no imp: lost 3 pls ins fnl f* **20/1**

02-0 6 2 ¾ **Chankillo**[32] 182 3-9-7 60 ... GeorgeBaker 2 — 53
(Mark H Tompkins) *chsd ldrs: nt clr run and shuffled bk jst over 2f out: rdn and tried to rally over 1f out: no prog fnl f* **7/2**[2]

60-4 7 2 ½ **Lady Author**[27] 217 3-8-7 46 oh1 ... MartinLane 10 — 34
(Richard Fahey) *in tch: hdwy to chse ldr 8f out: rdn and chsd wnr briefly ent fnl 2f: sn outpcd and wknd over 1f out* **25/1**

00-5 8 hd **Search And Rescue (USA)**[11] 428 3-9-3 56 ... HayleyTurner 3 — 43
(J W Hills) *dwlt: hld up in tch in rr: rdn and effrt over 1f out: no prog and n.d* **25/1**

6-55 9 hd **Showsinger**[16] 358 3-9-0 53 ... JoeFanning 11 — 40
(Richard Fahey) *chsd ldrs: hdwy to ld and set stdy gallop after 1f: rdn and hdd jst over 2f out: sn wknd* **20/1**

00-4 10 1 **Foster's Road**[25] 255 3-9-2 60 ...(v) CharlesBishop(5) 1 — 45
(Mick Channon) *t.k.h: chsd ldrs: lost pl but stl wl in tch towards rr 5f out: rdn and effrt on inner jst over 2f out: wknd over 1f out* **9/1**

2m 10.66s (4.06) **Going Correction** +0.05s/f (Slow) — **10** Ran SP% **114.3**
Speed ratings (Par 95): **85,82,82,81,81 79,77,76,76,75**
toteswingers:1&2:£5.90, 1&3:£6.60, 2&3:£15.10 CSF £30.85 CT £371.95 TOTE £5.10: £2.40, £2.30, £5.60; EX 31.50 Trifecta £567.90 Part won. Pool: £767.47 - 0.50 winning units..
Owner H R H Princess Haya Of Jordan **Bred** Darley **Trained** Newmarket, Suffolk

FOCUS
An ordinary handicap, run at a steady pace. The winner has been rated as improving 9lb on her handicap debut, and the runner-up helps set the level.
T/Plt: £71.50 to a £1 stake. Pool:£63,714.05 - 650.01 winning tickets T/Qpdt: £16.10 to a £1 stake. Pool:£5,253.69 - 241.40 winning tickets SP

558 KEMPTON (A.W) (R-H)
Thursday, February 16

OFFICIAL GOING: Standard
Wind: Light, across (away from stands) Weather: Fair

572 32REDBINGO.COM H'CAP — 6f (P)
5:15 (5:15) (Class 7) (0-50,56) 4-Y-0+ — **£1,455** (£433; £216; £108) **Stalls** Low

Form — RPR

00/5 1 **All About You (IRE)**[22] 297 6-9-3 50 ... AdamKirby 1 — 59
(John Butler) *chsd ldng pair: hrd rdn to cl fr over 2f out: led over 1f out: hld on* **4/7**[1]

-343 2 ¾ **Bobbyow**[8] 467 4-8-11 49 ... MarkCoumbe(5) 6 — 56
(Terry Clement) *hld up in rr: prog on inner jst over 2f out: styd on to take 2nd ins fnl f: nt rch wnr* **20/1**

4-56 3 nk **Metropolitan Chief**[13] 396 8-8-10 48 ... CharlesBishop(5) 5 — 54
(Paul Burgoyne) *t.k.h: hld up in last pair: looking for room over 2f out: prog wl over 1f out: styd on wl after: tk 3rd and clsd on ldng pair nr fin: too much to do* **25/1**

-342 4 1 ½ **Gorgeous Goblin (IRE)**[13] 396 5-9-2 49 ...(t) JimmyFortune 11 — 50
(David C Griffiths) *stdd s: hld up in last pair: brought wd and shkn up over 2f out: styd on after: nrst fin* **9/1**[3]

-000 5 nse **Rise To Glory (IRE)**[12] 430 4-8-12 45 ... NeilChalmers 3 — 46
(Shaun Harris) *chsd clr ldr: clsd w wnr fr 2f out: upsides over 1f out: nt qckn after: lost pl ins fnl f* **100/1**

2-42 6 1 ¼ **Royal Acclamation (IRE)**[21] 307 7-8-10 48 ...(p) DavidKenny(5) 4 — 45
(Michael Scudamore) *chsd ldng trio: rdn over 2f out: one pce and no real imp over 1f out* **8/1**[2]

0423 7 1 ¼ **Flow Chart (IRE)**[7] 483 5-9-1 48 ... JoeFanning 8 — 41
(Peter Grayson) *hld up in last trio: pushed along and no prog over 2f out: nvr on terms after* **12/1**

0-00 8 ½ **Whats Your Story**[21] 307 4-8-12 45 ...(b) ShaneKelly 2 — 36
(Murty McGrath) *t.k.h: hld up in midfield: shkn up over 2f out: no real imp over 1f out: fdd* **40/1**

-501 9 nk **Silly Billy (IRE)**[2] 551 4-9-4 56 6ex ... JemmaMarshall(5) 7 — 47
(Sylvester Kirk) *nvr bttr than midfield: u.p over 2f out: no prog over 1f out* **10/1**

0-01 10 10 **Royal Envoy (IRE)**[22] 297 9-9-1 48 ...(b) MichaelStainton 10
(Paul Howling) *pushed up to ld fr wd draw and sn at least 8 l clr: wknd rapidly and hdd over 1f out: t.o* **20/1**

1m 13.13s (0.03) **Going Correction** +0.025s/f (Slow) — **10** Ran SP% **118.3**
Speed ratings (Par 97): **100,99,98,96,96 94,93,92,92,78**
toteswingers:1&2:£8.80, 1&3:£4.90, 2&3:£29.50 CSF £20.40 CT £170.87 TOTE £1.60: £1.10, £2.40, £5.10; EX 17.80.
Owner Mrs H F Prendergast **Bred** Ballylinch Stud **Trained** Newmarket, Suffolk

FOCUS
A bottom-drawer handicap and straightforward enough form. The winner will be well treated after this on his old form.

573 32RED CASINO MEDIAN AUCTION MAIDEN FILLIES' STKS — 1m (P)
5:45 (5:48) (Class 5) 3-5-Y-0 — **£2,264** (£673; £336; £168) **Stalls** Low

Form — RPR

2 1 **Laugh Out Loud**[27] 231 3-8-9 0 ... ChrisCatlin 5 — 83+
(Mick Channon) *trckd ldng pair: quick move to ld over 2f out: pushed along firmly and drew rt away: fin w plenty lft* **1/2**[1]

0-4 2 10 **Play Street**[32] 185 3-8-9 0 ... LukeMorris 2 — 60
(Jonathan Portman) *led 150yds: trckd ldr: clsd to chal over 2f out: chsd wnr after but sn lft bhd* **14/1**

2-2 3 ¾ **Macy Anne (IRE)**[9] 464 3-8-10 0 ow1 ... JimCrowley 4 — 59
(Robert Mills) *hld up in 5th: prog 3f out to go 3rd 2f out: no ch w wnr sn after: plugged on* **4/1**[2]

6- 4 hd **Geanie Mac (IRE)**[175] 5418 3-8-9 0 ... ShaneKelly 3 — 58
(Tim Pitt) *chsd ldrs: rdn and struggling over 2f out: kpt on fnl f to press for 3rd fin* **66/1**

5 5 **How Fortunate** 4-10-0 0 ... NickyMackay 7 — 52
(David Elsworth) *s.i.s: mostly in 6th and nvr on terms w ldrs: bhd fnl 2f* **40/1**

4-23 **6** 5 **Darsan (IRE)**[2] 552 4-10-0 64 ....(p) TomMcLaughlin 1 41
(Phil McEntee) *dwlt but drvn to ld after 150yds: hdd & wknd qckly over 2f out* **8/1**[3]

7 3 ½ **Littlemissperfect** 4-9-7 0 .... LukeRowe(7) 8 33
(Richard Rowe) *v.s.i.s and virtually t.o after 1f: tried briefly to cl 3f out: sn wknd* **66/1**

1m 39.41s (-0.39) **Going Correction** +0.025s/f (Slow)
WFA 3 from 4yo 19lb 7 Ran SP% **109.9**
Speed ratings (Par 100): **102,92,91,91,86 81,77**
toteswingers:1&2:£2.30, 1&3:£1.10, 2&3:£1.40 CSF £8.30 TOTE £1.40: £1.20, £3.10; EX 9.40.
Owner Ann Black,M Al Qatami & K M Al Mudhaf **Bred** Norman Court Stud **Trained** West Ilsley, Berks

FOCUS
A weak maiden and a progressive winner.

574 32REDPOKER.COM H'CAP 1m (P)
6:15 (6:16) (Class 6) (0-65,64) 4-Y-0+ **£1,617** (£481; £240; £120) **Stalls** Low

Form RPR

-132 **1** **Qeethaara (USA)**[5] 537 8-9-2 62 ....(p) LukeMorris 13 71
(Mark Brisbourne) *hld up wl in rr early: worked way into midfield by 1/2-way: wnt 3rd 2f out: clsd over 1f out: drvn ahd last 100yds: hld on* **11/1**

34-3 **2** nk **Beetuna (IRE)**[41] 67 7-8-9 60 ....(p) MarkCoumbe(5) 14 68
(Oliver Sherwood) *hld up and sn detached in 13th: prog fr 3f out: swtchd to inner over 1f out: r.o wl to take 2nd nr fin and cl on wnr* **14/1**

50-0 **3** 1 **Prince Of Sorrento**[13] 403 5-9-0 60 .... JamieMackay 1 66
(John Akehurst) *racd freely: led: jnd 2f out: fought off chalr jst over 1f out: hdd and no ex last 100yds* **14/1**

01-1 **4** hd **Cheers**[34] 154 4-9-3 63 .... FrankieMcDonald 6 68+
(Oliver Sherwood) *hld up in midfield: racd wd after 3f: drvn over 2f out: styd on fr over 1f out: nvr quite able to chal* **9/2**[2]

44-4 **5** nk **Comadoir (IRE)**[25] 262 6-9-1 61 .... IanMongan 12 66
(Jo Crowley) *wl in rr: hanging and looking reluctant in last trio over 2f out: picked up on outer over 1f out: fin wl* **9/1**

0-13 **6** ½ **Fibs And Flannel**[14] 386 5-9-4 64 .... TomMcLaughlin 10 67
(Willie Musson) *dwlt: hld up wl in rr: stdy prog fr 3f out: rdn to cl on ldrs over 1f out: kpt on same pce fnl f* **33/1**

54-0 **7** 1 ¼ **Barista (IRE)**[17] 359 4-8-12 63 .... CharlesBishop(5) 2 64
(Brian Forsey) *fast away but heavily restrained into midfield: rdn and effrt over 2f out: kpt on but nvr able to threaten* **50/1**

10-0 **8** ½ **Mad Ginger Alice**[32] 183 4-8-9 62 .... JenniferFerguson(7) 8 61
(Olivia Maylam) *nvr beyond midfield: pushed along and no hdwy over 2f out: kpt on steadily fr over 1f out* **66/1**

62- **9** ½ **Automotive**[64] 7754 4-9-0 60 .... ShaneKelly 4 58
(Julia Feilden) *prom: rdn over 2f out: nt qckn over 1f out: steadily fdd* **11/2**[3]

10-0 **10** nk **Ensnare**[20] 328 7-9-2 62 .... StevieDonohoe 7 60
(John Butler) *sn trckd ldr: rdn to chal and upsides 2f out: nt qckn over 1f out: wknd fnl f* **11/4**[1]

3-43 **11** 1 **Jo Boy**[23] 287 5-9-2 62 ....(b[1]) HayleyTurner 5 57
(Michael Bell) *trckd ldrs: lost pl and pushed along 2f out: no imp after: wknd fnl f* **6/1**

0-02 **12** 5 **Scary Movie (IRE)**[13] 401 7-8-11 64 .... DarrenEgan(7) 3 48
(Ronald Harris) *slowest away: virtually t.o in last after 2f: nvr a factor: keeping on at fin* **16/1**

42P- **13** 16 **Irie Ute**[262] 2550 4-9-0 63 .... SophieDoyle(3) 9
(Sylvester Kirk) *t.k.h: prom on outer: wknd rapidly wl over 2f out: t.o* **50/1**

45-6 **14** 4 ½ **Red Yarn**[41] 60 5-9-2 62 ....(b) GeorgeBaker 11
(Joseph Tuite) *racd v wd in midfield: wknd rapidly 3f out: eased over 1f out: t.o* **28/1**

1m 39.4s (-0.40) **Going Correction** +0.025s/f (Slow) 14 Ran SP% **123.9**
Speed ratings (Par 101): **103,102,101,101,101 100,99,98,98,98 97,92,76,71**
toteswingers:1&2:£19.70, 1&3:£16.30, 2&3:£36.40 CSF £155.05 CT £2249.30 TOTE £11.80: £2.90, £5.10, £3.80; EX 210.80.
Owner Mark Brisbourne **Bred** Shadwell Farm LLC **Trained** Great Ness, Shropshire

FOCUS
A competitive-looking handicap for the grade. There was a sound pace on which suited the closers and the two outside stalls filled the first two places. The winner built on her recent form.
Automotive Official explanation: jockey said gelding had a breathing problem
Scary Movie(IRE) Official explanation: jockey said gelding never travelled

575 32REDBET.COM H'CAP 1m 4f (P)
6:45 (6:47) (Class 6) (0-60,59) 4-Y-0+ **£1,617** (£481; £240; £120) **Stalls** Centre

Form RPR

4/02 **1** **Asterales**[13] 395 5-8-8 46 .... JamieMackay 7 55
(Willie Musson) *hld up in last pair: long way off the pce: clsd fr 4f out: stdy prog gng easily over 2f out: swtchd to inner and led over 1f out: rdn and styd on wl* **8/1**

006- **2** 1 ¾ **Musashi (IRE)**[107] 7206 7-9-0 52 ....(b) JoeFanning 1 58
(Laura Mongan) *t.k.h: hld up in last pair: long way off the pce: clsd over 3f out: stdy prog to chal over 1f out: chsd wnr after: styd on but nt qckn* **11/1**

00-5 **3** 3 ½ **Time Square (FR)**[22] 296 5-9-7 59 ....(t) LukeMorris 4 59
(Tony Carroll) *trckd clr ldr and sn clr of rest: clsd 3f out: led 2f out but immediately drvn: hdd and one pce over 1f out* **7/4**[1]

-005 **4** 3 ¼ **Bilidn**[12] 433 4-8-13 54 .... MartinLane 3 49
(Noel Quinlan) *led and sn spreadeagled the field: c bk 3f out: hdd 2f out: steadily fdd* **20/1**

-211 **5** 3 **Black Iceman**[14] 389 4-9-1 59 .... SimonPearce(3) 2 49
(Lydia Pearce) *hld up in 4th and wl off the pce: wnt 3rd 1/2-way: clsd 3f out: drvn and nt qckn 2f out: fdd* **5/1**[3]

06-3 **6** ½ **Four Steps Back**[35] 130 5-8-12 50 .... HayleyTurner 5 40
(Mark Usher) *chsd clr ldng pair to 1/2-way: pushed along over 3f out: dropped to last pair and drvn over 2f out: no ch after* **6/1**

00-1 **7** 9 **Sylas Ings**[8] 468 4-9-1 56 6ex ....(v) IanMongan 6 31
(Pat Phelan) *hld up in last trio: long way off the pce: rdn and no prog over 3f out: wl bhd fnl 2f* **3/1**[2]

2m 35.39s (0.89) **Going Correction** +0.025s/f (Slow)
WFA 4 from 5yo+ 3lb 7 Ran SP% **116.5**
Speed ratings (Par 101): **98,96,94,92,90 90,84**
toteswingers:1&2:£9.40, 1&3:£4.30, 2&3:£7.00 CSF £89.91 TOTE £8.60: £3.00, £4.40; EX 63.40.
Owner W J Musson **Bred** Miss Nicola Gilbert **Trained** Newmarket, Suffolk

FOCUS
A moderate handicap and a tight-looking affair. The fourth set a decent pace and they were fairly strung out early, although the time was slow. The first two came from the back and the form is rated around the runner-up.
Sylas Ings Official explanation: jockey said gelding never travelled

576 32RED.COM FILLIES' H'CAP 6f (P)
7:15 (7:16) (Class 5) (0-70,70) 4-Y-0+ **£2,264** (£673; £336; £168) **Stalls** Low

Form RPR

-044 **1** **Absa Lutte (IRE)**[9] 461 9-9-6 69 .... GeorgeBaker 5 76+
(Michael Mullineaux) *t.k.h: hld up in last pair in slowly run event: pushed along and gd prog over 1f out to ld last 100yds: readily* **15/2**

2-42 **2** ½ **Liberal Lady**[23] 277 4-8-6 60 ....(e) RaulDaSilva(5) 2 65
(Ralph Smith) *racd freely but restrained in front and set modest pce: kicked on jst over 2f out: hdd and hld last 100yds* **7/2**[3]

-646 **3** nk **Mack's Sister**[8] 474 5-8-13 62 ....(p) ShaneKelly 3 66
(Dean Ivory) *hld up bhd ldrs: effrt whn pce lifted 2f out: wnt 2nd over 1f out to jst ins fnl f: nt qckn* **5/2**[1]

00-0 **4** 1 ¼ **Athwaab**[8] 473 5-8-8 62 .... CharlesBishop(5) 6 62
(Noel Chance) *t.k.h: hld up in last pair in slowly run event: swtchd ins and effrt over 1f out: nt qckn fnl f* **20/1**

-421 **5** nk **Sannibel**[6] 499 4-9-5 68 6ex .... LukeMorris 4 67
(Tony Carroll) *t.k.h: pressed ldr: nt qckn wl pce lifted 2f out: lost 2nd over 1f out: fdd* **3/1**[2]

0130 **6** 1 ¾ **Avonvalley**[13] 396 5-8-7 56 oh2 .... JoeFanning 7 49+
(Peter Grayson) *t.k.h: forced to r wd bhd ldrs: nt qckn 2f out: wl hld fnl f* **9/1**

0-46 **7** 1 ¾ **Black Baccara**[1] 560 5-9-4 70 ....(be) RyanClark(3) 1 58
(Phil McEntee) *t.k.h: hld up bhd ldng pair: nt qckn whn pce lifted 2f out: wl btn fnl f* **10/1**

1m 15.54s (2.44) **Going Correction** +0.025s/f (Slow) 7 Ran SP% **111.4**
Speed ratings (Par 100): **84,83,82,81,80 78,76**
toteswingers:1&2:£7.00, 1&3:£1.30, 2&3:£2.70 CSF £32.02 TOTE £9.20: £4.40, £2.30; EX 41.00.
Owner D & D Coatings Ltd **Bred** Ian Amond **Trained** Alpraham, Cheshire

FOCUS
A slowly run sprint handicap for fillies. Modest form and not a race to be positive about.

577 32RED H'CAP 2m (P)
7:45 (7:47) (Class 4) (0-85,86) 4-Y-0+ **£4,075** (£1,212; £606; £303) **Stalls** Low

Form RPR

-213 **1** **Exemplary**[12] 427 5-9-13 86 .... AdamKirby 5 96
(Mark Johnston) *trckd ldng pair: wnt 2nd 6f out: led 3f out and kicked clr: 5 l up over 1f out: in command after: eased nr fin* **4/1**[2]

32-2 **2** 1 **Dark Ranger**[29] 202 6-9-3 76 .... ShaneKelly 9 85+
(Tim Pitt) *hld up in last trio: stdy prog fr 3f out gng easily: wnt 2nd wl over 1f out but 5 l bhd wnr: clsd grad but nvr gng to get there* **11/8**[1]

4/5- **3** 4 ½ **Gilded Age**[20] 6023 6-8-10 69 ....(tp) HayleyTurner 3 72
(Chris Gordon) *racd in 6th: rdn 6f out: dropped to 8th and struggling bdly over 4f out: rallied over 2f out: wnt 3rd over 1f out: no ch but kpt gng* **25/1**

-441 **4** 7 **Nezhenka**[20] 332 5-9-12 85 .... JoeFanning 1 79
(Mark Johnston) *trckd ldrs: rdn to chse wnr over 2f out to wl over 1f out: wknd fnl f* **6/1**[3]

5-12 **5** 3 ¼ **Rosewood Lad**[20] 332 5-9-1 74 .... LukeMorris 7 64
(J S Moore) *trckd ldrs: rdn fr 5f out: easily lft bhd fr over 2f out* **10/1**

4/0- **6** 3 ½ **Tasheba**[26] 6690 7-9-7 80 ....(p) FergusSweeney 2 66
(Caroline Keevil) *led 4f: chsd ldr to 6f out: rdn and wknd over 2f out* **20/1**

4-46 **7** 6 **Bennelong**[21] 310 6-8-1 67 .... LukeRowe(7) 8 46
(Richard Rowe) *heavily restrained s and hld up in detached last: latched on to gp 5f out: wknd over 2f out* **12/1**

000- **8** 5 **Battleoftrafalgar**[31] 7803 5-9-4 77 ....(b) GeorgeBaker 4 50
(Michael Attwater) *pressed ldr: led after 4f: hdd 3f out: wknd qckly 2f out* **14/1**

00-0 **9** 99 **Magicalmysterytour (IRE)**[21] 310 9-8-13 72 .... JamieMackay 6
(Willie Musson) *a in last pair: wknd over 5f out: sn wl t.o* **16/1**

3m 28.12s (-1.98) **Going Correction** +0.025s/f (Slow) 9 Ran SP% **114.3**
Speed ratings (Par 105): **105,104,102,98,97 95,92,89,40**
toteswingers:1&2:£1.60, 1&3:£33.60, 2&3:£5.80 CSF £9.73 CT £116.33 TOTE £4.20: £1.70, £1.10, £4.20; EX 11.60.
Owner Dr Marwan Koukash **Bred** Darley **Trained** Middleham Moor, N Yorks

FOCUS
Not a bad staying handicap, but it was a tactical affair. The winner is rated back to his best but the form isn't entirely convincing.
Bennelong Official explanation: jockey said gelding hung right in straight
Magicalmysterytour(IRE) Official explanation: vet said gelding returned distressed

578 £32 FREE AT 32RED.COM H'CAP 7f (P)
8:15 (8:17) (Class 6) (0-55,55) 4-Y-0+ **£1,617** (£481; £240; £120) **Stalls** Low

Form RPR

00-1 **1** **Diplomatic (IRE)**[25] 264 7-9-4 55 .... LukeMorris 4 67
(Michael Squance) *hld up in midfield on inner: prog over 2f out: chsd ldr over 1f out: drvn to ld whn veered lft and bmpd runer-up 75yds out: styd on* **3/1**[1]

-226 **2** ¾ **Blueberry Fizz (IRE)**[15] 379 4-9-0 51 ow1 ....(v) AdamKirby 6 61
(John Ryan) *led 2f: pressed ldr: led 3f out: drvn 2 l clr over 1f out: hdd and bmpd last 75yds* **10/1**

50-0 **3** 1 ½ **Olynard (IRE)**[32] 183 6-9-4 55 .... GeorgeBaker 3 61
(Michael Mullineaux) *prom: chsd ldr over 2f out to over 1f out: styd on: nvr able to chal* **20/1**

0222 **4** 3 **Cairanne**[6] 503 4-8-7 47 .... RyanClark(3) 2 45
(Tom Keddy) *wl plcd bhd ldrs on inner: effrt over 2f out: one pce and no imp in 4th fnl f* **9/1**

04-3 **5** nse **Pastoral Jet**[15] 379 4-8-5 49 .... LukeRowe(7) 14 47+
(Richard Rowe) *hld up wl in rr and racd wd: pushed along on outer over 2f out: styd on fr over 1f out: nrst fin* **7/1**[3]

0620 **6** 1 ½ **Dingaan (IRE)**[8] 473 9-9-3 54 .... JoeFanning 11 48
(Peter Grayson) *stdd s: hld up wl in rr: sme prog and pushed along 2f out: no imp on ldrs over 1f out: kpt on* **12/1**

06- **7** hd **Lady Mango (IRE)**[190] 4911 4-8-10 54 .... DarrenEgan(7) 9 50+
(Ronald Harris) *hld up in midfield: shkn up and no prog at rr of main gp 2f out: kpt on but nvr on terms* **40/1**

0-23 **8** hd **Nacho Libre**[21] 313 7-9-4 55 ....(b) PaddyAspell 8 48
(Michael Easterby) *trckd ldrs on outer: lost pl 3f out: no imp 2f out: one pce after* **4/1**[2]

000- **9** 1 **Akarana (IRE)**[170] 5607 5-9-0 51 .... StevieDonohoe 1 41
(Willie Musson) *outpcd in last: detached and struggling tl styd on fr over 1f out: gng on at fin* **7/1**[3]

3-03 **10** ½ **Harvest Mist (IRE)**[15] 375 4-8-11 48 ....(p) HayleyTurner 5 37
(Michael Blanshard) *restless stalls: wl in tch bhd ldrs: effrt over 2f out: sn no prog: wknd fnl f* **16/1**

60-0 **11** ¾ **Dells Breezer**[20] 320 4-9-1 **52** ..... IanMongan 13 39
(Pat Phelan) *hld up in rr: effrt into midfield jst over 2f out: no hdwy after: wknd fnl f* **16/1**

6120 **12** 6 **My Best Man**[25] 264 6-9-3 **54** ..... (t) JimCrowley 10 24
(Tony Carroll) *a in rr: rdn and no prog over 2f out: wl btn after* **16/1**

0-06 **13** 4½ **Toms River Tess (IRE)**[21] 313 4-8-12 **49** ..... (p) JamieGoldstein 7
(Zoe Davison) *pressed ldrs tl wknd qckly over 2f out* **100/1**

00-6 **14** 1 **Tenancy (IRE)**[9] 456 8-8-10 **47** ..... NeilChalmers 12
(Shaun Harris) *pressed ldr: led after 2f to 3f out: wknd qckly* **66/1**

1m 25.87s (-0.13) **Going Correction** +0.025s/f (Slow) **14 Ran SP% 124.1**
Speed ratings (Par 101): **101,100,98,95,94 93,93,92,91,91 90,83,78,77**
toteswingers:1&2:£8.40, 1&3:£22.10, 2&3:£31.00 CSF £34.40 CT £533.99 TOTE £3.80: £1.70, £3.20, £7.10; EX 31.40.
Owner K Squance & R Favarulo **Bred** Darley **Trained** Newmarket, Suffolk

FOCUS
This looked wide open. There was a generous early pace on, but still few landed a serious blow. Modest form, the winner building on his latest C&D win.
T/Plt: £427.00 to a £1 stake. Pool:£64,104.38 - 109.59 winning tickets T/Qpdt: £103.50 to a £1 stake. Pool:£8,014.83 - 57.30 winning tickets JN

551 SOUTHWELL (L-H)

Thursday, February 16

OFFICIAL GOING: Standard to slow
Wind: Light across Weather: Cloudy

579 BLUE SQUARE WINTER CARNIVAL IPHONE APPRENTICE H'CAP 1m 3f (F)
1:50 (1:50) (Class 6) (0-60,60) 4-Y-0+ **£1,704** (£503; £251) **Stalls** Low

Form RPR

3-43 **1** **Favorite Girl (GER)**[13] 401 4-9-0 **60** ..... JackDuern(5) 3 68
(Michael Appleby) *t.k.h: trckd ldrs on inner: hdwy over 3f out: rdn to ld wl over 1f out: hung rt ins fnl f: kpt on* **6/1**

43-6 **2** ½ **Spartan King (IRE)**[43] 28 4-8-12 **53** ..... MichaelO'Connell 1 60
(Ian Williams) *dwlt and hld up in rr: stdy hdwy on outer over 4f out: effrt to chse ldrs 3f out: rdn to chal wl over 1f out: ev ch whn sltly hmpd ins fnl f: sn drvn and no ex* **7/2**[2]

5-14 **3** nk **Mister Frosty (IRE)**[5] 530 6-8-13 **57** 6ex ..... DarrenEgan(5) 5 63
(George Prodromou) *trckd ldng pair: hdwy to ld wl over 3f out: rdn over 2f out: hdd wl over 1f out: n.m.r and swtchd lft ins fnl f: kpt on* **2/1**[1]

052- **4** 9 **Thackeray**[104] 7271 5-9-0 **56** ..... LMcNiff(3) 6 46
(Chris Fairhurst) *t.k.h: trckd ldrs on outer hdwy over 4f out and sn cl up: rdn along wl over 2f out and grad wknd* **7/1**

-055 **5** 1½ **Dunaskin (IRE)**[6] 493 12-8-0 **46** ..... (b) ShirleyTeasdale(7) 7 33
(Richard Guest) *cl up: led after 2f: rdn along over 4f out: hdd wl over 3f out: wknd over 2f out* **12/1**

5-44 **6** 19 **Kingaroo (IRE)**[9] 453 6-8-11 **53** ..... RaulDaSilva(3) 4
(Garry Woodward) *led 2f: cl up tl rdn along over 4f out and sn wknd* **5/1**[3]

053- **7** ¾ **Ivan The Terrible (IRE)**[50] 7902 4-8-7 **53** ..... CharlesEddery(5) 2
(Richard Guest) *chsd ldrs: rdn along 1/2-way: sn lost pl and bhd* **20/1**

2m 28.06s (0.06) **Going Correction** +0.025s/f (Slow)
WFA 4 from 5yo+ 2lb **7 Ran SP% 111.5**
Speed ratings (Par 101): **100,99,99,92,91 77,77**
toteswingers:1&2:£4.10, 2&3:£1.60, 1&3:£3.10 CSF £25.77 TOTE £5.70: £2.80, £3.00; EX 33.30.
Owner Terry Pryke **Bred** Gestut Gorlsdorf **Trained** Danethorpe, Notts

FOCUS
A modest opener in which the pace wasn't strong yet the first three managed to pull clear in the home straight. The third is probably the best guide.

580 FOLLOW SOUTHWELL ON TWITTER H'CAP 5f (F)
2:20 (2:20) (Class 6) (0-60,60) 4-Y-0+ **£1,704** (£503; £251) **Stalls** High

Form RPR

2241 **1** **Canadian Danehill (IRE)**[3] 544 10-9-3 **56** 6ex ..... (e) FrederikTylicki 7 65
(Robert Cowell) *trckd ldrs: hdwy 2f out: rdn to chal and n.m.r ins fnl f: kpt on wl to ld nr fin* **4/1**[2]

4430 **2** ½ **First In Command (IRE)**[2] 551 7-8-12 **54** ..... (t) MichaelO'Connell(3) 8 61
(Daniel Mark Loughnane) *chsd ldr: hdwy wl over 1f out: rdn to ld ins fnl f: sn drvn: hdd and no ex towards fin* **3/1**[1]

621- **3** nk **Sandwith**[56] 7853 9-9-4 **57** ..... (p) LeeNewman 2 63
(George Foster) *a.p: effrt wl over 1f out: sn rdn and ev ch ent fnl f: sn drvn and no ex last 50yds* **11/2**[3]

-455 **4** 1 **Spic 'n Span**[6] 492 7-9-0 **60** ..... (v) DarrenEgan(7) 5 62
(Ronald Harris) *led: rdn over 1f out: hdd ins fnl f: sn edgd rt and one pce* **9/1**

-634 **5** 2½ **Bookiesindex Boy**[14] 380 8-9-6 **59** ..... (b) StephenCraine 3 52
(J R Jenkins) *hld up: hdwy to trck ldrs over 2f out: sn rdn and one pce* **6/1**

3443 **6** ½ **Ace Of Spies (IRE)**[14] 385 7-9-7 **60** ..... (b) JamesSullivan 6 52
(Conor Dore) *in tch: rdn along 2f out: sn one pce* **14/1**

1065 **7** 6 **Bird Dog**[2] 551 6-8-5 **51** ..... (v) DannyBrock(7) 4 21
(Phil McEntee) *in tch: rdn along over 2f out: sn wknd* **4/1**[2]

0-00 **8** 3½ **Take Root**[10] 445 4-9-0 **60** ..... (p) JackDuern(7) 1 17
(Reg Hollinshead) *dwlt: sn chsng ldrs on outer: rdn along over 2f out and sn wknd* **18/1**

59.02s (-0.68) **Going Correction** -0.10s/f (Stan) **8 Ran SP% 116.6**
Speed ratings (Par 101): **101,100,99,98,94 93,83,78**
toteswingers:1&2:£3.90, 2&3:£4.40, 1&3:£2.30 CSF £16.82 CT £66.60 TOTE £5.30: £1.90, £1.10, £2.00; EX 21.10 Trifecta £87.50 Pool: £657.52 - 5.56 winning units..
Owner T W Morley **Bred** Skymarc Farm Inc And Dr A J O'Reilly **Trained** Six Mile Bottom, Cambs

FOCUS
A low-grade handicap contested by the usual familiar names at this level, three of them having their second run this week. The pace took a furlong or so to really pick up. Straightforward form.

581 PLAY GOLF AT SOUTHWELL MEDIAN AUCTION MAIDEN STKS 1m 4f (F)
2:50 (2:50) (Class 5) 4-6-Y-0 **£2,264** (£673; £336; £168) **Stalls** Low

Form RPR

43 **1** **Candelita**[22] 300 5-8-8 0 ..... JoshBaudains(7) 3 63
(Jo Hughes) *trckd ldrs: hdwy on inner 3f out: swtchd rt over 2f out and sn chal: led 1 1/2f out: sn rdn clr: styd on strly* **7/2**[2]

04- **2** 2½ **Ace Serve**[251] 2871 4-8-9 0 ..... DominicFox(3) 9 59
(Oliver Sherwood) *trckd ldrs: hdwy and cl up 1/2-way: rdn over 2f out: drvn to chse wnr ent fnl f: no imp* **6/1**

6/0- **3** 3¾ **Toymaker**[283] 1950 5-9-6 65 ..... FrederikTylicki 7 58
(James Given) *cl up: led 1/2-way: rdn over 2f out: hdd 1 1/2f out: kpt on same pce* **11/8**[1]

0-00 **4** 1 **Yours**[12] 430 4-8-12 45 ..... PhillipMakin 5 51
(Kevin Ryan) *chsd ldrs: rdn along wl over 2f out: sn one pce* **16/1**

0/53 **5** 6 **Somerset Island (IRE)**[16] 369 4-9-3 55 ..... AndrewMullen 1 46
(Michael Smith) *chsd ldrs on inner: rdn along and outpcd over 4f out: plugged on u.p fnl 2f* **11/2**[3]

6 1 **Godwit** 4-8-9 0 ..... RyanClark(3) 4 40
(Eugene Stanford) *s.i.s and in rr: hdwy on outer 1/2-way: chsd ldrs over 3f out: sn rdn along and no imp fnl 2f* **10/1**

3 **7** 10 **Punta Baluarte**[46] 1 6-8-12 0 ..... DaleSwift(3) 8 24
(Julie Camacho) *a towards rr* **50/1**

0/ **8** 33 **Danbrook (IRE)**[502] 6566 4-9-3 0 ..... PJMcDonald 2
(George Moore) *a in rr: rdn along and bhd fr over 4f out* **40/1**

0- **9** 4 **Give Or Take**[63] 7766 4-9-3 0 ..... (p) WilliamCarson 6
(Christine Dunnett) *sn led: pushed along and hdd 1/2-way: sn wknd and bhd fnl 3f* **50/1**

2m 42.66s (1.66) **Going Correction** +0.025s/f (Slow)
WFA 4 from 5yo+ 3lb **9 Ran SP% 115.3**
Speed ratings: **95,93,90,90,86 85,78,56,54**
toteswingers:1&2:£2.60, 2&3:£2.70, 1&3:£2.20 CSF £24.51 TOTE £4.90: £1.50, £1.30, £1.60; EX 14.70 Trifecta £28.00 Pool: £756.71 - 19.97 winning units..
Owner Pedro Rosas **Bred** Pedro Rosas **Trained** Lambourn, Berks

FOCUS
A weak maiden run at an uneven gallop and in a slow time. There's some doubt over the worth of the form, the winner rated to a best view of her Lingfield effort.

582 SOUTHWELL-RACECOURSE.CO.UK H'CAP 1m 4f (F)
3:25 (3:27) (Class 5) (0-75,75) 4-Y-0+ **£2,264** (£673; £336; £168) **Stalls** Low

Form RPR

303- **1** **Stand Guard**[94] 7413 8-9-6 **73** ..... AdamKirby 2 82
(John Butler) *hld up in tch: gd hdwy 4f out: cl up 3f out: led over 2f out: rdn clr whn hung rt ent fnl f: kpt on strly* **5/2**[2]

44-1 **2** 1½ **Tricksofthetrade (IRE)**[9] 460 6-9-7 **74** 6ex ..... PJMcDonald 7 81
(Alan Swinbank) *trckd ldrs: hdwy to ld 4f out: jnd and rdn 3f out: hdd over 2f out: drvn and kpt on same pce appr fnl f* **11/8**[1]

5-34 **3** 5 **Switched Off**[21] 310 7-9-3 **73** ..... (p) MichaelO'Connell(3) 5 72
(Ian Williams) *hld up towards rr: stdy hdwy over 4f out: chsd ldng pair 3f out: rdn and ch 2f out: one pce appr fnl f* **9/2**[3]

-424 **4** 14 **Dazzling Valentine**[3] 548 4-9-1 **74** ..... (p) DominicFox(3) 4 51
(Alan Bailey) *cl up: led after 3f: rdn along and hdd 4f out: wknd 3f out* **6/1**

300/ **5** 2½ **Bee Sting**[519] 6091 8-8-10 **70** ..... (p) MatthewMcGhee(7) 1 43
(Lisa Williamson) *a towards rr: outpcd and bhd fr over 4f out* **66/1**

536- **6** 10 **Zamina (IRE)**[50] 7900 4-9-5 **75** ..... (t) StephenCraine 6 32
(Tim Vaughan) *chsd ldng pair: rdn along over 3f out: sn wknd* **25/1**

-240 **7** 95 **Bow River Arch (USA)**[19] 355 4-9-0 **70** ..... (p) WilliamCarson 3
(Peter Hiatt) *led 3f: cl up: rdn along 1/2-way: sn wknd and wl bhd fnl 3f* **8/1**

2m 39.33s (-1.67) **Going Correction** +0.025s/f (Slow)
WFA 4 from 6yo+ 3lb **7 Ran SP% 119.6**
Speed ratings (Par 103): **106,105,101,92,90 84,20**
toteswingers:1&2:£1.90, 2&3:£2.00, 1&3:£2.70 CSF £6.79 TOTE £3.80: £1.70, £1.30; EX 11.00.
Owner C Owen **Bred** Juddmonte Farms Ltd **Trained** Newmarket, Suffolk

FOCUS
An ordinary handicap run at a steady gallop and more of a test of speed than stamina. The form is not the most solid, with the winner rated back to something like last winter's form.
Bow River Arch(USA) Official explanation: jockey said filly ran flat

583 MEMBERSHIP OF SOUTHWELL GOLF CLUB CLAIMING STKS 6f (F)
3:55 (3:55) (Class 6) 3-Y-O **£1,704** (£503; £251) **Stalls** Low

Form RPR

6-62 **1** **Thorpe Bay**[20] 321 3-8-10 62 ..... (b) FrederikTylicki 4 66
(Mark Rimmer) *trckd ldrs: hdwy over 2f out: swtchd rt and effrt wl over 1f out: rdn to ld ent fnl f: sn clr and hung lft: kpt on strly* **8/1**

5234 **2** 3½ **One More Roman (IRE)**[5] 536 3-8-8 62 ..... (bt) DominicFox(3) 3 56
(Gay Kelleway) *s.i.s and bhd: rdn along 1/2-way: hdwy on wd outside 2f out: styd on to take 2nd ins fnl f* **5/2**[2]

-343 **3** 1 **Faraway**[17] 357 3-8-12 65 ..... (b[1]) WilliamCarson 1 54
(Ronald Harris) *cl up: rdn to ld wl over 1f out: drvn and hdd ent fnl f: sn wknd* **11/4**[3]

3603 **4** 4 **Ishiamiracle**[6] 491 3-8-6 65 ..... (p) LauraPike(5) 2 40
(Phil McEntee) *set str pce: rdn over 2f out: hdd wl over 1f out: sn wknd* **11/8**[1]

000- **5** 6 **After Timer (IRE)**[125] 6835 3-8-7 39 ..... (p) TomEaves 5 17
(Julie Camacho) *cl up: rdn along 1/2-way: sn wknd* **50/1**

1m 17.0s (0.50) **Going Correction** +0.025s/f (Slow) **5 Ran SP% 110.4**
Speed ratings (Par 95): **97,92,91,85,77**
CSF £27.99 TOTE £7.50: £2.60, £3.70; EX 27.50.Thorpe Bay was claimed by C. R. Dore for £4000.
Owner Con Donovan **Bred** Clive Dennett **Trained** Newmarket, Suffolk
■ Claretinthewood (8/1) was withdrawn on vet's advice. R4 applies, deduct 10p in the £.

FOCUS
Far less between the runners on official ratings than the betting suggested in what was an ordinary claimer. The pace was good without being overly strong. A much improved effort from the winner at face value, but this is perhaps not form to take too seriously.
After Timer(IRE) Official explanation: trainer's rep said filly was unsuited by the track

584 THOUSANDS OF SPORTS EXPERIENCES AT BLUESQ.COM H'CAP 1m (F)
4:25 (4:25) (Class 4) (0-85,81) 4-Y-0+ **£4,528** (£1,347; £673; £336) **Stalls** Low

Form RPR

00-3 **1** **Call To Reason (IRE)**[46] 5 5-9-7 **81** ..... TonyHamilton 9 91
(Ian Williams) *hld up in rr: gd hdwy over 2f out: led 1 1/2f out: rdn out* **5/1**[3]

0243 **2** 1½ **The Lock Master (IRE)**[3] 548 5-8-12 **79** ..... JackDuern(7) 3 86
(Michael Appleby) *trckd ldrs: rdn along and outpcd over 3f out: hdwy on inner 2f out: rdn to chse wnr ent fnl f: sn edgd rt and no imp* **11/4**[1]

11-4 **3** 1¼ **On The Cusp (IRE)**[44] 22 5-9-1 **75** ..... (p) WilliamCarson 5 79+
(Richard Guest) *set str pce: wd st: rdn 2f out: hdd 1 1/2f out and sn drvn: kpt on same pce fnl f* **10/1**

05-1 **4** 4 **Dubaianswer**[44] 22 4-9-6 **80** ..... StephenCraine 6 75
(Tony Coyle) *in tch: smooth hdwy to trck ldrs over 3f out: effrt to chse ldr over 2f out: rdn wl over 1f out and sn one pce* **15/2**

1-0 **5** shd **Son Vida (IRE)**[12] 432 4-9-6 **80** ..... PhillipMakin 8 75
(Mark Johnston) *chsd ldrs on outer: pushed along: lost pl and wd st: styd on fnl f* **6/1**

115- **6** 1 **Gritstone**[52] 7877 5-9-4 **81** ..... LeeTopliss(3) 4 73
(Richard Fahey) *trckd ldrs: hdwy to chse ldr over 3f out: sn rdn and wknd wl over 1f out* **4/1**[2]

0-60 7 2 3/4 **Levitate**[12] 426 4-8-11 **78**...(v) NoraLooby(7) 1 64
(Alan McCabe) *cl up on inner: rdn along 3f out: wknd 2f out* **20/1**
-403 8 3/4 **Community (USA)**[6] 494 4-8-0 **67** oh1... DannyBrock(7) 7 51
(Phil McEntee) *cl up: rdn along 3f out: wknd over 2f out* **40/1**
4142 9 1 **Pipers Piping (IRE)**[9] 463 6-8-5 **70**...(p) AmyScott(5) 2 52
(Alastair Lidderdale) *a in rr* **8/1**
1m 43.56s (-0.14) **Going Correction** +0.025s/f (Slow) **9** Ran SP% **116.8**
Speed ratings (Par 105): **101,99,98,94,94 93,90,89,88**
toteswingers:1&2:£2.70, 2&3:£3.30, 1&3:£8.00 CSF £19.39 CT £134.19 TOTE £6.80: £1.80, £1.60, £3.20; EX 22.10 Trifecta £138.70 Pool: £506.09 - 2.70 winning units..
Owner Dr Marwan Koukash **Bred** J Hanly, T Stewart & A Stroud **Trained** Portway, Worcs
■ Stewards' Enquiry : Jack Duern eight-day ban: used whip with excessive frequency (Mar 1-3,5-9)

FOCUS
A fairly useful handicap run at a good clip by and large, for all the pace steadied a bit after an early dash for the lead, and enough horses of interest at the head of affairs to think the form is reliable. The winner is rated back to her best.
Pipers Piping(IRE) Official explanation: jockey said gelding never travelled

585 PLAY ROULETTE AT BLUESQ.COM H'CAP 7f (F)
4:55 (4:55) (Class 5) (0-75,75) 4-Y-0+ **£2,264** (£673; £336; £168) **Stalls** Low

Form RPR
-232 1 **Mazovian (USA)**[6] 496 4-8-1 **62**... DannyBrock(7) 6 75
(Michael Chapman) *cl up: led 3f out: rdn 2f out: clr over 1f out: styd on strly* **13/2**[3]
-311 2 6 **Fluctuation (IRE)**[16] 370 4-8-9 **66**...(b) MichaelO'Connell(3) 5 63
(Ian Williams) *trckd ldrs: hdwy 1/2-way: chsd wnr over 2f out: rdn wl over 1f out: sn one pce* **2/1**[1]
1-31 3 2 1/4 **Andiamo Via**[16] 371 5-8-11 **65**... AndrewMullen 1 56
(Michael Smith) *sn outpcd and rdn along in rr: hdwy over 2f out: styd on u.p to take modest 3rd appr fnl f* **2/1**[1]
4-26 4 6 **Piceno (IRE)**[22] 304 4-9-4 **75**...(b) RyanPowell(3) 2 50
(Scott Dixon) *cl up: rdn along 1/2-way: sn outpcd* **4/1**[2]
2-45 5 1 **Striker Torres (IRE)**[10] 447 6-8-12 **69**...(v) DaleSwift(3) 3 41
(Ian McInnes) *s.i.s: a in rr* **14/1**
0-00 6 5 **Alpha Tauri (USA)**[1] 560 6-9-6 **74**...(t) WilliamCarson 4 32
(Richard Guest) *sn led and set str pce: rdn along and hdd 3f out: wknd qckly fnl 2f* **14/1**
1m 28.99s (-1.31) **Going Correction** +0.025s/f (Slow) **6** Ran SP% **113.3**
Speed ratings (Par 103): **108,101,98,91,90 84**
toteswingers:1&2:£1.90, 2&3:£1.20, 1&3:£3.50 CSF £20.31 TOTE £9.80: £4.80, £1.20; EX 24.00.
Owner Mrs M Chapman **Bred** Darley **Trained** Market Rasen, Lincs

FOCUS
Not an easy race to assess with several not at their best on the day and the runners finishing well strung out. The pace seemed sound and it was the pick of the round course times. The winner is rated to the best view of his old form.
T/Plt: £106.30 to a £1 stake. Pool of £57,818.94 - 396.80 winning tickets. T/Qpdt: £17.50 to a £1 stake. Pool of £5,474.66 - 231.30 winning tickets. JR

484 MEYDAN (L-H)
Thursday, February 16
OFFICIAL GOING: Tapeta - standard; turf - good

586a RANGE ROVER SPORT TROPHY (H'CAP) (TAPETA) 1m
2:30 (2:30) (95-105,105) 3-Y-0+
£42,580 (£14,193; £7,096; £3,548; £2,129; £1,419)

RPR
1 **Sooraah**[27] 245 5-8-13 102... RyanMoore 12 108
(William Haggas) *mid-div: smooth prog 2 1/2f out: led 110yds out: r.o wl* **12/1**
2 1 1/2 **Scarf (AUS)**[54] 5-9-0 104... SilvestreDeSousa 6 106
(Saeed Bin Suroor) *chsd ldrs: led 1 1/2f out: hdd 110yds out* **8/1**
3 2 1/2 **Canwinn (IRE)**[26] 261 6-8-13 102... WilliamBuick 2 99+
(D Selvaratnam, UAE) *in rr of mid-div: r.o fnl 2f: nrst fin* **11/2**[3]
4 1/2 **Yaa Wayl (IRE)**[42] 53 5-8-13 102...(vt) TedDurcan 8 98+
(Saeed Bin Suroor) *s.i.s: racd in rr: r.o wl fnl 1 1/2f: nrst fin* **12/1**
5 1/4 **The Rectifier (USA)**[27] 246 5-9-1 105... MickyFenton 13 99
(Jim Boyle) *sn led: hdd 1 1/2f out: kpt on same pce* **25/1**
6 1 3/4 **Finjaan**[27] 246 6-9-0 104...(b) RichardHills 11 94
(Doug Watson, UAE) *trckd ldrs: ev ch 2f out: one pce fnl 1 1/2f* **9/1**
7 2 1/2 **Banna Boirche (IRE)**[13] 416 6-8-5 101... ConorHoban(6) 4 85
(M Halford, Ire) *nvr bttr than mid-div* **14/1**
8 5 1/2 **Man Of Action (USA)**[26] 260 5-8-11 101...(v) MickaelBarzalona 9 73+
(Saeed Bin Suroor) *slowly away: nvr nr to chal* **5/1**[2]
9 1 **Red Gulch**[13] 416 5-8-13 102... FrankieDettori 3 72
(Mahmood Al Zarooni) *trckd ldrs tl wknd 2f out* **7/2**[1]
10 1 3/4 **Mabait**[27] 246 6-8-11 101... JamieSpencer 14 66
(David Simcock) *settled in rr: nvr able to chal* **25/1**
11 1 3/4 **Navajo Chief**[7] 489 5-8-13 102... KierenFallon 1 64
(Alan Jarvis) *mid-div: rdn 3f out: sn btn* **9/1**
12 1 1/4 **Energia Colonial (BRZ)**[20] 344 5-9-1 105... MircoDemuro 7 63
(Fabricio Borges, Sweden) *settled in rr: nvr nr to chal* **33/1**
13 5 1/2 **He'sminenotyours (USA)**[20] 344 6-9-1 105...(t) RichardMullen 5 51
(S Seemar, UAE) *chsd ldrs tl 4 1/2f out: sn wknd* **14/1**
14 8 **Happy Today (USA)**[20] 344 4-8-13 102...(vt) WayneSmith 10 30
(M Al Muhairi, UAE) *nvr bttr than mid-div* **12/1**
1m 36.66s (-0.84) **14** Ran SP% **128.3**
CSF: 109.75 TRICAST: 608.39.
Owner Mohd Jaber Abdullah **Bred** C R Mason **Trained** Newmarket, Suffolk

FOCUS
A good handicap. The field were taken along at a fair pace thanks to the The Rectifier.

NOTEBOOK
Sooraah was unsuited by a hold-up ride in a modestly run race when failing to beat a rival in the Group 2 Cape Verdi on her reappearance, but she was ridden closer to the pace on this notable drop in class and the surface evidently suited. She was always going well and was a thoroughly convincing winner. Her most realistic chance of following up will be if kept to handicaps, but her profile suggests she probably hasn't finished improving and her connections may prefer to chase some more black type, in which case the Group 3 Burj Nahaar over C&D on March 10 may be a suitable target.
Scarf(AUS), a multiple winner in Australia who won a handicap over there going just short of this trip as recently as December, shaped well on his Dubai debut. He was a bit keen early on and just didn't see it out as well as the winner, so perhaps he'll benefit from a slight drop in distance.
Canwinn(IRE) lacked the pace of the front two.
Yaa Wayl(IRE) was left with too much to do after missing the break and having to switch in the straight. He finished strongly.
The Rectifier(USA) ran much better than on the turf last time.
Man Of Action(USA) was beaten at odds-on in a turf handicap in January and on this occasion, not for the first time, proved awkward. He lost his chance with a slow start, and was then stuck much too wide when trying to recover. While not one to trust, he's better than he showed.
Red Gulch failed to build on his recent C&D third.
Navajo Chief couldn't dominate. (op 11-1)

587a JAGUAR XF TROPHY (H'CAP) (TAPETA) 1m 1f 110y
3:05 (3:05) (95-105,105) 3-Y-0+
£42,580 (£14,193; £7,096; £3,548; £2,129; £1,419)

RPR
1 **Zain Shamardal (IRE)**[6] 515 4-9-0 100...(t) RoystonFfrench 8 102
(A Al Raihe, UAE) *mid-div: smooth prog 2 1/2f out: r.o wl* **12/1**
2 1 **Jardim (BRZ)**[13] 416 6-9-3 102... KShea 14 102
(M F De Kock, South Africa) *settled in rr: r.o wl fnl 2 1/2f: nrst fin* **25/1**
3 1 1/4 **Start Right**[27] 246 5-9-2 101... KierenFallon 12 98
(Saeed Bin Suroor) *in rr of mid-div: led 1 1/2f out: hdd 1 1/2f out: one pce fnl 10yds* **4/1**[1]
4 1/4 **Royal Destination (IRE)**[27] 241 7-9-1 100...(vt) OlivierPeslier 3 97
(F Nass, Bahrain) *s.i.s: in rr of mid-div: r.o fnl 1 1/2f: nrst fin* **25/1**
5 1 **Sharaayeen**[6] 515 5-9-1 100... RichardHills 6 95
(A Al Raihe, UAE) *trckd ldrs: ev ch 2f out: one pce fnl f* **8/1**
6 1/2 **Prince D'Alienor (IRE)**[26] 260 4-9-2 102... GregoryBenoist 1 96
(X Nakkachdji, France) *in rr of mid-div: n.m.r 2 1/2f out: r.o same pce fnl 1 1/2f* **6/1**
7 1 **Wealthy (IRE)**[26] 260 5-9-0 99...(t) TedDurcan 13 91
(Saeed Bin Suroor) *settled in rr: nvr nr to chal* **14/1**
8 shd **Atlantic Brave**[20] 344 6-9-5 105...(vt) WayneSmith 2 96
(M Al Muhairi, UAE) *a mid-div* **8/1**
9 6 3/4 **Dubawi Star**[7] 489 4-8-11 98...(b) TadhgO'Shea 5 75
(John M Oxx, Ire) *trckd ldng pair: led 3 1/2f out: hdd 2f out* **14/1**
10 1/2 **Anaerobio (ARG)**[7] 489 5-9-2 101...(t) ChristopheSoumillon 4 78
(M F De Kock, South Africa) *in rr of mid-div: rdn 3f out: one pce fnl 1 1/2f* **11/2**[3]
11 6 1/2 **Nationalism**[21] 317 5-9-4 104... FrankieDettori 9 66
(Mahmood Al Zarooni) *slowly away: nvr able to chal* **9/2**[2]
12 16 1/2 **Critical Moment (USA)**[13] 420 5-9-1 100... WilliamBuick 10 30
(F Nass, Bahrain) *nvr bttr than mid-div* **25/1**
13 3 1/4 **Balducci**[13] 416 5-9-4 104...(tp) MircoDemuro 7 26
(Ernst Oertel, UAE) *sn led: hdd & wknd 3 1/2f out* **33/1**
14 dist **Canadian (IRE)**[21] 317 4-8-13 99...(p) PatCosgrave 11
(M bin Shafya, UAE) *trckd ldrs tl 4f out: wknd qckly* **25/1**
1m 58.16s (-0.84) **14** Ran SP% **129.4**
CSF: 300.43 TRICAST: 1437.66.
Owner Jaber Abdullah **Bred** Kevin & Meta Cullen **Trained** UAE

FOCUS
Not a strong race, but Balducci took them along at a good pace, going through the first three splits in 25.71, 49.49, and 1.14.19, and Start Right was in front when going 1.39.10 at the 1m point. Those held up were favoured.

NOTEBOOK
Zain Shamardal(IRE) was a bit short of room early in the back straight, and he also became tight for room on the final bend, but the latter bit of trouble helped him as it meant his challenge was delayed in this strongly run race. He was not obviously well handicapped, adding to the impression this wasn't a hot contest.
Jardim(BRZ), much like on his Dubai debut over 1m, did his best work late on and got closer this time. He was helped by the way the race unfolded, but maybe there will be more to come.
Start Right is hard to win with, but once again he's better than he showed. Back up in trip, he was stuck wide on the first bend (ended up covering more ground than those around him according to Trakus data) and was committed too soon. He'll be worth another try at this distance under a more patient ride, but won't mind a return to a strongly run 1m.
Royal Destination(IRE) was denied a clear run turning into the straight before running on, and this was better than of late, but considering how the race unfolded it's probably not a performance to go overboard about.
Sharaayeen had Zain Shamardal behind when successful at Jebel Ali last time, but on this occasion (5lb higher) he was compromised by racing closer to the pace than his old rival.
Dubawi Star made his move towards the lead prematurely and unsurprisingly paid for it.
Anaerobio(ARG) found little for pressure. He had been going to the right way, albeit gradually, but his recent form had been on turf (including when second to stablemate Mutahadee the previous week) and he was well beaten on his sole previous try on this surface.
Nationalism covered more ground than most, but he's a disappointing sort.

588a RANGE ROVER EVOQUE TROPHY (H'CAP) (TURF) 7f
3:45 (3:45) (100-116,116) 3-Y-0+
£67,741 (£22,580; £11,290; £5,645; £3,387; £2,258)

RPR
1 **Delegator**[166] 5707 6-9-2 111... FrankieDettori 13 114
(Saeed Bin Suroor) *mid-div: smooth prog 2f out: led fnl 55yds* **5/2**[1]
2 3/4 **Jaasoos (IRE)**[20] 344 8-9-1 110... KierenFallon 1 111
(D Selvaratnam, UAE) *trckd ldr: n.m.r 2 1/2f: led 1 1/2f out: hdd cl home* **16/1**
3 1 3/4 **Rerouted (USA)**[13] 420 4-8-9 105... ChristopheSoumillon 12 100+
(M F De Kock, South Africa) *in rr of mid-div: r.o wl fnl 2f: nrst fin* **3/1**[2]
4 1 1/4 **The Comedian (AUS)**[27] 6-8-11 107...(bt) VladDuric 9 99
(M Freedman, Singapore) *mid-div: r.o fnl 1 1/2f: nrst fin* **9/1**
5 1/2 **Kavango (IRE)**[35] 144 5-8-10 106... PatCosgrave 5 97
(M bin Shafya, UAE) *mid-div: r.o fnl 2f but nvr able to chal* **16/1**
6 3/4 **Captain Obvious (AUS)**[13] 420 7-9-6 116...(t) OChavez 2 105
(S Burridge, Singapore) *wl away: sn led: hdd 1 1/2f out: one pce fnl 110yds* **8/1**[3]
7 hd **Dohasa (IRE)**[13] 420 7-8-13 108... MircoDemuro 11 97
(Ismail Mohammed) *trckd ldrs: ev ch 3f out: wknd fnl 1 1/2f* **25/1**
8 1/4 **Spectacle Du Mars (FR)**[21] 315 5-9-0 109... GregoryBenoist 14 97
(X Nakkachdji, France) *settled in rr: nvr bttr than mid-div* **14/1**
9 nse **Redemptor**[21] 316 4-8-9 105... TedDurcan 10 92
(E Charpy, UAE) *nvr nr to chal* **33/1**
10 1 1/4 **Tamaathul**[7] 487 5-9-2 111...(t) TadhgO'Shea 15 96
(A Al Raihe, UAE) *settled in rr: nvr able to chal* **16/1**
11 3/4 **Dux Scholar**[110] 7170 4-9-3 112...(t) RyanMoore 7 95
(H J Brown, South Africa) *settled in rr: nvr nr to chal* **12/1**
12 2 1/4 **Five Cents**[6] 513 5-8-11 107... RoystonFfrench 6 83
(A Al Raihe, UAE) *trckd ldrs tl 3f out: sn wknd* **16/1**

13 2 **Barbecue Eddie (USA)**[7] 487 8-8-13 108...................(b) RichardHills 4 79
(Doug Watson, UAE) *chsd ldrs tl 2 1/2f out* **16/1**
14 nse **Ibn Battuta (USA)**[691] 1025 7-8-13 108........................ WayneSmith 16 79
(M Al Muhairi, UAE) *nvr bttr than mid-div* **25/1**
15 7 1/2 **Silver Ocean (USA)**[21] 315 4-8-13 108......................... WilliamBuick 3 59
(Niels Petersen, Norway) *trckd ldrs tl 2 1/2f out: wknd fnl f* **20/1**
16 5 1/4 **Colonial (IRE)**[42] 53 5-8-10 106............................ MickaelBarzalona 8 42
(Saeed Bin Suroor) *nvr able to chal* **25/1**
1m 25.31s (85.31) **16** Ran SP% **137.7**
CSF: 48.59 TRICAST: 141.34.
Owner Godolphin **Bred** Mrs P Good **Trained** Newmarket, Suffolk

FOCUS
A quality handicap and Captain Obvious set a fair pace, going 25.48, 49.69 and 1.13.27.

NOTEBOOK
Delegator had two key factors in his favour - a lenient official mark of 111 and this being his first run of the year. The winner is a Classic-placed horse who recorded an RPR of 123 as a 3yo, and he was awarded an RPR of 117 just four outings ago when taking last year's Group 2 Duke of York Stakes. That success came on his reappearance and he has now won first time out for the last four years. He had lost his way on his final two starts of 2011, but he was back in good enough form to take advantage of this handy mark on what was his handicap debut. It remains to be seen whether he can be as effective when back up in class and not so fresh. (op 11-4)
Jaasoos(IRE) saved plenty of ground with an inside trip and had every chance. He ran up to his best.
Rerouted(USA), who made rapid late headway in a 6f Tapeta Group 3 on his recent debut for Mike de Kock, went some way to confirming that promise, but he'd been left with plenty to do. He's handicapped to win when the race unfolds to suit. (op 4-1)
The Comedian(AUS), in good form in Singapore lately, showed himself competitively handicapped with a staying-on effort. (op 8-1)
Kavango(IRE) was a bit short of room through the early stages and did well to finish so close.
Redemptor did well to get so close after losing several lengths at the start.
Tamaathul ◆ was continually denied a clear run in the straight when attempting to stay on from a long way back. He should have finished a lot closer and this went some way to suggesting his second-place finish in a Group 3 the previous week might not have been a fluke. (op 14-1)
Dux Scholar ◆, having his first start since leaving Sir Michael Stoute, was another who got no run at all.

589a JAGUAR XJ TROPHY (H'CAP) (TAPETA) 6f
4:20 (4:20) (100-110,110) 3-Y-O+
£46,451 (£15,483; £7,741; £3,870; £2,322; £1,548)

RPR
1 **Happy Dubai (IRE)**[6] 513 5-9-0 105...................(t) SilvestreDeSousa 14 108+
(A Al Raihe, UAE) *trckd ldng pair: led 1 1/2f out: comf* **16/1**
2 1 1/2 **Kanaf (IRE)**[20] 346 5-8-13 104.. RichardHills 1 102
(M Al Muhairi, UAE) *in rr of mid-div: r.o wl fnl 1 1/2f: nrst fin* **13/2**
3 1 1/4 **Green Beret (IRE)**[13] 419 6-9-1 106........................(t) RoystonFfrench 5 100
(A Al Raihe, UAE) *mid-div: r.o fnl 1 1/2f: nrst fin* **11/1**
4 hd **Casual Glimpse**[103] 7295 4-8-11 102................ ChristopheSoumillon 10 96
(M F De Kock, South Africa) *settled in rr: r.o fnl 1 1/2f: nrst fin* **6/1**[3]
5 1/4 **Reynaldothewizard (USA)**[27] 244 6-9-3 108...........(t) RichardMullen 3 101
(S Seemar, UAE) *chsd ldrs: ev ch 2 1/2f out: one pce fnl 1 1/2f* **5/1**[2]
6 1 1/4 **Jimmy Styles**[13] 420 8-8-11 102....................................(p) RyanMoore 9 91
(Clive Cox) *nvr able to chal* **16/1**
7 3/4 **Internationaldebut (IRE)**[13] 419 7-8-10 101................. KierenFallon 4 88
(Paul Midgley) *mid-div: chsd ldrs 2 1/2f out: wknd fnl 1 1/2f* **14/1**
8 3/4 **Spin Cycle (IRE)**[42] 50 6-9-2 107...........................(t) FrankieDettori 12 91
(S Seemar, UAE) *sn led: hdd 1 1/2f out: wknd fnl f* **16/1**
9 1 **Warsaw (IRE)**[335] 7-9-2 107...(b) KShea 8 88
(M F De Kock, South Africa) *slowly away: sn rdn in rr: n.d* **16/1**
10 3 1/4 **Verde-Mar (BRZ)**[186] 5-9-5 110............................... ValmirDeAzeredo 13 81
(Fabricio Borges, Sweden) *nvr nr to chal* **20/1**
11 3 1/4 **As De Trebol (USA)**[21] 315 6-8-13 104......................... BFayosMartin 7 64
(M Delcher-Sanchez, Spain) *trckd ldrs tl 1 1/2f out: wknd fnl 110yds* **14/1**
12 2 1/4 **Ariete Arrollador**[21] 314 5-8-11 102......................... IoritzMendizabal 2 55
(G Arizkorreta Elosegui, Spain) *chsd ldrs tl 2 1/2f out: sn wknd* **3/1**[1]
13 6 3/4 **Silaah**[21] 314 8-8-13 104..(p) AdrianNicholls 6 35
(David Nicholls) *nvr bttr than mid-div* **14/1**
14 1 **Bay Knight (IRE)**[13] 416 6-9-3 108...........................(tp) PatCosgrave 11 36
(J S Moore) *chsd ldrs tl 3f out: sn wknd* **33/1**
1m 11.62s (0.02) **14** Ran SP% **128.9**
CSF: 124.70 TRICAST: 1,234.63.
Owner Ahmed Al Falasi **Bred** Waterford Hall Stud **Trained** UAE

FOCUS
Just an ordinary sprint handicap for a 100-110, but the winner is significantly better than the bare result. The lead was contested by Spin Cycle and As De Trebol, who between them set fractions of 24.62 and 47.74, and neither had much hope of sustaining their efforts. Consequently, plenty of those held up finished strongly, yet Happy Dubai, who sat no worse than third and was caught wide for most of the way, saw it out best.

NOTEBOOK
Happy Dubai(IRE) ◆ became the first horse to win over this C&D from stall 14 and the record of gates 12, 13 & 14 combined (allowing for non-runners) is now just 1-41. According to Trakus the winner covered more ground than the next four finishers, including five meters more than the runner-up, and his average speed was upwards of 0.5kph quicker than any of his rivals. After going about 4l clear halfway up the straight, he understandably got tired and the winning margin underplays his superiority. Happy Dubai was most progressive at last year's Carnival when he was successful three times on turf, but had mainly struggled this time. However, he shaped as though returning to form at Jebel Ali last time and is now well and truly back to his best. This was a Group-class performance and a rise in the weights will probably underestimate him. (op 20-1)
Kanaf(IRE), up 8lb for winning at Jebel Ali, had no obvious excuse.
Green Beret(IRE) hasn't had the Carnival that might have expected after his promising reappearance, but he made late headway after, as usual, travelling well.
Casual Glimpse stayed on from a long way back on his debut for Mike de Kock. He was suited by the pace scenario, but could build on this.
Reynaldothewizard(USA) wasn't good enough. (op 11-2)
As De Trebol(USA) was a long way below recent form despite the race unfolding to suit.

590a AL FAHIDI FORT SPONSORED BY AL TAYER MOTORS (GROUP 2) (TURF) 1m
4:55 (4:55) 3-Y-O+
£96,774 (£32,258; £16,129; £8,064; £4,838; £3,225)

RPR
1 **Viscount Nelson (USA)**[27] 243 5-9-0 113..........................(b) KShea 12 116+
(M F De Kock, South Africa) *in rr of mid-div: smooth prog 2 1/2f out: rdn to ld fnl 110yds* **8/1**
2 1/2 **Albaasil (IRE)**[21] 316 4-9-0 106... RichardHills 4 115
(Doug Watson, UAE) *mid-div: chsd ldrs 2 1/2f out: led 1 1/2f out: hdd fnl 110yds* **13/2**[3]
3 1 **Master Of Hounds (USA)**[7] 488 4-9-0 115....(t) ChristopheSoumillon 1 113
(M F De Kock, South Africa) *trckd ldr on rail: n.m.r 2 1/2f out: r.o fnl 1 1/2f* **4/1**[2]
4 1/2 **Derbaas (USA)**[7] 487 6-9-0 113.................................(t) TadhgO'Shea 11 112
(A Al Raihe, UAE) *chsd ldrs: led 2f out: hdd 1 1/2f out: no ex* **14/1**
5 1 **Time Prisoner (USA)**[21] 316 5-9-0 113.................. MickaelBarzalona 3 109
(Mahmood Al Zarooni) *mid-div: r.o same pce fnl 1 1/2f* **11/1**
6 2 1/2 **Marcret (ITY)**[21] 318 5-9-0 110... RyanMoore 13 104
(Marco Botti) *settled in rr: nvr nr to chal* **20/1**
7 1 1/2 **Rio De La Plata (USA)**[102] 7324 7-9-0 118.................(p) FrankieDettori 8 100
(Saeed Bin Suroor) *nvr bttr than mid-div* **6/4**[1]
8 nse **Laa Rayb (USA)**[11] 8-9-0 104..............................(t) WilliamBuick 6 100
(D Selvaratnam, UAE) *in rr of mid-div: n.d* **33/1**
9 nse **Dandy Boy (ITY)**[13] 416 6-9-0 101.. TedDurcan 7 100
(David Marnane, Ire) *settled in rr: nvr nr to chal* **33/1**
10 2 **Always Certain (AUS)**[27] 6-9-5 115.................................(p) VladDuric 2 100
(M Freedman, Singapore) *nvr bttr than mid-div* **20/1**
11 4 **Do It All (USA)**[27] 246 5-9-0 105...........................(t) SilvestreDeSousa 9 86
(Saeed Bin Suroor) *sn led: hdd & wknd 2f out* **50/1**
12 1/4 **Snaafy (USA)**[20] 344 8-9-0 108....................................(v) WayneSmith 10 54
(M Al Muhairi, UAE) *trckd ldr tl 2 1/2f out: wknd* **33/1**
13 14 **Maraheb**[13] 416 4-9-0 107..(t) RoystonFfrench 5 53
(A Al Raihe, UAE) *s.i.s: trckd ldrs tl wknd 2f out* **12/1**
1m 38.13s (98.13) **13** Ran SP% **127.4**
CSF: 58.61.
Owner Ms Partridge, M De Kock, C Haynes Et Al **Bred** Barronstown Stud **Trained** South Africa

FOCUS
A solid but unspectacular running of this Group 2. The pace was fair enough, with the lead contested and the sectionals 26.73, 50.48 and 1.14.35. The form is set around the third and eighth.

NOTEBOOK
Viscount Nelson(USA) was up against it last time on what was his first start since leaving Aidan O'Brien - he finished a 4l second to stablemate Mutahadee when conceding 10lb in a 1m1f handicap and that horse followed up with significant ease from 6lb higher. Back in Group company and down slightly in trip, he travelled well and found more off the bridle than has sometimes been the case. This exceptionally well-bred individual has looked something of an underachiever, but it's no surprise that Mike de Kock, who has done so well with other Ballydoyle cast-offs, seems to be getting the best from him, although interestingly he's only being leased to his current owners by team Coolmore.
Albaasil(IRE) was beaten narrowly into second off 104 on his recent Dubai debut, but he confirmed form with the close-up third from that race, Time Prisoner, on much worse terms, and it would surely be unwise to use him to hold the form down. He had progressed well in just a few runs for Sir Michael Stoute and evidently remains on the up.
Master Of Hounds(USA), back on turf and down in trip, travelled well but was short of room in the straight and just lacked the speed of the front two. The way he moved through the race suggests he's not one to give up on just yet, and you only need to look at the winner's profile to realise Mike de Kock knows how to get the best out of underachievers.
Derbaas(USA) won this last year but has yet to show his best this term.
Time Prisoner(USA) couldn't cope with the rise in class.
Rio De La Plata(USA), returning from a 102-day break with cheekpieces fitted, had a wide trip but basically just failed to fire.

591a RANGE ROVER TROPHY (H'CAP) (TURF) 1m 2f
5:30 (5:30) (100-119,119) 3-Y-O+
£67,741 (£22,580; £11,290; £5,645; £3,387; £2,258)

RPR
1 **Zanzamar (SAF)**[13] 416 5-8-10 109.............................(bt) RichardHills 9 114
(M F De Kock, South Africa) *in rr of mid-div: smooth prog 2 1/2f out: led fnl f: r.o wl* **20/1**
2 1 1/2 **Fallen Idol**[21] 319 5-8-9 108... WilliamBuick 11 110
(Saeed Bin Suroor) *in rr of mid-div: smooth prog 3f out: led 1 1/2f out: hdd fnl f* **7/1**[3]
3 3/4 **Al Shemali**[21] 319 8-8-5 102....................................(t) RoystonFfrench 4 105
(A Al Raihe, UAE) *mid-div: r.o fnl 1 1/2f: nrst fin* **7/1**[3]
4 1 **Shimraan (FR)**[138] 6558 5-9-6 119.. FrankieDettori 1 118
(Mahmood Al Zarooni) *mid-div: r.o fnl 2f: nrst fin* **3/1**[1]
5 hd **Rostrum (FR)**[21] 319 5-8-9 108.............................. MickaelBarzalona 16 106
(Mahmood Al Zarooni) *settled in rr: nvr able to chal* **16/1**
6 1/4 **Unusual Suspect (USA)**[107] 7218 8-9-0 112...............(v) RyanMoore 14 111
(Michael Kent, Australia) *settled in rr: r.o wl fnl 1 1/2f: nrst fin* **20/1**
7 3/4 **Trois Rois (FR)**[7] 484 7-8-5 104..................................(b) HarryBentley 3 100
(Ismail Mohammed) *slowly away: nvr able to chal* **33/1**
8 2 3/4 **Belgian Bill**[21] 317 4-8-5 104..(t) TedDurcan 8 96
(George Baker) *mid-div: smooth prog 2 1/2f out: led 1 1/2f out: sn hdd & wknd* **12/1**
9 1 3/4 **Quick Wit**[21] 319 5-8-6 105...................................... SilvestreDeSousa 6 92
(Saeed Bin Suroor) *trckd ldr tl wknd 3f out* **5/1**[2]
10 8 **Alrasm (IRE)**[27] 243 5-8-5 100... TadhgO'Shea 2 75
(E Charpy, UAE) *trckd ldrs tl wknd 3f out* **25/1**
11 2 3/4 **Dance And Dance (IRE)**[35] 144 6-8-11 110............. JamieSpencer 13 76
(Ed Vaughan) *settled in rr: nvr nr to chal* **10/1**
12 1 1/4 **Hot Six (BRZ)**[131] 6710 7-8-5 104.................................. MircoDemuro 7 67
(Fabricio Borges, Sweden) *Settled rr: n.d* **25/1**
13 2 1/2 **Sweet Ducky (USA)**[21] 315 4-8-7 104 ow2.....................(t) KUlubaev 10 65
(H J Brown, South Africa) *in rr of mid-div: nvr able to chal* **25/1**
14 6 1/4 **War Monger (USA)**[7] 489 8-8-5 101........................... RichardMullen 15 50
(Doug Watson, UAE) *trckd ldr: led 4f out: hdd 3f out* **33/1**
15 2 3/4 **Treble Jig (USA)**[20] 344 5-8-11 110.............................. WayneSmith 12 50
(M Al Muhairi, UAE) *sn led: hdd 4f out: sn wknd* **17/2**
2m 4.06s (124.06)
WFA 4 from 5yo+ 1lb **15** Ran SP% **126.8**
CSF: 150.02 TRICAST: 1,106.44. PLACEPOT: £922.00 to a £1 stake. Pool of £8,020.64 - 6.35 winning tickets. QUADPOT: £36.50 to a £1 stake. Pool of £919.30 - 18.60 winning tickets..
Owner Hamdan Al Maktoum **Bred** Danika Stud **Trained** South Africa

FOCUS
A race marred by runner-up Fallen Idol picking up what looked a serious injury. The quality of this handicap was good and they went a fair pace. Treble Jig took them along through the first half-mile at a fair pace, going 26.58 and 51.02, but he was soon beaten and the remaining fractions were cut out by War Monger, who went 1.15.11 and 1.39.91 before also dropping right away.

NOTEBOOK
Zanzamar(SAF) was well beaten in a 1m Tapeta handicap on his reappearance, but this time he was switched to turf and, perhaps crucially, a tongue-tie was added. He travelled well throughout and was back to his absolute best.
Fallen Idol sadly went badly wrong as he crossed the line.

Al Shemali reversed his reappearance form with Quick Wit and again showed enough to suggest he's handicapped to win.
Shimraan(FR) faced a tough task off 119 on his Dubai debut.
Rostrum(FR) doesn't look particularly well handicapped.

565 LINGFIELD (L-H)

Friday, February 17

OFFICIAL GOING: Standard

Wind: Moderate, behind Weather: Overcast

592 BET AT BLUE SQUARE APPRENTICE (S) STKS — 1m 4f (P)

1:45 (1:45) (Class 6) 4-Y-O+ — **£1,704** (£503; £251) **Stalls** Low

Form / RPR

-310 **1** **Ay Tay Tate (IRE)**[11] 452 6-9-10 65..............................(p) KieranO'Neill 3 70
(David C Griffiths) *mde all: set sedate pce: wnt 3 l clr 4f out: hrd rdn over 1f out: hld on u.p: all out* **7/2**[3]

02-1 **2** *1* **Eagle Nebula**[42] 57 8-9-3 68.................................... AccursioRomeo(7) 4 68
(Brett Johnson) *in tch: effrt and chsd wnr over 2f out: drvn to cl fnl f: a hld* **2/1**[2]

5032 **3** *½* **Kames Park (IRE)**[6] 535 10-9-5 69......................... CharlesEddery(5) 2 68
(Richard Guest) *dwlt: t.k.h in rr: effrt and wnt 3rd over 1f out: styd on: nt gng pce to rch wnr* **6/4**[1]

600- **4** *3¾* **Robby Bobby**[18] 7654 7-8-12 52.............................. CharlotteJenner(7) 1 57?
(Laura Mongan) *chsd ldrs tl outpcd fnl 2f* **33/1**

00/- **5** *6* **Cantabilly (IRE)**[17] 1756 9-9-2 55... RaulDaSilva(3) 6 47
(Ron Hodges) *chsd wnr tl wknd over 2f out* **9/1**

2m 34.83s (1.83) **Going Correction** 0.0s/f (Stan)
WFA 4 from 6yo+ 3lb — **5** Ran SP% **108.5**
Speed ratings (Par 101): **93,92,92,89,85**
CSF £10.57 TOTE £4.10: £1.50, £1.40; EX 10.40.The winner was bought in for 5,600gns
Owner Andrew Langan **Bred** Kelly's Vintage Partnership **Trained** Bawtry, S Yorks

FOCUS
A low-key start to the meeting and a reminder, were it needed, that the shape of the race can mean a whole lot more than handicap marks. It was slowly run and the form is shaky.

593 CYPRIUM BAR AT MARRIOTT LINGFIELD (S) STKS — 7f (P)

2:20 (2:20) (Class 6) 3-Y-O+ — **£1,704** (£503; £251) **Stalls** Low

Form / RPR

0023 **1** **Cyflymder (IRE)**[4] 550 6-9-8 60.. HayleyTurner 1 59
(David C Griffiths) *chsd clr ldr: clsd and rdn to take narrow ld jst ins fnl f: sn hdd: rallied to get up on line* **4/6**[1]

250- **2** *nse* **Catherines Call (IRE)**[316] 1200 5-9-3 75............................ LukeMorris 3 54
(Des Donovan) *hld up in 3rd: clsd w wnr ent fnl f: narrow ld 150yds out: hrd rdn: hdd on line* **15/8**[2]

1604 **3** *2¼* **Divine Rule (IRE)**[13] 422 4-9-7 53........................ CharlotteJenner(7) 5 59
(Laura Mongan) *led: sn 3 l clr: hdd & wknd ins fnl f* **16/1**

000- **4** *3¾* **Kyllachy Storm**[144] 6398 8-9-8 57.. GeorgeBaker 4 43
(Ron Hodges) *stdd s: t.k.h in rr: rdn over 1f out: no rspnse* **11/1**[3]

1m 24.24s (-0.56) **Going Correction** 0.0s/f (Stan) — **4** Ran SP% **109.0**
Speed ratings (Par 101): **103,102,100,96**
CSF £2.18 TOTE £1.80; EX 2.10.There was no bid for the winner.
Owner Steve Young **Bred** Miss Laura G F Ferguson **Trained** Bawtry, S Yorks

FOCUS
Another moderate seller and the form looks questionable. The winner did not need to match his recent efforts.

594 MIRROR PUNTERS CLUB H'CAP — 1m 5f (P)

2:50 (2:51) (Class 6) (0-65,65) 4-Y-O+ — **£1,704** (£503; £251) **Stalls** Low

Form / RPR

0401 **1** **El Libertador (USA)**[6] 530 6-9-2 57 6ex.........................(b) ShaneKelly 5 65
(Eric Wheeler) *hld up in rr: smooth hdwy on outer 3f out: drvn to ld over 1f out: all out* **11/2**

0/0- **2** *hd* **Henry San (IRE)**[32] 7236 5-9-10 65.................................. FergusSweeney 1 72
(Alan King) *trckd ldng pair: rdn to press wnr fnl f: kpt on wl nr fin* **9/4**[2]

-131 **3** *3½* **Maslak (IRE)**[14] 400 8-9-8 63... ChrisCatlin 2 65
(Peter Hiatt) *led: hrd rdn and hdd over 1f out: no ex* **5/4**[1]

23-1 **4** *hd* **Kishanda**[47] 1 4-9-4 63...(v) HayleyTurner 7 65
(Gay Kelleway) *chsd ldr tl ins fnl 2f: kpt on same pce* **5/1**[3]

6-00 **5** *2¼* **Perfect Shot (IRE)**[30] 202 6-9-8 63..................................(b) AmirQuinn 3 61
(Jim Best) *hld up in 5th: rdn and unable to chal fnl 2f* **14/1**

000- **6** *shd* **Bute Street**[109] 7195 7-8-13 54.................................... RichardKingscote 6 52
(Ron Hodges) *hld up in 4th: outpcd over 2f out: sn btn* **16/1**

0-46 **7** *5* **Vinces**[30] 200 8-8-5 51 oh6.......................................(p) RaulDaSilva(5) 4 42
(Tim McCarthy) *rrng bef stalls opened: t.k.h in 5th: rdn over 4f out: wknd 3f out* **16/1**

2m 48.5s (2.50) **Going Correction** 0.0s/f (Stan)
WFA 4 from 5yo+ 4lb — **7** Ran SP% **125.7**
Speed ratings (Par 101): **92,91,89,89,88 88,85**
toteswingers:1&2:£2.60, 1&3:£2.10, 2&3:£2.00 CSF £20.59 TOTE £5.20: £2.60, £2.10; EX 21.90.
Owner J L Day **Bred** Kingswood Farm **Trained** Lambourn, Berks

FOCUS
A moderate staying handicap. It was slowly run and the form is shaky. The winner is rated close to last winter's form.

595 BET AT BLUE SQUARE ON YOUR MOBILE MEDIAN AUCTION MAIDEN STKS — 1m 2f (P)

3:25 (3:27) (Class 6) 3-Y-O — **£1,704** (£503; £251) **Stalls** Low

Form / RPR

1 **Ed De Gas** 3-9-3 0.. ChrisCatlin 2 73+
(Rae Guest) *s.s: hld up in rr: gd hdwy to ld jst over 1f out: sn clr: readily* **33/1**

2 **2** *2* **Gabrial The Hero (USA)**[14] 399 3-9-3 0.............................. StevieDonohoe 7 69+
(David Simcock) *dwlt: plld hrd in 4th: chal and hung bdly rt 1f out: nt rcvr* **2/7**[1]

5 **3** *3¾* **Marmas**[14] 399 3-9-3 0... KieranO'Neill 8 61
(Marcus Tregoning) *hld up in 5th on outer: rdn 3f out: styd on same pce* **6/1**[3]

60 **4** *½* **Chronic Flame (TUR)**[6] 523 3-9-3 0.. HayleyTurner 3 60
(Marcus Tregoning) *prom tl no ex jst over 1f out* **11/2**[2]

00- **5** *1¼* **Run Of The Day**[130] 6742 3-8-12 0.. ShaneKelly 1 53
(Eve Johnson Houghton) *prom: drvn along and lost pl over 3f out: rallied on inner ent st: wknd fnl f* **50/1**

0-05 **6** *1½* **Masters Blazing**[18] 362 3-9-3 61.............................(p) TomMcLaughlin 5 55
(John Ryan) *led: rdn over 2f out: hdd & wknd jst over 1f out* **20/1**

0 **7** *35* **Khatella (IRE)**[6] 533 3-8-9 0... RyanPowell(3) 6
(John Flint) *dwlt: a in last pair: rdn 4f out: lost tch 3f out* **100/1**

2m 6.85s (0.25) **Going Correction** 0.0s/f (Stan) — **7** Ran SP% **118.1**
Speed ratings (Par 95): **99,97,94,94,93 91,63**
toteswingers:1&2:£4.40, 1&3:£8.00, 2&3:£1.50 CSF £45.79 TOTE £22.40: £10.20, £1.10; EX 40.40 Trifecta £317.60 Pool: £528.05 - 1.23 winning units..
Owner Can Artam **Bred** Canartam Ltd **Trained** Newmarket, Suffolk

FOCUS
A moderate and uncompetitive maiden in which odds-on backers got their fingers burnt. It was a muddling race and there were doubts over the bare form.

596 FOLLOW US ON TWITTER @LINGFIELDPARK H'CAP — 1m (P)

4:00 (4:00) (Class 4) (0-85,84) 3-Y-O — **£4,204** (£1,251; £625; £312) **Stalls** High

Form / RPR

1-31 **1** **Shabora (IRE)**[14] 398 3-9-4 84...................................... DominicFox(3) 4 92+
(Roger Varian) *dwlt: hdwy over 4f out: led 3f out: rdn 2 l clr 1f out: jst hld on* **9/2**[2]

11-1 **2** *nk* **Karma Chameleon**[32] 193 3-8-13 76................................... ShaneKelly 5 83+
(John Berry) *hld up in 6th: hdwy over 1f out: hrd rdn and r.o wl fnl f: clsng on wnr at fin* **5/1**[3]

64-1 **3** *1½* **Switzerland (IRE)**[34] 181 3-9-1 83................................ DarylByrne(5) 6 87
(Mark Johnston) *prom: led 6f out tl 3f out: kpt on same pce appr fnl f* **5/4**[1]

060- **4** *2½* **Santadelacruze**[59] 7835 3-8-6 69.. NickyMackay 7 67
(Gary Moore) *hld up in rr: pushed along and r.o fnl 2f: nrst fin* **66/1**

05-1 **5** *nk* **Dubai Sunshine (IRE)**[17] 369 3-9-5 82.......................... HayleyTurner 2 79
(Michael Bell) *t.k.h: trckd ldrs: rdn over 2f out: one pce* **13/2**

1-3 **6** *½* **Moderator**[14] 398 3-9-1 78.. FergusSweeney 3 74
(Gary Moore) *hld up in rr: pushed along and hdwy on outer 3f out: wknd 2f out* **12/1**

0-1 **7** *7* **Flash Crash**[42] 56 3-8-7 70.. JohnFahy 1 50
(Robert Cowell) *dwlt: hdwy to ld after 1f: hdd 6f out: wknd over 2f out* **9/1**

1m 37.7s (-0.50) **Going Correction** 0.0s/f (Stan) — **7** Ran SP% **111.8**
Speed ratings (Par 99): **102,101,100,97,97 96,89**
toteswingers:1&2:£2.90, 1&3:£1.90, 2&3:£2.50 CSF £25.72 CT £42.58 TOTE £5.30: £3.60, £1.90; EX 22.60 Trifecta £52.90 Pool: £761.95 - 10.64 winning units..
Owner Sheikh Ahmed Al Maktoum **Bred** Darley **Trained** Newmarket, Suffolk

FOCUS
The best race on the card by a long way with five of the seven runners last-time-out winners. The pace didn't really pick up until after about 3f, but the form still looks solid for the grade. The winner is progressing nicely.

597 GOLF MEMBERSHIP AT MARRIOTT LINGFIELD MAIDEN STKS — 6f (P)

4:35 (4:35) (Class 5) 3-Y-O+ — **£2,385** (£704; £352) **Stalls** Low

Form / RPR

0- **1** **Equation Of Time**[74] 7634 3-8-11 .... MartinLane 4 76
(David Flood) *stdd s: hld up in 5th: wd into st: hdwy over 1f out: led ins fnl f: rdn clr* **12/1**

3-22 **2** *2¾* **Derivatives (IRE)**[10] 457 3-8-6 70.................................. NickyMackay 8 63
(John Gosden) *prom: led 3f out tl ins fnl f: nt qckn* **1/1**[1]

064- **3** *3* **Conowen**[139] 6525 3-8-11 68... ShaneKelly 3 58
(William Jarvis) *chsd ldrs: effrt 2f out: no ex fnl f* **7/2**[3]

032- **4** *½* **Heartsong (IRE)**[189] 5017 3-8-6 67.................................... HayleyTurner 2 51
(John Gallagher) *led tl 3f out: wknd jst over 1f out* **11/4**[2]

50- **5** *shd* **Jane Lachatte (IRE)**[71] 7672 3-8-6 .... ChrisCatlin 7 51
(Stuart Williams) *dwlt: outpcd in rr: styd on fnl f* **33/1**

0-0 **6** *1* **Yalding Dancer**[22] 308 3-8-6 .... RichardThomas 6 48
(John Best) *stdd s: hld up in 6th: rdn 3f out: effrt on inner ent st: wknd over 1f out* **66/1**

6- **7** *1¼* **Elavssom (IRE)**[168] 5672 3-8-11 .... StevieDonohoe 1 49
(Jo Hughes) *outpcd: a in rr: lost tch 3f out* **20/1**

0 **8** *7* **Just Me'Lady**[36] 135 3-8-0 ow1.. JakePayne(7) 5 22
(Bill Turner) *trckd ldrs tl 3f out tl hung rt and wknd qckly 2f out* **66/1**

1m 11.19s (-0.71) **Going Correction** 0.0s/f (Stan) — **8** Ran SP% **117.3**
Speed ratings (Par 103): **104,100,96,95,95 94,92,83**
toteswingers:1&2:£4.70, 1&3:£6.30, 2&3:£1.30 CSF £25.06 TOTE £36.20: £4.30, £1.20, £1.10; EX 56.60 Trifecta £527.50 Part won. Pool: £712.87 - 1.23 winning units..
Owner Laurence Mann **Bred** Jenny Hall Bloodstock Ltd **Trained** Exning, Suffolk

FOCUS
Another modest maiden and a contested lead.
Just Me'Lady Official explanation: jockey said filly hung right on bends

598 PLAY RAINBOW RICHES AT BLUESQ.COM H'CAP — 7f (P)

5:05 (5:05) (Class 6) (0-60,60) 4-Y-O+ — **£1,704** (£503; £251) **Stalls** Low

Form / RPR

6064 **1** **Efistorm**[4] 550 11-9-7 60.. HayleyTurner 4 69
(Conor Dore) *chsd ldrs: rdn to ld 1f out: hld on wl nr fin: all out* **9/2**[3]

3214 **2** *hd* **Do More Business (IRE)**[6] 522 5-8-13 52......................(v) IanMongan 1 60
(Pat Phelan) *patiently rdn in rr: shkn up and hdwy over 1f out: rdn to chal ins fnl f: jst hld* **4/1**[2]

-455 **3** *3* **Cristaliyev**[13] 422 4-9-6 59.......................................(b) GeorgeBaker 6 59
(Jim Boyle) *trckd ldrs: rdn over 1f out: one pce fnl f* **7/2**[1]

00-0 **4** *hd* **Smoky Cloud (IRE)**[37] 123 5-9-7 60...........................(p) TomMcLaughlin 7 60
(Amy Weaver) *led tl 3f out: led again 2f out tl 1f out: no ex* **9/2**[3]

06-0 **5** *2¼* **Grand Honour (IRE)**[30] 203 6-8-10 49 oh1 ow3...............(p) ShaneKelly 2 43
(Paul Howling) *towards rr: drvn and sme hdwy fnl 2f: nvr rchd ldrs* **12/1**

5602 **6** *3¼* **Putin (IRE)**[7] 490 4-8-4 48...(bt) LauraPike(5) 3 33
(Phil McEntee) *awkward s: bmpd and hdwy 5f out: led 3f out tl 2f out: wknd over 1f out* **8/1**

-040 **7** *1¼* **Captainrisk (IRE)**[13] 424 6-9-5 58......................................(v) MartinLane 9 40
(Christine Dunnett) *chsd ldrs tl wknd over 2f out: btn whn hung rt fnl bnd* **16/1**

06-3 **8** *shd* **Saucy Buck (IRE)**[13] 422 4-9-7 60..............................(b) RobertHavlin 8 41
(Jamie Poulton) *t.k.h: towards rr and nt handling bnd after 2f: drvn along and btn whn rn wd fnl bnd* **9/2**[3]

1m 24.46s (-0.34) **Going Correction** 0.0s/f (Stan) — **8** Ran SP% **121.5**
Speed ratings (Par 101): **101,100,97,97,94 90,89,89**
toteswingers:1&2:£3.00, 1&3:£3.80, 2&3:£3.60 CSF £24.46 CT £72.73 TOTE £5.80: £1.10, £2.30, £1.30; EX 19.70 Trifecta £87.50 Pool: £693.61 - 5.86 winning units..
Owner Sean J Murphy **Bred** E Duggan And D Churchman **Trained** Hubbert's Bridge, Lincs

FOCUS
A moderate handicap, but despite a disputed lead the pair with the most stamina doubts fought out the finish. The winner is rated to his winter best.
T/Plt: £53.30 to a £1 stake. Pool:£39,413.58 - 539.33 winning tickets T/Qpdt: £11.20 to a £1 stake. Pool:£4,148.90 - 272.95 winning tickets LM

544 WOLVERHAMPTON (A.W) (L-H)

Friday, February 17

OFFICIAL GOING: Standard

Wind: Fresh, behind Weather: Overcast

599 BET AT BLUE SQUARE H'CAP 5f 20y(P)

5:15 (5:15) (Class 6) (0-60,60) 3-Y-O **£1,704** (£503; £251) **Stalls** Low

Form RPR

3-53 **1** **Wild Sauce**21 [326] 3-9-5 **58**......(b1) TomEaves 2 65
(Bryan Smart) *mde all: shkn up and edgd rt over 1f out: rdn ins fnl f: sn hung lft: all out* **5/21**

00-5 **2** *hd* **Chateau Lola**10 [455] 3-8-7 **46** oh1......(v) JoeFanning 1 52
(Derek Shaw) *chsd ldrs: pushed along 1/2-way: rdn to chse wnr fnl f: sn ev ch: r.o* **40/1**

000- **3** *1* **My Name Is Sam**78 [7593] 3-8-1 **47**...... DarrenEgan(7) 5 49
(Ronald Harris) *hld up: rdn 1/2-way: r.o wl ins fnl f: nt rch ldrs* **5/1**

-242 **4** *nk* **Magilini (IRE)**10 [455] 3-8-6 **50**......(b) DeanHeslop(5) 3 51
(David Barron) *wnt rt s: chsd wnr tl rdn over 1f out: styd on same pce ins fnl f* **4/13**

03-0 **5** *½* **Tuibama (IRE)**10 [455] 3-9-2 **55**...... PhillipMakin 6 54
(Ben Haslam) *hld up: hdwy u.p over 1f out: styd on* **16/1**

4-61 **6** *3¼* **Tiablo (IRE)**18 [357] 3-9-4 **60**...... RichardEvans(3) 4 47
(David Evans) *pushed along in rr early: hdwy 3f out: rdn over 1f out: no ex ins fnl f* **3/12**

53-2 **7** *19* **Rooknrasbryripple**9 [469] 3-8-10 **56**...... PhoebeCruse(7) 7
(Ralph Smith) *s.v.s: a wl bhd* **7/1**

1m 2.73s (0.43) **Going Correction** +0.225s/f (Slow) 7 Ran SP% **111.1**
Speed ratings (Par 95): **105,104,103,102,101 96,66**
toteswingers: 1&2 £7.70, 1&3 £2.80, 2&3 £19.70 CSF £81.17 CT £448.77 TOTE £5.40: £2.50, £7.10; EX 63.30.

Owner Richard Page **Bred** Ashbrittle Stud **Trained** Hambleton, N Yorks

FOCUS
The well-backed favourite put in a gritty display to hold off an outsider in this modest handicap. It was run in a fair time and the form looks sound.

600 WOLVERHAMPTON HOSPITALITY - A PLEASURE H'CAP 1m 5f 194y(P)

5:45 (5:46) (Class 6) (0-65,65) 4-Y-O+ **£1,704** (£503; £251) **Stalls** Low

Form RPR

-113 **1** **Magic Millie (IRE)**7 [493] 5-9-2 **60**...... AmyScott(5) 9 69
(Alastair Lidderdale) *chsd ldrs: rdn to ld ins fnl f: r.o* **9/23**

403- **2** *1¼* **Lakota Ghost (USA)**41 [7263] 4-9-1 **59**...... LukeMorris 2 66
(Seamus Durack) *a.p: chsd ldr over 3f out: rdn over 2f out: styd on* **3/12**

41-0 **3** *1½* **Dream Catcher (SWE)**36 [129] 9-9-10 **63**......(p) JoeFanning 1 68
(Jonjo O'Neill) *led: rdn over 1f out: hdd and unable qck ins fnl f*

06-0 **4** *4* **Redhotdoc**7 [500] 8-9-4 **64**...... MatthewMcGhee(7) 4 63
(Bill Moore) *s.i.s: hld up: hdwy over 2f out: nvr trbld ldrs* **12/1**

0004 **5** *10* **Nesnaas (USA)**11 [446] 11-8-0 **46** oh1...... NicoleNordblad(7) 6 31
(Alastair Lidderdale) *hld up: rdn over 2f out: n.d* **20/1**

00-0 **6** *3½* **Angelena Ballerina (IRE)**8 [480] 5-9-7 **63**...... NataliaGemelova(3) 3 44
(Dai Williams) *hld up: rdn over 3f out: wknd over 2f out* **66/1**

265- **7** *1½* **Amir Pasha (UAE)**28 [6155] 7-9-4 **64**......(p) KatieDowson(7) 7 42
(Micky Hammond) *chsd ldr tl pushed along over 2f out: wknd over 2f out* **20/1**

P-03 **8** *4* **War Of The Roses (IRE)**11 [452] 9-9-12 **65**...... TomEaves 8 38
(Roy Brotherton) *prom: rdn over 2f out: wknd over 1f out* **11/41**

0/ **9** *6* **Chaninbar (FR)**96 [162] 9-9-7 **60**...... StephenCraine 5 24
(Brendan Powell) *rel to r: a bhd: t.o* **11/1**

3m 6.61s (0.61) **Going Correction** +0.225s/f (Slow)
WFA 4 from 5yo+ 5lb 9 Ran SP% **115.1**
Speed ratings (Par 101): **107,106,105,103,97 95,94,92,88**
toteswingers:1&2:£3.40, 1&3:£3.30, 2&3:£3.30 CSF £17.91 CT £63.64 TOTE £6.90: £2.10, £1.20, £2.00; EX 22.60.

Owner Chris Beek Racing **Bred** John C Little **Trained** Lambourn, Berks

FOCUS
A low-grade staying handicap. It was run at a stop-start gallop and they finished well strung out behind the clear front three. The winner proved herself as good on Polytrack as Fibresand, and the second and third were close to their marks.

War Of The Roses(IRE) Official explanation: trainer said gelding lost its action behind

601 BET AT BLUE SQUARE ON YOUR MOBILE H'CAP 1m 4f 50y(P)

6:15 (6:15) (Class 4) (0-85,85) 4-Y-O+ **£4,204** (£1,251; £625; £312) **Stalls** Low

Form RPR

0-34 **1** **Brunston**13 [427] 6-9-7 **80**...... LukeMorris 5 91
(Brendan Powell) *hld up: hdwy over 3f out: rdn and hung lft 2f out: led ins fnl f: styd on wl* **11/13**

11 **2** *3¾* **Queen Of Denmark (USA)**7 [501] 4-9-9 **85** 6ex...... JoeFanning 6 91
(Mark Johnston) *a.p: chsd ldr over 3f out: led 2f out: sn rdn: hdd and no ex ins fnl f* **8/111**

-213 **3** *3¼* **Boa**6 [535] 7-8-11 **73**...... AmyRyan(3) 4 73
(Reg Hollinshead) *chsd ldr tl led 5f out: rdn and hdd 2f out: wknd ins fnl f* **20/1**

40-1 **4** *nse* **Accumulate**7 [500] 9-9-3 **76** 6ex......(p) AdamKirby 1 76
(Bill Moore) *chsd ldrs: outpcd over 3f out: styd on ins fnl f* **3/12**

-232 **5** *2¾* **Shabak Hom (IRE)**14 [402] 5-8-8 **72**...... MatthewCosham(5) 2 67
(David Evans) *hld up: pushed along 7f out: hdwy over 3f out: rdn and wknd 2f out* **25/1**

443- **6** *21* **Pertemps Networks**70 [7699] 8-9-4 **77**...... JamesSullivan 3 39
(Michael Easterby) *led 7f: rdn over 3f out: wknd over 2f out* **12/1**

2m 39.99s (-1.11) **Going Correction** +0.225s/f (Slow)
WFA 4 from 5yo+ 3lb 6 Ran SP% **107.5**
Speed ratings (Par 105): **112,109,107,107,105 91**
toteswingers:1&2:£2.00, 1&3:£4.40, 2&3:£3.40 CSF £18.14 TOTE £9.80: £3.40, £1.30; EX 21.90.

Owner Paul Frank Barry **Bred** Seasons Holidays **Trained** Upper Lambourn, Berks

FOCUS
A decent handicap. It was run at a fair pace and a revitalised runner forged clear from the unexposed hot favourite. The winner is rated back close to his old form.

Shabak Hom(IRE) Official explanation: jockey said gelding hung right-handed throughout

602 WOLVERHAMPTON HOLIDAY INN H'CAP 1m 4f 50y(P)

6:45 (6:45) (Class 7) (0-50,50) 4-Y-O+ **£1,704** (£503; £251) **Stalls** Low

Form RPR

0/0- **1** **Den Maschine**68 [5832] 7-9-2 **49**...... AdamKirby 6 65+
(Paul Rich) *a.p: chsd ldr over 3f out: led over 2f out: sn rdn clr: eased nr fin* **11/22**

203- **2** *5* **Easydoesit (IRE)**34 [6585] 4-8-2 **45**...... DarrenEgan(7) 2 52+
(Tony Carroll) *hld up: hdwy u.p over 1f out: wnt 2nd ins fnl f: no ch w wnr* **10/1**

3-21 **3** *1½* **Mayan Flight (IRE)**30 [200] 4-9-0 **50**...... DavidProbert 8 54
(Tony Carroll) *hld up in tch: rdn over 2f out: styd on same pce fr over 1f out* **11/81**

4200 **4** *nk* **Yossi (IRE)**10 [453] 8-8-9 **47**......(p) CharlesEddery(5) 7 51
(Richard Guest) *s.i.s: hld up: hdwy over 2f out: rdn over 1f out: styd on same pce* **25/1**

00-2 **5** *5* **Sacco D'Oro**10 [465] 6-9-0 **47**...... JoeFanning 12 43
(Michael Mullineaux) *hld up: hdwy over 4f out: rdn and wknd over 1f out* **18/1**

4450 **6** *½* **Grecian Goddess (IRE)**6 [530] 4-8-11 **50**...... MichaelO'Connell(3) 10 45
(John Ryan) *chsd ldrs: led over 3f out: rdn and hdd over 2f out: wknd fnl f* **16/1**

2-63 **7** *1¾* **Imperial Fong**6 [530] 4-8-11 **50**...... RyanClark(3) 1 42
(Chris Dwyer) *plld hrd and prom: rdn over 2f out: wknd over 1f out* **13/23**

24-6 **8** *2¾* **Red Flash (IRE)**17 [66] 5-9-0 **47**...... WilliamCarson 5 35
(David Bridgwater) *hld up: rdn over 3f out: wknd over 2f out* **12/1**

5-50 **9** *¾* **Rapturous Applause**15 [389] 4-9-0 **50**...... FrederikTylicki 4 37
(Micky Hammond) *hld up: plld hrd: a in rr: rdn and wknd over 2f out* **28/1**

000- **10** *8* **Without Equal**11 [7078] 6-9-1 **48**......(p) PJMcDonald 9 22
(Martin Todhunter) *s.i.s: hdwy to chse ldr over 9f out: led over 4f out: hdd over 3f out: sn rdn and wknd* **66/1**

050- **11** *½* **Josephine Malines**196 [3910] 8-8-7 **45**...... MatthewCosham(5) 3 18
(Richard Price) *led: hdd over 4f out: rdn and wknd over 2f out* **33/1**

40-0 **12** *4½* **Laura Land**10 [454] 6-8-13 **46**...... LukeMorris 11 12
(Mark Brisbourne) *dwlt: hld up: rdn over 3f out: sn wknd* **20/1**

2m 44.71s (3.61) **Going Correction** +0.225s/f (Slow)
WFA 4 from 5yo+ 3lb 12 Ran SP% **115.2**
Speed ratings (Par 97): **96,92,91,91,88 87,86,84,84,78 78,75**
toteswingers: 1&2 £9.00, 1&3 £1.80, 2&3 £3.30 CSF £53.60 CT £115.86 TOTE £7.00: £1.90, £2.30, £1.70; EX 65.20.

Owner Paul Morgan **Bred** York Stut & Stald Rainbow **Trained** Newport, Gwent

FOCUS
There was an emphatic winner of this steadily run handicap. It was no fluke and this rates a clear personal best on the Flat.

603 MIRROR PUNTERS CLUB CLAIMING STKS 1m 1f 103y(P)

7:15 (7:15) (Class 5) 4-Y-O+ **£2,264** (£673) **Stalls** Low

Form RPR

5262 **1** **Standpoint**4 [548] 6-8-11 79......(p) AmyRyan(3) 3 74+
(Reg Hollinshead) *mde all: set stdy pce tl qcknd over 2f out: shkn up over 1f out: styd on* **1/81**

4105 **2** *1¾* **Petomic (IRE)**11 [449] 7-8-7 60......(p) WilliamCarson 2 63
(Richard Guest) *chsd wnr: rdn over 2f out: edgd lft over 1f out: eased whn hld nr fin* **11/22**

2m 8.69s (6.99) **Going Correction** +0.225s/f (Slow) 2 Ran SP% **104.3**
Speed ratings (Par 103): **77,75**
TOTE £1.20.

Owner Moores Metals Ltd **Bred** Juddmonte Farms Ltd **Trained** Upper Longdon, Staffs

FOCUS
Just two runners lined-up in this claimer and the hot favourite made all in workmanlike style to improve his strike-rate to 3-39. Unconvincing form.

604 HOTEL & CONFERENCING AT WOLVERHAMPTON MAIDEN FILLIES' STKS 7f 32y(P)

7:45 (7:48) (Class 5) 3-Y-O+ **£2,264** (£673; £336; £168) **Stalls** High

Form RPR

1 **Rosby Waves (USA)** 3-8-7 0...... JoeFanning 7 70+
(Mark Johnston) *led 6f out: rdn and hung lft over 1f out: styd on* **3/11**

0- **2** *1¾* **Tooley Woods (IRE)**273 [2254] 3-8-7 0...... DavidProbert 5 64
(George Margarson) *a.p: chsd wnr 1/2-way: rdn and hung lft over 1f out: styd on same pce ins fnl f* **12/13**

0-4 **3** *3¼* **Moorside Magic**18 [358] 3-8-7 0...... PatrickMathers 4 55
(Richard Fahey) *led 1f: chsd wnr to 1/2-way: sn pushed along: rdn and swtchd rt over 1f out: no ex fnl f* **8/12**

4 *4* **Valiant Bee** 4-9-10 0...... AdamKirby 3 50
(Bill Moore) *prom: rdn over 2f out: wknd over 1f out* **22/1**

5 *14* **Chocolate Pursuits** 3-8-7 0...... RichardKingscote 6 22
(Tom Dascombe) *s.s: a in rr: wknd over 2f out* **12/13**

1m 32.59s (2.99) **Going Correction** +0.225s/f (Slow)
WFA 3 from 4yo 17lb 5 Ran SP% **55.8**
Speed ratings (Par 100): **91,89,85,80,64**
toteswinger: 1&2 £5.80 CSF £7.88 TOTE £3.70: £2.20, £1.02; EX 14.10.

Owner Sheikh Hamdan Bin Mohammed Al Maktoum **Bred** Darley **Trained** Middleham Moor, N Yorks

FOCUS
The hot favourite Infortual gave trouble at the start and refused to enter the stalls (4/5F, deduct 55p in the £ under R4). That left the way clear for a well-bred Mark Johnston-trained newcomer to dominate this minor maiden. It was steadily run and there is not much form to go on.

605 PLAY RAINBOW RICHES AT BLUESQ.COM H'CAP 7f 32y(P)

8:15 (8:16) (Class 5) (0-75,72) 3-Y-O **£2,264** (£505; £505; £168) **Stalls** High

Form RPR

-501 **1** **Homeward Strut**14 [407] 3-8-2 **58** oh6......(b) RaulDaSilva(5) 4 62
(Frank Sheridan) *a.p: led ins fnl f: rdn out* **5/1**

-131 **2** *½* **Speedy Yaki (IRE)**6 [536] 3-9-6 **71** 6ex......(t) StephenCraine 1 74
(Daniel Mark Loughnane) *hld up: hdwy over 1f out: rdn and ev ch ins fnl f: r.o* **5/22**

326 **2** *dht* **Henry Bee**15 [383] 3-9-6 **71**...... TonyHamilton 5 74
(Richard Fahey) *chsd ldr: led over 1f out: rdn and hdd ins fnl f: r.o* **4/13**

0-04 **4** *1¾* **Jawking**20 [352] 3-8-4 **60**...... MatthewCosham(5) 3 58
(David Evans) *led: rdn and hdd over 1f out: no ex ins fnl f* **16/1**

5-21 **5** 4 ½ **Somemothersdohavem**[18] 358 3-9-4 **72**.................... RyanPowell(3) 2 58
(John Ryan) *reluctant to go on to the crse and difficult to load into the stalls: hld up: rdn over 2f out: nt run on* **6/4**[1]

1m 32.12s (2.52) **Going Correction** +0.225s/f (Slow) **5** Ran SP% **111.1**
Speed ratings (Par 97): **94,93,93,91,86**
PL: HB £1.40, SY £0.90; EX: HS-HB £8.50, HS-SY £7.60; CSF: HS-HB £12.19, HS-SY £8.93; toteswingers: HS-HB £3.50, HS-SY £4.10 TOTE £4.80: £1.80.
Owner Mersey Racing, Bolingbroke Racing **Bred** Mickley Stud **Trained** Wolverhampton, W Midlands

FOCUS
There was a tight finish in this competitive handicap which involved three last-time-out winners. It was steadily run and the form might not prove all that solid, but there was no fluke about the winner.
Somemothersdohavem Official explanation: jockey said gelding never travelled
T/Plt: £19.30 to a £1 stake. Pool: £72,059.02. 2,713.59 winning tickets. T/Qpdt: £2.30 to a £1 stake. Pool: £7,768.65. 2,441.86 winning tickets. CR

606 - 615a (Foreign Racing) - See Raceform Interactive

586 MEYDAN (L-H)
Friday, February 17

OFFICIAL GOING: Tapeta - standard; turf - good

616a S O G LOGISTICS (H'CAP) (TAPETA) 7f
1:20 (1:20) (80-98,98) 3-Y-O+

£6,451 (£6,451; £1,612; £806; £483; £322)

RPR

1 **Tertio Bloom (SWE)**[22] 314 7-9-6 **98**................(t) Per-AndersGraberg 8 102
(Fabricio Borges, Sweden) *in rr of mid-div: rdn 3f out: led 1f out: jnd on line* **14/1**

1 *dht* **Capital Attraction (USA)**[28] 242 5-9-4 **96**.................. MircoDemuro 7 100
(Ernst Oertel, UAE) *mid-div: rdn 2 1/2f out: r.o wl fnl 1 1/2f: forced dead heat on line* **12/1**

3 ½ **Cinderkamp**[26] 4-9-1 **93**.. TedDurcan 11 96
(Doug Watson, UAE) *s.i.s: smooth prog 2 1/2f out: r.o wl fnl 1 1/2f: jst failed* **6/1**[2]

4 2 ¼ **Kaiss (USA)**[21] 344 5-9-1 **93**......................................(t) RichardMullen 9 90
(S Seemar, UAE) *in rr of mid-div: r.o fnl 2f: nrst fin* **25/1**

5 ¾ **Fityaan**[26] 4-9-0 **91**... RichardHills 5 87
(M Al Muhairi, UAE) *trckd ldr: led 2 1/2f out: hdd 1f out: no ex* **6/1**[2]

6 1 ½ **Hajoum (IRE)**[14] 420 6-9-3 **95**..............................(vt) RoystonFfrench 14 86
(A Al Raihe, UAE) *nvr bttr than mid-div* **16/1**

7 1 ¼ **Firestreak**[27] 260 7-9-6 **98**.......................................(t) WayneSmith 10 85
(M Al Muhairi, UAE) *trckd ldng pair: ev ch 3f: nt qckn fnl 1 1/2f* **9/1**

8 *hd* **Shamekh (GER)**[27] 259 4-8-11 **89**.............................. HarryBentley 12 76
(M Al Muhairi, UAE) *in rr of mid-div: n.d* **14/1**

9 *hd* **Bravo Echo**[27] 261 6-9-5 **97**.............................. SilvestreDeSousa 2 83
(Michael Attwater) *sn led: hdd 2 1/2f out: sn wknd* **16/1**

10 2 ¼ **Munaddam (USA)**[7] 513 10-9-6 **98**.............................. TadhgO'Shea 6 78
(E Charpy, UAE) *in rr of mid-div: n.d* **20/1**

11 ¾ **Spirit Of Sharjah (IRE)**[22] 317 7-9-6 **98**...................... RyanMoore 13 76
(Julia Feilden) *settled in rr: nvr nr to chal* **8/1**[3]

12 ¼ **Les Troyens**[42] 80 4-9-5 **97**.................................... MickaelBarzalona 3 74
(Saeed Bin Suroor) *nvr bttr than mid-div* **8/1**[3]

13 4 **League Champion (USA)**[7] 513 9-8-13 **90**...................... CSanchez 1 57
(M Ramadan, UAE) *chsd ldrs tl 4f out: sn wknd* **33/1**

14 1 ¾ **Al Aasifh (IRE)**[27] 261 4-9-6 **98**.............................. FrankieDettori 4 60
(Saeed Bin Suroor) *in rr of mid-div: nvr able to chal* **9/2**[1]

1m 24.8s (-0.40) **14** Ran SP% **123.3**
CSF: Tertio Bloom & Capital Attraction 86.26, CA & TB 85.02; TRICAST: TB/CA/C 567.36, CA/TB/C 562.40..
Owner H E Sheikh Sultan Bin Khalifa Al Nahyan **Bred** WinStar Farm LLC **Trained** United Arab Emirates
Owner Stall In Bloom **Bred** Triple Crown Bloomers Ab & Peter Frisk **Trained** Sweden

FOCUS
A dead heat in this ordinary handicap, in which the pace was a bit too strong. Bravo Echo took them along through the first half-mile, going 24.99 and 47.50, and Fityaan was in front when clocking 1.11.77 at the 6f point, but those last two sectionals were significantly quicker than in the earlier maiden, and the final time was 0.63 seconds faster.

NOTEBOOK
Tertio Bloom(SWE), a regular winner in Sweden, was helped by a better draw than on his first two starts in Dubai, but much of his form has come over shorter and he only just got the trip.
Capital Attraction(USA) was suited by this drop in distance after bizarrely trying 1m2f in good company last time, and this was a useful performance from 6lb higher than when winning over C&D two starts previously.
Cinderkamp, up 5lb for winning over 6f at Abu Dhabi, was sensibly dropped in from his wide stall, with the trip was a question mark. He was arguably a bit unlucky as he had to wait for a run at the top of the straight before finishing well from a long way back.
Kaiss(USA) stepped up significantly on his recent form.
Fityaan, just behind Cinderkamp last time, wasn't good enough.
Hajoum(IRE) ◆ probably isn't straightforward, but he was better than the bare result when winning over 6f here two starts previously (subsequently outclassed in Group 3) and this time, drawn widest, covered more ground than any of his rivals.
Al Aasifh(IRE) ran as though something was wrong.

617a BALANCHINE SPONSORED BY S O G OPERATIONS (GROUP 2) (F&M) (TURF) 1m 1f
1:55 (1:55) 3-Y-O

£77,419 (£25,806; £12,903; £6,451; £3,870; £2,580)

RPR

1 **Mahbooba (AUS)**[28] 245 5-9-0 113.................. ChristopheSoumillon 10 113+
(M F De Kock, South Africa) *mid-div: rdn 2 1/2f out: r.o wl fnl 1 1/2f: led 100yds out: comf* **8/11**[1]

2 2 ½ **First City**[28] 245 6-9-3 110.. RoystonFfrench 8 110
(A Al Raihe, UAE) *trckd ldng pair: led 1 1/2f out: hdd fnl 100yds: no ex* **9/2**[2]

3 ¼ **Reem (AUS)**[14] 416 5-9-0 100.. KShea 9 106
(M F De Kock, South Africa) *trckd ldr: led 5f out: hdd 1 1/2f out: kpt on same pce* **16/1**

4 2 ½ **Al Sharood**[28] 245 4-9-0 98.. TadhgO'Shea 3 101
(Doug Watson, UAE) *sn led: hdd 5f out: kpt on same pce* **33/1**

5 3 **Rhythm Of Light**[28] 245 4-9-0 107.............................. KierenFallon 6 95
(Tom Dascombe) *slowly away: settled in last: nvr a threat* **12/1**

6 1 **Hurricane Havoc (IRE)**[28] 245 4-9-0 100................(bt) KevinManning 4 93
(J S Bolger, Ire) *nvr bttr than mid-div* **20/1**

7 1 ¾ **Fanditha (IRE)**[28] 242 6-9-0 99.. TedDurcan 5 89
(Mick Channon) *settled in rr: hrd rdn 4 1/2f out: n.d* **50/1**

8 *nse* **Dysphonia (AUS)**[111] 6-9-0 112....................................(p) FrankieDettori 2 89
(Saeed Bin Suroor) *s.i.s: settled in rr: nvr able to chal* **5/1**[3]

9 2 ½ **Grafitti**[159] 5982 7-9-0 102.......................................(t) Per-AndersGraberg 7 84
(Niels Petersen, Norway) *settled in rr: rdn 4f out: n.d* **28/1**

10 8 **Marvada (IRE)**[28] 245 4-9-0 102.............................. SilvestreDeSousa 1 67
(K J Condon, Ire) *nvr bttr than mid-div* **33/1**

1m 50.27s (110.27) **10** Ran SP% **122.4**
CSF: 4.25.
Owner Sheikh Mohammed Bin Khalifa Al Maktoum **Bred** Sheikh Mohammed Bin Khalifa Al Maktoum **Trained** South Africa

FOCUS
A weak Group 2 in which Mahbooba reversed Cape Verdi form with First City and gained a clear-cut success, despite having a tough trip and looking uncomfortable under pressure. The gallop seemed okay judging by the sectionals (26.50, 49.07, 1.12.61 and 1.37.14), but the trio who finished directly behind the winner had filled the first three positions for most of the way and Mahbooba was the only runner to make up significant ground.

NOTEBOOK
Mahbooba(AUS) was unsuited by the pace, covered more ground than any of her rivals (according to Trakus) and also hung once under pressure. While clearly better than the bare result, it was an ugly performance - she needed a hard ride to be straightened up and go through with her effort - and it doesn't say much for the others that she was able to win. She also had a hard time on her previous start and might be best watched for now, especially as there is no opportunity for her to compete solely against her own sex for the remainder of the Carnival.
First City was always going to struggle to confirm form with Mahbooba over this extra furlong. Her head carriage was again a bit high at times and she wasn't at her best.
Reem(AUS) is not really up to this level.
Al Sharood may have found the trip stretching her. She has to be worth another try on an artificial surface considering her sire's record with his runners on non-turf tracks and that she's won both her starts off the grass.
Rhythm Of Light was held up last after missing the break and the pace scenario gave her no hope, but even so she's not at her best at the moment.
Dysphonia(AUS) improved to quite a smart level in Australia, but ran nowhere near her best form on her Dubai debit after a 111-day break. She was a bit keen early and might appreciate a return to shorter.

618a S O G FINANCE (H'CAP) (TAPETA) 1m 2f
2:35 (2:35) (80-98,97) 3-Y-O+

£9,677 (£3,225; £1,612; £806; £483; £322)

RPR

1 **Plantagenet (SPA)**[14] 421 5-9-6 **97**........................ IoritzMendizabal 12 105
(G Arizkorreta Elosegui, Spain) *in rr of mid-div: rdn to ld fnl 100yds: styd on* **20/1**

2 2 **Ahlaain (USA)**[35] 172 4-9-3 **95**.. AhmedAjtebi 2 99
(A Al Raihe, UAE) *trckd ldr: led 5f out: clr 4 1/2f out: tired fnl f: hdd last 100yds* **20/1**

3 3 ¼ **Jutland**[146] 6339 5-9-5 **96**.. TedDurcan 3 94
(Doug Watson, UAE) *trckd ldrs: rdn 2f out: r.o same pce* **16/1**

4 ¼ **Famusa**[22] 319 5-9-4 **95**.. RyanMoore 14 92
(Marco Botti) *sn led: hdd 5f out: kpt on same pce* **10/1**

5 *shd* **Dr Faustus (IRE)**[22] 317 7-9-1 **91**................................(t) KierenFallon 11 89
(Doug Watson, UAE) *settled in rr: r.o fnl 2f: nrst fin* **14/1**

6 ¼ **Trojan Nights (USA)**[27] 259 4-9-1 **93**........................ WayneSmith 8 89
(M Al Muhairi, UAE) *mid-div: chsd ldr 3f out: one pce fnl 1 1/2f* **5/1**[2]

7 1 **Clasp**[12] 10-9-2 **93**..(t) TadhgO'Shea 7 87
(Doug Watson, UAE) *a mid-div* **6/1**[3]

8 ¼ **Graymalkin (IRE)**[27] 259 5-9-1 **91**.....................................(b) PatCosgrave 1 86
(M bin Shafya, UAE) *settled in rr: nvr able to chal* **6/1**[3]

9 1 **Maali (IRE)**[5] 4-9-5 **97**..(b) RoystonFfrench 6 89
(A Al Raihe, UAE) *a mid-div* **10/1**

10 ¾ **Abjer (FR)**[22] 319 4-9-5 **97**.............................. SilvestreDeSousa 4 87
(Ismail Mohammed) *trckd ldr tl 2 1/2f out: sn wknd* **18/1**

11 *hd* **Royaaty (IRE)**[14] 421 6-9-2 **93**................................(p) MircoDemuro 13 83
(M bin Shafya, UAE) *nvr bttr than mid-div* **20/1**

12 10 ¼ **Glen Nevis (USA)**[14] 421 8-8-11 **95**..................(v) SaeedAlMazrooe(7) 9 64
(A Al Raihe, UAE) *settled in rr: hrd rdn 4 1/2f out: sn btn* **25/1**

13 4 **Emerald Wilderness (IRE)**[20] 354 8-9-5 **96**............(p) WilliamBuick 10 57
(Robert Cowell) *settled in rr: n.d* **3/1**[1]

14 1 ¾ **Espiritu (FR)**[27] 257 6-9-1 **91**..(b) XZiani 5 50
(G Al Marri, UAE) *settled in rr: chsd ldrs 2f out: sn btn* **25/1**

2m 5.05s (0.35)
WFA 4 from 5yo+ 1lb **14** Ran SP% **128.2**
CSF: 371.17; TRICAST: 6424.77. PLACEPOT: £1450.40 to a £1 stake. Pool of £2,185.64 - 1.10 winning tickets. QUADPOT: Part won. £173.10 to a £1 stake. Pool of £234.00 - 0.10 winning tickets. Pool of £210.60 carried forward..
Owner Roberto Whyte Guerra **Bred** Dehesa De Milagro **Trained** Spain

FOCUS
The three who finished directly behind the winner were always on or near the lead, so Plantagenet did well to stay on from off the pace. Famusa was in front at the quarter-mile point, clocking 27.16, but Ahlaain soon went clear and set the remaining fractions in 51.63, 1.15.62 and 1.39.94.

NOTEBOOK
Plantagenet(SPA) ◆ had been set far too much to do in a couple of modestly run races over further on turf earlier in the year, and here he won despite the race not unfolding to suit. Not only was the gallop slower than ideal, but he covered more ground than the next four finishers. His performance needs upgrading.
Ahlaain(USA) had his chance from the front.
Jutland was always well placed.
Famusa was in the correct place but wasn't good enough.
Trojan Nights(USA) was up 6lb for his recent win and had a wide trip.
Clasp travelled well under a hold-up ride, but didn't get the clearest of runs and the leaders weren't stopping.
Emerald Wilderness(IRE) had won his last three starts over this trip at Lingfield, but he had no hope of completing a four-timer considering how events unfolded. He's a bridle horse who is at his best chasing a hot pace, but that wasn't the case here and he was under pressure and extremely wide on the final bend when trying to make up ground on horses who weren't coming back.

592 LINGFIELD (L-H)

Saturday, February 18

OFFICIAL GOING: Standard

Wind: Strong, half behind Weather: Overcast, windy

619 FA CUP BETTING AT BLUESQ.COM CLAIMING STKS 1m (P)

1:10 (1:10) (Class 6) 3-Y-O **£1,704** (£503; £251) **Stalls** High

Form RPR

341 **1** **Clean Bowled (IRE)**[9] 479 3-8-10 65 (p) NedCurtis(7) 7 69
(Roger Curtis) *pressed ldrs on outer tl led over 3f out: readily wnt clr 3f out: pushed along and styd on wl fr over 1f out: eased towards fin* **11/4**[2]

2-32 **2** *1 3/4* **Crowning Star (IRE)**[9] 479 3-8-11 61 LukeMorris 3 58
(J S Moore) *hld up in tch: effrt to chse clr ldr over 2f out: drvn and edgd lft over 1f out: styd on same pce and a hld after* **13/8**[1]

-635 **3** *2* **Angel Cake (IRE)**[25] 288 3-8-5 48 (p) HayleyTurner 1 47
(Phil McEntee) *chsd ldng trio: rdn and chsd clr ldng pair 2f out: kpt on u.p fnl f: nvr gng pce to threaten ldrs* **20/1**

66-4 **4** *2 3/4* **Flying Pickets (IRE)**[48] 6 3-9-3 73 JohnFahy 4 53
(Alan McCabe) *v.s.a: hld up in last pair: rdn over 2f out: drvn and wnt modest 4th jst over 1f out: plugged on but nvr trbld ldrs* **7/2**[3]

-645 **5** *2* **Cat Queen**[7] 534 3-8-2 53 DominicFox(3) 6 36
(Gay Kelleway) *awkward leaving stalls: hld up in last pair: rdn and no prog over 2f out: wl hld fnl 2f* **10/1**

4636 **6** *5* **Meet Joe Black (IRE)**[16] 393 3-8-8 51 (v) MatthewCosham(5) 5 33
(David Evans) *pressed ldr tl rdn and unable qck over 3f out: wknd 2f out: wl bhd fnl f* **9/1**

-400 **7** *17* **Castalian Spring (IRE)**[4] 556 3-8-5 45 (tp) FrankieMcDonald 2
(Phil McEntee) *dwlt: sn rcvrd and led: rdn and hdd over 3f out: sn lost pl: wl bhd fnl 2f: eased ins fnl f: t.o* **200/1**

1m 38.36s (0.16) **Going Correction** -0.10s/f (Stan) **7** Ran SP% **111.3**
Speed ratings (Par 95): **95,93,91,88,86 81,64**
Tote Swingers: 1&2 £1.80, 1&3 £5.50, 2&3 £3.50 CSF £7.18 TOTE £3.30: £1.90, £1.80; EX 6.60.
Owner Richard Dean **Bred** Cathal Ennis **Trained** Lambourn, Berks
■ The first winner under rules for former Irish pony racing champion Ned Curtis, 16, son of trainer Roger.

FOCUS
A weak claimer but the time was 0.23 seconds faster than the following 3yo maiden.
Cat Queen Official explanation: jockey said filly became upset at start

620 BREATHE SPA AT LINGFIELD MARRIOTT MAIDEN STKS 1m (P)

1:40 (1:41) (Class 5) 3-Y-O **£2,385** (£704; £352) **Stalls** High

Form RPR

2 **1** **Roxelana (IRE)**[14] 429 3-8-12 0 JimmyFortune 9 72+
(Jeremy Noseda) *prom in main gp: rdn to chse clr ldr over 2f out: hrd drvn and styd on fr over 1f out: chal and edgd lft ins fnl f: led towards fin: all out* **8/11**[1]

24 **2** *hd* **Devote Myself (IRE)**[7] 523 3-8-12 0 MartinLane 8 71
(David Evans) *chsd ldr after 1f: clsd on ldr over 3f out: sn led and clr: rdn 2f out: drvn and edgd rt ins fnl f: hdd towards fin* **4/1**[2]

3 *3 1/4* **Icelander (USA)** 3-9-3 0 JoeFanning 7 69+
(Mark Johnston) *hld up in midfield: hdwy to chse ldng pair wl over 2f out: rdn wl over 2f out: unable qck ent fnl f: edgd lft and wknd ins fnl f* **5/1**[3]

0-3 **4** *2 3/4* **Arte Del Calcio**[19] 358 3-9-3 0 DavidProbert 4 63
(David Elsworth) *t.k.h: hld up in midfield: hdwy 3f out: rdn to chse ldng trio 2f out: no imp and outpcd over 1f out: wl hld fnl f* **6/1**

5-6 **5** *12* **First Glance**[28] 249 3-9-3 0 NeilChalmers 1 35
(Michael Appleby) *broke fast and led: sn hdd: prom in main gp: rdn and struggling over 2f out: wknd 2f out* **50/1**

05 **6** *1 1/2* **Jacasa Too**[24] 291 3-8-12 0 JamesMillman 5 27
(Rod Millman) *a towards rr: rdn and lost tch over 2f out* **100/1**

0- **7** *3 1/4* **The Quarterjack**[149] 6281 3-9-0 0 SimonPearce(3) 6 24
(Ron Hodges) *t.k.h: hld up in rr: rdn and sme hdwy over 2f out: wknd 2f out* **100/1**

05- **8** *24* **Dark Celt (IRE)**[199] 4675 3-9-3 0 ShaneKelly 3
(Tim Pitt) *racd freely: sn led and clr: hdd over 3f out and sn dropped out: wl bhd and eased fnl f: t.o* **66/1**

9 *65* **Brave Kiss** 3-8-12 0 NickyMackay 10
(David Elsworth) *s.i.s: a last: lost tch 3f out: wl t.o and eased fnl 2f* **20/1**

1m 38.59s (0.39) **Going Correction** -0.10s/f (Stan) **9** Ran SP% **119.1**
Speed ratings (Par 97): **94,93,90,87,75 74,71,47,**
Tote Swingers: 1&2 £1.70, 1&3 £2.40, 2&3 £3.10 CSF £4.08 TOTE £1.70: £1.02, £1.40, £2.00; EX 5.10 Trifecta £14.60 Pool; £564.78 - 28.61 winning units..
Owner P Makin **Bred** Stowell Park Stud **Trained** Newmarket, Suffolk

FOCUS
This was run in a time 0.23 seconds slower than the earlier 3yo claimer.
Arte Del Calcio Official explanation: jockey said gelding hung right
Brave Kiss Official explanation: vet said filly finished distressed

621 CLYDE GRIFFIN 50TH BIRTHDAY MEDIAN AUCTION MAIDEN STKS 5f (P)

2:15 (2:16) (Class 6) 3-Y-O **£1,704** (£503; £251) **Stalls** High

Form RPR

44- **1** **Available (IRE)**[129] 6787 3-8-12 0 HayleyTurner 4 70+
(Jim Boyle) *v free to post: chsd rivals: rdn ent fnl 2f: chal between horses jst ins fnl f: led fnl 100yds: styd on wl and sn in command* **5/2**[2]

3-2 **2** *2* **El McGlynn (IRE)**[9] 481 3-8-12 62 LukeMorris 2 62
(John O'Shea) *chsd ldr: rdn to chal 2f out: led wl over 1f out: hrd drvn over 1f out: hdd fnl 100yds: no ex* **6/4**[1]

5040 **3** *1* **Arabian Flight**[7] 518 3-8-12 58 KieranO'Neill 1 58
(John Bridger) *free to post: sn led: rdn and hdd wl over 1f out: stl ev ch u.p 1f out: no ex fnl 100yds* **3/1**[3]

58.45s (-0.35) **Going Correction** -0.10s/f (Stan) **3** Ran SP% **93.6**
Speed ratings (Par 95): **98,94,93**
CSF £4.92 TOTE £2.60; EX 3.60.
Owner M Khan X2 **Bred** Carrigbeg Stud & David Powell **Trained** Epsom, Surrey

FOCUS
Just the three runners after The Kicking Lord played up before the start was withdrawn, and it was a moderate race.

622 GET YOUR BET ON AT BLUE SQUARE H'CAP 1m (P)

2:50 (2:50) (Class 2) (0-100,102) 4-Y-O+ **£10,350** (£3,080; £1,539; £769) **Stalls** High

Form RPR

2-30 **1** **Night Lily (IRE)**[28] 254 6-8-13 92 WilliamCarson 3 101
(Paul D'Arcy) *hld up in midfield: swtchd rt and effrt u.p over 1f out: str chal ins fnl f: kpt on wl to ld last stride* **20/1**

2-25 **2** *shd* **Tarooq (USA)**[14] 426 6-8-4 88 RaulDaSilva(5) 7 97
(Richard Fahey) *chsd ldrs: chsd clr ldr 2f out: rdn and clsd over 1f out: led ins fnl f: kpt on wl tl hdd last stride* **5/1**[1]

36-3 **3** *1* **Mr Willis**[14] 426 6-9-0 93 MarcHalford 4 99
(Terry Clement) *hld up in midfield: rdn and effrt over 1f out: ev ch and edgd rt u.p ins fnl f: styd on same pce fnl 75yds* **7/1**[3]

21-4 **4** *nk* **Numeral (IRE)**[14] 426 4-8-7 86 KieranO'Neill 12 92
(Richard Hannon) *hld up in last quartet: rdn and hdwy on inner over 1f out: chsd ldrs ins fnl f: kpt on same pce fnl 75yds* **5/1**[1]

41-5 **5** *1 1/2* **Mia's Boy**[28] 254 8-9-5 101 RyanClark(3) 9 103
(Chris Dwyer) *hld up in last trio: hdwy u.p over 1f out: chsng ldrs whn nt clr run ins fnl f: kpt on same pce and no imp fnl 100yds* **7/1**[3]

1-42 **6** *3/4* **Lockantanks**[14] 426 5-9-0 93 LukeMorris 1 94
(Michael Appleby) *chsd ldrs: rdn 2f out: drvn and clsd on ldr over 1f out: unable qck 1f out: styd on same pce ins fnl f* **13/2**[2]

121- **7** *shd* **Loyalty**[63] 7801 5-9-9 102 (v) JoeFanning 2 102+
(Derek Shaw) *awkward leaving stalls: rdr lost iron and lost many l s: clsd and in tch in last pair 6f out: rdn and hdwy jst ins fnl f: styd on fnl 100yds: nvr trbld ldrs* **17/2**

-521 **8** *1/2* **Chilli Green**[3] 563 5-8-7 91 6ex (p) MatthewCosham(5) 10 90
(John Akehurst) *led at stdy gallop: pushed along and qcknd clr over 3f out: rdn and c bk to field over 1f out: hdd ins fnl f: fdd fnl 75yds* **12/1**

014- **9** *1 3/4* **Crystal Gal (IRE)**[147] 6370 5-9-7 100 IanMongan 8 95
(Lucy Wadham) *chsd ldr: allowed ldr to go clr over 3f out: rdn over 2f out: lost 2nd 2f out: wknd ent fnl f* **10/1**

-353 **10** *1 1/4* **Hazzard County (USA)**[14] 431 8-8-9 93 LauraPike(5) 6 85
(David Simcock) *hld up in last pair: rdn and effrt 1f out: kpt on: nvr trbld ldrs* **16/1**

3-10 **11** *nk* **Sunset Kitty (USA)**[21] 354 5-8-8 87 ShaneKelly 11 79
(Mike Murphy) *hld up in midfield on outer: lost pl bnd 2f out: rdn and no prog wl over 1f out: wl btn and eased wl ins fnl f* **14/1**

1m 35.55s (-2.65) **Going Correction** -0.10s/f (Stan) **11** Ran SP% **116.3**
Speed ratings (Par 109): **109,108,107,107,106 105,105,104,103,101 101**
Tote Swingers: 1&2 £22.60, 1&3 £34.30, 2&3 £8.20 CSF £116.01 CT £786.03 TOTE £22.30: £5.10, £2.40, £2.70; EX 145.20 Trifecta £459.00 Part won. Pool: £620.33 - 0.20 winning units..
Owner K Snell **Bred** Keith Wills **Trained** Newmarket, Suffolk
■ Stewards' Enquiry : Marc Halford three-day ban: careless riding (Mar 3,5,6)

FOCUS
A good, competitive handicap and they went a decent pace (time unsurprisingly much the best of four races at the trip).

NOTEBOOK
Night Lily(IRE) failed to beat a rival over C&D on her previous start, but here she returned to her very best form with a performance that was bordering on smart. (op 16-1)
Tarooq(USA)'s most recent race didn't unfold to suit (finished behind a few of these), but here he had a promising claimer aboard and this panned out more favourably. He ran up to his best. (op 9-2 tchd 4-1)
Mr Willis didn't build on his most recent effort when he closed well from off a modest pace (finished ahead of Tarooq), despite this time getting a good gallop to chase, but he initially made his challenge towards the inside rail, which isn't always ideal. (op 15-2 tchd 13-2)
Numeral(IRE) raced towards the inside rail for even longer, basically the duration of the straight. He had also compromised his chance with a slow start and may yet be capable of rating higher. (op 13-2)
Mia's Boy was denied a clear run when staying on in the straight, but didn't look unlucky. Official explanation: jockey said gelding suffered interference in runing (op 6-1)
Lockantanks finished ahead of today's runner-up, third and fourth when second in a muddling event over C&D last time, but he couldn't confirm form despite appearing to have his chance. (tchd 7-1)
Loyalty was a neck too good for Night Lily over C&D on his previous start, but here he lost his chance with an awkward start that caused Joe Fanning to lose an iron. In the circumstances he did well to finish so close. Official explanation: jockey said gelding jumped awkwardly causing him to lose and iron and be slowly away (op 8-1 tchd 9-1)
Chilli Green was sent clear before the straight. She was carrying a penalty for a win in a weaker race at Kempton three days earlier and couldn't sustain her bid. (op 16-1)
Hazzard County(USA) had a wide trip and his effort can be upgraded. (op 14-1)
Sunset Kitty(USA), who was taken widest of all into the straight, is another who did better than the bare facts suggest.

623 BLUE SQUARE SPRINT SERIES ROUND 7 H'CAP (QUALIFIER) (DIV I) 6f (P)

3:25 (3:26) (Class 5) (0-70,71) 4-Y-O+ **£2,726** (£805; £402) **Stalls** Low

Form RPR

0152 **1** **Waterloo Dock**[14] 424 7-9-3 66 (v) LukeMorris 1 73
(Michael Quinn) *chsd ldr tl sltly hmpd bnd 5f out: bustled along and chsd ldng pair after: drvn over 1f out: chsd ldr 1f out: kpt on wl to ld wl ins fnl f: hld on wl* **9/1**

-332 **2** *shd* **Cliffords Reprieve**[22] 320 4-8-11 60 (b) JimmyFortune 7 67
(Eric Wheeler) *in tch in midfield: effrt u.p over 1f out: styd on u.p and ev ch fnl 75yds: r.o but jst hld* **7/2**[1]

4-24 **3** *1/2* **Valmina**[7] 526 5-8-12 68 (t) GeorgeDowning(7) 10 73
(Tony Carroll) *hld up in last pair: rdn and gd hdwy jst ins fnl f: chal fnl 75yds: no ex and hld towards fin* **9/1**

-006 **4** *3/4* **Catalyze**[7] 526 4-9-4 67 (t) MartinHarley 6 70
(Richard Guest) *sn bustled up to ld: rdn clr 2f out: drvn 1f out: hdd and lost 3 pls wl ins fnl f* **9/2**[2]

0000 **5** *nk* **Memphis Man**[7] 526 9-8-3 57 oh1 ow1 MatthewCosham(5) 5 59
(David Evans) *taken down early: in tch in midfield: rdn ent fnl 2f: styd on same pce u.p fnl f* **33/1**

0321 **6** *1/2* **Nubar Boy**[7] 528 5-9-8 71 (v) MartinLane 9 71
(David Evans) *stdd s: hld up in last quartet: swtchd rt and effrt u.p over 1f out: styd on ins fnl f: nvr gng pce to rch ldrs* **11/2**[3]

00-0 **7** *1* **Brynfa Boy**[18] 371 6-9-1 64 (bt[1]) StephenCraine 8 61
(Daniel Mark Loughnane) *stdd s: hld up in rr: swtchd lft and hdwy jst over 1f out: drvn ins fnl f: one pce and no prog fnl 100yds* **20/1**

0-04 **8** *3/4* **Italian Tom (IRE)**[7] 528 5-9-0 70 DarrenEgan(7) 11 65
(Ronald Harris) *in tch in midfield: rdn and unable qck over 1f out: styd on same pce and no threat to ldrs fnl f* **16/1**

-546 **9** *1* **Joe Le Taxi (IRE)**[1] 458 4 -9-0**63** JoeFanning 4 60
(Mark Johnston) *short of room sn after s: hld up in rr: gd hdwy on inner over 1f out: rdn and no prog ins fnl f: eased fnl 50yds* **7/2**[1]

0000 **10** *7* **Royal Intruder**[7] 528 7 -8-7**56** oh1 WilliamCarson 3 25
(Richard Guest) *chsd ldr: rdn and unable qck ent fnl 2f: lost 2nd 1f out: fdd fnl 150yds* **25/1**

1m 10.95s (-0.95)**Going Correction** -0.10s/f (Stan) **10**Ran SP% **115.4**
Speed ratings (Par 103): **102,101,101,100,99 99,97,96,95,86**
Tote Swingers: 1&2 £3.70, 1&3 £9.10, 2&3 £7.60 CSF £39.24 CT £304.46 TOTE £9.10 : £2.40, £1.70, £2.70 ; EX 31.10 Trifecta £435.00 Part won. Pool: £587.85 - 0.63 winning units.
Owner M J Quinn **Bred** Norman Court Stud **Trained** Newmarket, Suffolk
■ Stewards' Enquiry : George Downing two-day ban: careless riding (Mar 3,5)

FOCUS
Round 7 of the Blue Square Sprint Series. The pace was brisk.

624 BLUE SQUARE SPRINT SERIES ROUND 7 H'CAP (QUALIFIER) (DIV II) 6f (P)

4:00 (4:00) (Class 5) (0-70,70) 4-Y-O+ **£2,726** (£805; £402) **Stalls** Low

Form RPR

3424 **1** **Gorgeous Goblin (IRE)**[7] 572 5 -8-7**56** oh7 (t) DavidProbert 8 64
(David C Griffiths) *hld up in tch in midfield: rdn and effrt on outer jst over 1f out: hdwy 1f out: chal fnl 100yds: r.o to ld last strides* **10/1**

2543 **2** *hd* **Captain Dimitrios**[7] 528 4 -8-10**64** (v) MatthewCosham(5) 7 71
(David Evans) *chsd ldr: rdn to ld 2f out: battled on wl u.p fr over 1f out: hdd and no ex last strides* **5/1**[3]

0-33 **3** *½* **My Lord**[22] 323 4 -8-11**67** DarrenEgan(7) 1 72
(Ronald Harris) *wnt rt s: t.k.h: hld up in midfield: rdn and hdwy on inner over 1f out: drvn and ev ch 1f out: unable qck wl ins fnl f* **10/1**

03-0 **4** *¾* **Hoover**[28] 251 4 -9-1**69** NathanAlison(5) 2 72
(Jim Boyle) *chsd ldrs: rdn and effrt 2f out: pressed ldrs 1f out: styd on same pce fnl 100yds* **9/2**[2]

065 **5** *1* **Clear Ice (IRE)**[22] 325 5 -9-4**67** (bt) ShaneKelly 11 67
(Gay Kelleway) *stdd and swtchd lft after s: hld up in rr: rdn and effrt over 1f out: swtchd rt 1f out: styd on ins fnl f: nvr gng pce to rch ldrs* **16/1**

-020 **6** *nk* **Rylee Mooch**[23] 311 4 -9-2**70** (e) CharlesEddery(5) 5 69
(Richard Guest) *chsd ldrs: rdn and unable qck over 1f out: kpt on same pce ins fnl f* **16/1**

0050 **7** *1 ¼* **Forty Proof (IRE)**[9] 498 4 -8-8**57** (be) KieranO'Neill 6 52
(Alan McCabe) *s.i.s: plld hrd: sn hld up in midfield: rdn and effrt jst over 1f out: hung lft and no imp ins fnl f* **16/1**

-450 **8** *¾* **Fantasy Fighter (IRE)**[14] 424 7 -8-2**56** oh1 RaulDaSilva(5) 3 48
(John E Long) *t.k.h: hld up in midfield on outer: rdn and lost pl bnd 2f out: rdn and no prog over 1f out* **7/1**

4633 **9** *nse* **Waabel**[14] 424 5 -8-12**61** MartinHarley 10 53
(Richard Guest) *a towards rr: bhd 1/2-way: rdn wl over 1f out: kpt on fnl f: n.d* **4/1**[1]

6-35 **10** *nk* **Royal Box**[19] 359 5 -8-11**60** RichardThomas 9 51
(David Evans) *a in rr: rdn ent fnl 2f: kpt on fnl f: n.d* **8/1**

125- **11** *2* **Dreams Of Glory**[171] 5615 4 -8-12**64** SimonPearce(3) 4 49
(Ron Hodges) *led tl rdn and hdd 2f out: wknd jst over 1f out* **16/1**

1m 11.19s (-0.71)**Going Correction** -0.10s/f (Stan) **11**Ran SP% **120.2**
Speed ratings (Par 103): **100,99,99,98,96 96,94,93,93,93 90**
Tote Swingers: 1&2 £8.40, 1&3 £8.40, 2&3 £9.20 CSF £60.76 CT £534.38 TOTE £12.40 : £3.40, £1.80, £3.90 ; EX 64.20 Trifecta £246.30 Pool: £928.87 - 2.79 winning units.
Owner K Humphries & Sons Roofing Contractors **Bred** S & L Humphries **Trained** Bawtry, S Yorks

FOCUS
The time was 0.24 seconds slower than the first division.
Dreams Of Glory Official explanation: jockey said colt hung right

625 CYPRIUM GRILL AT MARRIOTT LINGFIELD H'CAP 1m 4f (P)

4:35 (4:35) (Class 4) (0-85,81) 4-Y-O+ **£4,204** (£1,251; £625 ; £312) **Stalls** Low

Form RPR

3-23 **1** **Crunched**[22] 332 5 -9-3**77** (b[1]) ShaneKelly 1 84
(Tim Pitt) *mde all: rdn and clr 2f out: drvn ent fnl f: forged clr and in command fnl 100yds: styd on* **11/4**[2]

00-0 **2** *4 ½* **Battleoftrafalgar**[2] 577 5 -9-3**77** (b) GeorgeBaker 4 79
(Michael Attwater) *chsd wnr for 2f: chsd ldrs after: rdn over 3f out: chsd wnr again 2f out: rallied u.str.p and trying to chal ent fnl f: no ex and btn fnl 150yds: eased towards fin* **8/1**

1 **3** *9* **Belle Josephine**[12] 451 4 -8-7**70** JoeFanning 6 55
(Mark Johnston) *a in rr: rdn along and nvr gng fr 9f out: struggling and dropped to last 5f out: 4th and wl btn over 2f out: wnt poor 3rd ins fnl f* **6/5**[1]

23-1 **4** *2 ½* **Bert The Alert**[36] 149 4 -8-9**72** WilliamCarson 5 53
(Gary Moore) *t.k.h: chsd wnr after 2f: rdn and hung lft over 2f out: lost 2nd and btn 2f out: wknd over 1f out* **9/2**[3]

101- **5** *9* **Beau Fighter**[44] 1977 7 -8-13**73** FergusSweeney 3 40
(Gary Moore) *a in rr: lost tch over 3f out* **16/1**

2m 29.99s (-3.01)**Going Correction** -0.10s/f (Stan)
WFA 4 from 5yo+ 3lb **5**Ran SP% **107.3**
Speed ratings (Par 105): **106,103,97,95,89**
CSF £21.26 TOTE £4.00 : £2.20 , £4.70 ; EX 23.50 .
Owner Decadent Racing **Bred** D J And Mrs Deer **Trained** Newmarket, Suffolk

FOCUS
Not a competitive race with the favourite below form.
Battleoftrafalgar Official explanation: vet said gelding lost right-hind shoe

626 WEDDINGS AT LINGFIELD MARRIOTT HOTEL H'CAP 1m (P)

5:05 (5:05) (Class 5) (0-75,80) 4-Y-O+ **£2,385** (£704; £352) **Stalls** High

Form RPR

512- **1** **Push Me (IRE)**[66] 6924 5 -9-0**71** MichaelO'Connell(3) 8 80+
(Jamie Poulton) *in tch: rdn 2f out: hdwy over 1f out: led ins fnl f: r.o wl* **16/1**

-242 **2** *1 ¾* **Legal Legacy**[12] 448 6 -9-6**74** JimmyFortune 4 79+
(David C Griffiths) *fly-jmpd leaving stalls and slowly away: hld up in rr: c wd and effrt over 1f out: str run ins fnl f: wnt 2nd fnl 50yds: nvr gng to threaten wnr* **4/1**[1]

43-3 **3** *¾* **Tiradito (USA)**[24] 302 5 -9-5**73** (p) GeorgeBaker 2 76
(Michael Attwater) *chsd ldrs: rdn wl over 1f out: chsd ldr over 1f out: hrd drvn and ev ch 1f out: outpcd fnl 100yds* **11/1**

4-41 **4** *½* **I Confess**[7] 538 7 -9-12**80** (b) JoeFanning 11 82
(Geoffrey Harker) *chsd ldrs: rdn and unable qck over 1f out: kpt on same pce ins fnl f* **11/2**[2]

0005 **5** *nk* **Honey Of A Kitten (USA)**[5] 538 4 -8-12**66** RichardThomas 3 67
(David Evans) *in tch in midfield: pushed along over 4f out: rdn over 2f out: chsd ldrs and styd on same pce ins fnl f* **22/1**

-52 **6** *nk* **The Happy Hammer (IRE)**[94] 302 6 -8-10**67** RyanClark(3) 1 67
(Eugene Stanford) *hld up in last quartet: nt clr run ent fnl 2f: hdwy on inner and rdn over 1f out: kpt on same pce ins fnl f* **4/1**[1]

3011 **7** *½* **Satwa Laird**[10] 470 6 -9-5**73** HayleyTurner 7 72
(Conor Dore) *in tch in midfield: rdn and effrt whn n.m.r over 1f out: nvr much room and no real imp ins fnl f* **14/1**

-642 **8** *shd* **Mishrif (USA)**[7] 517 6 -9-6**74** (b) ShaneKelly 5 73
(J R Jenkins) *led: rdn ent fnl 2f: drvn and hrd pressed 1f out: hdd ins fnl f: wknd towards fin* **10/1**[3]

-111 **9** *¾* **Daniel Thomas (IRE)**[5] 403 10 -9-3**71** (tp) WilliamCarson 9 68
(Richard Guest) *dwlt: hld up in midfield on outer: effrt u.p over 1f out: no prog: styd on same pce fnl f* **11/2**[2]

-024 **10** *hd* **One Way Or Another (AUS)**[13] 447 9 -9-6**74** (b) LukeMorris 6 73
(David Evans) *t.k.h: hld up towards rr: effrt towards inner but nt clr run over 1f out: sme hdwy 1f out: nvr enough room ins fnl f and no prog: eased towards fin* **14/1**

000- **11** *2 ¼* **Taqaat (USA)**[117] 7054 4 -8-11**70** RaulDaSilva(5) 10 62
(Tim McCarthy) *chsd ldr: rdn and unable qck 2f out: lost 2nd over 1f out and wknd 1f out: wl btn and eased towards fin* **40/1**

0-00 **12** *4* **Guest Book (IRE)**[16] 391 5 -8-13**72** DavidKenny(5) 12 55
(Michael Scudamore) *v.s.a: in tch in last pair: rdn and no rspnse over 2f out: wknd wl over 1f out* **25/1**

1m 36.94s (-1.26)**Going Correction** -0.10s/f (Stan) **12**Ran SP% **118.0**
Speed ratings (Par 103): **102,100,99,99,98 98,97,97,96,96 94,90**
Tote Swingers: 1&2 £17.60, 1&3 £18.60, 2&3 £8.40 CSF £77.19 CT £763.17 TOTE £22.30 : £5.00, £2.00 , £3.50 ; EX 122.20 Trifecta £525.80 Part won. Pool: £710.59 - 0.10 winning units.
Owner Alex and Janet Card **Bred** Mrs Dolores Gleeson **Trained** Telscombe, E Sussex

FOCUS
A modest but competitive handicap.
One Way Or Another (AUS) Official explanation: jockey said gelding was denied a clear run
Guest Book (IRE) Official explanation: jockey said gelding was slowly away
T/Plt: £69.70 to a £1 stake. Pool:£62,877.72 - 657.64 winning tickets T/Qpdt: £41.60 to a £1 Pool:£3,281.77 - 58.24 w. tickets SP 627a Foreign Racing (See Raceform Interactive)

542 CAGNES-SUR-MER

Saturday, February 18

OFFICIAL GOING: Fibresand: standard

628a PRIX DES SEMBOULES (CONDITIONS) (3YO) (FIBRESAND) 1m (F)

12:30 (12:00) 3-Y-O **£12,083** (£4,833; £3,625 ; £2,416 ; £1,208)

RPR

1 **Roero (FR)** 3 -9-4**0** Francois-XavierBertras 2 81+
(F Rohaut, France) **3/1**[2]

2 *1* **Baby Cross**[29] 247 3 -9-4**0** IoritzMendizabal 5 79
(J-C Rouget, France) **3/5**[1]

3 *nk* **Swing Alone (IRE)**[8] 542 3 -8-11**0** MickaelForest 4 71
(Gay Kelleway) *s.i.s: racd 4th: pulling freely: rdn bef st: no ex u.p: styd on wl fnl f: clst at fin* **63/10**[3]

4 *1 ¾* **Questor (FR)**[43] 3 -8-10**0** ThibaultSpeicher(8) 3 74
(M Boutin, France) **12/1**

5 *¾* **Passior (FR)**[29] 247 3 -9-4**0** (p) ThomasMessina 1 72
(P Lenogue, France) **10/1**

1m 35.01s (95.01) **5**Ran SP% **118.0**
WIN (incl. 1 euro stake): 4.00. PLACES: 1.30, 1.10. SF: 5.50 .
Owner Haras De Saint Pair & F Rohaut **Bred** 6 C Racing Ltd **Trained** Sauvagnon, France

443 ST MORITZ (R-H)

Sunday, February 19

OFFICIAL GOING: Snow: frozen

629a GROSSER PREIS PRESTIGE - RENNBAHN BERLIN/HOPPEGRTEN (CONDITIONS) (4YO+) (SNOW) 6f 110y

11:40 (12:00) 4-Y-O+

£8,630 (£4,315; £3,082 ; £2,054 ; £1,027 ; £616)

RPR

1 **Le Big (GER)**[61] 8 -9-4**0** AndreBest 6
(P Schaerer, Switzerland) **17/10**[1]

2 *6* **Exchange**[7] 4 -9-4**0** FreddyDiFede 8
(A Schennach, Switzerland) **111/10**

3 *½* **Desert Strike**[29] 251 6 -8-11**0** JimCrowley 2
(Charles Hills) *led: pushed along whn pressed over 1 1/2f out: hdd nring fnl f: kpt on at one pce* **22/5**[3]

4 *2* **Shuffle Champ** 5 -8-11**0** (p) RobertHavlin 4
(M Weiss, Switzerland) **84/10**

5 *½* **Lodano (FR)**[364] 627 7 -9-2**0** SteveDrowne 10
(M Weiss, Switzerland) **7/2**[2]

6 *1 ½* **Lady Areia (GER)**[311] 6406 6 -8-6**0** StephaneLaurent 5
(K Klein, Switzerland) **184/10**

7 *5* **Rushing Dasher (GER)**[364] 627 10 -9-2**0** FrauNatalieFriberg 11
(Natalie Friberg, Switzerland) **124/10**

8 *1* **Florentiner (GER)**[60] 9 -8-11**0** EPedroza 3
(A Trybuhl, Germany) **32/5**

9 *2* **Divin Honor (FR)**[73] 5 -9-4**0** (p) FredericSpanu 9
(A Schaerer, Switzerland) **142/10**

10 *1 ¾* **Nordfalke (IRE)**[581] 4184 5 -8-9**0** KarinZwahlen 7
(A Schaerer, Switzerland) **133/10**

11 *10* **Boccalino (GER)**[124] 4 -9-6**0** (b) DPorcu 1
(P Schaerer, Switzerland) **114/10**

1m 22.0s (82.00) **11**Ran SP% **144.4**
PARI-MUTUEL (all including 1 chf stakes): WIN 2.70; PLACE 1.60, 3.30, 2.50; SF 29.00 .
Owner Philipp Sander **Bred** Gestut Wittekindshof **Trained** Switzerland

630a GUBELIN 73 GROSSER PREIS VON ST MORITZ (CONDITIONS) (4YO+) (SNOW) 1m 2f

1:25 (12:00) 4-Y-0+

£37,722 (£18,860; £13,472; £8,981; £4,490; £2,695)

RPR

1 African Art (USA)[14] [443] 6-8-11 0 FreddyDiFede 5 89
(P Schaerer, Switzerland) 159/10

2 2 ½ Flash Dance (GER)[95] 5-9-6 0 EPedroza 4 93
(A Wohler, Germany) 37/10[1]

3 3 ½ Schutzenjunker (GER)[352] [778] 7-8-11 0 (p) DPorcu 16 77
(P Schaerer, Switzerland) 63/1

4 1 ¾ Ziking (FR)[14] [444] 7-8-11 0 FredericSpanu 14 74
(A Schaerer, Switzerland) 128/10

5 2 Winterwind (IRE)[14] [443] 7-9-8 0 (p) GeorgBocskai 12 81
(Carmen Bocskai, Switzerland) 26/5[3]

6 1 ¼ Tarkheena Prince (USA)[120] [7045] 7-9-4 0 MEsposito 8 74
(C Von Der Recke, Germany) 177/10

7 1 Non Stop[261] 6-9-0 0 FabienLefebvre 9 68
(M Le Forestier, France) 244/10

8 1 ½ Pont Des Arts (FR)[14] [443] 8-9-6 0 MiguelLopez 3 71
(A Schaerer, Switzerland) 148/10

9 nk Keep Cool[98] [7409] 5-9-0 0 AndreBest 11 64
(Andreas Lowe, Germany) 36/5

10 2 Mascarpone (GER)[14] [443] 8-8-11 0 (p) RobertHavlin 6 57
(M Weiss, Switzerland) 26/1

11 nk Halling River (IRE)[14] [444] 5-8-11 0 SteveDrowne 15 57
(M Weiss, Switzerland) 145/10

12 ¾ Earl Of Winds (GER)[14] [443] 7-9-0 0 StephaneLaurent 7 58
(P Schaerer, Switzerland) 97/10

13 3 The Bells O Peover[14] [443] 4-8-10 0 (b) FrannyNorton 2 49
(Mark Johnston) *settled towards rr on ins: sme late prog: nvr on terms* 42/10[2]

14 dist Salut (GER)[196] 4-9-5 0 FilipMinarik 1
(P Schiergen, Germany) 73/10

15 nk Calypso Magic (IRE)[14] [443] 4-8-11 0 ow1 JimCrowley 10
(Linda Jewell) *chsd ldrs tl wknd over 3f out: t.o* 73/1

16 ½ Happy Wedding (IRE)[96] 6-9-5 0 (p) FabriceVeron 13
(H-A Pantall, France) 139/10

17 dist Licence To Till (USA)[14] [443] 5-9-6 0 JoeFanning 17
(Mark Johnston) *racd towards rr on outside: t.o fnl 2f* 205/10

2m 13.8s (133.80)
WFA 4 from 5yo+ 1lb 17 Ran SP% 143.4
PARI-MUTUEL (all including 1 chf stakes): WIN 16.90; PLACE 4.10, 2.30, 9.00; SF 52.30.
Owner Peter Aregger **Bred** Sean Gorman **Trained** Switzerland

631a GROSSER PREIS GUNTER SACHS MEMORIAL RACE (CONDITIONS) (4YO+) (SNOW) 1m 1f

1:50 (12:00) 4-Y-0+

£4,602 (£2,301; £1,643; £1,095; £547; £328)

RPR

1 Maverik[26] [280] 4-9-2 0 JimCrowley 3
(Ralph Beckett) *a.p: led 1/2-way: shkn up and qcknd 2 l clr over 1 1/2f out: r.o wl u.p fnl f* 17/5[2]

2 ¾ Hoist The Sail (IRE)[483] 4-9-6 0 EPedroza 9
(P Schaerer, Switzerland) 9/10[1]

3 6 Sentimento (ISR)[364] [629] 9-8-9 0 (p) MiguelLopez 6
(J D Hillis, Germany) 87/10

4 7 Niya (FR)[14] [444] 5-8-6 0 AndreBest 5
(P Schaerer, Switzerland) 128/10

5 2 ½ Rayo (CZE)[364] [629] 7-9-2 0 (p) SteveDrowne 8
(M Weiss, Switzerland) 19/2

6 dist Puro (CZE)[364] [629] 10-9-2 0 StephaneLaurent 11
(M Weiss, Switzerland) 201/10

7 10 Story Of Dubai[7] 5-8-13 0 RobertHavlin 2
(M Weiss, Switzerland) 23/5[3]

8 1 ¾ Still Standing (FR)[664] 5-8-5 0 ow2 (b) ChantalZollet 1
(Chantal Zollet, Switzerland) 115/10

9 4 Distinctive Image (USA)[156] 7-9-8 0 MEsposito 10
(C Von Der Recke, Germany) 32/1

10 dist Toughness Danon[7] 6-8-9 0 (b) FilipMinarik 7
(C Von Der Recke, Germany) 23/1

11 6 Spirit Of Xaar (IRE)[14] [444] 6-8-9 0 MarcHalford 4
(Linda Jewell) *chsd ldrs: wknd and bhd fnl 3f: t.o* 222/10

2m 2.61s (122.61) 11 Ran SP% 144.5
PARI-MUTUEL (all including 1 chf stakes): WIN 4.40; PLACE 1.50, 1.30, 1.90; SF 12.00.
Owner Athos, Cooper, Quinn, EPL **Bred** J G Davis & Star Pointe Ltd **Trained** Kimpton, Hants

599 WOLVERHAMPTON (A.W) (L-H)

Monday, February 20

OFFICIAL GOING: Standard
Wind: Fresh behind Weather: Overcast

632 GET YOUR BET ON BLUESQ.COM AMATEUR RIDERS' H'CAP 1m 4f 50y(P)

2:15 (2:16) (Class 6) (0-52,52) 4-Y-0+ £1,646 (£506; £253) Stalls Low

Form RPR

000- 1 Lil Ella (IRE)[38] [6236] 5-10-9 52 MrsFreyaBrewer(5) 10 62
(Patrick Holmes) *hld up: hdwy over 2f out: led 1f out: styd on wl* 28/1

40-4 2 5 Harare[49] [9] 11-10-7 50 (v) GemmaTutty(5) 6 53+
(Karen Tutty) *s.s: hld up: hdwy over 2f out: rdn over 1f out: styd on to go 2nd towards fin: no ch w wnr* 7/1

000- 3 1 ¼ Into The Light[29] [5609] 7-10-7 50 MrRLindsay(5) 8 50
(Philip Kirby) *mid-div: hdwy over 3f out: rdn over 1f out: styd on same pce* 11/1

33-0 4 nse My Mate Mal[10] [493] 8-10-5 50 (p) MissCScott(7) 3 50+
(William Stone) *chsd ldr tl led over 3f out: rdn and hdd 1f out: no ex ins fnl f* 5/1[3]

/0-5 5 ½ Arisea (IRE)[42] [105] 9-10-4 49 MissRebeccaSparkes(7) 4 48
(James Moffatt) *prom: n.m.r and lost pl 8f out: hdwy over 2f out: styd on: nt trble ldrs* 11/2

000- 6 ½ Mystified (IRE)[82] [6379] 9-10-4 49 MissAChadwick(7) 12 47
(Alan Berry) *prom: lost pl over 8f out: r.o ins fnl f* 66/1

-042 7 ¾ Carlton Scroop (FR)[13] [453] 9-10-9 52 (b) MissMBryant(5) 2 49
(Paddy Butler) *chsd ldrs: pushed along 7f out: rdn and ev ch fr over 1f out tl no ex ins fnl f* 4/1[1]

53/0 8 2 Benozzo Gozzoli[17] [395] 6-10-7 52 (t) MissCLBrown(7) 1 46
(Seamus Mullins) *led: hdd over 3f out: rdn over 1f out: n.m.r and wknd ins fnl f* 20/1

0-04 9 7 Magnitude[13] [454] 7-10-11 49 (b) MissSBrotherton 5 32
(Brian Baugh) *prom: rdn over 2f out: wknd over 1f out* 9/2[2]

040- 10 8 Northumberland[90] [7503] 6-10-8 51 MrOGarner(5) 9 21
(Owen Brennan) *prom: rdn over 3f out: wknd over 2f out* 50/1

0-00 11 6 Carr Hall (IRE)[14] [450] 9-10-9 52 MrCCarroll(5) 7 12
(Tony Carroll) *hld up: a in rr: bhd fr 1/2-way* 7/1

020/ 12 40 Dawn Mystery[1367] [2094] 8-10-5 50 MrAFrench(7) 11
(Alan Berry) *a in rr: bhd fr 1/2-way: eased fnl 2f: t.o* 50/1

2m 43.12s (2.02) **Going Correction** +0.10s/f (Slow) 12 Ran SP% 117.2
Speed ratings (Par 101): **97,93,92,92,92 92,91,90,85,80 76,49**
toteswingers:1&2:£21.50, 1&3:£45.60, 2&3:£14.60 CSF £204.80 CT £2309.32 TOTE £36.30: £8.40, £3.40, £4.30; EX 182.70 TRIFECTA Not won..
Owner Foulrice Park Racing Limited **Bred** K Maginn **Trained** Brandsby, N. Yorks
■ Stewards' Enquiry : Mr R Lindsay two-day ban: used whip with excessive frequency (Apr 1,21)

FOCUS
A moderate race run at a good pace, thanks to Benozzo Gozzoli. The winner had plummeted in the weights and the form is rated on the negative side.

633 SPONSOR A RACE BY CALLING 01902 390000 H'CAP 1m 141y(P)

2:45 (2:46) (Class 6) (0-55,55) 4-Y-0+ £1,704 (£503; £251) Stalls Low

Form RPR

60-3 1 Just Five (IRE)[10] [490] 6-9-2 55 (v) JamieSpencer 10 62
(John Weymes) *chsd ldrs: led 2f out: sn rdn: styd on* 8/1

-466 2 ½ Polar Auroras[5] [561] 4-9-2 55 (t) DavidProbert 13 61
(Tony Carroll) *prom: lost pl over 6f out: hdwy over 2f out: rdn and hung lft fr over 1f out: r.o* 13/2[3]

600- 3 nse Tanforan[145] [6452] 10-9-2 55 MickyFenton 7 61
(Brian Baugh) *prom: racd keenly: rdn over 1f out: r.o* 33/1

3-61 4 ¾ Cwmni[24] [334] 6-9-0 53 LukeMorris 2 58+
(Bryn Palling) *mid-div: outpcd over 3f out: hdwy: nt clr run and swtchd rt over 1f out: edgd lft: r.o* 6/1[2]

-033 5 1 ½ Just Timmy Marcus[14] [450] 6-9-0 53 (v) RussKennemore 1 54
(Brian Baugh) *hld up: hmpd wl over 7f out: hdwy 5f out: nt clr run and lost pl over 2f out: hdwy over 1f out: sn rdn: styd on same pce ins fnl f* 9/2[1]

360- 6 3 ¼ Princess Gail[80] [7610] 4-9-2 55 ShaneKelly 9 48
(Mark Brisbourne) *s.s: hmpd wl over 7f out: rdn over 1f out: no imp ins fnl f* 7/1

-451 7 1 ¾ Flying Applause[11] [477] 7-8-10 54 (bt) CharlesEddery(5) 3 43
(Roy Bowring) *s.s: hdwy to join ldr over 6f out: rdn over 2f out: wknd fnl f* 15/2

-000 8 1 Ryedale Dancer (IRE)[14] [448] 4-8-13 55 (tp) RobertLButler(3) 11 42
(Richard Guest) *chsd ldrs: rdn over 2f out: wknd fnl f* 50/1

10-0 9 ½ Roman Ruler (IRE)[21] [361] 4-9-2 55 PhillipMakin 4 41
(Chris Fairhurst) *led: rdn and hdd 2f out: wknd fnl f* 16/1

50-6 10 2 ½ Swinger[20] [369] 4-8-11 55 (t) MarkCoumbe(5) 5 35
(Scott Dixon) *hld up: hmpd wl over 7f out: bhd and rdn 1/2-way: n.d* 10/1

00-6 11 1 Ashgrove Nell (IRE)[11] [477] 4-9-2 55 (be) StephenCraine 6 33
(Daniel Mark Loughnane) *mid-div: hmpd wl over 7f out: sn lost pl: rdn and wknd over 2f out* 33/1

00-0 12 11 Pie Poudre[25] [306] 5-9-1 54 (p) TomEaves 12
(Roy Brotherton) *s.i.s: hdwy and edgd lft wl over 7f out: rdn over 2f out: wknd over 1f out* 8/1

1m 51.91s (1.41) **Going Correction** +0.10s/f (Slow) 12 Ran SP% 115.1
Speed ratings (Par 101): **97,96,96,95,94 91,90,89,88,86 85,75**
toteswingers:1&2:£8.90, 1&3:£27.30, 2&3:£34.90 CSF £56.68 CT £1641.21 TOTE £9.40: £2.60, £2.80, £10.30; EX 75.60 Trifecta £388.40 Part won. Pool: £524.96 - 0.10 winning units..
Owner Grange Park Racing & Partner **Bred** Rathbarry Stud **Trained** Middleham Moor, N Yorks
■ Stewards' Enquiry : David Probert three-day ban: careless riding (Mar 5-7)

FOCUS
A modest handicap run in a slow time. Several of these were squeezed for room on passing the winning post for the first time.
Swinger Official explanation: jockey said gelding never travelled
Pie Poudre Official explanation: jockey said gelding lost interest

634 HOTEL & CONFERENCING AT WOLVERHAMPTON (S) STKS 1m 141y(P)

3:20 (3:20) (Class 6) 4-Y-0+ £1,704 (£503; £251) Stalls Low

Form RPR

6-32 1 Red Somerset (USA)[26] [299] 9-9-0 72 KieranO'Neill 4 67
(Mike Murphy) *trckd ldrs: racd keenly: shkn up over 2f out: rdn to ld wl ins fnl f: r.o* 10/11[1]

-602 2 ¾ Ahlawy (IRE)[14] [449] 9-9-1 62 (t) RaulDaSilva(5) 6 71
(Frank Sheridan) *chsd ldr tl led over 2f out: rdn and hdd wl ins fnl f* 16/1

2523 3 ¾ Marvo[16] [423] 8-9-0 65 JoeFanning 7 63
(Mark H Tompkins) *hld up in tch: chsd ldr over 1f out: sn rdn and hung lft: nt run on* 4/1[2]

2515 4 1 ¾ Faithful Ruler (USA)[6] [553] 8-8-13 75 (p) DarrenEgan(7) 5 65
(Ronald Harris) *hld up: rdn: hung lft and styd on ins fnl f: nt trble ldrs* 6/1[3]

-002 5 4 ½ Ossie Ardiles (IRE)[9] [532] 4-9-0 51 (v) LukeMorris 2 49
(Michael Appleby) *chsd ldrs: rdn over 1f out: wknd fnl f* 28/1

404- 6 ½ Hail Tiberius[29] [3054] 5-9-0 67 (t) JamieSpencer 3 48
(Tim Walford) *led: rdn and hdd over 2f out: wknd fnl f* 4/1[2]

045- 7 3 ½ Escardo (GER)[169] [2600] 9-8-7 40 JoshBaudains(7) 1 40
(David Bridgwater) *hld up: rdn over 2f out: wknd over 1f out* 100/1

1m 50.91s (0.41) **Going Correction** +0.10s/f (Slow) 7 Ran SP% 117.0
Speed ratings (Par 101): **102,101,100,99,95 94,91**
toteswingers:1&2:£4.40, 1&3:£1.40, 2&3:£5.40 CSF £19.67 TOTE £2.50: £1.50, £7.20; EX 15.40.There was no bid for the winner. Hail Tiberius was claimed by M. Keighley for £6,000.
Owner M Murphy **Bred** Haras D'Etreham **Trained** Westoning, Beds

FOCUS
A modest seller, run a full second quicker than the earlier Class 6 handicap. The form is a bit dubious, limited by the runner-up.

635 DINE IN THE HORIZONS RESTAURANT MAIDEN STKS 1m 1f 103y(P)

3:55 (3:59) (Class 5) 3-Y-0+ £2,264 (£673; £336; £168) Stalls Low

Form RPR

5-3 1 Cape Savannah[30] [249] 3-8-5 0 NickyMackay 5 77
(David Simcock) *led 2f: chsd ldr tl led again over 3f out: rdn clr fr over 1f out* 11/4[2]

3- **2** *4 ½* **Croftamie**[110] 7232 3-8-0 0.................... JoeFanning 2 63
(Mark Johnston) *chsd wnr tl led over 7f out: hdd over 3f out: styd on same pce fr over 1f out* **11/8**[1]

3 *6* **Ruacana** 3-8-5 0.................... HayleyTurner 9 55+
(Michael Bell) *s.i.s: hld up: hdwy and nt clr run over 1f out: rdn to go 3rd nr fin: nvr nr to chal* **6/1**[3]

4 *nk* **Kata Rock (USA)**[175] 5-9-12 0.................... TomEaves 3 60?
(Brian Rothwell) *dwlt: hld up: hdwy over 3f out: wkng whn rdn and edgd rt over 1f out: lost 3rd nr fin* **50/1**

5 **5** *1 ¼* **Roughlyn**[24] 324 3-8-5 0.................... LukeMorris 1 52
(Kevin Ryan) *chsd ldrs: rdn over 2f out: wkng whn hung lft over 1f out* **11/1**

0 **6** *6* **Delightful Sleep**[5] 569 4-9-9 0.................... RichardEvans(3) 11 45
(David Evans) *hld up: hdwy over 2f out: hmpd wl over 1f out: sn wknd* **50/1**

0 **7** *1* **Ruby Doo**[20] 369 4-9-7 0.................... MartinHarley 8 38
(Alastair Lidderdale) *chsd ldrs tl wknd over 2f out* **80/1**

8 *1 ¼* **Star Bonita (IRE)** 3-8-0 0.................... MartinLane 6 29
(David Simcock) *s.s: rn green and a in rr* **11/1**

9 *2 ¼* **The Yank** 3-8-5 0.................... DavidProbert 7 30
(Tony Carroll) *hld up: hdwy 6f out: rdn over 2f out: wknd over 1f out* **25/1**

10 *½* **Maggie Pink** 3-7-11 0.................... DominicFox(3) 10 24
(Michael Appleby) *hld up: rdn over 3f out: wknd over 2f out* **40/1**

6- **11** *73* **Myfourthboy**[53] 7913 5-9-9 0.................... GaryBartley(3) 4
(Alan Berry) *in rr: pushed along over 6f out: rdn and wknd over 3f out: t.o* **100/1**

2m 2.85s (1.15) **Going Correction** +0.10s/f (Slow)
WFA 3 from 4yo+ 21lb **11 Ran SP% 112.2**
Speed ratings (Par 103): **98,94,88,88,87 81,81,79,77,77 12**
toteswingers:1&2:£1.50, 1&3:£3.30, 2&3:£2.80 CSF £6.25 TOTE £3.80: £1.20, £1.10, £2.00; EX 7.30 Trifecta £31.60 Pool: £1,069.14 - 24.98 winning units..
Owner John Cook **Bred** New England Stud, Lord Derby And P Vela **Trained** Newmarket, Suffolk

FOCUS
Not a strong race (time 2.17 seconds slower than following Class 6 handicap). The winner clearly improved but the runner-up probably didn't match her debut turf form.

636 STAY AT THE WOLVERHAMPTON HOLIDAY INN H'CAP 1m 1f 103y(P)
4:25 (4:25) (Class 6) (0-65,64) 4-Y-0+ **£1,704** (£503; £251) **Stalls** Low

Form RPR

3-10 **1** **Vanilla Rum**[28] 275 5-9-3 **60**.................... (b) JoeFanning 9 74
(John Mackie) *hld up: hdwy over 5f out: led over 1f out: edgd lft and r.o wl: eased nr fin* **7/2**[2]

1163 **2** *2 ¾* **Aviso (GER)**[5] 570 8-9-1 **63**.................... MatthewCosham(5) 10 71
(David Evans) *led 2f: chsd ldr tl led again over 2f out: rdn and hdd over 1f out: styd on same pce ins fnl f* **7/1**[3]

3511 **3** *2 ¼* **Warden Bond**[14] 450 4-9-0 **57**.................... (p) MartinLane 7 60
(William Stone) *hld up: hdwy over 1f out: styd on to go 3rd ins fnl f: nt trble ldrs* **7/1**[3]

0-40 **4** *1* **Nolecce**[13] 460 5-9-1 **61**.................... (p) RobertLButler(3) 5 62
(Richard Guest) *chsd ldrs: rdn over 2f out: hung lft and styd on same pce fr over 1f out* **22/1**

/54- **5** *nse* **Royal Etiquette (IRE)**[238] 3466 5-9-4 **61**.................... HayleyTurner 3 62
(Lawney Hill) *hld up: hdwy over 1f out: styd on: nvr trbld ldrs* **9/1**

14-0 **6** *2 ¼* **Kyle Of Bute**[21] 361 6-9-7 **64**.................... RussKennemore 11 60
(Brian Baugh) *hld up: hdwy over 3f out: rdn over 1f out: wknd ins fnl f* **14/1**

00-0 **7** *¾* **Strong Vigilance (IRE)**[31] 224 5-9-4 **61**.................... JamieSpencer 6 55
(Michael Bell) *dwlt: pushed along in rr early: in rr and drvn along over 2f out: kpt on ins fnl f: nvr on terms* **8/1**

2-03 **8** *2 ¾* **Merrjanah**[9] 531 4-8-13 **56**.................... PaddyAspell 4 45
(John Wainwright) *chsd ldrs: rdn over 2f out: wknd over 1f out* **40/1**

0-15 **9** *2 ¾* **Harrys Yer Man**[13] 453 8-8-12 **55**.................... ShaneKelly 2 38
(Mark Brisbourne) *hld up: effrt over 2f out: sn wknd* **11/1**

00/- **10** *4 ½* **Aegean King**[520] 6187 6-8-7 **50**.................... DavidProbert 1 23
(Michael Wigham) *chsd ldrs: n.m.r and lost pl 7f out: pushed along over 3f out: rdn and wknd over 2f out* **3/1**[1]

40-0 **11** *shd* **Master Of Song**[43] 97 5-8-12 **60**.................... (p) CharlesEddery(5) 8 33
(Roy Bowring) *led over 7f out: rdn and hdd over 2f out: wknd over 1f out* **33/1**

2m 0.68s (-1.02) **Going Correction** +0.10s/f (Slow) **11 Ran SP% 118.1**
Speed ratings (Par 101): **108,105,103,102,102 100,99,97,95,91 90**
toteswingers:1&2:£5.40, 1&3:£5.20, 2&3:£5.90 CSF £27.91 CT £164.94 TOTE £4.80: £1.30, £3.20, £1.30; EX 29.90 Trifecta £54.80 Pool: £564.29 - 7.61 winning units..
Owner Derbyshire Racing VI **Bred** Charley Knoll Partnership **Trained** Church Broughton , Derbys

FOCUS
A modest handicap run at a reasonable pace once the 11th went clear. The winner got back to his early 2011 form.
Aegean King Official explanation: jockey said gelding never travelled

637 FOLLOW US ON TWITTER @BLUESQ H'CAP 5f 20y(P)
5:00 (5:00) (Class 5) (0-75,73) 3-Y-0 **£2,264** (£673; £336; £168) **Stalls** Low

Form RPR

5144 **1** **Redair (IRE)**[12] 469 3-8-10 **67**.................... MatthewCosham(5) 2 73
(David Evans) *chsd ldrs: rdn to ld ins fnl f: rdr dropped whip sn after: edgd lft: r.o* **40/1**

10-1 **2** *½* **Gin Twist**[12] 469 3-9-3 **69**.................... (b) RichardKingscote 8 73
(Tom Dascombe) *hld up: hdwy 1/2-way: rdn and ev ch ins fnl f: r.o* **14/1**

621- **3** *¾* **Code Six (IRE)**[108] 7267 3-9-0 **66**.................... TomEaves 9 68
(Bryan Smart) *led: rdn and hdd ins fnl f: unable qck* **12/1**

2-21 **4** *2 ½* **Al Freej (IRE)**[11] 481 3-9-4 **73**.................... DominicFox(3) 5 66
(Roger Varian) *mid-div: pushed along 1/2-way: r.o ins fnl f: nt trble ldrs* **5/6**[1]

54-6 **5** *2 ¼* **Majestic Rose**[12] 469 3-9-1 **67**.................... MartinHarley 4 51
(Mick Channon) *prom tl outpcd over 3f out: styd on ins fnl f* **33/1**

500- **6** *nse* **Van Go Go**[205] 4558 3-8-8 **65**.................... MarkCoumbe(5) 7 49
(Scott Dixon) *sn outpcd: r.o ins fnl f: nvr nrr* **40/1**

51 **7** *1 ¼* **Cats Eyes**[19] 373 3-8-13 **65**.................... ShaneKelly 1 45
(Robert Cowell) *chsd ldrs: rdn over 1f out: wknd ins fnl f* **11/2**[2]

-113 **8** *nk* **Lady Caprice**[12] 469 3-9-1 **67**.................... (p) HayleyTurner 10 46
(Jane Chapple-Hyam) *w ldr: rdn and ev ch over 1f out: wknd ins fnl f* **12/1**

46-6 **9** *1 ½* **Darnathean**[19] 377 3-9-7 **73**.................... (b) LukeMorris 6 46
(Paul D'Arcy) *chsd ldrs: rdn 1/2-way: wknd over 1f out* **13/2**[3]

1m 2.29s (-0.01) **Going Correction** +0.10s/f (Slow) **9 Ran SP% 113.1**
Speed ratings (Par 97): **104,103,102,98,94 94,92,91,89**
toteswingers:1&2:£17.20, 1&3:£29.40, 2&3:£9.10 CSF £494.29 CT £7020.03 TOTE £60.50: £8.10, £2.90, £3.30; EX 407.70 Trifecta £1034.20 Part won. Pool: £1,397.69 - 0.20 winning units..
Owner J & J Potter & The late Mrs S Edwards **Bred** Noel O'Callaghan **Trained** Pandy, Monmouths

FOCUS
This looked an okay race for the grade - four of the nine runners had won last time. The pace seemed strong. There was a surprise winner rated in line with her recent form plus rider's claim.

638 THE BLACK COUNTRY'S ONLY RACECOURSE MAIDEN STKS 7f 32y(P)
5:30 (5:31) (Class 5) 3-Y-O+ **£2,264** (£673; £336; £168) **Stalls** High

Form RPR

62 **1** **Red Trump (IRE)**[21] 358 3-8-9 0.................... WilliamCarson 2 65+
(Charles Hills) *chsd ldrs: rdn to ld ins fnl f: r.o* **8/15**[1]

2 *hd* **Prime Run** 3-8-4 0.................... MartinLane 1 59+
(David Simcock) *s.i.s: hld up: hdwy over 1f out: rdn and ev ch ins fnl f: r.o* **10/3**[2]

0 **3** *1 ¾* **Charlcot**[31] 231 4-9-5 0.................... DarrenEgan(7) 4 65
(James Bethell) *sn led: hdd over 5f out: chsd ldrs: rdn over 1f out: styd on same pce ins fnl f* **8/1**[3]

00 **4** *2 ¾* **Burning Passion**[20] 369 3-8-9 0.................... JamesSullivan 5 52
(Michael Easterby) *chsd ldrs: rdn over 1f out: edgd lft and styd on same pce fnl f* **40/1**

0-0 **5** *½* **Henry George**[20] 369 3-8-9 0.................... JoeFanning 7 51
(Mark Johnston) *chsd ldrs: led over 5f out: rdn over 1f out: hdd and no ex ins fnl f* **10/1**

00- **6** *20* **Fantasy Hero**[188] 5142 3-8-9 0.................... LukeMorris 3
(Ronald Harris) *s.i.s: in rr: rdn 1/2-way: wknd over 2f out* **40/1**

1m 31.22s (1.62) **Going Correction** +0.10s/f (Slow)
WFA 3 from 4yo+ 17lb **6 Ran SP% 113.4**
Speed ratings (Par 103): **94,93,91,88,88 65**
toteswingers:1&2:£1.60, 1&3:£1.20, 2&3:£2.20 CSF £2.68 TOTE £2.00: £1.10, £1.80; EX 2.80.
Owner R J Arculli **Bred** Derek Veitch **Trained** Lambourn, Berks

FOCUS
An ordinary maiden (time 1.48 seconds slower than following Class 5 handicap). Dubious form, rated around the fourth, with the winner not needing to match his latest effort.

639 PLAY ROULETTE AT BLUESQ.COM/CASINO H'CAP 7f 32y(P)
6:00 (6:00) (Class 5) (0-70,70) 4-Y-0+ **£2,264** (£673; £336; £168) **Stalls** High

Form RPR

00-0 **1** **Bahamian Lad**[21] 359 7-9-2 **65**.................... (v[1]) GeorgeBaker 4 72
(Reg Hollinshead) *mde all: rdn over 1f out: sn hung lft: styd on* **8/1**

00-1 **2** *¾* **Hawk Moth (IRE)**[21] 359 4-9-4 **67**.................... ChrisCatlin 6 72+
(John Spearing) *hld up: shkn up over 2f out: rdn and r.o wl ins fnl f: wnt 2nd post: nt rch wnr* **4/1**[1]

-015 **3** *hd* **Fleetwoodsands (IRE)**[9] 528 5-9-7 **70**.................... (t) LukeMorris 8 74
(Milton Bradley) *s.i.s: hld up: hdwy over 1f out: r.o to go 3rd post* **8/1**

5-34 **4** *nse* **Dancing Maite**[10] 492 7-9-7 **70**.................... MartinLane 7 74
(Roy Bowring) *chsd ldr: rdn and ev ch over 1f out: styd on* **12/1**

-252 **5** *½* **Dunmore Boy (IRE)**[10] 498 4-8-11 **63**.................... (p) LeeTopliss(3) 2 66
(Richard Fahey) *chsd ldrs: rdn over 1f out: styd on* **8/1**

-030 **6** *1 ¼* **Chookie Avon**[33] 199 5-9-6 **69**.................... (p) JoeFanning 3 69
(Keith Dalgleish) *chsd ldrs: rdn over 1f out: styd on same pce ins fnl f* **4/1**[1]

04-1 **7** *hd* **July Days (IRE)**[16] 430 6-8-10 **59**.................... RussKennemore 5 58
(Brian Baugh) *s.i.s: hld up: rdn over 2f out: hdwy over 1f out: no ex ins fnl f* **9/2**[2]

2316 **8** *6* **Needwood Ridge**[14] 448 5-9-0 **68**.................... (bt) RaulDaSilva(5) 9 51
(Frank Sheridan) *chsd ldrs: rdn over 2f out: wknd over 1f out* **6/1**[3]

-444 **U** **Lucky Dan (IRE)**[11] 478 6-8-13 **65**.................... RobertLButler(3) 1
(Paul Green) *sddle slipped sn after s: a in rr: lost tch fr over 2f out: bhd whn uns rdr ins fnl f* **20/1**

1m 29.74s (0.14) **Going Correction** +0.10s/f (Slow) **9 Ran SP% 118.3**
Speed ratings (Par 103): **103,102,101,101,101 99,99,92,**
toteswingers:1&2:£7.10, 1&3:£15.10, 2&3:£8.30 CSF £41.05 CT £272.00 TOTE £12.20: £3.00, £3.20, £2.80; EX 49.80 Trifecta £515.00 Pool: £939.58 - 1.35 winning units..
Owner Graham Brothers Racing Partnership **Bred** J D Graham **Trained** Upper Longdon, Staffs

FOCUS
The first seven finished in a bit of a bunch and this doesn't look like strong form for the level. The winner is rated to his C&D form in November.
T/Plt: £832.20 to a £1 stake. Pool:£94,140.77 - 82.57 winning tickets T/Qpdt: £19.50 to a £1 stake. Pool:£11,289.39 - 427.10 winning tickets CR

579 SOUTHWELL (L-H)
Tuesday, February 21

OFFICIAL GOING: Standard
Wind: Miderate across Weather: Cloudy with sunnyperiods

640 PLACE ONLY BETTING AT BLUESQ.COM (S) STKS 6f (F)
1:50 (1:50) (Class 6) 3-Y-0+ **£1,704** (£503; £251) **Stalls** Low

Form RPR

-212 **1** **Ingleby Arch (USA)**[7] 553 9-9-8 75.................... LMcNiff(5) 1 78
(David Barron) *cl up: rdn along: outpcd and lost pl after 2f: hdwy wl over 1f out: rdn and n.m.r ent fnl f: styd on wl to ld last 75yds* **1/1**[1]

0552 **2** *1 ¼* **Punching**[11] 492 8-9-13 68.................... HayleyTurner 4 74
(Conor Dore) *cl up: led 2f out: rdn over 1f out: hdd and no ex last 75yds* **9/4**[2]

3236 **3** *1 ¾* **Pilgrim Dancer (IRE)**[15] 447 5-9-8 55.................... (v) StephenCraine 3 63
(Tony Coyle) *dwlt: hdwy and cl up after 2f: effrt 2f out: sn rdn and ev ch tl one pce ins fnl f* **10/1**

50-1 **4** *2* **Cape Of Storms**[33] 215 9-9-13 68.................... (b) TomEaves 2 62
(Roy Brotherton) *sn led: rdn along over 2f out: sn hdd: grad wknd ent fnl f* **4/1**[3]

1m 16.51s (0.01) **Going Correction** 0.0s/f (Stan) **4 Ran SP% 109.9**
Speed ratings (Par 101): **99,97,95,92**
CSF £3.59 TOTE £2.00; EX 2.80.There was no bid for winner.
Owner Dave Scott **Bred** Alexander-Groves Thoroughbreds **Trained** Maunby, N Yorks

FOCUS
Despite them going a strong pace from the outset in this seller, all the four runners were still in contention at the furlong marker. The first three are close to their recent marks.

641 GOLF AND RACING AT SOUTHWELL H'CAP 1m (F)
2:20 (2:20) (Class 6) (0-55,61) 3-Y-O **£1,704** (£503; £251) **Stalls** Low

Form RPR

0211 **1** **Samasana (IRE)**[7] 556 3-9-8 **61** 6ex.................... TonyHamilton 6 72
(Ian Wood) *led 2f: cl up: led again 2f out: sn rdn clr: styd on strly* **9/4**[2]

0-62 **2** 3 **Pelican Rock (IRE)**[14] 459 3-8-11 **50**..................(p) RichardKingscote 7 54
(Tom Dascombe) *trckd ldng pair: effrt over 2f out: sn rdn and hung lft: styd on to chse wnr over 1f out: no imp* **5/4**[1]

000- **3** 5 **Smart Affair**[161] 6019 3-8-11 **50** ow2.............................. JamesMillman 5 43
(Rod Millman) *dwlt: sn chsng ldrs: rdn along and outpcd over 3f out: styd on u.p fnl 2f: tk 3rd nr fin* **14/1**

033 **4** 1 **J J Leary (IRE)**[7] 556 3-8-12 **51**..............................(v) JamieSpencer 1 41
(Ian Williams) *cl up: led after 2f: rdn: edgd rt and hdd 2f out: sn drvn and wknd wl over 1f out* **4/1**[3]

03-0 **5** 13 **Canning Vale**[31] 255 3-8-13 **55**.............................. AdamBeschizza(3) 4 15
(Julia Feilden) *in tch: rdn along over 3f out: sn outpcd* **20/1**

60-6 **6** 8 **Angel Warrior (IRE)**[18] 407 3-9-2 **55**.............................. PJMcDonald 2
(Ben Haslam) *a in rr: rdn along and bhd fnl 3f* **14/1**

1m 44.16s (0.46) **Going Correction** 0.0s/f (Stan) **6** Ran SP% **113.3**
Speed ratings (Par 95): **97,94,89,88,75 67**
toteswingers:1&2:£1.20, 2&3:£3.80, 1&3:£5.80 CSF £5.55 TOTE £3.20: £2.00, £1.20; EX 5.60.
Owner Paddy Barrett **Bred** Patrick Cassidy **Trained** Upper Lambourn, Berks

FOCUS
This 3yo handicap was run at a strong gallop thanks to the frustrating J J Leary. The winner confirmed his recent form with the third and fourth despite being a lot worse off at the weights.

642 SOUTHWELL-RACECOURSE.CO.UK MAIDEN STKS 1m 3f (F)
2:50 (2:50) (Class 5) 3-Y-0+ **£2,385** (£704; £352) **Stalls** Low

Form RPR

020- **1** **Artisan**[39] 5311 4-9-9 65.............................. DaleSwift(3) 2 75
(Brian Ellison) *hld up in tch: hdwy to chse ldr 3f out: rdn 2f out: styd on u.p to ld last 75yds* **9/2**[2]

2-22 **2** 1 ½ **Cotton Trader (USA)**[25] 324 3-8-5 78......................(b[1]) NickyMackay 3 68
(John Gosden) *t.k.h: trckd ldr: cl up 1/2-way: led wl over 3f out: pushed clr wl over 2f out: rdn wl over 1f out: hung rt and wknd ent fnl f: hdd last 75yds* **2/5**[1]

50 **3** 6 **Dewala**[7] 552 3-7-11 0.............................. DominicFox(3) 4 52
(Michael Appleby) *led: rdn along 4f out: sn hdd and plugged on same pce fnl 3f* **66/1**

5 **4** 41 **Authentication**[36] 195 3-8-5 0.............................. JoeFanning 1
(Mark Johnston) *chsd ldng pair: pushed along bef 1/2-way: rdn and lost pl wl over 4f out: sn bhd* **5/1**[3]

2m 26.83s (-1.17) **Going Correction** 0.0s/f (Stan)
WFA 3 from 4yo 23lb **4** Ran SP% **107.8**
Speed ratings (Par 103): **104,102,98,68**
CSF £6.93 TOTE £7.20; EX 9.00.
Owner Dan Gilbert & Kristian Strangeway **Bred** Foursome Thoroughbreds **Trained** Norton, N Yorks

FOCUS
Just the four runners and a modest maiden, but the pace and time were fair. The winner deserves credit but the favourite was disappointing.

643 DINE IN THE PANTRY CLAIMING STKS 1m 6f (F)
3:25 (3:25) (Class 6) 4-Y-0+ **£1,704** (£503; £251) **Stalls** Low

Form RPR

31-1 **1** **La Estrella (USA)**[33] 213 9-9-10 89.............................. JamieSpencer 1 93+
(Don Cantillon) *trckd ldr: smooth hdwy to ld wl over 2f out: pushed clr wl over 1f out: easily* **1/6**[1]

030- **2** 5 **Halla San**[9] 3157 10-9-3 89.............................. LeeTopliss(3) 2 78
(Richard Fahey) *set stdy pce: rdn along over 3f out: hdd wl over 2f out: kpt on same pce* **8/1**[2]

-603 **3** 23 **Chookie Hamilton**[11] 500 8-9-5 73.............................. JoeFanning 3 60
(Keith Dalgleish) *trckd ldng pair: pushed along 4f out: rdn wl over 3f out: sn wknd and eased* **9/1**[3]

3m 12.0s (3.70) **Going Correction** 0.0s/f (Stan) **3** Ran SP% **106.8**
Speed ratings (Par 101): **89,86,73**
CSF £2.01 TOTE £1.30; EX 1.70.
Owner Don Cantillon **Bred** Five Horses Ltd And Theatrical Syndicate **Trained** Newmarket, Suffolk

FOCUS
An uncompetitive claimer, with doubts over the current form of the second and third. All three were eased to some extent.

644 PLAY GOLF BEFORE RACING AT SOUTHWELL H'CAP 1m 4f (F)
4:00 (4:00) (Class 6) (0-60,66) 4-Y-0+ **£1,704** (£503; £251) **Stalls** Low

Form RPR

-334 **1** **Newport Arch**[21] 366 4-9-0 **59**..........................(v) MichaelO'Connell(3) 6 69
(John Quinn) *a.p: effrt 3f out: rdn to chse ldrs wl over 1f out: sn drvn and styd on gamely to ld last 100yds* **11/2**

05-6 **2** 1 ¼ **Effervesce (IRE)**[47] 43 5-9-6 **59**................................(b[1]) JimCrowley 2 67
(David Pipe) *hld up in tch: smooth hdwy over 4f out: led 2f out: rdn and wandered over 1f out: drvn ins fnl f: hdd and no ex last 100yds* **2/1**[1]

-143 **3** 1 ½ **Mister Frosty (IRE)**[5] 579 6-9-5 **58**.............................. FrederikTylicki 3 64
(George Prodromou) *hld up towards rr: stdy hdwy over 4f out: rdn to chse ldrs over 2f out: drvn and one pce appr fnl f* **10/1**

6631 **4** 3 **Cloudy Start**[11] 493 6-9-7 **60**.............................. FergusSweeney 8 61
(Jamie Osborne) *prom: led after 2f: rdn along over 3f out: hdd 2f out and grad wknd appr fnl f* **10/1**

3-62 **5** 1 **Spartan King (IRE)**[5] 579 4-8-11 **53**.............................. JamieSpencer 4 53
(Ian Williams) *hld up in rr: hdwy on outer over 3f out: rdn along to chse ldrs over 2f out: sn no imp* **10/3**[2]

636- **6** nse **Seawood**[61] 7858 6-8-10 **49** ow1..............................(t) RussKennemore 7 49
(Roy Bowring) *trckd ldrs: hdwy and cl up 5f out: rdn along 3f out: grad wknd* **22/1**

3231 **7** 8 **Brunello**[7] 557 4-9-10 **66** 6ex..................................(v[1]) DanielTudhope 1 53
(David O'Meara) *in tch: rdn along over 4f out: sn wknd* **4/1**[3]

0-04 **8** 12 **Final Tune (IRE)**[11] 493 9-8-9 **51**.............................. RyanClark(3) 5 19
(Mandy Rowland) *led 2f: cl up: rdn along 4f out: wknd over 3f out* **33/1**

2m 40.99s (-0.01) **Going Correction** 0.0s/f (Stan)
WFA 4 from 5yo+ 3lb **8** Ran SP% **117.3**
Speed ratings (Par 101): **100,99,98,96,95 95,90,82**
toteswingers:1&2:£4.30, 2&3:£4.40, 1&3:£6.40 CSF £17.42 CT £108.90 TOTE £8.00: £1.70, £1.90, £2.40; EX 23.20 Trifecta £268.20 Pool: £659.84 - 1.82 winning units..
Owner Alan Mann **Bred** R P Williams **Trained** Settrington, N Yorks

FOCUS
Plenty of in-form horses lined up here, but the race was notable for the gamble on the Magnier, Tabor and Smith-owned Effervesce, who was narrowly thwarted. The winner recorded a 3lb personal best with the third setting the standard.

645 DOWNLOAD THE BLUE SQUARE BET APP H'CAP 5f (F)
4:35 (4:35) (Class 4) (0-85,84) 3-Y-0 **£4,095** (£1,225; £612; £306) **Stalls** High

Form RPR

00-1 **1** **Bella Ophelia (IRE)**[40] 135 3-8-2 **65** oh1...................... NickyMackay 1 73+
(Hughie Morrison) *wnt lft s: sn cl up: led over 2f out: rdn and edgd rt ent fnl f: kpt on* **11/10**[1]

2-61 **2** ¾ **Reve Du Jour (IRE)**[11] 491 3-8-2 **65** oh1.......................... LukeMorris 3 69
(Alan McCabe) *led: rdn along and hdd over 2f out: drvn ent fnl f: kpt on* **3/1**[3]

C034 **3** 4 **Ishiamiracle**[5] 503 3-8-2 **65** oh1..................................(p) HayleyTurner 2 55
(Phil McEntee) *prom: rdn along 1/2-way: kpt on same pce u.p fr over 1f out* **7/1**

436- **4** 4 **Bubbly Ballerina**[53] 7918 3-9-7 **84**..................................(p) JoeFanning 4 60
(Alan Bailey) *chsd ldng pair: rdn along 1/2-way: wknd wl over 1f out* **11/4**[2]

1m 0.55s (0.85) **Going Correction** +0.15s/f (Slow) **4** Ran SP% **111.8**
Speed ratings (Par 99): **99,97,91,85**
CSF £4.89 TOTE £1.50; EX 5.50.
Owner Mrs Belinda Scott & Partners **Bred** Tally-Ho Stud **Trained** East Ilsley, Berks

FOCUS
Four fillies lined up for this fairly modest 3yo sprint handicap. The first two are progressive but this is only fillies' form.

646 GET YOUR BET ON AT BLUESQ.COM H'CAP 1m (F)
5:10 (5:10) (Class 5) (0-70,70) 4-Y-0+ **£2,264** (£673; £336; £168) **Stalls** Low

Form RPR

2-53 **1** **St Oswald**[7] 553 4-9-2 **65**.............................. AndrewMullen 4 77
(David Nicholls) *trckd ldng pair: hdwy 3f out: led 1 1/2f out: sn rdn clr: styd on wl* **7/4**[1]

1/35 **2** 5 **D'Urberville**[19] 384 5-9-5 **68**.............................. FrederikTylicki 5 68
(J R Jenkins) *led: rdn 2f out: hdd 1 1/2f out: kpt on same pce* **3/1**[2]

4-15 **3** 2 ¾ **General Tufto**[28] 287 7-8-13 **62**..................................(b) MartinLane 6 56
(Charles Smith) *in tch: rdn along and outpcd wl over 3f out: styd on fnl 2f* **6/1**

21-6 **4** 9 **Rock Anthem (IRE)**[37] 183 8-9-1 **64**.............................. KieranO'Neill 1 37
(Mike Murphy) *dwlt and in rr: rdn along 3f out: plugged on fnl 2f: n.d* **10/3**[3]

056- **5** ½ **Thatcherite (IRE)**[112] 7213 4-9-7 **70**..........................(t) StephenCraine 3 42
(Tony Coyle) *in tch: hdwy to chse ldng pair 3f out: rdn over 2f out: wknd wl over 1f out* **13/2**

41-0 **6** 4 ½ **Reason To Believe (IRE)**[22] 361 4-9-0 **63**.................... PhillipMakin 2 24
(Ben Haslam) *cl up: rdn along over 3f out: sn wknd* **14/1**

1m 42.55s (-1.15) **Going Correction** 0.0s/f (Stan) **6** Ran SP% **118.7**
Speed ratings (Par 103): **105,100,97,88,87 83**
toteswingers:1&2:£2.00, 2&3:£2.80, 1&3:£4.00 CSF £7.89 TOTE £4.00: £2.20, £3.40; EX 10.80.
Owner Richard Jeffrey **Bred** Paul Hearson Bloodstock **Trained** Sessay, N Yorks

FOCUS
A run-of-the-mill handicap run at an even gallop. There were doubts over most of these and the form is not rated too positively.
T/Plt: £116.00 to a £1 stake. Pool of £54,681.44 - 343.89 winning tickets. T/Qpdt: £38.10 to a £1 stake. Pool of £3,182.70 - 61.70 winning tickets. JR

[572] KEMPTON (A.W) (R-H)
Wednesday, February 22

OFFICIAL GOING: Standard
Wind: Fresh, half behind Weather: Overcast

647 FREE ENTRY FOR BETDAQ MEMBERS H'CAP 5f (P)
5:30 (5:30) (Class 5) (0-75,79) 4-Y-0+ **£2,264** (£673; £336; £168) **Stalls** Low

Form RPR

15-3 **1** **Fair Passion**[12] 492 5-9-7 **75**.............................. DaneO'Neill 7 84
(Derek Shaw) *hld up bhd ldrs: prog over 1f out: clsd to ld last 150yds: rdn and r.o* **8/1**[3]

5-35 **2** 1 **Estonia**[7] 560 5-9-6 **74**.............................. ShaneKelly 3 81+
(Michael Squance) *s.i.s: sn in tch: prog on inner fr 2f out: stopped in run briefly 1f out: r.o to take 2nd last 100yds: no imp on wnr after* **9/2**[2]

3242 **3** 1 **Island Legend (IRE)**[7] 560 6-9-7 **75**..................(p) RichardKingscote 1 77
(Milton Bradley) *fast away: led: rdn over 1f out: hdd and fdd last 150yds* **11/8**[1]

-561 **4** ½ **Triple Dream**[7] 560 7-9-11 **79** 6ex........................(tp) RussKennemore 8 79
(Milton Bradley) *chsd ldng pair to 2f out: rdn and nt qckn and sn lost pl: kpt on again fnl f* **8/1**[3]

40-0 **5** 1 **Billy Red**[11] 525 8-9-5 **73**..(b) FergusSweeney 6 69
(J R Jenkins) *chsd ldr to 1f out: n.m.r sn after and fdd* **20/1**

-013 **6** nk **Novabridge**[12] 497 4-8-11 **65**..(b) PaddyAspell 2 60
(Neil Mulholland) *chsd ldrs: wnt 3rd 2f out: hanging and nt qckn over 1f out: fdd fnl f* **10/1**

6-00 **7** 1 **Baby Dottie**[14] 474 5-8-3 **62**.............................. JemmaMarshall(5) 4 54
(Pat Phelan) *settled in last pair: jst pushed along fr 2f out: one pce and no ch of rching ldrs* **20/1**

0003 **8** ¾ **Captain Scooby**[7] 560 6-8-11 **70**.............................. CharlesEddery(5) 5 59
(Richard Guest) *a in last pair: rdn and struggling 1/2-way: one pce after* **8/1**[3]

00-6 **9** 13 **Lucky Art (USA)**[26] 327 6-9-2 **75**.............................. JustinNewman(5) 9 17
(Conor Dore) *racd wd: chsd ldrs: rdn bef 1/2-way: wknd qckly 2f out: t.o* **20/1**

59.82s (-0.68) **Going Correction** +0.05s/f (Slow) **9** Ran SP% **117.0**
Speed ratings (Par 103): **107,105,103,103,101 100,99,98,77**
toteswingers:1&2:£9.60, 2&3:£1.70, 1&3:£4.80 CSF £43.00 CT £78.54 TOTE £9.90: £3.30, £1.80, £1.10; EX 64.70.
Owner The Whiteman Partnership **Bred** D R Tucker **Trained** Sproxton, Leics
■ Stewards' Enquiry : Dane O'Neill one-day ban: careless riding (7 Mar)

FOCUS
A couple of closers came to the fore here. The runner-up sets the standard.

648 BETDAQ MULTIPLES H'CAP 1m 2f (P)
6:00 (6:00) (Class 5) (0-75,75) 4-Y-0+ **£2,264** (£673; £336; £168) **Stalls** Low

Form RPR
3-01 **1** **John Louis**[25] 349 4-9-2 **71** JoeFanning 6 84
(Philip McBride) *mde all: mod pce but untrbld: kicked on over 2f out: maintained gallop after: unchal* **5/2**[1]
100- **2** 3 ½ **Silver Alliance**[125] 6978 4-9-2 **71** LukeMorris 7 77
(Julia Feilden) *chsd wnr after 1f: rdn over 2f out: styd on same pce and nvr able to chal* **10/1**
4-54 **3** 1 ¾ **Lisahane Bog**[21] 374 5-9-3 **71** (v) JohnFahy 1 74
(Peter Hedger) *chsd wnr 1f: racd in 3rd tl 3f out: sn drvn: chsd ldng pair again over 1f out: one pce* **11/2**[3]
00-0 **4** ½ **Edgewater (IRE)**[29] 280 5-9-0 **75** DarrenEgan(7) 3 77
(John Akehurst) *chsd ldng trio: outpcd and lost pl over 2f out: kpt on again fnl f to press for 3rd nr fin* **7/1**
6-63 **5** 1 ½ **Menadati (USA)**[21] 374 4-8-12 **67** TomMcLaughlin 9 66
(Peter Hiatt) *hld up in midfield: prog on outer to go 3rd 3f out: no imp 2f out: fdd over 1f out* **3/1**[2]
100- **6** 1 **Hurricane Spirit (IRE)**[64] 7831 8-9-7 **75** SteveDrowne 10 72
(Terry Clement) *t.k.h: hld up in 7th: plenty to do whn pce lifted over 2f out: one pce and n.d* **12/1**
4-22 **7** 1 ¼ **Hurricane Hymnbook (USA)**[25] 349 7-9-4 **72** StevieDonohoe 2 66
(Willie Musson) *blindfold off sltly late and dwlt: hld up: detached in last and pushed along over 2f out: modest late prog: nvr in it* **13/2**
00-0 **8** shd **Lord Theo**[13] 480 8-9-4 **72** RobertHavlin 8 66
(Nick Littmoden) *stdd s: hld up in last pair: rdn whn pce lifted over 2f out: nvr a threat* **100/1**
00-5 **9** 2 **Black Coffee**[13] 480 7-8-13 **67** (b) ShaneKelly 4 57
(Mark Brisbourne) *dwlt: chsd ldrs: rdn and struggling over 2f out: hanging wl over 1f out: wknd* **20/1**

2m 8.02s (0.02) **Going Correction** +0.05s/f (Slow)
WFA 4 from 5yo+ 1lb 9 Ran SP% **117.3**
Speed ratings (Par 103): **101,98,96,96,95 94,93,93,91**
toteswingers:1&2:£12.50, 1&3:£4.30, 2&3:£8.80 CSF £29.22 CT £128.49 TOTE £3.50: £1.30, £2.90, £2.00; EX 43.60.
Owner Four Winds Racing **Bred** Wood Farm Stud (Waresley) **Trained** Newmarket, Suffolk

FOCUS
The winner made all off an easy lead and it proved impossible to make up significant ground. The form is taken at face value.

649 BACK OR LAY AT BETDAQ.COM CLAIMING STKS 7f (P)
6:30 (6:30) (Class 6) 3-Y-0+ **£1,617** (£481; £240; £120) **Stalls** Low

Form RPR
-123 **1** **Marajaa (IRE)**[28] 299 10-9-13 81 StevieDonohoe 6 84+
(Willie Musson) *confidently rdn: hld up in last pair: smooth prog 2f out: led 120yds out: pushed clr* **1/1**[1]
021- **2** 1 ½ **Mambo Spirit (IRE)**[64] 7834 8-9-12 73 DaneO'Neill 4 79
(Tony Newcombe) *hld up in 4th: prog over 2f out: led wl over 1f out and wnt for home: hdd and readily hld last 120yds* **15/2**[3]
0-55 **3** 4 ½ **Last Sovereign**[21] 378 8-9-9 75 (b) MichaelO'Connell(3) 2 67
(Ollie Pears) *t.k.h: bmpd after 100yds: chsd ldng pair: wnt 2nd over 2f out and tried to chal: lft bhd by ldng pair fnl f* **4/1**[2]
-060 **4** 5 **Best Trip (IRE)**[7] 560 5-9-10 70 (t) FrannyNorton 3 51
(Richard Guest) *racd freely: led: shifted rt after 100yds: hdd & wknd rapidly wl over 1f out* **14/1**
01-0 **5** 2 ¼ **Whitechapel**[49] 31 5-9-10 70 DavidProbert 1 45
(Andrew Balding) *bdly hmpd against rail after 100yds: a in last pair: rdn over 2f out: wknd over 1f out* **4/1**[2]
0-06 **6** nk **Clone Devil (IRE)**[15] 466 3-8-3 44 FrankieMcDonald 5 34
(Alastair Lidderdale) *chsd ldr to over 2f out: wknd qckly* **150/1**

1m 26.09s (0.09) **Going Correction** +0.05s/f (Slow)
WFA 3 from 5yo+ 17lb 6 Ran SP% **109.1**
Speed ratings (Par 101): **101,99,94,88,85 85**
toteswingers:1&2:£1.50, 1&3:£1.30, 2&3:£4.00 CSF £8.76 TOTE £2.10: £1.20, £2.80; EX 7.00.
Owner W J Musson **Bred** Shadwell Estate Company Limited **Trained** Newmarket, Suffolk

FOCUS
A fair claimer, but it was straightforward for the winner who was best in. The form is not rated too positively.

650 BETDAQ MOBILE APPS MEDIAN AUCTION MAIDEN STKS 1m 3f (P)
7:00 (7:01) (Class 6) 3-5-Y-0 **£1,617** (£481; £240) **Stalls** Low

Form RPR
1 **Red Orator** 3-8-5 0 JoeFanning 3 74+
(Mark Johnston) *pressed ldr: wd bnd 3f out and rdn: narrow ld over 1f out: kpt on to draw clr fnl f* **6/4**[1]
3 **2** 3 ¼ **Munificence**[12] 502 3-8-5 0 ChrisCatlin 2 66
(Marco Botti) *led but pressed thrght: rdn 3f out: hdd over 1f out: one pce after* **13/8**[2]
20-6 **3** 1 **Oneiric**[25] 355 4-9-7 68 IanMongan 1 63
(Brett Johnson) *trckd ldng pair: rdn over 3f out: tried to chal 2f out: one pce after* **7/2**[3]

2m 22.42s (0.52) **Going Correction** +0.05s/f (Slow)
WFA 3 from 4yo 23lb 3 Ran SP% **100.3**
Speed ratings (Par 101): **100,97,96**
CSF £3.69 TOTE £2.10; EX 4.10.
Owner Newsells Park Stud **Bred** Newsells Park Stud **Trained** Middleham Moor, N Yorks

FOCUS
Only three runners and the time was 1.13 seconds slower than the following Class 6 handicap, which was a strongly run race. The winner is a likely improver but the bare form is shaky.

651 SKYSPORTS.COM H'CAP 1m 3f (P)
7:30 (7:32) (Class 6) (0-60,60) 4-Y-0+ **£1,617** (£481; £240; £120) **Stalls** Low

Form RPR
4406 **1** **Striding Edge (IRE)**[16] 452 6-8-11 **57** NicoleNordblad(7) 12 72
(Hans Adielsson) *hld up in 8th: smooth prog over 2f out: led over 1f out: pushed clr fnl f* **9/1**
5-21 **2** 2 ¼ **Trecase**[7] 558 5-8-5 **51** (t) DarrenEgan(7) 3 62
(Tony Carroll) *hld up in rr: prog on outer over 3f out to press ldrs over 2f out: hung lft after: chal and w wnr over 1f out: styd on same pce* **15/2**[3]
-435 **3** 7 **Land Hawk (IRE)**[16] 452 6-9-1 **57** SimonPearce(3) 5 55
(Lydia Pearce) *trckd ldrs: prog over 4f out: led wl over 2f out: sn drvn: hdd wl over 1f out: wl btn in 4th fnl f: snatched 3rd on post* **7/1**[2]
0-12 **4** hd **Fire In Babylon (IRE)**[31] 265 4-9-3 **58** (b[1]) JimCrowley 11 56
(Michael Wigham) *chsd ldr to over 6f out: styd prom: rdn to go 2nd over 2f out: led briefly wl over 1f out: easily lft bhd by ldng pair after: lost 3rd post* **7/4**[1]
0-36 **5** 2 ¼ **Safwaan**[11] 530 5-8-13 **52** StevieDonohoe 10 46
(Willie Musson) *hld up in last trio: last and pushed along over 2f out: passed wkng rivals after: rdn and styd on fnl f: no ch* **8/1**
50-4 **6** 1 ¼ **Port Hill**[20] 389 5-9-2 **55** ShaneKelly 9 47
(Mark Brisbourne) *prom: chsd ldr over 6f out to 3f out: sn wknd* **14/1**
-066 **7** ½ **Prince Of Thebes (IRE)**[11] 519 11-8-10 **54** (p) MarkCoumbe(5) 13 45
(Michael Attwater) *s.s: mostly in last trio: rdn 4f out: struggling after: prog to go modest 5th briefly ins fnl f: nvr a threat* **20/1**
040- **8** 2 ¼ **Agapanthus (GER)**[112] 6811 7-9-0 **53** (p) PaddyAspell 8 40
(Neil Mulholland) *s.v.s: sn in tch in last trio: urged along and no rspnse wl over 2f out: wl btn after* **50/1**
535- **9** hd **Gower Rules (IRE)**[161] 6052 4-9-5 **60** KieranO'Neill 4 46
(John Bridger) *led at gd pce: drvn and hdd wl over 2f out: sn wknd qckly* **16/1**
53-0 **10** ½ **Ivan The Terrible (IRE)**[6] 579 4-8-7 **53** CharlesEddery(5) 7 38
(Richard Guest) *stdd s: t.k.h and hld up in rr: rdn 4f out: struggling after* **40/1**
4/ **11** ½ **Petit Ecuyer (FR)**[34] 6-9-2 **55** GeorgeBaker 2 40
(Gary Moore) *wl in tch: cl enough over 3f out: lost grnd sn after: jst pushed along and dropped away* **14/1**
-334 **12** 10 **Beneath**[13] 477 5-9-5 **58** (b) DaneO'Neill 6 25
(Neil Mulholland) *prom: rdn over 3f out: wknd over 2f out: eased over 1f out: t.o* **9/1**
00-0 **13** 15 **Indus Valley (IRE)**[29] 276 5-9-1 **54** (b) MartinHarley 14
(Des Donovan) *hld up in tch: rdn over 3f out: sn wknd rapidly: t.o* **66/1**

2m 21.29s (-0.61) **Going Correction** +0.05s/f (Slow)
WFA 4 from 5yo+ 2lb 13 Ran SP% **121.6**
Speed ratings (Par 101): **104,102,97,97,95 94,94,92,92,92 91,84,73**
toteswingers:1&2:£16.20, 2&3:£14.60, 1&3:£12.60 CSF £74.41 CT £511.25 TOTE £11.20: £2.70, £2.10, £2.60; EX 83.00.
Owner Erik Penser **Bred** G Prendergast **Trained** Kingston Lisle, Oxon

FOCUS
A moderate handicap run at a good pace. The first two came clear and the winner is rated back to last year's best.

652 SKYSPORTS.COM RACING H'CAP 6f (P)
8:00 (8:00) (Class 4) (0-85,82) 4-Y-0+ **£4,075** (£1,212; £606; £303) **Stalls** Low

Form RPR
0-03 **1** **Clear Praise (USA)**[11] 525 5-9-3 **78** HayleyTurner 2 86
(Simon Dow) *hld up in 7th: prog over 2f out: rdn to ld over 1f out: styd on: jst hld on* **5/1**[2]
22-3 **2** shd **Arctic Lynx (IRE)**[28] 304 5-9-1 **76** GeorgeBaker 9 85+
(John Best) *hld up in last pair: effrt on outer over 1f out: forced way through sn after: fin wl: jst failed* **11/4**[1]
-202 **3** 1 **Earlsmedic**[27] 311 7-8-12 **76** (v) RyanClark(3) 4 81
(Stuart Williams) *hld up bhd ldrs gng wl: prog to ld over 1f out: immediately idled and hdd: nt qckn after: styd on nr fin* **11/2**[3]
-211 **4** 1 **Torres Del Paine**[29] 282 5-9-0 **75** KieranO'Neill 7 77
(Jimmy Fox) *dwlt: hld up in last pair: prog through rivals over 1f out: produced to chal ins fnl f: fnd nil* **5/1**[2]
600- **5** 3 ¾ **Roodee Queen**[63] 7847 4-9-3 **78** RichardKingscote 6 68
(Milton Bradley) *trckd ldng trio: rdn to chal 2f out: upsides over 1f out: sn wknd* **20/1**
0206 **6** 2 ¼ **Rylee Mooch**[4] 624 4-8-4 **70** (e) CharlesEddery(5) 8 52
(Richard Guest) *pushed up to ld and set str pce: hdd & wknd over 1f out* **25/1**
1-35 **7** ½ **Tislaam (IRE)**[28] 304 5-9-1 **76** (p) MartinHarley 10 57
(Alan McCabe) *trckd ldng pair: rdn over 2f out: sing to weaken whn bmpd jst over 1f out* **7/1**
-541 **8** ½ **Pick A Little**[22] 368 4-9-3 **78** SteveDrowne 1 57
(Michael Blake) *chsd ldrs: u.p over 2f out: sn btn* **10/1**
12-0 **9** ½ **Monsieur Jamie**[52] 3 4-9-6 **81** FrederikTylicki 5 59
(J R Jenkins) *pressed ldr to over 2f out: sn btn* **12/1**

1m 12.53s (-0.57) **Going Correction** +0.05s/f (Slow) 9 Ran SP% **113.3**
Speed ratings (Par 105): **105,104,103,102,97 94,93,92,92**
toteswingers:1&2:£4.00, 2&3:£4.10, 1&3:£5.00 CSF £18.73 CT £77.37 TOTE £6.20: £1.70, £1.40, £1.60; EX 20.10.
Owner Chua, Moore, Goalen & Warner **Bred** Juddmonte Farms Inc **Trained** Epsom, Surrey
■ Stewards' Enquiry : George Baker three-day ban: careless riding (7-9 Mar)

FOCUS
A fair, competitive handicap that was run at an overly strong pace and set it up for those held up. The winner is rated up a length on recent form.

653 ALL-WEATHER "HANDS AND HEELS" APPRENTICE SERIES H'CAP (RACING EXCELLENCE INITIATIVE) 1m (P)
8:30 (8:31) (Class 7) (0-50,49) 4-Y-0+ **£1,455** (£433; £216; £108) **Stalls** Low

Form RPR
26-4 **1** **Rigid**[39] 66 5-9-2 **48** GeorgeDowning 4 59
(Tony Carroll) *trckd ldrs: smooth prog to ld wl over 1f out: pushed along and drew clr* **7/1**[3]
3240 **2** 6 **Very Well Red**[12] 490 9-9-0 **49** ThomasGarner(3) 6 47
(Peter Hiatt) *prom: pushed along over 2f out: outpcd over 1f out: kpt on to take 2nd last 100yds* **13/2**[2]
00-0 **3** ½ **Ellielusive (IRE)**[12] 503 5-8-13 **45** JackDuern 7 42
(Mark Brisbourne) *towards rr: 9th over 3f out: prog on inner over 2f out: styd on fnl f to take 3rd nr fin* **25/1**
05-0 **4** ½ **Gambatte**[12] 503 5-8-13 **45** DarrenEgan 12 40+
(Tony Carroll) *stdd s: hld up in last quartet and wl off the pce: effrt on outer over 2f out: styd on: nrst fin* **16/1**
00-6 **5** ¾ **Rosy Dawn**[7] 558 7-8-8 **45** AccursioRomeo(5) 8 39
(Brett Johnson) *led: urged along over 2f out: hdd wl over 1f out: wknd and lost pls last 100yds* **14/1**
000- **6** 3 ¾ **Future Impact (IRE)**[98] 7429 4-9-1 **47** (v[1]) NoraLooby 9 32
(Pat Murphy) *mostly chsd ldr: chal and upsides 2f out: wknd over 1f out* **9/1**
000- **7** ½ **Inquisitress**[102] 7387 8-8-10 **45** JenniferFerguson(3) 11 29+
(John Bridger) *s.i.s: hld up in last quartet and wl off the pce: effrt on inner whn nt clr run over 2f out: no ch after* **12/1**
060- **8** ½ **Dune Island**[265] 2637 4-8-13 **45** JoshBaudains 14 28
(John Bridger) *a in midfield: pushed along and no prog 2f out* **50/1**
464- **9** ¾ **My Sister**[51] 6438 5-8-8 **45** RobertSpencer(5) 5 26
(Mark Usher) *sn hld up in last pair and wl off the pce: nvr a factor* **13/2**[2]

The Form Book Flat, Raceform Ltd, Compton, RG20 6NL

-050 **10** *nk* **Mi Regalo**[27] 312 4-8-12 **49**..............................(p) EvaMoscrop(5) 13 29
(Phil McEntee) *racd v wd: prom: lost grnd bnd 3f out: sn wknd* **16/1**

0-04 **11** *shd* **By Implication**[7] 561 4-8-13 **45**..............................(b) ThomasBrown 3 25
(Ed de Giles) *trckd ldrs: cl enough over 2f out: wknd over 1f out* **5/1**[1]

5004 **12** *6* **Le Reveur**[7] 558 10-8-13 **45**..............................(e) DannyBrock 1 11
(Richard Guest) *prom: pushed along 1/2-way: sn struggling: wknd over 2f out* **8/1**

00/0 **13** *15* **During The War (USA)**[7] 389 5-8-13 **48** ow1..........(b) JoshCrane(3) 2
(Chris Dwyer) *v.s.a: a in last pair: t.o* **66/1**

-0 **14** *12* **Noinformation (IRE)**[42] 125 5-8-12 **47**..............(b) IanBurns(3) 10
(Mark Michael McNiff, Ire) *a towards rr: wknd over 3f out: wl t.o* **15/2**

1m 41.36s (1.56) **Going Correction** +0.05s/f (Slow) **14** Ran SP% **122.1**
Speed ratings (Par 97): **94,88,87,87,86 82,82,81,80,80 80,74,59,47**
toteswingers:1&2:£7.80, 2&3:£21.00, 1&3:£57.70 CSF £52.26 CT £1098.53 TOTE £8.80: £3.00, £2.70, £7.10; EX 33.20.
Owner Mr & Mrs J B Bacciochi **Bred** Limestone And Tara Studs **Trained** Cropthorne, Worcs
■ Stewards' Enquiry : Accursio Romeo four-day ban: stop riding before the post (7-10 Mar)

FOCUS
A really moderate handicap and it had a messy look to it with these apprentice-ridden runners soon well spread out. Weak form, taken at face value.
T/Plt: £41.00 to a £1 stake. Pool of £65,452.75 - 1,163.62 winning tickets. T/Qpdt: £13.00 to a £1 stake. Pool of £6,625.83 - 376.57 winning tickets. JN

619 LINGFIELD (L-H)
Wednesday, February 22

OFFICIAL GOING: Standard
Wind: fairly strong, half behind Weather: dry, breezy

654 BET AND WATCH AT BLUESQ.COM CLAIMING STKS 5f (P)
1:45 (1:45) (Class 6) 4-Y-O+ **£1,704** (£503; £251) **Stalls** High

Form RPR

20/3 **1** **Brenin Taran**[32] 253 6-9-1 80.............................. MartinLane 1 79
(David Simcock) *taken down early: stdd s: hld up in tch: hdwy to chse ldng pair 1/2-way: rdn and effrt over 1f out: ev ch ins fnl f: r.o wl to ld towards fin* **15/8**[2]

-311 **2** *nk* **Drawnfromthepast (IRE)**[15] 456 7-9-1 82.............. JamieSpencer 3 78
(Jamie Osborne) *chsd ldng pair tl 1/2-way: swtchd rt and effrt wl over 1f out: drvn to chal jst ins fnl f: led fnl 100yds: hdd and no ex towards fin* **6/4**[1]

-220 **3** *1/2* **Mottley Crewe**[11] 527 5-9-9 85..............................(b) MartinHarley 4 84
(Richard Guest) *sn bustled along to ld: rdn 2f out: drvn jst ins fnl f: hdd fnl 100yds: styd on same pce after* **3/1**[3]

0500 **4** *3/4* **Forty Proof (IRE)**[4] 624 4-7-10 57..............................(b) NoraLooby(7) 2 61
(Alan McCabe) *taken down early: hld up in tch in last pair: pushed along ent fnl f: styd on fnl 100yds: nt clr run cl home* **20/1**

5404 **5** *3/4* **Decider (USA)**[12] 497 9-8-5 57..............................(v) LukeMorris 5 60
(Ronald Harris) *taken down early: t.k.h: pressed ldng after 1f tl hung rt and lost pl bnd 2f out: sn drvn: styd on same pce fnl f* **40/1**

57.41s (-1.39) **Going Correction** -0.10s/f (Stan) **5** Ran SP% **107.0**
Speed ratings (Par 101): **107,106,105,104,103**
CSF £4.75 TOTE £2.20: £1.10, £1.40; EX 4.80.
Owner Mrs Ann Simcock **Bred** D M I Simcock **Trained** Newmarket, Suffolk

FOCUS
A fair contest for the grade and a good winning time. The fourth and fifth limit the form.

655 LINGFIELD PARK OWNERS CLUB (S) STKS 1m 2f (P)
2:15 (2:15) (Class 6) 4-Y-O+ **£1,704** (£503; £251) **Stalls** Low

Form RPR

1110 **1** **Daniel Thomas (IRE)**[4] 626 10-9-6 71..............(tp) WilliamCarson 6 71+
(Richard Guest) *hld up in tch in last trio: nt clr run on ent fnl 2f: swtchd rt and stl nt clr run wl over 1f out: hmpd and swtchd sharply lft jst ins fnl f: qcknd and str run to ld fnl 50yds: sn in command* **7/2**[2]

204- **2** *1 1/4* **Enriching (USA)**[149] 6412 4-8-7 63.............................. DarrenEgan(7) 1 61
(Noel Quinlan) *led: stdd gallop after 2f: rdn and qcknd clr w rival 2f out: stl clr w rival and edgd rt ins fnl f: hdd fnl 50yds: nt pce of wnr and sn btn: hld on for 2nd* **9/2**[3]

02-5 **3** *shd* **Potentiale (IRE)**[19] 401 8-8-8 64..............(v) Leah-AnneAvery(7) 8 61
(J W Hills) *hld up in rr: hdwy on outer 3f out: wd bnd 2f out: pushed along and styd on to chse ldng pair jst ins fnl f: kpt on* **16/1**

5-53 **4** *1/2* **Ostentation**[7] 567 5-8-12 65..............................(p) MichaelO'Connell(3) 2 60
(Roger Teal) *w ldr: rdn and qcknd clr w ldr 2f out: stl ev ch and clr w ldr whn carried rt ins fnl f: no ex and lost 2 pls fnl 50yds* **16/1**

05-4 **5** *1/2* **Cheers Buddy (IRE)**[16] 449 4-9-0 68.............................. KieranO'Neill 5 59
(David C Griffiths) *t.k.h: chsd ldrs: rdn wl over 1f out: unable qck and edgd rt u.p jst over 1f out: styd on same pce ins fnl f* **12/1**

2162 **6** *4* **Alhaban (IRE)**[7] 567 6-9-6 65.............................. LukeMorris 9 56
(Ronald Harris) *chsd ldng trio: rdn over 2f out: swtchd rt and n.m.r over 1f out tl hmpd and lost pl jst ins fnl f: nt rcvr and n.d after* **7/1**

-006 **7** *hd* **Jordaura**[30] 275 6-9-1 73.............................. ShaneKelly 4 51
(Gay Kelleway) *hld up in tch in midfield: hdwy to chse ldrs 3f out: drvn and unable qck over 1f out: styng on same pce whn n.m.r jst ins fnl f: wl hld after* **2/1**[1]

1-26 **8** *2 1/2* **King's Colour**[39] 175 7-9-6 68.............................. DavidProbert 7 51
(Brett Johnson) *t.k.h: hld up in tch in last trio: pushed along over 2f out: rdn and swtchd rt over 1f out: sn no imp and wl hld fnl f* **8/1**

00 **9** *8* **Tiger Who**[22] 367 4-8-2 0.............................. NatashaEaton(7) 3 25
(David Flood) *t.k.h: hld up in midfield: rdn and dropped to rr 3f out: wl bhd fnl 2f* **100/1**

2m 6.08s (-0.52) **Going Correction** -0.10s/f (Stan)
WFA 4 from 5yo+ 1lb **9** Ran SP% **117.8**
Speed ratings (Par 101): **98,97,96,96,96 92,92,90,84**
toteswingers:1&2:£6.10, 1&3:£10.00, 2&3:£21.40 CSF £20.17 TOTE £3.70: £1.10, £2.10, £6.10; EX 33.80 Trifecta £465.80 Part won. Pool: £629.58 - 0.42 winning units..There was no bid for the winner.
Owner Rakebackmypoker.com **Bred** Lawn Stud **Trained** Stainforth, S Yorks

FOCUS
This seller was run at a steady gallop. The field were well bunched at halfway but despite the soft fractions the leaders were caught inside the final furlong. The winner rates better than the bare form.

656 LINGFIELDPARK.CO.UK H'CAP 1m 2f (P)
2:50 (2:57) (Class 5) (0-75,75) 3-Y-O **£2,385** (£704; £352) **Stalls** Low

Form RPR

14-5 **1** **Next Cry (USA)**[38] 184 3-9-2 **70**.............................. KieranO'Neill 3 75
(Richard Hannon) *chsd ldrs: rdn to chse ldr 2f out: drvn and chal 1f out: led ins fnl f: kpt on wl and forged ahd towards fin* **7/1**

0-13 **2** *1/2* **Good Morning Star (IRE)**[23] 362 3-9-4 **72**.............. JoeFanning 6 76
(Mark Johnston) *led: rdn and fnd ex 2f out: hdd ins fnl f: battled on gamely tl no ex and btn towards fin* **6/1**[3]

6-1 **3** *3* **Palmyra (IRE)**[10] 428 3-8-9 **63**.............................. MartinLane 2 61
(David Simcock) *dwlt: niggled along and nvr looked to be gng in rr: rdn over 3f out: 4th and wl hld u.p over 1f out: styd on ins fnl f to go 3rd nr fin: nvr threatened ldrs* **13/8**[1]

0-31 **4** *nk* **Bramshill Lass**[26] 324 3-9-6 **74**.............................. JimCrowley 7 71
(Amanda Perrett) *chsd ldr tl 2f out: sn u.p and fnd little: 3rd and btn 1f out: pushed along and one pce fnl f: lost 3rd nr fin* **9/2**[2]

51-5 **5** *4 1/2* **King Of Wing (IRE)**[39] 180 3-9-7 **75**.............................. WilliamCarson 1 63
(Jim Boyle) *pushed along early: in tch: rdn and fnd little 2f out: drvn and wknd over 1f out* **12/1**

2m 6.27s (-0.33) **Going Correction** -0.10s/f (Stan) **5** Ran SP% **90.8**
Speed ratings (Par 97): **97,96,94,93,90**
CSF £28.86 TOTE £6.60: £3.30, £1.10; EX 23.10.
Owner William Stobart **Bred** G Watts Humphrey Jr Et Al **Trained** East Everleigh, Wilts
■ King's Wharf (8/1, vet's advice at s) and Athletic (9/1, burst out of the stalls) were withdrawn. Deduct 20p in the £ under R4.

FOCUS
A typically muddling 1m2f handicap in which few were able to get into contention as the front two quickened rounding the home turn. The winner belatedly confirmed the promise of his Kempton win last year.

657 BET AT BLUE SQUARE MEDIAN AUCTION MAIDEN STKS 6f (P)
3:20 (3:28) (Class 6) 3-5-Y-O **£1,704** (£503; £251) **Stalls** Low

Form RPR

336- **1** **Performing Pocket (USA)**[159] 6126 3-8-9 77.............. JamieSpencer 1 66+
(David Simcock) *mde virtually: set stdy gallop: nudged along and qcknd wl over 1f out: r.o strly and wl clr ins fnl f: easily* **1/4**[1]

-534 **2** *4* **Flying Kitty**[7] 564 3-8-4 48.............................. KieranO'Neill 5 48
(John Bridger) *t.k.h: hld up in tch in rr: effrt u.p on inner over 1f out: chsd clr wnr ins fnl f: kpt on but no ch w wnr* **16/1**[3]

24-3 **3** *1/2* **Look At Me Now**[11] 524 3-8-9 67..............................(p) HayleyTurner 3 51
(Jim Boyle) *t.k.h: sn chsng wnr: rdn and unable qck wl over 1f out: no ch w wnr and styd on same pce u.p fnl f* **9/2**[2]

-340 **4** *nk* **Miakora**[11] 524 4-9-5 46.............................. ShaneKelly 2 49
(Michael Quinn) *broke fast: sn restrained and hld up in 3rd: chsd wnr over 2f out: rdn and unable qck wl over 1f out: wl hld 1f out: lost 2nd and kpt on same pce fnl f* **33/1**

1m 13.84s (1.94) **Going Correction** -0.10s/f (Stan)
WFA 3 from 4yo 15lb **4** Ran SP% **107.0**
Speed ratings (Par 101): **83,77,77,76**
CSF £5.23 TOTE £1.20; EX 3.90.
Owner M M Racing **Bred** Clarkland Farm **Trained** Newmarket, Suffolk

FOCUS
A weak, slowly run maiden and the form should be treated with some caution. The winner did not need to match his 2yo form.

658 CYPRIUM BAR AT MARRIOTT LINGFIELD H'CAP 6f (P)
3:55 (3:55) (Class 6) (0-65,65) 4-Y-O+ **£1,704** (£503; £251) **Stalls** Low

Form RPR

4213 **1** **Diamond Vine (IRE)**[18] 425 4-9-6 **65**..............................(p) LukeMorris 8 73
(Ronald Harris) *hld up in last trio: hdwy on outer 1/2-way: rdn wl over 1f out: drvn and styd on wl fnl f: led towards fin* **9/4**[1]

4050 **2** *3/4* **Riflessione**[14] 474 6-8-12 **64**..............................(v) DarrenEgan(7) 6 69
(Ronald Harris) *t.k.h and hung rt thrght: led: clr after 2f: rdn and stl hanging fr over 1f out: kpt on tl hdd wl ins fnl f: fin towards stands' rail* **16/1**

-654 **3** *hd* **Even Bolder**[14] 473 9-9-6 **65**.............................. ShaneKelly 1 70
(Eric Wheeler) *broke wl: sn restrained and hld up in midfield: swtchd lft and effrt wl over 1f out: hdwy u.p and ev ch ins fnl f: one pce towards fin* **7/2**[2]

301- **4** *hd* **Catalinas Diamond (IRE)**[95] 7488 4-9-3 **62**..............(t) SteveDrowne 5 66
(Pat Murphy) *hld up in midfield: rdn wl over 1f out: drvn and ev ch ins fnl f: kpt on same pce wl ins fnl f* **10/1**

3341 **5** *1 1/2* **Dvinsky (USA)**[11] 522 11-9-6 **65**..............................(b) TomMcLaughlin 7 64
(Paul Howling) *chsd ldr: rdn and effrt 2f out: unable qck over 1f out: styd on same pce ins fnl f* **8/1**

2-45 **6** *1 1/4* **Meia Noite**[12] 496 5-9-0 **59**..............................(p) MartinHarley 3 54
(Alan McCabe) *taken down early: hld up in last trio: drvn and effrt over 1f out: no imp fnl f* **13/2**

2-60 **7** *1/2* **Rio Royale (IRE)**[39] 179 6-8-10 **62**.............................. LukeRowe(7) 2 56
(Amanda Perrett) *stdd after s: hld up in rr: pushed along and effrt on inner over 1f out: styd on but nvr gng pce to chal* **4/1**[3]

1m 11.85s (-0.05) **Going Correction** -0.10s/f (Stan) **7** Ran SP% **112.4**
Speed ratings (Par 101): **96,95,94,94,92 90,90**
toteswingers:1&2:£9.60, 1&3:£2.50, 2&3:£11.50 CSF £37.50 CT £121.65 TOTE £3.60: £2.20, £8.70; EX 25.00 Trifecta £84.30 Pool: £744.26 - 6.53 winning units..
Owner Ridge House Stables Ltd **Bred** Michael O'Mahony **Trained** Earlswood, Monmouths

FOCUS
A moderate sprint handicap and the first four finished in a heap. Muddling form.

659 MARRIOTTLINGFIELDPARK.CO.UK H'CAP 6f (P)
4:30 (4:30) (Class 4) (0-85,84) 3-Y-O **£4,204** (£1,251; £625; £312) **Stalls** Low

Form RPR

-112 **1** **Pale Orchid (IRE)**[14] 471 3-9-7 **84**.............................. LukeMorris 4 94+
(David Evans) *hld up in last trio: hdwy to chse ldrs 2f out: swtchd lft and effrt wl over 1f out: drvn to chal 1f out: led fnl 75yds: r.o wl* **8/11**[1]

25-3 **2** *1 3/4* **Waseem Faris (IRE)**[28] 295 3-9-3 **80**.............................. MartinHarley 1 84
(Mick Channon) *in tch in midfield: effrt on to chse ldr 2f out: sn ev ch: drvn to ld 1f out: sn hrd pressed: hdd and nt pce of wnr fnl 75yds* **8/1**

-113 **3** *1 1/2* **Adranian (IRE)**[14] 471 3-9-2 **79**..............................(v) DavidProbert 2 78
(David C Griffiths) *led for 1f: pressed ldr after tl led again 3f out: rdn and edgd rt wl over 1f out: hdd 1f out: outpcd fnl 150yds* **16/1**

6-11 **4** *hd* **Sweet Ovation**[19] 394 3-8-4 **67** HayleyTurner 3 66
(Mark Usher) *stdd s: hld up in last: pushed along and sme hdwy on inner over 1f out: styd on same pce ins fnl f: pressing for 3rd cl home: nvr trbld ldrs* **7/1**[3]

012 **5** *2 ¼* **Abi Scarlet (IRE)**[13] 482 3-8-11 **74** RobertHavlin 5 65
(Hughie Morrison) *chsd ldrs: rdn and unable qck ent fnl 2f: hung lft and unable qck over 1f out: styd on same pce and n.d fnl f* **16/1**

-412 **6** *nk* **Chapellerie (IRE)**[11] 536 3-8-3 **66** WilliamCarson 7 56
(Richard Guest) *sn bustled along to press ldr: led after 1f tl 1/2-way: lost 2nd 2f out: wknd u.p ent fnl f* **11/1**

-112 **7** *9* **Oratorian (IRE)**[33] 230 3-9-4 **81** JimCrowley 6 43
(Sylvester Kirk) *hld up in last trio: rdn and struggling ist over 2f out: lost tch 2f out* **11/2**[2]

1m 10.29s (-1.61) **Going Correction** -0.10s/f (Stan) 7 Ran SP% **117.0**
Speed ratings (Par 99): **106,103,101,101,98 98,86**
toteswingers:1&2:£2.70, 1&3:£3.90, 2&3:£13.30 CSF £7.90 TOTE £1.90: £1.40, £2.00; EX 9.10.
Owner Mrs E Evans **Bred** Mrs A J Donnelly **Trained** Pandy, Monmouths

FOCUS
A competitive handicap run at a decent pace, and the clear pick of the three C&D times. The winner is progressive.

660 BET AT BLUE SQUARE ON YOUR MOBILE H'CAP 7f (P)
5:00 (5:00) (Class 6) (0-60,60) 3-Y-O **£1,704** (£503; £251) **Stalls** Low

Form RPR

4 **1** **Source Of Light (IRE)**[19] 404 3-9-5 **58** StephenCraine 13 63+
(Daniel Mark Loughnane) *hld up in tch in midfield: swtchd rt and effrt over 1f out: r.o wl u.p fnl f to ld fnl 50yds* **12/1**

46-3 **2** *½* **Purple Affair (IRE)**[11] 518 3-9-4 **60** RyanPowell(3) 12 64+
(J S Moore) *hld up in midfield: nt clr run wl over 1f out: swtchd rt 1f out: r.o strly u.p ins fnl f: snatched 2nd last stride* **6/1**[2]

-332 **3** *nse* **First Bid**[8] 556 3-9-7 **60** (b) FrederikTylicki 3 63
(James Given) *t.k.h early: hld up in tch: rdn and swtchd lft over 1f out: drvn to ld fnl 100yds: hung rt and sn hdd: no ex* **11/2**[1]

050- **4** *1 ¼* **King's Future**[90] 7530 3-9-7 **60** JimCrowley 6 60
(John Akehurst) *sn led: rdn 2f out: drvn and hrd pressed ent fnl f: hdd fnl 100yds: no ex and wknd fnl 75yds* **12/1**

4522 **5** *½* **Songbird Blues**[11] 518 3-9-0 **53** HayleyTurner 14 52+
(Mark Usher) *stdd and swtchd lft s: hld up in rr: hdwy and c wd over 1f out: styd on wl fnl f: nt rch ldrs* **6/1**[2]

00-4 **6** *½* **Emirates Jack (IRE)**[15] 459 3-8-13 **52** MartinLane 1 49
(David Simcock) *hld up in tch in midfield: rdn and effrt wl over 1f out: kpt on same pce u.p fnl f* **15/2**[3]

0312 **7** *¾* **Lana (IRE)**[9] 549 3-9-3 **56** KieranO'Neill 7 51
(David Evans) *t.k.h: hld up towards rr: hdwy on outer 3f out: rdn and effrt 2f out: no imp 1f out: styd on same pce fnl f* **11/2**[1]

1 **8** *nk* **Drinmoy Lad (IRE)**[41] 138 3-9-4 **57** MartinHarley 10 51
(Michael McElhone, Ire) *chsd ldrs: effrt to chse ldr 2f out: ev ch u.p over 1f out: wknd ins fnl f* **8/1**

60-0 **9** *¾* **Here Comes Jeanie**[41] 132 3-8-11 **50** JamieGoldstein 2 42
(Michael Madgwick) *hld up towards rr: rdn and hdwy towards inner over 1f out: no prog 1f out* **33/1**

6-55 **10** *¾* **Umph (IRE)**[25] 352 3-9-3 **56** (v) RichardThomas 11 46
(David Evans) *chsd ldrs on outer: rdn and struggling whn jostled wl over 1f out: wknd ins fnl f* **66/1**

505- **11** *nse* **Tectonic (IRE)**[95] 7483 3-9-0 **60** ow2 (p) JoshCrane(7) 9 50
(Chris Dwyer) *t.k.h: sn chsng ldr: unable qck 2f out: struggling whn jostled over 1f out: wknd ins fnl f* **10/1**

035- **12** *8* **Sea Anemone**[55] 7909 3-9-2 **55** DavidProbert 4 24
(Andrew Balding) *hld up in midfield: shuffled bk towards rr and rdn 2f out: no prog and btn 1f out: eased wl ins fnl f* **16/1**

4-03 **13** *hd* **Finalist**[19] 397 3-8-10 **56** (b) PaulBooth(7) 8 24
(Dean Ivory) *awkward s and slowly away: racd wd and a struggling: wl bhd 1f out* **40/1**

5660 **14** *5* **Sweetest Friend (IRE)**[7] 564 3-9-2 **55** (p) WilliamCarson 5
(J S Moore) *a in rr: rdn and struggling wl over 2f out: bhd 2f out* **66/1**

1m 24.97s (0.17) **Going Correction** -0.10s/f (Stan) 14 Ran SP% **120.9**
Speed ratings (Par 95): **95,94,94,92,92 91,90,90,89,88 88,79,79,73**
toteswingers:1&2:£34.00, 1&3:£29.00, 2&3:£6.40 CSF £81.59 CT £462.16 TOTE £21.80: £6.40, £3.00, £1.60; EX 121.70 Trifecta £549.60 Part won. Pool: £742.75 - 0.30 winning units..
Owner Mrs C Loughnane **Bred** Peter McCutcheon **Trained** Baldwin's Gate, Staffs

FOCUS
An ordinary 3-y-o handicap and the pace was on from the word go. The fourth sets the standard.
T/Plt: £37.40 to a £1 stake. Pool:£49,589.31 - 966.58 winning tickets T/Qpdt: £20.40 to a £1 stake. Pool:£4,390.57 - 158.52 winning tickets SP

628 CAGNES-SUR-MER
Wednesday, February 22

OFFICIAL GOING: Fibresand: standard

661a PRIX DE CAVAILLON (CLAIMER) (3YO COLTS & GELDINGS) (FIBRESAND) 1m 2f (D)
1:50 (12:00) 3-Y-O **£6,250** (£2,500; £1,875; £1,250; £625)

RPR

1 **Path Finder (FR)**[14] 476 3-9-0 0 (p) Francois-XavierBertras 3 69
(Reg Hollinshead) *broke wl: racd cl 2nd: sent to ld 2f out: threatened on all sides over 1f out: r.o wl u.p despite hd hanging to one side: readily* **9/2**[2]

2 *½* **King Of Song (FR)**[68] 3-8-9 0 (b) JulienAuge 9 63
(H-A Pantall, France) **44/5**

3 *1* **Flipou (FR)**[29] 290 3-8-9 0 IoritzMendizabal 2 61
(J-C Rouget, France) **2/1**[1]

4 *hd* **Together Again (FR)**[47] 3-8-9 0 (b) SebastienMaillot 4 61
(M Boutin, France) **35/1**

5 *snk* **Dollar King (GER)**[33] 247 3-8-4 0 (b) MarcLerner(5) 11 60
(Exors Of W Baltromei, Germany) **83/10**

6 *hd* **Pasco (BEL)**[14] 476 3-8-4 0 (p) CesarPasserat(5) 5 60
(F Vermeulen, France) **32/1**

7 *1 ¼* **Saroso (FR)**[106] 3-9-0 0 (b) MickaelForest 1 62
(W Walton, France) **17/2**

8 *8* **Potkol (FR)**[14] 476 3-8-9 0 (b) ThomasMessina 7 41
(C Boutin, France) **68/10**

9 *6* **Lord Bedarrides (FR)**[14] 476 3-9-0 0 (b) JohanVictoire 8 34
(J Heloury, France) **6/1**[3]

10 *4* **Abrasivo (ITY)**[14] 476 3-8-9 0 SUrru 6 21
(P Caravati, Italy) **44/1**

2m 5.1s (125.10) **10** Ran SP% **118.1**
WIN (incl. 1 euro stake): 5.50. PLACES: 1.60, 2.40, 1.50. DF: 29.20. SF: 67.70.
Owner John L Marriott **Bred** Mrs Kim Sundgren **Trained** Upper Longdon, Staffs

NOTEBOOK
Path Finder(FR) looked sure to be swamped at the furlong pole, but at the line was still half a length to the good.

647 KEMPTON (A.W) (R-H)
Thursday, February 23

OFFICIAL GOING: Standard
Wind: Virtually nil Weather: Sunny getting dark

662 32REDBINGO.COM H'CAP 7f (P)
5:20 (5:20) (Class 7) (0-50,50) 4-Y-O+ **£1,455** (£433; £216; £108) **Stalls** Low

Form RPR

226- **1** **Ereka (IRE)**[70] 7768 4-9-3 **50** LukeMorris 1 58
(John Best) *in tch: drvn and styd on over 2f out: chsd ldr over 1f out: led fnl 120yds: drvn out* **6/1**[3]

0-45 **2** *nk* **Meydan Style (USA)**[14] 483 6-8-12 **45** (p) NeilChalmers 6 52
(Richard Ford) *chsd ldrs 2f: drvn and one pce into mid-div 4f out: styd on again fr 2f out: r.o u.p ins fnl f: fin wl: nt quite get up* **12/1**

0-00 **3** *½* **Chandrayaan**[22] 375 5-8-9 **45** (v) SimonPearce(3) 11 51
(John E Long) *wnt rt s: sn chsng ldrs: rdn 2f out: kpt on to take 3rd clsng stages: nt quite gng pce of ldng duo* **14/1**

2262 **4** *nk* **Blueberry Fizz (IRE)**[7] 578 4-9-0 **50** (v) MichaelO'Connell(3) 8 55
(John Ryan) *led: drvn and hung rt 2f out: kpt on appr fnl f: hdd fnl 120yds: lost 2 pls clsng stages* **11/4**[2]

-212 **5** *¾* **Emerald Royal**[8] 561 4-9-2 **49** ShaneKelly 10 52+
(Eric Wheeler) *pushed rt s: in rr: hdwy 2f out: rdn and kpt on wl fnl 120yds: gng on cl home* **5/2**[1]

0-04 **6** *½* **Cavalry Guard (USA)**[22] 379 8-8-12 **45** (b) RichardKingscote 4 47
(Tim McCarthy) *chsd ldrs: wnt 2nd briefly 2f out: styd on tl wknd fnl 120yds* **16/1**

-002 **7** *2 ¼* **Wee Buns**[22] 379 7-8-12 **45** TomMcLaughlin 2 41
(Paul Burgoyne) *in rr: pushed along and hdwy 2f out: kpt on fnl f: nvr gng pce to rch ldrs* **16/1**

5/00 **8** *¾* **Omega Centauri**[21] 390 4-8-12 **45** SteveDrowne 5 39
(Ed McMahon) *chsd ldrs: rdn over 2f out: wknd 1f out* **25/1**

4310 **9** *1 ¼* **Lovat Lane**[8] 561 4-9-1 **48** ChrisCatlin 3 38
(Eve Johnson Houghton) *chsd ldrs: rdn over 3f out: sn outpcd: mod prog again ins fnl f* **8/1**

6-03 **10** *5* **Littleportnbrandy (IRE)**[13] 503 4-9-1 **48** (bt) WilliamCarson 13 25
(Richard Guest) *in rr: hung rt wl over 2f out: sn hanging lft and no ch* **20/1**

05-0 **11** *1 ½* **Magical Star**[28] 307 4-8-12 **45** DavidProbert 9 18
(Michael Wigham) *hmpd s: t.k.h: effrt over 2f out: nvr in contention and sn wknd* **25/1**

056- **12** *20* **Misshollygolightly**[200] 4819 4-8-12 **45** RussKennemore 7
(Brian Baugh) *chsd ldrs: rdn 3f out: wknd 3f out* **16/1**

1m 26.58s (0.58) **Going Correction** 0.0s/f (Stan) 12 Ran SP% **125.1**
Speed ratings (Par 97): **96,95,95,94,93 93,90,89,88,82 81,58**
toteswingers: 1&2 £11.90, 1&3 £17.20, 2&3 £36.70. CSF £78.27 CT £994.43 TOTE £8.20: £1.50, £4.70, £5.20; EX 133.40.
Owner Mrs A M Riney **Bred** Mrs A M Riney **Trained** Hucking, Kent

FOCUS
A very moderate handicap in which the pace was sound throughout. The winner raced close to the inside rail throughout. Straightforward form.
Emerald Royal ◆ Official explanation: jockey said gelding suffered interference at start

663 32REDPOKER.COM MEDIAN AUCTION MAIDEN STKS 7f (P)
5:50 (5:51) (Class 6) 3-5-Y-O **£1,617** (£481; £240; £120) **Stalls** Low

Form RPR

05- **1** **Lady Sylvia**[97] 7454 3-8-6 0 LukeMorris 7 66
(Joseph Tuite) *trckd ldr: led ins fnl 3f: narrowly hdd ins fnl 2f: led again 1f out: drvn and styd on strly ins fnl f* **5/1**[1]

0-5 **2** *3 ¼* **Diamond Marks (IRE)**[8] 565 3-8-11 0 JohnFahy 9 62
(John Gallagher) *in tch: chsd ldrs 3f out: rdn and slt ld ins fnl 2f: hdd 1f out: kpt on but nt gng pce of wnr ins fnl f* **33/1**[3]

60-0 **3** *5* **Stormin Gordon (IRE)**[40] 181 3-7-13 0 IanBurns(7) 1 44
(Noel Quinlan) *chsd ldrs: riddn and styd on to take one pce 3rd over 1f out* **50/1**

0- **4** *1 ¾* **Mulberry Brite**[213] 4388 4-9-9 0 TomMcLaughlin 10 45
(Karen George) *in rr: rdn and styd on one pce for wl hld 3rd over 1f out* **33/1**[3]

0 **5** *nk* **Scripturist**[26] 350 3-8-11 0 WilliamCarson 2 43
(William Jarvis) *in rr: pushed along over 3f out: modest prog fnl f* **12/1**[2]

-0 **6** *9* **Kiss My Heart**[22] 373 3-8-6 0 KieranO'Neill 4 14
(Peter Makin) *t.k.h: led: hdd ins fnl 3f: wknd qckly over 1f out* **33/1**[3]

1m 28.0s (2.00) **Going Correction** 0.0s/f (Stan)
WFA 3 from 4yo 17lb 6 Ran SP% **35.1**
Speed ratings (Par 101): **88,84,78,76,76 65**
toteswingers: 1&2 £1.60, 1&3 £5.50, 2&3 £26.30. CSF £9.58 TOTE £1.70: £1.10, £3.90; EX 10.60.
Owner David J Keast **Bred** Highclere Stud **Trained** Great Shefford, Berks

FOCUS
A depleted field and one in which very short-priced market leader Kalokagathia was withdrawn after going down in the stalls (1/4F, deduct 80p in the £ under R4). The form of this moderately run and most uncompetitive maiden is weak, rated around the winner, with the time slow. The winner raced towards the inside rail in the closing stages.

664 32REDBET.COM H'CAP (DIV I) 6f (P)
6:20 (6:20) (Class 6) (0-55,55) 4-Y-O+ **£1,617** (£481; £240; £120) **Stalls** Low

Form RPR

4-13 **1** **First Class**[34] 226 4-8-13 **50** DavidProbert 3 64+
(Rae Guest) *in rr: drvn and hdwy wl ins fnl 2f: styng on whn hmpd and pushed lft 1f out: rallied wl to ld fnl 30yds: drvn out* **6/4**[1]

6-0 **2** *nk* **Lady Mango (IRE)**[7] 578 4-9-3 **54** LukeMorris 4 67
(Ronald Harris) *in tch: hdwy on ins over 2f out: drvn to ld appr fnl f: sn hung lft: hdd and no ex fnl 30yds* **10/1**

6-05 **3** *2 ¾* **Grand Honour (IRE)**[6] 598 6-8-9 **46** oh1 (p) KieranO'Neill 6 50
(Paul Howling) *in rr: drvn and gd hdwy appr fnl f: pushed lft 1f out and lost momentum: rcvrd to take 3rd fnl 100yds: no imp on ldng duo* **14/1**

0-06 **4** *1 ¼* **Cheery Cat (USA)**[32] 267 8-9-4 **55** (b[1]) NeilChalmers 5 55
(Richard Ford) *chsd ldrs: rdn 2f out: styd on same pce fnl f* **14/1**

-602 **5** *nk* **Tamino (IRE)**[14] 483 9-8-11 **48** (b) FrankieMcDonald 2 47
(Alastair Lidderdale) *sn drvn to ld: hdd appr fnl f: sn pushed lft: wknd fnl 120yds* **8/1**[3]

6-62 **6** *1 ½* **Itsthursdayalready**[9] 551 5-9-2 **53** ShaneKelly 8 47
(Mark Brisbourne) *in tch: hdwy 2f out: styd on same pce appr fnl f* **9/2**[2]

20-0 **7** *hd* **Namir (IRE)**[13] 498 10-9-2 **53** (vt) FergusSweeney 1 47
(James Evans) *in rr: drvn 2f out: sme prog fnl f* **25/1**

03-4 **8** *hd* **Almaty Express**[13] 498 10-9-4 **55** (b) JamieSpencer 7 48
(John Weymes) *chsd ldr: rdn over 2f out chalng but u.p whn hmpd 1f out: nt rcvr and sn btn* **12/1**

5-64 **9** *5* **Queen Of Heaven (USA)**[29] 291 4-9-2 **53** SteveDrowne 12 30
(Peter Makin) *outpcd most of way* **16/1**

25-0 **10** *1 ½* **Flaxen Lake**[34] 232 5-9-3 **54** RichardKingscote 11 26
(Milton Bradley) *chsd ldrs over 4f* **12/1**

00/0 **11** *36* **Muktasb (USA)**[29] 297 11-8-9 **46** oh1 (v) WilliamCarson 10
(Richard Guest) *s.i.s: a in rr: wl bhd fnl 2f* **50/1**

1m 12.9s (-0.20) **Going Correction** 0.0s/f (Stan) **11** Ran SP% **118.8**
Speed ratings (Par 101): **101,100,96,95,94 92,92,92,85,83 35**
toteswingers: 1&2 £3.50, 1&3 £8.70, 2&3 £21.80. CSF £17.95 CT £160.45 TOTE £2.60: £1.40, £2.30, £5.10; EX 24.90.
Owner Brian Cooper And Miss Elaine Reffo **Bred** Amethyst Stud **Trained** Newmarket, Suffolk

FOCUS
A moderate handicap but a decent gallop teed the race up for those coming from just off the pace, although it was the slower division. The first two pulled a few lengths clear and the winner took a step forward.

665 32REDBET.COM H'CAP (DIV II) 6f (P)
6:50 (6:50) (Class 6) (0-55,55) 4-Y-0+ **£1,617** (£481; £240; £120) **Stalls** Low

Form RPR

4-63 **1** **Dorothy's Dancing (IRE)**[17] 445 4-9-3 **54** GeorgeBaker 8 69+
(Gary Moore) *t.k.h: hld up in rr: hdwy on ins appr fnl 2f: drvn to ld 1f out: pushed out clsng stages: readily* **9/2**[2]

20-0 **2** *nk* **Amazing Win (IRE)**[15] 474 4-9-2 **53** SamHitchcott 4 66
(Mick Channon) *chsd ldrs: rdn 2f out: styd on to chse wnr fnl 50yds: gng on u.p cl home but a hld by wnr* **6/1**[3]

4256 **3** *2* **Slatey Hen (IRE)**[13] 497 4-9-0 **51** (p) WilliamCarson 7 57
(Richard Guest) *chsd ldrs: drvn to take slt ld over 1f out: sn hdd: outpcd into 3rd fnl 150yds* **7/1**

00-0 **4** *½* **Avonlini**[24] 356 6-9-1 **52** RussKennemore 1 57
(Brian Baugh) *led tl hdd over 1f out: sn outpcd* **20/1**

4-06 **5** *2 ¼* **Demoiselle Bond**[28] 312 4-9-2 **53** SteveDrowne 10 51
(Lydia Richards) *chsd ldr tl rdn over 2f out: sn outpcd* **10/1**

03-4 **6** *hd* **Kipchak (IRE)**[46] 97 7-8-12 **54** (b) LucyKBarry[(5)] 11 51
(Conor Dore) *chsd ldrs: rdn and one pce over 2f out: kpt on again u.p clsng stages* **16/1**

4530 **7** *nse* **White Shift (IRE)**[15] 467 6-8-10 **47** (p) ShaneKelly 3 44
(Paul Howling) *mid-div: rdn and styd on same pce fr over 2f out: kpt on clsng stages* **13/2**

-563 **8** *2 ½* **Metropolitan Chief**[7] 572 8-8-6 **48** CharlesBishop[(5)] 6 37
(Paul Burgoyne) *in rr: swtchd: lft wl over 2f out: sn edging lft and one pce u.p* **8/1**

-056 **9** *5* **Sailing North (USA)**[12] 524 4-9-4 **55** DavidProbert 5 28
(Ronald Harris) *s.i.s: outpcd* **14/1**

-531 **10** *5* **Lisselton Cross**[14] 483 4-9-2 **53** (v) LukeMorris 9 10
(Martin Bosley) *a in rr* **4/1**[1]

1m 12.77s (-0.33) **Going Correction** 0.0s/f (Stan) **10** Ran SP% **115.8**
Speed ratings (Par 101): **102,101,98,98,95 95,94,91,84,78**
toteswingers: 1&2 £5.40, 1&3 £7.00, 2&3 £5.00. CSF £31.49 CT £186.73 TOTE £6.10: £2.30, £1.50, £3.20; EX 32.30.
Owner Tom Glynn **Bred** Patrick Carroll **Trained** Lower Beeding, W Sussex

FOCUS
Another moderate handicap in which the gallop was sound, and the time was a length quicker than division one. The winner raced close to the inside rail throughout and looked slightly better than the bare form.
Demoiselle Bond Official explanation: jockey said filly hung left
Sailing North(USA) Official explanation: jockey said gelding was slowly away
Lisselton Cross Official explanation: jockey said gelding never travelled

666 £32 FREE AT 32RED.COM H'CAP 1m (P)
7:20 (7:20) (Class 6) (0-55,55) 4-Y-0+ **£1,617** (£481; £240; £120) **Stalls** Low

Form RPR

34-4 **1** **Having A Ball**[50] 31 8-9-4 **55** ChrisCatlin 4 62
(Jonathan Portman) *trckd ldrs: drvn to ld 2f out: styd on wl u.p fnl f* **4/1**[1]

3130 **2** *½* **Querido (GER)**[12] 532 8-9-1 **55** (tp) RobertLButler[(3)] 2 61
(Paddy Butler) *chsd ldrs: rdn to go 2nd 1f out: styd on u.p fnl f: no imp on wnr clsng stages* **10/1**

6-65 **3** *½* **Teen Ager (FR)**[8] 561 8-8-13 **50** JohnFahy 5 55
(Paul Burgoyne) *in tch: hdwy and n.m.r over 1f out: rdn and styd on ins fnl f to take 3rd fnl 100yds: nt qckn clsng stages* **9/2**[2]

-005 **4** *1 ¼* **Shaws Diamond (USA)**[21] 386 6-9-0 **51** (v) DaneO'Neill 8 53
(Derek Shaw) *chsd ldrs: wnt 2nd wl over 1f out: styd on same pce u.p fnl f* **5/1**[3]

00-3 **5** *2 ¼* **Escape Artist**[8] 558 5-8-13 **50** KieranO'Neill 9 47
(John Bridger) *in rr: hdwy over 2f out: hanging rt u.p fr wl over 1f out: kpt on clsng stages* **10/1**

06-4 **6** *¾* **Luv U Noo**[27] 334 5-8-4 **46** oh1 JamesRogers[(5)] 6 41
(Brian Baugh) *slowly away: in rr: hdwy on ins and wl in tch 2f out: chsd ldrs u.p over 1f out: wknd fnl f* **10/1**

000- **7** *2* **Fault**[67] 7812 6-8-12 **54** AmyScott[(5)] 13 45
(Alastair Lidderdale) *sn pressing ldr: drvn to chal appr fnl 2f: wknd appr fnl f* **16/1**

0355 **8** *½* **Blue Noodles**[12] 532 6-9-0 **51** (p) PaddyAspell 7 40
(John Wainwright) *chsd ldrs: rdn over 2f out: wknd over 1f out* **12/1**

0-23 **9** *1 ¾* **Saktoon (USA)**[23] 370 4-8-13 **53** (v) DaleSwift[(3)] 14 38
(Derek Shaw) *in rr: rdn and hung rt whn sme prog over 2f out: no ch after* **12/1**

0/00 **10** *1* **Highcliffe**[12] 530 4-8-9 **46** oh1 (v[1]) RichardKingscote 3 29
(Martin Bosley) *outpcd most of way* **14/1**

-600 **11** *2* **Tunza The Lion**[14] 477 5-8-9 **46** oh1 NeilChalmers 11 25
(Richard Ford) *s.i.s: bhd most of way* **50/1**

000- **12** *1 ¾* **Alioonagh (USA)**[163] 6033 5-9-1 **52** LukeMorris 10 27
(Peter Makin) *sn led: hdd 2f out: sn wknd* **11/1**

1m 39.86s (0.06) **Going Correction** 0.0s/f (Stan) **12** Ran SP% **120.3**
Speed ratings (Par 101): **99,98,98,96,94 93,91,91,89,88 86,84**
toteswingers: 1&2 £7.20, 1&3 £3.60, 2&3 £9.90. CSF £45.16 CT £168.26 TOTE £5.40: £1.70, £3.40, £2.20; EX 52.50.
Owner P D Cundell **Bred** R G Percival **Trained** Compton, Berks

FOCUS
A moderate handicap run at a reasonable gallop, The winner raced towards the inside rail before edging towards the centre in the closing stages. The winner probably didn't need to improve much on his latest effort.
Shaws Diamond(USA) Official explanation: jockey said mare suffered interference leaving stalls

667 32RED CASINO H'CAP (LONDON MILE QUALIFIER) 1m (P)
7:50 (7:50) (Class 5) (0-75,75) 3-Y-O **£2,264** (£673; £336; £168) **Stalls** Low

Form RPR

40-6 **1** **Bareback (IRE)**[42] 127 3-9-2 **70** LukeMorris 10 74
(John Best) *led after 1f: set modest pce: drvn and qcknd over 2f out: hrd pressed in three-way chal fr over 1f out: kpt on gamely cl home* **9/1**

62-1 **2** *nk* **Majestic Zafeen**[39] 184 3-9-6 **74** FrankieMcDonald 3 77
(Alastair Lidderdale) *led 1f: t.k.h and trckd ldrs: drvn to chal wl over 1f out: styd upsides in three-way chal fnl f: no ex cl home* **11/2**[2]

2-22 **3** *nk* **Tenbridge**[22] 377 3-9-0 **68** (p) DaneO'Neill 5 70
(Derek Haydn Jones) *chsd ldrs: chal wl over 1f out and stl upsides in three-way chal thrght fnl f: no ex cl home* **11/2**[2]

-431 **4** *1 ¼* **Berlusca (IRE)**[10] 549 3-9-4 **72** 6ex ShaneKelly 7 71
(Mark Brisbourne) *chsd ldrs: rdn over 2f out: kpt on fnl f but nt gng pce of ldng trio* **9/2**[1]

4-15 **5** *hd* **Whipcrackaway (IRE)**[22] 377 3-8-8 **62** (p) JohnFahy 1 61+
(Peter Hedger) *broke wl: stdd in rr: hdwy on ins over 2f out: kpt on clsng stages: nt gng pce to rch ldrs* **15/2**[3]

004- **6** *½* **Graylyn Valentino**[64] 7837 3-8-10 **64** StevieDonohoe 4 62
(Robin Dickin) *in tch: rdn over 2f out: styd on ins fnl f: nt rch ldrs* **16/1**

50-1 **7** *2* **Four Better**[22] 377 3-9-6 **74** FergusSweeney 8 67
(Jamie Osborne) *sn chsng ldrs: rdn over 2f out: wknd fnl f* **9/2**[1]

24-5 **8** *1* **Mr Knightley (IRE)**[15] 471 3-9-7 **75** (b) StephenCraine 6 65
(Jim Boyle) *in tch: trckd ldrs and drvn over 2f out: wknd ins fnl f* **12/1**

0-25 **9** *2 ¼* **Biba Diva (IRE)**[20] 398 3-9-7 **75** (p) JamieSpencer 2 60
(Jeremy Noseda) *awkward s and bhd: swtchd lft and rdn 2f out: little imp on ldrs and wknd appr fnl f* **15/2**[3]

4-60 **10** *¾* **Nant Saeson (IRE)**[24] 362 3-8-12 **66** PaddyAspell 9 49
(John Wainwright) *outpcd most of way* **66/1**

1m 40.63s (0.83) **Going Correction** 0.0s/f (Stan) **10** Ran SP% **115.7**
Speed ratings (Par 97): **95,94,94,93,92 92,90,89,87,86**
toteswingers: 1&2 £23.70, 1&3 £12.60, 2&3 £3.80. CSF £57.43 CT £307.83 TOTE £11.80: £3.30, £2.50, £2.00; EX 87.50.
Owner Malt, Malcolm & Gabriel **Bred** L Fox **Trained** Hucking, Kent

FOCUS
A fair handicap containing several winners but a slow gallop means this bare form isn't reliable and those held up were at a disadvantage. The form is rated on the negative side. The winner raced centre-to-far side in the straight.
Whipcrackaway(IRE) ◆ Official explanation: jockey said gelding ducked left leaving stalls

668 32RED CONDITIONS STKS 1m 4f (P)
8:20 (8:20) (Class 4) 4-Y-0+ **£4,075** (£1,212; £606; £303) **Stalls** Centre

Form RPR

/46- **1** **Into Wain (USA)**[31] 1105 5-9-2 88 JamieSpencer 5 84
(Steve Gollings) *trckd clr ldr and 12 l down over 3f out: sn pushed along: styd on fr 2f out: jnd ldr ins fnl f: carried lft and styd on to ld nr fin* **7/4**[2]

6-13 **2** *½* **Uphold**[34] 223 5-9-2 80 (t[1]) DominicFox[(3)] 3 86
(Gay Kelleway) *led: sn clr and extending ld: stl 12 l clr over 3f out: rdn over 2f out: jnd ins fnl f: kpt on gamely: edgd lft and hdd nr fin* **12/1**

-021 **3** *5* **Layline (IRE)**[19] 427 5-9-7 92 ShaneKelly 1 80
(Gay Kelleway) *racd in 3rd bhd clr ldr: rdn 3f out: no imp on ldng duo and one pce fnl 2f* **6/4**[1]

4414 **4** *20* **Nezhenka**[7] 577 5-8-11 85 JoeFanning 4 38
(Mark Johnston) *in tch w chsng gp of 4 bhd clr ldr: rdn over 4f out: wknd over 3f out* **4/1**[3]

1131 **5** *33* **Magic Millie (IRE)**[6] 600 5-8-6 62 AmyScott[(5)] 2
(Alastair Lidderdale) *in tch w chsng gp of 4 bhd clr ldr: rdn and btn 5f out: t.o* **20/1**

2m 31.94s (-2.56) **Going Correction** 0.0s/f (Stan) **5** Ran SP% **108.8**
Speed ratings (Par 105): **108,107,104,91,69**
CSF £19.54 TOTE £2.80: £1.20, £5.90; EX 30.20.
Owner P J Martin **Bred** Don M Robinson **Trained** Scamblesby, Lincs

FOCUS
Not a competitive event but a useful conditions race in which the pack allowed the leader to establish a clear lead after a steadily run first couple of furlongs. The form is rated around the runner-up. The winner came down the centre.

669 32RED.COM H'CAP 7f (P)
8:50 (8:50) (Class 5) (0-75,75) 4-Y-0+ **£2,264** (£673; £336; £168) **Stalls** Low

Form RPR

5-12 **1** **Garstang**[27] 328 9-9-5 **73** NeilChalmers 2 84
(Richard Ford) *sn trcking ldr: led narrowly 2f out: pushed along and qcknd fnl f: readily* **15/2**

630- **2** *2 ½* **Jungle Bay**[110] 7299 5-8-12 **73** LewisWalsh[(7)] 7 77
(Jane Chapple-Hyam) *in tch: drvn and hdwy over 1f out: styd on fnl f to chse wnr fnl 150yds but no imp* **6/1**[3]

1331 **3** *2 ¼* **Lastkingofscotland (IRE)**[12] 517 6-9-5 **73** (b) GeorgeBaker 1 71
(Conor Dore) *led: drvn and narrowly hdd 2f out: styd pressing wnr tl over 1f out: wknd into 3rd fnl 150yds* **9/4**[1]

0-00 **4** *5* **Street Power (USA)**[33] 253 7-9-7 **75** (p) SteveDrowne 6 60
(Jeremy Gask) *stdd s: in rr: hdwy on ins to chse ldrs 2f out and disp 2nd wl over 1f out: wknd fnl f* **4/1**[2]

-504 **5** *1 ½* **May's Boy**[12] 517 4-9-2 **70** (p) DaneO'Neill 4 51
(Mark Usher) *chsd ldrs: rdn over 2f out: wknd wl over 1f out* **4/1**[2]

060- **6** *1 ¼* **Alfresco**[134] 6796 8-9-4 **72** (b) LukeMorris 5 49
(John Best) *sn bhd: rdn and little rspnse over 2f out* **16/1**

20-0 **7** *¾* **Rowan Spirit (IRE)**[23] 371 4-9-5 **73** ShaneKelly 3 48
(Mark Brisbourne) *chsd ldrs: rdn and wknd 2f out* **20/1**

000- **8** *8* **Crazy Chris**[127] 4707 7-9-0 **68** RichardKingscote 8 22
(Milton Bradley) *in rr and racd on outer: lost tch ins fnl 3f* **12/1**

1m 25.34s (-0.66) **Going Correction** 0.0s/f (Stan) **8** Ran SP% **115.2**
Speed ratings (Par 103): **103,100,97,91,90 88,87,78**
toteswingers: 1&2 £18.20, 1&3 £1.50, 2&3 £7.90. CSF £51.96 CT £135.18 TOTE £7.80: £2.10, £2.40, £1.10; EX 67.70.

Owner The Foulrice Twenty **Bred** Mrs S E Barclay **Trained** Garstang, Lancs

FOCUS

Mainly exposed performers in a fair handicap. The gallop was just an ordinary one and the winner came down the centre. He is rated to his best form sonce 2009.

T/Plt: £135.20 to a £1 stake. Pool:£67,022.22 - 361.76 winning tickets T/Qpdt: £19.70 to a £1 stake. Pool:£8,657.04 - 325.00 winning tickets ST

640 SOUTHWELL (L-H)

Thursday, February 23

OFFICIAL GOING: Standard

Wind: Moderate across Weather: Sunny periods

670 PLACE ONLY BETTING AT BLUESQ.COM H'CAP 7f (F)

2:10 (2:10) (Class 6) (0-65,68) 4-Y-0+ **£2,045** (£603; £302) **Stalls** Low

Form RPR

-104 **1** **Beachwood Bay**[23] 372 4-8-9 **60** JoshBaudains(7) 8 71
(Jo Hughes) *prom: smooth hdwy to ld over 2f out: pushed out fnl f* **4/1**[2]

4436 **2** 1 **Ace Of Spies (IRE)**[7] 580 7-9-2 **60** JamesSullivan 10 68
(Conor Dore) *towards rr: gd hdwy on outer 1/2-way: chsd ldrs over 2f out and sn rdn: chsd wnr over 1f out: kpt on same pce ins fnl f* **20/1**

0020 **3** 1 1/2 **Dickie Le Davoir**[15] 473 8-9-2 **63** (b) RobertLButler(3) 9 67
(Richard Guest) *dwlt and towards rr: hdwy 2f out: rdn to chse ldrs over 1f out: swtchd lft ent fnl f: kpt on* **16/1**

1-36 **4** 1 1/4 **Ace Master**[14] 478 4-9-3 **61** AmirQuinn 7 62
(Roy Bowring) *cl up: led after 2f: rdn along and hdd over 2f out: wknd over 1f out* **4/1**[2]

15-1 **5** 4 **Monte Cassino (IRE)**[44] 113 7-8-11 **55** (e) TomEaves 3 45
(Bryan Smart) *cl up: effrt 3f out: rdn along 2f out and grad wknd* **6/1**[3]

2321 **6** 2 3/4 **Mazovian (USA)**[7] 585 4-9-3 **68** 6ex DannyBrock(7) 1 50
(Michael Chapman) *chsd ldrs on inner: rdn along 2f out: sn no imp* **7/4**[1]

0-06 **7** 2 **Bonnie Prince Blue**[9] 551 9-8-10 **54** (b) PatrickMathers 2 31
(Ian McInnes) *sn rdn along and bhd tl sme late hdwy* **25/1**

05-2 **8** shd **Arachnophobia (IRE)**[21] 386 6-9-0 **65** (v) KirstenSmith(7) 6 42
(Martin Bosley) *dwlt: a in rr* **14/1**

03U- **9** 4 **Red Scintilla**[105] 7351 5-8-11 **55** (p) AndrewMullen 4 21
(Nigel Tinkler) *sn rdn along and a in rr* **33/1**

000- **10** 4 **Lucky Mellor**[90] 7535 5-9-2 **65** (b) ShaneBKelly(5) 5 20
(Barry Murtagh) *led 2f: cl up: rdn along 3f out: sn edgd lft and wknd* **33/1**

1m 30.01s (-0.29) **Going Correction** +0.075s/f (Slow) **10** Ran SP% **117.7**

Speed ratings (Par 101): **104,102,101,99,95 92,89,89,85,80**

toteswingers: 1&2 £21.70, 1&3 £11.00 2&3 £11.60. CSF £84.24 CT £846.34 TOTE £5.30: £1.90, £6.20, £4.20; EX 91.20 TRIFECTA Not won..

Owner B Parren & Jo Hughes **Bred** Bumble Bloodstock Ltd **Trained** Lambourn. Berks

FOCUS

This modest contest comprised a mix of in-form runners and some inconsistent ones. There were three vying for the lead from an early stage, setting a solid gallop, and it went to a horse stepping up in trip. Improved form from the winner.

Mazovian(USA) Official explanation: jockey said gelding ran flat

671 GOLF AND RACING AT SOUTHWELL (S) STKS 1m (F)

2:40 (2:41) (Class 6) 4-Y-0+ **£1,704** (£503; £251) **Stalls** Low

Form RPR

4451 **1** **Mcconnell (USA)**[8] 562 7-9-4 69 (b) MartinHarley 4 75
(Richard Guest) *trckd ldng pair: smooth hdwy over 2f out: rdn to chal over 1f out: kpt on to ld ins fnl f* **9/4**[2]

061- **2** 1 **River Ardeche**[68] 7710 7-9-4 68 JoeFanning 1 73
(Tracy Waggott) *led: rdn wl over 1f out and sn jnd: drvn and hdd ins fnl f: kpt on same pce* **14/1**[3]

00-4 **3** 5 **Trans Sonic**[9] 553 9-8-12 85 TomEaves 2 55
(David O'Meara) *chsd ldr: rdn along over 3f out: drvn over 2f out: sn hung lft and wknd* **1/2**[1]

-056 **4** 8 **Sofias Number One (USA)**[13] 490 4-8-12 57 (bt) MartinLane 3 37
(Roy Bowring) *sn rdn along and a in rr: bhd fnl 3f* **14/1**[3]

1m 43.32s (-0.38) **Going Correction** +0.075s/f (Slow) **4** Ran SP% **110.8**

Speed ratings (Par 101): **104,103,98,90**

CSF £22.50 TOTE £4.00; EX 11.00.There was no bid for the winner.

Owner Rakebackmypoker.com **Bred** Hall Et Al Farm **Trained** Stainforth, S Yorks

FOCUS

With the favourite running poorly, and the runner-up previously rated just 53, this took little winning. The first two are rated pretty much to their marks.

672 DINE IN THE PANTRY H'CAP 1m 4f (F)

3:10 (3:10) (Class 5) (0-70,67) 4-Y-0+ **£2,264** (£673; £336; £168) **Stalls** Low

Form RPR

5-12 **1** **Overrule (USA)**[11] 367 8-9-4 **64** (p) BarryMcHugh 8 75+
(Brian Ellison) *hld up towards rr: smooth hdwy over 4f out: trckd ldrs on bit and wdr st: led ent fnl f: sn clr: v easily* **7/2**[2]

-446 **2** 4 1/2 **Kingaroo (IRE)**[7] 579 6-8-7 **53** oh1 FrannyNorton 5 55
(Garry Woodward) *led 1f: cl up: led again 4f out: rdn over 2f out: drvn over 1f out: hdd ent fnl f: kpt on: no ch w wnr* **12/1**

0-45 **3** 1 1/4 **Jawaab (IRE)**[16] 460 8-9-7 **67** (e) MartinLane 3 67
(Richard Guest) *hld up and bhd: hdwy over 4f out: rdn to chse ldrs over 2f out: kpt on same pce: tk 3rd ins fnl f* **11/4**[1]

-223 **4** 1 1/4 **Arkaim**[21] 384 4-9-2 **65** (v) MickyFenton 4 63
(Pam Sly) *plld hrd: chsd ldrs: hdwy and cl up 3f out: ev ch over 2f out: sn rdn and wknd appr fnl f* **11/4**[1]

0555 **5** 12 **Dunaskin (IRE)**[7] 579 12-8-7 **53** oh8 (b) JamesSullivan 7 32
(Richard Guest) *cl up: led after 1f: rdn along 5f out: hdd over 4f out: wknd over 3f out* **28/1**

40-2 **6** 3 1/4 **Absolute Princess**[21] 381 4-8-9 **63** RaulDaSilva(5) 6 37
(Scott Dixon) *trckd ldng pair on inner: cl up over 3f out: sn rdn and wknd* **6/1**[3]

-460 **7** 46 **Bennelong**[7] 577 6-9-7 **67** AmirQuinn 2
(Richard Rowe) *in tch: rdn along 5f out: outpcd and bhd over 3f out: eased fnl 2f* **7/1**

10/0 **8** 24 **Stop On**[16] 460 7-8-10 **56** TonyHamilton 1
(Chris Grant) *a in rr: sn rdn along: outpcd and bhd fr 1/2-way: t.o fnl 3f* **40/1**

2m 41.38s (0.38) **Going Correction** +0.075s/f (Slow)

WFA 4 from 6yo+ 3lb **8** Ran SP% **115.9**

Speed ratings (Par 103): **101,98,97,96,88 86,55,39**

toteswingers: 1&2 £3.00, 1&3 £2.90, 2&3 £9.70. CSF £44.71 CT £131.51 TOTE £6.00: £3.10, £6.00, £2.70; EX 38.90 Trifecta £161.10 Pool: £435.61 - 2.00 winning units..

Owner Brian Ellison **Bred** Avalon Farms Inc **Trained** Norton, N Yorks

FOCUS

A decent gallop set this up perfectly for the strong-travelling winner. However, most of his opponents were either unpredictable types or out of form. The form is rated around the second.

Bennelong Official explanation: jockey said gelding ran flat

673 MIX BUSINESS WITH PLEASURE AT SOUTHWELL H'CAP 2m (F)

3:40 (3:40) (Class 5) (0-70,69) 4-Y-0+ **£2,385** (£704; £352) **Stalls** Low

Form RPR

2-22 **1** **Blackmore**[9] 555 5-9-12 **69** JoeFanning 3 78
(Julia Feilden) *led 1 1/2f: trckd ldr: pushed along 3f out: rdn wl over 1f out: styd on to ld ins fnl f: gamely* **9/4**[1]

/3-2 **2** 1/2 **Aaman (IRE)**[23] 366 6-9-10 **67** MartinLane 5 75
(Bernard Llewellyn) *cl up: led after 1 1/2f: rdn over 2f out: drvn over 1f out: hdd ins fnl f: kpt on* **11/4**[2]

1-06 **3** 7 **Three White Socks (IRE)**[16] 460 5-9-6 **63** (p) BarryMcHugh 7 63
(Brian Ellison) *hld up: hdwy on outer 6f out: rdn along to chse ldrs 3f out: wd st: drvn 2f out and kpt on same pce* **7/1**

0/5- **4** 1/2 **Rory Boy (USA)**[11] 6504 7-9-5 **62** (p) MichaelStainton 1 61
(Graeme McPherson) *trckd ldng pair on inner: pushed along 6f out: rdn and lost pl over 4f out: plugged on u.p fnl 2f* **5/1**[3]

44-3 **5** 10 **Salontyre (GER)**[9] 555 6-9-8 **65** (p) StevieDonohoe 6 52
(Bernard Llewellyn) *hld up in rr: sme hdwy 5f out: rdn along 4f out: sn btn* **10/1**

0-11 **6** 15 **Steady Gaze**[28] 309 7-9-11 **68** AmirQuinn 4 37
(Richard Rowe) *trckd ldrs: rdn along over 3f out: wknd 2f out* **12/1**

14-4 **7** 6 **C P Joe (IRE)**[27] 332 4-9-6 **69** (v) FrannyNorton 8 31
(Paul Green) *hld up: hdwy to trck ldrs 6f out: rdn along wl over 3f out: sn wknd* **7/1**

3m 44.91s (-0.59) **Going Correction** +0.075s/f (Slow)

WFA 4 from 5yo+ 6lb **7** Ran SP% **115.9**

Speed ratings (Par 103): **104,103,100,100,95 87,84**

toteswingers: 1&2 £1.90, 1&3 £4.20, 2&3 £5.60. CSF £8.91 CT £36.12 TOTE £2.50: £1.10, £3.20; EX 8.80 Trifecta £46.30 Pool: £629.22 - 10.05 winning units..

Owner Good Company Partnership **Bred** Juddmonte Farms Ltd **Trained** Exning, Suffolk

FOCUS

This was a fair contest for the surface and distance, with several coming into the race in decent form. The gallop was just an average one for the trip, which gave the pacemaking runner-up every chance. The first two came clear and the winner is rated back to his best.

Steady Gaze Official explanation: trainer's rep said gelding was unsuited by the Fibresand surface

674 BET AT BLUE SQUARE ON YOUR MOBILE H'CAP 1m (F)

4:10 (4:10) (Class 4) (0-85,84) 4-Y-0+ **£4,204** (£1,251; £625; £312) **Stalls** Low

Form RPR

5-14 **1** **Dubaianswer**[7] 584 4-9-3 **80** StephenCraine 9 91
(Tony Coyle) *trckd ldrs on outer: smooth hdwy and cl up 3f out: led 2f out: rdn ent fnl f and kpt on wl* **9/1**

06-0 **2** 1 3/4 **Mawaakef (IRE)**[40] 177 4-9-7 **84** FrederikTylicki 8 91
(J R Jenkins) *chsd ldrs: hdwy over 3f out and sn cl up: ev ch 2f out tl rdn and one pce ins fnl f* **5/1**[3]

16-5 **3** 2 1/4 **Greyfriarschorista**[26] 354 5-9-5 **82** BarryMcHugh 4 84
(Brian Ellison) *hld up towards rr: hdwy on inner 1/2-way: chsd ldng pair 2f out: sn rdn and kpt on same pce appr fnl f* **10/3**[1]

1 **4** 2 **Colour Guard**[13] 495 4-8-12 **75** JoeFanning 1 72+
(Mark Johnston) *awkward and lost grnd s: green in rr: hdwy 3f out: styd on fnl 2f: nrst fin* **7/2**[2]

2033 **5** 1 **Follow The Flag (IRE)**[9] 554 8-9-4 **81** (be) StevieDonohoe 7 76
(Alan McCabe) *towards rr: wd st: rdn and sme hdwy on outer wl over 1f out: n.d* **9/1**

-264 **6** 4 1/2 **Piceno (IRE)**[7] 585 4-8-7 **75** (p) RaulDaSilva(5) 6 60
(Scott Dixon) *chsd ldr: led after 1f and set str pce: rdn along 3f out: hdd 2f out and sn wknd* **12/1**

-115 **7** 1 3/4 **Aquarian Spirit**[19] 432 5-9-0 **77** PaulHanagan 5 58
(Richard Fahey) *in tch: effrt over 3f out: sn rdn and btn* **15/2**

1-43 **8** 11 **On The Cusp (IRE)**[7] 584 5-8-12 **75** (p) MartinHarley 3 30
(Richard Guest) *led 1f: cl up: rdn along over 3f out and sn wknd* **11/2**

1m 43.5s (-0.20) **Going Correction** +0.075s/f (Slow) **8** Ran SP% **116.8**

Speed ratings (Par 105): **104,102,100,98,97 92,90,79**

toteswingers: 1&2 £9.50, 1&3 £6.80, 2&3 £4.60. CSF £54.48 CT £184.27 TOTE £14.80: £5.30, £3.40, £1.40; EX 61.60 Trifecta £424.30 Pool: £590.59 - 1.03 winning units..

Owner C E Whiteley **Bred** Dave Curran & Eric Cantillon **Trained** Norton, N Yorks

FOCUS

A flyaway gallop set by the two leaders tested the others all the way, although the bare time was slower than the seller. A length personal best from the winner.

675 SOUTHWELL GOLF CLUB LADIES MAIDEN FILLIES' STKS 1m (F)

4:40 (4:42) (Class 5) 3-Y-0+ **£2,385** (£704; £352) **Stalls** Low

Form RPR

3-62 **1** **Cape Safari (IRE)**[23] 369 3-8-9 67 (p) MartinLane 3 66
(James Tate) *trckd ldrs: effrt over 2f out: rdn to ld jst over 1f out: kpt on* **5/6**[1]

23 **2** 1 1/4 **Scatter Dice (IRE)**[20] 399 3-8-9 0 FrannyNorton 5 63
(Mark Johnston) *cl up: led 3f out: rdn wl over 1f out: hdd appr fnl f: kpt on same pce* **7/2**[3]

-65 **3** 2 **Gabrial's Lexi (IRE)**[12] 533 3-8-9 0 PaulHanagan 1 59
(Richard Fahey) *chsd ldrs on inner: pushed along and sltly outpcd over 3f out: rdn and kpt on fnl 2f* **10/3**[2]

4 3 **Moorgate Lass** 4-10-0 0 MickyFenton 4 58
(Garry Woodward) *dwlt and in rr: gd hdwy on outer to join ldrs 3f out: wd st: rdn 2f out: ev ch tl wknd appr fnl f* **50/1**

5-46 **5** 9 **Phoenix Flame**[16] 454 4-9-7 50 (bt[1]) DannyBrock(7) 2 37
(Alan McCabe) *led: rdn along and hdd 3f out: sn wknd* **10/1**

1m 45.87s (2.17) **Going Correction** +0.075s/f (Slow)

WFA 3 from 4yo 19lb **5** Ran SP% **110.9**

Speed ratings (Par 100): **92,90,88,85,76**

CSF £4.16 TOTE £1.80: £1.30, £2.70; EX 4.20.

Owner Saif Ali **Bred** Rabbah Bloodstock Limited **Trained** Newmarket, Suffolk

FOCUS

A weak fillies' maiden. The pace wasn't testing, but they finished in a plausible order. The form is rated around the winner.

676 GET YOUR BET ON AT BLUESQ.COM H'CAP 1m (F)

5:10 (5:10) (Class 6) (0-60,61) 4-Y-0+ **£1,704** (£503; £251) **Stalls** Low

Form RPR

-010 **1** **St Ignatius**[23] 370 5-8-5 **51** (be) JackDuern(7) 2 62
(Michael Appleby) *sn led: rdn along over 2f out: hdd 1 1/2f out: rallied u.p ins fnl f to ld again last 40yds* **25/1**

0-21 **2** *nk* **Caledonia Prince**[13] 490 4-9-0 60........................(p) JoshBaudains(7) 8 70
(Jo Hughes) *trckd ldng pair: hdwy 3f out: led 1 1/2f out: rdn ins fnl f: edgd lft: hdd and no ex last 40yds* **5/4**[1]
/605 **3** *1 3/4* **Myraid**[9] 557 5-8-11 50........................ JamesSullivan 9 56
(Ruth Carr) *midfield: hdwy 3f out: chsd ldrs wl over 1f out and sn rdn: drvn and ch ent fnl f: kpt on same pce* **33/1**
2244 **4** *1 1/2* **Spacecraft (IRE)**[13] 490 5-8-5 51........................(b) DannyBrock(7) 3 54
(Christopher Kellett) *hld up towards rr: hdwy over 2f out: rdn wl over 1f out: styd on appr fnl f: nrst fin* **8/1**[3]
0-31 **5** *2 1/2* **Just Five (IRE)**[3] 633 6-9-3 61 6ex........................(v) RaulDaSilva(5) 10 58
(John Weymes) *trckd ldrs on outer: hdwy 3f out: rdn wl over 1f out: kpt on same pce appr fnl f* **8/1**[3]
06-0 **6** *1 3/4* **Exopuntia**[46] 96 6-8-10 52........................ AdamBeschizza(3) 7 45
(Julia Feilden) *chsd ldrs on inner: n.m.r and stmbld over 3f out: rdn wl over 2f out: sn one pce* **20/1**
-505 **7** *1/2* **Hilbre Court (USA)**[14] 477 7-8-8 52........................(p) DavidKenny(5) 12 44
(Brian Baugh) *in tch on outer: hdwy to chse ldrs over 2f out: sn rdn and no imp* **14/1**
504- **8** *3/4* **Kool Shuffle (GER)**[57] 7112 4-8-12 51........................(t) BarryMcHugh 4 41
(Tony Coyle) *hld up towards rr: effrt wl over 2f out: sn rdn and n.d* **7/2**[2]
035- **9** *6* **Brown Pete (IRE)**[57] 7890 4-9-5 58........................(b) MartinHarley 6 34
(Richard Guest) *cl up: rdn wl over 2f out: sn wknd* **12/1**
6026 **10** *4 1/2* **Putin (IRE)**[6] 598 4-8-3 47........................(bt) LauraPike(5) 5 13
(Phil McEntee) *cl up: rdn along over 3f out and sn wknd* **25/1**
-600 **11** *9* **Jay Jays Joy**[13] 490 4-8-3 49........................(v) NedCurtis(7) 11
(Paul Midgley) *s.i.s and a bhd* **50/1**
000- **12** *13* **Thrust Control (IRE)**[131] 6869 5-9-4 57........................ TomEaves 13
(Tracy Waggott) *in tch on wd outside: rdn along 1/2-way: sn wknd* **16/1**
336- **13** *40* **Fly By White (IRE)**[182] 5401 4-9-0 58........................ JustinNewman(5) 1
(Barry Murtagh) *a bhd: t.o fr over 3f out* **50/1**

1m 44.55s (0.85) **Going Correction** +0.075s/f (Slow) **13** Ran SP% **128.4**
Speed ratings (Par 101): **98,97,95,94,91 90,89,88,82,78 69,56,16**
toteswingers: 1&2 £11.30, 1&3 £65.10, 2&3 £26.80. CSF £57.94 CT £1231.72 TOTE £38.30: £7.60, £1.60, £8.10; EX 122.00 TRIFECTA Not won..
Owner Michael Appleby **Bred** Simon And Helen Plumbly **Trained** Danethorpe, Notts

FOCUS
The in-form runner-up was all the rage in this low-grade contest, but he found one to beat him. The form seems sound enough.
St Ignatius Official explanation: trainer said, regarding apparent improvement in form, that the gelding appeared to benefit from being able to dominate over a longer trip, having been outpaced last time.
T/Plt: £175.80 to a £1 stake. Pool:£60,506.18 - 251.23 winning tickets T/Qpdt: £6.20 to a £1 stake. Pool:£6,091.76 - 724.74 winning tickets JR

613 MEYDAN (L-H)
Thursday, February 23
OFFICIAL GOING: Tapeta: standard; turf: good
Rail on turf track moved out 12m from inside line.

677a SWAIDAN TRADING COMPANY - GOODYEAR (H'CAP) (TAPETA) 1m 1f 110y
2:30 (2:30) (100-110,110) 3-Y-0+
£46,451 (£15,483; £7,741; £3,870; £2,322; £1,548)

RPR
1 **Capponi (IRE)**[28] 317 5-9-6 110........................ FrankieDettori 2 115+
(Mahmood Al Zarooni) *trckd ldr: led 2 1/2f out: clr 1 1/2f out: comf* **2/1**[1]
2 *3* **Disa Leader (SAF)**[20] 416 7-9-4 108........................ JGeroudis 4 107
(M F De Kock, South Africa) *mid-div: rdn 2 1/2f out: ev ch 2f out: r.o same pce fnl 1 1/2f* **6/1**[3]
3 *1 3/4* **Vagabond Shoes (IRE)**[20] 416 5-9-6 110........................ OlivierPeslier 5 105
(Stephane Chevalier, UAE) *settled in rr: nvr nr to chal but r.o fnl 2f* **6/1**[3]
4 *1* **Sarrsar**[28] 317 5-9-5 109........................(vt) MickaelBarzalona 8 102
(Saeed Bin Suroor) *settled in last: nvr able to chal but r.o fnl 2f* **9/4**[2]
5 *1/2* **Royal Destination (IRE)**[7] 587 7-8-10 100........................(vt) WayneSmith 3 92
(F Nass, Bahrain) *trckd ldng duo: rdn 2 1/2f out: ev ch 2f out: wknd fnl 110yds* **16/1**
6 *2* **Rochdale**[14] 489 9-8-11 101........................(t) RoystonFfrench 6 89
(A Al Raihe, UAE) *settled in rr: nvr able to chal* **33/1**
7 *3/4* **Club Oceanic**[14] 489 4-8-10 101........................(v) SilvestreDeSousa 1 88
(Saeed Bin Suroor) *nvr bttr than mid-div* **9/1**
8 *6 1/2* **Navajo Chief**[7] 586 5-8-10 100........................ KierenFallon 7 73
(Alan Jarvis) *sn led: rdn 4f out: hdd & wknd 2 1/2f out* **16/1**

1m 58.82s (-0.18) **8** Ran SP% **117.4**
CSF: £15.17; TRICAST: £62.54.
Owner Sheikh Hamdan Bin Mohammed Al Maktoum **Bred** Darley **Trained** Newmarket, Suffolk

FOCUS
An ordinary handicap for a 100-110. The pace was slow (27.41, 53.09, 1.18.52 and 1.41.41) and early leader Navajo Chief should have lasted longer, even though this trip stretches him. A personal best from the winner.

NOTEBOOK
Capponi(IRE) had the race in the bag when sent clear early in the straight. He was helped by the run of the race and this wide-margin win off a mark of 110 surely flatters him.
Disa Leader(SAF) confirmed recent 1m form with Vagabond Shoes, having been the more forwardly placed of the pair, but he had given Capponi far too big a start and also covered nine meters more than that rival.
Vagabond Shoes(IRE) was a bit keen under restraint early on, but he was basically set an impossible task and got going too late, much like last time.
Sarrsar threw away a winning chance when edged out by Capponi last time, so it seems the plan was to produce him late this time. But even so, sitting last off such slow fractions gave the gelding no hope whatsoever.

678a SWAIDAN TRADING COMPANY - PEUGEOT (H'CAP) (TAPETA) 1m 3f
3:05 (3:05) (100-110,110) 3-Y-0+
£46,451 (£15,483; £7,741; £3,870; £2,322; £1,548)

RPR
1 **Jamr**[14] 484 4-8-10 104........................(v) PatCosgrave 9 106
(M bin Shafya, UAE) *mid-div: chsd ldrs 2 1/2f out: led 1 1/2f out: r.o wl* **3/1**[1]
2 *nk* **Spring Of Fame (USA)**[14] 484 6-9-5 110........................ MickaelBarzalona 7 112
(Saeed Bin Suroor) *in rr of mid-div: rdn 4f out: r.o wl fnl 2f: nrst fin* **7/2**[2]
3 *1* **Honour System (IRE)**[14] 484 5-9-0 105........................ SilvestreDeSousa 6 105
(Saeed Bin Suroor) *trckd ldr: ev ch whn n.m.r 1 1/2f out: one pce afterwards* **10/1**
4 *1/2* **Jardim (BRZ)**[7] 587 6-9-0 105........................ KShea 8 104
(M F De Kock, South Africa) *mid-div: rdn 3f out: r.o fnl 2f* **4/1**[3]
5 *3/4* **Fiery Lad (IRE)**[14] 484 7-8-9 100........................ WilliamBuick 2 98
(Luca Cumani) *a mid-div* **16/1**
6 *2 1/4* **Rostrum (FR)**[7] 591 5-9-1 106........................ FrankieDettori 1 100
(Mahmood Al Zarooni) *settled in rr: nvr nr to chal but r.o fnl 2f* **7/1**
7 *2* **Mikhail Glinka (IRE)**[14] 486 5-9-4 109........................(t) RyanMoore 4 99
(H J Brown, South Africa) *trckd ldr: ev ch 2f out: wknd fnl f* **10/1**
8 *2 1/4* **Nanton (USA)**[20] 421 10-8-11 102........................ TedDurcan 11 88
(E Charpy, UAE) *settled in rr: nvr nr to chal* **25/1**
9 *2 3/4* **Yaseer (IRE)**[13] 515 4-8-9 102........................ RichardHills 10 83
(E Charpy, UAE) *sn led: rdn 3f out: hdd & wknd fnl 1 1/2f* **25/1**
10 *2* **Kidnapped (AUS)**[175] 5659 6-8-9 100........................(v) KierenFallon 5 78
(Saeed Bin Suroor) *s.i.s: nvr able to chal* **16/1**
11 *6* **Durdlaz (IRE)**[33] 260 7-8-9 100........................(v) RichardMullen 3 67
(S Seemar, UAE) *nvr bttr than mid-div* **33/1**

2m 18.13s (-0.27)
WFA 4 from 5yo+ 2lb **11** Ran SP% **120.3**
CSF: £13.44; TRICAST: £95.25.
Owner Sheikh Mansoor bin Mohammed al Maktoum **Bred** J Knight And E Cantillon **Trained** United Arab Emirates

FOCUS
The went a modest pace (27.80, 52.33, 1.17.18, 1.42.25 and 2.06.09), with Yaseer taking them along for most of the way. The first two met last time out.

NOTEBOOK
Jamr tends to do little in front - he only just held on when completing a Dubai hat-trick two starts previously and was overhauled by Spring Of Fame after being committed too soon last time. On this occasion he was again clinging on at the line, having not helped himself by hanging left, and he only just reversed form with his old rival on 1lb better terms. He's now 4-5 since switching to Dubai and could continue to defy the handicapper, especially if his challenge can be delivered a bit later.
Spring Of Fame(USA) didn't travel as well as when winning last time - he was being niggled along from an early stage, much like when runner-up two starts previously. He finished well, and just failed despite covering two meters more than the winner, but the suspicion remains that headgear might help him focus better.
Honour System(IRE) was held when hampered by the winner against the inside rail late on. It might have cost him second, but probably didn't.
Jardim(BRZ), up 3lb for his second-place finish over slightly shorter here the previous week, had his chance but simply didn't pick up sufficiently. He should appreciate a drop in trip, but is not well handicapped.
Fiery Lad(IRE) travelled okay and this was an improvement on the form he showed on his first two starts after a lengthy absence.
Rostrum(FR) remains too high in the weights.

679a MEYDAN CLASSIC SPONSORED BY THE SAEED & MOHAMMED AL NABOODAH GROUP (LISTED RACE) (TURF) 1m
3:45 (3:45) 3-Y-O
£58,064 (£19,354; £9,677; £4,838; £2,903; £1,935)

RPR
1 **Burano (IRE)**[14] 485 3-8-8 97........................ FrankieDettori 3 99
(Brian Meehan) *mid-div: smooth prog 2f out: r.o wl fnl f: led cl home* **16/1**
2 *shd* **Entifaadha**[145] 6527 3-8-8 107........................ RichardHills 8 99
(William Haggas) *in rr of mid-div: r.o fnl 2f: led 1f out: hdd cl home* **2/1**[2]
3 *3/4* **Noor Zabeel (USA)**[14] 485 3-8-8 100........................ SilvestreDeSousa 9 97
(A Al Raihe, UAE) *in rr of mid-div: chsd ldrs 2f out: r.o fnl f: nrst fin* **14/1**
4 *nk* **Fiscal**[20] 417 3-8-8 97........................ AndreaAtzeni 12 97
(M Al Jahouri, UAE) *trckd ldng pair: ev ch 1f out: one pce fnl 110yds* **16/1**
5 *3/4* **Matusalen (SPA)**[123] 3-8-8 102........................ BFayosMartin 4 95
(M Delcher-Sanchez, Spain) *s.i.s: settled in rr: r.o fnl 1 1/2f* **8/1**[3]
6 *3 1/4* **Cash Luck (AUS)**[25] 4-9-4 112........................(b) VladDuric 2 84
(M Freedman, Singapore) *s.i.s: in rr of mid-div: chsd ldrs: ev ch 1 1/2f out: one pce fnl 110yds* **7/4**[1]
7 *1/2* **Factory Time (IRE)**[20] 417 3-8-8 100........................(t) RoystonFfrench 5 86
(A Al Raihe, UAE) *sn led: hdd & wknd 1f out* **10/1**
8 *2 1/4* **Energia Dust (BRZ)**[20] 417 4-9-4 96........................ Per-AndersGraberg 10 78
(Fabricio Borges, Sweden) *mid-div: rdn 4f out: n.d* **33/1**
9 *1/2* **Kenny Powers**[20] 417 3-8-8 97........................(t) KierenFallon 1 80
(Tom Dascombe) *trckd ldrs: ev ch 2f out: one pce fnl f* **12/1**
10 *11 1/2* **Old Pal (FR)**[20] 417 3-8-8 97........................(tp) WilliamBuick 11 53
(Niels Petersen, Norway) *trckd ldr tl 2 1/2f out: one pce fnl 1 1/2f* **33/1**
11 *3/4* **Cody Maverick (IRE)**[6] 613 3-8-8 88........................(bt) AhmedAjtebi 6 52
(A Al Raihe, UAE) *racd in rr: n.d* **66/1**
12 *7 1/4* **Strait Of Zanzibar (USA)**[20] 417 3-8-8 99........................(p) TadhgO'Shea 7 35
(K J Condon, Ire) *nvr nr to chal* **33/1**

1m 40.22s (100.22)
WFA 3 from 4yo 19lb **12** Ran SP% **126.3**
CSF: £50.49..
Owner Jonathan Harvey / Brian Meehan **Bred** Sir E J Loder **Trained** Manton, Wilts

FOCUS
Only the fourth running of the Meydan Classic and the form doesn't look strong. They finished in something of a bunch. Factory Time set a fair pace (26.43, 50.91 and 1.15.41).

NOTEBOOK
Burano(IRE) was set far too much to do when a staying-on fifth in the trial, before flopping in the UAE 2000 Guineas, but he was back on turf here and also had the ever-excellent Frankie Dettori taking over for the first time. He was blocked in by the third when rounding the turn into the straight and continued to find trouble for much of the closing stages, but he saved ground by making his bid towards the inside and got running room in time. His breeding suggests he might get a bit further and he could improve on this form in due course.
Entifaadha, absent since finishing fifth of 16 in a sales race at Newmarket in October, covered five meters more than Burano and would have won had he been able to get a clear run without going wide. It's doubtful he ran to his official mark of 107, but he's entitled to come on for the run. (op 9-4)
Noor Zabeel(USA) produced a sustained bid, but just wasn't good enough. Like the runner-up, he covered five metres more than the winner. This was an improvement on his Dubai debut when sixth in the Guineas, but it remains to be seen whether there's much more to come.
Fiscal looked a shrewd purchase out of John Gosden's yard at 10,000gns judged on his fourth-place finish in the trial, and he proved it here.
Matusalen(SPA), a prolific winner in Spain, was immediately behind after missing the break and had to use up plenty of energy to try and get into contention, before his effort unsurprisingly flattened out late on.
Cash Luck(AUS), a regular winner in Singapore, didn't help himself with a sluggish start but he saved much more ground than any of his rivals. He weakened late on and didn't get anywhere near his official mark of 112.
Factory Time(IRE), who made all in the 7f trial, again went from the front but couldn't sustain his bid over this longer trip.

Kenny Powers didn't build on the form he showed when runner-up in the trial.

680a UAE OAKS SPONSORED BY THE SAEED & MOHAMMED AL NABOODAH GROUP (GROUP 3) (FILLIES) (TAPETA) 1m 1f 110y
4:20 (4:20) 3-Y-O

£96,774 (£32,258; £16,129 ; £8,064 ; £4,838 ; £3,225)

RPR
1 **Falls Of Lora (IRE)**[44] 6564 3 -8-9104 MickaelBarzalona 3 104+
(Mahmood Al Zarooni) *mid-div: rdn 2 1/2f out: r.o wl fnl 1 1/2f: led 110yds out: comf* **7/2**[2]
2 2 3/4 **Mary Fildes (IRE)**[20] 418 3 -8-994 (p) JamesDoyle 5 99
(J S Moore) *sn ldr: t.k.h: clr 3 1/2f out: tired fnl 2f: hdd fnl 110yds* **33/1**
3 nk **Alsindi (IRE)**[20] 418 3 -8-9100 RoystonFfrench 2 98
(A Al Raihe, UAE) *mid-div: chsd ldr 3f out: kpt on same pce fnl 1 1/2f* **11/1**[3]
4 shd **Moon Spun (SAF)**[20] 418 4 -9-593 RyanMoore 4 96
(H J Brown, South Africa) *trckd ldr: rdn 4f out: kpt on same pce fnl 2f* **20/1**
5 1 1/2 **Pimpernel (IRE)**[20] 418 3 -8-9106 FrankieDettori 6 95
(Mahmood Al Zarooni) *settled in rr: nvr nr to chal* **4/9**[1]
6 12 1/2 **Colorful Notion (IRE)**[20] 418 3 -8-980 MircoDemuro 1 69
(Marco Botti) *racd in last: nvr nr to chal* **33/1**

2m 1.12s (2.12)
WFA 3 from 4yo 21lb **6**Ran SP% **110.5**
CSF: £84.70. .
Owner Godolphin **Bred** Darley **Trained** Newmarket, Suffolk

FOCUS
A disappointing turnout for the UAE Oaks - there was only one filly representing the southern hemisphere in a field of just six - and the race unfolded in bizarre fashion. The front-running Mary Fildes went at least 12l clear down the back straight, but the clock shows she was able to do so without setting a strong pace. Here are her sectionals along with the splits for the earlier slowly run C&D handicap in brackets: 27.93 (27.41), 52.06 (53.09), 1.17.34 (1.18.52) and 1.41.98 (1.41.41). The final time was 2.30 seconds slower than the handicap. The runner-up is the best guide to the form.

NOTEBOOK
Falls Of Lora (IRE)the only one of these who didn't contest the UAE 1000 Guineas, won despite being set an awful lot to do. She failed to beat a rival in the Prix Marcel Boussac when last seen, but that still represented her best RPR and maybe she has more to offer. The surface evidently suited, which is no surprise considering she's a daughter of Street Cry. (op 3-1)
Mary Fildes (IRE)could have been expected to hold on (touched 1.4 in running), but she's simply not bred for this trip and tired dramatically in the straight, edging right late on.
Alsindi(IRE) had stamina to prove, and she has also yet to convince on this surface. It's unclear what she achieved. (op 10-1)
Moon Spun (SAF)had been well beaten in the Guineas and again didn't offer much.
Pimpernel(IRE) was too keen when runner-up in the Guineas and again refused to drop her head. She is best watched until proving she will relax in her races. (op 1-2)

681a AL NABOODAH CONSTRUCTION GROUP (H'CAP) (TURF) 5f
4:55 (4:55) (100-116,116) 3-Y-O+

£67,741 (£22,580; £11,290 ; £5,645 ; £3,387 ; £2,258)

RPR
1 **Nocturnal Affair (SAF)**[20] 419 6 -8-9105 (t) RyanMoore 1 113
(David Marnane, Ire) *chsd ldrs: rdn 2f out: led 1f out: comf* **6/1**[1]
2 1 1/4 **Monsieur Joe (IRE)**[20] 419 5 -8-8104 WilliamBuick 13 107
(Robert Cowell) *in rr of mid-div: r.o wl fnl 1 1/2f: nrst fin* **13/2**[2]
3 3/4 **Inxile (IRE)**[20] 419 7 -9-5115 (p) AdrianNicholls 6 115
(David Nicholls) *sn led: hdd 1f out: kpt on same pce* **6/1**[1]
4 1 **Prohibit**[144] 6563 7 -9-6116 (p) JimCrowley 10 113
(Robert Cowell) *settled in rr: r.o fnl 1 1/2f: nrst fin* **7/1**[3]
5 nk **Seachantach (USA)**[20] 420 6 -8-5100 (t) RichardMullen 3 97
(S Seemar, UAE) *mid-div: kpt on same pce fnl 1 1/2f* **28/1**
6 nk **Green Beret (IRE)**[7] 589 6 -8-7102 (t) RoystonFfrench 2 98
(A Al Raihe, UAE) *mid-div: kpt on same pce fnl 1 1/2f* **10/1**
7 1 1/4 **Better Be The One (AUS)**[6] 6 -9-5115 (b) VladDuric 4 105
(M Freedman, Singapore) *chsd ldrs tl one pce 1 1/2f out* **6/1**[1]
8 3/4 **Invincible Ash (IRE)**[20] 419 7 -8-6101 (p) TadhgO'Shea 9 89
(M Halford, Ire) *nvr bttr than mid-div* **20/1**
9 1 1/2 **Humidor (IRE)**[20] 419 5 -8-10106 (t) PatCosgrave 11 88
(George Baker) *s.i.s: settled in rr: nvr able to chal* **10/1**
10 3/4 **Happy Dubai (IRE)**[7] 589 5 -9-4113 (t) SilvestreDeSousa 7 93
(A Al Raihe, UAE) *trckd ldr: nt qckn fnl 1 1/2f* **6/1**[1]
11 2 3/4 **Prinzde Glas (IRE)**[28] 314 5 -8-5100 (bt) MircoDemuro 8 70
(Stephane Chevalier, UAE) *trckd ldr tl 2f out: one pce fnl f* **33/1**
12 dist **Mar Adentro (FR)**[20] 419 6 -9-2111 (tp) ChristopheSoumillon 5
(R Chotard, France) *trckd ldr tl wknd 2 1/2f out* **10/1**

58.47s (58.47) **12**Ran SP% **121.4**
CSF: £44.49; TRICAST: £250.24. .
Owner Emma Bifova **Bred** T D Andrews **Trained** Bansha, Co Tipperary

FOCUS
A good sprint handicap in which the action unfolded up the middle of the track.

NOTEBOOK
Nocturnal Affair (SAF)didn't run to his best when fifth behind the likes of Monsieur Joe and Inxile over C&D last time, but clearly this was more like it. He may yet have more to offer.
Monsieur Joe (IRE)was seemingly found out by a 4lb rise for his recent win, but he still ran well and is entitled to be improving considering he's only a 5yo and has not been overraced. (op 6-1)
Inxile(IRE) showed his usual speed and kept on well. This was a fine performance off a mark of 115.
Prohibit made a promising return from a 144-day absence. His main aim is presumably the C&D Al Quoz Sprint on World Cup day, a race in which he was fifth last year.
Better Be The One (AUS)was third in the Al Quoz Sprint last year on his only previous visit to Dubai, and he's been in winning form in Singapore lately, so better could have been expected.
Happy Dubai (IRE)was better than the bare form when winning over 6f on Tapeta the previous week, but the handicapper took no chances, hammering him with an 8lb rise. He has won over C&D, but struggled this time.

682a AL NABOODAH CONSTRUCTION GROUP (CONDITIONS RACE) (TURF) 1m 1f
5:30 (5:30) 3-Y-O+

£38,709 (£12,903; £6,451 ; £3,225 ; £1,935 ; £1,290)

RPR
1 **City Style (USA)**[28] 318 6 -8-11111 MickaelBarzalona 3 112+
(Mahmood Al Zarooni) *settled in rr: rdn 2 1/2f out: smooth prog 1 1/2f out: led fnl f: comf* **2/1**[1]
2 2 **Rerouted (USA)**[7] 588 4 -8-11105 (b) ChristopheSoumillon 4 108
(M F De Kock, South Africa) *mid-div: rdn 3f out: r.o fnl 1 1/2f: nrst fin* **5/2**[2]
3 shd **Secrecy**[14] 489 6 -8-11108 (p) FrankieDettori 11 108
(Saeed Bin Suroor) *sn led: kicked clr 2f out: hdd fnl f* **11/2**
4 3/4 **Shamalgan (FR)**[14] 487 5 -9-2115 GregoryBenoist 1 111
(X Nakkachdji, France) *trckd ldrs: ev ch 1f out: one pce fnl 110yds* **12/1**
5 2 1/4 **Tajaaweed (USA)**[96] 7 -9-0110 RichardHills 7 104
(Doug Watson, UAE) *mid-div: chsd ldrs 2 1/2f out: nt qckn fnl f* **10/1**
6 3/4 **Hujaylea (IRE)**[20] 416 9 -8-11102 (p) TadhgO'Shea 6 100
(M Halford, Ire) *s.i.s: settled in rr: n.d* **33/1**
7 5 **Janood (IRE)**[62] 7868 4 -8-1193 (vt) PatCosgrave 9 89
(M bin Shafya, UAE) *in rr of mid-div: rdn 3 1/2f out: nvr able to chal* **33/1**
8 1 1/4 **Fanunalter**[42] 144 6 -8-11117 RyanMoore 2 87
(Marco Botti) *in rr of mid-div: chsd ldrs 2 1/2f out: wknd fnl f* **4/1**[3]
9 nk **Kingship Spirit (IRE)**[8] 6 -8-1190 (t) RoystonFfrench 8 86
(M Ramadan, UAE) *trckd ldrs tl 3f out: sn btn* **100/1**
10 2 1/4 **Mantoba**[34] 241 4 -8-1195 (bt) WilliamBuick 5 81
(Brian Meehan) *trckd ldrs: rdn 4 1/2f out: sn wknd* **33/1**

1m 53.49s (113.49) **10**Ran SP% **123.9**
CSF: £7.55. PLACEPOT: £123.10 to a £1 stake. Pool of £5,542.75 - 32.85 winning tickets. QUADPOT: £33.40 to a £1 stake. Pool of £510.80 - 11.30 winning tickets.
Owner Sheikh Hamdan Bin Mohammed Al Maktoum **Bred** Stoneside Stable **Trained** Newmarket, Suffolk

FOCUS
A good conditions race, although Secrecy set a sluggish pace, going 28.00, 52.90, 1.17.90 and 1.41.36. It was disappointing he couldn't hold on.

NOTEBOOK
City Style (USA)won the inaugural Meydan Classic (confusingly held at Nad Al Sheba) and here he was winning again on the same day that race was being staged for the fourth time. This was his fourth Carnival success in total and his second this year. His only defeat so far in 2012 came when runner-up to the Duty Free-bound Musir over C&D in January and he gave a nice boost to that form. He had 6lb in hand of Rerouted on official figures, but still did well to win considering he was held up in this slowly run race.
Rerouted(USA) ran another solid race, but this won't have helped his handicap mark.
Secrecy set a slow pace and could have been expected to hold on.
Shamalgan(FR) again ran nowhere near his official mark of 115.
Tajaaweed(USA) struggled on his first start since leaving the US.
Fanunalter was again disappointing, even though the race wasn't exactly run to suit.

654 LINGFIELD (L-H)
Friday, February 24

OFFICIAL GOING: Standard
Wind: medium, across Weather: dry, bright spells

683 BET AT BLUE SQUARE CLAIMING STKS 1m 2f (P)
1:40 (1:40) (Class 6) 3-Y-O **£1,704** (£503; £251) **Stalls** Low

Form RPR
3411 1 **Clean Bowled (IRE)**[6] 619 3 -8-1265 (p) NedCurtis(7) 4 76
(Roger Curtis) *hld up in last pair: smooth hdwy on inner over 2f out: pushed along to chal over 1f out: led ins fnl f: sn clr: easily* **8/13**[1]
-322 2 3 1/4 **Crowning Star (IRE)**[6] 619 3 -8-1261 LukeMorris 1 62
(J S Moore) *t.k.h early: hld up in 3rd: rdn to ld over 1f out: hdd ins fnl f: sn btn: eased towards fin* **2/1**[2]
0-46 3 6 **Nic Nok**[13] 534 3 -8-649 (b[1]) RaulDaSilva(5) 3 49
(Harry Dunlop) *hmpd s: t.k.h: sn rcvrd to chse ldr: led over 2f out: rdn and hdd over 1f out: sn wknd* **40/1**
63 4 12 **Cuore (IRE)**[17] 464 3 -9-10 FergusSweeney 6 29
(Jamie Osborne) *t.k.h early: hld up in last pair: rdn over 4f out: wknd 2f out* **12/1**[3]
0-50 5 12 **Search And Rescue (USA)**[9] 571 3 -9-356 JoeFanning 2
(J W Hills) *dwlt: sn led: hdd over 2f out: sn dropped out: bhd fnl 2f* **33/1**

2m 6.93s (0.33)**Going Correction** +0.10s/f (Slow) **5**Ran SP% **108.3**
Speed ratings (Par 95): **102,99,94,85,75**
CSF £1.96 TOTE £1.50 : £1.10 , £1.10 ; EX 1.90 .
Owner Richard Dean **Bred** Cathal Ennis **Trained** Lambourn, Berks

FOCUS
This claimer was run at a steady pace, and the two market leaders dominated the closing stages. Another improved effort at face value from the winner but the handicapper is unlikely to be kind.
Crowning Star (IRE) Official explanation: vet said gelding lost a right-hind shoe just after start

684 BREATHE SPA AT MARRIOTT LINGFIELD MEDIAN AUCTION MAIDEN STKS 1m (P)
2:15 (2:15) (Class 6) 3-4-Y-O **£1,704** (£503; £251) **Stalls** High

Form RPR
1 **Mafi (IRE)**[128] 6964 4 -9-1366 WilliamCarson 5 75
(Mark Hoad) *chsd ldrs on outer: rdn to chse ldr 2f out: ev ch but hanging lft over 1f out: led jst ins fnl f: sn hdd and awkward hd carriage u.p: led again fnl strides* **20/1**
2 hd **Legendary** 3 -8-80 LukeMorris 2 69
(Ed Vaughan) *s.i.s: in tch in rr: rdn and effrt on inner 2f out: ev ch 1f out: led fnl 100yds: kpt on tl hdd and no ex last strides* **9/1**
32 3 2 1/2 **Falcon's Reign (FR)**[20] 428 3 -8-80 ShaneKelly 1 63
(Jeremy Noseda) *pressed ldr on inner tl led over 4f out: rdn ent fnl 2f: hdd jst ins fnl f: no ex: wknd towards fin* **4/7**[1]
0 4 3/4 **Lanarkshire (IRE)**[25] 358 3 -8-80 JoeFanning 3 61
(Mark Johnston) *led tl over 4f out: rdn ent fnl 2f: sn unable qck: 4th and outpcd over 1f out: one pce and no threat to ldrs fnl f* **11/2**[2]
- 5 18 **Auntie Mabel** 3 -8-30 DavidProbert 4 15
(Andrew Balding) *niggled along thrght: rdn over 4f out: wknd and lost tch 2f out* **6/1**[3]

1m 37.71s (-0.49)**Going Correction** +0.10s/f (Slow)
WFA 3 from 4yo 19lb **5**Ran SP% **108.1**
Speed ratings (Par 101): **106,105,103,102,84**
CSF £151.94 TOTE £21.30 : £6.00 , £3.10 ; EX 88.70 .
Owner Mrs J E Taylor **Bred** Kilboy Estate **Trained** Lewes, E Sussex

FOCUS
Only five runners, but there was a shock 20-1 winner while the odds-on favourite disappointed. The winner is rated back towards something like his Irish form.

685 HOLLOW LANE H'CAP 1m (P)
2:50 (2:51) (Class 5) (0-70,70) 4-Y-O+ **£2,385** (£704; £352) **Stalls** High

Form RPR
0-12 1 **Twinkled**[9] 562 4 -8-1167 IanBurns(7) 10 72
(Michael Bell) *stdd s: hld up in last trio: pushed along 2f out: stl plenty to do and rdn jst over 1f out: str run ins fnl f to ld towards fin* **5/1**[2]

4-50 **2** ½ **Cativo Cavallino**[30] 301 9-9-1 **64** .... RichardThomas 8 68
(John E Long) *pressed ldrs on outer: rdn to ld 2f out: drvn over 1f out: kpt on wl u.p tl hdd and no ex towards fin* **7/1**[3]

4-3 **3** ½ **Jumeirah Liberty**[20] 428 4-8-13 **62** .... JamieGoldstein 4 65
(Zoe Davison) *hld up wl in tch in midfield: rdn and hdwy on inner wl over 1f out: ev ch 1f out: kpt on same pce fnl 100yds* **25/1**

60-0 **4** ¾ **Peadar Miguel**[15] 480 5-9-5 **68** .... GeorgeBaker 1 69
(Noel Quinlan) *trckd ldrs on inner: switching rt 2f out: drvn and chsd ldrs 1f out: unable qck and kpt on same pce fnl f* **4/1**[1]

000- **5** shd **Monsieur Broughton**[77] 7698 4-8-7 **56** .... JamieMackay 9 57
(Willie Musson) *stdd s: hld up in rr: hdwy over 1f out: swtchd lft jst ins fnl f: kpt on* **33/1**

5135 **6** shd **Shared Moment (IRE)**[9] 568 6-9-3 **66** ....(v) TomQueally 5 67
(John Gallagher) *in tch in midfield: rdn 2f out: drvn and chsd ldrs jst ins fnl f: styd on same pce fnl 100yds* **4/1**[1]

0-00 **7** 1 ¾ **Huzzah (IRE)**[33] 262 7-8-10 **59** .... MichaelStainton 2 56
(Paul Howling) *t.k.h: led: hdd and hmpd bnd 2f out: lost pl and sn rdn: styd on same pce fr over 1f out* **8/1**

4-50 **8** ½ **Salient**[9] 568 8-9-6 **69** .... JoeFanning 6 66
(Michael Attwater) *chsd ldr: rdn and ev ch wl over 1f out: unable qck ent fnl f: no ex and btn whn hmpd and snatched up ins fnl f* **8/1**

-525 **9** ¾ **Tuxedo**[13] 517 7-9-1 **64** .... WilliamCarson 7 58
(Peter Hiatt) *in tch in last trio: pushed along over 4f out: drvn over 1f out: no imp* **9/1**

00-0 **10** 6 **Taqaat (USA)**[6] 626 4-9-2 **70** ....(p) RaulDaSilva(5) 3 50
(Tim McCarthy) *in tch: pushed along over 2f out: wknd wl over 1f out: bhd fnl f* **12/1**

1m 37.67s (-0.53) **Going Correction** +0.10s/f (Slow) **10** Ran SP% **115.9**
Speed ratings (Par 103): **106,105,105,104,104 104,102,101,101,95**
Tote Swingers: 1&2 £9.20, 1&3 £7.20, 2&3 £27.50 CSF £39.66 CT £817.12 TOTE £5.90: £2.40, £3.60, £5.50; EX 43.40 Trifecta £617.70 Part won. Pool: £834.82 - 0.20 winning units..
Owner D W & L Y Payne **Bred** D W And L Y Payne And Barton Stud **Trained** Newmarket, Suffolk

FOCUS
A wide-open handicap, run at only a steady pace. It's doubtful the winner had to improve much.
Monsieur Broughton Official explanation: jockey said gelding was denied a clear run
Huzzah(IRE) Official explanation: jockey said gelding hung right throughout

686 GET YOUR BET ON AT BLUESQ.COM FILLIES' H'CAP 7f (P)
3:25 (3:25) (Class 4) (0-80,80) 4-Y-O+ **£4,204** (£1,251; £625; £312) **Stalls** Low

Form RPR
113- **1** **Triple Charm**[55] 7941 4-9-4 **77** ....(p) JamieSpencer 3 92
(Jeremy Noseda) *hld up in tch: rdn and chsd ldrs whn gallop qcknd over 2f out: chal 1f out: led ins fnl f: r.o wl: rdn out* **11/10**[1]

11-0 **2** 1 ¾ **Libys Dream (IRE)**[49] 83 4-9-7 **80** .... RichardKingscote 1 90
(Tom Dascombe) *wnt rt s: t.k.h: chsd ldr: jnd ldr and qcknd over 2f out: led over 1f out: hdd ins fnl f: one pce* **2/1**[2]

0663 **3** 2 ½ **Requisite**[9] 563 7-9-6 **79** ....(b) TonyHamilton 4 82
(Ian Wood) *hld up in tch: rdn and effrt in 4th jst over 2f out: swtchd rt and drvn jst over 1f out: nt pce of ldrs ins fnl f* **8/1**

3-01 **4** 1 ½ **Bavarian Princess (USA)**[13] 537 4-8-13 **72** .... MartinHarley 2 71
(Mrs K Burke) *pushed rt s: sn led at stdy gallop: rdn and qcknd whn jnd over 2f out: drvn and hdd over 1f out: wknd ins fnl f* **7/1**[3]

5-00 **5** 3 ¾ **Chevise (IRE)**[9] 563 4-9-5 **78** .... TomQueally 5 67
(Steve Woodman) *a last and nvr gng wl: rdn 3f out: lost tch 2f out* **14/1**

1m 25.38s (0.58) **Going Correction** +0.10s/f (Slow) **5** Ran SP% **111.2**
Speed ratings (Par 102): **100,98,95,93,89**
CSF £3.59 TOTE £2.30: £1.30, £1.20; EX 3.90.
Owner Bluehills Racing Limited **Bred** Hesmonds Stud Ltd **Trained** Newmarket, Suffolk

FOCUS
Another moderately run affair, and the winner deserves credit for an impressive performance in a race that wasn't run to suit. Fair form for the grade, rated around the runner-up.

687 MARRIOTTLINGFIELD.CO.UK H'CAP 6f (P)
4:00 (4:00) (Class 6) (0-60,60) 4-Y-O+ **£1,704** (£503; £251) **Stalls** Low

Form RPR
0453 **1** **Super Frank (IRE)**[21] 396 9-8-13 **52** ....(b) JamieGoldstein 2 60
(Zoe Davison) *prom in main gp: wnt 3rd but stl plenty to do 2f out: clsd on ldr jst ins fnl f: chal fnl 100yds: drvn ahd fnl 50yds: kpt on* **15/2**

6-00 **2** hd **Basle**[24] 372 5-9-4 **57** ....(t) ShaneKelly 7 64
(Gay Kelleway) *taken down early: chsd clr ldr: rdn over 1f out: drvn and clsd on ldr 1f out: ev ch fnl 100yds: kpt on* **12/1**

00-6 **3** ¾ **Efisio Princess**[44] 124 9-9-4 **57** .... RichardThomas 10 62
(John E Long) *led and crossed to rail: sn clr: stl wl clr and rdn over 1f out: edgd rt and coming bk to field 1f out: hdd fnl 75yds* **40/1**

4500 **4** ¾ **Fantasy Fighter (IRE)**[6] 624 7-8-13 **55** ....(p) AdamBeschizza(3) 4 57
(John E Long) *taken down early: t.k.h: hld up off the pce in midfield: rdn and effrt over 1f out: r.o u.p fnl f: nt rch ldrs* **9/2**[2]

3140 **5** ½ **Chjimes (IRE)**[13] 522 8-9-7 **60** ....(b) GeorgeBaker 5 61
(Conor Dore) *stdd s: hld up wl off the pce in rr: rdn and hdwy towards inner over 1f out: r.o ins fnl f: nt rch ldrs* **4/1**[1]

0-05 **6** shd **Anjomarba (IRE)**[42] 154 5-9-4 **57** .... TomQueally 6 57
(Conor Dore) *stdd s: hld up wll off the pce in last quartet: rdn and sme hdwy over 2f out: drvn over 1f out: r.o ins fnl f: nt rch ldrs* **5/1**[3]

-513 **7** ¾ **Welcome Approach**[14] 498 9-9-4 **57** .... JamieSpencer 8 55
(John Weymes) *stdd s: hedl up wl off the pce in last quartet: rdn and effrt on wd outside over 1f out: styd on fnl f: n.d* **5/1**[3]

4-02 **8** hd **Little Perisher**[25] 356 5-8-3 **49** ....(p) LeonnaMayor(7) 9 46
(Paul Howling) *racd off the pce in midfield: rdn: no prog and lost pl over 1f out: styd on ins fnl f: nvr trbld ldrs* **9/1**

-020 **9** 2 ¾ **Kucharova (IRE)**[9] 561 4-8-11 **55** ....(p) DavidKenny(5) 1 43
(Seamus Mullins) *prom in main gp: rdn in 4th 2f out: no imp: plugged on same pce and lost pls fnl f* **8/1**

1m 12.48s (0.58) **Going Correction** +0.10s/f (Slow) **9** Ran SP% **114.5**
Speed ratings (Par 101): **100,99,98,97,97 96,95,95,92**
Tote Swingers: 1&2 £16.80, 1&3 £32.50, 2&3 £34.10 CSF £91.61 CT £3344.93 TOTE £9.50: £2.90, £4.60, £7.80; EX 96.10 TRIFECTA Not won..
Owner M Sharp T Brightwell **Bred** A Butler **Trained** Hammerwood, E Sussex

FOCUS
A low-grade sprint handicap run at a scorching gallop and it played into the hands of Super Frank, who confirmed the promise of his last run to win in a driving finish. There are doubts over the form.

688 LINGFIELD PARK OWNERS CLUB MAIDEN STKS 1m 4f (P)
4:30 (4:30) (Class 5) 4-Y-O+ **£2,385** (£704; £352) **Stalls** Low

Form RPR
4-22 **1** **Broughton Sands**[27] 355 4-8-12 **66** .... JamieMackay 6 69
(Willie Musson) *t.k.h: hld up in midfield: hdwy over 2f out: rdn to chal over 1f out: led ins fnl f: styd on wl: rdn out* **2/1**[2]

233 **2** nk **Southern State (USA)**[9] 569 4-9-3 **0** .... JoeFanning 8 74
(Mark Johnston) *led over 10f out: stdd gallop 6f out: hdd 5f out: chsd ldrs after: cl 3rd and rdn 2f out: pressed ldrs on inner over 1f out: drvn and chsd wnr wl ins fnl f: one pce fnl 50yds* **6/4**[1]

22 **3** 1 **Red Shuttle**[18] 451 5-9-6 **0** ....(t) JamieSpencer 3 72
(Noel Quinlan) *t.k.h: hld up in last pair: hdwy to ld 5f out: rdn over 1f out: drvn and hdd ins fnl f: nt qckn and btn fnl 75yds* **11/2**

30- **4** 9 **Maher (USA)**[135] 6789 4-9-3 **68** .... ShaneKelly 2 58
(Evan Williams) *hld up in tch in rr: wnt 4th jst over 2f out: pushed along and no hdwy wl over 1f out: wl btn 1f out* **9/2**[3]

05-6 **5** 10 **Sondray**[43] 130 4-8-12 **53** ....(t) FergusSweeney 4 39
(Jo Crowley) *chsd ldr for 1f: wnt 2nd again 8f out tl 5f out: rdn: hld hd high and lost pl 3f out: bhd fnl 2f* **33/1**

0/ **6** hd **Thunderonthemount**[960] 3791 7-9-1 **0** .... JemmaMarshall(5) 5 41
(Michael Attwater) *t.k.h: led tl over 10f out: chsd ldr tl 8f out: lost pl 5f out: wknd over 2f out: sn bhd* **66/1**

2m 34.46s (1.46) **Going Correction** +0.10s/f (Slow)
WFA 4 from 5yo+ 3lb **6** Ran SP% **111.3**
Speed ratings (Par 103): **99,98,98,92,85 85**
Tote Swingers: 1&2 £1.70, 1&3 £2.00, 2&3 £1.50 CSF £5.28 TOTE £2.40: £1.10, £1.40; EX 7.20 Trifecta £17.90 Pool: £838.85 - 34.52 winning units..
Owner Broughton Thermal Insulation **Bred** Michael E Broughton **Trained** Newmarket, Suffolk

FOCUS
A modest maiden run at a muddling pace. The first two are rated to their recent C&D form.

689 PLAY ROULETTE AT BLUESQ.COM FILLIES' H'CAP 1m 2f (P)
5:00 (5:00) (Class 5) (0-70,69) 4-Y-O+ **£2,385** (£704; £352) **Stalls** Low

Form RPR
4-12 **1** **Sail Home**[25] 363 5-9-4 **69** .... AdamBeschizza(3) 4 73+
(Julia Feilden) *t.k.h: rdn and effrt 2f out: hdwy u.p 1f out: r.o wl to ld fnl 50yds: hld on cl home* **9/4**[1]

35-0 **2** nk **Isdaal**[29] 306 5-8-7 **55** oh1 ....(p) JoeFanning 3 58+
(Kevin Morgan) *t.k.h: hld up in tch in rr: rdn and effrt on outer over 1f out: r.o strly ins fnl f: wnt 2nd last stride* **6/1**

2106 **3** shd **Kai Mook**[9] 570 5-9-2 **64** .... SteveDrowne 7 67
(Roger Ingram) *led at stdy gallop: qcknd 2f out: rdn over 1f out: kpt on wl tl hdd and no ex fnl 50yds: lost 2nd last stride* **4/1**[2]

0-00 **4** nk **Mad Ginger Alice**[8] 574 4-8-8 **62** .... LauraPike(5) 5 64
(Olivia Maylam) *dwlt: sn rcvrd and t.k.h: jnd ldr over 8f out: rdn and ev ch wl over 1f out: unable qck ins fnl f: kpt on* **20/1**

136- **5** 2 ½ **Lady Barastar (IRE)**[123] 7062 4-9-4 **67** .... TomQueally 2 64
(Amanda Perrett) *stdd s: hld up in rr early: hdwy on outer to chse ldrs 8f out: rdn 2f out: unable qck over 1f out: styd on same pce and hld fnl f* **9/2**[3]

4-41 **6** 1 **Inpursuitoffreedom**[14] 494 5-9-6 **68** ....(v) JamieSpencer 6 63
(Philip McBride) *t.k.h: chsd ldrs early: stdd bk into last trio 8f out: rdn and effrt over 1f out: drvn and styd on same pce fnl f* **5/1**

6-04 **6** dht **Broughton Place**[21] 399 4-8-10 **59** .... JamieMackay 1 54
(Willie Musson) *t.k.h: chsd ldrs early: stdd into last trio 8f out: rdn and effrt over 1f out: no imp* **10/1**

2m 8.3s (1.70) **Going Correction** +0.10s/f (Slow)
WFA 4 from 5yo 1lb **7** Ran SP% **113.8**
Speed ratings (Par 100): **97,96,96,96,94 93,93**
Tote Swingers: 1&2 £4.30, 1&3 £3.30, 2&3 £2.80 CSF £16.07 TOTE £3.70: £2.30, £6.40; EX 19.80.
Owner Hoofbeats Racing Club **Bred** Juddmonte Farms Ltd **Trained** Exning, Suffolk

FOCUS
A moderate fillies' handicap run at a muddling pace, but a thrilling finish. Limited form.
T/Plt: £1,332.90 to a £1 stake. Pool: £60,438.17 - 33.10 winning tickets. T/Qpdt: £38.60 to a £1 stake. Pool: £7,311.90 - 139.96 winning tickets. SP

[632] WOLVERHAMPTON (A.W) (L-H)
Friday, February 24

OFFICIAL GOING: Standard
Wind: Light, across Weather: Overcast

690 BET AT BLUE SQUARE APPRENTICE H'CAP 5f 216y(P)
5:30 (5:30) (Class 7) (0-50,50) 4-Y-O+ **£1,704** (£503; £251) **Stalls** Low

Form RPR
0/0- **1** **Prigsnov Dancer (IRE)**[386] 401 7-8-12 **45** .... JakePayne 12 54
(Garry Woodward) *sn led: rdn jst over 1f out: sn edgd lft: kpt on wl towards fin* **20/1**

-004 **2** 1 ¼ **Odd Ball (IRE)**[15] 483 5-8-12 **45** .... ThomasBrown 6 50
(Lisa Williamson) *in rr: u.p 3f out: hdwy on wd outer over 1f out: r.o strly and edgd lft ins fnl f: wnt 2nd towards fin: nt rch wnr* **6/1**[3]

6-00 **3** 1 ¼ **Bint Elnadim (IRE)**[11] 550 4-8-12 **45** .... NoelGarbutt 1 49+
(Derek Shaw) *hld up: nt clr run over 1f out: sn swtchd rt: styd on ins fnl f: gng on at fin* **11/1**

460- **4** shd **Valdemar**[379] 482 6-8-9 **45** ....(v) DavidSimmonson(3) 11 46
(Alan Brown) *prom: pushed along 2f out: chalng for 2nd fnl f: styd on same pce* **33/1**

3-00 **5** shd **Tancred Spirit**[18] 445 4-8-7 **45** ....(v) NedCurtis(5) 9 46
(Paul Midgley) *chsd ldrs: pushed along over 2f out: chalng for 2nd ins fnl f: kpt on u.p but nt pce of wnr* **16/1**

6025 **6** ½ **Tamino (IRE)**[1] 664 9-8-12 **48** ....(b) JenniferFerguson(3) 4 47
(Alastair Lidderdale) *pushed along early: midfield: hdwy 2f out: chalng for 2nd fnl f: styd on sampe pce towards fin* **6/1**[3]

0040 **7** ½ **Bachelor Knight (IRE)**[15] 483 4-8-13 **49** .... JacobButterfield(3) 5 46
(Suzzanne France) *hld up: hdwy over 2f out: rdn ins fnl f: one pce* **8/1**

00-1 **8** ¾ **Avoncreek**[25] 356 8-9-3 **50** ....(v) NicoleNordblad 10 45
(Brian Baugh) *broke wl: racd keenly: lost pl after 1f: sn in midfield: rdn and no imp on ldrs fnl f* **9/2**[1]

600- **9** 1 ¼ **Colamandis**[77] 7696 5-8-5 **45** .... MatthewHopkins(7) 13 36
(Hugh McWilliams) *prom: rdn over 1f out: wknd ins fnl f* **100/1**

030- 10 *nk* **Wheatfield (IRE)**[112] 7274 8-8-11 **47** (t) LauraBarry(3) 2 37
(Thomas McGivern, Ire) *midfield: rdn over 1f out: outpcd fnl f* **20/1**

0554 11 *3* **Takajan (IRE)**[10] 551 5-9-3 **50** GeorgeDowning 7 31
(Mark Brisbourne) *hld up: hdwy over 4f out: pushed along and in tch 2f out: wknd over 1f out* **11/2**[2]

350- 12 *11* **Vintage Grape (IRE)**[185] 5344 4-8-13 **46** (b) JasonHart 8
(Eric Alston) *midfield: pushed along over 3f out: sn lost pl: n.d after* **15/2**

4/0- 13 *2 ¼* **Red Rani**[410] 113 7-8-12 **45** (v[1]) NoraLooby 3
(Reg Hollinshead) *s.i.s: pushed along thrght: a bhd* **20/1**

1m 15.48s (0.48) **Going Correction** -0.025s/f (Stan) **13** Ran SP% **117.4**
Speed ratings (Par 97): **95,93,91,91,91 90,90,89,87,87 83,68,65**
Tote Swingers: 1&2 £95.60, 1&3 £48.90, 2&3 £10.40 CSF £127.05 CT £1400.00 TOTE £65.00: £8.70, £3.20, £4.00; EX 282.00.

Owner J M Lacey **Bred** Tom Radley **Trained** Bolham, Notts

FOCUS
Low-grade stuff but a truly run race. The winner raced close to the inside rail throughout and showed his first real form since he was a 2yo.

Red Rani Official explanation: jockey said mare suffered interference leaving stalls

691 THE BLACK COUNTRY'S ONLY RACECOURSE H'CAP 5f 20y(P)
6:00 (6:04) (Class 7) (0-50,62) 4-Y-O+ **£1,704** (£503; £251) **Stalls** Low

Form RPR

30-5 1 **Lizzy's Dream**[35] 227 4-8-9 **45** JulieBurke(3) 9 52+
(Robin Bastiman) *in last and sn outpcd: stl in rr ent st wl over 1f out: swtchd lft jst over 1f out and hdwy: r.o strly ins fnl f: led towards fin* **9/2**[2]

-100 2 *½* **Deveze (IRE)**[16] 467 4-9-2 **49** (b) DaneO'Neill 2 54
(Milton Bradley) *trckd ldrs: led wl over 1f out: sn rdn and edgd rt: hdd towards fin* **14/1**

0-36 3 *nk* **Porthgwidden Beach (USA)**[16] 467 4-8-13 **46** (tp) ChrisCatlin 5 50
(Anthony Middleton) *trckd ldrs: effrt over 1f out: hung rt ent fnl f: styd on u.p* **8/1**

0-40 4 *¾* **Bygones For Coins (IRE)**[36] 214 4-8-5 **45** MatthewHopkins(7) 12 46
(Alan Berry) *hld up: swtchd lft and hdwy on inner over 1f out: chsd ldrs ins fnl f: kpt on* **100/1**

16-0 5 *hd* **Sally's Swansong**[11] 544 6-9-2 **49** (b) AndrewMullen 3 50
(Eric Alston) *hld up: hdwy on inner over 1f out: styng on in contention ins fnl f: no ex fnl 50yds* **15/2**

2411 6 *½* **Canadian Danehill (IRE)**[8] 580 10-10-1 **62** 12ex (e) FrederikTylicki 6 61+
(Robert Cowell) *in tch early: : pushed along and outpcd whn towards rr over 3f out: hdwy 1f out: styd on towards fin: nt quite pce to rch ldrs* **5/1**[3]

0-22 7 *nk* **Good Timin'**[11] 544 4-9-3 **50** LukeMorris 10 48
(David Brown) *hld up: rdn and hdwy over 1f out: kpt on ins fnl f: nt pce to rch ldrs* **3/1**[1]

0-45 8 *1 ¾* **Rio's Girl**[18] 445 5-9-0 **47** (bt) JamesSullivan 8 38
(Tony Coyle) *in tch on outer: effrt over 1f out: sn chsd ldrs: wknd fnl 150yds* **11/1**

60-0 9 *6* **Love Club**[11] 544 4-8-12 **45** MickyFenton 4 15
(Brian Baugh) *led early: prom: ev ch 2f out: rdn over 1f out: wknd jst ins fnl f* **14/1**

0-00 10 *¾* **Green Warrior**[16] 467 4-8-11 **47** (p) RobertLButler(3) 7 14
(Richard Guest) *prom: pushed along over 2f out: n.m.r whn wkng jst ins fnl f* **33/1**

00/0 11 *1 ½* **Skiddaw View**[35] 227 4-8-12 **45** (b[1]) TomEaves 1
(Alan Brown) *sn led: rdn and hdd over 1f out: wandered arnd whn wkng sn after* **50/1**

1m 2.54s (0.24) **Going Correction** -0.025s/f (Stan) **11** Ran SP% **110.3**
Speed ratings (Par 97): **97,96,95,94,94 93,92,90,80,79 76**
Tote Swingers: 1&2 £16.00, 1&3 £7.40, 2&3 £24.20 CSF £60.52 CT £466.37 TOTE £5.70: £1.90, £3.80, £2.40; EX 64.40.

Owner Mrs P Bastiman **Bred** Sheikh Abdulla Bin Isa Al-Khalifa **Trained** Cowthorpe, N Yorks

■ Stewards' Enquiry : Chris Catlin two-day ban: careless riding (Mar 9-10)

FOCUS
Not too many in-form types in a moderate handicap. The gallop was again sound and the winner edged towards the far rail the in the closing stages. The winner may do better but the bare form is shaky.

Good Timin' Official explanation: trainer said gelding finished distressed

692 WOLVERHAMPTON-RACECOURSE.CO.UK H'CAP 1m 141y(P)
6:30 (6:30) (Class 5) (0-70,70) 4-Y-O+ **£2,264** (£673; £336; £168) **Stalls** Low

Form RPR

2-33 1 **Moral Issue**[21] 403 4-9-0 **66** DaleSwift(3) 6 73
(Ian McInnes) *mde all: rdn and edgd rt over 1f out: r.o wl: a looked in command ins fnl f* **3/1**[1]

14-1 2 *1 ¼* **Violent Velocity (IRE)**[18] 449 9-9-0 **70** DavidSimmonson(7) 2 74
(John Quinn) *in tch: wnt 2nd jst under 2f out: rdn over 1f out: styd on but no real imp on wnr ins fnl f* **11/2**[2]

000- 3 *hd* **Forward Feline (IRE)**[91] 7537 6-8-13 **62** LukeMorris 5 66
(Bryn Palling) *hld up: rdn and hdwy over 1f out: styd on ins fnl f: nvr able to chal wnr* **20/1**

-455 4 *1 ½* **Striker Torres (IRE)**[8] 585 6-9-5 **68** TomEaves 4 68
(Ian McInnes) *hld up: hdwy on outer over 1f out: kpt on ins fnl f: nt pce to get to ldrs* **17/2**

305- 5 *nk* **Muftarres (IRE)**[118] 7175 7-8-10 **66** NedCurtis(7) 1 66
(Paul Midgley) *midfield: effrt over 1f out: one pce fnl 100yds: nvr able to chal* **11/1**

20- 6 *1 ¼* **Devonelli (IRE)**[14] 511 4-9-4 **67** PaddyAspell 3 64
(John Wainwright) *chsd ldrs: rdn over 1f out: wknd fnl 110yds* **15/2**[3]

500- 7 *5* **Coax**[43] 5725 4-9-2 **65** DanielTudhope 7 50
(Patrick Holmes) *chsd ldr: rdn over 2f out: lost 2nd jst under 2f out: wknd 1f out* **9/1**

002- 8 *nk* **Lifetime (IRE)**[32] 7722 4-9-6 **69** JohnFahy 8 53
(Brian Ellison) *in rr: rdn over 2f out: nvr on terms* **3/1**[1]

1m 50.58s (0.08) **Going Correction** -0.025s/f (Stan) **8** Ran SP% **110.8**
Speed ratings (Par 103): **98,96,96,95,95 94,89,89**
Tote Swingers: 1&2 £1.90, 1&3 £7.50, 2&3 £30.10 CSF £18.30 CT £261.04 TOTE £5.20: £1.70, £1.90, £3.30; EX 21.80.

Owner B Valentine **Bred** Redmyre Bloodstock Ltd **Trained** Catwick, E Yorks

FOCUS
A modest handicap in which the gallop was just an ordinary one. The winner came down the centre in the straight and is rated to his best.

693 JIM PARKER'S 80TH BIRTHDAY CELEBRATION MAIDEN STKS 1m 141y(P)
7:00 (7:02) (Class 5) 3-Y-O **£2,264** (£673; £336; £168) **Stalls** Low

Form RPR

1 **Rockgoat (IRE)** 3-9-3 0 NickyMackay 7 69
(Marco Botti) *w ldr: led 7f out: mde rest: rdn whn strly pressed ins fnl f: kpt pulling out more towards fin* **11/4**[1]

0- 2 *nk* **Hikma (USA)**[129] 6934 3-8-7 0 DarylByrne(5) 5 63
(Mark Johnston) *awkward leaving stalls: hdwy after 1f: wnt cl 2nd over 6f out: rdn over 1f out whn chalng strly: hld towards fin* **7/2**[2]

0 3 *3 ½* **Eastern Amour (IRE)**[13] 523 3-9-3 0 ChrisCatlin 2 60
(Marco Botti) *led: hdd 7f out: chsd ldrs fr 6f out: niggled along over 3f out: rdn over 2f out: edgd lft over 1f out: no imp ins fnl f* **5/1**[3]

535- 4 *1* **Auntie Joy**[220] 4178 3-8-12 66 JamesSullivan 6 53
(Michael Easterby) *hld up: pushed along 3f out: styd on ins fnl f: nt pce to rch ldrs* **12/1**

5 *nk* **Handy Chat (IRE)** 3-9-3 0 (p) MartinHarley 4 57?
(Des Donovan) *trckd ldrs: rdn over 2f out: nt clr run and swtchd rt over 1f out: one pce ins fnl f* **33/1**

00 6 *1* **Zenaad (USA)**[13] 523 3-9-3 0 DaneO'Neill 1 55
(Seamus Durack) *hld up: pushed along over 3f out: rdn over 2f out: no imp over 1f out* **9/1**

0- 7 *shd* **Feeling Good**[172] 5786 3-9-0 0 DaleSwift(3) 3 55+
(Brian Ellison) *hld up: pushed along over 2f out: nvr able to trble ldrs* **11/4**[1]

1m 53.27s (2.77) **Going Correction** -0.025s/f (Stan) **7** Ran SP% **112.9**
Speed ratings (Par 97): **86,85,82,81,81 80,80**
Tote Swingers: 1&2 £2.40, 1&3 £3.70, 2&3 £2.80 CSF £12.27 TOTE £3.50: £1.50, £3.20; EX 11.90.

Owner Giuliano Manfredini **Bred** Tullpark Limited **Trained** Newmarket, Suffolk

■ Stewards' Enquiry : Martin Harley two-day ban: used whip above shoulder (Mar 9-10)

FOCUS
Little strength in depth to this ordinary maiden in which the two market leaders pulled clear. The pace was just a moderate one and the winner raced towards the far side the in the straight. The form is rated cautiously.

694 GET YOUR BET ON AT BLUESQ.COM H'CAP 1m 1f 103y(P)
7:30 (7:30) (Class 4) (0-85,85) 4-Y-O+ **£4,204** (£1,251; £625; £312) **Stalls** Low

Form RPR

2-52 1 **Knowe Head (NZ)**[15] 480 5-8-8 **72** RichardKingscote 2 79
(James Unett) *led early: prom: led over 1f out: edgd rt fr 1f out: kpt on wl: in control towards fin* **7/2**[1]

30-0 2 *½* **Just Bond (IRE)**[31] 280 10-9-1 **82** DaleSwift(3) 4 88
(Geoffrey Oldroyd) *hld up: hdwy over 1f out: sn chsd wnr: styd on ins fnl f* **14/1**

0434 3 *¾* **Tevez**[13] 529 7-9-6 **84** MartinHarley 1 89
(Des Donovan) *in tch: effrt whn n.m.r and hmpd over 1f out: styd on ins fnl f: hld towards fin* **10/1**

-103 4 *1* **Thunderstruck**[22] 391 7-9-7 **85** (p) IanMongan 7 87
(Scott Dixon) *hld up: hdwy to go prom after 1f: wnt 2nd over 6f out: rdn over 2f out: lost 2nd over 1f out and nt qckn: styd on same pce ins fnl f* **9/2**[3]

40-0 5 *hd* **Snow Dancer (IRE)**[36] 216 8-8-12 **76** JamesSullivan 9 78
(Hugh McWilliams) *in rr: prog ins fnl f: styd on: nt pce to chal* **8/1**

00-2 6 *½* **Mullins Way (USA)**[22] 391 4-9-7 **85** StevieDonohoe 5 86
(Jo Hughes) *plld hrd: hld up in tch: outpcd wl over 1f out: kpt on towards fin: nt pce of ldrs* **5/1**

-400 7 *1 ¾* **Georgebernardshaw (IRE)**[11] 548 7-8-11 **75** WilliamCarson 8 72
(Richard Guest) *chsd ldrs: pushed along over 3f out: no ex fnl 100yds: eased towards fin* **28/1**

420- 8 *¾* **Prince Of Dance**[195] 5059 6-9-7 **85** JohnFahy 3 81
(Tom Tate) *hld up: hdwy on outer wl over 1f out: no imp ins fnl f* **4/1**[2]

113- 9 *1 ½* **Yorksters Prince (IRE)**[115] 7214 5-8-8 **72** ow1 (b) TomEaves 6 64
(Tony Coyle) *sn led: rdn and hdd over 1f out: wknd wl ins fnl f* **16/1**

1m 59.95s (-1.75) **Going Correction** -0.025s/f (Stan) **9** Ran SP% **113.3**
Speed ratings (Par 105): **106,105,104,104,103 103,101,101,99**
Tote Swingers: 1&2 £9.70, 1&3 £4.20, 2&3 £17.30 CSF £51.91 CT £443.87 TOTE £3.70: £1.10, £6.10, £4.10; EX 46.30.

Owner Lord Stuart J Stone **Bred** Glazeley Farms Trust **Trained** Tedsmore Hall, Shropshire

FOCUS
Mainly exposed sorts in a useful handicap. The gallop was an ordinary one and the winner came down the centre. The second and third set the standard.

695 HOTEL & CONFERENCING AT WOLVERHAMPTON CLASSIFIED CLAIMING STKS 1m 4f 50y(P)
8:00 (8:00) (Class 6) 4-Y-O+ **£1,704** (£503; £251) **Stalls** Low

Form RPR

1-54 1 **Thundering Home**[20] 433 5-8-10 65 (t) DavidKenny(5) 2 73
(George Baker) *hld up: hdwy over 3f out: wnt 2nd gng wl over 2f out: led over 1f out: r.o wl and in command fnl f* **5/2**[1]

0323 2 *3 ¼* **Kames Park (IRE)**[7] 592 10-8-10 70 RobertLButler(3) 5 66
(Richard Guest) *hld up in rr: hdwy over 2f out: kpt on to take 2nd ins fnl f: no imp on wnr* **4/1**[2]

6022 3 *5* **Ahlawy (IRE)**[4] 634 9-8-4 62 (t) RaulDaSilva(5) 6 54
(Frank Sheridan) *chsd ldr tl rdn over 2f out: one pce fnl f* **5/2**[1]

2004 4 *nse* **Yossi (IRE)**[7] 602 8-8-5 46 (p) WilliamCarson 4 50
(Richard Guest) *led: 6 l clr over 3f out: rdn and hdd over 1f out: no ex ins fnl f* **16/1**

00/5 5 *2 ¼* **Bee Sting**[8] 582 8-8-11 70 (p) LukeMorris 1 52
(Lisa Williamson) *trckd ldrs: rdn over 3f out: wknd over 2f out* **17/2**

5-30 6 *21* **Kidlat**[29] 310 7-8-8 67 (t) NicoleNordblad(7) 7 23
(Hans Adielsson) *plld hrd: sn prom: rdn and wknd 3f out: wl bhd after* **11/2**[3]

2m 39.21s (-1.89) **Going Correction** -0.025s/f (Stan) **6** Ran SP% **108.9**
Speed ratings (Par 101): **105,102,99,99,97 83**
Tote Swingers: 1&2 £2.40, 1&3 £2.00, 2&3 £1.90 CSF £11.91 TOTE £4.00: £2.00, £1.80; EX 11.60.

Owner George Baker **Bred** Rabbah Bloodstock Limited **Trained** Whitsbury, Hants

FOCUS
A modest event in which an ordinary gallop increased passing halfway. The winner raced centre-to-far side in the straight and the form is rated around him.

696 PLAY ROULETTE AT BLUESQ.COM H'CAP 5f 20y(P)
8:30 (8:32) (Class 6) (0-65,65) 4-Y-0+ **£1,704** (£503; £251) **Stalls** Low

Form RPR

4-62 **1** **Court Applause (IRE)**^{14} [497] 4-9-4 **62**.......................... GeorgeBaker 3 71
(William Muir) *chsd ldrs: r.o to ld wl ins fnl f: jst hld on towards fin* **5/1^{2}**

220- **2** *nk* **Silvanus (IRE)**^{146} [6537] 7-9-6 **64**.......................... MickyFenton 2 72
(Paul Midgley) *midfield: hdwy ins fnl f: r.o and pressed wnr towards fin* **22/1**

1-01 **3** *½* **Da'Quonde (IRE)**^{14} [497] 4-8-13 **57**.......................... TomEaves 6 63
(Bryan Smart) *chsd ldr: rdn over 1f out: ev ch wl ins fnl f: nt qckn towards fin* **3/1^{1}**

5064 **4** *1 ¼* **Twice Red**^{22} [385] 4-9-2 **60**.......................... DaneO'Neill 10 62
(Derek Shaw) *towards rr: pushed along over 2f out: hdwy over 1f out: styd on ins fnl f: nt rch ldrs* **13/2^{3}**

404- **5** *1 ¼* **Pitkin**^{58} [7896] 4-9-3 **61**.......................... PaddyAspell 8 59
(Michael Easterby) *chsd ldrs: rdn over 1f out: one pce ins fnl f* **9/1**

6621 **6** *½* **Shawkantango**^{17} [461] 5-9-4 **65**..........................(v) DaleSwift$^{(3)}$ 12 61
(Derek Shaw) *towards rr: rdn over 1f out: kpt on ins fnl f: nt pce to chal* **7/1**

20-3 **7** *½* **Spirit Of Coniston**^{17} [456] 9-8-9 **60**.......................... NedCurtis$^{(7)}$ 1 55
(Paul Midgley) *led: rdn over 1f out: hdd wl ins fnl f: wknd fnl 50yds* **14/1**

-650 **8** *hd* **Grand Stitch (USA)**^{14} [497] 6-8-7 **56**.......................... NeilFarley$^{(5)}$ 4 50
(Declan Carroll) *chsd ldrs: rdn over 1f out: wknd fnl 50yds* **16/1**

4050 **9** *3 ¼* **Elhamri**^{31} [287] 8-8-13 **62**.......................... LucyKBarry$^{(5)}$ 11 46
(Conor Dore) *a bhd: nvr on terms* **33/1**

406- **10** *1 ¼* **Juarla (IRE)**^{185} [5344] 4-9-5 **63**.......................... LukeMorris 5 43
(Ronald Harris) *midfield: rdn over 2f out: outpcd over 1f out: wknd fnl f* **10/1**

0-00 **11** *nse* **Brynfa Boy**^{6} [623] 6-9-6 **64**..........................(bt) StephenCraine 9 44
(Daniel Mark Loughnane) *midfield: outpcd over 1f out: wl btn fnl f* **12/1**

1m 1.58s (-0.72) **Going Correction** -0.025s/f (Stan) **11** Ran SP% **114.1**
Speed ratings (Par 101): **104,103,102,100,98 97,97,96,91,89 89**
Tote Swingers: 1&2 £17.30, 1&3 £2.60, 2&3 £19.50 CSF £105.01 CT £384.08 TOTE £6.30: £2.10, £10.00, £1.80; EX 97.60.
Owner John H W Finch Ian Knightley David Ross **Bred** James Waldron **Trained** Lambourn, Berks

FOCUS
A modest handicap run at a decent gallop throughout. The winner raced centre-to-far side in the straight. He reversed C&D form with the third and recorded a length personal best.
T/Plt: £240.80 to a £1 stake. Pool: £87,114.40 - 264.06 winning units. T/Qpdt: £10.70 to a £1 stake. Pool: £10,350.09 - 714.84 winning units. DO

697 - 708a (Foreign Racing) - See Raceform Interactive

683 LINGFIELD (L-H)
Saturday, February 25

OFFICIAL GOING: Standard
Wind: Light, across Weather: Fine, pleasant

709 BET ON TODAY'S FOOTBALL AT BLUESQ.COM MAIDEN STKS 1m 4f (P)
1:45 (1:46) (Class 5) 3-Y-O **£2,385** (£704; £352) **Stalls** Low

Form RPR

003- **1** **Rapid Heat Lad (IRE)**^{77} [7718] 3-9-3 60.......................... GeorgeBaker 6 73+
(Reg Hollinshead) *trckd ldng pair: wnt 2nd over 3f out: led wl over 1f out: shkn up and sn clr: eased fnl 75yds* **4/1^{2}**

2 **2** *5* **Za'Lan (USA)**^{11} [552] 3-9-3 0.......................... JoeFanning 1 64
(Mark Johnston) *led to 1/2-way: sn pushed along: dropped to 3rd over 3f out u.p: kpt on to chse wnr 1f out: no imp* **4/9^{1}**

05-2 **3** *nk* **Ctappers**^{17} [472] 3-8-12 65.......................... CharlesBishop$^{(5)}$ 3 62
(Mick Channon) *reminders in 5th after 3f: effrt to go 4th 3f out but nt on terms: kpt on fnl 2f: nrly snatched 2nd* **12/1^{3}**

0-40 **4** *2 ¾* **Foster's Road**^{10} [571] 3-9-3 58.......................... MartinHarley 4 58
(Mick Channon) *pressed ldr: led 1/2-way: rdn and hdd wl over 1f out: wknd* **40/1**

0 **5** *1 ½* **Dalmo**^{49} [84] 3-9-3 0.......................... ShaneKelly 5 56
(Gary Moore) *awkward to load into stalls: mostly in last: urged along 5f out: wnt 5th 3f out: nvr on terms but kpt on* **25/1**

0 **6** *67* **Noosa Boy**^{28} [350] 3-9-3 0.......................... LukeMorris 2
(Ronald Harris) *chsd ldng pair: rdn 5f out: wknd rapidly over 3f out: t.o* **20/1**

2m 31.55s (-1.45) **Going Correction** +0.025s/f (Slow) **6** Ran SP% **108.0**
Speed ratings (Par 97): **105,101,101,99,98 53**
Tote Swingers: 1&2 £1.10, 1&3 £1.90, 2&3 £1.30 CSF £5.73 TOTE £4.90: £1.90, £1.02; EX 8.90.
Owner Graham Brothers Racing Partnership **Bred** Roundhill Stud & Gleadhill House Stud Ltd **Trained** Upper Longdon, Staffs

FOCUS
There was a turn-up in this weak maiden as the runner-up ran a shocker. The form makes sense otherwise.

710 BLUE SQUARE SPRINT SERIES GRAND FINAL (H'CAP) 6f (P)
2:15 (2:16) (Class 4) 4-Y-O+ **£9,703** (£2,887; £1,443; £721) **Stalls** Low

Form RPR

-310 **1** **Aldermoor (USA)**^{10} [560] 6-8-12 **71**..........................(v^{1}) RyanClark$^{(3)}$ 4 82
(Stuart Williams) *settled in 8th: effrt on outer 2f out: hrd rdn over 1f out: r.o to ld ins fnl f: sn in command* **10/1**

0022 **2** *1 ¼* **Picansort**^{14} [528] 5-8-10 **66**..........................(v) ShaneKelly 10 73
(Peter Crate) *trckd ldng trio: effrt 2f out: drvn to ld over 1f out: hdd and outpcd ins fnl f* **7/1^{2}**

1-23 **3** *shd* **Hatta Stream (IRE)**^{14} [526] 6-9-5 **75**.......................... RobertHavlin 8 82
(Lydia Pearce) *chsd ldrs: pushed along 1/2-way: effrt over 1f out: clsd fnl f: outpcd last 100yds* **8/1**

2131 **4** *¾* **Diamond Vine (IRE)**^{3} [658] 4-9-1 **71** 6ex..........................(p) LukeMorris 7 76
(Ronald Harris) *wl in rr: pushed along bef 1/2-way: styd on u.p fr 2f out: nrst fin* **17/2**

6330 **5** *hd* **Waabel**^{7} [624] 5-8-5 **61**.......................... JohnFahy 11 65
(Richard Guest) *trckd ldng pair: wnt 2nd 1/2-way: drvn to chal and upsides over 1f out: nt qckn* **14/1**

1-12 **6** *nk* **Sulis Minerva (IRE)**^{14} [525] 5-9-5 **80**.......................... RaulDaSilva$^{(5)}$ 12 83+
(Jeremy Gask) *racd wd: hld up in midfield: gng easily 2f out: rdn and fnd nil over 1f out: kpt on nr fin* **4/1^{1}**

5432 **7** *nse* **Captain Dimitrios**^{7} [624] 4-8-4 **65**..........................(v) MatthewCosham$^{(5)}$ 1 68
(David Evans) *led: drvn and pressed 2f out: hdd over 1f out: one pce after* **17/2**

3216 **8** *nk* **Nubar Boy**^{7} [623] 5-9-1 **71**..........................(v) MartinLane 6 73
(David Evans) *stdd s and then s.i.s: mostly in last pair: effrt on wd outside 2f out: styd on: no ch* **14/1**

0120 **9** *nse* **The Strig**^{10} [563] 5-9-2 **72**.......................... WilliamCarson 3 74
(Stuart Williams) *chsd ldrs on inner: rdn 2f out: one pce u.p fnl f* **15/2^{3}**

-114 **10** *hd* **Speak The Truth (IRE)**^{35} [252] 6-8-9 **70**..........................(p) NathanAlison$^{(5)}$ 9 71
(Jim Boyle) *awkward s and lost grnd: mostly in last pair: effrt on wd outside 2f out: kpt on: no ch* **14/1**

-241 **11** *nk* **Haadeeth**^{14} [526] 5-9-3 **76**.......................... RichardEvans$^{(3)}$ 5 76
(David Evans) *wl in rr on inner: effrt 2f out: nt clr run over 1f out and swtchd lft: one pce after* **14/1**

1521 **12** *2 ¼* **Waterloo Dock**^{7} [623] 7-8-12 **68**..........................(v) ChrisCatlin 2 61
(Michael Quinn) *chsd ldr but shoved along to do so: lost 2nd 1/2-way: stl there over 1f out: wknd* **14/1**

1m 10.9s (-1.00) **Going Correction** +0.025s/f (Slow) **12** Ran SP% **118.9**
Speed ratings (Par 105): **107,105,105,104,103 103,103,103,103,102 102,99**
Tote Swingers: 1&2 £25.80, 1&3 £28.60, 2&3 £13.40 CSF £78.59 CT £604.64 TOTE £12.10: £4.90, £3.10, £3.60; EX 106.70 Trifecta £826.50 Part won. Pool: £1,116.92 - 0.10 winning units..
Owner Darren Hudson-Wood **Bred** Gulf Coast Farms LLC **Trained** Newmarket, Suffolk

FOCUS
The Blue Square Sprint Series, now in its second year, has really captured the imagination among owners and trainers. The nature of the competition meant this final was always going to be contested by a bang in-form bunch, and it followed seven competitive qualifying rounds. In short, it's a good initiative and those responsible for making it happen should be applauded. They went a good pace thanks to Captain Dimitrios and it was a surprisingly clean race. The time was only 0.69 seconds slower than the followed Listed contest. Solid form.
Haadeeth Official explanation: jockey said gelding had become upset in stalls

711 BLUESQ.COM CLEVES STKS (LISTED RACE) 6f (P)
2:50 (2:51) (Class 1) 4-Y-O+
£18,714 (£7,095; £3,550; £1,768; £887; £445) **Stalls** Low

Form RPR

21-1 **1** **Oasis Dancer**^{49} [89] 5-9-0 105.......................... JimCrowley 9 103
(Ralph Beckett) *racd on outer: hld up in tch: gng wl 2f out: rdn and prog over 1f out: led jst ins fnl f: drvn out to hold on* **6/5^{1}**

2-20 **2** *½* **Fratellino**^{35} [253] 5-9-0 92..........................(t) MartinHarley 3 101
(Alan McCabe) *a in ldng trio: rdn sn after 1/2-way: led over 1f out: hdd jst ins fnl f: styd on: jst hld* **25/1**

1-31 **3** *½* **Capone (IRE)**^{22} [405] 7-9-0 97.......................... ShaneKelly 6 99
(Scott Dixon) *hld up in last quartet: prog jst over 2f out: drvn over 1f out: chsd ldng pair ins fnl f: styd on but nvr quite able to chal* **6/1^{3}**

021- **4** *2 ¼* **Docofthebay (IRE)**^{105} [7392] 8-9-3 103..........................(b) IanMongan 5 95
(Scott Dixon) *s.i.s: hld up in last quartet: prog against rail over 1f out: styd on to take 4th ins fnl f: nt pce to threaten* **8/1**

01-4 **5** *1 ¼* **Sugar Beet**^{22} [405] 4-8-9 87.......................... LukeMorris 7 83
(Ronald Harris) *chsd ldrs in 6th: drvn over 2f out: kpt on to dispute 4th 1f out: fdd after* **33/1**

01-4 **6** *hd* **Googlette (IRE)**^{49} [89] 4-8-9 88.......................... JamieSpencer 11 83
(Ed Vaughan) *pressed ldr: rdn 2f out: fdd fnl f* **12/1**

4241 **7** *½* **Gorgeous Goblin (IRE)**^{7} [624] 5-8-9 58..........................(t) DavidProbert 8 81?
(David C Griffiths) *in tch in 7th: effrt but wdst of all bnd 2f out: n.d over 1f out* **100/1**

6633 **8** *1* **Requisite**^{1} [686] 7-8-9 79..........................(b) TonyHamilton 10 78
(Ian Wood) *settled in rr: last 1/2-way: effrt 2f out: no real prog* **66/1**

60- **9** *nse* **Roodle**^{175} [5702] 5-8-9 81..........................(b) TomQueally 2 78
(Eve Johnson Houghton) *dwlt: hld up in last quartet: rdn over 2f out: no real prog* **100/1**

66-3 **10** *1* **Dasho**^{30} [311] 4-9-0 82.......................... LucyKBarry 1 79
(Olivia Maylam) *led to over 1f out: wknd* **50/1**

0-11 **11** *3* **Palace Moon**^{14} [527] 7-9-0 103..........................(t) JoeFanning 4 70
(William Knight) *trckd ldrs on inner: rdn 2f out: dropped away over 1f out: b.b.v* **3/1^{2}**

1m 10.21s (-1.69) **Going Correction** +0.025s/f (Slow) **11** Ran SP% **115.8**
Speed ratings (Par 111): **112,111,110,107,106 105,105,103,103,102 98**
Tote Swingers: 1&2 £4.50, 1&3 £2.70, 2&3 £17.10 CSF £41.59 TOTE £2.30: £1.30, £7.30, £1.30; EX 30.20 Trifecta £115.50 Pool: £1,588.95 - 10.18 winning units..
Owner Mrs M E Slade **Bred** Whitsbury Manor Stud And Mrs M E Slade **Trained** Kimpton, Hants

FOCUS
A rough Listed race, run at an average pace. It's impossible to work out the exact level of the form - plenty of big-priced runners who were up against it as the weights finished close up - but it was competitive and they went a strong pace. The time was 0.69 seconds quicker than the earlier Class 4. The 1-2-3 was identical to when the same trio met on different terms in a C&D handicap on January 7. The winner did not need to match his figure in that race.

NOTEBOOK
Oasis Dancer had 13lb in hand over the runner-up on official figures and surely didn't have to be at his best to complete a hat-trick of wins over 6f on Polytrack, though he wasn't helped by being forced wide on the final turn. In total he's 3-4 at this trip, with the only defeat coming on Tapeta in Dubai. (op 11-8)
Fratellino was 7lb worse off with Oasis Dancer than when 2l behind that rival in January. He has probably upped his level, while the winner's level has dipped. (tchd 22-1)
Capone(IRE) fared best of those held up well off the pace, but could probably have done with an even stronger pace. (tchd 13-2)
Docofthebay(IRE) had been absent since winning over C&D at the same level last November and ran with promise. (op 12-1)
Gorgeous Goblin(IRE) was a 26-race maiden prior to a recent success, but is clearly well and truly improving. Yes, this is muddling form, but there's no doubt she ran well above her mark and that's despite having a tough, wide trip, notably into the straight.
Palace Moon had been resurgent lately, most recently winning over C&D off 98, but this time he was reported by the Vet to have bled from the nose. Official explanation: vet said gelding bled from the nose (op 5-2)

712 GET YOUR BET ON AT BLUESQUARE.COM WINTER DERBY TRIAL STKS (LISTED RACE) 1m 2f (P)
3:20 (3:20) (Class 1) 4-Y-O+
£18,714 (£7,095; £3,550; £1,768; £887; £445) **Stalls** Low

Form RPR

2-14 **1** **Junoob**^{28} [354] 4-8-13 95..........................(b) RichardKingscote 5 97+
(Tom Dascombe) *stdd s: hld up in last pair: stl there 2f out: str run on outer jst over 1f out: led last 50yds: won gng away* **3/1^{1}**

1-42 **2** 1 1/4 **Tinshu (IRE)**[28] 354 6 -8-12[94] (p) DaneO'Neill 8 93
(Derek Haydn Jones) *cl up: effrt 2f out: drvn over 1f out: clsd to ld wl ins fnl f but wnr sn swept by* **6/1**

21-0 **3** 1/2 **Loyalty**[7] 622 5 -9-0[102] (v) JimCrowley 7 94
(Derek Shaw) *hld up in rr: rdn and prog fr 2f out: styd on wl to take 3rd nr fin but outpcd by wnr* **9/2**[2]

0-2 **4** nk **King's Trail (JPN)**[29] 341 10 -9-0[90] TomQueally 9 93
(Takashi Kodama, Ire) *prog on outer to ld after 2f: racd keenly in front: drvn 2f out: kpt on w hd high tl hdd & wknd last 75yds* **28/1**

10-1 **5** nk **True To Form (IRE)**[1] 554 5 -9-0[92] (p) LukeMorris 4 92
(Ronald Harris) *cl up: rdn to dispute 2nd jst over 2f out: outpcd fnl f* **12/1**

24-1 **6** 3/4 **Tappanappa (IRE)**[31] 300 5 -9-0[79] (v[1]) DavidProbert 11 91
(Andrew Balding) *dwlt: hld up in midfield: prog to trck ldng pair 1/2-way: rdn to go 2nd 3f out: drvn and nt qckn over 1f out: fdd* **14/1**

310- **7** 3/4 **Our Joe Mac (IRE)**[83] 6163 5 -9-0[101] (p) PaulHanagan 3 89
(Richard Fahey) *t.k.h early: cl up: rdn over 2f out: nt qckn over 1f out: one pce after* **11/2**[3]

-442 **8** shd **Veroon (IRE)**[21] 432 6 -9-0[80] (p) FrederikTylicki 2 89?
(James Given) *nvr bttr than midfield: rdn over 2f out: one pce and no imp* **66/1**

-U11 **9** hd **Emma's Gift (IRE)**[14] 529 4 -8-8[92] (b) AdamBeschizza 1 84
(Julia Feilden) *hld up in midfield: lost pl on inner wl over 2f out: one pce and no prog over 1f out* **11/2**[3]

00-3 **10** 4 1/2 **Oceanway (USA)**[29] 341 4 -8-8[95] JoeFanning 6 75
(Mark Johnston) *led 2f: pressed ldr to 3f out: wknd qckly over 1f out* **9/1**

03-5 **11** 2 1/4 **Mister Green (FR)**[10] 570 6 -9-0[62] (bt) StephenCraine 10 75?
(David Flood) *s.s: a in last pair: wknd 2f out* **100/1**

2m 5.58s (-1.02) **Going Correction** +0.025s/f (Slow)
WFA 4 from 5yo+ 1lb **11**Ran SP% **118.5**
Speed ratings (Par 111): **105,104,103,103,103 102,101,101,101,98 96**
Tote Swingers: 1&2 £3.50, 1&3 £6.10, 2&3 £7.40 CSF £21.19 TOTE £3.90 : £1.60 , £2.10 , £1.80 ; EX 27.70 Trifecta £67.90 Pool: £1,073.22 - 67.90 winning units.
Owner Alan Solomon **Bred** Shadwell Estate Company Limited **Trained** Malpas, Cheshire

FOCUS
This trial has produced the Winter Derby winner five times since then turn of the millennium, with four of them going on to the main event following a victory. The latest running wasn't that strong a race and they went a slow pace. There are doubts over the bare form and several could be flattered.

NOTEBOOK
Junoob cost just 3,500gns out of John Dunlop's yard last October, and changed hands again for only £12,000 after winning the second of two claimers for Amy Weaver over this C&D in December. You won't find many shrewder claims, with the gelding having now progressed enough to take this Listed prize. He wasn't at his best when beaten off 95 here on his previous start, having been asked to lead, but return to hold-up tactics, as well as the re-fitting of blinkers, did the trick and he quickened up smartly under a confident ride. His change of pace should see him have a say in the Winter Derby itself. (op 9-2)
Tinshu(IRE) couldn't conform earlier form with Junoob but still ran well, especially considering she was carrying a 3lb penalty. (op 9-2)
Loyalty had an excuse last time (awkward start, jockey lost an iron) and this was more like it, although he probably didn't reach his best form. It seems 1m may be his optimum trip.
King's Trail (JPN) ex-Japanese but now based in Ireland, was responsible for the muddling pace and might be flattered. (op 25-1)
True To Form (IRE)was up in class and faced with different conditions after a win off 89 at Southwell, but he has won over 1m2f on Polytrack. He showed he was worth a shot at this level and may have more to offer. (op 14-1)
Tappanappa(IRE) was up dramatically in class after a 1m4f maiden win here, and had a visor on for the first time, but after that recent success Andrew Balding said the horse has a "decent race in him." The race didn't unfold to suit, as he had to make a forward move sooner than ideal owing to the lack of pace, and he was vulnerable to the closers. This wasn't a bad run in the circumstances and he could yet prove to be quite useful. (tchd 16-1)

713 BET AT BLUE SQUARE H'CAP 7f (P)
3:55 (3:56) (Class 5) (0-70,70) 4-Y-0+ **£2,385** (£704; £352) **Stalls** Low

Form RPR

06-6 **1** **Copperwood**[38] 205 7 -9-3[67] JoeFanning 1 74
(Mark Johnston) *trckd ldrs: shkn up and cl up over 1f out: pushed into ld last 100yds: readily* **11/2**[3]

0641 **2** 1/2 **Efistorm**[8] 598 11 -9-0[64] PaulHanagan 7 70
(Conor Dore) *racd freely: w ldr: led 2f out: hrd rdn over 1f out: hdd and one pce last 100yds* **10/1**

526 **3** 1/2 **The Happy Hammer (IRE)**[7] 626 6 -9-3[67] WilliamCarson 3 72
(Eugene Stanford) *in tch: prog to trck ldng pair 3f out: drvn to chal over 1f out: kpt on but hld ins fnl f* **11/4**[1]

5-30 **4** 1/2 **Showboating (IRE)**[35] 252 4 -9-6[70] (t) MartinHarley 5 73
(Alan McCabe) *dwlt: hld up in tch: trckd ldrs 2f out: n.m.r over 1f out: rdn and kpt on same pce fnl f* **17/2**

0-06 **5** 3/4 **Reposer (IRE)**[14] 528 4 -9-6[70] TomQueally 4 71
(Noel Quinlan) *led narrowly: hdd 2f out: fdd u.p fnl f* **16/1**

0-51 **6** 1 **Muhandis (IRE)**[16] 478 4 -9-3[67] (v) ChrisCatlin 2 66
(Nick Littmoden) *slowly away: hld up last: effrt on outer 3f out: plugged on but nvr on terms* **16/1**

1-15 **7** 1 **Cut And Thrust (IRE)**[34] 262 6 -8-7[64] NicoleNordblad[(7)] 6 60
(Mark Wellings) *hld up in rr: n.m.r wl over 2f out: shkn up and no prog over 1f out* **4/1**[2]

6-64 **8** 1 1/4 **Getcarter**[10] 568 6 -9-4[68] LukeMorris 8 61
(John Best) *stdd s: hld up in last pair: effrt on inner 2f out: sn no prog and btn* **4/1**[2]

1m 24.54s (-0.26) **Going Correction** +0.025s/f (Slow) **8**Ran SP% **113.4**
Speed ratings (Par 103): **102,101,100,100,99 98,97,95**
Tote Swingers: 1&2 £6.60, 1&3 £3.90, 2&3 £4.90 CSF £57.10 CT £182.55 TOTE £6.10 : £1.70 , £3.00, £1.40 ; EX 41.40 Trifecta £676.00 Pool: £1,032.28 - 1.13 winning units.
Owner Always Trying Partnership VIII (E) **Bred** Hertford Offset Press **Trained** Middleham Moor, N Yorks

FOCUS
Just a modest handicap and an ordinary gallop meant those who raced handily were favoured. Muddling form, with the runner-up probably the key.

714 GET YOUR BET ON AT BLUESQ.COM H'CAP 1m 5f (P)
4:30 (4:30) (Class 5) (0-75,74) 4-Y-0+ **£2,385** (£704; £352) **Stalls** Low

Form RPR

30-1 **1** **The Holyman (IRE)**[43] 150 4 -9-4[72] DaneO'Neill 7 80
(Jo Crowley) *mde all: dictated stdy pce tl wound it up fr wl over 2f out: drvn over 1f out: styd on* **6/4**[1]

20-5 **2** 1 1/4 **Sand Skier**[30] 310 5 -9-2[73] NicoleNordblad[(7)] 2 79
(Hans Adielsson) *mostly trckd ldng pair: wnt 2nd over 1f out and looked dangerous: shkn up and nt qckn fnl f* **9/2**[2]

3-26 **3** 2 1/4 **Sunset Place**[30] 309 5 -9-4[68] (p) RobertHavlin 1 71
(Jonathan Geake) *trckd wnr: shkn up and nt qckn wl over 1f out: sn lost 2nd and hld* **9/1**

0-02 **4** 1 **Quinsman**[15] 500 6 -9-5[72] RyanPowell[(3)] 8 74
(J S Moore) *hld up in last trio: outpcd over 2f out: plugged on fnl f to take 4th nr fin* **9/2**[2]

000- **5** 1 1/2 **Baharat (IRE)**[75] 2406 4 -8-12[66] (bt[1]) MartinHarley 4 65?
(Richard Guest) *trckd ldrs: outpcd over 2f out: nvr on terms after* **25/1**

0-30 **6** 1 1/2 **Kavaloti (IRE)**[14] 521 8 -9-6[70] (b) GeorgeBaker 5 67
(Gary Moore) *s.i.s: hld up in last trio: outpcd over 2f out: fdd* **9/1**

/20- **7** 3/4 **Cozy Tiger (USA)**[52] 1470 7 -9-10[74] StevieDonohoe 6 70
(Willie Musson) *hld up and sn last: outpcd fr 3f out: nvr on terms after* **7/1**[3]

2m 48.9s (2.90) **Going Correction** +0.025s/f (Slow)
WFA 4 from 5yo+ 4lb **7**Ran SP% **112.7**
Speed ratings (Par 103): **92,91,89,89,88 87,86**
Tote Swingers: 1&2 £2.30, 1&3 £3.90, 2&3 £6.30 CSF £8.16 CT £42.91 TOTE £2.20 : £1.30 , £2.60; EX 7.80 Trifecta £58.30 Pool: £1,114.26 - 14.12 winning units.
Owner Kilstone Limited **Bred** Old Carhue Stud **Trained** Whitcombe, Dorset

FOCUS
A modest handicap where the winner dictated at a steady pace. The runner-up sets the standard.

715 PLAY BLACKJACK AT BLUESQ.COM H'CAP 5f (P)
5:05 (5:05) (Class 4) (0-85,85) 4-Y-0+ **£4,204** (£1,251; £625 ; £312) **Stalls** High

Form RPR

0-51 **1** **Taajub (IRE)**[14] 525 5 -9-7[85] IanMongan 5 95
(Peter Crate) *chsd ldr: rdn wl over 1f out: styd on to ld last 100yds* **15/8**[1]

2143 **2** 3/4 **Desert Strike**[6] 629 6 -9-1[79] JimCrowley 3 86
(Charles Hills) *chsd ldrs: wnt 3rd wl over 1f out: drvn and styd on to take 2nd nr fin: unable to chal* **9/1**

-010 **3** 1/2 **Royal Bajan (USA)**[14] 525 4 -8-10[74] FrederikTylicki 4 79
(James Given) *led: drifted rt over 1f out: hdd and fdd last 100yds* **11/2**[3]

-352 **4** hd **Estonia**[3] 647 5 -8-9[73] ShaneKelly 7 77
(Michael Squance) *dwlt: hld up in 6th: rdn over 1f out: styd on ins fnl f: nrst fin* **5/1**[2]

400- **5** 1/2 **Baby Strange**[133] 6862 8 -9-7[85] JoeFanning 6 88
(Derek Shaw) *dwlt: hld up in last: off the pce 2f out: coaxed along and r.o fnl f: nrst fin* **7/1**

051- **6** nk **Diamond Charlie (IRE)**[67] 7833 4 -9-7[85] GeorgeBaker 1 87
(Simon Dow) *stdd s: hld up in last trio: effrt wl over 1f out: kpt on one pce after: n.d* **6/1**

06-0 **7** 3 3/4 **Highland Harvest**[14] 528 8 -8-8[72] MartinLane 2 60
(Jamie Poulton) *chsd ldrs: rdn over 2f out: wknd over 1f out* **25/1**

020- **8** nk **Berberana (IRE)**[131] 6913 4 -9-3[81] (t) JamieSpencer 8 68
(Jeremy Gask) *chsd ldrs on outer tl wknd 2f out* **16/1**

58.11s (-0.69) **Going Correction** +0.025s/f (Slow) **8**Ran SP% **113.3**
Speed ratings (Par 105): **106,104,104,103,102 102,96,95**
Tote Swingers: 1&2 £3.30, 1&3 £4.80, 2&3 £5.30 CSF £19.59 CT £78.34 TOTE £3.10 : £1.50 , £3.20, £2.80 ; EX 17.30 Trifecta £47.90 Pool: £1,331.35 - 20.54 winning units.
Owner Peter Crate **Bred** Rabbah Bloodstock Limited **Trained** Newdigate, Surrey

FOCUS
A fair sprint handicap, and straightforward form.
Diamond Charlie (IRE) Official explanation: jockey said gelding jumped awkwardly from stalls
T/Plt: £52.70 to a £1 stake. Pool: £81,552.00 - 1,127.53 winning tickets. T/Qpdt: £9.10 to a £1 stake. Pool: £4,856.00 - 390.93 winning tickets. JN

661 CAGNES-SUR-MER
Saturday, February 25

OFFICIAL GOING: Fibresand: standard

716a PRIX POLICEMAN (LISTED RACE) (3YO) (FIBRESAND) 1m 2f (D)
1:30 (12:00) 3-Y-0 **£22,916** (£9,166; £6,875 ; £4,583 ; £2,291)

RPR

1 **Saonois (FR)**[21] 3 -8-11[0] AntoineHamelin 2 112
(J-P Gauvin, France) **27/10**[1]

2 4 **Espero (FR)** 3 -8-11[0] IoritzMendizabal 8 104
(J-C Rouget, France) **9/2**

3 2 **Mobaco (FR)**[105] 7403 3 -9-2[0] FranckBlondel 6 105
(F Rossi, France) **14/5**[2]

4 1 1/2 **Sir Jade (FR)**[21] 3 -8-11[0] Pierre-CharlesBoudot 9 97
(J-M Capitte, France) **7/2**[3]

5 hd **Remus De La Tour (FR)**[26] 364 3 -8-11[0] LaurentDoreau 7 97
(K Borgel, France) **9/1**

6 1/2 **Swing Alone (IRE)**[7] 628 3 -8-11[0] MickaelForest 3 96
(Gay Kelleway) *racd towards rr on rail: proged to 5th bef st: rdn early in st: no ex u.p fnl 1 1/2f* **24/1**

7 5 **Glamour Star (GER)**[26] 365 3 -8-11[0] DavyBonilla 5 86
(Exors Of W Baltromei, Germany) **22/1**

8 19 **Correct**[149] 6484 3 -8-8[0] NicolasPerret 4 45
(K Borgel, France) **39/1**

9 dist **Private Riviera**[13] 542 3 -8-8[0] (b[1]) JohanVictoire 1
(C Boutin, France) **31/1**

1m 59.72s (119.72) **9**Ran SP% **117.7**
WIN (incl. 1 euro stake): 3.70. PLACES: 1.30, 1.80, 1.50. DF: 12.90. SF: 21.70
Owner P Treyve **Bred** Earl Haras De Nonant Le Pin **Trained** France 717a Foreign Racing (See RI)

690 WOLVERHAMPTON (A.W) (L-H)
Monday, February 27

OFFICIAL GOING: Standard
Wind: Light behind Weather: Overcast

718 BET AND WATCH AT BLUESQ.COM H'CAP 5f 20y (P)
2:30 (2:30) (Class 5) (0-75,81) 4-Y-0+ **£2,264** (£673; £336 ; £168) **Stalls** Low

Form RPR

-312 **1** **Greenhead High**[27] 371 4 -8-6[67] ShirleyTeasdale[(7)] 7 76
(David Nicholls) *chsd ldr: r.o to ld wl ins fnl f* **8/1**[3]

0-03 **2** hd **Kylladdie**[31] 325 5 -9-7[75] (b) JamieSpencer 4 83
(Steve Gollings) *trckd ldrs: racd keenly: rdn over 1f out: hung lft wl ins fnl f: r.o* **9/2**[1]

2030 **3** *shd* **Dancing Freddy (IRE)**[20] 458 5-9-3 **71**....................(tp) WilliamCarson 6 79
(Richard Guest) *led: rdn over 1f out: hdd wl ins fnl f* **9/1**
-215 **4** *2 3/4* **No Mean Trick (USA)**[17] 497 6-8-13 **67**........................ MickyFenton 3 65
(Paul Midgley) *prom: rdn 1/2-way: styd on same pce fnl f* **9/2**[1]
2-16 **5** *1/2* **Perlachy**[20] 461 8-8-13 **67**..(v) LukeMorris 5 63
(Ronald Harris) *mid-div: pushed along 3f out: hdwy over 1f out: nt trble ldrs* **12/1**
0064 **6** *3/4* **Catalyze**[9] 623 4-8-12 **66**..(t) MartinHarley 1 59
(Richard Guest) *s.s: hld up: r.o ins fnl f: nvr trbld ldrs* **7/1**[2]
0-33 **7** *1/2* **Tombi (USA)**[14] 545 8-9-4 **72**.. JoeFanning 11 63
(Keith Dalgleish) *s.i.s: hld up: r.o ins fnl f: nvr nrr* **8/1**[3]
5-31 **8** *3/4* **Fair Passion**[5] 647 5-9-13 **81** 6ex...................................... DaneO'Neill 8 70
(Derek Shaw) *hld up: rdn over 1f out: nvr trbld ldrs* **9/2**[1]
/14- **9** *9* **You'relikemefrank**[380] 523 6-9-3 **71**...........................(p) NeilChalmers 2 27
(Richard Ford) *chsd ldrs: rdn over 1f out: wknd fnl f* **22/1**

1m 1.92s (-0.38) **Going Correction** +0.05s/f (Slow) **9** Ran SP% **111.3**
Speed ratings (Par 103): **105,104,104,100,99 98,97,96,81**
toteswingers:1&2:£7.80, 2&3:£9.80, 1&3:£14.20 CSF £41.58 CT £321.90 TOTE £8.30: £2.60, £2.40, £3.50; EX 34.90 Trifecta £266.00 Part won. Pool £359.46 - 0.30 winning units..
Owner Charles Castle **Bred** Wyck Hall Stud Ltd **Trained** Sessay, N Yorks

FOCUS
Assessing likely underfoot conditions, clerk of the course Fergus Cameron said: "We turned the track over for the first time in ten days but we have triple power-mastered and rolled it and it should ride standard." The four non-runners in this opener had been due to start from stalls 9, 10, 12 and 13 respectively. It proved difficult to make up significant ground. The winner carried over his Southwell improvement.
Fair Passion Official explanation: trainer said mare finished distressed

719 WOLVERHAMPTON-RACECOURSE.CO.UK CLASSIFIED CLAIMING STKS 5f 216y(P)
3:00 (3:05) (Class 6) 4-Y-0+ **£1,704** (£503; £251) **Stalls** Low

Form RPR
5-04 **1** **Mother Jones**[14] 545 4-8-4 65.. HayleyTurner 4 69
(David Brown) *chsd ldrs: rdn to ld 1f out: r.o* **16/1**
0322 **2** *nk* **Steelcut**[20] 461 8-8-10 70..(p) JoeFanning 6 74
(David Evans) *s.i.s: hld up: hdwy over 2f out: rdn and ev ch whn hung lft ins fnl f: unable qck nr fin* **10/11**[1]
0-14 **3** *3 1/4* **Cape Of Storms**[6] 640 9-8-10 68..................................(b) LukeMorris 2 64
(Roy Brotherton) *led: rdn and hdd 1f out: styd on same pce* **5/1**[2]
-060 **4** *hd* **Whipphound**[19] 473 4-9-0 65.. ShaneKelly 5 67
(Mark Brisbourne) *s.i.s: hdwy over 4f out: rdn over 1f out: styd on* **6/1**[3]
030- **5** *3 1/4* **Sarah's Art (IRE)**[86] 7629 9-8-5 65...........................(vt[1]) RyanPowell(3) 1 51
(Gary Harrison) *s.i.s: rdn over 2f out: nvr on terms* **12/1**
405- **6** *6* **Bertie Southstreet**[171] 5895 9-8-8 64..............................(v) PJMcDonald 7 31
(Paul Midgley) *chsd ldr: rdn and ev ch 2f out: wknd over 1f out* **33/1**

1m 15.12s (0.12) **Going Correction** +0.05s/f (Slow) **6** Ran SP% **99.9**
Speed ratings (Par 101): **101,100,96,96,91 83**
toteswingers:1&2:£2.30, 2&3:£1.70, 1&3:£3.40 CSF £24.67 TOTE £12.80: £3.40, £1.30; EX 17.30 Trifecta £40.80 Pool £602.36 - 10.91 winning units..Mother Jones was claimed by P. D. Evans for £3,000.
Owner D H Brown **Bred** New Hall Stud **Trained** Averham Park, Notts
■ El Dececy was withdrawn (9/1, ref to ent stalls). R4 applies, deduct 10p in the £.

FOCUS
A modest claimer. The winner was the pick on last year's turf best and did not quite match that here, with the runner-up the best guide.
Sarah's Art(IRE) Official explanation: jockey said gelding never travelled

720 GREAT OFFERS AT WOLVERHAMPTON-RACECOURSE.CO.UK MAIDEN STKS 5f 216y(P)
3:30 (3:32) (Class 5) 3-Y-0+ **£2,264** (£673; £252; £252) **Stalls** Low

Form RPR
1 **Mon Ami Jolie (USA)** 4-9-10 0...................................... SeanLevey(3) 7 75+
(Richard Hannon) *s.s: hdwy over 2f out: hmpd over 1f out: rdn: hung lft and led wl ins fnl f: r.o* **1/1**[1]
660/ **2** *1 1/2* **Going French (IRE)**[532] 6026 5-9-13 0.......................... SamHitchcott 9 67
(Dai Burchell) *led: rdn over 1f out: hdd and unable qck wl ins fnl f* **50/1**
-222 **3** *1 1/2* **Derivatives (IRE)**[10] 597 3-8-7 70.. RobertHavlin 8 54
(John Gosden) *hld up: racd keenly: swtchd lft and hdwy over 1f out: r.o to dispute 3rd post* **6/4**[2]
3 *dht* **Ring For Baileys** 3-8-7 0.. FrannyNorton 3 54+
(Chris Dwyer) *s.s: hdwy 4f out: swtchd rt 2f out: sn rdn: styd on* **33/1**
36-0 **5** *hd* **Cerejeira (IRE)**[38] 231 4-9-8 54....................................(bt) ShaneKelly 2 57
(Eric Alston) *chsd ldrs: rdn and ev ch whn hung rt over 1f out: bmpd ins fnl f: no ex* **14/1**
5 **6** *3 3/4* **Demora**[39] 214 3-8-7 0.. NeilChalmers 6 41
(Michael Appleby) *plld hrd and prom: rdn and wknd over 1f out* **28/1**
6 **7** *shd* **Dear Ben**[49] 107 3-8-12 0.. WilliamCarson 1 46
(Brian Baugh) *hld up: hdwy over 1f out: nvr trbld ldrs* **33/1**
5 **8** *2 3/4* **Dancing Ellie Mae**[20] 462 3-8-7 0.................................... MartinLane 4 32
(Derek Shaw) *hld up: nvr on terms* **50/1**
6 **9** *7* **Windygoul Lad**[20] 462 3-8-12 0................................. AndrewMullen 10 14
(Keith Dalgleish) *racd keenly: trckd ldr 5f out: rdn over 2f out: wkng whn hung lft fr over 1f out* **25/1**
50- **10** *9* **Hurriya**[126] 7058 3-8-7 0.. JoeFanning 11
(Mark Johnston) *prom tl pushed along and wknd over 2f out* **7/1**[3]

1m 15.86s (0.86) **Going Correction** +0.05s/f (Slow)
WFA 3 from 4yo+ 15lb **10** Ran SP% **126.3**
Speed ratings (Par 103): **96,94,92,92,91 86,86,82,73,61**toteswingers:1&2:£19.80, 2&3:£7.10 (Derivatives), 1&3:£0.80 (D), 2&3:£29.30 (Ring For Baileys), 1&3:£5.90 (RFB); TOTE PLACE: Derivatives 0.50, Ring For Baileys 3.10; TRIFECTA: 389.40 (D), Not won (RFB). Pool £1,052.46. CSF £80.10 TOTE £2.30: £1.10, £13.00, £3.10; EX 1227 Trifecta £Owner Andrew Tinkler Bred.

FOCUS
This looked a modest maiden.The fifth could be the key to the form.

721 BET AT BLUE SQUARE ON YOUR MOBILE H'CAP 1m 4f 50y(P)
4:00 (4:00) (Class 5) (0-75,73) 4-Y-0+ **£2,264** (£673; £336; £168) **Stalls** Low

Form RPR
1-23 **1** **Country Road (IRE)**[24] 402 6-9-7 **73**............................(p) LukeMorris 6 82
(Michael Appleby) *led 1f: chsd ldr tl led again over 5f out: rdn clr over 1f out: eased nr fin* **13/2**
51-1 **2** *3* **Illustrious Forest**[21] 452 4-8-9 **71**.................................. JackDuern(7) 3 75
(John Mackie) *a.p: chsd ldr over 5f out tl rdn over 2f out: styd on same pce appr fnl f: wnt 2nd again nr fin* **11/8**[1]
2133 **3** *nk* **Boa**[10] 601 7-9-7 **73**.. HayleyTurner 4 77
(Reg Hollinshead) *chsd ldrs: wnt 2nd over 2f out: sn rdn: hung lft over 1f out: styd on same pce: lost 2nd nr fin* **11/2**[3]
35-1 **4** *8* **Honourable Knight (IRE)**[33] 296 4-9-0 **69**..............(be) DavidProbert 5 60
(Mark Usher) *hld up: hdwy over 4f out: rdn over 2f out: wknd over 1f out* **5/1**[2]
0-06 **5** *11* **Angelena Ballerina (IRE)**[10] 600 5-8-2 **59**.................... AmyScott(5) 1 32
(Dai Williams) *s.i.s: hld up and a in rr: pushed along and lost tch fr over 3f out* **66/1**
-460 **6** *2 1/2* **Ivory Jazz**[12] 563 5-9-4 **70**.. MartinHarley 7 39
(Richard Guest) *led after 1f: hdd over 5f out: wknd wl over 3f out* **16/1**
06-2 **P** **Royal Alcor (IRE)**[21] 452 5-8-12 **64**.........................(b) FrankieMcDonald 2
(Alastair Lidderdale) *s.i.s: hld up: sddle slipped 10f out: bhd fnl 6f: sn p.u* **5/1**[2]

2m 40.37s (-0.73) **Going Correction** +0.05s/f (Slow)
WFA 4 from 5yo+ 3lb **7** Ran SP% **111.5**
Speed ratings (Par 103): **104,102,101,96,89 87,**
toteswingers:1&2:£2.50, 2&3:£2.40, 1&3:£2.80 CSF £15.12 TOTE £9.70: £4.10, £1.30; EX 21.50.
Owner S Hussain & P O'Neill **Bred** Brittas House Stud & Lynch Bages & Samac **Trained** Danethorpe, Notts

FOCUS
Quite a competitive little heat, and it was run at a solid gallop thanks to Ivory Jazz. The winner rates back to his best.
Honourable Knight(IRE) Official explanation: jockey said colt hung left-handed
Royal Alcor(IRE) Official explanation: jockey said saddle slipped

722 DINE IN HORIZONS APPRENTICE H'CAP 1m 1f 103y(P)
4:30 (4:30) (Class 5) (0-70,70) 4-Y-0+ **£2,264** (£673; £336; £168) **Stalls** Low

Form RPR
0055 **1** **Honey Of A Kitten (USA)**[9] 626 4-9-1 **64**............... MatthewCosham 5 75
(David Evans) *sn chsng ldr: pushed along over 3f out: rdn to ld wl over 1f out: hung lft: r.o* **11/4**[2]
-311 **2** *1/2* **Patriotic (IRE)**[20] 463 4-9-0 **68**.. JoshCrane(5) 3 77
(Chris Dwyer) *a.p: rdn to chse wnr over 1f out: edgd lft: r.o* **7/2**[3]
0-50 **3** *4 1/2* **Black Coffee**[5] 648 7-9-1 **67**..................................(b) RachealKneller(3) 1 67
(Mark Brisbourne) *hld up in tch: rdn over 1f out: styd on same pce: wnt 3rd ins fnl f* **11/1**
-004 **4** *3 3/4* **Goal (IRE)**[12] 562 4-9-3 **66**..(t) RaulDaSilva 4 58
(Richard Guest) *trckd ldrs: plld hrd: rdn over 1f out: wknd fnl f* **25/1**
-006 **5** *hd* **Alpha Tauri (USA)**[11] 585 6-9-0 **68**..............................(t) NoraLooby(5) 6 60
(Richard Guest) *led: rdn and hdd wl over 1f out: wknd ins fnl f* **66/1**
1052 **6** *nk* **Petomic (IRE)**[10] 603 7-8-7 **59**..............................(p) CharlesEddery(3) 2 50
(Richard Guest) *s.i.s: hld up: n.d* **25/1**
-101 **7** *2* **Vanilla Rum**[7] 636 5-9-0 **66** 6ex....................................(b) JackDuern(3) 7 53
(John Mackie) *hld up: hdwy on outer over 3f out: rdn and wknd over 1f out* **2/1**[1]
0223 **8** *8* **Master Of Dance (IRE)**[20] 463 5-9-4 **70**..............(p) JustinNewman(3) 9 40
(Keith Dalgleish) *prom: rdn over 3f out: wknd over 2f out* **7/1**
066/ **9** *2 1/2* **Wind Star**[523] 6289 9-8-13 **62**.. DavidKenny 8 27
(Brendan Powell) *hld up: rdn and wknd over 2f out* **50/1**

2m 1.46s (-0.24) **Going Correction** +0.05s/f (Slow) **9** Ran SP% **114.2**
Speed ratings (Par 103): **103,102,98,95,95 94,93,85,83**
toteswingers:1&2:£3.80, 2&3:£6.70, 1&3:£6.70 CSF £12.25 CT £88.75 TOTE £2.90: £1.10, £1.40, £4.40; EX 15.90 Trifecta £175.40 Pool £1,313.51 - 5.54 winning units..
Owner Mrs E Evans **Bred** Kenneth L Ramsey And Sarah K Ramsey **Trained** Pandy, Monmouths

FOCUS
A modest handicap for apprentice riders, run at a fair pace. The first two were always prominent and finished clear. The winner did not need to match his winter best and the second notched a personal best.

723 RINGSIDE CONFERENCE SUITE - 700 THEATRE STYLE MAIDEN STKS 1m 1f 103y(P)
5:00 (5:00) (Class 5) 3-Y-0 **£2,264** (£673; £336; £168) **Stalls** Low

Form RPR
1 **Ogaritmo** 3-8-13 0 ow1.. AdamKirby 4 75
(Marco Botti) *chsd ldrs: shkn up to ld over 1f out: r.o* **9/4**[1]
3 **2** *1 1/2* **Ruacana**[7] 635 3-9-3 0.. JamieSpencer 1 76
(Michael Bell) *a.p: chsd ldr over 2f out: rdn and ev ch over 1f out: hung lft ins fnl f: styd on* **5/2**[2]
04-2 **3** *2 1/2* **Lionrock (FR)**[12] 565 3-9-3 67.. JoeFanning 6 71
(Mark Johnston) *led: rdn and hdd over 1f out: no ex ins fnl f* **9/4**[1]
4 *1 1/2* **Benbecula** 3-9-3 0.. KieranO'Neill 8 68+
(Richard Hannon) *s.i.s and hmpd s: bhd: hdwy over 2f out: rdn over 1f out: r.o: nt rch ldrs* **11/2**[3]
5 *3 3/4* **Ruby Glass (IRE)** 3-9-3 0...(b[1]) ShaneKelly 7 60?
(Brian Meehan) *wnt rt s: sn pushed along and rn green in rr: hdwy over 2f out: rdn over 1f out: wknd ins fnl f* **16/1**
0 **6** *20* **Maggie Pink**[7] 635 3-8-5 0.. JackDuern(7) 5
(Michael Appleby) *chsd ldr tl rdn and wknd over 1f out* **100/1**
7 *3* **Fa'Side Castle (IRE)** 3-9-3 0.. AndrewMullen 2
(Keith Dalgleish) *s.i.s: hld up: rdn and wknd over 2f out* **50/1**

2m 2.3s (0.60) **Going Correction** +0.05s/f (Slow) **7** Ran SP% **114.3**
Speed ratings (Par 97): **99,97,95,94,90 73,70**
toteswingers:1&2:£1.80, 2&3:£1.90, 1&3:£1.60 CSF £8.24 TOTE £3.90: £3.60, £1.10; EX 10.50 Trifecta £26.70 Pool £1,052.98 - 29.13 winning units..
Owner Dr Ornella Carlini Cozzi **Bred** Dr Ornella Cozzi Carlini **Trained** Newmarket, Suffolk

FOCUS
An interesting maiden which should throw up winners, although the bare form is no more than fair. The third is the best guide.

724 STAY AT THE WOLVERHAMPTON HOLIDAY INN MEDIAN AUCTION MAIDEN STKS 1m 141y(P)
5:30 (5:31) (Class 5) 3-4-Y-0 **£2,264** (£673; £336; £168) **Stalls** Low

Form RPR
3 **1** **Bint Alzain (IRE)**[34] 279 3-8-2 0...................................... LukeMorris 3 68+
(Gerard Butler) *s.s: hdwy over 6f out: shkn up over 1f out: rdn to ld ins fnl f: r.o* **11/4**[2]
052- **2** *1 1/4* **Duke Of Clarence (IRE)**[58] 7938 3-8-7 72..................... KieranO'Neill 2 70
(Richard Hannon) *w ldr: pushed along over 3f out: rdn to ld over 1f out: hdd ins fnl f: styd on same pce* **10/11**[1]
3 *nk* **Kudoz** 3-8-7 0.. JohnFahy 6 69+
(Clive Cox) *hld up: pushed along and hdwy over 2f out: rdn over 1f out: r.o* **9/2**[3]
04-0 **4** *8* **Kool Shuffle (GER)**[4] 676 4-9-9 51........................(t) BrianToomey(5) 5 57
(Tony Coyle) *led: rdn: edgd rt and hdd over 1f out: wknd fnl f* **22/1**
5 *6* **Green Mitas (ITY)** 3-8-2 0.. RaulDaSilva(5) 1 37
(Frank Sheridan) *s.s: a bhd* **14/1**

06 **6** *5* **Delightful Sleep**[7] 635 4-9-11 0... RichardEvans(3) 4 32
(David Evans) *chsd ldrs: rdn over 3f out: wknd wl over 1f out* **100/1**
0 **R** **Idarose (IRE)**[17] 502 3-7-13 0... DominicFox(3) 7
(Hugh McWilliams) *ref to r: tk no part* **150/1**
1m 51.68s (1.18) **Going Correction** +0.05s/f (Slow)
WFA 3 from 4yo 21lb **7** Ran SP% **109.9**
Speed ratings (Par 103): **96,94,94,87,82 77,**
toteswingers:1&2:£1.30, 2&3:£1.40, 1&3:£2.30 CSF £5.14 TOTE £2.30: £1.10, £1.20; EX 5.80.
Owner Asaad Al Banwan **Bred** Philip Brady **Trained** Newmarket, Suffolk
FOCUS
A muddling maiden which was not strong run. The winner matched her debut form and should do better.

725 PLAY BLACKJACK AT BLUESQ.COM H'CAP 1m 141y(P)
6:00 (6:00) (Class 6) (0-60,60) 4-Y-0+ **£1,704** (£503; £251) **Stalls** Low

Form RPR
2-35 **1** **Idol Deputy (FR)**[38] 224 6-9-0 **60**... RachealKneller(7) 4 75
(Mark Usher) *hld up: hdwy over 2f out: led on bit ins fnl f: shkn up and r.o wl* **4/1**[1]
5113 **2** *3* **Warden Bond**[7] 636 4-9-4 **57**...(p) MartinLane 8 65
(William Stone) *chsd ldrs: led over 1f out: rdn and hdd ins fnl f: styd on same pce* **4/1**[1]
0560 **3** *2* **The Which Doctor**[12] 559 7-9-5 **58**...(e) MartinHarley 7 61
(Richard Guest) *hld up: hdwy over 1f out: r.o: nt rch ldrs* **18/1**
-553 **4** *½* **Join Up**[16] 532 6-9-3 **56**... ShaneKelly 3 58
(Mark Brisbourne) *a.p: rdn over 1f out: styd on same pce fnl f* **8/1**
406- **5** *3¾* **Ra Junior (USA)**[159] 6262 6-9-0 **60**... NedCurtis(7) 10 54
(Paul Midgley) *hld up in tch: effrt over 2f out: wknd fnl f* **25/1**
006- **6** *nk* **See The Storm**[153] 6428 4-8-3 **49**... MatthewMcGhee(7) 2 42
(Lisa Williamson) *hld up in tch: rdn over 2f out: wknd fnl f* **40/1**
-425 **7** *½* **Symphonic Dancer (USA)**[17] 490 5-9-1 **54**... RussKennemore 13 46
(Brian Baugh) *led early: chsd ldr sn after: led over 3f out: rdn and hdd over 1f out: wknd fnl f* **10/1**
-601 **8** *nk* **Stamp Duty (IRE)**[16] 532 4-9-5 **58**... DuranFentiman 9 49
(Suzzanne France) *s.i.s: hld up: rdn over 2f out: nvr nrr* **11/1**
5-00 **9** *2¼* **Athenian Garden (USA)**[34] 289 5-9-2 **55**... WilliamCarson 6 41
(Richard Guest) *s.i.s: hld up: nvr on terms* **66/1**
-641 **10** *nk* **Marksbury**[16] 531 5-9-6 **59**... LukeMorris 5 44
(Mark Brisbourne) *hld up in tch: rdn over 1f out: wknd fnl f* **6/1**[2]
0-04 **11** *3¾* **Ergo (FR)**[31] 333 8-8-13 **52**...(b) PaddyAspell 1 29
(James Moffatt) *hld up: rdn and wknd over 2f out* **15/2**[3]
00/0 **12** *6* **Gifted Heir (IRE)**[16] 532 8-8-4 **48**... RaulDaSilva(5) 11
(Ray Peacock) *hld up: wknd over 2f out* **66/1**
2345 **13** *16* **Look For Love**[14] 550 4-8-7 **53**...(p) JackDuern(7) 12
(Reg Hollinshead) *sn pushed along to ld at a str pce: wknd and hdd over 3f out* **12/1**
1m 50.2s (-0.30) **Going Correction** +0.05s/f (Slow) **13** Ran SP% **116.8**
Speed ratings (Par 101): **103,100,98,98,94 94,94,93,91,91 88,82,68**
toteswingers:1&2:£3.30, 2&3:£14.20, 1&3:£20.90 CSF £17.72 CT £256.20 TOTE £5.60: £2.20, £1.10, £7.10; EX 21.70 Trifecta £238.00 Pool £1,309.45 - 4.07 winning units..
Owner Miss J C Blackwell **Bred** Sheikh Sultan Bin Khalifa Al Nayan **Trained** Upper Lambourn, Berks
FOCUS
With both Look For Love and Symphonic Dancer determined to make the running despite being drawn in the two outside stalls, the early pace was frantic. This eventually played into the hands of those ridden with patience. Good form for the grade, backed by the time.
Symphonic Dancer(USA) Official explanation: jockey said mare hung left-handed
T/Jkpt: Not won. T/Plt: £28.90 to a £1 stake. Pool £103,835.82 - 2,620.58 winning units. T/Qpdt: £9.80 to a £1 stake. Pool £7,515.86 - 562.40 winning units. CR

709 LINGFIELD (L-H)
Tuesday, February 28
OFFICIAL GOING: Standard
Wind: Virtually nil

726 BET BLUE SQUARE ON YOUR MOBILE APPRENTICE H'CAP 1m 2f (P)
2:10 (2:10) (Class 6) (0-65,64) 3-Y-O **£1,704** (£503; £251) **Stalls** Low

Form RPR
40-6 **1** **Captain Cardington (IRE)**[25] 398 3-9-10 **64**...(v1) MartinHarley 2 66
(Mick Channon) *hld up wl in tch: shkn up and effrt to chse ldr ent fnl 2f: drvn to ld 1f out: pricking ears and idling bdly ins fnl f: a jst doing enough to hold on* **13/2**[3]
66-6 **2** *½* **Excellent News (IRE)**[15] 549 3-9-6 **60**... RyanPowell 1 61
(J W Hills) *in tch in last trio and pushed along at times: rdn to chse ldrs 2f out: carried rt and chsd wnr ins fnl f: styd on u.p fnl 75yds* **14/1**
2-06 **3** *nse* **Chankillo**[13] 571 3-9-6 **60**... JohnFahy 7 61
(Mark H Tompkins) *hld up in tch in last trio: effrt and rdn over 1f out: swtchd rt ins fnl f: styd on strly u.p fnl 75yds: nt quite rch ldrs* **4/1**[2]
005- **4** *1* **Always Eager**[137] 6829 3-9-3 **60**... DarylByrne(3) 6 59
(Mark Johnston) *chsd ldr tl led 3f out: rdn wl over 1f out: hdd 1f out: stl pressing wnr but nt qckning whn hung rt ins fnl f: lost 2 pls fnl 100yds* **6/4**[1]
0-53 **5** *¾* **Saucy Cat (IRE)**[13] 571 3-8-11 **56**... HarveyMason(5) 5 53
(John Best) *racd wd: hld up in rr: hdwy over 2f out: rdn and no imp over 1f out: kpt on ins fnl f: nvr trbld ldrs* **7/1**
00-5 **6** *9* **Bojangle (IRE)**[14] 556 3-8-3 **46** ow1...(be1) JoshBaudains(3) 8 25
(Dominic Ffrench Davis) *t.k.h: chsd ldrs: rdn and lost pl jst over 2f out: bhd 1f out* **14/1**
1333 **7** *8* **Complex**[21] 466 3-9-2 **56**... MatthewCosham 4 19
(David Evans) *led tl hdd and rdn 3f out: dropped to rr 2f out: sn lost tch* **9/1**
03 **R** **Malt (IRE)**[19] 479 3-8-5 **45**...(be) RaulDaSilva 3
(Philip McBride) *ref to r* **33/1**
2m 7.34s (0.74) **Going Correction** +0.125s/f (Slow) **8** Ran SP% **112.1**
Speed ratings (Par 95): **102,101,101,100,100 92,86,**
toteswingers:1&2:£5.10, 2&3:£11.10, 1&3:£6.40 CSF £86.38 CT £406.59 TOTE £9.20: £1.50, £4.90, £1.40; EX 59.90 Trifecta £223.20 Pool: £742.19 - 2.46 winning units..
Owner Nick & Olga Dhandsa & John & Zoe Webster **Bred** Brian Williamson **Trained** West Ilsley, Berks
■ Stewards' Enquiry : Martin Harley two-day ban: used whip with excessive frequency, 2nd offence in 6 mths (Mar 13-14)
FOCUS
A weak apprentice handicap, though it was sound run. The winner is rated back to form.
Complex Official explanation: vet said filly pulled up lame

727 CYPRIUM BAR AT MARRIOTT LINGFIELD (S) STKS 1m 2f (P)
2:40 (2:40) (Class 6) 3-Y-O **£1,704** (£503; £251) **Stalls** Low

Form RPR
-562 **1** **Moment In The Sun**[13] 571 3-8-7 54... WilliamCarson 4 58+
(William Muir) *mde all: gng best over 2f out: rdn clr 2f out: edgd rt over 1f out: styd on wl* **11/8**[1]
-656 **2** *5* **Pink Evie**[21] 459 3-8-4 55...(p) DominicFox(3) 2 48
(Gay Kelleway) *dwlt: t.k.h: chsd ldrs: chsd wnr and rdn over 2f out: outpcd 2f out: styd on same pce and wl hld after* **5/1**[3]
634 **3** *4* **Cuore (IRE)**[4] 683 3-8-12 0...(b1) ShaneKelly 1 45
(Jamie Osborne) *chsd wnr tl 4f out: lost pl and nt clr run wl over 2f out: sn rdn and outpcd: no ch over 1f out: wnt 3rd nr fin* **15/2**
-145 **4** *½* **Anginola (IRE)**[15] 547 3-8-8 63...(v) MatthewCosham(5) 3 45
(David Evans) *in tch: rdn and hdwy on outer over 4f out: chsd wnr over 3f out tl over 2f out: 3rd and wl hld over 1f out: lost 3rd nr fin* **7/4**[2]
2m 7.99s (1.39) **Going Correction** +0.125s/f (Slow) **4** Ran SP% **106.9**
Speed ratings (Par 95): **99,95,91,91**
CSF £7.94 TOTE £2.80; EX 9.80.The winner was sold to David Flood for 6,800gns.
Owner Foursome Thoroughbreds **Bred** Foursome Thoroughbreds **Trained** Lambourn, Berks
FOCUS
An uncompetitive seller won in comprehensive fashion by Moment In The Sun. This could rate improved form at face value but the time was slow.

728 LINGFIELDPARK.CO.UK H'CAP 2m (P)
3:10 (3:10) (Class 5) (0-75,70) 4-Y-0+ **£2,385** (£704; £352) **Stalls** Low

Form RPR
13 **1** **Belle Josephine**[10] 625 4-9-6 **70**... JoeFanning 3 77
(Mark Johnston) *mde all: rn green and hung rt 6f out: rdn and grad increased gallop over 3f out: clr over 1f out: r.o wl and in command fnl f: eased towards fin* **4/1**
211- **2** *1* **The Absent Mare**[111] 7331 4-8-12 **62**... MartinLane 1 67
(Robin Dickin) *stdd s: hld up in last: hdwy on outer jst over 2f out: rdn over 1f out: chsd wnr fnl 75yds: r.o wl but no threat to wnr* **3/1**[3]
222 **3** *1¾* **Maison Brillet (IRE)**[24] 433 5-9-8 **69**...(p) RyanClark(3) 5 72
(Clive Drew) *hld up in tch: rdn and effrt over 2f out: chsd wnr 2f out: no imp and styd on same pce fnl f: lost 2nd fnl 75yds* **9/4**[1]
133- **4** *nse* **Cotton Grass**[55] 4175 4-8-12 **62**... JohnFahy 6 65
(Mark H Tompkins) *chsd ldng pair: rdn effrt over 2f out: unable qck u.p over 1f out: styd on same pce fnl f* **11/1**
1-00 **5** *8* **Kahfre**[17] 521 5-9-12 **70**...(be) DavidProbert 4 63
(Gary Moore) *chsd wnr: jnd wnr 6f out tl rdn and unable qck over 2f out: drvn and wknd wl over 1f out: eased towards fin* **5/2**[2]
3m 31.1s (5.40) **Going Correction** +0.125s/f (Slow)
WFA 4 from 5yo 6lb **5** Ran SP% **112.7**
Speed ratings (Par 103): **91,90,89,89,85**
CSF £16.48 TOTE £4.00: £2.30, £3.00; EX 11.60.
Owner Sheikh Hamdan Bin Mohammed Al Maktoum **Bred** Meon Valley Stud **Trained** Middleham Moor, N Yorks
FOCUS
Only the five runners, but a competitive affair nonetheless. Joe Fanning was allowed to dictate a pedestrian pace on the winner, who could be getting her act together. The form is rated around the third.
Kahfre Official explanation: jockey said gelding never travelled

729 BREATHE SPA AT MARRIOTT LINGFIELD H'CAP 7f (P)
3:40 (3:40) (Class 6) (0-60,60) 4-Y-0+ **£1,704** (£503; £251) **Stalls** Low

Form RPR
050- **1** **Buxton**[62] 7895 8-9-3 **56**...(t) MartinLane 6 63
(Roger Ingram) *stdd s: nudged along in rr early: clsd and nt clr run ent fnl 2f: gd hdwy jst over 1f out: led ins fnl f: drvn fnl 100yds: jst lasted* **7/1**
00-5 **2** *shd* **Sottovoce**[39] 225 4-9-5 **58**... JimCrowley 5 65
(Simon Dow) *hld up in tch: pushed along over 4f out: rdn and no prog over 2f out: hdwy and swtchd rt 1f out: chsd wnr fnl 100yds: styd on strly: jst failed* **14/1**
0-34 **3** *1½* **Prince Namid**[33] 312 10-9-1 **54**... LukeMorris 3 57
(Jonathen de Giles) *in tch: rdn and outpcd over 2f out: drvn and rallied over 1f out: nt clr run and swtchd lft 1f out: kpt on u.p fnl 100yds* **14/1**
-410 **4** *hd* **Fearless Poet (IRE)**[13] 561 4-8-13 **52**...(b) JoeFanning 8 54
(Bryan Smart) *chsd ldrs on outer: rdn and effrt 2f out: chsd wnr briefly jst ins fnl f: styd on same pce fnl 100yds* **4/1**[3]
6222 **5** *3* **Katmai River (IRE)**[20] 474 5-9-6 **59**...(v) SteveDrowne 4 53
(Mark Usher) *pressed ldr: ev ch and rdn 2f out: led over 1f out tl jst ins fnl f: wknd fnl 100yds* **2/1**[1]
-350 **6** *2¾* **Royal Box**[10] 624 5-9-0 **58**...(p) MatthewCosham(5) 2 45
(David Evans) *chsd ldrs: rdn and unable qck wl over 2f out: rallied u.p over 1f out: wknd ins fnl f* **3/1**[2]
1010 **7** *1¾* **Crocodile Bay (IRE)**[15] 550 9-9-1 **54**...(p) WilliamCarson 1 36
(Richard Guest) *led: rdn ent fnl 2f: drvn: edgd rt and hdd over 1f out: wknd fnl f* **8/1**
1m 25.39s (0.59) **Going Correction** +0.125s/f (Slow) **7** Ran SP% **115.3**
Speed ratings (Par 101): **101,100,99,98,95 92,90**
toteswingers:1&2:£15.50, 2&3:£10.80, 1&3:£11.10 CSF £94.12 CT £1330.04 TOTE £5.50: £4.40, £3.80; EX 83.70 Trifecta £488.80 Part won. Pool: £660.63 - 0.42 winning units..
Owner Peter J Burton **Bred** Sharon Ingram **Trained** Epsom, Surrey
FOCUS
There was plenty of competition for the lead on here and the front-runners rather cut each others' throats. The form is rated cautiously.

730 FOLLOW US ON TWITTER @BLUESQ MAIDEN STKS 7f (P)
4:10 (4:10) (Class 5) 3-Y-O+ **£2,385** (£704; £352) **Stalls** Low

Form RPR
1 **Alkadi (IRE)** 3-8-4 0... JoeFanning 5 69+
(Mark Johnston) *chsd ldr: rdn and chal over 1f out: led ins fnl f: r.o wl under hands and heels riding fnl 150yds* **11/8**[1]
4 **2** *1¾* **Sugar Prince (IRE)**[34] 298 3-8-9 0... ShaneKelly 2 69
(Tim Pitt) *led: rdn and clr w wnr jst over 2f out: drvn 1f out: sn hdd and one pce* **10/3**[3]
35- **3** *3½* **Gold Falcon (IRE)**[69] 7837 3-8-9 0... MartinLane 6 66+
(David Simcock) *stdd s: plld hrd early: hld up in last: trapped bhd rivals as ldrs qcknd clr jst over 2f out: stl last and hmpd wl over 1f out: hdwy between horses to go modest 3rd 1f out: r.o: n.d* **7/4**[2]
4 *5* **Fushicho** 3-8-9 0... JimCrowley 1 46
(Michael Wigham) *chsd ldrs: rdn and outpcd jst over 2f out: disputing 3rd but no ch w ldrs wl over 1f out: wknd fnl f* **16/1**

0-0 5 *nk* **The Quarterjack**[10] 620 3-8-6 0 .... SimonPearce(3) 3 45
(Ron Hodges) *t.k.h: hld up in tch: rdn and outpcd jst over 2f out: disputing 3rd and no threat to ldrs wl over 1f out: wknd fnl f* **100/1**

1m 25.92s (1.12) **Going Correction** +0.125s/f (Slow) 5 Ran SP% **108.4**
Speed ratings (Par 103): **98,96,92,86,85**
CSF £6.14 TOTE £2.10: £1.20, £1.10; EX 5.60.
Owner Sheikh Hamdan Bin Mohammed Al Maktoum **Bred** Darley **Trained** Middleham Moor, N Yorks

FOCUS
A modest maiden, although the winner could be anything. Despite the race being open to older horses, the five runners were all 3yos. The form is rated around the runner-up.

731 PLAY GOLF AT MARRIOTT LINGFIELD MAIDEN STKS 6f (P)
4:40 (4:41) (Class 5) 3-Y-O **£2,385** (£704; £352) **Stalls** Low

Form RPR
-433 1 **Fugitive Motel (IRE)**[13] 565 3-8-10 70 .... NicoleNordblad(7) 4 71
(Hans Adielsson) *mde all: t.k.h and set stdy gallop: qcknd clr 2f out: rdn over 1f out: kpt on and a gng to hold on* **5/1**[2]
426- 2 ½ **Traveller's Tales**[126] 7081 3-8-12 75 .... KieranO'Neill 1 64
(Richard Hannon) *chsd wnr: rdn: hung rt and outpcd 2f out: stl 4 l down 1f out: styd on and clsng on wnr fnl 100yds but nvr gng to quite get to wnr* **1/3**[1]
06 3 10 **Lyrical Gangster (IRE)**[34] 292 3-9-3 0 .... JimmyFortune 3 37
(Peter Chapple-Hyam) *s.i.s and short of room s: hld up in tch in rr: rdn and outpcd over 2f out: 3rd and no ch over 1f out* **8/1**[3]
4 3 **One Last Dream** 3-9-0 0 .... SimonPearce(3) 2 28
(Ron Hodges) *wnt rt s: v green and hung rt thrght: chsd ldrs tl hung bdly rt and lost pl bnd 2f out: wl bhd after* **50/1**

1m 14.41s (2.51) **Going Correction** +0.125s/f (Slow) 4 Ran SP% **104.8**
Speed ratings (Par 97): **88,87,74,70**
CSF £6.97 TOTE £5.40; EX 8.60.
Owner Hans Adielsson A B **Bred** Michael Begley **Trained** Kingston Lisle, Oxon

FOCUS
Another modest maiden and ity's likely the winner merely ran to form.

732 GET YOUR BET ON AT BLUESQ.COM H'CAP 1m (P)
5:10 (5:15) (Class 6) (0-60,60) 4-Y-0+ **£1,704** (£503; £251) **Stalls** High

Form RPR
3-46 1 **Kipchak (IRE)**[5] 665 7-9-1 54 ....(b) LukeMorris 8 66
(Conor Dore) *mounted on crse and taken down early: mde all: rdn ent fnl 2f: kpt on wl u.p fnl f: drvn out* **5/2**[1]
-524 2 ¾ **Penbryn (USA)**[17] 519 5-9-2 55 ....(v) SteveDrowne 6 65
(Nick Littmoden) *hld up in tch towards rr: hdwy to chse ldrs 2f out: rdn and hld hd awkwardly over 1f out: chsd wnr fnl 100yds: kpt on* **13/2**[3]
0-02 3 2 ½ **Gallantry**[33] 306 10-9-3 56 .... TomMcLaughlin 3 60
(Paul Howling) *dwlt: sn rcvrd and in midfield: rdn and effrt on inner 2f out: chsd wnr over 1f out: no imp and one pce fnl f* **7/1**
-454 4 1 ½ **Roman Flame**[24] 428 4-8-7 53 .... DannyBrock(7) 4 54
(Michael Quinn) *chsd ldrs: rdn and unable qck jst over 2f out: outpcd over 1f out: styd on same pce and no threat to wnr after* **25/1**
3-46 5 ½ **Dichoh**[33] 306 9-9-4 57 ....(p) GeorgeBaker 2 57
(Michael Madgwick) *hld up in rr: sltly hmpd 6f out: rdn and swtchd rt over 1f out: styd on ins fnl f: nvr trbld ldrs* **5/1**[2]
0-30 6 ½ **Princess Willow**[41] 203 4-9-0 53 .... RichardThomas 9 52
(John E Long) *fly-jmpd leaving stalls: in tch: rdn over 3f out: outpcd u.p ent fnl 2f: no threat to wnr fr over 1f out* **16/1**
4553 7 ½ **Cristaliyev**[11] 598 4-9-4 57 ....(v) JoeFanning 5 54
(Jim Boyle) *chsd wnr: rdn and unable qck 2f out: lost 2nd over 1f out: wknd fnl f* **7/1**
5-60 8 12 **Red Yarn**[12] 574 5-9-6 59 ....(b) LiamKeniry 7 29
(Joseph Tuite) *rdn along leaving stalls: in tch towards rr: rdn and struggling over 3f out: bhd and lost tch over 2f out: bhd and eased ins fnl f* **33/1**
404- 9 8 **Takhreej (IRE)**[186] 5432 4-9-7 60 .... ChrisCatlin 1
(Paul Rich) *in tch in last quartet: rdn 4f out: wknd over 2f out: wl bhd and eased ins fnl f* **5/2**[1]

1m 37.78s (-0.42) **Going Correction** +0.125s/f (Slow) 9 Ran SP% **124.8**
Speed ratings (Par 101): **107,106,103,102,101 101,100,88,80**
toteswingers:1&2:£6.70, 2&3:£4.90, 1&3:£5.80 CSF £21.72 CT £107.88 TOTE £5.10: £1.60, £2.10, £1.90; EX 23.80 Trifecta £88.90 Pool: £864.58 - 7.19 winning units..
Owner Liam Breslin **Bred** Miss Mary Davidson & Mrs Steffi Von Schilcher **Trained** Hubbert's Bridge, Lincs

FOCUS
A competitive closer featuring plenty of irresolute performers. It was well run and the form could be rated slightly higher.
Penbryn(USA) Official explanation: jockey said gelding hung left
Takhreej(IRE) Official explanation: jockey said gelding never travelled
T/Plt: £1,099.70 to a £1 stake. Pool £65,761.70 - 43.65 winning units. T/Qpdt: £191.70 to a £1 stake. Pool £4,922.21 - 19.00 winning units. SP

662 KEMPTON (A.W) (R-H)
Wednesday, February 29

OFFICIAL GOING: Standard
Wind: Virtually nil

733 FREE ENTRY FOR BETDAQ MEMBERS H'CAP 1m 2f (P)
5:35 (5:36) (Class 4) (0-85,85) 4-Y-0+ **£4,075** (£1,212; £606; £303) **Stalls** Low

Form RPR
00-2 1 **Dunhoy (IRE)**[18] 520 4-9-0 79 .... DaneO'Neill 3 87
(Tony Newcombe) *in rr but in tch: hdwy over 2f out: drvn to chal 1f out: styd upsides u.p tl tk slt ld fnl 30yds* **9/4**[1]
0-31 2 ½ **Megalala (IRE)**[28] 374 11-8-12 76 .... KieranO'Neill 1 83
(John Bridger) *led: drvn over 2f out: jnd 1f out: kpt on gamely tl narrowly hdd fnl 30yds* **5/1**
000- 3 1 ¼ **Sinfonico (IRE)**[109] 7393 4-9-3 85 ....(be[1]) SeanLevey(3) 4 90
(Richard Hannon) *in rr but in tch: hdwy on ins fr 2f out: nt clr run and swtchd lft 1f out: nt clr run again sn after and c lft again: no ex fnl 120yds* **10/3**[3]
541- 4 6 **Sakhee's Pearl**[71] 7831 6-8-13 77 .... LiamKeniry 6 70
(Jo Crowley) *chsd ldrs: rdn over 2f out: wknd over 1f out* **11/4**[2]
060- 5 1 **Kakapuka**[97] 7531 5-9-2 80 .... LukeMorris 2 71
(Anabel K Murphy) *chsd ldrs: wnt 2nd 3f out: rdn over 2f out: wknd qckly appr fnl f* **20/1**
412- 6 3 ½ **Ya Hafed**[29] 1286 4-8-8 73 .... ChrisCatlin 5 57
(Sheena West) *chsd ldrs tl rdn 3f out: wknd qckly* **16/1**

2m 4.79s (-3.21) **Going Correction** -0.175s/f (Stan)
WFA 4 from 5yo+ 1lb 6 Ran SP% **107.8**
Speed ratings (Par 105): **105,104,103,98,98 95**
toteswingers:1&2:£2.90, 1&3:£1.70, 2&3:£4.80 CSF £12.63 TOTE £3.70: £1.40, £1.90; EX 12.40.
Owner David Gilbert **Bred** Rossenarra Bloodstock Limited **Trained** Yarnscombe, Devon

FOCUS
The leader set a fair gallop and the form looks sound for the grade. The runner-up sets the standard.

734 BETDAQ MULTIPLES H'CAP 6f (P)
6:05 (6:05) (Class 6) (0-55,55) 3-Y-O **£1,617** (£481; £240; £120) **Stalls** Low

Form RPR
5342 1 **Flying Kitty**[7] 657 3-8-11 48 .... KieranO'Neill 4 53
(John Bridger) *in rr: drvn and hdwy on ins fr 2f out: str run to ld fnl 120yds: sn in command: readily* **10/1**
334 2 1 ¾ **J J Leary (IRE)**[8] 641 3-9-0 51 ....(v) FrannyNorton 6 51
(Ian Williams) *led after 2f: rdn 2f out: kpt on fr over 1f out: hdd and outpcd fnl 120yds: hld on wl for 2nd* **6/1**[2]
000- 3 ½ **Armiger**[144] 6695 3-9-2 53 .... GeorgeBaker 2 51+
(William Muir) *towards rr: hdwy 3f out: swtchd lft over 1f out: str run ins fnl f: fin wl to take 3rd cl home* **8/1**
55-0 4 *nk* **First Rebellion**[14] 564 3-8-10 47 .... DavidProbert 3 44
(Tony Carroll) *led 2f: styd chsng ldr: ev ch and rdn fr 2f out: styd on fnl f: one pce and lost 3rd cl home* **10/1**
00-3 5 *nk* **My Name Is Sam**[12] 599 3-8-10 47 .... LukeMorris 5 43
(Ronald Harris) *chsd ldrs: rdn over 1f out: styd on same pce thrght fnl f* **9/2**[1]
0-5 6 *shd* **George Fenton**[14] 564 3-8-9 46 ....(tp) ShaneKelly 11 42+
(Richard Guest) *chsd ldrs: rdn and ev ch fr 2f out: styd on same pce fnl f* **15/2**[3]
4452 7 1 **Marie's Fantasy**[14] 564 3-9-3 54 .... JamieGoldstein 10 47
(Zoe Davison) *s.i.s: in rr: rdn over 2f out: styd on fnl f: styng on whn n.m.r clsng stages* **12/1**
0-52 8 1 **Chateau Lola**[12] 599 3-8-12 49 ....(v) JoeFanning 8 38
(Derek Shaw) *in tch: rdn and hdwy to chse ldrs over 2f out: wknd ins fnl 120yds* **8/1**
40-0 9 1 **Gone By Sunrise**[28] 376 3-9-3 54 .... TonyHamilton 1 40
(Richard Fahey) *chsd ldrs on ins: rdn wl over 2f out: wknd fnl f* **8/1**
60-0 10 2 **Mandianna (IRE)**[25] 429 3-9-4 55 .... DaneO'Neill 9 35
(Jo Crowley) *outpcd most of way* **20/1**
500- 11 *nk* **Hatha Zain (IRE)**[166] 6118 3-8-9 46 oh1 .... RichardKingscote 7 25
(Milton Bradley) *outpcd most of way* **16/1**
006- 12 8 **Jeremy Sue**[63] 7898 3-8-9 46 oh1 .... FrankieMcDonald 12
(Derek Haydn Jones) *racd on outside: bhd most of way* **40/1**

1m 13.8s (0.70) **Going Correction** +0.175s/f (Slow) 12 Ran SP% **116.5**
Speed ratings (Par 95): **102,99,99,98,98 98,96,95,94,91 91,80**
toteswingers:1&2:£12.10, 1&3:£17.50, 2&3:£8.60 CSF £67.71 CT £509.68 TOTE £9.20: £3.30, £1.90, £4.00; EX 64.80.
Owner J J Bridger **Bred** Laundry Cottage Stud Farm **Trained** Liphook, Hants

FOCUS
An ordinary sprint handicap, but it was competitive and sound run. Fair form for the grade.
Jeremy Sue Official explanation: jockey said filly never travelled

735 BACK OR LAY AT BETDAQ.COM H'CAP 6f (P)
6:35 (6:35) (Class 5) (0-75,75) 4-Y-0+ **£2,264** (£673; £336; £84; £84) **Stalls** Low

Form RPR
0030 1 **Captain Scooby**[7] 647 6-8-13 70 .... RobertLButler(3) 7 77
(Richard Guest) *in tch: rdn and hdwy over 1f out: styd on strly to ld fnl 120yds: jst hld on* **22/1**
-040 2 *shd* **Italian Tom (IRE)**[11] 623 5-9-0 68 .... LukeMorris 4 75
(Ronald Harris) *in tch: chsd ldrs 2f out: sn rdn and one pce: styd on fnl f: pushed lft fnl 120yds: fin strly: jst failed* **6/1**[2]
36-1 3 ½ **The Wee Chief (IRE)**[25] 425 6-9-1 69 .... KieranO'Neill 5 74
(Jimmy Fox) *hld up in rr: hdwy on ins fr 2f out: styd on to chse ldrs ins fnl f: kpt on but nt quite rch wnr and one pce into 3rd clsng stages* **7/2**[1]
1133 4 *shd* **Dancing Welcome**[18] 537 6-9-7 75 ....(b) RichardKingscote 1 80
(Milton Bradley) *chsd ldr: rdn over 2f out: styd on same pce fnl f* **12/1**
32-5 4 *dht* **Rambo Will**[36] 282 4-9-2 70 .... DavidProbert 2 75
(J R Jenkins) *chsd ldrs: rdn 2f out: styd on fnl f: nvr quite gng pce to chal* **8/1**[3]
0-51 6 1 ½ **Zip Lock (IRE)**[21] 473 6-9-4 72 .... GeorgeBaker 9 72
(Olivia Maylam) *in rr: hdwy and rdn over 1f out: styd on fnl f: nt quite rch ldrs* **10/1**
0604 7 *nk* **Best Trip (IRE)**[7] 649 5-8-13 67 ....(t) WilliamCarson 8 66
(Richard Guest) *sn led at str pce: rdn and kpt on fr 2f out: hdd & wknd fnl 120yds* **8/1**[3]
-243 8 1 ½ **Valmina**[11] 623 5-9-0 68 ....(t) SteveDrowne 10 63
(Tony Carroll) *in tch: rdn 2f out: styd on fnl f: nvr gng pce to rch ldrs* **9/1**
3-46 9 *nk* **Sermons Mount (USA)**[18] 517 6-9-4 72 .... JohnFahy 3 66
(Paul Howling) *stdd s: in rr: rdn and sme hdwy over 1f out: nvr a threat* **11/1**
2525 10 4 ½ **Dunmore Boy (IRE)**[9] 639 4-8-9 63 ....(p) TonyHamilton 12 42
(Richard Fahey) *chsd ldrs: rdn over 2f out: wknd over 1f out* **16/1**
126- 11 1 ¼ **Gooseberry Bush**[160] 6276 5-8-13 67 .... LiamKeniry 11 42
(Gary Brown) *outpcd most of way* **50/1**
3-60 12 *nk* **Yankee Storm**[18] 526 7-9-1 72 ....(v) RyanClark(3) 6 46
(Michael Wigham) *chsd ldrs 4f* **6/1**[2]

1m 12.49s (-0.61) **Going Correction** +0.175s/f (Slow) 12 Ran SP% **120.3**
Speed ratings (Par 103): **111,110,110,110,110 108,107,105,105,99 97,97**
toteswingers:1&2:£52.90, 1&3:£18.30, 2&3:£3.80 CSF £151.26 CT £588.80 TOTE £31.80: £6.20, £2.90, £1.90; EX 301.80.
Owner Future Racing (Notts) Limited **Bred** Hellwood Stud Farm & Paul Davies (h'Gate) **Trained** Stainforth, S Yorks

FOCUS
There was a strong pace on here thanks to Best Trip, and the complexion of the race changed well inside the last as the closers took over. Sound if ordinary form.

736 BETDAQ MOBILE APPS H'CAP 1m (P)
7:05 (7:05) (Class 6) (0-65,65) 4-Y-0+ **£1,617** (£481; £240; £120) **Stalls** Low

Form RPR
1321 1 **Qeethaara (USA)**[13] 574 8-9-7 65 ....(p) LukeMorris 2 73
(Mark Brisbourne) *chsd ldrs: drvn and qcknd fnl f to take narrow ld fnl 120yds: hld on wl* **9/2**[2]

2-01 **2** *nk* **Warbond**[14] 561 4-8-13 **57** .... JamieGoldstein 6 64
(Michael Madgwick) *s.i.s: sn in tch: hdwy on ins fr 2f out: chal ins fnl f and upsides fnl 150yds: nt quite pce of wnr cl home* **7/2**[1]

3-50 **3** *nk* **Mister Green (FR)**[4] 712 6-9-4 **62** .... (bt) StephenCraine 7 68+
(David Flood) *in rr: stdy hdwy and travelling ok ins fnl 2f: rdn appr fnl f: fin wl: nt quite rch ldng duo* **9/2**[2]

0126 **4** *½* **Valley Tiger**[14] 559 4-9-5 **63** .... TonyHamilton 10 68
(Richard Fahey) *sn chsng ldr: chal wl over 2f out tl slt ld 1f out: hdd fnl 120yds: no ex* **12/1**

4-32 **5** *2* **Beetuna (IRE)**[13] 574 7-8-13 **62** .... (v) MarkCoumbe(5) 9 62
(Oliver Sherwood) *in rr: rdn over 2f out: styd on fnl f: nt pce to rch ldrs* **9/2**[2]

2P 0 **6** *shd* **Irie Ule**[13] 674 4-9-1 **62** .... SophieDoyle(3) 1 62
(Sylvester Kirk) *chsd ldrs: rdn over 2f out: wknd u.p ins fnl f* **50/1**

124- **7** *1* **Kielty's Folly**[210] 4666 8-8-13 **62** .... DavidKenny(5) 5 60
(Brian Baugh) *led: jnd wl over 2f out: hdd 1f out: sn btn* **8/1**[3]

050/ **8** *3¾* **Sun Dream**[870] 6728 5-8-13 **57** .... DavidProbert 4 46
(Tony Carroll) *s.i.s: in rr: rdn on ins over 2f out: nvr gng pce to get beyond mid-div* **25/1**

4-00 **9** *2* **Barista (IRE)**[13] 574 4-8-11 **60** .... CharlesBishop(5) 8 45
(Brian Forsey) *t.k.h in rr: effrt on outside wl over 2f out: nvr in contention and sn wknd* **14/1**

-000 **10** *1¾* **Bubbly Braveheart (IRE)**[14] 568 5-8-8 **57** .... (p) JemmaMarshall(5) 3 38
(Pat Phelan) *stdd s: in rr: racd on outer: a in rr* **16/1**

1m 41.81s (2.01) **Going Correction** +0.175s/f (Slow) **10** Ran SP% **113.9**
Speed ratings (Par 101): **96,95,95,94,92 92,91,88,86,84**
CSF £20.10 CT £75.79 TOTE £5.00: £1.80, £1.40, £1.70; EX 18.40.
Owner Mark Brisbourne **Bred** Shadwell Farm LLC **Trained** Great Ness, Shropshire

FOCUS
They went a steady early pace and it turned into a sprint up the straight. The form is not the most solid.

737 READ NICK LUCK IN RACING PLUS MAIDEN STKS 1m (P)
7:35 (7:35) (Class 5) 3-Y-O+ **£2,264** (£673; £336; £168) **Stalls** Low

Form RPR

3 **1** **Icelander (USA)**[11] 620 3-8-9 0 .... JoeFanning 4 72+
(Mark Johnston) *trckd ldrs on ins: pushed along wl over 1f out and sn in 2nd: styd on fnl f to ld fnl 150yds: kpt on strly* **6/4**[1]

53 **2** *1* **Strawberrymystique**[18] 533 4-9-9 0 .... AdamKirby 5 69
(Marco Botti) *chsd ldrs: pushed along 2f out: styd on to chse wnr fnl 50yds but no imp* **4/1**[2]

0 **3** *¾* **Dream Prospector**[15] 552 3-8-9 0 .... MartinLane 10 67
(James Tate) *led: rdn over 2f out: kpt on tl hdd fnl 150yds: one pce into 3rd fnl 50yds* **20/1**

5 **4** *¾* **How Fortunate**[13] 573 4-9-9 0 .... DaneO'Neill 11 66
(David Elsworth) *sn chsng ldr: rdn over 2f out: lost 2nd over 1f out: one pce ins fnl f* **33/1**

335 **5** *3¼* **Yajber (USA)**[18] 523 3-8-9 69 .... SteveDrowne 6 57
(Terry Clement) *chsd ldrs: rdn over 2f out: wknd 1f out* **9/2**[3]

6 *1¾* **Art News (IRE)** 3-8-9 0 .... AmirQuinn 9 53
(Gary Moore) *in rr: pushed along: over 2f out: kpt on fnl f but nvr a threat* **20/1**

7 *1½* **Lal Bhai** 4-10-0 0 .... ChrisCatlin 2 55
(Chris Down) *s.i.s: in rr: pushed along and effrt over 2f out: styd on same pce fnl f* **66/1**

6- **8** *1¼* **Salford Prince (IRE)**[142] 6754 4-10-0 0 .... JimmyFortune 3 52
(David Elsworth) *chsd ldrs: pushed along 3f out: wknd 2f out* **14/1**

04 **9** *1¾* **Cutting It Fine (IRE)**[32] 350 3-8-9 0 .... ShaneKelly 1 42
(Jeremy Noseda) *sn pushed along in rr: a bhd* **6/1**

10 *21* **Samuel George**[39] 5-10-0 0 .... LukeMorris 7
(Michael Blake) *s.i.s: a in rr: t.o* **100/1**

11 *32* **Night Symfonic** 3-8-4 0 .... WilliamCarson 8
(Brett Johnson) *s.i.s: in rr: hung lft and t.o fr over 2f out* **50/1**

1m 39.9s (0.10) **Going Correction** +0.175s/f (Slow)
WFA 3 from 4yo+ 19lb **11** Ran SP% **116.0**
Speed ratings (Par 103): **106,105,104,103,100 98,97,95,94,73 41**
toteswingers:1&2:£1.80, 1&3:£8.20, 2&3:£17.80 CSF £6.72 TOTE £2.50: £1.30, £1.40, £7.20; EX 8.60.
Owner Sheikh Hamdan Bin Mohammed Al Maktoum **Bred** Darley **Trained** Middleham Moor, N Yorks

FOCUS
Not much strength in depth to this maiden, but a promising winner. It was steadily run and the first four were always prominent. The form is rated around the runner-up.

738 EVENT MAGAZINE H'CAP 1m 4f (P)
8:05 (8:06) (Class 6) (0-65,65) 4-Y-O+ **£1,617** (£481; £240; £120) **Stalls** Centre

Form RPR

0-36 **1** **Sumani (FR)**[35] 303 6-9-1 **59** .... HayleyTurner 10 66
(Simon Dow) *mde all at stdy pce: drvn and qcknd over 2f out: chal fr 1f out: styd on gamely to assert fnl 75yds* **13/2**

2-13 **2** *½* **Shirataki (IRE)**[35] 296 4-9-4 **65** .... ChrisCatlin 2 71
(Peter Hiatt) *t.k.h: trckd ldrs: chal over 1f out: drvn to press wnr ins fnl f: outpcd fnl 75yds* **9/2**[2]

5-53 **3** *nk* **Laser Blazer**[21] 468 4-7-13 **51** .... (p) RaulDaSilva(5) 1 57
(Jeremy Gask) *t.k.h: trckd ldr: rdn whn pce qcknd over 2f out: styd on to disp 2nd ins fnl f but nvr quite gng pce to rch wnr* **13/2**

0-53 **4** *1½* **Time Square (FR)**[13] 575 5-9-1 **59** .... (t) LukeMorris 9 63
(Tony Carroll) *s.i.s: in rr: hdwy 6f out: chsd ldrs over 3f out: rdn and outpcd over 2f out: kpt on again ins fnl f* **12/1**

5-10 **5** *1½* **Jamarjo (IRE)**[26] 400 5-9-7 **65** .... JimmyFortune 8 66+
(Steve Gollings) *hld up in rr: pushed along whn pce qcknd over 2f out: styd on towards outside over 1f out: fin wl: nt rch ldrs* **6/1**[3]

4061 **6** *shd* **Striding Edge (IRE)**[7] 651 6-8-12 **63** 6ex .... NicoleNordblad(7) 7 64
(Hans Adielsson) *in tch: lost position 7f out: hdwy whn pce qcknd 2f out: styd on same pce ins fnl f* **7/2**[1]

6314 **7** *1* **Cloudy Start**[8] 644 6-8-9 **60** .... LeonnaMayor(7) 3 59
(Jamie Osborne) *in rr: pushed along and sme hdwy on ins over 2f out: nvr gng pce to rch ldrs* **12/1**

06-2 **8** *1¼* **Musashi (IRE)**[13] 575 7-8-11 **55** .... JoeFanning 11 52
(Laura Mongan) *s.i.s: in rr: pushed along over 2f out: nvr gng pce to get into contention* **20/1**

1063 **9** *1* **Kai Mook**[5] 689 5-9-5 **63** .... SteveDrowne 5 59
(Roger Ingram) *in tch: rdn over 2f out: nvr quite gng pce to rch ldrs: wknd fnl f* **11/1**

000- **10** *1* **If What And Maybe**[105] 7441 4-8-6 **56** .... (v) RyanPowell(3) 4 50
(John Ryan) *slowly away: in rr: hdwy to chse ldrs 4f out: rdn and wknd fr 2f out* **33/1**

2m 38.03s (3.53) **Going Correction** +0.175s/f (Slow)
WFA 4 from 5yo+ 3lb **10** Ran SP% **112.8**
Speed ratings (Par 101): **95,94,94,93,92 92,91,90,90,89**
toteswingers:1&2:£9.30, 1&3:£8.90, 2&3:£6.60 CSF £34.59 CT £196.44 TOTE £7.00: £2.60, £1.70, £2.50; EX 41.90.
Owner T G Parker **Bred** Christian Wattinne **Trained** Epsom, Surrey

FOCUS
A tactical race, dominated from the front by Hayley Turner aboard the winner. The form cannot be taken too literally.
Time Square(FR) Official explanation: jockey said gelding ran too freely
If What And Maybe Official explanation: jockey said gelding missed the break

739 JOCKEY CLUB VENUES FILLIES' H'CAP 7f (P)
8:35 (8:36) (Class 5) (0-70,68) 3-Y-O **£2,264** (£673; £336; £168) **Stalls** Low

Form RPR

-141 **1** **Clodhopper (IRE)**[14] 564 3-9-0 **61** .... JimCrowley 7 67+
(Jamie Osborne) *stdd s: hld up in rr: drvn whn pce qcknd 2f out: str run u.p fnl f to ld fnl 120yds: r.o strly* **9/4**[1]

1-30 **2** *1* **Chambles**[33] 322 3-8-12 **64** .... (t) DavidKenny(5) 1 67
(Andrew Reid) *broke wl: stdd towards rr after 2f: hdwy on ins 2f out: slt ld over 1f out: hdd and outpcd fnl 120yds* **4/1**[3]

651- **3** *nk* **Hill Of Dreams (IRE)**[62] 7909 3-9-0 **61** .... ShaneKelly 4 63
(Dean Ivory) *s.i.s: sn prom: chsd ldr after 2f: chal fr 2f out to 1f out: styd on same pce ins fnl f* **9/2**

-424 **4** *nk* **Millibar (IRE)**[33] 331 3-9-7 **68** .... (p) ChrisCatlin 5 69
(Nick Littmoden) *s.i.s: in rr: drvn and hdwy over 1f out: squeezed between horses 1f out: kpt on but nvr any ch w wnr* **10/1**

41 **5** *1¼* **Source Of Light (IRE)**[7] 660 3-9-3 **64** 6ex .... StephenCraine 3 62
(Daniel Mark Loughnane) *chsd ldrs: rdn over 1f out: styd on same pce u.p ins fnl f* **11/4**[2]

056 **6** *2½* **Jacasa Too**[11] 620 3-8-3 **50** .... (b[1]) LukeMorris 2 41
(Rod Millman) *t.k.h: led 1f: styd chsng ldrs: ev ch 2f out: wkng whn n.m.r 1f out* **40/1**

30-6 **7** *6* **Ionwy**[32] 352 3-8-8 **55** .... FrankieMcDonald 6 30
(Derek Haydn Jones) *led after 1f: rdn and hdd over 1f out: wkng whn hmpd sn after* **33/1**

1m 28.82s (2.82) **Going Correction** +0.175s/f (Slow) **7** Ran SP% **110.1**
Speed ratings (Par 94): **90,88,88,88,86 83,77**
toteswingers:1&2:£2.80, 1&3:£2.10, 2&3:£6.30 CSF £10.68 TOTE £3.40: £1.90, £2.00; EX 12.40.
Owner A Taylor **Bred** Yeomanstown Stud **Trained** Upper Lambourn, Berks
■ Stewards' Enquiry : Chris Catlin three-day ban: careless riding (Mar 14-16)

FOCUS
Not a bad little handicap but another steadily run race. The form is not rated too positively.
T/Jkpt: Not won. T/Plt: £55.30 to a £1 stake. Pool:£95,696.73 - 1,261.93 winning tickets T/Qpdt: £11.20 to a £1 stake. Pool:£9,740.00 - 642.00 winning tickets ST

[733]KEMPTON (A.W) (R-H)
Thursday, March 1

OFFICIAL GOING: Standard (polytrack)
Wind: virtually nil Weather: dry

740 32REDBINGO.COM H'CAP 6f (P)
5:40 (5:40) (Class 7) (0-50,50) 4-Y-O+ **£1,455** (£433; £216; £108) **Stalls** Low

Form RPR

-010 **1** **Royal Envoy (IRE)**[14] 572 9-9-1 **48** .... (p) MichaelStainton 3 57
(Paul Howling) *hld up in midfield: rdn and hdwy over 1f out: edgd rt and chal ins fnl f: led fnl 100yds: r.o wl* **12/1**

-020 **2** *1½* **Little Perisher**[6] 687 5-9-2 **49** .... (p) TomMcLaughlin 5 53
(Paul Howling) *led: rdn ent fnl 2f: hdd and no ex fnl 100yds* **14/1**

3432 **3** *hd* **Bobbyow**[14] 572 4-9-2 **49** .... GeorgeBaker 2 53
(Terry Clement) *chsd ldrs: rdn and effrt wl over 1f out: chsd ldr 1f out: chal and carried rt ins fnl f: styd on same pce fnl 100yds* **3/1**[1]

6-66 **4** *1½* **Hambleton**[17] 544 5-8-12 **50** .... (p) JustinNewman(5) 1 49
(Bryan Smart) *bustled along leaving stalls and sn chsng ldrs: rdn wl over 1f out: styd on same pce and a hld fnl f* **4/1**[2]

5630 **5** *½* **Metropolitan Chief**[7] 665 8-8-10 **48** .... CharlesBishop(5) 7 45
(Paul Burgoyne) *stdd s: hld up in midfield: nt clr run ent fnl 2f: swtchd lft and fnlly got clr run jst ins fnl f: styd on but nvr a threat* **16/1**

00-0 **6** *3½* **Sabys Gem (IRE)**[35] 306 4-9-3 **50** .... (b[1]) JimCrowley 10 36
(Michael Wigham) *s.i.s: niggled along early: in tch towards rr: rdn and effrt jst over 2f out: no imp* **9/2**[3]

63-0 **7** *½* **Hollie**[43] 203 4-9-3 **50** .... SteveDrowne 6 34
(Peter Makin) *chsd ldr tl 1f out: fdd ins fnl f* **8/1**

5540 **8** *1¾* **Takajan (IRE)**[6] 690 5-9-2 **49** .... LukeMorris 11 28
(Mark Brisbourne) *a towards rr: rdn and effrt on inner over 2f out: no prog over 1f out: wknd ins fnl f* **9/1**

000- **9** *1½* **Litotes**[120] 7229 4-9-3 **50** .... (p) ShaneKelly 9 24
(Michael Attwater) *dropped in bhd after s: a bhd: n.d* **25/1**

-030 **10** *½* **Littleportnbrandy (IRE)**[7] 662 4-9-1 **48** .... (b) MartinHarley 4 20
(Richard Guest) *rn wout declared tongue tie: chsd ldrs: rdn wl over 2f out: struggling and hmpd ent fnl 2f: wknd qckly wl over 1f out* **16/1**

1m 12.97s (-0.13) **Going Correction** -0.10s/f (Stan) **10** Ran SP% **114.3**
Speed ratings (Par 97): **96,94,93,91,91 86,85,83,81,80**
toteswingers:1&2:£11.40, 1&3:£5.90, 2&3:£4.30 CSF £163.68 CT £634.56 TOTE £11.20: £3.30, £3.90, £1.40; EX 57.80.
Owner James Esau **Bred** Northern Lights Bloodstock **Trained** Lee-On-The-Solent, Hants
■ Stewards' Enquiry : Tom McLaughlin two-day ban: careless riding (Mar 15-16)

FOCUS
A bottom-drawer sprint handicap, run at an average pace and the form makes sense.
Littleportnbrandy(IRE) Official explanation: trainer's rep said he had been unable to fit the tongue strap

741 32REDPOKER.COM H'CAP 1m 4f (P)
6:10 (6:11) (Class 7) (0-50,49) 4-Y-O+ **£1,455** (£433; £216; £108) **Stalls** Centre

Form RPR

6-00 **1** **Dolly Colman (IRE)**[23] 454 4-8-10 **45** .... RichardKingscote 11 54
(Michael Blake) *stdd s: hld up in rr: hdwy over 2f out: switching lft and gd hdwy over 1f out: chsd ldr 1f out: chal ins fnl f: styd on wl to ld towards fin* **14/1**

-000 **2** *hd* **Lytham (IRE)**[24] 450 11-9-2 **49** AdamKirby 7 58
(Tony Carroll) *hld up in tch: edgd out lft over 2f out: trckd ldr 2f out: rdn to ld over 1f out: drvn and hrd pressed ins fnl f: kpt on tl hdd and no ex towards fin* **8/1**

4-45 **3** *4 ½* **The Catenian (IRE)**[22] 468 4-8-10 **45** (v[1]) ShaneKelly 1 46
(John Butler) *stdd s: hld up in last quartet: rdn and gd hdwy on inner jst over 2f out: chsd ldng pair 1f out: no prog and outpcd fnl 150yds* **3/1**[1]

4-00 **4** *5* **Sing Alana Sing**[15] 569 4-8-3 **45** (t) JakePayne[(7)] 5 38
(Bill Turner) *chsd ldr tl led over 2f out: rdn 2f out: hdd over 1f out: wknd fnl f* **50/1**

0-04 **5** *1 ¼* **Olimamu (IRE)**[27] 395 5-8-9 **45** (vt[1]) SimonPearce[(3)] 8 36
(Lydia Pearce) *hld up in tch in midfield: rdn effrt over 2f out: drvn and chsng ldrs wl over 1f out: wknd 1f out* **20/1**

0-02 **6** *shd* **Diamond Twister (USA)**[15] 558 6-9-0 **47** (t) LukeMorris 12 38
(Lisa Williamson) *chsd ldrs: drvn and chsd ldr briefly jst over 2f out: wknd jst over 1f out* **7/1**[2]

0-35 **7** *¾* **Escape Artist**[7] 666 5-9-2 **49** KieranO'Neill 6 39
(John Bridger) *t.k.h early: hld up in tch: rdn 4f out: stl chsng ldrs u.p 2f out: wknd over 1f out* **7/1**[2]

556- **8** *2 ¾* **Always De One**[132] 5666 5-8-12 **45** JamieMackay 9 31
(K F Clutterbuck) *t.k.h early: in tch: stdd bk into midfield 8f out: rdn and no prog over 2f out: plugged on but no threat to ldrs fnl f* **66/1**

0-30 **9** *2 ½* **Farmers Hill**[36] 303 4-8-7 **45** RyanPowell[(3)] 2 27
(Mark Hoad) *chsd ldrs: rdn over 4f out: wknd ent fnl 2f* **10/1**

66-4 **10** *12* **It's Dubai Dolly**[22] 468 6-9-1 **48** (b) SteveDrowne 4 11
(Alastair Lidderdale) *led tl over 2f out: wknd qckly 2f out: wl bhd fnl f* **15/2**[3]

0-60 **11** *24* **Maxiyow (IRE)**[19] 519 4-8-7 **45** (t) DominicFox[(3)] 13
(Terry Clement) *hld up in rr: lost tch over 2f out: t.o fnl 2f* **66/1**

000/ **12** *2 ¾* **Nyetimber (USA)**[693] 1194 6-8-13 **46** ChrisCatlin 14
(Peter Hiatt) *chsd ldrs tl lost pl 5f out: bhd 3f out: t.o fnl 2f* **22/1**

U **Liberty Love (IRE)**[1295] 3862 7-8-12 **45** (b) MartinHarley 10
(Shaun Harley, Ire) *stdd s: hld up in last quartet: hdwy into midfield and stl gng wl whn clipped heels: stmbld and uns rdr over 2f out* **3/1**[1]

2m 33.98s (-0.52) **Going Correction** -0.10s/f (Stan)
WFA 4 from 5yo+ 2lb 13 Ran SP% **127.7**
Speed ratings (Par 97): **97,96,93,90,89 89,89,87,85,77 61,59,**
toteswingers:1&2:£44.20, 1&3:£8.50, 2&3:£8.90 CSF £124.85 CT £438.62 TOTE £19.50: £4.70, £2.70, £1.80; EX 272.00.
Owner K Corke **Bred** Miss Imelda O'Shaughnessy **Trained** Trowbridge, Wilts

FOCUS
Another bottom-level handicap and it looked wide open. They went a sound pace and two drew clear from 1f out.
Dolly Colman(IRE) Official explanation: trainer said, regarding apparent improvement in form, that the filly had benefited by the change of tactics and that the stable seemed to be coming into form.
Olimamu(IRE) Official explanation: jockey said mare was denied a clear run
It's Dubai Dolly Official explanation: jockey said mare had no more to give
Liberty Love(IRE) Official explanation: jockey said gelding accidentally clipped heels of Lytham app 2f out, stumbled and unseated.

742 32RED CASINO MEDIAN AUCTION MAIDEN STKS 6f (P)
6:40 (6:41) (Class 5) 3-5-Y-O **£2,264** (£673; £336; £168) **Stalls** Low

Form RPR

1 **Perfect Fantasy (IRE)** 3-8-5 0 JohnFahy 5 71+
(Clive Cox) *in tch in midfield: hdwy on inner over 2f out: led over 1f out: rn green 1f out: hld on wl fnl f* **9/4**[1]

32-4 **2** *nk* **Heartsong (IRE)**[13] 597 3-8-5 67 MartinLane 4 70
(John Gallagher) *led for 1f: chsd ldng pair: effrt over 2f out: rdn and ev ch over 1f out: sustained chal thrght fnl f: r.o but a jst hld* **3/1**[2]

3-22 **3** *5* **El McGlynn (IRE)**[12] 621 3-8-5 62 (p) LukeMorris 1 54
(John O'Shea) *led for 1f: chsd ldr after tl led again over 2f out: drvn and hdd over 1f out: wknd ins fnl f* **10/3**[3]

4 *1 ½* **Nothing's Simple** 3-8-5 0 LauraPike[(5)] 7 54
(Hugo Palmer) *s.i.s: outpcd in rr and pushed along thrght: kpt on fnl 2f: nvr trbld ldrs* **11/1**

0- **5** *1 ½* **Yarra Valley**[207] 4823 3-8-5 0 JamieMackay 2 44
(Willie Musson) *slowly away: wl bhd: pushed along and switching rt 2f out: kpt on: nvr on terms* **9/2**

0-0 **6** *6* **Buckley Boy**[27] 399 3-8-5 0 CharlesEddery[(5)] 3 30
(K F Clutterbuck) *pushed along early: led after 1f: rdn 1/2-way: hdd over 2f out: sn wknd: bhd fnl f* **40/1**

/0-0 **7** *6* **Mollyow (IRE)**[27] 399 4-8-12 47 (b[1]) HarryPoulton[(7)] 6
(Terry Clement) *in tch in midfield: rdn and struggling over 3f out: wl bhd fnl 2f* **33/1**

1m 13.42s (0.32) **Going Correction** -0.10s/f (Stan)
WFA 3 from 4yo 14lb 7 Ran SP% **110.7**
Speed ratings (Par 103): **93,92,85,83,81 73,65**
toteswingers:1&2:£1.20, 1&3:£1.70, 2&3:£2.00 CSF £8.59 TOTE £2.30: £1.50, £2.80; EX 12.00.
Owner John Drew & Ian M Brown **Bred** Eugene O'Donnell & Balmerino Bloodstock **Trained** Lambourn, Berks

FOCUS
Straightforward AW maiden form.

743 £32 FREE AT 32RED.COM H'CAP 1m (P)
7:10 (7:10) (Class 6) (0-60,60) 3-Y-O **£1,617** (£481; £240; £120) **Stalls** Low

Form RPR

040- **1** **Beauchamp Castle**[64] 7889 3-8-13 **59** (t) NicoleNordblad[(7)] 10 65+
(Hans Adielsson) *hld up in last quartet: swtchd lft and rdn over 2f out: hdwy over 1f out: r.o wl fnl f to ld fnl 75yds: sn in command: readily* **12/1**

05-0 **2** *1 ½* **Tectonic (IRE)**[8] 660 3-9-5 **58** (p) GeorgeBaker 6 60
(Chris Dwyer) *led: rdn ent fnl 2f: drvn and hdd over 1f out: kpt battling on and led again 150yds: hdd and nt pce of wnr fnl 75yds* **12/1**

-056 **3** *1 ¼* **Masters Blazing**[13] 595 3-9-7 **60** (p) AdamKirby 2 59
(John Ryan) *in tch in midfield: reminder 6f out: hdwy towards inner over 2f out: chsd ldrs 1f out: styd on same pce ins fnl f* **10/1**[3]

-465 **4** *shd* **Auntie Kathryn (IRE)**[36] 294 3-8-2 **46** RaulDaSilva[(5)] 7 45
(Stuart Williams) *chsd ldrs: rdn to press ldr 2f out: drvn ahd over 1f out: hdd and no ex ins fnl f: wknd towards fin* **10/1**[3]

000- **5** *1* **Song Of Joy (IRE)**[112] 7343 3-9-7 **60** (bt[1]) LukeMorris 4 57
(Paul D'Arcy) *s.i.s: rdn along early: bhd: effrt over 2f out: drvn and hdwy over 1f out: kpt on fnl 150yds but nvr gng pce to chal* **11/2**[2]

-550 **6** *2 ¾* **Umph (IRE)**[8] 660 3-9-3 **56** RichardThomas 3 46
(David Evans) *hld up in rr: hdwy towards inner 2f out: no imp 1f out: styd on same pce and wl hld fnl f* **25/1**

3120 **7** *shd* **Lana (IRE)**[8] 660 3-9-1 **59** MatthewCosham[(5)] 5 49
(David Evans) *in tch: rdn ent fnl 2f: chsd ldrs and drvn over 1f out: unable qck and wknd ins fnl f* **14/1**

0-55 **8** *1* **Waspy**[15] 571 3-8-7 **46** ChrisCatlin 8 34
(Ed Dunlop) *in tch: rdn and unable qck 2f out: drvn over 1f out: wknd ins fnl f* **12/1**

6-32 **9** *1 ¾* **Purple Affair (IRE)**[8] 660 3-9-4 **60** RyanPowell[(3)] 9 44
(J S Moore) *chsd ldrs: rdn and fnd little ent fnl 2f: edgd lft and wknd over 1f out* **5/4**[1]

-005 **10** *1 ¼* **Frock (IRE)**[19] 518 3-9-7 **60** JamieMackay 11 41
(Sylvester Kirk) *a in rr: rdn and no prog over 2f out: n.d* **16/1**

00-5 **11** *5* **Echo Of Thunder (IRE)**[43] 204 3-8-12 **51** SteveDrowne 1 20
(Nick Littmoden) *chsd ldrs: effrt u.p on inner jst over 2f out: wknd over 1f out: fdd fnl f* **33/1**

3-05 **12** *¾* **Canning Vale**[9] 641 3-9-2 **55** MartinHarley 13 23
(Julia Feilden) *pressed ldr tl drvn over 2f out: wknd wl over 1f out: bhd fnl f* **66/1**

1m 39.46s (-0.34) **Going Correction** -0.10s/f (Stan) 12 Ran SP% **121.9**
Speed ratings (Par 96): **97,95,94,94,93 90,90,89,87,86 81,80**
toteswingers:1&2:£18.50, 1&3:£14.70, 2&3:£16.30 CSF £149.85 CT £1528.27 TOTE £18.40: £3.70, £4.10, £2.30; EX 135.60.
Owner Erik Penser **Bred** Erik Penser **Trained** Kingston Lisle, Oxon

FOCUS
A weak 3-y-o handicap, run at a fair pace.
Purple Affair(IRE) Official explanation: jockey said gelding hung left

744 32REDBET.COM H'CAP 1m (P)
7:40 (7:41) (Class 6) (0-55,55) 4-Y-0+ **£1,617** (£481; £240; £120) **Stalls** Low

Form RPR

4 **1** **Esytopolishadimond (IRE)**[27] 413 5-8-10 **47** JimCrowley 12 56
(Michael J Browne, Ire) *hld up in midfield: swtchd lft and effrt over 2f out: hdwy u.p over 1f out: r.o wl fnl f to ld towards fin* **7/2**[1]

43-0 **2** *½* **Baby Driver**[56] 45 4-8-12 **49** DaneO'Neill 6 57
(Tony Newcombe) *chsd ldrs: wnt 2nd over 4f out: led 2f out and sn clr: drvn ins fnl f: edgd lft fnl 100yds: hdd and no ex towards fin* **8/1**

2125 **3** *¾* **Emerald Royal**[7] 662 4-9-0 **51** LukeMorris 3 57
(Eric Wheeler) *dwlt: bhd: hdwy on inner and rdn over 2f out: swtchd lft and r.o to chse ldrs 1f out: kpt on same pce u.p fnl 100yds* **5/1**[3]

-653 **4** *2 ½* **Teen Ager (FR)**[7] 666 8-8-12 **49** LiamKeniry 5 50
(Paul Burgoyne) *pushed along early: in tch in midfield: hdwy to chse ldrs and gng wl over 1f out: rdn to chse wnr over 1f out: no imp: wknd fnl 100yds* **15/2**

60-6 **5** *3* **Princess Gail**[10] 633 4-9-4 **55** ShaneKelly 4 49
(Mark Brisbourne) *hld up towards rr: hdwy towards inner over 2f out: swtchd lft over 1f out: drvn and no prog 1f out: wknd ins fnl f* **14/1**

00-3 **6** *1 ¼* **Tanforan**[10] 633 10-9-4 **55** RussKennemore 9 46
(Brian Baugh) *dwlt: towards rr: rdn and effrt over 2f out: no imp over 1f out* **14/1**

6-41 **7** *2 ¼* **Rigid**[8] 653 5-8-4 **48** GeorgeDowning[(7)] 2 34
(Tony Carroll) *in tch: rdn and unable qck jst over 2f out: wknd over 1f out: wl hld fnl f* **4/1**[2]

1302 **8** *1 ¾* **Querido (GER)**[7] 666 8-9-1 **55** (tp) RobertLButler[(3)] 14 37
(Paddy Butler) *hld up towards rr: rdn and effrt over 2f out: no imp: nvr trbld ldrs* **16/1**

00-0 **9** *shd* **Inquisitress**[8] 653 8-8-9 **46** oh1 KieranO'Neill 1 27
(John Bridger) *stdd after s: hld up in tch: rdn and effrt to chse ldr 2f out: drvn and no imp over 1f out: fdd 1f out* **33/1**

06-4 **10** *2 ¼* **Avalon Bay**[58] 21 4-8-12 **52** (t) RyanClark[(3)] 13 28
(Pat Eddery) *in tch on outer: lost pl and rdn wl over 2f out: sn struggling: no threat to ldrs fnl 2f* **20/1**

2402 **11** *½* **Very Well Red**[8] 653 9-8-12 **49** ChrisCatlin 10 24
(Peter Hiatt) *chsd ldr until over 4f out: rdn and losing pl over 3f out: bhd fnl 2f* **16/1**

0-00 **12** *¾* **Farmers Dream (IRE)**[21] 483 5-8-6 **46** oh1 DominicFox[(3)] 7 19
(Richard Price) *s.i.s: a in rr: n.d* **50/1**

0000 **13** *8* **Royal Intruder**[12] 623 7-9-2 **53** (e[1]) MartinHarley 8 8
(Richard Guest) *led and sn clr: hdd 2f out: fdd over 1f out: wl bhd fnl f* **25/1**

1m 38.53s (-1.27) **Going Correction** -0.10s/f (Stan) 13 Ran SP% **120.4**
Speed ratings (Par 101): **102,101,100,98,95 94,91,90,89,87 87,86,78**
toteswingers:1&2:£7.30, 1&3:£4.20, 2&3:£7.00 CSF £30.65 CT £147.26 TOTE £4.60: £1.60, £2.90, £2.10; EX 41.60.
Owner Michael J Browne **Bred** Oak Lodge Bloodstock **Trained** Cashel, Co. Tipperary

FOCUS
An ordinary handicap, run at a solid pace that suited the closers.

745 32RED H'CAP 1m 3f (P)
8:10 (8:10) (Class 4) (0-85,85) 4-Y-0+ **£4,075** (£1,212; £606; £303) **Stalls** Low

Form RPR

0-52 **1** **Sand Skier**[5] 714 5-8-2 **73** NicoleNordblad[(7)] 2 81
(Hans Adielsson) *hld up wl in tch: wnt 2nd over 2f out: rdn to ld wl over 1f out: edgd lft fr over 1f out: kpt on wl fnl f* **11/4**[2]

50-2 **2** *½* **Franco Is My Name**[26] 427 6-9-7 **85** JohnFahy 7 92
(Peter Hedger) *hld up in tch in last trio: hdwy to chse ldrs 2f out: rdn to press wnr jst over 1f out: carried lft but nt qckn u.p: hung lft and hld towards fin* **7/4**[1]

005- **3** *2 ¼* **Mataaleb**[172] 5963 5-9-2 **83** SimonPearce[(3)] 4 86
(Lydia Pearce) *t.k.h: hld up in last trio: nt clr run over 2f out: swtchd lft 2f out: drvn and hdwy over 1f out: chsd ldng pair ent fnl f: kpt on but no imp fnl f* **15/2**

26-6 **4** *6* **Brouhaha**[20] 501 8-9-0 **78** RichardKingscote 5 70
(Tom Dascombe) *hld up in last: rdn jst over 2f out: sme hdwy to go 4th 1f out: no imp fnl f* **13/2**[3]

620- **5** *8* **Scamperdale**[85] 7651 10-9-2 **80** RussKennemore 3 58
(Brian Baugh) *chsd ldr after 1f: rdn to ld and qcknd wl over 2f out: hdd wl over 1f out: sn outpcd: wknd 1f out* **33/1**

0-02 **6** *3 ¼* **Battleoftrafalgar**[12] 625 5-8-7 **76** (b) MarkCoumbe[(5)] 6 48
(Michael Attwater) *led at stdy gallop: hdd and rdn wl over 2f out: struggling jst over 2f out: wknd over 1f out* **10/1**

-140 **7** *3 ¼* **Shieldmaiden (USA)**[34] 342 4-9-0 **79** (b) JoeFanning 1 45
(Mark Johnston) *t.k.h: chsd ldrs: rdn and effrt on inner over 2f out: sn struggling: wknd wl over 1f out* **7/1**

2m 20.45s (-1.45) **Going Correction** -0.10s/f (Stan)
WFA 4 from 5yo+ 1lb 7 Ran SP% **112.7**
Speed ratings (Par 105): **101,100,99,94,88 86,84**
toteswingers:1&2:£2.30, 1&3:£5.30, 2&3:£3.10 CSF £7.72 TOTE £4.50: £1.70, £1.40; EX 9.40.
Owner Erik Penser **Bred** Rabbah Bloodstock Limited **Trained** Kingston Lisle, Oxon

FOCUS
This fair handicap was run at a modest pace and most took time to settle. The principals were clear at the finish.

746 32RED.COM H'CAP 7f (P)
8:40 (8:40) (Class 5) (0-75,75) 4-Y-0+ **£2,264** (£673; £336; £168) **Stalls** Low

Form RPR
124- **1** **Ducal**[82] 7716 4-9-7 **75** JohnFahy 3 88
(Mike Murphy) *hld up in last quartet: hdwy over 2f out: clsd to chse ldrs over 1f out: rdn to chal ins fnl f: r.o wl to ld fnl 50yds* **3/1**[1]
3-32 **2** ½ **Russian Ice**[22] 470 4-9-7 **75** (b) ShaneKelly 10 86
(Dean Ivory) *racd off the pce in midfield: hdwy to chse ldrs 2f out: drvn to chal ent fnl f: led ins fnl f: sn hrd pressed: kpt on tl hdd and no ex fnl 50yds* **8/1**[3]
/20- **3** 2¼ **Amazon Twilight**[257] 3172 4-9-4 **72** AdamKirby 4 77
(Brett Johnson) *chsd ldrs: rdn and effrt to chal 2f out: led jst over 1f out tl hdd ins fnl f: outpcd by ldng pair after: kpt on for clr 3rd* **12/1**
0-03 **4** 2¼ **She Ain't A Saint**[19] 520 4-9-4 **72** (b) LukeMorris 6 71
(Jane Chapple-Hyam) *chsd ldrs: rdn and chal on inner jst over 2f out: led wl over 1f out tl hdd jst over 1f out: wknd ins fnl f* **9/2**[2]
2-50 **5** 2¼ **Archelao (IRE)**[15] 570 4-9-0 **68** AmirQuinn 7 61
(Richard Rowe) *racd in midfield and pushed along: rdn and effrt over 2f out: kpt on steadily fr over 1f out: nvr gng pce to threaten ldrs* **20/1**
0203 **6** *nse* **Dickie Le Davoir**[7] 670 8-8-4 **63** (v) CharlesEddery(5) 13 56
(Richard Guest) *dwlt and swtchd rt after s: bhd: rdn and c wd wl over 2f out: styd on past btn horses fr over 1f out: nvr trbld ldrs* **20/1**
0-15 **7** ½ **Hip Hip Hooray**[36] 302 6-8-13 **67** KieranO'Neill 1 58
(Luke Dace) *dwlt: bhd: rdn and effrt whn nt clr run over 2f out: styd on past btn horses fr over 1f out: nvr trbld ldrs* **16/1**
3313 **8** ½ **Lastkingofscotland (IRE)**[7] 669 6-9-5 **73** (b) LiamKeniry 12 63
(Conor Dore) *racd freely: chsd ldr tl pushed ahd ent fnl 2f: hdd wl over 1f out: wknd ent fnl f: fdd* **8/1**[3]
3-33 **9** 1½ **Tiradito (USA)**[12] 626 5-9-5 **73** (p) GeorgeBaker 11 59
(Michael Attwater) *racd off the pce in midfield: rdn over 2f out: no prog: nvr trbld ldrs* **8/1**[3]
3-04 **10** 2½ **Hoover**[12] 624 4-9-0 **68** JimCrowley 9 47
(Jim Boyle) *in tch: rdn and unable qck over 2f out: wknd wl over 1f out: wl btn fnl f* **17/2**
/63- **11** ½ **Decimate**[170] 6034 4-9-2 **70** MartinHarley 2 48
(Andrew Reid) *in tch: rdn and unable qck wl over 2f out: wknd 2f out: wl btn fnl f* **33/1**
00-5 **12** *shd* **Perfect Ch'I (IRE)**[50] 124 5-8-13 **67** (t) JoeFanning 5 45
(Ian Wood) *led tl ent fnl 2f: sn wknd: fdd over 1f out* **14/1**
0110 **13** 1¼ **Satwa Laird**[12] 626 6-8-13 **72** DavidKenny(5) 8 46
(Conor Dore) *rdr struggling to remove hood s and slowly away: a bhd* **14/1**

1m 24.48s (-1.52) **Going Correction** -0.10s/f (Stan) **13** Ran SP% **126.4**
Speed ratings (Par 103): **104,103,100,98,95 95,95,94,92,89 89,89,87**
toteswingers:1&2:£9.10, 1&3:£13.80, 2&3:£17.40 CSF £28.16 CT £276.03 TOTE £2.70: £1.70, £2.70, £3.90; EX 33.60.
Owner The Icebreakers **Bred** Cheveley Park Stud Ltd **Trained** Westoning, Beds

FOCUS
A competitive handicap for the class, run at a solid pace.
Tiradito(USA) Official explanation: jockey said gelding hung left throughout
Satwa Laird Official explanation: jockey said it took three attempts to remove blindfold which was stuck on the bridle and gelding was slow away
T/Jkpt: Pool of £477,696.62 carried forward to Newbury, 2nd March T/Plt: £317.70 to a £1 stake. Pool:£116,040.55 - 266.62 winning tickets T/Qpdt: £101.80 to a £1 stake. Pool:£9,568.24 - 69.50 winning tickets SP

670 SOUTHWELL (L-H)
Thursday, March 1

OFFICIAL GOING: Standard
Wind: Virtually nil Weather: Fine and dry

747 LADBROKES MOBILE H'CAP 1m (F)
2:20 (4:25) (Class 5) (0-75,68) 3-Y-0 **£2,264** (£673; £336; £168) **Stalls** Low

Form RPR
40-2 **1** **Chatterati (USA)**[36] 291 3-9-7 **68** JoeFanning 4 79
(Mark Johnston) *trckd ldng pair on outer: hdwy 3f out: led wl over 1f out: rdn and styd on fnl f* **4/1**[3]
-313 **2** 2 **Availed Speaker (IRE)**[17] 547 3-9-1 **65** LeeTopliss(3) 3 71
(Richard Fahey) *cl up: led after 2f: hdd over 2f out and sn rdn: rallied to chse wnr appr fnl f: edgd rt and kpt on same pce last 100yds* **13/8**[1]
2111 **3** 2¼ **Samasana (IRE)**[9] 641 3-9-7 **68** 6ex TonyHamilton 5 69
(Ian Wood) *led 2f: cl up: rdn to ld again over 2f out: hdd wl over 1f out: sn drvn and one pce appr fnl f* **7/4**[2]
-033 **4** 3¼ **Outlaw Torn (IRE)**[19] 534 3-8-11 **58** (e) WilliamCarson 2 51
(Richard Guest) *hld up: hdwy over 3f out: sn rdn along and outpcd fnl 2f* **16/1**
23-4 **5** 2 **Bapak Pintar**[57] 32 3-9-5 **66** PaulMulrennan 1 55
(Kevin Ryan) *chsd ldrs on inner: rdn along over 3f out: sn outpcd* **15/2**

1m 44.0s (0.30) **Going Correction** 0.0s/f (Stan) **5** Ran SP% **112.1**
Speed ratings (Par 98): **98,96,93,90,88**
CSF £11.21 TOTE £5.00: £2.00, £1.10; EX 13.70.
Owner Sheikh Hamdan Bin Mohammed Al Maktoum **Bred** Darley **Trained** Middleham Moor, N Yorks

FOCUS
A modest small-field 3yo handicap run at a steady tempo and the winning time was comparatively slow.
Samasana(IRE) Official explanation: jockey said filly became upset at start

748 LADBROKES MOBILE CLAIMING STKS 7f (F)
2:50 (4:25) (Class 6) 3-Y-0 **£1,704** (£503; £251) **Stalls** Low

Form RPR
6-44 **1** **Flying Pickets (IRE)**[12] 619 3-9-5 **70** (be) JohnFahy 5 73
(Alan McCabe) *reminders s and sn cl up: led wl over 2f out: rdn and hung lft over 1f out: hdd ins fnl f: drvn and rallied to ld nr fin* **9/2**[3]
2342 **2** *nse* **One More Roman (IRE)**[14] 583 3-8-11 **61** (vt[1]) RobertWinston 4 65
(Gay Kelleway) *trckd ldrs on outer: hdwy over 2f out: chal wl over 1f out: sn rdn and carried hd high: slt ld ins fnl f: hdd and no ex nr fin* **7/2**[2]
3323 **3** 13 **First Bid**[8] 660 3-8-13 **63** (b) PaulMulrennan 2 32
(James Given) *chsd ldrs: rdn along 3f out: swtchd rt over 2f out and sn outpcd* **13/8**[1]
06-3 **4** 7 **Bengaline**[23] 462 3-8-6 **59** (b[1]) MarkCoumbe(5) 3 11
(Scott Dixon) *t.k.h: sn led: rdn along and hdd wl over 2f out: sn wknd* **10/1**
12-2 **5** 2 **Point At Issue (IRE)**[60] 6 3-9-5 **62** (b) AndrewMullen 1 14
(David Nicholls) *cl up on inner: rdn along after 2f out: sn lost pl and bhd* **7/2**[2]

1m 30.7s (0.40) **Going Correction** 0.0s/f (Stan) **5** Ran SP% **109.8**
Speed ratings (Par 96): **97,96,82,74,71**
CSF £19.84 TOTE £7.10: £4.00, £1.70; EX 23.20.
Owner Tariq Al Nisf **Bred** Richard Frayne **Trained** Averham Park, Notts

FOCUS
A competitive claimer on paper and they went a sensible gallop from the outset. The winning time was respectable for the grade.
Point At Issue(IRE) Official explanation: jockey said gelding was never travelling

749 SOUTHWELL-RACECOURSE.CO.UK H'CAP 5f (F)
3:20 (4:25) (Class 5) (0-75,70) 3-Y-0 **£2,264** (£673; £336; £168) **Stalls** High

Form RPR
0-11 **1** **Bella Ophelia (IRE)**[9] 645 3-9-6 **70** 6ex JimmyFortune 4 82+
(Hughie Morrison) *qckly away and stdd sn after s: trckd ldrs: hdwy to ld over 2f out: rdn clr over 1f out: kpt on strly* **11/8**[1]
-612 **2** 2¼ **Reve Du Jour (IRE)**[9] 645 3-8-11 **64** SeanLevey(3) 7 67
(Alan McCabe) *sn led: hdd over 2f out and sn rdn: drvn and kpt on ins fnl f* **7/1**
21-3 **3** ½ **Code Six (IRE)**[10] 637 3-9-2 **66** PaulMulrennan 1 67
(Bryan Smart) *chsd ldrs on outer: rdn along 2f out: kpt on same pce appr fnl f* **11/4**[2]
613- **4** 1 **Scrooby Doo**[129] 7067 3-9-1 **70** MarkCoumbe(5) 2 67
(Scott Dixon) *prom: rdn wl over 1f out: sn one pce* **13/2**[3]
4126 **5** ½ **Chapellerie (IRE)**[8] 659 3-9-2 **66** WilliamCarson 3 62
(Richard Guest) *s.i.s and bhd: swtchd lft to far rail bef 1/2-way: styd on u.p fr over 1f out: n.d* **10/1**
41-4 **6** ¾ **Chester'Slittlegem (IRE)**[46] 189 3-9-2 **66** JohnFahy 5 59
(Ed de Giles) *chsd ldrs: n.m.r and lost pl after 2f: bhd after* **20/1**
6205 **7** 3½ **Dawn Lightning**[22] 469 3-8-7 **64** (p) DarrenEgan(7) 6 44
(Alan McCabe) *chsd ldrs: rdn along 1/2-way: sn outpcd* **20/1**

1m 0.5s (0.80) **Going Correction** +0.25s/f (Slow) **7** Ran SP% **113.2**
Speed ratings (Par 98): **103,99,98,97,96 95,89**
CSF £11.58 TOTE £2.10: £1.30, £3.40; EX 5.50.
Owner Mrs Belinda Scott & Partners **Bred** Tally-Ho Stud **Trained** East Ilsley, Berks

FOCUS
A handicap that lacked strength in depth, but the pace was honest and the winner looks a useful filly on this surface.

750 LADBROKES MOBILE MEDIAN AUCTION MAIDEN STKS 5f (F)
3:50 (4:25) (Class 5) 3-4-Y-0 **£2,264** (£673; £336; £168) **Stalls** High

Form RPR
-200 **1** **Ladydolly**[16] 551 4-9-1 **51** (p) DarrenEgan(7) 3 63
(Roy Brotherton) *trckd ldrs: hdwy 2f out: led over 1f out: rdn out* **7/2**[3]
03-4 **2** 1 **How Sweet It Is (IRE)**[42] 214 3-8-9 **61** WilliamCarson 1 53
(James Bethell) *cl up on outer: ev ch 2f out: sn rdn and chsd wnr appr fnl f: no imp towards fin* **2/1**[1]
4-33 **3** 2½ **Look At Me Now**[8] 657 3-9-0 **67** (v) StephenCraine 6 49
(Jim Boyle) *dwlt: sn cl up: led 1/2-way: rdn 2f out: drvn and hdd over 1f out: wknd fnl f* **4/1**
600- **4** 4½ **Whip It In (IRE)**[128] 7072 3-8-3 **40** ow1 NedCurtis(7) 5 29
(Paul Midgley) *a towards rr* **33/1**
63- **5** 3¾ **Skystream (IRE)**[71] 7845 4-9-8 **52** TonyHamilton 4 21
(Ian Semple) *cl up: ev ch 2f out: sn rdn and wknd* **5/2**[2]
-655 **6** 6 **Miss Bloom**[31] 357 3-8-9 **35** AndrewMullen 2
(Garry Woodward) *cl up: rdn along and wkng whn hmpd and lost pl wl over 1f out* **50/1**

1m 1.19s (1.49) **Going Correction** +0.25s/f (Slow)
WFA 3 from 4yo 13lb **6** Ran SP% **109.0**
Speed ratings (Par 103): **98,96,92,85,79 69**
toteswingers:1&2:£1.80, 1&3:£2.60, 2&3:£1.40 CSF £10.27 TOTE £5.70: £2.90, £1.20; EX 12.50.
Owner P S J Croft **Bred** Paul Croft **Trained** Elmley Castle, Worcs

FOCUS
A low-class maiden for 3-4yos run a decent pace throughout, and the winning time was fair for the grade.

751 FOLLOW SOUTHWELL ON TWITTER H'CAP 1m 4f (F)
4:20 (4:25) (Class 4) (0-85,82) 4-Y-0+ **£4,204** (£1,251; £625; £312) **Stalls** Low

Form RPR
5-31 **1** **Admirable Duque (IRE)**[37] 285 6-9-0 **82** (be) JoshBaudains(7) 11 94+
(Dominic Ffrench Davis) *hld up in midfield: gd hdwy over 3f out: chsd ldng pair 2f out: rdn to ld and hung bdly lft appr fnl f: sn clr* **10/1**
2432 **2** 3¾ **The Lock Master (IRE)**[14] 584 5-9-5 **80** NeilChalmers 9 85
(Michael Appleby) *hld up in rr: stdy hdwy 5f out: slt ld 3f out and wd st: rdn 2f out: hdd and drvn appr fnl f: kpt on: no ch w wnr* **7/1**
0-52 **3** *nk* **Big Creek (IRE)**[46] 187 5-9-5 **80** JimmyFortune 8 84
(Jeremy Noseda) *hld up: stdy hdwy to trck ldrs 1/2-way: effrt to dispute ld wl over 2f out: sn rdn and ev ch tl drvn and one pce ent fnl f* **9/4**[1]
-453 **4** 1 **Jawaab (IRE)**[7] 672 8-8-0 **68** oh1 (e) DarrenEgan(7) 6 71
(Richard Guest) *hld up and bhd: hdwy 4f out: rdn along 3f out: styd on fnl 2f: nrst fin* **25/1**
0335 **5** 11 **Follow The Flag (IRE)**[7] 674 8-9-3 **81** (be) SeanLevey(3) 7 66
(Alan McCabe) *towards rr: pushed along 5f out: rdn and sme hdwy 3f out: n.d* **20/1**
4-12 **6** 2¼ **Tricksofthetrade (IRE)**[14] 582 6-9-2 **77** PJMcDonald 2 59
(Alan Swinbank) *cl up: led 4f out: rdn along and hdd 3f out: grad wknd fnl 2f* **4/1**[2]
1-05 **7** 12 **Son Vida (IRE)**[14] 584 4-9-1 **78** JoeFanning 1 40
(Mark Johnston) *led: rdn along and hdd 4f out: wknd over 3f out* **14/1**
01-5 **8** ½ **Union Island (IRE)**[18] 285 6-9-0 **78** DaleSwift(3) 3 40
(Brian Ellison) *chsd ldrs: rdn along over 4f out: sn wknd* **8/1**
1-32 **9** 11 **Mazij**[20] 501 4-9-0 **77** WilliamCarson 5 21
(Peter Hiatt) *chsd ldrs: rdn along 4f out: wknd 3f out* **5/1**[3]
01-5 **10** 10 **Beau Fighter**[12] 625 7-8-11 **72** (p) RobertWinston 4
(Gary Moore) *trckd ldrs: rdn along 5f out: sn wknd* **25/1**

The Form Book Flat, Raceform Ltd, Compton, RG20 6NL

43-6 **11** 3 ¾ **Pertemps Networks**[13] 601 8-9-2 77 PaddyAspell 10
(Michael Easterby) *chsd ldng pair: pushed along 1/2-way: wknd over 4f out* **50/1**

2m 38.75s (-2.25) **Going Correction** 0.0s/f (Stan)
WFA 4 from 5yo+ 2lb 11 Ran SP% **121.2**
Speed ratings (Par 105): **107,104,104,103,96 94,86,86,79,72 69**
toteswingers:1&2:£16.70, 1&3:£7.50, 2&3:£4.80 CSF £77.17 CT £217.27 TOTE £11.30: £3.60, £3.40, £1.50; EX 79.90 TRIFECTA Not won..
Owner Mrs J E Taylor **Bred** Airlie Stud And R N Clay **Trained** Lambourn, Berks

FOCUS
Son Vida and Tricksofthetrade set a strong pace and it was no surprise they weakened out of contention in a race where they finished well strung out.
Big Creek(IRE) Official explanation: jockey said saddle slipped

752 MEMBERSHIP OF SOUTHWELL GOLF CLUB H'CAP 6f (F)
4:50 (4:50) (Class 6) (0-65,65) 4-Y-0+ **£1,617** (£481; £240; £120) **Stalls** Low

Form				RPR
-313	**1**		**Prince Of Vasa (IRE)**[20] 496 5-9-4 62 AndrewMullen 9 (Michael Smith) *led: rdn along 2f out: jnd and drvn over 1f out: hdd narrowly ins fnl f: rallied gamely to ld again towards fin* **85/40**[1]	72
5460	**2**	*nk*	**Joe Le Taxi (IRE)**[12] 623 4-9-3 61 JoeFanning 5 (Mark Johnston) *trckd ldrs on inner: smooth hdwy over 2f out: chal over 1f out: rdn to ld narrowly ins fnl f: hdd and no ex towards fin* **4/1**[3]	70
4362	**3**	*2 ½*	**Ace Of Spies (IRE)**[7] 670 7-9-0 58 JimmyFortune 7 (Conor Dore) *trckd ldng pair: hdwy on outer and cl up 3f out: rdn over 2f out and ev ch tl drvn and one pce ent fnl f* **11/4**[2]	59
03-5	**4**	*2 ¼*	**Indian Arrow**[20] 498 4-8-11 58 DaleSwift(3) 8 (John Quinn) *dwlt: in tch on outer: hdwy and wd st: rdn to chse ldrs 2f out: no imp over 1f out* **12/1**	52
320	**5**	*8*	**Gracie's Gift (IRE)**[16] 551 10-8-8 52 (v) WilliamCarson 1 (Richard Guest) *towards rr and rdn along bef 1/2-way: sme hdwy over 2f out: sn edgd lft and n.d* **11/1**	20
-515	**6**	*¾*	**Ridgeway Hawk**[28] 385 4-8-11 60 (v) LeeNewnes(5) 3 (Mark Usher) *awkward s: sn rdn along and a towards rr* **8/1**	26
004-	**7**	*8*	**Whiskey Junction**[141] 6793 8-9-4 65 AdamBeschizza(3) 2 (Michael Quinn) *a towards rr* **16/1**	
200-	**8**	*10*	**Amno Dancer (IRE)**[272] 2692 5-8-12 56 TonyHamilton 4 (Ian Semple) *cl up on inner: rdn along 3f out: sn wknd* **25/1**	

1m 16.69s (0.19) **Going Correction** 0.0s/f (Stan) 8 Ran SP% **115.5**
Speed ratings (Par 101): **98,97,94,91,80 79,68,55**
toteswingers:1&2:£3.00, 1&3:£2.30, 2&3:£3.80 CSF £11.07 CT £23.30 TOTE £4.10: £2.40, £1.70, £1.90; EX 12.10 TRIFECTA Pool: £574.65 - 25.68 winning units..
Owner Mrs Sandra Smith **Bred** E O'Gorman **Trained** Kirkheaton, Northumberland

FOCUS
Not many got into this moderate handicap, and those that raced prominently dominated the finish.

753 LADBROKES APPRENTICE H'CAP 1m (F)
5:20 (5:20) (Class 5) (0-75,75) 4-Y-0+ **£2,264** (£673; £336; £168) **Stalls** Low

Form				RPR
14	**1**		**Colour Guard**[7] 674 4-9-7 75 DarylByrne 4 (Mark Johnston) *dwlt: sn trcking ldng pair: chal and green on outer over 3f out: sn rdn to ld 3f out: rn green 2f out: rdn clr appr fnl f: kpt on* **4/9**[1]	89+
066-	**2**	*3*	**Sir George (IRE)**[152] 6533 7-9-1 74 JacobButterfield(5) 6 (Ollie Pears) *cl up: disp ld 3f out and ev ch tl rdn wl over 1f out and kpt on same pce appr fnl f* **6/1**[2]	78
4000	**3**	*6*	**Georgebernardshaw (IRE)**[6] 694 7-9-1 72 DarrenEgan(3) 1 (Richard Guest) *in tch: rdn along over 3f out: plugged on same pce fnl 2f: n.d* **10/1**	62
-153	**4**	*5*	**General Tufto**[9] 646 7-8-5 62 (b) IanBurns(3) 2 (Charles Smith) *sn outpcd: a bhd* **8/1**[3]	41
0-00	**5**	*6*	**Amethyst Dawn (IRE)**[29] 378 6-8-13 70 (tp) NoelGarbutt(3) 3 (Andrew Reid) *led: rdn along 4f out: hdd 3f out and sn wknd* **16/1**	35

1m 44.09s (0.39) **Going Correction** 0.0s/f (Stan) 5 Ran SP% **109.6**
Speed ratings (Par 103): **98,95,89,84,78**
CSF £3.54 TOTE £1.70: £1.10, £2.00; EX 3.00.
Owner Sheikh Hamdan Bin Mohammed Al Maktoum **Bred** Meon Valley Stud **Trained** Middleham Moor, N Yorks

FOCUS
A modest handicap restricted to apprentice jockeys, run at a sensible gallop.
T/Plt: £55.70 to a £1 stake. Pool:£62,635.69 - 820.84 winning tickets T/Qpdt: £4.90 to a £1 stake. Pool:£5,464.67 - 819.54 winning tickets JR

677 MEYDAN (L-H)
Thursday, March 1

OFFICIAL GOING: Tapeta: standard; turf: round course - good; straight course - good to firm

754a AL DANA VISA INFINITE CARD (CONDITIONS RACE) (TURF) 7f
2:30 (2:30) 3-Y-0
£19,354 (£6,451; £3,225; £1,612; £967; £645)

			RPR
1		**Counterglow (IRE)**[169] 6055 3-8-9 89 FrankieDettori 4 (Mahmood Al Zarooni) *settled in rr: smooth prog 3f out: led cl home* **11/4**[1]	92+
2	*shd*	**Right To Dream (IRE)**[27] 417 3-8-9 97 (b) KierenFallon 7 (Brian Meehan) *trckd ldr: led 1 1/2f out: hdd cl home* **5/1**	92
3	*2*	**Colorful Notion (IRE)**[7] 680 3-8-5 80 MircoDemuro 1 (Marco Botti) *in rr of mid-div: kpt on same pce fnl 1 1/2f* **20/1**	83
4	*1 ¾*	**Factory Time (IRE)**[7] 679 3-8-9 100 (t) SilvestreDeSousa 6 (A Al Raihe, UAE) *sn led: hdd & wknd 1 1/2f out* **3/1**[2]	82
5	*shd*	**Moon Spun (SAF)**[7] 680 4-9-0 98 RyanMoore 3 (H J Brown, South Africa) *mid-div: chsd ldrs 2 1/2f out: nt qckn fnl 1 1/2f* **6/1**	75
6	*2 ¾*	**Fiscal**[7] 679 3-8-9 104 AndreaAtzeni 5 (M Al Jahouri, UAE) *mid-div: rdn 3f out: one pce fnl 1 1/2f* **7/2**[3]	74
7	*20*	**Bonne Idee (FR)**[53] 3-8-5 90 TadhgO'Shea 2 (E Charpy, UAE) *racd in rr: kpt on same pce fnl 1 1/2f* **25/1**	16

1m 25.82s (85.82)
WFA 3 from 4yo 16lb 7 Ran SP% **113.4**
CSF: £16.60..
Owner Godolphin **Bred** Colin Kennedy **Trained** Newmarket, Suffolk

FOCUS
Rail out 15m on turf track. Not a particularly strong race on the face of it.

NOTEBOOK
Counterglow(IRE) has been gelded since he finished third behind Graphic and Noor Zabeel in a conditions race at Kempton on his third start last year. Although he hadn't run this season, the runner-up from that race has run with credit in pattern races at this track, and on a line through that colt he was entitled to go well in this company. Brought with a challenge down the wide outside, he had to battle, but didn't flinch, unlike last year, and at the line his nose was just in front. (op 2-1)
Right To Dream(IRE) rallied when the winner drew up alongside, but was just denied on the line. He reversed C&D form with Factory Time, who was much better drawn than him the last time they met. (tchd 11-2)
Colorful Notion(IRE) looked to have a bit to find at this level but she ran well, appreciating the drop back in distance. She'd hgave finished closer but for running into the back of the weakening Factory Time with over a furlong to go.
Factory Time(IRE) did a bit too much early on out in front and didn't see his race out. He was weakening when hampered by the hanging Right To Dream. (op 4-1)
Moon Spun(SAF) was a shade disappointing but the drop back in trip proved to be against her.

755a AL DANA WEALTH (H'CAP) (TAPETA) 1m 2f
3:05 (3:05) (95-113,113) 3-Y-0+
£58,064 (£19,354; £9,677; £4,838; £2,903; £1,935)

			RPR
1		**Bronze Cannon (USA)**[21] 484 7-8-11 105 ow1(t) ChristopheSoumillon 2 (H J Brown, South Africa) *in rr of mid-div: smooth prog 3f out: led 1 1/2f out: comf* **10/1**	109+
2	*2 ¼*	**Sarrsar**[7] 677 5-9-2 109 (vt) MickaelBarzalona 6 (Saeed Bin Suroor) *in rr of mid-div: r.o fnl 1 1/2f: nrst fin* **7/1**	110
3	*2 ¼*	**Yaa Wayl (IRE)**[14] 586 5-8-9 102 (vt) TedDurcan 13 (Saeed Bin Suroor) *s.i.s: settled in rr: r.o fnl 1 1/2f: nrst fin* **16/1**	98
4	*hd*	**Sirvino**[21] 484 7-8-5 98 HarryBentley 12 (David Barron) *trckd ldrs: led 5f out: hdd 1 1/2f out: kpt on same pce* **14/1**	94
5	*¾*	**Jardim (BRZ)**[7] 678 6-8-10 104 KShea 5 (M F De Kock, South Africa) *settled in rr: nvr nr to chal but r.o fnl 2f* **9/1**	97
6	*hd*	**Nationalism**[14] 587 5-8-9 102 SilvestreDeSousa 1 (Mahmood Al Zarooni) *mid-div on rail: chsd ldrs 2f out: nt qckn fnl f* **16/1**	96
7	*1 ¼*	**Joshua Tree (IRE)**[21] 486 5-9-6 113 RyanMoore 14 (Marco Botti) *trckd ldrs: ev ch 4f out: wknd fnl 2f* **12/1**	104
8	*shd*	**Ottoman Empire (FR)**[21] 484 6-8-8 101 JamieSpencer 3 (David Simcock) *trckd ldrs: ev ch 1 1/2f out: wknd fnl 110yds* **9/2**[2]	92
9	*2 ¼*	**Alkimos (IRE)**[21] 486 4-8-9 102 FrankieDettori 4 (Saeed Bin Suroor) *nvr bttr than mid-div* **11/4**[1]	89
10	*1 ¼*	**Disa Leader (SAF)**[7] 677 7-9-1 108 JGeroudis 7 (M F De Kock, South Africa) *trckd ldrs: ev ch 2 1/2f out: wknd fnl 1 1/2f* **6/1**[3]	92
11	*9*	**Yaseer (IRE)**[7] 678 4-8-7 100 RichardHills 8 (E Charpy, UAE) *s.i.s: nvr able to chal* **33/1**	66
12	*5*	**Emerald Wilderness (IRE)**[13] 618 8-8-5 96 (p) RichardMullen 11 (Robert Cowell) *sn led: hdd 5f out: wknd fnl 2f* **16/1**	54
13	*9 ¼*	**Hurricane Havoc (IRE)**[13] 617 4-8-7 100 (bt) TadhgO'Shea 10 (J S Bolger, Ire) *settled in rr: n.d* **25/1**	38
14	*11 ½*	**Mantoba**[7] 682 4-8-5 95 (t) AdrianNicholls 9 (Brian Meehan) *settled in rr: struggling 4 1/2f out* **33/1**	13

2m 4.24s (-0.46) 14 Ran SP% **132.5**
CSF: £85.13; TRICAST: £1,152.30..
Owner Ramzan Kadyrov **Bred** Hascombe & Valiant Studs **Trained** South Africa

FOCUS
They went a solid gallop here, and it paid to be ridden with a bit of patience.

NOTEBOOK
Bronze Cannon(USA), who ran well over a furlong further last time, improved on that on this third run back from a break. He had a nice low draw, got a pitch in midfield racing one off the rail, found the gaps in the straight and picked up well for pressure. He looks to have run up to the best of his form over the past two years in success.
Sarrsar might not be the heartiest of battlers and seemingly needs to be delivered as late as possible, but not for the first time his rider gave away ground going wider than most (6m further than winner and 11m further than third according to Trakus).
Yaa Wayl(IRE) Thirsk maiden winner over 5f in 2009 and highly progressive at 3yo, winning three times between 7f-1m, the most significant of which came in a York Listed event in August 2010; won Newbury conditions race in 2011 and signs of encouragement in three outings at Meydan earlier this year
Sirvino eventually paid for going off too fast, although he deserves credit for being able to hang on for fourth place. (op 12-1)
Jardim(BRZ) made late ground up the rail in the straight but he seems to finish his races off like this never mind what distance he runs over. (op 8-1)
Nationalism, held up in midfield on the rail, had an ideal trip throughout and can have no excuses.
Joshua Tree(IRE), trying Tapeta for the first time, was drawn widest of all and as a result he ended up having racing wider than ideal. He shouldn't be judged too harshly on this. (op 14-1)
Ottoman Empire(FR) raced a little closer to the pace than was ideal and got tired in the closing stages, dropping out of the places inside the last.

756a ATTIJARI POINTS REWARDS PROGRAM (H'CAP) (TURF) 6f
3:45 (3:45) (100-111,111) 3-Y-0+
£67,741 (£22,580; £11,290; £5,645; £3,387; £2,258)

			RPR
1		**Soul (AUS)**[110] 5-9-3 109 FrankieDettori 10 (Saeed Bin Suroor) *trckd ldrs: smooth prog 3f out: led 1f out: comf* **4/1**[2]	113
2	*1 ¼*	**Invincible Ash (IRE)**[7] 681 7-8-9 101 (p) JamieSpencer 9 (M Halford, Ire) *settled in rr: r.o fnl 2f: nrst fin* **14/1**	101+
3	*nse*	**Al Sharood**[13] 617 4-8-10 102 KierenFallon 3 (Doug Watson, UAE) *wl away: trckd ldrs: led 2f out: hdd 1f out: kpt on same pce* **8/1**	102
4	*1 ½*	**Iver Bridge Lad**[27] 419 5-9-0 111 (b) MichaelO'Connell(5) 8 (John Ryan) *mid-div: chsd ldrs 3f out: kpt on same pce fnl f* **5/1**[3]	106
5	*shd*	**Dohasa (IRE)**[14] 588 7-9-1 107 RyanMoore 6 (Ismail Mohammed) *settled in rr: nvr nr to chal but r.o fnl 1 1/2f* **16/1**	102
6	*hd*	**Kanaf (IRE)**[14] 589 5-9-1 107 RichardHills 4 (M Al Muhairi, UAE) *s.i.s: mid-div: kpt on same pce fnl 1 1/2f* **7/2**[1]	101
7	*¾*	**Jimmy Styles**[14] 589 8-8-9 101 (p) TedDurcan 5 (Clive Cox) *mid-div: chsd ldrs 3f out: one pce fnl 1 1/2f* **8/1**	93
8	*½*	**Seachantach (USA)**[7] 681 6-8-8 100 (t) RichardMullen 7 (S Seemar, UAE) *nvr bttr than mid-div* **14/1**	90
9	*5*	**Regal Parade**[27] 416 8-8-13 105 AdrianNicholls 1 (David Nicholls) *trckd ldrs tl wknd 1 1/2f out* **8/1**	79
10	*1 ½*	**Bay Knight (IRE)**[14] 589 6-8-11 104 (t) JamesDoyle 2 (J S Moore) *wl away: sn led: hdd & wknd 2f out* **33/1**	72

11 10 ¼ **Redemptor**14 588 4-8-11 104.....................................(t) TadhgO'Shea 11 39
(E Charpy, UAE) *nvr bttr than mid-div* **22/1**

1m 11.21s (71.21) **11** Ran SP% **118.7**
CSF: £59.65; TRICAST: £434.46..

Owner Godolphin **Bred** Woodlands Stud **Trained** Newmarket, Suffolk

FOCUS
Quite a competitive handicap.

NOTEBOOK
Soul(AUS) took a 6.5f Listed event on his last start for his previous trainer in Australia and has a Group 2 win on his CV from earlier in his career. Bought by Godolphin after his last win, he made a pleasing debut for his new connections and looks the type who could quite easily step up into Group company in Europe this season. All three of his previous wins had come with cut in the ground, two of them on heavy, and so there might be more improvement to come when he gets to race on an easier surface. (op 7-2)
Invincible Ash(IRE) had been disappointing in three starts since running well behind Addictive Dream on her return to Meydan earlier this year, but this was better. She travelled well off the pace and, had she got a clear run, would have finished closer. The sixth furlong was a plus. (op 16-1)
Al Sharood, dropping back in trip having not got home over 1m plus, was never far away but was being pushed along some way out. She responded well, though.
Iver Bridge Lad had to give weight all round and ran a solid enough race back up in distance.
Dohasa(IRE) is fully exposed and ran about as well as could be expected.
Kanaf(IRE) was disappointing back on turf. It looks like the Tapeta surface suits him better than turf now and, having had only four starts on dirt/synthetics, he's still open to improvement back on those surfaces.
Jimmy Styles perhaps ran a little better for the switch back to turf, but he continues to be hard to place.

757a CBD WORLD MASTERCARD (H'CAP) (TAPETA) 7f
4:20 (4:20) (100-111,112) 3-Y-0+

£67,741 (£22,580; £11,290; £5,645; £3,387; £2,258)

RPR

1 **Barbecue Eddie (USA)**14 588 8-9-2 108.................(b) TadhgO'Shea 4 110
(Doug Watson, UAE) *s.i.s: mid-div: r.o wl fnl 1 1/2f: led fnl 110yds: comf* **16/1**

2 ¾ **Finjaan**14 586 6-8-10 102...(bt) KierenFallon 11 102
(Doug Watson, UAE) *mid-div: chsd ldrs 2 1/2f out: ev ch 110yds out: nt qckn fnl 55yds* **16/1**

3 ½ **Montmorency (IRE)**40 261 6-8-8 100.......................(vt) HarryBentley 5 99
(S Seemar, UAE) *trckd ldrs: led 1 1/2f out: hdd fnl 110yds* **20/1**

4 nse **Canwinn (IRE)**14 586 6-8-10 102.................................... JamesDoyle 2 101
(D Selvaratnam, UAE) *trckd ldrs: ev ch 1 1/2f out: one pce fnl 110yds* **7/1**2

5 1 ¾ **Scarf (AUS)**14 586 5-9-1 107... FrankieDettori 9 101
(Saeed Bin Suroor) *trckd ldrs: ev ch 1 1/2f out: one pce fnl f* **5/2**1

6 hd **Snaafy (USA)**14 590 8-8-13 105.................................(v) WayneSmith 3 98
(M Al Muhairi, UAE) *in rr of mid-div: r.o fnl 1 1/2f: nrst fin* **25/1**

7 nse **Tamaathul**14 588 5-9-5 111..(t) RichardHills 6 104
(A Al Raihe, UAE) *s.i.s: nvr bttr than mid-div* **12/1**3

8 2 **The Comedian (AUS)**14 588 6-9-1 107.......................(bt) VladDuric 12 95
(M Freedman, Singapore) *settled in rr: nvr able to chal* **7/1**2

9 ¾ **Ip Man (NZ)**27 417 4-9-3 112..(bt) OChavez 10 99
(S Burridge, Singapore) *mid-div: rdn 4f out: sn btn* **7/1**2

10 4 **Casual Glimpse**6 706 4-8-11 103 ow1............. ChristopheSoumillon 7 77
(M F De Kock, South Africa) *nvr bttr than mid-div* **7/1**2

11 ¼ **Silaah**14 589 8-8-4 102... ShirleyTeasdale(6) 1 76
(David Nicholls) *sn led: hdd & wknd 1 1/2f out* **33/1**

12 1 ¾ **Reynaldothewizard (USA)**14 589 6-9-1 107.........(t) RichardMullen 14 76
(S Seemar, UAE) *in rr of mid-div: nvr nr to chal* **16/1**

13 4 ¼ **Warsaw (IRE)**14 589 7-9-1 107..(b) KShea 8 65
(M F De Kock, South Africa) *s.i.s: a in rr* **25/1**

14 17 **The Rectifier (USA)**14 586 5-8-11 104......................... MickyFenton 13 15
(Jim Boyle) *nvr bttr than mid-div* **14/1**

1m 24.37s (-0.83) **14** Ran SP% **126.0**
CSF: £249.72; TRICAST: £5,098.92..

Owner Hamdan Al Maktoum **Bred** Margaret Addis **Trained** United Arab Emirates

FOCUS
A very competitive heat.

NOTEBOOK
Barbecue Eddie(USA) saved ground scraping paint until straightening up for home (only Canwinn and Tamaathul from the next nine home travelled a shorter distance according to Trakus), and he found just enough for pressure to hold off Finjaan. The return to Tapeta clearly suited.
Finjaan comes out of the race as the best horse, as he travelled 5m further than the winner and his average speed was 0.2kph faster. A 7f specialist, he appreciated the drop back in trip.
Montmorency(IRE) tracked the leader for much of the race before taking over early in the straight, but he couldn't quite see it out.
Canwinn(IRE) enjoyed a ground-saving trip and had every chance. (op 6-1 tchd 13-2)
Scarf(AUS), back a furlong in distance, travelled well into the race but it was a little disappointing he didn't find more for pressure. He covered as much ground as the runner-up.
Snaafy(USA) needs them to go off really fast up front over this distance, and the pace wasn't that hot this time.
Tamaathul had a nice trip, saving ground on the inside, and just wasn't good enough. His current mark - a result of finishing a shock second in a Group 3 last month - doesn't make things easy.

758a ZABEEL MILE SPONSORED BY COMMERCIAL BANK OF DUBAI (GROUP 2) (TURF) 1m
4:55 (4:55) 3-Y-0+

£96,774 (£32,258; £16,129; £8,064; £4,838; £3,225)

RPR

1 **Do It All (USA)**14 590 5-9-2 100...........................(t) SilvestreDeSousa 9 110
(Saeed Bin Suroor) *sn led: kicked clr 2f out: r.o wl* **33/1**

2 1 ¾ **Derbaas (USA)**14 590 6-9-2 113..................................(t) RichardHills 6 106+
(A Al Raihe, UAE) *trckd ldrs: ev ch 1f out: nt qckn fnl 110yds* **9/1**

3 hd **Dux Scholar**14 588 4-9-2 112......................................(vt) RyanMoore 10 106+
(H J Brown, South Africa) *mid-div: smooth prog 2 1/2f out: ev ch 1 1/2f out: nt qckn fnl 110yds* **13/2**3

4 ½ **Sandagiyr (FR)**21 487 4-9-2 112............................ FrankieDettori 11 104+
(Saeed Bin Suroor) *mid-div: chsd ldrs 3f out: nt qckn fnl 1 1/2f* **5/1**2

5 ½ **Jaasoos (IRE)**14 588 8-9-2 112...................................... KierenFallon 1 103+
(D Selvaratnam, UAE) *mid-div on rail: rdn 3f out: chsd ldrs 1 1/2f out: wknd fnl 110yds* **8/1**

6 shd **Dark Matter (AUS)**21 485 4-8-10 113............................(t) TedDurcan 2 103+
(S Burridge, Singapore) *trckd ldng duo: ev ch 2f out: one pce fnl 1 1/2f* **11/1**

7 2 ¼ **Viscount Nelson (USA)**14 590 5-9-5 116...........................(b) KShea 7 101+
(M F De Kock, South Africa) *settled in rr: nvr nr to chal* **13/8**1

8 ½ **Ibn Battuta (USA)**14 588 7-9-2 108.............................. WayneSmith 12 97+
(M Al Muhairi, UAE) *settled in rr: nvr nr to chal* **40/1**

9 2 **Always Certain (AUS)**14 590 6-9-2 115.........................(p) VladDuric 3 92+
(M Freedman, Singapore) *in rr of mid-div: nvr able to chal* **25/1**

10 4 **Fanunalter**7 682 6-9-2 115...(p) MircoDemuro 8 83+
(Marco Botti) *s.i.s: settled in last: n.d* **16/1**

11 2 ¼ **Gingerbread Man (AUS)**18 5-9-2 116..........................(t) OpieBosson 5 78+
(Ranji Marsh, Singapore) *nvr bttr than mid-div* **11/1**

12 3 ½ **Laa Rayb (USA)**14 590 8-9-2 104.................................(t) JamesDoyle 4 70+
(D Selvaratnam, UAE) *settled in rr: n.d* **33/1**

1m 38.98s (98.98) **12** Ran SP% **123.9**
CSF: £311.32..

Owner Godolphin **Bred** Winsong Farms **Trained** Newmarket, Suffolk

FOCUS
A competitive race run at a steady pace.

NOTEBOOK
Do It All(USA) got into this Group 2 race as a reserve and, with nothing else wanting to go on, Silvestre de Sousa was granted an uncontested lead aboard the outsider. It was virtually impossible to make a case for the horse beforehand (beaten 13 lengths by Viscount Nelson over C&D last time) but he is a confirmed front-runner and, with nothing hassling him, he was able to go a pace to suit himself. He found plenty when put under pressure in the straight, but this has to go down as a race cleverly stolen by de Sousa.
Derbaas(USA) tracked the winner throughout and was well enough placed turning in. He got to within a length of the winner before being shrugged off.
Dux Scholar covered more ground than most. (op 7-1)
Sandagiyr(FR) was forced to cover plenty of ground from his wide draw.
Jaasoos(IRE) enjoyed a ground-saving trip.
Dark Matter(AUS) enjoyed a ground-saving trip in what was a very steadily run race. (op 10-1)
Viscount Nelson(USA) was set an impossible task considering the lack of pace in the race, and although he stayed on late he had no chance of getting seriously involved. (op 7-4)

759a NAD AL SHEBA TROPHY SPONSORED BY ATTIJARI AL ISLAMI (GROUP 3) (TURF) 1m 6f 11y
5:30 (5:30) 3-Y-0+

£77,419 (£25,806; £12,903; £6,451; £3,870; £2,580)

RPR

1 **Fox Hunt (IRE)**27 421 5-9-4 113...................................(v) FrankieDettori 6 118
(Mahmood Al Zarooni) *trckd ldng trio: led 2f out: r.o wl: comf* **13/8**1

2 2 ½ **Opinion Poll (IRE)**138 6857 6-9-5 116.................... MickaelBarzalona 11 117
(Mahmood Al Zarooni) *settled in rr: smooth prog 6f out: chsd wnr 2f out: nt qckn fnl f* **10/3**2

3 1 ¼ **Jakkalberry (IRE)**81 7729 6-9-2 117..................................(t) RyanMoore 5 111
(Marco Botti) *mid-div: r.o fnl 2f: nrst fin* **15/2**3

4 2 ½ **Modun (IRE)**121 7218 5-9-4 112.................................. SilvestreDeSousa 4 109
(Saeed Bin Suroor) *trckd ldng trio: ev ch 3f out: kpt on same pce fnl 1 1/2f* **8/1**

5 ¾ **Irish Flame (SAF)**21 486 6-9-2 112.................... ChristopheSoumillon 8 106
(M F De Kock, South Africa) *mid-div: rdn 3 1/2f out: nvr able to chal* **8/1**

6 ½ **Glen's Diamond**27 421 4-8-11 104.............................. JamieSpencer 10 105
(Richard Fahey) *settled in rr: r.o fnl 2f: nrst fin* **14/1**

7 hd **Electrolyser (IRE)**27 421 7-9-2 109.................................. TedDurcan 2 105
(Clive Cox) *trckd ldrs: ev ch 3f out: one pce fnl 1 1/2f* **33/1**

8 1 ¾ **Mashoor (FR)**27 5-9-2 110.. RobertoPerez 1 103
(B Al Shaibani, Saudi Arabia) *sn led: rdn 4f out: hdd & wknd 2f out* **25/1**

9 1 ¼ **Kasbah Bliss (FR)**151 6562 10-9-7 115......................... GeraldMosse 12 106
(F Doumen, France) *settled in rr: nvr nr to chal* **10/1**

10 3 ¼ **Averroes (IRE)**27 421 5-9-2 105.................................... MircoDemuro 3 96
(Ernst Oertel, UAE) *trckd ldrs: ev ch 2 1/2f out: wknd fnl 1 1/2f* **20/1**

11 10 **Rostrum (FR)**7 678 5-9-2 106.. KierenFallon 7 82
(Mahmood Al Zarooni) *in rr of mid-div: n.d* **16/1**

12 dist **Manjakani**27 421 4-8-11 100.. TadhgO'Shea 9
(Ismail Mohammed) *in rr of mid-div: n.d* **33/1**

3m 1.09s (181.09)
WFA 4 from 5yo+ 4lb **12** Ran SP% **131.3**
CSF: £7.32. PLACEPOT: Part won: £5,203.50 to a £1 stake. Pool £7,128.15 - 0.50 winning tickets. QUADPOT: Part won. £389.60 to a £1 stake. Pool £526.60 - 0.40 winning tickets..

Owner Sheikh Hamdan Bin Mohammed Al Maktoum **Bred** Ballylinch Stud **Trained** Newmarket, Suffolk

FOCUS
A good quality Group 3 race and the form should work out.

NOTEBOOK
Fox Hunt(IRE) impressed in winning a handicap over the C&D last time and had no trouble coping with the rise in class. Never too far off the pace, he took over early in the straight and, while strongly pressed by Opinion Poll, found extra for pressure and was actually drawing further clear at the finish. He's an improving stayer and the Dubai Gold Cup, run over 2m on World Cup night, should suit him down to the ground. (op 7-4)
Opinion Poll(IRE) lacked the recent outing of the winner and also had to give him 1lb. This was a perfectly respectable effort in the circumstances and, granted some improvement, he too will go to the Dubai Gold Cup with strong claims. (op 3-1)
Jakkalberry(IRE), last seen finishing seventh in the Hong Kong Vase, wasn't given a hard race on his return to action. He seemed to get the trip well enough, but the Sheema Classic is presumably his target on World Cup night.
Modun(IRE) trailed in last in the Melbourne Cup on his debut for Godolphin, but he'd apparently been going well in training in recent weeks and this was a far more promising effort. He's not up to the class of the first three, though.
Irish Flame(SAF) was well backed to put behind him a rather disappointing effort on his return here last month, and he did improve on that run, but the first three were too strong. (op 9-1)
Glen's Diamond, patiently ridden, ran on late from the back but still finished further behind Fox Hunt, who was 3lb better off at the weights with him, than he did last time.
Electrolyser(IRE) had a nice run through the race next to the rail and had no excuse.
Kasbah Bliss(FR), who might have won a Champion Hurdle had his trainer seen the light, plugged on without getting competitive. He hadn't run since October so is fully entitled to come on for this. (op 8-1 tchd 9-1)
Averroes(IRE) was worse off at the weights with Fox Hunt here than when beaten easily by him over the C&D last time. He's just not up to this class. (op 16-1)

[726]LINGFIELD (L-H)

Friday, March 2

OFFICIAL GOING: Standard

Wind: light, across Weather: dry

760 CYPRIUM BAR AT MARRIOTT LINGFIELD (S) STKS 1m (P)

2:10 (2:10) (Class 6) 4-Y-0+ **£1,704** (£503; £251) **Stalls** High

Form RPR

-321 **1** **Red Somerset (USA)**[11] 634 9-9-4 72 KieranO'Neill 8 75
(Mike Murphy) *dropped in bhd after 1f: pushed along and nt clr run 2f out: sn swtchd rt: str run over 1f out: drvn and r.o wl to ld fnl 100yds: eased cl home* **10/3**[3]

1626 **2** ¾ **Alhaban (IRE)**[9] 655 6-9-4 65 LukeMorris 7 73
(Ronald Harris) *in tch in midfield: rdn and effrt over 2f out: drvn and hdwy to chse ldrs over 1f out: kpt on to chse wnr wl ins fnl f: no imp* **8/1**

1101 **3** nse **Daniel Thomas (IRE)**[9] 655 10-9-4 70 (tp) WilliamCarson 3 73
(Richard Guest) *dwlt: hdwy into midfield 6f out: switching to outer and rdn over 2f out: styd on u.p ins fnl f* **11/4**[2]

5-23 **4** 1 **Hierarch (IRE)**[16] 568 5-8-12 63 HayleyTurner 4 65
(David Simcock) *chsd ldrs tl pushed along to go 2nd over 3f out: rdn to ld ent fnl 2f: hdd over 1f out: styd on same pce ins fnl f* **5/2**[1]

-260 **5** nse **King's Colour**[9] 655 7-9-1 68 SeanLevey(3) 6 70
(Brett Johnson) *chsd ldrs: rdn and effrt to chal wl over 1f out: led jst over 1f out tl fnl 100yds: wknd towards fin* **12/1**

5603 **6** 9 **The Which Doctor**[4] 725 7-8-13 58 (e) DuilioDaSilva(5) 5 50
(Richard Guest) *sn bustled along to ld: hdd and rdn ent fnl 2f: wknd fnl f* **16/1**

-534 **7** 11 **Ostentation**[9] 655 5-8-12 62 (p) DaneO'Neill 1 18
(Roger Teal) *chsd ldr tl over 3f out: lost pl and rdn jst over 2f out: btn and eased ent fnl f* **9/1**

060/ **8** 2 **Persian Buddy**[637] 2714 6-8-12 57 StevieDonohoe 2 14
(Jamie Poulton) *s.i.s: a in rr: lost tch over 2f out* **150/1**

1m 37.31s (-0.89) **Going Correction** +0.125s/f (Slow) **8** Ran SP% **113.7**
Speed ratings (Par 101): **109,108,108,107,107 98,87,85**
Tote Swingers: 1&2 £4.30, 1&3 £2.30, 2&3 £5.90 CSF £29.54 TOTE £4.30: £2.10, £2.90, £1.10; EX 24.70 Trifecta £72.00 Pool: £842.71 - 8.66 winning units..There was no bid for the winner.

Owner M Murphy **Bred** Haras D'Etreham **Trained** Westoning, Beds

FOCUS
They went a decent pace in this seller and the 72-rated winner came from some way back to prevail in a bunch finish.

761 FOREST ROW H'CAP 1m (P)

2:45 (2:45) (Class 6) (0-65,64) 4-Y-0+ **£1,704** (£503; £251) **Stalls** High

Form RPR

0231 **1** **Cyflymder (IRE)**[14] 593 6-9-4 62 HayleyTurner 1 69
(David C Griffiths) *mde all: rdn and qcknd wl over 1f out: drvn and kpt on wl ins fnl f: hld on cl home: all out* **3/1**[2]

0-00 **2** shd **Ensnare**[15] 574 7-9-3 61 StevieDonohoe 3 68
(John Butler) *chsd ldrs early: stdd into last pair after 6f out: rdn and hdwy jst over 1f out: chal wnr ins fnl f: r.o wl: jst failed* **8/1**

4-22 **3** 2 **Princess Lexi (IRE)**[16] 568 5-9-2 60 JimCrowley 6 62
(William Knight) *chsd ldrs: rdn and effrt 2f out: drvn and unable qck over 1f out: styd on same pce fnl f* **13/8**[1]

4265 **4** ¾ **Lutine Charlie (IRE)**[16] 562 5-9-5 63 (p) LukeMorris 7 63
(Ronald Harris) *stdd and dropped in bhd after s: t.k.h hdwy to chse ldrs after 2f: drvn and effrt wl over 1f out: chsd wnr but unable qck over 1f out: styd on same pce fnl f* **10/1**

-136 **5** ½ **Fibs And Flannel**[15] 574 5-9-6 64 TonyCulhane 5 63
(Willie Musson) *hld up wl in tch in last: nt asked for effrt tl rdn 1f out: no imp fnl 100yds* **7/2**[3]

6361 **6** 1½ **Jonnie Skull (IRE)**[21] 503 6-8-7 58 (vt) DannyBrock(7) 2 54
(Phil McEntee) *t.k.h: chsd ldr: rdn 2f out: lost 2nd over 1f out: wknd ins fnl f* **20/1**

1m 38.61s (0.41) **Going Correction** +0.125s/f (Slow) **6** Ran SP% **110.3**
Speed ratings (Par 101): **102,101,99,99,98 97**
Tote Swingers: 1&2 £2.90, 1&3 £4.00, 2&3 £2.20 CSF £24.90 TOTE £3.40: £1.90, £3.50; EX 26.00.

Owner Steve Young **Bred** Miss Laura G F Ferguson **Trained** Bawtry, S Yorks

FOCUS
The well-backed winner got an easy lead and just held on in this tactical handicap.
Fibs And Flannel Official explanation: trainer said gelding bled

762 PATRICIA HILL MEMORIAL MAIDEN STKS 1m 4f (P)

3:20 (3:21) (Class 5) 3-Y-0+ **£2,385** (£704; £352) **Stalls** Low

Form RPR

22 **1** **Za'Lan (USA)**[6] 709 3-8-5 0 FrannyNorton 4 57+
(Mark Johnston) *mde all: set stdy gallop tl rdn and qcknd clr over 1f out: in command and rdn hands and heels fnl f: pressed towards fin but a doing enough* **2/7**[1]

05 **2** nk **Dalmo**[6] 709 3-8-7 0 ow2 ShaneKelly 5 59
(Gary Moore) *chsd ldr: rdn over 2f out: outpcd and drvn over 1f out: styd on ins fnl f: pressing wnr towards fin: a hld* **6/1**[2]

3 2¼ **Faraway Land (USA)** 4-9-4 0 AdamBeschizza(3) 6 51+
(Julia Feilden) *wnt rt s: hld up in last: rdn and no imp wl over 1f out: rn green and edgd lft over 1f out: hdwy 1f out: styd wl on ins fnl f: wnt 3rd towards fin* **9/1**[3]

6 **4** nk **Icy Quiet**[18] 546 4-9-7 0 StevieDonohoe 3 51
(Tobias B P Coles) *in tch: rdn and unable qck 2f out: drvn and styd on same pce fr over 1f out: lost 3rd towards fin* **33/1**

5 1½ **Life Of Laughter (USA)**[58] 4-9-12 0 JamieMackay 2 54
(Willie Musson) *chsd ldrs: rdn and unable qck wl over 1f out: styd on same pce fr over 1f out* **16/1**

2m 39.68s (6.68) **Going Correction** +0.125s/f (Slow)
WFA 3 from 4yo 23lb **5** Ran SP% **110.9**
Speed ratings (Par 103): **82,81,80,80,79**
CSF £2.58 TOTE £1.30: £1.10, £1.80; EX 2.50.

Owner Sheikh Hamdan Bin Mohammed Al Maktoum **Bred** Darley **Trained** Middleham Moor, N Yorks

FOCUS
The hot favourite had to work quite hard to get the job done in this slowly run maiden but he still looked green and could go on to better things.

763 TANDRIDGE H'CAP 5f (P)

3:50 (3:50) (Class 5) (0-70,70) 4-Y-0+ **£2,385** (£704; £352) **Stalls** High

Form RPR

264- **1** **Ability N Delivery**[28] 408 7-9-0 63 (p) JimCrowley 1 75
(Michael J Browne, Ire) *sn chsng ldr: rdn and clsd over 1f out: drvn ahd ins fnl f: sn clr and r.o strly: readily* **5/1**

3322 **2** 3 **Cliffords Reprieve**[13] 623 4-8-12 61 (b) JimmyFortune 6 62+
(Eric Wheeler) *t.k.h: hld up in midfield: nt clr run and shuffled bk to rr bnd wl over 1f out: rallied 1f out: r.o wl ins fnl f to snatch 2nd last stride: no ch w wnr* **5/2**[1]

0-11 **3** shd **Jimmy Ryan (IRE)**[49] 152 11-9-1 69 (t) RaulDaSilva(5) 4 70
(Tim McCarthy) *taken down early and led to s: chsd ldrs: outpcd bnd 2f out: rdn and rallied 1f out: styd on ins fnl f: wnt 3rd cl home* **9/2**[3]

30-5 **4** nse **Atlantic Beach**[39] 272 7-9-4 67 (b) LiamKeniry 9 68
(Milton Bradley) *stdd s: hld up in rr: hdwy on inner 2f out: swtchd rt over 1f out: r.o to go 2nd wl ins fnl f: no imp and lost 2 pls cl home* **22/1**

0-00 **5** ¾ **Ice Trooper**[20] 526 4-9-6 69 (b[1]) DaneO'Neill 7 67
(Linda Stubbs) *taken down early: sn led: rdn over 1f out: hdd jst ins fnl f: sn btn: wknd and lost 3 pls wl ins fnl f* **3/1**[2]

1405 **6** ½ **Chjimes (IRE)**[7] 687 8-8-11 60 (b) HayleyTurner 3 56
(Conor Dore) *t.k.h: hld up in midfield: rdn and effrt 1f out: kpt on but no ch w wnr* **8/1**

460 **7** 2¼ **Black Baccara**[15] 576 5-8-12 68 (be) DannyBrock(7) 5 56
(Phil McEntee) *stdd after s: hld up in last trio: rdn and effrt on inner over 1f out: no prog ins fnl f: nvr trbld ldrs: eased towards fin* **25/1**

0-04 **8** 1¾ **Athwaab**[15] 576 5-8-6 60 CharlesBishop(5) 2 42
(Noel Chance) *taken down early: dwlt and jostled leaving stalls: sn rdn along and rcvrd to r in midfield: rdn to chse ldng pair 2f out: no prog: wknd ins fnl f* **9/1**

0502 **9** 2½ **Riflessione**[9] 658 6-9-1 64 (v) LukeMorris 10 37
(Ronald Harris) *chsd ldrs on outer: drvn and unable qck wl over 1f out: wknd ent fnl f* **16/1**

58.87s (0.07) **Going Correction** +0.125s/f (Slow) **9** Ran SP% **123.6**
Speed ratings (Par 103): **104,99,99,98,97 96,93,90,86**
Tote Swingers: 1&2 £2.90, 1&3 £4.00, 2&3 £2.20 CSF £19.33 CT £63.75 TOTE £7.20: £2.50, £1.70, £1.10; EX 18.10 Trifecta £57.40 Pool: £57.40 - 1,271.69 winning units..

Owner Michael J Browne **Bred** Mrs C F Van Straubenzee & Miss A Gibson Fleming **Trained** Cashel, Co. Tipperary

FOCUS
They went a decent pace in this sprint handicap but the two prominent runners were given plenty of rope by the rest and the hold-up performers couldn't get involved.

764 MARSH GREEN H'CAP 7f (P)

4:25 (4:25) (Class 5) (0-75,75) 3-Y-0 **£2,385** (£704; £352) **Stalls** Low

Form RPR

-211 **1** **Kickingthelilly**[20] 518 3-9-6 74 ChrisCatlin 3 81
(Rae Guest) *chsd ldr: rdn to ld over 1f out: in command ins fnl f: rdn out* **15/8**[2]

5011 **2** 1¾ **Homeward Strut**[14] 605 3-8-2 61 (b) RaulDaSilva(5) 2 63
(Frank Sheridan) *chsd ldrs: n.m.r and swtchd rt over 1f out: rdn to chse wnr and hung lft ins fnl f: no imp* **11/2**[3]

4-50 **3** 3 **Mr Knightley (IRE)**[8] 667 3-9-2 75 (b) NathanAlison(5) 1 69
(Jim Boyle) *t.k.h: led: rdn 2f out: hdd over 1f out: wknd ins fnl f* **15/2**

-651 **4** 2½ **Boots And Spurs**[16] 565 3-9-7 75 (v) LukeMorris 4 62
(Mrs K Burke) *a last: rdn over 4f out: nvr gng wl after: drvn over 2f out: no rspnse and wl hld over 1f out* **6/5**[1]

1m 25.02s (0.22) **Going Correction** +0.125s/f (Slow) **4** Ran SP% **107.4**
Speed ratings (Par 98): **103,101,97,94**
CSF £11.00 TOTE £2.10; EX 4.60.

Owner Tony Hirschfeld **Bred** Tony Hirschfeld & L K Piggott **Trained** Newmarket, Suffolk

FOCUS
Three last-time-out winners lined-up in this small-field handicap which was run at a strong pace.
Boots And Spurs Official explanation: jockey said gelding never travelled

765 BREATHE SPA AT MARRIOTT LINGFIELD H'CAP 7f (P)

5:00 (5:00) (Class 4) (0-85,81) 4-Y-0+ **£4,204** (£1,251; £625; £312) **Stalls** Low

Form RPR

-420 **1** **Titan Triumph**[27] 426 8-9-6 80 (t) JimCrowley 11 84
(William Knight) *stdd and dropped in bhd after s: t.k.h: hld up in rr: hdwy on inner over 1f out: chsd ldrs ins fnl f: drvn and r.o wl fnl 100yds to ld on post* **11/2**[2]

-504 **2** nse **Dozy Joe**[16] 563 4-9-4 81 (p) SeanLevey(3) 3 85
(Ian Wood) *led and set stdy gallop: rdn and qcknd wl over 1f out: battled on gamely u.p tl hdd on post* **6/1**[3]

3-43 **3** ¾ **Caldercruix (USA)**[24] 458 5-8-11 76 (v) RaulDaSilva(5) 9 78
(James Evans) *t.k.h: w ldr: rdn over 1f out: stl ev ch ins fnl f: unable qck and hld fnl 75yds* **11/4**[1]

550- **4** 1½ **Sos Brillante (CHI)**[100] 7516 7-9-0 79 MarkCoumbe(5) 10 77
(Terry Clement) *t.k.h: hld up in tch in midfield: rdn and effrt whn swtchd rt over 1f out: kpt on ins fnl f: nt pce to rch ldrs* **9/1**

62-1 **5** 1¼ **Aqua Ardens (GER)**[24] 457 4-9-3 77 StephenCraine 4 71
(George Baker) *chsd ldrs: rdn and effrt to chal 2f out: drvn: flashed tail and could nt qckn over 1f out: one pce and hld fnl f* **8/1**

-006 **6** ½ **Majuro (IRE)**[16] 563 8-9-3 77 (t) TonyCulhane 8 70
(Richard Guest) *t.k.h: hld up in last pair: swtchd to outer over 2f out: rdn and effrt wl over 1f out: no imp tl styd on ins fnl f: nvr trbld ldrs* **13/2**

-060 **7** shd **Frequency**[37] 304 5-9-2 76 (b) JimmyFortune 6 69
(Keith Dalgleish) *t.k.h: hld up wl in tch in midfield: rdn and unable qck over 1f out: one pce and no threat to ldrs fnl f* **11/2**[2]

000- **8** 1¼ **Cuthbert (IRE)**[134] 6980 5-8-7 67 (v) HayleyTurner 5 56
(William Jarvis) *dwlt: sn rcvrd and chsd ldrs on inner: rdn wl over 1f out: wknd ins fnl f* **12/1**

1m 27.06s (2.26) **Going Correction** +0.125s/f (Slow) **8** Ran SP% **113.9**
Speed ratings (Par 105): **92,91,91,89,87 87,87,85**
Tote Swingers: 1&2 £6.50, 1&3 £4.30, 2&3 £3.90 CSF £37.84 CT £109.90 TOTE £7.50: £1.70, £2.40, £1.60; EX 33.10 Trifecta £205.10 Pool: £1,025.60 - 3.70 winning units..

Owner Canisbay Bloodstock **Bred** Hesmonds Stud Ltd **Trained** Patching, W Sussex

FOCUS
Not a strong handicap for the grade and it was run at a very steady pace and a number of runners pulled hard in the early stages.

766 LINGFIELDPARK.CO.UK H'CAP 1m (P)
5:30 (5:30) (Class 6) (0-65,65) 3-Y-O £1,704 (£503; £251) Stalls High

Form RPR
3222 1 **Crowning Star (IRE)**[7] 683 3-9-2 **60** LukeMorris 2 63
(J S Moore) *chsd ldr: rdn to chal 2f out: drvn to ld 1f out: styd on wl* **9/4**[2]
0-50 2 ¾ **Emma Jean (IRE)**[46] 191 3-8-2 **51** oh6 (t) RaulDaSilva(5) 5 52
(Frank Sheridan) *chsd ldng pair: rdn and effrt on inner wl over 1f out: kpt on u.p and chsd wnr wl ins fnl f: hld towards fin* **20/1**
33-4 3 nk **Stag Hill (IRE)**[16] 571 3-8-13 **57** LiamKeniry 1 57
(Sylvester Kirk) *led: jnd and rdn 2f out: hdd 1f out: no ex: lost 2nd and styd on same pce wl ins fnl f:* **2/1**[1]
60-1 4 8 **Jericho (IRE)**[24] 462 3-9-7 **65** JimCrowley 6 47
(Jamie Osborne) *chsd ldng trio: rdn and stl plenty to do over 2f out: no prog and wl btn over 1f out* **9/4**[2]
5 2 **Hugenot (IRE)**[49] 161 3-9-7 **65** StevieDonohoe 3 42
(Tobias B P Coles) *t.k.h early: stdd after s and hld up in rr: rdn and struggling 3f out: bhd fnl 2f* **10/1**[3]
1m 38.95s (0.75) **Going Correction** +0.125s/f (Slow) **5** Ran SP% **108.7**
Speed ratings (Par 96): **101,100,99,91,89**
CSF £33.86 TOTE £1.90: £1.10, £8.50; EX 33.80.
Owner Ray Styles & J S Moore **Bred** Summerhill Bloodstock **Trained** Upper Lambourn, Berks

FOCUS
A minor handicap run at just a fair pace.
Jericho(IRE) Official explanation: trainer's rep had no explanation for the poor form shown.
T/Plt: £23.80 to a £1 stake. Pool: £70,184.22 - 2,149.05 winning tickets. T/Qpdt: £5.50 to a £1 stake. Pool: £5,577.33 - 746.45 winning tickets. SP

718 WOLVERHAMPTON (A.W) (L-H)
Friday, March 2

OFFICIAL GOING: Standard
Wind: Light, behind Weather: Overcast

767 NAME A RACE TO ENHANCE YOUR BRAND APPRENTICE H'CAP 1m 4f 50y(P)
5:40 (5:40) (Class 6) (0-55,55) 4-Y-0+ £1,704 (£503; £251) Stalls Low

Form RPR
002- 1 **Holden Eagle**[94] 7573 7-8-13 **55** IanBurns(3) 1 66
(Tony Newcombe) *led: hdd over 9f out: chsd ldr tl led again over 3f out: rdn and edgd rt over 1f out: styd on* **6/1**[3]
-562 2 nk **Corvette**[25] 446 4-8-10 **54** ThomasBrown(3) 10 65
(Michael Appleby) *hld up: hdwy 4f out: chsd wnr over 1f out: sn rdn and edgd rt: styd on* **7/1**
253- 3 3 ¼ **Ishismart**[44] 5267 8-8-8 **50** NicoleNordblad(3) 11 55
(Reg Hollinshead) *hld up: hdwy over 2f out: rdn and hung lft ins fnl f: no ex* **9/1**
450- 4 4 ½ **Colliers Castle (IRE)**[155] 6476 6-8-9 **55** MatthewMcGhee(7) 6 53
(Lisa Williamson) *prom: lost pl 9f out: pushed along over 3f out: styd on ins fnl f* **25/1**
0044 5 nse **Yossi (IRE)**[7] 695 8-8-4 **46** (p) NoraLooby(3) 8 44
(Richard Guest) *prom: chsd wnr over 3f out: ev ch over 2f out: wknd fnl f* **8/1**
-255 6 ½ **Satwa Ballerina**[20] 519 4-8-7 **51** (b) NatashaEaton(3) 5 48
(Mark Rimmer) *chsd ldrs: edgd lft over 2f out: wknd over 1f out* **20/1**
0-46 7 ¾ **Port Hill**[9] 651 5-9-2 **55** RachealKneller 9 51
(Mark Brisbourne) *hld up: hdwy over 2f out: wknd over 1f out* **5/1**[2]
8 ¾ **Gap Of Dunloe (IRE)**[140] 6855 4-8-10 **54** JoshBaudains(3) 12 49+
(Evan Williams) *hld up: hmpd over 2f out: n.d* **9/4**[1]
0-25 9 2 ½ **Sacco D'Oro**[14] 602 6-8-5 **47** NoelGarbutt(3) 3 38
(Michael Mullineaux) *hld up: bhd fnl 6f: hmpd over 2f out* **33/1**
060- 10 13 **Dubara Reef (IRE)**[64] 7914 5-8-7 **46** (p) LukeRowe 7 16
(Paul Green) *prom: pushed along 7f out: wknd 3f out* **14/1**
60-5 F **Deferto Delphi**[29] 390 5-8-2 **46** oh1 (b) LauraBarry(5) 4
(Barry Murtagh) *plld hrd: trckd ldr tl led over 9f out: clr 6f out: hdd over 3f out: sn pushed along: looked hld whn hmpd and fell over 2f out: fatally injured* **25/1**
2m 40.04s (-1.06) **Going Correction** 0.0s/f (Stan)
WFA 4 from 5yo+ 2lb **11** Ran SP% **117.4**
Speed ratings (Par 101): **103,102,100,97,97 97,96,96,94,85**
toteswingers:1&2:£4.80, 1&3:£15.00, 2&3:£10.40 CSF £45.03 CT £379.05 TOTE £7.80: £2.20, £3.70, £3.00; EX 30.30.
Owner The About A Fortnight Partnership **Bred** A G Newcombe & M Patel **Trained** Yarnscombe, Devon
■ Stewards' Enquiry : Thomas Brown five-day ban: careless riding (Mar 16-17,19-21)

FOCUS
A moderate handicap run at a steady pace until the free running Deferto Delphi pulled his way to the front with a circuit to go. He was weakening through the field when unfortunately he fell over two out and was fatally injured.

768 WOLVERHAMPTON-RACECOURSE.CO.UK CLAIMING STKS 5f 20y(P)
6:10 (7:03) (Class 5) 3-Y-O £2,264 (£673; £336; £168) Stalls Low

Form RPR
1441 1 **Redair (IRE)**[11] 637 3-8-3 67 MatthewCosham(5) 1 72
(David Evans) *s.i.s: sn pushed along in rr: hdwy 2f out: rdn to ld over 1f out: r.o* **4/7**[1]
44-1 2 1 ¼ **Available (IRE)**[13] 621 3-8-10 70 NickyMackay 2 69
(Jim Boyle) *chsd ldr: pushed along 1/2-way: rdn and ev ch over 1f out: styd on* **15/8**[2]
- 3 hd **Morocco Moon** 3-8-10 0 MartinLane 4 68
(Tim Pitt) *s.i.s: sn prom: rdn and ev ch over 1f out: styd on* **16/1**[3]
4 5 **Shake Baby Shake** 3-8-4 0 WilliamCarson 3 44
(Bill Turner) *led: rdn: edgd rt and hdd over 1f out: wknd ins fnl f* **33/1**
6556 5 16 **Miss Bloom**[1] 750 3-7-13 35 RyanPowell(3) 5
(Garry Woodward) *chsd ldrs: pushed along and hung rt over 3f out: wknd 2f out* **150/1**
1m 2.23s (-0.07) **Going Correction** 0.0s/f (Stan) **5** Ran SP% **107.9**
Speed ratings (Par 98): **100,98,97,89,64**
CSF £1.75 TOTE £1.60: £1.10, £1.10; EX 1.90.
Owner J & J Potter & The late Mrs S Edwards **Bred** Noel O'Callaghan **Trained** Pandy, Monmouths

FOCUS
Laura Barry was taken to hospital after her fall in the opener. The replacement ambulance wasn't available, resulting in the second race being delayed by almost an hour.

769 ENJOY THE PUNTERS PACKAGE GROUP OFFER H'CAP 5f 216y(P)
6:40 (7:29) (Class 6) (0-65,65) 3-Y-O £1,704 (£503; £251) Stalls Low

Form RPR
2 1 **Russian Bullet**[50] 138 3-9-4 **62** GeorgeBaker 5 67
(Jamie Osborne) *led: hdd 5f out: w ldr: rdn to ld over 1f out: r.o* **9/4**[1]
5-06 2 ¾ **Maria Montez**[21] 499 3-8-12 **56** MartinLane 8 58
(J W Hills) *hld up: hdwy over 1f out: ran and r.o wl ins fnl f: nt rch wnr* **40/1**
51-2 3 nk **Hey Fiddle Fiddle (IRE)**[34] 352 3-9-6 **64** WilliamCarson 3 65
(Charles Hills) *dwlt: hld up: hdwy over 2f out: rdn over 1f out: r.o to go 3rd post* **7/2**[2]
-145 4 nse **M J Woodward**[28] 407 3-8-9 **58** DarylByrne(5) 6 58
(Paul Green) *chsd wnr tl led 5f out: rdn and hdd over 1f out: ev ch ins fnl f: unable qck towards fin* **12/1**
-616 5 1 ¾ **Tiablo (IRE)**[14] 599 3-8-10 **59** MatthewCosham(5) 7 54
(David Evans) *hld up: nt clr run 2f out: swtchd rt and hdwy over 1f out: r.o: nt rch ldrs* **10/1**
000- 6 1 **Vexillum (IRE)**[118] 7294 3-9-7 **65** SamHitchcott 4 57
(Mick Channon) *hld up in tch: rdn over 2f out: styd on same pce fnl f* **13/2**[3]
244- 7 ¾ **Towbee**[177] 5817 3-8-9 **60** DavidSimmonson(7) 1 49
(Michael Easterby) *s.s: bhd: r.o ins fnl f: nvr nrr* **8/1**
4246 8 ¾ **Prince Gabrial (IRE)**[21] 491 3-9-0 **58** FrannyNorton 2 45
(Kevin Ryan) *prom and sn pushed along: rdn over 2f out: wknd ins fnl f* **17/2**
50-4 9 7 **Pressure Drop (IRE)**[22] 482 3-9-0 **65** JoshBaudains(7) 9 29
(Jo Hughes) *trckd ldrs: racd keenly: rdn and wknd over 2f out* **14/1**
23-5 10 nk **Ambitious Icarus**[21] 491 3-9-2 **63** RobertLButler(3) 11 27
(Richard Guest) *plld hrd and prom: rdn and wknd 2f out* **16/1**
02-4 11 11 **Forever Janey**[42] 228 3-8-4 **48** DavidProbert 12
(Paul Green) *chsd ldrs: rdn over 2f out: wknd over 1f out* **33/1**
1m 15.89s (0.89) **Going Correction** 0.0s/f (Stan) **11** Ran SP% **122.7**
Speed ratings (Par 96): **94,93,92,92,90 88,87,86,77,77 62**
toteswingers:1&2:£25.50, 1&3:£2.00, 2&3:£29.50 CSF £110.18 CT £333.70 TOTE £4.60: £1.60, £10.60, £1.80; EX 94.30.
Owner Martyn and Elaine Booth **Bred** Cranford Bloodstock Uk Ltd **Trained** Upper Lambourn, Berks

FOCUS
A modest 3yo handicap, that lacked any strength in depth.

770 HORIZONS RESTAURANT MEDIAN AUCTION MAIDEN STKS 7f 32y(P)
7:10 (7:53) (Class 5) 3-5-Y-O £2,264 (£673; £336; £168) Stalls High

Form RPR
1 **Warfare** 3-8-7 0 PJMcDonald 5 71+
(Kevin Ryan) *dwlt: bhd: gd hdwy over 2f out: led and hung lft fr over 1f out: rdn out* **7/1**[3]
425- 2 1 ¾ **Sunley Pride**[119] 7258 3-8-7 75 SamHitchcott 10 66
(Mick Channon) *chsd ldrs: rdn and ev ch whn hung lft over 1f out: styd on same pce ins fnl f* **8/11**[1]
3 1 **Compton Prince** 3-8-7 0 JohnFahy 2 63
(Clive Cox) *led 1f: chsd ldrs: led wl over 1f out: sn rdn and hdd: hmpd sn after: kpt on* **15/2**
2 4 ½ **Lord Paget**[21] 499 3-8-4 0 AmyRyan(3) 1 66+
(Reg Hollinshead) *hld up: hdwy over 2f out: hmpd over 1f out: styd on* **4/1**[2]
0/ 5 2 ¾ **Director's Dream (IRE)**[509] 6770 4-8-11 0 (b[1]) NatashaEaton(3) 6 56?
(Mark Rimmer) *led 6f out: sn clr: hdd wl over 1f out: hmpd and no ex jst over 1f out* **50/1**
6 2 ¾ **The Bendy Fella (IRE)** 4-9-4 0 LeeNewnes(5) 4 53
(Mark Usher) *sn outpcd: nvr nrr* **25/1**
4 7 6 **Moorgate Lass**[8] 675 4-9-4 0 MickyFenton 8 32
(Garry Woodward) *chsd clr ldr over 5f out: hmpd and wknd over 2f out* **16/1**
- 8 2 ½ **Glennten** 3-8-4 0 SophieDoyle(3) 9 24
(Sylvester Kirk) *hld up: bhd fnl 4f* **50/1**
6- 9 3 ¾ **Midnite Motivation**[85] 7673 3-8-2 0 DavidProbert 7
(Derek Shaw) *hld up: rdn and wknd over 2f out* **33/1**
10 43 **Ozz** 3-7-13 0 DominicFox(3) 3
(Frank Sheridan) *s.s: outpcd: t.o* **40/1**
1m 31.19s (1.59) **Going Correction** 0.0s/f (Stan)
WFA 3 from 4yo 16lb **10** Ran SP% **121.2**
Speed ratings (Par 103): **90,88,86,86,83 80,73,70,66,16**
toteswingers:1&2:£2.30, 1&3:£5.70, 2&3:£2.20 CSF £12.69 TOTE £5.40: £2.00, £1.20, £2.20; EX 20.10.
Owner Guy Reed **Bred** G Reed **Trained** Hambleton, N Yorks
■ Stewards' Enquiry : Sam Hitchcott two-day ban: careless riding (Mar 16-17)

FOCUS
A moderate maiden run at an average pace. The winner came wide into the straight but hung left and finished on the inside rail.

771 HOTEL & CONFERENCING AT WOLVERHAMPTON H'CAP 1m 1f 103y(P)
7:40 (8:17) (Class 5) (0-75,75) 4-Y-0+ £2,587 (£770; £384; £192) Stalls Low

Form RPR
-162 1 **Postscript (IRE)**[20] 538 4-9-0 **68** FrannyNorton 8 80
(Ian Williams) *a.p: rdn to ld ins fnl f: r.o* **4/1**[2]
-243 2 1 ¾ **McCool Bannanas**[20] 538 4-8-10 **64** RichardKingscote 2 72
(James Unett) *trckd ldrs: racd keenly: rdn ins fnl f: styd on* **8/1**
0551 3 hd **Honey Of A Kitten (USA)**[4] 722 4-8-5 **64** MatthewCosham(5) 7 72
(David Evans) *chsd ldr tl 7f out: remained handy: wnt 2nd again over 3f out: pushed along to ld over 2f out: rdn over 1f out: hdd and unable qck ins fnl f* **13/8**[1]
0-43 4 1 **Hidden Glory**[22] 480 5-9-7 **75** (b) PaulMulrennan 1 80
(James Given) *hld up: hdwy over 2f out: rdn ins fnl f: styd on same pce* **10/1**
4244 5 8 **Dazzling Valentine**[15] 582 4-8-12 **73** NatashaEaton(7) 3 62
(Alan Bailey) *hld up: rdn over 2f out: sn wknd* **16/1**
0 6 ¾ **Sublime Talent (IRE)**[18] 548 6-9-2 **70** (t) AdamKirby 4 57
(Evan Williams) *hld up: rdn and wknd over 2f out* **33/1**
00-2 7 2 **Silver Alliance**[9] 648 4-9-3 **71** GeorgeBaker 5 54
(Julia Feilden) *trckd ldrs: plld hrd: led 7f out: rdn and hdd over 2f out: wknd fnl f* **5/1**[3]

4-23 **8** *6* **Mighty Clarets (IRE)**[9] 268 5 -9-169 RobertWinston 6 39
(Barry Leavy) *led: hdd 7f out: chsd ldr to over 3f out: rdn and wknd over 2f out* **11/2**
2m 0.52s (-1.18)**Going Correction** 0.0s/f (Stan) **8**Ran SP% **119.2**
Speed ratings (Par 103): **105,103,103,102,95 94,92,87**
toteswingers: 1&2 £6.80, 1&3 £4.50, 2&3 £3.10 CSF £37.29 CT £72.63 TOTE £4.50 : £1.90, £1.70, £1.50 ; EX 40.40 .
Owner Dr Marwan Koukash **Bred** Darley **Trained** Portway, Worcs

FOCUS
A fair handicap in which the first four pulled a long way clear.

772 STAY AT THE WOLVERHAMPTON HOLIDAY INN H'CAP 2m 119y (P)
8:10 (8:43) (Class 6) (0-60,60) 4-Y-0+ **£1,704** (£503; £251) **Stalls** Low

Form RPR
-023 **1** **Blue Cossack (IRE)**[16] 566 4 -9-257 DavidProbert 7 66
(Mark Usher) *a.p: rdn to ld ins fnl f: edgd lft: styd on* **6/1**[3]
53-5 **2** *nk* **Uncut Stone (IRE)**[31] 366 4 -9-560 (b) PaulMulrennan 10 68
(Peter Niven) *a.p: rdn over 1f out: edgd lft ins fnl f: styd on wl nr fin* **8/1**
5/2- **3** *nse* **Sainglend**[14] 7087 7 -9-656 PJMcDonald 13 64
(Paul Rich) *chsd ldrs: rdn and ev ch ins fnl f: styd on* **10/3**[1]
-302 **4** *1 1/4* **Six Of Clubs**[16] 566 6 -8-1356 (b) JakePayne[(7)] 12 63
(Bill Turner) *hld up: hdwy 11f out: chsd ldr over 3f out: led wl over 1f out: sn rdn: hdd and unable qck ins fnl f* **8/1**
000- **5** *6* **Needwood Park**[65] 6618 4 -8-849 WilliamCarson 8 48
(Ray Craggs) *led at stdy pce tl qcknd 6f out: rdn and hdd wl over 1f out: wknd ins fnl f* **33/1**
0-31 **6** *4 1/2* **Waldsee (GER)**[16] 566 7 -9-858 AdamKirby 4 52
(Paul Rich) *hld up: pushed along over 6f out: hdwy over 4f out: rdn over 3f out: wknd over 1f out* **4/1**[2]
6-04 **7** *1/2* **Redhotdoc**[14] 600 8 -9-360 (b[1]) MatthewMcGhee[(7)] 5 53
(Bill Moore) *s.s: hdwy over 3f out: rdn and wknd over 2f out* **18/1**
0-00 **8** *4* **Blackstone Vegas**[21] 500 6 -9-558 DaleSwift[(3)] 9 47
(Derek Shaw) *mid-div: lost pl over 6f out: drvn along whn nt clr run over 3f out: n.d after* **4/1**[2]
-550 **9** *1/2* **Lucky Diva**[25] 446 5 -8-1053 (p) RyanWhile[(7)] 6 41
(Bill Turner) *hld up: rdn and wknd over 3f out* **40/1**
-150 **10** *nk* **Prince Charlemagne (IRE)**[16] 566 9 -8-1152(p) MatthewCosham[(5)] 11 40
(Dr Jeremy Naylor) *hld up: hdwy over 3f out: rdn and wknd over 2f out* **40/1**
3200 **11** *10* **Delorain (IRE)**[16] 566 9 -8-1349 (p) MartinLane 3 25
(William Stone) *chsd ldr tl rdn over 5f out: wknd over 3f out* **33/1**
3m 41.86s (0.06)**Going Correction** 0.0s/f (Stan)
WFA 4 from 5yo+ 5lb **11**Ran SP% **115.6**
Speed ratings (Par 101): **99,98,98,98,95 93,93,91,90,90 86**
toteswingers:1&2:£9.80, 1&3:£4.90, 2&3:£10.80 CSF £50.64 CT £184.90 TOTE £5.40 : £2.20, £3.20, £2.50 ; EX 40.70 .
Owner Reg Brookes & Richard Jurd **Bred** Morgan Ferris **Trained** Upper Lambourn, Berks

FOCUS
A competitive staying handicap for the grade. The pace was muddling and the winner came down the centre of the track.
Uncut Stone (IRE) Official explanation: jockey said gelding hung left-handed

773 SPONSOR A RACE BY CALLING 01902 390000 H'CAP 1m 1f 103y (P)
8:40 (9:10) (Class 7) (0-50,50) 4-Y-0+ **£1,704** (£503; £251) **Stalls** Low

Form RPR
60-3 **1** **Cabal**[22] 477 5 -9-047 (b) DanielTudhope 5 56
(Andrew Crook) *hld up: hdwy over 1f out: rdn to ld ins fnl f: r.o* **11/2**[3]
-040 **2** *2* **By Implication**[9] 653 4 -8-1245 (b) JohnFahy 7 50
(Ed de Giles) *hld up: hdwy over 4f out: rdn over 1f out: edgd rt ins fnl f: styd on* **10/1**
-500 **3** *1* **Tous Les Deux**[38] 276 9 -8-947 MatthewCosham[(5)] 11 50
(Dr Jeremy Naylor) *hld up: rdn and r.o wl ins fnl f: nt rch ldrs* **16/1**
-262 **4** *1 1/4* **My Mate Les (IRE)**[30] 390 4 -9-350 DavidProbert 3 50
(Tony Carroll) *a.p: rdn and ev ch ins fnl f: no ex* **7/2**[2]
0000 **5** *3/4* **Kirstys Lad**[22] 477 10 -8-1245 RichardKingscote 10 44
(Michael Mullineaux) *chsd ldr tl led over 1f out: sn rdn: hdd and no ex ins fnl f* **33/1**
0200 **6** *1 1/4* **Hathaway (IRE)**[16] 559 5 -8-1050 RachealKneller[(7)] 2 46
(Mark Brisbourne) *hld up: hdwy over 1f out: sn rdn: wknd towards fin* **9/1**
-066 **7** *hd* **Granny Anne (IRE)**[20] 531 4 -9-148 (p) WilliamCarson 9 44
(Paul D'Arcy) *chsd ldrs: rdn over 1f out: wknd ins fnl f* **7/1**
006- **8** *nk* **Clear Spring (IRE)**[79] 7750 4 -8-1245 NickyMackay 8 40
(John Spearing) *prom: nt clr run over 1f out: nt rcvr* **14/1**
0-06 **9** *2 3/4* **Forbidden (IRE)**[23] 468 9 -8-1147 (t) AmyRyan[(3)] 12 36
(Ian McInnes) *hld up: rdn over 2f out: n.d* **16/1**
-040 **10** *3/4* **Misere**[17] 551 4 -8-1346 PaulMulrennan 1 34
(Kevin Ryan) *led: rdn and hdd over 1f out: wknd fnl f* **11/1**
3-56 **11** *1* **Wing N Prayer (IRE)**[35] 334 5 -9-047 (p) PaddyAspell 4 33
(John Wainwright) *chsd ldrs: rdn over 1f out: wknd fnl f* **33/1**
2224 **12** *2* **Cairanne**[15] 578 4 -8-1046 RyanClark[(3)] 6 27
(Tom Keddy) *hld up: rdn and wknd over 2f out* **3/1**[1]
2m 2.55s (0.85)**Going Correction** 0.0s/f (Stan) **12**Ran SP% **126.8**
Speed ratings (Par 97): **96,94,93,92,91 90,90,87,86 86,84**
toteswingers:1&2:£16.50, 1&3:£17.90, 2&3:£37.50 CSF £64.21 CT £850.88 TOTE £5.90 : £2.50, £3.80, £6.20 ; EX 95.50 .
Owner Leeds Plywood And Doors Ltd **Bred** Cheveley Park Stud Ltd **Trained** Middleham Moor, N Yorks

FOCUS
A wide-open handicap, in which most of the field seemed to have a chance with 1f left to run.
Clear Spring (IRE) Official explanation: jockey said colt was denied a clear run
Misere Official explanation: jockey said filly hung right-handed
Cairanne Official explanation: trainer said filly never travelled
T/Plt: £18.00 to a £1 stake. Pool: £85,641.63. 3,459.64 winning tickets. T/Qpdt: £5.60 to a £1 stake. Pool: £10,037.99. 1,307.09 winning tickets. CR

774 - (Foreign Racing) - See Raceform Interactive

697 DUNDALK (A.W) (L-H)
Friday, March 2

OFFICIAL GOING: Standard

775a HARP LAGER SOCIAL CLUB H'CAP 6f (P)
6:50 (6:50) (47-65,65) 4-Y-0+ **£4,025** (£933; £408 ; £233)

RPR
1 **Charismas Birthday (IRE)**[21] 504 4 -8-547 (b) LeighRoche[(5)] 6 56
(Philip M Byrne, Ire) *mde virtually all: strly pressed and jnd briefly 2f out: kpt on wl u.p fnl f* **8/1**
2 *1* **Naoise (IRE)**[7] 700 4 -9-455 (t) KevinManning 8 61
(J S Bolger, Ire) *trckd ldrs: 6th 1/2-way: rdn to go 4th over 1f out: kpt on same pce fnl f wout threatening wnr* **4/1**[2]
3 *nk* **Cailin Coillteach**[7] 700 4 -9-1263 FergalLynch 13 68+
(W McCreery, Ire) *mid-div: 8th 1/2-way: rdn into 6th over 1f out: kpt on fnl f wout rching wnr* **6/1**[3]
4 *1 3/4* **Gala Spirit (IRE)**[18] 550 5 -9-455 (p) WayneLordan 12 54
(Peter Niven) *chsd ldrs: 4th 1/2-way: 3rd and rdn over 1f out: no ex ins fnl f* **8/1**
5 *nk* **Rose Garnet (IRE)**[49] 163 4 -9-152 (t) GaryCarroll 14 50
(David Marnane, Ire) *hld up towards rr: sme hdwy on outer fr 2f out: 8th 1f out: kpt on* **17/2**
6 *1/2* **Primalova (IRE)**[28] 408 6 -9-763 (t) RonanWhelan[(5)] 1 60
(William J Fitzpatrick, Ire) *prom on inner: 3rd 1/2-way: hdwy to dispute briefly 2f out: sn rdn and hdd: no ex ins fnl f: wknd* **16/1**
7 *1* **Daring Man (IRE)**[152] 6560 7 -9-462 RossCoakley[(7)] 7 55
(Denis W Cullen, Ire) *trckd ldr in 2nd: rdn in 3rd 2f out: no ex and wknd fnl f* **9/1**
8 *nk* **Alvar (USA)**[21] 504 4 -8-1148 ShaneFoley 3 41
(M Halford, Ire) *chsd ldrs: 5th 1/2-way: drvn along fr early st: no imp fr over 1f out: wknd* **10/3**[1]
9 *nse* **Red Army Blues (IRE)**[14] 610 4 -9-1165 EmmetMcNamara[(3)] 11 57
(G M Lyons, Ire) *towards rr and nvr a factor* **12/1**
10 *1/2* **Desert Al (IRE)**[21] 504 9 -8-1047 (b) DeclanMcDonogh 4 38
(Owen Weldon, Ire) *mid-div: chsd ldrs on inner early st: no ex fr over 1f out* **16/1**
11 *1/2* **The Yellow Bin (IRE)**[28] 409 4 -8-547 (b[1]) ConorHoban[(5)] 10 36
(S Donohoe, Ire) *in rr of mid-div: rdn early st and no ex fr over 1f out* **33/1**
12 *nk* **Curl Cat (USA)**[21] 511 6 -9-960 (bt) RoryCleary 2 48
(Thomas Cleary, Ire) *s.i.s and a in rr* **20/1**
13 *2 1/2* **The Gnathologist (IRE)**[98] 5189 7 -8-949 ow2. AndrewPThornton[(3)] 9 29
(Donal Kinsella, Ire) *chsd ldrs: 7th 1/2-way: no ex under 2f out* **50/1**
14 *17* **Khelino (IRE)**[84] 7700 4 -10-065 PatSmullen 5
(Rodger Sweeney, Ire) *a towards rr: eased whn btn fnl f* **10/1**
1m 11.9s (71.90) **14**Ran SP% **138.3**
CSF £45.53 CT £229.54 TOTE £13.60 : £4.20, £2.50, £2.50 ; DF 64.20 .
Owner Mrs Michael Byrne **Bred** Michael M Byrne **Trained** Dove Grove, Birr, Co Offaly,

FOCUS
This low grade handicap produced a first career win for the winner.

NOTEBOOK
Charismas Birthday (IRE) benefited from a positive front-running ride. The winner had hinted more to come when stepping up on previous form in third on her last visit here. She got into a nice rhythm up front from her low draw and under a good drive stuck to her task well.
Naoise(IRE) had won over 7f here last month and was fancied to run well again. He was done no favours with his wide draw but to his credit he plugged on well under pressure on the outer. He won't mind a step back up in trip on this evidence. (op 5/1 tchd 11/2)
Cailin Coillteach had finished on front of the first two when she won a couple of times over this trip and 7f last month. She put up a good performance off her revised rating from her unfavourable wide draw and still looks on a competitive mark. (op 5/1)
Gala Spirit (IRE) had proved a disappointing favourite over a furlong longer at Wolverhampton last month. This was better from the Invincible Spirit filly who looked another who wants a bit further than this. (op 6/1)
Rose Garnet (IRE) ran another consistent race when staying on well inside the final furlong without threatening. (op 8/1)
Alvar(USA) came under pressure when they straightened for home and found little under pressure. (op 13/2 tchd 3/1)

776a-780a Foreign Racing (See Raceform Interactive)

760 LINGFIELD (L-H)
Saturday, March 3

OFFICIAL GOING: Standard
Wind: Fresh, half behind Weather: Becoming sunny by race 3

781 HEY, HEY WE'RE THE MONKEES H'CAP 6f (P)
1:40 (1:40) (Class 6) (0-55,57) 4-Y-0+ **£1,704** (£503; £251) **Stalls** Low

Form RPR
6-02 **1** **Lady Mango (IRE)**[9] 664 4 -9-457 LukeMorris 6 66
(Ronald Harris) *mid-div: rdn 3f out: hdwy over 1f out: str run to ld fnl strides* **11/2**[3]
2624 **2** *hd* **Blueberry Fizz (IRE)**[9] 662 4 -9-053 (v) AdamKirby 12 61
(John Ryan) *prom: led over 2f out: hrd rdn and kpt on fnl f: hdd fnl strides* **9/2**[2]
-030 **3** *nk* **Overwhelm**[26] 445 4 -9-255 (t) MartinHarley 2 62
(Andrew Reid) *towards rr: hdwy on inner ent st: str chal fnl f: kpt on* **9/1**
-000 **4** *1 1/4* **Microlight**[28] 424 4 -8-1251 (b) RichardThomas 3 54
(John E Long) *prom: hrd rdn over 1f out: one pce ins fnl f* **20/1**
0560 **5** *1 1/2* **Sailing North (USA)**[9] 665 4 -9-255 (p) WilliamCarson 1 53
(Ronald Harris) *dwlt: rdn along and sn in midfield: effrt and hrd rdn 2f out: one pce appr fnl f* **33/1**
0-02 **6** *1/2* **Amazing Win (IRE)**[9] 665 4 -9-255 SamHitchcott 4 52
(Mick Channon) *bhd: rdn and sme hdwy over 1f out: nvr nrr* **4/1**[1]
3-35 **7** *nk* **Mr Skipiton (IRE)**[21] 522 7 -9-053 DaneO'Neill 7 49
(Terry Clement) *chsd ldrs: rdn over 2f out: wknd jst over 1f out* **9/2**[2]
4531 **8** *nk* **Super Frank (IRE)**[9] 687 9 -9-255 (b) JamieGoldstein 9 50
(Zoe Davison) *s.s: bhd: v wd and effrt ent st: nt rch ldrs* **11/1**
6043 **9** *1 3/4* **Divine Rule (IRE)**[15] 593 4 -8-955 (b) CharlotteJenner[(7)] 8 44
(Laura Mongan) *in tch on outer: rn wd bnd into st: sn btn* **15/2**
-600 **10** *2 3/4* **Prize Point**[22] 498 6 -9-255 (b[1]) StevieDonohoe 5 35
(Tom Gretton) *led tl over 2f out: hrd rdn and wknd over 1f out* **33/1**

0-04 **11** *16* **Hand Painted**[24] 470 6-9-2 **55**....(b[1]) JohnFahy 10
(Anthony Middleton) *s.s: a bhd: rdn and n.d fnl 2f* **50/1**

1m 11.59s (-0.31) **Going Correction** +0.05s/f (Slow) **11** Ran SP% **114.5**
Speed ratings (Par 101): **104,103,103,101,99 99,98,98,95,92 70**
toteswingers:1&2:£4.00, 2&3:£10.70, 1&3:£12.40 CSF £28.43 CT £222.68 TOTE £6.90: £2.80, £2.10, £4.10; EX 29.90 Trifecta £250.90 Pool: £373.06 - 1.10 winning units..
Owner L Scadding & Mrs S Peachey-Scadding **Bred** Mount Coote Stud **Trained** Earlswood, Monmouths

FOCUS
A moderate sprint handicap, with recent winning form thin on the ground, and just 6lb covered the 11 runners.
Super Frank(IRE) Official explanation: jockey said gelding was slowly away
Prize Point Official explanation: trainer said gelding had a breathing problem

782 IN MEMORY OF DAVY JONES (S) STKS 5f (P)
2:15 (2:15) (Class 6) 4-Y-0+ **£1,704** (£503; £251) **Stalls** High

Form RPR
4045 **1** **Decider (USA)**[10] 654 9-9-0 57....(b) LukeMorris 1 64
(Ronald Harris) *pressed ldr: hrd rdn over 1f out: kpt on to ld fnl 75yds* **7/1[2]**
2203 **2** *nk* **Mottley Crewe**[10] 654 5-9-5 85....(b) MartinHarley 4 68
(Richard Guest) *led: hrd rdn ins fnl f: hdd and nt qckn fnl 75yds* **1/7[1]**
2604 **3** *6* **Pharoh Jake**[24] 467 4-9-0 47.... KieranO'Neill 2 41
(John Bridger) *chsd ldng pair: rdn 3f out: outpcd fnl 2f* **33/1[3]**
-060 **4** *¾* **Toms River Tess (IRE)**[16] 578 4-8-9 45....(b[1]) JamieGoldstein 3 34
(Zoe Davison) *sn last: rdn and n.d fnl 2f* **80/1**

58.25s (-0.55) **Going Correction** +0.05s/f (Slow) **4** Ran SP% **104.2**
Speed ratings (Par 101): **106,105,95,94**
CSF £8.33 TOTE £8.50; EX 11.00.Mottley Crewe was claimed by A. J. McCabe for £6,000. There was no bid for the winner.
Owner Robert Bailey **Bred** Green Willow Farms **Trained** Earlswood, Monmouths

FOCUS
A poor seller and complete horror show for those punters willing to take odds of 1-7 about the favourite.
Mottley Crewe Official explanation: trainer's rep said, regarding running, that the gelding was unsuited by the slower early pace.

783 LINGFIELD PARK OWNERS CLUB H'CAP 5f (P)
2:50 (2:50) (Class 6) (0-55,58) 4-Y-0+ **£1,704** (£503; £251) **Stalls** High

Form RPR
2563 **1** **Slatey Hen (IRE)**[9] 665 4-8-11 **50**....(p) WilliamCarson 1 59
(Richard Guest) *mde all: hrd rdn over 1f out: kpt on wl* **8/1[3]**
-631 **2** *1 ¾* **Dorothy's Dancing (IRE)**[9] 665 4-9-5 **58**.... GeorgeBaker 2 61
(Gary Moore) *plld hrd: chsd ldng pair: wnt 2nd ent st: nt qckn fnl f* **8/11[1]**
-363 **3** *1 ¾* **Porthgwidden Beach (USA)**[8] 691 4-8-7 **46**....(tp) ChrisCatlin 5 42
(Anthony Middleton) *chsd wnr tl ent st: kpt on same pce* **16/1**
1002 **4** *¾* **Deveze (IRE)**[8] 691 4-8-12 **51** ow1....(b) DaneO'Neill 4 45
(Milton Bradley) *hld up in rr: effrt and wnt 4th ent st: nt pce to chal* **10/1**
0600 **5** *2 ¾* **Mandy's Hero**[21] 522 4-8-11 **55**.... MarkCoumbe(5) 6 39
(Olivia Maylam) *hld up mainly 5th: outpcd and btn 2f out* **20/1**
-220 **6** *½* **Good Timin'**[8] 691 4-8-11 **50**.... HayleyTurner 7 32
(David Brown) *t.k.h in rr: rdn and n.d fnl 2f* **7/2[2]**

58.83s (0.03) **Going Correction** +0.05s/f (Slow) **6** Ran SP% **111.0**
Speed ratings (Par 101): **101,98,95,94,89 89**
toteswingers:1&2:£1.90, 2&3:£4.00, 1&3:£4.60 CSF £14.12 CT £87.43 TOTE £9.50: £2.90, £1.10; EX 11.10 Trifecta £189.60 Pool: £556.05 - 2.17 winning units..
Owner Rakebackmypoker.com **Bred** Shane Doyle **Trained** Stainforth, S Yorks
■ Stewards' Enquiry : Mark Coumbe five-day ban: used whip when out of contention (Mar 17,19-22)

FOCUS
A moderate sprint handicap and the winning time was 0.58 seconds slower than the seller.
Dorothy's Dancing(IRE) Official explanation: trainer's rep had no explanation for the poor form shown

784 MUSKY JELLYBABY MAIDEN FILLIES' STKS 1m (P)
3:20 (3:21) (Class 5) 3-Y-0+ **£2,385** (£704; £352) **Stalls** High

Form RPR
0-2 **1** **Hikma (USA)**[8] 693 3-8-6.... FrannyNorton 4 67
(Mark Johnston) *chsd ldrs: str chal fnl f: led on line* **11/4[2]**
242 **2** *shd* **Devote Myself (IRE)**[14] 620 3-8-6 66.... RichardThomas 8 66
(David Evans) *in tch on outer: wnt 2nd 2f out: led ins fnl f: kpt on wl u.p: hdd on line* **9/4[1]**
3 *1 ½* **Cockney Sparrow** 3-8-6.... LukeMorris 7 62
(Peter Chapple-Hyam) *free to post: led: rdn and hdd ins fnl f: no ex fnl 75yds* **8/1**
-3 **4** *2 ¾* **Barbarella Blue (IRE)**[38] 291 3-8-6.... ChrisCatlin 1 55+
(Marco Botti) *in tch: rdn and lost pl 3f out: styd on fnl f* **5/1[3]**
5 *1 ¼* **Redinessence (IRE)** 4-9-10.... JamieMackay 5 58
(Willie Musson) *dwlt: bhd: pushed along and styd on fnl 2f: nvr nrr* **40/1**
6-4 **6** *nk* **Geanie Mac (IRE)**[16] 573 3-8-6.... MartinLane 3 52
(Tim Pitt) *prom tl hrd rdn and wknd wl over 1f out* **40/1**
0 **7** *2 ¾* **Morilles**[21] 533 3-8-6.... JohnFahy 10 45
(Clive Cox) *wnt rt s: prom: rdn over 2f out: wknd over 1f out* **11/1**
8 *1 ½* **Norse Song** 3-8-6.... NickyMackay 6 41
(David Elsworth) *s.s: a towards rr* **16/1**
5- **9** *½* **Johanna Fosie (IRE)**[187] 5537 3-8-7 ow1.... SamHitchcott 2 41
(Mick Channon) *t.k.h towards rr: rdn 3f out: sn btn* **7/1**
10 *8* **Bright Girl (IRE)** 4-9-3.... NatashaEaton(7) 9 27
(Mark Rimmer) *a bhd: no ch fnl 2f* **50/1**

1m 39.89s (1.69) **Going Correction** +0.05s/f (Slow)
WFA 3 from 4yo 18lb **10** Ran SP% **118.8**
Speed ratings (Par 100): **93,92,91,88,87 87,84,82,82,74**
toteswingers:1&2:£2.20, 2&3:£3.70, 1&3:£17.00 CSF £9.48 TOTE £5.50: £3.50, £1.10, £5.70; EX 10.80 Trifecta £44.30 Pool: £623.86 - 10.40 winning units..
Owner Sheikh Hamdan Bin Mohammed Al Maktoum **Bred** Darley **Trained** Middleham Moor, N Yorks

FOCUS
Not a strong fillies' maiden and it was crucial to race handily.
Norse Song Official explanation: trainer's rep said filly did not face the kickback; jockey said filly ran green

785 MIKE LILLEY 60TH BIRTHDAY H'CAP 1m (P)
3:55 (3:55) (Class 3) (0-95,93) 4-Y-0+ **£6,792** (£2,021; £1,010; £505) **Stalls** High

Form RPR
2-11 **1** **Forceful Appeal (USA)**[35] 351 4-8-11 **83**.... HayleyTurner 10 91
(Simon Dow) *t.k.h: trckd ldr: led 2f out: rdn out* **11/2[3]**
2-21 **2** *1* **George Guru**[21] 520 5-8-9 **86**.... MarkCoumbe(5) 9 91+
(Michael Attwater) *hld up in rr: rdn and gd hdwy 1f out: fin wl to snatch 2nd* **9/2[2]**
0-15 **3** *shd* **True To Form (IRE)**[7] 712 5-9-6 **92**....(p) LukeMorris 2 97
(Ronald Harris) *chsd ldrs: hrd rdn wl over 1f out: r.o ins fnl f* **8/1**
2-01 **4** *nk* **Amitola (IRE)**[28] 426 5-9-5 **91**.... JimmyFortune 8 95
(David Barron) *led tl 2f out: kpt on u.p fnl f* **7/1**
1-44 **5** *2* **Numeral (IRE)**[14] 622 4-9-0 **86**.... RichardHughes 3 86
(Richard Hannon) *chsd ldng pair: one pce appr fnl f* **2/1[1]**
6-33 **6** *hd* **Mr Willis**[14] 622 6-9-7 **93**.... SteveDrowne 7 92
(Terry Clement) *mid-div: rdn and styd on fr over 1f out: unable to chal* **15/2**
-216 **7** *¾* **Shifting Star (IRE)**[28] 426 7-8-13 **88**.... SeanLevey(3) 1 86
(John Bridger) *chsd ldrs on inner: no ex over 1f out* **20/1**
-000 **8** *1 ¼* **Spirit Of Xaar (IRE)**[13] 631 6-8-7 **79** oh4.... FrannyNorton 4 74
(Linda Jewell) *a towards rr* **125/1**
040- **9** *nk* **First Post (IRE)**[161] 6339 5-9-0 **86**.... DaneO'Neill 5 80
(Derek Haydn Jones) *a bhd* **14/1**
200- **10** *¾* **Nelson's Bounty**[129] 7110 5-8-10 **82**.... WilliamCarson 11 74
(Paul D'Arcy) *mid-div on outer: outpcd fnl 2f* **14/1**
0104 **11** *2 ¾* **Bawaardi (IRE)**[28] 431 6-8-3 **80**.... MatthewCosham(5) 6 66
(David Evans) *a bhd* **25/1**

1m 37.82s (-0.38) **Going Correction** +0.05s/f (Slow) **11** Ran SP% **125.0**
Speed ratings (Par 107): **103,102,101,101,99 99,98,97,97,96 93**
toteswingers:1&2:£4.30, 2&3:£10.30, 1&3:£10.50 CSF £32.08 CT £208.96 TOTE £7.90: £2.30, £2.10, £2.90; EX 19.70 Trifecta £400.20 Pool: £1,054.80 - 1.95 winning units..
Owner Simon Caunce **Bred** Juddmonte Farms Inc **Trained** Epsom, Surrey

FOCUS
The best race on the card by some way and a field worthy of the prize, but the early pace didn't look at all strong and the hold-up horses were at a disadvantage as a result.

NOTEBOOK
Forceful Appeal(USA) ◆ was bidding for a hat-trick off a mark 4lb higher than when beating a subsequent winner over C&D last time. Always travelling well, he was in the ideal position on the shoulder of the leader as things panned out and after taking over before the 2f pole, was never going to be caught. He has done nothing but improve since arriving from France and could well go on to even better things. (op 6-1 tchd 5-1)
George Guru ◆, 4lb higher than when beating a subsequent winner at Kempton last month, probably emerges with most credit from this race. Held up well off the ordinary pace, he travelled well on the inside before edging out approaching the home bend. He enjoyed a clear run, but the leaders were quickening from the front off the turn and he did remarkably well to power home for second. He should be able to find compensation soon. (op 4-1 tchd 5-1)
True To Form(IRE) has proved a revelation on sand this winter and should have found this easier than the Listed contest he took part in here seven days earlier. Another to race handily, he had every chance over the last 2f but was inclined to hang away to his left in the straight and was never doing quite enough. (op 11-1)
Amitola(IRE), up another 3lb after her all-the-way success over C&D last month, was again gifted an uncontested lead but the winner served it up to her from some way out and, despite keeping on, she lost two places in the dying strides. She may be best over 7f. (tchd 15-2)
Numeral(IRE) has done well on Polytrack this winter and occupied a decent early position here, but he couldn't quicken sufficiently when asked. He may also be better over 7f and remains 5lb above his last winning mark. (op 11-4 tchd 3-1)
Mr Willis, a five-time winner here, came into this on a losing run of 17 but was only beaten just over a length in a stronger contest over C&D last time. Another to travel well in midfield, he stayed on without offering a threat and would have preferred a stronger gallop. (op 7-1 tchd 8-1)
Shifting Star(IRE) finished behind three of these over C&D last month and didn't help himself by racing keenly early, despite the removal of the blinkers. (op 16-1)

786 LINGFIELDPARK.CO.UK H'CAP 1m 4f (P)
4:30 (4:30) (Class 5) (0-70,70) 4-Y-0+ **£2,385** (£704; £352) **Stalls** Low

Form RPR
40-0 **1** **Spiritual Art**[17] 570 6-9-4 **67**....(b) TomMcLaughlin 7 74
(Luke Dace) *trckd ldr: led 2f out: rdn out* **16/1**
2-12 **2** *1 ¼* **Eagle Nebula**[15] 592 8-9-4 **67**.... AdamKirby 2 72
(Brett Johnson) *chsd ldng pair: rdn to chal over 1f out: nt qckn ins fnl f* **3/1[2]**
3232 **3** *¾* **Kames Park (IRE)**[8] 695 10-8-12 **66**.... CharlesEddery(5) 6 70
(Richard Guest) *stdd s: t.k.h in rr: effrt and rdn 2f out: styd on to take 3rd nr fin* **6/1**
2-23 **4** *shd* **Broughtons Paradis (IRE)**[39] 281 6-9-4 **67**.... StevieDonohoe 4 71
(Willie Musson) *hld up in 6th: wnt 4th 3f out: rdn to press ldrs over 1f out: one pce* **2/1[1]**
1313 **5** *1 ¾* **Maslak (IRE)**[15] 594 8-9-0 **63**.... ChrisCatlin 3 64
(Peter Hiatt) *led tl 2f out: no ex fnl f* **4/1[3]**
4- **6** *3 ½* **Scribe (IRE)**[91] 7630 4-9-5 **70**.... RichardThomas 1 65
(David Evans) *hld up in 5th: rdn and losing tch 3f out: n.d after* **9/1**
0 **7** *16* **Eurhythmic (IRE)**[35] 355 5-9-4 **70**.... RobertLButler(3) 5 40
(Jim Old) *in tch in 4th: hrd rdn over 3f out: wknd over 2f out* **33/1**

2m 33.36s (0.36) **Going Correction** +0.05s/f (Slow)
WFA 4 from 5yo+ 2lb **7** Ran SP% **111.4**
Speed ratings (Par 103): **100,99,98,98,97 95,84**
toteswingers:1&2:£12.60, 2&3:£2.50, 1&3:£10.30 CSF £60.38 TOTE £28.70: £10.50, £1.30; EX 95.70.
Owner Miss Ruth Kennedy **Bred** R Haim **Trained** Five Oaks, W Sussex

FOCUS
The way this ordinary handicap was going to be run was fairly predictable, though the result less so. The pace didn't look that strong.

787 FOLLOW US ON TWITTER @LINGFIELDPARK H'CAP 1m 2f (P)
5:05 (5:05) (Class 5) (0-75,70) 3-Y-O **£2,385** (£704; £352) **Stalls** Low

Form RPR
100- **1** **Sheila's Buddy**[115] 7336 3-9-0 **65**.... LiamKeniry 8 72
(J S Moore) *s.s: towards rr: wd bnd into st: gd hdwy over 1f out: r.o to ld fnl 100yds* **20/1**
60-4 **2** *1 ¾* **Santadelacruze**[15] 596 3-9-0 **65**.... TomQueally 2 68
(Gary Moore) *in tch in 4th: rdn to press ldr ins fnl f: one pce fnl 100yds* **7/2[2]**
0-31 **3** *shd* **News Desk**[17] 571 3-9-1 **66**.... RobertHavlin 3 69
(John Gosden) *chsd ldng pair: drvn to ld 1f out: hdd and nt qckn fnl 100yds* **7/4[1]**
0-34 **4** *2 ¼* **Arte Del Calcio**[14] 620 3-9-2 **67**.... DaneO'Neill 6 65
(David Elsworth) *hld up in 5th: rdn over 2f out: btn whn n.m.r over 1f out: kpt on fnl f* **7/2[2]**
4-06 **5** *1 ¼* **King's Wharf (IRE)**[21] 523 3-8-11 **67**.... MatthewCosham(5) 4 63
(David Evans) *led: qcknd 3f out: hdd & wknd 1f out* **10/1[3]**
004- **6** *hd* **Kelpie Blitz (IRE)**[143] 6792 3-9-1 **66**.... MickyFenton 7 61
(Seamus Durack) *chsd ldr: rdn to chal over 1f out: wknd ent fnl f* **16/1**

1-55 **7** 2 1/2 **King Of Wing (IRE)**[10] 656 3 -9-5 70........................(v[1]) WilliamCarson 1 60
(Jim Boyle) *a towards rr: hrd rdn and nt trble ldrs fnl 2f* **16/1**
621- **8** 11 **Priestley's Reward (IRE)**[28] 7117 3 -8-10 68................ LukeRowe(7) 5 36
(Mrs K Burke) *s.s: hld up off the pce in last: sme hdwy 4f out: wknd over 2f out* **10/1**[3]
2m 6.79s (0.19) **Going Correction** +0.05s/f (Slow) **8**Ran SP% **115.5**
Speed ratings (Par 98): **101,99,99,97,96 96,94,85**
toteswingers:1&2:£21.50, 2&3:£2.20, 1&3:£14.00 CSF £89.82 CT £190.86 TOTE £14.20 : £2.40 , £1.80, £1.10 ; EX 80.50 Trifecta £264.20 Pool: £1,064.15 - 2.98 winning units.
Owner Ray Styles **Bred** Mrs Anita R Dodd **Trained** Upper Lambourn, Berks
FOCUS
A modest handicap and the early pace was ordinary.
T/Plt: £410.90 to a £1 stake. Pool £69,169.69 - 122.86 winning units. T/Qpdt: £13.10 to a £1 stake. Pool £5,601.20 - 314.40 winning units. LM

[754] MEYDAN (L-H)
Saturday, March 3
OFFICIAL GOING: Tapeta: standard; turf: good

792a AL DANA WEALTH (H'CAP) (TURF) 1m 2f
4:55 (4:55) (100-112,112) 3-Y-O+
£67,741 (£22,580; £11,290 ; £5,645 ; £3,387 ; £2,258)

RPR
1 **Simon De Montfort (IRE)**[182] 5711 5 -8-10 104....... MickaelBarzalona 4 109
(Mahmood Al Zarooni) *settled in rr: smooth prog 3f out: n.m.r 1 1/2f: r.o wl once clr: led fnl 55yds* **4/1**[2]
2 1 **Mikhail Glinka (IRE)**[9] 678 5 -9-2 109....................(vt) RoystonFfrench 5 113
(H J Brown, South Africa) *trckd ldr: led 2f out: hdd fnl 55yds* **16/1**
3 2 1/4 **Anaerobio (ARG)**[16] 587 5 -8-8 101.............................(t) MircoDemuro 3 101
(M F De Kock, South Africa) *sn led: hdd 2f out: kpt on same pce* **10/1**
4 2 **Quick Wit**[16] 591 5 -8-11 105.............................. SilvestreDeSousa 12 100
(Saeed Bin Suroor) *mid-div: chsd ldrs 2 1/2f out: kpt on same pce fnl 1 1/2f* **12/1**
5 1 1/4 **Marcret (ITY)**[16] 590 5 -9-1 108........................ RyanMoore 10 101
(Marco Botti) *s.i.s: settled in rr: r.o wl fnl 2f* **10/1**
6 nse **Rerouted (USA)**[9] 682 4 -9-1 108...(b) KShea 1 101
(M F De Kock, South Africa) *trckd ldng pair: ev ch 1 1/2f: nt qckn fnl f* **5/1**[3]
7 2 1/4 **Grand Vent (IRE)**[272] 2751 4 -9-5 112............................ FrankieDettori 6 100
(Saeed Bin Suroor) *nvr bttr than mid-div* **13/8**[1]
8 2 **Trois Rois (FR)**[16] 591 7 -8-9 102.............................(b) TadhgO'Shea 11 86
(Ismail Mohammed) *in rr of mid-div: n.d* **25/1**
9 shd **Unusual Suspect (USA)**[16] 591 8 -9-5 112...............(v) JamieSpencer 7 96
(Michael Kent, Australia) *settled in rr: nvr nr to chal* **12/1**
10 1 1/4 **Masterofthe rolls (IRE)**[23] 489 4 -8-10 104..................... KierenFallon 8 85
(Saeed Bin Suroor) *in rr of mid-div: nvr able to chal* **7/1**
11 shd **Summit Surge (IRE)**[37] 319 8 -9-0 107.........................(t) JamesDoyle 9 89
(Luca Cumani) *in rr of mid-div: nvr able to chal* **20/1**
12 hd **Grafitti**[15] 617 7 -8-9 102...(t) Per-AndersGraberg 2 83
(Niels Petersen, Norway) *in rr of mid-div: rdn 4f out: sn btn* **33/1**
2m 3.93s (123.93) **12**Ran SP% **138.3**
CSF: £77.05; TRICAST: £647.86.
Owner Godolphin **Bred** Darley **Trained** Newmarket, Suffolk
FOCUS
Rail out 15m on turf track. The feature 1m2f handicap was a wide-open affair.
NOTEBOOK
Simon De Montfort (IRE) returning from a six-month absence, won in impressive fashion despite giving the leaders a start and being held in for a couple of strides when beginning his run. A classy performer at his best, he's won first time out for the last four seasons, including over C&D last season and when in this form isn't far short of Group 1 standard. (op 9-2)
Mikhail Glinka (IRE) had run well on his first two starts at the carnival this year, prior to disappointing last time out. He returned to form in a first-time visor only being beaten by a classier rival. His yard is starting to come into form and should continue to pick up prize money over the next few weeks.
Anaerobio(ARG) bounced back to form returned to turf. He benefitted from dictating a modest tempo in front. (op 8-1 tchd 9-1)
Quick Wit, racing off a 5lb higher mark than when winning over C&D two start back, ran a respectable race without ever looking like threatening the first three.
Rerouted(USA), 3lb higher than when finishing runner-up off 3lb lower over 1f shorter last week, ran poorly. He needs to come down in trip and in the weights if he's going to be winning.
Grand Vent (IRE) was another to disappoint. Strong in the market on his UAE debut and first start since being beaten in the French Derby last June. He was never near enough to mount a challenge. Despite being lightly raced he doesn't look anything special.

788a - 791a & 793a - 799a (Foreign Racing) - See Raceform Interactive

[781] LINGFIELD (L-H)
Monday, March 5
OFFICIAL GOING: Standard
Wind: Strong, half against Weather: Fine

800 SUMMER EVENINGS AT LINGFIELD PARK CLAIMING STKS 6f (P)
2:30 (2:30) (Class 6) 4-Y-O+ **£1,704** (£503; £251) **Stalls** Low

Form RPR
3112 **1** **Drawnfromthepast (IRE)**[12] 654 7 -9-1 79.................. GeorgeBaker 4 82
(Jamie Osborne) *hld up in last: prog on outer wl over 1f out: cajoled along and r.o to ld last 50yds* **13/8**[1]
1211 **2** 3/4 **Hinton Admiral**[21] 545 8 -9-0 75.. JoeFanning 5 78
(Keith Dalgleish) *awkward s: sn chsd ldr: shkn up to ld jst over 1f out: hdd and nt qckn last 50yds* **13/8**[1]
5210 **3** 2 **Waterloo Dock**[9] 710 7 -8-12 68..............................(v) LukeMorris 1 70
(Michael Quinn) *led: urged along over 2f out: hdd jst over 1f out: one pce* **10/1**[3]
0240 **4** 1 1/4 **One Way Or Another (AUS)**[5] 626 9 -8-11 73........(b) HayleyTurner 2 65
(David Evans) *stdd s: trckd ldng pair: pushed along 2f out: nt qckn and wl hld over 1f out* **7/2**[2]
1m 12.15s (0.25) **Going Correction** +0.10s/f (Slow) **4**Ran SP% **107.5**
Speed ratings (Par 101): **102,101,98,96**
CSF £4.46 TOTE £3.20 ; EX 3.00 .
Owner Mark Benton **Bred** D And Mrs D Veitch **Trained** Upper Lambourn, Berks

FOCUS
Straightforward form with the first three pretty much to their marks.

801 DOWNLOAD THE NEW MARRIOTT GOLF APP (S) STKS 6f (P)
3:00 (3:01) (Class 6) 3-Y-O **£1,704** (£503; £251) **Stalls** Low

Form RPR
3-33 **1** **Superplex**[25] 481 3 -8-13 63..(p) JimmyFortune 2 69
(John Quinn) *w.w in rr: prog on inner 2f out to ld over 1f out: hung rt but drvn clr* **4/1**[2]
0-46 **2** 2 3/4 **Miss Purity Pinker (IRE)**[23] 536 3 -8-8 60.............(v) RichardThomas 6 55+
(David Evans) *pressed ldrs: led over 3f out: carried wd by loose horse bnd 2f out: sn hdd: tried to rally 1f out: outpcd* **14/1**
3433 **3** 1 1/4 **Faraway**[18] 583 3 -9-5 63...(b) LukeMorris 7 62
(Ronald Harris) *w.w: prog over 2f out: cl up over 1f out: outpcd after* **4/1**[2]
4-65 **4** 6 **Majestic Rose**[14] 637 3 -9-0 65.. MartinHarley 4 38
(Mick Channon) *uns rdr and bolted to post: stdd s: hld up in last: rdn bef 1/2-way: no ch: tk remote 4th fnl f* **5/1**[3]
-621 **5** 3/4 **Thorpe Bay**[18] 583 3 -9-5 66...(b) HayleyTurner 5 41
(Conor Dore) *s.i.s: t.k.h early: hld up bhd ldrs: pushed along and could nt qckn 2f out: wknd qckly fnl f* **13/8**[1]
50-0 **6** 4 1/2 **Tumbleowtashoes**[19] 565 3 -8-10 24........................... RyanPowell(3) 3 20
(John Ryan) *led after 1f to over 3f out: sn rdn: lft disputing ld wl over 1f out: wknd qckly* **100/1**
0403 **U** **Arabian Flight**[16] 621 3 -8-8 58.. KieranO'Neill 1
(John Bridger) *taken down early: led 1f: cl up whn uns rdr wl over 3f out* **6/1**
1m 12.32s (0.42) **Going Correction** +0.10s/f (Slow) **7**Ran SP% **116.7**
Speed ratings (Par 96): **101,97,95,87,86 80,**
toteswingers:1&2:£10.70, 2&3:£10.10, 1&3:£2.70 CSF £56.70 TOTE £4.40 : £1.90 , £7.50 ; EX 63.60 Trifecta £599.20 Pool: £915.12- 1.13 winning units. .There was no bid for the winner.
Owner Allan Stennett **Bred** Mickley Stud, Stennett, Hillside Racing **Trained** Settrington, N Yorks
FOCUS
An eventful seller, and ordinary form for the grade. The winner is rated back towards his early 2yo form.
Miss Purity Pinker (IRE) Official explanation: jockey said filly suffered interference in running by loose horse

802 FURLONGS & FAIRWAYS H'CAP 5f (P)
3:30 (3:30) (Class 6) (0-60,59) 3-Y-O **£1,704** (£503; £251) **Stalls** High

Form RPR
4520 **1** **Marie's Fantasy**[5] 734 3 -9-2 54.................................. JamieGoldstein 3 60
(Zoe Davison) *hld up in 5th: pushed along 1/2-way: prog on wd outside over 1f out: r.o to ld last 75yds* **11/2**
35-0 **2** 3/4 **Betty Brook (IRE)**[23] 524 3 -9-6 58................................ SteveDrowne 4 61
(Nick Littmoden) *trckd ldng pair: gng strly: wnt 2nd wl over 1f out: shkn up to chal ent fnl f: fnd little* **7/1**
0-35 **3** nk **My Name Is Sam**[5] 734 3 -8-9 47.. LukeMorris 5 49
(Ronald Harris) *mde most: drvn and jnd 1f out: hdd and no ex last 75yds* **2/1**[1]
563- **4** 1 1/4 **Chicarito**[108] 7452 3 -9-7 59..(p) JohnFahy 1 56
(John Gallagher) *hld up in 4th: gng wl 2f out: rdn and nt qckn over 1f out: kpt on same pce after* **9/2**[3]
5-04 **5** 1/2 **First Rebellion**[5] 734 3 -8-4 47.. RaulDaSilva(5) 2 43
(Tony Carroll) *pressed ldr to wl over 1f out: rdn and nt qckn after: eased whn hld nr fin* **3/1**[2]
000- **6** 5 **Maltease Ah**[122] 7267 3 -9-5 57...(t) MartinHarley 7 35
(Andrew Reid) *stdd s fr wd draw: hld up in last: effrt on inner whn n.m.r 2f out: wknd over 1f out* **20/1**
59.92s (1.12) **Going Correction** +0.10s/f (Slow) **6**Ran SP% **109.2**
Speed ratings (Par 96): **95,93,93,91,90 82**
toteswingers:1&2:£4.80, 2&3:£1.90, 1&3:£2.90 CSF £39.10 TOTE £6.80 : £4.00 , £1.50 ; EX 37.60.
Owner David J Bearman **Bred** Mesnil, Mount Coote, New England Stud **Trained** Hammerwood, E Sussex
FOCUS
A weak 3yo sprint handicap, run at a decent pace. Limited but sound form.

803 BREATHE SPA AT LINGFIELD MARRIOTT H'CAP 1m 4f (P)
4:00 (4:00) (Class 5) (0-75,74) 3-Y-O **£2,385** (£704; £352) **Stalls** Low

Form RPR
22-2 **1** **Quixote**[49] 196 3 -8-10 63.. HayleyTurner 5 70
(Clive Brittain) *trckd ldng trio: wnt 3rd 3f out and chsd ldr 2f out: pushed into ld over 1f out: hrd pressed and drvn last 100yds: hld on wl* **4/1**[2]
-653 **2** hd **Gabrial's Lexi (IRE)**[11] 675 3 -8-8 61............................ FrannyNorton 1 67
(Richard Fahey) *hld up in 5th: steadily clsd fr over 2f out: wnt 2nd ins fnl f and clsd on wnr: could nt qckn last strides* **8/1**
4-51 **3** 2 1/4 **Next Cry (USA)**[12] 656 3 -9-7 74.. KieranO'Neill 3 76
(Richard Hannon) *trckd ldng pair to 3f out: effrt on inner whn nt clr run briefly 2f out: styd on to take 3rd fnl f: nt gng pce to chal* **2/1**[1]
-404 **4** 1 1/2 **Foster's Road**[9] 709 3 -8-5 58..(v) ChrisCatlin 7 58
(Mick Channon) *trckd ldr: led wl over 2f out and kicked on: hdd and fdd over 1f out* **20/1**
02-1 **5** 11 **Quiet Appeal (IRE)**[46] 217 3 -8-3 56................................. JoeFanning 6 38
(Mark Johnston) *led at fair pce: hdd wl over 2f out: wknd qckly wl over 1f out* **9/2**[3]
150- **6** 1/2 **Grand Gold**[143] 6829 3 -9-7 74.. GeorgeBaker 4 56
(Seamus Durack) *hld up in last pair: rdn over 4f out: sn struggling: wl bhd fnl 2f* **25/1**
530- **7** 12 **Shivsingh**[161] 6399 3 -8-9 67.. CharlesBishop(5) 2 29
(Mick Channon) *hld up in last pair: rdn and wknd over 3f out: t.o* **10/1**
0-61 **8** 2 **Captain Cardington (IRE)**[7] 726 3 -8-11 64..............(v) MartinHarley 8 23
(Mick Channon) *hld up in 6th: pushed along over 4f out: wknd qckly 3f out: t.o* **15/2**
2m 33.54s (0.54) **Going Correction** +0.10s/f (Slow) **8**Ran SP% **112.1**
Speed ratings (Par 98): **102,101,100,99,92 91,83,82**
toteswingers:1&2:£6.10, 2&3:£4.60, 1&3:£2.60 CSF £34.11 CT £80.11 TOTE £3.00 : £1.10 , £2.40, £2.00 ; EX 33.20 Trifecta £121.00 Pool: £873.60 - 5.34 winning units.
Owner C E Brittain **Bred** Mr & Mrs R & P Scott **Trained** Newmarket, Suffolk

FOCUS
This moderate 3-y-o handicap was run at an average pace and the first pair were nicely clear at the finish. It was not a bad race for the grade and the form is sound, rated around the fourth.

804 GREAT OFFERS ON GOLF MEMBERSHIP CLAIMING STKS 1m 2f (P)
4:30 (4:30) (Class 6) 4-Y-O+ **£1,704** (£503; £251) **Stalls** Low

Form RPR
-111 **1** **Munsarim (IRE)**^{31} [402] 5-9-5 86.....(b) JoeFanning 7 84+
(Keith Dalgleish) *t.k.h: sn trckd ldr: led wl over 2f out: hung bdly rt fr over 1f out and ended up against nr side rail but in n.d fnl f* **8/15**^{1}

2445 **2** *3 ½* **Dazzling Valentine**^{3} [771] 4-8-1 73..... NatashaEaton$^{(7)}$ 3 66
(Alan Bailey) *hld up in 4th: prog to chse wnr 2f out: kpt on but no imp fnl f* **9/2**^{2}

00-6 **3** *1 ¼* **Hurricane Spirit (IRE)**^{12} [648] 8-8-13 73..... SteveDrowne 1 68
(Terry Clement) *hld up in last trio: rdn and effrt on inner over 2f out: kpt on same pce: no threat* **12/1**

5250 **4** *nse* **Tuxedo**^{10} [685] 7-8-13 62..... WilliamCarson 4 68
(Peter Hiatt) *led 1f: trckd ldng pair: nt qckn over 2f out: tried to renew effrt over 1f out: wl hld whn short of room nr fin* **33/1**

1413 **5** *½* **Spinning Ridge (IRE)**^{28} [449] 7-8-13 71.....(v) LukeMorris 5 67
(Ronald Harris) *hld up in last pair: effrt over 2f out: hrd rdn and one pce fnl f: no threat* **15/2**^{3}

5-45 **6** *3 ¼* **Cheers Buddy (IRE)**^{12} [655] 4-8-11 64..... HayleyTurner 2 59
(David C Griffiths) *led after 1f: shkn up and hdd wl over 2f out: fdd over 1f out* **20/1**

3050 **7** *4 ½* **Sienna Blue**^{21} [550] 4-8-0 57..... JakePayne$^{(7)}$ 8 46
(Bill Turner) *stdd s and s.i.s: hld up in last: brief effrt 2f out: sn wknd* **80/1**

2m 7.65s (1.05) **Going Correction** +0.10s/f (Slow) 7 Ran SP% **111.8**
Speed ratings (Par 101): **99,96,95,95,94 92,88**
toteswingers:1&2:£1.60, 2&3:£4.40, 1&3:£2.80 CSF £3.01 TOTE £1.80: £1.30, £1.60; EX 3.80 Trifecta £16.00 Pool: £1037.51 - 47.85 winning units..
Owner Joseph Leckie & Sons Ltd **Bred** Shadwell Estate Company Limited **Trained** Carluke, S Lanarks

■ Stewards' Enquiry : Natasha Eaton two-day ban: careless riding (Mar 19-20)

FOCUS
A 1m2f claimer that was run at a steady pace and developed into a sprint around 3f out. Not form to be too sure about and the winner did not need to match his best.

805 BOOK BIRTHDAY PARTIES AT LINGFIELD PARK MAIDEN STKS 1m (P)
5:00 (5:01) (Class 5) 3-Y-O+ **£2,385** (£704; £352) **Stalls** High

Form RPR
0- **1** **Solemn Oath (USA)**^{138} [6951] 3-8-10 0..... LukeMorris 6 75+
(Ed Vaughan) *t.k.h: trckd ldng pair: shkn up 2f out: r.o to ld jst ins fnl f: sn in command: readily* **6/4**^{1}

566- **2** *2 ¼* **Haymarket**^{150} [6675] 3-8-10 73..... JoeFanning 2 70
(Mark Johnston) *led 1f: trckd ldr: rdn 2f out: tried to chal over 1f out: one pce fnl f* **11/4**^{2}

53 **3** *½* **Marmas**^{17} [595] 3-8-10 0..... KieranO'Neill 1 69
(Marcus Tregoning) *pushed up to ld after 1f: rdn 2f out: hdd and one pce jst ins fnl f* **8/1**^{3}

2 **4** *nk* **Prime Run**^{14} [638] 3-8-5 0..... MartinLane 4 63
(David Simcock) *t.k.h: trckd ldng pair: rdn 2f out: nt qckn over 1f out: one pce after* **11/4**^{2}

5 *9* **Multifac'Eted** 3-8-2 0..... RyanPowell$^{(3)}$ 7 41
(J S Moore) *slowly away and veered rt: sn in tch in last pair: shkn up and outpcd fr over 2f out: fdd* **33/1**

00- **6** *½* **Glens Wobbly**^{158} [6473] 4-10-0 0..... RobertHavlin 5 45
(Jonathan Geake) *hld up in 5th: shkn up over 2f out: sn lft wl bhd by ldrs* **100/1**

0-6 **7** *4 ½* **One Cool Dancer (IRE)**^{19} [565] 3-8-5 0..... JohnFahy 3 29
(John Gallagher) *sn in last: struggling fr 1/2-way* **100/1**

1m 39.39s (1.19) **Going Correction** +0.10s/f (Slow)
WFA 3 from 4yo 18lb 7 Ran SP% **109.4**
Speed ratings (Par 103): **98,95,95,94,85 85,80**
toteswingers:1&2:£1.10, 2&3:£3.20, 1&3:£2.40 CSF £5.30 TOTE £1.60: £1.10, £2.40; EX 5.70.
Owner Gold Rush Thoroughbreds **Bred** John Antonelli **Trained** Newmarket, Suffolk

FOCUS
A modest maiden. It was steadily run and there are one or two doubts over the form. The race is rated around the third and fourth.

806 WINTER DERBY COMING SOON FILLIES' H'CAP 6f (P)
5:30 (5:30) (Class 5) (0-75,75) 4-Y-O+ **£2,385** (£704; £352) **Stalls** Low

Form RPR
31- **1** **Haamaat (IRE)**^{112} [7411] 4-9-2 73..... AdamBeschizza$^{(3)}$ 2 86+
(William Haggas) *hld up in last: rapid prog to join ldrs over 2f out: sn shkn up: r.o to ld over 1f out: sn wl in command* **4/6**^{1}

01-4 **2** *1 ¾* **Catalinas Diamond (IRE)**^{12} [658] 4-8-8 62.....(t) SteveDrowne 5 69
(Pat Murphy) *hld up in last pair: prog over 1f out to chse wnr ins fnl f: shkn up and styd on but no imp* **14/1**

006- **3** *1 ½* **Secret Queen**^{257} [3283] 5-8-8 62.....(v^1) LukeMorris 8 65
(Martin Hill) *t.k.h: trckd ldng pair: rdn 2f out: kpt on one pce after* **12/1**

1334 **4** *hd* **Dancing Welcome**^{5} [735] 6-9-7 75.....(b) RichardKingscote 7 77
(Milton Bradley) *mde most to over 1f out: fdd fnl f* **5/1**^{2}

2410 **5** *1 ¼* **Gorgeous Goblin (IRE)**^{9} [711] 5-9-2 70.....(t) JimmyFortune 3 68
(David C Griffiths) *t.k.h: trckd ldr: disp ld on inner gng wl 2f out: shkn up and wknd tamely over 1f out* **11/2**^{3}

-002 **6** *nk* **Basle**^{10} [687] 5-8-7 61 oh2.....(t) ShaneKelly 1 58
(Gay Kelleway) *hld up: in last pair fr 1/2-way: jst pushed along over 1f out: taken to outer and styd on nr fin: nvr remotely involved* **16/1**

1m 12.86s (0.96) **Going Correction** +0.10s/f (Slow) 6 Ran SP% **112.3**
Speed ratings (Par 100): **97,94,92,92,90 90**
toteswingers:1&2:£3.70, 2&3:£13.60, 1&3:£4.10 CSF £11.72 CT £61.49 TOTE £1.90: £1.40, £5.40; EX 8.10 Trifecta £71.40 Pool: £988.14 - 10.23 winning units..
Owner Hamdan Al Maktoum **Bred** Hunscote House Farm Stud **Trained** Newmarket, Suffolk

FOCUS
An ordinary fillies' handicap. The winner did it well considering and there should be more to come.
T/Plt: £218.40 to a £1 stake. Pool of £85,794.17 - 286.66 winning tickets. T/Qpdt: £11.10 to a £1 stake. Pool of £8,355.96 - 553.05 winning tickets. JN

^{747}SOUTHWELL (L-H)
Tuesday, March 6

OFFICIAL GOING: Standard
Wind: Virtually nil Weather: Fine and dry

807 CHAMPIONS LEAGUE BETTING WITH FREEBETTING.CO.UK H'CAP 7f (F)
2:10 (2:10) (Class 6) (0-52,52) 4-Y-O+ **£1,704** (£503; £251) **Stalls** Low

Form RPR
0-60 **1** **Tenancy (IRE)**^{19} [578] 8-8-11 47 oh1 ow1.....(b) RobertWinston 6 55
(Shaun Harris) *qckly away: mde all rdn clr wl over 1f out: edgd rt ins fnl f: kpt on wl towards fin* **20/1**

-060 **2** *½* **Bonnie Prince Blue**^{12} [670] 9-8-11 50..... DaleSwift$^{(3)}$ 8 57
(Ian McInnes) *chsd ldrs on outer and sn pushed along: rdn and outpcd 1/2-way: swtchd lft and hdwy on inner 2f out: sn rdn and styd on to chse wnr ent fnl f: kpt on* **8/1**

0042 **3** *1 ½* **Odd Ball (IRE)**^{11} [690] 5-8-8 47..... AmyRyan$^{(3)}$ 4 50
(Lisa Williamson) *dwlt and sn swtchd to outer: hdwy 3f out: rdn to chse wnr wl over 1f out: kpt on same pce* **5/1**^{3}

50-0 **4** *4 ½* **Sopran Nad (ITY)**^{22} [550] 8-8-10 51.....(b) RaulDaSilva$^{(5)}$ 7 42
(Frank Sheridan) *chsd wnr: rdn along over 2f out: drvn and wknd wl over 1f out* **10/3**^{2}

4104 **5** *2* **Fearless Poet (IRE)**^{7} [729] 4-9-2 52.....(b) TomEaves 2 37
(Bryan Smart) *dwlt: sn rdn along and in tch: drvn 2f out and sn btn* **5/4**^{1}

0-00 **6** *2 ½* **Mnarani (IRE)**^{25} [503] 5-8-10 46.....(b) ChrisCatlin 3 25
(James Evans) *t.k.h: chsd ldng pair: rdn over 2f out and sn wknd* **9/1**

000/ **7** *22* **Royal Crest**^{571} [5024] 6-8-10 46 oh1.....(b) JoeFanning 1
(Andrew Crook) *chsd ldrs on inner: rdn along 3f out: sn wknd* **33/1**

1m 30.38s (0.08) **Going Correction** -0.05s/f (Stan) 7 Ran SP% **113.0**
Speed ratings (Par 101): **97,96,94,89,87 84,59**
toteswingers:1&2:£12.10, 1&3:£7.10, 2&3:£4.20 CSF £160.48 CT £930.14 TOTE £39.20: £13.00, £4.30; EX 105.50 Trifecta £169.50 Pool: £973.60 - 4.25 winning units..
Owner Wilf Hobson **Bred** G A E And J Smith Bloodstock Ltd **Trained** Carburton, Notts

FOCUS
A very poor handicap and a difficult winner to predict. Shaky form, rated around the third and fourth.
Tenancy(IRE) Official explanation: trainer said, regarding apparent improvement in form, that the gelding was an inconsistent sort but was a course specialist.
Fearless Poet(IRE) Official explanation: jockey said gelding never travelled

808 FREE BETTING WITH FREEBETTING.CO.UK H'CAP 5f (F)
2:40 (2:40) (Class 5) (0-75,71) 4-Y-O+ **£2,264** (£673; £336; £168) **Stalls** High

Form RPR
0303 **1** **Dancing Freddy (IRE)**^{8} [718] 5-9-7 71.....(tp) WilliamCarson 3 81
(Richard Guest) *dwlt: sn trcking ldrs: hdwy to ld over 2f out: rdn over 1f out: drvn ins fnl f: kpt on wl* **4/1**^{1}

0-44 **2** *½* **Love You Louis**^{20} [560] 6-9-6 70..... JoeFanning 2 78
(J R Jenkins) *led: hdd over 2f out: cl up and rdn over 1f out: ev ch tl edgd rt and no ex wl ins fnl f* **13/2**^{3}

210- **3** *1 ¼* **Wreningham**^{66} [7940] 7-8-9 62..... RyanClark$^{(3)}$ 5 66
(Pat Eddery) *prom: cl up 1/2-way: rdn to chal over 1f out: sn edgd lft: ev ch tl drvn and one pce fnl 100yds* **14/1**

5522 **4** *hd* **Punching**^{14} [640] 8-9-4 68..... HayleyTurner 4 71
(Conor Dore) *trckd ldrs: hdwy and cl up 2f out: rdn and n.m.r over 1f out: kpt on u.p fnl f* **7/1**

-405 **5** *nk* **La Capriosa**^{28} [461] 6-8-11 61.....(p) RobertWinston 1 63
(Scott Dixon) *dwlt: sn cl up on wd outside: rdn along 2f out: kpt on same pce appr fnl f* **16/1**

2154 **6** *nk* **No Mean Trick (USA)**^{8} [718] 6-9-3 67..... MickyFenton 9 68+
(Paul Midgley) *chsd ldrs on stands' rail: pushed along and outpcd over 2f out: sn swtchd lft and rdn: styd on ins fnl f* **4/1**^{1}

6216 **7** *shd* **Shawkantango**^{11} [696] 5-8-12 65.....(v) DaleSwift$^{(3)}$ 6 65+
(Derek Shaw) *s.i.s and sn rdn in rr: swtchd lft after 1f: drvn 1/2-way: hdwy over 1f out: styd on strly fnl f: nrst fin* **15/2**

2-26 **8** *nk* **Soopacal (IRE)**^{35} [371] 7-8-12 65.....(p) LeeTopliss$^{(3)}$ 10 64
(Brian Ellison) *chsd ldrs: rdn along 2f out: kpt on same pce* **5/1**^{2}

4213 **9** *1* **Suddenly Susan (IRE)**^{28} [461] 4-9-1 70.....(b) RaulDaSilva$^{(5)}$ 7 66
(Scott Dixon) *prom: rdn along over 2f out: grad wknd* **8/1**

20-0 **10** *8* **Legal Eagle (IRE)**^{35} [371] 7-9-3 70.....(p) RobertLButler$^{(3)}$ 8 37
(Paul Green) *chsd ldrs: rdn along bef 1/2-way: sn wknd* **33/1**

59.39s (-0.31) **Going Correction** +0.025s/f (Slow) 10 Ran SP% **120.9**
Speed ratings (Par 103): **103,102,100,99,99 98,98,98,96,83**
toteswingers:1&2:£5.20, 1&3:£15.40, 2&3:£21.30 CSF £31.42 CT £339.49 TOTE £6.50: £2.00, £1.50, £4.20; EX 43.50 Trifecta £243.20 Pool: £759.33 - 2.31 winning units..
Owner Rakebackmypoker.com **Bred** Vincent Duignan **Trained** Stainforth, S Yorks

FOCUS
An ordinary sprint handicap, but a competitive one and it favoured those to race handily. The winner is rated to his winter best.

809 HORSE RACING FREE BETS WITH FREEBETTING.CO.UK (S) STKS 1m 3f (F)
3:10 (3:11) (Class 6) 4-Y-O+ **£1,704** (£503; £251) **Stalls** Low

Form RPR
0-43 **1** **Trans Sonic**^{12} [671] 9-8-8 72.....(p) DeclanCannon$^{(3)}$ 4 82
(David O'Meara) *disp ld tl led over 3f out: rdn clr over 2f out: kpt on strly fnl f* **7/1**^{3}

03-1 **2** *7* **Stand Guard**^{19} [582] 8-9-1 79..... AdamKirby 1 73
(John Butler) *in tch: pushed along 1/2-way: hdwy to chse ldng pair over 3f out: rdn to chse wnr over 2f out: sn drvn and hung rt over 1f out: no imp fnl f* **4/11**^{1}

00-6 **3** *13* **Norton Girl**^{56} [113] 4-8-7 38 ow2..... PatrickMathers 6 41
(Tracy Waggott) *chsd ldng pair: rdn along 4f out: drvn wl over 2f out: plugged on to take poor 3rd ins fnl f* **100/1**

100- **4** *1* **Clara Zetkin**^{46} [237] 4-8-5 75..... MartinLane 5 39
(Patrick Michael Verling, Ire) *hld up in rr: hdwy over 4f out: rdn along 3f out: plugged on fnl 2f: n.d* **16/1**

61-2 **5** *¾* **River Ardeche**^{12} [671] 7-9-1 69..... JoeFanning 2 46
(Tracy Waggott) *slt ld: rdn along over 4f out: hdd over 3f out: wknd fnl 2f: hung bdly rt and lost poor 3rd ins fnl f* **5/1**^{2}

600- **6** *15* **Brave Enough (USA)**^{76} [7850] 5-8-4 46.....(tp) NedCurtis$^{(7)}$ 3 15
(Roger Curtis) *in tch: rdn along 5f out: sn outpcd and bhd* **33/1**

7 20 **Liver Bird**[240] 4-8-10 0 MickyFenton 7
(Paul Midgley) *in tch: rdn along over 4f out: sn wknd and bhd* **40/1**
2m 25.6s (-2.40) **Going Correction** -0.05s/f (Stan)
WFA 4 from 5yo+ 1lb 7 Ran SP% **114.7**
Speed ratings (Par 101): **106,100,91,90,90 79,64**
toteswingers:1&2:£1.60, 1&3:£15.30, 2&3:£15.60 CSF £10.17 TOTE £4.70: £2.10, £1.10; EX 13.20.There was no bid for the winner.
Owner Mrs Lynne Lumley **Bred** I A Balding **Trained** Nawton, N Yorks
■ Stewards' Enquiry : Patrick Mathers three-day ban: weighed in 2lb heavy (Mar 20-22)
FOCUS
An uncompetitive seller and a result that would have surprised many. The pace was decent thanks to a contested lead. It's hard to know what this form amounts to.

810 EXCLUSIVE FREE BETTING WITH FREEBETTING.CO.UK H'CAP 1m 6f (F)
3:40 (3:44) (Class 5) (0-75,75) 4-Y-0+ **£2,385** (£704; £352) **Stalls** Low

Form RPR
11-6 **1** **Storm Hawk (IRE)**[21] 555 5-9-7 **73** (b) RyanClark(3) 2 84
(Pat Eddery) *hld up in rr: hdwy on outer 5f out: led 3f out and sn rdn clr: styd on strly fnl f* **3/1**[2]
11-1 **2** 2 3/4 **Mediterranean Sea (IRE)**[33] 381 6-9-10 **73** FrederikTylicki 6 80
(J R Jenkins) *hld up: stdy hdwy over 4f out: effrt to chse wnr 2f out: sn rdn and no imp fnl f* **7/4**[1]
-105 **3** 7 **First Rock (IRE)**[21] 555 6-9-0 **68** GarryWhillans(5) 3 65
(Alan Swinbank) *t.k.h early: prom: led 4f out: hdd 3f out and sn rdn: kpt on one pce fnl 2f* **9/2**[3]
-500 **4** 3 3/4 **Irish Jugger (USA)**[41] 296 5-8-12 **60** ow1 (b[1]) JamesMillman 5 53
(Rod Millman) *hld up in rr: hdwy over 4f out: rdn to chse ldrs 3f out: sn one pce* **10/1**
1315 **5** 3/4 **Magic Millie (IRE)**[12] 668 5-8-12 **66** AmyScott(5) 4 57
(Alastair Lidderdale) *trckd ldrs: hdwy to ld 1/2-way: hdd 4f out and sn rdn: wknd wl over 2f out* **20/1**
360- **6** 1 3/4 **Cotton King**[184] 5761 5-9-12 **75** (vt) StevieDonohoe 7 63
(Tobias B P Coles) *led to 1/2-way: prom tl rdn along over 3f out and sn wknd* **5/1**
04-2 **7** 31 **Ace Serve**[19] 581 4-8-9 **65** DominicFox(3) 1
(Oliver Sherwood) *cl up: rdn along over 5f out: sn wknd* **20/1**
3m 7.84s (-0.46) **Going Correction** -0.05s/f (Stan)
WFA 4 from 5yo+ 4lb 7 Ran SP% **114.8**
Speed ratings (Par 103): **99,97,93,91,90 89,72**
toteswingers:1&2:£2.20, 1&3:£2.60, 2&3:£2.80 CSF £8.76 TOTE £4.00: £2.60, £1.70; EX 9.50.
Owner Storm Hawk Partnership **Bred** Rodger O'Dwyer **Trained** Nether Winchendon, Bucks
FOCUS
An ordinary staying handicap and the pace was steady until picking up just before halfway. The winner got back on track with the second rated to the best view of his previous form.

811 SOUTHWELL-RACECOURSE.CO.UK H'CAP 1m 4f (F)
4:10 (4:15) (Class 6) (0-60,60) 4-Y-0+ **£1,704** (£503; £251) **Stalls** Low

Form RPR
440- **1** **Light The City (IRE)**[168] 6236 5-9-1 **54** JamesSullivan 9 62
(Ruth Carr) *cl up: led over 3f out: jnd and rdn over 2f out: drvn and styd on wl fnl f* **13/2**
005- **2** 1 3/4 **Nippy Nikki**[82] 7774 4-8-9 **50** PaddyAspell 8 55
(John Norton) *chsd ldrs: rdn along over 3f out: drvn on inner wl over 1f out: kpt on fnl f* **28/1**
66-6 **3** 1 1/2 **Rubi Dia**[54] 136 5-9-2 **60** JustinNewman(5) 7 63
(Kevin M Prendergast) *trckd ldrs: hdwy 4f out: chal over 2f out: sn rdn and ev ch tl drvn and one pce ent fnl f* **11/4**[2]
0-14 **4** 1 3/4 **Mustajed**[21] 557 11-9-4 **57** (b) JamesMillman 3 57
(Rod Millman) *hld up in rr: hdwy 3f out: sn rdn and kpt on fnl 2f: nt rch ldrs* **8/1**
0045 **5** nse **Nesnaas (USA)**[7] 600 11-8-0 **46** oh1 NicoleNordblad(7) 5 46
(Alastair Lidderdale) *hld up in rr: hdwy 3f out: sn rdn and kpt on fnl 2f: nt rch ldrs* **25/1**
0-00 **6** 7 **Tayarat (IRE)**[13] 493 7-8-2 **46** oh1 (bt) DanielleMcCreery(5) 4 35
(Michael Chapman) *s.i.s: a in rr* **25/1**
4462 **7** 3/4 **Kingaroo (IRE)**[6] 672 6-9-0 **53** FrannyNorton 10 41
(Garry Woodward) *led: rdn along and hdd over 3f out: sn wknd* **9/2**[3]
-004 **8** 1 1/4 **Yours**[19] 581 4-9-3 **58** PhillipMakin 6 44
(Kevin Ryan) *chsd ldrs: rdn along wl over 3f out: sn wknd* **16/1**
26/6 **9** 2 **Bluecrop Boy**[29] 446 8-8-7 **46** oh1 (be) FrankieMcDonald 1 29
(Dominic Ffrench Davis) *in tch: rdn along over 4f out: sn wknd* **20/1**
0-44 **10** 1 1/2 **Magic Haze**[28] 460 6-9-0 **56** RyanPowell(3) 2 36
(Sally Hall) *hld up: a towards rr* **5/2**[1]
2m 39.72s (-1.28) **Going Correction** -0.05s/f (Stan)
WFA 4 from 5yo+ 2lb 10 Ran SP% **119.6**
Speed ratings (Par 101): **102,100,99,98,98 93,93,92,91,90**
toteswingers:1&2:£28.60, 1&3:£4.50, 2&3:£15.20 CSF £178.64 CT £621.61 TOTE £7.80: £1.60, £10.30, £1.70; EX 293.10 TRIFECTA Not won..
Owner Atkins Legal Services **Bred** Rabbah Bloodstock Limited **Trained** Huby, N Yorks
FOCUS
A moderate handicap, but sound form. Straightforward form with the winner the best guide.
Kingaroo(IRE) Official explanation: jockey said gelding had no more to give
Magic Haze Official explanation: jockey said gelding never travelled

812 GET LIVE FOOTBALL SCORES AT FOOTBALLSCORES.COM H'CAP 1m (F)
4:40 (4:44) (Class 4) (0-85,82) 4-Y-0+ **£4,204** (£1,251; £625; £312) **Stalls** Low

Form RPR
141 **1** **Colour Guard**[5] 753 4-9-0 **75** JoeFanning 7 93+
(Mark Johnston) *trckd ldr: pushed along 3f out: hdwy to chal over 2f out: rdn to ld wl over 1f out: clr appr fnl f: eased towards fin* **11/8**[1]
211- **2** 3 1/2 **Beautiful Day**[81] 7782 4-9-5 **80** PhillipMakin 6 88
(Kevin Ryan) *led: rdn and jnd over 2f out: hdd wl over 1f out: kpt on same pce* **4/1**[3]
3355 **3** 1 1/4 **Follow The Flag (IRE)**[5] 751 8-9-5 **80** (b) JohnFahy 8 85
(Alan McCabe) *in tch: hdwy over 2f out: rdn to chse ldng pair wl over 1f out: drvn and no imp appr fnl f* **20/1**
3-02 **4** 1 3/4 **Masai Moon**[20] 563 8-9-7 **82** JamesMillman 1 83
(Rod Millman) *chsd ldng pair: rdn along on inner 3f out: kpt on same pce fnl 2f* **16/1**
4511 **5** nk **Mcconnell (USA)**[12] 671 7-8-9 **75** (b) DuilioDaSilva(5) 5 75
(Richard Guest) *hld up in rr: hdwy wl over 2f out: sn rdn and no imp fr over 1f out* **12/1**
51- **6** 2 1/4 **Great Expectations**[68] 7913 4-9-0 **75** SteveDrowne 3 70
(J R Jenkins) *hld up towards rr: hdwy 3f out: sn rdn and btn wl over 1f out* **5/2**[2]
054- **7** 22 **Mozayada (USA)**[278] 2653 8-8-11 **72** RobertWinston 4 17
(Mel Brittain) *chsd ldrs: rdn along 1/2-way: sn wknd* **50/1**
03-0 **8** 7 **King Of Windsor (IRE)**[34] 374 5-9-0 **75** PaulMulrennan 9
(Keith Dalgleish) *a towards rr* **16/1**
1m 41.34s (-2.36) **Going Correction** -0.05s/f (Stan) 8 Ran SP% **116.9**
Speed ratings (Par 105): **109,105,104,102,102 99,77,70**
toteswingers:1&2:£2.20, 1&3:£5.40, 2&3:£12.20 CSF £7.48 CT £74.73 TOTE £2.10: £1.10, £1.40, £4.70; EX 7.20 Trifecta £31.00 Pool: £1,028.66 - 24.52 winning units..
Owner Sheikh Hamdan Bin Mohammed Al Maktoum **Bred** Meon Valley Stud **Trained** Middleham Moor, N Yorks
FOCUS
A decent handicap with a progressive winner who was 7lb well in. The second is progressive too but the third limits to some extent.

813 SOUTHWELL RACECOURSE FOR CONFERENCES H'CAP 6f (F)
5:10 (5:12) (Class 6) (0-60,60) 4-Y-0+ **£1,704** (£503; £251) **Stalls** Low

Form RPR
0500 **1** **Elhamri**[11] 696 8-9-7 **60** HayleyTurner 1 71
(Conor Dore) *trckd ldng pair: hdwy 1/2-way: led 2f out: rdn over 1f out: drvn out* **5/1**[3]
-626 **2** 1 1/2 **Itsthursdayalready**[12] 664 5-9-2 **55** ShaneKelly 2 61
(Mark Brisbourne) *chsd ldrs: hdwy 2f out: rdn to chse wnr ent fnl f and ev ch tl drvn and one pce last 100yds* **9/2**[2]
43-0 **3** nk **Caramelita**[54] 139 5-9-7 **60** (v) FrederikTylicki 4 65
(J R Jenkins) *hld up in tch: hdwy over 2f out: rdn to chse wnr over 1f out: kpt on same pce* **11/2**
06-3 **4** 1 **Bond Blade**[35] 372 4-9-1 **57** DaleSwift(3) 6 59
(Geoffrey Oldroyd) *dwlt and pushed along in rr: hdwy on outer over 2f out: sn rdn and styd on fnl f: nrst fin* **3/1**[1]
0256 **5** 3/4 **Tamino (IRE)**[11] 690 9-8-8 **47** (b) FrankieMcDonald 7 47
(Alastair Lidderdale) *led: rdn along 3f out: hdd 2f out and grad wknd appr fnl f* **18/1**
30-0 **6** 1/2 **Lindoro**[54] 139 7-8-12 **56** JustinNewman(5) 8 54
(Kevin M Prendergast) *cl up: rdn wl over 2f out and ev ch tl drvn and wknd over 1f out* **9/2**[2]
-236 **7** 8 **Transmit (IRE)**[42] 289 5-9-5 **58** (b) DuranFentiman 3 30
(Tim Easterby) *chsd ldrs on inner: rdn along wl over 2f out: grad wknd* **15/2**
0-60 **8** 4 1/2 **Wishbone (IRE)**[39] 329 5-9-5 **58** TonyCulhane 5 16
(Jo Hughes) *dwlt: a in rr* **25/1**
1m 16.34s (-0.16) **Going Correction** -0.05s/f (Stan) 8 Ran SP% **114.3**
Speed ratings (Par 101): **99,97,96,95,94 93,82,76**
CSF £27.67 CT £127.30 TOTE £8.10: £2.70, £1.60, £2.50; EX 27.40 Trifecta £88.80 Pool: £785.51 - 6.54 winning units..
Owner Chris Marsh **Bred** Highfield Stud Ltd **Trained** Hubbert's Bridge, Lincs
FOCUS
Another moderate handicap to end the card, but the form is sound.
T/Plt: £336.00 to a £1 stake. Pool:£72,646.77 - 157.80 winning tickets T/Qpdt: £15.20 to a £1 stake. Pool:£6,757.80 - 328.50 winning tickets JR

794 CHANTILLY (R-H)
Tuesday, March 6
OFFICIAL GOING: Polytrack: standard

814a PRIX MEYDAN GOLF COURSE (CONDITIONS) (4YO+) (POLYTRACK) 6f 110y
1:20 (12:00) 4-Y-0+ **£20,833** (£8,333; £6,250; £4,166; £2,083)

RPR
1 **Myasun (FR)**[89] 7678 5-8-11 0 JohanVictoire 8 103
(C Baillet, France) **12/5**[1]
2 snk **Spectacle Du Mars (FR)**[19] 588 5-9-0 0 GregoryBenoist 7 106
(X Nakkachdji, France) **7/2**[2]
3 1 **Kalahari Gold (IRE)**[126] 7221 7-8-11 0 Francois-XavierBertras 12 100
(F Rohaut, France) **5/1**[3]
4 snk **Rodrigo De Torres**[171] 6145 5-8-11 0 MartinHarley 5 100
(Mrs K Burke) *racd in midfield: gd prog early in st to go 3rd 2f out: no ex u.p: styd on fnl f* **101/1**
5 nk **Mariol (FR)**[103] 7534 9-9-0 0 IoritzMendizabal 1 102
(Robert Collet, France) **14/1**
6 nse **Izalia (FR)**[191] 5532 4-8-10 0 FranckBlondel 2 98
(F Rossi, France) **9/1**
7 hd **Chopouest (FR)**[76] 5-8-11 0 FredericSpanu 10 98
(T Castanheira, France) **18/1**
8 1 **Le Big (GER)**[16] 629 8-9-0 0 AndreBest 9 98
(M Rolland, France) **21/1**
9 3 1/2 **Sunday Nectar (IRE)**[207] 5028 4-8-8 0 Roberto-CarlosMontenegro 4 82
(X Thomas-Demeaulte, France) **47/1**
10 4 **Waitress (USA)**[105] 7509 4-8-8 0 MickaelBarzalona 6 70
(H-A Pantall, France) **83/10**
0 **Nova Neyev (FR)**[59] 4-8-11 0 StephaneBreux 3
(P Capelle, France) **67/1**
0 **Valle (USA)**[89] 7678 4-8-13 0 ow2 ChristopheSoumillon 11
(M Delcher-Sanchez, Spain) **14/1**
1m 17.77s (77.77) 12 Ran SP% **116.7**
WIN (incl. 1 euro stake): 3.40. PLACES: 1.30, 1.60, 1.70. DF: 7.60. SF: 14.00.
Owner Ecurie Jarlan **Bred** Sarl Ecurie Jarlan **Trained** France

815a PRIX DE LA GRANGE DES BOIS (CLAIMER) (5YO+) (POLYTRACK) 1m
3:55 (12:00) 5-Y-0+ **£7,916** (£3,166; £2,375; £1,583; £791)

RPR
1 **Settebellezze (FR)**[212] 5-9-1 0 TonyPiccone 3 84
(J Rossi, France) **13/1**
2 shd **Sea Fight (USA)**[59] 6-8-11 0 (p) YannickLetondeur 11 80
(N Clement, France) **13/1**
3 2 **Barzini (GER)**[71] 5-9-5 0 RonanThomas 6 83
(J Phelippon, France) **11/1**
4 3/4 **Up And Coming (IRE)**[67] 8-9-1 0 ThomasHuet 4 78
(J E Pease, France) **7/1**[3]
5 2 **Samardal (FR)**[67] 5-9-4 0 JohanVictoire 9 76
(N Minner, Belgium) **9/2**[2]

6 nse **Celebrity Choice (IRE)**296 5-9-1 0 .... ChristopheSoumillon 5 73
(M Gentile, France) 2/1[1]
7 1 **Bold Marc (IRE)**59 92 10-8-11 0 ....(p) MartinHarley 8 67
(Mrs K Burke) *broke wl: sn ld: clr ld ent st: rdn and stl clr 2f out: hdd 1 1/2f out: grad wknd ins fnl f* 21/1
8 6 **Babylone (IRE)**64 5-9-4 0 .... FranckBlondel 2 60
(Mlle S-V Tarrou, France) 9/1
9 6 **Arrivederla (IRE)**43 6-8-8 0 .... Pierre-CharlesBoudot 7 36
(C Boutin, France) 10/1
10 2 **Ocanelle (FR)**120 5-8-8 0 ....(b[1]) SylvainRuis 1 31
(F Sanchez, France) 45/1
0 **Fedora (IRE)**24 537 6-9-3 0 .... IoritzMendizabal 10
(Olivia Maylam) *a towards rr: rdn early in st: no rspnse: eased* 18/1
1m 38.66s (98.66) 11 Ran SP% 117.7
WIN (incl. 1 euro stake): 14.00. PLACES: 3.30, 4.20, 3.60. DF: 68.10. SF: 104.70.
Owner Penelope S A R L **Bred** Penelope S.A.R.L. **Trained** France

740 KEMPTON (A.W) (R-H)
Wednesday, March 7

OFFICIAL GOING: Standard
Wind: Strong, against Weather: Fine but changeable

816 FREE BETDAQ CHELTENHAM PREVIEW HERE TONIGHT MEDIAN AUCTION MAIDEN STKS 1m 2f (P)
5:30 (5:31) (Class 5) 3-Y-O £2,264 (£673; £336; £168) Stalls Low

Form RPR
52-2 1 **Duke Of Clarence (IRE)**9 724 3-9-3 72 ....(b[1]) RichardHughes 7 71
(Richard Hannon) *trckd ldr after 2f: moved up to chal over 3f out and pair sn clr: led jst over 1f out: pushed along and readily drew clr* 5/4[1]
0- 2 4 1/2 **Distant Love (IRE)**223 4471 3-8-12 0 .... JimmyFortune 6 59
(Andrew Balding) *led: set mod gallop: pressed and increased the pce over 3f out: sn clr in ldng pair: hdd jst over 1f out: no answer to wnr and eased last 100yds* 11/8[2]
06 3 2 3/4 **Brandy Snapping**25 533 3-8-12 0 .... TomMcLaughlin 4 52
(Mark Brisbourne) *mostly in 5th: pushed along over 4f out: effrt to go 3rd ins fnl f: styd on but no ch* 66/1
4 1 **Findeln** 3-8-12 0 .... DaneO'Neill 8 50
(Eve Johnson Houghton) *dwlt: pushed up into 4th after 3f: rdn over 3f out: tried to chal for 3rd over 1f out: one pce* 16/1
0-0 5 nk **Corn Maiden**51 195 3-8-9 0 .... RyanClark(3) 1 49
(Phil McEntee) *awkward to s: sn in last pair: rdn over 4f out: struggling over 2f out: styd on fr over 1f out* 25/1
0 6 2 **The Yank**16 635 3-9-3 0 .... LukeMorris 5 50
(Tony Carroll) *trckd ldr 2f: chsd ldng pair after: rdn and wl outpcd fr over 3f out: wknd fnl f* 25/1
7 3 1/4 **Let's Confer** 3-8-7 0 .... MarkCoumbe(5) 9 38
(Michael Attwater) *s.s: rn green in last: struggling fr 4f out: nvr a factor* 16/1
8 1 3/4 **Optimism** 3-8-12 0 .... WilliamCarson 3 35
(William Muir) *s.s: mostly in 6th: rdn over 3f out: no prog and sn btn: wknd over 1f out* 11/1[3]
2m 10.85s (2.85) **Going Correction** +0.075s/f (Slow) 8 Ran SP% 115.8
Speed ratings (Par 98): **91,87,85,84,84 82,79,78**
toteswingers:1&2:£1.10, 1&3:£14.80, 2&3:£26.70 CSF £3.19 TOTE £1.90: £1.10, £1.20, £4.40; EX 4.10 Trifecta £31.60 Pool: £11,659.76 - 273.03 winning units..
Owner D Dixon J Stunt J Fiyaz **Bred** Corduff Stud Ltd & J F Gribomont **Trained** East Everleigh, Wilts

FOCUS
A weak 3-y-o maiden, run at a moderate pace.

817 BETDAQ CHELTENHAM PREVIEW WITH PADDY BRENNAN H'CAP 1m 2f (P)
6:00 (6:01) (Class 2) (0-100,96) 4-Y-0+
£9,835 (£2,945; £1,472; £736; £368; £184) Stalls Low

Form RPR
-153 1 **True To Form (IRE)**4 785 5-9-3 92 ....(p) LukeMorris 4 100
(Ronald Harris) *hld up in tch: wnt 4th over 4f out: wound up over 2f out: r.o over 1f out to ld last 100yds: sn clr* 9/4[2]
-300 2 1 1/4 **Licence To Till (USA)**17 630 5-9-7 96 .... JoeFanning 6 101
(Mark Johnston) *led: rdn and jnd over 1f out: narrowly hdd fnl f: kpt on but outpcd last 100yds* 11/4[3]
0-00 3 shd **Fanditha (IRE)**19 617 6-9-5 94 ....(v[1]) MartinHarley 3 99
(Mick Channon) *trckd ldng pair: wnt 2nd over 4f out: chal 2f out: upsides over 1f out but hanging: drvn into narrow ld fnl f but finding little: hdd last 100yds: lost 2nd post* 14/1
00-3 4 3/4 **Sinfonico (IRE)**7 733 4-8-10 85 ....(e[1]) RichardHughes 1 89
(Richard Hannon) *hld up bhd ldrs: pushed along 2f out: tried to cl 1f out: stl pushed along and swtchd lft: nrst fin* 2/1[1]
-100 5 3 **Sunset Kitty (USA)**18 622 5-8-11 86 .... ShaneKelly 2 84
(Mike Murphy) *led 3f: chsd ldr to over 4f out: styd cl up tl wknd fnl f* 11/1
040- 6 3/4 **Taaresh (IRE)**14 7908 7-8-7 82 oh2 .... TomQueally 5 78
(Kevin Morgan) *hld up in rr but in tch: shkn up 2f out: no prog over 1f out: wl hld after* 33/1
-653 7 11 **Tartan Trip**25 529 5-8-0 82 oh1 ....(b) JoeyHaynes(7) 7 56
(Andrew Balding) *restless stalls: rrd whn they opened and lost 15 l: rcvrd and in tch after 3f: wknd 4f out* 10/1
2m 6.07s (-1.93) **Going Correction** +0.075s/f (Slow) 7 Ran SP% 117.8
Speed ratings (Par 109): **110,109,108,108,105 105,96**
toteswingers:1&2:£2.40, 1&3:£6.50, 2&3:£5.80 CSF £9.40 TOTE £3.00: £1.60, £1.90; EX 9.00.
Owner David & Gwyn Joseph **Bred** Sir E J Loder **Trained** Earlswood, Monmouths

FOCUS
A fair handicap, run at an uneven pace.

NOTEBOOK
True To Form(IRE) landed a fourth course success with a game effort. He moved kindly through the race and found plenty when asked to get on top inside the final furlong. He's won at all four AW tracks and this rates a career-best effort, so perhaps there will be something suitable for him next at Lingfield's Winter Derby meeting later this month.
Licence To Till(USA), well beaten in two outings on snow in Switzerland last month, would have no doubt gone closer had he made this more of a test. He is where the handicapper wants him, though. (tchd 3-1)
Fanditha(IRE) had been campaigned on her last three outings. She ran better in a first-time visor and put it up to the second off the home turn, in the process compromising that one's finishing effort. It remains to be seen whether she backs this up, however. (op 12-1)
Sinfonico(IRE) ran a sound race on his return from a break over C&D a week earlier and went in a first-time eyeshield here, which saw him prove free beforehand. He never looked like hitting the front this time, though, and may have found it coming that bit too soon. (op 3-1 tchd 10-3)
Tartan Trip Official explanation: jockey said that the gelding missed the break

818 CHELTENHAM TIPS AT TONIGHT'S BETDAQ PREVIEW H'CAP 1m 2f (P)
6:30 (6:30) (Class 6) (0-65,65) 4-Y-0+ £1,617 (£481; £240; £120) Stalls Low

Form RPR
-404 1 **Nolecce**10 636 5-8-13 60 ....(p) RobertLButler(3) 4 69
(Richard Guest) *wl plcd on inner: prog to chse ldr over 2f out: led over 1f out: edgd lft but hld on in fin* 8/1
3-42 2 1/2 **Cane Cat (IRE)**21 559 5-9-1 59 ....(t) JoeFanning 7 67
(Tony Carroll) *hld up in last pair: stl there 2f out: rapid prog on outer over 1f out: wnt 2nd last 100yds and clsd on wnr: too much to do* 15/2
1441 3 3/4 **Wisecraic**21 567 5-9-6 64 .... LiamKeniry 10 69
(J S Moore) *t.k.h: hld up bhd ldrs on inner: effrt to go 3rd 2f out: styd on but nvr able to chal: fin 4th: plcd 3rd* 10/1
2234 4 1 1/2 **Arkaim**13 672 4-9-6 64 ....(v) MickyFenton 1 66
(Pam Sly) *led: sn t.k.h and clr after 3f: hdd and fdd over 1f out: fin 5th: plcd 4th* 8/1
-020 5 1 1/4 **Scary Movie (IRE)**20 574 7-9-6 64 ....(p) LukeMorris 2 63
(Ronald Harris) *dwlt: rn in snatches thrght: early reminders yet gng strly at rr of field 2f out: styd on late: fin 6th: plcd 5th* 12/1
22-0 6 1 **Edgware Road**19 224 4-9-7 65 ....(b) JimCrowley 6 62
(Paul Rich) *squeezed out after 150yds: hld up after and dropped to last pair: tried to weave through over 1f out: nt pce to threaten: fin 7th: plcd 6th* 5/1[1]
4-45 7 1 1/4 **Comadoir (IRE)**20 574 6-9-3 61 .... DaneO'Neill 13 56
(Jo Crowley) *hld up in rr: swift move to midfield on wd outside over 5f out but sn lost pl: prog again over 2f out through rivals: wknd over 1f out: fin 8th: plcd 7th* 11/1
54-5 8 1/2 **Royal Etiquette (IRE)**16 636 5-9-2 60 .... HayleyTurner 12 54
(Lawney Hill) *trckd ldrs: racd wd fr 1/2-way: lost pl over 2f out: sn btn: fin 9th: plcd 8th* 7/1[3]
0-63 9 shd **Oneiric**14 650 4-9-5 63 .... AdamKirby 3 56
(Brett Johnson) *chsd ldr: drvn over 3f out: lost 2nd and wknd over 2f out: fin 10th: plcd 9th* 11/1
5530 10 5 **Cristaliyev**8 732 4-8-13 57 ....(p) StephenCraine 5 40
(Jim Boyle) *t.k.h: trckd ldrs early: lost pl 1/2-way: no prog over 1f out: fin 11th: plcd 10th* 33/1
60-0 11 13 **Dune Island**14 653 4-8-7 51 oh6 .... KieranO'Neill 8
(John Bridger) *hld up: rapid prog on outer to press ldrs over 5f out: wknd over 3f out: t.o: fin 12th: plcd 11th* 125/1
1-42 D 3/4 **Beggers Belief**42 296 4-9-7 65 ....(b) WilliamCarson 9 71
(Eric Wheeler) *hld up in last quartet: prog over 2f out: r.o fr over 1f out: wnt 3rd last 100yds: nvr quite able to chal: fin 3rd: disqualified and plcd last: jockey weighed in light* 6/1[2]
2m 7.96s (-0.04) **Going Correction** +0.075s/f (Slow) 12 Ran SP% 114.6
Speed ratings (Par 101): **103,102,101,100,99 98,97,97,96,92 82,102**
toteswingers:1&2:£13.40, 1&12:£12.80, 2&12:£2.20 CSF £64.54 CT £606.74 TOTE £13.40: £4.40, £1.30, £4.00; EX 78.90 Trifecta £2651.50 Part won. Pool: £3,583.15 - 0.93 winning units..
Owner Future Racing (Notts) Limited **Bred** Hedsor Stud **Trained** Stainforth, S Yorks
■ Stewards' Enquiry : William Carson four-day ban: weighed in light (22-24 March)

FOCUS
This seemed wide open. It was run at an ordinary pace and the form is rated around the runner-up.

819 BETDAQ FOR CHELTENHAM FESTIVAL VALUE BETTING H'CAP 6f (P)
7:00 (7:00) (Class 6) (0-65,65) 4-Y-0+ £1,617 (£481; £240; £120) Stalls Low

Form RPR
-026 1 **Amazing Win (IRE)**4 781 4-8-11 55 .... SamHitchcott 2 66
(Mick Channon) *cl up: led 2f out: rdn and kpt on wl enough to hold on fnl f* 15/2
0644 2 1 1/4 **Twice Red**12 696 4-9-1 59 .... DaneO'Neill 7 66
(Derek Shaw) *hld up bhd ldrs: swtchd to far rail and effrt 2f out: chsd wnr fnl f: styd on but a hld* 9/2[2]
4602 3 nse **Joe Le Taxi (IRE)**6 752 4-9-3 61 .... JoeFanning 1 68
(Mark Johnston) *led: hanging lft and hdd 2f out: nt qckn over 1f out: styd on but nvr really threatened wnr after* 6/4[1]
-103 4 1 1/4 **Belinsky (IRE)**28 473 5-9-4 62 .... JimCrowley 10 65
(Julie Camacho) *trckd ldrs: cl enough in 4th over 1f out: drvn and nt qckn after* 8/1
3415 5 2 1/4 **Dvinsky (USA)**14 658 11-9-7 65 ....(b) TomMcLaughlin 11 61
(Paul Howling) *rousted along to go prom fr wd draw: lost pl u.p 2f out: n.d after* 16/1
160- 6 shd **Doctor Hilary**80 7811 10-9-1 59 ....(v) RobertHavlin 12 54
(Mark Hoad) *hld up and racd on outer: shkn up and nt qckn 2f out: nt on terms after* 33/1
06-0 7 1/2 **Juarla (IRE)**12 696 4-9-2 60 .... LukeMorris 3 54
(Ronald Harris) *hld up in last trio: sme prog over 2f out: rchd 5th over 1f out but nt on terms: fdd* 20/1
50-0 8 3/4 **Invigilator**36 372 4-8-12 56 .... MartinLane 5 47
(Derek Shaw) *stdd s: hld up in last pair: bustled along over 2f out: couple of reminders fnl f: nvr involved* 25/1
1553 9 1 **Vhujon (IRE)**25 517 7-9-2 60 .... RobbieFitzpatrick 4 48
(Peter Grayson) *t.k.h: hld up in last: urged along and no prog over 2f out* 7/1[3]
4215 10 3/4 **Sannibel**20 576 4-9-7 65 .... TomQueally 8 51
(Tony Carroll) *pressed ldr to over 2f out: sn lost pl and btn* 10/1
1m 13.19s (0.09) **Going Correction** +0.075s/f (Slow) 10 Ran SP% 120.1
Speed ratings (Par 101): **102,100,100,98,95 95,94,93,92,91**
toteswingers:1&2:£4.10, 1&3:£3.40, 2&3:£2.80 CSF £41.56 CT £80.81 TOTE £8.20: £2.50, £2.20, £1.30; EX 53.00 Trifecta £250.70 Pool: £3,738.61 - 11.03 winning units.
Owner M Channon **Bred** J Repard **Trained** West Ilsley, Berks

FOCUS
An ordinary sprint handicap that looked more open than the betting indicated. There was a sound pace on, but still it paid to race handily.

820 HAPPY 75TH BIRTHDAY ROY CHRISMAS H'CAP 1m 4f (P)
7:30 (7:30) (Class 5) (0-75,73) 4-Y-0+ £2,264 (£673; £336; £168) Stalls Centre

Form RPR
-132 1 **Shirataki (IRE)**7 738 4-8-11 65 .... ChrisCatlin 2 74
(Peter Hiatt) *hld up in 3rd: sudden move and qcknd to ld over 3f out: at least 2 l clr after: advantage dwindled nr fin but a holding on* 2/1[2]

12-4 **2** *nk* **Shalambar (IRE)**[25] 521 6-8-13 **65** LukeMorris 3 73
(Tony Carroll) *trckd ldr: moving up to chal whn wnr shot past over 3f out: chsd him after: no imp tl clsd last 150yds: a jst hld* **6/1**

/-14 **3** *3 ¾* **Copper Canyon**[21] 570 4-9-2 **73** RyanPowell(3) 1 75
(J S Moore) *hld up last: outpcd whn wnr qckned over 3f out: struggling after: tk 3rd last strides* **7/2**[3]

2332 **4** *nk* **Southern State (USA)**[12] 688 4-9-4 **72** (b[1]) JoeFanning 4 74
(Mark Johnston) *led and untrbld at mod pce: hdd over 3f out and ct flat-footed: sn dropped bk to 3rd: tried to rally 2f out: wknd fnl f: lost 3rd last strides* **7/4**[1]

2m 36.82s (2.32) **Going Correction** +0.075s/f (Slow)
WFA 4 from 6yo 2lb 4 Ran SP% **106.2**
Speed ratings (Par 103): **95,94,92,92**
CSF £12.04 TOTE £2.70; EX 14.40.
Owner P W Hiatt **Bred** Deerfield Farm **Trained** Hook Norton, Oxon

FOCUS
This tight-looking handicap proved a highly tactical affair and the form is worth treating with caution.
Copper Canyon Official explanation: jockey said that the gelding hung right

821 GOFFS READY-TO-RUN SALE APRIL 3RD H'CAP (LONDON MILE QUALIFIER) 1m (P)
8:00 (8:01) (Class 5) (0-70,70) 4-Y-0+ **£2,264** (£673; £336; £168) **Stalls** Low

Form RPR

012- **1** **Zaheeb**[70] 7890 4-8-13 **62** WilliamCarson 6 71
(Dave Morris) *mde all and untrbld ld: rdn and hung lft over 2f out: stened out and styd on stoutly fr over 1f out* **9/1**

06-0 **2** *¾* **Junket**[42] 302 5-9-7 **70** JoeFanning 9 77+
(Dr Jon Scargill) *hld up in last quartet: nt clr run over 2f out: sed to run on over 1f out: fin wl to take 2nd and cl on wnr nr fin* **9/1**

6-16 **3** *¾* **Rezwaan**[21] 568 5-9-5 **68** (be) ShaneKelly 3 74
(Murty McGrath) *hld up towards rr: prog on inner over 2f out: rdn and tried to cl over 1f out: hrd drvn and styd on to take 3rd last strides* **5/2**[1]

1-64 **4** *nk* **Rock Anthem (IRE)**[15] 646 8-9-0 **63** KieranO'Neill 5 68
(Mike Murphy) *chsd wnr 1f and again wl over 2f out: drvn and tried to chal over 1f out: hld after: lost pls nr fin* **12/1**

-503 **5** *hd* **Mister Green (FR)**[7] 736 6-8-13 **62** (bt) StephenCraine 1 67
(David Flood) *t.k.h: hld up in midfield: effrt over 2f out: styd on fr over 1f out but nvr able to chal* **4/1**[2]

3442 **6** *2 ¼* **Storm Runner (IRE)**[21] 559 4-8-6 **58** RyanPowell(3) 2 57
(George Margarson) *sn restrained towards rr: effrt over 2f out: kpt on fr over 1f out but r already unfolded* **6/1**[3]

-150 **7** *nk* **Hip Hip Hooray**[6] 746 6-9-4 **67** LukeMorris 11 66
(Luke Dace) *hld up in last quartet: taken to outer over 2f out: r already unfolded whn tried to make grnd over 1f out: nrst fin* **9/1**

105- **8** *¾* **West Leake (IRE)**[105] 7517 6-9-5 **68** LiamKeniry 10 65
(Paul Burgoyne) *t.k.h: hld up in last pair: sme prog on inner fr over 2f out: rdn over 1f out: wknd fnl f* **25/1**

4-41 **9** *2* **Having A Ball**[13] 666 8-8-9 **58** ChrisCatlin 12 50
(Jonathan Portman) *pushed up to chse wnr after 1f: lost 2nd u.p wl over 2f out: sn btn* **14/1**

650- **10** *4 ½* **L'Hirondelle (IRE)**[117] 7362 8-9-1 **69** MarkCoumbe(5) 4 51
(Michael Attwater) *racd wd: nt gng wl towards rr sn after 1/2-way: wl btn over 2f out* **10/1**

1-03 **11** *¾* **With Hindsight (IRE)**[34] 381 4-9-7 **70** RussKennemore 8 50
(Michael Scudamore) *chsd ldrs: u.p over 2f out: sn wknd* **20/1**

000- **12** *2 ¾* **Dinner Date**[399] 381 10-9-4 **70** RyanClark(3) 7 44
(Tom Keddy) *trckd ldrs: shkn up and wknd over 2f out* **40/1**

1m 38.89s (-0.91) **Going Correction** +0.075s/f (Slow) 12 Ran SP% **127.4**
Speed ratings (Par 103): **107,106,105,105,105 102,102,101,99,95 94,91**
toteswingers:1&2:£11.90, 1&3:£6.70, 2&3:£7.80 CSF £92.26 CT £274.24 TOTE £8.90: £3.20, £3.90, £1.30; EX 100.40 Trifecta £445.40 Part won. Pool: £601.89 - 0.10 winning units..
Owner Stuart Wood **Bred** Theakston Stud **Trained** Baxter's Green, Suffolk

FOCUS
A competitive handicap, run at a fair pace.
L'Hirondelle(IRE) Official explanation: jockey said that the gelding was never travelling
With Hindsight(IRE) Official explanation: jockey said that the gelding ran free

822 GET WELL SOON BRODDERS H'CAP 1m (P)
8:30 (8:31) (Class 7) (0-50,50) 4-Y-0+ **£1,533** (£452; £226) **Stalls** Low

Form RPR

50-3 **1** **Holyfield Warrior (IRE)**[21] 561 8-8-11 **49** MarkCoumbe(5) 9 56
(Michael Attwater) *hld up in last pair: nt clr run and swtchd lft 2f out: rdn and styd on fr over 1f out to pass toiling rivals and ld last 50yds* **13/2**[3]

006- **2** *½* **Chez Vrony**[86] 7741 6-8-12 **45** WilliamCarson 8 51
(Dave Morris) *racd wd: in tch: rdn over 2f out: styd on to ld jst over 1f out: idled in front: hdd last 50yds* **16/1**

0-65 **3** *shd* **Rosy Dawn**[14] 653 7-8-12 **45** ShaneKelly 7 50+
(Brett Johnson) *tried to match strides w ldr tl unable to do so wl over 2f out: hmpd sn after: rallied fnl f: kpt on: fin 4th: promoted to 3rd* **33/1**

00-4 **4** *¾* **Henry's Hero**[7] 375 6-8-8 **46** RaulDaSilva(5) 3 50
(Chris Dwyer) *led at gd pce but pressed: shrugged off rival over 2f out: drvn and hdd wl over 1f out: kpt on fnl f: fin 3rd: disqualified and plcd 4th* **16/1**

6534 **5** *hd* **Teen Ager (FR)**[6] 744 8-9-3 **50** LiamKeniry 2 53
(Paul Burgoyne) *hld up towards rr: smooth prog over 1f out: brought to chal over 1f out: rdn and fnd nil* **5/1**[2]

3-02 **5** *dht* **Baby Driver**[6] 744 4-9-2 **49** DaneO'Neill 5 52
(Tony Newcombe) *t.k.h: trckd ldrs: rdn to ld narrowly wl over 1f out: idled and hdd jst over 1f out: nt qckn after* **11/10**[1]

0-03 **7** *2 ¼* **Ellielusive (IRE)**[14] 653 5-8-12 **45** TomMcLaughlin 6 43
(Mark Brisbourne) *broke on terms: t.k.h and sn restrained: last after 3f: rdn and racd alone on inner fnl 2f: no imp* **25/1**

5-04 **8** *1* **Gambatte**[14] 653 5-8-12 **45** LukeMorris 4 41
(Tony Carroll) *s.i.s: hld up in last trio: rdn over 2f out: no prog and wl btn over 1f out* **8/1**

0-00 **9** *3 ¼* **Inquisitress**[6] 744 8-8-12 **45** KieranO'Neill 1 33
(John Bridger) *prom: looked poised to chal over 2f out: wknd rapidly over 1f out* **18/1**

1m 40.38s (0.58) **Going Correction** +0.075s/f (Slow) 9 Ran SP% **112.5**
Speed ratings (Par 97): **100,99,98,98,98 98,96,95,91**
toteswingers:1&2:£25.40, 1&3:£27.10, 2&3:£23.60 CSF £99.68 CT £2083.80 TOTE £8.60: £2.10, £4.70, £4.70; EX 113.80 TRIFECTA Not won..
Owner The AJ Syndicate **Bred** A Malone **Trained** Epsom, Surrey
■ Stewards' Enquiry : Raul Da Silva one-day ban: careless riding (21 Mar)

FOCUS
A tight bottom-drawer handicap, run at a good pace.

T/Plt: £82.50 to a £1 stake. Pool:£68,728.87 - 607.93 winning tickets T/Qpdt: £37.10 to a £1 stake. Pool:£6,876.80 - 137.13 winning tickets JN

[800]LINGFIELD (L-H)
Wednesday, March 7

OFFICIAL GOING: Standard
Wind: fresh, across Weather: rain, clearing up in afternoon, breezy

823 WORLD HORSE WELFARE CELEBRATES 85 YEARS H'CAP 5f (P)
2:10 (2:10) (Class 6) (0-60,60) 4-Y-0+ **£1,704** (£503; £251) **Stalls** High

Form RPR

4056 **1** **Chjimes (IRE)**[5] 763 8-9-6 **59** (b) HayleyTurner 3 68
(Conor Dore) *in tch and travelling wl: effrt to join ldr wl over 1f out: pushed ahd ent fnl f: r.o wl: comf* **2/1**[1]

6060 **2** *1 ¾* **Sherjawy (IRE)**[25] 522 8-9-5 **58** JamieGoldstein 4 61
(Zoe Davison) *broke wl: pressed ldrs tl rdn and sltly outpcd ent fnl 2f: swtchd lft and rallied u.p 1f out: chsd wnr ins fnl f: no imp* **11/2**

6206 **3** *1 ¾* **Dingaan (IRE)**[20] 578 9-9-0 **53** RobbieFitzpatrick 6 50
(Peter Grayson) *bhd: hdwy u.p ent fnl f: kpt on but no threat to wnr* **16/1**

0-13 **4** *½* **Silver Linnet (IRE)**[23] 544 5-9-5 **58** (p) AdamKirby 1 53
(John Butler) *sn led: rdn ent fnl 2f: hdd ent fnl f: wknd fnl 100yds* **11/4**[2]

-053 **5** *1 ¾* **Grand Honour (IRE)**[13] 664 6-8-7 **46** oh1 (p) KieranO'Neill 2 35
(Paul Howling) *in tch: rdn 3f out: unable qck over 1f out: one pce and wl hld fnl f* **13/2**

4554 **6** *1 ½* **Spic 'n Span**[20] 580 7-9-6 **59** (v) LukeMorris 5 42
(Ronald Harris) *pressed ldr on outer: rdn and unable qck wl over 1f out: wknd fnl f* **5/1**[3]

58.61s (-0.19) **Going Correction** +0.025s/f (Slow) 6 Ran SP% **111.3**
Speed ratings (Par 101): **102,99,96,95,92 90**
toteswingers:1&2:£3.60, 1&3:£6.20, 2&3:£14.70 CSF £13.11 TOTE £2.80: £1.90, £2.60; EX 15.80.
Owner Mrs Louise Marsh **Bred** Morgan O'Flaherty **Trained** Hubbert's Bridge, Lincs

FOCUS
There was a fair gallop on here, with three taking each other on in front.

824 BETFRED "STILL TREBLE ODDS ON LUCKY 15" CLAIMING STKS 1m 4f (P)
2:40 (2:40) (Class 6) 4-Y-0+ **£1,704** (£503; £251) **Stalls** Low

Form RPR

1013 **1** **Daniel Thomas (IRE)**[5] 760 10-9-1 71 (tp) WilliamCarson 1 71
(Richard Guest) *dwlt: sn chsd ldng pair: rdn over 2f out: nt clr run on inner and swtchd rt jst over 1f out: r.o wl fnl 100yds to ld last strides* **5/1**[3]

-231 **2** *hd* **Country Road (IRE)**[9] 721 6-9-3 73 (p) LukeMorris 2 73
(Michael Appleby) *led: rdn and jnd wl over 2f out: hdd 2f out: stl ev ch and drvn over 1f out: battled on gamely u.p to ld again fnl 50yds: hdd and no ex last strides* **1/1**[1]

-122 **3** *nk* **Eagle Nebula**[4] 786 8-9-3 67 AdamKirby 3 72
(Brett Johnson) *chsd ldr: jnd ldr and rdn wl over 2f out: drvn and ld narrowly 2f out: battled on wl tl hdd and no ex fnl 50yds* **6/1**

-541 **4** *nk* **Thundering Home**[12] 695 5-9-3 69 (t) JoeFanning 5 72
(George Baker) *hld up in tch: rdn and effrt to chse ldrs jst over 2f out: kpt on u.p and ev ch ins fnl f: unable qck towards fin* **3/1**[2]

-630 **5** *33* **Imperial Fong**[19] 602 4-7-13 50 RaulDaSilva(5) 4
(Chris Dwyer) *stdd s: hld up in tch in last pair: rdn and lost tch over 3f out: wl bhd over 1f out* **40/1**

2m 34.65s (1.65) **Going Correction** +0.025s/f (Slow)
WFA 4 from 5yo+ 2lb 5 Ran SP% **108.4**
Speed ratings (Par 101): **95,94,94,94,72**
CSF £10.25 TOTE £6.50: £2.20, £1.10; EX 9.40.
Owner Rakebackmypoker.com **Bred** Lawn Stud **Trained** Stainforth, S Yorks

FOCUS
They went steady early before beginning to sprint running down the hill.

825 LINGFIELD PARK OWNERS CLUB H'CAP 1m 5f (P)
3:10 (3:12) (Class 5) (0-70,68) 4-Y-0+ **£2,385** (£704; £352) **Stalls** Low

Form RPR

3101 **1** **Ay Tay Tate (IRE)**[19] 592 6-9-4 **65** (p) KieranO'Neill 2 72
(David C Griffiths) *mde all: rdn ent fnl 2f: drvn over 1f out: battled on v gamely and hld on wl fnl f* **5/1**[2]

4011 **2** *nk* **El Libertador (USA)**[19] 594 6-9-1 **62** (b) ShaneKelly 1 68
(Eric Wheeler) *hld up in last trio: hdwy 3f out: 5th and rdn over 1f out: no imp tl hdwy ins fnl f: swtchd rt fnl 75yds: r.o wl to snatch 2nd last stride* **11/2**[3]

4-34 **3** *nse* **Prince Blue**[42] 303 5-8-8 **55** oh2 ow1 SamHitchcott 3 61
(John E Long) *pressed ldr thrght: drvn and ev ch fr 2f out: unable qck and hld fnl f: lost 2nd last stride* **11/2**[3]

550- **4** *½* **Talbot Green**[209] 4974 4-8-8 **58** WilliamCarson 9 63
(William Muir) *in tch in midfield: chsd ldng trio and drvn over 2f out: unable qck over 1f out: rallied jst ins fnl f: styng on wl whn carried rt wl ins fnl f: nt quite rch ldrs* **12/1**

4353 **5** *1* **Land Hawk (IRE)**[14] 651 6-8-7 **57** SimonPearce(3) 5 62
(Lydia Pearce) *chsd ldng pair: rdn wl over 1f out: trying to chal between horses but nvr quite enough room fr 1f out: squeezed out and hmpd wl ins fnl f: nt rcvr: eased cl home* **4/1**[1]

-306 **6** *4* **Kavaloti (IRE)**[11] 714 8-9-7 **68** (b) AmirQuinn 8 66
(Gary Moore) *s.i.s and rdn along early: racd in last trio: rdn 5f out: no prog: last and wl hld 2f out: styd on fnl f: nvr trbld ldrs* **14/1**

1/0- **7** *1 ½* **Calzaghe (IRE)**[77] 7850 8-8-9 **56** LukeMorris 4 52
(Martin Hill) *racd in midfield: rdn 5f out: no imp u.p over 2f out: plugged on fnl f but no threat to ldrs* **25/1**

62-0 **8** *4 ½* **Mr Plod**[32] 433 7-8-9 **56** (p) MartinHarley 7 45
(Andrew Reid) *stdd and dropped in bhd after s: a in rr: rdn and no prog over 2f out: n.d* **9/1**

-263 **9** *9* **Sunset Place**[11] 714 5-9-6 **67** (p) RobertHavlin 6 42
(Jonathan Geake) *chsd ldrs: rdn and no prog over 2f out: wknd wl over 1f out: wl bhd fnl f* **5/1**[2]

2m 46.3s (0.30) **Going Correction** +0.025s/f (Slow)
WFA 4 from 5yo+ 3lb 9 Ran SP% **112.3**
Speed ratings (Par 103): **100,99,99,99,98 96,95,92,87**
toteswingers:1&2:£3.40, 1&3:£5.20, 2&3:£2.80 CSF £31.43 CT £154.19 TOTE £6.90: £3.10, £2.70, £2.40; EX 23.30 Trifecta £67.00 Pool: £608.03 - 6.71 winning units..
Owner O C Racing **Bred** Kelly's Vintage Partnership **Trained** Bawtry, S Yorks
■ Stewards' Enquiry : Shane Kelly one-day ban: careless riding (21 Mar)

FOCUS
This looked an open handicap beforehand.

Land Hawk(IRE) Official explanation: jockey said that the gelding was denied a clear run

826 BETFRED "THE HOME OF GOALS GALORE" H'CAP — 1m 2f (P)
3:40 (3:40) (Class 5) (0-70,69) 4-Y-0+ — **£2,385** (£704; £352) **Stalls** Low

Form — RPR

-221 **1** **Abigails Angel**[21] 559 5-9-3 **66** .... AdamKirby 2 — 72
(Brett Johnson) *chsd ldr tl 7f out: styd chsng ldrs: rdn and switching rt 2f out: drvn to chal and rdr dropped rein ins fnl f: led fnl 100yds: drvn out* **3/1**[2]

33-3 **2** *hd* **Conducting**[39] 349 4-9-5 **68** .... (p) ShaneKelly 8 — 74
(Gay Kelleway) *in tch in midfield: rdn and effrt to chal 2f out: sn led and drvn: hrd drvn and hdd fnl 100yds: r.o but a jst hld* **5/1**

2-53 **3** *1 1/4* **Potentiale (IRE)**[14] 655 8-8-7 **63** .... (v) Leah-AnneAvery(7) 3 — 67
(J W Hills) *in tch in rr: hdwy and swtchd rt jst over 1f out: styd on to chse ldng pair fnl 100yds: no imp after* **8/1**

33-4 **4** *2 1/2* **Minsky Mine (IRE)**[25] 535 5-9-4 **67** .... (p) LukeMorris 9 — 66
(Michael Appleby) *chsd ldrs: wnt 2nd 7f out: ev ch and rdn 2f out: drvn and no ex over 1f out: wknd ins fnl f* **4/1**[3]

00-5 **5** *4 1/2* **Baharat (IRE)**[11] 714 4-9-0 **63** .... (bt) MartinHarley 4 — 53
(Richard Guest) *taken down early: sn led: hrd pressed and rdn ent fnl 2f: hdd over 1f out: wknd 1f out: eased wl ins fnl f* **14/1**

0-00 **6** *3 3/4* **Lord Theo**[14] 648 8-9-6 **69** .... RobertHavlin 5 — 51
(Nick Littmoden) *hld up in last pair: rdn and no prog over 2f out: sn outpcd and wl btn fnl 2f* **16/1**

-635 **7** *19* **Menadati (USA)**[14] 648 4-9-3 **66** .... WilliamCarson 7 — 10
(Peter Hiatt) *t.k.h early: in tch in last trio: drvn and no rspnse 4f out: lost tch 3f out: wl bhd fnl 2f: t.o* **11/4**[1]

2m 6.08s (-0.52) **Going Correction** +0.025s/f (Slow) **7** Ran SP% **112.0**
Speed ratings (Par 103): **103,102,101,99,96 93,78**
toteswingers:1&2:£2.60, 1&3:£3.90, 2&3:£4.00 CSF £17.50 CT £105.31 TOTE £3.90: £2.20, £1.50; EX 10.80 Trifecta £40.00 Pool: £598.09 - 11.04 winning units..
Owner B R Johnson **Bred** P Balding **Trained** Epsom, Surrey

FOCUS
A classic Lingfield finish.
Menadati(USA) Official explanation: jockey said that the gelding stopped quickly

827 BETFRED "THE BONUS KING" MAIDEN STKS — 7f (P)
4:10 (4:11) (Class 5) 3-Y-0 — **£2,385** (£704; £352) **Stalls** Low

Form — RPR

5- **1** **Incendiary (IRE)**[125] 7248 3-8-10 0 .... NoelGarbutt(7) 2 — 76
(Hugo Palmer) *hld up in tch: rdn and effrt over 1f out: qcknd and str run to ld jst ins fnl f: r.o strly* **33/1**

55- **2** *2* **Ghost Train (IRE)**[190] 5596 3-9-3 0 .... JoeFanning 7 — 71
(Mark Johnston) *chsd ldr: rdn and ev ch 2f out: drvn and led 1f out: sn hdd: styd on same pce* **5/1**[3]

5- **3** *1/2* **Dartford (USA)**[109] 7493 3-9-3 0 .... RobertHavlin 4 — 69
(John Gosden) *hld up in tch: rdn and effrt 2f out: hdwy over 1f out: styd on steadily ins fnl f: wnt 3rd fnl 75yds: nvr gng pce to threaten ldrs* **5/4**[1]

353- **4** *1 1/4* **Emman Bee (IRE)**[126] 7223 3-8-12 62 .... MartinLane 6 — 61
(John Gallagher) *led: rdn 2f out: drvn and hdd 1f out: outpcd ins fnl f* **9/1**

5 *2 1/2* **Petersboden** 3-9-3 0 .... FergusSweeney 8 — 59
(Michael Blanshard) *in tch: hdwy to chse ldrs on outer over 2f out: rdn and outpcd 2f out: no threat to ldrs but plugged on ins fnl f* **100/1**

444- **6** *hd* **Elite**[109] 7491 3-8-12 66 .... MartinHarley 10 — 54
(Mick Channon) *in tch: rdn to chse ldng pair 2f out: unable qck u.p over 1f out: wknd fnl f* **8/1**

323 **7** *1 3/4* **Falcon's Reign (FR)**[12] 684 3-9-3 72 .... ShaneKelly 9 — 54
(Jeremy Noseda) *trckd ldrs: rdn 2f out: drvn and fnd nil over 1f out: wknd fnl f: eased towards fin* **3/1**[2]

05 **8** *11* **Scriptturist**[13] 663 3-9-3 0 .... WilliamCarson 1 — 24
(William Jarvis) *sn dropped to rr and rdn after 2f: lost tch over 2f out* **66/1**

9 *1/2* **Saharan Air (IRE)** 3-9-3 0 .... StephenCraine 3 — 23
(George Baker) *v.s.a: rn v green and rdn along thrght: nvr gng pce: lost tch over 2f out* **25/1**

0 **10** *52* **Payback (GER)**[25] 523 3-9-3 0 .... AdamKirby 5
(John Butler) *t.k.h: hld up in midfield: lost pl 4f out: lost tch 3f out: wl t.o fnl 2f* **66/1**

1m 24.18s (-0.62) **Going Correction** +0.025s/f (Slow) **10** Ran SP% **118.0**
Speed ratings (Par 98): **104,101,101,99,96 96,94,82,81,22**
toteswingers:1&2:£19.00, 1&3:£14.60, 2&3:£22.80 CSF £189.39 TOTE £49.10: £7.10, £3.50, £1.20; EX 183.90 Trifecta £540.70 Part won. Pool: £730.76 - 0.10 winning units..
Owner Derek Iceton **Bred** Limestone & Tara Studs **Trained** Newmarket, Suffolk

FOCUS
A modest maiden.
Falcon's Reign(FR) Official explanation: jockey said that the colt hung left in the closing stages
Payback(GER) Official explanation: jockey said that the gelding hung right

828 BREATHE SPA AT LINGFIELD MARRIOTT H'CAP — 7f (P)
4:40 (4:40) (Class 6) (0-60,62) 4-Y-0+ — **£1,704** (£503; £251) **Stalls** Low

Form — RPR

0-03 **1** **Prince Of Sorrento**[20] 574 5-9-7 **60** .... StevieDonohoe 2 — 73+
(John Akehurst) *chsd ldr tl led wl over 3f out: wnt clr on bridle over 2f out: in n.d fnl 2f: rdn over 1f out: eased towards fin* **15/8**[1]

-003 **2** *3* **Chandrayaan**[13] 662 5-8-4 **46** .... (v) SimonPearce(3) 3 — 51
(John E Long) *in tch in midfield: rdn and effrt on inner 2f out: kpt on u.p to go 2nd ins fnl f: no ch w wnr* **11/1**

50-1 **3** *1* **Buxton**[8] 729 8-9-9 **62** 6ex .... (t) MartinLane 10 — 64
(Roger Ingram) *stdd and dropped in bhd after s: bhd: rdn 4f out: styd on u.p fnl f: snatched 3rd last stride: nvr trbld ldrs* **8/1**

-056 **4** *nse* **Anjomarba (IRE)**[12] 687 5-9-2 **55** .... HayleyTurner 7 — 57
(Conor Dore) *led tl 4f out: rdn and outpcd by wnr over 2f out: no threat and plugged on same pce: lost 2 pls ins fnl f* **7/1**

0400 **5** *1 3/4* **Captainrisk (IRE)**[19] 598 6-8-11 **57** .... (v) DanielHarris(7) 5 — 54
(Christine Dunnett) *chsd ldrs: rdn over 2f out: 3rd and wl outpcd 2f out: wl hld and plugged on same pce fr over 1f out* **33/1**

4-10 **6** *1/2* **July Days (IRE)**[16] 639 6-9-6 **59** .... RussKennemore 4 — 55
(Brian Baugh) *taken down early: hld up in midfield: rdn over 3f out: sme hdwy u.p over 1f out: plugged on but n.d* **6/1**[3]

0-52 **7** *3/4* **Sottovoce**[8] 729 4-9-5 **58** .... JimCrowley 9 — 52
(Simon Dow) *chsd ldrs: rdn and struggling over 2f out: outpcd and wl hld 2f out: wknd over 1f out* **7/2**[2]

-200 **8** *1 1/2* **My Jeanie (IRE)**[32] 422 8-8-1 **47** oh1 ow1 .... LeonnaMayor(7) 8 — 37
(Jimmy Fox) *t.k.h: hld up in last pair: rdn and struggling 3f out: n.d* **25/1**

56-0 **9** *5* **Fleetwoodmaxi (USA)**[45] 262 5-9-4 **57** .... FergusSweeney 6 — 34
(Peter Makin) *a towards rr: rdn 4f out: lost tch 3f out* **33/1**

1m 24.36s (-0.44) **Going Correction** +0.025s/f (Slow) **9** Ran SP% **113.0**
Speed ratings (Par 101): **103,99,98,98,96 95,94,93,87**
toteswingers:1&2:£5.80, 1&3:£5.00, 2&3:£5.70 CSF £23.00 CT £132.06 TOTE £3.20: £2.10, £3.00, £3.80; EX 29.40 Trifecta £286.20 Part won. Pool: £386.76 - 0.10 winning units..
Owner John Akehurst **Bred** Mrs P Akhurst **Trained** Epsom, Surrey

FOCUS
A moderate handicap but a taking performance from the winner.

829 ALL WEATHER "HANDS AND HEELS" APPRENTICE SERIES H'CAP (PART OF THE RACING EXCELLENCE INITIATIVE) — 1m (P)
5:10 (5:12) (Class 6) (0-55,58) 4-Y-0+ — **£1,704** (£503; £251) **Stalls** High

Form — RPR

-461 **1** **Kipchak (IRE)**[8] 732 7-9-5 **58** 6ex .... (b) NoelGarbutt 3 — 69
(Conor Dore) *mde all: rdn over 1f out: styd on wl and asserted ins fnl f: pushed out* **7/2**[2]

5350 **2** *2* **Jackie Love (IRE)**[21] 561 4-8-5 **47** .... (v) JenniferFerguson(3) 2 — 53
(Olivia Maylam) *hld up in rr: rdn and hdwy wl over 1f out: chsd ldng trio ent fnl f: styd on wl to go 2nd wl ins fnl f: no threat to wnr* **12/1**

5242 **3** *3/4* **Penbryn (USA)**[8] 732 5-9-2 **55** .... (v) JackDuern 6 — 60
(Nick Littmoden) *s.i.s: sn pushed along: hdwy on outer into midfield 5f out: chsd wnr 2f out: swtchd ins and hdwy to press wnr 1f out: awkward hd carriage and no ex ins fnl f: wknd fnl 100yds* **15/8**[1]

6-40 **4** *2* **Avalon Bay**[6] 744 4-8-8 **52** .... (b) DavidWarren(5) 4 — 52
(Pat Eddery) *t.k.h: hdwy to chse wnr after 1f tl 2f out: 3rd and unable qck over 1f out: wknd ins fnl f* **8/1**

0200 **5** *3 1/2* **Kucharova (IRE)**[12] 687 4-9-0 **53** .... ThomasBrown 1 — 45
(Seamus Mullins) *prom in main gp: rdn and outpcd wl over 2f out: plugged on same pce and no threat to ldrs fnl 2f* **8/1**

2624 **6** *1 1/4* **My Mate Les (IRE)**[5] 773 4-8-11 **50** .... GeorgeDowning 7 — 39
(Tony Carroll) *chsd ldrs tl rdn and no imp over 2f out: 5th and wl btn over 1f out: wknd 1f out* **5/1**[3]

3-55 **7** *3 1/2* **Gay Gallivanter**[35] 375 4-8-7 **46** oh1 .... DannyBrock 5 — 27
(Michael Quinn) *chsd wnr for 1f: sn rdn and steadily lost pl: bhd wl over 1f out* **14/1**

0400 **8** *24* **Hot Tub**[21] 561 4-8-4 **46** oh1 .... (v[1]) DanielHarris(3) 9
(Christine Dunnett) *racd on outer: a towards rr: last and struggling over 3f out: sn lost tch: wl bhd and eased fr over 1f out: t.o* **33/1**

1m 38.46s (0.26) **Going Correction** +0.025s/f (Slow) **8** Ran SP% **113.2**
Speed ratings (Par 101): **99,97,96,94,90 89,86,62**
toteswingers:1&2:£7.70, 1&3:£1.70, 2&3:£5.50 CSF £43.08 CT £99.95 TOTE £3.10: £2.00, £2.90, £1.40; EX 48.10 Trifecta £131.70 Pool: £1,237.18 - 6.95 winning units..
Owner Liam Breslin **Bred** Miss Mary Davidson & Mrs Steffi Von Schilcher **Trained** Hubbert's Bridge, Lincs

FOCUS
An ordinary contest.
T/Plt: £50.90 to a £1 stake. Pool:£62,075.01 - 889.99 winning tickets T/Qpdt: £12.70 to a £1 stake. Pool:£5,649.61 - 328.24 winning tickets SP

807 SOUTHWELL (L-H)
Thursday, March 8

OFFICIAL GOING: Standard
Wind: Virtually nil Weather: Cloudy

830 FREE BETTING WITH FREEBETTING.CO.UK (S) STKS — 1m 4f (F)
2:20 (2:20) (Class 6) 4-Y-0+ — **£1,704** (£503; £251) **Stalls** Low

Form — RPR

-121 **1** **Overrule (USA)**[14] 672 8-9-5 76 .... (p) BarryMcHugh 2 — 73+
(Brian Ellison) *trckd ldrs: wd st and smooth hdwy to ld wl over 2f out: cleverly* **1/2**[1]

3135 **2** *3/4* **Maslak (IRE)**[5] 786 8-9-5 63 .... ChrisCatlin 3 — 67
(Peter Hiatt) *led: rdn along and hdd 3f out: sn drvn and sltly outpcd: rallied to take 2nd ins fnl f: kpt on* **9/2**[3]

0060 **3** *3 1/4* **Jordaura**[15] 655 6-8-13 70 .... RobertWinston 5 — 57
(Gay Kelleway) *hld up in rr: gd hdwy 4f out: sn cl up: rdn to ld briefly 3f out: sn hdd and drvn: one pce appr fnl f* **4/1**[2]

120- **4** *7* **Davana**[345] 1032 6-8-8 54 .... LukeMorris 4 — 41
(Colin Teague) *chsd ldr: rdn along wl over 3f out and sn wknd* **20/1**

20/0 **5** *30* **Dawn Mystery**[17] 632 8-8-3 45 ow2 .... (b) MatthewHopkins(7) 6
(Alan Berry) *dwlt: sn chsng ldng pair: rdn along over 4f out and sn wknd* **100/1**

2m 40.89s (-0.11) **Going Correction** -0.125s/f (Stan) **5** Ran SP% **110.6**
Speed ratings (Par 101): **95,94,92,87,67**
CSF £3.25 TOTE £1.90: £1.02, £2.90; EX 3.40.There was no bid for the winner.
Owner Brian Ellison **Bred** Avalon Farms Inc **Trained** Norton, N Yorks

FOCUS
An uncompetitive seller run at an average pace and the runners spurned the inside rail over the last 1m. The second sets the level.

831 HORSE RACING FREE BETS WITH FREEBETTING.CO.UK H'CAP — 6f (F)
2:50 (2:50) (Class 6) (0-52,52) 4-Y-0+ — **£1,704** (£503; £251) **Stalls** Low

Form — RPR

3-65 **1** **Only Ten Per Cent (IRE)**[37] 370 4-9-0 **50** .... FrederikTylicki 9 — 65+
(J R Jenkins) *towards rr and pushed along 1/2-way: hdwy on inner 2f out: rdn over 1f out: led appr fnl f: kpt on strly* **9/4**[1]

230 **2** *3* **Flow Chart (IRE)**[21] 572 5-8-11 **47** .... RobbieFitzpatrick 6 — 53
(Peter Grayson) *chsd ldrs: hdwy over 2f out: rdn to ld over 1f out: hdd appr fnl f and kpt on same pce* **10/1**

0602 **3** *3* **Bonnie Prince Blue**[2] 807 9-8-11 **50** .... (e[1]) DaleSwift(3) 5 — 47
(Ian McInnes) *outpcd and bhd: hdwy on inner 2f out: sn rdn and styd on strly fnl f: nrst fin* **11/2**[2]

3205 **4** *nse* **Gracie's Gift (IRE)**[7] 752 10-8-11 **52** .... (v) CharlesEddery(5) 7 — 49
(Richard Guest) *dwlt: sn chsng ldrs: hdwy over 2f out: sn rdn and one pce appr fnl f* **9/1**

2565 **5** *nse* **Tamino (IRE)**[2] 813 9-8-4 **47** .... (b) LeonnaMayor(7) 8 — 44
(Alastair Lidderdale) *prom: chsd ldr 1/2-way: rdn 2f out: one pce and edgd lft appr fnl f* **9/1**

5400 **6** *4* **Takajan (IRE)**[7] 740 5-8-11 **47** .... (b[1]) LukeMorris 3 — 32
(Mark Brisbourne) *led: rdn 2f out: sn hdd and grad wknd* **13/2**[3]

-306 **7** *1 1/2* **Tawseef (IRE)**[27] 503 4-8-11 **47** .... (b) TomEaves 4 — 27
(Roy Brotherton) *s.i.s: a in rr* **10/1**

-500 **8** *8* **Young Simon**[38] 356 5-8-11 **47** .... (v) JoeFanning 2
(George Margarson) *chsd ldrs on inner: rdn along 1/2-way: sn btn* **7/1**

306- **9** *6* **Indian Dumaani**140 6982 5-8-12 **48**............................ WilliamCarson 12
(David Bridgwater) *chsd ldrs on wd outside: rdn along and wd st: sn wknd* **16/1**

4-00 **10** *hd* **Morermaloke**55 155 4-9-1 **51**....................................(p) PJMcDonald 10
(Ian McInnes) *chsd ldrs: rdn along 1/2-way: wd st and sn wknd* **28/1**

1m 15.02s (-1.48) **Going Correction** -0.125s/f (Stan) 10 Ran SP% **119.5**
Speed ratings (Par 101): **104,100,96,95,95 90,88,77,69,69**
toteswingers:1&2:£4.50, 1&3:£3.20, 2&3:£11.10 CSF £27.08 CT £114.95 TOTE £3.30: £1.30, £2.60, £1.60; EX 28.60 Trifecta £281.40 Pool: £658.03 - 1.73 winning units..
Owner B Silkman **Bred** Sandro Garavelli **Trained** Royston, Herts

FOCUS
A very moderate 46-52 sprint with recent winning form conspicuous by its absence. The winner did it well and the form has been given a chance.

832 FREE CASINO OFFERS AT FREEBETTING.CO.UK H'CAP 1m (F)
3:25 (3:25) (Class 6) (0-55,55) 3-Y-O **£1,704** (£503; £251) **Stalls** Low

Form RPR

-622 **1** **Pelican Rock (IRE)**16 641 3-8-11 **50**.................... RichardKingscote 2 59+
(Tom Dascombe) *cl up: led after 2f: hdd over 4f out: effrt to ld again over 2f out: sn rdn clr: eased ins fnl f* **1/1**1

340- **2** *2* **Bountiful Catch**105 7530 3-8-12 **51**................................. MickyFenton 7 54
(Pam Sly) *dwlt: hdwy on outer to join ldrs after 1f: led bef 1/2-way: rdn along and hdd over 2f out: kpt on u.p fnl f: no ch w wnr* **6/1**3

3-30 **3** *7* **Rhyme Royal**30 459 3-8-10 **49** ow1........................... PaulMulrennan 3 36
(James Given) *in tch: rdn along wl over 2f out: sn one pce* **14/1**

-550 **4** *3 3/4* **Waspy**7 743 3-8-7 **46**... ChrisCatlin 1 25
(Ed Dunlop) *led 2f: cl up: rdn along and outpcd over 3f out: kpt on u.p appr fnl f* **11/1**

060- **5** *3* **Compton Monarch**199 5316 3-8-0 **46** oh1.............. NicoleNordblad(7) 6 18
(Hans Adielsson) *towards rr: pushed along wl over 3f out: rdn wl over 2f out: nvr a factor* **7/2**2

0-60 **6** *3/4* **Tigresa (IRE)**41 336 3-9-2 **55**... JoeFanning 5 26
(Mark Johnston) *chsd ldrs: rdn wl over 2f out: sn wknd* **10/1**

1m 43.8s (0.10) **Going Correction** -0.125s/f (Stan) 6 Ran SP% **110.6**
Speed ratings (Par 96): **94,92,85,81,78 77**
toteswingers:1&2:£2.00, 1&3:£2.80, 2&3:£6.40 CSF £7.26 TOTE £2.30: £1.10, £3.70; EX 8.30.
Owner Laurence A Bellman **Bred** Daniel Chassagneux **Trained** Malpas, Cheshire

FOCUS
A poor 46-55 handicap contested by six maidens and not a race to dwell on. The front pair had the race to themselves from a long way out. The winner rates a small personal best.

833 FREE BINGO OFFERS AT FREEBETTING.CO.UK MEDIAN AUCTION MAIDEN STKS 1m (F)
3:55 (3:55) (Class 6) 3-5-Y-O **£1,704** (£503; £251) **Stalls** Low

Form RPR

550- **1** **Jacob McCandles**186 5761 5-9-7 **64**.................................. LMcNiff(5) 5 66+
(David Barron) *t.k.h early: trckd ldrs: hdwy 3f out: led wl over 1f out: shkn up and kpt on wl fnl f* **3/1**2

04- **2** *2* **Lithograph (USA)**140 6977 3-8-3 **0**.................................... JoeFanning 9 47
(Mark Johnston) *prom: led wl over 2f out: sn rdn and hdd wl over 1f out: chsd wnr and edgd lft jst ins fnl f: kpt on same pce* **11/2**3

52-4 **3** *1 1/4* **Thackeray**21 579 5-9-12 **55**.. DuranFentiman 8 55
(Chris Fairhurst) *prom: led after 2f: rdn along and hdd wl over 2f out: drvn and one pce appr fnl f* **15/2**

0-35 **4** *2 1/4* **Handsome King**23 552 5-9-12 **64**............................(p) FrederikTylicki 3 50
(J R Jenkins) *led 2f: trckd ldrs on inner: effrt 3f out: sn rdn: carried hd high and one pce* **11/4**1

5 *2 1/4* **Black Dragon**20 4-9-5 **0**..(t) NatashaEaton(7) 6 45
(Mark Rimmer) *s.i.s and bhd: rapid hdwy on outer to join ldrs over 3f out: rdn 2f out: sn one pce* **8/1**

6 *18* **Wilander** 3-8-8 **0**... TomEaves 4
(Gay Kelleway) *chsd ldrs: rdn along 3f out: sn wknd* **33/1**

06 **7** *13* **Gold Deal (IRE)**23 552 3-8-8 **0**...(t) LeeNewman 2
(Deborah Sanderson) *chsd ldrs: rdn along over 3f out: sn wknd* **20/1**

55 **8** *1* **Roughlyn**17 635 3-8-5 **0**.. JulieBurke(3) 7
(Kevin Ryan) *prom: rdn along over 3f out: sn wknd* **11/2**3

1m 43.31s (-0.39) **Going Correction** -0.125s/f (Stan)
WFA 3 from 4yo+ 18lb 8 Ran SP% **113.0**
Speed ratings (Par 101): **96,94,92,90,88 70,57,56**
toteswingers:1&2:£5.70, 1&3:£6.00, 2&3:£3.60 CSF £19.39 TOTE £5.70: £2.40, £2.50, £3.60; EX 21.90 Trifecta £138.00 Pool: £854.31 - 4.58 winning units..
Owner Harrowgate Bloodstock Ltd **Bred** Tibthorpe Stud **Trained** Maunby, N Yorks

FOCUS
A weak maiden and being won by a 5yo suggests this isn't great form behind the winner. The time also limits the form.

834 EXCLUSIVE BETTING OFFERS AT FREEBETTING.CO.UK H'CAP 7f (F)
4:30 (4:30) (Class 5) (0-75,75) 4-Y-O+ **£2,264** (£673; £336; £168) **Stalls** Low

Form RPR

5251 **1** **Imprimis Tagula (IRE)**23 553 8-9-4 **72**...................(v) SamHitchcott 10 81
(Alan Bailey) *trckd ldrs: cl up 3f out: effrt 2f out: rdn to ld over 1f out: drvn out* **7/1**

560- **2** *1/2* **Nezami (IRE)**161 6478 7-9-0 **68**.. MickyFenton 8 76
(Paul Midgley) *led: rdn over 2f out: hdd over 1f out: kpt on wl u.p fnl f* **33/1**

0414 **3** *1* **Ezra Church (IRE)**27 496 5-9-2 **75**............................. DeanHeslop(5) 6 80
(David Barron) *cl up: rdn over 2f out and ev ch tl drvn and one pce ent fnl f* **13/2**3

41-1 **4** *1 1/4* **Myboyalfie (USA)**27 496 5-9-6 **74**...........................(v) FrederikTylicki 4 76
(J R Jenkins) *in tch: pushed along 1/2-way: hdwy to chse ldrs and n.m.r 2f out: sn swtchd lft and rdn: kpt on same pce* **2/1**1

1240 **5** *nse* **Avonrose**30 458 5-9-7 **75**.. PhillipMakin 7 77
(Derek Shaw) *trckd ldrs: hdwy 3f out: rdn 2f out: one pce appr fnl f* **12/1**

01-4 **6** *5* **Katy's Secret**37 368 5-8-13 **70**.................................... RyanPowell(3) 11 60
(William Jarvis) *dwlt: hdwy on outer to chse ldrs over 3f out: wd st: sn rdn and btn* **11/1**

-313 **7** *1 1/4* **Andiamo Via**21 585 5-8-11 **65**.. PJMcDonald 2 51
(Michael Smith) *dwlt: a towards rr* **9/2**2

3216 **8** *3* **Mazovian (USA)**14 670 4-8-11 **68**............................ RobertLButler(3) 3 47
(Michael Chapman) *prom: rdn along wl over 2f out: grad wknd* **10/1**

2036 **9** *4 1/2* **Dickie Le Davoir**7 746 8-8-4 **63**............................(b) CharlesEddery(5) 5 31
(Richard Guest) *dwlt: a towards rr* **14/1**

13-0 **10** *13* **Yorksters Prince (IRE)**13 694 5-9-0 **68**...................(b) BarryMcHugh 1
(Tony Coyle) *a in rr* **20/1**

1m 27.77s (-2.53) **Going Correction** -0.125s/f (Stan) 10 Ran SP% **116.8**
Speed ratings (Par 103): **109,108,107,105,105 100,98,95,90,75**
toteswingers:1&2:£22.30, 1&3:£7.70, 2&3:£33.00 CSF £205.51 CT £1570.05 TOTE £10.80: £2.50, £10.90, £2.40; EX 248.10 TRIFECTA Not won..
Owner Middleham Park Racing XLI & Alan Bailey **Bred** Glashare House Stud **Trained** Newmarket, Suffolk

FOCUS
Quite a competitive handicap for the money and those that raced prominently were at an advantage. Sound form with the winner slowly returning to form.

835 MEMBERSHIP OF SOUTHWELL GOLF CLUB H'CAP 5f (F)
5:00 (5:01) (Class 4) (0-85,85) 4-Y-O+ **£4,204** (£1,251; £625; £312) **Stalls** High

Form RPR

1-36 **1** **Six Wives**26 525 5-8-13 **77**... RobertWinston 5 86
(Scott Dixon) *prom: chsd ldr after 2f: rdn to ld appr fnl f: kpt on wl* **9/2**2

1-16 **2** *1 1/4* **Cadeaux Pearl**44 286 4-9-1 **82**..................................(b) RyanPowell(3) 6 87
(Scott Dixon) *led: rdn wl over 1f out: hdd appr fnl f: kpt on* **12/1**

000- **3** *2 1/4* **Waking Warrior**143 6917 4-9-1 **79**.................................... PhillipMakin 9 75
(Kevin Ryan) *trckd ldrs: hdwy 2f out: sn rdn and edgd lft over 1f out: drvn and no imp fnl f* **7/2**1

-310 **4** *nk* **Fair Passion**10 718 5-9-1 **79**... DaneO'Neill 2 74
(Derek Shaw) *dwlt: hdwy to trck ldrs 1/2-way: n.m.r and swtchd lft over 1f out: sn rdn and kpt on same pce* **10/1**

020- **5** *3* **Haajes**124 7298 8-8-11 **82**.. NedCurtis(7) 4 67+
(Paul Midgley) *towards rr: rdn along over 2f out: styd on appr fnl f: nrst fin* **22/1**

0-20 **6** *1 1/4* **West Coast Dream**44 286 5-9-7 **85**.................................. TomEaves 1 65
(Roy Brotherton) *prom on outer: rdn along 2f out: edgd rt over 1f out: sn wknd* **12/1**

2032 **7** *nse* **Mottley Crewe**5 782 5-9-7 **85**....................................(b) MartinHarley 10 65
(Des Donovan) *chsd ldrs: rdn 2f out: sn btn: wnt wrong after line: fatally injured* **6/1**

00-5 **8** *1/2* **Baby Strange**12 715 8-9-6 **84**... MartinLane 3 62+
(Derek Shaw) *s.i.s and swtchd lft after s: wl bhd tl sme late hdwy* **12/1**

-340 **9** *72* **Sir Geoffrey (IRE)**26 525 6-9-1 **79**............................(b) FrederikTylicki 11
(Scott Dixon) *chse ldrs: rdn along over 2f out: sn lost pl and bhd whn heavily eased fnl f: b.b.v* **9/1**

2-00 **R** **Monsieur Jamie**15 652 4-9-1 **79**................................ PaulMulrennan 7
(J R Jenkins) *ref to r and tk no part* **11/2**3

58.06s (-1.64) **Going Correction** -0.20s/f (Stan) 10 Ran SP% **116.6**
Speed ratings (Par 105): **105,103,99,98,94 92,92,91, ,**
toteswingers:1&2:£4.70, 1&3:£5.50, 2&3:£10.10 CSF £57.29 CT £211.15 TOTE £6.10: £2.50, £3.30, £1.70; EX 47.30 Trifecta £727.10 Part won. Pool: £982.60 - 0.50 winning units..
Owner Sexy Six Partnership **Bred** Cheveley Park Stud Ltd **Trained** Babworth, Notts

FOCUS
This looked a decent sprint handicap, but the start proved crucial. The first two set the level.
Baby Strange Official explanation: jockey said gelding was slowly away
Sir Geoffrey(IRE) Official explanation: trainer said gelding bled from the nose

836 LADY MEMBERS OF SOUTHWELL GOLF CLUB APPRENTICE H'CAP 1m 3f (F)
5:30 (5:30) (Class 5) (0-75,67) 4-Y-O+ **£2,385** (£704; £352) **Stalls** Low

Form RPR

3/22 **1** **Hunters Belt (IRE)**2 460 8-9-6 **67**..................................... JasonHart 4 75
(Noel Wilson) *hld up in tch: hdwy on outer over 4f out: led wl over 2f out: rdn wl over 1f out: drvn out* **13/8**1

-431 **2** *1* **Favorite Girl (GER)**21 579 4-8-8 **63**......................... RichardOliver(7) 1 69
(Michael Appleby) *trckd ldr on inner: hdwy to ld over 3f out: hdd wl over 2f out: sn hung bdly rt: ev ch whn wandered bdly ins fnl f: no ex towards fin* **11/4**2

352- **3** *2 3/4* **Tobrata**93 7647 6-9-0 **61**.. JoshBaudains 5 65
(Mel Brittain) *trckd ldr: pushed along: n.m.r and outpcd over 3f out: swtchd rt and rdn over 2f out: no imp fnl f* **13/8**1

4030 **4** *13* **Community (USA)**21 584 4-8-9 **64**.............................. EvaMoscrop(7) 3 45
(Phil McEntee) *t.k.h: led: rdn along and hdd over 3f out: sn outpcd* **20/1**3

2m 25.07s (-2.93) **Going Correction** -0.125s/f (Stan)
WFA 4 from 6yo+ 1lb 4 Ran SP% **107.6**
Speed ratings (Par 103): **105,104,102,92**
CSF £6.29 TOTE £2.30; EX 7.50.
Owner R A Fisher & John Blair **Bred** Charlie Purcell **Trained** Middleham, N Yorks

FOCUS
A messy four-runner apprentice handicap and the form means little. A minor personal best from the winner.
T/Plt: £25.80 to a £1 stake. Pool:£63,751.81 - 1,797.66 winning tickets T/Qpdt: £15.40 to an £1 stake. Pool:£5,192.08 - 248.43 winning tickets JR

767 WOLVERHAMPTON (A.W) (L-H)
Thursday, March 8

OFFICIAL GOING: Standard
Wind: Fresh behind Weather: Cloudy with sunny spells

837 BET ON YOUR MOBILE WITH FREEBETTING.CO.UK H'CAP 7f 32y(P)
5:40 (5:41) (Class 7) (0-50,50) 4-Y-O+ **£1,704** (£503; £251) **Stalls** High

Form RPR

0423 **1** **Odd Ball (IRE)**2 807 5-8-11 **47**.. AmyRyan(3) 7 56+
(Lisa Williamson) *dwlt: hld up: hdwy over 1f out: rdn and r.o to ld nr fin* **10/3**1

-000 **2** *nk* **Ad Vitam (IRE)**28 483 4-8-13 **46**............................(vt) MichaelStainton 6 54
(Micky Hammond) *chsd ldrs: rdn and n.m.r over 1f out: led wl ins fnl f: hdd nr fin* **5/1**3

6305 **3** *1 1/4* **Metropolitan Chief**7 740 8-9-0 **47**..................................... JohnFahy 1 52
(Paul Burgoyne) *chsd ldrs: led 1f out: sn rdn: hdd and unable qck wl ins fnl f* **8/1**

0400 **4** *1/2* **Bachelor Knight (IRE)**13 690 4-8-8 **48**............... JacobButterfield(7) 2 52
(Suzzanne France) *mid-div: hdwy and nt clr run over 1f out: styd on* **22/1**

0/0- **5** *hd* **The Bay Bandit**201 5267 5-9-3 **50**..................................... AdamKirby 4 57+
(John Butler) *hld up: nt clr run fr over 1f out tl r.o wl towards fin: nvr nr to chal* **6/1**

0300 **6** *nk* **Littleportnbrandy (IRE)**7 740 4-8-9 **47**................(b) DuilioDaSilva(5) 8 49
(Richard Guest) *w ldr tl pushed along to ld 2f out: rdn and hdd 1f out: styd on same pce ins fnl f* **33/1**

5-00 **7** *nse* **Flaxen Lake**^{14} 664 5-9-3 **50**..(p) LukeMorris 12 52
(Milton Bradley) *hld up: rdn over 2f out: hdwy over 1f out: styd on* **18/1**

-100 **8** *½* **Clerical (USA)**^{27} 503 6-9-2 **49**..(e^{1}) ShaneKelly 9 50
(Robert Cowell) *a.p: rdn over 1f out: styd on same pce ins fnl f* **14/1**

040- **9** *1 ¾* **Avon Light**^{139} 6999 4-9-2 **49**..(p) LiamKeniry 5 46
(Milton Bradley) *led: rdn and hdd 1f out: no ex ins fnl f* **22/1**

-452 **10** *1 ½* **Meydan Style (USA)**^{14} 662 6-9-0 **47**.......................(p) NeilChalmers 11 40
(Richard Ford) *hld up: hdwy 4f out: rdn over 1f out: no ex* **9/2**^{2}

-505 **11** *3 ¼* **Poppy Golightly**^{27} 503 5-8-11 **49**.......................... NeilFarley$^{(5)}$ 10 34
(Declan Carroll) *mid-div: hdwy over 2f out: rdn and wknd over 1f out* **10/1**

1m 31.61s (2.01) **Going Correction** +0.175s/f (Slow) **11** Ran SP% **116.0**
Speed ratings (Par 97): **95,94,93,92,92 92,92,91,89,87 84**
Tote Swingers: 1&2 £6.70, 1&3 £4.30, 2&3 £15.80 CSF £18.80 CT £125.64 TOTE £3.10: £1.10, £5.50, £3.40; EX 31.20 Trifecta £450.00 Pool: £2,505.84 - 4.12 winning units..
Owner Mrs S Morris **Bred** Ms S Pettigrew & J Jamieson **Trained** Saighton, Cheshire
■ Stewards' Enquiry : John Fahy caution: careless riding.

FOCUS
A minor handicap, but the winner can be marked up because he came from some way back in a steadily run race and the fifth looked unlucky. Low-grade form.
The Bay Bandit Official explanation: jockey said gelding was denied a clear run
Meydan Style(USA) Official explanation: trainer said gelding finished stiff behind

838 FREE BETS ON YOUR MOBILE WITH FREEBETTING.CO.UK MAIDEN FILLIES' STKS 7f 32y(P)
6:10 (6:13) (Class 5) 3-Y-0+ **£2,264** (£673; £336; £168) **Stalls** High

Form RPR
0-5 **1** **Yarra Valley**^{7} 742 3-8-8 0.. ChrisCatlin 6 68
(Willie Musson) *hld up: hdwy over 2f out: rdn to ld and hung lft ins fnl f: drvn out* **16/1**

2 *½* **Trail Of Tears (IRE)** 3-8-8 0.. RobertHavlin 3 67+
(John Gosden) *chsd ldr tl led wl over 1f out: sn rdn and hung lft: hdd ins fnl f: r.o* **9/4**^{1}

0- **3** *2* **Vena Amoris (USA)**^{139} 6985 3-8-8 0.......................... JoeFanning 7 62
(Mark Johnston) *prom: pushed along 1/2-way: ev ch 1f out: styd on same pce* **11/4**^{2}

4 *4* **Swift Act** 3-8-8 0.. LukeMorris 4 52+
(Ronald Harris) *sn pushed along towards rr: hdwy over 1f out: wknd ins fnl f* **33/1**

5 *hd* **Chuckle** 3-8-8 0.. NickyMackay 1 52+
(Marco Botti) *chsd ldrs: shkn up and swtchd lft over 1f out: wknd ins fnl f* **3/1**^{3}

6 *1 ¾* **Big Sylv (IRE)** 3-8-8 0.. LiamJones 9 47
(James Unett) *s.i.s: hld up: hdwy over 2f out: hmpd wl over 1f out: wknd fnl f* **66/1**

456 **7** *2 ½* **Meia Noite**^{15} 658 5-9-10 57..(v^{1}) ShaneKelly 5 47
(Alan McCabe) *sn led: rdn and hdd wl over 1f out: wknd fnl f* **10/1**

64- **8** *7* **Coupland Lass (IRE)**^{278} 2723 4-9-10 0.......................... JamieMackay 10 30
(Willie Musson) *s.s: bhd: nvr nr to chal* **16/1**

5 **9** *24* **Chocolate Pursuits**^{20} 604 3-8-8 0.......................... RichardKingscote 2
(Tom Dascombe) *chsd ldrs tl rdn: hung rt and wknd over 2f out* **28/1**

1m 31.15s (1.55) **Going Correction** +0.175s/f (Slow)
WFA 3 from 4yo+ 16lb **9** Ran SP% **111.2**
Speed ratings (Par 100): **98,97,95,90,90 88,85,77,50**
Tote Swingers: 1&2 £5.40, 1&3 £15.10, 2&3 £1.90 CSF £49.49 TOTE £17.00: £4.10, £1.30, £2.00; EX 66.10 Trifecta £655.70 Pool: £6,123.57 - 6.91 winning units..
Owner W J Musson **Bred** Denford Stud Ltd **Trained** Newmarket, Suffolk

FOCUS
The first three pulled clear in what was probably a fair fillies' maiden. The form could be rated higher.
Coupland Lass(IRE) Official explanation: jockey said, regarding running and riding, that his orders were to drop the filly in, keep it balanced and get it to finish in the best possible position, it had suffered a fracture last year which kept it in its box for most of the winter, but had been working well recently and was thought forward enough to run, it was slowly away, asked for an effort on home bend, but tired quickly approaching final furlong and ands felt it prudent not to persist.
Chocolate Pursuits Official explanation: jockey said filly ran green

839 STAY AT THE WOLVERHAMPTON HOLIDAY INN (S) STKS 5f 216y(P)
6:40 (6:41) (Class 6) 4-Y-0+ **£1,704** (£503; £251) **Stalls** Low

Form RPR
05-6 **1** **Bertie Southstreet**^{10} 719 9-9-0 64..(b) MickyFenton 2 66
(Paul Midgley) *hld up in tch: shkn up to ld 1f out: rdn out* **14/1**

50-2 **2** *2* **Catherines Call (IRE)**^{20} 593 5-8-9 74.......................... DavidProbert 4 55
(Des Donovan) *a.p: chsd ldr over 4f out: rdn and ev ch 1f out: styd on same pce* **1/1**^{1}

3616 **3** *3 ¼* **Jonnie Skull (IRE)**^{6} 761 6-9-6 58..(vt) LukeMorris 1 56
(Phil McEntee) *plld hrd: trckd ldr tl over 4f out: remained handy: rdn over 2f out: styd on same pce fr over 1f out* **5/1**^{3}

100/ **4** *1* **Sundae**^{840} 7454 8-9-0 78.. AdamKirby 3 47
(K F Clutterbuck) *set stdy pce tl qcknd over 2f out: rdn and hdd 1f out: wknd wl ins fnl f* **2/1**^{2}

1m 16.23s (1.23) **Going Correction** +0.175s/f (Slow) **4** Ran SP% **106.7**
Speed ratings (Par 101): **98,95,91,89**
CSF £28.48 TOTE £10.50; EX 26.60.Ther was no bid for the winner.
Owner J D Walker **Bred** B Whitehouse **Trained** Westow, N Yorks

FOCUS
The outsider finished well from off the steady pace to spring a surprise and register a ninth win in this small-field seller. The winner and third help set the level.
Bertie Southstreet Official explanation: trainer said, regarding apparent improvement in form, that the gelding may have benefited from the re-application of blinkers in a weaker contest.
Sundae Official explanation: jockey said gelding moved poorly in final furlong

840 BETTING ON YOUR MOBILE AT FREEBETTING.CO.UK CLAIMING STKS 1m 141y(P)
7:10 (7:10) (Class 6) 3-Y-0 **£1,704** (£503; £251) **Stalls** Low

Form RPR
4111 **1** **Clean Bowled (IRE)**^{13} 683 3-8-13 72..........................(p) NedCurtis$^{(7)}$ 3 76
(Roger Curtis) *sn chsng ldr: led 3f out: pushed along over 1f out: reminder and hung lft ins fnl f: comf* **8/13**^{1}

-441 **2** *1 ¾* **Flying Pickets (IRE)**^{7} 748 3-9-1 70..(be) JohnFahy 1 66
(Alan McCabe) *chsd ldrs: rdn over 2f out: hung rt and lft ins fnl f: styd on* **4/1**^{2}

-066 **3** *hd* **Aiaam Al Wafa (IRE)**^{23} 556 3-7-11 53 ow1............(p) DannyBrock$^{(7)}$ 6 54
(Phil McEntee) *hld up: hdwy over 1f out: sn rdn: styd on* **33/1**

-522 **4** *2 ½* **Siouxies Dream**^{26} 534 3-8-8 56.. LukeMorris 4 53
(Michael Appleby) *prom: chsd wnr over 2f out: sn rdn: no ex ins fnl f* **9/2**^{3}

60-0 **5** *19* **Kuwait Moon**^{58} 114 3-8-2 43.. NoraLooby$^{(7)}$ 5
(Alan McCabe) *led: pushed along and hdd 3f out: wknd wl over 1f out* **66/1**

00-0 **6** *3 ¼* **Hatha Zain (IRE)**^{8} 734 3-8-10 42.......................... RichardKingscote 2
(Milton Bradley) *hld up: plld hrd: rdn and wknd over 2f out* **50/1**

1m 52.62s (2.12) **Going Correction** +0.175s/f (Slow) **6** Ran SP% **106.5**
Speed ratings (Par 96): **97,95,95,93,76 73**
.Aiaam Al Wafa was subject to a friendly claim. Clean Bowled was also subject to a friendly claim.\n\x\x
Owner Richard Dean **Bred** Cathal Ennis **Trained** Lambourn, Berks

FOCUS
A progressive performer had no trouble justifying odds-on favouritism in this steadily run claimer. Straightforward form.

841 FREE BETTING ON YOUR MOBILE WITH FREEBETTING.CO.UK H'CAP 1m 141y(P)
7:40 (7:40) (Class 4) (0-85,82) 3-Y-O **£4,204** (£1,251; £625; £312) **Stalls** Low

Form RPR
10-2 **1** **Come On Blue Chip (IRE)**^{34} 398 3-9-7 **82**.......................(b) AdamKirby 1 92
(Paul D'Arcy) *hld up: hdwy to ld 1f out: sn rdn clr: readily* **5/2**^{2}

4314 **2** *4 ½* **Berlusca (IRE)**^{14} 667 3-8-11 **72**.......................... TomMcLaughlin 2 73
(Mark Brisbourne) *hld up: swtchd rt and hdwy over 1f out: styd on same pce ins fnl f* **12/1**

1 **3** *¾* **Rosby Waves (USA)**^{20} 604 3-8-11 **72**.......................... JoeFanning 7 71
(Mark Johnston) *a.p: chsd ldr over 2f out: rdn to ld and hung lft over 1f out: hdd 1f out: no ex ins fnl f* **7/1**

1-12 **4** *nk* **Karma Chameleon**^{20} 596 3-9-4 **79**.......................... ShaneKelly 3 83+
(John Berry) *chsd ldrs: cl up whn hmpd and lost pl over 1f out: nt rcvr* **2/1**^{1}

0-61 **5** *1 ¾* **Bareback (IRE)**^{14} 667 3-8-12 **73**.......................... LukeMorris 6 68
(John Best) *led early: chsd ldr: rdn whn hmpd over 1f out: styd on same pce* **10/1**

221- **6** *1* **Presburg (IRE)**^{160} 6506 3-9-5 **80**.......................... LiamKeniry 5 73
(Joseph Tuite) *dwlt: hld up: rdn over 3f out: wknd fnl f* **13/2**^{3}

105- **7** *1 ¼* **Stellar Express (IRE)**^{131} 7167 3-8-7 **75**.......................... JackDuern$^{(7)}$ 4 65
(Michael Appleby) *sn led: clr over 6f out: rdn over 2f out: wkng whn hdd over 1f out* **16/1**

1m 50.02s (-0.48) **Going Correction** +0.175s/f (Slow) **7** Ran SP% **110.4**
Speed ratings (Par 100): **109,105,104,104,102 101,100**
Tote Swingers: 1&2 £6.20, 1&3 £3.50, 2&3 £6.40 CSF £29.05 TOTE £3.00: £1.60, £3.70; EX 26.50.
Owner Blue Chip Feed Ltd **Bred** Gerry Flannery Developments **Trained** Newmarket, Suffolk

FOCUS
A competitive handicap. Breakaway leader Stellar Express set a strong pace but the favourite ran into severe traffic problems stuck on the inside and the winner stormed clear out wide. A personal best from the winner and the fourth is rated 3l better than the bare facts.
Rosby Waves(USA) Official explanation: jockey said filly hung left-handed closing stages
Stellar Express(IRE) Official explanation: jockey said filly hung left-handed throughout

842 THE BLACK COUNTRY'S ONLY RACECOURSE FILLIES' H'CAP 1m 141y(P)
8:10 (8:10) (Class 5) (0-70,63) 4-Y-O+ **£2,264** (£673; £336; £168) **Stalls** Low

Form RPR
600- **1** **Maz**^{80} 7816 4-9-4 **60**.. JoeFanning 2 70+
(Alan Bailey) *chsd ldr tl led wl over 1f out: shkn up ins fnl f: styd on wl* **9/2**^{3}

4662 **2** *2 ¾* **Polar Auroras**^{17} 633 4-9-0 **56**..(t) DavidProbert 3 60
(Tony Carroll) *a.p: rdn to chse wnr and hung lft over 1f out: styd on same pce ins fnl f* **7/2**^{2}

100- **3** *½* **Wiseman's Diamond (USA)**^{162} 6452 7-9-7 **63**..........(b) MickyFenton 1 66
(Paul Midgley) *prom: pushed along over 3f out: styd on same pce ins fnl f* **16/1**

00-3 **4** *1 ¾* **Forward Feline (IRE)**^{13} 692 6-9-6 **62**.......................... LukeMorris 8 62
(Bryn Palling) *hld up: rdn over 2f out: styd on same pce fnl f* **10/3**^{1}

-236 **5** *hd* **Darsan (IRE)**^{21} 573 4-9-7 **63**.......................... TomMcLaughlin 7 62
(Phil McEntee) *s.s: hld up: r.o ins fnl f: nvr nrr* **9/1**

6410 **6** *1* **Marksbury**^{10} 725 5-9-3 **59**.. ShaneKelly 5 56
(Mark Brisbourne) *hld up: hdwy over 2f out: rdn over 1f out: wknd ins fnl f* **11/2**

5260 **7** *2 ¾* **Monadreen Dancer**^{28} 478 4-9-0 **56**.......................... StephenCraine 6 47
(Daniel Mark Loughnane) *hld up: nt clr run over 2f out: rdn over 1f out: n.m.r fnl f: n.d* **11/1**

00-0 **8** *½* **Crazy Chris**^{14} 669 7-9-6 **62**.. LiamKeniry 4 52
(Milton Bradley) *led: clr 7f out: rdn and hdd wl over 1f out: edgd lft and wknd fnl f* **18/1**

1m 52.27s (1.77) **Going Correction** +0.175s/f (Slow) **8** Ran SP% **108.3**
Speed ratings (Par 100): **99,96,96,94,94 93,91,90**
Tote Swingers: 1&2 £3.90, 1&3 £16.70, 2&3 £3.50 CSF £18.37 CT £175.21 TOTE £3.40: £1.70, £1.50, £3.60; EX 23.10 Trifecta £232.80 Pool: £638.79 - 2.03 winning units..
Owner AB Racing Limited **Bred** Alan Bailey **Trained** Newmarket, Suffolk

FOCUS
The top weight was 7lb lower than the ceiling of the weights in this 0-70 handicap. Modest but solid form. The winner did the job in good style and may have more to offer.

843 FOOTBALL SCORES ON YOUR MOBILE WITH FOOTBALLSCORES.COM H'CAP 1m 1f 103y(P)
8:40 (8:41) (Class 6) (0-60,60) 4-Y-O+ **£1,704** (£503; £251) **Stalls** Low

Form RPR
60-0 **1** **Whodathought (IRE)**^{34} 400 4-9-6 **59**..........................(b) AdamKirby 2 70
(Paul Rich) *hld up: hdwy u.p over 2f out: drvn to ld ins fnl f: r.o* **10/1**

-315 **2** *1 ½* **Just Five (IRE)**^{14} 676 6-9-0 **58**..........................(v) RaulDaSilva$^{(5)}$ 8 66
(John Weymes) *chsd ldrs: led over 1f out: rdn and hdd ins fnl f: styd on same pce* **9/2**^{2}

000- **3** *2 ½* **Count Ceprano (IRE)**^{70} 7904 8-9-1 **57**.......................... SimonPearce$^{(3)}$ 1 60
(Lydia Pearce) *hld up: hdwy over 1f out: wnt 3rd ins fnl f: nt trble ldrs* **8/1**

50-6 **4** *2* **Swish Dish (CAN)**^{26} 532 5-8-7 **46** oh1.......................... PJMcDonald 5 44
(Micky Hammond) *led: hdd over 7f out: chsd ldrs: rdn over 2f out: no ex fnl f* **33/1**

6010 **5** *1 ½* **Stamp Duty (IRE)**^{10} 725 4-9-2 **58**.......................... DaleSwift$^{(3)}$ 4 53
(Suzzanne France) *hld up: hdwy over 2f out: rdn over 1f out: wknd ins fnl f* **11/2**^{3}

0/0- **6** *1 ¾* **Jobekani (IRE)**^{240} 3952 6-8-5 **47** oh1 ow1..........(p) AmyRyan$^{(3)}$ 7 39
(Lisa Williamson) *hld up: rdn over 1f out: styd on ins fnl f: nvr nrr* **50/1**

-150 **7** *¾* **Harrys Yer Man**^{17} 636 8-9-1 **54**.. ShaneKelly 12 44
(Mark Brisbourne) *dwlt: hdwy over 7f out: rdn over 1f out: wknd fnl f* **11/1**

50/0 **8** *1* **Pahente**^{22} 561 4-9-0 **53**.. LukeMorris 10 43
(Tony Carroll) *hld up: rdn over 1f out: nvr on terms* **33/1**

0-00 **9** 1 ¼ **Strong Vigilance (IRE)**17 636 5-9-4 **57** .... JoeFanning 11 42
(Michael Bell) *pushed along towards rr early: hdwy to ld over 7f out: rdn over 2f out: hdd over 1f out: wknd and eased fnl f* **3/1**1

6000 **10** 1 ¼ **Tunza The Lion**14 666 5-8-7 **46** oh1 .... NeilChalmers 9 29
(Richard Ford) *hld up: rdn over 1f out: a in rr* **80/1**

5050 **11** 7 **Hilbre Court (USA)**14 676 7-8-11 **50** ....(p) RussKennemore 13 18
(Brian Baugh) *chsd ldr: hung rt over 3f out: rdn over 2 out: wknd over 1f out: eased* **10/1**

020/ **12** 5 **Claimant (IRE)**333 4022 5-9-0 **60** .... JackDuern(7) 3 17
(Michael Appleby) *mid-div: rdn and wknd over 2f out* **8/1**

0-0 **13** 52 **King Of Connacht**55 160 9-8-7 **46** oh1 ....(p) LiamJones 6
(Mark Wellings) *hld up: rdn and wknd over 2f out: t.o* **66/1**

2m 1.96s (0.26) **Going Correction** +0.175s/f (Slow) **13** Ran SP% **118.6**
Speed ratings (Par 101): **105,103,101,99,98 96,96,95,94,93 86,82,36**
Tote Swingers: 1&2 £11.50, 1&3 £17.90, 2&3 £9.10 CSF £52.97 CT £386.59 TOTE £14.30: £3.90, £1.80, £3.70; EX 73.60 Trifecta £519.40.
Owner L M Power **Bred** Meadowlands Stud **Trained** Newport, Gwent
■ Stewards' Enquiry : P J McDonald three-day ban: careless riding (Mar 22-24)

FOCUS
A modest handicap. The pace was strong and they finished well strung out. Sound but limited form.
T/Plt: £737.00 to a £1 stake. Pool: £82,754.05 - 81.96 winning tickets. T/Qpdt: £102.40 to a £1 stake. Pool: £7,932.30 - 57.30 winning tickets. CR

837 WOLVERHAMPTON (A.W) (L-H)

Friday, March 9

OFFICIAL GOING: Standard
Wind: Moderate, across Weather: Cloudy

844 SIX NATIONS BETTING WITH FREEBETTING.CO.UK H'CAP 5f 20y(P)
5:50 (5:50) (Class 5) (0-70,69) 4-Y-0+ **£2,264** (£673; £336; £168) **Stalls** Low

Form RPR

2066 **1** **Rylee Mooch**16 652 4-9-1 **68** ....(e) CharlesEddery(5) 3 77
(Richard Guest) *mde all: rdn ins fnl f: kpt on wl: in command towards fin* **7/1**2

00-0 **2** 1 ¼ **Tom Sawyer**45 282 4-9-0 **62** ....(v1) PaulMulrennan 9 67
(Julie Camacho) *midfield: rdn over 1f out: hdwy ins fnl f: r.o: gng on at fin: tk 2nd post* **16/1**

2155 **3** shd **Blown It (USA)**35 406 6-9-7 **69** .... JoeFanning 2 73
(Keith Dalgleish) *chsd ldrs: rdn to take 2nd 1f out: kpt on ins fnl f: no real imp on wnr: lost 2nd post* **7/2**1

40-0 **4** nk **Methaaly (IRE)**36 387 9-9-3 **65** ....(be) RichardKingscote 1 68
(Michael Mullineaux) *midfield and niggled along: hdwy over 1f out: styd on ins fnl f: nt quite pce of ldrs* **16/1**

2123 **5** hd **Rightcar**27 522 5-8-9 **57** .... RobbieFitzpatrick 7 59
(Peter Grayson) *hld up: rdn and hdwy over 1f out: kpt on ins fnl f: nt quite pce of ldrs* **9/1**

243- **6** shd **Dispol Grand (IRE)**164 6427 6-8-8 **63** .... NedCurtis(7) 8 65
(Paul Midgley) *chsd ldrs 3 wd: pushed along over 2f out: nt qckn over 1f out: edgd lft and styd on same pce ins fnl f* **25/1**

25-0 **7** shd **Dreams Of Glory**20 624 4-8-11 **62** .... SimonPearce(3) 5 64
(Ron Hodges) *w wnr: rdn and lost 2nd 1f out: edgd rt ins fnl f: no ex fnl 50yds* **10/1**

0-54 **8** ½ **Atlantic Beach**7 763 7-9-5 **67** ....(b) LiamKeniry 6 67
(Milton Bradley) *hld up: hdwy 1f out: styd on ins fnl f: one pce and n.m.r fnl 75yds* **9/1**

20-2 **9** ½ **Silvanus (IRE)**14 696 7-9-5 **67** .... MickyFenton 11 65
(Paul Midgley) *hld up: pushed along bhd wall of runners over 1f out: no imp* **8/1**

4116 **10** ½ **Canadian Danehill (IRE)**14 691 10-8-11 **59** ....(e) WilliamCarson 4 55
(Robert Cowell) *chsd ldrs: pushed along over 2f out: btn whn n.m.r wl ins fnl f: eased towards fin* **7/1**2

333 **11** 1 ¼ **My Lord**20 624 4-8-12 **67** .... DarrenEgan(7) 10 59
(Ronald Harris) *a outpcd and bhd* **15/2**3

1m 1.91s (-0.39) **Going Correction** +0.025s/f (Slow) **11** Ran SP% **114.8**
Speed ratings (Par 103): **104,102,101,101,101 100,100,99,99,98 96**
toteswingers: 1&2 £21.30, 1&3 £5.50, 2&3 £13.30. CSF £110.14 CT £465.14 TOTE £9.10: £3.20, £2.90, £1.60; EX 181.90.
Owner Katie Hughes,Julie McCarlie,Sheila White **Bred** Mrs Sheila White **Trained** Stainforth, S Yorks
■ Stewards' Enquiry : Ned Curtis one-day ban: careless riding (Mar 23)

FOCUS
This was competitive enough, but the winner was allowed a softish lead and that proved crucial. The runner-up ran well in the circumstances.
Dreams Of Glory Official explanation: jockey said colt hung right-handed
Silvanus(IRE) Official explanation: jockey said gelding was denied a clear run
Canadian Danehill(IRE) Official explanation: jockey said gelding was denied a clear run

845 NAME A RACE TO ENHANCE YOUR BRAND H'CAP 5f 216y(P)
6:20 (6:20) (Class 6) (0-55,54) 3-Y-O **£1,704** (£503; £251) **Stalls** Low

Form RPR

3342 **1** **J J Leary (IRE)**9 734 3-8-12 **50** ....(v) FrannyNorton 3 59+
(Ian Williams) *mde all: r.o wl fr over 1f out: a in command* **5/2**1

0-56 **2** 1 ¾ **George Fenton**9 734 3-8-8 **46** ....(tp) MartinLane 11 49+
(Richard Guest) *hld up: rdn and hdwy over 1f out: styd on ins fnl f: tk 2nd towards fin: nt rch wnr* **7/1**3

05-6 **3** ¾ **Bitter Lemon**64 40 3-9-2 **54** .... FergusSweeney 8 55
(Tony Newcombe) *chsd wnr: rdn and outpcd by wnr 1f out: lost 2nd towards fin* **25/1**

2424 **4** ¾ **Magilini (IRE)**21 599 3-9-0 **52** ....(b) LeeNewman 10 50
(David Barron) *in tch: rdn over 1f out: styd on same pce ins fnl f* **15/2**

40-0 **5** ½ **Trending (IRE)**23 564 3-8-13 **51** ....(p) AdamKirby 13 49+
(Jeremy Gask) *stdd s: hld up: rdn and hdwy over 1f out: styd on towards fin: nt pce to get to ldrs* **18/1**

00-5 **6** ½ **After Timer (IRE)**22 583 3-8-7 **45** ....(b1) BarryMcHugh 4 40
(Julie Camacho) *midfield: hdwy 2f out: rdn to chse ldrs over 1f out: no ex fnl 100yds* **66/1**

404- **7** 1 **Celestial Dawn**135 7103 3-9-2 **54** .... LukeMorris 6 46
(John Weymes) *midfield: rdn over 3f out: no imp fnl f* **8/1**

-046 **8** ½ **Very First Blade**23 564 3-8-12 **50** .... ShaneKelly 7 41
(Mark Brisbourne) *midfield: pushed along over 3f out: wknd over 1f out* **15/2**

3-05 **9** 1 ½ **Tuibama (IRE)**21 599 3-9-1 **53** .... PhillipMakin 5 39
(Ben Haslam) *racd keenly: trckd ldrs: rdn over 1f out: wknd ins fnl f* **10/1**

00-0 **10** 2 ½ **Brian's Best**31 455 3-8-7 **45** .... NeilChalmers 1 24
(Richard Ford) *hld up: nt clr run over 1f out: nvr on terms* **100/1**

0-40 **11** nk **Romany Spirit (IRE)**24 556 3-9-2 **54** .... TomEaves 12 32
(Jason Ward) *chsd ldrs tl rdn and wknd over 1f out* **40/1**

000- **12** 12 **Bonnie Blade**70 7925 3-8-9 **47** ....(v1) LiamJones 2
(James Unett) *chsd ldrs: n.m.r over 2f out: sn wknd* **40/1**

00-3 **13** 41 **Armiger**9 734 3-9-1 **53** .... WilliamCarson 9
(William Muir) *midfield: pushed along over 3f out: wknd over 2f out: eased whn wl btn wl over 1f out: t.o* **5/1**2

1m 15.54s (0.54) **Going Correction** +0.025s/f (Slow) **13** Ran SP% **117.9**
Speed ratings (Par 96): **97,94,93,92,92 91,90,89,87,84 83,67,12**
toteswingers: 1&2 £4.30, 1&3 £12.20, 2&3 £21.20. CSF £19.02 CT £370.54 TOTE £2.80: £1.20, £2.70, £6.20; EX 20.60.
Owner Dr Marwan Koukash **Bred** Con Marnane **Trained** Portway, Worcs

FOCUS
This was similarly run to the first race, with the winner dictating and pinching it off the home turn. Weakish form.
Tuibama(IRE) Official explanation: jockey said gelding ran too freely
Armiger Official explanation: trainer's rep had no explanation for the poor form shown

846 RUGBY BETTING WITH FREEBETTING.CO.UK H'CAP 1m 4f 50y(P)
6:50 (6:50) (Class 2) (0-100,95) 4-Y-O£9,955 (£2,979; £1,489; £745; £371) **Stalls** Low

Form RPR

11-1 **1** **William Haigh (IRE)**68 5 4-9-5 **95** .... PJMcDonald 7 102
(Alan Swinbank) *prom: chsd ldr over 6f out: led 2f out: rdn over 1f out: r.o ins fnl f: a doing enough cl home* **9/4**1

0213 **2** ¾ **Layline (IRE)**15 668 5-9-4 **92** .... ShaneKelly 3 98
(Gay Kelleway) *trckd ldrs: lost pl 6f out but stl hld up: plld wd and hdwy wl over 1f out: r.o to take 2nd wl ins fnl f: clsd on wnr but a hld cl home* **15/2**

-341 **3** 1 **Brunston**21 601 6-8-13 **87** .... LukeMorris 5 91
(Brendan Powell) *hld up: tk clsr order 6f out: rdn to take 2nd 1f out: lost 2nd wl ins fnl f: one pce cl home* **7/2**3

112 **4** 4 **Queen Of Denmark (USA)**21 601 4-8-12 **88** .... JoeFanning 4 86
(Mark Johnston) *trckd ldrs: led 8f out: hdd 2f out: wknd ins fnl f* **3/1**2

6-53 **5** 1 ¼ **Greyfriarschorista**15 674 5-8-8 **82** .... BarryMcHugh 6 78
(Brian Ellison) *led at stdy pce: hdd 8f out: remained prom: rdn over 1f out: wknd ins fnl f* **15/2**

/00- **6** 3 ½ **Memory Cloth**167 6335 5-8-10 **87** .... DaleSwift(3) 8 78
(Brian Ellison) *hld up: rdn over 2f out: wl outpcd over 1f out* **14/1**

/00- **7** ¾ **Almail (USA)**181 5932 6-9-6 **94** .... FergusSweeney 2 84
(Jamie Osborne) *hld up in rr: u.p over 2f out: wl outpcd over 1f out* **33/1**

2m 40.26s (-0.84) **Going Correction** +0.025s/f (Slow)
WFA 4 from 5yo+ 2lb **7** Ran SP% **111.1**
Speed ratings (Par 109): **103,102,101,99,98 96,95**
toteswingers: 1&2 £2.70, 1&3 £2.70, 2&3 £4.30. CSF £18.56 CT £54.20 TOTE £3.30: £1.70, £2.90; EX 20.50.
Owner Shropshire Wolves II **Bred** Mrs C L Weld **Trained** Melsonby, N Yorks

FOCUS
A generous prize attracted a good field, but the pace was disappointingly slack. Further improvement from the progressive winner, with the runner-up rated to his best.

NOTEBOOK
William Haigh(IRE) maintained his splendid run on AW tracks, and it is even more to his credit that he has now recorded three wins apiece on the two differing surfaces. He has continued to defy the handicapper even though he doesn't win by far (his last four have all been by three-quarters of a length), and he will be an interesting contender in decent races this summer if he can transfer his improvement to grass. (op 5-2 tchd 11-4)
Layline(IRE), more at home back among handicappers after a foray into conditions company last time, ran a fine race in defeat. He travelled strongly and saw it out well, but the winner is in the sort of form that made him hard to beat. (op 8-1)
Brunston, capable of winning off this mark at his peak, showed his is not far off his best again. He is a decent AW performer these days. (tchd 5-2)
Queen Of Denmark(USA), forced to do the donkey work after the first 4f to improve a poor early tempo, was on a tough mark considering her lack of experience. (op 5-2 tchd 10-3)
Greyfriarschorista, trying 1m4f for the first time, looks better at 1m or 1m1f. (op 8-1 tchd 10-1)
Memory Cloth, patiently ridden over this longer trip, didn't convince that 1m4f is what he needs. (op 16-1)

847 THE BLACK COUNTRY'S ONLY RACECOURSE MEDIAN AUCTION MAIDEN STKS 1m 4f 50y(P)
7:20 (7:22) (Class 6) 3-5-Y-O **£1,704** (£503; £251) **Stalls** Low

Form RPR

503- **1** **Aldo**175 6135 5-9-7 62 .... LeonnaMayor(7) 4 70
(Alastair Lidderdale) *hld up: rdn to take 2nd and abt 4 l down over 2f out: clsd over 1f out: r.o to ld ins fnl f: in command towards fin* **11/2**3

00- **2** 2 ¼ **What's The Point**272 2930 4-9-12 0 .... TomEaves 1 67
(Ollie Pears) *led at stdy pce: rdn and abt 4 l clr over 2f out: hung rt over 1f out: sn reduced advantage: hdd ins fnl f: no ex fnl 100yds* **33/1**

5-23 **3** 3 ½ **Ctappers**13 709 3-8-5 65 .... JoeFanning 5 58
(Mick Channon) *trckd ldrs: dropped to rr after 4f: hdwy over 3f out: rdn and chsd ldrs over 2f out: sn no imp* **9/4**1

32 **4** 7 **Munificence**16 650 3-8-5 0 .... NickyMackay 7 48
(Marco Botti) *racd keenly: hld up: hdwy to go prom after 4f: rdn 3f out: wknd over 2f out* **9/4**1

6 **5** 1 ½ **Godwit**22 581 4-9-7 0 .... RichardKingscote 2 44
(Eugene Stanford) *prom tl rdn and wknd over 2f out* **33/1**

00-4 **6** 27 **Never Satisfied**42 324 3-8-5 68 .... WilliamCarson 8
(Charles Hills) *prom: pushed along 5f out: wknd 3f out* **4/1**2

6562 **7** 1 ½ **Pink Evie**10 727 3-8-0 55 ....(p) LukeMorris 6
(Gay Kelleway) *hld up: hdwy to chse ldrs after 4f: rdn over 3f out: sn wknd* **25/1**

2m 40.2s (-0.90) **Going Correction** +0.025s/f (Slow)
WFA 3 from 4yo 23lb 4 from 5yo 2lb **7** Ran SP% **106.7**
Speed ratings (Par 101): **104,102,100,95,94 76,75**
toteswingers: 1&2 £15.00, 1&3 £2.90, 2&3 £8.90. CSF £130.55 TOTE £4.50: £2.80, £11.30; EX 165.50.
Owner Entertainments Committee **Bred** Mrs Pamela Donald **Trained** Lambourn, Berks

FOCUS
This was an ordinary maiden at best, and the pace was pedestrian, so there was little to get excited about. The winner limits the form and the second improved given the run of the race.

848 FREE BETTING WITH FREEBETTING.CO.UK H'CAP 1m 141y (P)
7:50 (7:53) (Class 7) (0-50,50) 4-Y-0+ £1,704 (£503; £251) Stalls Low

Form RPR
000- 1 **Douze Points (IRE)**[71] 7911 6 -9-148 AdamKirby 2 64+
(John Butler) *walked to post: awkward leaving stalls: hld up: last whn nt clr run ent st wl over 1f out: hdwy and swtchd lft appr fnl f: r.o to ld fnl 120yds: sn in command: eased down towards fin* 11/10[1]
-665 2 2 **Avon Supreme**[27] 530 4 -9-350 ShaneKelly 1 57
(Gay Kelleway) *midfield: swtchd lft and hdwy over 1f out: styd on ins fnl f: wnt 2nd fnl 75yds: no ch w wnr* 6/1[3]
-025 3 1 1/4 **Baby Driver**[2] 822 4 -9-249 FergusSweeney 11 53
(Tony Newcombe) *led: rdn and hdd fnl 120yds: no ex cl home* 5/1[2]
06-6 4 nk **See The Storm**[11] 725 4 -8-949 MatthewMcGhee(7) 6 52
(Lisa Williamson) *trckd ldrs: effrt over 1f out: one pce fnl 110yds* 33/1
0-05 5 1/2 **Dubonny**[32] 450 5 -8-745 (t) RaulDaSilva(5) 7 47
(Frank Sheridan) *trckd ldrs: n.m.r whn u.p over 1f out: styd on same pce ins fnl f* 12/1
0005 6 1/2 **Kirstys Lad**[7] 773 10 -8-1245 RichardKingscote 3 46
(Michael Mullineaux) *midfield: rdn over 1f out: kpt on same pce ins fnl f* 20/1
2444 7 1/2 **Spacecraft (IRE)**[15] 676 5 -8-1050 (b) DannyBrock(7) 13 50
(Christopher Kellett) *hld up in rr: rdn over 1f out: kpt on u.p ins fnl f: no imp* 11/1
6-46 8 1 **Luv U Noo**[15] 666 5 -8-1245 (p) RussKennemore 10 43
(Brian Baugh) *hld up: rdn and hdwy over 1f out: swtchd lft 150yds out: kpt on u.p* 20/1
000- 9 hd **Duneen Dream (USA)**[102] 7571 7 -9-350 DavidProbert 12 47
(Nikki Evans) *prom: rdn over 2f out: wknd ins fnl f* 25/1
0-00 10 7 **Fortunelini**[42] 328 7 -8-1050 DarrenEgan(7) 5 31
(Frank Sheridan) *hld up: effrt over 2f out: no imp: wknd over 1f out* 40/1
-060 11 2 1/4 **Forbidden (IRE)**[7] 773 9 -9-047 (vt) TomEaves 4 23
(Ian McInnes) *hld up: nt clr run over 1f out: sn rdn: nvr on terms* 40/1
0/00 12 5 **Gifted Heir (IRE)**[11] 725 8 -9-148 (p) JoeFanning 8 12
(Ray Peacock) *prom: rdn and wkng whn n.m.r wl over 1f out: bhd fnl f* 66/1

1m 50.77s (0.27) **Going Correction** +0.025s/f (Slow) 12Ran SP% 117.3
Speed ratings (Par 97): **99,97,96,95,95 94,94,93,93,87 85,80**
toteswingers: 1&2 £3.10, 1&3 £2.80, 2&3 £4.60. CSF £6.77 CT £24.99 TOTE £1.50 : £1.40, £2.00, £1.90; EX 9.20.
Owner J Butler **Bred** Tally-Ho Stud **Trained** Newmarket, Suffolk

FOCUS
This selling-class race, run at a decent gallop for the grade, was won by a remarkable late surge from a generously handicapped contender who had fallen from grace in the last six months. He rates better than the bare facts.
Gifted Heir (IRE) Official explanation: jockey said gelding moved poorly

849 MIRROR PUNTERS CLUB H'CAP 2m 119y (P)
8:20 (8:21) (Class 5) (0-75,75) 4-Y-0+ £2,264 (£673; £336 ; £168) Stalls Low

Form RPR
60-6 1 **Cotton King**[3] 810 5 -9-1275 (bt[1]) StevieDonohoe 3 83
(Tobias B P Coles) *hld up: nt clr run 2f out: hdwy on inner wl over 1f out: sn led: hrd pressed cl home: jst did enough* 7/1
-221 2 nse **Blackmore**[15] 673 5 -9-1073 JoeFanning 8 81
(Julia Feilden) *a.p: led over 2f out: rdn and hdd over 1f out: rallied wl ins fnl f: jst hld* 5/2[1]
50-0 3 1 **Russian George (IRE)**[93] 192 6 -9-1073 (tp) RobertWinston 9 80
(Steve Gollings) *s.i.s: hld up: rdn and hdwy on outer over 2f out: sn ev ch: nt qckn over 1f out: styd on ins fnl f but a hld* 7/2[3]
5/50 4 2 3/4 **Sam Lord**[28] 500 8 -9-1073 PaddyAspell 7 77
(James Moffatt) *trckd ldrs for 1f: hld up: rdn 3f out: hdwy and styd on ins fnl f: nt rch front trio* 33/1
1-03 5 1 3/4 **Dream Catcher (SWE)**[21] 600 9 -9-164 (p) DavidProbert 1 66
(Jonjo O'Neill) *prom: rdn over 1f out: one pce and no imp ins fnl f* 14/1
-434 6 4 **Hidden Glory**[7] 771 5 -9-1275 (b) PaulMulrennan 6 72
(James Given) *hld up in rr: rdn and hdwy to chse ldrs over 1f out: no imp: wknd fnl 150yds* 9/1
/65- 7 2 3/4 **Sansili**[153] 5784 5 -8-1059 (p) WilliamCarson 4 53
(Peter Bowen) *handy: pushed along 4f out: wknd over 1f out* 25/1
3-01 8 8 **Fantino**[36] 392 6 -9-063 (t) RobertHavlin 2 47
(Pat Murphy) *led: rdn and hdd over 2f out: wknd wl over 1f out* 12/1
3-52 9 hd **Uncut Stone (IRE)**[7] 772 4 -8-761 ow1 (b) TomEaves 5 45
(Peter Niven) *hld up: hdwy to go prom after 2f: rdn and wknd 3f out* 3/1[2]

3m 39.96s (-1.84) **Going Correction** +0.025s/f (Slow)
WFA 4 from 5yo+ 5lb 9Ran SP% 119.4
Speed ratings (Par 103): **105,104,104,103,102 100,99,95,95**
toteswingers: 1&2 £4.60, 1&3 £8.90, 2&3 £2.30. CSF £25.78 CT £74.01 TOTE £11.50 : £3.90, £2.60, £1.50 ; EX 33.80.
Owner Mrs Sarah Hamilton **Bred** Meon Valley Stud **Trained** Newmarket, Suffolk

FOCUS
After a routine gallop for the distance, the finish was contested by two runners with contrasting recent form. The winner is rated back to his best.
Uncut Stone (IRE) Official explanation: trainer's rep said, regarding running, that the race may have come too soon for the gelding.

850 HORSE RACING FREE BETS WITH FREEBETTING.CO.UK H'CAP 1m 4f 50y (P)
8:50 (8:51) (Class 6) (0-65,65) 4-Y-0+ £1,704 (£503; £251) Stalls Low

Form RPR
02-1 1 **Holden Eagle**[7] 767 7 -8-455 IanBurns(7) 2 64
(Tony Newcombe) *led: hdd over 5f out: remained w ldr: rdn 3f out: regained ld ins fnl f: styd on: in control towards fin* 7/2[1]
-105 2 1/2 **Jamarjo (IRE)**[9] 738 5 -9-765 RobertWinston 9 73
(Steve Gollings) *w ldr: led over 5f out: rdn and hdd ins fnl f: styd on: hld cl home* 9/2[2]
/40- 3 1 3/4 **Reset City**[230] 4341 6 -9-765 (t) StevieDonohoe 3 70
(Ian Williams) *racd keenly in midfield: hdwy over 1f out: styd on ins fnl f: no imp on front duo* 12/1
3341 4 shd **Newport Arch**[17] 644 4 -9-464 (v) JoeFanning 1 69
(John Quinn) *trckd ldrs: rdn over 1f out: styd on same pce ins fnl f* 7/2[1]
3140 5 2 **Cloudy Start**[9] 738 6 -8-960 LeonnaMayor(7) 6 62
(Jamie Osborne) *s.s: hld up: hdwy over 3f out: rdn on wd outside over 2f out: styd on u.p ins fnl f: nt trble ldrs* 12/1
64-0 6 1/2 **Delagoa Bay (IRE)**[30] 468 4 -8-551 oh6 LukeMorris 10 52
(Sylvester Kirk) *hld up: niggled along over 4f out: rdn and hdwy over 1f out: kpt on ins fnl f: nt trble ldrs* 40/1
6-2P 7 1 3/4 **Royal Alcor (IRE)**[11] 721 5 -9-664 (b) FrankieMcDonald 4 62
(Alastair Lidderdale) *midfield: hdwy 6f out: prom 5f out: chalng u.p 2f out: rdn over 1f out: wknd ins fnl f* 9/1
0445 8 hd **Yossi (IRE)**[7] 767 8 -8-451 oh4 (p) DeclanCannon(3) 8 49
(Richard Guest) *trckd ldrs: rdn over 2f out: no imp over 1f out: wknd ins fnl f* 22/1
200- 8 dht **Hallstatt (IRE)**[102] 7570 6 -9-765 (t) PaulMulrennan 5 63
(John Mackie) *trckd ldrs: rdn and outpcd over 2f out: no imp after* 14/1
00-6 10 2 1/2 **Prince Freddie**[21] 433 4 -9-565 TomEaves 11 59
(Roy Brotherton) *hld up: rdn over 2f out: nvr a threat* 28/1
2115 11 3 1/2 **Black Iceman**[22] 575 4 -8-958 SimonPearce(3) 7 46
(Lydia Pearce) *midfield: pushed along 3f out: wknd over 2f out* 6/1[3]

2m 42.93s (1.83) **Going Correction** +0.025s/f (Slow)
WFA 4 from 5yo+ 2lb 11Ran SP% 119.2
Speed ratings (Par 101): **94,93,92,92,91 90,89,89,89,87 85**
toteswingers: 1&2 £5.30, 1&3 £10.00, 2&3 £11.20. CSF £18.88 CT £172.93 TOTE £5.10 : £1.80, £1.50, £4.60 ; EX 22.10.
Owner The About A Fortnight Partnership **Bred** A G Newcombe & M Patel **Trained** Yarnscombe, Devon

FOCUS
This was run at a modest pace and it paid to be handy. Modest, straightforward form.
Royal Alcor (IRE) Official explanation: jockey said gelding ran too free early
T/Jkpt: Part won. £25,000.00 to a £1 stake. Pool of £12,326.45 - 0.50 winning tickets. T/Plt: £558.50 to a £1 stake. Pool of £106,277.07 - 138.90 winning tickets. T/Qpdt: £137.50 to a £1 stake. Pool of £10,642.75 - 57.24 winning tickets. DO

851a - 864a (Foreign Racing) - See Raceform Interactive

116 DEAUVILLE (R-H)
Friday, March 9
OFFICIAL GOING: Fibresand: standard

865a PRIX DE LA VIE (CLAIMER) (3YO) (FIBRESAND) 6f 110y
3:55 (12:00) 3-Y-0 £7,916 (£3,166; £2,375 ; £1,583 ; £791)

RPR
1 **Worth**[44] 295 3 -8-130 (b) ThomasHenderson(3) 5 80
(Barry Brennan) *chsd ldr fr s: hrd rdn fr over 1 1/2f out: tk ld 150yds out: strly chal fnl 50yds: jst hld on* 36/5
2 nse **Picante (IRE)**[67] 17 3 -8-80 (p) AnthonyCrastus 12 72
(C Boutin, France) 15/2
3 3 1/2 **Majestic Speed (IRE)**[61] 211 3 -8-110 (p) FranckBlondel 10 65
(Rod Collet, France) 10/1
4 shd **Darnathean**[18] 637 3 -8-110 (b) IoritzMendizabal 6 65
(Paul D'Arcy) *broke fast: sn established clr: u.p over 1f out: hdd 150yds out: styd on wl fnl 100yds: lost 3rd cl home* 10/1
5 snk **Elusive Storm (FR)**[52] 3 -8-80 Francois-XavierBertras 9 61
(F Rohaut, France) 14/1
6 snk **Class Monitor**[67] 17 3 -8-110 JulienAuge 7 64
(Mrs K Burke) *racd towards rr: r.o wl u.p fnl 1 1/2f: clst at fin* 33/10[1]
7 1 1/4 **Moonlight Diamond (IRE)**[249] 3 -9-10 TheoBachelot 11 64
(U Suter, France) 72/1
8 hd **Yun (FR)**[73] 3 -8-80 (b) JohanVictoire 2 56
(C Baillet, France) 14/1
9 2 **Gag (FR)**[7] 3 -8-110 FlavienPrat 1 54
(M Nigge, France) 36/1
10 3 1/2 **Talawa (FR)**[163] 3 -8-30 (p) JeremyBonin(5) 4 41
(J Clais, France) 78/1
0 **Khanbaligh (FR)**[84] 7814 3 -8-30 MarcLerner(5) 13
(C Lerner, France) 53/1
0 **Carols Blizzard (USA)**[9] 3 -9-10 (b[1]) StephanePasquier 3
(G Botti, Italy) 48/10[2]
0 **Saltamontes**[63] 3 -9-20 (p) ThomasHuet 8
(S Cerulis, France) 6/1[3]

1m 18.2s (78.20) 13Ran SP% 117.4
WIN (incl. 1 euro stake): 8.20. PLACES: 3.00, 2.80, 3.40. DF: 32.50. SF: 64.10.
Owner Marcus Foley **Bred** Miss P A Zygmant **Trained** Upper Lambourn, Berks

844 WOLVERHAMPTON (A.W) (L-H)
Saturday, March 10
OFFICIAL GOING: Standard
Wind: Fresh behind Weather: Overcast

866 NEW WILLIAM HILL IPHONE APP LADY WULFRUNA STKS (LISTED RACE) 7f 32y (P)
2:20 (2:21) (Class 1) 4-Y-0+
£19,848 (£7,525; £3,766 ; £1,876 ; £941 ; £472) Stalls High

Form RPR
1-02 1 **Libys Dream (IRE)**[15] 686 4 -8-1281 RichardKingscote 2 97
(Tom Dascombe) *chsd ldrs: rdn over 1f out: r.o to ld wl ins fnl f* 16/1
-200 2 hd **Belgian Bill**[23] 591 4 -9-3102 (t) PaulHanagan 3 102
(George Baker) *chsd ldrs: led over 1f out: rdn: edgd lft and hdd wl ins fnl f* 7/2[1]
3-23 3 1 1/2 **Clockmaker (IRE)**[49] 254 6 -9-396 DuranFentiman 6 98
(Tim Easterby) *racd keenly: trckd ldr 6f out: led over 2f out: rdn and hdd over 1f out: styd on same pce ins fnl f* 5/1[2]
-301 4 1 1/2 **Night Lily (IRE)**[21] 622 6 -8-1295 WilliamCarson 5 89
(Paul D'Arcy) *mid-div: pushed along and hdwy over 2f out: rdn over 1f out: r.o* 9/1
21-4 5 1 1/2 **Docofthebay (IRE)**[14] 711 8 -9-6103 (b) IanMongan 8 93+
(Scott Dixon) *hld up: hdwy u.p over 1f out: r.o: nt rch ldrs* 5/1[2]
-313 6 1 **Capone (IRE)**[14] 711 7 -9-397 ShaneKelly 12 88+
(Scott Dixon) *hld up: rdn over 1f out: styd on: nt trble ldrs* 6/1[3]
010- 7 shd **Celtic Sultan (IRE)**[37] 7076 8 -9-382 MickyFenton 4 88
(Paul Midgley) *sn led: rdn and hdd over 2f out: wknd ins fnl f* 66/1
255- 8 1 **Elshabakiya (IRE)**[119] 7392 4 -8-12101 JoeFanning 11 80
(Clive Brittain) *hld up: rdn over 1f out: n.d* 13/2
040- 9 nk **Cochabamba (IRE)**[102] 7578 4 -8-1293 DaneO'Neill 10 80
(Roger Teal) *hld up: rdn over 2f out: n.d* 18/1

60-0 **10** *1 ½* **Roodle**[14] 711 5-8-12 80.........(b) TomQueally 1 76
(Eve Johnson Houghton) *mid-div: rdn over 2f out: wknd over 1f out* **150/1**

-426 **11** *2 ¼* **Lockantanks**[21] 622 5-9-3 93......... LukeMorris 9 80
(Michael Appleby) *prom: rdn over 2f out: wknd wl over 1f out* **16/1**

-141 **12** *1 ¾* **Dubaianswer**[16] 674 4-8-12 87......... StephenCraine 7 66
(Tony Coyle) *hld up: wknd over 2f out* **25/1**

1m 27.26s (-2.34) **Going Correction** -0.025s/f (Stan) **12** Ran SP% **116.2**
Speed ratings (Par 111): **112,111,110,108,106 105,105,104,103,102 99,97**
toteswingers: 1&2 £9.40, 1&3 £6.00, 2&3 £4.30. CSF £69.58 TOTE £17.70: £5.10, £1.50, £2.10; EX 109.00 TRIFECTA Not won..
Owner Ms A Quinn **Bred** Irish National Stud **Trained** Malpas, Cheshire

FOCUS
The five previous winners of this contest had been aged between six and eight, but this was one for the youngsters in comparative terms and something of a turn up. They didn't go much of the pace which counted against the hold-up horses, whilst the draw played its part too with the first four starting from the six lowest stalls. Pace was favoured on the day. The winner is on an upward curve.

NOTEBOOK
Libys Dream(IRE) was a winner over C&D on her last visit here, but seemed to have it all to do on these terms as she had upwards of 20lb to find with the majority of her rivals. However, she is a progressive filly, whilst racing close to the steady pace undoubtedly helped, and she took full advantage when the gap appeared inside the last furlong. (tchd 14-1)
Belgian Bill, back from three starts at Meydan, hadn't run over a trip this short since September 2010. He looked to have done everything right, racing close to the pace from his good draw before hitting the front over a furlong out, but the filly grabbed him late on. (op 6-1)
Clockmaker(IRE) was another to race up with the pace, but may not have helped himself by taking a grip and although in front on the turn for home, couldn't see his race out. He has proved most consistent this winter. (op 9-2)
Night Lily(IRE) did best of those held up, but she has gained all eight of her wins over 1m and could have done with a much stronger gallop over this trip. (op 7-1)
Docofthebay(IRE), narrowly beaten by Dunelight in this race last year, had a 3lb penalty to carry on account of his Listed success at Lingfield in November and was another to get going too late. (op 6-1)
Capone(IRE), whose seven wins have all been over 6f, does stay this far but he had no choice than to be dropped out from the widest stall and by the time he got into gear the race was over. (tchd 7-1)
Celtic Sultan(IRE), making his debut for the yard after 137 days off, set the pace as he often does and stayed in the thick of the action for longer than might have been expected, especially as he was worst in on these terms. He may have been flattered by the way the race was run, but should be able to find easier tasks than this. (op 80-1)
Elshabakiya(IRE), reappearing from 119 days off, can go well fresh and has twice finished runner-up at this level. She was best in on these terms, but saw too much daylight from her wide draw and is now 0-12. (op 6-1)

867 DOWNLOAD WILLIAM HILL FROM THE APP-STORE H'CAP 7f 32y(P)
2:55 (2:56) (Class 4) (0-85,83) 3-Y-O **£4,204** (£1,251; £625; £312) **Stalls** High

Form RPR

4-13 **1** **Switzerland (IRE)**[22] 596 3-9-7 83......... JoeFanning 7 105+
(Mark Johnston) *hld up in tch: chsd ldr wl over 2f out: led over 1f out: shkn up and c clr fnl f: easily* **13/8**[1]

-211 **2** *8* **Gabrial's Bounty (IRE)**[30] 482 3-8-12 74......... FrannyNorton 6 73
(Mick Channon) *s.i.s: sn pushed along to chse ldrs: rdn over 2f out: styd on to go 2nd wl ins fnl f: no ch w wnr* **9/2**[2]

640- **3** *shd* **Shamaal Nibras (USA)**[157] 6623 3-9-6 82......... KieranO'Neill 3 81
(Richard Hannon) *prom: nt clr run and lost pl wl over 2f out: r.o ins fnl f* **5/1**[3]

1133 **4** *1* **Adranian (IRE)**[17] 659 3-9-2 78.........(v) DavidProbert 5 74
(David C Griffiths) *chsd ldrs tl led 1/2-way: rdn and hdd over 1f out: wknd ins fnl f* **5/1**[3]

16R- **5** *1* **Daraa (IRE)**[134] 7135 3-8-13 75......... BrettDoyle 10 69
(Clive Brittain) *s.i.s: hld up: plld hrd: hdwy over 2f out: sn rdn: styd on same pce fr over 1f out* **33/1**

36-1 **6** *¾* **Performing Pocket (USA)**[17] 657 3-9-1 77......... MartinLane 8 69
(David Simcock) *hld up: rdn over 2f out: nvr trbld ldrs* **12/1**

3262 **7** *1* **Henry Bee**[22] 605 3-8-11 73......... PaulHanagan 9 62
(Richard Fahey) *in rr: hdwy u.p over 1f out: wknd ins fnl f* **20/1**

1265 **8** *1 ¾* **Chapellerie (IRE)**[9] 749 3-8-3 65 ow1......... WilliamCarson 4 50
(Richard Guest) *chsd ldr tl rdn 1/2-way: wknd over 2f out* **20/1**

010- **9** *1 ¾* **Forest Edge (IRE)**[112] 7491 3-8-11 73......... RichardThomas 1 53
(David Evans) *led to 1/2-way: rdn and wknd wl over 1f out: eased ins fnl f* **33/1**

1m 28.04s (-1.56) **Going Correction** -0.025s/f (Stan) **9** Ran SP% **112.7**
Speed ratings (Par 100): **107,97,97,96,95 94,93,91,89**
CSF £8.10 CT £28.75 TOTE £2.20: £1.10, £1.80, £2.00; EX 11.90.
Owner Sheikh Majid Bin Mohammed al Maktoum **Bred** Rabbah Bloodstock Limited **Trained** Middleham Moor, N Yorks

FOCUS
They went a fair pace in this and few ever got into it. This was all about the winner who looks much improved. the form has a solid feel in behind.

868 WILLIAM HILL LINCOLN TRIAL H'CAP 1m 141y(P)
3:30 (3:30) (Class 2) (0-105,100) 4-Y-O+
£18,675 (£5,592; £2,796; £1,398; £699; £351) **Stalls** Low

Form RPR

0-43 **1** **Nazreef**[14] 266 5-9-4 94.........(bt) RobertWinston 10 103
(Hughie Morrison) *chsd ldr: led over 1f out: sn rdn: jst hld on* **14/1**

006- **2** *shd* **Kingscroft (IRE)**[168] 6326 4-8-12 88......... JoeFanning 1 96
(Mark Johnston) *chsd ldrs: rdn and ev ch ins fnl f: styd on* **16/1**

1-55 **3** *hd* **Mia's Boy**[21] 622 8-9-10 100......... GeorgeBaker 7 108
(Chris Dwyer) *hld up: nt clr run over 2f out: hdwy over 1f out: rdn ins fnl f: r.o* **11/2**[3]

005- **4** *1 ¼* **Prime Exhibit**[126] 7295 7-9-2 95......... LeeTopliss(3) 6 100
(Richard Fahey) *hld up in tch: rdn over 1f out: styd on* **9/1**

-252 **5** *nk* **Tarooq (USA)**[21] 622 6-9-0 90......... PaulHanagan 5 94
(Richard Fahey) *trckd ldrs: plld hrd: shkn up over 1f out: rdn and hung lft ins fnl f: styd on* **4/1**[1]

-014 **6** *hd* **Amitola (IRE)**[7] 785 5-9-1 91......... PhillipMakin 4 95
(David Barron) *led: rdn and hdd over 1f out: styd on same pce ins fnl f* **16/1**

000- **7** *1 ½* **Light From Mars**[168] 6335 7-9-5 95......... FrannyNorton 8 96
(John Quinn) *plld hrd and prom: rdn over 2f out: styd on same pce ins fnl f* **12/1**

1-03 **8** *1* **Loyalty**[14] 712 5-9-10 100.........(v) DaneO'Neill 2 98
(Derek Shaw) *hld up: pushed along over 3f out: hdwy u.p over 1f out: nt trble ldrs* **9/2**[2]

330- **9** *hd* **Pintura**[168] 6339 5-9-9 99......... JimmyFortune 9 97
(David Simcock) *hld up: rdn over 2f out: styd on: nt trble ldrs* **12/1**

/0-2 **10** *½* **Reve De Nuit (USA)**[69] 5 6-9-8 98......... TomQueally 13 95
(Alan McCabe) *hld up: rdn over 1f out: nvr on terms* **20/1**

000- **11** *2 ¼* **Final Drive (IRE)**[364] 846 6-9-9 99......... StevieDonohoe 3 90
(John Butler) *s.i.s: hld up: n.d* **25/1**

3002 **12** *nk* **Licence To Till (USA)**[3] 817 5-9-6 96......... AdamKirby 11 87
(Mark Johnston) *chsd ldrs: rdn over 2f out: wknd fnl f* **9/1**

030- **13** *7* **The Tichborne (IRE)**[226] 4472 4-8-13 89......... WilliamCarson 12 64
(Roger Teal) *hld up: rdn over 2f out: wknd over 1f out* **20/1**

1m 49.22s (-1.28) **Going Correction** -0.025s/f (Stan) **13** Ran SP% **120.8**
Speed ratings (Par 109): **104,103,103,102,102 102,100,99,99,99 97,97,90**
toteswingers:1&2:£0.00, 2&3:£22.80, 1&3:£24.30 CSF £216.03 CT £1440.19 TOTE £10.10: £4.40, £3.80, £2.20; EX 158.50 Trifecta £654.70 Part won. Pool: £884.62 - 0.64 winning units..
Owner Deborah Collett & M J Watson **Bred** M J Watson **Trained** East Ilsley, Berks

FOCUS
No winner of this race in 15 previous runnings has gone on to win the Doncaster handicap, though the 1997 Lincoln winner Kuala Lipis finished fourth in the inaugural running, 2000 winner John Ferneley finished third, whilst Very Wise had to be pulled up after the start here before winning the big race in 2007 when it was run at Newcastle. The 2001 Lincoln winner Nimello did win at this meeting, but only the consolation race for those that didn't get into the trial. Nine of these are entered at Doncaster. The pace was solid enough without being break-neck. The winner looks as good as ever and the form makes plenty of sense.

NOTEBOOK
Nazreef was never far off the pace. Back on sand after finishing 60l behind Grumeti in the Grade 2 Dovecote Novices' Hurdle at Kempton last month, he was sent to the front over a furlong from home but had to really knuckle down in order to hold off the runner-up and may have been headed for a few strides. However, with Winston at his strongest he had his head down where it mattered. He is entered for the Lincoln and was cut to a general 20-1 with most firms, but would appear to have little chance of getting in.
Kingscroft(IRE), returning from 168 days off and back off his last winning mark, was travelling better than anything just behind the leaders turning in and it looked as though his effort had been timed just right, but he was just worried out of it. This was the longest trip he had tried, but it would be churlish to blame a lack of stamina for this cracking effort in defeat. (op 14-1)
Mia's Boy's record here before this read 12241 with his last win coming by a nose over Loyalty over this trip in December. Ridden much more patiently than the first two, his rider had little choice than to make his run up the inside after turning in, but it's never easy to make a sustained run up the rail here so in view of how narrowly he was beaten he covered himself in glory with this performance. (op 5-1)
Prime Exhibit, returning from 126 days off, finished third in this race last year off this mark following a longer absence. He made his move rounding the home bend, but had to go four-wide in order to do so, which was far from ideal, and he could never quite find enough on reaching the straight. (op 8-1)
Tarooq(USA) is now 8lb higher than when winning over C&D in November, but his chance was compromised here by him taking too strong a hold in a handy position early. This was still a creditable effort under the circumstances. (op 5-1)
Amitola(IRE) likes to go from the front and had his own way out in front. He wasn't shaken off until well inside the last furlong and this was a good effort over a trip probably right on the limit of his stamina. (op 14-1)
Light From Mars, winner of last season's Newbury Spring Cup and in the same ownership as the runner-up, ran a fair race on his return from 168 days off, but he has won following a longer layoff in the past so it remains to be seen which way he goes from this. (tchd 16-1)
Loyalty has been in superb form on Polytrack in recent months with his mark shooting up 21b between September and February, but he was held by Mia's Boy on C&D running in December and never landed a meaningful blow here. (op 5-1 tchd 4-1)

869 BEST ODDS GUARANTEED WITH WILLIAMHILL.COM MOBILE MAIDEN STKS 1m 141y(P)
4:05 (4:05) (Class 5) 3-Y-O+ **£2,264** (£673; £336; £168) **Stalls** Low

Form RPR

2 **1** **Legendary**[15] 684 3-8-8 0......... LukeMorris 10 79+
(Ed Vaughan) *hld up: hdwy over 2f out: led 1f out: edgd lft: rdn out* **9/2**[3]

2422 **2** *3* **Devote Myself (IRE)**[7] 784 3-8-3 70......... MartinLane 8 68
(David Evans) *a.p: pushed along to ld 2f out: rdn and hdd 1f out: styd on same pce* **15/2**

42 **3** *5* **Attain**[28] 523 3-8-5 0......... AdamBeschizza(3) 7 62
(Julia Feilden) *hld up: hdwy u.p over 1f out: r.o to go 3rd post: nvr nrr* **7/2**[2]

\- **4** *shd* **Star For Life (USA)** 3-8-8 0......... PaulHanagan 6 62
(Mikael Magnusson) *prom: chsd ldr over 3f out: ev ch 2f out: wkng whn edgd rt ins fnl f* **6/1**

3- **5** *shd* **Navaho Spirit**[185] 5834 3-8-1 0......... NatashaEaton(7) 3 62
(Terry Clement) *chsd ldr tl over 3f out: rdn over 1f out: styd on same pce* **22/1**

0/ **6** *shd* **Marster Parkes**[639] 2882 4-10-0 0......... TomEaves 4 68
(John Quinn) *sn prom: rdn over 2f out: wknd fnl f* **50/1**

7 *1 ¼* **Dropzone (USA)** 3-8-8 0......... TomQueally 5 59
(Marco Botti) *s.s: hld up: drvn along over 3f out: nvr on terms* **13/8**[1]

454- **8** *3 ¾* **Intiqaal (IRE)**[227] 4441 5-10-0 0.........(t) PhillipMakin 2 57+
(Derek Shaw) *s.i.s: hld up: a in rr* **50/1**

4 **9** *10* **Valiant Bee**[22] 604 4-9-9 0......... AdamKirby 1 31
(Bill Moore) *led: pushed along and hdd 2f out: sn wknd* **100/1**

0 **10** *3* **Lal Bhai**[10] 737 4-10-0 0......... DaneO'Neill 9 30
(Chris Down) *prom: rdn over 3f out: hung rt and wknd over 2f out* **100/1**

1m 50.28s (-0.22) **Going Correction** -0.025s/f (Stan)
WFA 3 from 4yo+ 20lb **10** Ran SP% **114.8**
Speed ratings (Par 103): **99,96,91,91,91 91,90,87,78,75**
toteswingers:1&2:£1.10, 2&3:£3.60, 1&3:£2.20 CSF £35.83 TOTE £8.60: £2.10, £2.90, £1.30; EX 36.80.
Owner Mrs Doreen M Swinburn **Bred** Genesis Green Stud Ltd **Trained** Newmarket, Suffolk

FOCUS
A weak maiden but it was run at a sound pace. The first pair pulled clear and the winner did it well.
Valiant Bee Official explanation: jockey said filly ran too freely

870 WILLIAMHILL.COM CLASSIFIED CLAIMING STKS 5f 20y(P)
4:40 (4:40) (Class 5) 4-Y-O+ **£2,264** (£673; £336; £168) **Stalls** Low

Form RPR

3222 **1** **Steelcut**[12] 719 8-8-2 70.........(p) MartinLane 2 72
(David Evans) *hld up: hdwy 1/2-way: nt clr run over 1f out: led ins fnl f: r.o wl* **15/8**[1]

0301 **2** *2 ¼* **Captain Scooby**[10] 735 6-9-2 73......... RobertLButler(3) 4 81
(Richard Guest) *outpcd: r.o to go 2nd wl ins fnl f: no ch w wnr* **11/1**

-260 **3** *nk* **Soopacal (IRE)**[4] 808 7-8-6 65......... BarryMcHugh 1 67
(Brian Ellison) *led early: chsd ldrs: rdn and ev ch ins fnl f: styd on same pce* **7/2**[3]

03-2 **4** 1/2 **Angelo Poliziano**[64] 62 6-8-2 70..............................(p) PaulHanagan 5 61
(Ann Duffield) *prom: pushed along 1/2-way: rdn and hung lft ins fnl f: no ex* **5/2**[2]

0451 **5** 2 **Decider (USA)**[7] 782 9-8-2 59..(b) LukeMorris 3 54
(Ronald Harris) *sn chsng ldr: rdn 1/2-way: btn whn hmpd ins fnl f* **8/1**

-005 **6** 1 **Ice Trooper**[8] 763 4-8-8 68..(b) TomEaves 6 56
(Linda Stubbs) *sn led: rdn over 1f out: hdd & wknd ins fnl f* **12/1**

1m 1.22s (-1.08) **Going Correction** -0.025s/f (Stan) 6 Ran SP% **112.7**
Speed ratings (Par 103): **107,103,102,102,98 97**
CSF £22.74 TOTE £2.40: £1.30, £1.80; EX 12.90.
Owner Shropshire Wolves 3 **Bred** Mrs B Skinner **Trained** Pandy, Monmouths

FOCUS
A routine claimer. The pace was good and the form is soild for the grade.
Decider(USA) Official explanation: jockey said gelding suffered interference in closing stages

871 WILLIAM HILL APP - DOWNLOAD TODAY! H'CAP 5f 216y(P)
5:15 (5:16) (Class 2) (0-100,97) 4-Y-0+

£9,960 (£2,982; £1,491; £745; £372; £187) **Stalls** Low

Form RPR

-122 **1** **Alben Star (IRE)**[36] 405 4-9-2 92.................................. PaulHanagan 7 104+
(Richard Fahey) *chsd ldrs: nt clr run over 2f out: rdn over 1f out: r.o to ld post* **4/1**[1]

26-1 **2** shd **Whaileyy (IRE)**[44] 311 4-9-2 92....................................(b) AdamKirby 12 104
(Marco Botti) *chsd ldr tl led over 1f out: rdn and edgd rt ins fnl f: hdd post* **4/1**[1]

010- **3** 2 1/4 **Courageous (IRE)**[147] 6865 6-8-11 87........................(t) WilliamCarson 9 92
(Kevin Ryan) *led: rdn and hdd over 1f out: styd on same pce ins fnl f* **25/1**

6514 **4** 1 **Piscean (USA)**[28] 527 7-8-12 91..................................... RyanClark(3) 8 93+
(Tom Keddy) *hld up: hdwy u.p over 1f out: r.o: nt rch ldrs* **9/1**

260- **5** 1 **Dubai Dynamo**[147] 6862 7-9-0 90.. PJMcDonald 2 89+
(Ruth Carr) *s.i.s: hld up: stl last over 1f out: r.o wl ins fnl f* **28/1**

-311 **6** hd **Woolfall Sovereign (IRE)**[46] 286 6-8-11 87.............. BarryMcHugh 13 85+
(George Margarson) *hld up: hdwy over 2f out: rdn over 1f out: styd on* **8/1**[3]

-063 **7** shd **Five Star Junior (USA)**[28] 527 6-9-1 91..................... JamesSullivan 5 89+
(Linda Stubbs) *hld up: r.o u.p ins fnl f: nt rch ldrs* **15/2**[2]

-202 **8** shd **Fratellino**[14] 711 5-9-4 97..(t) DeclanCannon(3) 3 95
(Alan McCabe) *chsd ldrs: rdn over 2f out: styd on same pce fr over 1f out* **9/1**

1-45 **9** 1 1/2 **Sugar Beet**[14] 711 4-8-11 87... LukeMorris 6 80
(Ronald Harris) *in rr: rdn over 2f out: n.d* **33/1**

500- **10** nk **Crown Choice**[210] 5032 7-9-4 94.................................. FrederikTylicki 1 86
(Paul Midgley) *mid-div: hdwy over 2f out: rdn over 1f out: wknd ins fnl f* **8/1**[3]

236- **11** nk **Mass Rally (IRE)**[126] 7295 5-9-1 91.................................. TomEaves 4 82
(Michael Dods) *s.i.s: a in rr* **11/1**

0-00 **12** 1 1/2 **Colonel Mak**[46] 286 5-9-5 95.. LeeNewman 11 82
(David Barron) *prom: pushed along over 3f out: rdn and edgd lft over 1f out: wknd fnl f* **33/1**

402- **13** 4 **Mac Gille Eoin**[113] 7456 8-8-11 87..................................... JohnFahy 10 62
(John Gallagher) *chsd ldrs: rdn over 1f out: hmpd and wknd sn after* **50/1**

1m 13.11s (-1.89) **Going Correction** -0.025s/f (Stan) 13 Ran SP% **117.5**
Speed ratings (Par 109): **111,110,107,106,105 104,104,104,102,102 101,99,94**
toteswingers:1&2:£2.70, 2&3:£22.50, 1&3:£32.80 CSF £16.82 CT £355.19 TOTE £4.20: £1.80, £2.10, £8.90; EX 20.50.
Owner J K Shannon & M A Scaife **Bred** Rathasker Stud **Trained** Musley Bank, N Yorks

FOCUS
A cracking sprint handicap run at a strong pace. The form looks rock-solid and the front pair are sprinters to follow. The winner is progressive.

NOTEBOOK
Alben Star(IRE) ◆ has returned from a long absence in decent form on Polytrack and this was his best effort to date. Having travelled well behind the leaders, he briefly became short of room turning for home and by the time they reached the straight he had a few lengths to make up on the leaders, but he produced an electrifying burst of speed to grab the race on the line. Still unexposed, he is one to watch out for in high-class sprint handicaps back on turf. (tchd 7-2)
Whaileyy(IRE) ◆ was able to take a handy position and he looked the have the race won when getting the better of the leader over a furlong out, but the winner came from out of the clouds to deny him. Raised 10lb after bolting up in first-time blinkers at Kempton in his previous start, this was a mighty effort from stall 12 and he too should make a name for himself this coming turf season. (op 5-1)
Courageous(IRE) ◆, making his AW debut after 147 days off, took a couple of lengths out of his rivals breaking from the stalls and only the front pair were able to get past him. He has no great record fresh, so this has to go down as a highly encouraging reappearance. (tchd 28-1)
Piscean(USA) was making a rare appearance over 7f when winning here two starts back. Again doing his best work late, he looks worth another go over the longer trip. (op 15-2)
Dubai Dynamo ◆, returning from 147 days off, has won fresh before but usually needs a run. Racing over a trip this short for the first time in two years, he was completely outpaced early but finished well and is worth watching out for returned to further. (op 40-1)
Woolfall Sovereign(IRE), winner of three of his previous four starts including twice over C&D, stayed on from over a furlong out but he faced a stiff task from the outside stall. (tchd 17-2)
Five Star Junior(USA) could only make modest late progress and is now 0-30 at Class 2 level or above. (op 7-1 tchd 6-1)
Fratellino was put up 5lb after running a 105-rated rival to half a length in a Lingfield Listed contest last time and was up against it as soon as he was denied his usual front-running role. (op 8-1)

872 WILLIAM HILL - HOME OF BETTING H'CAP 1m 5f 194y(P)
5:45 (5:45) (Class 4) (0-85,81) 4-Y-0+ **£4,204** (£1,251; £625; £312) **Stalls** Low

Form RPR

3-11 **1** **Chabada (JPN)**[47] 271 4-9-8 80.................................. JimmyFortune 3 89+
(Ian Williams) *mde all: set stdy pce tl qcknd over 3f out: pushed clr over 1f out: comf* **5/6**[1]

30-2 **2** 2 1/4 **Halla San**[18] 643 10-9-12 80... PaulHanagan 7 86
(Richard Fahey) *chsd wnr: pushed along over 3f out: rdn over 1f out: styd on same pce* **20/1**

52-3 **3** 2 1/4 **Where's Susie**[52] 202 7-9-11 79....................................... DaneO'Neill 1 82
(Michael Madgwick) *chsd ldrs: rdn over 3f out: styd on same pce fnl f* **13/2**[3]

0-61 **4** nse **Cotton King**[1] 849 5-9-13 81 6ex...............................(bt) StevieDonohoe 8 84
(Tobias B P Coles) *hld up: rdn over 2f out: hung lft over 1f out: r.o ins fnl f: nvr nrr* **13/2**[3]

4322 **5** 1 **The Lock Master (IRE)**[9] 751 5-9-5 80......................... JackDuern(7) 5 81
(Michael Appleby) *chsd ldrs: rdn over 2f out: styd on same pce fr over 1f out* **6/1**[2]

000- **6** 1 1/4 **Arizona John (IRE)**[155] 6676 7-8-11 68..................... DeclanCannon(3) 4 67
(John Mackie) *s.i.s: hld up: hdwy u.p over 1f out: no ex ins fnl f* **22/1**

223 **7** 1 1/2 **Maison Brillet (IRE)**[11] 728 5-8-11 68.........................(p) RyanClark(3) 2 65
(Clive Drew) *prom: rdn over 2f out: wknd fnl f* **20/1**

100- **8** 2 **Action Front (USA)**[226] 4473 4-9-7 79.............................. MartinLane 6 74
(Derek Shaw) *hld up: rdn 3f out: wknd over 1f out* **33/1**

3m 6.91s (0.91) **Going Correction** -0.025s/f (Stan)
WFA 4 from 5yo+ 4lb 8 Ran SP% **112.3**
Speed ratings (Par 105): **96,94,93,93,92 92,91,90**
toteswingers:1&2:£4.10, 2&3:£6.80, 1&3:£1.50 CSF £23.61 CT £70.08 TOTE £2.00: £1.10, £3.90, £1.30; EX 17.80.
Owner Dr Marwan Koukash **Bred** Flaxman Holdings Limited **Trained** Portway, Worcs
■ Stewards' Enquiry : Jack Duern four day ban: used whip above permitted level (Mar 24,26-28)

FOCUS
A fair staying handicap, but not the greatest test of stamina and the order hardly changed. The winner proved different class, dictating on a day when pace held up very well.
T/Jkpt: Not won. T/Plt: £59.80 to a £1 stake. Pool of £99,042.94 - 1,208.71 winning tickets.
T/Qpdt: £22.10 to a £1 stake. Pool of £5,345.60 - 178.70 winning tickets. CR

[788]MEYDAN (L-H)
Saturday, March 10

OFFICIAL GOING: Tapeta: standard; turf: good

873a AL BASTAKIYA SPONSORED BY EMIRATES (LISTED RACE) (TAPETA) 1m 1f 110y
1:05 (1:05) 3-Y-O

£96,774 (£32,258; £16,129; £8,064; £4,838; £3,225)

RPR

1 **Mickdaam (IRE)**[30] 485 3-8-9 109 ow1.............. ChristopheSoumillon 1 112+
(M F De Kock, South Africa) *trckd ldng pair: led 1 1/2f out: r.o wl* **6/4**[1]

2 2 1/4 **Surfer (USA)**[30] 485 3-8-8 102....................................... RichardMullen 8 106
(S Seemar, UAE) *mid-div: r.o fnl 2f: nrst fin* **16/1**

3 1 1/2 **Counterglow (IRE)**[9] 754 3-8-8 98.............................. FrankieDettori 7 103
(Mahmood Al Zarooni) *mid-div: chsd ldrs 3f out: ev ch 1 1/2f out: one pce fnl 100yds* **8/1**[3]

4 3/4 **Prepared**[58] 142 3-8-8 98.. SilvestreDeSousa 12 101+
(A Al Raihe, UAE) *s.i.s: settled in rr: r.o fnl 2f* **25/1**

5 2 **Spoil The Fun (FR)**[40] 364 3-8-8 101..........................(t) MircoDemuro 13 97
(C Ferland, France) *trckd ldrs: ev ch 2 1/2f out: one pce fnl 1 1/2f* **16/1**

6 1/4 **Cash Luck (AUS)**[16] 679 4-9-4 112...............................(bt) VladDuric 2 94
(M Freedman, Singapore) *mid-div: chsd ldrs 3f out: kpt on same pce fnl 1 1/2f* **12/1**

7 5 **Kinglet (USA)**[30] 485 3-8-8 109.............................. MickaelBarzalona 5 86
(Mahmood Al Zarooni) *settled in last: nvr able to chal* **2/1**[2]

8 1 3/4 **Matusalen (SPA)**[16] 679 3-8-8 102............................... BFayosMartin 9 82
(M Delcher-Sanchez, Spain) *settled in rr: nvr able to chal* **20/1**

9 1 **Energia Dust (BRZ)**[16] 679 4-9-4 95................. Per-AndersGraberg 11 78
(Fabricio Borges, Sweden) *in rr of mid-div: n.d* **40/1**

10 3/4 **Noor Zabeel (USA)**[16] 679 3-8-8 104........................ RoystonFfrench 3 79
(A Al Raihe, UAE) *nvr bttr than mid-div* **16/1**

11 14 **Mary Fildes (IRE)**[16] 680 3-8-4 99.........................(p) TadhgO'Shea 14 46
(J S Moore) *sn led: rdn 3 1/2f out: hdd 2 1/2f out: wknd qckly* **20/1**

12 11 1/2 **Old Pal (FR)**[16] 679 3-8-8 94..(t) TedDurcan 6 27
(Niels Petersen, Norway) *nvr bttr than mid-div* **66/1**

13 2 **Fiscal**[9] 754 3-8-8 104.. AndreaAtzeni 10 22
(M Al Jahouri, UAE) *in rr of mid-div: nvr able to chal* **33/1**

1m 59.76s (0.76)
WFA 3 from 4yo 20lb 13 Ran SP% **130.0**
CSF: £29.35.
Owner Sheikh Mohammed Bin Khalifa Al Maktoum **Bred** Victor Stud Bloodstock Ltd **Trained** South Africa

FOCUS
Rail out 12m on turf track. The middle leg of the UAE Triple Crown, but it was a weak race for the class. Mary Fildes was asked to repeat the tactics that saw her fluke second in the C&D Oaks, but she was pursued by the aptly named Spoil The Fun and set quicker fractions this time. Here are her splits to the 6f point, with the times she clocked in the Oaks in brackets: 26.68 (27.93), 50.20 (52.06) and 1.14.90 (1.17.34).

NOTEBOOK
Mickdaam(IRE) had been shaping as though he'd appreciate a step up to this sort of trip, notably when a closing second to Kinglet in the Guineas, but it's doubtful he really had to improve. If this is more or less the standard required in the UAE Derby then clearly he'll take all the beating, but the suspicion is that race will be significantly tougher.
Surfer(USA) yet again found himself poorly placed. He covered 12 meters more than the winner and had the highest average speed of all.
Counterglow(IRE) found this tougher than the 7f turf conditions race he won here on his reappearance, and he ran about as well as could have been expected under these different conditions. He doesn't look anything special, but seems to be going the right way.
Prepared ◆ caught the eye when just behind Mickdaam in the 7f Guineas Trial, but had been off since. This was a promising return as he fared best of those held up, whilst giving the impression he'll be sharper for the run. He could go well at a price in the UAE Derby, provided the standard required isn't significantly higher than was the case here.
Spoil The Fun(FR) chased the clear early leader but he wasn't good enough to sustain his bid.
Kinglet(USA) scraped home in the Guineas, but he's not bred for this longer trip. He wasn't helped by a hold-up ride and meeting trouble when trying to stay on, and basically had plenty against him.

874a MAHAB AL SHIMAAL SPONSORED BY SKYWARDS (GROUP 3) (TAPETA) 6f
1:40 (1:40) 3-Y-O+

£77,419 (£25,806; £12,903; £6,451; £3,870; £2,580)

RPR

1 **Krypton Factor**[36] 420 4-9-5 112.................................(b) KierenFallon 11 118+
(F Nass, Bahrain) *trckd ldrs: led 1 1/2f out: r.o wl* **5/1**[3]

2 2 1/2 **Hitchens (IRE)**[36] 420 7-9-5 113........................... SilvestreDeSousa 9 110
(David Barron) *mid-div: r.o fnl 1 1/2f but no ch w wnr* **3/1**[1]

3 1/2 **August Rush (SAF)**[238] 6-9-5 110...............................(t) RyanMoore 7 108
(H J Brown, South Africa) *trckd ldrs: ev ch 1f out: nt qckn fnl f* **12/1**

4 1 **Global City (IRE)**[49] 261 6-9-5 100.......................(t) MickaelBarzalona 5 105+
(Saeed Bin Suroor) *mid-div: r.o fnl 1 1/2f: nrst fin* **10/1**

5 1/4 **Addictive Dream (IRE)**[58] 141 5-9-5 112..................... AdrianNicholls 4 104
(David Nicholls) *sn led: rdn 2f out: hdd & wknd 1 1/2f out* **7/2**[2]

6 1 1/2 **Jaasoos (IRE)**[9] 758 8-9-5 112.. JamesDoyle 3 99
(D Selvaratnam, UAE) *mid-div: n.m.r 3f out: kpt on same pce fnl 1 1/2f* **12/1**

7 1 1/4 **Alazeyab (USA)**[15] 706 6-9-5 107 ....(vt) TadhgO'Shea 2 95
(A Al Raihe, UAE) *trckd ldrs: ev ch 3f out: one pce fnl 1 1/2f* **25/1**
8 1/4 **Iver Bridge Lad**[9] 756 5-9-5 111 ....(b) MichaelO'Connell 1 94
(John Ryan) *a mid-div* **6/1**
9 1/4 **Green Beret (IRE)**[16] 681 6-9-5 106 ....(t) RoystonFfrench 13 94
(A Al Raihe, UAE) *nvr bttr than mid-div* **33/1**
10 2 1/2 **Kanaf (IRE)**[9] 756 5-9-5 107 .... RichardHills 6 86
(M Al Muhairi, UAE) *settled in rr: nvr able to chal* **14/1**
11 1 3/4 **Right To Dream (IRE)**[9] 754 3-8-9 97 ....(b) FrankieDettori 12 88
(Brian Meehan) *racd in rr: n.d* **20/1**
12 1 1/2 **Ergiyas (USA)**[155] 6-9-5 108 .... KUlubaev 10 75
(H J Brown, South Africa) *nvr bttr than mid-div* **25/1**
13 9 1/4 **Seachantach (USA)**[9] 756 6-9-5 100 ....(vt) RichardMullen 8 46
(S Seemar, UAE) *nvr bttr than mid-div* **66/1**

1m 11.56s (-0.04)
WFA 3 from 4yo+ 14lb **13** Ran SP% **126.2**
CSF: £20.38.
Owner Fawzi Abdulla Nass **Bred** Lady Fairhaven **Trained** Bahrain

FOCUS
A trial for the Golden Shaheen, but not a particularly strong Group 3 sprint. The third and fourth set the standard.

NOTEBOOK
Krypton Factor overcame a wide draw and travelling furthest of the first eight home. On his previous start he'd got involved in a war up front, but this time he sat a little off the pace and saw his race out strongly in the straight, easily reversing C&D form with Hitchens, whom he was meeting on the same terms, in the process. He'd have probably won even more comfortably had he enjoyed a ground-saving trip, and is better than the bare form suggests. One would imagine he'll likely take his chance in the Golden Shaheen now and, while the company might prove a bit hot for him there, he should acquit himself with credit.
Hitchens(IRE) didn't have the ideal trip either, for although he travelled 2m less than the winner, he went further than the next six home, so it wasn't a bad effort. The winner reversed recent C&D form with him quite easily, though.
August Rush(SAF) was last seen winning a turf Grade 1 sprint in South Africa in July. Debuting for a new trainer, he had every chance at the top of the straight but couldn't quite go through with his challenge, and perhaps he just blew up. He might be of more interest next time.
Global City(IRE), held up as usual, saved ground on the rail and finished his race off fairly well, but he's not up to this class and he ran about as well as could have been expected.
Addictive Dream(IRE), who won twice on Polytrack earlier in his career, was chasing a hat-trick following wins in handicap company on turf. Once again he set out to make all, but he found it tougher holding off this class of opposition.
Jaasoos(IRE) was being pushed along and was also hampered on the turn in, and it looked as though he found this trip a little on the short side.
Alazeyab(USA), disappointing in his previous two starts, ran a bit better dropped back in distance, but he did have a perfect trip.
Iver Bridge Lad was another hampered on the turn in, but it's hard to say he'd have finished much closer with a clear run.

875a MEYDAN SPRINT SPONSORED BY EMIRATES SKY CARGO (CONDITIONS RACE) (TURF) 5f

2:15 (2:15) 3-Y-O+

£67,741 (£22,580; £11,290; £5,645; £3,387; £2,258)

RPR
1 **Invincible Ash (IRE)**[9] 756 7-8-9 101 ....(p) JamieSpencer 2 110
(M Halford, Ire) *in rr of mid-div: rdn 2f out: r.o wl fnl 1 1/2f: led 100yds out* **20/1**
2 shd **Sole Power**[90] 7730 5-9-0 115 .... JohnnyMurtagh 14 115
(Edward Lynam, Ire) *in rr of mid-div: r.o wl fnl 1 1/2f: nrst fin* **15/2**
3 1/2 **Nocturnal Affair (SAF)**[16] 681 6-9-0 112 ....(t) RyanMoore 5 113
(David Marnane, Ire) *mid-div: chsd ldrs 1 1/2f out: ev ch 100yds out: nt qckn fnl f* **6/1**[3]
4 shd **Monsieur Joe (IRE)**[16] 681 5-9-0 106 .... PatCosgrave 7 113
(Robert Cowell) *trckd ldrs: ev ch 2 1/2f out: nt qckn fnl f* **14/1**
5 1 1/2 **Inxile (IRE)**[16] 681 7-9-0 115 ....(p) AdrianNicholls 8 107
(David Nicholls) *sn led: hdd 1 1/2f out: kpt on same pce* **8/1**
6 1 **Al Sharood**[9] 756 4-8-9 102 .... TadhgO'Shea 4 99
(Doug Watson, UAE) *trckd ldrs: led 1 1/2f out: hdd 100yds out: kpt on same pce* **33/1**
7 1 **War Artist (AUS)**[161] 6520 9-9-0 113 .... KShea 9 100
(M F De Kock, South Africa) *mid-div: r.o same pce fnl 1 1/2f* **12/1**
8 1/2 **Margot Did (IRE)**[160] 6563 4-8-9 113 .... HayleyTurner 10 93
(Michael Bell) *trckd ldr: ev ch 3f out: one pce fnl 2f* **7/1**
9 1/4 **Prohibit**[16] 681 7-9-0 116 ....(p) JimCrowley 11 97
(Robert Cowell) *nvr bttr than mid-div* **4/1**[2]
10 2 **Mar Adentro (FR)**[16] 681 6-9-0 110 ....(tp) ChristopheSoumillon 12 90
(R Chotard, France) *in rr of mid-div: nvr able to chal* **16/1**
11 1/2 **Moonreach (IRE)**[15] 705 5-9-0 90 ....(b) RichardMullen 6 88
(S Seemar, UAE) *nvr bttr than mid-div* **40/1**
12 shd **Murbeh (IRE)**[7] 791 4-9-0 96 ....(t) RichardHills 1 88
(A Al Raihe, UAE) *nvr bttr than mid-div* **33/1**
13 3 1/2 **Regally Ready (USA)**[61] 5-9-0 117 ....(vt) FrankieDettori 3 75
(Steven Asmussen, U.S.A) *chsd ldrs tl wknd 2f out* **7/2**[1]
14 8 1/2 **Rock Jock (IRE)**[15] 705 5-9-0 102 ....(b) OlivierPeslier 13 45+
(E Charpy, UAE) *v.s.a: nvr involved* **40/1**
15 14 **Munaddam (USA)**[22] 616 10-9-0 95 .... AndreaAtzeni 15
(R Bouresly, Kuwait) *n.d* **50/1**

59.28s (59.28) **15** Ran SP% **129.6**
CSF: £166.63.
Owner P J Condron **Bred** Mrs Sandra Maye **Trained** Doneany, Co Kildare

FOCUS
A trial for the Al Quoz Sprint (now a Group 1), run over the C&D on World Cup night. The leaders set a good gallop here and the first three came from well off the pace. The winner is rated to her best and the runner-up to his Abbaye form.

NOTEBOOK
Invincible Ash(IRE) hadn't been at her best this year but showed more last time when a fast-finishing second over 6f, and the drop back to the minimum (Group 3 winner over the trip at the Curragh last summer) proved no problem off what was a decent gallop. She did need every yard of the trip to get up but, while a stiffer track probably suits her ideally, she was fourth in the Al Quoz Sprint last year, and presumably that race will once again be her target now.
Sole Power, off the track since running in the Hong Kong Sprint in December, travelled through the race like the best horse. He quickened up well to lead in the centre of the track, but was just denied close home by the filly, who challenged towards the far rail. He's fully entitled to come on for the run and should be a player in the Al Quoz Sprint (well beaten in it last year on reappearance).
Nocturnal Affair(SAF), winner of a handicap over the C&D last time, had the race run to suit once again, and had no excuse. He's probably a good marker for the form.
Monsieur Joe(IRE) raced a little closer to the pace than has often been the case, but put up another good effort in defeat.
Inxile(IRE), who's been in good form in similar company, did best of those who pressed the pace. He was never given much peace out in front, though, and ultimately helped set things up for the closers.
Al Sharood coped well with the drop in trip and ran right up to her best after disputing it for much of the way.
War Artist(AUS), who was keeping on well late after getting outpaced, hadn't run since October so he should come on for this. He was second in the Al Quoz Sprint last year and, while it promises to be a tougher event this time around now that it has Group 1 status, this will have served its purpose in prepping him for another tilt.
Margot Did(IRE) showed plenty of pace before fading. She was another reappearing following an absence, and better should be expected next time.
Prohibit, fifth in the Al Quoz Sprint last year, was a little disappointing considering he had the benefit of a recent outing. On his best form he would have had every chance in this company. His connections will be hoping he'll come on more for this outing than for his reappearance.
Regally Ready(USA), who beat Bated Breath last autumn when taking a Canadian Grade 1, and then followed up in the Breeders' Cup Turf Sprint, was very disappointing, being pushed along some way out. This wasn't his true form, and perhaps the change in headgear (normally wears blinkers, but this time had a tongue-tie and visor on) was partly to blame.

876a BURJ NAHAAR SPONSORED BY EMIRATES SKY CARGO (GROUP 3) (TAPETA) 1m

2:50 (2:50) 3-Y-O+

£77,419 (£25,806; £12,903; £6,451; £3,870; £2,580)

RPR
1 **African Story**[30] 487 5-9-0 113 .... FrankieDettori 4 117+
(Saeed Bin Suroor) *trckd ldrs: led 1 1/2f out: r.o wl: comf* **5/1**[2]
2 4 **Snaafy (USA)**[9] 757 8-9-0 104 ....(v) RichardHills 12 108
(M Al Muhairi, UAE) *trckd ldr: ev ch 1 1/2f out: kpt on same pce fnl 100yds* **33/1**
3 shd **Musir (AUS)**[44] 318 6-9-0 117 .... ChristopheSoumillon 1 108
(M F De Kock, South Africa) *mid-div on rail: swtchd out 3f out: r.o fnl 2f: nrst fin* **8/11**[1]
4 1 1/2 **Kavango (IRE)**[23] 588 5-9-0 105 .... PatCosgrave 5 104
(M bin Shafya, UAE) *trckd ldng pair: ev ch 3f out: kpt on same pce fnl 2f* **50/1**
5 2 3/4 **Le Drakkar (AUS)**[44] 318 7-9-0 110 ....(b) CSanchez 14 98
(A bin Huzaim, UAE) *sn led: hdd 1 1/2f out: wknd fnl 100yds* **50/1**
6 shd **Vagabond Shoes (IRE)**[16] 677 5-9-0 110 .... OlivierPeslier 8 98
(Stephane Chevalier, UAE) *trckd ldrs: ev ch 2 1/2f out: one pce fnl 1 1/2f* **20/1**
7 2 1/2 **Rajsaman (FR)**[44] 318 5-9-0 119 ....(b) RoystonFfrench 3 92+
(A Al Raihe, UAE) *nvr able to chal* **10/1**
8 1/2 **Dysphonia (AUS)**[22] 617 6-8-9 112 ....(p) SilvestreDeSousa 7 86+
(Saeed Bin Suroor) *nvr bttr than mid-div* **20/1**
9 1 **Sooraah**[23] 586 5-8-9 109 .... JamieSpencer 13 84+
(William Haggas) *settled in rr: nvr able to chal* **14/1**
10 2 **Maraheb**[23] 590 4-9-0 107 ....(t) TadhgO'Shea 9 84+
(A Al Raihe, UAE) *nvr bttr than mid-div* **20/1**
11 9 1/4 **Jardim (BRZ)**[9] 755 6-9-0 104 .... KShea 10 63+
(M F De Kock, South Africa) *racd in rr: n.d* **33/1**
12 1 **Gitano Hernando**[293] 2340 6-9-0 118 .... RichardHughes 11 60+
(H J Brown, South Africa) *in rr of mid-div: n.d* **12/1**
13 4 1/2 **Silver Ocean (USA)**[23] 588 4-9-0 105 .... KierenFallon 6 50+
(Niels Petersen, Norway) *s.i.s: settled in rr: n.d* **40/1**
14 6 1/4 **Dux Scholar**[9] 758 4-9-0 112 ....(vt) RyanMoore 2 36+
(H J Brown, South Africa) *nvr nr to chal* **9/1**[3]

1m 35.93s (-1.57) **14** Ran SP% **134.5**
CSF: £177.46.
Owner Godolphin **Bred** Darley **Trained** Newmarket, Suffolk

FOCUS
The favourite was well below form and this wasn't a strong Group 3, but the winner is progressing. The sectionals were quick (25.48, 47.72 and 1.11.49), but it proved hard to make up significant ground. The form is rated around the runner-up and fourth.

NOTEBOOK
African Story ◆ would have won the Group 3 Firebreak Stakes over C&D last time granted a clear run, and had that been the case he'd now be 3-3 on Tapeta in Dubai. He was helped by Musir's below-par performance, but this still looked a career best and he could be tough to beat in the Godolphin Mile on the World Cup card, with there possibly even more to come.
Snaafy(USA) was beaten off 105 over 7f here the previous week, but this trip suits better and he has plenty of really smart form to his name, notably winning this race on the Nad Al Sheba dirt in 2009. Although not as good as he was, this was a respectable performance behind the improving winner.
Musir(AUS) had a surprisingly tough trip from stall one, being taken wide before the turn into the straight (ended up covering eight meters more than the winner according to Trakus), and he'd also raced further back than those who finished ahead of him, but he basically failed to pick up as well as his jockey might have expected. He was a bit flat after two Group wins already this year, but could bounce back on World Cup day, where he'll have the choice of the Godolphin Mile and the Duty Free.
Kavango(IRE) again showed he's capable of smart form and he remains lightly raced for his age, but he's still not quite up to this level.
Sooraah needed the leaders to come back, which they didn't.
Gitano Hernando needs more of a test and wasn't suited by the way the race unfolded.

877a DUBAI CITY OF GOLD SPONSORED BY SKYWARDS (GROUP 2) (TURF) 1m 4f 11y

3:30 (3:30) 3-Y-O+

£96,774 (£32,258; £12,096; £12,096; £4,838; £3,225)

RPR
1 **Mikhail Glinka (IRE)**[7] 792 5-9-0 110 ....(vt) RoystonFfrench 1 115
(H J Brown, South Africa) *sn led: kicked clr 3f out: r.o wl: jst hld on* **14/1**
2 1 **Cavalryman**[139] 7049 6-9-0 111 .... OlivierPeslier 8 114+
(Saeed Bin Suroor) *in rr of mid-div: r.o wl fnl 2f: nrst fin* **20/1**
3 1/2 **Campanologist (USA)**[90] 7729 7-9-0 116 .... KierenFallon 2 113
(Saeed Bin Suroor) *trckd ldrs: ev ch 2 1/2f out: r.o same pce fnl 1 1/2f* **10/1**[3]
3 dht **Songcraft (IRE)**[30] 486 4-8-11 115 .... SilvestreDeSousa 12 112+
(Saeed Bin Suroor) *mid-div: r.o fnl 1 1/2f but nvr able to chal* **4/1**[2]
5 3 **Zanzamar (SAF)**[23] 591 5-9-0 113 ....(bt) RichardHills 9 108
(M F De Kock, South Africa) *in rr of mid-div: r.o one pce fnl 1 1/2f* **12/1**
6 hd **Joshua Tree (IRE)**[9] 755 5-9-0 113 .... JohnnyMurtagh 7 108
(Marco Botti) *trckd ldrs: ev ch 3f out: nt qckn fnl 1 1/2f* **14/1**
7 3 1/2 **Topclas (FR)**[13] 6-9-0 102 ....(vt) PatCosgrave 3 102
(M bin Shafya, UAE) *in rr of mid-div: n.d but r.o fnl 1 1/2f* **66/1**
8 shd **Shimraan (FR)**[23] 591 5-9-0 119 .... FrankieDettori 10 102
(Mahmood Al Zarooni) *trckd ldrs: ev ch 3f out: wknd fnl f* **10/3**[1]

9 *1 ¾* **Viscount Nelson (USA)**[9] 758 5-9-0 116 KShea 15 99
(M F De Kock, South Africa) *settled in rr: nvr able to chal* **10/1**[3]

10 *1 ¾* **Laajooj (IRE)**[30] 486 4-8-11 111 MickaelBarzalona 16 96
(Mahmood Al Zarooni) *in rr of mid-div: n.d* **12/1**

11 *¼* **Indian Days**[188] 5776 7-9-0 113 AlanMunro 11 96
(James Given) *trckd ldrs: ev ch 3f out: wknd fnl 1 1/2f* **12/1**

12 *1 ¼* **Dubai Prince (IRE)**[30] 488 4-8-11 112 (bt) AhmedAjtebi 13 93
(Mahmood Al Zarooni) *slowly away: n.d* **14/1**

13 *5* **Bronze Cannon (USA)**[9] 755 7-9-0 109 (t) RyanMoore 4 86
(H J Brown, South Africa) *nvr bttr than mid-div* **12/1**

14 *2* **Unusual Suspect (USA)**[7] 792 8-9-0 112 (v) JamieSpencer 14 83
(Michael Kent, Australia) *settled in rr: rdn 6f out: sn btn* **25/1**

15 *18 ¼* **Once More Dubai (USA)**[30] 484 7-9-0 105 (bt) TedDurcan 5 54
(Saeed Bin Suroor) *s.i.s: nvr nr to chal* **33/1**

16 *5* **Kreem**[36] 4-8-11 113 RobertoPerez 6 45
(B Al Shaibani, Saudi Arabia) *mid-div: rdn and wknd 3f out* **20/1**

2m 33.68s (153.68)
WFA 4 from 5yo+ 2lb **16** Ran SP% **129.8**
CSF: £285.77.
Owner Ramzan Kadyrov **Bred** Paulyn Ltd **Trained** South Africa

FOCUS
A trial for the Sheema Classic but how much bearing it will have on that Group 1 contest is debatable. A slight personal best from the winner, who made all.

NOTEBOOK
Mikhail Glinka(IRE) made every yard for a shock success. Although beaten in a handicap over 1m2f by Simon De Montfort last time, that was an improved effort from him (matched previous career-best RPR), and the addition of a visor seemed to be the difference. The headgear was once again in place here and, soon out in front, he was able to dictate a pace to suit himself. While he was challenged at the top of the straight, he's a strong stayer, Royston Ffrench had kept something in reserve and he was able to hold off the closers with a length to spare. He'll find repeating the trick in the Sheema Classic much tougher, but he deserves to take his chance.
Cavalryman ◆ is the one to take from the race as he did best of those held up off the pace and according to Trakus he travelled 11m further than the winner and 12m further than the third. It was also his first outing since finishing fifth in the Prix Royal-Oak last autumn, and one would expect him to come on for it. Fifth in the 2010 Sheema Classic, it's not hard to see him at least matching that effort on World Cup night.
Campanologist(USA), returning from a three-month absence, was never far off the pace and had every chance turning in. He kept on but lacked the finishing speed of the runner-up. That said, he's also entitled to benefit from the outing.
Songcraft(IRE), unbeaten in his previous four starts and stepping up to Group company for the first time, wasn't done many favours by Zanzamar hanging into him early in the straight but he kept on well once in the clear. Like the runner-up, he travelled a good deal further than the winner and third, and he looks to be still on the upgrade.
Zanzamar(SAF) didn't seem to get home over this longer trip and should be suited by a return to 1m2f.
Joshua Tree(IRE), back on turf, can't have many excuses as he was never too far off the pace in a race dominated throughout by the leader.
Topclas(FR) enjoyed one of the best ground-saving trips of the field, albeit having been held up well off the pace.
Shimraan(FR), unusually for a Dettori-ridden horse, got trapped wide throughout. The race wasn't really run to suit his style of running and he ended up racing closer to the pace than usual.
Indian Days failed to make the most of racing nearer the front, but probably needed the run having been absent since September.

878a AL MAKTOUM CHALLENGE R3 SPONSORED BY EMIRATES (GROUP 1) (TAPETA) 1m 2f
4:05 (4:05) 3-Y-0+

£154,838 (£51,612; £25,806; £12,903; £7,741; £5,161)

RPR

1 **Capponi (IRE)**[16] 677 5-9-0 113 AhmedAjtebi 7 120+
(Mahmood Al Zarooni) *trckd ldrs: led 2f out: r.o wl: comf* **9/1**

2 *4* **Silver Pond (FR)**[90] 7729 5-9-0 117 (t) OlivierPeslier 12 112
(Doug Watson, UAE) *trckd ldrs: ev ch 1 1/2f out: kpt on same pce fnl f* **12/1**

3 *½* **Prince Bishop (IRE)**[30] 488 5-9-0 117 (v) FrankieDettori 3 111
(Saeed Bin Suroor) *slowly away: trckd ldr: ev ch 1 1/2f out: nt qckn fnl f* **9/1**

4 *2* **Monterosso**[350] 1002 5-9-0 121 (t) MickaelBarzalona 1 107+
(Mahmood Al Zarooni) *mid-div: chsd ldrs 3f out: one pce fnl f* **5/1**[3]

5 *2* **Richard's Kid (USA)**[30] 488 7-9-0 113 (bt) RichardMullen 6 103+
(S Seemar, UAE) *racd in rr: r.o wl fnl 1 1/2f* **20/1**

6 *shd* **Fly Down (USA)**[36] 5-9-0 117 (t) COspina 11 103+
(B Al Subaie, Saudi Arabia) *settled in rr: nvr nr to chal but r.o fnl 2f* **20/1**

7 *¾* **Haatheq (USA)**[30] 488 5-9-0 112 RichardHills 5 101+
(A Al Raihe, UAE) *in rr of mid-div: kpt on same pce fnl 1 1/2f* **12/1**

8 *4 ¼* **Irish Flame (SAF)**[9] 759 6-9-0 110 KShea 14 92+
(M F De Kock, South Africa) *in rr of mid-div: n.d* **28/1**

9 *1 ¼* **Al Shemali**[9] 8-9-0 111 (t) RoystonFfrench 4 90+
(A Al Raihe, UAE) *in rr of mid-div: nvr able to chal* **25/1**

10 *4* **Treble Jig (USA)**[23] 591 5-9-0 110 WayneSmith 8 82
(M Al Muhairi, UAE) *sn led: hdd & wknd 2f out* **40/1**

11 *12 ½* **Mendip (USA)**[30] 488 5-9-0 115 KierenFallon 9 57+
(Saeed Bin Suroor) *in rr of mid-div: nvr able to chal* **5/1**[3]

12 *2 ½* **Bold Silvano (SAF)**[30] 487 6-9-0 118 ChristopheSoumillon 2 52+
(M F De Kock, South Africa) *nvr bttr than mid-div* **7/2**[1]

13 *13 ½* **Biondetti (USA)**[30] 488 4-9-0 110 (t) SilvestreDeSousa 13 25+
(Mahmood Al Zarooni) *in rr of mid-div: n.d* **12/1**

14 *dist* **Green Destiny (IRE)**[147] 6861 5-9-0 119 RyanMoore 10 +
(H J Brown, South Africa) *a in rr* **9/2**[2]

2m 3.05s (-1.65) **14** Ran SP% **136.1**
CSF: £119.24.
Owner Sheikh Hamdan Bin Mohammed Al Maktoum **Bred** Darley **Trained** Newmarket, Suffolk

FOCUS
A race with a classy roll of honour, so no great surprise it's now a Group 1, but it is essentially a trial for the Dubai World Cup and it's not satisfactory that such a contest has top-level status. Plenty have attempted the double, but only Dubai Millennium (2000), Street Cry (2002) and Electrocutionist (2006) have taken this en-route to World Cup glory. This year's contest was ruined by an apparent pace and/or track bias. Just like in some of the earlier Tapeta races, it proved difficult to make up significant ground - at halfway the first four finishers were 2nd, 3rd, 4th and 5th respectively. Treble Jig took the field to the 6f point in sectionals of 26.99, 50.62, 1.13.74. The progressive winner posted a personal best mark.

NOTEBOOK
Capponi(IRE)'s last start in Britain came when he finished tenth in the 2010 Cambridgeshire off just 104. Clearly he's made huge progress lately, this win following on from a couple of handicap wins off 105 and most recently 110, and the idea he was flattered last time was blatantly wrong. However, this latest victory, and the ease with which it was achieved, is hard to take seriously. Not only was he well placed, but his closest rival is a stayer, the third looks ungenuine, and the fourth hadn't run for a year. Maybe he'll prove in the Dubai World Cup he's now genuinely top class, but that's doubtful.
Silver Pond(FR) ◆ covered six meters more than the winner and lacked that one's pace. He was going the right way towards the end of last year and there should be more to come when he goes back up in trip - basically this was a nice trial for the Sheema Classic.
Prince Bishop(IRE) didn't look keen from the start, having to be rushed up after missing the break, and then being awkward under pressure in the straight.
Monterosso won the Dubai City Of Gold when making his reappearance on this card last year, but he hadn't been seen since, meaning he had a longer absence to overcome this time, and he lacked the required sharpness. He should come on for the run, but it's highly doubtful he'll improve on last year's third in the World Cup and maybe he's another who will go for the Sheema Classic instead.
Richard's Kid(USA) covered more ground than the first four, including nine meters more than the winner, but still fared best of those held up. He was also better than he showed in the second round of this Challenge, but it's still difficult to see him winning the World Cup.
Fly Down(USA) needs more of a stamina test, so this wasn't a bad run in the circumstances.
Mendip(USA), winner of the second round, was eased in the straight and something may have been amiss.
Bold Silvano(SAF) flopped in the Firebreak Stakes on his recent return from a lengthy absence and he did nothing here to suggest his old ability remains, even allowing for the race not being run to suit. Interestingly, he's been strong in the market on both his starts this year, but he's a horse with much to prove.
Green Destiny(IRE) ran a shocker on his first start since leaving William Haggas. Maybe he'll do better back on turf, but he's joined a trainer whose runners are hard to predict.

879a JEBEL HATTA SPONSORED BY EMIRATES (GROUP 1) (TURF) 1m 1f
4:40 (4:40) 3-Y-0+

£116,129 (£38,709; £19,354; £9,677; £5,806; £3,870)

RPR

1 **Master Of Hounds (USA)**[23] 590 4-9-0 115 (t) KShea 14 115
(M F De Kock, South Africa) *wl away: sn led: kicked clr 2 1/2f out: r.o wl: hld on gamely* **16/1**

2 *¾* **City Style (USA)**[16] 682 6-9-0 112 MickaelBarzalona 2 113
(Mahmood Al Zarooni) *trckd ldrs: ev ch 2f out: r.o fnl f: nrst fin* **13/2**[3]

3 *1 ¼* **Mutahadee (IRE)**[30] 489 4-9-0 116 ChristopheSoumillon 9 111+
(M F De Kock, South Africa) *settled in rr: n.m.r 2 1/2f out: r.o fnl 1 1/2f: nrst fin* **13/8**[1]

4 *¾* **Secrecy**[16] 682 6-9-0 108 (p) KierenFallon 13 109
(Saeed Bin Suroor) *trckd ldr: ev ch 2 1/2f out: one pce fnl 1 1/2f* **33/1**

5 *1 ¼* **Derbaas (USA)**[9] 758 6-9-0 113 (t) TadhgO'Shea 7 106+
(A Al Raihe, UAE) *trckd ldrs: ev ch 3f out: kpt on same pce fnl 1 1/2f* **33/1**

6 *¾* **Wigmore Hall (IRE)**[147] 6861 5-9-0 117 JamieSpencer 8 105+
(Michael Bell) *in rr of mid-div: r.o same pce fnl 2f* **8/1**

7 *1 ¼* **Albaasil (IRE)**[23] 590 4-9-0 115 RichardHills 4 102+
(Doug Watson, UAE) *in rr of mid-div: kpt on same pce fnl 1 1/2f* **16/1**

8 *1 ¾* **River Jetez (SAF)**[210] 5073 9-8-9 115 PatCosgrave 12 93+
(M F De Kock, South Africa) *in rr of mid-div: nvr able to chal* **20/1**

9 *½* **Presvis**[44] 318 8-9-0 120 RyanMoore 3 97+
(Luca Cumani) *settled in last: n.d* **11/2**[2]

10 *½* **Dubawi Gold**[90] 7731 4-9-0 117 RichardHughes 11 96+
(Richard Hannon) *settled in rr: nvr able to chal* **8/1**

11 *1 ¼* **First City**[22] 617 6-8-9 110 RoystonFfrench 10 89+
(A Al Raihe, UAE) *trckd ldrs tl 3f out: wknd fnl 1 1/2f* **25/1**

12 *1 ¼* **Pisco Sour (USA)**[30] 488 4-9-0 113 SilvestreDeSousa 1 91+
(Saeed Bin Suroor) *trckd ldng pair tl rdn and wknd 3f out* **20/1**

13 *1 ¼* **Rio De La Plata (USA)**[23] 590 7-9-0 118 (p) FrankieDettori 6 88+
(Saeed Bin Suroor) *in rr of mid-div: nvr able to chal* **12/1**

14 *16 ½* **Ibn Battuta (USA)**[9] 758 7-9-0 107 WayneSmith 5 54+
(M Al Muhairi, UAE) *nvr bttr than mid-div* **66/1**

1m 51.96s (111.96) **14** Ran SP% **129.2**
CSF: £116.33. PLACEPOT: £67.00 to a £1 stake. Pool of £4,065.12 - 44.23 winning tickets.QUADPOT: £18.00 to a £1 stake. Pool of £333.28 - 13.64 winning tickets..
Owner Sheikh Mohammed Bin Khalifa Al Maktoum **Bred** Silk And Scarlet Syndicate **Trained** South Africa

FOCUS
Just like the third round of the Al Maktoum Challenge, the Jebel Hatta acts as a prep race for a bigger target (the Dubai Duty Free), yet it now has Group 1 status. In another similarity with the preceding race, the form is muddling as the pace scenario suited those prominent, and in particular, the front-running winner.

NOTEBOOK
Master Of Hounds(USA) had the widest draw, but he was able to get to the front without overexerting himself and fractions of 27.20, 52.22, 1.16.75 and 1.39.83 represented a dawdle. While he has to be considered flattered by the bare form, that's not to say he can't go on from this. He was having only the 13th start of his career, and more specifically this was just his fourth outing since joining Mike de Kock, and his second since being fitted with a tongue-tie. Now that he's ended a losing run dating back to a 2010 maiden, he might gain in confidence and he is obviously worth his place in the Duty Free.
City Style(USA) deserves credit for getting closest to the front-running winner and remains on the up.
Mutahadee(IRE) ◆ closed impressively, quickening up much better than a few other classy types who were ridden with similar restraint. He proved he's up to this sort of level after a couple of easy handicap wins off 105 and most recently 111, and his chance in the Duty Free will be obvious.
Secrecy raced in second for much of the way and is a bit flattered.
Derbaas(USA) had his chance.
Wigmore Hall(IRE) won this race on his reappearance last year but the way the race unfolded gave him little hope of repeating the trick. Even so, he didn't quicken anywhere near as well as Mutahadee.
River Jetez(SAF) made an adequate return from 210 days off.
Presvis ◆ had no chance. Everyone knows Luca Cumani's charge is a confirmed hold-up performer, but it was still surprising to see him almost detached from the other runners on turning into the straight. He couldn't possibly win from such a position, but did make late progress to pass a few rivals and showed a bit of the old sparkle that was missing on his reappearance. This should put him spot on for when he bids to defend his Duty Free title at the end of the month.
Dubawi Gold did not fire, but he had excuses as he was held up off the slow pace, didn't get the clearest of runs and was unproven beyond 1m. He could still have a good season.

880 - 882a (Foreign Racing) - See Raceform Interactive

830 SOUTHWELL (L-H)

Tuesday, March 13

OFFICIAL GOING: Standard

Wind: Virtually nil Weather: overcast

883 "CHAMPION HURDLE FREE BETS WITH FREEBETTING.CO.UK" H'CAP 6f (F)

1:55 (1:55) (Class 4) (0-85,82) 4-Y-O+ **£4,204** (£1,251; £625; £312) **Stalls** Low

Form RPR

-433 **1** **Caldercruix (USA)**[11] 765 5-8-10 **76**........................(v) RaulDaSilva(5) 10 90
(James Evans) *cl up: rdn to chal over 2f out: led wl over 1f out: clr ins fnl f* **4/1**[2]

5224 **2** *4* **Punching**[7] 808 8-8-7 **68**.. HayleyTurner 7 70
(Conor Dore) *led: rdn along over 2f out: hdd wl over 1f out: sn drvn and one pce fnl f* **5/1**[3]

-544 **3** *1* **Close To The Edge (IRE)**[28] 554 4-9-6 **81**...................... ShaneKelly 8 80
(Alan McCabe) *sn in tch: hdwy to chse ldrs 1/2-way: rdn wl over 1f out: edgd lft and kpt on same pce appr fnl f* **13/2**

000- **4** *1 ½* **Klynch**[140] 7076 6-9-7 **82**...(b) PJMcDonald 4 77+
(Ruth Carr) *towards rr: hdwy and wd st: rdn 2f out: styd on appr fnl f: nrst fin* **20/1**

2130 **5** *hd* **Suddenly Susan (IRE)**[7] 808 4-8-9 **70**........................(b) LukeMorris 6 64
(Scott Dixon) *chsd ldng pair: rdn along over 2f out: one pce fr over 1f out* **9/1**

000- **6** *6* **Gallagher**[140] 7074 6-9-2 **77**... JamesSullivan 2 53
(Ruth Carr) *towards rr: hdwy and in tch 1/2-way: rdn over 2f out and sn wknd* **10/1**

6023 **7** *1 ¼* **Joe Le Taxi (IRE)**[6] 819 4-8-3 **64**..................................... JoeFanning 1 36
(Mark Johnston) *in tch on inner: rdn along bef 1/2-way: sn wknd* **7/2**[1]

151- **8** *nk* **Toby Tyler**[154] 6778 6-9-4 **79**...(v) MickyFenton 9 50
(Paul Midgley) *dwlt and towards rr: hdwy and wd st: rdn over 2f out: edgd lft and wknd wl over 1f out* **14/1**

-233 **9** *1 ¼* **Hatta Stream (IRE)**[17] 710 6-8-13 **77**........................ SimonPearce(3) 3 45
(Lydia Pearce) *chsd ldrs on inner: rdn along 1/2-way: sn wknd* **15/2**

1m 14.03s (-2.47) **Going Correction** -0.20s/f (Stan) **9** Ran SP% **114.5**
Speed ratings (Par 105): **108,102,101,99,99 91,89,89,87**
toteswingers:1&2:£5.10, 1&3:£4.80, 2&3:£5.30 CSF £24.12 CT £126.19 TOTE £4.80: £1.70, £1.70, £2.60; EX 29.30 Trifecta £309.10 Part won. Pool: £417.81 - 0.84 winning units..
Owner David Mantle **Bred** Bjorn Nielsen **Trained** Broadwas, Worcs

FOCUS
A fair sprint handicap and the best race on the card. Not many got into it.
Joe Le Taxi(IRE) Official explanation: jockey said gelding never travelled

884 ENJOY THE CHELTENHAM FESTIVAL WITH FREEBETTING.CO.UK CLASSIFIED CLAIMING STKS 1m (F)

2:30 (2:30) (Class 6) 4-Y-O+ **£1,704** (£503; £251) **Stalls** Low

Form RPR

0101 **1** **St Ignatius**[19] 676 5-8-0 55 ow2.................................(be) JackDuern(7) 2 65+
(Michael Appleby) *chsd ldr: rdn along wl over 2f out: styd on wl fr over 1f out: chal and edgd lft ins fnl f: sn led and styd on strly* **4/1**

0065 **2** *3 ½* **Alpha Tauri (USA)**[15] 722 6-8-12 65.......................... DuilioDaSilva(5) 3 67
(Richard Guest) *led: qcknd clr over 3f out: rdn wl over 1f out: wknd ent fnl f: sn hdd and one pce* **11/1**

1365 **3** *3 ¼* **Fibs And Flannel**[11] 761 5-8-6 63.............................(p) JamieMackay 4 49
(Willie Musson) *hld up in tch: hdwy 3f out: rdn over 2f out: kpt on same pce* **10/3**[3]

3623 **4** *nk* **Ace Of Spies (IRE)**[12] 752 7-8-2 62................................. LukeMorris 6 44
(Conor Dore) *chsd ldrs: pushed along 3f out: rdn over 2f out: sn one pce* **3/1**[2]

-430 **5** *1 ¼* **Jo Boy**[26] 574 5-8-6 61... HayleyTurner 1 46
(Michael Bell) *chsd ldng pair on inner: rdn over 2f out: sn wknd* **2/1**[1]

000- **6** *12* **Catcher Of Dreams (IRE)**[274] 2990 6-8-4 40...........(tp) FrannyNorton 5 17
(George Foster) *dwlt: a towards rr* **66/1**

1m 41.21s (-2.49) **Going Correction** -0.20s/f (Stan) **6** Ran SP% **111.2**
Speed ratings (Par 101): **104,100,97,96,95 83**
toteswingers:1&2:£4.90, 1&3:£2.10, 2&3:£3.30 CSF £42.30 TOTE £4.60: £2.50, £3.80; EX 24.20.St Ignatius was claimed by Mr A. Bailey for £4,500
Owner Dallas Racing **Bred** Simon And Helen Plumbly **Trained** Danethorpe, Notts

FOCUS
A moderate classified claimer, but there was no hanging about.

885 CHELTENHAM FESTIVAL FREE BETS WITH FREEBETTING.CO.UK MAIDEN STKS 6f (F)

3:05 (3:05) (Class 5) 3-Y-O **£2,385** (£704; £352) **Stalls** Low

Form RPR

352- **1** **Half A Billion (IRE)**[143] 7038 3-9-0 68........................... LeeTopliss(3) 3 75
(Michael Dods) *t.k.h early and carried hd high: chsd ldng pair: smooth hdwy on outer to ld 2f out: rdn clr fnl f* **9/4**[2]

3 **2** *6* **Ring For Baileys**[15] 720 3-8-12 0................................... FrannyNorton 1 52
(Chris Dwyer) *cl up on inner: led after 2f: jnd and rdn over 2f out: sn hdd: rallied u.p over 1f out: one pce fnl f* **5/2**[3]

255- **3** *3 ¼* **One Kool Dude**[153] 6800 3-8-10 64.................................. IanBurns(7) 4 47
(Michael Bell) *dwlt: sn outpcd and rdn along in rr bef 1/2-way: styd on fr wl over 1f out to take remote 3rd ins fnl f* **5/1**

0- **4** *2 ½* **Young Freddie (IRE)**[144] 6983 3-9-3 0........................... TomEaves 2 40
(Bryan Smart) *led 2f: cl up: rdn along over 2f out: sn edgd rt and wknd wl over 1f out* **2/1**[1]

1m 15.56s (-0.94) **Going Correction** -0.20s/f (Stan) **4** Ran SP% **109.3**
Speed ratings (Par 98): **98,90,85,82**
CSF £8.10 TOTE £3.50; EX 6.50.
Owner I Galletley, B Stenson, M Dods **Bred** Mount Coote Stud **Trained** Denton, Co Durham

FOCUS
A moderate maiden with three of the four runners returning from lengthy absences.

886 FREE HORSE RACING BETS WITH FREEBETTING.CO.UK (S) STKS 7f (F)

3:45 (3:45) (Class 6) 3-Y-O+ **£1,704** (£503; £251) **Stalls** Low

Form RPR

-050 **1** **Son Vida (IRE)**[12] 751 4-9-8 72...................................... JoeFanning 1 78
(Mark Johnston) *dwlt and swtchd to outer after s: smooth hdwy and cl up 1/2-way: led wl over 2f out: rdn clr appr fnl f: edgd lft and styd on* **15/8**[2]

2121 **2** *3 ¾* **Ingleby Arch (USA)**[21] 640 9-9-9 73.......................... LMcNiff(5) 3 74
(David Barron) *chsd ldr: pushed along 1/2-way rdn to chse wnr wl over 1f out: sn drvn and no imp* **8/15**[1]

6163 **3** *5* **Jonnie Skull (IRE)**[5] 839 6-9-7 57...........................(vt) DannyBrock(7) 4 61
(Phil McEntee) *led: rdn along and jnd 1/2-way: hdd wl over 2f out and grad wknd* **16/1**[3]

3U-0 **4** *13* **Red Scintilla**[19] 670 5-9-3 53.......................................(p) AndrewMullen 2 16
(Nigel Tinkler) *chsd ldng pair on inner: rdn along 1/2-way: sn outpcd* **50/1**

1m 29.14s (-1.16) **Going Correction** -0.20s/f (Stan) **4** Ran SP% **107.9**
Speed ratings (Par 101): **98,93,88,73**
CSF £3.24 TOTE £2.20; EX 3.70.The winner was sold to Mr A. Bailey for 6,600gns
Owner Jim McGrath, Roger & Dianne Trevitt **Bred** John Fielding **Trained** Middleham Moor, N Yorks

FOCUS
An uncompetitive claimer, but something of a turn-up.

887 CHELTENHAM FESTIVAL FREE BETTING WITH FREEBETTING.CO.UK H'CAP 5f (F)

4:25 (4:25) (Class 6) (0-60,60) 4-Y-O+ **£1,704** (£503; £251) **Stalls** High

Form RPR

4302 **1** **First In Command (IRE)**[26] 580 7-9-2 **55**....................(t) ShaneKelly 12 68+
(Daniel Mark Loughnane) *trckd ldrs: smooth hdwy to ld 2f out: rdn ins fnl f and kpt on* **11/2**[3]

-122 **2** *½* **Argentine (IRE)**[35] 456 8-9-7 **60**....................................(b) TomEaves 4 70
(Ian Semple) *trckd ldrs on bit: smooth hdwy 2f out: chal over 1f out: sn rdn and kpt on same pce fnl f* **5/2**[1]

6442 **3** *1 ¼* **Twice Red**[6] 819 4-9-3 **59**.. LeeTopliss(3) 9 65
(Derek Shaw) *towards rr: pushed along bef 1/2-way: hdwy wl over 1f out: styd on wl fnl f: nrst fin* **5/1**[2]

21-3 **4** *1 ¼* **Sandwith**[26] 580 9-8-13 **57**...(p) LMcNiff(5) 3 58
(George Foster) *prom: rdn 2f out: sn edgd lft and wknd appr fnl f* **7/1**

0-30 **5** *shd* **Spirit Of Coniston**[18] 696 9-8-12 **58**.............................. NedCurtis(7) 2 59
(Paul Midgley) *prom: rdn along 2f out: sn edgd lft and kpt on same pce* **12/1**

5631 **6** *¾* **Slatey Hen (IRE)**[10] 783 4-9-2 **55**...........................(p) WilliamCarson 10 53
(Richard Guest) *chsd ldrs: led bef 1/2-way: rdn and hdd 2f out: wknd ent fnl f* **12/1**

1160 **7** *6* **Canadian Danehill (IRE)**[4] 844 10-9-6 **59**..................(e) JoeFanning 5 35
(Robert Cowell) *in tch: n.m.r and lost pl after 1f: n.d after* **7/1**

50-0 **8** *shd* **Fashion Icon (USA)**[40] 380 6-9-1 **57**....................(b) DeclanCannon(3) 1 33
(David O'Meara) *cl up on wd outside: rdn along over 2f out and grad wknd* **33/1**

0-00 **9** *6* **Miss Polly Plum**[32] 498 5-9-1 **57**.................................(p) RyanClark(3) 6 11
(Chris Dwyer) *dwlt: a towards rr* **20/1**

5546 **10** *2* **Spic 'n Span**[6] 823 7-9-6 **59**...(v) LukeMorris 13
(Ronald Harris) *dwlt: chsd ldrs to 1/2-way: sn wknd* **16/1**

060- **11** *1 ¾* **Chosen One (IRE)**[153] 6802 7-9-4 **57**........................... JamesSullivan 8
(Ruth Carr) *led: rdn along and hdd bef 1/2-way: sn wknd* **25/1**

0/00 **12** *3 ½* **Skiddaw View**[18] 691 4-8-7 **46** oh1.............................. AndrewMullen 11
(Alan Brown) *dwlt: towards rr: bhd fr 1/2-way* **100/1**

59.47s (-0.23) **Going Correction** 0.0s/f (Stan) **12** Ran SP% **119.4**
Speed ratings (Par 101): **101,100,98,96,96 94,85,85,75,72 69,63**
toteswingers:1&2:£3.60, 1&3:£4.60, 2&3:£3.40 CSF £19.03 CT £76.12 TOTE £6.80: £2.60, £1.10, £1.60; EX 24.50 Trifecta £227.00 Pool: £567.57 - 1.85 winning units..
Owner Mrs C Loughnane **Bred** Peter And Mrs McCutcheon **Trained** Baldwin's Gate, Staffs

FOCUS
A moderate sprint handicap and the first six pulled a long way clear of the rest.

888 BIGGEST FREE BETS WITH FREEBETTING.CO.UK H'CAP 1m 4f (F)

5:05 (5:06) (Class 5) (0-75,78) 4-Y-O+ **£2,264** (£673; £336; £168) **Stalls** Low

Form RPR

3414 **1** **Newport Arch**[4] 850 4-8-8 **64**.............................(v) MichaelO'Connell(3) 4 76+
(John Quinn) *trckd ldr: hdwy to chal on bit 3f out: led 2f out: pushed out fnl f: easily* **7/4**[1]

11-0 **2** *3* **Maven**[54] 216 4-9-5 **72**.. DuranFentiman 5 78
(Tim Easterby) *trckd ldng pair: pushed along and sltly outpcd 4f out: hdwy over 2f out: rdn to chal over 1f out: kpt on same pce fnl f* **7/1**

-431 **3** *1 ¼* **Trans Sonic**[7] 809 9-9-10 **78** 6ex...................(p) DeclanCannon(3) 2 82
(David O'Meara) *led: rdn along over 3f out: hdd 2f out: sn drvn and one pce fr over 1f out* **11/4**[3]

2042 **4** *hd* **Turjuman (USA)**[9] 557 7-8-13 **64**.............................(v[1]) KierenFallon 1 67
(Alan Bailey) *dwlt and rdn along s: rn in snatches: in tch: hdwy to trck ldng pair 4f out: rdn along and outpcd 3f out: styd on u.p appr fnl f* **2/1**[2]

2m 37.89s (-3.11) **Going Correction** -0.20s/f (Stan)
WFA 4 from 7yo+ 2lb **4** Ran SP% **108.9**
Speed ratings (Par 103): **102,100,99,99**
CSF £12.44 TOTE £2.40; EX 14.20.
Owner Alan Mann **Bred** R P Williams **Trained** Settrington, N Yorks

FOCUS
An ordinary middle-distance handicap.

889 COMPARE FREE BETS WITH FREEBETTING.CO.UK APPRENTICE H'CAP 1m 4f (F)

5:40 (5:40) (Class 6) (0-60,60) 4-Y-O+ **£1,704** (£503; £251) **Stalls** Low

Form RPR

0260 **1** **Putin (IRE)**[19] 676 4-8-2 **46** oh1.................................(bt) DannyBrock(3) 4 52
(Phil McEntee) *led: rdn along 3f out: hdd and cl up 2f out: rallied to ld again ent fnl f: sn drvn: hung rt and kpt on gamely towards fin* **20/1**

0-00 **2** *¾* **Visions Of Johanna (USA)**[31] 530 7-8-5 **49**............... DarrenEgan(5) 5 54
(Richard Guest) *chsd wnr: hdwy 4f out: cl up 3f out: rdn and slt ld 2f out: sn hdd: rallied to ld again over 1f out: hdd ent fnl f: sn n.m.r and kpt on u.p towards fin* **5/1**[2]

00-3 **3** *1* **Revolving World (IRE)**[35] 453 9-8-2 **46** oh1..............(t) NoelGarbutt(5) 6 49
(Lee James) *dwlt and in rr: hdwy on wd outside over 5f out: chsd wnr over 3f out: rdn to chal over 2f out: led briefly wl over 1f out: sn hdd: drvn and n.m.r ins fnl f: one pce* **15/2**[3]

-040 **4** *hd* **Magnitude**[22] 632 7-8-9 **48**..(v) LMcNiff 8 51
(Brian Baugh) *in tch: hdwy to chse ldrs 4f out: rdn wl over 2f out: styng on whn n.m.r and swtchd lft ent fnl f: nrst fin* **12/1**

1405 **5** *¾* **Cloudy Start**[4] 850 6-9-4 **60**.. LeonnaMayor(3) 2 62+
(Jamie Osborne) *hld up towards rr: pushed along over 4f out and rr whn sltly hmpd over 3f out: styd on fnl 2f: nvr a factor* **11/8**[1]

-040 **6** *5* **Final Tune (IRE)**[21] 644 9-8-7 **49**............................... CharlesBishop(3) 3 43
(Mandy Rowland) *in tch: effrt over 4f out: sn rdn along: edgd lft over 3f out and sn bhd* **16/1**

0/55 **7** *11* **Bee Sting**[18] 695 8-9-2 **55**...(p) ShaneBKelly 9 33
(Lisa Williamson) *a towards rr* **5/1**[2]

50-4 **U** **Colliers Castle (IRE)**[11] [767] 6-8-7 **53**................. MatthewMcGhee(7) 1
(Lisa Williamson) *chsd ldrs: rdn along 4f out: wkng whn n.m.r: stmbld and uns rdr over 3f out* **17/2**

2m 40.84s (-0.16) **Going Correction** -0.20s/f (Stan)
WFA 4 from 6yo+ 2lb **8** Ran SP% **116.1**
Speed ratings (Par 101): **92,91,90,90,90 86,79,**
toteswingers:1&2:£9.80, 1&3:£8.20, 2&3:£6.00 CSF £117.99 CT £834.54 TOTE £21.20: £4.90, £1.10, £2.60; EX 131.20 Trifecta £598.60 Part won. Pool: £809.04 - 0.64 winning units..
Owner Steve Jakes **Bred** D Llewelyn & J Runeckles **Trained** Newmarket, Suffolk
■ Stewards' Enquiry : Charles Bishop six-day ban: careless riding (Mar 27-31,Apr 1)

FOCUS
This was a poor race and with the pace slackening noticeably before halfway, the time was almost three seconds slower than the preceding contest.
T/Plt: £380.60 to a £1 stake. Pool:£48,431.12 - 92.89 winning tickets T/Qpdt: £38.30 to a £1 stake. Pool:£3,333.22 - 64.36 winning tickets JR

816 KEMPTON (A.W) (R-H)

Wednesday, March 14

OFFICIAL GOING: Standard
Wind: virtually nil Weather: dry

890 FREE ENTRY FOR BETDAQ MEMBERS H'CAP 5f (P)
5:50 (5:51) (Class 5) (0-75,75) 4-Y-O+ **£2,264** (£673; £336; £168) **Stalls** Low

Form RPR

2423 **1** **Island Legend (IRE)**[21] [647] 6-9-7 **75**.............................(p) DaneO'Neill 3 83
(Milton Bradley) *mde all: rdn over 1f out: kpt on wl u.p fnl f* **11/8**[1]

422 **2** ¾ **Liberal Lady**[27] [576] 4-8-7 **61** oh1..................................(e) LukeMorris 1 66
(Ralph Smith) *sn chsng wnr: rdn wl over 1f out: drvn and kpt on fnl f* **11/2**[3]

0222 **3** ½ **Picansort**[18] [710] 5-9-0 **68**.. ShaneKelly 7 72
(Peter Crate) *hld up off the pce: rdn to chse ldng trio 1/2-way: rdn over 1f out: swtchd lft jst ins fnl f: r.o wl fnl 100yds: nt rch ldrs* **9/4**[2]

600 **4** ¾ **Black Baccara**[12] [763] 5-8-8 **65**..................................(be) RyanClark(3) 4 66
(Phil McEntee) *hld up off the pce: hdwy and lft chsng ldng pair 3f out: rdn ent fnl f: styd on same pce fnl 150yds* **20/1**

2160 **5** nk **Shawkantango**[8] [808] 5-8-9 **66** ow1...................(v) MichaelO'Connell(3) 6 66+
(Derek Shaw) *awkward leaving stalls and slowly away: bhd: hdwy on inner but stl plenty to do over 1f out: styd on wl fnl f: nt rch ldrs* **8/1**

00-0 **6** 4 ½ **Ingleby Star (IRE)**[40] [406] 7-8-12 **71**..........................(p) JustinNewman(5) 2 55
(Ian McInnes) *chsd ldrs: hung lft and nt handle bnd over 3f out: lost pl and bhd 1/2-way: no ch fnl 2f* **16/1**

0-60 **7** 3 ½ **Lucky Art (USA)**[21] [647] 6-8-11 **70**.................................. LucyKBarry(5) 5 41
(Conor Dore) *racd in midfield tl wnt wd and lost pl bnd 3f out: bhd fnl 2f* **16/1**

59.48s (-1.02) **Going Correction** -0.075s/f (Stan) **7** Ran SP% **115.9**
Speed ratings (Par 103): **105,103,103,101,101 94,88**
toteswingers: 1&2 £1.60, 1&3 £1.10, 2&3 £1.20 CSF £9.95 TOTE £1.90: £1.10, £3.70; EX 10.60.

Owner J M Bradley **Bred** Jerome Casey **Trained** Sedbury, Gloucs

FOCUS
A modest handicap in which the first pair filled the front two positions pretty much throughout.

891 BETDAQ MULTIPLES H'CAP 1m 2f (P)
6:20 (6:24) (Class 6) (0-60,66) 4-Y-O+ **£1,617** (£481; £240; £120) **Stalls** Low

Form RPR

00-0 **1** **Flag Of Glory**[43] [366] 5-9-4 **57**.. WilliamCarson 12 65
(Peter Hiatt) *sn led and mde rest: rdn jst over 2f out: drvn and kpt on wl fnl f* **14/1**

-350 **2** ¾ **Escape Artist**[13] [741] 5-8-8 **47**... KieranO'Neill 4 54+
(John Bridger) *t.k.h: hld up in last trio: nt clr run wl over 1f out: hdwy and swtchd rt 1f out: r.o wl to chse wnr wl ins fnl f: nvr quite gng to rch wnr* **10/1**

4-50 **3** ½ **Royal Etiquette (IRE)**[7] [818] 5-9-7 **60**.............................. DaneO'Neill 8 66
(Lawney Hill) *hld up in last trio: rdn and effrt on outer 2f out: drvn and hdwy over 1f out: kpt on wl fnl f: nvr quite gng to rch wnr* **5/2**[1]

4041 **4** 1 ¼ **Nolecce**[7] [818] 5-9-10 **66** 6ex.....................................(p) RobertLButler(3) 2 69
(Richard Guest) *chsd wnr tl 8f out: rdn to chse wnr again 2f out: drvn and unable qck over 1f out: lost 2 pls fnl 100yds* **10/3**[2]

-422 **5** nk **Cane Cat (IRE)**[7] [818] 5-9-3 **59**..........................(t) MichaelO'Connell(3) 13 62
(Tony Carroll) *hld up in rr: c wd and effrt wl over 1f out: hdwy u.p jst over 1f out: kpt on fnl f: nt rch ldrs* **7/2**[3]

300- **6** 1 **Market Puzzle (IRE)**[131] [7263] 5-8-12 **58**...............(p) RachealKneller(7) 5 59
(Mark Brisbourne) *in tch: pushed along and effrt to chse ldrs 1f out: kpt on same pce under hands and heels riding fnl f* **25/1**

0-01 **7** ½ **Whodathought (IRE)**[6] [843] 4-9-5 **65** 6ex..................(b) DarrenEgan(7) 9 65
(Paul Rich) *chsd wnr 8f out tl 2f out: drvn and no ex over 1f out: wknd ins fnl f* **8/1**

P-06 **8** 1 **Irie Ute**[14] [736] 4-9-4 **60**... SophieDoyle(3) 7 58
(Sylvester Kirk) *chsd ldrs: rdn and effrt wl over 1f out: drvn and unable qck ent fnl f: wknd ins fnl f* **33/1**

550 **9** 1 ½ **Gay Gallivanter**[7] [829] 4-8-7 **46** oh1..............................(p) LukeMorris 11 41
(Michael Quinn) *in tch in midfield: rdn and unable qck over 1f out: wknd jst ins fnl f* **33/1**

-023 **10** 2 **Gallantry**[15] [732] 10-9-3 **56**... TomMcLaughlin 1 47
(Paul Howling) *hld up in last quartet: hdwy on inner 3f out: rdn and no prog over 1f out: wknd ins fnl f* **16/1**

/0-0 **11** 4 ½ **Expensive Legacy**[47] [334] 5-8-4 **46** oh1.................... RossAtkinson(3) 6 29
(Tor Sturgis) *chsd ldrs: rdn 3f out: wknd over 1f out: bhd fnl f* **66/1**

2m 7.74s (-0.26) **Going Correction** -0.075s/f (Stan) **11** Ran SP% **117.8**
Speed ratings (Par 101): **98,97,97,96,95 94,94,93,92,90 87**
toteswingers:1&2:£33.40, 1&3:£8.80, 2&3:£6.80 CSF £134.25 CT £413.01 TOTE £23.90: £5.00, £3.10, £1.20; EX 201.50.
Owner N D Edden **Bred** Follow The Flag Partnership **Trained** Hook Norton, Oxon

FOCUS
A moderate handicap.
Flag Of Glory Official explanation: trainer said, regarding apparent improvement in form, that the gelding was suited by the drop in trip.
Cane Cat(IRE) Official explanation: jockey said mare hung left throughout

892 BACK OR LAY AT BETDAQ.COM MEDIAN AUCTION MAIDEN STKS 6f (P)
6:50 (6:51) (Class 6) 3-5-Y-O **£1,617** (£481; £240; £120) **Stalls** Low

Form RPR

63-0 **1** **Justbookies Dotnet**[33] [491] 3-9-0 65............................(v) IanMongan 10 69
(Louise Best) *sn chsng ldr and clr of field: rdn 2f out: drvn and clsd on ldr 1f out: led fnl 100yds: styd on wl* **20/1**

04- **2** 1 ¼ **Nevaeh**[84] [7838] 3-8-9 0.. LukeMorris 5 60
(Pat Eddery) *racd off the pce in midfield: rdn over 2f out: drvn and clsd on ldrs ent fnl f: kpt on u.p to go 2nd towards fin* **7/1**[3]

4 **3** ½ **Big Wave (IRE)**[32] [533] 4-9-9 0.. ShaneKelly 11 59
(Jane Chapple-Hyam) *wnt lft s: sn led and set fast gallop: stl clr and rdn over 1f out: hdd fnl 100yds: no ex and lost 2nd towards fin* **11/2**[2]

300- **4** ½ **Electric Qatar**[209] [5216] 3-9-0 90................................. RichardKingscote 1 62
(Tom Dascombe) *burst out of stalls early: sn restrained and hld up in 3rd: t.k.h: rdn wl over 1f out: clsd u.p 1f out: edgd lft and fnd little ins fnl f: one pce* **1/3**[1]

-5 **5** 1 **Auntie Mabel**[19] [684] 3-8-9 0... DavidProbert 9 54
(Andrew Balding) *racd off the pce in midfield: rdn over 2f out: clsd u.p over 1f out: kpt on ins fnl f* **25/1**

6 ½ **Langley Vale** 3-9-0 0.. DaneO'Neill 7 58+
(Roger Teal) *racd off the pce in midfield: rdn and no prog over 2f out: 6th and wl hld 2f out: styd on wl ins fnl f: gng on fin* **33/1**

4 **7** 5 **Nothing's Simple**[13] [742] 3-8-9 0.................................... LauraPike(5) 8 43
(Hugo Palmer) *s.i.s: racd wl off the pce in rr: sme hdwy 2f out: nvr trbld ldrs* **25/1**

8 ¾ **Ghazeer (IRE)** 3-8-11 0.................................... MichaelO'Connell(3) 12 41
(Derek Shaw) *v.s.a: wl bhd: sme hdwy fnl 2f: n.d* **33/1**

00- **9** 3 ½ **Adelindus**[139] [7118] 3-8-9 0... SteveDrowne 3 25
(Ed Vaughan) *racd off the pce in midfield: rdn and outpcd over 2f out: wl btn 2f out: wknd* **25/1**

6 **10** 2 ¾ **The Bendy Fella (IRE)**[12] [770] 4-9-9 0........................ LeeNewnes(5) 6 26
(Mark Usher) *a wl bhd: nvr on terms* **33/1**

0 **11** 31 **Night Symfonic**[14] [737] 3-8-9 0.................................... WilliamCarson 2
(Brett Johnson) *s.i.s: a bhd: t.o and eased ins fnl f* **50/1**

1m 12.85s (-0.25) **Going Correction** -0.075s/f (Stan)
WFA 3 from 4yo 14lb **11** Ran SP% **130.0**
Speed ratings (Par 101): **98,96,95,95,93 93,86,85,80,77 35**
toteswingers:1&2:£11.20, 1&3:£16.70, 2&3:£4.70 CSF £152.73 TOTE £46.50: £6.20, £2.70, £1.80; EX 197.80.
Owner Louise Best Racing & Martyn Cruse **Bred** Dxb Bloodstock Ltd **Trained** Hollingbourne, Kent

FOCUS
The favourite's below-par performance means this is just modest form.

893 BETDAQ MOBILE APPS H'CAP (DIV I) 6f (P)
7:20 (7:20) (Class 5) (0-75,75) 4-Y-O+ **£2,264** (£673; £336; £168) **Stalls** Low

Form RPR

3130 **1** **Lastkingofscotland (IRE)**[13] [746] 6-9-4 **72**.................(b) LukeMorris 2 80
(Conor Dore) *chsd ldr: rdn and qcknd to ld 2f out: drvn and edgd rt jst ins fnl f: kpt on wl* **9/1**

145- **2** 1 **Black Cadillac (IRE)**[266] [3271] 4-8-9 **63**.......................... DavidProbert 8 68
(Andrew Balding) *in tch: rdn and effrt ent fnl 2f: chsd wnr over 1f out: pressing wnr ins fnl f: one pce fnl 100yds* **14/1**

30-2 **3** ½ **Jungle Bay**[20] [669] 5-9-5 **73**.. AdamKirby 4 78
(Jane Chapple-Hyam) *stdd s: hld up in rr: stl plenty to do whn swtchd ins and effrt 2f out: gd hdwy over 1f out: disputing 2nd and running on whn nt enough room and eased towards fin* **13/8**[1]

30-3 **4** 1 ¼ **Bond Fastrac**[50] [282] 5-9-3 **74**... DaleSwift(3) 1 74
(Geoffrey Oldroyd) *in tch in midfield: effrt u.p 3f out: chsd ldrs 1f out: styng on same pce whn nt clr run ins fnl f* **7/1**[3]

1140 **5** 2 ¾ **Speak The Truth (IRE)**[18] [710] 6-8-11 **70**...............(p) NathanAlison(5) 6 62
(Jim Boyle) *t.k.h: hld up in rr: rdn and effrt over 2f out: styd on fnl f: nvr trbld ldrs* **16/1**

1200 **6** nse **The Strig**[18] [710] 5-9-3 **71**.. WilliamCarson 10 62
(Stuart Williams) *chsd ldr: carried lft wl over 2f out: rdn and unable qck ent fnl 2f: wknd jst over 1f out* **10/1**

00-0 **7** ½ **Local Singer (IRE)**[48] [311] 4-9-6 **74**............................. TomMcLaughlin 5 64
(Paul Howling) *in tch in midfield: rdn and unable qck ent fnl 2f: wknd jst over 1f out* **28/1**

60-6 **8** 1 **Alfresco**[20] [669] 8-9-2 **70**..(b) GeorgeBaker 3 57
(John Best) *led: c towards centre st: rdn and hdd 2f out: wknd over 1f out* **25/1**

21-2 **9** 2 ½ **Mambo Spirit (IRE)**[21] [649] 8-9-7 **75**................................. DaneO'Neill 9 54
(Tony Newcombe) *t.k.h: hld up in rr: rdn and no prog over 2f out: wknd wl over 1f out* **6/1**[2]

410- **10** 7 **Qubuh (IRE)**[86] [7819] 4-8-13 **67**.. ShaneKelly 7 25
(Linda Stubbs) *in tch in midfield: rdn and no prog over 2f out: sn wknd* **7/1**[3]

1m 11.71s (-1.39) **Going Correction** -0.075s/f (Stan) **10** Ran SP% **116.3**
Speed ratings (Par 103): **106,104,104,102,98 98,97,96,93,83**
toteswingers:1&2:£31.70, 1&3:£5.20, 2&3:£8.90 CSF £126.52 CT £313.57 TOTE £11.00: £2.40, £5.20, £1.50; EX 109.20.
Owner Mrs Jennifer Marsh **Bred** Baronrath Stud **Trained** Hubbert's Bridge, Lincs

FOCUS
The time was the quickest of four races at the trip, including 0.55 seconds faster than the other division.
Jungle Bay Official explanation: jockey said he stopped riding gelding before line as he was concerned of running into back of winner.

894 RACING PLUS, OUT EVERY DAY FOR CHELTENHAM H'CAP 1m (P)
7:50 (7:50) (Class 5) (0-70,69) 4-Y-O+ **£2,264** (£673; £336; £168) **Stalls** Low

Form RPR

-031 **1** **Prince Of Sorrento**[7] [828] 5-9-4 **66** 6ex.......................... JamieMackay 3 75+
(Lee Carter) *hld up wl in tch: trckd ldrs and travelling strly over 1f out: rdn to chal and qcknd clr w rival 1f out: led fnl 100yds: a jst doing enough after and rdn out* **5/2**[1]

5035 **2** nk **Mister Green (FR)**[7] [821] 6-9-1 **63**................................(bt) JamesDoyle 4 71
(David Flood) *hld up in tch: swtchd ins 2f out: hdwy to trck ldrs on bridle over 1f out: led and qcknd clr w wnr 1f out: hdd fnl 100yds: a jst hld after* **5/2**[1]

-505 **3** 4 ½ **Archelao (IRE)**[13] [746] 4-9-6 **68**.. AmirQuinn 8 66
(Richard Rowe) *hld up in tch towards rr: nt clr run ent fnl 2f: rdn and outpcd by ldng pair jst over 1f out: kpt on to snatch 3rd last stride* **7/1**[3]

30-0 **4** *shd* **Quite A Catch (IRE)**[47] 330 4-9-4 **66**........................(v) StephenCraine 7 63
(Jonathan Portman) *chsd ldr tl led jst over 2f out: rdn wl over 1f out: hdd 1f out and immediately outpcd: lost 3rd last stride* **16/1**

-502 **5** *2 1/4* **Cativo Cavallino**[19] 685 9-9-3 **65**.............................. RichardThomas 6 57
(John E Long) *in tch on outer: rdn and unable qck over 2f out: plugged on same pce and wl hld fnl 2f* **8/1**

33 **6** *1 1/4* **Jumeirah Liberty**[19] 685 4-9-0 **62**.............................. JamieGoldstein 1 51
(Zoe Davison) *chsd ldrs: rdn and effrt on inner 2f out: outpcd jst over 1f out: wknd fnl f* **12/1**

3211 **7** *4* **Qeethaara (USA)**[14] 736 8-9-6 **68**..............................(p) LukeMorris 9 48
(Mark Brisbourne) *stdd s: hld up in rr: effrt on inner 2f out: no imp over 1f out: wknd fnl f* **9/2**[2]

-065 **8** *3 1/4* **Reposer (IRE)**[18] 713 4-9-6 **68**.............................. RobbieFitzpatrick 2 41
(Noel Quinlan) *led tl jst over 2f out: sn outpcd: wknd over 1f out* **18/1**

1m 38.34s (-1.46) **Going Correction** -0.075s/f (Stan) 8 Ran SP% **117.8**
Speed ratings (Par 103): **104,103,99,99,96 95,91,88**
toteswingers:1&2:£2.40, 1&3:£6.00, 2&3:£6.80 CSF £8.84 CT £38.55 TOTE £4.70: £1.30, £1.40, £2.50; EX 9.60.
Owner John Akehurst **Bred** Mrs P Akhurst **Trained** Epsom, Surrey

FOCUS
Modest form.

895 "BET LATE AT CHELTENHAM" H'CAP 1m 4f (P)
8:20 (8:20) (Class 6) (0-55,55) 4-Y-0+ **£1,617** (£481; £240; £120) **Stalls** Centre

Form RPR

-004 **1** **Khun John (IRE)**[28] 559 9-9-4 **55**.............................. JamieMackay 6 63
(Willie Musson) *hld up in midfield: rdn and effrt to chse ldr over 1f out: led 1f out: styd on wl: rdn out* **5/2**[2]

-533 **2** *1* **Laser Blazer**[14] 738 4-8-13 **52**..............................(p) JimCrowley 4 58
(Jeremy Gask) *chsd ldrs: rdn over 2f out: drvn and chsd ldng pair over 1f out: kpt on to chse wnr fnl 100yds: no imp* **9/4**[1]

0-00 **3** *1 1/2* **Bengal Tiger**[50] 276 6-9-0 **51**.............................. DavidProbert 8 55
(Tony Carroll) *chsd ldr: rdn to ld over 1f out: hdd 1f out: no ex and lost 2nd fnl 100yds: one pce* **13/2**

-453 **4** *1/2* **The Catenian (IRE)**[13] 741 4-8-7 **46** oh1..............................(v) ShaneKelly 5 49
(John Butler) *hld up in rr: hdwy on inner to chse ldrs over 1f out: shkn up 1f out: sn rdn and fnd nil: no imp fnl 100yds* **5/1**[3]

-001 **5** *3 3/4* **Dolly Colman (IRE)**[13] 741 4-8-10 **49**.............................. RichardKingscote 2 46
(Michael Blake) *hld up in rr: rdn and hdwy over 1f out: no imp fnl f* **7/1**

6-36 **6** *1 1/2* **Four Steps Back**[27] 575 5-8-13 **50**.............................. LiamKeniry 3 45
(Mark Usher) *hld up in last trio: rdn and effrt 2f out: no prog and outpcd over 1f out: wknd fnl f* **20/1**

-300 **7** *1/2* **Farmers Hill**[13] 741 4-8-7 **46** oh1..............................(b) WilliamCarson 7 40
(Mark Hoad) *led: rdn and hdd over 1f out: wknd u.p over 1f out* **25/1**

-045 **8** *1 1/4* **Olimamu (IRE)**[13] 741 5-8-6 **46** oh1..............................(vt) SimonPearce(3) 9 38
(Lydia Pearce) *in tch in midfield: rdn and unable qck over 2f out: outpcd 2f out and n.d after* **20/1**

402- **9** *3/4* **Suhailah**[134] 7206 6-8-8 **50**.............................. MarkCoumbe(5) 10 41
(Michael Attwater) *chsd ldrs: rdn over 2f out: drvn wl over 1f out: wknd over 1f out* **16/1**

2m 35.43s (0.93) **Going Correction** -0.075s/f (Stan)
WFA 4 from 5yo+ 2lb 9 Ran SP% **121.1**
Speed ratings (Par 101): **93,92,91,91,88 87,87,86,85**
toteswingers:1&2:£1.20, 1&3:£4.70, 2&3:£5.20 CSF £8.80 CT £33.24 TOTE £4.20: £1.50, £1.20, £2.70; EX 10.90.
Owner The Strawberries To A Donkey Partnership **Bred** Sti Engineering Srl **Trained** Newmarket, Suffolk

FOCUS
A moderate race.

896 BETDAQ MOBILE APPS H'CAP (DIV II) 6f (P)
8:50 (8:50) (Class 5) (0-75,75) 4-Y-0+ **£2,264** (£673; £336; £168) **Stalls** Low

Form RPR

-553 **1** **Last Sovereign**[21] 649 8-9-3 **74**..............................(b) MichaelO'Connell(3) 9 88
(Ollie Pears) *rdr late removing hood and dwlt: sn rcvrd and led after 1f: clr 1/2-way: rdn further clr 2f out: coming bk to rivals ins fnl f but nvr gng to be ct: eased towards fin* **7/1**

3012 **2** *1 1/4* **Captain Scooby**[4] 870 6-9-2 **73**.............................. RobertLButler(3) 5 81
(Richard Guest) *hld up wl in rr: rdn and hdwy over 1f out: kpt on u.p fnl f: wnt 2nd towards fin: nvr looked like getting to wnr* **11/2**[3]

0402 **3** *hd* **Italian Tom (IRE)**[14] 735 5-9-2 **70**.............................. LukeMorris 3 77
(Ronald Harris) *t.k.h: led for 1f: chsd ldrs: rdn to chse clr ldr over 1f out: kpt on and clsng on wnr ins fnl f: nvr gng to rch wnr: lost 2nd towards fin* **11/4**[1]

0/5- **4** *2 1/4* **Indian Art (IRE)**[168] 6467 6-9-1 **72**.............................. SeanLevey(3) 4 73
(Sylvester Kirk) *racd in midfield: rdn and no rspnse jst over 2f out: styd on ins fnl f: no ch w wnr* **5/1**[2]

0153 **5** *2* **Fleetwoodsands (IRE)**[23] 639 5-9-3 **71**..............................(t) LiamKeniry 8 66
(Milton Bradley) *t.k.h: chsd ldr over 4f out: rdn and no prog jst over 2f out: lost 2nd over 1f out: wknd fnl f* **10/1**

5410 **6** *1* **Pick A Little**[21] 652 4-9-7 **75**.............................. SteveDrowne 2 67
(Michael Blake) *chsd ldrs for 2f: steadily lost pl: rdn and no rspnse over 2f out: one pce and wl hld fnl 2f* **5/1**[2]

/40- **7** *1* **Bahri Sheen (IRE)**[340] 1236 4-8-13 **67**.............................. JimCrowley 1 56
(John Best) *hld up towards rr: rdn jst over 2f out: plugged on: nvr trbld ldrs* **16/1**

-460 **8** *1* **Sermons Mount (USA)**[14] 735 6-9-2 **70**.............................. JohnFahy 6 56
(Paul Howling) *hld up in rr: rdn and no hdwy over 2f out: n.d* **10/1**

63-0 **9** *3 1/4* **Decimate**[13] 746 4-8-8 **67**.............................. DavidKenny(5) 10 43
(Andrew Reid) *a in rr: wd and rdn bnd 3f out: no prog: n.d* **33/1**

1m 12.26s (-0.84) **Going Correction** -0.075s/f (Stan) 9 Ran SP% **114.9**
Speed ratings (Par 103): **102,100,100,97,94 93,91,90,86**
toteswingers:1&2:£4.50, 1&3:£5.80, 2&3:£16.10 CSF £44.95 CT £132.38 TOTE £8.30: £2.50, £1.90, £1.10; EX 33.70.
Owner Richard Walker **Bred** Gestut Hof Ittlingen & Cheveley Park Stud Ltd **Trained** Norton, N Yorks

FOCUS
The time was 0.55 seconds slower than the first division.
Fleetwoodsands(IRE) Official explanation: jockey said gelding ran too freely

897 "GETTING OUT STKS AT CHELTENHAM" H'CAP 6f (P)
9:20 (9:20) (Class 4) (0-85,78) 3-Y-0 **£4,075** (£1,212; £606; £303) **Stalls** Low

Form RPR

132- **1** **Marford Missile (IRE)**[315] 1806 3-9-7 **78**................ RichardKingscote 4 82+
(Tom Dascombe) *stdd and dropped in bhd after s: hld up in rr: rdn and effrt 2f out: swtchd lft jst ins fnl f: r.o wl to ld nr fin* **5/2**[2]

1334 **2** *nk* **Adranian (IRE)**[4] 867 3-9-7 **78**..............................(v) DavidProbert 2 81
(David C Griffiths) *led: rdn over 1f out: kpt on wl u.p tl hdd and no ex nr fin* **13/8**[1]

2-42 **3** *1* **Heartsong (IRE)**[13] 742 3-9-0 **71**.............................. JohnFahy 1 71
(John Gallagher) *chsd ldrs: wnt 2nd over 2f out: effrt u.p over 1f out: kpt on same pce ins fnl f* **7/1**[3]

6-16 **4** *5* **Performing Pocket (USA)**[4] 867 3-9-6 **77**.............................. JimCrowley 3 62
(David Simcock) *t.k.h: chsd ldr tl over 2f out: wknd u.p 2f out* **5/2**[2]

1m 12.8s (-0.30) **Going Correction** -0.075s/f (Stan) 4 Ran SP% **107.7**
Speed ratings (Par 100): **99,98,97,90**
CSF £6.88 TOTE £2.40; EX 6.20.
Owner The MHS 4x10 Partnership **Bred** Miss Mary Davidson & Mrs Steffi Von Schilcher **Trained** Malpas, Cheshire

T/Plt: £138.80 to a £1 stake. Pool:£78,737.64 - 413.94 winning tickets T/Qpdt: £20.70 to a £1 stake. Pool:£7,295.87 - 259.68 winning tickets SP

883 SOUTHWELL (L-H)
Wednesday, March 14

OFFICIAL GOING: Standard
Wind: Virtually nil Weather: Heavily overcast

898 ENJOY THE CHELTENHAM FESTIVAL WITH FREEBETTING.CO.UK H'CAP 5f (F)
1:55 (1:55) (Class 6) (0-65,65) 3-Y-0 **£1,704** (£503; £251) **Stalls** High

Form RPR

-520 **1** **Chateau Lola**[14] 734 3-8-5 **49**..............................(v) JoeFanning 6 54
(Derek Shaw) *prom: cl up 1/2-way: effrt to chal over 1f out: led ins fnl f: kpt on* **8/1**

6122 **2** *nk* **Reve Du Jour (IRE)**[13] 749 3-9-4 **65**.............................. SeanLevey(3) 3 69
(Alan McCabe) *led: rdn wl over 1f out: edgd lft ent fnl f: sn hdd and kpt on same pce* **6/4**[1]

06-0 **3** *2* **Jeremy Sue**[14] 734 3-8-2 **46** oh1..............................(b[1]) FrankieMcDonald 4 43
(Derek Haydn Jones) *dwlt: in rr and swtchd lft after 1f: hdwy to chse ldrs over 2f out: sn rdn and kpt on fnl f* **50/1**

104- **4** *1 1/2* **Phoenix Clubs (IRE)**[171] 6384 3-9-7 **65**.............................. BarryMcHugh 2 56
(Paul Midgley) *chsd ldrs: rdn along 2f out: kpt on same pce* **8/1**

1454 **5** *1* **M J Woodward**[12] 769 3-9-1 **59**.............................. LukeMorris 8 47
(Paul Green) *chsd ldrs: rdn along 2f out: sn one pce* **7/2**[3]

-562 **6** *shd* **George Fenton**[5] 845 3-8-2 **46** oh1..............................(tp) WilliamCarson 7 33
(Richard Guest) *towards rr and sn pushed along: rdn along 1/2-way: kpt on fr over 1f out* **10/3**[2]

-030 **7** *3/4* **Lady Nickandy (IRE)**[53] 250 3-8-9 **53**..............................(v) RoystonFfrench 1 38
(Karen Tutty) *cl up: rdn along 1/2-way: grad wknd fr wl over 1f out* **16/1**

0-04 **8** *6* **Script**[34] 481 3-8-1 **48** oh1 ow2.............................. JulieBurke(3) 5 11
(Alan Berry) *a in rr: rdn along 1/2-way: sn outpcd* **50/1**

58.97s (-0.73) **Going Correction** -0.225s/f (Stan) 8 Ran SP% **117.3**
Speed ratings (Par 96): **96,95,92,89,88 88,86,77**
toteswingers: 1&2 £3.40, 1&3 £20.00, 2&3 £18.80 CSF £21.05 CT £576.52 TOTE £7.00: £2.40, £1.10, £10.70; EX 32.20 TRIFECTA Not won..
Owner Basingstoke Commercials **Bred** Basingstoke Commercials **Trained** Sproxton, Leics

FOCUS
A moderate sprint handicap.

899 "CHAMPION CHASE FREE BETS" WITH FREEBETTING.CO.UK H'CAP 7f (F)
2:30 (2:31) (Class 5) (0-75,78) 4-Y-0+ **£2,264** (£673; £336; £168) **Stalls** Low

Form RPR

3112 **1** **Fluctuation (IRE)**[27] 585 4-9-0 **67**..............................(v) FrannyNorton 3 77
(Ian Williams) *trckd ldrs: hdwy over 2f out: rdn to chal ent fnl f: styd on wl to ld nr fin* **3/1**[2]

-531 **2** *nk* **St Oswald**[22] 646 4-9-7 **74**.............................. AdrianNicholls 1 83
(David Nicholls) *hld up in rr: hdwy on inner wl over 2f out: rdn to take slt ld over 1f out: drvn and edgd rt ins fnl f: hdd and no ex towards fin* **4/1**[3]

1041 **3** *2* **Beachwood Bay**[20] 670 4-8-5 **65**.............................. JoshBaudains(7) 5 69
(Jo Hughes) *trckd ldrs: hdwy 3f out: chal wl over 1f out: sn rdn and ev ch tl one pce ins fnl f* **5/2**[1]

2646 **4** *1 3/4* **Piceno (IRE)**[20] 674 4-9-6 **73**..............................(b) RobertWinston 4 73
(Scott Dixon) *sn led: rdn along wl over 2f out: drvn and hdd over 1f out: sn wknd and edgd lft fnl f* **7/1**

462- **5** *nse* **Dream Win**[271] 3112 6-9-5 **72**.............................. BarryMcHugh 6 72
(Brian Ellison) *hld up: hdwy on outer 3f out: rdn and ev ch 2f out: edgd lft and wknd appr fnl f* **12/1**

2511 **6** *5* **Imprimis Tagula (IRE)**[6] 834 8-9-11 **78** 6ex................(v) KierenFallon 2 65
(Alan Bailey) *trckd ldr: pushed along 3f out: rdn 2f out and sn btn* **5/2**[1]

1m 27.48s (-2.82) **Going Correction** -0.25s/f (Stan) 6 Ran SP% **122.3**
Speed ratings (Par 103): **106,105,103,101,101 95**
toteswingers: 1&2 £2.30, 1&3 £2.10, 2&3 £3.60 CSF £16.98 TOTE £5.20: £3.00, £1.60; EX 15.50.
Owner J Tredwell **Bred** Corduff Stud & T J Rooney **Trained** Portway, Worcs

FOCUS
They seemed to go reasonable pace in this ordinary handicap.
Imprimis Tagula(IRE) Official explanation: trainer had no explanation for the poor form shown

900 CHELTENHAM FESTIVAL FREE BETS WITH FREEBETTING.CO.UK H'CAP 1m (F)
3:05 (3:06) (Class 5) (0-70,70) 4-Y-0+ **£2,264** (£673; £336; £168) **Stalls** Low

Form RPR

6-61 **1** **Copperwood**[18] 713 7-9-7 **70**.............................. JoeFanning 2 84+
(Mark Johnston) *trckd ldrs: smooth hdwy 3f out: led wl over 1f out: pushed out* **13/2**

/352 **2** *2 1/2* **D'Urberville**[22] 646 5-9-5 **68**.............................. FrederikTylicki 5 74
(J R Jenkins) *towards rr: pushed along and hdwy 3f out: rdn to chse ldrs 2f out: edgd lft and kpt on fnl f to take 2nd nr fin* **11/4**[2]

-212 **3** *1/2* **Caledonia Prince**[20] 676 4-8-7 **63**..............................(p) JoshBaudains(7) 8 67
(Jo Hughes) *cl up: led 1/2-way: wd st and sn rdn: hdd wl over 1f out: kpt on same pce: lost 2nd towards fin* **6/4**[1]

4611 **4** *2 3/4* **Kipchak (IRE)**[7] 829 7-8-10 **59**..............................(b) HayleyTurner 4 57
(Conor Dore) *sn led: hdd 1/2-way: cl up and ev ch over 2f out tl wknd wl over 1f out* **6/1**[3]

35-0 **5** *2 3/4* **Brown Pete (IRE)**[20] 676 4-8-0 **56** oh1..............................(tp) NoraLooby(7) 1 48
(Richard Guest) *clsd up on inner: rdn along over 3f out and sn wknd* **20/1**

00-0 **6** *8* **Thrust Control (IRE)**[20] 676 5-8-9 **58** oh3 ow2................ TomEaves 6 33
(Tracy Waggott) *chsd ldrs: rdn along over 3f out: sn wknd* **40/1**

604- 7 3 ½ **Excuse Me**[93] 7739 4-8-8 57.........................(t) PJMcDonald 7 24+
(Kevin Ryan) *s.i.s: a bhd* **16/1**
000- 8 17 **Hab Reeh**[187] 5902 4-8-9 58......................... JamesSullivan 3
(Ruth Carr) *chsd ldrs: rdn along wl over 3f out: sn wknd and bhd* **7/1**
1m 41.61s (-2.09) **Going Correction** -0.25s/f (Stan) **8** Ran SP% **119.9**
Speed ratings (Par 103): **100,97,97,94,91 83,80,63**
toteswingers: 1&2 £3.20, 1&3 £3.40, 2&3 £2.10 CSF £26.06 CT £42.00 TOTE £7.20: £1.60, £1.10, £1.60; EX 34.30 Trifecta £71.90 Pool: £1,003.41 - 10.32 winning units..
Owner Always Trying Partnership VIII (E) **Bred** Hertford Offset Press **Trained** Middleham Moor, N Yorks

FOCUS
Another modest handicap.
Excuse Me Official explanation: jockey said gelding reared as stalls opened

901 BIGGEST FREE BETS WITH FREEBETTING.CO.UK (S) STKS 1m (F)
3:45 (3:45) (Class 6) 3-Y-O £1,704 (£503; £251) Stalls Low

Form RPR
00-3 1 **Smart Affair**[22] 641 3-8-7 46......................... AndreaAtzeni 2 55+
(Rod Millman) *in rr and sn pushed along: rdn along 1/2-way: hdwy 3f out: wd st: chsd ldrs 2f out: styd on wl u.p appr fnl f: led last 50yds* **14/1**
6221 2 1 ½ **Pelican Rock (IRE)**[6] 832 3-9-4 50......................... StephenCraine 7 62
(Tom Dascombe) *cl up: led 1/2-way: rdn clr 2f out: drvn ins fnl f: wknd and hdd last 50yds* **6/4**[1]
3422 3 1 ¾ **One More Roman (IRE)**[13] 748 3-9-4 63..............(vt) RobertWinston 3 58
(Gay Kelleway) *trckd ldrs: hdwy to chse ldr 3f out: rdn wl over 1f out: kpt on same pce u.p fnl f* **5/2**[2]
0334 4 6 **Outlaw Torn (IRE)**[13] 747 3-8-13 57.....................(e) CharlesEddery(5) 5 45
(Richard Guest) *chsd ldrs on inner: rdn along 3f out: sn outpcd* **16/1**
5-02 5 2 ¼ **Tectonic (IRE)**[13] 743 3-8-12 59.........................(p) MartinDwyer 6 34
(Chris Dwyer) *led to 1/2-way: cl up tl rdn wl over 2f out and grad wknd* **5/2**[2]
060- 6 3 ¼ **Brave One (IRE)**[142] 7058 3-8-7 0......................... AdrianNicholls 4 24
(David Nicholls) *dwlt: swtchd to outer sn after s: hdwy on outer 1/2-way: cl up 3f out: wd st: sn rdn and wknd 2f out* **20/1**
7 20 **Hurricane Hugo (IRE)**[33] 505 3-8-12 0.........................(p) TomEaves 1
(Ian Semple) *in rr: rdn along 1/2-way: sn outpcd and bhd* **12/1**[3]
1m 42.45s (-1.25) **Going Correction** -0.25s/f (Stan) **7** Ran SP% **122.1**
Speed ratings (Par 96): **96,94,92,86,84 81,61**
toteswingers: 1&2 £4.30, 1&3 £3.40, 2&3 £1.80 CSF £38.63 TOTE £17.20: £7.80, £2.10; EX 44.50.The winner was sold to Alan Bailey for 3,000gns. Pelican Rock was claimed by Mr A. Crook for £5,000.
Owner Rod Millman Racing Club **Bred** T E Pocock **Trained** Kentisbeare, Devon

FOCUS
A poor seller.

902 COMPARE FREE BETS WITH FREEBETTING.CO.UK H'CAP 1m 6f (F)
4:25 (4:25) (Class 5) (0-75,75) 4-Y-O+ £2,432 (£842) Stalls Low

Form RPR
214- 1 **Priceless Art (IRE)**[10] 7900 7-9-12 75......................... PJMcDonald 4 80+
(Alan Swinbank) *trckd ldng pair: hdwy to ld over 4f out: pushed wl clr fnl 2f: unchal* **15/8**[2]
-063 2 11 **Three White Socks (IRE)**[20] 673 5-8-13 62..............(b[1]) BarryMcHugh 2 62
(Brian Ellison) *trckd ldr tl led after 6f: rdn along and hdd over 4f out: sn outpcd* **3/1**[3]
/26- P **Palawi (IRE)**[18] 5857 5-9-4 67......................... TomEaves 1
(John Quinn) *led tl p.u lame after 6f: fatally injured* **1/1**[1]
3m 6.44s (-1.86) **Going Correction** -0.25s/f (Stan) **3** Ran SP% **109.8**
Speed ratings (Par 103): **95,88,**
CSF £6.76 TOTE £3.20; EX 3.40.
Owner Matthew Green & David Manasseh **Bred** Lady Bamford **Trained** Melsonby, N Yorks

FOCUS
Just the three runners, but no shortage of drama.

903 FREE HORSE RACING BETS WITH FREEBETTING.CO.UK MAIDEN STKS 7f (F)
5:05 (5:06) (Class 5) 3-Y-O+ £2,264 (£673; £336; £168) Stalls Low

Form RPR
1 **Minstrels Gallery (IRE)** 3-8-12 0......................... FrederikTylicki 6 81+
(J R Jenkins) *trckd ldng pair: hdwy and cl up over 2f out: rdn to chal wl over 1f out: led ins fnl f: styd on wl towards fin* **85/40**[2]
004- 2 ½ **Hamis Al Bin (IRE)**[227] 4571 3-8-12 69......................... JoeFanning 4 79
(Mark Johnston) *led 2f: cl up: led again wl over 2f out: sn jnd and rdn wl over 1f out: drvn and hdd ins fnl f: no ex towards fin* **8/15**[1]
65 3 14 **Dilizan (IRE)**[41] 383 3-8-12 0......................... BarryMcHugh 3 42
(Brian Ellison) *in rr: hdwy 3f out: rdn over 2f out: styd on: nvr a factor* **10/1**
04-2 4 1 ¾ **Orwellian**[58] 194 3-8-12 59.........................(p) TomEaves 1 38
(Bryan Smart) *cl up on inner: led after 2f: rdn along over 3f out: hdd wl over 2f out and sn wknd* **7/1**[3]
406- 5 1 **Eqtiraab (IRE)**[137] 7158 4-9-7 59......................... JacobButterfield(7) 5 41
(Tony Coyle) *chsd ldrs: rdn along 1/2-way: sn outpcd* **33/1**
030- 6 2 ¾ **Spread Boy (IRE)**[89] 7781 5-9-7 45......................... MatthewHopkins(7) 8 34
(Alan Berry) *a towards rr* **100/1**
1m 27.35s (-2.95) **Going Correction** -0.25s/f (Stan)
WFA 3 from 4yo+ 16lb **6** Ran SP% **122.8**
Speed ratings (Par 103): **106,105,89,87,86 83**
toteswingers: 1&2 £1.60, 1&3 £2.30, 2&3 £1.50 CSF £4.03 TOTE £3.40: £1.20, £1.20; EX 6.50 Trifecta £26.80 Pool: £512.77 - 14.15 winning units..
Owner The Three Honest Men **Bred** Morecool Stud **Trained** Royston, Herts

FOCUS
A weak maiden and the front pair had the race to themselves from a long way out. There was a huge gap back to the rest.

904 FREE BETTING WITH FREEBETTING.CO.UK H'CAP 6f (F)
5:40 (5:42) (Class 6) (0-60,66) 4-Y-O+ £1,704 (£503; £251) Stalls Low

Form RPR
0-05 1 **Strictly Pink (IRE)**[47] 323 4-9-6 59......................... KierenFallon 3 68
(Alan Bailey) *cl up: led wl over 2f out: rdn over 1f out: drvn ins fnl f: jst hld on* **9/2**[3]
5001 2 nse **Elhamri**[8] 813 8-9-13 66 6ex......................... HayleyTurner 7 75
(Conor Dore) *in tch: hdwy to trck ldrs 1/2-way: effrt to chal over 1f out: rdn ins fnl f: drvn and kpt on towards fin: jst hld* **3/1**[2]
5156 3 1 ½ **Ridgeway Hawk**[13] 752 4-9-6 59.........................(v) RobertHavlin 4 63
(Mark Usher) *outpcd and in rr: wd st and sn rdn: styd on wl fr over 1f out: nrst fin* **9/1**

2054 4 nk **Gracie's Gift (IRE)**[6] 831 10-8-6 50.........................(v) CharlesEddery(5) 8 53
(Richard Guest) *chsd ldrs: hdwy 2f out: rdn to chse ldng pair ins fnl f: sn one pce* **11/1**
6262 5 1 **Itsthursdayalready**[8] 813 5-8-9 55......................... JackDuern(7) 1 55
(Mark Brisbourne) *chsd ldrs on inner: rdn along 2f out: drvn and no imp fnl f* **9/4**[1]
6345 6 2 **Bookiesindex Boy**[27] 580 8-9-4 57.........................(b) FrederikTylicki 6 51
(J R Jenkins) *cl up: effrt on bit and ev ch 2f out: rdn over 1f out: sn wknd* **8/1**
-210 7 ¾ **Cut The Cackle (IRE)**[32] 526 6-9-2 60.................(bt) DuilioDaSilva(5) 5 52
(Richard Guest) *outpcd and bhd fr 1/2-way* **15/2**
6500 8 6 **Grand Stitch (USA)**[18] 606 6-0-10 64......................... NeilFarley(5) 2 28
(Declan Carroll) *led: rdn along 1/2-way: sn hdd & wknd* **16/1**
1m 15.25s (-1.25) **Going Correction** -0.25s/f (Stan) **8** Ran SP% **121.0**
Speed ratings (Par 101): **98,97,95,95,94 91,90,82**
toteswingers: 1&2 £3.00, 1&3 £8.30, 2&3 £7.20 CSF £19.66 CT £120.74 TOTE £4.50: £1.80, £1.60, £4.40; EX 20.40 Trifecta £136.00 Pool: £814.74 - 4.43 winning units..
Owner A J H **Bred** Tally-Ho Stud **Trained** Newmarket, Suffolk

FOCUS
A moderate sprint handicap to end, but the pace was solid.
T/Plt: £46.50 to a £1 stake. Pool: £57,551.04. 902.82 winning tickets. T/Qpdt: £8.70 to a £1 stake. Pool: £2,985.82. 251.94 winning tickets. JR

866 WOLVERHAMPTON (A.W) (L-H)
Thursday, March 15

OFFICIAL GOING: Standard
Wind: Light, behind. Weather: Overcast

905 "WORLD HURDLE FREE BETS" WITH FREEBETTING.CO.UK H'CAP 5f 20y(P)
5:45 (5:49) (Class 5) (0-75,73) 3-Y-O £2,264 (£673; £336; £168) Stalls Low

Form RPR
4411 1 **Redair (IRE)**[13] 768 3-9-0 71......................... MatthewCosham(5) 6 83
(David Evans) *hld up: hdwy over 1f out: rdn to ld and edgd rt ins fnl f: r.o wl* **6/1**
44-0 2 2 ¼ **Towbee**[13] 769 3-8-7 59.........................(b[1]) JamesSullivan 1 62
(Michael Easterby) *w ldr tl led over 3f out: rdn: hung rt and hdd ins fnl f: sn hung lft: styd on same pce* **9/2**[2]
164- 3 2 ¼ **Beau Mistral (IRE)**[174] 6293 3-9-4 73......................... RobertLButler(3) 2 68
(Paul Green) *chsd ldrs: rdn over 1f out: styd on same pce fnl f* **20/1**
-056 4 1 ¾ **Miserere Mei (IRE)**[41] 394 3-8-0 55.........................(e) DeclanCannon(3) 9 44
(Richard Guest) *hld up: hdwy 1/2-way: rdn over 1f out: wknd ins fnl f* **33/1**
566- 5 ¾ **Molly Jones**[153] 6843 3-9-2 68......................... DaneO'Neill 8 54
(Derek Haydn Jones) *s.s: bhd: rdn over 1f out: r.o ins fnl f: nvr nrr* **14/1**
0-12 6 nk **Gin Twist**[24] 637 3-9-5 71.........................(b) RichardKingscote 4 56
(Tom Dascombe) *s.v.s: rdn over 1f out: r.o ins fnl f: nvr on terms* **3/1**[1]
002- 7 1 ¾ **Alnair (IRE)**[97] 7692 3-8-4 61......................... NeilFarley(5) 5 40
(Declan Carroll) *chsd ldrs: rdn over 1f out: wknd fnl f* **14/1**
1-33 8 2 ¼ **Code Six (IRE)**[14] 749 3-9-0 66......................... TomEaves 3 37
(Bryan Smart) *led: hdd over 3f out: rdn over 1f out: sn wknd* **9/2**[2]
1 9 1 ¾ **Russian Bullet**[13] 769 3-9-0 66......................... FergusSweeney 11 31
(Jamie Osborne) *chsd ldrs: rdn over 1f out: sn wknd* **5/1**[3]
310- 10 8 **Rusty Rocket (IRE)**[159] 6699 3-9-7 73......................... LukeMorris 7
(Paul Green) *prom: pushed along over 3f out: wknd 1/2-way* **12/1**
1m 2.0s (-0.30) **Going Correction** -0.025s/f (Stan) **10** Ran SP% **121.0**
Speed ratings (Par 98): **101,97,93,91,89 89,86,82,80,67**
Tote Swingers:1&2:£5.20, 2&3:£21.60, 1&3:£11.50 CSF £34.57 CT £531.28 TOTE £5.00: £1.60, £2.10, £6.40; EX 33.60 Trifecta £493.70 Pool £4,577.15 - 6.86 winning units..
Owner J & J Potter & The late Mrs S Edwards **Bred** Noel O'Callaghan **Trained** Pandy, Monmouths

FOCUS
A competitive sprint handicap run at a solid pace with the field well grouped turning for home. The winner was back to her 2yo peak and the form is straightforward behind.
Gin Twist Official explanation: jockey said filly planted itself in stalls and missed the break
Alnair(IRE) Official explanation: jockey said gelding hung right-handed
Rusty Rocket(IRE) Official explanation: jockey said colt hung right-handed

906 ENJOY THE CHELTENHAM FESTIVAL WITH FREEBETTING.CO.UK (S) STKS 1m 141y(P)
6:15 (6:15) (Class 6) 4-Y-O+ £1,704 (£503; £251) Stalls Low

Form RPR
3211 1 **Red Somerset (USA)**[13] 760 9-9-4 72......................... KieranO'Neill 3 84
(Mike Murphy) *chsd ldrs: rdn over 2f out: led 1f out: drvn out* **6/4**[2]
4452 2 nk **Dazzling Valentine**[10] 804 4-8-7 71......................... JoeFanning 4 72
(Alan Bailey) *hld up: hdwy 2f out: nt clr run and swtchd rt jst over 1f out: rdn and ev ch ins fnl f: r.o* **6/5**[1]
5115 3 3 ¼ **Mcconnell (USA)**[9] 812 7-9-4 75.........................(b) WilliamCarson 5 76
(Richard Guest) *s.i.s: racd keenly and sn prom: chsd clr ldr 3f out: rdn 2f out: styd on same pce fnl f* **15/2**[3]
0-26 4 ½ **Absolute Princess**[21] 672 4-8-4 62......................... RyanPowell(3) 2 64
(Scott Dixon) *chsd ldr tl led over 4f out: pushed clr over 3f out: rdn and hung lft over 1f out: sn hdd: no ex ins fnl f* **25/1**
5154 5 2 **Faithful Ruler (USA)**[24] 634 8-8-11 70.................(p) DarrenEgan(7) 6 71
(Ronald Harris) *hld up: rdn over 2f out: styd on same pce fr over 1f out* **12/1**
-000 6 19 **Portrush Storm**[40] 430 7-7-8 37......................... JohnFahy 1 20
(Ray Peacock) *led: hdd over 4f out: rdn and wknd over 2f out* **100/1**
1m 49.96s (-0.54) **Going Correction** -0.025s/f (Stan) **6** Ran SP% **109.7**
Speed ratings (Par 101): **101,100,97,97,95 78**
Tote Swingers:1&2:£1.50, 2&3:£2.20, 1&3:£1.10 CSF £3.43 TOTE £2.40: £1.10, £1.50; EX 4.10.The winner was bought in for 3,750gns. Dazzling Valentine was the subject of a friendly claim.
Owner M Murphy **Bred** Haras D'Etreham **Trained** Westoning, Beds

FOCUS
A fairly competitive event for this grade but the form may not be as good as it looks on paper.

907 FREE HORSE RACING BETS WITH FREEBETTING.CO.UK H'CAP 1m 1f 103y(P)
6:45 (6:45) (Class 4) (0-85,85) 4-Y-O+ £4,204 (£1,251; £625; £312) Stalls Low

Form RPR
3112 1 **Patriotic (IRE)**[17] 722 4-8-4 73 ow1......................... RaulDaSilva(5) 2 86+
(Chris Dwyer) *a.p: shkn up over 1f out: led ins fnl f: r.o wl* **4/1**[2]
2621 2 2 ½ **Standpoint**[27] 603 6-8-11 82.........................(p) JackDuern(7) 9 88
(Reg Hollinshead) *sn chsng ldr: led over 2f out: rdn over 1f out: hdd and unable qck ins fnl f* **11/1**
40-0 3 shd **First Post (IRE)**[12] 785 5-9-7 85......................... DaneO'Neill 7 91
(Derek Haydn Jones) *a.p: rdn over 1f out: styd on* **12/1**

15-6 **4** 1 **Gritstone**[28] 584 5-9-2 **80** PaulHanagan 5 84
(Richard Fahey) *a.p: chsd ldr over 2f out: rdn over 1f out: no ex ins fnl f* **7/2**[1]
52-0 **5** 3 **Chosen Forever**[56] 216 7-8-12 **79** DaleSwift(3) 13 77
(Geoffrey Oldroyd) *hld up: rdn over 2f out: r.o ins fnl f: nvr nrr* **14/1**
1034 **6** ½ **Thunderstruck**[12] 694 7-9-6 **84** (p) IanMongan 4 82
(Scott Dixon) *s.i.s: pushed along early in rr: hdwy u.p over 1f out: nvr trbld ldrs* **9/1**
-000 **7** 1½ **Calypso Magic (IRE)**[25] 630 4-9-2 **80** LukeMorris 6 75
(Linda Jewell) *hld up in tch: racd keenly: rdn over 1f out: styd on same pce* **50/1**
-121 **8** ½ **Twinkled**[20] 685 4-8-0 **71** IanBurns(7) 3 65
(Michael Bell) *s.i.s: hld up: rdn over 1f out: nvr on terms* **14/1**
1-20 **9** 1¾ **West End Lad**[31] 548 9-9-1 **79** (b) RussKennemore 10 69
(Roy Bowring) *mid-div: hdwy u.p over 2f out: wknd fnl f* **14/1**
4420 **10** 4 **Veroon (IRE)**[19] 712 6-9-2 **80** (p) FrederikTylicki 11 63
(James Given) *hld up: rdn over 2f out: n.d* **13/2**[3]
4343 **11** 3½ **Tevez**[20] 694 7-9-6 **84** DavidProbert 1 60
(Des Donovan) *hld up: rdn over 2f out: a in rr* **11/1**
16- **12** 5 **Dubai Bay (FR)**[172] 6383 4-8-9 **73** MickyFenton 12 40
(Paul Midgley) *led 7f: sn rdn and wknd* **20/1**
024- **13** ½ **Calaf**[170] 6429 4-8-11 **75** TonyHamilton 8 41
(Richard Fahey) *plld hrd and prom: rdn over 3f out: wknd over 2f out* **14/1**

2m 0.02s (-1.68) **Going Correction** -0.025s/f (Stan) **13** Ran SP% **123.3**
Speed ratings (Par 105): **106,103,103,102,100 99,98,97,96,92 89,85,84**
Tote Swingers:1&2:£7.60, 2&3:£29.10, 1&3:£8.20 CSF £49.68 CT £502.22 TOTE £3.80: £1.30, £3.10, £4.20; EX 50.30 Trifecta £324.10 Pool £2,185.54 - 4.99 winning units..
Owner M M Foulger **Bred** Darley **Trained** Six Mile Bottom, Cambs

FOCUS
A moderate handicap run at a steady pace, with the first four home racing prominently throughout. The winner is progressive and has every chance of rating higher.
Calypso Magic(IRE) Official explanation: vet said gelding finished lame in front

908 FREE BETTING WITH FREEBETTING.CO.UK MAIDEN STKS 1m 1f 103y(P)
7:15 (7:19) (Class 5) 3-Y-0+ **£2,264** (£673; £336; £168) **Stalls** Low

Form RPR
1 **Modernism** 3-8-7 0 JoeFanning 5 78+
(Mark Johnston) *chsd ldr tl led over 2f out: shkn up ins fnl f: styd on* **11/2**[3]
32 **2** 1 **Ruacana**[17] 723 3-8-7 0 HayleyTurner 13 76
(Michael Bell) *hld up: hdwy over 2f out: rdn over 1f out: r.o to go 2nd post: nt rch wnr* **3/1**[2]
04- **3** nk **Eshaab (USA)**[169] 6462 3-8-7 0 PaulHanagan 8 75
(Ed Dunlop) *mid-div: hdwy over 6f out: rdn and edgd lft over 1f out: styd on* **8/11**[1]
4 shd **Fleeting Image** 3-8-2 0 FrannyNorton 2 70+
(Alan Bailey) *chsd ldrs: shkn up over 1f out: styd on* **12/1**
5 9 **Raamz (IRE)**[27] 5-9-8 0 MartinDwyer 9 56+
(Kevin Morgan) *hld up: hdwy u.p and hung lft over 1f out: hmpd ins fnl f: n.d* **50/1**
03 **6** 2 **Eastern Amour (IRE)**[20] 693 3-8-7 0 AndreaAtzeni 11 52
(Marco Botti) *chsd ldrs: rdn over 2f out: wkng whn hung lft fnl f* **10/1**
64 **7** 4 **Icy Quiet**[13] 762 4-9-8 0 MickyFenton 7 44
(Tobias B P Coles) *mid-div: rdn over 3f out: wknd 2f out* **40/1**
8 ¾ **David's Folly (IRE)** 3-8-2 0 LukeMorris 1 37
(Bryn Palling) *s.s: a in rr* **66/1**
9 1¼ **Magical Marvin** 3-8-7 0 NeilChalmers 10 39
(Michael Appleby) *in rr: rdn and wknd over 2f out* **80/1**
4 **10** 3½ **Kata Rock (USA)**[24] 635 5-9-13 0 BarryMcHugh 4 37
(Brian Rothwell) *sn led: rdn and hdd over 2f out: n.m.r and wknd sn after* **33/1**
06 **11** 1¼ **Maggie Pink**[17] 723 3-7-13 0 DominicFox(3) 12 24
(Michael Appleby) *hld up: a in rr: wknd 3f out* **100/1**
0 **12** 11 **Fa'Side Castle (IRE)**[17] 723 3-8-7 0 AndrewMullen 6
(Keith Dalgleish) *chsd ldrs: rdn over 3f out: sn wknd* **80/1**
13 48 **Leototo** 5-9-13 0 IanMongan 3
(Linda Jewell) *s.s: pushed along and hung lft fnl 6f: a in rr: lost tch fnl 4f: t.o* **100/1**

2m 1.17s (-0.53) **Going Correction** -0.025s/f (Stan)
WFA 3 from 4yo+ 20lb **13** Ran SP% **128.4**
Speed ratings (Par 103): **101,100,99,99,91 89,86,85,84,81 80,70,27**
Tote Swingers:1&2:£3.80, 2&3:£1.40, 1&3:£3.00 CSF £23.89 TOTE £7.70: £2.10, £1.30, £1.10; EX 27.90 Trifecta £85.70 Pool £3,628.86 - 31.31 winning units..
Owner Sheikh Hamdan Bin Mohammed Al Maktoum **Bred** Darley **Trained** Middleham Moor, N Yorks

FOCUS
A fair maiden, run at a steady pace and won in good style by a Mark Johnston newcomer. The form is rated around the second.

909 COMPARE FREE BETS WITH FREEBETTING.CO.UK H'CAP 1m 141y(P)
7:45 (7:46) (Class 5) (0-70,69) 4-Y-0+ **£2,264** (£673; £336; £168) **Stalls** Low

Form RPR
56-5 **1** **Thatcherite (IRE)**[23] 646 4-9-6 **68** (t) StephenCraine 8 78
(Tony Coyle) *s.i.s: hld up: hdwy over 2f out: rdn to ld wl ins fnl f: r.o* **6/1**[3]
6262 **2** nk **Alhaban (IRE)**[13] 760 6-9-7 **69** LukeMorris 7 78
(Ronald Harris) *mid-div: hdwy 1/2-way: rdn over 1f out: led ins fnl f: sn hdd: hung lft: r.o* **9/2**[2]
-331 **3** 4 **Moral Issue**[20] 692 4-9-4 **69** DaleSwift(3) 3 69+
(Ian McInnes) *w ldr tl led over 5f out: rdn over 1f out: hdd ins fnl f: btn whn hmpd sn after* **2/1**[1]
1264 **4** 1¼ **Valley Tiger**[15] 736 4-9-1 **63** PaulHanagan 6 60
(Richard Fahey) *dwlt: hld up: hdwy u.p over 1f out: nvr trbld ldrs* **6/1**[3]
4-06 **5** 6 **Kyle Of Bute**[24] 636 6-9-1 **63** RussKennemore 5 46
(Brian Baugh) *chsd ldrs: rdn over 2f out: wknd fnl f* **7/1**
6-00 **6** 11 **Smirfy's Silver**[45] 361 8-8-12 **60** RichardKingscote 1 18
(Michael Mullineaux) *led 3f: rdn over 3f out: wknd 2f out* **16/1**
-260 **7** 1½ **Justcallmehandsome**[41] 403 10-9-1 **63** (v) HayleyTurner 2 18
(Dominic Ffrench Davis) *dwlt: hld up: rdn over 2f out: n.d* **8/1**
550- **8** 27 **Loyal N Trusted**[142] 7084 4-8-12 **60** WilliamCarson 4
(Richard Price) *chsd ldrs: rdn over 3f out: wknd over 2f out* **16/1**

1m 49.73s (-0.77) **Going Correction** -0.025s/f (Stan) **8** Ran SP% **115.5**
Speed ratings (Par 103): **102,101,98,97,91 81,80,56**
Tote Swingers:1&2:£7.50, 2&3:£3.50, 1&3:£6.10 CSF £33.42 CT £73.10 TOTE £9.10: £2.80, £1.30, £1.10; EX 45.20 Trifecta £275.40 Pool £2,940.84 - 7.90 winning units..
Owner Brian Kerr & Tony Coyle **Bred** Taroka Equine Investments **Trained** Norton, N Yorks

FOCUS
This handicap was run at a fierce early pace that suited those coming from behind. A personal best from the winner and the form could be rated a few pounds higher.

910 BIGGEST FREE BETS WITH FREEBETTING.CO.UK H'CAP 5f 20y(P)
8:15 (8:15) (Class 7) (0-50,50) 4-Y-0+ **£1,704** (£503; £251) **Stalls** Low

Form RPR
0-51 **1** **Lizzy's Dream**[20] 691 4-9-2 **49** LeeNewman 1 64+
(Robin Bastiman) *sn chsng ldrs: led over 1f out: rdn clr fnl f* **1/1**[1]
-664 **2** 2¾ **Hambleton**[14] 740 5-9-2 **49** (p) TomEaves 5 52
(Bryan Smart) *s.i.s: hld up: nt clr run 1/2-way: hdwy over 1f out: r.o to go 2nd wl ins fnl f: no ch w wnr* **5/1**[2]
3633 **3** 1¾ **Porthgwidden Beach (USA)**[12] 783 4-8-6 **46** (tp) NoelGarbutt(7) 2 43
(Anthony Middleton) *led: rdn: edgd rt and hdd over 1f out: no ex ins fnl f* **7/1**[3]
0024 **4** ½ **Deveze (IRE)**[12] 783 4-9-3 **50** (b) RichardKingscote 9 45+
(Milton Bradley) *stdd s: hld up: hdwy over 1f out: nt trble ldrs* **9/1**
005- **5** ¾ **Autocracy**[231] 4461 5-9-3 **50** (tp) JohnFahy 8 42
(Daniel Kubler) *prom: rdn over 1f out: no ex fnl f* **20/1**
0-00 **6** nk **Love Club**[20] 691 4-8-9 **45** RyanPowell(3) 4 36
(Brian Baugh) *chsd ldrs: rdn 1/2-way: no ex fnl f* **33/1**
05-3 **7** ½ **The Magic Of Rio**[67] 95 6-8-12 **45** HayleyTurner 10 34
(John Balding) *chsd ldrs: rdn over 1f out: wknd ins fnl f* **16/1**
4006 **8** 3¾ **Takajan (IRE)**[7] 831 5-8-13 **46** (b) LukeMorris 7 22
(Mark Brisbourne) *prom: rdn 1/2-way: wknd over 1f out* **10/1**
030- **9** 2½ **Dolly Bay**[97] 7693 4-9-3 **50** JoeFanning 6 20
(Julia Feilden) *s.i.s: outpcd: sme hdwy over 1f out: wknd fnl f* **20/1**
0650 **10** 3½ **Bird Dog**[28] 580 6-8-10 **50** (v) DannyBrock(7) 11
(Phil McEntee) *prom: rdn 1/2-way: wknd wl over 1f out* **14/1**

1m 2.38s (0.08) **Going Correction** -0.025s/f (Stan) **10** Ran SP% **123.3**
Speed ratings (Par 97): **98,93,90,90,88 88,87,81,77,71**
Tote Swingers:1&2:£3.90, 2&3:£5.70, 1&3:£4.80 CSF £6.41 CT £26.20 TOTE £1.30: £1.10, £1.70, £2.70; EX 7.60 Trifecta £14.80 Pool £325.47 - 16.23 winning units..
Owner Mrs P Bastiman **Bred** Sheikh Abdulla Bin Isa Al-Khalifa **Trained** Cowthorpe, N Yorks

FOCUS
A low-grade handicap, but the winner is improving and may cope with a rise in grade. The runner-up sets a solid enough standard.
Porthgwidden Beach(USA) Official explanation: jockey said filly hung right on final bend

911 CHELTENHAM FESTIVAL FREE BETS WITH FREEBETTING.CO.UK H'CAP (DIV I) 5f 216y(P)
8:45 (8:46) (Class 5) (0-70,70) 4-Y-0+ **£2,264** (£673; £336; £168) **Stalls** Low

Form RPR
3305 **1** **Waabel**[19] 710 5-8-12 **61** WilliamCarson 8 75+
(Richard Guest) *hld up: drvn along 1/2-way: hdwy over 1f out: led ins fnl f: rdn out* **5/2**[1]
0604 **2** 2¼ **Whipphound**[17] 719 4-9-2 **65** LukeMorris 1 72
(Mark Brisbourne) *mid-div: hdwy over 2f out: led over 1f out: rdn: edgd lft and hdd ins fnl f: styd on same pce* **11/2**
-041 **3** 2½ **Mother Jones**[17] 719 4-9-2 **65** HayleyTurner 10 64
(David Evans) *chsd ldrs: rdn and ev ch over 1f out: no ex ins fnl f* **5/1**[3]
14-0 **4** ¾ **You'relikemefrank**[17] 718 6-9-5 **68** (p) NeilChalmers 5 64
(Richard Ford) *hld up: hdwy over 1f out: styd on same pce fnl f* **25/1**
04-5 **5** 1 **Pitkin**[20] 696 4-8-11 **60** PaddyAspell 3 53
(Michael Easterby) *hld up in tch: rdn over 1f out: styd on same pce* **7/2**[2]
5020 **6** ½ **Riflessione**[13] 763 6-8-8 **64** (b) DarrenEgan(7) 7 56
(Ronald Harris) *chsd ldr tl led 2f out: rdn: edgd rt and hdd over 1f out: wknd ins fnl f* **14/1**
010/ **7** 2½ **Tagula Breeze (IRE)**[929] 5421 6-9-1 **67** DaleSwift(3) 2 51
(Ian McInnes) *trckd ldrs: plld hrd: rdn and hung lft over 1f out: wknd fnl f* **20/1**
0-05 **8** 7 **Billy Red**[22] 647 8-9-7 **70** (b) FergusSweeney 9 31
(J R Jenkins) *led 4f: sn rdn: n.m.r over 1f out: wknd fnl f* **6/1**
26-0 **9** 6 **Gooseberry Bush**[15] 735 5-8-13 **62** LiamKeniry 6
(Gary Brown) *dwlt: outpcd: bhd fr 1/2-way* **22/1**

1m 14.7s (-0.30) **Going Correction** -0.025s/f (Stan) **9** Ran SP% **116.8**
Speed ratings (Par 103): **101,98,94,93,92 91,88,79,71**
Tote Swingers:1&2:£5.60, 2&3:£3.90, 1&3:£1.90 CSF £16.30 CT £64.43 TOTE £4.40: £1.60, £2.00, £1.30; EX 24.60 Trifecta £132.60 Pool £340.55 - 1.90 winning units..
Owner Rakebackmypoker.com **Bred** Shadwell Estate Company Limited **Trained** Stainforth, S Yorks

FOCUS
A messy sprint handicap run at a strong pace in which the field were well grouped turning for home. The winner was well treated on last spring's form.
Riflessione Official explanation: jockey said gelding hung right-handed

912 CHELTENHAM FESTIVAL FREE BETS WITH FREEBETTING.CO.UK H'CAP (DIV II) 5f 216y(P)
9:15 (9:17) (Class 5) (0-70,69) 4-Y-0+ **£2,264** (£673; £336; £168) **Stalls** Low

Form RPR
4320 **1** **Captain Dimitrios**[19] 710 4-8-12 **65** (v) MatthewCosham(5) 7 74
(David Evans) *w ldr tl led wl over 1f out: sn hdd: rallied to ld wl ins fnl f: r.o* **13/2**[3]
0-04 **2** shd **Methaaly (IRE)**[6] 844 9-9-3 **65** (be) RichardKingscote 6 74
(Michael Mullineaux) *hld up in tch: rdn over 1f out: edgd lft ins fnl f: r.o* **11/1**
0005 **3** 1½ **Memphis Man**[26] 623 9-8-7 **55** RichardThomas 5 59
(David Evans) *s.i.s: hld up: rdn over 1f out: r.o ins fnl f: wnt 3rd nr fin: nt rch ldrs* **25/1**
1553 **4** hd **Blown It (USA)**[6] 844 6-9-7 **69** JoeFanning 3 73
(Keith Dalgleish) *chsd ldrs: led over 1f out: sn rdn: hdd and unable qck wl ins fnl f* **4/1**[2]
330 **5** nse **My Lord**[6] 844 4-8-12 **67** DarrenEgan(7) 9 70
(Ronald Harris) *prom: rdn over 1f out: styd on* **14/1**
3222 **6** ¾ **Cliffords Reprieve**[13] 763 4-8-13 **61** (b) WilliamCarson 4 62
(Eric Wheeler) *hld up: r.o ins fnl f: n.m.r towards fin: nt rch ldrs* **4/1**[2]
-050 **7** ¾ **Steel City Boy (IRE)**[63] 139 9-8-10 **58** LukeMorris 2 57
(Garry Woodward) *led: hdd wl over 1f out: no ex ins fnl f* **33/1**
444U **8** hd **Lucky Dan (IRE)**[24] 639 6-9-0 **65** RobertLButler(3) 1 63
(Paul Green) *s.i.s: hld up: rdn over 1f out: nvr trbld ldrs* **25/1**
-630 **9** 1½ **Powerful Pierre**[35] 478 5-8-13 **64** (v) LeeTopliss(3) 10 58
(Ian McInnes) *s.i.s: sn pushed along and prom: rdn over 2f out: styd on same pce fr over 1f out* **33/1**

5-11 **10** 2½ **Consistant**[34] [498] 4-9-0 **62**.................................... AdamKirby 8 48
(Brian Baugh) *dwlt: hld up: rdn over 2f out: n.d* **13/8**[1]
1m 14.77s (-0.23) **Going Correction** -0.025s/f (Stan) **10** Ran SP% **120.0**
Speed ratings (Par 103): **100,99,97,97,97 96,95,95,93,89**
Tote Swingers:1&2:£11.70, 2&3:£13.20, 1&3:£22.10 CSF £73.26 CT £1676.73 TOTE £10.00: £3.10, £4.60, £3.60; EX 62.60 TRIFECTA Not won..
Owner Wayne Clifford **Bred** W G H Barrons **Trained** Pandy, Monmouths

FOCUS
A competitive sprint handicap, run at a strong pace. Straightforward form.
Consistant Official explanation: jockey said gelding had no more to give
T/Plt: £21.30 to a £1 stake. Pool £97,053.57. 3,323.48 winning tickets T/Qpdt: £4.20 to a £1 stake. Pool £8,369.49. 1,453.08 winning tickets CR

913 - (Foreign Racing) - See Raceform Interactive

865 DEAUVILLE (R-H)
Thursday, March 15
OFFICIAL GOING: Fibresand: standard

914a PRIX MONTENICA (LISTED RACE) (3YO COLTS & GELDINGS) (FIBRESAND) 6f 110y
3:05 (12:00) 3-Y-O **£22,916** (£9,166; £6,875; £4,583; £2,291)

RPR
1 **Lord Sinclair (USA)**[32] 3-9-2 0.................................... ThierryThulliez 3 103
(F Chappet, France) **9/2**[2]
2 *snk* **Robert Le Diable (FR)**[32] [542] 3-9-2 0............. Pierre-CharlesBoudot 6 102
(D Prod'Homme, France) **53/10**[3]
3 *2* **Vaniloquio (IRE)**[112] [7533] 3-9-2 0............. Christophe-PatriceLemaire 2 96
(N Clement, France) **6/4**[1]
4 *shd* **Hurry Up George**[77] [7906] 3-9-2 0.................................... JimCrowley 8 96
(Ralph Beckett) *broke wl to r cl 3rd on outer: rdn early in st: picked up wl: u.p ent fnl f: styd on wl wout threatening ldrs: lost 3rd on line* **17/2**
5 *1¾* **Paris Blue (FR)**[112] [7533] 3-9-2 0.................................... MaximeGuyon 7 91
(J-L Pelletan, France) **13/1**
6 *½* **Happy Sun Percy**[13] 3-9-2 0.................................... StephanePasquier 5 89
(G Doleuze, France) **8/1**
7 *1¾* **Paraggi**[114] [7508] 3-9-2 0.................................... GregoryBenoist 1 84
(M Delzangles, France) **14/1**
8 *3* **Sea Trial (FR)**[112] [7533] 3-9-2 0.................................... JohanVictoire 4 76
(Mme C Head-Maarek, France) **13/1**
1m 18.5s (78.50) **8** Ran SP% **116.6**
WIN (incl. 1 euro stake): 5.50. PLACES: 1.60, 1.50, 1.20. DF: 10.50. SF: 23.80.
Owner Ecurie Des Clos **Bred** Mme C Morange **Trained** France

823 LINGFIELD (L-H)
Friday, March 16
OFFICIAL GOING: Standard
Wind: light breeze behind Weather: cloudy

915 GOLD CUP FREE BETS WITH FREEBETTING.CO.UK CLASSIFIED CLAIMING STKS 1m 2f (P)
1:55 (1:55) (Class 6) 4-Y-O+ **£1,704** (£503; £251) **Stalls** Low

Form RPR
0-63 **1** **Hurricane Spirit (IRE)**[11] [804] 8-8-3 73.................... NatashaEaton(7) 3 72
(Terry Clement) *trckd ldrs: led 2f out: in command ent fnl f: pushed out* **5/1**
0131 **2** *2* **Daniel Thomas (IRE)**[9] [824] 10-8-12 70.................(tp) WilliamCarson 1 70
(Richard Guest) *trckd ldrs: sltly outpcd 2f out: wnt 2nd ent fnl f: r.o wl but a being hld* **7/4**[1]
6-20 **3** *6* **Musashi (IRE)**[16] [738] 7-8-12 54.................................(b) SteveDrowne 5 58
(Laura Mongan) *hld up bhd ldrs: pushed along over 4f out: nvr gng pce to get on terms: wnt 3rd ins fnl f* **33/1**
4414 **4** *2* **Wisecraic**[9] [818] 5-8-12 64...(p) LiamKeniry 4 54
(J S Moore) *prom: chal 2f out: sn hld in disp 2nd: fdd ins fnl f* **5/2**[2]
000 **5** *nk* **Whodunit (UAE)**[30] [570] 8-9-2 66.................................(b) LukeMorris 2 57
(Peter Hiatt) *led: rdn over 3f out: hdd 2f out: fdd ins fnl f* **7/2**[3]
2m 4.9s (-1.70) **Going Correction** -0.05s/f (Stan) **5** Ran SP% **106.8**
Speed ratings (Par 101): **104,102,97,96,95**
CSF £13.34 TOTE £7.30: £2.30, £1.50; EX 13.50.Hurricane Spirit was claimed by Hans Adielsson for £5,000.
Owner The Little House Partnership **Bred** Knocktoran Stud **Trained** Newmarket, Suffolk

FOCUS
An ordinary claimer run at what looked a steady enough pace, but won with a bright change of gear two out from Hurricane Spirit.

916 FREE HORSE RACING BETS WITH FREEBETTING.CO.UK CLAIMING STKS 7f (P)
2:30 (2:30) (Class 6) 3-Y-O **£1,704** (£503; £251) **Stalls** Low

Form RPR
403U **1** **Arabian Flight**[11] [801] 3-8-2 58.................................... KieranO'Neill 2 62
(John Bridger) *hld up bhd front 3: rdn 3f out: no imp tl str run ent fnl f: led fnl 100yds: won gng away* **8/1**
4412 **2** *1½* **Flying Pickets (IRE)**[8] [840] 3-9-3 72..............................(be) JohnFahy 4 73
(Alan McCabe) *hld up bhd front 3: rdn and hdwy over 1f out: ev ch ent fnl f: kpt on but no ex fnl 100yds* **4/1**[3]
4331 **3** *½* **Fugitive Motel (IRE)**[17] [731] 3-8-6 73.................... NicoleNordblad(7) 5 68
(Hans Adielsson) *racd freely: led: rdn over 1f out: sn jnd: no ex whn hdd fnl 100yds* **5/4**[1]
5506 **4** *4½* **Umph (IRE)**[15] [743] 3-8-7 52.......................................(v) RichardThomas 1 49
(David Evans) *trckd ldr: rdn 2f out: kpt on same pce fnl f* **20/1**
-503 **5** *½* **Mr Knightley (IRE)**[14] [764] 3-9-2 73.......................(b) NathanAlison(5) 3 62
(Jim Boyle) *racd keenly: trckd ldr: rdn 2f out: kpt on same pce fnl f* **5/2**[2]
1m 25.19s (0.39) **Going Correction** -0.05s/f (Stan) **5** Ran SP% **108.9**
Speed ratings (Par 96): **95,93,92,87,87**
CSF £37.16 TOTE £10.40: £3.40, £1.50; EX 36.70.
Owner Mrs Liz Gardner **Bred** Mr & Mrs A E Pakenham **Trained** Liphook, Hants

FOCUS
Run-of-the-mill claiming form.

917 FREE BETTING WITH FREEBETTING.CO.UK H'CAP 7f (P)
3:05 (3:05) (Class 5) (0-70,70) 3-Y-O **£2,385** (£704; £352) **Stalls** Low

Form RPR
4-23 **1** **Lionrock (FR)**[18] [723] 3-9-4 67.................................... JoeFanning 8 72
(Mark Johnston) *led after 1f: kpt on wl fnl f: rdn out* **5/2**[2]
000- **2** *½* **Scouting For Girls**[233] [4446] 3-8-7 56 oh1...................... PaulHanagan 4 59
(Jim Boyle) *trckd ldrs: nudged along over 3f out: styd on to go 2nd ins fnl f: clsng on wnr at fin* **8/1**
31 **3** *½* **Bint Alzain (IRE)**[18] [724] 3-9-7 70.................................... LukeMorris 2 71
(Gerard Butler) *hld up: rdn and hdwy on inner to chse wnr over 1f out: kpt on same pce fnl f* **5/1**[3]
4244 **4** *½* **Millibar (IRE)**[16] [739] 3-9-5 68.................................(p) SteveDrowne 5 68
(Nick Littmoden) *led for 1f: chsd wnr: rdn 2f out: kpt on same pce fnl f* **16/1**
053- **5** *3¼* **Shamardeliah (IRE)**[93] [7757] 3-9-7 70.................................... KierenFallon 3 61
(James Tate) *racd keenly in tch: rdn 2f out: nt pce to get on terms* **2/1**[1]
1200 **6** *3* **Lana (IRE)**[15] [743] 3-8-8 57.................................... RichardThomas 7 40
(David Evans) *racd keenly: trckd ldrs: fdd ins fnl f* **20/1**
605- **7** *shd* **Musically**[219] [4913] 3-9-4 67.................................... TonyCulhane 6 50
(Mick Channon) *hld up: rdn over 2f out: nvr a danger* **8/1**
1m 25.2s (0.40) **Going Correction** -0.05s/f (Stan) **7** Ran SP% **111.4**
Speed ratings (Par 98): **95,94,93,93,89 86,86**
toteswingers:1&2:£4.40, 1&3:£2.40, 2&3:£5.90 CSF £21.25 CT £89.12 TOTE £1.90: £1.10, £5.90; EX 19.40 Trifecta £129.30.
Owner Sheikh Hamdan Bin Mohammed Al Maktoum **Bred** M Daguzan-Garros & Rolling Hills Farm **Trained** Middleham Moor, N Yorks

FOCUS
One or two promising types in here and, with more to come from a few of these, this could be useful form for the grade despite the winner being allowed to dictate on his own terms out in front (time was virtually identical to previous claimer).

918 COMPARE FREE BETS WITH FREEBETTING.CO.UK MAIDEN STKS 1m (P)
3:45 (3:46) (Class 5) 3-Y-O **£2,385** (£704; £352) **Stalls** High

Form RPR
3 **1** **Margate**[49] [331] 3-8-12 0.................................... MichaelHills 4 78
(Charles Hills) *mde all: kicked clr 2f out: in command after: comf* **7/2**[2]
23 **2** *2¾* **Imtithal (IRE)**[34] [523] 3-8-12 0.................................... MartinLane 6 71
(James Tate) *hld up: rdn and hdwy over 1f out: styd on to go 2nd towards fin: a being hld by wnr* **8/1**
00- **3** *nk* **Estedaama (IRE)**[199] [5583] 3-8-12 0.................................... PaulHanagan 5 70
(Marcus Tregoning) *hld up: pushed along 3f out: sn outpcd: styd on strly fr over 1f out: wnt 3rd towards fin* **11/1**
62- **4** *1¼* **Dynastic**[142] [7094] 3-9-3 0.................................... RyanMoore 1 72
(Richard Hannon) *trckd ldrs: pushed along to chse wnr over 2f out: sn drvn and hld: no ex whn lost 2 pls towards fin* **11/10**[1]
5 *1* **Danube River** 3-8-12 0.................................... JoeFanning 3 65
(Mark Johnston) *trckd ldrs: rdn over 3f out: styd on same pce fr over 1f out* **14/1**
406- **6** *nk* **Tight Lipped (IRE)**[189] [5876] 3-9-3 76.................................... LukeMorris 7 69
(James Eustace) *prom: rdn over 3f out: one pce fr over 1f out* **15/2**[3]
30- **7** *1½* **Inffiraaj (IRE)**[147] [6984] 3-8-12 0.................................... TonyCulhane 9 61
(Mick Channon) *hld up: rdn over 2f out: nt pce to get involved* **33/1**
5- **8** *5* **Beckfield Point**[188] [5919] 3-9-3 0.................................(t) SteveDrowne 2 54
(Stuart Williams) *mid-div: rdn over 2f out: wknd fnl f* **100/1**
9 *4½* **Tom Red** 3-9-3 0.................................... IanMongan 8 43
(Dean Ivory) *little slowly away: towards rr: rdn over 3f out: wknd 2f out* **50/1**
1m 37.72s (-0.48) **Going Correction** -0.05s/f (Stan) **9** Ran SP% **113.6**
Speed ratings (Par 98): **100,97,96,95,94 94,92,87,83**
toteswingers:1&2:£3.40, 1&3:£6.00, 2&3:£14.80 CSF £30.56 TOTE £5.20: £1.50, £1.50, £3.70; EX 21.50 Trifecta £568.70.
Owner K Abdulla **Bred** Juddmonte Farms Ltd **Trained** Lambourn, Berks

FOCUS
Some promising types on show and a maiden that should throw up future winners.

919 FOOTBALL FREE BETS WITH FREEBETTING.CO.UK FILLIES' H'CAP 1m (P)
4:25 (4:25) (Class 5) (0-70,72) 4-Y-O+ **£2,385** (£704; £352) **Stalls** High

Form RPR
2211 **1** **Abigails Angel**[9] [826] 5-9-6 72 6ex.................................... MarkCoumbe(5) 7 80
(Brett Johnson) *trckd ldr: rdn 2f out: str chal ins fnl f: all out whn led on nod line* **7/2**
114- **2** *nse* **Methayel (IRE)**[128] [7334] 4-9-7 68.................................... BrettDoyle 6 76
(Clive Brittain) *led: rdn over 1f out: kpt on whn pressed ins fnl f: all out whn hdd on nod line* **10/3**[3]
1356 **3** *1¾* **Shared Moment (IRE)**[21] [685] 6-8-11 65............(v) NicoleNordblad(7) 2 69
(John Gallagher) *trckd ldr: rdn 2f out: kpt on same pce fnl f* **3/1**[2]
165- **4** *2¾* **National Hope (IRE)**[140] [7137] 4-9-6 67..........................(t) KierenFallon 1 64
(George Baker) *s.i.s: in last pair: pushed along over 4f out: rdn to chse ldrs 2f out: sn one pce* **9/4**[1]
-204 **5** *2¾* **Bold Ring**[49] [323] 6-9-1 65.................................... SophieDoyle(3) 3 56
(Eric Wheeler) *cl up: rdn over 2f out: one pce fr over 1f out* **12/1**
560 **6** *7* **Meia Noite**[8] [838] 5-8-3 57...(p) NoraLooby(7) 5 31
(Alan McCabe) *hld up: rdn over 2f out: nvr any imp* **40/1**
1m 38.58s (0.38) **Going Correction** -0.05s/f (Stan) **6** Ran SP% **111.2**
Speed ratings (Par 100): **96,95,94,91,88 81**
toteswingers:1&2:£5.00, 1&3:£52.10, 2&3:£31.40 CSF £15.16 CT £36.20 TOTE £2.70: £1.10, £3.40; EX 13.70 Trifecta £17.90.
Owner B R Johnson **Bred** P Balding **Trained** Epsom, Surrey

FOCUS
A cracking finish to this fillies' handicap.

920 GET FREE BETS WITH FREEBETTING.CO.UK H'CAP 1m (P)
5:05 (5:05) (Class 5) (0-75,78) 3-Y-O **£2,385** (£704; £352) **Stalls** High

Form RPR
1111 **1** **Clean Bowled (IRE)**[8] [840] 3-9-5 78 6ex.......................(p) NedCurtis(7) 6 83
(Roger Curtis) *trckd ldrs: swooped to ld ent fnl f: kpt on wl: readily* **6/1**[3]
40-1 **2** *1* **Beauchamp Castle**[15] [743] 3-8-5 64.....................(t) NicoleNordblad(7) 1 67
(Hans Adielsson) *steadily away: in last pl making prog whn lost pl coming wd fnl bnd: sn rdn: styd on to chse wnr ins fnl f: drifted lft: hld fnl 75yds* **3/1**[2]

432- **3** *2* **Altona (IRE)**[143] 7081 3-9-5 **71**.. TonyCulhane 4 69
(Mick Channon) *in last pair: rdn 2f out: hdwy over 1f out: styd on to go 3rd ins fnl f* **11/1**

0-21 **4** *1 ¾* **Hikma (USA)**[13] 784 3-9-5 **71**.. JoeFanning 5 65
(Mark Johnston) *sn prom: rdn and ev ch over 1f out: no ex fnl f* **11/8**[1]

1113 **5** *hd* **Samasana (IRE)**[15] 747 3-9-2 **68**.. MartinDwyer 3 62
(Ian Wood) *led: rdn 2f out: hdd ent fnl f: no ex* **12/1**

353- **6** *2 ¾* **Ermyn Flyer**[127] 7342 3-7-13 **56**.............................. JemmaMarshall(5) 7 44
(Pat Phelan) *racd keenly: trckd ldrs: rdn 2f out: wknd over 1f out* **16/1**

-615 **7** *hd* **Bareback (IRE)**[8] 841 3-9-7 **73**.. SteveDrowne 2 60
(John Best) *trckd ldr: rdn over 2f out: fdd ins fnl f* **9/1**

1m 38.31s (0.11) **Going Correction** -0.05s/f (Stan) **7** Ran SP% **113.3**
Speed ratings (Par 98): **97,96,94,92,92 89,89**
toteswingers:1&2:£2.40, 1&3:£5.20, 2&3:£5.30 CSF £23.85 TOTE £4.30: £1.60, £1.80; EX 18.30.
Owner Richard Dean **Bred** Cathal Ennis **Trained** Lambourn, Berks
■ Stewards' Enquiry : Nicole Nordblad one-day ban: careless riding (Mar 30)

FOCUS
A competitive-looking little handicap run at what appeared a reasonable gallop.

921 RUGBY FREE BETS WITH FREEBETTING.CO.UK MAIDEN STKS 1m 4f (P)
5:40 (5:40) (Class 5) 3-Y-O **£2,385** (£704; £352) **Stalls** Low

Form RPR

0 **1** **Bordoni (USA)**[34] 523 3-9-3 0.. JoeFanning 4 86
(Mark Johnston) *trckd ldrs: chal over 2f out: sn rdn: led ins fnl f: styd on wl* **8/11**[1]

4 **2** *2 ¼* **Benbecula**[18] 723 3-9-3 0.. RyanMoore 6 82
(Richard Hannon) *racd keenly: jnd ldr after 1f tl rn sltly wd on bnd after 2f: trckd ldr: led 4f out: qcknd pce whn jnd over 2f out: sn rdn: no ex whn hdd ins fnl f: edgd rt whn hld* **7/4**[2]

0-46 **3** *17* **Never Satisfied**[7] 847 3-8-12 68......................(b1) MatthewLawson(5) 3 55
(Charles Hills) *led tl 4f out: outpcd by front pair over 2f out: no ch after* **20/1**

0 **4** *2 ¼* **Star Bonita (IRE)**[25] 635 3-8-12 0.. MartinLane 5 46
(David Simcock) *in tch: rdn 4f out: outpcd over 2f out: no ch after* **50/1**

600- **5** *7* **Witty Buck**[298] 2355 3-9-3 40.. JohnFahy 2 40
(Alan McCabe) *awkward leaving stalls: struggling 4f out: a in rr* **80/1**

5 **6** *43* **Ruby Glass (IRE)**[18] 723 3-9-3 0................................(b) MartinDwyer 1
(Brian Meehan) *in tch: rdn 4f out: btn over 2f out: eased* **14/1**[3]

2m 31.21s (-1.79) **Going Correction** -0.05s/f (Stan) **6** Ran SP% **108.9**
Speed ratings (Par 98): **103,101,90,88,84 55**
CSF £2.00 TOTE £1.90: £1.10, £1.60; EX 2.60.
Owner Sheikh Hamdan Bin Mohammed Al Maktoum **Bred** Darley **Trained** Middleham Moor, N Yorks

FOCUS
Not much depth to this maiden and the two that dominated the market did so in the race, coming a long way clear in the straight and both look nice prospects.
T/Plt: £125.80 to a £1 stake. Pool:£61,746.91 - 358.21 winning tickets T/Qpdt: £26.70 to a £1 stake. Pool:£3,555.20 - 98.30 winning tickets TM

905 WOLVERHAMPTON (A.W) (L-H)
Friday, March 16

OFFICIAL GOING: Standard
Wind: Fresh behind Weather: Overcast

922 COMPARE FREE BETS WITH FREEBETTING.CO.UK APPRENTICE H'CAP 1m 1f 103y(P)
5:50 (5:53) (Class 5) (0-70,70) 4-Y-O+ **£2,264** (£673; £336; £168) **Stalls** Low

Form RPR

000- **1** **Prohibition (IRE)**[217] 5002 6-8-4 **56** oh4.......................... AmyScott(3) 8 63
(Alastair Lidderdale) *s.s: hld up and bhd: hdwy over 1f out: rdn and r.o to ld towards fin* **20/1**

010- **2** *hd* **Jack's Revenge (IRE)**[150] 6936 4-9-4 **70**................(tp) DavidKenny(3) 10 77
(George Baker) *hld up: hdwy u.p over 1f out: swtchd lft ins fnl f: r.o wl* **11/1**

504- **3** *½* **Ollon (USA)**[147] 7003 4-8-9 **58**.. MichaelMetcalfe 2 64
(Mrs K Burke) *a.p: chsd ldr over 2f out: rdn over 1f out: ev ch wl ins fnl f: r.o* **4/1**[2]

3-00 **4** *nk* **Yorksters Prince (IRE)**[8] 834 5-9-2 **68**..................(b) ShaneBKelly(3) 3 73
(Tony Coyle) *led: rdn over 2f out: hdd towards fin* **25/1**

1010 **5** *1 ¾* **Vanilla Rum**[18] 722 5-9-5 **68**..................................(b) MichaelO'Connell 4 69
(John Mackie) *hld up in tch: hmpd and lost pl 7f out: hdwy 2f out: rdn over 1f out: edgd lft ins fnl f: styd on* **4/1**[2]

2432 **6** *¾* **McCool Bannanas**[14] 771 4-8-11 **65**.......................... NathanAlison(5) 5 65
(James Unett) *trckd ldrs: plld hrd: rdn over 1f out: styd on* **10/3**[1]

4-6 **7** *3 ¾* **Scribe (IRE)**[13] 786 4-8-13 **65**.......................... MatthewCosham(3) 11 57
(David Evans) *chsd ldr tl pushed along over 4f out: rdn over 2f out: styng on same pce whn hmpd and eased ins fnl f* **12/1**

0526 **8** *nk* **Petomic (IRE)**[9] 722 7-8-4 **58**................................(p) CharlesEddery(5) 1 49
(Richard Guest) *sn prom: rdn over 3f out: wknd fnl f* **25/1**

0304 **9** *6* **Community (USA)**[8] 836 4-8-10 **64**.......................... LeonnaMayor(5) 7 43
(Phil McEntee) *s.i.s: hld up: rdn over 3f out: wknd over 2f out* **50/1**

-004 **10** *¾* **Mad Ginger Alice**[21] 689 4-8-5 **61**.......................... JenniferFerguson(7) 6 38
(Olivia Maylam) *hld up: hdwy 1/2-way: rdn and wknd over 2f out* **14/1**

-503 **11** *8* **Black Coffee**[18] 722 7-8-11 **65**................................(b) RachealKneller(5) 9 25
(Mark Brisbourne) *prom: chsd ldr over 4f out tl rdn wl over 2f out: sn wknd* **5/1**[3]

2m 1.45s (-0.25) **Going Correction** +0.05s/f (Slow) **11** Ran SP% **116.9**
Speed ratings (Par 103): **103,102,102,102,100 99,96,96,90,90 83**
toteswingers:1&2:£62.10, 2&3:£9.80, 1&3:£20.30 CSF £214.08 CT £1068.40 TOTE £43.90: £8.40, £3.00, £2.60; EX 445.20.
Owner Chris Beek Racing **Bred** Kevin Buckley **Trained** Lambourn, Berks

FOCUS
This apprentice handicap was was run at a steady pace, with four virtually in a line approaching the post.

923 SIX NATIONS FREE BETS WITH FREEBETTING.CO.UK H'CAP 1m 1f 103y(P)
6:20 (6:20) (Class 6) (0-60,59) 3-Y-O **£1,704** (£503; £251) **Stalls** Low

Form RPR

-612 **1** **Moataz (USA)**[52] 288 3-9-7 **59**.. FrannyNorton 8 67
(Mark Johnston) *led over 8f out: clr fr over 1f out: comf* **9/4**[1]

3-43 **2** *3 ¾* **Stag Hill (IRE)**[14] 766 3-9-4 **56**.. LiamKeniry 11 56
(Sylvester Kirk) *a.p: chsd wnr over 5f out: rdn over 2f out: styd on same pce fnl f* **3/1**[2]

006- **3** *1 ¼* **Cool Fantasy (IRE)**[122] 7422 3-9-4 **56**......................(b) WilliamCarson 7 53
(Paul D'Arcy) *hld up: rdn and hung lft over 2f out: hdwy over 1f out: r.o to go 3rd post: nvr nrr* **18/1**

-502 **4** *nk* **Emma Jean (IRE)**[14] 766 3-8-8 **51**............................(t) RaulDaSilva(5) 5 48
(Frank Sheridan) *trckd ldr over 8f out: plld hrd: lost 2nd over 5f out: rdn over 2f out: no ex fnl f* **12/1**

00-4 **5** *nse* **Martha's Way**[42] 407 3-8-13 **51**.. PaddyAspell 10 48
(Michael Easterby) *prom: rdn over 2f out: styd on u.p* **5/1**[3]

060- **6** *shd* **Skyeron**[209] 5270 3-8-1 **46**.. RachealKneller(7) 2 42
(Mark Brisbourne) *hld up: hdwy over 3f out: rdn over 1f out: styd on same pce ins fnl f* **28/1**

0663 **7** *2 ¼* **Aiaam Al Wafa (IRE)**[8] 840 3-8-8 **53**..................(p) LeonnaMayor(7) 12 45
(Phil McEntee) *s.i.s: hld up: styd on ins fnl f: nvr nrr* **22/1**

0-46 **8** *½* **Emirates Jack (IRE)**[23] 660 3-8-7 **50**.. LauraPike(5) 1 41
(David Simcock) *mid-div: lost pl over 4f out: rdn over 2f out: no imp* **6/1**

6353 **9** *nk* **Angel Cake (IRE)**[27] 619 3-9-0 **52**................................(p) HayleyTurner 9 42
(Phil McEntee) *s.i.s: hld up: rdn over 3f out: n.d* **14/1**

05-5 **10** *1 ¾* **My New Angel (IRE)**[43] 393 3-8-4 **45**.................. AdamBeschizza(3) 6 31
(Paul Green) *hld up: rdn over 3f out: n.d* **33/1**

00-0 **11** *10* **Silver Native (IRE)**[57] 217 3-8-7 **45**.. ShaneKelly 3 10
(Mike Murphy) *led 1f: chsd ldrs: rdn over 3f out: wknd over 2f out* **50/1**

2m 2.53s (0.83) **Going Correction** +0.05s/f (Slow) **11** Ran SP% **119.0**
Speed ratings (Par 96): **98,94,93,93,93 93,91,90,90,88 80**
toteswingers:1&2:£2.50, 2&3:£17.90, 1&3:£12.80 CSF £8.64 CT £97.32 TOTE £3.60: £1.60, £2.10, £4.60; EX 11.20.
Owner Dr Marwan Koukash **Bred** Stonestreet Thoroughbred Holdings LLC **Trained** Middleham Moor, N Yorks

FOCUS
A minor handicap run at a moderate gallop. The winner, who dictated from the front, came down the centre in the straight.

924 FOOTBALL BETTING WITH FREEBETTING.CO.UK H'CAP 1m 4f 50y(P)
6:50 (6:50) (Class 7) (0-50,50) 4-Y-O+ **£1,704** (£503; £251) **Stalls** Low

Form RPR

-002 **1** **Visions Of Johanna (USA)**[3] 889 7-8-11 **49**........... DuilioDaSilva(5) 7 61
(Richard Guest) *a.p: chsd ldr over 3f out: led over 2f out: clr fr over 1f out: comf* **5/2**[1]

-213 **2** *4* **Mayan Flight (IRE)**[28] 602 4-9-1 **50**.. DavidProbert 1 56+
(Tony Carroll) *hld up: hdwy 6f out: nt clr run fr over 3f out tl wl over 1f out: rdn to chse wnr ins fnl f: no imp* **11/4**[2]

06-0 **3** *2 ¼* **Swords**[38] 453 10-8-7 **45**................................(p) RaulDaSilva(5) 6 47
(Ray Peacock) *chsd ldrs: pushed along over 4f out: rdn over 2f out: styd on same pce fr over 1f out* **80/1**

3-00 **4** *2* **Ivan The Terrible (IRE)**[23] 651 4-8-12 **50**............... RobertLButler(3) 8 49
(Richard Guest) *hld up: nt clr run over 2f out: hdwy u.p over 1f out: styd on: nt trble ldrs* **25/1**

53-3 **5** *3* **Ishismart**[14] 767 8-9-3 **50**.. HayleyTurner 9 44
(Reg Hollinshead) *prom: lost pl after 2f: in rr and pushed along 7f out: nt clr run over 2f out: hdwy u.p over 1f out: wknd ins fnl f* **6/1**[3]

4-06 **6** *2* **Delagoa Bay (IRE)**[7] 850 4-8-10 **45**.. LiamKeniry 5 36
(Sylvester Kirk) *hld up: pushed along 8f out: nt clr run over 2f out: nvr nr to chal* **11/1**

4450 **7** *7* **Yossi (IRE)**[7] 850 8-8-13 **46**................................(p) FrannyNorton 3 26
(Richard Guest) *led: rdn and hdd over 2f out: wknd over 1f out* **15/2**

6004 **8** *shd* **It's Me And You**[39] 451 4-8-11 **46**......................(vt1) JamesSullivan 12 26
(Michael Easterby) *s.s: hdwy to chse ldrs after 1f: rdn over 2f out: wknd wl over 1f out* **9/1**

0-06 **9** *12* **Just Zak**[43] 390 7-8-5 **45**.. GarethEdwards(7) 2
(Garry Woodward) *hld up: rdn and wknd over 2f out: t.o* **50/1**

4506 **10** *14* **Grecian Goddess (IRE)**[28] 602 4-8-11 **49**....(p) MichaelO'Connell(3) 10
(John Ryan) *hld up: hdwy over 5f out: rdn whn hmpd over 2f out: sn wknd: t.o* **14/1**

150- **11** *44* **Golan Heights (IRE)**[270] 3240 6-8-5 **45**..................(b) DarrenEgan(7) 11
(Adrian McGuinness, Ire) *chsd ldr tl rdn over 3f out: wknd over 2f out: t.o* **25/1**

2m 41.81s (0.71) **Going Correction** +0.05s/f (Slow)
WFA 4 from 6yo+ 2lb **11** Ran SP% **117.2**
Speed ratings (Par 97): **99,96,94,93,91 90,85,85,77,68 38**
toteswingers:1&2:£1.90, 2&3:£80.20, 1&3:£49.90 CSF £9.09 CT £424.39 TOTE £3.40: £1.90, £1.20, £15.60; EX 13.30.
Owner Willie McKay & Brian Carey **Bred** David S Milch **Trained** Stainforth, S Yorks

FOCUS
This uncompetitive handicap was run at a messy pace.
Grecian Goddess(IRE) Official explanation: jockey said filly stopped quickly

925 EURO 2012 FREE BETS WITH FREEBETTING.CO.UK MAIDEN STKS 5f 20y(P)
7:20 (7:20) (Class 5) 3-Y-O+ **£2,264** (£673; £336; £168) **Stalls** Low

Form RPR

-3 **1** **Morocco Moon**[14] 768 3-8-7 0.. ShaneKelly 6 66
(Tim Pitt) *mde all: shkn up over 1f out: r.o wl: eased nr fin* **9/4**[2]

2223 **2** *2 ¼* **Derivatives (IRE)**[18] 720 3-8-7 70.. NickyMackay 5 58
(John Gosden) *chsd ldrs: rdn to chse wnr ins fnl f: no imp* **11/10**[1]

300- **3** *1 ¼* **Economic Crisis (IRE)**[178] 6232 3-8-0 55........... MatthewHopkins(7) 2 53
(Alan Berry) *w wnr tl rdn over 1f out: edgd lft and no ex ins fnl f* **50/1**

5605 **4** *3* **Sailing North (USA)**[13] 781 4-9-3 53......................(tp) DarrenEgan(7) 4 57
(Ronald Harris) *edgd lft s: chsd ldrs: rdn 1/2-way: styd on same pce appr fnl f* **25/1**

00/ **5** *2 ¾* **Dikanta**[496] 7345 4-9-10 0.. HayleyTurner 3 47
(Robert Cowell) *s.i.s and hmpd s: hdwy over 3f out: rdn 1/2-way: wknd over 1f out* **14/1**

4 **6** *4 ½* **Shake Baby Shake**[14] 768 3-8-0 0.. JakePayne(7) 1 16
(Bill Turner) *hld up: plld hrd: wknd 1/2-way* **40/1**

7 *2* **Caboodle** 3-8-7 0.. RichardKingscote 7
(Tom Dascombe) *s.i.s: sn outpcd* **9/2**[3]

1m 2.36s (0.06) **Going Correction** +0.05s/f (Slow)
WFA 3 from 4yo 12lb **7** Ran SP% **111.5**
Speed ratings (Par 103): **101,97,95,90,86 79,75**
toteswingers:1&2:£1.10, 2&3:£8.30, 1&3:£15.20 CSF £4.78 TOTE £3.40: £1.50, £1.20; EX 6.00.
Owner Saintly Racing **Bred** R J Cornelius **Trained** Newmarket, Suffolk

FOCUS
A maiden with little strength in depth. The winner set a steady pace and once again came down the centre of the track in the straight.

926 GRAND NATIONAL FREE BETS WITH FREEBETTING.CO.UK H'CAP (DIV I) 7f 32y (P)
7:50 (7:50) (Class 6) (0-55,55) 4-Y-0+ **£1,704** (£503; £251) **Stalls** High

Form RPR
0/51 **1** **All About You (IRE)**[29] 572 6 -9-0**53** AdamKirby 8 74
(John Butler) *hld up: hdwy over 2f out: shkn up to ld over 1f out: rdn clr ins fnl f* **11/8**[1]
0335 **2** *6* **Just Timmy Marcus**[25] 633 6 -9-0**53** RussKennemore 12 58
(Brian Baugh) *hld up: nt clr run over 2f out: hdwy over 1f out: rdn to go 2nd ins fnl f: no ch w wnr* **11/1**
3450 **3** *½* **Look For Love**[18] 725 4 -8-6**52** (p) JackDuern(7) 4 56
(Reg Hollinshead) *chsd ldrs: rdn and ev ch over 1f out: no ex ins fnl f* **16/1**
400- **4** *¾* **Whitstable Native**[164] 6610 4 -9-2**55** LukeMorris 7 57
(Joseph Tuite) *hld up: nt clr run over 2f out: rdn over 1f out: styd on: nt trbld ldrs* **11/1**
0264 **5** *nk* **Fantasy Fry**[43] 386 4 -9-2**55** GeorgeBaker 5 56
(David Evans) *mid-div: hdwy over 2f out: rdn over 1f out: styd on same pce fnl f* **9/2**[2]
0564 **6** *1* **Anjomarba (IRE)**[9] 828 5 -9-2**55** HayleyTurner 3 53
(Conor Dore) *chsd ldr: rdn and ev ch over 1f out: no ex fnl f* **8/1**[3]
0-00 **7** *2* **Roman Ruler (IRE)**[25] 633 4 -8-9**53** LMcNiff(5) 6 46
(Chris Fairhurst) *hld up: rdn over 1f out: nvr nrr* **33/1**
4-04 **8** *nk* **Kool Shuffle (GER)**[8] 724 4 -8-12**51** BarryMcHugh 10 43
(Tony Coyle) *chsd ldrs: rdn over 2f out: wknd over 1f out* **25/1**
0/5- **9** *½* **Vantaa (IRE)**[402] 454 4 -9-2**55** RobertWinston 11 46
(Mrs K Burke) *s.i.s: hld up: swtchd rt over 1f out: nvr trbld ldrs* **14/1**
0100 **10** *¾* **Crocodile Bay (IRE)**[7] 729 9 -9-1**54** (b) FrannyNorton 2 43
(Richard Guest) *chsd ldrs: rdn over 2f out: n.m.r and wknd over 1f out* **16/1**
5655 **11** *2 ¼* **Tamino (IRE)**[8] 831 9 -8-3**47** (b) AmyScott(5) 1 29
(Alastair Lidderdale) *led: rdn and hdd over 1f out: wknd fnl f* **16/1**
/0-0 **12** *¾* **Secret Hero**[7] 856 6 -8-4**50** (b) DarrenEgan(7) 9 30
(Adrian McGuinness, Ire) *hld up: rdn 1/2-way: sn wknd* **20/1**

1m 28.73s (-0.87) **Going Correction** +0.05s/f (Slow) **12**Ran SP% **123.9**
Speed ratings (Par 101): **106,99,98,97,97 96,93,93,93,92 89,88**
toteswingers:1&2:£8.30, 2&3:£13.70, 1&3:£10.10 CSF £18.66 CT £193.00 TOTE £2.90 : £1.20, £3.50, £5.00 ; EX 28.20 .
Owner Mrs H F Prendergast **Bred** Ballylinch Stud **Trained** Newmarket, Suffolk

FOCUS
This uncompetitive handicap was run at a solid pace with the field well grouped entering the straight.

927 GRAND NATIONAL FREE BETS WITH FREEBETTING.CO.UK H'CAP (DIV II) 7f 32y (P)
8:20 (8:22) (Class 6) (0-55,55) 4-Y-0+ **£1,704** (£503; £251) **Stalls** High

Form RPR
/0-5 **1** **The Bay Bandit**[8] 837 5 -8-11**50** AdamKirby 2 58+
(John Butler) *hld up: pushed along over 2f out: hdwy u.p and nt clr run over 1f out: hrd rdn to ld post* **4/5**[1]
-000 **2** *shd* **Huzzah (IRE)**[21] 685 7 -9-2**55** MichaelStainton 5 63
(Paul Howling) *chsd ldr 6f out tl led over 2f out: rdn over 1f out: hdd post* **3/1**[2]
5026 **3** *1 ½* **Monsieur Pontaven**[41] 430 5 -9-0**53** (b) LeeNewman 11 57
(Robin Bastiman) *s.i.s: hld up: hdwy over 1f out: rdn and hung rt ins fnl f: r.o* **16/1**
00-0 **4** *nse* **Fault**[22] 666 6 -8-13**52** FergusSweeney 10 56
(Alastair Lidderdale) *hld up: hdwy over 2f out: rdn over 1f out: r.o* **25/1**
-230 **5** *½* **Nacho Libre**[29] 578 7 -9-1**54** (b) PaddyAspell 7 56
(Michael Easterby) *prom: nt clr run 2f out: rdn over 1f out: styd on* **8/1**[3]
3006 **6** *½* **Littleportnbrandy (IRE)**[8] 837 4 -8-7**46** (b) WilliamCarson 6 47
(Richard Guest) *hld up: hdwy over 1f out: sn rdn: styd on* **33/1**
000- **7** *3* **Eyes On**[282] 2827 4 -8-11**55** (t) RaulDaSilva(5) 12 48
(Frank Sheridan) *hld up: hdwy 2f out: sn rdn: styd on* **33/1**
00-0 **8** *2* **Amno Dancer (IRE)**[5] 752 5 -9-1**54** TomEaves 4 42
(Ian Semple) *plld hrd and prom: rdn over 1f out: hmpd and wknd ins fnl f* **50/1**
1200 **9** *nse* **My Best Man**[29] 578 6 -9-0**53** (t) DavidProbert 9 40
(Tony Carroll) *hld up: rdn over 1f out: n.d* **33/1**
453- **10** *½* **Sairaam (IRE)**[163] 6626 6 -9-0**53** RobertWinston 8 39
(Charles Smith) *prom: rdn over 2f out: wknd ins fnl f* **12/1**
44-0 **11** *11* **Jaldarshaan (IRE)**[52] 289 5 -9-2**55** (v[1]) LukeMorris 1 11
(Colin Teague) *led: rdn and hdd over 2f out: wknd and eased over 1f out* **12/1**

1m 30.07s (0.47) **Going Correction** +0.05s/f (Slow) **11**Ran SP% **127.6**
Speed ratings (Par 101): **99,98,97,97,96 95,92,90,90,89 77**
toteswingers:1&2:£2.70, 2&3:£10.40, 1&3:£2.70 CSF £3.44 CT £25.89 TOTE £1.70 : £1.20, £1.60, £3.70 ; EX 7.50 .
Owner J Butler **Bred** Darley **Trained** Newmarket, Suffolk
■ Stewards' Enquiry : Adam Kirby two-day ban: used whip above the permitted level (Mar 30-31)

FOCUS
An honest gallop. This was an ordinary handicap, but it produced a thrilling finish with the two market leaders dominating.
Jaldarshaan(IRE) Official explanation: trainer said mare would not face the first-time visor

928 HORSE RACING FREE BETS WITH FREEBETTING.CO.UK H'CAP 2m 119y (P)
8:50 (8:51) (Class 4) (0-85,88) 4-Y-0+ **£4,204** (£1,251; £625 ; £312) **Stalls** Low

Form RPR
1-31 **1** **Rasheed**[34] 521 4 -9-2**80** NickyMackay 3 91
(John Gosden) *trckd ldrs: wnt 2nd over 3f out: led over 2f out: rdn clr fr over 1f out: styd on strly* **13/8**[1]
-024 **2** *7* **Quinsman**[20] 714 6 -8-12**71** LiamKeniry 6 74
(J S Moore) *hld up: hdwy over 2f out: rdn over 1f out: styd on same pce: wnt 2nd ins fnl f* **14/1**
056- **3** *1 ¼* **English Summer**[174] 6333 5 -10-1**88** AdamKirby 4 90
(Mark Johnston) *prom: chsd wnr over 2f out: rdn over 1f out: wknd ins fnl f* **2/1**[2]
-125 **4** *1 ½* **Rosewood Lad**[29] 577 5 -9-0**73** LukeMorris 2 73
(J S Moore) *chsd ldr tl wnt upsides 1/2-way: led over 4f out: rdn and hdd over 2f out: wknd over 1f out* **11/2**
-132 **5** *120* **Uphold**[22] 668 5 -9-1**083** (t) RobertWinston 1
(Gay Kelleway) *racd keenly: led at stdy pce tl jnd and qcknd 1/2-way: hdd over 4f out: sn pushed along and hung lft: rdn and wknd over 2f out: t.o* **9/2**[3]

3m 40.93s (-0.87) **Going Correction** +0.05s/f (Slow)
WFA 4 from 5yo+ 5lb **5**Ran SP% **111.7**
Speed ratings (Par 105): **104,100,100,99,**
CSF £22.17 TOTE £3.30 : £2.20, £6.50 ; EX 20.10 .
Owner Ms Rachel D S Hood **Bred** Miss K Rausing And Mrs S M Rogers **Trained** Newmarket, Suffolk

FOCUS
This 2m handicap was run at a crawl with the race developing into a 2f sprint turning for home.
Uphold Official explanation: jockey said gelding ran too freely and hung left-handed under pressure

929 FREE BETTING WITH FREEBETTING.CO.UK H'CAP 1m 141y (P)
9:20 (9:21) (Class 6) (0-55,55) 4-Y-0+ **£1,704** (£503; £251) **Stalls** Low

Form RPR
026- **1** **One Of Twins**[23] 7005 4 -8-8**54** DavidSimmonson(7) 13 67
(Michael Easterby) *mde all: rdn over 2f out: drvn out* **12/1**
300/ **2** *2 ¼* **Forever Hope**[63] 165 5 -8-13**52** BarryMcHugh 9 60
(Tony Coyle) *a.p: chsd wnr 4f out: rdn over 1f out: styd on same pce ins fnl f* **9/1**
-614 **3** *1 ¼* **Cwmni**[25] 633 6 -9-0**53** LukeMorris 6 58
(Bryn Palling) *prom: rdn over 2f out: styd on same pce ins fnl f* **4/1**[1]
0-65 **4** *1 ¼* **Princess Gail**[15] 744 4 -9-0**53** ShaneKelly 7 55
(Mark Brisbourne) *chsd ldrs: rdn over 1f out: styd on same pce fnl f* **8/1**
0002 **5** *1* **Ad Vitam (IRE)**[8] 837 4 -8-8**47** ow1 (vt) MichaelStainton 5 47
(Micky Hammond) *s.i.s: hld up: styd on u.p fr over 1f out: nvr nrr* **5/1**[2]
5534 **6** *shd* **Join Up**[18] 725 6 -8-9**55** RachealKneller(7) 12 55
(Mark Brisbourne) *prom: rdn over 1f out: styd on same pce* **6/1**[3]
4020 **7** *¾* **Very Well Red**[15] 744 9 -8-8**47** WilliamCarson 1 45
(Peter Hiatt) *chsd ldr over 4f: rdn over 2f out: no ex fr over 1f out* **12/1**
0-36 **8** *1 ¼* **Tanforan**[15] 744 10 -9-2**55** RussKennemore 11 50
(Brian Baugh) *hmpd sn after s: hld up: rdn over 2f out: nvr trbld ldrs* **16/1**
000- **9** *6* **Bertie Blu Boy**[88] 7820 4 -8-13**55** RobertLButler(3) 10 36
(Paul Green) *hld up: a in rr* **28/1**
-065 **10** *2 ¾* **Angelena Ballerina (IRE)**[18] 721 5 -8-11**55** (v) AmyScott(5) 8 30
(Dai Williams) *hld up: pushed along over 3f out: a in rr* **20/1**
0-03 **11** *¾* **Olynard (IRE)**[29] 578 6 -9-2**55** GeorgeBaker 4 28
(Michael Mullineaux) *hld up: a in rr* **5/1**[2]

1m 51.27s (0.77) **Going Correction** +0.05s/f (Slow) **11**Ran SP% **118.2**
Speed ratings (Par 101): **98,96,94,93,92 92,92,91,85,83 82**
toteswingers:1&2:£25.40, 2&3:£10.40, 1&3:£5.40 CSF £116.14 CT £523.77 TOTE £14.60 : £4.00, £3.30, £1.80 ; EX 145.00 .
Owner Clark Industrial Services Partnership **Bred** Clark Industrial Services Partnership **Trained** Sheriff Hutton, N Yorks

FOCUS
A solid gallop was set by the winner who was booted straight into the lead, and it was another race on the card where those that raced prominently were favoured.
T/Plt: £28.40 to a £1 stake. Pool £87,932.44 - 2,257.88 winning units. T/Qpdt: £2.60 to a £1 stake. Pool £8,113.61 - 2,284.39 winning units. CR

930a-936a Foreign Racing (See RI)

[922] WOLVERHAMPTON (A.W) (L-H)
Saturday, March 17

OFFICIAL GOING: Standard
Wind: Light behind Weather: Overcast

937 COMPARE FREE BETS WITH FREEBETTING.CO.UK H'CAP 1m 5f 194y (P)
5:50 (5:50) (Class 6) (0-60,60) 4-Y-0+ **£1,704** (£503; £251) **Stalls** Low

Form RPR
5622 **1** **Corvette**[15] 767 4 -9-4**58** LukeMorris 2 65
(Michael Appleby) *a.p: shkn up over 2f out: rdn to ld and edgd rt ins fnl f: styd on* **9/4**[1]
2333 **2** *1* **Leyte Gulf (USA)**[14] 392 9 -9-9**59** DaneO'Neill 5 64
(Chris Bealby) *hld up: rdn over 2f out: hdwy over 1f out: r.o u.p to go 2nd towards fin: nt rch wnr* **7/2**[2]
-316 **3** *¾* **Waldsee (GER)**[15] 772 7 -9-8**58** AdamKirby 7 62
(Paul Rich) *chsd ldrs: pushed along 7f out: rdn over 2f out: styd on same pce ins fnl f* **9/2**[3]
02- **4** *nk* **Polly Holder (IRE)**[312] 5209 4 -9-5**59** (b[1]) WilliamCarson 6 62
(Paul D'Arcy) *led 1f: chsd ldr: rdn over 2f out: styd on same pce ins fnl f* **11/2**
00-0 **5** *½* **If What And Maybe**[17] 738 4 -8-10**53** (v) MichaelO'Connell(3) 4 55
(John Ryan) *s.i.s: pushed along to ld after 1f: rdn over 2f out: hdd and unable qck ins fnl f* **11/1**
-005 **6** *6* **Perfect Shot (IRE)**[29] 594 6 -9-10**60** (b) AmirQuinn 1 54
(Jim Best) *hld up: rdn over 2f out: wknd fnl f* **8/1**
660- **7** *nk* **Carnelian (IRE)**[103] 6504 5 -8-10**46** oh1 TomEaves 3 40
(Ian Semple) *hld up: nt clr run over 2f out: wknd over 1f out* **40/1**

3m 4.36s (-1.64) **Going Correction** 0.0s/f (Stan)
WFA 4 from 5yo+ 4lb **7**Ran SP% **108.4**
Speed ratings (Par 101): **104,103,103,102,102 99,98**
Tote Swingers: 1&2 £1.30, 1&3 £4.70, 2&3 £3.20 CSF £9.07 TOTE £2.90 : £2.80, £2.40 ; EX 5.40.
Owner Tom Cunnane **Bred** Newsells Park Stud **Trained** Danethorpe, Notts

FOCUS
A steadily run race with the field well grouped leaving the back.

938 SIX NATIONS FREE BETS WITH FREEBETTING.CO.UK H'CAP (DIV I) 5f 216y (P)
6:20 (6:21) (Class 6) (0-52,53) 4-Y-0+ **£1,704** (£503; £251) **Stalls** Low

Form RPR
0-06 **1** **Sabys Gem (IRE)**[16] 740 4 -8-11**47** (b) ShaneKelly 3 57
(Michael Wigham) *hld up: racd keenly: hdwy and nt clr run over 1f out: rdn to ld nr fin* **8/1**
0005 **2** *nk* **Rise To Glory (IRE)**[29] 572 4 -8-10**46** oh1 NeilChalmers 1 55
(Shaun Harris) *mid-div: hdwy over 2f out: led over 1f out: rdn and hdd ins fnl f: r.o* **15/2**
-350 **3** *hd* **Mr Skipiton (IRE)**[14] 781 7 -9-2**52** (b[1]) LukeMorris 11 60
(Terry Clement) *trckd ldrs: rdn to ld ins fnl f: hdd nr fin* **5/1**[2]
0-04 **4** *2 ½* **Avonlini**[23] 665 6 -9-0**50** RussKennemore 2 50
(Brian Baugh) *trckds ldrs: rdn over 1f out: styd on same pce ins fnl f* **11/2**[3]

 The Form Book Flat, Raceform Ltd, Compton, RG20 6NL

6023 **5** ½ **Bonnie Prince Blue**[9] 831 9-9-0 **53**.................................. DaleSwift(3) 4 51
(Ian McInnes) *sn pushed along in rr: rdn over 1f out: hung lft and r.o ins fnl f: nvr nrr* **15/2**

0202 **6** 1 **Little Perisher**[16] 740 5-8-13 **49**............................(p) MichaelStainton 12 44
(Paul Howling) *trckd ldr: plld hrd: sddle slipped sn after s: led wl over 1f out: sn rdn and hdd: no ex ins fnl f* **7/1**

40-0 **7** 2½ **Avon Light**[9] 837 4-8-12 **48**..(p) LiamKeniry 8 35
(Milton Bradley) *mid-div: hdwy over 2f out: sn rdn: styd on same pce fr over 1f out* **14/1**

0066 **8** 1 **Littleportnbrandy (IRE)**[1] 927 4-8-10 **46** oh1.........(b) WilliamCarson 6 30
(Richard Guest) *hld up: rdn over 1f out: nvr on terms* **12/1**

000/ **9** *hd* **Yanza**[811] 7852 6-8-11 **52**.. RaulDaSilva(5) 5 35
(Pam Ford) *led: rdn and hdd wl over 1f out: wknd and eased ins fnl f* **50/1**

-103 **10** 1¾ **Cheyenne Red (IRE)**[32] 551 6-9-2 **52**........................... PhillipMakin 9 30
(Michael Herrington) *prom: rdn over 2f out: wknd fnl f* **9/2**[1]

1m 15.01s (0.01) **Going Correction** 0.0s/f (Stan) **10** Ran SP% **113.7**
Speed ratings (Par 101): **99,98,98,95,94 93,89,88,88,85**
Tote Swingers: 1&2 £9.40, 1&3 £12.10, 2&3 £11.00 CSF £64.94 CT £336.65 TOTE £10.80: £3.90, £3.10, £1.10; EX 93.80.
Owner S Osman & D Hassan **Bred** Calley House Uk **Trained** Newmarket, Suffolk

FOCUS
Not form to get excited about.
Sabys Gem(IRE) Official explanation: trainer said, regarding apparent improvement in form, that the gelding requires cover which he was able to find on this occasion.
Little Perisher Official explanation: jockey said saddle slipped

939 SIX NATIONS FREE BETS WITH FREEBETTING.CO.UK H'CAP (DIV II) 5f 216y(P)
6:50 (6:50) (Class 6) (0-52,52) 4-Y-0+ **£1,704** (£503; £251) **Stalls** Low

Form RPR
3-40 **1** **Almaty Express**[23] 664 10-9-2 **52**...............................(b) KieranO'Neill 10 61
(John Weymes) *chsd ldr: rdn to ld over 1f out: hung lft wl ins fnl f: jst hld on* **6/1**[3]

416- **2** *nk* **Sleights Boy (IRE)**[192] 5824 4-8-12 **51**.................(v) DeclanCannon(3) 13 59
(Ian McInnes) *a.p: rdn over 2f out: edgd lft and chsd wnr wl ins fnl f: r.o* **40/1**

302 **3** 1 **Flow Chart (IRE)**[9] 831 5-8-11 **47**........................... RobbieFitzpatrick 3 52
(Peter Grayson) *mid-div: hdwy over 2f out: rdn and hung lft ins fnl f: r.o* **7/1**

-064 **4** ¾ **Diamond Fire (IRE)**[36] 503 8-8-10 **46** oh1......................(t) ShaneKelly 5 51+
(Adrian McGuinness, Ire) *hld up: hdwy over 1f out: running on whn n.m.r and eased nr fin* **12/1**

-000 **5** 1 **Flaxen Lake**[9] 837 5-8-12 **48**...(p) LukeMorris 4 47
(Milton Bradley) *hld up: pushed along 4f out: rdn and r.o fr over 1f out: nvr nrr* **7/1**

660 **6** 4 **Jolie Etoile**[36] 499 4-8-10 **46** oh1.................................. DavidProbert 11 32
(Tony Carroll) *prom: rdn over 1f out: no ex fnl f* **25/1**

/0-1 **7** 1¾ **Prigsnov Dancer (IRE)**[22] 690 7-9-1 **51**........................ MickyFenton 9 32
(Garry Woodward) *led: rdn and hdd over 1f out: btn whn hmpd ins fnl f* **7/2**[1]

4503 **8** ¾ **Look For Love**[1] 926 4-8-9 **52**......................................(p) JackDuern(7) 8 30
(Reg Hollinshead) *sn pushed along in rr: rdn over 2f out: nvr on terms* **5/1**[2]

0004 **9** ½ **Microlight**[14] 781 4-9-0 **50**.....................................(b) RichardThomas 12 27
(John E Long) *s.i.s: rdn over 2f out: sn wknd* **10/1**

63-5 **10** ¾ **Skystream (IRE)**[16] 750 4-9-2 **52**...................................(p) TomEaves 1 26
(Ian Semple) *chsd ldrs: rdn and hung lft over 1f out: wknd ins fnl f* **16/1**

0060 **11** 5 **Takajan (IRE)**[2] 910 5-8-5 **46** oh1.............................. JamesRogers(5) 7
(Mark Brisbourne) *hld up in tch: plld hrd: rdn and wknd over 2f out* **25/1**

005 **12** 8 **Tancred Spirit**[22] 690 4-8-5 **48** oh1 ow2.......................(v) NedCurtis(7) 2
(Paul Midgley) *hld up: a in rr: wknd over 2f out* **14/1**

1m 14.8s (-0.20) **Going Correction** 0.0s/f (Stan) **12** Ran SP% **117.6**
Speed ratings (Par 101): **101,100,99,98,96 91,89,88,87,86 79,69**
Tote Swingers: 1&2 £80.30, 1&3 £6.90, 2&3 £66.50 CSF £229.80 CT £1744.01 TOTE £8.70: £2.90, £11.00, £2.00; EX 432.70.
Owner Highmoor Racing 4 & Tag Racing **Bred** P G Airey **Trained** Middleham Moor, N Yorks

FOCUS
Few got into this.
Diamond Fire(IRE) Official explanation: jockey said, regarding running and riding, that his orders were, as the gelding is a particularly difficult ride who requires coaxing to do his best, to drop in and make a run as late as possible, it was unable to settle behind the leaders and it showed signs of hanging right in home straight when asked to quicken and was blocked closing stages which he reported at scales.

940 MICK HEMMINGS BECOMES A PENSIONER CLAIMING STKS 5f 216y(P)
7:20 (7:22) (Class 5) 3-Y-0 **£2,264** (£673; £336; £168) **Stalls** Low

Form RPR
6165 **1** **Tiablo (IRE)**[15] 769 3-8-5 58.. LukeMorris 5 61
(David Evans) *chsd ldrs: pushed along over 2f out: rdn over 1f out: r.o to ld wl ins fnl f* **7/1**[2]

2-42 **2** 1¼ **The Dancing Lord**[56] 250 3-8-5 68................................ RyanWhile(7) 1 64
(Bill Turner) *led: hdd over 2f out: rdn whn rdr dropped whip over 1f out: led ins fnl f: sn hung rt and hdd: styd on same pce* **7/1**[2]

-462 **3** ½ **Miss Purity Pinker (IRE)**[12] 801 3-8-5 59....................(v) MartinLane 2 55
(David Evans) *chsd ldr tl led over 2f out: rdn over 1f out: hdd ins fnl f: hmpd sn after: styd on same pce* **16/1**

4-12 **4** ½ **Available (IRE)**[15] 768 3-8-7 69.. NickyMackay 6 56
(Jim Boyle) *chsd ldrs: pushed along 1/2-way: styd on towards fin* **13/8**[1]

40-6 **5** 2¼ **Wish Again (IRE)**[39] 455 3-8-10 56................................. AdrianNicholls 4 52
(David Nicholls) *trckd ldrs: hmpd over 2f out: sn rdn: styd on same pce fnl f* **10/1**[3]

0 **6** ¾ **Ozz**[15] 770 3-8-2 0..(bt[1]) RaulDaSilva(5) 3 46
(Frank Sheridan) *s.i.s: sn outpcd: r.o under tender handling ins fnl f: nvr nr to chal* **100/1**

1m 15.41s (0.41) **Going Correction** 0.0s/f (Stan) **6** Ran SP% **79.1**
Speed ratings (Par 98): **97,95,94,94,91 90**
Tote Swingers: 1&2 £2.20, 1&3 £2.70, 2&3 £4.10 CSF £23.60 TOTE £6.20: £3.10, £1.20; EX 24.90.
Owner Mrs E Evans **Bred** Hyde Park Stud **Trained** Pandy, Monmouths
■ Superplex was withdrawn (9/4, arrived at the s without cheekpieces). Deduct 30p in the £ under R4.
■ Stewards' Enquiry : Ryan While two-day ban: careless riding (Mar 31-Apr 1)

FOCUS
Quite a competitive claimer run at a good gallop but but it produced the slowest time of the three 6f races on the card.

941 GREAT OFFERS AT WOLVERHAMPTON-RACECOURSE.CO.UK (S) STKS 7f 32y(P)
7:50 (7:52) (Class 6) 4-Y-0+ **£1,704** (£503; £251) **Stalls** High

Form RPR
-330 **1** **Tombi (USA)**[19] 718 8-8-12 71.. JoeFanning 7 76
(Keith Dalgleish) *hld up: racd keenly: hdwy over 1f out: r.o to ld towards fin* **20/1**

315- **2** ¾ **Dialogue**[119] 7492 6-8-12 87... JimmyFortune 3 74
(Ollie Pears) *a.p: shkn up over 2f out: rdn to ld ins fnl f: hdd towards fin* **4/6**[1]

-240 **3** 1 **Unlimited**[40] 447 10-8-12 72.. DavidProbert 1 71
(Tony Carroll) *hld up: hdwy over 1f out: nt clr run ins fnl f: r.o* **40/1**

1040 **4** 2¼ **Bawaardi (IRE)**[14] 785 6-9-4 79... AdamKirby 2 71
(David Evans) *chsd ldrs: rdn over 1f out: ev ch ins fnl f: styd on same pce* **7/2**[2]

4135 **5** 1¼ **Spinning Ridge (IRE)**[12] 804 7-9-4 70.........................(v) LukeMorris 5 68
(Ronald Harris) *prom: chsd ldr over 4f out: rdn over 1f out: no ex ins fnl f* **22/1**

2600 **6** 1¾ **Monadreen Dancer**[9] 842 4-8-8 54 ow1.......................... ShaneKelly 6 53
(Daniel Mark Loughnane) *led: clr 1/2-way: rdn over 1f out: hdd & wknd ins fnl f* **100/1**

50-3 **7** 6 **Khajaaly (IRE)**[40] 448 5-8-12 73...................................... PaulHanagan 4 41
(Julia Feilden) *hld up in tch: racd keenly: wknd over 1f out* **5/1**[3]

1m 29.4s (-0.20) **Going Correction** 0.0s/f (Stan) **7** Ran SP% **111.4**
Speed ratings (Par 101): **101,100,99,96,95 93,86**
Tote Swingers: 1&2 £3.90, 1&3 £14.00, 2&3 £10.10 CSF £32.99 TOTE £15.00: £6.40, £1.40; EX 38.70.No bid for the winner. Dialogue sold to Mr D. Nicholls for £6,000.
Owner Gordon McDowall **Bred** Sun Valley Farm **Trained** Carluke, S Lanarks

FOCUS
A fair claimer.
Khajaaly(IRE) Official explanation: jockey said gelding never travelled

942 FOOTBALL FREE BETS WITH FREEBETTING.CO.UK H'CAP 7f 32y(P)
8:20 (8:21) (Class 5) (0-70,74) 4-Y-0+ **£2,264** (£673; £336; £168) **Stalls** High

Form RPR
0306 **1** **Chookie Avon**[26] 639 5-9-2 **68**.......................................(p) JoeFanning 5 75
(Keith Dalgleish) *a.p: racd keenly: chsd ldr over 2f out: shkn up over 1f out: rdn to ld nr fin* **13/2**[3]

3121 **2** *nse* **Greenhead High**[19] 718 4-9-4 **70**................................ AdrianNicholls 8 77
(David Nicholls) *led: rdn over 1f out: hdd nr fin* **4/1**[1]

600- **3** *hd* **Smalljohn**[86] 7857 6-9-1 **67**..(v) TomEaves 3 73
(Bryan Smart) *chsd ldr tl pushed along over 2f out: rdn over 1f out: r.o* **5/1**[2]

0/ **4** 1 **One For Joules (IRE)**[154] 5126 5-9-0 **66**......................... LukeMorris 6 70
(Michael Scudamore) *s.i.s: hld up: hdwy over 1f out: sn rdn: r.o: nt rch ldrs* **12/1**

-024 **5** *shd* **Wigram's Turn (USA)**[35] 538 7-9-1 **67**.........................(t) PaddyAspell 7 70
(Michael Easterby) *prom: rdn over 1f out: styd on same pce ins fnl f* **9/1**

5045 **6** 1¾ **May's Boy**[23] 669 4-8-8 **67**....................................(p) RachealKneller(7) 11 66
(Mark Usher) *sn mid-div: hdwy over 2f out: rdn over 1f out: styd on same pce ins fnl f* **20/1**

0-12 **7** *shd* **Hawk Moth (IRE)**[26] 639 4-9-2 **68**................................. ChrisCatlin 12 66
(John Spearing) *s.i.s: hld up: nt clr run over 1f out: r.o ins fnl f: nvr trbld ldrs* **13/2**[3]

-030 **8** *shd* **With Hindsight (IRE)**[10] 821 4-8-12 **69**...................... DavidKenny(5) 1 67
(Michael Scudamore) *mid-div: nt clr run over 2f out: hdwy over 1f out: no ex ins fnl f* **33/1**

2430 **9** ½ **Valmina**[17] 735 5-9-2 **68**..(t) SteveDrowne 4 65
(Tony Carroll) *s.i.s: hdwy over 1f out: no ex ins fnl f* **14/1**

-600 **10** 1¼ **Yankee Storm**[17] 735 7-9-1 **70**.....................................(v) RyanClark(3) 9 63
(Michael Wigham) *hld up: rdn over 1f out: n.d* **16/1**

1m 29.25s (-0.35) **Going Correction** 0.0s/f (Stan) **10** Ran SP% **101.3**
Speed ratings (Par 103): **102,101,101,100,100 98,98,98,97,96**
Tote Swingers: 1&2 £2.90, 1&3 £5.60, 2&3 £4.90 CSF £24.62 CT £90.03 TOTE £7.50: £2.30, £1.70, £1.60; EX 25.40.
Owner Carleton Boys Of Carlisle **Bred** D And J Raeburn **Trained** Carluke, S Lanarks
■ Bahamian Lad was withdrawn on vet's advice (11/2, deduct 15p in the £ under R4).

FOCUS
A competitive race for the grade but it proved impossible to come from off the pace with the front three filling those positions throughout.

943 HORSE AND SPORTS TIPS @ RELAYMAN.COM MEDIAN AUCTION MAIDEN STKS 1m 141y(P)
8:50 (8:51) (Class 5) 3-Y-0 **£2,264** (£673; £336; £168) **Stalls** Low

Form RPR
1 **Hajras (IRE)** 3-9-3 0.. PaulHanagan 1 76+
(Mark Johnston) *s.i.s: hld up: pushed along over 5f out: hdwy 2f out: shkn up to ld ins fnl f: r.o wl* **4/9**[1]

-065 **2** 2¼ **King's Wharf (IRE)**[14] 787 3-9-3 65.................................. AdamKirby 3 66
(David Evans) *led: rdn over 1f out: hdd and unable qck ins fnl f* **6/1**[3]

-0 **3** ½ **Glennten**[15] 770 3-9-3 0.. LiamKeniry 2 65
(Sylvester Kirk) *chsd ldrs: rdn over 1f out: styd on same pce ins fnl f* **66/1**

4 2½ **Torero** 3-9-3 0.. PhillipMakin 6 59
(Kevin Ryan) *hld up: styd on fr over 1f out: nvr trbld ldrs* **14/1**

5 **5** *shd* **Green Mitas (ITY)**[19] 724 3-8-12 0.............................. RaulDaSilva(5) 9 59
(Frank Sheridan) *s.s: hld up: hdwy over 1f out: nvr trbld ldrs* **33/1**

24 **6** 2¼ **Lord Paget**[15] 770 3-9-3 0... GeorgeBaker 7 54
(Reg Hollinshead) *chsd ldr tl rdn over 1f out: wknd ins fnl f* **4/1**[2]

35-4 **7** 1¾ **Auntie Joy**[22] 693 3-8-12 64.. JamesSullivan 5 45
(Michael Easterby) *prom: rdn over 2f out: wknd over 1f out* **12/1**

60 **8** *hd* **Windygoul Lad**[19] 720 3-9-3 0.. AndrewMullen 4 49
(Keith Dalgleish) *hld up: rdn and hung lft over 2f out: wknd over 1f out* **25/1**

1m 50.9s (0.40) **Going Correction** 0.0s/f (Stan) **8** Ran SP% **126.2**
Speed ratings (Par 98): **98,96,95,93,93 91,89,89**
Tote Swingers: 1&2 £2.50, 1&3 £38.90, 2&3 £29.80 CSF £4.65 TOTE £1.50: £1.02, £1.70, £13.20; EX 5.90.
Owner Hamdan Al Maktoum **Bred** Shadwell Estate Company Limited **Trained** Middleham Moor, N Yorks
■ Paul Hanagan's first winner as retained rider to Hamdan Al Maktoum.

FOCUS
Those with experience set only a modest standard.

Windygoul Lad Official explanation: jockey said gelding ran too free

944 GRAND NATIONAL FREE BETS WITH FREEBETTING.CO.UK H'CAP 1m 4f 50y (P)
9:20 (9:20) (Class 5) (0-70,69) 4-Y-0+ **£2,264** (£673; £336 ; £168) **Stalls** Low

Form RPR
600- **1** **Saint Thomas (IRE)**[38] 7200 5 -8-11**62**............... MichaelO'Connell(3) 3 69
(John Mackie) *hld up: hdwy over 1f out: r.o to ld wl ins fnl f: edgd lft towards fin* **5/1**[3]
006- **2** *nk* **White Diamond**[51] 7215 5 -8-13**68**.................................... JackDuern(7) 6 74
(Michael Appleby) *chsd ldr after 2f: rdn and ev ch ins fnl f: r.o* **16/1**
0223 **3** *3/4* **Ahlawy (IRE)**[22] 695 9 -9-2**69**.....................................(t) RaulDaSilva(5) 2 74
(Frank Sheridan) *chsd ldr 2f: remained handy: rdn over 1f out: r.o* **11/1**
-534 **4** *hd* **Time Square (FR)**[17] 738 5 -8-11**59**.................................(t) LukeMorris 5 63
(Tony Carroll) *hld up: plld hrd: hdwy over 2f out: rdn and ev ch fr over 1f out: no ex towards fin* **4/1**[2]
5414 **5** *hd* **Thundering Home**[10] 824 5 -9-2**69**............................(t) DavidKenny(5) 7 73
(George Baker) *a.p: led 2f out: sn rdn: hdd wl ins fnl f* **2/1**[1]
1352 **6** *7* **Maslak (IRE)**[9] 830 8 -9-1**63**.................................... ChrisCatlin 4 56
(Peter Hiatt) *led at stdy pce tl qcknd over 4f out: rdn and hdd 2f out: wknd ins fnl f* **4/1**[2]
3155 **7** *1/2* **Magic Millie (IRE)**[1] 810 5 -8-11**64**............................ AmyScott(5) 1 56
(Alastair Lidderdale) *s.i.s: hld up: hdwy over 5f out: chsd ldr over 3f out: rdn over 1f out: wknd fnl f* **8/1**

2m 44.39s (3.29) **Going Correction** 0.0s/f (Stan) 7Ran SP% **115.3**
Speed ratings (Par 103): **89,88,88,88,88 83,83**
Tote Swingers: 1&2 £49.10, 1&3 £19.10, 2&3 £12.00 CSF £76.18 TOTE £4.70 : £2.40 , £3.80 ; EX 112.70.
Owner P Riley **Bred** S Coughlan **Trained** Church Broughton , Derbys

FOCUS
A steadily run affair in which there was only a couple of lengths covering the whole field two furlongs out and just over a length separated the first five at the finish, so the form isn't strong.
T/Plt: £411.10 to a £1 stake. Pool: £86,806.26 - 154.12 winning tickets. T/Qpdt: £70.80 to a £1 stake. Pool: £7,881.94 - 82.34 w. tickets. CR

945a-952a & 954a-957a Foreign Racing (See RI)

880 SAINT-CLOUD (L-H)
Saturday, March 17

OFFICIAL GOING: Turf: soft

953a PRIX EXBURY (GROUP 3) (4YO+) (TURF) 1m 2f
1:30 (12:00) 4-Y-O+ **£33,333** (£13,333; £10,000 ; £6,666 ; £3,333)

RPR
1 **Chinchon (IRE)**[259] 3655 7 -8-11**0**................................. OlivierPeslier 2 110
(C Laffon-Parias, France) *settled in rr: last ent st: smooth prog on wd outside over 2f out: r.o wl to take ld 150yds out: sn clr: comf* **8/5**[1]
2 *3/4* **War Is War (IRE)**[14] 794 4 -8-9**0**................................ ThomasHuet 5 106
(E J O'Neill, France) *settled in 2nd on ins: disp ld after 1f tl hdd 2 1/2f out: shkn up to take ld again 2f out: r.o wl: hdd 150yds out: styd on wl* **30/1**
3 *3/4* **Saga Dream (FR)**[53] 6903 6 -8-11**0**.............................. ThierryJarnet 1 107
(F Lemercier, France) *settled in 5th on ins: rdn over 1 1/2f out: wnt 4th ent fnl f: styd on wl: tk 3rd cl home* **11/2**[3]
4 *hd* **Tryst**[14] 794 7 -8-9**0**.. FranckBlondel 4 104
(J E Hammond, France) *settled in rr: swtchd to ins rail ent st: picked up wl: wnt 3rd 1f out: r.o wl: lost 3rd cl home* **44/5**
5 *1/2* **Kya One (FR)**[24] 4 -8-8**0**.................................... IoritzMendizabal 3 102
(Y De Nicolay, France) *settled in 6th: gd prog over 1 1/2f out: n.m.r 1f out: picked up wl ins fnl f: r.o wl* **15/1**
6 *1/2* **Tip Toe (FR)**[97] 7733 5 -8-9**0**................................ SebastienMaillot 8 102
(F Doumen, France) *settled in 5th on outside: rdn 2f out: no ex: styd on one pce fnl f* **13/1**
7 *snk* **Don Bosco (FR)**[14] 5 -8-9**0**...................................... GregoryBenoist 9 102
(D Smaga, France) *led early pulling hrd for 1f: settled in 3rd: rdn over 2f out: no ex: styd on one pce fnl 1 1/2f* **7/2**[2]
8 *6* **Amazing Beauty (GER)**[34] 543 5 -8-6**0**.......................... MaximeGuyon 7 87
(M Figge, Germany) *racd in 2nd on settling: disp ld after 1f tl led u.p over 2 1/2f out: hdd over 2f out: grad fdd fnl 1 1/2f* **9/1**
9 *10* **Pump Pump Boy (FR)**[9] 4 -8-9**0**................................ JohanVictoire 6 70
(M Pimbonnet, France) *racd in 5th towards outside: rdn over 2 1/2f out: no ex: grad fdd: eased ins fnl f* **30/1**

2m 8.1s (-7.90) 9Ran SP% **116.1**
WIN (incl. 1 euro stake): 2.60. PLACES: 1.70, 5.00, 1.90. DF: 50.40. SF: 65.90
Owner Sarl Darpat France **Bred** Zubieta Ltd **Trained** Chantilly, France

890 KEMPTON (A.W) (R-H)
Monday, March 19

OFFICIAL GOING: Standard
Wind: light, across Weather: dry and bright

958 BHEST RACING TO SCHOOL H'CAP 5f (P)
2:50 (2:51) (Class 5) (0-70,70) 4-Y-0+ **£2,264** (£673; £336 ; £168) **Stalls** Low

Form RPR
6004 **1** **Black Baccara**[5] 890 5 -8-13**65**................................(be) RyanClark(3) 2 73
(Phil McEntee) *in tch: travelling wl and waiting for gap over 1f out: rdn and qcknd to chal 1f out: drvn ahd ins fnl f: kpt on wl u.p* **9/1**
5530 **2** *1/2* **Vhujon (IRE)**[12] 819 7 -8-10**59**........................... RobbieFitzpatrick 4 65
(Peter Grayson) *in tch in midfield: rdn 1/2-way: swtchd lft over 1f out: styd on wl u.p ins fnl f* **20/1**
0602 **3** *3/4* **Sherjawy (IRE)**[12] 823 8 -8-9**58**.............................. JamieGoldstein 7 61
(Zoe Davison) *in tch in midfield: rdn 1/2-way: drvn 1f out: styd on u.p fnl 150yds* **12/1**
45-2 **4** *shd* **Black Cadillac (IRE)**[5] 893 4 -9-0**63**.......................... DavidProbert 9 66
(Andrew Balding) *dwlt and bumping match w rival sn after s: hanging rt in rr: rdn over 2f out: hanging rt and forced to go between horses ent fnl f: r.o wl fnl 100yds: nt rch ldrs* **9/4**[1]
5-00 **5** *3/4* **Dreams Of Glory**[10] 844 4 -8-10**62**.......................... SimonPearce(3) 6 62
(Ron Hodges) *chsd ldrs: rdn wl over 1f out: hanging rt and unable qck over 1f out: rdr dropped whip and styd on same pce ins fnl f* **16/1**
0561 **6** *nk* **Chjimes (IRE)**[12] 823 8 -9-1**64**................................(b) HayleyTurner 5 63
(Conor Dore) *sn led: rdn over 1f out: drvn and hdd ins fnl f: no ex* **10/1**
2-54 **7** *1 1/4* **Rambo Will**[19] 735 4 -9-7**70**...................................... ShaneKelly 8 65
(J R Jenkins) *dwlt and barging match sn after s: hld up in last trio: rdn wl over 1f out: hung rt and styd on same pce fnl f* **4/1**[2]
60/2 **8** *hd* **Going French (IRE)**[21] 720 5 -9-0**63**............................ LukeMorris 3 57
(Dai Burchell) *led briefly: chsd ldr tl ent fnl f: wknd ins fnl f: btn whn n.m.r and eased towards fin* **9/1**
0136 **9** *3 1/2* **Novabridge**[26] 647 4 -9-2**65**.....................................(b) AdamKirby 1 46
(Neil Mulholland) *dwlt: a bhd: n.d* **5/1**[3]

(-0.50) **Going Correction** +0.025s/f (Slow) 9Ran SP% **114.9**
Speed ratings (Par 103): **105,104,103,102,101 101,99,98,93**
toteswingers:1&2:£26.20 2&3:£27.90, 1&3:£12.60 CSF £167.13 CT £2157.60 TOTE £10.00 : £2.90, £4.90 , £2.80 ; EX 252.00 Trifecta £506.80 Pool: £1027.45 - 1.50 winning units.
Owner Eventmaker Racehorses **Bred** Peter Balding **Trained** Newmarket, Suffolk

FOCUS
A modest sprint handicap in which they went a strong pace. The winner is rated back to her best.

959 32RED.COM MEDIAN AUCTION MAIDEN STKS 1m 2f (P)
3:20 (3:21) (Class 5) 3-5-Y-O **£2,264** (£673; £336 ; £168) **Stalls** Low

Form RPR
3 **1** **Cockney Sparrow**[16] 784 3 -8-3**0**.................................. LukeMorris 1 72
(Peter Chapple-Hyam) *chsd ldr for 2f: chsd ldrs after: rdn over 4f out: ev ch and hrd drvn over 1f out: led ins fnl f: forged clr fnl 100yds: rdn out* **4/1**[3]
052- **2** *2 1/4* **Beau Duke (IRE)**[99] 5672 3 -8-8**68**............................ DavidProbert 2 73
(Andrew Balding) *led tl 7f out: rdn to ld again but hung lft and rn wd bnd 2f out: drvn and edgd rt over 1f out: hdd ins fnl f: btn fnl 100yds: wknd towards fin* **11/8**[1]
3 *2 1/4* **Plus Fours (USA)**3 -8-8**0**..(p) TomQueally 4 68
(Amanda Perrett) *dwlt: in tch in last pair: rdn over 4f out: hdwy u.p on inner to press ldrs over 1f out: outpcd jst ins fnl f: wknd fnl 75yds* **10/1**
0-42 **4** *3* **Santadelacruze**[16] 787 3 -8-8**66**................................ FergusSweeney 3 62
(Gary Moore) *chsd ldrs: rdn over 3f out: unable qck 2f out: wknd ent fnl f* **6/1**
223 **5** *nk* **Red Shuttle**[24] 688 5 -10-0**70**.....................................(t) AdamKirby 5 65
(Noel Quinlan) *hld up in tch: hdwy to chse ldr and t.k.h 8f out: led 7f out and flashed tail: hdd and rdn 2f out: wknd jst over 1f out* **7/2**[2]
0- **6** *6* **Minstrel Lad**[291] 2650 4 -10-0**0**................................ TomMcLaughlin 6 53
(Lydia Pearce) *hld up in tch in last pair: rdn over 3f out: wknd over 1f out* **66/1**

2m 7.99s (-0.01) **Going Correction** +0.025s/f (Slow)
WFA 3 from 4yo+ 20lb 6Ran SP% **109.2**
Speed ratings (Par 103): **101,99,97,95,94 89**
CSF £9.39 TOTE £3.50 : £1.50 , £1.80 ; EX 9.00 .
Owner P Cunningham **Bred** P Cunningham **Trained** Newmarket, Suffolk

FOCUS
A modest maiden. The form doesn't look worth a great deal, with the early pace slow. The time was 1.47 seconds slower than the following older-horse Class 5 handicap. The runner-up looks the best guide.
Santadelacruze Official explanation: trainer said colt lost a right-fore shoe

960 £32 FREE AT 32RED.COM H'CAP 1m 2f (P)
3:50 (3:51) (Class 5) (0-75,75) 4-Y-0+ **£2,264** (£673; £336 ; £168) **Stalls** Low

Form RPR
2504 **1** **Tuxedo**[14] 804 7 -8-9**63**...(b) LukeMorris 1 72
(Peter Hiatt) *chsd ldrs: effrt u.p over 1f out: led fnl 75yds: r.o wl: rdn out* **11/1**
132- **2** *1/2* **Woop Woop (IRE)**[84] 7878 4 -9-4**75**.............................. RyanPowell(3) 7 83
(Ian Williams) *chsd ldrs: wnt 2nd 7f out: led over 1f out: drvn ent fnl f: hdd fnl 75yds: kpt on gamely but a hld* **6/1**[2]
6-61 **3** *3/4* **Casual Mover (IRE)**[33] 570 4 -9-7**75**............................ SteveDrowne 6 81
(John Best) *in tch: rdn and effrt to chse ldrs over 2f out: drvn and hdwy to press ldrs 1f out: styd on same pce fnl 100yds* **5/4**[1]
-543 **4** *1* **Lisahane Bog**[26] 648 5 -9-2**70**.....................................(v) MartinLane 2 74
(Peter Hedger) *hld up in tch in last trio: rdn and effrt on inner over 1f out: swtchd lft ins fnl f: kpt on u.p but nt gng pce to rch ldrs* **13/2**[3]
3-32 **5** *2 1/4* **Conducting**[12] 826 4 -9-2**70**.......................................(p) ShaneKelly 9 70
(Gay Kelleway) *led over 8f out: rdn ent fnl 2f: drvn and hdd over 1f out: wknd ins fnl f* **15/2**
00-4 **6** *2 1/4* **Clara Zetkin**[13] 809 4 -9-4**72**................................. TomMcLaughlin 4 67
(Michael Wigham) *wnt lft at s and v.s.a: hld up in rr: hdwy over 1f out: rdn and styd on same pce fnl f* **50/1**
041/ **7** *3 1/4* **Managua**[581] 5161 6 -9-6**74**.. DaneO'Neill 3 63
(Barry Brennan) *in tch on midfield: rdn and unable qck over 2f out: wknd over 1f out* **14/1**
1632 **8** *nse* **Aviso (GER)**[7] 636 8 -8-6**65**.................................. MatthewCosham(5) 8 53
(David Evans) *hld up in last trio: rdn and effrt on outer over 2f out: no imp and no threat to ldrs fnl 2f* **11/1**
022- **9** *3 1/4* **Persian Herald**[142] 7160 4 -9-4**72**................................ MartinDwyer 5 54
(William Muir) *led tl over 8f out: lost 2nd 7f out: rdn and lost pl over 2f out: wknd wl over 1f out: bhd fnl f* **16/1**

2m 6.52s (-1.48) **Going Correction** +0.025s/f (Slow) 9Ran SP% **115.0**
Speed ratings (Par 103): **106,105,105,104,102 100,98,97,95**
CSF £75.01 CT £140.78 TOTE £10.70 : £3.40 , £1.40 , £1.80 ; EX 95.30 Trifecta £254.20 Pool: £1065.08 - 3.10 winning units.
Owner Phil Kelly **Bred** Gainsborough Stud Management Ltd **Trained** Hook Norton, Oxon

FOCUS
A modest handicap. The winner continued his minor progress, as did the second.
Casual Mover (IRE)◆ Official explanation: jockey said colt was never travelling

961 32REDBET.COM H'CAP 1m 4f (P)
4:20 (4:20) (Class 6) (0-60,58) 4-Y-0+ **£1,617** (£481; £240 ; £120) **Stalls** Centre

Form RPR
5-02 **1** **Isdaal**[24] 689 5 -9-4**56**... JoeFanning 6 66
(Kevin Morgan) *hld up in last pair: hdwy over 4f out: chsd clr ldr wl over 2f out: led over 1f out: sn clr and styd on wl* **3/1**[2]
/021 **2** *3* **Asterales**[32] 575 5 -9-0**52**...................................... JamieMackay 7 57
(Willie Musson) *stdd and dropped in bhd after s: wl off the pce in rr: hdwy over 3f out: wnt modest 3rd over 2f out: rdn wl over 1f out: kpt on fnl f: wnt 2nd on post: no threat to wnr* **15/8**[1]
35-0 **3** *nse* **Gower Rules (IRE)**[26] 651 4 -9-4**58**............................ KieranO'Neill 1 63
(John Bridger) *chsd ldr for 2f: wnt 2nd again 6f out: led 5f out and sn clr: rdn over 2f out: hdd over 1f out: no ex and btn 1f out: styd on same pce and lost 2nd on post* **4/1**[3]

50-4 **4** *28* **Counterparty**[35] 546 4-9-3 **57** .... FergusSweeney 5 17
(Alan King) *restless in stalls: hld up off the pce in midfield: rdn and no rspnse 4f out: sn lost tch* **14/1**

600- **5** *5* **Curlew (IRE)**[136] 7263 6-9-5 **57** .... JamesMillman 2
(Chris Down) *t.k.h: chsd ldr 10f out tl wl over 2f out: sn wknd and wl bhd fnl 2f* **12/1**

3340 **6** *28* **Beneath**[26] 651 5-9-4 **56** ....(b) AdamKirby 4
(Neil Mulholland) *rdn along leaving stalls and led after 1f: sn clr: hdd 5f out: lost pl qckly and last 4f out: lost tch and t.o fnl 3f* **5/1**

2m 34.25s (-0.25) **Going Correction** +0.025s/f (Slow)
WFA 4 from 5yo+ 2lb **6** Ran SP% **110.8**
Speed ratings (Par 101): **101,99,98,80,76 58**
toteswingers:1&2:£1.70, 2&3:£2.00, 1&3:£2.50 CSF £8.81 TOTE £5.00: £2.30, £1.70; EX 9.30.
Owner Roemex Ltd **Bred** Shadwell Estate Company Limited **Trained** Gazeley, Suffolk

FOCUS
A moderate race run at an overly strong pace, and they finished strung out. The first two came from the back and the winner is rated up 3lb on his earlier form.

962 32RED H'CAP 7f (P)
4:50 (4:50) (Class 3) (0-95,95) 4-Y-0+ **£6,663** (£1,982; £990; £495) **Stalls** Low

Form RPR

5144 **1** **Piscean (USA)**[9] 871 7-9-3 **91** .... GeorgeBaker 5 101
(Tom Keddy) *hld up in last quartet: gd hdwy over 1f out: rdn and qcknd to ld 1f out: r.o wl: comf* **13/2**[3]

000 **2** *1* **Bravo Echo**[31] 616 6-9-7 **95** .... JimCrowley 12 103
(Michael Attwater) *stdd and dropped in bhd after s: t.k.h: hld up in rr: hdwy into midfield 1/2-way: rdn over 1f out: chsd wnr ins fnl f: r.o wl for clr 2nd but unable to threaten wnr* **16/1**

5210 **3** *1 ¼* **Chilli Green**[30] 622 5-8-6 **87** ....(p) DarrenEgan(7) 10 91
(Lee Carter) *pressed ldrs on outer: ev ch u.p 2f out: chsd wnr but outpcd 1f out: styd on same pce after* **10/1**

-110 **4** *½* **Prince Of Burma (IRE)**[44] 426 4-9-0 **88** ....(b) IanMongan 11 91
(Jeremy Gask) *hld up in midfield: swtchd to outer and rdn over 2f out: no imp tl styd on wl ins fnl f: no threat to wnr* **15/2**

300- **5** *hd* **Crown Counsel (IRE)**[135] 7295 4-8-12 **86** .... JoeFanning 1 88
(Mark Johnston) *led: rdn and hrd pressed over 2f out: hdd and unable qck 1f out: styd on same pce fnl f* **4/1**[1]

3530 **6** *nse* **Hazzard County (USA)**[30] 622 8-8-11 **92** .... AliceHaynes(7) 9 94
(David Simcock) *stdd s: hld up in rr: rdn and effrt on inner 2f out: hdwy over 1f out: kpt on ins fnl f* **16/1**

342- **7** *½* **Jack My Boy (IRE)**[136] 7262 5-8-7 **81** oh2......................(v) MartinLane 2 82
(David Evans) *chsd ldrs: drvn 2f out: pressed ldrs but unable qck over 1f out: styd on same pce and hld ins fnl f* **25/1**

00-6 **8** *1 ¼* **Reignier**[57] 266 5-9-2 **90** ....(p) MartinHarley 6 88
(Mrs K Burke) *t.k.h: hld up in midfield: n.m.r over 2f out: swtchd lft and rdn over 1f out: kpt on but no threat to ldrs* **16/1**

-510 **9** *½* **Seek The Fair Land**[37] 527 6-9-1 **94** ....(b) NathanAlison(5) 13 90
(Jim Boyle) *broke wl and sn crossed over to chse ldr: ev ch u.p 2f out: no ex ent fnl f: wknd ins fnl f* **20/1**

-010 **10** *shd* **Ocean Legend (IRE)**[33] 563 7-8-9 **83** .... TomQueally 7 79
(Tony Carroll) *in tch in midfield: rdn and unable qck over 2f out: one pce and no threat to ldrs fr over 1f out* **25/1**

50-6 **11** *hd* **Greensward**[58] 254 6-9-1 **89** .... KieranO'Neill 3 84
(Mike Murphy) *awkward leaving stalls and s.i.s: rcvrd and in midfield after 2f: rdn and effrt on inner 2f out: no prog: styng on same pce and hld whn nt clr run and hmpd ins fnl f* **6/1**[2]

5042 **12** *1 ¼* **Dozy Joe**[17] 765 4-8-8 **82** ....(p) LukeMorris 4 74
(Ian Wood) *in tch in midfield: rdn 3f out: drvn and unable qck 2f out: styd on same pce and no threat to ldrs fr over 1f out* **8/1**

0630 **13** *¾* **Five Star Junior (USA)**[9] 871 6-9-2 **90** .... JamesSullivan 8 80
(Linda Stubbs) *t.k.h: hld up in last quartet: rdn and no prog ent fnl 2f: n.d* **11/1**

1m 24.91s (-1.09) **Going Correction** +0.025s/f (Slow) **13** Ran SP% **118.0**
Speed ratings (Par 107): **107,105,104,103,103 103,103,101,101,100 100,99,98**
toteswingers:1&2:£26.20, 2&3:£33.70, 1&3:£8.00 CSF £101.63 CT £1055.86 TOTE £3.80: £1.10, £6.60, £4.20; EX 103.20 Trifecta £409.30 Pool: £691.39 - 1.25 winning units..
Owner Andrew Duffield **Bred** Connie And John Iacuone **Trained** Newmarket, Suffolk
■ Stewards' Enquiry : Nathan Alison one-day ban; did not keep straight leaving stalls (2nd Apr)

FOCUS
A good, competitive handicap, but it was a modestly run and was set up nicely for a horse with sprint speed. The winner is getting closer to his old best.

NOTEBOOK
Piscean(USA) was keen early on but saved enough to outpace his rivals, helped by the next two finishers having wide trips. While his latest win was gained over this distance, that race unfolded in similar circumstances and his pace (formerly an out-and-out sprinter) is a useful asset when the emphasis is on speed rather than stamina. (op 11-2)
Bravo Echo ◆ was better than he showed on occasions in Dubai and he ran a fine race on his first start back in Britain. He conceded loads of ground out wide (not helped by stalls 12) and did well to get so close. (tchd 20-1)
Chilli Green ◆, much like the runner-up, was caught wide and otherwise would have finished closer. She has more to offer and is one to keep on side. (op 9-1 tchd 8-1)
Prince Of Burma(IRE), returning from 44 days off, wasn't helped by stall 11 and is capable of a bit better. (op 9-1)
Crown Counsel(IRE) set what looked an ordinary gallop and it was disappointing he didn't see his race out better, but he might have needed this after 135 days off. (op 9-2)
Greensward found disappointingly little for pressure and was well held when short of room late on. (op 5-1 tchd 9-2)

963 32REDCASINO H'CAP 2m (P)
5:20 (5:21) (Class 5) (0-70,67) 4-Y-0+ **£2,264** (£673; £336; £168) **Stalls** Low

Form RPR

5-46 **1** **Frederick William**[33] 569 4-9-4 **64** ....(p) DaneO'Neill 3 73
(Chris Gordon) *hld up in tch: trckd ldrs 4f out: led over 2f out and sn rdn clr: in n.d fr over 1f out: rdn out* **11/1**

11-2 **2** *3 ½* **The Absent Mare**[20] 728 4-9-3 **63** .... MartinLane 9 68+
(Robin Dickin) *stdd and dropped in bhd after s: stl 9th and plenty to do whn rdn over 2f out: hdwy over 1f out: chsd clr wnr 1f out: r.o but nvr gng to rch wnr* **11/4**[1]

-000 **3** *3 ½* **Blackstone Vegas**[17] 772 6-9-1 **56** .... JoeFanning 5 57
(Derek Shaw) *stdd s: hld up towards rr: rdn and effrt over 2f out: chsd clr wnr briefly jst over 1f out: 3rd and wl hld fnl f* **11/1**

0231 **4** *3 ¼* **Blue Cossack (IRE)**[17] 772 4-9-1 **61** .... DavidProbert 1 58
(Mark Usher) *chsd ldrs: rdn over 2f out: drvn and nt gng pce of wnr 2f out: modest 2nd briefly over 1f out: 4th and wl btn fnl f* **6/1**

660- **5** *2 ¾* **Dalhaan (USA)**[19] 5318 7-9-12 **67** .... IanMongan 8 61
(Luke Dace) *chsd ldr: rdn and ev ch 3f out: nt gng pce of wnr ent fnl 2f: wknd over 1f out* **14/1**

3066 **6** *2* **Kavaloti (IRE)**[12] 825 8-9-12 **67** ....(b) GeorgeBaker 10 58
(Gary Moore) *hld up in tch towards rr: rdn and fnd little over 2f out: wl btn over 1f out* **4/1**[2]

-361 **7** *8* **Sumani (FR)**[19] 738 6-9-7 **62** .... HayleyTurner 4 44
(Simon Dow) *led: rdn and hdd over 2f out: nt gng pce of wnr 2f out: lost 2nd over 1f out: sn btn: eased ins fnl f* **9/2**[3]

212- **8** *1 ¼* **Kadouchski (FR)**[24] 4712 8-9-1 **63** .... HannahNunn(7) 2 43
(John Berry) *t.k.h: hld up in midfield: lost pl 4f out: wknd over 2f out: wl btn and eased ins fnl f* **20/1**

0112 **9** *4 ½* **El Libertador (USA)**[12] 825 6-9-7 **62** ....(b) JimmyFortune 7 37
(Eric Wheeler) *hld up in midfield: wknd over 2f out: virtually p.u ins fnl f* **12/1**

0/0 **10** *8* **Chaninbar (FR)**[31] 600 9-9-0 **55** ....(v) LukeMorris 6 20
(Brendan Powell) *v rel to r and sn t.o: consented to run after 2f: clsd and tagged on to bk of the field 12f out: rdn 5f out: lost tch over 3f out: eased over 1f out: t.o* **50/1**

3m 31.87s (1.77) **Going Correction** +0.025s/f (Slow)
WFA 4 from 6yo+ 5lb **10** Ran SP% **116.9**
Speed ratings (Par 103): **96,94,92,90,89 88,84,83,81,77**
CSF £41.51 CT £350.87 TOTE £11.30: £3.60, £1.50, £4.50; EX 57.30 TRIFECTA Not won..
Owner Mrs Kate Digweed **Bred** D J Weston **Trained** Morestead, Hants
■ Stewards' Enquiry : Jimmy Fortune two-day ban; careless riding (2nd-3rd Apr)

FOCUS
The finish was dominated by those held up, suggesting Sumani went off too fast. The winner is rated back to his 3yo best.
El Libertador(USA) Official explanation: jockey said gelding ran too freely

964 OLLY MURS LIVE 17.08.12 H'CAP 6f (P)
5:50 (5:51) (Class 6) (0-60,59) 4-Y-0+ **£1,617** (£481; £240; £120) **Stalls** Low

Form RPR

5130 **1** **Welcome Approach**[24] 687 9-9-4 **56** .... LukeMorris 8 64
(John Weymes) *stdd and dropped in bhd after s: hld up towards rr: rdn and hdwy over 1f out: running on whn swtchd rt and bmpd rival ins fnl f: led fnl 75yds: r.o wl: eased cl home* **10/1**

0101 **2** *¾* **Royal Envoy (IRE)**[18] 740 9-9-0 **52** ....(p) MichaelStainton 6 58
(Paul Howling) *in tch in midfield: rdn and edging rt wl over 1f out: hdwy u.p jst ins fnl f: r.o wl u.p to snatch 2nd on post* **8/1**

00-4 **3** *nse* **Kyllachy Storm**[31] 593 8-9-4 **56** .... GeorgeBaker 1 62
(Ron Hodges) *chsd ldr: rdn over 2f out: drvn and led ins fnl f: sn hdd and one pce: lost 2nd on post* **14/1**

3-54 **4** *¾* **Indian Arrow**[18] 752 4-9-4 **56** .... JimmyFortune 9 62+
(John Quinn) *hld up in last quartet: rdn and hung rt 2f out: hdwy and nt clr run ins fnl f: swtchd rt and r.o wl fnl 75yds* **7/2**[2]

5004 **5** *nk* **Forty Proof (IRE)**[26] 654 4-9-0 **57** ....(v) MatthewCosham(5) 3 59
(David Evans) *t.k.h: chsd ldrs: rdn over 2f out: pressing ldrs but unable qck whn bmpd ins fnl f: styd on same pce fnl 100yds* **9/2**[3]

050- **6** *2 ¼* **Bold Diva**[265] 3495 7-9-3 **55** ....(v) DavidProbert 7 50
(Tony Carroll) *in tch in midfield: rdn and effrt on inner over 2f out: no ex ent fnl f: wknd fnl 100yds* **12/1**

3456 **7** *nse* **Bookiesindex Boy**[5] 904 8-9-5 **57** ....(b) TonyCulhane 4 52
(J R Jenkins) *led: clr 1/2-way: rdn over 1f out: coming bk to field 1f out: hdd ins fnl f: wknd fnl 100yds* **11/1**

5310 **8** *¾* **Super Frank (IRE)**[16] 781 9-9-3 **55** ....(b) JamieGoldstein 2 48
(Zoe Davison) *awkward in stalls and slowly away: a towards rr: rdn and effrt on inner 2f out: no imp* **16/1**

60-6 **9** *nk* **Doctor Hilary**[12] 819 10-9-6 **58** ....(v) RobertHavlin 11 50
(Mark Hoad) *a towards rr: rdn and no imp over 2f out: nvr trbld ldrs* **20/1**

62-0 **10** *2 ½* **Automotive**[32] 574 4-9-7 **59** .... JoeFanning 5 43
(Julia Feilden) *chsd ldrs: rdn and no ex 2f out: wknd over 1f out: fdd ins fnl f* **11/4**[1]

1m 13.18s (0.08) **Going Correction** +0.025s/f (Slow) **10** Ran SP% **120.6**
Speed ratings (Par 101): **100,99,98,97,97 94,94,93,93,89**
toteswingers:1&2:£4.10, 2&3:£9.30, 1&3:£22.00 CSF £90.44 CT £1166.60 TOTE £9.80: £2.70, £3.40, £3.50; EX 27.70 Trifecta £272.30 Pool: £747.02 - 2.03 winning units..
Owner T A Scothern & Tag Racing **Bred** P Wyatt And Ranby Hall **Trained** Middleham Moor, N Yorks

FOCUS
A modest handicap The race was set up for those ridden with restraint, and the winner showed his best form since last winter.
Indian Arrow ◆ Official explanation: jockey said colt was denied a clear run
Super Frank(IRE) Official explanation: jockey said gelding jumped awkwardly leaving stalls
T/Jkpt: Not won. T/Plt: £156.80 to a £1 stake. Pool of £100,765.42 - 468.95 winning tickets. T/Qpdt: £10.90 to a £1 stake. Pool of £7,402.25 - 500.95 winning tickets. SP

COMPIEGNE (L-H)
Monday, March 19
OFFICIAL GOING: Turf: very soft

965a PRIX D'AIGUISY (CLAIMER) (5YO+) (GENTLEMAN RIDERS) (TURF) 1m
3:25 (12:00) 5-Y-0+ **£6,666** (£2,666; £2,000; £1,333; £666)

RPR

1 **Sequoia (FR)**[56] 7-11-0 0 .... MrJean-PhilippeBoisgontier 5 78
(P Monfort, France) **11/5**[1]

2 *3 ½* **Bernando (FR)**[128] 8-10-6 0 .... MrMikaelMescam 2 62
(J Phelippon, France) **26/1**

3 *1 ½* **Miami Gator (IRE)**[184] 6150 5-10-10 0 ....(b) MrDHDunsdon 1 63
(Mrs K Burke) *broke smartly to ld: hdd after 2f: relegated to 3rd ent st: rdn 2f out: styd on wl fnl f* **11/2**

4 *nk* **Bold Marc (IRE)**[13] 815 10-10-6 0 ....(p) MrSWalker 4 58
(Mrs K Burke) *racd in 2nd for 2f: relegated to 4th bef st: u.p over 1 1/2f out: styd on wl fnl f* **31/1**

5 *1 ½* **Gioia (FR)**[72] 5-10-2 0 .... MrThibaudMace(5) 3 55
(Mme S Adet, France) **24/1**

6 *¾* **Barzini (GER)**[13] 815 5-11-0 0 .... MrFlorentGuy 7 61
(J Phelippon, France) **23/10**[2]

7 *8* **Nightdance Victor (GER)**[137] 7256 5-10-6 0 .... MrDennisSchiergen 6 34
(P Schiergen, Germany) **43/10**[3]

8 *8* **Cape Velvet (IRE)**[9] 8-10-2 0 .... MrArthurHoyeau 8 12
(Mme J Bidgood, France) **17/2**
1m 38.99s (98.99) **8** Ran SP% **117.2**
WIN (incl. 1 euro stake): 3.20. PLACES: 1.50, 3.00, 2.30. DF: 21.80. SF: 38.70.
Owner Ecurie Grand'Ouest **Bred** Ronchalon Racing Ltd & B & C & Mlle I Jousset **Trained** France

[958]KEMPTON (A.W) (R-H)

Tuesday, March 20

OFFICIAL GOING: Standard
Wind: Virtually nil Weather: Sunny spells

966 WORTHINGTON'S H'CAP 1m 2f (P)
2:40 (2:42) (Class 6) (0-60,59) 4-Y-0+ £1,617 (£481; £240; £120) Stalls Low

Form RPR
-625 1 **Spartan King (IRE)**[28] 644 4-9-2 **54** .... JamieSpencer 4 61
(Ian Williams) *v.s.a: sn rcvrd and in tch off mod pce: rapid hdwy to ld over 4f out and qcknd fr 3f out: drvn over 1f out: hrd pressed clsng stages but a jst doing enough* **3/1**[1]
-503 2 *shd* **Royal Etiquette (IRE)**[6] 891 5-9-7 **59** .... DaneO'Neill 7 66
(Lawney Hill) *chsd ldrs: rdn along as pce qcknd 3f out: styd on to chse wnr fnl 120yds: gng on clsng stages but a jst hld* **3/1**[1]
200- 3 *hd* **Tinkerbell Will**[106] 7640 5-8-11 **49** .... RichardThomas 9 55
(John E Long) *chsd ldrs: drvn to chse wnr over 3f out: kpt on u.p fnl f: narrowly lost 2nd fnl 120yds but kpt on: nt qckn clsng stages* **20/1**
4544 4 *2 1/4* **Roman Flame**[21] 732 4-8-13 **51** .... KieranO'Neill 6 53
(Michael Quinn) *led at mod pce: hdd over 4f out: lost 2nd over 3f out: styd chsng ldrs tl wknd fnl 120yds* **12/1**[3]
045- 5 *hd* **Endaxi Mana Mou**[138] 7246 4-8-5 **48** .... RosieJessop(5) 1 50
(Peter Charalambous) *chsd ldrs tl outpcd 4f out: drvn over 2f out: styd on fnl f but no imp* **20/1**
0-54 6 *2 1/4* **Ermyntrude**[55] 305 5-9-3 **55** .... IanMongan 10 52
(Pat Phelan) *in rr: drvn over 2f out: kpt on fnl f: nvr any ch* **8/1**[2]
-046 7 *hd* **Broughton Place**[25] 689 4-9-5 **57** .... StevieDonohoe 8 54
(Willie Musson) *chsd ldr tl over 4f out: wknd over 2f out* **16/1**
5003 8 *2* **Tous Les Deux**[18] 773 9-8-9 **47** .... MichaelStainton 3 40
(Dr Jeremy Naylor) *in rr: rdn and effrt on outer over 2f out: nvr gng pce to get into contention* **33/1**
060/ 9 *11* **Our Georgie Girl**[1009] 2978 5-8-7 **45** .... AndreaAtzeni 2 16
(Rod Millman) *chsd ldrs to 1/2-way* **66/1**
2m 10.02s (2.02) **Going Correction** +0.05s/f (Slow) **9** Ran SP% **88.6**
Speed ratings (Par 101): **93,92,92,90,90 89,88,87,78**
Tote Swingers: 1&2 £1.70, 1&3 £6.40, 2&3 £7.10 CSF £6.07 CT £54.95 TOTE £3.00: £1.10, £1.10, £6.40; EX 8.50 Trifecta £56.00 Pool: £234.21 - 3.09 winning units..
Owner Jamie Robert Roberts **Bred** Tareq Al Mazeedi **Trained** Portway, Worcs
■ Stewards' Enquiry : Dane O'Neill two-day ban; used whip above permitted level (3rd,4th Apr)

FOCUS
This moderate handicap lost plenty of its interest when the gambled-on Trecase refused to enter the stalls. A rather muddling race in which the runner-up sets the form standard.

967 CARLING H'CAP (LONDON MILE QUALIFIER) 1m (P)
3:10 (3:10) (Class 5) (0-70,69) 4-Y-0+ £2,264 (£673; £336; £168) Stalls Low

Form RPR
2622 1 **Alhaban (IRE)**[5] 909 6-9-7 **69** .... LukeMorris 5 79
(Ronald Harris) *in tch: hdwy 2f out: sn drvn: led 1f out: styd on strly clsng stages: comf* **4/1**[2]
1500 2 *3* **Hip Hip Hooray**[13] 821 6-9-4 **66** .... IanMongan 7 69
(Luke Dace) *in rr: hdwy and rdn over 1f out: styd on fnl f to take 2nd fnl 30yds but no ch w wnr* **11/1**
030- 3 *shd* **Afkar (IRE)**[117] 7532 4-9-7 **69** .... BrettDoyle 3 72
(Clive Brittain) *led 2f: styd chsng ldrs: rdn and ev ch appr fnl f: kpt on clsng stages but no ch w wnr* **6/1**
12-1 4 *nk* **Zaheeb**[13] 821 4-9-4 **66** .... WilliamCarson 8 68
(Dave Morris) *chsd ldrs: slt ld 2f out: jnd over 1f out and sn hdd: kpt on u.p fnl 120yds* **2/1**[1]
-012 5 *nk* **Warbond**[20] 736 4-8-11 **59** .... JamieGoldstein 6 61
(Michael Madgwick) *s.i.s: in rr: hdwy on ins 2f out: ev ch 1f out: styd on same pce fnl 120yds* **11/2**[3]
606- 6 *1/2* **Arctic Mirage**[175] 6434 4-9-1 **63** .... DaneO'Neill 1 63
(Michael Blanshard) *chsd ldrs: drvn and ev ch 1f out one pce u.p fnl 120yds* **25/1**
00-0 7 *1* **Dinner Date**[13] 821 10-9-0 **65** .... RyanClark(3) 11 63
(Tom Keddy) *in tch: drvn and hdwy over 1f out: one pce ins fnl f* **33/1**
-163 8 *2* **Rezwaan**[13] 821 5-9-6 **68** .... (p) FrankieMcDonald 10 62
(Murty McGrath) *in rr: rdn and hung rt fr 2f out: no ch after* **8/1**
-002 9 *1/2* **Ensnare**[18] 761 7-9-1 **63** .... StevieDonohoe 2 55
(Willie Musson) *in rr tl styd on fnl f* **14/1**
05-0 10 *6* **West Leake (IRE)**[13] 821 6-9-5 **67** .... LiamKeniry 12 46
(Paul Burgoyne) *led after 2f: hdd 2f out: hung rt and sn wknd* **20/1**
1m 39.42s (-0.38) **Going Correction** +0.05s/f (Slow) **10** Ran SP% **120.7**
Speed ratings (Par 103): **103,100,99,99,99 98,97,95,95,89**
Tote Swingers: 1&2 £9.70, 1&3 £6.70, 2&3 £17.50 CSF £47.78 CT £267.83 TOTE £4.00: £1.40, £3.50, £1.30; EX 48.40 Trifecta £137.60 Pool: £728.94 - 3.92 winning units..
Owner Robert Bailey **Bred** Eimear Mulhern **Trained** Earlswood, Monmouths

FOCUS
There wasn't much pace on in this ordinary handicap and it saw a blanket finish. It's possible the form is not all it seems but the winner is accorded a small personal best.
Ensnare Official explanation: jockey said regarding running and riding of gelding that his instructions were to jump out get him in a postition where he was travelling get him in a position he was travelling nicely. He added that gelding had banged his head leaving the stalls, which had been reported in the weighing room. He further stated that gelding was never able to go the early pace and failed to pick up.

968 COORS LIGHT H'CAP 2m (P)
3:40 (3:40) (Class 6) (0-55,55) 4-Y-0+ £1,617 (£481; £240; £120) Stalls Low

Form RPR
4-22 1 **Broughtons Bandit**[39] 493 5-9-0 **48** .... StevieDonohoe 3 57
(Willie Musson) *hld up in rr: hdwy over 2f out: rdn to ld appr fnl f: drvn out clsng stages* **7/2**[2]
0054 2 *nk* **Bilidn**[31] 575 4-8-12 **51** .... ChrisCatlin 10 59
(Noel Quinlan) *t.k.h: trckd ldrs: chal fr over 4f out tl slt ld ins fnl 3f: hdd 2f out: styd pressing ldrs: chsd wnr ins fnl f but no imp clsng stages* **3/1**[1]
05-3 3 *hd* **Captain Sharpe**[24] 557 4-9-2 **55** .... (p) MartinLane 7 63
(Bernard Llewellyn) *chsd ldrs: drvn and outpcd over 4f out: hdwy u.p wl over 1f out: styd on wl clsng stages to dispute 2nd fnl 120yds: kpt on but no imp on wnr clsng stages* **14/1**
-003 4 *5* **Bengal Tiger**[6] 895 6-8-10 **51** .... GeorgeDowning(7) 1 53
(Tony Carroll) *chsd ldrs: led 2f out: sn rdn: hdd over 1f out: wknd ins fnl f* **14/1**
/0-0 5 *5* **Calzaghe (IRE)**[13] 825 8-9-6 **54** .... (v) LukeMorris 6 50
(Martin Hill) *hld up in rr: sme hdwy 3f out: nvr rchd ldrs: btn fr 2f out* **16/1**
250/ 6 *1* **Mymateeric**[444] 7213 6-8-9 **46** oh1 .... SimonPearce(3) 4 41
(Lydia Pearce) *chsd ldrs: rdn over 2f out: sn btn* **50/1**
00-6 7 *2 1/4* **Bute Street**[32] 594 7-9-3 **51** .... GeorgeBaker 9 43
(Ron Hodges) *hld up in rr: sme prog over 2f out: nvr nr ldrs* **13/2**
051- 8 *1 3/4* **Hamilton Hill**[147] 7087 5-9-6 **54** .... JimCrowley 11 44
(Dai Burchell) *chsd ldr tl led in front 1/2-way: hdd ins fnl 3f: wknd rapidly over 1f out* **7/1**
500 9 *9* **Chhota Naa**[36] 546 4-8-7 **51** .... (p) RaulDaSilva(5) 5 30
(Harry Dunlop) *a towards rr* **16/1**
-060 10 *8* **Raghdaan**[42] 454 5-8-12 **46** oh1 .... (t) WilliamCarson 12 16
(Peter Hiatt) *in tch: hdwy 1/2-way: wknd 3f out* **25/1**
1500 11 *7* **Prince Charlemagne (IRE)**[18] 772 9-9-3 **51** .... (p) MichaelStainton 2 12
(Dr Jeremy Naylor) *t.k.h: in tch tl wknd qckly 4f out* **20/1**
025- U **Who Loves Ya Baby**[94] 7800 4-8-8 **52** .... RosieJessop(5) 8
(Peter Charalambous) *led: lft rein broke, rn out and uns rdr 1/2-way* **11/2**[3]
3m 31.43s (1.33) **Going Correction** +0.05s/f (Slow)
WFA 4 from 5yo+ 5lb **12** Ran SP% **124.1**
Speed ratings (Par 101): **98,97,97,95,92 92,91,90,85,81 78,**
Tote Swingers: 1&2 £3.40, 1&3 £5.20, 2&3 £11.90 CSF £14.88 CT £137.25 TOTE £5.40: £1.40, £1.10, £4.60; EX 16.20 Trifecta £108.60 Pool: £721.08 - 4.91 winning units..
Owner Broughton Thermal Insulation **Bred** M E Broughton **Trained** Newmarket, Suffolk

FOCUS
There was drama in this weak staying handicap as the front-running Who Loves Ya Baby ducked out going into the back straight and sent his rider crashing into the far rail. The race was steadily run and the principals ultimately pulled clear in a tight finish. It's doubtful if this is form to be too positive about.

969 GOFFS READY-TO-RUN SALE APRIL 3RD MAIDEN STKS 6f (P)
4:10 (4:12) (Class 5) 3-Y-0+ £2,264 (£673; £336; £168) Stalls Low

Form RPR
336- 1 **Yeeoow (IRE)**[137] 7273 3-8-13 **75** .... MartinHarley 8 75+
(Mrs K Burke) *trckd ldr: led 2f out: drvn clr fnl f: readily* **7/2**[2]
0- 2 *1* **Willies Wonder (IRE)**[206] 5480 3-8-13 0 .... MichaelHills 10 70+
(Charles Hills) *t.k.h: trckd ldrs: chsd wnr ins fnl 2f: kpt on but no imp ins fnl f* **3/1**[1]
3 *1 1/4* **Choice Words (USA)** 4-9-12 0 .... KieranO'Neill 7 70
(Emma Lavelle) *in rr: hdwy: n.m.r: drvn and green 2f out: styd on to take 3rd fnl f: kpt on but no imp on ldng duo* **10/1**
3 4 *1* **Compton Prince**[18] 770 3-8-13 0 .... JohnFahy 6 63
(Clive Cox) *chsd ldrs: drvn over 2f out: kpt on same pce fnl f* **16/1**
5 *nk* **Cooler Climes** 3-8-13 0 .... TomQueally 9 62+
(Pat Eddery) *s.i.s: in rr: pushed along hung rt and green over 2f out: drvn over 1f out: styd on fnl f: gng on cl home* **12/1**
6 *1 1/2* **Finesse** 3-8-8 0 .... JimCrowley 2 52
(Ralph Beckett) *towards rr: pushed along over 2f out: kpt on clsng stages but nvr gng pce to get into contention* **8/1**
50 7 *3/4* **Marinus (IRE)**[55] 298 3-8-13 0 .... LiamKeniry 3 55
(Sylvester Kirk) *t.k.h: in tch: effrt on ins fr 2f out: nvr in tch over 1f out: wknd ins fnl f* **16/1**
6- 8 *3* **Invincible Beauty (IRE)**[181] 6252 3-8-8 0 .... LukeMorris 11 40
(Seamus Durack) *in rr: riddn and effrt to get in bhd ldrs 2f out: sn btn* **50/1**
2- 9 *2 3/4* **Hannibal Hayes (USA)**[251] 3984 3-8-13 0 .... RyanMoore 1 36
(Jeremy Noseda) *plld hrd: chsd ldrs: rdn and wknd over 2f out* **6/1**[3]
4 10 *6* **One Last Dream**[21] 731 3-8-10 0 .... SimonPearce(3) 4 17
(Ron Hodges) *in rr most of way* **100/1**
42 11 *5* **Sugar Prince (IRE)**[21] 730 3-8-13 0 .... JamieSpencer 5
(Tim Pitt) *led tl hdd 2f out: sn eased* **6/1**[3]
1m 12.79s (-0.31) **Going Correction** +0.05s/f (Slow)
WFA 3 from 4yo 13lb **11** Ran SP% **118.4**
Speed ratings (Par 103): **104,102,101,99,99 97,96,92,88,80 73**
Tote Swingers: 1&2 £4.20, 1&3 £10.40, 2&3 £5.60 CSF £14.53 TOTE £5.40: £1.70, £1.10, £4.40; EX 17.70 Trifecta £384.10 Pool: £988.00 - 1.90 winning units..
Owner R Lee & Mrs E Burke **Bred** Arctic Tack Stud **Trained** Middleham Moor, N Yorks

FOCUS
A modest maiden but it should throw up its share of future winners. The form choice winner looks the best initial guide.
One Last Dream Official explanation: jockey said gelding ran green
Sugar Prince(IRE) Official explanation: jockey said saddle slipped

970 KEMPTON PARK (SUPPORTED BY BETFAIR) FILLIES' H'CAP 6f (P)
4:40 (4:40) (Class 5) (0-70,70) 3-Y-0+ £2,264 (£673; £336; £168) Stalls Low

Form RPR
2-20 1 **Dressed In Lace**[62] 201 3-9-0 **69** .... IanMongan 3 73
(Jo Crowley) *chsd ldrs: wnt 2nd 2f out: hrd drvn to take narrow ld fnl 120yds: hld on all out* **9/2**[2]
1-42 2 *nk* **Catalinas Diamond (IRE)**[15] 806 4-9-6 **62** .... (t) SteveDrowne 5 69
(Pat Murphy) *chsd ldrs: drvn to go 3rd over 1f out: styd on u.p fnl f: tk 2nd clsng stages but nt quite rch wnr* **8/1**
0261 3 *hd* **Amazing Win (IRE)**[13] 819 4-9-5 **61** .... TonyCulhane 4 67
(Mick Channon) *led: drvn along over 1f out: hdd fnl 120yds: no ex and lost 2nd clsng stages* **3/1**[1]
1-46 4 *1 1/2* **Chester'Slittlegem (IRE)**[19] 749 3-8-10 **65** .... JohnFahy 2 63
(Ed de Giles) *in rr: rdn and hdwy appr fnl f: kpt on clsng stages: nt rch ldrs* **14/1**
2100 5 *nk* **Cut The Cackle (IRE)**[6] 904 6-9-4 **60** .... (bt) WilliamCarson 9 61
(Richard Guest) *in rr: drvn and hdwy over 1f out: styd on wl clsng stages* **7/1**[3]
604- 6 *nk* **Rockme Cockney**[138] 7248 3-8-5 **65** .... RaulDaSilva(5) 7 61
(Jeremy Gask) *chsd ldrs: rdn 3f out: one pce 2f out: kpt on again clsng stages* **10/1**
06-3 7 *nk* **Secret Queen**[15] 806 5-9-4 **60** .... (v) LukeMorris 8 59
(Martin Hill) *s.i.s: in rr: drvn and hdwy fnl f: nt rch ldrs* **7/1**[3]
12-3 8 *1/2* **Sunny Side Up (IRE)**[70] 112 3-8-8 **63** .... TonyHamilton 11 56
(Richard Fahey) *trckd ldr: chal 4f out to 3f out: wknd 2f out* **8/1**
320- 9 *nk* **Shes Rosie**[235] 4486 4-10-0 **70** .... RussKennemore 10 66
(John O'Shea) *chsd ldrs: rdn over 2f out: wknd over 1f out* **14/1**

0-06 **10** *6* **Yalding Dancer**[32] 597 3-8-3 **58**................................ RichardThomas 1 31
(John Best) *outpcd* **66/1**

1m 13.35s (0.25) **Going Correction** +0.05s/f (Slow)
WFA 3 from 4yo+ 13lb **10** Ran SP% **114.3**
Speed ratings (Par 100): **100,99,99,97,96 96,96,95,95,87**
Tote Swingers: 1&2 £4.20, 1&3 £4.60, 2&3 £6.00 CSF £39.52 CT £123.80 TOTE £6.40: £4.40, £3.80, £1.10; EX 51.00 Trifecta £212.80 Pool: £681.65 - 2.37 winning units..

Owner Mrs Liz Nelson **Bred** R F And S D Knipe **Trained** Whitcombe, Dorset

FOCUS
It paid to race handily in this modest fillies' sprint handicap. The form makes a fair bit of sense amongst the first four.

Shes Rosie Official explanation: jockey said filly ran too freely

971 KEMPTON.CO.UK (SUPPORTED BY BETFAIR) H'CAP 1m 4f (P)
5:10 (5:10) (Class 4) (0-85,84) 4-Y-O+ **£4,528** (£1,347; £673; £336) **Stalls** Centre

Form RPR

4-16 **1** **Tappanappa (IRE)**[24] 712 5-9-7 **84**............................(v) DavidProbert 2 93+
(Andrew Balding) *trckd ldrs: pushed along to ld wl over 1f out: styd on strly fnl f* **9/4**[1]

0-22 **2** *2 ¾* **Halla San**[10] 872 10-9-5 **82**... TonyHamilton 6 87
(Richard Fahey) *chsd ldrs: drvn 2f out: chsd wnr jst ins fnl f: kpt on but no imp* **16/1**

2-33 **3** *3 ¼* **Where's Susie**[10] 872 7-9-2 **79**.. DaneO'Neill 3 80+
(Michael Madgwick) *in rr: drvn and hdwy fr 2f out: styd on wl fnl f: tk 3rd clsng stages but no imp on ldng duo* **8/1**

610- **4** *½* **Saint Helena (IRE)**[200] 5693 4-8-12 **77**............................. LukeMorris 1 76
(Harry Dunlop) *led 1f: styd chsng ldrs: drvn to dispute 2nd wl over 1f out: wknd fnl 120yds: dropped to 4th clsng stages* **10/1**

05-3 **5** *1* **Mataaleb**[19] 745 5-9-3 **83**... SimonPearce(3) 10 80
(Lydia Pearce) *chsd ldrs: wnt 2nd 6f out: chal fr 4 out tl led wl over 2f out: hdd wl over 1f out: wknd ins fnl f* **7/1**[3]

004- **6** *2 ¾* **Highlife Dancer**[155] 6916 4-8-8 **73**...................................... ChrisCatlin 4 66
(Mick Channon) *in rr: rdn 3f out: sme prog fnl f* **25/1**

461- **7** *nse* **Daring Indian**[93] 7806 4-8-10 **75**.................................. StevieDonohoe 5 68
(Ian Williams) *in rr: hdwy 3f out: sn rdn: one pce fnl 2f* **7/1**[3]

40-5 **8** *¾* **Pandorica**[57] 275 4-8-6 **71**... MartinLane 8 63
(Bernard Llewellyn) *mid-div: rdn 3f out: sn btn* **33/1**

100- **9** *3* **Yes Chef**[155] 6922 5-9-2 **79**... JamesMillman 7 66
(Rod Millman) *led after 1f: jnd 4f out: hdd wl over 2f out: wknd qckly* **7/2**[2]

20-5 **10** *¾* **Scamperdale**[19] 745 10-9-0 **77**................................. RussKennemore 9 63
(Brian Baugh) *in rr: effrt 3f out: nvr rchd ldrs: sn wknd* **25/1**

2m 32.61s (-1.89) **Going Correction** +0.05s/f (Slow)
WFA 4 from 5yo+ 2lb **10** Ran SP% **114.7**
Speed ratings (Par 105): **108,106,104,103,103 101,101,100,98,98**
Tote Swingers: 1&2 £9.40, 1&3 £4.70, 2&3 £5.80 CSF £39.39 CT £247.40 TOTE £3.10: £1.10, £2.30, £3.20; EX 27.20 Trifecta £68.90 Pool: £999.96 - 10.73 winning units..

Owner McMahon/Gorell/Pausewang **Bred** P Monaghan, J Collins & G Dillon **Trained** Kingsclere, Hants

FOCUS
A fair handicap. It was run at an uneven pace, but the form still makes sense. There could be more to come from the winner.

Daring Indian Official explanation: jockey said gelding ran too freely

972 KEMPTON PARK (SUPPORTED BY BETFAIR) H'CAP 7f (P)
5:40 (5:40) (Class 6) (0-60,60) 4-Y-O+ **£1,617** (£481; £240; £120) **Stalls** Low

Form RPR

3050 **1** **Spin Again (IRE)**[40] 478 7-9-7 **60**........................... RichardKingscote 9 75
(Daniel Kubler) *trckd ldr: led over 2f out: pushed out fnl f: comf* **14/1**

0-11 **2** *4* **Diplomatic (IRE)**[33] 578 7-9-7 **60**...................................... AdamKirby 7 64+
(Michael Squance) *in rr: drvn over 2f out: styd on wl fnl f: tk 2nd last strides but no ch w wnr* **13/8**[1]

064- **3** *½* **Fortunate Bid (IRE)**[123] 7463 6-9-5 **58**.......................(p) TonyHamilton 3 61
(Linda Stubbs) *in tch: hdwy on ins 2f out: drvn to dispute 2nd ins fnl f: nt rch wnr: styd on same pce* **12/1**

-021 **4** *nse* **Lady Mango (IRE)**[17] 781 4-9-6 **59**................................... LukeMorris 5 62
(Ronald Harris) *chsd ldrs: rdn 2f out: styd on fnl f: gng on clsng stages* **9/2**[2]

1633 **5** *½* **Jonnie Skull (IRE)**[7] 886 6-9-3 **56**...........................(vt) JamieSpencer 8 57
(Phil McEntee) *led: rdn and hdd over 2f out: lost 2nd fnl 120yds: wknd clsng stages* **12/1**

0-13 **6** *1 ¾* **Buxton**[13] 828 8-9-7 **60**...(t) MartinLane 4 57
(Roger Ingram) *in rr: hdwy on ins over 1f out: kpt on same pce ins fnl f* **14/1**

2142 **7** *nk* **Do More Business (IRE)**[32] 598 5-9-2 **55**..................(v) IanMongan 13 51
(Alison Batchelor) *chsd ldrs: rdn 2f out: wknd ins fnl f* **16/1**

26-1 **8** *½* **Ereka (IRE)**[26] 662 4-9-0 **53**.. SteveDrowne 1 47
(John Best) *chsd ldrs: rdn 2f out: wknd ins fnl f* **10/1**[3]

3053 **9** *½* **Metropolitan Chief**[12] 837 8-8-8 **47**.................................... JohnFahy 6 40
(Paul Burgoyne) *t.k.h: chsd ldrs: rdn over 2f out: wknd fnl f* **25/1**

-060 **10** *1* **Custom House (IRE)**[45] 425 4-9-3 **56**................(b) RichardThomas 11 46
(John E Long) *slowly away: in rr: effrt 3f out: nvr rchd ldrs: btn over 1f out* **28/1**

65-4 **11** *2 ¼* **Hubood**[57] 273 4-9-4 **57**.. BrettDoyle 2 41
(Clive Brittain) *s.i.s: bhd most of way* **10/1**[3]

50/0 **12** *10* **Sun Dream**[20] 736 5-9-1 **54**... TomQueally 12
(Tony Carroll) *slowly away: a in rr* **50/1**

1m 25.4s (-0.60) **Going Correction** +0.05s/f (Slow) **12** Ran SP% **118.3**
Speed ratings (Par 101): **105,100,99,99,99 97,96,96,95,94 92,80**
Tote Swingers: 1&2 £7.30, 1&3 £26.30, 2&3 £6.30 CSF £36.32 CT £305.50 TOTE £21.50: £5.50, £1.40, £3.50; EX 62.90 Trifecta £1007.60 Pool: £1,361.82 - 1.00 winning units..

Owner David Dacosta **Bred** Barry Lyons **Trained** Whitsbury, Hants
■ The first winner for trainer Daniel Kubler.

FOCUS
This modest handicap looked competitive for the class. It was yet another race where racing handily proved an advantage. The winner is rated back to something like last winter's form.

T/Jkpt: Not won. T/Plt: £50.60 to a £1 stake. Pool of £89,885.72 - 1,294.64 winning tickets. T/Qpdt: £9.00 to a £1 stake. Pool of £4,864.73 - 396.83 winning tickets. ST

[898]SOUTHWELL (L-H)
Tuesday, March 20

OFFICIAL GOING: Standard
Wind: Moderate behind Weather: Fine and dry

973 FREE BETTING ON MOBILE WITH FREEBETTING.CO.UK APPRENTICE H'CAP 1m (F)
2:20 (2:20) (Class 6) (0-60,59) 3-Y-O **£1,704** (£503; £251) **Stalls** Low

Form RPR

5-50 **1** **My New Angel (IRE)**[4] 923 3-8-2 **45**.....................(be[1]) DarrenEgan(5) 2 51
(Paul Green) *hld up: hdwy 3f out: swtchd rt and effrt to chal wl over 1f out: rdn to take slt ld and flashed tail ent fnl f: edgd lft and kpt on* **16/1**

503 **2** *1 ½* **Dewala**[28] 642 3-8-13 **54**... JackDuern(3) 3 57
(Michael Appleby) *led: rdn along wl over 2f out: drvn and hdd ent fnl f: kpt on same pce* **4/1**[3]

310- **3** *5* **Percythepinto (IRE)**[131] 7342 3-9-7 **59**..........................(t) DavidKenny 6 51
(George Baker) *trckd ldng pair: cl up 3f out: rdn over 2f out: one pce fr over 1f out* **7/4**[1]

05-4 **4** *nse* **Always Eager**[21] 726 3-9-4 **59**....................................... DarylByrne(3) 4 50
(Mark Johnston) *cl up: rdn along over 3f out: btn 2f out* **15/8**[2]

04-4 **5** *hd* **Ferdy (IRE)**[71] 108 3-8-7 **45**.................................... MatthewLawson 1 36
(Paul Green) *chsd ldrs on inner: rdn along 1/2-way and sn outpcd: swtchd wd over 2f out: plugged on appr fnl f* **8/1**

1m 41.94s (-1.76) **Going Correction** -0.40s/f (Stan) **5** Ran SP% **108.1**
Speed ratings (Par 96): **92,90,85,85,85**
CSF £71.98 TOTE £17.80: £8.30, £1.90; EX 87.00.

Owner C J Dingwall **Bred** Mrs Noelle Walsh **Trained** Lydiate, Merseyside

FOCUS
A poor race and a difficult winner to predict. With the two market leaders both a bit disappointing this is not a race to be too positive about.

My New Angel(IRE) Official explanation: trainer representative said regarding apparent improvement in form filly appeared to have benefited from the first time eye-shield and blinkers.

974 MIRROR PUNTERS CLUB MEDIAN AUCTION MAIDEN STKS 1m (F)
2:50 (2:50) (Class 6) 3-5-Y-O **£1,704** (£503; £251) **Stalls** Low

Form RPR

1 **Clayton** 3-8-10 0 ow1.. PhillipMakin 4 87+
(Kevin Ryan) *trckd ldr: cl up whn green and pushed along briefly 3f out: led on bit wl over 2f out: sn rn green and shkn up wl over 1f out: sn rdn clr: easily* **1/1**[1]

32-3 **2** *9* **Frosty Friday**[68] 137 4-9-7 62..................................... FrederikTylicki 6 62
(J R Jenkins) *trckd ldrs on outer: hdwy and cl up 3f out: rdn over 2f out: kpt on same pce: no ch w wnr* **11/4**[2]

3 *2 ¾* **Time For Harry** 5-9-5 0.. DannyBrock(7) 1 61
(Phil McEntee) *led: rdn along 3f out: hdd wl over 2f out: kpt on same pce fr wl over 1f out* **33/1**

4 *9* **Ossie's Dancer** 3-8-9 0.. JoeFanning 2 35
(Robert Cowell) *s.i.s and towards rr: hdwy over 3f out: sn rdn and nvr nr ldrs* **14/1**

0/5 **5** *14* **Director's Dream (IRE)**[18] 770 4-9-7 0......................... FrannyNorton 7
(Mark Rimmer) *dwlt: a in rr: bhd fnl 3f* **14/1**

5 **6** *1* **Multifac'Eted**[15] 805 3-8-1 0.. RyanPowell(3) 3
(J S Moore) *a towards rr: bhd fnl 3f* **40/1**

2365 **7** *1 ¾* **Darsan (IRE)**[12] 842 4-9-7 61...................................... RobertWinston 5
(Phil McEntee) *chsd ldrs: rdn along wl over 3f out: sn wknd and bhd* **5/1**[3]

1m 41.26s (-2.44) **Going Correction** -0.40s/f (Stan)
WFA 3 from 4yo+ 17lb **7** Ran SP% **112.0**
Speed ratings (Par 101): **96,87,84,75,61 60,58**
Tote Swingers: 1&2 £1.70, 1&3 £6.80, 2&3 £9.20 CSF £3.69 TOTE £3.10: £2.40, £1.10; EX 4.90.

Owner Guy Reed **Bred** G Reed **Trained** Hambleton, N Yorks

FOCUS
A weak and uncompetitive maiden, but the favourite proved different class. The winning time was 0.68 seconds faster than the opening handicap. The winner impressed and looks useful, but overall the form is weak, rated around the runner-up.

975 FREE BETTING OFFERS AT FREEBETTING.CO.UK H'CAP 6f (F)
3:20 (3:22) (Class 5) (0-70,70) 3-Y-O **£2,264** (£673; £336; £168) **Stalls** Low

Form RPR

1222 **1** **Reve Du Jour (IRE)**[6] 898 3-9-2 **65**............................... JimmyFortune 4 73
(Alan McCabe) *qckly away: mde all: rdn over 1f out: kpt on* **2/1**[1]

1-33 **2** *1 ½* **Man Of My Word**[40] 482 3-9-3 **66**............................(p) RobertWinston 3 69
(Scott Dixon) *chsd ldrs on inner: hdwy over 2f out: rdn to chse wnr appr fnl f: sn drvn and kpt on* **9/2**[2]

13-4 **3** *1 ¾* **Scrooby Doo**[19] 749 3-9-4 **70**.. BillyCray(3) 7 67
(Scott Dixon) *chsd wnr: rdn to chal and hung lft 2f out: drvn and one pce appr fnl f* **10/1**[3]

2-25 **4** *5* **Point At Issue (IRE)**[19] 748 3-8-13 **62**.....................(b) AdrianNicholls 8 43
(David Nicholls) *chsd ldrs: rdn along over 2f out: sn one pce* **10/1**[3]

004- **5** *6* **Bartley**[102] 7686 3-9-6 **69**... TomEaves 1 31
(Bryan Smart) *sn rdn along and a outpcd in rr* **20/1**

55-2 **6** *1 ¾* **Ghost Train (IRE)**[13] 827 3-9-7 **70**.................................. JoeFanning 2 26
(Mark Johnston) *in tch: rdn along 1/2-way: sn btn* **2/1**[1]

5-54 **7** *1 ¼* **Essexvale (IRE)**[42] 462 3-8-4 **56** oh7.............................. JulieBurke(3) 6
(Alan Berry) *sn outpcd and a in rr* **100/1**

1m 15.34s (-1.16) **Going Correction** -0.40s/f (Stan) **7** Ran SP% **108.8**
Speed ratings (Par 99): **91,89,86,80,72 69,68**
Tote Swingers: 1&2 £2.00, 1&3 £3.40, 2&3 £4.20 CSF £10.27 CT £60.71 TOTE £3.20: £1.90, £1.70; EX 11.60.

Owner Mrs Z Wentworth **Bred** John Jones **Trained** Averham Park, Notts

FOCUS
Just a fair sprint handicap and there was always likely to be plenty of pace on. The form seems sound enough, rated around the second and third.

Ghost Train(IRE) Official explanation: jockey said gelding never travelled

976 MOBILE FREE BETS WITH FREEBETTING.CO.UK (S) STKS 1m 4f (F)
3:50 (3:51) (Class 6) 4-Y-O+ **£1,704** (£503; £251) **Stalls** Low

Form RPR

4313 **1** **Trans Sonic**[7] 888 9-9-5 79.......................................(p) DanielTudhope 7 83
(David O'Meara) *mde all: pushed clr 3f out: styd on: easily* **4/7**[1]

0603 **2** *12* **Jordaura**[12] 830 6-8-13 67.. RobertWinston 4 60
(Gay Kelleway) *hld up in rr: hdwy 1/2-way: rdn to chse wnr over 2f out: drvn wl over 1f out: sn no imp* **3/1**[2]

0-42 **3** *5* **Harare**[29] 632 11-8-6 50....(v) GemmaTutty(7) 2 50
(Karen Tutty) *bhd hdwy over 3f out: rdn 2f out: styd on to take poor 3rd nr fin* **10/1**

4 *shd* **Polurrian (IRE)**[12] 5-8-13 0....(b) RobertHavlin 3 50
(Charles Egerton) *trckd wnr: effrt 4f out: rdn along over 3f out: sn one pce: lost poor 3rd nr fin* **8/1**[3]

20-4 **5** *17* **Davana**[12] 830 6-8-9 50 ow1.... RobbieFitzpatrick 5 19
(Colin Teague) *prom: pushed along 1/2-way: rdn and wknd over 4f out* **14/1**

6 *14* **Skiddaw Secret**[75] 5-8-8 0.... TomEaves 1
(John Weymes) *a towards rr: outpcd and bhd fnl 4f* **28/1**

0-0 **7** *1 ½* **Give Or Take**[33] 581 4-8-11 0.... AdrianNicholls 8
(Christine Dunnett) *in rr: rdn along bef 1/2-way: sn bhd* **80/1**

00- **8** *13* **Reveal The Light**[245] 4185 5-8-5 45.... RyanPowell(3) 6
(Garry Woodward) *in tch: hdwy 5f out: rdn along over 3f out: sn wknd and bhd* **20/1**

2m 36.03s (-4.97) **Going Correction** -0.40s/f (Stan)
WFA 4 from 5yo+ 2lb **8** Ran SP% **125.0**
Speed ratings (Par 101): **100,92,88,88,77 67,66,58**
Tote Swingers: 1&2 £1.50, 1&3 £3.50, 2&3 £2.30 CSF £2.92 TOTE £1.60: £1.02, £1.20, £2.80; EX 3.20.The winner was bought in for 6,250gns. Polurrian was claimed by R G Fell for £6,000.
Owner Mrs Lynne Lumley **Bred** I A Balding **Trained** Nawton, N Yorks

FOCUS
About as uncompetitive a seller as you can get with half the field beaten passing the winning post on the first circuit. The form is rated around the winner.

977 FREE BETTING WITH FREEBETTING.CO.UK H'CAP 5f (F)
4:20 (4:20) (Class 4) (0-85,81) 3-Y-0 **£4,095** (£1,225; £612; £306; £152) **Stalls** High

Form RPR
24-4 **1** **Wicked Wench**[72] 99 3-8-9 **69**.... RobbieFitzpatrick 2 83
(Jo Hughes) *dwlt: hdwy on outer after 1f: cl up 1/2-way: rdn along 2f out: kpt on to ld ent fnl f: styd on strly* **9/1**

23-4 **2** *2 ½* **Bookiesindexdotnet**[73] 86 3-8-2 **69**.... DarrenEgan(7) 1 74
(J R Jenkins) *cl up: rdn to ld wl over 1f out: hdd ent fnl f: kpt on same pce* **17/2**[3]

-111 **3** *½* **Bella Ophelia (IRE)**[19] 749 3-9-3 **77**.... JimmyFortune 5 80
(Hughie Morrison) *cl up: effrt to chal 2f out: sn rdn and ev ch tl drvn and one pce ins fnl f* **8/13**[1]

012- **4** *6* **I'll Be Good**[146] 7103 3-9-7 **81**.... JoeFanning 4 63
(Robert Johnson) *trckd ldrs: effrt 2f out: sn rdn and no imp* **7/2**[2]

0343 **5** *2 ¾* **Ishiamiracle**[28] 645 3-7-11 **64** ow1....(p) DannyBrock(7) 3 36
(Phil McEntee) *led: rdn along over 2f out: sn hdd & wknd* **20/1**

57.55s (-2.15) **Going Correction** -0.325s/f (Stan) **5** Ran SP% **109.4**
Speed ratings (Par 100): **104,100,99,89,85**
CSF £69.80 TOTE £9.40: £3.80, £3.50; EX 58.10.
Owner James Hearne **Bred** Rainsbrook Bloodstock **Trained** Lambourn, Berks

FOCUS
A small field, but a decent 3yo sprint handicap and a bit of a turn-up. The winner posted a 6lb personal best in a good time.

978 FOLLOW SOUTHWELL ON TWITTER H'CAP 1m 3f (F)
4:50 (4:50) (Class 5) (0-75,75) 4-Y-0+ **£2,264** (£673; £336; £168) **Stalls** Low

Form RPR
3324 **1** **Southern State (USA)**[13] 820 4-9-2 **71**.... JoeFanning 6 79
(Mark Johnston) *trckd ldrs on inner: hdwy 3f out: effrt wl over 1f out: sn rdn: edgd rt ins fnl f: styd on to ld last 50yds* **9/2**[3]

4141 **2** *¾* **Newport Arch**[7] 888 4-8-12 **70** 6ex....(v) MichaelO'Connell(3) 9 77
(John Quinn) *trckd ldrs: smooth hdwy 3f out and sn cl up: led wl over 1f out: rdn ins fnl f: hdd and no ex last 50yds* **4/1**[2]

4312 **3** *¾* **Favorite Girl (GER)**[12] 836 4-8-3 **65** ow1.... JackDuern(7) 3 70
(Michael Appleby) *cl up: led after 3f: rdn along over 2f out: hdd wl over 1f out: ev ch tl drvn and one pce ins fnl f* **7/1**

1-12 **4** *3 ½* **Mediterranean Sea (IRE)**[14] 810 6-9-7 **75**.... FrederikTylicki 5 74
(J R Jenkins) *hld up towards rr: pushed along over 3f out: hdwy over 2f out: sn rdn and kpt on: nt rch ldrs* **11/4**[1]

02-0 **5** *9* **Lifetime (IRE)**[25] 692 4-8-13 **68**.... BarryMcHugh 1 51
(Brian Ellison) *sn led: hdd after 3f: cl up: rdn along 3f out: grad wknd* **9/1**

4346 **6** *2* **Hidden Glory**[11] 849 5-9-6 **74**....(b) PaulMulrennan 7 53
(James Given) *hld up: hdwy over 3f out: sn rdn along and n.d* **11/2**

40-1 **7** *1* **Light The City (IRE)**[14] 811 5-8-7 **61** oh1.... JamesSullivan 8 38
(Ruth Carr) *prom: rdn along wl over 3f out and sn wknd* **16/1**

3-00 **8** *18* **King Of Windsor (IRE)**[14] 812 5-9-5 **73**.... TomEaves 4 18
(Keith Dalgleish) *a in rr* **40/1**

2m 23.13s (-4.87) **Going Correction** -0.40s/f (Stan)
WFA 4 from 5yo+ 1lb **8** Ran SP% **111.1**
Speed ratings (Par 103): **101,100,99,97,90 89,88,75**
Tote Swingers: 1&2 £3.70, 1&3 £5.50, 2&3 £4.90 CSF £21.45 CT £117.65 TOTE £5.40: £1.80, £2.40, £2.00; EX 23.40.
Owner Sheikh Hamdan Bin Mohammed Al Maktoum **Bred** Edward P Evans **Trained** Middleham Moor, N Yorks

FOCUS
Quite a competitive handicap, but they didn't go much of a pace. A small step up from the winner, and solid enough form.

979 DINE IN THE PANTRY H'CAP 5f (F)
5:20 (5:20) (Class 6) (0-55,61) 4-Y-0+ **£1,704** (£503; £251) **Stalls** High

Form RPR
3021 **1** **First In Command (IRE)**[7] 887 7-9-8 **61** 6ex....(t) ShaneKelly 1 72+
(Daniel Mark Loughnane) *trckd ldrs: smooth hdwy on outer wl over 1f out: cl up on bit ent fnl f: qcknd to ld last 100yds: easily* **5/6**[1]

5-30 **2** *2 ¼* **The Magic Of Rio**[5] 910 6-8-4 **46** oh1.... RyanPowell(3) 4 49
(John Balding) *led: rdn over 1f out: hdd last 100yds: kpt on: no ch w wnr* **10/1**

2001 **3** *¾* **Ladydolly**[19] 750 4-8-9 **55**....(p) DarrenEgan(7) 2 55
(Roy Brotherton) *chsd ldrs: hdwy and cl up 2f out: rdn to chal over 1f out: one pce fnl f* **9/2**[2]

-404 **4** *3 ¾* **Bygones For Coins (IRE)**[25] 691 4-8-7 **46** oh1.... JoeFanning 5 33
(Alan Berry) *cl up: rdn along 2f out: grad wknd* **20/1**

0-00 **5** *4* **Namir (IRE)**[26] 664 10-8-7 **51**....(bt) DavidKenny(5) 7 23
(James Evans) *chsd ldrs: rdn along 2f out: sn wknd* **28/1**

50-0 **6** *1 ¼* **Egyptian Lord**[78] 8 9-8-8 **47** oh1 ow1....(b) RobbieFitzpatrick 6 15
(Peter Grayson) *chsd ldrs: rdn over 2f out: sn wknd* **100/1**

0-10 **7** *nk* **Prignsov Dancer (IRE)**[3] 939 7-8-12 **51**.... RobertWinston 3 18
(Garry Woodward) *dwlt and towards rr: pushed along 1/2-way: rdn and swtchd lft wl over 1f out: n.d* **6/1**[3]

420- **8** *4* **Inde Country**[99] 7737 4-8-9 **55**....(t) JackDuern(7) 8
(Nicky Vaughan) *racd nr stands' rail: chsd ldrs: rdn along 2f out: sn wknd* **16/1**

58.49s (-1.21) **Going Correction** -0.325s/f (Stan) **8** Ran SP% **111.2**
Speed ratings (Par 101): **96,92,91,85,78 76,76,69**
Tote Swingers: 1&2 £2.30, 1&3 £1.90, 2&3 £6.10 CSF £9.52 CT £23.64 TOTE £2.20: £1.10, £2.50, £1.10; EX 11.10.
Owner Mrs C Loughnane **Bred** Peter And Mrs McCutcheon **Trained** Baldwin's Gate, Staffs

FOCUS
A weak sprint handicap to end the card and the result was never really in doubt. Those that raced towards the centre of the track were again favoured. The form is rated around the runner-up.
Prignsov Dancer(IRE) Official explanation: jockey said gelding jumped awkardly leaving stalls
T/Plt: £146.30 to a £1 stake. Pool of £860,507.38 - 301.83 winning tickets. T/Qpdt: £16.20 to a £1 stake. Pool of £4,774.31 - 217.68 winning tickets. JR

980 - (Foreign Racing) - See Raceform Interactive

966 KEMPTON (A.W) (R-H)
Wednesday, March 21

OFFICIAL GOING: Standard
Wind: Moderate, across (towards stands) Weather: Fine, pleasant

981 WIN BIG WITH BETDAQ MULTIPLES MEDIAN AUCTION MAIDEN STKS 7f (P)
5:20 (5:21) (Class 5) 3-5-Y-0 **£2,264** (£673; £336; £168) **Stalls** Low

Form RPR
1 **Dellbuoy** 3-8-6 0.... JemmaMarshall(5) 6 74+
(Pat Phelan) *s.i.s: rn green in last early: gd prog over 2f out to join ldr over 1f out: shkn up to ld narrowly but decisively last 100yds* **20/1**

53-4 **2** *nk* **Emman Bee (IRE)**[14] 827 3-8-6 62.... MartinLane 2 68
(John Gallagher) *trckd ldrs: prog to ld over 1f out: sn jnd: r.o but hdd and hld last 100yds* **4/1**[2]

062- **3** *4 ½* **Viola Da Gamba (IRE)**[213] 5299 3-8-6 74....[1] HayleyTurner 4 56
(William Knight) *led after 1f: hanging lft and reminder 4f out and again over 3f out: rdn over 2f out: hdd and nt qckn over 1f out: sn outpcd* **5/4**[1]

50- **4** *nse* **King Vahe (IRE)**[92] 7835 3-8-11 0.... JimCrowley 8 61
(Alan Jarvis) *trckd ldr over 5f out: rdn to chal over 2f out: nt qckn wl over 1f out: fdd* **8/1**[3]

0 **5** *3 ¾* **Ghazeer (IRE)**[7] 892 3-8-11 0.... JoeFanning 1 51
(Derek Shaw) *led 1f: cl up tl wknd wl over 1f out* **12/1**

04- **6** *nk* **Bashama**[223] 4963 4-9-7 0.... BrettDoyle 3 50
(Clive Brittain) *in tch: pushed along and no prog over 2f out: wknd over 1f out* **8/1**[3]

5 **7** *1 ¾* **Petersboden**[14] 827 3-8-11 0.... FergusSweeney 7 45
(Michael Blanshard) *hld up: gng wl enough on outer over 2f out: shkn up and wknd over 1f out* **9/1**

60 **8** *nse* **The Bendy Fella (IRE)**[7] 892 4-9-7 0.... LeeNewnes(5) 5 50
(Mark Usher) *s.i.s: in tch in rr: shkn up and no prog over 2f out: wknd* **100/1**

1m 26.4s (0.40) **Going Correction** -0.025s/f (Stan)
WFA 3 from 4yo 15lb **8** Ran SP% **110.1**
Speed ratings (Par 103): **96,95,90,90,86 85,83,83**
toteswingers: 1&2 £12.20, 1&3 £6.90, 2&3 £1.50. CSF £91.10 TOTE £23.90: £4.40, £1.10, £1.30; EX 86.60.
Owner Tony Smith **Bred** Ermyn Lodge Stud Limited **Trained** Epsom, Surrey

FOCUS
Racing took place on the outer course. A weak maiden that went to sole newcomer in the line-up, with the favourite disappointing.
Ghazeer(IRE) Official explanation: jockey said gelding hung left

982 BACK OR LAY AT BETDAQ.COM H'CAP 7f (P)
5:55 (5:56) (Class 5) (0-75,75) 3-Y-0 **£2,264** (£673; £336; £168) **Stalls** Low

Form RPR
452- **1** **Manomine**[97] 7763 3-8-9 **63**.... BrettDoyle 4 69
(Clive Brittain) *blindfold off sltly late and dwlt: sn chsd ldrs in 5th: shkn up over 2f out: prog over 1f out: styd on wl to ld last 50yds* **7/2**[2]

26-2 **2** *½* **Traveller's Tales**[22] 731 3-9-5 **73**.... RyanMoore 6 77
(Richard Hannon) *trckd ldng pair: rdn to chal fr 2f out: drvn ahd last 150yds: hdd and outpcd fnl 50yds* **9/2**[3]

0-52 **3** *¾* **Diamond Marks (IRE)**[27] 663 3-8-9 **63**.... JohnFahy 10 65
(John Gallagher) *carried lft s: t.k.h: sn trckd ldng trio: poised to chal gng best jst over 2f out: rdn and hanging over 1f out but sn upsides: nt qckn ins fnl f* **25/1**

050- **4** *shd* **Rogue Reporter (IRE)**[162] 6771 3-8-11 **68**.... RyanClark(3) 9 70
(Stuart Williams) *carried lft s: hld up in last and wl off the pce: pushed along and sme prog over 2f out: styd on wl fnl f: nrly snatched 3rd* **16/1**

640- **5** *½* **Compton Target (IRE)**[81] 7937 3-8-0 **61**....(t) NicoleNordblad(7) 1 61
(Hans Adielsson) *hld up in midfield: styd on inner in st: shkn up 2f out: trying to cl 1f out: pushed along and kpt on same pce last 150yds* **15/2**

4-41 **6** *shd* **Burnhope**[46] 429 3-9-7 **75**.... LukeMorris 7 75
(Scott Dixon) *wnt lft s: racd freely: led: hrd pressed 2f out: hdd and fdd last 150yds* **3/1**[1]

-302 **7** *nk* **Chambles**[21] 739 3-8-6 **65**....(t) DavidKenny(5) 2 64
(Andrew Reid) *difficult to load into stalls: restless in them and dwlt: settled in 7th: rdn over 2f out: nt qckn and no imp tl styd on last 150yds* **8/1**

420- **8** *2* **Ocean Myth**[205] 5562 3-9-2 **70**.... NickyMackay 5 64
(Jonathan Portman) *chsd ldr and clr of rest to over 2f out: tried to chal 2f out: impeded jst ins fnl f and wknd* **25/1**

650- **9** *½* **Zuzu Angel (IRE)**[209] 5409 3-8-11 **65**.... JimCrowley 8 58
(William Knight) *carried lft s: hld up in last trio: styd on inner in st: reminder over 1f out: nvr involved* **8/1**

5 **10** *2* **Hugenot (IRE)**[19] 766 3-8-11 **65**.... StevieDonohoe 3 52
(Tobias B P Coles) *a in last trio: struggling in last over 2f out* **40/1**

1m 26.45s (0.45) **Going Correction** -0.025s/f (Stan) **10** Ran SP% **115.4**
Speed ratings (Par 98): **96,95,94,94,93 93,93,91,90,88**
toteswingers: 1&2 £1.50, 1&3 £12.60, 2&3 £12.20. CSF £19.03 CT £344.85 TOTE £3.30: £1.60, £2.60, £4.70; EX 20.60.
Owner Mrs C E Brittain **Bred** C R Mason **Trained** Newmarket, Suffolk
■ Brett Doyle's first winner in Britain for more than four years.
■ Stewards' Enquiry : John Fahy one-day ban: careless riding (Apr 4)

FOCUS
The pace appeared fair for this modest handicap. Sound if ordinary form.

Rogue Reporter(IRE) Official explanation: jockey said colt was denied a clear run

983 BETDAQ MOBILE APPS MEDIAN AUCTION MAIDEN STKS 1m 4f (P)
6:25 (6:26) (Class 6) 3-5-Y-0 **£1,617** (£481; £240) **Stalls** Centre

Form RPR

220- **1** **Billy Buttons**[163] 6749 4-9-12 82 DavidProbert 1 67
(Andrew Balding) *mde all: coaxed along and looked in command over 1f out: rdn fnl f and limited rspnse: jst hld on* **1/5**[1]

-233 **2** *shd* **Ctappers**[12] 847 3-8-6 63 ChrisCatlin 4 64
(Mick Channon) *hld up in last: rdn over 3f out and looked in trble: rallied to go 2nd over 1f out: clsd on wnr fnl f: jst failed* **4/1**[2]

3 *11* **Total Obsession**[7] 5-9-9 0 (b[1]) RobertHavlin 3 43
(Mark Hoad) *trckd wnr: rdn to chal over 2f out: lost 2nd and wknd over 1f out* **66/1**[3]

2m 36.97s (2.47) **Going Correction** -0.025s/f (Stan)
WFA 3 from 4yo 22lb 4 from 5yo 2lb **3** Ran SP% **104.8**
Speed ratings (Par 101): **90,89,82**
CSF £1.23 TOTE £1.20; EX 1.10.
Owner W V & Mrs E S Robins **Bred** Mrs Shirley Robins **Trained** Kingsclere, Hants

FOCUS
Perhaps not the performance some were expecting from a 1-5 shot, but he didn't need to match his best in this weak race.

984 BETDAQ MOBILE APPS H'CAP 1m 3f (P)
6:55 (6:58) (Class 6) (0-55,54) 4-Y-O+ **£1,617** (£481; £240; £120) **Stalls** Low

Form RPR

443- **1** **Spartan Spirit (IRE)**[324] 1769 4-9-3 **54** JimmyFortune 1 74+
(Hughie Morrison) *t.k.h: hld up in 5th: smooth prog to ld jst over 2f out: cruised clr over 1f out: eased last 75yds* **10/11**[1]

5332 **2** *2 ½* **Laser Blazer**[7] 895 4-9-1 **52** (p) JimCrowley 7 61
(Jeremy Gask) *trckd ldng pair: wnt 2nd 3f out: tried to chal over 2f out but wnr sn breezed by: unavailing chse after and flattered by proximity* **4/1**[2]

0002 **3** *1 ½* **Lytham (IRE)**[20] 741 11-9-2 **52** AdamKirby 3 58
(Tony Carroll) *hld up in 6th: rdn and prog over 2f out: wnt 3rd jst over 1f out: kpt on but no ch* **7/1**[3]

3502 **4** *2* **Escape Artist**[7] 891 5-8-11 **47** KieranO'Neill 4 50
(John Bridger) *hld up in last pair: cajoled along fr 4f out: nvr on terms but plugged on to take 4th fnl f* **9/1**

0-05 **5** *5* **If What And Maybe**[4] 937 4-8-13 **53** (v) MichaelO'Connell(3) 8 47
(John Ryan) *drvn to ld and set fair pce: hdd jst over 2f out: immediately btn: wknd fnl f* **14/1**

650- **6** *3 ½* **Rasam Aldaar**[17] 6052 4-9-2 **53** (tp) HayleyTurner 6 40
(Neil King) *trckd ldng trio: rdn over 4f out: sn lost pl: no ch whn impeded over 2f out* **14/1**

0420 **7** *9* **Carlton Scroop (FR)**[30] 632 9-8-13 **52** ow1 (v[1]) RobertLButler(3) 5 23
(Paddy Butler) *a in last pair: struggling fnl 3f: sn bhd* **20/1**

0000 **8** *17* **Tunza The Lion**[13] 843 5-8-9 **45** NeilChalmers 9
(Richard Ford) *t.k.h: chsd ldr to 3f out: wknd rapidly: t.o* **66/1**

2m 20.72s (-1.18) **Going Correction** -0.025s/f (Stan)
WFA 4 from 5yo+ 1lb **8** Ran SP% **114.5**
Speed ratings (Par 101): **103,101,100,98,95 92,85,73**
toteswingers: 1&2 £1.70, 1&3 £3.20, 2&3 £2.70. CSF £4.68 CT £15.23 TOTE £1.60: £1.02, £1.10, £2.80; EX 6.50.
Owner Thurloe Thoroughbred XXVIII **Bred** Swordlestown Stud **Trained** East Ilsley, Berks

FOCUS
A weak handicap made up of exposed performers, the obvious exception being the hot favourite. He was value for further and is clearly much improved this year.

985 SKYSPORTS.COM H'CAP (DIV I) 6f (P)
7:25 (7:25) (Class 6) (0-55,55) 4-Y-O+ **£1,617** (£481; £240; £120) **Stalls** Low

Form RPR

6242 **1** **Blueberry Fizz (IRE)**[18] 781 4-9-0 **54** (v) MichaelO'Connell(3) 12 62
(John Ryan) *chsd ldr: led jst bef 1/2-way: hrd rdn over 1f out: hld on nr fin: all out* **7/2**[1]

-500 **2** *½* **Jemimaville (IRE)**[42] 467 5-8-9 **46** oh1 (v) LiamJones 7 52
(Giles Bravery) *trckd ldrs: rdn to go 2nd wl over 1f out: clsd on wnr grad fnl f: nt qckn last 100yds* **16/1**

-064 **3** *1 ¾* **Cheery Cat (USA)**[27] 664 8-9-2 **53** (b) NeilChalmers 3 53
(Richard Ford) *chsd ldrs in 6th: pushed along over 3f out: effrt u.p over 2f out: kpt on to take 3rd last 75yds* **6/1**[3]

0604 **4** *nk* **Toms River Tess (IRE)**[18] 782 4-8-9 **46** oh1 (b) JamieGoldstein 6 45
(Zoe Davison) *racd in 8th and off the pce: wd bnd 3f out: prog 2f out: styd on but nvr able to chal* **66/1**

0/6- **5** *hd* **Spoof Master (IRE)**[434] 123 8-8-7 **47** (t) SimonPearce(3) 9 46
(Lydia Pearce) *chsd ldng pair: wnt 2nd over 2f out to wl over 1f out: no ex fnl f* **25/1**

6606 **6** *1* **Jolie Etoile**[4] 939 4-8-9 **46** oh1 HayleyTurner 8 42
(Tony Carroll) *hld up in 9th and wl off the pce: rdn and sme prog over 2f out: kpt on same pce fr over 1f out* **14/1**

2063 **7** *2 ½* **Dingaan (IRE)**[14] 823 9-9-1 **52** RobbieFitzpatrick 10 40
(Peter Grayson) *hld up in 10th and wl off the pce: effrt on outer over 2f out: plugged on but nvr on terms* **8/1**

0303 **8** *6* **Overwhelm**[18] 781 4-8-13 **55** (t) DavidKenny(5) 1 23
(Andrew Reid) *v s.i.s and lost all ch: wl bhd in last: nvr a factor* **4/1**[2]

04-0 **9** *nk* **Finn's Rainbow**[69] 139 4-9-4 **55** (p) LukeMorris 4 22
(John Weymes) *taken down early and steadily to post: nt on terms in 7th: struggling and no prog over 2f out: wknd* **11/1**

6054 **10** *1* **Sailing North (USA)**[5] 925 4-8-9 **53** (b[1]) DarrenEgan(7) 2 17
(Ronald Harris) *led at str pce but hdd and in trble bef 1/2-way: wknd 2f out* **15/2**

205- **11** *3 ¼* **Mark Anthony (IRE)**[155] 6939 5-9-3 **54** (p) RobertWinston 11
(Shaun Harris) *racd wd: chsd ldrs to 1/2-way: wknd and sn bhd* **8/1**

1m 12.9s (-0.20) **Going Correction** -0.025s/f (Stan) **11** Ran SP% **116.7**
Speed ratings (Par 101): **100,99,97,96,96 95,91,83,83,81 77**
toteswingers: 1&2 £1.70, 1&3 £3.20, 2&3 £2.70. CSF £60.61 CT £333.12 TOTE £3.50: £1.10, £8.70, £1.50; EX 61.60.
Owner Dr R A & Mrs J L Dixon **Bred** Patrick J Corbet **Trained** Newmarket, Suffolk

FOCUS
The first division of an open handicap, although it perhaps wasn't as competitive as it looked on paper. They went a good gallop. It's doubtful the winner had to improve much.

Overwhelm Official explanation: jockey said filly missed the break

986 SKYSPORTS.COM H'CAP (DIV II) 6f (P)
7:55 (7:55) (Class 6) (0-55,55) 4-Y-O+ **£1,617** (£481; £240; £120) **Stalls** High

Form RPR

236- **1** **Running Mate (IRE)**[175] 6444 5-9-4 **55** (t) IanMongan 9 67
(Jo Crowley) *hld up towards rr: prog on outer jst over 2f out: rdn to ld jst ins fnl f: sn in command* **10/3**[1]

1306 **2** *1 ½* **Avonvalley**[34] 576 5-9-3 **54** RobbieFitzpatrick 7 61
(Peter Grayson) *hld up towards rr: swtchd to inner and prog 2f out: cl enough over 1f out: styd on same pce to take 2nd last 100yds* **11/1**

0-00 **3** *1* **Invigilator**[14] 819 4-9-2 **53** JoeFanning 8 57
(Derek Shaw) *hld up in midfield: prog on outer over 2f out: led over 1f out to jst ins fnl f: fdd* **6/1**[3]

0052 **4** *1* **Rise To Glory (IRE)**[4] 938 4-8-9 **46** oh1 RobertWinston 2 47
(Shaun Harris) *trckd ldng pair: led briefly wl over 1f out: outpcd after* **7/2**[2]

500 **5** *1* **Mi Regalo**[28] 653 4-8-9 **46** oh1 (v) LukeMorris 5 43
(Phil McEntee) *chsd ldr: chal 2f out: hanging and fnd nil: btn over 1f out* **14/1**

0535 **6** *¾* **Grand Honour (IRE)**[14] 823 6-8-9 **46** oh1 (p) ShaneKelly 6 41
(Paul Howling) *trckd ldrs: poised to chal 2f out but others sn wnt by: unable to respond after* **14/1**

6000 **7** *1* **Prize Point**[18] 781 6-9-1 **52** (bt) StevieDonohoe 1 44
(Tom Gretton) *led to wl over 1f out: steadily wknd* **25/1**

2000 **8** *1 ¼* **My Best Man**[5] 927 6-9-2 **53** (t) AdamKirby 10 41
(Tony Carroll) *wl in rr: hrd rdn and no prog over 2f out: n.d over 1f out* **8/1**

0-00 **9** *¾* **Dells Breezer**[34] 578 4-8-7 **49** (v[1]) JemmaMarshall(5) 4 34
(Pat Phelan) *chsd ldng quartet: rdn and cl enough wl over 1f out: wknd* **12/1**

6043 **10** *½* **Pharoh Jake**[18] 782 4-8-10 **47** KieranO'Neill 11 31
(John Bridger) *sn in last pair: effrt on inner over 2f out: no prog over 1f out: wknd* **20/1**

3100 **11** *10* **Super Frank (IRE)**[2] 964 9-9-4 **55** (b) JamieGoldstein 3
(Zoe Davison) *rel to r: swvd lft and rdr lost irons: brief effrt to get ito it 1/2-way: sn btn: t.o* **12/1**

1m 12.7s (-0.40) **Going Correction** -0.025s/f (Stan) **11** Ran SP% **116.4**
Speed ratings (Par 101): **101,99,97,96,95 94,92,91,90,89 76**
toteswingers: 1&2 £15.00, 1&3 £5.40, 2&3 £34.90. CSF £40.05 CT £212.87 TOTE £5.30: £1.70, £2.80, £1.20; EX 60.10.
Owner Kilstone Limited **Bred** Paul Ennis **Trained** Whitcombe, Dorset
■ Stewards' Enquiry : Jemma Marshall two-day ban: careless riding (Apr 4-5)

FOCUS
As in division one the pace was decent and the winning time was slightly quicker. It appeared an advantage to come from off the pace. Sound form, rated around the second and third.

Super Frank(IRE) Official explanation: jockey said gelding missed the break

987 SKYSPORTS.COM RACING H'CAP (LONDON MILE QUALIFIER) 1m (P)
8:25 (8:26) (Class 4) (0-80,78) 4-Y-O+ **£4,075** (£1,212; £606; £303) **Stalls** Low

Form RPR

10- **1** **Qaraaba**[179] 6330 5-9-4 **76** GeorgeBaker 8 87
(Seamus Durack) *dropped out in last: gd prog fr 2f out following runner-up through: rdn and r.o fnl f to ld last stride* **9/1**

104- **2** *shd* **Zafeen's Pearl**[123] 7486 5-9-4 **76** ShaneKelly 13 87+
(Dean Ivory) *hld up wl in rr: gd prog jst over 2f out and swtchd to inner: stl on bridle 1f out: shkn up and qcknd to ld last 150yds but move nt decisive: rdn and hdd post* **5/1**[1]

210- **3** *3* **Dr Red Eye**[133] 7339 4-9-2 **77** BillyCray(3) 5 81
(Scott Dixon) *led 1f: chsd ldr: chal again 2f out: w ldr over 1f out tl ins fnl f: sn outpcd* **14/1**

540- **4** *nk* **Islesman**[117] 7542 4-9-6 **78** RobertWinston 1 81
(Heather Main) *trckd ldng pair: rdn to ld over 1f out: sn jnd: hdd and easily outpcd last 150yds* **8/1**

-312 **5** *3 ¼* **Megalala (IRE)**[21] 733 11-9-5 **77** KieranO'Neill 10 73
(John Bridger) *led after 1f and set str pce: urged along over 3f out: hdd over 1f out: fdd* **10/1**

1 **6** *1 ¼* **Mafi (IRE)**[26] 684 4-9-3 **75** RobertHavlin 2 68
(Mark Hoad) *chsd ldrs in 6th: rdn over 2f out: nt pce to prog after* **11/1**

2422 **7** *¾* **Legal Legacy**[32] 626 6-9-3 **75** HayleyTurner 11 66
(David C Griffiths) *s.i.s: hld up in last trio: rdn over 2f out: n.d whn hmpd over 1f out: plugged on* **13/2**[3]

0000 **8** *½* **Spirit Of Xaar (IRE)**[18] 785 6-9-3 **75** FrannyNorton 6 65
(Linda Jewell) *t.k.h: hld up in midfield: rdn over 2f out: no prog and wl btn over 1f out* **33/1**

112- **9** *nk* **Ellie In The Pink (IRE)**[152] 6997 4-9-5 **77** JimCrowley 7 66
(Alan Jarvis) *t.k.h: hld up towards rr: rdn over 2f out: wl hld whn nt clr run over 1f out: fdd* **11/2**[2]

250- **10** *1 ¼* **Cocohatchee**[194] 5892 4-9-1 **73** IanMongan 3 60
(Pat Phelan) *t.k.h: hld up towards rr: rdn and no prog over 2f out: wl btn over 1f out* **33/1**

-121 **11** *2 ¼* **Garstang**[27] 669 9-9-6 **78** NeilChalmers 4 59
(Richard Ford) *chsd ldng pair: drvn and hanging over 2f out: sn wknd* **11/1**

236- **12** *3 ½* **Silenceofthewind (USA)**[186] 6148 5-9-6 **78** (t) MartinHarley 9 51
(Mrs K Burke) *racd wd in midfield: u.p over 2f out: sn btn* **10/1**

-034 **13** *¾* **She Ain't A Saint**[20] 746 4-9-0 **72** (b) LukeMorris 12 44
(Jane Chapple-Hyam) *chsd ldrs in 5th: rdn over 3f out: wknd over 2f out* **10/1**

1m 37.48s (-2.32) **Going Correction** -0.025s/f (Stan) **13** Ran SP% **123.0**
Speed ratings (Par 105): **110,109,106,106,103 102,101,100,100,99 97,93,92**
toteswingers: 1&2 £12.50, 1&3 £33.20, 2&3 £14.10. CSF £55.15 CT £659.78 TOTE £12.00: £5.50, £3.20, £9.50; EX 80.70.
Owner P A Deal **Bred** Shadwell Estate Company Limited **Trained** Baydon, Wilts

FOCUS
Plenty of pace on for this 1m handicap and it was no surprise to see the finishers dominate. The form seems sound.

988 ALL NEW RACING PLUS OUT NOW H'CAP 1m (P)
8:55 (8:55) (Class 7) (0-50,50) 4-Y-O+ **£1,455** (£433; £216; £108) **Stalls** Low

Form RPR

4231 **1** **Odd Ball (IRE)**[13] 837 5-9-0 **50** AmyRyan(3) 9 61
(Lisa Williamson) *s.s: hld up in last pair: gd prog on inner over 2f out: hung lft but led last 150yds: rdn out* **5/1**[2]

3502 **2** *2 ¼* **Jackie Love (IRE)**[14] 829 4-8-8 **48** (b) JenniferFerguson(7) 13 54
(Olivia Maylam) *t.k.h: hld up but sn in 7th: effrt over 2f out: styd on to take 3rd fnl f and 2nd last 50yds: no threat to wnr* **12/1**

0253 **3** ½ **Baby Driver**[12] 848 4-9-3 **50** HayleyTurner 12 55
(Tony Newcombe) *trckd ldr after 2f: led over 3f out: gng easily over 2f out: idled bdly and drvn over 1f out: hdd and btn last 150yds* **7/2**[1]
-654 **4** ½ **Rosy Dawn**[14] 822 7-8-12 **45** ShaneKelly 8 49
(Brett Johnson) *hld up in rr: rdn over 2f out on outer: kpt on fr over 1f out to take 4th nr fin: n.d* **14/1**
4520 **5** 1 **Meydan Style (USA)**[13] 837 6-9-0 **47** NeilChalmers 1 48
(Richard Ford) *trckd ldrs disputing 5th: rdn and tried to cl fr 2f out: one pce fnl f* **12/1**
-404 **6** 2½ **Avalon Bay**[14] 829 4-9-3 **50** (b) AdamKirby 2 46
(Pat Eddery) *chsd ldr 2f: rdn to go 2nd again briefly 2f out: wknd fnl f* **13/2**[3]
3-00 **7** 3¼ **Kenswick**[70] 125 5-8-5 **45** (b) GeorgeDowning(7) 4 33
(Pat Eddery) *hld up wl in rr: wd bnd 3f out: struggling after: no ch over 1f out* **33/1**
320- **8** 2 **Gee Major**[107] 7640 5-9-3 **50** LukeMorris 7 34
(Nicky Vaughan) *chsd ldrs disputing 5th: rdn and no prog over 2f out: wknd over 1f out* **7/2**[1]
06-0 **9** 5 **Clear Spring (IRE)**[19] 773 4-8-12 **45** NickyMackay 10 17
(John Spearing) *chsd ldng pair: rdn and wknd 2f out: eased fnl f* **11/1**
000- **10** *shd* **Titan Diamond (IRE)**[119] 7524 4-8-6 **46** RachealKneller(7) 11 18
(Mark Usher) *racd wd towards rr: wknd 2f out* **40/1**
2601 **11** 7 **Putin (IRE)**[8] 889 4-8-12 **45** (bt) LiamJones 6
(Phil McEntee) *led to over 3f out: wknd rapidly 2f out: t.o* **10/1**

1m 38.82s (-0.98) **Going Correction** -0.025s/f (Stan) **11 Ran SP% 119.3**
Speed ratings (Par 97): **103,100,100,99,98 96,93,91,86,85 78**
toteswingers: 1&2 £11.20, 1&3 £4.30, 2&3 £9.50. CSF £64.71 CT £240.10 TOTE £7.30: £2.50, £2.40, £2.00; EX 32.70.
Owner Mrs S Morris **Bred** Ms S Pettigrew & J Jamieson **Trained** Saighton, Cheshire

FOCUS
A low-grade handicap and the closers again benefited. Solid form, the second and third setting a sound standard.
T/Jkpt: £9,302.30 to a £1 stake. Pool of £72,060.69 - 5.50 winning tickets. T/Plt: £18.40 to a £1 stake. Pool of £73,520.44 - 2,912.36 winning tickets. T/Qpdt: £5.50 to a £1 stake. Pool of £6,677.62 - 895.20 winning tickets. JN

981 KEMPTON (A.W) (R-H)

Thursday, March 22

OFFICIAL GOING: Standard
Wind: Moderate, across (towards stands) Weather: Fine

989 32REDBINGO.COM CLAIMING STKS 1m (P)
6:00 (6:00) (Class 6) 4-Y-0+ **£1,617** (£481; £240; £120) **Stalls** Low

Form RPR
1063 **1** **April Fool**[43] 470 8-8-10 73 (b) DarrenEgan(7) 6 86
(Ronald Harris) *fast away: mde all and nvr less than 3 l clr: shkn up and drew rt away over 1f out* **15/2**[3]
2111 **2** 10 **Red Somerset (USA)**[7] 906 9-8-13 72 KieranO'Neill 4 59
(Mike Murphy) *v awkward leaving stalls and lost many l as wnr blasted off: hld up in last: rdn 1/2-way: laboured prog fr 2f out: tk modest 2nd nr fin* **11/8**[1]
5053 **3** 1 **Archelao (IRE)**[8] 894 4-9-5 68 AmirQuinn 1 63
(Richard Rowe) *trckd wnr: shkn up 2f out: sn wl outpcd and no ch: lost 2nd nr fin* **12/1**
-464 **4** 1 **Aquilifer (IRE)**[54] 351 4-9-5 72 ShaneKelly 2 60
(Mrs K Burke) *trckd ldng pair but nt on terms w them: pushed along and no imp over 2f out: rdn and lost 3rd last 150yds* **10/1**
500- **5** 1½ **Moynahan (USA)**[124] 7492 7-9-5 78 (bt) JimmyFortune 3 57
(Paul Cole) *hld up in 4th and off the pce: rdn over 2f out: no prog and wl btn over 1f out* **9/4**[2]
050- **6** 9 **Tipsy Girl**[216] 5240 4-8-10 73 RobertWinston 5 27
(Denis Coakley) *hld up in 5th: dropped in last and btn over 2f out: t.o* **10/1**

1m 37.37s (-2.43) **Going Correction** -0.05s/f (Stan) **6 Ran SP% 110.5**
Speed ratings (Par 101): **110,100,99,98,96 87**
toteswingers:1&2:£1.70, 2&3:£1.70, 1&3:£6.80 CSF £17.83 TOTE £7.30: £3.10, £1.10; EX 15.70.Red Somerset was subject to a friendly claim. Tipsy Girl was claimed by R. S. Hoskins for £8000.
Owner S & A Mares **Bred** Miss B Swire **Trained** Earlswood, Monmouths

FOCUS
A fairly competitive race of its type, at least on paper, but it was turned into a procession by the fast-starting winner. At face value this is up there with his best turf form, but the effort has been rated more conservatively.

990 32RED CASINO MEDIAN AUCTION MAIDEN FILLIES' STKS 1m (P)
6:30 (6:30) (Class 5) 3-5-Y-0 **£2,264** (£673; £336; £168) **Stalls** Low

Form RPR
5- **1** **Lady Macduff (IRE)**[156] 6935 3-8-11 0 JoeFanning 1 82
(Mark Johnston) *led 1f: trckd ldr to 1/2-way and again wl over 2f out: pushed into ld over 1f out: readily* **9/2**[2]
62- **2** 2 **Safarjal (IRE)**[155] 6950 3-8-11 0 PaulHanagan 6 78
(Charles Hills) *led after 1f and set mod pce: shkn up and hdd over 1f out: nt qckn and wl hld fnl f* **4/9**[1]
03- **3** 2 **Dutch Diamond**[145] 7165 3-8-11 0 NickyMackay 3 73
(John Gosden) *hld up in tch: chsd ldng pair over 2f out: pushed along and no imp but styd on steadily* **6/1**[3]
0- **4** 10 **Pearls From Sydney**[203] 5655 3-8-11 0 StevieDonohoe 7 50
(Paul Cole) *hld up in tch: shkn up and wknd over 2f out: sn bhd* **33/1**
5 1¾ **Russian Rumba (IRE)** 3-8-11 0 RichardKingscote 4 46
(Jonathan Portman) *cl up: trckd ldr 1/2-way to wl over 2f out: sn wknd qckly* **50/1**
6 2¾ **Goodie Goodie** 3-8-11 0 DavidProbert 2 40
(Sylvester Kirk) *hld up: a in last: rn green and struggling fr 1/2-way: wknd over 2f out* **40/1**

1m 39.97s (0.17) **Going Correction** -0.05s/f (Stan) **6 Ran SP% 109.1**
Speed ratings (Par 100): **97,95,93,83,81 78**
toteswingers:1&2:£1.20, 2&3:£1.10, 1&3:£1.70 CSF £6.60 TOTE £3.80: £1.80, £1.10; EX 8.60.
Owner Sheikh Hamdan Bin Mohammed Al Maktoum **Bred** Mrs E Thompson **Trained** Middleham Moor, N Yorks

FOCUS
An interesting fillies' maiden, featuring three runners with promising form and a couple of nicely-bred newcomers. There are doubts over the form but the first three finished clear.

Goodie Goodie Official explanation: jockey said filly ran green

991 32RED.COM H'CAP 7f (P)
7:00 (7:00) (Class 5) (0-75,76) 4-Y-0+ **£2,264** (£673; £336; £168) **Stalls** Low

Form RPR
-004 **1** **Street Power (USA)**[28] 669 7-9-0 **72** RaulDaSilva(5) 4 84
(Jeremy Gask) *stdd s: t.k.h: hld up in last pair: taken to outer and sustained prog fr over 2f out to ld last 150yds: drew away* **15/2**
0-50 **2** 2 **Perfect Ch'I (IRE)**[21] 746 5-8-11 **64** MartinLane 7 71
(Ian Wood) *mde most: clr after 3f: rdn over 2f out: hdd and one pce last 150yds* **25/1**
0352 **3** ¾ **Mister Green (FR)**[8] 894 6-8-9 **62** (bt) LukeMorris 1 67
(David Flood) *settled in 7th: shkn up 2f out: prog jst over 1f out: drvn and r.o to take 3rd nr fin* **5/1**[3]
1100 **4** ¾ **Satwa Laird**[21] 746 6-9-5 **72** HayleyTurner 5 75
(Conor Dore) *chsd ldrs: pushed along bef 1/2-way: effrt 2f out: styd on same pce fr over 1f out* **16/1**
0-30 **5** ¾ **Big Bay (USA)**[40] 517 6-9-5 **72** (b) ChrisCatlin 2 73
(Jane Chapple-Hyam) *trckd ldng trio: effrt against far rail 2f out: rdn and styd on same pce after* **20/1**
-611 **6** 1¼ **Copperwood**[8] 900 7-9-9 **76** 6ex JoeFanning 11 73
(Mark Johnston) *hld up in 8th and towards outside: rdn and nt qckn 2f out: kpt on fnl f: nt gng pce to threaten* **9/2**[2]
4155 **7** 1¾ **Dvinsky (USA)**[15] 819 11-8-11 **64** (b) ShaneKelly 3 56
(Paul Howling) *mostly chsd ldr to over 1f out: wknd ins fnl f* **33/1**
6420 **8** 2 **Mishrif (USA)**[33] 626 6-9-6 **73** (b) PaulHanagan 6 60
(J R Jenkins) *hld up in last trio: shkn up and detached fr main gp in 10th 2f out: keeping on at fin: nvr involved* **13/2**
0103 **9** *nk* **Royal Bajan (USA)**[26] 715 4-9-7 **74** PaulMulrennan 8 60
(James Given) *t.k.h: trckd ldng pair: disp 2nd over 2f out to over 1f out: wknd rapidly* **14/1**
-330 **10** *hd* **Tiradito (USA)**[21] 746 5-9-6 **73** (p) GeorgeBaker 10 59
(Michael Attwater) *stdd s fr wd draw and hld up last: hanging lft bnd 3f out and reminders: bhd after: keeping on at fin* **10/1**
20-3 **11** ½ **Amazon Twilight**[21] 746 4-9-5 **72** IanMongan 9 56
(Brett Johnson) *trckd ldng quartet: drvn and no prog over 2f out: sn wknd* **7/2**[1]

1m 24.65s (-1.35) **Going Correction** -0.05s/f (Stan) **11 Ran SP% 115.4**
Speed ratings (Par 103): **105,102,101,101,100 98,96,94,94,93 93**
toteswingers:1&2:£122.30, 2&3:£32.50, 1&3:£13.50 CSF £179.85 CT £1041.34 TOTE £8.90: £3.50, £9.60, £1.60; EX 257.70.
Owner Horses First Racing Limited **Bred** John Hawkins **Trained** Sutton Veny, Wilts

FOCUS
This looked a competitive handicap, in which few could be confidently discounted, and it was well run. The winner is rated back towards hios form of this time last year.

992 £32 FREE AT 32RED.COM H'CAP 1m 4f (P)
7:30 (7:30) (Class 5) (0-70,70) 4-Y-0+ **£2,264** (£673; £336; £168) **Stalls** Centre

Form RPR
2-42 **1** **Shalambar (IRE)**[15] 820 6-9-1 **65** JimCrowley 5 73
(Tony Carroll) *led after 1f and set mod pce: wound it up wl over 3f out: hrd pressed and drvn 2f out: styd on wl to assert fnl f* **4/1**[3]
5-14 **2** 2½ **Honourable Knight (IRE)**[24] 721 4-9-3 **69** (v) DavidProbert 2 73
(Mark Usher) *settled in last pair: pushed along 4f out: effrt u.p 2f out: kpt on to take 2nd fnl f: no imp on wnr* **11/4**[2]
0-01 **3** 1¼ **Spiritual Art**[19] 786 6-9-6 **70** (b) TomMcLaughlin 3 72
(Luke Dace) *led at slow pce for 1f: trckd wnr to 8f out and again over 2f out: sn chalng: hld and lost 2nd fnl f: fdd* **6/1**
1052 **4** 1 **Jamarjo (IRE)**[13] 850 5-9-4 **68** RobertWinston 6 68
(Steve Gollings) *cl up: trckd wnr after 4f: drvn and nt qckn over 2f out: lost pl and one pce after* **6/1**
-030 **5** 4½ **War Of The Roses (IRE)**[34] 600 9-9-0 **64** TomEaves 4 57
(Roy Brotherton) *stdd s: hld up in last: pushed along and detached fr rest over 3f out: nvr on terms after* **16/1**
1321 **6** ¾ **Shirataki (IRE)**[15] 820 4-9-1 **67** ChrisCatlin 1 59
(Peter Hiatt) *hld up in 4th and t.k.h after 3f: rdn and nt qckn 2f out: hld after: wknd fnl f* **5/2**[1]

2m 33.61s (-0.89) **Going Correction** -0.05s/f (Stan)
WFA 4 from 5yo+ 2lb **6 Ran SP% 109.7**
Speed ratings (Par 103): **100,98,97,96,93 93**
toteswingers:1&2:£3.00, 2&3:£4.80, 1&3:£2.20 CSF £14.63 TOTE £4.00: £2.40, £2.10; EX 20.50.
Owner B J Millen **Bred** His Highness The Aga Khan's Studs S C **Trained** Cropthorne, Worcs

FOCUS
Just a modest handicap, with the top weight rated 70, but competitive nonetheless. The second and third set the standard.

993 32REDPOKER.COM H'CAP 1m 3f (P)
8:00 (8:01) (Class 6) (0-60,59) 3-Y-0 **£1,617** (£481; £240; £120) **Stalls** Low

Form RPR
-535 **1** **Saucy Cat (IRE)**[23] 726 3-9-4 **56** LukeMorris 8 63
(John Best) *sn trckd ldrs in 5th: prog over 2f out: led jst over 1f out: hanging lft u.p but styd on wl* **13/2**
200- **2** 1 **Courtesy Call (IRE)**[141] 7223 3-9-7 **59** JoeFanning 4 64
(Mark Johnston) *settled in midfield disputing 6th: rdn over 3f out: no prog tl wl over 1f out: styd on to take 2nd last 100yds: unable to chal* **11/4**[1]
00-5 **3** 1¼ **Midnight Sequel**[57] 292 3-8-7 **45** MartinLane 9 48
(Michael Blake) *hld up in last trio: effrt on outer over 2f out: hanging u.p and hd to one side but styd on fr over 1f out to take 3rd last strides* **25/1**
5621 **4** ½ **Moment In The Sun**[23] 727 3-9-6 **58** JimmyFortune 1 60
(David Flood) *mde most: edgd lft whn drvn 2f out: hdd jst over 1f out: fdd nr fin* **11/2**[3]
-025 **5** 1 **Tectonic (IRE)**[8] 901 3-9-7 **59** (p) GeorgeBaker 2 59
(Chris Dwyer) *mostly trckd ldr tl rdn and nt qckn wl over 1f out: fdd ins fnl f* **5/1**[2]
000- **6** *nse* **Blue Pencil**[104] 7685 3-8-4 **45** RyanPowell(3) 3 45
(Roger Curtis) *trckd ldng pair: hrd rdn and nt qckn over 2f out: one pce after* **40/1**
00-5 **7** 3 **Run Of The Day**[34] 595 3-9-3 **55** ShaneKelly 10 50
(Eve Johnson Houghton) *v wd first 2f: dropped in and hld up in last pair after: reminder over 1f out: hanging lft and nvr remotely involved* **33/1**
45-4 **8** *nk* **Ice Loch**[57] 294 3-8-11 **49** DaneO'Neill 7 43
(Michael Blanshard) *a abt same pl: rdn over 2f out: outpcd after* **17/2**
-303 **9** 2½ **Rhyme Royal**[14] 832 3-8-9 **47** PaulMulrennan 5 37
(James Given) *trckd ldng trio: rdn over 3f out: wknd 2f out* **10/1**

03-3 **10** *3 3/4* **Pearl Frost**[76] 56 3-9-5 **57**...(b) IanMongan 11 40
(Laura Mongan) *s.i.s: a in last pair: rdn 4f out: bhd over 2f out* **8/1**

00-3 **11** *18* **Leading Star**[43] 472 3-8-8 **46**... ChrisCatlin 6
(Michael Madgwick) *racd wd thrght: in tch in midfield tl wknd over 3f out: t.o* **20/1**

2m 22.47s (0.57) **Going Correction** -0.05s/f (Stan) **11** Ran SP% **116.8**
Speed ratings (Par 96): **95,94,93,93,92 92,90,89,88,85 72**
toteswingers:1&2:£3.70, 2&3:£24.60, 1&3:£26.10 CSF £23.48 CT £425.20 TOTE £6.90: £2.30, £1.10, £8.10; EX 23.70.
Owner Mrs A M Riney **Bred** Mrs A M Riney **Trained** Hucking, Kent

FOCUS
A low-grade handicap, in which the top weight was rated just 59, but the form looks sound. The race is rated around the second, fourth and fifth.

994 32RED H'CAP (LONDON MILE QUALIFIER) 1m (P)
8:30 (8:31) (Class 4) (0-85,80) 3-Y-O **£4,075** (£1,212; £606) **Stalls** Low

Form RPR

212- **1** **Rio Grande**[102] 7725 3-9-4 **77**...(p) PaulHanagan 2 85
(Ann Duffield) *racd freely: mde all: had other pair in trble sn after 1/2-way: clr over 2f out: rdn and maintain ld fr over 1f out* **11/8**[1]

114- **2** *6* **Titus Star (IRE)**[97] 7786 3-8-13 **72**... LukeMorris 4 66
(J S Moore) *chsd wnr: rdn fr 1/2-way: outpcd and no ch fnl 2f* **11/8**[1]

-621 **3** *2 1/4* **Cape Safari (IRE)**[28] 675 3-8-10 **69**...(p) MartinLane 3 58
(James Tate) *chsd wnr: rdn over 3f out: outpcd and no ch over 2f out: fdd* **7/2**[2]

1m 39.91s (0.11) **Going Correction** -0.05s/f (Stan) **3** Ran SP% **106.4**
Speed ratings (Par 100): **97,91,88**
CSF £3.48 TOTE £2.10; EX 3.00.
Owner Sir Robert Ogden **Bred** Haras Du Mezeray & Ronchalon Racing **Trained** Constable Burton, N Yorks

FOCUS
A poor turnout numerically but, on paper, an open handicap. The winner is worth more at face value but this form is unconvincing.

995 32REDBET.COM H'CAP 1m (P)
9:00 (9:00) (Class 6) (0-60,60) 4-Y-O+ **£1,617** (£481; £240; £120) **Stalls** Low

Form RPR

/0-3 **1** **Toymaker**[35] 581 5-9-7 **60**... PaulMulrennan 9 73
(James Given) *trckd ldrs in 6th: prog 2f out: rdn to ld 1f out: drvn clr and r.o wl* **12/1**

0230 **2** *2* **Gallantry**[8] 891 10-9-3 **56**... ShaneKelly 7 64
(Paul Howling) *hld up in last trio: stdy prog on inner over 2f out: rdn and r.o to take 2nd last 100yds: no ch to chal* **14/1**

1253 **3** *1 1/2* **Emerald Royal**[21] 744 4-8-12 **51**...(b[1]) LukeMorris 11 56
(Eric Wheeler) *s.i.s: dropped in fr wd draw and hld up last: drvn 2f out: styd on fr over 1f out to take 3rd last strides* **9/2**[2]

4 *nk* **Yes Mam (IRE)**[334] 1535 4-8-7 **46** oh1... FrannyNorton 1 50
(Tom Tate) *w ldr: led 1/2-way: drvn 2f out: hdd and nt qckn 1f out: fdd last 100yds* **7/2**[1]

6-30 **5** *nk* **Saucy Buck (IRE)**[34] 598 4-9-3 **59**... MichaelO'Connell(3) 5 62
(Jamie Poulton) *hld up in rr: rdn and prog fr 2f out: kpt on fnl f: nt gng pce to threaten* **16/1**

-465 **6** *nk* **Dichoh**[23] 732 9-9-3 **56**... GeorgeBaker 3 58
(Michael Madgwick) *trckd ldrs on inner: rdn and nt qckn wl over 1f out: one pce after* **12/1**

00-5 **7** *1/2* **Monsieur Broughton**[27] 685 4-9-3 **56**... StevieDonohoe 2 58
(Willie Musson) *hld up in midfield: prog over 2f out to chse ldrs over 1f out: nt qckn after: 5th and hld whn no room and lost pls nr fin* **6/1**[3]

-450 **8** *2 1/2* **Comadoir (IRE)**[15] 818 6-9-7 **60**... IanMongan 12 56
(Jo Crowley) *racd on outer: trckd ldrs: effrt to dispute 2nd over 2f out: wknd over 1f out* **9/2**[2]

0-00 **9** *2 1/2* **Pie Poudre**[31] 633 5-9-0 **53**...(b) TomEaves 8 43
(Roy Brotherton) *hld up in last pair: rdn and sme prog 2f out: wknd over 1f out* **50/1**

4 **10** *5* **Apple Blossom Time (IRE)**[59] 274 5-9-0 **53**... DaneO'Neill 4 31
(Derek Haydn Jones) *t.k.h: trckd ldng pair: disp 2nd briefly over 2f out: sn wknd* **8/1**

0-00 **11** *3 1/4* **Dune Island**[15] 818 4-8-7 **46** oh1...(v[1]) KieranO'Neill 6 17
(John Bridger) *led to 1/2-way: wknd qckly over 2f out* **66/1**

/40- **12** *9* **Night Sky**[243] 4337 5-9-7 **60**... TomQueally 10
(Tony Carroll) *racd wd in midfield: rdn over 3f out: sn wknd: t.o* **20/1**

1m 38.46s (-1.34) **Going Correction** -0.05s/f (Stan) **12** Ran SP% **120.1**
Speed ratings (Par 101): **104,102,100,100,99 99,99,96,94,89 85,76**
toteswingers:1&2:£23.10, 2&3:£7.60, 1&3:£9.50 CSF £168.41 CT £880.43 TOTE £9.10: £4.90, £5.40, £1.80; EX 99.30.
Owner Antoniades Family **Bred** A G Antoniades **Trained** Willoughton, Lincs

FOCUS
A modest finale, in which the top weight was rated 60. The form looks sound, rated around the second.
Monsieur Broughton Official explanation: jockey said gelding was denied a clear run
T/Plt: £35.60 to a £1 stake. Pool of £69690.86 - 1429.02 winning tickets. T/Qpdt: £18.50 to a £1 stake. Pool of £6759.66 - 269.80 winning tickets. JN

937 WOLVERHAMPTON (A.W) (L-H)
Thursday, March 22

OFFICIAL GOING: Standard
Wind: Light against Weather: Fine

996 HORSE RACING FREE BETS WITH FREEBETTING.CO.UK H'CAP 5f 20y(P)
2:00 (2:00) (Class 6) (0-65,71) 4-Y-O+ **£1,704** (£503; £251) **Stalls** Low

Form RPR

1605 **1** **Shawkantango**[8] 890 5-9-6 **64**...(v) JoeFanning 9 74
(Derek Shaw) *dwlt and wnt rt s: hdwy 1/2-way: rdn to ld ins fnl f: edgd lft: r.o wl* **9/2**[2]

0041 **2** *2 1/4* **Black Baccara**[3] 958 5-9-10 **71** 6ex...(be) RyanClark(3) 8 73
(Phil McEntee) *hld up: hdwy over 1f out: rdn to chse wnr ins fnl f: styd on same pce* **14/1**

1235 **3** *1/2* **Rightcar**[13] 844 5-8-13 **57**... RobbieFitzpatrick 4 57
(Peter Grayson) *hld up: hdwy over 1f out: rdn and edgd rt ins fnl f: styd on same pce* **8/1**

4515 **4** *1/2* **Decider (USA)**[12] 870 9-9-1 **59**...(v) LukeMorris 3 57
(Ronald Harris) *alwyas prom: rdn over 1f out: styd on* **12/1**

43-6 **5** *hd* **Dispol Grand (IRE)**[13] 844 6-8-12 **63**... NedCurtis(7) 5 61
(Paul Midgley) *led to 1/2-way: rdn over 1f out: styd on same pce fnl f* **12/1**

6316 **6** *1* **Slatey Hen (IRE)**[9] 887 4-8-6 **55**...(p) DuilioDaSilva(5) 1 49
(Richard Guest) *sn chsng ldr: led 1/2-way: rdn over 1f out: hdd and no ex ins fnl f* **15/2**[3]

2603 **7** *shd* **Soopacal (IRE)**[12] 870 7-9-5 **63**... BarryMcHugh 6 57
(Brian Ellison) *sn pushed along to chse ldrs: rdn over 1f out: no ex fnl f* **9/2**[2]

0-02 **8** *nk* **Tom Sawyer**[13] 844 4-9-4 **62**...(v) PaulMulrennan 7 55
(Julie Camacho) *prom: rdn over 1f out: no ex fnl f* **4/1**[1]

5616 **9** *2 1/4* **Chjimes (IRE)**[3] 958 8-9-6 **64**...(b) HayleyTurner 2 48
(Conor Dore) *hld up: hdwy 1/2-way: rdn over 1f out: wknd fnl f* **9/1**

1m 2.42s (0.12) **Going Correction** +0.05s/f (Slow) **9** Ran SP% **111.3**
Speed ratings (Par 101): **101,97,96,95,95 93,93,93,89**
toteswingers:1&2:£11.30, 2&3:£6.70, 1&3:£6.70 CSF £61.25 CT £475.46 TOTE £4.90: £2.00, £1.70, £1.80; EX 70.50 Trifecta £620.60 Pool: £1056.74 - 1.26 winning units..
Owner Shawthing Racing Partnership **Bred** Derek Shaw **Trained** Sproxton, Leics
■ Stewards' Enquiry : Duilio Da Silva caution: careless riding.

FOCUS
They went a furious early pace in this moderate sprint with a three-way contested lead between Slatey Hen, Dispol Grand and Soopacal. It did none of them any favours, however, merely setting the race up for the hold-up horses. The first three home occupied the last three places earlier in the contest. The form is rated around the second.
Tom Sawyer Official explanation: jockey said gelding ran flat

997 FREE BETTING WITH FREEBETTING.CO.UK H'CAP 5f 216y(P)
2:35 (2:36) (Class 5) (0-75,80) 4-Y-O+ **£2,587** (£770; £384; £192) **Stalls** Low

Form RPR

00-4 **1** **My Kingdom (IRE)**[76] 54 6-9-3 **71**...(t) JamieSpencer 7 81
(Ian Williams) *hld up: swtchd lft and hdwy over 1f out: str run to ld post* **8/1**

3051 **2** *shd* **Waabel**[7] 911 5-8-13 **67** 6ex... MartinHarley 12 77
(Richard Guest) *chsd ldrs: rdn to chse ldr over 1f out: r.o to ld towards fin: hdd post* **6/1**[2]

5531 **3** *1 1/4* **Last Sovereign**[8] 896 8-9-9 **80** 6ex...(b) MichaelO'Connell(3) 9 86
(Ollie Pears) *sn led: clr 1/2-way: rdn over 1f out: hdd and no ex towards fin* **10/1**

2405 **4** *1/2* **Avonrose**[14] 834 5-9-6 **74**... PhillipMakin 11 78
(Derek Shaw) *hld up: hdwy over 2f out: rdn and edgd lft fnl f: r.o* **16/1**

0-65 **5** *1 1/4* **Restless Bay (IRE)**[69] 157 4-9-7 **75**...(p) ChrisCatlin 13 75
(Reg Hollinshead) *in rr: hdwy over 1f out: sn rdn: r.o: nt rch ldrs* **9/1**

400- **6** *1/2* **Florio Vincitore (IRE)**[157] 6920 5-8-9 **63**... BarryMcHugh 1 62
(Brian Ellison) *hld up: rdn over 1f out: r.o ins fnl f: nrst fin* **7/1**[3]

313- **7** *2* **Mata Hari Blue**[163] 6779 6-9-3 **71**...(t) RussKennemore 8 63
(John Holt) *prom: chsd ldr over 2f out tl rdn over 1f out: no ex fnl f* **28/1**

2000 **8** *2 1/4* **Loyal Royal (IRE)**[40] 526 9-8-7 **61**...(bt) RichardKingscote 10 46
(Milton Bradley) *s.i.s: hld up: r.o ins fnl f: nvr nrr* **16/1**

0600 **9** *1* **Frequency**[20] 765 5-9-7 **75**...(b) JoeFanning 6 57
(Keith Dalgleish) *mid-div: nt clr run over 2f out: rdn over 1f out: wknd fnl f* **8/1**

1212 **10** *11* **Greenhead High**[5] 942 4-9-2 **70**... AdrianNicholls 2 17
(David Nicholls) *chsd ldrs: hmpd 5f out: pushed along 1/2-way: wknd over 1f out* **11/4**[1]

500- **11** *7* **Nine Before Ten (IRE)**[170] 6615 4-8-11 **70**...(t) DuilioDaSilva(5) 4
(Richard Guest) *chsd ldr tl rdn over 2f out: wknd over 1f out* **40/1**

010/ **12** *5* **Whiteoak Lady (IRE)**[897] 6596 7-8-10 **64**... FrannyNorton 5
(John Spearing) *dwlt: outpcd* **50/1**

1m 14.63s (-0.37) **Going Correction** +0.05s/f (Slow) **12** Ran SP% **114.4**
Speed ratings (Par 103): **104,103,102,101,99 99,96,93,92,77 68,61**
toteswingers:1&2:£7.90, 2&3:£7.20, 1&3:£12.20 CSF £52.66 CT £492.36 TOTE £8.90: £2.70, £2.50, £3.10; EX 59.70 Trifecta £302.90 Pool: £1920.16 - 4.69 winning units..
Owner Dr Marwan Koukash **Bred** Irish National Stud **Trained** Portway, Worcs

FOCUS
A modest sprint handicap, but a dramatic finish. It was well run and the form is solid. The winner had slipped to a good mark.

998 THE BLACK COUNTRY'S ONLY RACECOURSE H'CAP 1m 4f 50y(P)
3:05 (3:05) (Class 6) (0-65,65) 3-Y-O **£1,704** (£503; £251) **Stalls** Low

Form RPR

6-62 **1** **Excellent News (IRE)**[23] 726 3-9-3 **61**... SebSanders 7 65
(J W Hills) *hld up in tch: rdn over 3f out: led 1f out: styd on wl* **10/1**[3]

30-0 **2** *4* **Shivsingh**[17] 803 3-9-7 **65**...(v[1]) ChrisCatlin 3 63
(Mick Channon) *sn pushed along in rr: hdwy over 2f out: styd on u.p to go 2nd post: no ch w wnr* **33/1**

6630 **3** *nk* **Aiaam Al Wafa (IRE)**[6] 923 3-8-5 **56**...(p) DannyBrock(7) 6 53
(Phil McEntee) *chsd ldr tl rdn over 1f out: styd on same pce fnl f* **28/1**

6121 **4** *1 1/2* **Moataz (USA)**[6] 923 3-9-7 **65** 6ex... JoeFanning 4 60
(Mark Johnston) *led: edgd rt and hdd 1f out: wknd ins fnl f* **8/13**[1]

-230 **5** *3/4* **Cotes Du Rhone (IRE)**[43] 472 3-8-2 **46** oh1...(v) LukeMorris 1 40
(David Evans) *s.i.s: hld up in tch: rdn over 5f out: sn outpcd: styd on ins fnl f* **12/1**

6532 **6** *4* **Gabrial's Lexi (IRE)**[17] 803 3-9-7 **65**... TonyHamilton 2 52
(Richard Fahey) *chsd ldrs: rdn over 3f out: wknd 2f out* **7/2**[2]

2m 42.77s (1.67) **Going Correction** +0.05s/f (Slow) **6** Ran SP% **107.3**
Speed ratings (Par 96): **96,93,93,92,91 88**
toteswingers:1&2:£9.80, 2&3:£19.40, 1&3:£7.20 CSF £193.72 TOTE £7.60: £3.00, £3.70; EX 46.70.
Owner Andrew Motion & Partners **Bred** Lynch Bages Ltd & Samac Ltd **Trained** Upper Lambourn, Berks

FOCUS
A modest handicap run at an ordinary pace. There are doubts over the form with the top two in the market both disappointing.

999 FREE BETS ON YOUR MOBILE AT FREEBETTING.CO.UK (S) STKS 1f 103y(P)
3:40 (3:40) (Class 6) 4-Y-O+ **£1,704** (£503; £251) **Stalls** Low

Form RPR

-535 **1** **Greyfriarschorista**[13] 846 5-8-12 80... BarryMcHugh 2 82+
(Brian Ellison) *mde all: clr 2f out: comf* **2/5**[1]

2233 **2** *3 3/4* **Ahlawy (IRE)**[5] 944 9-8-7 69...(t) RaulDaSilva(5) 1 74
(Frank Sheridan) *chsd ldrs: rdn to go 2nd over 2f out: hung lft over 1f out: no imp* **11/2**[2]

1153 **3** *7* **Mcconnell (USA)**[7] 906 7-9-4 73...(b) MartinHarley 3 65
(Richard Guest) *s.i.s: hld up: racd keenly: rdn over 2f out: wkng whn wnt 3rd wl over 1f out* **9/1**

1545 **4** *3 3/4* **Faithful Ruler (USA)**[7] 906 8-9-4 70...(p) LukeMorris 4 60
(Ronald Harris) *chsd wnr tl rdn over 2f out: wknd wl over 1f out* **8/1**[3]

2m 1.42s (-0.28) **Going Correction** +0.05s/f (Slow) **4** Ran SP% **107.9**
Speed ratings (Par 101): **103,99,93,90**
CSF £2.98 TOTE £1.40; EX 2.50.The winner was bought by W Mckay for 8,000gns.

Owner Koo's Racing Club **Bred** Castlemartin Stud And Skymarc Farm **Trained** Norton, N Yorks
FOCUS
An uncompetitive seller. The winner was the clear form pick and the second looks the bset guide.

1000 MIRROR PUNTERS CLUB H'CAP 1m 1f 103y(P)
4:15 (4:15) (Class 5) (0-70,70) 4-Y-O+ **£2,264** (£673; £336; £168) **Stalls** Low

Form RPR
532 **1** **Strawberrymystique**[22] 737 4-9-3 **66**.............................. AdamKirby 4 76
(Marco Botti) *chsd ldr tl led over 2f out: rdn over 1f out: sn edgd lft: styd on* **15/8**[1]
00-3 **2** 2 ¼ **Count Ceprano (IRE)**[14] 843 8-8-5 **57**..................... SimonPearce(3) 9 62
(Lydia Pearce) *hld up: hdwy over 1f out: rdn to go 2nd wl ins fnl f: nt trble wnr* **16/1**
04-3 **3** ½ **Ollon (USA)**[6] 922 4-8-9 **58**..(p) MartinHarley 3 62
(Mrs K Burke) *chsd ldrs: rdn over 1f out: styd on* **3/1**[2]
0-52 **4** 1 ½ **Edgeworth (IRE)**[36] 570 6-9-4 **67**..................................(p) ChrisCatlin 8 68
(David Bridgwater) *hld up: r.o ins fnl f: nvr nr to chal* **5/1**[3]
5030 **5** ½ **Black Coffee**[6] 922 7-9-2 **65**...(b) LukeMorris 5 65
(Mark Brisbourne) *prom: rdn over 2f out: styd on same pce fr over 1f out* **14/1**
2644 **6** 1 **Valley Tiger**[7] 909 4-9-0 **63**.. TonyHamilton 1 61
(Richard Fahey) *led: hdd over 2f out: sn rdn: wknd fnl f* **14/1**
5-30 **7** 2 ¾ **John Potts**[48] 403 7-9-5 **68**.. RussKennemore 6 60
(Brian Baugh) *hld up: rdn over 2f out: sn wknd* **7/1**
54-0 **8** 3 ¾ **Intiqaal (IRE)**[12] 869 5-8-12 **61**...(t) PhillipMakin 7 45
(Derek Shaw) *hld up: rdn and wknd over 2f out* **20/1**

2m 1.52s (-0.18) **Going Correction** +0.05s/f (Slow) **8 Ran SP% 112.9**
Speed ratings (Par 103): **102,100,99,98,97 96,94,91**
toteswingers:1&2:£5.90, 2&3:£7.80, 1&3:£2.00 CSF £33.25 CT £86.55 TOTE £2.30: £1.10, £4.10, £1.70; EX 24.70 Trifecta £81.10 Pool: £4579.55 - 41.77 winning units..
Owner Two For One Partnership **Bred** Newsells Park Stud **Trained** Newmarket, Suffolk
FOCUS
A modest handicap and the pace was ordinary. The second and third set the standard.

1001 RINGSIDE ENTERTAINMENT MAIDEN STKS 1m 141y(P)
4:50 (4:51) (Class 5) 3-Y-O+ **£2,264** (£673; £336; £168) **Stalls** Low

Form RPR
04-2 **1** **Hamis Al Bin (IRE)**[8] 903 3-8-9 69............................... FrannyNorton 8 81
(Mark Johnston) *chsd ldr 2f: remained handy: rdn to ld 1f out: r.o: eased nr fin* **2/1**[1]
0- **2** 3 ¾ **Cape Samba**[223] 4996 3-8-9 0....................................... JamieSpencer 10 73
(Peter Chapple-Hyam) *a.p: chsd ldr over 6f out: rdn over 2f out: sn ev ch: styd on same pce ins fnl f* **2/1**[1]
-222 **3** hd **Cotton Trader (USA)**[30] 642 3-8-9 77........................(b) RobertHavlin 5 72
(John Gosden) *led: rdn and hdd 1f out: styd on same pce* **9/4**[2]
0 **4** 1 **Dropzone (USA)**[12] 869 3-8-9 0..................................... AndreaAtzeni 3 70
(Marco Botti) *s.i.s: sn pushed along to chse ldrs: rdn over 3f out: outpcd over 2f out: styd on fnl f* **10/1**[3]
5 **5** 10 **Redinessence (IRE)**[19] 784 4-9-9 0........................... JamieMackay 1 42
(Willie Musson) *hld up: nvr trbld ldrs* **33/1**
6 3 ¼ **Bridal Medic** 3-8-9 0... BarryMcHugh 2 40
(John Mackie) *prom: rdn over 3f out: wknd wl over 1f out* **33/1**
0- **7** 16 **Serendipity Blue**[199] 5786 3-8-4 0................................ DuranFentiman 6
(John Weymes) *s.s: sn pushed along in rr: lost tch fnl 3f: t.o* **50/1**
8 1 ¼ **Diggers Daydream (IRE)** 4-10-0 0............................ JamesSullivan 4
(Lisa Williamson) *s.i.s: hld up: wknd over 2f out: t.o* **150/1**

1m 50.06s (-0.44) **Going Correction** +0.05s/f (Slow)
WFA 3 from 4yo 19lb **8 Ran SP% 115.0**
Speed ratings (Par 103): **103,99,99,98,89 86,72,71**
toteswingers:1&2:£1.60, 2&3:£1.80, 1&3:£1.20 CSF £6.28 TOTE £4.30: £1.60, £1.90, £1.10; EX 8.20 Trifecta £13.30 Pool: £7776.98 - 431.25 winning units..
Owner Ahmed Jaber **Bred** Mrs H Owen **Trained** Middleham Moor, N Yorks
■ Stewards' Enquiry : Jamie Spencer one-day ban: careless riding (Apr 5)
FOCUS
A modest maiden dominated by the form horses. A tricky race to pin down through the third, but the time was reasonable.
Diggers Daydream(IRE) Official explanation: jockey said gelding ran freely early

1002 FREE BETTING DEALS AT FREEBETTING.CO.UK H'CAP 1m 141y(P)
5:20 (5:20) (Class 6) (0-65,65) 4-Y-O+ **£1,704** (£503; £251) **Stalls** Low

Form RPR
4326 **1** **McCool Bannanas**[6] 922 4-9-7 **65**................................... AdamKirby 2 74
(James Unett) *chsd ldrs: led 1f out: drvn out* **3/1**[1]
364 **2** 1 **Spin Cast**[36] 567 4-9-4 **62**... JamieSpencer 8 68
(Ian Williams) *hld up: hdwy and nt clr run over 1f out: swtchd rt ins fnl f: r.o to go 2nd nr fin: nt rch wnr* **4/1**[2]
-621 **3** 1 **Piccolo Express**[38] 550 6-9-5 **63**................................ RussKennemore 9 67
(Brian Baugh) *hld up: plld hrd: hdwy over 1f out: styd on* **9/1**
4-55 **4** ½ **Pitkin**[7] 911 4-9-2 **60**.. JamesSullivan 5 63
(Michael Easterby) *prom: racd keenly: rdn over 1f out: styd on* **9/1**
-264 **5** 1 ¼ **Absolute Princess**[7] 906 4-9-1 **62**...............................(p) BillyCray(3) 3 62
(Scott Dixon) *sn led: clr 5f out: rdn and hung lft over 1f out: sn hdd and no ex* **16/1**
2600 **6** 1 **Justcallmehandsome**[7] 909 10-9-0 **63**..................(v) LucyKBarry(5) 12 61
(Dominic Ffrench Davis) *s.i.s: hld up: r.o ins fnl f: nvr nrr* **20/1**
3152 **7** nk **Just Five (IRE)**[14] 843 6-9-3 **61**.................................(v) PhillipMakin 6 58
(John Weymes) *hld up: rdn over 2f out: kpt on: nt trble ldrs* **11/2**[3]
06-5 **8** hd **Ra Junior (USA)**[24] 725 6-8-8 **59**................................. NedCurtis(7) 4 56
(Paul Midgley) *prom: rdn over 2f out: nt clr run over 1f out: swtchd rt and no ex ins fnl f* **9/1**
24-0 **9** nk **Kielty's Folly**[22] 736 8-8-11 **60**.................................. JamesRogers(5) 1 56
(Brian Baugh) *chsd ldr: rdn over 2f out: nt clr run over 1f out: no ex ins fnl f* **14/1**
600- **10** 6 **Catallout (IRE)**[143] 7198 4-9-5 **63**.............................. DanielTudhope 11 45
(Declan Carroll) *hld up: a in rr: wknd over 2f out* **28/1**
0-00 **11** ¾ **Crazy Chris**[14] 842 7-8-11 **58**.....................................(t) RyanClark(3) 10 38
(Milton Bradley) *chsd ldrs: rdn over 2f out: wknd over 1f out* **18/1**

1m 50.85s (0.35) **Going Correction** +0.05s/f (Slow) **11 Ran SP% 116.4**
Speed ratings: **100,99,98,97,96 95,95,95,95,89 89**
toteswingers:1&2:£3.60, 2&3:£5.30, 1&3:£7.20 CSF £14.31 CT £98.30 TOTE £3.50: £1.10, £2.20, £2.10; EX 15.80 Trifecta £42.50 Pool: £5377.51 - 93.46 winning units..
Owner Mark Sheehy & Malcolm Hall **Bred** M Sheehy **Trained** Tedsmore Hall, Shropshire
■ Stewards' Enquiry : Billy Cray 1st incident, caution: careless riding. (2nd) one-day ban: careless riding (Apr 5)
FOCUS
A moderate handicap to end the card, but run at a strong pace. The winner did not need to improve much if at all.
Piccolo Express Official explanation: jockey said gelding hung right throughout
Just Five(IRE) Official explanation: jockey said gelding hung right throughout
T/Plt: £339.50 to a £1 stake. Pool of £52,475.55 - 112.83 winning tickets. T/Qpdt: £54.50 to a £1 stake. Pool of £3,281.34 - 44.50 winning tickets. CR

915 LINGFIELD (L-H)
Friday, March 23

OFFICIAL GOING: Standard
Wind: virtually nil Weather: warm and sunny

1003 ALL WEATHER "HANDS AND HEELS" APPRENTICE SERIES FINAL H'CAP (RACING EXCELLENCE INITIATIVE) 1m 5f (P)
2:00 (2:00) (Class 5) (0-75,75) 4-Y-O+ **£2,385** (£704; £352) **Stalls** Low

Form RPR
6033 **1** **Chookie Hamilton**[20] 643 8-9-4 **72**................................ NoelGarbutt 4 79
(Keith Dalgleish) *chsd ldrs: rdn and effrt to chse ldr wl over 1f out: led 1f out: kpt on wl* **10/1**
0242 **2** 1 **Quinsman**[7] 928 6-9-0 **71**.. AliceHaynes(3) 3 77
(J S Moore) *stdd s: t.k.h: hld up in tch in rr: rdn over 3f out: hdwy to chse ldng pair wl over 1f out: chsd wnr wl ins fnl f: no imp towards fin* **11/4**[2]
3526 **3** 1 **Maslak (IRE)**[6] 944 8-8-9 **63**....................................... JackDuern 2 67
(Peter Hiatt) *led and set stdy gallop: qcknd over 4f out: rdn over 1f out: hdd 1f out: styd on same pce fnl f* **7/1**
134- **4** 6 **Zafranagar (IRE)**[20] 7734 7-9-2 **70**............................. GeorgeDowning 6 65
(Tony Carroll) *t.k.h: hld up in tch: stdd into last pair 10f out: hdwy to chse ldrs and rdn over 4f out: wknd over 1f out* **7/2**[3]
2212 **5** hd **Blackmore**[14] 849 5-9-7 **75**... DarrenEgan 1 70
(Julia Feilden) *rdr struggling to remove hood and slowly away: sn rcvrd and in tch: chsd ldrs 10f out: rdn and dropped to last pair 5f out: struggling over 2f out: wknd wl over 1f out* **2/1**[1]
43-5 **6** ¾ **The Winged Assasin (USA)**[42] 63 6-8-13 **67**................(t) IanBurns 5 61
(Shaun Lycett) *chsd ldr: rdn over 4f out: ev ch 3f out tl unable qck 2f out: wknd over 1f out* **14/1**

2m 48.17s (2.17) **Going Correction** 0.0s/f (Stan)
WFA 4 from 5yo+ 3lb **6 Ran SP% 110.5**
Speed ratings (Par 103): **93,92,91,88,87 87**
Tote Swingers: 1&2 £3.90, 1&3 £6.10, 2&3 £3.20 CSF £36.29 TOTE £13.00: £5.60, £1.10; EX 53.80.
Owner Raeburn Brick Limited **Bred** D And J Raeburn **Trained** Carluke, S Lanarks
FOCUS
They crawled early on and some of these were keen. The race is rated around the third, but this isn't reliable form.
Chookie Hamilton Official explanation: trainer said, regarding apparent iprovement in form, that the gelding was better suited by the Polytrack surface
Blackmore Official explanation: jockey said gelding lunged forward in stalls, his hand slipped off the blind and was slow to start

1004 2ND BARRY GURR MEMORIAL MAIDEN FILLIES' STKS 7f (P)
2:30 (2:30) (Class 5) 3-Y-O+ **£2,385** (£704; £352) **Stalls** Low

Form RPR
050- **1** **Jumeirah Palm Star**[235] 4614 3-8-9 66.......................... KieranO'Neill 4 75
(Richard Hannon) *t.k.h early: dropped in bhd ldng pair after 1f: rdn to chse ldr jst over 2f out: kpt on to press wnr 1f out: led wl ins fnl f: r.o wl* **2/1**[2]
3- **2** ½ **Shame On You (IRE)**[139] 7293 3-8-9 0............................ MichaelHills 1 74
(Charles Hills) *dwlt: sn rcvrd to ld: looked to be gng best whn rdr looked over wrong shoulder and c centre st: rdn and pressed ent fnl f: hdd and no ex wl ins fnl f* **8/11**[1]
0-3 **3** 13 **Vena Amoris (USA)**[15] 838 3-8-9 0................................. JoeFanning 3 45
(Mark Johnston) *chsd ldr: shkn up over 4f out: rdn and struggling in 3rd jst over 2f out: wknd wl over 1f out* **11/2**[3]
64-0 **4** 6 **Coupland Lass (IRE)**[15] 838 4-9-10 0.......................... StevieDonohoe 6 28
(Willie Musson) *s.i.s: a off the pce in last pair: no ch over 2f out* **40/1**
0 **5** 2 ¼ **Bright Girl (IRE)**[20] 784 4-9-3 0.............................. NatashaEaton(7) 5 22
(Mark Rimmer) *a off the pce in last pair: hung lft and lost tch over 2f out* **100/1**

1m 24.52s (-0.28) **Going Correction** 0.0s/f (Stan)
WFA 3 from 4yo 15lb **5 Ran SP% 110.1**
Speed ratings (Par 100): **101,100,85,78,76**
CSF £3.80 TOTE £2.80: £1.10, £1.30; EX 4.70.
Owner Hamed Rashed Bin Ghadayer **Bred** Plantation Stud **Trained** East Everleigh, Wilts
FOCUS
Hard to know the exact worth of the form, but it's probably no better than fair, rated around the runner-up. The first two finished well clear.
Bright Girl(IRE) Official explanation: jockey said filly hung left

1005 MARRIOTT PLAY & STAY CLAIMING STKS 6f (P)
3:00 (3:00) (Class 6) 4-Y-O+ **£1,704** (£503; £251) **Stalls** Low

Form RPR
3201 **1** **Captain Dimitrios**[8] 912 4-8-8 65.......................(v) MatthewCosham(5) 6 81
(David Evans) *mde all: rdn wl over 1f out: drvn and battled on gamely fnl f* **6/1**[2]
2112 **2** ¾ **Hinton Admiral**[18] 800 8-8-13 75.................................... JoeFanning 5 79
(Keith Dalgleish) *taken down early: chsd ldng pair: wnt 2nd over 3f out: rdn and unable qck over 1f out: styd on same pce u.p ins fnl f* **7/4**[1]
-051 **3** nse **Strictly Pink (IRE)**[9] 904 4-8-8 59.............................. CathyGannon 4 73
(Alan Bailey) *chsd wnr tl over 3f out: rdn 2f out: drvn and kpt on same pce fnl f* **10/1**
1121 **4** ½ **Drawnfromthepast (IRE)**[18] 800 7-9-3 79................ JamieSpencer 2 81
(Jamie Osborne) *stdd s: hld up in 4th pl: rdn and effrt over 1f out: fnd little and no real imp: drvn ins fnl f: kpt on towards fin but nvr gng pce to threaten wnr* **7/4**[1]
366- **5** 4 ½ **Jake The Snake (IRE)**[282] 3045 11-9-0 84...................... JimCrowley 1 63
(Tony Carroll) *stdd s: hld up in rr: clsd and in tch 2f out: rdn and no hdwy over 1f out: wknd ins fnl f* **8/1**[3]

1m 11.35s (-0.55) **Going Correction** 0.0s/f (Stan) **5 Ran SP% 107.2**
Speed ratings (Par 101): **103,102,101,101,95**
.Captain Dimitrios claimed by Mr A. J. D. Lidderdale for £6,000. Hinton Admiral\n\x\x claimed by Mr C. R. Dore for £6,000. Jake The Snake (IRE) claimed by Mr Willie McKay for £7,000.
Owner Wayne Clifford **Bred** W G H Barrons **Trained** Pandy, Monmouths

FOCUS
Form to treat with caution as Captain Dimitrios made all and it proved difficult to make up significant ground. It is rated around the winner and third.

1006 WORLD HORSE WELFARE CELEBRATES 85 YEARS H'CAP 5f (P)
3:35 (3:35) (Class 6) (0-60,60) 3-Y-O **£1,704** (£503; £251) **Stalls** High

Form RPR
450- **1** **Persidha**[144] 7196 3-9-5 **60**........(v[1]) JoeFanning 5 67
(Derek Shaw) *chsd clr ldr: rdn and effrt over 1f out: clsd on ldr 1f out: chal under hands and heels riding ins fnl f: led fnl 75yds: sn in command* **6/1**
63-4 **2** ¾ **Chicarito**[18] 802 3-9-3 **58**........(p) MartinDwyer 1 62
(John Gallagher) *led: sn clr and set str gallop: rdn over 1f out: hdd and no ex fnl 75yds* **11/4[1]**
5201 **3** *nk* **Marie's Fantasy**[18] 802 3-9-2 **57**........ JamieGoldstein 4 60
(Zoe Davison) *chsd ldng pair: rdn over 2f out: drvn over 1f out: kpt on u.p ins fnl f* **7/2[2]**
-062 **4** *2* **Maria Montez**[21] 769 3-9-3 **58**........ MartinLane 3 54
(J W Hills) *dwlt: a in last pair: rdn wl over 2f out: kpt on ins fnl f: nvr gng pce to threaten ldrs* **11/4[1]**
045 **5** ½ **Strike A Pose (IRE)**[41] 524 3-9-0 **55**........ CathyGannon 2 49
(David Evans) *dwlt: hld up in 4th pl: rdn and effrt over 1f out: kpt on same pce fnl f* **4/1[3]**

58.77s (-0.03) **Going Correction** 0.0s/f (Stan) **5** Ran SP% **109.8**
Speed ratings (Par 96): **100,98,98,95,94**
CSF £22.32 TOTE £5.30: £2.80, £3.20; EX 23.30.
Owner K Panos **Bred** Theobalds Stud **Trained** Sproxton, Leics

FOCUS
A moderate sprint handicap in which the pace horses dominated throughout. The time was fair and the winner is rated back to her 2yo best.

1007 LINGFIELD PARK OWNERS CLUB H'CAP 6f (P)
4:10 (4:10) (Class 4) (0-85,84) 4-Y-O+ **£4,204** (£1,251; £625; £312) **Stalls** Low

Form RPR
240- **1** **Another Try (IRE)**[180] 6378 7-9-4 **81**........ PaulHanagan 6 88
(Alan Jarvis) *t.k.h: sn pressing ldr: ev ch and rdn ent fnl 2f: kpt on u.p ins fnl f to ld last stride* **6/1**
2410 **2** *shd* **Haadeeth**[27] 710 5-8-8 **76**........ MatthewCosham[(5)] 1 82
(David Evans) *t.k.h: chsd ldrs on inner: rdn to ld over 1f out: kpt on wl fnl f tl hdd last stride* **8/1**
2330 **3** *shd* **Hatta Stream (IRE)**[10] 883 6-8-11 **77**........ SimonPearce[(3)] 2 83
(Lydia Pearce) *in tch: rdn and effrt over 1f out: pressed ldrs ins fnl f: kpt on wl towards fin* **11/2[3]**
2160 **4** *nse* **Nubar Boy**[27] 710 5-8-7 **70**........(v) ShaneKelly 5 76
(David Evans) *stdd s: hld up in tch in last pair: hdwy on inner over 1f out: rdn and pressing ldrs ins fnl f: kpt on wl* **9/1**
0-50 **5** *nk* **Baby Strange**[15] 835 8-9-7 **84**........ JoeFanning 7 89
(Derek Shaw) *t.k.h: hld up in last pair: rdn and hdwy over 1f out: pressing ldrs ins fnl f: no ex towards fin* **4/1[1]**
-032 **6** *1* **Kylladdie**[25] 718 5-9-0 **77**........(b) JamieSpencer 10 79
(Steve Gollings) *chsd ldrs: hdwy to join ldrs over 2f out: ev ch and rdn wl over 1f out: unable qck 1f out: styd on same pce fnl f* **9/2[2]**
1432 **7** *nk* **Desert Strike**[27] 715 6-9-3 **80**........ JimCrowley 4 81
(Charles Hills) *t.k.h: hld up wl in tch in midfield: rdn over 2f out: hdwy ent fnl f: styng on whn n.m.r ins fnl f: unable to chal* **6/1**
6000 **8** 1¾ **Frequency**[1] 997 5-8-12 **75**........(b) PaulMulrennan 8 70
(Keith Dalgleish) *hld up wl in tch: hdwy to chse ldrs on outer wl over 2f out: rdn 2f out: no ex ent fnl f: wknd ins fnl f* **12/1**
00-5 **9** *1* **Roodee Queen**[30] 652 4-9-0 **77**........ LiamKeniry 3 69
(Milton Bradley) *broke fast and led: rdn wl over 1f out: hdd over 1f out: wknd ins fnl f* **16/1**

1m 11.62s (-0.28) **Going Correction** 0.0s/f (Stan) **9** Ran SP% **116.8**
Speed ratings (Par 105): **101,100,100,100,100 98,98,96,94**
Tote Swingers: 1&2 £9.70, 1&3 £6.60, 2&3 £10.10 CSF £53.66 CT £282.58 TOTE £6.30: £1.80, £1.90, £2.90; EX 60.50 Trifecta £872.90 Part won. Pool: £1,179.71 - 0.30 winning units..
Owner The Twyford Partnership **Bred** Jarvis Associates **Trained** Twyford, Bucks

FOCUS
A competitive sprint handicap, but the pace was modest (time 0.27 seconds slowe than earlier claimer) and they finished in a heap. Straightforward form.

1008 BREATHE SPA AT LINGFIELD MARRIOTT H'CAP 1m 2f (P)
4:45 (4:45) (Class 3) (0-95,92) 4-Y-O+ **£6,663** (£1,982; £990; £495) **Stalls** Low

Form RPR
51- **1** **Eshtibaak (IRE)**[163] 6804 4-9-2 **87**........ PaulHanagan 1 98
(John Gosden) *hld up in last pair: rdn and hdwy to chse ldrs 2f out: drew clr w rival ent fnl f: kpt on to ld last strides* **8/13[1]**
1411 **2** *shd* **Colour Guard**[17] 812 4-9-0 **85**........ JoeFanning 3 95
(Mark Johnston) *broke fast and led tl hdd 5f out: rdn to ld again wl over 1f out: drew clr w wnr ent fnl f: drvn ins fnl f: hdd last strides* **11/4[2]**
00-0 **3** *7* **Almail (USA)**[14] 846 6-9-3 **88**........ FergusSweeney 2 84
(Jamie Osborne) *s.i.s: bhd: clsd and in tch 7f out: rdn and chsd ldng pair wl over 1f out: outpcd over 1f out: wknd fnl f* **66/1**
U110 **4** 2¼ **Emma's Gift (IRE)**[27] 712 4-9-4 **92**........(b) AdamBeschizza[(3)] 6 84
(Julia Feilden) *hld up in tch: cl clsd and chse ldrs 2f out: sn rdn and wknd* **8/1[3]**
1111 **5** ¾ **Munsarim (IRE)**[18] 804 5-9-1 **86**........(b) PaulMulrennan 5 76+
(Keith Dalgleish) *t.k.h: chsd ldr tl led 5f out and dashed clr: hung bdly rt and v wd bnd 4f out: hdd wl over 1f out: sn dropped out* **10/1**

2m 4.84s (-1.76) **Going Correction** 0.0s/f (Stan) **5** Ran SP% **110.3**
Speed ratings (Par 107): **107,106,101,99,98**
CSF £2.57 TOTE £1.60: £1.10, £2.20; EX 2.70.
Owner Hamdan Al Maktoum **Bred** P D Savill **Trained** Newmarket, Suffolk

FOCUS
The pace was modest, but this looks strong form from the first two, who are progressive, coming clear.

NOTEBOOK
Eshtibaak(IRE) looked pretty decent when winning a Nottingham maiden over this trip when last seen in October and he confirmed that promise, although this relative speed test wasn't ideal and he only just wore down the bang in-form, progressive runner-up. There should be more to come. (op 11-10)
Colour Guard had raced exclusively at Southwell, winning three of his four starts at up to 1m, and he progressed again under these different conditions. He should go on progressing, although he will have to prove himself as effective on turf. (op 9-4 tchd 3-1)
Almail(USA) travelled well to a point but was left behind by a couple of improvers, despite taking a shorter route into the straight. (op 50-1)
Emma's Gift(IRE), who was weak in the market, ran nowhere near form. (op 6-1)
Munsarim(IRE) had won his last four starts, but has shown a tendency to hang right and did so this time when leaving the back straight - he started racing much too freely and went extremely wide on the bend. After rejoining the main field he again hung right on the final turn, albeit not so badly, and carried the first two finishers a bit wide. He had also sweated up. Official explanation: jockey said gelding hung right (op 15-2)

1009 BET AT BLUE SQUARE H'CAP 1m (P)
5:20 (5:24) (Class 6) (0-55,55) 4-Y-O+ **£1,704** (£503; £251) **Stalls** High

Form RPR
00-1 **1** **Prohibition (IRE)**[7] 922 6-8-13 **52**........ PaulHanagan 3 59+
(Alastair Lidderdale) *hld up in last pair: rdn and hdwy over 1f out: drvn and chal ins fnl f: r.o wl to ld cl home* **5/2[1]**
024- **2** ½ **Bedibyes**[147] 7144 4-9-2 **55**........ JimCrowley 1 61
(Richard Mitchell) *hld up in last pair: hdwy and nt clr run 2f out: rdn and effrt on inner over 1f out: drvn and pressed ldrs ins fnl f: kpt on: wnt 2nd last strides* **12/1**
255- **3** *hd* **Byrd In Hand (IRE)**[162] 6816 5-8-12 **54**........ SeanLevey[(3)] 9 59
(John Bridger) *t.k.h: chsd ldrs: rdn and effrt to ld wl over 1f out: drvn and hrd pressed ins fnl f: hdd and no ex cl home* **6/1[3]**
3020 **4** ½ **Querido (GER)**[22] 744 8-9-2 **55**........(tp) JoeFanning 6 59
(Paddy Butler) *chsd ldrs: rdn and chsd ldr wl over 1f out: ev ch ins fnl f: unable qck towards fin* **7/1**
5346 **5** ½ **Join Up**[7] 929 6-9-2 **55**........ ShaneKelly 2 58
(Mark Brisbourne) *hld up in tch in midfield: nt clr run 2f out: swtchd rt and effrt u.p over 1f out: drvn and pressed ldrs ins fnl f: styd on same pce fnl 100yds* **9/1**
5022 **6** ¾ **Jackie Love (IRE)**[2] 988 4-8-9 **48**........(v) CathyGannon 7 49
(Olivia Maylam) *dwlt: t.k.h: hld up in tch in midfield: rdn and hdwy over 1f out: styng on and chsng ldrs whn nt clr run fnl 100yds* **11/2[2]**
626- **7** 1½ **Rainsborough**[143] 7203 5-8-13 **52**........(p) JohnFahy 11 50
(Peter Hedger) *hld up in tch towards rr on outer: rdn and effrt over 1f out: styd on same pce ins fnl f* **16/1**
0200 **8** 3½ **Very Well Red**[7] 929 9-8-8 **47**........ ChrisCatlin 8 37
(Peter Hiatt) *chsd ldr: rdn and unable qck 2f out: sn lost 2nd and wknd over 1f out* **10/1**
-601 **9** *3* **Tenancy (IRE)**[17] 807 8-8-12 **51**........(b) NeilChalmers 5 34
(Shaun Harris) *broke fast and led: rdn and hdd wl over 1f out: sn wknd* **25/1**
0-31 **10** 1½ **Holyfield Warrior (IRE)**[16] 822 8-8-7 **51**........ MarkCoumbe[(5)] 10 30
(Michael Attwater) *in tch on outer: rdn and lost pl jst over 2f out: wknd over 1f out* **10/1**

1m 37.73s (-0.47) **Going Correction** 0.0s/f (Stan) **10** Ran SP% **116.3**
Speed ratings (Par 101): **102,101,101,100,100 99,98,94,91,90**
Tote Swingers: 1&2 £6.90, 1&3 £4.40, 2&3 £12.70 CSF £34.74 CT £169.29 TOTE £3.80: £1.70, £3.70, £3.10; EX 34.00 Trifecta £245.20 Pool: £1,169.70 - 3.53 winning units..
Owner Chris Beek Racing **Bred** Kevin Buckley **Trained** Lambourn, Berks

FOCUS
A moderate race run at a fair pace and resulting in a bunch finish. The winner did not need to match his Wolverhampton win.
Jackie Love(IRE) Official explanation: jockey said filly was denied a clear run closing stages
Holyfield Warrior(IRE) Official explanation: jockey said gelding ran flat
T/Plt: £136.30 to a £1 stake. Pool: £55,508.87 - 297.09 winning tickets. T/Qpdt: £56.50 to a £1 stake. Pool: £4,360.95 - 57.10 winning tickets. SP

996 WOLVERHAMPTON (A.W) (L-H)
Friday, March 23

OFFICIAL GOING: Standard
Wind: Light, against Weather: Fine

1010 FREE BETTING WITH FREEBETTING.CO.UK H'CAP 5f 216y(P)
5:40 (5:40) (Class 6) (0-60,60) 3-Y-O **£1,704** (£503; £251) **Stalls** Low

Form RPR
5626 **1** **George Fenton**[9] 898 3-8-8 **47**........(tp) MartinHarley 5 58
(Richard Guest) *chsd ldrs: rdn over 2f out: led ins fnl f: drvn out* **11/4[2]**
3430 **2** ¾ **Lord Buffhead**[51] 376 3-8-4 **46**........ DeclanCannon[(3)] 2 55
(Richard Guest) *led: rdn over 1f out: hdd ins fnl f: styd on* **12/1**
3421 **3** *nk* **J J Leary (IRE)**[14] 845 3-9-3 **56**........(v) FrannyNorton 6 64
(Ian Williams) *chsd ldr: rdn and ev ch fr over 1f out: styd on* **11/8[1]**
-353 **4** *8* **My Name Is Sam**[18] 802 3-8-8 **47**........ LukeMorris 7 29
(Ronald Harris) *sn pushed along in rr: sme hdwy u.p over 2f out: wknd over 1f out* **7/2[3]**
5-00 **5** *3* **Rainbow Riches (IRE)**[58] 294 3-8-7 **53** ow3........ NedCurtis[(7)] 8 26
(Roger Curtis) *prom: rdn over 3f out: wknd over 1f out* **16/1**
0-56 **6** *2* **After Timer (IRE)**[14] 845 3-8-8 **47** oh1 ow1........(b) TomEaves 4
(Julie Camacho) *s.i.s: sn outpcd* **22/1**
00-4 **7** *nk* **Whip It In (IRE)**[22] 750 3-8-7 **46** oh1........ BarryMcHugh 3
(Paul Midgley) *s.i.s: sn outpcd* **40/1**

1m 14.75s (-0.25) **Going Correction** -0.05s/f (Stan) **7** Ran SP% **111.4**
Speed ratings (Par 96): **99,98,97,86,82 80,79**
toteswingers: 1&2 £6.10, 1&3 £1.60, 2&3 £2.90 CSF £32.33 CT £59.83 TOTE £3.10: £1.40, £8.20; EX 26.10.
Owner Maze Rattan Limited **Bred** R P Williams **Trained** Stainforth, S Yorks
■ Stewards' Enquiry : Martin Harley two-day ban: used whip above permitted level (Apr 7-8)

FOCUS
A weak handicap, but interesting, tactically, nonetheless. The first three finished clear and the form is rated around the runner-up.

1011 BET ON YOUR MOBILE WITH FREEBETTING.CO.UK H'CAP 1m 5f 194y(P)
6:10 (6:10) (Class 5) (0-75,74) 4-Y-O+ **£2,264** (£673; £336; £168) **Stalls** Low

Form RPR
230- **1** **Veloce (IRE)**[163] 6798 4-8-10 **62**........ FrannyNorton 8 73
(Ian Williams) *set stdy pce tl qcknd over 4f out: hdd over 2f out: rallied to ld post* **10/3[2]**
00-0 **2** *nse* **Hallstatt (IRE)**[14] 850 6-8-11 **62**........(t) MichaelO'Connell[(3)] 6 73
(John Mackie) *a.p: chsd wnr over 3f out: led over 2f out: rdn over 1f out: r.o: hdd post* **9/1**
2241 **3** *7* **Bold Adventure**[15] 465 8-8-7 **55**........ JamieMackay 7 56
(Willie Musson) *s.i.s: hld up: r.o ins fnl f: wnt 3rd nr fin: nrr nrr* **5/1**
1333 **4** *nk* **Boa**[25] 721 7-9-10 **72**........ HayleyTurner 1 73
(Reg Hollinshead) *chsd ldrs: rdn over 2f out: wknd fnl f: lost 3rd nr fin* **4/1[3]**
351- **5** ½ **Hit The Switch**[6] 7415 6-9-3 **65**........(p) TomQueally 4 65
(Jennie Candlish) *chsd wnr tl pushed along over 3f out: rdn over 2f out: wknd over 1f out* **13/2**

0-03 **6** *1* **Russian George (IRE)**[14] 849 6-9-12 **74**..............(tp) RobertWinston 2 73
(Steve Gollings) *hld up: rdn over 2f out: wknd over 1f out* **11/4**[1]

64-0 **7** *1 ½* **Inside Knowledge (USA)**[50] 392 6-8-7 **55**.................... LukeMorris 5 52
(Garry Woodward) *hld up: hdwy u.p 2f out: wknd over 1f out* **25/1**

4/0- **8** *12* **Lileo (IRE)**[119] 7536 5-9-1 **63**.................................... MichaelStainton 3 43
(Nikki Evans) *hld up: pushed along over 5f out: wknd over 2f out* **50/1**

3m 3.29s (-2.71) **Going Correction** -0.05s/f (Stan)
WFA 4 from 5yo+ 4lb **8** Ran SP% **115.6**
Speed ratings (Par 103): **105,104,100,100,100 99,99,92**
toteswingers: 1&2 £7.10, 1&3 £6.60, 2&3 £4.80 CSF £33.44 CT £148.44 TOTE £4.10: £1.20, £4.60, £1.10; EX 29.70.
Owner Dr Marwan Koukash **Bred** J Jamgotchian **Trained** Portway, Worcs

FOCUS
Modest form. The winner has not really progressed and the second is rated back to form.

1012 EXCLUSIVE FREE BETS AT FREEBETTING.CO.UK H'CAP 7f 32y(P)
6:40 (6:41) (Class 6) (0-55,56) 3-Y-O **£1,704** (£503; £251) **Stalls** High

Form RPR

000- **1** **Johnny Cavagin**[129] 7422 3-9-2 **55**...........................(t) RobertWinston 7 63
(Richard Guest) *a.p: rdn over 2f out: styd on u.p to ld wl ins fnl f: hung lft: kpt on* **16/1**

5024 **2** *nk* **Emma Jean (IRE)**[7] 923 3-8-12 **51**.............................(t) LukeMorris 6 58
(Frank Sheridan) *hld up: hdwy u.p over 1f out: r.o wl* **10/1**

0-45 **3** *¾* **Martha's Way**[7] 923 3-8-12 **51**.................................. PaddyAspell 1 56
(Michael Easterby) *led: rdn and edgd lft over 1f out: hdd wl ins fnl f* **14/1**

4654 **4** *1* **Auntie Kathryn (IRE)**[22] 743 3-8-0 **46** oh1...................... IanBurns(7) 5 48
(Stuart Williams) *hld up: swtchd rt over 2f out: hdwy over 1f out: hung lft fnl f: r.o: nt rch ldrs* **11/2**[3]

0-05 **5** *hd* **Trending (IRE)**[14] 845 3-8-10 **49**...............................(p) TomQueally 4 51
(Jeremy Gask) *s.i.s: hld up: hdwy over 1f out: nt clr run ent fnl f: swtchd lft: sn hrd rdn: styd on same pce* **7/1**

06-1 **6** *3 ¾* **Sudden Wish (IRE)**[79] 38 3-9-1 **54**............................ FrannyNorton 9 52+
(Alan Bailey) *hld up: hmpd over 2f out: hdwy and nt clr run over 1f out: swtchd rt: hmpd ins fnl f: eased* **10/3**[1]

5225 **7** *nse* **Songbird Blues**[30] 660 3-9-0 **53**................................ DavidProbert 2 44
(Mark Usher) *s.i.s: hld up: hdwy over 2f out: rdn to chse ldr over 1f out: no ex ins fnl f* **7/2**[2]

24-0 **8** *1* **Johnson's Cat (IRE)**[60] 270 3-8-11 **53**.................... RobertLButler(3) 8 42
(Richard Guest) *hld up: rdn over 1f out: no ex fnl f* **16/1**

503- **9** *8* **Spoken Words**[184] 6260 3-9-0 **56** ow3.......................... GaryBartley(3) 3 23
(Hugh McWilliams) *prom: chsd ldr 1/2-way tl rdn and wknd over 1f out* **14/1**

0-60 **10** *4* **Bellinda**[58] 294 3-8-7 **46** oh1................................. FrankieMcDonald 10
(Martin Bosley) *chsd ldr to 1/2-way: wknd over 2f out* **66/1**

05-3 **11** *3 ¼* **Diva Donkey (IRE)**[42] 495 3-9-0 **53**.............................. TomEaves 11
(Bryan Smart) *chsd ldrs tl wknd over 2f out* **16/1**

1m 29.7s (0.10) **Going Correction** -0.05s/f (Stan) **11** Ran SP% **114.7**
Speed ratings (Par 96): **97,96,95,94,94 90,90,88,79,75 71**
toteswingers: 1&2 £46.80, 1&3 £30.10, 2&3 £24.10 CSF £162.84 CT £2329.43 TOTE £30.20: £7.60, £2.40, £6.40; EX 382.50.
Owner A Bell **Bred** A Bell **Trained** Stainforth, S Yorks
■ Stewards' Enquiry : Luke Morris one-day ban: careless riding (Apr 7)

FOCUS
There were a few unexposed sorts and it was one of the handicap debutants that came home in front. The form is rated through the second and third.
Johnny Cavagin Official explanation: trainer said, regarding apparent improvement in form, that the gelding had benefited from maturing and strengthening over the winter.
Trending(IRE) Official explanation: jockey said he felt obliged, as a precaution, to ease the gelding final strides, being concerned of running out of room on the inside rail.
Sudden Wish(IRE) Official explanation: jockey said filly was denied a clear run

1013 DINE IN THE HORIZONS RESTAURANT H'CAP 1m 1f 103y(P)
7:10 (7:11) (Class 5) (0-75,73) 3-Y-O **£2,385** (£704; £352) **Stalls** Low

Form RPR

3132 **1** **Availed Speaker (IRE)**[22] 747 3-9-0 **66**....................... TonyHamilton 3 69
(Richard Fahey) *trckd ldr: racd keenly: hmpd and lost pl 7f out: led over 1f out: rdn and edgd lft ins fnl f: jst hld on* **3/1**[2]

1- **2** *shd* **Apothecary**[100] 7757 3-9-7 **73**.................................... NickyMackay 1 76+
(John Gosden) *hld up: hdwy: nt clr run and swtchd rt 1f out: r.o wl* **6/5**[1]

00-1 **3** *nse* **Zain Princess (IRE)**[41] 534 3-8-9 **61**............................ LukeMorris 6 64
(Gerard Butler) *hld up: hdwy over 1f out: rdn and hmpd sn after: r.o wl* **5/1**[3]

0-31 **4** *1 ¼* **Cool Hand Luke (IRE)**[45] 464 3-9-2 **68**................ RichardKingscote 2 68
(Tom Dascombe) *led over 2f: chsd ldrs: shkn up over 2f out: rdn over 1f out: styd on* **8/1**

1 **5** *1* **Rockgoat (IRE)**[28] 693 3-9-2 **73**.............................. AntiocoMurgia(5) 5 71
(Marco Botti) *s.i.s: hdwy to ld 7f out: rdn and hdd over 1f out: styd on same pce ins fnl f* **8/1**

5-40 **6** *8* **Auntie Joy**[6] 943 3-8-12 **64**....................................... PaddyAspell 4 45
(Michael Easterby) *prom: chsd ldr over 5f out tl rdn over 2f out: wknd over 1f out* **50/1**

2m 2.59s (0.89) **Going Correction** -0.05s/f (Stan) **6** Ran SP% **111.3**
Speed ratings (Par 98): **94,93,93,92,91 84**
toteswingers: 1&2 £1.10, 1&3 £2.50, 2&3 £1.90 CSF £6.88 TOTE £4.50: £2.20, £1.30; EX 9.00.
Owner Dr Marwan Koukash **Bred** D Veitch, E McEvoy & P Costigan **Trained** Musley Bank, N Yorks
■ Stewards' Enquiry : Nicky Mackay one-day ban: careless riding (Apr 7)

FOCUS
They went very steady early and it was a bit of a messy race. The form wouldn't be the most solid but does make enough sense.
Auntie Joy Official explanation: jockey said filly hung right-handed throughout

1014 GREAT OFFERS AT WOLVERHAMPTON-RACECOURSE.CO.UK H'CAP 1m 1f 103y(P)
7:40 (7:41) (Class 7) (0-50,55) 4-Y-O+ **£1,704** (£503; £251) **Stalls** Low

Form RPR

-365 **1** **Safwaan**[30] 651 5-9-3 **50**.. JamieMackay 8 57
(Willie Musson) *trckd ldrs: plld hrd: wnt 2nd over 2f out: led over 1f out: sn rdn: jst hld on* **2/1**[1]

2240 **2** *hd* **Cairanne**[21] 773 4-8-9 **45**....................................... RyanClark(3) 4 52
(Tom Keddy) *hld up: racd keenly: hdwy over 1f out: r.o wl* **16/1**

25-6 **3** *hd* **So Is She (IRE)**[7] 96 4-9-3 **50**...........................(be) FrannyNorton 3 57
(Alan Bailey) *s.i.s: hld up: hdwy and hmpd over 1f out: r.o wl ins fnl f* **14/1**

000 **4** *hd* **Lean Machine**[37] 561 5-9-3 **50**.................................(p) LukeMorris 2 56
(Ronald Harris) *hld up: hdwy and nt clr run over 1f out: swtchd rt and sn rdn: r.o* **12/1**

00-0 **5** *1 ¾* **Duneen Dream (USA)**[14] 848 7-9-1 **48**........................ DavidProbert 6 50
(Nikki Evans) *hld up: hdwy over 1f out: r.o: nt rch ldrs* **20/1**

-000 **6** *2* **Carr Hall (IRE)**[32] 632 9-9-2 **49**................................. TomQueally 13 47
(Tony Carroll) *prom: rdn over 2f out: no ex ins fnl f* **40/1**

400/ **7** *1 ¼* **Lady Brickhouse**[501] 7381 5-8-13 **46** ow1........................ AdamKirby 7 41
(Michael Squance) *hld up: shkn up over 1f out: r.o ins fnl f: nvr nrr* **14/1**

0021 **8** *2 ¼* **Visions Of Johanna (USA)**[7] 924 7-9-3 **55** 6ex...... DuilioDaSilva(5) 11 45
(Richard Guest) *chsd ldrs: rdn over 2f out: wknd fnl f* **11/4**[2]

4440 **9** *shd* **Spacecraft (IRE)**[14] 848 5-9-2 **49**..........................(b) NickyMackay 12 39
(Christopher Kellett) *s.i.s: sn prom: chsd ldr 5f out tl rdn over 2f out: wknd fnl f* **12/1**

6-64 **10** *¾* **See The Storm**[14] 848 4-9-1 **48**.................................. TomEaves 5 37
(Lisa Williamson) *prom: rdn over 2f out: wknd fnl f* **16/1**

-055 **11** *2 ¼* **Dubonny**[14] 848 5-8-7 **45**.................................(bt[1]) RaulDaSilva(5) 10 29
(Frank Sheridan) *led: rdn and hdd over 1f out: wknd and eased ins fnl f* **9/1**[3]

262/ **12** *1 ½* **Cape Schanck**[366] 8-8-10 **50**................................... LewisWalsh(7) 9 31
(Alan Coogan) *hld up: bhd fnl 3f* **20/1**

2m 2.04s (0.34) **Going Correction** -0.05s/f (Stan) **12** Ran SP% **122.4**
Speed ratings (Par 97): **96,95,95,95,93 92,91,89,88,88 86,84**
toteswingers: 1&2 £8.70, 1&3 £8.20, 2&3 £24.40 CSF £37.63 CT £377.89 TOTE £2.80: £1.20, £7.50, £5.40; EX 52.60.
Owner Libertys **Bred** Shadwell Estate Company Limited **Trained** Newmarket, Suffolk

FOCUS
There was a gamble landed here. A weak handicap rated through the runner-up.
Dubonny Official explanation: jockey said mare had no more to give

1015 LIVE FOOTBALL SCORES FOOTBALLSCORES.COM H'CAP 5f 20y(P)
8:10 (8:10) (Class 4) (0-85,84) 4-Y-O+ **£4,204** (£1,251; £625; £312) **Stalls** Low

Form RPR

4231 **1** **Island Legend (IRE)**[9] 890 6-9-4 **81** 6ex.....................(p) DaneO'Neill 4 89
(Milton Bradley) *mde all: rdn and hung lft over 1f out: r.o* **9/2**[2]

0/31 **2** *½* **Brenin Taran**[30] 654 6-9-3 **80**................................... MartinLane 3 86
(David Simcock) *hood removed sltly late: s.i.s: hdwy over 3f out: chsd wnr and nt clr run over 1f out: swtchd rt: r.o* **7/2**[1]

3 *1 ¼* **Head Space (IRE)**[181] 6364 4-9-3 **80**............................ TomEaves 1 82
(Ruth Carr) *hld up: r.o wl ins fnl f: nt rch ldrs* **33/1**

0661 **4** *hd* **Rylee Mooch**[14] 844 4-8-4 **72**...........................(e) CharlesEddery(5) 6 73
(Richard Guest) *s.i.s: hld up: hdwy over 1f out: r.o* **16/1**

0122 **5** *shd* **Captain Scooby**[9] 896 6-8-10 **73**............................. MartinHarley 9 74+
(Richard Guest) *sn outpcd: rdn 1/2-way: r.o ins fnl f: nrst fin* **8/1**

4-00 **6** *¾* **Volcanic Dust (IRE)**[72] 120 4-9-0 **77**..................... RichardKingscote 2 75
(Milton Bradley) *hld up: plld hrd: hdwy over 1f out: styd on* **10/1**

-162 **7** *½* **Cadeaux Pearl**[15] 835 4-9-4 **84**...........................(b) RyanPowell(3) 5 80
(Scott Dixon) *chsd wnr tl rdn over 1f out: no ex ins fnl f* **6/1**[3]

21-6 **8** *½* **Red Cape (FR)**[77] 62 9-9-4 **81**............................(b) JamesSullivan 10 75
(Ruth Carr) *chsd ldrs: rdn over 1f out: no ex ins fnl f* **20/1**

3104 **9** *½* **Fair Passion**[15] 835 5-9-2 **79**................................... AdamKirby 8 72
(Derek Shaw) *hood removed sltly late: s.i.s: hld up: plld hrd and hung lft: rdn over 1f out: nvr trbld ldrs* **6/1**[3]

-361 **10** *1 ½* **Six Wives**[15] 835 5-9-6 **83**..................................... RobertWinston 7 70
(Scott Dixon) *chsd ldrs: pushed along 1/2-way: rdn over 1f out: wknd ins fnl f* **8/1**

1m 1.42s (-0.88) **Going Correction** -0.05s/f (Stan) **10** Ran SP% **113.9**
Speed ratings (Par 105): **105,104,102,101,101 100,99,98,98,95**
toteswingers: 1&2 £5.00, 1&3 £29.00, 2&3 £17.00 CSF £20.09 CT £387.23 TOTE £4.40: £1.50, £1.70, £10.10; EX 16.70.
Owner J M Bradley **Bred** Jerome Casey **Trained** Sedbury, Gloucs
■ Stewards' Enquiry : Ryan Powell caution: careless riding.

FOCUS
This race was won after a furlong, when it became clear Island Legend was not going to be taken on in front. The winner is rated back to his best at face value.
Fair Passion Official explanation: jockey said mare hung left

1016 HORSE RACING FREE BETS WITH FREEBETTING.CO.UK MAIDEN FILLIES' STKS 5f 216y(P)
8:40 (8:42) (Class 5) 3-Y-O+ **£2,264** (£673; £336; £168) **Stalls** Low

Form RPR

2- **1** **Dreaming Of Rubies**[191] 6045 3-8-9 0...........................(t) TomEaves 3 71
(Ben Haslam) *mde all: rdn over 1f out: jst hld on* **13/2**[3]

04-2 **2** *nk* **Nevaeh**[9] 892 3-8-9 0... LukeMorris 7 70
(Pat Eddery) *a.p: pushed along 1/2-way: rdn to chse wnr over 1f out: r.o* **4/1**[2]

2 **3** *2 ¼* **Trail Of Tears (IRE)**[15] 838 3-8-9 0.............................. RobertHavlin 5 63
(John Gosden) *chsd wnr: hung rt over 2f out: rdn over 1f out: styd on same pce ins fnl f* **4/5**[1]

4 *2* **Catflap (IRE)** 3-8-9 0.. NickyMackay 2 56
(Derek Haydn Jones) *chsd ldrs: rdn over 1f out: no ex ins fnl f* **25/1**

5 *nk* **Princess Steph (IRE)** 3-8-9 0............................... RichardKingscote 8 55
(Heather Main) *s.i.s: r.o ins fnl f: nvr nrr* **16/1**

53- **6** *½* **Millymonkin**[154] 6985 3-8-9 0.................................. JamesSullivan 4 54
(Michael Easterby) *hld up: hdwy over 1f out: nt trble ldrs* **16/1**

0- **7** *2 ¼* **Verge (IRE)**[315] 2049 3-8-9 0.................................... TedDurcan 9 47
(Ed Vaughan) *sn outpcd: nt clr run and swtchd lft over 1f out: nvr nrr* **10/1**

6 **8** *nk* **Big Sylv (IRE)**[15] 838 3-8-9 0.................................... LiamJones 11 46
(James Unett) *chsd ldrs: pushed along 1/2-way: wknd over 1f out* **33/1**

40 **9** *2 ¾* **Valiant Bee**[13] 869 4-9-8 0...................................... AdamKirby 1 41
(Bill Moore) *hld up: nvr on terms* **50/1**

6-0 **10** *11* **Midnite Motivation**[21] 770 3-8-9 0.............................. DavidProbert 6
(Derek Shaw) *mid-div: hdwy over 2f out: sn wknd* **100/1**

1m 14.76s (-0.24) **Going Correction** -0.05s/f (Stan)
WFA 3 from 4yo+ 13lb **10** Ran SP% **119.5**
Speed ratings (Par 100): **99,98,95,92,92 91,88,88,84,70**
toteswingers: 1&2 £5.40, 1&3 £2.40, 2&3 £2.30 CSF £32.87 TOTE £7.10: £1.60, £1.80, £1.10; EX 43.60.
Owner Middleham Park Racing XXVII **Bred** New England, Myriad And Watership Down **Trained** Middleham Moor, N Yorks

FOCUS
A modest maiden but a welcome winner for Ben Haslam, who's been stuck on the cold list for a while. The favourite disappointed and the form is not rated too positively.
T/Plt: £921.20 to a £1 stake. Pool: £83,732.14. 66.35 winning tickets. T/Qpdt: £137.20 to a £1 stake. Pool: £9,566.32. 51.57 winning tickets. CR

1003**LINGFIELD** (L-H)

Saturday, March 24

OFFICIAL GOING: Standard

Wind: light, across Weather: warm and sunny

1031 BET AT BLUE SQUARE MAIDEN STKS 1m 2f (P)

1:50 (1:54) (Class 5) 3-Y-O+ **£3,067** (£905; £453) **Stalls** Low

Form RPR

6- **1** **Dark Stranger (USA)**[143] 7233 3-8-7 0 .... WilliamBuick 1 82+
(John Gosden) *str: lw: rn green thrght: nudged along in midfield: 5th and rdn 2f out: hdwy and edgd lft 1f out: styd on strly fnl 150yds: wnt 2nd wl ins fnl f: led nr fin* **4/1**[3]

42 **2** ½ **Benbecula**[8] 921 3-8-7 0 .... KieranO'Neill 2 81
(Richard Hannon) *w'like: swtg: rn green thrght: led: hung bdly rt and wd bnd after 1f: rdn and qcknd clr 2f out: stl wl clr 1f out: rn green fnl 150yds: edgd rt and hdd nr fin* **11/4**[2]

552- **3** 1 ½ **Hefner (IRE)**[155] 6994 3-8-7 83 .... JamieSpencer 6 78
(Richard Hannon) *t.k.h early: hld up in tch: rdn and effrt in 4th 2f out: sn outpcd but chsd clr wnr over 1f out: racd awkwardly u.p but clsd ins fnl f: nvr gng to rch ldr and n.m.r nr fin* **5/2**[1]

4222 **4** 3 **Devote Myself (IRE)**[14] 869 3-8-2 71 .... CathyGannon 11 67
(David Evans) *chsd ldr tl carried v wd bnd after 1f: sn rcvrd to chse ldrs: rdn and outpcd 2f out: plugged on same pce but no threat to ldrs after* **16/1**

4 **5** ½ **Beggar's Banquet (IRE)**[71] 147 3-8-7 0 .... TedDurcan 10 71
(George Baker) *w'like: str: s.i.s: hld up in rr: c wd and hdwy wl over 1f out: styd on steadily ins fnl f: nvr threatened ldrs* **14/1**

6 3 ½ **Ultimate Destiny** 3-8-7 0 .... MartinLane 9 64
(Ralph Beckett) *leggy: s.i.s: sn rcvrd and in midfield: lost pl and rdn over 4f out: plugged on but no threat to ldrs fnl 2f* **50/1**

66-2 **7** ½ **Haymarket**[19] 805 3-8-7 72 .... JoeFanning 4 63
(Mark Johnston) *w'like: scope: tall: lw: chsd ldrs tl carried v wd bnd after 1f: sn rcvrd and chsd ldrs 8f out: pressed ldr 3f out tl rdn and outpcd 2f out: lost 2nd over 1f out: fdd fnl f* **15/2**

8 1 **Arctic Galaxy (CAN)** 3-8-7 0 .... RobertHavlin 5 61+
(John Gosden) *w'like: str: scope: bit bkwd: rn green thrght: s.i.s: in tch towards rr: hdwy into midfield 8f out: rdn over 3f out: outpcd and btn 2f out: plugged on same pce after* **20/1**

6 **9** 11 **Art News (IRE)**[24] 737 3-8-7 0 .... LukeMorris 3 39
(Gary Moore) *str: chsd ldrs: lft 2nd 9f out tl 8f out: chsd ldrs after: rdn 5f out: wknd over 2f out: wl bhd over 1f out* **20/1**

06- **10** 6 **Kingshill Lad (IRE)**[100] 7769 3-8-0 0 ....(t) NatashaEaton(7) 7 27
(Terry Clement) *leggy: uns rdr and galloped loose bef s: rrd s and slowly away: a bhd: lost tch 3f out* **200/1**

0-0 **11** 5 **Estee Will**[50] 399 5-9-8 0 .... RichardThomas 8 16
(John E Long) *leggy: unf: sn rdn along in midfield: hmpd and pushed rt sn after s: dropped in rr and nt gng wl 8f out: lost tch 3f out: t.o* **300/1**

2m 4.9s (-1.70) **Going Correction** 0.0s/f (Stan)
WFA 3 from 5yo 20lb 11 Ran SP% **111.9**
Speed ratings (Par 103): **106,105,104,102,101 98,98,97,88,84 80**
toteswingers:1&2:£2.90, 2&3:£2.40, 1&3:£3.30 CSF £13.96 TOTE £5.00: £1.50, £1.70, £1.50; EX 15.40 Trifecta £34.00 Pool: £1371.27 - 29.84 winning units..
Owner H R H Princess Haya Of Jordan **Bred** Darley **Trained** Newmarket, Suffolk

FOCUS

A decent maiden with the third setting a good standard. There's more to come from the winner.
Benbecula Official explanation: jockey said colt hung right

1032 BLUESQUARE.COM SPRING CUP (LISTED RACE) 7f (P)

2:25 (2:25) (Class 1) 3-Y-O

£22,684 (£8,600; £4,304; £2,144; £1,076; £540) **Stalls** Low

Form RPR

411- **1** **Gusto**[154] 7019 3-9-3 105 .... RyanMoore 2 111
(Richard Hannon) *lw: mde all and dictated stdy gallop: rdn and qcknd 2f out: edgd out rt fr over 1f out: r.o wl and in command ins fnl f: rdn out* **9/4**[1]

5-20 **2** 1 **Kenny Powers**[30] 679 3-9-1 98 ....(t) RichardKingscote 8 106
(Tom Dascombe) *hld up in tch: rdn and effrt whn edgd lft over 1f out: drvn and str run fnl f: chsd wnr fnl 50yds: r.o but readily hld* **18/1**

166- **3** 1 ¼ **Bannock (IRE)**[144] 7220 3-9-3 110 .... JoeFanning 10 105
(Mark Johnston) *chsd ldrs on outer: chsd wnr 2f out: rdn wl over 1f out: styd on same pce u.p fnl f: lost 2nd fnl 50yds* **11/2**[3]

1121 **4** 4 **Pale Orchid (IRE)**[31] 659 3-8-10 91 .... LukeMorris 3 87
(David Evans) *hld up in tch: rdn and effrt whn swtchd lft over 1f out: wnt 4th 1f out: no imp and styd on same pce after* **13/2**

000- **5** 1 ½ **Gatepost (IRE)**[188] 6196 3-9-1 102 .... JamieSpencer 1 88
(Mick Channon) *dwlt: sn rcvrd and chsd ldrs: rdn and effrt wl over 1f out: fnd little u.p and btn 1f out: wl hld and plugged on same pce after* **10/3**[2]

050- **6** ½ **Crown Dependency (IRE)**[189] 6162 3-9-1 100 .... DaneO'Neill 11 87
(Richard Hannon) *stdd and dropped in bhd after s: hld up in tch in last pair: stuck bhd a wall of horses 2f out: hdwy u.p over 1f out: kpt on fnl f: nvr trbld ldrs* **11/1**

2111 **7** nk **Kickingthelilly**[22] 764 3-8-10 79 .... ChrisCatlin 6 81
(Rae Guest) *dwlt: hld up in tch towards rr: swtchd lft and effrt over 1f out: styd on same pce after: nvr trbld ldrs* **22/1**

8 shd **Arbitrageur (IRE)**[15] 853 3-9-1 0 .... TomQueally 7 86?
(Donal Kinsella, Ire) *unf: s.i.s: hld up in tch in rr: effrt and n.m.r on inner over 1f out: rdn and styd on same pce after: nvr trbld ldrs* **150/1**

310- **9** ½ **Big Note (IRE)**[198] 5849 3-9-1 94 ....[1] JimmyFortune 5 84
(Andrew Balding) *swtg: plld hrd: hld up wl in tch: rdn and unable qck whn barging match w rival and pushed wd bnd 2f out: sn outpcd and n.d over 1f out* **18/1**

040- **10** 1 ¼ **Boris Grigoriev (IRE)**[198] 5849 3-9-1 101 .... PaulHanagan 9 81
(Michael Easterby) *w wnr tl rdn and unable qck ent fnl 2f: wknd over 1f out: fdd ins fnl f* **28/1**

0-1 **11** 1 ¼ **Equation Of Time**[36] 597 3-9-1 82 .... MartinLane 4 78
(David Flood) *taken down early: t.k.h: chsd ldrs: rdn and unable qck whn barging match w rival 2f out: wknd over 1f out: fdd ins fnl f* **28/1**

1m 23.93s (-0.87) **Going Correction** 0.0s/f (Stan) 11 Ran SP% **113.3**
Speed ratings (Par 106): **104,102,101,96,95 94,94,94,93,92 90**
toteswingers:1&2:£9.90, 2&3:£15.40, 1&3:£2.80 CSF £42.56 TOTE £3.10: £1.80, £5.20, £1.70; EX 47.40 Trifecta £172.00 Pool: £1330.12 - 5.72 winning units..
Owner Highclere Thoroughbred Racing-Rock Sand **Bred** New England, Mount Coote & P Barrett **Trained** East Everleigh, Wilts

FOCUS

The winner continued his 2yo progress and this rates a personal best. The form seems sound enough.

NOTEBOOK

Gusto was representing a stable that has sent out a couple of Group 1 performers to win this race in recent years, namely Paco Boy and Dubawi Gold. It'll be a surprise if he rises to that sort of level, but he's clearly a smart colt and won this well having been up there the whole way. The extra furlong proved no problem to him and the Free Handicap might be the right sort of race for him, followed by the Jersey Stakes. (op 11-4 tchd 7-4)

Kenny Powers, back from Meydan where he ran well over this trip in the first of his two starts, before finding a mile beyond him next time, was staying on well at the finish. He had a bit to find with the winner at the weights so this was a perfectly satisfactory effort. (op 20-1)

Bannock(IRE) was best in at the weights but, along with Pale Orchid, was the most exposed runner in the line-up. It didn't look to be the trip that beat him. (op 5-1 tchd 9-2)

Pale Orchid(IRE), who's probably best over 6f, has been progressive this winter but this was another step up in class. She didn't run badly but wasn't helped by having to challenge hard against the inside rail. (op 11-2)

Gatepost(IRE), whose season tailed off after a promising start last year, didn't seem to get home. He might be one for decent sprint handicaps later in the season, but could do with dropping a few pounds first. (op 4-1 tchd 9-2)

Crown Dependency(IRE), gelded over the winter, is another for whom valuable sprint handicaps are likely to be the targets later in the year. (op 12-1 tchd 16-1)

Kickingthelilly, who is only rated 79 but has had a good winter, ran above herself. (op 20-1)

Equation Of Time Official explanation: jockey said colt ran too free

1033 GET YOUR BET ON AT BLUE SQUARE HEVER SPRINT STKS (LISTED RACE) 5f (P)

2:55 (2:55) (Class 1) 4-Y-O+

£18,714 (£7,095; £3,550; £1,768; £887; £445) **Stalls** High

Form RPR

2020 **1** **Fratellino**[14] 871 5-9-0 95 ....(t) MartinHarley 1 105
(Alan McCabe) *taken down early: chsd ldrs: wnt 2nd 2f out: rdn to chal over 1f out: drvn to ld 1f out: r.o wl ins fnl f* **11/1**

1- **2** ½ **Spirit Quartz (IRE)**[167] 4-9-0 110 .... JamieSpencer 7 103
(Robert Cowell) *stdd s: t.k.h: hld up in tch in rr: hdwy on outer over 1f out: r.o wl but edging lft ins fnl f: wnt 2nd towards fin: nvr quite getting to wnr* **16/1**

103- **3** ¾ **Bajan Tryst (USA)**[105] 7721 6-9-0 97 .... PhillipMakin 10 101
(Kevin Ryan) *in tch in midfield: swtchd rt and effrt 2f out: hdwy u.p 1f out: chse wnr fnl 75yds: kpt on but lost 2nd towards fin* **25/1**

060- **4** ¾ **Blue Jack**[237] 4573 7-9-0 94 ....(v) RichardKingscote 2 98
(Tom Dascombe) *t.k.h: hld up in tch in last trio: rdn and gd hdwy on inner over 1f out: chsd ldrs and drvn ins fnl f: styd on same pce fnl 100yds* **16/1**

300- **5** nk **Medicean Man**[161] 6858 6-9-0 108 ....(p) PaulHanagan 3 99+
(Jeremy Gask) *lw: hld up in last pair: switching rt and effrt over 1f out: styng whn nt clr run and carried lft ins fnl f: styd on fnl 75yds: nvr able to chal* **9/2**[3]

210- **6** nk **Noble Storm (USA)**[240] 4468 6-9-0 108 .... MartinLane 6 96
(Ed McMahon) *sn led and racd freely: rdn and hdd 1f out: no ex: lost 2nd fnl 75yds: wknd towards fin* **7/2**[2]

1-11 **7** 1 ½ **Oasis Dancer**[28] 711 5-9-3 105 .... JimCrowley 8 93
(Ralph Beckett) *lw: chsd ldrs on outer: rdn and effrt wl over 1f out unable qck u.p 1f out: wknd ins fnl f* **5/2**[1]

540- **8** hd **Borderlescott**[259] 3874 10-9-0 111 .... RyanMoore 5 90
(Robin Bastiman) *broke fast and led briefly: chsd ldrs tl lost pl 1/2-way: rdn and outpcd wl over 1f out: no threat to ldrs but kpt on again ins fnl f* **13/2**

1-13 **9** ¾ **Even Stevens**[60] 286 4-9-0 96 .... LukeMorris 4 87
(Scott Dixon) *chsd ldr after 1f tl 2f out: drvn and no ex over 1f out: wknd ins fnl f* **14/1**

58.84s (0.04) **Going Correction** 0.0s/f (Stan) 9 Ran SP% **112.9**
Speed ratings (Par 111): **99,98,97,95,95 94,92,92,90**
toteswingers:1&2:£10.60, 2&3:£17.50, 1&3:£51.70 CSF £165.53 TOTE £13.80: £2.50, £2.90, £6.30; EX 144.10 Trifecta £695.40 Part won. Pool: £939.85 -0.40 winning units..
Owner Sale Of The Century **Bred** Llety Stud **Trained** Averham Park, Notts

FOCUS

This looked quite competitive but not all these are at their best over 5f, and it left the door open for a bit of a shock. The form cannot be taken too literally but the winner rates a length personal best.

NOTEBOOK

Fratellino had a bit to find on the book, but he's at his best over the minimum trip, had a good draw, and after breaking well enough to bag the ideal position tracking the leader on the rail, the race could not have gone any smoother for him. He nipped through on the inside turning in and just had enough in hand to hold off the closers, who hadn't enjoyed such a dream run. This was his day and he'll be lucky to have things fall so kindly again. (op 10-1 tchd 9-1)

Spirit Quartz(IRE) ◆, winner of four of his nine starts including a Group 3 race when trained in Italy, had been gelded since he last ran. Held up in rear and wider than ideal, he got a bump from Bajan Tryst heading into the bend into the straight, which caused him to lose his footing slightly, but once straightened up he finished his race off really well, albeit while hanging left. He looks a good recruit to the yard, and the Abernant Stakes might be a suitable target. (op 14-1)

Bajan Tryst(USA) wasn't ideally drawn and got caught wide much of the way. He ran a sound race in the circumstances, especially as he's probably more effective over 6f. (tchd 22-1 and 33-1)

Blue Jack enjoyed a ground-saving trip but lacked the pace to get seriously involved in the closing stages. This was still a good effort at the weights though.

Medicean Man, who kept the runner-up company out the back early, didn't get much of a clear run in the straight and shaped better than his position suggests. He'll be better suited by a return to a stiffer track.

Noble Storm(USA) didn't settle in front and gave himself no chance of getting home. (tchd 3-1)

Oasis Dancer, who has two verdicts over the winner over 6f earlier this year, was caught wide and outpaced from the turn in. (op 11-4 tchd 3-1)

Borderlescott was the highest rated horse in the race but he's now a 10yo, he was restricted to just three starts last year, and it looks like his best days are now well behind him. (tchd 7-1)

1034 BLUE SQUARE WINTER DERBY (GROUP 3) 1m 2f (P)

3:25 (3:26) (Class 1) 4-Y-O+

£56,710 (£21,500; £10,760; £5,360; £2,690; £1,350) **Stalls** Low

Form RPR

120- **1** **Premio Loco (USA)**[168] 6693 8-9-5 113 .... GeorgeBaker 11 115
(Chris Wall) *lw: broke wl and chsd ldr tl 5f out: styd trcking ldrs: swtchd rt and effrt to chal 1f out: rdn to ld ins fnl f: r.o wl* **5/1**[2]

001- **2** ½ **Cai Shen (IRE)**[199] 5829 4-9-0 105 .... JamieSpencer 13 109
(Richard Hannon) *lw: in tch: rdn and effrt on outer bnd wl over 1f out: hdwy and edgd lft over 1f out: ev ch ins fnl f: kpt on but hld by wnr fnl 100yds: wnt 2nd last strides* **4/1**[1]

620- **3** *hd* **Circumvent**[98] 7802 5-9-0 98 JimmyFortune 12 109
(Paul Cole) *chsd ldrs: wnt 2nd 5f out: rdn to ld over 1f out: sn hrd pressed and drvn 1f out: hdd ins fnl f: kpt on u.p: lost 2nd last strides* **16/1**

634- **4** *2 1/4* **Black Spirit (USA)**[189] 6161 5-9-0 104 (t) AdamKirby 6 104
(Clive Cox) *lw: chsd ldrs: rdn and effrt 2f out: pressing ldrs but unable qck u.p 1f out: outpcd by ldng trio and one pce ins fnl f* **6/1**[3]

-010 **5** *nk* **Sooraah**[14] 876 5-8-11 108 RyanMoore 4 101+
(William Haggas) *lw: t.k.h early: hmpd sn after s: hld up in tch in last quartet: nt clr run and edging lft over 1f out: hdwy u.p 1f out: r.o fnl f: nvr able to chal* **7/1**

015- **6** *3/4* **Riggins (IRE)**[122] 7516 8-9-0 98 J-PGuillambert 9 102
(Ed Walker) *in tch in midfield: n.m.r ent fnl 2f: effrt u.p 1f out: kpt on same pce ins fnl f* **18/1**

526- **7** *1 3/4* **Vivacious Vivienne (IRE)**[22] 777 6-8-11 102 LukeMorris 10 96
(Donal Kinsella, Ire) *lw: dwlt: sn bustled along and rcvrd to r in tch: rdn and unable qck ent fnl 2f: wknd 1f out* **14/1**

1100 **8** *nk* **Emerald Wilderness (IRE)**[23] 755 8-9-0 95 (p) JimCrowley 5 98
(Robert Cowell) *hld up in tch in last quartet: swtchd rt and hdwy ent fnl f: styd on fnl f: nvr trbld ldrs* **16/1**

10-0 **9** *1 1/4* **Our Joe Mac (IRE)**[28] 712 5-9-0 101 (v1) TonyHamilton 8 95
(Richard Fahey) *led: rdn and hdd over 1f out: btn 1f out: fdd ins fnl f* **28/1**

-141 **10** *nse* **Junoob**[28] 712 4-9-0 95 (b) RichardKingscote 2 95
(Tom Dascombe) *in tch in midfield on inner: hmpd sn after s: nvr looked to travelling that wl: pushed along over 4f out: effrt whn short of room and hmpd bnd wl over 1f out: drvn and sme hdwy over 1f out: wknd ins fnl f* **4/1**[1]

-200 **11** *1* **Lyssio (GER)**[44] 484 5-9-0 98 [1] TomQueally 7 93
(Michael Attwater) *swtg: chsd ldrs: rdn and unable qck ent fnl 2f: losing pl whn sltly hmpd wl over 1f out: sn wknd* **50/1**

045- **12** *2 1/4* **Myplacelater**[183] 6301 5-8-11 102 PaulHanagan 3 86
(Richard Fahey) *hld up in last pair: rdn and no hdwy over 1f out: n.d* **10/1**

-030 **13** *5* **Loyalty**[14] 868 5-9-0 97 (v) JoeFanning 1 79
(Derek Shaw) *stdd s: hld up in last pair: rdn and no hdwy over 1f out: wl btn and eased wl ins fnl f* **20/1**

2m 3.49s (-3.11) **Going Correction** 0.0s/f (Stan) **13** Ran SP% **126.4**
Speed ratings (Par 113): **112,111,111,109,109 108,107,107,106,106 105,103,99**
toteswingers:1&2:£4.80, 2&3:£13.20, 1&3:£12.90 CSF £26.40 TOTE £6.30: £2.40, £1.70, £5.00; EX 34.50 Trifecta £1056.30 Pool: £3040.48 - 2.13 winning units..
Owner Bernard Westley **Bred** Kidder, Cole & Griggs **Trained** Newmarket, Suffolk

FOCUS
A good Winter Derby featuring seven horses rated above 100, and it was the highest rated horse in the field who came out on top. It was typically not strongly run, but the form makes sense amongst the principals.

NOTEBOOK
Premio Loco(USA) defied a 5lb penalty to win. He'd done all his previous winning at up to a mile, but had had very few chances to prove his stamina beyond that distance, and he was only beaten a nose in this very race back in 2009, so it shouldn't have been a concern. Although drawn out in stall 11, he got out of the stalls quickly and was able to cross over without much difficulty and take up a position tracking the leader on the rail. From that moment on the race went perfectly for him as he got the split early in the straight and quickened up nicely. Although a multiple winner on turf, his record on Polytrack is excellent, having now won six of his eight starts. (op 13-2 tchd 7-1 and 9-2)
Cai Shen(IRE) ◆, in contrast to the winner, had a tough trip, stuck wide throughout having been drawn out in stall 13. He quickened up well to get into contention in the straight, but, were Trakus data available, one would probably find that he had travelled a good deal further than Premio Loco. He didn't really improve a great deal from his reappearance win last year but hopefully he can build on this, as he clearly has the ability to score in pattern company. (op 5-1)
Circumvent, like the winner, overcame his wide draw with a fast break, and he was well placed throughout as a result. This was a solid effort and he probably wasn't far off his best.
Black Spirit(USA), gelded over the winter, enjoyed a rails run for much of the race and, although squeezed up a touch just inside the last, didn't really have any excuses. He might not be the easiest to place this year. (op 8-1)
Sooraah struggled to get into the race from behind and could have done with them going harder up front and setting the race up for a closer. (op 6-1 tchd 15-2)
Riggins(IRE) is not really up to winning at this level and is better over a mile anyway. (op 16-1 tchd 22-1)
Vivacious Vivienne(IRE), who ran Fame And Glory to half a length over 1m6f at Leopardstown last spring, got outpaced when the race got serious. (op 12-1 tchd 11-1)
Emerald Wilderness(IRE) didn't run well out in Dubai and it was asking a lot for him to bounce back in a competitive race like this. (op 18-1)
Junoob has been in cracking form here but this was a step up in class and his style of running makes him a hostage to fortune. Hampered on the first bend, he got another bump on the turn into the straight, and soon had the white flag out. (op 9-2)
Myplacelater was double her SP on Betfair at the off and never threatened from off the pace on her debut for Richard Fahey. (op 11-1 tchd 16-1)

1035 GET YOUR BET ON AT BLUE SQUARE H'CAP — 1m (P)
4:00 (4:01) (Class 2) (0-100,100) 4-Y-0+ **£10,221** (£3,041; £1,519; £759) **Stalls** High

Form RPR

-212 **1** **George Guru**[21] 785 5-8-4 **88** ow1 MarkCoumbe(5) 6 98+
(Michael Attwater) *t.k.h: chsd ldrs: led gng wl 2f out: rdn clr and edgd lft over 1f out: r.o wl and in command fnl f: eased towards fin* **13/8**[1]

640- **2** *1 3/4* **Axiom**[140] 7295 8-9-7 **100** J-PGuillambert 2 104
(Ed Walker) *hld up in tch: rdn and effrt wl over 1f out: n.m.r briefly ent fnl f: chsd clr wnr fnl 100yds: r.o but no threat to wnr* **8/1**

0-20 **3** *hd* **Reve De Nuit (USA)**[14] 868 6-9-4 **97** MartinHarley 5 101
(Alan McCabe) *t.k.h: hld up in tch: rdn and effrt wl over 1f out: edgd lft u.p 1f out: rn u.p but no threat to wnr* **7/1**

60-5 **4** *1 1/4* **Dubai Dynamo**[14] 871 7-8-11 **90** HayleyTurner 3 91
(Ruth Carr) *chsd ldr: rdn and unable qck 2f out: styd on same pce u.p fr over 1f out* **9/2**[3]

005- **5** *3/4* **Hung Parliament (FR)**[143] 7234 4-9-1 **94** RichardKingscote 1 93
(Tom Dascombe) *in tch: rdn 3f out: styd on and swtchd rt 1f out: kpt on u.p fnl f but no threat to wnr* **14/1**

06-2 **6** *nk* **Kingscroft (IRE)**[14] 868 4-8-11 **90** JoeFanning 7 88
(Mark Johnston) *led: hdd 2f out: rdn and nt gng pce of wnr whn sltly hmpd over 1f out: btn jst ins fnl f and lost 4 pls fnl 100yds:* **7/2**[2]

4201 **7** *5* **Titan Triumph**[22] 765 8-8-2 **86** oh4 (t) MatthewCosham(5) 4 73
(William Knight) *stdd s: t.k.h: hld up in last pair: rdn and effrt jst over 2f out: no prog and wl hld 1f out* **20/1**

00-0 **8** *1/2* **Final Drive (IRE)**[14] 868 6-9-4 **97** StevieDonohoe 8 83
(John Butler) *stdd s: hld up in last pair: rdn and effrt over 2f out: no hdwy and wl hld over 1f out* **33/1**

1m 37.08s (-1.12) **Going Correction** 0.0s/f (Stan) **8** Ran SP% **116.5**
Speed ratings (Par 109): **105,103,103,101,101 100,95,95**
toteswingers:1&2:£3.90, 2&3:£7.90, 1&3:£3.50 CSF £16.19 CT £73.82 TOTE £2.90: £1.40, £2.00, £1.80; EX 20.80 Trifecta £151.50 Pool: £2049.59 - 10.01 winning units..
Owner T M Jones **Bred** T M Jones **Trained** Epsom, Surrey

FOCUS
They went quite steady here and the winner's turn of foot proved decisive. Not strong form for the grade, and a bit muddling. The winner is progressive.

NOTEBOOK
George Guru has been progressive on this surface over the winter and continues to improve, winning here off effectively a 2lb higher mark (including 1lb overweight) than when an unfortunate second over the C&D last time. The fact that they went an ordinary gallop early played into his hands as he can quicken well, and it'll be interesting to see if he can translate this form to turf as he's only run on Polytrack so far. (op 6-4 tchd 5-4 and 15-8)
Axiom stayed on for second behind the easy winner. His consistency does him few favours with the handicapper. (op 11-1 tchd 14-1)
Reve De Nuit(USA) could have done with a stronger pace as he didn't settle early and that probably blunted his finishing effort. (op 9-1)
Dubai Dynamo is another who was unsuited by the way the race was run. A hold-up performer at his best coming late, he ended up racing closer to the pace than ideal and was readily outpaced from the turn in. (op 6-1 tchd 4-1)
Hung Parliament(FR), gelded over the winter following a disappointing 3yo campaign, never threatened from off the pace, but he's well handicapped on his juvenile form and might yet bounce back when switched to the turf. (tchd 16-1)
Kingscroft(IRE), who has made all on more than one occasion in the past, set out to do so again. He was easily seen off by the winner off the home turn, though, and this was a disappointing effort considering his promising return in the Lincoln Trial a fortnight earlier. (tchd 4-1)

1036 FOLLOW US ON TWITTER @BLUESQ MAIDEN STKS — 1m (P)
4:35 (4:35) (Class 5) 3-Y-0+ **£3,067** (£905; £453) **Stalls** High

Form RPR

3- **1** **Forgotten Hero (IRE)**[157] 6951 3-8-10 0 MichaelHills 2 91+
(Charles Hills) *mde and racd keenly: squeezed along and readily qcknd clr over 1f out: eased towards fin: v easily* **4/5**[1]

034- **2** *6* **Hazaz (IRE)**[147] 7167 3-8-10 100 BrettDoyle 7 76
(Clive Brittain) *lw: hld up in last trio: rdn and effrt to chse wnr 2f out: sn outpcd and wl hld 1f out: jst hld on for 2nd* **6/4**[2]

\- **3** *nse* **Valley Of Destiny** 3-8-10 0 RyanMoore 1 76+
(Richard Hannon) *w'like: bit bkwd: s.i.s: rn green and rdn along early: racd in last trio: rdn and outpcd ent fnl 2f: 5th and wl hld over 1f out: no ch w wnr but styd on wl ins fnl f: nrly snatched 2nd* **14/1**[3]

00- **4** *7* **Bevis Marks (USA)**[192] 6059 3-8-10 0 JoeFanning 5 59
(Mark Johnston) *lw: chsd ldng pair: rdn 4f out: wknd u.p wl over 1f out: 4th and wl btn 1f out* **25/1**

0 **5** *1* **Norse Song**[21] 784 3-8-5 0 NickyMackay 4 52
(David Elsworth) *leggy: chsd ldr: clsd and pressed ldr jst over 2f out: sn rdn and outpcd: 3rd and wl btn 1f out: wknd fnl f* **66/1**

6-0 **6** *36* **Salford Prince (IRE)**[24] 737 4-9-13 0 JimmyFortune 6
(David Elsworth) *awkward leaving stalls: t.k.h: hld up in rr: lost tch over 2f out: t.o and virtually p.u ins fnl f* **33/1**

1m 36.83s (-1.37) **Going Correction** 0.0s/f (Stan)
WFA 3 from 4yo 17lb **6** Ran SP% **110.5**
Speed ratings (Par 103): **106,100,99,92,91 55**
toteswingers:1&2:£1.10, 2&3:£2.50, 1&3:£1.30 CSF £2.11 TOTE £1.50: £1.20, £1.10; EX 2.40.
Owner J Hanson,Cavendish InvLtd,Sir A Ferguson **Bred** James Burns And A Moynan **Trained** Lambourn, Berks

FOCUS
The betting made this a two-horse race but in reality only one horse mattered from a long way out. The winner looks very useful but the bare form is hard to pin down.

1037 BET AT BLUE SQUARE ON YOUR MOBILE H'CAP — 1m 4f (P)
5:10 (5:10) (Class 3) (0-95,95) 4-Y-0+ **£6,792** (£2,021; £1,010; £505) **Stalls** Low

Form RPR

230- **1** **Viking Storm**[190] 6130 4-8-5 **81** oh5 LukeMorris 1 89
(Harry Dunlop) *t.k.h: chsd ldrs: rdn and effrt to chal over 1f out: drvn 1f out: led ins fnl f: r.o wl* **7/2**[2]

201- **2** *3/4* **Right Stuff (FR)**[101] 7753 9-9-2 **90** RyanMoore 6 97
(Gary Moore) *chsd ldrs tl hdwy to ld 9f out: rdn and fnd ex wl over 1f out: hrd pressed 1f out: hdd and styd on same pce ins fnl f* **6/1**[3]

56-3 **3** *5* **English Summer**[8] 928 5-8-13 **87** JoeFanning 4 86
(Mark Johnston) *led tl 9f out: chsd ldr: rdn 2f out: unable qck and outpcd by ldng pair 1f out: no ch w ldrs but battled on to hold on for 3rd ins fnl f* **5/2**[1]

2132 **4** *shd* **Layline (IRE)**[15] 846 5-9-7 **95** ShaneKelly 5 94
(Gay Kelleway) *taken down early: chsd ldrs: rdn and pressed ldrs 2f out: nt pce of ldng pair and btn 1f out: battling for 3rd and kpt on same pce fnl f* **5/2**[1]

0/05 **5** *1/2* **Smokey Oakey (IRE)**[22] 529 8-8-7 **81** oh2 PaulHanagan 2 79
(Mark H Tompkins) *hld up in tch: rdn over 2f out: c wd and drvn over 1f out: outpcd by ldng pair and btn 1f out: kpt on and pressing for placings fnl f* **16/1**

12- **6** *9* **O Ma Lad (IRE)**[200] 5804 4-8-2 **81** oh1 SophieDoyle(3) 3 65
(Sylvester Kirk) *stdd s: hld up in detached last: rdn and no hdwy over 3f out: nvr on terms* **8/1**

2m 30.86s (-2.14) **Going Correction** 0.0s/f (Stan)
WFA 4 from 5yo+ 2lb **6** Ran SP% **110.6**
Speed ratings (Par 107): **107,106,103,103,102 96**
toteswingers:1&2:£3.00, 2&3:£2.40, 1&3:£2.20 CSF £23.23 TOTE £4.70: £2.10, £3.20; EX 26.10.
Owner Be Hopeful Partnership **Bred** Charlie Wyatt **Trained** Lambourn, Berks

FOCUS
They were going along quite steadily in front until Ryan Moore decided to inject some pace into the race aboard Right Stuff. A fair handicap but the form is not entirely convincing with the winner 5lb wrong.

NOTEBOOK
Viking Storm was quite keen early but settled once Right Stuff went on and the pace picked up. He quickened up well when he got the split in the straight and this has to go down as a personal-best, as he was 5lb out of the handicap and therefore effectively racing off a career-high mark. (op 5-1)
Right Stuff(FR) kicked on entering the straight and tried to nick the race, but he couldn't shake off the winner and was eventually done for a bit of toe, which is not surprising considering he's a two-miler really. (op 9-2)
English Summer is another who stays a good deal further than this. (tchd 9-4 and 11-4)
Layline(IRE) was a little disappointing considering that the way the race was run should have suited him, but he's on a career-high mark now and perhaps the handicapper has him for the time being. (tchd 9-4 and 11-4)
Smokey Oakey(IRE), who was 2lb out of the handicap, hasn't shown much on the Flat for some time. (op 11-1)
O Ma Lad(IRE), who finished lame on his final start last year, was behind throughout and has a bit to prove now. Official explanation: jockey said gelding moved poorly throughout; vet said gelding returned sore (op 9-1 tchd 7-1)

T/Plt: £144.60 to a £1 stake. Pool:£123,153.24 - 621.72 winning tickets T/Qpdt: £59.70 to a £1 stake. Pool:£5,395.66 - 66.88 winning tickets SP

1038 - 1039a (Foreign Racing) - See Raceform Interactive

CURRAGH (R-H)

Sunday, March 25

OFFICIAL GOING: Yielding (soft in places)

1040a THE IRISH FIELD H'CAP 6f

3:30 (3:31) 3-Y-0+ **£11,104** (£3,245; £1,537; £512)

RPR

1 **Croisultan (IRE)**[168] 6733 6-9-12 104 PatSmullen 6 108
(D K Weld, Ire) *w.w: hdwy to chse ldrs fr over 1f out: r.o wl fnl f to ld nr line* **5/1**[2]

2 *nk* **Maarek**[182] 6388 5-9-5 97 SeamieHeffernan 8 100
(David Peter Nagle, Ire) *sn trckd ldrs: in front wl over 1f out: kpt on wl fnl f: hdd nr line* **9/2**[1]

3 *1 1/4* **Glor Na Mara (IRE)**[128] 7469 4-9-0 92 (t) KevinManning 1 91
(J S Bolger, Ire) *w.w: prog fr 1/2-way: ev ch fr 1 1/2f out: no imp and kpt on same pce ins fnl f* **10/1**

4 *shd* **Six Of Hearts**[149] 7149 8-9-6 103 SamJames(5) 10 102
(Cecil Ross, Ire) *trckd ldrs: no imp u.p and kpt on same pce fr 1f out* **12/1**

5 *1 3/4* **Jeannie Galloway (IRE)**[189] 6189 5-8-9 87 PaulHanagan 3 80
(Richard Fahey) *cl up: no imp u.p and kpt on same pce fr 1f out* **5/1**[2]

6 *1/2* **Mountain Coral (IRE)**[23] 776 8-8-4 82 NGMcCullagh 7 74
(F Oakes, Ire) *chsd ldrs: no imp u.p and kpt on same pce fr over 1f out* **9/1**

7 *nse* **Knock Stars (IRE)**[128] 7468 4-8-7 85 BenCurtis 4 76
(Patrick Martin, Ire) *w.w: rdn to chse ldrs and no imp fr over 1f out: kpt on same pce* **20/1**

8 *nk* **Colour Of Love (IRE)**[142] 7262 4-8-9 87 (b) ChrisHayes 2 77
(W McCreery, Ire) *towards rr for much: kpt on same pce fr 1 1/2f out* **16/1**

9 *1 3/4* **Great Huzzar (IRE)**[260] 3883 4-8-7 85 WayneLordan 5 70
(T Stack, Ire) *w.w: prog 1/2-way: sn prom: no ex fr 1f out* **5/1**[2]

10 *7* **Luisant**[149] 7149 9-8-12 90 FranBerry 11 52
(J A Nash, Ire) *led: jnd fr 2f out: sn hdd and no ex* **8/1**[3]

11 *1* **My Girl Anna (IRE)**[16] 851 5-8-4 82 oh2 RoryCleary 9 41
(Muredach Kelly, Ire) *trckd ldrs: wknd fr over 1f out* **8/1**[3]

1m 17.71s (2.21) **Going Correction** +0.70s/f (Yiel) **11 Ran SP% 127.8**
Speed ratings: **109,108,106,106,104 103,103,103,101,91 90**
CSF £30.50 CT £233.41 TOTE £6.90: £2.80, £2.10, £2.20; DF 47.80.
Owner Brunabonne Syndicate **Bred** D G Iceton **Trained** The Curragh, Co Kildare
■ Stewards' Enquiry : Paul Hanagan severe caution: failed to keep a straight line until passing the marker poles

FOCUS
A competitive sprint though not many look to have much scope to improve. The winner rates back to his best.

NOTEBOOK
Croisultan(IRE), having his first run for Dermot Weld and backed to reflect the manner of his work at home, got there in the end. Pat Smullen had to wait for a gap, which came just in time. An established Pattern-level performer for Liam McAteer, Croisultan can provide Dermot Weld with a reliable runner in sprint races at Group 3 or Listed level. It was a fine performance to win this off 104. (op 7/1)
Maarek gave a brave performance and just failed. He was probably in front long enough but the slight ease in conditions favoured him and this was highly encouraging with a view to the campaign ahead. (op 5/1 tchd 11/2)
Glor Na Mara(IRE) was really weak in the market and impressed with his attitude under pressure. Given the yard form, the drift in the betting was alarming and it will be interesting to see how Jim Bolger places him. (op 8/1)
Six Of Hearts travelled powerfully and made a pleasing return to action. One imagines that, like the winner, he will go for the Cork Stakes. He finished ninth in that Listed event in 2010 but is a different proposition now. (op 14/1)
Jeannie Galloway(IRE) looked to have every chance and had no more to offer in the closing stages. (op 5/1 tchd 9/2)
Mountain Coral(IRE) was a little out of his depth at this level at this stage of his career. (op 8/1)
My Girl Anna(IRE) Official explanation: jockey said mare lost its action and weakened quickly

1041a LODGE PARK STUD EUROPEAN BREEDERS FUND PARK EXPRESS STKS (GROUP 3) (F&M) 1m

4:00 (4:01) 3-Y-0+ **£43,333** (£12,666; £6,000; £2,000)

RPR

1 **Chrysanthemum (IRE)**[196] 5976 4-9-11 103 (b[1]) WayneLordan 8 110
(David Wachman, Ire) *sn trckd ldrs: t.k.h: rdn to ld over 1f out: styd on wl* **8/1**

2 *1 1/2* **Twirl (IRE)**[140] 7316 3-8-9 RyanMoore 5 103+
(A P O'Brien, Ire) *w.w: prog to chse ldrs fr 2f out: rdn in pursuit of wnr and no imp ins fnl f: kpt on same pce* **7/4**[1]

3 *1 1/4* **Princess Sinead (IRE)**[182] 6389 3-8-9 105 ShaneFoley 3 100
(Mrs John Harrington, Ire) *w.w towards rr: prog to chse ldrs fr 2f out: no imp u.p and on wout threatening fnl f* **7/1**

4 *1 1/2* **Kissable (IRE)**[168] 6736 4-9-11 102 ChrisHayes 9 101
(Kevin Prendergast, Ire) *chsd ldrs: struggling fr 2f out: sn no imp: kpt on same pce* **14/1**

5 *1/2* **Janey Muddles (IRE)**[161] 6898 3-8-9 100 KevinManning 7 95
(J S Bolger, Ire) *mid-div: sme hdwy 2f out: sn no imp u.p: kpt on same pce* **12/1**

6 *1 1/2* **Aaraas**[147] 7185 3-8-9 98 DeclanMcDonogh 6 92
(Kevin Prendergast, Ire) *w.w towards rr: kpt on same pce u.p wout threatening fr 2f out* **14/1**

7 *2 1/4* **Crystal Gal (IRE)**[36] 622 5-9-11 IanMongan 12 91
(Lucy Wadham) *prom: struggling fr 2f out: sn no imp: kpt on same pce* **20/1**

8 *3/4* **Libys Dream (IRE)**[15] 866 4-9-11 RichardKingscote 2 89
(Tom Dascombe) *sn mid-div: no imp fr 2f out* **12/1**

9 *4 1/4* **Homecoming Queen (IRE)**[142] 7283 3-8-9 106 CO'Donoghue 11 75
(A P O'Brien, Ire) *led: pressed fr 2f out: hdd and no ex fr over 1f out* **6/1**[3]

10 *6 1/2* **Miranda's Girl (IRE)**[23] 777 7-9-11 79 (b) RoryCleary 10 64
(Thomas Cleary, Ire) *sn chsd ldrs: 5th 1/2-way: no ex fr 2f out* **66/1**

11 *9* **Anam Allta (IRE)**[175] 6561 4-10-0 110 PatSmullen 4 47
(D K Weld, Ire) *sn trckd ldrs: 5th 3f out: no ex fr 2f out* **9/2**[2]

1m 47.26s (1.26) **Going Correction** +0.20s/f (Good)
WFA 3 from 4yo+ 17lb **11 Ran SP% 127.4**
Speed ratings: **102,100,99,97,97 95,93,92,88,82 73**
CSF £24.26 TOTE £12.40: £3.20, £1.30, £2.10; DF 37.70.
Owner Michael Tabor **Bred** Pegasus Breeding Ltd **Trained** Goolds Cross, Co Tipperary

FOCUS
A really interesting Park Express in which the form looks really reliable and the pace was good. It rates a better than average renewal. It is possible that the best prospect in the race finished second, but that is taking nothing away from the winner.

NOTEBOOK
Chrysanthemum(IRE) has a decent record when fresh, winning a Listed race easily on her juvenile debut and running a useful race in the Guineas last term. She recalled all that class with a sparkling display. Wayne Lordan settled her as best he could and what was notable throughout was how powerfully she travelled in first-time blinkers. Lordan had to get serious with her in the final furlong and the favourite looked a big threat but Chrysanthemum found plenty and was quite a convincing winner. She relishes an ease in the ground and that restricts her somewhat. One assumes she will come back for the Pretty Polly, in which she finished third last year, later this term. David Wachman, trainer: "She likes an ease in the ground and a horse who was third in a Group 1 last year was entitled to win that. She will appreciate going further and the blinkers helped. We'll look at the Mooresbridge Stakes." (op 9/1 tchd 10/1)
Twirl(IRE), a sister to Misty For Me, who was the talking horse, drifted in the betting and ran as if she needed the race. Ryan Moore had to niggle at her to keep her in contention and she seemed to get her second wind to stay on nicely. Her trainer's runners in the previous races did not set the world alight and Twirl will surely improve for this, for all that it is hard to see her beating Maybe if they clash over a mile. Given her inexperience, this was a perfectly satisfactory effort. Aidan O'Brien, trainer: "She ran a lovely race and I was delighted. Hopefully, she'll improve for it." (op 6/4)
Princess Sinead(IRE) had solid form as a juvenile and performed well without really threatening. She has trained on and connections ought to be able to get more black-type placing for her. (op 8/1 tchd 9/1)
Kissable(IRE) really needs further and, without a success since her juvenile days, she ran a creditable race. This was an encouraging start to the campaign.
Janey Muddles(IRE) had plenty on her plate in this company and ran a fair race.
Anam Allta(IRE) was the big disappointment and presumably something was amiss, as she has been really consistent and was one of the first beaten. Official explanation: jockey said filly travelled well before weakening quickly in the latter stages (op 4/1)

1043a WWW.THETOTE.COM IRISH LINCOLNSHIRE (PREMIER H'CAP) 1m

5:00 (5:01) 4-Y-0+

£30,000 (£9,500; £4,500; £1,500; £1,000; £500)

RPR

1 **Sharestan (IRE)**[259] 3894 4-9-4 97 JohnnyMurtagh 14 112+
(John M Oxx, Ire) *chsd ldrs: prog into 2nd over 1f out: led and styd on wl ins fnl f* **3/1**[1]

2 *2 3/4* **Ansaab**[149] 7154 4-8-4 83 ChrisHayes 9 92
(Kevin Prendergast, Ire) *chsd ldrs: clsd up fr 3f out: led appr fnl f: hdd and kpt on same pce ins fnl f* **7/1**[3]

3 *nk* **Sikara (IRE)**[162] 6884 4-8-9 95 ShaneGray(7) 3 103
(T Stack, Ire) *chsd ldrs: 7th early: mod 3rd and kpt on same pce fr over 1f out* **6/1**[2]

4 *1 1/4* **Parkers Mill (IRE)**[308] 2331 4-9-0 93 WayneLordan 7 98
(T Stack, Ire) *sn mid-div: kpt on wout threatening u.p fr over 1f out* **12/1**

5 *3 1/2* **Hujaylea (IRE)**[31] 682 9-9-4 102 (p) ConorHoban(5) 10 99
(M Halford, Ire) *w.w: rdn to chse ldrs and no imp fr over 1f out: kpt on same pce* **16/1**

6 *2 1/2* **Scottish Boogie (IRE)**[57] 4134 5-7-11 83 oh4 RossCoakley(7) 16 74
(C Byrnes, Ire) *sn trckd ldrs: 3rd fr 3f out: no imp fr over 1f out* **14/1**

7 *1 1/2* **Toufan Express**[16] 854 10-7-11 83 oh4 (b) SamanthaBell(7) 11 71
(Adrian McGuinness, Ire) *prom early: sn chsd ldrs: no imp and kpt on same pce fr over 1f out* **25/1**

8 *2 1/2* **Defining Year (IRE)**[147] 7187 4-9-12 105 ShaneFoley 4 87
(M Halford, Ire) *w.w: kpt on same pce u.p wout threatening fr over 1f out* **14/1**

9 *5 1/2* **Drombeg Dawn (IRE)**[194] 6040 6-8-4 83 BenCurtis 6 52
(A J McNamara, Ire) *chsd ldrs: no imp u.p and kpt on same pce fr 2f out* **12/1**

10 *1 3/4* **Whipless (IRE)**[30] 703 4-8-8 87 (b) RoryCleary 18 52
(J S Bolger, Ire) *prom: sn led: hdd fr 1/2-way: styd cl up tl no ex appr fnl f* **25/1**

11 *2* **Take It To The Max**[147] 7189 5-9-1 97 (p) LeeTopliss(3) 19 58
(Richard Fahey) *prom: in front 1/2-way: jnd fr 3f out: no ex appr fnl f* **8/1**

12 *1 3/4* **If Per Chance (IRE)**[44] 506 7-8-4 83 (tp) FergalLynch 17 40
(John Joseph Hanlon, Ire) *w.w: kpt on same pce fr over 2f out* **20/1**

13 *5* **Windsor Palace (IRE)**[221] 5183 7-9-2 95 (b[1]) JPO'Brien 8 40
(A P O'Brien, Ire) *chsd ldrs: 9th early: no ex 2f out* **10/1**

14 *3/4* **Solent Ridge (IRE)**[16] 854 7-7-11 83 oh1 GaryPhillips(7) 5 27
(G M Lyons, Ire) *chsd ldrs: 8th early: no ex 2f out* **50/1**

15 *3 3/4* **Prince Of Fire (GER)**[30] 703 7-8-6 85 NGMcCullagh 1 20
(C F Swan, Ire) *chsd ldrs: dropped bhd fr over 2f out* **11/1**

16 *2 3/4* **Northern Rocked (IRE)**[140] 7318 6-9-2 98 ShaneGorey(3) 13 27+
(D K Weld, Ire) *sn chsd ldrs and taken wd: struggling 1/2-way: sn no imp* **33/1**

17 *7 1/2* **Arabian Spirit**[148] 7161 7-8-7 86 PaulHanagan 2
(Richard Fahey) *chsd ldrs: 6th early: no ex 2f out* **14/1**

18 *9 1/2* **Font Of Wisdom (IRE)**[242] 4453 4-9-1 94 PatSmullen 15 +
(D K Weld, Ire) *sn chsd ldrs and taken wd: struggling over 3f out: sn no ex* **9/1**

1m 45.69s (-0.31) **Going Correction** +0.20s/f (Good) **18 Ran SP% 148.9**
Speed ratings: **109,106,105,104,101 98,97,94,89,87 85,83,78,77,74 71,63,54**
CSF £26.76 TOTE £3.80: £1.60, £2.70, £2.20, £3.00; DF 52.30.
Owner H H Aga Khan **Bred** H H Aga Khan Studs S C **Trained** Currabeg, Co Kildare

FOCUS
John Oxx's patience reaped a big-race dividend with Sharestan, who proved in another league to these rivals. The form looks reliable, with the first four unexposed and clear.

NOTEBOOK
Sharestan(IRE) looked a bit raw when asked to get to the front and that was understandable as he was having just his third start. Once he got there, he had the race sewn up and, given the rating he carried here, he was clearly a Pattern-class performer running in a handicap. He will now try Listed level and he ought to be at home in at least that class. He ought to thrive over another couple of furlongs, though it is true that he has - like many Shamardals - a liking for an ease. This 4yo's story still has chapters to be written. John Oxx, trainer: "I thought this fellow might be too inexperienced. He was injured at two and, while he won his maiden last year and ran well afterwards, I just felt that he was not fully over the injury, so I left him off. I expect he'll step up to Listed level now and I'll look at the Heritage Stakes at Leopardstown. I still think he is green. He could step up in trip and certainly likes an ease, so we'll see how he handles fast ground." (op 7/2)
Ansaab excelled himself. His trainer opined pre-race that he would need the outing but the market was really strong about his chance and he justified that, giving best close home. A consistent sort, he relishes big fields and is also ground-versatile. He ought to have a fruitful campaign. (op 14/1)
Sikara(IRE) is quite high in the weights but still seemingly progressive. She was strong at the finish here.
Parkers Mill(IRE) is another interesting sort for the year whose mark will not make him all that easy to place. He is far from exposed and would probably prefer better ground.

Hujaylea(IRE), fresh from Dubai, ran his usual honest race and is a bit in no man's land off 102 at this stage of his career.
Scottish Boogie(IRE) ran his race and probably has little scope off this mark.
Toufan Express was running on the spot at the finish. He gave an honest performance. (op 33/1)
Drombeg Dawn(IRE) Official explanation: trainer said mare was found to be in season post-race which was confirmed by the vet
Prince Of Fire(GER) Official explanation: jockey said gelding did not act on today's ground and hung in running
Font Of Wisdom(IRE), who was around twice his SP on the exchanges near the off, was extremely disappointing. (op 8/1)

1042 - 1044a (Foreign Racing) - See Raceform Interactive

1031 LINGFIELD (L-H)

Monday, March 26

OFFICIAL GOING: Standard
Wind: Moderate, half against Weather: Sunny, warm

1045 WILLIAMHILLBINGO.COM JACKPOT SURPRISE (S) STKS 1m (P)

2:15 (2:15) (Class 6) 3-Y-O+ £1,704 (£503; £251) Stalls High

Form RPR
1112 1 **Red Somerset (USA)**[4] 989 9-10-0 75 KieranO'Neill 6 79
(Mike Murphy) *t.k.h: hld up in last trio: shkn up and prog on outer over 1f out: led last 100yds: sn clr: comf* 6/5[1]
0/60 2 1 ½ **Slam**[44] 535 7-9-8 70 (p) JimCrowley 7 69
(Robert Cowell) *trckd ldr after 2f: effrt to ld wl over 1f out: narrowly hdd 1f out: one pce* 7/2[2]
1355 3 shd **Spinning Ridge (IRE)**[9] 941 7-10-0 70 (v) LukeMorris 5 75
(Ronald Harris) *t.k.h: trckd ldrs: produced to take narrow advantage 1f out: urged along and fnd little: hdd last 100yds* 9/2[3]
6032 4 3 **Jordaura**[6] 976 6-9-8 67 (t) RobertWinston 4 62
(Gay Kelleway) *racd wd: hld up in last trio: effrt to chse ldrs over 1f out: nt qckn and wl hld fnl f* 6/1
-463 5 3 **Nic Nok**[31] 683 3-8-7 51 ow2 (b) MartinDwyer 2 52?
(Harry Dunlop) *led to wl over 1f out: wknd qckly fnl f* 33/1
060- 6 1 ½ **Diplomasi**[108] 7698 4-9-8 57 BrettDoyle 3 52
(Clive Brittain) *hld up in last trio: rdn 2f out: no prog and sn btn: b.b.v* 12/1
000- 7 ½ **Polly Adler**[202] 5816 5-8-12 26 JemmaMarshall(5) 1 46?
(Alastair Lidderdale) *trckd ldr 2f: styd cl up tl wknd over 1f out* 66/1
1m 38.95s (0.75) **Going Correction** +0.10s/f (Slow)
WFA 3 from 4yo+ 17lb 7 Ran SP% 112.3
Speed ratings (Par 101): **100,98,98,95,92 90,90**
toteswingers:1&2:£1.70, 2&3:£2.20, 1&3:£2.40 CSF £5.35 TOTE £2.10: £1.50, £1.60; EX 6.30.The winner was bought in for 5,600gns.
Owner M Murphy **Bred** Haras D'Etreham **Trained** Westoning, Beds

FOCUS
A fair seller, but they didn't go that quick and the time was 0.56 seconds slower than the following Class 6 handicap. Not form to be confident about.
Diplomasi Official explanation: trainer's rep said gelding bled

1046 I WON £116K ON WILLIAMHILLBINGO.COM H'CAP 1m (P)

2:45 (2:47) (Class 6) (0-65,63) 3-Y-O £1,704 (£503; £251) Stalls High

Form RPR
3-42 1 **Emman Bee (IRE)**[5] 981 3-8-13 62 DarrenEgan(7) 6 70
(John Gallagher) *hld up disputing 5th: clsd on ldrs over 2f out: wnt 2nd jst over 1f out: drvn and styd on to ld last 100yds* 7/2[1]
04-6 2 ½ **Graylyn Valentino**[32] 667 3-9-6 62 BrettDoyle 2 69
(Robin Dickin) *racd keenly: led: kicked on whn pressed 2f out: hdd and one pce last 100yds* 13/2
6-16 3 hd **Sudden Wish (IRE)**[3] 1012 3-8-12 54 CathyGannon 8 61+
(Alan Bailey) *hld up in last quartet: gng strly but stl there 2f out: rdn over 1f out: r.o wl fnl f: too much to do* 9/2[2]
-320 4 ¾ **Purple Affair (IRE)**[25] 743 3-9-7 63 LukeMorris 4 68
(J S Moore) *hld up on inner disputing 5th: effrt 2f out: hanging lft u.p over 1f out but wnt 3rd briefly fnl f: one pce* 6/1[3]
0563 5 ¾ **Masters Blazing**[25] 743 3-9-3 59 (v[1]) AdamKirby 5 62
(John Ryan) *trckd ldng pair: rdn and effrt to try to chal 2f out: nt qckn over 1f out: one pce* 8/1
50-0 6 ¾ **Hurriya**[28] 720 3-8-10 52 JoeFanning 10 56+
(Mark Johnston) *s.i.s: hld up in last quartet: prog on inner whn nt clr run over 1f out and hmpd sn after: nt rcvr but styd on* 25/1
-432 7 1 **Stag Hill (IRE)**[10] 923 3-9-0 56 LiamKeniry 1 55
(Sylvester Kirk) *trckd ldrs: cl up and rdn wl over 1f out: fdd ins fnl f* 7/1
03U1 8 shd **Arabian Flight**[10] 916 3-9-3 59 KieranO'Neill 12 58
(John Bridger) *stdd fr wd draw and hld up in last pair: effrt 2f out: rdn and one pce over 1f out* 20/1
51-3 9 nk **Hill Of Dreams (IRE)**[26] 739 3-9-5 61 ShaneKelly 9 59
(Dean Ivory) *mostly chsd ldr: tried to chal 2f out: nt qckn over 1f out: wknd fnl f* 16/1
50-4 10 1 ¾ **King's Future**[33] 660 3-9-4 60 StevieDonohoe 11 54
(Lee Carter) *stdd fr wd draw and hld up in last pair: rdn and no prog 2f out* 25/1
6-22 11 1 ¼ **Athletic**[68] 209 3-9-7 63 MartinDwyer 3 54
(Andrew Reid) *hld up disputing 5th: drvn 3f out: wknd over 1f out* 14/1
1m 38.39s (0.19) **Going Correction** +0.10s/f (Slow) 11 Ran SP% 116.6
Speed ratings (Par 96): **103,102,102,101,100 100,99,98,98,96 95**
toteswingers:1&2:£8.70, 2&3:£10.30, 1&3:£5.40 CSF £25.19 CT £104.28 TOTE £3.70: £1.80, £2.70, £1.70; EX 34.30 Trifecta £412.10 Pool: £623.86 - 1.12 winning units..
Owner Mark Benton **Bred** O Bourke **Trained** Chastleton, Oxon

FOCUS
A moderate but competitive handicap. The weinner is rated in line with a best view of her previous form.
Purple Affair(IRE) Official explanation: jockey said gelding hung left
Hurriya ◆ Official explanation: jockey said filly was denied a clear run

1047 GET £25 FREE ON WILLIAMHILLBINGO.COM H'CAP 1m 5f (P)

3:15 (3:16) (Class 6) (0-60,59) 4-Y-O+ £1,704 (£503; £251) Stalls Low

Form RPR
-343 1 **Prince Blue**[19] 825 5-9-3 55 RichardThomas 7 62
(John E Long) *trckd ldr: pushed up to ld wl over 1f out: idled and shkn up fnl f: hld on* 9/2[3]
5004 2 ¾ **Irish Jugger (USA)**[20] 810 5-9-6 58 (b) JamesMillman 4 62
(Rod Millman) *hld up in last trio: pushed along wl over 2f out and no immediate rspnse: grad clsd fr over 1f out: wnt 2nd ins fnl f: nt quite able to chal* 10/1
-211 3 ½ **Celtic Charlie (FR)**[14] 530 7-9-0 52 [1] IanMongan 3 56
(Pat Phelan) *trckd ldng trio: rdn over 3f out: outpcd over 2f out: kpt on again fnl f* 7/4[1]
5-65 4 nk **In The Long Grass (IRE)**[19] 446 4-8-4 45 (v) JoeFanning 1 48
(Jim Boyle) *led at fair pce: rdn and hdd wl over 1f out: fdd ins fnl f* 20/1
3535 5 1 ¼ **Land Hawk (IRE)**[19] 825 6-9-2 57 SimonPearce(3) 6 58
(Lydia Pearce) *trckd ldng pair: cl up and gap appeared on inner wl over 1f out: nt qckn then wknd fnl f* 7/2[2]
1433 6 8 **Mister Frosty (IRE)**[34] 644 6-9-7 59 RobertWinston 5 48
(Gay Kelleway) *hld up in last trio: suddenly off the bridle wl over 3f out: bhd fnl 2f* 7/1
000- 7 2 ¼ **Barbirolli**[184] 6356 10-8-8 46 MartinLane 2 32
(William Stone) *hld up in last trio: rdn wl over 3f out: sn struggling and bhd* 50/1
2m 45.95s (-0.05) **Going Correction** +0.10s/f (Slow)
WFA 4 from 5yo+ 3lb 7 Ran SP% 114.8
Speed ratings (Par 101): **104,103,103,103,102 97,95**
CSF £47.16 TOTE £5.20: £2.50, £6.40; EX 50.50.
Owner Downlands Racing **Bred** Downlands Racing **Trained** Caterham, Surrey

FOCUS
A moderate staying handicap and the field were taken along by In The Long Grass. A small personal best from the winner.
Irish Jugger(USA) Official explanation: trainer said gelding lost off-fore shoe

1048 PLAY MOBILE BINGO WITH WILLIAMHILLBINGO.COM MAIDEN STKS 6f (P)

3:45 (3:45) (Class 5) 3-Y-O £2,385 (£704; £352) Stalls Low

Form RPR
1 **Valbchek (IRE)** 3-9-3 0 JohnnyMurtagh 1 84+
(Jeremy Noseda) *t.k.h: hld up in tch: wnt 2nd over 1f out but running green: lft in ld sn after: nudged along and sn clr* 4/11[1]
2 2 ¾ **Pashan Garh** 3-9-0 0 RyanClark(3) 7 68
(Pat Eddery) *wl in tch on outer: rdn 2f out: wnt 2nd fnl f: kpt on but no ch w wnr* 25/1
60- 3 3 ½ **Lazeez (USA)**[177] 6529 3-8-12 0 BrettDoyle 6 52
(Clive Brittain) *chsd ldr: rdn over 2f out: lost 2nd over 1f out: outpcd after* 16/1
4 4 ½ **Exkaliber** 3-8-12 0 RaulDaSilva(5) 3 43
(Jeremy Gask) *cl up: rdn 2f out: wknd qckly fnl f* 14/1[3]
40 5 6 **Nothing's Simple**[12] 892 3-8-10 0 NoelGarbutt(7) 4 23
(Hugo Palmer) *s.s: bdly outpcd in last pair and a detached* 66/1
6 1 **Give Us A Belle (IRE)** 3-9-3 0 IanMongan 2 20
(Christine Dunnett) *dwlt: bdly outpcd in last pair and a detached* 100/1
2- U **Aurens (IRE)**[96] 7837 3-9-0 0 AdamBeschizza(3) 5 72
(Brian Gubby) *racd freely: led: tried to kick on 2f out: hung rt over 1f out then swvd bdly rt and uns rdr sn after* 7/2[2]
1m 13.17s (1.27) **Going Correction** +0.10s/f (Slow) 7 Ran SP% 114.4
Speed ratings (Par 98): **95,91,86,80,72 71,**
toteswingers:1&2:£4.10, 2&3:£7.20, 1&3:£2.50 CSF £15.35 TOTE £1.30: £1.10, £7.10; EX 11.50.
Owner Richard Keen & Paul Smith **Bred** Kildaragh Stud **Trained** Newmarket, Suffolk

FOCUS
An uncompetitive maiden run in a time 0.62 seconds slower than the following Class 5 fillies' handicap. The winner looks a fair bit better than the bare form, which is complicated by the unseater who would probably have finished second.
Give Us A Belle(IRE) Official explanation: trainer said gelding did not face the kickback

1049 INSTANT PLAY SLOTS ON WILLIAMHILLBINGO.COM FILLIES' H'CAP 6f (P)

4:15 (4:15) (Class 5) (0-75,75) 4-Y-O+ £2,385 (£704; £352) Stalls High

Form RPR
0513 1 **Strictly Pink (IRE)**[3] 1005 4-8-7 61 CathyGannon 2 71
(Alan Bailey) *mde all: rdn wl over 1f out: styd on u.p ins fnl f* 11/4[1]
6-30 2 ½ **Secret Queen**[6] 970 5-8-7 61 oh1 (v) LukeMorris 1 69
(Martin Hill) *sltly awkward s: sn trckd ldng trio: rdn to go 2nd jst over 1f out and threatened to cl on wnr: nvr finding enough ins fnl f* 4/1[3]
2613 3 2 **Amazing Win (IRE)**[6] 970 4-8-7 61 ChrisCatlin 4 63
(Mick Channon) *hld up in tch: urged along and outpcd wl over 1f out: styd on fnl f to take 3rd nr fin* 10/3[2]
1-40 4 ½ **Caledonia Princess**[44] 528 6-9-5 73 JimCrowley 5 73
(Stuart Williams) *pressed wnr: nt qckn 2f out: lost 2nd and one pce jst over 1f out* 7/1
441 5 1 **Absa Lutte (IRE)**[39] 576 9-9-3 71 GeorgeBaker 3 68
(Michael Mullineaux) *hld up in last: effrt but outpcd wl over 1f out: one pce and no imp* 9/2
-005 6 4 ½ **Chevise (IRE)**[31] 686 4-9-0 75 DarrenEgan(7) 6 58
(Steve Woodman) *racd on outer: pressed ldng pair to over 2f out: sn btn* 8/1
1m 12.55s (0.65) **Going Correction** +0.10s/f (Slow) 6 Ran SP% 111.5
Speed ratings (Par 100): **99,98,95,95,93 87**
toteswingers:1&2:£3.00, 2&3:£2.80, 1&3:£1.60 CSF £13.76 TOTE £3.90: £2.00, £1.90; EX 15.80.
Owner A J H **Bred** Tally-Ho Stud **Trained** Newmarket, Suffolk
■ Cathy Gannon's first winner since she broke her leg in October.

FOCUS
It proved difficult to make up ground in this ordinary fillies' handicap, as it did through the card. The winner built slightly on her recent form.

1050 OVER £1M JACKPOT ON WILLIAMHILLBINGO.COM H'CAP 7f (P)

4:45 (4:46) (Class 5) (0-70,70) 4-Y-O+ £2,385 (£704; £352) Stalls Low

Form RPR
0-22 1 **Catherines Call (IRE)**[18] 839 5-9-0 70 DannyBrock(7) 11 80
(Des Donovan) *trckd ldr: effrt to ld 2f out: drvn clr over 1f out: in command after* 14/1
000- 2 1 ½ **Not My Choice (IRE)**[131] 7428 7-9-1 64 (t) DavidProbert 4 70
(David C Griffiths) *led at gd pce: hdd 2f out and sn outpcd by wnr: styd on ins fnl f* 9/2[1]
305 3 1 ¾ **My Lord**[11] 912 4-8-11 67 DarrenEgan(7) 2 68
(Ronald Harris) *chsd ldng pair: outpcd fr 2f out: kpt on same pce ins fnl f to hold on for 3rd* 8/1
1405 4 hd **Speak The Truth (IRE)**[12] 893 6-9-6 69 (p) MartinDwyer 6 70
(Jim Boyle) *chsd ldrs disputing 4th: rdn and outpcd 2f out: hanging lft but kpt on ins fnl f* 16/1
645- 5 nk **Dear Maurice**[132] 7424 8-8-11 67 (t) NoelGarbutt(7) 3 67
(Tobias B P Coles) *dwlt: sn chsd ldrs in 6th: outpcd 2f out: bmpd along and styd on fnl f* 16/1

6412 **6** ½ **Efistorm**[30] 713 11-9-2 **65**.......... HayleyTurner 12 64
(Conor Dore) *hld up in 9th and off the pce: shkn up and r.o fnl f: nvr any ch* **6/1**[2]
0230 **7** ½ **Joe Le Taxi (IRE)**[13] 883 4-9-0 **63**.......... JoeFanning 1 60
(Mark Johnston) *chsd ldrs disputing 4th: rdn and outpcd 2f out: nt on terms after* **13/2**[3]
-150 **8** ½ **Cut And Thrust (IRE)**[30] 713 6-9-0 **63**.......... AdamKirby 9 59
(Mark Wellings) *hld up in 8th and off the pce: effrt whn nt clr run over 1f out: kpt on but no ch* **9/1**
6000 **9** *nk* **Yankee Storm**[9] 942 7-9-2 **68**..........(b) RyanClark(3) 10 63
(Michael Wigham) *hld up wl off the pce in last quartet: swtchd lft jst over 1f out: rdn and late prog fnl f: nvr in contention* **14/1**
4600 **10** ½ **Sermons Mount (USA)**[12] 896 6-9-6 **69**.......... JohnFahy 14 63
(Paul Howling) *s.i.s: hld up wl off the pce in rr and racd wd: styd on fnl f: nvr in contention* **33/1**
6463 **11** ¾ **Mack's Sister**[39] 576 5-8-12 **61**..........(p) LukeMorris 5 53
(Dean Ivory) *in tch in 7th: outpcd and pushed along 2f out: nvr on terms after* **8/1**
00-1 **12** *nk* **Super Duplex**[56] 276 5-9-2 **65**.......... IanMongan 13 56
(Pat Phelan) *hld up wl off the pce in last quartet: sme late prog but nvr in contention* **8/1**
020- **13** *1* **Llewellyn**[174] 6617 4-9-2 **65**.......... GeorgeBaker 7 53
(Jim Boyle) *hld up wl off the pce in rr: jst pushed along on inner fnl 2f: no prog* **16/1**
00-0 **14** *8* **Cuthbert (IRE)**[24] 765 5-8-10 **64**..........(v) MarkCoumbe(5) 8 31
(William Jarvis) *slowly away: rousted along and mostly in last: t.o* **20/1**

1m 24.77s (-0.03) **Going Correction** +0.10s/f (Slow) **14** Ran SP% **127.8**
Speed ratings (Par 103): **104,102,100,100,99 99,98,98,97,97 96,95,94,85**
toteswingers:1&2:£23.10, 2&3:£8.10, 1&3:£19.60 CSF £80.53 CT £577.92 TOTE £19.90: £4.40, £2.60, £2.70; EX 160.10 TRIFECTA Not won..
Owner Philip Mclaughlin **Bred** K Maginn **Trained** Exning, Suffolk

FOCUS
They were surprisingly well strung out from an early stage and those held up couldn't get involved. This is form to treat with caution, but the winner is rated back towards her best.
Cuthbert(IRE) Official explanation: jockey said gelding missed the break

1051 FREE BINGO EVERY MONDAY ON WILLIAMHILLBINGO.COM H'CAP 1m 2f (P)
5:15 (5:15) (Class 5) (0-70,70) 4-Y-0+ **£2,385** (£704; £352) **Stalls** Low

Form RPR
5233 **1** **Marvo**[35] 634 8-9-1 **64**..........(b) JoeFanning 6 71
(Mark H Tompkins) *hld up: wnt 3rd 3f out gng strly: effrt on inner to ld wl over 1f out: drvn and styd on* **3/1**[3]
-325 **2** 1¾ **Conducting**[7] 960 4-9-7 **70**..........(p) RobertWinston 5 73
(Gay Kelleway) *trckd ldr after 2f: brought to chal on outer as wnr slipped by on inner 2f out: chsd him after: nt qckn fnl f* **5/2**[2]
5434 **3** 3¾ **Lisahane Bog**[7] 960 5-9-7 **70**..........(b) JohnFahy 3 66
(Peter Hedger) *trckd ldr 2f: styd cl up tl drvn and struggling 3f out: kpt on to take 3rd again fnl f: no imp on ldng pair* **2/1**[1]
5024 **4** ¾ **Escape Artist**[5] 984 5-8-7 **56** oh8.......... KieranO'Neill 1 50
(John Bridger) *t.k.h: hld up: rdn over 3f out and sn struggling: wl adrift 2f out: styd on fnl f* **10/1**
06-0 **5** *2* **Abriachan**[72] 176 5-9-2 **65**.......... AdamKirby 2 55
(Noel Quinlan) *led: rdn and hdd wl over 1f out: wknd fnl f* **6/1**

2m 6.78s (0.18) **Going Correction** +0.10s/f (Slow) **5** Ran SP% **110.3**
Speed ratings (Par 103): **103,101,98,98,96**
CSF £10.86 TOTE £3.70: £1.80, £2.10; EX 10.90.
Owner M P Bowring **Bred** Mystic Meg Limited **Trained** Newmarket, Suffolk

FOCUS
A modest, steadily run handicap that probably took little winning.
T/Plt: £55.60 to a £1 stake. Pool of £88,900.75 - 1,166.75 winning tickets. T/Qpdt: £47.30 to a £1 stake. Pool of £5,920.03 - 92.60 winning tickets. JN

973 SOUTHWELL (L-H)
Tuesday, March 27

OFFICIAL GOING: Standard
Wind: Virtually nil Weather: Fine and dry

1052 FREE CASINO BETTING WITH FREEBETTING.CO.UK H'CAP 1m (F)
2:30 (2:30) (Class 6) (0-65,65) 4-Y-0+ **£1,704** (£503; £251) **Stalls** Low

Form RPR
2123 **1** **Caledonia Prince**[13] 900 4-9-5 **63**..........(p) JoeFanning 10 74
(Jo Hughes) *trckd ldrs: hdwy 3f out: led 1 1/2f out: sn rdn and kpt on wl fnl f* **7/4**[1]
2635 **2** 1½ **Mataajir (USA)**[47] 478 4-9-5 **63**.......... MartinLane 1 71
(Derek Shaw) *prom: led 3f out: rdn 2f out: hdd 1 1/2f out: drvn and kpt on fnl f* **2/1**[2]
1534 **3** *2* **General Tufto**[26] 753 7-9-2 **60**..........(b) RobbieFitzpatrick 9 63
(Charles Smith) *sn bhd and rdn along: hdwy on inner 3f out: chsd ldng pair over 1f out: drvn and no imp fnl f* **11/1**
204- **4** *nk* **Bring Sweets (IRE)**[37] 5210 5-8-9 **53**.......... BarryMcHugh 11 56
(Brian Ellison) *in tch: hdwy on outer 3f out: rdn to chse ldrs 2f out: no imp fnl f* **16/1**
6053 **5** *3* **Myraid**[33] 676 5-8-7 **51** oh1.......... JamesSullivan 6 47
(Ruth Carr) *in tch: hdwy to trck ldrs 1/2-way: pushed along 3f out: rdn over 2f out and kpt on same pce* **8/1**[3]
504- **6** *shd* **Moheebb (IRE)**[150] 7178 8-9-7 **65**..........(b) PJMcDonald 4 61
(Ruth Carr) *towards rr: hdwy over 2f out: sn rdn and kpt on fnl f: nvr nr ldrs* **16/1**
04-0 **7** *hd* **Takhreej (IRE)**[13] 732 4-9-0 **58**.......... LukeMorris 2 53
(Paul Rich) *chsd ldrs: rdn along over 3f out: wknd over 2f out* **20/1**
04-0 **8** 4½ **Dunseverick (IRE)**[64] 269 4-9-4 **62**.......... TonyCulhane 7 47
(Jo Hughes) *cl up: rdn along over 3f out: drvn and wknd wl over 1f out* **12/1**
021- **9** *18* **Funky Munky**[17] 7159 7-8-10 **54**..........(p) PaulMulrennan 8
(Alistair Whillans) *in tch: rdn along 1/2-way: wknd over 3f out: sn bhd* **25/1**
3040 **10** *8* **Community (USA)**[11] 922 4-8-8 **59**..........(b[1]) DannyBrock(7) 5
(Phil McEntee) *dwlt: rapid hdwy to ld after 1f: rdn along over 3f out: sn hdd & wknd* **28/1**

1m 41.7s (-2.00) **Going Correction** -0.20s/f (Stan) **10** Ran SP% **120.7**
Speed ratings (Par 101): **102,100,98,98,95 95,94,90,72,64**
toteswingers:1&2:£1.80, 2&3:£6.30, 1&3:£4.30 CSF £5.44 CT £29.78 TOTE £3.20: £1.50, £1.40, £2.00; EX 6.10 Trifecta £35.40 Pool: £593.44 - 12.40 winning units..
Owner Isla & Colin Cage **Bred** Mrs I M Cage And C J Cage **Trained** Lambourn, Berks

FOCUS
A fair race for the class, the first two having good records here. The winner is back on an upward curve.
Dunseverick(IRE) Official explanation: jockey said that the gelding hung badly left

1053 FREE ONLINE BINGO AT FREEBETTING.CO.UK MAIDEN STKS 1m (F)
3:00 (3:02) (Class 5) 3-Y-O **£2,385** (£704; £352) **Stalls** Low

Form RPR
04 **1** **Lanarkshire (IRE)**[32] 684 3-9-3 0.......... JoeFanning 9 76
(Mark Johnston) *cl up: effrt over 2f out: rdn wl over 1f out: styd on to ld ins fnl f* **4/1**[3]
0-0 **2** ¾ **Feeling Good**[32] 693 3-9-3 0.......... BarryMcHugh 6 74
(Brian Ellison) *trckd ldrs on inner: hdwy 3f out: rdn wl over 1f out: styd on ins fnl f: nrst fin* **16/1**
06- **3** *nk* **Supaheart**[157] 7030 3-8-12 0.......... RobertWinston 12 68
(Hughie Morrison) *cl up: effrt wl over 2f out: rdn to ld wl over 1f out: hdd ins fnl f: kpt on same pce* **5/2**[2]
4 *nse* **Outback (IRE)**[144] 7276 3-9-3 79.......... TomEaves 5 73
(Ann Duffield) *led: rdn along wl over 2f out: hdd wl over 1f out: edgd rt and one pce ent fnl f* **13/8**[1]
064- **5** *11* **Fisher**[139] 7336 3-9-3 66.......... AdrianNicholls 11 48
(David Nicholls) *chsd ldrs: rdn along wl over 2f out: sn one pce* **14/1**
00- **6** ½ **Lady Kashaan (IRE)**[155] 7058 3-8-12 0.......... PJMcDonald 2 42
(Alan Swinbank) *towards rr: hdwy 3f out: rdn over 2f out and sn no imp* **33/1**
4 **7** 2½ **Ossie's Dancer**[7] 974 3-9-3 0.......... ShaneKelly 10 41
(Robert Cowell) *racd wd: in midfield: effrt 3f out: sn rdn and no hdwy* **33/1**
8 *5* **Haywain** 3-9-3 0.......... PhillipMakin 7 29
(Kevin Ryan) *sn pushed along to chse ldrs: rdn along wl over 3f out and sn wknd* **9/1**
9 *2* **Highway Warrior** 3-8-12 0.......... MartinLane 8 20
(Kevin M Prendergast) *a in rr* **66/1**
10 ½ **Meljana (IRE)** 3-8-12 0.......... GarryWhillans(5) 3 24
(Alan Swinbank) *s.i.s: a bhd* **50/1**
11 *13* **Jawbreakeronastick** 3-9-3 0.......... RussKennemore 1
(John Stimpson) *midfield: rdn along wl over 3f out: sn outpcd and bhd* **100/1**
6-0 **12** *42* **Elavssom (IRE)**[39] 597 3-9-3 0.......... TonyCulhane 4
(Jo Hughes) *sn rdn along in rr: bhd bef 1/2-way: t.o and virtually p.u wl over 2f out* **50/1**

1m 42.06s (-1.64) **Going Correction** -0.20s/f (Stan) **12** Ran SP% **121.5**
Speed ratings (Par 98): **100,99,98,98,87 87,84,79,77,77 64,22**
toteswingers:1&2:£11.20, 2&3:£7.90, 1&3:£12.90 CSF £63.34 TOTE £4.50: £1.20, £3.50, £1.90; EX 68.40 Trifecta £160.70 Pool: £790.87 - 3.64 winning units..
Owner Sheikh Hamdan Bin Mohammed Al Maktoum **Bred** Victor Stud Bloodstock Ltd **Trained** Middleham Moor, N Yorks

FOCUS
An interesting maiden and there wasn't much separating the first four at the line, with the rest well beaten, but the form is probably just fair. The time was reasonable.
Supaheart Official explanation: jockey said that the filly hung right in the final three furlongs

1054 FREE ONLINE CASINOS AT FREEBETTING.CO.UK H'CAP 5f (F)
3:30 (3:30) (Class 6) (0-60,66) 4-Y-0+ **£1,704** (£503; £251) **Stalls** High

Form RPR
0211 **1** **First In Command (IRE)**[7] 979 7-9-13 **66** 6ex..........(t) ShaneKelly 7 76
(Daniel Mark Loughnane) *trckd ldrs: pushed along 2f out: rdn and n.m.r over 1f out: drvn ins fnl f: led nr fin* **10/11**[1]
000- **2** *nk* **Lesley's Choice**[105] 7744 6-9-7 **60**..........(b) AdamKirby 5 69
(Paul Rich) *cl up: led 1/2-way: rdn over 1f out: drvn and hung rt ins fnl f: hdd and no ex nr fin* **3/1**[2]
4560 **3** *nk* **Bookiesindex Boy**[8] 964 8-9-2 **55**..........(b) FrederikTylicki 2 63
(J R Jenkins) *prom: chal on bit wl over 1f out and ev ch tl rdn and nt qckn wl ins fnl f* **8/1**
1-34 **4** *2* **Sandwith**[14] 887 9-8-13 **57**..........(p) LMcNiff(5) 4 58
(George Foster) *prom: effrt 2f out: sn rdn and kpt on same pce fnl f* **7/1**[3]
3166 **5** *4* **Slatey Hen (IRE)**[5] 996 4-8-11 **55**..........(p) DuilioDaSilva(5) 10 41
(Richard Guest) *hld up: effrt and nt clr run wl over 1f out: sn swtchd lft and n.m.r: rdn and no imp fnl f* **16/1**
60-0 **6** 3½ **Chosen One (IRE)**[14] 887 7-9-2 **55**.......... JamesSullivan 1 29
(Ruth Carr) *cl up on outer: rdn along over 2f out: sn wknd* **50/1**
0-00 **7** ½ **Fashion Icon (USA)**[14] 887 6-9-1 **54**.......... DanielTudhope 8 26
(David O'Meara) *slt ld to 1/2-way: sn rdn along and wknd wl over 1f out* **25/1**
615- **8** *5* **Ever Roses**[214] 5433 4-9-6 **59**..........(v) MickyFenton 9 13
(Paul Midgley) *cl up: rdn along over 2f out: sn wknd* **40/1**

59.5s (-0.20) **Going Correction** 0.0s/f (Stan) **8** Ran SP% **115.1**
Speed ratings (Par 101): **101,100,100,96,90 84,84,76**
toteswingers:1&2:£2.00, 2&3:£3.60, 1&3:£2.20 CSF £3.69 CT £12.28 TOTE £1.90: £1.10, £2.10, £1.60; EX 4.80 Trifecta £22.40 Pool: £661.27 - 21.83 winning units..
Owner Mrs C Loughnane **Bred** Peter And Mrs McCutcheon **Trained** Baldwin's Gate, Staffs

FOCUS
A moderate but compelling sprint handicap. Fair form for the grade. The winner's best form since 2009.

1055 FREE BETTING WITH FREEBETTING.CO.UK MEDIAN AUCTION MAIDEN STKS 1m 4f (F)
4:00 (4:00) (Class 5) 3-5-Y-O **£2,385** (£704; £352) **Stalls** Low

Form RPR
634- **1** **Juno The Muffinman (IRE)**[165] 6825 3-8-5 73.......... RichardKingscote 1 79
(Tom Dascombe) *chsd ldr: led over 4f out: pushed along and rn wd st: rdn clr and hung rt to stands' rails ins fnl 2f: kpt on* **5/6**[1]
030- **2** *10* **Aliante**[187] 6275 3-8-0 72.......... JoeFanning 5 61
(Mark Johnston) *chsd ldng pair: hdwy 4f out: cl up whn bmpd wl over 2f out: sn rdn and hung bdly lft to inner wl over 1f out: one pce after* **6/4**[2]
05-2 **3** *10* **Nippy Nikki**[21] 811 4-9-6 52.......... PaddyAspell 4 44
(John Norton) *in tch: rdn along and outpcd 5f out: hdwy 3f out: poor 3rd and plugged on same pce fnl 2f* **10/1**[3]
-463 **4** *20* **Never Satisfied**[11] 921 3-8-5 62..........(b) WilliamCarson 2 15
(Charles Hills) *set str pce: rdn along 5f out: hdd over 4f out: wknd 3f out* **16/1**
5 *63* **Berwaaz (GER)**[28] 4-9-11 0.......... ShaneKelly 3
(Andrew Crook) *dwlt and in rr: pushed along after 4f: hdwy on outer 5f out: rdn along 4f out: sn wknd and bhd whn eased ins fnl 2f* **150/1**

2m 40.25s (-0.75) **Going Correction** -0.20s/f (Stan)
WFA 3 from 4yo 22lb **5** Ran SP% **110.2**
Speed ratings (Par 103): **94,87,80,67,25**
CSF £2.32 TOTE £1.70: £1.10, £2.40; EX 2.50.

Owner Manor House Stables LLP **Bred** D Harron, Ederidge Ltd & Glenvale Stud **Trained** Malpas, Cheshire

FOCUS

A bizarre race as the winner hung badly right around the final bend, momentarily carrying Aliante wide, and ended up against the stands' rail, while the runner-up hung in the opposite direction once switched and ended up on the far rail. Tricky form to pin down.

Berwaaz(GER) Official explanation: jockey said that the gelding had a breathing problem

1056 FOOTBALL SCORES ON YOUR MOBILE AT FOOTBALLSCORES.COM H'CAP 1m 6f (F)

4:30 (4:30) (Class 3) (0-95,89) 4-Y-0+ **£6,792** (£2,021; £1,010 ; £505) **Stalls** Low

Form RPR

1-61 **1** **Storm Hawk (IRE)**[21] [810] 5 -8-13[79] (b) RyanClark(3) 4 88
(Pat Eddery) *s.i.s and bhd: hdwy on outer over 5f out: led 2f out: rdn over 1f out: edgd lft and drvn ins fnl f: hld on gamely* **5/1**[3]

160- **2** *nse* **Boss's Destination**[193] [6115] 5 -9-1[78] PJMcDonald 5 87
(Alan Swinbank) *trckd ldrs: hdwy over 2f out: rdn to chse wnr over 1f out: drvn to chal ins fnl f and ev ch: edgd rt and no ex nr line* **10/1**

4-11 **3** *1 1/4* **Captain Bellamy (USA)**[12] [555] 4 -8-10[77] RobertWinston 9 84
(Hughie Morrison) *trckd ldrs: hdwy 3f out: rdn over 2f out: drvn and chsd ldng pair ins fnl f: no imp* **3/1**[1]

65-4 **4** *2 1/4* **Bedouin Bay**[32] [285] 5 -8-10[76] (p) DeclanCannon(3) 7 80
(Alan McCabe) *prom: led over 3f out: sn rdn and hdd 2f out: drvn and one pce appr fnl f* **14/1**

100- **5** *3* **Sherman McCoy**[169] [6749] 6 -9-5[82] JamesMillman 1 82
(Rod Millman) *led: rdn along 5f out: hdd jst over 3f out: grad wknd fnl 2f* **33/1**

3225 **6** *1 1/4* **The Lock Master (IRE)**[7] [872] 5 -9-3[80] LukeMorris 8 78
(Michael Appleby) *hld up in tch: effrt over 4f out: rdn wl over 2f out: sn no imp* **13/2**

12- **7** *6* **Taikoo**[44] [6832] 7 -9-2[86] ChristianSewell(7) 6 76
(Hughie Morrison) *hld up: a towards rr* **16/1**

-311 **8** *1* **Admirable Duque (IRE)**[26] [751] 6 -9-5[89] (be) DarrenEgan(7) 3 77
(Dominic Ffrench Davis) *t.k.h early: hld up: a towards rr* **6/1**

1/1- **9** *10* **Marsh Warbler**[41] [7070] 5 -9-0[77] BarryMcHugh 2 51
(Brian Ellison) *trckd ldrs: cl up on inner after 3f: rdn along 5f out: sn wknd and bhd fnl 3f* **9/2**[2]

3m 4.33s (-3.97) **Going Correction** -0.20s/f (Stan)
WFA 4 from 5yo+ 4lb **9**Ran SP% 112.0
Speed ratings (Par 107): **103,102,102,100,99 98,95,94,88**
toteswingers:1&2:£9.10, 2&3:£5.10, 1&3:£2.80 CSF £51.55 CT £172.98 TOTE £4.90 : £1.60 , £3.10, £1.30 ; EX 48.60 Trifecta £342.00 Pool: £1035.30 - 2.24 winning units.
Owner Storm Hawk Partnership **Bred** Rodger O'Dwyer **Trained** Nether Winchendon, Bucks

FOCUS

A good staying handicap with plenty proven here and/or in form. The winner continues to progress on the surface.

NOTEBOOK

Storm Hawk (IRE)improved his record at the track 4-5, defying a mark 6lb higher than last time. His only defeat here came when he challenged towards the inside and faced loads of kickback, but he was taken wide this time and had just enough left late on after moving into the race going easily. (op 6-1)

Boss's Destination, returning from 193 days off, showed himself to be a useful sort on Fibresand on his first try on the surface. He's relatively lightly raced and open to more improvement. tchd 14-1)

Captain Bellamy (USA)had Storm Hawk behind when winning over 2m here last time, but today's winner had an excuse on that occasion. Raised 6lb, he came up just short. (op 11-4)

Bedouin Bay ran well in hot company on this return to the Flat. (op 12-1)

Sherman McCoy hadn't been seen for 169 days, but has gone well fresh before. This was his first try on Fibresand, though, and he should do better in due course. (op 28-1)

Admirable Duque (IRE)had won his two previous starts here, but he struggled on this rise in class off 7lb higher than last time. (op 9-2)

Marsh Warbler was reported to have finished distressed over hurdles last time and he ran here as though something was again amiss. (op 4-1 tchd 5-1)

1057 GREAT OFFERS AT SOUTHWELL-RACECOURSE.CO.UK H'CAP 2m (F)

5:00 (5:00) (Class 6) (0-65,65) 4-Y-0+ **£1,704** (£503; £251) **Stalls** Low

Form RPR

0-00 **1** **Carnac (IRE)**[42] [555] 6 -9-1[54] (p) ShaneKelly 3 63
(Alan McCabe) *trckd ldrs: hdwy on outer to trck ldr 1/2-way: effrt 4f out and sn led: rdn clr over 2f out: kpt on wl* **9/2**

2-4 **2** *8* **Polly Holder (IRE)**[10] [937] 4 -9-1[59] (p) WilliamCarson 4 58
(Paul D'Arcy) *mde most tl rdn along 4f out and sn hdd: drvn over 2f out: kpt on same pce* **11/4**[2]

514- **3** *5* **River Dragon (IRE)**[97] [7914] 7 -9-12[65] BarryMcHugh 5 58
(Tony Coyle) *cl up: rdn along over 5f out: outpcd and mod 3rd fr wl over 3f out* **2/1**[1]

532- **4** *1 3/4* **Lady Bluesky**[57] [7163] 9 -9-5[63] GarryWhillans(5) 2 54
(Alistair Whillans) *trckd ldrs: rdn along and lost pl over 5f out: plugged on u.p fnl 3f* **7/2**[3]

450/ **5** *26* **Ice And Fire**[1037] [1273] 13 -8-0[46] oh1 (b) NoelGarbutt(7) 6
(John Stimpson) *in tch: rdn along over 4f out: sn wknd* **66/1**

3-14 **6** *21* **Kishanda**[20] [594] 4 -8-12[63] (v) IanBurns(7) 1
(Gay Kelleway) *trckd ldrs on inner: rdn along over 4f out: sn wknd and bhd* **12/1**

3m 42.02s (-3.48) **Going Correction** -0.20s/f (Stan)
WFA 4 from 6yo+ 5lb **6**Ran SP% 109.6
Speed ratings (Par 101): **100,96,93,92,79 69**
toteswingers:1&2:£2.50, 2&3:£1.80, 1&3:£1.90 CSF £16.36 TOTE £4.90 : £2.10 , £2.40 ; EX 18.40.
Owner A J McCabe & Charles Wentworth **Bred** Kilfrush Stud **Trained** Averham Park, Notts

FOCUS

A moderate, uncompetitive staying handicap and they finished strung out, despite the early pace being slow. The winner is rated back to last year's best but there are doubts over what he beat.

1058 GOLF AND RACING AT SOUTHWELL H'CAP 7f (F)

5:30 (5:30) (Class 5) (0-70,70) 3-Y-0 **£2,264** (£673; £336 ; £168) **Stalls** Low

Form RPR

001- **1** **Daddy Warbucks (IRE)**[165] [6835] 3 -9-5[68] AdrianNicholls 3 75
(David Nicholls) *cl up on inner: led 1/2-way: rdn wl over 1f out: strly pressed and drvn ins fnl f: styd on gamely* **8/1**

4122 **2** *3/4* **Flying Pickets (IRE)**[11] [916] 3 -9-7[70] (be) JohnFahy 5 75
(Alan McCabe) *trckd ldrs: hdwy on inner 3f out: cl up wl over 1f out: rdn to challenge and ev ch ins fnl f: no ex towards fin* **13/8**[1]

1135 **3** *1/2* **Samasana (IRE)**[11] [920] 3 -9-5[68] TonyHamilton 6 72
(Ian Wood) *cl up: chal on outer 2f out: sn rdn and ev ch tl drvn and one pce ins fnl f* **5/1**[3]

00-2 **4** *3 1/2* **Dansili Dutch (IRE)**[16] [491] 3 -8-7[61] DeanHeslop(5) 7 55
(David Barron) *in tch: rdn along and outpcd wl over 2f out: styd on u.p fnl f: n.d* **4/1**[2]

2650 **5** *2 3/4* **Chapellerie (IRE)**[17] [867] 3 -8-13[62] WilliamCarson 8 49
(Richard Guest) *dwlt: a towards rr* **11/1**

5224 **6** *1* **Siouxies Dream**[19] [840] 3 -8-7[56] (p) LukeMorris 4 40
(Michael Appleby) *led: hdd 1/2-way: rdn along wl over 2f out and sn wknd* **9/1**

211- **7** *1 1/2* **Tweet Lady**[199] [5945] 3 -9-6[69] JamesMillman 1 49
(Rod Millman) *a in rr* **14/1**

1m 27.72s (-2.58) **Going Correction** -0.20s/f (Stan) **7**Ran SP% 110.9
Speed ratings (Par 98): **106,105,104,100,97 96,94**
toteswingers:1&2:£4.00, 2&3:£1.70, 1&3:£6.60 CSF £20.19 CT £68.81 TOTE £6.70 : £2.50 , £2.40; EX 18.60 Trifecta £230.30 Pool: £585.18 - 1.88 winning units.
Owner Martin Love **Bred** Edmond Kent **Trained** Sessay, N Yorks

FOCUS

A modest handicap in which the front three pulled clear in a decent time. The form has been rated fairly positively.

Tweet Lady Official explanation: jockey said that the filly became restive in the stalls and resented the kick-back

T/Jkpt: £10,000.00 to a £1 stake. Pool of £20,546.14 - 2.50 winning tickets. T/Plt: £16.50 to a £1 stake. Pool of £72,404.09 - 3,201.99 winning tickets. T/Qpdt: £6.90 to a £1 stake. Pool of £4,947.52 - 524.16 w. tickets. JR 1059a-1060a Foreign Racing (See Raceform Interactive)

989 KEMPTON (A.W) (R-H)

Wednesday, March 28

OFFICIAL GOING: Standard

Wind: Light, against Weather: Sunny, warm

1061 WIN BIG WITH BETDAQ MULTIPLES H'CAP 5f (P)

5:40 (5:40) (Class 6) (0-65,62) 4-Y-0+ **£1,617** (£481; £240 ; £120) **Stalls** Low

Form RPR

546- **1** **Howyadoingnotsobad (IRE)**[121] [7567] 4 -8-11[57] RaulDaSilva(5) 7 68
(Karen George) *mde all: rdn and edgd lft fr over 1f out: asserted ins fnl f* **4/1**[1]

10-3 **2** *1 1/2* **Wreningham**[22] [808] 7 -9-4[62] (p) RyanClark(3) 9 68
(Pat Eddery) *chsd wnr: trying to chal whn carried lft fr over 1f out: nt qckn fnl f* **8/1**

-040 **3** *1 1/4* **Athwaab**[26] [763] 5 -8-12[58] MatthewLawson(5) 1 59
(Noel Chance) *chsd ldng pair: rdn on inner over 1f out: nt qckn and no imp* **10/1**

506- **4** *3/4* **Sarangoo**[118] [7591] 4 -9-6[61] CathyGannon 5 59
(Malcolm Saunders) *dwlt: detached in last pair: pushed along over 1f out: r.o fnl f to take 4th nr fin: nvr in contention* **10/1**

6323 **5** *3/4* **Porthgwidden Beach (USA)**[13] [910] 4 -8-0[48] oh3.(tp) DarrenEgan(7) 2 44
(Anthony Middleton) *chsd ldrs disputing 4th: rdn and no imp over 1f out: n.d after* **12/1**

6023 **6** *shd* **Sherjawy (IRE)**[9] [958] 8 -9-3[58] JamieGoldstein 6 53
(Zoe Davison) *sn racd wd: disp 6th: no prog over 1f out: nvr in contention* **9/2**[2]

0045 **7** *3/4* **Forty Proof (IRE)**[9] [964] 4 -8-11[57] MatthewCosham(5) 4 50
(David Evans) *hld up disputing 6th: shkn up over 1f out: no real prog and nvr in contention* **5/1**[3]

-003 **8** *1 1/4* **Invigilator**[7] [986] 4 -8-12[53] JoeFanning 3 41
(Derek Shaw) *t.k.h early: n.m.r after 1f: chsd ldrs disputing 4th: nt qckn over 1f out: fdd* **4/1**[1]

0630 **9** *3* **Dingaan (IRE)**[7] [985] 9 -8-11[52] RobbieFitzpatrick 8 29
(Peter Grayson) *stdd s: hld up in last and detached: pushed along on outer over 1f out: eased last 100yds* **25/1**

59.54s (-0.96) **Going Correction** -0.15s/f (Stan) **9**Ran SP% 115.7
Speed ratings (Par 101): **101,98,96,95,94 94,92,90,86**
toteswingers: 1&2 £6.10, 1&3 £12.70, 2&3 £4.60 CSF £36.35 CT £300.92 TOTE £7.30 : £2.90 , £1.40, £2.40 ; EX 52.10 .
Owner Ten Four Fun **Bred** J G Reid **Trained** Higher Eastington, Devon
■ Stewards' Enquiry : Ryan Clark three-day ban: careless riding (11-13 April)

FOCUS

This low-grade sprint handicap was run at a sound pace with plenty driven along turning for home. It paid to race up with the pace as the first three home were always in those positions. The time was decent and the winner has been accorded a pesonal best.

Athwaab Official explanation: jockey said that the mare hung left

1062 BACK OR LAY AT BETDAQ.COM H'CAP 1m 2f (P)

6:10 (6:10) (Class 6) (0-60,62) 3-Y-O **£1,617** (£481; £240 ; £120) **Stalls** Low

Form RPR

4044 **1** **Foster's Road**[23] [803] 3 -9-5[57] (v) MartinHarley 3 64
(Mick Channon) *trckd ldrs in 6th and cl up: rdn and prog over 1f out: led jst ins fnl f: styd on* **7/1**[3]

300- **2** *1/2* **Lady Mandy**[144] [7292] 3 -8-10[48] PaulHanagan 6 54
(Richard Fahey) *sn pushed along in 7th and nvr gng sweetly: effrt u.p on outer wl over 1f out: r.o to take 2nd last 100yds: clsng on wnr fin* **11/4**[1]

0-20 **3** *1 1/2* **Green Legacy (USA)**[57] [255] 3 -9-6[58] SebSanders 2 61
(Amanda Perrett) *trckd ldng pair: drvn to chal on inner 1f out: chsd wnr to last 100yds: one pce* **9/1**

5351 **4** *1* **Saucy Cat (IRE)**[9] [993] 3 -9-10[62] 6ex LukeMorris 4 63
(John Best) *trckd ldng trio: gng wl enough over 2f out: rdn and tried to chal over 1f out: nt qckn* **9/2**[2]

00-2 **5** *1 1/2* **Courtesy Call (IRE)**[9] [993] 3 -9-7[59] JoeFanning 5 57
(Mark Johnston) *pressed ldr: rdn to take narrow ld 2f out: hdd & wknd jst ins fnl f* **11/4**[1]

-050 **6** *2 3/4* **Canning Vale**[27] [743] 3 -8-11[49] CathyGannon 9 42
(Julia Feilden) *hld up in last trio: pushed along over 3f out: brought wd in st: sme prog over 1f out: n.d* **50/1**

0255 **7** *2* **Tectonic (IRE)**[6] [993] 3 -9-2[59] (p) RaulDaSilva(5) 1 48
(Chris Dwyer) *led: rdn and narrowly hdd 2f out: wknd qckly fnl f* **9/1**

40-2 **8** *6* **Bountiful Catch**[20] [832] 3 -9-0[52] MickyFenton 8 29
(Pam Sly) *t.k.h: trckd ldrs on outer in 5th: rdn over 2f out: wknd over 1f out* **14/1**

00-5 **9** *31* **Classy Lass**[55] [382] 3 -8-7[45] MartinLane 10
(Derek Shaw) *v.s.a: in tch in last trio tl wknd 3f out: t.o* **66/1**

000- **10** *nk* **Jenndale**[124] 7540 3-8-7 **45**....(p) ChrisCatlin 7
(Chris Dwyer) *plld hrd for 2f and hld up last: nt gng wl after: t.o over 1f out* **50/1**

2m 7.7s (-0.30) **Going Correction** -0.15s/f (Stan) 10 Ran SP% **116.1**
Speed ratings (Par 96): **95,94,93,92,91 89,87,82,58,57**
toteswingers: 1&2 £5.40, 1&3 £9.40, 2&3 £6.70 CSF £26.35 CT £177.28 TOTE £6.30: £1.90, £1.10, £1.80; EX 48.20.
Owner Dave and Gill Hedley **Bred** G Hedley & Mike Channon Bloodstock Limited **Trained** West Ilsley, Berks

FOCUS
A modest 3yo handicap, run at a fair pace. The third and fourth set the standard.
Classy Lass Official explanation: jockey said that the filly hung badly right

1063 BETDAQ MOBILE APPS H'CAP 5f (P)
6:40 (6:40) (Class 5) (0-75,75) 3-Y-O **£2,264** (£673; £336; £168) **Stalls** Low

Form RPR
3-42 **1** **Bookiesindexdotnet**[8] 977 3-8-8 **69**.... DarrenEgan(7) 6 76
(J R Jenkins) *mde all: pressed 2f out: sn asserted: pushed out and wl in command fnl f* **11/2**
21- **2** *1 1/4* **Lesotho (IRE)**[263] 3855 3-9-6 **74**.... AdamKirby 7 77
(Noel Quinlan) *chsd wnr: chal and upsides 2f out: nt qckn sn after: wl hld fnl f* **15/8**[1]
4213 **3** *2* **J J Leary (IRE)**[5] 1010 3-8-2 **56**....(v) FrannyNorton 4 51
(Ian Williams) *chsd ldng pair: rdn and one pce over 1f out* **7/2**[2]
200- **4** *2 3/4* **Mitie Mouse**[207] 5701 3-9-7 **75**.... JimCrowley 3 60
(Mike Murphy) *hld up in last trio: prog to take 4th wl over 1f out: sn rdn and no imp* **4/1**[3]
45-5 **5** *3/4* **Macdonald Mor (IRE)**[81] 84 3-9-6 **74**.... TomMcLaughlin 5 57
(Michael Wigham) *a in last trio: nvr a factor* **20/1**
215- **6** *3/4* **Blodwen Abbey**[138] 7364 3-9-5 **73**.... LiamJones 2 53
(James Unett) *s.i.s: t.k.h and sn chsd ldng trio: wknd over 1f out* **8/1**
3313 **7** *2 1/4* **Fugitive Motel (IRE)**[12] 916 3-8-12 **73**.... NicoleNordblad(7) 1 45
(Hans Adielsson) *a in last trio: struggling fr 1/2-way* **9/1**

59.7s (-0.80) **Going Correction** -0.15s/f (Stan) 7 Ran SP% **118.3**
Speed ratings (Par 98): **100,98,94,90,89 88,84**
toteswingers: 1&2 £2.20, 1&3 £3.80, 2&3 £3.00 CSF £17.13 TOTE £5.70: £1.90, £2.50; EX 19.80.
Owner Bookmakers Index Ltd **Bred** D R Tucker **Trained** Royston, Herts

FOCUS
This sprint handicap was run at a sensible pace and, as was the case with the first race on the card, dominated by those able to race up with the early gallop. The winner is rated in line with the best view of her Southwell run.

1064 BETDAQ CASINO GAMES CLASSIFIED CLAIMING STKS 7f (P)
7:10 (7:10) (Class 6) 4-Y-O+ **£1,617** (£481; £240; £120) **Stalls** Low

Form RPR
3553 **1** **Spinning Ridge (IRE)**[2] 1045 7-9-1 70....(v) LukeMorris 2 76
(Ronald Harris) *dwlt: hld up in 4th bhd clr ldr: prog to hd chsng gp over 1f out and sn led: drvn out* **11/4**[2]
2403 **2** *1* **Unlimited**[11] 941 10-8-9 72.... JimCrowley 6 67
(Tony Carroll) *hld up in last bhd clr ldr: urged along over 2f out: styd on to take 2nd last 100yds: a hld* **5/1**
/5-4 **3** *1/2* **Indian Art (IRE)**[14] 896 6-8-10 71.... SeanLevey(3) 5 70
(Sylvester Kirk) *hld up in 3rd bhd clr ldr: rdn over 2f out: chal wl over 1f out: sn rdn and one pce* **2/1**[1]
12-0 **4** *1* **Cheylesmore (IRE)**[77] 119 4-9-3 72....(v) WilliamCarson 3 71
(Stuart Williams) *t.k.h: trckd clr ldr: rdn and lost 2nd over 1f out: nt qckn and wl hld after* **3/1**[3]
3-40 **5** *7* **Finefrenzyrolling (IRE)**[20] 4-8-2 60 ow2....(b) LukeRowe(7) 1 44
(Mrs K Burke) *led and sn abt 10 l clr: styd on inner in st: wknd and hdd over 1f out* **12/1**

1m 24.82s (-1.18) **Going Correction** -0.15s/f (Stan) 5 Ran SP% **109.4**
Speed ratings (Par 101): **100,98,98,97,89**
toteswingers: 1&2 £8.70 CSF £15.82 TOTE £6.60: £3.10, £1.10; EX 11.20.
Owner Robert & Nina Bailey **Bred** Eddie O'Leary **Trained** Earlswood, Monmouths

FOCUS
A small turnout for this claiming event. They went a strong pace. There are the usual doubts over the grade and the form is rated around the winner.

1065 RACING PLUS OUT EVERY SATURDAY MAIDEN STKS 1m 3f (P)
7:40 (7:40) (Class 5) 3-Y-O+ **£2,264** (£673; £336; £168) **Stalls** Low

Form RPR
4/ **1** **Splendid Light**[530] 6883 4-9-13 0.... WilliamBuick 9 84+
(John Gosden) *green in preliminaries: mde all and racd keenly: jnd over 1f out: pushed along and edgd lft: fnd plenty and a holding on: cleverly* **8/11**[1]
20- **2** *nk* **Niceofyoutotellme**[242] 4535 3-8-8 0 ow1.... JimCrowley 6 81+
(Ralph Beckett) *trckd ldrs: smooth prog to go 2nd over 2f out: sn chalng: rdn and w wnr 1f out: r.o wl but a hld* **11/4**[2]
62-4 **3** *10* **Dynastic**[12] 918 3-8-7 77.... KieranO'Neill 4 62
(Richard Hannon) *prom: chsd wnr 5f out to over 2f out: sn wl outpcd* **5/1**[3]
05- **4** *3/4* **Dicey Vows (USA)**[154] 7111 4-9-13 0.... DavidProbert 2 64
(Alan Jarvis) *hld up in last trio: effrt whn nt clr run wl over 2f out: sn outpcd: kpt on fr over 1f out* **33/1**
5 *3/4* **Plumbago Blue** 3-8-2 0.... AndreaAtzeni 10 54
(Marco Botti) *dwlt: sn trckd ldrs: rdn 4f out disputing 4th on outer: outpcd over 2f out: kpt on* **16/1**
6 *3 1/2* **Smarty Time**[11] 5-9-6 0.... SeanLevey(3) 1 51
(John Bridger) *dwlt: hld up last: effrt on inner 3f out: sn outpcd but sme prog 2f out* **100/1**
7 *3 1/2* **Sweet Vera**[11] 7-9-9 0.... MartinLane 3 45
(Shaun Harris) *a in midfield: wl outpcd fr over 2f out* **100/1**
0/6 **8** *18* **Thunderonthemount**[33] 688 7-9-9 0.... JemmaMarshall(5) 7 17
(Michael Attwater) *mostly chsd wnr to 5f out: sn rdn: wknd qckly over 2f out: t.o* **66/1**
00 **9** *8* **Lal Bhai**[18] 869 4-9-13 0.... DaneO'Neill 5
(Chris Down) *hld up in last trio: rdn 4f out: sn wknd: t.o* **66/1**
6-54 **10** *3 3/4* **Redclue (IRE)**[46] 534 3-8-7 58....(v1) ChrisCatlin 8
(Miss Louise Allan) *in tch in midfield to 4f out: wknd rapidly: t.o* **33/1**

2m 19.28s (-2.62) **Going Correction** -0.15s/f (Stan)
WFA 3 from 4yo 21lb 4 from 5yo+ 1lb 10 Ran SP% **118.0**
Speed ratings (Par 103): **103,102,95,94,94 91,89,76,70,67**
toteswingers: 1&2 £1.20, 1&3 £1.40, 2&3 £2.00 CSF £2.87 TOTE £1.70: £1.40, £1.20, £1.10; EX 3.10.
Owner George Strawbridge **Bred** George Strawbridge **Trained** Newmarket, Suffolk

FOCUS
This interesting maiden was run at a sensible pace, with the first two home pulling right away from the field up the straight, in the style of decent types. There is some doubt what the bare form is worth with the third disappointing.

1066 GOFFS READY-TO-RUN SALE APRIL 3RD H'CAP 7f (P)
8:10 (8:10) (Class 4) (0-85,83) 4-Y-O+ **£4,075** (£1,212; £606; £303) **Stalls** Low

Form RPR
24-1 **1** **Ducal**[27] 746 4-9-4 **80**.... JohnFahy 4 91
(Mike Murphy) *trckd ldrs: prog to ld jst over 2f out: drvn and hrd pressed fr over 1f out: styd on wl* **3/1**[2]
411/ **2** *1/2* **Dubarshi**[510] 7317 4-9-6 **82**.... DaneO'Neill 8 92
(Jo Crowley) *hld up disputing 5th: clsd on ldrs gng wl 2f out: pressed wnr over 1f out: styd on but a jst hld* **8/1**
31-1 **3** *hd* **Haamaat (IRE)**[23] 806 4-9-4 **80**.... PaulHanagan 10 89
(William Haggas) *t.k.h: hld up fr wd draw and disp 7th: prog on outer wl over 1f out: wnt 3rd fnl f and looked dangerous: nt qckn last 100yds* **9/4**[1]
100- **4** *nse* **Intercept (IRE)**[131] 7457 4-9-2 **78**.... WilliamBuick 11 87
(John Gosden) *stdd s fr wd draw: t.k.h and hld up in last trio: plld out wd and shkn up 2f out: prog over 1f out: r.o fnl f: clsng at fin* **15/2**
-024 **5** *2 1/4* **Masai Moon**[22] 812 8-9-4 **80**.... JamesMillman 7 83
(Rod Millman) *trckd ldr: moved up to chal over 2f out: nt qckn w wnr sn after: wknd fnl f* **14/1**
0041 **6** *1 1/2* **Street Power (USA)**[6] 991 7-8-11 **78** 6ex.... RaulDaSilva(5) 3 79+
(Jeremy Gask) *hld up in last trio: pushed along and trying to make prog whn short of room over 1f out: one pce after* **9/2**[3]
0100 **7** *shd* **Ocean Legend (IRE)**[9] 962 7-9-7 **83**.... AdamKirby 6 85+
(Tony Carroll) *hld up in midfield disputing 5th: looking for room 2f out: cl up but looked hld whn nt clr run jst over 1f out: eased* **16/1**
0420 **8** *hd* **Dozy Joe**[9] 962 4-9-6 **82**.... MartinLane 9 80
(Ian Wood) *prom: rdn over 2f out: styd chsng ldrs tl wknd fnl f* **20/1**
010- **9** *7* **Polar Annie**[170] 6747 7-9-4 **80**.... LukeMorris 5 59
(Malcolm Saunders) *led at gd pce to jst over 2f out: wknd rapidly over 1f out* **40/1**
340- **10** *13* **Rajeh (IRE)**[181] 6485 9-9-4 **80**.... RobbieFitzpatrick 1 24
(Peter Grayson) *dropped to last after 2f and sn struggling: t.o 3f out* **66/1**

1m 24.59s (-1.41) **Going Correction** -0.15s/f (Stan) 10 Ran SP% **118.1**
Speed ratings (Par 105): **102,101,101,101,98 96,96,96,88,73**
toteswingers: 1&2 £5.00, 1&3:£2.40, 2&3:£5.00 CSF £27.29 CT £65.19 TOTE £5.00: £2.00, £3.20, £1.10; EX 29.80.
Owner The Icebreakers **Bred** Cheveley Park Stud Ltd **Trained** Westoning, Beds

FOCUS
A competitive 7f handicap, run at a steady pace. The first four were all unexposed/progressive and the winner built on his previous solid C&D run.

1067 AMIGO H'CAP 7f (P)
8:40 (8:40) (Class 6) (0-60,60) 3-Y-O **£1,617** (£481; £240; £120) **Stalls** Low

Form RPR
5064 **1** **Umph (IRE)**[12] 916 3-8-13 **52**....(b1) CathyGannon 9 63
(David Evans) *mde all: sn clr and spreadeagled field: drvn over 2f out and looked vulnerable briefly: sn extended ld again: unchal* **12/1**
004- **2** *4 1/2* **Parque Atlantico**[88] 7938 3-8-7 **46** oh1....(v1) DavidProbert 1 45
(Andrew Balding) *awkward s: rousted along in last quartet: prog on inner fr 2f out: styd on wl to take 2nd nr fin: no ch w wnr* **10/1**
6544 **3** *3/4* **Auntie Kathryn (IRE)**[5] 1012 3-8-2 **46** oh1.... RaulDaSilva(5) 5 43
(Stuart Williams) *trckd ldrs: rdn over 2f out: styd on to chse clr wnr ins fnl f: lost 2nd nr fin* **7/2**[1]
040- **4** *1* **Vicgernic**[107] 7735 3-8-8 **47**....(p) FergusSweeney 6 41
(Gary Moore) *hld up in 7th and off the pce: rdn over 2f out: styd on wl fr over 1f out: nvr involved* **20/1**
0-03 **5** *3/4* **Stormin Gordon (IRE)**[34] 663 3-8-1 **47**....(p) DarrenEgan(7) 7 39
(Noel Quinlan) *chsd clr wnr: tried to cl over 2f out: sn no imp: lost 2nd and fdd ins fnl f* **33/1**
4223 **6** *1* **One More Roman (IRE)**[14] 901 3-9-0 **60**....(vt) IanBurns(7) 10 49
(Gay Kelleway) *hld up in last quartet and wl off the pce: bmpd along over 2f out: styd on fr over 1f out: no ch* **9/1**
400- **7** *nk* **Elusive Island (USA)**[208] 5681 3-9-5 **58**.... PaulHanagan 4 47
(Ann Duffield) *awkward s: t.k.h and sn trckd ldrs: rdn and no prog 2f out: fdd fnl f* **4/1**[2]
3421 **8** *1 3/4* **Flying Kitty**[28] 734 3-9-2 **55**.... KieranO'Neill 8 39
(John Bridger) *stdd s: hld up in last quartet and wl off the pce: rdn over 2f out: sme prog over 1f out: n.d and fdd last 100yds* **13/2**[3]
000- **9** *nse* **Medam**[134] 7421 3-8-11 **50**.... MartinLane 11 34
(Shaun Harris) *heavily restrained s: hld up in last and a long way off the pce: rdn on outer over 2f out: kpt on fr over 1f out: no ch* **40/1**
300- **10** *hd* **True Prince (USA)**[147] 7222 3-9-1 **54**.... JimCrowley 2 37
(Amanda Perrett) *chsd ldrs: rdn sn after 1/2-way: no prog 2f out: wknd fnl f* **7/2**[1]
0566 **11** *5* **Jacasa Too**[28] 739 3-8-7 **46** oh1....(b) LukeMorris 3 16
(Rod Millman) *chsd ldrs: rdn over 2f out: wknd wl over 1f out* **25/1**

1m 25.95s (-0.05) **Going Correction** -0.15s/f (Stan) 11 Ran SP% **118.5**
Speed ratings (Par 96): **94,88,88,86,86 84,84,82,82,82 76**
toteswingers: 1&2 £25.90, 1&3:£4.60, 2&3:£8.50 CSF £121.10 CT £524.03 TOTE £12.50: £3.20, £3.10, £2.60; EX 166.10.
Owner Mrs E Evans **Bred** Tally-Ho Stud **Trained** Pandy, Monmouths
■ Stewards' Enquiry : Cathy Gannon two-day ban: used whip in the incorrect place (11-12 Apr)

FOCUS
A modest if competitive looking handicap, run at a decent pace. The winner made all and was back to something like his early 2yo best.
T/Jkpt: Not won. T/Plt: £59.60 to a £1 stake. Pool: £76,899.25. 940.47 winning tickets. T/Qpdt: £4.60 to a £1 stake. Pool: £8,173.20. 1,297.65 winning tickets. JN

1045 LINGFIELD (L-H)
Wednesday, March 28

OFFICIAL GOING: Standard
Wind: Virtually nil Weather: Sunny and warm

1068 PRESTIGE HERITAGE MAIDEN STKS 7f (P)
2:30 (2:30) (Class 5) 3-Y-O **£2,385** (£704; £352) **Stalls** Low

Form RPR
30- **1** **Anaconda (FR)**[226] 5130 3-9-3 0.... RichardKingscote 2 89+
(Tom Dascombe) *mde all: shkn up and qcknd wl clr over 1f out: eased towards fin: v easily* **8/15**[1]

450- **2** *6* **Cryptic Choice (IRE)**[202] 5849 3-9-3 75 RobertWinston 1 70
(Charles Hills) *stdd s: chsd ldrs: rdn and effrt to chse wnr 2f out: drvn and btn over 1f out: hld on for modest 2nd cl home* **4/1**[2]
3 *hd* **Morocco** 3-9-3 0 WilliamBuick 4 69+
(John Gosden) *sn chsng wnr: shkn up: rn green and dropped to 3rd bnd 2f out: no ch w wnr but kpt on again ins fnl f to press for modest 2nd cl home* **9/2**[3]
4 *9* **Tatty** 3-8-12 0 MartinLane 5 40
(Ian Wood) *a same pl: rdn and struggling over 2f out: wknd 2f out: sn bhd* **33/1**
5-0 **5** *1* **Beckfield Point**[12] 918 3-9-0 0 (t) RyanClark(3) 3 42
(Stuart Williams) *stdd s: a last: rdn and struggling over 2f out: wknd 2f out: sn bhd* **50/1**

1m 24.52s (-0.28) **Going Correction** +0.025s/f (Slow) 5 Ran SP% **108.3**
Speed ratings (Par 98): **102,95,94,84,83**
CSF £2.89 TOTE £1.30: £1.70, £1.20; EX 3.20.
Owner The MHS 8X8 Partnership **Bred** Haras Du Quesnay **Trained** Malpas, Cheshire

FOCUS
Not a strong race and there are doubts over the bare form, but the winner is potentially useful.

1069 PLATERS AND STAMPERS (S) STKS 6f (P)
3:00 (3:00) (Class 6) 3-Y-O+ **£1,704** (£503; £251) **Stalls** Low

Form RPR
0646 **1** **Catalyze**[30] 718 4-9-9 65 (t) WilliamCarson 2 68
(Richard Guest) *racd off the pce in 4th: rdn and effrt on inner 2f out: drvn and hdwy over 1f out: led ins fnl f: hrd pressed after but a jst holding rival: drvn out* **1/1**[1]
0206 **2** *nk* **Riflessione**[13] 911 6-9-7 63 (v) DarrenEgan(7) 5 72
(Ronald Harris) *led for 1f: chsd ldr after: rdn 2f out: drvn and kpt on to chal 1f out: ev ch ins fnl f: nt qckn u.p towards fin* **14/1**
66-5 **3** *2* **Jake The Snake (IRE)**[5] 1005 11-9-9 84 MartinHarley 4 61
(Richard Guest) *rdn leaving stalls to go prom: led after 1f: rdn 3f out: 4 l clr 2f out: drvn and wandered u.p over 1f out: hdd and styd on same pce ins fnl f* **4/1**[2]
2103 **4** *3/4* **Waterloo Dock**[23] 800 7-9-7 68 (v) DannyBrock(7) 1 63
(Michael Quinn) *sn rdn along: chsd ldng pair: drvn over 2f out: plugged on same pce fr over 1f out* **4/1**[2]
-540 **5** *1 1/4* **Atlantic Beach**[19] 844 7-10-0 67 (b) LukeMorris 3 59
(Milton Bradley) *sn outpcd in last and rdn along: kpt on fnl f but nvr any threat to ldrs* **13/2**[3]

1m 11.91s (0.01) **Going Correction** +0.025s/f (Slow) 5 Ran SP% **110.0**
Speed ratings (Par 101): **100,99,96,95,94**
CSF £15.36 TOTE £2.00: £1.90, £1.70; EX 13.60.There was no bid for the winner.
Owner Willie McKay **Bred** The Hon Robert Hanson **Trained** Stainforth, S Yorks
■ Stewards' Enquiry : William Carson seven-day ban: overuse of whip (11-14 April, 16-18 Apri)

FOCUS
A fascinating betting heat primarily involving the two Willie McKay-owned runners, and those who heeded the market moves were rewarded.

1070 COOK, CREATE, INSPIRE H'CAP 6f (P)
3:30 (3:30) (Class 6) (0-60,60) 4-Y-O+ **£1,704** (£503; £251) **Stalls** Low

Form RPR
6312 **1** **Dorothy's Dancing (IRE)**[25] 783 4-9-5 58 GeorgeBaker 6 71
(Gary Moore) *chsd ldr: led gng strly wl over 1f out: rdn clr ent fnl f: in command fnl f: comf* **5/2**[1]
0005 **2** *2 3/4* **Flaxen Lake**[11] 939 5-8-8 47 (p) LukeMorris 2 52
(Milton Bradley) *chsd ldrs: rdn over 2f out: drvn over 1f out: chsd clr wnr jst ins fnl f: styd on same pce and no imp* **9/1**
3062 **3** *hd* **Avonvalley**[7] 986 5-9-1 54 RobbieFitzpatrick 11 58
(Peter Grayson) *awkward leaving stalls and s.i.s: bhd: c wd bnd 2f out: styd on wl u.p ins fnl f: pressing for 2nd cl home: no ch w wnr* **14/1**
0530 **4** *1/2* **Metropolitan Chief**[8] 972 8-8-8 47 JohnFahy 9 49
(Paul Burgoyne) *hld up in midfield: rdn and effrt on inner over 1f out: styd on same pce and no imp fnl 150yds* **25/1**
0600 **5** *1* **Custom House (IRE)**[8] 972 4-9-3 56 DaneO'Neill 8 55
(John E Long) *bhd: swtchd ins and effrt u.p over 1f out: kpt on fnl f: no threat to wnr* **9/1**
643- **6** *nse* **Luisa Tetrazzini (IRE)**[225] 5139 6-8-9 53 MarkCoumbe(5) 1 52
(Terry Clement) *dwlt: in tch towards rr: effrt u.p over 1f out: kpt on ins fnl f: no threat to wnr* **20/1**
1012 **7** *1/2* **Royal Envoy (IRE)**[9] 964 9-8-13 52 MichaelStainton 7 49
(Paul Howling) *in tch in midfield: rdn and unable qck wl over 1f out: styd on same pce and no threat to wnr fr over 1f out* **8/1**[3]
2421 **8** *nse* **Blueberry Fizz (IRE)**[7] 985 4-9-0 60 6ex (v) DarrenEgan(7) 12 57
(John Ryan) *chsd ldng trio: rdn and unable qck 2f out: outpcd and btn 1f out: wknd ins fnl f* **6/1**[2]
244- **9** *1/2* **True Satire**[109] 7717 4-9-0 60 LewisWalsh(7) 10 56
(Jane Chapple-Hyam) *racd on outer: in tch towards rr: bmpd over 3f out: rdn and no prog 2f out: plugged on same pce fnl f* **6/1**[2]
6550 **10** *1/2* **Tamino (IRE)**[12] 926 9-8-2 46 oh1 (b) JemmaMarshall(5) 4 40
(Alastair Lidderdale) *taken down early: t.k.h: hld up towards rr: swtchd rt and hdwy over 3f out: rdn and fnd nil wl over 1f out: plugged on same pce and n.d after* **20/1**
0-63 **11** *1* **Efisio Princess**[33] 687 9-9-4 57 RichardThomas 3 48
(John E Long) *sn led: rdn and hdd wl over 1f out: lost 2nd jst ins fnl f: wknd fnl 100yds* **12/1**

1m 12.06s (0.16) **Going Correction** +0.025s/f (Slow) 11 Ran SP% **116.0**
Speed ratings (Par 101): **99,95,95,94,93 93,92,92,91,90 89**
toteswingers: 1&2 £7.00, 1&3 £7.70, 2&3 £15.20 CSF £24.27 CT £269.57 TOTE £3.40: £1.50, £2.50, £4.60; EX 26.10 Trifecta £151.60 Pool: £1,065.37 - 5.20 winning units..
Owner Tom Glynn **Bred** Patrick Carroll **Trained** Lower Beeding, W Sussex

FOCUS
A moderate handicap run in a time 0.15 seconds slower than the earlier seller. The form is rated around the second and the third.
True Satire Official explanation: jockey said filly suffered interference in running
Efisio Princess Official explanation: jockey said that that the mare hung right throughout

1071 CUSHIONSMART H'CAP 1m 4f (P)
4:00 (4:00) (Class 5) (0-75,74) 4-Y-O+ **£2,385** (£704; £352) **Stalls** Low

Form RPR
-143 **1** **Copper Canyon**[21] 820 4-9-4 73 LukeMorris 4 83
(J S Moore) *racd off the pce in 5th: clsd on ldrs 4f out: chsng ldrs but hld in over 2f out: edgd out rt and bmpd rival jst over 2f out: edgd rt and pushed rival wdr bnd wl over 1f out: drvn to ld 1f out: styd on wl* **2/1**[1]
3-10 **2** *3 3/4* **Kiss A Prince**[24] 275 6-9-7 74 (b) ShaneKelly 7 78
(Dean Ivory) *stdd and dropped in bhd after s: hdwy on outer to chse ldrs 3f out: pushed rt ent fnl 2f: pushed wdr bnd wl over 1f out: lost pl: rallied u.p 1f out and chsd wnr ins fnl f: no imp* **4/1**[3]
1011 **3** *1* **Ay Tay Tate (IRE)**[21] 825 6-8-13 66 (p) KieranO'Neill 5 68
(David C Griffiths) *led for 1f: chsd ldng pair after 10f out: rdn over 3f out: drvn and ev ch ent fnl f: outpcd by wnr fnl f: kpt on* **10/3**[2]
30-0 **4** *nk* **Timocracy**[42] 570 7-9-0 67 RobertHavlin 6 69
(Alastair Lidderdale) *led after 1f: rdn over 2f out: hdd 1f out: sn outpcd by wnr and btn: kpt on same pce* **10/1**
321- **5** *1 3/4* **Moresweets 'n Lace**[315] 2204 5-9-4 71 GeorgeBaker 3 70
(Gary Moore) *hld up off the pce in last pair: clsd on ldrs 4f out: rdn and no prog over 1f out: styng on same pce and wl hld whn nt clr run wl ins fnl f* **8/1**
0-04 **6** *2* **Edgewater (IRE)**[35] 648 5-9-7 74 StevieDonohoe 1 70
(Lee Carter) *chsd ldrs: swtchd rt and hdwy 4f out: chsd ldr 3f out: rdn and ev ch ent fnl 2f: no ex and btn 1f out: wknd fnl f* **12/1**
4534 **7** *5* **Jawaab (IRE)**[27] 751 8-8-8 66 (e) CharlesEddery(5) 2 54
(Richard Guest) *pushed along leaving stalls: chsd ldr 10f out: upsides ldrs and rdn 5f out: struggling 3f out: wknd 2f out* **12/1**

2m 30.36s (-2.64) **Going Correction** +0.025s/f (Slow)
WFA 4 from 5yo+ 2lb 7 Ran SP% **112.0**
Speed ratings (Par 103): **109,106,105,105,104 103,99**
toteswingers: 1&2 £2.20, 1&3 £1.80, 2&3 £2.70 CSF £9.73 TOTE £3.70: £1.90, £2.20; EX 9.00.
Owner Gary B Watts **Bred** Snailwell Stud Co Ltd **Trained** Upper Lambourn, Berks

FOCUS
A fair handicap run at a reasonable pace. The winner was less exposed than most of these and the second ran just about his best race of the winter.

1072 POTS AND PANS MEDIAN AUCTION MAIDEN STKS 5f (P)
4:30 (4:30) (Class 5) 3-Y-O **£2,385** (£704; £352) **Stalls** High

Form RPR
043- **1** **Red Senor (IRE)**[244] 4462 3-9-3 71 WilliamCarson 3 73
(Charles Hills) *chsd ldr: led on bit ent fnl f: sn rdn clr: comf* **15/8**[1]
04- **2** *2 3/4* **Christopher Chua (IRE)**[251] 4240 3-8-12 0 DavidKenny(5) 4 63
(Simon Dow) *s.i.s: in tch in last pl: rdn and hdwy on inner over 1f out: chsd wnr 1f out: kpt on but no ch w wnr* **33/1**
325- **3** *1* **Samba Night (IRE)**[163] 6919 3-9-3 68 LukeMorris 2 59
(James Eustace) *hld up in tch: rdn and effrt wl over 1f out: 3rd and styd on same pce fnl f* **9/2**
0-02 **4** *2 3/4* **Chart**[56] 376 3-9-3 60 LeeNewman 1 49
(William Jarvis) *chsd ldng pair tl rdn and unable qck over 1f out: btn 1f out: wknd ins fnl f* **7/2**[3]
420 **5** *3 1/2* **Sugar Prince (IRE)**[8] 969 3-9-3 0 RobertHavlin 5 37
(Tim Pitt) *led tl rdn and hdd ent fnl f: sn wknd* **2/1**[2]

59.74s (0.94) **Going Correction** +0.025s/f (Slow) 5 Ran SP% **111.5**
Speed ratings (Par 98): **93,88,87,82,77**
CSF £41.46 TOTE £2.40: £1.20, £7.30; EX 40.80.
Owner R J Arculli **Bred** E O'Leary **Trained** Lambourn, Berks

FOCUS
A weak maiden run in a time 1.09 seconds slower than the following Class 5 handicap for older horses. The winner is a small improver as rated, though there is some doubt over the form.

1073 PRESTIGE BANKER H'CAP 5f (P)
5:00 (5:00) (Class 5) (0-75,75) 4-Y-O+ **£2,385** (£704; £352) **Stalls** High

Form RPR
-050 **1** **Billy Red**[13] 911 8-8-13 67 (b) FergusSweeney 3 76
(J R Jenkins) *stmbld sltly leaving stalls: pressed ldr: rdn wl over 1f out: led ent fnl f: kpt on wl: rdn out* **12/1**
64-1 **2** *1* **Ability N Delivery**[19] 851 7-9-3 71 (p) JimCrowley 6 76
(Michael J Browne, Ire) *hld up in last pair: rdn and effrt on outer wl over 1f out: hdwy 1f out: chsd wnr wl ins fnl f: no imp* **5/1**[3]
3524 **3** *1/2* **Estonia**[32] 715 5-9-7 75 AdamKirby 4 79
(Michael Squance) *dwlt: racd in last pair: hdwy and swtchd rt 1f out: chsd ldrs and kpt on same pce fnl 100yds* **5/2**[2]
-621 **4** *1/2* **Court Applause (IRE)**[33] 696 4-8-12 66 MartinDwyer 1 68
(William Muir) *chsd ldrs: drvn over 1f out: chsd wnr 1f out: one pce and lost 2 pls wl ins fnl f* **5/1**[3]
000- **5** *1 3/4* **Befortyfour**[193] 6177 7-9-4 72 (t) MartinHarley 7 68
(Richard Guest) *chsd ldrs: rdn: edgd lft and unable qck wl over 1f out: one pce and no imp whn n.m.r ins fnl f* **5/4**[1]
00-0 **6** *2* **Nine Before Ten (IRE)**[6] 997 4-8-11 70 DuilioDaSilva(5) 2 58
(Richard Guest) *sn led: rdn wl over 1f out: hdd ent fnl f: wknd fnl 150yds* **22/1**

58.65s (-0.15) **Going Correction** +0.025s/f (Slow) 6 Ran SP% **118.4**
Speed ratings (Par 103): **102,100,99,98,96 92**
toteswingers: 1&2 £5.30, 1&3 £4.40, 2&3 £2.90 CSF £72.33 CT £202.61 TOTE £14.70: £3.70, £3.20; EX 41.50 Trifecta £226.50 Pool: £777.66 - 2.54 winning units..
Owner Mrs Irene Hampson **Bred** D R Tucker **Trained** Royston, Herts

FOCUS
The main focus of attention in this modest sprint handicap was the heavily supported Befortyfour. It was well run and the winner did not need to match his winter best.

1074 HARRISON H'CAP 7f (P)
5:30 (5:30) (Class 6) (0-60,66) 4-Y-O+ **£1,704** (£503; £251) **Stalls** Low

Form RPR
0501 **1** **Spin Again (IRE)**[8] 972 7-9-13 66 6ex RichardKingscote 11 75
(Daniel Kubler) *in tch on outer: hdwy to chse ldr 2f out: rdn to ld jst over 1f out: clr and in command ins fnl f: a gng to hold on: rdn out* **11/10**[1]
0032 **2** *1/2* **Chandrayaan**[21] 828 5-8-4 46 (v) SimonPearce(3) 10 54
(John E Long) *in tch: rdn and effrt to chse ldng trio 2f out: unable qck and sltly outpcd over 1f out: rallied u.p fnl f: wnt 2nd fnl 75yds: clsng towards fin but nvr quite getting to wnr* **7/2**[2]
0-04 **3** *3 3/4* **Fault**[12] 927 6-8-12 51 (t) FergusSweeney 1 49
(Alastair Lidderdale) *chsd ldrs tl lost pl and dropped towards rr over 3f out: swtchd rt and nt clr run over 2f out: 6th and hdwy over 1f out: no ch w ldrs but r.o wl fnl f: wnt 3rd cl home* **13/2**[3]
1000 **4** *1/2* **Crocodile Bay (IRE)**[12] 926 9-8-8 52 (p) CharlesEddery(5) 9 49
(Richard Guest) *chsd ldr tl led after 2f: rdn 2f out: hdd and no ex jst over 1f out: wknd fnl 100yds* **14/1**
6006 **5** *2* **Monadreen Dancer**[11] 941 4-9-1 54 ShaneKelly 3 45
(Daniel Mark Loughnane) *in tch: rdn and effrt 2f out: sn no imp u.p: wknd ent fnl f* **8/1**
0660 **6** *2 1/2* **Littleportnbrandy (IRE)**[11] 938 4-8-7 46 oh1 WilliamCarson 5 30
(Richard Guest) *s.i.s: niggled along in rr: sme hdwy fnl f: n.d* **20/1**

6-00 **7** *6* **Gooseberry Bush**^{13} 911 5-9-4 **57**.................................... LiamKeniry 8 25
(Gary Brown) *stdd s: t.k.h: hld up in last pair: rdn no hdwy 2f out: nvr on terms* **25/1**

00-0 **8** *1 ¼* **Litotes**^{27} 740 4-8-5 **49** ow1..(p) MarkCoumbe$^{(5)}$ 7 14
(Michael Attwater) *chsd ldr over 4f out tl 2f out: wknd ent fnl f: fdd and eased wl ins fnl f* **33/1**

0020 **9** *2* **Wee Buns**^{34} 662 7-8-7 **46** oh1...(p) JohnFahy 4
(Paul Burgoyne) *led for 2f: chsd ldrs: rdn and struggling 2f out: wknd over 1f out: wl bhd and eased wl ins fnl f* **16/1**

1m 24.76s (-0.04) **Going Correction** +0.025s/f (Slow) **9** Ran SP% **118.4**
Speed ratings (Par 101): **101,100,96,95,93 90,83,82,79**
toteswingers: 1&2 £1.70, 1&3 £3.00, 2&3 £2.60 CSF £4.94 CT £17.44 TOTE £2.60: £1.50, £2.60, £1.70; EX 6.00 Trifecta £23.30 Pool: £1,025.32 - 32.53 winning units..
Owner David Dacosta **Bred** Barry Lyons **Trained** Whitsbury, Hants

FOCUS
A moderate handicap, but an improving winner whis is rated pretty much back to last winter's form.
T/Plt: £116.50 to a £1 stake. Pool: £59,045.76. 369.76 winning tickets. T/Qpdt: £30.60 to a £1 stake. Pool £4,686.57. 113.23 winning tickets. SP

1075 - 1081a (Foreign Racing) - See Raceform Interactive

1061 KEMPTON (A.W) (R-H)

Thursday, March 29

OFFICIAL GOING: Standard
Wind: Light, against Weather: Sunny, warm

1082 32REDBINGO.COM CLASSIFIED CLAIMING STKS 6f (P)
5:55 (5:55) (Class 6) 3-Y-O+ **£1,617** (£481; £240; £120) **Stalls** Low

Form RPR

2221 **1** **Steelcut**^{19} 870 8-9-2 70..(p) MatthewCosham$^{(5)}$ 3 76
(David Evans) *s.s: t.k.h and sn hld up in 4th: smooth prog to ld jst over 1f out: pushed out: comf* **9/4**^{2}

4032 **2** *2 ¼* **Unlimited**^{1} 1064 10-9-7 72.. NeilCallan 1 68
(Tony Carroll) *t.k.h: trckd ldr 1f: restrained: effrt to chal over 1f out: chsd wnr fnl f: easily hld* **11/2**^{3}

3U10 **3** *2* **Arabian Flight**^{3} 1046 3-8-8 59.. KieranO'Neill 5 58
(John Bridger) *trckd ldr after 1f: rdn over 2f out: led briefly over 1f out: sn outpcd* **8/1**

3301 **4** *1 ¼* **Tombi (USA)**^{12} 941 8-9-7 74... JimmyFortune 4 58
(Keith Dalgleish) *hld up and sn last: outpcd over 2f out: shkn up and nvr on terms after: fin lame* **5/4**^{1}

0-06 **5** *nk* **Jimmy The Lollipop (IRE)**^{47} 518 3-8-9 62.................(b) LiamKeniry 2 58
(Neil Mulholland) *led: set modest pce tl wound it up over 3f out: hdd and fdd over 1f out* **14/1**

1m 12.57s (-0.53) **Going Correction** -0.025s/f (Stan)
WFA 3 from 8yo+ 13lb **5** Ran SP% **108.4**
Speed ratings (Par 101): **102,99,96,94,94**
CSF £13.80 TOTE £3.10: £1.10, £3.60; EX 8.80.Jimmy The Lollipop (IRE) claimed by Mr Ian Williams for £7,000.
Owner Shropshire Wolves 3 **Bred** Mrs B Skinner **Trained** Pandy, Monmouths

FOCUS
An uncompetitive claimer, run at a steady gallop which suited the winner who quickened away from his rivals impressively. He's rated up slightly on his recent form.
Tombi(USA) Official explanation: vet said gelding returned lame

1083 32REDBET.COM H'CAP 1m 3f (P)
6:25 (6:25) (Class 6) (0-65,65) 4-Y-O+ **£1,617** (£481; £240; £120) **Stalls** Low

Form RPR

045- **1** **The Blue Dog (IRE)**^{251} 4275 5-9-1 **59**........................... AndreaAtzeni 4 71
(Michael Wigham) *trckd ldng trio: prog to go 2nd wl over 1f out: sn clsd on ldr: pushed firmly into ld last 150yds: styd on wl* **12/1**^{3}

43-1 **2** *1* **Spartan Spirit (IRE)**^{8} 984 4-9-1 **60** 6ex....................... JimmyFortune 7 70
(Hughie Morrison) *led: drew 2 l clr 2f out and looked in command: urged along and pressed jst over 1f out w hd high: hdd and nt qckn last 150yds* **1/4**^{1}

4500 **3** *6* **Yossi (IRE)**^{13} 924 8-8-4 **51** oh6...............................(b) DeclanCannon$^{(3)}$ 1 50
(Richard Guest) *chsd ldr to over 8f out: wnt 2nd again wl over 2f out to wl over 1f out: wknd fnl f* **25/1**

0/00 **4** *nk* **Pahente**^{21} 843 4-7-13 **51**... DarrenEgan$^{(7)}$ 6 50
(Tony Carroll) *dwlt: hld up wl off the pce in last pair: rdn over 3f out and struggling: styd on wl fnl 2f: nrly snatched 3rd* **25/1**

0616 **5** *7* **Striding Edge (IRE)**^{29} 738 6-9-0 **65**..................... NicoleNordblad$^{(7)}$ 2 51
(Hans Adielsson) *hld up off the pce in last quartet: shkn up over 2f out: nvr on terms* **7/1**^{2}

60/0 **6** *5* **Persian Buddy**^{27} 760 6-8-10 **54**................................... RobertWinston 5 31
(Jamie Poulton) *dwlt: t.k.h: hld up in last pair and wl off the pce: rdn over 3f out: no prog* **66/1**

0-55 **7** *1* **Baharat (IRE)**^{18} 826 4-9-2 **61**....................................(bt) WilliamCarson 3 36
(Richard Guest) *rrd s: t.k.h: hld up off the pce in last quartet: rdn over 3f out: no prog* **20/1**

-423 **8** *2* **Beggers Belief**^{22} 818 4-9-6 **65**......................................(b) SebSanders 8 37
(Eric Wheeler) *prog to chse ldr over 8f out: rdn over 3f out: lost 2nd wl over 2f out: wknd qckly* **7/1**^{2}

2m 20.33s (-1.57) **Going Correction** -0.025s/f (Stan)
WFA 4 from 5yo+ 1lb **8** Ran SP% **126.6**
Speed ratings (Par 101): **104,103,98,98,93 89,89,87**
Tote Swingers: 1&2 £2.60, 1&3 £40.60, 2&3 £7.00 CSF £17.07 CT £122.02 TOTE £28.90: £3.40, £1.02, £9.20; EX 40.30.
Owner R Carson **Bred** Mervyn Stewkesbury **Trained** Newmarket, Suffolk

FOCUS
A moderate handicap which centred on the well-in runner-up, but he was a bit below par. The winner is rated back to his best.

1084 32RED CASINO FILLIES' H'CAP 7f (P)
6:55 (6:55) (Class 5) (0-70,70) 4-Y-O+ **£2,264** (£673; £336; £168) **Stalls** Low

Form RPR

2110 **1** **Qeethaara (USA)**^{15} 894 8-9-5 **68**...................................(p) LukeMorris 4 76
(Mark Brisbourne) *trckd ldr: upsides gng easily fr over 2f out tl stoked up ent fnl f: fnd enough to ld and assert fnl 100yds* **9/2**^{2}

-502 **2** *1* **Perfect Ch'l (IRE)**^{7} 991 5-9-1 **64**................................... MartinLane 3 69
(Ian Wood) *led at decent pce: rdn and jnd by wnr over 2f out: hdd and one pce last 100yds* **5/4**^{1}

1005 **3** *nse* **Cut The Cackle (IRE)**^{9} 970 6-8-10 **59**...................(bt) WilliamCarson 1 64
(Richard Guest) *hld up in last: rdn 2f out: no prog tl r.o ins fnl f: fin wl and nrly snatched 2nd* **6/1**

622 **4** *½* **Polar Auroras**^{21} 842 4-8-7 **56**..(t) DavidProbert 5 60
(Tony Carroll) *hld up in 4th: rdn 3f out: chsd ldng pair over 1f out: kpt on but no imp fnl f: lost 3rd nr fin* **11/2**^{3}

606- **5** *1 ¼* **Cahala Dancer (IRE)**^{183} 6468 4-8-11 **60**......................... KieranO'Neill 2 60
(Roger Teal) *chsd ldng pair but nvr gng w much verve: lost 3rd and btn over 1f out* **11/2**^{3}

1m 25.97s (-0.03) **Going Correction** -0.025s/f (Stan) **5** Ran SP% **107.7**
Speed ratings (Par 100): **99,97,97,97,95**
CSF £10.18 TOTE £4.80: £1.70, £1.60; EX 10.30.
Owner Mark Brisbourne **Bred** Shadwell Farm LLC **Trained** Great Ness, Shropshire

FOCUS
A modest small-field fillies' handicap that looked pretty straightforward on paper, but a steady-enough tempo produced a bunched finish, and a game if slightly unexpected winner in an average time for the grade. An improved effort from the winner.

1085 £32 FREE AT 32RED.COM H'CAP 2m (P)
7:25 (7:25) (Class 5) (0-75,74) 4-Y-O+ **£2,264** (£673; £336; £168) **Stalls** Low

Form RPR

1-22 **1** **The Absent Mare**^{10} 963 4-8-10 **63**................................... LukeMorris 5 71+
(Robin Dickin) *hld up last: effrt 4f out: drvn over 3f out: prog on outer to ld over 1f out: styd on* **11/8**^{1}

-036 **2** *1 ¼* **Russian George (IRE)**^{6} 1011 6-9-5 **74**.....................(tp) DarrenEgan$^{(7)}$ 7 80
(Steve Gollings) *hld up in 5th: rdn over 3f out: prog on inner to ld briefly wl over 1f out: kpt on same pce after* **9/2**^{3}

/5-3 **3** *2 ¼* **Gilded Age**^{21} 577 6-9-6 **68**..(tp) DaneO'Neill 1 71
(Chris Gordon) *led: set modest pce tl jnd after 7f: racd hrd fr over 4f out: beat off rival over 2f out: hdd and one pce wl over 1f out* **8/1**

612- **4** *7* **Ministry**^{59} 6356 4-8-13 **66**... FergusSweeney 4 61
(Gary Moore) *t.k.h: hld up in 4th tl moved up to join ldr after 7f: racd hrd disputing ld fr over 4f out tl btn off jst over 2f out: wknd fnl f* **4/1**^{2}

243- **5** *7* **Handles For Forks (IRE)**^{178} 6584 4-9-4 **71**................. TonyCulhane 3 58
(Mick Channon) *trckd ldrs: drvn over 3f out: wknd over 2f out* **8/1**

-315 **6** *6* **Vertueux (FR)**^{20} 566 7-8-13 **61**... NeilCallan 6 40
(Tony Carroll) *trckd ldr 7f: drvn over 4f out: sn struggling and btn* **11/1**

3m 30.2s (0.10) **Going Correction** -0.025s/f (Stan)
WFA 4 from 6yo+ 5lb **6** Ran SP% **110.8**
Speed ratings (Par 103): **98,97,96,92,89 86**
Tote Swingers: 1&2 £2.20, 1&3 £2.90, 2&3 £5.80 CSF £7.59 TOTE £2.10: £1.30, £1.70; EX 8.80.
Owner J C Clemmow **Bred** Beautiful Losers Bloodstock & R Hobson **Trained** Atherstone on Stour, Warwicks

FOCUS
With no natural front-runner in the field the pace was predictably steady and they were still tightly bunched turning out of the back straight. The winner made her challenge up the centre of the track and rates a small personal best.

1086 32RED.COM MAIDEN STKS 1m (P)
7:55 (7:58) (Class 5) 3-Y-O **£2,264** (£673; £336; £168) **Stalls** Low

Form RPR

56- **1** **Grey Mirage**^{148} 7232 3-9-3 0... AdamKirby 7 82+
(Marco Botti) *led after 1f: mde rest: shkn up and wl in command over 1f out: pushed out last 150yds* **10/11**^{1}

5-3 **2** *2 ¼* **Dartford (USA)**^{22} 827 3-9-3 0.. RobertHavlin 2 75
(John Gosden) *led 1f: dropped to 3rd after 2f: rdn to chse wnr 2f out: styd on but no imp* **5/1**^{3}

3 *½* **Red Ramesses (IRE)** 3-9-3 0... LukeMorris 1 74
(John Best) *hld up in tch: rdn over 3f out: prog to go 4th wl over 2f out: styd on to take 3rd fnl f: pressed runner-up nr fin* **16/1**

532- **4** *1 ¼* **Peter Anders**^{149} 7210 3-9-3 73.. JoeFanning 9 71
(Mark Johnston) *chsd wnr after 2f: rdn and lost 2nd 2f out: one pce after* **5/2**^{2}

5 *1* **Trend Is My Friend (USA)** 3-9-3 0..................................... NeilCallan 5 69+
(Amanda Perrett) *v green in preliminaries: dwlt: hld up in last pair: effrt 3f out: hanging and green over 2f out: kpt on fr over 1f out* **12/1**

0 **6** *7* **Tom Red**^{13} 918 3-9-3 0... KieranO'Neill 8 53
(Dean Ivory) *restrained into last sn after s: brief effrt over 3f out: sn lft bhd* **100/1**

3-5 **7** *5* **Navaho Spirit**^{19} 869 3-9-3 0... MarcHalford 6 41
(Terry Clement) *t.k.h early: chsd ldng trio tl wknd rapidly over 2f out* **33/1**

0 **8** *8* **Saharan Air (IRE)**^{22} 827 3-9-3 0...................................... LiamKeniry 4 23
(George Baker) *hld up: struggling fr 1/2-way: sn bhd* **66/1**

1m 39.22s (-0.58) **Going Correction** -0.025s/f (Stan) **8** Ran SP% **116.6**
Speed ratings (Par 98): **101,98,98,97,96 89,84,76**
Tote Swingers: 1&2 £1.20, 1&3 £7.30, 2&3 £7.60 CSF £6.26 TOTE £2.20: £1.10, £1.02, £9.40; EX 6.70.
Owner Scuderia Vittadini Srl **Bred** Grundy Bloodstock Srl **Trained** Newmarket, Suffolk

FOCUS
An interesting 3-y-o maiden with some decent proven form up against a very well-backed potential improver from the Marco Botti yard. The winning time was fair compared with later handicaps and the form is rated around the second and fourth.
Trend Is My Friend(USA) Official explanation: jockey said colt hung left and ran green

1087 32RED H'CAP 1m (P)
8:25 (8:25) (Class 4) (0-85,85) 4-Y-O+ **£4,075** (£1,212; £606; £303) **Stalls** Low

Form RPR

050- **1** **Ashva (USA)**^{245} 4467 4-9-1 **79**... AdamKirby 9 90+
(Michael Dods) *hld up in rr: plld out and effrt on outer wl over 1f out: gd prog and qcknd up smartly to ld last 150yds: sn clr* **11/4**^{2}

1005 **2** *2 ¼* **Sunset Kitty (USA)**^{22} 817 5-9-7 **85**................................. ShaneKelly 5 90
(Mike Murphy) *hld up in last pair: plld out and effrt over 1f out following wnr: r.o fnl f to take 2nd last strides* **10/1**^{3}

0-35 **3** *½* **Den's Gift (IRE)**^{47} 520 8-8-9 **78**................................(b) LucyKBarry$^{(5)}$ 7 82
(Clive Cox) *led after 1f: kicked on 3f out: hdd and outpcd last 150yds: lost 2nd last strides* **16/1**

6221 **4** *¾* **Alhaban (IRE)**^{9} 967 6-9-0 **78** 6ex..................................... LukeMorris 4 80
(Ronald Harris) *chsd ldrs: pushed along fr 1/2-way: effrt u.p 2f out: one pce* **10/1**^{3}

6530 **5** *1* **Tartan Trip**^{22} 817 5-9-3 **81**..(v) DavidProbert 8 81
(Andrew Balding) *racd wd: hld up in tch: smooth prog over 2f out: chsd ldr over 1f out: sn rdn and nt qckn: wknd ins fnl f* **12/1**

-414 **6** *¾* **I Confess**^{40} 626 7-9-2 **80**..(b) RobertWinston 3 78
(Geoffrey Harker) *prom: drvn to chse ldr over 2f out: no imp: lost pl fr over 1f out* **16/1**

11- **7** *hd* **Ancient Greece**^{184} 6435 5-8-12 **76**..................................(t) DaneO'Neill 1 74
(George Baker) *snatched up on inner over 6f out and dropped to last pair: effrt on inner over 2f out: no prog 1f out: outpcd* **33/1**

4112 **8** *1* **Colour Guard**[6] 1008 4-9-7 **85** .... JoeFanning 6 80
(Mark Johnston) *fast away: led 1f: trckd ldr: rdn and nt qckn over 2f out: sn lost pl and btn* 5/4[1]

0/0- **9** *11* **Bramshaw (USA)**[353] 1269 5-9-2 **80** .... NeilCallan 2 50
(Amanda Perrett) *chsd ldrs: n.m.r over 6f out: wknd over 2f out: t.o* 12/1

1m 38.14s (-1.66) **Going Correction** -0.025s/f (Stan) **9** Ran SP% **119.4**
Speed ratings (Par 105): **107,104,104,103,102 101,101,100,89**
Tote Swingers: 1&2 £5.50, 1&3 £15.10, 2&3 £11.60 CSF £31.73 CT £384.19 TOTE £3.90: £1.60, £1.20, £3.50; EX 38.40.
Owner Andrew Tinkler **Bred** Brook Stud Bloodstock Ltd **Trained** Denton, Co Durham

FOCUS
A competitive handicap run at a strong gallop. A taking winner, with the form rated around the third and fourth.
Ancient Greece Official explanation: jockey said gelding suffered interference in running
Bramshaw(USA) Official explanation: jockey said gelding suffered interference in running

1088 32REDPOKER.COM H'CAP 1m (P)
8:55 (8:55) (Class 6) (0-60,60) 4-Y-0+ **£1,617** (£481; £240; £120) **Stalls** Low

Form RPR

-305 **1** **Saucy Buck (IRE)**[7] 995 4-9-6 **59** .... NeilCallan 7 68
(Jamie Poulton) *trckd ldng trio: prog jst over 2f out gng wl: led jst over 1f out: drvn and hld on wl* 12/1

-112 **2** *½* **Diplomatic (IRE)**[9] 972 7-9-7 **60** .... LukeMorris 3 68
(Michael Squance) *trckd ldng pair: drvn over 2f out: kpt on u.p to take 2nd nr fin: a hld* 2/1[1]

0-51 **3** *½* **The Bay Bandit**[13] 927 5-9-0 **53** ....(e[1]) AdamKirby 10 60
(John Butler) *hld up disputing 7th: effrt on outer over 2f out: drvn and styd on fr over 1f out: nvr quite able to chal* 11/4[2]

6036 **4** *nse* **The Which Doctor**[27] 760 7-8-12 **56** ....(e) DuilioDaSilva(5) 2 63
(Richard Guest) *t.k.h: hld up disputing 7th: eye-catching prog on inner fr 2f out: jst pushed along and styd on fnl f: eased last two strides* 16/1

2005 **5** *shd* **Kucharova (IRE)**[22] 829 4-8-12 **51** .... LiamKeniry 4 58
(Seamus Mullins) *led: drvn 2f out: hdd jst over 1f out: kpt on same pce after* 20/1

5345 **6** *1* **Teen Ager (FR)**[22] 822 8-8-10 **49** ....(p) JohnFahy 5 53
(Paul Burgoyne) *t.k.h: trckd ldr: nt qckn 2f out: sn lost 2nd: fdd ins fnl f* 12/1

-410 **7** *½* **Having A Ball**[22] 821 8-9-4 **57** .... ChrisCatlin 8 60
(Jonathan Portman) *trckd ldrs disputing 5th: rdn over 2f out: one pce and nvr able to threaten fr over 1f out* 14/1

0-50 **8** *nk* **Monsieur Broughton**[7] 995 4-9-3 **56** .... JamieMackay 9 58
(Willie Musson) *hld up in last pair: plenty to do whn effrt 2f out: sn rdn: styd on last 150yds: nrst fin* 13/2[3]

51-5 **9** *1 ¼* **Karate (IRE)**[63] 306 4-8-13 **59** ....(t) NicoleNordblad(7) 11 58
(Hans Adielsson) *t.k.h: sn hld up in last and wl off the pce: effrt on inner 2f out: no prog 1f out* 14/1

-040 **10** *2 ¼* **Gambatte**[22] 822 5-8-0 **46** oh1 .... DarrenEgan(7) 12 40
(Tony Carroll) *t.k.h: hld up in last trio: drvn and no prog 2f out* 40/1

540- **11** *hd* **Merito**[163] 6940 4-9-0 **58** .... MatthewCosham(5) 1 52
(David Evans) *chsd ldrs disputing 5th: rdn over 2f out: wknd over 1f out* 40/1

1m 40.15s (0.35) **Going Correction** -0.025s/f (Stan) **11** Ran SP% **117.6**
Speed ratings (Par 101): **97,96,96,95,95 94,94,94,92,90 90**
Tote Swingers: 1&2 £8.20, 1&3 £10.30, 2&3 £2.00 CSF £35.65 CT £89.14 TOTE £19.60: £6.90, £1.10, £1.30; EX 62.20.
Owner Surrey Elite **Bred** T Sherman **Trained** Telscombe, E Sussex
■ Stewards' Enquiry : Luke Morris two-day ban: used whip above permitted level (Apr 12-13)

FOCUS
A lowly handicap but reportedly a few with morning money riding on the outcome. This was a typical Kempton handicap run at a fair gallop and a bunched finish. The winner's best effort since his 2yo peak.
T/Plt: £58.70 to a £1 stake. Pool: £56,898.31 - 707.18 winning tickets. T/Qpdt: £20.40 to a £1 stake. Pool: £6,512.55 - 235.88 winning tickets. JN

1010 WOLVERHAMPTON (A.W) (L-H)
Thursday, March 29

OFFICIAL GOING: Standard
Wind: Fresh across Weather: Fine

1089 GET FREE BETS AT FREEBETTING.CO.UK MAIDEN STKS 5f 20y(P)
2:30 (2:32) (Class 5) 3-Y-0+ **£2,264** (£673; £336; £168) **Stalls** Low

Form RPR

32 **1** **Ring For Baileys**[16] 885 3-8-4 0 .... RaulDaSilva(5) 1 61
(Chris Dwyer) *led 1f: w ldr tl led again 2f out: styd on wl* 13/2[3]

4044 **2** *3* **Bygones For Coins (IRE)**[9] 979 4-9-0 43 .... MatthewHopkins(7) 6 55?
(Alan Berry) *led 4f out: pushed along and hdd 2f out: lost 2nd over 1f out: styd on same pce: wnt 2nd again post* 100/1

023- **3** *nk* **Come On Dave (IRE)**[177] 6598 3-9-0 75 .... AndrewMullen 5 54
(David Nicholls) *trckd ldrs: plld hrd: wnt 2nd over 1f out: rdn ins fnl f: nt run on: lost 2nd post* 9/2[2]

245- **4** *3 ¼* **Tahnee Mara (IRE)**[183] 6449 3-8-9 70 .... PhillipMakin 3 37
(Kevin Ryan) *prom and sn pushed along: rdn 1/2-way: styd on same pce appr fnl f* 8/11[1]

060- **5** *2 ¾* **My Pearl (IRE)**[188] 6293 3-9-0 59 .... PaulMulrennan 2 32
(Kevin Ryan) *s.i.s: sn pushed along and a in rr: bhd fr 1/2-way* 8/1

6 *nk* **Noble Bounty** 3-8-11 0 .... JulieBurke(3) 4 31
(Kevin Ryan) *s.i.s: rn green in rr: bhd fr 1/2-way* 20/1

1m 2.26s (-0.04) **Going Correction** +0.075s/f (Slow)
WFA 3 from 4yo 12lb **6** Ran SP% **106.3**
Speed ratings (Par 103): **103,98,97,92,88 87**
Tote Swingers: 1&2 £7.20, 1&3 £1.30, 2&3 £10.50 CSF £214.78 TOTE £5.30: £2.00, £21.10; EX 90.60.
Owner G R Bailey Ltd (Baileys Horse Feeds) **Bred** P And Mrs A G Venner **Trained** Six Mile Bottom, Cambs

FOCUS
An uncompetitive maiden in which the AW debutants didn't show much and the runners were in similar positions all the way. However, the pace was solid enough. Unconvincing form, rated around the exposed runner-up.

1090 WATCH THE BIG MATCH AT RILEYS (S) STKS 5f 20y(P)
3:00 (3:04) (Class 6) 3-Y-0 **£1,704** (£503; £251) **Stalls** Low

Form RPR

-126 **1** **Gin Twist**[14] 905 3-8-13 71 ....(b) RichardKingscote 3 70
(Tom Dascombe) *hld up in tch: rdn to ld ins fnl f: r.o* 1/2[1]

-223 **2** *½* **El McGlynn (IRE)**[28] 742 3-8-7 62 ....(p) LukeMorris 8 62
(John O'Shea) *broke wl: stdd and lost pl 4f out: hdwy over 1f out: led ins fnl f: sn rdn and hdd: kpt on* 11/2[3]

0300 **3** *5* **Lady Nickandy (IRE)**[15] 898 3-8-6 50 ....(v) GemmaTutty(7) 1 50
(Karen Tutty) *led 4f out: hdd & wknd ins fnl f* 20/1

4623 **4** *shd* **Miss Purity Pinker (IRE)**[12] 940 3-8-7 59 ....(v) CathyGannon 7 44
(David Evans) *led 1f: chsd ldr: rdn over 1f out: styd on same pce* 4/1[2]

0-00 **5** *4* **Brian's Best**[20] 845 3-8-12 33 .... NeilChalmers 5 34
(Richard Ford) *prom: pushed along 1/2-way: wknd over 1f out* 100/1

540 **6** *nse* **Essexvale (IRE)**[9] 975 3-8-0 49 ....(b[1]) MatthewHopkins(7) 2 29
(Alan Berry) *chsd ldr: pushed along over 1f out: wknd fnl f* 66/1

46 **7** *14* **Shake Baby Shake**[13] 925 3-8-0 0 .... JakePayne(7) 6
(Bill Turner) *s.i.s: hdwy wl over 3f out: sn pushed along and hung rt: wknd 1/2-way* 40/1

1m 3.12s (0.82) **Going Correction** +0.075s/f (Slow) **7** Ran SP% **111.7**
Speed ratings (Par 96): **96,95,87,87,80 80,58**
Tote Swingers: 1&2 £1.50, 1&3 £2.90, 2&3 £4.00 CSF £3.47 TOTE £1.50: £1.10, £1.30; EX 3.60 Trifecta £21.10 Pool: £888.36 - 31.08 winning units..There was no bid for the winner.
Owner Manor House Stables LLP **Bred** Highclere Stud **Trained** Malpas, Cheshire

FOCUS
A weak seller. The first two were a cut above the rest on official ratings, so the result was predictable.

1091 FREE BETTING WITH FREEBETTING.CO.UK H'CAP 5f 216y(P)
3:35 (3:35) (Class 4) (0-80,79) 4-Y-0+ **£4,528** (£1,347; £673; £336) **Stalls** Low

Form RPR

300- **1** **Jarrow (IRE)**[186] 6382 5-9-6 **78** .... JoeFanning 8 93
(David Nicholls) *a.p: led over 1f out: edgd rt: clr fnl f: readily* 6/1

263 **2** *4 ½* **The Happy Hammer (IRE)**[33] 713 6-8-9 **67** .... WilliamCarson 2 68
(Eugene Stanford) *hld up: hdwy over 1f out: r.o to go 2nd post: no ch w wnr* 12/1

000- **3** *hd* **Julius Geezer (IRE)**[164] 6913 4-9-7 **79** .... RichardKingscote 6 79
(Tom Dascombe) *chsd ldr: rdn over 1f out: no ex ins fnl f: lost 2nd post* 5/1[2]

1301 **4** *1* **Lastkingofscotland (IRE)**[15] 893 6-9-3 **75** ....(b) LukeMorris 7 72
(Conor Dore) *chsd ldrs: drvn along 1/2-way: styd on same pce fr over 1f out* 5/1[2]

-655 **5** *1* **Restless Bay (IRE)**[7] 997 4-9-3 **75** ....(p) ChrisCatlin 1 69
(Reg Hollinshead) *hld up: rdn over 1f out: styd on ins fnl f: nvr nrr* 11/2[3]

1-20 **6** *1 ¾* **Mambo Spirit (IRE)**[15] 893 8-9-2 **74** .... DaneO'Neill 9 62
(Tony Newcombe) *chsd ldrs: rdn over 1f out: wknd ins fnl f* 18/1

1225 **7** *½* **Captain Scooby**[6] 1015 6-8-13 **74** .... RobertLButler(3) 4 60
(Richard Guest) *broke wl enough: lost pl 5f out: n.d after* 12/1

433- **8** *6* **Escape To Glory (USA)**[199] 6003 4-9-7 **79** ....(v[1]) PaulHanagan 3 46
(Mikael Magnusson) *sn led: clr 4f out: hdd over 1f out: wknd fnl f* 3/1[1]

00-6 **9** *1* **Gallagher**[16] 883 6-9-2 **74** .... JamesSullivan 5 38
(Ruth Carr) *s.i.s: outpcd* 33/1

1m 13.88s (-1.12) **Going Correction** +0.075s/f (Slow) **9** Ran SP% **111.6**
Speed ratings (Par 105): **110,104,103,102,101 98,98,90,88**
Tote Swingers: 1&2 £13.10, 1&3 £7.40, 2&3 £11.80 CSF £71.13 CT £379.48 TOTE £7.40: £2.50, £2.30, £2.10; EX 87.50 TRIFECTA Not won..
Owner Dab Hand Racing **Bred** Derek Veitch **Trained** Sessay, N Yorks

FOCUS
The pace was frantic thanks to the tearaway front-runner, though the main body of the field largely ignored him. The winner is rated back to at least his best at face value.

1092 BUSCADOR H'CAP 1m 4f 50y(P)
4:10 (4:10) (Class 6) (0-60,60) 4-Y-0+ **£1,704** (£503; £251) **Stalls** Low

Form RPR

/0-1 **1** **Den Maschine**[20] 602 7-9-7 **60** .... AdamKirby 5 72
(Paul Rich) *a.p: rdn over 2f out: edgd rt and styd on u.p to ld wl ins fnl f* 5/4[1]

2-11 **2** *nk* **Holden Eagle**[20] 850 7-9-0 **60** .... IanBurns(7) 7 71
(Tony Newcombe) *chsd ldr tl led over 5f out: pushed along and hdd wl over 1f out: edgd rt: styd on to ld wl ins fnl f: sn hdd: kpt on* 4/1[3]

00-5 **3** *1 ¾* **Needwood Park**[16] 772 4-8-8 **49** .... MartinDwyer 11 59+
(Ray Craggs) *a.p: chsd ldr over 5f out: rdn to ld wl over 1f out: hdd and hmpd wl ins fnl f: no ex* 22/1

0650 **4** *6* **Angelena Ballerina (IRE)**[13] 929 5-8-9 **51** .... NataliaGemelova(3) 8 50
(Dai Williams) *s.i.s: hld up: hdwy over 9f out: pushed along over 4f out: rdn and wknd over 1f out* 40/1

-423 **5** *1* **Harare**[9] 976 11-8-4 **50** ....(v) GemmaTutty(7) 9 47
(Karen Tutty) *dwlt: hld up: hdwy over 2f out: wknd over 1f out* 22/1

6/0 **6** *1 ½* **Wind Star**[31] 722 9-9-0 **58** ....(t) MarkCoumbe(5) 6 53
(Brendan Powell) *hld up: hdwy over 2f out: rdn and wknd over 1f out* 12/1

20/0 **7** *nk* **Claimant (IRE)**[21] 843 5-8-11 **57** .... JackDuern(7) 4 52
(Michael Appleby) *hld up: rdn over 2f out: hung lft fnl f: nvr on terms* 28/1

-124 **8** *19* **Fire In Babylon (IRE)**[36] 651 4-9-3 **58** .... ShaneKelly 3 22
(Michael Wigham) *hld up: pushed along over 3f out: rdn and wknd over 2f out* 3/1[2]

00-5 **9** *18* **Always Dixie (IRE)**[79] 111 5-8-7 **46** oh1 .... JoeFanning 1
(Andrew Crook) *hld up: rdn and wknd 3f out: t.o* 66/1

00-0 **10** *30* **Hab Reeh**[15] 900 4-8-13 **54** ....(t) JamesSullivan 2
(Ruth Carr) *led: clr 10f out tl over 6f out: hdd over 5f out: sn rdn: wknd 3f out: t.o* 40/1

2m 42.31s (1.21) **Going Correction** +0.075s/f (Slow)
WFA 4 from 5yo+ 2lb **10** Ran SP% **115.7**
Speed ratings (Par 101): **98,97,96,92,91 90,90,78,66,46**
Tote Swingers: 1&2 £2.00, 1&3 £7.80, 2&3 £9.80 CSF £5.81 CT £70.53 TOTE £3.00: £1.30, £1.10, £4.50; EX 6.50 Trifecta £88.60 Pool: £855.78 - 7.14 winning units..
Owner Paul Morgan **Bred** York Stut & Stald Rainbow **Trained** Newport, Gwent

FOCUS
This was contested by a mixed bunch, but the first two both came into the race in good form. The third's proximity is a worry.
Claimant(IRE) Official explanation: vet said gelding finished lame

1093 HORSERACING FREE BETS WITH FREEBETTING.CO.UK H'CAP 1m 1f 103y(P)
4:40 (4:41) (Class 5) (0-75,75) 3-Y-0 **£2,264** (£673; £336; £168) **Stalls** Low

Form RPR

1 **1** **Ed De Gas**[41] 595 3-9-7 **75** .... ChrisCatlin 3 85
(Rae Guest) *dwlt: hld up: hdwy and swtchd lft over 1f out: shkn up to ld ins fnl f: r.o* 5/2[2]

12- **2** *¾* **Koko Loca (IRE)**[134] 7436 3-9-5 **73** .... MartinHarley 5 81
(Marco Botti) *a.p: chsd ldr over 2f out: rdn to ld wl over 1f out: hdd ins fnl f: styd on* 7/4[1]

010- **3** 2 **Bounty Seeker (USA)**[155] 7095 3-9-7 75 JoeFanning 1 79
(Mark Johnston) *led 1f: chsd ldr tl led over 2f out: rdn and hdd wl over 1f out: hmpd 1f out: styd on same pce* **9/2**[3]

04-6 **4** 1 1/4 **Kelpie Blitz (IRE)**[26] 787 3-8-11 65 MickyFenton 6 66
(Seamus Durack) *hld up: hdwy over 2f out: ev ch over 1f out: edgd lft and no ex ins fnl f* **12/1**

-513 **5** 4 1/2 **Next Cry (USA)**[24] 803 3-9-3 74 SeanLevey(3) 7 66
(Richard Hannon) *prom: pushed along 1/2-way: rdn over 2f out: edgd lft and wknd fnl f* **5/1**

6303 **6** 19 **Aiaam Al Wafa (IRE)**[7] 998 3-8-0 61 oh6 (p) DannyBrock(7) 4
(Phil McEntee) *pushed along to ld over 8f out: rdn and hdd over 2f out: wknd over 1f out* **33/1**

2m 1.0s (-0.70) **Going Correction** +0.075s/f (Slow) 6 Ran SP% **110.4**
Speed ratings (Par 98): **106,105,103,102,98 81**
Tote Swingers: 1&2 £1.60, 1&3 £3.10, 2&3 £2.70 CSF £7.03 TOTE £3.50: £2.40, £1.60; EX 5.90.
Owner R A Pegum **Bred** Canartam Ltd **Trained** Newmarket, Suffolk
■ Stewards' Enquiry : Chris Catlin caution: careless riding.

FOCUS
This was a decent race of its type, with lightly raced horses of some potential filling the first two places. Both showed improvment, with the next two close to their marks.

1094 FREE CASINO BETS AT FREEBETTING.CO.UK H'CAP 1m 1f 103y(P)
5:15 (5:15) (Class 5) (0-75,75) 4-Y-0+ £2,264 (£673; £336; £168) Stalls Low

Form RPR

0105 **1** **Vanilla Rum**[13] 922 5-8-13 67 (b) FrannyNorton 3 77
(John Mackie) *chsd ldrs: rdn to ld 1f out: edgd lft: r.o* **4/1**[1]

0305 **2** 2 **Black Coffee**[7] 1000 7-8-10 64 (b) ShaneKelly 4 70
(Mark Brisbourne) *s.i.s: hld up: hdwy over 1f out: r.o to go 2nd wl ins fnl f: nt rch wnr* **8/1**

060- **3** 1 **Laughing Jack**[47] 6976 4-9-0 75 GeorgeDowning(7) 10 79
(Tony Carroll) *hld up: rdn over 1f out: r.o ins fnl f: nrst fin* **20/1**

214- **4** 1/2 **Sciampin**[180] 6538 4-8-12 71 TobyAtkinson(5) 1 74
(Marco Botti) *led: rdn and hdd 1f out: styd on same pce* **9/2**[2]

4-60 **5** shd **Scribe (IRE)**[13] 922 4-8-8 62 (v[1]) RichardThomas 7 64
(David Evans) *chsd ldr: rdn and ev ch over 1f out: styd on same pce fnl f* **12/1**

66-2 **6** 1 **Sir George (IRE)**[28] 753 7-8-13 74 JacobButterfield(7) 6 74
(Ollie Pears) *s.i.s: hld up: hdwy over 1f out: styd on: nt rch ldrs* **5/1**[3]

-222 **7** 2 1/2 **Zenarinda**[48] 494 5-8-13 67 PaulHanagan 9 62
(Mark H Tompkins) *trckd ldrs: racd keenly: rdn over 2f out: hung lft and wknd fnl f* **7/1**

000- **8** 2 1/2 **Sir Bruno (FR)**[232] 4921 5-9-6 74 RichardKingscote 2 64
(Bryn Palling) *hld up: hdwy over 3f out: rdn and wknd over 1f out* **8/1**

0003 **9** 1 3/4 **Georgebernardshaw (IRE)**[28] 753 7-8-13 70 RobertLButler(3) 8 56
(Richard Guest) *hld up: hdwy over 5f out: rdn over 2f out: sn wknd* **14/1**

4/ **10** 9 **Silent Decision (USA)**[683] 2148 6-9-7 75 (p) ChrisCatlin 5 42
(John Stimpson) *prom: pushed along 5f out: wknd over 3f out* **14/1**

2m 1.43s (-0.27) **Going Correction** +0.075s/f (Slow) 10 Ran SP% **115.4**
Speed ratings (Par 103): **104,102,101,100,100 99,97,95,93,85**
Tote Swingers: 1&2 £5.30, 1&3 £22.00, 2&3 £36.10 CSF £35.75 CT £569.20 TOTE £4.20: £1.70, £2.60, £7.30; EX 13.30 Trifecta £640.50 Part won. Pool: £865.59 - 0.10 winning units..
Owner Derbyshire Racing VI **Bred** Charley Knoll Partnership **Trained** Church Broughton , Derbys

FOCUS
The pace was a decent one, which helped the winner's finishing effort, but it was still a likeable performance. He's rated a bit closer to his old form.

1095 FREE ONLINE BINGO AT FREEBETTING.CO.UK H'CAP (DIV I) 1m 141y(P)
5:45 (5:45) (Class 6) (0-52,56) 4-Y-0+ £1,704 (£503; £251) Stalls Low

Form RPR

2311 **1** **Odd Ball (IRE)**[8] 988 5-9-3 56 6ex AmyRyan(3) 3 67+
(Lisa Williamson) *dwlt: hld up: swtchd lft and hdwy over 1f out: r.o to ld wl ins fnl f: sn clr* **85/40**[1]

-000 **2** 2 3/4 **Kenswick**[8] 988 5-8-10 46 oh1 (b) CathyGannon 1 50
(Pat Eddery) *led: rdn and hdd over 2f out: rallied to ld ins fnl f: sn hdd and unable qck* **20/1**

5444 **3** hd **Roman Flame**[9] 966 4-9-1 51 FrannyNorton 2 55
(Michael Quinn) *chsd ldrs: rdn over 2f out: edgd rt and ev ch ins fnl f: styd on same pce* **11/1**

-654 **4** 1/2 **Princess Gail**[13] 929 4-9-2 52 TomMcLaughlin 9 55
(Mark Brisbourne) *s.i.s: hld up: hdwy over 1f out: r.o: nt rch ldrs* **7/1**

0645 **5** 3/4 **Aggbag**[47] 531 8-8-3 46 oh1 (p) RichardOliver(7) 7 47
(Michael Appleby) *hld up: rdn over 1f out: r.o ins fnl f: nvr nrr* **25/1**

405- **6** 3/4 **Danceyourselfdizzy (IRE)**[175] 6659 4-8-3 46 DannyBrock(7) 12 45
(Phil McEntee) *swtchd lft sn after s: chsd ldr tl led over 2f out: rdn and edgd rt fr over 1f out: hdd ins fnl f: wknd towards fin* **28/1**

300- **7** hd **Rasteau (IRE)**[103] 7800 4-8-7 46 RyanClark(3) 8 45
(Tom Keddy) *pushed along in rr early: hld up: styd on ins fnl f: nvr nrr* **25/1**

-000 **8** 1 **Roman Ruler (IRE)**[13] 926 4-9-0 50 PhillipMakin 6 47
(Chris Fairhurst) *chsd ldrs: rdn over 2f out: no ex fnl f* **13/2**[3]

000- **9** 2 1/4 **Boga (IRE)**[177] 6602 5-8-3 46 GemmaTutty(7) 11 37
(Karen Tutty) *mid-div: hdwy over 5f out: rdn and wknd fnl f* **80/1**

-460 **10** 1 **Luv U Noo**[20] 848 5-8-10 46 oh1 RussKennemore 4 38
(Brian Baugh) *s.i.s: hld up: nt clr run wl over 1f out: n.d* **20/1**

00-0 **11** 1/2 **Eyes On**[13] 927 4-8-11 52 (t) RaulDaSilva(5) 10 40
(Frank Sheridan) *hld up: rdn over 2f out: wknd over 1f out* **20/1**

6652 **12** 4 1/2 **Avon Supreme**[20] 848 4-9-2 52 ShaneKelly 5 30
(Gay Kelleway) *prom: rdn over 3f out: wknd over 1f out* **9/2**[2]

0056 **13** 12 **Kirstys Lad**[20] 848 10-8-10 46 oh1 RichardKingscote 13
(Michael Mullineaux) *prom: rdn over 3f out: wknd over 2f out* **16/1**

1m 51.54s (1.04) **Going Correction** +0.075s/f (Slow) 13 Ran SP% **116.9**
Speed ratings (Par 101): **98,95,95,94,94 93,93,92,90,89 89,85,74**
Tote Swingers: 1&2 £9.50, 1&3 £4.60, 2&3 £14.50 CSF £52.60 CT £335.48 TOTE £2.30: £1.10, £3.30, £4.50; EX 32.80 Trifecta £290.60 Pool: £534.24 - 1.36 winning units..
Owner Mrs S Morris **Bred** Ms S Pettigrew & J Jamieson **Trained** Saighton, Cheshire
■ Stewards' Enquiry : Danny Brock one-day ban: failed to ride to draw (Apr 12)

FOCUS
This was a low-grade race, and the improving winner made some unreliable rivals look pedestrian. The form is taken at face value and there could be more to come from her.
Luv U Noo Official explanation: jockey said mare was denied a clear run
Avon Supreme Official explanation: jockey said filly hung left

1096 FREE ONLINE BINGO AT FREEBETTING.CO.UK H'CAP (DIV II) 1m 141y(P)
6:15 (6:16) (Class 6) (0-52,52) 4-Y-0+ £1,704 (£503; £251) Stalls Low

Form RPR

0-31 **1** **Cabal**[27] 773 5-9-2 52 (b) DanielTudhope 11 65
(Andrew Crook) *hld up: swtchd rt and hdwy over 1f out: r.o to ld wl ins fnl f: readily* **6/1**[3]

505- **2** 1 3/4 **Goldstorm**[175] 6653 4-8-11 47 RussKennemore 1 56
(Brian Baugh) *s.i.s: hld up: pushed along over 3f out: hdwy over 1f out: rdn and ev ch ins fnl f: edgd lft: styd on same pce* **12/1**

2402 **3** 1 1/4 **Cairanne**[6] 1014 4-8-7 46 oh1 RyanClark(3) 8 52
(Tom Keddy) *s.s: hld up: hdwy over 1f out: r.o to go 3rd post: nt trble ldrs* **11/2**[2]

00-0 **4** hd **Titan Diamond (IRE)**[8] 988 4-8-3 46 RachealKneller(7) 9 52
(Mark Usher) *a.p: led ins fnl f: sn rdn and hdd: styd on same pce: lost 3rd post* **33/1**

106- **5** 3 **Downtown Boy (IRE)**[194] 6153 4-9-1 51 PaddyAspell 5 50
(Ray Craggs) *led: rdn over 1f out: hdd and no ex ins fnl f* **25/1**

5500 **6** 1/2 **Gay Gallivanter**[15] 891 4-8-10 46 oh1 (p) FrannyNorton 6 43
(Michael Quinn) *chsd ldr: rdn over 1f out: wknd fnl f* **20/1**

/0-6 **7** nk **Jobekani (IRE)**[21] 843 6-8-7 46 oh1 (p) AmyRyan(3) 10 43
(Lisa Williamson) *hld up: hdwy over 1f out: hung lft and wknd ins fnl f* **25/1**

0550 **8** nse **Dubonny**[6] 1014 5-8-5 46 oh1 (t) RaulDaSilva(5) 2 43
(Frank Sheridan) *chsd ldrs: wnt 2nd over 2f out: rdn and ev ch ins fnl f: wknd towards fin* **16/1**

5030 **9** 2 **Look For Love**[12] 939 4-8-8 51 JackDuern(7) 7 43
(Reg Hollinshead) *trckd ldrs: plld hrd: rdn over 2f out: hmpd over 1f out: wknd fnl f* **10/1**

00-6 **10** 7 **Libre**[76] 160 12-8-10 46 oh1 MartinDwyer 13 22
(Violet M Jordan) *hld up: rdn over 2f out: a in rr* **66/1**

055- **11** 6 **Russian Winter**[124] 7561 4-8-10 46 JamesSullivan 12
(Tim Etherington) *s.s: a bhd* **40/1**

41 **12** 3 3/4 **Esytopolishadimond (IRE)**[6] 1019 5-9-2 52 PaulHanagan 4
(Michael J Browne, Ire) *chsd ldrs: pushed along over 2f out: nt clr run sn after: wknd and eased wl over 1f out* **9/4**[1]

1m 51.48s (0.98) **Going Correction** +0.075s/f (Slow) 12 Ran SP% **102.4**
Speed ratings (Par 101): **98,96,95,95,92 92,91,91,89,83 78,75**
Tote Swingers: 1&2 £13.10, 1&3 £5.10, 2&3 £10.00 CSF £51.77 CT £305.94 TOTE £3.60: £1.10, £5.10, £2.00; EX 79.00 Trifecta £236.70 Pool: £403.19 - 1.26 winning units..
Owner Leeds Plywood And Doors Ltd **Bred** Cheveley Park Stud Ltd **Trained** Middleham Moor, N Yorks
■ Cwmni was withdrawn after bolting to post (7/1, deduct 10p in the £ under R4).
■ Stewards' Enquiry : Daniel Tudhope three-day ban: careless riding (Apr 12-14)
Racheal Kneller two-day ban: careless riding (Apr 12-13)
Russ Kennemore two-day ban: careless riding (Apr 12-13)

FOCUS
A similar time to division one. Like the first division, the winner was in a different league from the rest, but there is some doubt over the strenghth of the form.
T/Plt: £322.10 to a £1 stake. Pool: £62,005.00 - 140.49 winning tickets. T/Qpdt: £33.00 to a £1 stake. Pool: £6,170.00 - 137.99 winning tickets. CR

1097 - 1103a (Foreign Racing) - See Raceform Interactive

1068 LINGFIELD (L-H)
Friday, March 30

OFFICIAL GOING: Standard
Wind: Almost nil Weather: Sunny and warm

1104 SUMMER NIGHTS AT LINGFIELD PARK CLAIMING STKS 1m 5f (P)
2:20 (2:20) (Class 6) 4-Y-0+ £1,704 (£503; £251) Stalls Low

Form RPR

5340 **1** **Ostentation**[28] 760 5-8-11 60 JoeFanning 1 59
(Roger Teal) *cl up in 3rd: effrt 2f out: qcknd to ld 1f out: drvn along and edgd lft: hld on nr fin* **5/1**[3]

2422 **2** nk **Quinsman**[7] 1003 6-9-8 71 LukeMorris 4 70
(J S Moore) *hld up in rr: effrt and sltly wd on bnd into st: wnt 2nd and clsd on wnr ins fnl f: jst hld* **4/5**[1]

50-4 **3** 1 3/4 **Talbot Green**[23] 825 4-9-3 57 MartinDwyer 2 65
(William Muir) *sn trcking ldr: chal 2f out: one pce ent fnl f* **7/1**

502- **4** 1 **Shy**[185] 6438 7-8-9 64 (b) CathyGannon 3 55
(Rod Millman) *led: rdn and hdd 1f out: 2nd and hld whn squeezed on rail and snatched up ins fnl f* **7/2**[2]

2m 46.01s (0.01) **Going Correction** +0.025s/f (Slow)
WFA 4 from 5yo+ 3lb 4 Ran SP% **106.9**
Speed ratings (Par 101): **100,99,98,98**
CSF £9.53 TOTE £5.70; EX 8.70.The winner was claimed by A. J. D. Lidderdale for £3,000.
Owner John Morton **Bred** Wellsummers Stud **Trained** Ashtead, Surrey
■ Stewards' Enquiry : Joe Fanning two-day ban: careless riding (Apr 13-14)

FOCUS
Normally this would be put down as a nondescript claimer, but it was made much more interesting by the presence of the two jockeys battling for the Winter Jockeys' Championship on its final day and, in a race run at an ordinary pace, the pair fought out the finish. Muddling form, limited by the third.

1105 BREATHE SPA AT MARRIOTT LINGFIELD CLASSIFIED CLAIMING STKS 1m 2f (P)
2:50 (2:50) (Class 6) 4-Y-0+ £1,704 (£503; £251) Stalls Low

Form RPR

0533 **1** **Archelao (IRE)**[8] 989 4-9-2 67 AmirQuinn 2 74
(Richard Rowe) *in tch in 4th: led briefly 3f out: styd on to ld again ins fnl f: drvn clr* **13/2**

5041 **2** 2 1/4 **Tuxedo**[11] 960 7-8-10 63 (b) LukeMorris 1 64
(Peter Hiatt) *chsd ldng pair: rdn to ld over 2f out: hdd and one pce ins fnl f* **7/2**[2]

4144 **3** 1 1/2 **Wisecraic**[14] 915 5-8-8 63 LiamKeniry 3 59
(J S Moore) *hld up in rr: hdwy over 2f out: styd on same pce fr over 1f out* **4/1**[3]

1312 **4** 1 **Daniel Thomas (IRE)**[14] 915 10-8-9 70 (tp) WilliamCarson 5 58
(Richard Guest) *s.s and rdn early: towards rr: effrt and wnt 4th 2f out: no imp* **1/1**[1]

006 **5** 15 **Apassionforfashion**[57] 381 4-8-6 34 (e) LiamJones 6 25
(Mark Rimell) *t.k.h: trckd ldr tl 3f out: sn wknd* **150/1**

000/ **6** *65* **Hot Cherry**[1802] 1232 8-8-8 44 .... JohnFahy 4
(H Edward Haynes) *led tl wknd 3f out* **100/1**

2m 5.75s (-0.85) **Going Correction** +0.025s/f (Slow) **6** Ran SP% **107.2**
Speed ratings (Par 101): **104,102,101,100,88 36**
toteswingers: 1&2 £2.20, 1&3 £2.10, 2&3 £1.20 CSF £26.49 TOTE £6.30: £2.00, £2.10; EX 26.10.
Owner Miss Victoria Baalham **Bred** Mount Coote Stud And M H Dixon **Trained** Sullington, W Sussex
■ Stewards' Enquiry : Amir Quinn two-day ban: used whip above permitted level (Apr 13-14)

FOCUS
In reality this was only a four-runner claimer, though at least the two outsiders made sure the pace was honest. The winner is rated back to his maiden best.

1106 LAURENCE WRIGHT RETIREMENT H'CAP — 1m 2f (P)
3:25 (3:26) (Class 6) (0-60,63) 4-Y-0+ — **£1,704** (£503; £251) **Stalls** Low

Form RPR
000- **1** **Russian Storm**[116] 7640 4-8-2 **46** .... JemmaMarshall(5) 1 54
(Pat Phelan) *t.k.h: prom: drvn to join ldr 1f out: jst got up fnl 50yds* **5/1**[3]

0-01 **2** *hd* **Flag Of Glory**[16] 891 5-9-7 **60** .... WilliamCarson 3 67
(Peter Hiatt) *led: jnd and hrd rdn ent fnl f: narrowly hdd fnl 50yds: kpt on wl* **9/2**[2]

050- **3** *1 ½* **The Ducking Stool**[112] 7695 5-8-7 **46** oh1 .... CathyGannon 9 50
(Julia Feilden) *chsd ldrs: effrt and tried to chal over 1f out: one pce fnl f* **12/1**

0-32 **4** *½* **Count Ceprano (IRE)**[8] 1000 8-9-1 **57** .... SimonPearce(3) 11 60
(Lydia Pearce) *in tch: rdn over 2f out: styd on fnl f* **15/2**

-021 **5** *1 ¼* **Isdaal**[11] 961 5-9-3 **63** 6ex ow1 .... MichaelJMurphy(7) 2 64+
(Kevin Morgan) *chsd ldrs: rdn and outpcd over 2f out: kpt on fnl f* **7/2**[1]

343/ **6** *nk* **Second To Nun (IRE)**[636] 3683 6-8-8 **47** .... FergusSweeney 8 47
(Michael Blanshard) *prom: wnt 2nd 6f out tl over 1f out: no ex* **33/1**

4621 **7** *1 ¾* **Cantor**[48] 519 4-9-5 **58** .... (b) WilliamBuick 4 55
(Giles Bravery) *a abt same pl: rdn and no hdwy fnl 3f* **9/2**[2]

-026 **8** *3* **Diamond Twister (USA)**[29] 741 6-8-7 **46** .... (t) LukeMorris 5 37
(Lisa Williamson) *s.i.s: towards rr: rdn over 3f out: nvr trbld ldrs* **12/1**

0660 **9** *1 ½* **Prince Of Thebes (IRE)**[37] 651 11-8-9 **53** .... (p) MarkCoumbe(5) 7 41
(Michael Attwater) *s.s: bhd: mod effrt on outer 4f out: sn rdn and wknd* **10/1**

00-6 **10** *14* **Glens Wobbly**[25] 805 4-8-11 **50** .... RobertHavlin 12
(Jonathan Geake) *a in rr gp: drvn along and n.d fnl 3f* **80/1**

2m 6.68s (0.08) **Going Correction** +0.025s/f (Slow) **10** Ran SP% **115.7**
Speed ratings (Par 101): **100,99,98,98,97 97,95,93,92,80**
toteswingers: 1&2 £6.40, 1&3 £13.00, 2&3 £13.70 CSF £27.55 CT £256.32 TOTE £7.10: £2.20, £2.00, £4.60; EX 41.20.
Owner Ermyn Lodge Stud **Bred** Ermyn Lodge Stud Limited **Trained** Epsom, Surrey
■ Stewards' Enquiry : Jemma Marshall two-day ban: used whip above permitted level (Apr 13-14)

FOCUS
A moderate handicap and it paid to race handily. The winning time was nearly a second slower than the preceding claimer. The form is not entirely convincing.
Russian Storm Official explanation: trainer's rep said, regarding apparent improvement in form, that since it's last run, the filly has recovered from an abscess on its lung.

1107 BARRY O'CONNOR CELEBRATION BIRTHDAY MAIDEN FILLIES' STKS — 1m 2f (P)
4:00 (4:01) (Class 5) 3-Y-0+ — **£2,385** (£704; £352) **Stalls** Low

Form RPR
5 **1** **Danube River**[14] 918 3-8-6 .... JoeFanning 7 68+
(Mark Johnston) *mde all: in command whn edgd rt and rn green over 1f out: rdn out* **9/4**[2]

060- **2** *4* **Lady Romanza (IRE)**[195] 6152 3-8-1 42 .... JemmaMarshall(5) 8 60
(Brendan Powell) *prom: chsd wnr over 3f out: hrd rdn and nt qckn appr fnl f* **33/1**

3 *3* **Red Hand (USA)** 3-8-7 ow1 .... WilliamBuick 2 55+
(John Gosden) *dwlt: hld up in rr: hdwy over 2f out: drvn to chse ldrs over 1f out: no ex* **8/11**[1]

5 **4** *½* **Raamz (IRE)**[15] 908 5-9-5 .... MichaelJMurphy(7) 4 57
(Kevin Morgan) *chsd ldrs: clsd up on outer over 2f out: no ex over 1f out* **12/1**

4 **5** *2* **Findeln**[23] 816 3-8-6 .... CathyGannon 5 49
(Eve Johnson Houghton) *mid-div: rdn and outpcd 3f out: sn btn* **8/1**[3]

0 **6** *1 ¾* **Optimism**[23] 816 3-8-6 .... MartinDwyer 6 46
(William Muir) *dwlt: t.k.h in rr: rdn and n.d fnl 3f* **20/1**

00-0 **7** *2 ½* **Polly Adler**[4] 1045 5-9-12 26 .... FergusSweeney 1 45
(Alastair Lidderdale) *chsd wnr tl over 3f out: wknd over 2f out* **66/1**

0 **8** *13* **Littlemissperfect**[43] 573 4-9-12 .... JamieGoldstein 3 19
(Richard Rowe) *towards rr: rdn over 4f out: sn last and struggling* **66/1**

2m 6.39s (-0.21) **Going Correction** +0.025s/f (Slow)
WFA 3 from 4yo+ 20lb **8** Ran SP% **118.2**
Speed ratings (Par 100): **101,97,95,95,93 92,90,79**
toteswingers: 1&2 £15.50, 1&3 £1.10, 2&3 £12.00 CSF £73.01 TOTE £2.80: £1.10, £6.80, £1.10; EX 102.70 Trifecta £167.30 Pool: £1,385.99 - 6.13 winning units..
Owner Sheikh Hamdan Bin Mohammed Al Maktoum **Bred** Darley **Trained** Middleham Moor, N Yorks
■ This double for Joe Fanning secured him the AW jockeys' title after a fine tussle with Luke Morris.

FOCUS
Again those that raced up with the pace were at an advantage. A weak and uncompetitive fillies' maiden and with the runner-up rated just 42, it's not hard to hold deep reservations over the strength of the form. The pace and the time were slow.
Littlemissperfect Official explanation: trainer said filly did not face the kickback

1108 LINGFIELD PARK OWNERS CLUB H'CAP — 1m (P)
4:30 (4:30) (Class 5) (0-70,70) 4-Y-0+ — **£2,385** (£704; £352) **Stalls** High

Form RPR
144- **1** **Snow Trooper**[195] 6167 4-9-7 **70** .... ShaneKelly 8 78
(Dean Ivory) *t.k.h: in tch on outer: drvn to chal 1f out: edgd lft: got up fnl 50yds* **13/2**

-500 **2** *nk* **Salient**[35] 685 8-9-4 **67** .... J-PGuillambert 6 74
(Michael Attwater) *led: hrd rdn over 1f out: kpt on wl u.p: jst hdd fnl 50yds* **22/1**

3653 **3** *nk* **Fibs And Flannel**[17] 884 5-8-13 **62** .... JamieMackay 7 69
(Willie Musson) *towards rr: swtchd outside and effrt over 1f out: fin wl to snatch 3rd* **12/1**

2311 **4** *nk* **Cyflymder (IRE)**[28] 761 6-9-2 **65** .... KieranO'Neill 9 71
(David C Griffiths) *chsd ldrs: drvn to chal over 1f out: nt qckn ins fnl f* **11/2**[3]

5025 **5** *1 ½* **Cativo Cavallino**[16] 894 9-9-1 **64** .... RichardThomas 5 66
(John E Long) *hld up in rr: rdn and styd on fnl 2f: hung lft in st: nvr nrr* **14/1**

1-05 **6** *½* **Whitechapel**[37] 649 5-9-6 **69** .... JohnFahy 4 70
(Daniel Kubler) *t.k.h: pressed ldrs tl no ex over 1f out* **8/1**

1210 **7** *1 ¼* **Twinkled**[15] 907 4-9-0 **70** .... IanBurns(7) 10 68
(Michael Bell) *t.k.h: prom: pressed ldr over 3f out tl over 1f out: fading whn n.m.r ent fnl f* **10/3**[1]

3523 **8** *2 ½* **Mister Green (FR)**[8] 991 6-9-4 **67** .... (bt) LukeMorris 2 60
(David Flood) *in tch on rail: rdn 3f out: sn btn* **7/2**[2]

3563 **9** *½* **Shared Moment (IRE)**[14] 919 6-9-2 **65** .... (v) MartinDwyer 3 57
(John Gallagher) *dwlt: in rr: hmpd on rail 5f out: rdn 3f out: a bhd* **11/1**

1m 38.34s (0.14) **Going Correction** +0.025s/f (Slow) **9** Ran SP% **112.2**
Speed ratings (Par 103): **100,99,99,99,97 97,95,93,92**
toteswingers: 1&2 £23.00, 1&3 £12.00, 2&3 £27.20 CSF £129.19 CT £1652.53 TOTE £8.70: £3.00, £6.90, £3.60; EX 171.20 TRIFECTA Not won..
Owner K B Taylor **Bred** Ashridge Farm Stud **Trained** Radlett, Herts
■ Stewards' Enquiry : J-P Guillambert two-day ban: used whip above permitted level (Apr 13-14)

FOCUS
A competitive if modest handicap and the pace was ordinary. The form is rated around the runner-up.
Shared Moment(IRE) Official explanation: trainer said mare was in season

1109 FOLLOW US ON TWITTER @LINGFIELDPARK H'CAP — 7f (P)
5:05 (5:05) (Class 4) (0-85,78) 3-Y-O — **£4,204** (£1,251; £625; £312) **Stalls** Low

Form RPR
0-10 **1** **Four Better**[36] 667 3-9-3 **74** .... FergusSweeney 7 80
(Jamie Osborne) *hld up in rr: hdwy and hung lft over 1f out: drvn to chal ins fnl f: led nr fin* **12/1**

2112 **2** *hd* **Gabrial's Bounty (IRE)**[20] 867 3-9-4 **75** .... MartinHarley 2 80
(Mick Channon) *cl up in 3rd: led jst over 1f out: hrd rdn and kpt on wl fnl f: hdd nr fin* **8/1**[3]

221- **3** *2 ¾* **Galician**[127] 7526 3-9-7 **78** .... JoeFanning 5 79+
(Mark Johnston) *hld up in 4th: shkn up whn hmpd over 1f out: styd on fnl f* **8/11**[1]

5-1 **4** *1 ¼* **Incendiary (IRE)**[23] 827 3-8-11 **75** .... NoelGarbutt(7) 3 69
(Hugo Palmer) *hld up in 5th: briefly nt clr run on inner on home turn: rdn to chse ldrs over 1f out: no ex fnl f* **10/3**[2]

231- **5** *2 ¾* **Lady Gibraltar**[119] 7597 3-9-6 **77** .... (v) JimmyFortune 1 64
(Alan Jarvis) *led after 1f tl wknd jst over 1f out* **12/1**

340- **6** *6* **Eightfold**[165] 6921 3-8-10 **67** .... MartinDwyer 6 38
(Seamus Durack) *led 1f then chsd ldr tl wl over 1f out: last and wkng whn bmpd appr fnl f* **33/1**

1m 24.43s (-0.37) **Going Correction** +0.025s/f (Slow) **6** Ran SP% **110.4**
Speed ratings (Par 100): **103,102,99,98,95 88**
toteswingers: 1&2 £4.60, 1&3 £2.70, 2&3 £1.90 CSF £93.59 TOTE £14.10: £3.60, £1.30; EX 91.00.
Owner C Woollett P Hearn & Mr & Mrs J Wilson **Bred** Lordship Stud **Trained** Upper Lambourn, Berks

FOCUS
Not a bad little handicap, featuring some progressive 3yos. The pace was decent but the form is ordinary enough with both the third and fourth below their maiden wins.

1110 GOLF & RACING AT LINGFIELD MARRIOTT H'CAP — 6f (P)
5:35 (5:35) (Class 5) (0-75,70) 3-Y-O — **£2,385** (£704; £352) **Stalls** Low

Form RPR
026- **1** **Dishy Guru**[106] 7765 3-9-3 **70** .... FergusSweeney 2 81
(Michael Blanshard) *trckd ldrs in 3rd: nipped through on inner to ld ent st: sn clr: rdn out* **11/2**

-31 **2** *1* **Morocco Moon**[14] 925 3-9-1 **68** .... ShaneKelly 1 75
(Tim Pitt) *t.k.h: led tl hdd and outpcd by wnr ent st: kpt on but hld after* **11/4**[2]

-124 **3** *1 ¾* **Available (IRE)**[13] 940 3-9-2 **69** .... WilliamBuick 5 70
(Jim Boyle) *hld up in last: wnt 4th 2f out: no imp over 1f out* **8/1**

-331 **4** *hd* **Superplex**[25] 801 3-9-0 **67** .... (p) JimmyFortune 4 68
(John Quinn) *hld up in 4th: effrt on rail and drvn along over 1f out: no imp* **7/4**[1]

3-01 **5** *2 ¾* **Justbookies Dotnet**[16] 892 3-9-1 **68** .... (v) IanMongan 3 60
(Louise Best) *pressed ldr: rdn 2f out: wd on home turn and qckly btn ent st* **9/2**[3]

1m 12.3s (0.40) **Going Correction** +0.025s/f (Slow) **5** Ran SP% **107.7**
Speed ratings (Par 98): **98,96,94,94,90**
CSF £19.72 TOTE £7.50: £3.60, £2.30; EX 16.70.
Owner Clifton Partners **Bred** J W Ford **Trained** Upper Lambourn, Berks

FOCUS
A modest sprint handicap for 3yos. The winner is up a length on his 2yo form.
T/Plt: £3,930.80 to a £1 stake. Pool: £56,539.51. 10.50 winning tickets. T/Qpdt: £459.70 to a £1 stake. Pool: £6,648.13. 10.70 winning tickets. LM

1089 WOLVERHAMPTON (A.W) (L-H)
Friday, March 30

OFFICIAL GOING: Standard
Wind: Cloudy with sunny spells Weather: Fresh across

1111 GRAND NATIONAL FREE BETS WITH FREEBETTING.CO.UK MEDIAN AUCTION MAIDEN STKS — 5f 216y(P)
5:55 (6:00) (Class 6) 3-5-Y-O — **£1,704** (£503; £251) **Stalls** Low

Form RPR
55-0 **1** **Elshabakiya (IRE)**[20] 866 4-9-8 100 .... NeilCallan 7 80+
(Clive Brittain) *trckd ldrs: led wl over 1f out: clr fnl f: easily* **1/10**[1]

06 **2** *5* **Ozz**[13] 940 3-8-7 0 ow3 .... (bt) MatthewCosham(5) 6 53
(Frank Sheridan) *prom: pushed along 1/2-way: wnt 2nd and edgd lft ins fnl f: no ch w wnr* **33/1**[3]

246 **3** *2 ¼* **Lord Paget**[13] 943 3-8-7 68 .... JackDuern(7) 4 48
(Reg Hollinshead) *hld up: hdwy over 1f out: wnt 3rd ins fnl f: nvr any ch* **12/1**[2]

00/5 **4** *1 ½* **Dikanta**[14] 925 4-9-13 45 .... FrederikTylicki 2 47
(Robert Cowell) *sn led: hdd wl over 1f out: wknd fnl f* **40/1**

60 **5** *1 ¼* **Dear Ben**[32] 720 3-9-0 0 .... RussKennemore 3 39
(Brian Baugh) *hld up: plld hrd: rdn over 2f out: wknd over 1f out* **33/1**[3]

00- **6** *8* **Ewenny Star**[93] 7889 3-8-2 0 .... DarrenEgan(7) 1
(Bryn Palling) *racd keenly: trckd ldr tl rdn 1/2-way: wknd wl over 1f out* **200/1**

006- **7** 3 1/4 **Right Credentials**[260] 4018 4-9-8 25 .... NeilChalmers 5
(Richard Ford) *hld up: lost tch over 2f out* **200/1**
1m 15.6s (0.60) **Going Correction** -0.075s/f (Stan)
WFA 3 from 4yo 13lb **7** Ran SP% **107.9**
Speed ratings (Par 101): **93,86,83,81,79 69,64**
toteswingers:1&2:£1.80, 2&3:£1.50, 1&3:£1.20 CSF £7.93 TOTE £1.10: £1.02, £10.40; EX 6.50.
Owner Saeed Manana **Bred** Rabbah Bloodstock Limited **Trained** Newmarket, Suffolk

FOCUS
An uncompetitive maiden won easily by the 100-rated Elshabakiya. The time was slow and the bare form is a bit shaky.
Dear Ben Official explanation: jockey said gelding ran too freely

1112 WOLVERHAMPTON-RACECOURSE.CO.UK H'CAP 1m 5f 194y(P)
6:25 (6:27) (Class 6) (0-60,66) 4-Y-0+ **£1,704** (£503; £251) **Stalls** Low

Form RPR
0542 **1** **Bilidn**[10] 968 4-8-11 **51** .... ChrisCatlin 9 64
(Noel Quinlan) *hld up in tch: plld hrd: rdn to chse ldr 2f out: styd on u.p to ld nr fin* **9/4**[1]
0-11 **2** *hd* **Den Maschine**[1] 1092 7-9-9 **66** 6ex .... DarrenEgan(7) 10 78
(Paul Rich) *a.p: chsd ldr 10f out tl led over 3f out: rdn and edgd rt fr over 1f out: hdd nr fin* **4/1**[2]
643- **3** 3/4 **White Deer (USA)**[157] 7075 8-9-3 **53** ....(p) RobertWinston 5 64
(Geoffrey Harker) *hld up: hdwy over 3f out: rdn over 1f out: styd on* **8/1**[3]
54-4 **4** *10* **Mecox Bay (IRE)**[80] 111 5-9-0 **50** .... PaulHanagan 12 47
(Jennie Candlish) *hld up: drvn along over 2f out: hung lft over 1f out: n.d* **8/1**[3]
0-4U **5** *hd* **Colliers Castle (IRE)**[17] 889 6-9-0 **53** .... AmyRyan(3) 2 50
(Lisa Williamson) *hld up: styd on ins fnl f: n.d* **18/1**
303- **6** *nk* **Famagusta**[112] 7688 5-8-7 **46** oh1 ....(v) AdamBeschizza(3) 3 43
(Peter Charalambous) *chsd ldr 4f: remained handy: rdn over 2f out: wknd over 1f out* **25/1**
4534 **7** 1 1/2 **The Catenian (IRE)**[16] 895 4-8-6 **46** oh1 ....(v) MartinLane 6 40
(John Butler) *hld up: shkn up over 1f out: nvr nr to chal* **8/1**[3]
25-U **8** 3 1/2 **Who Loves Ya Baby**[10] 968 4-8-7 **52** .... RosieJessop(5) 1 42
(Peter Charalambous) *led: pushed along and hdd over 3f out: wknd over 1f out* **8/1**[3]
50-0 **9** 3 1/2 **Josephine Malines**[42] 602 8-8-7 **48** oh1 ow2(bt[1]) MatthewCosham(5) 13 33
(Richard Price) *hld up: bhd fnl 3f* **66/1**
-366 **10** *5* **Four Steps Back**[16] 895 5-8-12 **48** .... DavidProbert 4 26
(Mark Usher) *prom: rdn over 3f out: wknd over 2f out* **16/1**
6-03 **11** *17* **Swords**[14] 924 10-8-10 **46** oh1 ....(p) FrannyNorton 11
(Ray Peacock) *prom: pushed along over 4f out: sn hung rt: wknd 3f out: t.o* **33/1**
3m 3.2s (-2.80) **Going Correction** -0.075s/f (Stan)
WFA 4 from 5yo+ 4lb **11** Ran SP% **114.6**
Speed ratings (Par 101): **105,104,104,98,98 98,97,95,93,90 81**
toteswingers:1&2:£2.60, 2&3:£4.60, 1&3:£5.00 CSF £10.19 CT £59.60 TOTE £3.70: £1.40, £1.30, £2.60; EX 12.00.
Owner Patrick Wilmott **Bred** Meon Valley Stud **Trained** Newmarket, Suffolk
■ Stewards' Enquiry : Chris Catlin nine-day ban: used whip above permitted level (Apr 13-14,16-21,23)

FOCUS
A moderate handicap. It was run in a fair time for the grade and saw decent efforts from the front three to pull clear.
Swords Official explanation: jockey said gelding hung badly right-handed

1113 HORSERACING FREE BETS WITH FREEBETTING.CO.UK MAIDEN STKS 1m 4f 50y(P)
6:55 (6:56) (Class 5) 3-Y-0+ **£2,264** (£673; £336; £168) **Stalls** Low

Form RPR
1 **Bob's World** 3-8-5 0 .... FrannyNorton 9 79+
(Jennie Candlish) *s.i.s: hld up: hdwy over 2f out: rdn to ld and hung rt ins fnl f: r.o* **20/1**
04-3 **2** 2 1/2 **Eshaab (USA)**[15] 908 3-8-5 77 .... PaulHanagan 8 75+
(Ed Dunlop) *a.p: chsd ldr over 2f out: led over 1f out: sn rdn: hdd and unable qck ins fnl f* **4/11**[1]
63- **3** 1 3/4 **Cloudy Spirit**[17] 7630 7-9-8 0 .... TonyCulhane 2 69+
(Reg Hollinshead) *chsd ldr tl led over 8f out: hdd over 1f out: styd on same pce ins fnl f* **7/1**[2]
4 *nk* **Nice Rose** 3-8-0 0 .... MartinLane 7 67+
(Mark Johnston) *hld up: pushed along and hdwy 3f out: rdn over 1f out: styd on same pce ins fnl f* **7/1**[2]
000- **5** *12* **Bells Of Berlin**[179] 6572 3-8-5 35 .... AndrewMullen 10 52
(Alan McCabe) *chsd ldrs: rdn over 2f out: wknd over 1f out* **28/1**
65 **6** 1 1/4 **Godwit**[21] 847 4-9-6 0 .... RichardKingscote 4 47
(Eugene Stanford) *led over 3f: chsd ldr tl rdn over 2f out: wknd over 1f out* **25/1**
5 **7** *hd* **Life Of Laughter (USA)**[28] 762 4-9-11 0 .... StevieDonohoe 6 52
(Willie Musson) *s.i.s: hld up: nvr on terms* **16/1**[3]
0/ **8** 2 3/4 **Tiger Girl**[965] 4792 5-9-8 0 .... ChrisCatlin 5 43
(Noel Quinlan) *s.i.s: hld up: rdn and wknd over 2f out* **66/1**
0 **9** *6* **David's Folly (IRE)**[15] 908 3-8-0 0 .... JamesSullivan 11 31
(Bryn Palling) *hld up: a in rr: rdn and wknd 3f out* **80/1**
0 **10** *17* **Magical Marvin**[15] 908 3-8-5 0 .... NeilChalmers 1
(Michael Appleby) *chsd ldrs: pushed along 5f out: wknd 3f out: t.o* **100/1**
636/ **11** *5* **Rebel Woman**[320] 6-9-3 45 .... MatthewLawson(5) 3
(Mrs A Corson, Jersey) *hld up: rdn over 3f out: sn wknd: t.o* **100/1**
2m 40.21s (-0.89) **Going Correction** -0.075s/f (Stan)
WFA 3 from 4yo 22lb 4 from 5yo+ 2lb **11** Ran SP% **121.0**
Speed ratings (Par 103): **99,97,96,95,87 87,87,85,81,69 66**
toteswingers:1&2:£4.60, 2&3:£2.10, 1&3:£12.60 CSF £28.16 TOTE £32.90: £6.30, £1.02, £1.50; EX 65.80.
Owner Bob Cant **Bred** Robert J Cant **Trained** Basford Green, Staffs

FOCUS
A weakish maiden run in a time 1.31 seconds slower than the following Class 4 handicap. The runner-up was a bit disappointing but the winner was no fluke on the day.

1114 FREE BETTING WITH FREEBETTING.CO.UK H'CAP 1m 4f 50y(P)
7:25 (7:25) (Class 4) (0-85,82) 4-Y-0+ **£4,204** (£1,251; £625; £312) **Stalls** Low

Form RPR
1-12 **1** **Illustrious Forest**[32] 721 4-8-8 **71** .... FrannyNorton 7 85+
(John Mackie) *chsd ldr over 10f out: led over 2f out: shkn up ins fnl f: readily* **13/8**[1]
0331 **2** 1 3/4 **Chookie Hamilton**[7] 1003 8-8-4 **72** .... DarrenEgan(7) 2 81
(Keith Dalgleish) *s.i.s: hld up: hdwy over 2f out: rdn to go 2nd ins fnl f: no ch w wnr* **9/2**[3]
-320 **3** *5* **Mazij**[29] 751 4-8-13 **76** .... WilliamCarson 5 77
(Peter Hiatt) *led 1f: chsd ldrs: rdn to chse wnr over 1f out: edgd rt: no ex ins fnl f* **3/1**[2]
3-60 **4** 1/2 **Pertemps Networks**[29] 751 8-9-0 **75** .... JamesSullivan 8 75
(Michael Easterby) *hld up: hdwy over 1f out: styd on same pce fnl f* **25/1**
250/ **5** *1* **Legend Erry (IRE)**[1382] 3104 8-8-7 **68** .... RichardKingscote 1 67
(Venetia Williams) *hld up: effrt over 1f out: no ex fnl f* **8/1**
610- **6** 4 1/2 **Lieutenant Kojak**[154] 7137 4-8-2 **70** .... RosieJessop(5) 4 61
(Peter Charalambous) *hld up: plld hrd: effrt over 1f out: wknd fnl f* **18/1**
430- **7** *7* **Zennor**[36] 6470 5-9-7 **82** ....(p) StephenCraine 3 62
(Tom Symonds) *led 1f out: rdn and hdd over 2f out: wknd over 1f out* **16/1**
042/ **8** *56* **King Kenny**[214] 7-9-0 **80** .... MatthewLawson(5) 6
(Mrs A Corson, Jersey) *chsd ldrs: pushed along over 3f out: wknd over 2f out: t.o* **20/1**
2m 38.9s (-2.20) **Going Correction** -0.075s/f (Stan)
WFA 4 from 5yo+ 2lb **8** Ran SP% **112.1**
Speed ratings (Par 105): **104,102,99,99,98 95,90,53**
toteswingers:1&2:£2.10, 2&3:£3.10, 1&3:£1.70 CSF £8.79 CT £19.00 TOTE £2.60: £1.10, £2.30, £1.10; EX 9.10.
Owner Derbyshire Racing VII **Bred** Norman A Blyth **Trained** Church Broughton , Derbys

FOCUS
An ordinary handicap. The winner resumed his progress and the second ran probably his best race of the winter.

1115 FREE CASINO BETTING WITH FREEBETTING.CO.UK CLASSIFIED STKS 5f 216y(P)
7:55 (7:56) (Class 5) 3-Y-O **£2,264** (£673; £336; £168) **Stalls** Low

Form RPR
5-26 **1** **Ghost Train (IRE)**[10] 975 3-9-0 70 .... NeilCallan 5 71
(Mark Johnston) *led 5f out: shkn up over 1f out: rdn and hung rt ins fnl f: styd on* **11/2**[3]
2232 **2** 1 1/4 **Derivatives (IRE)**[14] 925 3-9-0 67 .... NickyMackay 2 67
(John Gosden) *s.i.s: hld up: rdn over 1f out: r.o to go 2nd nr fin: nt trble wnr* **4/1**[2]
-464 **3** *nk* **Chester'Slittlegem (IRE)**[10] 970 3-8-9 65 .... RaulDaSilva(5) 1 66
(Ed de Giles) *chsd ldrs: rdn over 1f out: nt clr run ins fnl f: styd on same pce: lost 2nd nr fin* **12/1**
015- **4** *2* **Winter Hill**[230] 5052 3-9-0 66 .... RichardKingscote 3 60
(Tom Dascombe) *hld up in tch: rdn over 1f out: styd on same pce* **8/11**[1]
3-43 **5** 1 3/4 **Scrooby Doo**[10] 975 3-8-11 70 .... BillyCray(3) 4 54
(Scott Dixon) *led 1f: remained w wnr tl pushed along over 2f out: no ex fnl f* **12/1**
1m 14.51s (-0.49) **Going Correction** -0.075s/f (Stan) **5** Ran SP% **108.7**
Speed ratings (Par 98): **100,98,97,95,92**
CSF £25.78 TOTE £7.00: £2.50, £2.00; EX 18.30.
Owner A D Spence **Bred** E Puerari, Oceanic B/Stock & Riviera Eq **Trained** Middleham Moor, N Yorks

FOCUS
An interesting little classified event, and although the favourite flopped, this looked a nice enough performance from Ghost Train. Straightforward form at face value.

1116 ENJOY THE PUNTERS PACKAGE GROUP OFFER H'CAP 5f 216y(P)
8:25 (8:25) (Class 5) (0-70,75) 4-Y-0+ **£2,264** (£673; £336; £168) **Stalls** Low

Form RPR
2011 **1** **Captain Dimitrios**[7] 1005 4-9-13 **75** 6ex ....(v) PaulHanagan 7 84
(Alastair Lidderdale) *broke wl and led early: trckd ldr: racd keenly: led over 1f out: rdn and edgd lft ins fnl f: r.o* **8/1**
5534 **2** 3/4 **Blown It (USA)**[15] 912 6-9-7 **69** ....(b) NeilCallan 2 76
(Keith Dalgleish) *a.p: chsd wnr ins fnl f: sn ev ch: rdn: edgd lft and nt qckn* **5/1**[2]
0512 **3** *nk* **Waabel**[8] 997 5-9-5 **67** .... WilliamCarson 8 73
(Richard Guest) *hld up: hdwy over 1f out: r.o: nt rch ldrs* **6/4**[1]
-000 **4** 1 1/4 **Guest Book (IRE)**[41] 626 5-9-0 **67** .... DavidKenny(5) 11 69
(Michael Scudamore) *s.i.s: outpcd: r.o wl ins fnl f: nrst fin* **18/1**
6042 **5** 1 1/4 **Whipphound**[15] 911 4-9-3 **65** .... LukeMorris 6 63
(Mark Brisbourne) *prom: rdn over 1f out: styd on same pce fnl f* **11/2**[3]
1305 **6** 1/2 **Suddenly Susan (IRE)**[17] 883 4-9-3 **68** ....(b) BillyCray(3) 9 64
(Scott Dixon) *sn led: rdn and hdd over 1f out: no ex ins fnl f* **12/1**
-143 **7** 1 1/4 **Cape Of Storms**[32] 719 9-8-10 **65** ....(b) DarrenEgan(7) 5 57
(Roy Brotherton) *mid-div: rdn over 2f out: styd on same pce fnl f* **16/1**
4-04 **8** 2 3/4 **You'relikemefrank**[15] 911 6-9-5 **67** ....(p) NeilChalmers 3 50
(Richard Ford) *trckd ldrs: plld hrd: rdn over 1f out: wknd ins fnl f* **25/1**
-042 **9** 1/2 **Methaaly (IRE)**[15] 912 9-9-6 **68** ....(be) RichardKingscote 1 50
(Michael Mullineaux) *hld up: rdn over 2f out: wknd fnl f* **10/1**
1m 14.14s (-0.86) **Going Correction** -0.075s/f (Stan) **9** Ran SP% **114.9**
Speed ratings (Par 103): **102,101,100,98,97 96,94,91,90**
toteswingers:1&2:£5.00, 2&3:£3.00, 1&3:£2.40 CSF £47.45 CT £92.93 TOTE £5.70: £2.20, £1.50, £1.10; EX 30.30.
Owner C S J Beek **Bred** W G H Barrons **Trained** Lambourn, Berks

FOCUS
A modest sprint handicap. The form is rated around the runner-up.

1117 FREE BINGO BETTING WITH FREEBETTING.CO.UK H'CAP 7f 32y(P)
8:55 (8:55) (Class 5) (0-75,79) 4-Y-0+ **£2,264** (£673; £336; £168) **Stalls** High

Form RPR
000- **1** **Amazing Star (IRE)**[11] 6658 7-9-7 **75** .... DanielTudhope 8 84
(Declan Carroll) *hld up: hdwy over 2f out: swtchd rt over 1f out: rdn to ld nr fin* **6/1**[2]
0631 **2** 1/2 **April Fool**[8] 989 8-9-4 **79** 6ex ....(b) DarrenEgan(7) 3 87
(Ronald Harris) *led: rdn over 1f out: hdd nr fin* **11/4**[1]
1004 **3** *2* **Satwa Laird**[8] 991 6-9-4 **72** .... LukeMorris 2 75
(Conor Dore) *a.p: rdn over 1f out: edgd lft and styd on same pce ins fnl f* **13/2**[3]
230- **4** *nse* **Justbookie Dot Com (IRE)**[127] 7531 4-9-5 **73** ....(v) PadraigBeggy 7 75
(David Evans) *chsd ldrs: rdn over 1f out: styd on same pce ins fnl f* **9/1**
0-01 **5** 1 1/2 **Bahamian Lad**[39] 639 7-9-0 **68** ....(v) TonyCulhane 5 66
(Reg Hollinshead) *chsd ldr: rdn over 1f out: no ex ins fnl f* **6/1**[2]
0-00 **6** 1/2 **All Right Now**[62] 351 5-9-2 **70** .... AndreaAtzeni 10 67
(Derek Haydn Jones) *s.i.s: hld up: hdwy over 1f out: nt trble ldrs* **10/1**
4106 **7** *hd* **Pick A Little**[16] 896 4-9-2 **73** .... RyanClark(3) 4 70
(Michael Blake) *s.i.s: hld up: r.o ins fnl f: nvr nrr* **16/1**

1535 **8** 3 1/4 **Fleetwoodsands (IRE)**[16] 896 5 -9-371......................(t) LiamKeniry 12 59
(Milton Bradley) *hld up: rdn over 1f out: n.d* **8/1**
000- **9** 3 1/2 **Da Ponte**[195] 6167 4 -9-275.. DavidKenny(5) 11 53
(Michael Scudamore) *prom: rdn over 2f out: wknd over 1f out* **25/1**
5306 **10** nk **Opus Maximus (IRE)**[46] 548 7 -9-674........................ StephenCraine 1 51
(Conor Dore) *hld up: rdn over 2f out: wknd over 1f out* **8/1**
1m 28.42s (-1.18)**Going Correction** -0.075s/f (Stan) 10Ran SP%**119.6**
Speed ratings (Par 103): **103,102,100,100,98 97,97,93,89,89**
toteswingers:1&2:£8.60, 2&3:£5.40, 1&3:£6.00 CSF £23.49 CT £116.45 TOTE £8.90 : £2.80, £2.10, £1.70 ; EX 51.80 .
Owner K McConnell **Bred** Glending Bloodstock **Trained** Sledmere, E Yorks

FOCUS
An ordinary handicap in which confirmed front-runner April Fool seemed to gradually increase the pace. The form has a sound look to it.
T/Plt: £3.90 to a £1 stake. Pool £79,209.65 - 14,646.28 winning units. T/Qpdt: £2.90 to a £1 stake. Pool £6,705.44 - 1,674.01 winning units. CR

1017 DUNDALK (A.W) (L-H)
Friday, March 30

OFFICIAL GOING: Standard

1118a IRISH STALLION FARMS EUROPEAN BREEDERS FUND 2YO AUCTION MAIDEN 5f (P)
6:15 (6:16) 2-Y-O **£7,187** (£1,666; £729 ; £416)

RPR
1 **Verbal Honesty (IRE)**2 -8-8... RoryCleary 5 73+
(J S Bolger, Ire) *chsd ldrs: 3rd 1/2-way: rdn to ld 1f out: kpt on wl u.p fnl f* **9/2**[3]
2 hd **Angela's Dream (IRE)**2 -8-11...................................... NGMcCullagh 2 75+
(G M Lyons, Ire) *dwlt: sn chsd ldrs: 4th 1/2-way: rdn 2f out: u.p in 5th 1f out: kpt on wl fnl f: pressed wnr clsng stages* **10/1**
3 nk **Versilia Gal (IRE)**2 -8-8... BenCurtis 6 71
(Patrick Martin, Ire) *hld up towards rr: rdn 2f out: styd on in 4th 1f out: kpt on fnl f* **20/1**
4 nk **Gathering Power (IRE)**[6] 1038 2 -8-11........................ WayneLordan 4 73
(Edward Lynam, Ire) *prom and disp: 2nd 1/2-way: led 2f out: rdn and hdd 1f out: no ex fnl f: kpt on same pce* **10/11**[1]
5 3/4 **Toccata Blue (IRE)**2 -9-2... GaryCarroll 3 76
(G M Lyons, Ire) *hld up towards rr: rdn 2f out: styd on into 3rd 1f out: no ex ins fnl f* **13/2**
6 8 **Tiger Sunset (IRE)**2 -8-13.. PatSmullen 1 40
(J S Moore) *led and disp: rdn and hdd 2f out: wknd over 1f out* **7/2**[2]
1m 1.43s (61.43) 6Ran SP%**120.0**
CSF £48.07 TOTE £6.50 : £2.80, £8.10 ; DF 20.30 .
Owner Mrs J S Bolger **Bred** D H W Dobson **Trained** Coolcullen, Co Carlow

FOCUS
A fairly nondescript race, particularly because five of them finished within a length of each other. The time was slow and the form in all probability is ordinary.

NOTEBOOK
Verbal Honesty (IRE)was keen and green early on but the penny dropped with her in the straight and she ran on well having got a shade of first run on the second and third. It was a pretty decent performance and she'll improve. How she'll fare against winners is the question. (op 4/1)
Angela's Dream (IRE)ran well and she should pick up a similar race here before long. She did her best work at the finish once realising that she had to go between horses inside the last but was just unable to peg back the winner. An extra furlong would also suit.
Versilia Gal (IRE)was a little fractious in the stalls, seemed to struggle for a good bit of the way due mostly to greenness but she persisted and kept on well inside the last. She's one of the more obvious potential improvers.
Gathering Power (IRE)showed no progression. Prominent the whole way, she still betrayed what would have been called greenness on her first run as she ran around a bit on the rail and didn't see out her race to any great effect. One would imagine she'll improve and perhaps this came a bit quick. Or maybe not. Time will tell. (op 11/10)
Toccata Blue (IRE)kept plugging away, wasn't beaten far and is sure to benefit a good deal for the experience. (op 6/1)
Tiger Sunset (IRE) sent to Ireland for his debut, was well held. (op 7/2 tchd 100/30)

1119 - 1124a (Foreign Racing) - See Raceform Interactive

FONTAINEBLEAU
Friday, March 30

OFFICIAL GOING: Turf: soft

1125a PRIX DES TROIS PIGNONS (CONDITIONS) (3YO) (TURF) 6f
12:45 (12:00) 3-Y-O **£14,166** (£5,666; £4,250 ; £2,833 ; £1,416)

RPR
1 **Huma Bird**[201] 5961 3 -8-100.. FabriceVeron 1 99
(H-A Pantall, France) **138/10**
2 1 1/2 **Mister Ryan (FR)**[104] 3 -8-100.................................. MaximeGuyon 2 94
(H-A Pantall, France) **11/2**
3 1/2 **Barbayam**[15] 913 3 -8-70.. FlavienPrat 3 89
(F Head, France) **2/1**[1]
4 2 **Bay Shore (IRE)**[239] 4843 3 -8-100.......................... IoritzMendizabal 7 86
(J-C Rouget, France) **9/2**[3]
5 1 1/2 **Judas Jo (FR)**[154] 7135 3 -8-100................................ JohanVictoire 5 81?
(Gay Kelleway) *swvd at s: settled 4th: rdn over 2f out: no ex: styd on one pce fnl f* **21/1**
6 1 3/4 **Bandidazo (USA)**[127] 7533 3 -9-00................... Pierre-CharlesBoudot 8 80
(A Fabre, France) **53/10**
7 1 1/2 **Antalia (FR)**[140] 7385 3 -8-90.......................... ThomasHenderson(6) 6 76
(J-C Rouget, France) **4/1**[2]
8 10 **Secret Wishes (FR)**[88] 3 -8-100.................................... TheoBachelot 4 39
(Mlle S-V Tarrou, France) **45/1**
1m 10.0s (70.00) 8Ran SP%**116.2**
WIN (incl. 1 euro stake): 14.80. PLACES: 3.10, 2.10, 1.50. DF: 25.20. SF: 55.60 .
Owner Sheikh Mohammed **Bred** Darley **Trained** France

1127a PRIX DE MONTEREAU (H'CAP) (3YO) (TURF) 1m 2f
3:25 (12:00) 3-Y-O **£12,500** (£5,000; £3,750 ; £2,500 ; £1,250)

RPR
1 **Mouhjim (FR)**[13] 3 -8-30 ow1.. AntoineHamelin 2 77
(Mme P Butel, France) **41/5**
2 3/4 **Dylans Verse (IRE)**[21] 3 -8-110..............................(p) JulienAuge 6 84
(P Monfort, France) **3/1**[1]
3 nk **Pink Anabella (FR)**[27] 3 -8-100...................................... AlexisBadel 1 82
(J-M Beguigne, France) **73/10**
4 1 3/4 **Marmaris (FR)**[21] 3 -8-90.. TonyPiccone 3 77
(C Lerner, France) **78/10**
5 1 1/2 **Dinnar (FR)**[70] 247 3 -8-80.. MaximeGuyon 11 73
(Mario Hofer, Germany) **9/2**[2]
6 2 **Chief Hawkeye (IRE)**[65] 3 -8-50 ow1............................ AllanBonnefoy 9 66
(J-V Toux, France) **22/1**
7 3 **Uma De Synthe (FR)**[88] 3 -8-80.................................. AnthonyCrastus 5 63
(A Bonin, France) **40/1**
8 5 **Quand Reverraije (FR)**[10] 3 -8-90................................ ThomasHuet 7 54
(F Doumen, France) **12/1**
9 snk **Swing Alone (IRE)**[34] 716 3 -9-100............................ IoritzMendizabal 10 69
(Gay Kelleway) *broke wl towards outside: racd 5th but pulling hrd: gd prog on outside towards st: rdn over 2f out: no ex: fdd fnl f* **5/1**[3]
10 7 **Xpo Universel (FR)**[64] 3 -8-100.................................... TheoBachelot 4 41
(F Doumen, France) **20/1**
11 **Filiatra (FR)**[174] 3 -8-40.. AurelienLemaitre 12 35
(F Head, France) **21/1**
2m 8.0s (128.00) 11Ran SP%**117.9**
WIN (incl. 1 euro stake): 9.20. PLACES: 2.70, 1.60, 2.60. DF: 17.30. SF: 46.90 .
Owner Jean Rollin **Bred** B Gouin **Trained** France

1126a (Foreign Racing) - See Raceform Interactive

DONCASTER (L-H)
Saturday, March 31

OFFICIAL GOING: Good (watered; 7.1 (overall), 7.7 (middle - far side), 7.8 (middle - stands' side))
Wind: moderate across Weather: Overcast

1128 WILLIAM HILL SPRING MILE (H'CAP) 1m (S)
2:05 (2:07) (Class 3) 4-Y-O+
£24,900 (£7,456; £3,728 ; £1,864 ; £932 ; £468)**Stalls** High

Form RPR
020- **1** **Norse Blues**[150] 7227 4 -9-385...................................... LeeNewman 2 95
(Sylvester Kirk) *prom: rdn to ld over 1f out: drvn and kpt on wl fnl f* **50/1**
005- **2** 1 3/4 **Kyllachy Star**[189] 6326 6 -9-390.................................. ShaneBKelly(5) 7 96
(Richard Fahey) *midfield: pushed along and hdwy over 2f out: kpt on: wnt 2nd towards fin* **25/1**
114- **3** shd **Mont Ras (IRE)**[266] 3877 5 -9-587................................ DanielTudhope 8 93
(David O'Meara) *w ldr: rdn to ld over 2f out: hdd over 1f out: kpt on: lost 2nd towards fin* **10/1**
500- **4** nk **Captain Bertie (IRE)**[147] 7295 4 -9-284.......................... RobertWinston 12 97+
(Charles Hills) *midfield: short of room and lost pl over 3f out: short of room again over 2f out and dropped to rr: swtchd rt over 1f out: r.o strly: hung lft fnl 100yds: wnt 4th post: unlucky* **13/2**[1]
1104 **5** 1/2 **Prince Of Burma (IRE)**[7] 962 4 -9-688..........................(b) IanMongan 6 92
(Jeremy Gask) *hld up: hdwy over 2f out: sn rdn: kpt on one pce* **20/1**
053- **6** 1/2 **Redvers (IRE)**[161] 7023 4 -9-688...................................... JimmyFortune 1 91
(Ed Vaughan) *hld up: hdwy over 2f out: sn rdn: kpt on one pce* **16/1**
051- **7** 3/4 **Shamdarley (IRE)**[176] 6674 4 -9-385.............................. PhillipMakin 16 86+
(Michael Dods) *hld up: briefly tight for room over 2f out: pushed along and hdwy over 1f out: kpt on fnl f* **7/1**[2]
0-03 **8** 1 1/4 **First Post (IRE)**[6] 907 5 -9-486...................................... ShaneKelly 21 84
(Derek Haydn Jones) *in tch: rdn over 2f out: sn one pce* **20/1**
332- **9** 3 1/4 **Weapon Of Choice (IRE)**[75] 6704 4 -9-789........................ ChrisCatlin 22 80
(Stuart Kittow) *prom: rdn 3f out: sn one pce: wknd fnl f* **16/1**
000- **10** 1 1/2 **Snow Bay**[176] 6672 6 -9-688...................................... AndrewMullen 19 75
(David Nicholls) *led narrowly: pushed along whn hdd over 2f out: wknd over 1f out* **12/1**
113- **11** shd **Perfect Cracker**[92] 7928 4 -9-688.................................. JohnFahy 9 75
(Clive Cox) *in tch: rdn over 2f out: no imp* **20/1**
100- **12** 1 **Kiwi Bay**[147] 7295 7 -9-789.. TomEaves 17 74
(Michael Dods) *hld up: pushed along over 3f out: nvr threatened ldrs* **33/1**
-203 **13** 1/2 **Reve De Nuit (USA)**[1035] 6 -9-587...................................... PatSmullen 18 71
(Alan McCabe) *in tch: rdn over 2f out: wknd over 1f out* **12/1**
3430 **14** 1 3/4 **Tevez**[16] 907 7 -9-284...(p) CathyGannon 20 64
(Des Donovan) *s.i.s: hld up: hdwy to chse ldrs over 2f out: wknd over 1f out* **33/1**
002- **15** 3/4 **Kay Gee Be (IRE)**[157] 7110 8 -9-587................................ TonyHamilton 14 65
(Richard Fahey) *midfield: rdn over 2f out: sn no imp* **12/1**
000- **16** 2 3/4 **Leviathan**[196] 6163 5 -9-789...................................... DaneO'Neill 13 60
(Tony Newcombe) *hld up: pushed along and brief hdwy over 2f out: wknd over 1f out* **8/1**[3]
50-0 **17** 1 3/4 **Arabian Spirit**[6] 1043 7 -9-186...................................... LeeTopliss(3) 11 53
(Richard Fahey) *hld up in tch: nvr threatened* **28/1**
0-26 **18** 3/4 **Mullins Way (USA)**[36] 694 4 -9-385.............................. RobbieFitzpatrick 5 51
(Jo Hughes) *chsd ldrs: rdn over 2f out: wknd over 1f out* **28/1**
10-0 **19** 3 1/4 **Pat's Legacy (USA)**[56] 431 6 -8-1186.......................... JoshBaudains(7) 4 44
(Jo Hughes) *prom: rdn over 2f out: sn wknd* **28/1**
6-26 **20** 18 **Kingscroft (IRE)**[7] 1035 4 -9-688.................................... NeilCallan 10
(Mark Johnston) *trckd ldrs: losing pl whn short of room 3f out: wknd over 2f out* **25/1**
00-5 **21** 3 **Crown Counsel (IRE)**[12] 962 4 -9-789.............................. JoeFanning 15
(Mark Johnston) *chsd ldrs: pushed along over 3f out: sn wknd* **14/1**
10-3 **22** 24 **Miami Gator (IRE)**[2] 965 5 -9-287..........................(v) MichaelMetcalfe(3) 3
(Mrs K Burke) *w ldr: lost pl 4f out: sn wknd: eased* **50/1**
1m 38.59s (-0.71)**Going Correction** +0.025s/f (Good) 22Ran SP%**129.7**
Speed ratings (Par 107): **104,102,102,101,101 100,100,98,95,94 94,93,92,90,90 87,85,84,81,63 60,36**
toteswingers:1&2:£146.10, 1&3:£36.20, 2&3:£64.90 CSF £1005.52 CT £12725.03 TOTE £106.00: £21.00, £6.50, £2.80, £2.00 ; EX 3572.50 Trifecta £1944.10 Part won. Pool: £2,627.19 - 0.20 winning units. .
Owner J C Smith **Bred** Littleton Stud **Trained** Upper Lambourn, Berks

FOCUS

The usual cavalry charge for the highest-rated 22 horses that missed the cut for the Lincoln itself, but instead of splitting into two or more groups the entire field raced as a bunch down the centre of the track. Under the circumstances there was always likely to be trouble. Eight of the last ten winners had been 4yos and eight of the previous nine winners hadn't raced since the previous year, trends which continue following this running. The form makes a fair bit of sense, but the fourth was unlucky. The winner is rated up a length on his 3yo form.

NOTEBOOK

Norse Blues's success would have been a major shock to most punters. Racing for the first time since November, he had given no indication that a searching mile like this suits him with his best previous efforts either coming over shorter or around a bend. He didn't look particularly well handicapped either, but there was no faulting the way he kept on finding a bit more after leading over a furlong from home and the conclusion must be that he has just improved from three to four. It will be interesting to see if he can build on this, even though this was a tasty prize to win.

Kyllachy Star missed the cut for the Lincoln by one, so found himself off top weight here, though his capable apprentice took off a handy 5lb. He finished 11th in this race last year having already had a run, but he had dropped 4lb below his last winning mark and ran a blinder in defeat, keeping on all the way to the line after creeping closer passing the 3f pole. He deserves to find a nice handicap and would be of interest if returning to Chester, where he has won twice. (op 22-1)

Mont Ras(IRE) hadn't been seen since July, but he made a winning return after a longer absence last year and then went on to complete a hat-trick. The subject of good market support through the week though a drifter on course, he helped share the early pace along with Snow Bay and Miami Gator, but lasted much longer than that pair and didn't lose the advantage until the winner collared him over a furlong out. He remains unexposed and his trainer believes he may improve throughout the season. (op 8-1)

Captain Bertie(IRE) ◆ had been gelded since ending the last turf season disappointingly and was very well backed here. He held a fair position in the middle of the field early, but met every bit of trouble going between the 3f and 2f poles as weakening rivals fell back into his lap. He soon faced an impossible task, but once seeing daylight he finished with such a rattle that it's hard to believe he wouldn't have gone close to winning with a clear run. He deserves to gain compensation. (op 9-1)

Prince Of Burma(IRE) did well on Polytrack at the start of the year and as a result was 10lb higher than when last on turf, but he finished strongly against the far rail having been in rear early and this effort suggests he can carry on the good work back on the grass. (op 25-1)

Redvers(IRE), racing for a new yard on this first start since October, was trying 1m for the first time off a new career-high mark. Another to stay on well towards the far side of the field, he had no more to offer in the last 50 yards, but it's probably worth giving him the benefit of the doubt with regard to his stamina.

Shamdarley(IRE), 6lb higher than when winning over 1m2f at York on his most recent start last October, was another to get caught up in the melee coming to the last 2f. There was no way back from there, but he did stay on and it may be that he needs the longer trip now. The Zetland Gold Cup could be his sort of race. (op 15-2 tchd 8-1 and 6-1)

First Post(IRE) made a promising move from midfield over 2f out, but not for the first time then started to hang. (tchd 22-1)

Leviathan, gelded since last seen in September, was back down to his last winning mark and better might have been expected considering the positive vibes coming from the yard plus the market support. (op 12-1)

Miami Gator(IRE) Official explanation: jockey said gelding never travelled

1129 NEW WILLIAM HILL IPHONE APP CAMMIDGE TROPHY (LISTED RACE) 6f

2:40 (2:41) (Class 1) 3-Y-O+

£18,714 (£7,095; £3,550; £1,768; £887; £445) **Stalls** High

Form	Pos	Dist	Horse	Jockey	RPR
433-	**1**		**The Cheka (IRE)**[182] 6521 6-9-2 108 (Eve Johnson Houghton) *trckd ldrs: hdwy 2f out: rdn to chal ins fnl f: styd on to ld last 50yds* **12/1**	(p) NeilCallan 11	113
0060	**2**	*3/4*	**Jimmy Styles**[30] 756 8-9-2 100 (Clive Cox) *t.k.h early: cl up: effrt wl over 1f out: rdn to ld ent fnl f: hdd and nt qckn last 50yds* **12/1**	(p) JohnFahy 10	111
342-	**3**	*2*	**Mayson**[147] 7298 4-9-2 100 (Richard Fahey) *led: rdn along wl over 1f out: hdd ent fnl f: kpt on same pce* **13/2**	TonyHamilton 12	105
114-	**4**	*1 1/4*	**Royal Rock**[168] 6858 8-9-7 112 (Chris Wall) *hld up in rr: hdwy over 2f out: rdn over 1f out: styd on fnl f: nrst fin* **10/1**	ChrisCatlin 4	106
2000	**5**	*hd*	**Internationaldebut (IRE)**[44] 589 7-9-2 103 (Paul Midgley) *hld up in rr: hdwy on outer wl over 2f out: rdn to chse ldrs over 1f out: one pce fnl f* **20/1**	FrederikTylicki 3	100
40-0	**6**	*1*	**Boris Grigoriev (IRE)**[7] 1032 3-8-3 98 (Michael Easterby) *chsd ldrs: rdn along over 2f out: sn one pce* **80/1**	JamesSullivan 13	93
303-	**7**	*1/2*	**High Standing (USA)**[182] 6534 7-9-2 103 (Jeremy Gask) *hld up in tch: hdwy over 2f out: rdn to chse ldrs over 1f out: sn no imp* **25/1**	[1] IanMongan 6	95
1-46	**8**	*nk*	**Googlette (IRE)**[35] 711 4-8-11 87 (Ed Vaughan) *chsd ldrs: rdn along 2f out: sn wknd* **66/1**	PhillipMakin 9	89
111-	**9**	*1/2*	**Sirius Prospect (USA)**[147] 7298 4-9-5 110 (Dean Ivory) *hld up in rr: effrt and n.m.r over 2f out: sn swtchd lft and rdn: n.d* **9/4**[1]	ShaneKelly 8	96+
000-	**10**	*1*	**Waffle (IRE)**[189] 6332 6-9-2 102 (David Barron) *a towards rr* **11/2**[3]	FranBerry 5	89+
030-	**11**	*7*	**Pabusar**[183] 6500 4-9-2 102 (Ralph Beckett) *wnt lft s: a in rr* **33/1**	PatSmullen 2	67
0201	**12**	*1*	**Fratellino**[7] 1033 5-9-5 92 (Alan McCabe) *prom: pushed along 1/2-way: sn rdn and wknd* **33/1**	(t) JimmyFortune 7	67
50-4	**13**	*2 1/4*	**Sos Brillante (CHI)**[29] 765 7-8-11 78 (Terry Clement) *a towards rr: outpcd and bhd fnl 2f* **150/1**	LiamJones 1	52
66-3	**14**	*6*	**Bannock (IRE)**[7] 1032 3-8-6 108 (Mark Johnston) *cl up on inner: rdn along wl over 2f out: sn wknd* **5/1**[2]	JoeFanning 14	36

1m 11.71s (-1.89) **Going Correction** +0.025s/f (Good)

WFA 3 from 4yo+ 13lb **14** Ran SP% **118.5**

Speed ratings (Par 111): **113,112,109,107,107 106,105,105,104,103 93,92,89,81**

toteswingers:1&2:£29.60, 1&3:£16.00, 2&3:£9.50 CSF £137.91 TOTE £11.50: £3.80, £3.60, £2.50; EX 92.10 Trifecta £555.40 Pool: £3,588.14 - 4.78 winning units..

Owner Anthony Pye-Jeary And Mel Smith **Bred** James Robert Mitchell **Trained** Blewbury, Oxon

FOCUS

A decent edition of this Listed race, which has gone to subsequent Group 1 winners La Cucaracha and Les Arcs since 2005. The pace was on the stands' side and the first three came out of the four highest-numbered stalls. Not many got involved and the form makes sense amongst the principals. The winner and third are rated to form with the second to his mark in this last year.

NOTEBOOK

The Cheka(IRE), soon chasing the pace after a slightly slow start, picked up inside the last to win a shade readily. A classy performer who avoided a penalty for his Group 3 win last May, he was just the pick on BHA figures. This was his first run over a sprint trip on his 20th racecourse appearance, and he is clearly well at home over a truly run 6f, which extends his options for the remainder of the season. (op 9-1)

Jimmy Styles, last year's winner, made a good fist of following up in what looked a better renewal of this race. Fit from a four-race Dubai campaign, he travelled well and took over entering the final furlong, but could not hold off the winner. This was a sound run, but he's not easy to place successfully. (tchd 11-1)

Mayson showed bright pace alongside the rail but had to give best at the furlong pole. This was an encouraging reappearance from this relatively lightly raced 4yo, who has made the frame in each of the five Listed races he's contested without managing to win one. He can put that right, perhaps on easier ground. (op 7-1)

Royal Rock, sixth in this last year, was penalised for a Group 3 win in the autumn. Running on late, he did best of those who came from off the pace and also of those drawn low. He should win a race or two again this year. (op 8-1)

Internationaldebut(IRE) was another to finish well on the unfavoured side having come here fully fit after running in Dubai. (tchd 16-1)

Boris Grigoriev(IRE), one of only two 3yos in the line-up, was the first off the bridle but stuck on for sixth. He was favourably drawn and may have been flattered. (tchd 66-1)

High Standing(USA), fitted with a new form of headgear, ran a respectable race on his debut for the yard. (tchd 33-1)

Sirius Prospect(USA) won his last four races of 2011, culminating in a victory over Mayson in this grade over C&D in November, and improved his official rating by 30lb during the year. After proving a little reluctant to enter the stalls, he failed to spark and was never seen with a chance, but he was running on when it was all over. Bated Breath, beaten favourite in this last year, went on to establish himself as a Group 1 horse, and Sirius Prospect may yet do likewise. He is well worth another chance. (tchd 2-1)

Waffle(IRE) did not get a clear run when trying to pick up heading towards the furlong pole but is not the type to make too many excuses for. (op 8-1)

Bannock(IRE) was a smart 2yo and fit from a run at Lingfield, but he ran poorly here from what looked a favourable berth against the stands' rail. (op 7-1)

1130 WILLIAM HILL LINCOLN (HERITAGE H'CAP) 1m (S)

3:15 (3:16) (Class 2) 4-Y-O+

£62,250 (£18,640; £9,320; £4,660; £2,330; £1,170) **Stalls** High

Form	Pos	Dist	Horse	Jockey	RPR
000-	**1**		**Brae Hill (IRE)**[210] 5699 6-9-1 **95** (Richard Fahey) *prom: led over 3f out: rdn over 2f out: kpt on u.p fnl f: jst hld on* **25/1**	TonyHamilton 12	104
35-1	**2**	*shd*	**Mull Of Killough (IRE)**[70] 254 6-9-2 **96** (Jane Chapple-Hyam) *hld up in tch: pushed along over 2f out: hdwy over 1f out: r.o strly fnl f: jst failed* **10/1**[3]	ShaneKelly 21	105+
540-	**3**	*1*	**Fury**[164] 6955 4-9-1 **98** (William Haggas) *midfield: pushed along wl over 2f out: hdwy over 1f out: drvn and kpt on wl fnl f: wnt 3rd post* **8/1**[2]	AdamBeschizza(3) 9	104
011-	**4**	*hd*	**Edinburgh Knight (IRE)**[129] 7516 5-9-10 **104** (Paul D'Arcy) *dwlt: hld up in tch: pushed along and hdwy over 2f out: chsd wnr over 1f out: kpt on: lost 3rd post* **11/1**	PatSmullen 2	110
452-	**5**	*2 1/4*	**Eton Forever (IRE)**[203] 5929 5-9-9 **103** (Roger Varian) *trckd ldrs: rdn over 2f out: ev ch appr fnl f: no ex fnl 100yds* **11/2**[1]	NeilCallan 7	104
156-	**6**	*1*	**Askaud (IRE)**[122] 7584 4-9-3 **97** (Scott Dixon) *hld up: rdn and hdwy 2f out: kpt on: nvr threatened ldrs* **40/1**	(p) IanMongan 1	96
430-	**7**	*hd*	**Barren Brook**[176] 6672 5-8-10 **90** (Michael Easterby) *dwlt: racd keenly hld up: hdwy over 2f out: kpt on one pce: nvr threatened ldrs* **20/1**	JamesSullivan 6	88
123-	**8**	*1/2*	**Stevie Thunder**[164] 6955 7-8-12 **95** (Ian Williams) *in tch: wnt prom 3f out: rdn over 2f out: no ex fnl f* **16/1**	RyanClark(3) 4	92
0-54	**9**	*1 3/4*	**Dubai Dynamo**[7] 1035 7-8-10 **90** (Ruth Carr) *s.i.s: racd keenly: hld up in midfield: rdn over 2f out: kpt on one pce* **33/1**	CathyGannon 16	83
0-60	**10**	*hd*	**Man Of Action (USA)**[44] 586 5-9-7 **101** (Saeed Bin Suroor) *sn pushed along towards rr: bhd tl late hdwy* **16/1**	(b1) RobertHavlin 20	93
040-	**11**	*1*	**Shavansky**[161] 7029 8-8-11 **91** (Rod Millman) *midfield: rdn over 2f out: sn one pce: nvr threatened ldrs* **25/1**	JamesMillman 11	81
301-	**12**	*shd*	**Don't Call Me (IRE)**[196] 6150 5-9-1 **95** (David Nicholls) *chsd ldrs: wknd over 1f out* **20/1**	(t) PaulQuinn 17	85
-343	**13**	*2 1/4*	**Start Right**[44] 587 5-9-7 **101** (Saeed Bin Suroor) *hld up: nvr threatened* **8/1**[2]	(v1) DaneO'Neill 18	86
30-0	**14**	*3/4*	**Pintura**[21] 868 5-9-5 **99** (David Simcock) *chsd ldrs: rdn 3f out: wknd over 1f out* **22/1**	JimmyFortune 13	82
33-6	**15**	*1 1/4*	**Field Of Dream**[71] 246 5-9-6 **100** (Jamie Osborne) *midfield: rdn over 3f out: sn no imp* **28/1**	PhillipMakin 5	80
-233	**16**	*2 3/4*	**Clockmaker (IRE)**[21] 866 6-9-2 **96** (Tim Easterby) *w ldr: rdn 3f out: sn wknd* **33/1**	DavidAllan 10	70
0146	**17**	*3/4*	**Amitola (IRE)**[21] 868 5-8-11 **91** (David Barron) *prom: rdn over 2f out: wknd over 1f out* **50/1**	LeeNewman 3	63
00-0	**18**	*1 3/4*	**Light From Mars**[21] 868 7-9-1 **95** (John Quinn) *midfield: rdn over 2f out: sn btn* **14/1**	TomEaves 19	63
120-	**19**	*3 3/4*	**Smarty Socks (IRE)**[161] 7023 8-9-8 **102** (David O'Meara) *hld up: nvr threatened* **20/1**	DanielTudhope 22	61
5-	**20**	*1/2*	**Cocozza (USA)**[222] 5332 4-9-5 **99** (Marco Botti) *awkward leaving stalls: racd keenly: sn led narrowly: hdd over 3f out: sn wknd* **14/1**	JoeFanning 15	57
-553	**21**	*5*	**Mia's Boy**[21] 868 8-9-2 **101** (Chris Dwyer) *midfield: pushed along 1/2-way: wknd over 2f out* **14/1**	RaulDaSilva(5) 14	48
0-00	**22**	*1 3/4*	**Lowther**[55] 315 7-9-3 **97** (David Nicholls) *chsd ldrs: wknd over 2f out* **40/1**	(b) AndrewMullen 8	40

1m 37.36s (-1.94) **Going Correction** +0.025s/f (Good) **22** Ran SP% **129.3**

Speed ratings (Par 109): **110,109,108,108,106 105,105,104,103,102 101,101,99,98,97 94,93,92,88,87 82,81**

toteswingers:1&2:£52.40, 1&3:£31.00, 2&3:£21.50 CSF £228.84 CT £2252.70 TOTE £34.10: £8.70, £3.40, £2.40, £2.90; EX 409.90 Trifecta £6795.00 Pool: £22,037.96 - 2.40 winning units..

Owner Dr Marwan Koukash **Bred** James Doyle **Trained** Musley Bank, N Yorks

■ Stewards' Enquiry : Tony Hamilton two-day ban: used whip above permitted level (Apr 14,16)

FOCUS

An up-to-scratch renewal of this historic race, although the bottomweights got in off a mark of 90, lower than for several years. As in the Spring Mile the field raced in one group down the centre of the track. There were no real hard-luck stories and the draw did not look to have a significant effect, with the winner drawn in the centre, the runner-up coming from 21, and the next half-dozen from single-figure stalls. The time was quick, over a second faster than the Spring Mile. Brae Hill bettered last year's effort in this race, the runner-up rates better than ever and the third was back to something like his best.

NOTEBOOK

Brae Hill(IRE), runner-up to Sweet Lightning 12 months ago and racing off the same mark here, went one better with a game success. Tracking the pace down the centre, he struck for home early enough and just held on. He lost his way after taking the Bunbury Cup at Newmarket under a brave ride last summer, but does go well fresh. It would be no surprise to see him aimed at something at the Chester May meeting. (tchd 22-1)

Mull Of Killough(IRE), who raced on the stands' side of the group, finished well and would have won in another stride. His rider felt that he would have got there if he'd had something to carry him into the race. A recent Lingfield winner, he had been third in this race two years ago off an identical mark when trained by Richard Fahey. (op 12-1)
Fury, last year's 2000 Guineas fifth, looked potentially very well treated off 98 on this handicap debut, but had plenty to prove after failing to beat a rival on his final three starts last term. Gelded during the winter, he was reported to have been working well by his trainer, who has landed this race three times. The grey travelled nicely and ran on after being switched to the far side of the pack, just lacking the pace to trouble the winner. The ground was quicker than ideal for him and he looks back to something like his best, well capable of making his mark in Listed company. (op 13-2 tchd 6-1)
Edinburgh Knight(IRE), racing from a career-high mark after successive wins at Ascot and Kempton (Listed race) in the autumn, had every chance but his big weight just told late on. He goes well fresh and looked to stay the mile well enough.
Eton Forever(IRE) took the Spring Mile a year ago and clearly likes the sort of test these big-field handicaps provide. Always well placed, he was in there fighting at the furlong pole but could not quite quicken up. While this was another solid effort, he has been held three times from this mark since his victory 12 months ago. (op 13-2)
Askaud(IRE), one of just two females in the race, was 10lb higher than when last in a handicap and made late progress towards the far side of the group. She won't mind a return to further. (op 33-1)
Barren Brook was staying on after a tardy start and remains generally progressive. He is ideally suited by a stiffer test. (tchd 22-1)
Stevie Thunder ran well but is currently operating from a career-high mark.
Dubai Dynamo was not discredited by any means and can race off a pound lower mark in future.
Man Of Action(USA), tried in a change of headgear, is by no means straightforward and was never nearer after being slow to break. (tchd 14-1)
Start Right, who was a pound well in, failed to figure in a first-time visor. (op 12-1)
Field Of Dream had reportedly been working well in Dubai and had some smart form for another trainer last year, but he ran a lacklustre race.
Light From Mars, last year's Newbury Spring Cup winner, is well handicapped on that form, but was unable to build on his Lincoln Trial effort.
Cocozza(USA) dropped away rather tamely after holding a slender lead towards the stands' side of the group. Formerly with John Oxx, he was having just the sixth run of his life and perhaps lacked experience at this stage of his career. He could have done with some cut in the ground too. (op 11-1)

1131 DOWNLOAD WILLIAM HILL FROM THE APP STORE BROCKLESBY CONDITIONS STKS 5f

3:50 (3:51) (Class 4) 2-Y-O **£6,469** (£1,925; £962; £481) **Stalls** High

Form				RPR
1		**My Boy Bill** 2-8-11 0 ... PaddyAspell 10	78+
		(Michael Easterby) *dwlt and hld up in rr: bhd after 2f: hdwy 2f out: swtchd lft over 1f out: str run ent fnl f: led nr fin* **7/1**
2	½	**Well Acquainted (IRE)** 2-8-11 0 ... JohnFahy 1	76+
		(Clive Cox) *hld up: gd hdwy on outer wl over 1f out: rdn to ld ins fnl f: hdd and no ex nr fin* **12/1**
3	nk	**Mayfield Girl (IRE)** 2-8-6 0 ... DuranFentiman 9	70+
		(Mel Brittain) *dwlt: sn chsng ldrs: hdwy to ld over 1f out: rdn and hdd ins fnl f: kpt on* **33/1**
4	2¼	**Just Past Andover (IRE)** 2-8-11 0 ... DaneO'Neill 12	67
		(Bill Turner) *slt ld on stands' rail: rdn and hdd wl over 1f out: kpt on same pce* **6/1**[3]
5	nk	**Lucky Lodge** 2-8-11 0 ... DavidAllan 5	66
		(Mel Brittain) *chsd ldrs: rdn along 2f out: kpt on same pce* **40/1**
6	¾	**Perfect Words (IRE)** 2-8-11 0 ... ChrisCatlin 8	63
		(Mick Channon) *midfield: effrt over 2f out: sn rdn and kpt on same pce* **18/1**
7	1	**Lady Poppy** 2-8-6 0 ... AndrewMullen 6	55
		(George Moore) *cl up: rdn along over 2f out: grad wknd* **9/1**
8	2½	**Heavy Metal** 2-8-11 0 ... JoeFanning 3	51
		(Mark Johnston) *prom: rdn along over 2f out: sn wknd* **5/1**[2]
9	2½	**Emperor's Daughter** 2-8-7 0 ow1 ... ShaneKelly 11	38
		(Tim Pitt) *dwlt: a towards rr* **33/1**
10	2¾	**Maypole Joe (IRE)** 2-8-11 0 ... CathyGannon 7	32
		(David Evans) *towards rr: rdn along bef 1/2-way: nvr a factor* **14/1**
11	1	**Marvelino** 2-8-8 0 ... RyanClark(3) 4	28
		(Pat Eddery) *cl up: rdn over 2f out: sn wknd* **11/4**[1]
12	2¾	**Deepest Blue** 2-8-11 0 ... PhillipMakin 2	18
		(Jamie Osborne) *a towards rr* **8/1**

1m 0.14s (-0.36) **Going Correction** +0.025s/f (Good) **12 Ran SP% 119.2**
Speed ratings (Par 94): **103,102,101,98,97 96,94,90,86,82 80,76**
toteswingers:1&2:£19.60, 1&3:£66.80, 2&3:£39.70 CSF £87.18 TOTE £8.90: £2.90, £4.00, £7.70; EX 98.50 Trifecta £1338.60 Pool: £2,424.08 - 1.34 winning units..
Owner Mrs L Ward **Bred** Cheveley Park Stud Ltd **Trained** Sheriff Hutton, N Yorks

FOCUS
The first 2yo race on turf of the new season and some notable efforts, not least from the winner, whilst there should be races to be won with some those in behind. The pace was strong but this was probably an ordinary renewal.

NOTEBOOK
My Boy Bill ◆ is an already-gelded 65,000gns half-brother to five winners including the Lincoln winner Penitent, but although well backed beforehand his supporters must have been concerned to see him miss the break and then race in a detached last until halfway. His rider switched him out wide over a furlong out. He still had plenty to do then, but just took off to grab the front pair close to the line and won a little cheekily. As a February foal he may have been a bit more forward than a few of his rivals, but this was still a taking debut and he should get another furlong in due course. (op 10-1)
Well Acquainted(IRE) ◆ ran a debut full of promise, especially as he proved friendless in the market. Having worked hard to nail the leader inside the last 20 yards, he was unfortunate to find the winner nailing them both close to the line. A 30,000GBP yearling out of a winner at up to 1m3f in Canada, he was the oldest in the field being a January foal, but this trip would have been sharp enough on pedigree and he should go one better eventually. (op 8-1 tchd 14-1)
Mayfield Girl(IRE) ◆, a 10,500gns half-sister to five winners at up to 1m2f, missed the break but was soon up there amongst the leaders and looked the likely winner after hitting the front over a furlong out, but she was cut down by the front pair close to the line. She should find a race. (op 25-1)
Just Past Andover(IRE), a 9,500GBP colt out of a winner at up to 7f, represented the yard responsible for four of the last ten winners of this race. He showed good speed under the stands' rail throughout and looks to have a future. (op 5-1)
Lucky Lodge, a stablemate of the third though retained for just 2,000GBP as a yearling, is a half-brother to a 6f winner out of a 5f winner. He also showed definite signs of promise on this debut. (op 25-1)
Perfect Words(IRE), retained for 6,000euros as a yearling, is a half-brother to three winners including one over hurdles. This late-April foal was just about the youngest in the field and was off the bridle at halfway, but he is entitled to have benefited from the experience. (op 16-1)
Heavy Metal, first foal of a Grade 1 winning sprinter in South Africa, attracted market support and raced prominently early, but faded disappointingly over a furlong from home. (op 8-1)
Marvelino, a 13,000GBP half-brother to two winning sprinters, represented the yard responsible for one of the better recent winners of this race in Hearts Of Fire, but having shown decent early speed the way he stopped so quickly was worrying. (op 3-1)

1132 HARRIET POWELL MAIDEN STKS 1m 2f 60y

4:20 (4:20) (Class 5) 3-Y-O **£2,911** (£866; £432; £216) **Stalls** Low

Form				RPR
2-2	1		**Zaina (IRE)**[49] [533] 3-8-12 0 ... DaneO'Neill 2	86
		(Gerard Butler) *midfield: pushed along and hdwy over 2f out: led appr fnl f: kpt on wl* **14/1**
2	1¼	**Minimise Risk** 3-9-3 0 ... JimmyFortune 13	90+
		(Andrew Balding) *midfield: hdwy over 3f out: rdn 2f out: cl up whn short of room appr fnl f: kpt on wl but nt rch wnr* **9/1**
25-	3	5	**Lelaps (USA)**[150] [7233] 3-9-3 0 ... NeilCallan 12	79
		(Marco Botti) *prom: led over 3f out: sn rdn: hdd appr fnl f: edgd rt: no ex* **10/1**
62-	4	hd	**Theturnofthesun (IRE)**[174] [6726] 3-9-3 0 ... RobertHavlin 9	78
		(John Gosden) *in tch: pushed along over 3f out: kpt on one pce* **5/1**[3]
5	2¼	**Last Shadow** 3-9-3 0 ... PhillipMakin 3	74
		(William Muir) *hld up: pushed along over 2f out: kpt on over 1f out: nrst fin* **50/1**
26-	6	1	**Kaafel (IRE)**[172] [6768] 3-9-3 0 ... RobertWinston 11	72
		(Charles Hills) *trckd ldrs: rdn 3f out: ev ch over 1f out: wknd fnl f* **3/1**[2]
7	¾	**Falkland (IRE)** 3-9-3 0 ... NickyMackay 10	70
		(John Gosden) *hld up: hdwy on outer 3f out: kpt on one pce over 1f out* **8/1**
42-	8	8	**Sir Graham Wade (IRE)**[180] [6572] 3-9-3 0 ... JoeFanning 7	54
		(Mark Johnston) *led: hdd over 3f out: wknd over 1f out* **9/4**[1]
0-	9	2¾	**Mr Snoozy**[253] [4292] 3-9-3 0 ... GrahamGibbons 4	49
		(Tim Walford) *in tch: rdn over 3f out: wknd over 2f out* **33/1**
0-0	10	2¼	**Medlaur**[46] [552] 3-8-12 0 ... PaulMulrennan 8	39
		(James Given) *hld up: n.d* **150/1**
5-0	11	11	**Johanna Fosie (IRE)**[28] [784] 3-8-12 0 ... ChrisCatlin 5	17
		(Mick Channon) *hld up: a towards rr* **50/1**
330-	12	8	**Sehnsucht (IRE)**[266] [3861] 3-9-3 77 ... ShaneKelly 1
		(Alan McCabe) *hld up in midfield: wknd over 3f out* **20/1**
13	1¼	**Razzle Dazzle 'Em** 3-8-12 0 ... DuilioDaSilva(5) 6
		(Shaun Harris) *midfield: wknd over 3f out* **80/1**

2m 10.47s (1.07) **Going Correction** +0.075s/f (Good) **13 Ran SP% 122.8**
Speed ratings (Par 98): **98,97,93,92,91 90,89,83,81,79 70,64,63**
toteswingers:1&2:£12.70, 1&3:£12.30, 2&3:£15.70 CSF £132.26 TOTE £16.50: £4.00, £2.60, £3.50; EX 103.50 Trifecta £1795.40 Part won. Pool: £2,426.24 - 0.62 winning units..
Owner Asaad Al Banwan **Bred** Miss J Murphy **Trained** Newmarket, Suffolk

FOCUS
Probably just a fair maiden overall, but winners should emerge from it. The first two pulled clear late on and there's a chance their form is worth a bit more. The time was not bad compared with the later handicaps.
Sehnsucht(IRE) Official explanation: jockey said colt never travelled

1133 WILLIAM HILL APP - DOWNLOAD TODAY! H'CAP (DIV I) 1m 2f 60y

4:55 (4:56) (Class 4) (0-85,85) 4-Y-O+ **£5,175** (£1,540; £769; £384) **Stalls** Low

Form				RPR
0-1	1		**Qaraaba**[10] [987] 5-9-3 **81** ... DaneO'Neill 2	93
		(Seamus Durack) *hld up towards rr: stdy hdwy over 3f out: trckd ldrs on bit 2f out: rdn and qckd to ld jst ins fnl f: comf* **4/1**[1]
0-31	2	1½	**Reachforthebucks**[47] [548] 4-9-4 **82** ... ShaneKelly 4	91
		(Jane Chapple-Hyam) *hld up towards rr: stdy hdwy 4f out: rdn to chse ldrs 2f out: chal appr fnl f and ev ch tl drvn and one pce ins fnl f* **5/1**[2]
-521	3	1¾	**Knowe Head (NZ)**[36] [694] 5-8-9 **73** ... LiamJones 17	79
		(James Unett) *hld up: stdy hdwy over 4f out: chal 2f out: rdn and led briefly appr fnl f: sn hdd and one pce* **25/1**
000-	4	nk	**Embsay Crag**[14] [6773] 6-8-7 **71** oh3 ... CathyGannon 9	76
		(Kate Walton) *hld up in rr: hdwy on wd outside over 2f out: sn rdn and styd on fnl f: nrst fin* **12/1**
1-	5	shd	**The Fun Crusher**[336] [1692] 4-9-2 **80** ... DavidAllan 11	85
		(Tim Easterby) *hld up towards rr: hdwy over 3f out: rdn wl over 1f out: kpt on fnl f: nrst fin* **11/1**[3]
4200	6	¾	**Veroon (IRE)**[16] [907] 6-9-1 **79** ... (p) PaulMulrennan 13	83
		(James Given) *hld up: hdwy 1/2-way: trckd ldrs 3f out: effrt and rt clr run 2f out: sn swtchd rt and rdn: styng on whn nt clr run over 1f out: no imp after* **20/1**
510-	7	1¾	**Landaman (IRE)**[178] [6632] 4-9-4 **82** ... JoeFanning 6	82
		(Mark Johnston) *in tch: hdwy to trck ldrs 1/2-way: effrt 3f out: rdn to ld 2f out: hdd appr fnl f and sn wknd* **4/1**[1]
222-	8	7	**Yojimbo (IRE)**[159] [7050] 4-9-5 **83** ... ChrisCatlin 10	70
		(Mick Channon) *trckd ldr: cl up 4f out: led 3f out: sn rdn and hdd 2f out: grad wknd* **11/1**[3]
5-64	9	1	**Gritstone**[16] [907] 5-8-12 **79** ... LeeTopliss(3) 8	64
		(Richard Fahey) *in tch: rdn along over 3f out: sn no imp* **12/1**
3P0/	10	½	**Kaolak (USA)**[44] [3633] 6-9-7 **85** ... DanielTudhope 14	69
		(Jim Goldie) *trckd ldng pair: effrt over 3f out: sn rdn and wknd* **16/1**
610-	11	4½	**Imaginary World (IRE)**[188] [6383] 4-9-0 **78** ... (be) RobertWinston 7	54
		(Alan McCabe) *a towards rr* **16/1**
1-02	12	1¾	**Maven**[18] [888] 4-8-8 **72** ... DuranFentiman 5	44
		(Tim Easterby) *trckd ldrs on inner: hdwy 4f out: cl up 3f out: sn rdn and wknd fnl 2f* **20/1**
325-	13	1½	**Beat Of The Blues**[120] [7600] 4-8-6 **77** ... JackDuern(7) 12	47
		(Michael Appleby) *s.i.s: sn chsng ldrs: rdn along 1/2-way and sn wknd* **33/1**
11/4	14	9	**City Ground (USA)**[8] [501] 5-8-7 **78** ... DavidSimmonson(7) 1	31
		(Michael Easterby) *led: rdn along 1/2-way: hdd 4f out: wknd wl over 2f out* **20/1**
540-	15	3½	**Ailsa Craig (IRE)**[175] [6708] 6-8-11 **75** ... TonyHamilton 16	21
		(Edwin Tuer) *trckd ldrs: hdwy on outer and cl up 1/2-way: sn rdn and wknd 4f out* **25/1**
040/	16	59	**Indian Ocean (IRE)**[1253] [6973] 6-9-7 **85** ... TomEaves 15
		(Brian Rothwell) *a in rr: t.o fnl 3f* **33/1**

2m 9.39s (-0.01) **Going Correction** +0.075s/f (Good) **16 Ran SP% 128.3**
Speed ratings (Par 105): **103,101,100,100,100 99,98,92,91,91 87,86,85,77,75 27**
toteswingers:1&2:£4.30, 1&3:£26.60, 2&3:£23.70 CSF £21.79 CT £463.00 TOTE £4.30: £1.40, £1.80, £7.60, £3.10; EX 24.60 Trifecta £930.90 Pool: £1,937.39 - 1.54 winning units..
Owner P A Deal **Bred** Shadwell Estate Company Limited **Trained** Baydon, Wilts

FOCUS
A decent handicap, but the prominent racers may have done too much early as none of the leading bunch figured in the finish. It looked a better race than division II despite being slightly slower. Improvement from the first two.

Beat Of The Blues Official explanation: jockey said gelding stumbled on bend turning into straight

1134 WILLIAM HILL APP - DOWNLOAD TODAY! H'CAP (DIV II) 1m 2f 60y
5:30 (5:30) (Class 4) (0-85,85) 4-Y-0+ **£5,175** (£1,540; £769; £384) **Stalls** Low

Form RPR

-200 **1** **West End Lad**[16] 907 9-8-13 **77**.............................(b) RussKennemore 9 88
(Roy Bowring) *swtchd lft s: hld up in rr: pushed along over 2f out: gd hdwy over 1f out: led ins fnl f: sn clr* **33/1**

24-0 **2** 4 1/2 **Calaf**[16] 907 4-9-1 **79**.. TonyHamilton 5 81
(Richard Fahey) *in tch: rdn over 2f out: led over 1f out: hdd ins fnl f: no ch w wnr* **10/1**

33-1 **3** nk **Alfred Hutchinson**[68] 273 4-8-8 **75**........................ DaleSwift(3) 10 77
(Geoffrey Oldroyd) *hld up in midfield: pushed along and rapid hdwy on outer over 2f out: kpt on one pce over 1f out* **8/1**

660- **4** 3/4 **Mcbirney (USA)**[163] 6976 5-9-0 **78**........................... NeilCallan 11 78
(Paul D'Arcy) *midfield: hdwy 3f out: rdn over 1f out: kpt on ins fnl f* **13/2**[2]

0-21 **5** 1 1/2 **Dunhoy (IRE)**[31] 733 4-9-4 **82**.............................. DaneO'Neill 7 80
(Tony Newcombe) *hld up in midfield: hdwy over 2f out: sn rdn: kpt on* **4/1**[1]

130- **6** nk **Judicious**[162] 6989 5-9-1 **79**.............................. RobertWinston 14 76+
(Geoffrey Harker) *hld up in rr: on bridle whn swtchd to inner over 2f out: stl on bit whn swtchd to outer 1f out: r.o: nvr nrr: lame* **14/1**

510- **7** 1/2 **Jonny Lesters Hair (IRE)**[182] 6533 7-9-7 **85**.................. DavidAllan 12 81
(Tim Easterby) *led: rdn whn hdd over 1f out: no ex* **14/1**

6212 **8** 3 **Standpoint**[16] 907 6-8-11 **82**...............................(p) JackDuern(7) 6 72
(Reg Hollinshead) *midfield: pushed along over 3f out: wknd over 1f out* **14/1**

304- **9** 3 1/4 **Good Boy Jackson**[175] 6708 4-9-3 **81**........................ PhillipMakin 4 65
(Kevin Ryan) *prom: rdn over 3f out: wknd over 2f out* **7/1**[3]

10-3 **10** 1 **Dr Red Eye**[10] 987 4-8-5 **72**................................ BillyCray(3) 15 54
(Scott Dixon) *in tch: rdn over 3f out: sn no imp* **14/1**

040- **11** 1/2 **Souter Point (USA)**[215] 4423 6-8-13 **77**..................... AndrewMullen 1 58
(Peter Salmon) *in tch on inner: pushed along over 3f out: wknd over 1f out* **50/1**

530- **12** 11 **Tres Coronas (IRE)**[171] 6803 5-9-7 **85**........................ LeeNewman 8 45
(David Barron) *midfield: rdn over 3f out: sn wknd* **9/1**

200- **13** 1/2 **Amazing Blue Sky**[138] 7413 6-8-10 **74**........................ JamesSullivan 2 34
(Ruth Carr) *prom: rdn over 3f out: sn wknd* **25/1**

164- **14** 1 3/4 **Hail Bold Chief (USA)**[198] 6078 5-8-7 **71** oh1.................. TomEaves 16 27
(Alan Swinbank) *hld up: nvr threatened* **20/1**

641- **15** 6 **Tiger Webb**[151] 7214 4-9-4 **82**.............................. PaulMulrennan 3 27
(Michael Easterby) *trckd ldrs: wknd qckly over 3f out* **16/1**

066- **16** 147 **Audacious**[233] 4959 4-9-2 **80**............................... JimmyFortune 13
(Michael Quinn) *midfield: rdn over 4f out: sn btn: eased* **28/1**

2m 8.6s (-0.80) **Going Correction** +0.075s/f (Good) **16** Ran SP% **125.5**
Speed ratings (Par 105): **106,102,102,101,100 100,99,97,94,93 93,84,84,82,78**
toteswingers:1&2:£49.10, 1&3:£49.10, 2&3:£17.10 CSF £331.00 CT £2927.55 TOTE £46.60: £6.50, £3.70, £3.00, £1.80; EX 920.50 TRIFECTA Not won..
Owner K Nicholls **Bred** Keith Nicholls **Trained** Edwinstowe, Notts

FOCUS
No more than a fair handicap, run at a decent gallop and in a time 0.79 seconds quicker than the previous division. There was a shortage of unexposed or progressive types and the form is ordinary. The winner looks better than ever at the age of nine.
Judicious ◆ Official explanation: jockey said, regarding running and riding, that his orders were to drop in from a wide draw, get the gelding settled and try to get a run in the straight, it was unhappy on what he felt was loose ground and he was denied a clear run in the straight; vet said gelding returned lame.
Dr Red Eye Official explanation: trainer said gelding was unsuited by the good ground

1135 UNIVERSALRECYCLINGCOMPANY.CO.UK APPRENTICE H'CAP 1m 2f 60y
6:05 (6:08) (Class 5) (0-70,70) 4-Y-0+ **£2,911** (£866; £432; £216) **Stalls** Low

Form RPR

34-4 **1** **Zafranagar (IRE)**[8] 1003 7-9-1 **69**........................ GeorgeDowning(5) 17 80
(Tony Carroll) *hld up towards rr: gd hdwy over 3f out: chal wl over 1f out: sn rdn and styd on to ld last 100yds* **10/1**

3553 **2** 1 **Follow The Flag (IRE)**[25] 812 8-8-13 **67**...............(be) NoraLooby(5) 16 77
(Alan McCabe) *hld up in tch: gd hdwy over 3f out: led wl over 2f out: rdn and edgd rt wl over 1f out: sn jnd and drvn: hdd and no ex last 100yds* **12/1**

306- **3** 5 **Cottam Donny**[166] 6918 4-8-8 **62**.............................. JasonHart(5) 6 62
(Mel Brittain) *in tch: hdwy 4f out: rdn to chse ldrs over 2f out: drvn to chse ldng pair and edgd lft ent fnl f: sn one pce* **9/1**

004- **4** nk **Veiled Applause**[166] 6918 9-9-2 **70**............................ KevinLundie(5) 5 69
(John Quinn) *hld up towards rr: hdwy 3f out: rdn to chse ldrs 2f out: kpt on fnl f: nrst fin* **6/1**[1]

-004 **5** 3 1/4 **Yorksters Prince (IRE)**[15] 922 5-9-2 **70**...........(b) JacobButterfield(5) 1 63
(Tony Coyle) *trckd ldrs: hdwy over 3f out: rdn to chse ldr over 2f out: sn rdn and wkng whn sltly hmpd ent fnl f* **8/1**[3]

400- **6** nk **Tribal Myth (IRE)**[144] 6093 5-8-12 **68**........................ PaulMcGiff(7) 14 61
(Kevin Ryan) *hld up: hdwy over 4f out: chsd ldrs over 2f out: sn rdn and kpt on same pce* **28/1**

230- **7** 3 1/4 **Sartingo (IRE)**[192] 6263 5-9-4 **67**............................ GarryWhillans 2 54
(Alan Swinbank) *hld up: hdwy over 3f out: rdn to chse ldrs 2f out: sn no imp* **15/2**[2]

060- **8** 1 **Pertuis (IRE)**[39] 3042 6-9-0 **70**............................. KatieDowson(7) 8 55
(Micky Hammond) *a towards rr* **25/1**

200- **9** 3/4 **Sharp Sovereign (USA)**[138] 7413 6-9-0 **66**........... JustinNewman(3) 12 49
(Ian McInnes) *prom: rdn along over 4f out and sn wknd* **25/1**

26-1 **10** hd **One Of Twins**[15] 929 4-8-6 **60**........................... DavidSimmonson(5) 3 43
(Michael Easterby) *led 2f: chsd ldr: rdn along over 3f out and sn wknd* **9/1**

-533 **11** 4 **Potentiale (IRE)**[24] 826 8-8-7 **63**......................(v) Leah-AnneAvery(7) 15 38
(J W Hills) *hld up: hdwy 3f out: rdn over 2f out: n.d* **11/1**

520- **12** 3 **Hits Only Jude (IRE)**[94] 7901 9-8-1 **57**..................... MichaelKenny(7) 10 27
(Declan Carroll) *nvr nr ldrs* **33/1**

15-2 **13** 5 **Dialogue**[14] 941 6-8-11 **67**................................ JordanNason(7) 7 27
(David Nicholls) *nvr a factor* **8/1**[3]

3131 **14** 10 **Trans Sonic**[11] 976 9-9-6 **69**.............................(p) ShaneBKelly 18 10
(David O'Meara) *chsd ldrs: led after 2f and sn clr: rdn along 4f out: hdd wl over 2f out and sn wknd* **10/1**

2645 **15** 7 **Absolute Princess**[9] 1002 4-8-4 **56** oh4..................(p) DannyBrock(3) 19
(Scott Dixon) *a towards rr: bhd fnl 3f* **25/1**

6464 **16** 44 **Piceno (IRE)**[17] 899 4-9-7 **70**............................... RaulDaSilva 13
(Scott Dixon) *prom: rdn along over 4f out: sn lost pl and bhd* **16/1**

2m 10.75s (1.35) **Going Correction** +0.075s/f (Good) **16** Ran SP% **126.3**
Speed ratings (Par 103): **97,96,92,91,89 89,86,85,85,84 81,79,75,67,61 26**
toteswingers:1&2:£41.50, 1&3:£21.00, 2&3:£49.00 CSF £121.22 CT £1144.15 TOTE £11.40: £2.80, £3.80, £3.00, £2.20; EX 143.10 TRIFECTA Not won..
Owner Paul Downing **Bred** His Highness The Aga Khan's Studs S C **Trained** Cropthorne, Worcs

FOCUS
A competitive race for this apprentice handicap, but the form looks ordinary. The winner's best run since coming to Britain. They went a decent pace early.
T/Jkpt: Not won. T/Plt: £3,911.60 to a £1 stake. Pool:£215,139.56 - 40.15 winning tickets T/Qpdt: £228.40 to a £1 stake. Pool:£11,954.58 - 38.73 winning tickets AS

1082 KEMPTON (A.W) (R-H)
Saturday, March 31

OFFICIAL GOING: Standard
Wind: Fresh, against Weather: Cloudy

1136 WILLIAMHILL.COM MAIDEN FILLIES' STKS 5f (P)
1:50 (1:51) (Class 5) 2-Y-0 **£2,911** (£866; £432; £216) **Stalls** Low

Form RPR

1 **Woodland Mill (IRE)** 2-9-0 0.................................... PaulHanagan 5 71+
(Richard Fahey) *trckd ldng trio: pushed along and prog to ld jst over 1f out: wl in command fnl f* **5/1**[3]

2 1 3/4 **Ceiling Kitty** 2-9-0 0...................................... RichardKingscote 9 66+
(Tom Dascombe) *slowly away: sn rchd midfield: 7th 1/2-way: rdn and prog over 1f out: styd on wl to take 2nd last strides* **11/4**[1]

3 hd **Poetic Princess** 2-9-0 0....................................... TonyCulhane 8 63
(Jo Hughes) *chsd ldrs: 6th 1/2-way: rdn and prog over 1f out: chsd wnr ins fnl f: kpt on but lost 2nd last strides* **25/1**

4 3/4 **Red Star Lady (IRE)** 2-9-0 0.................................. MartinHarley 6 60
(Mrs K Burke) *pressed ldng pair: v wd bnd 2f out: nt qckn over 1f out: one pce after* **7/2**[2]

5 1 1/4 **Bheleyf (IRE)** 2-9-0 0.. LukeMorris 4 56
(Joseph Tuite) *mde most: wd bnd 2f out: hdd jst over 1f out: wknd fnl f* **10/1**

6 1 1/2 **Sally Bruce** 2-8-7 0...................................... JenniferFerguson(7) 12 50+
(Olivia Maylam) *racd wd early fr outside draw: towards rr: 8th 1/2-way: shkn up and kpt on fr over 1f out* **100/1**

7 hd **Dreamy Ciara** 2-9-0 0.. PadraigBeggy 11 50+
(David Evans) *rousted along in 9th after 2f and struggling to stay in tch: kpt on fr over 1f out* **16/1**

8 3/4 **Relay** 2-9-0 0.. KieranO'Neill 1 47
(Richard Hannon) *plenty of tail-swishing: urged along to press ldr: wknd jst over 1f out* **13/2**

9 1/2 **Cherryred Girl (IRE)** 2-9-0 0.................................... LiamKeniry 3 45
(J S Moore) *s.i.s: rcvrd to chse ldrs and 5th 1/2-way: pushed along and fdd over 1f out* **20/1**

10 6 **Vanessa** 2-9-0 0.. FrannyNorton 10 24
(Mick Channon) *hmpd after 1f: v wd bnd sn after: bhd rest of way* **11/1**

11 8 **Lively Little Lady** 2-8-9 0............................... MatthewLawson(5) 7
(Mrs A Corson, Jersey) *slowly away: a in rr: t.o* **25/1**

1m 1.29s (0.79) **Going Correction** -0.075s/f (Stan) **11** Ran SP% **115.6**
Speed ratings (Par 89): **90,87,86,85,83 81,80,79,78,69 56**
toteswingers:1&2:£3.40, 1&3:£16.20, 2&3:£15.00 CSF £17.98 TOTE £5.60: £1.80, £1.40, £6.20; EX 20.70 Trifecta £434.10 Part won. Pool: £586.69 - 0.62 winning units..
Owner Peter Timmins **Bred** Mrs Sandra McCarthy **Trained** Musley Bank, N Yorks

FOCUS
The first two-year-old race of the season, confined to fillies this year, and most likely just fair form given the pedigrees of the horses involved. The field were soon strung out more on account of collective inexperience than a strong gallop, but finished compressed in a modest time. The winner will have more to offer.

NOTEBOOK
Woodland Mill(IRE), the most costly among the field at £20,000Y, is bred to be speedy, being a sister to 2-y-o 6f winner What About You as well as two other winners out of a 5f/6f winner. She was always travelling well close up on the rail and asserted readily under little more than a strong drive to win comfortably despite edging left. She clearly knew her job well but is entitled to improve. (op 4-1)
Ceiling Kitty ◆, a half-sister to her stable's 2011 2-y-o 5f winner Van Go Go, shaped well after fluffing the start and showed enough to think she can win an early-season maiden. She might have struggled to beat the winner even with a prompt break, but she's better than the distance back to the rest might suggest and will surely have learnt plenty. (op 3-1 tchd 4-1)
Poetic Princess, a very cheaply-bought half-sister to the modest handicapper Bentley, shaped well without ever really threatening to land a blow and given her purchase price is going to be more favourably treated in maiden auctions.
Red Star Lady(IRE), the fourth foal of a sprinting half-sister to top miler Dick Turpin, was well backed and showed plenty of speed. She's a bit better than this seeing as she was forced wide by the eventual fifth, and is another whose sales price will get her into weaker maidens than this. (op 6-1 tchd 10-3)
Bheleyf(IRE) is out of a maiden that stayed 1m2f but she didn't look short of speed herself, for all she rather spoiled her effort by hanging and looking a tricky ride on the home turn. (op 8-1)
Sally Bruce, who is out of a half-sister to the Middle Park runner-up Holborn, never really threatened.
Dreamy Ciara, a half-sister to 1m/1m2f handicapper Ridgeway Jazz, looked greener than most of her stable's youngsters do first time and was soon in a very poor position. The penny dropped late on, however, and she'll likely be a different proposition next time. (op 25-1)
Relay was weak the market and this half-sister to two winners faded after disputing the early lead on the rail. (op 9-2)

1137 WILLIAM HILL APP-DOWNLOAD TODAY! MAGNOLIA STKS (LISTED RACE) 1m 2f (P)
2:20 (2:21) (Class 1) 4-Y-0+
£18,714 (£7,095; £3,550; £1,768; £887; £445) **Stalls** Low

Form RPR

/24- **1** **Arctic Cosmos (USA)**[167] 6910 5-8-13 **110**................(p) WilliamBuick 3 113+
(John Gosden) *mde all: wound it up fr 4f out: stretched clr over 2f out: in n.d after: eased nr fin* **5/4**[1]

-422 **2** 6 **Tinshu (IRE)**[35] 712 6-8-11 **93**.............................(p) FergusSweeney 4 99
(Derek Haydn Jones) *hld up last: prog over 3f out but outpcd: styd on to take 2nd jst ins fnl f: no ch w wnr* **8/1**

046- **3** 1 3/4 **Hurricane Higgins (IRE)**[249] 4411 4-8-13 **101**................ FrannyNorton 6 98
(Mark Johnston) *in tch: outpcd and rdn over 3f out: struggling after: styd on fr over 1f out to take 3rd last stride* **10/3**[2]

0-24 **4** *hd* **King's Trail (JPN)**[35] 712 10-8-13 92 .... SebSanders 1 97
(Takashi Kodama, Ire) *t.k.h: cl up: chsd wnr 1/2-way: outpcd fr 3f out: no ch after: lost pl ins fnl f* **20/1**

433/ **5** *9* **Fair Trade**[547] 6529 5-8-13 0 .... PaulHanagan 2 79
(Hughie Morrison) *plld v hrd: mostly chsd wnr to 1/2-way: struggling over 3f out: wknd* **7/2**[3]

-336 **6** *1 1/4* **Mr Willis**[28] 785 6-8-13 92 .... MarcHalford 5 77
(Terry Clement) *in tch: outpcd and rdn over 3f out: wknd wl over 1f out* **25/1**

2m 4.15s (-3.85) **Going Correction** -0.075s/f (Stan) **6** Ran SP% **109.5**
Speed ratings (Par 111): **112,107,105,105,98 97**
toteswingers:1&2:£1.80, 1&3:£1.60, 2&3:£2.90 CSF £11.51 TOTE £1.80: £1.10, £3.20; EX 6.40.
Owner Rachel Hood and RJH Geffen **Bred** Sheridan & Iadora Farm **Trained** Newmarket, Suffolk

FOCUS
An uncompetitive Listed race which revolved around whether former St Leger winner Arctic Cosmos would be found out by the trip. He wasn't, and the race turned into something of a non-event. He only needed to repeat last year's form.

NOTEBOOK
Arctic Cosmos(USA) was tackling a shorter-than-ideal trip on his seasonal reappearance. He had run well forcing the pace on his first run of the season last year in the Cumberland Lodge Stakes and in the absence of any regular front runner here his rider sensibly took him to the front on a a track that by and large works against those held up. The race was good as over once he stepped up the gallop leaving the far straight and he cantered past the post with as much in hand as his best form entitled him to have. He's still lightly raced for one of his age and seems certain to win another pattern race or two before long with perhaps the Yorkshire Cup the most appealing spring objective, though his trainer is probably more mindful of prize money than prestige and probably has a bigger North American target in mind later on. (op Evens tchd 11-8)
Tinshu(IRE) continues in good form and second place here was some consolation for being eliminated from the Winter Derby, but she was never in the same league as the winner and it's doubtful second place represents improved form given she'd finished a similar distance ahead of King's Trail last time (op 7-1 tchd 13-2)
Hurricane Higgins(IRE) had been gelded since 2011 when he'd started to look temperamental in good company over 1m4f, but the fact he'd won first time out before made him of interest after his long break. He ran in snatches, however, consenting to stay on late only when the race was over and though this trip is in the sharp side for him too he remains one to tread warily with. (op 9-2)
King's Trail(JPN) didn't adopt the front-running tactic he had last time but didn't seem any less effective for it and this is probably as good as he is. (op 16-1)
Fair Trade still looks the quirky hard-pulling underachiever he was for David Elsworth when last seen in 2010. Being gelded since then doesn't look to have settled him down at all and he was a spent force a long way from home, albeit at a trip he has still to prove himself at. Official explanation: jockey said gelding ran too free (op 9-2)
Mr Willis has had his limitations exposed off a mark of 93 in handicaps this year but even so ran no sort of race.

1138 WILLIAM HILL-THE HOME OF BETTING MAIDEN STKS 7f (P)
2:55 (2:55) (Class 5) 3-Y-0+ £2,911 (£866; £432; £216) Stalls Low

Form RPR

222- **1** **Glen Moss (IRE)**[180] 6579 3-8-13 81 .... PaulHanagan 2 88
(Charles Hills) *t.k.h: trckd ldng pair: rdn to ld on inner over 1f out: clr fnl f: pushed out* **6/1**[3]

4- **2** *3 1/4* **Bartolomeu**[268] 3755 3-8-13 0 .... AndreaAtzeni 3 79
(Marco Botti) *free to post: trckd ldrs: rdn in cl 4th 2f out: styd on to take 2nd last 140yds: no ch w wnr* **11/10**[1]

3 *3/4* **Trade Commissioner (IRE)** 4-10-0 0 .... WilliamBuick 6 77+
(John Gosden) *s.i.s: prog fr last trio to go 5th 2f out but nt on terms: shkn up over 1f out: styd on wl to take 3rd nr fin* **12/1**

034- **4** *1 1/4* **Impel (IRE)**[156] 7126 3-8-10 76 .... SeanLevey(3) 10 74
(Richard Hannon) *trckd ldr: chal over 2f out: upsides over 1f out: fdd fnl f* **4/1**[2]

3 **5** *4 1/2* **Choice Words (USA)**[11] 969 4-10-0 0 .... MickyFenton 7 67
(Emma Lavelle) *led to over 1f out: wknd fnl f* **16/1**

200- **6** *nk* **Jay Bee Blue**[162] 6995 3-8-10 75 .... SophieDoyle(3) 5 61
(J S Moore) *wl in rr: pushed along 3f out: sn outpcd: kpt on fr over 1f out* **50/1**

05 **7** *5* **Ghazeer (IRE)**[10] 981 3-8-13 0 .... MartinLane 8 48
(Derek Shaw) *in tch in midfield: outpcd over 2f out: wknd over 1f out* **100/1**

8 *10* **Thrasos (IRE)** 3-8-13 0 .... LiamKeniry 9 21
(Jo Crowley) *racd wd: trckd ldrs tl wknd qckly over 2f out* **50/1**

5 **9** *2 3/4* **Mayforde Jack**[67] 283 3-8-13 0 .... TonyCulhane 1 13
(Jo Hughes) *hld up: hmpd and snatched up after 1f: bhd rest of way* **80/1**

00- **10** *39* **Dance With Me (IRE)**[182] 6527 3-8-13 0 .... DavidProbert 4
(Andrew Balding) *s.i.s: hmpd after 1f: in tch to 1/2-way: wknd rapidly: t.o* **13/2**

1m 24.43s (-1.57) **Going Correction** -0.075s/f (Stan)
WFA 3 from 4yo 15lb **10** Ran SP% **115.0**
Speed ratings (Par 103): **105,101,100,99,93 93,87,76,73,28**
toteswingers:1&2:£2.40, 1&3:£5.80, 2&3:£4.00 CSF £12.76 TOTE £4.80: £1.60, £1.30, £2.80; EX 13.70 Trifecta £27.60 Pool: £1,139.23 - 30.44 winning units..
Owner John C Grant **Bred** Rathbarry Stud **Trained** Lambourn, Berks

FOCUS
A fair maiden that went the way of the one with the best form, though the eventual third looks the better long-term prospect. The pace wasn't strong and it paid to race handily. The winner is rated back to last year's debut form.
Thrasos(IRE) Official explanation: jockey said colt ran green at start

1139 WILLIAMHILL.COM ROSEBERY H'CAP 1m 3f (P)
3:30 (3:32) (Class 2) (0-105,99) 4-Y-0+
£18,675 (£5,592; £2,796; £1,398; £699; £351) Stalls Low

Form RPR

210- **1** **Charles Camoin (IRE)**[289] 3069 4-9-1 **90** .... LiamKeniry 3 98
(Sylvester Kirk) *wl plcd in midfield on inner: prog over 2f out to cl on ldrs over 1f out: drvn and styd on wl to ld narrowly last 75yds* **15/2**[3]

066- **2** *nk* **Fork Handles**[259] 4108 4-9-1 **90** .... MartinHarley 2 98
(Mick Channon) *wl plcd in midfield: prog over 2f out and sn trckd ldrs: rdn to ld jst over 1f out: styd on but hdd last 75yds* **33/1**

314- **3** *1* **Ramona Chase**[188] 6375 7-8-6 **85** .... (t) MarkCoumbe(5) 12 91
(Michael Attwater) *hld up in midfield: 9th and gng strly over 3f out: prog 2f out: styd on wl fnl f to take 3rd nr fin* **25/1**

324- **4** *3/4* **Romeo Montague**[161] 7017 4-8-11 **86** .... TomMcLaughlin 8 91
(Ed Dunlop) *hld up in last quartet: stdy prog on inner over 2f out: clsd on ldrs 1f out and sn in 3rd: one pce last 75yds* **20/1**

0020 **5** *1/2* **Licence To Till (USA)**[21] 868 5-9-7 **95** .... FrannyNorton 6 99
(Mark Johnston) *led after 1f to 7f out: styd prom: rdn to ld briefly over 1f out: fdd ins fnl f* **16/1**

1/ **6** *1/2* **Starluck (IRE)**[15] 769 7-9-8 **96** .... SebSanders 4 99
(David Arbuthnot) *prom: 4th over 4f out: drvn on outer to try to chal over 1f out: one pce over 1f out* **12/1**

3413 **7** *nk* **Brunston**[22] 846 6-9-0 **88** .... LukeMorris 14 90
(Brendan Powell) *wl in rr: pushed along 5f out: nt gng wl and drvn 3f out: styd on fr over 1f out: nrst fin* **16/1**

-431 **8** *1/2* **Nazreef**[21] 868 5-9-9 **97** .... (t) DarryllHolland 13 98
(Hughie Morrison) *w ldrs: led 7f out to wl over 2f out: wknd fnl f* **16/1**

300- **9** *nk* **Fattsota**[112] 7719 4-9-4 **93** .... AndreaAtzeni 11 94
(Marco Botti) *towards rr: rdn and effrt 3f out: nvr gng pce to latch on to ldng gp* **16/1**

-304 **10** *1 1/2* **Sirvino**[30] 755 7-9-5 **98** .... LMcNiff(5) 16 96
(David Barron) *prom on outer: chsd ldr 5f out: wd bnd 3f out: sn drvn to take narrow ld: hdd & wknd over 1f out* **16/1**

030- **11** *nk* **Reflect (IRE)**[247] 4473 4-9-0 **89** .... KieranO'Neill 5 87
(Richard Hannon) *led 1f: trckd ldrs after: cl enough 2f out: steadily wknd* **5/1**[2]

51-1 **12** *nk* **Eshtibaak (IRE)**[8] 1008 4-9-5 **94** .... PaulHanagan 7 95+
(John Gosden) *in tch in midfield whn hmpd and lost pl after 2f: dropped to rr: 13th 4f out: tried to cl on ldng gp over 1f out: no ch and eased last 100yds* **11/4**[1]

0-22 **13** *1 3/4* **Franco Is My Name**[30] 745 6-8-10 **87** .... (p) HarryBentley(3) 1 81
(Peter Hedger) *settled in midfield on inner: rdn over 2f out and nt on terms w ldrs: no real imp over 1f out: wknd fnl f* **16/1**

400- **14** *2 3/4* **Jehanbux (USA)**[238] 4777 4-8-12 **90** .... SeanLevey(3) 15 79
(Richard Hannon) *stdd s: dropped in fr wd draw and hld up in last pair: no prog over 3f out* **20/1**

0/0- **15** *20* **Hillview Boy (IRE)**[224] 5285 8-9-8 **96** .... WilliamBuick 9 49
(Jim Goldie) *dwlt: hld up in last pair: no prog over 3f out: sn bhd: t.o* **20/1**

1-11 **16** *12* **William Haigh (IRE)**[22] 846 4-9-10 **99** .... PJMcDonald 10 30
(Alan Swinbank) *chsd ldrs on outer: drvn 5f out: wknd over 3f out: t.o* **17/2**

2m 18.81s (-3.09) **Going Correction** -0.075s/f (Stan)
WFA 4 from 5yo+ 1lb **16** Ran SP% **129.7**
Speed ratings (Par 109): **108,107,107,106,106 105,105,105,104,103 103,103,102,100,85 76**
toteswingers:1&2:£67.10, 1&3:£74.60, 2&3:£117.50 CSF £254.93 CT £5860.31 TOTE £9.60: £2.80, £4.40, £7.20, £5.70; EX 430.10 TRIFECTA Not won..
Owner Chris Wright & The Hon Mrs J M Corbett **Bred** Pat Grogan **Trained** Upper Lambourn, Berks
■ Stewards' Enquiry : Darryll Holland two-day ban: careless riding (Apr 14,16)

FOCUS
A competitive handicap as it so often is and one that saw a multitude of horses in a line inside the last after an uneven early gallop picked up going down the far side. There was a bunch finish and the form may not be reliable. The winner is rated up a length on his 3yo form.

NOTEBOOK
Charles Camoin(IRE) ◆ hadn't been seen since Royal Ascot but he had been progressive prior to that and there was little concern about his going well first time out as he had shown last year. Dropped out, he came with a steady run to lead very late on, much as he did when winning at the Derby meeting last year, and he looks the sort that will do even better tried again over 1m4f. It will be surprising if there isn't quite a lot more to come from him given his unexposed profile and the handicapper will probably struggle to keep tabs on him for a while yet. (op 11-1)
Fork Handles won first time out as a youngster and finished third in the Cheshire Oaks on her reappearance last year, so a bold display in the face of a more realistic assignment than she has often faced was no surprise. She'll be just as effective back at 1m2f given the chance in a handicap.
Ramona Chase was fourth in this race last year off a mark of 81 so this represents a very good effort and he'll have to merit very close consideration if he goes to Epsom next for the City and Suburban next month.
Romeo Montague hasn't always looked straightforward but he didn't do a lot wrong here and his effort is probably all the more promising given that he was much more poorly placed turning for home than the trio that beat him. Like Ramona Chase, he handles switchback tracks very well (won at Brighton last year and second at Epsom) so he'll be another to consider in the City and Suburban
Licence To Till(USA) fared better than he has most starts this season and even showed ahead very briefly approaching the last but he's going to need to find something less competitive before he gets his head back in front.
Starluck(IRE) looked an interesting contender on his first run on the Flat since winning here in 2010, having looked unlucky in the County Hurdle at Cheltenham off a mark of 150 last month, but he was always well placed and didn't seem to have any excuses. (op 11-1)
Nazreef looked to find the trip beyond him, for all he ran without his usual blinkers. Official explanation: jockey said gelding had no more to give (op 14-1)
Reflect(IRE) ran as though he needed his first race since Goodwood last July, dropping out after being a bit fresh early and then losing his place turning out of the back straight. He had some decent form behind some unexposed sorts in the middle of last year ad isn't one to give up on yet. (op 9-1)
Eshtibaak(IRE)'s effort off a 7lb higher mark than his last win is best ignored to a large degree as he was impeded early on and soon in a poor position as a result. He made up some late ground without being knocked about unduly, but it's worth pointing out that the form of his latest win had already been let down. Official explanation: jockey said colt suffered interference on first bend (op 3-1 tchd 7-2)
Hillview Boy(IRE) Official explanation: jockey said gelding hung left
William Haigh(IRE) was clearly not himself. (op 15-2 tchd 9-1)

1140 NEW WILLIAM HILL IPHONE APP CONDITIONS STKS 7f (P)
4:05 (4:05) (Class 4) 4-Y-0+ £5,175 (£1,540; £769; £384) Stalls Low

Form RPR

1-2 **1** **Primaeval**[70] 261 6-9-0 100 .... (v) StevieDonohoe 1 105+
(James Fanshawe) *hld up in 5th: smooth prog 2f out: rdn to take narrow ld jst over 1f out: drvn and hld on wl* **11/10**[1]

60-4 **2** *1/2* **Rodrigo De Torres**[25] 814 5-9-0 97 .... MartinHarley 6 104
(Mrs K Burke) *led: set mod pce to 1/2-way: drvn 2f out: hdd jst over 1f out: edgd rt ins fnl f: styd on but a hld* **28/1**

1221 **3** *hd* **Alben Star (IRE)**[21] 871 4-9-0 98 .... PaulHanagan 3 103
(Richard Fahey) *t.k.h: trckd ldr to over 1f out: styd on fnl f: a hld* **5/2**[2]

-110 **4** *3/4* **Palace Moon**[35] 711 7-9-0 102 .... (t) LukeMorris 5 101
(William Knight) *hld up in last pair: prog on inner 2f out: wnt 4th fnl f: styd on but nvr able to chal* **7/1**[3]

002 **5** *1 3/4* **Bravo Echo**[12] 962 6-9-0 98 .... J-PGuillambert 4 99
(Michael Attwater) *t.k.h: racd wd: hld up in 4th: effrt 2f out: hrd rdn and cl up 1f out: eased whn btn last 100yds* **7/1**[3]

40-0 **6** *3/4* **Cochabamba (IRE)**[21] 866 4-8-9 90 .... LiamKeniry 7 90
(Roger Teal) *hld up in last pair: rdn over 2f out: no prog* **25/1**

5100 **7** *1 1/2* **Seek The Fair Land**[12] 962 6-8-9 93 .... (b) NathanAlison(5) 2 91
(Jim Boyle) *trckd ldng pair to 2f out: steadily fdd* **33/1**

1m 24.98s (-1.02) **Going Correction** -0.075s/f (Stan) **7** Ran SP% **111.4**
Speed ratings (Par 105): **102,101,101,100,98 97,95**
toteswingers:1&2:£5.60, 1&3:£1.40, 2&3:£8.00 CSF £36.54 TOTE £2.00: £1.30, £6.70; EX 25.60.

Owner The Foncey Syndicate **Bred** Stowell Park Stud **Trained** Newmarket, Suffolk
FOCUS
A useful minor event but one that turned out to be as messily run as it promised to be beforehand and the winning margin doesn't reflect the winner's superiority after a sprint finish. The winner and third are close to their marks as rated.
Bravo Echo Official explanation: jockey said gelding was denied a clear run

1141 DOWNLOAD WILLIAM HILL FROM THE APP-STORE H'CAP 6f (P)
4:40 (4:41) (Class 3) (0-90,89) 4-Y-O+ **£8,409** (£2,502; £1,250; £625) Stalls Low

Form				RPR
004-	1		**Shropshire (IRE)**205 5852 4-9-0 **87** MatthewLawson(5) 5 (Charles Hills) *hld up in last pair: brought to outer and prog jst over 2f out: drvn to cl on ldrs fnl f: styd on to ld post* **6/13**	96
523-	2	shd	**New Leyf (IRE)**128 7631 6-9-6 **88** J-PGuillambert 8 (Ed Walker) *hld up in rr: prog over 2f out: pressed ldr ent fnl f: drvn to ld last 75yds: hdd post* **11/22**	97
130-	3	½	**Tagula Night (IRE)**174 6723 6-9-5 **87** PaulHanagan 6 (Dean Ivory) *t.k.h: trckd ldng pair: wnt 2nd 2f out: drvn to ld 1f out: hdd and no ex last 75yds* **16/1**	94
13-1	4	1½	**Triple Charm**36 686 4-9-2 **84** (p) WilliamBuick 12 (Jeremy Noseda) *dropped in fr wd draw and hld up last: shkn up over 2f out: styd on fnl 2f to take 4th last strides: nrst fin* **6/13**	87+
10-3	5	nk	**Courageous (IRE)**21 871 6-9-5 **87** (t) WilliamCarson 2 (Kevin Ryan) *trckd ldr: led over 2f out: hdd and fdd 1f out* **13/2**	89
120-	6	2	**Farlow (IRE)**205 5852 4-9-5 **87** RichardKingscote 1 (Ralph Beckett) *in tch on inner: rdn and effrt 2f out: no imp whn edgd lft fnl f: fdd* **10/31**	82
500-	7	hd	**Arctic Feeling (IRE)**189 6347 4-8-11 **86** LauraBarry(7) 4 (Richard Fahey) *hld up in last trio: pushed along fr over 2f out: kpt on but nvr on terms* **11/1**	81
02-0	8	2	**Mac Gille Eoin**21 871 8-9-3 **85** LukeMorris 11 (John Gallagher) *sweating: chsd ldrs: rdn and effrt on outer 2f out: no prog 1f out: wknd* **33/1**	73
510-	9	½	**Sacrosanctus**206 5830 4-9-2 **87** HarryBentley(3) 3 (Scott Dixon) *trckd ldrs: disp 2nd jst over 2f out to wl over 1f out: hrd rdn and wknd* **12/1**	74
020-	10	10	**We Have A Dream**156 7127 7-9-5 **87** MartinDwyer 7 (William Muir) *in tch in midfield: rdn over 2f out: sn wknd* **28/1**	42
-511	11	9	**Taajub (IRE)**35 715 5-9-7 **89** SebSanders 9 (Peter Crate) *racd wd and hanging lft: chsd ldrs to 1/2-way: eased whn no ch over 1f out: t.o* **10/1**	15
030-	12	hd	**Button Moon (IRE)**182 6531 4-9-2 **84** (p) MartinLane 10 (Ian Wood) *led to over 2f out: wknd rapidly: t.o* **33/1**

1m 11.52s (-1.58) **Going Correction** -0.075s/f (Stan) 12 Ran SP% **120.7**
Speed ratings (Par 107): **107,106,106,104,103 101,100,98,97,84 72,71**
toteswingers:1&2:£7.10, 1&3:£23.80, 2&3:£13.70 CSF £39.09 CT £507.35 TOTE £7.10: £2.40, £2.00, £4.00; EX 39.00 Trifecta £782.50 Part won. Pool: £1,057.47 - 0.40 winning units..
Owner The Hon Mrs J M Corbett & C Wright **Bred** Tally-Ho Stud **Trained** Lambourn, Berks
■ Stewards' Enquiry : J-P Guillambert two-day ban: used whip above permitted level (Apr 16-17)
FOCUS
Quite a useful sprint handicap that was run at a strong pace and the first two came from well back. The winner is rated back to his best with the second running as well as ever.
NOTEBOOK
Shropshire(IRE) has a good first-time-out record - he won on his debut as a juvenile and was third to Frankel in the Greenham last year - and he added to that with a game success on his first start since being gelded, one that probably underestimates the worth of this effort as despite being favoured to a degree by the run of the race, it almost seemed he did it despite making up his ground too quickly. He's lightly raced for his age and might be interesting in one of the big 6f turf handicaps later this summer. (op 5-1 tchd 9-2)
New Leyf(IRE) isn't the most straightforward (naughty at the start here) but he's given his running on all starts since joining this yard. That said, a return to 7f might just suit him on the Polytrack. (op 13-2)
Tagula Night(IRE) is another with a good first-time-out record and he ran well considering he was without his usual headgear on his first outing since leaving Walter Swinburn and raced much closer to the pace than the trio in the frame beside him. He goes well at Goodwood, so might be worth looking out for there before too long.
Triple Charm's latest form had been franked by the runner-up winning a Listed contest since but though she didn't fare as well herself here she can be partly excused as she got rather detached in rear having been dropped in from her outside stall, only to finish with a rattle. The likelihood is that she is still well handicapped. (op 7-2)
Courageous(IRE) did well to last so long considering he was so close to the good gallop early on. (op 5-1)
Farlow(IRE) won first time out last season but never promised to repeat that effort despite a trouble-free passage on the inside rail. (op 5-1)
Arctic Feeling(IRE) looked rusty on her first run of the year, pushed along before halfway. (op 20-1 tchd 22-1)
Mac Gille Eoin Official explanation: jockey said horse hung left
Taajub(IRE) Official explanation: jockey said gelding hung left

1142 BEST ODDS GUARANTEED @ WILLIAMHILL.COM H'CAP (LONDON MILE QUALIFIER) 1m (P)
5:10 (5:11) (Class 4) (0-85,85) 3-Y-O **£5,175** (£1,540; £769; £384) Stalls Low

Form				RPR
423-	1		**Savanna Days (IRE)**195 6187 3-8-12 **76** MartinHarley 2 (Mick Channon) *hld up in 4th gng wl: prog jst over 2f out: rdn to ld over 1f out: clr fnl f: styd on* **5/13**	83
1111	2	1¾	**Clean Bowled (IRE)**15 920 3-8-13 **84** (p) NedCurtis(7) 3 (Roger Curtis) *hld up in 6th: swtchd sharply lft jst over 2f out: pushed along and r.o fr over 1f out: tk 2nd nr fin* **8/1**	87
614-	3	¾	**Gabrial's Gift (IRE)**188 6373 3-9-6 **84** WilliamBuick 1 (David Simcock) *t.k.h: sn trckd ldr: chal and w wnr over 1f out: nt qckn and hld fnl f: lost 2nd nr fin* **2/11**	85
2-12	4	1½	**Majestic Zafeen**37 667 3-8-12 **76** PaulHanagan 7 (Alastair Lidderdale) *led: hanging lft bnd over 4f out to over 3f out: hdd over 1f out: one pce* **7/1**	74
-124	5	6	**Karma Chameleon**23 841 3-9-1 **79** SebSanders 5 (John Berry) *hld up in 5th: rdn and effrt over 2f out: no imp over 1f out: wknd fnl f* **7/22**	63
016-	6	3¼	**Fennell Bay (IRE)**164 6957 3-8-8 **72** FrannyNorton 6 (Mark Johnston) *trckd ldng pair: shkn up over 2f out: sn lost pl and btn* **13/2**	48
004-	7	6	**Sir Glanton (IRE)**199 6055 3-9-7 **85** LiamKeniry 8 (Amanda Perrett) *hld up last: shkn up and lost tch over 2f out: t.o* **12/1**	47

1m 38.18s (-1.62) **Going Correction** -0.075s/f (Stan) 7 Ran SP% **116.9**
Speed ratings (Par 100): **105,103,102,101,95 91,85**
toteswingers:1&2:£6.70, 1&3:£3.60, 2&3:£4.30 CSF £44.83 CT £105.85 TOTE £7.00: £3.50, £2.70; EX 44.00 Trifecta £92.50 Pool: £1,540.41 - 12.32 winning units..
Owner Jon and Julia Aisbitt **Bred** Gestut Etzean **Trained** West Ilsley, Berks
FOCUS
A fair handicap to end proceedings, though disappointing perhaps there weren't more unexposed types on show given the higher rating band than most handicaps of its type so far this year. The pace wasn't strong and the form is rated around the fourth.
Majestic Zafeen Official explanation: jockey said filly hung left throughout
T/Plt: £159.40 to a £1 stake. Pool:£71,921.04 - 329.35 winning tickets T/Qpdt: £73.30 to a £1 stake. Pool:£4,095.19 - 41.34 winning tickets JN

945 MEYDAN (L-H)
Saturday, March 31

OFFICIAL GOING: Tapeta: standard; turf: good
The 2.45pm was re-run at the end of the card (7.25pm GB time) after the original running was stopped and declared void (Fox Hunt fatally injured)

1143a GODOLPHIN MILE SPONSORED BY ETISALAT (GROUP 2) (TAPETA) 1m
2:10 (2:10) 3-Y-O+
£387,096 (£129,032; £64,516; £32,258; £19,354; £12,903)

			RPR
1		**African Story**21 876 5-9-0 117 FrankieDettori 3 (Saeed Bin Suroor) *trckd ldr: smooth prog 3f out: led 1 1/2f out: comf* **5/61**	121+
2	4	**Viscount Nelson (USA)**21 877 5-9-0 116 (b) KShea 12 (M F De Kock, South Africa) *s.i.s: settled in rr: r.o fnl 2f: nrst fin* **12/1**	112+
3	1¾	**Red Jazz (USA)**249 4412 5-9-0 112 MichaelHills 8 (Charles Hills) *sn led: hdd 1 1/2f out: kpt on gamely* **10/13**	108
4	¼	**Richard's Kid (USA)**21 878 7-9-0 112 (bt) RichardMullen 1 (S Seemar, UAE) *racd in rr: r.o fnl 1 1/2f: nrst fin* **33/1**	107+
5	½	**Haatheq (USA)**21 878 5-9-0 112 TadhgO'Shea 13 (A Al Raihe, UAE) *mid-div: kpt on same pce fnl 1 1/2f* **25/1**	106
6	¾	**First City**21 879 6-8-9 110 RoystonFfrench 4 (A Al Raihe, UAE) *t.k.h: mid-div: chsd ldrs 3f out: kpt on same pce fnl 1 1/2f* **25/1**	99
7	½	**Shamalgan (FR)**37 682 5-9-0 115 GregoryBenoist 5 (X Nakkachdji, France) *nvr bttr than mid-div* **28/1**	103
8	shd	**Sandagiyr (FR)**30 758 4-9-0 111 MickaelBarzalona 2 (Saeed Bin Suroor) *nvr bttr than mid-div* **11/1**	103
9	¾	**Derbaas (USA)**21 879 6-9-0 113 (t) RichardHills 6 (A Al Raihe, UAE) *in rr of mid-div: nvr able to chal* **20/1**	101
10	hd	**Dux Scholar**21 876 4-9-0 111 GlynSchofield 9 (H J Brown, South Africa) *nvr bttr than mid-div* **33/1**	101
11	shd	**Snaafy (USA)**21 876 8-9-0 109 (v) WayneSmith 11 (M Al Muhairi, UAE) *trckd ldrs: ev ch 1 1/2f out: wknd fnl 110yds* **33/1**	100
12	18¼	**Do It All (USA)**30 758 5-9-0 116 (t) SilvestreDeSousa 10 (Saeed Bin Suroor) *trckd ldrs tl wknd 2f out* **12/1**	58
P		**Western Aristocrat (USA)**124 7572 4-9-0 113 RyanMoore 7 (Jeremy Noseda) *a in rr: p.u 4f out* **6/12**

1m 37.52s (0.02) **Going Correction** +0.30s/f (Slow) **13** Ran SP% **126.4**
Speed ratings: **111,107,105,104,104 103,103,103,102,102 102,83,**
CSF £11.87; TRICAST £69.35.
Owner Godolphin **Bred** Darley **Trained** Newmarket, Suffolk
FOCUS
The time was 0.13 seconds quicker than last year, but 0.95 seconds off the 2010 running and the general feeling was that the Tapeta track was riding on the slow side. A reasonable field lined up and the winner is a really smart, likeable type, but it would probably be unwise to get too carried away. The form is rated around the third and fourth and African Story fits with previous winnes of this race.
NOTEBOOK
African Story had just about the ideal trip in tracking an ordinary pace (set by Red Jazz), whereas three of the next four finishers were held up, two of them having missed the break. He would be 4-4 (all on Tapeta) since switching from France to Dubai had he enjoyed a clear run in the Firebreak Stakes on February 9 and has made significant progress on this surface. It will be interesting to see if he can prove as effective back on grass. (op Evens)
Viscount Nelson(USA), off the turf for the first time, did well to get so close considering he was left with a lot to do after missing the break and came widest of all into the straight. There was a suggestion he could be aimed at the Cox Plate. (op 11-1)
Red Jazz(USA), third in this last year, was having his first start for 249 days, but he won the 2010 Free Handicap off an even longer break. He couldn't make the most of being allowed to dominate and seems better suited by 7f.
Richard's Kid(USA) was unsuited by the drop in distance. He ran on from a long way back after a sluggish start and can do better. It was reported beforehand he could be set to return to the US with former trainer Bob Baffert.
Haatheq(USA) was held from his wide draw and wasn't good enough to get involved. (op 20-1)
First City, trying Tapeta for the first time, was keen early.
Do It All(USA), a shock winner of the Zabeel Mile on turf last time, presumably has a problem. (op 11-1)
Western Aristocrat(USA), who never looked happy after a slow start, seemed to lose his action completely at around halfway and was pulled up sharply. He was apparently taken back to the stabling area in a van, but initial reports suggested he wasn't seriously injured.

1144a DUBAI GOLD CUP SPONSORED BY AL TAYER MOTORS (GROUP 3) (TURF) 2m
2:45 (7:25) 3-Y-O+
£387,096 (£129,032; £64,516; £32,258; £19,354; £12,903)

			RPR
1		**Opinion Poll (IRE)**30 759 6-9-0 116 FrankieDettori 10 (Mahmood Al Zarooni) *mid-div: smooth prog to ld 2f out: r.o wl* **10/111**	116
2	¾	**Joshua Tree (IRE)**21 877 5-9-0 113 JohnnyMurtagh 5 (Marco Botti) *in rr of mid-div: r.o fnl 1 1/2f: nrst fin* **16/1**	115
3	shd	**Zanzamar (SAF)**21 877 5-8-13 113 (t) RichardHills 12 (M F De Kock, South Africa) *settled in rr: r.o fnl 3 1/2f: nrst fin* **18/1**	114
4	1¼	**Averroes (IRE)**30 759 5-9-0 104 PatCosgrave 4 (Ernst Oertel, UAE) *mid-div: chsd ldrs 3 1/2f out: one pce fnl 1 1/2f* **50/1**	114
5	¼	**Kasbah Bliss (FR)**30 759 10-9-0 115 Christophe-PatriceLemaire 13 (F Doumen, France) *in rr of mid-div: kpt on same pce fnl 1 1/2* **14/1**	113
6	6	**Irish Flame (SAF)**21 878 6-9-0 108 KShea 6 (M F De Kock, South Africa) *trckd ldr tl 3f out: sn wknd* **33/1**	107
7	¼	**Barbican**122 7584 4-8-8 111 RyanMoore 2 (Alan Bailey) *nvr bttr than mid-div* **9/22**	105

8 8 1/2 **Unusual Suspect (USA)**[21] 877 8-9-0 112......................(v) CNakatani 3 97
(Michael Kent, Australia) *mid-div: smooth prog to ld 4f out: hdd 2f out: wknd fnl f* **33/1**

9 *dist* **Mikhail Glinka (IRE)**[21] 877 5-9-0 115......................(vt) GlynSchofield 8
(H J Brown, South Africa) *trckd ldr tl wknd 3f out* **8/1**[3]

10 *dist* **Makani Bisty (JPN)**[27] 5-9-0 110..............................(b) FutoshiKomaki 1
(Yoshito Yahagi, Japan) *sn led: hdd 4f out: no ex* **11/1**

F **Bronze Cannon (USA)**[21] 877 7-9-0 109..........................(t) KUlubaev 7
(H J Brown, South Africa) *settled in rr: broke leg and fell 6f out: fatally injured* **33/1**

P **Grand Vent (IRE)**[28] 792 4-8-8 112.......................... MickaelBarzalona 9
(Saeed Bin Suroor) *trckd ldrs: p.u 6f out: fatally injured* **16/1**

3m 23.73s (203.73)
WFA 4 from 5yo+ 5lb **12** Ran SP% **124.5**
CSF: £19.74 TRICAST: £189.89.
Owner Godolphin **Bred** Darley **Trained** Newmarket, Suffolk
■ The last ride of Richard Hills's career.

FOCUS

This stayers' event, a new addition to the World Cup card, was stopped before halfway as a result of Fox Hunt suffering a fatal leg injury early on. He lay in a dangerous position, on the racing line not far beyond the turn into the straight, so there was no option but to bring the race to a halt. Controversially, the race was re-run at the end of the card, almost five hours later, and with Bronze Cannon and Grand Vent both breaking legs, the Japanese-trained Makani Bisty stopping as though shot leaving the back straight, having led the field for much of the way (just as he did in the first running of the race), and Mikhail Glinka being eased right off in the straight, it's hard to come to any other conclusion than that the race should not have been run.

NOTEBOOK

Opinion Poll(IRE), who only found Fame And Glory too good in the Ascot Gold Cup last year, was a worthy winner. He'd run a promising race behind Fox Hunt on his reappearance, and Dettori had switched to ride him instead this time. Taking up the running turning in, he quickly established a gap on the rest and, while he got tired in the closing stages, he was never going to be caught. He should again be a big player in the Cup races back in Europe this season. (op evens)
Joshua Tree(IRE), whose only previous start beyond 1m4f came when fifth in the 2010 St Leger, ran a great race. Held up towards the back, he found his path blocked at the top of the straight and by the time he got into full flight the winner had gone beyond recall. Nevertheless, he showed he has the stamina for 2m, and the Cup races offer up a new avenue for him. (op 14-1)
Zanzamar(SAF) had a big stamina question mark hanging over him, but he got this half-mile longer trip well. Like the runner-up he was given a waiting ride, but unlike him he had a clear run at the winner down the outside. (op 16-1)
Averroes(IRE) finished well behind Opinion Poll in the Nad Al Sheba Trophy, but this was better. How reliable the form is must be open to question, however.
Kasbah Bliss(FR) loomed up travelling well at the top of the straight, but when the button was pressed there was nothing there. He's the type that needs everything to fall just right.
Irish Flame(SAF) was slightly inconvenienced when Makani Bisty dropped quickly back through the field leaving the back straight, but didn't look to get home.
Barbican, who has long looked a stayer in the making, didn't look particularly comfortable on the track in the straight and is easily forgiven this. He was progressive last season and hopefully he can get back on track when returning to Europe. (tchd 5-1)
Unusual Suspect(USA), who wasn't disgraced in the Melbourne Cup last year, went to the front apparently going well leaving the back straight, but he was joined by the winner on turning in and soon fell in a hole.

1145a UAE DERBY SPONSORED BY THE SAEED & MOHAMMED AL NABOODAH GROUP (GROUP 2) (TAPETA) 1m 1f 110y

3:25 (3:25) 3-Y-O

£774,193 (£258,064; £129,032; £64,516; £38,709; £25,806)

RPR

1 **Daddy Long Legs (USA)**[147] 7306 3-8-9 117.................. CO'Donoghue 7 115
(A P O'Brien, Ire) *trckd ldrs: led 2 1/2f out: r.o wl: comf* **7/1**[3]

2 1 1/4 **Yang Tse Kiang (FR)**[25] 3-8-9 108.................................. ThierryJarnet 8 112+
(R Chotard, France) *in rr of mid-div: r.o wl fnl 2f: nrst fin* **16/1**

3 3/4 **Wrote (IRE)**[147] 7301 3-8-9 115.. RyanMoore 13 111
(A P O'Brien, Ire) *trckd ldrs: ev ch 1 1/2f out: nt qckn fnl 55yds* **11/4**[1]

4 1 1/4 **Mickdaam (IRE)**[21] 873 3-8-9 112...................... ChristopheSoumillon 6 110+
(M F De Kock, South Africa) *s.i.s: in rr of mid-div: n.m.r 3f out: r.o fnl 1 1/2f: nrst fin* **9/2**[2]

5 1 1/4 **Red Duke (USA)**[175] 6689 3-8-9 112.................................. TomQueally 12 106
(John Quinn) *in rr of mid-div: r.o fnl 1 1/2f but nvr able to chal* **11/1**

6 3 1/2 **Balada Sale (ARG)**[140] 4-9-1 107.............. Christophe-PatriceLemaire 4 99
(P Bary, France) *trckd ldrs: ev ch 2 1/2f out: one pce fnl 1 1/2f* **10/1**

7 1 **Lucky Chappy (IRE)**[41] 3-8-9 106..(t) AGarcia 1 97
(H Graham Motion, U.S.A) *nvr bttr than mid-div* **11/1**

8 6 3/4 **Burano (IRE)**[37] 679 3-8-9 107... KierenFallon 2 83
(Brian Meehan) *trckd ldrs tl 2 1/2f out: one pce fnl 1 1/2f* **25/1**

9 1/2 **Kinglet (USA)**[21] 873 3-8-9 107.. FrankieDettori 9 82
(Mahmood Al Zarooni) *racd in rr: n.d* **16/1**

10 3 1/2 **Falls Of Lora (IRE)**[37] 680 3-8-5 104.................... MickaelBarzalona 10 71
(Mahmood Al Zarooni) *slowly away: nvr nr to chal* **20/1**

11 2 3/4 **Maritimer (CAN)**[125] 3-8-9 106......................................(t) GlynSchofield 3 69
(H J Brown, South Africa) *trckd ldng pair tl 2 1/2f out: sn btn* **20/1**

12 1 1/2 **Helmet (AUS)**[28] 796 4-9-5 119.................................(tp) KerrinMcEvoy 14 69+
(Peter Snowden, Australia) *wl away: sn led: hdd & wknd 2 1/2f out* **9/1**

13 2 3/4 **Entifaadha**[37] 679 3-8-9 107..(b) RichardHills 11 60
(William Haggas) *settled in rr: nvr able to chal* **14/1**

14 16 1/2 **Genten (USA)**[42] 3-8-9 106.. CraigAWilliams 5 26
(Yoshito Yahagi, Japan) *nvr bttr than mid-div* **33/1**

1m 58.35s (-0.65) **Going Correction** +0.30s/f (Slow)
WFA 3 from 4yo 19lb **14** Ran SP% **127.8**
Speed ratings: **114,113,112,111,110 107,106,101,101,98 96,94,92,79**
CSF: £115.09; TRICAST: £393.34.
Owner Michael Tabor & Derrick Smith & Mrs John Magnier **Bred** Woodford Thoroughbreds LLC **Trained** Ballydoyle, Co Tipperary

FOCUS

The UAE Derby had only ever been won by Saeed Bin Suroor (seven times) and Mike de Kock (five), but Aidan O'Brien hadn't had a runner in the race until last year when he sent out Master Of Hounds to finish second and Alexander Pope (now called Packing Tycoon) to take sixth. This time around the O'Brien-trained runners finished first and third, and it's clear Ballydoyle's presence gives this fixture a significant boost. There was only a modest pace. The form is rated around the progressive first two.

NOTEBOOK

Daddy Long Legs(USA) didn't face the kickback in the Breeders' Cup Juvenile when last seen, but prior to that he'd won the Royal Lodge and he confirmed Newmarket form with Wrote in game fashion. He was helped by the run of the race for a lot of the way, but was probably left clear sooner than ideal and he did well to run on so strongly - that's despite having sweated up beforehand. It was suggested afterwards he'll now be aimed at the Kentucky Derby (Master Of Hounds ran fifth at Churchill Downs after finishing runner-up in this), and while it remains to be seen whether dirt is his surface, his pedigree offers hope.
Yang Tse Kiang(FR) was difficult to weigh up after winning a four-runner conditions race at Chantilly on his reappearance, but that at least proved he could both act on a synthetic surface and stay this trip. He travelled nicely off the pace, and the suspicion is his rider thought he had everything covered early in the straight, but the winner was too strong. (op 14-1)
Wrote(IRE), last year's Breeders' Cup Juvenile Turf winner, made a promising reappearance. He looked a big threat turning into the straight, but he'd covered more ground than the winner and got tired. There should be plenty more to come, but he's surely one to avoid if he follows Daddy Long Legs to the US Triple Crown as he is not bred for dirt. (op 4-1)
Mickdaam(IRE) didn't help himself with a slow start but may well have finished in the first three granted a clear run, and he should get further. (op 11-2)
Red Duke(USA), returning from 175 days off, was caught a bit wide and got tired in the straight. He might have needed the run and/or failed to stay, and the impression is we've yet to see the best of him. (op 10-1)
Balada Sale(ARG) had been winning by wide margins in Argentina, including their 1000 Guineas and Oaks. The only filly in the line-up, she wasn't ridden as handily as usual and just kept on at the one pace. She can probably do better.
Lucky Chappy(IRE), fourth behind Wrote from a wide draw at the Breeders' Cup, has been in good form in the US recently but he failed to give his true running. He started sluggishly and that set the tone. (op 12-1)
Burano(IRE) found this tougher than the Meydan Classic (1m, turf) he won last time.
Kinglet(USA), the UAE 2000 Guineas winner, has lost his way since going up in trip. (op 14-1)
Falls Of Lora(IRE) won a bizarre running of the UAE Oaks but never recovered from a slow start this time. (op 16-1)
Helmet(AUS) refused to settle in front and was beaten before the turn. He looked really good in Australia earlier in his career, but he seems to be going the wrong way now. (op 10-1)

1146a AL QUOZ SPRINT SPONSORED BY EMIRATES NBD (GROUP 1) (TURF) 5f

4:00 (4:00) 3-Y-O+

£387,096 (£129,032; £64,516; £32,258; £19,354; £12,903)

RPR

1 **Ortensia (AUS)**[133] 7-8-9 112...................................(b) CraigAWilliams 10 115+
(Paul Messara, Australia) *settled in rr: smooth prog 2f out: led fnl 110yds* **6/1**[2]

2 1 1/4 **Sole Power**[21] 875 5-9-0 115...................................... JohnnyMurtagh 14 115
(Edward Lynam, Ire) *settled in rr: smooth prog 2f out: r.o fnl f* **11/2**[1]

3 *nk* **Joy And Fun (NZ)**[55] 9-9-0 117..(p) BrettDoyle 6 114
(D Cruz, Hong Kong) *slowly away: in rr of mid-div: r.o wl fnl f: nrst fin* **6/1**[2]

4 *nk* **Monsieur Joe (IRE)**[21] 875 5-9-0 112................................. PatCosgrave 1 113
(Robert Cowell) *sn led: hdd fnl 110yds: kpt on same pce* **20/1**

5 *hd* **August Rush (SAF)**[21] 874 6-9-0 110.........................(t) GlynSchofield 8 112
(H J Brown, South Africa) *trckd ldr: ev ch ins fnl f: nt qckn fnl 110yds* **22/1**

6 *shd* **Nocturnal Affair (SAF)**[21] 875 6-9-0 112.....................(t) RyanMoore 5 112
(David Marnane, Ire) *mid-div: r.o fnl 1 1/2f: nrst fin* **8/1**[3]

7 3/4 **Invincible Ash (IRE)**[21] 875 7-8-9 111.....................(p) JamieSpencer 7 104
(M Halford, Ire) *settled in rr: nvr nr to chal* **12/1**

8 1/2 **Secret Asset (IRE)**[140] 7392 7-9-0 114.......................... GeorgeBaker 13 107
(Jane Chapple-Hyam) *nvr able to chal* **25/1**

9 *shd* **Better Be The One (AUS)**[37] 681 6-9-0 115.............(b) KierenFallon 12 107
(M Freedman, Singapore) *nvr bttr than mid-div* **16/1**

10 1/2 **Margot Did (IRE)**[21] 875 4-8-9 114................................ HayleyTurner 15 100
(Michael Bell) *chsd ldrs: ev ch 2f out: nt qckn fnl f* **9/1**

11 1 3/4 **War Artist (AUS)**[21] 875 9-9-0 113.. KShea 9 99
(M F De Kock, South Africa) *nvr bttr than mid-div* **14/1**

12 *shd* **A Shin Virgo (JPN)**[28] 5-8-9 108................................. YuichiFukunaga 4 94
(Ken Kozaki, Japan) *nvr able to chal* **25/1**

13 2 1/4 **Prohibit**[21] 875 7-9-0 115...(p) JimCrowley 11 91
(Robert Cowell) *nvr bttr than mid-div* **12/1**

14 2 3/4 **Regally Ready (USA)**[21] 875 5-9-0 117..........................(vt) CNakatani 3 81
(Steven Asmussen, U.S.A) *trckd ldrs tl 2f out: wknd fnl f* **20/1**

15 1 1/2 **Addictive Dream (IRE)**[21] 874 5-9-0 112.................... AdrianNicholls 2 75
(David Nicholls) *trckd ldrs: ev ch 2 1/2f out: wknd fnl f* **8/1**[3]

57.98s (57.98) **15** Ran SP% **125.7**
CSF: £37.08; TRICAST: £212.51.
Owner A D N Fraser, Miss A C N Fraser & Ms E J H Ridley **Bred** L D Rhodes **Trained** Australia

FOCUS

Only the second time this has been run over 5f, and having been upgraded from a Group 2 race last year the organisers were rewarded with an ultra-competitive field, featuring nine individual Group/Grade 1 winners, albeit none with more than one win at the top level to his/her name. It was certainly a much weaker Group 1 than the Golden Shaheen, reflected in the prize money on offer, which was half that of the Tapeta race and identical to that put up for the Godolphin Mile and Gold Cup. As anticipated there was a strong gallop on, which suited those ridden with patience, and the final time (57.98) was just 0.34sec outside the track record. Ortensia is rated to her mark, with the second and fourth to recent C&D best.

NOTEBOOK

Ortensia(AUS) continued the trend of horses bred in the southern hemisphere having an edge in this division, highlighted by their success in Europe and in this race in the past. Winner of both previous starts for her current stable, including a Group 1 last time out, she had to prove her effectiveness over the minimum trip, but the blinkers she used to wear for her previous yard were back on, and with the leaders going quick it was always going to set up nicely for her closing style. Once switched to the outside she ran on strongly, and she was going further clear at the line. Royal Ascot could well be on the agenda this summer, and the King's Stand (where she will avoid Black Caviar) looks the obvious target.
Sole Power had conditions (fast ground, fast pace) to suit and got a good lead into the race from Margot Did. He had every chance, reversed form with Invincible Ash from three weeks earlier, and was simply beaten by a better rival. (op 6-1)
Joy And Fun(NZ), winner of this race two years ago when it was run as a Group 3 over 6f, took his first Group 1 when successful at Sha Tin last time. Having anticipated the start, he missed the break and was ridden along to regain the lost ground. A mid-race move to briefly hit the front also didn't help his cause, and all in all connections can count themselves a little unlucky that things didn't pan out a little kinder.
Monsieur Joe(IRE), fourth in the trial, has a record of steady improvement here over the winter (joined current stable before shipping out) and this was another career-best. Considering he was up there the whole way disputing the lead, he did very well to hang on to fourth place, and it'll be interesting to see if he can transfer his improved form back to Europe this summer, as he could be a big player in some of the top sprints, especially the Nunthorpe, if he does. (op 14-1)
August Rush(SAF) ran well behind Krypton Factor (winner of the Golden Shaheen later on the card) on Tapeta last time, and was fully entitled to have come on for that outing, his first since July. Never too far off the pace, he posted a good effort in a race run to suit those ridden out the back.
Nocturnal Affair(SAF) wasn't beaten far in the trial for this race three weeks earlier, but this required more and, while he ran a decent race, he wasn't quite up to the required standard.
Invincible Ash(IRE), fourth in this race last year and winner of the trial last time out, wasn't best away, but that's not a problem with her as she's a hold-up performer anyway. Having originally raced up the centre of the track, she eventually challenged towards the far rail, had her momentum slightly checked when Joy And Fun crossed in front of her, and came up a little short. (op 11-1)

Secret Asset(IRE), whose narrow defeat in the Abbaye stands out from the rest of his form, was nevertheless back over his ideal trip, having raced over 6f in his final two starts last year. He ran about as well as could be expected. (op 22-1)
Better Be The One(AUS), third in this race last year, was struggling to go the pace some way out and, while he was closing at the death, he was never in the hunt.
Margot Did(IRE) showed good speed to a furlong and a half out, but in common with most of the other pacesetters she paid the price inside the last. This ground was probably plenty quick enough for her. (op 10-1)
War Artist(AUS), runner-up in this last year, is now a 9yo and looks to have lost a step.
A Shin Virgo(JPN) was never a threat.
Prohibit followed up his disappointing efforts in the trial with a sub-par performance in the main event.
Regally Ready(USA) was also disappointing. (op 14-1)
Addictive Dream(IRE) was another who paid the price for taking the field along at a strong gallop.

1147a DUBAI GOLDEN SHAHEEN SPONSORED BY GULF NEWS (GROUP 1) (TAPETA) — 6f

4:35 (4:35) 3-Y-0+

£774,193 (£258,064; £129,032; £64,516; £38,709; £25,806)

RPR

1 **Krypton Factor**[21] [874] 4-9-0 117 ....(b) KierenFallon 5 123
(F Nass, Bahrain) *trckd ldr: rdn 2f out: led 110yds out: r.o wl* **13/2**

2 2 1/4 **Rocket Man (AUS)**[27] 7-9-0 125 .... FCoetzee 1 116
(Patrick Shaw, Singapore) *wl away: disp str pce: led 2 1/2f out: hdd 110yds out: no ex* **3/1**[1]

3 2 **Lucky Nine (IRE)**[27] 5-9-0 118 ....(b) BrettPrebble 12 109
(C Fownes, Hong Kong) *mid-div: chsd ldrs 2 1/2f out: one pce fnl f* **13/2**

4 1 1/2 **Hitchens (IRE)**[21] [874] 7-9-0 113 .... SilvestreDeSousa 6 105
(David Barron) *mid-div: r.o fnl 1 1/2f* **14/1**

5 3 1/4 **Giant Ryan (USA)**[147] [7302] 6-9-0 115 ....(t) WMartinez 3 94
(Bisnath Parboo, U.S.A) *wl away: disp str pce: hdd 2 1/2 out: kpt on same pce fnl f* **16/1**

6 hd **The Factor (USA)**[35] 4-9-0 117 ....(t) RBejarano 7 94+
(Bob Baffert, U.S.A) *nt travel early: passed btn rivals late on* **4/1**[3]

7 1/2 **Inxile (IRE)**[21] [875] 7-9-0 113 ....(p) AdrianNicholls 10 92
(David Nicholls) *trckd ldrs tl wknd fnl f* **40/1**

8 1 **Russian Rock (IRE)**[22] [861] 5-9-0 108 .... WayneSmith 4 89
(M Al Muhairi, UAE) *nvr bttr than mid-div* **40/1**

9 2 3/4 **Happy Dubai (IRE)**[32] 5-9-0 112 ....(t) JohnnyMurtagh 2 80
(A Al Raihe, UAE) *trckd ldrs: ev ch 1 1/2f out: one pce fnl f* **33/1**

10 1 **Sepoy (AUS)**[35] 4-8-11 123 .... KerrinMcEvoy 9 74
(Peter Snowden, Australia) *ct wd and keen early: nvr travelled* **7/2**[2]

11 3/4 **Iver Bridge Lad**[21] [874] 5-9-0 108 ....(b) MichaelO'Connell 8 74
(John Ryan) *slowly away: a in rr* **50/1**

12 2 **Soul (AUS)**[30] [756] 5-9-0 113 .... FrankieDettori 11 68
(Saeed Bin Suroor) *nvr bttr than mid-div* **14/1**

1m 10.79s (-0.81) **Going Correction** +0.30s/f (Slow) **12** Ran SP% **122.9**
Speed ratings: **117,114,111,109,105 104,104,102,99,97 96,94**
CSF: £26.77; TRICAST: £137.95.
Owner Fawzi Abdulla Nass **Bred** Lady Fairhaven **Trained** Bahrain

FOCUS
It was a shame The Factor and Sepoy failed to give their true running, but this was still a high-class sprint. The winner produced a step up, with the second to his mark.

NOTEBOOK
Krypton Factor had the ideal trip just in behind the pacesetters. He's progressed significantly since returned to sprinting at the Carnival, including taking the Group 3 Mahab Al Shimaal from a poor draw last time, and he could yet have more to offer. However, he may struggle to confirm form with Rocket Man should they meet on that one's home patch in the KrisFlyer International Sprint at Kranji in May. (op 15/2)
Rocket Man(AUS) ran an absolutely huge race in defeat. According to Trakus the 400m split was the quickest in the history of Meydan and he was one of those responsible, duelling with Giant Ryan from the off. The US speedster understandably dropped away, and Rocket Man should also have faded, but he kept on remarkably well for second.
Lucky Nine(IRE), last year's Hong Kong Sprint winner who was again successful at the top level last time, wasn't helped by a wide draw but looked third best on the day. (op 7-1)
Hitchens(IRE) actually defeated Krypton Factor earlier in the year, but he was no match for that rival on his previous start, or this time. He ran an admirable race nonetheless.
Giant Ryan(USA) paid for helping set the rapid early fractions along with the runner-up. (op 14-1 tchd 20-1)
The Factor(USA) has shown in the US that he's capable of going ridiculously fast fractions, but he just wasn't on his game this time. He struggled badly early on before running on all too late. (op 9-2)
Inxile(IRE) ran about as well as could have been expected from a double-figure stall. (op 33-1)
Russian Rock(IRE), who has shown improved form at Jebel Ali lately, notably winning a Listed race last time, was outclassed back at Meydan.
Sepoy(AUS) is one of the best sprinters in Australia, but he was trying this surface for the first time and, keen early, he basically never looked happy.

1148a DUBAI DUTY FREE SPONSORED BY DUBAI DUTY FREE (GROUP 1) (TURF) — 1m 1f

5:25 (5:25) 3-Y-0+

£1,935,483 (£645,161; £322,580; £161,290; £96,774; £64,516)

RPR

1 **Cityscape**[111] [7731] 6-9-0 121 .... JamesDoyle 11 126
(Roger Charlton) *trckd ldrs: kicked clr 2 1/2f out: r.o wl: comf* **8/1**[3]

2 4 1/4 **Mutahadee (IRE)**[21] [879] 4-9-0 116 .... ChristopheSoumillon 10 117
(M F De Kock, South Africa) *in rr of mid-div: r.o fnl 2f: nrst fin* **9/2**[2]

3 hd **City Style (USA)**[21] [879] 6-9-0 113 .... MickaelBarzalona 13 117
(Mahmood Al Zarooni) *mid-div: r.o fnl 2f: nrst fin* **25/1**

4 1 1/4 **Wigmore Hall (IRE)**[21] [879] 5-9-0 117 .... JamieSpencer 15 114
(Michael Bell) *settled in rr: nvr able to chal but r.o fnl 1 1/2f* **20/1**

5 1/4 **Xtension (IRE)**[34] 5-9-0 118 .... JeffLloyd 9 114
(J Moore, Hong Kong) *in rr of mid-div: r.o fnl 1 1/2f* **16/1**

6 1 3/4 **Musir (AUS)**[21] [876] 6-9-0 117 .... KShea 5 110
(M F De Kock, South Africa) *trckd ldrs: ev ch 2 1/2f out: one pce fnl 1 1/2f* **14/1**

7 hd **Ambitious Dragon (NZ)**[34] 6-9-0 122 ....(b) DouglasWhyte 4 110
(A T Millard, Hong Kong) *nvr bttr than mid-div* **2/1**[1]

8 1 **Delegator**[44] [588] 6-9-0 116 .... FrankieDettori 6 108
(Saeed Bin Suroor) *nvr bttr than mid-div* **22/1**

9 1/2 **Dark Shadow (JPN)**[48] 5-9-0 121 ....(p) YuichiFukunaga 7 107
(Noriyuki Hori, Japan) *nvr bttr than mid-div* **10/1**

10 1/4 **Rajsaman (FR)**[21] [876] 5-9-0 117 ....(b) RoystonFfrench 3 106
(A Al Raihe, UAE) *s.i.s: n.d* **66/1**

11 2 **Green Destiny (IRE)**[21] [878] 5-9-0 119 ....(t) GlynSchofield 1 102
(H J Brown, South Africa) *nvr able to chal* **40/1**

12 1 3/4 **California Memory (USA)**[34] 6-9-0 120 .... MatthewChadwick 8 98
(A S Cruz, Hong Kong) *in rr of mid-div: nvr able to chal* **16/1**

13 6 3/4 **Rio De La Plata (USA)**[21] [879] 7-9-0 118 ....(v) SilvestreDeSousa 14 84
(Saeed Bin Suroor) *trckd ldrs tl wknd 3f out* **40/1**

14 14 **Presvis**[21] [879] 8-9-0 120 .... RyanMoore 12 54
(Luca Cumani) *slowly away: a in rr* **20/1**

15 dist **Await The Dawn (USA)**[147] [7305] 5-9-0 121 .... JPO'Brien 2
(A P O'Brien, Ire) *sn led: hdd & wknd 2 1/2f out* **8/1**[3]

1m 48.65s (108.65) **15** Ran SP% **125.3**
CSF: £41.86; TRICAST: £895.11.
Owner K Abdulla **Bred** Juddmonte Farms Ltd **Trained** Beckhampton, Wilts
■ Dubawi Gold was withdrawn on vet's advice after kicking the back of the stalls.

FOCUS
A competitive race on paper, featuring seven individual Group/Grade 1 winners, and only 9lb covering the entire field. With no confirmed pace in the race a tactical affair looked likely, but Joseph O'Brien sent Await The Dawn on and set a reasonable gallop. A personal best from Cityscape in a track record, and he rates a better than average winner of this.

NOTEBOOK
Cityscape closely followed the pace-setter and when he stopped quickly rounding the turn into the straight, Doyle had no option but to take up the running. Kicking on once in line for home, he quickly pulled out a lead of six or seven lengths, and while that gap was closed down a little as the line approached, he won easily in a course record, beating the previous time by 0.09sec. It's hard to know where this performance came from, as on the face of it it looks a big step up on his previous efforts, but fast ground is clearly not a problem to him any longer, he showed that in Hong Kong as well, and winning over this slightly longer trip opens up the possibility of going 1m2f with him now. He'll have plenty of options, both in Europe and overseas (Roger Charlton mentioned the possibility of Singapore, and going back to Hong Kong), but of course being in the same ownership as Frankel reduces his choices in Britain to some degree.
Mutahadee(IRE) narrowly reversed Jebel Hatta form with City Style while confirming form with Wigmore Hall, Presvis, and Rio De La Plata. He didn't enjoy the greatest trip, being trapped wider than ideal throughout and only going in pursuit of the winner after he'd stolen a march. He could now go for the Singapore Cup. (op 6-1)
City Style(USA) also didn't get the best of trips and didn't get going until it was too late.
Wigmore Hall(IRE), third to Presvis in this race last year, was drawn widest of all. Dropped in towards the back as usual, when the winner kicked for home he had yet to be asked for an effort. Switched to the outer, he had far too much ground to make up inside the final furlong and a half, and while he stayed on he was never in a position to challenge for the places. His rider felt the ground was quicker than ideal. (op 14-1)
Xtension(IRE) finished narrowly behind Cityscape when third in the Hong Kong Mile, but he never saw which way he went this time. One small consolation is that, for the first time in seven meetings, he finished in front of his old rival Ambitious Dragon.
Musir(AUS), who is just as effective on turf as he is on Tapeta, tracked the leader, saving ground on the rail, but couldn't match the winner's acceleration from the top of the straight. He had every chance. (op 12-1)
Ambitious Dragon(NZ) was a well-backed favourite and simply didn't run his race. He got stirred up in the paddock beforehand and in the race itself he wouldn't settle in the early stages. Winner of five Group 1 races at Sha Tin in Hong Kong, he has a smart turn of foot on his day, but just couldn't utilise it here having wasted energy early. (op 5-2)
Delegator travelled well into the straight but found little extra once straightened for home. His stamina for this trip had been the question mark and he certainly didn't improve for the longer distance. (op 20-1)
Dark Shadow(JPN), who put up a good effort in defeat in his prep race at Kyoto, looked to hold sound claims, but he was another who had a wide trip and he didn't help his cause by hanging left in the straight.
Rajsaman(FR) never threatened, although he was done no favours when the weakening Await The Dawn got in his way on the bend into the straight. (op 50-1)
Green Destiny(IRE) was another who enjoyed a ground-saving trip on the inside and had no real excuse. (op 33-1)
California Memory(USA) was inconvenienced to an even greater extent, as the Ballydoyle horse fell back into his path. (op 12-1)
Presvis was held up in last place and looking for a way through when Await The Drawn dropped back, becoming another hampered in the same incident. (op 16-1)
Await The Dawn(USA) set a reasonable gallop, but stopped quickly rounding the turn into the straight. (op 9-1)

1149a DUBAI SHEEMA CLASSIC PRESENTED BY LONGINES (GROUP 1) (TURF) — 1m 4f 11y

6:00 (6:00) 3-Y-0+

£1,935,483 (£645,161; £322,580; £161,290; £96,774; £64,516)

RPR

1 **Cirrus Des Aigles (FR)**[28] [794] 6-9-0 128 .... OlivierPeslier 8 125
(Mme C Barande-Barbe, France) *trckd ldrs: led 4 1/2f out: kicked clr 1 1/2f out: r.o wl* **11/4**[2]

2 1/4 **St Nicholas Abbey (IRE)**[147] [7305] 5-9-0 124 .... JPO'Brien 9 125+
(A P O'Brien, Ire) *mid-div: chsd ldrs 2 1/2f out: r.o fnl 1 1/2f: nrst fin* **9/4**[1]

3 3 1/2 **Jakkalberry (IRE)**[30] [759] 6-9-0 117 ....(t) RyanMoore 7 119
(Marco Botti) *s.i.s: in rr of mid-div: r.o fnl 1 1/2f: nrst fin* **33/1**

4 1/2 **Treasure Beach**[167] [6910] 4-8-13 120 .... JamieSpencer 6 119
(A P O'Brien, Ire) *trckd ldng pair: ev ch 3f out: nt qckn fnl 1 1/2f* **8/1**

5 1 1/4 **Mahbooba (AUS)**[43] [617] 5-8-9 113 .... KShea 4 111
(M F De Kock, South Africa) *nvr bttr than mid-div* **20/1**

6 1 1/2 **Beaten Up**[161] [7027] 4-8-13 119 .... JohnnyMurtagh 3 115
(William Haggas) *nvr bttr than mid-div* **7/2**[3]

7 2 **Cavalryman**[21] [877] 6-9-0 113 .... FrankieDettori 5 110
(Saeed Bin Suroor) *settled in rr: nvr able to chal* **14/1**

8 1/2 **Songcraft (IRE)**[21] [877] 4-8-13 115 ....(v) SilvestreDeSousa 1 111
(Saeed Bin Suroor) *trckd ldng pair: rdn 3 1/2f out: wknd fnl 2f* **16/1**

9 2 1/2 **Shimraan (FR)**[21] [877] 5-9-0 119 .... MickaelBarzalona 10 106
(Mahmood Al Zarooni) *broke awkwardly: settled in rr: nvr able to chal* **33/1**

10 dist **Bold Silvano (SAF)**[21] [878] 6-9-0 118 ....(t) ChristopheSoumillon 2
(M F De Kock, South Africa) *sn led: hdd 4 1/2f out: wknd 2 1/2f out* **16/1**

2m 31.3s (151.30)
WFA 4 from 5yo+ 2lb **10** Ran SP% **119.8**
CSF: £9.46; TRICAST: £162.63.
Owner Jean-Claude-Alain Dupouy & Xavier Niel **Bred** M Yvon Lelimouzin & M Benoit Deschamps **Trained** France

FOCUS
With Champion Stakes winner Cirrus Des Aigles, Breeders' Cup Turf winner St Nicholas Abbey, Irish Derby winner Treasure Beach and up-and-comer Beaten Up in the line-up, the race looked pretty much up to standard, and the form looks solid. However a cautious view has been taken of the race. They went quite steady early.

NOTEBOOK

Cirrus Des Aigles(FR) was always well placed on the leader's shoulder. Taking over early in the straight, he was able to get first run on the runner-up, and that proved crucial. He was previously considered something of a 1m2f specialist, but he'd won over this sort of trip on more than one occasion in the past and clearly stamina is not a problem for him, although his turn of foot is more effective when the early pace is sedate. He had originally been scheduled to run in the World Cup, but when he was turned over on the AW at Chantilly on his reappearance (only 1-8 on synthetics), he was rerouted to this race. That proved a wise decision.

St Nicholas Abbey(IRE) was impressive at the Breeders' Cup, but he got to use Lasix there, and he lacked a previous outing this term (beaten on reappearance last two seasons). He stays this trip well so the lack of early pace counted against him, and allowing a horse as good as Cirrus Des Aigles to get first run in the straight was always going to mean he would be up against it. He closed him right down close home, but just came up short. The Coronation Cup, which he won last year, looks an obvious target for him once again. (op 11-4)

Jakkalberry(IRE), in a similar position to St Nicholas Abbey turning in, couldn't match his closing speed, but still ran on well. The Melbourne Cup is apparently the long-term plan for him. (op 28-1)

Treasure Beach is a dual Group 1 winner, but he very much looked the stable's second string here. Having tracked the winner for most of the race, he had his chance in the straight, but couldn't match that one's acceleration. He might have to head back to America and Canada in search of Group 1 success this year.

Mahbooba(AUS), who had more on her plate back against the boys, didn't settle that well early on. She could have done with a stronger pace as her finishing effort looked to be compromised. (op 16-1)

Beaten Up was another who was keen through the early stages and didn't finish as he can. This was only his fourth ever start and it might just have been all too much for him at this stage of his career, but he remains a gelding of great potential, and he's not one to give up on.

Cavalryman didn't shape badly in the Dubai City Of Gold last time out, but he made little progress from off the pace in the straight here, and looked rather uncomfortable on the ground.

Songcraft(IRE), who has had a good winter at Meydan, dropped right out in the straight.

Shimraan(FR) hasn't lived up to expectations in Dubai. (op 25-1)

Bold Silvano(SAF) had been intended to run in the World Cup. A beaten favourite in both his starts on the Tapeta (excuse latest) since returning from injury, he dropped out quickly from the turn in on this return to the turf, and perhaps the application of a tongue-tie for the first time hinted at a breathing problem.

1150a DUBAI WORLD CUP SPONSORED BY EMIRATES AIRLINE (GROUP 1) (TAPETA) — 1m 2f

6:40 (6:40) 3-Y-O+

£3,870,967 (£1,290,322; £645,161; £322,580; £193,548; £129,032)

RPR

1 — **Monterosso**^{21} [878] 5-9-0 121 ....(t) MickaelBarzalona 8 — 126
(Mahmood Al Zarooni) *mid-div: smooth prog 2 1/2f out: led 1 1/2f out: r.o wl: comf* **20/1**

2 — 3 — **Capponi (IRE)**^{21} [878] 5-9-0 122 .... AhmedAjtebi 11 — 120
(Mahmood Al Zarooni) *trckd ldrs: led 2f out: hdd 1 1/2f out: kpt on same pce* **11/1**

3 — ½ — **Planteur (IRE)**^{202} [5988] 5-9-0 122 .... RyanMoore 6 — 119
(Marco Botti) *s.i.s: settled in rr: r.o fnl 2f: nrst fin* **14/1**

4 — ½ — **So You Think (NZ)**^{147} [7308] 6-9-0 126 .... JPO'Brien 4 — 118
(A P O'Brien, Ire) *trckd ldrs: ev ch 2f out: nt qckn fnl f* **5/4**^{1}

5 — 2¼ — **Zazou (GER)**^{28} [794] 5-9-0 118 .... OlivierPeslier 3 — 114
(W Hickst, Germany) *in rr of mid-div: r.o fnl 2f* **12/1**

6 — 1 — **Eishin Flash (JPN)**^{97} [7873] 5-9-0 120 .... Christophe-PatriceLemaire 2 — 112
(Hideaki Fujiwara, Japan) *settled in rr: nvr nr to chal but r.o fnl 1 1/2f* **14/1**

7 — hd — **Prince Bishop (IRE)**^{21} [878] 5-9-0 116 ....(v) FrankieDettori 12 — 111
(Saeed Bin Suroor) *settled in rr: n.d* **33/1**

8 — nk — **Master Of Hounds (USA)**^{21} [879] 4-9-0 115 ..(t) ChristopheSoumillon 1 — 111
(M F De Kock, South Africa) *in rr of mid-div: nvr able to chal* **20/1**

9 — 1 — **Royal Delta (USA)**^{35} 4-8-9 119 .... JLezcano 7 — 104
(William Mott, U.S.A) *trckd ldrs: seriously hmpd by wkng rival 3f out: nt rcvr* **10/1**

10 — 3¼ — **Smart Falcon (JPN)**^{66} 7-9-0 118 .... YutakaTake 5 — 102
(Ken Kozaki, Japan) *stmbld s: racd in rr: nvr nr to chal* **13/2**^{2}

11 — ½ — **Mendip (USA)**^{21} [878] 5-9-0 115 .... SilvestreDeSousa 13 — 101
(Saeed Bin Suroor) *settled in rr: hmpd fnl bnd: nvr nr to chal* **33/1**

12 — 8¼ — **Game On Dude (USA)**^{55} 5-9-0 122 ....(bt) ChantalSutherland 14 — 85
(Bob Baffert, U.S.A) *mid-div: chsd ldrs 3f out: one pce fnl 1 1/2f* **8/1**^{3}

13 — 4 — **Transcend (JPN)**^{41} 6-9-0 121 ....(t) ShinjiFujita 10 — 77
(Takayuki Yasuda, Japan) *sn led: hdd 2f out: sn btn* **20/1**

2m 2.67s (-2.03) **Going Correction** +0.30s/f (Slow) — **13** Ran SP% **127.5**
Speed ratings: **120,117,117,116,115 114,114,113,113,110 110,103,100**
CSF: £224.74 TRICAST: £3198.78. Placepot: £424.70 to a £1 stake. Pool of: £20656.00- 35.50 winning tickets. Quadpot: £83.20 to a £1 stake. Pool of £1081 - 9.60 winning tickets..
Owner Godolphin **Bred** Darley **Trained** Newmarket, Suffolk

FOCUS

Just like the previous two runnings of the World Cup at Meydan, there was no standout performer and it was again a messy race, with the gallop only modest. The pace might not have been quite as slow as in the last couple of years (final time quicker than those two races), but that's not saying much and the hold-up horses still had little hope. It remains the case that no horse at a single-figure price has finished in the first three since the race moved from Nad Al Sheba and the winning standard in recent seasons has been below the level one would expect of the world's richest race. Some might enjoy the spectacle, but it's a nightmare for punters. Monterosso posted a personal best.

NOTEBOOK

Monterosso could have had a case made for him as he ran third in last year's race and seemingly needed the run on his only start since then when fourth in a C&D Group 1 on Super Saturday. Plus it should be remembered he's a Royal Ascot winner and went off favourite for an Irish Derby (when with Mark Johnston), but in winning this he hasn't suddenly proved he's top class and that surely defeats the object of the race. His rider celebrated early as usual (and was later unseated when continuing to soak it up on his return to the winner's enclosure), but this time he was on a horse who was well clear. It will be interesting to see if Monterosso can build on this elsewhere.

Capponi(IRE) made it a 1-2 for Godolphin. He had today's winner behind when taking the third round of the Al Maktoum Challenge over C&D last time, but that one has clearly progressed past him and his limitations were exposed. (op 12-1)

Planteur(IRE) deserves a deal of credit for getting so close as he sweated up, started awkwardly and was then caught wider and further back than ideal. This was a really promising debut for the Marco Botti yard after a 202-day break and it's hoped he goes on from it, unlike after he won the Prix Ganay last year.

So You Think(NZ) was heavily gambled shortly before the off, but he again failed to justify the hype. He has proved time and again he's high class on his day, but he's never convinced as a real top notcher - not in the northern hemisphere anyway - and it's got to be doubtful he'll ever reach such heights after this display. Despite having been well placed, he looked laboured under pressure and was one-paced. (op 6-4)

Zazou(GER) defeated Cirrus Des Aigles (won the Sheema Classic earlier on this card) in a Polytrack conditions race on his return, but he could never get seriously involved this time.

Eishin Flash(JPN), who returned to his best when second to Orfevre in the Arima Kinen last time, found this an insufficient stamina test. He raced towards the rear having leapt as the stalls opened and then just plugged on having taken the shortest route.

Prince Bishop(IRE) didn't get the best of trips, racing off the modest pace and being caught wide for some of the way.

Master Of Hounds(USA) struggled. He was allowed an easy lead when winning the Group 1 Jebel Hatta (1m1f, turf) and this was a lot tougher.

Royal Delta(USA) was an intriguing contender for Bill Mott, who trained Cigar to win the inaugural running in 1996 and had sent out only one runner in the race since then. However, last year's Ladies' Classic winner lost her chance when seriously hampered by Transcend, who weakened rapidly just before the straight.

Smart Falcon(JPN) is the best dirt performer in Japan, but we never got the chance to see what he's really made of as he got upset in the stalls and then stumbled soon after the start. He ended up well behind and had no chance.

Mendip(USA) found trouble when already struggling on the final bend.

Game On Dude(USA) had a tough, wide trip from stall 14.

Transcend(JPN) had been bustled up to help take the field along, but his rider never looked at ease, appearing to want to slow the pace down the back straight despite having company, and something may have been amiss when the horse dropped away.

1128 DONCASTER (L-H)

Sunday, April 1

OFFICIAL GOING: Good (watered; 7.1 (overall), 7.7 (middle - far side), 7.8 (middle -stands' side))

Wind: light 1/2 against Weather: fine and sunny

1154 AJA GENTLEMAN AMATEUR RIDERS' H'CAP — 1m 4f

1:35 (1:35) (Class 5) (0-70,70) 4-Y-O+ — **£2,807** (£870; £435; £217) **Stalls** Low

Form — RPR

00-6 — 1 — **Arizona John (IRE)**^{22} [872] 7-10-10 **66** .... MrDHDunsdon 9 — 78+
(John Mackie) *trckd ldrs: smooth hdwy over 3f out: led on bit wl over 2f out: rdn ins fnl f: kpt on* **5/1**^{1}

-524 — 2 — ½ — **Edgeworth (IRE)**^{10} [1000] 6-10-8 **67** .... MrMJJSmith(3) 15 — 77
(David Bridgwater) *hld up towards rr: hdwy over 3f out: n.m.r wl over 2f out: effrt to chse ldrs wl over 1f out: sn rdn and styd on wl fnl f* **10/1**

066- — 3 — ¾ — **Zaplamation (IRE)**^{103} [6295] 7-9-13 **60** .... MrFMitchell(5) 2 — 69
(John Quinn) *midfield: hdwy to trck ldrs over 4f out: effrt wl over 2f out: rdn to chse wnr over 1f out: kpt on same pce fnl f* **6/1**^{2}

06-2 — 4 — 7 — **White Diamond**^{15} [944] 5-10-9 **68** .... MrStephenHarrison(3) 7 — 66
(Michael Appleby) *cl up: led wl over 3f out: rdn and hdd wl over 2f out: grad wknd appr fnl f* **12/1**

-554 — 5 — nse — **Pitkin**^{10} [1002] 4-9-11 **59** .... MrWEasterby(5) 16 — 57
(Michael Easterby) *midfield: hdwy over 3f out: rdn to chse ldrs over 2f out: kpt on same pce* **8/1**^{3}

-030 — 6 — 1¼ — **Merrjanah**^{41} [636] 4-9-6 **56** oh1 .... MrAFrench(7) 1 — 52
(John Wainwright) *hld up towards rr: hdwy over 4f out: n.m.r wl over 2f out: sn swtchd rt and styd on appr fnl f: nt rch ldrs* **33/1**

-401 — 7 — nk — **Jeer (IRE)**^{50} [535] 8-10-12 **68** .... MrOGreenall 3 — 63
(Michael Easterby) *hld up in rr: hdwy 3f out: rdn over 2f out: sn no imp* **6/1**^{2}

600- — 8 — ¾ — **Hurakan (IRE)**^{181} [6592] 6-10-6 **65** .... MrMPrice(3) 4 — 59
(Richard Price) *hld up towards rr: hdwy over 3f out: sn rdn along and n.d* **16/1**

310- — 9 — ½ — **Kodicil (IRE)**^{152} [7215] 4-10-9 **66** .... MrSWalker 10 — 59
(Tim Walford) *t.k.h: chsd ldng pair: pushed along over 3f out: sn rdn and btn over 2f out* **5/1**^{1}

2-20 — 10 — 4½ — **Northern Spy (USA)**^{67} [302] 8-10-2 **63** .... MrJCoffill-Brown(5) 8 — 49
(Simon Dow) *in tch: hdwy on inner to chse ldrs 1/2-way: rdn along 3f out: sn wknd* **16/1**

00-1 — 11 — 1¼ — **Lil Ella (IRE)**^{41} [632] 5-9-13 **60** .... MrNSlatter(5) 11 — 44
(Patrick Holmes) *hld up: a towards rr* **16/1**

0/5- — 12 — 5 — **Sedgwick**^{362} [1150] 10-10-9 **68** .... MrMEnnis(3) 12 — 44
(Shaun Harris) *in tch: rdn along over 3f out: sn wknd* **25/1**

6504 — 13 — 11 — **Angelena Ballerina (IRE)**^{3} [1092] 5-9-7 **56** oh5 .... MrLMichael(7) 6 — 14
(Dai Williams) *chsd ldrs: rdn along 4f out: sn wknd* **40/1**

005- — 14 — 12 — **Stadium Of Light (IRE)**^{211} [5738] 5-9-10 **57** .... MrOGarner(5) 17
(John Harris) *sn led: rdn along over 4f out: hdd wl over 3f out and sn wknd* **40/1**

2302 — 15 — 3¾ — **Gallantry**^{10} [995] 10-9-9 **58** .... MrJBromley(7) 5
(Paul Howling) *hld up: a in rr* **28/1**

/00- — 16 — 11 — **Ladies Best**^{184} [3730] 8-10-9 **70** ....(p) MrGeorgeHenderson(5) 14
(John Harris) *a in rr: bhd fnl 3f* **25/1**

2m 35.19s (0.29) **Going Correction** +0.10s/f (Good)
WFA 4 from 5yo+ 1lb — **16** Ran SP% **126.4**
Speed ratings (Par 103): **103,102,102,97,97 96,96,95,95,92 91,88,81,73,70 63**
toteswingers:1&2:£18.60, 1&3:£8.80, 2&3:£15.20 CSF £53.01 CT £316.38 TOTE £7.10: £1.70, £3.50, £1.90, £2.30; EX 69.50 Trifecta £198.50 Pool: £627.87 - 2.34 winning units..
Owner Derbyshire Racing **Bred** Abergwaun Farms **Trained** Church Broughton , Derbys

FOCUS

Good ground for a second day straight and GoingStick readings suggested there was little between to the two sides (7.7 far side - 7.8 stands' side). Trainer Alan McCabe, who walked the track, felt it had "tightened up a bit" since the previous day. They went a steady pace in this amateur riders' handicap, yet three were able to draw clear, with the money horses coming to the fore.

1155 CROWNHOTEL-BAWTRY.COM MAIDEN STKS — 7f

2:10 (2:11) (Class 5) 3-Y-O — **£2,911** (£866; £432; £216) **Stalls** High

Form — RPR

2- — 1 — **Born To Surprise**^{185} [6483] 3-9-3 0 .... JamieSpencer 12 — 94+
(Michael Bell) *hld up in rr: gd hdwy to ld over 1f out: qcknd clr: impressive* **7/4**^{1}

40- — 2 — 5 — **Star Date (IRE)**^{158} [7101] 3-9-3 0 .... NickyMackay 8 — 77+
(Gerard Butler) *hld up in rr: styd on fnl 2f: tk 2nd jst ins fnl f: no ch w wnr* **16/1**

3 — ½ — **Mutafaakir (IRE)** 3-9-3 0 .... PaulHanagan 9 — 76+
(John Gosden) *dwlt: mid-div: effrt over 2f out: hung lft: kpt on to take 3rd last 150yds* **11/2**

00- — 4 — 3¼ — **Chester Aristocrat**^{318} [2214] 3-9-3 0 .... DavidAllan 2 — 67
(Eric Alston) *s.i.s: t.k.h: sn trcking ldrs: outpcd over 2f out: kpt on fnl f* **100/1**

5 — ¾ — **Malingering** 3-9-3 0 .... MartinLane 6 — 65
(Hugo Palmer) *s.s: in rr tl styd on fnl 2f* **66/1**

04- — 6 — 1 — **Take Two**^{149} [7257] 3-9-3 0 .... RussKennemore 7 — 62
(John O'Shea) *t.k.h: led after 2f: hdd over 2f out: wknd fnl f* **40/1**

44- **7** ½ **Sequoia**[250] 4414 3-9-3 0 RobertWinston 11 61
(Charles Hills) *trckd ldrs: led over 2f out: hdd & wknd over 1f out* **3/1**[2]
00- **8** *shd* **Vite (IRE)**[152] 7209 3-9-3 0 PaulMulrennan 5 61
(Deborah Sanderson) *chsd ldrs: t.k.h: wknd over 1f out* **150/1**
04- **9** *shd* **Nordic Quest (IRE)**[134] 7494 3-9-3 0 LukeMorris 1 60
(Gerard Butler) *in rr: swtchd rt after 1f: kpt on fnl 2f: nvr a factor* **12/1**
0- **10** ¾ **Highland Duke (IRE)**[197] 6160 3-9-3 0 AdamKirby 14 58
(Clive Cox) *chsd ldrs: t.k.h: wknd over 1f out* **9/2**[3]
060- **11** ¾ **So Cheeky**[95] 7889 3-8-12 55 AndrewMullen 10 51
(Peter Salmon) *chsd ldrs: wknd over 1f out* **200/1**
12 7 **Icewan** 3-9-3 0 MickyFenton 13 37
(Paul Midgley) *s.i.s: sn pushed along in rr: bhd fnl 2f* **150/1**
13 2 ½ **Common Cents** 3-8-10 0 DarrenEgan(7) 3 31
(Ronald Harris) *chsd ldrs on outer: lost pl 2f out* **80/1**
0- **14** 6 **Penang Pegasus**[170] 6828 3-9-3 0 DanielTudhope 4
(David O'Meara) *led 2f: lost pl over 2f out* **20/1**

1m 27.04s (0.74) **Going Correction** +0.075s/f (Good) **14 Ran SP% 121.2**
Speed ratings (Par 98): **98,92,91,88,87 86,85,85,85,84 83,75,72,65**
toteswingers:1&2:£7.30, 1&3:£3.90, 2&3:£10.30 CSF £34.44 TOTE £3.30: £1.60, £3.70, £1.80; EX 39.10 Trifecta £267.10 Pool: £934.95 - 2.59 winning units..
Owner Dr Ali Ridha **Bred** Rabbah Bloodstock Limited **Trained** Newmarket, Suffolk

FOCUS
Probably just an ordinary maiden, but hard not to be taken with the effort of the winner. The winning time was quicker than both older-horse handicaps over the trip.

1156 DOWNLOAD WILLIAM HILL FROM THE APP STORE H'CAP (DIV I) 7f
2:45 (2:47) (Class 4) (0-85,85) 4-Y-O+ **£5,175** (£1,540; £769; £384) **Stalls** High

Form RPR
400- **1** **Karaka Jack**[158] 7110 5-9-3 **81** AdrianNicholls 16 89
(David Nicholls) *trckd ldrs: pushed along 1/2-way: sn rdn and outpcd: hdwy wl over 1f out: swtchd lft and drvn ent fnl f: styd on strly to ld last 75yds* **16/1**
10-0 **2** ¾ **Celtic Sultan (IRE)**[22] 866 8-9-4 **82** MickyFenton 19 88
(Paul Midgley) *trckd ldrs: hdwy over 2f out: rdn to chse ldr over 1f out: drvn to chal ins fnl f and ev ch tl no ex last 75yds* **20/1**
14-2 **3** *shd* **Sound Amigo (IRE)**[47] 554 4-9-2 **80** PJMcDonald 17 86
(Ollie Pears) *prom: cl up 1/2-way: led wl over 2f out: rdn over 1f out: hdd and no ex last 75yds* **9/1**[3]
64-0 **4** ¾ **Thunderball**[71] 253 6-9-7 **85** (p) NeilCallan 8 89
(Scott Dixon) *in tch: hdwy over 2f out: rdn to chse ldng pair over 1f out: drvn and ch ent fnl f: kpt on same pce* **28/1**
12-0 **5** *nk* **Ellie In The Pink (IRE)**[11] 987 4-8-13 **77** KierenFallon 10 80
(Alan Jarvis) *midfield: pushed along wl over 2f out: rdn and hdwy wl over 1f out: n.m.r and swtchd rt ent fnl f: kpt on u.p towards fin* **4/1**[1]
21-3 **6** ½ **Aerodynamic (IRE)**[88] 36 5-8-12 **76** PaddyAspell 4 78+
(Michael Easterby) *hld up in rr: hdwy over 2f out: rdn over 1f out: styd on wl fnl f: nrst fin* **16/1**
02-5 **7** ½ **Musnad (USA)**[20] 273 4-8-7 **71** oh1 BarryMcHugh 6 71
(Brian Ellison) *t.k.h: hld up towards rr: hdwy over 2f out: rdn and n.m.r over 1f out: kpt on fnl f: nrst fin* **20/1**
0404 **8** 1 ¼ **Bawaardi (IRE)**[15] 941 6-8-13 **82** MatthewCosham(5) 22 79
(David Evans) *in tch towards stands' rail: hdwy over 2f out: rdn to chse ldrs over 1f out: kpt on same pce fnl f* **25/1**
0-23 **9** ¾ **Jungle Bay**[18] 893 5-8-3 **74** LewisWalsh(7) 13 69
(Jane Chapple-Hyam) *chsd ldrs: rdn along 2f out: wknd appr fnl f* **12/1**
000- **10** *nk* **Amazing Amoray (IRE)**[198] 6113 4-9-1 **79** PhillipMakin 2 73
(David Barron) *towards rr: hdwy 2f out: sn rdn and styd on fnl f: nt rch ldrs* **20/1**
000- **11** *nk* **Sonning Rose (IRE)**[184] 6495 4-8-10 **74** TonyCulhane 20 67
(Mick Channon) *stdd s and hld up towards rr: hdwy over 2f out: rdn and n.m.r over 1f out: kpt on: nt rch ldrs* **20/1**
025- **12** 1 ½ **Little Black Book (IRE)**[202] 6003 4-9-1 **79** LukeMorris 1 68
(Gerard Butler) *midfield: hdwy 1/2-way: rdn to chse ldrs over 2f out: wknd over 1f out* **8/1**[2]
230- **13** ½ **Rio Cobolo (IRE)**[169] 6869 6-8-3 **74** ShirleyTeasdale(7) 18 62
(David Nicholls) *prom: cl up 1/2-way: led briefly 3f out: sn rdn and hdd over 2f out: wknd over 1f out* **50/1**
300- **14** 2 **Oratory (IRE)**[163] 6989 6-9-0 **78** RobertWinston 7 60
(Geoffrey Harker) *dwlt and sltly hmpd s: towards rr: hdwy over 2f out: rdn and n.m.r wl over 1f out: n.d* **14/1**
101- **15** ¾ **Silvery Moon (IRE)**[199] 6078 5-9-5 **83** DavidAllan 15 63
(Tim Easterby) *chsd ldrs: rdn wl over 2f out: sn wknd* **11/1**
016- **16** ½ **Al Muheer (IRE)**[239] 4810 7-9-0 **78** (b) JamesSullivan 21 57
(Ruth Carr) *in tch: rdn along wl over 2f out: sn wknd* **40/1**
-414 **17** ½ **Viva Ronaldo (IRE)**[50] 520 6-9-0 **85** GeorgeChaloner(7) 3 63
(Richard Fahey) *a towards rr* **14/1**
263/ **18** ¾ **Jalors (IRE)**[536] 6849 4-8-0 **71** oh1 DarrenEgan(7) 9 47
(Ronald Harris) *nvr a factor* **50/1**
501- **19** 12 **Count Bertoni (IRE)**[190] 6355 5-9-1 **79** (b) DanielTudhope 11 22
(David O'Meara) *prom: rdn along 1/2-way: sn wknd* **25/1**
0-06 **20** *nse* **Zacynthus (IRE)**[64] 354 4-9-5 **83** MartinHarley 5 26
(Alan McCabe) *a bhd* **11/1**
160- **21** ¾ **Barkston Ash**[219] 5450 4-9-0 **78** DuranFentiman 14 19
(Eric Alston) *chsd ldrs: rdn along wl over 2f out: sn wknd* **28/1**
100- **22** 3 **Polish World (USA)**[162] 7023 8-9-0 **85** NedCurtis(7) 12 18
(Paul Midgley) *led: rdn along 1/2-way: hdd 3f out and sn wknd* **40/1**

1m 27.48s (1.18) **Going Correction** +0.075s/f (Good) **22 Ran SP% 133.0**
Speed ratings (Par 105): **96,95,95,94,93 93,92,91,90,90 89,88,87,85,84 83,83,82,68,68 67,64**
toteswingers:1&2:£60.10, 1&3:£16.50, 2&3:£14.40 CSF £315.53 CT £3079.53 TOTE £18.70: £5.40, £4.30, £3.10, £7.90; EX 471.10 TRIFECTA Not won..
Owner M Mackay & S Bruce **Bred** Tarworth Bloodstock Investments Ltd **Trained** Sessay, N Yorks

FOCUS
The first division of this fair handicap, in which the runners raced in one group centre-to stands' side. The time was 2.40 seconds slower than division two.
Zacynthus(IRE) Official explanation: jockey said gelding lost its action

1157 NEW WILLIAM HILL IPHONE APP H'CAP 6f
3:20 (3:21) (Class 2) (0-100,100) 4-Y-O+ **£12,938** (£3,850; £1,924; £962) **Stalls** High

Form RPR
-000 **1** **Colonel Mak**[22] 871 5-9-0 **98** LMcNiff(5) 15 107
(David Barron) *chsd ldrs towards stands' side: led over 1f out: kpt on wl* **33/1**
100- **2** 1 ¾ **Advanced**[148] 7295 9-8-12 **94** AmyRyan(3) 11 97
(Kevin Ryan) *in tch: drvn over 2f out: kpt on wl to chse wnr jst fnl f* **20/1**
000- **3** *hd* **King Of Jazz (IRE)**[211] 5699 4-9-3 **96** JamieSpencer 4 99+
(Michael Bell) *towards rr: hdwy on outer 2f out: kpt on wl fnl f* **10/1**
1-45 **4** 1 **Docofthebay (IRE)**[22] 866 8-9-0 **93** (b) RobertWinston 3 93
(Scott Dixon) *mid-div: hdwy over 2f out: kpt on same pce fnl f* **8/1**[3]
020- **5** *hd* **Fitz Flyer (IRE)**[228] 5180 6-8-7 **93** ShirleyTeasdale(7) 19 92
(David Nicholls) *racd stands' side: w ldr: kpt on same pce fnl f* **33/1**
500- **6** ½ **El Viento (FR)**[163] 6987 4-8-9 **91** LeeTopliss(3) 10 88
(Richard Fahey) *hld up in rr: hdwy 2f out: kpt on wl ins fnl f: struck over hd by rival's whip nr fin* **28/1**
/00- **7** 1 **Sunraider (IRE)**[302] 2706 5-8-8 **87** MickyFenton 18 81
(Paul Midgley) *chsd ldrs towards stands' side: one pce fnl 2f* **50/1**
416- **8** *hd* **Nasri**[183] 6521 6-9-4 **97** DarryllHolland 20 90
(David Nicholls) *racd stands' side: led: hdd over 1f out: fdd* **7/1**[2]
400- **9** ½ **Ancient Cross**[170] 6706 8-9-7 **100** (t) PaulMulrennan 17 92
(Michael Easterby) *squeezed out s: hld up in rr: hdwy over 2f out: kpt on fnl f: nvr a threat* **20/1**
240- **10** ½ **Confessional**[162] 7018 5-9-5 **98** (be) DavidAllan 5 88
(Tim Easterby) *chsd ldrs on outer: wknd fnl 100yds* **16/1**
000- **11** ½ **Imperial Djay (IRE)**[197] 6148 7-8-10 **89** PJMcDonald 13 78
(Ruth Carr) *swvd lft s: in rr: kpt on fnl 2f: nvr a factor* **50/1**
046- **12** *nse* **Johannes (IRE)**[156] 7149 9-8-8 **87** TonyHamilton 1 76
(Richard Fahey) *prom: effrt over 2f out: fdd over 1f out* **20/1**
250- **13** *hd* **Damika (IRE)**[206] 5852 9-8-9 **88** MichaelStainton 16 76
(David Brown) *rrd s: sn mid-div: nvr a factor* **40/1**
000- **14** 2 ½ **Star Rover (IRE)**[102] 7847 5-8-4 **88** ow1 (v) MatthewCosham(5) 21 68
(David Evans) *racd stands' side: chsd ldrs: wknd over 1f out* **28/1**
300- **15** ½ **Swilly Ferry (USA)**[162] 7018 5-8-8 **87** AdrianNicholls 22 65
(David Nicholls) *mid-div towards stands' side: nvr a factor* **12/1**
210- **16** 1 ¼ **Marine Commando**[162] 7018 4-8-13 **92** PaulHanagan 14 66
(Richard Fahey) *mid-div: effrt over 2f out: wknd over 1f out* **12/1**
160- **17** ¾ **Desert Law (IRE)**[183] 6522 4-9-5 **98** JimmyFortune 8 70
(Andrew Balding) *hld up in mid-div: hdwy over 2f out: chsng ldrs over 1f out: sn wknd* **5/1**[1]
00-0 **18** *nk* **Crown Choice**[22] 871 7-9-0 **93** FrederikTylicki 6 64
(Paul Midgley) *chsd ldrs on outer: lost pl 2f out* **12/1**
106- **19** 1 ½ **Elusive Prince**[184] 6500 4-8-12 **91** (v) LeeNewman 7 57
(David Barron) *toward rr: short-lived effrt on outer 2f out* **33/1**
300- **20** ½ **No Hubris (USA)**[205] 5879 5-8-11 **90** JamesSullivan 9 55
(Ruth Carr) *s.i.s: a in rr* **33/1**
350- **21** 14 **Joe Packet**[176] 6706 5-9-7 **100** StephenCraine 2 20
(Jonathan Portman) *chsd ldrs on outside: lost pl over 2f out: eased whn bhd* **33/1**
065- **22** 6 **Wildcat Wizard (USA)**[336] 1720 6-8-11 **90** NeilCallan 12
(David Nicholls) *s.i.s: swtchd rt after 1f and racd towards stands' side: bhd fnl 2f: eased* **20/1**

1m 12.7s (-0.90) **Going Correction** +0.075s/f (Good) **22 Ran SP% 125.3**
Speed ratings (Par 109): **109,106,106,105,104 104,102,102,101,101 100,100,100,96,96 94,93,93,91,90 71,63**
toteswingers:1&2:£85.40, 1&3:£42.70, 2&3:£13.40 CSF £570.82 CT £7017.62 TOTE £44.60: £8.00, £5.40, £3.80, £1.90; EX 743.90 TRIFECTA Not won..
Owner Norton Common Farm Racing,O'Kane,Murphy **Bred** Peter Baldwin **Trained** Maunby, N Yorks

FOCUS
All the early pace was stands' side in this sprint handicap.

NOTEBOOK
Colonel Mak, below his best on Polytrack earlier in the year, was well positioned tracking the speed stands' side and always looked the winner having kicked well over 1f out. A very useful sprinter on his day, his rating will elevate to the low 100s following this, which may make life difficult.
Advanced is 4lb above his last winning mark but kept responding and the 9yo is likely to pay his way once more this season. (op 28-1)
King Of Jazz(IRE), making his debut for the yard, finished well and did enough to suggest he can win at the distance, even if 7f is preferred. (op 11-1)
Docofthebay(IRE) made a satisfactory return to turf and should again pay his way this season.
Fitz Flyer(IRE) was soon prominent stands' side and made a good start for his new yard.
El Viento(FR) fared best of the Richard Fahey trio and looks to have more to give as a 4yo.
Sunraider(IRE) is below his last winning mark and made a nice start for his new yard, showing up well stands' side. (op 66-1)
Nasri was soon duelling for the lead from his high draw and should benefit from the outing. (op 11-1)
Ancient Cross made some late headway but is quite high in the handicap.
Swilly Ferry(USA) didn't offer much on this first start for Dandy Nicholls, but can improve. (op 10-1)
Marine Commando was weak in the market made no show on this season reappearance. (op 10-1 tchd 9-1)
Desert Law(IRE) refused to settle on this seasonal reappearance and gave himself no chance. This run should have taken the fizz out of him and he deserves another chance. (tchd 9-2)

1158 BEST ODDS GUARANTEED AT WILLIAMHILL.COM DONCASTER MILE STKS (LISTED RACE) 1m (R)
3:55 (3:55) (Class 1) 4-Y-O+ **£19,536** (£7,388; £3,692; £1,844) **Stalls** Low

Form RPR
531- **1** **Penitent**[188] 6416 6-8-12 108 DanielTudhope 4 96
(David O'Meara) *trckd ldrs: hdwy and cl up whn sltly hmpd 2f out: chal over 1f out: rdn to ld ent fnl f: kpt on* **5/1**[3]
203- **2** *hd* **Questioning (IRE)**[176] 6693 4-8-12 107 (p) WilliamBuick 7 94+
(John Gosden) *trckd ldrs: hdwy 3f out: cl up and ev ch whn hmpd 2f out: sn swtchd rt and rdn: styd on wl fnl f: fin 3rd: plcd 2nd* **3/1**[2]
2-60 **3** ¾ **St Moritz (IRE)**[80] 145 6-8-12 106 AdrianNicholls 8 94
(David Nicholls) *hld up in rr: swtchd to outer and effrt over 2f out: rdn to ld and hung bdly lft 2f out: drvn and hdd ent fnl f: kpt on: fin 2nd: disqualified and plcd 3rd* **5/1**[3]
0400 **4** 1 ¼ **Navajo Chief**[38] 677 5-8-12 100 KierenFallon 3 90
(Alan Jarvis) *trckd ldr: effrt and cl up 3f out: rdn and ev ch whn sltly hmpd 2f out: sn drvn and one pce fnl f* **12/1**
140- **5** 2 ¼ **Side Glance**[169] 6860 5-8-12 115 JimmyFortune 1 85
(Andrew Balding) *led: jnd and rdn along 3f out: hdd 2f out: sn n.m.r and wknd over 1f out* **5/4**[1]
4220 **6** *nk* **Legal Legacy**[11] 987 6-8-12 74 AndrewMullen 6 84?
(David C Griffiths) *hld up: sme hdwy over 2f out: sn rdn and n.d* **100/1**
6-51 **7** 10 **Thatcherite (IRE)**[17] 909 4-8-12 74 (t) StephenCraine 2 60
(Tony Coyle) *trckd ldrs: effrt 3f out: sn rdn and wknd over 2f out* **100/1**

1410 **8** *15* **Dubaianswer**[22] 866 4-8-7 82 BarryMcHugh 5 19
(Tony Coyle) *trckd ldrs: effrt and cl up on outer over 3f out: sn rdn and wknd* **50/1**

1m 39.04s (-0.66) **Going Correction** +0.075s/f (Good) **8** Ran SP% **114.4**
Speed ratings (Par 111): **106,105,105,103,101 101,91,76**
toteswingers:1&3:£4.80, 1&2:£2.80, 3&2:£2.80 CSF £20.40 TOTE £6.00: £1.90, £1.10, £2.10; EX 23.20 Trifecta £138.80 Pool: £2,474.70 - 13.19 winning units.
Owner Middleham Park Racing XVII **Bred** Cheveley Park Stud Ltd **Trained** Nawton, N Yorks
■ Stewards' Enquiry : Adrian Nicholls two-day ban: careless riding (Apr 16-17)

FOCUS
The pace appeared a fairly even one in this Listed contest, yet things got quite tight in the final 2f, and the first four were separated by just over a length. There was 2lb between the first three on ratings.

NOTEBOOK
Penitent, the 2010 Lincoln winner, struggled to find himself at this sort of level last season, but he's since left William Haggas and turned in an improved effort on this reappearance. He'll need more to win at Group 3 level, however. (op 13-2)
Questioning(IRE), placed in a Group 3 at Newmarket on his final outing last season, stayed on having been hampered, but one couldn't say he was unlucky. He had cheekpieces back on and isn't the easiest to win with. (op 7-2)
St Moritz(IRE), last year's winner, didn't have the race go to plan. He wasn't best away and had to come from further back than ideal. He crossed a couple of the runners when sweeping into the lead and, despite sticking on pluckily, it was understandable why he was demoted to third. He can win again at this level. (op 6-1)
Navajo Chief, out of luck in Dubai earlier this year, ran a solid race and showed last season he's capable of winning a handicap from this sort of mark. (tchd 14-1)
Side Glance ended last year contesting a couple of Group 1s. Allowed to stride on, he was quickly beaten once headed and clearly failed to give his running. (op 10-11)

1159 STOBART DONCASTER SHIELD (CONDITIONS STKS) 1m 4f
4:30 (4:30) (Class 2) 4-Y-0+ **£12,938** (£3,850; £1,924; £962) **Stalls** Low

Form RPR
046- **1** **Eternal Heart (IRE)**[169] 6857 4-8-13 103 JoeFanning 4 99
(Mark Johnston) *trckd ldr: effrt over 3f out: led narrowly over 2f out: hdd 1f out: rallied to regain ld last 100yds: hld on wl* **5/2**[2]
413/ **2** *½* **King Of Wands**[592] 5218 6-9-0 107 WilliamBuick 2 98
(John Gosden) *hld up in last: eased outside over 2f out: led narrowly 1f out: sn rdn and hung lft: hdd ins fnl f: no ex towards fin* **5/4**[1]
1410 **3** *hd* **Junoob**[8] 1034 4-9-5 99 (b) RichardKingscote 3 104
(Tom Dascombe) *stdd s: sn trcking ldrs: hdwy to trck ldrs over 2f out: upsides over 1f out: no ex clsng stages* **9/1**
14- **4** *7* **Just Lille (IRE)**[156] 7136 9-8-9 88 (p) PaulHanagan 5 82
(Ann Duffield) *led: qcknd pce over 4f out: hdd over 2f out: wknd fnl 2f* **16/1**
-161 **5** *6* **Tappanappa (IRE)**[12] 971 5-9-0 91 (v) DavidProbert 1 77
(Andrew Balding) *hld up: hdwy over 5f out: rdn over 2f out: edgd lft and wknd over 1f out* **4/1**[3]

2m 31.86s (-3.04) **Going Correction** +0.10s/f (Good)
WFA 4 from 5yo+ 1lb **5** Ran SP% **108.9**
Speed ratings (Par 109): **114,113,113,108,104**
CSF £5.90 TOTE £3.30: £2.00, £1.50; EX 5.60.
Owner Mrs Joan Keaney **Bred** Mrs Joan Keaney **Trained** Middleham Moor, N Yorks
■ Stewards' Enquiry : William Buick caution: careless riding.

FOCUS
A cracking finish to this conditions event.

NOTEBOOK
Eternal Heart(IRE), a half-brother to Yavana's Pace, gutting it out in a fashion typical of runners from the yard. A triple winner early last season, he was Group 3-placed over 2m and this trip is an absolute minimum. The fact he didn't run as a 2yo suggests he can continue to progress this year and he'll presumably take the cup route, with the Henry II Stakes at Sandown in May a possible early season target. (op 3-1 tchd 10-3)
King Of Wands, a progressive sort in 2009/10, looked to be coming with a winning run from 2f out, but he didn't knuckle down as hard as the winner and probably just needed this first run in 592 days. He should improve and can probably be aimed at similar races to the winner. (tchd Evens)
Junoob, progressive on the AW this winter, ran a huge race at the weights, but won't be easy to place and races such as this often don't provide him with the decent pace that suits. (op 7-1)
Just Lille(IRE)'s last two wins have been in claimers and she was always likely to struggle here. (op 14-1)
Tappanappa(IRE) found little and looked awkward. His two wins have been on Polytrack and he's clearly not doing on the track what he does at home, as he is well thought of by his trainer. (tchd 7-2 and 9-2)

1160 EQUINITY POWERED BY GARMIN H'CAP 1m 2f 60y
5:05 (5:05) (Class 3) (0-90,85) 3-Y-O **£8,409** (£2,502; £1,250; £625) **Stalls** Low

Form RPR
1- **1** **Kingsdesire (IRE)**[115] 7673 3-9-7 85 (t) AdamKirby 9 95+
(Marco Botti) *hld up in rr: smooth hdwy over 4f out: trckd ldrs on bit over 2f out: n.m.r and swtchd rt wl over 1f out: sn led: rdn and kpt on wl fnl f* **6/1**[3]
140- **2** *¾* **Goldoni (IRE)**[211] 5709 3-9-5 83 DavidProbert 6 92
(Andrew Balding) *a.p: effrt 3f out: sn rdn and led briefly 2f out: sn hdd: kpt on wl u.p fnl f* **10/1**
623- **3** *2¼* **Hallmark Star**[135] 7454 3-9-0 78 DaneO'Neill 1 83
(Gerard Butler) *trckd ldrs: rdn along and sltly outpcd 2f out: styd on fnl f* **14/1**
40-1 **4** *½* **Ex Oriente (IRE)**[85] 84 3-9-0 78 WilliamBuick 5 83+
(John Gosden) *prom: led over 5f out: rdn along and hdd wl over 3f out: kpt on same pce fnl 2f* **16/1**
12- **5** *½* **Montaser (IRE)**[197] 6144 3-9-2 80 JamieSpencer 2 83+
(David Simcock) *hld up in rr: hdwy on outer wl over 2f out: rdn and styd on wl fnl f: nrst fin* **5/1**[2]
50-6 **6** *nk* **Grand Gold**[27] 803 3-8-3 72 oh1 ow1 (t) MatthewLawson(5) 4 74
(Seamus Durack) *chsd ldrs: rdn along wl over 2f out: sn one pce* **50/1**
166- **7** *1½* **Mcvicar**[174] 6753 3-8-9 73 TonyCulhane 7 72
(Mick Channon) *hld up in rr: hdwy wl over 2f out: rdn and kpt on fnl f: nt rch ldrs* **33/1**
510- **8** *hd* **Indepub**[162] 7021 3-9-0 78 PhillipMakin 10 77
(Kevin Ryan) *hld up towards rr: sme hdwy wl over 2f out: sn rdn and n.d* **33/1**
1- **9** *1¾* **Attenborough (USA)**[241] 4714 3-9-2 80 RyanMoore 11 75
(Jeremy Noseda) *hld up in tch: hdwy to trck ldrs over 4f out: effrt 3f out: shkn up and hld whn n.m.r and sltly hmpd 2f out: sn wknd* **13/8**[1]
1 **10** *2¼* **Modernism**[17] 908 3-9-2 80 JoeFanning 3 71
(Mark Johnston) *led: hdd over 5f out: cl up and led again wl over 3f out: sn rdn: hdd 2f out and sn wknd* **6/1**[3]
205- **11** *8* **The Blue Banana (IRE)**[163] 6986 3-8-13 77 TonyHamilton 8 52
(Edwin Tuer) *a in rr* **20/1**

2m 10.45s (1.05) **Going Correction** +0.10s/f (Good) **11** Ran SP% **117.6**
Speed ratings (Par 102): **99,98,96,96,95 95,94,94,92,91 84**
toteswingers:1&2:£10.40, 1&3:£10.80, 2&3:£20.10 CSF £61.74 CT £810.05 TOTE £6.10: £2.40, £3.20, £3.20; EX 77.90 Trifecta £1486.20 Part won. Pool: £2,008.41 - 0.42 winning units..
Owner Giuliano Manfredini **Bred** Mrs Cherry Faeste **Trained** Newmarket, Suffolk
■ Stewards' Enquiry : Adam Kirby one-day ban: careless riding (Apr 16)

FOCUS
A good-quality 3yo handicap run at just an ordinary gallop.

NOTEBOOK
Kingsdesire(IRE) looked useful winning making a winning debut over 1m at Kempton and his superior speed was what won him the race. This is as far as he wants to go and there should be more to come, with there likely to be options at Newmarket's Craven and Guineas meetings over the next few weeks. (op 11-2 tchd 13-2)
Goldoni(IRE) was never far away and stuck on well. He was trying to come back at the winner and could have done with more of a test at the distance. (tchd 9-1 and 12-1)
Hallmark Star kept grinding away without being able to quicken and a stiffer test will suit the son of Nayef in future. He can win from this sort of mark. (op 16-1)
Ex Oriente(IRE) looked on a high enough mark following his Lingfield maiden win but was well placed throughout and ran well. (op 12-1)
Montaser(IRE) was unable to find room for much of the straight but finished strongly down the outer once the race was all over. He wasn't best placed given the way the race unfolded and looks capable of winning something similar. (op 8-1)
Grand Gold ran well from 2lb wrong and will find easier opportunities.
Attenborough(USA) looked plenty short enough from a mark of 80 on this handicap debut, but one would still have expected a more prominent showing. He held every chance. (op 6-4 tchd 11-8 and 7-4)
Modernism was beaten off readily having made the early running. It was only his second start and he probably deserves another chance. (op 13-2 tchd 5-1)

1161 DOWNLOAD WILLIAM HILL FROM THE APP STORE H'CAP (DIV II) 7f
5:35 (5:36) (Class 4) (0-85,85) 4-Y-0+ **£5,175** (£1,540; £769; £384) **Stalls** High

Form RPR
000- **1** **Mujaadel (USA)**[159] 7076 7-8-10 74 (p) AndrewMullen 12 84
(David Nicholls) *s.i.s: swtchd rt after 1f: gd hdwy stands' side over 2f out: led jst ins fnl f: kpt on towards fin* **16/1**
160- **2** *¾* **Layla's Hero (IRE)**[190] 6331 5-9-7 85 (p) JamieSpencer 22 93+
(John Quinn) *hld up towards rr: stdy hdwy over 2f out: sn nt clr run: gd hdwy and bmpd over 1f out: upsides last 100yds: no ex* **6/1**[1]
200- **3** *½* **Defence Council (IRE)**[102] 7846 4-9-0 78 PaulHanagan 13 84
(Mel Brittain) *in rr: hdwy over 2f out: styd on wl fnl f* **12/1**
000- **4** *1* **Azrael**[246] 4550 4-9-7 85 MartinHarley 20 89
(Alan McCabe) *chsd ldrs stands' side: led over 2f out: hdd jst ins fnl f: kpt on same pce* **14/1**
1-20 **5** *hd* **Global Village (IRE)**[54] 458 7-9-0 78 KierenFallon 11 86+
(Brian Ellison) *in rr div: hdwy and nt clr run over 2f out: swtchd lft over 1f out: keeping on wl last 75yds whn nt clr run and snatched up* **8/1**[2]
4331 **6** *hd* **Caldercruix (USA)**[19] 883 5-9-1 84 (v) RaulDaSilva(5) 14 86
(James Evans) *chsd ldrs: upsides over 1f out: kpt on same pce* **11/1**
450- **7** *nse* **Silverware (USA)**[175] 6727 4-8-13 77 TomEaves 19 79
(Linda Stubbs) *chsd ldrs stands' side: kpt on one pce over 1f out* **33/1**
110- **8** *½* **George Baker (IRE)**[197] 6174 5-9-1 79 WilliamBuick 21 80
(George Baker) *mid-div stands' side: sn drvn along: styd on wl appr fnl f* **14/1**
616- **9** *1¼* **Apollo D'Negro (IRE)**[197] 6167 4-8-10 74 (v) JohnFahy 4 72
(Clive Cox) *chsd ldrs on outer: upsides over 1f out: fdd jst ins fnl f* **11/1**
60-2 **10** *1¼* **Nezami (IRE)**[24] 834 7-8-7 71 oh1 RussKennemore 10 65
(Paul Midgley) *chsd ldrs: drvn and outpcd 3f out: hmpd over 1f out: kpt on fnl f* **20/1**
421- **11** *3½* **Sam Nombulist**[148] 7299 4-9-0 81 AmyRyan(3) 17 66
(Richard Whitaker) *dwlt: sn in tch: outpcd over 3f out: edgd rt: nvr a threat* **9/1**[3]
4105 **12** *½* **Gorgeous Goblin (IRE)**[27] 806 5-8-7 71 oh4 (t) DavidProbert 7 54
(David C Griffiths) *mid-div: drvn over 2f out: wknd over 1f out* **50/1**
241- **13** *2¼* **Switchback**[194] 6234 4-8-13 77 PaulMulrennan 15 54
(Michael Easterby) *dwlt: nvr a factor* **33/1**
406- **14** *shd* **Collateral Damage (IRE)**[274] 3620 9-9-0 78 DavidAllan 1 55
(Tim Easterby) *mid-div: on outer: effrt 3f out: wknd over 1f out* **25/1**
106- **15** *4½* **Illustrious Prince (IRE)**[159] 7076 5-8-11 80 NeilFarley(5) 6 45
(Declan Carroll) *chsd ldrs on outer: wknd over 1f out* **33/1**
004- **16** *3¾* **George Benjamin**[239] 4810 5-8-11 75 AdrianNicholls 8 30
(David Nicholls) *mid-div: brief effrt on outer over 2f out: sn wknd* **12/1**
112- **17** *1¾* **Beckermet (IRE)**[155] 7171 10-9-7 85 PJMcDonald 18 35
(Ruth Carr) *w ldrs: wknd over 2f out* **28/1**
1121 **18** *shd* **Fluctuation (IRE)**[18] 899 4-8-7 71 (v) FrannyNorton 9 21
(Ian Williams) *a towards rr* **14/1**
004- **19** *3¼* **Roninski (IRE)**[120] 7628 4-9-0 83 (t) JustinNewman(5) 5 24
(Deborah Sanderson) *chsd ldrs on outer: lost pl over 2f out* **28/1**
500- **20** *1½* **Rigolleto (IRE)**[165] 6948 4-9-4 82 TonyCulhane 2 19
(Mick Channon) *mid-div on outer: effrt over 2f out: sn wknd* **14/1**
5351 **21** *12* **Greyfriarschorista**[10] 999 5-9-2 80 WilliamCarson 16
(Richard Guest) *mde most: hdd over 2f out: wkng whn heavily eased over 1f out* **16/1**

1m 27.08s (0.78) **Going Correction** +0.075s/f (Good) **21** Ran SP% **132.2**
Speed ratings (Par 105): **98,97,96,95,95 94,94,94,92,91 87,86,84,84,79 74,72,72,68,67 53**
CSF £104.61 CT £1264.98 TOTE £28.80: £5.60, £1.80, £3.00, £4.60; EX 257.50 TRIFECTA Not won..
Owner W R B Racing 49 **Bred** Lawrence Goichman **Trained** Sessay, N Yorks
■ Stewards' Enquiry : Kieren Fallon three-day ban: careless riding (Apr 16-18)

FOCUS
As in the first division the field gathered centre-to-stands' side. The pace was decent and the time was 2.40 seconds faster than the earlier heat.
Greyfriarschorista Official explanation: jockey said gelding was denied a clear run and lost its action

T/Jkpt: Not won. T/Plt: £251.80 to a £1 stake. Pool:£133,443.12 - 386.78 winning tickets T/Qpdt: £46.20 to a £1 stake. Pool:£8,854.90 - 141.61 winning tickets JR

1059 SAINT-CLOUD (L-H)

Sunday, April 1

OFFICIAL GOING: Turf: good

1163a PRIX EDMOND BLANC-TOP 14 ORANGE (GROUP 3) (4YO+) (TURF) 1m

2:50 (12:00) 4-Y-O+ **£33,333** (£13,333; £10,000 ; £6,666 ; £3,333)

RPR

1 **Moonwalk In Paris (FR)**39 4 -8-110 ChristopheSoumillon 7 113
(J-C Rouget, France) *hld up in rr: qcknd wl early in st: str run ent fnl f. hung lft: appeared to cause interference to horses ins fnl f: tk ld 50yds out: r.o wl* **7/4**1

2 ½ **Evaporation (FR)**151 7239 5 -8-80 FlavienPrat 1 109
(C Laffon-Parias, France) *settled in 3rd on ins: r.o wl appr fnl f: wnt 3rds 50yds out: got up for 2nd fnl strides* **12/1**

3 snk **No Risk At All (FR)**33 880 5 -8-110 GaetanMasure 5 112
(J-P Gallorini, France) *settled in 2nd on outer: rdn to ld 2f out: r.o wl: hdd 50yds out: lost 2nd fnl strides* **13/2**

4 snk **Zinabaa (FR)**154 7193 7 -9-00 YannickLetondeur 2 114
(M Mace, France) *settled in 5th: mde gd prog 2f out: r.o wl ent fnl f: no room to chal ldrs: had to be swtchd to outside: fin strly: unlucky* **16/1**

5 4 **Celebrissime (IRE)**22 880 7 -8-130 ow2 OlivierPeslier 6 104
(F Head, France) *settled in 6th: wnt 4th 2f out: rdn but no ex: suffered interference ent fnl f: styd on one pce* **9/4**2

6 3½ **Quentindemontargis (FR)**12 5 -8-110 SylvainRuis 3 94
(C Boutin, France) *sn led: stl in front ent st: hdd 2f out: no ex: styd on at one pce* **20/1**

7 1 **Sandy's Charm (FR)**182 6568 4 -8-100 Francois-XavierBertras 4 91
(F Rohaut, France) *settled in 3rd: rdn but no ex 2f out: fdd* **9/2**3

1m 40.6s (-6.90) 7Ran SP% 117.0
WIN (incl. 1 euro stake): 2.40. PLACES: 1.80, 5.10. SF: 20.30
Owner SARL Ecurie J-L Tepper **Bred** Neustrian Associates & Dandy's Farm **Trained** Pau, France

NOTEBOOK
Moonwalk In Paris (FR) vaulted straight from a conditions race success on the AW into contention for the best Group races over 1m after coming with an irresistible run to claim the prize. Connections had to survive a lengthy inquiry after the front four all got a little tight for room in the final furlong. He may return for the Prix du Muguet in a month's time.

1162a Foreign Racing (See Raceform Interactive)

REDCAR (L-H)

Monday, April 2

OFFICIAL GOING: Good to firm (8.5)
Wind: Virtually nil Weather: Overcast

1164 GATES ARE OPEN AND WE'RE RACING MAIDEN AUCTION STKS 5f

2:15 (2:17) (Class 5) 2-Y-O **£2,264** (£673; £336 ; £168) Stalls Centre

Form RPR

1 **Lothian Countess** 2 -8-40 JamesSullivan 1 65
(George Foster) *prom: cl up 1/2-way: led wl over 1f out: rdn and kpt on wl ins fnl f* **66/1**

2 ½ **All Fur Coat** 2 -8-110 TonyCulhane 7 70
(Jo Hughes) *towards rr: pushed along and hdwy over 2f out: rdn over 1f out: styd on ins fnl f:* **10/3**1

3 ¾ **Out Of The Blocks** 2 -8-90 RichardKingscote 5 65
(Tom Dascombe) *towards rr and pushed along 1/2-way: hdwy on outer wl over 1f out: styd on ins fnl f* **13/2**

4 1¼ **Kryena's Rose** 2 -8-40 ChrisCatlin 4 55
(Mick Channon) *cl up: chal 2f out: sn rdn and ev ch tl wknd ent fnl f* **7/2**2

5 nse **Caught Napping** 2 -8-20 JakePayne(7) 2 60
(Bill Turner) *led: rdn along 2f out: sn hdd and grad wknd appr fnl f* **12/1**

6 4½ **Midnight Dream (FR)** 2 -8-120 TomEaves 8 45
(Linda Stubbs) *dwlt: in tch: pushed along 1/2-way: sn rdn: rn green and wandered: wknd wl over 1f out* **4/1**3

7 1½ **Zero Rated (IRE)** 2 -8-70 DavidAllan 3 34+
(Tim Easterby) *sn outpcd and a in rr* **13/2**

8 1¾ **Amourous (IRE)** 2 -8-40 DuranFentiman 6 24+
(Tim Easterby) *sn outpcd and a in rr* **10/1**

9 6 **Babylon Candle** 2 -8-120 PJMcDonald 10 8
(Lisa Williamson) *cl up on outer: effrt over 2f out: sn rdn and wknd over 1f out* **25/1**

1m 0.87s (2.27) **Going Correction** +0.20s/f (Good) 9Ran SP% 114.1
Speed ratings (Par 92): **89,88,87,85,84 77,75,72,62**
toteswingers:1&2:£25.10, 2&3:£5.70, 1&3:£26.40 CSF £274.12 TOTE £55.10 : £8.00 , £1.50 , £2.10; EX 415.70 TRIFECTA Not won. .
Owner A G Foster **Bred** Llety Stud **Trained** Haddington, East Lothian

FOCUS
No form to go on, but they were a relatively cheap bunch and it went to the outsider of the field. The time was 0.47 seconds quicker than the following juvenile seller. The winner was quite professional but this is probably just modest early-season form.

NOTEBOOK
Lothian Countess, a £2,200 purchase, is a half-sister to a few winners at up to 1m4f. She showed good speed throughout and clearly knew what was required, winning tidily. This March foal was co-bottom weight and might find it tough to follow up.
All Fur Coat, a £12,000 purchase, is a half-sister to a 6f winner and her dam won over the same trip. She's a compact March foal and was doing her best work at the finish. (op 11-4 tchd 7-2)
Out Of The Blocks cost only 2,500gns and didn't appeal on pedigree, but he's from a good stable and showed ability, keeping on after being bumped at the start. (op 9-2)
Kryena's Rose, a 5,500gns half-sister a couple of 6f winners, showed speed but didn't have much room in the closing stages and was easily intimidated. She's not that big, but is a late April foal. (tchd 3-1 and 4-1)
Caught Napping unseated his rider coming out of the paddock, but was quickly reunited with Jake Payne. A £1,500 purchase, he's a half-brother to a 1m winner and has a bit of size about him. He's an April foal and may need more time. (op 9-1 tchd 14-1)
Midnight Dream (FR) a March foal, cost 9,000euros but has already been gelded. He's a half-brother to a 1m winner and 1m1f scorer, and needed the experience over a trip on the short side. (op 9-2 tchd 7-2)
Amourous(IRE) got upset in the stalls and that can't have helped her chance. (op 14-1)

1165 REDCAR RACECOURSE CHEAPEST ADMISSION IN BRITAIN (S) STKS 5f

2:45 (2:47) (Class 6) 2-Y-O **£1,704** (£503; £251) Stalls Centre

Form RPR

1 **Severn Bore** 2 -8-50 JakePayne(7) 2 61
(Bill Turner) *sn led: rdn appr fnl f: kpt on wl* **9/1**

2 ¾ **Suivez L'Argent** 2 -8-40 JulieBurke(3) 3 53+
(Joseph Tuite) *in tch: sn pushed along: green: outpcd and bhd 1/2-way: rdn and hdwy over 1f out: styd on strly fnl f* **14/1**

0 3 ¾ **Vanessa**2 1136 2 -8-70 ChrisCatlin 1 50
(Mick Channon) *prom: cl up 1/2-way: chal wl over 1f out: sn rdn and ev ch tl no ex last 150yds* **9/4**2

0 4 4½ **Cherryred Girl (IRE)**2 1136 2 -8-40 RyanPowell(3) 4 32
(J S Moore) *cl up: rdn along 2f out: wknd over 1f out* **9/2**3

5 1 **Khyber Bridge** 2 -8-120 TonyCulhane 5 33
(Jo Hughes) *chsd ldrs: rdn along over 2f out: sn wknd* **6/1**

6 ¾ **Mad Jazz** 2 -8-70 BarryMcHugh 6 25
(Tony Coyle) *wnt bdly rt s and s.i.s: hdwy to chse ldrs 1/2-way: sn rdn: edgd lft and wknd fnl 2f* **2/1**1

1m 1.34s (2.74) **Going Correction** +0.20s/f (Good) 6Ran SP% 113.2
Speed ratings (Par 90): **86,84,83,76,74 73**
toteswingers:1&2:£2.80, 2&3:£4.50, 1&3:£2.90 CSF £111.37 TOTE £7.10 : £3.50 , £4.80 ; EX 27.40.There was no bid for the winner.
Owner Richard Jeffrey **Bred** T M M Partnership **Trained** Sigwells, Somerset

FOCUS
This is likely to prove moderate form - the time was 0.47 seconds slower than the earlier weak-looking juvenile maiden - but the third and fourth had the benefit of previous experience, so the front two deserve credit. The form is rated as standard for the grade.

NOTEBOOK
Severn Bore, a March foal out of a 6f winner, knew his job. He might win again at a similar level. (op 13-2)
Suivez L'Argent, not sold at 800gns last October, is a half-sister to a 1m3f-1m4f winner, as well as a successful hurdler, and is an April foal, so this was an encouraging enough debut. She was outpaced for most of the way but finished strongly. (op 8-1 tchd 16-1)
Vanessa, who is by St Leger winner Sixties Icon, had every chance but didn't finish well enough. She was turned out only two days after making her debut at Kempton. (op 7-2)
Cherryred Girl (IRE) finished 6l ahead of Vanessa at Kempton two days earlier, but here she faded after showing speed. (op 4-1 tchd 7-2)
Mad Jazz, a 1,500gns daughter of Sir Percy, had reportedly been to Southwell for racecourse practice and went off favourite, but she was never competitive after swerving right on leaving the stalls. (tchd 4-1 in a place)

1166 BECOME AN ANNUAL BADGE HOLDER TODAY MEDIAN AUCTION MAIDEN STKS 7f

3:15 (3:19) (Class 5) 3-Y-O **£2,264** (£673; £336 ; £168) Stalls Centre

Form RPR

25-2 1 **Sunley Pride**31 770 3 -9-372 MartinHarley 7 79
(Mick Channon) *trckd ldrs: smooth hdwy 3f out: led on bit over 2f out: rdn ins fnl f: kpt on* **11/4**3

35- 2 nk **Lady Loch**235 4961 3 -8-120 PaulHanagan 2 73
(Richard Fahey) *led: jnd and pushed along 3f out: hdd and sltly outpcd over 2f out: rallied u.p fnl f: styd on wl towards fin* **5/4**1

3- 3 9 **Midnight Tryst**168 6912 3 -8-120 SilvestreDeSousa 1 49
(Ann Duffield) *t.k.h: trckd ldrs: effrt wl over 2f out: sn rdn and one pce fr wl over 1f out* **9/4**2

4 4½ **Brother Superior** 3 -9-30 DuranFentiman 3 42
(Tim Easterby) *a in rr* **25/1**

5 1½ **Julier Pass (IRE)**246 4585 3 -9-10 ow1 GaryBartley(3) 5 39
(Hugh McWilliams) *cl up: chal briefly over 3f out: sn rdn and wknd over 2f out* **28/1**

0- 6 14 **Solange (IRE)**161 7058 3 -8-120 DavidAllan 4
(Tim Easterby) *prom: rdn along 1/2-way: sn wknd* **50/1**

1m 26.67s (2.17) **Going Correction** +0.20s/f (Good) 6Ran SP% 111.1
Speed ratings (Par 98): **95,94,84,79,77 61**
toteswingers:1&2:£1.10, 2&3:£1.40, 1&3:£1.50 CSF £6.47 TOTE £3.10 : £1.10 , £1.50 ; EX 5.80 .
Owner James Sunley **Bred** Sunley Stud **Trained** West Ilsley, Berks

FOCUS
An ordinary maiden in which the front two finished well clear. The time wasn't bad and the winner may improve on this.

1167 JOHN SMITH'S REDCAR STRAIGHT-MILE CHAMPIONSHIP (H'CAP) (QUALIFIER) 1m

3:45 (3:46) (Class 5) (0-75,75) 3-Y-O **£2,264** (£673; £336 ; £168) Stalls Centre

Form RPR

000- 1 **Wolf Spirit (IRE)**186 6484 3 -8-963 JamesSullivan 1 70
(Ruth Carr) *hld up in tch: hdwy on outer wl over 2f out: chal over 1f out: led briefly ent fnl f: sn rdn and hdd: rallied to ld again last 50yds* **20/1**

020- 2 ½ **Nameitwhatyoulike**178 6670 3 -9-075 DavidSimmonson(7) 6 80
(Michael Easterby) *trckd ldrs: hdwy to ld wl over 1f out: rdn and hdd briefly ent fnl f: sn led again tl hdd and no ex last 50yds* **6/1**3

-600 3 3 **Nant Saeson (IRE)**9 667 3 -9-270 PaddyAspell 4 68
(John Wainwright) *hld up in rr: hdwy wl over 2f out: rdn to chse ldrs ent fnl f: kpt on same pce* **33/1**

3-45 4 shd **Bapak Pintar**32 747 3 -8-1165 PhillipMakin 9 65+
(Kevin Ryan) *trckd ldrs: rdn along and outpcd wl over 2f out: wandered and n.m.r over 1f out: kpt on ins fnl f* **16/1**

252- 5 ¾ **Ghalaa (IRE)**201 6047 3 -8-1266 PaulHanagan 10 62
(Mark Johnston) *cl up: led over 3f out: sn rdn and hdd 2f out: grad wknd appr fnl f* **3/1**1

604- 6 ¾ **Sygnature**212 5727 3 -9-169 PJMcDonald 8 63
(Alan Swinbank) *led: pushed along and hdd over 3f out: sn rdn and one pce* **3/1**1

2-30 7 nk **Sunny Side Up (IRE)**13 970 3 -8-862 TonyHamilton 2 56
(Richard Fahey) *hld up: hdwy 3f out: rdn over 2f out: sn no imp* **7/1**

53-5 8 2¼ **Shamardeliah (IRE)**17 917 3 -9-169 KierenFallon 7 57
(James Tate) *trckd ldrs: hdwy 3f out: chsd ldng pair over 2f out: sn rdn and btn over 1f out* **11/2**2

11-4 9 16 **Maybeagrey**77 193 3 -9-270 DuranFentiman 5 20
(Tim Easterby) *dwlt and towards rr: sme hdwy 3f out: sn rdn and nvr a factor* **7/1**

1m 40.41s (2.41) **Going Correction** +0.20s/f (Good) 9Ran SP% 118.3
Speed ratings (Par 98): **95,94,91,91,90 89,89,87,71**
toteswingers:1&2:£23.70, 2&3:£30.60, 1&3:£47.50 CSF £138.05 CT £3971.13 TOTE £21.30 : £7.80, £2.60 , £15.10 ; EX 155.90 Trifecta £1034.90 Part won. Pool: £1398.53 - 0.63 winning units..

Owner Michael Hill **Bred** Con Marnane **Trained** Huby, N Yorks

FOCUS

An ordinary handicap run at a good pace. The winner was well in on last year's debut form and the second is accorded a length personal best.

Bapak Pintar Official explanation: jockey said colt hung both ways

1168 COME RACING AGAIN ON EASTER MONDAY H'CAP 6f

4:15 (4:16) (Class 4) (0-85,85) 3-Y-0+ **£3,234** (£962; £481; £240) **Stalls** Centre

Form RPR

000- **1** **Arganil (USA)**[108] 7793 7-9-11 **82** PhillipMakin 13 93
(Kevin Ryan) *hld up in rr: hdwy over 2f out: chsd ldrs over 1f out: rdn to ld ins fnl f: kpt on strly* **25/1**

053- **2** ¾ **Whozthecat (IRE)**[118] 7643 5-9-3 **79** (v) NeilFarley(5) 15 88
(Declan Carroll) *hld up: hdwy 2f out: sn rdn: styd on to chse wnr ins fnl f: no imp towards fin* **9/1**

354- **3** 2¼ **Hamoody (USA)**[277] 3535 8-9-7 **85** ShirleyTeasdale(7) 11 86
(David Nicholls) *midfield: smooth hdwy to trck ldrs over 2f out: led over 1f out: sn rdn: hdd and one pce fnl f* **16/1**

0360 **4** *nk* **Dickie Le Davoir**[25] 834 8-9-2 **76** (p) RobertLButler(3) 3 76
(Richard Guest) *in rr: swtchd lft and hdwy on outer 2f out: sn rdn and styd on fnl f: nrst fin* **33/1**

00-4 **5** *nk* **Klynch**[20] 883 6-9-10 **81** (b) PJMcDonald 6 80
(Ruth Carr) *towards rr: swtchd lft and hdwy 2f out: sn rdn and styd on fnl f: nrst fin* **20/1**

000- **6** *hd* **Able Master (IRE)**[207] 5852 6-9-11 **82** DanielTudhope 10 81+
(David O'Meara) *in tch: pushed along over 2f out: sn rdn: styd on fnl f: nrst fin* **7/1**[3]

51-0 **7** 3 **Toby Tyler**[20] 883 6-9-8 **79** (v) MickyFenton 8 68
(Paul Midgley) *in rr: hdwy 2f out: sn rdn and kpt on appr fnl f: nt rch ldrs* **20/1**

1-60 **8** *hd* **Red Cape (FR)**[10] 1015 9-9-9 **80** (b) JamesSullivan 7 69
(Ruth Carr) *chsd ldrs: rdn along over 2f out: grad wknd* **16/1**

143- **9** *nk* **Caranbola**[200] 6094 6-9-7 **78** RobertWinston 14 66
(Mel Brittain) *prom: rdn along 2f out: grad wknd* **12/1**

002- **10** ¾ **Tabaret**[179] 6655 9-8-11 **71** oh6 AmyRyan(3) 2 56
(Richard Whitaker) *prom: cl up 1/2-way: rdn and ev ch 2f out: wknd appr fnl f* **25/1**

000- **11** 1 **Mr Optimistic**[199] 6112 4-9-7 **81** LeeTopliss(3) 4 63
(Richard Fahey) *nvr nr ldrs* **9/2**[1]

243- **12** 1 **Fast Shot**[160] 7074 4-9-6 **82** AdamCarter(5) 12 61
(Tim Easterby) *prom: rdn 2f out: wknd over 1f out* **10/1**

400- **13** 1¼ **Another Citizen (IRE)**[160] 7076 4-9-5 **76** DavidAllan 9 51
(Tim Easterby) *chsd ldrs: rdn along wl over 2f out: sn wknd* **12/1**

420- **14** *nse* **Solar Spirit (IRE)**[191] 6346 7-9-3 **74** SilvestreDeSousa 5 49
(Tracy Waggott) *led: rdn along over 2f out: hdd & wknd wl over 1f out* **15/2**

040- **15** 7 **Arry's Orse**[168] 6917 5-9-2 **73** AdrianNicholls 1 25
(David Nicholls) *in tch: rdn along over 2f out: sn wknd* **6/1**[2]

1m 12.24s (0.44) **Going Correction** +0.20s/f (Good) **15** Ran SP% **123.1**

Speed ratings (Par 105): **105,104,101,100,100 99,95,95,95,94 92,91,89,89,80**

toteswingers:1&2:£46.90, 2&3:£43.40, 1&3:£69.10 CSF £226.28 CT £2226.19 TOTE £32.40: £8.40, £3.80, £5.70; EX 344.00 TRIFECTA Not won..

Owner M & Mrs C McGeever **Bred** Colt Neck Stables, Llc **Trained** Hambleton, N Yorks

FOCUS

A fair and typically competitive sprint handicap. The form could work out well in the next few weeks. It's been rated around the winner's turf best from last year.

Arry's Orse Official explanation: jockey said gelding hung right throughout

1169 BOOK TICKETS ON-LINE @ REDCARRACING.CO.UK APPRENTICE CLAIMING STKS 6f

4:45 (4:45) (Class 6) 3-4-Y-0 **£1,704** (£503; £251) **Stalls** Centre

Form RPR

-254 **1** **Point At Issue (IRE)**[13] 975 3-8-12 60 (b) MichaelO'Connell 7 69
(David Nicholls) *chsd ldrs: rdn along wl over 2f out: styd on to chse ldr ent fnl f: drvn to ld last 100yds: kpt on wl* **6/1**[3]

23-3 **2** 3¼ **Come On Dave (IRE)**[4] 1089 3-8-12 75 ShirleyTeasdale(4) 3 63+
(David Nicholls) *chsd ldr: led 1/2-way: clr wl over 1f out: rdn ent fnl f: wknd qckly and hdd last 100yds* **5/2**[1]

0056 **3** 2 **Ice Trooper**[23] 870 4-9-10 66 (p) AmyRyan 9 55
(Linda Stubbs) *chsd ldng pair: rdn along 2f out: kpt on same pce fnl f* **3/1**[2]

006- **4** 7 **Brunswick Vale (IRE)**[195] 6232 3-8-5 39 (b[1]) NedCurtis(4) 4 27
(Paul Midgley) *in rr and sn pushed along: hdwy 3f out: plugged on fnl 2f: nvr nr ldrs* **14/1**

-400 **5** 3½ **Romany Spirit (IRE)**[24] 845 3-8-3 52 LukeRowe(4) 5 14
(Jason Ward) *in rr: rdn along and bhd 1/2-way: sme late hdwy* **25/1**

-422 **6** 5 **The Dancing Lord**[16] 940 3-8-9 67 RyanWhile(4) 1
(Bill Turner) *led: pushed along and hdd 1/2-way: sn rdn and wknd* **5/2**[1]

44-6 **7** 3½ **Running Water**[73] 227 4-9-2 44 DarylByrne(4) 2
(Hugh McWilliams) *rrd s and s.i.s: a in rr* **33/1**

000 **8** 1¼ **Green Warrior**[38] 691 4-9-6 60 (e) CharlesEddery(4) 8
(Richard Guest) *in tch: rdn along 1/2-way: sn outpcd and bhd* **12/1**

1m 12.92s (1.12) **Going Correction** +0.20s/f (Good)

WFA 3 from 4yo 12lb **8** Ran SP% **117.6**

Speed ratings (Par 101): **100,95,93,83,79 72,67,66**

toteswingers:1&2:£3.40, 2&3:£2.50, 1&3:£3.40 CSF £22.09 TOTE £6.30: £1.50, £1.40, £1.30; EX 22.70 Trifecta £74.40 Pool: £1076.08 - 10.70 winning units..

Owner David Fish **Bred** Lynn Lodge Stud **Trained** Sessay, N Yorks

■ Stewards' Enquiry : Shirley Teasdale two-day ban: used whip above permitted level (Apr 16-17)

FOCUS

A modest claimer run at a strong pace. The time was relatively good but there are doubts over the form given the grade. It has been rated around the winner.

Running Water Official explanation: jockey said filly reared at start

1170 FOLLOW REDCARRACING ON FACEBOOK & TWITTER FILLIES' H'CAP 1m 2f

5:15 (5:16) (Class 5) (0-70,67) 3-Y-0+ **£2,264** (£673; £336; £168) **Stalls** Low

Form RPR

232 **1** **Scatter Dice (IRE)**[39] 675 3-8-6 **64** SilvestreDeSousa 3 79
(Mark Johnston) *set stdy pce: qcknd 3f out: rdn clr 2f out: styd on strly* **7/2**[3]

40-3 **2** 7 **Reset City**[24] 850 6-9-12 **65** (t) JamieSpencer 2 70
(Ian Williams) *hld up in rr: smooth hdwy to trck ldrs over 3f out: effrt to chse wnr wl over 1f out: sn rdn and no imp* **3/1**[2]

613- **3** 1½ **Sweetnessandlight**[95] 7915 3-8-7 **65** MichaelStainton 1 63
(Jason Ward) *trckd ldrs: pushed along 3f out: rdn and sltly outpcd over 2f out: n.m.r on inner over 1f out: styd on fnl f* **7/1**

550- **4** 2 **No Time To Cry**[142] 7398 3-8-0 **58** JamesSullivan 4 52
(Ann Duffield) *chsd ldng pair on inner: pushed along 3f out: rdn 2f out: sn wknd* **5/1**

312- **5** 1½ **Painted Tail (IRE)**[181] 6601 5-10-0 **67** PJMcDonald 7 62
(Alan Swinbank) *trckd wnr: effrt over 3f out: rdn along over 2f out: drvn and one pce fr wl over 1f out* **5/2**[1]

-560 **6** 6 **Wing N Prayer (IRE)**[31] 773 5-9-0 **53** oh8 PaddyAspell 5 36
(John Wainwright) *hld up: a in rr* **40/1**

000- **7** 2 **Graceful Act**[170] 6799 4-9-0 **56** DaleSwift(3) 6 35
(Ron Barr) *trckd ldrs: hdwy on outer over 3f out: rdn along over 2f out: sn wknd* **16/1**

2m 9.21s (2.11) **Going Correction** +0.20s/f (Good)

WFA 3 from 4yo+ 19lb **7** Ran SP% **113.3**

Speed ratings (Par 100): **99,93,92,90,89 84,83**

toteswingers:1&2:£3.30, 2&3:£3.90, 1&3:£4.30 CSF £14.15 TOTE £4.50: £3.00, £1.50; EX 11.00.

Owner Sheikh Hamdan Bin Mohammed Al Maktoum **Bred** Darley **Trained** Middleham Moor, N Yorks

FOCUS

A modest handicap. Improvement from the winner at face value.

T/Jkpt: Not won. T/Plt: £919.50 to a £1 stake. Pool of £87,423.62 - 69.40 winning tickets. T/Qpdt: £86.50 to a £1 stake. Pool of £7,931.77 - 67.80 winning tickets. JR

814 CHANTILLY (R-H)

Monday, April 2

OFFICIAL GOING: Polytrack : standard

1171a PRIX DE LA TRAVERSIERE (MAIDEN) (UNRACED 3YO COLTS & GELDINGS) (POLYTRACK) 1m 1f 110y

2:20 (12:00) 3-Y-0 **£10,000** (£4,000; £3,000; £2,000; £1,000)

RPR

1 **Hi Ya Pal (USA)** 3-9-2 0 ThierryThulliez 7 86
(N Clement, France) **108/10**

2 *shd* **Kalamos (USA)** 3-9-2 0 StephanePasquier 15 86
(P Bary, France) **68/10**

3 1¼ **Bolingbroke (IRE)** 3-9-2 0 MaximeGuyon 12 83
(A Fabre, France) **43/10**[1]

4 4 **Elasyaaf (FR)** 3-9-2 0 ChristopheSoumillon 10 75
(J E Hammond, France) **78/10**

5 2 **Tolka (IRE)** 3-9-2 0 TheoBachelot 8 71
(S Wattel, France) **29/1**

6 *snk* **Al Nawras** 3-9-2 0 AurelienLemaitre 1 71
(F Head, France) **15/1**

7 ½ **Siberian Freeze (IRE)** 3-8-8 0 Georges-AntoineAnselin(8) 9 70
(N Clement, France) **61/1**

8 1½ **Passarinho (IRE)** 3-9-2 0 JulienAuge 11 67
(H-A Pantall, France) **26/1**

9 *hd* **Berabani (FR)** 3-9-2 0 Christophe-PatriceLemaire 3 66
(M Delzangles, France) **9/2**[2]

10 *nk* **Little Power (FR)** 3-9-2 0 SylvainRuis 6 66
(J-P Carvalho, Germany) **43/1**

0 **Comedy Award (USA)** 3-9-2 0 Pierre-CharlesBoudot 14
(A Fabre, France) **18/1**

0 **Neverendings Story (FR)** 3-9-2 0 AlexisBadel 2
(R Laplanche, France) **46/1**

0 **Ironstone (IRE)** 3-9-2 0 GregoryBenoist 4
(M Delzangles, France) **5/1**[3]

0 **Rob Gold (FR)** 3-9-2 0 FlavienPrat 5
(T Clout, France) **27/1**

0 **Gangsterbanksters (FR)** 3-9-2 0 MichaelMetcalfe 13
(Mrs K Burke) *rdn fr s to gain position cl to ldrs: dropped bk to 6th bef st: rdn over 2 1/2f out: no ex: grad fdd* **58/1**

2m 1.2s (121.20) **15** Ran SP% **116.2**

WIN (incl. 1 euro stake): 11.80. PLACES: 3.50, 3.00, 2.50. DF: 38.30. SF: 94.90.

Owner Waterville Lake Stables LLC **Bred** Waterville Lake Stables Llc **Trained** Chantilly, France

1172a PRIX DE LA FU MADAME (CLAIMER) (4YO) (POLYTRACK) 1m 1f 110y

2:55 (12:00) 4-Y-0 **£7,916** (£3,166; £2,375; £1,583; £791)

RPR

1 **Divin Leon (FR)**[6] 4-9-4 0 Christophe-PatriceLemaire 17 86
(M Boutin, France) **74/10**[2]

2 1¾ **Alphorn (FR)**[24] 4-9-5 0 TonyPiccone 11 83
(Y Barberot, France) **12/1**

3 ½ **Bearheart (IRE)**[91] 16 4-9-2 0 (p) GregoryBenoist 14 79
(P Monfort, France) **9/1**

4 *hd* **Polimere (FR)**[107] 4-8-6 0 MathieuTavaresDaSilva(5) 7 74
(E Libaud, France) **16/1**

5 *hd* **Eros De La Luna (FR)**[6] 4-8-7 0 SoufyaneMoulin(8) 13 77
(C Boutin, France) **57/1**

6 1¾ **Casquito (IRE)**[17] 4-8-11 0 (b) TheoBachelot 10 70
(U Suter, France) **9/1**

7 *shd* **Storming Honor (SPA)**[27] 4-8-11 0 (p) JohanVictoire 12 69
(L A Urbano-Grajales, France) **4/1**[1]

8 ½ **Dorade Rose (FR)**[24] 4-9-2 0 (b) FlavienPrat 3 73
(D Smaga, France) **8/1**[3]

9 *snk* **Yosha (IRE)**[11] 4-9-5 0 ThierryJarnet 6 76
(P Demercastel, France) **9/1**

10 *snk* **Toronto (FR)**[17] 4-8-8 0 (p) MaximeGuyon 2 65
(P Monfort, France) **10/1**

0 **Ollon (USA)**[11] 1000 4-9-1 0 MichaelMetcalfe 4
(Mrs K Burke) *racd midfield on inner rail: began to make prog 3f out: short of room on rail 2f out: had to be stdd: lost all ch: dropped towards rr fnl f* **16/1**

0 **Masaraat (FR)**[11] 4-9-0 0 (p) AntoineCoutier(5) 15
(F Vermeulen, France) **33/1**

0 **Khalini (FR)**[150] 4-8-8 0 (p) AntoineHamelin(3) 8
(Y Gourraud, France) **40/1**

0 **Nijisky Girl (FR)**[357] 4-8-11 0 JulienAuge 1
(Y-M Porzier, France) **84/1**

0 **All By Myself**[10] 4-8-10 0 StevanBourgois(8) 16
(Robert Collet, France) **47/1**
0 **Ty Bolide (FR)**[20] 4-8-11 0 AllanBonnefoy 5
(F Sanchez, France) **105/1**
0 **Iron Will (FR)** 4-9-5 0 (b) DPorcu 9
(E Kurdu, Germany) **24/1**
2m 0.2s (120.20) **17** Ran SP% **116.9**
WIN (incl. 1 euro stake): 8.40. PLACES: 2.80, 4.10, 3.70. DF: 41.30. SF: 86.10.
Owner K Chehboub & B Chehboub **Bred** K Chehboub & B Chehboub **Trained** France

1052 SOUTHWELL (L-H)
Tuesday, April 3

OFFICIAL GOING: Standard
Wind: Light behind Weather: Overcast

1173 32RED CASINO MEDIAN AUCTION MAIDEN STKS 6f (F)
2:20 (2:20) (Class 6) 3-5-Y-0 **£1,704** (£503; £251) **Stalls** Low

Form				RPR
632-	1		**Untold Melody**[182] [6598] 3-8-9 68 PhillipMakin 5	55
			(Kevin Ryan) *cl up: led after 2f: rdn along wl over 1f out: drvn ins fnl f and kpt on wl* **11/10**[1]	
0-4	2	1	**Pearls From Sydney**[12] [990] 3-8-9 0 StevieDonohoe 4	52
			(Paul Cole) *trckd ldrs: hdwy over 2f out and sn rdn: swtchd lft ent fnl f: styd on wl towards fin* **20/1**	
04-0	3	nk	**Celestial Dawn**[25] [845] 3-8-9 51 LukeMorris 1	51
			(John Weymes) *led 2f: cl up: rdn along wl over 2f out: sltly outpcd over 1f out: kpt on wl towards fin* **14/1**	
00/2	4	1 ½	**Forever Hope**[18] [929] 5-9-4 53 LeeTopliss(3) 6	49
			(Tony Coyle) *cl up on outer: chal over 2f out: sn rdn and ev ch tl wknd ins fnl f* **7/1**	
04	5	8	**Adili (IRE)**[61] [383] 3-9-0 0 BarryMcHugh 2	26+
			(Brian Ellison) *sn rdn along and outpcd in rr: wl bhd 1/2-way: styd on fnl 2f: nvr a factor* **7/2**[2]	
	6	3	**Dartrix** 3-8-9 0 TomEaves 7	11
			(Michael Dods) *wnt rt and s.i.s: a in rr* **9/2**[3]	
0	7	4	**Diggers Daydream (IRE)**[12] [1001] 4-9-9 0 AmyRyan(3) 3	
			(Lisa Williamson) *cl up on inner: rdn along 1/2-way: sn wknd* **80/1**	

1m 16.36s (-0.14) **Going Correction** -0.025s/f (Stan)
WFA 3 from 4yo+ 12lb **7** Ran SP% **113.2**
Speed ratings (Par 101): **99,97,97,95,84 80,75**
toteswingers: 1&2 £3.30, 1&3 £3.00, 2&3 £12.70. CSF £26.36 TOTE £2.10: £1.50, £8.30; EX 17.60.
Owner Hambleton Racing XIX **Bred** J Jamgotchian **Trained** Hambleton, N Yorks

FOCUS
A weak maiden unlikely to produce too many future winners. The winner's task was eased by poor runs from her main market rivals and she didn't need to match her 2yo form.

1174 32REDPOKER.COM (S) STKS 1m 4f (F)
2:50 (2:50) (Class 6) 4-Y-0+ **£1,704** (£503) **Stalls** Low

Form				RPR
1211	1		**Overrule (USA)**[26] [830] 8-9-5 76 (p) BarryMcHugh 3	69+
			(Brian Ellison) *led 1f: trckd ldr tl led again on bit 3f out: sn clr: hrd hld* **1/12**[1]	
5555	2	6	**Dunaskin (IRE)**[40] [672] 12-9-0 44 (b) CharlesEddery(5) 1	48
			(Richard Guest) *t.k.h early: led after 1f: rdn along and hdd 3f out: sn outpcd* **7/1**[2]	

2m 44.36s (3.36) **Going Correction** -0.025s/f (Stan)
WFA 4 from 8yo+ 1lb **2** Ran SP% **104.8**
Speed ratings (Par 101): **87,83**
TOTE £1.10.The winner was sold to Fran Harper for 6,000gns.
Owner Brian Ellison **Bred** Avalon Farms Inc **Trained** Norton, N Yorks

FOCUS
The two non-runners reduced this seller to an uneven match with 32lb separating the pair. Overrule was value at least double the margin but did not need to match his recent efforts.

1175 £32 FREE AT 32RED.COM H'CAP 1m 6f (F)
3:20 (3:20) (Class 5) (0-75,75) 4-Y-0+ **£2,385** (£704; £352) **Stalls** Low

Form				RPR
55-0	1		**Shifting Gold (IRE)**[49] [555] 6-8-10 64 (bt) AmyRyan(3) 7	70
			(Kevin Ryan) *in rr: pushed along after 4f: hdwy on outer and in tch 1/2-way: rdn along: outpcd and bhd 4f out: wd st: hdwy on wd outside wl over 1f out: styd on strly u.p fnl f to ld last 50yds* **9/2**[2]	
0632	2	¾	**Three White Socks (IRE)**[20] [902] 5-8-6 60 ow1 (p) PaulPickard(3) 3	65
			(Brian Ellison) *hld up in rr: pushed along and outpcd over 4f out: hdwy over 2f out: rdn to chse ldrs wl over 1f out: drvn to chal wl ins fnl f: ev ch tl no ex last 50yds* **7/1**	
-124	3	nk	**Mediterranean Sea (IRE)**[14] [978] 6-9-10 75 FrederikTylicki 5	80
			(J R Jenkins) *trckd ldrs on inner: pushed along and sltly outpcd over 4f out: hdwy 3f out: rdn to ld 1 1/2f out: drvn and edgd rt ins fnl f: hdd and no ex last 50yds* **15/8**[1]	
054-	4	¾	**Ginger Grey (IRE)**[15] [6767] 5-8-12 63 ow1 (b) DanielTudhope 8	67
			(David O'Meara) *hld up in tch: hdwy to trck ldrs 5f out: effrt 3f out: rdn to chse ldr over 1f out: drvn and kpt on same pce fnl f* **16/1**	
-001	5	7	**Carnac (IRE)**[7] [1057] 6-8-9 60 6ex (p) ShaneKelly 1	54
			(Alan McCabe) *sn led: hdd over 8f out: cl up: rdn along over 3f out: sn drvn and grad wknd fnl 2f* **6/1**[3]	
5003	6	3 ¼	**Yossi (IRE)**[5] [1083] 8-8-2 56 oh11 (p) DeclanCannon(3) 2	46
			(Richard Guest) *cl up: led over 8f out: rdn along over 3f out: hdd wl over 1f out and sn wknd* **20/1**	
104-	7	2 ¼	**Gosforth Park**[116] [7689] 6-8-6 57 DuranFentiman 6	43
			(Mel Brittain) *trckd ldrs: rdn along 3f out: sn wknd* **6/1**[3]	
0-10	8	10	**Light The City (IRE)**[14] [978] 5-8-9 60 JamesSullivan 4	32
			(Ruth Carr) *trckd ldng pair: pushed along over 4f out: rdn 3f out and sn wknd* **14/1**	

3m 6.7s (-1.60) **Going Correction** -0.025s/f (Stan) **8** Ran SP% **111.3**
Speed ratings (Par 103): **103,102,102,101,97 96,94,89**
toteswingers: 1&2 £5.20, 1&3 £3.00, 2&3 £3.50. CSF £33.73 CT £75.33 TOTE £4.60: £1.70, £1.40, £1.40; EX 36.00 Trifecta £115.50 Pool: £574.74 - 3.68 winning units..
Owner Hambleton Racing Ltd VIII **Bred** Watership Down Stud **Trained** Hambleton, N Yorks

FOCUS
An ordinary staying handicap, but a dramatic race and a thrilling finish. The first two home were never travelling from an early stage, but their riders' persistence eventually paid off. The winner showed similar form as to when winning off this mark over C&D last July.

1176 32RED H'CAP 6f (F)
3:50 (3:50) (Class 4) (0-80,78) 3-Y-0 **£4,075** (£1,212; £606; £303) **Stalls** Low

Form				RPR
0125	1		**Abi Scarlet (IRE)**[41] [659] 3-9-3 74 HayleyTurner 5	84
			(Hughie Morrison) *trckd ldr: cl up 3f out: rdn to ld wl over 1f out: styd on strly fnl f* **7/2**[2]	
52-1	2	1 ¼	**Half A Billion (IRE)**[21] [885] 3-8-13 73 LeeTopliss(3) 4	79
			(Michael Dods) *trckd ldr: effrt over 2f out: sn rdn and sltly outpcd over 1f out: kpt on ins fnl f: tk 2nd nr line* **2/1**[1]	
2221	3	hd	**Reve Du Jour (IRE)**[14] [975] 3-8-13 70 ShaneKelly 7	75
			(Alan McCabe) *led: jnd and rdn along over 2f out: hdd wl over 1f out: drvn and one pce fnl f: lost 2nd nr line* **7/2**[2]	
-332	4	10	**Man Of My Word**[14] [975] 3-8-7 67 (p) BillyCray(3) 2	40
			(Scott Dixon) *in rr: sn rdn along and outpcd: styd on u.p fnl 2f: nvr a factor* **12/1**	
12-4	5	3	**I'll Be Good**[14] [977] 3-9-7 78 JoeFanning 6	42
			(Robert Johnson) *trckd ldrs: rdn along 2f out: sn wknd* **9/1**	
440-	6	12	**Al Shaqab (IRE)**[200] [6111] 3-9-6 77 (p) PhillipMakin 1	
			(Kevin Ryan) *sn rdn along in rr: bhd fr 1/2-way* **5/1**[3]	

1m 15.3s (-1.20) **Going Correction** -0.025s/f (Stan) **6** Ran SP% **112.1**
Speed ratings (Par 100): **107,105,105,91,87 71**
toteswingers: 1&2 £2.60, 1&3 £3.30, 2&3 £1.80. CSF £10.92 TOTE £6.50: £5.40, £1.10; EX 11.80.
Owner The Boot Inn Partnership **Bred** Henry O'Callaghan **Trained** East Ilsley, Berks

FOCUS
A fair little sprint handicap with five of the six runners previous course winners, and the first three pulled a long way clear of the others. The pace was decent and the winner posted a personal best.

1177 32RED.COM H'CAP 6f (F)
4:20 (4:20) (Class 5) (0-75,73) 4-Y-0+ **£2,264** (£673; £336; £168) **Stalls** Low

Form				RPR
2160	1		**Mazovian (USA)**[26] [834] 4-8-8 67 DannyBrock(7) 9	79
			(Michael Chapman) *cl up: led after 1f: rdn wl over 1f out: drvn ins fnl f and kpt on gamely* **7/1**	
2242	2	1 ¾	**Punching**[21] [883] 8-9-2 68 LukeMorris 4	74
			(Conor Dore) *led 1f: cl up: chal over 2f out: sn rdn and ev ch tl drvn and no ex ins fnl f* **9/2**[2]	
0012	3	2 ¼	**Elhamri**[20] [904] 8-9-1 67 HayleyTurner 3	66
			(Conor Dore) *chsd ldrs: rdn along and hdwy 2f out: styd on ins fnl f: nrst fin* **15/2**	
3131	4	hd	**Prince Of Vasa (IRE)**[33] [752] 5-9-0 66 AndrewMullen 2	64
			(Michael Smith) *chsd ldrs on inner: effrt over 2f out: sn rdn and no imp appr fnl f* **3/1**[1]	
3056	5	1	**Suddenly Susan (IRE)**[4] [1116] 4-8-13 68 (b) BillyCray(3) 6	63+
			(Scott Dixon) *repeatedly bmpd and hmpd s: sn squeezed out and in rr: hdwy to chse ldrs bef 1/2-way: rdn over 2f out and kpt on same pce* **7/1**	
0-34	6	shd	**Bond Fastrac**[20] [893] 5-9-4 73 DaleSwift(3) 7	68
			(Geoffrey Oldroyd) *bmpd and hmpd s: sn in rr: wd st and hdwy 2f out: sn rdn and no imp* **6/1**[3]	
13-0	7	5	**Mata Hari Blue**[12] [997] 6-9-4 70 (t) RussKennemore 8	49
			(John Holt) *chsd ldng pair: rdn wl over 2f out: grad wknd* **9/1**	
0-00	8	5	**Rowan Spirit (IRE)**[40] [669] 4-9-5 71 ShaneKelly 1	34
			(Mark Brisbourne) *a in rr* **16/1**	
405-	9	½	**Choc'A'Moca (IRE)**[162] [7065] 5-8-9 61 (v) MickyFenton 5	22
			(Paul Midgley) *wnt rt and almost uns rdr s: a in rr* **25/1**	

1m 15.12s (-1.38) **Going Correction** -0.025s/f (Stan) **9** Ran SP% **114.0**
Speed ratings (Par 103): **108,105,102,102,101 100,94,87,86**
toteswingers: 1&2 £6.50, 1&3 £14.70, 2&3 £2.90. CSF £37.97 CT £244.45 TOTE £12.70: £3.80, £1.10, £4.40; EX 56.30 Trifecta £216.90 Pool: £1,117.04 - 3.81 winning units..
Owner Mrs M Chapman **Bred** Darley **Trained** Market Rasen, Lincs

FOCUS
A modest sprint handicap and a rough race with all sorts of argy-bargy exiting the stalls involving Suddenly Susan, Bond Fastrac and Choc'a'moca. The first two horses home held those positions throughout, having avoided the early melee. The winne is back to the form of his February win here.

1178 CALL 01636 814481 TO SPONSOR A RACE H'CAP 7f (F)
4:50 (4:50) (Class 6) (0-60,60) 4-Y-0+ **£1,704** (£503; £251) **Stalls** Low

Form				RPR
-651	1		**Only Ten Per Cent (IRE)**[26] [831] 4-9-4 57 FrederikTylicki 10	75+
			(J R Jenkins) *cl up: led 3f out: pushed clr wl over 1f out: shkn up ins fnl f: rdn and kpt on nr fin* **7/4**[1]	
6234	2	nk	**Ace Of Spies (IRE)**[21] [884] 7-9-7 60 HayleyTurner 14	72
			(Conor Dore) *midfield: hdwy 3f out: rdn to chse wnr fr over 1f out: styd on wl fnl f: jst hld* **8/1**[3]	
6335	3	2 ½	**Jonnie Skull (IRE)**[14] [972] 6-8-9 55 (vt) DannyBrock(7) 13	60
			(Phil McEntee) *towards rr: hdwy wl over 2f out: sn rdn and kpt on fnl f: nrst fin* **16/1**	
1563	4	3 ½	**Ridgeway Hawk**[20] [904] 4-9-6 59 (v) RobertHavlin 8	55
			(Mark Usher) *sn rdn along and bhd: wd st: hdwy wl over 1f out: edgd lft ins fnl f: kpt on: nrst fin* **9/1**	
50-6	5	1 ¼	**Bold Diva**[15] [964] 7-9-1 54 (v) LukeMorris 9	46
			(Tony Carroll) *dwlt and towards rr: hdwy 3f out: rdn to chse ldrs over 2f out: one pce fr over 1f out* **12/1**	
2645	6	1 ½	**Fantasy Fry**[18] [926] 4-8-9 53 MatthewCosham(5) 2	41
			(David Evans) *dwlt and towards rr: hdwy on inner wl over 2f out: sn rdn and no imp* **7/1**[2]	
3023	7	1	**Flow Chart (IRE)**[17] [939] 5-8-9 48 ow1 RobbieFitzpatrick 1	34
			(Peter Grayson) *cl up on inner: rdn wl over 2f out and grad wknd* **16/1**	
0-06	8	1	**Lindoro**[28] [813] 7-9-0 53 BarryMcHugh 11	36
			(Kevin M Prendergast) *towards rr: hdwy 3f out: rdn over 2f out: n.d* **10/1**	
0004	9	2 ¾	**Crocodile Bay (IRE)**[6] [1074] 9-8-8 52 (p) CharlesEddery(5) 5	28
			(Richard Guest) *slt ld: rdn and hdd 3f out: sn wknd* **25/1**	
42/-	10	2 ¾	**Dolly Royal (IRE)**[552] [6460] 7-9-4 57 JoeFanning 4	25
			(Robert Johnson) *dwlt: a in rr* **20/1**	
00/0	11	1 ¾	**Lady Brickhouse**[11] [1014] 5-8-7 46 oh1 AndreaAtzeni 6	
			(Michael Squance) *a towards rr* **18/1**	
6010	12	¾	**Tenancy (IRE)**[11] [1009] 8-8-12 51 (b) RobertWinston 12	
			(Shaun Harris) *cl up on outer: rdn along 1/2-way: sn wknd* **22/1**	
000-	13	1 ½	**Viking Dancer**[199] [6159] 5-8-13 52 PJMcDonald 3	9
			(Ruth Carr) *a in rr* **25/1**	

60-4 **14** *14* **Valdemar**[39] 690 6-8-7 **46** oh1 ....(v) AndrewMullen 7
(Alan Brown) *midfield: rdn along 3f out: sn wknd* **50/1**

1m 30.24s (-0.06) **Going Correction** -0.025s/f (Stan) **14** Ran SP% **122.5**
Speed ratings (Par 101): **99,98,95,91,90 88,87,86,83,80 78,77,75,59**
toteswingers: 1&2 £3.60, 1&3 £9.60, 2&3 £13.40. CSF £14.40 CT £169.36 TOTE £2.00: £1.10, £1.70, £6.80; EX 17.70 Trifecta £165.70 Pool: £580.29 - 2.59 winning units..
Owner B Silkman **Bred** Sandro Garavelli **Trained** Royston, Herts

FOCUS
A moderate handicap, full of the usual suspects. The pace was good and the winner looked better than the bare form.

1179 FOLLOW SOUTHWELL ON TWITTER H'CAP 1m (F)
5:20 (5:21) (Class 6) (0-55,55) 4-Y-0+ **£1,704** (£503; £251) **Stalls** Low

Form				RPR
/535	**1**		**Somerset Island (IRE)**[47] 581 4-9-2 **55** ....(p) AndrewMullen 13 (Michael Smith) *prom: effrt and cl up 2f out: sn rdn: styd on u.p to ld last 100yds: jst hld on* **10/1**	63
5-05	**2**	*nse*	**Brown Pete (IRE)**[20] 900 4-8-9 **53** ....(e[1]) DuilioDaSilva(5) 7 (Richard Guest) *s.i.s and bhd: hdwy over 2f out: rdn over 1f out: styd on strly: jst failed* **8/1**[3]	61
0235	**3**	*3/4*	**Bonnie Prince Blue**[17] 938 9-8-11 **53** .... DaleSwift(3) 3 (Ian McInnes) *dwlt and towards rr: hdwy over 2f out: sn rdn: swtchd lft ent fnl f: styd on strly: nrst fin* **14/1**	59
4400	**4**	*1/2*	**Spacecraft (IRE)**[11] 1014 5-8-9 **48** ....(b) JoeFanning 2 (Christopher Kellett) *dwlt and in rr: stdy hdwy over 3f out: wd st: led wl over 1f out and sn rdn: drvn and hdd ins fnl f: wknd towards fin* **9/2**[1]	53
00-0	**5**	*3*	**Bertie Blu Boy**[18] 929 4-8-10 **52** .... RobertLButler(3) 10 (Paul Green) *chsd ldrs: hdwy to ld 3f out: rdn and hdd wl over 1f out: kpt on same pce* **33/1**	50
0535	**6**	*2 1/2*	**Myraid**[7] 1052 5-8-11 **50** .... JamesSullivan 12 (Ruth Carr) *midfield: hdwy and in tch over 3f out: rdn wl over 2f out: sn btn* **9/2**[1]	42
6010	**7**	*1*	**Putin (IRE)**[13] 988 4-8-3 **49** ....(bt) LeonnaMayor(7) 9 (Phil McEntee) *prom: rdn along 3f out: wknd fnl 2f* **10/1**	39
6-05	**8**	*1/2*	**Thank You Joy**[67] 333 4-8-12 **51** ....(v) FrederikTylicki 4 (J R Jenkins) *dwlt and towards rr tl sme late hdwy* **12/1**	40
500/	**9**	*7*	**Woteva**[850] 7650 6-8-2 **48** .... EvaMoscrop(7) 14 (Nigel Tinkler) *chsd ldrs on outer: wknd wl over 3f out* **66/1**	21
0025	**10**	*hd*	**Ad Vitam (IRE)**[18] 929 4-8-9 **48** ....(vt) MichaelStainton 5 (Micky Hammond) *dwlt: a towards rr* **7/1**[2]	20
06-5	**11**	*7*	**Downtown Boy (IRE)**[5] 1096 4-8-12 **51** .... PaddyAspell 8 (Ray Craggs) *chsd ldrs: rdn along over 3f out: sn wknd* **12/1**	
350-	**12**	*7*	**It's A Mans World**[316] 2348 6-8-12 **51** .... RobertWinston 1 (Kevin M Prendergast) *a in rr* **25/1**	
0-00	**13**	*1 1/4*	**Hab Reeh**[5] 1092 4-9-1 **54** ....(bt) PJMcDonald 11 (Ruth Carr) *sn led: rdn along and hdd 3f out: sn wknd* **25/1**	
40	**14**	*29*	**Apple Blossom Time (IRE)**[12] 995 5-8-11 **50** ....(b[1]) AndreaAtzeni 6 (Derek Haydn Jones) *chsd ldrs on inner: rdn along wl over 3f out: sn wknd and bhd whn eased fnl 2f* **8/1**[3]	

1m 43.63s (-0.07) **Going Correction** -0.025s/f (Stan) **14** Ran SP% **123.4**
Speed ratings (Par 101): **99,98,98,97,94 92,91,90,83,83 76,69,68,39**
toteswingers: 1&2 £11.00, 1&3 £15.20, 2&3 £22.50. CSF £87.28 CT £1173.61 TOTE £12.20: £3.80, £3.40, £4.20; EX 116.00 Trifecta £426.20 Pool: £1,002.20 - 1.74 winning units..
Owner David Armstrong **Bred** W J Kennedy **Trained** Kirkheaton, Northumberland

FOCUS
Another moderate handicap. Unusually for the track, three of the first four home came from a long way back, with the pace quite strong. As in the previous contest, the race went to a less-exposed type. The winner built on his C&D maiden form.
T/Plt: £15.40 to a £1 stake. Pool of £56,968.80 - 2,694.55 winning tickets. T/Qpdt: £8.80 to a £1 stake. Pool of £4,491.76 - 377.35 winning tickets. JR

1104 LINGFIELD (L-H)
Wednesday, April 4

OFFICIAL GOING: Standard
Wind: Cloudy Weather: Light, across

1180 LINGFIELDPARK.CO.UK MEDIAN AUCTION MAIDEN FILLIES' STKS 1m (P)
2:00 (2:01) (Class 5) 3-4-Y-0 **£2,264** (£673; £336; £168) **Stalls** High

Form				RPR
05-	**1**		**Moment In Time (IRE)**[169] 6933 3-8-13 0 .... MartinLane 5 (David Simcock) *trckd ldr's slow pce: shkn up to ld wl over 1f out: styd on fnl f* **11/10**[1]	67+
00-	**2**	*1*	**White Flight**[165] 7030 3-8-13 0 .... LeeNewman 6 (Jonathan Portman) *hld up in 4th: effrt over 2f out: shkn up to chse wnr fnl f: styd on but nvr really threatened* **16/1**	63
62-3	**3**	*1 1/4*	**Viola Da Gamba (IRE)**[14] 981 3-8-13 73 .... JimCrowley 1 (William Knight) *led: set v mod pce to 3f out: rdn 2f out: sn hdd and nt qckn: one pce* **11/4**[2]	60
0-	**4**	*2 1/2*	**Indian Blossom**[177] 6742 3-8-13 0 .... LukeMorris 2 (Harry Dunlop) *stdd s: hld up bhd ldng pair: nt qckn and outpcd 2f out: wl hld after* **4/1**[3]	54
5	**5**	*3/4*	**Russian Rumba (IRE)**[13] 990 3-8-13 0 .... RichardKingscote 4 (Jonathan Portman) *hld up last: pushed along and outpcd fr 2f out: n.d after* **12/1**	52

1m 41.93s (3.73) **Going Correction** +0.05s/f (Slow) **5** Ran SP% **107.9**
Speed ratings (Par 100): **83,82,80,78,77**
CSF £17.58 TOTE £2.40: £2.10, £10.30; EX 18.90.
Owner Mrs Julia Annable **Bred** L K I Bloodstock Ltd **Trained** Newmarket, Suffolk

FOCUS
A modest fillies' maiden run at a slow pace. The winner has more to offer, but the third disappointed.

1181 LINGFIELD MARRIOTT HOTEL & COUNTRY CLUB CLAIMING STKS 7f (P)
2:30 (2:30) (Class 6) 3-Y-0+ **£1,704** (£503; £251) **Stalls** Low

Form				RPR
5306	**1**		**Hazzard County (USA)**[16] 962 8-9-9 91 .... LauraPike(5) 4 (David Simcock) *hld up in 3rd: moved up to chal on outer over 2f out: led over 1f out: sn in command: comf* **6/4**[1]	88+
1122	**2**	*1 3/4*	**Hinton Admiral**[12] 1005 8-9-10 75 .... HayleyTurner 1 (Conor Dore) *trckd ldr: led 2f out: rdn and hdd over 1f out: styd on but readily hld* **9/4**[2]	79
540-	**3**	*3 1/2*	**Barolo Top (IRE)**[173] 6829 3-8-7 75 .... RichardKingscote 2 (Tom Dascombe) *hld up in last: lft bhd by others over 2f out: shuffled along to take 3rd fnl f: sn eased* **3/1**[3]	62
0000	**4**	*3/4*	**Calypso Magic (IRE)**[20] 907 4-9-11 77 .... LukeMorris 3 (Linda Jewell) *led to 2f out: sn btn* **15/2**	69

1m 26.78s (1.98) **Going Correction** +0.05s/f (Slow)
WFA 3 from 4yo+ 14lb **4** Ran SP% **107.5**
Speed ratings (Par 101): **90,88,84,83**
CSF £5.07 TOTE £1.50; EX 4.30.Barolo Top was claimed by Mr T. Gould for £5,000. Hazzard County was claimed by Mr P. D. Evans for £12,000.
Owner Khalifa Dasmal **Bred** Cho, Llc **Trained** Newmarket, Suffolk

FOCUS
Only four runners and the pace was slow (time 2.12 seconds slower than the following maiden), but it was a fair claimer.

1182 LINGFIELDPARK.CO.UK MAIDEN STKS 7f (P)
3:00 (3:01) (Class 5) 3-Y-0 **£2,385** (£704; £352) **Stalls** Low

Form				RPR
6-	**1**		**Muarrab**[253] 4414 3-9-3 0 .... PaulHanagan 14 (Ed Dunlop) *trckd ldrs: prog on outer to go 3rd over 2f out: sn chalng: shkn up to ld over 1f out: forged away* **13/8**[1]	81
5	**2**	*1 3/4*	**Cooler Climes**[15] 969 3-9-3 0 .... LukeMorris 7 (Pat Eddery) *trckd ldr: led jst over 2f out: rdn and hdd over 1f out: styd on but readily hld* **9/4**[2]	77
5	**3**	*5*	**Princess Steph (IRE)**[12] 1016 3-8-12 0 .... RichardKingscote 6 (Heather Main) *trckd ldng trio on inner: outpcd fr 2f out: wnt 3rd jst over 1f out: no ch* **10/1**[3]	58
6-	**4**	*1/2*	**Cyrus Sod**[162] 7083 3-9-3 0 .... TomMcLaughlin 11 (Ed Dunlop) *hld up in rr: outpcd fr over 2f out: pushed along and prog over 1f out: styd on fnl f* **16/1**	62
	5	*nk*	**Tharawal (IRE)** 3-9-3 0 .... MarcHalford 5 (Terry Clement) *dwlt: wl in rr: outpcd over 2f out: pushed along and prog over 1f out: styd on fnl f* **100/1**	61
06-	**6**	*3 1/4*	**Kogershin (USA)**[165] 7025 3-8-12 0 .... KieranO'Neill 9 (Marcus Tregoning) *settled in midfield: effrt and rchd 6th jst over 2f out but already outpcd: one pce after* **10/1**[3]	47
	7	*1 1/2*	**Collectable**[173] 6850 3-8-12 0 .... LeeNewman 13 (Jonathan Portman) *trckd ldng pair on outer to over 2f out: steadily wknd* **80/1**	43
00-	**8**	*1/2*	**Kai**[200] 6160 3-9-3 0 .... HayleyTurner 3 (Michael Bell) *led to jst over 2f out: wknd over 1f out* **16/1**	47
	9	*6*	**Perfect Policy** 3-8-12 0 .... JimCrowley 1 (Ralph Beckett) *dwlt: nvr beyond midfield: pushed along on inner 3f out: wknd and eased over 1f out* **20/1**	25
-	**10**	*nse*	**Fauran (IRE)** 3-8-12 0 .... NeilCallan 8 (Clive Brittain) *t.k.h: trckd ldrs: urged along 3f out: wknd 2f out* **12/1**	25
40	**11**	*1 3/4*	**One Last Dream**[15] 969 3-9-0 0 .... SimonPearce(3) 12 (Ron Hodges) *fractious in preliminaries: nvr beyond midfield on outer: outpcd over 2f out: wknd over 1f out* **100/1**	26
5-	**12**	*7*	**Triple Salchow**[146] 7345 3-8-12 0 .... FrankieMcDonald 10 (Alastair Lidderdale) *s.s: hld up wl in rr: nvr a factor: t.o* **40/1**	
	13	*9*	**Lion's Maid** 3-8-7 0 .... MarkCoumbe(5) 4 (Michael Attwater) *dwlt: a in last: t.o* **100/1**	

1m 24.66s (-0.14) **Going Correction** +0.05s/f (Slow) **13** Ran SP% **117.9**
Speed ratings (Par 98): **102,100,94,93,93 89,87,87,80,80 78,70,60**
toteswingers:1&2:£2.00, 1&3:£6.50, 2&3:£6.30 CSF £4.88 TOTE £3.00: £1.10, £1.10, £2.70; EX 7.00 Trifecta £47.60 Pool: £661.44 - 10.27 winning units..
Owner Hamdan Al Maktoum **Bred** Stratford Place Stud **Trained** Newmarket, Suffolk

FOCUS
The front two were well fancied and look to have run to decent level, but there was little depth on paper.
Tharawal(IRE) Official explanation: jockey said colt ran green
One Last Dream Official explanation: jockey said gelding hung right

1183 DISCOVER RACING DAY AT LINGFIELD PARK (S) STKS 6f (P)
3:30 (3:30) (Class 6) 3-Y-0+ **£1,704** (£503; £251) **Stalls** Low

Form				RPR
1261	**1**		**Gin Twist**[6] 1090 3-8-9 71 ....(b) RichardKingscote 3 (Tom Dascombe) *hld up in 4th: clsd on ldrs gng wl 2f out: asked to ld ins fnl f: edgd rt but sn in command: comf* **4/5**[1]	64+
1034	**2**	*1 1/4*	**Waterloo Dock**[7] 1069 7-9-12 68 ....(v) LukeMorris 4 (Michael Quinn) *wnt rt s: chsd ldr: rdn to cl 2f out: led over 1f out on outer: hdd and nudged ins fnl f: sn btn* **7/4**[2]	68
0430	**3**	*4 1/2*	**Pharoh Jake**[14] 986 4-9-7 46 .... KieranO'Neill 2 (John Bridger) *trckd ldng pair: tried to chal on inner over 1f out: sn lft bhd* **16/1**[3]	49
6044	**4**	*1*	**Toms River Tess (IRE)**[14] 985 4-9-2 44 ....(b) JamieGoldstein 1 (Zoe Davison) *led at str pce: hdd and fdd over 1f out* **16/1**[3]	41
00	**5**	*61*	**Just Me'Lady**[47] 597 3-8-1 0 .... DominicFox(3) 5 (Bill Turner) *impeded s: sn struggling: t.o bef 1/2-way* **33/1**	

1m 11.79s (-0.11) **Going Correction** +0.05s/f (Slow)
WFA 3 from 4yo+ 12lb **5** Ran SP% **106.6**
Speed ratings (Par 101): **102,100,94,93,11**
CSF £2.20 TOTE £1.70: £1.20, £1.10; EX 2.00.The winner was brought in for 7,600gns.
Owner Manor House Stables LLP **Bred** Highclere Stud **Trained** Malpas, Cheshire

FOCUS
An uncompetitive seller in which Toms River Tess took them along at a good pace. The winner did not need to match her winter form.

1184 MIRROR PUNTERS CLUB H'CAP 2m (P)
4:00 (4:00) (Class 6) (0-60,60) 4-Y-0+ **£1,704** (£503; £251) **Stalls** Low

Form				RPR
3024	**1**		**Six Of Clubs**[14] 772 6-9-7 **57** ....(b) KierenFallon 3 (Bill Turner) *patiently rdn in midfield: prog over 2f out: clsd to ld ins fnl f: drvn out* **10/3**[1]	65
0-43	**2**	*1 1/2*	**Talbot Green**[5] 1104 4-9-3 **57** .... MartinDwyer 10 (William Muir) *trckd ldrs: prog on outer 3f out: led 2f out: drvn and hdd ins fnl f: one pce* **5/1**[3]	64
4055	**3**	*nk*	**Cloudy Start**[22] 889 6-9-3 **60** .... LeonnaMayor(7) 2 (Jamie Osborne) *hld up in 8th: prog on inner over 3f out: chsd ldrs 2f out: styd on same pce after* **10/1**	66
1-50	**4**	*1/2*	**Galiotto (IRE)**[13] 566 6-9-9 **59** ....(v) RyanMoore 4 (Gary Moore) *settled in midfield: rdn 5f out: keeping on u.p whn n.m.r over 2f out: rallied fnl f: nrst fin* **13/2**	65

0-60 **5** *3 ¾* **Bute Street**^{15} [968] 7-8-13 **49** .... RichardKingscote 1 50
(Ron Hodges) *trckd ldng pair: wnt 2nd over 4f out: gng strly over 3f out: lost pl over 2f out: fdd* **14/1**

5340 **6** *4 ½* **The Catenian (IRE)**^{5} [1112] 4-8-7 **47** oh1 ow1................(p) ShaneKelly 5 43
(John Butler) *stdd s: hld up in last trio: gng wl enough over 3f out: sme prog over 2f out but only 7th: nvr on terms* **7/1**

2113 **7** *2* **Celtic Charlie (FR)**^{9} [1047] 7-9-2 **52**.................................... IanMongan 7 45
(Pat Phelan) *taken down early: led to 2f out: steadily wknd* **4/1**^{2}

50/6 **8** *nk* **Mymateeric**^{15} [968] 6-8-7 **46** oh1 .... SimonPearce$^{(3)}$ 11 39
(Lydia Pearce) *hld up in last trio: rdn over 4f out: no prog and wl btn over 2f out* **40/1**

000/ **9** *4 ½* **Sahara Sunshine**^{78} [6775] 7-9-0 **50**............................ FergusSweeney 8 38
(Laura Mongan) *stdd s: hld up in last: lft bhd over 3f out: shkn up over 1f out: nvr remotely involved* **66/1**

0056 **10** *3 ½* **Perfect Shot (IRE)**^{18} [937] 6-9-5 **58**.......................... RobertLButler$^{(3)}$ 6 41
(Jim Best) *hld up in midfield: shkn up and wknd over 3f out: sn bhd* **25/1**

2-60 **11** *hd* **Henry Holmes**^{71} [278] 9-8-12 **48**.. LukeMorris 9 31
(Lydia Richards) *chsd ldr to over 4f out: sn wknd* **14/1**

3m 24.91s (-0.79) **Going Correction** +0.05s/f (Slow)
WFA 4 from 6yo+ 4lb **11** Ran SP% **115.8**
Speed ratings (Par 101): **103,102,102,101,99 97,96,96,94,92 92**
toteswingers:1&2:£5.30, 1&3:£9.70, 2&3:£10.70 CSF £19.29 CT £150.31 TOTE £5.70: £1.60, £2.10, £3.00; EX 24.10 Trifecta £132.50 Pool: £601.66 - 3.36 winning units..
Owner Gongolfin **Bred** R V Young **Trained** Sigwells, Somerset

FOCUS
A moderate handicap run at an ordinary pace. The winner travels well and may do better, with the next three close to their marks.
Sahara Sunshine Official explanation: jockey said mare reared leaving stalls
Henry Holmes Official explanation: vet said gelding had been struck into left-hind

1185 GREAT DEALS ON ANNUAL MEMBERSHIP H'CAP 5f (P)
4:30 (4:30) (Class 6) (0-65,64) 4-Y-0+ **£1,704** (£503; £251) **Stalls** High

Form RPR

3121 **1** **Dorothy's Dancing (IRE)**^{7} [1070] 4-9-8 **64** 6ex................. RyanMoore 2 72
(Gary Moore) *chsd ldng trio: wnt 3rd over 2f out and 2nd over 1f out: hrd rdn and styd on to ld last 100yds* **11/8**^{1}

00-2 **2** *¾* **Lesley's Choice**^{8} [1054] 6-9-4 **60**.............................(v) JamesDoyle 5 65
(Paul Rich) *chsd ldrs in 5th: pushed along 1/2-way: plld out and drvn 1f out: styd on to take 2nd post* **5/1**^{2}

0236 **3** *nse* **Sherjawy (IRE)**^{7} [1061] 8-9-2 **58**.............................(b) JamieGoldstein 1 63
(Zoe Davison) *w ldr: led after 2f: drvn over 1f out: hdd and one pce last 100yds* **10/1**

-300 **4** *nk* **Welsh Inlet (IRE)**^{68} [320] 4-9-4 **60**............................... KieranO'Neill 3 64
(John Bridger) *hld up in 7th: pushed along on inner 1/2-way: drvn and effrt over 1f out: styd on but nvr quite able to chal* **10/1**

6160 **5** *nk* **Chjimes (IRE)**^{13} [996] 8-9-7 **63**.............................(b) HayleyTurner 7 66
(Conor Dore) *hld up in 6th: brought wd bnd 2f out and pushed along: styd on and reminder ins fnl f: nrst fin* **8/1**^{3}

-005 **6** *4* **Dreams Of Glory**^{16} [958] 4-9-2 **61**.............................. SimonPearce$^{(3)}$ 4 49
(Ron Hodges) *led 2f: pressed ldr tl wknd over 1f out* **10/1**

-000 **7** *shd* **Baby Dottie**^{42} [647] 5-9-3 **59**... IanMongan 6 47
(Pat Phelan) *s.i.s: hld up in last and racd wd: detached fr rest 1/2-way: pushed along and nvr on terms after* **5/1**^{2}

0000 **8** *2 ¼* **Prize Point**^{14} [986] 6-8-9 **51** oh2 ow2.......................(bt) StevieDonohoe 8 31
(Tom Gretton) *racd on outer: pressed ldng pair to 1/2-way: wknd 2f out* **25/1**

58.84s (0.04) **Going Correction** +0.05s/f (Slow) **8** Ran SP% **117.7**
Speed ratings (Par 101): **101,99,99,99,98 92,92,88**
toteswingers:1&2:£2.50, 1&3:£2.80, 2&3:£4.70 CSF £8.80 CT £50.68 TOTE £2.80: £1.40, £1.70, £2.90; EX 6.90 Trifecta £30.90 Pool: £1,054.83 - 25.24 winning units..
Owner Tom Glynn **Bred** Patrick Carroll **Trained** Lower Beeding, W Sussex

FOCUS
A moderate sprint handicap run at a good pace. The form is rated around the third.

1186 CYPRIUM BAR AT LINGFIELD MARRIOTT H'CAP 1m 2f (P)
5:00 (5:00) (Class 4) (0-85,84) 4-Y-0+ **£4,075** (£1,212; £606; £303) **Stalls** Low

Form RPR

1- **1** **Camborne**^{147} [7327] 4-9-3 **80**... RobertHavlin 7 92+
(John Gosden) *s.s: hld up in last trio: prog and wd bnd 2f out: rdn and r.o to ld last 150yds: decisively* **5/1**^{3}

3125 **2** *1 ½* **Megalala (IRE)**^{14} [987] 11-9-0 **77**................................... KieranO'Neill 9 83
(John Bridger) *led at gd pce: drvn over 1f out: hdd and outpcd last 150yds: styd on* **12/1**

-523 **3** *¾* **Big Creek (IRE)**^{34} [751] 5-9-3 **80**..................................... RyanMoore 2 85
(Jeremy Noseda) *trckd ldng trio: effrt 2f out: hrd rdn to go 2nd briefly 1f out: outpcd after* **11/4**^{1}

110- **4** *3* **Kyllachy Spirit**^{189} [6439] 4-9-7 **84**..................................... ShaneKelly 8 83
(William Knight) *trckd ldng pair: wnt 2nd over 2f out: drvn and no imp over 1f out: wknd fnl f* **8/1**

-046 **5** *2 ¾* **Edgewater (IRE)**^{7} [1071] 5-8-11 **74**..........................(v^{1}) StevieDonohoe 1 67
(Lee Carter) *settled in midfield: outpcd in 6th over 2f out: nt qckn and no imp after* **16/1**

3466 **6** *2 ¼* **Hidden Glory**^{15} [978] 5-8-9 **72**..................................(b) PaulMulrennan 3 61
(James Given) *trckd ldrs in 5th: shkn up and cl enough 2f out: wknd qckly fnl f* **8/1**

31-0 **7** *3 ¾* **Epsom Salts**^{77} [202] 7-8-13 **76**... IanMongan 4 57
(Pat Phelan) *s.s: hld up last and racd wd: sme late hdwy: nvr a factor* **20/1**

013- **8** *1 ¼* **Bahamian Music (IRE)**^{249} [4553] 5-9-4 **81**......................... LukeMorris 5 60
(Ed Vaughan) *chsd ldr to over 2f out: wknd qckly over 1f out* **16/1**

100- **9** *1* **Watered Silk**^{187} [6497] 4-9-3 **80**...................................... HayleyTurner 10 57
(Marcus Tregoning) *dwlt: hld up in last trio: pushed along over 3f out: nvr in contention* **9/1**

3241 **10** *8* **Southern State (USA)**^{15} [978] 4-8-12 **75**......................... KierenFallon 6 36
(Mark Johnston) *rousted along after 1f: in tch but nvr gng that wl: wknd over 3f out: eased over 1f out: t.o* **4/1**^{2}

2m 3.44s (-3.16) **Going Correction** +0.05s/f (Slow) **10** Ran SP% **119.8**
Speed ratings (Par 105): **114,112,112,109,107 105,102,101,101,94**
toteswingers:1&2:£7.10, 1&3:£3.30, 2&3:£10.70 CSF £65.22 CT £200.45 TOTE £5.80: £1.80, £3.50, £1.10; EX 87.10 Trifecta £386.40 Pool: £1,039.33 - 1.99 winning units..
Owner H R H Princess Haya Of Jordan **Bred** Southill Stud **Trained** Newmarket, Suffolk

FOCUS
A fair handicap run at an honest pace. The form is rated around the runner-up and third.
T/Plt: £9.60 to a £1 stake. Pool:£55,466.34 - 4,181.43 winning tickets T/Qpdt: £2.40 to a £1 stake. Pool:£4,640.22 - 1,398.73 winning tickets JN

1111 WOLVERHAMPTON (A.W) (L-H)
Wednesday, April 4

OFFICIAL GOING: Standard
Wind: Fresh against Weather: Overcast

1187 32RED H'CAP 5f 20y(P)
5:30 (5:30) (Class 5) (0-75,76) 4-Y-0+ **£2,264** (£673; £336; £168) **Stalls** Low

Form RPR

0413 **1** **Mother Jones**^{20} [911] 4-8-7 **65**.............................. MatthewCosham$^{(5)}$ 8 73
(David Evans) *chsd ldrs: rdn over 1f out: r.o to ld post* **8/1**

020- **2** *shd* **Speightowns Kid (USA)**^{223} [5419] 4-9-5 **72**................... WilliamBuick 5 80
(Matthew Salaman) *led: rdn and hung rt fr over 1f out: hdd post* **9/2**^{2}

5342 **3** *½* **Blown It (USA)**^{5} [1116] 6-9-2 **69**...................................(v^{1}) JoeFanning 3 75
(Keith Dalgleish) *hld up: hdwy 1/2-way: nt clr run over 1f out: shkn up ins fnl f: kpt on* **3/1**^{1}

3-24 **4** *1 ½* **Angelo Poliziano**^{25} [870] 6-9-0 **67**........................(p) SilvestreDeSousa 2 68
(Ann Duffield) *chsd ldrs: rdn over 1f out: styd on same pce ins fnl f* **11/2**

1546 **5** *nk* **No Mean Trick (USA)**^{29} [808] 6-8-13 **66**...................... MickyFenton 10 66
(Paul Midgley) *w ldr: rdn and ev ch over 1f out: no ex ins fnl f* **11/2**

6051 **6** *½* **Shawkantango**^{13} [996] 5-9-0 **70**.................................(v) DaleSwift$^{(3)}$ 4 68
(Derek Shaw) *sn outpcd: r.o ins fnl f: nrst fin* **5/1**^{3}

1314 **7** *¾* **Diamond Vine (IRE)**^{39} [710] 4-8-11 **71**......................(p) DarrenEgan$^{(7)}$ 7 66
(Ronald Harris) *s.i.s: outpcd: r.o ins fnl f: nvr nrr* **14/1**

0412 **8** *1 ¾* **Black Baccara**^{13} [996] 5-9-1 **71**..................................(be) RyanClark$^{(3)}$ 1 60
(Phil McEntee) *hld up in tch: rdn over 1f out: wknd ins fnl f* **12/1**

1m 2.21s (-0.09) **Going Correction** +0.15s/f (Slow) **8** Ran SP% **116.1**
Speed ratings (Par 103): **106,105,105,102,102 101,100,97**
toteswingers:1&2:£8.20, 1&3:£4.60, 2&3:£3.80 CSF £44.46 CT £134.93 TOTE £13.80: £3.60, £1.50, £1.30; EX 52.20 Trifecta £591.00 Pool: £902.56 - 1.13 winning units..
Owner Mike Nolan **Bred** New Hall Stud **Trained** Pandy, Monmouths

FOCUS
A cold evening and there was a strong headwind facing the runners in the straight. The opening race was a fair sprint handicap. The pace was not very strong and there was a tight finish. The winner is rated up a length on her winter form.

1188 32RED.COM FILLIES' MAIDEN AUCTION STKS 5f 20y(P)
6:00 (6:00) (Class 5) 2-Y-O **£2,264** (£673; £336; £168) **Stalls** Low

Form RPR

0 **1** **Dreamy Ciara**^{4} [1136] 2-8-4 0.. CathyGannon 1 71
(David Evans) *mde all: rdn over 1f out: styd on* **9/4**^{2}

3 **2** *nk* **Poetic Princess**^{4} [1136] 2-8-4 0... JoeFanning 7 70
(Jo Hughes) *chsd wnr: rdn over 1f out: r.o* **1/1**^{1}

3 *6* **Jamnean** 2-8-6 0 ow1.. RussKennemore 4 50
(John Holt) *chsd ldrs: pushed along 1/2-way: wknd fnl f* **14/1**

4 *2 ¼* **Windsor Rose (IRE)** 2-8-6 0.. FrannyNorton 6 42
(Mark Brisbourne) *sn pushed along in rr: hdwy 1/2-way: wknd wl over 1f out* **9/1**^{3}

5 *1* **Shop Til You Drop** 2-8-4 0.. RichardThomas 8 38
(David Evans) *chsd ldrs: pushed along 1/2-way: sn wknd* **22/1**

6 *4 ½* **Schottische** 2-8-4 0.. AndreaAtzeni 3 20
(Derek Haydn Jones) *sn outpcd* **14/1**

7 *2* **Myzamour** 2-8-1 0.. RyanPowell$^{(3)}$ 5 13
(J S Moore) *s.s: outpcd* **14/1**

1m 3.58s (1.28) **Going Correction** +0.15s/f (Slow) **7** Ran SP% **115.1**
Speed ratings (Par 89): **95,94,84,81,79 72,69**
toteswingers:1&2:£1.60, 1&3:£5.80, 2&3:£4.30 CSF £4.91 TOTE £4.90: £2.10, £1.10; EX 5.30 Trifecta £84.60 Pool: £927.72 - 8.11 winning units..
Owner Mrs Emma Ambrose **Bred** Mrs S M Shone **Trained** Pandy, Monmouths

FOCUS
The two runners with experience dominated this fillies' auction maiden and there was a big gap back to the third. There was little depth to this maiden.

NOTEBOOK
Dreamy Ciara finished over 3l behind Poetic Princess in a 5f Kempton maiden four days earlier, but she looked much more streetwise under a forcing ride this time and showed a good attitude to reverse her debut form. This looked an ordinary race but she is a half-sister to four-time AW handicap winner Ridgeway Jazz (at up to 9.4f) and should continue to progress with time and distance. (op 4-1)
Poetic Princess, a very cheaply bought half-sister to prolific minor AW handicap winner Bentley, started her career with a creditable 25-1 third in a 5f Kempton fillies' maiden on Saturday. She was strong in the market turned out quickly and gave it a decent try but couldn't quite get to grips with the front-running winner. (op 4-5)
Jamnean, a half-sister to an exposed 65-rated maiden, showed a bit of ability on her debut and should improve for the experience. (tchd 12-1 and 16-1)
Windsor Rose(IRE), a 6,000gns half-sister to a minor 6f minor maiden winner Pendle Lady, looked inexperienced before plugging on for a remote fourth on debut. (op 17-2 tchd 8-1 and 10-1)
Shop Til You Drop ran green and was never involved on her first start. (op 20-1)

1189 32RED CASINO H'CAP 1m 4f 50y(P)
6:30 (6:31) (Class 6) (0-60,65) 4-Y-0+ **£1,704** (£503; £251) **Stalls** Low

Form RPR

000- **1** **Maid Of Meft**^{176} [6780] 5-9-3 **58**.. JoeFanning 7 68
(Keith Dalgleish) *hld up: hdwy over 3f out: rdn over 2f out: led over 1f out: styd on wl* **15/8**^{1}

-066 **2** *2 ¼* **Delagoa Bay (IRE)**^{19} [924] 4-8-4 **46** oh1........................... CathyGannon 2 52
(Sylvester Kirk) *hld up: hdwy over 1f out: r.o to go 2nd nr fin: no ch w wnr* **12/1**

0210 **3** *shd* **Visions Of Johanna (USA)**^{12} [1014] 7-8-10 **56**......... DuilioDaSilva$^{(5)}$ 10 62
(Richard Guest) *a.p: chsd ldr over 4f out: led over 2f out: rdn and hdd over 1f out: styd on same pce ins fnl f: lost 2nd nr fin* **15/2**

100- **4** *1 ½* **Iguacu**^{277} [3637] 8-8-13 **54**... SilvestreDeSousa 3 57
(Richard Price) *hld up: hdwy over 2f out: rdn over 1f out: styd on same pce ins fnl f* **25/1**

45-1 **5** *3* **The Blue Dog (IRE)**^{6} [1083] 5-9-10 **65** 6ex......................... AndreaAtzeni 5 64
(Michael Wigham) *prom: lost pl over 4f out: rdn and edgd lft over 2f out: styd on same pce* **3/1**^{2}

554- **6** *1 ½* **Flying Phoenix**^{42} [7211] 4-9-2 **58**..................................... KellyHarrison 9 54
(Dai Burchell) *chsd ldr over 7f: remained handy: rdn over 2f out: wknd fnl f* **16/1**

-460 **7** *1 ¼* **Port Hill**^{33} [767] 5-8-11 **52**... TomMcLaughlin 1 46
(Mark Brisbourne) *plld hrd: led: rdn and hdd over 2f out: wknd ins fnl f* **7/1**^{3}

560- **8** *2 ½* **Mahfal (FR)**^{23} [6493] 4-9-4 **60**..(t) BarryMcHugh 6 50
(Brian Ellison) *prom: pushed along over 3f out: wknd over 2f out* **12/1**

-030 **9** *7* **Swords**[5] 1112 10 -8-0**46** oh1 .... (p) RaulDaSilva(5) 11 25
(Ray Peacock) *dwlt: hld up: racd wd 6f out: lost tch fr over 3f out* **50/1**
400 **10** *2 1/2* **Valiant Bee**[12] 1016 4 -8-8**50** .... ChrisCatlin 8 25
(Bill Moore) *hld up: racd keenly: hdwy 6f out: rdn and hung lft over 2f out: sn wknd* **25/1**

2m 43.33s (2.23)**Going Correction** +0.15s/f (Slow)
WFA 4 from 5yo+ 1lb **10**Ran SP% **115.0**
Speed ratings (Par 101): **98,96,96,95,93 92,91,89,85,83**
toteswingers:1&2:£5.80, 1&3:£2.40, 2&3:£10.80 CSF £25.32 CT £139.65 TOTE £2.70 : £1.10, £5.30, £1.20 ; EX 36.00 Trifecta £144.20 Pool: £1185.37 - 6.08 winning units.
Owner Gordon McDowall **Bred** Ian Murray Tough **Trained** Carluke, S Lanarks
■ Stewards' Enquiry : Raul Da Silva five-day ban: used whip when out of contention (Apr 18-21,tbn)

FOCUS
They went a steady pace in this handicap and a gamble was landed in good style by a well-handicapped runner who was returning for a new yard. The form looks sound.
Swords Official explanation: jockey said gelding hung badly right-handed

1190 £32 FREE AT 32RED.COM H'CAP 1m 1f 103y (P)
7:00 (7:01) (Class 5) (0-75,75) 3-Y-O **£2,264** (£673; £336 ; £168) **Stalls** Low

Form RPR
1-2 **1** **Apothecary**[12] 1013 3 -9-7**75** .... WilliamBuick 9 84+
(John Gosden) *mde all: rdn and hung rt ins fnl f: r.o* **9/4**[1]
0-13 **2** *nk* **Zain Princess (IRE)**[12] 1013 3 -8-9**63** .... NickyMackay 8 71
(Gerard Butler) *hld up: hdwy 6f out: chsd wnr over 3f out: rdn over 1f out: hmpd ins fnl f: r.o* **10/1**
0-12 **3** *1 3/4* **Beauchamp Castle**[19] 920 3 -8-7**68** .... (t) NicoleNordblad(7) 5 72+
(Hans Adielsson) *plld hrd and prom: hmpd and stmbld over 6f out: hdwy and hung rt over 2f out: rdn over 1f out: styd on* **9/1**
112- **4** *1/2* **Spirit Of The Law (IRE)**[193] 6345 3 -9-3**71** .... JamieSpencer 10 74
(Ed Dunlop) *sn chsng ldrs: rdn over 1f out: no ex ins fnl f* **10/3**[2]
21-0 **5** *1/2* **Priestley's Reward (IRE)**[32] 787 3 -8-13**67** .... RobertWinston 4 69
(Mrs K Burke) *mid-div: hmpd over 6f out: hdwy u.p 2f out: sn rdn: styd on same pce fnl f* **40/1**
52-1 **6** *1 1/4* **Manomine**[14] 982 3 -8-13**67** .... BrettDoyle 6 67
(Clive Brittain) *chsd ldrs: edgd lft over 6f out: pushed along over 3f out: rdn over 2f out: styd on same pce fr over 1f out* **6/1**[3]
321- **7** *3 3/4* **Equity Card (FR)**[169] 6928 3 -9-6**74** .... SilvestreDeSousa 3 66
(Mark Johnston) *chsd wnr tl pushed along over 3f out: rdn over 1f out: wknd fnl f* **7/1**
400- **8** *1* **Travis County (IRE)**[210] 5825 3 -9-4**72** .... BarryMcHugh 7 62
(Brian Ellison) *s.i.s: hld up: a in rr* **20/1**
32-3 **9** *6* **Altona (IRE)**[19] 920 3 -9-3**71** .... MartinHarley 1 48
(Mick Channon) *hld up: hmpd over 6f out: wknd over 2f out* **11/1**

2m 4.68s (2.98)**Going Correction** +0.15s/f (Slow) **9**Ran SP% **115.3**
Speed ratings (Par 98): **92,91,90,89,89 88,84,83,78**
toteswingers:1&2:£2.70, 2&3:£8.50, 1&3:£6.90 CSF £26.04 CT £171.33 TOTE £4.30 : £1.90, £2.20, £2.80 ; EX 23.40 Trifecta £72.70 Pool: £1122.43 - 11.42 winnning units.
Owner H R H Princess Haya Of Jordan **Bred** Cliveden Stud Ltd **Trained** Newmarket, Suffolk
■ Stewards' Enquiry : William Buick caution: careless riding

FOCUS
An interesting handicap for 3-y-os. The pace was steady but there was a lot to like about the performance of the progressive winner, who improved a little as did the runner-up. The fifth sets the standard.
Altona(IRE) Official explanation: trainer's rep said filly was unsuited by the slow early pace

1191 32REDPOKER.COM H'CAP 1m 141y (P)
7:30 (7:30) (Class 6) (0-65,65) 4-Y-O+ **£1,704** (£503; £251) **Stalls** Low

Form RPR
1520 **1** **Just Five (IRE)**[13] 1002 6 -8-11**60** .... (v) RaulDaSilva(5) 11 71
(John Weymes) *led: hdd over 7f out: chsd ldrs tl led over 1f out: rdn out* **20/1**
00-1 **2** *3* **Douze Points (IRE)**[26] 848 6 -9-3**61** .... AdamKirby 6 65+
(John Butler) *hld up: pushed along and hdwy over 2f out: rdn and swtchd rt over 1f out: hung lft and r.o: no ch w wnr* **8/13**[1]
1-50 **3** *1 1/2* **Karate (IRE)**[6] 1088 4 -8-8**59** .... (t) NicoleNordblad(7) 5 60
(Hans Adielsson) *hld up: hdwy over 3f out: nt clr run and swtchd lft ins fnl f: styd on* **28/1**
50-0 **4** *1 1/4* **Loyal N Trusted**[20] 909 4 -8-13**57** .... SilvestreDeSousa 8 55
(Richard Price) *a.p: rdn over 1f out: no ex ins fnl f* **33/1**
6352 **5** *1 1/2* **Mataajir (USA)**[8] 1052 4 -9-5**63** .... MartinLane 13 57
(Derek Shaw) *led over 7f out: rdn and hdd over 1f out: hung rt and no ex ins fnl f* **11/2**[2]
030- **6** *1/2* **Mr Chocolate Drop (IRE)**[96] 7930 8 -8-11**60** .... (t) NathanAlison(5) 2 53
(Mandy Rowland) *hld up: plld hrd: r.o ins fnl f: nvr nrr* **50/1**
6251 **7** *nk* **Spartan King (IRE)**[15] 966 4 -8-13**57** .... JamieSpencer 12 49
(Ian Williams) *prom: chsd ldr over 6f out: rdn and ev ch wl over 1f out: wkng whn hmpd ins fnl f* **10/1**[3]
6006 **8** *hd* **Justcallmehandsome**[13] 1002 10 -8-13**62** ow1 .... LucyKBarry(5) 9 54
(Dominic Ffrench Davis) *hld up: nvr on terms* **25/1**
0-34 **9** *1 1/2* **Forward Feline (IRE)**[27] 842 6 -9-4**62** .... RobertWinston 3 51
(Bryn Palling) *hld up: rdn over 2f out: n.d* **28/1**
04-6 **10** *1* **Bashama**[14] 981 4 -9-3**61** .... BrettDoyle 10 47
(Clive Brittain) *chsd ldrs: rdn over 3f out: wknd over 2f out* **33/1**
030- **11** *2 3/4* **Climaxfortackle (IRE)**[166] 6990 4 -9-7**65** .... JoeFanning 4 45
(Derek Shaw) *s.i.s: a in rr* **10/1**[3]

1m 51.18s (0.68)**Going Correction** +0.15s/f (Slow) **11**Ran SP% **118.8**
Speed ratings (Par 101): **102,99,98,96,95 95,94,94,93,92 90**
toteswingers:1&2:£1.60, 2&3:£2.40, 1&3:£1.50 CSF £31.69 CT £424.63 TOTE £34.40 : £5.30, £1.50, £8.10 ; EX 54.70 TRIFECTA Not won.
Owner Grange Park Racing & Partner **Bred** Rathbarry Stud **Trained** Middleham Moor, N Yorks

FOCUS
The hot favourite didn't get the run of things and couldn't reel in a rival who got first run in this strongly run handicap. The pace held up pretty well through the card.
Mataajir(USA) Official explanation: jockey said gelding hung right-handed

1192 SPONSOR A RACE BY CALLING 01902 390000 MEDIAN AUCTION MAIDEN STKS 1m 141y (P)
8:00 (8:00) (Class 6) 3-5-Y-O **£1,704** (£503; £251) **Stalls** Low

Form RPR
03-3 **1** **Dutch Diamond**[13] 990 3 -8-4**73** .... NickyMackay 4 70
(John Gosden) *a.p: chsd ldr over 5f out: led over 1f out: rdn and hdd ins fnl f: rallied to ld nr fin* **1/1**[1]
366- **2** *1/2* **Benzanno (IRE)**[195] 6268 3 -8-9**73** .... DavidProbert 7 74
(Andrew Balding) *plld hrd and a.p: rdn to ld ins fnl f: hung lft: edgd rt and hdd nr fin* **5/2**[2]
0652 **3** *3 1/2* **King's Wharf (IRE)**[18] 943 3 -8-9**67** .... PadraigBeggy 8 66
(David Evans) *led: rdn over 2f out: hdd over 1f out: no ex ins fnl f* **6/1**[3]
-03 **4** *3/4* **Glennten**[18] 943 3 -8-9**0** .... LiamKeniry 2 64
(Sylvester Kirk) *chsd ldr 3f out: remained handy: shkn up over 1f out: styd on same pce* **7/1**
5 *1 1/4* **Ty Gwr** 3 -8-9**0** .... MartinLane 5 61
(David Simcock) *s.s: hld up: plld hrd: hdwy over 1f out: wknd ins fnl f* **20/1**
6 *21* **Khamseen** 5 -9-7**0** .... DavidKenny(5) 3
(Karen George) *s.s: a in rr: wknd over 2f out* **50/1**

1m 52.42s (1.92)**Going Correction** +0.15s/f (Slow)
WFA 3 from 5yo 17lb **6**Ran SP% **112.1**
Speed ratings (Par 101): **97,96,93,92,91 73**
toteswingers:1&2:£1.60, 2&3:£2.40, 1&3:£1.50 CSF £3.68 TOTE £2.40 : £2.20 , £2.00 ; EX 5.50 Trifecta £20.00 Pool: £458.23 - 16.94 winning units.
Owner Mrs P Robinson G Philipps & Ms R Hood **Bred** Serpentine Bloodstock Et Al **Trained** Newmarket, Suffolk

FOCUS
The two 73-rated market leaders pulled clear in this steadily run maiden. The form is fairly weak, rated around the third and fourth.

1193 HUGH HENNESSEY MEMORIAL FILLIES' H'CAP 7f 32y (P)
8:30 (8:30) (Class 5) (0-70,70) 4-Y-O+ **£2,264** (£673; £336 ; £168) **Stalls** High

Form RPR
4106 **1** **Marksbury**[27] 842 5 -8-8**57** .... MartinLane 7 65
(Mark Brisbourne) *chsd ldr tl led over 1f out: pushed out* **5/1**[3]
3-03 **2** *3/4* **Caramelita**[29] 813 5 -8-11**60** .... (v) FrederikTylicki 3 66
(J R Jenkins) *stdd s: hld up: hdwy over 2f out: rdn over 1f out: r.o to go 2nd wl ins fnl f: could nt quite rch wnr* **11/4**[2]
306- **3** *2 1/4* **Mawjoodah**[123] 7629 4 -9-7**70** .... BarryMcHugh 2 70
(Brian Ellison) *led: rdn and hdd over 1f out: no ex ins fnl f* **5/2**[1]
0053 **4** *1 3/4* **Cut The Cackle (IRE)**[8] 1084 6 -8-10**59** .... (bt) WilliamCarson 4 54
(Richard Guest) *hld up in tch: pushed along 1/2-way: outpcd 2f out: styd on towards fin* **5/2**[1]
-230 **5** *6* **Saktoon (USA)**[41] 666 4 -8-0**56** oh3 .... (v) DarrenEgan(7) 1 35
(Derek Shaw) *trckd ldrs: racd keenly: rdn over 2f out: sn wknd* **9/1**

1m 30.27s (0.67)**Going Correction** +0.15s/f (Slow) **5**Ran SP% **110.5**
Speed ratings (Par 100): **102,101,98,96,89**
CSF £18.88 TOTE £8.80 : £3.30 , £1.20 ; EX 16.60 .
Owner Wayne Hennessey **Bred** Dunchurch Lodge Stud Company **Trained** Great Ness, Shropshire

FOCUS
A fillies' handicap weakened by two withdrawals. The pace was steady and the form does not look strong. The winner is rated back to her best.
T/Jkpt: Not won. T/Plt: £12.00 to a £1 stake. Pool of £98,913.90 - 6,014.14 winning tickets. T/Qpdt: £5.10 to a £1 stake. Pool of £8,490.63 - 1,228.69 winning tickets. CR

1194 - 1200a (Foreign Racing) - See Raceform Interactive

FOLKESTONE (R-H)
Thursday, April 5

OFFICIAL GOING: Good to firm (firm in places on straight course; good in places on round course) changing to good to firm on straight course after race 1 (2.10)
fresh, acrossovercast, chilly

1201 HYDER-COLLINS EASTER CHICKS MEDIAN AUCTION MAIDEN STKS 5f
2:10 (2:10) (Class 6) 3-Y-O **£2,385** (£704; £352) **Stalls** High

Form RPR
-423 **1** **Heartsong (IRE)**[22] 897 3 -8-12**70** .... MartinLane 4 73
(John Gallagher) *w ldr tl led 3f out: nudged along and qcknd clr 1f out: eased towards fin: easily* **7/4**[1]
-55 **2** *4* **Auntie Mabel**[22] 892 3 -8-12**0** .... DavidProbert 2 59
(Andrew Balding) *in tch in rr: rdn 1/2-way: hdwy u.p and n.m.r jst over 1f out: chsd wnr jst ins fnl f: sn outpcd by wnr but kpt on for 2nd* **13/2**
00-6 **3** *1 1/4* **Vexillum (IRE)**[34] 769 3 -9-3**62** .... MartinHarley 3 59
(Mick Channon) *led for 2f: pressed wnr after: rdn and unable qck over 1f out: nt pce of wnr and lost 2nd: jst ins fnl f: one pce after* **15/8**[2]
20- **4** *21* **Subtle Knife**[160] 7135 3 -8-12**0** .... WilliamCarson 1 25
(Giles Bravery) *pushed along: pressed ldrs: rdn and unable qck ent fnl 2f: btn ent fnl f: eased ins fnl f* **3/1**[3]

1m 0.83s (0.83)**Going Correction** +0.25s/f (Good) **4**Ran SP% **109.5**
Speed ratings (Par 96): **103,96,94,61**
CSF £11.88 TOTE £2.00 ; EX 6.60 .
Owner Colin Rashbrook **Bred** Gerry And John Rowley **Trained** Chastleton, Oxon

FOCUS
This was undeniably a weak maiden. The winner is rated in line with a best view of her previous form.

1202 BET TOTEPOOL TEXT TOTE TO 89660 MAIDEN STKS 5f
2:40 (2:40) (Class 5) 2-Y-O **£2,385** (£704; £352) **Stalls** High

Form RPR
1 **Judy In Disguise** 2 -8-5**0** .... RyanWhile(7) 4 75
(Bill Turner) *dwlt and short of room leaving stalls: towards rr: swtchd rt and pushed along 1/2-way: hdwy to ld over 1f out: clr 1f out: r.o strly: readily* **5/1**[3]
6 **2** *4 1/2* **Perfect Words (IRE)**[7] 1131 2 -9-3**0** .... MartinHarley 2 64
(Mick Channon) *chsd ldrs: rdn and effrt over 1f out: chsd clr wnr 1f out: kpt on but no imp* **6/5**[1]
3 *1 1/2* **Marchwood** 2 -9-3**0** .... LiamKeniry 5 58
(J S Moore) *led: rdn and hdd over 1f out: wknd ins fnl f* **17/2**
0 **4** *2 3/4* **Relay**[5] 1136 2 -8-12**0** .... KieranO'Neill 1 44
(Richard Hannon) *stdd s: bhd: rdn ent fnl 2f: sme hdwy ent fnl f: nvr trbld ldrs* **9/2**[2]
0 **5** *2* **Maypole Joe (IRE)**[7] 1131 2 -9-3**0** .... CathyGannon 3 41
(David Evans) *pressed ldr tl 2f out: struggling whn short of room jst over 1f out: sn wknd* **11/2**
6 *hd* **Missing Agent** 2 -8-12**0** .... MatthewCosham(5) 6 41
(David Evans) *in tch but sn rdn along: wknd wl over 1f out: bhd fnl f* **22/1**

1m 1.32s (1.32)**Going Correction** +0.25s/f (Good) **6**Ran SP% **110.6**
Speed ratings (Par 92): **99,91,89,85,81 81**
CSF £11.14 TOTE £7.20 : £3.60 , £1.10 ; EX 14.30 .
Owner Mrs Tracy Turner **Bred** Mrs Hugh Maitland-Jones **Trained** Sigwells, Somerset
■ Ryan While's first winner. He's the grandson of Bill Turner.

FOCUS
Three of the six runners had previous experience in this ordinary maiden, but a newcomer blew them away.

NOTEBOOK
Judy In Disguise ◆ is a January foal, so was comfortably the oldest in the field. Despite a slow start and being forced to make her effort well wide of her rivals, she produced an impressive turn of foot to hit the front over a furlong out and bounded clear to give her rider (the trainer's grandson) his first win on his 14th ride. There is a bit of stamina on the dam's side of the filly's pedigree and the way she won this suggests that another furlong wouldn't be a problem. (op 17-2 tchd 9-1)
Perfect Words(IRE) represented the Brocklesby form having finished sixth of the 12 runners at Doncaster, but by the time he was asked for this effort the filly had got first run on him and there was nothing he could do about it. (op 10-11 tchd 5-6)
Marchwood, a 7,000GBP colt out of a half-sister to three winners including the useful sprinter High Voltage, showed some ability on this debut and may be able to pick up a similar maiden before too long. (op 9-1 tchd 12-1)
Relay had the plum draw on her Kempton debut, but didn't get home after racing prominently and there was a lot of tail-swishing. She didn't appear to repeat that trait here, but neither did she show much improvement. (tchd 4-1)
Maypole Joe(IRE) finished over 8l behind Perfect Words in the Brocklesby and barely reduced the margin. (op 17-2)
Missing Agent was struggling from some way out. (op 16-1)

1203 LIVE POOL INFORMATION AT TOTEPOOL.COM H'CAP — 6f
3:10 (3:10) (Class 4) (0-85,82) 4-Y-0+ **£4,528** (£1,347; £673; £336) **Stalls** High

Form RPR
655- **1** **Kingswinford (IRE)**[101] 7876 6-9-2 **77** .... CathyGannon 1 85
(David Evans) *w ldr tl led ent fnl 2f: drvn wl over 1f out: hrd pressed thrght fnl f: hld on wl u.p: all out* **16/1**
321- **2** *nse* **Seeking Magic**[172] 6895 4-9-7 **82** .... AdamKirby 4 90
(Clive Cox) *taken down early: t.k.h: stdd s and hld up in rr: swtchd rt and hdwy wl over 1f out: rdn to chal and edgd lft 1f out: drvn and ev ch thrght fnl f: a jst hld* **1/2**[1]
264- **3** *6* **Perfect Pastime**[171] 6917 4-9-6 **81** .... PatCosgrave 2 70
(Jim Boyle) *chsd ldrs: pushed along 4f out: rdn and ev ch jst over 2f out: unable qck and n.m.r ent fnl f: wknd* **9/2**[2]
0-50 **4** *1 1/4* **Roodee Queen**[13] 1007 4-9-2 **77** .... LiamKeniry 5 62
(Milton Bradley) *t.k.h: chsd ldrs: rdn and effrt wl over 1f out: wknd jst over 1f out* **17/2**[3]
0-00 **5** *3 3/4* **Local Singer (IRE)**[22] 893 4-9-2 **77** .... TomMcLaughlin 8 50
(Paul Howling) *led tl ent fnl 2f: wknd qckly over 1f out* **12/1**
1m 13.34s (0.64) **Going Correction** +0.25s/f (Good) 5 Ran SP% **108.9**
Speed ratings (Par 105): **105,104,96,95,90**
CSF £24.91 TOTE £11.60: £10.10, £1.10; EX 19.70 Trifecta £48.00 Pool: £500.19 - 7.71 winning units..
Owner J E Abbey **Bred** J Costello **Trained** Pandy, Monmouths

FOCUS
This race was affected by three non-runners and the front pair pulled clear, but it still produced a bit of a shock. The form is rated around the winner and the second ran as well as ever at face value.

1204 FOLLOW TOTEPOOL ON FACEBOOK AND TWITTER H'CAP — 5f
3:40 (3:40) (Class 4) (0-80,80) 4-Y-0+ **£4,528** (£1,347; £673; £336) **Stalls** High

Form RPR
4102 **1** **Haadeeth**[13] 1007 5-8-13 **77** .... MatthewCosham(5) 8 83
(David Evans) *taken down early: hld up in tch: hdwy and nt clr run over 1f out: swtchd rt 1f out: rdn and r.o wl to ld nr fin* **6/1**[3]
-031 **2** *1/2* **Clear Praise (USA)**[43] 652 5-9-0 **73** .... HayleyTurner 6 77
(Simon Dow) *taken down early: chsd ldrs: ev ch wl over 1f out: pushed ahd jst ins fnl f: hrd pressed and drvn fnl 75yds: hdd and no ex nr fin* **10/3**[2]
5614 **3** *1 1/2* **Triple Dream**[43] 647 7-8-12 **71** ....(tp) LiamKeniry 5 70
(Milton Bradley) *hld up in last pair: hdwy over 1f out: nt clr run ent fnl f: swtchd rt fnl 150yds: r.o but unable to chal* **13/2**
0-32 **4** *1* **Wreningham**[8] 1061 7-8-7 **66** oh4 .... LukeMorris 3 62
(Pat Eddery) *sn led: rdn over 1f out: hdd jst ins fnl f: one pce fnl 100yds* **11/1**
604- **5** *nk* **Scarlet Rocks (IRE)**[97] 7919 4-8-9 **68** ....(p) CathyGannon 7 63
(David Evans) *sn pushed along: in tch towards rr: rdn and effrt wl over 1f out: nt clr run and sltly hmpd ent fnl f: styd on fnl 100yds* **8/1**
-126 **6** *hd* **Sulis Minerva (IRE)**[40] 710 5-9-2 **80** .... RaulDaSilva(5) 1 74
(Jeremy Gask) *chsd ldrs on outer: rdn and edgd rt wl over 1f out: unable qck u.p ent fnl f: wknd fnl 100yds* **13/2**
1214 **7** *3 1/4* **Drawnfromthepast (IRE)**[13] 1005 7-9-6 **79** .... JamieSpencer 4 63
(Jamie Osborne) *w ldr: rdn and unable qck whn n.m.r over 1f out: btn whn n.m.r ins fnl f: eased towards fin* **11/4**[1]
1m 0.71s (0.71) **Going Correction** +0.25s/f (Good) 7 Ran SP% **110.1**
Speed ratings (Par 105): **104,103,100,99,98 98,93**
toteswingers:1&2:£5.10, 2&3:£5.00, 1&3:£6.70 CSF £24.26 CT £124.37 TOTE £9.60: £4.70, £3.20; EX 36.10 Trifecta £110.20 Pool: £792.38 - 5.32 winning units..
Owner A Whelan **Bred** Bolton Grange **Trained** Pandy, Monmouths

FOCUS
A fair sprint handicap in which all seven runners had been given campaigns on the AW since they were last on turf. Ordinary early-season handicap form, with the winner rated back to his best.
Triple Dream Official explanation: jockey said gelding was denied a clear run

1205 CLAYDON HORSE EXERCISERS H'CAP — 1m 4f
4:10 (4:10) (Class 5) (0-75,74) 4-Y-0+ **£2,385** (£704; £352) **Stalls** High

Form RPR
220- **1** **Dove Cottage (IRE)**[188] 6503 10-8-8 **61** oh3 ow1 .... FergusSweeney 3 67
(Stuart Kittow) *taken down early: mde all: rdn 2f out: battled on gamely fr over 1f out: a holding rival fnl 100yds* **5/1**[3]
516- **2** *nk* **Iron Condor**[125] 5837 5-9-7 **74** .... LukeMorris 4 80
(James Eustace) *chsd ldng trio: wnt 3rd wl over 2f out: drvn 2f out: chsd wnr jst ins fnl f and sn ev ch: unable qck u.p and hld fnl 100yds* **7/2**[2]
3216 **3** *8* **Shirataki (IRE)**[14] 992 4-8-13 **67** .... ChrisCatlin 6 60
(Peter Hiatt) *t.k.h: chsd ldrs: wnt 2nd over 3f out: rdn and ev ch wl over 1f out: unable qck u.p: wknd ins fnl f* **11/2**
630- **4** *3* **Swift Blade (IRE)**[171] 6924 4-9-0 **68** .... JamieSpencer 1 56
(Lady Herries) *stdd s: hld up off the pce in last pair: clsd 4f out: 4th and asked for effrt wl over 1f out: fnd nil and wl btn 1f out* **3/1**[1]
330- **5** *6* **Bussa**[106] 7734 4-9-2 **70** .... CathyGannon 2 48
(David Evans) *s.i.s: racd off the pce in rr: clsd 4f out: effrt u.p over 2f out: edgd rt and wknd over 1f out* **16/1**
3610 **6** *17* **Sumani (FR)**[17] 963 6-8-9 **62** .... HayleyTurner 7 13
(Simon Dow) *chsd ldr: pushed along 6f out: rdn and lost 2nd over 3f out: wknd over 2f out: wl bhd and eased ins fnl f* **3/1**[1]
2m 40.48s (-0.42) **Going Correction** +0.05s/f (Good)
WFA 4 from 5yo+ 1lb 6 Ran SP% **110.2**
Speed ratings (Par 103): **103,102,97,95,91 80**
CSF £21.70 TOTE £5.30: £1.60, £3.30; EX 18.60.
Owner Reg Gifford **Bred** D R Tucker **Trained** Blackborough, Devon

FOCUS
A modest middle-distance handicap. The winner seemingly ran his best race for two years, but had the run of things.
Sumani(FR) Official explanation: jockey said gelding ran flat

1206 CLAYDON HORSE EXERCISERS MAIDEN STKS — 1m 1f 149y
4:40 (4:41) (Class 5) 3-Y-0+ **£2,385** (£704; £352) **Stalls** Centre

Form RPR
00-3 **1** **Estedaama (IRE)**[20] 918 3-8-4 72 .... PaulHanagan 11 73+
(Marcus Tregoning) *chsd ldrs: rdn over 3f out: drvn and styd on over 1f out: swtchd rt 1f out: led fnl 100yds: styd on wl and gng away at fin* **3/1**[1]
232 **2** *2 1/4* **Imtithal (IRE)**[20] 918 3-8-4 72 .... JoeFanning 7 68
(James Tate) *chsd ldrs: ev ch u.p wl over 1f out: led over 1f out: hdd fnl 100yds: no ex* **11/2**[3]
0- **3** *3/4* **Hunt A Mistress (IRE)**[166] 7025 3-8-4 0 .... LukeMorris 8 66+
(Paul Cole) *t.k.h: chsd ldr: ev ch whn hung lft bnd jst over 2f out: continued to hang and racing on stands' rail but stl chsng ldrs over 1f out: styd on same pce fnl f* **7/2**[2]
5- **4** *3/4* **Schoolmaster**[147] 7354 4-10-0 0 .... AdamKirby 10 73
(Giles Bravery) *hld up in midfield: clsd on ldrs 4f out: rdn and effrt jst over 2f out: chsd ldr briefly ent fnl f: no ex u.p ins fnl f* **20/1**
5 *3 3/4* **Muzhil (IRE)** 3-8-5 0 ow1 .... BrettDoyle 1 58
(Clive Brittain) *s.i.s: bhd: clsd on ldrs 4f out: hdwy and rdn wl over 1f out: no imp and styd on same pce fnl f* **20/1**
2223 **6** *4 1/2* **Cotton Trader (USA)**[14] 1001 3-8-9 74 ....(b) WilliamBuick 9 55
(John Gosden) *led: rdn wl over 1f out: hdd over 1f out: fnd little u.p and btn 1f out: fdd and eased fnl 100yds* **3/1**[1]
0- **7** *4* **Lady Burlesque (IRE)**[138] 7494 3-8-4 0 .... ChrisCatlin 3 39
(Mick Channon) *sn pushed along and struggling in last trio: nvr on terms* **50/1**
300- **8** *3/4* **Polydamos**[148] 7329 3-8-9 75 .... JamieSpencer 2 50
(Harry Dunlop) *chsd ldrs: lost pl and rdn 4f out: rallied and hdwy to chse ldrs over 2f out: wknd u.p jst over 1f out: fdd and eased fnl 75yds* **13/2**
9 *3/4* **Geordie Boy** 3-8-4 0 .... RaulDaSilva(5) 5 41
(Sheena West) *v.s.a: a bhd* **66/1**
0- **10** *46* **Mount Mayday (IRE)**[232] 5170 3-8-9 0 ....(t) WilliamCarson 4
(Stuart Williams) *stdd s: hld up towards rr: hdwy 8f out: jnd ldrs 4f out: hung lft and rdn 3f out: wknd rapidly: wl t.o and eased ins fnl f* **50/1**
2m 6.06s (1.16) **Going Correction** +0.05s/f (Good)
WFA 3 from 4yo+ 19lb 10 Ran SP% **115.9**
Speed ratings (Par 103): **97,95,94,94,91 87,84,83,83,46**
toteswingers:1&2:£3.80, 2&3:£5.20, 1&3:£4.10 CSF £18.70 TOTE £4.50: £2.00, £1.60, £2.00; EX 15.80 Trifecta £84.90 Pool: £1006.25 - 8.77 winning units..
Owner Hamdan Al Maktoum **Bred** Shadwell Estate Company Limited **Trained** Lambourn, Berks

FOCUS
Quite an interesting maiden for the track but only ordinary form. The winner built on her reappearance promise.
Hunt A Mistress(IRE) Official explanation: jockey said filly hung left in straight
Geordie Boy Official explanation: jockey said gelding was slowly away

1207 FOLKESTONE TOWN CENTRE MANAGEMENT JUBILEE EVENTS H'CAP — 1m 1f 149y
5:10 (5:21) (Class 6) (0-65,65) 4-Y-0+ **£1,704** (£503; £251) **Stalls** Centre

Form RPR
133- **1** **Tidal Run**[252] 4476 4-9-7 **65** .... WilliamBuick 4 73+
(Mick Channon) *hld up in midfield: rdn and effrt over 2f out: chsng ldrs and swtchd rt over 1f out: led ins fnl f: drvn and drew clr fnl 75yds* **10/3**[2]
00-6 **2** *2 1/2* **Market Puzzle (IRE)**[22] 891 5-8-5 **56** ....(p) RachealKneller(7) 7 59
(Mark Brisbourne) *chsd ldrs: hdwy to press ldrs and carried lft over 1f out: pushed along to chse ldr fnl 100yds: fnd little and one pce* **15/2**[3]
5-40 **3** *1 1/2* **Hubood**[16] 972 4-8-11 **55** .... BrettDoyle 3 55
(Clive Brittain) *chsd ldr tl 7f out: rdn and effrt to chal whn carried lft over 1f out: n.m.r 1f out: no ex and outpcd fnl 100yds* **12/1**
-012 **4** *1* **Flag Of Glory**[6] 1106 5-9-2 **60** .... WilliamCarson 9 58
(Peter Hiatt) *rdn leaving stalls: led after 1f: edgd lft u.p over 1f out: hdd ins fnl f: wknd fnl 75yds* **6/4**[1]
0-00 **5** *1 1/4* **Taqaat (USA)**[41] 685 4-8-13 **62** .... RaulDaSilva(5) 1 57
(Tim McCarthy) *t.k.h: chsd ldrs for 2f: hld up in midfield after: rdn and no imp wl over 1f out: styd on same pce and wl hld ins fnl f* **10/1**
5002 **6** *2 3/4* **Hip Hip Hooray**[16] 967 6-9-5 **63** .... IanMongan 10 53
(Luke Dace) *hld up in rr: rdn and effrt over 1f out: swtchd rt and no prog 1f out: nvr trbld ldrs* **8/1**
0040 **7** *3/4* **Mad Ginger Alice**[20] 922 4-8-8 **59** .... JenniferFerguson(7) 2 47
(Olivia Maylam) *dwlt and rdn along leaving stalls: dashed up to chse ldr 7f out: rdn and ev ch whn carried lft over 1f out: unable qck and struggling whn short of room 1f out: wknd ins fnl f* **14/1**
40-0 **8** *10* **Merito**[7] 1088 4-8-9 **58** ....(v[1]) MatthewCosham(5) 5 25
(David Evans) *t.k.h: hld up in last pair: rdn and short-lived effrt ent fnl 2f: sn wknd* **20/1**
2m 6.8s (1.90) **Going Correction** +0.05s/f (Good) 8 Ran SP% **114.2**
Speed ratings (Par 101): **94,92,90,90,89 86,86,78**
toteswingers:1&2:£3.70, 2&3:£9.70, 1&3:£7.50 CSF £28.27 CT £265.20 TOTE £4.20: £1.30, £1.50, £4.00; EX 19.80 Trifecta £119.60 Pool: £1112.22 - 6.88 winning units..
Owner M Channon **Bred** Barry Walters Farms **Trained** West Ilsley, Berks
■ Stewards' Enquiry : William Carson two-day ban: careless riding (Apr 19-20)

FOCUS
A moderate handicap to end the card, though the early pace was fair. Pretty ordinary form, but there's a chance the winner will do better.
T/Jkpt: Not won. T/Plt: £59.80 to a £1 stake. Pool of £73,215.76 - 892.34 winning tickets. T/Qpdt: £24.10 to a £1 stake. Pool of £5,493.56 - 167.99 winning tickets. SP

MAISONS-LAFFITTE (R-H)

Thursday, April 5

OFFICIAL GOING: Turf: good to soft

1208a PRIX DJEBEL (GROUP 3) (3YO COLTS & GELDINGS) (TURF) 7f (S)

1:20 (12:00) 3-Y-O £33,333 (£13,333; £10,000; £6,666; £3,333)

RPR

1 **French Fifteen (FR)**[158] [7192] 3-9-2 0............................ OlivierPeslier 7 116
(N Clement, France) *towards rr: stdy prog on outer fr over 3f out: rdn to chal over 2f out: led jst over 1f out: hung lft ins fnl f: kpt on* **53/10**[2]

2 *nk* **Abtaal (USA)**[182] [6660] 3-9-2 0............................ ChristopheSoumillon 2 115
(J-C Rouget, France) *midfield on inner: shkn up to improve over 3f out: rdn 1 1/2f out: slt stumble over 1f out: r.o ins fnl f but nt rch wnr* **1/1**[1]

3 *1 ½* **Hermival (IRE)**[145] 3-9-2 0............................ Christophe-PatriceLemaire 8 111
(M Delzangles, France) *hld up in last: rdn to try and improve over 3f out: briefly outpcd over 2f out: gd hdwy u.p fr 1 1/2f out: wnt 3rd ins fnl f* **15/1**

4 *2 ½* **Rockinante (FR)**[180] [6692] 3-9-2 0............................ RyanMoore 4 104
(Richard Hannon) *midfield on outer: impr to chal 3f out: rdn to ld over 2f out: hdd over 1f out: outpcd by ldng trio ins fnl f* **12/1**

5 *snk* **Al Malek (FR)**[18] 3-9-2 0............................ MaximeGuyon 6 104
(Mario Hofer, Germany) *trckd ldrs on inner: 2nd gng wl over 3f out: rdn over 2f out: awkward u.p and lost pls over 1f out: kpt on again ins fnl f* **11/2**[3]

6 *shd* **Lord Sinclair (USA)**[21] [914] 3-9-2 0............................ ThierryThulliez 1 104
(F Chappet, France) *hld up on inner: rdn 2 1/2f out: kpt one pce fnl 2f* **12/1**

7 *nk* **Paris Blue (FR)**[21] [914] 3-9-2 0............................ BriceRaballand 3 103
(J-L Pelletan, France) *hld up: rdn 2f out: outpcd fr over 1 1/2f out: kpt on ins fnl f* **55/1**

8 *½* **Veneto (FR)**[11] 3-9-2 0............................ ThierryJarnet 9 101
(B De Montzey, France) *trckd ldrs on outer: lost pl 3f out: rdn over 2f out: steadily fdd ins fnl 1 1/2f* **23/1**

9 *6* **Salure**[18] 3-9-2 0............................ DarioVargiu 5 85
(B Grizzetti, Italy) *sn led: rdn over 2f out: hdd & wknd 2f out: eased whn btn* **14/1**

10 *3 ½* **Amaan (USA)**[33] 3-9-2 0............................ IoritzMendizabal 10 76
(J-C Rouget, France) *pressed ldr: rdn over 2f out: wknd over 1 1/2f out: eased ins fnl f* **31/1**

1m 26.6s (-1.40) **Going Correction** 0.0s/f (Good) **10** Ran SP% **118.6**
Speed ratings: **108,107,105,103,102 102,102,101,95,91**
WIN (incl. 1 euro stake): 6.30. PLACES: 1.60, 1.20, 2.50. DF: 4.20. SF: 10.50..
Owner H H Sheikh Abdullah Bin Khalifa Al Thani **Bred** Mme G & G Forien **Trained** Chantilly, France

FOCUS
A good edition of the Djebel, although the third limits the form.

NOTEBOOK
French Fifteen(FR), a Group 1 scorer in the Criterium International last year, was given a patient ride by Peslier and despite looking a bit green after quickening he held Abtaal, who finished three lengths clear of him in a Group 3 at Saint-Cloud in October. This did his 2000 Guineas prospects no harm and he is likely to head to Newmarket rather than the equivalent race at Longchamp.
Abtaal(USA) beat French Fifteen when they met in the autumn. Representing a trainer with a good record in this event, he was finishing well and may not have been best suited by the drop back to 7f.
Hermival(IRE) won a heavy-ground maiden in November and this was a big step up.
Rockinante(FR) ran respectably in this company and his trainer regards him as a Jersey or Italian Guineas type. He should improve on this.

1209a PRIX IMPRUDENCE (GROUP 3) (3YO FILLIES) (TURF) 7f (S)

1:50 (12:00) 3-Y-O £33,333 (£13,333; £10,000; £6,666; £3,333)

RPR

1 **Mashoora (IRE)**[170] [6941] 3-9-0 0............................ ChristopheSoumillon 9 111+
(J-C Rouget, France) *hld up in last pair: gd prog on outer fr over 2f out: rdn to chal over 1f out: led jst ins fnl f: sn clr: pushed out hands and heels w jockey looking rnd fnl 150yds: heavily eased fnl 50yds: v cheekily* **19/10**[1]

2 *nk* **Belle De Lune (FR)**[21] [913] 3-9-0 0............................ BriceRaballand 8 108+
(J-L Pelletan, France) *midfield on inner: rdn to improve fr over 1 1/2f out: r.o to go 2nd wl ins fnl f: flattered by proximity to wnr* **60/1**

3 *snk* **Nadeaud (FR)**[21] [913] 3-9-0 0............................ ThierryJarnet 7 108
(D Guillemin, France) *trckd ldr on outer: led over 2 1/2f out: rdn over 1 1/2f out: hdd jst ins fnl f: no ex: lost 2nd fnl 50yds* **17/2**

4 *½* **Restiadargent (FR)**[156] [7220] 3-9-0 0............................ MaximeGuyon 3 107
(H-A Pantall, France) *trckd ldr in centre: t.k.h: rdn to try and chal fr 2f out: kpt on one pce* **14/5**[2]

5 *1* **Topeka (IRE)**[156] [7219] 3-9-0 0............................ IoritzMendizabal 5 104
(Robert Collet, France) *midfield on outer: rdn to chal fr over 1 1/2f out: no ex and fdd ins fnl f* **7/2**[3]

6 *1 ¾* **Tibaldi (FR)**[156] [7219] 3-9-0 0............................ JohanVictoire 4 99
(Mme C Head-Maarek, France) *hld up in last: rdn 2f out: outpcd over 1f out: nt given hrd time one btn ins fnl f* **19/1**

7 *2* **Tribune (FR)**[21] [913] 3-9-0 0............................ OlivierPeslier 1 94
(J-C Rouget, France) *trckd ldr on inner: rdn and qckly btn 1 1/2f out: wknd and eased ins fnl f* **83/10**

8 *¾* **Ruby's Day**[226] [5365] 3-9-0 0............................ ThomasHuet 2 92
(E J O'Neill, France) *midfield: rdn over 2f out: wknd: eased ins fnl f* **43/1**

9 *dist* **Misedargent (FR)**[111] [7814] 3-9-0 0............................ FabriceVeron 6
(H-A Pantall, France) *led: rdn 3f out: hdd 2 1/2f out: qckly wknd: t.o* **27/1**

1m 26.5s (-1.50) **Going Correction** 0.0s/f (Good) **9** Ran SP% **116.8**
Speed ratings: **108,107,107,106,105 103,101,100,**
WIN (incl. 1 euro stake): 2.90. PLACES: 1.70, 7.90, 2.40. DF: 74.50. SF: 100.70..
Owner Hamdan Al Maktoum **Bred** Grangecon Stud **Trained** Pau, France

FOCUS
The winner was eased a length. The form fits the race averages, rated round the fifth and eighth.

NOTEBOOK
Mashoora(IRE) put this to bed in a matter of strides just over a furlong out before easing right down. With three furlongs left to run it was apparent Soumillon was very confident and travelling strongly. He finally let the filly down in the final two furlongs and she quickened clear impressively, though Belle De Lune, the only horse travelling in a manner to suggest she could pose a threat, was caught in a pocket behind. Value for a greater margin of victory, she looks a lively player for the Newmarket Guineas.
Belle De Lune(FR), the only runner travelling in a manner to suggest she could pose a threat, was caught in a pocket behind tiring horses and was denied a run. Once getting out in the clear she closed down on the winner rapidly, going down by just a neck, but she was flattered by the distance as Soumillon eased his mount down with 50 yards to run.

1210 - (Foreign Racing) - See Raceform Interactive

[1136]KEMPTON (A.W) (R-H)

Saturday, April 7

OFFICIAL GOING: Standard
Wind: Moderate, across (towards stand) Weather: Cloudy

1211 BETFRED THE BONUS KING BINGO/BRITISH STALLION STUDS E B F MAIDEN STKS 5f (P)

1:35 (1:35) (Class 5) 2-Y-O £3,946 (£1,174; £586; £293) **Stalls** Low

Form RPR

1 **Baileys Jubilee** 2-8-12............................ SilvestreDeSousa 7 84+
(Mark Johnston) *pressed ldr: rdn to ld ent st: sn clr: readily* **9/1**

0 2 *4* **Marvelino**[7] [1131] 2-9-3............................ DaneO'Neill 5 75
(Pat Eddery) *chsd ldng pair: rdn to take 2nd ent fnl f: no ch w wnr* **11/2**[3]

3 *1 ¼* **Mosstang (IRE)** 2-9-3............................ MartinDwyer 9 70
(Robert Mills) *chsd ldrs: pushed along and one pce fnl 2f* **25/1**

4 *1 ¼* **Lyric Ace (IRE)** 2-9-3............................ KieranO'Neill 4 66+
(Richard Hannon) *short of room sn after s: rn green: in tch: rdn and styd on same pce fnl 2f* **5/6**[1]

5 *hd* **Coconut Kisses** 2-8-12............................ PaulMulrennan 10 60
(Bill Turner) *led tl ent st: wknd and lost 2nd ent fnl f* **33/1**

6 *2 ½* **Lea Valley Black** 2-9-3............................ RichardKingscote 2 56
(Tom Dascombe) *in tch tl outpcd 2f out* **20/1**

7 *shd* **Chilworth Icon** 2-9-3............................ ChrisCatlin 1 56
(Mick Channon) *s.s: last tl rdn and modest hdwy fnl 2f* **20/1**

8 *nse* **Hats Off** 2-9-3............................ LukeMorris 6 55
(John Best) *sn rdn along in modest 7th: n.d fnl 2f* **5/1**[2]

9 *3 ¼* **Fortinbrass (IRE)** 2-9-3............................ JimCrowley 8 44
(Ralph Beckett) *s.s: rdn along: a bhd* **14/1**

10 *17* **Modern Society** 2-9-3............................ BrettDoyle 3
(Andrew Reid) *a towards rr: no ch fnl 2f* **80/1**

59.92s (-0.58) **Going Correction** -0.15s/f (Stan) **10** Ran SP% **120.8**
Speed ratings (Par 92): **98,91,89,87,87 83,83,83,77,50**
toteswingers:1&2:£5.00, 1&3:£22.70, 2&3:£20.20 CSF £55.79 TOTE £9.70: £2.40, £1.90, £7.30; EX 37.30 Trifecta £333.10 Part won. Pool: £450.16 - 0.36 winning units..
Owner G R Bailey Ltd (Baileys Horse Feeds) **Bred** P And Mrs A G Venner **Trained** Middleham Moor, N Yorks

FOCUS
Only one of these had race experience.

NOTEBOOK
Baileys Jubilee, a £19,000 half-sister to a 1m winner, out of a (Listed placed) 1m winner, knew her job better than most and saw the race out really well. She's an April foal, so there should be more to come. (op 12-1 tchd 8-1)
Marvelino was a disappointing favourite in the Brocklesby a week earlier. He travelled well enough but just lacked the winner's end-race speed.
Mosstang(IRE), a 6,000euros January foal, was never that far and showed ability.
Lyric Ace(IRE), a £23,000 February foal, is bred to be fast and precocious. He must have been showing plenty at home to go off so short, but he ran green after soon losing his position and only began to get the idea when the race was as good as over. There should be a lot better to come. (op 10-11 tchd 6-5, 5-4 in places)
Coconut Kisses ◆, an April foal who is bred to sprint, showed good speed to lead from the widest gate before her exertions told. Her natural pace should see her win a race.
Chilworth Icon is a May foal by a St Leger winner in Sixties Icon, but she's out of a 7f-1m nursery winner. She missed the break and was outpaced, but kept on reasonably well. (op 16-1)

1212 BETFRED GOALS GALORE H'CAP (LONDON MILE QUALIFIER) 1m (P)

2:05 (2:05) (Class 2) (0-105,100) 4-Y-0+ £12,938 (£3,850; £1,924; £962) **Stalls** Low

Form RPR

4310 1 **Nazreef**[7] [1139] 5-9-3 **96**............................(vt[1]) DarryllHolland 11 108
(Hughie Morrison) *prom: led after 2f: hung lft and hdd 2f out: regained ld over 1f out: rdn clr* **11/1**

323- 2 *3* **Double Dealer**[161] [7168] 4-8-12 **91**............................ FrankieDettori 6 96
(Mahmood Al Zarooni) *chsd ldrs: rdn 2f out: hmpd and swtchd rt over 1f out: kpt on to take 2nd ins fnl f* **10/3**[1]

210- 3 *1 ¼* **Highland Knight (IRE)**[253] [4494] 5-9-3 **96**............................(t) DavidProbert 1 98
(Andrew Balding) *prom: led 2f out: edgd lft and hdd over 1f out: one pce* **7/1**[2]

-311 4 *shd* **Maverik**[48] [631] 4-8-5 **84**............................ RichardKingscote 7 86
(Ralph Beckett) *led 2f: chsd ldrs: rdn and swtchd rt 2f out: kpt on same pce* **7/1**[2]

636- 5 *¾* **Chapter And Verse (IRE)**[147] [7393] 6-8-11 **90**............................ RyanMoore 9 90
(Mike Murphy) *towards rr: rdn and styd on fnl 2f: nvr nrr* **11/1**

426- 6 *¾* **Extraterrestrial**[160] [7189] 8-8-5 **91**............................ LauraBarry[(7)] 14 89+
(Richard Fahey) *t.k.h: hld up in last: shkn up and hdwy over 1f out: fin wl* **25/1**

5-0 7 *hd* **Cocozza (USA)**[7] [1130] 4-9-3 **96**............................ AdamKirby 5 94
(Marco Botti) *in rr of midfield: hdwy 2f out: no imp fnl f* **9/1**

15-6 8 *3 ¾* **Riggins (IRE)**[14] [1034] 8-9-5 **98**............................ J-PGuillambert 13 87
(Ed Walker) *in tch tl hrd rdn and btn 2f out* **8/1**[3]

30-0 9 *½* **The Tichborne (IRE)**[28] [868] 4-8-8 **87**............................ JamesDoyle 4 75
(Roger Teal) *chsd ldrs: hrd rdn 2f out: wknd over 1f out* **33/1**

120- 10 *½* **Golden Tempest (IRE)**[190] [6495] 4-8-8 **87**............................ ShaneKelly 12 74
(Eve Johnson Houghton) *a mid-div: rdn and btn 2f out* **25/1**

010- 11 *hd* **Fantasy Gladiator**[147] [7393] 6-8-6 **85**............................(p) PaulHanagan 10 71
(Robert Cowell) *mid-div: lost pl 3f out: n.d after* **12/1**

40-2 12 *½* **Axiom**[14] [1035] 8-9-0 **100**............................ MichaelJMurphy[(7)] 3 85
(Ed Walker) *hld up in rr: hdwy 2f out: wknd 1f out* **10/1**

0-00 13 *nse* **Final Drive (IRE)**[14] [1035] 6-9-0 **93**............................(t) StevieDonohoe 2 78
(John Butler) *s.i.s: bhd tl hdwy 2f out: wknd over 1f out* **50/1**

140- 14 *½* **Capaill Liath (IRE)**[197] [6302] 4-8-10 **89**............................(p) PaulMulrennan 8 73
(Kevin Ryan) *in tch tl wknd 2f out* **25/1**

1m 36.75s (-3.05) **Going Correction** -0.15s/f (Stan) **14** Ran SP% **119.1**
Speed ratings (Par 109): **109,106,104,104,103 103,102,99,98,98 98,97,97,96**
toteswingers:1&2:£6.30, 1&3:£18.60, 2&3:£5.80 CSF £44.37 CT £292.69 TOTE £14.30: £4.00, £1.40, £2.90; EX 56.60 Trifecta £252.60 Pool: £1,109.46 - 3.25 winning units..
Owner Deborah Collett & M J Watson **Bred** M J Watson **Trained** East Ilsley, Berks

FOCUS
A good, competitive handicap, but the form is a bit muddling.

NOTEBOOK
Nazreef dictated a gallop to suit himself under a superb front-running jockey. He went left under pressure and the field were spread out across the track in the closing stages. He was entitled to take this, being only 2lb higher than when landing the Lincoln Trial on his penultimate start, and he appreciated the drop in trip having contested the Rosebery the previous week, but he looks a bit flattered by the bare result. He had the help of a first-time visor. (tchd 10-1 and 12-1)

Double Dealer, his trainer's first runner in Britain this year, didn't get the clearest of runs (ended up against the stands' rail) and had little chance with the well-ridden winner. It was a good run in the circumstances, but he showed a high carriage and doesn't really appeal as the type to take too short a price about. (op 7-2 tchd 4-1)
Highland Knight(IRE) looked potentially smart last season but hadn't been seen since July. This was a promising enough return. (op 8-1)
Maverik gained his latest win on the snow at St Moritz and was 8lb higher than when successful over C&D in January, but that form worked out well. He was nicely placed but wasn't good enough. (op 13-2 tchd 11-2)
Chapter And Verse(IRE), returning from a 147-day break, didn't have the race run to suit and ran about as well as could have been expected. (tchd 12-1)
Extraterrestrial ◆ made a promising return from a 160-day break, going on at the finish having been held up off the muddling gallop.
Riggins(IRE) had a wide trip. (tchd 9-1)
The Tichborne(IRE) Official explanation: jockey said that the gelding hung left

1213 BETFRED MOBILE SPORTS SNOWDROP FILLIES' STKS (LISTED RACE) 1m (P)

2:40 (2:41) (Class 1) 4-Y-0+

£18,714 (£7,095; £3,550; £1,768; £887; £445) **Stalls** Low

Form / RPR

130- **1** **Captivator**[154] 7296 5-8-12 94 KierenFallon 6 104
(James Fanshawe) *hld up in handy 5th: nt clr run over 2f out: rdn to take narrow ld jst ins fnl f: all out* **7/1**[3]

113- **2** *shd* **Law Of The Range**[253] 4497 5-8-12 104 AdamKirby 5 104
(Marco Botti) *led 1f: chsd ldr: led 2f out tl jst ins fnl f: rallied wl: ev ch nr fin: kpt on gamely* **7/4**[1]

0105 **3** *3* **Sooraah**[14] 1034 5-8-12 106 RyanMoore 11 97
(William Haggas) *chsd ldrs: rdn over 2f out: one pce appr fnl f* **3/1**[2]

51- **4** *2* **Raasekha**[258] 4356 4-8-12 90 PaulHanagan 4 93+
(Charles Hills) *fly-jmpd s: towards rr: drvn along over 2f out: styd on to take 4th over 1f out: no imp* **9/1**

3014 **5** *2* **Night Lily (IRE)**[28] 866 6-8-12 94 WilliamCarson 10 88
(Paul D'Arcy) *t.k.h: sn stdd into last: rdn and styd on fr over 1f out: nt rch ldrs* **8/1**

0-06 **6** *nk* **Cochabamba (IRE)**[7] 1140 4-8-12 90 FrankieDettori 8 87
(Roger Teal) *t.k.h: sn stdd bk into midfield: rdn and no hdwy fnl 2f* **16/1**

5-01 **7** *½* **Elshabakiya (IRE)**[8] 1111 4-8-12 100 BrettDoyle 9 86
(Clive Brittain) *t.k.h: mid-div on outer: rdn and hung rt over 2f out: nt pce to chal* **14/1**

8 *1 ¼* **Provisional**[231] 4-8-12 0 JamesDoyle 7 83
(Martyn Meade) *towards rr: rdn over 2f out: n.d* **66/1**

0-40 **9** *1 ½* **Sos Brillante (CHI)**[7] 1129 7-8-12 78 (b[1]) LukeMorris 1 80
(Terry Clement) *t.k.h in rr: hdwy into midfield after 2f: rdn over 2f out: wknd wl over 1f out* **100/1**

521- **10** *hd* **Hayaku (USA)**[180] 6750 4-8-12 77 (bt) JimCrowley 3 79
(Ralph Beckett) *led after 1f tl 2f out: wknd over 1f out* **33/1**

1104 **11** *4 ½* **Emma's Gift (IRE)**[15] 1008 4-8-12 90 (b) AdamBeschizza 2 69
(Julia Feilden) *plld hrd: prom tl hrd rdn and wknd 2f out* **20/1**

1m 36.96s (-2.84) **Going Correction** -0.15s/f (Stan) **11** Ran SP% **117.7**
Speed ratings (Par 108): **108,107,104,102,100 100,100,98,97,97 92**
toteswingers:1&2:£3.30, 1&3:£4.40, 2&3:£2.30 CSF £19.19 TOTE £7.40: £2.20, £1.30, £1.10; EX 23.00 Trifecta £86.10 Pool: £1,279.27 - 10.99 winning units..
Owner Lord Vestey **Bred** Stowell Park Stud **Trained** Newmarket, Suffolk

FOCUS
A reasonable fillies' Listed contest, although the pace was ordinary and those held up couldn't get involved.

NOTEBOOK
Captivator had previously shown her best form over 1m2f. It was a career best by some way and there may be even more to come when she goes back up in trip. (op 10-1)
Law Of The Range hadn't been seen since finishing third in the Group 3 Oaks Tree Stakes at last year's Glorious Goodwood meeting, but she was reported by her trainer to be "fit and ready". This was a promising enough return. (op 2-1)
Sooraah was ridden closer to the pace than usual, with the gallop not as strong as she would have liked, and consequently her finishing kick wasn't quite so effective. It was suggested before this might be her last run before going to stud. (op 11-4 tchd 5-2)
Raasekha had been absent since making all in an Ascot maiden last July. She needed a blanket for stalls entry and lost ground when starting awkwardly, but she shaped really nicely, going on at the finish to fare best of those held up, despite not being given a hard time. (op 8-1)
Night Lily(IRE) was second in this last year, but she was hopelessly placed this time and had no chance. (op 7-1)

1214 BETFRED THE BONUS KING QUEEN'S PRIZE (H'CAP) 2m (P)

3:15 (3:15) (Class 2) (0-105,98) 4-Y-0+

£12,450 (£3,728; £1,864; £932; £466; £234) **Stalls** Low

Form / RPR

001- **1** **Thimaar (USA)**[190] 6499 4-9-3 **93** PaulHanagan 12 105
(John Gosden) *led: drvn along and jnd 2f out: forged ahd ins fnl f: rdn out* **4/1**[2]

011- **2** *1* **Gulf Of Naples (IRE)**[162] 7139 4-9-0 **90** SilvestreDeSousa 8 101
(Mark Johnston) *trckd ldrs: wnt 2nd 7f out: jnd wnr and wandered 2f out: kpt on u.p: worn down ins fnl f* **10/3**[1]

-222 **3** *7* **Halla San**[18] 971 10-8-12 **84** PatrickMathers 9 86
(Richard Fahey) *mid-div: styd on u.p fnl 3f: wnt 3rd ins fnl f: nt trble first 2* **33/1**

01-2 **4** *1* **Right Stuff (FR)**[14] 1037 9-9-7 **93** RyanMoore 3 94
(Gary Moore) *prom: rdn over 2f out: no ch w first 2* **6/1**

-311 **5** *4 ½* **Rasheed**[22] 928 4-8-11 **87** WilliamBuick 6 83
(John Gosden) *mid-div: effrt and drvn along 3f out: no imp* **5/1**[3]

040- **6** *½* **Hawk Mountain (UAE)**[70] 5883 7-9-2 **88** LukeMorris 1 83
(John Quinn) *in tch: rdn 4f out: btn wl over 2f out* **25/1**

4-16 **7** *2* **First Avenue**[63] 427 7-8-8 **80** KieranO'Neill 7 73
(Laura Mongan) *towards rr: rdn over 3f out: nvr nr ldrs* **20/1**

0-00 **8** *3* **Montaff**[64] 421 6-9-12 **98** JamesDoyle 2 87
(Mick Channon) *towards rr: mod effrt 3f out: n.d* **14/1**

-611 **9** *6* **Storm Hawk (IRE)**[11] 1056 5-8-9 **84** (b) RyanClark[(3)] 11 66
(Pat Eddery) *stdd s: hld up in last: rdn 3f out: a bhd* **18/1**

430- **10** *½* **Enroller (IRE)**[11] 7297 7-9-2 **88** (t) MartinDwyer 14 69
(William Muir) *plld hrd: chsd wnr tl 7f out: wknd over 4f out: sn bhd* **40/1**

B00- **11** *2 ¼* **Activate**[196] 6333 5-9-6 **92** PaulMulrennan 5 71
(Kevin Ryan) *a bhd: no ch fnl 3f* **8/1**

6-33 **12** *nk* **English Summer**[14] 1037 5-9-0 **86** JamieSpencer 4 64
(Mark Johnston) *chsd ldrs: rdn 4f out: wknd over 2f out* **16/1**

220- **13** *47* **Kiama Bay (IRE)**[154] 7297 6-9-12 **98** StevieDonohoe 10 20
(John Quinn) *mid-div on outer tl rn v wd on bnd 4f out: sn t.o* **18/1**

3m 24.36s (-5.74) **Going Correction** -0.15s/f (Stan)
WFA 4 from 5yo+ 4lb **13** Ran SP% **122.2**
Speed ratings (Par 109): **108,107,104,103,101 101,100,98,95,95 94,93,70**
toteswingers:1&2:£3.30, 1&3:£41.60, 2&3:£36.70 CSF £17.37 CT £398.32 TOTE £4.80: £2.00, £1.90, £10.40; EX 19.20 Trifecta £746.30 Pool: £2,087.88 - 2.07 winning units..
Owner Hamdan Al Maktoum **Bred** Shadwell Farm LLC **Trained** Newmarket, Suffolk

FOCUS
This looks really strong form, a couple of improvers who are both entered in the Yorkshire Cup finishing clear, and the track record was lowered.

NOTEBOOK
Thimaar(USA) was thought good enough to contest the Great Voltigeur last season, albeit he was well beaten, and won his final start of the campaign when upped to this trip for the first time in an Ascot handicap. He's now a gelding and resumed off just 4lb higher, and he confirmed staying is very much his game. There should be more to come when he gets on a proper galloping course, and he could yet be a Group horse. He's reportedly going for the Sagaro Stakes next. (op 9-2)
Gulf Of Naples(IRE) ◆ confirmed himself a smart sort in the making. He didn't make his debut until late July last season, but he won three of his five starts (the latest off 87) and shaped nicely after a 162-day break. There were clear signs he's sill green as he wandered a bit under pressure and he's open to loads of improvement. He can develop into a proper Cup horse in time. (op 4-1 tchd 9-2)
Halla San won't always run into two such promising types. In this form he can end a losing run dating back to 2008. (op 28-1)
Right Stuff(FR) had finished second in this race for the last two years. He wasn't good enough but helps give the form a solid look. (op 7-1)
Rasheed had won three of his last four starts, but he was up another 7lb and couldn't cope with the rise. (op 9-2)
Hawk Mountain(UAE), back on the Flat, shaped nicely after a 70-day break. (op 22-1 tchd 20-1)
Kiama Bay(IRE) Official explanation: jockey said that the gelding hung left throughout

1215 BETFRED "WHEN BOTH TEAMS SCORE" FILLIES' CONDITIONS STKS 1m (P)

3:45 (3:47) (Class 2) 3-Y-O

£12,450 (£3,728; £1,864; £932; £466; £234) **Stalls** Low

Form / RPR

21 **1** **Laugh Out Loud**[51] 573 3-8-12 80 WilliamBuick 9 92+
(Mick Channon) *hld up in rr: rdn and hdwy over 1f out: r.o to ld fnl 75yds* **6/1**[2]

216- **2** *1* **Way Too Hot**[168] 7028 3-8-12 90 AdamKirby 1 90
(Clive Cox) *travelled wl in tch: hdwy 2f out: rdn to press ldrs over 1f out: kpt on to take 2nd nr fin* **9/1**[3]

213- **3** *nk* **Esentepe (IRE)**[161] 7169 3-8-12 92 RyanMoore 5 89
(Richard Hannon) *chsd ldrs: led over 1f out: drvn along fnl f: hdd and nt qckn fnl 75yds* **12/1**

10- **4** *¾* **Tactfully (IRE)**[161] 7169 3-8-12 85 MickaelBarzalona 7 88+
(Mahmood Al Zarooni) *bhd: rdn over 2f out: gd late hdwy* **6/1**[2]

205- **5** *nse* **Arsaadi (IRE)**[189] 6526 3-8-12 92 PaulHanagan 10 87
(William Haggas) *in tch: rdn over 2f out: edgd rt ins fnl f: cl 4th and styng on whn short of room fnl 100yds* **10/1**

1- **6** *1* **Witnessed**[224] 5464 3-8-12 82 FrankieDettori 3 85
(Mahmood Al Zarooni) *chsd ldr: led after 2f tl over 1f out: wknd ins fnl f* **3/1**[1]

624- **7** *hd* **Bana Wu**[182] 6691 3-8-12 102 DavidProbert 4 85
(Andrew Balding) *prom: rdn 2f out: no ex over 1f out* **6/1**[2]

2-1 **8** *1 ¼* **Appealing (IRE)**[92] 61 3-8-12 79 SilvestreDeSousa 2 82
(Marco Botti) *settled off the pce in 7th: effrt 2f out: no imp over 1f out* **10/1**

062- **9** *1 ¾* **Semayyel (IRE)**[168] 7028 3-8-12 97 BrettDoyle 8 78
(Clive Brittain) *led 2f: prom tl wknd jst over 1f out* **14/1**

106- **10** *3 ½* **Dreamwriter (USA)**[168] 7019 3-8-12 90 KieranO'Neill 6 70
(Richard Hannon) *a in rr: rdn over 2f out: sn struggling* **16/1**

1m 38.02s (-1.78) **Going Correction** -0.15s/f (Stan) **10** Ran SP% **116.3**
Speed ratings (Par 101): **102,101,100,99,99 98,98,97,95,92**
CSF £58.74 TOTE £5.60: £2.10, £2.90, £2.60; EX 55.80 Trifecta £803.00 Pool: £1,117.76 - 1.03 winning units..
Owner Ann Black,M Al Qatami & K M Al Mudhaf **Bred** Norman Court Stud **Trained** West Ilsley, Berks

FOCUS
This looked a decent conditions race, with a case to be made for several of the runners, but the pace seemed modest (time the slowest of four races at the trip) and they finished well bunched behind the winner.

NOTEBOOK
Laugh Out Loud ◆ had plenty of confidence behind her in the market and she showed she's pretty smart. She was a bit keen under restraint, racing further back than ideal, but she produced a sustained finishing kick and the winning margin probably underplays her superiority. There should be more to come in a strongly run race and she's an interesting outsider for the 1000 Guineas. She's generally available at 66-1. (op 11-2 tchd 4-1)
Way Too Hot travelled just about best of all but she couldn't resist the winner's late bid and might have needed this after a 168-day break. She has a progressive profile and has more to offer. (op 10-1)
Esentepe(IRE) made a respectable reappearance and should pay her way at around Listed level. (op 11-1)
Tactfully(IRE) was given too much to do and just plugged on without threatening. She might not be anything special, for all that she looked so promising when making a winning debut, but she may be capable of a bit better. (op 9-1)
Arsaadi(IRE), having her first start since leaving Ed Dunlop, might have been around a length closer had she not run out of room late on. Paul Hanagan reported the filly hung right-handed in the closing stages and was denied a clear run. Official explanation: jockey said that the filly hung right-handed in the closing stages and was denied a clear run (op 15-2)
Witnessed didn't put up much of a fight once challenged. She looked a good prospect when winning her sole start last season, denying today's third in a Beverley maiden, but this performance leaves her with something to prove. (op 9-2)
Bana Wu was weak in the market and offered little on her first start since finishing fourth in the Group 2 Rockfel. (op 11-2 tchd 5-1)

1216 BETFRED "DOUBLE DELIGHT" CONDITIONS STKS (C&G) 1m (P)

4:20 (4:20) (Class 2) 3-Y-O

£12,450 (£3,728; £1,864; £932; £466; £234) **Stalls** Low

Form / RPR

13- **1** **Eastern Sun (IRE)**[231] 5276 3-8-12 0 WilliamBuick 6 103
(John Gosden) *wd early: chsd ldrs: led 5f out: rdn and hld on wl fr over 1f out* **3/1**[1]

10- **2** *1 ¾* **Miblish**[189] 6527 3-8-12 79......(t) BrettDoyle 2 98
(Clive Brittain) *sn led: hdd 5f out: hrd rdn 2f out: kpt on to regain 2nd ins fnl f* **8/1**[1]

332- **3** *1 ¼* **Leqqaa (USA)**[171] 6952 3-8-12 95...... PaulHanagan 4 95
(Mark Johnston) *broke best: sn lost pl and rdn: rallied into 2nd over 3f out: one pce appr fnl f* **3/1**[1]

0-43 **4** *¾* **Mehdi (IRE)**[58] 485 3-9-4 102......(t) ShaneKelly 1 99
(Brian Meehan) *cl up: rdn 2f out: one pce* **10/3**[2]

421- **5** *½* **Lord Ofthe Shadows (IRE)**[171] 6952 3-9-4 98...... RyanMoore 5 98
(Richard Hannon) *hld up in last pair: rdn over 2f out: nt pce to chal* **6/1**[3]

064- **6** *4* **Red Seventy**[171] 6952 3-8-12 99...... PatDobbs 3 83
(Richard Hannon) *hld up in last pair: effrt 2f out: sn wknd* **7/1**

1m 37.08s (-2.72) **Going Correction** -0.15s/f (Stan) **6** Ran SP% **111.0**
Speed ratings (Par 104): **107,105,104,103,102 98**
toteswingers:1&2:£5.40, 1&3:£2.50, 2&3:£5.40 CSF £25.67 TOTE £3.70: £1.70, £4.00; EX 33.70 TRIFECTA Not won..
Owner Prince AA Faisal & Rachel Hood **Bred** Saad Bin Mishrif **Trained** Newmarket, Suffolk

FOCUS
Hard to know the exact worth of this form.

NOTEBOOK
Eastern Sun(IRE) hadn't been seen since finishing third in the Solario Stakes and made a nice comeback. He looks a smart prospect. (op 4-1)
Miblish, fitted with a tongue-tie for the first time on his return from a 189-day break, showed himself much better than his official mark of 79 suggests and would surely have been better off going for a handicap. He holds a number of big-race entries.
Leqqaa(USA) made just an adequate return from 171 days off (op 7-2 tchd 5-2)
Mehdi(IRE), back from Dubai, has yet to convince on artificial surfaces. (tchd 9-4 and 7-2)
Lord Ofthe Shadows(IRE) had Leqqaa behind when winning at Newmarket on his final start of 2011, but he couldn't confirm form on his return to action. (op 9-2 tchd 7-1)

1217 BETFRED "HAT TRICK HEAVEN" H'CAP 7f (P)
4:55 (4:55) (Class 3) (0-95,90) 3-Y-O

£8,092 (£2,423; £1,211; £605; £302; £152) **Stalls** Low

Form RPR

40-3 **1** **Shamaal Nibras (USA)**[28] 867 3-9-0 **83**...... RyanMoore 1 90
(Richard Hannon) *plld hrd: chsd ldrs: led 2f out: rdn out* **16/1**

142- **2** *1* **Amazing Storm (IRE)**[179] 6766 3-9-5 **88**...... PatDobbs 3 92
(Richard Hannon) *stdd s: plld hrd: hdwy to chse ldrs after 2f: hung bdly lft fr 2f out: kpt on to take 2nd fnl 100yds* **11/1**

13- **3** *¾* **Hadaj**[275] 3776 3-9-7 **90**...... BrettDoyle 7 92
(Clive Brittain) *prom: rdn whn n.m.r and sltly lost pl 2f out: rallied and nt clr run over 1f out: r.o ins fnl f* **14/1**

1- **4** *½* **Solar Deity (IRE)**[143] 7431 3-9-1 **84**...... AdamKirby 11 85+
(Marco Botti) *hld up towards rr: hdwy to chal ins fnl 2f: one pce ins fnl f* **11/8**[1]

160- **5** *3* **Red Larkspur (IRE)**[259] 4312 3-9-0 **83**...... DaneO'Neill 8 76
(Roger Teal) *hld up in tch: rdn and styd on same pce fnl 2f* **33/1**

21-3 **6** *shd* **Galician**[8] 1109 3-8-9 **78**...... SilvestreDeSousa 2 70+
(Mark Johnston) *mid-div: rdn over 3f out: hdwy over 1f out: no imp fnl f* **3/1**[2]

000- **7** *1 ½* **Church Music (IRE)**[189] 6518 3-9-7 **90**...... DarryllHolland 4 78
(Michael Scudamore) *plld hrd: w ldr: hrd rdn and outpcd 2f out: btn whn n.m.r over 1f out* **40/1**

060- **8** *1 ¼* **Charitable Act (FR)**[168] 7026 3-9-4 **87**...... MartinDwyer 9 72
(William Muir) *in rr: effrt into midfield 2f out: no further prog* **20/1**

104- **9** *2* **Ghostwriting (USA)**[178] 6788 3-9-7 **90**...... WilliamBuick 10 69
(John Gosden) *stdd s: hld up in last: mod effrt 2f out: n.d* **7/1**[3]

240- **10** *1 ¾* **Hot Sugar (USA)**[189] 6524 3-8-11 **80**...... PaulMulrennan 6 55
(Kevin Ryan) *sn led and restrained in front: set weak pce: hdd & wknd 2f out* **25/1**

514- **11** *1 ¾* **Basantee**[155] 7259 3-8-10 **79**...... RichardKingscote 5 49
(Tom Dascombe) *towards rr: rdn 3f out: sn struggling* **33/1**

1m 25.92s (-0.08) **Going Correction** -0.15s/f (Stan) **11** Ran SP% **117.4**
Speed ratings (Par 102): **94,92,92,91,88 87,86,84,82,80 78**
toteswingers:1&2:£8.20, 1&3:£17.80, 2&3:£15.80 CSF £166.12 CT £2556.47 TOTE £15.90: £3.40, £2.40, £3.10; EX 107.80.
Owner Tariq S Al Tayer **Bred** Andrew Cowen & Gary Tolchin **Trained** East Everleigh, Wilts

FOCUS
A good 3yo handicap, but the pace seemed a bit muddling and the field were spread out across the track in the closing stages.

NOTEBOOK
Shamaal Nibras(USA) improved a good deal on the form he showed on his reappearance at Wolverhampton with quite a useful performance, despite being keen. He should have more to offer. (op 14-1 tchd 18-1)
Amazing Storm(IRE) did remarkably well to finish so close. He pulled hard and then hung over towards the stands' rail in the straight, yet found only one too good. If he can ever learn to settle then he could be quite decent. Official explanation: jockey said that the colt ran too free and hung left (tchd 10-1 and 14-1)
Hadaj hadn't been seen since finishing third behind Harbour Watch in a 6f conditions race at the Newmarket July meeting. He would have finished closer with a better run through and this was a promising return. (op 16-1)
Solar Deity(IRE), a C&D maiden winner on his debut last November, was well backed to follow up and he travelled nicely, but his finishing effort was tame. (op 5-4 tchd 6-5, 7-4 in a place)
Red Larkspur(IRE) ran well after an absence of 259 days.
Galician was a bit disappointing, not building on earlier promise. (tchd 7-2)
T/Plt: £400.70 to a £1 stake. Pool:£101,693.20 - 185.23 winning tickets T/Qpdt: £42.00 to a £1 stake. Pool:£6,670.54 - 117.39 winning tickets LM

MUSSELBURGH (R-H)
Saturday, April 7

OFFICIAL GOING: Good to soft (soft in places; 5.8)
Wind: Virtually nil Weather: Overcast

1218 BETFRED "WHEN BOTH TEAMS SCORE" E B F MAIDEN STKS 5f
2:10 (2:10) (Class 5) 2-Y-O **£3,881** (£1,155; £577; £288) **Stalls** High

Form RPR

1 **Storm Moon (USA)** 2-9-3 0...... JoeFanning 3 81+
(Mark Johnston) *qckly away and sn led: rdn and qcknd clr over 1f out: pushed out* **5/1**[3]

4 **2** *2 ½* **Just Past Andover (IRE)**[7] 1131 2-8-12 0...... CharlesBishop(5) 2 72
(Bill Turner) *chsd ldrs: hdwy and edgd lft 2f out: sn rdn and kpt on same pce appr fnl f* **11/4**[2]

3 *hd* **Polski Max** 2-9-3 0...... TonyHamilton 8 71+
(Richard Fahey) *sltly hmpd s: sn chsng ldrs: rdn along wl over 1f out: kpt on same pce* **15/8**[1]

4 *shd* **Someone's Darling** 2-8-12 0...... DanielTudhope 9 66
(Jim Goldie) *wnt rt s: in rr: hdwy to chse ldrs and swtchd rt wl over 1f out: sn rdn and kpt on same pce* **33/1**

5 *10* **Jordanstown** 2-9-3 0...... PhillipMakin 6 35+
(Kevin Ryan) *sltly hmpd s and rr tl styd on fnl 2f: n.d* **13/2**

6 *5* **Rated** 2-9-3 0...... SamHitchcott 5 17
(Mick Channon) *a in rr* **33/1**

7 *7* **Majestic Jess (IRE)** 2-9-3 0...... StephenCraine 10
(Tom Dascombe) *cl up on inner: rdn along 1/2-way: wkng whn bmpd 2f out and bhd after* **9/1**

8 *2* **Princess In Exile** 2-8-12 0...... LeeNewman 4
(George Foster) *a towards rr* **14/1**

9 *hd* **Red Style (IRE)** 2-9-3 0...... MickyFenton 7
(Paul Midgley) *sltly hmpd and wnt rt s: in tch: rdn along 1/2-way and sn wknd* **40/1**

1m 1.33s (0.93) **Going Correction** +0.15s/f (Good) **9** Ran SP% **116.4**
Speed ratings (Par 92): **98,94,93,93,77 69,58,55,54**
toteswingers:1&2:£3.20, 1&3:£3.30, 2&3:£1.70 CSF £19.08 TOTE £4.30: £1.70, £1.20, £1.20; EX 23.40.
Owner Sheikh Hamdan Bin Mohammed Al Maktoum **Bred** Darley **Trained** Middleham Moor, N Yorks

FOCUS
Following 5mm of overnight rain the going was eased to good to soft, soft in places (GoingStick 5.8), and Joe Fanning, after riding the winner of the first, said it was 'a bit tacky', while Phil Makin said it was 'good to soft'.

NOTEBOOK
Storm Moon(USA) knew his job, as he broke quickly from stall three, crossed over to the stands' rail, travelled strongly and won comfortably. He should go on from this, and it's worth noting that his trainer, who sent out the winner of the juvenile maiden at Kempton half an hour earlier, seems to have his 2yos pretty forward. (op 8-1)
Just Past Andover(IRE) had the huge benefit of a previous outing, having finished fourth in the Brocklesby a week earlier. Drawn worst of all, he wasn't best away and always playing catch-up from then on, but he kept on for second and gives the form substance. (op 7-2 tchd 5-2)
Polski Max, a March foal out of a 5f 2yo winner, was being niggled along from some way out but he kept on well, and the outing should bring him on. (op 13-8 tchd 9-4)
Someone's Darling, whose yard is not known for 2yo winners, looked to be staying on to challenge for a place, but she edged right in the closing stages, which might have cost her third. The experience will have done her good. (op 22-1)
Jordanstown, hampered and towards the rear early on, was well held. (op 7-1 tchd 8-1)
Rated was pretty clueless throughout. (op 40-1)
Majestic Jess(IRE) knew his job and showed bright early pace along the stands' rail, but he came under pressure with over 2f to run and then became short of room as he weakened. This ground might not have suited him and he could do better next time. (tchd 17-2 and 10-1)

1219 BETFRED THE BONUS KING WHISTLEJACKET CONDITIONS STKS 5f
2:45 (2:45) (Class 2) 3-Y-O+ **£12,938** (£3,850; £1,924; £962) **Stalls** High

Form RPR

323- **1** *shd* **Hamish McGonagall**[209] 5985 7-9-7 114...... DavidAllan 1 112
(Tim Easterby) *cl up: rdn over 1f out: sn chal and ev ch whn carried rt across trck ins fnl f: jst hld: fin 2nd, shd: plcd 1st* **7/2**[1]

260- **2** **Bear Behind (IRE)**[189] 6535 3-8-2 97...... HayleyTurner 6 99
(Tom Dascombe) *led: rdn along wl over 1f out: drvn and hung consistently rt ins fnl f: jst hld on: fin 1st: disqualified and plcd 2nd* **7/2**[1]

/40- **3** *2 ¾* **Excel Bolt**[168] 7018 4-8-13 95...... TomEaves 8 94
(Bryan Smart) *chsd ldrs on inner: rdn along wl over 1f out: kpt on same pce fnl f* **8/1**[3]

140- **4** *¾* **Shoshoni Wind**[213] 5827 4-9-0 96...... PhillipMakin 5 92
(Kevin Ryan) *towards rr: hdwy 2f out: sn rdn to chse ldrs over 1f out: no imp fnl f* **8/1**[3]

40-0 **5** *2 ¼* **Borderlescott**[14] 1033 10-8-13 109...... NeilCallan 2 83
(Robin Bastiman) *chsd ldrs: rdn along wl over 1f out: sn wknd* **7/2**[1]

450- **6** *1 ½* **Captain Dunne (IRE)**[188] 6563 7-8-13 107......(p) DuranFentiman 4 78
(Tim Easterby) *trckd ldrs: effrt 2f out: sn rdn and wknd over 1f out* **6/1**[2]

013- **7** *28* **Mister Manannan (IRE)**[200] 6233 5-9-2 98...... AdrianNicholls 3
(David Nicholls) *dwlt a: bhd and eased fr wl over 1f out* **8/1**[3]

59.73s (-0.67) **Going Correction** +0.15s/f (Good)
WFA 3 from 4yo+ 11lb **7** Ran SP% **114.3**
Speed ratings (Par 109): **110,111,106,105,101 99,54**
toteswingers:2&1:£2.70, 2&3:£8.30, 1&3:£4.60 CSF £15.59 TOTE £2.60: £1.10, £2.40; EX 18.80 Trifecta £274.40 Pool: £567.49 - 1.53 winning units..
Owner Reality Partnerships I **Bred** J P Coggan And Whitsbury Manor Stud **Trained** Great Habton, N Yorks
■ Stewards' Enquiry : Hayley Turner one-day ban: careless riding (21 April)

FOCUS
The pace held up in this conditions race.

NOTEBOOK
Hamish McGonagall was recording his fifth win from seven starts over this C&D, and repeating last year's success in the race. It's hard to quibble with the decision of the stewards to award him the race, as he was prevented from keeping a straight line and was only beaten narrowly. (op 3-1)
Bear Behind(IRE), the only 3yo in the field, would have been better off at the weights with Hamish McGonagall had this been a handicap, and he looked to have his limitations exposed at two, but this might be a signal that last year's sprinting 2yos will hold their own against their elders this year. He finished first past the post, but carried Hamish McGonagall across the track, and the stewards ruled that that had cost the latter victory. (op 5-1 tchd 11-2)
Excel Bolt, gelded over the winter, tracked the leader on the rail and kept on well on ground plenty soft enough for him. He ran poorly on both starts last year, but was a good 2yo (third in Norfolk) and this was a return to form. (op 9-1)
Shoshoni Wind faced no easy task at the weights, but she won first time up last year and can clearly go well fresh. She ran about as well as could be expected. (op 9-1 tchd 11-1)
Borderlescott was best in at the weights but this performance added to the evidence that he's probably now on the decline. (op 4-1 tchd 10-3 and 9-2 in places)
Captain Dunne(IRE) didn't help his cause by failing to settle. (op 9-2)
Mister Manannan(IRE) was awkward from the stalls and trapped out wide afterwards. Eased some way out, presumably something was amiss (reported to have never been travelling). Official explanation: jockey said that the gelding was never travelling (tchd 17-2)

1220 BETFRED "GOALS GALORE" H'CAP 7f 30y
3:20 (3:21) (Class 3) (0-95,95) 4-Y-O+ **£8,409** (£2,502; £1,250; £625) **Stalls** Low

Form RPR

60-0 **1** **Justonefortheroad**[97] 5 6-9-5 **93**...... FrederikTylicki 8 103
(Richard Fahey) *hld up in rr: smooth hdwy 3f out: trckd ldrs 2f out: rdn and qcknd ent fnl f: led last 100yds* **12/1**

0111 **2** 2 1/2 **Captain Dimitrios**[8] 1116 4-8-2 **79**......................(v) NataliaGemelova(3) 1 82
(Alastair Lidderdale) *cl up: led after 1f: rdn along over 2f out: drvn over 1f out: hdd and no ex ins fnl f* **16/1**

05-4 **3** 1 1/4 **Prime Exhibit**[28] 868 7-8-12 **89**.. LeeTopliss(3) 7 89
(Richard Fahey) *in tch: hdwy on outer over 2f out: rdn to chse ldng pair over 1f out: kpt on same pce ins fnl f* **9/2**[2]

500- **4** *hd* **Parisian Pyramid (IRE)**[154] 7295 6-9-4 **92**...................... PhillipMakin 2 91
(Kevin Ryan) *trckd ldrs: hdwy over 2f out: rdn to chse ldr over 1f out: one pce ins fnl f* **9/2**[2]

60-2 **5** 2 1/2 **Layla's Hero (IRE)**[6] 1161 5-8-8 **85**..................(p) MichaelO'Connell(3) 11 78
(John Quinn) *hld up: hdwy over 2f out: sn rdn and kpt on fnl f: nrst fin* **7/2**[1]

00-0 **6** *hd* **Polish World (USA)**[6] 1156 8-8-11 **85**............................ MickyFenton 5 77
(Paul Midgley) *chsd ldng pair: effrt 3f out: rdn over 2f out: drvn and wknd ent fnl f* **33/1**

21-5 **7** 1/2 **Jeannie Galloway (IRE)**[13] 1040 5-8-13 **87**................. TonyHamilton 6 78
(Richard Fahey) *in tch on inner: hdwy over 2f out: rdn wl over 1f out: no imp* **5/1**[3]

003- **8** 8 **Castles In The Air**[175] 6862 7-9-2 **95**.......................... ShaneBKelly(5) 4 64
(Richard Fahey) *a in rr* **15/2**

24-0 **9** 1 1/4 **Oil Strike**[63] 431 5-8-11 **85**.. JamesSullivan 10 51
(Michael Easterby) *led 1f: cl up: rdn 3f out: drvn over 2f out and sn wknd* **20/1**

100- **10** 11 **Silver Bullitt**[115] 7759 4-8-5 **79**..(b1) JoeFanning 9 15
(Mark Johnston) *chsd ldrs: rdn along 3f out: sn wknd* **25/1**

201- **11** 13 **Amenable (IRE)**[173] 6917 5-8-11 **85**............................ AdrianNicholls 3
(David Nicholls) *midfield: pushed along 3f out: sn wknd* **16/1**

1m 30.0s (1.00) **Going Correction** +0.325s/f (Good) **11** Ran SP% **118.0**
Speed ratings (Par 107): **107,104,102,102,99 99,98,89,88,75 60**
toteswingers:1&2:£22.30, 1&3:£11.4, 2&3:£15.70 CSF £183.39 CT £1019.77 TOTE £16.00: £4.60, £4.50, £1.80; EX 366.70.
Owner The Pontoon Partnership **Bred** Wellsummers Farm & Hammarsfield B'Stock **Trained** Musley Bank, N Yorks

FOCUS
They went a strong pace early here, Oil Strike and Captain Dimitrios taking each other on in front.

NOTEBOOK
Justonefortheroad, who was detached in last place early on, found them coming back to him in the straight. With 2f to run he was clearly going best, but had to wait for a gap to appear, and when it did he quickened up well to score. Even allowing for the race being run to suit, he did it easily, and he might have even more to offer. A return to 1m will suit him in a more sensibly run race. (op 14-1 tchd 16-1)
Captain Dimitrios had the best draw and tried to make the most of it, but he was taken on in front and that probably cost him victory. It was a good effort to hold on to second in the circumstances, and clearly 7f is no problem to him on a sharp track. (op 14-1)
Prime Exhibit was squeezed up and then got caught wider than ideal on the turn into the straight, but he stayed on well in the closing stages. He doesn't find winning easy. (op 7-2)
Parisian Pyramid(IRE) is on a long losing run but he was well supported, and this was a promising return to action. (op 6-1)
Layla's Hero(IRE) was a bit disappointing considering his good effort at Doncaster six days earlier. This might have come too soon. (op 4-1)
Polish World(USA) chased the two early leaders and, after briefly threatening to take a hand, didn't see his race out. Quicker ground suits him better. (op 25-1)
Jeannie Galloway(IRE) had won on both her previous visits here, but she was a bit disappointing this time, failing to pick up despite enjoying a rails run from midfield. (op 6-1 tchd 9-2)
Oil Strike Official explanation: jockey said that the gelding ran too free

1221 BETFRED ROYAL MILE (HANDICAP STKS) 1m
3:50 (3:51) (Class 2) (0-100,95) 3-Y-O
£31,125 (£9,320; £4,660; £2,330; £1,165; £585) **Stalls** Low

Form RPR

240- **1** **Chapter Seven**[203] 6170 3-8-11 **85**.............................. FrederikTylicki 11 89+
(Richard Fahey) *stdd s: sn swtchd rt and hld up in rr: hdwy on inner over 2f out: rdn ent fnl f: styd on wl to ld last 50yds* **12/1**

204- **2** *nk* **Evervescent (IRE)**[189] 6535 3-8-11 **85**....................... GrahamGibbons 2 88
(J S Moore) *trckd ldrs: hdwy 3f out: rdn to ld wl over 1f out: drvn ent fnl f: hdd and no ex last 50yds* **9/1**

231- **3** 1/2 **Kinloch Castle**[156] 7240 3-8-8 **82**................................ AdrianNicholls 12 84
(Mark Johnston) *cl up: effrt to chal 3f out: rdn 2f out and ev ch tl drvn and no ex ins fnl f* **9/1**

1110 **4** 1 3/4 **Kickingthelilly**[14] 1032 3-8-9 **83**................................. RobertWinston 10 81
(Rae Guest) *hld up in rr: hdwy on outer over 2f out: rdn to chse ldrs over 1f out: styd on ins fnl f* **20/1**

-131 **5** 1/2 **Switzerland (IRE)**[28] 867 3-9-7 **95**.............................. JoeFanning 4 92
(Mark Johnston) *trckd ldrs: hdwy 3f out: rdn 2f out: drvn and one pce ins fnl f* **10/3**[1]

21-1 **6** 3/4 **Bronze Angel (IRE)**[84] 180 3-8-13 **87**.......................... HayleyTurner 8 82
(Marcus Tregoning) *hld up towards rr: hdwy wl over 2f out: swtchd rt and rdn wl over 1f out: kpt on same pce fnl f* **5/1**[2]

110- **7** *shd* **Gabrial (IRE)**[298] 3012 3-9-1 **89**...................................... TonyHamilton 7 84+
(Richard Fahey) *hld up: hdwy wl over 2f out: rdn and n.m.r over 1f out: swtchd lft and kpt on fnl f: nrst fin* **8/1**

140- **8** 1 **Queens Revenge**[287] 3402 3-9-4 **92**.................................. DavidAllan 1 84
(Tim Easterby) *hld up in rr: hdwy 3f out: rdn wl over 1f out: no imp fnl f* **33/1**

110- **9** 2 1/4 **Cravat**[173] 6914 3-9-3 **91**.. PJMcDonald 6 78
(Mark Johnston) *chsd ldrs: effrt and cl up 3f out: rdn along over 2f out: wknd over 1f out* **11/1**

110- **10** 3 **Zakreet**[176] 6829 3-8-11 **85**.. PhillipMakin 3 65
(Kevin Ryan) *led: rdn along 3f out: hdd wl over 1f out and grad wknd* **11/1**

-311 **11** 7 **Shabora (IRE)**[50] 596 3-9-1 **89**.. NeilCallan 5 53
(Roger Varian) *chsd ldrs: rdn along 3f out: wknd 2f out* **13/2**[3]

346- **12** *shd* **Shamrocked (IRE)**[196] 6336 3-8-10 **84**.......................... SamHitchcott 9 48
(Mick Channon) *hld up: hdwy on outer and in tch 3f out: rdn along over 2f out and sn wknd* **25/1**

1m 43.34s (2.14) **Going Correction** +0.325s/f (Good) **12** Ran SP% **120.1**
Speed ratings (Par 104): **102,101,101,99,98 98,98,97,94,91 84,84**
toteswingers:1&2:£22.60, 1&3:£27.50, 2&3:£19.20 CSF £114.49 CT £1048.02 TOTE £20.40: £6.10, £3.60, £4.10; EX 151.50 Trifecta £464.90 Part won. Pool: £628.32 - 0.10 winning units..
Owner T G & Mrs M E Holdcroft **Bred** Bearstone Stud **Trained** Musley Bank, N Yorks
■ Stewards' Enquiry : Graham Gibbons two-day ban: use of whip (21 & 23 Apr)

FOCUS
A good handicap, won last year by Glen's Diamond, who went on to win in Group 3 company.

NOTEBOOK
Chapter Seven, representing last year's winning yard, was dropped in at the tail of the field and was fortunate to have a gap open up nicely for him on the rail, so that he was able to stay on strongly unimpeded. While things fell kindly for him in the race itself, this was still a step up on his 2yo efforts, and the extra distance was clearly in his favour. Richard Fahey had said beforehand that the colt had done very well physically over the winter, and there could easily be more to come from him. (op 16-1)
Evervescent(IRE), like the winner, had his stamina to prove, but he got it well having tracked the leader on the rail. Placed in Listed company and fourth in the Two-Year-Old Trophy last year, he's on a workable mark. (op 14-1)
Kinloch Castle, who bolted up in a Southwell maiden on his final start at two, kept the leader company up front and kept on for pressure. One of the least experienced in the line-up, he should have more improvement in him. (op 14-1)
Kickingthelilly, running on turf for the first time, was out the back with the winner for much of the race and had a nice clear run down the outside in the straight. She was competing off a 9lb higher mark than when last successful so this was a good effort. (op 22-1 tchd 18-1)
Switzerland(IRE), raised 12lb for his Wolverhampton stroll, was a market drifter. Briefly denied a clear run, he got out soon enough but was simply one-paced under pressure. Perhaps the mile stretched him a bit. (op 11-4 tchd 4-1)
Bronze Angel(IRE), back on turf and chasing a hat-trick, eventually crossed to the rail in the straight and followed the winner through. He was a non-runner due to soft ground on an occasion last year, and presumably a quicker surface than he had here will suit him in future.
Gabrial(IRE) got bumped about and was continually denied a clear run in the straight, so it's probably not worth reading too much into his finishing position. (op 15-2)
Zakreet made all over a mile on soft ground at Ayr last autumn, but having made the early running here he disappointingly dropped out with over a furlong to run. (op 12-1 tchd 10-1)
Shabora(IRE) is by Cape Cross and presumably this ground wasn't to her liking. (op 15-2)

1222 BETFRED STILL TREBLE ODDS ON LUCKY 15'S H'CAP 1m 1f
4:25 (4:26) (Class 6) (0-65,63) 4-Y-O+ **£2,264** (£673; £336; £168) **Stalls** Low

Form RPR

401/ **1** **Shamarlane**[497] 7605 5-9-3 **59**.. TomEaves 7 68
(Clive Mulhall) *t.k.h early: trckd ldrs: hdwy 3f out: led wl over 1f out: rdn ins fnl f and kpt on strly* **8/1**

-311 **2** 1 3/4 **Cabal**[9] 1096 5-9-2 **58**..(b) DanielTudhope 3 63
(Andrew Crook) *trckd ldrs on inner: hdwy over 2f out: n.m.r and swtchd lft over 1f out: sn rdn and kpt on ins fnl f* **9/2**[2]

002- **3** *hd* **Seldom (IRE)**[192] 6452 6-9-7 **63**.................................... RobertWinston 6 67
(Mel Brittain) *t.k.h and jinked lft after 100yds: trckd ldr: effrt to ld over 2f out: rdn and hdd wl over 1f out: kpt on same pce fnl f* **7/2**[1]

0-11 **4** *nk* **Prohibition (IRE)**[15] 1009 6-9-2 **58**.................................... JoeFanning 4 62
(Alastair Lidderdale) *stdd s and hld up in rr: smooth hdwy over 3f out: trckd ldrs gng wl 2f out: n.m.r and swtchd lft over 1f out: sn rdn and kpt on* **9/2**[2]

300- **5** 3/4 **Naafetha (IRE)**[179] 6777 4-9-1 **57**...................................... LeeNewman 9 59
(George Foster) *led: rdn along 3f out: sn hdd and grad wknd appr fnl f* **18/1**

5356 **6** 1 1/4 **Myraid**[4] 1179 5-8-8 **50**... JamesSullivan 1 49
(Ruth Carr) *trckd ldrs: effrt 3f out: rdn along 2f out: sn drvn and no imp* **6/1**[3]

132- **7** 1/2 **La Bacouetteuse (FR)**[100] 7105 7-9-5 **61**.........................(p) DavidAllan 2 59
(Iain Jardine) *hld up: a in rr* **9/2**[2]

030- **8** *nk* **Nicholas Pocock (IRE)**[128] 7003 6-8-12 **57**...................... DaleSwift(3) 8 54
(Ian McInnes) *hld up in tch: hdwy on outer over 2f out: rdn along wl over 1f out: sn btn* **20/1**

60-0 **9** 15 **Carnelian (IRE)**[21] 937 5-8-7 **49** oh4.......................... DuranFentiman 5 13
(Ian Semple) *a towards rr: outpcd and bhd fr over 2f out* **50/1**

1m 59.94s (6.04) **Going Correction** +0.325s/f (Good) **9** Ran SP% **114.2**
Speed ratings (Par 101): **86,84,84,84,83 82,81,81,68**
toteswingers:1&2:£8.50, 1&3:£7.40, 2&3:£4.40 CSF £43.34 CT £150.38 TOTE £13.30: £3.60, £2.10, £1.10; EX 62.80.
Owner Mrs C M Mulhall **Bred** John M Troy **Trained** Scarcroft, W Yorks

FOCUS
Just an ordinary handicap run at a modest early pace, but the winner scored with authority.

1223 BETFRED "DOUBLE DELIGHT" E B F MAIDEN STKS 1m 4f 100y
5:00 (5:00) (Class 4) 3-Y-O+ **£5,175** (£1,540; £769; £384) **Stalls** Low

Form RPR

05-2 **1** **Key Gold**[91] 84 3-8-2 72.. JoeFanning 1 69+
(Mark Johnston) *mde all: rdn over 2f out: kpt on wl fnl f* **1/2**[1]

4 **2** 2 1/4 **Torero**[21] 943 3-8-7 0... PJMcDonald 3 70
(Kevin Ryan) *t.k.h: trckd wnr: effrt 3f out: rdn and wandered over 1f out: hung rt and no imp fnl f* **3/1**[2]

30- **3** 10 **Greyhope**[202] 6187 3-8-4 0.. JulieBurke(3) 5 55
(Lucinda Russell) *s.i.s and bhd: hdwy 5f out: rdn along wl over 2f out: plugged on: n.d* **7/1**[3]

0 **4** 1/2 **Sweet Vera**[10] 1065 7-9-9 0.. RobertWinston 2 51
(Shaun Harris) *trckd ldng pair: rdn along over 3f out: hung lft and outpcd fnl 2f* **40/1**

54- **5** 13 **Lady Gargoyle**[161] 7158 4-9-8 0.. DanielTudhope 4 31
(Jim Goldie) *in tch: rdn along and outpcd over 3f out: sn bhd* **25/1**

2m 50.77s (8.77) **Going Correction** +0.325s/f (Good)
WFA 3 from 4yo 21lb 4 from 7yo 1lb **5** Ran SP% **110.5**
Speed ratings (Par 105): **83,81,74,74,65**
CSF £2.30 TOTE £1.60: £1.10, £1.50; EX 2.10.
Owner Jaber Abdullah **Bred** Newsells Park Stud **Trained** Middleham Moor, N Yorks

FOCUS
This didn't look likely to take much winning.

1224 BETFRED THE BONUS KING BINGO H'CAP 7f 30y
5:35 (5:36) (Class 6) (0-65,64) 4-Y-O+ **£2,264** (£673; £336; £168) **Stalls** Low

Form RPR

000- **1** **Nadeen (IRE)**[123] 7646 5-9-7 **64**...................................... AndrewMullen 4 74
(Michael Smith) *dwlt: hld up towards rr: hdwy 3f out: str run on inner over 1f out: led ent fnl f: rdn out* **3/1**[1]

062 **2** 1 1/4 **Resplendent Alpha**[58] 477 8-8-6 **56**.......................... LeonnaMayor(7) 10 63
(Alastair Lidderdale) *hld up and bhd: hdwy on wd outside over 2f out: rdn to chse ldrs over 1f out: edgd rt ins fnl f: kpt on* **11/1**

400- **3** 1/2 **Monel**[193] 6426 4-8-12 **55**.. DanielTudhope 7 61
(Jim Goldie) *in tch: hdwy over 2f out: rdn to chse ldrs wl over 1f out: drvn and kpt on fnl f* **8/1**

05-0 **4** 1/2 **Mark Anthony (IRE)**[17] 985 5-9-3 **60**.....................(p) RobertWinston 3 64
(Shaun Harris) *led and set str pce: rdn over 2f out: drvn: edgd rt and hdd ent fnl f: sn wknd* **20/1**

2305 **5** 2 1/4 **Nacho Libre**^{22} [927] 7-8-10 **53**........(b) PaddyAspell 5 51
(Michael Easterby) *chsd ldrs: hdwy 3f out: rdn 2f out: drvn and kpt on same pce appr fnl f* **8/1**
2120 **6** 1 1/4 **Greenhead High**^{16} [997] 4-9-5 **62**........ AdrianNicholls 9 60
(David Nicholls) *trckd ldng pair: tk clsr order over 2f out: rdn whn n.m.r over 1f out: kpt on same pce* **9/2**^{2}
0263 **7** 1 1/2 **Monsieur Pontaven**^{22} [927] 5-8-8 **51**........(b) LeeNewman 12 42
(Robin Bastiman) *hld up towards rr: sme hdwy fnl 2f: nvr a factor* **7/1**^{3}
-043 **8** 1/2 **Fault**^{10} [1074] 6-8-12 **55**........(t) PhillipMakin 6 44
(Alastair Lidderdale) *chsd ldr: hdwy 3f out: sn cl up: rdn 2f out and sn wknd* **17/2**
64-3 **9** 1 **Fortunate Bid (IRE)**^{18} [972] 6-9-1 **58**........(p) TonyHamilton 1 45
(Linda Stubbs) *in tch: rdn along wl over 2f out: sn no hdwy* **7/1**^{3}
320- **10** 3 1/4 **Hellbender (IRE)**^{217} [5725] 6-8-13 **61**........ LMcNiff(5) 8 39
(George Foster) *hld up: a bhd* **12/1**

1m 31.81s (2.81) **Going Correction** +0.325s/f (Good) **10** Ran SP% **121.7**
Speed ratings (Par 101): **96,94,94,93,90 89,87,87,86,82**
toteswingers:1&2:£10.40, 1&3:£8.50, 2&3:£19.20 CSF £39.52 CT £254.06 TOTE £5.00: £2.00, £4.90, £4.10; EX 45.40.
Owner Miss Rebecca Smith **Bred** Rabbah Bloodstock Limited **Trained** Kirkheaton, Northumberland
■ Stewards' Enquiry : Paddy Aspell two-day ban: careless riding (21-24 April)

FOCUS
A modest handicap run at a good early gallop, and the principals came from off the pace.

1225 - 1234a (Foreign Racing) - See Raceform Interactive

1218 MUSSELBURGH (R-H)
Sunday, April 8

OFFICIAL GOING: Good to soft (5.8)
Wind: Moderate, against Weather: Overcast

1235 BETFRED "HAT TRICK HEAVEN" (S) STKS — 5f
1:50 (1:51) (Class 5) 2-Y-O £3,234 (£962; £481; £240) Stalls High

Form RPR
03 **1** **Vanessa**^{6} [1165] 2-8-2 0........ CharlesBishop(5) 2 63+
(Mick Channon) *qckly away: mde all: rdn clr wl over 1f out: kpt on* **5/4**^{1}
6 **2** 5 **Mad Jazz**^{6} [1165] 2-8-7 0........ BarryMcHugh 5 45
(Tony Coyle) *chsd wnr: rdn along 2f out: outpcd appr fnl f* **9/4**^{2}
3 4 **Red Koko (IRE)** 2-8-7 0........ PJMcDonald 3 34+
(George Moore) *in tch: hdwy to chse ldng pair 1/2-way: rdn along 2f out: edgd lft and outpcd over 1f out* **11/2**
4 5 **Maggies Gem (IRE)** 2-8-7 0........ RussKennemore 4 13
(Paul Midgley) *wnt rt s: in tch: rdn along 1/2-way: sn outpcd* **5/1**^{3}

1m 2.92s (2.52) **Going Correction** +0.20s/f (Good) **4** Ran SP% **107.3**
Speed ratings (Par 92): **87,79,72,64**
CSF £4.24 TOTE £1.90; EX 3.90.The winner was sold to J. Goldie for £5,500.
Owner Norman Court Stud I **Bred** Mike Channon Ltd And Norman Court Stud **Trained** West Ilsley, Berks

FOCUS
No rain overnight and a stiff breeze led to the going being given as good to soft all around, although the GoingStick at 7am read the same as the previous day (5.8). Russ Kennemore, returning after the first, reported that the ground was on "the slow side of good, and a bit dead". With the only colt in the field declared a non-runner, this was effectively a fillies' seller.

NOTEBOOK
Vanessa had Mad Jazz well behind her when third at Redcar six days earlier, and had no trouble confirming the form. She made a good start, grabbed the rail, and was always in full control thereafter, but it's not worth going overboard as this was a modest contest. She was bought at the auction by Jim Goldie for £5,500. (op 11-10 tchd 11-8)
Mad Jazz was a well-backed favourite before trailing in last of six at Redcar on her debut, and she was again pretty strong in the market considering she had over six lengths to make up with Vanessa on that effort. As it was she only made slight inroads into that deficit. (op 11-4)
Red Koko(IRE), who showed signs of inexperience beforehand, showed up well to halfway before dropping away. She should benefit from this. (op 7-2)
Maggies Gem(IRE) ran green throughout. Official explanation: jockey said that the filly hung right throughout (op 9-1)

1236 BETFRED THE BONUS KING H'CAP (DIV I) — 5f
2:20 (2:20) (Class 4) (0-85,88) 4-Y-O+ £3,357 (£3,357; £769; £384) Stalls High

Form RPR
102- **1** **Go Go Green (IRE)**^{165} [7104] 6-8-10 **72**........ KierenFallon 7 77
(Jim Goldie) *trckd ldrs: cl up after 2f: led wl over 1f out and sn rdn: edgd lft and drvn jst ins fnl f: edgd rt last 75yds and jnd on line* **8/1**
1112 **1** dht **Captain Dimitrios**^{1} [1220] 4-9-3 **79**........(v) PaulHanagan 8 84
(Alastair Lidderdale) *led: jnd 1/2-way: rdn and hdd wl over 1f out: cl up and edgd sltly rt over 1f out: sn n.m.r on inner and bmpd jst ins fnl f: rallied strly to join ldr on line* **3/1**^{1}
20-5 **3** 1 3/4 **Haajes**^{31} [835] 8-9-6 **82**........ MickyFenton 2 81
(Paul Midgley) *towards rr: hdwy over 2f out: rdn and styd on fnl f: tk 3rd nr line* **8/1**
0-06 **4** nse **Ingleby Star (IRE)**^{25} [890] 7-8-13 **78**........(p) PaulPickard(3) 9 77
(Ian McInnes) *cl up: pushed along after 2f: rdn wl over 1f out: kpt on same pce: lost 3rd nr line* **14/1**
00- **5** 1 **Crimson Knot (IRE)**^{166} [7073] 4-8-2 **71**........ MatthewHopkins(7) 6 66
(Alan Berry) *cl up: rdn along wl over 1f out: wknd fnl f* **17/2**
000- **6** hd **Baldemar**^{183} [6703] 7-9-2 **83**........ ShaneBKelly(5) 3 77+
(Richard Fahey) *in tch: rdn along 2f out: kpt on same pce* **14/1**
265- **7** 2 **Boundaries**^{174} [6917] 4-9-0 **76**........(v) DavidAllan 1 63
(Tim Easterby) *prom on wd outside: rdn along over 2f out: sn wknd* **9/1**
-112 **8** 13 **Upper Lambourn (IRE)**^{61} [458] 4-8-13 **75**........ BarryMcHugh 10
(Brian Ellison) *sn outpcd and a bhd* **13/2**^{3}
00-1 **U** **Arganil (USA)**^{6} [1168] 7-9-9 **88** 6ex........(p) AmyRyan(3) 4
(Kevin Ryan) *rrd and uns rdr s* **7/2**^{2}

1m 1.42s (1.02) **Going Correction** +0.20s/f (Good) **9** Ran SP% **116.6**
Speed ratings (Par 105): **99,99,96,96,94 94,91,70,** WIN: CD £1.70 , GGG £3.70; PL: CD £1.10, GGG £2.90, H £3.10; EX: CD-GGG £16.50, GGG-CD £14.10; CSF: CD-GGG £13.92, GGG-CD £16.30; TRICAST: CD-GGG-H £88.38, GGG-CD-H £101.77; toteswingers toteswingers: 1&2 £5.30, 1&3 (CD) £6.60, 1&3 (GGG) £8.20 TOTE £027: £0Owner, £Chris Beek Racing, £Bred, £W G H BarronsTrained Lambourn, Berks.
Owner Jim Goldie Racing Club **Bred** Edmond And Richard Kent **Trained** Uplawmoor, E Renfrews

FOCUS
There wasn't a hectic early pace on.

1237 BETFRED THE BONUS KING H'CAP (DIV II) — 5f
2:50 (2:56) (Class 4) (0-85,84) 4-Y-O+ £5,175 (£1,540; £769; £384) Stalls High

Form RPR
164- **1** **Mayoman (IRE)**^{205} [6112] 7-8-13 **76**........ DanielTudhope 1 88
(David O'Meara) *in tch on outer: hdwy 1/2-way: rdn to ld appr fnl f: styd on strly* **4/1**^{1}
360- **2** 3/4 **Rothesay Chancer**^{165} [7104] 4-8-10 **73**........ LeeNewman 10 82
(Jim Goldie) *cl up: rdn along wl over 1f out: kpt on u.p fnl f* **5/1**^{2}
006- **3** 1 3/4 **Highland Warrior**^{236} [5148] 13-8-4 **67**........ PaulHanagan 3 70
(Paul Midgley) *in rr and sn pushed along: hdwy on outer wl over 1f out: sn rdn and styd on fnl f: nrst fin* **20/1**
000- **4** 3/4 **Lost In Paris (IRE)**^{214} [5831] 6-9-6 **83**........(p) DavidAllan 6 83
(Tim Easterby) *chsd ldrs: effrt 2f out: sn rdn and one pce ent fnl f* **11/2**^{3}
305- **5** 3/4 **Bronze Beau**^{174} [6913] 5-9-4 **81**........(t) JamesSullivan 4 78
(Linda Stubbs) *prom: cl up after 2f: rdn to ld wl over 1f out: hdd appr fnl f and sn wknd* **16/1**
1222 **6** 3/4 **Argentine (IRE)**^{26} [887] 8-8-2 **65** oh2........(b) DuranFentiman 8 60
(Ian Semple) *dwlt and in rr: sme hdwy over 1f out: n.d* **16/1**
3423 **7** hd **Blown It (USA)**^{4} [1187] 6-8-8 **71**........ JoeFanning 7 65+
(Keith Dalgleish) *trckd ldrs: effrt whn n.m.r over 1f out and again ins fnl f: no ch after* **11/2**^{3}
465- **8** 6 **Crimea (IRE)**^{197} [6350] 6-9-7 **84**........ AdrianNicholls 9 56
(David Nicholls) *led: rdn along 2f out: sn hdd & wknd* **5/1**^{2}

1m 1.33s (0.93) **Going Correction** +0.20s/f (Good) **8** Ran SP% **100.6**
Speed ratings (Par 105): **100,98,96,94,93 92,92,82**
toteswingers: 1&2 £2.60, 1&3 £8.90, 2&3 £12.50 CSF £18.15 CT £214.59 TOTE £4.20: £1.50, £1.50, £5.50; EX 19.70 Trifecta £216.50 Pool: £330.68 - 1.13 winning units..
Owner Tom Tuohy **Bred** James Cosgrove **Trained** Nawton, N Yorks

FOCUS
A false start was originally called here after Rasaman burst his stall. He was withdrawn (11/2, deduct 15p in the £ under R4) and the second running of the race favoured those who had done the least amount of running first time around. As such, the form is slightly dubious. The winning time was 0.91sec slower than the first division.
Blown It(USA) Official explanation: jockey said that the gelding was denied a clear run

1238 BETFRED "THE HOME OF GOALS GALORE" MAIDEN STKS — 7f 30y
3:20 (3:22) (Class 5) 3-Y-O+ £2,911 (£866; £432; £216) Stalls Low

Form RPR
0- **1** **President Lincoln (USA)**^{275} [3833] 4-10-0 79........ GrahamGibbons 6 82
(Declan Carroll) *trckd ldrs: hdwy wl over 2f out: rdn to ld jst over 1f out: wandered and hung rt ins fnl f: kpt on* **7/2**^{3}
2 1 3/4 **Jack Dexter** 3-9-0 0........ DanielTudhope 2 72
(Jim Goldie) *dwlt and in rr: gd hdwy wl over 2f out: swtchd rt over 1f out: rdn and ev ch on inner whn rn green jst ins fnl f: kpt on same pce* **22/1**
00- **3** 5 **Forget Me Not Lane (IRE)**^{155} [7293] 3-9-0 0........ PhillipMakin 1 59
(Kevin Ryan) *towards rr: hdwy over 2f out: swtchd to outer and rdn wl over 1f out: styd on fnl f* **9/1**
4 1 1/2 **Pursuit of Passion** 4-9-9 0........ TonyHamilton 4 55
(Richard Fahey) *s.i.s and bhd: hdwy 2f out: styd on fnl f: nrst fin* **18/1**
04- **5** 1 **Gran Canaria Queen**^{187} [6598] 3-8-9 0........ BarryMcHugh 7 47
(Ian Semple) *led: rdn along over 2f out: hdd over 1f out: sn hung lft and wknd* **33/1**
600 **6** 3/4 **Windygoul Lad**^{22} [943] 3-9-0 0........ AndrewMullen 5 50
(Keith Dalgleish) *a towards rr* **50/1**
3- **7** nse **Three Darlings (IRE)**^{183} [6702] 3-8-9 0........ AdrianNicholls 9 45
(David Nicholls) *cl up: effrt wl over 2f out: sn rdn and disp ld tl drvn and wknd over 1f out* **12/5**^{2}
62- **8** 1 **Hawks Reef**^{155} [7293] 3-9-0 0........ PaulHanagan 3 47
(Richard Fahey) *trckd ldrs on inner: pushed along 3f out: rdn 2f out and sn btn* **6/4**^{1}
/00- **9** 2 **Mr Khan**^{354} [1494] 4-9-11 49........ JulieBurke(3) 8 47
(Linda Perratt) *plld hrd: chsd ldrs: rdn over 2f out: sn wknd* **66/1**

1m 32.51s (3.51) **Going Correction** +0.35s/f (Good)
WFA 3 from 4yo 14lb **9** Ran SP% **117.6**
Speed ratings (Par 103): **93,91,85,83,82 81,81,80,78**
toteswingers: 1&2 £11.30, 1&3 £6.20, 2&3 £17.80 CSF £76.87 TOTE £3.80: £1.10, £5.40, £1.50; EX 65.80 Trifecta £415.60 Pool: £330.68 - 1.36 winning units..
Owner M Stewart **Bred** Claiborne Farm **Trained** Sledmere, E Yorks

FOCUS
Just an ordinary maiden.

1239 BETFRED MUSSELBURGH GOLD CUP (HANDICAP STKS) — 1m 6f
3:50 (3:52) (Class 4) (0-85,84) 4-Y-O+ £12,938 (£3,850; £1,924; £962) Stalls Low

Form RPR
3/3- **1** **Shubaat**^{205} [6130] 5-9-7 **83**........ NeilCallan 1 94
(Roger Varian) *cl up on inner: led after 3f: hdd and cl up 1/2-way: led again over 4f out: rdn over 2f out: hdd wl over 1f out: drvn and styd on to ld appr fnl f: r.o wl* **3/1**^{2}
023- **2** 3 **Pittodrie Star (IRE)**^{36} [7577] 5-9-4 **80**........ DanielTudhope 8 87
(David O'Meara) *in tch: hdwy 4f out: chsd wnr 3f out: rdn to ld wl over 1f out: drvn and hdd ent fnl f: no ex* **16/1**
110- **3** 1 3/4 **Lexington Bay (IRE)**^{165} [7102] 4-9-5 **84**........ PaulHanagan 5 89+
(Richard Fahey) *chsd ldrs whn hmpd and lost pl after 2 1/2f: towards rr: hdwy 3f out: rdn to chse ldrs wl over 1f out: kpt on u.p fnl f: nrst fin* **11/4**^{1}
126- **4** 4 1/2 **Jeu De Vivre (IRE)**^{163} [7136] 4-9-2 **81**........ SilvestreDeSousa 11 79+
(Mark Johnston) *hld up towards rr: hdwy over 3f out: chsd ldrs whn sltly hmpd wl over 1f out: drvn and one pce fnl f* **6/1**^{3}
220- **5** 7 **Persian Peril**^{161} [6989] 8-9-8 **84**........ PJMcDonald 6 72
(Alan Swinbank) *trckd ldrs: effrt over 3f out: rdn along over 2f out: grad wknd* **28/1**
110- **6** 1 3/4 **Unknown Rebel (IRE)**^{154} [5724] 4-8-13 **81**........(p) AmyRyan(3) 10 67
(Kevin Ryan) *led tl rn wd bnd after 3f: chsd ldng pair: rdn along 3f out: sn wknd* **18/1**
256- **7** 3 3/4 **Red Jade**^{52} [7017] 7-9-7 **83**........ PhillipMakin 4 64
(Mrs K Burke) *in tch on inner: rdn along 4f out: drvn and wknd wl over 2f out* **12/1**
422- **8** 5 **Meetings Man (IRE)**^{218} [5724] 5-9-3 **79**........ TomEaves 12 53
(Micky Hammond) *hld up towards rr: hdwy on outer and in tch 1/2-way: rdn along 4f out and n.d* **16/1**
P0/0 **9** 3 3/4 **Kaolak (USA)**^{8} [1133] 6-9-7 **83**........ KierenFallon 9 52
(Jim Goldie) *hld up and bhd: hdwy on wd outside over 3f out: rdn 2f out and sn wknd* **16/1**

010- **10** 1 **Hollins**[157] 6171 8-9-4 **80** .... FrederikTylicki 7 47
(Micky Hammond) *in rr: wl bhd and outpcd 4f out: kpt on fnl 2f: nvr a factor* **25/1**

1431 **11** 6 **Copper Canyon**[11] 1071 4-9-2 **81** .... GrahamGibbons 2 40
(J S Moore) *cl up: led after 6f: hdd over 4f out: prom tl rdn along over 2f out and sn wknd* **8/1**

440- **12** 65 **Unex Renoir**[178] 6822 4-8-13 **83** ....(p) MarkCoumbe(5) 3
(Michael Attwater) *midfield: hdwy and in tch over 4f out: rdn along over 3f out: sn wknd and bhd whn eased wl over 1f out* **18/1**

3m 8.11s (2.81) **Going Correction** +0.35s/f (Good)
WFA 4 from 5yo+ 3lb **12** Ran SP% **120.2**
Speed ratings (Par 105): **105,103,102,99,95 94,92,89,87,87 83,46**
toteswingers: 1&2 £10.30, 1&3 £3.20, 2&3 £13.10 CSF £51.81 CT £150.02 TOTE £3.40: £1.50, £5.90, £1.40; EX 46.20 Trifecta £847.30 Part won. Pool: £1,145.05 0.96 winning units..
Owner Sheikh Ahmed Al Maktoum **Bred** Darley **Trained** Newmarket, Suffolk

FOCUS
The result of this race was decided early on.
Copper Canyon Official explanation: jockey said that the gelding lost its action
Unex Renoir Official explanation: jockey said that the gelding was never travelling

1240 BETFRED TREBLE ODDS ON LUCKY 15 H'CAP 1m 6f
4:25 (4:25) (Class 6) (0-60,64) 4-Y-0+ **£2,264** (£673; £336; £168) **Stalls** Low

Form RPR

633- **1** **Ad Value (IRE)**[159] 7212 4-9-0 **56** .... PJMcDonald 8 67
(Alan Swinbank) *trckd ldng pair: cl up over 4f out: led 3f out: rdn clr over 1f out: kpt on* **11/4**[2]

445/ **2** 1 ½ **Ministerofinterior**[35] 3382 7-9-0 **53** ....(t) FrederikTylicki 7 62
(Richard Ford) *trckd ldrs on inner: pushed along and sltly outpcd over 3f out: rdn and hdwy 2f out: swtchd rt and drvn to chse wnr ins fnl f: kpt on* **2/1**[1]

3401 **3** 5 **Ostentation**[9] 1104 5-9-8 **61** .... PaulHanagan 11 63
(Alastair Lidderdale) *hld up: gd hdwy 6f out: trckd ldrs over 4f out: rdn to chse wnr wl over 2f out: drvn and one pce appr fnl f* **9/2**[3]

5552 **4** shd **Dunaskin (IRE)**[5] 1174 12-8-7 **46** oh1 ....(b) WilliamCarson 4 48
(Richard Guest) *cl up: rdn along over 3f out: chsd ldrs whn n.m.r: hmpd and lost pl 2f out: styd on u.p fnl f* **16/1**

0-10 **5** ¾ **Lil Ella (IRE)**[7] 1154 5-9-7 **60** .... DanielTudhope 5 61
(Patrick Holmes) *hld up in rr: hdwy 6f out: chsd ldrs 3f out: rdn over 2f out: drvn and one pce fr wl over 1f out* **9/1**

5/5- **6** 1 ¾ **Knox Overstreet**[12] 335 4-9-4 **60** .... SamHitchcott 1 59
(Mick Channon) *hld up towards rr: hdwy to chse ldrs over 4f out: rdn 3f out: drvn and no imp fr over 2f out* **12/1**

640- **7** 3 **Abernethy (IRE)**[73] 7720 4-8-1 **46** oh1 ....(t) JulieBurke(3) 2 40
(Linda Perratt) *hld up and bhd: sme hdwy 3f out: sn rdn along and nvr a factor* **25/1**

000- **8** 3 **Rare Coincidence**[32] 5167 11-8-8 **47** .... TomEaves 9 37
(Alan Berry) *sn led: rdn along over 4f out: hdd 3f out: sn wknd* **25/1**

0/0- **9** 19 **Northern Acres**[16] 5311 6-9-4 **57** .... PaulMulrennan 6 21
(Sue Bradburne) *a in rr* **33/1**

260- **10** 134 **Oh Landino (GER)**[283] 2733 7-8-7 **46** oh1 .... LeeNewman 10
(Jim Goldie) *chsd ldrs: rdn along and lost pl 6f out: sn bhd* **20/1**

3m 10.13s (4.83) **Going Correction** +0.35s/f (Good)
WFA 4 from 5yo+ 3lb **10** Ran SP% **117.2**
Speed ratings (Par 101): **100,99,96,96,95 94,93,91,80,**
toteswingers: 1&2 £3.40, 1&3 £3.70, 2&3 £3.60 CSF £8.22 CT £23.31 TOTE £3.50: £1.30, £1.20, £2.00; EX 10.10 Trifecta £44.40 Pool: £942.59 - 15.70 winning units..
Owner Mrs V McGee **Bred** Michael Dalton **Trained** Melsonby, N Yorks

FOCUS
A moderate staying contest, run in a time 2.02sec slower than the 0-85 Musselburgh Gold Cup earlier on the card.
Oh Landino(GER) Official explanation: jockey said that the gelding had a breathing problem

1241 BETFRED 4 TIMES THE ODDS ON LUCKY 31 H'CAP 7f 30y
4:55 (4:59) (Class 5) (0-75,74) 3-Y-0 **£2,911** (£866; £432; £216) **Stalls** Low

Form RPR

332- **1** **Joshua The First**[162] 7157 3-9-2 **69** .... JoeFanning 10 75
(Keith Dalgleish) *hld up in tch: gd hdwy 3f out: led over 1f out: sn rdn and styd on wl* **15/2**

1 **2** 1 ¼ **Alkadi (IRE)**[40] 730 3-9-4 **71** .... SilvestreDeSousa 5 74
(Mark Johnston) *hld up in tch: hdwy over 2f out: rdn to chse ldrs and edgd rt over 1f out: stmbld sltly jst ins fnl f: kpt on wl u.p towards fin* **4/1**[2]

4-11 **3** nk **Laffan (IRE)**[89] 112 3-9-7 **74** .... PhillipMakin 2 76+
(Kevin Ryan) *plld hrd: chsd ldng pair: unbalanced bnd after 2f: pushed along and n.m.r over 2f out: rdn over 1f out: styd on ins fnl f* **4/1**[2]

022- **4** 1 ½ **Colbyor**[156] 7267 3-9-2 **69** .... PaulHanagan 4 67
(Richard Fahey) *chsd ldrs: hdwy 3f out: rdn to ld briefly wl over 1f out: sn hdd: edgd rt and one pce* **11/2**[3]

351- **5** 1 ¼ **Tinzapeas**[167] 7056 3-9-5 **72** .... SamHitchcott 9 67
(Mick Channon) *in tch: hdwy on inner over 3f out: rdn to chse ldrs 2f out: drvn and one pce appr fnl f* **14/1**

01-1 **6** 1 ¾ **Daddy Warbucks (IRE)**[12] 1058 3-9-4 **71** .... AdrianNicholls 7 63
(David Nicholls) *cl up: chal 3f out: rdn to dispute ld over 2f out: drvn and hld whn n.m.r and hmpd appr fnl f* **7/2**[1]

053- **7** 1 ¼ **Rock Canyon (IRE)**[101] 7907 3-8-9 **62** .... PaulMulrennan 1 49
(Linda Perratt) *slt ld: rdn and edgd lft 2f out: sn hdd: drvn appr fnl f and grad wknd* **33/1**

6505 **8** 1 **Chapellerie (IRE)**[12] 1058 3-8-8 **61** .... WilliamCarson 8 45
(Richard Guest) *s.i.s and bhd: hdwy on wd outside 3f out: rdn over 2f out and sn wknd* **14/1**

430- **9** 6 **Rano Pano (USA)**[204] 6144 3-8-2 **55** .... JamesSullivan 11 23
(Brian Ellison) *a in rr* **28/1**

360- **10** nse **Fayr Fall (IRE)**[169] 7021 3-9-5 **72** .... DuranFentiman 6 40
(Tim Easterby) *dwlt: a in rr* **18/1**

3-30 **11** 9 **Burnwynd Spirit (IRE)**[61] 459 3-7-13 **55** oh4 .... DominicFox(3) 3
(Ian Semple) *chsd ldrs: rdn along over 3f out: wknd over 2f out* **66/1**

1m 32.34s (3.34) **Going Correction** +0.35s/f (Good) **11** Ran SP% **115.9**
Speed ratings (Par 98): **94,92,92,90,89 87,85,84,77,77 67**
toteswingers: 1&2 £4.40, 1&3 £6.00, 2&3 £3.30 CSF £36.51 CT £141.45 TOTE £8.80: £2.30, £1.40, £1.90; EX 34.30 Trifecta £138.50 Pool: £1,452.52 - 7.76 winning units..
Owner newkeylets **Bred** P Docherty **Trained** Carluke, S Lanarks

Daddy Warbucks(IRE) Official explanation: jockey said that the gelding hung left
Rock Canyon(IRE) Official explanation: jockey said that the gelding hung left
Burnwynd Spirit(IRE) Official explanation: jockey said that the gelding hung left

1242 BETFRED 5 TIMES THE ODDS ON LUCKY 63 H'CAP 5f
5:30 (5:30) (Class 6) (0-60,60) 4-Y-0+ **£2,264** (£673; £336; £168) **Stalls** High

Form RPR

005- **1** **Boucher Garcon (IRE)**[158] 7230 4-8-2 **46** .... NeilFarley(5) 5 57
(Declan Carroll) *prom: led after 1f: rdn clr wl over 1f out: kpt on strly* **8/1**

65-6 **2** 1 **Mercers Row**[80] 215 5-9-7 **60** .... SilvestreDeSousa 10 67
(Noel Wilson) *dwlt and towards rr: hdwy 2f out: sn rdn: styd on wl fnl f* **13/2**[3]

6-05 **3** ½ **Cerejeira (IRE)**[41] 720 4-9-1 **54** ....(t) DavidAllan 9 59
(Eric Alston) *chsd ldrs: rdn along wl over 1f out: drvn and kpt on fnl f* **10/1**

6030 **4** 1 ½ **Soopacal (IRE)**[17] 996 7-9-5 **58** ....(t) BarryMcHugh 7 58
(Brian Ellison) *chsd ldrs: rdn 2f out: n.m.r over 1f out: kpt on same pce fnl f* **4/1**[1]

-344 **5** 1 **Sandwith**[12] 1054 9-8-12 **56** ....(p) LMcNiff(5) 8 52+
(George Foster) *towards rr: hdwy 1/2-way: swtchd rt and effrt to chse ldrs on outer over 1f out: sn rdn and no imp* **5/1**[2]

160- **6** ½ **Here Now And Why (IRE)**[132] 7566 5-9-4 **57** ....(p) TomEaves 6 51
(Ian Semple) *cl up: effrt to chse wnr wl over 1f out: sn rdn and wknd ins fnl f* **5/1**[2]

0442 **7** 1 ½ **Bygones For Coins (IRE)**[10] 1089 4-8-4 **50** .... MatthewHopkins(7) 12 39
(Alan Berry) *in rr: hdwy whn bdly hmpd wl over 1f out: sn swtchd rt and kpt on fnl f* **20/1**

-305 **8** 2 **Spirit Of Coniston**[26] 887 9-8-10 **56** .... NedCurtis(7) 11 38
(Paul Midgley) *led 1f: chsd ldrs: rdn along 2f out: sn wknd* **13/2**[3]

5500 **9** 5 **Tamino (IRE)**[11] 1070 9-8-7 **46** oh1 ....(b) JoeFanning 3 10
(Alastair Lidderdale) *in tch: effrt to chse ldrs over 2f out: sn rdn and wknd* **12/1**

000 **10** 2 ½ **Green Warrior**[6] 1169 4-9-2 **60** ....(p) CharlesEddery(5) 2 15
(Richard Guest) *a in rr* **25/1**

026- **11** 4 ½ **Triskaidekaphobia**[165] 7100 9-8-7 **49** ....(t) DominicFox(3) 1
(Wilf Storey) *a towards rr* **22/1**

3-50 **12** 1 ½ **Skystream (IRE)**[22] 939 4-8-11 **50** ....(b1) TonyHamilton 4
(Ian Semple) *cl up: rdn along 1/2-way: sn wknd* **33/1**

1m 1.25s (0.85) **Going Correction** +0.20s/f (Good) **12** Ran SP% **123.8**
Speed ratings (Par 101): **101,99,98,96,94 93,91,88,80,76 69,66**
toteswingers: 1&2 £14.50, 1&3 £20.00, 2&3 £14.10 CSF £59.01 CT £550.22 TOTE £8.90: £3.20, £2.80, £3.90; EX 74.40 Trifecta £564.80 Pool: £946.55 - 1.24 winning units..
Owner M Cunningham & P Cunningham **Bred** N Hartery **Trained** Sledmere, E Yorks

FOCUS
A moderate sprint handicap, but the winning time was faster than both divisions of the 0-85 handicaps earlier on the card.
T/Jkpt: £1,499.30 to a £1 stake. Pool: £155,213.77. 73.50 winning tickets. T/Plt: £72.80 to a £1 stake. Pool: £78,321.88. 785.19 winning tickets. T/Qpdt: £11.80 to a £1 stake. Pool: £5,347.70. 334.55 winning tickets. JR

1243 - (Foreign Racing) - See Raceform Interactive

LONGCHAMP (R-H)
Sunday, April 8

OFFICIAL GOING: Turf: good

1244a PRIX LA FORCE (GROUP 3) (3YO) (TURF) 1m 2f
1:30 (12:00) 3-Y-0 **£33,333** (£13,333; £10,000; £6,666; £3,333)

RPR

1 **Saonois (FR)**[43] 716 3-9-2 0 .... AntoineHamelin 3 109+
(J-P Gauvin, France) *settled 4th under restraint: wnt 3rd on rail ent fnl f: r.o strly ent fnl f but short of room: fnd split between ldrs in fnl 25yds: got up on line* **7/2**[2]

2 shd **Saint Loup (FR)**[30] 3-9-2 0 .... GregoryBenoist 6 109
(J-C Rouget, France) *sent to ld after 100yds: led into st: hdd over 1 1/2f out: rallied wl u.str ride 100yds out: grabbed ld 50yds out: r.o strly u.p: hdd on line* **14/1**

3 snk **Beauvoir (IRE)**[30] 3-9-2 0 .... Christophe-PatriceLemaire 4 109
(J-C Rouget, France) *led for 100yds: settled in 2nd under restraint: rdn to ld over 1 1/2f out: gng wl: hdd 50yds out: r.o wl* **8/15**[1]

4 6 **Psyche (FR)**[6] 3-8-13 0 .... ThierryJarnet 2 94
(C Boutin, France) *settled in rr: no ex ent fnl 1 1/2f: r.o fnl f to go 4th cl home* **16/1**

5 1 **Tifongo (FR)**[22] 951 3-9-2 0 ....(p) MaximeGuyon 5 95
(H-A Pantall, France) *settled 3rd on outer: rdn over 1 1/2f out: r.o: no ex ent fnl f: lost 4th cl home* **8/1**[3]

6 5 **Loverdose (USA)**[57] 3-9-2 0 ....(p) JohanVictoire 1 85
(F Vermeulen, France) *settled 5th: rdn but no ex early in st: nvr a factor* **20/1**

2m 4.65s (0.65) **6** Ran SP% **115.9**
WIN (incl. 1 euro stake): 4.40. PLACES: 3.80, 10.90. SF: 34.20.
Owner Pascal Treyve **Bred** Earl Haras De Nonant Le Pin **Trained** France

FOCUS
The form fits the race averages, rated around the third to his mark.

NOTEBOOK
Saonois(FR), a Listed winner on sand in February, got up late to land the biggest career success for both trainer and jockey. He may go for the Prix Greffulhe and then the Jockey Club.
Beauvoir(IRE) took up the running but could not hold on, and was pipped by his pacemaker for second.

1245a PRIX D'HARCOURT (GROUP 2) (4YO+) (TURF) 1m 2f
2:40 (12:00) 4-Y-0+ **£61,750** (£23,833; £11,375; £7,583; £3,791)

RPR

1 **Giofra**[163] 7156 4-8-8 0 .... MaximeGuyon 1 118
(A De Royer-Dupre, France) *settled 3rd: several l off ldrs: rdn early in st: qcknd wl to take ld 1 1/2f out: sn clr: comf* **4/1**[2]

2 3 **Vadamar (FR)**[119] 7729 4-9-1 0 .... Christophe-PatriceLemaire 2 119
(A De Royer-Dupre, France) *settled wl in rr: rdn early in st: swtchd to outside: r.o wl fnl 1 1/2f but no ch w wnr* **11/10**[1]

3 4 **Saga Dream (FR)**[22] 953 6-8-11 0 .... ThierryJarnet 4 107
(F Lemercier, France) *settled 5th: styd on u.p fnl 2f: wnt 3rd fnl 50yds* **11/2**[3]

4 ½ **War Is War (IRE)**[22] 953 4-8-11 0 .... ThomasHuet 5 106
(E J O'Neill, France) *led after 50yds: set gd pce: hdd 1 1/2f out: styd on wl u.p ins fnl f: lost 3rd fnl 50yds* **14/1**

5 2 ½ **Vodkato (FR)**[123] 7668 4-8-11 0 .... StephanePasquier 3 101
(S Wattel, France) *settled 4th: rdn but no ex in st: wnt 5th fnl 50yds* **13/2**

6 nk **Poet**[147] 7409 7-8-11 0 LukeMorris 6 100
(Clive Cox) *led for first 50yds: settled cl 2nd on outer: rdn early in st: no ex: styd on one pce fnl 1 1/2f: lost 5th fnl 50yds* **7/1**

2m 1.35s (-2.65) **6** Ran SP% **115.5**
WIN (incl. 1 euro stake): 5.20. PLACES: 2.10, 1.70. SF: 11.00..
Owner Haras De La Perelle **Bred** Haras De La Perelle **Trained** Chantilly, France

FOCUS
The form makes sense, rated around the runner-up.

NOTEBOOK
Giofra comprehensively outpointed her more experienced stablemate on only her fourth racecourse start, confirming the abundant promise she had shown on her final start last at three.
Vadamar(FR) stayed on well in second having been held up by Christophe Lemaire but could not get to his stablemate. He will step back up to 1m4f for his next start.
Poet helped set a generous pace alongside War Is War, but was unable to match strides with the closers on ground which had dried out beyond his optimum conditions.

1164 REDCAR (L-H)
Monday, April 9

OFFICIAL GOING: Good to soft (good in places; 6.8)
Wind: Moderate half behind Weather: Cloudy, drizzle from race 4 onwards

1246 MARKET CROSS JEWELLERS FILLIES' H'CAP 5f
2:00 (2:00) (Class 5) (0-75,72) 4-Y-0+ **£2,264** (£673; £336; £168) **Stalls** Centre

Form RPR
-013 **1** **Da'Quonde (IRE)**[45] 696 4-8-7 **58** TomEaves 10 69
(Bryan Smart) *prom: led 3f out: drvn appr fnl f: kpt on wl* **11/2**[3]
312- **2** 2 **Bailadeira**[133] 7566 4-8-7 **58** JamesSullivan 4 62
(Tim Etherington) *trckd ldrs: rdn over 2f out: kpt on but no ch w wnr* **8/1**
460- **3** shd **Red Roar (IRE)**[152] 7341 5-8-11 **65** BarryMcHugh(3) 9 69
(Alan Berry) *in tch: pushed along over 2f out: rdn over 1f out: kpt on* **8/1**
-450 **4** hd **Rio's Girl**[45] 691 5-7-13 **53** oh1 (bt) DominicFox(3) 8 56
(Tony Coyle) *prom: rdn over 2f out: kpt on one pce* **14/1**
20-0 **5** 3/4 **Shes Rosie**[20] 970 4-9-4 **69** RussKennemore 7 69
(John O'Shea) *sn pushed along and reminders towards rr: kpt on fnl f: nrst fin* **13/2**
161- **6** 1 **Song Of Parkes**[201] 6261 5-9-7 **72** DavidAllan 6 69
(Eric Alston) *dwlt: sn pushed along in rr: sme hdwy over 1f out: kpt on fnl f: nvr threatened ldrs* **7/2**[2]
312- **7** 3 3/4 **Mecca's Team**[267] 4124 4-9-0 **65** PaulMulrennan 1 48
(Michael Dods) *prom: pushed along and outpcd 1/2-way: wknd fnl f* **3/1**[1]
-000 **8** 1/2 **Fashion Icon (USA)**[13] 1054 6-7-13 **53** oh2 (b) DeclanCannon(3) 11 34
(David O'Meara) *chsd ldrs: wknd fnl f* **22/1**
050- **9** 1 1/4 **Nomoreblondes**[166] 7106 8-9-4 **69** (v) MickyFenton 3 46
(Paul Midgley) *led: hdd 3f out: sn rdn: wknd over 1f out* **12/1**
040/ **10** 16 **She Who Dares Wins**[696] 2087 12-8-2 **53** oh8 DuranFentiman 2
(Lee James) *sn pushed along to keep in tch: bhd over 2f out* **100/1**

59.87s (1.27) **Going Correction** +0.275s/f (Good) **10** Ran SP% **117.9**
Speed ratings (Par 100): **100,96,96,96,95 93,87,86,84,59**
toteswingers: 1&2 £6.00, 1&3 £10.50, 2&3 £17.90. CSF £49.59 CT £363.65 TOTE £7.30: £2.20, £3.00, £2.50; EX 37.10.
Owner The Barber Girls **Bred** Gestut Sohrenhof **Trained** Hambleton, N Yorks

FOCUS
After 40mm rain over the last seven days the ground was described as 'just on the easy side of good'. A modest fillies' sprint handicap and they raced in one group towards the centre. The runner-up is rated to her turf mark.
Song Of Parkes Official explanation: jockey said mare missed the break

1247 KELSEY ALDERSON DESIGNED TODAY'S RACECARD COVER H'CAP 2m 4y
2:35 (2:35) (Class 6) (0-65,64) 4-Y-0+ **£1,617** (£481; £240; £120) **Stalls** Low

Form RPR
100- **1** **Zefooha (FR)**[15] 7107 8-9-10 **62** (p) GrahamGibbons 9 73+
(Tim Walford) *trckd ldng pair: led on bit wl over 2f out: pushed arnd 4 l clr over 1f out: eased fnl f: readily* **4/1**[3]
/53- **2** 1 3/4 **Dan's Heir**[317] 2496 10-8-10 **51** DominicFox(3) 4 54
(Wilf Storey) *midfield: pushed along and hdwy on outer over 3f out: kpt on: wnt 2nd nr fin: no ch w wnr* **5/1**
14-3 **3** hd **River Dragon (IRE)**[13] 1057 7-9-12 **64** BarryMcHugh 7 67
(Tony Coyle) *w ldr: led narrowly over 4f out: hdd wl over 2f out: sn no ch w wnr: kpt on one pce: lost 2nd nr fin* **2/1**[1]
530- **4** 2 **Dechiper (IRE)**[11] 5790 10-8-9 **47** RobertWinston 10 48
(Robert Johnson) *in tch: rdn over 3f out: kpt on one pce* **14/1**
500- **5** 1 1/4 **Manager Mick (IRE)**[252] 4611 4-8-3 **45** PatrickMathers 6 44
(John Norton) *hld up: rdn over 4f out: no initial hdwy: kpt on over 1f out: nvr threatened ldrs* **25/1**
33/6 **6** 5 **Painted Sky**[59] 500 9-9-11 **63** PaddyAspell 8 56
(Donald McCain) *in tch: pushed along over 3f out: sn one pce: wknd over 1f out* **7/2**[2]
000- **7** 4 1/2 **I Got Music**[10] 7075 5-8-9 **47** (b) TomEaves 1 35
(Keith Reveley) *hld up in rr: pushed along over 5f out: nvr threatened* **12/1**
00-6 **8** 29 **Mystified (IRE)**[49] 632 9-8-7 **48** JulieBurke(3) 2
(Alan Berry) *led: rdn whn hdd over 4f out: sn wknd* **20/1**
000- **9** 8 **Carlton Mac**[21] 939 7-8-7 **45** (p) AdrianNicholls 5
(Simon Griffiths) *hld up: pushed along 10f out: bhd over 4f out* **33/1**

3m 41.15s (9.75) **Going Correction** +0.60s/f (Yiel)
WFA 4 from 5yo+ 4lb **9** Ran SP% **118.1**
Speed ratings (Par 101): **99,98,98,97,96 93,91,77,73**
toteswingers: 1&2 £4.30, 1&3 £3.60, 2&3 £3.30. CSF £24.31 CT £51.55 TOTE £4.50: £2.50, £2.50, £1.10; EX 23.10.
Owner Shaun Conway **Bred** Darley Stud Management Co Ltd **Trained** Sheriff Hutton, N Yorks

FOCUS
The two pacesetters took each other on from a long way out in this modest stayers' handicap. The runner-up is rated to last year's C&D form and the race may be worth a little more than face value.

1248 RACING UK ON SKY 432 (S) STKS 7f
3:10 (3:10) (Class 6) 3-Y-0+ **£1,617** (£481; £240; £120) **Stalls** Centre

Form RPR
2-36 **1** **Zomerlust**[55] 553 10-9-2 80 (v) MichaelO'Connell(3) 9 61
(John Quinn) *prom: led 4f out: rdn over 1f out: kpt on* **4/6**[1]
000- **2** 1 1/2 **Carnival Dream**[119] 7740 7-9-0 38 RussKennemore 8 52
(Hugh McWilliams) *chsd ldrs: rdn over 2f out: kpt on: nvr quite rch wnr* **66/1**
U-04 **3** 2 3/4 **Red Scintilla**[27] 886 5-8-11 53 (p) DeclanCannon(3) 11 45
(Nigel Tinkler) *midfield: pushed along and outpcd 4f out: hdwy 2f out: wnt 3rd jst ins fnl f: kpt on* **12/1**
465- **4** 2 1/4 **Rub Of The Relic (IRE)**[226] 5470 7-9-5 53 (v) BarryMcHugh 2 44
(Paul Midgley) *hld up in rr: pushed along over 4f out: bhd tl kpt on fr over 1f out: wnt 4th fnl 50yds* **12/1**
50-0 **5** 1 1/4 **Vintage Grape (IRE)**[45] 690 4-9-0 45 DavidAllan 12 35
(Eric Alston) *chsd ldrs: rdn over 3f out: one pce* **20/1**
-405 **6** 3/4 **Finefrenzyrolling (IRE)**[12] 1064 4-8-7 62 (b) LukeRowe(7) 3 33
(Mrs K Burke) *led: hdd 4f out: remained prom tl wknd fnl f* **9/2**[2]
344- **7** 1 1/4 **En Fuego**[191] 6536 5-9-5 50 PaulQuinn 10 35
(Geoffrey Harker) *hld up: pushed along over 4f out: nvr threatened* **9/1**[3]
0-0 **8** 4 **Pivotal Prospect**[90] 114 4-9-0 0 RoystonFfrench 1 19
(Tracy Waggott) *prom: rdn over 3f out: wknd over 1f out* **25/1**
000- **9** 1 1/4 **Illawalla**[129] 7610 4-9-2 35 GaryBartley(3) 6 21
(Hugh McWilliams) *hld up: nvr threatened* **100/1**
006/ **10** 24 **Labretella (IRE)**[15] 4707 5-9-0 38 (t) RobertWinston 4
(Robert Johnson) *midfield: pushed along over 4f out: sn wknd: eased over 1f out* **50/1**
500- **11** 22 **King Bertolini (IRE)**[178] 6834 5-8-12 42 MatthewHopkins(7) 5
(Alan Berry) *slowly away: sn pushed along in rr: a wl bhd* **66/1**
20-0 **12** 4 1/2 **Inde Country**[20] 979 4-9-0 48 (t) GrahamGibbons 7
(Nicky Vaughan) *hld up: pushed along over 4f out: sn btn: eased over 1f out* **28/1**

1m 27.41s (2.91) **Going Correction** +0.275s/f (Good) **12** Ran SP% **121.5**
Speed ratings (Par 101): **94,92,89,86,85 84,82,78,76,49 24,19**
toteswingers: 1&2 £16.00, 1&3 £3.20, 2&3 £54.50. CSF £92.83 TOTE £1.60: £1.10, £14.40, £2.10; EX 53.70.There was no bid for the winner.
Owner Mrs S Quinn **Bred** The Lavington Stud **Trained** Settrington, N Yorks
■ Stewards' Enquiry : Luke Rowe caution: failed to take all reasonable and permissable measures to obtain best possible placing.

FOCUS
Plenty of no-hopers in this selling race which on official figures was at the mercy of the odds-on favourite. The runner-up is rated to his est form of the past year.

1249 JOHN SMITH'S REDCAR STRAIGHT-MILE CHAMPIONSHIP (H'CAP) (QUALIFIER) 1m
3:45 (3:45) (Class 4) (0-85,85) 4-Y-0+ **£4,204** (£1,251; £625; £312) **Stalls** Centre

Form RPR
112- **1** **Abidhabidubai**[202] 6234 4-8-10 **74** TomEaves 2 82
(John Quinn) *hld up in tch: smooth hdwy over 2f out: rdn to ld appr fnl f: kpt on wl* **9/1**[3]
113- **2** 1 **Invincible Hero (IRE)**[205] 6173 5-9-0 **78** DanielTudhope 19 84
(Declan Carroll) *prom: led over 3f out: rdn over 2f out: hdd appr fnl f: kpt on* **5/1**[2]
100- **3** 3/4 **Blues Jazz**[173] 6949 6-8-11 **80** GarryWhillans(5) 6 84
(Ian Semple) *trckd ldrs: pushed along over 3f out: ev ch over 1f out: kpt on one pce* **16/1**
-260 **4** hd **Mullins Way (USA)**[9] 1128 4-9-5 **83** TonyCulhane 7 87
(Jo Hughes) *in tch: pushed along and outpcd over 3f out: hdwy over 1f out: kpt on fnl f* **14/1**
0-02 **5** 1 1/4 **Just Bond (IRE)**[45] 694 10-9-2 **83** DaleSwift(3) 12 84
(Geoffrey Oldroyd) *dwlt: hld up: briefly short of room 2f out: hdwy over 1f out: kpt on: nrst fin* **12/1**
420- **6** 1 1/4 **Dolphin Rock**[199] 6302 5-9-6 **84** LeeNewman 3 82
(David Barron) *trckd ldrs: rdn over 2f out: sn one pce* **9/2**[1]
0-35 **7** shd **Elijah Pepper (USA)**[67] 391 7-8-9 **73** GrahamGibbons 1 71
(David Barron) *dwlt: hld up: hdwy into midfield over 2f out: sn rdn: kpt on fnl f: nt rch ldrs* **12/1**
06-0 **8** 3/4 **Collateral Damage (IRE)**[8] 1161 9-9-0 **78** (t) DavidAllan 4 74
(Tim Easterby) *hld up in midfield: rdn over 2f out: sme hdwy over 1f out: one pce fnl f* **9/1**[3]
1150 **9** 1 1/2 **Aquarian Spirit**[46] 674 5-8-13 **77** TonyHamilton 10 70
(Richard Fahey) *chsd ldrs: rdn over 2f out: wknd ins fnl f* **12/1**
010- **10** 1 1/4 **European Dream (IRE)**[16] 7558 9-9-1 **82** (p) RobertLButler(3) 20 72
(Richard Guest) *s.i.s: hld up in rr: pushed along over 3f out: nvr threatened* **20/1**
04-6 **11** 1/2 **Moheebb (IRE)**[13] 1052 8-9-0 **78** (b) PJMcDonald 9 67
(Ruth Carr) *midfield: rdn over 3f out: nvr threatened* **14/1**
203- **12** 5 **Fazza**[178] 6831 5-8-11 **75** PaulMulrennan 17 52
(Edwin Tuer) *chsd ldrs: rdn over 2f out: wknd over 1f out* **14/1**
0-00 **13** 5 **Pat's Legacy (USA)**[9] 1128 6-9-0 **85** (t) JoshBaudains(7) 15 51
(Jo Hughes) *midfield: rdn over 3f out: wknd over 1f out* **16/1**
000- **14** 2 1/4 **Quite Sparky**[218] 5757 5-9-4 **82** JamesSullivan 18 42
(Mike Sowersby) *hld up: a towards rr* **50/1**
500- **15** 23 **File And Paint (IRE)**[191] 6533 4-8-10 **74** ow1 NeilCallan 16
(Lawrence Mullaney) *midfield: rdn over 3f out: sn wknd: eased* **16/1**
16-0 **16** 6 **Dubai Bay (FR)**[25] 907 4-8-7 **71** RussKennemore 8
(Paul Midgley) *led: hdd over 3f out: sn wknd* **28/1**
610- **17** 25 **Lady Sledmere (IRE)**[202] 6234 4-8-8 **72** MickyFenton 14
(Paul Midgley) *midfield: wknd qckly over 3f out: eased* **28/1**

1m 40.36s (2.36) **Going Correction** +0.275s/f (Good) **17** Ran SP% **129.2**
Speed ratings (Par 105): **99,98,97,97,95 94,94,93,92,90 90,85,80,78,55 49,24**
toteswingers: 1&2 £3.90, 1&3 £34.70, 2&3 £23.30. CSF £54.12 CT £765.97 TOTE £9.90: £2.00, £1.10, £6.20, £4.60; EX 64.40.
Owner Nigel S Cooper **Bred** Brightwalton Stud **Trained** Settrington, N Yorks

FOCUS
A competitive qualifier for Redcar's straight mile championship final in October. Again they raced in one group towards the centre of the track. The first two showed improvement with the third and fourth setting the level.
Dubai Bay(FR) Official explanation: jockey said filly lost its action
Lady Sledmere(IRE) Official explanation: trainer said filly had a breathing problem

1250 WIN A VIP DAY OUT @ REDCARRACING.CO.UK MAIDEN STKS 1m 1f
4:20 (4:23) (Class 5) 3-Y-0+ **£2,264** (£673; £336; £168) **Stalls** Low

Form RPR
3- **1** **Cameron Highland (IRE)**[166] 7109 3-8-11 0 NeilCallan 4 91+
(Roger Varian) *t.k.h early: trckd ldr: led over 6f out: clr on bit 3f out: pushed out fnl f: easily* **6/5**[1]
0- **2** 8 **Sunpass**[159] 7232 3-8-11 0 MarcHalford 10 71+
(John Gosden) *t.k.h early: hld up: pushed along and stdy hdwy fr over 3f out: angled towards outer 2f out: wnt 2nd appr fnl f: kpt on: no ch w wnr* **13/2**[3]
04 **3** 2 **Dropzone (USA)**[18] 1001 3-8-11 0 AndreaAtzeni 1 66
(Marco Botti) *trckd ldrs: rdn over 3f out: kpt on one pce* **11/1**

	4	2	**Border Bandit (USA)**[162] 4-10-0 0 .... PatrickMathers 6 (Tracy Waggott) *s.i.s: sn midfield: pushed along and hdwy over 3f out: kpt on: wnt 4th post* **100/1**	66
5-	5	shd	**Daliance (IRE)**[252] 4624 3-8-11 0 .... RichardKingscote 13 (Tom Dascombe) *in tch: pushed along and hdwy to chse ldr over 2f out: wknd ins fnl f* **2/1**[2]	62
2-	6	7	**Cosmic Halo**[244] 4875 3-8-6 0 .... BarryMcHugh 14 (Richard Fahey) *in tch: rdn over 3f out: wknd over 2f out* **14/1**	41
	7	9	**Bollin Nancy** 3-8-6 0 .... DuranFentiman 11 (Tim Easterby) *hld up: pushed along over 4f out: sme late hdwy: nvr threatened* **50/1**	22
	8	1 1/4	**Hulwa (USA)** 3-8-6 0 .... RoystonFfrench 5 (Tracy Waggott) *midfield: wknd over 3f out* **100/1**	19
0/6	9	1 1/4	**Marster Parkes**[30] 869 4-10-0 0 .... TomEaves 9 (John Quinn) *racd keenly in tch: rdn over 3f out: wknd over 1f out* **40/1**	25
	10	3	**Under Par** 4-9-2 0 .... DavidSimmonson(7) 8 (Michael Easterby) *midfield: wknd over 4f out* **66/1**	13
40	11	5	**Kata Rock (USA)**[25] 908 5-10-0 0 .... PaddyAspell 3 (Brian Rothwell) *led: hdd over 6f out: wknd over 3f out* **66/1**	
0-	12	9	**Actor (IRE)**[173] 6954 3-8-11 0 .... JamesSullivan 2 (John Weymes) *dwlt: hld up: a towards rr* **66/1**	
0-	13	9	**Cara's Delight (AUS)**[168] 7063 5-9-9 0 .... LeeNewman 7 (Frederick Watson) *midfield: rdn over 5f out: wknd over 3f out* **200/1**	
0R	14	7	**Idarose (IRE)**[42] 724 3-8-8 0 ow2 .... RussKennemore 12 (Hugh McWilliams) *hld up: a bhd* **200/1**	

1m 57.72s (4.72) **Going Correction** +0.60s/f (Yiel)
WFA 3 from 4yo+ 17lb **14** Ran SP% **119.0**
Speed ratings (Par 103): **103,95,94,92,92 86,78,76,75,73 68,60,52,46**
toteswingers: 1&2 £2.70, 1&3 £3.10, 2&3 £4.80. CSF £9.81 TOTE £2.10: £1.30, £1.30, £2.40; EX 10.30.
Owner H R H Sultan Ahmad Shah **Bred** Epona Bloodstock Ltd **Trained** Newmarket, Suffolk

FOCUS
Steady rain was starting to get into the ground ahead of this maiden in which only five could be seriously fancied beforehand. The level is fluid with the third rated 6lb off his latest mark.

1251 BUY YOUR TICKETS ON-LINE @ REDCARRACING.CO.UK H'CAP 7f
4:55 (4:55) (Class 5) (0-70,68) 4-Y-O+ £2,264 (£673; £336; £168) **Stalls** Centre

Form				RPR
632-	1		**Le Chat D'Or**[178] 6840 4-9-1 62 .... (t) PaulMulrennan 7 (Michael Dods) *trckd ldrs: pushed along 3f out: rdn to ld appr fnl f: kpt on wl* **4/1**[1]	73+
000-	2	1 1/4	**Broctune Papa Gio**[181] 6777 5-8-12 62 .... DeclanCannon(3) 10 (Keith Reveley) *in tch: rdn and hdwy to ld narrowly wl over 1f out: hdd appr fnl f: kpt on but a hld by wnr* **9/1**	70
336-	3	2	**Free Art**[204] 6192 4-9-6 67 .... RobertWinston 3 (Geoffrey Harker) *hld up in midfield: pushed along over 3f out: hdwy over 1f out: wnt 3rd jst ins fnl f: kpt on* **12/1**	69
562-	4	1 3/4	**Hayek**[168] 7057 5-8-10 62 .... (b) AdamCarter(5) 6 (Tim Easterby) *hld up: pushed along over 3f out: hdwy over 1f out: kpt on* **11/1**	60
000-	5	1	**Maggie Mey (IRE)**[170] 7024 4-9-7 68 .... MickyFenton 1 (Paul Midgley) *led: rdn whn hdd wl over 1f out: wknd ins fnl f* **8/1**	63
233-	6	3 1/2	**Petsas Pleasure**[166] 7112 6-9-3 64 .... PJMcDonald 4 (Ollie Pears) *hld up in rr: sme late hdwy: nvr threatened ldrs* **5/1**[3]	49
1231	7	3 1/2	**Caledonia Prince**[13] 1052 4-8-3 57 .... (p) JoshBaudains(7) 12 (Jo Hughes) *midfield: hdwy to chse ldrs over 2f out: wknd over 1f out* **9/2**[2]	33
201-	8	4 1/2	**Hoppy's Flyer (FR)**[168] 7063 4-9-5 66 .... RussKennemore 8 (Paul Midgley) *racd keenly in tch: wknd 2f out* **16/1**	30
5250	9	1/2	**Dunmore Boy (IRE)**[40] 735 4-9-2 63 .... TonyHamilton 2 (Richard Fahey) *chsd ldrs: wknd over 2f out* **16/1**	25
000-	10	hd	**Fama Mac**[168] 7063 5-8-7 54 oh6 .... JamesSullivan 9 (Neville Bycroft) *prom: rdn over 3f out: sn edgd lft: wknd over 1f out: eased ins fnl f* **16/1**	
300-	11	11	**Media Stars**[178] 6833 7-8-8 55 .... TomEaves 5 (Robert Johnson) *hld up: a towards rr* **40/1**	
412-	12	34	**Whispered Times (USA)**[194] 6453 5-9-7 68 .... PatrickMathers 11 (Tracy Waggott) *v.s.a: a wl bhd* **16/1**	

1m 28.13s (3.63) **Going Correction** +0.275s/f (Good) **12** Ran SP% **118.0**
Speed ratings (Par 103): **90,88,86,84,83 79,75,70,69,69 56,17**
toteswingers: 1&2 £9.40, 1&3 £9.20, 2&3 £24.60. CSF £39.94 CT £407.16 TOTE £4.40: £1.80, £2.60, £4.00; EX 48.00.
Owner Calum Stewart Anne Gillespie **Bred** Dr A Gillespie **Trained** Denton, Co Durham

FOCUS
The rain was persisting and conditions looked to be bordering on soft in this modest handicap. The winner is rated in line with last year's C&D form.
Caledonia Prince Official explanation: jockey said gelding missed the break

1252 FOLLOW REDCARRACING ON FACEBOOK & TWITTER H'CAP 5f
5:30 (5:32) (Class 6) (0-65,64) 3-Y-O £1,617 (£481; £240; £120) **Stalls** Centre

Form				RPR
4-02	1		**Towbee**[25] 905 3-9-3 60 .... (b) JamesSullivan 2 (Michael Easterby) *in tch: led on bit 2f out: pushed clr appr fnl f: kpt on wl* **3/1**[2]	71
04-4	2	2	**Phoenix Clubs (IRE)**[26] 898 3-9-7 64 .... BarryMcHugh 1 (Paul Midgley) *hld up: pushed along 1/2-way: hdwy over 1f out: briefly short of room appr fnl f: kpt on wl: wnt 2nd fnl 50yds* **9/1**	68+
564	3	1 1/4	**Miserere Mei (IRE)**[25] 905 3-8-7 53 .... (p) DeclanCannon(3) 11 (Richard Guest) *in tch: rdn 1/2-way: hdwy to chse wnr over 1f out: kpt on one pce: lost 2nd fnl 50yds* **20/1**	52
0-40	4	2 1/2	**Pressure Drop (IRE)**[38] 769 3-9-5 62 .... TonyCulhane 10 (Jo Hughes) *led: rdn whn hdd 2f out: no ex fnl f* **14/1**	52
1-	5	nse	**Dancheur (IRE)**[180] 6800 3-9-3 63 .... MichaelMetcalfe(3) 7 (Mrs K Burke) *s.i.s: hld up: pushed along 1/2-way: kpt on one pce: nvr threatened ldrs* **11/8**[1]	53+
300-	6	3/4	**Made In The Shade**[168] 7059 3-8-10 53 .... MickyFenton 4 (Paul Midgley) *chsd ldr: rdn 2f out: sn no imp* **16/1**	40
104-	7	nk	**Elusive Bonus (IRE)**[188] 6597 3-9-0 57 .... DanielTudhope 3 (David O'Meara) *chsd ldr: rdn 2f out: sn no imp* **9/2**[3]	43
5406	8	7	**Essexvale (IRE)**[11] 1090 3-8-0 50 oh1 .... (b) MatthewHopkins(7) 9 (Alan Berry) *hld up: rdn 1/2-way: nvr on terms* **66/1**	11
306-	9	7	**Hopes Rebellion**[268] 4079 3-8-6 56 .... (v[1]) JasonHart(7) 8 (Declan Carroll) *prom: pushed along and lost pl 1/2-way: wknd over 1f out* **14/1**	

1m 0.35s (1.75) **Going Correction** +0.275s/f (Good) **9** Ran SP% **120.8**
Speed ratings (Par 96): **97,93,91,87,87 86,86,74,63**
toteswingers: 1&2 £4.00, 1&3 £6.00, 2&3 £8.30. CSF £31.87 CT £475.58 TOTE £4.60: £1.60, £1.50, £4.30; EX 28.10.
Owner Mrs A Jarvis **Bred** Mrs A Jarvis **Trained** Sheriff Hutton, N Yorks
■ Stewards' Enquiry : Jason Hart five-day ban: used whip above shoulder height without giving gelding time to respond (Apr 23-27)

FOCUS
A low-grade 3-y-o sprint handicap. The runner-up is possibly better than the bare form with the third to her AW mark.
Hopes Rebellion Official explanation: trainer said gelding was unsuited by the good to soft (soft in places) ground
T/Jkpt: £5,555.50 to a £1 stake. Pool: £25,000. 4.50 winning tickets. T/Plt: £34.40 to a £1 stake. Pool: £51,496.65. 1,091.46 winning tickets. T/Qpdt: £5.30 to a £1 stake. Pool: £3,017.03. 417.83 winning tickets. AS

WARWICK (L-H)
Monday, April 9

OFFICIAL GOING: Good to soft changing to soft (good to soft in places) after race 2 (2.45) changing to soft after race 5 (4.30)
Wind: Fresh, behind Weather: Wet

1253 CALL STAR SPORTS ON 0800 521 321 (S) STKS 5f
2:10 (2:10) (Class 6) 2-Y-O £1,617 (£481; £240; £120) **Stalls** Low

Form				RPR
1	1		**Severn Bore**[7] 1165 2-8-9 0 .... DarrenEgan(7) 1 (Bill Turner) *mde all: rdn 2f out: r.o wl and edgd lft ins fnl f: wl in command whn wnt rt fnl strides* **5/2**[2]	65
5	2	3	**Shop Til You Drop**[5] 1188 2-8-6 0 .... RichardThomas 5 (David Evans) *wnt rt s: chsd ldrs: rdn and nt qckn 2f out: kpt on for press to take 2nd wl ins fnl f: no imp on wnr* **8/1**	44
2	3	1	**Suivez L'Argent**[7] 1165 2-8-3 0 .... HarryBentley(3) 2 (Joseph Tuite) *w wnr tl rdn 2f out: lost 2nd and faltered wl ins fnl f: styd on same pce towards fin* **9/4**[1]	41
	4	nk	**Black Eider** 2-8-6 0 .... CathyGannon 6 (John Spearing) *wnt rt s and s.i.s: hld up: hdwy 2f out: edgd rt whn chalng for pls over 1f out: kpt on same pce wl ins fnl f* **9/1**	40
	5	2 1/2	**Silicon Valley** 2-8-6 0 .... JohnFahy 7 (Dominic Ffrench Davis) *wnt rt s and s.i.s: towards rr: pushed along 1/2-way: sn outpcd: kpt on steadily wl ins fnl f: nt pce to get competitive* **33/1**	31
04	6	2	**Relay**[4] 1202 2-8-6 0 .... KieranO'Neill 4 (Richard Hannon) *chsd ldrs: rdn 2f out: sn edgd lft: j. path over 1f out: wknd fnl f* **4/1**[3]	23
6	7	7	**Missing Agent**[4] 1202 2-8-11 0 .... PadraigBeggy 3 (David Evans) *dwlt: a outpcd and bhd* **16/1**	3

1m 3.75s (4.15) **Going Correction** +0.60s/f (Yiel) **7** Ran SP% **109.3**
Speed ratings (Par 90): **90,85,83,83,79 75,64**
toteswingers: 1&2 £5.50, 1&3 £1.20, 2&3 £3.80 CSF £20.34 TOTE £2.70: £1.30, £6.20; EX 21.40.The winner was bought in for 5,800gns.
Owner Richard Jeffrey **Bred** T M M Partnership **Trained** Sigwells, Somerset

FOCUS
A modest seller to start the card with five of the seven runners having previous racecourse experience but the form is very moderate. Even allowing for the type of race, the winning time was still slow, which suggests the going was testing.

NOTEBOOK
Severn Bore was penalised for beating Suivez L'Argent in a similar event at Redcar seven days earlier (third horse has won since), but despite hanging away to his left late on he gained a more emphatic success here. His trainer was of the opinion that the easier ground was the reason for that, but having won two sellers he will have to be stepped up in class now. He was retained for 5,800gns at the auction.
Shop Til You Drop finished a well-beaten fifth of seven in a Wolverhampton maiden five days earlier, but despite the drop in grade this was probably a step forward. She should be able to win a seller. (op 15-2 tchd 7-1)
Suivez L'Argent was beaten less than a length by Severn Bore at Redcar and had a 5lb pull, but despite holding every chance she was comfortably held late on. Perhaps the easier ground wasn't in her favour.
Black Eider, an 800gns half-sister to a 1m3f selling winner, missed the break but then travelled well off the pace and there was a modicum of promise in this effort. A bit further wouldn't come amiss in due course. (op 10-1 tchd 12-1)

1254 STARSPORTSBET.CO.UK H'CAP 6f
2:45 (2:46) (Class 5) (0-75,75) 4-Y-O+ £2,264 (£673; £336; £168) **Stalls** Low

Form				RPR
000-	1		**Divine Call**[193] 6478 5-9-4 72 .... MartinLane 4 (Milton Bradley) *mde all: edgd rt fr 2f out: rdn over 1f out: r.o: in command towards fin* **16/1**	85
0-41	2	1	**My Kingdom (IRE)**[18] 997 6-9-7 75 .... (t) JimmyFortune 16 (Ian Williams) *hld up: hdwy under 2f out: chsd wnr fnl f: styd on: hld towards fin* **6/1**[2]	85+
1604	3	1 1/2	**Nubar Boy**[17] 1007 5-8-12 71 .... (v) MatthewCosham(5) 2 (David Evans) *midfield: hdwy 2f out: rdn and tried to chal over 1f out: nt qckn ins fnl f: styd on but nt pce of front 2 after* **20/1**	76
141-	4	1/2	**Paradise Spectre**[187] 6634 5-9-2 73 .... HarryBentley(3) 13 (Mrs K Burke) *in rr div early: hdwy into midfield 1/2-way: rdn 2f out: hdwy to chse ldrs over 1f out: kpt on ins fnl f* **8/1**[3]	76
0425	5	1 3/4	**Whipphound**[10] 1116 4-8-11 65 .... (p) ShaneKelly 10 (Mark Brisbourne) *midfield: hdwy 1/2-way: rdn 2f out: styd on same pce ins fnl f* **20/1**	63
4023	6	3 1/4	**Italian Tom (IRE)**[26] 896 5-8-13 74 .... DarrenEgan(7) 7 (Ronald Harris) *dwlt: sn chsd ldrs: pushed along over 2f out: kpt on same pce fnl f* **14/1**	61
5131	7	nk	**Strictly Pink (IRE)**[14] 1049 4-8-11 65 .... CathyGannon 9 (Alan Bailey) *chsd ldrs: rdn 2f out: one pce fnl f* **6/1**[2]	51
3140	8	5	**Diamond Vine (IRE)**[5] 1187 4-9-3 71 .... (p) KierenFallon 14 (Ronald Harris) *in rr div: sn niggled along: rdn and hdwy 2f out: no imp over 1f out: eased whn btn ins fnl f* **18/1**	41
330-	9	2 1/2	**Northern Bolt**[181] 6778 7-8-13 67 .... PadraigBeggy 6 (Ian McInnes) *edgy in stalls: towards rr: kpt on ins fnl f: nt pce to trble ldrs* **11/1**	29

402- **10** 2 **Brave Dream**[187] 6634 4-8-11 **65** PhillipMakin 11 21
(Kevin Ryan) *in tch: lost pl 1/2-way: outpcd after* **16/1**
6000 **11** 1 ¾ **Sermons Mount (USA)**[14] 1050 6-8-13 **67** JohnFahy 5 17
(Paul Howling) *w wnr tl over 2f out: sn rdn: wknd over 1f out* **25/1**
533- **12** hd **Mon Visage**[224] 5542 4-9-5 **73** TedDurcan 3 23
(Chris Wall) *midfield: effrt on inner over 2f out: wknd over 1f out* **5/1**[1]
1060 **13** ½ **Pick A Little**[10] 1117 4-9-0 **71** RyanClark(3) 15 19
(Michael Blake) *in rr: pushed along after 2f: nvr on terms* **16/1**
635- **14** 1 **Volito**[163] 7172 6-8-11 **65** SamHitchcott 1 10
(Anabel K Murphy) *s.s and wnt rt s: in rr: pushed along after 2f: nvr able to trble ldrs* **40/1**
-012 **15** 7 **Sole Danser (IRE)**[58] 522 4-9-5 **73** LiamKeniry 12
(Milton Bradley) *in tch on outer: rdn over 2f out: sn wknd* **10/1**
455- **16** 2 **Bermondsey Bob (IRE)**[182] 6752 6-8-11 **65** WilliamCarson 8
(John Spearing) *dwlt: sn prom: rdn over 2f out: sn wknd* **25/1**

1m 14.92s (3.12) **Going Correction** +0.60s/f (Yiel) **16** Ran SP% **123.0**
Speed ratings (Par 103): **103,101,99,99,96 92,91,85,81,79 76,76,76,74,65 62**
toteswingers: 1&2 £21.90, 1&3 £32.30, 2&3 £74.90 CSF £102.37 CT £2045.65 TOTE £27.20: £5.70, £1.70, £5.70, £3.20; EX 165.50 TRIFECTA Not won..
Owner E A Hayward **Bred** Cheveley Park Stud Ltd **Trained** Sedbury, Gloucs

FOCUS
A modest if competitive sprint handicap. The draw didn't seem make much difference with the main action unfolding towards the nearside rail. The third is rated to his old turf form.
Pick A Little Official explanation: trainer said, gelding was unsuited by the good to soft ground.
Volito Official explanation: jockey said gelding was slowly away

1255 FOLLOW US ON TWITTER @STARSPORTS_BET CONDITIONS STKS 6f
3:20 (3:20) (Class 3) 4-Y-0+ **£6,663** (£1,982; £990; £495) **Stalls** Low

Form RPR
603- **1** **New Planet (IRE)**[254] 4526 4-8-8 100 TomQueally 3 100
(John Quinn) *chsd ldr: led over 1f out: edgd rt ins fnl f and rdn clr: r.o wl* **9/4**[2]
660- **2** 2 ¾ **Bathwick Bear (IRE)**[170] 7018 4-8-8 88 PadraigBeggy 4 91
(David Evans) *led: rdn and hdd over 1f out: wl hld by wnr ins fnl f* **9/1**
405- **3** nk **Mac's Power (IRE)**[171] 6987 6-8-8 100 (t[1]) KierenFallon 1 90
(James Fanshawe) *hld up in rr: effrt to chse ldrs over 1f out: kpt on to chal for 2nd ins fnl f but no imp on wnr* **11/10**[1]
40-1 **4** 3 ¾ **Another Try (IRE)**[17] 1007 7-8-8 83 DavidProbert 2 78
(Alan Jarvis) *racd keenly: chsd ldrs tl rdn and wknd over 1f out* **18/1**
3116 **5** 10 **Woolfall Sovereign (IRE)**[30] 871 6-8-8 87 JoeFanning 6 46
(George Margarson) *hld up: pushed along 2f out: toiling fnl f* **6/1**[3]

1m 14.81s (3.01) **Going Correction** +0.75s/f (Yiel) **5** Ran SP% **107.9**
Speed ratings (Par 107): **109,105,104,99,86**
toteswingers: 1&2 £14.10 CSF £19.52 TOTE £3.30: £2.00, £4.10; EX 20.00.
Owner Ross Harmon **Bred** Mrs Diane Williams **Trained** Settrington, N Yorks

FOCUS
Again the runners gradually migrated towards the nearside rail in the straight. For the third race in a row, it paid to race at the sharp end and the first two held those positions throughout. The form is rated around the first two.

NOTEBOOK
New Planet(IRE) ◆, gelded since last seen nine months earlier, travelled well behind the leader and found plenty when asked to go and win his race. It will be interesting to see what the handicapper does with him, but this was only his eighth start and he could well be a Group-class sprinter in the making. (tchd 2-1 and 5-2)
Bathwick Bear(IRE) appeared to run a blinder here as he split two horses rated 12lb above him, but he was undoubtedly helped by being out in front and is now on a losing run of 20. (op 10-1 tchd 11-1)
Mac's Power(IRE), third in last season's Stewards' Cup amongst other smart efforts in defeat, had a first-time hood alongside the usual tongue-tie for this reappearance. He appeared to disappoint, but he was keen enough at the back of the field early and will be much happier back in bigger fields in strongly run handicaps. (tchd 11-8 in a place)
Another Try(IRE) made a successful reappearance on Polytrack last month, but had a lot to do on these terms and was well held. (op 14-1 tchd 20-1)
Woolfall Sovereign(IRE) was having only his fourth start on turf having been in good form on the AW since last on grass. He too had bit to find at the weights, but still ran poorly. (op 11-2 tchd 9-2)

1256 CALL 08000 521321 FOR ALL AINTREE PRICES MAIDEN STKS (DIV I) 7f 26y
3:55 (3:56) (Class 5) 3-Y-0 **£2,264** (£673; £336; £168) **Stalls** Low

Form RPR
5- **1** **Flexible Flyer**[182] 6751 3-9-3 0 DarryllHolland 8 77
(Hughie Morrison) *hld up: shkn up 1/2-way: hdwy over 2f out: sn chsd ldr: r.o to ld fnl 110yds: pushed out* **4/1**[2]
0-2 **2** 1 ¼ **Willies Wonder (IRE)**[20] 969 3-9-3 0 MichaelHills 4 74
(Charles Hills) *racd keenly: led: brought wd ent st over 2f out: rdn over 1f out: hdd fnl 110yds: hld towards fin* **11/10**[1]
3 3 ¼ **Charles Tyrwhitt** 3-9-3 0 KierenFallon 11 65
(George Baker) *in tch: effrt 2f out: nt qckn over 1f out: kpt on same pce and n.d to front 2 ins fnl f* **12/1**
4 ¾ **Black Mascara (IRE)** 3-8-12 0 PatDobbs 10 58
(Richard Hannon) *bhd: rdn and hdwy 2f out: kpt on same pce and no imp fr over 1f out* **12/1**
0- **5** 2 ½ **Clowance Keys**[288] 3424 3-9-3 0 JamesMillman 5 56
(Rod Millman) *in tch: rdn over 1f out and edgd lft: one pce* **33/1**
0- **6** 3 ½ **Looks Like Rain**[269] 4061 3-8-12 0 HayleyTurner 3 42
(Michael Bell) *chsd ldr to 1/2-way: wknd 2f out* **16/1**
6- **7** 1 ¼ **Royal Dutch**[145] 7431 3-9-3 0 CathyGannon 2 43
(Denis Coakley) *hld up: pushed along 2f out: nvr a threat* **7/1**[3]
00- **8** 3 ¼ **Silence Is Easy**[151] 7344 3-8-12 0 MartinDwyer 7 29
(William Muir) *racd keenly: prom: rdn 2f out: wknd over 1f out* **12/1**
9 33 **Seventeen Seventy** 3-8-10 0 JordanTaylor(7) 6
(Alan Coogan) *a bhd: t.o after 3f: eased whn wl btn fnl f* **100/1**
0-06 **10** 5 **Symphony Of Space**[66] 404 3-8-12 40 ShaneKelly 9
(Alan McCabe) *chsd ldrs: wknd 1/2-way: eased whn wl btn over 1f out: t.o* **100/1**

1m 29.44s (4.84) **Going Correction** +0.85s/f (Soft) **10** Ran SP% **114.0**
Speed ratings (Par 98): **106,104,100,100,97 93,91,88,50,44**
toteswingers: 1&2 £1.80, 1&3 £8.20, 2&3 £4.20 CSF £8.46 TOTE £5.70: £1.90, £1.10, £1.90; EX 12.00 Trifecta £92.50 Pool £654.42 - 5.23 winning units..
Owner A J Struthers, J F Dean & Mrs J Scott **Bred** Glebe Stud **Trained** East Ilsley, Berks

FOCUS
This was a modest maiden, though there's probably more to come from the winner. The form is a bit fluid with little to go on.
Symphony Of Space Official explanation: trainer said filly was unsuited by the soft (good to soft in places) ground

1257 CALL 08000 521321 FOR ALL AINTREE PRICES MAIDEN STKS (DIV II) 7f 26y
4:30 (4:31) (Class 5) 3-Y-0 **£2,264** (£673; £336; £168) **Stalls** Low

Form RPR
022- **1** **Verse Of Love**[207] 6102 3-9-3 71 CathyGannon 3 79
(David Evans) *mde all: rdn over 1f out: r.o: edgd lft towards fin and a doing enough whn pressed* **6/1**
-3 **2** ½ **Valley Of Destiny**[16] 1036 3-9-3 0 KieranO'Neill 2 78
(Richard Hannon) *trckd ldrs: rdn over 1f out: tk 2nd wl ins fnl f: pressed wnr towards fin: styd on but hld* **4/1**[2]
03- **3** 5 **Stepturn**[241] 5017 3-9-3 0 DaneO'Neill 4 65
(George Baker) *w wnr: rdn and stl ev ch over 1f out: nt qckn ins fnl f: lost 2nd: no ex fnl 100yds* **28/1**
440- **4** 2 ¼ **Engrossing**[143] 7454 3-9-3 79 NickyMackay 7 58
(David Elsworth) *trckd ldrs: rdn over 1f out: one pce* **7/1**
22- **5** nk **Discression**[275] 3878 3-9-3 0 PhillipMakin 10 58
(Kevin Ryan) *midfield: pushed along over 2f out: sn outpcd: no imp after* **11/8**[1]
6 2 ½ **Pursue** 3-9-3 0 LiamJones 6 51
(William Haggas) *midfield: rdn 3f out: sn outpcd* **5/1**[3]
7 5 **Outside Art** 3-8-7 0 JamesRogers(5) 9 32
(Gary Harrison) *hld up: pushed along 4f out: kpt on whn running green over 1f out: nvr able to trble ldrs* **66/1**
0- **8** 6 **Absolutely Me (IRE)**[170] 7025 3-8-12 0 LiamKeniry 1 16
(Dominic Ffrench Davis) *midfield: rdn 2f out: wknd over 1f out* **80/1**
9 1 **Sushi** 3-8-12 0 TedDurcan 8 13
(Rae Guest) *hld up: pushed along over 2f out: nvr on terms* **16/1**
10 7 **Buds Bruvver** 3-9-3 0 AdamKirby 11
(Brian Baugh) *a bhd: nvr on terms* **66/1**
0 **11** 7 **Roundelay**[75] 291 3-8-12 0 WilliamCarson 5
(Anthony Carson) *a bhd: edgd lft whn n.d over 1f out* **100/1**

1m 29.87s (5.27) **Going Correction** +0.85s/f (Soft) **11** Ran SP% **120.1**
Speed ratings (Par 98): **103,102,96,94,93 90,85,78,77,69 61**
toteswingers: 1&2 £4.30, 1&3 £13.30, 2&3 £10.80 CSF £30.56 TOTE £7.70: £2.80, £2.60, £5.00; EX 38.00 Trifecta £325.80 Pool £678.20 - 1.54 winning units..
Owner Bathwick Gold Partnership **Bred** Mrs S Clifford **Trained** Pandy, Monmouths

FOCUS
Normal service was resumed with those that raced up with the pace holding a significant advantage. The winning time was 0.43 seconds slower than the first division. The runner-up is to his debut form although the fourth and fifth were both disappointing.
Outside Art Official explanation: vet said filly lost a near-fore shoe

1258 ANY AINTREE HORSE TO WIN £50,000 H'CAP 1m 2f 188y
5:05 (5:08) (Class 4) (0-85,85) 4-Y-0+ **£4,075** (£1,212; £606; £303) **Stalls** Low

Form RPR
260- **1** **Miss Aix**[139] 7510 4-9-1 **79** HayleyTurner 8 86
(Michael Bell) *prom: brought wd ent st over 2f out: led under 2f out: sn rdn: r.o wl and in control towards fin* **7/2**[2]
5532 **2** 2 ¾ **Follow The Flag (IRE)**[9] 1135 8-8-7 **71** (be) ShaneKelly 1 73
(Alan McCabe) *a.p: rdn 3f out: wnt 2nd wl over 1f out: sn edgd rt: ev ch ent fnl f: no ex fnl 75yds* **8/1**
000- **3** 1 ¾ **Ingleby Spirit**[24] 6163 5-9-4 **85** LeeTopliss(3) 12 84
(Richard Fahey) *hld up: rdn and outpcd over 3f out: prog over 1f out: styd on ins fnl f: nt pce to trble front 2* **4/1**[3]
00-0 **4** 1 ½ **Yes Chef**[20] 971 5-8-12 **76** JamesMillman 3 72
(Rod Millman) *led: rdn over 2f out: hdd under 2f out: one pce fr over 1f out* **14/1**
265- **5** ½ **Anton Dolin (IRE)**[179] 6822 4-9-3 **81** TedDurcan 7 76
(John Dunlop) *midfield: hdwy 5f out: effrt to chse ldrs over 2f out: one pce fnl f* **9/1**
100- **6** 2 **Carter**[220] 5685 6-8-10 **77** RyanClark(3) 9 69
(Ian Williams) *hld up: rdn 2f out: kpt on over 1f out: no imp on ldrs* **25/1**
6-64 **7** 10 **Brouhaha**[39] 745 8-8-9 **76** HarryBentley(3) 2 50
(Tom Dascombe) *midfield: rdn over 2f out: wknd over 1f out* **18/1**
21-5 **8** 20 **Refractor (IRE)**[85] 187 4-8-11 **75** MartinLane 13
(James Fanshawe) *plld hrd: hld up: rdn 2f out: nvr a threat* **11/2**
10-0 **9** 7 **Landaman (IRE)**[9] 1133 4-9-2 **80** JoeFanning 5
(Mark Johnston) *plld hrd: hld up: rdn 3f out: wknd over 2f out* **3/1**[1]

2m 30.35s (9.25) **Going Correction** +0.975s/f (Soft) **9** Ran SP% **119.5**
Speed ratings (Par 105): **105,103,101,100,100 98,91,77,71**
toteswingers: 1&2 £7.70, 1&3 £3.00, 2&3 £7.20 CSF £32.91 CT £118.81 TOTE £5.00: £1.90, £2.10, £2.20; EX 48.50 Trifecta £311.60 Part won. Pool £421.09 - 0.40 winning units..
Owner J L C Pearce **Bred** J L C Pearce **Trained** Newmarket, Suffolk
■ Stewards' Enquiry : Shane Kelly two-day ban: used whip above permitted level (Apr 23-24)

FOCUS
This was a fair handicap and again you needed to be prominent. The runner-up confirmed his latest Doncaster form.

1259 VISIT STARSPORTSBET.CO.UK FOR ALL TEAM BLOGS H'CAP (DIV I) 1m 22y
5:40 (5:42) (Class 6) (0-60,60) 3-Y-0 **£1,704** (£503; £251) **Stalls** Low

Form RPR
050- **1** **Our Phylli Vera (IRE)**[191] 6524 3-9-2 **55** DaneO'Neill 5 59
(Harry Dunlop) *prom: led over 2f out: sn rdn: kpt on ins fnl f: hld on wl towards fin* **8/1**[3]
005- **2** nk **My Boy Ginger**[195] 6432 3-9-7 **60** JamesMillman 6 63+
(Rod Millman) *hld up: hdwy u.p over 2f out: r.o to take 2nd wl ins fnl f: pressed wnr towards fin: jst hld* **20/1**
540- **3** 1 ½ **Pius Parker (IRE)**[172] 6972 3-9-6 **59** JohnFahy 1 59
(John Gallagher) *trckd ldrs: rdn over 2f out: wnt 2nd wl over 1f out: nt qckn: lost 2nd wl ins fnl f: no ex towards fin* **17/2**
000- **4** 2 ½ **Divine Success (IRE)**[201] 6260 3-9-2 **58** LeeTopliss(3) 15 52
(Richard Fahey) *racd keenly: a.p: rdn over 3f out: styd on same pce fr over 1f out and no imp on ldrs* **14/1**
50-0 **5** 1 ½ **Gadreel (IRE)**[84] 191 3-8-4 **46** oh1 RyanPowell(3) 12 37
(Anthony Middleton) *hld up: pushed along 3f out: hdwy u.p over 1f out: sn swtchd lft: styd on ins fnl f: unable to trble ldrs* **33/1**
60-5 **6** 2 ¼ **My Pearl (IRE)**[11] 1089 3-9-2 **55** PhillipMakin 2 41
(Kevin Ryan) *trckd ldrs: rdn and outpcd over 3f out: sn btn* **8/1**[3]
001- **7** nk **Mick Slates (IRE)**[158] 7242 3-8-9 **53** NeilFarley(5) 9 38
(Declan Carroll) *awkward s: in rr: sme hdwy u.p over 1f out: briefly nt clr run ins fnl f: one pce and no imp after* **6/1**[1]

000- **8** *nk* **Highly Likely (IRE)**[182] 6757 3-8-11 **50**.............................. TedDurcan 4 34+
(John Dunlop) *hld up in midfield: wknd over 2f out: eased whn btn ins fnl f* **7/1**[2]

006- **9** *1* **Artful Lady (IRE)**[189] 6579 3-8-11 **50**.............................. TomQueally 14 32
(George Margarson) *hld up: pushed along on wd outside over 2f out: nvr able to get on terms* **14/1**

000- **10** *¾* **Applaudere**[117] 7757 3-8-10 **49**.............................. FergusSweeney 11 29
(Jamie Osborne) *midfield: rdn 2f out: sn btn* **33/1**

4-00 **11** *½* **Johnson's Cat (IRE)**[17] 1012 3-8-11 **50**.............................. WilliamCarson 3 29
(Richard Guest) *led: hdd over 2f out: sn rdn: wknd fnl f* **8/1**[3]

04-2 **12** *1 ¾* **Parque Atlantico**[12] 1067 3-8-7 **46** oh1..............................(v) DavidProbert 10 21
(Andrew Balding) *midfield: rdn and wknd over 3f out* **6/1**[1]

0-40 **13** *30* **King's Future**[14] 1046 3-9-6 **59**.............................. StevieDonohoe 13
(Loo Cartor) *trokd ldrs: rdn over 3f out: sn wknd: t.o* **14/1**

405 **14** *4* **Nothing's Simple**[14] 1048 3-9-2 **55**.............................. MichaelHills 8
(Hugo Palmer) *a bhd: struggling over 3f out: eased whn wl btn 2f out: t.o* **16/1**

1m 50.0s (9.00) **Going Correction** +0.975s/f (Soft) **14** Ran SP% **121.5**
Speed ratings (Par 96): **94,93,92,89,88 85,85,85,84,83 83,81,51,47**
toteswingers: 1&2 £23.10, 1&3 £20.70, 2&3 £15.00 CSF £162.97 CT £1400.15 TOTE £12.50: £4.20, £8.40, £3.90; EX 203.10 TRIFECTA Not won..
Owner Kieron Drake & Simon Withers **Bred** Awbeg Stud **Trained** Lambourn, Berks

FOCUS
A moderate handicap in which only one of these had won a race before, although the winner looks an improver.
Our Phylli Vera(IRE) Official explanation: trainer said, regarding apparent improvement in form, that the filly was suited by the softer ground and longer trip and had strengthened up over the winter.
Gadreel(IRE) Official explanation: trainer's rep said gelding was unsuited by the soft ground
Mick Slates(IRE) Official explanation: jockey said gelding became unbalanced
Highly Likely(IRE) Official explanation: jockey said gelding had no more to give

1260 VISIT STARSPORTSBET.CO.UK FOR ALL TEAM BLOGS H'CAP (DIV II) 1m 22y
6:15 (6:15) (Class 6) (0-60,60) 3-Y-O **£1,704** (£503; £251) **Stalls** Low

Form RPR

5635 **1** **Masters Blazing**[14] 1046 3-9-5 **58**..............................(v) AdamKirby 1 71+
(John Ryan) *midfield: hdwy 4f out: rdn to ld over 1f out: styd on wl to draw clr ins fnl f: eased cl home* **9/2**[2]

000- **2** *7* **Mexican Wave**[214] 5861 3-8-7 **46** oh1.............................. HayleyTurner 7 43
(Michael Bell) *racd keenly: trckd ldrs: rdn 3f out: kpt on to take 2nd fnl 110yds: no imp on wnr* **9/2**[2]

440- **3** *3* **Coach Montana (IRE)**[116] 7763 3-9-2 **55**.............................. GeorgeBaker 6 45
(Jane Chapple-Hyam) *trckd ldrs: rdn over 2f out: nt qckn: styd on same pce fnl f* **10/3**[1]

260- **4** *1 ½* **Doc Hill**[159] 7223 3-8-8 **47**.............................. FergusSweeney 11 34
(Michael Blanshard) *led: rdn and hdd over 1f out: no ex wl ins fnl f* **16/1**

50 **5** *½* **Hugenot (IRE)**[19] 982 3-9-7 **60**.............................. StevieDonohoe 14 45
(Tobias B P Coles) *hld up: pushed along over 2f out: styd on u.p fnl f: nvr able to trble ldrs* **33/1**

04-0 **6** *2 ½* **Sleepy Lucy**[89] 121 3-8-7 **51**.............................. CharlesEddery(5) 4 31
(Richard Guest) *hld up: hdwy 3f out: rdn to chse ldrs over 2f out: one pce over 1f out* **20/1**

10-3 **7** *9* **Percythepinto (IRE)**[20] 973 3-9-6 **59**..............................(t) PatCosgrave 12 18
(George Baker) *prom: rdn 2f out: sn wknd* **16/1**

00-5 **8** *6* **Song Of Joy (IRE)**[39] 743 3-9-6 **59**..............................(bt) WilliamCarson 5
(Paul D'Arcy) *pushed along jst after s: bhd: rdn and no imp 2f out: eased whn wl btn fnl f* **7/1**

6366 **9** *12* **Meet Joe Black (IRE)**[51] 619 3-8-11 **50**..............................(v) PadraigBeggy 8
(David Evans) *rdn along jst after s: a towards rr and nvr travelled wl* **20/1**

-606 **10** *10* **Tigresa (IRE)**[32] 832 3-8-11 **50**.............................. JoeFanning 13
(Mark Johnston) *handy on outer: effrt 3f out: wknd 2f out* **22/1**

0-30 **11** *5* **Armiger**[31] 845 3-9-0 **53**.............................. MartinDwyer 9
(William Muir) *s.v.s: a bhd* **16/1**

060- **12** *5* **Chater Garden (IRE)**[179] 6817 3-8-13 **52**.............................. KierenFallon 10
(Alan Jarvis) *in tch: rdn 4f out: wknd over 3f out* **6/1**[3]

1m 50.24s (9.24) **Going Correction** +0.975s/f (Soft) **12** Ran SP% **120.7**
Speed ratings (Par 96): **92,85,82,80,80 77,68,62,50,40 35,30**
toteswingers: 1&2 £4.10, 1&3 £4.50, 2&3 £3.60 CSF £24.12 CT £77.77 TOTE £6.10: £1.80, £2.10, £1.70; EX 35.70 Trifecta £197.70 Pool £435.61 - 1.63 winning units..
Owner Masters Stud & Partner **Bred** D R Botterill **Trained** Newmarket, Suffolk

FOCUS
This race had double the number of previous winners of division one, though that isn't saying much. The winning time was 0.24 seconds slower. The form is tentatively rated.
T/Plt: £180.60 to a £1 stake. Pool: £38,165.18 154.19 winning tickets. T/Qpdt: £30.90 to a £1 stake. Pool: £1,971.73. 47.10 winning tickets. DO

YARMOUTH (L-H)
Monday, April 9

OFFICIAL GOING: Good (good to soft in places) changing to good to soft (soft in places) after race 1 (2.25)
Wind: Fresh, across. Weather: Overcast

1261 BURLINGTON PALM HOTEL MAIDEN STKS 1m 3y
2:25 (2:29) (Class 5) 3-Y-O+ **£2,264** (£673; £336; £168) **Stalls** Centre

Form RPR

1 **Falcon In Flight** 3-8-7 0.............................. ChrisCatlin 5 86+
(Jeremy Noseda) *hld up in tch: led over 2f out: pushed clr fnl f* **10/1**[3]

42- **2** *7* **Debating Society (IRE)**[208] 6064 3-8-13 0 ow1.............................. RyanMoore 1 76+
(Sir Michael Stoute) *hld up: rdn over 3f out: hdwy over 2f out: chsd wnr fnl f: styd on same pce* **6/1**[2]

3 *4* **Gravitate** 3-8-12 0.............................. WilliamBuick 15 66+
(John Gosden) *sn pushed along in rr: hdwy over 2f out: wknd fnl f* **11/1**

4 *3* **Rufus Stone (USA)** 4-9-13 0.............................. LukeMorris 4 63
(Jane Chapple-Hyam) *chsd ldrs: rdn over 2f out: wknd wl over 1f out* **66/1**

2- **5** *¾* **Periphery (USA)**[173] 6951 3-8-12 0.............................. FrankieDettori 10 57
(Mahmood Al Zarooni) *chsd ldr: rdn and ev ch over 1f out: wknd fnl f* **1/1**[1]

6 *3 ¾* **Al Sirat**[24] 6-9-6 0.............................. JackDuern(7) 7 53
(Michael Appleby) *mid-div: hdwy over 3f out: rdn and wknd wl over 1f out* **200/1**

35- **7** *1* **Vertibes**[116] 7766 4-9-13 0.............................. SebSanders 9 50
(Marcus Tregoning) *sn pushed along in rr: nvr nrr* **28/1**

0- **8** *1 ½* **Desert Red (IRE)**[168] 7052 3-8-7 0.............................. SilvestreDeSousa 3 38
(Michael Bell) *mid-div: effrt 1/2-way: wknd over 2f out* **25/1**

0- **9** *4 ½* **Thawabel (IRE)**[182] 6745 3-8-7 0.............................. TadhgO'Shea 12 27
(Marcus Tregoning) *hdwy over 6f out: rdn and wknd over 2f out* **28/1**

10 *4* **Darwinian** 3-8-4 0.............................. AdamBeschizza(3) 14 18
(Dave Morris) *sn outpcd* **150/1**

11 *nse* **Extremely Alert** 3-8-12 0.............................. JamieSpencer 2 23+
(Michael Bell) *s.s: hdwy over 3f out: wknd 2f out* **20/1**

4- **12** *3* **Mutasadder (USA)**[171] 6993 3-8-12 0..............................(b[1]) PaulHanagan 6 16
(Roger Varian) *led: racd keenly: clr 6f out: hdd & wknd over 2f out* **6/1**[2]

13 *50* **L'Ile Rousse** 3-8-2 0.............................. RaulDaSilva(5) 16
(Chris Dwyer) *chsd ldrs tl wknd 1/2-way: t.o* **200/1**

1m 44.76s (4.16) **Going Correction** +0.45s/f (Yiel)
WFA 3 from 4yo+ 15lb **13** Ran SP% **114.7**
Speed ratings (Par 103): **97,90,86,83,82 78,77,76,71,67 67,64,14**
Tote Swingers:1&2:£7.20, 2&3:£5.50, 1&3:£12.90 CSF £62.18 TOTE £12.30: £2.60, £1.90, £2.90; EX 95.90.
Owner Saeed Suhail **Bred** Rabbah Bloodstock Limited **Trained** Newmarket, Suffolk

FOCUS
An interesting maiden and it was won impressively by Falcon In Flight, who quickened clear after travelling best. The runner-up sets the level for now.

1262 DIGIBET.COM H'CAP 1m 3y
3:00 (3:01) (Class 5) (0-75,74) 4-Y-O+ **£2,264** (£673; £336; £84; £84) **Stalls** Centre

Form RPR

056- **1** **Barwick**[143] 7453 4-9-6 **73**.............................. WilliamBuick 9 81
(Mark H Tompkins) *chsd ldrs: led over 1f out: rdn and hung lft ins fnl f: r.o* **6/1**[3]

300- **2** *nk* **Batgirl**[198] 6355 5-9-5 **72**.............................. FrankieDettori 6 79
(John Berry) *hld up in tch: rdn and ev ch whn hmpd ins fnl f: r.o* **8/1**

202- **3** *2 ½* **Tilsworth Glenboy**[211] 5969 5-9-2 **69**.............................. RyanMoore 5 70
(J R Jenkins) *hld up: hdwy over 2f out: rdn and hung lft ins fnl f: styd on same pce* **4/1**[2]

2-14 **4** *5* **Zaheeb**[20] 967 4-8-10 **66**.............................. AdamBeschizza(3) 7 56
(Dave Morris) *w ldr tl led 3f out: rdn and hdd over 1f out: sn hung lft: wknd ins fnl f* **9/1**

1121 **4** *dht* **Patriotic (IRE)**[25] 907 4-9-0 **72**.............................. RaulDaSilva(5) 1 62
(Chris Dwyer) *hld up: hdwy over 2f out: rdn over 1f out: wkng whn rdr dropped reins ins fnl f* **9/4**[1]

3060 **6** *4 ½* **Opus Maximus (IRE)**[10] 1117 7-9-0 **72**.............................. DavidKenny(5) 3 51
(Conor Dore) *chsd ldrs: rdn over 2f out: sn wknd* **20/1**

0/1- **7** *17* **Scottish Star**[425] 471 4-9-7 **74**.............................. LukeMorris 2 14
(James Eustace) *hld up: rdn and wknd over 2f out* **17/2**

30-3 **8** *shd* **Afkar (IRE)**[20] 967 4-9-2 **69**.............................. BrettDoyle 8 9
(Clive Brittain) *led 5f: rdn and wknd over 1f out* **9/1**

0000 **9** *6* **Spirit Of Xaar (IRE)**[19] 987 6-9-5 **72**.............................. SebSanders 4
(Linda Jewell) *w ldr over 4f: rdn and wknd over 2f out* **14/1**

1m 43.6s (3.00) **Going Correction** +0.45s/f (Yiel) **9** Ran SP% **118.1**
Speed ratings (Par 103): **103,102,100,95,95 90,73,73,67**
Tote Swingers:1&2:£7.80, 2&3:£9.00, 1&3:£7.60 CSF £54.30 CT £218.36 TOTE £8.10: £4.10, £3.20, £1.90; EX 53.60.
Owner Steve Ashley **Bred** Dullingham Park **Trained** Newmarket, Suffolk
■ Stewards' Enquiry : William Buick one-day ban: careless riding (Apr 23)

FOCUS
Just a modest handicap and Barwick had to survive a stewards' enquiry after drifting left late on and carrying Batgirl towards the far rail. The runner-up sets the standard.

1263 MATTHEW CLARK H'CAP 7f 3y
3:35 (3:35) (Class 6) (0-65,65) 4-Y-O+ **£1,617** (£481; £240; £120) **Stalls** Centre

Form RPR

210- **1** **Caldermud (IRE)**[174] 6938 5-9-7 **65**..............................(t) RyanMoore 11 75
(Olivia Maylam) *hld up: hdwy over 1f out: r.o u.p to ld wl ins fnl f* **11/2**

316- **2** *1* **Viking Rose (IRE)**[182] 6764 4-9-7 **65**.............................. LukeMorris 1 72
(James Eustace) *chsd ldr tl led over 2f out: rdn: edgd rt and hdd wl ins fnl f* **9/2**[2]

650- **3** *¾* **Yakama (IRE)**[110] 7843 7-8-10 **54**..............................(p) TomMcLaughlin 5 59
(Christine Dunnett) *hld up: hdwy: nt clr run and swtchd lft over 1f out: r.o* **25/1**

5230 **4** *1* **Mister Green (FR)**[10] 1108 6-9-1 **59**..............................(bt) JamesDoyle 7 61
(David Flood) *hld up: hdwy over 2f out: rdn over 1f out: styd on same pce ins fnl f* **9/1**

4005 **5** *shd* **Captainrisk (IRE)**[33] 828 6-8-7 **56**..............................(v) RaulDaSilva(5) 9 58
(Christine Dunnett) *chsd ldrs: rdn over 2f out: styd on same pce fnl f* **16/1**

0-60 **6** *2 ¼* **Doctor Hilary**[21] 964 10-8-11 **55**..............................(v) ChrisCatlin 3 51
(Mark Hoad) *hld up: rdn over 2f out: hdwy over 1f out: nt trble ldrs* **22/1**

060 **7** *nk* **Irie Ute**[26] 891 4-9-0 **58**.............................. JamieSpencer 6 53
(Sylvester Kirk) *hld up: nt clr run and swtchd rt over 1f out: nt trble ldrs* **11/1**

04-0 **8** *shd* **Whiskey Junction**[39] 752 8-9-5 **63**.............................. SebSanders 8 58
(Michael Quinn) *led over 4f: sn rdn: no ex ins fnl f* **20/1**

0/55 **9** *1 ½* **Director's Dream (IRE)**[20] 974 4-8-12 **56**..............................(b) PaulHanagan 2 47
(Mark Rimmer) *mid-div: rdn over 2f out: edgd lft over 1f out: wknd fnl f* **25/1**

2300 **10** *1* **Joe Le Taxi (IRE)**[14] 1050 4-9-4 **62**.............................. SilvestreDeSousa 4 50
(Mark Johnston) *chsd ldrs: rdn 1/2-way: wknd fnl f* **5/1**[3]

5011 **11** *hd* **Spin Again (IRE)**[12] 1074 7-9-7 **65**.............................. WilliamBuick 12 53
(Daniel Kubler) *chsd ldrs: rdn over 1f out: fnl f* **11/4**[1]

005- **12** *67* **Tortilla (IRE)**[103] 7902 4-8-0 **51** oh3..............................(b) DannyBrock(7) 10
(Des Donovan) *s.s: sn drvn along in rr: wknd 3f out: t.o* **40/1**

1m 30.93s (4.33) **Going Correction** +0.45s/f (Yiel) **12** Ran SP% **120.4**
Speed ratings (Par 101): **93,91,91,89,89 87,86,86,85,83 83,7**
Tote Swingers:1&2:£7.30, 2&3:£33.00, 1&3:£33.80 CSF £28.67 CT £589.70 TOTE £7.20: £3.10, £2.40, £8.40; EX 38.60.
Owner The Hookfield Racing Club **Bred** P J B O Callaghan **Trained** Epsom, Surrey
■ Stewards' Enquiry : Raul Da Silva two-day ban: used whip above permitted level (Apr 23-24)

FOCUS
A moderate but competitive handicap and straightforward form rated around the placed horses.
Spin Again(IRE) Official explanation: trainer said gelding was unsuited by the good to soft (soft in places) ground

1264 AVENUE PUB BEATTY ROAD H'CAP 7f 3y
4:10 (4:10) (Class 4) (0-85,82) 3-Y-O **£4,075** (£1,212; £606; £303) **Stalls** Centre

Form RPR

623- **1** **Fourth Of June (IRE)**[150] 7367 3-9-2 **77**.............................. PaulHanagan 3 83
(Ed Dunlop) *trckd ldrs: racd keenly: led over 1f out: sn rdn: r.o* **13/2**

321- **2** *nk* **Grizzle**[165] 7126 3-9-7 **82**.............................. FrankieDettori 1 87
(Mahmood Al Zarooni) *hld up: swtchd lft and hdwy over 1f out: rdn and ev ch ins fnl f: r.o* **13/8**[1]

514- **3** ½ **The Noble Ord**[223] 5584 3 -8-12**73** RyanMoore 5 77
(Sylvester Kirk) *chsd ldrs: rdn over 1f out: r.o* **4/1**[2]

06-6 **4** 1 ¾ **Tight Lipped (IRE)**[4] 918 3 -8-13**74** LukeMorris 6 73
(James Eustace) *chsd ldr: rdn and ev ch over 1f out: styd on same pce ins fnl f* **12/1**

-261 **5** 1 ½ **Ghost Train (IRE)**[10] 1115 3 -8-10**71** SilvestreDeSousa 4 66
(Mark Johnston) *led: swtchd to r on stands' side rail 1/2-way: rdn and hdd over 1f out: edgd lft: no ex ins fnl f* **6/1**

5-15 **6** ½ **Dubai Sunshine (IRE)**[52] 596 3 -9-7**82** JamieSpencer 2 76
(Michael Bell) *hld up: rdn over 1f out: styd on same pce fnl f* **5/1**[3]

1m 30.1s (3.50) **Going Correction** +0.45s/f (Yiel) **6**Ran SP% **110.1**
Speed ratings (Par 100): **98,97,97,95,93 92**
Tote Swingers:1&2:£3.70, 2&3:£1.50, 1&3:£6.50 CSF £16.89 TOTE £6.60 : £3.60 , £1.30 ; EX 22.30.
Owner Mrs Susan Roy **Bred** Con Marnane **Trained** Newmarket, Suffolk

FOCUS
A fair 3-y-o handicap but soundly run and the runner-up is an improver.

1265 ODDSCHECKER.COM MEDIAN AUCTION MAIDEN STKS 1m 2f 21y
4:45 (4:45) (Class 6) 3-5-Y-O £1,617 (£481; £240 ; £120) **Stalls** Low

Form RPR

53- **1** **Samba King**[178] 6825 3 -8-9**0** MickaelBarzalona 4 78+
(Mahmood Al Zarooni) *mde all: rdn over 1f out: styd on wl* **5/2**[2]

332- **2** 3 ½ **Zaeem**[168] 7060 3 -8-9**78** FrankieDettori 6 71+
(Mahmood Al Zarooni) *chsd wnr 2f: remained handy: wnt 2 again 2f out: rdn and hung lft ins fnl f: no ex* **1/1**[1]

3 ¾ **Kashgar** 3 -8-9**0** JamieSpencer 2 70+
(Michael Bell) *chsd ldrs: shkn up over 2f out: nt clr run and swtchd lft over 1f out: styd on same pce ins fnl f* **7/1**[3]

4 ¾ **Joe The Coat** 3 -8-9**0** PaulHanagan 1 68
(Mark H Tompkins) *dwlt and awkward leaving stalls: hld up: hdwy over 1f out: styd on same pce ins fnl f* **22/1**

5- **5** 1 **Bonnet De Douche (IRE)**[167] 7083 3 -8-4**0** LukeMorris 3 61
(Peter Chapple-Hyam) *hld up in tch: n.m.r over 2f out: rdn over 1f out: styd on same pce fnl f* **14/1**

0 **6** 3 ¼ **Arctic Galaxy (CAN)**[16] 1031 3 -8-9**0** WilliamBuick 5 60
(John Gosden) *prom: chsd wnr 8f out tl pushed along 2f out: wknd ins fnl f* **10/1**

2m 14.59s (4.09) **Going Correction** +0.45s/f (Yiel) **6**Ran SP% **111.2**
Speed ratings (Par 101): **101,98,97,97,96 93**
Tote Swingers:1&2:£1.40, 2&3:£1.90, 1&3:£2.20 CSF £5.25 TOTE £4.20 : £1.60 , £1.40 ; EX 5.90.
Owner Godolphin **Bred** Darley **Trained** Newmarket, Suffolk

FOCUS
Probably an ordinary maiden, but a likeable winner and the fourth and fifth are probably the keys to the longer-term standard.

1266 ODDSCHECKER.MOBI H'CAP 1m 2f 21y
5:20 (5:20) (Class 5) (0-75,75) 4-Y-0+ £2,264 (£673; £336 ; £168) **Stalls** Low

Form RPR

642 **1** **Spin Cast**[18] 1002 4 -8-9**63** JamieSpencer 1 68
(Ian Williams) *led: rdn and hdd ins fnl f: rallied to ld nr fin* **9/2**[3]

011- **2** hd **Glass Mountain (IRE)**[172] 6969 4 -9-6**74** JackMitchell 4 79+
(James Fanshawe) *a.p: nt clr run fr over 2f out tl over 1f out: rdn to ld ins fnl f: n.m.r thereafter: hdd nr fin* **3/1**[1]

0-20 **3** 1 ¾ **Silver Alliance**[38] 771 4 -9-1**69** LukeMorris 6 71
(Julia Feilden) *chsd ldrs: rdn over 1f out: styd on same pce ins fnl f* **12/1**

04-6 **4** 1 ½ **Highlife Dancer**[20] 971 4 -9-3**71** MartinHarley 7 70
(Mick Channon) *chsd wnr tl reminder over 1f out: nudged along and styd on same pce fnl f* **5/1**

6-02 **5** 1 **Junket**[33] 821 5 -9-4**72** RyanMoore 5 69
(Dr Jon Scargill) *s.i.s: hld up in tch: rdn over 1f out: styd on* **7/2**[2]

3252 **6** nk **Conducting**[14] 1051 4 -9-2**70** (p) MickaelBarzalona 8 66
(Gay Kelleway) *hld up: rdn over 1f out: styd on: nt pce to chal* **9/1**

25-0 **7** 5 **Beat Of The Blues**[9] 1133 4 -8-13**74** JackDuern[(7)] 2 60
(Michael Appleby) *s.i.s: hld up: rdn over 3f out: wknd over 2f out* **14/1**

230- **8** ½ **Jewelled**[199] 6302 6 -9-7**75** SebSanders 3 60
(Lady Herries) *hld up: hdwy over 3f out: wknd fnl f* **9/1**

0-00 **9** 16 **Give Or Take**[20] 976 4 -8-2**61** oh16 RaulDaSilva[(5)] 9 14
(Christine Dunnett) *hld up: rdn over 3f out: wknd over 2f out* **80/1**

2m 15.83s (5.33) **Going Correction** +0.45s/f (Yiel) **9**Ran SP% **117.7**
Speed ratings (Par 103): **96,95,94,93,92 92,88,87,75**
Tote Swingers:1&2:£3.40, 2&3:£7.80, 1&3:£12.70 CSF £18.81 CT £152.99 TOTE £3.70 : £1.30 , £1.10, £4.50 ; EX 23.40 .
Owner Dr Marwan Koukash **Bred** P W Harris **Trained** Portway, Worcs

FOCUS
A modest handicap.

1267 BEST ODDS@ODDSCHECKER.COM H'CAP 1m 3f 101y
5:55 (5:56) (Class 6) (0-65,70) 3-Y-0 £1,617 (£481; £240 ; £120) **Stalls** Low

Form RPR

2321 **1** **Scatter Dice (IRE)**[7] 1170 3 -9-13**70** 6ex SilvestreDeSousa 1 78+
(Mark Johnston) *mde all: rdn clr fr over 1f out: comf* **8/11**[1]

-063 **2** 3 **Chankillo**[41] 726 3 -9-4**61** WilliamBuick 4 63
(Mark H Tompkins) *chsd wnr: rdn over 1f out: styd on same pce fnl f* **9/2**[2]

0-05 **3** 3 **Corn Maiden**[33] 816 3 -8-4**54** LewisWalsh[(7)] 3 50
(Phil McEntee) *prom: rdn over 3f out: outpcd over 2f out: rallied over 1f out: hung lft and no ex fnl f* **50/1**

052 **4** 3 ½ **Dalmo**[38] 762 3 -9-7**64** RyanMoore 2 55
(Gary Moore) *chsd ldrs: rdn over 2f out: wknd fnl f* **13/2**[3]

06-3 **5** 25 **Cool Fantasy (IRE)**[24] 923 3 -8-13**56** (b) LukeMorris 5
(Paul D'Arcy) *hld up in tch: rdn and hung lft over 4f out: wknd 3f out: t.o* **10/1**

6214 **6** 43 **Moment In The Sun**[18] 993 3 -9-1**58** JamesDoyle 6
(David Flood) *s.i.s: hld up: hdwy over 3f out: sn wknd and eased: t.o* **17/2**

2m 33.43s (4.73) **Going Correction** +0.45s/f (Yiel) **6**Ran SP% **111.0**
Speed ratings (Par 96): **100,97,95,93,74 43**
Tote Swingers:1&2:£1.50, 2&3:£31.30, 1&3:£4.20 CSF £4.22 TOTE £1.60 : £1.10 , £2.00 ; EX 4.10.
Owner Sheikh Hamdan Bin Mohammed Al Maktoum **Bred** Darley **Trained** Middleham Moor, N Yorks

FOCUS
Not a bad race for the grade as Scatter Dice is well handicapped and the runner-up also looks reasonably weighted.
Moment In The Sun Official explanation: jockey said filly lost its action
T/Plt: £102.00 to a £1 stake. Pool £47,070.78. 336.71 winning tickets. T/Qpdt: £12.80 to a £1 stake. Pool £3,099.55. 177.84 w. tickets. CR

1268a Foreign Racing (See RI)

PONTEFRACT (L-H)
Tuesday, April 10

OFFICIAL GOING: Good (7.4)
Wind: fresh 1/2 behind Weather: overcast, breezy

1269 "HIGHLY COMMENDED" PONTEFRACT LOYALTY CARD H'CAP (DIV I) 1m 4y
2:20 (2:21) (Class 5) (0-70,70) 4-Y-0+ £2,385 (£704; £352) **Stalls** Low

Form RPR

0-31 **1** **Toymaker**[19] 995 5 -9-4**67** PaulMulrennan 3 81+
(James Given) *trckd ldrs: smooth hdwy over 2f out: led over 1f out: rdn clr: readily* **9/2**[1]

605- **2** 3 ¼ **First Class Favour (IRE)**[160] 7235 4 -9-1**64** DavidAllan 12 71
(Tim Easterby) *t.k.h in midfield: swtchd ins over 3f out: hdwy over 2f out: tk 2nd last 100yds: no imp* **16/1**

00-3 **3** 2 ½ **Wiseman's Diamond (USA)**[33] 842 7 -8-13**62** (b) MickyFenton 5 63
(Paul Midgley) *trckd ldrs: plld outside over 1f out: styd on wl to take 3rd last 50yds* **18/1**

-456 **4** 2 **Cheers Buddy (IRE)**[36] 804 4 -8-11**60** BarryMcHugh 1 57
(Tony Coyle) *in tch: effrt over 2f out: one pce over 1f out* **8/1**[3]

511- **5** hd **Eastward Ho**[111] 7848 4 -8-13**62** MichaelStainton 13 58
(Jason Ward) *w ldr: led over 2f out: hdd over 1f out: wknd last 150yds* **20/1**

20-0 **6** 2 ½ **Hits Only Jude (IRE)**[10] 1135 9 -8-0**56** (v) MichaelKenny[(7)] 7 46
(Declan Carroll) *s.i.s: hdwy over 2f out: nvr nr ldrs* **14/1**

052- **7** 1 ¾ **Indieslad**[171] 7024 4 -9-6**69** TonyHamilton 4 55+
(Ann Duffield) *trckd ldrs: t.k.h: effrt over 2f out: wknd fnl f* **9/2**[1]

30-5 **8** 2 **Praxios**[95] 65 4 -9-2**65** DanielTudhope 2 50
(Noel Wilson) *s.i.s: hdwy on ins over 2f out: nvr trbld ldrs* **33/1**

2360 **9** ½ **Transmit (IRE)**[35] 813 5 -8-8**57** GrahamGibbons 14 38
(Tim Easterby) *s.i.s: sme hdwy 2f out: nvr a factor* **50/1**

50-1 **10** 1 ¼ **Jacob McCandles**[33] 833 5 -8-12**66** LMcNiff[(5)] 6 44
(David Barron) *in rr: effrt on outer over 3f out: hung lft and lost pl over 1f out* **5/1**[2]

050- **11** 2 ¼ **Cara's Request (AUS)**[178] 6867 7 -9-0**70** ShirleyTeasdale[(7)] 10 43
(David Nicholls) *led: hdd over 2f out: wknd fnl f* **20/1**

3313 **12** 2 **Moral Issue**[26] 909 4 -9-3**69** DaleSwift[(3)] 11 37
(Ian McInnes) *chsd ldrs: effrt over 2f out: wknd over 1f out* **10/1**

0412 **13** 17 **Tuxedo**[11] 1105 7 -9-3**66** (b) WilliamCarson 8
(Peter Hiatt) *mid-div: lost pl over 1f out: sn eased and wl bhd: lame* **20/1**

004- **14** 30 **Five Hearts**[239] 5120 4 -8-9**58** WilliamBuick 9
(Mark H Tompkins) *in rr: hung lft and lost pl over 2f out: heavily eased over 1f out: t.o* **9/1**

1m 48.12s (2.22) **Going Correction** +0.35s/f (Good) **14**Ran SP% **120.2**
Speed ratings (Par 103): **102,98,96,94,94 91,89,87,87,86 83,81,64,34**
Tote Swingers: 1&2 £17.90, 1&3 £10.60, 2&3 £50.50 CSF £71.26 CT £1230.97 TOTE £3.90 : £1.70, £4.50 , £2.90 ; EX 102.10 TRIFECTA Not won. .
Owner Antoniades Family **Bred** A G Antoniades **Trained** Willoughton, Lincs

FOCUS
Just a modest handicap, but a really likeable winner.
Tuxedo Official explanation: trainer said gelding finished lame right-fore

1270 HIGH-RISE MEDIAN AUCTION MAIDEN STKS 1m 2f 6y
2:50 (2:53) (Class 4) 3-Y-O £4,075 (£1,212; £606 ; £303) **Stalls** Low

Form RPR

20-2 **1** **Niceofyoutotellme**[13] 1065 3 -9-3**83** JimCrowley 4 84+
(Ralph Beckett) *hld up in mid-div: hdwy 4f out: led over 1f out: smoothly* **8/11**[1]

3 **2** 1 ¼ **Kudoz**[43] 724 3 -9-3**0** JohnFahy 3 74
(Clive Cox) *hld up in mid-div: effrt over 2f out: wnt 2nd 1f out: kpt on wl: no imp* **13/2**[2]

64-5 **3** 10 **Fisher**[14] 1053 3 -8-10**64** ShirleyTeasdale[(7)] 5 54
(David Nicholls) *mid-div: hdwy over 2f out: kpt on to take modest 3rd last 100yds* **28/1**

4 2 ½ **Sarmatian Knight (IRE)** 3 -9-0**0** RyanPowell[(3)] 12 49
(Ian Williams) *in rr: hdwy 3f out: kpt on fnl f* **50/1**

3- **5** hd **Mighty Motive**[116] 7783 3 -9-3**0** GrahamGibbons 13 49
(John Mackie) *led 2f: chsd ldr: led over 2f out: hdd over 1f out: sn wknd* **28/1**

6 **6** hd **Bridal Medic**[19] 1001 3 -9-0**0** MichaelO'Connell[(3)] 8 48
(John Mackie) *s.i.s: hdwy over 2f out: nvr nr ldrs* **66/1**

00- **7** 4 ½ **Derek The Diamond**[153] 7329 3 -9-3**0** NeilChalmers 6 39
(Michael Appleby) *led after 2f: hdd over 2f out: wknd fnl f* **200/1**

0- **8** 3 ½ **Red Alex**[302] 2983 3 -9-3**0** JamesSullivan 10 32
(James Given) *in rr: nvr on terms* **100/1**

542- **9** 1 ¼ **Scarlet Whispers**[201] 6275 3 -8-12**75** MickyFenton 11 25
(Pam Sly) *hld up in rr: hdwy 4f out: lost pl 2f out* **7/1**[3]

0 **10** 8 **Haywain**[14] 1053 3 -9-3**0** PhillipMakin 1 14
(Kevin Ryan) *sn chsng ldrs: wknd 2f out* **33/1**

11 15 **Eanans Bay (IRE)** 3 -9-3**0** WilliamBuick 2
(Mark H Tompkins) *s.i.s: in rr: wl bhd whn eased over 1f out* **16/1**

4- **12** 3 ¼ **Rosselli (IRE)**[150] 7398 3 -9-3**0** PaulHanagan 7
(Mrs K Burke) *chsd ldrs: lost pl over 2f out: bhd whn eased ins fnl f* **13/2**[2]

00- **13** 78 **Goodfellows Quest (IRE)**[250] 4714 3 -9-3**0** (p) TonyHamilton 9
(Ann Duffield) *chsd ldrs: rdn and lost pl 3f out: t.o whn eased 2f out: virtually p.u* **100/1**

2m 18.35s (4.65) **Going Correction** +0.35s/f (Good) **13**Ran SP% **118.7**
Speed ratings (Par 100): **95,94,86,84,83 83,80,77,76,69 57,55,**
Tote Swingers: 1&2 £12.70, 1&3 £2.50, 2&3 £7.80 CSF £5.41 TOTE £1.90 : £1.10 , £1.60 , £6.10 ; EX 5.50 Trifecta £49.80 Pool: £928.51 - 13.77 winning units. .
Owner R Roberts **Bred** Minster Stud **Trained** Kimpton, Hants

FOCUS
An uncompetitive maiden.

1271 DALBY STAND H'CAP 6f
3:20 (3:23) (Class 3) (0-95,95) 3-Y-0
£7,470 (£2,236; £1,118 ; £559 ; £279 ; £140) **Stalls** Low

Form RPR

000- **1** **Es Que Love (IRE)**[192] 6535 3 -8-11**85** SilvestreDeSousa 2 100
(Mark Johnston) *mde all: wnt clr over 2f out: kpt on: lasted home* **4/1**[2]

136-1 **2** 1 **Yeeoow (IRE)**[21] 969 3 -8-0**77** oh1 ow1 HarryBentley[(3)] 5 89
(Mrs K Burke) *chsd ldrs: wnt 2nd last 75yds: kpt on wl* **12/1**

650- **3** *1 1/4* **Springinmystep (IRE)**[186] 6670 3-8-6 **80** .... JamesSullivan 9 88
(Michael Dods) *chsd ldrs: wnt 2nd 3f out: kpt on fnl f* **25/1**

021- **4** *6* **Right Result (IRE)**[192] 6539 3-8-7 **81** ow1 .... GrahamGibbons 14 70+
(James Bethell) *swtchd lft s: in rr: hdwy whn n.m.r over 2f out: kpt on fnl f* **16/1**

505- **5** *2 3/4* **Mitchum**[207] 6111 3-8-6 **80** .... LeeNewman 6 60
(David Barron) *chsd ldrs: wknd over 1f out* **20/1**

051- **6** *2 1/2* **Byronic Hero**[176] 6912 3-8-5 **79** .... BarryMcHugh 12 51+
(Jedd O'Keeffe) *s.i.s: in rr: kpt on fnl 2f: nvr nr ldrs* **25/1**

211- **7** *nse* **Mezzotint (IRE)**[117] 7765 3-8-11 **85** .... AdamKirby 1 57+
(Marco Botti) *gave problems gng to s: mid-div: stmbld over 2f out: kpt on fnl f: nvr a factor* **3/1**[1]

01- **8** *shd* **Jinkor Noble**[190] 6579 3-8-8 **82** .... JohnFahy 16 54
(Clive Cox) *mid-div on outer: effrt over 2f out: wknd over 1f out* **12/1**

331- **9** *2 3/4* **Indego Blues**[206] 6152 3-8-4 **78** .... PaulQuinn 15 41
(David Nicholls) *in rr on outer: sme hdwy over 1f out: hung lft: nvr on terms* **20/1**

0-06 **10** *2* **Boris Grigoriev (IRE)**[10] 1129 3-9-7 **95** .... PaddyAspell 8 51
(Michael Easterby) *in rr: hung lft 2f out: nvr a factor* **20/1**

114- **11** *3* **Ralphy Boy (IRE)**[241] 5061 3-8-9 **90** .... ShirleyTeasdale(7) 13 37
(David Nicholls) *chsd ldrs on outer: edgd lft over 2f out: wknd over 1f out* **33/1**

053- **12** *3/4* **Parc De Launay**[165] 7138 3-9-1 **89** .... JamieSpencer 4 33
(Tom Tate) *t.k.h in rr: effrt on outer 2f out: nvr on terms* **11/2**[3]

422- **13** *5* **See Clearly**[178] 6864 3-8-4 **78** .... DuranFentiman 7
(Tim Easterby) *chsd ldrs: lost pl over 2f out* **40/1**

105- **14** *1* **Bop It**[165] 7138 3-8-8 **82** .... TomEaves 11
(Bryan Smart) *in tch on outer: stmbld and lost pl 2f out* **20/1**

440- **15** *42* **Worthington (IRE)**[236] 5216 3-8-12 **86** .... PaulHanagan 3 +
(Richard Fahey) *chsd ldrs: bdly hmpd over 2f out: eased and sn bhd: t.o: virtually p.u* **14/1**

1m 17.58s (0.68) **Going Correction** +0.175s/f (Good) **15** Ran SP% **120.4**
Speed ratings (Par 102): **102,100,99,91,87 84,83,83,80,77 73,72,65,64,8**
Tote Swingers: 1&2 £12.60, 1&3 £34.00, 2&3 £75.70 CSF £43.46 CT £1098.92 TOTE £3.90: £1.20, £4.50, £7.60; EX 66.10 Trifecta £523.10 Part won. Pool: £706.95 - 0.31 winning units..
Owner Crone Stud Farms Ltd **Bred** Newhall Ltd **Trained** Middleham Moor, N Yorks
■ Stewards' Enquiry : Shirley Teasdale two-day ban: careless riding (Apr 24-25)

FOCUS
This looked a strong sprint handicap, but nothing could live with the well-backed Es Que Love, who was able to get an uncontested lead from stall two.

NOTEBOOK
Es Que Love(IRE) didn't build on his maiden win last year, but an improved performance was expected judging by the market and he had this won some way out. While he was helped by the run of the race, he's clearly progressed to a pretty decent level. (op 9-2)
Yeeoow(IRE) would have found this a lot tougher than the Kempton maiden he won on his reappearance, but he ran a fine race. He was 1lb out of the handicap and carried 1lb overweight. (op 9-1)
Springinmystep(IRE) shaped nicely after a six-month break. With normal improvement he can win off this sort of mark. (op 33-1)
Right Result(IRE), another who carried 1lb overweight, fared best of those from off the pace, finishing well once in the clear. He was last seen winning a Polytrack maiden for John Quinn in October and had since been sold for 32,000gns. (op 14-1)
Mitchum shaped well enough after a 207-day break. (op 18-1)
Byronic Hero, returning from a 176-day absence, was second best of those who got behind. (op 20-1)
Mezzotint(IRE) won his last two starts of 2011 on Polytrack, but he couldn't justify strong market support on this return. He played up beforehand, couldn't get a worthwhile position from the inside stall and seemed to stumble in the straight. His starting price suggests a lot better was expected, and he had previously looked promising. (op 9-2)
Boris Grigoriev(IRE), weak in the market, didn't get the smoothest of trips and finished up well held. Official explanation: trainer said gelding had a breathing problem (op 14-1)
Parc De Launay had been gelded since he was last seen in October, but things didn't really pan out for him here and he was well beaten. (op 5-1 tchd 6-1)
Bop It, a half-brother to Hoof It, was having his first run as a gelding but was really weak in the market. He met serious trouble early on and that cost him any chance. (op 14-1)
Worthington(IRE) Official explanation: jockey said filly suffered interference in running

1272 JAMAICAN FLIGHT H'CAP — 2m 1f 216y
3:50 (3:51) (Class 5) (0-75,74) 4-Y-0+ — **£2,385** (£704; £352) **Stalls** Low

Form RPR

63-3 **1** **Cloudy Spirit**[11] 1113 7-9-3 **65** .... TonyCulhane 5 76
(Reg Hollinshead) *in rr: hdwy 6f out: sn drvn: wnt 2nd over 2f out: rdn to ld over 1f out: styd on wl* **5/2**[1]

5/2- **2** *2 1/4* **Ambrose Princess (IRE)**[248] 4806 7-9-10 **72** ....(p) JimCrowley 13 80
(Michael Scudamore) *led after 1f: hdd over 1f out: kpt on same pce* **10/1**

026- **3** *1 3/4* **Rosairlie (IRE)**[26] 7331 4-8-9 **62** .... TomEaves 2 68
(Micky Hammond) *mid-div: hdwy 4f out: wnt 3rd over 1f out: kpt on same pce* **22/1**

0003 **4** *hd* **Blackstone Vegas**[22] 963 6-8-7 **55** .... MartinLane 1 61
(Derek Shaw) *in rr: hdwy 3f out: tk 4th 1f out: kpt on same pce* **8/1**[3]

60-0 **5** *7* **Dubara Reef (IRE)**[10] 767 5-8-7 **55** oh2 ....(p) JamesSullivan 6 53
(Paul Green) *led 1f: chsd ldrs: wknd appr fnl f* **40/1**

402- **6** *1/2* **Riptide**[41] 6915 6-9-12 **74** ....(v) JamieGoldstein 3 72
(Michael Scudamore) *hld up in rr: hdwy on outside 6f out: sn chsng ldrs: hung lft and wknd over 1f out* **9/1**

200- **7** *8* **Tarantella Lady**[38] 6155 4-8-13 **66** .... AndrewMullen 9 55
(George Moore) *mid-div: drvn 5f out: lost pl 3f out* **50/1**

143- **8** *shd* **Jeu De Roseau (IRE)**[178] 6451 8-9-7 **69** .... JamieSpencer 8 58
(Chris Grant) *chsd ldrs: wknd over 1f out* **9/1**

010- **9** *1/2* **Descaro (USA)**[129] 7075 6-9-11 **73** .... SilvestreDeSousa 14 61
(David O'Meara) *hld up in rr: sme hdwy on outer over 2f out: nvr a factor* **5/1**[2]

25/3 **10** *hd* **Akarshan (IRE)**[40] 546 7-9-5 **67** .... TonyHamilton 15 55
(Evan Williams) *chsd ldrs: drvn 5f out: lost pl over 2f out* **20/1**

/05- **11** *1 1/2* **High Ransom**[50] 7075 5-9-1 **63** ....(p) FrederikTylicki 7 49
(Micky Hammond) *a in rr: nvr on terms* **14/1**

/504 **12** *1 1/4* **Sam Lord**[32] 849 8-9-10 **72** .... PaddyAspell 11 57
(James Moffatt) *in rr: t.k.h: hdwy 6f out: lost pl over 2f out: fin lame* **16/1**

65-0 **13** *53* **Sansili**[32] 849 5-8-9 **57** ....(p) WilliamCarson 12
(Peter Bowen) *mid-div: drvn over 4f out: lost pl over 2f out: sn eased: t.o over 1f out: virtually p.u* **22/1**

33-4 **14** *25* **Cotton Grass**[42] 728 4-8-8 **61** .... WilliamBuick 10
(Mark H Tompkins) *chsd ldrs: hmpd 3f out: wknd over 2f out: bhd whn heavily eased over 1f out: virtually p.u* **12/1**

4m 12.61s (16.41) **Going Correction** +0.35s/f (Good)
WFA 4 from 5yo+ 5lb **14** Ran SP% **123.5**
Speed ratings (Par 103): **77,76,75,75,72 71,68,68,67,67 67,66,43,32**
Tote Swingers: 1&2 £7.20, 1&3 £15.70, 2&3 £33.30 CSF £27.09 CT £472.27 TOTE £3.60: £1.70, £3.70, £5.40; EX 31.80 Trifecta £433.10 Part won. Pool: £585.32 - 0.31 winning units..
Owner Mrs Norma Harris **Bred** Mrs Norma Harris **Trained** Upper Longdon, Staffs

FOCUS
A fair staying handicap and a reasonable winner.
Sam Lord Official explanation: trainer said gelding finished lame left-fore
Cotton Grass Official explanation: jockey said filly had no more to give having been hampered

1273 PADDOCK PACKAGE H'CAP — 1m 2f 6y
4:25 (4:26) (Class 2) (0-105,96) 4-Y-0+
£7,684 (£7,684; £1,770; £885; £442; £222) **Stalls** Low

Form RPR

300- **1** **Deauville Flyer**[199] 6333 6-9-1 **90** .... GrahamGibbons 2 95
(Tim Easterby) *in rr: reminders over 5f out: hdwy over 2f out: led nr fin: jnd on line* **20/1**

325- **1** *dht* **Mirrored**[181] 6803 6-8-12 **87** .... DuranFentiman 6 92
(Tim Easterby) *hld up in rr: hdwy over 2f out: styd on to chal wl ins fnl f: dead-heated on line* **9/1**

053- **3** *1/2* **Northside Prince (IRE)**[127] 6803 6-8-9 **89** .... GarryWhillans(5) 4 93+
(Alan Swinbank) *chsd ldrs: drvn 3f out: styd on to ld ins fnl f: hdd and no ex nr line* **7/1**

35-4 **4** *7* **Suits Me**[38] 793 9-9-7 **96** .... JamieSpencer 1 86+
(David Barron) *led 2f: swtchd wd bnd over 5f out: upsides over 2f out: hung lft and led over 1f out: hdd & wknd ins fnl f* **9/2**[2]

4/1 **5** *2* **Splendid Light**[13] 1065 4-8-11 **86** .... WilliamBuick 8 72+
(John Gosden) *t.k.h: w ldr: led after 2f: hdd over 1f out: wknd fnl 100yds* **7/4**[1]

425- **6** *nk* **Beaumont's Party (IRE)**[17] 6163 5-9-5 **94** .... JimmyFortune 3 79
(Chris Grant) *mid-div: kpt on fnl 2f: nvr on terms* **25/1**

0205 **7** *27* **Licence To Till (USA)**[10] 1139 5-8-10 **85** .... SilvestreDeSousa 9 16+
(Mark Johnston) *chsd ldrs: wknd wl over 1f out: sn heavily eased: t.o* **15/2**

103- **8** *6* **Kinyras (IRE)**[193] 6497 4-8-13 **88** .... JamesSullivan 5
(Michael Easterby) *in rr: bhd fnl 3f: t.o* **25/1**

2030 **9** *3* **Reve De Nuit (USA)**[10] 1128 6-8-10 **85** .... AndrewMullen 10
(Alan McCabe) *chsd ldrs: drvn over 3f out: sn lost pl and bhd: t.o* **33/1**

422- **10** *9* **Las Verglas Star (IRE)**[208] 6080 4-8-13 **88** .... PaulHanagan 7
(Richard Fahey) *anticipated s and missed break: drvn over 3f out: sn bhd: t.o* **6/1**[3]

2m 16.66s (2.96) **Going Correction** +0.35s/f (Good) **10** Ran SP% **118.5**
Speed ratings (Par 109): **102,102,101,96,94 94,72,67,65,58**WIN: Deauville Flyer £15.00, Mirrored £7.20: Place: DF £8.10, Mirrored £3.70 Northside Prince £3.10 EX: DF/M £106.60, M/DF £87.36 CSF: DF/M £91.62, M/DF £87.36 TRICAST: DF/M/NP £701.28 M/DF/NP £669.18. Tote Swingers: DF&M £35.00, DF&NP £9.90, M&NP £31.70.27 CSF £Owner CT £Middleham Park Racing XXX TOTE £Bred: £Millsec Limited, £Trained, £Great Habton, N Yorks.
Owner Mr And Mrs J D Cotton **Bred** Harts Farm And Stud **Trained** Great Habton, N Yorks
■ Stewards' Enquiry : Graham Gibbons two-day ban: used whip above permitted level (Apr 24-25)

FOCUS
The pace was much too strong, with the free-going Splendid Light leading ahead of confirmed front-runner Suits Me. That helped set the race up nicely for those held up and a couple of Tim Easterby-trained runners shared the prize.

NOTEBOOK
Deauville Flyer's latest success had been gained over 2m, so it helped that the quick gallop brought his stamina into play. He had been off for 199 days and may have more to offer, especially when back up in distance, but the bare result flatters him. (op 25-1)
Mirrored hadn't been seen for six months, but he has won when fresh in the past, so is not sure to find significant improvement for this run. (op 25-1)
Northside Prince(IRE), a beaten favourite on his hurdling debut when last seen in December, ran a fine race on his return to the Flat as he had sat closer to the overly quick gallop than the first two finishers. (op 8-1)
Suits Me was taken wide once it was clear he couldn't get his own way (presumably doesn't like company), but it didn't help him to save anything for the finish and he was spent early in the straight. This performance is easily excused. (op 6-1)
Splendid Light, surprisingly turned out just two weeks after overcoming a lengthy absence to win a Polytrack maiden (runner-up won earlier on this card), but it's impossible to know whether or not he bounced as he simply went off too fast. Just like last time, he was quite headstrong, so he was again sent to the front, but he had no chance of sustaining such a quick pace. It's hoped this doesn't set him back, as he had looked a nice prospect. (op 13-8 tchd 2-1)
Las Verglas Star(IRE) Official explanation: jockey said gelding missed the break having anticipated the start

1274 PONTEFRACT-RACES.CO.UK MAIDEN FILLIES' STKS — 6f
4:55 (4:57) (Class 5) 3-Y-0 — **£2,385** (£704; £352) **Stalls** Low

Form RPR

24- **1** **Lisiere (IRE)**[186] 6673 3-9-0 **0** .... PaulHanagan 11 82
(Mrs K Burke) *mde virtually all: edgd lft and drew clr appr fnl f* **7/4**[1]

2 *6* **Bessichka** 3-9-0 **0** .... JimmyFortune 9 63
(Simon Dow) *sn chsng ldrs: kpt on same pce to take 2nd last 100yds* **8/1**

6 **3** *2 1/2* **Dartrix**[7] 1173 3-9-0 **0** .... TomEaves 6 55+
(Michael Dods) *s.i.s: hdwy and edgd rt over 1f out: styd on ins fnl f: tk 3rd nr fin* **25/1**

6 **4** *1* **Finesse**[21] 969 3-9-0 **0** .... JimCrowley 12 52
(Ralph Beckett) *chsd ldrs: kpt on one pce over 1f out* **7/2**[2]

5 *nk* **Elegant Girl (IRE)** 3-9-0 **0** .... DavidAllan 5 51+
(Tim Easterby) *chsd ldrs: one pce fnl 2f* **20/1**

23 **6** *nk* **Trail Of Tears (IRE)**[18] 1016 3-9-0 **0** .... WilliamBuick 8 50
(John Gosden) *chsd ldrs: fdd over 1f out* **6/1**[3]

7 *1 1/4* **Sherry Cherie (IRE)** 3-9-0 **0** .... PatrickMathers 4 46+
(Richard Fahey) *ponied to s: s.i.s: kpt on fnl 2f: nvr a factor* **33/1**

0-2 **8** *2 3/4* **Tooley Woods (IRE)**[53] 604 3-9-0 **0** .... DavidProbert 3 37
(George Margarson) *chsd ldrs: upsides over 2f out: wknd over 1f out* **11/1**

9 *3/4* **Toodeloo** 3-9-0 **0** .... PhillipMakin 2 34
(Kevin Ryan) *mid-div: effrt over 2f out: sn wknd* **20/1**

10 *4* **Irish Girls Spirit (IRE)** 3-9-0 **0** .... MickyFenton 7 22
(Paul Midgley) *mid-div: effrt on outer over 2f out: sn wknd* **66/1**

0 **11** *hd* **Caboodle**[25] 925 3-9-0 **0** .... StephenCraine 1 21
(Tom Dascombe) *mid-div: hdwy on inner over 2f out: lost pl over 1f out* **25/1**

0- 12 *hd* **Al Dain (IRE)**[203] 6232 3-9-0 0.. TonyHamilton 10 20
(Kevin Ryan) *in rr: bhd fnl 2f* **40/1**

1m 19.41s (2.51) **Going Correction** +0.175s/f (Good) 12 Ran SP% **116.4**
Speed ratings (Par 95): **90,82,78,77,76 76,74,71,70,64 64,64**
Tote Swingers: 1&2 £4.60, 1&3 £10.10, 2&3 £24.30 CSF £14.43 TOTE £2.70: £1.30, £2.20, £5.90; EX 13.70 Trifecta £76.10 Pool: £1,222.03 - 11.88 winning units..
Owner David & Yvonne Blunt **Bred** Swordlestown Stud **Trained** Middleham Moor, N Yorks

FOCUS
An ordinary fillies' maiden.

1275 RACING ON MONDAY 23RD APRIL H'CAP — 1m 2f 6y
5:25 (5:26) (Class 5) (0-75,75) 4-Y-O+ £2,385 (£704; £352) Stalls Low

Form RPR
001- 1 **Media Hype**[285] 3559 5-9-2 **70**.. PhillipMakin 7 86+
(Mrs K Burke) *s.i.s: hdwy over 3f out: led appr fnl f: edgd lft and forged clr: eased towards fin* **9/1**

0113 2 *5* **Ay Tay Tate (IRE)**[13] 1071 6-8-12 **66**........................(p) JimmyFortune 1 72
(David C Griffiths) *chsd ldrs: kpt on to take 2nd last 75yds: no ch w wnr* **7/1**[3]

000- 3 *1/2* **Doctor Zhivago**[199] 6346 5-9-5 **73**.. TomEaves 4 78
(Ian McInnes) *hld up in mid-div: hdwy 3f out: nt clr run 2f out: styd on fnl f* **14/1**

04-4 4 *nk* **Veiled Applause**[10] 1135 9-8-12 **69**..................... MichaelO'Connell(3) 10 73
(John Quinn) *mid-div: effrt over 2f out: kpt on fnl f* **13/2**[2]

021- 5 *1 1/4* **Brockfield**[140] 7506 6-9-2 **70**.. SilvestreDeSousa 3 72
(Mel Brittain) *led: hdd appr fnl f: wknd towards fin* **7/2**[1]

30-0 6 *1/2* **Sartingo (IRE)**[10] 1135 5-8-6 **65**................................ GarryWhillans(5) 11 66
(Alan Swinbank) *in rr: hmpd bnd after 2f: hung lft and kpt on fnl 2f: nvr nr ldrs* **20/1**

060- 7 *1 3/4* **Gala Casino Star (IRE)**[166] 7130 7-8-12 **73**............... JordanNason(7) 2 70
(Geoffrey Harker) *s.i.s: kpt on fnl 2f: nvr nr ldrs* **33/1**

123- 8 *nse* **Odin's Raven (IRE)**[260] 4382 7-9-4 **75**........................ PaulPickard(3) 12 72
(Brian Ellison) *s.i.s: kpt on fnl 2f: nvr nr ldrs* **20/1**

61-0 9 *shd* **Daring Indian**[21] 971 4-9-4 **75**.. RyanPowell(3) 17 72
(Ian Williams) *in rr: nt clr run over 2f out: kpt on fnl f* **10/1**

502- 10 *1/2* **Tapis Libre**[161] 7215 4-8-7 **68**................................ DavidSimmonson(7) 14 64
(Michael Easterby) *mid-div: effrt over 2f out: nvr a factor* **25/1**

000- 11 *2* **Camerooney**[191] 6302 9-9-7 **75**.. BarryMcHugh 9 67
(Brian Ellison) *chsd ldrs: wknd over 1f out* **20/1**

2256 12 *3 1/2* **The Lock Master (IRE)**[14] 1056 5-8-13 **67**.................. NeilChalmers 16 52
(Michael Appleby) *in rr: nvr on terms* **25/1**

031- 13 *3 1/2* **Spanish Plume**[144] 7453 4-9-7 **75**................................ GrahamGibbons 8 53
(Reg Hollinshead) *chsd ldrs: lost pl over 1f out* **14/1**

050- 14 *6* **Goldenveil (IRE)**[144] 7453 4-9-2 **70**.................................... PaulHanagan 15 36
(Richard Fahey) *mid-div: effrt over 2f out: sn wknd* **10/1**

60-0 15 *11* **Pertuis (IRE)**[10] 1135 6-9-1 **69**..................................(p) FrederikTylicki 13 13
(Micky Hammond) *mid-div on outer: lost pl over 2f out: sn bhd* **33/1**

00-0 16 *4* **Amazing Blue Sky**[10] 1134 6-9-5 **73**.................................... JamesSullivan 5
(Ruth Carr) *t.k.h: trckd ldrs: wknd over 2f out* **20/1**

0346 17 *65* **Thunderstruck**[26] 907 7-9-0 **68**..(p) IanMongan 6
(Scott Dixon) *chsd ldrs on outer: hmpd bnd after 2f: lost pl over 2f out: bhd and eased over 1f out: virtually p.u: hopelessly t.o* **16/1**

2m 16.71s (3.01) **Going Correction** +0.35s/f (Good) 17 Ran SP% **127.2**
Speed ratings (Par 103): **101,97,96,96,95 94,93,93,93,93 91,88,85,81,72 69,17**
Tote Swingers: 1&2 £14.40, 1&3 £24.40, 2&3 £18.90 CSF £64.39 CT £893.12 TOTE £10.70: £3.30, £2.20, £3.40, £2.50; EX 105.80 Trifecta £457.60 Part won. Pool: £618.46 - 0.60 winning tickets..
Owner Light Valley Stud & Mrs E Burke **Bred** Meon Valley Stud **Trained** Middleham Moor, N Yorks

FOCUS
A modest handicap run at a good pace.
Sartingo(IRE) Official explanation: jockey said gelding suffered interference on first bend

1276 "HIGHLY COMMENDED" PONTEFRACT LOYALTY CARD H'CAP (DIV II) — 1m 4y
5:55 (5:55) (Class 5) (0-70,69) 4-Y-O+ £2,385 (£704; £352) Stalls Low

Form RPR
2-43 1 **Thackeray**[33] 833 5-8-9 **57**.. KellyHarrison 6 67
(Chris Fairhurst) *t.k.h in rr: hdwy on inner over 2f out: chsd ldrs over 1f out: edgd rt: styd on to ld clsng stages* **20/1**

4554 2 *1 1/4* **Striker Torres (IRE)**[46] 692 6-9-4 **66**.....................(v) FrederikTylicki 12 73
(Ian McInnes) *s.i.s: hdwy 3f out: sn chsng ldrs: led over 1f out: hdd and no ex last 40yds* **10/1**

0030 3 *1/2* **Georgebernardshaw (IRE)**[12] 1094 7-8-13 **61**........... WilliamCarson 3 67
(Richard Guest) *chsd ldrs: swtchd rt 2f out: styd on fnl f* **5/1**[3]

-020 4 *4* **Maven**[10] 1133 4-9-7 **69**.. DuranFentiman 4 66
(Tim Easterby) *chsd ldrs: edgd lft over 1f out: one pce* **7/1**

1-25 5 *1 1/2* **River Ardeche**[35] 809 7-9-7 **69**.. MartinLane 1 62
(Tracy Waggott) *w ldr: led after 2f: hdd over 1f out: one pce* **14/1**

02-3 6 *5* **Seldom (IRE)**[3] 1222 6-9-1 **63**.. SilvestreDeSousa 7 45
(Mel Brittain) *mid-div: effrt over 2f out: nvr nr ldrs* **11/4**[1]

000- 7 *5* **Cono Zur (FR)**[172] 6990 5-9-4 **66**.. JamesSullivan 5 36
(Ruth Carr) *led 2f: w ldr: wknd over 1f out* **4/1**[2]

000- 8 *3 3/4* **Idealism**[195] 6453 5-8-7 **55** oh10.. LeeNewman 14 17
(Micky Hammond) *in rr: hdwy over 3f out: wknd over 1f out* **66/1**

9 *3 1/4* **Snooker (GER)**[12] 6-9-3 **65**.. PaulHanagan 11 19
(Rose Dobbin) *in rr: drvn 3f out: nvr a factor* **16/1**

423- 10 *4* **Deep Applause**[205] 6192 4-9-0 **62**.. TomEaves 13
(Michael Dodds) *s.i.s: hdwy 3f out: wknd over 1f out* **20/1**

054- 11 *1/2* **Munaawib**[188] 6633 4-8-8 **59**..(bt) HarryBentley(3) 9
(David C Griffiths) *sn chsng ldrs: lost pl over 2f out* **33/1**

0045 12 *3 3/4* **Yorksters Prince (IRE)**[10] 1135 5-9-7 **69**.................(b) BarryMcHugh 10
(Tony Coyle) *mid-div: hdwy on outer to chse ldrs over 4f out: lost pl over 2f out* **14/1**

1m 48.07s (2.17) **Going Correction** +0.35s/f (Good) 12 Ran SP% **118.1**
Speed ratings (Par 103): **103,101,101,97,95 90,85,82,78,74 74,70**
Tote Swingers: 1&2 £23.20, 1&3 £15.20, 2&3 £5.80 CSF £199.74 CT £1184.35 TOTE £25.40: £5.70, £4.40, £2.00; EX 190.80 TRIFECTA Not won..
Owner Mrs C A Arnold **Bred** Mrs R D Peacock **Trained** Middleham Moor, N Yorks

FOCUS
The second leg of a modest handicap.
T/Jkpt: £2,777.70 to a £1 stake. Pool: £25,000.00 - 9.00 winning tickets. T/Plt: £348.60 to a £1 stake. Pool: £95,084.00 - 199.06 winning tickets. T/Qpdt: £5,097.00 to a £1 stake. Pool: £5,097.00 - 39.70 winning tickets. WG

[1173]SOUTHWELL (L-H)
Tuesday, April 10

OFFICIAL GOING: Standard
Wind: Fresh across Weather: Fine and dry

1277 £32 FREE AT 32RED.COM MAIDEN STKS — 5f (F)
2:00 (2:01) (Class 5) 2-Y-O £2,264 (£673; £336; £168) Stalls High

Form RPR
1 **Somethingboutmary** 2-8-9 0.. AmyRyan(3) 4 68+
(Kevin Ryan) *wnt lft s: green: hung lft and outpcd after 2f: hdwy on outer wl over 1f out: sn rdn and green: styd on wl fnl f to ld last 50yds* **4/1**[3]

2 *1/2* **Stripped Bear (IRE)** 2-8-12 0.. StephenCraine 2 66
(Tom Dascombe) *trckd ldr: cl up 1/2-way: chal 2f out: rdn to ld ent fnl f: hdd and no ex last 50yds* **9/2**

3 *2* **Crystal Cove** 2-9-3 0.. RobertWinston 3 64
(Tim Easterby) *led: jnd and shkn up 2f out: rdn and hdd ent fnl f: kpt on same pce* **11/4**[2]

4 *4* **Hillbilly Boy (IRE)** 2-8-10 0.. DarrenEgan(7) 1 50
(Bill Turner) *s.i.s and rdn along in rr: hdwy and in tch 1/2-way: sn rdn and btn wl over 1f out* **85/40**[1]

5 *1* **Lady Raffa** 2-8-9 0.. LeeTopliss(3) 5 41
(Michael Dodds) *chsd ldrs: rdn along over 2f out: sn wknd* **16/1**

5 6 *4 1/2* **Khyber Bridge**[8] 1165 2-9-3 0.. TonyCulhane 6 30
(Jo Hughes) *chsd ldng pair: rdn along 1/2-way: sn wknd* **16/1**

59.94s (0.24) **Going Correction** -0.15s/f (Stan) 6 Ran SP% **108.6**
Speed ratings (Par 92): **92,91,88,81,80 72**
Tote Swingers: 1&2 £2.40, 1&3 £2.80, 2&3 £3.30 CSF £20.41 TOTE £4.90: £1.70, £2.70; EX 19.00.
Owner Wildcard Racing Syndicate **Bred** Stuart Thom & Paul Rock **Trained** Hambleton, N Yorks

FOCUS
The first 2-y-o race of the season on Fibresand and a modest affair, but the winner can go on. The form is fluid at this stage.

NOTEBOOK
Somethingboutmary ◆, out of a sister to the 1000 Guineas third Super Sleuth and by a sire with a fair record here, is a January foal and was the oldest in the field, but she still showed her inexperience, missing the break and than racing green towards the far side of the track. However, she still managed to pick these off without her rider having to go for absolutely everything and there is probably even better to come. (op 7-2)
Stripped Bear(IRE), an 18,000GBP half-sister to a 7f juvenile winner, showed good speed and had every chance, but no sooner had she got the better of the leader than the winner pounced. An ordinary early-season event can come her way. (op 4-1)
Crystal Cove, out of a winning half-sister to nine winners by a sire with a 28% strike-rate here, like the winner is a January foal and he showed decent speed out in front until collared entering the last furlong. He obviously possesses some ability. (op 10-3 tchd 5-2)
Hillbilly Boy(IRE), retained for 15,000GBP as a yearling out of a winning sprinter, would have been the stable's representative in the Brocklesby had sore shins not kept him away from Doncaster. However, he completely missed the kick and that is usually fatal over this straight 5f. (op 11-4 tchd 3-1)

1278 32REDPOKER.COM MEDIAN AUCTION MAIDEN STKS — 7f (F)
2:30 (2:32) (Class 6) 3-4-Y-O £1,704 (£503; £251) Stalls Low

Form RPR
066- 1 **Kingscombe (USA)**[131] 7593 3-8-13 56.. CathyGannon 4 63
(Pat Eddery) *cl up: rdn to ld over 1f out: drvn ins fnl f and kpt on gamely* **9/4**[2]

03 2 *1/2* **Charlcot**[50] 638 4-9-13 0.. KierenFallon 2 67
(James Bethell) *trckd ldrs: hdwy 3f out: chal wl over 1f out: sn rdn and ev ch tl no ex last 100yds* **15/2**

4-03 3 *8* **Celestial Dawn**[7] 1173 3-8-3 51.. RaulDaSilva(5) 1 35
(John Weymes) *cl up on inner: led after 3f: rdn along over 2f out: drvn and hdd over 1f out: sn one pce* **9/1**

0-42 4 *3 1/4* **Pearls From Sydney**[7] 1173 3-8-9 0 ow1..................... StevieDonohoe 8 28
(Paul Cole) *trckd ldrs: swtchd rt to outer and effrt 2f out: sn rdn and edgd lft wl over 1f out: sn one pce* **11/2**[3]

4 5 *2 1/2* **Fushicho**[42] 730 3-8-13 0.. DarryllHolland 6 25
(Michael Wigham) *sn rdn along and outpcd in rr: bhd 1/2-way: swtchd wd 2f out and sme late hdwy* **50/1**

350- 6 *1/2* **Daddyow**[10] 4385 4-9-13 65.. FergusSweeney 3 29
(Tim Vaughan) *in tch: hdwy on outer and cl up 3df out: rdn over 2f out: edgd lft wl over 1f out and sn wknd* **20/1**

600- 7 *5* **Choisirez (IRE)**[197] 6399 3-8-8 57.. PadraigBeggy 7
(David Evans) *sn rdn along and a bhd* **25/1**

0- 8 *1 1/4* **Adverse (IRE)**[226] 5514 3-8-8 0.. HayleyTurner 9
(Michael Bell) *led 3f: cl up: rdn along over 3f out and sn wknd* **7/4**[1]

1m 31.35s (1.05) **Going Correction** +0.025s/f (Slow)
WFA 3 from 4yo 14lb 8 Ran SP% **114.9**
Speed ratings (Par 101): **95,94,85,81,78 78,72,71**
Tote Swingers: 1&2 £0.00, 1&3 £6.90, 2&3 £7.20 CSF £19.00 TOTE £4.40: £2.50, £2.00, £2.50; EX 25.30.
Owner P W Middleton **Bred** Juddmonte Farms Inc **Trained** Nether Winchendon, Bucks

FOCUS
A moderate maiden with the winner rated just 56.

1279 32RED CASINO CLAIMING STKS — 6f (F)
3:00 (3:01) (Class 6) 3-Y-O+ £1,704 (£503; £251) Stalls Low

Form RPR
2422 1 **Punching**[7] 1177 8-9-3 68.. HayleyTurner 7 75
(Conor Dore) *mde all: rdn and qcknd 2f out: kpt on wl u.p fnl f* **5/2**[2]

-100 2 *1 1/2* **Ghostwing**[63] 458 5-9-8 80.. FergusSweeney 5 75
(James Evans) *trckd ldrs: hdwy on outer over 2f out: rdn and carried hd high over 1f out: sn edgd lft and kpt on same pce* **11/4**[3]

2062 3 *nk* **Riflessione**[13] 1069 6-8-10 67..(v) DarrenEgan(7) 4 69
(Ronald Harris) *cl up: rdn along 2f out: drvn over 1f out: sn one pce* **8/1**

300- 4 *1 3/4* **Beat The Bell**[207] 6112 7-8-13 81.. DeanHeslop(5) 3 67
(David Barron) *trckd ldrs: effrt wl over 2f out: rdn wl over 1f out: hld whn n.m.r and squeezed out ins fnl f* **15/8**[1]

0123 5 *1/2* **Elhamri**[7] 1177 8-9-2 67.. LiamKeniry 2 61
(Conor Dore) *trckd ldrs: effrt over 2f out: sn n.m.r and swtchd rt to outer: rdn over 1f out and no imp fnl f* **12/1**

/00- 6 5 **Orpen Wide (IRE)**147 6236 10-9-2 44........................(bt) AnnStokell(5) 6 50
(Michael Chapman) *dwlt: a in rr* **125/1**
1m 16.33s (-0.17) **Going Correction** +0.025s/f (Slow) 6 Ran SP% **109.6**
Speed ratings (Par 101): **102,100,99,97,96 89**
Tote Swingers: 1&2 £1.10, 1&3 £1.90, 2&3 £11.40 CSF £9.29 TOTE £4.40: £2.70, £1.10; EX 10.30.
Owner Liam Breslin **Bred** Cheveley Park Stud Ltd **Trained** Hubbert's Bridge, Lincs
■ Stewards' Enquiry : Fergus Sweeney one-day ban: careless riding (Apr 24)

FOCUS
A moderate claimer and, not for the first time in races like this, official ratings were turned on their head.

1280 ATR GRAND NATIONAL MICROSITE NOW LIVE H'CAP 6f (F)
3:30 (3:30) (Class 6) (0-60,60) 4-Y-0+ **£1,704** (£503; £251) **Stalls** Low

Form RPR
2342 1 **Ace Of Spies (IRE)**7 1178 7-9-7 60................................ HayleyTurner 1 73
(Conor Dore) *cl up on inner: chal over 2f out: rdn to ld 1f out: styd on strly* **2/1**1
-302 2 5 **The Magic Of Rio**21 979 6-8-7 46 oh1.......................... CathyGannon 6 43
(John Balding) *led: rdn along and jnd over 2f out: hdd 1f out and kpt on same pce* **11/2**
0544 3 ½ **Gracie's Gift (IRE)**27 904 10-8-10 49........................(v) KierenFallon 5 44
(Richard Guest) *chsd ldrs: wd st and sn rdn along: drvn over 1f out: styd on fnl f* **4/1**2
4055 4 2½ **La Capriosa**35 808 6-9-7 60....................................(b1) RobertWinston 8 47
(Scott Dixon) *prom: rdn and ch over 2f out: sn drvn and one pce fr over 1f out* **7/1**
600- 5 4½ **Gentleman Is Back (USA)**193 6505 4-9-7 60.................. LiamKeniry 2 33
(Ed de Giles) *trckd ldrs: effrt wl over 2f out: sn rdn and wknd* **14/1**
040- 6 5 **Gracie's Games**177 6889 6-8-13 55..........................(v) SophieDoyle(3) 3 12
(Richard Price) *in tch: rdn along on inner wl over 2f out: sn wknd* **25/1**
6-00 7 6 **Juarla (IRE)**34 819 4-8-12 58................................. DarrenEgan(7) 4
(Ronald Harris) *a in rr: outpcd and bhd fr 1/2-way* **9/2**3
003- 8 1¾ **Charles Parnell (IRE)**218 5787 9-9-0 53......................(p) JoeFanning 7
(Simon Griffiths) *dwlt: a bhd* **25/1**
1m 16.37s (-0.13) **Going Correction** +0.025s/f (Slow) 8 Ran SP% **113.8**
Speed ratings (Par 101): **101,94,93,90,84 77,69,67**
Tote Swingers: 1&2 £3.00, 1&3 £2.60, 2&3 £4.70 CSF £13.22 CT £39.06 TOTE £4.30: £1.40, £3.80, £2.50; EX 11.00.
Owner Mrs Louise Marsh **Bred** Gainsborough Stud Management Ltd **Trained** Hubbert's Bridge, Lincs

FOCUS
A moderate sprint handicap. The winning time was fractionally slower than the claimer.

1281 32RED.COM H'CAP 1m 4f (F)
4:05 (4:05) (Class 5) (0-75,73) 3-Y-0 **£2,385** (£704; £352) **Stalls** Low

Form RPR
6213 1 **Cape Safari (IRE)**19 994 3-9-1 67...............................(p) KierenFallon 2 75+
(James Tate) *trckd ldrs: hdwy over 3f out: chsd ldr whn n.m.r on inner wl over 1f out: sn rdn and styd on to ld jst ins fnl f: sn edgd rt and styd on strly* **5/1**3
2-21 2 2 **Quixote**36 803 3-9-2 68.. HayleyTurner 3 72
(Clive Brittain) *led 1f: cl up: led again over 4f out: rdn and hung lft wl over 1f out: drvn and hdd jst ins fnl f: sn no ex* **9/4**1
-311 3 ¾ **Spartilla**62 472 3-8-13 65.. PaulMulrennan 5 68
(James Given) *trckd ldrs: hdwy over 3f out: rdn 2f out and kpt on same pce appr fnl f* **5/2**2
1 4 14 **Red Orator**48 650 3-9-7 73... JoeFanning 1 53
(Mark Johnston) *stmbld and reminders s: hdwy on inner to ld after 1f: rdn along 1/2-way: hdd over 4f out: wknd over 3f out* **5/2**2
45-4 5 6 **Minnie Diva (IRE)**91 114 3-8-10 65.............................. JulieBurke(3) 4 36
(Kevin Ryan) *prom: rdn along and lost pl after 3f: sn in rr and bhd fr over 4f out* **16/1**
2m 39.56s (-1.44) **Going Correction** +0.025s/f (Slow) 5 Ran SP% **110.5**
Speed ratings (Par 98): **105,103,103,93,89**
CSF £16.61 TOTE £9.80: £8.70, £2.10; EX 18.30.
Owner Saif Ali **Bred** Rabbah Bloodstock Limited **Trained** Newmarket, Suffolk

FOCUS
An ordinary middle-distance handicap for 3yos, though four of the five runners had recent winning form.

1282 32RED H'CAP 2m (F)
4:35 (4:35) (Class 4) (0-85,85) 4-Y-0+ **£4,075** (£1,212; £606; £303) **Stalls** Low

Form RPR
60-2 1 **Boss's Destination**14 1056 5-9-8 81............................. PJMcDonald 10 89+
(Alan Swinbank) *hld up in rr: stdy hdwy over 5f out: jnd ldrs over 3f out: led 2f out and sn rdn: idled ent fnl f: kpt on wl* **3/1**2
12-0 2 1¼ **Taikoo**14 1056 7-9-12 85.. RobertWinston 3 90
(Hughie Morrison) *led 5f: cl up: rdn over 3f out and ev ch tl sltly outpcd and swtchd rt over 1f out: rallied ins fnl f* **12/1**
5-44 3 ½ **Bedouin Bay**14 1056 5-8-13 75....................................(p) SeanLevey(3) 9 79
(Alan McCabe) *cl up: led after 5f: rdn along 3f out: hdd 2f out: drvn and ev ch tl no ex ins fnl f* **9/1**
0 4 6 **Bocamix (FR)**22 500 6-8-11 70......................................(t) KierenFallon 6 69
(Andrew Crook) *hld up in midfield: hdwy 4f out: rdn to chse ldrs over 2f out: drvn and no imp ent fnl f: hld whn eased fnl 100yds* **33/1**
26-4 5 56 **Jeu De Vivre (IRE)**2 1239 4-9-4 81.................................. JoeFanning 7 11
(Mark Johnston) *hld up: sme hdwy and in tch over 5f out: sn rdn along and wknd 4f out* **7/1**3
-113 6 6 **Captain Bellamy (USA)**14 1056 4-9-2 79..................... DarryllHolland 8
(Hughie Morrison) *prom: chsd ldng pair 1/2-way: rdn along 5f out: drvn 3f out and sn wknd* **13/8**1
2125 7 4½ **Blackmore**18 1003 5-9-2 75.. CathyGannon 2
(Julia Feilden) *towards rr: rdn along after 5f: sn outpcd and bhd: t.o fnl 4f* **17/2**
2/ 8 2½ **Sambulando (FR)**430 621 9-8-6 70............................... RaulDaSilva(5) 4
(Frank Sheridan) *dwlt and sn pushed along to chse ldrs: rdn along and lost pl bef 1/2-way: t.o fnl 4f* **100/1**
54-4 9 1½ **Ginger Grey (IRE)**7 1175 5-8-4 66 oh4..................(b) DeclanCannon(3) 5
(David O'Meara) *chsd ldrs: rdn along and lost pl 1/2-way: t.o fnl 4f* **16/1**
3m 44.72s (-0.78) **Going Correction** +0.025s/f (Slow)
WFA 4 from 5yo+ 4lb 9 Ran SP% **113.6**
Speed ratings (Par 105): **102,101,101,98,70 67,64,63,62**
Tote Swingers: 1&2 £7.60, 1&3 £5.00, 2&3 £20.50 CSF £37.95 CT £288.60 TOTE £4.20: £1.20, £8.30, £2.10; EX 41.80.
Owner G H Bell **Bred** Overbury Stallions Ltd **Trained** Melsonby, N Yorks

FOCUS
A reminder that 2m around here in a strongly run race is one of the greatest stamina tests in racing, on the Flat or over jumps. Bedouin Bay and Taikoo were responsible for the relentless early pace (the field was well strung out with a circuit left) and credit to both horses for still making the frame.
Captain Bellamy(USA) Official explanation: jockey said gelding never travelled
Blackmore Official explanation: jockey said gelding hung right
Sambulando(FR) Official explanation: jockey said gelding had no more to give

1283 VISIT ATTHERACES.COM/NATIONAL H'CAP 7f (F)
5:05 (5:06) (Class 6) (0-55,57) 4-Y-0+ **£1,704** (£503; £251) **Stalls** Low

Form RPR
2353 1 **Bonnie Prince Blue**7 1179 9-8-11 53...........................(b) DaleSwift(3) 9 66
(Ian McInnes) *towards rr: wd st: gd hdwy over 2f out: rdn over 1f out: led appr fnl f: sn clr* **15/2**3
0230 2 3¾ **Flow Chart (IRE)**7 1178 5-8-8 47.............................. RobbieFitzpatrick 8 50
(Peter Grayson) *towards rr: hdwy wl over 2f out: rdn to chse ldrs over 1f out: styd on fnl f: tk 2nd nr line* **8/1**
4004 3 shd **Spacecraft (IRE)**7 1179 5-8-9 48.................................... JoeFanning 1 51
(Christopher Kellett) *in rr: hdwy wl over 2f out: swtchd rt and rdn wl over 1f out: kpt on fnl f* **7/2**1
3353 4 hd **Jonnie Skull (IRE)**7 1178 6-9-2 55..............................(vt) KierenFallon 6 57
(Phil McEntee) *prom: chsd ldr over 2f out: sn rdn and ch tl drvn and one pce appr fnl f: lost 2nd nr line* **7/2**1
000- 5 3 **Blue Charm**196 6430 8-8-11 50.................................... PJMcDonald 2 44
(Ian McInnes) *in tch: hdwy to chse ldrs over 2f out: sn rdn and one pce* **20/1**
0100 6 ¾ **Tenancy (IRE)**7 1178 8-8-12 51.................................... RobertWinston 4 43
(Shaun Harris) *led: rdn over 2f out: drvn over 1f out: hdd & wknd appr fnl f* **20/1**
0-00 7 3½ **Eyes On**12 1095 4-8-4 48..(tp) RaulDaSilva(5) 14 31
(Frank Sheridan) *prom: rdn along wl over 2f out: sn wknd* **20/1**
6456 8 hd **Fantasy Fry**7 1178 4-9-0 53...(t) CathyGannon 7 35
(David Evans) *chsd ldrs: hdwy over 2f out: sn rdn and wknd wl over 1f out* **9/2**2
0040 9 6 **Crocodile Bay (IRE)**7 1178 9-8-7 51..................(p) CharlesEddery(5) 13 17
(Richard Guest) *prom: chsd ldr 1/2-way: rdn wl over 2f out and sn wknd* **25/1**
0-60 10 1½ **Swinger**50 633 4-8-11 53..(t) BillyCray(3) 12 15
(Scott Dixon) *prom: rdn along wl over 2f out: sn wknd* **9/1**
000- 11 11 **Indian Giver**197 6415 4-9-1 57 ow2................................ GaryBartley(3) 3
(Hugh McWilliams) *in rr: wd st: a bhd* **33/1**
0 12 33 **Liver Bird**35 809 4-8-11 50......................................(b1) RussKennemore 5
(Paul Midgley) *chsd ldrs on inner: n.m.r and hmpd 4f out: sn lost pl and bhd whn eased fnl 3f* **33/1**
1m 30.37s (0.07) **Going Correction** +0.025s/f (Slow) 12 Ran SP% **119.5**
Speed ratings (Par 101): **100,95,95,95,91 91,87,86,80,78 65,28**
Tote Swingers: 1&2 £11.10, 1&3 £4.30, 2&3 £6.20 CSF £59.23 CT £252.51 TOTE £8.00: £2.20, £3.50, £1.30; EX 56.90.
Owner Michael Hardcastle **Bred** George Joseph Hicks **Trained** Catwick, E Yorks
■ Stewards' Enquiry : Robbie Fitzpatrick two-day ban: used whip above permitted level (Apr 24-25)

FOCUS
A very moderate handicap with the two top weights rated just 55.
Indian Giver Official explanation: jockey said filly would not face the kickback
Liver Bird Official explanation: jockey said gelding hung badly left-handed
T/Plt: £105.50 to a £1 stake. Pool: £58,699.00 - 405.87 winning tickets. T/Qpdt: £23.70 to a £1 stake. Pool: £4,767.00 - 148.68 winning tickets. JR

1261 YARMOUTH (L-H)
Tuesday, April 10

OFFICIAL GOING: Good to soft (soft in places; 6.6)
Wind: Fresh across Weather: Cloudy with sunny spells

1284 NORFOLK RACING CLUB/BLUES PROPERTY MAIDEN AUCTION STKS 5f 43y
2:10 (2:10) (Class 6) 2-Y-0 **£1,617** (£481; £240; £120) **Stalls** Centre

Form RPR
1 **Mossgo (IRE)** 2-9-2 0.. LukeMorris 4 77+
(John Best) *chsd ldr tl led 1/2-way: edgd lft over 1f out: rdn out* **6/1**3
3 2 2 **Out Of The Blocks**8 1164 2-8-9 0.............................. RichardKingscote 5 63
(Tom Dascombe) *a.p: pushed along 1/2-way: rdn to chse wnr fnl f: styd on same pce* **4/5**1
3 1¾ **Reberty Lee** 2-8-9 0.. TomQueally 3 57
(Noel Quinlan) *s.i.s: pushed along in rr early: hdwy 1/2-way: rdn over 1f out: no ex ins fnl f* **11/2**2
4 1¼ **Eloquent Star (IRE)** 2-8-8 0 ow2......................... MatthewCosham(5) 2 56+
(David Evans) *s.i.s: sn pushed along to chse ldrs: rdn 1/2-way: no ex fnl f* **15/2**
6 5 3 **Sally Bruce**10 1136 2-7-11 0.................................... JenniferFerguson(7) 1 36
(Olivia Maylam) *led to 1/2-way: wknd ins fnl f* **17/2**
1m 6.94s (4.24) **Going Correction** +0.225s/f (Good) 5 Ran SP% **107.5**
Speed ratings (Par 90): **75,71,69,67,62**
CSF £10.91 TOTE £7.00: £2.50, £1.10; EX 11.40.
Owner Hucking Horses V **Bred** Louis Robinson **Trained** Hucking, Kent

FOCUS
This was an ordinary juvenile maiden. The field kept more towards the stands' rail and the second sets the level, although the form is a little guessy.

NOTEBOOK
Mossgo(IRE) made most and readily scored at the first time of asking. He knew his job from the gates and, despite wanting to hang left 1f out, knuckled down professionally under pressure inside the final furlong. He has some scope about him and is likely to come on nicely for the outing, so he could just bag a novice event at this early stage of the season. (op 13-2 tchd 5-1)
Out Of The Blocks was placed on his debut in a weak maiden at Redcar last week. As there was no strong support for his rivals he got heavily backed to put his previous experience to good use, but he ultimately still proved too green. This cheap purchase will do well to win a maiden. (op Evens tchd 6-5)
Reberty Lee's half-brother, Sensei, landed a gamble when winning on his debut for this stable two years ago. He travelled kindly off the pace, but proved laboured when asked for an effort and perhaps a sounder surface would help. (op 4-1)
Eloquent Star(IRE) ◆'s rider put up 2lb overweight. Already gelded, he proved very easy to back and was the first beaten. However, there was something to like about his finishing effort and it's a decent bet he'll show plenty more next time out. (op 7-1 tchd 6-1 and 8-1)

Sally Bruce showed up early before weakening and looks plating-class. (op 8-1 tchd 10-1)

1285 NORFOLK RACING CLUB/EAST ANGLIAN AIR AMBULANCE MEDIAN AUCTION MAIDEN STKS 6f 3y
2:40 (2:40) (Class 5) 3-4-Y-O **£2,264** (£673; £336; £168) **Stalls** Centre

Form				RPR
43	1		**Big Wave (IRE)**27 892 4-9-7 0 ShaneKelly 2 (Jane Chapple-Hyam) *plld hrd: w ldr tl led 2f out: shkn up ins fnl f: r.o* **11/4**2	67
0-	2	1 3/4	**Silver Lace (IRE)**157 7292 3-8-9 0 TedDurcan 1 (Chris Wall) *s.i.s: hld up: hdwy over 1f out: rdn to chse wnr ins fnl f: r.o* **10/1**3	58+
	3	2 1/2	**Kashmiri Star** 3-8-9 0 LukeMorris 6 (Michael Quinn) *prom: pushed along over 2f out: styd on same pce fnl f* **28/1**	50
05-	4	3/4	**Indiana Guest (IRE)**208 6099 3-9-0 0 TomQueally 3 (George Margarson) *s.i.s: hld up: racd keenly: hdwy 2f out: rdn over 1f out: no ex fnl f* **14/1**	53
6	5	1 1/2	**Give Us A Belle (IRE)**15 1048 3-9-0 0 TomMcLaughlin 4 (Christine Dunnett) *s.i.s: sn prom: rdn over 1f out: wknd ins fnl f* **150/1**	48
33-	6	2 3/4	**Knight Vision**299 3082 3-9-0 0 AdrianNicholls 5 (David Nicholls) *led: rdn and hdd 2f out: wknd ins fnl f* **4/5**1	39
640-	7	3/4	**Mucky Molly**123 7690 4-9-2 55 MarkCoumbe(5) 7 (Olivia Maylam) *prom: pushed along 1/2-way: rdn over 1f out: wknd fnl f* **12/1**	35

1m 16.31s (1.91) **Going Correction** +0.225s/f (Good)
WFA 3 from 4yo 12lb 7 Ran SP% **109.8**
Speed ratings (Par 103): **96,93,90,89,87 83,82**
Tote Swingers: 1&2 £2.80, 1&3 £4.90, 2&3 £15.20 CSF £27.00 TOTE £3.80: £1.80, £2.50; EX 32.00.
Owner Philip Carney **Bred** P De Vere Hunt **Trained** Dalham, Suffolk

FOCUS
A moderate maiden.
Knight Vision Official explanation: trainer's rep had no explanation for the poor form shown

1286 NORFOLK RACING CLUB/M.D. THOMPSON ELECTRICAL H'CAP 1m 3f 101y
3:10 (3:10) (Class 5) (0-70,71) 4-Y-0+ **£2,264** (£673; £336; £168) **Stalls** Centre

Form				RPR
224-	1		**Colinca's Lad (IRE)**114 7805 10-9-1 66 RosieJessop(5) 6 (Peter Charalambous) *mde virtually all: clr 6f out: rdr dropped whip 2f out: pushed out* **5/1**3	78
001-	2	6	**Grandad Mac**196 6437 4-9-1 61 ShaneKelly 3 (Jane Chapple-Hyam) *s.i.s: hld up: hdwy to chse wnr over 3f out: rdn over 2f out: styd on same pce* **11/8**1	63
0524	3	nk	**Jamarjo (IRE)**19 992 5-9-7 67 TomQueally 1 (Steve Gollings) *prom: rdn over 2f out: styd on same pce* **12/1**	68
33-1	4	9	**Tidal Run**5 1207 4-9-11 71 6ex MartinHarley 5 (Mick Channon) *hld up: hdwy over 3f out: rdn and wknd over 1f out* **9/4**2	57
0414	5	1 1/4	**Nolecce**27 891 5-9-1 64 (p) RobertLButler(3) 7 (Richard Guest) *hld up: hung lft over 4f out: hdwy over 3f out: rdn and wknd wl over 1f out* **10/1**	48
413-	6	4	**Royal Defence (IRE)**182 6769 6-9-1 61 PatCosgrave 4 (Michael Quinn) *chsd wnr 8f: sn rdn and wknd* **20/1**	38

2m 31.74s (3.04) **Going Correction** +0.10s/f (Good) 6 Ran SP% **111.1**
Speed ratings (Par 103): **92,87,87,80,79 77**
Tote Swingers: 1&2 £2.40, 1&3 £3.50, 2&3 £3.70 CSF £12.11 TOTE £3.80: £1.70, £2.20; EX 15.90.
Owner P Charalambous **Bred** Peter Charles **Trained** Newmarket, Suffolk

FOCUS
This looked competitive, but the winner hosed up.
Nolecce Official explanation: jockey said gelding hung left

1287 NORFOLK RACING CLUB/OAKLEY HORSEBOXES APPRENTICE (S) STKS 1m 2f 21y
3:40 (3:40) (Class 6) 3-Y-O **£1,617** (£481; £240; £120) **Stalls** Low

Form				RPR
1-5	1		**Final Delivery**83 209 3-9-2 72 DavidKenny 1 (George Baker) *hld up: hdwy 1/2-way: rdn to ld over 1f out: hung lft wl ins fnl f: kpt on* **4/9**1	58
00-0	2	1 3/4	**Imperial Stargazer**62 472 3-8-13 55 (v1) CharlesBishop(3) 5 (Mick Channon) *chsd ldr: rdn over 3f out: ev ch over 1f out: hung lft ins fnl f: styd on same pce* **6/1**3	54
3660	3	6	**Meet Joe Black (IRE)**1 1260 3-9-2 50 (v) MatthewCosham 3 (David Evans) *dwlt: reminders sn after s: hdwy to ld over 8f out: rdn and hdd over 1f out: hld whn hmpd ins fnl f: eased* **12/1**	47
006-	4	12	**April Leyf (IRE)**173 6977 3-8-8 36 JackDuern(3) 2 (Mark Brisbourne) *led: hdd over 8f out: chsd ldrs: rdn over 4f out: wknd over 3f out* **33/1**	13
60-6	5	dist	**Skyeron**25 923 3-8-8 45 RachealKneller(3) 4 (Mark Brisbourne) *hld up in tch: plld hrd: sddle slipped sn after s: lost tch fr over 4f out: t.o* **9/2**2	

2m 15.69s (5.19) **Going Correction** +0.10s/f (Good) 5 Ran SP% **112.4**
Speed ratings (Par 96): **83,81,76,67,**
CSF £3.87 TOTE £1.60: £1.10, £1.80; EX 3.00.There was no bid for the winner.
Owner M Khan X2 **Bred** Mallalieu Bloodstock Ltd **Trained** Whitsbury, Hants
■ Stewards' Enquiry : Charles Bishop one-day ban: careless riding (Apr 24)

FOCUS
A muddling 3-y-o seller.
Skyeron Official explanation: jockey said saddle slipped

1288 NORFOLK RACING CLUB/HAMLYN FINANCIAL SERVICES H'CAP 1m 1f
4:15 (4:18) (Class 5) (0-70,70) 3-Y-O **£2,264** (£673; £336; £168) **Stalls** Low

Form				RPR
113	1		**Miss Cato**68 393 3-8-12 61 ChrisCatlin 10 (Rae Guest) *mde all: rdn over 1f out: styd on wl* **6/1**3	74
4-64	2	2 3/4	**Kelpie Blitz (IRE)**12 1093 3-9-1 64 GeorgeBaker 9 (Seamus Durack) *hld up: hdwy and hmpd 2f out: rdn to chse wnr fnl f: hung lft: styd on* **7/2**1	71
003-	3	3 1/4	**My Guardian Angel**273 3954 3-9-4 67 TomQueally 2 (Mark H Tompkins) *prom: pushed along 1/2-way: rdn over 2f out: no ex fnl f* **9/1**	67
002-	4	3/4	**Harry Buckle**151 7369 3-9-6 69 LukeMorris 7 (Philip McBride) *hld up: hdwy over 3f out: sn rdn: no ex fnl f* **13/2**	67
006-	5	14	**Darrow (IRE)**225 5564 3-9-7 70 ShaneKelly 4 (William Knight) *chsd ldrs: rdn and edgd lft 2f out: sn wknd* **9/2**2	37
05-0	6	7	**Musically**25 917 3-9-3 66 MartinHarley 1 (Mick Channon) *hld up: hdwy over 3f out: rdn whn hmpd 2f out: sn wknd and eased* **25/1**	18
-220	7	11	**Athletic**15 1046 3-8-5 61 DavidWarren(7) 11 (Andrew Reid) *s.i.s: sn chsng wnr: wknd over 2f out: t.o* **33/1**	
0-10	8	3 1/2	**Flash Crash**53 596 3-9-5 68 PatCosgrave 3 (Robert Cowell) *chsd ldrs: rdn over 3f out: wknd over 2f out: t.o* **20/1**	
040-	9	16	**Denton Dancer**160 7222 3-8-13 62 (p) TedDurcan 6 (James Eustace) *s.i.s: hld up: rdn and wknd over 4f out: t.o* **50/1**	
0-33	10	35	**Vena Amoris (USA)**18 1004 3-8-13 62 NeilCallan 5 (Mark Johnston) *sn pushed along and prom: lost pl 7f out: bhd fnl 5f: t.o* **25/1**	

1m 57.0s (1.20) **Going Correction** +0.10s/f (Good) 10 Ran SP% **95.4**
Speed ratings (Par 98): **98,95,92,92,79 73,63,60,46,15**
Tote Swingers: 1&2 £2.80, 1&3 £6.70, 2&3 £4.90 CSF £15.92 CT £83.13 TOTE £3.90: £1.10, £1.90, £2.90; EX 16.80.
Owner A H Bennett **Bred** A H Bennett **Trained** Newmarket, Suffolk

FOCUS
This moderate 3yo handicap proved a lively betting heat. Fair form.
Vena Amoris(USA) Official explanation: jockey said filly never travelled

1289 NORFOLK RACING CLUB/PLANTDRIVE LTD H'CAP 6f 3y
4:45 (4:46) (Class 4) (0-80,79) 4-Y-0+ **£4,075** (£1,212; £606; £303) **Stalls** Centre

Form				RPR
425-	1		**Ray Of Joy**242 5018 6-9-6 78 TomQueally 3 (J R Jenkins) *hld up: hdwy over 1f out: r.o u.p to ld nr fin* **10/1**	86
231-	2	1/2	**Oh So Spicy**183 6752 5-9-0 72 TedDurcan 2 (Chris Wall) *hld up in tch: rdn and ev ch fr over 1f out: r.o* **10/3**1	78
33-0	3	hd	**Escape To Glory (USA)**12 1091 4-9-7 79 (v) GeorgeBaker 6 (Mikael Magnusson) *hld up: hdwy over 2f out: rdn to ld and hung lft 1f out: hdd nr fin* **8/1**	84
0326	4	hd	**Kylladdie**18 1007 5-9-5 77 (b) LukeMorris 9 (Steve Gollings) *stall opened fractionally early: led 1f: chsd ldrs: led wl over 1f out: rdn and hdd 1f out: r.o* **12/1**	82
3604	5	1/2	**Dickie Le Davoir**8 1168 8-9-1 76 (b) RobertLButler(3) 4 (Richard Guest) *hld up: swtchd lft and hdwy over 1f out: r.o* **16/1**	79
42-0	6	4	**Jack My Boy (IRE)**22 962 5-9-2 79 (b) MatthewCosham(5) 7 (David Evans) *led 5f out: rdn and hdd wl over 1f out: wknd and eased wl ins fnl f* **7/2**2	69
2250	7	3/4	**Captain Scooby**12 1091 6-9-6 78 MartinHarley 1 (Richard Guest) *chsd ldrs: rdn over 2f out: wknd fnl f* **12/1**	66
212-	8	1/2	**Comrade Bond**161 7213 4-8-12 70 NeilCallan 10 (Mark H Tompkins) *chsd ldrs: rdn over 1f out: wknd ins fnl f* **9/2**3	56
040-	9	nk	**Rough Rock (IRE)**157 7299 7-9-1 73 KieranO'Neill 5 (Chris Dwyer) *sn pushed along and prom: rdn over 2f out: wknd fnl f* **20/1**	58
3303	10	hd	**Hatta Stream (IRE)**18 1007 6-8-8 69 SimonPearce(3) 8 (Lydia Pearce) *dwlt: rdn over 2f out: n.d* **12/1**	54

1m 14.94s (0.54) **Going Correction** +0.225s/f (Good) 10 Ran SP% **117.4**
Speed ratings (Par 105): **105,104,104,103,103 97,96,96,95,95**
Tote Swingers: 1&2 £7.80, 1&3 £11.30, 2&3 £4.10 CSF £43.70 CT £287.03 TOTE £15.60: £5.10, £1.40, £2.40; EX 56.10.
Owner Robin Stevens **Bred** D R Tucker **Trained** Royston, Herts

FOCUS
A wide-open sprint handicap. There was a solid pace on and the first five came clear in a very tight finish down the centre of the track.

1290 DIGIBET.COM H'CAP 5f 43y
5:15 (5:15) (Class 5) (0-75,73) 4-Y-0+ **£2,264** (£673; £336; £168) **Stalls** Centre

Form				RPR
023-	1		**Bouncy Bouncy (IRE)**181 6802 5-9-2 68 (t) GeorgeBaker 6 (Michael Bell) *hld up: hdwy over 1f out: rdn to ld wl ins fnl f: r.o: readily* **3/1**2	79+
051-	2	1 1/4	**Style And Panache (IRE)**167 7106 4-9-2 73 MatthewCosham(5) 1 (David Evans) *chsd ldr: rdn and ev ch fr over 1f out tl unable qck wl ins fnl f* **10/3**3	79
-442	3	1/2	**Love You Louis**35 808 6-9-6 72 TomQueally 4 (J R Jenkins) *led: rdn over 1f out: edgd rt and hdd wl ins fnl f* **11/4**1	76
445-	4	2 1/4	**Danzoe (IRE)**125 7649 5-8-9 61 LukeMorris 3 (Christine Dunnett) *prom: pushed along 1/2-way: rdn over 1f out: styd on same pce fnl f* **15/2**	57
634-	5	3/4	**Liberty Ship**221 5680 7-9-4 70 RoystonFfrench 7 (Mark Buckley) *chsd ldrs: swtchd rt 1f out: rdn and nt clr run ins fnl f: no ex* **7/1**	63
344-	6	1 3/4	**Magical Speedfit (IRE)**180 6815 7-8-13 72 RichardOld(7) 9 (George Margarson) *hld up: effrt and hmpd over 1f out: wknd fnl f* **12/1**	59
0/0-	7	4 1/2	**Speedyfix**231 5355 5-8-11 63 (v) TomMcLaughlin 10 (Christine Dunnett) *hld up in tch: plld hrd: rdn: hung lft and wknd over 1f out* **33/1**	34

1m 3.96s (1.26) **Going Correction** +0.225s/f (Good) 7 Ran SP% **109.6**
Speed ratings (Par 103): **98,96,95,91,90 87,80**
Tote Swingers: 1&2 £3.20, 1&3 £1.20, 2&3 £4.90 CSF £12.25 CT £26.43 TOTE £3.90: £2.30, £1.30; EX 12.90.
Owner Mrs A Scotney Mrs D Asplin A Symonds **Bred** Ms Adelaide Foley & Roger O'Callaghan **Trained** Newmarket, Suffolk

FOCUS
A strongly run sprint handicap and sound form.
T/Plt: £33.00 to a £1 stake. Pool: £53,587.00 - 1,185.36 winning tickets. T/Qpdt: £7.40 to a £1 stake. Pool: £4,172.00 - 415.05 winning tickets. CR

1291 - (Foreign Racing) - See Raceform Interactive

CATTERICK (L-H)
Wednesday, April 11

OFFICIAL GOING: Good (good to soft in places) changing to good to soft (good in places) after race 4 (3:30)
Wind: Light across Weather: Sunshine and showers

1292 CATTERICK FLAT SEASON STARTS TODAY H'CAP 5f
2:00 (2:00) (Class 6) (0-60,60) 3-Y-O **£2,045** (£603; £302) **Stalls** Low

Form				RPR
600-	1		**Oneniteinheaven (IRE)**210 6043 3-8-12 54 MichaelO'Connell(3) 5 (Jane Chapple-Hyam) *trckd ldng pair: hdwy and cl up 2f out: rdn to chal over 1f out: drvn whn rdr dropped whip fnl 50yds: styd on to ld post* **4/1**1	60
0-65	2	shd	**Wish Again (IRE)**25 940 3-9-5 58 (p) AdrianNicholls 7 (David Nicholls) *led: rdn wl over 1f out: jnd appr fnl f and sn drvn: kpt on tl hdd and no ex nr line* **5/1**3	64

504- **3** 2¼ **Majestic Breeze (IRE)**[200] 6352 3-8-11 **50** BarryMcHugh 2 48
(Brian Ellison) *trckd ldrs: hdwy whn nt clr run and swtchd rt appr fnl f: sn rdn and kpt on* **9/2**[2]

-050 **4** 1 **Tuibama (IRE)**[33] 845 3-9-0 **53** (p) PJMcDonald 1 47
(Ben Haslam) *cl up on inner: rdn along 2f out: ev ch tl drvn and one pce appr fnl f* **5/1**[3]

00-3 **5** hd **Economic Crisis (IRE)**[26] 925 3-8-9 **55** MatthewHopkins(7) 6 48
(Alan Berry) *rrd s and s.i.s: hdwy to chse ldrs 1/2-way: rdn on inner whn n.m.r and hmpd over 1f out: kpt on same pce* **9/1**

4302 **6** 1½ **Lord Buffhead**[19] 1010 3-8-11 **55** CharlesEddery(5) 8 43
(Richard Guest) *chsd ldrs: hdwy on outer 2f out: sn rdn and one pce* **13/2**

4545 **7** 1¾ **M J Woodward**[28] 898 3-9-1 **59** (v) DarylByrne(5) 3 41
(Paul Green) *chsd ldrs: n.m.r and swtchd rt after 1f: rdn along bef 1/2-way and sn outpcd* **5/1**[3]

-005 **8** 11 **Brian's Best**[13] 1090 3-8-7 **46** oh1 NeilChalmers 9
(Richard Ford) *sn outpcd and a bhd* **80/1**

1m 1.87s (2.07) **Going Correction** +0.475s/f (Yiel) **8** Ran SP% **112.7**
Speed ratings (Par 96): **102,101,98,96,96 93,91,73**
toteswingers:1&2:£5.30, 1&3:£4.00, 2&3:£4.30 CSF £23.43 CT £92.30 TOTE £4.60: £3.00, £1.10, £2.40; EX 27.50.
Owner Mrs A Cantillon **Bred** Johnny Kent **Trained** Dalham, Suffolk

FOCUS
A modest start to the Flat season at Catterick.

1293 HAPPY 40TH BIRTHDAY KIRSTEN LAWRENCE H'CAP 7f
2:30 (2:33) (Class 5) (0-75,75) 4-Y-0+ **£2,264** (£673; £336; £168) **Stalls** Centre

Form RPR

20-0 **1** **Solar Spirit (IRE)**[9] 1168 7-9-6 **74** RobertWinston 3 86
(Tracy Waggott) *t.k.h: trckd ldrs on inner: hdwy 2f out: chsd ldr over 1f out: rdn ent fnl f: styd on wl to ld nr fin* **10/1**

004- **2** ½ **Madam Macie (IRE)**[169] 7076 5-9-7 **75** GrahamGibbons 11 86
(David O'Meara) *led: rdn clr wl over 1f out: drvn ins fnl f: hdd and no ex nr fin* **5/2**[1]

012- **3** 5 **Viking Warrior (IRE)**[179] 6867 5-8-13 **67** TomEaves 5 64
(Michael Dods) *in tch: hdwy 3f out: rdn to chse ldng pair wl over 1f out: sn edgd lft and kpt on same pce* **10/1**

410- **4** hd **Timeless Elegance (IRE)**[269] 4126 5-9-7 **75** LeeNewman 14 72
(David Barron) *sn chsng ldr: rdn 2f out and sn edgd rt: drvn and one pce fr over 1f out* **10/1**

003- **5** nse **Chosen Character (IRE)**[170] 7050 4-9-7 **75** (t) StephenCraine 7 71
(Tom Dascombe) *towards rr: hdwy over 2f out: rdn wl over 1f out: kpt on fnl f* **9/1**[3]

30-0 **6** 3 **Rio Cobolo (IRE)**[10] 1156 6-9-6 **74** AdrianNicholls 13 62
(David Nicholls) *towards rr: hdwy 3f out: rdn and n.m.r wl over 1f out: sn no imp* **14/1**

650- **7** ½ **Diman Waters (IRE)**[220] 5760 5-9-5 **73** TedDurcan 9 60
(Eric Alston) *t.k.h: trckd ldng pair: rdn along over 2f out: sn wknd* **12/1**

162- **8** nk **Icy Blue**[180] 6830 4-9-4 **75** AmyRyan(3) 12 61
(Richard Whitaker) *dwlt and towards rr tl sme hdwy on outer fnl 2f: nvr a factor* **16/1**

6116 **9** nse **Copperwood**[20] 991 7-8-9 **68** DarylByrne(5) 6 54
(Mark Johnston) *dwlt: a in rr* **17/2**[2]

150- **10** 1½ **Insolenceofoffice (IRE)**[153] 7349 4-8-8 **62** (p) NeilChalmers 8 44
(Richard Ford) *a towards rr* **50/1**

3061 **11** ½ **Chookie Avon**[25] 942 5-9-3 **71** (p) JamesSullivan 4 52
(Keith Dalgleish) *a towards rr* **10/1**

003- **12** 1½ **Lizzie (IRE)**[172] 7024 4-8-12 **66** (b) DavidAllan 1 43
(Tim Easterby) *midfield: n.m.r on inner bef 1/2-way: sn lost pl and bhd* **9/1**[3]

010- **13** 5 **No Quarter (IRE)**[199] 6381 5-8-9 **63** PatrickMathers 15 26
(Tracy Waggott) *chsd ldrs on outer: rdn along 1/2-way: sn wknd* **50/1**

1m 28.08s (1.08) **Going Correction** +0.475s/f (Yiel) **13** Ran SP% **119.6**
Speed ratings (Par 103): **103,102,96,96,96 93,92,92,92,90 89,88,82**
toteswingers:1&2:£7.20, 1&3:£15.00, 2&3:£5.70 CSF £35.04 CT £273.25 TOTE £14.40: £4.00, £1.60, £2.40; EX 45.60.
Owner Christopher James Allan **Bred** Paul Hensey **Trained** Spennymoor, Co Durham
■ Stewards' Enquiry : David Allan caution: careless riding.

FOCUS
A competitive handicap for the level, run at a good gallop.

1294 GORACING.CO.UK CLAIMING STKS 7f
3:00 (3:00) (Class 6) 3-Y-0+ **£1,704** (£503; £251) **Stalls** Centre

Form RPR

04-0 **1** **George Benjamin**[10] 1161 5-9-12 75 AndrewMullen 10 80
(David Nicholls) *hld up in tch: smooth hdwy over 2f out: rdn to ld ins fnl f: kpt on strly* **9/2**[3]

440- **2** 1¾ **No Poppy (IRE)**[169] 7076 4-9-2 77 AdamCarter(5) 9 70
(Tim Easterby) *towards rr: hdwy whn nt clr run and swtchd wd 2f out: sn rdn and styd on to chse ldng pair ent fnl f: edgd lft and kpt on: nt rch wnr* **4/1**[2]

040- **3** nk **Tajneed (IRE)**[79] 9-10-0 100 AdrianNicholls 1 76
(David Nicholls) *cl up: led 4f out: rdn wl over 1f out: hdd & wknd ins fnl f* **6/5**[1]

4005 **4** 2¼ **Romany Spirit (IRE)**[9] 1169 3-8-0 52 JamesSullivan 7 51
(Jason Ward) *chsd ldng pair: rdn along 2f out: drvn and kpt on same pce appr fnl f* **66/1**

0-06 **5** nk **Thrust Control (IRE)**[28] 900 5-9-3 51 JacobButterfield(7) 3 65?
(Tracy Waggott) *led 3f: cl up: rdn along over 2f out and grad wknd* **33/1**

00-0 **6** 2 **Boga (IRE)**[13] 1095 5-9-0 44 BarryMcHugh 5 50
(Karen Tutty) *chsd ldrs on inner: rdn along over 2f out: grad wknd* **100/1**

005- **7** 3¾ **Ursula (IRE)**[206] 6189 6-9-4 76 MichaelMetcalfe(3) 4 47
(Mrs K Burke) *chsd ldrs on inner: rdn along over 2f out: sn wknd* **9/2**[3]

225- **8** 1¼ **Baybshambles (IRE)**[293] 3307 8-9-7 57 DaleSwift(3) 6 46
(Ron Barr) *s.i.s: a bhd* **20/1**

/00- **9** hd **Penton Hook**[35] 5441 6-9-5 55 (p) PaddyAspell 8 41
(Barry Murtagh) *chsd ldrs on outer: rdn along bef 1/2-way: sn wknd and bhd* **200/1**

1m 29.08s (2.08) **Going Correction** +0.25s/f (Good)
WFA 3 from 4yo+ 14lb **9** Ran SP% **112.5**
Speed ratings (Par 101): **98,96,95,93,92 90,86,84,84**
toteswingers:1&2:£3.40, 1&3:£2.40, 2&3:£2.10 CSF £21.38 TOTE £9.00: £1.90, £1.20, £1.02; EX 24.10.George Benjamin was claimed by Kieran Burke for £10,000.
Owner C M & M A Scaife **Bred** Mascalls Stud **Trained** Sessay, N Yorks

FOCUS
The favourite didn't appear to stay the trip.

1295 PIN POINT RECRUITMENT H'CAP 1m 3f 214y
3:30 (3:36) (Class 4) (0-80,80) 4-Y-0+ **£4,075** (£1,212; £606; £303) **Stalls** Low

Form RPR

200- **1** **Chilly Filly (IRE)**[207] 6172 6-9-7 **80** BarryMcHugh 8 89
(Brian Ellison) *trckd ldrs: hdwy and cl up 3f out: rdn to chal over 1f out: styd on wl to ld last 50yds* **7/1**[3]

0-61 **2** hd **Arizona John (IRE)**[10] 1154 7-8-10 **72** 6ex DeclanCannon(3) 7 81
(John Mackie) *trckd ldrs: hdwy 4f out: led 3f out: rdn over 1f out: drvn and edgd rt ins fnl f: hdd and no ex towards fin* **13/2**[2]

00-4 **3** 2¼ **Embsay Crag**[11] 1133 6-8-10 **69** KellyHarrison 1 74
(Kate Walton) *hld up towards rr: hdwy 3f out: rdn to chse ldrs 2f out: styd on fnl f: nrst fin* **7/1**[3]

242- **4** 1 **Sohcahtoa (IRE)**[166] 7139 6-8-8 **72** LMcNiff(5) 2 75
(David Barron) *hld up and bhd: hdwy over 2f out: rdn wl over 1f out: styd on wl fnl f: nrst fin* **7/1**[3]

551- **5** 2¼ **Patavium (IRE)**[25] 4982 9-9-4 **77** JamesSullivan 10 77
(Edwin Tuer) *chsd ldrs: hdwy 3f out: rdn over 2f out and kpt on same pce* **14/1**

325- **6** 1¾ **Rio's Rosanna (IRE)**[159] 7272 5-9-5 **78** RobertWinston 15 75
(Richard Whitaker) *stdd s and sn swtchd lft to inner: hld up in rr: hdwy wl over 2f out: rdn over 1f out: kpt on: nrst fin* **11/2**[1]

140- **7** 9 **Lady Amakhala**[242] 5035 4-9-2 **76** AndrewMullen 6 59
(George Moore) *hld up in rr: hdwy over 2f out: sn rdn and nvr nr ldrs* **10/1**

415- **8** 9 **Dark Dune (IRE)**[124] 7699 4-9-0 **74** DavidAllan 14 42
(Tim Easterby) *in tch on outer: rdn along to chse ldng pair 3f out: drvn 2f out and sn wknd* **12/1**

031- **9** 4 **Cape Rising (IRE)**[254] 4611 5-9-4 **77** PJMcDonald 12 39
(Alan Swinbank) *prom: chsd clr ldr after 3f: rdn along over 3f out: wknd over 2f out* **11/1**

/51- **10** 4½ **Jack Dawkins (USA)**[393] 858 7-8-9 **68** AdrianNicholls 3 23
(David Nicholls) *in tch: hdwy on inner to chse ldrs over 2f out: rdn wl over 1f out and sn wknd* **22/1**

1310 **11** 3¾ **Trans Sonic**[11] 1135 9-8-4 **68** (b) ShaneBKelly(5) 13 17
(David O'Meara) *led and sn clr: rdden along 4f out: hdd & wknd 3f out* **25/1**

144- **12** 1¾ **Pintrada**[256] 4530 4-9-2 **76** TedDurcan 9 22
(James Bethell) *rrd s and s.i.s: a in rr* **11/1**

360- **13** 22 **Jewelled Dagger (IRE)**[76] 7002 8-8-11 **73** MichaelO'Connell(3) 5
(Sharon Watt) *chsd ldrs: pushed along 1/2-way: sn lost pl and bhd fr over 3f out* **80/1**

220- **14** 2¾ **Sally Friday (IRE)**[209] 6086 4-9-1 **75** TomEaves 11
(Edwin Tuer) *chsd ldrs: rdn along 4f out: sn wknd* **25/1**

2m 41.05s (2.15) **Going Correction** +0.25s/f (Good)
WFA 4 from 5yo+ 1lb **14** Ran SP% **119.6**
Speed ratings (Par 105): **102,101,100,99,98 97,91,85,82,79 76,75,61,59**
toteswingers:1&2:£10.90, 1&3:£18.00, 2&3:£5.20 CSF £49.63 CT £336.54 TOTE £8.70: £2.60, £2.60, £3.00; EX 78.90.
Owner Dan Gilbert **Bred** Moyglare Stud Farm Ltd **Trained** Norton, N Yorks

FOCUS
There was a good pace set by Trans Sonic, who had blinkers back on, and he predictably didn't get home. It paid to be handy entering the home straight.

1296 RACINGUK.COM MAIDEN STKS 5f 212y
4:00 (4:02) (Class 5) 3-Y-0+ **£2,264** (£673; £336; £168) **Stalls** Low

Form RPR

32- **1** **Alive And Kicking**[320] 2479 4-10-0 70 TedDurcan 11 76
(James Bethell) *cl up on outer: effrt to chal over 1f out: rdn ins fnl f: kpt on to ld nr line* **10/3**[2]

02- **2** nk **Cone Donkey (IRE)**[160] 7248 3-8-11 0 TomEaves 2 67
(Bryan Smart) *led: jnd 2f out and sn rdn along: drvn and edgd rt ins fnl f: hdd and nt qckn nr line* **7/1**

03- **3** 6 **Zaffy (IRE)**[284] 3611 3-8-11 0 DavidAllan 5 48
(Tim Easterby) *chsd ldrs: rdn along wl over 2f out: kpt on same pce u.p appr fnl f* **5/1**[3]

0- **4** 2¼ **Hadrians Rule (IRE)**[335] 2033 3-9-2 0 DuranFentiman 4 46
(Tim Easterby) *trckd ldr: cl up 1/2-way: rdn wl over 1f out and ev ch whn edgd lft and hmpd: wknd ent fnl f* **2/1**[1]

5 ½ **John Coffey (IRE)** 3-9-2 0 AdrianNicholls 10 44
(David Nicholls) *s.i.s and bhd: gd hdwy 2f out: chsd ldrs and green appr fnl f: kpt on same pce* **12/1**

0- **6** 3½ **Joy To The World (IRE)**[196] 6440 3-8-6 0 NeilFarley(5) 7 28
(Paul Cole) *a towards rr* **17/2**

50/ **7** 1 **Yas Marina (USA)**[544] 6883 4-9-11 0 DeclanCannon(3) 6 33
(David O'Meara) *a towards rr* **25/1**

8 2¼ **Striking Cat** 3-8-11 0 BarryMcHugh 8 17
(Brian Ellison) *hld up: hdwy and in tch on outer 3f out: sn rdn and wknd* **40/1**

203- **9** 20 **Busy Bimbo (IRE)**[168] 7103 3-8-4 57 MatthewHopkins(7) 3
(Alan Berry) *chsd ldrs on inner: rdn along whn stmbld 3f out: sn wknd* **25/1**

1m 16.53s (2.93) **Going Correction** +0.25s/f (Good)
WFA 3 from 4yo 12lb **9** Ran SP% **113.9**
Speed ratings (Par 103): **90,89,81,78,77 73,71,68,42**
toteswingers:1&2:£3.60, 1&3:£2.80, 2&3:£5.00 CSF £25.80 TOTE £3.80: £1.60, £1.40, £2.60; EX 21.20.
Owner M J Dawson **Bred** M J Dawson **Trained** Middleham Moor, N Yorks

FOCUS
Only a modest maiden, but a few could be given a chance if running up to their best form. The first four were all making their seasonal debut.

1297 YORKSHIRE-OUTDOORS.CO.UK H'CAP 1m 5f 175y
4:30 (4:30) (Class 5) (0-75,70) 4-Y-0+ **£2,264** (£673; £336; £168) **Stalls** Low

Form RPR

304- **1** **Golden Future**[149] 5504 9-8-10 **61** FrancescaWolter(7) 10 72
(Peter Niven) *hld up in midfield: smooth hdwy on outer 2f out: led jst ins fnl f: edgd lft and kpt on strly* **25/1**

023- **2** 2¼ **Hi Dancer**[8] 6870 9-8-6 **53** DeclanCannon(3) 6 61
(Ben Haslam) *trckd ldrs: hdwy over 3f out: rdn 2f out and ev ch tl drvn and one pce ins fnl f* **2/1**[1]

302- **3** 3½ **Mohawk Ridge**[169] 7075 6-9-9 **70** LeeTopliss(3) 2 73
(Michael Dods) *led 1f: prom: effrt over 2f out and sn swtchd lft: rdn and slt ld over 1f out: drvn: edgd lft and hdd ins fnl f: sn wknd* **3/1**[2]

223- **4** *¾* **Danceintothelight**[25] 6157 5-9-4 **62**............................ KellyHarrison 12 64
(Micky Hammond) *hld up and bhd: hdwy over 3f out: rdn 2f out: kpt on appr fnl f: nrst fin* **10/1**

0-02 **5** *nk* **Hallstatt (IRE)**[19] 1011 6-9-4 **65**...........................(t) MichaelO'Connell(3) 8 67
(John Mackie) *cl up: led 3f out: rdn 2f out: drvn and hdd over 1f out: grad wknd* **6/1**[3]

43-3 **6** *6* **White Deer (USA)**[12] 1112 8-9-4 **62**.........................(p) RobertWinston 3 55
(Geoffrey Harker) *hld up towards rr: smooth hdwy 4f out: trckd ldrs and ev ch whn swtchd wd to outer wl over 1f out: sn no imp and eased fnl f* **8/1**

60-0 **7** *½* **Mahfal (FR)**[7] 1189 4-8-13 **60**....................................(b) BarryMcHugh 9 53
(Brian Ellison) *hld up towards rr: pushed along: hdwy and in tch 1/2-way: rdn 5f out: sn wknd* **25/1**

5340 **8** *6* **Jawaab (IRE)**[14] 1071 8-9-2 **65**...........................(e) CharlesEddery(5) 4 49
(Richard Guest) *cl up: led after 1f: rdn along 4f out: hdd 3f out and sn wknd* **25/1**

5263 **9** *2¾* **Maslak (IRE)**[19] 1003 8-8-11 **62**............................ MatthewHopkins(7) 7 42
(Peter Hiatt) *chsd ldrs: rdn along over 4f out: sn wknd* **20/1**

65-0 **10** *9* **Amir Pasha (UAE)**[8] 600 7-8-9 **60**..........................(p) KatieDowson(7) 5 28
(Micky Hammond) *in tch on inner: pushed along over 5f out: sn lost pl and bhd* **20/1**

456- **11** *5* **Bavarian Nordic (USA)**[124] 7689 7-8-11 **55**..................... TomEaves 11 16
(Richard Whitaker) *s.i.s: a in rr: bhd fnl 3f* **40/1**

3m 10.75s (7.15) **Going Correction** +0.475s/f (Yiel)
WFA 4 from 5yo+ 3lb **11** Ran SP% **116.3**
Speed ratings (Par 103): **89,87,85,85,85 81,81,77,76,71 68**
toteswingers:1&2:£12.90, 1&3:£14.60, 2&3:£2.80 CSF £69.48 CT £205.14 TOTE £29.00: £7.60, £1.20, £1.10; EX 123.10.
Owner The Little Ice Club **Bred** Larksborough Stud Limited **Trained** Barton-le-Street, N Yorks

FOCUS
These are the types of horses that will probably clash quite often at this sort of distance, so it remains to be seen how reliable this form will be.

1298 CATTERICKBRIDGE.CO.UK APPRENTICE H'CAP 5f
5:00 (5:01) (Class 6) (0-65,65) 4-Y-0+ **£2,045** (£603; £302) **Stalls** Low

Form RPR

05-1 **1** **Boucher Garcon (IRE)**[3] 1242 4-8-5 **52** 6ex..................... NeilFarley(3) 4 69
(Declan Carroll) *mde all: sn clr: shkn up and r.o strly fnl f: unchal* **13/8**[1]

3-65 **2** *4* **Dispol Grand (IRE)**[20] 996 6-9-1 **62**............................ LMcNiff(3) 15 65
(Paul Midgley) *towards rr: hdwy on wd outside over 2f out: rdn and kpt on to chse wnr ins fnl f: no imp* **11/1**

052- **3** *nk* **Kyzer Chief**[313] 2667 7-8-12 **59**.. ShaneBKelly(3) 7 61
(Ron Barr) *prom centre: hdwy 2f out: rdn to chse wnr over 1f out: kpt on same pce fnl f* **16/1**

15-0 **4** *nk* **Ever Roses**[15] 1054 4-9-1 **59**.....................................(v) MichaelO'Connell 1 60
(Paul Midgley) *wnt rt s and racd towards far side: in rr: hdwy 2f out: sn rdn and kpt on fnl f: nrst fin* **40/1**

44U0 **5** *nk* **Lucky Dan (IRE)**[27] 912 6-9-1 **64**................................ DarylByrne(5) 9 64
(Paul Green) *in rr: rdn along 1/2-way: hdwy on wd outside wl over 1f out: styd on fnl f: nrst fin* **12/1**

4504 **6** *1¼* **Rio's Girl**[2] 1246 5-8-3 **52**..(bt) ShirleyTeasdale(5) 3 47
(Tony Coyle) *wnt rt s: racd towards far side and in tch: rdn along 2f out and no hdwy* **17/2**[2]

0-06 **7** *¾* **Chosen One (IRE)**[15] 1054 7-8-9 **53**................................ JulieBurke 11 46
(Ruth Carr) *towards rr: hdwy 2f out: rdn over 1f out: styd on fnl f: nrst fin* **33/1**

05-0 **8** *2½* **Sharp Shoes**[100] 8 5-8-11 **62**..................................(p) LauraBarry(7) 13 46
(Ann Duffield) *chsd ldrs: rdn along 2f out: sn wknd* **25/1**

6-40 **9** *nk* **Luscivious**[75] 327 8-8-8 **52**...(bt) RyanPowell 5 34
(Scott Dixon) *racd centre: chsd ldrs: rdn 2f out: sn wknd* **16/1**

030- **10** *3¾* **Ballarina**[205] 6213 6-8-10 **59**.. JasonHart(5) 2 28
(Eric Alston) *hmpd s: racd towards far side and sn chsng wnr: rdn along 2f out and grad wknd appr fnl f* **9/1**[3]

110- **11** *½* **Prince James**[138] 7535 5-8-8 **59**........................... DavidSimmonson(7) 10 26
(Michael Easterby) *dwlt and sltly hmpd s: sn outpcd and wl bhd 1/2-way: sme late hdwy* **12/1**

303- **12** *½* **Cross Of Lorraine (IRE)**[183] 6778 9-9-6 **64**.................(b) LeeTopliss 6 29
(Chris Grant) *chsd ldrs: rdn along 1/2-way: sn wknd* **16/1**

10/0 **13** *¾* **Tagula Breeze (IRE)**[27] 911 6-9-4 **65**..................... GarryWhillans(3) 12 28
(Ian McInnes) *a towards rr* **20/1**

00-0 **14** *2¼* **Royal Blade (IRE)**[72] 356 5-8-7 **58**........................ MatthewHopkins(7) 14 13
(Alan Berry) *a towards rr* **66/1**

0000 **15** *1¾* **Fashion Icon (USA)**[2] 1246 6-8-7 **51**........................(b) DeclanCannon 8
(David O'Meara) *racd centre: in tch: rdn along 2f out: sn wknd* **22/1**

1m 1.95s (2.15) **Going Correction** +0.475s/f (Yiel) **15** Ran SP% **119.8**
Speed ratings (Par 101): **101,94,94,93,93 91,89,85,85,79 78,77,76,73,70**
toteswingers:1&2:£5.00, 1&3:£7.10, 2&3:£17.60 CSF £17.48 CT £227.88 TOTE £2.30: £1.50, £2.20, £3.70; EX 22.30.
Owner M Cunningham & P Cunningham **Bred** N Hartery **Trained** Sledmere, E Yorks

FOCUS
The field were spread right across the course once in line for home, but it was soon apparent that the favourite was going to win.
Prince James Official explanation: jockey said gelding suffered interference at start and never travelled
T/Jkpt: Not won. T/Plt: £14.00 to a £1 stake. Pool:£62,670.08 - 3,247.38 winning tickets T/Qpdt: £3.80 to a £1 stake. Pool:£4,502.15 - 857.47 winning tickets JR

1211 KEMPTON (A.W) (R-H)
Wednesday, April 11

OFFICIAL GOING: Standard
Wind: Moderate, across, Races 1-2; strong against, Races 3-4; moderate, half against, remainder Weather: Mostly fine but cloudy; raining race 4.

1299 WIN BIG WITH BETDAQ MULTIPLES APPRENTICE H'CAP 1m 2f (P)
5:30 (5:30) (Class 6) (0-60,60) 4-Y-0+ **£1,617** (£481; £240; £120) **Stalls** Low

Form RPR

00-0 **1** **Addikt (IRE)**[92] 110 7-9-7 **60**.......................... WilliamTwiston-Davies 3 71
(Michael Scudamore) *hld up disputing 8th: stdy prog over 2f out: wl-timed effrt to ld over 1f out: sn in command* **15/8**[1]

5-63 **2** *2¼* **So Is She (IRE)**[19] 1014 4-8-11 **50**..............................(be) IanBurns 9 57
(Alan Bailey) *dwlt: settled in last pair: pushed along 1/2-way: 10th over 2f out: gd prog on inner after: styd on to take 2nd ins fnl f: n.d to wnr* **8/1**

-503 **3** *3¼* **Karate (IRE)**[7] 1191 4-9-5 **58**.......................................(t) NicoleNordblad 7 58
(Hans Adielsson) *hld up in rr: prog over 2f out: chsd ldrs over 1f out but sn outpcd: pushed along and kpt on one pce to take 3rd ins fnl f* **11/2**[2]

0006 **4** *1¼* **Carr Hall (IRE)**[19] 1014 9-8-8 **47**................................ GeorgeDowning 6 45
(Tony Carroll) *hld up in midfield: prog on inner 3f out: led briefly wl over 1f out: wknd fnl f* **12/1**

0260 **5** *2¾* **Diamond Twister (USA)**[12] 1106 6-8-2 **46** oh1..........(t) KevinLundie(5) 4 38
(Lisa Williamson) *s.i.s: sn prom: lft in ld over 3f out: hdd & wknd wl over 1f out* **20/1**

-546 **6** *1½* **Ermyntrude**[22] 966 5-8-12 **54**.. NedCurtis(3) 5 43
(Pat Phelan) *racd on outer: chsd ldrs: pushed along and nt qckn 3f out: edgd rt and wknd over 1f out* **8/1**

20-0 **7** *4½* **Gee Major**[21] 988 5-8-11 **50**.. ThomasBrown 8 30
(Nicky Vaughan) *chsd ldr: lft disputing ld over 3f out: sn rdn: lost 2nd and wknd 2f out* **12/1**

-360 **8** *2¼* **Bull Five**[82] 224 5-9-7 **60**...(v[1]) MichaelJMurphy 2 36
(Nick Littmoden) *chsd ldrs: rdn over 2f out: wknd qckly over 1f out* **15/2**[3]

-030 **9** *7* **Harvest Mist (IRE)**[55] 578 4-8-8 **47**............................... NoelGarbutt 12 9
(Shaun Lycett) *racd wd and forced even wdr bnd over 7f out: a in rr: struggling over 3f out* **16/1**

232- **10** *1½* **Oliver's Gold**[47] 3742 4-9-2 **58** ow2........................(p) ThomasGarner(3) 10 17
(Shaun Harris) *dwlt: racd wd thrght: nvr bttr than midfield: wknd qckly over 2f out* **14/1**

630/ **11** *2* **Navajo Nation (IRE)**[382] 429 6-8-13 **57**........................ RyanWhile(5) 11 12
(Bill Turner) *prom in chsng gp: wknd rapidly 3f out: wl bhd over 1f out* **50/1**

0-00 **12** *23* **Polly Adler**[12] 1107 5-8-3 **47** oh1 ow1............................(b[1]) JacobMoore(5) 1
(Alastair Lidderdale) *mde most: hung bdly lft and hdd bnd over 3f out: rdr then dropped whip: continued on wd outside and t.o* **33/1**

2m 6.73s (-1.27) **Going Correction** -0.125s/f (Stan) **12** Ran SP% **121.8**
Speed ratings (Par 101): **100,98,95,94,92 91,87,85,80,79 77,59**
toteswingers:1&2:£5.70, 2&3:£4.90, 1&3:£3.90 CSF £17.36 CT £74.84 TOTE £2.20: £1.10, £2.70, £2.90; EX 21.50 Trifecta £88.90 Pool: £448.56 - 3.73 winning units..
Owner Good Breed Limited **Bred** Deerpark Stud **Trained** Bromsash, H'fords

FOCUS
A moderate handicap restricted to apprentice riders. The pace was overly strong thanks to Polly Alder, who was much too keen in first-time blinkers and failed to handle the turn out of the back straight.
Gee Major Official explanation: vet said gelding was struck into behind
Polly Adler Official explanation: jockey said mare hung badly left throughout

1300 BACK OR LAY AT BETDAQ.COM H'CAP 5f (P)
6:00 (6:00) (Class 5) (0-70,70) 4-Y-0+ **£2,264** (£673; £336; £168) **Stalls** Low

Form RPR

46-1 **1** **Howyadoingnotsobad (IRE)**[14] 1061 4-8-10 **64**........ RaulDaSilva(5) 1 78
(Karen George) *fast away: mde all: shkn up and asserted wl over 1f out: unchal after* **2/1**[1]

0-30 **2** *2½* **Amazon Twilight**[20] 991 4-9-7 **70**.................................. RyanMoore 2 74
(Brett Johnson) *s.i.s: rousted along to go prom: rdn and styd on to take 2nd wl ins fnl f: no ch w wnr* **11/4**[2]

2363 **3** *nk* **Sherjawy (IRE)**[7] 1185 8-8-9 **58**................................(b) JamieGoldstein 4 61
(Zoe Davison) *chsd wnr to over 3f out and again over 1f out: no imp: lost 2nd wl ins fnl f* **12/1**

0-20 **4** *2* **Silvanus (IRE)**[33] 844 7-9-4 **67**...................................... MickyFenton 8 63
(Paul Midgley) *restrained s: hld up and last for 2f: pushed along and prog 2f out: wnt 4th ins fnl f: nvr remotely involved* **10/1**

2211 **5** *1½* **Steelcut**[13] 1082 8-9-2 **70**...(p) MatthewCosham(5) 7 60
(David Evans) *chsd ldrs: rdn 1/2-way: outpcd over 1f out: no ch whn nt clr run ins fnl f* **9/2**[3]

5603 **6** *¾* **Bookiesindex Boy**[15] 1054 8-8-3 **57** ow1..................(b) DuilioDaSilva(5) 6 45
(J R Jenkins) *chsd wnr over 3f out: tried to chal 2f out: outpcd sn after: wknd fnl f* **12/1**

554- **7** *1½* **Leadenhall Lass (IRE)**[146] 7448 6-9-6 **69**.................. FergusSweeney 5 51
(Pat Phelan) *stdd s: hld up in last trio: pushed along 2f out: nvr remotely on terms* **16/1**

0300 **8** *5* **With Hindsight (IRE)**[25] 942 4-9-0 **68**......................... DavidKenny(5) 9 32
(Michael Scudamore) *outpcd in last after 2f: bhd rest of way* **33/1**

59.13s (-1.37) **Going Correction** -0.125s/f (Stan) **8** Ran SP% **111.5**
Speed ratings (Par 103): **105,101,100,97,94 93,91,83**
toteswingers:1&2:£3.00, 1&3:£3.30, 2&3:£6.30 CSF £7.11 CT £46.68 TOTE £3.10: £1.40, £1.10, £3.30; EX 8.50 Trifecta £26.60 Pool: £670.01 - 18.61 winning units..
Owner Ten Four Fun **Bred** J G Reid **Trained** Higher Eastington, Devon

FOCUS
An uncompetitive sprint handicap.

1301 BETDAQ MOBILE APPS MEDIAN AUCTION MAIDEN STKS 1m 3f (P)
6:30 (6:33) (Class 6) 3-5-Y-0 **£1,617** (£481; £240; £120) **Stalls** Low

Form RPR

503- **1** **Expense Claim (IRE)**[203] 6244 3-8-8 75......................... MartinDwyer 4 79+
(Andrew Balding) *trckd ldng pair: clsd to ld over 2f out: pushed along and in command after: eased nr fin* **5/4**[1]

2 *1¼* **Pistol (IRE)** 3-8-8 0.. RyanMoore 7 77+
(Sir Michael Stoute) *difficult to load into stalls: dwlt: sn in 5th: shkn up over 3f out: prog and firmly drvn over 2f out: chsd wnr over 1f out: styd on but nvr able to chal* **11/8**[2]

00- **3** *8* **Hector's Chance**[173] 6994 3-8-8 0................................... JamesDoyle 1 62
(Heather Main) *t.k.h: trckd ldr: led 3f out to over 2f out: pushed along and wl outpcd after* **20/1**

03- **4** *1¾* **Totom Chief**[126] 7650 3-8-8 0...................................... JamieGoldstein 2 59
(Gay Kelleway) *trckd ldng pair: shkn up over 2f out: sn wl outpcd* **9/1**[3]

0-6 **5** *3½* **Minstrel Lad**[23] 959 4-9-11 0..................................... SimonPearce(3) 9 56
(Lydia Pearce) *stdd s: hld up in last: shkn up 3f out: sme prog 2f out: nvr on terms* **66/1**

- **6** *2½* **Call Me April**[21] 4-9-9 0... TomMcLaughlin 6 46
(Karen George) *awkward to load into stalls: dwlt: settled in 7th: sme prog to take 5th jst over 2f out: pushed along and no hdwy after: fdd fnl f* **12/1**

6 **7** *1½* **Smarty Time**[14] 1065 5-9-6 0....................................... SeanLevey(3) 8 44
(John Bridger) *a abt same pl: rdn over 3f out: sn btn* **25/1**

40 **8** *6* **Ossie's Dancer**[15] 1053 3-8-8 0...................................... ShaneKelly 3 35
(Robert Cowell) *in tch in midfield: wknd over 2f out* **33/1**

3 **9** *25* **Total Obsession**[21] 983 5-9-9 0.................................(b) RobertHavlin 5
(Mark Hoad) *led at fair pce: hdd 3f out: wknd v rapidly: t.o* **66/1**

2m 19.89s (-2.01) **Going Correction** -0.125s/f (Stan)
WFA 3 from 4yo+ 20lb **9** Ran SP% **118.8**
Speed ratings (Par 101): **102,101,95,94,91 89,88,84,66**
toteswingers:1&2:£1.10, 1&3:£6.30, 2&3:£5.50 CSF £3.15 TOTE £2.20: £1.02, £1.40, £5.30; EX 3.60 Trifecta £50.40 Pool: £789.07 - 11.58 winning units..

Owner Another Bottle Racing 2 **Bred** Glending Bloodstock **Trained** Kingsclere, Hants

FOCUS

Not much strength in depth to this maiden, but the first two in the market finished well clear and the time was 1.73 seconds quicker than the later Class 6 handicap.

1302 BETDAQ CASINO GAMES H'CAP 1m 4f (P)

7:00 (7:00) (Class 3) (0-95,86) 3-Y-O **£6,411** (£1,919; £959; £479; £239) **Stalls** Centre

Form RPR

62-4 1 **Theturnofthesun (IRE)**[11] 1132 3-8-13 **78**... RobertHavlin 4 84
(John Gosden) *mde all: grad increased pce fr 1/2-way: gng best over 2f out: rdn over 1f out: edgd lft and rt but a holding on* **4/1**[3]

01 2 *nk* **Bordoni (USA)**[26] 921 3-9-7 **86**... SilvestreDeSousa 5 92
(Mark Johnston) *trckd wnr: pushed along over 3f out: drvn and no imp 2f out: styd on and clsd nr fin: a hld* **7/4**[1]

321- 3 *1* **Cherry Street**[191] 6572 3-9-5 **84**... JimmyFortune 3 88
(Andrew Balding) *rrd s: t.k.h: hld up in 4th: effrt on outer over 2f out: disp 2nd over 1f out: kpt on same pce* **5/2**[2]

431- 4 *1 1/2* **Flying Trader (USA)**[117] 7786 3-8-7 **72**... LukeMorris 2 74
(Jane Chapple-Hyam) *trckd ldng pair: shkn up 3f out: tried to mount a chal wl over 1f out: fdd ins fnl f* **5/1**

1112 5 *3/4* **Clean Bowled (IRE)**[11] 1142 3-8-13 **85**...(p) NedCurtis(7) 1 85
(Roger Curtis) *settled in last: effrt on inner over 2f out: nt qckn wl over 1f out: wl hld fnl f* **11/1**

2m 34.0s (-0.50) **Going Correction** -0.125s/f (Stan) **5** Ran SP% **109.9**

Speed ratings (Par 102): **96,95,95,94,93**

CSF £11.42 TOTE £4.90: £2.10, £1.30; EX 12.40.

Owner RJH Geffen and Rachel Hood **Bred** B Gleeson & Balmerino Bloodstock **Trained** Newmarket, Suffolk

FOCUS

A fair race, but the well-ridden winner set a modest pace in an uncontested lead, and the field finished in a bit if a bunch.

NOTEBOOK

Theturnofthesun(IRE), up in trip on his handicap debut, wandered a bit under pressure, but that was no bad thing as the runner-up was inconvenienced, and he was always holding on. There may be more to come as he continues to learn his job. (op 5-1)

Bordoni(USA) ◆ looked a strong stayer when justifying market support in a 1m4f Lingfield maiden on his second start, and this wasn't enough of a test for him. He still looked green, but kept staying on, despite having to switch in order to get a clear run, and he could progress past the winner in due course, especially if they meet in a more truly run race. (op 11-10)

Cherry Street, absent since winning a 1m2f Pontefract maiden in October, just didn't pick up well enough. He's entitled to come on for the run. (op 4-1 tchd 9-4)

Flying Trader(USA), who hadn't been seen since winning a nursery off 5lb lower over an extended 1m at Wolverhampton in December, shaped okay but didn't prove his stamina. (op 6-1 tchd 13-2)

Clean Bowled(IRE) was another with stamina to prove, and anyway he probably found this company a bit hot. (op 15-2)

1303 SKYSPORTS.COM H'CAP 1m 3f (P)

7:30 (7:32) (Class 6) (0-60,60) 3-Y-O **£1,617** (£360; £360; £120) **Stalls** Low

Form RPR

0-53 1 **Midnight Sequel**[20] 993 3-8-7 **46** oh1... MartinLane 3 51
(Michael Blake) *trckd ldrs in 6th: rdn and prog to chse ldr jst over 2f out: chal over 1f out: styd on dourly to ld last 100yds* **11/2**[3]

200- 2 *nk* **Always Ends Well (IRE)**[179] 6864 3-9-7 **60**... SilvestreDeSousa 4 64
(Mark Johnston) *won battle for ld and set gd pce: drvn 2f out: kpt on wl but hdd last 100yds* **4/1**[2]

031- 2 *dht* **Better Be Mine (IRE)**[196] 6460 3-8-13 **52**... RyanMoore 11 56
(John Dunlop) *hld up in 7th: prog over 2f out: drvn over 1f out: str chal fnl f: nt qckn last 100yds* **3/1**[1]

040- 4 *1* **Rocco Breeze (IRE)**[224] 5634 3-8-4 **48**... RaulDaSilva(5) 7 50
(Philip McBride) *settled in midfield in 8th: rdn wl over 2f out: prog wl over 1f out: kpt on same pce fnl f* **15/2**

05-0 5 *1 1/4* **Dark Celt (IRE)**[53] 620 3-8-8 **47** oh1 ow1...[1] RobertHavlin 1 47
(Tim Pitt) *stdd s: dropped out in last: brought wd and promising prog jst over 2f out: rdn to cl on ldrs 1f out: fdd last 150yds* **16/1**

5-00 6 *2 1/4* **Johanna Fosie (IRE)**[11] 1132 3-9-2 **55**... SamHitchcott 2 51
(Mick Channon) *t.k.h early: trckd ldng pair to over 2f out: nt qckn sn after: fdd fnl f* **20/1**

-540 7 *2* **Redclue (IRE)**[14] 1065 3-9-3 **56**...(p) AdamKirby 9 48
(Miss Louise Allan) *settled in last trio: rdn 3f out: kpt on fnl 2f but nt pce to threaten* **14/1**

430- 8 *1 1/2* **Daring Damsel (IRE)**[184] 6760 3-9-6 **59**... HayleyTurner 5 49
(Paul Cole) *chsd ldrs in 5th: rdn over 4f out: steadily wknd fnl 2f* **16/1**

030- 9 *3 3/4* **Strictly Mine**[184] 6760 3-9-0 **53**... JimCrowley 12 36
(Jonathan Portman) *tried to ld but forced to chse ldr: shkn up over 2f out: wknd tamely sn after* **12/1**

000- 10 *3/4* **Shek O Lad**[208] 6110 3-8-10 **49**... RichardMullen 14 31
(Alan Jarvis) *racd wd: chsd ldng trio: rdn 5f out: wknd over 2f out* **20/1**

00-0 11 *1* **Adelindus**[28] 892 3-9-0 **53**... LukeMorris 10 33
(Ed Vaughan) *hld up in 9th: rdn 3f out: no prog and sn btn* **16/1**

000- 12 *112* **Ben Croy**[140] 7521 3-9-2 **55**... ShaneKelly 13
(Murty McGrath) *awkward s: hld up in last trio: wknd 4f out: virtually p.u fnl 2f* **14/1**

2m 21.62s (-0.28) **Going Correction** -0.125s/f (Stan) **12** Ran SP% **120.3**

Speed ratings (Par 96): **96,95,95,95,94 92,91,89,87,86 85**, PL: BBM £1.30, AEW £1.70; EX: MS-BBM £10.80, MS-AEW £14.10; CSF: MS-BBM £11.32, MS-AEW £14.09; TRICAST: MS-BBM-AEW £36.65, MS-AEW-BBM £39.09; toteswingers:1&2 (BBM):£2.30, 1&2 (AEW):£5.60, 2&3:£1.20 TOTE £7.10: £1.90 TRIFECTA 13-1-8 £127 Owner.

FOCUS

Not a bad race for the grade in which Always Ends Well seemed to set a reasonable gallop.

1304 RACING PLUS-BUY IT EVERY SATURDAY H'CAP (LONDON MILE QUALIFIER) 1m (P)

8:00 (8:01) (Class 4) (0-85,82) 3-Y-O **£4,075** (£1,212; £606; £303) **Stalls** Low

Form RPR

142- 1 **Kid Suitor (IRE)**[180] 6826 3-9-2 **80**... SeanLevey(3) 9 87
(Richard Hannon) *t.k.h: hld up in 5th: plld out and prog 2f out: rdn to ld 1f out: styd on wl* **9/1**

016- 2 *1 1/4* **Bank On Me**[165] 7167 3-9-5 **80**... JimmyFortune 4 84
(Philip McBride) *hld up in 6th: prog on inner 2f out: pushed up to chal 1f out: stl jst pushed along and styd on same pce to take 2nd last stride* **14/1**

021- 3 *nse* **California English (IRE)**[119] 7751 3-9-2 **77**... AdamKirby 3 81
(Marco Botti) *trckd ldr: shkn up 2f out: brought to chal and upsides 1f out: nt qckn w wnr after: lost 2nd last stride* **9/4**[1]

31-3 4 *2 1/2* **Kinloch Castle**[4] 1221 3-9-7 **82**... SilvestreDeSousa 5 80
(Mark Johnston) *trckd ldng pair: shkn up 3f out: sn lost pl and outpcd: styd on again fnl f* **11/4**[2]

120- 5 *nk* **Tingo In The Tale (IRE)**[175] 6957 3-9-3 **78**... JamesDoyle 8 76
(David Arbuthnot) *hld up in 7th: taken to outer and pushed along over 2f out: sme late prog but nvr involved* **12/1**

531- 6 *1 1/4* **Holly Martins**[168] 7094 3-8-10 **78**...(t) NicoleNordblad(7) 7 73
(Hans Adielsson) *led: 2 l clr over 2f out: hdd & wknd 1f out: eased* **14/1**

610- 7 *1 1/2* **Mr Maynard**[173] 6995 3-9-2 **77**... RyanMoore 2 68
(Sir Michael Stoute) *trckd ldng pair: rdn and nt qckn 2f out: lost pl and steadily fdd* **4/1**[3]

124- 8 *3/4* **Tidy Affair (IRE)**[151] 7390 3-9-7 **82**... ShaneKelly 10 72
(Murty McGrath) *hld up in last: pushed along fr over 2f out: nvr involved* **40/1**

1m 38.32s (-1.48) **Going Correction** -0.125s/f (Stan) **8** Ran SP% **110.9**

Speed ratings (Par 100): **102,100,100,98,97 96,95,94**

toteswingers:1&2:£27.70, 1&3:£5.80, 2&3:£4.80 CSF £115.38 CT £368.80 TOTE £12.00: £2.30, £2.80, £1.50; EX 216.90 Trifecta £251.40 Pool: £526.60 - 1.55 winning units..

Owner Byerley Thoroughbred Racing **Bred** Brian Dolan **Trained** East Everleigh, Wilts

FOCUS

A fair 3yo handicap and the pace, set by Holly Martins for a lot of the way, seemed just ordinary.

1305 SKYSPORTS.COM RACING H'CAP (DIV I) 6f (P)

8:30 (8:31) (Class 5) (0-70,70) 4-Y-O+ **£2,264** (£673; £336; £168) **Stalls** Low

Form RPR

4423 1 **Twice Red**[29] 887 4-8-7 **61**... RaulDaSilva(5) 6 71
(Mandy Rowland) *disp 3rd bhd clr ldng pair: rdn over 2f out: clsd on inner to ld jst ins fnl f: idled but hld on* **13/2**[2]

-540 2 *hd* **Rambo Will**[23] 958 4-9-7 **70**... DavidProbert 11 79
(J R Jenkins) *chsd clr ldr and clr of rest: clsd to ld over 1f out: hdd jst ins fnl f: kpt on wl: jst hld* **8/1**

1034 3 *1/2* **Belinsky (IRE)**[35] 819 5-8-13 **62**... JimCrowley 7 69
(Julie Camacho) *disp 3rd bhd clr ldrs: rdn over 2f out: clsd to chal 1f out: nt qckn last 150yds* **12/1**

600- 4 *1 1/2* **Flashbang**[166] 7137 4-9-1 **64**... SilvestreDeSousa 10 67
(Paul Cole) *prom in chsng gp: rdn over 2f out: kpt on to take 4th fnl f: unable to chal* **9/1**

5-00 5 *3/4* **West Leake (IRE)**[22] 967 6-9-2 **65**... LiamKeniry 8 65
(Paul Burgoyne) *sn off the pce in 7th: effrt over 2f out: kpt on to take 5th fnl f: nt pce to threaten* **16/1**

0002 6 *1/2* **Huzzah (IRE)**[26] 927 7-8-8 **57**... MichaelStainton 4 56
(Paul Howling) *sn wl off the pce in last trio: rdn and no prog over 2f out: kpt on fnl f* **15/2**

06-6 7 *hd* **Arctic Mirage**[22] 967 4-8-13 **62**... DaneO'Neill 1 60
(Michael Blanshard) *sn off the pce in 9th: rdn and no prog over 2f out: kpt on fnl f* **7/1**[3]

004- 8 *1/2* **Homeboy (IRE)**[300] 3075 4-9-5 **68**... HayleyTurner 9 64
(Marcus Tregoning) *sn off the pce in 6th: rdn and struggling in rr over 2f out: kpt on late* **13/2**[2]

-422 9 *1/2* **Catalinas Diamond (IRE)**[22] 970 4-9-0 **63**...(t) RobertHavlin 12 58
(Pat Murphy) *rrd bdly s and lost many l: ct up at rr over 4f out but wl off the pce: nvr able to threaten* **12/1**

4630 10 *2* **Mack's Sister**[16] 1050 5-8-11 **60**...(p) LukeMorris 2 48
(Dean Ivory) *reluctant to enter stalls: awkward s: drvn in 8th after 2f: nvr a factor* **6/1**[1]

0403 11 *1 1/2* **Athwaab**[14] 1061 5-8-4 **58** ow1... MatthewLawson(5) 3 42
(Noel Chance) *taken down early: a bhd: rdn in last over 3f out* **25/1**

1360 12 *2* **Novabridge**[23] 958 4-9-1 **64**...(b) AdamKirby 5 41
(Neil Mulholland) *blasted off in front and sn 6 l clr: wknd rapidly and hdd over 1f out* **20/1**

1m 12.11s (-0.99) **Going Correction** -0.125s/f (Stan) **12** Ran SP% **116.2**

Speed ratings (Par 103): **101,100,100,98,97 96,96,95,94,92 90,87**

toteswingers:1&2:£5.40, 1&3:£4.20, 2&3:£19.80 CSF £56.55 CT £619.58 TOTE £6.50: £1.90, £3.90, £4.60; EX 86.00 TRIFECTA Not won..

Owner Miss M E Rowland **Bred** Baroness Bloodstock & Redmyre Bloodstock **Trained** Lower Blidworth, Notts

FOCUS

Division one of a modest sprint handicap and the runners were soon well strung out, with Novabridge, who has yet to win beyond 5f, setting an unsustainable pace in a clear lead. Those prominent in the chasing pack dominated the finish, and the hold-up horses could never get into contention.

Catalinas Diamond(IRE) Official explanation: jockey said filly missed the break

1306 SKYSPORTS.COM RACING H'CAP (DIV II) 6f (P)

9:00 (9:00) (Class 5) (0-70,69) 4-Y-O+ **£2,264** (£673; £336; £168) **Stalls** Low

Form RPR

5-24 1 **Black Cadillac (IRE)**[23] 958 4-9-2 **64**... JimmyFortune 3 80
(Andrew Balding) *pressed ldr and a gng wl: led over 2f out: shkn up and drew clr fnl f: decisively* **7/4**[1]

6133 2 *3* **Amazing Win (IRE)**[16] 1049 4-9-0 **62**... SamHitchcott 1 68
(Mick Channon) *trckd ldrs: wnt 2nd on inner 2f out: tried to chal over 1f out: brushed aside fnl f* **8/1**

336- 3 *1 1/4* **Links Drive Lady**[172] 7024 4-9-4 **66**... ShaneKelly 4 68
(Dean Ivory) *chsd ldrs: rdn over 2f out: kpt on to take 3rd 1f out: no imp after* **11/2**[3]

5304 4 *2 1/4* **Metropolitan Chief**[14] 1070 8-8-2 **55** oh9... RaulDaSilva(5) 7 50
(Paul Burgoyne) *t.k.h: trckd ldng pair: nt qckn 2f out: outpcd and lost 3rd 1f out* **40/1**

1550 5 *1 3/4* **Dvinsky (USA)**[20] 991 11-9-1 **63**...(b) TomMcLaughlin 10 52
(Paul Howling) *chsd ldrs: nt qckn 2f out: outpcd over 1f out* **20/1**

0-10 6 *1 1/2* **Super Duplex**[16] 1050 5-9-3 **65**... IanMongan 2 49
(Pat Phelan) *dwlt: hld up in last trio: abt to be asked for effrt whn hmpd wl over 1f out: kpt on after: no ch* **12/1**

3-00 7 *nk* **Decimate**[28] 896 4-8-7 **62**... DavidWarren(7) 9 45
(Andrew Reid) *racd freely: led but kpt off the rail: hdd over 2f out: sn fdd* **40/1**

521- 8 *1/2* **Royal Selection (IRE)**[139] 7525 4-8-12 **60**... TadhgO'Shea 6 42
(Karen George) *impeded s: towards rr: rdn over 2f out: edgd rt wl over 1f out: no prog* **14/1**

000- 9 *1* **Bilko Pak (IRE)**[135] 7566 4-8-5 **58**... MarkCoumbe(5) 12 37
(Brendan Powell) *s.s: wl in rr: sme prog on inner 1/2-way: no hdwy fnl 2f* **40/1**

/23- 10 *nk* **Oh My Days (IRE)**[383] 971 4-9-0 **62**... AdamKirby 5 40
(Clive Cox) *wnt lft s: plld hrd and hld up in midfield: shkn up and nt qckn 2f out: wl btn after* **9/2**[2]

006- **11** *2 ½* **Kings 'n Dreams**[174] 6980 5-9-0 **69**.................................. PaulBooth(7) 8 39
(Dean Ivory) *dwlt: a in rr: bmpd along outer 2f out and no prog* **16/1**

000- **12** *8* **Mary's Pet**[118] 7767 5-8-9 **57**.................................. LukeMorris 11
(Lee Carter) *a towards rr: wknd 2f out* **40/1**

1m 12.13s (-0.97) **Going Correction** -0.125s/f (Stan) **12** Ran SP% **115.8**
Speed ratings (Par 103): **101,97,95,92,90 88,87,86,85,85 81,71**
toteswingers:1&2:£4.10, 1&3:£1.90, 2&3:£14.70 CSF £14.87 CT £62.58 TOTE £2.70: £1.10, £2.50, £1.70; EX 12.10 Trifecta £231.70 Pool: £579.28 - 1.85 winning units..
Owner N Botica **Bred** John Foley & Miss Ann Aungier **Trained** Kingsclere, Hants

FOCUS
The time was almost identical to the strongly run first leg.
T/Plt: £7.20 to a £1 stake. Pool: £62,496.99. 6,258.94 winning tickets. T/Qpdt: £3.10 to a £1 stake. Pool: £5,459.19. 1,293.00 winning tickets. JN

1180 LINGFIELD (L-H)
Wednesday, April 11

OFFICIAL GOING: Standard
Wind: light half-behind Weather: sunny periods early with rain from 3.30

1307 EUROPA QUALITY PRINT CLASSIFIED CLAIMING STKS 6f (P)
1:50 (1:50) (Class 6) 3-Y-O+ **£1,704** (£503; £251) **Stalls** Low

Form RPR

5123 **1** **Waabel**[12] 1116 5-9-3 70.................................. DuilioDaSilva(5) 1 69
(Richard Guest) *mde all: rdn 2 l clr jst over 1f out: jst hld on: all out* **2/1**[1]

1605 **2** *shd* **Chjimes (IRE)**[7] 1185 8-9-3 63.................................(b) HayleyTurner 5 63
(Conor Dore) *hld up in tch: rdn and stdy prog fr 2f out: kpt on wl ins fnl f: only jst failed* **8/1**

U103 **3** *¾* **Arabian Flight**[13] 1082 3-8-6 59.................................. KieranO'Neill 7 59
(John Bridger) *hld up in tch: outpcd in last pair over 2f out: r.o strly ent fnl f: nrst fin* **16/1**

2013 **4** *1 ¼* **Marie's Fantasy**[19] 1006 3-8-9 57 ow1.......................... JamieGoldstein 6 58
(Zoe Davison) *hld up in tch: rdn 2f out: disp 2nd briefly ent fnl f: kpt on same pce* **40/1**

3053 **5** *½* **My Lord**[16] 1050 4-8-12 66.................................. DarrenEgan(7) 4 57
(Ronald Harris) *trckd ldrs: rdn to dispute 2nd on outer over 2f out: no ex fnl f* **7/2**[2]

4054 **6** *¾* **Speak The Truth (IRE)**[16] 1050 6-9-1 68................(p) NathanAlison(5) 8 56
(Jim Boyle) *wnt rt s: bhd: styd on fnl f: n.d* **9/2**[3]

6-00 **7** *2* **Highland Harvest**[46] 715 8-9-8 70.................................. MartinLane 3 52
(Jamie Poulton) *trckd ldrs: rdn over 2f out: fdd fnl f* **10/1**

0342 **8** *4* **Waterloo Dock**[7] 1183 7-9-4 67.................................. LukeMorris 2 35
(Michael Quinn) *chsd ldr: pushed along over 3f out: fdd wl over 1f out: eased whn btn fnl f* **7/1**

1m 11.68s (-0.22) **Going Correction** -0.05s/f (Stan)
WFA 3 from 4yo+ 12lb **8** Ran SP% **114.8**
Speed ratings (Par 101): **99,98,97,96,95 94,91,86**
toteswingers:1&2:£5.20, 1&3:£4.40, 2&3:£13.70 CSF £19.11 TOTE £4.60: £1.20, £3.10, £5.60; EX 15.60.
Owner Rakebackmypoker.com **Bred** Shadwell Estate Company Limited **Trained** Stainforth, S Yorks

FOCUS
This classified claimer was run at a solid pace and the form makes sense.
Speak The Truth(IRE) Official explanation: jockey said gelding was slowly away

1308 PREMIER SHOWFREIGHT MAIDEN AUCTION STKS 5f (P)
2:20 (2:20) (Class 6) 2-Y-O **£1,704** (£503; £251) **Stalls** High

Form RPR

5 **1** **Caught Napping**[9] 1164 2-8-2 0.................................. DarrenEgan(7) 3 66+
(Bill Turner) *trckd ldrs: rdn to ld over 1f out: edgd lft: kpt on: comf* **11/4**[2]

62 **2** *1 ¾* **Perfect Words (IRE)**[6] 1202 2-8-6 0.......................... CharlesBishop(5) 2 62
(Mick Channon) *chsd ldrs: rdn over 2f out: kpt on to go 2nd ins fnl f: nt pce of wnr* **9/4**[1]

3 *1 ¾* **Fiducia** 2-8-11 0.................................. HayleyTurner 7 56+
(Simon Dow) *dwlt: in last pair but sn trcking ldng trio: rn green whn pushed along over 2f out: kpt on fnl f but nvr gng pce to threaten* **9/2**[3]

3 **4** *½* **Jamnean**[7] 1188 2-8-6 0 ow2.................................. RussKennemore 1 49
(John Holt) *led: rdn and hdd over 1f out: no ex whn lost 2 pls ins fnl f* **12/1**

5 *1 ¾* **Otto The First** 2-9-2 0.................................. LukeMorris 5 53
(John Best) *rn green: dwlt: sn pushed along in last: nvr threatened* **11/4**[2]

59.49s (0.69) **Going Correction** -0.05s/f (Stan) **5** Ran SP% **110.0**
Speed ratings (Par 90): **92,89,86,85,82**
CSF £9.30 TOTE £4.00: £3.30, £1.10; EX 7.80.
Owner E A Brook **Bred** Whitson Bloodstock Limited **Trained** Sigwells, Somerset

FOCUS
An ordinary juvenile maiden rated around the second and fourth.

NOTEBOOK
Caught Napping showed the clear benefit of his Redcar debut nine days previously and stepped up markedly on that form with a ready success. He didn't appear to be doing that much out in front, so should have some more to offer and he's already recouped more than his £1,500 price tag. It was his yard's fourth 2-y-o winner this term. (op 9-2)
Perfect Words(IRE) set the standard on his two previous efforts, but had finished behind two of the winner's stablemates in both outings. He lacked anything like that rival's turn of foot on this switch to Polytrack and, while this was too sharp, he will do very well to win a maiden. (tchd 5-2)
Fiducia, bred to get further, didn't go unbacked for this racecourse debut but she lost out through inexperience. She recovered from a tardy start, but lacked the know-how to challenge when asked for an effort and should come on plenty. (op 4-1 tchd 5-1)
Jamnean showed decent early speed, but paid for such exertions before the final furlong and looks plating-class. (op 15-2)
Otto The First, whose yard struck with its second 2-y-o winner of 2012 the previous day, looked well beforehand and met support. He blew the start, however, and ran distinctly green thereafter. (tchd 5-2)

1309 CHARTPLAN H'CAP (DIV I) 1m (P)
2:50 (2:51) (Class 6) (0-55,55) 4-Y-O+ **£1,704** (£503; £251) **Stalls** High

Form RPR

00-1 **1** **Russian Storm**[12] 1106 4-8-11 **50**.................................. FergusSweeney 1 63
(Pat Phelan) *trckd ldrs: pushed along to ld ent fnl f: sn clr: comf* **7/1**

-513 **2** *2 ¾* **The Bay Bandit**[13] 1088 5-9-0 **53**.................................(e) ChrisCatlin 2 60
(John Butler) *mid-div: rdn over 2f out: hdwy and swtchd rt over 1f out: styd on to go 2nd ins fnl f: no ch w wnr* **13/2**

3465 **3** *1* **Join Up**[19] 1009 6-9-1 **54**.................................. ShaneKelly 9 59
(Mark Brisbourne) *t.k.h: trckd ldrs: rdn 2f out: chsd wnr briefly jst ins fnl f: kpt on same pce* **6/1**[3]

0120 **4** *1* **Royal Envoy (IRE)**[14] 1070 9-8-13 **52**.......................... MichaelStainton 6 54
(Paul Howling) *led: rdn 2f out: hdd ent fnl f: no ex* **20/1**

004 **5** *2 ¼* **Lean Machine**[19] 1014 5-8-11 **50**.................................(p) LukeMorris 5 47
(Ronald Harris) *trckd ldrs: rdn over 2f out: one pce fr over 1f out* **13/2**

-500 **6** *nk* **Monsieur Broughton**[13] 1088 4-9-2 **55**.......................... StevieDonohoe 8 52
(Willie Musson) *s.i.s: in last: rdn wl over 2f out: c wd ent st: styd on but nvr a danger* **9/2**[1]

4656 **7** *2* **Dichoh**[20] 995 9-9-2 **55**.................................(p) GeorgeBaker 12 47
(Michael Madgwick) *mid-div: rdn over 2f out: sn btn* **11/2**[2]

2305 **8** *shd* **Saktoon (USA)**[7] 1193 4-9-0 **53**.................................(v) MartinLane 3 45
(Derek Shaw) *mid-div: rdn 3f out: sn btn* **50/1**

00-4 **9** *½* **Whitstable Native**[26] 926 4-9-1 **54**.............................. PaulHanagan 11 45
(Joseph Tuite) *trckd ldrs: rdn over 2f out: wknd ent fnl f* **6/1**[3]

0244 **10** *shd* **Escape Artist**[16] 1051 5-8-9 **48**.................................. KieranO'Neill 7 38
(John Bridger) *s.i.s: in last pair: effrt on inner 2f out: wknd 1f out* **10/1**

1m 37.14s (-1.06) **Going Correction** -0.05s/f (Stan) **10** Ran SP% **117.1**
Speed ratings (Par 101): **103,100,99,98,96 95,93,93,93,93**
toteswingers:1&2:£2.10, 1&3:£5.00, 2&3:£4.50 CSF £52.23 CT £297.68 TOTE £8.50: £3.30, £2.50, £1.10; EX 22.20.
Owner Ermyn Lodge Stud **Bred** Ermyn Lodge Stud Limited **Trained** Epsom, Surrey

FOCUS
This moderate handicap was a wide-open affair. It was run at a fair enough pace.

1310 CHARTPLAN H'CAP (DIV II) 1m (P)
3:20 (3:20) (Class 6) (0-55,55) 4-Y-O+ **£1,704** (£503; £251) **Stalls** High

Form RPR

0430 **1** **Fault**[4] 1224 6-8-11 **50**.................................. BrettDoyle 8 58
(Alastair Lidderdale) *racd keenly: mid-div: c wd ent st: sn rdn: styd on fr over 1f out: fin strly to ld fnl 40yds* **16/1**

55-3 **2** *½* **Byrd In Hand (IRE)**[19] 1009 5-8-13 **55**.......................... SeanLevey(3) 7 62
(John Bridger) *prom early: trckd ldr over 6f out: rdn to ld over 1f out: no ex whn hdd fnl 40yds* **6/1**[2]

143- **3** *½* **Ymir**[378] 1045 6-9-1 **54**.................................(t) J-PGuillambert 12 60
(Michael Attwater) *trckd ldrs: rdn over 2f out: kpt on to go 2nd briefly ins fnl f: no ex towards fin* **20/1**

0322 **4** *½* **Chandrayaan**[14] 1074 5-8-6 **48**.................................(v) SimonPearce(3) 9 53
(John E Long) *hld up towards rr: gd hdwy on inner fnl bnd: sn rdn: styd on* **8/1**[3]

000- **5** *1 ¼* **Mac Tiernan (IRE)**[114] 7820 5-9-0 **53**.......................... JimmyFortune 4 55
(Ed de Giles) *prom early: trckd ldrs after 2f: rdn jst over 2f out: one pce fr over 1f out* **11/8**[1]

0204 **6** *nk* **Querido (GER)**[19] 1009 8-8-13 **55**.......................(tp) RobertLButler(3) 5 56
(Paddy Butler) *mid-div: rdn and hdwy to chse ldrs wl over 1f out: one pce fnl f* **20/1**

/21- **7** *½* **Belle Noverre (IRE)**[33] 855 8-8-12 **51**.......................... ChrisCatlin 11 51
(John Butler) *s.i.s: racd wd thrght: towards rr of midfield: styd on fnl f but nvr able to get on terms* **10/1**

0055 **8** *1 ¼* **Kucharova (IRE)**[13] 1088 4-8-13 **51** ow1.......................... IanMongan 6 49
(Seamus Mullins) *prom for 2f: sn in midfield: rdn over 3f out: nt a danger after* **16/1**

2533 **9** *1 ¼* **Emerald Royal**[20] 995 4-8-11 **50**.................................(b) LukeMorris 1 44
(Eric Wheeler) *s.i.s: bhd: pushed along and stdy prog fr 3f out: styng on but looking hld whn nt clr run jst ins fnl f: eased after* **8/1**[3]

05-6 **10** *1 ¼* **Danceyourselfdizzy (IRE)**[13] 1095 4-8-0 **46** oh1.....(p) DannyBrock(7) 3 37
(Phil McEntee) *led: pushed 3 l clr over 2f out: hdd over 1f out: wknd* **25/1**

6/64 **11** *2 ½* **Josie's Dream (IRE)**[61] 495 4-8-7 **53**.......................... JoshBaudains(7) 2 39
(Jo Hughes) *mid-div early: struggling towards rr fr over 3f out* **20/1**

00-5 **12** *hd* **Curlew (IRE)**[23] 961 6-9-0 **53**.................................. DaneO'Neill 10 38
(Chris Down) *a towards rr* **50/1**

1m 37.56s (-0.64) **Going Correction** -0.05s/f (Stan) **12** Ran SP% **119.6**
Speed ratings (Par 101): **101,100,100,99,98 97,97,96,94,93 91,91**
toteswingers:1&2:£23.70, 1&3:£26.40, 2&3:£25.10 CSF £101.98 CT £1980.37 TOTE £31.10: £4.90, £1.80, £7.60; EX 128.30.
Owner Chris Beek Racing **Bred** Mrs A M Vestey **Trained** Lambourn, Berks

FOCUS
The second division of the 1m handicap and another wide-open event.
Belle Noverre(IRE) Official explanation: jockey said, regarding running and riding, that his orders were to be positive and get a handy position, the mare anticipated the start and was slowly away, it was not his intention to race wide but had no choice, and was unable to lay up with the early pace which, in his opinion, was overly fast, at the 2f mark he asked for an effort and it kept on past beaten horses; trainer said the mare had only been with him for 30 days and felt that it needed further.

1311 OCEAN PARTNERSHIP PRINT FILLIES' H'CAP 1m (P)
3:50 (3:50) (Class 5) (0-75,74) 4-Y-O+ **£2,385** (£704; £352) **Stalls** High

Form RPR

260- **1** **Ssafa**[240] 5101 4-9-3 **70**.................................. SebSanders 4 76
(J W Hills) *trckd ldr: rdn to ld ent fnl f: hld on wl fnl 120yds: all out* **7/2**[2]

1101 **2** *½* **Qeethaara (USA)**[13] 1084 8-9-4 **71**.......................(p) LukeMorris 2 76
(Mark Brisbourne) *trckd ldrs: rdn over 1f out: styd on to press wnr fnl 120yds: hld nring fin* **7/2**[2]

30-0 **3** *½* **Climaxfortackle (IRE)**[7] 1191 4-8-12 **65**.......................... MartinLane 1 69
(Derek Shaw) *s.i.s: in last pair but wl in tch: rdn over 1f out: styd on but nt pce to quite get on terms* **14/1**

610- **4** *¾* **Midas Moment**[191] 6583 4-9-7 **74**.................................. MartinDwyer 5 76
(William Muir) *trckd ldrs: rdn jst over 2f out: kpt on same pce fnl f* **6/1**[3]

340- **5** *½* **Zing Wing**[255] 4584 4-9-4 **71**.................................. JimmyFortune 8 72
(Paul Cole) *hld up in last 2 but wl in tch: rdn 2f out: nt pce to chal* **11/8**[1]

2045 **6** *¾* **Bold Ring**[26] 919 6-8-8 **64**.................................. SophieDoyle(3) 6 63
(Eric Wheeler) *led: rdn 2f out: hdd 1f out: no ex* **10/1**

1m 38.31s (0.11) **Going Correction** -0.05s/f (Stan) **6** Ran SP% **116.6**
Speed ratings (Par 100): **97,96,96,95,94 94**
toteswingers:1&2:£1.70, 1&3:£5.80, 2&3:£4.40 CSF £16.85 CT £152.06 TOTE £5.70: £4.70, £3.20; EX 25.70.
Owner Prolinx Limited **Bred** Newsells Park Stud **Trained** Upper Lambourn, Berks

FOCUS
A modest fillies' handicap, run at an average pace and it saw a host of chances 1f out.

1312 RUDRIDGE MAIDEN STKS 1m 2f (P)
4:20 (4:21) (Class 5) 3-Y-O **£2,385** (£704; £352) **Stalls** Low

Form RPR

62- **1** **Almuftarris (USA)**[209] 6100 3-9-3 0.................................. PaulHanagan 1 81
(Ed Dunlop) *wnt sltly rt s: trckd ldrs: rdn to ld ent fnl f: sn hrd pressed: hld on wl: all out* **1/1**[1]

4- **2** *nk* **Commend**[169] 7080 3-9-3 0 .... RyanMoore 2 80+
(Sir Michael Stoute) *slowly away and hmpd s: sn mid-div: pushed along and hdwy 2f out: rdn for str chal thrght fnl f: kpt on: hld fnl strides* **9/2**[3]

323- **3** *3* **Yaa Salam**[175] 6954 3-9-3 78 .... SilvestreDeSousa 9 74
(Mahmood Al Zarooni) *mid-div: rdn over 2f out: swtchd rt ent fnl f: sn wnt 3rd: styd on but nt gng pce of ldng pair* **7/2**[2]

62- **4** *1* **Ruscello (IRE)**[183] 6772 3-9-3 0 .... J-PGuillambert 7 72+
(Ed Walker) *racd keenly: trckd ldrs: rdn over 2f out: c wdst ent st: kpt on same pce* **12/1**

5-32 **5** *nk* **Dartford (USA)**[13] 1086 3-9-3 73 .... RobertHavlin 5 71
(John Gosden) *trckd ldrs: rdn over 2f out: kpt on same pce fr over 1f out* **8/1**

630- **6** *½* **Poetic Power (IRE)**[162] 7309 3-9-3 75 .... NickyMackay 4 70
(David Elsworth) *led: rdn over 2f out: hdd ent fnl f: no ex* **33/1**

00- **7** *5* **Silver Samba**[191] 6588 3-8-12 0 .... JimmyFortune 10 55
(Andrew Balding) *s.i.s: rdn over 3f out: a towards rr* **66/1**

6 **8** *1* **Ultimate Destiny**[18] 1031 3-9-3 0 .... JimCrowley 3 58
(Ralph Beckett) *bmpd s: mid-div: nudged along whn dropped to rr 1/2-way: rdn over 3f out: wknd over 1f out* **20/1**

60 **9** *¾* **Art News (IRE)**[18] 1031 3-9-3 0 .... (b¹) GeorgeBaker 6 57
(Gary Moore) *a towards rr* **66/1**

423 **10** *1 ½* **Attain**[32] 869 3-9-3 73 .... LukeMorris 8 54
(Julia Feilden) *sn trcking ldrs: rdn 3f out: hung lft whn btn over 1f out* **20/1**

2m 5.39s (-1.21) **Going Correction** -0.05s/f (Stan) **10** Ran SP% **124.7**
Speed ratings (Par 98): **102,101,99,98,98 97,93,93,92,91**
toteswingers:1&2:£3.30, 1&3:£1.90, 2&3:£3.60 CSF £6.07 TOTE £2.60: £1.30, £2.40, £1.70; EX 12.50.

Owner Hamdan Al Maktoum **Bred** Shadwell Farm LLC **Trained** Newmarket, Suffolk

FOCUS
Two useful colts came nicely clear from a fair yardstick in third here, in what was an above-average 3-y-o maiden for the track.

1313 EUROPA QUALITY PRINT H'CAP 7f (P)
4:50 (4:52) (Class 5) (0-70,70) 3-Y-O **£2,385** (£704; £352) **Stalls** Low

Form RPR

363- **1** **Tigers Tale (IRE)**[181] 6817 3-8-11 **60** .... (v) JamesDoyle 10 72
(Roger Teal) *sn led: rdn clr ent fnl f: styd on strly* **5/1**[3]

-231 **2** *3 ¾* **Lionrock (FR)**[26] 917 3-9-7 **70** .... SilvestreDeSousa 6 72
(Mark Johnston) *trckd ldrs: rdn wl over 1f out: sn swtchd rt: styd on to go 2nd fnl 120yds: no ch w wnr* **13/8**[1]

56-0 **3** *1* **Princess Maya**[75] 322 3-8-12 **61** .... DaneO'Neill 2 60
(Jo Crowley) *in tch: rdn 2f out: styd on fnl f: edgd sltly rt: wnt 3rd towards fin* **14/1**

-015 **4** *hd* **Justbookies Dotnet**[12] 1110 3-9-5 **68** .... (v) IanMongan 4 66
(Louise Best) *broke wl: racd keenly: trckd ldr: rdn 2f out: kpt on same pce ins fnl f* **25/1**

4643 **5** *½* **Chester'Slittlegem (IRE)**[12] 1115 3-9-3 **66** .... KieranO'Neill 9 63
(Ed de Giles) *mid-div: rdn over 2f out: styd on fnl f* **16/1**

006- **6** *shd* **Xinbama (IRE)**[208] 6132 3-9-6 **69** .... SebSanders 3 66+
(J W Hills) *stdd s: in last pair: pushed along and clsng whn nt clr run over 1f out: running on again whn short of room fnl 75yds: nvr any ch* **14/1**

40-6 **7** *¾* **Eightfold**[12] 1109 3-9-2 **65** .... (t) GeorgeBaker 5 60
(Seamus Durack) *stdd s: in last pair: nudged along and hdwy fr wl over 1f out: sn rdn: styng on but hld whn v short of room fnl 50yds* **25/1**

020- **8** *hd* **Welsh Royale**[160] 7252 3-9-0 **63** .... JimCrowley 1 57
(William Muir) *hld up towards rr: hdwy on inner 2f out: rdn in tch but nt clr run on rails thrght most of fnl f* **25/1**

323- **9** *¾* **Khazium (IRE)**[195] 6484 3-9-6 **69** .... (p) LukeMorris 11 61
(Pat Eddery) *rdn over 2f out: sme late prog but mainly towards rr* **4/1**[2]

2322 **10** *½* **Derivatives (IRE)**[12] 1115 3-9-4 **67** .... NickyMackay 8 58
(John Gosden) *mid-div: rdn 2f out: nvr threatened: fdd ins fnl f* **6/1**

410- **11** *5* **Subtle Embrace (IRE)**[216] 5840 3-8-10 **66** .... DarrenEgan(7) 12 43
(Harry Dunlop) *trckd ldrs: effrt over 2f out: wknd over 1f out* **33/1**

1m 25.16s (0.36) **Going Correction** -0.05s/f (Stan) **11** Ran SP% **122.7**
Speed ratings (Par 98): **95,90,89,89,88 88,87,87,86,86 80**
toteswingers:1&2:£2.80, 1&3:£9.80, 2&3:£6.00 CSF £13.55 CT £115.49 TOTE £9.20: £2.40, £1.10, £5.00; EX 20.90.

Owner B Kitcherside & Big Cat Partnership **Bred** Butlersgrove Stud **Trained** Ashtead, Surrey

FOCUS
Not a bad 3-y-o handicap for the class.

1314 TAG WORLDWIDE FILLIES' H'CAP 1m 2f (P)
5:20 (5:20) (Class 5) (0-75,72) 4-Y-O+ **£2,385** (£704; £352) **Stalls** Low

Form RPR

200- **1** **Cala Santanyi**[277] 3873 4-9-7 **72** .... LukeMorris 2 81
(Gerard Butler) *trckd ldrs: rdn wl over 1f out: led jst ins fnl f: styd on wl* **1/1**[1]

323- **2** *¾* **Chatterer (IRE)**[185] 6729 4-9-7 **72** .... HayleyTurner 5 79
(Marcus Tregoning) *trckd ldr: led over 2f out: sn rdn: hdd jst ins fnl f: kpt on but no ex* **7/2**[3]

030- **3** *2 ½* **Entrance**[114] 7816 4-8-7 **58** oh2 .... PaulHanagan 3 60
(Julia Feilden) *squeezed out s: racd in 5th: nudged along 4f out: c wd and rdn over 2f out: no imp tl styd on ent fnl f: wnt 3rd sn after* **16/1**

21-5 **4** *2* **Moresweets 'n Lace**[14] 1071 5-9-5 **70** .... GeorgeBaker 4 68
(Gary Moore) *trckd ldrs: effrt over 1f out: no ex whn lost 3rd ins fnl f* **9/4**[2]

610- **5** *2 ¾* **Ela Gonda Mou**[140] 7513 5-8-9 **65** .... RosieJessop(5) 1 58
(Peter Charalambous) *led: rdn and hdd over 2f out: fdd fnl f* **16/1**

2m 5.46s (-1.14) **Going Correction** -0.05s/f (Stan) **5** Ran SP% **114.8**
Speed ratings (Par 100): **102,101,99,97,95**
CSF £5.25 TOTE £1.80: £1.10, £1.30; EX 6.40.

Owner The Distaff 3 **Bred** Aston Mullins Stud **Trained** Newmarket, Suffolk

FOCUS
A moderate fillies' handicap, run at an average pace.

T/Plt: £30.60 to a £1 stake. Pool:£60,541.66 - 1,439.67 winning tickets T/Qpdt: £20.00 to a £1 stake. Pool:£5,736.03 - 212.15 winning tickets TM

NOTTINGHAM (L-H)
Wednesday, April 11

OFFICIAL GOING: Good to soft
Wind: Light against Weather: Sunshine and showers

1315 E B F BETFRED "WILL THEY WON'T THEY" NOVICE STKS 5f 13y
2:10 (2:10) (Class 4) 2-Y-O **£4,528** (£1,347; £673; £336) **Stalls** High

Form RPR

01 **1** **Dreamy Ciara**[7] 1188 2-8-11 0 .... PadraigBeggy 4 75
(David Evans) *mde all: edgd lft thrght: rdn over 1f out: styd on gamely* **2/1**[2]

2 *1* **Black Monk (IRE)** 2-9-0 0 .... PatDobbs 2 71
(Richard Hannon) *chsd wnr: shkn up over 1f out: sn ev ch: rdr dropped whip sn after: unable qck nr fin* **8/11**[1]

3 *2* **Yes Two** 2-9-0 0 .... JamesMillman 3 67
(Rod Millman) *chsd ldrs: outpcd 3f out: rallied and hung lft over 1f out: styd on same pce ins fnl f* **9/1**[3]

4 *9* **Frosted Off** 2-9-0 0 .... LiamJones 1 35
(John Spearing) *s.i.s: outpcd* **16/1**

1m 3.34s (2.34) **Going Correction** +0.375s/f (Good) **4** Ran SP% **107.1**
Speed ratings (Par 94): **96,94,91,76**
CSF £3.81 TOTE £3.10; EX 3.50.

Owner Mrs Emma Ambrose **Bred** Mrs S M Shone **Trained** Pandy, Monmouths

FOCUS
Races on inner coursed and distances as advertised. The ground had dried out a touch to good to soft all round, with a GoingStick reading of 6.8, but there was a heavy shower, including some hail, before the first race. The inside track was in use for the first time in a while and there was a bit of a headwind in the straight. The form will take time to settle but at the moment is rated an average renewal.

NOTEBOOK
Dreamy Ciara's previous experience made a difference in this novice race, bouncing out quickly, grabbing the stands' rail and seeing off the challenge of the favourite in the closing stages. It'll be a surprise if she finishes in front of the runner-up, whose rider dropped his whip, if they ever meet again. David Evans, who was winning this race for the fourth time in the last five years, said she wouldn't be sharp enough for the Lily Agnes. It's worth noting her sire made a good start with his 2-y-os last year, notching nine winners from 21 individual runners. (op 7-4 tchd 13-8)
Black Monk(IRE) lacked the previous experience of the winner, didn't have the rail to help and his rider dropped his whip with a furlong and a half to run, just as he was about to give him a reminder for the first time. All those factors contributed to him not making a winning debut, but he should soon be going one better. (tchd 4-5 and 5-6 in places)
Yes Two began to lose touch with the first two with 2f to run but rallied late and will be of more interest next time with this experience under his belt. (op 14-1)
Frosted Off was slowly away and struggled throughout. (op 18-1 tchd 14-1)

1316 BETFRED "GOALS GALORE" CONDITIONS STKS 5f 13y
2:40 (2:41) (Class 3) 3-Y-O+
£6,411 (£1,919; £959; £479; £239; £120) **Stalls** High

Form RPR

/30- **1** **Jonny Mudball**[332] 2138 6-9-1 105 .... (t) RichardKingscote 2 96
(Tom Dascombe) *chsd ldr: shkn up over 1f out: r.o to ld post* **15/8**[2]

100- **2** *shd* **Foxy Music**[172] 7018 8-9-1 87 .... PatCosgrave 6 96
(Eric Alston) *led: rdn ins fnl f: hdd post* **40/1**

000- **3** *2 ¼* **Tax Free (IRE)**[207] 6145 10-9-8 94 .... KierenFallon 5 95
(David Nicholls) *chsd ldrs: pushed along 1/2-way: styd on same pce wl ins fnl f: eased whn hld nr fin* **10/1**

200- **4** *2 ¼* **Liberty Lady (IRE)**[262] 4357 5-8-10 95 .... TomQueally 3 75
(Des Donovan) *s.i.s: sn pushed along in rr: hdwy over 1f out: sn rdn: no ex ins fnl f* **10/1**

525- **5** *4* **Triple Aspect (IRE)**[284] 3644 6-9-1 108 .... LiamJones 4 65
(Jeremy Gask) *chsd ldrs: shkn up over 1f out: wknd ins fnl f* **5/1**[3]

230- **6** *1* **Dinkum Diamond (IRE)**[193] 6520 4-9-10 106 .... WilliamBuick 1 71
(Henry Candy) *s.i.s and edgd lft s: sn prom: pushed along and hung lft 1/2-way: wknd over 1f out* **7/4**[1]

1m 1.32s (0.32) **Going Correction** +0.375s/f (Good) **6** Ran SP% **108.4**
Speed ratings (Par 107): **112,111,108,104,98 96**
toteswingers:1&2:£10.60, 1&3:£2.90, 2&3:£17.10 CSF £51.33 TOTE £2.00: £1.40, £15.00; EX 72.10.

Owner Woodgate Family **Bred** Mrs P A Reditt And M J Reditt **Trained** Malpas, Cheshire
■ Stewards' Enquiry : Pat Cosgrave two-day ban: used whip above permitted level (Apr 25-26)

FOCUS
A race that seemed to confirm something of a bias towards the stands' side rail, as there was almost a shock result.

NOTEBOOK
Jonny Mudball, who was absent for most of last year with an injury, has been gelded since last seen. Entitled to have needed this, he eventually wore down the leader, while racing one off the rail, and a return to a stiffer track ought to suit him. Perhaps the Palace House Stakes (dead-heated for third last year) will once again be his early target. (op 9-4)
Foxy Music made most of the running on the rail and only being denied right on the line. He came into the race with a mark of 87, while the winner is officially rated 18lb superior. Undoubtedly he was turned out fit and well (has won first time out in the past), but still, it's likely this form flatters him, and hopefully the handicapper doesn't take it too literally. (op 25-1)
Tax Free(IRE), who tracked the leader on the rail, kept on reasonably well without threatening the first two. He's needed his reappearance run in recent years and should come on for it. (op 12-1 tchd 9-1)
Liberty Lady(IRE), out the back for much of the race, stayed on late. (op 9-1 tchd 8-1)
Triple Aspect(IRE) has switched stables and is another who's been gelded since he last ran, but this was a little disappointing. (op 9-2 tchd 4-1)
Dinkum Diamond(IRE)'s trainer said beforehand that the colt had missed a fair bit of work, and in the race itself he was caught widest of all throughout. All things considered, it would be hasty to read too much into his performance. (tchd 13-8 and 2-1)

1317 BETFRED THE BONUS KING H'CAP 5f 13y
3:10 (3:13) (Class 4) (0-85,84) 3-Y-O **£4,075** (£1,212; £606; £303) **Stalls** High

Form RPR

10-0 **1** **Rusty Rocket (IRE)**[27] 905 3-8-8 **71** .... PaulMulrennan 9 76
(Paul Green) *chsd ldrs: outpcd over 1f out: rallied to ld nr fin* **33/1**

421- **2** *nse* **Personal Touch**[162] 7210 3-8-10 **73** .... TonyHamilton 5 78
(Richard Fahey) *s.i.s: sn pushed along in rr: hdwy and nt clr run fnl f: swtchd lft wl ins fnl f: sn ev ch: r.o* **13/2**[3]

000- **3** *½* **Signifer (IRE)**[159] 7261 3-9-6 **83** .... MartinHarley 8 86
(Mick Channon) *chsd ldrs: rdn to ld wl ins fnl f: hdd nr fin* **20/1**

2-45 **4** *hd* **I'll Be Good**[8] 1176 3-9-4 **81** ... JoeFanning 10 83
(Robert Johnson) *hld up: hdwy over 1f out: rdn and ev ch wl ins fnl f: styd on* **20/1**

43-1 **5** *1* **Red Senor (IRE)**[14] 1072 3-8-10 **78** ... MatthewLawson(5) 7 77
(Charles Hills) *s.i.s: hdwy over 1f out: rdn ins fnl f: styd on* **12/1**

223- **6** *¾* **Lupo D'Oro (IRE)**[152] 7359 3-9-1 **78** ... AdamKirby 11 74
(John Best) *hld up: rdn over 1f out: swtchd rt sn after: r.o towards fin* **7/1**

250- **7** *½* **Tip Top Gorgeous (IRE)**[187] 6670 3-9-1 **78** ... DanielTudhope 4 72
(David O'Meara) *hld up: hdwy over 1f out: sn rdn and edgd lft: nt trble ldrs* **11/1**

3-32 **8** *hd* **Come On Dave (IRE)**[9] 1169 3-8-8 **71** ow1 ... KierenFallon 1 64
(David Nicholls) *led towards centre: clr whn hung rt fr 1/2 way: rdn over 1f out: hdd and no ex wl ins fnl f* **9/1**

21-2 **9** *3½* **Lesotho (IRE)**[14] 1063 3-8-12 **75** ... TomQueally 3 56
(Noel Quinlan) *chsd ldrs: rdn over 1f out: wknd ins fnl f* **6/1**[2]

512- **10** *¾* **Ashpan Sam**[159] 7261 3-8-10 **73** ... LiamJones 2 51
(John Spearing) *s.i.s: sn mid-div: rdn over 1f out: wknd fnl f* **14/1**

110- **11** *½* **Royal Award**[193] 6518 3-9-4 **81** ... NeilCallan 12 57
(Ian Wood) *chsd ldrs: rdn over 1f out: wknd ins fnl f* **11/2**[1]

100- **12** *2* **Airborne Again (IRE)**[256] 4536 3-9-6 **83** ... FrankieDettori 6 52
(Harry Dunlop) *chsd ldrs tl rdn and wknd over 1f out* **11/1**

31- **13** *1¼* **Knocker Knowles (IRE)**[232] 5347 3-9-7 **84** ... PadraigBeggy 13 49
(David Evans) *s.i.s: sn pushed along in rr: wknd over 1f out* **11/1**

1m 2.72s (1.72) **Going Correction** +0.375s/f (Good) **13** Ran SP% **117.3**
Speed ratings (Par 100): **101,100,100,99,98 97,96,95,90,89 88,85,83**
toteswingers:1&2:£51.20, 1&3:£136.80, 2&3:£33.20 CSF £227.53 CT £4401.30 TOTE £55.40: £14.00, £3.60, £8.10; EX 396.70 TRIFECTA Not won..
Owner Seven Stars Racing **Bred** Mike Hyde **Trained** Lydiate, Merseyside

FOCUS
A competitive sprint and the complexion of the race changed inside the last.
Rusty Rocket(IRE) Official explanation: trainer's rep said, regarding apparent improvement in form, as reported last time, the colt hung right but on this occasion, it benefited from racing on turf.

1318 BETFRED BARRY HILLS "FURTHER FLIGHT" STKS (LISTED RACE) 1m 6f 15y
3:40 (3:42) (Class 1) 4-Y-0+
£19,848 (£7,525; £3,766; £1,876; £941; £472) **Stalls** Low

Form RPR

0-60 **1** **Electrolyser (IRE)**[41] 759 7-9-0 109 ... AdamKirby 6 110
(Clive Cox) *mde all: rdn and edgd rt over 1f out: styd on wl* **16/1**

613- **2** *2* **Zuider Zee (GER)**[122] 7733 5-9-0 105 ... WilliamBuick 5 107
(John Gosden) *chsd ldrs: rdn over 4f out: outpcd over 3f out: rallied fnl f: wnt 2nd post* **8/1**

400- **3** *hd* **Dandino**[235] 5284 5-9-0 112 ... KierenFallon 7 107
(James Fanshawe) *hld up: hdwy over 3f out: rdn to chse wnr over 2f out: styd on same pce ins fnl f: lost 2nd post* **2/1**[1]

306- **4** *1* **Blue Bajan (IRE)**[215] 5884 10-9-0 111 ... DanielTudhope 2 106
(David O'Meara) *hld up: hdwy 5f out: rdn over 2f out: styd on* **10/1**

253- **5** *¾* **Solar Sky**[194] 6498 4-8-11 100 ... TomQueally 4 104
(Sir Henry Cecil) *prom: lost pl 6f out: swtchd rt and r.o ins fnl f* **5/1**[2]

46-1 **6** *shd* **Eternal Heart (IRE)**[10] 1159 4-8-11 103 ... JoeFanning 1 104
(Mark Johnston) *chsd ldrs: rdn over 2f out: no ex fnl f* **5/1**[2]

102- **7** *4* **Parlour Games**[161] 7226 4-8-11 97 ... FrankieDettori 8 99
(Mahmood Al Zarooni) *prom: chsd wnr briefly over 2f out: wknd over 1f out* **6/1**[3]

45-0 **8** *nk* **Myplacelater**[18] 1034 5-8-9 103 ... JamieSpencer 3 93
(Richard Fahey) *hld up: effrt over 2f out: wknd over 1f out* **20/1**

145- **9** *17* **Address Unknown**[210] 6074 5-9-0 102 ... NeilCallan 9 75
(Ian Williams) *chsd wnr tl rdn and wknd over 2f out* **66/1**

3m 7.61s (1.31) **Going Correction** +0.075s/f (Good)
WFA 4 from 5yo+ 3lb **9** Ran SP% **113.3**
Speed ratings (Par 111): **102,100,100,100,99 99,97,97,87**
toteswingers:1&2:£15.50, 1&3:£4.50, 2&3:£4.20 CSF £134.49 TOTE £20.50: £5.20, £3.40, £2.00; EX 79.60 Trifecta £521.20 Part won. Pool: £704.36 - 0.70 winning units..
Owner Mr And Mrs P Hargreaves **Bred** Darley **Trained** Lambourn, Berks

FOCUS
Most of these were making their seasonal reappearance.

NOTEBOOK
Electrolyser(IRE), who was third best in at the weights and race-fit from taking in a couple of races in Dubai, including a Group 3 last time out, was one of the exceptions, and he made the most of it, making every yard of the running to record his first win since September 2009. Not hassled in front, he was able to set a pace to suit himself, found plenty when asked to kick clear in the straight, and simply looked to appreciate this drop in class. The Sagaro Stakes could be next. (op 18-1)
Zuider Zee(GER) ◆, last year's November Handicap winner, stayed on well after getting outpaced. A disputed lead and a stronger gallop would have helped his cause, and he should come on for this. (op 6-1)
Dandino was the one to beat strictly on the ratings, but he hadn't run since August and was debuting for a new stable having failed to make the track over the winter when with Nicky Henderson. He put up a perfectly respectable effort for a reappearance run, especially as he was held up quite a way off the pace. (op 7-2)
Blue Bajan(IRE) is another who could have done with the leader being taken on in front. (op 14-1 tchd 16-1)
Solar Sky, who didn't get the clearest of runs in the straight, ran as though a return to 2m will be in his favour. He looks the type who could have more to offer this season. (op 7-2 tchd 11-2)
Eternal Heart(IRE), a winner over 1m4f at Doncaster ten days earlier, had his stamina to prove. He didn't convince on that front, but perhaps the ground was softer than he would like. (tchd 4-1 and 6-1)
Parlour Games was a little keen early and, after being brought to challenge, his effort petered out quite quickly. (op 9-2)

1319 BETFRED MOBILE H'CAP (DIV I) 1m 2f 50y
4:10 (4:11) (Class 5) (0-70,70) 3-Y-0 **£2,264** (£673; £336; £168) **Stalls** Low

Form RPR

-155 **1** **Whipcrackaway (IRE)**[48] 667 3-8-13 **62** ... JohnFahy 12 71
(Peter Hedger) *prom: lost pl 8f out: hdwy over 2f out: r.o u.p to ld wl ins fnl f* **7/1**

606- **2** *1¾* **Nicholascopernicus (IRE)**[130] 7627 3-9-1 **64** ... PatCosgrave 9 70
(Ed Walker) *hdwy to chse ldrs over 8f out: rdn to ld over 2f out: hdd wl ins fnl f* **9/2**[1]

0-66 **3** *1* **Grand Gold**[10] 1160 3-9-2 **70** ... (t) MatthewLawson(5) 8 74
(Seamus Durack) *hld up: hdwy over 2f out: rdn and hung lft fr over 1f out: styd on* **6/1**[2]

550 **4** *2¾* **Roughlyn**[34] 833 3-8-8 **57** ... FrederikTylicki 10 56
(Kevin Ryan) *led: propped and hdd 8f out: chsd ldrs: rdn over 3f out: no ex ins fnl f* **20/1**

405- **5** *4* **Fleur De La Vie (IRE)**[126] 7650 3-8-8 **60** ... HarryBentley(3) 11 51
(Ralph Beckett) *chsd ldr 8f out: led over 3f out: rdn and hdd over 2f out: wknd over 1f out* **8/1**

050- **6** *1* **Spirit Na Heireann (IRE)**[206] 6187 3-9-2 **65** ... TonyHamilton 3 54
(Richard Fahey) *hld up: hdwy over 3f out: sn outpcd: n.d after* **6/1**[2]

-314 **7** *6* **Cool Hand Luke (IRE)**[19] 1013 3-9-4 **67** ... RichardKingscote 4 45
(Tom Dascombe) *chsd ldrs: rdn over 3f out: wknd over 1f out* **7/1**

000- **8** *2¼* **Fine Kingdom**[183] 6774 3-8-9 **58** ... (p) PaulMulrennan 6 32
(Michael Dods) *s.i.s: sme hdwy 1/2-way: rdn over 4f out: wknd over 2f out* **22/1**

0-50 **9** *8* **Run Of The Day**[20] 993 3-8-7 **56** oh1 ... (v[1]) RoystonFfrench 5 14
(Eve Johnson Houghton) *sn pushed along in rr: bhd fr 1/2-way* **40/1**

600- **10** *13* **Bajan Hero**[195] 6489 3-8-12 **61** ... PadraigBeggy 1
(David Evans) *sn pushed along in rr: bhd fr 1/2-way* **50/1**

1214 **11** *½* **Moataz (USA)**[20] 998 3-9-7 **70** ... JamieSpencer 7
(Mark Johnston) *chsd ldrs: led 8f out: hdd over 3f out: wknd over 2f out* **13/2**[3]

045- **12** *4½* **It's A Girl Thing (IRE)**[131] 7599 3-9-5 **68** ... KierenFallon 2
(George Baker) *s.i.s: a towards rr: eased fr over 2f out* **14/1**

2m 15.49s (1.19) **Going Correction** +0.075s/f (Good) **12** Ran SP% **116.4**
Speed ratings (Par 98): **98,96,95,93,90 89,84,83,76,66 65,62**
toteswingers:1&2:£9.10, 1&3:£13.30, 2&3:£9.20 CSF £36.21 CT £202.29 TOTE £12.10: £3.40, £1.80, £2.10; EX 47.80 Trifecta £330.00 Part won. Pool: £445.95 - 0.60 winning units..
Owner P R Hedger **Bred** Kilfrush Stud **Trained** Dogmersfield, Hampshire

FOCUS
This was run at a good pace and those ridden with a bit of patience were favoured.

1320 BETFRED MOBILE H'CAP (DIV II) 1m 2f 50y
4:40 (4:40) (Class 5) (0-70,70) 3-Y-0 **£2,264** (£673; £336; £168) **Stalls** Low

Form RPR

040- **1** **Dorry K (IRE)**[182] 6807 3-8-11 **65** ... DeanHeslop(5) 10 72
(David Barron) *hld up: hdwy 4f out: r.o to ld wl ins fnl f* **14/1**

00-1 **2** *hd* **Sheila's Buddy**[39] 787 3-9-7 **70** ... LiamKeniry 9 76
(J S Moore) *hld up: hdwy over 1f out: rdn and r.o wl: nt quite get up* **13/2**[3]

563- **3** *1½* **Neil's Pride**[266] 4194 3-8-7 **56** ... FrederikTylicki 8 60
(Richard Fahey) *hld up: hdwy over 4f out: sn pushed along: r.o* **7/2**[1]

600- **4** *nk* **Fine Altomis**[203] 6259 3-8-7 **56** oh3 ... PaulMulrennan 3 59
(Michael Dods) *chsd ldr tl over 5f out: wnt 2nd again over 3f out: rdn and ev ch wl ins fnl f: unable qck towards fin* **14/1**

052- **5** *1½* **Joyful Spirit (IRE)**[184] 6753 3-8-12 **61** ... WilliamBuick 12 61
(John Dunlop) *sn led: rdn and edgd lft over 1f out: hdd and no ex wl ins fnl f* **11/2**[2]

-610 **6** *1½* **Captain Cardington (IRE)**[37] 803 3-9-3 **66** ... (v) MartinHarley 1 63
(Mick Channon) *a.p: rdn and n.m.r over 1f out: no ex ins fnl f* **20/1**

064- **7** *9* **Renegotiate**[181] 6812 3-9-4 **67** ... (v[1]) DavidProbert 11 47
(Andrew Balding) *hld up: effrt over 2f out: sn wknd* **13/2**[3]

400- **8** *3¼* **Maliha (IRE)**[202] 6275 3-8-13 **62** ... PhillipMakin 7 36
(Kevin Ryan) *chsd ldrs tl rdn and wknd over 2f out* **20/1**

36-3 **9** *1¼* **Chelsea Mick**[86] 193 3-9-1 **69** ... JustinNewman(5) 5 41
(John Mackie) *hld up: hdwy over 5f out: rdn over 3f out: wknd over 2f out* **9/1**

00-4 **10** *33* **Bevis Marks (USA)**[18] 1036 3-8-11 **60** ... JoeFanning 6
(Mark Johnston) *prom: chsd ldr over 5f out tl rdn over 3f out: wknd over 2f out: t.o* **10/1**

500 **11** *3¾* **Marinus (IRE)**[22] 969 3-8-13 **62** ... DarryllHolland 2
(Sylvester Kirk) *hld up: j. path 8f out: wknd and eased fnl 3f: t.o* **11/1**

2m 15.95s (1.65) **Going Correction** +0.075s/f (Good) **11** Ran SP% **114.6**
Speed ratings (Par 98): **96,95,94,94,93 92,84,82,81,54 51**
toteswingers:1&2:£15.80, 1&3:£13.60, 2&3:£4.90 CSF £99.63 CT £390.56 TOTE £12.50: £4.00, £1.70, £2.20; EX 88.30 Trifecta £251.40 Part won. Pool: £339.74 - 0.73 winning units..
Owner Twinacre Nurseries Ltd **Bred** Twinacre Nurseries Ltd **Trained** Maunby, N Yorks

FOCUS
The slower of the two divisions by 0.46sec.
Marinus(IRE) Official explanation: trainer said gelding did not appear to handle the track

1321 BETFRED MOBILE CASINO H'CAP 1m 75y
5:10 (5:10) (Class 3) (0-95,91) 4-Y-0+ **£6,663** (£1,982; £990; £495) **Stalls** Centre

Form RPR

021- **1** **Neutrafa (IRE)**[165] 7160 4-8-8 **81** ... HarryBentley(3) 15 97
(John Mackie) *hld up: hdwy over 3f out: led 2f out: sn clr: easily* **13/2**[3]

300- **2** *3¾* **Certral**[221] 5702 4-8-6 **79** ow3 ... PaulPickard(3) 13 86
(Brian Ellison) *s.i.s: hld up: nt clr run fr over 2f out tl swtchd rt over 1f out: r.o to go 2nd wl ins fnl f: no ch w wnr* **25/1**

100- **3** *1½* **Stage Attraction (IRE)**[165] 7168 4-9-1 **85** ... DavidProbert 11 89
(Andrew Balding) *a.p: rdn over 2f out: styd on same pce fnl f* **16/1**

010- **4** *½* **Oriental Scot**[165] 7168 5-9-0 **84** ... FrankieDettori 8 87
(William Jarvis) *hld up: hdwy over 2f out: rdn over 1f out: styd on same pce fnl f* **6/1**[2]

226- **5** *hd* **Robemaker**[165] 7168 4-9-7 **91** ... WilliamBuick 5 93
(John Gosden) *hld up: pushed along and nt clr run over 2f out: hdwy over 1f out: r.o: nt rch ldrs* **5/1**[1]

6-02 **6** *¾* **Mawaakef (IRE)**[48] 674 4-9-1 **85** ... FrederikTylicki 10 86
(J R Jenkins) *chsd ldrs: rdn over 2f out: no ex fnl f* **15/2**

40-0 **7** *4½* **Shavansky**[11] 1130 8-9-6 **90** ... JamesMillman 6 80
(Rod Millman) *s.i.s: hld up: hdwy over 2f out: wknd fnl f* **10/1**

0-34 **8** *3* **Sinfonico (IRE)**[35] 817 4-9-0 **84** ... (e) PatDobbs 9 67
(Richard Hannon) *prom: rdn over 2f out: wknd over 1f out* **11/1**

1045 **9** *1½* **Prince Of Burma (IRE)**[11] 1128 4-9-3 **87** ... (b) PatCosgrave 12 67
(Jeremy Gask) *hld up: hdwy over 3f out: rdn: edgd lft and wknd wl over 1f out* **12/1**

/62- **10** *5* **Chiswick Bey (IRE)**[336] 2003 4-9-6 **90** ... TonyHamilton 3 58
(Richard Fahey) *prom: rdn and nt clr run over 2f out: sn wknd* **16/1**

500- **11** *3¼* **Masked Dance (IRE)**[133] 7586 5-9-4 **88** ... (p) NeilCallan 1 49
(Scott Dixon) *led: hdd & wknd 2f out* **50/1**

0-31 **12** *7* **Call To Reason (IRE)**[55] 584 5-9-2 **86** ... JamieSpencer 4 31
(Ian Williams) *hld up: hdwy 4f out: nt clr run over 2f out: sn wknd: t.o* **8/1**

221- **13** *1¾* **Change The Subject (USA)**[105] 7894 4-8-9 **79** ... JoeFanning 2 20
(Peter Salmon) *dwlt: hld up: hmpd 7f out: hdwy 1/2-way: wknd over 2f out: t.o* **28/1**

214- **14** *2¾* **Orbit The Moon (IRE)**[307] 2834 4-9-1 **85** ... (t) PaulMulrennan 14 20
(Michael Dods) *hld up: wkng whn hmpd wl over 2f out: t.o* **33/1**

-060 **15** 1 ¾ **Zacynthus (IRE)**[10] 1156 4-8-13 **83**....................(tp) JohnFahy 7 14
(Alan McCabe) *prom: racd keenly: trckd ldr 6f out tl rdn over 3f out: wknd over 2f out: t.o* **50/1**

1m 46.5s (-3.10) **Going Correction** -0.20s/f (Firm) 15 Ran SP% **118.2**
Speed ratings (Par 107): **107,103,101,101,101 100,95,92,91,86 83,76,74,71,69**
toteswingers:1&2:£50.00, 1&3:£32.10, 2&3:£102.90 CSF £168.09 CT £1559.02 TOTE £8.80: £3.70, £10.90, £6.80; EX 292.50 TRIFECTA Not won..
Owner Tony Ashley **Bred** Twelve Oaks Stud & Deerpark Stud **Trained** Church Broughton , Derbys
■ Stewards' Enquiry : Jamie Spencer caution: careless riding

FOCUS
Zacynthus and Masked Dance took each other on in front here and the race was set up for a closer.

NOTEBOOK
Neutrafa(IRE) ◆ was poorly drawn and got caught a bit wide around the turn, but she cruised through the race and quickened clear from 2f out. She won with real authority, is clearly miles ahead of the handicapper and a quick reappearance will have to be considered, as she'll pay for this with a steep rise in the weights. That said, black type will no doubt be her connections' main aim this season. (op 8-1)
Certral travelled well out the back and, suited by the way the race was run, came through to take second behind the impressive winner. She coped with the ground well but a faster surface suits her best. (op 33-1 tchd 40-1)
Stage Attraction(IRE) kept on well from midfield. He likes to get his toe in so the bit of dig he had here was in his favour. (op 18-1 tchd 20-1)
Oriental Scot tracked the winner through but lacked her acceleration. (op 7-1 tchd 9-2)
Robemaker benefited from the strong pace up front and was another who stayed on from the rear, despite not enjoying the clearest of runs. (op 9-2)
Mawaakef(IRE) chased the two leaders and did best of those that raced prominently, so deserves a little extra credit. His trainer's in good form at the moment. (op 8-1 tchd 9-1)
Call To Reason(IRE) didn't get the smoothest of passages in the straight, and his rider didn't persevere in a lost cause. (op 7-1 tchd 13-2)

1322 BETFRED MOBILE LOTTO H'CAP 1m 75y
5:40 (5:44) (Class 5) (0-75,75) 3-Y-O **£2,264** (£673; £336; £168) **Stalls** Centre

Form RPR
521- **1** **The Giving Tree (IRE)**[182] 6807 3-9-4 72.................... WilliamBuick 1 82
(Sylvester Kirk) *hld up: hdwy over 2f out: led over 1f out: rdn and edgd lft ins fnl f: r.o* **6/1**[3]
500- **2** 1 ¾ **Uncle Roger (IRE)**[174] 6972 3-8-12 66.................... NeilCallan 6 72
(Eve Johnson Houghton) *hld up in tch: hmpd over 5f out: rdn and ev ch over 1f out: styd on same pce ins fnl f* **16/1**
215- **3** ¾ **Mistress Of Rome**[182] 6806 3-8-9 63.................... PaulMulrennan 10 67
(Michael Dods) *chsd ldrs: rdn over 2f out: r.o* **9/1**
01- **4** nk **Al Jabreiah**[174] 6973 3-9-0 68.................... LiamJones 2 72
(William Haggas) *hld up: nt clr run 2f out: hdwy over 1f out: r.o: nt rch ldrs* **9/1**
505- **5** ½ **Drummond**[215] 5891 3-9-4 72.................... JohnFahy 14 74
(Clive Cox) *led: hdd over 6f out: chsd ldr tl led again over 2f out: rdn and hdd over 1f out: no ex ins fnl f* **15/2**
653 **6** 2 ½ **Dilizan (IRE)**[28] 903 3-8-8 65.................... PaulPickard(3) 8 62
(Brian Ellison) *hld up: hdwy over 2f out: rdn over 1f out: no ex fnl f* **14/1**
550- **7** 3 **Camrock Star (IRE)**[118] 7763 3-8-9 63....................(v) PadraigBeggy 5 53
(David Evans) *mid-div: hmpd over 5f out: rdn over 3f out: wknd over 1f out* **40/1**
64-3 **8** nk **Beau Mistral (IRE)**[27] 905 3-9-4 72.................... PhillipMakin 7 61
(Paul Green) *hld up: pushed along over 2f out: nvr trbld ldrs* **16/1**
330- **9** 3 **It's A Privilege**[145] 7454 3-9-2 75.................... JamesRogers(5) 9 57
(Ralph Beckett) *s.s: sn drvn along: rapid hdwy to ld over 6f out: hdd over 2f out: wknd over 1f out* **16/1**
010- **10** ½ **Wyndham Wave**[195] 6484 3-9-2 70.................... JamesMillman 3 51
(Rod Millman) *hld up: hdwy over 3f out: nt clr run over 2f out: sn wknd* **20/1**
050- **11** 1 **Paladin (IRE)**[200] 6334 3-9-4 72.................... MickaelBarzalona 4 51
(Mahmood Al Zarooni) *chsd ldrs: rdn over 2f out: wknd fnl f* **5/1**[2]
506- **12** 18 **Brailsford (IRE)**[182] 6805 3-9-4 72.................... FrankieDettori 13
(Mahmood Al Zarooni) *sn prom: hung lft 2f out: sn wknd and eased* **3/1**[1]

1m 49.49s (-0.11) **Going Correction** -0.20s/f (Firm) 12 Ran SP% **119.2**
Speed ratings (Par 98): **92,90,89,89,88 86,83,82,79,79 78,60**
toteswingers:1&2:£11.50, 1&3:£9.40, 2&3:£16.80 CSF £98.64 CT £875.86 TOTE £7.00: £2.30, £6.20, £2.70; EX 93.70 Trifecta £666.10 Part won. Pool: £900.22 - 0.45 winning units..
Owner Knockainey Stud **Bred** Knockainey Stud & Storway Ltd **Trained** Upper Lambourn, Berks

FOCUS
No more than a fair handicap.
It's A Privilege Official explanation: jockey said gelding became upset in stalls and was slowly away
Brailsford(IRE) Official explanation: jockey said he had no explanation for the poor form shown
T/Plt: £650.70 to a £1 stake. Pool:£50,725.66 - 56.90 winning tickets T/Qpdt: £92.90 to a £1 stake. Pool:£6,080.06 - 48.40 winning tickets CR

1201 FOLKESTONE (R-H)
Thursday, April 12

OFFICIAL GOING: Good to soft (good in places) changing to soft after race 1 (2:10) abandoned after race 2 (2.45) due to unsafe ground
Wind: almost nil Weather: rain and cold

1330 CALL STAR SPORTS 08000 521 321 MEDIAN AUCTION MAIDEN STKS 5f
2:10 (2:10) (Class 6) 2-Y-O **£1,704** (£503; £251) **Stalls** High

Form RPR
6 **1** **Rated**[5] 1218 2-9-3 0.................... MartinHarley 3 71
(Mick Channon) *settled 3rd: pushed along 2f out: produced to ld on inner 1f out: hanging rt but asserted u.p fnl 100yds* **3/1**[2]
3 **2** 1 ¾ **Marchwood**[7] 1202 2-9-3 0.................... LiamKeniry 2 65
(J S Moore) *chsd ldr: pushed along and led 2f out: drvn and hdd 1f out: duelled for ld tl no ex fnl 100yds* **10/11**[1]
3 6 **Ladweb** 2-9-3 0.................... IanMongan 4 43
(John Gallagher) *slow away: in last and running green: rdn along 3f out: btn 2f out: kpt on to take poor 3rd fnl 100yds* **14/1**
23 **4** 1 ¾ **Suivez L'Argent**[3] 1253 2-8-5 0.................... JacobMoore(7) 5 32
(Joseph Tuite) *led: rdn and hdd 2f out: dropped away whn n.m.r and sn btn: dropped last fnl 100yds* **10/3**[3]

1m 4.4s (4.40) **Going Correction** +0.65s/f (Yiel) 4 Ran SP% **107.1**
Speed ratings (Par 90): **90,87,77,74**
CSF £6.15 TOTE £4.10; EX 7.00.
Owner M Channon **Bred** Mike Channon Bloodstock Ltd **Trained** West Ilsley, Berks

FOCUS
An ordinary juvenile maiden, in which those with form had reached only modest levels, and it was run in driving rain. The form is given a token rating through the runner-up but is limited.

NOTEBOOK
Rated, always in rear on his sole previous run, showed marked improvement. Third in the early stages, he squeezed through a gap up the stands' rail with 2f left and asserted soon afterwards. Considering his pedigree, he should continue to progress, especially when given the chance to try longer distances. (op 4-1)
Marchwood, third here on his debut a week previously, probably performed to a similar level again. Always chasing the pace, he led briefly at the 2f marker, but could not handle the winner in the closing stages. He may need to drop to a claimer in order to notch a victory. (tchd 5-6 and Evens)
Ladweb, an inexpensive sprint-bred newcomer, was very green in the early stages. He got the hang of things in the second half of the race, though, and plugged on gamely. (op 12-1)
Suivez L'Argent, in the frame on her two earlier starts, led until beyond halfway. She folded quickly, however, and even though the ground and weather may have been a factor here, does not appear to be progressing. (op 11-4 tchd 7-2)

1331 STARSPORTSBET.CO.UK H'CAP 6f
2:45 (2:48) (Class 5) (0-75,75) 3-Y-O **£3,234** (£962; £481; £240) **Stalls** High

Form RPR
26-1 **1** **Dishy Guru**[13] 1110 3-9-7 **75**.................... LiamKeniry 14 82
(Michael Blanshard) *cl up: swtchd rt ins fnl 2f: produced to chal over 1f out: drvn along to ld 1f out battled on wl* **17/2**
000- **2** ½ **Mayo Lad (IRE)**[197] 6463 3-8-11 **65**.................... RyanMoore 7 70+
(Richard Hannon) *midfield: swtchd rt and rdn to chse ldrs over 1f out: pressed wnr ins fnl f: no ex cl home* **11/4**[1]
323- **3** 1 **School Fees**[227] 5562 3-9-6 **74**.................... MartinHarley 11 76
(Henry Candy) *mounted outside paddock: disp ld against nrside rail: rdn and hdd ins fnl f: no ex cl home* **5/1**[2]
440- **4** 7 **Light Burst (USA)**[184] 6768 3-8-9 **63**.................... SilvestreDeSousa 4 43+
(Mahmood Al Zarooni) *cl up: pushed along 2f out: drvn to press ldrs over 1f out: wknd ins fnl f* **7/1**[3]
050- **5** 1 ¼ **Star Kingdom (IRE)**[132] 7597 3-9-0 **68**.................... MartinDwyer 3 44
(Robert Mills) *disp ld tl rdn and hdd over 1f out: drvn and no ex ins fnl f* **22/1**
2-12 **6** 2 ¼ **Welease Bwian (IRE)**[76] 326 3-8-11 **65**....................(t) JamesDoyle 10 33+
(Stuart Williams) *in rr: rdn along 3f out: swtchd rt and effrt 2f out: mod late hdwy wout threatening ldrs* **20/1**
-523 **7** ¾ **Diamond Marks (IRE)**[22] 982 3-8-10 **64**.................... JamieSpencer 2 30+
(John Gallagher) *in tch on outer: pushed along and ev ch over 1f out: wknd and eased ins fnl f* **20/1**
400- **8** 11 **Amis Reunis**[192] 6590 3-9-1 **72**.................... DominicFox(3) 8
(Anthony Carson) *in rr thrght: drvn 4f out: struggling and wl btn 2f out* **18/1**
040- **9** 1 ¼ **Foot Tapper**[159] 7293 3-8-13 **67**.................... TedDurcan 13
(Chris Wall) *slow away: a in rr: pushed along and wknd over 2f out* **12/1**
6R-5 **10** 6 **Daraa (IRE)**[33] 867 3-9-6 **74**.................... BrettDoyle 5
(Clive Brittain) *midfield on outer: pushed along over 2f out: fdd and wl btn 1f out* **25/1**
-214 **11** ½ **Al Freej (IRE)**[52] 637 3-9-5 **73**.................... NeilCallan 6
(Roger Varian) *dwlt: midfield: drvn and effrt over 3f out: wknd 2f out* **5/1**[2]

1m 20.67s (7.97) **Going Correction** +1.30s/f (Soft) 11 Ran SP% **113.7**
Speed ratings (Par 98): **98,97,96,86,85 82,81,66,64,56 56**
toteswingers:1&2:£6.20, 2&3:£3.40, 1&3:£7.30 CSF £29.12 CT £133.33 TOTE £11.60: £3.70, £1.30, £2.20; EX 45.60.
Owner Clifton Partners **Bred** J W Ford **Trained** Upper Lambourn, Berks

FOCUS
With 6mm of rain falling during and following the opener, the ground was officially changed to soft prior to this event. Some jockeys, however, called it heavy. On paper, this was an ultra-competitive handicap. It was run, like the first race, in a downpour and the meeting was abandoned after this race due to waterlogging, so it is probably best not to be too positive about the form.

1332 FOLLOW US ON TIWTTER @STARSPORTS.BET (S) STKS 7f (S)
() (Class 6) 3-Y-O £

1333 ANN CLARK MAIDEN STKS 7f (S)
() (Class 5) 3-Y-O+ £

1334 CALL 08000 521 321 FOR ALL AINTREE PRICES H'CAP 1m 7f 92y
() (Class 5) (0-70,) 4-Y-O+ £

1335 BRITAIN'S NUMBER ONE TEXT BETTING SERVICE H'CAP 1m 4f
() (Class 4) (0-85,) 4-Y-O+ £

1336 BACK ANY AINTREE HORSE TO WIN £50,000 APPRENTICE H'CAP 1m 4f
() (Class 6) (0-60,) 4-Y-O+ £

T/Plt: £11.60 to a £1 stake. Pool:£46,219.36 - 2,898.63 winning tickets CS

1187 WOLVERHAMPTON (A.W) (L-H)
Thursday, April 12

OFFICIAL GOING: Standard
Wind: Almost nil Weather: Sunny

1337 LADBROKES BET ON YOUR MOBILE H'CAP 5f 216y(P)
5:55 (5:57) (Class 6) (0-60,60) 3-Y-O **£1,704** (£503; £251) **Stalls** Low

Form RPR
1 **Phebes Wish (IRE)**[158] 7317 3-8-7 **46**....................(t) JamesSullivan 7 59
(John C McConnell, Ire) *t.k.h early: in tch: smooth hdwy over 2f out: rdn to ld over 1f out: edgd lft: rdn and kpt on fnl f* **6/1**
-055 **2** nk **Trending (IRE)**[20] 1012 3-8-4 **48**....................(b[1]) RaulDaSilva(5) 4 60
(Jeremy Gask) *plld hrd: hld up towards rr: hdwy over 1f out: edgd lft and chsd wnr ins fnl f: clsng at fin* **9/2**[3]
003- **3** 1 ¼ **Art Dzeko**[308] 2831 3-9-6 **59**.................... DavidAllan 1 67
(Tim Easterby) *bhd: pushed along 1/2-way: hdwy over 1f out: kpt on fnl f: no imp towards fin* **7/2**[2]
0624 **4** 1 ½ **Maria Montez**[20] 1006 3-9-5 **58**.................... MartinLane 8 61
(J W Hills) *hld up: drvn and hdwy on outside wl over 1f out: no imp ins fnl f* **10/1**
3534 **5** ½ **My Name Is Sam**[20] 1010 3-8-1 **47**....................(v[1]) DarrenEgan(7) 5 49
(Ronald Harris) *set decent gallop: qcknd clr over 2f out: sn rdn: hdd over 1f out: sn no ex* **11/1**

6-03 **6** *2* **Jeremy Sue**[29] 898 3-8-7 **46** oh1 (b) AndreaAtzeni 11 41
(Derek Haydn Jones) *sn chsng ldr fr wd draw: rdn and lost 2nd 2f out: btn fnl f* **33/1**

505- **7** *hd* **Kathleensluckylad (IRE)**[139] 7540 3-9-7 **60** PhillipMakin 6 55
(Kevin Ryan) *chsd ldrs: drvn along and outpcd over 2f out: n.d after* **3/1**[1]

0455 **8** *7* **Strike A Pose (IRE)**[20] 1006 3-9-1 **54** PadraigBeggy 10 26
(David Evans) *hld up in tch on outside: drvn and struggling over 2f out: btn over 1f out* **22/1**

5-63 **9** *3* **Bitter Lemon**[34] 845 3-9-0 **53** TomMcLaughlin 3
(Tony Newcombe) *hld up on ins: drvn and outpcd over 2f out: sn btn* **10/1**

004- **10** *5* **Hawaiian Freeze**[273] 3993 3-8-9 **48** ChrisCatlin 9
(John Stimpson) *racd wd in rr: lost tch 1/2-way: nvr on terms* **66/1**

1m 15.0s **Going Correction** +0.05s/f (Slow) **10** Ran SP% **115.0**
Speed ratings (Par 96): **102,101,99,97,97 94,94,85,81,74**
Tote Swingers:1&2:£7.00, 2&3:£5.00, 1&3:£6.40 CSF £32.14 CT £111.95 TOTE £7.70: £2.30, £1.40, £2.20; EX 36.80 Trifecta £155.40.
Owner Derek Kierans **Bred** C M Farrell **Trained** Stamullen, Co Meath

FOCUS
A modest handicap but a few of these had yet to really show their hand. The third to his juvenile form looks the best guide.
Phebes Wish(IRE) Official explanation: trainer said, regarding apparent improvement in form, that the gelding was better suited by the all weather surface and shorter trip, it had also been gelded over the winter.
Bitter Lemon Official explanation: jockey said filly never travelled

1338 LADBROKES BET IN PLAY H'CAP 1m 5f 194y(P)
6:25 (6:25) (Class 6) (0-65,65) 4-Y-0+ **£1,704** (£503; £251) **Stalls** Low

Form RPR

-605 **1** **Bute Street**[8] 1184 7-8-8 **49** RichardKingscote 6 59
(Ron Hodges) *chsd ldrs: hdwy 1/2-way: led over 4f out: clr over 2f out: drvn and kpt on strly* **9/1**

-112 **2** *3* **Holden Eagle**[14] 1092 7-9-3 **65** IanBurns(7) 2 71
(Tony Newcombe) *chsd ldr to 1/2-way: drvn and outpcd over 3f out: rallied to chse clr wnr 2f out: kpt on fnl f: nvr able to chal* **15/2**[3]

51-5 **3** *1 1/4* **Hit The Switch**[20] 1011 6-9-9 **64** (p) TomQueally 1 68
(Jennie Candlish) *t.k.h early: led: rdn and hdd over 4f out: rallied: outpcd fr 2f out* **8/1**

6221 **4** *nk* **Corvette**[26] 937 4-8-11 **62** JackDuern(7) 5 66
(Michael Appleby) *hld up in last: effrt whn nt clr run on ins over 3f out: sn rdn along: kpt on fnl f: nrst fin* **7/2**[2]

0-1 **5** *14* **Maid Of Meft**[8] 1189 5-9-9 **64** 6ex JoeFanning 7 56
(Keith Dalgleish) *taken down early to post: dwlt: sn prom: hdwy 1/2-way: rdn over 4f out: wknd 2f out: eased whn no ch fnl f* **4/5**[1]

0305 **P** **War Of The Roses (IRE)**[21] 992 9-9-7 **62** TomEaves 8
(Roy Brotherton) *hld up in tch: outpcd and hung lft 4f out: lost tch 2f out: p.u and dismntd 1f out* **25/1**

3m 4.72s (-1.28) **Going Correction** +0.05s/f (Slow)
WFA 4 from 5yo+ 3lb **6** Ran SP% **114.5**
Speed ratings (Par 101): **105,103,102,102,94**
Tote Swingers:1&2:£4.90, 2&3:£4.30, 1&3:£4.90 CSF £71.57 CT £564.17 TOTE £10.70: £2.20, £3.70; EX 63.50.
Owner J W Mursell **Bred** J W Mursell **Trained** Charlton Mackrell, Somerset

FOCUS
Some in-form horses here but ordinary form rated through the runner-up.
Maid Of Meft Official explanation: jockey said mare ran flat
War Of The Roses(IRE) Official explanation: jockey said gelding pulled up lame

1339 ATR GRAND NATIONAL MICROSITE NOW LIVE (S) STKS 1m 4f 50y(P)
6:55 (6:55) (Class 6) 4-Y-0+ **£1,704** (£503; £251) **Stalls** Low

Form RPR

3-12 **1** **Stand Guard**[37] 809 8-9-6 78 TomQueally 2 83
(John Butler) *t.k.h: in tch: stdy hdwy over 3f out: chsd ldr over 2f out: shkn up to ld ins fnl f: comf* **4/7**[1]

02-4 **2** *5* **Shy**[13] 1104 7-8-9 63 (b) AndreaAtzeni 6 64
(Rod Millman) *led: rdn and qcknd over 2f out: hdd ins fnl f: kpt on same pce* **5/1**[3]

3 *11* **Gay Sloane (IRE)**[104] 6321 8-9-0 75 JimmyFortune 3 51
(John Coombe) *cl up: wnt 2nd over 4f out to over 2f out: sn struggling* **9/2**[2]

000- **4** *3/4* **Guga (IRE)**[134] 7113 6-8-11 56 (v) MichaelO'Connell(3) 4 50
(John Mackie) *t.k.h: in tch: stdy hdwy over 4f out: rdn and wknd over 2f out* **22/1**

5 *13* **Tulia De Gravelle (FR)**[23] 5-8-9 0 RichardMullen 7 24
(Philip Hobbs) *sn chsng ldr: drvn along over 4f out: wknd over 2f out: t.o* **40/1**

-060 **6** *25* **Just Zak**[27] 924 7-9-0 40 (b) PaulMulrennan 5
(Garry Woodward) *dwlt: hld up: drvn and outpcd over 5f out: lost tch over 3f out: t.o* **150/1**

2m 40.11s (-0.99) **Going Correction** +0.05s/f (Slow)
WFA 4 from 5yo+ 1lb **6** Ran SP% **106.0**
Speed ratings (Par 101): **105,101,94,93,85 68**
Tote Swingers:1&2:£1.30, 2&3:£1.60, 1&3:£1.20 CSF £3.18 TOTE £1.60: £1.10, £2.10; EX 2.40.
Owner J Butler **Bred** Juddmonte Farms Ltd **Trained** Newmarket, Suffolk

FOCUS
A weak race in which the winner is the best guide, despite not needing to match recent form to score.

1340 MIRROR PUNTERS CLUB MEDIAN AUCTION MAIDEN STKS 1m 4f 50y(P)
7:25 (7:26) (Class 5) 3-5-Y-O **£2,264** (£673; £336; £168) **Stalls** Low

Form RPR

1 **Natasha Rostova** 3-8-2 0 DavidProbert 1 67+
(Andrew Balding) *missed break: plld hrd in tch: hdwy to ld over 3f out: rdn and rn green 2f out: kpt on strly* **12/1**[2]

55 **2** *5* **Green Mitas (ITY)**[26] 943 3-8-2 0 RaulDaSilva(5) 3 61
(Frank Sheridan) *chsd ldrs: drvn and outpcd over 3f out: hung lft and chsd clr wnr over 1f out: kpt on: no imp* **20/1**[3]

02- **3** *7* **My Destination (IRE)**[181] 6825 3-8-7 0 (p) MickaelBarzalona 2 52
(Mahmood Al Zarooni) *t.k.h: led at stdy gallop: rdn and hdd over 3f out: fnd little and lost 2nd over 1f out* **1/9**[1]

4 *18* **Daisy Daze**[16] 4-9-5 0 RichardEvans(3) 4 16
(David Evans) *chsd ldr to over 3f out: sn rdn and outpcd: btn fnl 2f* **100/1**

2m 46.51s (5.41) **Going Correction** +0.05s/f (Slow)
WFA 3 from 4yo 21lb **4** Ran SP% **103.5**
Speed ratings (Par 103): **83,79,75,63**
CSF £104.70 TOTE £10.10; EX 42.50.
Owner J C & S R Hitchins **Bred** J C & S R Hitchins **Trained** Kingsclere, Hants

FOCUS
Just the four runners but a real bombshell. The runner-up looks the best guide but not a race to be too positive about.

1341 ATTHERACES.COM/NATIONAL CLAIMING STKS 1m 1f 103y(P)
7:55 (7:55) (Class 5) 4-Y-0+ **£2,385** (£704; £352) **Stalls** Low

Form RPR

1115 **1** **Munsarim (IRE)**[20] 1008 5-9-2 86 (b) JoeFanning 1 88
(Keith Dalgleish) *t.k.h: hld up in tch: hdwy and shkn up to ld over 1f out: drifted rt ins fnl f: kpt on wl* **1/1**[1]

02-0 **2** *3/4* **Kay Gee Be (IRE)**[12] 1128 8-9-5 87 PaulHanagan 5 89
(Richard Fahey) *t.k.h: led 1f: chsd ldr: drvn and ev ch over 2f out: wnt 2nd ins fnl f: kpt on u.p* **9/4**[2]

2120 **3** *1/2* **Standpoint**[12] 1134 6-8-8 82 (p) JackDuern(7) 3 84
(Reg Hollinshead) *cl up: led over 2f out to over 1f out: kpt on same pce ins fnl f* **7/2**[3]

6320 **4** *3* **Aviso (GER)**[7] 960 8-8-8 64 PadraigBeggy 2 71
(David Evans) *prom: effrt and drvn over 2f out: no ex over 1f out* **28/1**

065 **5** *19* **Apassionforfashion**[13] 1105 4-8-3 34 (be) LiamJones 4 26
(Mark Rimell) *stdd s: t.k.h and led after 1f: hdd over 2f out: sn rdn and wknd: t.o* **200/1**

2m 2.71s (1.01) **Going Correction** +0.05s/f (Slow) **5** Ran SP% **106.9**
Speed ratings (Par 103): **97,96,95,93,76**
CSF £3.27 TOTE £1.40: £1.10, £1.80; EX 4.00.Munsarim was claimed by Richard Fahey for £13,000.
Owner Joseph Leckie & Sons Ltd **Bred** Shadwell Estate Company Limited **Trained** Carluke, S Lanarks

FOCUS
The gallop looked fairly decent here but the winner did not need to improve on recent figures with the placed horses below their best.

1342 LADBROKES.COM H'CAP 1m 141y(P)
8:25 (8:25) (Class 5) (0-75,75) 4-Y-0+ **£2,587** (£770; £384; £192) **Stalls** Low

Form RPR

1121 **1** **Red Somerset (USA)**[17] 1045 9-9-7 **75** KieranO'Neill 3 83
(Mike Murphy) *hld up on ins: gd hdwy over 1f out: kpt on wl fnl f: led towards fin* **8/1**

366- **2** *1/2* **Angelic Upstart (IRE)**[306] 2935 4-9-7 **75** JimmyFortune 11 82
(Andrew Balding) *led at ordinary gallop: rdn and qcknd wl over 1f out: kpt on: hdd and no ex towards fin* **4/1**[1]

640- **3** *nse* **Great Shot**[174] 6997 4-9-4 **72** LiamKeniry 6 79
(Sylvester Kirk) *plld hrd: prom: effrt and rdn 2f out: kpt on ins fnl f* **9/2**[2]

025- **4** *hd* **Whitby Jet (IRE)**[217] 5856 4-9-6 **74** ShaneKelly 5 81+
(Ed Vaughan) *s.i.s: hld up in last pl: gd hdwy on outside over 1f out: kpt on fnl f: nrst fin* **9/1**

3111 **5** *1 1/2* **Odd Ball (IRE)**[14] 1095 5-8-6 **63** AmyRyan(3) 1 66+
(Lisa Williamson) *hld up: rdn and effrt on outside wl over 1f out: kpt on fnl f: nvr able to chal* **5/1**[3]

0606 **6** *1/2* **Opus Maximus (IRE)**[3] 1262 7-8-13 **72** DavidKenny(5) 2 74
(Conor Dore) *hld up towards rr: rdn and hdwy over 1f out: kpt on fnl f: nt pce to chal* **25/1**

-006 **7** *1 1/4* **All Right Now**[13] 1117 5-9-1 **69** AndreaAtzeni 4 68
(Derek Haydn Jones) *t.k.h: trckd ldrs: drvn over 2f out: no ex fnl f* **12/1**

0043 **8** *nk* **Satwa Laird**[13] 1117 6-9-4 **72** GeorgeBaker 8 70
(Conor Dore) *t.k.h: trckd ldr 2f: cl up: rdn 2f out: wknd ins fnl f* **16/1**

5531 **9** *1/2* **Spinning Ridge (IRE)**[15] 1064 7-8-12 **73** (v) DarrenEgan(7) 12 70
(Ronald Harris) *plld hrd in midfield on outside: n.m.r briefly 2f out: effrt over 1f out: sn outpcd* **25/1**

2206 **10** *nk* **Legal Legacy**[11] 1158 6-9-6 **74** AndrewMullen 7 71
(David C Griffiths) *plld hrd: prom: chsd ldr after 2f to over 1f out: sn btn* **9/1**

4/0 **11** *4* **Silent Decision (USA)**[14] 1094 6-9-4 **72** (p) LiamJones 9 59
(John Stimpson) *hld up towards rr: rdn along over 3f out: struggling fnl 2f* **66/1**

5513 **12** *1 1/4* **Honey Of A Kitten (USA)**[16] 771 4-9-2 **70** PadraigBeggy 10 54
(David Evans) *t.k.h: cl up on outside tl rdn and wknd over 1f out* **10/1**

1m 50.68s (0.18) **Going Correction** +0.05s/f (Slow) **12** Ran SP% **117.8**
Speed ratings (Par 103): **101,100,100,100,99 98,97,97,96,96 92,91**
Tote Swingers:1&2:£7.60, 2&3:£16.00, 1&3:£25.80 CSF £39.06 CT £167.26 TOTE £9.50: £3.50, £1.20, £2.80; EX 57.20.
Owner M Murphy **Bred** Haras D'Etreham **Trained** Westoning, Beds

FOCUS
A competitive handicap run at a good clip and the winner ran close to his best of the last year, while the third is rated to form.
Whitby Jet(IRE) Official explanation: jockey said gelding suffered interference at start

1343 LADBROKES H'CAP 5f 20y(P)
8:55 (8:55) (Class 6) (0-60,58) 4-Y-0+ **£1,704** (£503; £251) **Stalls** Low

Form RPR

0030 **1** **Invigilator**[15] 1061 4-9-0 **51** JoeFanning 6 61+
(Derek Shaw) *hld up: pushed along and plenty to do 1/2-way: gd hdwy on outside over 1f out: styd on strly fnl f: led post* **9/2**[1]

0013 **2** *nse* **Ladydolly**[23] 979 4-8-11 **53** (p) RaulDaSilva(5) 9 61
(Roy Brotherton) *trckd ldrs: rdn to ld over 1f out: kpt on fnl f: hdd post* **11/1**

5154 **3** *1* **Decider (USA)**[21] 996 9-9-0 **58** (b) DarrenEgan(7) 3 62
(Ronald Harris) *led at decent gallop: rdn and hdd over 1f out: kpt on same pce fnl f* **5/1**[2]

0500 **4** *nse* **Steel City Boy (IRE)**[28] 912 9-9-5 **56** GrahamGibbons 4 60
(Garry Woodward) *chsd ldr: effrt and rdn 2f out: kpt on same pce fnl f* **5/1**[2]

2353 **5** *3* **Rightcar**[21] 996 5-9-6 **57** RobbieFitzpatrick 7 50
(Peter Grayson) *dwlt and swtchd lft s: hld up: hdwy on ins 2f out: no imp ins fnl f* **5/1**[2]

6642 **6** *1/2* **Hambleton**[28] 910 5-8-13 **50** (p) TomEaves 5 41
(Bryan Smart) *in tch: drvn and outpcd 1/2-way: no imp fr over 1f out* **6/1**[3]

00/0 **7** *1 1/2* **Yanza**[26] 938 6-8-10 **50** AmyRyan(3) 1 36
(Pam Ford) *prom: drvn and outpcd over 2f out: sn wknd* **20/1**

0450 **8** *hd* **Forty Proof (IRE)**[15] 1061 4-9-4 **55** (bt) PadraigBeggy 10 40
(David Evans) *dwlt: bhd on outside: struggling 1/2-way: nvr on terms* **17/2**

0/54 **9** *1 1/2* **Dikanta**[13] 1111 4-9-1 **52** TomQueally 2 32
(Robert Cowell) *towards rr: struggling 1/2-way: nvr on terms* **14/1**

000- 10 11 **Haafhd Decent (IRE)**249 4826 4-8-11 **51**............ NataliaGemelova(3) 8
(Dai Williams) *midfield on outside: struggling after 2f: no ch after: t.o* **66/1**
1m 2.39s (0.09) **Going Correction** +0.05s/f (Slow) **10** Ran SP% **114.2**
Speed ratings (Par 101): **101,100,99,99,94 93,91,90,88,70**
Tote Swingers:1&2:£9.40, 2&3:£9.50, 1&3:£7.20 CSF £53.15 CT £262.21 TOTE £6.90: £2.90, £3.40, £2.10; EX 43.90 TRIFECTA Not won..
Owner Derek Shaw **Bred** Granham Farm And P Hearson Bloodstock **Trained** Sproxton, Leics

FOCUS
No hiding place here and the pace held up so the winner did well to come from behind. The next three home help to set the level.
T/Plt: £248.80 to a £1 stake. Pool:£66,716.14. 195.70 winning tickets T/Qpdt: £23.80 to a £1 stake. Pool:£7,153.05. 222.40 winning tickets RY

1344 - 1351a (Foreign Racing) - See Raceform Interactive

LEICESTER (R-H)
Friday, April 13

OFFICIAL GOING: Soft
Wind: almost nil Weather: overcast and light rain

1352 BET TOTEPLACEPOT TEXT TOTE TO 89660 MEDIAN AUCTION MAIDEN STKS 5f 2y
2:20 (2:20) (Class 5) 2-Y-O **£2,587** (£770; £384; £192) **Stalls** High

Form RPR
4 1 **Lyric Ace (IRE)**6 1211 2-9-3 0.............................. RyanMoore 3 88+
(Richard Hannon) *broke wl: mde all: pushed along to assert 2f out: powered clr ins fnl f: impressive* **15/8**2
2 5 **Effie B** 2-8-12 0.. MartinHarley 1 65+
(Mick Channon) *slowly away and green early: pushed along and hdwy 2f out: kpt on to chse ldng pair over 1f out: stdy prog to take 2nd ins fnl f: no ch w wnr* **33/1**
2 3 1 **Well Acquainted (IRE)**13 1131 2-9-3 0.................. AdamKirby 6 66
(Clive Cox) *in tch: pushed along to chse wnr 2f out: no ch w wnr 1f out: wknd and lost 2nd ins fnl f* **13/8**1
4 6 **Lord Ashley (IRE)** 2-9-3 0........................ RichardKingscote 4 45
(Tom Dascombe) *in tch: pushed along over 2f out: no imp and wknd over 1f out* **20/1**
5 2 ½ **Letstalkaboutmoney (IRE)** 2-9-3 0..................... JimCrowley 5 36
(Mrs K Burke) *dwlt: a in rr and running green: pushed along thrght: btn over 2f out* **5/1**3
3 6 25 **Mosstang (IRE)**6 1211 2-9-3 0............................ MartinDwyer 2
(Robert Mills) *chsd ldr: pushed along over 3f out: wknd 2f out: sn wl btn and heavily eased ins fnl f: t.o* **8/1**
1m 4.42s (4.42) **Going Correction** +0.825s/f (Soft) **6** Ran SP% **108.4**
Speed ratings (Par 92): **97,89,87,77,73 33**
toteswingers:1&2:£8.60, 2&3:£2.50, 1&3:£1.02 CSF £45.21 TOTE £2.40: £1.20, £7.10; EX 49.60.
Owner Byerley Thoroughbred Racing **Bred** Rathasker Stud **Trained** East Everleigh, Wilts

FOCUS
False rail from the round course bend all the way up to the winning post increased distances by 7m on round course. An ordinary maiden, but the three that had already raced before had all shown ability and the winner was impressive, although the third ran below his Brocklesby form.

NOTEBOOK
Lyric Ace(IRE) ◆ started odds-on favourite when just behind Mosstang on his Kempton debut six days earlier, but showed here why he was so popular on his debut with an impressive all-the-way success. The testing ground obviously didn't bother him and he should win more races. (op 9-4 tchd 5-2)
Effie B had been withdrawn from her intended debut at Folkestone the previous day due to a bruised foot. She didn't have a lot to recommend her on pedigree, being a half-sister to a winning juvenile plater, but despite proving friendless in the market she ran a race full of promise. Slow to break and soon in last place way off the pace, she stayed on very nicely past beaten horses over the last 2f and it will be a surprise if she can't go one better before too long. (op 20-1)
Well Acquainted(IRE) was only just beaten in the Brocklesby on his debut and travelled as well as anything behind the leaders here, but once the gun was put to his head the response was very disappointing. The slower ground may have been to blame, but despite several placings in the meantime the Brocklesby form is now 0-6. (tchd 7-4)
Lord Ashley(IRE), a 36,000euros colt, saw plenty of daylight on the outside before fading, but there is plenty of stamina on the dam's side of his pedigree, so he should progress given time and a longer trip. (op 22-1)
Letstalkaboutmoney(IRE), a half-brother to a winning sprinter, was always struggling. (op 11-2 tchd 4-1)
Mosstang(IRE) ran way below his Kempton form, being eased off over a furlong out with his rider looking down. His rider reported that the colt lost his action, whilst the trainer's representative subsequently reported that he was coughing post-race. Official explanation: jockey said colt lost its action; trainer's rep said colt was found to be coughing. (op 5-1 tchd 9-2)

1353 BET TOTEPOOL TEXT TOTE TO 89660 (S) STKS 5f 218y
2:55 (2:56) (Class 6) 3-Y-O **£1,811** (£539; £269; £134) **Stalls** High

Form RPR
65- 1 **Ficelle (IRE)**143 7505 3-8-9 0......................... MartinHarley 6 62
(Mrs K Burke) *in rr early and racd w hd to one side: pushed along 3f out: styd on ins fnl 2f: led 1f out: kpt on wl* **14/1**
-404 2 4 **Pressure Drop (IRE)**4 1252 3-9-0 62.................. TonyCulhane 5 55
(Jo Hughes) *unruly in preliminaries: led tl hdd 4f out: regained ld over 2f out: drvn along and hdd 1f out: sn no ch w wnr* **9/1**
3233 3 2 ¼ **First Bid**43 748 3-9-5 66.............................(b) PaulMulrennan 4 52
(James Given) *chsd ldr: led 4f out: hdd and pushed along over 2f out: grad wknd and btn ins fnl f* **9/2**3
2541 4 1 **Point At Issue (IRE)**11 1169 3-9-5 60..................(b) AdrianNicholls 1 49
(David Nicholls) *cl up: rdn and reminders over 3f out: wknd and btn wl over 1f out* **9/2**3
6215 5 2 ¼ **Thorpe Bay**39 801 3-9-5 67............................ HayleyTurner 2 42
(Conor Dore) *in tch: rdn 3f out: no rspnse and btn over 1f out* **11/4**2
-344 6 8 **Arte Del Calcio**41 787 3-9-0 66.......................... DaneO'Neill 3 18
(David Elsworth) *slowly away: rdn along over 3f out: drvn and no ch 2f out: btn and eased ins fnl f* **9/4**1
1m 19.76s (6.76) **Going Correction** +0.925s/f (Soft) **6** Ran SP% **110.5**
Speed ratings (Par 96): **91,85,82,81,78 67**
toteswingers:1&2:£24.10, 2&3:£6.60, 1&3:£11.70 CSF £118.43 TOTE £22.20: £10.10, £8.10; EX 166.70.The winner was sold to R Harris for 4,800gns.
Owner D Simpson & Mrs E Burke **Bred** Tally-Ho Stud **Trained** Middleham Moor, N Yorks

FOCUS
A moderate seller and a bit of a turn-up with the winner possibly in the best place nearest the rail.

1354 BET TOTEQUADPOT TEXT TOTE TO 89660 H'CAP 7f 9y
3:30 (3:30) (Class 4) (0-85,85) 4-Y-O+ **£4,528** (£1,347; £673; £336) **Stalls** High

Form RPR
-205 1 **Global Village (IRE)**12 1161 7-9-0 **78**.................. KierenFallon 16 91+
(Brian Ellison) *in rr: on inner whn pushed along 3f out: n.m.r 2f out and lft w plenty to do: swtchd rt and kpt on over 1f out: surged through to ld ins fnl f* **9/2**1
550- 2 1 ¼ **Gouray Girl (IRE)**174 7031 5-9-5 **83**...................... DaneO'Neill 12 92
(Henry Candy) *midfield on inner: n.m.r 2f out: rdn and kpt on to press ldrs 1f out: unable to go w wnr wl ins fnl f* **5/1**2
0-25 3 ½ **Layla's Hero (IRE)**6 1220 5-9-7 **85**....................(v1) JamieSpencer 2 93+
(John Quinn) *slowly away and swtchd lft to inner: rdn and last 2f out: swtchd rt and drvn over 1f out: kpt on to chse ldrs 1f out: no ex cl home* **7/1**3
4300 4 1 ¼ **Tevez**13 1128 7-9-4 **82**.. MartinHarley 10 87
(Des Donovan) *midfield on outer: rdn along 2f out: kpt on fr over 1f out: one pce* **16/1**
51-6 5 ½ **Great Expectations**38 812 4-8-8 **72**.................... FrederikTylicki 3 75+
(J R Jenkins) *in tch: rdn to ld 2f out: drvn and hdd ins fnl f: wknd and no ex cl home* **9/1**
00-1 6 3 **Amazing Star (IRE)**14 1117 7-9-3 **81**.................. GrahamGibbons 11 79
(Declan Carroll) *midfield: pushed along whn stmbld over 2f out: pushed along and short of room over 1f out: drvn and no ex fnl f* **22/1**
355- 7 ½ **Russian Rave**201 6378 6-9-1 **79**.......................... StephenCraine 9 73
(Jonathan Portman) *midfield: drvn and effrt over 2f out: wknd over 1f out* **20/1**
441- 8 1 **Ted's Brother (IRE)**174 7024 4-8-7 **76**.................. CharlesEddery(5) 6 68
(Richard Guest) *in rr: effrt to chse ldrs: drvn and wknd ins fnl f* **16/1**
00-4 9 7 **Intercept (IRE)**16 1066 4-9-2 **80**......................... WilliamBuick 13 54
(John Gosden) *cl up: rdn and grad wknd fnl 2f: btn wl ins fnl f* **7/1**3
041- 10 3 **Ventura Sands (IRE)**210 6116 4-8-8 **72**.................. PaulHanagan 1 38
(Richard Fahey) *taken to post early: keen bhd ldrs: pushed along 2f out and grad wknd* **14/1**
600- 11 nk **Hail Promenader (IRE)**230 5495 6-8-9 **76**............. DominicFox(3) 7 41
(Anthony Carson) *a in rr: rdn and no imp 2f out* **50/1**
003- 12 3 ½ **Galatian**161 7262 5-9-0 **78**................................. JamesMillman 8 34
(Rod Millman) *in tch: rdn 3f out: wknd fnl 2f* **20/1**
0025 13 shd **Bravo Echo**13 1140 6-9-4 **82**................................ JimCrowley 14 38
(Michael Attwater) *led: rdn and hdd 2f out: sn wknd* **20/1**
300- 14 4 ½ **Flynn's Boy**231 5450 4-9-0 **78**............................ HayleyTurner 4 22
(Rae Guest) *cl up tl rdn 3f out: wknd qckly fnl 2f* **7/1**3
1210 15 19 **Fluctuation (IRE)**12 1161 4-8-4 **71**.....................(v) RyanPowell(3) 5
(Ian Williams) *in rr: rdn 4f out: drvn and struggling 3f out: t.o* **33/1**
1m 31.8s (5.60) **Going Correction** +0.925s/f (Soft) **15** Ran SP% **124.3**
Speed ratings (Par 105): **105,103,103,101,101 97,97,95,87,84 84,80,79,74,53**
toteswingers:1&2:£9.80, 2&3:£10.50, 1&3:£3.70 CSF £24.20 CT £164.89 TOTE £3.30: £2.20, £2.00, £2.40; EX 21.70.
Owner Jack Racing Melksham **Bred** Kilfrush Stud **Trained** Norton, N Yorks

FOCUS
A competitive handicap, but quite a rough race. Three horses disputed the early lead, but none of them figured in the finish. The first two home raced close to the stands' rail throughout, which was definitely an advantage. The third, to last year's reappearance mark, looks the best guide.

1355 TOTEPOOL MOBILE TEXT TOTE TO 89660 H'CAP 1m 3f 183y
4:05 (4:06) (Class 5) (0-70,73) 3-Y-O **£2,587** (£770; £384; £192) **Stalls** Low

Form RPR
2131 1 **Cape Safari (IRE)**3 1281 3-9-10 **73** 6ex...................(p) KierenFallon 2 84
(James Tate) *in tch: pressed ldrs 3f out: rdn to ld ins fnl 2f: duelled for ld and a looked to be holding rival ins fnl f* **11/4**1
050- 2 hd **Party Line**195 6526 3-9-0 **63**............................. SilvestreDeSousa 8 73
(Mark Johnston) *pressed ldr: pushed along 3f out: led briefly ins fnl 2f: ev ch and duelling for ld wl over 1f out: edgd out cl home* **5/1**2
000- 3 1 ¾ **Like Clockwork**177 6951 3-8-4 **56** oh4..................... SimonPearce(3) 3 63
(Mark H Tompkins) *towards rr: rdn over 3f out: hdwy and chsd ldrs over 2f out: kpt on but nt gng pce of ldng duo ins fnl f* **16/1**
560- 4 5 **Spanish Fork (IRE)**183 6812 3-9-6 **69**...................... MartinHarley 5 68
(Mick Channon) *hld up: rdn 3f out: drvn and struggling fnl 2f: one pce* **8/1**
050- 5 13 **Flashman**154 7369 3-8-13 **62**................................ PaulHanagan 4 40
(Richard Fahey) *unruly bef s: t.k.h bhd ldrs: pushed along 3f out: wknd over 2f out: wl btn ins fnl f* **11/4**1
35-4 6 10 **Fine Resolve**98 56 3-9-4 **67**................................ JimmyFortune 1 29
(Andrew Balding) *in rr: rdn 3f out: rdn and no imp fnl 3f* **11/2**3
332 7 21 **Time To Dance**63 502 3-9-7 **70**.............................. LiamKeniry 6
(Joseph Tuite) *led tl rdn and hdd over 2f out: sn wknd and btn: eased and t.o fnl f* **10/1**
2m 49.86s (15.96) **Going Correction** +1.15s/f (Soft) **7** Ran SP% **111.5**
Speed ratings (Par 98): **92,91,90,87,78 72,58**
toteswingers:1&2:£1.60, 2&3:£0.00, 1&3:£11.60 CSF £15.86 CT £175.26 TOTE £2.90: £1.30, £4.50; EX 10.90.
Owner Saif Ali **Bred** Rabbah Bloodstock Limited **Trained** Newmarket, Suffolk

FOCUS
They only went a steady early pace in this middle-distance handicap and it developed into a 4f sprint, but they still finished well spread out behind the front pair. The winner confirmed recent improvement, although there are one or two doubts about the form.

1356 FREE RACING POST FORM AT TOTEPOOL.COM CONDITIONS STKS 5f 218y
4:40 (4:40) (Class 3) 3-Y-O **£7,115** (£2,117; £1,058) **Stalls** High

Form RPR
214- 1 **Accession (IRE)**174 7019 3-9-4 96......................... AdamKirby 4 96+
(Clive Cox) *chsd ldr: pushed along to ld ins fnl 2f: rdn along and pressed ins fnl f: on top cl home* **4/9**1
10-0 2 hd **Big Note (IRE)**20 1032 3-9-4 94........................ JimmyFortune 1 95
(Andrew Balding) *last and tk v t.k.h: wnt 2nd u.p ins fnl 2f: pressed ldr under stern driving ins fnl f: hld cl home* **11/4**2
040- 3 12 **Luv U Forever**168 7155 3-8-13 94........................ TonyCulhane 2 61
(Jo Hughes) *led tl rdn and hdd ins fnl 2f: dropped away tamely 1f out* **8/1**3
1m 20.83s (7.83) **Going Correction** +1.025s/f (Soft) **3** Ran SP% **107.0**
Speed ratings (Par 102): **88,87,71**
CSF £1.94 TOTE £1.30; EX 2.20.
Owner Brighthelm Racing **Bred** Corduff Stud Ltd **Trained** Lambourn, Berks

FOCUS
Not surprisingly this three-runner conditions event developed into a game of cat and mouse. The form is muddling and best rated around the first two.

NOTEBOOK

Accession(IRE) didn't run at all badly when fourth in a Doncaster Listed event when last seen in October, but although he managed to make a winning return it was far from easy and he had to be kept right up to his work to hold on. He was already proven with some cut, but these conditions would have been more demanding and he can probably do better back on a sounder surface. (op 8-13 tchd 8-11)

Big Note(IRE) had twice been found out in better company since winning two of his first three starts at two and was the only one of the trio to have had a recent run, but he did his chances little good by taking a keen hold in last place early. In view of how close he came to winning, it could be argued he might have done so had he settled better, but the winner probably has the greater scope in the longer term. (tchd 9-4 and 3-1)

Luv U Forever was strictly the one to beat on these terms having run well in Pattern company on a few occasions, but she had 11 starts at two and was easily brushed aside after making the running to over a furlong out. (op 9-2)

1357 FOLLOW TOTEPOOL ON FACEBOOK AND TWITTER MAIDEN FILLIES' STKS — 7f 9y

5:15 (5:22) (Class 5) 3-Y-O — £2,587 (£770; £384; £192) Stalls High

Form — RPR

1 **Moonstone Magic** 3-9-0 0 ... JimCrowley 4 — 103
(Ralph Beckett) *midfield: hdwy 4f out: pushed along to ld over 1f out: kpt on strly: impressive* **16/1**

35-2 2 *8* **Lady Loch**[11] [1166] 3-9-0 0 ... PaulHanagan 17 — 79
(Richard Fahey) *midfield: drvn 3f out: no immediate rspnse: plugged on fr over 1f out: no ch w wnr: nabbed 2nd on nod* **11/2**

32- 3 *hd* **Ladyship**[235] [5323] 3-9-0 0 ... RyanMoore 8 — 78
(Sir Michael Stoute) *midfield: rdn 3f out: drvn along and drifted rt ins fnl 2f: chsd wnr over 1f out: sn btn: lost 2nd on nod* **2/1**[1]

5- 4 *6* **Negin**[260] [4471] 3-9-0 0 ... WilliamBuick 10 — 60
(Ed Dunlop) *in tch: rdn and chsd ldr over 2f out: led briefly over 1f out: drvn and wknd fnl f* **5/1**[3]

5 *3* **Newington** 3-8-11 0 ... SimonPearce(3) 2 — 51
(Lydia Pearce) *in rr and slow away: rn green: pushed along 4f out: stdy prog fnl 3f: keeping on cl home: nt wout promise* **150/1**

6 *2 1/4* **Pretty Primo (IRE)** 3-9-0 0 ... PatDobbs 9 — 45
(Richard Hannon) *led: rdn and hdd over 1f out: grad wknd* **25/1**

2- 7 *1 1/2* **Srinagar Girl**[169] [7124] 3-9-0 0 ... TomQueally 14 — 40
(Sir Henry Cecil) *in tch: rdn over 3f out: drvn and one pce 2f out: no ex fnl f* **10/3**[2]

55 8 *3 1/4* **Russian Rumba (IRE)**[9] [1180] 3-9-0 0 ... RichardKingscote 18 — 30
(Jonathan Portman) *midfield: rdn over 2f out: sn one pce* **33/1**

05 9 *5* **Norse Song**[20] [1036] 3-9-0 0 ... MarcHalford 1
(David Elsworth) *cl up: rdn and ev ch 2f out: wknd 1f out* **100/1**

52- 10 *1* **Cheworee**[279] [3865] 3-9-0 0 ... NickyMackay 15
(David Elsworth) *in tch: hdwy to chse ldrs 4f out: rdn and grad wknd ins fnl 2f* **14/1**

00- 11 *3 1/4* **Art Of Gold**[185] [6776] 3-9-0 0 ... FergusSweeney 11
(Amy Weaver) *in rr: rdn and no imp fnl 2f* **200/1**

0- 12 *4* **Sangrail**[210] [6131] 3-9-0 0 ... KierenFallon 7
(William Muir) *cl up: rdn over 2f out: sn btn and wknd* **33/1**

06- 13 *8* **Shamakat**[184] [6800] 3-9-0 0 ... TedDurcan 6
(Rae Guest) *towards rr: struggling 2f out: t.o* **33/1**

00- 14 *13* **Silent Laughter**[175] [6991] 3-9-0 0 ... LeeNewman 12
(Jonathan Portman) *cl up: rdn and lost pl 3f out: t.o* **200/1**

50- 15 *2 1/4* **Pindrop**[282] [3736] 3-9-0 0 ... AdamKirby 3
(Clive Cox) *in tch: rdn 4f out: struggling fnl 2f* **40/1**

00- 16 *10* **Kittens**[154] [7369] 3-9-0 0 ... PhillipMakin 13
(William Muir) *in rr: drvn and struggling 4f out: t.o fnl 2f* **80/1**

17 *3* **Felona E Serona** 3-8-9 0 ... LauraPike(5) 5
(Laura Young) *a in rr: struggling fnl 3f: t.o* **100/1**

0-4 18 *6* **Archina (IRE)**[100] [34] 3-9-0 0 ... JimmyFortune 16
(Andrew Balding) *in tch: rdn 3f out: sn wknd: t.o* **33/1**

1m 32.38s (6.18) **Going Correction** +1.025s/f (Soft) — 18 Ran SP% **123.9**
Speed ratings (Par 95): **105,95,95,88,85 82,81,77,71,70 66,62,53,38,35 24,20,13**
toteswingers:1&2:£19.30, 2&3:£4.10, 1&3:£10.60 CSF £97.27 TOTE £20.80: £4.90, £3.00, £1.10; EX 167.50.
Owner Lady Marchwood **Bred** Lady Marchwood **Trained** Kimpton, Hants

FOCUS

This fillies' maiden wasn't as competitive as the numbers would suggest and they finished well spread out, but it was a most taking performance from the winner. The placed horses set a fair standard but the runner-up is rated 10lb off her best in the conditions.

1358 PLAY TOTESCOOP6 TOMORROW AT TOTEPOOL.COM H'CAP — 1m 60y

5:45 (5:48) (Class 5) (0-70,70) 4-Y-O+ — £2,587 (£770; £384; £192) Stalls Low

Form — RPR

4510 1 **Flying Applause**[53] [633] 7-9-4 67 ... (bt) AndreaAtzeni 3 — 79
(Roy Bowring) *cl up: rdn to chse ldr over 2f out: drvn to ld 1f out: kpt on wl* **25/1**

240- 2 *3 1/4* **Save The Bees**[189] [6674] 4-9-0 70 ... JasonHart(7) 6 — 75+
(Declan Carroll) *in tch: hdwy to chse ldrs 3f out: rdn 2f out: drvn and chsd wnr ins fnl f: jst won battle for 2nd post* **8/1**

5002 3 *shd* **Salient**[14] [1108] 8-9-2 68 ... KierenFox(3) 2 — 72
(Michael Attwater) *led: drvn and pressed strly over 1f out: hdd 1f out: sn no ch w wnr and lost 2nd post* **22/1**

2560 4 *1 1/2* **The Lock Master (IRE)**[3] [1275] 5-9-4 67 ... NeilChalmers 1 — 68
(Michael Appleby) *midfield: hdwy to chse ldr 2f out: sn one pce* **7/1**[3]

-416 5 *1 1/4* **Inpursuitoffreedom**[49] [689] 5-9-2 68 ... (v) AdamBeschizza(3) 12 — 66
(Philip McBride) *in rr: hdwy on ins 3f out: pushed along over 2f out: kpt on one pce fnl f* **16/1**

050- 6 *3* **Bloodsweatandtears**[175] [6990] 4-9-7 70 ... JimCrowley 10 — 61
(William Knight) *in rr: rdn 3f out: plugged on one pce 2f out: no ex ins fnl f: nvr a threat* **9/2**[2]

0-30 7 *1 1/4* **Dr Red Eye**[13] [1134] 4-9-4 70 ... MichaelO'Connell(3) 5 — 58
(Scott Dixon) *cl up: rdn and ev ch 2f out: drifted lft and wknd u.p fnl f* **7/2**[1]

041- 8 *9* **Xpres Maite**[108] [7884] 9-8-11 60 ... (b) FergusSweeney 13 — 27
(Roy Bowring) *cl up: rdn over 4f out: wknd and btn fnl 2f* **14/1**

3522 9 *5* **D'Urberville**[30] [900] 5-9-5 68 ... FrederikTylicki 4 — 24
(J R Jenkins) *midfield: hdwy 3f out: rdn and bmpd over 2f out: struggling and btn after* **9/1**

430- 10 *7* **Mini's Destination**[186] [6748] 4-9-0 63 ... PhillipMakin 7
(John Holt) *in rr: rdn 3f out: hmpd over 2f out: drvn and one pce after* **10/1**

0/3- 11 *14* **Amba**[151] [7411] 6-9-2 65 ... DavidProbert 9
(Des Donovan) *in tch: rdn over 3f out: struggling whn drifted lft over 2f out: sn eased* **25/1**

0-04 12 *7* **Quite A Catch (IRE)**[30] [894] 4-9-5 68 ... (v) LeeNewman 11
(Jonathan Portman) *midfield: rdn 4f out: struggling whn short of room 2f out: eased after* **20/1**

65-4 13 *22* **National Hope (IRE)**[28] [919] 4-9-2 65 ... (tp) KierenFallon 14
(George Baker) *in tch: rdn along 3f out: wknd ins fnl 2f* **16/1**

-430 14 *80* **On The Cusp (IRE)**[50] [674] 5-9-7 70 ... (p) MartinHarley 8
(Richard Guest) *rdn to go prom: lost pl after 2f: dropped away 5f out: t.o* **12/1**

1m 53.55s (8.45) **Going Correction** +1.15s/f (Soft) — 14 Ran SP% **126.0**
Speed ratings (Par 103): **103,99,99,98,96 93,92,83,78,71 57,50,28,**
toteswingers:1&2:£54.30, 2&3:£19.60, 1&3:£37.80 CSF £214.46 CT £4469.32 TOTE £38.80: £8.30, £3.90, £6.10; EX 348.80.
Owner K Nicholls **Bred** G H Beeby And Viscount Marchwood **Trained** Edwinstowe, Notts

FOCUS

A modest handicap to end the card and a few of these took wayward courses in the home straight. The winner, third and fourth were all well placed so the runner-up deserves credit for this effort.

Salient Official explanation: jockey said gelding lost a front shoe

On The Cusp(IRE) Official explanation: jockey said gelding never travelled

T/Plt: £602.60 to a £1 stake. Pool:£50,191.11 - 60.80 winning tickets. T/Qpdt: £6.40 to a £1 stake. Pool of £5,239.41 - 597.49 winning tickets. CS

1337 WOLVERHAMPTON (A.W) (L-H)

Friday, April 13

OFFICIAL GOING: Standard

Wind: fresh against Weather: dry

1359 £32 FREE AT 32RED.COM H'CAP — 7f 32y(P)

5:55 (5:56) (Class 6) (0-60,60) 3-Y-O — £1,704 (£503; £251) Stalls High

Form — RPR

2236 1 **One More Roman (IRE)**[16] [1067] 3-9-6 59 ... (bt) NeilCallan 9 — 66
(Gay Kelleway) *mid-div: hdwy fr 2f out: swtchd lft ins fnl f: r.o wl to ld nring fin: rdn out* **14/1**

2460 2 *hd* **Prince Gabrial (IRE)**[42] [769] 3-9-1 57 ... AmyRyan(3) 4 — 63
(Kevin Ryan) *trckd ldrs: rdn to chse ldr over 2f out: led ins fnl f: edgd rt: hdd nring fin* **14/1**

000- 3 *1* **Love Grows Wild (USA)**[281] [3761] 3-9-3 56 ... HayleyTurner 10 — 60+
(Michael Bell) *little slowly away: towards rr: nudged along at times: rdn 2f out: sn swtchd rt: r.o: wnt 3rd wl ins fnl f: nrst fin* **3/1**[1]

0641 4 *1 1/4* **Umph (IRE)**[16] [1067] 3-9-7 60 ... (b) CathyGannon 2 — 60
(David Evans) *prom: led over 3f out: rdn 2 l clr jst over 2f out: no ex whn hdd ins fnl f* **15/2**[3]

0242 5 *1/2* **Emma Jean (IRE)**[21] [1012] 3-8-9 53 ... (t) RaulDaSilva(5) 8 — 52
(Frank Sheridan) *mid-div: rdn to chse ldrs 2f out: kpt on same pce fnl f* **10/1**

006- 6 *nk* **Titus Bolt (IRE)**[168] [7132] 3-9-6 59 ... StephenCraine 6 — 57+
(Jim Boyle) *s.i.s: towards rr: rdn over 2f out: styd on fr over 1f out: nvr trbld ldrs* **3/1**[1]

00-1 7 *1/2* **Johnny Cavagin**[21] [1012] 3-9-5 58 ... (t) RobertWinston 7 — 55
(Richard Guest) *mid-div: rdn over 2f out: styd on but nt gng pce to get on terms* **11/2**[2]

050- 8 *1 3/4* **Wrapped Up**[128] [7666] 3-9-2 55 ... JamesDoyle 12 — 47
(Heather Main) *hld up towards rr: c wd whn rdn ent st: styd on but nvr gng pce to get on terms* **33/1**

01-0 9 *hd* **Mick Slates (IRE)**[4] [1259] 3-8-9 53 ... NeilFarley(5) 3 — 45
(Declan Carroll) *s.i.s: sn pushed along to chse ldrs: rdn over 3f out: wknd jst over 1f out* **17/2**

030- 10 *4 1/2* **Kylin**[174] [7030] 3-9-7 60 ... GeorgeBaker 11 — 39
(Olivia Maylam) *a towards rr* **16/1**

4-24 11 *2 1/4* **Orwellian**[30] [903] 3-9-5 58 ... (b) TomEaves 5 — 31
(Bryan Smart) *racd keenly: trckd ldrs: rdn over 2f out: wknd ent fnl f* **12/1**

303- 12 *10* **Dylan's Dream (IRE)**[182] [6835] 3-9-2 55 ... DavidAllan 1
(Tim Easterby) *led tl over 3f out: wknd 2f out* **33/1**

1m 29.51s (-0.09) **Going Correction** +0.025s/f (Slow) — 12 Ran SP% **129.6**
Speed ratings (Par 96): **101,100,99,98,97 97,96,94,94,89 86,75**
toteswingers:1&2:£15.10, 2&3:£11.40, 1&3:£9.80 CSF £213.17 CT £771.45 TOTE £13.70: £3.20, £6.90, £1.30; EX 342.00 TRIFECTA Not won..
Owner Miss Gay Kelleway **Bred** Mrs Fitriani Hay **Trained** Exning, Suffolk
■ Stewards' Enquiry : Neil Callan two-day ban: careless riding (Apr 27-28)

FOCUS

Some of these look destined to do better and the form looks sound enough rated around the runner-up, fourth and fifth.

Johnny Cavagin Official explanation: jockey said gelding was hampered on bend

1360 32RED CASINO CLAIMING STKS — 1m 141y(P)

6:25 (6:25) (Class 6) 3-Y-O+ — £1,617 (£481; £240; £120) Stalls Low

Form — RPR

5-43 1 **Indian Art (IRE)**[16] [1064] 6-9-6 68 ... SeanLevey(3) 1 — 75
(Sylvester Kirk) *trckd ldrs: rdn 3f out: led over 1f out: asserted fnl f: readily* **10/3**[2]

5310 2 *3* **Spinning Ridge (IRE)**[1] [1342] 7-9-3 73 ... (v) DarrenEgan(7) 5 — 69
(Ronald Harris) *hld up: smooth hdwy fr over 2f out: trcking ldrs travelling best jst over 1f out: sn rdn to chse wnr but a being readily hld* **2/1**[1]

2332 3 *1 3/4* **Ahlawy (IRE)**[22] [999] 9-9-3 68 ... (t) RaulDaSilva(5) 7 — 63
(Frank Sheridan) *led for over 2f: trckd ldr: rdn wl over 2f out: lost 2nd jst ins fnl f: kpt on same pce* **4/1**

/602 4 *nk* **Slam**[18] [1045] 7-9-8 67 ... (p) JamieSpencer 3 — 63
(Robert Cowell) *trckd ldr: led after 2f: rdn over 2f out: hdd over 1f out: no ex fnl f* **7/2**[3]

003- 5 *2* **Dr Albert**[109] [7879] 3-8-4 60 ... (t) SilvestreDeSousa 6 — 53
(Frank Sheridan) *hld up in tch: rdn over 3f out: one pce fnl 2f* **12/1**

6455 6 *4 1/2* **Aggbag**[15] [1095] 8-8-13 43 ... (p) RichardOliver(7) 4 — 46
(Michael Appleby) *trckd ldrs: rdn 3f out: wknd over 1f out* **33/1**

7 *16* **Trio Of Trix** 3-8-9 0 ow3 ... TomMcLaughlin 2
(Malcolm Saunders) *s.i.s: sn struggling: a in rr: t.o* **28/1**

1m 50.44s (-0.06) **Going Correction** +0.025s/f (Slow)
WFA 3 from 5yo+ 17lb — 7 Ran SP% **112.7**
Speed ratings (Par 101): **101,98,96,96,94 90,76**
toteswingers:1&2:£2.20, 2&3:£1.60, 1&3:£2.90 CSF £10.12 TOTE £3.80: £2.70, £2.10; EX 9.40 Trifecta £75.50 Pool: £537.90 - 5.27 winning units..
Owner R Hannon **Bred** Michael Woodlock And Seamus Kennedy **Trained** Upper Lambourn, Berks

FOCUS
Quite a competitive little claimer and run at a strong gallop in the conditions, but the form still looks muddling.

1361 ENJOY THE PUNTERS PACKAGE GROUP OFFER H'CAP 2m 119y(P)
6:55 (6:55) (Class 6) (0-60,60) 4-Y-0+ £1,704 (£503; £251) Stalls Low

Form RPR
0553 **1** **Cloudy Start**[9] 1184 6-9-3 **60** LeonnaMayor(7) 2 67
(Jamie Osborne) *little slowly away: sn mid-div: rdn wl over 2f out: hdwy over 1f out: styd on strly fnl f: led fnl 75yds* **6/1**[3]
-221 **2** ½ **Broughtons Bandit**[24] 968 5-9-3 **53** StevieDonohoe 8 59
(Willie Musson) *hld up: hdwy fr 3f out: rdn 2f out: styd on to ld v briefly fnl 75yds: no ex* **2/1**[1]
3163 **3** 2 **Waldsee (GER)**[27] 937 7-9-8 **50** JamesDoyle 5 62
(Paul Rich) *trckd ldrs: rdn over 3f out: chal over 2f out: led over 1f out: no ex whn hdd fnl 75yds* **13/2**
-4U5 **4** 2 **Colliers Castle (IRE)**[14] 1112 6-8-11 **50** AmyRyan(3) 9 51
(Lisa Williamson) *hld up: rdn 4f out: no imp tl styd on fnl f: snatched 4th fnl strides* **8/1**
3332 **5** nk **Leyte Gulf (USA)**[27] 937 9-9-10 **60** (p) DaneO'Neill 1 61
(Chris Bealby) *in tch: trckd ldrs 3f out: rdn over 2f out: styd on same pce: lost 4th fnl strides* **8/1**
-432 **6** 2 **Talbot Green**[9] 1184 4-9-3 **57** MartinDwyer 3 55
(William Muir) *trckd ldr: led over 8f out: rdn and hdd over 1f out: fdd ins fnl f* **7/2**[2]
7 14 **Greenmeetic (IRE)**[4] 5-8-5 **46** oh1 RaulDaSilva(5) 7 28
(Frank Sheridan) *t.k.h: hld up: hdwy to trck ldr 8f out: rdn 3f out: wknd 2f out* **22/1**
/550 **8** 2½ **Bee Sting**[31] 889 8-8-6 **49** (p) ShirleyTeasdale(7) 4 28
(Lisa Williamson) *in tch: rdn over 3f out: wknd 2f out* **33/1**
/0-0 **9** 33 **Lileo (IRE)**[21] 1011 5-9-5 **55** MichaelStainton 6
(Nikki Evans) *led for over 8f: rdn 5f out: wknd over 3f out: t.o* **50/1**

3m 46.4s (4.60) **Going Correction** +0.025s/f (Slow)
WFA 4 from 5yo+ 4lb 9 Ran SP% **114.6**
Speed ratings (Par 101): **90,89,88,87,87 86,80,79,63**
toteswingers:1&2:£4.40, 2&3:£5.40, 1&3:£8.90 CSF £17.98 CT £80.59 TOTE £8.10: £2.70, £1.40, £2.90; EX 21.10 Trifecta £202.30 Part won. Pool: £273.38 - 0.80 winning units..
Owner Steve Jakes **Bred** Juddmonte Farms Ltd **Trained** Upper Lambourn, Berks

FOCUS
A competitive contest despite the grade, with several of the runners coming into this in good form. The form is rated around the winner and third with another step up for the second.

1362 32RED H'CAP 5f 20y(P)
7:25 (7:25) (Class 4) (0-85,85) 4-Y-0+ £4,204 (£1,251; £625; £312) Stalls Low

Form RPR
00-0 **1** **Arctic Feeling (IRE)**[13] 1141 4-8-13 **84** LauraBarry(7) 7 92
(Richard Fahey) *chsd ldrs: rdn and edgd lft over 1f out: led narrowly jst ins fnl f: sn hrd pressed: hld on* **9/2**[2]
1040 **2** shd **Fair Passion**[21] 1015 5-8-13 **77** NeilCallan 3 84
(Derek Shaw) *chsd ldrs: rdn over 2f out: swtchd lft over 1f out: str chal upsides thrght fnl f: jst hld* **9/2**[2]
026- **3** 1 **Wooden King (IRE)**[134] 7594 7-8-9 **73** TomMcLaughlin 5 76
(Malcolm Saunders) *chsd ldr: rdn over 2f out: led narrowly briefly jst ins fnl f: kpt on but no ex* **18/1**
310- **4** nk **Mappin Time (IRE)**[210] 6113 4-9-4 **82** (p) DavidAllan 6 84
(Tim Easterby) *s.i.s: sn pushed along in last 3 but in tch: drvn 2f out: r.o fnl f: fin wl* **9/1**
-505 **5** 1¼ **Baby Strange**[21] 1007 8-9-6 **84** MartinLane 2 82
(Derek Shaw) *sn pushed along bhd ldrs: drvn over 2f out: nvr gng pce to get on terms* **7/1**[3]
3 **6** 2 **Head Space (IRE)**[21] 1015 4-9-2 **80** TomEaves 1 71
(Ruth Carr) *slowly away: in last 3 but in tch: rdn over 2f out: kpt on but nvr any imp on ldrs* **7/1**[3]
2311 **7** ½ **Island Legend (IRE)**[21] 1015 6-9-7 **85** (p) DaneO'Neill 4 74
(Milton Bradley) *led: rdn 2f out: narrowly hdd whn squeezed up on rails jst ins fnl f: no ex* **7/4**[1]

1m 1.12s (-1.18) **Going Correction** +0.025s/f (Slow) 7 Ran SP% **113.0**
Speed ratings (Par 105): **110,109,108,107,105 102,101**
toteswingers:1&2:£5.90, 2&3:£11.20, 1&3:£10.10 CSF £24.24 TOTE £3.10: £1.20, £2.40; EX 16.80.
Owner Percy / Green Racing 2 **Bred** John McEnery **Trained** Musley Bank, N Yorks

FOCUS
They went a good pace in this sprint and the first two set the level.

1363 32RED.COM MAIDEN FILLIES' STKS 1m 1f 103y(P)
7:55 (7:56) (Class 5) 3-Y-0+ £2,264 (£673; £336; £168) Stalls Low

Form RPR
5- **1** **Bon Allumage**[169] 7118 3-8-9 0 TomQueally 4 74+
(Sir Henry Cecil) *broke wl: led for 3f: trckd ldr: rdn and drifted rt fr over 1f out: led ent fnl f: r.o wl: readily* **5/2**[1]
45- **2** 2 **Candycakes (IRE)**[231] 5444 3-8-9 0 JamieSpencer 9 70+
(Michael Bell) *s.i.s: sn rcvrd: led after 3f: rdn 2f out: hdd ent fnl f: nt gng pce of wnr* **4/1**[3]
4 **3** ½ **Fleeting Image**[29] 908 3-8-9 0 CathyGannon 3 69
(Alan Bailey) *in tch: rdn 2f out to chse ldrs: kpt on ins fnl f* **5/1**
4 shd **Indian Petal** 3-8-9 0 MickaelBarzalona 7 69+
(Mahmood Al Zarooni) *racd keenly: hld up: pushed along and hdwy fr 2f out: kpt on ins fnl f: improve* **3/1**[2]
56- **5** nk **Porcini**[196] 6506 3-8-6 0 AdamBeschizza(3) 6 68
(Philip McBride) *mid-div: rdn over 2f out: swtchd lft to chse ldrs over 1f out: kpt on same pce* **50/1**
30- **6** ¾ **Supreme Luxury (IRE)**[185] 6776 3-8-6 0 AmyRyan(3) 13 68+
(Kevin Ryan) *racd keenly: hld up: hdwy whn short of room ent fnl f: kpt on same pce whn clr run fnl 150yds* **20/1**
220- **7** 2 **Arley Hall**[244] 5029 3-8-9 72 TonyHamilton 1 62
(Richard Fahey) *mid-div: rdn over 2f out: effrt over 1f out: one pce fnl f* **9/1**
4 **8** shd **Swift Act**[36] 838 3-8-2 0 DarrenEgan(7) 5 62
(Ronald Harris) *in tch: rdn over 2f out to chse ldrs: no ex fnl 120yds* **80/1**
54 **9** hd **Raamz (IRE)**[14] 1107 5-9-5 0 MichaelJMurphy(7) 10 66
(Kevin Morgan) *mid-div: rdn whn carried wd ent st: sn one pce* **33/1**
-34 **10** 2¼ **Barbarella Blue (IRE)**[41] 784 3-8-9 0 AndreaAtzeni 8 59
(Marco Botti) *trckd ldrs: rdn over 2f out: fdd ins fnl f* **16/1**
55 **11** 12 **Redinessence (IRE)**[22] 1001 4-9-12 0 JamieMackay 2 36
(Willie Musson) *stdd s: a in rr: wknd wl over 1f out* **80/1**
6- **12** 6 **Silent Ambition**[202] 6322 3-8-9 0 LiamJones 11
(Mark Brisbourne) *little slowly away: a towards rr* **66/1**

2m 2.93s (1.23) **Going Correction** +0.025s/f (Slow)
WFA 3 from 4yo+ 17lb 12 Ran SP% **119.7**
Speed ratings (Par 100): **95,93,92,92,92 91,89,89,89,87 77,71**
toteswingers:1&2:£3.10, 2&3:£4.00, 1&3:£3.70 CSF £12.32 TOTE £4.80: £2.00, £3.00, £1.70; EX 19.40 Trifecta £47.60 Pool: £324.51 - 5.04 winning units..
Owner Ennismore Racing I **Bred** Ennismore Racing I **Trained** Newmarket, Suffolk

FOCUS
An interesting fillies' maiden with plenty of top stables represented. The slow pace limits things and the form is tricky to pin down.
Barbarella Blue(IRE) Official explanation: jockey said filly hung right

1364 HORIZONS RESTAURANT, THE PLACE TO DINE CLASSIFIED STKS 1m 1f 103y(P)
8:25 (8:25) (Class 6) 3-Y-0 £1,704 (£503; £251) Stalls Low

Form RPR
000- **1** **Topanga Canyon**[205] 6245 3-9-0 62 (v[1]) LiamKeniry 8 76
(Andrew Balding) *mde all: kicked clr 2f out: sn wl in command: comf* **15/2**
422- **2** 2½ **Naseem Alyasmeen (IRE)**[219] 5818 3-9-0 65 MartinHarley 5 71
(Mick Channon) *trckd ldrs: rdn over 2f out: chsd wnr over 1f out: kpt on for clr 2nd but no ch w wnr* **4/1**[2]
05-1 **3** 5 **Lady Sylvia**[50] 663 3-8-11 65 HarryBentley(3) 3 61
(Joseph Tuite) *trckd ldrs: rdn over 2f out: kpt on same pce* **4/1**[2]
324- **4** 1¼ **Dubious Escapade (IRE)**[167] 7157 3-9-0 65 SilvestreDeSousa 7 58
(Ann Duffield) *hdwy to chse wnr after 1f: rdn whn short of room over 2f out: keeping on at same pce whn hung lft fr over 1f out* **6/1**[3]
000- **5** nk **Symphony Star (IRE)**[195] 6526 3-9-0 65 JimCrowley 2 57+
(Paul D'Arcy) *in tch: rdn whn outpcd in last pair over 2f out: styd on fnl f* **10/3**[1]
5326 **6** shd **Gabrial's Lexi (IRE)**[22] 998 3-9-0 65 JamieSpencer 4 57
(Richard Fahey) *in tch: hdwy after 3f to trck wnr: rdn whn wnr kicked clr 2f out: lost 2nd over 1f out: fdd ins fnl f* **15/2**
0-14 **7** 1¼ **Jericho (IRE)**[42] 766 3-9-0 65 FergusSweeney 1 54
(Jamie Osborne) *awkward leaving stalls: last but in tch: rdn 3f out: nvr a threat* **8/1**

2m 3.29s (1.59) **Going Correction** +0.025s/f (Slow) 7 Ran SP% **112.0**
Speed ratings (Par 96): **93,90,86,85,84 84,83**
toteswingers:1&2:£5.70, 2&3:£3.90, 1&3:£3.70 CSF £35.73 TOTE £9.10: £4.80, £3.10; EX 35.50 Trifecta £188.90 Part won. Pool: £255.33 - 0.63 winning units..
Owner Mick and Janice Mariscotti **Bred** Honeypuddle Stud **Trained** Kingsclere, Hants

FOCUS
A modest handicap and again a steady gallop but it was turned into a rout by Topanga Canyon. The runner-up looks the best guide to the level.
Topanga Canyon Official explanation: trainer's rep said, regarding apparent improvement in form, that the gelding has matured and strengthened over the winter, its first run since being gelded and appeared to benefit from the first-time visor.
Dubious Escapade(IRE) Official explanation: jockey said filly hung left

1365 32REDPOKER.COM H'CAP 1m 141y(P)
8:55 (8:55) (Class 6) (0-65,65) 3-Y-0 £1,704 (£503; £251) Stalls Low

Form RPR
2221 **1** **Crowning Star (IRE)**[42] 766 3-9-4 **62** (t) NeilCallan 7 73
(Gay Kelleway) *trckd ldr: led wl over 1f out: sn shkn up to go clr: pushed out: readily* **3/1**[1]
-464 **2** 7 **Casa Bex**[62] 518 3-9-6 **64** (t) JimmyFortune 6 59
(Philip McBride) *hld up: rdn and hdwy over 2f out: styd on to go 2nd ins fnl f: no ch w wnr* **3/1**[1]
344 **3** ¾ **Outlaw Torn (IRE)**[30] 901 3-8-6 **55** (e) CharlesEddery(5) 4 48
(Richard Guest) *led: rdn and hdd wl over 1f out: sn no ch w wnr: no ex whn lost 2nd ins fnl f* **22/1**
300- **4** 1¼ **Represent (IRE)**[164] 7205 3-9-4 **62** MartinHarley 9 52
(Mick Channon) *hld up travelling wl in last: stdy prog on outer fr over 2f out: rdn wl over 1f out: styd on but nvr gng pce to get on terms* **8/1**
205- **5** 3¾ **Thecornishcowboy**[168] 7140 3-9-1 **62** MichaelO'Connell(3) 3 44
(John Ryan) *chsd ldrs: rdn over 2f out: wknd jst over 1f out* **9/1**
060 **6** nse **Maggie Pink**[29] 908 3-8-0 **51** oh6 JackDuern(7) 8 33
(Michael Appleby) *mid-div: rdn and hdwy over 2f out: wknd jst over 1f out* **66/1**
036 **7** 5 **Eastern Amour (IRE)**[29] 908 3-9-7 **65** (b[1]) AdamKirby 2 35
(Marco Botti) *mid-div: struggling 5f out: wknd 2f out* **4/1**[2]
2-23 **8** 2¼ **Macy Anne (IRE)**[57] 573 3-9-5 **63** MartinDwyer 5 28
(Robert Mills) *s.i.s: struggling 3f out: a towards rr* **12/1**
50-0 **9** ½ **Zuzu Angel (IRE)**[23] 982 3-9-5 **63** JimCrowley 1 27
(William Knight) *chsd ldrs: rdn over 3f out: wknd jst over 2f out* **7/1**[3]

1m 49.43s (-1.07) **Going Correction** +0.025s/f (Slow) 9 Ran SP% **117.1**
Speed ratings (Par 96): **105,98,98,97,93 93,89,87,86**
toteswingers:1&2:£3.10, 2&3:£14.00, 1&3:£9.40 CSF £12.07 CT £165.83 TOTE £4.00: £2.60, £1.10, £6.80; EX 12.90 Trifecta £154.60 Pool: £263.34 - 1.26 winning units..
Owner Countrywide Classics Limited **Bred** Summerhill Bloodstock **Trained** Exning, Suffolk

FOCUS
A modest race with the winner rated back to his juvenile best, although the placed horses are rated below their winter form.
T/Plt: £161.90 to a £1 stake. Pool of £67,674.43 - 305.04 winning tickets. T/Qpdt: £36.80 to a £1 stake. Pool of £8,376.16 - 168.22 winning tickets. TM

1366 - 1372a (Foreign Racing) - See Raceform Interactive

1307 LINGFIELD (L-H)
Saturday, April 14

OFFICIAL GOING: Standard
Wind: light across Weather: mild wih a light breeze

1373 GRAND NATIONAL FREE BETS AT FREEBETTING.CO.UK H'CAP 7f (P)
2:00 (2:06) (Class 3) (0-95,95) 4-Y-0+ £8,409 (£2,502; £1,250; £625) Stalls Low

Form RPR
025- **1** **My Freedom (IRE)**[203] 6335 4-9-4 **92** FrankieDettori 12 108
(Saeed Bin Suroor) *midfield on outer: swtchd lft and rdn over 1f out: surged through on inner to ld 1f out: sn in n.d: impressive* **7/2**[1]
030- **2** 3½ **Naabegha**[182] 6862 5-8-13 **87** PatCosgrave 10 93
(Ed de Giles) *squeezed out s and in rr: t.k.h: hdwy over 3f out: effrt to chse ldrs over 1f out: r.o wl and tk 2nd cl home: no ch w wnr* **22/1**
303- **3** hd **The Confessor**[161] 7295 5-9-2 **90** DaneO'Neill 3 96
(Henry Candy) *led: rdn and hdd 1f out: sn no ch w wnr and lost 2nd cl home* **7/2**[1]

00-4 **4** *1* **Azrael**[13] 1161 4-8-11 **85** MartinHarley 4 88
(Alan McCabe) *pressed ldr: rdn and ev ch 2f out: grad wknd ins fnl f* **13/2**[2]
020- **5** *½* **Corporal Maddox**[188] 6723 5-8-12 **86** StevieDonohoe 5 88
(Jamie Osborne) *in rr: pushed along 2f out: one pce and no threat ins fnl f* **22/1**
1000 **6** *hd* **Seek The Fair Land**[14] 1140 6-8-12 **91** NathanAlison(5) 14 92
(Jim Boyle) *hld up: stl in rr whn rdn 2f out: plugged on one pce: nvr a threat* **22/1**
024- **7** *1 ¾* **Honeymead (IRE)**[210] 6148 4-8-13 **87** FrederikTylicki 1 83
(Richard Fahey) *in rr: rdn over 2f out: no ch and btn fnl f: one pce* **12/1**
0-14 **8** *hd* **Another Try (IRE)**[5] 1255 7-8-9 **83** DavidProbert 7 79
(Alan Jarvis) *in tch: pushed along over 1f out: struggling ins fnl f* **11/1**[3]
1460 **9** *1 ¼* **Amitola (IRE)**[14] 1130 5-9-3 **91** RyanMoore 9 83
(David Barron) *wd: cl up: rdn 2f out: wknd wl over 1f out* **13/2**[2]
300- **10** *½* **Space Station**[203] 6341 6-8-12 **86** NeilCallan 2 77
(Simon Dow) *stmbld s: in tch: rdn and ev ch over 1f out: wknd ins fnl f* **18/1**
015- **11** *hd* **Bronze Prince**[231] 5474 5-9-6 **94** JimCrowley 8 85+
(Michael Attwater) *midfield: lost pl over 2f out: pushed along and effrt whn short of room wl over 1f out: sn lost ch and eased* **14/1**
0-60 **12** *hd* **Greensward**[26] 962 6-8-7 **88** DarrenEgan(7) 11 78
(Mike Murphy) *slowly away and detached in last: rdn and no ch over 2f out* **14/1**

1m 22.71s (-2.09) **Going Correction** -0.075s/f (Stan) **12** Ran SP% **118.8**
Speed ratings (Par 107): **108,104,103,102,102 101,99,99,98,97 97,97**
toteswingers:1&2:£44.30, 2&3:£21.50, 1&3:£2.00 CSF £92.62 CT £288.04 TOTE £3.50: £2.00, £8.80, £1.70; EX 95.00 TRIFECTA Not won..
Owner Godolphin **Bred** Skymarc Farm **Trained** Newmarket, Suffolk

FOCUS
A competitive handicap run at a decent pace thanks to a disputed lead, but there was only one horse in it at the end. The form lloks sound enough rated around those in the frame behind the winner.

NOTEBOOK
My Freedom(IRE) ◆ was reappearing after an absence of 231 days and has been known to hang, but the gelding operation seems to have worked the oracle judging by this effort. It took him a while to get in from his wide draw, but travelled really nicely once he did and when switched towards the inside rail to lead inside the last furlong, produced a telling turn of foot to go clear. He looks more than capable of winning even better prizes than this. (op 4-1 tchd 9-2 and 10-3)
Naabegha ◆, making his AW debut after a 182-day absence, ran a blinder considering he missed the break but he finished with quite a rattle and can only go on from here. (tchd 25-1)
The Confessor was racing for the first time since November, but has a good record fresh and this was another decent effort. He was given little peace up front by Azrael, but hung in there until the winner swamped him from the furlong pole. (op 9-2)
Azrael was making his AW debut having run a blinder on his return from a long absence at Doncaster earlier this month and this was another good effort under a prominent ride. (op 8-1 tchd 10-1)
Corporal Maddox was another making his AW debut after 188 days off but, although he is now on a losing run of 16, he was staying on nicely at the end having been given a bit to do. (op 28-1)
Seek The Fair Land, a triple C&D winner, had excuses for three defeats since winning over 6f here in January and was also staying on down the wide outside from well off the pace, but he was up against several rivals who were unexposed on the surface in this contest. (op 25-1 tchd 28-1 and 20-1)
Amitola(IRE) is a confirmed front-runner, but couldn't lead this time and didn't run up to her best as a result. (op 8-1 tchd 6-1)
Bronze Prince, picked up for 50,000gns by current connections, had been gelded since his final start for John Gosden last August and can be forgiven this, as he was trying for the same gap as the winner coming to the last furlong, but came off second best in that battle. (op 17-2)
Greensward had a coming together with the runner-up exiting the stalls and soon found himself in a detached last. (op 9-1 tchd 16-1)

1374 BETTER GRAND NATIONAL ODDS AT FREEBETTING.CO.UK H'CAP 1m 4f (P)
2:30 (2:30) (Class 2) (0-105,100) 4-Y-0+ **£12,938** (£3,850; £1,924; £962) **Stalls** Low

Form RPR
010- **1** **Midsummer Sun**[185] 6803 4-9-3 **94** IanMongan 3 106+
(Sir Henry Cecil) *racd wd: t.k.h in tch: rdn to ld over 1f out: hrd drvn and fnd plenty for press ins fnl f: wnt clr in impressive fashion* **4/1**[3]
052- **2** *2* **Ithoughtitwasover (IRE)**[197] 6497 4-9-0 **91** KierenFallon 7 99
(Mark Johnston) *midfield: nudged along 5f out: drvn to chse ldrs 2f out: kpt on fr over 1f out but no threat to easy wnr* **3/1**[1]
51- **3** *1* **Royal Peculiar**[269] 4208 4-8-10 **87** TomQueally 10 94
(Sir Henry Cecil) *t.k.h in rr: taken to outer and hdwy 3f out: rdn and styd on 2f out: carried hd awkwardly and tk 3rd fnl f* **5/1**
5-35 **4** *1 ¾* **Mataaleb**[25] 971 5-8-6 **82** TadhgO'Shea 6 86
(Lydia Pearce) *in rr: rdn 3f out: c wd into st and drvn: kpt on one pce ins fnl f: no threat to ldrs* **16/1**
406- **5** *1 ½* **Buthelezi (USA)**[197] 6498 4-9-9 **100** RobertHavlin 4 102
(John Gosden) *sn led: rdn and hdd over 2f out: wknd fnl f* **7/2**[2]
354- **6** *5* **Twin Soul (IRE)**[170] 7129 4-9-3 **94** DavidProbert 5 88
(Andrew Balding) *midfield: rdn 5f out: struggling and btn 2f out* **12/1**
-220 **7** *¾* **Franco Is My Name**[14] 1139 6-8-11 **87** (p) JohnFahy 9 79
(Peter Hedger) *t.k.h in rr: hdwy 3f out: effrt and short of room 2f out: rdn and one pce over 1f out* **16/1**
0-03 **8** *2* **Almail (USA)**[22] 1008 6-8-10 **86** FergusSweeney 1 75
(Jamie Osborne) *in tch: rdn and short of room 3f out: lost pl 2f out: sn btn* **50/1**
0-30 **9** *¾* **The Bells O Peover**[55] 630 4-8-11 **88** (b) NeilCallan 2 76
(Mark Johnston) *cl up: led over 2f out: drvn and hdd over 1f out: wknd and btn ins fnl f* **18/1**
660- **10** *1 ½* **Bridle Belle**[210] 6151 4-8-10 **87** FrederikTylicki 8 73
(Richard Fahey) *towards rr of midfield: pushed along over 3f out: struggling fnl 2f* **14/1**

2m 27.97s (-5.03) **Going Correction** -0.075s/f (Stan) course record
WFA 4 from 5yo+ 1lb **10** Ran SP% **117.2**
Speed ratings (Par 109): **113,111,111,109,108 105,105,103,103,102**
toteswingers:1&2:£3.30, 2&3:£3.20, 1&3:£4.20 CSF £16.52 CT £61.32 TOTE £4.80: £2.10, £1.60, £1.60; EX 21.20 Trifecta £117.30 Pool: £600.92 - 3.79 winning units..
Owner K Abdulla **Bred** Juddmonte Farms Ltd **Trained** Newmarket, Suffolk

FOCUS
A strong middle-distance handicap, run at a decent pace resulting in a new course record. The form looks solid rated around the runner-up and fourth.

NOTEBOOK
Midsummer Sun ◆ was having his first outing since October and remains lightly raced, but was deserted by Tom Queally in favour of Royal Peculiar. He didn't have the best of trips either, always being stuck on the outside of the leaders and seeing plenty of daylight, but he found plenty when sent for home off the final bend and, with further progress likely, looks set for a good season. (op 6-1)
Ithoughtitwasover(IRE) was making his AW debut after 197 days off and didn't do a lot wrong, but despite doing his best to get on terms with the winner in the home straight couldn't make much impression on him. (op 9-2 tchd 11-4)
Royal Peculiar ◆ was the least exposed in the field with this only his third start and he had plenty of subsequent winners behind when winning a C&D maiden last July. Having his first start since, he made a promising move running down to the home bend, but he still displayed signs of greenness in the home straight and is likely to come on a good deal, both for the run and the added experience. (op 4-1)
Mataaleb ◆ has been running better this year and this was another good effort back in this stronger company. Given a lot to do, he was doing some good late work down the outside and remains lightly raced for a 5-y-o. He is worth looking out for back in slightly lesser grade. (op 14-1)
Buthelezi(USA) was making his AW debut and having his first start since September, but had been gelded in the meantime and won first time out last year. However, having been ridden into the early lead he looked awkward once headed over 3f out and though he tried to hang in there, was beaten in the home straight. He has a bit to prove. (op 5-1 tchd 11-2)
Twin Soul(IRE) was last seen finishing a close fourth in a fillies' Listed event here last October, but a 15lb hike for that meant she was 26lb higher than when completing a Polytrack hat-trick early last year, and she was under the pump to maintain her position a good 5f out here. (op 7-1)
The Bells O Peover Official explanation: jockey said gelding hung left throughout

1375 FREE GRAND NATIONAL BETS AT FREEBETTING.CO.UK INTERNATIONAL TRIAL STKS (LISTED RACE) 1m (P)
3:05 (3:05) (Class 1) 3-Y-O **£18,714** (£7,095; £3,550; £1,768; £887) **Stalls** High

Form RPR
005- **1** **Talwar (IRE)**[175] 7020 3-9-0 107 RyanMoore 3 99
(Jeremy Noseda) *chsd ldr and keen: rdn and briefly outpcd 2f out: chal wd and styd on wl 1f out: led fnl 75yds: won gng away* **10/11**[1]
411- **2** *1* **Prince Alzain (USA)**[110] 7879 3-9-0 88 DaneO'Neill 6 96
(Gerard Butler) *hld up: 3rd and rdn 2f out: effrt and swtchd to inner over 1f out: drvn and led 1f out: hdd fnl 75yds* **2/1**[2]
3 *2 ½* **Masterel (ITY)**[128] 3-9-0 92 AdamKirby 1 90
(Marco Botti) *taken steadily to post: sn led and established clr advantage: rdn 2f out: drvn along and emptied 1f out: sn btn* **8/1**[3]
1- **4** *3 ¼* **Spykes Bay (USA)**[176] 7000 3-9-0 72 JimCrowley 4 82
(Mrs K Burke) *hld up: rdn over 2f out: sn struggling and no imp ins fnl f* **12/1**
15- **5** *3* **Viola D'Amour (IRE)**[265] 4372 3-8-9 78 RichardKingscote 5 70
(Tom Dascombe) *hld up: pushed along 4f out: rdn along and no ch over 2f out* **22/1**

1m 36.84s (-1.36) **Going Correction** -0.075s/f (Stan) **5** Ran SP% **108.9**
Speed ratings (Par 106): **103,102,99,96,93**
CSF £2.85 TOTE £1.80: £1.40, £1.10; EX 3.10.
Owner Vimal Khosla **Bred** Philip And Mrs Jane Myerscough **Trained** Newmarket, Suffolk

FOCUS
This Listed contest has been won by some smart performers such as Castle Gandolfo in 2002 and Dubawi Gold last year, but the winners in between didn't really set the world alight. The form is a bit muddling with the winner not needing to run to his best juvenile mark to score.

NOTEBOOK
Talwar(IRE) had upwards of 15lb in hand of his four rivals based on official ratings, but he disappointed in all three starts after easily winning the Group 3 Solario and had never raced on the AW before. Given a lead by the runaway Masterel, he briefly looked in trouble turning for home but he kept at it and, making his effort on the traditionally favoured centre of the track, found enough to grab the race well inside the last furlong. As game as this success was, he didn't beat the runner-up as comfortably as the 19lb between them would suggest and he may not be the easiest to place from now on. If he is to win another race on turf, he is likely to need some cut and is now to be aimed at the Italian 2000 Guineas. (op 6-5)
Prince Alzain(USA), a dual winner at Wolverhampton towards the end of last year including when flooring the winner's long odds-on stablemate Harvard N Yale, looked to have been produced at the right time when leading against the rail inside the last furlong, but the winner may have been on the quicker part of the track and nailed him close home. (op 7-4)
Masterel(ITY), twice a winner from four starts in Italy including in Listed company, went off hard in front and it briefly looked as though he might have stolen it, but he emptied once in line for home. He can win races here when ridden with a little more restraint. (op 10-1 tchd 12-1)
Spykes Bay(USA), not seen since making a winning debut in a Wolverhampton maiden last October (couple of subsequent winners behind), is rated just 72 so faced a massive task and it's hard to know what this will do to his mark. (op 10-1 tchd 15-2)
Viola D'Amour(IRE) hadn't been seen since disappointing in a German Listed event last July and was the first beaten. (op 12-1)

1376 FREE HORSE RACING BETS AT FREEBETTING.CO.UK MAIDEN STKS 6f (P)
3:40 (3:40) (Class 5) 3-Y-O **£2,911** (£866; £432; £216) **Stalls** Low

Form RPR
5- **1** **Khubala (IRE)**[185] 6787 3-9-3 0 RyanMoore 10 72+
(Ed Dunlop) *cl up: hdwy 2f out: pushed along and kpt on 1f out: rdn to ld ins fnl f* **5/2**[2]
4 **2** *1* **Catflap (IRE)**[22] 1016 3-8-12 0 NickyMackay 6 64
(Derek Haydn Jones) *led: pushed along over 1f out: rdn and hdd ins fnl f: nt gng pce of wnr cl home* **14/1**
6 **3** *1* **Langley Vale**[31] 892 3-9-3 0 SebSanders 11 66
(Roger Teal) *t.k.h in midfield: hdwy 2f out: rdn and kpt on to go 3rd ins fnl f* **14/1**
4 *¾* **Jocasta Dawn** 3-8-12 0 FergusSweeney 12 58+
(Henry Candy) *towards rr: pushed along and hdwy over 1f out: kpt on nicely ins fnl f: fin wl: nt wout promise* **33/1**
4- **5** *nse* **Mrs Huffey**[161] 7292 3-8-12 0 DaneO'Neill 4 58+
(Henry Candy) *hld up: pushed along 2f out: hdwy and nt clr run over 1f out: kpt on one pce* **6/5**[1]
4- **6** *1 ½* **Whatsofunny (IRE)**[184] 6818 3-8-12 0 NeilCallan 9 53
(Roger Varian) *in tch: pushed along and effrt 2f out: drvn and no imp ins fnl f* **5/1**[3]
4 **7** *2 ½* **Exkaliber**[19] 1048 3-9-3 0 IanMongan 3 50
(Jeremy Gask) *in tch: hdwy 2f out: ev ch and rdn 1f out: drvn and no ex ins fnl f: sn btn* **20/1**
00- **8** *hd* **Madame Feu**[181] 6892 3-8-12 0 HayleyTurner 2 45
(Henry Candy) *cl up: pushed along and lost pl 2f out: wknd and btn 1f out* **33/1**
000- **9** *3* **Aubrietia**[173] 7056 3-8-12 0 TedDurcan 5 35
(Ed Vaughan) *towards rr thrght: rdn and struggling 2f out* **50/1**
10 *¾* **Mystical Witch** 3-8-9 0 DominicFox(3) 7 33
(Christine Dunnett) *slowly away and green in rr: nvr on terms* **125/1**

1m 14.23s (2.33) **Going Correction** -0.075s/f (Stan) **10** Ran SP% **117.4**
Speed ratings (Par 98): **81,79,78,77,77 75,71,71,67,66**
toteswingers:1&2:£11.20, 2&3:£9.10, 1&3:£24.40 CSF £34.38 TOTE £3.30: £1.10, £3.80, £4.10; EX 32.40.
Owner Miss P Araci **Bred** James F Hanly **Trained** Newmarket, Suffolk

FOCUS
A modest maiden run at a pedestrian pace, but several of these are entitled to improve. The placed horses are probably the best guides.

1377 FREEBETTING.CO.UK ON EVERY UK RACE MEETING MEDIAN AUCTION MAIDEN STKS — 7f (P)
4:45 (4:46) (Class 6) 3-5-Y-0 — **£2,181** (£644; £322) **Stalls** Low

Form — RPR

4-2 **1** **Bartolomeu**[14] 1138 3-8-12 0 .... AdamKirby 4 — 78+
(Marco Botti) *mde jst abt all: rdn 2f out: strly pressed ins fnl f: battled on wl and jst hld on* **4/6**[1]

362- **2** *hd* **Jack Of Diamonds (IRE)**[171] 7095 3-8-12 76 .... JackMitchell 1 — 77
(Roger Teal) *in tch: rdn along 3f out: str run on inner to chse wnr 1f out: duelled for ld and jst edgd out cl home* **4/1**[3]

40- **3** *½* **Sandbetweenourtoes (IRE)**[307] 2953 3-8-12 0 .... ShaneKelly 3 — 76
(Brian Meehan) *ponied to s: rdn along early to chse ldr: pressed ldr 4f out: rdn 2f out: wknd 1f out: plugged on one pce ins fnl f* **3/1**[2]

4 *13* **Evanescent (IRE)** 3-8-12 0 .... MartinHarley 2 — 40
(Alan McCabe) *hld up: rdn along 4f out: no ch and one pce fnl 2f* **33/1**

50 **5** *2* **Petersboden**[24] 981 3-8-12 0 .... FergusSweeney 5 — 35
(Michael Blanshard) *a in rr: pushed along and outpcd 5f out: struggling fnl 3f* **66/1**

1m 24.52s (-0.28) **Going Correction** -0.075s/f (Stan) — **5** Ran SP% **109.4**
Speed ratings (Par 101): **98,97,97,82,80**
CSF £3.72 TOTE £1.50: £1.10, £1.70; EX 3.40.
Owner H E Sheikh Sultan Bin Khalifa Al Nahyan **Bred** Sheikh Sultan Bin Khalifa Al Nayhan **Trained** Newmarket, Suffolk
■ Stewards' Enquiry : Adam Kirby two-day ban: used whip above permitted level (Apr 28,30)
Jack Mitchell four-day ban: used whip above permitted level (Apr 28,30,May 1-2)

FOCUS
A modest maiden and little covered the three market principals at the line. The runner-up sets the standard.

1378 LADBROKES ODDS ON FOR SUCCESS GAME ON H'CAP — 7f (P)
5:15 (5:18) (Class 5) (0-70,70) 4-Y-0+ — **£3,067** (£905; £453) **Stalls** Low

Form — RPR

0000 **1** **Yankee Storm**[19] 1050 7-9-3 66 ....(b) RyanMoore 9 — 76
(Michael Wigham) *midfield: hdwy on outer over 1f out: pushed along and r.o wl 1f out: led fnl 75yds* **10/1**

50-0 **2** *1 ½* **L'Hirondelle (IRE)**[38] 821 8-9-4 67 ....(p) NeilCallan 4 — 73
(Michael Attwater) *bhd ldrs: pushed along on inner over 1f out: rdn to press ldrs 1f out: led ins fnl f: hdd fnl 75yds* **11/1**

0311 **3** *¾* **Prince Of Sorrento**[31] 894 5-9-7 70 .... JamieMackay 6 — 74
(Lee Carter) *slowly away: sn pushed along and in midfield: wd ent st: drvn to chse ldrs jst over 1f out: kpt on and battled for pls* **3/1**[1]

553- **4** *nk* **Proper Charlie**[254] 4709 4-9-2 65 .... JimCrowley 14 — 68
(William Knight) *in rr: hdwy 2f out: pushed along and kpt on wl 1f out: fin wl and pressed for pls* **14/1**

5022 **5** *1* **Perfect Ch'I (IRE)**[16] 1084 5-9-3 66 .... JamesDoyle 2 — 66
(Ian Wood) *disp ld tl led over 1f out: hdd ins fnl f: fdd cl home* **14/1**

2632 **6** *nse* **The Happy Hammer (IRE)**[16] 1091 6-9-4 67 .... GeorgeBaker 13 — 67
(Eugene Stanford) *in rr: effrt over 2f out: hdwy to chse ldrs over 1f out: kpt on one pce* **9/2**[2]

-302 **7** *2* **Secret Queen**[19] 1049 5-9-0 63 ....(v) FergusSweeney 5 — 58
(Martin Hill) *hld up: hdwy over 2f out: drvn and effrt 1f out: no ex and fdd cl home* **16/1**

0456 **8** *nk* **May's Boy**[28] 942 4-9-2 65 ....(p) DaneO'Neill 3 — 59
(Mark Usher) *cl up: disp ld after 1f: rdn and wknd over 1f out* **10/1**

-040 **9** *nk* **Hoover**[44] 746 4-9-4 67 .... PatCosgrave 12 — 60
(Jim Boyle) *in rr: rdn and effrt on inner 2f out: hdwy and chsd ldrs over 1f out: no ex and fdd ins fnl f* **11/1**

63/0 **10** *nk* **Jalors (IRE)**[13] 1156 4-8-11 67 .... DarrenEgan(7) 1 — 59
(Ronald Harris) *cl up: shuffled bk 3f out: pushed along 2f out: effrt over 1f out: no ex ins fnl f* **33/1**

0255 **11** *1 ¼* **Cativo Cavallino**[15] 1108 9-9-1 64 .... RichardThomas 11 — 53
(John E Long) *in rr: rdn 2f out: sn no imp* **25/1**

010- **12** *1 ¼* **Blue Deer (IRE)**[122] 7754 4-9-2 65 .... StevieDonohoe 7 — 51
(Lee Carter) *midfield on outer: pushed along and no hdwy fnl 2f* **50/1**

00-2 **13** *¾* **Not My Choice (IRE)**[19] 1050 7-9-4 67 ....(t) MichaelStainton 10 — 51
(David C Griffiths) *disp ld after 1f: rdn along and 3rd ent st: fdd after* **6/1**[3]

0020 **14** *10* **Ensnare**[25] 967 7-9-0 63 .... TonyCulhane 8 — 20
(Willie Musson) *in rr thrght: rdn and no hdwy fnl 3f* **25/1**

1m 23.62s (-1.18) **Going Correction** -0.075s/f (Stan) — **14** Ran SP% **124.1**
Speed ratings (Par 103): **103,101,100,100,98 98,96,96,95,95 94,92,91,80**
toteswingers:1&2:£13.70, 2&3:£5.40, 1&3:£10.80 CSF £115.13 CT £419.92 TOTE £11.80: £5.10, £3.20, £1.30; EX 81.90.
Owner R L Maynard **Bred** Mark Johnston Racing Ltd **Trained** Newmarket, Suffolk

FOCUS
A modest handicap and another race run at a fair pace thanks to a contested lead and the form looks pretty solid.

1379 LADBROKES SHOPS ARE OPEN TONIGHT H'CAP — 1m 2f (P)
5:45 (5:45) (Class 6) (0-60,59) 4-Y-0+ — **£2,181** (£644; £322) **Stalls** Low

Form — RPR

2423 **1** **Penbryn (USA)**[38] 829 5-9-6 58 ....(v) GeorgeBaker 13 — 66
(Nick Littmoden) *hld up and racd wd: hdwy 2f out: drvn and hanging lft over 1f out whn pressing ldr: kpt on to ld cl home* **11/2**[3]

-114 **2** *nk* **Prohibition (IRE)**[7] 1222 6-8-13 58 .... LeonnaMayor(7) 5 — 65
(Alastair Lidderdale) *hld up: nt clr run 2f out: hdwy on ins over 1f out: drvn and led 1f out: hdd cl home* **6/1**

3-20 **3** *2* **Regal Rave (USA)**[90] 188 5-8-13 51 ....(p) JohnFahy 3 — 54
(Peter Hedger) *hld up: hdwy on outer over 2f out: rdn and kpt on 1f out: hung sltly lft but fin wl* **11/1**

50-3 **4** *1 ¼* **The Ducking Stool**[15] 1106 5-8-8 46 .... NickyMackay 11 — 47
(Julia Feilden) *in tch: hdwy 2f out: rdn and ev ch over 1f out: no ex ins fnl f* **14/1**

26-0 **5** *2 ½* **Rainsborough**[22] 1009 5-8-13 51 ....(p) NeilCallan 7 — 52
(Peter Hedger) *hld up: hdwy ins fnl 4f: rdn 2f out: effrt whn bdly hmpd and stmbld 1f out: lost all ch* **20/1**

-055 **6** *nk* **If What And Maybe**[24] 984 4-8-13 51 ....(v) AdamKirby 2 — 46
(John Ryan) *drvn along to ld: hrd rdn 2f out: hdd 1f out: folded tamely ins fnl f* **8/1**

06-5 **7** *2 ¼* **Cahala Dancer (IRE)**[16] 1084 4-9-5 57 .... JamesDoyle 6 — 47
(Roger Teal) *hld up: rdn 2f out: no ch ins fnl f* **12/1**

4023 **8** *1 ¾* **Cairanne**[16] 1096 4-8-6 47 ow2 .... RyanClark(3) 14 — 34
(Tom Keddy) *cl up: drvn 3f out: struggling fnl f* **11/1**

000- **9** *2* **Matavia Bay (IRE)**[173] 7055 4-9-7 59 .... DavidProbert 1 — 42
(Alan Jarvis) *cl up: rdn over 2f out: wknd over 1f out* **5/1**[2]

0460 **10** *10* **Broughton Place**[25] 966 4-9-2 54 .... StevieDonohoe 9 — 17
(Willie Musson) *bhd: nvr on terms* **20/1**

0000 **11** *3 ¼* **Bubbly Braveheart (IRE)**[45] 736 5-9-3 55 .... IanMongan 4 — 11
(Pat Phelan) *midfield: rdn along 3f out: wknd and btn fnl 2f* **9/2**[1]

0-00 **12** *4 ½* **Estee Will**[21] 1031 5-8-7 45 .... RichardThomas 10
(John E Long) *in tch: lost pl 4f out: struggling after* **80/1**

003- **13** *1 ½* **Notabadlad**[233] 5406 5-9-7 59 .... HayleyTurner 8 — 3
(Simon Dow) *in rr: wnt midfield after 3f: rdn 3f out: sn no ch and btn* **12/1**

2m 4.97s (-1.63) **Going Correction** -0.075s/f (Stan) — **13** Ran SP% **125.1**
Speed ratings (Par 101): **103,102,101,100,98 97,96,94,93,85 82,78,77**
toteswingers:1&2:£6.10, 2&3:£6.70, 1&3:£10.80 CSF £39.67 CT £364.71 TOTE £6.10: £2.30, £2.40, £3.90; EX 46.20.
Owner Mrs K Graham, N Littmoden, A Highfield **Bred** Kilboy Estate Inc **Trained** Newmarket, Suffolk
■ Stewards' Enquiry : Leonna Mayor two-day ban: used whip above permitted level (Apr 28,30)

FOCUS
A moderate handicap, but run at a decent pace. The form is rated around the placed horses.
T/Plt: £38.20 to a £1 stake. Pool of £65,397.04 - 1,249.66 winning tickets. T/Qpdt: £21.60 to a £1 stake. Pool of £2,880.39 - 98.61 winning tickets. CS

NEWCASTLE (L-H)
Saturday, April 14

OFFICIAL GOING: Soft (heavy in places; 4.7)
Wind: Fresh, half against Weather: Cloudy, showers

1380 DELOITTE MAIDEN FILLIES' STKS — 1m 4f 93y
1:35 (1:35) (Class 5) 3-4-Y-0 — **£2,911** (£866; £432; £216) **Stalls** Centre

Form — RPR

4 **1** **Nice Rose**[15] 1113 3-8-7 0 .... SilvestreDeSousa 4 — 78
(Mark Johnston) *mde all: clr over 4f out: pushed out fnl 2f: unchal* **2/1**[1]

632- **2** *4 ½* **Agadir Summer**[155] 7360 4-9-13 74 .... MartinLane 2 — 72
(David Simcock) *chsd ldrs: effrt and chsd (clr) wnr over 3f out: kpt on fnl f: nt gng pce to chal* **2/1**[1]

/50- **3** *16* **Starstuded (IRE)**[166] 7198 4-9-13 61 ....(t) GrahamGibbons 5 — 47
(Martyn Meade) *hld up in tch: effrt and disp 2nd pl over 3f out: rdn and outpcd fr over 2f out* **10/1**[3]

04- **4** *8* **See Emily Play (IRE)**[186] 6776 3-8-7 0 ....(b¹) WilliamBuick 1 — 32
(John Gosden) *chsd wnr: rdn and outpcd over 4f out: wknd 3f out* **5/2**[2]

5 *18* **Hurricane Rita (IRE)** 4-9-13 0 .... PJMcDonald 3
(Alan Swinbank) *hld up: rdn along over 3f out: sn wknd* **16/1**

3m 5.2s (19.60) **Going Correction** +1.475s/f (Soft)
WFA 3 from 4yo 21lb — **5** Ran SP% **110.2**
Speed ratings (Par 100): **93,90,79,74,62**
CSF £6.32 TOTE £3.20: £1.30, £2.10; EX 4.90.
Owner Ahmed Jaber **Bred** Miss K Rausing **Trained** Middleham Moor, N Yorks

FOCUS
Testing conditions and it was still raining when the runners jumped off for this opening race. The form needs treating with caution as Nice Rose was allowed too big a lead and galloped on relentlessly to record a time over three seconds slower than the later Class 5 handicap.

1381 32REDBET.COM FOR GRAND NATIONAL BETTING H'CAP — 1m 2f 32y
2:10 (2:11) (Class 4) (0-85,87) 4-Y-0+ — **£5,175** (£1,540; £769; £384) **Stalls** Centre

Form — RPR

30-0 **1** **Tres Coronas (IRE)**[14] 1134 5-9-6 84 .... GrahamGibbons 9 — 92
(David Barron) *rrd in stalls: hld up: smooth hdwy over 2f out: effrt and chsd ldr over 1f out: led last 100yds: drvn out* **6/1**[3]

40-0 **2** *1* **Ailsa Craig (IRE)**[14] 1133 6-8-9 73 .... JamesSullivan 6 — 79
(Edwin Tuer) *hld up: effrt and hdwy over 2f out: rdn and chsd wnr wl ins fnl f: r.o* **20/1**

2001 **3** *1 ¼* **West End Lad**[14] 1134 9-9-7 85 ....(b) RussKennemore 4 — 88
(Roy Bowring) *led: rdn and 3 l clr over 2f out: hdd last 100yds: kpt on same pce* **8/1**

005- **4** *½* **Oneofapear (IRE)**[257] 4608 6-9-1 79 .... PJMcDonald 3 — 81
(Alan Swinbank) *hld up in midfield: effrt over 2f out: kpt on fnl f: nt gng pce to chal* **33/1**

300- **5** *4 ½* **Silver Grey (IRE)**[161] 7296 5-9-3 81 .... PaulHanagan 5 — 74
(Martyn Meade) *chsd ldrs: rdn 3f out: effrt and wnt 2nd briefly over 1f out: wknd ins fnl f* **8/1**

611- **6** *½* **Miss Blink**[206] 6263 5-8-10 74 .... LeeNewman 11 — 66
(Robin Bastiman) *hld up: shkn up over 2f out: edgd lft: kpt on steadily fnl 2f: nvr nr to chal* **25/1**

10-0 **7** *1 ¾* **Jonny Lesters Hair (IRE)**[14] 1134 7-9-6 84 .... DavidAllan 14 — 73
(Tim Easterby) *chsd ldr to over 1f out: drvn and wknd ins fnl f* **12/1**

003- **8** *1 ¼* **King Kurt (IRE)**[210] 6151 4-9-4 82 .... PhillipMakin 7 — 68
(Kevin Ryan) *t.k.h: hld up in tch: hung lft and outpcd wl over 2f out: n.d after* **11/1**

4-02 **9** *nk* **Calaf**[14] 1134 4-9-1 79 .... JamieSpencer 8 — 64
(Richard Fahey) *plld hrd in tch: pushed along and edgd lft over 2f out: wknd over 1f out* **5/1**[2]

552- **10** *1 ½* **Blue Destination**[28] 5242 4-8-13 80 .... MichaelO'Connell(3) 13 — 62
(John Quinn) *midfield: drvn and outpcd over 3f out: n.d after* **16/1**

350- **11** *10* **Harvey's Hope**[16] 6451 6-8-5 74 .... ShaneBKelly(5) 16 — 36
(Keith Reveley) *hld up: rdn along over 3f out: sn wknd* **25/1**

1051 **12** *9* **Vanilla Rum**[16] 1094 5-8-8 72 ....(b) RobertWinston 2 — 16
(John Mackie) *hld up on ins: stdy hdwy over 5f out: rdn and wknd fr 3f out* **16/1**

1-1 **13** *7* **Camborne**[10] 1186 4-9-9 87 .... WilliamBuick 17 — 17
(John Gosden) *dwlt: sn in tch: rdn over 2f out: wknd over 1f out: eased* **4/1**[1]

41-0 **14** *12* **Tiger Webb**[14] 1134 4-8-9 80 .... DavidSimmonson(7) 10
(Michael Easterby) *hld up: rdn over 3f out: sn struggling* **66/1**

063- **15** *½* **Look Left**[190] 6674 4-9-2 80 .... MartinLane 15
(David Simcock) *s.i.s: hld up: struggling over 3f out: sn btn* **20/1**

41-0 **16** *56* **Switchback**[13] 1161 4-8-13 77 .... PaulMulrennan 12
(Michael Easterby) *midfield: lost pl qckly 5f out: lost tch fnl 3f* **40/1**

2m 24.8s (12.90) **Going Correction** +1.475s/f (Soft) — **16** Ran SP% **125.1**
Speed ratings (Par 105): **107,106,105,104,101 100,99,98,98,96 88,81,76,66,66 21**
CSF £128.27 CT £988.71 TOTE £9.70: £2.20, £5.60, £1.90, £6.70; EX 217.80 TRIFECTA Not won..
Owner J Cringan & D Pryde **Bred** Denis McDonnell **Trained** Maunby, N Yorks

FOCUS
A fair handicap in which West End Lad seemed to set a good pace considering the conditions. The winner is a track specialist and is rated to his best.

Camborne Official explanation: trainer's rep said gelding was unsuited by the soft (heavy in places) ground

1382 32RED H'CAP — 1m 4f 93y

2:45 (2:45) (Class 5) (0-70,70) 4-Y-0+ — **£2,911** (£866; £432; £216) **Stalls** Centre

Form — RPR

2-05 **1** — **Lifetime (IRE)**[25] 978 4-9-2 **66** ..... BarryMcHugh 1 — 79
(Brian Ellison) *dwlt: sn trcking ldrs: effrt over 2f out: led over 1f out: sn hung lft: styd on strly fnl f* — **11/2**[3]

050- **2** 5 — **Goodness**[15] 3044 4-9-4 **68** ..... (t) SilvestreDeSousa 10 — 74
(David O'Meara) *led: rdn and hdd whn hmpd and snatched up appr fnl f: kpt on same pce* — **16/1**

023- **3** 1 ½ — **Pokfulham (IRE)**[147] 7163 6-9-2 **65** ..... (v) LeeNewman 2 — 68
(Jim Goldie) *midfield: hdwy and cl up 4f out: effrt and rdn 2f out: kpt on same pce fnl f* — **13/2**

002- **4** 3 ½ — **Madrasa (IRE)**[165] 7212 4-8-9 **59** ..... (t) TomEaves 4 — 56
(Keith Reveley) *hld up: pushed along over 3f out: styd on fnl 2f: nvr able to chal* — **9/1**

205- **5** 3 — **Dzesmin (POL)**[18] 6775 10-8-12 **61** ..... (p) JamieSpencer 8 — 54
(Richard Guest) *dwlt: hld up: smooth hdwy and ev ch over 2f out: sn rdn and edgd lft: wknd 1f out* — **9/2**[2]

060- **6** 3 ¾ — **Magic Echo**[126] 7713 8-9-5 **68** ..... PhillipMakin 6 — 55
(George Foster) *hld up: pushed along over 3f out: no imp fnl 2f* — **25/1**

550- **7** 6 — **Silver Tigress**[173] 7062 4-8-7 **57** ..... PJMcDonald 5 — 34
(George Moore) *dwlt: hld up: rdn and hdwy over 3f out: wknd over 1f out* — **7/1**

112- **8** 12 — **Vittachi**[130] 7461 5-8-10 **64** ..... GarryWhillans(5) 11 — 22
(Alistair Whillans) *hld up on outside: struggling over 3f out: btn fnl 2f* — **10/1**

000- **9** 14 — **Srimenanti**[134] 7608 4-8-6 **56** oh4 ..... (p) JamesSullivan 7
(Brian Rothwell) *prom: outpcd over 4f out: btn fnl 3f* — **50/1**

410- **10** 1 ½ — **Grey Command (USA)**[242] 5149 7-9-6 **69** ..... RobertWinston 3
(Mel Brittain) *cl up: rdn 5f out: wknd over 3f out* — **14/1**

1412 **11** 28 — **Newport Arch**[25] 978 4-9-3 **70** ..... (v) MichaelO'Connell(3) 9
(John Quinn) *hld up in tch: struggling over 4f out: sn btn: t.o* — **4/1**[1]

3m 1.89s (16.29) **Going Correction** +1.475s/f (Soft)
WFA 4 from 5yo+ 1lb — **11** Ran SP% **116.8**
Speed ratings (Par 103): **104,100,99,97,95 92,88,80,71,70 51**
toteswingers:1&2:£5.60, 2&3:£42.40, 1&3:£9.20 CSF £89.15 CT £587.23 TOTE £6.60: £2.60, £4.40, £2.40; EX 143.80 TRIFECTA Not won..
Owner Koo's Racing Club **Bred** Lynn Lodge Stud And Foxtale Farm **Trained** Norton, N Yorks
■ Stewards' Enquiry : Barry McHugh three-day ban: careless riding (Apr 28,30,May 1)

FOCUS
A weak handicap in which Goodness ran a game race from the front, keeping on well having set what looked a fair enough pace. the winner is rated back to his 3-y-o best.

1383 32REDPOKER.COM H'CAP — 5f

3:20 (3:22) (Class 6) (0-60,60) 4-Y-0+ — **£2,070** (£616; £307; £153) **Stalls** Low

Form — RPR

0516 **1** — **Shawkantango**[10] 1187 5-9-4 **60** ..... (v) DaleSwift(3) 14 — 70
(Derek Shaw) *dwlt: sn in tch centre: led that gp over 2f out: drvn and overall ldr wl ins fnl f: r.o* — **9/1**

5-11 **2** ¾ — **Boucher Garcon (IRE)**[3] 1298 4-8-8 **52** 6ex ..... NeilFarley(5) 5 — 60+
(Declan Carroll) *sn pushed along to ld (overall ldr) far side gp: rdn 2f out: hdd wl ins fnl f: kpt on* — **11/10**[1]

6-05 **3** ¾ — **Sally's Swansong**[50] 691 6-8-8 **47** ..... (b) GrahamGibbons 11 — 52
(Eric Alston) *dwlt: hld up centre: hdwy over 1f out: kpt on fnl f: nrst fin* — **20/1**

010- **4** 2 — **Fair Bunny**[151] 7419 5-8-12 **51** ..... (b) SilvestreDeSousa 9 — 49
(Alan Brown) *cl up in centre: ev ch over 2f out to over 1f out: sn one pce* — **12/1**

0304 **5** 3 ½ — **Soopacal (IRE)**[6] 1242 7-9-5 **58** ..... (t) BarryMcHugh 13 — 43
(Brian Ellison) *led centre to over 2f out: sn rdn and kpt on same pce* — **11/2**[2]

006- **6** 1 — **Drumpellier (IRE)**[164] 7230 5-8-7 **46** oh1 ..... (p) PJMcDonald 15 — 28
(Simon West) *cl up centre: ev ch 1/2-way: outpcd fr 2f out* — **33/1**

1030 **7** 1 — **Cheyenne Red (IRE)**[28] 938 6-8-12 **51** ..... PhillipMakin 10 — 29
(Michael Herrington) *in tch centre: effrt and rdn over 2f out: no imp fr over 1f out* — **16/1**

040- **8** 3 ¼ — **Dotty Darroch**[193] 6618 4-8-13 **52** ..... LeeNewman 12 — 18
(Robin Bastiman) *cl up centre: drvn and outpcd 1/2-way: n.d after* — **25/1**

142- **9** nk — **Duke Of Rainford**[246] 5019 5-8-12 **51** ..... TomEaves 7 — 16
(Michael Herrington) *dwlt: hld up centre: rdn 2f out: nvr on terms* — **20/1**

12-2 **10** 1 ¼ — **Bailadeira**[5] 1246 4-9-5 **58** ..... JamesSullivan 2 — 19
(Tim Etherington) *prom far side: rdn and edgd rt over 2f out: sn outpcd* — **13/2**[3]

330- **11** 2 — **Hardrock Diamond**[232] 5433 4-8-8 **47** ..... PaulMulrennan 6
(Ian Semple) *in tch far side: drvn 1/2-way: sn btn* — **25/1**

366- **12** 7 — **Lady By Red (IRE)**[210] 6156 4-8-11 **53** ..... LeeTopliss(3) 4
(David Thompson) *chsd far side ldr to over 2f out: sn rdn and btn* — **50/1**

000- **13** 8 — **Cottam Stella**[154] 7399 4-8-8 **47** ow1 ..... DavidAllan 1
(Mel Brittain) *sn struggling far side: no ch fr 1/2-way* — **33/1**

1m 4.86s (3.76) **Going Correction** +0.80s/f (Soft) — **13** Ran SP% **125.0**
Speed ratings (Par 101): **101,99,98,95,89 88,86,81,80,78 75,64,51**
toteswingers:1&2:£4.50, 2&3:£17.40, 1&3:£28.80 CSF £18.59 CT £224.62 TOTE £10.50: £3.10, £1.40, £5.50; EX 28.60 Trifecta £282.50 Part won. Pool: £381.82 - 0.50 winning units..
Owner Shawthing Racing Partnership **Bred** Derek Shaw **Trained** Sproxton, Leics
■ Stewards' Enquiry : Dale Swift two-day ban: used whip above permitted level (Apr 28,30)

FOCUS
The winner, third and fourth were drawn in double figures in this moderate sprint and the third is rated close to form.

1384 32RED CASINO H'CAP — 7f

3:55 (3:55) (Class 6) (0-65,65) 4-Y-0+ — **£2,070** (£616; £307; £153) **Stalls** Low

Form — RPR

524 **1** — **Rise To Glory (IRE)**[24] 986 4-8-7 **51** oh3 ..... DuranFentiman 13 — 60
(Shaun Harris) *t.k.h: in tch: hdwy to chal over 1f out: led ins fnl f: drvn out* — **40/1**

20-0 **2** 1 ½ — **Hellbender (IRE)**[7] 1224 6-8-11 **60** ..... LMcNiff(5) 12 — 65
(George Foster) *sn cl up: led over 2f out: rdn and hdd ins fnl f: kpt on same pce* — **16/1**

300- **3** nk — **Jupiter Fidius**[108] 7099 5-8-6 **57** ..... GemmaTutty(7) 5 — 61+
(Karen Tutty) *hld up: stdy hdwy on outside 1/2-way: effrt over 1f out: kpt on fnl f to take 3rd cl home* — **16/1**

3114 **4** hd — **Cyflymder (IRE)**[15] 1108 6-9-7 **65** ..... JamieSpencer 8 — 68
(David C Griffiths) *in tch: effrt and drvn over 1f out: kpt on same pce wl ins fnl f* — **11/2**[2]

00-6 **5** 1 — **Florio Vincitore (IRE)**[23] 997 5-8-13 **57** ..... BarryMcHugh 6 — 60
(Brian Ellison) *prom: drvn over 2f out: sn edgd lft: rallied ins fnl f: hld whn n.m.r cl home* — **10/3**[1]

000- **6** 2 — **Steel Stockholder**[186] 6777 6-9-2 **60** ..... RobertWinston 9 — 56
(Mel Brittain) *t.k.h: in tch: effrt and rdn over 2f out: no ex fnl f* — **16/1**

2/-0 **7** 4 — **Dolly Royal (IRE)**[11] 1178 7-8-11 **55** ..... PaulMulrennan 2 — 40
(Robert Johnson) *hld up: pushed along over 2f out: kpt on fnl f: nvr able to chal* — **33/1**

550- **8** 6 — **Lady Gar Gar**[120] 7782 4-9-0 **61** ..... DaleSwift(3) 3 — 31
(Geoffrey Oldroyd) *prom: drvn and outpcd over 2f out: sn btn* — **6/1**[3]

530- **9** 18 — **Labroc (IRE)**[143] 7515 4-8-11 **55** ..... PJMcDonald 7
(Alan Swinbank) *bhd: struggling 3f out: nvr on terms* — **20/1**

005- **10** 1 ¾ — **Alluring Star**[165] 7213 4-8-13 **64** ..... DavidSimmonson(7) 11
(Michael Easterby) *led to over 2f out: sn rdn and btn* — **17/2**

3525 **11** ¾ — **Mataajir (USA)**[10] 1191 4-9-5 **63** ..... MartinLane 10
(Derek Shaw) *chsd ldng gp: struggling 3f out: sn btn* — **6/1**[3]

0413 **12** 6 — **Beachwood Bay**[31] 899 4-9-6 **64** ..... SilvestreDeSousa 4
(Jo Hughes) *in tch: rdn along 3f out: sn lost pl and struggling* — **7/1**

1m 34.35s (6.55) **Going Correction** +0.80s/f (Soft) — **12** Ran SP% **117.9**
Speed ratings (Par 101): **94,92,91,91,90 88,83,76,56,54 53,46**
toteswingers:1&2:£49.60, 2&3:£0.00, 1&3:£49.60 CSF £570.14 CT £10370.06 TOTE £60.60: £10.60, £3.90, £5.00; EX 238.90.
Owner S A Harris **Bred** Bryan Ryan **Trained** Carburton, Notts

FOCUS
A modest handicap and a surprise result but the form makes sense at face value.

1385 £32 FREE AT 32RED.COM MAIDEN STKS — 1m 2f 32y

5:00 (5:00) (Class 5) 3-Y-0+ — **£2,911** (£866; £432; £216) **Stalls** Centre

Form — RPR

5- **1** — **Gabrial The Great (IRE)**[199] 6447 3-8-9 0 ..... JamieSpencer 2 — 83
(Michael Bell) *sn chsng ldr: clr of rest after 4f: rdn: hung lft and led over 2f out: carried hd high: drvn clr fnl f* — **4/7**[1]

2- **2** 8 — **Widyaan (IRE)**[143] 7520 3-8-9 0 ..... (b[1]) PaulHanagan 4 — 72
(John Gosden) *t.k.h early: led: clr w wnr after 4f: hdd over 2f out: rallied: no ex fnl f: eased whn btn* — **7/2**[2]

3 7 — **Swinging Sultan**[55] 5-10-0 0 ..... PaulMulrennan 8 — 58
(Keith Reveley) *s.i.s: hld up: stdy hdwy to chse clr ldrs 4f out: no imp fnl 2f* — **7/1**[3]

0-0 **4** 2 ½ — **Mr Snoozy**[14] 1132 3-8-9 0 ..... GrahamGibbons 7 — 49
(Tim Walford) *t.k.h in rr: struggling 1/2-way: kpt on fnl 2f: nvr on terms* — **20/1**

04 **5** hd — **Sweet Vera**[7] 1223 7-9-9 0 ..... PaddyAspell 6 — 48
(Shaun Harris) *chsd ldng pair to 4f out: sn drvn and outpcd: n.d after* — **33/1**

6 4 ½ — **Cruachan (IRE)** 3-8-9 0 ..... TomEaves 1 — 40
(Ian Semple) *s.i.s: sn midfield: outpcd 1/2-way: n.d after* — **22/1**

7 27 — **Entihaa** 4-10-0 0 ..... PJMcDonald 3
(Alan Swinbank) *hld up in tch: struggling over 4f out: sn btn: t.o* — **18/1**

0-0 **8** 8 — **Penang Pegasus**[13] 1155 3-8-9 0 ..... RobertWinston 10
(David O'Meara) *t.k.h in rr: struggling 1/2-way: sn btn: t.o* — **18/1**

6/ **9** 85 — **Masra**[41] 6257 9-9-11 0 ..... LeeTopliss(3) 9
(David Thompson) *hld up: outpcd 1/2-way: sn btn: t.o* — **100/1**

2m 28.09s (16.19) **Going Correction** +1.475s/f (Soft)
WFA 3 from 4yo+ 19lb — **9** Ran SP% **121.9**
Speed ratings (Par 103): **94,87,82,80,79 76,54,48,**
toteswingers:1&2:£1.10, 2&3:£3.50, 1&3:£2.00 CSF £2.91 TOTE £1.70: £1.10, £1.10, £1.60; EX 2.20.
Owner Dr Marwan Koukash **Bred** Sarl Elevage Du Haras De Bourgeauville **Trained** Newmarket, Suffolk

FOCUS
An uncompetitive maiden, but this was harder work for Gabrial The Great than the winning margin suggests. The form is rated through the runner-up with doubts over the rest.
Masra Official explanation: vet said gelding finished distressed

1386 ST JAMES PLACE H'CAP — 1m 3y(S)

5:30 (5:30) (Class 6) (0-60,58) 3-Y-0 — **£2,070** (£616; £307; £153) **Stalls** Low

Form — RPR

006- **1** — **Kian's Joy**[163] 7240 3-8-8 **45** ..... BarryMcHugh 2 — 53
(Jedd O'Keeffe) *hld up: hdwy to ld over 2f out: sn rdn and rn green: edgd lft and kpt on wl ins fnl f* — **16/1**

300- **2** 1 ½ — **Rosie's Lady (IRE)**[193] 6611 3-9-0 **51** ..... RobertWinston 7 — 56
(David O'Meara) *w ldr: led briefly over 2f out: sn rdn and rallied: kpt on same pce ins fnl f* — **7/2**[3]

00-6 **3** ¾ — **Lady Kashaan (IRE)**[18] 1053 3-8-12 **49** ..... PJMcDonald 1 — 52
(Alan Swinbank) *prom: effrt and rdn over 2f out: kpt on ins fnl f* — **9/1**

0-06 **4** 12 — **Hurriya**[19] 1046 3-9-1 **52** ..... SilvestreDeSousa 3 — 28
(Mark Johnston) *led: rdn and hdd over 2f out: sn outpcd* — **12/5**[1]

614- **5** shd — **Red Tyke (IRE)**[163] 7242 3-9-0 **51** ..... TomEaves 6 — 26
(John Quinn) *prom: drvn and outpcd 3f out: n.d after* — **5/2**[2]

010- **6** 8 — **Lady Advocate (IRE)**[173] 7051 3-9-7 **58** ..... (b) DavidAllan 8 — 15
(Tim Easterby) *in tch: rdn and edgd towards stands' rail over 2f out: sn outpcd* — **9/1**

250- **7** 22 — **Champagne Valley**[193] 6611 3-9-3 **54** ..... AndrewMullen 4
(Sharon Watt) *in tch to 1/2-way: sn rdn and wknd: t.o* — **20/1**

00-0 **8** 1 ¾ — **Medam**[17] 1067 3-8-10 **47** ..... PaddyAspell 5
(Shaun Harris) *t.k.h: trckd ldrs tl rdn and wknd over 3f out: t.o* — **20/1**

1m 51.8s (8.40) **Going Correction** +0.80s/f (Soft) — **8** Ran SP% **115.6**
Speed ratings (Par 96): **90,88,87,75,75 67,45,43**
toteswingers:1&2:£20.00, 2&3:£6.70, 1&3:£20.00 CSF £72.19 CT £543.57 TOTE £23.30: £4.40, £1.80, £1.40; EX 310.00.
Owner Jenny & Ray Butler **Bred** Lady Herries **Trained** Middleham Moor, N Yorks

FOCUS
The first three finished well clear in this moderate handicap. The runner-up sets the level rated to the best of his juvenile form.
Kian's Joy ◆ Official explanation: trainer said, regarding apparent improvement in form, that the gelding had strengthened up having had a 163-day break.
Medam Official explanation: trainer said filly was unsuited by the soft (heavy in places) ground
T/Plt: £368.10 to a £1 stake. Pool of £57,665.33 - 114.35 winning tickets. T/Qpdt: £50.80 to a £1 stake. Pool of £3,669.59 - 53.40 winning tickets. RY

1359 **WOLVERHAMPTON (A.W)** (L-H)
Saturday, April 14

OFFICIAL GOING: Standard
Wind: Fresh, against Weather: Cloudy

1387 HIGH MOOR RACING SAYS THANKS - ALMATY EXPRESS H'CAP 5f 216y(P)
6:15 (6:15) (Class 6) (0-55,55) 4-Y-0+ **£2,070** (£616; £307; £153) **Stalls** Low

Form RPR
-044 **1** **Avonlini**[28] 938 6-8-7 **49** HarryBentley(3) 11 58
(Brian Baugh) *w ldr: rdn 2f out: led 1f out: hld on wl u.p* **16/1**
5646 **2** ½ **Anjomarba (IRE)**[29] 926 5-9-0 **53** LukeMorris 7 60
(Conor Dore) *chsd ldrs: blkd over 4f out: rdn over 2f out: chsd wnr ins fnl f: r.o* **17/2**
3352 **3** *hd* **Just Timmy Marcus**[29] 926 6-9-0 **53** RussKennemore 8 60
(Brian Baugh) *dwlt: sn in tch: rdn and hdwy over 1f out: kpt on ins fnl f* **8/1**
0-00 **4** 1 ¼ **Amno Dancer (IRE)**[29] 927 5-8-11 **50** FrederikTylicki 12 53
(Ian Semple) *trckd ldrs: effrt wl over 1f out: kpt on same pce ins fnl f* **25/1**
-401 **5** ½ **Almaty Express**[28] 939 10-9-2 **55** (b) KieranO'Neill 10 56
(John Weymes) *slt ld: rdn 2f out: hdd 1f out: sn no ex* **6/1**[2]
0643 **6** ½ **Cheery Cat (USA)**[24] 985 8-8-12 **51** (b) NeilChalmers 1 51
(Richard Ford) *in tch: effrt and rdn 2f out: kpt on ins fnl f* **16/1**
460- **7** *nk* **Perfect Honour (IRE)**[108] 7897 6-8-3 **49** DannyBrock(7) 2 48
(Des Donovan) *dwlt: hld up on ins: pushed along and hdwy over 1f out: nvr able to chal* **16/1**
0053 **8** *hd* **Memphis Man**[30] 912 9-9-2 **55** PadraigBeggy 4 53
(David Evans) *bhd: drvn along 1/2-way: hdwy fnl f: kpt on: nrst fin* **16/1**
0623 **9** 1 **Avonvalley**[17] 1070 5-9-1 **54** RobbieFitzpatrick 9 49
(Peter Grayson) *racd wd in midfield: drvn and c wd st: nvr rchd ldrs* **18/1**
061 **10** *nk* **Sabys Gem (IRE)**[28] 938 4-8-12 **51** (b) BrettDoyle 6 45
(Michael Wigham) *hld up: pushed along over 2f out: no imp over 1f out: eased whn hld ins fnl f* **3/1**[1]
16-2 **11** 2 ½ **Sleights Boy (IRE)**[28] 939 4-8-11 **53** (v) DeclanCannon(3) 3 39
(Ian McInnes) *prom: blkd on ins over 4f out: rdn and lost pl over 2f out: n.d after* **7/1**[3]
4560 **12** *shd* **Fantasy Fry**[4] 1283 4-8-13 **52** CathyGannon 5 37
(David Evans) *bhd: drvn and outpcd over 2f out: nvr on terms* **15/2**

1m 14.69s (-0.31) **Going Correction** +0.025s/f (Slow) **12** Ran SP% **117.8**
Speed ratings (Par 101): **103,102,102,100,99 99,98,98,97,96 93,93**
Tote Swingers: 1&2 £23.50, 1&3 £17.30, 2&3 £13.00 CSF £144.94 CT £1182.28 TOTE £22.60: £5.10, £2.00, £3.30; EX 115.50 TRIFECTA Not won..
Owner J H Chrimes **Bred** J H Chrimes **Trained** Audley, Staffs
■ Stewards' Enquiry : Kieran O'Neill three-day ban: careless riding (Apr 28,30,May 1)

FOCUS
Only a low-grade handicap but plenty came into the race in reasonable heart. That said, there was plenty of scrimmaging early with little getting into the race from behind. The form is rated around the placed horses.
Sleights Boy(IRE) Official explanation: jockey said gelding suffered interference shortly after start

1388 32RED.COM MAIDEN FILLIES' STKS 5f 20y(P)
6:45 (6:47) (Class 5) 2-Y-0 **£2,911** (£866; £432; £216) **Stalls** Low

Form RPR
5 **1** **Coconut Kisses**[7] 1211 2-9-0 0 KierenFallon 3 67
(Bill Turner) *mde all: shkn up and qcknd over 1f out: kpt on wl fnl f: unchal* **4/1**[3]
2 1 ½ **Back In The Frame** 2-9-0 0 RichardKingscote 4 62+
(Tom Dascombe) *s.i.s: bhd and outpcd: hdwy on ins to chse (clr) wnr ins fnl f: r.o* **4/1**[3]
3 2 ¼ **Lexi The Princess (IRE)** 2-9-0 0 JimmyFortune 2 54+
(Kevin Ryan) *s.i.s: rn green in rr: hdwy on outside over 1f out: kpt on fnl f: nt pce to chal* **10/3**[2]
4 **4** *shd* **Windsor Rose (IRE)**[10] 1188 2-9-0 0 TomMcLaughlin 5 53
(Mark Brisbourne) *sn pushed along: chsd wnr to over 1f out: sn outpcd* **22/1**
5 ½ **Until It Sleeps** 2-8-7 0 NoraLooby(7) 1 51
(Alan McCabe) *plld hrd: cl up: chsd wnr over 1f out to ins fnl f: sn outpcd* **33/1**
2 **6** 5 **Stripped Bear (IRE)**[4] 1277 2-9-0 0 StephenCraine 6 33
(Tom Dascombe) *unruly bef s and in stalls: fly j. s: in tch: drvn along 1/2-way: wknd wl over 1f out* **2/1**[1]
7 2 ¼ **Sixties Queen** 2-9-0 0 LiamJones 8 25
(Alan Bailey) *sn in tch: drvn along after 2f: hung lft and wknd fr 2f out* **14/1**
8 16 **Symphony Of Light** 2-8-11 0 RyanPowell(3) 7
(Dai Burchell) *missed break: a struggling: lost tch after 2f: t.o* **50/1**

1m 3.53s (1.23) **Going Correction** +0.025s/f (Slow) **8** Ran SP% **112.3**
Speed ratings (Par 89): **91,88,85,84,84 76,72,46**
Tote Swingers: 1&2 £4.00, 1&3 £4.30, 2&3 £3.10 CSF £19.45 TOTE £4.00: £1.30, £1.40, £1.10; EX 19.40 Trifecta £50.40 Pool: £328.06 - 4.81 winning units..
Owner P Venner **Bred** P And Mrs Venner And Trickledown Stud **Trained** Sigwells, Somerset

FOCUS
Probably just a fair maiden, but one run at a good pace. The winner's experience proved vital but the next two home are better longer-term prospects and should rate higher in time.

NOTEBOOK
Coconut Kisses had shown plenty of speed on her debut (fourth then has won well at Leicester since) and proved too professional for a couple that took a while to get the hang of things. She had the race won turning into the straight and looks a 5f performer through and through, though she'll be doing well to confirm form with the second and third again with the emphasis less on speed. (op 7-2 tchd 3-1 and 9-2)
Back In The Frame ◆ a £40,000 Dutch Art filly who is a half-sister to Coventry Stakes third St Barths, wasn't as strong in the market as her stable-companion but shaped well after taking a while to realise what was required, going on well close home under considerate handling. She should be up to winning a similar event next time. (tchd 7-2)
Lexi The Princess(IRE) is a 28,000gns yearling Super Sprint entry whose winning relations include the useful dual 5f 2-y-o winner Dozy She wasn't as sharp as that one (who won on her debut for the same yard) but she came home nicely widest of all and is sure to be a lot sharper next time. (op 9-2)
Windsor Rose(IRE) had clearly learned from her debut over C&D but only threatened briefly and probably needs dropping to claiming company. (op 25-1 tchd 28-1)
Until It Sleeps the first foal of a maiden who stayed 1m4f; couldn't find a buyer as a yearling but she travelled smoothly enough for the most part and looked to have a bit more ability than the result suggests. She might be worth looking out for if dropped in grade next time.
Stripped Bear(IRE) looked to set the standard on her Southwell debut second but she gave trouble beforehand as well as in the stalls and never looked happy. This clearly wasn't her running. (tchd 15-8 and 9-4)

1389 £32 FREE AT 32RED.COM MEDIAN AUCTION MAIDEN STKS 5f 20y(P)
7:15 (7:15) (Class 6) 3-4-Y-0 **£2,070** (£616; £307; £153) **Stalls** Low

Form RPR
2232 **1** **El McGlynn (IRE)**[16] 1090 3-8-10 62 LukeMorris 6 61
(John O'Shea) *in tch: hdwy over 1f out: led ins fnl f: rdn and r.o wl* **7/2**[3]
40- **2** ¾ **Kyllachy Dancer**[161] 7293 3-8-10 0 LiamKeniry 1 58
(John Quinn) *wnt rt s: cl up: effrt over 1f out: ev ch ent fnl f: kpt on: hld nr fin* **13/8**[1]
062 **3** 1 **Ozz**[15] 1111 3-8-10 0 (bt) CathyGannon 3 54
(Frank Sheridan) *trckd ldrs: effrt and rdn 2f out: kpt on same pce fnl f* **20/1**
353- **4** ½ **Missile Attack (IRE)**[182] 6874 4-9-12 59 FrederikTylicki 2 63
(Ian Semple) *led: rdn and hdd ins fnl f: edgd rt and kpt on same pce* **5/1**
634- **5** *nk* **Wiltshire Life (IRE)**[136] 7583 3-8-5 64 RaulDaSilva(5) 5 52
(Jeremy Gask) *prom on outside: effrt over 2f out: kpt on same pce fnl f* **3/1**[2]
56 **6** 2 **Demora**[47] 720 3-8-10 0 NeilChalmers 4 44
(Michael Appleby) *t.k.h: hld up in tch: rdn and outpcd after 2f: kpt on fnl f: nvr rchd ldrs* **28/1**

1m 2.37s (0.07) **Going Correction** +0.025s/f (Slow)
WFA 3 from 4yo 11lb **6** Ran SP% **110.2**
Speed ratings (Par 101): **100,98,97,96,95 92**
Tote Swingers: 1&2 £1.10, 1&3 £4.50, 2&3 £14.20 CSF £9.26 TOTE £3.90: £1.40, £1.10; EX 8.90.
Owner Michael G McGlynn **Bred** Michael Lyons Jnr **Trained** Elton, Gloucs

FOCUS
A weak maiden with the bunch finish rather underlining it didn't take much winning. The pace only really picked up shortly before halfway. The third and fourth are the best guide to the level.

1390 BRINDLEY HONDA FLEET H'CAP 1m 4f 50y(P)
7:45 (7:45) (Class 5) (0-70,70) 3-Y-0 **£2,911** (£866; £432; £216) **Stalls** Low

Form RPR
2121 **1** **Gabrial's King (IRE)**[67] 466 3-9-0 **63** JimmyFortune 2 69+
(Ian Williams) *hld up in 3rd: waited for split between rivals 2f out: led 1f out: rdn clr* **1/1**[1]
6523 **2** 2 ¾ **King's Wharf (IRE)**[10] 1192 3-9-3 **66** PadraigBeggy 4 67
(David Evans) *t.k.h: sn led: set modest pce: qcknd 4f out: drvn along over 2f out: hdd 1f out: sn outpcd* **9/1**
221 **3** 2 ¾ **Za'Lan (USA)**[43] 762 3-9-7 **70** KierenFallon 1 67
(Mark Johnston) *pressed ldr tl no ex appr fnl f* **11/4**[2]
-621 **4** 7 **Excellent News (IRE)**[23] 998 3-9-5 **68** SebSanders 3 53
(J W Hills) *stdd s: plld hrd in last: effrt and hrd rdn 3f out: wknd wl over 1f out* **7/2**[3]

2m 49.3s (8.20) **Going Correction** +0.025s/f (Slow) **4** Ran SP% **108.9**
Speed ratings (Par 98): **73,71,69,64**
CSF £9.66 TOTE £1.80; EX 11.30.
Owner Dr Marwan Koukash **Bred** Danella Partnership **Trained** Portway, Worcs

FOCUS
Two regular front runners in opposition but neither really wanted to press on and that turned what was promised to be an interesting handicap into an unsatisfactory game of cat and mouse. The runner-up is the best guide to the level.

1391 32RED H'CAP 1m 1f 103y(P)
8:15 (8:15) (Class 5) (0-70,68) 4-Y-0+ **£2,911** (£866; £432; £216) **Stalls** Low

Form RPR
066- **1** **Aldedash (USA)**[226] 5641 4-9-7 **68** KierenFallon 1 78
(James Fanshawe) *hld up in 5th: rdn 3f out: wnt 2nd 2f out: led over 1f out: rdn clr* **2/1**[1]
1011 **2** 2 ½ **St Ignatius**[32] 884 5-8-10 **64** NatashaEaton(7) 8 69
(Alan Bailey) *t.k.h: prom: rdn and lost pl over 2f out: rallied over 1f out: kpt on same pce* **11/1**
-065 **3** *shd* **Kyle Of Bute**[30] 909 6-9-0 **61** CathyGannon 5 66
(Brian Baugh) *dwlt: hld up in rr: rdn and hdwy over 1f out: styd on fnl f* **13/2**
6533 **4** 1 ¼ **Fibs And Flannel**[15] 1108 5-9-1 **62** JamieMackay 4 65
(Willie Musson) *hld up towards rr: hdwy on ins rail ent st: n.m.r and one pce fnl f* **13/2**
3052 **5** *hd* **Black Coffee**[16] 1094 7-9-4 **65** (b) ShaneKelly 2 67
(Mark Brisbourne) *hld up in rr: struggling to stay in tch 2f out: sme late hdwy* **6/1**[3]
3261 **6** 7 **McCool Bannanas**[23] 1002 4-9-7 **68** LiamJones 7 55
(James Unett) *plld hrd: chsd ldrs: rn wd bnd 7f out: led 4f out tl wknd over 1f out* **11/2**[2]
604- **7** 3 ¼ **Spirit Of Gondree (IRE)**[199] 6468 4-9-2 **63** RichardKingscote 9 43
(Milton Bradley) *led 2f: chsd ldr and plld hrd: lost 2nd 2f out: wknd over 1f out* **16/1**
6446 **8** 2 **Valley Tiger**[23] 1000 4-8-13 **60** JimmyFortune 3 36
(Richard Fahey) *t.k.h: led after 2f tl 4f out: wknd over 1f out* **8/1**

2m 2.35s (0.65) **Going Correction** +0.025s/f (Slow) **8** Ran SP% **115.0**
Speed ratings (Par 103): **98,95,95,94,94 88,85,83**
Tote Swingers: 1&2 £13.00, 1&3 £7.40, 2&3 £13.80 CSF £26.03 CT £122.22 TOTE £1.90: £1.50, £3.00, £1.80; EX 28.80 TRIFECTA Not won..
Owner Axom (XXVII) **Bred** Morgan's Ford Farm **Trained** Newmarket, Suffolk
■ Stewards' Enquiry : Natasha Eaton caution: careless riding.

FOCUS
Just a fair handicap but the winner looked a cut above the opposition and could yet go on to better things. The gallop was steady and several pulled their chance away. The form is limited, with the third the best guide.
McCool Bannanas Official explanation: jockey said gelding ran too free

1392 BUY YOUR CIVIC FROM BRINDLEY HONDA H'CAP 7f 32y(P)
8:45 (8:46) (Class 5) (0-75,75) 3-Y-0 **£2,911** (£866; £432; £216) **Stalls** High

Form RPR
21- **1** **Haaf A Sixpence**[140] 7559 3-9-7 **75** JimCrowley 2 82
(Ralph Beckett) *in tch: effrt on ins rail and rdn to ld 1f out: jst hld on* **7/2**[3]
051- **2** *nk* **Johnno**[166] 7197 3-9-7 **75** SebSanders 10 83+
(J W Hills) *hld up in rr: effrt on outer 3f out: str run fnl f: clsng at fin* **11/4**[1]
0112 **3** ½ **Homeward Strut**[43] 764 3-8-3 **62** (b) RaulDaSilva(5) 9 67
(Frank Sheridan) *broke best: trckd ldr and t.k.h: chal ins fnl f: kpt on* **14/1**
065- **4** 1 ½ **Raffinn**[196] 6539 3-8-12 **66** LiamKeniry 7 67
(Sylvester Kirk) *t.k.h in rr: rdn and hdwy over 1f out: styd on fnl f* **25/1**
05-0 **5** *nk* **Stellar Express (IRE)**[37] 841 3-9-0 **75** JackDuern(7) 1 75
(Michael Appleby) *sn led: hdd and no ex 1f out* **20/1**

313 **6** 1 ½ **Bint Alzain (IRE)**[29] 917 3-9-3 71........................... LukeMorris 4 67
(Gerard Butler) *trckd ldrs and gng wl tl rdn and wknd jst over 1f out* **7/1**

12 **7** nk **Alkadi (IRE)**[6] 1241 3-9-3 71.. KierenFallon 5 66
(Mark Johnston) *chsd ldrs: rdn over 2f out: sn outpcd* **3/1**[2]

1312 **8** ¾ **Speedy Yaki (IRE)**[57] 605 3-9-5 73...........................(bt) ShaneKelly 6 66
(Daniel Mark Loughnane) *hld up towards rr: hrd rdn 2f out: n.d* **14/1**

250- **9** 3 ¼ **Silvas Romana (IRE)**[161] 7294 3-9-4 72.................. TomMcLaughlin 3 57
(Mark Brisbourne) *mid-div: rdn over 3f out: wknd over 2f out* **28/1**

306- **10** 1 ½ **Purley Queen (IRE)**[143] 7514 3-8-5 62...................... SophieDoyle(3) 8 42
(Sylvester Kirk) *a bhd* **28/1**

1m 28.8s (-0.80) **Going Correction** +0.025s/f (Slow) **10** Ran SP% **115.2**
Speed ratings (Par 98): **105,104,104,102,102 100,99,99,95,93**
Tote Swingers: 1&2 £3.30, 1&3 £6.90, 2&3 £10.60 CSF £12.64 CT £117.25 TOTE £5.60: £1.60, £2.10, £5.40; EX 16.00 Trifecta £102.20 Pool: £364.92 - 2.64 winning units..
Owner Melody Racing **Bred** Melody Bloodstock **Trained** Kimpton, Hants

FOCUS
Quite an interesting handicap but it again turned into something of tactical affair on account of a less-than-true gallop which was ultimately the difference between a narrow defeat and a cosy win for the eventual runner-up, who might have been a little unlucky.

1393 32RED CASINO H'CAP 5f 20y(P)
9:15 (9:15) (Class 6) (0-65,65) 3-Y-O **£2,070** (£616; £307; £153) **Stalls** Low

Form RPR
2133 **1** **J J Leary (IRE)**[17] 1063 3-8-13 57............................(b[1]) JimmyFortune 3 64
(Ian Williams) *mde all: drvn to hold on fnl f* **6/1**[3]

321 **2** ¾ **Ring For Baileys**[16] 1089 3-8-13 62........................... RaulDaSilva(5) 2 66
(Chris Dwyer) *trckd ldng pair: rdn to chal 1f out: kpt on u.p* **6/5**[1]

50-1 **3** 1 **Persidha**[22] 1006 3-9-6 64..(v) JimCrowley 1 64
(Derek Shaw) *hld up in last: hdwy and hrd rdn over 1f out: kpt on* **3/1**[2]

1651 **4** 1 ¾ **Tiablo (IRE)**[28] 940 3-9-6 64.................................... CathyGannon 4 58
(David Evans) *trckd ldr: rdn 2f out: sn outpcd* **9/1**

5201 **5** 2 **Chateau Lola**[31] 898 3-8-8 52.....................................(v) MartinLane 5 39
(Derek Shaw) *dwlt: hld up in 4th: hrd rdn and btn over 1f out* **6/1**[3]

1m 2.4s (0.10) **Going Correction** +0.025s/f (Slow) **5** Ran SP% **109.0**
Speed ratings (Par 96): **100,98,97,94,91**
CSF £13.55 TOTE £5.30: £3.00, £1.70; EX 8.60.
Owner Dr Marwan Koukash **Bred** Con Marnane **Trained** Portway, Worcs

FOCUS
Four last-time-out winners in opposition but that doesn't mean it's strong form and it went to the one that wasn't. The winner improved on previous form with the third slightly below her latest mark.
T/Plt: £156.60 to a £1 stake. Pool: £66,975.75 - 2.64 winning tickets. T/Qpdt: £10.20 to a £1 stake. Pool: £7,684.72 - 553.58 winning tickets. RY

1394 - 1400a (Foreign Racing) - See Raceform Interactive

1075 LEOPARDSTOWN (L-H)
Sunday, April 15

OFFICIAL GOING: Good

1401a LEOPARDSTOWN 2,000 GUINEAS TRIAL STKS (GROUP 3) (C&G) 1m
2:55 (2:55) 3-Y-O **£25,729** (£7,520; £3,562; £1,187)

RPR
1 **Furner's Green (IRE)**[18] 1077 3-9-3 110.......................... JPO'Brien 4 107+
(A P O'Brien, Ire) *trckd ldr in 3rd: prog early st and chal 1f out whn struck on hd by rival's whip: sn led and kpt on wl* **4/6**[1]

2 2 ¾ **Akeed Wafi (IRE)**[204] 6365 3-9-3 .... JohnnyMurtagh 1 101
(John M Oxx, Ire) *trckd ldr in 2nd: hdwy to chal early st and led under 2f out: strly pressed and hdd ins fnl f: no imp on wnr* **7/4**[2]

3 4 ½ **Vault (IRE)**[18] 1077 3-9-3 97...............................(b[1]) SeamieHeffernan 3 91
(A P O'Brien, Ire) *led: strly pressed early st and hdd under 2f out: sn dropped to 3rd and no ex fnl f* **16/1**[3]

4 3 ¾ **Tiger At Heart (IRE)** 3-9-3 .... KevinManning 2 82?
(J S Bolger, Ire) *dwlt and settled in rr: pushed along appr st and sn no imp: no threat fr 2f out* **16/1**[3]

1m 41.97s (0.77) **Going Correction** +0.30s/f (Good) **4** Ran SP% **108.1**
Speed ratings: **108,105,100,97**
CSF £2.06 TOTE £1.40; DF 1.30.
Owner Derrick Smith **Bred** Whisperview Trading Ltd **Trained** Ballydoyle, Co Tipperary

FOCUS
With just four runners, tactics were always going play a crucial part in this Guineas trial. The winner did it well.

NOTEBOOK
Furner's Green(IRE) benefited most when coming off a decent pace. Ballydoyle were responsible for two runners and outsider Vault broke smartly to set a decent pace. It looked briefly like a good race would develop when the runner-up hit the front. However, when Joseph O'Brien asked the favourite to quicken he duly raised his game and settled the race in a matter of strides after receiving an accidental crack to his head from the whip of the runner-up's rider. While Aidan O'Brien didn't nominate his next target he clearly likes this son of Dylan Thomas and said a Guineas followed by the French Derby was in his mind for the colt. (op 8/13)
Akeed Wafi(IRE) had shown improvement from his eyecatching course debut effort to win his maiden at Gowran last September. He was fancied to make the favourite work but after taking over from the pacemaker in the straight he was soon struggling when more was needed. He should be sharper with this seasonal debut effort behind him. (op 7/4 tchd 6/4)
Vault(IRE) did his job well ensuring a descent gallop.
Tiger At Heart(IRE) was easy to back. The son of Teofilo, out of a half-sister to Mr Greeley, was settled at the rear and never looked like imposing his presence when the race unfolded. He should be more competitive when his sights are lowered. (op 12/1)

1403a LEOPARDSTOWN 1,000 GUINEAS TRIAL STKS (GROUP 3) (FILLIES) 7f
4:00 (4:01) 3-Y-O **£25,729** (£7,520; £3,562; £1,187)

RPR
1 **Homecoming Queen (IRE)**[21] 1041 3-9-0 105............ CO'Donoghue 1 109
(A P O'Brien, Ire) *mde all: rdn early st and strly pressed fr 1f out: kpt on best u.p fnl 100yds* **8/1**

2 nk **Fire Lily (IRE)**[196] 6564 3-9-0 111.............................. WayneLordan 6 108+
(David Wachman, Ire) *settled on outer in 7th: sme hdwy into 5th appr st: gd prog to chal 1f out: rdn and nt match wnr fnl 100yds* **7/4**[1]

3 ¾ **Up (IRE)**[11] 1195 3-9-0 107.. JPO'Brien 8 106+
(A P O'Brien, Ire) *hld up towards rr: last and rdn 2f out: hdwy on outer fr over 1f out: kpt on ins fnl f wout rching first 2* **9/2**[2]

4 ¾ **Remember Alexander**[203] 6389 3-9-0 105.................. ShaneFoley 3 104
(Mrs John Harrington, Ire) *trckd ldr in 3rd: 2nd and rdn 2f out: no imp in 4th fnl f: kpt on one pce* **13/2**

5 nse **After (IRE)**[203] 6389 3-9-0 99.. SeamieHeffernan 5 104+
(A P O'Brien, Ire) *towards rr: rdn ent st and sme hdwy over 1f out: wnt 5th ins fnl f and kpt on same pce* **25/1**

6 1 ¾ **Rubina (IRE)**[217] 5974 3-9-0 105..............................(t) JohnnyMurtagh 9 99
(John M Oxx, Ire) *trckd ldr in 2nd: 3rd and rdn 2f out: no ex fnl f* **8/1**

7 nk **Janey Muddles (IRE)**[21] 1041 3-9-0 100..................... KevinManning 2 98
(J S Bolger, Ire) *mid-div on inner: 6th 1/2-way: no imp fr over 1f out* **10/1**

8 hd **Bulbul (IRE)**[182] 6897 3-9-0 .... DeclanMcDonogh 7 98
(Kevin Prendergast, Ire) *trckd ldrs in 4th racing keenly: rdn early st and 3rd over 1f out: no ex ins fnl f: wknd* **5/1**[3]

9 2 **Ishvana (IRE)**[21] 1042 3-9-0 97.. PatSmullen 4 93
(A P O'Brien, Ire) *mid-div: 7th ent st: sn dropped to rr and no ex* **12/1**

1m 30.98s (2.28) **Going Correction** +0.425s/f (Yiel) **9** Ran SP% **127.4**
Speed ratings: **103,102,101,100,100 98,98,98,96**
CSF £24.87 TOTE £12.50: £3.40, £1.30, £1.50; DF 55.50.
Owner Mrs John Magnier & Michael Tabor & Derrick Smith **Bred** Tower Bloodstock **Trained** Ballydoyle, Co Tipperary

FOCUS
The winner, who ran a lot at two, is rated to her best.

NOTEBOOK
Homecoming Queen(IRE) had a very busy juvenile campaign and made her eighth start when winning a nursery at Fairyhouse off a mark of 72. She was subsequently placed at Group 3 level and was successful in a Listed event at the Curragh before finishing in rear at the Breeders' Cup (slowly into stride). She was having her second run of the season here and, with front-running tactics again employed, she saw off her rivals after setting a moderate pace. She quickened early in the straight and won despite edging right under pressure inside the final furlong. A tough and genuine type, she hardly figures among her trainer's better three-year-old fillies, although she will be allowed to take her chance at Group 1 level next time. Official explanation: trainer said, regarding the apparent improvement in form shown, that filly was having its first outing of the year at The Curragh last time and that it was over 1m on slower ground; he reported that filly became very tired late on in that race over the trip on that ground but that today it had obviously improved for having its first run of the season (op 12/1)
Fire Lily(IRE), a winner at Group 3 level and with solid Group 1 form in the book having run second in both the Moyglare Stud Stakes and the Prix Marcel Boussac, looked the likely winner when arriving with her effort over 1f out. Soon vying for the lead, she briefly edged right away from the whip and could raise no extra towards the finish. (op 7/4 tchd 15/8)
Up(IRE), fourth in the Breeders' Cup Juvenile Fillies in November, had finished second when odds-on in a four-runner event at Dundalk on her reappearance 11 days previously. Held up in rear, she had work to do when the tempo increased early in the straight and ran on quite well, giving the impression that there will be better to come when she goes back up in trip. (op 5/1)
Remember Alexander had a Group 3 win at this trip over Dewhurst Stakes winner Parish Hall to her credit last season before failing to build on that form on her two subsequent starts. Always close up, she failed to quicken when the pace increased but kept on to the line. She can improve. (op 8/1 tchd 6/1)
After(IRE), another of the Aidan O'Brien-trained quartet, a maiden winner over 6f, had been a shade disappointing after running second to Fire Lily in the Group 3 Anglesey Stakes. She made headway from behind and can be expected to come on from the run.

1404a P.W. MCGRATH MEMORIAL BALLYSAX STKS (GROUP 3) 1m 2f
4:35 (4:35) 3-Y-O **£25,729** (£7,520; £3,562; £1,187)

RPR
1 **Light Heavy (IRE)**[18] 1077 3-9-3 ....(tp) KevinManning 2 113+
(J S Bolger, Ire) *trckd ldrs in 3rd: hdwy in st to chal and led 1f out: rdn to assert and styd on wl: comf* **3/1**[3]

2 2 ½ **Call To Battle (IRE)**[161] 7320 3-9-3 105...................... JohnnyMurtagh 5 108+
(John M Oxx, Ire) *settled in 6th on outer: rdn in 5th ent st: kpt on u.p to go 2nd wl ins fnl f* **2/1**[2]

3 1 ½ **Tower Rock (IRE)**[161] 7320 3-9-3 101....................... SeamieHeffernan 1 105
(A P O'Brien, Ire) *trckd ldr in 2nd: drvn along ent st: no imp on wnr ins fnl f and dropped to 3rd clsng stages* **20/1**

4 1 ¾ **Athens (IRE)**[203] 6391 3-9-3 98...................................... CO'Donoghue 7 101
(A P O'Brien, Ire) *led: rdn ent st: strly pressed and hdd 1f out: no ex* **12/1**

5 nse **David Livingston (IRE)**[203] 6391 3-9-8 114....................... JPO'Brien 4 106
(A P O'Brien, Ire) *settled in 4th: pushed along ent st: no imp in 5th over 1f out: kpt on one pce* **7/4**[1]

6 ½ **Hit The Jackpot (IRE)**[18] 1077 3-9-3 94............................ PatSmullen 6 100
(D K Weld, Ire) *chsd ldrs: 6th 1/2-way: rdn along appr st: kpt on one pce u.p in st* **12/1**

7 13 **While You Wait (IRE)**[168] 7185 3-9-3 .... RoryCleary 3 74
(J S Bolger, Ire) *a in rr: drvn along sn after 1/2-way and lost tch bef st* **40/1**

2m 8.04s (-0.16) **Going Correction** +0.30s/f (Good) **7** Ran SP% **117.3**
Speed ratings: **112,110,108,107,107 106,96**
CSF £9.88 TOTE £3.40: £1.50, £1.80; DF 9.70.
Owner Mrs J S Bolger **Bred** J S Bolger **Trained** Coolcullen, Co Carlow

FOCUS
Former winners of this Derby trial include Galileo, High Chaparral, Yeats and Fame And Glory. The race produced another potential star when the winner supplemented his recent course win in a good time.

NOTEBOOK
Light Heavy(IRE) supplemented his recent course win. Successful in a conditions race over C&D last month, he was settled in third here as a good pace was set up front. He picked up admirably when they straightened for home to lead a furlong out and saw the trip out well. He was cut to 12-1 (from 50) for the Investec Derby but he doesn't hold an entry for the Epsom Classic and his trainer said the Irish equivalent would be his big-race target in June. He is going the right way and is clearly well regarded by his trainer. (op 5/2)
Call To Battle(IRE) was backed to make a winning start to his season. A dual winner last term, the Eyrefield Stakes winner over a furlong shorter last November galloped to the line but never looked like reeling in the winner. (op 5/2)
Tower Rock(IRE) finished best of the Ballydoyle trio. Winner of a 1m Navan maiden winner in soft ground last October, he finished behind the runner-up in Listed company here on his final start last season. This was a pleasing return and improvement is expected.
Athens(IRE) reversed form with the disappointing David Livingston.
David Livingston(IRE) was the principal stable fancy. The manner of his all-the-way Beresford Stakes victory over odds-on Akeed Mofeed last September looked solid but he was held up here. He had a bit to do in these underfoot conditions but failed to quicken when asked and his rider soon accepted the situation. (op 7/4 tchd 6/4)
Hit The Jackpot(IRE) never looked like getting involved. (op 12/1 tchd 11/1)
While You Wait(IRE), stablemate of the winner, was beaten before halfway.

1402 - 1406a (Foreign Racing) - See Raceform Interactive

[1243]LONGCHAMP (R-H)

Sunday, April 15

OFFICIAL GOING: Turf: good to soft

1407a PRIX DE LA GROTTE (GROUP 3) (3YO FILLIES) (TURF) 1m

2:40 (12:00) 3-Y-0 **£33,333** (£13,333; £10,000; £6,666; £3,333)

RPR

1 **Beauty Parlour**[198] 3-9-0 0 ChristopheSoumillon 3 114+
(E Lellouche, France) *settled in 4th: mde smooth prog to chal for ld over 1 1/2f out: tk ld 1f out: sn wnt clr: comf* **2/1**[1]

2 4 1/2 **Woven Lace**[24] 3-9-0 0 MaximeGuyon 1 104
(A Fabre, France) *settled in 2nd: rdn 2f out: tk ld 1 1/2f out: hdd 1f out: styd on wl* **6/1**

3 2 **Miss Carmie (FR)**[27] 3-9-0 0 ThierryJarnet 2 99
(Mlle S-V Tarrou, France) *settled towards rr: u.p ent st: r.o wl fr 1 1/2f out: got up for 3rd cl home* **25/1**

4 hd **Mandistana (FR)**[168] 3-9-0 0 Christophe-PatriceLemaire 6 99
(A De Royer-Dupre, France) *settled in 3rd: rdn 1 1/2f out: no ex: styd on one pce fnl f: lost 3rd cl home* **7/2**[3]

5 1 3/4 **Kendam (FR)**[19] 1059 3-9-0 0 MickaelBarzalona 7 95
(H-A Pantall, France) *settled towards rr: wnt 4th early in st: styd on fnl f* **14/1**

6 nk **Zantenda**[196] 6564 3-9-0 0 OlivierPeslier 4 94
(F Head, France) *sn led: hdd over 1 1/2f out: rdn but no ex: styd on* **11/4**[2]

7 1 1/2 **Rajastani (IRE)**[180] 6941 3-9-0 0 StephanePasquier 5 90
(S Wattel, France) *settled in rr: rdn but no ex fr 1 1/2f out: styd on* **12/1**

1m 37.82s (-0.58) **Going Correction** +0.075s/f (Good) **7 Ran SP% 114.7**
Speed ratings: **105,100,98,98,96 96,94**
WIN (incl. 1 euro stake): 2.50. PLACES: 1.70, 3.00. SF: 13.20.
Owner Ecurie Wildenstein **Bred** Dayton Investments Ltd **Trained** Lamorlaye, France

FOCUS
The winning time was 2.91sec quicker than the colts' trial that followed. The race has been rated based on the average rating for placed horses in this race.

NOTEBOOK
Beauty Parlour, who won both her starts in conditions races at two by lengthy margins, made an impressive return to action, pulling right away in the closing stages to win easily. Her trainer desribed her as "something out of the ordinary" and on this evidence she's going to be hard to beat in the Pouliches, while her pedigree suggests that the Prix de Diane trip will, if anything, be even more to her liking.
Woven Lace justified being supplemented into this on the back of an AW maiden win, although she had no chance with the easy winner.
Miss Carmie(FR) looks to have run up to her best in picking up pieces late and taking third without ever threatening the first two.
Mandistana(FR), a five-length winner of her maiden last back-end, was a shade disappointing, but she has a middle-distance pedigree (by Azamour out of a 1m4f Group 3 winning mare) and ought to do better when upped in distance.
Zantenda, third in the Marcel Boussac, took them along but dropped out rather disappointingly inside the final 2f. It could be that she'll be a sprinter this term, but at the moment there has to be a question about whether she has trained on.

1408a PRIX DE FONTAINEBLEAU (GROUP 3) (3YO COLTS) (TURF) 1m

3:10 (12:00) 3-Y-0 **£33,333** (£13,333; £10,000; £6,666; £3,333)

RPR

1 **Dragon Pulse (IRE)**[218] 5951 3-9-2 0 GregoryBenoist 6 116
(M Delzangles, France) *settled in 5th: picked up wl u.p fr 1 1/2f out: r.o strly fnl 100yds: got up on line* **9/2**[3]

2 shd **Dabirsim (FR)**[196] 6565 3-9-2 0 ChristopheSoumillon 4 116+
(C Ferland, France) *racd in 4th on outer pulling hrd: cruised to ld 1f out: sn clr: u.p 50yds out: r.o: ct on line* **4/6**[1]

3 2 1/2 **Sofast (FR)**[196] 6565 3-9-2 0 OlivierPeslier 1 110
(F Head, France) *sn led: rdn 2f out: hdd 1f out: r.o wl fnl f* **4/1**[2]

4 1 1/4 **Vaniloquio (IRE)**[31] 914 3-9-2 0 Christophe-PatriceLemaire 2 107
(N Clement, France) *settled in cl 2nd on outer of ldr: rdn over 1 1/2f out: no ex: styd on fnl f* **20/1**

5 2 1/2 **Historic Find**[164] 3-9-2 0 MaximeGuyon 3 101
(A Fabre, France) *settled in cl 3rd on rail: rdn over 1 1/2f out: nt qckn: styd on fnl f* **10/1**

6 4 **Coup De Theatre (FR)**[19] 1060 3-9-2 0 RonanThomas 5 92
(P Van De Poele, France) *settled in rr: rdn early in st: no ex: nvr a factor* **14/1**

1m 40.73s (2.33) **Going Correction** +0.075s/f (Good) **6 Ran SP% 118.7**
Speed ratings: **91,90,88,87,84 80**
WIN (incl. 1 euro stake): 7.90. PLACES: 2.10, 1.20. SF: 16.50.
Owner Tan Kai Chah **Bred** J F Tuthill & Mrs A W F Whitehead **Trained** France

FOCUS
The winning time was slow, 2.91sec off that which the fillies recorded in the Prix de la Grotte earlier on the card. Nevertheless, the first two are Group 1 class and the winner has been rated to his mark.

NOTEBOOK
Dragon Pulse(IRE) had some smart form in Ireland last season when trained by Jessica Harrington, including finshing runner-up to Power in the National Stakes on his last start. Making his debut for Mikael Delzangles, he settled well in rear but looked to have little chance of picking up the eventual runner-up when brought wide with his challenge in the straight. He quickened up impressively, seeing out every inch of the 1m, to put his head in front on the line. He's 16-1 for the 2,000 Guineas, and would warrant plenty of respect if travelling over, but connections seem inclined to keep him at home, and he's likely to have his work cut out confirming form with the runner-up in the Poulains.
Dabirsim(FR), Europe's joint-champion juvenile, on the back of an unbeaten campaign that included successes in the Morny and Jean Luc Lagardere, was keen under restraint attempting 1m for the first time. He hit the front swinging on the bridle, with Christophe Soumillon (partnering the horse for the first time) taking several looks over his shoulders. Unfortunately he took too long to spot the winner over his left shoulder and once he realised the danger and brought his mount under pressure, there was insufficient response to hold on. He has clearly trained on well and whether kept at this trip for the Poulains (still his intended target) or dropped back to sprinting, he will be a horse that lights up this season.
Sofast(FR), runner-up to Dabirsim in the Lagardere, looked fit for this return to action. He raced prominently but couldn't quicken with the front pair. Perhaps a further step up in trip will see him in a better light, but he was comprehensively beaten here.
Historic Find Off the mark at just the second attempt for Andre Fabre over 1m at Saint-cloud (heavy ground); well held but some late progress on return to action in Longchamp Group 3 in April 2012; longer trips may well suit.

CAPANNELLE (R-H)

Sunday, April 15

OFFICIAL GOING: Turf: heavy

1409a PREMIO CARLO CHIESA (GROUP 3) (3YO+ FILLIES AND MARES) (TURF) 6f

3:50 (12:00) 3-Y-0+ **£23,333** (£10,266; £5,600; £2,800)

RPR

1 **Noble Hachy**[28] 3-8-5 0 CristianDemuro 3 98
(L Riccardi, Italy) *midfield: impr to trck ldrs gng wl 3f out: shkn up to chal 2f out: rdn to ld jst ins fnl f: r.o* **19/20**[1]

2 1 1/2 **Malikayah (IRE)**[28] 4-9-3 0 SSulas 8 96
(D Camuffo, Italy) *prom on outer: prog to chal gng wl over 2f out: sn led: hdd jst ins fnl f: nt pce of wnr fnl 150yds: kpt on* **45/1**

3 3 **Adamantina**[175] 4-9-3 0 CColombi 2 87
(E Botti, Italy) *midfield on inner: rdn to try and improve over 2f out: outpcd over 1 1/2f out: r.o to go 3rd ins fnl 100yds: no ch w ldng pair* **18/5**[2]

4 1/2 **Bettolle (ITY)**[126] 3-8-5 0 CDiStasio 7 82
(P Cadeddu, Italy) *pressed ldr: briefly led 2 1/2f out: rdn and hdd over 2f out: kpt on one pce fnl 1 1/2f: lost 3rd fnl 100yds* **28/1**

5 2 **Extra (ITY)**[21] 4-9-3 0 PAragoni 9 79
(L Riccardi, Italy) *midfield on outer: rdn to try and chal over 1 1/2f out: outpcd over 1f out: kpt on ins fnl f* **119/10**

6 1 **Star Kodiak (IRE)**[175] 3-8-5 0 APolli 5 72
(A Di Dio, Italy) *led: rdn 3f out: hdd 2 1/2f out: no ex over 1f out: fdd ins fnl f* **56/10**[3]

7 4 **Golconde (IRE)**[25] 3-8-5 0 DarioVargiu 12 60
(G Botti, Italy) *towards rr: rdn and outpcd 2 1/2f out: plugged on ins fnl 1 1/2f* **32/5**

8 2 1/2 **Lady Story (IRE)**[204] 6371 3-8-5 0 SDiana 6 52
(Giuseppe Ligas, Italy) *midfield: rdn over 2f out: no ex ins fnl f: fdd* **50/1**

9 8 **Belly To Belly (IRE)**[175] 3-8-6 0 FabioBranca 11 27
(S Botti, Italy) *hld up in last pair: rdn to try and improve on wd outside over 2f out: no ex and qckly btn over 1f out: eased: t.o* **6/1**

10 3 1/2 **Desert Version**[28] 4-9-3 0 GBietolini 1 18
(S Botti, Italy) *prom early: rdn and lost pl over 2f out: sn wknd: eased whn btn: t.o* **6/1**

11 hd **Rebecca Wawa** 3-8-6 0 CFiocchi 4 15
(Manila Illuminati, Italy) *a towards rr: nvr a factor: t.o* **196/10**

12 2 **Ami Ami Chair**[539] 4-9-3 0 GMarcelli 10 11
(D Ducci, Italy) *prom on outer: rdn and wknd fr over 2f out: eased wl over 1f out: t.o* **90/1**

1m 10.5s (0.20)
WFA 3 from 4yo 12lb **12 Ran SP% 151.5**
WIN (incl. 1 euro stake): 1.95. PLACES: 1.37, 4.27, 1.72. DF: 32.94.
Owner Allevamento La Nuova Sbarra **Bred** Allavemento La Nuova Sbarra **Trained** Italy

DUSSELDORF (R-H)

Sunday, April 15

OFFICIAL GOING: Turf: soft

1410a FRUHJAHRS-MEILE-PREIS DER BESITZERVEREINIGUNG (GROUP 3) (4YO+) (TURF) 1m

4:00 (12:00) 4-Y-0+

£26,666 (£9,166; £4,583; £2,500; £1,666; £1,250)

RPR

1 **Alianthus (GER)**[175] 7048 7-9-4 0 ADeVries 1 116
(J Hirschberger, Germany) *mde all: rdn to extend advantage 2f out: kpt on wl ins fnl 1 1/2f: being clsd down at fin* **1/2**[1]

2 1/2 **Indomito (GER)**[161] 7323 6-9-0 0 EFrank 4 111
(A Wohler, Germany) *towards rr on inner: swtchd to outer and rdn to try and improve over 2f out: r.o to go 2nd ins fnl f: clsng at fin* **16/1**

3 3 1/2 **Empire Storm (GER)**[175] 7048 5-9-0 0 EPedroza 7 103
(A Wohler, Germany) *midfield on outer: rdn over 2f out: kpt on one pce fr over 1 1/2f out: wnt 3rd fnl 50yds* **48/10**[2]

4 nk **Neatico (GER)**[154] 7409 5-9-0 0 AStarke 2 102
(P Schiergen, Germany) *midfield on inner: rdn on turn into st: kpt on one pce ins fnl 2f: lost 3rd fnl 50yds* **56/10**[3]

5 2 1/2 **Sanjii Danon (GER)**[273] 4138 6-8-11 0 APietsch 3 94
(G Geisler, France) *hld up in last: prog on outer on turn into st: rdn over 2f out: kpt on one pce fnl 1 1/2f: wnt 5th last strides* **89/10**

6 hd **Point Blank (GER)**[182] 6905 4-9-0 0 THellier 5 96
(Mario Hofer, Germany) *trckd ldr: rdn to try and chal on turn into st: no ex over 1f out: fdd ins fnl f: lost 5th last strides* **69/10**

7 1/2 **Eigelstein**[175] 4-9-0 0 FilipMinarik 6 95
(P Schiergen, Germany) *midfield: rdn and lost pl on turn into st: last and outpcd over 1 1/2f out: plugged on ins fnl f* **12/1**

1m 40.39s (-0.77) **7 Ran SP% 135.4**
WIN (incl. 10 euro stake): 15. PLACES: 10, 15, 11. SF: 247.
Owner Gestut Schlenderhan **Bred** Gestut Karlshof **Trained** Germany

WINDSOR (R-H)

Monday, April 16

OFFICIAL GOING: Good (good to firm in places; 8.1)
Wind: Almost nil Weather: Fine

1411 EUROPEAN BREEDERS' FUND MAIDEN STKS 5f 10y

2:00 (2:00) (Class 5) 2-Y-0 **£3,234** (£962; £481; £240) **Stalls** Low

Form RPR

1 **Baddilini** 2-9-3 0 GeorgeBaker 3 81+
(Alan Bailey) *pressed ldng pair: led over 1f out: shkn up and flashed tail but readily asserted last 150yds* **3/1**[2]

	2	1 ¼	**Ouzinkie (IRE)** 2-9-3 0 ... MartinHarley 8 (Mick Channon) *hld up in rr: smooth prog to trck ldrs 1/2-way: looking for room 2f out: rdn and styd on wl fnl f: tk 2nd last strides* **14/1**	75+
	3	hd	**Regal Dan (IRE)** 2-9-3 0 ... MichaelHills 5 (Charles Hills) *trckd ldrs: pushed up to chal on outer over 1f out: readily hld by wnr ins fnl f: lost 2nd last strides* **4/1**[3]	74
0	4	1 ¼	**Fortinbrass (IRE)**[9] 1211 2-9-3 0 ... JimCrowley 2 (Ralph Beckett) *w ldr to over 1f out: rdn and one pce fnl f* **14/1**	69
	5	nk	**Vestibule** 2-8-12 0 ... CathyGannon 4 (Eve Johnson Houghton) *trckd ldrs: shkn up over 1f out: one pce after* **16/1**	63
6	6	¾	**Lea Valley Black**[9] 1211 2-9-3 0 ... RichardKingscote 1 (Tom Dascombe) *mde most against nr side rail to over 1f out: steadily fdd* **7/1**	66
	7	2 ½	**Meringue Pie** 2-9-3 0 ... RyanMoore 6 (Richard Hannon) *chsd ldrs: rdn and no imp 2f out: wknd over 1f out* **2/1**[1]	58+
	8	2 ¼	**World Freight Girl** 2-8-12 0 ... ShaneKelly 9 (Dean Ivory) *dwlt: sn pushed along: a in rr* **50/1**	43
	9	1 ¼	**Fletcher Christian** 2-9-3 0 ... NeilCallan 10 (John Gallagher) *s.i.s: sn pushed along in rr: nvr on terms* **25/1**	44
0	10	25	**Modern Society**[9] 1211 2-9-3 0 ... MartinDwyer 7 (Andrew Reid) *struggling after 2f: t.o* **100/1**	

1m 1.05s (0.75) **Going Correction** +0.05s/f (Good) **10** Ran SP% **116.8**
Speed ratings (Par 92): **96,94,93,91,91 90,86,82,80,40**
toteswingers:1&2:£7.60, 2&3:£9.70, 1&3:£2.90 CSF £43.87 TOTE £4.10: £1.10, £4.70, £1.70; EX 49.70 Trifecta £313.40 Pool: £470.23 - 1.11 winning units..
Owner Mrs A Shone & Mrs V Hubbard **Bred** Mrs A R Ruggles **Trained** Newmarket, Suffolk

FOCUS
Top bend dolled out 4yds from normal configuration adding 14yds to races of one mile and over. A typical early-season juvenile maiden for the track. This is a strong event on race averages and the winner may do a good bit better. The time was decent.

NOTEBOOK
Baddilini, a February foal who cost 14,000GBP, proved positive in the market throughout the day and certainly knew his job, travelling well and readily asserting. Although bred for further, being a brother to a Ribblesdale third, he's clearly quite precocious and will seemingly head to Chester for the Lily Agnes. (op 4-1)
Ouzinkie(IRE), half-brother to a 5f-1m winner, cost 20,000gns and made a really pleasing debut, travelling strongly having recovered from a sluggish start. He should win something similar.
Regal Dan(IRE) is all about speed, being a half-brother to useful 5f winners Star Rover and Jamesway, and he made a satisfactory debut. Normal progress can see him winning a maiden. (tchd 9-2)
Fortinbrass(IRE) fared best of those with previous experience. (op 12-1 tchd 11-1)
Vestibule, half-sister to a 4.5f winner in the US, showed ability and will find easier opportunities against her own sex. (op 25-1)
Lea Valley Black failed to confirm debut form with Fortinbrass. (op 9-1)
Meringue Pie, who went for 60,000euros, was beaten at half way. He should leave this form behind in time. (op 15-8 tchd 7-4 and 9-4)

1412 ROYAL WINDSOR RACING CLUB CLASSIFIED STKS 6f
2:30 (2:30) (Class 5) 3-Y-O **£2,264** (£673; £336; £168) **Stalls** Low

Form				RPR
055-	1		**Charlotte Rosina**[196] 6590 3-9-0 75 ... SebSanders 1 (Roger Teal) *racd freely: mde all against nr side rail: clr and rdn over 1f out: styd on wl* **13/2**[3]	81
10-0	2	3 ¼	**Forest Edge (IRE)**[37] 867 3-9-0 71 ... PadraigBeggy 5 (David Evans) *s.i.s: sn pushed along: hanging lft fr 1/2-way and u.p: prog to go 2nd 1f out: no imp on wnr* **25/1**	70
510-	3	nk	**Serene Oasis (IRE)**[177] 7028 3-9-0 75 ... MartinHarley 4 (Mick Channon) *cl up: chsd wnr 2f out: no imp and lost 2nd 1f out: kpt on* **5/1**[2]	69
614-	4	1	**Little China**[157] 7364 3-9-0 75 ... MartinDwyer 3 (William Muir) *t.k.h: hld up bhd ldrs: shkn up 2f out: no prog fnl f* **12/1**	66
34-4	5	1	**Impel (IRE)**[16] 1138 3-9-0 75 ... RyanMoore 7 (Richard Hannon) *a in rr: in last and u.p 1/2-way: nt gng pce to threaten* **1/1**[1]	63
6-1	6	¾	**Pettochside**[102] 41 3-9-0 74 ... JimCrowley 6 (Stuart Williams) *mostly chsd wnr to 2f out: wknd fnl f* **15/2**	60
443-	7	½	**Iced Opal**[206] 6293 3-9-0 71 ... DaneO'Neill 2 (Michael Blanshard) *settled in rr: rdn and no prog 2f out* **14/1**	59

1m 13.01s (0.01) **Going Correction** +0.05s/f (Good) **7** Ran SP% **110.0**
Speed ratings (Par 98): **101,96,96,94,93 92,91**
toteswingers:1&2:£6.50, 2&3:£15.10, 1&3:£3.10 CSF £124.25 TOTE £5.50: £3.30, £6.40; EX 87.80.
Owner Edward Hyde **Bred** Edward Hyde **Trained** Ashtead, Surrey
■ Stewards' Enquiry : Padraig Beggy seven-day ban: used whip above permitted level (Apr 30-May 6)

FOCUS
This looked much more competitive than the market implied and it turned into an old school Windsor contest, with the winner making all against the stands' rail. The race has not been rated too positively. The winner was back to her 2yo best.

1413 ANNUAL BADGE £264 ON SALE NOW CLAIMING STKS 1m 2f 7y
3:00 (3:00) (Class 6) 3-Y-O **£1,617** (£481; £240; £120) **Stalls** Centre

Form				RPR
3036	1		**Aiaam Al Wafa (IRE)**[18] 1093 3-8-4 54 ...(p) SilvestreDeSousa 3 (Phil McEntee) *hld up in last early: effrt and plenty to do over 3f out: rdn and clsd fr over 2f out: led last 150yds: drvn out* **7/1**	59
1-05	2	½	**Priestley's Reward (IRE)**[12] 1190 3-9-5 66 ... RobertWinston 2 (Mrs K Burke) *cl up: chsd ldr over 3f out: sn rdn: no imp tl clsd w wnr over 1f out: nrly upsides jst ins fnl f: nt qckn* **11/8**[1]	73
6-32	3	2	**Masters Club**[86] 255 3-8-11 66 ...(v[1]) JamesDoyle 5 (John Ryan) *led: gng bttr than rest over 2f out: rdn over 1f out: hdd & wknd last 150yds* **7/2**[2]	61
-215	4	¾	**Somemothersdohavem**[59] 605 3-8-11 70 ...(p) MichaelO'Connell[(3)] 1 (John Ryan) *loaded into stalls minutes bef the rest: chsd ldr to over 3f out: carried hd to one side after: stl in tch over 1f out: fnd nil* **6/1**[3]	63
0-	5	16	**Trove (IRE)**[149] 7494 3-9-0 0 ... RobertHavlin 4 (Mark Hoad) *in tch tl wknd wl over 2f out: t.o* **10/1**	31
520-	6	14	**Aljosan**[250] 4907 3-8-5 50 ... CathyGannon 6 (David Evans) *rdn to stay in tch bef 1/2-way: wknd over 3f out: wl t.o* **12/1**	

2m 9.11s (0.41) **Going Correction** -0.075s/f (Good) **6** Ran SP% **107.9**
Speed ratings (Par 96): **95,94,93,92,79 68**
CSF £15.85 TOTE £7.00: £3.10, £1.20; EX 15.70.
Owner Steve Jakes **Bred** Rabbah Bloodstock Limited **Trained** Newmarket, Suffolk

FOCUS
A weak claimer run at just an ordinary gallop, though the time wasn't bad compared with the maidens. The winner is rated up slightly on her recent form.

1414 WINDSOR VEHICLE LEASING WVL.COM MAIDEN STKS (DIV I) 1m 2f 7y
3:30 (3:31) (Class 5) 3-Y-O **£2,264** (£673; £336; £168) **Stalls** Centre

Form				RPR
4-	1		**Rosslyn Castle**[215] 6059 3-9-3 0 ... JamesDoyle 1 (Roger Charlton) *trckd ldrs: wnt 2nd wl over 2f out: led over 1f out: pushed along and readily drew clr* **1/1**[1]	86+
02-	2	3 ¾	**Ace Of Valhalla**[149] 7494 3-9-3 0 ... TomQueally 6 (Sir Henry Cecil) *mde most: hdd over 1f out: wl outpcd after: styd on* **3/1**[2]	76
	3	3	**Scottish Vespers (IRE)** 3-9-3 0 ... RyanMoore 10 (Sir Michael Stoute) *prom: shkn up and rn green 3f out: outpcd fr 2f out but kpt on* **8/1**[3]	70
00	4	nse	**Morilles**[44] 784 3-8-12 0 ... AdamKirby 4 (Clive Cox) *trckd ldrs in 5th: shkn up 3f out: outpcd fr 2f out and edgd rt: pushed along and pressed for 3rd fnl f* **25/1**	65
00-	5	1 ½	**Curly Come Home**[166] 7232 3-8-13 0 ow1 ... SebSanders 7 (Chris Wall) *in tch in 6th: outpcd fr over 2f out: kpt on* **50/1**	63
0-	6	nk	**Just When**[180] 6954 3-9-3 0 ... JimmyFortune 8 (Andrew Balding) *hld up in rr: pushed along whn nt clr run over 2f out: kpt on ins fnl f* **10/1**	66
00-	7	1 ¾	**Brundon**[212] 6168 3-8-12 0 ... DaneO'Neill 5 (Henry Candy) *hld up in rr: shkn up over 3f out: no prog over 2f out: sn outpcd* **33/1**	58
	8	2 ¼	**Aegaeus** 3-9-3 0 ... GeorgeBaker 3 (Ed Dunlop) *stdd s: hld up and mostly in last: shuffled along and no prog over 2f out* **14/1**	58
06	9	27	**Tom Red**[18] 1086 3-9-3 0 ... ShaneKelly 2 (Dean Ivory) *w ldr to 4f out: wknd rapidly wl over 2f out: eased and t.o* **66/1**	

2m 8.45s (-0.25) **Going Correction** -0.075s/f (Good) **9** Ran SP% **112.1**
Speed ratings (Par 98): **98,95,92,92,91 91,89,87,66**
toteswingers:1&2:£1.40, 2&3:£2.30, 1&3:£3.60 CSF £3.63 TOTE £1.90: £1.40, £1.40, £1.80; EX 4.20 Trifecta £17.10 Pool: £1030.48 - 44.45 winning units..
Owner Lady Rothschild **Bred** Carwell Equities Ltd **Trained** Beckhampton, Wilts

FOCUS
By far the stronger of the two divisions, certainly the one with more depth, and the time was almost two seconds quicker. The market principals pulled clear. The form is set around the race averages and the winner was value for extra.

1415 WINDSOR VEHICLE LEASING WVL.COM MAIDEN STKS (DIV II) 1m 2f 7y
4:00 (4:00) (Class 5) 3-Y-O **£2,264** (£673; £336; £168) **Stalls** Centre

Form				RPR
06-	1		**Man Of Plenty**[180] 6954 3-9-3 0 ... DaneO'Neill 8 (John Dunlop) *mostly trckd ldng pair: shkn up 3f out and hanging briefly: clsd over 1f out: led jst ins fnl f: a holding runner-up after* **7/1**	70+
0	2	nk	**Falkland (IRE)**[16] 1132 3-9-3 0 ... WilliamBuick 2 (John Gosden) *led after 3f: rdn and hdd over 2f out: hrd drvn and upsides ins fnl f: nt qckn* **4/6**[1]	69+
0	3	3	**Geordie Boy**[11] 1206 3-8-12 0 ... RaulDaSilva[(5)] 9 (Sheena West) *hld up but sn trckd ldng trio: prog to ld over 2f out: hung bdly lft wl over 1f out: hdd and fdd jst ins fnl f* **33/1**	63
	4	3 ¾	**Savida (IRE)** 3-8-12 0 ... RyanMoore 3 (Sir Michael Stoute) *led 3f: shkn up and rn green fr 1/2-way: steadily outpcd fr over 2f out* **9/2**[2]	51+
06	5	1 ½	**The Yank**[40] 816 3-8-10 0 ... GeorgeDowning[(7)] 5 (Tony Carroll) *hld up in last: stdy prog on outer over 3f out: chsd ldrs 2f out: outpcd after* **50/1**	53
00-	6	4	**Micquus (IRE)**[166] 7233 3-9-3 0 ... NeilChalmers 6 (Andrew Balding) *a abt same pl: outpcd fr over 2f out* **25/1**	45
	7	¾	**Interlocking (USA)** 3-8-12 0 ... TomQueally 1 (Sir Henry Cecil) *chsd ldrs but pushed along and rn green after 4f: steadily wknd fnl 3f* **6/1**[3]	38+
0	8	3	**Brave Kiss**[58] 620 3-8-12 0 ... FergusSweeney 7 (Mark Gillard) *a in rr: lost tch w ldrs 3f out* **80/1**	32
00-	9	6	**Delishuss**[164] 7257 3-8-12 0 ... MartinLane 10 (Dominic Ffrench Davis) *a in rr: bhd fnl 3f* **66/1**	20

2m 10.51s (1.81) **Going Correction** -0.075s/f (Good) **9** Ran SP% **116.4**
Speed ratings (Par 98): **89,88,86,83,82 78,78,75,71**
toteswingers:1&2:£2.50, 2&3:£7.70, 1&3:£9.20 CSF £12.09 TOTE £6.30: £1.90, £1.10, £5.50; EX 15.20 Trifecta £428.10 Pool: £1261.19 - 2.18 winning units..
Owner Bluehills Racing Limited **Bred** Hesmonds Stud Ltd **Trained** Arundel, W Sussex

FOCUS
Only four could be given a chance in what was clearly the weaker of the two divisions. The form is shaky with the third a doubt. The time was almost two seconds slower than division I. The field raced more towards the centre down the straight.

1416 STANDING SIRE WHATACAPER.COM H'CAP 1m 67y
4:30 (4:31) (Class 4) (0-85,85) 4-Y-O+ **£4,851** (£1,443; £721; £360) **Stalls** Low

Form				RPR
102-	1		**Moone's My Name**[175] 7054 4-9-1 79 ... JimCrowley 3 (Ralph Beckett) *trckd ldrs: smooth prog over 2f out: led over 1f out: drew clr fnl f: easily* **9/2**[2]	94+
256-	2	4	**Ree's Rascal (IRE)**[152] 7439 4-9-1 79 ... PatCosgrave 10 (Jim Boyle) *hld up in midfield: prog 2f out: rdn to chse wnr jst ins fnl f: no ch* **11/1**[3]	84
045-	3	½	**Borug (USA)**[175] 7053 4-9-7 85 ... SebSanders 9 (James Tate) *hld up in last trio: stl there over 2f out: making prog whn nt clr run twice over 1f out: rdn and styd on wl fnl f* **16/1**	89+
00-5	4	½	**Moynahan (USA)**[25] 989 7-9-0 78 ...(b) JimmyFortune 7 (Paul Cole) *hld up in rr: pushed along over 2f out: prog over 1f out: styd on to take 4th nr fin* **20/1**	81
04-2	5	nk	**Zafeen's Pearl**[26] 987 5-9-2 80 ... ShaneKelly 1 (Dean Ivory) *dwlt: sn rcvrd and trckd ldrs in 6th: effrt over 2f out: rdn and nt qckn wl over 1f out: outpcd after* **9/2**[2]	82
400-	6	hd	**Duster**[170] 7168 5-9-7 85 ... RyanMoore 4 (Hughie Morrison) *led to over 1f out: steadily fdd* **3/1**[1]	87
40-4	7	½	**Islesman**[26] 987 4-8-12 76 ... WilliamBuick 11 (Heather Main) *hld up in last trio: taken to wd outside and prog over 2f out: chsd ldrs over 1f out: pushed along and outpcd after* **12/1**	77
400-	8	hd	**Uncle Fred**[180] 6949 7-9-0 78 ... FergusSweeney 5 (Patrick Chamings) *hld up towards rr: nudged along over 2f out: stuck bhd rivals over 1f out: nvr nr ldrs* **14/1**	78+

440- **9** *hd* **Benandonner (USA)**[170] 7168 9-9-7 **85** NeilCallan 8 85
(Mike Murphy) *free to post: t.k.h: trckd ldr to 2f out: steadily fdd* **14/1**

131- **10** *¾* **Starwatch**[218] 5969 5-9-4 **85** SeanLevey(3) 13 83
(John Bridger) *hld up in last trio: pushed along over 2f out: kpt on fr over 1f out but no threat* **20/1**

234- **11** *2 ¼* **Ezdeyaad (USA)**[226] 5734 8-9-4 **82** GeorgeBaker 2 75
(Ed Walker) *trckd ldrs: pushed along fr over 2f out: steadily lost pl fr over 1f out* **33/1**

2214 **12** *nse* **Alhaban (IRE)**[18] 1087 6-8-12 **76** LukeMorris 12 69
(Ronald Harris) *trckd ldrs: rdn over 2f out: losing pl whn rdr dropped whip over 1f out* **25/1**

/10- **13** *½* **Odin (IRE)**[362] 1485 4-8-13 **77** NickyMackay 14 71
(David Elsworth) *hld up wl in rr: taken to outer and sme prog over 2f out: fdd over 1f out: eased* **25/1**

260- **14** *6* **Aciano (IRE)**[247] 5056 4-9-1 **79** DaneO'Neill 6 57
(Brendan Powell) *prom tl wknd qckly over 2f out* **20/1**

1m 43.09s (-1.61) **Going Correction** -0.075s/f (Good) **14** Ran SP% **121.5**
Speed ratings (Par 105): **105,101,100,100,99 99,99,98,98,97 95,95,95,89**
toteswingers:1&2:£15.00, 2&3:£42.50, 1&3:£18.60 CSF £47.50 CT £760.17 TOTE £5.90: £2.00, £3.50, £5.80; EX 76.40 TRIFECTA Not won..
Owner McDonagh Murphy And Nixon **Bred** Baroness Bloodstock & Tweenhills Stud **Trained** Kimpton, Hants

FOCUS
What had looked quite a competitive handicap, run at a good pace, was won with ease by Moone's My Name who has clearly improved. The form is rated through the second.
Alhaban(IRE) Official explanation: jockey said gelding suffered interference in runing
Odin(IRE) Official explanation: jockey said gelding hung right

1417 SKYBET.COM H'CAP 5f 10y
5:00 (5:01) (Class 4) (0-85,85) 4-Y-0+ **£4,851** (£1,443; £721; £360) **Stalls** Low

Form RPR

-450 **1** **Sugar Beet**[37] 871 4-9-7 **85** LukeMorris 7 94
(Ronald Harris) *towards rr and sn pushed along: prog u.p fr 2f out: styd on to ld last 100yds: jst hld on* **14/1**

3-03 **2** *shd* **Escape To Glory (USA)**[6] 1289 4-9-1 **79** WilliamBuick 6 88
(Mikael Magnusson) *hld up wl in rr: stdy prog against rail fr 2f out: rdn and r.o fnl f: jst failed* **6/1**[2]

500- **3** *1 ¼* **Solemn**[191] 6703 7-9-4 **82** (b) DaneO'Neill 3 86
(Milton Bradley) *chsd ldrs: rdn and effrt over 1f out: styd on to ld briefly ins fnl f: outpcd last 75yds* **14/1**

1266 **4** *1 ¼* **Sulis Minerva (IRE)**[11] 1204 5-8-8 **77** RaulDaSilva(5) 2 77
(Jeremy Gask) *hld up wl in rr: stdy prog and looking for room fr wl over 1f out: swtiched lft ins fnl f: r.o but no ch* **16/1**

315- **5** *½* **Pearl Blue (IRE)**[205] 6327 4-9-4 **82** GeorgeBaker 13 80+
(Chris Wall) *in tch on outer: effrt to press ldrs over 1f out: fdd ins fnl f* **6/1**[2]

4320 **6** *¾* **Desert Strike**[24] 1007 6-8-3 **72** MatthewLawson(5) 5 67+
(Charles Hills) *taken steadily to post: dwlt: hld up wl in rr: effrt 2f out: nt clr run more than once after: styd on* **14/1**

044- **7** *½* **Sutton Veny (IRE)**[130] 7675 6-9-7 **85** AdamKirby 16 78+
(Jeremy Gask) *dropped in fr wd draw and hld up wl in rr: effrt 2f out: repeatedly denied clr run after: fin wl but no ch* **13/2**[3]

004- **8** *½* **Avonmore Star**[171] 7138 4-8-13 **77** RyanMoore 15 69+
(Richard Hannon) *hld up in rr fr wd draw: effrt on outer 2f out: no prog fnl f* **9/2**[1]

300- **9** *nk* **Taurus Twins**[184] 6865 6-9-4 **82** (b) SilvestreDeSousa 4 72
(Richard Price) *led and racd against nr side rail: gng strly 2f out: hdd & wknd ins fnl f* **17/2**

3610 **10** *2 ½* **Six Wives**[24] 1015 5-9-0 **78** RobertWinston 8 59
(Scott Dixon) *mostly chsd ldr: hrd rdn over 1f out: wknd fnl f* **25/1**

300- **11** *nk* **Alpha Delta Whisky**[208] 6246 4-8-9 **73** TomQueally 10 53
(John Gallagher) *prom: rdn 1/2-way: wknd over 1f out* **25/1**

-006 **12** *1* **Volcanic Dust (IRE)**[24] 1015 4-9-4 **82** RichardKingscote 9 59
(Milton Bradley) *stdd s: hld up wl in rr: effrt 2f out: no prog whn nt clr run 1f out* **33/1**

51-2 **13** *1* **Style And Panache (IRE)**[6] 1290 4-8-9 **73** (p) CathyGannon 11 46
(David Evans) *prom: rdn 2f out: wkng whn hmpd 1f out* **6/1**[2]

1620 **14** *4* **Cadeaux Pearl**[24] 1015 4-9-2 **83** (b) RyanPowell(3) 12 42
(Scott Dixon) *free to post: prom to 1/2-way: wknd rapidly* **20/1**

59.92s (-0.38) **Going Correction** +0.05s/f (Good) **14** Ran SP% **126.2**
Speed ratings (Par 105): **105,104,102,100,100 98,98,97,96,92 92,90,89,82**
toteswingers:1&2:£19.70, 2&3:£17.00, 1&3:£40.00 CSF £96.19 CT £1236.48 TOTE £23.80: £5.30, £2.00, £6.00; EX 199.90 Trifecta £624.60 Part won. Pool: £844.11 - 0.63 winning units..
Owner Ridge House Stables Ltd **Bred** Coln Valley Stud **Trained** Earlswood, Monmouths

FOCUS
Those drawn in single figures dominated this sprint handicap. They went quick up front and it paid to come from off the pace. The winner carried on her AW improvement.

1418 SKYBET MOBILE FOR IPHONE & ANDROID H'CAP 1m 3f 135y
5:30 (5:30) (Class 5) (0-75,75) 4-Y-0+ **£2,264** (£673; £336; £168) **Stalls** Centre

Form RPR

0-04 **1** **Timocracy**[19] 1071 7-8-5 **66** LeonnaMayor(7) 14 73
(Alastair Lidderdale) *mde virtually all: hrd pressed fr over 2f out: urged along and hld on gamely nr fin* **12/1**

0-32 **2** *shd* **Reset City**[14] 1170 6-8-11 **65** SilvestreDeSousa 12 72
(Ian Williams) *t.k.h: hld up in midfield: prog over 2f out: drvn to chal over 1f out: w wnr last 100yds: jst pipped* **15/2**

410- **3** *1* **Star Commander**[226] 5716 4-9-6 **75** NeilCallan 7 80
(Mark H Tompkins) *trckd ldrs: effrt to chal over 2f out: nt qckn over 1f out: one pce* **9/2**[1]

-221 **4** *1 ½* **Broughton Sands**[52] 688 4-9-0 **69** ShaneKelly 16 72
(Willie Musson) *trckd ldrs: prog to chal over 2f out: nt qckn over 1f out: one pce after* **14/1**

210- **5** *1 ¼* **Shades Of Grey**[158] 7346 5-8-13 **67** AdamKirby 1 67
(Clive Cox) *trckd ldrs: nt qckn over 2f out: sn outpcd: kpt on again fnl f* **5/1**[2]

-421 **6** *7* **Shalambar (IRE)**[25] 992 6-9-2 **70** JimCrowley 15 59
(Tony Carroll) *prom: disp 2nd and drvn 3f out: sn lost pl: wknd over 1f out* **10/1**

526- **7** *1 ½* **Beat Route**[121] 7803 5-8-10 **64** JohnFahy 2 50
(Michael Attwater) *settled in midfield: snatched up 7f out: no prog over 2f out: n.d after* **10/1**

-630 **8** *hd* **Oneiric**[40] 818 4-8-7 **67** MarkCoumbe(5) 10 53
(Brett Johnson) *dwlt: hld up in last pair: effrt 3f out: plugged on but nvr a threat* **33/1**

-220 **9** *¾* **Hurricane Hymnbook (USA)**[33] 648 7-9-4 **72** JamieMackay 8 56
(Willie Musson) *blindfold late off and slowest away: hld up in last and appeared to r awkwardly: sme late prog: nvr in it* **20/1**

2163 **10** *1 ¾* **Shirataki (IRE)**[11] 1205 4-8-10 **65** LukeMorris 6 46
(Peter Hiatt) *t.k.h: prom: cl up 3f out: wknd 2f out* **16/1**

320- **11** *hd* **Filun**[230] 5580 7-9-4 **72** StephenCraine 4 53
(Anthony Middleton) *hld up towards rr on inner: sme prog 3f out: shkn up and no hdwy 2f out: wknd* **33/1**

400- **12** *3* **Amistress**[194] 6632 4-9-3 **72** CathyGannon 13 48
(Eve Johnson Houghton) *t.k.h: hld up in tch: rdn 3f out: no prog and wknd 2f out* **13/2**[3]

230 **13** *17* **Maison Brillet (IRE)**[37] 872 5-8-13 **67** (p) RobertHavlin 9 14
(Clive Drew) *hld up towards rr: effrt on outer 3f out: wknd qckly 2f out: t.o* **33/1**

4366 **14** *9* **The Mongoose**[CC] 538 4-9-0 **69** PadraigBeggy 11
(David Evans) *hld up towards rr: hmpd 7f out: a in rr after: t.o* **20/1**

41/0 **15** *19* **Managua**[28] 960 6-9-3 **71** DaneO'Neill 3
(Barry Brennan) *w wnr to over 3f out: wknd rapidly: t.o* **20/1**

2m 28.43s (-1.07) **Going Correction** -0.075s/f (Good)
WFA 4 from 5yo+ 1lb **15** Ran SP% **121.5**
Speed ratings (Par 103): **100,99,99,98,97 92,91,91,91,89 89,87,76,70,57**
toteswingers:1&2:£20.30, 2&3:£9.90, 1&3:£17.00 CSF £90.11 CT £470.95 TOTE £12.10: £2.60, £2.30, £2.60; EX 88.80 Trifecta £498.10 Pool: £807.75 - 1.20 winning units..
Owner B S Hicks **Bred** Gainsborough Stud Management Ltd **Trained** Lambourn, Berks
■ Stewards' Enquiry : Leonna Mayor seven-day ban: used whip above permitted level (May 1-7)

FOCUS
Few got into this from off the pace, the early gallop being just ordinary. Modest form with the winner rated to last year's best.
Broughton Sands Official explanation: jockey said filly suffered interference in running
T/Plt: £171.30 to a £1 stake. Pool of £84,544.28 - 360.15 winning tickets. T/Qpdt: £17.90 to a £1 stake. Pool of £7320.63 - 30192 winning tickets. JN

1387 WOLVERHAMPTON (A.W) (L-H)
Monday, April 16

OFFICIAL GOING: Standard
Wind: Light half- behind Weather: Cloudy with sunny spells

1419 32RED CASINO CLAIMING STKS 7f 32y(P)
2:15 (2:15) (Class 6) 3-Y-O **£1,704** (£503; £251) **Stalls** High

Form RPR

334- **1** **Poker Hospital**[143] 7539 3-8-9 70 ow1 (p) JamieSpencer 4 66
(George Baker) *a.p: chsd ldr 1/2-way: shkn up to ld over 1f out: edgd rt: rdn out* **7/2**[2]

1123 **2** *3 ½* **Homeward Strut**[2] 1392 3-9-7 62 (b) JoeFanning 3 68
(Frank Sheridan) *s.i.s: hdwy 4f out: rdn to chse wnr fnl f: hung lft and styd on same pce* **7/4**[1]

125- **3** *nk* **Annie Walker (IRE)**[184] 6864 3-9-6 65 PaulQuinn 2 66
(David Nicholls) *led 1f: chsd ldr to 1/2-way: rdn over 1f out: styd on* **7/1**

6414 **4** *3 ¼* **Umph (IRE)**[3] 1359 3-8-12 60 (b) MatthewCosham(5) 1 55
(David Evans) *chsd ldrs: pushed along 1/2-way: styd on same pce fnl 2f* **5/1**[3]

3130 **5** *1* **Fugitive Motel (IRE)**[19] 1063 3-8-6 72 NicoleNordblad(7) 5 48
(Hans Adielsson) *led 6f out: rdn and hdd over 1f out: wknd ins fnl f* **8/1**

041- **6** *1 ¼* **Guava**[128] 7718 3-8-9 66 DarrenEgan(7) 6 48
(Frank Sheridan) *s.i.s: hld up: shkn up and hung lft over 1f out: nvr on terms* **13/2**

1m 29.43s (-0.17) **Going Correction** -0.05s/f (Stan) **6** Ran SP% **112.2**
Speed ratings (Par 96): **98,94,93,89,88 87**
toteswingers:1&2:£1.70, 2&3:£2.20, 1&3:£3.40 CSF £10.07 TOTE £4.40: £1.50, £1.50; EX 7.20.Poker Hospital was claimed by J Stimpson for £6000.
Owner George Baker **Bred** Sir Eric Parker **Trained** Whitsbury, Hants

FOCUS
A moderate claimer. The winner probably only had to run to her winter AW form, with the runner-up the best guide.
Umph(IRE) Official explanation: jockey said gelding missed the break

1420 £32 FREE AT 32RED.COM MAIDEN STKS 5f 216y(P)
2:45 (2:47) (Class 5) 3-Y-O+ **£2,264** (£673; £336; £168) **Stalls** High

Form RPR

00- **1** **Jamhara**[201] 6458 3-8-12 0 BrettDoyle 8 62
(Clive Brittain) *chsd ldr: pushed along over 2f out: r.o to ld towards fin* **17/2**[3]

0/20 **2** *¾* **Going French (IRE)**[28] 958 5-10-0 62 (t) SamHitchcott 9 67
(Dai Burchell) *led: rdn over 1f out: hdd towards fin* **6/1**[2]

2 **3** *¾* **Pashan Garh**[21] 1048 3-9-3 0 TedDurcan 4 62
(Pat Eddery) *chsd ldrs: pushed along over 2f out: rdn and hung lft over 1f out: r.o to go 3rd post* **7/4**[1]

5 **4** *nse* **Julier Pass (IRE)**[14] 1166 3-9-0 0 GaryBartley(3) 3 62
(Hugh McWilliams) *chsd ldrs: rdn over 1f out: styd on same pce ins fnl f: lost 3rd post* **50/1**

5 *3* **Sir Maximilian (IRE)** 3-9-3 0 JamieSpencer 10 52+
(Ed Dunlop) *s.i.s: hld up: racd keenly: hdwy over 1f out: nt trble ldrs* **7/4**[1]

6 *2 ¼* **Temple Road (IRE)** 4-10-0 0 RussKennemore 2 48
(Milton Bradley) *s.s: hld up: hdwy over 2f out: rdn: hung rt and wknd fnl f* **66/1**

60 **7** *1 ½* **Big Sylv (IRE)**[24] 1016 3-8-12 0 LiamJones 6 35
(James Unett) *prom: rdn over 2f out: wknd over 1f out* **66/1**

0-0 **8** *2* **Verge (IRE)**[24] 1016 3-8-12 0 RichardMullen 1 29
(Ed Vaughan) *mid-div: rdn over 2f out: wknd wl over 1f out* **14/1**

9 *2* **Petrarchan** 4-10-0 0 (t) LiamKeniry 7 30
(Milton Bradley) *s.s: rdn over 2f out: a in rr* **20/1**

10 *5* **Craniac** 5-10-0 0 JoeFanning 5 14
(Frank Sheridan) *s.s: rdn over 2f out: a in rr* **33/1**

1m 15.04s (0.04) **Going Correction** -0.05s/f (Stan)
WFA 3 from 4yo+ 11lb **10** Ran SP% **116.9**
Speed ratings (Par 103): **97,96,95,94,90 87,85,83,80,73**
toteswingers:1&2:£4.20, 2&3:£2.70, 1&3:£3.30 CSF £55.97 TOTE £7.80: £2.10, £2.00, £1.20; EX 43.50.
Owner Saeed Manana **Bred** Rabbah Bloodstock Limited **Trained** Newmarket, Suffolk

FOCUS
A weak sprint maiden where it paid to race handily and the form should be treated with some caution.The form is rated around the runner-up.
Sir Maximilian(IRE) Official explanation: jockey said colt ran green

Temple Road(IRE) Official explanation: jockey said gelding hung right in home straight

1421 32RED H'CAP 1m 5f 194y(P)
3:15 (3:15) (Class 4) (0-85,84) 4-Y-0+ **£4,204** (£1,251; £625; £312) **Stalls** Low

Form RPR
001- **1** **Al Khawaneej**[244] 5141 4-9-3 **79** ... JamieSpencer 5 88+
(David Simcock) *hld up: hdwy over 1f out: r.o to ld wl ins fnl f: comf* **5/1**[3]
23-2 **2** *1* **Pittodrie Star (IRE)**[8] 1239 5-9-6 **80** ... DanielTudhope 8 87
(David O'Meara) *a.p: chsd ldr over 3f out: rdn to ld 1f out: hdd and unable qck wl ins fnl f* **11/4**[2]
2-35 **3** *hd* **Wild Desert (FR)**[16] 202 7-9-9 **83** ... SamHitchcott 3 89
(Charlie Longsdon) *chsd ldr tl led over 4f out: rdn and hdd 1f out: styd on same pce wl ins fnl f* **16/1**
4222 **4** *1 1/4* **Quinsman**[17] 1104 6-8-12 **72** ... LiamKeniry 4 77
(J S Moore) *a.p: rdn over 1f out: styd on same pce fnl f* **9/1**
-614 **5** *2 1/4* **Cotton King**[37] 872 5-9-6 **80** ... (bt) StevieDonohoe 6 81
(Tobias B P Coles) *hld up: hdwy over 2f out: rdn over 1f out: no ex fnl f* **6/1**
2304 **6** *25* **Mister Green (FR)**[7] 1263 6-7-12 **65** ... (t) DarrenEgan(7) 1 31
(David Flood) *chsd ldrs tl rdn and wknd 2f out* **25/1**
40-0 **7** *1 1/2* **Rajeh (IRE)**[19] 1066 9-9-4 **78** ... RobbieFitzpatrick 7 42
(Peter Grayson) *s.i.s: hld up and a in rr: lost tch fnl 3f* **66/1**
311- **8** *15* **Covert Decree**[219] 5938 4-9-3 **84** ... LucyKBarry(5) 2 27+
(Clive Cox) *led: racd keenly: clr 10f out tl hung rt 7f out: hdd over 4f out: wknd over 2f out: t.o* **2/1**[1]

3m 2.77s (-3.23) **Going Correction** -0.05s/f (Stan)
WFA 4 from 5yo+ 2lb **8** Ran SP% **112.2**
Speed ratings (Par 105): **107,106,106,105,104 90,89,80**
toteswingers:1&2:£3.50, 2&3:£5.60, 1&3:£10.20 CSF £18.39 CT £199.73 TOTE £5.60: £1.90, £1.60, £1.90; EX 19.90.
Owner Ahmad Al Shaikh **Bred** Cliveden Stud Ltd **Trained** Newmarket, Suffolk

FOCUS
A competitive staying handicap, run at a sound pace. The form makes sense at face value with the second and third fitting in.
Covert Decree Official explanation: jockey said filly ran too free

1422 DOWNLOAD OUR IPHONE APP MEDIAN AUCTION MAIDEN STKS 1m 141y(P)
3:45 (3:45) (Class 5) 3-5-Y-0 **£2,264** (£673; £336; £168) **Stalls** Low

Form RPR
1 **Main Line** 3-8-13 0 ... TedDurcan 6 76+
(David Lanigan) *hld up: hdwy over 1f out: led ins fnl f: r.o wl* **10/1**
6- **2** *1 1/4* **Sareeah (IRE)**[130] 7672 3-8-8 0 ... BrettDoyle 3 68
(Clive Brittain) *hmpd s: sn prom: rdn to ld over 1f out: hdd and unable qck ins fnl f* **4/1**[2]
52-2 **3** *3* **Beau Duke (IRE)**[28] 959 3-8-13 72 ... (v[1]) LiamKeniry 1 66
(Andrew Balding) *edgd rt s: led: rdn and hdd over 1f out: edgd lft and no ex ins fnl f* **1/1**[1]
60- **4** *3/4* **Tantamount**[166] 7232 3-8-10 0 ... HarryBentley(3) 2 65
(Roger Charlton) *hmpd s: sn prom: chsd ldr over 3f out: rdn over 1f out: no ex ins fnl f* **5/1**[3]
56 **5** *7* **Ruby Glass (IRE)**[31] 921 3-8-13 0 ... (b) JamieSpencer 11 48
(Brian Meehan) *prom: rdn over 1f out: wknd fnl f* **12/1**
5 **6** *1 1/4* **Handy Chat (IRE)**[52] 693 3-8-6 0 ... DannyBrock(7) 9 46
(Des Donovan) *chsd ldr 5f: rdn over 2f out: wknd over 1f out* **20/1**
7 *1 1/2* **Little Bucks** 3-8-10 0 ... DeclanCannon(3) 5 42
(Alan McCabe) *hmpd s: hld up: rdn and nt clr run over 2f out: sn wknd* **33/1**
0 **8** *7* **Jawbreakeronastick**[20] 1053 3-8-13 0 ... RussKennemore 10 26
(John Stimpson) *hld up: plld hrd: bhd fnl 3f* **150/1**
9 *8* **Gravie** 4-9-9 0 ... FrederikTylicki 7
(Brian Baugh) *hld up: lost tch fnl 3f* **66/1**
00 **10** *22* **Diggers Daydream (IRE)**[13] 1173 4-10-0 0 ... SamHitchcott 4
(Lisa Williamson) *hmpd s: hld up: plld hrd: hdwy over 5f out: rdn and wknd wl over 2f out: t.o* **200/1**
11 *62* **Captain Cavallo** 5-10-0 0 ... TonyCulhane 8
(Nicky Vaughan) *s.s: outpcd: t.o* **80/1**

1m 50.0s (-0.50) **Going Correction** -0.05s/f (Stan)
WFA 3 from 4yo+ 15lb **11** Ran SP% **115.0**
Speed ratings (Par 103): **100,98,96,95,89 88,86,80,73,54**
CSF £47.40 TOTE £10.50: £2.00, £1.60, £1.10; EX 56.60.
Owner William McAlpin **Bred** Greenwood Lodge Farm Inc **Trained** Upper Lambourn, Berks

FOCUS
A modest maiden, run at a fair pace. it was a bit muddling and the favourite disappointed, but the winner looks sure to improve.
Diggers Daydream(IRE) Official explanation: jockey said gelding ran too freely

1423 32RED.COM FILLIES' H'CAP 1m 141y(P)
4:15 (4:15) (Class 5) (0-70,67) 4-Y-0+ **£2,587** (£770; £384; £192) **Stalls** Low

Form RPR
212- **1** **Love Your Looks**[150] 7453 4-9-6 **66** ... TonyCulhane 7 74
(Mike Murphy) *chsd ldr 7f out tl led over 2f out: shkn up over 1f out: edgd lft: drvn out* **6/4**[1]
0230 **2** *1 3/4* **Cairanne**[2] 1379 4-8-0 **53** oh8 ... DarrenEgan(7) 5 57
(Tom Keddy) *s.i.s: hld up: hdwy over 1f out: r.o to go 2nd wl ins fnl f: nt rch wnr* **11/1**
12-5 **3** *1 1/2* **Painted Tail (IRE)**[14] 1170 5-9-7 **67** ... JamieSpencer 4 68
(Alan Swinbank) *chsd ldr tl led over 7f out: rdn and hdd over 2f out: no ex ins fnl f* **2/1**[2]
4-60 **4** *1/2* **Bashama**[12] 1191 4-8-12 **58** ... BrettDoyle 1 57
(Clive Brittain) *led: hdd over 7f out: chsd ldrs: rdn over 2f out: styd on same pce fr over 1f out* **20/1**
0300 **5** *1/2* **Harvest Mist (IRE)**[5] 1299 4-8-7 **53** oh6 ... RussKennemore 2 51
(Shaun Lycett) *hld up: rdn over 1f out: nvr trbld ldrs* **20/1**
2-32 **6** *1 1/2* **Frosty Friday**[27] 974 4-9-2 **62** ... FrederikTylicki 8 57
(J R Jenkins) *sn chsng ldrs: rdn over 2f out: wknd ins fnl f* **9/2**[3]
655 **R** **Apassionforfashion**[4] 1341 4-8-7 **53** oh8 ... (p) LiamJones 3
(Mark Rimell) *ref to r* **66/1**

1m 51.49s (0.99) **Going Correction** -0.05s/f (Stan) **7** Ran SP% **110.9**
Speed ratings (Par 100): **93,91,90,89,89 87,**
toteswingers:1&2:£3.20, 2&3:£2.50, 1&3:£1.70 CSF £17.20 CT £31.47 TOTE £2.40: £1.20, £3.40; EX 17.50.
Owner M Murphy **Bred** Ellis Stud And Bellow Hill Stud **Trained** Westoning, Beds

FOCUS
A moderate fillies' handicap, which was steadily run. The winner continues on the upgrade but there are doubts over the form with the second 8lb wrong.

1424 ENJOY THE PUNTERS PACKAGE GROUP OFFER H'CAP 1m 1f 103y(P)
4:45 (4:45) (Class 6) (0-60,60) 3-Y-O **£1,704** (£503; £251) **Stalls** Low

Form RPR
5-44 **1** **Always Eager**[27] 973 3-9-6 **59** ... JoeFanning 9 66
(Mark Johnston) *a.p: chsd ldr 6f out: led 2f out: rdn and edgd lft ins fnl f: r.o* **7/1**
0-65 **2** *1* **Skyeron**[6] 1287 3-8-7 **46** oh1 ... LiamJones 2 50
(Mark Brisbourne) *led: hdd over 7f out: remained handy: rdn to chse wnr over 1f out: r.o* **33/1**
005- **3** *2 1/2* **No Plan B (IRE)**[158] 7342 3-9-2 **55** ... FrederikTylicki 1 54
(Noel Quinlan) *a.p: rdn over 1f out: styd on* **6/1**[2]
4-20 **4** *nse* **Parque Atlantico**[7] 1259 3-8-7 **46** oh1 ... (v) LiamKeniry 4 45
(Andrew Balding) *a.p: rdn over 2f out: edgd lft: styd on* **14/1**
000- **5** *1/2* **Melodrama (IRE)**[170] 7165 3-9-3 **56** ... (b[1]) TedDurcan 10 54
(David Lanigan) *hld up in tch: rdn over 2f out: hung lft over 1f out: styd on* **10/1**
2146 **6** *3/4* **Moment In The Sun**[7] 1267 3-8-12 **58** ... (b[1]) DarrenEgan(7) 3 54+
(David Flood) *s.i.s: hld up: nt clr run fr over 1f out tl wl ins fnl f: nvr nr to chal* **16/1**
000- **7** *1/2* **Chocolat Chaud (IRE)**[188] 6776 3-9-7 **60** ... StevieDonohoe 6 55+
(J W Hills) *s.i.s: hld up: rdn over 2f out: r.o ins fnl f: nvr nrr* **8/1**
030- **8** *nk* **Single Girl (IRE)**[237] 5343 3-9-1 **54** ... LeeNewman 12 49
(Jonathan Portman) *prom: rdn over 2f out: no ex fnl f* **20/1**
05-2 **9** *1* **My Boy Ginger**[7] 1259 3-9-7 **60** ... JamesMillman 5 53
(Rod Millman) *hld up: rdn whn hmpd over 1f out: n.d* **7/2**[1]
0606 **10** *1 1/4* **Maggie Pink**[3] 1365 3-8-2 **48** oh1 ow2 ... JackDuern(7) 7 38
(Michael Appleby) *s.i.s: hld up: hdwy wl over 1f out: hmpd and wknd sn after* **50/1**
334- **11** *3 1/4* **Bursting Bubbles (IRE)**[130] 7673 3-9-5 **58** ... TomMcLaughlin 11 41
(Ed Dunlop) *sn pushed along in rr: rdn and hung rt over 2f out: sn wknd* **13/2**[3]
500- **12** *9* **Gabrial's Layla (IRE)**[149] 7493 3-8-13 **52** ... JamieSpencer 8 16
(Mark Johnston) *led over 7f out: rdn and hdd 2f out: wkng whn hmpd over 1f out: eased* **13/2**[3]

2m 1.49s (-0.21) **Going Correction** -0.05s/f (Stan) **12** Ran SP% **118.1**
Speed ratings (Par 96): **98,97,94,94,94 93,93,93,92,91 88,80**
toteswingers:1&2:£20.80, 2&3:£31.90, 1&3:£7.40 CSF £221.53 CT £1470.23 TOTE £7.80: £2.50, £7.40, £2.90; EX 194.20.
Owner Always Trying Partnership VIII (E) **Bred** Miss K Rausing **Trained** Middleham Moor, N Yorks

FOCUS
A weak 3-y-o handicap on paper, but there were plenty of potential improvers lurking. The winner beltedly built on his early 2yo form.
Moment In The Sun Official explanation: jockey said filly was denied a clear run

1425 32REDPOKER.COM APPRENTICE H'CAP 1m 1f 103y(P)
5:15 (5:15) (Class 6) (0-55,55) 4-Y-0+ **£1,704** (£503; £251) **Stalls** Low

Form RPR
-632 **1** **So Is She (IRE)**[5] 1299 4-8-11 **50** ... (be) NatashaEaton 3 59
(Alan Bailey) *prom: hmpd and lost pl after 1f: hld up in tch: rdn over 1f out: edgd lft and r.o to ld nr fin* **5/2**[1]
1500 **2** *1/2* **Harrys Yer Man**[39] 843 8-8-13 **52** ... JackDuern 13 60
(Mark Brisbourne) *s.i.s: hld up: hdwy over 1f out: r.o wl to go 2nd nr fin: nt rch wnr* **12/1**
045 **3** *1/2* **Lean Machine**[5] 1309 5-8-11 **50** ... (p) DarrenEgan 9 57
(Ronald Harris) *trckd ldrs: racd keenly: led over 6f out: clr over 2f out: rdn over 1f out: hdd nr fin* **8/1**
4443 **4** *4 1/2* **Roman Flame**[18] 1095 4-8-11 **50** ... DannyBrock 7 48
(Michael Quinn) *chsd ldrs: rdn over 1f out: no ex fnl f* **16/1**
320- **5** *1 1/2* **Naledi**[194] 3910 8-8-4 **48** ... JacobButterfield(5) 2 42
(Richard Price) *prom: hmpd and lost pl after 1f: hdwy over 1f out: edgd lft: nt trble ldrs* **20/1**
0002 **6** *1 1/2* **Kenswick**[18] 1095 5-8-7 **46** oh1 ... (v) CharlesBishop 10 37
(Pat Eddery) *led: hdd over 6f out: chsd ldr: rdn over 2f out: wknd fnl f* **9/1**
00-0 **7** *1 3/4* **Rasteau (IRE)**[18] 1095 4-8-7 **46** oh1 ... LukeRowe 11 34
(Tom Keddy) *hld up: rdn over 2f out: nvr on terms* **18/1**
30-0 **8** *1/2* **Nicholas Pocock (IRE)**[9] 1222 6-9-2 **55** ... JustinNewman 1 41
(Ian McInnes) *prom: hmpd and lost pl after 1f: n.d after* **16/1**
-403 **9** *12* **Hubood**[11] 1207 4-8-12 **54** ... JoshBaudains(3) 8 15
(Clive Brittain) *mid-div: rdn and wknd over 2f out* **13/2**[3]
6143 **10** *2 1/4* **Cwmni**[31] 929 6-8-10 **52** ... ThomasBrown(3) 12
(Bryn Palling) *hld up: hdwy over 4f out: rdn and wknd wl over 1f out* **11/1**
043- **11** *1 3/4* **Tigerbill**[191] 6698 4-9-0 **53** ... (t) DarylByrne 5
(Nicky Vaughan) *s.i.s: hdwy over 6f out: rdn and wknd over 2f out* **11/2**[2]
0402 **12** *24* **By Implication**[45] 773 4-8-4 **46** oh1 ... (b) IanBurns(3) 4
(Ed de Giles) *prom: rdn over 3f out: wknd over 2f out* **8/1**

2m 0.74s (-0.96) **Going Correction** -0.05s/f (Stan) **12** Ran SP% **127.3**
Speed ratings (Par 101): **102,101,101,97,95 94,92,92,81,79 78,56**
toteswingers:1&2:£13.60, 2&3:£22.20, 1&3:£8.20 CSF £38.12 CT £226.95 TOTE £4.20: £1.60, £4.70, £2.60; EX 69.00.
Owner Allan McNamee **Bred** Bayview Properties Ltd **Trained** Newmarket, Suffolk
■ Stewards' Enquiry : Charles Bishop nine-days ban: careless riding (Apr 30-May 8)

FOCUS
A weak handicap, run at a solid pace and the principals finished clear of the remainder. The winner confirmed C&D form with the third.
Hubood Official explanation: trainer's rep said filly bled from the nose
T/Jkpt: £33,772.90 to a £1 stake. Pool of £499,459.47 - 10.50 winning tickets. T/Plt: £43.20 to a £1 stake. Pool of £94,543.61 - 1,594.25 winning tickets. T/Qpdt: £17.90 to a £1 stake. Pool of £7,320.63 - 301.92 winning tickets. CR

1208 MAISONS-LAFFITTE (R-H)

Monday, April 16

OFFICIAL GOING: Turf: good

1426a PRIX SIGY (LISTED RACE) (3YO) (TURF) 6f (S)

2:20 (12:00) 3-Y-O **£22,916** (£9,166; £6,875; £4,583; £2,291)

RPR

1 **Gusto**[23] 1032 3-9-1 0 OlivierPeslier 10 108
(Richard Hannon) *broke wl towards outside: racd promly: rdn over 2f out: chal for ld 100yds out: looked hld: rallied wl u.p 25yds out: got up to take ld cl home* **11/5**[1]

2 *snk* **Carnoustie (FR)**[32] 913 3-8-8 0 ThierryThulliez 11 101
(N Clement, France) *fin 3rd, snk & nse: plcd 2nd* **16/1**

3 *1 1/4* **Reech Band**[22] 3-8-8 0 IoritzMendizabal 4 97
(D De Watrigant, France) *fin 4th: plcd 3rd* **20/1**

4 *nse* **Huma Bird**[17] 1125 3-8-8 0 MaximeGuyon 5 101
(H-A Pantall, France) *fin 2nd, snk: disqualified and plcd 4th* **12/1**

5 *shd* **Nagham (IRE)**[275] 4094 3-8-8 0 StephanePasquier 3 97
(Kevin Ryan) *broke wl towards stands' rail to r bhd ldrs: r.o wl fnl f to go 4th: no ex fnl 50yds* **12/1**

6 *1 1/4* **Tibaldi (FR)**[11] 1209 3-8-11 0 JohanVictoire 1 96
(Mme C Head-Maarek, France) **11/1**

7 *snk* **Tycoon's Garden (FR)**[146] 7508 3-8-11 0 Christophe-PatriceLemaire 8 95
(E Lellouche, France) **30/1**

8 *1* **Aviator (FR)**[168] 3-8-11 0 AlexisBadel 7 92
(Mme M Bollack-Badel, France) **23/1**

9 *1/2* **Calahorra (FR)**[167] 7220 3-8-11 0 ChristopheSoumillon 2 90
(C Baillet, France) **14/1**

10 *1/2* **Mister Ryan (FR)**[17] 1125 3-8-11 0 GeraldMosse 14 89
(H-A Pantall, France) **9/1**[2]

0 **Arabian Falcon**[171] 7155 3-8-11 0 FranckBlondel 15
(A Kleinkorres, Germany) **69/1**

0 **Dont Teutch (FR)**[167] 7220 3-9-1 0 GregoryBenoist 16
(D Smaga, France) **10/1**[3]

0 **Sotka**[272] 4191 3-8-8 0 ThierryJarnet 17
(F-H Graffard, France) **29/1**

0 **Small Frida (FR)**[32] 913 3-8-8 0 (b) Pierre-CharlesBoudot 12
(Mme Pia Brandt, France) **21/1**

0 **Paris Blue (FR)**[11] 1208 3-8-11 0 BriceRaballand 9
(J-L Pelletan, France) **31/1**

0 **Gaazaal (IRE)**[15] 3-8-8 0 AurelienLemaitre 6
(F Head, France) **14/1**

1m 12.4s (-1.00) **16** Ran SP% **117.9**
WIN (incl. 1 euro stake): 3.20. PLACES: 1.90, 3.60, 4.80. DF: 29.90. SF: 44.80.
Owner Highclere Thoroughbred Racing-Rock Sand **Bred** New England, Mount Coote & P Barrett **Trained** East Everleigh, Wilts

NOTEBOOK
Gusto travelled smoothly before leading, than rallied gamely to get back up. He may go for the Jersey Stakes.
Huma Bird got short of room as things tightened up on the rail.

1277 SOUTHWELL (L-H)

Tuesday, April 17

OFFICIAL GOING: Standard

Wind: Fresh across Weather: Cloudy with sunny periods

1427 MEMBERSHIP OF SOUTHWELL GOLF CLUB MEDIAN AUCTION MAIDEN STKS 1m (F)

2:10 (2:10) (Class 6) 3-5-Y-O **£1,704** (£503; £251) **Stalls** Low

Form RPR

022- 1 **Silver Blaze**[189] 6774 3-8-6 85 PJMcDonald 3 77
(Alan Swinbank) *cl up: effrt 3f out: rdn to chal 2f out: led over 1f out: kpt on strly* **6/4**[2]

440- 2 *2 3/4* **Gunner Will (IRE)**[179] 6986 3-8-8 78 ow2 JamieSpencer 5 73
(George Baker) *led: rdn along and edgd lft 2f out: hdd wl over 1f out: one pce fnl f* **1/1**[1]

5 3 *1 3/4* **Ty Gwr**[13] 1192 3-8-6 0 MartinLane 4 67
(David Simcock) *t.k.h: chsd ldng pair: effrt on outer 3f out: rdn 2f out and ch tl wknd appr fnl f* **25/1**

0- 4 *25* **Bridgehampton**[222] 5851 3-8-6 0 HayleyTurner 6 +
(Michael Bell) *s.i.s: sn rdn along: a bhd* **11/2**[3]

5 *15* **July Specialists** 3-8-0 0 ow2 DeclanCannon(3) 1
(Richard Guest) *chsd ldrs: rdn along over 3f out and sn wknd* **66/1**

1m 42.88s (-0.82) **Going Correction** -0.125s/f (Stan) **5** Ran SP% **110.7**
Speed ratings (Par 101): **99,96,94,69,54**
CSF £3.36 TOTE £3.20: £1.20, £1.10; EX 3.40.
Owner Mrs I Gibson **Bred** Southill Stud **Trained** Melsonby, N Yorks

FOCUS
A bright, dry afternoon and quite a brisk tail wind in the home straight. No older horses in this maiden and there were just three still in serious contention turning in. The time was slow and the form is not rated as high as it might have been.

1428 MIRROR PUNTERS CLUB FILLIES' H'CAP 5f (F)

2:40 (2:43) (Class 5) (0-70,69) 4-Y-O+ **£2,264** (£673; £336; £168) **Stalls** High

Form RPR

1050 1 **Gorgeous Goblin (IRE)**[16] 1161 5-9-3 **65** (t) DavidProbert 5 76
(David C Griffiths) *trckd ldrs: smooth hdwy 2f out: rdn to ld appr fnl f: edgd lft and kpt on* **7/2**[2]

0131 2 *1 3/4* **Da'Quonde (IRE)**[8] 1246 4-9-2 **64** 6ex TomEaves 3 69
(Bryan Smart) *slt ld: rdn wl over 1f out: hdd appr fnl f: kpt on same pce* **5/4**[1]

413- 3 *nk* **Bobby's Doll**[233] 5517 5-9-0 **69** GeorgeanBuckell(7) 1 73
(Terry Clement) *in tch: rdn along: outpcd and bhd after 2f: hdwy on wd outside wl over 1f out: kpt on u.p to chse ldng pair ins fnl f: nrst fin* **11/1**

026 4 *1* **Basle**[43] 806 5-8-4 **59** (t) DannyBrock(7) 7 59
(Gay Kelleway) *chsd ldrs on outer: hdwy 2f out: rdn and edgd lft ent fnl f: one pce* **11/1**

140- 5 *9* **Imaginary Diva**[197] 6580 6-9-2 **64** JamieSpencer 6 32
(George Margarson) *cl up: rdn along 2f out: sn wknd* **15/2**

0-06 6 *1/2* **Nine Before Ten (IRE)**[20] 1073 4-9-5 **67** MartinHarley 2 33
(Richard Guest) *dwlt: sn trcking ldrs: effrt and cl up 1/2-way: sn rdn and wknd wl over 1f out* **25/1**

0554 7 *1 1/4* **La Capriosa**[7] 1280 6-8-12 **60** (b) RobertWinston 4 22
(Scott Dixon) *cl up: rdn along over 2f out: sn wknd* **13/2**[3]

58.33s (-1.37) **Going Correction** -0.175s/f (Stan) **7** Ran SP% **112.3**
Speed ratings (Par 100): **103,100,99,98,83 82,80**
CSF £7.95 TOTE £4.10: £2.50, £1.30; EX 7.40.
Owner K Humphries & Sons Roofing Contractors **Bred** S & L Humphries **Trained** Bawtry, S Yorks

FOCUS
A modest fillies' sprint handicap. Not easy form to rate with the favourite a bit disappointing.

1429 SOUTHWELL-RACECOURSE.CO.UK CLAIMING STKS 1m 3f (F)

3:10 (3:10) (Class 6) 4-Y-0+ **£1,704** (£503; £251) **Stalls** Low

Form RPR

51-0 1 **Jack Dawkins (USA)**[6] 1295 7-9-3 68 PaulQuinn 5 80+
(David Nicholls) *trckd ldr: hdwy and cl up 5f out: led 4f out: clr wl over 2f out: easily* **5/1**[2]

3100 2 *9* **Trans Sonic**[6] 1295 9-9-1 79 (p) DanielTudhope 3 60
(David O'Meara) *set str pce: jnd 5f out: hdd 4f out and sn rdn: kpt on same pce fnl 2f: no ch w wnr* **2/1**[1]

00-3 3 *5* **Doctor Zhivago**[7] 1275 5-9-3 73 TomEaves 7 53
(Ian McInnes) *in tch: pushed along over 5f out: sn rdn and plugged on same pce* **2/1**[1]

4 4 *1 1/4* **Polurrian (IRE)**[28] 976 5-8-12 0 DeclanCannon(3) 8 49
(David O'Meara) *hld up towards rr: hdwy 5f out: rdn along 3f out: plodded on same pce* **25/1**

2630 5 *17* **Maslak (IRE)**[6] 1297 8-8-13 62 LukeMorris 6 16
(Peter Hiatt) *chsd ldng pair: rdn along bef 1/2-way: outpcd and bhd fr over 4f out* **8/1**[3]

0042 6 *8* **Irish Jugger (USA)**[22] 1047 5-8-11 58 ow2 (b) JamesMillman 1
(Rod Millman) *hld up: effrt over 5f out: sn rdn along and nvr a factor* **8/1**[3]

0/0- 7 *16* **Centre Stage**[322] 2596 4-8-13 0 DavidProbert 4
(Michael Appleby) *a towards rr: outpcd and bhd fnl 4f* **40/1**

2m 23.5s (-4.50) **Going Correction** -0.125s/f (Stan) **7** Ran SP% **111.8**
Speed ratings (Par 101): **111,104,100,99,87 81,70**
toteswingers:1&2:£2.70, 2&3:£1.80, 1&3:£2.50 CSF £14.75 TOTE £5.50: £3.10, £1.90; EX 16.80 Trifecta £48.00 Pool: £720.52 - 11.10 winning units..
Owner The Three K's **Bred** Clovelly Farms **Trained** Sessay, N Yorks

FOCUS
They went a strong pace and official ratings were turned upside down. The level is hard to pin down with the second and third both clearly below form

1430 DINE AT SOUTHWELL RACECOURSE (S) STKS 6f (F)

3:40 (3:40) (Class 6) 4-Y-0+ **£1,704** (£503; £251) **Stalls** Low

Form RPR

4221 1 **Punching**[7] 1279 8-9-4 69 HayleyTurner 4 76
(Conor Dore) *mde all: rdn wl over 1f out: kpt on gamely ins fnl f* **2/1**[1]

1235 2 *3/4* **Elhamri**[7] 1279 8-9-4 67 LiamKeniry 1 74
(Conor Dore) *chsd ldrs on inner: hdwy 2f out: sn rdn: kpt on ins fnl f* **16/1**

3421 3 *hd* **Ace Of Spies (IRE)**[7] 1280 7-9-4 62 LukeMorris 3 73
(Conor Dore) *chsd ldrs: rdn along and sltly outpcd bef 1/2-way: hdwy wl over 1f out: styd on u.p fnl f* **5/2**[3]

6-53 4 *1 1/4* **Jake The Snake (IRE)**[20] 1069 11-8-7 80 DuilioDaSilva(5) 6 63
(Richard Guest) *cl up: rdn along and edgd rt wl over 1f out: drvn and one pce ent fnl f* **6/1**

00-4 5 *2* **Beat The Bell**[7] 1279 7-8-7 81 DeanHeslop(5) 7 57
(David Barron) *prom on outer: rdn along 2f out: drvn appr fnl f and kpt on same pce* **9/4**[2]

03-0 6 *2 1/2* **Charles Parnell (IRE)**[7] 1280 9-8-12 53 (p) MichaelStainton 2 49
(Simon Griffiths) *dwlt: a in rr* **66/1**

1m 16.44s (-0.06) **Going Correction** -0.125s/f (Stan) **6** Ran SP% **114.3**
Speed ratings (Par 101): **95,94,93,92,89 86**
toteswingers:1&2:£3.90, 2&3:£3.20, 1&3:£1.70 CSF £32.75 TOTE £3.20: £1.40, £5.20; EX 15.90 Trifecta £29.30 Pool: £851.24 - 21.45 winning units..The winner was bought in for 6,250gns. Beat The Bell was claimed by J Osborne for £6,000.
Owner Liam Breslin **Bred** Cheveley Park Stud Ltd **Trained** Hubbert's Bridge, Lincs

FOCUS
The first three home were all trained by Conor Dore. Straightforward form with the first three close to their marks.

1431 SPORTS360.CO.UK H'CAP 7f (F)

4:10 (4:10) (Class 4) (0-85,83) 4-Y-0+ **£4,075** (£1,212; £606; £303) **Stalls** Low

Form RPR

224- 1 **Powerful Presence (IRE)**[160] 7339 6-9-3 **79** DanielTudhope 7 91
(David O'Meara) *cl up: led wl over 2f out: rdn over 1f out: kpt on wl towards fin* **3/1**[1]

0245 2 *nk* **Masai Moon**[20] 1066 8-9-3 **79** (b) JamesMillman 8 90
(Rod Millman) *hld up in tch: hdwy on outer wl over 1f out: rdn and styd on to chal ins fnl f: ev ch tl no ex towards fin* **13/2**[3]

00-6 3 *1/2* **Memory Cloth**[39] 846 5-9-6 **82** BarryMcHugh 1 92
(Brian Ellison) *trckd ldrs on inner: effrt over 2f out: rdn over 1f out: sn ev ch: edgd rt ent fnl f: kpt on* **12/1**

0060 4 *nk* **All Right Now**[5] 1342 5-8-7 **69** AndreaAtzeni 9 78
(Derek Haydn Jones) *prom: rdn along 2f out: drvn and n.m.r ent fnl f: kpt on same pce* **9/2**[2]

-400 5 *5* **Sos Brillante (CHI)**[10] 1213 7-9-2 **78** LukeMorris 2 74
(Terry Clement) *in tch: rdn along 3f out: drvn wl over 1f out and no imp* **22/1**

4-23 6 *shd* **Sound Amigo (IRE)**[16] 1156 4-9-6 **82** PJMcDonald 6 77
(Ollie Pears) *t.k.h early: trckd ldrs: effrt and swtchd lft 2f out: sn rdn and no imp* **3/1**[1]

1601 7 *nk* **Mazovian (USA)**[14] 1177 4-8-4 **73** DannyBrock(7) 5 67
(Michael Chapman) *led: rdn along 3f out: sn hdd and grad wknd fr over 1f out* **9/1**

0-45 8 *1* **Klynch**[15] 1168 6-9-4 **80** (b) JamesSullivan 4 72
(Ruth Carr) *racd wd: a in rr* **22/1**

0600 9 *6* **Zacynthus (IRE)**[6] 1321 4-9-4 **83** (bt[1]) DeclanCannon(3) 3 59
(Alan McCabe) *sn rdn along and a in rr* **14/1**

1m 27.6s (-2.70) **Going Correction** -0.125s/f (Stan) **9** Ran SP% **114.6**
Speed ratings (Par 105): **110,109,109,108,103 102,102,101,94**
toteswingers:1&2:£2.90, 2&3:£18.40, 1&3:£10.10 CSF £22.77 CT £200.34 TOTE £4.70: £1.40, £2.90, £3.50; EX 21.70 Trifecta £352.70 Pool: £791.35 - 1.66 winning units..
Owner The Lawton Bamforth Partnership **Bred** Corduff Stud **Trained** Nawton, N Yorks

FOCUS
A competitive handicap run at a strong pace and there was little between the first four home at the line. Interesting form with the winner recording a personal best.

1432 SPORTS 360 THE SPORTS ADVERTISING SPECIALISTS H'CAP 1m 3f (F)
4:40 (4:40) (Class 6) (0-65,65) 4-Y-0+ **£1,704** (£503; £251) **Stalls** Low

Form RPR
4620 **1** **Kingaroo (IRE)**[42] 811 6-8-9 **53** LukeMorris 9 61
(Garry Woodward) *trckd ldr: cl up 1/2-way: effrt to chal 3f out: rdn to ld 2f out: drvn and styd on wl ins fnl f* **8/1**
4013 **2** 2 1/4 **Ostentation**[9] 1240 5-9-3 **61** BrettDoyle 8 65+
(Alastair Lidderdale) *trckd ldrs: hdwy to chse ldng pair 3f out: rdn and n.m.r whn unbalanced wl over 1f out: sn chsng wnr: edgd lft and no imp ins fnl f* **13/8**[1]
00-2 **3** 3 **What's The Point**[39] 847 4-9-7 **65** (p) TomEaves 7 64+
(Ollie Pears) *led: rdn along 3f out: hdd 2f out: sn drvn and one pce* **3/1**[2]
0324 **4** 1 1/2 **Jordaura**[22] 1045 6-9-4 **62** (e[1]) RobertWinston 2 58
(Gay Kelleway) *hld up in rr: hdwy over 3f out: rdn over 2f out: plugged on: nt rch ldrs* **5/1**[3]
00-0 **5** 3 1/4 **Sharp Sovereign (USA)**[17] 1135 6-9-1 **62** DaleSwift(3) 5 52
(Ian McInnes) *chsd ldrs: rdn along 5f out: sn wknd* **8/1**
33 **6** *hd* **Revolving World (IRE)**[35] 889 9-8-7 **51** oh5 (t) RussKennemore 3 41
(Lee James) *s.i.s and bhd: hdwy on outer and in tch 1/2-way: rdn over 4f out: drvn and wknd over 3f out* **14/1**
4145 **7** 7 **Nolecce**[7] 1286 5-9-3 **64** (e[1]) DeclanCannon(3) 1 41
(Richard Guest) *in tch: rdn along over 4f out: sn wknd* **8/1**
54-0 **8** 8 **Munaawib**[7] 1276 4-9-1 **59** (vt[1]) DavidProbert 6 22
(David C Griffiths) *chsd ldng pair: rdn along over 4f out and sn wknd* **18/1**

2m 26.63s (-1.37) **Going Correction** -0.125s/f (Stan) **8** Ran SP% **125.0**
Speed ratings (Par 101): **99,97,95,94,91 91,86,80**
toteswingers:1&2:£4.80, 2&3:£1.80, 1&3:£3.90 CSF £23.62 CT £52.21 TOTE £12.30: £3.60, £1.60, £1.10; EX 40.10 Trifecta £45.50 Pool: £994.86 - 16.15 winning units..
Owner J Pownall **Bred** Kevin Walsh **Trained** Bolham, Notts
FOCUS
A modest handicap run at a sound pace. The winner stepped up on his winter efforts but the form is not entirely convincing.

1433 PLAY GOLF AT SOUTHWELL APPRENTICE H'CAP 1m 6f (F)
5:10 (5:10) (Class 5) (0-70,62) 4-Y-0+ **£2,385** (£704; £352) **Stalls** Low

Form RPR
0015 **1** **Carnac (IRE)**[14] 1175 6-9-10 **60** (p) NoraLooby 4 68
(Alan McCabe) *trckd ldng pair: cl up 4f out: led 3f out and sn rdn clr: easily* **15/8**[1]
5524 **2** 8 **Dunaskin (IRE)**[9] 1240 12-8-9 **45** (b) JasonHart 6 42
(Richard Guest) *cl up: pushed along to ld 4f out: rdn and hdd 3f out: drvn and plugged on fnl 2f: no ch w wnr* **13/2**
/40- **3** 5 **King's Road**[224] 5804 7-9-9 **59** (t) WilliamTwiston-Davies 1 49
(Anabel K Murphy) *trckd ldrs on inner: chsd ldng pair over 3f out: rdn 2f out and plugged on same pce* **7/2**[2]
5-23 **4** 7 **Nippy Nikki**[21] 1055 4-8-11 **52** DavidSimmonson(3) 2 32
(John Norton) *in rr and pushed along after 4f: hdwy 1/2-way: trckd ldrs on inner over 4f out: sn rdn and outpcd over 3f out* **9/2**[3]
3534 **5** 5 **Jonnie Skull (IRE)**[7] 1283 6-8-12 **55** (tp) RobJFitzpatrick(7) 3 28
(Phil McEntee) *led: rdn along and hdd 4f out: sn wknd* **8/1**
/04- **6** 31 **Al Shababiya (IRE)**[47] 7244 5-9-12 **62** (p) GeorgeDowning 5
(Alison Thorpe) *in rr and rdn along after 4f: bhd fr 1/2-way* **9/1**

3m 9.84s (1.54) **Going Correction** -0.125s/f (Stan)
WFA 4 from 5yo+ 2lb **6** Ran SP% **109.6**
Speed ratings (Par 103): **90,85,82,78,75 58**
toteswingers:1&2:£2.60, 2&3:£4.70, 1&3:£1.70 CSF £13.71 TOTE £2.40: £1.70, £2.80; EX 13.00.
Owner A J McCabe & Charles Wentworth **Bred** Kilfrush Stud **Trained** Averham Park, Notts
FOCUS
A weak apprentice handicap. It's doubtful if the winner's effort can be taken at face value.
T/Plt: £29.60 to a £1 stake. Pool of £64,353.57 - 1,582.04 winning tickets. T/Qpdt: £21.00 to a £1 stake. Pool of £4,692.83 - 164.72 winning tickets. JR

1268 SAINT-CLOUD (L-H)
Tuesday, April 17
OFFICIAL GOING: Turf: good to soft changing to soft after race 2 (1.20)

1434a PRIX PENELOPE (GROUP 3) (3YO FILLIES) (TURF) 1m 2f 110y
1:50 (12:00) 3-Y-0 **£33,333** (£13,333; £10,000; £6,666; £3,333)

RPR
1 **Waldlerche**[159] 3-9-0 0 MaximeGuyon 4 106
(A Fabre, France) *sn led: gng wl: surrendered ld towards end of bkstretch w over 3f to r: regained ld over 2 1/2f out as field swtchd to stands' rail: r.o strly: nvr threatened: comf: eased fnl 25yds* **2/1**[1]
2 3/4 **Crecy**[31] 952 3-9-0 0 IoritzMendizabal 7 105
(Y Fouin, France) *racd towards rr: gd prog fr 2 1/2f out: qcknd wl ent fnl 1 1/2f to go 2nd: r.o wl u.p wout threatening ldr: all out to hold 2nd cl home fr rallying Rjwa* **9/1**
3 *hd* **Rjwa (IRE)**[42] 3-9-0 0 Francois-XavierBertras 6 105
(F Rohaut, France) *racd 2nd on outside of ldr: 3rd ent st: r.o wl u.p on stands' side: rallied fnl f to jst miss 2nd cl home* **23/10**[2]
4 3 **Brocottes (FR)**[157] 7405 3-9-0 0 Christophe-PatriceLemaire 1 99
(N Clement, France) *racd 3rd: dropped bk to 4th bef st: rdn but no ex fr over 2f out: styd on fnl f* **33/10**[3]
5 1/2 **Rose Vista (FR)**[19] 3-9-0 0 AntoineHamelin 5 98
(J-L Guillochon, France) *at rr of field fr s: styd on wl fr over 2 1/2f out wout threatening ldrs* **13/1**
6 1 1/2 **Mirandola (FR)**[31] 952 3-9-0 0 Pierre-CharlesBoudot 3 95
(Y De Nicolay, France) *racd 4th: dropped bk to 5th bef st: rdn but no ex fr 2 1/2f out: styd on fnl 1 1/2f* **28/1**
7 12 **Joly Berengere (FR)**[28] 3-9-0 0 OlivierPeslier 2 71
(M Cesandri, France) *racd 5th: sent through to ld on inner rail bef end of bkstretch as rest of field racd wd: led into st: hdd 2 1/2f out: u.p fr 2f out: no ex: fdd* **11/1**

2m 19.8s (0.20) **7** Ran SP% **115.8**
WIN (incl. 1 euro stake): 3.00. PLACES: 2.00, 3.40. SF: 14.30.
Owner Gestut Bernried **Bred** Newsells Park Stud **Trained** Chantilly, France

NOTEBOOK
Waldlerche showed class and a little courage to maintain her 100 per cent record. A half-sister by Monsun to Masked Marvel, she was adding to her sole success at two. She set very modest early fractions, with several of his rivals forced to fight their mounts in an attempt to settle. Having briefly ceded the lead, she moved smoothly to take control 2f from home, and galloped all the way to the line. She is engaged in the Prix Saint-Alary and the Prix de Diane.

BEVERLEY (R-H)
Wednesday, April 18
OFFICIAL GOING: Good to soft (good in places) changing to soft after race 2 (2:10)

1435 ANDY TAYLOR SNR IS 70 TODAY MAIDEN AUCTION STKS (DIV I) 5f
1:40 (1:42) (Class 5) 2-Y-0 **£2,296** (£683; £341; £170) **Stalls** Low

Form RPR
1 **Ingleby Royale** 2-8-4 0 PatrickMathers 1 70
(Richard Fahey) *trckd ldrs on inner: hdwy 2f out: rdn over 1f out: styd on ins fnl f to ld last 75yds* **11/1**
4 **2** *nk* **Hillbilly Boy (IRE)**[8] 1277 2-8-8 0 DuilioDaSilva(5) 8 78
(Bill Turner) *wnt lft s: cl up: rdn to ld appr fnl f: sn drvn and edgd lft and rt: hdd and no ex last 75yds* **7/1**[3]
3 4 1/2 **Twilight Pearl** 2-8-7 0 ow1 DavidAllan 4 56+
(Tim Easterby) *prom: effrt 2f out: sn rdn and one pce fr over 1f out* **16/1**
2 **4** 1/2 **Ceiling Kitty**[18] 1136 2-8-11 0 RichardKingscote 2 58
(Tom Dascombe) *led: rdn along 2f out: edgd lft and hdd appr fnl f: sn hung lft and wknd* **9/4**[1]
3 **5** 1 3/4 **Mayfield Girl (IRE)**[18] 1131 2-8-8 0 RobertWinston 5 49
(Mel Brittain) *dwlt and towards rr: hdwy 2f out: sn rdn and styd on fnl f: nrst fin* **9/4**[1]
4 **6** 6 **Kryena's Rose**[16] 1164 2-8-1 0 CharlesBishop(5) 6 25
(Mick Channon) *chsd ldrs: rdn along over 2f out: sn wknd* **13/2**[2]
7 11 **Secret Destination** 2-8-4 0 BarryMcHugh 10
(Brian Ellison) *dwlt: a towards rr* **10/1**
8 *shd* **Dream Vale (IRE)** 2-8-4 0 DuranFentiman 9
(Tim Easterby) *sltly hmpd s and towards rr: sme hdwy and midfield 1/2-way: sn rdn along and wknd* **50/1**
9 10 **Special Report (IRE)** 2-8-8 0 DeclanCannon(3) 7
(Nigel Tinkler) *sn outpcd and a in rr* **50/1**
10 18 **Moss The Boss (IRE)** 2-8-9 0 MickyFenton 11
(Paul Midgley) *racd wd: in tch: pushed along 1/2-way: sn outpcd and bhd* **28/1**

1m 7.37s (3.87) **Going Correction** +0.725s/f (Yiel) **10** Ran SP% **118.0**
Speed ratings (Par 92): **98,97,90,89,86 77,59,59,43,14**
toteswingers:1&2:£20.80, 1&3:£25.10, 2&3:£15.60 CSF £85.69 TOTE £12.80: £4.10, £1.10, £4.90; EX 111.90.
Owner Percy Green Racing 4 & Partner **Bred** W Davis **Trained** Musley Bank, N Yorks
FOCUS
There was persistent rain at the course all morning, changing the official going to Good to soft, good in places. Four were taken out prior to the race but this still looked quite an interesting maiden, run at a solid pace with the field well strung out a long way from home.
NOTEBOOK
Ingleby Royale, well drawn in stall 1, did not get the best of breaks against some more experienced rivals but showed decent early pace to sit behind the leaders. He picked up well at the 2f marker and showed a willing attitude to hold off Hillbilly Boy inside the final furlong. His pedigree suggests he will want further in time so the rain-softened ground will have helped, but this was still a likeable debut. (op 12-1 tchd 10-1)
Hillbilly Boy(IRE)'s trainer's early-season 2yos are always worth noting and this one stepped up on his debut effort when fourth at Southwell, chasing the winner all the way to the line. He raced wide throughout but showed a willing attitude and his astute handler should find a race for this one. (op 9-1)
Twilight Pearl, related to some juvenile winners, was under pressure some way out but stayed on well on the testing ground, suggesting a step up in trip might suit.
Ceiling Kitty had the race run to suit from stall 2 but the well-supported favourite weakened inside the final furlong. She should be seen to better effect on quicker ground. (op 15-8)
Mayfield Girl(IRE)'s form, when third in the Brocklesby, has taken a knock recently and while she was not helped by a slow start, it was disappointing she could not finish closer. (op 5-2)
Kryena's Rose, running here from four possible entries in the next five days, showed early speed before fading and is another who looked unsuited by the going. (op 8-1)

1436 ROWAN LODGE (S) STKS 1m 100y
2:10 (2:10) (Class 6) 3-Y-0+ **£1,681** (£500; £250; £125) **Stalls** Low

Form RPR
4-12 **1** **Violent Velocity (IRE)**[54] 692 9-9-9 74 MichaelO'Connell(3) 6 79
(John Quinn) *trckd ldrs: hdwy 3f out: swtchd rt to inner 2f out: styd on to ld appr fnl f: rdn out* **9/4**[1]
00/0 **2** 1 **Woteva**[15] 1179 6-8-8 46 (p) EvaMoscrop(7) 7 66
(Nigel Tinkler) *led 1 1/2f: cl up: rdn to ld 2f out: hdd appr fnl f: kpt on* **40/1**
05- **3** 8 **Fu Fic Fas**[272] 4245 3-8-1 0 FrankieMcDonald 2 44
(Paul Fitzsimons) *midfield: hdwy over 3f out: rdn wl over 2f out: styd on u.p appr fnl f: n.d* **14/1**
-255 **4** 1/2 **River Ardeche**[8] 1276 7-9-6 69 RobertWinston 12 51
(Tracy Waggott) *trckd ldng pair: hdwy and cl up 4f out: led 3f out and wd to stands' rail: rdn and hdd 2f out: grad wknd* **5/1**[3]
6-50 **5** 3 1/2 **Ra Junior (USA)**[27] 1002 6-8-13 57 NedCurtis(7) 3 43
(Paul Midgley) *towards rr: hdwy 3f out: rdn over 2f out: plugged on: nvr nr ldrs* **8/1**
6 1 1/2 **Lucky For Some**[26] 5-8-10 0 DeanHeslop(5) 1 35
(Marjorie Fife) *dwlt and in rr: hdwy and wd st: rdn along on stands' rail over 2f out: plugged on: nvr nr ldrs* **100/1**
040- **7** 4 1/2 **Penderyn**[167] 7247 5-9-1 41 RobbieFitzpatrick 13 25
(Charles Smith) *led after 1 1/2f: rdn along and hdd 3f out: sn wknd* **100/1**
-400 **8** 1 3/4 **Kheskianto (IRE)**[68] 490 6-9-1 45 (b) RussKennemore 8 21
(Michael Chapman) *dwlt: a in rr* **100/1**
3510 **9** 5 **Greyfriarschorista**[17] 1161 5-9-7 78 DuilioDaSilva(5) 4 20
(Richard Guest) *chsd ldrs: rdn along wl over 2f out: sn wknd* **3/1**[2]
503- **10** 10 **Rowan Lodge (IRE)**[211] 6236 10-9-6 58 (b) PJMcDonald 9
(Ollie Pears) *midfield: rdn along over 3f out: sn wknd* **10/1**
5606 **11** 4 1/2 **Wing N Prayer (IRE)**[16] 1170 5-8-8 45 (p) DanielleMooney(7) 10
(John Wainwright) *a in rr* **50/1**

2331 **12** *11* **Marvo**[23] [1051] 8-9-12 68..................(b) TedDurcan 5
(Mark H Tompkins) *in tch: hdwy 4f out: rdn wl over 2f out and sn wknd* **5/1**[3]

1m 55.78s (8.18) **Going Correction** +1.10s/f (Soft)
WFA 3 from 4yo+ 14lb 12 Ran SP% **123.3**
Speed ratings (Par 101): **103,102,94,93,90 88,84,82,77,67 62,51**
toteswingers:1&2:£29.30, 1&3:£9.00, 2&3:£35.40 CSF £108.21 TOTE £2.70: £1.70, £7.40, £2.70; EX 146.20.The winner was bought in for £4,200.
Owner Mrs S Quinn **Bred** Miss Jill Finegan **Trained** Settrington, N Yorks

FOCUS
An average seller run at a decent gallop on a testing surface (officially changed to Soft after this race).
Marvo Official explanation: jockey said gelding had no more to give

1437 ANDY TAYLOR SNR IS 70 TODAY MAIDEN AUCTION STKS (DIV II) 5f
2:45 (2:49) (Class 5) 2-Y-O **£2,296** (£683; £341; £170) **Stalls** Low

Form RPR
1 **Tharawal Lady (IRE)** 2-8-8 0.................. LukeMorris 9 74
(John Quinn) *chsd ldrs: led jst ins fnl f: styd on wl* **16/1**
0 **2** *2 1/4* **Red Style (IRE)**[11] [1218] 2-8-9 0.................. MickyFenton 3 67
(Paul Midgley) *led: hdd jst ins fnl f: no ex* **25/1**
3 *2* **Inchy Coo** 2-8-11 0.................. DavidAllan 1 62
(Tim Easterby) *dwlt: in rr: hdwy over 1f out: styd on wl ins fnl f: will do bttr* **7/1**
4 *1 1/4* **Jubilee Games** 2-8-11 0.................. TonyHamilton 5 57
(Richard Fahey) *chsd ldrs: kpt on same pce appr fnl f* **11/2**[2]
622 **5** *nk* **Perfect Words (IRE)**[7] [1308] 2-8-4 0.................. CharlesBishop(5) 13 54
(Mick Channon) *hld up: hdwy on wd outside to chse ldrs over 2f out: kpt on one pce over 1f out* **13/2**[3]
6 *3/4* **Al Khisa (IRE)** 2-8-5 0.................. AmyRyan(3) 6 50
(Kevin Ryan) *wnt lft s: sn drvn along: kpt on fnl 2f: nvr nr ldrs* **10/1**
7 *5* **Miss Penny Arcade** 2-8-4 0.................. JoeFanning 10 30+
(Keith Dalgleish) *chsd ldrs: wknd over 1f out* **8/1**
8 *3 1/2* **Mount Seymour (IRE)** 2-8-8 0.................. DeclanCannon(3) 2 23
(Nigel Tinkler) *mid-div: hdwy to chse ldrs over 2f out: wknd over 1f out* **33/1**
9 *3 3/4* **Dha Chara (IRE)** 2-8-13 0.................. GrahamGibbons 7 11
(Reg Hollinshead) *hmpd s: drvn and sme hdwy over 2f out: sn wknd* **4/1**[1]
0 **10** *1* **Zero Rated (IRE)**[16] [1164] 2-8-6 0.................. DuranFentiman 8
(Tim Easterby) *chsd ldrs: wknd 2f out* **14/1**
11 *1 1/4* **Only For You** 2-8-4 0.................. JamesSullivan 11
(Alan Brown) *s.s: swtchd rt after s: a bhd* **50/1**
5 **12** *3 1/4* **Lucky Lodge**[18] [1131] 2-8-9 0.................. RobertWinston 12
(Mel Brittain) *dwlt: in rr: sme hdwy and swtchd wd outside 2f out: sn wknd* **4/1**[1]

1m 8.86s (5.36) **Going Correction** +0.925s/f (Soft) 12 Ran SP% **122.7**
Speed ratings (Par 92): **94,90,87,85,84 83,75,69,63,62 60,55**
toteswingers:1&2:£51.60, 1&3:£21.50, 2&3:£15.50 CSF £371.43 TOTE £27.10: £6.90, £10.20, £2.10; EX 893.00.
Owner Highfield Racing **Bred** Rathbarry Stud **Trained** Settrington, N Yorks

FOCUS
Due to the persistent heavy rain, the going had changed to Soft prior to the third race. As in the first division of this maiden, the pace was solid but the field were more well grouped approaching the final furlong.

NOTEBOOK
Tharawal Lady(IRE), who is closely related to smart sprinter Knot In Wood, made an encouraging debut. Always travelling well just behind the pace, she picked up nicely before battling on well to beat Red Style, who had the benefit of a previous run. The winner was giving John Quinn a quick double and while the handler is capable of readying one first time out, there should be more to come from this filly. (op 14-1)
Red Style(IRE) had shown little on her debut when last of nine at Musselburgh but this was a much-improved effort, for a yard which has yet to hit form. She was keen enough in front but quickened well and looks capable of landing a similar contest.
Inchy Coo, whose stablemate Twilight Pearl had run well in the first division of this maiden, stayed on well. Like her stablemate, she was outpaced early before staying on well into third and is bred to be better over further. (op 8-1 tchd 13-2)
Jubilee Games was under pressure 2f from home and stayed on well enough into fourth. She will come on for this. (op 9-2 tchd 6-1)
Perfect Words(IRE) was the most experienced in the field and stayed on well enough, but will probably be seen to better effect once handicapped. (op 11-2)
Dha Chara(IRE) was well supported throughout the day and looked good in the paddock but was never able to get competitive. (op 11-2 tchd 7-1)
Lucky Lodge was well beaten and is another to have let the Brocklesby form down. Official explanation: jockey said colt ran flat (op 9-2 tchd 7-2)

1438 PAT AND GRAHAM ROBERTS RUBY WEDDING H'CAP 5f
3:20 (3:27) (Class 3) (0-95,95) 4-Y-O+ **£7,115** (£2,117; £1,058; £529) **Stalls** Low

Form RPR
101- **1** **Magical Macey (USA)**[215] [6112] 5-9-3 91..........(b) GrahamGibbons 14 104
(David Barron) *trckd ldr: hdwy to ld over 1f out: rdn ins fnl f and kpt on strly* **20/1**
213- **2** *1* **Doc Hay (USA)**[165] [7298] 5-9-2 90.................. JoeFanning 6 99+
(Keith Dalgleish) *towards rr: hdwy 1/2-way: swtchd rt wl over 1f out: rdn and styd on to chse wnr ins fnl f: no imp towards fin* **15/2**[3]
5055 **3** *2 3/4* **Baby Strange**[5] [1362] 8-8-10 87.................. MichaelO'Connell(3) 7 87
(Derek Shaw) *midfield: pushed along and sltly outpcd 1/2-way: hdwy to chse ldrs whn swtchd lft ent fnl f: kpt on: nrst fin* **12/1**
346- **4** *1 3/4* **Hazelrigg (IRE)**[179] [7018] 7-8-12 86..........(be) DanielTudhope 3 79
(Tim Easterby) *trckd ldrs on inner: hdwy 2f out: rdn over 1f out: kpt on same pce* **7/1**[2]
0-35 **5** *nk* **Courageous (IRE)**[18] [1141] 6-8-12 86..........(t) FrederikTylicki 2 78
(Kevin Ryan) *led: rdn along 2f out: hdd appr fnl f and sn wknd* **13/2**[1]
330- **6** *3/4* **Racy**[179] [7018] 5-9-6 94.................. PhillipMakin 12 83
(Kevin Ryan) *prom: effrt 2f out: sn rdn and grad wknd appr fnl f* **7/1**[2]
00-0 **7** *1 1/2* **Sunraider (IRE)**[17] [1157] 5-8-13 87.................. MickyFenton 9 71
(Paul Midgley) *towards rr: hdwy wl over 1f out: sn rdn: kpt on fnl f: nvr rchd ldrs* **12/1**
040- **8** *3* **Cocktail Charlie**[179] [7018] 4-8-13 87.................. DavidAllan 8 60
(Tim Easterby) *midfield: effrt on inner 2f out: sn rdn and no imp* **9/1**
120- **9** *2 3/4* **Marvellous Value (IRE)**[180] [6987] 7-9-4 92.................. PaulMulrennan 10 55
(Michael Dods) *midfield: effrt 1/2-way: rdn 2f out and sn no hdwy* **9/1**
30-3 **10** *1* **Tagula Night (IRE)**[18] [1141] 6-9-0 88.................. TedDurcan 13 48
(Dean Ivory) *midfield: effrt 2f out: sn rdn and n.d* **11/1**
10-0 **11** *nk* **Marine Commando**[17] [1157] 4-9-3 91.................. TonyHamilton 1 50
(Richard Fahey) *a in rr* **12/1**
104- **12** *1 3/4* **Valery Borzov (IRE)**[165] [7295] 8-9-0 93.................. ShaneBKelly(5) 5 45
(Richard Fahey) *s.i.s: a in rr* **15/2**[3]
260- **13** *13* **Master Rooney (IRE)**[186] [6865] 6-8-13 87.................. RoystonFfrench 15
(Bryan Smart) *prom: rdn along 2f out: sn wknd* **20/1**

1m 7.2s (3.70) **Going Correction** +0.925s/f (Soft) 13 Ran SP% **122.8**
Speed ratings (Par 107): **107,105,101,98,97 96,94,89,84,83 82,80,59**
toteswingers:1&2:£14.40, 1&3:£11.90, 2&3:£17.20 CSF £167.66 CT £1955.26 TOTE £30.10: £10.40, £1.90, £4.60; EX 182.40.
Owner K J Alderson **Bred** Silver Springs Stud Farm Inc & Mrs J Costelloe **Trained** Maunby, N Yorks

FOCUS
A competitive 5f handicap for older horses was the feature on the card. They went a strong gallop from the outset on testing ground and it appeared particularly difficult to make up ground from behind under the prevailing conditions. They raced up the middle of the track and the draw looks much less significant than usual.

NOTEBOOK
Magical Macey(USA) won fresh from a similar break at Wolverhampton in April last year, and, having finished last season on very good terms with himself, reappeared in similar vein on his first start since taking a lesser-grade handicap off 6lb lower over this 5f trip on good to soft ground at Ayr last September. Re-plated beforehand, he flashed out of the gates, was always prominent and deserves real credit for a determined success. He has a good strike-rate over the minimum trip and looks set for further success if faced with similar conditions this season. (op 16-1)
Doc Hay(USA) was fancied under suitable conditions for an in-form yard and did best of those that didn't race prominently. This was a good seasonal reappearance and he looks likely to come on from it. (op 11-2 tchd 8-1)
Baby Strange drifted in the market which was surprising considering he arrived in form with reasonable each-way claims. He was another who made headway late on and will be of interest in similar grade off this sort of mark on better ground over 1f further this spring. (op 9-1 tchd 8-1)
Hazelrigg(IRE) was returning from a six-month break having performed well on better ground in a better race at Doncaster last October. He looks likely to benefit from this outing on better ground at up to 6f in the near future. (op 8-1 tchd 9-1)
Courageous(IRE) arrived in form but raced prominently and appeared to pay the price when one-paced late in the race. (tchd 7-1)
Racy returned from a break since October with a decent effort and, despite a modest strike-rate, remains of interest off a mark of 94 at up to 6f on better ground. (tchd 5-1)
Sunraider(IRE) progressed from his seasonal reappearance over 1f further at Doncaster this month and is another to take out of this race when stepped back up to 6f on better ground.
Tagula Night(IRE) Official explanation: jockey said gelding had no more to give
Master Rooney(IRE) Official explanation: trainer's rep said gelding was unsuited by the soft ground

1439 HORSEMEN'S GROUP BONUS FILLIES' STKS (H'CAP) 1m 1f 207y
3:55 (3:55) (Class 5) (0-70,69) 4-Y-O+ **£2,296** (£683; £341; £170) **Stalls** Low

Form RPR
110- **1** **Smart Step**[168] [7235] 4-9-5 67.................. JoeFanning 2 74
(Mark Johnston) *set stdy pce: qcknd 4f out: rdn 2f out: drvn and edgd lft ins fnl f: hld on gamely* **4/1**[1]
0204 **2** *nk* **Maven**[8] [1276] 4-9-7 69.................. DavidAllan 1 76
(Tim Easterby) *hld up in tch: hdwy 3f out: n.m.r and rdn wl over 1f out: swtchd rt to inner and drvn to chal ins fnl f: kpt on* **13/2**[2]
140- **3** *1 1/2* **Sangar**[194] [6674] 4-9-3 68.................. MichaelO'Connell(3) 9 72
(Ollie Pears) *trckd ldng pair on outer: hdwy over 2f out: rdn to chal over 1f out: drvn and ev ch whn edgd rt ent fnl f: no ex last 100yds* **4/1**[1]
0-03 **4** *3/4* **Climaxfortackle (IRE)**[7] [1311] 4-9-2 64.................. NickyMackay 7 66
(Derek Shaw) *trckd ldrs: effrt over 2f out and sn rdn: kpt on u.p ent fnl f: no imp* **12/1**
300- **5** *1 1/2* **Maybeme**[187] [6838] 6-8-3 58.................. TerenceFury(7) 8 57
(Neville Bycroft) *hld up towards rr: hdwy on outer and in tch 1/2-way: effrt wl over 2f out: rdn to chse ldrs over 1f out: kpt on same pce appr fnl f* **12/1**
040- **6** *6* **Spey Song (IRE)**[152] [7458] 4-9-7 69.................. GrahamGibbons 3 56
(James Bethell) *trckd ldrs: effrt 3f out: rdn over 2f out: grad wknd fr over 1f out* **7/1**[3]
0306 **7** *3/4* **Merrjanah**[17] [1154] 4-8-2 55.................. LeonnaMayor(5) 5 41
(John Wainwright) *hld up: a towards rr* **9/1**
3112 **8** *4* **Cabal**[11] [1222] 5-8-11 59..........(b) DanielTudhope 4 37
(Andrew Crook) *hld up in tch: hdwy wl over 2f out: sn rdn and btn* **7/1**[3]
6-5F **9** *13* **American Lover (FR)**[103] [66] 5-8-9 57 ow2.................. PaddyAspell 10 9
(John Wainwright) *a in rr* **25/1**
060- **10** *2 1/4* **Cosmic Moon**[215] [6116] 4-9-0 62.................. TonyHamilton 6 9+
(Richard Fahey) *t.k.h: cl up: sddle slipped bef 1/2-way: rdn wl over 2f out: sn wknd and eased* **7/1**[3]

2m 21.4s (14.40) **Going Correction** +1.30s/f (Soft) 10 Ran SP% **120.1**
Speed ratings (Par 100): **94,93,92,91,90 85,85,82,71,69**
toteswingers:1&2:£4.50, 1&3:£4.20, 2&3:£7.20 CSF £30.93 CT £112.84 TOTE £3.80: £1.80, £2.60, £2.10; EX 33.30.
Owner S R Counsell **Bred** Hascombe And Valiant Studs **Trained** Middleham Moor, N Yorks

FOCUS
This handicap looked competitive before the start and the field was well grouped at the 2f pole.
Cabal Official explanation: trainer said mare was unsuited by the soft ground
Cosmic Moon Official explanation: jockey said saddle slipped

1440 RACING UK H'CAP 1m 1f 207y
4:30 (4:32) (Class 4) (0-80,79) 3-Y-O **£4,140** (£1,232; £615; £307) **Stalls** Low

Form RPR
331- **1** **Sparkling Portrait**[130] [7709] 3-9-6 78.................. TonyHamilton 5 90
(Richard Fahey) *hld up in tch on inner: swtchd lft and gd hdwy 2f out: led ent fnl f: sn rdn and hld on wl* **10/3**[2]
546- **2** *nk* **Rocktherunway (IRE)**[184] [6911] 3-8-12 73.................. DaleSwift(3) 9 84
(Michael Dods) *hld up in rr: hdwy on wd outside over 3f out: rdn over 1f out: chal ins fnl f and ev ch tl drvn and no ex towards fin* **16/1**
10-0 **3** *5* **Indepub**[17] [1160] 3-9-1 76.................. AmyRyan(3) 3 77
(Kevin Ryan) *cl up: led after 2f: rdn over 2f out: drvn over 1f out: hdd ent fnl f: grad wknd* **12/1**
426- **4** *3 1/2* **Act Your Shoe Size**[186] [6864] 3-9-5 77.................. PhillipMakin 4 71
(Keith Dalgleish) *chsd ldrs: hdwy over 2f out: sn rdn and kpt on same pce* **25/1**
1- **5** *3/4* **Gabrial's Star**[213] [6187] 3-9-6 78.................. FrannyNorton 10 71
(Bryan Smart) *hld up in rr: hdwy wl over 2f out: rdn wl over 1f out: kpt on fnl f: nt rch ldrs* **3/1**[1]
134- **6** *1* **Deepsand (IRE)**[179] [7021] 3-9-7 79.................. DavidAllan 7 70
(Tim Easterby) *hld up: n.m.r and hmpd on inner 4f out: hdwy 2f out: sn rdn and kpt on same pce appr fnl f* **6/1**
00-1 **7** *3 1/2* **Wolf Spirit (IRE)**[16] [1167] 3-8-9 67.................. JamesSullivan 1 51
(Ruth Carr) *trckd ldrs on inner: hdwy over 2f out: rdn wl over 1f out and sn ev ch tl wknd appr fnl f* **20/1**

66-0 **8** *2 ¾* **Mcvicar**[17] 1160 3-9-0 72 TonyCulhane 2 50
(Mick Channon) *hld up: a towards rr* **16/1**

0-21 **9** *23* **Captivity**[68] 502 3-9-0 72 JoeFanning 8
(Mark Johnston) *trckd ldrs: hdwy over 3f out: rdn over 2f out and sn wknd* **14/1**

431- **10** *4 ½* **Sir Trevor (IRE)**[209] 6278 3-9-3 75 RichardKingscote 11
(Tom Dascombe) *led 2f: cl up rdn along wl over 2f out: sn wknd* **10/1**

333- **11** *10* **Mizbah**[182] 6957 3-9-5 77 TedDurcan 6
(Saeed Bin Suroor) *trckd ldrs: hdwy on outer 3f out: rdn wl over 2f out: sn wknd* **9/2**[3]

2m 21.35s (14.35) **Going Correction** +1.30s/f (Soft) 11 Ran SP% **124.4**
Speed ratings (Par 100): **94,93,89,86,86 85,82,80,62,58 50**
toteswingers:1&2:£15.90, 1&3:£9.60, 2&3:£31.70 CSF £59.67 CT £596.78 TOTE £4.80: £2.00, £7.20, £3.40; EX 65.60.
Owner Mike Browne **Bred** Dukes Stud & Overbury Stallions Ltd **Trained** Musley Bank, N Yorks

FOCUS
An interesting 3yo handicap run at a sensible gallop on the prevailing soft ground. The favourite had won three of the four previous runnings of this contest and another horse prominent in the betting, reportedly well fancied by his in-form trainer, landed the spoils.

1441 WHISTLEJACKETS REAL ALE BAR STKS (H'CAP) 7f 100y
5:05 (5:07) (Class 5) (0-70,70) 3-Y-O **£2,296** (£683; £341; £170) **Stalls** Low

Form RPR

056- **1** **Ardmay (IRE)**[211] 6230 3-9-4 67 PhillipMakin 12 84+
(Kevin Ryan) *hld up towards rr: gd hdwy wl over 2f out: led wl over 1f out: clr ins fnl f: comf* **11/2**[2]

555 **2** *6* **Ma Kellys (IRE)**[69] 481 3-8-10 59 BarryMcHugh 15 61
(Micky Hammond) *towards rr: hdwy over 2f out: sn rdn and styd on strly appr fnl f: tk 2nd nr line* **14/1**

604- **3** *shd* **Only Orsenfoolsies**[176] 7072 3-8-11 60 FrederikTylicki 6 62
(Micky Hammond) *in tch: effrt 3f out: sn rdn and sltly outpcd: styd on wl u.p appr fnl f:* **25/1**

063- **4** *½* **Hi There (IRE)**[181] 6973 3-9-0 63 TonyHamilton 4 64+
(Richard Fahey) *dwlt and towards rr: gd hdwy 3f out: rdn 2f out: chsd wnr ent fnl f: kpt on same pce: lost 2nd towards fin* **15/2**

203- **5** *5* **Blue Shoes (IRE)**[165] 7294 3-9-2 65 DuranFentiman 3 53
(Tim Easterby) *cl up on inner: led after 3f: rdn and hdd wl over 1f out: wknd fnl f* **8/1**

003- **6** *2* **Alabanda (IRE)**[186] 6864 3-9-5 68 DavidAllan 13 51
(Tim Easterby) *sn led: hdd after 3f: cl up tl rdn 2f out and grad wknd* **13/2**[3]

-406 **7** *1 ¼* **Auntie Joy**[26] 1013 3-8-10 59 PaddyAspell 1 39
(Michael Easterby) *in tch on inner: effrt over 2f out: sn rdn and btn* **25/1**

2312 **8** *½* **Lionrock (FR)**[7] 1313 3-9-7 70 JoeFanning 16 49
(Mark Johnston) *prom on wd outside: effrt 3f out: rdn over 2f out: sn wknd* **7/2**[1]

-300 **9** *½* **Sunny Side Up (IRE)**[16] 1167 3-8-6 60 ShaneBKelly(5) 10 37
(Richard Fahey) *t.k.h: chsd ldrs tl wknd over 2f out* **10/1**

033- **10** *2* **Sir Windsorlot (IRE)**[176] 7072 3-8-11 63 MichaelO'Connell(3) 9 35
(John Quinn) *dwlt: a towards rr* **13/2**[3]

504- **11** *10* **Baltic Bomber (IRE)**[197] 6599 3-8-11 60 JamesSullivan 7
(John Quinn) *prom: rdn along 3f out: sn wknd* **10/1**

04-5 **12** *30* **Bartley**[29] 975 3-9-2 65 RoystonFfrench 14
(Bryan Smart) *t.k.h: chsd ldrs: rdn along 3f out: sn wknd* **25/1**

1m 43.21s (9.41) **Going Correction** +1.30s/f (Soft) 12 Ran SP% **123.5**
Speed ratings (Par 98): **98,91,91,90,84 82,81,80,79,77 66,31**
toteswingers:1&2:£24.20, 1&3:£19.60, 2&3:£22.40 CSF £81.52 CT £1790.45 TOTE £7.70: £2.90, £7.20, £6.70; EX 112.70.
Owner A C Henson **Bred** Tom Kelly **Trained** Hambleton, N Yorks

FOCUS
There were four taken out due to the changing ground but this handicap was still run at a sound gallop, as plenty vied for the lead early and it suited those coming from off the pace.
Ardmay(IRE) Official explanation: trainer's rep said, regarding apparent improvement in form, that the gelding had matured over the winter and was suited by the soft ground.

1442 RACING HERE AGAIN NEXT THURSDAY H'CAP 1m 4f 16y
5:40 (5:40) (Class 5) (0-75,79) 3-Y-O **£2,296** (£683; £341; £170) **Stalls** Low

Form RPR

31 **1** **Cockney Sparrow**[30] 959 3-9-3 71 LukeMorris 1 85
(Peter Chapple-Hyam) *trckd ldr: chal over 3f out: led over 2f out: pushed clr over 1f out: eased clsng stages* **5/1**[3]

1311 **2** *7* **Cape Safari (IRE)**[5] 1355 3-9-11 79 12ex (p) JamesDoyle 4 81
(James Tate) *trckd ldrs: effrt 3f out: sn outpcd: kpt on fnl f to take modest 2nd nr fin* **9/4**[1]

-132 **3** *½* **Good Morning Star (IRE)**[56] 656 3-9-7 75 JoeFanning 6 76
(Mark Johnston) *set stdy pce: stepped up gallop over 4f out: hdd over 2f out: edgd lft ins fnl f: wknd and lost 2nd nr line* **9/4**[1]

440- **4** *31* **Tallevu (IRE)**[182] 6957 3-9-5 73 RichardKingscote 7 28
(Tom Dascombe) *t.k.h early: swtchd wd and pushed along 8f out: lost pl over 5f out: bhd fnl 3f: t.o* **11/2**

106- **5** *25* **Holy Roman Warrior (IRE)**[214] 6144 3-9-7 75 TonyHamilton 5
(Richard Fahey) *t.k.h in rr: hdwy to trck ldrs 5f out: lost pl over 2f out: sn bhd: wl t.o* **9/2**[2]

2m 59.57s (19.77) **Going Correction** +1.30s/f (Soft) 5 Ran SP% **111.8**
Speed ratings (Par 98): **86,81,81,60,43**
CSF £16.82 TOTE £3.90: £1.10, £2.00; EX 15.30.
Owner P Cunningham **Bred** P Cunningham **Trained** Newmarket, Suffolk

FOCUS
A decent early-season 3yo handicap for the grade and the form looks worth taking seriously. They went a sensible gallop given the trip on soft ground.
T/Plt: £5,527.30 to a £1 stake. Pool:£60,573.31 - 8.00 winning tickets T/Qpdt: £189.90 to a £1 stake. Pool:£7,289.77 - 28.40 winning tickets JR

1299 KEMPTON (A.W) (R-H)
Wednesday, April 18

OFFICIAL GOING: Standard
Wind: mild breeze across Weather: overcast with rain at times

1443 WIN BIG WITH BETDAQ MULTIPLES MEDIAN AUCTION MAIDEN FILLIES' STKS 1m 3f (P)
6:05 (6:05) (Class 6) 3-5-Y-O **£1,617** (£481; £240; £120) **Stalls** Low

Form RPR

30-0 **1** **Daring Damsel (IRE)**[7] 1303 3-8-9 59 (b[1]) StevieDonohoe 2 63
(Paul Cole) *mde all: rdn over 2f out: sn drifted lft: styd on wl fnl f* **14/1**

5- **2** *4* **Ice On Fire**[160] 7344 3-8-9 0 ShaneKelly 4 56+
(Philip McBride) *hld up towards rr: hdwy fr over 3f out: rdn to chse ldrs over 2f out: swtchd rt over 1f out: r.o: wnt 2nd ins fnl f* **3/1**[1]

00- **3** *2* **Kozmina Bay**[233] 5537 3-8-9 0 LeeNewman 5 52
(Jonathan Portman) *trckd ldrs early: midfield over 7f out: hdwy over 4f out: rdn over 3f out: chsd wnr 2f out tl no ex fnl f* **25/1**

00- **4** *2 ½* **Manbaa (USA)**[197] 6603 3-8-9 0 TadhgO'Shea 6 48
(John Dunlop) *trckd ldrs: rdn over 3f out: kpt on same pce fnl 2f* **5/1**

-000 **5** *1 ½* **Polly Adler**[7] 1299 5-10-0 40 (v[1]) MatthewDavies 10 48
(Alastair Lidderdale) *hld up towards rr: hdwy fr 4f out: outpcd 3f out: styd on ins fnl f* **25/1**

660- **6** *2* **Downton Abbey (IRE)**[183] 6928 3-8-9 60 KieranO'Neill 8 41
(Richard Hannon) *trckd ldrs: rdn over 3f out: fdd ins fnl f* **6/1**

00 **7** *18* **Littlemissperfect**[19] 1107 4-10-0 0 JamieGoldstein 3
(Richard Rowe) *little slowly away: sn mid-div: rdn over 3f out: sn wknd* **80/1**

00- **8** *1 ¾* **Ladram Bay (IRE)**[191] 6743 3-8-9 0 CathyGannon 7
(Jonathan Portman) *mid-div: struggling in last 3 whn squeezed out over 4f out: wknd over 3f out* **66/1**

5-5 **9** *4* **Bonnet De Douche (IRE)**[9] 1265 3-8-9 0 NeilCallan 1
(Peter Chapple-Hyam) *in tch: rdn over 3f out: wknd over 2f out* **4/1**[3]

0-2 **10** *10* **Distant Love (IRE)**[42] 816 3-8-9 0 DavidProbert 9
(Andrew Balding) *trckd wnr: rdn over 3f out: wknd over 2f out: eased ins fnl f* **7/2**[2]

0 **11** *31* **Lion's Maid**[14] 1182 3-8-5 0 ow1 MarkCoumbe(5) 11
(Michael Attwater) *hmpd sn after s: a towards rr: wknd over 3f out* **66/1**

2m 21.72s (-0.18) **Going Correction** -0.05s/f (Stan)
WFA 3 from 4yo+ 19lb 11 Ran SP% **116.8**
Speed ratings (Par 98): **98,95,93,91,90 89,76,74,72,64 42**
toteswingers:1&2:£5.90, 1&3:£18.50, 2&3:£21.20 CSF £54.10 TOTE £10.20: £2.90, £2.10, £10.70; EX 83.20 TRIFECTA Not won..
Owner Sisters Syndicate **Bred** Summerhill Bloodstock **Trained** Whatcombe, Oxon
■ Stewards' Enquiry : Shane Kelly two-day ban: careless riding (May 2-3)
Kieran O'Neill three-day ban: careless riding (May 2-4)

FOCUS
A weak fillies' maiden and unforgiving form which has been rated fairly negatively.
Distant Love(IRE) Official explanation: trainer's rep said filly had a breathing problem

1444 BACK OR LAY AT BETDAQ.COM CLASSIFIED CLAIMING STKS 6f (P)
6:35 (6:35) (Class 6) 3-Y-O **£1,617** (£481; £240; £120) **Stalls** Low

Form RPR

10 **1** **Russian Bullet**[34] 905 3-8-10 66 FergusSweeney 5 63
(Jamie Osborne) *racd keenly: trckd ldr: rdn to ld over 1f out: sn edgd rt: kpt on: jst hld on* **13/8**[1]

1033 **2** *nse* **Arabian Flight**[7] 1307 3-8-9 59 KieranO'Neill 7 62
(John Bridger) *walked to s: hld up in last of 5 in tch: hdwy whn swtchd rt 2f out: sn rdn: str run ins fnl f on far rails: narrowly denied* **9/2**[3]

6234 **3** *1 ¾* **Miss Purity Pinker (IRE)**[20] 1090 3-8-5 59 (v) CathyGannon 2 52
(David Evans) *led: rdn over 2f out: hdd over 1f out: sn sltly hmpd: kpt on same pce fnl f* **9/1**

0134 **4** *1 ½* **Marie's Fantasy**[7] 1307 3-8-9 57 NeilCallan 1 52
(Zoe Davison) *trckd ldrs: rdn over 2f out: kpt on same pce* **8/1**

6514 **5** *4 ½* **Tiablo (IRE)**[4] 1393 3-8-6 64 MartinLane 6 34
(David Evans) *trckd ldrs: rdn 3f out: sn one pce* **5/2**[2]

1m 12.83s (-0.27) **Going Correction** -0.05s/f (Stan) 5 Ran SP% **106.0**
Speed ratings (Par 96): **99,98,96,94,88**
CSF £8.39 TOTE £2.20: £1.50, £1.10; EX 8.30.
Owner Martyn and Elaine Booth **Bred** Cranford Bloodstock Uk Ltd **Trained** Upper Lambourn, Berks

FOCUS
A modest claimer. The winner was best in and didn't have to match his win two starts ago.

1445 BETDAQ MOBILE APPS H'CAP 6f (P)
7:05 (7:05) (Class 5) (0-70,70) 3-Y-O **£2,264** (£673; £336; £168) **Stalls** Low

Form RPR

010- **1** **Larwood (IRE)**[153] 7445 3-9-4 67 DaneO'Neill 5 84
(Henry Candy) *squeezed out s: last: hdwy over 2f out: qcknd up wl to ld jst over 1f out: r.o strly: easily* **11/4**[1]

-552 **2** *4 ½* **Auntie Mabel**[13] 1201 3-8-9 58 DavidProbert 3 61
(Andrew Balding) *trckd ldrs: rdn to ld jst ins 2f out: edgd lft and hdd jst over 1f out: nt pce of wnr* **7/1**

40-5 **3** *1 ¼* **Compton Target (IRE)**[28] 982 3-8-5 61 (t) NicoleNordblad(7) 2 60
(Hans Adielsson) *travelled wl in mid-div: hdwy 2f out: sn rdn: kpt on but nt pce to chal* **9/2**[2]

650- **4** *3 ½* **Esprit Danseur**[206] 6372 3-9-5 68 PatCosgrave 6 55
(Jim Boyle) *mid-div: mounting chal whn nt clr run 2f out: sn rdn: kpt on same pce* **16/1**

20-0 **5** *1 ¼* **Ocean Myth**[28] 982 3-9-5 68 LeeNewman 7 51
(Jonathan Portman) *trckd ldrs: rdn and ev ch 2f out: kpt on same pce fr over 1f out* **20/1**

100- **6** *1 ½* **Sanad (IRE)**[228] 5708 3-9-4 70 DominicFox(3) 11 49
(Anthony Carson) *towards rr: rdn over 3f out: sme late prog: nvr a factor* **16/1**

66-5 **7** *nse* **Molly Jones**[34] 905 3-9-4 67 FergusSweeney 8 45
(Derek Haydn Jones) *in tch: rdn wl over 2f out: wknd ent fnl f* **16/1**

25-3 **8** *1 ¼* **Samba Night (IRE)**[21] 1072 3-9-3 66 NeilCallan 4 40
(James Eustace) *mid-div: rdn 3f out: wknd over 1f out* **9/1**

403- **9** *¾* **Little Rainbow**[177] 7056 3-9-4 67 AdamKirby 10 39
(Clive Cox) *w ldr: rdn and ev ch 2f out: wknd fnl f* **13/2**

0154 **10** *4 ½* **Justbookies Dotnet**[7] 1313 3-9-5 68 (v) IanMongan 1 26
(Louise Best) *led: rdn and hdd wl over 1f out: sn wknd* **6/1**[3]

1m 12.13s (-0.97) **Going Correction** -0.05s/f (Stan) 10 Ran SP% **117.4**
Speed ratings (Par 98): **104,98,96,91,90 88,87,86,85,79**
toteswingers:1&2:£4.20, 1&3:£4.30, 2&3:£4.10 CSF £22.45 CT £84.94 TOTE £3.50: £1.80, £3.50, £1.10; EX 28.70 Trifecta £55.70 Pool: £569.31 - 7.56 winning units.
Owner Six Too Many **Bred** Celbridge Estates Ltd **Trained** Kingston Warren, Oxon
■ Stewards' Enquiry : David Probert one-day ban: careless riding (May 2)

FOCUS
The pace was good and this looks decent form for the grade. The winner was much improved and the form is rated at face value.

1446 BETDAQ CASINO GAMES H'CAP 2m (P)
7:35 (7:35) (Class 3) (0-95,89) 4-Y-O+ **£6,663** (£1,982; £990; £495) **Stalls** Low

Form RPR

001- **1** **Old Hundred (IRE)**[222] 5883 5-9-12 89 (v) HayleyTurner 4 101
(James Fanshawe) *travelled wl: hld up in mid-div: hdwy 3f out: sn swtchd lft: led 2f out: drifted rt and rdn fnl f: styd on wl* **10/3**[2]

10-3 **2** *nk* **Lexington Bay (IRE)**[10] 1239 4-9-0 **84** .... LeeTopliss(3) 6 95
(Richard Fahey) *in tch: nudged along fr over 6f out: snatched up on rails 4f out: rdn to chal 2f out: ev ch thrght fnl f: hld towards fin* **15/2**[3]

342- **3** *8* **Palazzo Bianco**[174] 7120 4-9-5 **86** .... StevieDonohoe 7 87
(John Gosden) *trckd ldrs: rdn over 3f out: nt pce to get involved: wnt 3rd ent fnl f* **10/11**[1]

00-0 **4** *6* **Action Front (USA)**[39] 872 4-8-8 **75** .... MartinLane 1 69
(Derek Shaw) *hld up: rdn to chse ldrs over 2f out: nt pce to get on terms* **50/1**

0-4 **5** *shd* **Saint Helena (IRE)**[29] 971 4-8-8 **75** .... DavidProbert 3 71
(Harry Dunlop) *led for 1f: trckd ldrs: trying to mount effrt whn nt clr run over 2f out tl jst over 1f out: styd on but no ch after* **14/1**

1124 **6** *2 ¾* **Queen Of Denmark (USA)**[40] 846 4-9-7 **88** .... NeilCallan 8 79
(Mark Johnston) *led after 1f tl 12f out: trckd clr ldr: rdn and ev ch briefly jst over 2f out: fdd fnl f* **12/1**

1-00 **7** *6* **Epsom Salts**[14] 1186 7-8-13 **76** .... IanMongan 2 60
(Pat Phelan) *in tch: hdwy to ld after 4f: sn qcknd pce and clr: rdn and hdd 2f out: wknd jst over 1f out* **25/1**

6110 **8** *21* **Storm Hawk (IRE)**[11] 1214 5-9-4 **84** .... (b) RyanClark(3) 5 42
(Pat Eddery) *dwlt: bhd: effrt to cl on outer 5f out: btn 3f out: eased fr 2f out* **16/1**

3m 28.29s (-1.81) **Going Correction** -0.05s/f (Stan)
WFA 4 from 5yo+ 4lb **8** Ran SP% **113.3**
Speed ratings (Par 107): **102,101,97,94,94 93,90,79**
toteswingers:1&2:£3.30, 1&3:£1.70, 2&3:£2.20 CSF £27.79 CT £38.77 TOTE £4.90: £1.10, £1.10, £1.80; EX 24.40 Trifecta £58.80 Pool: £561.16 - 7.06 winning units.
Owner Lael Stable **Bred** Lael Stables **Trained** Newmarket, Suffolk

FOCUS
The gallop seemed a bit muddling, and even when Epsom Salts injected some pace, going into a clear lead, he was basically ignored. However, a couple of the likelier types still pulled well clear. Both improved and there's a chance the form is worth a bit more.

NOTEBOOK
Old Hundred(IRE) hadn't been seen since taking the Mallard Stakes last September, but he resumed off only 3lb higher, was a winner on his only previous try over this C&D, and had also won on his 2011 reappearance. He was keen early and didn't find as much as had looked likely when produced with his challenge, going right under pressure, but he was always doing just enough. It would be unfair to be too critical as he still did enough to draw a long way clear of all bar the runner-up, and as far as his handicap mark goes it's no bad thing that his latest two victories have been gained only narrowly. (op 9-2)
Lexington Bay(IRE), who would have gone close at Musselburgh on his reappearance granted a clear run, recovered from being short of room about half a mile out here, and had his chance. He was well clear of the others and is a stayer on the up. (op 6-1)
Palazzo Bianco, lightly raced and previously progressive, was heavily backed to make a winning reappearance, but he was the subject of a late jockey change and was caught wider than ideal for a lot of the way. He seemed unsuited by the muddling tempo, never getting into a convincing rhythm, and is worth another chance. (op 6-5)
Action Front(USA) offered more than when making his debut for this yard the previous month.
Saint Helena(IRE) had stamina to prove, but she ran well in the face of a stiff task, especially as she didn't enjoy the clearest of runs. (op 12-1 tchd 11-1)
Queen Of Denmark(USA) was struck into. Official explanation: vet said filly was struck into (op 8-1)

1447 RACING PLUS OUT EVERY SATURDAY H'CAP 1m (P)
8:05 (8:06) (Class 6) (0-60,60) 4-Y-O+ **£1,617** (£481; £240; £120) **Stalls** Low

Form RPR

30-6 **1** **Mr Chocolate Drop (IRE)**[14] 1191 8-9-6 **59** .... (t) AdamKirby 5 68
(Mandy Rowland) *in tch: rdn to ld over 2f out: hld on v gamely thrght fnl f: drvn out* **5/1**[2]

0-04 **2** *nk* **Loyal N Trusted**[14] 1191 4-9-3 **56** .... JimCrowley 9 64
(Richard Price) *hld up towards rr: hdwy over 2f out: rdn to press wnr wl over 1f out: ev ch thrght fnl f: hld towards fin* **5/1**[2]

0125 **3** *¾* **Warbond**[29] 967 4-9-6 **59** .... JamieGoldstein 13 66+
(Michael Madgwick) *hld up: hdwy fr 2f out: sn rdn: wnt 3rd ins fnl f: styd on: clsng at fin* **4/1**[1]

220- **4** *1* **Annes Rocket (IRE)**[187] 6848 7-9-4 **60** .... SeanLevey(3) 3 64
(Jimmy Fox) *hld up: hdwy over 2f out: rdn to chse ldng pair over 1f out: hung lft and no ex whn lost 3rd ins fnl f* **9/1**

400- **5** *¾* **Prince Of Passion (CAN)**[169] 7208 4-9-6 **59** .... NeilCallan 4 62
(Derek Shaw) *hld up towards rr: rdn over 2f out: swtchd lft wl over 1f out: styd on wl fnl f* **11/1**

5033 **6** *nk* **Karate (IRE)**[7] 1299 4-8-12 **58** .... (t) NicoleNordblad(7) 1 60+
(Hans Adielsson) *mid-div on inner: nowhere to go bhd wkng horse fr 3f out and dropped to rr: kpt on but no ch after fr over 1f out* **6/1**[3]

4-00 **7** *1 ¼* **Kielty's Folly**[27] 1002 8-9-5 **58** .... PaulMulrennan 7 57
(Brian Baugh) *broke wl: sn stdd bhd ldr: rdn over 2f out: fdd ins fnl f* **13/2**

0-43 **8** *½* **Henry's Hero**[9] 822 6-8-7 **46** oh1 .... (b) CathyGannon 8 44
(Chris Dwyer) *sn led: rdn and hdd over 2f out: fdd fnl f* **16/1**

3020 **9** *nk* **Gallantry**[17] 1154 10-9-5 **58** .... TomMcLaughlin 6 55
(Paul Howling) *s.i.s: sn in tch: outpcd fr 2f out* **12/1**

010/ **10** *31* **Lily Lily**[807] 371 5-9-3 **59** .... (p) RyanClark(3) 2
(Natalie Lloyd-Beavis) *trckd ldr: rdn over 3f out: sn wknd: t.o* **33/1**

1m 39.51s (-0.29) **Going Correction** -0.05s/f (Stan) **10** Ran SP% **115.8**
Speed ratings (Par 101): **99,98,97,96,96 95,94,94,93,62**
toteswingers:1&2:£10.00, 1&3:£5.70, 2&3:£7.10 CSF £30.02 CT £112.24 TOTE £4.50: £1.20, £2.90, £1.80; EX 30.00 Trifecta £250.90 Part won. Pool: £339.11 - 0.93 winning units..
Owner Miss M E Rowland **Bred** P J Munnelly **Trained** Lower Blidworth, Notts

FOCUS
A moderate handicap run at just an ordinary gallop. Straightforward form, the winner rated to his best.
Karate(IRE) ◆ Official explanation: jockey said gelding was denied a clear run

1448 BOOK FOR MASCOT GRAND NATIONAL 07.05.12 H'CAP 1m 4f (P)
8:35 (8:35) (Class 6) (0-60,55) 3-Y-O **£1,617** (£481; £240; £120) **Stalls** Centre

Form RPR

2-15 **1** **Quiet Appeal (IRE)**[44] 803 3-9-7 **55** .... SilvestreDeSousa 6 59
(Mark Johnston) *racd keenly: trckd ldrs: rdn over 2f out: led over 1f out: kpt on gamely fnl f: hld on wl* **5/1**[3]

40-4 **2** *nk* **Rocco Breeze (IRE)**[7] 1303 3-9-0 **48** .... WilliamBuick 3 52
(Philip McBride) *little slowly away: sn trcking ldrs: rdn over 2f out: chal ent fnl f: kpt on but a being jst hld* **2/1**[1]

00-6 **3** *2 ¼* **Blue Pencil**[27] 993 3-8-8 **45** .... RyanPowell(3) 1 45
(Roger Curtis) *trckd ldrs: rdn wl over 2f out: sn hung lft: kpt on same pce* **16/1**

00-2 **4** *½* **Lady Mandy**[21] 1062 3-9-3 **51** .... StevieDonohoe 4 50
(Richard Fahey) *sn nudged along in rr: hrd rdn fr 3f out: styd on fnl f: nvr a danger* **11/4**[2]

0-00 **5** *nk* **Medlaur**[18] 1132 3-8-11 **45** .... PaulMulrennan 5 44
(James Given) *hld up: rdn wl over 2f out: no imp tl styd on fnl f: nvr a threat* **14/1**

000- **6** *4 ½* **La Confession**[225] 5813 3-9-4 **52** .... DavidProbert 2 44
(Rae Guest) *hld up in tch: rdn over 2f out: swtchd rt to chse ldrs over 1f out: fdd ins fnl f* **8/1**

0-02 **7** *1 ½* **Imperial Stargazer**[8] 1287 3-9-7 **55** .... (v) MatthewDavies 8 44
(Mick Channon) *hld up in tch: rdn to chse ldrs over 2f out: wknd fnl f* **25/1**

0-05 **8** *10* **Henry George**[58] 638 3-9-7 **55** .... NeilCallan 7 28
(Mark Johnston) *sn led: rdn and hdd over 1f out: sn wknd* **14/1**

2m 36.75s (2.25) **Going Correction** -0.05s/f (Stan) **8** Ran SP% **110.8**
Speed ratings (Par 96): **90,89,88,87,87 84,83,77**
toteswingers:1&2:£2.20, 1&3:£11.40, 2&3:£4.40 CSF £14.43 CT £138.26 TOTE £7.00: £2.20, £1.70, £4.10; EX 15.90 Trifecta £248.50 Pool: £423.29 - 1.26 winning units.
Owner T T Bloodstock **Bred** Corduff Stud Ltd & T J Rooney **Trained** Middleham Moor, N Yorks
■ Stewards' Enquiry : William Buick two-day ban: used whip above permitted level (May 2-3)

FOCUS
A weak handicap about which it's hard to draw many positives. The pace was no more than fair and the form is rated around the fisrt three.
Medlaur Official explanation: jockey said filly hung left throughout
La Confession Official explanation: jockey said filly hung right

1449 INTERACTIVE H'CAP 6f (P)
9:05 (9:06) (Class 4) (0-85,85) 3-Y-O **£4,075** (£1,212; £606; £303) **Stalls** Low

Form RPR

6-12 **1** **Dark Castle**[84] 295 3-8-13 77 .... LiamKeniry 8 89+
(Sylvester Kirk) *trckd ldrs: shkn up to ld over 1f out: r.o wl fnl f: readily* **2/1**[1]

11-0 **2** *2* **Mezzotint (IRE)**[8] 1271 3-9-7 85 .... [1] AdamKirby 6 91
(Marco Botti) *hld up: rdn and hdwy 2f out: r.o to take 2nd ins fnl f: no ch w wnr* **2/1**[1]

531- **3** *1 ¼* **Sky Crossing**[129] 7724 3-8-11 75 .... PaulMulrennan 5 77
(James Given) *led: rdn whn edgd lft and hdd over 1f out: no ex ins fnl f* **10/1**

064- **4** *1 ¾* **Amphora**[215] 6123 3-8-7 71 .... DavidProbert 3 67
(Andrew Balding) *hld up: rdn and hdwy 2f out: sn chsng ldrs: kpt on same pce fnl f* **7/1**[2]

00-4 **5** *4 ½* **Mitie Mouse**[21] 1063 3-8-10 74 .... NeilCallan 2 56
(Mike Murphy) *chsd ldrs: rdn over 2f out: fdd fnl f* **16/1**

102- **6** *1* **Toffee Tart**[200] 6524 3-8-13 77 .... SebSanders 4 56
(J W Hills) *hld up: rdn over 2f out: nvr any imp* **9/1**[3]

31-5 **7** *nk* **Lady Gibraltar**[19] 1109 3-8-12 76 .... (v) JimCrowley 7 54
(Alan Jarvis) *in tch: effrt on outer over 2f out: wknd 1f out* **16/1**

410- **8** *1 ½* **Red Mischief (IRE)**[240] 5324 3-8-8 72 .... JohnFahy 1 45
(Harry Dunlop) *chsd ldrs: rdn over 2f out: wknd over 1f out* **40/1**

1m 11.58s (-1.52) **Going Correction** -0.05s/f (Stan) **8** Ran SP% **112.5**
Speed ratings (Par 100): **108,105,103,101,95 94,93,91**
toteswingers:1&2:£1.70, 1&3:£3.60, 2&3:£6.60 CSF £5.43 CT £28.36 TOTE £3.20: £1.20, £1.50, £3.70; EX 6.70 Trifecta £39.50 Pool: £564.59 - 10.56 winning units.
Owner Ms Carol Cleary **Bred** Hedsor Stud **Trained** Upper Lambourn, Berks

FOCUS
The time was the quickest of three races at the trip. This was a decent little handicap and a fairly positive view has been taken of the form.
T/Plt: £19.80 to a £1 stake. Pool:£64,386.29 - 2,362.00 winning tickets T/Qpdt: £4.70 to a £1 stake. Pool:£7,402.14 - 1,146.15 winning tickets TM

NEWMARKET (R-H)
Wednesday, April 18

OFFICIAL GOING: Good (8.3)
Wind: fairly strong, against Weather: rain

1450 ALEX SCOTT MAIDEN STKS (C&G) 7f
1:50 (1:55) (Class 4) 3-Y-O **£4,528** (£1,347; £673; £336) **Stalls** Low

Form RPR

1 **Cogito (USA)** 3-9-0 0 .... MartinDwyer 5 91+
(Brian Meehan) *chsd ldr: rdn and effrt to chal over 1f out: led ent fnl f: pushed out and r.o wl: comf* **14/1**

2 *2 ¾* **Nine Realms** 3-9-0 0 .... LiamJones 11 84+
(William Haggas) *hld up in last quartet: rdn and stl plenty to do 2f out: swtchd lft over 1f out: styd on wl fnl f: wnt 2nd towards fin: no threat to wnr* **25/1**

2-5 **3** *¾* **Periphery (USA)**[9] 1261 3-9-0 0 .... (t) MickaelBarzalona 3 82
(Mahmood Al Zarooni) *led: rdn wl over 1f out: drvn and hdd ent fnl f: nt pce of wnr and one pce fnl f: lost 2nd towards fin* **9/2**[2]

3 **4** *hd* **Mutafaakir (IRE)**[17] 1155 3-9-0 0 .... (tp) TadhgO'Shea 9 81+
(John Gosden) *stdd s: t.k.h: hld up in last quartet: rdn over 1f out: styd on wl ins fnl f: wnt 4th cl home: no threat to wnr* **7/1**

25- **5** *¾* **Poole Harbour (IRE)**[285] 3793 3-9-0 0 .... PatDobbs 12 79
(Richard Hannon) *in tch in midfield: rdn and effrt wl over 1f out: kpt on same pce ins fnl f* **11/2**[3]

6 *½* **Courage (IRE)** 3-9-0 0 .... RyanMoore 4 78+
(Sir Michael Stoute) *in tch in midfield: rdn and effrt 2f out: no imp tl kpt on ins fnl f: no threat to wnr* **8/1**

42- **7** *1* **Qannaas (USA)**[173] 7133 3-9-0 0 .... PaulHanagan 2 75
(Charles Hills) *hld up in tch: rdn and effrt wl over 1f out: unable qck and no imp 1f out: wknd ins fnl f* **4/1**[1]

8 *2* **Hometown Glory** 3-9-0 0 .... ShaneKelly 1 70
(Brian Meehan) *chsd ldrs: swtchd lft and effrt over 1f out: unable qck and btn 1f out: wknd fnl f* **50/1**

32- **9** *2* **Flaxen Flare (IRE)**[176] 7080 3-9-0 0 .... JimmyFortune 8 65
(Andrew Balding) *chsd ldrs: rdn and unable qck wl over 1f out: btn 1f out: wknd fnl f* **9/2**[2]

5 **10** *2 ½* **Malingering**[17] 1155 3-9-0 0 .... MartinLane 6 58
(Hugo Palmer) *hld up in midfield: rdn and struggling ent fnl 2f: wknd over 1f out* **40/1**

3- **11** *1 ½* **Paddyfrommenlo (IRE)**[147] 7520 3-9-0 0 .... SebSanders 13 54
(J W Hills) *awkward leaving stalls and s.i.s: in tch towards rr: rdn and struggling over 2f out: wknd wl over 1f out* **16/1**

12 *20* **Moss Hill** 3-9-0 0 .... MichaelHills 7
(Charles Hills) *s.i.s: sn rdn along in rr: lost tch over 2f out: wl bhd and eased ins fnl f* **66/1**

0 **13** ½ **Seventeen Seventy**[9] 1256 3-9-0 0........................ SilvestreDeSousa 10
(Alan Coogan) *in tch towards rr: rdn and struggling 1/2-way: bhd fnl 2f: eased ins fnl f* **200/1**

1m 29.07s (3.67) **Going Correction** +0.40s/f (Good) **13** Ran SP% **118.1**
Speed ratings (Par 100): **95,91,91,90,89 89,88,85,83,80 79,56,55**
toteswingers:1&2:£85.60, 1&3:£18.70, 2&3:£47.30 CSF £325.73 TOTE £14.90: £3.20, £7.80, £1.60; EX 433.20 TRIFECTA Not won..
Owner Reddam Racing Llc **Bred** Lazy Lane Farms Inc **Trained** Manton, Wilts

FOCUS
Far side track used with stalls on far side. There was 1.5mm of rain the previous day but following a dry night and less than a millimetre of rain in the morning the ground was given as good (GoingStick 8.3). A strong headwind promised to make things tough for front-runners, but in this opening maiden the early pace wasn't strong and the winner and third were prominent throughout. This is usually a good maiden and the winner looks well above average.
Mutafaakir(IRE) Official explanation: jockey said colt hung right

1451 EQUESTRIANARTUK.COM CONDITIONS STKS 5f
2:25 (2:26) (Class 3) 2-Y-O **£6,469** (£1,925; £962; £481) **Stalls** Low

Form RPR

1 **1** **Baileys Jubilee**[11] 1211 2-8-10 0.............................. SilvestreDeSousa 1 93+
(Mark Johnston) *chsd ldr: cruised upside ldr over 2f out: led over 1f out: rdn and qcknd clr jst over 1f out: r.o strly: easily* **2/5**[1]

2 8 **Lucky Beggar (IRE)** 2-8-9 0.. MichaelHills 4 64+
(Charles Hills) *wnt lft s and s.i.s: rn green and t.k.h: hld up: swtchd rt over 3f out: rdn wl over 1f out: kpt on to chse clr wnr ins fnl f: n.d* **13/2**[3]

011 **3** 4½ **Dreamy Ciara**[7] 1315 2-8-10 0.. PadraigBeggy 2 48
(David Evans) *sn led: jnd and rdn over 2f out: hdd and drvn over 1f out: sn outpcd and btn: lost 2nd and fdd ins fnl f* **6/1**[2]

4 8 **Tahaf (IRE)** 2-8-9 0.. BrettDoyle 3 34+
(Clive Brittain) *s.i.s and pushed along early: hdwy to chse ldrs over 3f out: rdn and unable qck over 1f out: eased ent fnl f: virtually p.u ins fnl f: sddle slipped* **16/1**

1m 1.72s (2.62) **Going Correction** +0.40s/f (Good) **4** Ran SP% **104.9**
Speed ratings (Par 96): **95,82,75,62**
CSF £3.10 TOTE £1.40; EX 3.20.
Owner G R Bailey Ltd (Baileys Horse Feeds) **Bred** P And Mrs A G Venner **Trained** Middleham Moor, N Yorks

FOCUS
This event has been contested by some smart juveniles in the past decade, among them Golden Jubilee winner Art Connoisseur and the Group winners Cool Creek, Gilded and Monsieur Chevalier. The last three named were trained by Richard Hannon, who had won five of the most recent eight runnings but surprisingly was not represented this year. Those with experience have tended to dominate this race, and so it was again. It's tricky to pin down the level of the form but Baileys Jubilee looks a smart juvenile.

NOTEBOOK
Baileys Jubilee, one of two to have run previously, really knew her job first time on the Polytrack at Kempton and the form has been boosted by subsequent wins from the fourth and fifth. The manner of this follow-up victory was most impressive, the filly travelling smoothly before quickening right away through the final furlong, and she will prove hard to beat in the first part of the season. The Listed Marygate Stakes at York's May meeting looks an obvious target and, even at this stage, she could be a Queen Mary type. (op 4-9 tchd 1-2 in place)
Lucky Beggar(IRE) raced freely when seeing daylight on the outer but settled better when found a bit of cover. Coming through for a well beaten second, this half-brother to the useful current 3yo Kingsdesire will have no problem winning a maiden and will get 6f when required. There could be a race at Chester for him. (op 6-1 tchd 7-1)
Dreamy Ciara, on her toes beforehand, arrived on a hat-trick, but the form of her wins at Wolverhampton and Nottingham did not quite match Baileys Jubilee's debut effort. From the yard successful in this race 12 months ago, she set the pace but had no answers when the favourite eased past and came home well held. She's a tough filly who should win again, but obviously has her limitations. (op 11-2 tchd 5-1)
Tahaf(IRE), who is by Authorized and is a half-brother to Fillies' Mile and Ribblesdale winner Hibaayeb, doesn't have a pedigree associated with early 2yos. Needing to be stoked up after a slow start, he was never closer than third and was allowed to come home in his own time once demoted to last place, Brett Doyle subsequently reporting that the saddle had slipped. The colt will improve on this over longer trips later down the line. Official explanation: jockey said saddle slipped (op 14-1)

1452 £150,000 TATTERSALLS MILLIONS 3-Y-O SPRINT 6f
3:00 (3:00) (Class 2) 3-Y-O **£81,150** (£36,885; £14,760; £7,365; £4,440; £2,955) **Stalls** Low

Form RPR

1 **1** **Valbchek (IRE)**[23] 1048 3-9-3 0.. RyanMoore 3 100+
(Jeremy Noseda) *in tch in midfield: rdn and effrt 2f out: hdwy u.p over 1f out: drvn to ld ins fnl f: edgd lft: fnd ex and hld on wl towards fin* **10/3**[1]

163- **2** ½ **Swiss Spirit**[193] 6705 3-9-3 98.. WilliamBuick 15 99+
(David Elsworth) *stdd s and wnt lft s: hld up towards rr: rdn and effrt 2f out: hdwy on outer over 1f out: r.o wl and str chal ins fnl f: hld towards fin* **10/1**

116- **3** 1¾ **Tidentime (USA)**[214] 6170 3-9-3 92.................................. MartinHarley 4 93
(Mick Channon) *in tch: effrt u.p wl over 1f out: drvn and edgd out lft over 1f out: kpt on wl fnl f* **33/1**

1-4 **4** 2¼ **Solar Deity (IRE)**[11] 1217 3-9-3 84.................................. AdamKirby 5 86+
(Marco Botti) *in tch in midfield: rdn and outpcd on downhill run wl over 1f out: rallied 1f out: styd on wl ins fnl f* **12/1**

5 ½ **Van Ellis** 3-9-3 0.. NeilCallan 9 84+
(Mark Johnston) *w ldrs: led 2f out: sn rdn: edgd rt u.p 1f out: hdd ins fnl f: no ex: wknd fnl 100yds* **40/1**

6-1 **6** 1¼ **Muarrab**[14] 1182 3-9-3 81.. PaulHanagan 7 80
(Ed Dunlop) *chsd ldrs: rdn and chsd ldr wl over 1f out: unable qck u.p: wknd ins fnl f* **14/1**

344- **7** ½ **Balty Boys (IRE)**[193] 6688 3-9-3 110.............................. MichaelHills 12 79
(Charles Hills) *pressed ldr and racd towards centre: rdn 2f out: sn outpcd: wknd ins fnl f* **4/1**[2]

321- **8** ½ **Samitar**[200] 6526 3-8-12 111.. JamieSpencer 6 72
(Mick Channon) *led tl hdd and rdn 2f out: unable qck and losing pl whn n.m.r over 1f out: wknd 1f out* **10/3**[1]

010- **9** ¾ **Jacob Cats**[235] 5479 3-9-3 80.. PatDobbs 14 75
(Richard Hannon) *in tch in midfield on outer: rdn ent fnl 2f: edgd rt and outpcd wl over 1f out: n.d after* **50/1**

02- **10** 4½ **Out Do**[249] 5051 3-9-3 0.. FrankieDettori 13 67+
(Luca Cumani) *in tch in midfield: rdn and unable qck 2f out: outpcd and edgd rt on downhill run wl over 1f out: sn wknd* **16/1**

044- **11** *nk* **Philipstown**[192] 6724 3-9-3 73.. DaneO'Neill 1 59
(Richard Hannon) *in tch towards rr: rdn 3f out: sn struggling and wknd 2f out* **100/1**

510- **12** 4 **Wahylah (IRE)**[200] 6526 3-8-12 82.................................. BrettDoyle 11 41
(Clive Brittain) *chsd ldrs: rdn and unable qck over 2f out: sn wknd* **33/1**

13 ¾ **Nocturn** 3-9-3 0.. JimmyFortune 8 44
(Jeremy Noseda) *s.i.s: a in rr: rdn and struggling 1/2-way: bhd fnl 2f* **33/1**

550- **14** 4½ **Orders From Rome (IRE)**[214] 6170 3-9-3 83............(b[1]) TomQueally 10 30
(Eve Johnson Houghton) *in tch towards rr: rdn and struggling wl over 2f out: sn wknd and bhd* **66/1**

1315 **15** 7 **Switzerland (IRE)**[11] 1221 3-9-3 95.............................. SilvestreDeSousa 2
(Mark Johnston) *in tch towards rr: struggling u.p 3f out: sn wknd and bhd* **8/1**[3]

1m 14.14s (1.94) **Going Correction** +0.40s/f (Good) **15** Ran SP% **122.3**
Speed ratings (Par 104): **103,102,100,97,96 94,94,93,92,86 85,80,79,73,64**
toteswingers:1&2:£10.30, 1&3:£35.30, 2&3:£71.80 CSF £36.64 TOTE £5.10: £1.60, £3.20, £10.30; EX 43.50 TRIFECTA Not won..
Owner Richard Keen & Paul Smith **Bred** Kildaragh Stud **Trained** Newmarket, Suffolk

FOCUS
As usual with these valuable sales races, there was a mix of ability on show, and the big money on offer meant that not all of the runners were competing over their optimum distance. The winner built on his AW debut win and there's nothing that obviously limits the form.

NOTEBOOK
Valbchek(IRE) looked a promising colt when scoring on his debut at Lingfield and, while this required more and he lacked the experience of some of his rivals, he was well supported. He carried his head a bit high on his debut, and did so again here, despite the addition of a noseband, but he seems genuine enough as he found plenty for pressure and gamely saw off the runner-up's challenge. He deserves to take his chance in Pattern company now, and the Listed Carnarvon Stakes, which his trainer mentioned post-race, looks an ideal short-term target. (op 5-2)
Swiss Spirit is from a very successful sprinting family and, given his size, looked very much the type to do a lot better this year than at two. His stable hasn't been firing in the winners and he looked backward beforehand, so he was fully entitled to need this, but he ran a stormer, finishing strongly down the (possibly unfavoured) outside to take second. He should come on plenty for this and has the potential to make a Pattern-class sprinter. (tchd 11-1)
Tidentime(USA), whose last two starts at two came over 7f, was dropping back in distance. He got a nice lead on the far rail off his stablemate Samitar, didn't get the clearest of runs around 2f out, but kept on well, and a return to further ought to suit him.
Solar Deity(IRE), running on turf for the first time, got a bit unbalanced running into the Dip but was putting in some good work at the finish. He was another dropping back in trip for the money, but will be suited by a return to 7f. (tchd 14-1)
Van Ellis isn't bred to be a sprinter at all, being by Shamardal out of a mare who was third in the Park Hill, so this has to go down as a huge effort on his racecourse debut. He took over going well inside the final 2f but just couldn't hang on inside the last. There should be plenty of improvement to come from him, especially over a longer trip. (op 50-1)
Muarrab came here race-fit having made a winning return on the AW a fortnight earlier. Never too far away on the far side, he had every chance. (op 16-1)
Balty Boys(IRE), who had a wind operation over the winter, was prominent throughout, but raced towards the centre of the track, which was probably not the ideal place to be. He edged right as he weakened. (op 6-1 tchd early 7-1)
Samitar, who looked fit beforehand but has not grown much, was the one to beat on the ratings, but she showed when runner-up in the Fillies' Mile here last year that she stays well so there had to be a question mark over her being as effective over this trip. Ridden positively to try and make her stamina tell, she was being pushed along from some way out and ultimately disappointed. There has to be a question mark over whether she's trained on, especially as her connections chose to chase the bucks rather than Group race glory, and this was hardly the ideal Guineas trial. (op 7-2 tchd 3-1)
Jacob Cats, noisy in the paddock, was probably inconvenienced by having to race more towards the centre of the track. (op 66-1)
Out Do, another who raced wider than ideal, didn't really handle the Dip particularly well. He can go the handicap route now and will be of more interest in that sphere.
Orders From Rome(IRE) was on his toes beforehand.
Switzerland(IRE) struggled to go the pace back in distance and was beaten a long way out. He has still to prove he's not just a Polytrack horse. (tchd 10-1)

1453 BET AT BLUESQUARE.COM EUROPEAN FREE H'CAP (LISTED RACE) 7f
3:35 (3:35) (Class 1) 3-Y-O **£18,714** (£7,095; £3,550; £1,768; £887; £445) **Stalls** Low

Form RPR

652- **1** **Telwaar**[249] 5044 3-8-11 100.. WilliamBuick 3 102+
(Peter Chapple-Hyam) *stdd s: confidently rdn and hld up in last: stl gng wl over 1f out: plld out and asked for effrt ent fnl f: qcknd and str run to ld fnl 50yds* **9/2**[2]

6-30 **2** ½ **Bannock (IRE)**[18] 1129 3-9-7 110.............................. SilvestreDeSousa 6 110
(Mark Johnston) *led and set stdy gallop: hdd 4f out: led again: rdn and qcknd 2f out: battled on gamely u.p tl hdd and no ex fnl 50yds* **12/1**

34-2 **3** 1¼ **Hazaz (IRE)**[25] 1036 3-8-11 100.. BrettDoyle 7 97
(Clive Brittain) *chsd ldrs: hdwy to join ldrs 3f out: rdn and ev ch 2f out: edgd rt u.p over 1f out: kpt on same pce ins fnl f* **14/1**

402- **4** 1¼ **Redact (IRE)**[214] 6162 3-9-6 109.. PatDobbs 2 103
(Richard Hannon) *chsd ldrs: rdn and effrt 2f out: keeping on same pce and n.m.r jst ins fnl f: styd on same pce after* **7/1**[3]

13- **5** ½ **Zumbi (IRE)**[245] 5181 3-8-12 101.. RyanMoore 4 93+
(Sir Michael Stoute) *in tch in last pair: rdn and unable qck over 1f out: keeping on whn nt clr run: swtchd lft ins fnl f: styd on fnl 100yds* **10/11**[1]

000- **6** 1 **West Leake Diman (IRE)**[179] 7019 3-9-4 107.............. FrankieDettori 5 97
(Charles Hills) *stdd s: t.k.h: in tch: rdn and unable qck wl over 1f out: styd on same pce after* **14/1**

500- **7** 1 **B Fifty Two (IRE)**[193] 6688 3-9-2 105.............................. SebSanders 1 92
(J W Hills) *w ldr tl led 4f out: hdd and rdn 2f out: outpcd jst over 1f out: wknd ins fnl f* **16/1**

1m 28.03s (2.63) **Going Correction** +0.40s/f (Good) **7** Ran SP% **110.0**
Speed ratings (Par 106): **100,99,98,96,96 94,93**
toteswingers:1&2:£3.50, 1&3:£7.20, 2&3:£9.50 CSF £50.02 TOTE £5.60: £3.10, £3.10; EX 65.00.
Owner Ziad A Galadari **Bred** Galadari Sons Stud Company Limited **Trained** Newmarket, Suffolk

FOCUS
The Free Handicap is not a race that has had a great bearing on the Classics in recent times, although 2003 winner Indian Haven went on to take the Irish Guineas. Mystiko won this race and the 2000 Guineas in 1991, and four years later Harayir, second here, won the 1000 Guineas. This was still a decent Listed event, but it was steadily run and the time compares unfavourably with the Nell Gwyn. There are one or two doubts over the form, with the favourite failing to fire and both the second and third coming here on the back of a disappointing recent run, but the race has been rated at face value.

NOTEBOOK

Telwaar, runner-up to Fencing in the Washington Singer at Newbury on his last start in August, has yet to race at higher than Listed level. Covered up at the back of the field, shielded from the headwind, he came with a strong burst down the outside to cut down the leaders and clearly possesses a decent turn of foot. He's not in the Newmarket Guineas and, while he holds an entry in the French version, his trainer believes the colt will prove best at this trip, with the Jersey Stakes at Royal Ascot the likely target. Ouqba won both races in 2009 and Red Jazz nearly did likewise a year later. A strongly run race suits Telwaar, who is ideally served by faster ground than this. (op 4-1 tchd 7-2 and 5-1 in a place)

Bannock(IRE) made the running and fought off a couple of other prominent racers before succumbing to the winner down his outer. Returning to form after finishing last against his elders in the Cammidge Trophy at Doncaster, he clearly gets 7f but his Duke Of York Stakes entry suggests he is viewed as a sprinter. (op 11-1)

Hazaz(IRE)'s third in the Horris Hill Stakes in the autumn stood out amongst his 2yo form, and he was well beaten in a Polytrack maiden on his previous outing this term. He ran well from up with the pace and his chance wasn't helped by his jockey losing his whip late on. Likely to prove difficult to place successfully, he did best of the three 2,000 Guineas entries in this line-up. (tchd 18-1)

Redact(IRE), runner-up in the Mill Reef Stakes on his final start, remains with Richard Hannon after a lucrative deal to sell him to the Far East fell through. Lacking the pace to mount an effective challenge, he was slightly short of room inside the final furlong but it didn't cost him a place. He's worth another try at this trip and faster ground will help. (op 13-2 tchd 6-1 and 9-1 in a place)

Zumbi(IRE), a rare runner in this race for his powerful stable, was disappointing. Third in the Acomb Stakes at York on the second of his two juvenile runs, he looked potentially well treated for this reappearance, with improvement expected. Held up, he did not pick up when he needed to but did run on all too late when switched off the rail. His Guineas entry looks unrealistic but he will improve on this when tackling a mile and may warrant another chance. Official explanation: jockey said colt was denied a clear run (op 11-10 tchd 6-5 early)

West Leake Diman(IRE)'s challenge fizzled out and he may not have stayed. As in the Middle Park Stakes he finished a length ahead of B Fifty Two. (op 16-1)

B Fifty Two(IRE), whose Deauville second to Dabirsim has been made to look good, failed to see out the seventh furlong here after racing up with the pace. (tchd 20-1)

1454 LANWADES STUD NELL GWYN STKS (GROUP 3) (FILLIES) 7f

4:10 (4:11) (Class 1) 3-Y-O

£31,190 (£11,825; £5,918; £2,948; £1,479; £742) **Stalls** Low

Form — RPR

13-3 **1** **Esentepe (IRE)**[11] [1215] 3-8-12 92 .... PatDobbs 2 99
(Richard Hannon) *chsd ldr: rdn to ld over 1f out: kpt on gamely ins fnl f: all out* **28/1**

331- **2** *nk* **Nayarra (IRE)**[192] [6740] 3-9-1 106 .... MartinDwyer 7 101
(Mick Channon) *chsd ldrs: rdn 2f out: chsd wnr jst over 1f out: kpt on gamely u.p and pressing wnr towards fin* **20/1**

226- **3** *½* **Lily's Angel (IRE)**[235] [5472] 3-8-12 99 .... PaulHanagan 12 97
(Richard Fahey) *in tch: rdn and effrt 2f out: styd on u.p to chse ldng pair ins fnl f: kpt on wl towards fin* **9/1**

1- **4** *shd* **Starscope**[172] [7164] 3-8-12 87 ....[1] WilliamBuick 10 96+
(John Gosden) *hld up in last trio: rdn and effrt 2f out: hdwy over 1f out: styd on wl ins fnl f: gng on fin but nvr quite getting to ldrs* **7/1**[3]

100- **5** *shd* **Lady Gorgeous**[207] [6337] 3-8-12 90 .... MartinHarley 8 96
(Mick Channon) *hld up in tch: rdn and unable qck 2f out: rallied ent fnl f: kpt on u.p ins fnl f* **22/1**

025- **6** *1 ½* **Sunday Times**[193] [6691] 3-8-12 109 .... TomQueally 13 92
(Peter Chapple-Hyam) *stdd s: hld up in rr: rdn and effrt on outer 2f out: hdwy 1f out: styd on wl ins fnl f: nvr gng pce to rch ldrs* **15/2**

016- **7** *2* **What's Up (IRE)**[215] [6128] 3-8-12 75 .... JamieSpencer 3 87
(Kevin Ryan) *stdd s: in bhd: rdn 1/2-way: drvn over 1f out: prog ent fnl f: styd on to pass btn horses fnl f: nvr trbld ldrs* **100/1**

14- **8** *¾* **Minidress**[208] [6296] 3-8-12 97 .... MickaelBarzalona 5 85+
(Mahmood Al Zarooni) *hld up off the pce in midfield: rdn and effrt whn hung rt wl over 1f out: keeping on but stl plenty to do whn nt clr run and swtchd rt 1f out: kpt on but nvr able to chal* **9/1**

126- **9** *½* **Russelliana**[270] [4312] 3-8-12 104 .... RyanMoore 6 83
(Sir Michael Stoute) *in tch in midfield: rdn and unable qck ent fnl 2f: styd on one pce and no threat to ldrs fr over 1f out* **10/1**

1- **10** *nse* **Muaamara**[173] [7132] 3-8-12 77 .... SamHitchcott 4 83
(Mick Channon) *chsd ldng trio: rdn and effrt wl over 1f out: unable qck u.p over 1f out: wknd ins fnl f* **16/1**

1-25 **11** *nk* **Pimpernel (IRE)**[55] [680] 3-8-12 105 .... FrankieDettori 11 82
(Mahmood Al Zarooni) *taken down early: stdd s: t.k.h: hld up in rr: rdn and effrt 2f out: no imp: kpt on fnl f but nvr trbld ldrs* **3/1**[1]

140- **12** *1 ¾* **Regal Realm**[193] [6691] 3-8-12 102 .... JimmyFortune 9 78
(Jeremy Noseda) *hld up off the pce towards rr: clsd and effrt 2f out: sn rdn and unable qck: wknd ins fnl f: eased towards fin* **5/1**[2]

322- **13** *6* **Excelette (IRE)**[173] [7135] 3-8-12 98 .... TomEaves 1 61
(Bryan Smart) *led tl rdn and hdd over 1f out: sn btn: fdd ins fnl f* **20/1**

1m 27.6s (2.20) **Going Correction** +0.40s/f (Good) **13** Ran SP% **119.2**
Speed ratings (Par 105): **103,102,102,101,101 100,97,97,96,96 96,94,87**
toteswingers:1&2:£22.00, 1&3:£27.40, 2&3:£12.80 CSF £479.01 TOTE £39.90: £8.40, £5.90, £1.90; EX 406.40 Trifecta £921.20 Part won. Pool: £1,244.95 - 0.60 winning units..

Owner Middleham Park Racing XXXVIII **Bred** Peter Kelly And Ms Wendy Daly **Trained** East Everleigh, Wilts

FOCUS

Only one winner (Speciosa in 2006) has taken the Nell Gwyn and followed up in the Guineas in the last 25 years, so for all that this is a recognised trial for the first fillies' Classic, it has generally been of little guide. With 28-1 outsider Esentepe winning what looked an ordinary renewal this time around it's highly unlikely that that trend is about to be bucked. The time was 0.43sec quicker than the Free Handicap and the form looks sound, if limited for the grade.

NOTEBOOK

Esentepe(IRE), one of only two in the race with the benefit of race-fitness, bounced out well, tracked the leader on the far rail and, once taking over, kept on strongly to hold off the closers. It's most likely that this was her Guineas and, as she's not entered for the main event, connections are likely to head a different route, with the Musidora possibly next up. She did at least give a boost to the form of her Kempton reappearance, which was won in pleasing fashion by Laugh Out Loud, and that filly might be a shade overpriced at 66-1 for the Guineas. (op 25-1 tchd 33-1)

Nayarra(IRE) broke her maiden in an Italian Group 1 on her final start at two and so had to carry a 3lb penalty here. Beaten only a neck, she comes out of this as the best filly in the race, and is fully entitled to take her chance in the Guineas, for which she's 50-1, and the return to a mile ought to suit. It'll be a surprise if she's good enough to play a serious hand, though. (op 25-1 tchd 28-1 in a place)

Lily's Angel(IRE) had plenty of racing at two, the best of her efforts being a second to Discourse in the Sweet Solera. Racing more towards the centre of the track, which was a disadvantage, she saw her race out well to narrowly edge third place. It was a sound effort but she probably has her limitations. (op 15-2 tchd 7-1)

Starscope impressed in taking a back-end maiden here, but it was rather disconcerting to see her fitted with a hood on her return. Nevertheless, she took the eye in doing best of those held up off the pace, and although she had the far rail to help, her relative lack of experience was evident. Not knocked about but running on strongly at the finish, she'll appreciate another furlong (now best-priced 25-1 for the Guineas) and, while the Guineas might come a bit soon for her, she looks the best long-term prospect of these. (op 8-1)

Lady Gorgeous, slightly on her toes beforehand, looks to have improved over the winter, appeared to need every yard of this trip (dam is a half-sister to smart middle-distance stayer/2m hurdler I´m Supposin) and she should be all the better for this reappearance. (op 20-1 tchd 25-1 in a place)

Sunday Times had strong claims on the ratings and did travel well, albeit towards the unfavoured centre, but she struggled to land a blow on the principals, who mostly raced prominently throughout. There's plenty of speed in her pedigree and it's possible she'll prove happier back over sprint distances. (tchd 8-1)

What's Up(IRE), who is now with Kevin Ryan, was on her toes beforehand. Taking a big step up in class, she trailed the field for much of the race, but weaved between horses late and was putting in her best work at the finish. She threatens to improve plenty for another furlong and, while she might have blown her mark of 75, she looks up to picking up black type when getting to race over a bit further.

Minidress, whose pedigree suggests she'll be wanting further than 7f this year (dam won at up to 1m4f and is out of a successful middle-distance family), was a little unlucky in running, but she was another to confirm that her stable's runners are badly needing their reappearances. (op 10-1)

Russelliana looked a promising 2yo prior to a disappointing effort in the Princess Margaret Stakes, but she was lame in one of her hind legs after that race, and her connections decided to rough her off for the season. There wasn't a great deal of encouragement to take from this, but she was a bit dull in her coat, should come on for the run and ought to be suited by another furlong. (op 8-1 tchd 15-2)

Muaamara was up there a long way before weakening inside the last. She lacked experience for this, didn't run badly in the circumstances and is entitled to improve for the run. (op 20-1 tchd 14-1)

Pimpernel(IRE), runner-up in the Rockfel last term, proved a little disappointing out in Dubai this winter, and this was even worse. Having gone to post early, she found little for pressure in the race itself and carried her head high, which isn't a great combination. (op 9-2)

Regal Realm, winner of the Prestige Stakes last year, was held in a couple of starts in Group 2 company afterwards and had something to prove here. Again disappointing, the excuse that she raced furthest away from the favoured far rail seems a shade hollow. (op 9-2 tchd 11-2 in a place)

1455 BLUE SQUARE FEILDEN STKS (LISTED RACE) 1m 1f

4:45 (4:47) (Class 1) 3-Y-O

£18,714 (£7,095; £3,550; £1,768; £887; £445) **Stalls** Low

Form — RPR

143- **1** **Stipulate**[184] [6914] 3-8-13 91 .... TomQueally 4 108+
(Sir Henry Cecil) *t.k.h: hld up in tch: gng best and waiting for gap wl over 1f out: pushed along and qcknd to ld jst over 1f out: sn clr and r.o strly fnl f* **8/1**

210- **2** *4 ½* **Mister Music**[184] [6914] 3-8-13 90 .... JimmyFortune 6 98
(Richard Hannon) *led and set stdy gallop: rdn and qcknd ent fnl 2f: hdd jst over 1f out: sn outpcd and no ch w wnr fnl f: kpt on to hold 2nd* **28/1**

114- **3** *1* **Producer**[179] [7026] 3-8-13 100 .... RyanMoore 1 96
(Richard Hannon) *chsd ldrs: rdn and effrt wl over 1f out: outpcd by wnr and btn 1f out: kpt on same pce* **4/1**[2]

10- **4** *nk* **Oxford Charley (USA)**[179] [7026] 3-8-13 85 .... MickaelBarzalona 2 95
(Mikael Magnusson) *stdd s: t.k.h: hld up in rr: plld out over 2f out: rdn and effrt 2f out: sme hdwy u.p over 1f out: no ch w wnr and styd on same pce fnl f* **16/1**

1- **5** *¾* **Jungle Beat (IRE)**[278] [4054] 3-8-13 0 .... WilliamBuick 3 93+
(John Gosden) *hld up in tch: rdn and effrt on far rail 2f out: nt clr run and shuffled bk over 1f out: sn swtchd lft: no ch w wnr but plugged on fnl f* **9/2**[3]

12- **6** *shd* **Perennial**[193] [6692] 3-8-13 105 .... MichaelHills 7 93
(Charles Hills) *t.k.h: chsd ldr: rdn and nt qckn 2f out: wandered lft u.p over 1f out: one pce and wl hld fnl f* **5/4**[1]

01- **7** *4* **Pembrey**[182] [6954] 3-8-13 83 .... FrankieDettori 5 84
(Mahmood Al Zarooni) *stdd s: t.k.h: hld up in tch: hdwy to chse ldrs 3f out: sn rdn: wknd over 1f out: wl btn and eased wl ins fnl f* **8/1**

1m 56.62s (4.92) **Going Correction** +0.40s/f (Good) **7** Ran SP% **114.2**
Speed ratings (Par 106): **94,90,89,88,88 88,84**
toteswingers:1&2:£5.30, 1&3:£5.40, 2&3:£8.20 CSF £174.23 TOTE £8.60: £3.80, £5.80; EX 129.40.

Owner K Abdulla **Bred** Juddmonte Farms Ltd **Trained** Newmarket, Suffolk

FOCUS

A race which has produced a few Classic pointers over the years. Erhaab, second in this in 1994, was the last Feilden runner to win the Derby, while Bollin Eric, third in 2002, took the St Leger. Rebel Rebel and Olympian Odyssey were beaten in this before placing in the 2000 Guineas while Rumoush, the 2010 winner, finished third in that year's Oaks. This looked a reasonable edition, but the pace was very steady to halfway and a number of these were keen as a consequence. The form is a bit muddling but the winner at least is up to scratch for the race.

NOTEBOOK

Stipulate ran out a fluent winner, waited with and keen once again before picking his way through to lead and running on strongly. Beaten in a couple of Listed races last year after his winning debut, his trainer putting those defeats down to immaturity, he looks more the finished article now and is clearly a smart colt. He does not hold a Derby entry, but he merits a crack at a Group race now, with the Dee Stakes at Chester over an extended 1m2f a possible target. He's in the Dante too. While he acts on a sound surface, his action suggests he would also handle easy conditions. (tchd 10-1)

Mister Music had a good first season but was below par behind Stipulate on his final start at Pontefract. He has a likeable attitude to racing and stuck on well for second after making the running, but the winner was much too strong. He is largely consistent and could win a race at this level. (op 33-1)

Producer made a satisfactory reappearance. He appeared to stay the longer trip, albeit in a falsely run race, but all his juvenile wins were over Epsom's undulating 7f and the Surrey Stakes, a Listed race over that C&D at the Derby meeting, could be a suitable target. (op 9-2 tchd 5-1)

Oxford Charley(USA) had been behind Producer in the Horris Hill on his second start at two. Back up in trip, he was squeezed leaving the stalls and, after being held up in last, was switched to the outside for his effort. He did run on, but never really looked to be helping his rider and a serious challenge didn't materialise. The impression he leaves is that the best has yet to be seen of him. (op 12-1)

Jungle Beat(IRE) had made a good impression when winning at Newbury on his only run at two, when his immediate victim was Farhaan, who went on to beat Mister Music at Salisbury. He was caught flat-footed when some pace was injected into the race and then found his passage on the fence blocked, never really looking like troubling the leaders. This Derby entry had reportedly been coltish in the paddock and may not have been in the best frame of mind for this assignment. (op 7-2 tchd 5-1 and 11-2 in a place)

Perennial's second in the Group 3 Autumn Stakes here set the standard on form and he had 5lb in hand on adjusted BHA ratings. After tracking the leaders, he produced a rather tame effort when the pressure was on. This Derby and Dante entry has something to prove now, but it's probably too soon to be writing him off. (op 6-4)

Pembrey's maiden-race win when last seen six months ago gave him plenty to find on form, and he was not up to the task. He should come on for the run, though, for while he looked well in his coat he looked as though the outing would do him good. (op 10-1 tchd 7-1)

1456 GET YOUR BETS ON AT BLUESQUARE.COM MAIDEN STKS 1m 2f
5:20 (5:23) (Class 4) 3-Y-O £4,528 (£1,347; £673; £336) Stalls Low

Form				RPR
3-	1		**Model Pupil**[214] 6160 3-9-3 0 MichaelHills 9 (Charles Hills) *hld up towards rr: hdwy over 2f out: pushed along and qcknd to ld wl over 1f out: drvn and hdd fnl 100yds: battled bk gamely to ld again cl home* 6/1[2]	96+
2-	2	nse	**Shantaram**[222] 5891 3-9-3 0 WilliamBuick 6 (John Gosden) *chsd ldrs: gng wl but stuck bhd a wall of horses ent fnl 2f: swtchd lft and gd hdwy over 1f out: rdn to ld fnl 100yds: sn drvn and fnd little: hdd cl home* 5/4[1]	96+
	3	4	**Yazdi (IRE)** 3-9-3 0 MickaelBarzalona 4 (Brian Meehan) *hld up towards rr: rdn and looked to be struggling over 3f out: styd on and hdwy over 1f out: wnt 3rd ins fnl f: kpt on* 25/1	88
	4	1 1/4	**Sash Of Honour (IRE)** 3-9-3 0 RyanMoore 11 (Sir Michael Stoute) *hld up towards rr: rdn and effrt over 2f out: hdwy over 1f out: no threat to ldng pair but kpt on ins fnl f* 20/1	85
	5	1	**Suraj** 3-9-3 0 JamieSpencer 5 (Michael Bell) *stdd s: hld up in rr: clsd and in tch whn nt clr run ent fnl 2f: swtchd lft and hdwy over 1f out: kpt on steadily under hands and heels riding fnl f* 20/1	83+
23-3	6	6	**Yaa Salam**[7] 1312 3-9-3 78 (p) SilvestreDeSousa 7 (Mahmood Al Zarooni) *in tch: rdn and effrt to ld 2f out: sn hdd and unable qck: edgd rt u.p over 1f out: wknd fnl f* 10/1	71
6-	7	1 1/4	**All That Rules**[147] 7521 3-9-3 0 TomQueally 10 (Sir Henry Cecil) *pressed ldrs: rdn and unable qck ent fnl 2f: wknd over 1f out* 9/1	69
2-	8	7	**Shuja (USA)**[180] 6983 3-9-3 0 FrankieDettori 3 (Saeed Bin Suroor) *hld up in tch in midfield: stl gng wl enough whn nt clr run 2f out: shuffled bk and swtchd lft over 1f out: lost any ch and n.d after* 15/2[3]	55+
333-	9	1 1/2	**Humungosaur**[181] 6970 3-9-3 90 PatDobbs 8 (Richard Hannon) *rrd as stalls opened: sn rcvrd and pressing ldrs: rdn over 2f out: wknd wl over 1f out: fdd over 1f out* 14/1	52
0-	10	3 1/2	**Rainbow Gold**[235] 5475 3-9-3 0 PaulHanagan 2 (Mark Johnston) *led tl rdn and hdd 2f out: sn wknd and fdd fnl f* 14/1	45
	11	80	**Soho Spirit** 3-8-12 0 RobertHavlin 1 (James Toller) *midfield: wkng whn rdn 1/2-way: lost pl 4f out: t.o fr 2f out* 50/1	

2m 9.45s (3.65) **Going Correction** +0.40s/f (Good) 11 Ran SP% **118.2**
Speed ratings (Par 100): **101,100,97,96,95 91,90,84,83,80 16**
toteswingers:1&2:£3.00, 1&3:£22.40, 2&3:£9.60 CSF £13.25 TOTE £9.70: £2.70, £1.10, £6.70; EX 17.60 Trifecta £951.90 Part won. Pool: £1,286.43 - 0.33 winning units..
Owner K Abdulla **Bred** Juddmonte Farms Ltd **Trained** Lambourn, Berks

FOCUS
Always a good maiden, this looked an informative race on paper and, with a sound pace on and the first two drawing clear, the form looks solid. Winners should come from it.

1457 BET AT BLUESQUARE.COM ON YOUR MOBILE H'CAP 6f
5:55 (5:56) (Class 2) (0-100,100) 3-Y-O £12,938 (£3,850; £1,924; £962) Stalls Low

Form				RPR
00-1	1		**Es Que Love (IRE)**[8] 1271 3-8-12 **91** 6ex SilvestreDeSousa 2 (Mark Johnston) *mde all: readily wnt clr over 1f out: in command and rdn ins fnl f: tiring towards fin but in n.d* 10/3[1]	99
160-	2	2	**Sans Loi (IRE)**[200] 6524 3-8-5 **84** ow1 MartinDwyer 14 (Alan McCabe) *taken down early: hld up in rr: rdn and effrt wl over 1f out: kpt on wl ins fnl f: wnt 2nd cl home: no threat to wnr* 12/1	86
316-	3	nk	**Heeraat (IRE)**[228] 5715 3-8-9 **88** PaulHanagan 9 (William Haggas) *hld up in midfield: hdwy and squeezed between horses 2f out: drvn and chsd clr wnr ent fnl f: kpt on: lost 2nd cl home* 10/1	89
535-	4	nk	**Responsive**[207] 6340 3-8-7 **86** ow1 DarryllHolland 16 (Hughie Morrison) *hld up in midfield: rdn and effrt 2f out: hdwy and edging rt fr over 1f out: kpt on u.p but no threat to wnr* 9/1	86
105-	5	1/2	**Alejandro (IRE)**[215] 6114 3-8-9 **95** LauraBarry(7) 1 (Richard Fahey) *mostly chsd wnr: rdn 1/2-way: outpcd by wnr over 1f out: lost 2nd ent fnl f and kpt on same pce after* 25/1	93
42-2	6	1	**Amazing Storm (IRE)**[11] 1217 3-8-12 **91** PatDobbs 4 (Richard Hannon) *stdd s: t.k.h: hld up in tch: rdn and effrt wl over 1f out: kpt on same pce ins fnl f* 13/2[2]	86
141-	7	1/2	**Heyward Girl (IRE)**[173] 7138 3-8-4 **83** AndreaAtzeni 15 (Robert Eddery) *chsd ldrs: rdn jst over 2f out: unable qck over 1f out: styd on same pce* 22/1	77
321-	8	2	**Desert Philosopher**[172] 7174 3-8-4 **83** MickaelBarzalona 11 (Kevin Ryan) *in tch: rdn and unable qck over 2f out: outpcd and drvn wl over 1f out: n.d but plugged on u.p fnl f* 12/1	70
210-	9	1/2	**Top Cop**[223] 5849 3-8-13 **92** JimmyFortune 12 (Andrew Balding) *hld up in tch in midfield: rdn and effrt wl over 2f out: no imp and styd on same pce fr over 1f out* 7/1[3]	78
153-	10	1/2	**Dam Beautiful**[284] 3884 3-8-11 **93** JulieBurke(3) 6 (Kevin Ryan) *chsd ldrs: rdn jst over 2f out: unable qck wl over 1f out: wknd ins fnl f* 25/1	77
400-	11	nk	**North Star Boy (IRE)**[200] 6535 3-9-4 **97** RyanMoore 5 (Richard Hannon) *stdd s: hld up towards rr: rdn and effrt wl over 1f out: kpt on u.p fnl f: n.d* 14/1	80
110-	12	2	**Ballesteros**[179] 7019 3-9-0 **93** JamieSpencer 8 (Brian Meehan) *taken down early: stdd s: hld up in rr: rdn and effrt over 1f out: no imp: eased towards fin* 10/1	70
215-	13	3 1/2	**Indian Tinker**[196] 6625 3-8-3 **82** JohnFahy 3 (Robert Cowell) *stdd s: hld up towards rr: rdn and no prog wl over 1f out: n.d* 28/1	47
610-	14	6	**Gung Ho Jack**[194] 6670 3-8-4 **83** LiamJones 13 (John Best) *in tch tl 1/2-way: sn rdn and struggling: wknd wl over 1f out: bhd fnl f* 33/1	29
00-5	15	1/2	**Gatepost (IRE)**[25] 1032 3-9-7 **100** MartinHarley 7 (Mick Channon) *in tch towards rr: rdn and wknd wl over 2f out: bhd fnl f* 11/1	45
314-	16	1	**Marygold**[200] 6524 3-8-0 **82** HarryBentley(3) 10 (Lee Carter) *chsd ldrs tl jst over 2f out: wknd over 1f out: fdd fnl f* 25/1	23

1m 13.96s (1.76) **Going Correction** +0.40s/f (Good) 16 Ran SP% **129.8**
Speed ratings (Par 104): **104,101,100,100,99 98,97,95,94,93 93,90,86,78,77 76**
toteswingers:1&2:£18.60, 1&3:£10.70, 2&3:£42.50 CSF £43.57 CT £402.23 TOTE £4.00: £1.40, £3.90, £2.80, £3.00; EX 62.40 Trifecta £811.40 Part won. Pool: £1,096.62 - 0.60 winning units..
Owner Crone Stud Farms Ltd **Bred** Newhall Ltd **Trained** Middleham Moor, N Yorks

FOCUS
Won in successive years recently by Group 1 performers Sakhee's Secret and Prohibit, this was a good sprint handicap which is sure to yield plenty of winners over the coming months. Form to be fairly positive about. The field spread across the track.

NOTEBOOK
Es Que Love(IRE) held a race-fitness edge over the majority of his rivals, having easily won a Pontefract handicap last week. A pound well in under the penalty, he confirmed himself a young sprinter on the upgrade with a taking victory, coasting along at the head of affairs near the far rail and finding plenty once let down. He was essentially disappointing at two, but had held some big-race entries at one stage and is beginning to realise his potential now. He will be up to contesting Listed races before long but there could still be more to come from him in handicap company before then. (op 4-1 tchd 9-2 in a place)
Sans Loi(IRE), who had been held up, delivered his run on the opposite flank of the track to the winner and was closing the gap late on. Twice found wanting in Group 2 company at two, he should pay his way in strongly run sprint handicaps this year. (op 10-1)
Heeraat(IRE) ◆ had disappointed in a Group 3 on Polytrack on his final start at two but had looked useful when winning his maiden by 11l at Pontefract previously. In contrast to the first two he raced down the centre. After travelling nicely he ran on willingly once coming off the bridle, but the winner was too good. There is a decent prize to be won with him at some stage. (tchd 8-1)
Responsive, whose trainer has a decent record in this event, ran on through the final furlong, edging to her right all the while and ending up near the far side. Dropped 4lb since her last run at two, she will be worth another try over 7f. (op 12-1)
Alejandro(IRE) raced up with the winner on the far side and stuck on for pressure. Gelded during the winter, he was suited by the return to 6f.
Amazing Storm(IRE) again raced keenly but settled by halfway and did stick on down the far side. This was only his second race at a trip this short. (op 11-2 tchd 7-1)
Heyward Girl(IRE) could not dominate in this company but still ran a decent race, showing plenty of speed from her high draw. (op 20-1 tchd 25-1)
Top Cop did not produce a great deal when let down but he is not the type to give up on yet. (op 15-2)
Ballesteros was 11lb higher than when winning at Windsor in October and never figured on this reappearance, but he could be worth another chance. (op 9-1)
T/Plt: £5,470.80 to a £1 stake. Pool:£84,685.26 - 11.30 winning tickets T/Qpdt: £946.50 to a £1 stake. Pool:£7,034.91 - 5.50 winning tickets SP

1458 - 1465a (Foreign Racing) - See Raceform Interactive

1450 NEWMARKET (R-H)
Thursday, April 19

OFFICIAL GOING: Good to soft (8.0)
Wind: fresh, half behind Weather: dry

1466 NGK SPARK PLUGS/BRITISH STALLION STUDS E B F MAIDEN FILLIES' STKS 5f
1:50 (1:51) (Class 4) 2-Y-O £4,528 (£1,347; £673; £336) Stalls High

Form				RPR
	1		**Tassel** 2-9-0 0 RyanMoore 2 (Richard Hannon) *chsd ldr: rdn and rn green over 1f out: chal 1f out: led ins fnl f: styd on wl* 6/5[1]	83+
2	2	1 1/4	**All Fur Coat**[17] 1164 2-9-0 0 TonyCulhane 5 (Jo Hughes) *led: rdn over 1f out: drvn and hdd ins fnl f: no ex* 10/1	78
	3	1/2	**Graphic Guest** 2-9-0 0 SamHitchcott 9 (Mick Channon) *in tch: rdn wl over 1f out: drvn ent fnl f: chsd ldng pair ins fnl f: kpt on* 5/1[2]	76+
	4	1	**Royal Steps (IRE)** 2-9-0 0 KierenFallon 1 (James Tate) *chsd ldrs and racd wd of rivals: rdn and unable qck over 1f out: styd on under pce ins fnl f* 15/2	73
	5	1 1/2	**Lady Of The House (IRE)** 2-8-11 0 AmyRyan(3) 3 (Kevin Ryan) *in tch: rdn 1/2-way: effrt u.p over 1f out: no imp* 12/1	67
	6	1 1/4	**Mrs Warren** 2-9-0 0 MichaelHills 7 (Charles Hills) *stdd s: hld up in rr: rdn and effrt whn unbalanced on downhill run wl over 1f out: kpt on but no threat to ldrs fnl f* 7/1[3]	63
	7	3/4	**Seraphima** 2-9-0 0 LiamJones 8 (Alan Bailey) *in tch: rn green and wnt rt 2f out: sn rdn and wknd over 1f out* 14/1	60
	8	8	**Cernanova (IRE)** 2-9-0 0 TedDurcan 4 (Hugo Palmer) *dwlt: bhd: lost tch 1/2-way* 50/1	31

1m 0.03s (0.93) **Going Correction** +0.175s/f (Good) 8 Ran SP% **111.8**
Speed ratings (Par 91): **99,97,96,94,92 90,89,76**
toteswingers:1&2:£2.60, 1&3:£2.10, 2&3:£4.00 CSF £13.71 TOTE £2.00: £1.10, £2.00, £2.00; EX 11.30 Trifecta £32.20 Pool: £813.03 - 18.66 winning units.
Owner Highclere Thoroughbred Racing - Herbert Jones **Bred** Mrs Susan Field **Trained** East Everleigh, Wilts

FOCUS
Far side track used with stalls on stands' side. The quality of this maiden has varied significantly in recent years, but smart winners include Wunders Dream (Molecombe and Flying Childers), Flashy Wings (Queen Mary and Lowther) and Silk Blossom (Lowther), while Habaayib was third in 2010 before taking the Albany.

NOTEBOOK
Tassel, a £42,000 February foal, is from a family the stable knows well. She's a sister to a 5f-6f juvenile winner, as well as a half-sister to a few other winners, and her dam made a successful debut over 6f at two. There was loads of money around for her and she put up a fair performance to make a winning start, doing well to get the better of a filly who had plenty in her favour. Her connections think she could be Royal Ascot material. (tchd 11-10 and 5-4)
All Fur Coat is probably a bit flattered as she was the only runner with experience (second when favourite for her debut at Redcar) and had the benefit of the stands' rail. (op 8-1)
Graphic Guest, an 80,000gns April foal, is a half-sister to a few winners, including 5f-1m scorer (including Listed) Fourpenny Lane, and she made a pleasing debut. She's open to plenty of improvement. (op 11-2 tchd 6-1)
Royal Steps(IRE), a 36,000euros February foal, out of a 7f winner who was Listed placed at 1m3f, was drawn widest and wasn't helped by being isolated towards the middle of the track. She ran well in the circumstances. (op 8-1 tchd 7-1)
Lady Of The House(IRE), an 18,000gns February foal, showed ability.
Mrs Warren, a January foal, had her sales price increase from 20,000gns to £45,000. Charlie Hills said she had been "going nicely at home but probably isn't as forward as the colts we have run and is more of a leggy individual". She was soon behind and didn't seem to handle the Dip, so there should be plenty more to come. (op 11-1)
Seraphima, a 20,000gns February foal out of a 1m juvenile winner, shaped a bit better than her finishing position suggests. (op 12-1 tchd 16-1)

1467 SWAN AT LAVENHAM WOOD DITTON STKS 1m
2:25 (2:28) (Class 4) 3-Y-O £5,175 (£1,540; £769; £384) Stalls High

Form				RPR
	1	1 3/4	**Mukhadram** 3-9-3 0 PaulHanagan 10 (William Haggas) *hld up in tch: rdn and effrt wl over 1f out: hdwy u.p over 1f out: chsd wnr ins fnl f: no imp* 7/2[1]	83+

2 *shd* **Fluctuate (USA)** 3-9-3 0 .... NickyMackay 20 83+
(John Gosden) *hld up towards rr: rdn and hdwy wl over 1f out: chsd ldrs u.p ent fnl f: kpt on same pce fnl 150yds* **20/1**

3 *1* **Hill Street (IRE)** 3-9-3 0 .... WilliamBuick 14 81+
(John Gosden) *chsd ldr tl 5f out: styd prom: chsd wnr again over 2f out: rdn wl over 1f out: no ex 1f out: styd on same pce and lost 2 pls ins fnl f* **4/1**[2]

4 *2 1/4* **Bunraku** 3-8-12 0 .... MichaelHills 8 71+
(Charles Hills) *hld up towards rr: hdwy over 3f out: chsd ldrs and rn green u.p over 1f out: edgd rt and wknd jst ins fnl f* **33/1**

- 5 *2 1/2* **Straight Shot (IRE)** 3-9-3 0 .... (t) ShaneKelly 17 70
(Brian Meehan) *stdd s: hld up in tch: rdn 3f out: hdwy and rn green wl over 1f out: edgd rt and no imp 1f out* **40/1**

6 *3/4* **Viewpoint (IRE)** 3-9-3 0 .... PatDobbs 9 68+
(Richard Hannon) *in tch in midfield: rdn and unable qck 3f out: sme hdwy over 1f out: no imp 1f out but kpt on fnl f* **12/1**

- 7 *1/2* **Capitol Gain (IRE)** 3-9-3 0 .... MartinDwyer 5 67
(Brian Meehan) *pressed ldrs: led 3f out tl over 2f out: rdn and unable qck ent fnl 2f: wknd jst over 1f out* **50/1**

8 *hd* **Mawasem** 3-9-3 0 .... TadhgO'Shea 1 67+
(Sir Michael Stoute) *stdd s: hld up in rr: pushed along and hdwy whn swtchd rt ent fnl f: styd on fnl f: nvr trbld ldrs* **25/1**

9 *1/2* **Mawhub** 3-9-3 0 .... MickaelBarzalona 13 66
(Saeed Bin Suroor) *hld up in tch: rdn and unable qck 2f out: wknd u.p over 1f out* **14/1**

10 *1/2* **Sheikhzayedroad** 3-9-3 0 .... MartinLane 6 64+
(David Simcock) *stdd s: t.k.h early: hld up in rr: pushed along and sme hdwy over 1f out: kpt on fnl f: nvr trbld ldrs* **25/1**

11 *1/2* **Tenure** 3-9-3 0 .... RyanMoore 19 63+
(Sir Michael Stoute) *hld up in tch in rr: rdn and effrt whn rn green wl over 1f out: no imp: nvr trbld ldrs* **9/1**

12 *1* **Wildomar** 3-9-3 0 .... JohnnyMurtagh 16 61+
(Jeremy Noseda) *in tch: rdn and struggling ent fnl 2f: wknd over 1f out* **22/1**

13 *4 1/2* **Sky Khan** 3-9-3 0 .... JamieSpencer 7 51
(Ed Dunlop) *dwlt: sn rcvrd and chsng ldrs: rdn over 2f out: sn struggling and wknd 2f out* **14/1**

14 *1 3/4* **Encouraging (IRE)** 3-9-3 0 .... DaneO'Neill 2 47
(David Elsworth) *v.s.a: in rr: rdn and effrt on stands' rail wl over 1f out: no imp: wknd over 1f out* **80/1**

15 *1 1/4* **Roserrow** 3-9-3 0 .... JimmyFortune 3 44
(Andrew Balding) *in tch in midfield: pushed along after 2f: struggling 3f out: bhd fnl 2f* **20/1**

16 *2 1/4* **Omar Khayyam** 3-9-3 0 .... (t) DavidProbert 11 38
(Andrew Balding) *in tch in midfield rdn and struggling 3f out: sn lost pl: bhd over 1f out* **12/1**

17 *1* **Morlotti** 3-8-10 0 .... JordanTaylor(7) 12 36
(Luca Cumani) *chsd ldrs tl led 1/2-way: hdwy hdd 3f out: wknd wl over 1f out: fdd* **66/1**

D **Mariner's Cross (IRE)** 3-9-3 0 .... FrankieDettori 15 87+
(Mahmood Al Zarooni) *led tl 1/2-way: chsd ldrs tl led again over 2f out: rdn over 1f out: styd on wl ins fnl f: gng away at fin* **6/1**[3]

1m 39.26s (0.66) **Going Correction** +0.175s/f (Good) **18** Ran SP% **126.9**
Speed ratings (Par 100): **101,101,100,97,95 94,94,93,93,92 92,91,86,85,83 81,80,103**
toteswingers:1&2:£5.70, 1&3:£31.20, 2&3:£24.50 CSF £24.80 TOTE £7.60: £2.70, £2.10, £7.20; EX 35.00 Trifecta £454.90 Part won. Pool: £614.77 - 0.41 winning units..
Owner Hamdan Al Maktoum **Bred** Wardall Bloodstock **Trained** Newmarket, Suffolk

FOCUS
Often a contest that doesn't work out as well as expected, but the field looked a bit deeper than usual and the race should produce its share of winners. They early gallop was an ordinary one and little got into it from off the pace, the main action ultimately unfolding towards the stands' rail, having started off more down the middle of the track. The time was 1.82secs slower than the Craven, and the form is fluid rated around averages.

1468 £250,000 TATTERSALLS MILLIONS 3-Y-O TROPHY 1m 2f
3:00 (3:03) (Class 2) 3-Y-O

£135,275 (£55,350; £24,625; £12,275; £6,150; £2,450) **Stalls** High

Form RPR

513- **1** **Rougemont (IRE)**[173] 7167 3-9-3 85 .... PatDobbs 14 109
(Richard Hannon) *hld up in tch: rdn and effrt to ld ent 2f out: drvn over 1f out: styd on gamely u.p and a jst holding runner-up fnl f* **10/1**[3]

6214 **2** *1/2* **Mickdaam (IRE)**[19] 1145 3-9-3 112 .... JamieSpencer 5 108
(Richard Fahey) *chsd ldr: rdn to ld 3f out: hdd ent fnl 2f: battled on gamely u.p and ev ch after: a jst hld fnl f* **5/1**[2]

05-5 **3** *3 1/4* **Arsaadi (IRE)**[12] 1215 3-8-12 92 .... AhmedAjtebi 6 96
(William Haggas) *t.k.h: chsd ldr: rdn ev ch wl over 1f out: no ex 1f out: wknd ins fnl f* **16/1**

4 *3* **Amira's Prince (IRE)**[25] 1044 3-9-3 0 .... WayneLordan 3 95+
(David Wachman, Ire) *in tch in midfield: rdn and effrt over 2f out: chsd ldng trio: u.p over 1f out: btn ent fnl f: wknd* **5/1**[2]

151- **5** *4* **Coupe De Ville (IRE)**[201] 6527 3-9-3 105 .... RyanMoore 8 87
(Richard Hannon) *chsd ldrs: rdn and effrt ent fnl 2f: edgd rt and btn over 1f out: wknd ent fnl f* **7/2**[1]

24- **6** *2 3/4* **Alkazim (IRE)**[22] 1077 3-9-3 95 .... KierenFallon 7 82
(David Wachman, Ire) *in tch: rdn and unable qck jst over 2f out: wknd u.p wl over 1f out: 6th and wl btn fnl f* **12/1**

40-1 **7** *2 3/4* **Chapter Seven**[12] 1221 3-9-3 90 .... FrederikTylicki 1 76
(Richard Fahey) *in tch in midfield: rdn and struggling over 3f out: n.d after: plugged on fr over 1f out* **25/1**

100- **8** *shd* **Rock Supreme (IRE)**[201] 6527 3-9-3 79 .... JohnnyMurtagh 9 76
(Richard Hannon) *led tl hdd and rdn 3f out: wknd 2f out: 7th and wl btn ent fnl f* **28/1**

004- **9** *1* **Daghash**[181] 6986 3-9-3 79 .... BrettDoyle 11 74
(Clive Brittain) *t.k.h: chsd ldrs tl rdn and wknd over 2f out: wl btn over 1f out* **100/1**

422 **10** *7* **Benbecula**[26] 1031 3-9-3 85 .... KieranO'Neill 12 60
(Richard Hannon) *t.k.h: hld up in rr: rdn and litte rspnse over 3f out: bhd fnl 2f* **33/1**

41- **11** *8* **Handsome Man (IRE)**[177] 7083 3-9-3 80 .... FrankieDettori 10 44
(Saeed Bin Suroor) *chsd ldrs: rdn and no rspnse ent fnl 3f: wl btn 2f out: eased ins fnl f: t.o* **14/1**

21- **12** *4 1/2* **Ellaal**[183] 6951 3-9-3 85 .... TadhgO'Shea 4 35
(Charles Hills) *a bhd: lost tch over 3f out: t.o and eased ins fnl f* **14/1**

5-20 **13** *nk* **Entifaadha**[19] 1145 3-9-3 107 .... PaulHanagan 2 34
(William Haggas) *t.k.h: hld up in tch: rdn and btn 3f out: wl bhd and eased over 1f out: t.o* **5/1**[2]

0-14 **14** *6* **Ex Oriente (IRE)**[18] 1160 3-9-3 78 .... (b) WilliamBuick 13 22
(John Gosden) *hld up in rr: rdn and no rspnse over 4f out: wl bhd fnl 2f: eased over 1f out: t.o* **40/1**

2m 3.54s (-2.26) **Going Correction** +0.175s/f (Good) **14** Ran SP% **121.9**
Speed ratings (Par 104): **116,115,113,110,107 105,103,102,102,96 90,86,86,81**
toteswingers:1&2:£12.60, 1&3:£28.80, 2&3:£23.50 CSF £57.80 TOTE £12.10: £3.90, £2.00, £5.60; EX 90.40 Trifecta £917.10 Part won. Pool: £1,239.40 - 0.50 winning units. .
Owner Mrs J Wood **Bred** Mrs Clodagh McStay **Trained** East Everleigh, Wilts

■ Stewards' Enquiry : Jamie Spencer caution: careless riding.

FOCUS
Plenty of suspect stayers and a strong pace saw the field finish strung out behind the front two. It's hard to know if Mickdaam ran right up to his Dubai form, but he probably wasn't far off it and if that's the case then the level is pretty decent amongst the principals. The main action unfolded against the stands' rail and the third and fourth are rated pretty much to their marks.

NOTEBOOK
Rougemont(IRE) had Mickdaam behind when making a successful debut over 7f at the July course. He didn't really go on from that, his only subsequent win coming in a three-runner conditions event, but he's bred to improve with time and this was a huge improvement on his juvenile efforts. Having the rail to race against arguably made the difference, but in fairness he had travelled strongly and there looked no fluke in this. It remains to be seen where he goes from here but, while he could go be one for a Derby trial, it remains to be seen whether he's best fresh. (op 14-1)
Mickdaam(IRE), who was fourth in the UAE Derby less than three weeks earlier, had an unhelpful draw and didn't travel that strongly but kept plugging on, confirming the impression made in Dubai that he'll stay further. He coped okay with the switch from Tapeta to easy turf, and probably has more to offer, but he's been quite busy. (op 9-2 tchd 11-2 in a place)
Arsaadi(IRE) might have been a touch closer had she not been squeezed for room late on. She had shaped well behind Laugh Out Loud over 1m on Polytrack on her reappearance, and her performance here gives another boost to the form of Mick Channon's filly. (tchd 18-1)
Amira's Prince(IRE) looked decent when winning a 1m maiden at the Curragh on his reappearance (runner-up won next time), but he wasn't sure to be suited by this longer trip. He travelled well, but didn't see it out. (op 9-2 tchd 4-1)
Coupe De Ville(IRE) was a likeable juvenile, winning four of his six starts, including a Listed contest at 1m, and a 7f sales race here, but he wasn't sure to stay. Despite being well placed, he just didn't pick up. (op 9-2 tchd 5-1 in a place)
Alkazim(IRE) was yet another doubtful stayer, and he was the stable's second string. He travelled enthusiastically but had nothing left when it mattered. (op 10-1)
Entifaadha struggled when fitted with blinkers in the UAE Derby and this was another poor showing. He has gone the wrong way. (op 13-2)

1469 CONNAUGHT ACCESS FLOORING ABERNANT STKS (LISTED RACE) 6f
3:35 (3:36) (Class 1) 3-Y-O+

£18,714 (£7,095; £3,550; £1,768; £887; £445) **Stalls** High

Form RPR

42-3 **1** **Mayson**[19] 1129 4-9-5 100 .... PaulHanagan 3 114
(Richard Fahey) *chsd ldng pair: jnd ldrs gng wl over 1f out: rdn and qcknd to ld ent fnl f: r.o strly* **4/1**[2]

0602 **2** *3 1/2* **Jimmy Styles**[19] 1129 8-9-5 105 .... (p) JohnFahy 11 103
(Clive Cox) *led: rdn 2f out: edgd rt u.p over 1f out: hdd ent fnl f: nt pce of wnr but battled on gamely to hold 2nd* **15/2**

0005 **3** *1 1/2* **Internationaldebut (IRE)**[19] 1129 7-9-5 101 .... FrederikTylicki 6 98
(Paul Midgley) *hld up in tch: rdn and effrt over 1f out: r.o u.p ins fnl f: wnt 3rd nr fin* **25/1**

203- **4** *nk* **Cheviot (USA)**[193] 6733 6-9-5 100 .... (p) TomEaves 4 97
(Ian Semple) *pressed ldr: ev ch and rdn wl over 2f out: nt pce of wnr 1f out: duelling for 2nd after tl wknd fnl 50yds* **40/1**

03-1 **5** *1/2* **New Planet (IRE)**[10] 1255 4-9-5 100 .... TomQueally 5 95
(John Quinn) *chsd ldng trio: rdn and sltly outpcd over 1f out: styd on same pce u.p and no threat to wnr fnl f* **13/2**

122- **6** *1/2* **Elusivity (IRE)**[181] 6987 4-9-5 95 .... JamieSpencer 7 94
(Brian Meehan) *hld up in last trio: rdn and effrt over 1f out: kpt on fnl f but no ch w wnr* **7/1**

03-0 **7** *nk* **High Standing (USA)**[19] 1129 7-9-5 102 .... RyanMoore 10 97+
(Jeremy Gask) *in tch in midfield: rdn and unable qck over 1f out: styng on same pce and no ch w wnr whn squeezed for room and eased wl ins fnl f* **16/1**

11-0 **8** *shd* **Sirius Prospect (USA)**[19] 1129 4-9-9 110 .... ShaneKelly 1 97
(Dean Ivory) *in tch in midfield: rdn and effrt wl over 1f out: drvn and styd on same pce fr over 1f out* **11/2**[3]

450- **9** *nk* **Genki (IRE)**[187] 6858 8-9-5 114 .... (v) GeorgeBaker 8 92
(Roger Charlton) *stdd s: hld up in rr: rdn and effrt over 1f out: kpt on fnl f but no ch w wnr* **3/1**[1]

100- **10** *1 3/4* **Tiddliwinks**[229] 5707 6-9-5 102 .... NeilCallan 9 86
(Kevin Ryan) *rdr struggling to remove hood at s and slowly away: in tch in last trio: rdn ent fnl 2f: no prog whn n.m.r over 1f out: n.d* **20/1**

1m 11.86s (-0.34) **Going Correction** +0.175s/f (Good) **10** Ran SP% **114.9**
Speed ratings (Par 111): **109,104,102,101,101 100,100,100,99,97**
toteswingers:1&2:£6.50, 1&3:£17.30, 2&3:£25.50 CSF £32.64 TOTE £4.60: £1.40, £3.60, £5.60; EX 41.40 Trifecta £633.30 Pool: £1,035.63 - 1.21 winning units..
Owner David W Armstrong **Bred** Highfield Farm Llp **Trained** Musley Bank, N Yorks

FOCUS
An unsatisfactory race, with the pace being very steady for the trip, and the closers were at a significant disadvantage. The form is rated around the first two.

NOTEBOOK
Mayson, who settled better than in the past, was ideally positioned given the way the race unfolded and his superior acceleration carried him clear. He'd made a promising reappearance at Doncaster and is obviously progressing, but won't always have things falling so kindly. He'll now head for the Duke of York, for which he's 10-1 from 20-1 with Ladbrokes. (op 5-1)
Jimmy Styles, one place ahead of the winner at Doncaster, was soon in front on the rail and stuck on without being able to match the winner for speed. (op 8-1 tchd 7-1)
Internationaldebut(IRE) did best of those coming from off the speed, but was never in with a chance of winning.
Cheviot(USA) was soon on the speed and ran above market expectations. He'll be mainly contesting top sprint handicaps/Listed contests this season. (tchd 50-1)
New Planet(IRE), winner of a minor 6f conditions race at Warwick on his reappearance, couldn't quicken and would have preferred a stronger gallop. (op 8-1 tchd 9-1)
Elusivity(IRE) was a highly consistent and progressive 3yo, but being a hold-up performer the lack of a gallop was no good to him on this first crack at Pattern level. He can rate better than the bare form and ought to make his mark in this grade. (op 8-1 tchd 13-2)
Sirius Prospect(USA) was stuck wide with no cover and the race wasn't run to suit. (op 9-2 tchd 6-1)
Genki(IRE) was another unsuited by the lack of pace. (op 11-4 tchd 5-2)

Tiddliwinks was slowly away after the blind was removed late and then quickly done with having been short of room late. Official explanation: jockey said he was distracted by another unruly runner and was slow to remove the blind. (op 22-1 tchd 25-1)

1470 NOVAE BLOODSTOCK INSURANCE CRAVEN STKS (GROUP 3) (C&G) 1m

4:10 (4:11) (Class 1) 3-Y-O

£31,190 (£11,825; £5,918; £2,948; £1,479; £742) **Stalls** High

Form RPR

415- **1** **Trumpet Major (IRE)**[194] 6689 3-9-1 114 RyanMoore 12 114
(Richard Hannon) *chsd ldrs: pushed along 4f out: hdwy u.p to ld and edgd rt over 1f out: gng clr and continued edging rt fr 1f out: styd on strly: rdn out* **9/2**[3]

221- **2** *5* **Crius (IRE)**[210] 6270 3-8-12 113 PatDobbs 10 100
(Richard Hannon) *pressed ldrs and racd against stands' rail: led ent fnl 2f: hdd and drvn over 1f out: no ch w wnr fnl f but kpt on for 2nd* **4/1**[2]

13-1 **3** *1 1/2* **Eastern Sun (IRE)**[12] 1216 3-8-12 103 WilliamBuick 3 96+
(John Gosden) *racd in centre thrght: led tl ent fnl 2f: rdn and ev ch wl over 1f out: outpcd by wnr and btn 1f out: duelled for 2nd tl no ex fnl 100yds* **6/1**

012- **4** *2* **Ptolemaic**[185] 6914 3-8-12 93 (v) TomEaves 9 91
(Bryan Smart) *t.k.h: chsd ldrs: rdn and effrt ent fnl 2f: drvn and pressed ldrs briefly wl over 1f out: unable qck and sn outpcd: 4th and btn 1f out: plugged on* **50/1**

1- **5** *2 1/4* **Mighty Ambition (USA)**[215] 6160 3-8-12 0 FrankieDettori 11 86+
(Mahmood Al Zarooni) *stdd s: t.k.h and hld up in rr: pushed along and hdwy 1/2-way: rdn and no prog in 5th whn edgd rt over 1f out: wl hld fnl f* **7/2**[1]

601- **6** *1* **Campanology**[201] 6525 3-8-12 90 JohnnyMurtagh 8 84
(Richard Hannon) *hld up in midfield: rdn and struggling wl over 2f out: no ch w ldrs but rallied over 1f out: kpt on fnl f* **20/1**

1 **7** *1/2* **Minstrels Gallery (IRE)**[36] 903 3-8-12 78 FrederikTylicki 13 83
(J R Jenkins) *in tch in midfield: rdn and struggling 1/2-way: sn outpcd and no threat to ldrs fnl 2f: plugged on again ins fnl f* **20/1**

2-1 **8** *2* **Born To Surprise**[18] 1155 3-8-12 92 JamieSpencer 7 78+
(Michael Bell) *awkward as stalls opened and v.s.a: racd in centre tl 5f out: hld up bhd: stl plenty to do whn rdn and sme prog wl over 1f out: nvr on terms: eased towards fin* **15/2**

1- **9** *3/4* **Beaufort Twelve**[174] 7133 3-8-12 83 HarryBentley 5 77
(William Jarvis) *racd in centre tl 5f out: hld up towards rr: rdn and struggling 1/2-way: bhd and no ch fnl 2f* **14/1**

10-2 **10** *1 3/4* **Miblish**[12] 1216 3-8-12 97 (t) BrettDoyle 1 72
(Clive Brittain) *in tch: rdn and struggling wl over 2f out: wknd u.p 2f out* **28/1**

41- **11** *14* **Rayvin Black**[276] 4159 3-8-12 79 TedDurcan 6 40
(Mark H Tompkins) *a in rr: rdn and struggling 1/2-way: lost tch 3f out: t.o* **33/1**

3-1 **12** *1 3/4* **Forgotten Hero (IRE)**[26] 1036 3-8-12 92 MichaelHills 2 36+
(Charles Hills) *racd in centre tl 5f out: plld hrd chsd ldrs tl rdn and wknd jst over 2f out: eased fr over 1f out: t.o* **10/1**

1m 37.44s (-1.16) **Going Correction** +0.175s/f (Good) **12** Ran SP% **120.1**
Speed ratings (Par 108): **112,107,105,103,101 100,99,97,97,95 81,79**
toteswingers:1&2:£4.80, 1&3:£8.30, 2&3:£6.50 CSF £21.60 TOTE £5.40: £2.40, £1.50, £3.10; EX 17.60 Trifecta £128.70 Pool: £1,461.76 - 8.40 winning units..
Owner John Manley **Bred** John Cullinan **Trained** East Everleigh, Wilts

FOCUS

The last horse to win the Craven and follow up in the Guineas was Haafhd in 2004, but 2009 winner Delegator subsequently finished runner-up to Sea The Stars, and last year's race was won by Native Khan, who was then third to Frankel. This year's race was not as informative as it might have been, with the much-hyped Most Improved withdrawn owing to lameness, and a few of these were inconvenienced by racing up the middle before joining the main bunch towards the stands' side. The time was 1.82 seconds quicker than the Wood Ditton and the placed horses set the level, although both slightly below their best.

NOTEBOOK

Trumpet Major(IRE) had a patchy profile as a juvenile, but he did go off favourite for the same Newbury maiden his stable had won the previous year with Canford Cliffs, albeit he managed only third, and he later won the Champagne Stakes. His final run came in a muddling Dewhurst when he finished a close fifth (just behind Most Improved), and clearly he's done well from two to three. This was a strong-staying performance, as he was under pressure a fair way out, and Ryan Moore suggested he might find one with too much speed in the Guineas, but it was still a very smart effort considering he was conceding 3lb all round. He handled the easy ground well (not as soft as when he flopped in the Solario), but shouldn't mind a return to a quicker surface and his ability to handle this track is an obvious plus. (tchd 6-1)

Crius(IRE)'s win in the Group 3 Somerville Tattersall Stakes worked out exceptionally well, but he didn't really build on it here. He was helped by racing against the stands' rail, and there was a suggestion afterwards that he could go abroad for his Guineas. (op 5-1 tchd 7-2)

Eastern Sun(IRE) ◆ ended up on his own towards the middle of the track. He always looked to be in a good rhythm, much like when winning a Polytrack conditions event from the front on his reappearance, so it's hard to know if he was inconvenienced, but he hammered the other runners who started off up the middle. There should be plenty more to come. (op 7-1)

Ptolemaic came into this officially rated only 93, and he was keen enough for his first run in over six months, but he has a progressive profile. (op 40-1)

Mighty Ambition(USA) is talented but perhaps quirky. He briefly looked a threat when first picking up for pressure, but he carried his head high (like when winning on his only juvenile start) and wandered under pressure, and his run flattened out. It's likely he'll come on fitness-wise and he has the ability to do better. (op 9-2 tchd 10-3)

Campanology ran about as well as could have been expected. (op 25-1)

Minstrels Gallery(IRE), who only had a Southwell maiden win to his name (runner-up successful next time), showed himself to be decent. (op 28-1 tchd 33-1)

Born To Surprise probably didn't beat much at Doncaster on his reappearance, but he's better than he showed here as he raced away from the main action throughout after missing the break. (tchd 9-1)

Forgotten Hero(IRE) wasn't helped by racing away from the main action and was much too keen. Official explanation: jockey said colt ran too free (op 7-1)

1471 WEATHERBYS EARL OF SEFTON STKS (GROUP 3) 1m 1f

4:45 (4:48) (Class 1) 4-Y-O+

£31,190 (£11,825; £5,918; £2,948; £1,479; £742) **Stalls** High

Form RPR

03-3 **1** **Questioning (IRE)**[18] 1158 4-8-12 107 (p) WilliamBuick 10 115
(John Gosden) *hld up in tch: rdn and hdwy between horses 2f out: chal 1f out: racing awkwardly but sustained duel w runner-up fnl f: edgd rt u.p and drvn to ld cl home* **10/1**

110- **2** *hd* **Twice Over**[187] 6861 7-8-12 125 TomQueally 1 115
(Sir Henry Cecil) *hld up in tch: hdwy to ld 2f out: sn rdn: hrd pressed and drvn ent fnl f: kpt on gamely u.p tl hdd and no ex cl home* **6/5**[1]

042- **3** *1 3/4* **Beatrice Aurore (IRE)**[179] 7047 4-8-9 111 RyanMoore 6 108
(John Dunlop) *hld up in tch: rdn and hdwy wl over 1f out: edgd rt and chal 1f out: no ex and btn fnl 100yds* **6/1**[3]

244- **4** *1 1/4* **Afsare**[228] 5776 5-8-12 110 JamieSpencer 8 108+
(Luca Cumani) *rrd s and s.i.s: hld up in rr: hdwy 4f out: rdn and chsd ldrs over 1f out: kpt on same pce ins fnl f* **16/1**

110/ **5** *4* **Titus Mills (IRE)**[544] 7081 4-8-12 103 MartinDwyer 3 99
(Brian Meehan) *led tl rdn and hdd 2f out: wknd over 1f out* **50/1**

424- **6** *2 3/4* **Tazahum (USA)**[209] 6298 4-8-12 114 PaulHanagan 5 93
(Sir Michael Stoute) *t.k.h: chsd ldrs: rdn and unable qck over 1f out: wknd ent fnl f: fdd* **13/2**

115- **7** *1 3/4* **Prince Siegfried (FR)**[211] 6247 6-8-12 112 FrankieDettori 9 90
(Saeed Bin Suroor) *t.k.h: chsd ldrs: rdn 3f out: sn lost pl and bhd 2f out: wknd* **12/1**

104- **8** *6* **Albaqaa**[194] 6693 7-8-12 100 KieranO'Neill 4 74
(P J O'Gorman) *stdd s: t.k.h: hld up in rr: rdn and no rspnse over 2f out: sn bhd* **66/1**

100- **9** *1* **Ransom Note**[130] 7732 5-9-3 116 MichaelHills 7 81
(Charles Hills) *w ldr tl rdn and unable qck ent fnl 2f: wkng whn short of room over 1f out: eased fnl f* **5/1**[2]

1m 50.62s (-1.08) **Going Correction** +0.175s/f (Good) **9** Ran SP% **115.9**
Speed ratings (Par 113): **111,110,109,108,104 102,100,95,94**
toteswingers:1&2:£4.60, 1&3:£6.90, 2&3:£3.50 CSF £22.50 TOTE £9.10: £2.60, £1.10, £1.70; EX 30.10 Trifecta £119.00 Pool: £2,428.32 - 15.09 winning units..
Owner H R H Princess Haya Of Jordan **Bred** Fortbarrington Stud **Trained** Newmarket, Suffolk
■ Stewards' Enquiry : William Buick caution: careless riding.

FOCUS

Sound form for the grade, even with the runner-up below his best. The pace was fair and the placings remained unaltered following a short stewards' enquiry. The third and fourth are rated close to their marks in an ordinary renewal.

NOTEBOOK

Questioning(IRE), who may have been a tad unfortunate at Doncaster on his return, sat on the rail for much of the way, and being the only race-fit participant proved a decisive edge. He drifted right close home, not helping the runner-up, and the result may have been different but for that. Whether he's up to winning a Group 2 remains to be seen. (op 12-1)

Twice Over, who looked big and well beforehand, was below form but his trainer had warned he would need the run, and both seeing plenty of daylight a good bit off the rail and being carried right late on may have made the difference between victory and defeat. He should again be competitive in some of the lesser Group 1s this season, but it seems likely any victories will come below that level. (op 10-11 tchd 5-6)

Beatrice Aurore(IRE), narrowly denied in an Italian Group 1 on her final outing last season, looks to have resumed her progressive profile at four judging by this effort, keeping on centre-field. (op 8-1)

Afsare, who has been gelded over the winter, travelled well but once in the clear and asked to pick up his effort flattened out. His peak runs last season came at 1m4f and he could have done with more of a test at the distance, so it's possible there's more to come from the 5-y-o. (op 25-1 tchd 28-1)

Titus Mills(IRE), off since finishing last in the 2010 Racing Post Trophy, showed up well for a long way and is entitled to come on plenty. His next run will tell us more.

Tazahum(USA) looked the type to fare better at four, but his yard has yet to hit form and, having taken a good grip, it was no surprise to see him weaken. (op 8-1 tchd 10-1)

Prince Siegfried(FR) was yet another from the yard to finish well held. (op 14-1)

Ransom Note, last year's winner, looked vulnerable this time round under a 5lb penalty, but even so this was disappointing, as he was eased late after becoming short of room. (tchd 9-2 and 11-2)

1472 ROSSDALES MAIDEN FILLIES' STKS 7f

5:20 (5:23) (Class 4) 3-Y-O **£4,528** (£1,347; £673; £336) **Stalls** High

Form RPR

5- **1** **Perfect Step (IRE)**[262] 4614 3-9-0 0 NeilCallan 13 87
(Roger Varian) *racd in centre: chsd ldr: rdn to ld over 1f out: kpt on gamely u.p fnl f: drvn out* **14/1**

22- **2** *1/2* **Riot Of Colour**[209] 6291 3-9-0 0 JimCrowley 9 86+
(Ralph Beckett) *racd in centre: chsd ldrs: rdn to chal over 1f out: ev ch after: no ex and btn towards fin: 2nd of 15 in gp* **8/1**[3]

62- **3** *5* **Salacia (IRE)**[173] 7165 3-9-0 0 FrankieDettori 12 72
(Mahmood Al Zarooni) *racd in centre: overall ldr: rdn and forged clr w 2 rivals wl over 1f out: hdd over 1f out: wknd fnl f: 3rd of 15 in gp* **9/4**[1]

4 *2 3/4* **Anya** 3-9-0 0 J-PGuillambert 18 65
(Ed Walker) *racd in stands' side trio: swishing tail early: chsd overall ldrs tl rdn and outpcd wl over 1f out: wl hld but plugged on fnl f: 1st of 3 in gp* **100/1**

2- **5** *1/2* **Isatis**[161] 7344 3-9-0 0 TomQueally 17 63+
(Sir Henry Cecil) *racd in centre: in tch: rdn and unable ent fnl 2f: outpcd wl over 1f out and no ch w ldrs after: 4th of 15 in gp* **10/1**

6 *hd* **Aarti (IRE)** 3-9-0 0 JohnnyMurtagh 7 63+
(William Haggas) *racd in centre: in tch: effrt u.p ent fnl 2f: outpcd and btn wl over 1f out: plugged on: 5th of 15 in gp* **25/1**

7 *3/4* **Furbelow** 3-9-0 0 JimmyFortune 15 61+
(Jeremy Noseda) *racd in centre: rdn and unable qck jst over 2f out: outpcd and btn wl over 1f out: plugged on: 6th of 15 in gp* **16/1**

24- **8** *1/2* **More Than Words (IRE)**[160] 7359 3-9-0 0 PatDobbs 1 59+
(Richard Hannon) *racd in centre: hld up in midfield: rdn and effrt jst over 2f out: stlng but stl plenty to do whn hmpd over 1f out: n.d but plugged on fnl f: 7th of 15 in gp* **25/1**

9 *1/2* **Shy Rosa (USA)** 3-9-0 0 HayleyTurner 4 58
(Marcus Tregoning) *racd in centre: in tch in midfield: rdn over 3f out: outpcd over 2f out and no threat to ldrs after: plugged on: 8th of 15 in gp* **66/1**

10 *3/4* **Junior Diary (USA)** 3-9-0 0 MartinDwyer 8 56
(Brian Meehan) *racd in centre: towards rr: rdn and struggling over 3f out: plugged on to pass btn horses fnl f: n.d: 9th of 15 in gp* **66/1**

- **11** *3/4* **Central Line (USA)** 3-9-0 0 MickaelBarzalona 11 54
(Mahmood Al Zarooni) *racd in centre: chsd ldrs: rdn and unable qck ent fnl 2f: wknd u.p over 1f out: 10th of 15 in gp* **18/1**

0- **12** *3/4* **Bassara (IRE)**[184] 6934 3-9-0 0 TedDurcan 20 52
(Chris Wall) *racd in stands' side trio: in tch in midfield: rdn over 2f out: wknd wl over 1f out: 2nd of 3 in gp* **9/1**

13 *1 3/4* **Indian Moon** 3-9-0 0 StevieDonohoe 16 47
(Tobias B P Coles) *racd in centre: in tch in centre: rdn and struggling 3f out: wknd over 2f out: 11th of 15 in gp* **100/1**

3-2 **14** *nk* **Shame On You (IRE)**[27] 1004 3-9-0 0 DarryllHolland 2 46
(Charles Hills) *racd in centre: hld up towards rr: rdn and short-lived effrt over 2f out: no prog and wl hld over 1f out: 12th of 15 in gp* **15/2**[2]

15 *1 ¼* **Eltiqaa (IRE)** 3-9-0 0 WilliamBuick 10 43
(John Gosden) *racd in centre: s.i.s: a bhd: swtchd lft and rdn 3f out: no prog and no ch fnl 2f: 13th of 15 in gp* **28/1**

16 *6* **Nawarah** 3-9-0 0 SebSanders 19 27
(Michael Wigham) *racd in stands' side trio: a towards rr overall: wl bhd fnl 2f: 3rd of 3 in gp* **100/1**

4- **17** *16* **It's My Time**[178] 7058 3-9-0 0 MartinLane 14
(David Simcock) *racd in centre: s.i.s: sn pushed along and rcvrd to r in midfield: wknd over 3f out: t.o and eased fnl f: 14th of 15 in gp* **33/1**

3- **18** *1 ¾* **Qaadira (USA)**[177] 7080 3-9-0 0 [1] PaulHanagan 3
(John Gosden) *racd in centre: a bhd: lost tch 3f out: t.o and eased fnl f: 15th of 15 in gp* **17/2**

4- **P** **El Diamante (FR)**[314] 2880 3-9-0 0 RyanMoore 5
(Richard Hannon) *racd in centre: a towards rr: rdn and struggling 4f out: lost action and eased over 2f out: p.u and dismntd over 1f out* **16/1**

1m 25.79s (0.39) **Going Correction** +0.175s/f (Good) **19** Ran SP% **127.0**
Speed ratings (Par 97): **104,103,97,94,94 93,92,92,91,90 90,89,87,86,85 78,60,58,**
toteswingers:1&2:£20.70, 1&3:£13.50, 2&3:£6.10 CSF £117.99 TOTE £18.10: £4.90, £3.20, £2.00; EX 140.60 Trifecta £300.40 Pool: £812.06 - 2.00 winning units..
Owner Clipper Logistics **Bred** Epona Bloodstock Ltd **Trained** Newmarket, Suffolk

FOCUS
This fillies' maiden was dominated by those with previous experience, with the interesting newcomers failing to step up. The main action unfolded up the middle of the track, but three runners raced towards the possibly favoured stands' rail. The first two were clear and look above average.
Qaadira(USA) Official explanation: jockey said filly never travelled
El Diamante(FR) Official explanation: jockey said filly lost its action

1473 TURFTV H'CAP 1m 2f
5:50 (5:54) (Class 3) (0-95,90) 3-Y-O **£9,703** (£2,887; £1,443; £721) **Stalls** High

Form RPR
11- **1** **Main Sequence (USA)**[183] 6957 3-9-6 **89** TedDurcan 3 98+
(David Lanigan) *stdd s: hld up in rr: rdn and hdwy nrest stands' rail wl over 1f out: led jst ins fnl f: flashed tail u.p: r.o: rdn out* **2/1**[1]

213- **2** *½* **Ahzeemah (IRE)**[176] 7095 3-8-11 **80** (p) FrankieDettori 5 88
(Saeed Bin Suroor) *w ldrs: rdn and ev ch over 1f out: kpt on u.p and pressing wnr thrght fnl f: a jst hld* **9/1**

122- **3** *1 ¾* **Clare Island Boy (IRE)**[219] 6031 3-8-13 **85** SeanLevey(3) 7 89
(Richard Hannon) *led tl over 5f out: pushed along to ld again 3f out: hrd pressed and drvn wl over 1f out: hdd jst ins fnl f: no ex and btn fnl 75yds* **17/2**

51- **4** *4 ½* **Aazif (IRE)**[193] 6726 3-8-13 **82** PaulHanagan 8 77
(John Dunlop) *hld up in tch: hdwy to join ldrs ent fnl 2f: ev ch u.p over 1f out tl 1f out: wknd ins fnl f* **4/1**[3]

311- **5** *¾* **Finbar**[149] 7501 3-8-13 **82** FrederikTylicki 4 76
(James Given) *t.k.h: hld up in tch: hdwy to press ldrs 3f out: drvn wl over 1f out: unable qck and btn ent fnl f: wknd* **20/1**

515- **6** *1* **Martin Chuzzlewit (IRE)**[229] 5709 3-9-7 **90** RyanMoore 2 82+
(Sir Michael Stoute) *hld up in tch tl hdwy to ld over 5f out: hdd 3f out: wknd u.p over 1f out* **10/3**[2]

52-3 **7** *nse* **Hefner (IRE)**[26] 1031 3-9-0 **83** PatDobbs 6 74
(Richard Hannon) *t.k.h: chsd ldrs: rdn and unable qck ent fnl 2f: wknd over 1f out* **16/1**

433- **8** *4 ½* **Sound Advice**[217] 6077 3-9-2 **85** NeilCallan 1 67
(Keith Dalgleish) *t.k.h: hld up in tch: rdn and lost pl over 3f out: wknd ent fnl 2f: bhd fnl f* **16/1**

2m 6.37s (0.57) **Going Correction** +0.175s/f (Good) **8** Ran SP% **113.5**
Speed ratings (Par 102): **104,103,102,98,98 97,97,93**
toteswingers:1&2:£5.20, 1&3:£6.00, 2&3:£9.30 CSF £20.81 CT £124.36 TOTE £2.80: £1.40, £2.20, £2.20; EX 21.90 Trifecta £174.70 Pool: £835.74 - 3.54 winning units..
Owner Niarchos Family **Bred** Flaxman Holdings Ltd **Trained** Upper Lambourn, Berks

FOCUS
A good-quality 3yo handicap, as is often the case, although the lack of early pace resulted in it turning into something of a 3f dash. Both the winner and fourth deserve to have their efforts upgrading. The time was just under three seconds slower than the sales race earlier on the card and the form is muddling. The placed horses are rated as improvers but had the run of the race so might also limit the form.

NOTEBOOK
Main Sequence(USA), 10lb higher than when readily making a successful handicap debut at the course last October, retained his unbeaten record in workmanlike fashion, but he deserves rating better than the bare form considering he was held up in a race not run to suit and then appeared to idle. Ending up near the stands' rail, he flashed his tail when struck with the whip, as had been the case on his previous victory, but seems genuine and this clearly talented son of Aldebaran, recently supplemented into the Derby (given a 25-1 quote by Ladbrokes), will now head to York for a crack at the Dante. It's hard to see him winning that race, however. (tchd 5-2)
Ahzeemah(IRE) fared considerably better than the remainder of his stablemates had done at the two-day meeting, although he was well placed throughout. (op 11-1 tchd 8-1)
Clare Island Boy(IRE) probably ran a career-best on this seasonal reappearance, although like the runner-up he was well positioned to do so. (op 9-1 tchd 8-1)
Aazif(IRE) ◆, a half-brother to 2m Group winner Akmal as well as two other winners at 1m5f plus, looked all about galloping when winning his maiden at two, and he was given little chance here the way the pace unfolded. He should leave this form behind. (op 7-2 tchd 9-2)
Finbar, 15lb higher than when winning on his handicap debut, was keen on this first start in 149 days and didn't get home. It was his first try at 1m2f. (op 22-1 tchd 25-1)
Martin Chuzzlewit(IRE) was another disappointment for Sir Michael Stoute, being readily outpaced when the tempo quickened, only to plod on again late. He's surely capable of better. (op 7-2 tchd 3-1)
Hefner(IRE) was keen and seemed to find this a bit competitive on his handicap debut. (op 14-1)
T/Jkpt: Not won. T/Plt: £120.60 to a £1 stake. Pool:£87,691.72 - 530.69 winning tickets T/Qpdt: £40.20 to a £1 stake. Pool:£5,848.80 - 107.50 winning tickets SP

RIPON (R-H)
Thursday, April 19

OFFICIAL GOING: Soft (6.9)
Wind: moderate 1/2 against Weather: damp, cold and windy, becoming fine

1474 E B F EAT SLEEP & DRINK AT NAGS HEAD PICKHILL MAIDEN STKS 5f
2:10 (2:10) (Class 5) 2-Y-O **£3,557** (£1,058; £529; £264) **Stalls** High

Form RPR
1 **Run Fat Lass Run** 2-8-12 0 PhillipMakin 4 74+
(Kevin Ryan) *chsd ldrs: outpcd 3f out: hdwy over 1f out: r.o to ld last 75yds* **8/1**

2 *1* **Botanic Garden** 2-9-3 0 RichardMullen 1 75+
(David Brown) *swvd rt s: sn w ldrs: led over 1f out: hdd ins fnl f: no ex* **2/1**[1]

3 *1 ½* **Fly Fisher (IRE)** 2-9-3 0 TonyHamilton 8 70
(Richard Fahey) *s.i.s: sn outpcd: hdwy over 1f out: styd on to take 3rd nr line* **7/1**

4 *½* **Annie Gogh** 2-8-12 0 DavidAllan 2 63+
(Tim Easterby) *w ldrs: drvn over 2f out: one pce over 1f out* **5/2**[2]

0 **5** *7* **Lady Poppy**[19] 1131 2-8-12 0 AndrewMullen 6 38
(George Moore) *led: hdd over 1f out: sn wknd* **9/2**[3]

6 *3* **Royal Jenray** 2-9-0 0 MichaelO'Connell(3) 3 32
(Jedd O'Keeffe) *dwlt: sn drvn along and outpcd: nvr on terms* **12/1**

7 *32* **Sound Affects** 2-8-12 0 GrahamGibbons 5
(Alan Brown) *w ldrs: wknd 2f out: wl bhd whn heavily eased fnl f: t.o* **40/1**

1m 5.64s (4.94) **Going Correction** +0.975s/f (Soft) **7** Ran SP% **113.8**
Speed ratings (Par 92): **99,97,95,94,83 78,27**
toteswingers:1&2:£4.30, 1&3:£4.80, 2&3:£2.70 CSF £24.24 TOTE £8.60: £4.40, £1.70; EX 20.10.
Owner S C B Limited **Bred** Mrs C R Philipson & Mrs H G Lascelles **Trained** Hambleton, N Yorks

FOCUS
Rail around bend from back straight to home straight moved out 4m adding 12yds to distances on Round course. Only a small field for this juvenile maiden but some big northern yards were represented and it produced an impressive winner.

NOTEBOOK
Run Fat Lass Run was friendless in the market but she proved those negative vibes all wrong, picking up strongly once they came into the dip, and won with her ears pricked. The daughter of Sakhee is already looking a bargain buy at only 4,000gns and, despite showing plenty of speed over this minimum trip, probably won't come into her own until tackling further. (op 15-2)
Botanic Garden, unlike the winner, had been well supported and he looked the likeliest scorer at the two pole as he ranged upsides Lady Poppy. However, he is a nice moving individual and may have been better suited by a quicker surface. He should have no problem landing a similar race in the near future. (op 15-8 tchd 5-2)
Fly Fisher(IRE) was the real eyecatcher of the race, running on late having been badly outpaced at halfway. He had drifted markedly in the betting and will have learnt plenty from this experience. (tchd 6-1)
Annie Gogh, whose trainer has farmed this race in recent seasons, was unable to add to his long list of successes. She was by no means disgraced but appeared green throughout and didn't help her cause when hanging out into the centre of the course. (op 10-3 tchd 9-4)
Lady Poppy, whose Brocklesby form has taken several knocks, was firmly put in her place. She showed plenty of dash but was ultimately no match for the principals. (tchd 5-1)

1475 RIPON SILVER BOWL CONDITIONS STKS 1m 1f 170y
2:45 (2:45) (Class 3) 4-Y-O+ **£6,616** (£1,980; £990; £495) **Stalls** Low

Form RPR
214- **1** **Jet Away**[173] 7170 5-9-10 114 IanMongan 5 99
(Sir Henry Cecil) *t.k.h in 3rd: chal over 3f out: rdn over 2f out: styd on to ld last 50yds* **1/1**[1]

025- **2** *1 ½* **New Hampshire (USA)**[148] 7523 4-9-0 89 LeeTopliss(3) 2 89
(Tony Coyle) *led: hdd over 3f out: led over 2f out: hung bdly lft: almost collided w outside rail jst ins fnl f: hdd and no ex last 50yds* **22/1**

460- **3** *5* **Wannabe King**[208] 6335 6-9-0 93 (v[1]) RobertWinston 3 76
(Geoffrey Harker) *stdd s: t.k.h in last: trcking ldrs over 3f out: effrt and swtchd rt 2f out: wknd fnl 100yds: eased nr fin* **12/1**[3]

34-4 **4** *4 ½* **Black Spirit (USA)**[26] 1034 5-9-0 102 (t) AdamKirby 1 66
(Clive Cox) *trckd wnr: led over 3f out: hdd over 2f out: wknd 1f out: eased nr fin* **11/10**[2]

2m 15.14s (9.74) **Going Correction** +0.75s/f (Yiel) **4** Ran SP% **109.7**
Speed ratings (Par 107): **91,89,85,82**
CSF £16.08 TOTE £1.80; EX 14.10.
Owner K Abdulla **Bred** Juddmonte Farms Ltd **Trained** Newmarket, Suffolk

FOCUS
An intriguing conditions' contest despite the small field and the market had this down as a match between the two horses who stood out on adjusted official ratings. They went a sensible gallop on testing ground but the form looks muddling and not form to be confident about.

NOTEBOOK
Jet Away was returning from a near six-month break and attempting to defy a 10lb penalty for two wins in similar contests over this 1m2f trip last season, including when fresh on his seasonal reappearance at Lingfield last May. He raced a tad keenly in third as the field went in single file at a respectable tempo down the back straight, but he soon showed his class once the race began in earnest coming out of the dip, and it was taking how powerfully he finished this race. Admittedly, he was entitled to beat the outsider who finished second by much further on the book, but circumstances conspired against impressive winning margins, and connections must be pleased with this seasonal reappearance. (op 6-5 tchd 5-4)
New Hampshire(USA), last seen finishing fifth off 89 in a Lingfield handicap over this trip in November, set a steady tempo up front before trying to steal the race 2f out. Once asked for that effort he began to drift towards the stands' rail, nearly colliding with it just inside the furlong marker, but he still finished a very respectable second on this first start for new trainer Tony Coyle. He has been gelded since last season and it will be interesting to see if he is flattered by the bare form in the future. (op 20-1 tchd 25-1)
Wannabe King was returning from a seven-month break in a first-time visor, but couldn't repeat his seasonal reappearance success last April on his first start for new trainer Geoffrey Harker. A return to 1m on better ground will suit. (op 9-1)
Black Spirit(USA) failed to build on his fourth at Lingfield in the Group 3 Winter Derby last month. This was a disappointing effort as he could have been expected to give the winner a run for his money on these terms under the prevailing conditions. (op 6-5 tchd 5-4 and Evens)

1476 PPR FOUNDATION H'CAP (DIV I) 6f
3:20 (3:20) (Class 4) (0-85,85) 4-Y-O+ **£4,204** (£1,251; £625; £312) **Stalls** High

Form RPR
4-04 **1** **Thunderball**[18] 1156 6-9-7 **85** (p) IanMongan 12 96
(Scott Dixon) *mid-div: hdwy and swtchd rt over 1f out: styd on to ld last 75yds* **8/1**

320- **2** *1* **Spinatrix**[185] 6913 4-9-2 **80** PaulMulrennan 4 88
(Michael Dods) *swtchd lft after s: led: hung rt over 1f out: hdd and no ex wl ins fnl f* **13/2**

4- **3** *¾* **Jedward (IRE)**[183] 6960 5-8-11 **78** LeeTopliss(3) 14 84+
(Richard Fahey) *stdd s: hld up towards rr: hdwy over 2f out: nt clr run: chsng ldrs 1f out: kpt on same pce* **5/1**[2]

6045 **4** *1 ¾* **Dickie Le Davoir**[9] 1289 8-8-6 **75** (b) DuilioDaSilva(5) 15 75
(Richard Guest) *mid-div: hdwy to chse ldrs 2f out: styd on same pce fnl f* **12/1**

43-0 **5** *8* **Caranbola**[17] 1168 6-8-13 **77** RobertWinston 9 51
(Mel Brittain) *chsd ldrs: wknd over 1f out: eased towards fin* **14/1**

040- **6** *1 ½* **Mandalay King (IRE)**[177] 7074 7-8-8 **75** JulieBurke(3) 10 45
(Marjorie Fife) *in rr: hdwy over 2f out: wknd over 1f out* **28/1**

234/ **7** ½ **Ertikaan**[573] 6321 5-8-12 **83** DarrenEgan(7) 13 51
(Ronald Harris) *chsd ldrs: wknd over 1f out* **20/1**
321- **8** 1¼ **Little Jimmy Odsox (IRE)**[210] 6283 4-9-0 **78** DavidAllan 7 42
(Tim Easterby) *mid-div: effrt over 2f out: wkng whn hmpd over 1f out* **6/1**[3]
-600 **9** 2¾ **Red Cape (FR)**[17] 1168 9-9-0 **78** (b) JamesSullivan 3 33
(Ruth Carr) *w ldr: wknd over 1f out* **25/1**
060- **10** ¾ **Lady Royale**[194] 6703 4-9-1 **82** DaleSwift(3) 5 35
(Geoffrey Oldroyd) *rrd s: a towards rr* **33/1**
00-6 **11** 1¼ **Able Master (IRE)**[17] 1168 6-9-3 **81** SilvestreDeSousa 1 30
(David O'Meara) *wnt rt s: mid-div: drvn over 2f out: wkng whn hmpd over 1f out* **7/2**[1]
00-0 **12** ½ **Swilly Ferry (USA)**[18] 1157 5-9-7 **85** AdrianNicholls 11 32
(David Nicholls) *stdd s: hld up detached in last: nvr on terms* **12/1**
000- **13** 1½ **Tallahasse (IRE)**[265] 4516 4-8-13 **82** GarryWhillans(5) 2 24
(Alan Swinbank) *chsd ldrs: edgd lft and wknd 2f out* **25/1**

1m 18.45s (5.45) **Going Correction** +0.975s/f (Soft) **13 Ran SP% 118.5**
Speed ratings (Par 105): **102,100,99,97,86 84,84,82,78,77 76,75,73**
toteswingers:1&2:£10.50, 1&3:£4.40, 2&3:£7.10 CSF £54.50 CT £300.05 TOTE £6.40: £1.50, £3.10, £2.50; EX 70.10.
Owner Paul J Dixon **Bred** Mrs Yvette Dixon **Trained** Babworth, Notts
■ Stewards' Enquiry : Ian Mongan one-day ban: careless riding (May 3)

FOCUS
A competitive sprint handicap run on rain-softened ground, and won in gritty fashion. The winner ran his best race since early summer last year.
Able Master(IRE) Official explanation: trainer's rep had no explanation for the poor form shown

1477 RIPON "COCK O' NORTH" H'CAP 1m
3:55 (3:55) (Class 3) (0-95,89) 3-Y-O **£6,616** (£1,980; £990; £495; £246) **Stalls** Low

Form RPR
1 **1** **Hajras (IRE)**[33] 943 3-8-8 **76** JoeFanning 9 86+
(Mark Johnston) *sn chsg ldrs: rdn and wnt 2nd appr fnl f: styd on wl to ld last 50yds* **5/2**[1]
350- **2** ½ **Dance The Rain**[181] 6986 3-8-8 **76** RoystonFfrench 10 84
(Bryan Smart) *trckd ldrs: led over 2f out: hdd last 50yds* **28/1**
340- **3** 3½ **Satanic Beat (IRE)**[180] 7021 3-8-9 **77** PaulMulrennan 8 77
(Jedd O'Keeffe) *w ldr: led over 3f out: hdd over 2f out: styd on same pce fnl f* **7/1**[3]
411- **4** *hd* **Mr Spiggott (IRE)**[188] 6829 3-9-1 **83** FrannyNorton 11 83+
(Mick Channon) *s.i.s: swtchd rt after s: hdwy over 2f out: chsng ldrs over 1f out: kpt on same pce* **4/1**[2]
142- **5** 3¼ **Bountiful Girl**[217] 6077 3-8-11 **79** TonyHamilton 3 71
(Richard Fahey) *t.k.h: trckd ldrs: wknd over 1f out* **12/1**
05-0 **6** 2¼ **The Blue Banana (IRE)**[18] 1160 3-8-7 **75** JamesSullivan 1 62
(Edwin Tuer) *mid-div: hdwy to chse ldrs 4f out: fdd over 1f out* **20/1**
04-0 **7** 2 **Ghostwriting (USA)**[12] 1217 3-9-7 **89** RobertHavlin 2 72
(John Gosden) *trckd ldrs: nt clr run over 2f out: fdd over 1f out* **16/1**
11- **8** 2 **Just Fabulous**[236] 5487 3-9-5 **87** PJMcDonald 6 65
(George Moore) *led: hdd over 3f out: wknd over 2f out* **8/1**
241- **9** ¾ **Choisan (IRE)**[176] 7101 3-8-12 **80** DavidAllan 12 56
(Tim Easterby) *sn chsng ldrs: lost pl over 1f out* **8/1**
10-0 **10** 2 **Zakreet**[12] 1221 3-9-3 **85** PhillipMakin 4 57
(Kevin Ryan) *s.i.s: towards rr: t.k.h: drvn 3f out: nvr a factor* **12/1**
16- **11** 8 **For Shia And Lula (IRE)**[152] 7491 3-8-7 **75** PadraigBeggy 5 28
(Daniel Mark Loughnane) *hld up in rr: bhd fnl 3f* **66/1**
064- **12** 38 **Commissar**[252] 4964 3-9-2 **89** AntiocoMurgia(5) 7
(Mahmood Al Zarooni) *s.s: in last: bhd and rdn over 2f out: eased over 1f out: sn t.o* **16/1**

1m 46.83s (5.43) **Going Correction** +0.75s/f (Yiel) **12 Ran SP% 120.1**
Speed ratings (Par 102): **102,101,98,97,94 92,90,88,87,85 77,39**
CSF £86.93 TOTE £2.50: £1.30, £7.00, £2.80; EX 88.30.
Owner Hamdan Al Maktoum **Bred** Shadwell Estate Company Limited **Trained** Middleham Moor, N Yorks

FOCUS
The betting suggested this was a wide open early season 3-y-o handicap and the testing ground made any concrete predictions even harder to justify. Trends suggested the market had chosen the correct favourite, though, as his trainer had won two of the previous three runnings, most notably with Monterosso in 2010, who scaled Dubai World Cup heights in March. This race was run at a genuine gallop and was a proper test under the conditions. The runner-up looks the key to the form, backed up by the third.

NOTEBOOK
Hajras(IRE) won his maiden in good fashion over an extended 1m at Wolverhampton on debut last month. This colt by Dubai Destination is out of a Zafonic mare which suggested an initial rating of 76 was very workable entering handicap company. There was a good deal of substance on show in this success, so when combined with such a flashy pedigree there must be every chance that he can climb through the ranks this season, and on better ground he may prove an even tougher nut to crack. (tchd 3-1)
Dance The Rain ◆ deserves credit for finishing best of those that raced prominently and in being the only one to give the winner something significant to think about. She obviously goes well fresh, as she won on her debut at Doncaster last July, and this was a decent return from a six-month break. She is another with a taking pedigree, one which suggested she may handle soft ground, and she seemed to enjoy the surface. There will be handicaps to be won with her against her own sex off this sort of mark under similar conditions. (op 25-1 tchd 33-1)
Satanic Beat(IRE) returned from a six-month break having been gelded in the meantime. He raced prominently before fading into third and probably needed the outing. A return to 7f may prove ideal. (op 14-1)
Mr Spiggott(IRE) won his last two juvenile starts over 6f/1m at Newcastle and Haydock on soft and heavy ground, and is another who was entitled to need his first start since October. He has a tendency to start slowly which was again in evidence, but this was a very respectable reappearance and, being by Intikhab, he's open to considerable improvement when faced with fast ground for the first time since his debut at Yarmouth last August. (op 9-2)
Bountiful Girl should benefit from this seasonal reappearance, particularly if dropped back to 7f, as when successful at Thirsk on good to soft ground last August. (op 11-1)
Commissar Official explanation: trainer's rep said colt was unsuited by the soft ground

1478 PPR FOUNDATION H'CAP (DIV II) 6f
4:30 (4:30) (Class 4) (0-85,85) 4-Y-O+ **£4,204** (£1,251; £625; £312) **Stalls** High

Form RPR
43-0 **1** **Fast Shot**[17] 1168 4-9-3 **81** DavidAllan 3 93
(Tim Easterby) *trckd ldrs far side: led over 1f out: styd on strly fnl 100yds: 1st of 4 that gp* **14/1**
563- **2** 1¾ **Trade Secret**[140] 7595 5-8-9 **73** RobertWinston 11 79
(Mel Brittain) *hld up towards rr: gd hdwy to ld stands' side over 1f out: styd on same pce last 75yds* **16/1**
1-00 **3** 1¼ **Toby Tyler**[17] 1168 6-9-0 **78** (v) MickyFenton 10 80
(Paul Midgley) *in rr: effrt and nt clr run 2f out: swtchd lft over 1f out: styd on wl ins fnl f* **12/1**
104- **4** 1¼ **Misplaced Fortune**[180] 7031 7-9-0 **85** DanielleMooney(7) 15 83
(Nigel Tinkler) *led stands' side: edgd rt and hdd over 1f out: kpt on same pce* **25/1**
-600 **5** ¾ **Levitate**[63] 584 4-8-12 **76** (v) AndrewMullen 7 72
(Alan McCabe) *dwlt: in rr: hdwy over 2f out: hung rt over 1f out: nvr rchd ldrs* **16/1**
2500 **6** ½ **Captain Scooby**[9] 1289 6-8-9 **78** DuilioDaSilva(5) 1 72
(Richard Guest) *chsd ldrs far side: hdwy and chal over 1f out: one pce: 2nd of 4 that gp* **25/1**
000- **7** 1¾ **Lucky Numbers (IRE)**[167] 7262 6-9-4 **82** SilvestreDeSousa 4 71
(David O'Meara) *chsd ldr far side: drvn over 2f out: one pce: 3rd of 4 that gp* **9/4**[1]
154- **8** *nse* **Saucy Brown (IRE)**[246] 5163 6-8-11 **82** ShirleyTeasdale(7) 12 71
(David Nicholls) *w ldrs: wknd over 1f out* **12/1**
00-0 **9** 1 **Mr Optimistic**[17] 1168 4-8-13 **80** LeeTopliss(3) 13 65
(Richard Fahey) *chsd ldrs stands' side: wknd over 1f out* **16/1**
00-3 **10** ¾ **Waking Warrior**[42] 835 4-9-1 **79** PhillipMakin 8 62
(Kevin Ryan) *chsd ldrs: effrt over 2f out: wknd over 1f out* **8/1**[3]
12-0 **11** 3¼ **Beckermet (IRE)**[18] 1161 10-9-7 **85** PJMcDonald 2 58
(Ruth Carr) *led quartet far side: hdd & wknd over 1f out: last of 4 in gp* **16/1**
000- **12** 2¼ **Kellys Eye (IRE)**[237] 5434 5-8-13 **80** (p) DaleSwift(3) 14 45
(Deborah Sanderson) *chsd ldrs: drvn over 2f out: wknd over 1f out* **6/1**[2]
00-0 **13** 5 **Another Citizen (IRE)**[17] 1168 4-8-11 **75** JamesSullivan 6 24
(Tim Easterby) *mid-div: hdwy over 2f out: sn rdn: lost pl wl over 1f out* **18/1**
54-3 **14** 2½ **Hamoody (USA)**[17] 1168 8-9-7 **85** AdrianNicholls 9 26
(David Nicholls) *chsd ldrs stands' side: wknd over 1f out: eased towards fin* **14/1**

1m 18.3s (5.30) **Going Correction** +0.975s/f (Soft) **14 Ran SP% 121.4**
Speed ratings (Par 105): **103,100,99,97,96 95,93,93,91,90 86,83,76,73**
toteswingers:1&2:£32.50, 1&3:£29.60, 2&3:£20.40 CSF £222.83 CT £2823.12 TOTE £16.20: £4.10, £5.40, £3.30; EX 305.80.
Owner Ontoawinner & Partners **Bred** Whitsbury Manor Stud & Pigeon House Stud **Trained** Great Habton, N Yorks

FOCUS
This didn't look as strong as the first division on paper but it produced an emphatic winner. The form is rated around the first two.

1479 RACING GREEN DESIGNER MENSWEAR MAIDEN STKS 1m
5:05 (5:09) (Class 5) 3-Y-O **£2,587** (£770; £384; £192) **Stalls** Low

Form RPR
1 **Hawaiian Storm** 3-8-9 0 MichaelMetcalfe(3) 2 72
(Mrs K Burke) *chsd ldrs: led over 2f out: drvn out* **50/1**
2 1½ **Vital Calling** 3-9-3 0 LeeNewman 14 73
(David Barron) *trckd ldrs: wnt 2nd over 1f out: styd on same pce* **15/2**
3 4 **Friendsinlowplaces** 3-8-12 0 LMcNiff(5) 3 64+
(David Barron) *s.i.s: t.k.h: sn bhd: hdwy and swtchd lft over 2f out: rn green: styd on strly fnl f: tk 3rd nr fin: will improve* **14/1**
3 **4** 1½ **Gravitate**[10] 1261 3-9-3 0 RobertHavlin 4 61
(John Gosden) *w ldr: ev ch tl wknd fnl f* **2/1**[1]
65- **5** *nk* **No Dominion (IRE)**[190] 6805 3-9-3 0 PaulMulrennan 12 60+
(James Given) *in rr: hdwy over 3f out: nt clr run over 2f out: kpt on one pce* **40/1**
6 2¾ **Go On Gilbert** 3-9-3 0 PaddyAspell 5 54
(John Wainwright) *in rr: hdwy over 4f out: one pce fnl 2f* **100/1**
0-02 **7** 1½ **Feeling Good**[23] 1053 3-9-3 70 BarryMcHugh 10 50
(Brian Ellison) *drvn to ld: hdd over 2f out: wknd over 1f out* **11/4**[2]
0 **8** 2½ **Icewan**[18] 1155 3-9-3 0 MickyFenton 6 44
(Paul Midgley) *gave problems at s: s.i.s and in rr: hung bdly rt over 2f out: kpt on ins fnl f* **66/1**
9 1 **Lothair (IRE)** 3-9-3 0 PJMcDonald 7 42
(Alan Swinbank) *in tch: effrt over 2f out: wknd over 1f out* **25/1**
326- **10** 4½ **Saffa Hill (IRE)**[237] 5454 3-9-3 76 DavidAllan 15 32+
(Tim Easterby) *racd wd 1st 2f: in rr: drvn and sme hdwy over 3f out: lost pl and hmpd 2f out* **4/1**[3]
62- **11** 2¾ **Going Grey (IRE)**[138] 7627 3-9-3 0 TonyHamilton 1 26
(Richard Fahey) *chsd ldrs: lost pl over 2f out* **12/1**
0- **12** 44 **Master Chipper**[211] 6259 3-9-0 0 LeeTopliss(3) 8
(Michael Dods) *mid-div: sn drvn along: hdwy over 3f out: lost pl over 2f out: eased over 1f out: virtually p.u: t.o* **33/1**
0 **U** **Meljana (IRE)**[23] 1053 3-8-12 0 GarryWhillans(5) 9
(Alan Swinbank) *slowly away: swvd bdly lft s and uns rdr* **100/1**

1m 49.56s (8.16) **Going Correction** +0.75s/f (Yiel) **13 Ran SP% 120.8**
Speed ratings (Par 98): **89,87,83,82,81 78,77,74,73,69 66,22,**
toteswingers:1&2:£49.40, 1&3:£95.40, 2&3:£12.60 CSF £389.66 TOTE £60.10: £13.30, £2.60, £4.60; EX 630.00.
Owner The Storm Partnership **Bred** J A And Mrs Duffy **Trained** Middleham Moor, N Yorks

FOCUS
An average early season 3-y-o maiden run at a respectable gallop considering the testing surface, but not surprisingly the time was around 3 secs slower than the better-class 3-y-o handicap earlier on the card. The form is fluid with the form horses not at their best.

1480 MALOSA MEDICAL APPRENTICE H'CAP 5f
5:40 (5:41) (Class 5) (0-70,70) 4-Y-O+ **£2,587** (£770; £384; £192) **Stalls** High

Form RPR
3-00 **1** **Mata Hari Blue**[16] 1177 6-9-3 **68** (t) GeorgeDowning(3) 2 77
(John Holt) *dwlt: sn chsng ldrs: edgd rt over 1f out and ended up towards far side: styd on to ld last 100yds* **9/2**[1]
623 **2** 1¾ **Riflessione**[9] 1279 6-9-2 **67** (v) DarrenEgan(3) 3 70
(Ronald Harris) *led: edgd rt after s: hdd over 3f out: ended up far side: no ex last 100yds: tk 2nd nr fin* **15/2**
06-3 **3** *nk* **Highland Warrior**[11] 1237 13-8-11 **67** NedCurtis(8) 7 69
(Paul Midgley) *trckd ldrs: t.k.h: edgd rt over 1f out and ended up towards far side: kpt on same pce last 100yds* **6/1**[2]
520- **4** ½ **Just For Mary**[183] 6960 8-8-11 **69** (be) LauraSimpson(10) 10 69
(Daniel Mark Loughnane) *dwlt: in rr: racd towards stands' side: kpt on fnl 2f: nrst fin* **7/1**
3400 **5** *shd* **Sir Geoffrey (IRE)**[42] 835 6-9-6 **68** (b) DannyBrock 5 67
(Scott Dixon) *w ldrs: led over 3f out: edgd rt over 1f out and ended up far side: hdd and no ex last 100yds* **13/2**[3]
25-0 **6** 2¼ **Baybshambles (IRE)**[8] 1294 8-8-9 **57** GeorgeChaloner 6 48
(Ron Barr) *rrd s: outpcd in rr: kpt on fnl f: nvr a threat* **9/1**
130- **7** 7 **Novalist**[176] 7100 4-8-8 **56** (b) DarylByrne 4 22
(Robin Bastiman) *half rrd s: sn chsng ldrs: lost pl over 1f out* **14/1**

52-3 **8** 1 3/4 **Kyzer Chief**[8] 1298 7-8-6 **59**.................................... DavidSimmonson(5) 1 19
(Ron Barr) *rrd s: sn w ldrs: wknd over 2f out* **9/1**
40-0 **F** **Arry's Orse**[17] 1168 5-9-2 **70**.................................... ShirleyTeasdale(6) 11
(David Nicholls) *hld up: hdwy over 3f out: lost pl over 1f out: bhd whn fell 1f out: fatally injured* **9/2**[1]
1m 5.19s (4.49) **Going Correction** +0.975s/f (Soft) **9** Ran SP% **114.9**
Speed ratings (Par 103): **103,100,99,98,98 95,83,81,**
wingers:1&2:£5.50, 2&3:£6.20, 1&3:£6.70 CSF £38.10 CT £204.50 TOTE £4.10: £1.40, £2.80, £2.50; EX 34.80.
Owner M J Golding **Bred** R T And Mrs Watson **Trained** Peckleton, Leics
■ Stewards' Enquiry : George Downing four-day ban: used whip above permitted level (May 3-4,7-8)
FOCUS
A strongly run, if modest sprint handicap with the placed horses setting the level of the form.
Kyzer Chief Official explanation: jockey said gelding reared as gates opened
T/Plt: £5,815.70 to a £1 stake. Pool:£64,530.47 - 8.10 winning tickets T/Qpdt: Part won. £4,170.30 to a £1 stake. Pool:£5,643.68 - 0.80 winning tickets. WG

1419 WOLVERHAMPTON (A.W) (L-H)

Thursday, April 19

OFFICIAL GOING: Standard
Wind: Fresh across Weather: Showers

1481 32RED CASINO H'CAP 5f 216y(P)
6:05 (6:11) (Class 6) (0-65,70) 4-Y-0+ **£1,704** (£503; £251) **Stalls** Low

Form RPR
6300 **1** **Powerful Pierre**[35] 912 5-9-2 **63**.............................(b) DeclanCannon(3) 5 73
(Ian McInnes) *hld up: hdwy over 2f out: rdn over 1f out: rdr dropped whip wl ins fnl f: r.o to ld post* **33/1**
-241 **2** *nse* **Black Cadillac (IRE)**[8] 1306 4-9-12 **70** 6ex...................... DavidProbert 2 80
(Andrew Balding) *trckd ldrs: nt clr run 4f out: rdn to ld wl ins fnl f: hdd post* **5/6**[1]
/202 **3** 1 1/2 **Going French (IRE)**[3] 1420 5-9-4 **62**...........................(t) SamHitchcott 10 67
(Dai Burchell) *chsd ldr tl rdn to ld over 1f out: hdd and unable qck wl ins fnl f* **14/1**[3]
1/0- **4** 1 1/4 **Spice Run**[378] 1198 9-9-0 **63**.................................... LeonnaMayor(5) 11 64
(Alastair Lidderdale) *hld up: hdwy over 2f out: rdn over 1f out: styd on* **22/1**
-110 **5** *shd* **Consistant**[35] 912 4-9-4 **62**.. RussKennemore 6 63
(Brian Baugh) *stdd s: hld up: hdwy over 1f out: rdn and r.o ins fnl f: nt rch ldrs* **16/1**
1310 **6** 1/2 **Strictly Pink (IRE)**[10] 1254 4-9-7 **65**................................ CathyGannon 7 64
(Alan Bailey) *prom: pushed along over 2f out: styd on same pce ins fnl f* **15/2**[2]
015- **7** 1 1/2 **Full Shilling (IRE)**[184] 6940 4-8-13 **60**............................ RyanClark(3) 4 54
(John Spearing) *hld up: hmpd over 2f out: r.o ins fnl f: nvr nrr* **25/1**
1430 **8** *shd* **Cape Of Storms**[20] 1116 9-9-5 **63**................................(b) JamesDoyle 12 57
(Roy Brotherton) *led: racd wd tl jnd main gp 4f out: rdn and hdd over 1f out: no ex ins fnl f* **25/1**
06-4 **9** *nk* **Sarangoo**[22] 1061 4-9-3 **61**.. TomMcLaughlin 13 54
(Malcolm Saunders) *s.i.s: sn mid-div: swtchd lft over 2f out: hdwy u.p over 1f out: nt trble ldrs* **25/1**
4255 **10** 2 3/4 **Whipphound**[10] 1254 4-9-7 **65**...(p) LiamJones 1 49
(Mark Brisbourne) *chsd ldrs: rdn over 1f out: wknd ins fnl f* **14/1**[3]
5302 **11** 1 1/4 **Vhujon (IRE)**[31] 958 7-9-3 **61**.................................... RobbieFitzpatrick 8 40
(Peter Grayson) *hld up: rdn over 2f out: nvr on terms* **22/1**
0-00 **12** 6 **Legal Eagle (IRE)**[44] 808 7-9-4 **65**.........................(p) RobertLButler(3) 3 25
(Paul Green) *s.s: a bhd* **40/1**
320- **13** 9 **Arch Walker (IRE)**[178] 7065 5-9-5 **63**.................................. LukeMorris 9
(John Weymes) *prom tl rdn and wknd over 2f out* **16/1**
1m 14.6s (-0.40) **Going Correction** -0.025s/f (Stan) **13** Ran SP% **117.0**
Speed ratings (Par 101): **101,100,98,97,97 96,94,94,93,90 88,80,68**
CSF £56.31 CT £477.79 TOTE £50.60: £8.70, £1.10, £2.60; EX 108.00 TRIFECTA Not won..
Owner Richard Mustill **Bred** Hedsor Stud **Trained** Catwick, E Yorks
FOCUS
A modest handicap run at a reasonable gallop. The winner came down the centre in the straight and the third to his recent best helps set the standard.

1482 HOLIDAY INN WOLVERHAMPTON (S) STKS 5f 20y(P)
6:35 (6:40) (Class 6) 3-Y-O **£1,704** (£503; £251) **Stalls** Low

Form RPR
5345 **1** **My Name Is Sam**[7] 1337 3-8-12 47..............................(b[1]) CathyGannon 3 57
(Ronald Harris) *sn pushed along to ld: rdn over 1f out: edgd lft ins fnl f: styd on u.p* **7/1**[3]
1243 **2** 1/2 **Available (IRE)**[20] 1110 3-8-13 68..................................... PatCosgrave 6 56
(Jim Boyle) *chsd ldrs: rdn 1/2-way: edgd lft ins fnl f: styd on u.p to go 2nd towards fin* **13/8**[1]
2321 **3** 1/2 **El McGlynn (IRE)**[5] 1389 3-8-13 62.................................... LukeMorris 1 54
(John O'Shea) *a.p: rdn to chse wnr over 1f out: n.m.r ins fnl f: styd on same pce* **13/8**[1]
-300 **4** 1 1/2 **Burnwynd Spirit (IRE)**[11] 1241 3-8-9 51..................... DeclanCannon(3) 2 48
(Ian Semple) *s.i.s: sn chsng wnr: rdn 1/2-way: lost 2nd over 1f out: styd on same pce* **28/1**
2155 **5** 3 1/4 **Thorpe Bay**[6] 1353 3-8-13 67.. DavidKenny(5) 4 42
(Conor Dore) *hld up: rdn 1/2-way: nvr trbld ldrs* **11/2**[2]
1m 2.56s (0.26) **Going Correction** -0.025s/f (Stan) **5** Ran SP% **107.5**
Speed ratings (Par 96): **96,95,94,92,86**
.There was no bid for the winner. Available was claimed by J. Mackie for £6,000.\n\x\x
Owner Ridge House Stables Ltd **Bred** Summerville B'Stock & Herringswell Manor **Trained** Earlswood, Monmouths
FOCUS
A modest and uncompetitive seller in which the gallop was sound but not form to be too confident about. The winner edged towards the far rail late on.

1483 LIKE US ON FACEBOOK WOLVERHAMPTON RACECOURSE H'CAP 5f 20y(P)
7:05 (7:10) (Class 6) (0-62,62) 4-Y-O+ **£1,704** (£503; £251) **Stalls** Low

Form RPR
0-22 **1** **Lesley's Choice**[15] 1185 6-9-4 **62**....................................(b) JamesDoyle 4 71
(Paul Rich) *chsd ldr: pushed along 1/2-way: rdn over 1f out: styd on u.p to ld nr fin* **11/4**[1]
4015 **2** 1/2 **Almaty Express**[5] 1387 10-8-11 **55**..................................(b) LukeMorris 2 62
(John Weymes) *led: rdn and edgd lft over 1f out: hdd nr fin* **7/2**[2]
3535 **3** 2 **Rightcar**[7] 1343 5-8-13 **57**.. RobbieFitzpatrick 3 57+
(Peter Grayson) *hld up: hmpd wl over 3f out: r.o u.p ins fnl f: nt rch ldrs* **8/1**
150- **4** 1 1/4 **Ginzan**[190] 6802 4-9-3 **61**... TomMcLaughlin 8 56
(Malcolm Saunders) *chsd ldrs: edgd lft sn after s:* **9/1**
5-61 **5** 1 **Bertie Southstreet**[42] 839 9-9-4 **62**.......................(b) RussKennemore 5 54
(Paul Midgley) *trckd ldrs: racd keenly: hmpd wl over 3f out: rdn over 1f out: no ex ins fnl f* **15/2**
100- **6** 2 3/4 **Francis Albert**[129] 7737 6-8-13 **57**............................. RichardKingscote 7 39
(Michael Mullineaux) *hld up: rdn 1/2-way: wknd over 1f out* **20/1**
3633 **7** 1 1/4 **Sherjawy (IRE)**[8] 1300 8-9-0 **58**............................(b) JamieGoldstein 1 35
(Zoe Davison) *sn pushed along in rr: n.d* **6/1**[3]
5460 **8** *hd* **Spic 'n Span**[37] 887 7-8-12 **56**..(b) CathyGannon 6 33
(Ronald Harris) *hld up: plld hrd: rdn and wknd over 1f out* **10/1**
1m 1.63s (-0.67) **Going Correction** -0.025s/f (Stan) **8** Ran SP% **109.9**
Speed ratings (Par 101): **104,103,100,98,96 92,90,89**
toteswingers:1&2:£2.30, 2&3:£5.50, 1&3:£3.20 CSF £11.30 CT £60.33 TOTE £3.60: £1.70, £1.40, £2.30; EX 10.90 Trifecta £49.50 Pool: £513.96 - 7.68 winning units..
Owner L M Power **Bred** B C Allen **Trained** Newport, Gwent
FOCUS
Exposed performers in an ordinary handicap. Although the gallop was sound, those up with the pace held the edge and the winner came down the centre. The form is rated through the runner-up to the best of the last year's form.

1484 £32 FREE AT 32RED.COM MAIDEN STKS 1m 4f 50y(P)
7:35 (7:40) (Class 5) 3-Y-0+ **£2,264** (£673; £336; £168) **Stalls** Low

Form RPR
0- **1** **Kuda Huraa (IRE)**[369] 1407 4-9-12 0.............................. AndreaAtzeni 4 80+
(Roger Varian) *chsd ldrs: rdn over 2f out: led 1f out: styd on* **5/2**[2]
225- **2** 1 1/4 **Hyperlink (IRE)**[214] 6187 3-8-7 73....................................... JoeFanning 1 76
(Mark Johnston) *chsd ldr: rdn over 2f out: ev ch 1f out: edgd lft: styd on same pce ins fnl f* **11/8**[1]
4-32 **3** 3/4 **Eshaab (USA)**[20] 1113 3-8-7 76....................................... TadhgO'Shea 8 75
(Ed Dunlop) *led: rdn over 2f out: sn edgd lft: hdd 1f out: styd on same pce* **5/2**[2]
5- **4** 15 **Bollistick**[146] 7536 6-9-13 0.. RichardKingscote 5 53
(Michael Mullineaux) *mid-div: rdn over 3f out: wknd over 2f out* **200/1**
5 6 **Ghaabesh (IRE)**[186] 5-9-13 66...(t) TomEaves 2 43
(Donald McCain) *prom tl rdn and wknd over 2f out* **25/1**
6 *nk* **Al Faylasoof (USA)** 3-8-7 0.. SamHitchcott 7 41+
(David Simcock) *sn pushed along and rn v green in rr: lost tch fr over 3f out* **22/1**[3]
0/0 **7** 13 **Tiger Girl**[20] 1113 5-9-3 0.. AntiocoMurgia(5) 3 17
(Noel Quinlan) *hld up: rdn over 3f out: sn wknd: eased over 1f out: t.o* **200/1**
8 1 1/4 **On Command (IRE)**[26] 4-9-12 0...................................... DaneO'Neill 6 20
(Don Cantillon) *s.i.s: hld up: wknd over 3f out: eased over 1f out: t.o* **40/1**
2m 39.91s (-1.19) **Going Correction** -0.025s/f (Stan)
WFA 3 from 4yo 20lb 4 from 5yo+ 1lb **8** Ran SP% **110.9**
Speed ratings (Par 103): **102,101,100,90,86 86,77,76**
toteswingers:1&2:£1.10, 2&3:£1.70, 1&3:£1.30 CSF £5.88 TOTE £2.90: £1.10, £1.10, £1.40; EX 7.50 Trifecta £20.40 Pool: £864.04 -31.20 winning units..
Owner Mrs Fitri Hay **Bred** Healing Music Partnership **Trained** Newmarket, Suffolk
FOCUS
A fair maiden in which the three market leaders pulled clear when an ordinary tempo increased in the last three furlongs. The winner raced just off the inside rail in the straight and the placed horses set the standard.
Al Faylasoof(USA) Official explanation: jockey said colt ran green

1485 32RED FILLIES' H'CAP 1m 4f 50y(P)
8:05 (8:10) (Class 5) (0-70,70) 4-Y-0+ **£2,587** (£770; £384; £192) **Stalls** Low

Form RPR
4522 **1** **Dazzling Valentine**[35] 906 4-9-2 **66**.................................... LiamJones 2 73
(Alan Bailey) *chsd ldrs: rdn over 1f out: styd on to ld post* **7/2**[2]
0/4 **2** *shd* **One For Joules (IRE)**[33] 942 5-8-12 **66**....................... DavidKenny(5) 5 72
(Michael Scudamore) *hld up: hdwy over 3f out: chsd ldr over 2f out: sn rdn: styd on u.p to ld wl ins fnl f: hdd post* **5/2**[1]
5-15 **3** *nk* **The Blue Dog (IRE)**[15] 1189 5-9-2 **65**................................. AndreaAtzeni 3 71
(Michael Wigham) *chsd ldr tl led wl over 2f out: rdn over 1f out: hdd wl ins fnl f styd on* **9/2**[3]
00-1 **4** 6 **Zefooha (FR)**[10] 1247 8-9-5 **68** 6ex...........................(p) GrahamGibbons 1 64
(Tim Walford) *led: rdn and hdd wl over 2f out: wknd fnl f* **9/2**[3]
0-50 **5** 3/4 **Pandorica**[30] 971 4-9-4 **68**.. MartinLane 8 63
(Bernard Llewellyn) *chsd ldrs: rdn over 2f out: wknd fnl f* **12/1**
0- **6** 3/4 **Lisselan Pleasure (USA)**[122] 7823 5-9-2 **65**..................... LukeMorris 6 59
(Bernard Llewellyn) *s.s: hld up: rdn over 3f out: wknd fnl f* **15/2**
160- **7** 7 **Amana (USA)**[258] 4747 8-9-4 **70**.. RyanClark(3) 4 53
(Mark Brisbourne) *hld up: nt clr run over 2f out: rdn and wknd over 1f out* **16/1**
2m 42.21s (1.11) **Going Correction** -0.025s/f (Stan)
WFA 4 from 5yo+ 1lb **7** Ran SP% **112.5**
Speed ratings (Par 100): **95,94,94,90,90 89,85**
toteswingers:1&2:£1.10, 2&3:£3.10, 1&3:£3.60 CSF £12.26 CT £38.12 TOTE £5.70: £1.50, £1.10; EX 12.50 Trifecta £34.50 Pool: £624.71 - 13.38 winning units..
Owner The Glenbuccaneers **Bred** Chippenham Lodge Stud Ltd **Trained** Newmarket, Suffolk
FOCUS
A modest fillies handicap in which the gallop was an ordinary one to the straight. The first three pulled clear and the winner raced close to the inside rail. The first two look on good marks while the third sets the level of the form.

1486 32RED.COM H'CAP 1m 1f 103y(P)
8:35 (8:41) (Class 5) (0-70,68) 3-Y-O **£2,264** (£673; £336; £168) **Stalls** Low

Form RPR
-132 **1** **Zain Princess (IRE)**[15] 1190 3-9-5 **66**.............................. NickyMackay 6 75
(Gerard Butler) *hld up and bhd: hdwy to ld over 2f out: rdn clr over 1f out: styd on* **11/2**[3]
00-1 **2** 1 3/4 **Topanga Canyon**[6] 1364 3-9-7 **68** 6ex...........................(v) LiamKeniry 1 73+
(Andrew Balding) *led 1f: chsd ldrs: rdn to chse wnr over 1f out: styd on u.p* **7/2**[2]
305- **3** 5 **Landown Littlerock**[173] 7177 3-8-8 **62**............................. JackDuern(7) 3 57
(Reg Hollinshead) *chsd ldrs: rdn over 2f out: styng on same pce whn hung lft ins fnl f* **33/1**
600- **4** 1 **Madame St Clair (IRE)**[264] 4552 3-9-5 **66**......................... MartinDwyer 2 58+
(Brian Meehan) *prom: pushed along 1/2-way: lost pl over 3f out: hdwy and nt clr run over 1f out: nt trble ldrs* **6/1**

052- 5 hd **Aleksandar**[176] 7109 3-9-7 **68** KierenFallon 8 60
(Luca Cumani) *hmpd s: hld up: hdwy over 3f out: rdn and ev ch over 2f out: wknd fnl f* **3/1**[1]

040- 6 3 ¼ **Saint Irene**[203] 6489 3-9-2 **63** DaneO'Neill 4 48
(Michael Blanshard) *hld up: effrt over 2f out: wknd over 1f out* **22/1**

042- 7 4 **Frederickthegreat**[143] 7569 3-9-5 **66** (t) DarryllHolland 5 43
(Hughie Morrison) *prom: chsd ldr over 6f out tl led over 3f out: rdn and hdd over 2f out: wkng whn hung lft over 1f out* **7/2**[2]

00-2 8 28 **Always Ends Well (IRE)**[8] 1303 3-8-13 **60** JoeFanning 7
(Mark Johnston) *led over 8f out: rdn and hdd over 3f out: wknd 2f out: t.o* **8/1**

2m 1.0s (-0.70) **Going Correction** -0.025s/f (Stan) **8** Ran SP% **117.5**
Speed ratings (Par 98): **102,100,96,95,94 92,88,63**
toteswingers:1&2:£4.80, 2&3:£13.10, 1&3:£24.30 CSF £25.85 CT £586.39 TOTE £4.60: £1.10, £1.60, £8.60; EX 17.60 Trifecta £177.70 Pool: £720.52 - 3.00 winning units..
Owner Darren Hudson-Wood **Bred** Star Pointe Ltd & Miss J Elmes **Trained** Newmarket, Suffolk

FOCUS
A modest handicap run at a fair gallop and the form could be worth a little more than rated. The winner edged towards the far rail in the closing stages.

1487 32REDPOKER.COM H'CAP 7f 32y(P)
9:05 (9:10) (Class 6) (0-60,60) 4-Y-0+ **£1,704** (£503; £251) **Stalls** High

Form RPR

4-00 1 **Intiqaal (IRE)**[28] 1000 5-9-5 **58** (t) JoeFanning 3 70
(Derek Shaw) *hld up: hdwy over 1f out: r.o to ld wl ins fnl f: sn clr* **13/2**[3]

200- 2 2 ¼ **Cadmium Loch**[203] 6479 4-9-0 **60** JackDuern(7) 7 66
(Reg Hollinshead) *chsd ldr tl led over 2f out: rdn over 1f out: hdd and unable qck wl ins fnl f* **12/1**

4-30 3 hd **Fortunate Bid (IRE)**[12] 1224 6-9-2 **58** (p) MichaelO'Connell(3) 11 63
(Linda Stubbs) *hld up: racd keenly: hdwy over 1f out: r.o: nt rch ldrs* **16/1**

-600 4 hd **Sergeant Troy (IRE)**[65] 557 4-9-3 **56** (t) PatCosgrave 5 61
(George Baker) *s.i.s: sn pushed along into mid-div: hdwy u.p over 2f out: r.o* **7/4**[1]

0/24 5 2 **Forever Hope**[16] 1173 5-9-0 **53** BarryMcHugh 9 52
(Tony Coyle) *a.p: rdn to chse ldr over 1f out: no ex ins fnl f* **12/1**

3523 6 1 **Just Timmy Marcus**[5] 1387 6-9-0 **53** RussKennemore 8 50
(Brian Baugh) *hld up: hdwy over 1f out: styd on same pce ins fnl f* **13/2**[3]

0-40 7 nk **Whitstable Native**[8] 1309 4-9-1 **54** LukeMorris 12 50
(Joseph Tuite) *hld up: racd keenly: rdn over 1f out: r.o: nt trble ldrs* **25/1**

1061 8 ½ **Marksbury**[15] 1193 5-9-7 **60** MartinLane 4 55
(Mark Brisbourne) *hld up in tch: rdn over 2f out: n.m.r wl over 1f out: sn wknd* **17/2**

6436 9 1 **Cheery Cat (USA)**[5] 1387 8-8-12 **51** (v) KierenFallon 1 43
(Richard Ford) *led: pushed along and hdd over 2f out: sn rdn: wknd fnl f* **6/1**[2]

-000 10 ¾ **Pie Poudre**[28] 995 5-8-11 **50** (b) TomEaves 6 40
(Roy Brotherton) *s.i.s: a in rr* **40/1**

24-0 11 1 ¾ **This Ones For Eddy**[98] 128 7-9-7 **60** GrahamGibbons 2 45
(John Balding) *chsd ldrs: rdn over 2f out: wknd fnl f* **12/1**

1m 29.58s (-0.02) **Going Correction** -0.025s/f (Stan) **11** Ran SP% **123.1**
Speed ratings (Par 101): **99,96,96,95,93 92,92,91,90,89 87**
toteswingers:1&2:£22.60, 2&3:£33.10, 1&3:£37.90 CSF £85.90 CT £1241.88 TOTE £11.00: £3.10, £2.30, £5.80; EX 106.60 Trifecta £698.30 Part won. Pool: £943.74 - 0.62 winning units..
Owner Market Avenue Racing Club Ltd **Bred** Airlie Stud **Trained** Sproxton, Leics

FOCUS
A moderate handicap in which the gallop was a reasonable one and the form looks straightforward, rated around those in the frame behind the winner. The winner came down the centre.
T/Plt: £20.40 to a £1 stake. Pool of £84,065.69 - 3,006.68 winning tickets. T/Qpdt: £7.60 to a £1 stake. Pool of £7,641.99 - 742.54 winning tickets. CR

1488 - 1490a (Foreign Racing) - See Raceform Interactive

BATH (L-H)
Friday, April 20

OFFICIAL GOING: Good to soft (good in places; 6.4)
Wind: quite strong at times against Weather: cloudy with sunny periods

1491 R & R ICES FILLIES' H'CAP 1m 2f 46y
5:00 (5:00) (Class 4) (0-80,80) 4-Y-0+ **£3,428** (£1,020; £509; £254) **Stalls** Low

Form RPR

361- 1 **Night And Dance (IRE)**[160] 7401 4-9-4 **77** JohnFahy 6 88
(Clive Cox) *racd keenly: trckd ldr: rdn to ld over 1f out: kpt on wl fnl f* **7/2**[2]

3-14 2 2 **Tidal Run**[10] 1286 4-8-11 **70** LukeMorris 3 77
(Mick Channon) *trckd ldr: pressed ldr over 3f out: rdn over 2f out: ev ch briefly over 1f out: kpt on same pce fnl f* **11/2**[3]

241- 3 2 **Lady Rosamunde**[357] 1659 4-9-2 **75** (p) TadhgO'Shea 5 78
(Marcus Tregoning) *trckd ldrs: rdn over 2f out: styd on ins fnl f: wnt 3rd towards fin* **15/2**

210- 4 ½ **Destiny Of Dreams**[182] 6996 4-9-7 **80** DaneO'Neill 4 82
(Jo Crowley) *led: rdn whn pressed over 2f out: hdd over 1f out: sn hld: no ex whn lost 2 pls fnl 120yds* **7/2**[2]

211- 5 30 **Carinya (IRE)**[170] 7236 4-9-5 **78** GeorgeBaker 2 52
(Amy Weaver) *hld up bhd ldrs: tk clsr order 4f out: outpcd over 2f out: eased whn btn fnl f* **15/8**[1]

2m 16.47s (5.47) **Going Correction** +0.325s/f (Good) **5** Ran SP% **106.4**
Speed ratings (Par 102): **91,89,87,87,63**
CSF £20.03 TOTE £4.80: £1.90, £2.40; EX 16.50.
Owner H E Sheikh Sultan Bin Khalifa Al Nahyan **Bred** Round Hill Stud **Trained** Lambourn, Berks

FOCUS
Following a drying day the going was good to soft, good in places. They went a fair pace in this fillies' handicap. The favourite was disappointing but the unexposed winner scored with something in hand, while the runner-up is rated more in line with her Folkestone win.
Carinya(IRE) Official explanation: trainer said filly had a breathing problem

1492 PERI LTD MEDIAN AUCTION MAIDEN STKS 5f 161y
5:30 (5:34) (Class 5) 3-4-Y-0 **£2,264** (£673; £336; £168) **Stalls** Centre

Form RPR

244- 1 **Lethal Force (IRE)**[268] 4424 3-9-0 **105** JohnFahy 2 90+
(Clive Cox) *trckd ldrs: led over 1f out: shkn up briefly to draw clr ent fnl f: easily* **30/100**[1]

5- 2 9 **Captain Kendall (IRE)**[291] 3686 3-9-0 **0** PadraigBeggy 5 61
(David Evans) *chsd ldrs: rdn over 2f out: styd on to go 2nd towards fin: no ch w wnr* **16/1**[3]

3-42 3 ½ **Chicarito**[28] 1006 3-9-0 **59** NeilCallan 7 59
(John Gallagher) *led: rdn over 2f out: hdd over 1f out: sn hld by wnr: no ex whn lost 2nd towards fin* **16/1**[3]

6- 4 1 ½ **Allegra Byron**[228] 5779 3-8-9 **0** LukeMorris 4 49
(Jonathan Portman) *outpcd in last but in tch: nvr able to get on terms: wnt 4th ent fnl f* **50/1**

036- 5 1 ¾ **Emperor Vespasian**[182] 6992 3-9-0 **82** LiamKeniry 3 48
(Andrew Balding) *trckd ldrs: pushed along over 3f out: rdn over 2f out: wknd ent fnl f* **8/1**[2]

2-U R **Aurens (IRE)**[25] 1048 3-8-11 **0** AdamBeschizza(3) 8
(Brian Gubby) *reluctant to go to s: ref to r: tk no part* **8/1**[2]

1m 12.96s (1.76) **Going Correction** +0.325s/f (Good)
WFA 3 from 4yo 11lb **6** Ran SP% **112.9**
Speed ratings (Par 103): **101,89,88,86,84**
toteswingers:1&2:£1.80, 1&3:£1.60, 2&3:£6.90 CSF £7.17 TOTE £1.30: £1.02, £8.10; EX 6.40 Trifecta £23.90 Pool: £497.74 - 15.39 winning units..
Owner Alan G Craddock **Bred** Declan Johnson **Trained** Lambourn, Berks

FOCUS
One of the highest rated maidens in training had no trouble cashing in on a golden opportunity in this auction maiden. The third is the best guide to the level.

1493 EVENTS BAR MANAGEMENT H'CAP 5f 11y
6:00 (6:00) (Class 4) (0-85,85) 3-Y-O **£3,428** (£1,020; £509; £254) **Stalls** Centre

Form RPR

200- 1 **Fanrouge (IRE)**[202] 6518 3-9-7 **85** TomMcLaughlin 2 92
(Malcolm Saunders) *in last pair and in tch: pushed along fr over 3f out: rdn over 2f out: no imp tl str run fnl f: led fnl stride* **14/1**

161- 2 hd **Royal Reyah**[167] 7294 3-8-7 **71** FergusSweeney 1 77
(Stuart Kittow) *led: rdn whn hrd pressed fr over 2f out: kpt on gamely: hdd fnl stride* **9/4**[1]

00-3 3 ½ **Signifer (IRE)**[9] 1317 3-9-5 **83** MartinHarley 7 87
(Mick Channon) *prom: rdn upsides ldr fr 2f out: ev ch fnl f: no ex fnl 40yds* **11/4**[2]

4111 4 1 ¾ **Redair (IRE)**[36] 905 3-8-9 **78** MatthewCosham(5) 5 76
(David Evans) *unsettled in stalls: trckd ldrs: rdn over 2f out: kpt on same pce* **7/1**

21- 5 ¾ **Gabbiano**[128] 7749 3-9-3 **81** PatCosgrave 8 76
(Jeremy Gask) *wnt rt s: racd keenly: trckd ldrs: rdn in cl 3rd whn hung bdly lft fr over 1f out: unable to be rdn out and lost 2 pls fnl 120yds* **7/2**[3]

100- 6 2 ½ **Kyanight (IRE)**[216] 6169 3-8-9 **73** JohnFahy 3 59
(Clive Cox) *hld up in tch: rdn over 2f out: nvr gng pce to get on terms* **7/1**

1m 4.29s (1.79) **Going Correction** +0.325s/f (Good) **6** Ran SP% **111.3**
Speed ratings (Par 100): **98,97,96,94,92 88**
toteswingers:1&2:£4.70, 1&3:£3.70, 2&3:£1.80 CSF £44.94 CT £111.99 TOTE £18.80: £5.40, £1.10; EX 42.30 TRIFECTA Not won..
Owner Chris Scott **Bred** Silk Fan Syndicate **Trained** Green Ore, Somerset

FOCUS
A decent handicap with the winner progressive and the third setting the standard. The pace was not very strong but the winner came from a long way back to pick off the two pacesetters.
Redair(IRE) Official explanation: jockey said filly hung left throughout
Gabbiano Official explanation: jockey said gelding hung left throughout

1494 E B F AND WHITSBURY MANOR STUD LANSDOWN FILLIES' STKS (LISTED RACE) 5f 11y
6:30 (6:31) (Class 1) 3-Y-O+
£18,714 (£7,095; £3,550; £1,768; £887; £445) **Stalls** Centre

Form RPR

440- 1 **Beyond Desire**[201] 6563 5-9-0 **101** NeilCallan 7 102
(Roger Varian) *wnt to s early: mde all: rdn clr 1f out: jst hld on* **3/1**[2]

313- 2 hd **Caledonia Lady**[202] 6518 3-8-8 **104** HayleyTurner 11 101
(Jo Hughes) *hld up: hdwy fr wl over 1f out: sn rdn: chal for 2nd ent fnl f: r.o wl fnl 120yds: jst failed* **7/1**[3]

4501 3 1 ¾ **Sugar Beet**[4] 1417 4-9-0 **85** DarrenEgan 8 95
(Ronald Harris) *hld up: rdn and hdwy fr over 1f out: r.o wl fnl f: wnt 3rd towards fin* **25/1**

1214 4 ¾ **Pale Orchid (IRE)**[27] 1032 3-8-4 **91** CathyGannon 6 88
(David Evans) *trckd wnr: rdn over 2f out: kpt on at same pce fnl f: lost 2nd fnl 120yds: lost 3rd towards fin* **25/1**

156- 5 1 **Night Carnation**[188] 6858 4-9-0 **108** JimmyFortune 10 89
(Andrew Balding) *mid-div: swtchd rt wl over 1f out: sn rdn to chse ldrs: kpt on same pce fnl f* **13/8**[1]

042- 6 ¾ **Sioux Rising (IRE)**[189] 6854 6-9-0 **98** FrederikTylicki 9 86
(Richard Fahey) *mid-div: rdn over 2f out: nt pce to get involved: hung lft ins fnl f* **12/1**

30-0 7 1 ½ **Button Moon (IRE)**[20] 1141 4-9-0 **84** MartinDwyer 2 83
(Ian Wood) *trckd wnr: hmpd ins 1st f: rdn over 2f out: keeping on at same pce and hld whn squeezed up fnl f* **66/1**

000- 8 13 **Perfect Tribute**[188] 6858 4-9-0 **102** LukeMorris 3 34
(Clive Cox) *wnt to s early: sn pushed along in rr: wknd ent fnl f* **8/1**

060- U **Astrophysical Jet**[202] 6522 5-9-0 **100** GrahamGibbons 4 83
(Ed McMahon) *mid-div: rdn over 2f out: no imp: bdly hmpd whn uns rdr nring fin* **10/1**

2611 U **Gin Twist**[16] 1183 3-8-4 **71** (b) RichardKingscote 5 72?
(Tom Dascombe) *hmpd ins 1st f: sn pushed along in midfield: rdn over 2f out: wknd fnl f: hmpd and uns rdr nring fin* **50/1**

1m 2.69s (0.19) **Going Correction** +0.325s/f (Good)
WFA 3 from 4yo+ 10lb **10** Ran SP% **114.6**
Speed ratings (Par 108): **111,110,107,106,105 103,101,80, ,**
toteswingers:1&2:£4.50, 1&3:£13.90, 2&3:£18.10 CSF £22.99 TOTE £2.80: £1.70, £2.20, £5.50; EX 27.00 Trifecta £434.10 Part won. Pool: £586.74 - 0.10 winning units..
Owner Clipper Logistics **Bred** Pinnacle Bloodstock **Trained** Newmarket, Suffolk
■ Stewards' Enquiry : Frederik Tylicki seven-day ban: careless riding (May 4-10)

FOCUS
Five of the runners were rated between 100 and 108 in this fillies' Listed race. The pace was strong and a well-backed 5-y-o dominated. The fourm makes sense rated around the first four. There was a nasty incident when Astrophysical Jet seemed to clip heels and nearly fall when held in the closing stages, which caused Gin Twist to sweve and unseat her rider.

NOTEBOOK
Beyond Desire won first time out in her first two seasons and was a creditable sixth in a Listed race on her return last year. She was strongly supported in her bid to add to her impressive comeback record and showed a good attitude to hang on after setting a decent pace in front. She is a free-going type with plenty of natural speed and she posted a string a frame efforts on fast ground in Group company last summer. (op 9-2)
Caledonia Lady took a while to hit top gear on her comeback run but she finished fast and gave the winner a scare. Her highlight in 2011 was a 5f Listed win on good to soft ground at Ayr in September but she also went close in the Group 2 Flying Childers. This 3-y-o filly still has some potential after nine runs and could make a big impact in Group company this season. (tchd 13-2)

Sugar Beet posted a career-best effort when narrowly winning a Windsor handicap off 85 earlier in the week, and she deserves plenty of credit for staying on for third behind two much higher rated rivals on this second run in Listed company. (op 20-1)

Pale Orchid(IRE) showed progressive form winning a maiden and two handicaps on Polytrack this year, but she has come up short in Listed company on her last two starts. (op 20-1 tchd 28-1)

Night Carnation was a much-improved triple winner last year, including a 5f Group 3 success at Sandown in July. She had leading form claims back against her own sex in Listed company but put a dent in her chance by taking a strong hold and couldn't find a finishing kick on her return from six months off. (op 5-4)

Sioux Rising(IRE), a 98-rated 6-y-o mare, couldn't land a major blow over a trip sharper than ideal on her return from six months off. (tchd 11-1)

1495 E.B.F./AJK PREMIER FOOD COURTS MEDIAN AUCTION MAIDEN STKS — 5f 11y

7:00 (7:01) (Class 5) 2-Y-O — **£3,340** (£986; £493) **Stalls** Centre

Form — RPR

0 **1** — **Chilworth Icon**[13] [1211] 2-9-3 0 ... MartinHarley 8 — 84+
(Mick Channon) *trckd ldrs: rdn to ld over 1f out: r.o: readily* **11/2**[3]

32 **2** 2 **Poetic Princess**[16] [1188] 2-8-12 0 ... TonyCulhane 2 — 70
(Jo Hughes) *broke wl: trckd ldrs: outpcd wl over 2f out: hdwy over 1f out: r.o to go 2nd ins fnl f: no ch w wnr* **6/1**

3 1 1/4 **Citius (IRE)** 2-9-0 0 ... SeanLevey(3) 3 — 70+
(Richard Hannon) *in tch: outpcd wl over 2f out: hdwy over 1f out: r.o to go 3rd ins fnl f* **5/2**[2]

4 3 **Indian Affair** 2-9-3 0 ... RussKennemore 10 — 60
(Milton Bradley) *sn prom: rdn and ev ch over 2f out: no ex fnl f* **66/1**

42 **5** 3 **Just Past Andover (IRE)**[13] [1218] 2-8-10 0 ... DarrenEgan(7) 9 — 49
(Bill Turner) *led at decent pce: rdn 2f out: hdd over 1f out: fdd fnl f* **2/1**[1]

6 **6** 4 **Tiger Sunset (IRE)**[21] [1118] 2-9-3 0 ... NeilCallan 6 — 34
(J S Moore) *mid-div: rdn wl over 2f out: wknd fnl f* **12/1**

7 6 **Baltic Gin (IRE)** 2-8-12 0 ... TomMcLaughlin 4 — 8+
(Malcolm Saunders) *s.i.s: a towards rr* **20/1**

8 3 **I'm Watching** 2-8-12 0 ... KierenFallon 1
(George Baker) *sn outpcd in rr: wknd over 1f out* **12/1**

9 1 **Icanboogie** 2-9-3 0 ... TadhgO'Shea 5
(Karen George) *dwlt bdly: a bhd* **40/1**

1m 4.85s (2.35) **Going Correction** +0.325s/f (Good) — **9** Ran SP% **115.7**
Speed ratings (Par 92): **94,90,88,84,79 72,63,58,56**
toteswingers:1&2:£4.70, 1&3:£5.10, 2&3:£3.60 CSF £37.69 TOTE £8.70: £3.00, £2.00, £1.10; EX 29.30 Trifecta £458.40 Part won. Pool: £619.49 - 0.72 winning units..

Owner 7Rus **Bred** Norman Court Stud **Trained** West Ilsley, Berks

FOCUS
An average maiden, but the winner did the job well from one the main form contenders, and a Richard Hannon-trained newcomer showed promise in third. The runner-up is the best guide to the level at this stage.

NOTEBOOK
Chilworth Icon, a May foal, was never involved in a 5f Kempton maiden on debut, but he looked a different proposition here, tracking the leaders before showing a turn of foot to score with something in hand. By St Leger winner Sixties Icon and out of a 7f/1m 2-y-o winner, it is very encouraging that he has delivered at this trip at this stage of his career, and he should have plenty of scope for progress as he goes up in distance. (op 13-2)

Poetic Princess had leading claims on her close second behind a subsequent winner in a 5f Wolverhampton maiden fillies event on her second start, but she got tapped for speed at a crucial stage before staying on well after the winner had got away. (op 11-2 tchd 7-1)

Citius(IRE) ◆, who was well-backed, looked inexperienced but showed quite a bit of promise working his way into third on this debut. A £72,000 Iffraaj half-brother to fairly useful 1m2f Irish winner Azamata, he should learn a lot from this initial experience and should go close in a similar race next time. (op 3-1)

Indian Affair cost just 800gns as a foal but this half-brother to four winners in the US showed some speed and ability on this debut, and can be marked up a bit because he took a strong hold and looked very green. Official explanation: jockey said colt ran green

Just Past Andover(IRE) had decent form claims on his 6-1 fourth in the Brocklesby and second on slow ground at Musselburgh early this month. Sent off a strong favourite, he dictated the pace but was comfortably overhauled before weakening in a disappointing run. (tchd 7-4 and 9-4 in places)

1496 UHY PEACHEYS H'CAP — 2m 1f 34y

7:30 (7:30) (Class 6) (0-65,64) 4-Y-O+ — **£1,617** (£481; £240; £120) **Stalls** Centre

Form — RPR

45/2 **1** — **Ministerofinterior**[12] [1240] 7-9-1 53 ... (t) FrederikTylicki 5 — 68
(Richard Ford) *mid-div: dropped to last trio over 4f out: hdwy over 3f out: rdn whn swtchd rt over 1f out: led fnl 120yds: styd on strly* **13/8**[1]

4-35 **2** 2 **Salontyre (GER)**[11] [673] 6-9-11 63 ... (p) NeilCallan 11 — 76
(Bernard Llewellyn) *trckd ldrs: rdn over 2f out: led wl over 1f out: no ex whn hdd fnl 120yds* **10/3**[2]

6051 **3** 8 **Bute Street**[8] [1338] 7-9-2 54 6ex ... RichardKingscote 6 — 57
(Ron Hodges) *led: kicked clr over 3f out: hdd over 1f out: hld on for 3rd but no ex fnl f* **8/1**

005/ **4** 3/4 **Mae Cigan (FR)**[410] [1756] 9-9-0 52 ... DaneO'Neill 10 — 55
(Michael Blanshard) *hld up: rdn and stdy prog fr 4f out: wnt 4th ins fnl f: nvr trbld ldrs* **14/1**

0241 **5** 1 1/4 **Six Of Clubs**[16] [1184] 6-9-9 61 ... (b) KierenFallon 8 — 62
(Bill Turner) *hld up: hdwy fr 4f out: rdn 3f out: wnt 4th over 1f out: no ex whn lost 4th ins fnl f* **11/2**[3]

5040 **6** 20 **Angelena Ballerina (IRE)**[19] [1154] 5-8-9 50 ... NataliaGemelova(3) 1 — 27
(Dai Williams) *racd keenly: trckd ldr: rdn over 4f out: wknd 3f out: t.o* **40/1**

1254 **7** 4 1/2 **Rosewood Lad**[35] [928] 5-9-12 64 ... LukeMorris 2 — 36
(J S Moore) *chsd ldrs: rdn over 4f out: wknd over 3f out: t.o* **8/1**

000- **8** 19 **Nobbys Girl**[315] [2873] 7-8-0 45 ... DarrenEgan(7) 4
(Ronald Harris) *hld up: rdn over 4f out: wknd over 3f out: t.o* **40/1**

0/60 **9** 7 **Thunderonthemount**[23] [1065] 7-8-2 45 ... JemmaMarshall(5) 7
(Michael Attwater) *wnt to s early: hld up and a last: wknd over 3f out: t.o* **66/1**

3m 59.31s (7.41) **Going Correction** +0.325s/f (Good) — **9** Ran SP% **111.8**
Speed ratings (Par 101): **95,94,90,89,89 79,77,68,65**
toteswingers:1&2:£1.70, 1&3:£3.60, 2&3:£3.10 CSF £6.55 CT £30.42 TOTE £3.00: £1.20, £1.70, £2.20; EX 9.30 Trifecta £49.00 Pool: £839.11 - 12.66 winning units..

Owner D E Simpson & R Farrington-Kirkham **Bred** Deerfield Farm **Trained** Garstang, Lancs

FOCUS
The two market leaders pulled a long way clear in this minor staying handicap and the form looks solid, rated around the principals.

1497 TOYOTA WORLD BRISTOL H'CAP — 5f 161y

8:00 (8:02) (Class 6) (0-60,60) 4-Y-O+ — **£1,617** (£481; £240; £120) **Stalls** Centre

Form — RPR

4300 **1** — **Valmina**[34] [942] 5-9-6 59 ... (t) NeilCallan 11 — 77
(Tony Carroll) *towards rr: hdwy fr 3f out: rdn 2f out: r.o to ld jst ins fnl f: hld on: all out* **8/1**

3344 **2** hd **Dancing Welcome**[46] [806] 6-9-2 55 ... (b) RichardKingscote 15 — 72
(Milton Bradley) *chsd ldrs: rdn to ld wl over 1f out: hdd jst ins fnl f: kpt on gamely: jst hld* **5/1**[1]

200- **3** 6 **Trade Centre**[199] [6609] 7-8-5 51 ... TimClark(7) 12 — 49
(Milton Bradley) *mid-div: rdn over 2f out: kpt on to go 3rd ins fnl f: no ch w ldng pir* **12/1**

1332 **4** 1 3/4 **Amazing Win (IRE)**[9] [1306] 4-9-5 58 ... SamHitchcott 17 — 50
(Mick Channon) *mid-div: rdn and hdwy over 2f out to chse ldrs: kpt on same pce fnl f* **8/1**

000- **5** 2 **Quadra Hop (IRE)**[161] [7371] 4-8-11 50 ... DavidProbert 10 — 35
(Bryn Palling) *trckd ldrs: wnt prom 3f out: sn rdn: kpt on same pce fr over 1f out* **20/1**

-000 **6** nk **Juarla (IRE)**[10] [1280] 4-9-5 58 ... (tp) LukeMorris 14 — 42
(Ronald Harris) *s.i.s: sn mid-div: rdn over 2f out: kpt on same pce: nvr threatened ldrs* **20/1**

220- **7** nk **My Meteor**[191] [6802] 5-9-7 60 ... DaneO'Neill 1 — 43+
(Tony Newcombe) *hld up towards rr: styd on fr over 1f out: nvr a threat* **9/1**

0052 **8** 1/2 **Flaxen Lake**[23] [1070] 5-8-11 53 ... (p) SeanLevey(3) 3 — 35
(Milton Bradley) *a mid-div* **16/1**

0-43 **9** 1 1/2 **Kyllachy Storm**[32] [964] 8-9-3 56 ... GeorgeBaker 13 — 33
(Ron Hodges) *disp ld for 2f: sn rdn: wknd jst over 1f out* **6/1**[2]

610 **10** 1 3/4 **Sabys Gem (IRE)**[6] [1387] 4-8-12 51 ... (b) JimCrowley 9 — 22
(Michael Wigham) *towards rr: sme late prog: nvr a factor* **7/1**[3]

400- **11** 1/2 **Scommettitrice (IRE)**[305] [3226] 4-8-11 50 ... (b) PadraigBeggy 16 — 19
(David Evans) *rdr lost iron leaving stalls: mid-div on outer: effrt over 2f out: wknd fnl f* **28/1**

10/0 **12** 1 3/4 **Whiteoak Lady (IRE)**[29] [997] 7-9-5 58 ... MartinHarley 5 — 21
(John Spearing) *mid-div tl wknd over 1f out* **25/1**

056- **13** 2 1/4 **Brandywell Boy (IRE)**[176] [7123] 9-9-5 58 ... JamesDoyle 2 — 14
(Dominic Ffrench Davis) *mid-div: rdn over 2f out: wknd over 1f out* **28/1**

00-0 **14** 1 **Haafhd Decent (IRE)**[8] [1343] 4-8-9 51 ... NataliaGemelova(3) 4
(Dai Williams) *disp ld tl wknd over 2f out* **66/1**

1543 **15** 1 **Decider (USA)**[8] [1343] 9-8-7 53 ... (b) DarrenEgan(7) 7
(Ronald Harris) *disp ld tl wknd over 2f out* **14/1**

40-0 **16** 2 3/4 **Mucky Molly**[10] [1285] 4-9-2 55 ... (v[1]) CathyGannon 8
(Olivia Maylam) *a outpcd in rr* **20/1**

520- **17** 7 **Miss Firefly**[240] [5394] 7-9-3 56 ... J-PGuillambert 6
(Ron Hodges) *chsd ldrs tl wknd over 2f out* **20/1**

1m 13.58s (2.38) **Going Correction** +0.325s/f (Good) — **17** Ran SP% **127.2**
Speed ratings (Par 101): **97,96,88,86,83 83,82,82,80,77 77,74,71,70,69 65,56**
toteswingers:1&2:£4.90, 1&3:£13.00, 2&3:£13.90 CSF £43.47 CT £499.62 TOTE £8.90: £2.40, £2.00, £3.50, £2.60; EX 54.60 Trifecta £334.50 Pool: £637.97 - 1.40 winning units..
Owner Mayden Stud **Bred** Mayden Stud, J A And D S Dewhurst **Trained** Cropthorne, Worcs

FOCUS
A modest big-field handicap but it was a run at a decent pace and the first two finished a long way clear. The winner is rated to his winter AW form.
Juarla(IRE) Official explanation: jockey said colt suffered interference in running
T/Plt: £82.80 to a £1 stake. Pool:£51,635.44 - 455.00 winning tickets T/Qpdt: £27.70 to a £1 stake. Pool:£6,391.17 - 170.42 winning tickets TM

NEWBURY (L-H)

Friday, April 20

OFFICIAL GOING: Soft (4.6)
Wind: Virtually nil Weather: Overcast

1498 DUBAI DUTY FREE H'CAP — 5f 34y

1:35 (1:36) (Class 2) (0-110,108) 4-Y-O+
£11,205 (£3,355; £1,677; £838; £419; £210) **Stalls** Centre

Form — RPR

260- **1** — **Mirza**[171] [7221] 5-8-7 94 oh3 ... DavidProbert 3 — 103
(Rae Guest) *trckd ldrs: drvn along 1/2-way: led 1f out: rdn out* **7/2**[2]

60-4 **2** 1 1/4 **Blue Jack**[27] [1033] 7-8-7 94 ... (v) RichardKingscote 5 — 98
(Tom Dascombe) *in tch drvn and hdwy over 1f out: styd on to chse wnr fnl 120yds: no imp* **6/1**[3]

000- **3** 1 1/4 **Lui Rei (ITY)**[223] [5927] 6-8-7 94 oh2 ... JimCrowley 7 — 94
(Robert Cowell) *slowly away: drvn and hdwy between horses 1f out: kpt on to take 3rd fnl 75yds but no imp on ldng duo* **9/1**

000- **4** 1 **Cheveton**[167] [7295] 8-8-7 94 oh3 ... PaulHanagan 6 — 90
(Richard Price) *rrd in stalls: sn in tch: rdn 1/2-way: styd on same pce fr over 1f out* **13/2**

50-6 **5** 1/2 **Captain Dunne (IRE)**[13] [1219] 7-9-6 107 ... TedDurcan 1 — 101
(Tim Easterby) *led tl hdd jst ins fnl 2f: btn ins fnl f* **9/1**

40-0 **6** 1/2 **Confessional**[19] [1157] 5-8-10 97 ... (be) DavidAllan 2 — 89
(Tim Easterby) *chsd ldr tl led jst ins fnl 2f: wknd ins fnl f* **5/2**[1]

00-5 **7** 1 3/4 **Medicean Man**[27] [1033] 6-9-4 108 ... (p) HarryBentley(3) 8 — 94
(Jeremy Gask) *in tch: pushed along 1/2-way sn outpcd* **7/1**

1m 5.59s (4.19) **Going Correction** +0.90s/f (Soft) — **7** Ran SP% **110.9**
Speed ratings (Par 109): **102,100,98,96,95 94,92**
toteswingers:1&2:£4.00, 2&3:£17.40, 1&3:£10.80 CSF £22.93 CT £164.02 TOTE £5.00: £2.60, £1.90; EX 28.30 Trifecta £409.20 Part won. Pool: £553.04 - 0.92 winning units..
Owner C J Mills **Bred** C J Mills **Trained** Newmarket, Suffolk

FOCUS
Rail realignment increased distances on Round course by 8 metres. Following heavy showers all week and prior to racing the going was described as Soft. The time was pretty slow and jockeys after the first reported it was riding somewhere between soft and heavy. This high-class sprint often throws up performers that are capable of holding their own in Pattern company, the best recent winner of this being Kyllachy. That said, most of these were pretty exposed and some getting towards the veteran stage. A slight persoanl best from the winner with the runner-up confirming his recent AW return.

NOTEBOOK

Mirza ◆ was well backed on this seasonal return and duly justified the support. He was 3lb out of the handicap, which meant he was 9lb above his last winning mark but scored here in a manner which suggests he is on the upgrade. He is arguably better at 6f, so this gives further encouragement that there might be more to come. (op 6-1)

Blue Jack was easy in the market, but he won the corresponding race two years ago and clearly likes the track as he came through to chase home the winner. He has dropped to a decent mark as well, being 11lb lower than for his first run last year. (op 4-1 tchd 7-2)

Lui Rei(ITY), making his seasonal debut having been gelded during the winter, totally blew the start (this was later confirmed by his rider) but was noted staying on steadily in the closing stages. He is another who is well handicapped on his best form, having been 3lb wrong here, and will not mind racing over another furlong. Official explanation: jockey said gelding was slowly away (op 11-1 tchd 12-1)

Cheveton half-reared as the stalls opened and then saw plenty of daylight. He will come on for this but in recent years has not hit winning form until the second half of the season. (op 6-1 tchd 7-1)

Captain Dunne(IRE) made the running but gradually faded after being headed by stable companion Confessional over a furlong out. Epsom's fast 5f and fast ground represent his ideal conditions. (op 10-1)

Confessional was sent off favourite and looked sure to be involved when coming through to lead, but faded in the last furlong. (op 11-4 tchd 3-1)

Medicean Man had a lot to find with today's second compared with their recent Lingfield running and dropped away after seeing plenty of daylight early. He seems to save his best for Ascot. (op 5-1)

1499 COMPTON BEAUCHAMP ESTATES LTD E B F MAIDEN STKS 5f 34y

2:10 (2:10) (Class 4) 2-Y-O £4,528 (£1,347; £673; £336) **Stalls** Centre

Form	Pos	Dist	Horse	Jockey	RPR
	1		**Englishman** 2-9-3 0 (Charles Hills) *t.k.h: stdd in rr: rapid hdwy appr fnl f: str run to ld in clsng stages: won gng away* **9/2**[2]	MichaelHills 4	86+
	2	*1*	**Smoothtalkinrascal (IRE)** 2-9-3 0 (Brian Meehan) *trckd ldr: led 2f out: drvn and hung lft ins fnl f: hdd and outpcd in clsng stages* **8/1**	ShaneKelly 6	81+
	3	*¾*	**Dust Whirl** 2-9-3 0 (Richard Hannon) *sn led: hdd 2f out: styd chsng ldr but no imp fr over 1f out: one pce into 3rd in clsng stages* **17/2**	PatDobbs 8	79
	4	*½*	**Sign Of The Zodiac (IRE)** 2-9-3 0 (Richard Hannon) *chsd ldrs: drvn along 1/2-way: styd on same pce ins fnl f* **5/1**[3]	RyanMoore 11	77+
	5	*nk*	**Cay Verde** 2-9-3 0 (Mick Channon) *towards rr: pushed along 1/2-way: styd on wl in clsng stages: nt rch ldrs* **28/1**	MatthewDavies 10	76
	6	*hd*	**Edged Out** 2-8-12 0 (Bryn Palling) *in rr and pushed along 1/2-way: hdwy 1f out: swtchd lft and str run fnl 120yds: fin wl* **50/1**	LukeMorris 7	70+
	7	*hd*	**Premier Steps (IRE)** 2-8-12 0 (Tom Dascombe) *in tch: pushed along to chse ldrs 1/2-way: kpt on ins fnl f* **16/1**	RichardKingscote 9	69
	8	*¾*	**Inka Surprise (IRE)** 2-9-3 0 (Ralph Beckett) *hld up in rr: gd hdwy over 1f out: trckd ldrs ins fnl f: no ex in clsng stages* **4/1**[1]	JimCrowley 5	72
	9	*2*	**Carlton Blue (IRE)** 2-9-3 0 (Paul Cole) *chsd ldrs: rdn 1/2-way: wknd ins fnl f* **17/2**	JimmyFortune 2	64
	10	*1*	**Bungle Inthejungle** 2-9-3 0 (Mick Channon) *unruly paddock: towards rr: rdn 2f out hung lft and no ch fr over 1f out* **16/1**	MartinHarley 3	61
	11	*8*	**Fils Anges (IRE)** 2-9-3 0 (Michael Bell) *in tch: rdn to chse ldrs 1/2-way: sn wknd* **7/1**	JamieSpencer 1	32

1m 7.61s (6.21) **Going Correction** +0.90s/f (Soft) **11** Ran SP% **116.7**

Speed ratings (Par 94): **86,84,83,82,81 81,81,80,76,75 62**

toteswingers:1&2:£8.60, 2&3:£13.80, 1&3:£9.00 CSF £40.15 TOTE £5.80: £2.40, £3.30, £2.70; EX 51.70 Trifecta £329.80 Pool: £637.34 - 1.43 winning units..

Owner P Winkworth **Bred** Peter Winkworth **Trained** Lambourn, Berks

FOCUS

Subsequent Royal Ascot winner Winker Watson was probably the best recent winner of this juvenile maiden. A field of newcomers and a stiff test in the conditions at this stage of the season, and there was quite a bunched finish. The time was 2.02secs slower than the mature sprinters in the opening race, not a bad time in the circumstances and the averages for this race are good but the close finish raises doubts.

NOTEBOOK

Englishman ◆, from a family full of speed, tracked the pace before losing his pitch at halfway. He had only one behind him inside the last 2f but picked up really well and hit the front late on. He should be sharper next time and could well follow up. (tchd 5-1)

Smoothtalkinrascal(IRE) ◆, whose dam scored first time out as a juvenile, looked like emulating her when striking the front entering the final furlong but then edged left due to a combination of greenness and tiredness once in front, and was run down by the strong-finishing winner. His trainer's runners generally improve for an outing and he should soon gain compensation. (op 7-1)

Dust Whirl is bred to be speedy and showed plenty of pace up the centre and stuck to his task once headed. There should be races in him on this evidence. (op 8-1 tchd 9-1)

Sign Of The Zodiac(IRE), a half-brother to Brae Hill and several other speedy types, was noisy in the parade ring but travelled nicely for a long way, then looked set to drop away over a furlong out before staying on again when ridden. He should improve for the outing. (tchd 9-2)

Cay Verde was held up and, despite not looking entirely happy on the ground, kept on steadily and can come on for the experience. (op 33-1)

Edged Out, one of two fillies in the line-up, was the first off the bridle and out the back at halfway, but ran on really well in the closing stages. Her dam won on her juvenile debut and there is plenty of speed in this filly's pedigree.

Premier Steps(IRE), a half-sister to five winners, tracked the pace and only faded late on. (op 20-1 tchd 14-1)

Inka Surprise(IRE) was sent off favourite despite having a pedigree that suggests he might need longer trips in time. He travelled quite well into the race but could not find an extra gear in the last furlong. (tchd 7-2)

Fils Anges(IRE) attracted support but, after showing up prominently early, dropped away in the second half of the race. (op 9-1)

1500 DUBAI DUTY FREE FULL OF SURPRISES H'CAP 7f (S)

2:40 (2:41) (Class 3) (0-95,92) 3-Y-O

£6,536 (£1,957; £978; £489; £244; £122) **Stalls** Centre

Form	Pos	Dist	Horse	Jockey	RPR
001-	**1**		**Gregorian (IRE)**[182] 6983 3-9-3 **88** (John Gosden) *disp 2nd: drvn to a slt advantage ins fnl f: narrowly hdd fnl 120yds: rallied u.p to ld again last strides* **3/1**[2]	WilliamBuick 8	101+
01-	**2**	*hd*	**Tartiflette**[167] 7292 3-8-7 **78** oh1 (Ed McMahon) *trckd ldrs: chal between horses travelling wl appr fnl f: slt advantage fnl 120yds: sn rdn hdd last strides* **14/1**	GrahamGibbons 1	90
313-	**3**	*2½*	**Van Der Art**[182] 6995 3-8-13 **84** (Alan Jarvis) *t.k.h and sn led: jnd 1f out and narrowly hdd sn after: styd upsides tl wknd fnl 120yds* **25/1**	KierenFallon 13	90
1-	**4**	*¾*	**Aljamaaheer (IRE)**[185] 6935 3-9-3 **88** (Roger Varian) *plld hrd: chsd ldrs: pushed along and hdwy 2 out: nvr quite gng pce to rch ldng trio: kpt on same pce ins fnl f* **5/4**[1]	PaulHanagan 9	92+
112-	**5**	*2¾*	**Red Quartet (IRE)**[182] 6995 3-8-10 **81** (Robert Eddery) *in rr hdwy over 2f out: styd on one pce to take 5th ins fnl f* **16/1**	AndreaAtzeni 4	78
31-	**6**	*1¾*	**I'm So Glad**[257] 4823 3-8-7 **78** (Mick Channon) *disp 2nd: rdn over 2f out: wknd over 1f out* **28/1**	MartinHarley 5	70
61-	**7**	*2¼*	**Usain Colt**[182] 6991 3-9-2 **87** (Richard Hannon) *t.k.h: pushed along and sme prog over 2f out: nvr rchd ldrs and sn wknd* **7/1**[3]	RyanMoore 3	73
310-	**8**	*9*	**Self Centred**[181] 7028 3-9-0 **85** (Charles Hills) *t.k.h: a in rr* **25/1**	MichaelHills 7	48
110-	**9**	*6*	**Elusive Flame**[210] 6296 3-9-0 **85** (David Elsworth) *s.i.s: plld hrd: a towards rr* **25/1**	JamieSpencer 10	32
16-	**10**	*1¼*	**Newnton Lodge**[192] 6766 3-8-12 **83** (Roger Charlton) *t.k.h: a towards rr* **16/1**	JamesDoyle 14	27

1m 31.65s (5.95) **Going Correction** +0.90s/f (Soft) **10** Ran SP% **115.4**

Speed ratings (Par 102): **102,101,98,98,94 92,90,80,73,71**

toteswingers:1&2:£7.50, 2&3:£20.20, 1&3:£8.60 CSF £40.69 CT £905.30 TOTE £3.80: £1.60, £3.80, £3.70; EX 53.20 Trifecta £735.10 Part won. Pool of £993.41 - 0.10 winning units..

Owner H R H Princess Haya Of Jordan **Bred** Rathasker Stud **Trained** Newmarket, Suffolk

FOCUS

Often a decent handicap - the subsequent Britannia winner featured among the beaten runners in 2008 and '09. This year's race was steadily run, unsurprisingly considering the ground, and nothing got involved form off the pace. The first two improved from their maiden wins while the third stepped up on her juvenile form.

NOTEBOOK

Gregorian(IRE) looked awkward when winning a Doncaster maiden on his final start at two, having sweated up and carried his head high, but he's evidently matured well, and this ground suited considering he has a knee action. His head was again a touch high, but his attitude couldn't be faulted. There should be more to come, although it's doubtful he'd want conditions too quick. (op 4-1)

Tartiflette, who won a 6f Doncaster maiden on the second of two juvenile starts, showed herself well handicapped (even from 1lb out of the weights), but she didn't knuckle down as well as the winner. She was kidded into contention between rivals, but ran green under pressure. There should be improvement forthcoming, but she has to prove she's going the right way mentally. (tchd 12-1)

Van Der Art was responsible for the steady pace. This was a pleasing return from a six-month break.

Aljamaaheer(IRE) looked a decent prospect when winning a 6f Yarmouth maiden on his sole start at two, and he holds a 2000 Guineas entry, but couldn't justify strong market support on this return. He was basically too keen considering both the ground and his lack of race-fitness, and he'll be worth another chance. (op 10-11)

Red Quartet(IRE) couldn't confirm earlier C&D form with Van Der Art, but this was a promising enough return from 182 days off as the way the race unfolded gave him little hope. (op 20-1)

I'm So Glad, last seen winning a 6f maiden on fast ground in August, holds a Group 3 entry in Ireland, but this ground was probably a bit too testing.

Usain Colt looked useful when winning an extended 6f maiden here on the second of his two juvenile starts (form has already been franked), but he raced keenly on much softer ground this time. He's easily excused. (op 8-1)

Newnton Lodge remains a headstrong sort. However, he could prove a different proposition in a big-field, strongly run race, and it's worth remembering subsequent Britannia winner Fifteen Love, who represented the same owner/trainer combination, failed to beat a rival in this race on similarly testing ground in 2008. (op 20-1 tchd 25-1)

1501 COLN VALLEY STUD BRIDGET MAIDEN FILLIES' STKS 7f (S)

3:15 (3:16) (Class 4) 3-Y-O £4,528 (£1,347; £673; £336) **Stalls** Centre

Form	Pos	Dist	Horse	Jockey	RPR
	1		**Sentaril** 3-9-0 0 (William Haggas) *in tch: hdwy to chse clr ldr ins fnl 2f: qcknd to ld ins fnl f: wnt wl clr fnl 120yds: impressive* **15/2**[3]	JohnnyMurtagh 5	101+
	2	*8*	**Ensejaam (CAN)** 3-9-0 0 (Charles Hills) *led: stl 4 l clr 2f out: drvn and qcknd sn after: hdd by wnr ins fnl f and sn easily outpcd but stl wl clr of remainder* **12/1**	TadhgO'Shea 8	77
	3	*5*	**Love Tatoo (IRE)** 3-9-0 0 (Andrew Balding) *hld up in rr: stdy hdwy over 2f out: styd on wl ins fnl f to take wl hld 3rd fnl strides* **16/1**	JimmyFortune 19	64+
	4	*nk*	**Light Zabeel (USA)** 3-9-0 0 (Mick Channon) *chsd ldr but no ch fr over 2f out and sn dropped to 3rd: no ch w ldng duo fr over 1f out but kpt on tl ct for 3rd last strides* **16/1**	MartinHarley 12	63
	5	*2½*	**Radioactive** 3-9-0 0 (Ralph Beckett) *in tch: pushed along 3f out: styd on fnl 2f but nvr any ch* **8/1**	JimCrowley 15	57
	6	*2½*	**Divine Pamina (IRE)** 3-9-0 0 (Jim Boyle) *in rr: pushed along and green over 2f out: styd on ins fnl f* **33/1**	TomQueally 17	50+
	7	*1¼*	**Revelette (USA)** 3-9-0 0 (Charles Hills) *mid-div and pushed along 3f out: styd on fnl 2f* **10/1**	MichaelHills 11	47
	8	*shd*	**Sputnik Sweetheart** 3-9-0 0 (Richard Hannon) *s.i.s: hdwy and wl in tch 1/2-way: drvn: green and edgd rt over 2f out: stl green and kpt on same pce* **8/1**	PatDobbs 13	46+
	9	*½*	**Lashyn (USA)** 3-9-0 0 (Sir Michael Stoute) *chsd ldrs: rdn 3f out: wknd ins fnl 2f* **7/1**[2]	RyanMoore 7	45
	10	*5*	**Blissamore** 3-9-0 0 (Hughie Morrison) *in rr: rdn 3f out: sme prog over 2f out: nvr in contention and wknd sn after* **33/1**	DarryllHolland 2	32
	11	*3*	**Selfara** 3-9-0 0 (Roger Charlton) *slowly away and wnt rt s: towards rr most of way* **7/1**[2]	JamesDoyle 20	24
	12	*1½*	**Manaar (USA)** 3-9-0 0 (John Gosden) *chsd ldrs tl rdn and lost pl 1/2-way: no ch after* **9/2**[1]	PaulHanagan 9	20
	13	*1¾*	**Rum Punch** 3-9-0 0 (Eve Johnson Houghton) *chsd ldrs: bmpd and wknd over 2f out* **33/1**	CathyGannon 14	16
	14	*7*	**Ishi** 3-9-0 0 (Rod Millman) *a in rr* **66/1**	JamesMillman 16	
	15	*1*	**Haraqaan** 3-9-0 0 (Clive Brittain) *racd wd fr 1/2-way and sn bhd* **50/1**	BrettDoyle 1	
	16	*½*	**Doyle's Dream** 3-9-0 0 (Michael Madgwick) *chsd ldrs: rdn: green and wknd 1/2-way* **100/1**	JamieGoldstein 6	
	17	*9*	**Witchy Moments (IRE)** 3-8-9 0 (Paul Cole) *pushed wd after 3f: sn wl bhd* **16/1**	DuilioDaSilva(5) 4	

18 16 **Big Old Unit** 3-9-0 0 RichardKingscote 18
(Tom Dascombe) *sn rdn: green and bhd* **33/1**

1m 32.18s (6.48) **Going Correction** +0.90s/f (Soft) 18 Ran SP% **127.8**
Speed ratings (Par 97): **98,88,83,82,79 77,75,75,74,69 65,64,62,54,52 52,42,23**
toteswingers:1&2:£17.20, 2&3:£35.00, 1&3:£27.60 CSF £94.00 TOTE £8.60: £3.10, £3.90, £5.40; EX 119.30 Trifecta £367.30 Part won. Pool: £496.47 - 0.10 winning units..
Owner Lael Stable **Bred** Lael Stables **Trained** Newmarket, Suffolk

FOCUS
This fillies' maiden has gone to a subsequent Group-race winner three times in the last eight years, notably Promising Lead, who was successful at the highest level. The form is obviously fluid but the winner rates as above average.
Haraqaan Official explanation: jockey said filly hung left

1502 WHITLEY STUD MAIDEN FILLIES' STKS (DIV I) 1m 2f 6y
3:50 (3:51) (Class 4) 3-Y-O **£4,528** (£1,347; £673; £336) **Stalls** Low

Form RPR
1 **Vow** 3-9-0 0 JohnnyMurtagh 15 88+
(William Haggas) *in rr: pushed along 5f out: hdwy 3f out: styd on strly and 3rd 1f out: chsd ldrs 100yds out: fin wl to ld last 50yds* **11/2**
246- 2 1 **Everlong**[224] 5885 3-9-0 89 [1] JamieSpencer 2 86
(Peter Chapple-Hyam) *led: drvn 3 l clr jst ins fnl f: hdd and no ex in clsng stages* **4/1**[2]
- 3 4 ½ **Devine Guest (IRE)** 3-9-0 0 MartinHarley 11 77
(Mick Channon) *mid-div: hdwy over 3f out: chsng ldr over 1f out: kpt on same pce* **33/1**
0-3 4 3 ¾ **Hunt A Mistress (IRE)**[15] 1206 3-9-0 0 JimmyFortune 9 70
(Paul Cole) *chsd ldrs: wknd fnl f* **10/1**
0- 5 1 ¼ **Young Lou**[153] 7493 3-9-0 0 RoystonFfrench 7 67
(Robin Dickin) *gave problems in stalls: hmpd s: sn chsng ldrs: wknd over 1f out* **100/1**
0- 6 2 ½ **Sequence (IRE)**[170] 7233 3-9-0 0 RyanMoore 3 62+
(Sir Michael Stoute) *trckd ldrs: effrt over 3f out: wknd over 1f out* **9/1**
45 7 1 ¼ **Findeln**[21] 1107 3-9-0 0 CathyGannon 5 60
(Eve Johnson Houghton) *chsd ldrs: wknd over 1f out* **100/1**
8 2 **Amaraja (GER)** 3-9-0 0 TomQueally 12 56+
(Sir Henry Cecil) *in rr: hdwy on wd outside over 2f out: nvr nr ldrs* **5/1**[3]
5- 9 7 **Gallipot**[181] 7025 3-9-0 0 WilliamBuick 10 42+
(John Gosden) *trckd ldrs: effrt over 3f out: wknd 2f out* **7/2**[1]
5- 10 5 **Vickers Vimy**[140] 7598 3-9-0 0 JimCrowley 6 32
(Ralph Beckett) *hmpd s: t.k.h towards rr: effrt over 3f out: nvr a factor* **20/1**
11 15 **Eight Letters (USA)** 3-9-0 0 HayleyTurner 14
(Michael Bell) *in rr: drvn 4f out: bhd fnl 2f* **40/1**
12 26 **Runway Girl (IRE)** 3-9-0 0 JamesDoyle 13
(Roger Charlton) *hld up in rr: nvr a factor: bhd fnl 2f: t.o* **25/1**
13 20 **Four Leaves (IRE)** 3-9-0 0 AdamKirby 8
(Marco Botti) *mid-div: drvn over 3f out: bhd 2f out: eased: t.o* **16/1**
06 14 57 **Optimism**[21] 1107 3-9-0 0 MartinDwyer 1
(William Muir) *chsd ldrs: drvn 4f out: wknd over 2f out: bhd whn eased over 1f out: hopelessly t.o* **100/1**

2m 20.37s (11.57) **Going Correction** +1.325s/f (Soft) 14 Ran SP% **116.2**
Speed ratings (Par 97): **106,105,101,98,97 95,94,93,87,83 71,50,34,**
toteswingers:1&2:£6.30, 2&3:£26.10, 1&3:£51.40 CSF £25.34 TOTE £6.40: £2.60, £1.50, £9.80; EX 29.60 Trifecta £490.90 Part won. Pool: £663.44 - 0.50 winning units..
Owner Highclere Thoroughbred Racing-Pocahontas **Bred** J B Haggas **Trained** Newmarket, Suffolk

FOCUS
A maiden that's been won by a couple of Oaks winners in recent years, Eswarah in 2005 and Dancing Rain last season. Both Islington and Folk Opera also took this en-route to top-level honours. The form looks decent with the time good and the runner-up sets the standard.

1503 WHITLEY STUD MAIDEN FILLIES' STKS (DIV II) 1m 2f 6y
4:25 (4:26) (Class 4) 3-Y-O **£4,528** (£1,347; £673; £336) **Stalls** Low

Form RPR
3- 1 **Inchina**[181] 7030 3-9-0 0 JamesDoyle 11 80
(Roger Charlton) *mde all: qcknd 2f out: shkn up and edgd lft and rt ins fnl f: drvn and asserted fnl 120yds* **2/1**[1]
3 2 ½ **Red Hand (USA)**[21] 1107 3-9-0 0 WilliamBuick 10 79
(John Gosden) *trckd wnr thrght: drvn over 2f out: styd on and effrt ins fnl f: outpcd fnl 120yds but hld on wl for 2nd in clsng stages* **16/1**
62-2 3 nk **Safarjal (IRE)**[29] 990 3-9-0 77 [1] PaulHanagan 14 78+
(Charles Hills) *hld up in rr: hdwy fr 2f out: drvn and styd on fnl f to take 3rd fnl 120yds: clsng on 2nd nr fin but no imp on wnr* **8/1**[3]
4 2 **Momentary** 3-9-0 0 HayleyTurner 2 74
(Michael Bell) *trckd ldrs: drvn: edgd lft and styd on to take 3rd ins fnl 2f: sn no imp: wknd into 4th fnl 120yds* **25/1**
5 ¾ **Caphene** 3-9-0 0 TedDurcan 4 73+
(John Dunlop) *s.i.s: in rr: pushed along and green on ins over 3f out: kpt on fnl f but nvr any ch* **25/1**
6 ½ **Require** 3-9-0 0 KierenFallon 5 72+
(Luca Cumani) *trckd ldrs: pushed along over 2f out: styd on same pce fr over 1f out* **9/1**
4- 7 22 **Popular**[176] 7118 3-9-0 0 TomQueally 6 28
(Sir Henry Cecil) *disp 2nd to 3f out: wknd over 2f out* **9/4**[2]
0- 8 4 **Despatch**[182] 6985 3-9-0 0 JimCrowley 12 20
(Ralph Beckett) *in rr: shkn up on outside over 3f out: no imp and sn wknd* **9/1**
9 ½ **Cape Alex** 3-9-0 0 BrettDoyle 7 19
(Clive Brittain) *slowly away: green and in rr: tried to cl on main gp over 3f out: sn wknd* **40/1**

2m 24.8s (16.00) **Going Correction** +1.325s/f (Soft) 9 Ran SP% **111.2**
Speed ratings (Par 97): **89,88,88,86,86 85,68,64,64**
toteswingers:1&2:£6.90, 2&3:£5.60, 1&3:£4.10 CSF £32.48 TOTE £3.00: £1.20, £3.20, £2.40; EX 31.70 Trifecta £109.60 Pool of £839.34 - 5.66 winning units..
Owner A E Oppenheimer **Bred** Hascombe And Valiant Studs **Trained** Beckhampton, Wilts

FOCUS
The second division of what is so often a red-hot fillies' maiden. The winner improved on her debut while the placed horses set the standard.

1504 DUBAI DUTY FREE GOLF WORLD CUP CONDITIONS STKS 1m 2f 6y
4:55 (4:56) (Class 3) 3-Y-O **£6,536** (£1,957; £978; £489) **Stalls** Low

Form RPR
110- 1 **Ekthiaam (IRE)**[195] 6689 3-9-3 100 PaulHanagan 6 112
(Roger Varian) *hld up in 4th: stdy hdwy 3f out: trckd ldr over 2f out: led over 1f out: drvn clr ins fnl f: comf* **11/4**[2]
01- 2 5 **Wrotham Heath**[191] 6805 3-8-13 87 TomQueally 2 98
(Sir Henry Cecil) *t.k.h: led: hdd over 5f out: led again over 3f out: drvn and hdd over 1f out: outpcd by wnr ins fnl f* **10/11**[1]
61- 3 8 **Halling's Quest**[179] 7066 3-8-13 0 DarryllHolland 3 82
(Hughie Morrison) *chsd ldr: led over 5f out: hdd over 3f out: wknd 2f out* **7/1**
1- 4 23 **Gold Rally (USA)**[189] 6828 3-8-13 0 FrankieDettori 5 36
(Mahmood Al Zarooni) *chsd ldrs in 3rd: rdn 4f out: hung lft fr 3f out and sn btn: eased fnl f* **9/2**[3]

2m 20.9s (12.10) **Going Correction** +1.325s/f (Soft) 4 Ran SP% **109.7**
Speed ratings (Par 102): **104,100,93,75**
CSF £5.82 TOTE £4.00; EX 6.50.
Owner Hamdan Al Maktoum **Bred** Bernard Cooke **Trained** Newmarket, Suffolk

FOCUS
A conditions event that's been contested by loads of smart types over the years, the most notable in recent times being Light Shift, who won en-route to taking the 2007 Epsom Oaks. This year's race rather fell apart, as the keen-going runner-up and the third did too much too soon, and Gold Rally completely flopped. The form looks muddling but has been treated at something like face value for the moment.

NOTEBOOK
Ekthiaam(IRE) struggled in the Dewhurst when last seen, but he'd previously won a maiden here and followed up in the same Doncaster conditions event that Frankel had won the previous year. He's done well physically from two to three and settled better than when last seen, travelling nicely throughout. No future target was nominated by connections, but he's likely to stay at this trip and holds a Dante entry. In the longer term, he could be one for the Hampton Court at Royal Ascot. (op 10-3)
Wrotham Heath looked pretty good when winning a 1m Nottingham maiden on his final outing at two, and these conditions looked made for a horse with such a powerful, round action, but he was simply too keen. Interestingly, while Sir Henry Cecil had won this race twice in the last five years, his two most recent runners were both beaten before going on to win at Group level, namely Father Time (King Edward VII Stakes) and Bullet Train (Lingfield Derby Trial). (tchd 5-6)
Halling's Quest was up in class and trip after a 1m Southwell maiden win last October, and he went off plenty fast enough. It's probably significant he was thought good enough to run in this race and he'll be worth another try. (op 8-1 tchd 11-1)
Gold Rally(USA) created a good impression when winning a 1m maiden at Haydock on testing ground last year, but he's not exactly bred for such conditions and struggled this time. That said, his yard's runners really are hit and miss at the moment. (op 4-1 tchd 5-1)

1505 DREWEATTS 1759 H'CAP 2m
5:25 (5:26) (Class 4) (0-85,83) 4-Y-O+ **£4,528** (£1,347; £673; £336) **Stalls** Low

Form RPR
5-33 1 **Gilded Age**[22] 1085 6-8-10 67 (tp) SamHitchcott 7 77
(Chris Gordon) *led: rdn whn jnd fr over 3f out: stl hrd pressed fr 2f out tl asserted gamely in clsng stages* **25/1**
-160 2 ½ **First Avenue**[13] 1214 7-9-1 79 CharlotteJenner(7) 4 88
(Laura Mongan) *in tch: trckd wnr 4f out: str chal fr over 3f out and stl upsides thrght fnl f tl no ex in clsng stages* **14/1**
201- 3 shd **Blazing Field**[187] 6893 4-9-1 76 AdamKirby 2 85
(Clive Cox) *chsd ldrs: wnt 3rd 3f out: styd on to chal ins fnl f: kpt on in clsng stages to press for 2nd but a jst hld by wnr* **5/1**[2]
/0-2 4 14 **Henry San (IRE)**[49] 594 5-8-12 69 SilvestreDeSousa 10 61
(Alan King) *in tch chsd ldrs 1/2-way: rdn 3f out and sn btn* **8/1**
0/0- 5 nk **Natural High (IRE)**[37] 5954 7-9-10 81 JamesDoyle 13 73
(Paul Rich) *chsd ldrs tl wknd qckly over 3f out* **15/2**
12-6 6 3 ¾ **O Ma Lad (IRE)**[27] 1037 4-8-11 75 SophieDoyle(3) 11 63
(Sylvester Kirk) *in rr: hdwy and hung rt fr 3f out: no ch after* **16/1**
054- 7 shd **Roberto Pegasus (USA)**[187] 6893 6-9-4 75 IanMongan 8 63
(Pat Phelan) *chsd ldrs tl wknd fr 3f out* **7/2**[1]
100- 8 14 **L Frank Baum (IRE)**[189] 6832 5-9-6 77 (p) MartinLane 1 48
(Bernard Llewellyn) *nvr rchd ldrs: rdn and bhd fnl 4f* **7/1**
451- 9 3 ¼ **Hidden Valley**[187] 6891 4-8-12 73 (v) DavidProbert 5 40
(Andrew Balding) *in tch to 1/2-way: bhd fnl 4f* **13/2**[3]
-221 10 shd **The Absent Mare**[22] 1085 4-8-6 67 RoystonFfrench 6 34
(Robin Dickin) *s.i.s: in rr: hdwy and in tch 5f out: chsd ldrs 4f out: wknd 3f out* **14/1**
6/0- 11 11 **Spirit Of Adjisa (IRE)**[97] 4423 8-9-12 83 PaulHanagan 14 36
(Tim Vaughan) *chsd ldr to 5f out: wknd 3f out* **14/1**

3m 53.68s (21.68) **Going Correction** +1.325s/f (Soft)
WFA 4 from 5yo+ 4lb 11 Ran SP% **117.3**
Speed ratings (Par 105): **98,97,97,90,90 88,88,81,80,79 74**
toteswingers:1&2:£47.00, 2&3:£15.50, 1&3:£20.40 CSF £336.17 CT £2041.53 TOTE £37.60: £8.70, £4.90, £2.60; EX 386.10 TRIFECTA Not won..
Owner Draper Edmonds Draper **Bred** Darley **Trained** Morestead, Hants

FOCUS
Not many of these coped with such a demanding test and the front three finished well clear but this is not form to take too literally.
O Ma Lad(IRE) Official explanation: jockey said gelding hung right in home straight
T/Jkpt: £18,204.70 to a £1 stake. Pool of £76,921.56 - 3.00 winning tickets. T/Plt: £701.50 to a £1 stake. Pool of £90,617.66 - 94.29 winning tickets. T/Qpdt: £128.90 to a £1 stake. Pool of £7819.64 - 44.86 winning tickets. ST

1498 NEWBURY (L-H)
Saturday, April 21
OFFICIAL GOING: Soft (good to soft in places; 5.1)

1506 DUBAI DUTY FREE TENNIS CHAMPIONSHIPS MAIDEN STKS (DIV I) 1m (S)
1:30 (1:32) (Class 4) 3-Y-O **£5,175** (£1,540; £769; £384) **Stalls** Centre

Form RPR
2- 1 **Noble Mission**[179] 7082 3-9-3 0 [1] TomQueally 10 98+
(Sir Henry Cecil) *t.k.h early: trckd ldrs: led travelling wl 1f out: sn clr: easily* **3/1**[1]
6- 2 3 ¾ **Dream Tune**[183] 6993 3-9-3 0 AdamKirby 1 89+
(Clive Cox) *hld up in mid-div: gd hdwy over 2f out: styd on wl to take 2nd fnl 120yds but no imp on wnr* **6/1**[3]
5- 3 5 **Captain Cat (IRE)**[183] 6994 3-9-3 0 JamesDoyle 4 77
(Roger Charlton) *trckd ldrs: wnt 2nd 3f out: led 2f out: hdd 1f out: sn one pce: lost 2nd fnl 120yds* **9/1**
4 1 ½ **Gold Show** 3-8-12 0 MartinHarley 8 69
(Mick Channon) *in rr: hdwy fr 2f out: styd on wl fnl f: nt rch ldrs* **40/1**
5 nk **On My Own (TUR)** 3-9-3 0 HayleyTurner 3 73
(Marcus Tregoning) *in tch: pushed along over 2f out: styd on fnl f: nt a danger* **22/1**
00- 6 6 **Wreaths Of Empire (IRE)**[183] 6993 3-9-3 0 PatDobbs 12 60+
(Richard Hannon) *chsd ldr to 3f out: sn rdn: wknd 2f out* **25/1**

7 1 1/4 **Dick Bos** 3-9-3 0 JimmyFortune 2 57+
(Peter Chapple-Hyam) *t.k.h in rr: hdwy fr 3f out: in tch 2f out: sn outpcd* **16/1**

8 hd **Essell** 3-8-12 0 SamHitchcott 5 51
(Mick Channon) *chsd ldrs: rdn over 2f out: sn wknd* **80/1**

9 2 1/4 **Fly On By** 3-9-3 0 DaneO'Neill 9 51
(Henry Candy) *s.i.s: sn drvn in rr: nvr gng pce to get into contention* **80/1**

32- 10 1 1/2 **Cappielow Park**[162] 7367 3-9-3 0 KierenFallon 14 48
(William Jarvis) *disp 2nd: rdn over 2f out: sn btn* **8/1**

11 hd **Seventh Sign** 3-9-3 0 PaulHanagan 13 47+
(William Haggas) *slowly away: bhd most of way* **9/1**

3- 12 15 **Ibtahaj**[206] 6447 3-9-3 0 FrankieDettori 6
(Saeed Bin Suroor) *led: c to stands' side over 3f out: hdd 2f out and wknd qckly* **9/2**[2]

13 3/4 **Modern Tutor** 3-9-3 0 RyanMoore 7
(Sir Michael Stoute) *s.i.s: bhd most of way* **12/1**

63- 14 15 **Berengar (IRE)**[226] 5861 3-9-3 0 MartinDwyer 11
(Brian Meehan) *mid-div early: bhd fnl 3f* **16/1**

1m 47.29s (7.59) **Going Correction** +1.00s/f (Soft) 14 Ran SP% **121.1**
Speed ratings (Par 100): **102,98,93,91,91 85,84,84,81,80 80,65,64,49**
Tote Swingers: 1&2 £4.10, 1&3 £5.80, 2&3 £8.90 CSF £19.76 TOTE £3.10: £1.60, £2.70, £2.60; EX 18.00 Trifecta £281.60 Pool: £506.13 - 1.33 winning units..
Owner K Abdulla **Bred** Juddmonte Farms Ltd **Trained** Newmarket, Suffolk

FOCUS
The rail from the 1m point to the 5f point on the round course had been moved out six metres to provide fresh ground. As a consequence, the round course was 15 metres longer than standard. Martin Harley described the ground as "dead", and Adam Kirby said it was "soft". Often a good maiden and this latest running should produce plenty of nice winners. They started off up the middle of the track, but gradually edged over to the stands' rail at around halfway. This is usually a good maiden and has been rated as such.
Dick Bos Official explanation: jockey said colt ran too free
Modern Tutor Official explanation: jockey said colt was slowly away

1507 DUBAI DUTY FREE FINEST SURPRISE STKS (REGISTERED AS THE JOHN PORTER STAKES) (GROUP 3) 1m 4f 5y
2:00 (2:05) (Class 1) 4-Y-0+ **£31,190** (£11,825; £5,918; £2,948; £1,479) **Stalls** Low

Form RPR

243- 1 **Harris Tweed**[231] 5711 5-8-12 115 LiamJones 3 118
(William Haggas) *mde all: pushed along over 2f out: styd on strly thrght fnl f: unchal* **6/4**[1]

550- 2 5 **Allied Powers (IRE)**[223] 5990 7-8-12 107 JamieSpencer 7 110
(Michael Bell) *hld up in 5th: hdwy to go 3rd 4f out: chsd wnr 2f out: rdn and edgd lft over 1f out: sn no imp: kpt on hands and heels whn wl hld fnl 120yds* **7/1**

/62- 3 3 **Bridge Of Gold (USA)**[371] 1403 6-8-12 106 PaulHanagan 1 105
(Mikael Magnusson) *chsd ldrs: wnt 2nd 4f out: rdn 3f out and no imp: dropped to 3rd 2f out and sn no ch* **11/2**[3]

13/ 4 dist **Eye Of The Tiger (GER)**[692] 2574 7-8-12 112 TomQueally 5
(Barney Curley) *loose bef s: chsd ldr: rdn 5f out: wknd qckly 4f out: virtually p.u over 3f out* **22/1**

24-1 5 86 **Arctic Cosmos (USA)**[21] 1137 5-8-12 111 (p) WilliamBuick 4
(John Gosden) *s.i.s: racd in cl 4th: rdn 4f out: sn btn: virtually p.u over 3f out* **13/8**[2]

2m 44.02s (8.52) **Going Correction** +1.00s/f (Soft)
WFA 4 from 5yo+ 1lb 5 Ran SP% **110.3**
Speed ratings (Par 113): **111,107,105, ,**
CSF £12.03 TOTE £2.70: £1.60, £3.50; EX 13.20.
Owner B Haggas **Bred** J B Haggas **Trained** Newmarket, Suffolk

FOCUS
This was a real test and it only concerned three of the five runners in the closing stages. The winner is rated to his best with the runner-up close to last year's form.

NOTEBOOK
Harris Tweed, who was returning from a 231-day absence, took them along at a reasonable pace considering the conditions and galloped on relentlessly, recording his first success since 2010 and his first in Group company. He relishes soft round and took this in the manner of a horse who will be well suited by a return to staying trips. The Yorkshire Cup is the obvious target provided conditions aren't too quick, and the Melbourne Cup is a possible long-term goal. (tchd 7-4)
Allied Powers(IRE), fourth in this last year, was having his first start since being gelded. He travelled strongly but the winner wasn't stopping and he couldn't seriously threaten that rival once off the bridle, edging left under pressure. This was his first start for 223 days and he's entitled to come on for it. (op 11-1 tchd 12-1)
Bridge Of Gold(USA), absent since finishing second in this race last year, travelled nicely enough but could find no extra for pressure and ran like a horse in need of the outing. (op 7-1 tchd 5-1)
Eye Of The Tiger(GER) was a Group 2 winner in Germany but he hadn't been seen since May 2010. Fitted with a cross noseband, he got loose beforehand and was enthusiastic in the race itself, before offering nothing at all once off the bridle. His official mark of 112 will soon be history and he's best left alone until contesting low-grade handicaps. (op 16-1 tchd 25-1)
Arctic Cosmos(USA) has been lightly raced since winning the 2010 St Leger and, while he did win a weak 1m2f Listed race at Kempton on his reappearance, he ran poorly here. There were a number of possible excuses, including the bounce factor and the testing ground, but he'll be difficult to support with confidence next time. Official explanation: trainer said horse was unsuited by the soft (good to soft in places) ground (op 6-4 tchd 11-8)

1508 DUBAI DUTY FREE STKS (REGISTERED AS THE FRED DARLING STAKES) (GROUP 3) (FILLIES) 7f (S)
2:35 (2:35) (Class 1) 3-Y-0
£31,190 (£11,825; £5,918; £2,948; £1,479; £742) **Stalls** Centre

Form RPR

1 1 **Moonstone Magic**[8] 1357 3-9-0 85 JimCrowley 1 109
(Ralph Beckett) *hld up in rr but in tch: gd hdwy to trck ldrs over 2f out: led 1f out drvn clr ins fnl f: edgd rt: comf* **7/2**[2]

123- 2 3 3/4 **Radio Gaga**[176] 7135 3-9-0 91 RichardMullen 2 99
(Ed McMahon) *trckd ldrs: chal 3f out: led over 2f out: sn drvn: hdd 1f out: sn outpcd by wnr and hung rt but kpt on for clr 2nd* **10/1**

14- 3 9 **Electrelane**[151] 7508 3-9-0 96 NeilCallan 3 76
(Ralph Beckett) *pressed ldr: led over 3f out: rdn and hdd over 2f out: outpcd by ldng duo wl over 1f out but kpt on to hold 3rd* **10/1**

430- 4 3 1/2 **Switcher (IRE)**[225] 5885 3-9-0 99 RichardKingscote 5 67
(Tom Dascombe) *in tch: rdn and outpcd over 2f out: styd on again fnl f to take mod 4th clsng stages* **8/1**

115- 5 1 **Best Terms**[210] 6337 3-9-0 115 RyanMoore 7 64
(Richard Hannon) *t.k.h early: led tl hdd over 3f out: styd disputing wl-hld 3rd over 1f out: wknd fnl f* **5/2**[1]

1- 6 2 **Brick Tops**[168] 7293 3-9-0 80 JamieSpencer 8 59
(David Simcock) *s.i.s: drvn and hdwy fr 3f out: disp wl hld 3rd over 1f out: wknd fnl f* **12/1**

106- 7 1 1/4 **Villeneuve**[176] 7135 3-9-0 87 MartinDwyer 4 55
(William Muir) *sn towards rr: drvn and hdwy fr 3f out: jst bhd ldrs u.p wl over 1f out: sn wknd* **40/1**

415- 8 8 **Roger Sez (IRE)**[196] 6705 3-9-0 109 (b) DavidAllan 9 35
(Tim Easterby) *chsd ldrs tl wknd over 2f out* **15/2**

13- 9 4 1/2 **Fillionaire**[182] 7028 3-9-0 96 MartinHarley 6 23
(Mick Channon) *chsd ldrs: rdn 3f out: sn btn* **6/1**[3]

1m 31.56s (5.86) **Going Correction** +1.00s/f (Soft) 9 Ran SP% **116.3**
Speed ratings (Par 105): **106,101,91,87,86 84,82,73,68**
Tote Swingers: 1&2 £9.20, 1&3 £4.00, 2&3 £11.90 CSF £38.54 TOTE £4.90: £1.90, £3.50, £3.40; EX 48.20 TRIFECTA Part won. Pool: £1,275.85 - 0.30 winning units..
Owner Lady Marchwood **Bred** Lady Marchwood **Trained** Kimpton, Hants

FOCUS
The last winner of the Fred Darling to follow up in the 1000 Guineas was Wince back in 1999, and there's little chance that will change this year unless Moonstone Magic is supplemented (would cost £30,000 on April 30) and the ground at Newmarket comes up soft. This doesn't look strong form, but the time was 0.76 seconds quicker than the Greenham.

NOTEBOOK
Moonstone Magic, who had made a successful debut on similar ground at Leicester just eight days earlier, put up a smart performance to readily account for the runner-up with the pair well clear. It remains to be seen where she goes next, and she's not certain to get 1m, but she's a big filly who's open to more improvement. (op 4-1)
Radio Gaga improved on the form she showed over 6f last year. She's entered in the Guineas, but was outstayed by the winner here and probably won't get much further for now. (op 14-1)
Electrelane won on her debut over 7f on soft ground, so conditions suited, but she wasn't good enough on this return from a five-month break. (tchd 9-1)
Switcher(IRE) failed to beat a rival in the May Hill when last seen and this wasn't an obviously encouraging return, as she was keen early and only ran on when the race was as good as over. (tchd 9-1)
Best Terms won the Queen Mary and Lowther last year, but struggled in the Cheveley Park on her final juvenile outing and she's hasn't grown much over the winter. The ground and the trip were both question marks here and she gave herself no chance by refusing to settle. (tchd 9-4 and 11-4)
Brick Tops, who won a 6f Doncaster maiden on soft ground for Ralph Beckett last year, missed the break and never got involved. Official explanation: vet said filly returned lame (op 9-1)
Roger Sez(IRE) had the ground to suit but was unproven at the trip and offered nothing after a 196-day break. (op 6-1 tchd 11-2)
Fillionaire presumably didn't handle the ground. (op 15-2 tchd 8-1)

1509 AON GREENHAM STKS (GROUP 3) (C&G) 7f (S)
3:10 (3:10) (Class 1) 3-Y-0 **£31,190** (£11,825; £5,918; £2,948; £1,479) **Stalls** Centre

Form RPR

150- 1 **Caspar Netscher**[168] 7301 3-9-0 114 ShaneKelly 6 110
(Alan McCabe) *stdd s: trcking ldrs in 3rd: impr and swtchd rt wl over 1f out: drvn to ld ins fnl f: styd on strly* **3/1**[2]

222- 2 1 **Boomerang Bob (IRE)**[293] 3669 3-9-0 105 SebSanders 3 107
(J W Hills) *t.k.h early and stdd towards rr: hdwy over 2f out to ld wl over 1f out: hdd ins fnl f: kpt on but nt pce of wnr* **20/1**

114- 3 1 3/4 **Bronterre**[196] 6689 3-9-0 114 RyanMoore 4 103
(Richard Hannon) *plld hrd early: trckd ldr: led ins fnl 3f: rdn and hdd wl over 1f out: styd on same pce ins fnl f* **8/11**[1]

010- 4 18 **Rebellious Guest**[196] 6688 3-9-0 99 TomQueally 1 56
(George Margarson) *t.k.h early: a in rr: lost tch fnl 2f* **9/1**

310- 5 18 **Spiritual Star (IRE)**[196] 6689 3-9-0 109 JimmyFortune 5
(Andrew Balding) *led tl hdd ins fnl 3f: wknd 2f out: sn eased whn no ch* **8/1**[3]

1m 32.32s (6.62) **Going Correction** +1.00s/f (Soft) 5 Ran SP% **108.8**
Speed ratings (Par 108): **102,100,98,78,57**
CSF £43.21 TOTE £3.70: £1.50, £3.10; EX 38.60.
Owner Charles Wentworth **Bred** Meon Valley Stud **Trained** Averham Park, Notts

FOCUS
Last year the brilliant Frankel became the first horse since Wollow in 1976 to win the Greenham and follow up in the 2000 Guineas. The form of this latest running looks relatively weak, and the time was 0.76 seconds slower than the Fred Darling, suggesting the form may not prove to be reliable.

NOTEBOOK
Caspar Netscher, last year's Gimcrack and Mill Reef winner, looked to win in spite of the testing ground. He was too keen in the Breeders' Cup Juvenile Turf when last seen, and was again a touch headstrong through the early stages here, but he soon settled better than the favourite. Once under pressure he looked rather laboured, but he did enough to record his third Group-race success. He deserves to take his chance in the Guineas (generally 25-1), but he'll need to improve markedly on this performance, and while quicker going will help him, the longer trip probably won't. (op 7-2 tchd 4-1)
Boomerang Bob(IRE), last year's Norfolk runner-up, reportedly picked up an injury after finishing second in a Chantilly Group 3 in July, and he was untested beyond 5f, but this was a fine reappearance. It's hard to say he didn't get the trip as he was entitled to need the run. While he'd be a prime candidate to bounce if out again any time soon, there could be more to come in the long term. John Hills said the colt will be aimed at a Guineas, and mentioned both Newmarket and France. (op 16-1)
Bronterre ◆ had been the choice of Richard Hughes over recent Craven winner Trumpet Major in the Dewhurst, and finished one place ahead of his stablemate in fourth that day, but he was nowhere near that form on this return. He has a Listed win on easy ground to his name, but conditions were more demanding here and he gave himself no hope by racing too keenly, much like the same stable's runner in the Fred Darling. While this was hardly an ideal trial, he'll still be worth his place in the Guineas as he should be a different proposition granted a stronger pace against a bigger field. (op 4-6)
Rebellious Guest had stamina to prove and pulled hard. (op 10-1 tchd 11-1)
Spiritual Star(IRE) flopped when supplemented for the Dewhurst last season, and this was a disappointing return. He presumably disliked the ground. (op 15-2)

1510 BERRY BROS & RUDD MAGNUM SPRING CUP (H'CAP) 1m (S)
3:45 (3:48) (Class 2) (0-105,99) 4-Y-0+
£24,900 (£7,456; £3,728; £1,864; £932; £468) **Stalls** Centre

Form RPR

00-4 1 **Captain Bertie (IRE)**[21] 1128 4-8-7 85 WilliamCarson 7 98
(Charles Hills) *trckd ldrs: led 2f out: hung rt u.p fr 1f out: hld on wl clsng stages* **7/1**[3]

40-3 2 nk **Fury**[21] 1130 4-9-7 99 KierenFallon 21 111
(William Haggas) *hld up in rr: hdwy fr 3f out: chsd wnr 1f out: carried rt u.p jst ins fnl f: continued to edge rt: no ex clsng stages* **6/1**[1]

2051 3 1 1/2 **Global Village (IRE)**[8] 1354 7-8-8 86 PaulHanagan 8 95
(Brian Ellison) *mid-dvision: hdwy over 2f out: rdn to take 3rd ins fnl f: kpt on but no imp on ldng duo clsng stages* **14/1**

00-1 **4** 2 **Karaka Jack**[20] 1156 5-8-7 **85**.......... TadhgO'Shea 11 89
(David Nicholls) *in rr: pushed along and hdwy ins fnl 2f: edging lft and styd on wl fnl f to take 4th clsng stages* **33/1**

111- **5** 1 **Emilio Largo**[276] 4214 4-9-0 **92**.......... TomQueally 13 94
(Sir Henry Cecil) *in tch: drvn to chse ldrs fr 2f out on one pce whn hmpd ins fnl f: sn no ex* **16/1**

40-0 **6** 1 ¾ **Capaill Liath (IRE)**[14] 1212 4-8-8 **89**..........(p) JulieBurke(3) 9 87
(Kevin Ryan) *led: hdd 2f out: styd pressing wnr tl over 1f out: wknd ins fnl f* **66/1**

14-3 **7** nk **Mont Ras (IRE)**[21] 1128 5-8-10 **88**.......... WilliamBuick 2 85+
(David O'Meara) *trckd ldrs: rdn and effrt 2f out: nvr quite gng pce to get on terms: no ex fnl f* **16/1**

3114 **8** ½ **Maverik**[14] 1212 4-8-6 **84**.......... JimCrowley 14 80+
(Ralph Beckett) *chsd ldrs: rdn 2f out: wknd ins fnl f* **33/1**

310- **9** 4 ½ **Vainglory (USA)**[182] 7029 8-8-9 **92**.......... LauraPike(5) 5 77
(David Simcock) *in rr: styd on fnl 2f: nvr a threat* **66/1**

5-12 **10** 3 ¾ **Mull Of Killough (IRE)**[21] 1130 6-9-7 **99**.......... ShaneKelly 23 76+
(Jane Chapple-Hyam) *in rr: styd on ins fnl f: nvr any ch* **11/1**

-340 **11** 1 **Sinfonico (IRE)**[10] 1321 4-8-4 **82**.......... KieranO'Neill 12 57
(Richard Hannon) *in rr: hdwy over 2f out: one pce fr over 1f out and nvr any ch* **40/1**

310- **12** 2 ¾ **Labarinto**[217] 6163 4-9-5 **97**.......... RyanMoore 17 65
(Sir Michael Stoute) *nvr gng pce to get into contention* **12/1**

0-00 **13** 1 ¼ **Pintura**[21] 1130 5-9-3 **95**.......... JamieSpencer 10 60
(David Simcock) *in rr: hdwy fr 3f out and in tch over 2f out: sn rdn and no imp: eased whn no ch fnl f* **14/1**

10-4 **14** ½ **Oriental Scot**[10] 1321 5-8-3 **84**.......... HarryBentley(3) 18 48
(William Jarvis) *s.i.s: nvr gng pce to get beyond mid-div:* **14/1**

10-3 **15** 1 ¾ **Highland Knight (IRE)**[14] 1212 5-9-4 **96**..........(t) DavidProbert 4 56
(Andrew Balding) *chsd ldrs: rdn 3f out: wknd qckly over 2f out* **20/1**

2121 **16** 6 **George Guru**[28] 1035 5-8-10 **93**.......... MarkCoumbe(5) 19 39+
(Michael Attwater) *chsd ldrs 5f* **25/1**

620- **17** ¾ **Cruiser**[201] 6574 4-8-7 **85**.......... MartinDwyer 16 30
(William Muir) *in tch: rdn 1/2-way: sn btn* **33/1**

140- **18** 6 **Dubawi Sound**[175] 7168 4-8-10 **88**.......... NeilCallan 20 19
(Roger Varian) *in tch: rdn over 3f out: sn wknd* **13/2**[2]

0-00 **19** 22 **The Tichborne (IRE)**[14] 1212 4-8-7 **85**.......... LukeMorris 6
(Roger Teal) *pressed ldrs tl wknd qckly over 2f out: eased whn no ch fnl f* **33/1**

/20- **20** 9 **Heddwyn (IRE)**[308] 3156 5-8-10 **88**.......... HayleyTurner 22
(Marcus Tregoning) *s.i.s: in rr: rdn and dropped away fnl 3f: eased fnl f* **12/1**

3101 **21** 24 **Nazreef**[14] 1212 5-8-9 **87**..........(vt) DarryllHolland 15
(Hughie Morrison) *chsd ldrs: rdn over 3f out and sn btn: eased fnl f* **16/1**

11-0 **22** 12 **Take It To The Max**[27] 1043 5-9-0 **97**..........(p) ShaneBKelly(5) 3
(Richard Fahey) *chsd ldrs to 1/2-way: wknd 3f out: eased whn no ch fnl f* **33/1**

1m 45.79s (6.09) **Going Correction** +1.00s/f (Soft) **22** Ran SP% **130.2**
Speed ratings (Par 109): **109,108,107,105,104 102,102,101,97,93 92,89,88,87,86 80,79,73,51,42 18,6**
Tote Swingers: 1&2 £14.70, 1&3 £6.20, 2&3 £94.50 CSF £45.20 CT £606.61 TOTE £8.10: £2.40, £1.90, £3.70, £5.90; EX 43.20 TRIFECTA Pool: £4,133.94 - 5.40 winning units..
Owner A L R Morton **Bred** Glending Bloodstock **Trained** Lambourn, Berks
■ Stewards' Enquiry : William Carson one-day ban: careless riding (May 7)

FOCUS
Traditionally a hot handicap and competitive, and often a follow-up race for horses that contested the Lincoln Handicap at Doncaster. That was the case again this year, with the second and third from that contest re-opposing. In recent runnings a double-figure draw has proved essential, but that did not prove to be the case this time. The field initially raced in two groups before merging after a couple of furlongs up the centre of the track, and they finished well strung out in the conditions. the first two are rated back to the best of their early 3-y-o form with the fourth helping to set the level.

NOTEBOOK
Captain Bertie(IRE), fourth in the Spring Mile last time on his first run since being gelded, had previously shown he could handle soft ground and, after being produced to lead at around the quarter-mile pole, showed plenty of resolution to hold off the runner-up. He has run well at Chester in the past and could be aimed there if a suitable race presents itself. (op 13-2)
Fury, a good third in the Lincoln on his first run in a handicap and first start since being gelded, handled the softer ground and was produced with what looked a winning run entering the final furlong. However, the winner refused to be denied. The operation has clearly had a positive effect though, and there should be races to be won this season. He handles faster ground as well and races such as the Victoria and Royal Hunt Cups could figure in his programme. (tchd 11-2)
Global Village(IRE) ◆, in good form at 6-7f this winter, translated it to turf last time, winning on soft ground. Racing off 8lb higher here, he kept on without troubling the principals, proving he gets this far in the process. The Victoria Cup could be on the cards for him. (op 16-1)
Karaka Jack made a winning reappearance over 7f at Doncaster and stays this trip. He had a bit to prove on the surface off 4lb higher but stayed on and is clearly in good heart at present.
Emilio Largo progressed really well last summer; proving fully effective at 7f, but he stays this trip and handles fast and soft ground. Racing off 6lb above his last winning mark, he was never far away but was unable to pick up in the latter stages. He should come on for the outing. (op 14-1)
Capaill Liath(IRE) finished last behind Nazreef on his reappearance, but that was his first try on the all-weather and he ran much better here. He led for a long way and did not drop away once headed.
Mont Ras(IRE) did really well for this trainer last summer, winning three of his five starts but going up 26lb as a result, and finished a close third in the Spring Mile on his reappearance. He travelled well just behind the leaders but, unproven on soft ground, he faded in the closing stages.
Maverik, in good form on Polytrack and snow since joining this yard over the winter, showed up for a good way and looks as if he is still on the upgrade.
Vainglory(USA), well suited by 1m on a sound surface but has handled soft ground in the past, stayed on steadily and should benefit from the outing.
Mull Of Killough(IRE) had been in good form for his new trainer this spring, being touched off in the Lincoln last time, but was held up early here and did not really pick up under pressure in the ground. (op 9-1)
Labarinto, quietly progressive last season, was another who was held up and failed to get involved.
George Guru had never raced on turf before, but this consistent performer on Polytrack travelled strongly for a fair way and is probably worth a try on better ground.
Dubawi Sound impressed when making a winning debut over C&D at this meeting last year with plenty of subsequent winners behind, but did not reappear until the autumn when he failed to fire, being too keen in his races. He was in trouble soon after halfway here and has something to prove now. (op 9-1)
Nazreef's trainer reported that the gelding was unsuited by the ground. Official explanation: trainer said gelding was unsuited by the soft (good to soft places) ground

1511 BATHWICK TYRES MAIDEN STKS 1m 3f 5y
4:20 (4:22) (Class 4) 3-Y-O **£5,175** (£1,540; £769; £384) **Stalls** Low

Form RPR

2 **1** **Minimise Risk**[21] 1132 3-9-3 0.......... JamieSpencer 13 92+
(Andrew Balding) *trckd ldr travelling strly: led on bit 2f out: rdn and edgd rt ins fnl f: all out* **15/8**[1]

5- **2** hd **Uriah Heep (FR)**[176] 7133 3-9-3 0.......... RyanMoore 10 91+
(Sir Michael Stoute) *trckd ldrs: effrt over 2f out: chsd wnr over 1f out: carried rt ins fnl f: jst hld* **9/2**[3]

3 7 **Synchronicity (IRE)** 3-9-3 0.......... DaneO'Neill 12 79
(Richard Hannon) *s.i.s: hdwy 8f out: drvn 4f out: hung lft: styd on fnl f: tk modest 3rd towards fin* **16/1**

53 **4** 2 ¼ **Touch Gold (IRE)**[180] 7060 3-9-3 0.......... TomQueally 14 75
(Sir Henry Cecil) *led: hdd 2f out: fdd and lost 3rd clsng stages* **4/1**[2]

5 1 ½ **Rule Book (IRE)** 3-9-3 0.......... JimmyFortune 1 72
(Richard Hannon) *s.i.s: hdwy to trck ldrs after 2f: drvn over 3f out: one pce fnl 2f* **28/1**

6 ¾ **Sign Manual** 3-9-3 0.......... HayleyTurner 8 71
(Michael Bell) *unruly s: sn trcking ldrs: drvn over 3f out: one pce fnl 2f* **20/1**

2- **7** 4 **King Of Dudes**[161] 7398 3-9-3 0.......... IanMongan 5 63
(Sir Henry Cecil) *in rr: hdwy on ins over 3f out: sn chsng ldrs: wknd fnl f* **6/1**

03- **8** 8 **Venegazzu (IRE)**[203] 6529 3-9-3 0.......... RobertHavlin 2 49
(Peter Chapple-Hyam) *trckd ldrs: drvn over 3f out: lost pl over 1f out* **8/1**

9 20 **Imperial Ruby** 3-9-3 0.......... MartinHarley 6
(Mick Channon) *s.s: in rr: drvn 4f out: sn bhd: t.o* **40/1**

2m 34.37s (13.17) **Going Correction** +1.00s/f (Soft) **9** Ran SP% **114.9**
Speed ratings (Par 100): **92,91,86,85,84 83,80,74,60**
Tote Swingers: 1&2 £1.80, 1&3 £6.70, 2&3 £14.50 CSF £10.03 TOTE £2.90: £1.30, £1.60, £3.10; EX 10.30 Trifecta £79.90 Pool: £1,175.66 - 10.88 winning units..
Owner Mrs Fitri Hay **Bred** Highclere Stud And Balmerino Bloodstock **Trained** Kingsclere, Hants

FOCUS
The best recent winner of this maiden was Hala Bek, who later finished fourth in the Epsom Derby. A couple of useful prospects pulled well clear in this latest running and the fourth helps to set the level.

1512 DUBAI DUTY FREE TENNIS CHAMPIONSHIPS MAIDEN STKS (DIV II) 1m (S)
4:55 (4:55) (Class 4) 3-Y-O **£5,175** (£1,540; £769; £384) **Stalls** Centre

Form RPR

55- **1** **Forest Row**[183] 6991 3-9-3 0.......... AdamKirby 4 91+
(Clive Cox) *trckd ldrs: drvn to ld 2f out: rdn clr fnl f: readily* **9/2**[2]

2 2 ¾ **Lucanin** 3-9-3 0.......... RyanMoore 14 82+
(Sir Michael Stoute) *s.i.s: in rr: hdwy over 2f out: swtchd rt: 1f out: green but styd on to chse wnr fnl 120yds but no imp* **4/1**[1]

3 1 **Border Legend** 3-9-3 0.......... JamesDoyle 1 80+
(Roger Charlton) *t.k.h: green: trckd ldrs: drvn to chse wnr 1f out: no imp and one pce fnl f: dropped to 3rd fnl 120yds* **4/1**[1]

5- **4** 3 **Petaluma**[288] 3813 3-8-12 0.......... MartinHarley 12 68
(Mick Channon) *in rr: pushed along over 2f out: hdwy over 1f out: styd on clsng stages but nvr a threat* **15/2**

00- **5** hd **Underwritten**[171] 7232 3-9-3 0.......... JimmyFortune 5 73
(Andrew Balding) *led: rdn and hdd 2f out: styd disputing 2nd to 1f out: sn wknd* **33/1**

00- **6** 2 ¾ **Surrey Dream (IRE)**[194] 6751 3-9-3 0.......... SebSanders 3 66?
(Roger Teal) *pressed ldrs: rdn over 2f out: styd disputing 2nd to 1f out: wknd sn after* **66/1**

7 ½ **Wasabi (IRE)** 3-8-12 0.......... TedDurcan 8 60?
(John Berry) *in rr: pushed along over 2f out: sme hdwy ins fnl f* **66/1**

0- **8** nk **Rock Band**[206] 6462 3-9-3 0.......... PatDobbs 6 64+
(Richard Hannon) *s.i.s: in rr: drvn over 2f out: styd on fnl f: nvr a threat* **14/1**

9 ½ **Bitter Harvest** 3-9-3 0.......... JamieSpencer 2 63+
(Michael Bell) *in rr: pushed along over 2f out: sme late prog* **20/1**

5- **10** 9 **Energize (FR)**[171] 7232 3-9-3 0.......... JimCrowley 9 43
(Richard Hannon) *chsd ldrs to 2f out: sn rdn and wknd* **7/1**[3]

11 2 **Regal Art** 3-9-3 0.......... FergusSweeney 10 38
(Jo Crowley) *in tch: pushed along over 2f out: sn wknd* **33/1**

12 2 **Fuzzy Logic (IRE)** 3-9-3 0.......... WilliamBuick 11 33
(William Muir) *bhd most of way* **20/1**

13 10 **London Silver** 3-9-3 0.......... DaneO'Neill 13 10
(Henry Candy) *s.i.s: bhd most of way* **33/1**

3 **14** 40 **Red Ramesses (IRE)**[23] 1086 3-9-3 0.......... LiamJones 7
(John Best) *plld hrd: chsd ldrs: rdn and wknd rapidly wl over 2f out* **17/2**

1m 48.41s (8.71) **Going Correction** +1.00s/f (Soft) **14** Ran SP% **121.0**
Speed ratings (Par 100): **96,93,92,89,89 86,85,85,85,76 74,72,62,22**
Tote Swingers: 1&2 £7.10, 1&3 £6.10, 2&3 £2.30 CSF £21.28 TOTE £7.00: £2.40, £2.10, £1.20; EX 26.90 TRIFECTA Pool: £919.51 - 15.61 winning units..
Owner The Bodkins **Bred** Mette Campbell-Andenaes **Trained** Lambourn, Berks

FOCUS
The second division of this maiden looked a decent enough contest and is rated through the fourth and the race averages. The sixth and seventh might limit the form in the long term.
Bitter Harvest Official explanation: jockey said gelding hung right

1513 DUBAI DUTY FREE MILLENNIUM MILLIONAIRE H'CAP 1m 2f 6y
5:25 (5:25) (Class 4) (0-85,85) 4-Y-O+ **£5,175** (£1,540; £769; £192; £192) **Stalls** Low

Form RPR

101- **1** **Stand To Reason (IRE)**[276] 4215 4-9-4 **82**.......... WilliamBuick 8 95+
(Mikael Magnusson) *trckd ldrs: upsides over 2f out: led over 1f out: readily* **4/1**[2]

100- **2** 3 **Always The Lady**[168] 7296 4-9-3 **81**.......... AdamKirby 7 88
(Clive Cox) *chsd ldrs: led 3f out: hdd over 1f out: styd on same pce* **12/1**

-215 **3** 2 **Dunhoy (IRE)**[21] 1134 4-9-4 **82**.......... DaneO'Neill 16 85
(Tony Newcombe) *mid-div: drvn 3f out: kpt on over 1f out: tk 3rd nr fin* **16/1**

-312 **4** ½ **Reachforthebucks**[21] 1133 4-9-6 **84**.......... JamesDoyle 14 86+
(Jane Chapple-Hyam) *trckd ldrs: cl 3rd 2f out: wknd and lost 3rd clsng stages* **10/3**[1]

642- **4** dht **Ashiri (IRE)**[264] 4617 4-9-3 **81**.......... JamieSpencer 3 83+
(David Simcock) *in rr: effrt 3f out: kpt on fnl f* **12/1**

020- **6** 9 **Fanny May**[191] 6822 4-9-7 **85**.......... JimmyFortune 15 69
(Denis Coakley) *led 1f: trckd ldrs: t.k.h: wknd over 1f out* **11/1**

512- **7** *1* **Saborido (USA)**[339] 2190 6-9-4 **82** .... JimCrowley 12 64
(Amanda Perrett) *in rr: kpt on fnl f: nvr a factor* **25/1**

5322 **8** *3 ½* **Follow The Flag (IRE)**[12] 1258 8-8-8 **72** ....(be) ShaneKelly 2 47
(Alan McCabe) *led after 1f: hdd 3f out: edgd rt and grad wknd* **14/1**

120- **9** *6* **Hot Spice**[182] 7017 4-9-2 **80** .... TedDurcan 1 43
(John Dunlop) *chsd ldrs: wknd 2f out* **8/1**

-613 **10** *4 ½* **Casual Mover (IRE)**[33] 960 4-8-12 **76** .... LiamJones 11 30
(John Best) *mid-div: effrt over 3f out: lost pl 2f out* **16/1**

1-00 **11** *2 ¼* **Daring Indian**[11] 1275 4-8-7 **74** .... RyanPowell(3) 5 24
(Ian Williams) *trckd ldrs: t.k.h: lost pl over 2f out* **16/1**

60-4 **12** *2 ½* **Mcbirney (USA)**[21] 1134 5-8-13 **77** .... RyanMoore 10 22
(Paul D'Arcy) *in rr: effrt over 3f out: sn wknd* **5/1**[3]

-UUU **13** *4 ½* **Final Drive (IRE)**[14] 1212 6-8-13 **77** ....(t) FergusSweeney 13 13
(John Butler) *s.i.s: a in rr* **33/1**

2m 17.63s (8.83) **Going Correction** +1.00s/f (Soft) **13** Ran SP% **125.7**
Speed ratings (Par 105): **104,101,100,99,99 92,91,88,84,80 78,76,73**
Tote Swingers: 1&2 £8.10, 1&3 £37.80, 2&3 £44.60 CSF £54.84 CT £722.00 TOTE £3.80: £1.70, £3.00, £5.60; EX 45.00 TRIFECTA Part won. Pool: £706.16 - 0.41 winning units..
Owner B Nielsen & Eastwind Racing & M Trussell **Bred** Coleman Bloodstock Limited **Trained** Upper Lambourn, Berks

FOCUS
A decent, competitive handicap in which it has often paid to side with unexposed, progressive types from major stables, as in the case of the previous two winners, Forte Dei Marmi and Modun. The early pace was steady and the principals came up the centre of the track in the straight. The form is treated positively with the third rated close to his best.
T/Plt: £143.40 to a £1 stake. Pool of £116,426.69 - 592.62 winning tickets. T/Qpdt: £34.70 to a £1 stake. Pool of £6,549.88 - 139.65 winning tickets. ST

1315 NOTTINGHAM (L-H)
Saturday, April 21

OFFICIAL GOING: Soft (heavy in places; 6.2)

1514 YOUR RELIABLE BET DG TAXIS 01159500500 FILLIES' H'CAP 5f 13y
5:30 (5:30) (Class 5) (0-75,75) 3-Y-O **£3,234** (£962; £481; £120; £120) **Stalls** High

Form RPR

4231 **1** **Heartsong (IRE)**[16] 1201 3-8-9 **70** .... DarrenEgan(7) 1 87
(John Gallagher) *rrd s and slowly away: hld up: hdwy over 2f out: rdn to ld 2f out: hung lft over 1f out but sn clr: eased nr fin* **5/1**[2]

221- **2** *8* **First Fast Now (IRE)**[249] 5147 3-8-7 **64** .... DeclanCannon(3) 9 52
(Nigel Tinkler) *in tch: rdn over 2f out: kpt on one pce: wnt 2nd ins fnl f: no ch w wnr* **7/1**

006- **3** *¾* **Middleton Flyer (IRE)**[169] 7261 3-9-0 **68** .... RussKennemore 7 54
(Paul Midgley) *chsd ldrs: rdn over 2f out: plugged on: wnt 3rd post* **8/1**

45-4 **4** *shd* **Tahnee Mara (IRE)**[23] 1089 3-8-11 **68** ....(p) AmyRyan(3) 3 53
(Kevin Ryan) *led: rdn whn hdd 2f out: sn no ch w wnr: plugged on fnl f* **13/2**

3212 **4** *dht* **Ring For Baileys**[7] 1393 3-8-11 **65** .... AndreaAtzeni 4 50
(Chris Dwyer) *prom: rdn over 1f out: sn one pce: no ex towards fin* **11/2**[3]

635- **6** *2 ¼* **Copper Falls**[123] 7830 3-8-2 **56** .... FrankieMcDonald 6 33
(Brendan Powell) *prom: rdn over 2f out: wknd over 1f out* **8/1**

110- **7** *2* **Lexington Spirit (IRE)**[312] 3014 3-9-0 **75** .... LauraBarry(7) 2 45
(Richard Fahey) *chsd ldrs: rdn wl over 2f out: sn struggling* **5/2**[1]

2015 **8** *½* **Chateau Lola**[7] 1393 3-7-13 **56** oh4 ....(v) DominicFox(3) 5 24
(Derek Shaw) *hld up: rdn 3f out: a towards rr* **28/1**

1m 4.51s (3.51) **Going Correction** +0.675s/f (Yiel) **8** Ran SP% **112.1**
Speed ratings (Par 95): **98,85,84,83,83 80,77,76**
toteswingers: 1&2 £10.30, 1&3 £10.10, 2&3 £5.90. CSF £37.89 CT £274.00 TOTE £6.60: £2.60, £2.10, £4.40; EX 38.40.
Owner Colin Rashbrook **Bred** Gerry And John Rowley **Trained** Chastleton, Oxon

FOCUS
There was some fair past form among the runners in this race, but it's possible that some of them weren't at their best in the conditions. The winner raced in the centre, with others in the stands' side half of the track, so there is some doubt about the form.

1515 RONALDINHO'S 60TH SUMMER CELEBRATION MAIDEN STKS 5f 13y
6:00 (6:00) (Class 5) 2-Y-O **£2,911** (£866; £432; £216) **Stalls** High

Form RPR

2 **1** **Effie B**[8] 1352 2-8-7 0 .... CharlesBishop(5) 4 80+
(Mick Channon) *w ldr: led over 2f out: pushed clr over 1f out: kpt on wl: easily* **7/4**[1]

2 *7* **Golac** 2-9-3 0 .... SamHitchcott 2 60+
(Mick Channon) *chsd ldng pair: pushed along over 2f out: wnt 2nd appr fnl f: kpt on: no ch w wnr* **5/1**

3 *1 ½* **Bapak Bangsawan** 2-9-0 0 .... AmyRyan(3) 5 54+
(Kevin Ryan) *dwlt: sn pushed along towards rr: sme hdwy over 2f out: rdn over 1f out: kpt on one pce* **3/1**[3]

4 *nk* **Marshland** 2-9-3 0 .... RoystonFfrench 3 53+
(Mark Johnston) *led narrowly: hdd over 2f out: sn pushed along: no ex fnl f* **11/4**[2]

5 *17* **Top Boy** 2-9-0 0 .... DaleSwift(3) 1
(Derek Shaw) *veered lft s: sn outpcd in rr: hdwy to briefly chse ldrs over 2f out: rdn and hung lft over 1f out: wknd qckly* **14/1**

1m 4.62s (3.62) **Going Correction** +0.675s/f (Yiel) **5** Ran SP% **111.4**
Speed ratings (Par 92): **98,86,84,83,56**
CSF £10.92 TOTE £1.80: £1.02, £4.60; EX 12.30.
Owner R Bastian **Bred** R Bastian **Trained** West Ilsley, Berks

FOCUS
This juvenile event was lacking in numbers, unsurprising in view of the testing ground, but there were some reasonable winning pedigrees in the line-up. The winner raced against the stands' side rail and the winner had the edge on experience, but it is hard to set the level with confidence.

NOTEBOOK
Effie B had the advantage of a previous race over her four rivals. A precocious sort, she handled the soft ground well on that occasion, and her experience helped her leave the others standing. (op 2-1 tchd 9-4)
Golac, a 7,500GBP yearling, was no match for his stablemate, who went off at a shorter price. However, this half-brother to two sprinters showed enough to suggest he can hold his own in routine company. (op 6-1)
Bapak Bangsawan, a half-brother to three winners, is a May foal so there should be quite a bit more to come. Improvement can be expected as he matures. (op 11-4 tchd 5-2)
Marshland is likely to stay further in due course, and this half-brother to four winners can step up on this debut when facing the right test. (tchd 3-1)
Top Boy, a half-brother to two winning juveniles, is bred to be speedy, but he was green and the ground may have been against him. A 42,000gns yearling, he needs another chance to show what he can do. (op 11-1 tchd 9-1)

1516 BDN CONSTRUCTION H'CAP 5f 13y
6:30 (6:31) (Class 6) (0-65,67) 4-Y-0+ **£2,264** (£673; £336; £168) **Stalls** High

Form RPR

-652 **1** **Dispol Grand (IRE)**[10] 1298 6-8-11 **62** .... NedCurtis(7) 1 72
(Paul Midgley) *prom: led over 1f out: drvn and kpt on fnl f: jst hld on* **11/1**

5161 **2** *shd* **Shawkantango**[7] 1383 5-9-6 **67** ....(v) DaleSwift(3) 4 77
(Derek Shaw) *chsd ldrs: rdn over 2f out: kpt on fnl f: jst failed* **7/2**[2]

0301 **3** *2 ¾* **Invigilator**[9] 1343 4-8-9 **53** .... WilliamCarson 5 53
(Derek Shaw) *dwlt and bmpd s: hld up in rr: stl wl bhd over 2f out: hdwy over 1f out: kpt on: edgd rt fnl 50yds: no threat to ldng pair* **9/1**[3]

40-6 **4** *1 ¼* **Gracie's Games**[11] 1280 6-8-2 **53** ....(v) DarrenEgan(7) 7 49
(Richard Price) *wnt lft s: sn wl adrift: bhd tl kpt on fr over 1f out: sltly short of room 50yds out: nvr threatened ldrs* **14/1**

4323 **5** *nk* **Bobbyow**[51] 740 4-8-4 **51** oh2 .... DominicFox(3) 3 45
(Terry Clement) *chsd ldrs: rdn over 2f out: one pce: no ex ins fnl f* **20/1**

-112 **6** *2 ¼* **Boucher Garcon (IRE)**[7] 1383 4-8-13 **64** .... JasonHart(7) 10 50
(Declan Carroll) *led: rdn whn hdd over 1f out: wknd* **1/1**[1]

5004 **7** *1 ¼* **Steel City Boy (IRE)**[9] 1343 9-8-12 **56** .... LiamKeniry 8 38
(Garry Woodward) *chsd ldrs: wknd over 1f out* **12/1**

-060 **8** *4 ½* **Chosen One (IRE)**[10] 1298 7-8-7 **51** .... PaulMulrennan 9 17
(Ruth Carr) *prom: lost pl over 2f out: wknd over 1f out* **12/1**

1m 4.2s (3.20) **Going Correction** +0.675s/f (Yiel) **8** Ran SP% **117.4**
Speed ratings (Par 101): **101,100,96,94,93 90,88,81**
toteswingers: 1&2 £5.00, 1&3 £6.60, 2&3 £3.30. CSF £50.73 CT £371.00 TOTE £8.30: £3.20, £2.20, £1.70; EX 59.60.
Owner T W Midgley **Bred** Martyn J McEnery **Trained** Westow, N Yorks

FOCUS
This was a moderate sprint, but at least plenty of these experienced performers had previous form in the soft. The form is rated around the first two.

1517 HF H'CAP 1m 75y
7:00 (7:00) (Class 6) (0-65,70) 3-Y-O **£2,264** (£673; £336; £168) **Stalls** Centre

Form RPR

15-3 **1** **Mistress Of Rome**[10] 1322 3-9-5 **63** .... PaulMulrennan 9 71
(Michael Dods) *trckd ldrs: pushed along over 3f out: hdwy to chse ldr over 1f out: kpt on wl: led nr fin* **9/4**[1]

-421 **2** *nk* **Emman Bee (IRE)**[26] 1046 3-9-0 **65** .... DarrenEgan(7) 13 73
(John Gallagher) *trckd ldrs: led over 2f out: rdn 4 l clr over 1f out: flashed tail: no ex fnl 100yds: hdd nr fin* **11/2**[2]

0-60 **3** *3 ¾* **Eightfold**[10] 1313 3-9-5 **63** ....(t) GeorgeBaker 16 62
(Seamus Durack) *hld up in rr: hdwy on outer over 2f out: kpt on to go 3rd fnl 100yds: no threat to ldng pair* **10/1**

0-63 **4** *1 ¼* **Vexillum (IRE)**[16] 1201 3-9-2 **60** .... SamHitchcott 12 56
(Mick Channon) *prom: led over 5f out: hdd 3f out: kpt on one pce* **12/1**

0-20 **5** *1 ¼* **Bountiful Catch**[24] 1062 3-8-8 **52** .... LiamKeniry 1 45
(Pam Sly) *racd keenly: led: hdd over 5f out: led again 3f out: sn hdd: one pce* **16/1**

50-0 **6** *4 ½* **Camrock Star (IRE)**[10] 1322 3-9-2 **60** ....(v) PadraigBeggy 11 43
(David Evans) *racd keenly in tch: rdn over 3f out: sn no imp on ldrs* **16/1**

5-40 **7** *2 ½* **Ice Loch**[30] 993 3-8-7 **51** oh4 ....(b) FrankieMcDonald 7 28
(Michael Blanshard) *hld up in rr: briefly short of room over 1f out: kpt on fnl f: nrst fin* **28/1**

13-3 **8** *hd* **Sweetnessandlight**[19] 1170 3-9-6 **64** .... MichaelStainton 8 41
(Jason Ward) *midfield: rdn over 3f out: sn no imp* **8/1**[3]

30-0 **9** *1 ½* **Rano Pano (USA)**[13] 1241 3-8-5 **52** .... PaulPickard(3) 6 25
(Brian Ellison) *hld up in midfield: rdn over 2f out: no imp* **22/1**

05-5 **10** *8* **Thecornishcowboy**[8] 1365 3-9-1 **59** ....(v[1]) KirstyMilczarek 15 14
(John Ryan) *midfield: hdwy to chse ldrs over 3f out: wknd 2f out* **18/1**

04-6 **11** *1 ¾* **Rockme Cockney**[32] 970 3-9-5 **63** .... IanMongan 2 14
(Jeremy Gask) *midfield on inner: rdn over 3f out: sn wknd* **11/1**

006- **12** *2* **Moody Dancer**[177] 7124 3-9-7 **65** .... MartinDwyer 4 11
(William Muir) *hld up in midfield: rdn over 2f out: sn wknd* **16/1**

6060 **13** *½* **Tigresa (IRE)**[12] 1260 3-8-7 **51** oh5 .... RoystonFfrench 10
(Mark Johnston) *midfield: wknd over 2f out* **50/1**

060 **14** *20* **Gold Deal (IRE)**[44] 833 3-8-10 **54** ....(t) RussKennemore 14
(Deborah Sanderson) *hld up: a towards rr* **40/1**

1m 51.66s (2.06) **Going Correction** +0.175s/f (Good) **14** Ran SP% **117.5**
Speed ratings (Par 96): **96,95,91,90,89 84,82,82,80,72 71,69,68,48**
toteswingers: 1&2 £10.30, 1&3 £10.10, 2&3 £5.90. CSF £12.15 CT £107.17 TOTE £3.10: £1.30, £1.80, £3.80; EX 16.70.
Owner Kevin Kirkup **Bred** Dr A Gillespie **Trained** Denton, Co Durham

FOCUS
A mixed bunch contested this routine second-season handicap. Surprisingly for a race over 1m here, the first four all came from the outside half of the draw. The form is a bit fluid with the third doing well coming from the rear.

1518 DG TAXIS GETTING YOU HOME SAFELY MEDIAN AUCTION MAIDEN STKS 1m 2f 50y
7:30 (7:34) (Class 6) 3-Y-O **£2,264** (£673; £336; £168) **Stalls** Low

Form RPR

5 **1** **Last Shadow**[21] 1132 3-9-3 0 .... GeorgeBaker 3 76
(William Muir) *in tch: rdn over 2f out: styd on wl fr over 1f out: led fnl 100yds* **7/2**[1]

0- **2** *1 ¼* **Palus San Marco (IRE)**[301] 3401 3-9-3 0 .... RobertHavlin 6 74
(Peter Chapple-Hyam) *trckd ldr: chal over 2f out: rdn to ld over 1f out: kpt on: hdd fnl 100yds* **6/1**

3 *2 ¼* **Secrets Away (IRE)** 3-8-12 0 .... AndreaAtzeni 12 64
(Marco Botti) *led: rdn whn hdd over 1f out: jinked lft and hit rail sn after: no ex ins fnl f* **4/1**[2]

0 **4** *2 ½* **Gangsterbanksters (FR)**[19] 1171 3-9-3 0 .... WilliamCarson 11 65
(Mrs K Burke) *midfield: rdn over 3f out: kpt on one pce* **8/1**

025- **5** *nk* **Ballyheigue (IRE)**[208] 6400 3-9-3 73 .... MartinDwyer 5 64
(Brian Meehan) *trckd ldr: pushed along and outpcd 3f out: plugged on* **6/1**

00- **6** *2* **Choral Bee**[171] 7233 3-8-7 0 .... AmyScott(5) 1 55
(Henry Candy) *midfield: pushed along 3f out: sn one pce* **18/1**

7 *8* **Morning Coat** 3-9-3 0 .... SilvestreDeSousa 7 45
(Mahmood Al Zarooni) *slowly away: hld up: pushed along over 3f out: sn no imp* **9/2**[3]

00- **8** *½* **Ayla's Emperor**[169] 7257 3-8-12 0 .... MartinHarley 2 39
(Mick Channon) *midfield: rdn over 3f out: wknd over 2f out* **16/1**

- 9 7 **Play Tiger (FR)** 3-9-3 0 LiamKeniry 10 31
(David Simcock) *dwlt: hld up in midfield: pushed along over 3f out: wknd over 2f out* **16/1**

2m 23.58s (9.28) **Going Correction** +0.575s/f (Yiel) **9** Ran SP% **117.1**
Speed ratings (Par 96): **85,84,82,80,79 78,71,71,65**
toteswingers: 1&2 £4.50, 1&3 £5.80, 2&3 £6.20. CSF £25.18 TOTE £5.10: £1.50, £2.20, £2.20; EX 27.00.
Owner M J Caddy **Bred** Newsells Park Stud **Trained** Lambourn, Berks

FOCUS
There wasn't much experience in the line-up, and the general lack of soft-ground form makes it hard to weigh up, but what previous form there was suggests this was just a routine maiden. The level is again fluid although the first two are improvers.

1519 THINK TAXI THINK DG 01159500500 H'CAP 1m 2f 50y
8:00 (8:00) (Class 6) (0-65,68) 3-Y-O **£2,264** (£673; £336; £168) **Stalls** Low

Form RPR
22-2 1 **Naseem Alyasmeen (IRE)**^{8} [1364] 3-9-9 **67** MartinHarley 10 72
(Mick Channon) *midfield: rdn to chse ldr over 2f out: kpt on fnl f: led towards fin* **10/3**^{2}
1131 2 ¾ **Miss Cato**^{11} [1288] 3-9-10 **68** WilliamCarson 6 72
(Rae Guest) *trckd ldrs: pushed along to ld over 3f out: looked in command over 1f out: drvn and no ex ins fnl f: hdd towards fin* **9/4**^{1}
-454 3 nk **Bapak Pintar**^{19} [1167] 3-9-4 **65** AmyRyan$^{(3)}$ 7 68
(Kevin Ryan) *led narrowly: hdd over 3f out: sn rdn: kpt on* **10/1**
6351 4 ½ **Masters Blazing**^{12} [1260] 3-9-8 **66** KirstyMilczarek 2 68
(John Ryan) *hld up: pushed along over 3f out: hdwy over 1f out: kpt on fnl f* **8/1**
066- 5 1½ **Cheviot Quest (IRE)**^{205} [6487] 3-8-11 **58** HarryBentley$^{(3)}$ 8 57
(William Jarvis) *midfield: pushed along and outpcd over 3f out: kpt on fr over 1f out* **13/2**^{3}
4-62 6 2¼ **Graylyn Valentino**^{26} [1046] 3-9-5 **63** BrettDoyle 9 58
(Robin Dickin) *trckd ldrs: rdn over 3f out: wknd ins fnl f* **9/1**
444- 7 5 **Bathwick Street**^{206} [6460] 3-8-11 **55** PadraigBeggy 1 40
(David Evans) *in tch: pushed along over 3f out: sn btn* **16/1**
002- 8 6 **Shredding (IRE)**^{133} [7708] 3-8-9 **53** RoystonFfrench 5 27
(Ed Vaughan) *w ldr: rdn over 3f out: sn wknd* **18/1**
156- 9 2 **Remember Rocky**^{171} [7223] 3-8-6 **57** DarrenEgan$^{(7)}$ 4 27
(Steve Gollings) *hld up: wknd over 4f out* **8/1**
500- 10 17 **More Bottle (IRE)**^{170} [7242] 3-8-4 **51** oh1 DominicFox$^{(3)}$ 11
(Tom Tate) *hld up: a towards rr* **25/1**

2m 20.93s (6.63) **Going Correction** +0.575s/f (Yiel) **10** Ran SP% **123.5**
Speed ratings (Par 96): **96,95,95,94,93 91,87,82,81,67**
toteswingers: 1&2 £2.70, 1&3 £5.20, 2&3 £5.40. CSF £12.04 CT £72.00 TOTE £4.50: £1.50, £1.30, £3.20; EX 6.40.
Owner Jaber Abdullah **Bred** Patrick Byrnes **Trained** West Ilsley, Berks

FOCUS
The finish of this race was fought out by two fillies carrying big weights. The form makes sense despite the ground.
Graylyn Valentino Official explanation: jockey said gelding hung right
T/Plt: £31.10 to a £1 stake. Pool:£43,022.60 - 1,008.85 winning tickets T/Qpdt: £4.90 to a £1 stake. Pool:£4,581.03 - 688.26 winning tickets AS

THIRSK (L-H)
Saturday, April 21

OFFICIAL GOING: Soft (good to soft in places; 6.9)
Wind: Virtually nil Weather: Showers

1520 THIRSKRACECOURSE.NET H'CAP (DIV I) 7f
2:10 (2:11) (Class 5) (0-75,78) 4-Y-O+ **£3,101** (£915; £458) **Stalls** Low

Form RPR
040- 1 **The Osteopath (IRE)**^{164} [7339] 9-9-6 **74** PJMcDonald 9 86
(John Davies) *towards rr: hdwy over 2f out: rdn and n.m.r over 1f out: styd on strly fnl f to ld nr line* **28/1**
00-6 2 hd **Steel Stockholder**^{7} [1384] 6-8-7 **61** oh3 SilvestreDeSousa 1 72
(Mel Brittain) *trckd ldr: hdwy to ld over 2f out: rdn clr jst over 1f out: drvn ins fnl f: hdd and no ex nr line* **12/1**
12-3 3 1¾ **Viking Warrior (IRE)**^{10} [1293] 5-8-13 **67** TomEaves 2 74
(Michael Dods) *trckd ldrs: hdwy 3f out: rdn over 1f out: kpt on fnl f* **9/1**
4640 4 1½ **Piceno (IRE)**^{21} [1135] 4-9-0 **68** (p) RobertWinston 6 71
(Scott Dixon) *rrd and lost several l s: bhd tl hdwy 1/2-way: effrt over 2f out: rdn and n.m.r wl over 1f out: kpt on appr fnl f: nrst fin* **11/1**
40-2 5 nse **Save The Bees**^{8} [1358] 4-8-11 **70** NeilFarley$^{(5)}$ 13 73
(Declan Carroll) *hld up in rr: gd hdwy on wd outside wl over 2f out: rdn to chse ldrs over 1f out: kpt on same pce* **6/1**^{3}
11-2 6 1½ **Beautiful Day**^{46} [812] 4-8-12 **66** PhillipMakin 8 65
(Kevin Ryan) *chsd ldng pair: hdwy 3f out: chal 2f out and ev ch tl rdn and wknd over 1f out* **4/1**^{1}
62-4 7 ¾ **Hayek**^{12} [1251] 5-8-4 **63** ow1 (b) AdamCarter$^{(5)}$ 10 60
(Tim Easterby) *hld up towards rr: hdwy wl over 2f out: sn rdn and nvr nr ldrs* **14/1**
006- 8 1 **Bella Noir**^{182} [7033] 5-9-1 **72** (v) MichaelMetcalfe$^{(3)}$ 11 66
(Mrs K Burke) *hld up: hdwy 3f out: rdn to chse ldrs and hung lft wl over 1f out: sn wknd* **8/1**
00-5 9 6 **Maggie Mey (IRE)**^{12} [1251] 4-8-13 **67** MickyFenton 12 46
(Paul Midgley) *led: rdn along and hdd over 2f out: sn wknd* **14/1**
400- 10 4½ **Northern Fling**^{168} [7299] 8-9-4 **72** (v^{1}) LeeNewman 5 39
(Jim Goldie) *a towards rr* **12/1**
00-1 11 nk **Divine Call**^{12} [1254] 5-9-10 **78** MartinLane 7 44
(Milton Bradley) *trckd ldrs: effrt 3f out: rdn along over 2f out and sn wknd* **9/2**^{2}
321- 12 31 **Salik Tag (USA)**^{217} [6156] 4-8-13 **67** (t) AdrianNicholls 3
(David Nicholls) *in tch: hdwy to chse ldrs 3f out: rdn along over 2f out: hld whn hmpd over 1f out: sn bhd and eased* **14/1**

1m 32.21s (5.01) **Going Correction** +0.80s/f (Soft) **12** Ran SP% **120.7**
Speed ratings (Par 103): **103,102,100,99,99 97,96,95,88,83 82,47**
toteswingers: 1&2 £55.70, 1&3 £12.10, 2&3 £8.90. CSF £337.69 CT £3319.26 TOTE £25.40: £7.10, £3.40, £2.50; EX 330.70.
Owner Kevin Kirkup **Bred** Joe Rogers **Trained** Piercebridge, Durham

FOCUS
The opener was run at a frantic pace and the winner is rated to his best form of the last couple of years, with the fourth close to his turf best.

Piceno(IRE) Official explanation: jockey said gelding accidentally lost cheek piece approaching final furlong

1521 RACING UK MEDIAN AUCTION MAIDEN STKS 6f
2:40 (2:48) (Class 5) 3-4-Y-O **£2,943** (£875; £437; £218) **Stalls** High

Form RPR
2 1 **Jack Dexter**^{13} [1238] 3-9-0 0 DanielTudhope 5 85+
(Jim Goldie) *midfield: hdwy on outer whn sltly hmpd 2f out: sn chsng ldr: rdn to chal over 1f out: styd on to ld ins fnl f* **7/2**^{2}
5- 2 2½ **Gowanharry (IRE)**^{241} [5367] 3-8-9 0 PaulMulrennan 12 72
(Michael Dods) *led: pushed along 2f out: jnd and rdn over 1f out: hdd and one pce ins fnl f* **3/1**^{1}
440- 3 1¼ **On The Hoof**^{197} [6670] 3-9-0 70 JamesSullivan 9 73
(Michael Easterby) *in tch on stands' rail: hdwy to chse ldrs 2f out: rdn over 1f out: kpt on same pce* **13/2**
4 hd **Ta Ajabb** 3-8-11 0 AdamBeschizza$^{(3)}$ 6 72+
(William Haggas) *s.i.s and green: green and sn rdn along in rr: hdwy 1/2-way: chsd ldrs over 1f out: kpt on same pce* **6/1**^{3}
5 7 **Imperial Legend (IRE)** 3-9-0 0 AdrianNicholls 10 50
(David Nicholls) *chsd ldng pair: rdn over 2f out: grad wknd fr over 1f out* **16/1**
5 6 2¾ **Elegant Girl (IRE)**^{11} [1274] 3-8-9 0 DuranFentiman 3 36
(Tim Easterby) *in tch: hdwy to chse ldrs over 2f out: sn rdn and wknd over 1f out* **10/1**
7 shd **Rich Again (IRE)** 3-9-0 0 RobertWinston 2 41
(James Bethell) *wnt bdly lft s: in rr and sn swtchd rt to stands' rail: sme late hdwy* **16/1**
4 8 7 **Pursuit of Passion**^{13} [1238] 4-8-13 0 GeorgeChaloner$^{(7)}$ 7 13
(Richard Fahey) *dwlt and a in rr* **10/1**
6 9 4 **Noble Bounty**^{23} [1089] 3-9-0 0 PhillipMakin 4
(Kevin Ryan) *in tch: pushed along 1/2-way: sn hung lft and wknd* **40/1**
10 ½ **Warrick Brown** 3-9-0 0 TomEaves 11
(Tim Easterby) *a towards rr* **25/1**
4- 11 2 **Cried For You (IRE)**^{270} [4406] 3-8-4 0 AdamCarter$^{(5)}$ 8
(Tim Easterby) *led to s: cl up: rdn along over 2f out: sn hung lft and wknd* **16/1**
12 4½ **Olympian Diamond (IRE)** 4-9-6 0 BarryMcHugh 1
(Brian Rothwell) *wnt bdly lft s: a bhd* **80/1**

1m 17.02s (4.32) **Going Correction** +0.775s/f (Yiel)
WFA 3 from 4yo 11lb **12** Ran SP% **118.2**
Speed ratings (Par 103): **102,98,97,96,87 83,83,74,68,68 65,59**
toteswingers: 1&2 £5.10, 1&3 £5.30, 2&3 £5.60. CSF £14.16 TOTE £3.60: £1.10, £1.80, £2.20; EX 16.70.
Owner Jim Goldie Racing Club **Bred** Jim Goldie **Trained** Uplawmoor, E Renfrews

FOCUS
An average maiden for 3-4yo with very little form on show as the twelve runners only had fourteen career starts between them, and the third horse home made up eight of those. They went a solid gallop from the outset, racing a couple of lanes off the stands' rail, producing a proper test at the trip on soft ground. The placed horses set the level.

1522 MARKET CROSS JEWELLERS H'CAP 7f
3:15 (3:15) (Class 3) (0-90,90) 4-Y-O+ **£8,506** (£2,531; £1,265; £632) **Stalls** Low

Form RPR
001- 1 **Tariq Too**^{223} [5970] 5-9-2 **85** GeorgeBaker 10 96+
(Amy Weaver) *hld up in rr: smooth hdwy 3f out: led wl over 1f out: rdn clr ent fnl f: styd on* **17/2**^{3}
00-0 2 2¼ **Kiwi Bay**^{21} [1128] 7-9-6 **89** TomEaves 2 94
(Michael Dods) *chsd ldng pair: hdwy on inner and cl up 3f out: led over 2f out: rdn and hdd 1 1/2f out: drvn and kpt on fnl f* **16/1**
-540 3 ½ **Dubai Dynamo**^{21} [1130] 7-9-5 **88** JamesSullivan 8 92
(Ruth Carr) *hld up towards rr: hdwy wl over 2f out: rdn over 1f out: styd on fnl f: nrst fin* **10/1**
-260 4 2 **Kingscroft (IRE)**^{21} [1128] 4-9-5 **88** SilvestreDeSousa 6 87
(Mark Johnston) *midfield: gd hdwy 3f out: chal 2f out: sn rdn and one pce fr over 1f out* **10/1**
00-0 5 nk **Imperial Djay (IRE)**^{20} [1157] 7-9-5 **88** PJMcDonald 4 86
(Ruth Carr) *hld up: hdwy over 2f out: rdn wl over 1f out: kpt on fnl f: nrst fin* **14/1**
21-0 6 1 **Sam Nombulist**^{20} [1161] 4-8-12 **81** TonyCulhane 13 76
(Richard Whitaker) *midfield: hdwy on outer wl over 2f out: sn rdn along and edgd lft wl over 1f out: no imp appr fnl f* **12/1**
402- 7 ½ **Pravda Street**^{140} [6542] 7-9-4 **87** BarryMcHugh 3 81
(Brian Ellison) *midfield whn hmpd on inner 1/2-way: sn towards rr: hdwy 2f out: sn rdn and no imp* **12/1**
1121 8 ¾ **Captain Dimitrios**^{13} [1236] 4-8-10 **84** (v) LeonnaMayor$^{(5)}$ 11 76
(Alastair Lidderdale) *sn led: wd st and rdn along 3f out: hdd over 2f out and grad wknd* **9/1**
006- 9 2 **Point North (IRE)**^{182} [7023] 5-9-0 **83** DanielTudhope 5 70
(John Balding) *hld up and bhd: sme hdwy over 2f out: nvr a factor* **12/1**
306- 10 3 **Hot Rod Mamma (IRE)**^{171} [7234] 5-9-7 **90** GrahamLee 1 69
(Dianne Sayer) *s.i.s: a towards rr* **20/1**
53-2 11 nk **Whozthecat (IRE)**^{19} [1168] 5-8-8 **82** (v) NeilFarley$^{(5)}$ 9 60
(Declan Carroll) *chsd ldrs: rdn along wl over 2f out: sn wknd* **12/1**
5-43 12 1¼ **Prime Exhibit**^{14} [1220] 7-9-2 **88** (v^{1}) LeeTopliss$^{(3)}$ 12 63
(Richard Fahey) *awkward s: t.k.h and sn chsng ldrs: hdwy and cl up 3f out: rdn over 2f out and sn wknd* **11/2**^{1}
00-0 13 10 **Masked Dance (IRE)**^{10} [1321] 5-9-2 **85** (b) RobertWinston 14 34
(Scott Dixon) *chsd ldrs: cl up 1/2-way: rdn along wl over 2f out: sn wknd* **16/1**
36-0 14 5 **Mass Rally (IRE)**^{42} [871] 5-9-7 **90** (v) PaulMulrennan 7 26
(Michael Dods) *a in rr* **13/2**^{2}

1m 31.97s (4.77) **Going Correction** +0.875s/f (Soft) **14** Ran SP% **121.4**
Speed ratings (Par 107): **107,104,103,101,101 100,99,98,96,92 92,91,79,74**
toteswingers: 1&2 not won, 1&3 £3.40, 2&3 not won. CSF £138.65 CT £1430.33 TOTE £6.00: £2.40, £6.10, £3.50; EX 192.30.
Owner Bringloe Clarke Spain Hensby Partridge **Bred** D R Botterill **Trained** Newmarket, Suffolk

FOCUS
A wide open, competitive handicap. The pace was honest from the off and the winner was impressive, the form looks solid, rated through the runner-up.

NOTEBOOK
Tariq Too made a pleasing debut for his new yard after 223 days off the track, and such was the ease in which he travelled throughout the race he could be called the winner some way from home. Patiently ridden in rear, he started to pick up once in the straight and when hitting the front before the final furlong it was all over. This win came off a 6lb higher mark than when scoring on his final start last season and he looks progressive. He's been gelded, and given that he's only lightly raced he could still be open to improvement, particularly when getting his favoured soft ground. (tchd 8-1 and 9-1)

Kiwi Bay produced one of his better efforts away from Redcar, where he has won four times, and was unlucky to bump into such a progressive rival. He handled the ground well and stuck to his task up the far rail, but the winner was far too good for him. (op 22-1)
Dubai Dynamo was down in class after a creditable effort in the Lincoln, but there was a doubt about him in the testing conditions as all his previous wins had been on a sound surface. This was unfounded, and back down in trip he stayed on really well after making his challenge up the centre of the track. (op 9-1)
Kingscroft(IRE), down in trip after finishing well beaten in the Spring Mile, plugged on for fourth and looks in the grip of the handicapper at present. (op 17-2)
Imperial Djay(IRE), a dual C&D winner, stepped up on his seasonal debut and appreciated the return to this longer trip. His trainer is likely to find another winning opportunity for him.
Sam Nombulist improved for the fitting of a visor last season, but the headgear has been left off on both starts this term. He was forced to race wide from stall 10 and made his challenge up the centre of the track before keeping on all the way to the line. This wasn't a bad effort and he may be of interest next time especially if the headgear is reapplied. (op 14-1 tchd 11-1)
Pravda Street had a couple of spins over hurdles during the winter, and returned to the Flat 11lb higher than his last winning mark. He was one paced in the final furlong and looks a shade high in the wieghts at present. (op 14-1 tchd 11-1)
Captain Dimitrios showed his customary early pace, but couldn't keep up the gallop over a trip that stretches him. He'll be suited by a return to sprinting. (op 17-2)
Prime Exhibit was a disappointing favourite. The first-time visor had no effect and he hasn't won on turf now since August 2009. Official explanation: jockey said gelding ran too free (op 5-1)
Mass Rally(IRE) Official explanation: jockey said gelding stopped quickly

1523 MICHAEL FOSTER MEMORIAL E B F CONDITIONS STKS 7f

3:50 (3:50) (Class 3) 4-Y-0+

£11,205 (£3,355; £1,677; £838; £419; £210) **Stalls** Low

Form				RPR
0-01	**1**		**Justonefortheroad**[14] 1220 6-9-0 99 ...... TonyHamilton 5 (Richard Fahey) *hld up in tch: hdwy over 2f out: rdn to chse ldng pair ent fnl f: drvn and styd on wl to ld nr line* **5/1**[3]	104
0-42	**2**	*shd*	**Rodrigo De Torres**[21] 1140 5-9-0 98 ...... PhillipMakin 1 (Mrs K Burke) *trckd ldr: hdwy to ld wl over 2f out: rdn over 1f out: drvn ins fnl f: hdd on line* **11/1**	104
20-0	**3**	*1*	**Smarty Socks (IRE)**[21] 1130 8-9-0 102 ...... DanielTudhope 4 (David O'Meara) *dwlt and in rr: hdwy on outer wl over 2f out: rdn wl over 1f out: kpt on fnl f* **6/1**	101+
25-1	**4**	*¾*	**My Freedom (IRE)**[7] 1373 4-9-0 100 ...... SilvestreDeSousa 7 (Saeed Bin Suroor) *hld up in tch: hdwy on inner over 2f out: rdn to chal over 1f out: ev ch tl edgd lft and one pce last 100yds* **5/4**[1]	99
001-	**5**	*2 ¼*	**Xilerator (IRE)**[217] 6148 5-9-0 98 ...... AdrianNicholls 6 (David Nicholls) *led: rdn along 3f out: sn hdd and grad wknd* **7/2**[2]	94
0-00	**6**	*¾*	**Crown Choice**[20] 1157 7-9-0 91 ...... FrederikTylicki 2 (Paul Midgley) *chsd ldrs: rdn along wl over 2f out: grad wknd* **20/1**	92
/65-	**7**	*11*	**Charles De Mille**[151] 2394 4-9-0 0 ...... AndrewMullen 3 (George Moore) *chsd ldrs: rdn along over 3f out: sn wknd* **100/1**	63

1m 32.0s (4.80) **Going Correction** +0.875s/f (Soft) 7 Ran SP% **111.7**
Speed ratings (Par 107): **107,106,105,104,102 101,88**
toteswingers: 1&2 £3.00, 1&3 £2.70, 2&3 not won.. CSF £53.21 TOTE £4.90: £2.40, £4.10; EX 67.10.
Owner The Pontoon Partnership **Bred** Wellsummers Farm & Hammarsfield B'Stock **Trained** Musley Bank, N Yorks

FOCUS
An informative conditions' stakes for 4-yos plus that looked very tight on paper with only 3lb covering five of the seven-runner field according to adjusted official ratings. They went a decent gallop on soft ground and this was a proper test under the conditions which produced a cracking finish. These races are rarely that solid though and the runner-up looks the best guide to the level.

NOTEBOOK
Justonefortheroad represented his in-form trainer Richard Fahey with only a few pounds to find on the book. He arrived in peak form, after quickening from off the pace to win a decent 7f Musselburgh handicap on good to soft ground a fortnight ago (RPR 104), and he utilised identical tactics here under an expertly-timed ride from Tony Hamilton. This 6-y-o son of Domedriver is versatile as regards ground at up to 1m, and looks capable of further success in this grade or slightly better this season, as he is clearly thriving. (tchd 11-2)
Rodrigo De Torres advertised the excellent current form of his yard by reproducing his promising 7f Polytrack form at Chantilly and Kempton from March. He looked all over the winner well inside the final furlong, but was grabbed on the line, and on this evidence there is a decent handicap to be won with him over this trip on better ground this season. (tchd 12-1)
Smarty Socks(IRE) has a tendency to start slowly, which was again in evidence, but he made up most of the ground to finish a close third. He progressed significantly from his reappearance when third from last in the Lincoln, and will once again be a player in strong 7f handicap company on decent ground this term. (op 5-1)
My Freedom(IRE) didn't disgrace himself in fourth, but a return to better ground on turf or a Polytrack surface will suit. (op 13-8)
Xilerator(IRE) will come on from this satisfactory reappearance from a seven-month break. (op 3-1)

1524 THIRSK RACECOURSE CONFERENCE & WEDDING CENTRE H'CAP 5f

4:25 (4:25) (Class 3) (0-95,95) 3-Y-0 **£8,506** (£2,531; £1,265; £632) **Stalls** High

Form				RPR
101-	**1**		**Free Zone**[178] 7103 3-8-13 87 ...... TomEaves 1 (Bryan Smart) *prom: led after 1f and sn swtchd rt to stands' rail: rdn over 1f out: kpt on strly* **9/2**[3]	97
-454	**2**	*2 ½*	**I'll Be Good**[10] 1317 3-8-2 83 ...... MatthewHopkins(7) 2 (Robert Johnson) *trckd wnr: effrt 2f out and nt clr run on inner: swtchd lft and rdn ent fnl f: kpt on: no imp on wnr* **7/1**	84
5-32	**3**	*2 ¼*	**Waseem Faris (IRE)**[59] 659 3-8-8 82 ...... TonyCulhane 8 (Mick Channon) *in tch: hdwy to chse wnr 1/2-way: rdn along wl over 1f out: one pce* **3/1**[1]	75
240-	**4**	*2 ½*	**Kool Henry (IRE)**[203] 6535 3-8-13 87 ...... DanielTudhope 6 (David O'Meara) *led 1f: prom: rdn along 1/2-way and sn wknd* **10/3**[2]	71
625-	**5**	*½*	**Last Bid**[236] 5558 3-9-7 95 ...... DuranFentiman 4 (Tim Easterby) *a towards rr* **10/1**	77
510-	**6**	*¾*	**Amadeus Denton (IRE)**[224] 5922 3-8-11 85 ...... TonyHamilton 3 (Michael Dods) *dwlt sltly and n.m.r s: towards rr: hdwy over 2f out: sn rdn and btn over 1f out* **12/1**	64
53-0	**7**	*nse*	**Parc De Launay**[11] 1271 3-8-13 87 ...... MickyFenton 5 (Tom Tate) *prom: rdn along 1/2-way: sn wknd* **9/2**[3]	66

1m 2.83s (3.23) **Going Correction** +0.775s/f (Yiel) 7 Ran SP% **113.7**
Speed ratings (Par 102): **105,101,97,93,92 91,91**
toteswingers: 1&2 £1.10, 1&3 £5.50, 2&3 £4.70. CSF £34.76 CT £107.94 TOTE £4.70: £2.70, £2.70; EX 15.30.
Owner Fromthestables.com Racing **Bred** R G Levin **Trained** Hambleton, N Yorks

FOCUS
This didn't look a strong handicap, but the winner impressed in victory under a fine tactical ride. The runner-up is the best guide to the form.

NOTEBOOK
Free Zone got to the lead from his wide draw, and once he'd been angled to grab the stands' rail he wasn't for catching. A triple winner over 5f/6f last season, including on easy ground, he's been gelded since his last run and had the field well stretched out at the line. He showed a good attitude too and pulled out more when briefly threatened inside the final furlong, suggesting he can win more races especially if allowed to dominate. (op 4-1)
I'll Be Good is exposed, but both his wins came on soft ground and he was suited by the conditions. This was a good effort but the winner was too good for him. (tchd 15-2)
Waseem Faris(IRE), a firm-ground maiden winner on his debut and generally consistent since, ran his race but may appreciate the return to a sounder surface. (op 7-2 tchd 11-4)
Kool Henry(IRE), another gelded since his last run, likes to race prominently but couldn't match the early pace of some of his rivals, on his first start for 203 days. (op 4-1 tchd 3-1)
Last Bid landed a hat-trick of 5f wins last season, but she was unproven in the conditions. She was outpaced in rear at the halfway stage but ran on inside the final furlong, and should come on for this first run since a 236-day layoff. She's not one to give up on and will be suited by a return to a quicker surface. (op 8-1)
Amadeus Denton(IRE) travelled okay on the heels of the leaders, but couldn't quicken in ground that was probably too slow for him. (op 14-1)
Parc De Launay didn't step up from a disappointing seasonal debut and although he had some solid form last year, he has something to prove now. (tchd 5-1)

1525 THIRSK PAVILION DINE & RACE £74.95 H'CAP 1m 4f

5:00 (5:00) (Class 5) (0-75,75) 4-Y-0+ **£2,943** (£875; £437; £218) **Stalls** Low

Form				RPR
4-44	**1**		**Veiled Applause**[11] 1275 9-8-12 69 ...... MichaelO'Connell(3) 2 (John Quinn) *in tch on inner: gd hdwy 3f out: led wl over 1f out: rdn clr ent fnl f: kpt on wl* **14/1**	81+
0-00	**2**	*2*	**Amazing Blue Sky**[11] 1275 6-9-3 71 ...... JamesSullivan 7 (Ruth Carr) *a.p: cl up 1/2-way: led over 2f out: rdn and hdd wl over 1f out: kpt on u.p fnl f* **25/1**	77
100-	**3**	*2 ¼*	**Alsahil (USA)**[70] 6676 6-9-1 74 ...... GarryWhillans(5) 5 (Micky Hammond) *a.p: effrt 3f out: sn rdn: kpt on same pce fr over 1f out* **22/1**	76
0-43	**4**	*nk*	**Embsay Crag**[10] 1295 6-9-1 69 ...... KellyHarrison 11 (Kate Walton) *hld up in rr: hdwy on outer 5f out: chsd ldrs over 3f out: rdn and ev ch over 2f out: drvn and one pce fr over 1f out* **6/1**[2]	71
10-0	**5**	*¾*	**Grey Command (USA)**[7] 1382 7-8-13 67 ...... RobertWinston 3 (Mel Brittain) *hld up towards rr: hdwy 3f out: rdn along wl over 2f out: kpt on: nrst fin* **33/1**	68
136-	**6**	*1 ¾*	**Korngold**[224] 5938 4-9-2 71 ...... PhillipMakin 9 (John Dunlop) *hld up towards rr: hdwy over 4f out: rdn along and in tch over 2f out: sn no imp* **13/8**[1]	69
3400	**7**	*1 ½*	**Jawaab (IRE)**[10] 1297 8-8-8 62 ......(e) AndrewMullen 4 (Richard Guest) *chsd ldrs: rdn along over 3f out: sn one pce* **33/1**	58
0-06	**8**	*½*	**Sartingo (IRE)**[11] 1275 5-8-11 65 ...... PJMcDonald 8 (Alan Swinbank) *a in rr* **17/2**	60
50-2	**9**	*2 ½*	**Goodness**[7] 1382 4-9-1 70 ...... DanielTudhope 10 (David O'Meara) *chsd ldrs: rdn along over 3f out: grad wknd* **8/1**[3]	61
1132	**10**	*11*	**Ay Tay Tate (IRE)**[11] 1275 6-8-13 67 ......(p) TonyCulhane 1 (David C Griffiths) *led: rdn along 4f out: hdd over 2f out: sn wknd* **11/1**	40
300-	**11**	*5*	**King Of The Celts (IRE)**[100] 6674 4-9-4 73 ...... TomEaves 12 (Tim Easterby) *in tch: hdwy on outer to chse ldrs 5f out: rdn along 3f out: sn wknd* **16/1**	38
2410	**12**	*39*	**Southern State (USA)**[17] 1186 4-9-6 75 ...... SilvestreDeSousa 6 (Mark Johnston) *in tch: rdn along 1/2-way: sn wknd: bhd and eased fnl 2f* **8/1**[3]	

2m 47.81s (11.61) **Going Correction** +1.05s/f (Soft)
WFA 4 from 5yo+ 1lb 12 Ran SP% **120.1**
Speed ratings (Par 103): **103,101,100,99,99 98,97,96,95,87 84,58**
toteswingers: 1&2 £27.20, 1&3 £27.20, 2&3 not won. CSF £329.01 CT £7409.00 TOTE £16.80: £4.20, £6.10, £10.40; EX 314.50.
Owner Far 2 Many Sues **Bred** P J McCalmont **Trained** Settrington, N Yorks

FOCUS
An average handicap for older horses run at a decent tempo throughout and a winning time around sixteen seconds slower than standard illustrates the attritional ground conditions. A hefty April shower greeted the field as they entered the home straight, at which point the winner was coming right back on the bridle. He is rated to last summer's form with the runner-up in line with his best marks at the trip.
Jawaab(IRE) Official explanation: jockey said gelding hung left-handed in straight

1526 THOMAS LORD H'CAP 6f

5:35 (5:36) (Class 5) (0-70,68) 4-Y-0+ **£2,943** (£875; £437; £218) **Stalls** High

Form				RPR
510-	**1**		**Half A Crown (IRE)**[158] 7420 7-8-6 60 ...... HannahNunn(7) 12 (Peter Salmon) *cl up: led on bit over 2f out: pushed clr over 1f out: kpt on wl* **22/1**	74
000-	**2**	*4 ½*	**Besty**[199] 6634 5-8-11 58 ...... MickyFenton 13 (Paul Midgley) *in tch: hdwy 1/2-way: chsd ldrs 2f out: sn rdn and chsd wnr appr fnl f: no imp* **8/1**	58
00-0	**3**	*½*	**Fama Mac**[12] 1251 5-8-7 54 oh6 ...... JamesSullivan 11 (Neville Bycroft) *in rr: stdy hdwy over 2f out: rdn to chse ldrs over 1f out: kpt on fnl f: nrst fin* **9/1**	52
30-0	**4**	*1 ¾*	**Northern Bolt**[12] 1254 7-9-4 65 ......(b) PatrickMathers 4 (Ian McInnes) *sluggish s and reminders in rr: hdwy over 2f out: sn rdn and styd on appr fnl f: nrst fin* **9/1**	57
154-	**5**	*4*	**Meandmyshadow**[179] 7073 4-9-7 68 ...... FrederikTylicki 14 (Alan Brown) *led: rdn along 1/2-way: hdd over 2f out: sn drvn and wknd over 1f out* **10/1**	48
103-	**6**	*1 ¼*	**Secret City (IRE)**[180] 7064 6-9-4 65 ...... DanielTudhope 5 (Robin Bastiman) *towards rr: hdwy 2f out: rdn and kpt on appr fnl f: n.d* **16/1**	41
1314	**7**	*½*	**Prince Of Vasa (IRE)**[18] 1177 5-9-5 66 ...... AndrewMullen 1 (Michael Smith) *chsd ldrs on wd outside: cl up 1/2-way: rdn over 2f out and sn wknd* **7/1**[3]	40
0000	**8**	*3*	**Kwik Time**[77] 430 4-8-7 54 oh9 ...... LeeNewman 3 (Robin Bastiman) *towards rr: hdwy whn n.m.r and swtchd lft wl over 1f out: sn rdn and n.d* **66/1**	18
10-0	**9**	*1 ¼*	**Qubuh (IRE)**[38] 893 4-9-5 66 ...... TonyHamilton 6 (Linda Stubbs) *nvr bttr than midfield* **25/1**	26
05-0	**10**	*1 ½*	**Choc'A'Moca (IRE)**[18] 1177 5-8-13 60 ......(v) BarryMcHugh 2 (Paul Midgley) *dwlt: a towards rr* **20/1**	16
1206	**11**	*3 ¼*	**Greenhead High**[14] 1224 4-8-13 60 ...... AdrianNicholls 15 (David Nicholls) *in tch: hdwy to chse ldrs 1/2-way: rdn along 2f out and sn wknd* **13/2**[2]	
250-	**12**	*5*	**Commanche Raider (IRE)**[193] 6779 5-9-7 68 ......(p) TomEaves 9 (Michael Dods) *a bhd* **14/1**	

5-04 **13** *3 ¼* **Mark Anthony (IRE)**[14] 1224 5-8-12 **59**...................(p) RobertWinston 10
(Shaun Harris) *chsd ldrs: rdn along 1/2-way: sn lost pl and bhd* **5/1**[1]

-000 **14** *9* **Rowan Spirit (IRE)**[18] 1177 4-9-4 **68**.............................(p) RyanClark(3) 8
(Mark Brisbourne) *prom: rdn along bef 1/2-way: sn wknd* **10/1**

000- **15** *9* **Spanish Acclaim**[213] 6266 5-9-2 **63**................................. PJMcDonald 7
(Ruth Carr) *cl up: rdn along bef 1/2-way: sn wknd and bhd fnl 2f* **16/1**

1m 17.56s (4.86) **Going Correction** +0.90s/f (Soft) **15** Ran SP% **124.7**
Speed ratings (Par 103): **103,97,96,94,88 87,86,82,80,78 74,67,63,51,39**
toteswingers: 1&2 £32.30, 1&3 £32.30, 2&3 £14.40. CSF £188.07 CT £1136.00 TOTE £26.30: £8.40, £2.50, £6.00; EX 203.70.
Owner Viscount Environmental **Bred** Burns Farm Stud **Trained** Kirk Deighton, W Yorks

FOCUS
Only a moderate handicap where it proved best to race up with the pace off what was only a steady gallop. The advantage of a high draw was highlighted with the first three home coming out of stalls 12,13 and 11, and the form is hard to pin down.
Mark Anthony(IRE) Official explanation: trainer said, regarding running, that the gelding was unable to dominate

1527 THIRSKRACECOURSE.NET H'CAP (DIV II) 7f
6:05 (6:05) (Class 5) (0-75,74) 4-Y-O+ **£3,101** (£915; £458) **Stalls** Low

Form RPR

0U6- **1** **Just The Tonic**[176] 7141 5-9-0 **67**....................................... PhillipMakin 2 74
(Marjorie Fife) *in tch: hdwy to chse ldrs wl over 2f out: led wl over 1f out: sn clr* **20/1**

0303 **2** *3 ¾* **Georgebernardshaw (IRE)**[11] 1276 7-8-9 **62**................ KellyHarrison 4 59
(Richard Guest) *trckd ldr: hdwy and cl up 1/2-way: led wl over 2f out: rdn and hdd wl over 1f out: sn drvn and kpt on same pce* **10/3**[1]

10-0 **3** *4* **Calypso Cay**[98] 176 4-9-0 **67**....................................... AndrewMullen 12 54
(Peter Salmon) *led: rdn along 3f out: sn hdd: drvn and one pce fr wl over 1f out* **22/1**

0-20 **4** *2* **Nezami (IRE)**[20] 1161 7-9-2 **69**.. MickyFenton 9 50
(Paul Midgley) *dwlt and in rr: hdwy 3f out: rdn 2f out: styd on same pce* **9/2**[2]

346- **5** *2* **Tamasou (IRE)**[239] 5455 7-9-7 **74**.................................. AdrianNicholls 7 50
(Ed McMahon) *chsd ldrs: hdwy 3f out: rdn 2f out: sn drvn and wknd* **11/2**

160- **6** *2 ¾* **Keys Of Cyprus**[179] 7074 10-8-12 **72**......................... ShirleyTeasdale(7) 8 41
(David Nicholls) *midfield: hdwy and in tch over 3f out: sn rdn and wknd 2f out* **6/1**

10-0 **7** *2* **No Quarter (IRE)**[10] 1293 5-8-9 **62**............................. RobertWinston 10 26
(Tracy Waggott) *hld up in rr: hdwy on wd outside wl over 2f out: rdn and edgd lft wl over 1f out: n.d* **14/1**

000- **8** *nse* **Talent Scout (IRE)**[190] 6830 6-9-0 **67**.......................... DuranFentiman 1 31
(Tim Walford) *a in rr* **12/1**

605- **9** *nk* **Iceblast**[214] 6234 4-9-0 **67**.. JamesSullivan 5 30
(Michael Easterby) *hld up: a towards rr* **5/1**[3]

040- **10** *27* **Touch Tone**[262] 4670 5-9-4 **71**.. DanielTudhope 6
(David Thompson) *prom: cl up 1/2-way: rdn along wl over 2f out: sn wknd* **14/1**

1m 34.53s (7.33) **Going Correction** +1.05s/f (Soft) **10** Ran SP% **117.7**
Speed ratings (Par 103): **100,95,91,88,86 83,81,81,80,49**
toteswingers: 1&2 not won, 1&3 not won, 2&3 not won. CSF £86.77 CT £1556.53 TOTE £21.60: £4.40, £1.20, £5.10; EX 153.20.
Owner R W Fife **Bred** West Dereham Abbey Stud **Trained** Stillington, N Yorks

FOCUS
A modest handicap for older horses to conclude proceedings with a winning time significantly slower than the first division which began the meeting four hours earlier. The form is rated at face value through the runner-up.
Nezami(IRE) Official explanation: jockey said gelding reared as gates opened
T/Plt: £9,810.20 to a £1 stake. Pool of £55,770.84 - 4.15 winning tickets. T/Qpdt: £333.60 to a £1 stake. Pool of £3,517.11 - 7.80 winning tickets. JR

1481 WOLVERHAMPTON (A.W) (L-H)
Saturday, April 21

OFFICIAL GOING: Standard
Wind: Fresh across Weather: Showers

1528 £32 FREE AT 32RED.COM AMATEUR RIDERS' H'CAP 5f 216y(P)
6:15 (6:15) (Class 6) (0-60,60) 4-Y-O+ **£2,107** (£648; £324) **Stalls** Low

Form RPR

0/0- **1** **Enjoyment**[296] 3541 5-10-7 **60**.. MissDLenge(7) 1 72
(Alan McCabe) *sn led: clr over 1f out: pushed out* **14/1**

000- **2** *1* **Foreign Rhythm (IRE)**[193] 6778 7-10-9 **60**.................... MissVBarr(5) 8 69
(Ron Barr) *hld up: hdwy over 2f out: r.o to go 2nd ins fnl f: no ch w wnr* **33/1**

1665 **3** *2 ¼* **Slatey Hen (IRE)**[25] 1054 4-10-7 **53**.............................(p) MissZoeLilly 9 55
(Richard Guest) *prom: lost pl 5f out: hdwy over 2f out: styd on* **25/1**

-544 **4** *1 ½* **Indian Arrow**[33] 964 4-10-10 **56**.. MrSWalker 5 53
(John Quinn) *s.i.s: sn prom: chsd wnr over 1f out: sn rdn and edgd rt: no ex fnl f* **7/4**[1]

3004 **5** *6* **Welsh Inlet (IRE)**[17] 1185 4-10-7 **60**.............................. MrAJones(7) 10 38
(John Bridger) *s.i.s: sn prom: pushed along and hung rt fr over 2f out: sn wknd* **16/1**

0000 **6** *¾* **Loyal Royal (IRE)**[30] 997 9-10-8 **59**...........................(bt) MissHDavies(5) 4 34
(Milton Bradley) *s.i.s: hld up: hdwy and carried rt 2f out: nvr trbld ldrs* **9/1**[3]

0530 **7** *1* **Memphis Man**[7] 1387 9-10-8 **54**................................. MrFWindsorClive 7 26
(David Evans) *sn pushed along and prom: rdn over 2f out: sn wknd* **14/1**

0105 **8** *¾* **Stamp Duty (IRE)**[44] 843 4-10-6 **57**...................... MrAaronJames(5) 12 27
(Suzzanne France) *hld up: hdwy and carried rt 2f out: n.d* **11/1**

500 **9** *1 ¼* **Forty Proof (IRE)**[9] 1343 4-10-2 **53**.........................(bt) MrFMitchell(5) 13 19
(David Evans) *chsd wnr tl rdn and wknd over 1f out* **18/1**

3006 **10** *½* **Rapid Water**[70] 522 6-10-4 **57** ow1.............................. MissELOwen(7) 11 21
(Pat Eddery) *mid-div: lost pl over 3f out: in rr whn hmpd 2f out: bhd whn swtchd lft over 1f out* **20/1**

24-0 **11** *1* **Loves Theme (IRE)**[48] 102 4-10-5 **58**..................(p) MissAlexOwen(7) 2 19
(Alan Bailey) *chsd ldrs: rdn over 2f out: sn wknd* **12/1**

3506 **12** *¾* **Royal Box**[53] 729 5-10-3 **56**.. MissMLEvans(7) 6 15
(David Evans) *chsd ldrs: lost pl over 3f out: wknd over 2f out* **12/1**

1301 **P** **Welcome Approach**[33] 964 9-10-6 **59**........................ MrEKingsley(7) 3
(John Weymes) *hld up: p.u over 3f out: fatally injured* **17/2**[2]

1m 15.17s (0.17) **Going Correction** -0.125s/f (Stan) **13** Ran SP% **116.6**
Speed ratings (Par 101): **93,91,88,86,78 77,76,75,73,73 71,70,**
toteswingers: 1&2 £95.90, 1&3 £88.80, 2&3 £143.90. CSF £411.54 CT £11151.59 TOTE £14.70: £5.00, £12.20, £3.90; EX 180.40 TRIFECTA Not won..
Owner A J McCabe **Bred** Whatton Manor Stud **Trained** Averham Park, Notts

FOCUS
A modest handicap that wasn't run at the overly strong pace these races often are, but even so few ever got competitive with plenty not helping themselves by running very wide on the home turn.
Welsh Inlet(IRE) Official explanation: jockey said saddle slipped

1529 32RED CASINO H'CAP 5f 216y(P)
6:45 (6:46) (Class 6) (0-65,68) 3-Y-O **£2,181** (£644; £322) **Stalls** Low

Form RPR

00-2 **1** **Mayo Lad (IRE)**[9] 1331 3-9-10 **68**.. KieranO'Neill 5 76+
(Richard Hannon) *sn pushed along in rr: rdn over 2f out: str run and hung lft ins fnl f: led nr fin* **9/4**[1]

1232 **2** *nk* **Homeward Strut**[5] 1419 3-9-6 **64**...................................(b) LukeMorris 10 71
(Frank Sheridan) *prom: lost pl over 4f out: hdwy u.p over 1f out: led wl ins fnl f: hdd nr fin* **11/2**[3]

643 **3** *1 ¼* **Miserere Mei (IRE)**[12] 1252 3-8-3 **52**........................(p) DuilioDaSilva(5) 3 55
(Richard Guest) *led over 5f out: hdd over 4f out: chsd ldr tl rdn to ld over 1f out: hdd and unable qck wl ins fnl f* **22/1**

0552 **4** *hd* **Trending (IRE)**[9] 1337 3-8-8 **52**...................................(b) JamieMackay 2 54
(Jeremy Gask) *hld up in tch: plld hrd: rdn and swtchd rt ins fnl f: r.o* **11/1**

55-3 **5** *nk* **One Kool Dude**[39] 885 3-9-5 **63**.....................................(v[1]) KierenFallon 1 64
(Michael Bell) *sn pushed along to chse ldrs: led over 4f out: rdn and hdd over 1f out: styd on same pce ins fnl f* **8/1**

40-2 **6** *hd* **Absent Amy (IRE)**[70] 524 3-9-6 **64**.............................. StevieDonohoe 8 64+
(Willie Musson) *hld up: shkn up over 2f out: running on whn hmpd ins fnl f: nvr nr to chal* **12/1**

-021 **7** *1* **Towbee**[12] 1252 3-9-3 **68**.......................................(b) DavidSimmonson(7) 12 65
(Michael Easterby) *dwlt: hdwy over 2f out: rdn whn hmpd ins fnl f: sn hung rt: styd on same pce* **10/1**

0-13 **8** *1 ¾* **Persidha**[7] 1393 3-9-6 **64**...(v) MartinLane 7 56
(Derek Shaw) *led early: chsd ldrs: rdn over 1f out: styd on same pce fnl f* **12/1**

600- **9** *1* **Pendle Lady (IRE)**[170] 7252 3-9-1 **59**.......................... TomMcLaughlin 6 47
(Mark Brisbourne) *sn pushed along in rr: nvr on terms* **66/1**

044- **10** *½* **Classic Falcon (IRE)**[185] 6946 3-9-1 **62**.................... AdamBeschizza(3) 4 49
(William Haggas) *trckd ldrs: racd keenly: rdn over 1f out: wknd ins fnl f* **9/2**[2]

004- **11** *7* **Courtland King (IRE)**[184] 6975 3-9-2 **65**............(t) MatthewCosham(5) 9 29
(David Evans) *prom: rdn over 2f out: wknd over 1f out* **33/1**

1m 14.67s (-0.33) **Going Correction** -0.125s/f (Stan) **11** Ran SP% **117.0**
Speed ratings (Par 96): **97,96,94,94,94 94,92,90,89,88 79**
toteswingers: 1&2 £5.00, 1&3 £6.60, 2&3 £3.30. CSF £14.00 CT £220.92 TOTE £2.10: £1.10, £1.40, £4.70; EX 16.60 Trifecta £259.80 Part won. Pool: £351.14 - 0.20 winning units..
Owner Middleham Park Racing IX & James Pak **Bred** Redpender Stud Ltd **Trained** East Everleigh, Wilts
■ Stewards' Enquiry : Luke Morris two-day ban: used whip above permitted level (May 7-8)

FOCUS
A more interesting race of its type than many at this trip in this grade and it looks reliable form. The pace was strong and favoured those ridden with restraint.

1530 DOWNLOAD OUR IPHONE APP (S) STKS 1m 141y(P)
7:15 (7:15) (Class 6) 3-Y-O+ **£2,181** (£644; £322) **Stalls** Low

Form RPR

5100 **1** **Greyfriarschorista**[3] 1436 5-10-0 78................................. KierenFallon 5 74
(Richard Guest) *mde all: clr over 3f out: shkn up over 1f out: styd on* **11/8**[1]

0322 **2** *1 ¼* **Unlimited**[23] 1082 10-9-9 70... NeilCallan 7 67
(Tony Carroll) *hld up: hdwy 3f out: rdn to go 2nd over 2f out: r.o: nt rch wnr* **9/2**[2]

3323 **3** *2* **Ahlawy (IRE)**[8] 1360 9-10-0 68..(t) LukeMorris 3 67
(Frank Sheridan) *chsd ldrs: rdn over 2f out: styd on* **7/1**[3]

0-00 **4** *2* **Hackett (IRE)**[66] 558 4-9-2 46.....................(b) WilliamTwiston-Davies(7) 4 57
(Shaun Lycett) *hld up: rdn over 2f out: r.o ins fnl f: nvr nrr* **20/1**

-644 **5** *½* **Rock Anthem (IRE)**[45] 821 8-10-0 63.............................. KieranO'Neill 8 61
(Mike Murphy) *hld up: rdn over 1f out: r.o: nvr trbld ldrs* **9/2**[2]

0-05 **6** *3 ½* **Aglaja**[74] 466 3-8-0 42...(p) SophieDoyle(3) 2 40
(Frank Sheridan) *chsd wnr 2f: remained handy: rdn over 2f out: wknd over 1f out* **25/1**

6024 **7** *11* **Slam**[8] 1360 7-9-9 65...(p) PatCosgrave 6 23
(Robert Cowell) *prom: chsd wnr over 6f out tl rdn and wknd over 2f out* **7/1**[3]

4050 **8** *15* **Nothing's Simple**[12] 1259 3-8-1 50..............................(b[1]) NoelGarbutt(7) 1
(Hugo Palmer) *prom: pushed along 1/2-way: wknd 3f out: t.o* **25/1**

1m 50.16s (-0.34) **Going Correction** -0.125s/f (Stan)
WFA 3 from 4yo+ 15lb **8** Ran SP% **115.9**
Speed ratings (Par 101): **96,94,93,91,90 87,78,64**
toteswingers: 1&2 £1.50, 1&3 £2.10, 2&3 £4.50. CSF £7.64 TOTE £1.80: £1.10, £1.80, £2.80; EX 9.50 Trifecta £10.80 Pool: £319.13 - 21.80 winning units..The winner was sold to C Beek racing for 6000gns
Owner Willie McKay **Bred** Castlemartin Stud And Skymarc Farm **Trained** Stainforth, S Yorks

FOCUS
A wide variety of abilities on show in an uncompetitive seller. The pace was uneven with the winner dictating.

1531 32RED FILLIES' H'CAP 1m 141y(P)
7:45 (7:46) (Class 5) (0-70,70) 3-Y-O **£2,911** (£866; £432; £216) **Stalls** Low

Form RPR

01-4 **1** **Al Jabreiah**[10] 1322 3-9-5 **68**.. LiamJones 3 75+
(William Haggas) *hld up: hdwy over 1f out: rdn and edgd lft ins fnl f: r.o to ld towards fin* **7/2**[1]

1 **2** *1 ¼* **Frosty Berry**[99] 159 3-9-3 **66**.. NickyMackay 4 70
(Marco Botti) *chsd ldrs: shkn up to ld over 1f out: rdn ins fnl f: hdd towards fin* **5/1**

060- **3** *¾* **Princess Caetani (IRE)**[203] 6526 3-9-7 **70**........................ MartinLane 2 75+
(David Simcock) *hld up: swtchd rt and hdwy over 1f out: sn rdn: hmpd ins fnl f: r.o: nt rch ldrs* **9/2**[3]

11-0 **4** *hd* **Tweet Lady**[25] 1058 3-9-6 **69**... JamesMillman 9 71
(Rod Millman) *chsd ldr tl led over 2f out: rdn and hdd over 1f out: styd on* **18/1**

00-3 **5** *nk* **Love Grows Wild (USA)**[8] 1359 3-8-7 **56**.................... JamieSpencer 8 57
(Michael Bell) *a.p: rdn over 2f out: styd on* **4/1**[2]

53-1 **6** *1* **Boudoir (IRE)**[97] 185 3-9-7 **70**.. KieranO'Neill 5 69
(Richard Hannon) *hld up: hdwy over 1f out: sn rdn: styd on same pce ins fnl f* **4/1**[2]

41-6 **7** *1 ¼* **Guava**[5] 1419 3-9-3 **66**... LukeMorris 1 62
(Frank Sheridan) *hld up: hdwy over 2f out: rdn over 1f out: no ex ins fnl f* **14/1**

0-00 **8** *8* **Medam**[7] 1386 3 -8-857 oh11 ow1 RobbieFitzpatrick 7 35
(Shaun Harris) *sn led: rdn: hung rt and hdd over 2f out: wknd over 1f out* **100/1**
06-6 **9** *5* **Kogershin (USA)**[17] 1182 3 -9-366 TadhgO'Shea 6 32
(Marcus Tregoning) *hld up: rdn over 2f out: wknd wl over 1f out* **20/1**
1m 50.27s (-0.23) **Going Correction** -0.125s/f (Stan) 9Ran SP% 114.8
Speed ratings (Par 95): **96,94,94,94,93 92,91,84,80**
toteswingers: 1&2 £5.60, 1&3 £4.50, 2&3 £5.90. CSF £21.12 CT £79.14 TOTE £5.30 : £1.40, £1.50, £2.10 ; EX 32.30 Trifecta £73.30 Pool: £325.92 - 3.29 winning units.
Owner Mohammed Jaber **Bred** Rabbah Bloodstock Limited **Trained** Newmarket, Suffolk
FOCUS
An interesting fillies handicap containing plenty that looked open to improvement. It was run at a good pace and it looks good form for the grade.

1532 32RED.COM MAIDEN FILLIES' STKS 1m 1f 103y (P)
8:15 (8:16) (Class 5) 3-Y-O+ **£2,911** (£866; £432 ; £216) **Stalls** Low

Form RPR
2- **1** **Shestheman**[186] 6933 3 -8-100 TedDurcan 6 80+
(David Lanigan) *a.p: pushed along over 2f out: chsd ldr over 1f out: rdn to ld wl ins fnl f: r.o* **11/2**
43 **2** *1 1/2* **Fleeting Image**[8] 1363 3 -8-30 NatashaEaton(7) 10 77
(Alan Bailey) *led: rdn over 1f out: hdd and unable qck wl ins fnl f* **16/1**
064- **3** *1 1/2* **Aniseed (IRE)**[186] 6933 3 -8-1078 KierenFallon 11 74
(William Haggas) *chsd ldrs: rdn and hung rt over 1f out: styd on* **5/1**3
4 *hd* **Sound Hearts (USA)** 3 -8-100 NeilCallan 4 73+
(Roger Varian) *s.i.s: sn mid-div: hdwy over 2f out: rdn and edgd lft over 1f out: styd on* **11/4**2
3- **5** *shd* **Epoque (USA)**[217] 6168 3 -8-100 TomQueally 1 73
(Sir Henry Cecil) *chsd ldr tl rdn over 1f out: styd on same pce fnl f* **9/4**1
540- **6** *3* **Specific (IRE)**[193] 6776 3 -8-1070 MickaelBarzalona 12 67
(Mahmood Al Zarooni) *chsd ldrs: rdn over 2f out: wknd fnl f* **12/1**
7 *3 1/4* **Bite Of The Cherry** 3 -8-100 StevieDonohoe 9 60+
(Michael Bell) *hld up: styd on appr fnl f: nvr nrr* **66/1**
5 **8** *1 3/4* **Plumbago Blue**[24] 1065 3 -8-100 NickyMackay 2 56
(Marco Botti) *prom: rdn over 2f out: n.m.r over 1f out: wknd fnl f* **33/1**
0- **9** *3 1/2* **Still I'm A Star (IRE)**[186] 6933 3 -8-100 JamieSpencer 5 49+
(David Simcock) *hld up: nvr on terms* **20/1**
54- **10** *1 1/4* **News Show**[186] 6934 3 -8-100 MartinLane 7 46
(David Simcock) *s.i.s: hld up: a in rr* **50/1**
05 **11** *7* **Bright Girl (IRE)**[29] 1004 4 -9-80 (b[1]) AdamBeschizza(3) 3 35
(Mark Rimmer) *hld up: rdn over 3f out: sn wknd* **80/1**
12 *3 1/2* **Bashaash (USA)** 3 -8-100 TadhgO'Shea 8 24
(Ed Dunlop) *s.i.s: a in rr* **40/1**
1m 58.95s (-2.75) **Going Correction** -0.125s/f (Stan)
WFA 3 from 4yo 15lb 12Ran SP% 117.9
Speed ratings (Par 100): **107,105,104,104,104 101,98,96,93,92 86,83**
toteswingers: 1&2 £28.70, 1&3 £6.50, 2&3 £38.30. CSF £81.48 TOTE £4.80 : £1.20 , £4.80 , £2.20; EX 56.40 Trifecta £281.60 Part won. Pool: £380.61 - 0.82 winning units.
Owner The Kathryn Stud **Bred** The Kathryn Stud **Trained** Upper Lambourn, Berks
■ Stewards' Enquiry : Stevie Donohoe caution: entered wrong stall
FOCUS
No more than a fair maiden despite the stables represented and unlikely there were any potential stars on show. The pace wasn't strong and it paid to be handy.

1533 FIND US ON FACEBOOK WOLVERHAMPTON RACECOURSE H'CAP 1m 1f 103y (P)
8:45 (8:47) (Class 6) (0-65,65) 4-Y-O+ **£2,181** (£644; £322) **Stalls** Low

Form RPR
332- **1** **Ishikawa (IRE)**[22] 5380 4 -8-1256 FergusSweeney 10 71
(Alan King) *prom: rdn over 2f out: hung lft over 1f out: styd on u.p to ld ins fnl f: sn clr* **7/1**
00-0 **2** *3 3/4* **Hurakan (IRE)**[20] 1154 6 -9-765 JamesDoyle 11 72
(Richard Price) *chsd ldr: rdn to ld over 1f out: hdd and unable qck ins fnl f* **7/1**
-324 **3** *4* **Count Ceprano (IRE)**[12] 1106 8 -8-1158 SimonPearce(3) 3 57
(Lydia Pearce) *mid-div: rdn over 3f out: styd on fr over 1f out: nvr able to chal* **14/1**
0132 **4** *nse* **Ostentation**[4] 1432 5 -9-260 MickaelBarzalona 7 58
(Alastair Lidderdale) *chsd ldrs: led 2f out: rdn and hdd over 1f out: wknd ins fnl f* **4/1**1
1142 **5** *hd* **Prohibition (IRE)**[7] 1379 6 -9-361 KierenFallon 8 59
(Alastair Lidderdale) *s.i.s: hld up: rdn over 1f out: r.o ins fnl f: nvr trbld ldrs* **9/2**2
4225 **6** *1* **Cane Cat (IRE)**[38] 891 5 -9-361 (t) LukeMorris 1 57
(Tony Carroll) *hld up: rdn over 2f out: styd on fr over 1f out: nvr trbld ldrs* **9/1**
10-5 **7** *1/2* **Ela Gonda Mou**[10] 1314 5 -8-1261 RosieJessop(5) 4 56
(Peter Charalambous) *led: clr over 6f out: hdd 2f out: wknd fnl f* **16/1**
5334 **8** *1* **Fibs And Flannel**[7] 1391 5 -9-462 JamieMackay 6 55
(Willie Musson) *s.i.s: hld up: rdn over 2f out: nvr on terms* **11/2**3
005- **9** *1* **Valdaw**[276] 4200 4 -9-159 NeilCallan 5 50
(Tony Carroll) *hld up: rdn over 2f out: a in rr* **22/1**
0525 **10** *3 1/4* **Black Coffee**[7] 1391 7 -9-765 (b) ShaneKelly 2 49
(Mark Brisbourne) *s.i.s: hld up: rdn over 2f out: nvr on terms* **11/1**
202- **11** *1* **Arashi**[282] 4024 6 -9-765 (v) MartinLane 9 47
(Derek Shaw) *hld up: effrt over 2f out: wknd wl over 1f out* **16/1**
1m 59.72s (-1.98) **Going Correction** -0.125s/f (Stan) 11Ran SP% 119.7
Speed ratings (Par 101): **103,99,96,96,95 95,94,93,92,89 89**
toteswingers: 1&2 £11.80, 1&3 £17.20, 2&3 £8.70. CSF £56.43 CT £678.11 TOTE £6.60 : £1.40 , £3.10, £4.40 ; EX 64.00 Trifecta £748.20 Part won. Pool: £1,011.15 - 0.62 winning units.
Owner ROA Racing Partnership V **Bred** Ken Carroll **Trained** Barbury Castle, Wilts
■ Stewards' Enquiry : Jamie Mackay caution: entered wrong stall
FOCUS
A run-of-the-mill race for the grade with recent winning form thin on the ground. The pace was strong but the majority of the field were content to sit well back and few got into it.

1534 32REDPOKER.COM H'CAP 1m 4f 50y (P)
9:15 (9:15) (Class 6) (0-60,59) 4-Y-O+ **£2,181** (£644; £322) **Stalls** Low

Form RPR
1 **Teak (IRE)**[195] 5222 5 -8-954 GeorgeDowning(7) 2 65
(Ian Williams) *a.p: nt clr run over 2f out: rdn to ld 1f out: r.o wl* **9/2**2
2103 **2** *2 1/2* **Visions Of Johanna (USA)**[7] 1189 7 -9-557 KierenFallon 5 64
(Richard Guest) *hld up: hdwy over 2f out: led over 1f out: sn rdn and hdd: styd on same pce ins fnl f* **7/2**1
0041 **3** *2 1/2* **Khun John (IRE)**[38] 895 9 -9-759 StevieDonohoe 3 62
(Willie Musson) *hld up: hdwy over 2f out: led wl over 1f out: sn rdn and hdd: no ex ins fnl f* **9/2**2

1150 **4** *4* **Black Iceman**[43] 850 4 -9-157 SimonPearce(3) 7 54
(Lydia Pearce) *hld up: nt clr run over 2f out: hdwy and nt clr run over 1f out: nvr trbld ldrs* **14/1**
3660 **5** *shd* **Four Steps Back**[22] 1112 5 -8-146 RachealKneller(7) 6 42
(Mark Usher) *hld up: sme hdwy over 1f out: nvr nrr* **25/1**
/004 **6** *2* **Pahente**[23] 1083 4 -8-1049 NeilCallan 10 42
(Tony Carroll) *chsd ldrs: rdn over 3f out: wknd over 1f out* **10/1**
,5U0- **7** *1 1/2* **Into The Wind**[188] 6894 5 -9-254 JamesMillman 9 45
(Rod Millman) *hld up: rdn over 2f out: n.d* **25/1**
4600 **8** *nk* **Port Hill**[17] 1189 5 -8-1250 ShaneKelly 1 40
(Mark Brisbourne) *led 1f: chsd ldrs: rdn over 2f out: wknd fnl f* **13/2**3
5-03 **9** *2* **Gower Rules (IRE)**[33] 961 4 -9-659 KieranO'Neill 11 46
(John Bridger) *led after 1f: hdd 9f out: chsd ldr tl rdn over 2f out: wknd over 1f out* **9/1**
45-5 **10** *7* **Endaxi Mana Mou**[32] 966 4 -8-347 RosieJessop(5) 12 23
(Peter Charalambous) *plld hrd and prom: led 9f out: clr over 6f out: hdd wl over 1f out: sn wknd* **28/1**
344- **11** *13* **Disturbia (IRE)**[169] 7263 4 -8-746 LukeMorris 4
(Olivia Maylam) *mid-div: pushed along 1/2-way: wknd over 2f out: t.o* **16/1**
00-4 **12** *4 1/2* **Iguacu**[17] 1189 8 -9-153 JamesDoyle 8
(Richard Price) *hld up: wknd over 2f out: t.o* **14/1**
2m 39.06s (-2.04) **Going Correction** -0.125s/f (Stan)
WFA 4 from 5yo+ 1lb 12Ran SP% 121.4
Speed ratings (Par 101): **101,99,97,95,94 93,92,92,91,86 77,74**
toteswingers: 1&2 £3.10, 1&3 £5.20, 2&3 £6.60. CSF £20.66 CT £77.19 TOTE £5.50 : £1.50 , £1.90, £2.60 ; EX 26.70 Trifecta £71.90 Pool: £830.91 - 8.54 winning units.
Owner Farranamanagh **Bred** Michael Morrissey **Trained** Portway, Worcs
FOCUS
A modest handicap to finish with and little of interest behind the first three. Once again there was no hanging around but the clear leader was ignored.
T/Plt: £1,143.30 to a £1 stake. Pool of £67,908.89 - 43.36 winning tickets. T/Qpdt: £28.40 to a £1 stake. Pool of £8,337.73 - 217.20 winning tickets. CR

1535 - 1537a (Foreign Racing) - See Raceform Interactive

NAAS (L-H)
Saturday, April 21
OFFICIAL GOING: Good to yielding (yielding to places)

1538a WOODLANDS STKS (LISTED RACE) 5f
3:40 (3:40) 3-Y-O+ **£21,666** (£6,333; £3,000 ; £1,000)

RPR
1 **Santo Padre (IRE)**[14] 1226 8 -9-998 FergalLynch 1 109
(David Marnane, Ire) *chsd ldrs in 5th: rdn to ld 1f out: styd on wl fnl f* **12/1**
2 *2 1/2* **Spirit Quartz (IRE)**[28] 1033 4 -9-12 PatSmullen 4 103
(Robert Cowell) *cl up: 3rd for much: no imp and kpt on same pce fr 1f out* **6/4**1
3 *1/2* **Katla (IRE)**[14] 1226 4 -9-9101 WJLee 3 98
(J F Grogan, Ire) *sn narrow ldr: hdd and no imp fr 1f out: kpt on same pce* **3/1**2
4 *1 1/4* **The Reaper (IRE)**[14] 1226 4 -9-12101 (b) JohnnyMurtagh 2 97
(G M Lyons, Ire) *sn cl up: on terms fr 1/2-way: no imp and kpt on same pce fr 1f out* **9/2**3
5 *nk* **Balmont Mast (IRE)**[14] 1226 4 -9-998 ShaneFoley 5 93
(Edward Lynam, Ire) *chsd ldrs last of the 6: niggled along 1/2-way: no imp and kpt on fr over 1f out* **5/1**
6 *2 1/4* **Oor Jock (IRE)**[20] 4 -9-993 MichaelHussey 6 88
(John Patrick Shanahan, Ire) *trckd ldrs: cl 4th for much: no imp and kpt on same pce fr over 1f out* **9/1**
1m 1.53s (-0.47) 6Ran SP% 117.5
CSF £32.39 TOTE £14.90 : £5.30, £1.30 ; DF 82.80 .
Owner Victor Partnership **Bred** Victor Stud Bloodstock & Brendan Cummins **Trained** Bansha, Co Tipperary
FOCUS
The winner looked back to his best here.
NOTEBOOK
Santo Padre (IRE) returned to his best in quite emphatic fashion. Tucked in behind the leaders, who didn't go at a breakneck speed, he was switched to the far side to find daylight and when asked to quicken he left them for dead up the hill. It was impressive and it was good to see the horse back to his best. Even given the conditions though it was a slow time and that might just temper the visual impression ever so slightly. (op 14/1)
Spirit Quartz (IRE) ran as if he would have preferred to get a lead. He didn't really but he had no answer to the extra gear exhibited by the winner. (op 6/4 tchd 5/4)
Katla(IRE) showed speed without going flat out and kept going inside the last furlong. She was also left behind by the winner and in a race that wasn't entirely satisfactory she ran more or less to her mark. (op 9/4)
The Reaper (IRE) is really a 6f horse anyway but he struggled to get into any kind of rhythm on ground, which would have been softer than ideal. (op 11/2)
Balmont Mast (IRE) doesn't really look good enough on current evidence to be good enough for this grade but he did some reasonable late work. (op 4/1)
Oor Jock (IRE) dropped away inside the last having shown speed. (op 20/1)

1539a - 1548a (Foreign Racing) - See Raceform Interactive

1038 CURRAGH (R-H)
Sunday, April 22
OFFICIAL GOING: Straight course - yielding; round course - good to yielding changing to soft on all courses after race 4 (3.50)

1549a BIG BAD BOB GLADNESS STKS (GROUP 3) 7f
4:20 (4:22) 4-Y-O+ **£32,500** (£9,500; £4,500 ; £1,500)

RPR
1 **Excelebration (IRE)**[190] 6860 4 -9-7126 JPO'Brien 5 124+
(A P O'Brien, Ire) *trckd ldrs: 4th 1/2-way: smooth hdwy to ld over 1f out: qcknd clr fnl f: v easily* **2/7**1
2 *3 1/4* **Croisultan (IRE)**[15] 1226 6 -9-1106 PatSmullen 3 103
(D K Weld, Ire) *hld up in rr: hdwy into 3rd over 1f out: kpt on same pce to go 2nd fnl f but no ch w easy wnr* **10/1**3
3 *3/4* **Windsor Palace (IRE)**[28] 1043 7 -9-194 (b) SeamieHeffernan 4 101?
(A P O'Brien, Ire) *led: strly pressed and hdd briefly 2 1/2f out: kpt on u.p tl hdd again over 1f out: sn no ch w easy wnr and dropped to 3rd fnl f* **25/1**

The Form Book Flat, Raceform Ltd, Compton, RG20 6NL

4 4 1/2 **Billyford (IRE)**[9] 1370 7 -9-193 JohnnyMurtagh 2 89
(Liam Roche, Ire) *trckd ldrs: 5th 1/2-way: 4th 2f out: rdn and no ex fr 1f out: eased whn btn clsng stages* **16/1**
5 11 **Kargali (IRE)**[238] 5526 7 -9-195 (t) KevinManning 6 59
(Luke Comer, Ire) *chsd ldrs in 3rd: drvn along 3f out and no ex fr 2f out: wknd* **40/1**
6 9 **Beacon Lodge (IRE)**[219] 6129 7 -9-1 FranBerry 1 35
(David Nicholls) *trckd ldr racing freely: led briefly 2 1/2f out: sn rdn and no ex: wknd* **5/1**[2]
1m 31.37s (0.57)**Going Correction** +0.275s/f (Good) **6**Ran SP% **115.7**
Speed ratings: **107,103,102,97,84 74**
CSF £4.74 TOTE £1.10 : £1.02 , £5.10 ; DF 4.60 .
Owner Derrick Smith **Bred** Owenstown Stud **Trained** Ballydoyle, Co Tipperary
FOCUS
An easy win for a horse rated 20lb higher than his closest rival.
NOTEBOOK
Excelebration(IRE)'s first start for new connections couldn't have gone more smoothly. He travelled well in the soft ground and, when asked to go and win his race, he left the opposition for dead while only doing a half speed himself. The engine proved intact and he heads to what is looking like an exciting renewal of the Lockinge next month. (op 1/4 tchd 3/10)
Croisultan(IRE) appreciated the rain that fell and ran on pretty well inside the last furlong or so. He was beaten very easily by the winner as one would expect, but it was a creditable effort and banished the memory of his poor effort at Cork two weeks earlier. (op 12/1)
Windsor Palace (IRE)is a valuable pacemaker and did his job in setting it up for his stablemate. A share of the spoils was a bonus. (op 28/1)
Billyford(IRE) found this a bit different than racing against handicappers at Dundalk and it's fair to say that he floundered a bit in conditions he wouldn't have encountered in some time. (op 20/1)
Kargali(IRE) was always likely to struggle. (op 33/1)
Beacon Lodge (IRE)had a good early position but went from travelling to finding nothing in just a few strides. Official explanation: jockey said gelding ran too free; vet said gelding was found to be blowing hard post-race (op 11/2)

1550 - 1552a & 1555a (Foreign Racing) - See Raceform Interactive

KREFELD (R-H)
Sunday, April 22

OFFICIAL GOING: Turf: good to soft

1553a PREIS DER SWK - DR BUSCH-MEMORIAL (GROUP 3) (3YO) (TURF) 1m 110y
3:30 (3:44) 3-Y-O
£26,666 (£9,166; £4,583 ; £2,500 ; £1,666 ; £1,250)

RPR
1 **Amaron**[189] 6901 3 -9-20 DavyBonilla 8 108
(Andreas Lowe, Germany) *broke fast: in ldng gp at first: checked sltly bkstretch: tk ld again bef the fnl turn over 2 1/2f out: led into st: r.o wl: repelled ev chal: r.o wl to line* **58/10**
2 hd **Energizer (GER)**[168] 7325 3 -9-20 ADeVries 5 108
(J Hirschberger, Germany) *broke slowly: settled in midfield: shkn up early in the st: tk sme time to find his feet: qcknd wl over 1 1/2f out: fin strly* **15/1**
3 1/2 **Auenturm (GER)** 3 -9-20 FrederikTylicki 2 107
(Uwe Ostmann, Germany) *broke fast: briefly led: then checked and settled in the ldng gp: looked btn early st: rallied wl whn asked: r.o wl ins fnl f: battled it out w the two ldrs to the line* **87/10**
4 1 1/4 **Pastorius (GER)**[168] 7325 3 -9-20 THellier 6 104
(Mario Hofer, Germany) *broke slowly: allowed to settle: sn began picking up horses in the bkstretch on the outside: a.p: r.o wl in the st: unable to chal first three* **18/5**[2]
5 3 1/2 **Kolonel (GER)**[238] 3 -9-20 EPedroza 7 96
(A Wohler, Germany) *broke fast: prom: racd keenly: led briefly in bk st: settled wl to come through in st: chal ldr: wknd fnl f* **57/10**
6 4 **Pakal (GER)**[175] 7192 3 -9-20 OlivierPeslier 10 88
(W Figge, Germany) *broke wl: settled in midfield: shkn up upon ent the st: r.o wl but unable to chal for ld and wknd* **23/5**[3]
7 hd **Girolamo (GER)**[35] 3 -9-20 AStarke 1 87
(P Schiergen, Germany) *broke wl but then lost stride: bkmarker in the bkstretch: allowed to find his rhythm: nursed along through fnl turn: shkn up in st: responded wl: styd on* **14/5**[1]
8 hd **Red Ghost (GER)**3 -9-20 (b) EFrank 4 87
(S Smrczek, Germany) *prom at first: cl up tl 1/2-way down the bkstretch: qckly wknd* **34/1**
9 9 **Lycidas (GER)**[155] 7494 3 -9-20 (b) StevieDonohoe 3 67
(Tobias B P Coles) *broke fast: prom in the early stages: r.o wl in midfield: rdn but no ex in the st* **162/10**
10 13 **World's Flash (GER)**[252] 3 -9-20 FabienLefebvre 9 38
(Andreas Lowe, Germany) *broke wl: settled in ldng gp: led briefly arnd 1st bnd: sn wknd* **36/5**
1m 50.42s (3.82) **10**Ran SP% **133.0**
WIN (incl. 10 euro stake): 68. PLACES: 24, 40, 32. SF: 440
Owner Gestut Winterhauch **Bred** Genesis Green Stud Ltd **Trained** Germany

SAN SIRO (R-H)
Sunday, April 22

OFFICIAL GOING: Turf: soft

1554a PREMIO AMBROSIANO (GROUP 3) (4YO+) (TURF) 1m 2f
2:55 (12:00) 4-Y-O+ **£23,333** (£10,266; £5,600 ; £2,800)

RPR
1 **Saratoga Black (IRE)**[315] 2982 5 -8-110 FabioBranca 4 114
(B Grizzetti, Italy) *trckd ldr in clr 2nd: shkn up to chal over 2 1/2f out: rdn to ld over 2f out: qcknd clr over 1 1/2f out: kpt on ins fnl f: comf* **27/8**[3]
2 1 1/2 **Estejo (GER)**[14] 8 -8-110 PierantonioConvertino 1 111
(R Rohne, Germany) *midfield: prog to chal gng wl 2 1/2f out: rdn and outpcd by eventual wnr over 1 1/2f out: wnt 2nd over 1f out: r.o ins fnl f: nrst fin* **7/10**[1]
3 1 3/4 **Frankenstein**[28] 5 -8-110 MircoDemuro 2 108
(B Grizzetti, Italy) *hld up in last pair on inner: rdn over 2 1/2f out: kpt on one pce fr over 1 1/2f* **21/10**[2]
4 2 1/2 **Iryklon (POL)**[189] 6905 6 -8-110 LManiezzi 5 103
(Vaclav Luka II, Czech Republic) *hld up in last pair on outer: rdn over 3f out: outpcd over 2 1/2f out: kpt on to go 4th ins fnl f* **7/1**
5 4 **Gasquet (ITY)**[424] 661 6 -8-110 CColombi 3 95
(Gianfranco Verricelli, Italy) *led: over 3 l clr on turn into st: rdn over 2 1/2f out: hdd over 2f out: no ex and wknd: eased ins fnl f* **28/1**
2m 9.5s (2.80) **5**Ran SP% **129.9**
WIN (incl. 1 euro stake): 4.37. PLACES: 1.56, 1.28. DF: 7.72
Owner Lino Scarpellini **Bred** John Neary **Trained** Italy

1269 PONTEFRACT (L-H)
Monday, April 23

OFFICIAL GOING: Soft (good to soft in places) changing to soft (heavy in places) after race 2 (2:45)
Wind: Virtually nil Weather: Overcast

1556 BHEST RACING TO SCHOOL MAIDEN FILLIES' STKS 5f
2:15 (2:16) (Class 5) 2-Y-O **£2,385** (£704; £352) **Stalls** Low

Form RPR
1 **Jadanna (IRE)** 2 -9-00 PaulMulrennan 9 76+
(James Given) *wnt rt s: sn swtchd markedly lft to inner: trckd ldrs: swtchd rt and effrt to chal ent fnl f: rdn: rn green and edgd lft: sn led: styd on strly* **16/1**
2 2 3 **Back In The Frame**[9] 1388 2 -9-00 RichardKingscote 1 65
(Tom Dascombe) *cl up on inner: slt ld over 2f out and sn rdn: hdd and one pce ins fnl f* **2/1**[1]
0 3 3/4 **Princess In Exile**[16] 1218 2 -9-00 LeeNewman 3 63+
(George Foster) *cl up: effrt 2f out: sn rdn and ev ch tl kpt on same pce ins fnl f* **25/1**
4 1 1/2 **Excel Yourself (IRE)**2 -9-00 KierenFallon 2 57+
(James Tate) *hmpd and in rr after 1f: hdwy on inner 2f out: rdn over 1f out: kpt on: nrst fin* **9/2**[3]
5 1 3/4 **Lasilia (IRE)** 2 -9-00 PhillipMakin 8 51+
(Kevin Ryan) *dwlt: hdwy to chse ldrs 1/2-way: effrt wl over 1f out: sn rdn and one pce* **10/3**[2]
6 1 1/4 **Mace The Ace** 2 -9-00 AndrewMullen 5 46
(David C Griffiths) *sn rdn along and outpcd in rr: bhd 1/2-way: styd on fr over 1f out* **33/1**
34 7 3 1/4 **Jamnean**[12] 1308 2 -9-00 RussKennemore 6 35+
(John Holt) *chsd ldrs: rdn along over 2f out: sn wknd* **14/1**
5 8 2 3/4 **Lady Raffa**[13] 1277 2 -9-00 TomEaves 7 25
(Michael Dods) *a towards rr* **12/1**
9 3 1/4 **Modern Lady** 2 -8-110 DeclanCannon(3) 4 13
(Richard Guest) *slt ld: rdn along 1/2-way: sn hdd & wknd* **15/2**
1m 9.02s (5.72)**Going Correction** +0.975s/f (Soft) **9**Ran SP% **113.4**
Speed ratings (Par 89): **93,88,87,84,81 79,74,70,65**
toteswingers:1&2:£7.30, 1&3:£24.10, 2&3:£14.00 CSF £47.47 TOTE £22.50 : £4.20 , £1.30 , £7.00; EX 53.20 TRIFECTA Not won. .
Owner Danethorpe Racing Partnership **Bred** Rathasker Stud **Trained** Willoughton, Lincs
FOCUS
After 40mm of rain in the last week and 6mm over the previous 24 hours the ground was genuinely soft according to the riders in the opener. This was a modest 2yo fillies' maiden with the form pitched at the top end of the race averages. The first two both look the types to do better.
NOTEBOOK
Jadanna(IRE) ◆, drawn widest of all, was switched inside after the start. She gradually worked her way into contention and, moved outside to make her finishing effort, ultimately won going away. The way this well-bred filly came home, 6f will suit her even better on less testing ground.
Back In The Frame, slowly away when runner-up first time on Polytrack at Wolverhampton, knew her job here but she was outgunned by the winner. She can surely find an opening in the next few weeks. (op 9-4 tchd 15-8)
Princess In Exile, well beaten first time, travelled strongly but seemed not to quite get home in the end in the testing conditions. (op 28-1)
Excel Yourself (IRE) a well-made sister to a Gimcrack runner-up, missed a beat at the start. She kept on in her own time in the home straight and this will have taught her plenty. (op 7-2)
Lasilia(IRE), speedily bred, was pulled wide for a run once in line for home but didn't get home. Less testing conditions will see her in a more favourable light. (op 7-2 tchd 4-1)
Modern Lady, half-sister to a couple of juvenile winners, was backed at long odds to make a winning debut. Fitted with a rug for stalls entry, she showed bags of toe until stopping to nothing in the final furlong. Much better ground will aid her cause. (tchd 8-1)

1557 PONTEFRACT'S GOT TALENT NIGHT ON 1ST JUNE H'CAP 1m 4f 8y
2:45 (2:45) (Class 4) (0-80,78) 3-Y-O **£4,840** (£1,429; £714) **Stalls** Low

Form RPR
322 1 **Ruacana**[39] 908 3 -9-677 HayleyTurner 7 90
(Michael Bell) *hld up in rr: stdy hdwy over 3f out: effrt on inner over 2f out: rdn to ld wl over 1f out: drvn out* **11/2**
23-3 2 1 3/4 **Hallmark Star**[22] 1160 3 -9-778 DaneO'Neill 1 88
(Gerard Butler) *cl up: rdn to ld over 2f out: drvn and hdd wl over 1f out: kpt on u.p fnl f* **10/3**[1]
452- 3 3 3/4 **Singalat**[131] 7752 3 -9-576 PaulMulrennan 6 80
(James Given) *hld up in rr: hdwy 4f out: rdn to chse ldrs 2f out: kpt on same pce appr fnl f* **16/1**
310- 4 3 **Winner's Wish**[187] 6957 3 -9-475 PaulHanagan 5 74
(Jeremy Noseda) *trckd ldrs: hdwy on outer and cl up 4f out: rdn along 3f out: sn one pce* **7/2**[2]
100- 5 8 **Moon Trip**[226] 5931 3 -9-475 SilvestreDeSousa 4 61
(Mark Johnston) *mde most tl rdn along and hdd wl over 2f out: sn drvn and wknd* **8/1**
1211 6 59 **Gabrial's King (IRE)**[9] 1390 3 -8-1269 JamieSpencer 3
(Ian Williams) *hld up towards rr: sme hdwy 5f out: rdn along over 3f out: sn wknd and bhd whn eased fnl 2f* **11/2**
221- 7 3/4 **Amoralist**[186] 6977 3 -9-778 KierenFallon 2
(Ed Dunlop) *trckd ldng pair: hdwy and cl up over 3f out: sn rdn and wknd: bhd and eased over 1f out* **9/2**[3]
2m 53.77s (12.97)**Going Correction** +1.10s/f (Soft) **7**Ran SP% **111.2**
Speed ratings (Par 100): **100,98,96,94,89 49,49**
toteswingers:1&2:£4.00, 1&3:£8.40, 2&3:£6.40 CSF £22.75 TOTE £5.50 : £2.50 , £1.40 ; EX 19.20.
Owner Sheikh Marwan Al Maktoum **Bred** Darley **Trained** Newmarket, Suffolk
FOCUS
A competitive 3yo middle-distance handicap in which they kept away from the inside rail and ended up on the stands' side in the home straight. The two leaders took each other on and the pace was unrelenting. In the ever deteriorating ground the time was over 18secs outside the RP Standard. The form is not rated too postively but the winner is accorded a 5lb personal best.

Gabrial's King(IRE) Official explanation: trainer's rep said gelding was unsuited by the soft (heavy in places) ground

1558 RIU PALACE MELONERAS H'CAP 6f

3:15 (3:16) (Class 2) (0-100,99) 4-Y-O+

£11,827 (£3,541; £1,770; £885; £442; £222) **Stalls** Low

Form RPR

026- **1** **Seal Rock**[185] 6987 4-9-3 **95**.................................... DaneO'Neill 1 104
(Henry Candy) *trckd ldrs on inner: hdwy and cl up 2f out: rdn to ld over 1f out: styd on wl towards fin* **9/2**[1]

60-1 **2** *1* **Mirza**[3] 1498 5-9-5 97 6ex.................................... WilliamCarson 2 103
(Rae Guest) *led gp on inner: prom tl led 2f out: sn rdn and hdd over 1f out: kpt on wl u.p fnl f* **5/1**[2]

40-3 **3** *½* **Tajneed (IRE)**[12] 1294 9-8-5 **90**.................... ShirleyTeasdale[(7)] 5 94
(David Nicholls) *cl up on inner: effrt over 2f out: rdn wl over 1f out: one pce ent fnl f* **16/1**

400- **4** *nse* **Osteopathic Remedy (IRE)**[199] 6672 8-8-13 **91**............... TomEaves 4 95
(Michael Dods) *cl up on inner: rdn along 2f out: drvn appr fnl f and kpt on same pce* **20/1**

00-4 **5** *5* **Parisian Pyramid (IRE)**[16] 1220 6-8-13 **91**.................. JamieSpencer 9 79+
(Kevin Ryan) *racd wd and overall ldr: pushed along and hdd over 2f out: sn rdn and btn wl over 1f out* **15/2**

010- **6** *3¾* **Coolminx (IRE)**[192] 6854 5-8-11 **89**.............................. PaulHanagan 13 65+
(Richard Fahey) *racd wd: prom: chsd ldr 1/2-way: rdn along 2f out: grad wknd* **12/1**

65-0 **7** *4½* **Wildcat Wizard (USA)**[22] 1157 6-8-10 **88**................ MichaelO'Connell 3 49
(David Nicholls) *dwlt: chsd ldrs on inner: rdn along over 2f out: sn wknd* **40/1**

04-1 **8** *1¾* **Shropshire (IRE)**[23] 1141 4-8-7 **90**...................... MatthewLawson[(5)] 15 46
(Charles Hills) *racd wd: hld up towards rr: hdwy 2f out: sn rdn and plugged on: nvr a factor* **12/1**

400- **9** *¾* **Victoire De Lyphar (IRE)**[268] 4534 5-9-7 **99**............. AndrewMullen 17 52
(David Nicholls) *racd wd: hld up towards rr: sme late hdwy* **25/1**

-454 **10** *½* **Docofthebay (IRE)**[22] 1157 8-9-1 **93**........................(b) RobertWinston 7 45
(Scott Dixon) *racd wd: hld up towards rr: hdwy over 2f out: rdn wl over 1f out: no imp* **10/1**

000- **11** *1* **Grissom (IRE)**[185] 6987 6-8-13 **91**................................ DavidAllan 11 40
(Tim Easterby) *racd wd: prom: rdn along 2f out: sn wknd* **28/1**

2330 **12** *10* **Clockmaker (IRE)**[23] 1130 6-9-0 **92**.................... DuranFentiman 12
(Tim Easterby) *racd wd: a in rr* **14/1**

00-0 **13** *1¾* **No Hubris (USA)**[22] 1157 5-8-10 **88**............................ PJMcDonald 10
(Ruth Carr) *racd wd: chsd ldr to 1/2-way: sn wknd* **66/1**

16-0 **14** *2* **Nasri**[22] 1157 6-9-5 **97**.. KierenFallon 6
(David Nicholls) *racd wd: hld up towards rr: sme hdwy over 2f out: sn rdn and n.d* **6/1**[3]

-006 **15** *½* **Crown Choice**[2] 1523 7-8-13 **91**..................................... FrederikTylicki 8
(Paul Midgley) *racd wd: chsd ldrs: rdn along 1/2-way: sn wknd* **25/1**

614- **16** *10* **Citrus Star (USA)**[159] 7433 5-9-5 **97**............................ PhillipMakin 16
(Chris Wall) *dwlt: racd wd: a in rr* **22/1**

000- **17** *23* **Fred Willetts (IRE)**[241] 5450 4-8-11 **89**....................... LeeNewman 14
(David Barron) *racd wd: a in rr* **22/1**

1m 22.64s (5.74) **Going Correction** +1.10s/f (Soft) **17 Ran SP% 126.5**
Speed ratings (Par 109): **105,103,103,102,96 91,85,82,81,81 79,66,64,61,60 47,16**
toteswingers:1&2:£4.30, 1&3:£23.10, 2&3:£23.10 CSF £23.88 CT £277.82 TOTE £6.50: £1.30, £2.20, £4.30, £4.70; EX 31.10 Trifecta £639.80 Pool: £1,037.65 - 1.20 winning units..
Owner P A Deal **Bred** Mrs A D Bourne **Trained** Kingston Warren, Oxon

FOCUS
The ground was changed to soft, heavy in places ahead of this highly competitive and quite valuable Class 2 sprint handicap. Six of the 17 runners stuck to the far rail and they filled the first five places. The stands' side is the place to be on soft ground at the back end after the track has been watered in the summer, but the majority who chose to race wide here made the wrong call. A step up from the winner with the second running to his Newbury form.

NOTEBOOK
Seal Rock, who had won first time out in each of his two previous seasons, was having just his ninth career start. He came through between horses on the turn in and in the end wore down the runner-up. Rated 95 here, he is sure to be a candidate for all the top 6f handicaps this time. (op 11-2)
Mirza, 3lb out of the handicap when scoring over 5f at Newbury three days earlier, was in effect just 3lb higher under his 6lb penalty. He took the other five along on the inside but did not see out the extra furlong as well as the winner. He's ground dependent and after Newbury will be a few pounds higher in the ratings when he reappears. (tchd 9-2 and 11-2)
Tajneed(IRE), back with his previous handler after an abortive spell in France, was dropped 10lb after finishing only third in a 7f claimer at Catterick. He is now 7lb below his last winning mark in 2010. He loves soft ground and connections will be keen to find another opportunity for him soon.
Osteopathic Remedy(IRE), fourth in this last year from a 6lb higher mark, has recorded all eight of his handicap wins over a mile.
Parisian Pyramid(IRE) ◆, who led throughout of those who raced on the hare rail, is back on his last winning mark which was in 2010. He is clearly at the top of his game and in this ownership will no doubt head next for Chester. (op 8-1)
Coolminx(IRE), who took last year's Bronze Cup at Ayr from a 6lb lower mark, finished clear second-best of those who raced wide. (op 16-1)

1559 PONTEFRACT MARATHON H'CAP 2m 5f 122y

3:45 (3:45) (Class 5) (0-75,74) 4-Y-O+

£2,264 (£673; £336; £168) **Stalls** Low

Form RPR

040- **1** **Mr Crystal (FR)**[25] 6915 8-9-7 **69**............................ FrederikTylicki 3 78
(Micky Hammond) *hld up in tch: hdwy on inner 4f out: pushed along over 3f out: effrt to chse ldr wl over 1f out: rdn and slt advantage appr fnl f: sn drvn and hld on gamely towards fin* **9/2**[2]

02-6 **2** *shd* **Riptide**[13] 1272 6-9-11 **73**.......................................(p) JamieGoldstein 9 82
(Michael Scudamore) *led: jnd 5f out: rdn along and hdd briefly 3f out: led again over 2f out: drvn and hdd jst over 1f out: rallied gamely ins fnl f: jst failed* **5/1**[3]

10-0 **3** *18* **Descaro (USA)**[13] 1272 6-9-10 **72**.............................. DanielTudhope 8 65
(David O'Meara) *trckd ldr: smooth hdwy and cl up 5f out: effrt to ld briefly 3f out: rdn along and hdd over 2f out: sn drvn and plugged on same pce* **11/2**

05-0 **4** *1½* **High Ransom**[13] 1272 5-8-12 **60**................................(p) PJMcDonald 5 51
(Micky Hammond) *trckd ldrs: effrt 4f out: rdn along 3f out: drvn and plugged on one pce fnl 2f* **5/1**[3]

6- **5** *3¼* **Mutiska (IRE)**[19] 1198 5-9-2 **64**................................ SilvestreDeSousa 7 52+
(J C Hayden, Ire) *hld up in tch: hdwy over 3f out: chsd ldrs over 2f out: sn rdn and hung lft: no imp after* **7/2**[1]

/00- **6** *13* **Mistoffelees**[52] 2810 6-9-12 **74**....................................(t) PaulMulrennan 6 51
(James Given) *hld up: a in rr* **16/1**

04-6 **7** *10* **Al Shababiya (IRE)**[6] 1433 5-8-9 **57**............................(v[1]) HayleyTurner 2 25
(Alison Thorpe) *chsd ldrs: rdn along over 4f out: sn wknd and bhd* **10/1**

610- **8** *9* **Baan (USA)**[114] 7564 9-9-0 **62**.. PaulHanagan 4 22
(James Eustace) *hld up: a towards rr: bhd fnl 3f* **10/1**

5m 30.07s (39.07) **Going Correction** +1.10s/f (Soft) **8 Ran SP% 113.2**
Speed ratings (Par 103): **72,71,65,64,63 58,55,52**
toteswingers:1&2:£4.30, 1&3:£5.60, 2&3:£4.70 CSF £26.60 CT £124.56 TOTE £5.70: £2.00, £1.90, £2.10; EX 25.60 Trifecta £224.20 Pool: £494.00 - 1.63 winning units..
Owner Champagne Ascent Partnership **Bred** Gerard Schence **Trained** Middleham Moor, N Yorks

FOCUS
After 4mm fell in less than an hour the sun came out to play ahead of this marathon. The pace was very steady until the final three-quarters of a mile, but having to climb the Pontefract hill twice made this a severe test. The time was over 49secs slower than the RP Standard. The form is not easy to assess, but has been rated round the first two, who finished clear.

1560 SUBSCRIBE ONLINE @ RACINGUK.COM MAIDEN STKS 6f

4:15 (4:16) (Class 5) 3-Y-O+

£2,385 (£704; £352) **Stalls** Low

Form RPR

03- **1** **Intense Pink**[196] 6758 3-8-9 0.. PaulHanagan 8 93+
(Chris Wall) *trckd ldrs: hdwy to ld 1 1/2f out: sn clr: unchal* **3/1**[2]

2 *14* **Stir Trader (IRE)** 3-9-0 0.. JamesDoyle 5 53
(Roger Charlton) *midfield: hdwy to chse ldrs 2f out: sn rdn and styd on fnl f: no ch w wnr* **8/1**

623- **3** *1¾* **Tortoni (IRE)**[175] 7197 3-9-0 75.. PhillipMakin 11 48
(Kevin Ryan) *chsd ldrs: rdn 2f out: edgd lft over 1f out: kpt on fnl f* **7/1**[3]

0-22 **4** *nk* **Willies Wonder (IRE)**[14] 1256 3-9-0 72.......................... RobertWinston 4 47
(Charles Hills) *in tch: hdwy to chse ldrs wl over 1f out: sn rdn and one pce* **7/4**[1]

0-0 **5** *¾* **Adverse (IRE)**[13] 1278 3-8-9 0.. HayleyTurner 13 40
(Michael Bell) *towards rr: hdwy 2f out: kpt on appr fnl f: nvr a factor* **25/1**

00- **6** *hd* **Lucky Mark (IRE)**[331] 2485 3-9-0 0................................... LeeNewman 7 44
(Deborah Sanderson) *led: rdn along over 2f out: hdd 1 1/2f out: grad wknd* **66/1**

7 *¾* **Compton Time** 3-8-11 0.. LeeTopliss[(3)] 2 42
(Michael Dods) *in tch: rdn along 1/2-way and sn wknd* **50/1**

8 *1¼* **Taizong (IRE)** 3-9-0 0.. StevieDonohoe 3 38
(Ian Williams) *a towards rr* **20/1**

326- **9** *1* **Star City (IRE)**[220] 6110 3-9-0 71.. TomEaves 10 35
(Michael Dods) *t.k.h: stmbld sltly after s and towards rr: sn in tch: hdwy to chse ldrs 2f out: sn rdn and btn* **9/1**

44 **10** *7* **Linroyale Boy (USA)**[69] 552 4-9-11 0................................ PJMcDonald 9 17
(Alan Swinbank) *dwlt: a bhd* **25/1**

11 *2* **Beaurepaire Kid** 3-8-9 0... DeanHeslop[(5)] 1
(David Barron) *dwlt: sn chsng ldrs on inner: cl up 1/2-way: rdn along 2f out and sn wknd* **16/1**

12 *2½* **Baileys Bigishu** 3-9-0 0... PaulMulrennan 6
(James Given) *a in rr* **40/1**

0 **13** *14* **Under Par**[14] 1250 4-8-13 0.................................. DavidSimmonson[(7)] 12
(Michael Easterby) *chsd ldrs on wd outside: rdn along 1/2-way: sn wknd* **100/1**

1m 21.43s (4.53) **Going Correction** +1.10s/f (Soft)
WFA 3 from 4yo 11lb **13 Ran SP% 120.2**
Speed ratings (Par 103): **113,94,92,91,90 90,89,87,86,77 74,71,52**
toteswingers:1&2:£6.00, 1&3:£5.40, 2&3:£5.60 CSF £25.70 TOTE £3.90: £1.20, £2.70, £2.50; EX 31.70 Trifecta £203.10 Pool: £620.43 - 2.26 winning units..
Owner D S Lee **Bred** Jeremy Green & Sons & Cheveley Park Stud **Trained** Newmarket, Suffolk

FOCUS
Plenty of dead wood in this sprint maiden but a facile winner who made light of the testing conditions. The winner's time was much quicker than the earlier 88-99 sprint handicap. She looks very useful, although the remainder look modest.

1561 PICNIC PACKAGE - NEW FOR 2012 H'CAP 1m 4y

4:45 (4:45) (Class 5) (0-75,74) 4-Y-O+

£2,385 (£704; £352) **Stalls** Low

Form RPR

5101 **1** **Flying Applause**[10] 1358 7-9-3 **73**..............................(bt) LeeTopliss[(3)] 5 83
(Roy Bowring) *hmpd s and bhd: gd hdwy on wd outside 3f out: chal over 1f out: rdn to ld ent fnl f: drvn and styd on wl fnl 100yds* **9/1**

252/ **2** *nk* **Edmaaj (IRE)**[590] 5936 4-9-4 **71**.................................... DanielTudhope 10 80
(David O'Meara) *hld up and bhd: hdwy whn nt clr run over 2f out: effrt to chse ldrs over 1f out: rdn to chal ent fnl f: sn hung rt and ev ch tl drvn and no ex last 50yds* **9/1**

03-5 **3** *6* **Chosen Character (IRE)**[12] 1293 4-9-7 **74**.......(vt) RichardKingscote 12 70
(Tom Dascombe) *hld up in rr: hdwy over 2f out: rdn to chse ldrs over 1f out: styng on whn hit in face by oppenents whip jst ins fnl f: kpt on same pce after* **8/1**

62-0 **4** *3¾* **Icy Blue**[12] 1293 4-9-4 **74**... AmyRyan[(3)] 8 61
(Richard Whitaker) *midfield: hdwy to chse ldrs over 2f out: rdn wl over 1f out: kpt on same pce fnl f* **10/1**

351- **5** *1¾* **Watts Up Son**[145] 7235 4-8-13 **71**.................................(t) NeilFarley[(5)] 2 54+
(Declan Carroll) *cl up on inner: led over 2f out: sn rdn: hdd ent fnl f and sn wknd* **14/1**

1-14 **6** *3* **Myboyalfie (USA)**[46] 834 5-9-7 **74**...........................(v) FrederikTylicki 7 50
(J R Jenkins) *towards rr: hdwy whn n.m.r 2f out: sn rdn and no imp appr fnl f* **15/2**[3]

6066 **7** *12* **Opus Maximus (IRE)**[11] 1342 7-9-3 **70**........................... HayleyTurner 13 18
(Conor Dore) *hld up towards rr: sme hdwy on wd outside 2f out: sn rdn and nvr a factor* **18/1**

05-2 **8** *9* **First Class Favour (IRE)**[13] 1269 4-8-13 **66**...................... DavidAllan 4
(Tim Easterby) *wnt lft s: midfield: rdn along over 3f out: nvr a factor* **11/2**[1]

21-5 **9** *3¼* **Brockfield**[13] 1275 6-9-3 **70**.. RobertWinston 9
(Mel Brittain) *midfield: hdwy and in tch 2f out: sn rdn and btn* **7/1**[2]

4460 **10** *3* **Valley Tiger**[9] 1391 4-8-7 **60** oh1..................................... PaulHanagan 3
(Richard Fahey) *a in rr* **22/1**

4300 **11** *hd* **On The Cusp (IRE)**[10] 1358 5-8-10 **68**....................(p) DuilioDaSilva[(5)] 6
(Richard Guest) *led: rdn along and hdd 3f out: sn wknd* **40/1**

210- **12** *hd* **Diablo Dancer**[232] 5760 4-9-4 **71**................................ DuranFentiman 14
(Tim Walford) *chsd ldrs: rdn along over 2f out: sn wknd* **14/1**

00-0 **13** *21* **Camerooney**[13] 1275 9-9-3 **73**.................................. PaulPickard[(3)] 16
(Brian Ellison) *cl up: rdn along 3f out: wknd qckly: bhd and eased wl over 1f out* **22/1**

2-04 **14** *75* **Cheylesmore (IRE)**[26] 1064 4-9-4 **71**...................(v) WilliamCarson 11
(Stuart Williams) *chsd ldrs: rdn along 1/2-way: sn wknd: bhd and eased fnl 2f* **33/1**

021- **U** **Law To Himself (IRE)**^{174} [7215] 5-9-3 **70**........................ PJMcDonald 1
(Alan Swinbank) *uns rdr s* **8/1**

1m 54.92s (9.02) **Going Correction** +1.225s/f (Soft) **15** Ran SP% **123.6**
Speed ratings (Par 103): **103,102,96,92,91 88,76,67,63,60 60,60,39,,**
toteswingers:1&2:£7.30, 1&3:£18.90, 2&3:£19.00 CSF £85.86 CT £705.86 TOTE £8.40: £3.20, £3.30, £2.80; EX 91.50 Trifecta £508.60 Part won. Pool: £687.37 - 0.91 winning units..
Owner K Nicholls **Bred** G H Beeby And Viscount Marchwood **Trained** Edwinstowe, Notts

FOCUS
The heavy rain returned ahead of this modest, but wide-open handicap which seemed to be run at a very strong pace. Five were almost in a line but the first two were clear at the line. The first three home came from well off the pace. The winner is rated back to his old best.
Watts Up Son Official explanation: jockey said gelding hung right

1562 NRC DAY ON WEDNESDAY 2ND MAY APPRENTICE H'CAP — 1m 2f 6y
5:15 (5:15) (Class 5) (0-70,70) 4-Y-0+ £2,385 (£704; £352) Stalls Low

Form RPR
02-0 **1** **Tapis Libre**^{13} [1275] 4-8-13 **67**................................ DavidSimmonson$^{(5)}$ 1 76
(Michael Easterby) *mde all: rdn 2f out: kpt on gamely fnl f* **15/2**
421 **2** *1 ¾* **Spin Cast**^{14} [1266] 4-9-0 **66**.. GeorgeDowning$^{(3)}$ 6 71
(Ian Williams) *in tch: hdwy to chse ldrs 3f out: rdn over 1f out: kpt on fnl f* **3/1**^{1}
622 **3** *shd* **Resplendent Alpha**^{16} [1224] 8-8-4 **56**...................... NicoleNordblad$^{(3)}$ 9 61
(Alastair Lidderdale) *hld up in rr: gd hdwy on wd outside 2f out: rdn to chse ldrs over 1f out: kpt on same pce ins fnl f* **7/1**
4666 **4** *2 ¾* **Hidden Glory**^{19} [1186] 5-9-7 **70**..................................(b) GeorgeChaloner 2 69
(James Given) *trckd ldrs: hdwy on inner over 2f out: rdn to chal over 1f out and ev ch tl wknd ins fnl f* **4/1**^{2}
3244 **5** *¾* **Jordaura**^{6} [1432] 6-9-4 **67**... DannyBrock 3 65
(Gay Kelleway) *hld up in rr: hdwy 3f out: rdn to chse ldrs over 1f out: sn no imp* **5/1**^{3}
360- **6** *¾* **Operateur (IRE)**^{206} [6503] 4-8-8 **60**.................................. LauraBarry$^{(3)}$ 7 56
(Ben Haslam) *cl up: rdn along 3f out: wknd wl over 1f out* **16/1**
0-62 **7** *½* **Market Puzzle (IRE)**^{18} [1207] 5-8-7 **56**.......................(p) RachealKneller 5 51
(Mark Brisbourne) *trckd ldrs: effrt 3f out: rdn along over 2f out: sn btn* **7/1**
5-00 **8** *4 ½* **Amir Pasha (UAE)**^{12} [1297] 7-8-2 **58**.........................(p) KatieDowson$^{(7)}$ 8 44
(Micky Hammond) *hld up: a in rr* **20/1**
0-00 **9** *46* **Pertuis (IRE)**^{13} [1275] 6-8-11 **65**.................................. ConorHarrison$^{(5)}$ 4
(Micky Hammond) *hld up: hmpd 7f out: rdn along 4f out and sn bhd* **9/1**

2m 28.12s (14.42) **Going Correction** +1.225s/f (Soft) **9** Ran SP% **119.1**
Speed ratings (Par 103): **91,89,89,87,86 86,85,82,45**
CSF £31.30 CT £169.34 TOTE £6.60: £2.90, £1.10, £3.10; EX 47.90 Trifecta £388.90 Part won. Pool: £525.60 - 0.82 winning units..
Owner Carpet Kings Syndicate **Bred** Sedgecroft Stud **Trained** Sheriff Hutton, N Yorks
■ Stewards' Enquiry : George Downing three-day ban: careless riding (May 9-11)

FOCUS
The rain continued to fall ahead of this modest apprentice handicap. The form is not entirely convincing, but is taken at face value for now.
T/Plt: £117.40 to a £1 stake. Pool:£71,208.68 - 442.52 winning tickets T/Qpdt: £21.60 to a £1 stake. Pool:£5,005.73 - 171.05 winning tickets JR

1411 WINDSOR (R-H)
Monday, April 23

OFFICIAL GOING: Soft (6.0)
Top bend dolled out 4yds from normal configuration adding 14yds to races of 1m and over. Rest at normal configuration and track at maximum width.
Wind: Moderate, against Weather: Overcast, drizzly, cold

1563 DAVISBAKERYCARIBBEAN.COM MAIDEN AUCTION FILLIES' STKS — 5f 10y
5:25 (5:26) (Class 5) 2-Y-0 £2,264 (£673; £336; £168) Stalls Low

Form RPR
1 **Threes Grand** 2-8-4 0.. NickyMackay 1 71
(Scott Dixon) *w ldrs: rdn 2f out: led jst over 1f out: edgd lft fnl f: jst hld on* **7/1**
2 *shd* **Uncomplicated** 2-8-10 0... PatCosgrave 4 77
(Jim Boyle) *dwlt sltly and shkn up sn after s: prog to join ldrs 1/2-way: led briefly over 1f out: pressed wnr after: kpt on wl nr fin: jst failed* **16/1**
5 **3** *1 ½* **Vestibule**^{7} [1411] 2-8-4 0... JohnFahy 6 66
(Eve Johnson Houghton) *trckd ldrs: effrt 2f out: trying to chal against far rail fr 1f out: n.m.r last 100yds and eased off nr fin* **5/2**^{1}
4 *1 ½* **Ishi Honest** 2-8-6 0... DavidProbert 2 62+
(Mark Usher) *sn pushed along: struggling in last pair 1/2-way: styd on fnl f: nrst fin* **14/1**
5 **5** *2 ¼* **Bheleyf (IRE)**^{23} [1136] 2-8-3 0... HarryBentley$^{(3)}$ 5 54
(Joseph Tuite) *racd freely: led to over 1f out: sn wknd* **9/2**^{3}
6 *hd* **Lucky Suit (IRE)** 2-8-8 0 ow2.. RyanMoore 9 55
(Richard Hannon) *w ldng pair: rdn over 2f out: wknd wl over 1f out* **7/2**^{2}
0 **7** *¾* **Myzamour**^{19} [1188] 2-8-4 0... TadhgO'Shea 8 48
(J S Moore) *rn green and early reminder: in tch 1/2-way: rdn and wknd 2f out* **50/1**
8 *3 ½* **Close Together (IRE)** 2-8-6 0... MartinDwyer 3 38+
(Robert Mills) *v.s.i.s: a in last and nvr on terms* **12/1**

1m 6.83s (6.53) **Going Correction** +1.10s/f (Soft) **8** Ran SP% **103.7**
Speed ratings (Par 89): **91,90,88,86,82 82,80,75**
toteswingers:1&2:£8.30, 1&3:£1.60, 2&3:£8.30 CSF £87.84 TOTE £8.60: £1.40, £5.50, £1.10; EX 104.80 Trifecta £1054.60 Pool: £3,178.06 - 2.23 winning units..
Owner Paul J Dixon **Bred** Mrs Fiona Denniff **Trained** Babworth, Notts
■ Birdie Queen was withdrawn (12/1, unruly in stalls). Deduct 5p in the £ under R4.
■ Stewards' Enquiry : Nicky Mackay two-day ban: careless riding (May 7-8)

FOCUS
The top bend was dolled out four yards from normal configuration, adding 14 yards to race distances of 1m plus. As usual when the ground is testing, they raced towards the far side in the straight. This didn't look a strong maiden. The third looks the best guide.

NOTEBOOK
Threes Grand, a £3,000 half-sister to a 6f winner, showed a good attitude to make a successful start. She was getting weight from most of her rivals and probably only had to run to a modest level, but there might be more to come. (op 11-2)
Uncomplicated, a 16,000euros half-sister to a 1m winner out of a 6f winner, was conceding weight all round and showed plenty of ability after starting slowly. She didn't have a great deal of room late on, but was always just held. (op 20-1)
Vestibule didn't build significantly on the form she showed on her debut over C&D a week earlier. She was held when a bit short of room against the far rail late on. (op 11-4 tchd 9-4)
Ishi Honest, a 6,5000gns January foal, kept on quite nicely and this was an encouraging debut. (op 20-1 tchd 25-1)
Bheleyf(IRE) didn't see it out after racing freely. (op 5-1 tchd 6-1)
Lucky Suit(IRE), a 10,000euros February foal, out of a 7f winner, carried 2lb overweight and didn't show a great deal. (op 11-4)

1564 DAVISBAKERYCARIBBEAN.COM H'CAP — 6f
5:55 (5:55) (Class 5) (0-75,75) 4-Y-0+ £2,264 (£673; £336; £168) Stalls Low

Form RPR
013- **1** **Rafaaf (IRE)**^{194} [6801] 4-9-4 **73**.. AndreaAtzeni 5 84
(Robert Eddery) *settled in 10th: prog on outer over 1f out: rdn to ld ins fnl f: styd on wl* **10/1**^{3}
015- **2** *¾* **Highland Colori (IRE)**^{260} [4817] 4-9-4 **73**....................... DavidProbert 9 82
(Andrew Balding) *pressed ldr: rdn 2f out: drvn to ld 1f out: sn hdd: styd on but a hld* **13/2**^{2}
146- **3** *½* **Midnight Rider (IRE)**^{208} [6442] 4-9-5 **74**.......................... TedDurcan 14 81
(Chris Wall) *settled in midfield: rdn and effrt over 1f out: styd on to take 3rd wl ins fnl f* **10/1**^{3}
124- **4** *1* **Interakt**^{215} [6246] 5-9-0 **72**... HarryBentley$^{(3)}$ 16 76
(Joseph Tuite) *pressed ldrs: rdn to chal over 1f out: nrly upsides jst ins fnl f: no ex* **12/1**
1000 **5** *1 ¼* **Ocean Legend (IRE)**^{26} [1066] 7-9-6 **75**......................... JimmyFortune 1 75
(Tony Carroll) *in tch: effrt towards outer over 1f out: styd on same pce fnl f: nvr able to chal* **14/1**
105- **6** *shd* **Emiratesdotcom**^{157} [7457] 6-9-6 **75**.................................. LiamKeniry 4 74
(Milton Bradley) *hld up in last: stl there over 1f out: prog and one reminder fnl f: styng on whn eased last strides* **16/1**
3206 **7** *nse* **Desert Strike**^{7} [1417] 6-9-3 **72**... DarryllHolland 7 71
(Charles Hills) *taken steadily to post: t.k.h: hld up in last trio: stl there over 1f out: prog and couple of reminders fnl f: keeping on whn eased last strides* **16/1**
120- **8** *½* **Seamus Shindig**^{190} [6895] 10-8-12 **72**............................ AmyScott$^{(5)}$ 10 70
(Henry Candy) *led: stdy pce to 1/2-way: hdd & wknd 1f out* **16/1**
2023 **9** *½* **Earlsmedic**^{61} [652] 7-9-2 **74**..(v) RyanClark$^{(3)}$ 6 70
(Stuart Williams) *hld up in last trio: wdst of all and shkn up over 1f out: one pce and nvr on terms* **16/1**
06-0 **10** *1* **Kings 'n Dreams**^{12} [1306] 5-9-3 **72**.................................(b) JimCrowley 8 65
(Dean Ivory) *s.i.s: t.k.h and sn cl up: wknd over 1f out* **11/1**
-504 **11** *shd* **Roodee Queen**^{18} [1203] 4-9-6 **75**.................................. RussKennemore 3 68
(Milton Bradley) *pressed ldng pair: rdn and sing to weaken whn hmpd jst ins fnl f* **33/1**
-230 **12** *nk* **Jungle Bay**^{22} [1156] 5-9-5 **74**... GeorgeBaker 13 66
(Jane Chapple-Hyam) *trckd ldrs: cl up gng wl whn looking for room 2f out: shkn up and fdd over 1f out* **11/4**^{1}
6043 **13** *¾* **Nubar Boy**^{14} [1254] 5-8-11 **71**............................(v) MatthewCosham$^{(5)}$ 11 60
(David Evans) *t.k.h: cl up tl wknd over 1f out* **14/1**
1002 **14** *1 ½* **Ghostwing**^{13} [1279] 5-9-6 **75**... FergusSweeney 2 59
(James Evans) *hld up in wl in rr: shkn up towards outer over 1f out: no prog* **14/1**

1m 19.5s (6.50) **Going Correction** +1.10s/f (Soft) **14** Ran SP% **120.7**
Speed ratings (Par 103): **100,99,98,97,95 95,95,94,93,92 92,91,90,88**
toteswingers:1&2:£8.40, 1&3:£17.70, 2&3:£12.30 CSF £73.79 CT £698.24 TOTE £8.00: £3.20, £2.60, £5.20; EX 73.40 Trifecta £867.40 Pool: £1,406.60 - 1.20 winning units..
Owner Aitken & Phillips **Bred** Oscar Stud **Trained** Newmarket, Suffolk
■ Stewards' Enquiry : Andrea Atzeni two-day ban: careless riding (May 7-8)

FOCUS
A competitive sprint handicap. Again, they ended up towards the far side, although the winner made his move up the middle. The winner resumed his latter 3yo improvement with the next two close to their 3yo marks.

1565 SKYBET.COM H'CAP — 1m 67y
6:25 (6:26) (Class 4) (0-85,85) 3-Y-0 £4,851 (£1,443; £721; £360) Stalls Low

Form RPR
033- **1** **Paloma's Prince (IRE)**^{187} [6953] 3-8-11 **75**..................... PatCosgrave 9 81
(Jim Boyle) *trckd ldr: sustained chal fr over 3f out: drvn to ld jst over 1f out: styd on* **33/1**
21-6 **2** *½* **Presburg (IRE)**^{46} [841] 3-9-2 **80**....................................... LiamKeniry 14 85
(Joseph Tuite) *hld up in midfield: prog 4f out: pressed ldng pair fr 2f out against far rail: tried to chal over 1f out: styd on* **33/1**
200- **3** *shd* **Perfect Delight**^{205} [6526] 3-8-13 **77**................................... JohnFahy 2 82
(Clive Cox) *led: hrd pressed fr over 3f out: hdd jst over 1f out: styd on but jst hld* **11/1**
500- **4** *1* **Jack Who's He (IRE)**^{184} [7021] 3-9-1 **84**............... MatthewCosham$^{(5)}$ 8 87
(David Evans) *in tch in midfield: rdn over 2f out: styd on fr over 1f out: tk 4th ins fnl f: clsng at fin* **14/1**
263- **5** *2 ¼* **Dutch Master**^{165} [7350] 3-8-11 **75**................................ JimmyFortune 12 73
(Andrew Balding) *trckd ldrs: effrt and cl up 2f out: fdd over 1f out* **25/1**
132- **6** *2* **Ocean Tempest**^{129} [7786] 3-9-1 **79**............................... KirstyMilczarek 5 72
(John Ryan) *awkward s: hld up in midfield: rdn and effrt over 2f out: no imp over 1f out* **33/1**
1 **7** *5* **Basseterre (IRE)**^{93} [249] 3-8-13 **77**.................................. MichaelHills 7 58
(Charles Hills) *restless in stalls and missed the break: mostly in last pair: effrt on outer 3f out: threatened to cl on ldrs over 1f out: sn wknd* **2/1**^{1}
213- **8** *1* **Tidal Way (IRE)**^{202} [6606] 3-9-3 **81**................................. MartinHarley 10 60
(Mick Channon) *cl up: rdn over 2f out: wknd wl over 1f out* **9/1**^{3}
01- **9** *1 ¾* **Napoleon's Muse (IRE)**^{217} [6215] 3-8-13 **77**.................. JimCrowley 13 52
(Ralph Beckett) *a in rr: detached in last 4f out: rdn 3f out: nvr on terms* **14/1**
121- **10** *5* **Venetian View (IRE)**^{180} [7095] 3-9-7 **85**......................... GeorgeBaker 1 49
(Gary Moore) *stdd s: hld up in rr: shkn up wl over 2f out: no prog: wknd over 1f out* **12/1**
231- **11** *12* **Sheikh The Reins (IRE)**^{166} [7329] 3-9-3 **81**...................... LukeMorris 4 17
(John Best) *trckd ldng pair: pushed along 4f out: wknd u.p 2f out: t.o* **25/1**
31- **12** *1 ½* **Duke Of Firenze**^{236} [5618] 3-9-2 **80**.................................. RyanMoore 11 13
(Sir Michael Stoute) *hld up in rr: effrt over 3f out: rdn and no prog 2f out: sn wknd rapidly: t.o* **9/4**^{2}

1m 52.99s (8.29) **Going Correction** +1.10s/f (Soft) **12** Ran SP% **120.0**
Speed ratings (Par 100): **102,101,101,100,98 96,91,90,88,83 71,69**
toteswingers:1&2:£76.40, 1&3:£74.90, 2&3:£76.40 CSF £831.98 CT £12236.16 TOTE £51.20: £13.40, £13.50, £4.10; EX 942.40 TRIFECTA Not won..
Owner Serendipity Syndicate 2006 **Bred** Skymarc Farm **Trained** Epsom, Surrey

FOCUS
Most of these were returning from a break, and the front two in the betting underperformed, so the form looks just ordinary. The first three all improved on their 2yo form. The pace held up well and the runners gradually edged over to the far rail in the straight.
Jack Who's He(IRE) Official explanation: jockey said gelding hung left

Basseterre(IRE) Official explanation: jockey said colt was slowly away

1566 READING POST H'CAP 1m 3f 135y
6:55 (6:55) (Class 4) (0-80,79) 4-Y-O+ £4,204 (£1,251; £625; £312) Stalls Centre

Form RPR

240- **1** **Kleitomachos (IRE)**[190] 6891 4-9-0 73 IanMongan 7 83
(Stuart Kittow) *hld up in 4th: prog to chse clr ldr over 3f out: taken to far rail over 2f out: styd on dourly to ld ins fnl f* **5/1**[3]

24-1 **2** *1 3/4* **Colinca's Lad (IRE)**[13] 1286 10-8-11 74 RosieJessop(5) 8 81
(Peter Charalambous) *led at gd pce: clr 4f out: styd centre fr 3f out: tired 2f out: hdd ins fnl f* **9/2**[2]

2214 **3** *12* **Broughton Sands**[7] 1418 4-8-10 69 JimmyFortune 6 56
(Willie Musson) *hld up in 6th: wl off the pce 5f out: prog to go 3rd over 2f out but nowhere nr ldng pair: tried to cl over 1f out: wknd and eased fnl f* **8/1**

234- **4** *18* **Achalas (IRE)**[137] 7677 4-9-5 78 (t) WilliamBuick 4 34
(Heather Main) *trckd ldng pair: wnt 2nd 1/2-way tl over 3f out: sn wknd and wl bhd* **6/1**

5331 **5** *40* **Archelao (IRE)**[24] 1105 4-9-0 72 ow1 AmirQuinn 1
(Richard Rowe) *t.k.h: chsd ldr to 1/2-way: wknd over 3f out: eased and wl t.o* **25/1**

-142 **6** *22* **Honourable Knight (IRE)**[32] 992 4-8-11 70 (v) DavidProbert 5
(Mark Usher) *a in last pair: rdn and wknd 5f out: sn wl t.o* **16/1**

121- **7** *12* **Snow Hill**[223] 6024 4-9-6 79 GeorgeBaker 3
(Chris Wall) *hld up in 5th: rdn and wknd over 4f out: eased over 2f out: wl t.o* **11/8**[1]

2m 41.04s (11.54) **Going Correction** +1.10s/f (Soft)
WFA 4 from 10yo 1lb 7 Ran SP% **112.1**
Speed ratings (Par 105): **105,103,95,83,57 42,34**
toteswingers:1&2:£2.30, 1&3:£25.80, 2&3:£11.30 CSF £26.38 CT £174.12 TOTE £7.10: £3.10, £2.30; EX 40.50 Trifecta £194.30 Pool: £5,864.08 - 22.33 winning units..
Owner Eric Gadsden **Bred** Carrigbeg Stud Co Ltd **Trained** Blackborough, Devon

FOCUS
Most of these struggled in the ground and this only concerned two runners in the straight. The form od the first two could be underrated.
Snow Hill Official explanation: jockey said gelding stopped quickly

1567 WINDSOR VEHICLE LEASING MAIDEN STKS 1m 2f 7y
7:25 (7:26) (Class 5) 3-Y-O £2,264 (£673; £336; £168) Stalls Centre

Form RPR

06- **1** **Opinion (IRE)**[187] 6953 3-9-3 0 RichardMullen 9 87+
(Sir Michael Stoute) *hld up in midfield: off the pce over 4f out but sn prog: chsd ldr over 2f out: shkn up and clsd to ld ins fnl f: styd on wl* **12/1**

2 *2* **Biographer** 3-9-3 0 TedDurcan 3 83+
(David Lanigan) *hld up in midfield: off the pce over 4f out but sn prog: pushed along and styd on fnl 2f: tk 2nd last 75yds* **11/2**[2]

0- **3** *1 1/4* **Fearless Dream**[237] 5583 3-8-12 0 WilliamBuick 15 75
(John Gosden) *led: pressed over 3f out but sn kicked clr: tired fr 2f out: hdd ins fnl f* **6/1**[3]

00- **4** *2* **Rye House (IRE)**[181] 7083 3-9-3 0 RyanMoore 6 76+
(Sir Michael Stoute) *hld up wl in rr: wl off the pce over 4f out: gd prog wl over 3f out: rdn 2f out: kpt on same pce after* **8/1**

0-2 **5** *1/2* **Cape Samba**[32] 1001 3-9-3 0 MartinDwyer 5 75
(Peter Chapple-Hyam) *t.k.h: prom: rdn over 2f out: one pce after and nvr able to chal* **5/1**[1]

06 **6** *6* **Arctic Galaxy (CAN)**[14] 1265 3-9-3 0 RobertHavlin 11 63+
(John Gosden) *hld up in rr: nt on terms fr 1/2-way: nudged along and styd on in encouraging style fr 3f out: nrst fin* **16/1**

0- **7** *1* **Attwaal (IRE)**[173] 7232 3-9-3 0 NeilCallan 7 61+
(Roger Varian) *trckd ldrs: prog to dispute 3rd over 3f out: sn rdn: wknd 2f out* **10/1**

8 *4 1/2* **Almost Gemini (IRE)** 3-9-3 0 JamieSpencer 14 52
(Roger Varian) *mostly chsd ldr to over 2f out: floundering and wknd after* **6/1**[3]

9 *1/2* **Chapelle du Roi (USA)** 3-9-3 0 DaneO'Neill 2 51+
(David Lanigan) *s.i.s: hld up in last: sme prog 3f out but hanging bdly: nvr on terms* **16/1**

505- **10** *5* **Thecornishcockney**[187] 6952 3-9-3 68 MichaelO'Connell 8 41
(John Ryan) *ponied to s: sn prom: rdn over 3f out: wknd over 2f out* **20/1**

00- **11** *2 1/4* **Sea Fret**[184] 7025 3-8-12 0 DarryllHolland 4 32
(Hughie Morrison) *chsd ldng pair: rdn over 3f out: wknd over 2f out* **33/1**

12 *4* **Magma** 3-8-12 0 JimmyFortune 10 24
(Andrew Balding) *a wl in rr: struggling over 4f out* **25/1**

00- **13** *7* **Hard Road**[173] 7233 3-9-3 0 SebSanders 1 15
(Chris Wall) *wl in rr: pushed along firmly and struggling over 4f out: t.o* **40/1**

00 **14** *11* **Magical Marvin**[24] 1113 3-9-3 0 NeilChalmers 13
(Michael Appleby) *prom 3f: sn lost pl bdly: wl in rr 4f out: t.o* **200/1**

15 *15* **Pick Three** 3-9-3 0 GeorgeBaker 12
(Roger Charlton) *nvr bttr than midfield: struggling over 4f out: t.o* **16/1**

2m 19.77s (11.07) **Going Correction** +1.10s/f (Soft) 15 Ran SP% **120.6**
Speed ratings (Par 98): **99,97,96,94,94 89,88,85,84,80 79,75,70,61,49**
toteswingers:1&2:£14.60, 1&3:£20.20, 2&3:£9.00 CSF £72.92 TOTE £13.90: £5.60, £1.20, £3.20; EX 106.30 Trifecta £1239.20 Part won. Pool: £1,674.67 - 0.41 winning units..
Owner Highclere Thoroughbred Racing-Herring **Bred** Ballylinch Stud **Trained** Newmarket, Suffolk

FOCUS
Plenty of powerful connections were represented and this maiden ought to produce a few winners. The form is rated around the race averages plus the fifth and sixth. They raced far side in the closing stages.
Chapelle du Roi(USA) Official explanation: jockey said colt hung left

1568 SKYBET MOBILE FOR IPHONE & ANDROID H'CAP 1m 3f 135y
7:55 (7:55) (Class 5) (0-70,70) 3-Y-O £2,264 (£673; £336; £168) Stalls Centre

Form RPR

04-0 **1** **Nordic Quest (IRE)**[22] 1155 3-9-6 69 LukeMorris 7 77
(Gerard Butler) *t.k.h: trckd ldrs: effrt over 3f out: rdn to chal over 2f out: led over 1f out: styd on wl* **11/4**[1]

030- **2** *3 3/4* **Wayne Manor (IRE)**[195] 6772 3-9-1 64 JimCrowley 8 65
(Ralph Beckett) *led to 8f out: trckd ldr: rdn to ld again wl over 2f out: hdd and one pce over 1f out* **9/2**[2]

2154 **3** *2* **Somemothersdohavem**[7] 1413 3-9-7 70 (p) MichaelO'Connell 5 68
(John Ryan) *t.k.h: led 8f out to wl over 2f out: steadily fdd over 1f out* **14/1**

-663 **4** *1 1/2* **Grand Gold**[12] 1319 3-9-7 70 (t) GeorgeBaker 4 65
(Seamus Durack) *hld up: stdy prog fr 1/2-way gng wl: jnd ldrs over 3f out: rdn over 2f out: nt qckn and fdd after* **11/4**[1]

60-2 **5** *1* **Lady Romanza (IRE)**[24] 1107 3-8-9 63 JemmaMarshall(5) 6 57
(Brendan Powell) *t.k.h: sn stdd into last pair: wl off the pce 4f out: rdn and plugged on after: nvr able to land a blow* **20/1**

60-4 **6** *4* **Spanish Fork (IRE)**[10] 1355 3-9-4 67 MartinHarley 2 54
(Mick Channon) *hld up in last: pushed along 1/2-way and lost tch: wl bhd 4f out: kpt on steadily fnl 2f* **13/2**

025- **7** *3 1/2* **Dovils Date**[291] 3780 3-9-3 66 JamesMillman 1 47
(Rod Millman) *trckd ldrs: lost pl and pushed along 5f out: wknd over 3f out* **6/1**[3]

600- **8** *90* **Enjoying (IRE)**[147] 7569 3-8-11 60 (b) PadraigBeggy 3
(David Evans) *t.k.h: prom: rdn 4f out and gave up: wl t.o* **20/1**

2m 44.35s (14.85) **Going Correction** +1.10s/f (Soft) 8 Ran SP% **115.3**
Speed ratings (Par 98): **94,91,90,89,88 85,83,23**
toteswingers:1&2:£4.50, 1&3:£11.90, 2&3:£12.50 CSF £15.49 CT £141.27 TOTE £2.80: £1.10, £2.50, £4.90; EX 16.70 Trifecta £112.00 Pool: £665.95 - 4.40 winning units..
Owner A D Spence **Bred** Gestut Wittekindshof **Trained** Newmarket, Suffolk

FOCUS
Once more the runners ended up far side in the straight. The time was reasonable compared with the earlier handicap considering the ground had worsened. A clear personal best from the winner.
T/Jkpt: Not won. T/Plt: £1,954.80 to a £1 stake. Pool:£98,815.59 - 36.90 winning tickets T/Qpdt: £598.10 to a £1 stake. Pool:£6,628.12 - 8.20 winning tickets JN

1569 - (Foreign Racing) - See Raceform Interactive

1490 LONGCHAMP (R-H)
Monday, April 23

OFFICIAL GOING: Turf: very soft changing to heavy after race 2 (12.50)

1570a PRIX NOAILLES (GROUP 2) (3YO COLTS & FILLIES) (TURF) 1m 2f 110y
1:50 (12:00) 3-Y-O £61,750 (£23,833; £11,375; £7,583; £3,791)

RPR

1 **Hard Dream (IRE)**[37] 3-9-2 0 StephanePasquier 5 111
(F Rohaut, France) *settled in 2nd on outside of ldr: chsd clr ldr fr 2f out: r.o wl fnl f: chal ldr 100yds out: tk ld 50yds out: r.o wl* **7/1**[3]

2 *1 1/2* **Tifongo (FR)**[15] 1244 3-9-2 0 ChristopheSoumillon 1 108
(H-A Pantall, France) *led fr s: set slow pce: rdn to go clr over 2f out: r.o wl: st clr 1f out: chal 100yds out: hdd 50yds out: styd on wl* **9/1**

3 *1 1/2* **Valdo Bere (FR)**[22] 1162 3-9-2 0 ThierryJarnet 2 105+
(E Leenders, France) *settled in 3rd on ins: dropped bk to 4th bef st: chsd ldrs fr 2f out: wnt 3rd 1f out: styd on wl fnl f* **9/1**

4 *3* **Loi (IRE)**[190] 6902 3-9-2 0 OlivierPeslier 6 99+
(J-M Beguigne, France) *settled in 4th on outside: dropped bk to 5th bef st: wnt 3rd briefly early in st: no ex fr over 1 1/2f out: styd on fnl f* **4/5**[1]

5 *5* **Quart De Rhum (FR)**[22] 3-9-2 0 IoritzMendizabal 4 89
(Y Fouin, France) *at rr of field fr s: rdn to go 3rd on outside bef st: u.p to chse ldrs over 2f out: no ex: wknd* **33/1**

6 *8* **Lidari (FR)**[37] 951 3-9-2 0 Christophe-PatriceLemaire 3 74
(J-C Rouget, France) *settled in 5th: dropped bk to rr of field bef st: rdn but no rspnse in st: wknd* **3/1**[2]

2m 29.37s (19.17) 6 Ran SP% **116.0**
WIN (incl. 1 euro stake): 5.60. PLACES: 2.90, 3.50. SF: 41.90.
Owner Pandora Stud LLC **Bred** Ecurie Des Monceaux **Trained** Sauvagnon, France

FOCUS
The form, rated through the runner-up, fits the averages for the Noailles.

NOTEBOOK
Hard Dream(IRE) continued his improvement, although he was helped by being handy in a race in which few got involved. (tchd 13/2)

1330 FOLKESTONE (R-H)
Tuesday, April 24

1571 Meeting Abandoned - Waterlogged

1427 SOUTHWELL (L-H)
Tuesday, April 24

OFFICIAL GOING: Standard
Wind: Almost nil Weather: Cloudy

1578 32REDBET.COM APPRENTICE CLAIMING STKS 1m (F)
5:00 (5:00) (Class 6) 3-Y-O+ £1,704 (£503; £251) Stalls Low

Form RPR

0304 **1** **Bold Marc (IRE)**[36] 965 10-9-2 68 ConorHarrison(5) 9 78
(Mrs K Burke) *led 1f: pressed ldr: led over 4f out: pushed along and drew clr fr over 2f out* **12/1**

0-00 **2** *8* **Arabian Spirit**[24] 1128 7-9-11 83 LauraBarry(3) 1 67
(Richard Fahey) *prom: effrt and chsd wnr over 3f out: sn rdn: no imp fr 2f out* **7/2**[3]

1533 **3** *1 1/4* **Mcconnell (USA)**[33] 999 7-9-6 70 (b) DannyBrock 7 56
(Richard Guest) *chsd ldrs: drvn and effrt over 3f out: no ex fr 2f out* **11/4**[1]

6-26 **4** *3/4* **Sir George (IRE)**[26] 1094 7-9-11 73 WilliamTwiston-Davies(3) 3 62
(Ollie Pears) *s.i.s: hld up in tch: drvn and outpcd over 3f out: n.d after* **10/3**[2]

2100 **5** *2* **Fluctuation (IRE)**[11] 1354 4-9-4 71 (v) GeorgeDowning(3) 4 50
(Ian Williams) *hld up in tch: outpcd over 3f out: styd alone far rail ent st: nvr on terms* **11/4**[1]

032- **6** *7* **Lakeman (IRE)**[216] 4944 6-9-7 60 (be) JustinNewman 6 34
(Brian Ellison) *hld up towards rr on outside: struggling over 3f out: sn btn* **9/1**

-600 **7** *1/2* **Vogarth**[70] 553 8-9-0 39 (b) EvaMoscrop(5) 2 31
(Michael Chapman) *dwlt: plld hrd and led after 1f: hdd over 4f out: wknd wl over 2f out* **50/1**

1m 41.9s (-1.80) **Going Correction** -0.20s/f (Stan) 7 Ran SP% **118.3**
Speed ratings (Par 101): **101,93,91,91,89 82,81**
toteswingers:1&2:£4.40, 1&3:£6.40, 2&3:£4.10 CSF £56.05 TOTE £15.80: £3.90, £2.40; EX 42.50.
Owner Mrs Elaine M Burke **Bred** Eamon D Delany **Trained** Middleham Moor, N Yorks
■ Conor Harrison's first winner in Britain, to go with five in Ireland.

FOCUS
A moderate claimer, run at a decent pace and just the fastest of the three C&D races. The form is rated around the winner's form last year with doubts over the rest.

1579 BRITISH STALLION STUDS 32RED.COM E B F NOVICE STKS 5f (F)
5:30 (5:30) (Class 5) 2-Y-O £3,622 (£1,078; £538; £269) Stalls High

Form RPR
1 1 **Storm Moon (USA)**[17] 1218 2-9-5 0 JoeFanning 5 90+
(Mark Johnston) *mde all: shkn up and edgd lft over 1f out: qckndd clr fnl f: eased towards fin: readily* 4/11[1]
0 2 2 3/4 **Secret Destination**[6] 1435 2-8-9 0 BarryMcHugh 1 64
(Brian Ellison) *chsd wnr: drvn over 2f out: edgd lft over 1f out: kpt on same pce fnl f* 14/1[3]
1 3 2 1/2 **Woodland Mill (IRE)**[24] 1136 2-8-9 0 ShaneBKelly(5) 4 60
(Richard Fahey) *t.k.h: trckd ldrs: effrt and drvn over 1f out: sn outpcd* 5/2[2]
4 12 **Hellolini** 2-8-9 0 LeeNewman 2 12
(Robin Bastiman) *s.i.s: sn in tch: drvn and outpcd 1/2-way: sn struggling* 33/1

59.89s (0.19) **Going Correction** -0.15s/f (Stan) 4 Ran SP% **111.5**
Speed ratings (Par 92): **92,87,83,64**
CSF £6.95 TOTE £1.50; EX 4.90.
Owner Sheikh Hamdan Bin Mohammed Al Maktoum **Bred** Darley **Trained** Middleham Moor, N Yorks

FOCUS
The winner basically outclassed these and was value for a wider margin. He is potentially very useful but there are tougher tasks ahead.

NOTEBOOK
Storm Moon(USA) made it two wins from as many starts with another taking success. Trainer Mark Johnston has hit the ground running with his 2yos and this son of Invincible Spirit made it 4-6 juvenile winners for the yard so far in 2012. He has a lot of early speed and is evidently versatile regards underfoot conditions, something that will hold him in decent stead as the year progresses. This marks him down as a very likely candidate for the Listed National Stakes at Sandown next month, often a stepping stone for Royal Ascot in June, but there is also the Lily Agnes at Chester to consider, a test that could really suit. (op 4-9)
Secret Destination was firmly outclassed, but this was an awful lot better than her debut effort at Beverley last week and she has some scope. (op 16-1 tchd 9-1)
Woodland Mill(IRE) looked useful when winning at Kempton on her debut last month, but she didn't find anything when let down on this contrasting surface. She's probably worth another chance.
Hellolini, whose dam won over this trip at two, was struggling before halfway and the run was much needed.

1580 32RED CASINO H'CAP 1m 4f (F)
6:00 (6:00) (Class 6) (0-60,60) 4-Y-O+ £1,704 (£503; £251) Stalls Low

Form RPR
5242 1 **Dunaskin (IRE)**[7] 1433 12-8-2 46 oh1 (b) DuilioDaSilva(5) 5 53
(Richard Guest) *t.k.h: pressed ldr: led over 6f out: mde rest: rdn and edgd rt fr 2f out: kpt on wl fnl f* 14/1
1324 2 2 1/4 **Ostentation**[3] 1533 5-9-0 60 (b[1]) KatiaScallan(7) 3 63
(Alastair Lidderdale) *t.k.h: in tch on ins: lost pl 1/2-way: rallied over 2f out: chsd wnr ins fnl f: r.o* 2/1[1]
04-4 3 nk **Bring Sweets (IRE)**[28] 1052 5-9-0 53 BarryMcHugh 7 56
(Brian Ellison) *hld up on outside: hdwy to chse wnr over 2f out: effrt and rdn over 1f out: hung lft and lost 2nd ins fnl f: no ex* 2/1[1]
4336 4 6 **Mister Frosty (IRE)**[29] 1047 6-9-6 59 NeilCallan 4 52
(Gay Kelleway) *trckd ldrs: wnt 2nd 5f out to over 2f out: rdn and wknd over 1f out* 4/1[2]
4235 5 2 1/4 **Harare**[26] 1092 11-8-3 49 (v) GemmaTutty(7) 2 38
(Karen Tutty) *prom: drvn along 4f out: hung lft and wknd over 2f out* 25/1
5/5- 6 16 **Lava Steps (USA)**[456] 103 6-8-10 49 DanielTudhope 8 13
(David O'Meara) *led to over 6f out: rdn and outpcd over 4f out: wknd 3f out: eased whn no ch fnl 2f* 6/1[3]
/00- 7 nk **Key Decision (IRE)**[130] 7787 8-8-7 46 oh1 (t) JohnFahy 1 9
(C Moore, Ire) *hld up: drvn along over 4f out: wknd over 3f out* 16/1

2m 39.56s (-1.44) **Going Correction** -0.20s/f (Stan) 7 Ran SP% **117.3**
Speed ratings (Par 101): **96,94,94,90,88 78,77**
toteswingers:1&2:£4.60, 1&3:£2.90, 2&3:£1.50 CSF £44.15 CT £83.91 TOTE £11.80: £4.40, £1.90; EX 22.70.
Owner Mrs Alison Guest **Bred** J P And Miss M Mangan **Trained** Stainforth, S Yorks

FOCUS
A weak handicap, run at a fair pace and rated on the negative side. The principals finished clear.

1581 32RED H'CAP 6f (F)
6:30 (6:30) (Class 4) (0-85,85) 4-Y-O+ £4,075 (£1,212; £606; £303) Stalls Low

Form RPR
2452 1 **Masai Moon**[7] 1431 8-9-1 79 (b) JamesMillman 3 91
(Rod Millman) *w ldrs: led 3f out: rdn along over 2f out: drew clr fnl f* 7/2[2]
10-4 2 4 **Mappin Time (IRE)**[11] 1362 4-9-4 82 (p) DavidAllan 6 81
(Tim Easterby) *prom: drvn and chsd wnr over 2f out: kpt on fnl f: nvr able to chal* 3/1[1]
0501 3 hd **Gorgeous Goblin (IRE)**[7] 1428 5-8-7 71 6ex (t) TedDurcan 4 70
(David C Griffiths) *hld up: effrt and rdn on outside over 1f out: edgd lft: no imp fnl f* 7/1
2352 4 nk **Elhamri**[7] 1430 8-8-7 71 oh5 KirstyMilczarek 2 69
(Conor Dore) *in tch: effrt whn hmpd over 2f out: sn rdn and rallied over 1f out: kpt on same pce* 14/1
6010 5 nse **Mazovian (USA)**[7] 1431 4-8-2 73 DannyBrock(7) 1 70
(Michael Chapman) *cl up on ins: ev ch 3f out: drvn and kpt on same pce fr over 1f out* 10/1
1-50 6 4 **Jeannie Galloway (IRE)**[17] 1220 5-9-2 85 ShaneBKelly(5) 5 70
(Richard Fahey) *led to 3f out: rdn and hung lft over 2f out: sn wknd* 4/1[3]
16P- 7 1 3/4 **Eastern Hills**[131] 7771 7-8-8 79 (p) NoraLooby(7) 9 58
(Alan McCabe) *dwlt: sn prom on outside: drvn along 3f out: wknd over 1f out* 11/1
3031 8 2 1/2 **Dancing Freddy (IRE)**[49] 808 5-8-11 75 (tp) MartinHarley 7 46
(Richard Guest) *hld up in tch: effrt and drvn 2f out: sn wknd* 8/1
-00R 9 20 **Monsieur Jamie**[47] 835 4-9-1 79 FrederikTylicki 8
(J R Jenkins) *s.i.s: sn in tch on outside: struggling after 2f: sn lost tch: t.o* 12/1

1m 14.55s (-1.95) **Going Correction** -0.20s/f (Stan) 9 Ran SP% **122.6**
Speed ratings (Par 105): **105,99,99,99,98 93,91,87,61**
toteswingers:1&2:£2.80, 1&3:£3.20, 2&3:£4.00 CSF £15.52 CT £72.48 TOTE £3.40: £1.90, £1.60, £2.70; EX 15.00.
Owner Rod Millman Racing Club **Bred** Mrs B A Matthews **Trained** Kentisbeare, Devon

FOCUS
A competitive sprint handicap for the grade and a clear-cut success for the winner. He is rated in line with his best form in the past year.

Elhamri Official explanation: jockey said gelding suffered interference

1582 £32 FREE AT 32RED.COM H'CAP 1m (F)
7:05 (7:05) (Class 5) (0-70,70) 3-Y-O £2,264 (£673; £336; £168) Stalls Low

Form RPR
16-6 1 **Fennell Bay (IRE)**[24] 1142 3-9-7 70 JoeFanning 3 79
(Mark Johnston) *led 1f: chsd ldr: effrt and rdn 2f out: sn edgd lft: styd on wl fnl f: led nr fin* 85/40[2]
443 2 1/2 **Outlaw Torn (IRE)**[11] 1365 3-8-2 56 oh3 (e) DuilioDaSilva(5) 1 64
(Richard Guest) *t.k.h: led after 1f: rdn over 2f out: styd on fnl f: hdd nr fin* 7/1
2211 3 6 **Crowning Star (IRE)**[11] 1365 3-9-7 70 (t) NeilCallan 4 64
(Gay Kelleway) *prom on outside: effrt over 2f out: edgd lft and no ex appr fnl f* 11/10[1]
00-0 4 2 3/4 **Travis County (IRE)**[20] 1190 3-9-7 70 BarryMcHugh 5 58
(Brian Ellison) *s.i.s: hld up in tch: stdy hdwy over 3f out: sn rdn: edgd lft and wknd over 1f out* 9/2[3]
6-05 5 9 **Inya House**[73] 536 3-8-4 56 oh5 DeclanCannon(3) 2 23
(Nigel Tinkler) *trckd ldrs on ins: drvn and outpcd over 3f out: btn fnl 2f* 22/1

1m 41.96s (-1.74) **Going Correction** -0.20s/f (Stan) 5 Ran SP% **114.6**
Speed ratings (Par 98): **100,99,93,90,81**
CSF £16.91 TOTE £2.40: £1.20, £3.80; EX 10.60.
Owner Sheikh Hamdan Bin Mohammed Al Maktoum **Bred** J R Wills **Trained** Middleham Moor, N Yorks

FOCUS
This moderate 3yo handicap was a tight affair the top three all going off a mark of 70. The first pair finished well clear of the rest in a driving finish, and both improved.

1583 32REDPOKER.COM H'CAP 1m (F)
7:40 (7:40) (Class 6) (0-60,59) 4-Y-O+ £1,704 (£503; £251) Stalls Low

Form RPR
65-4 1 **Rub Of The Relic (IRE)**[15] 1248 7-9-1 53 (v) BarryMcHugh 2 62
(Paul Midgley) *mde all: rdn and hrd pressed over 2f out: styd on wl fnl f* 10/1
3566 2 1 **Myraid**[17] 1222 5-8-10 48 (b[1]) JamesSullivan 4 55
(Ruth Carr) *t.k.h: trckd ldrs: hdwy and ev ch over 2f out: sn rdn: edgd rt and kpt on same pce ins fnl f* 6/1[2]
00-6 3 2 3/4 **Orpen Wide (IRE)**[14] 1279 10-8-12 50 (bt) RussKennemore 1 50
(Michael Chapman) *cl up: rdn and ev ch 3f out: one pce fr 2f out* 50/1
666- 4 nk **Kyllachykov (IRE)**[182] 7084 4-8-7 45 LeeNewman 5 45
(Robin Bastiman) *prom: rdn over 3f out: no imp whn hung bdly lft over 2f out: kpt on fnl f: nvr able to chal* 8/1
0-06 5 1/2 **Hits Only Jude (IRE)**[14] 1269 9-9-0 59 (v) MichaelKenny(7) 3 58
(Declan Carroll) *sn pushed along and prom on ins: outpcd whn bmpd over 2f out: plugged on fnl f: no imp* 7/1[3]
0-65 6 10 **Bold Diva**[21] 1178 7-8-7 52 (v) GeorgeDowning(7) 9 28
(Tony Carroll) *s.i.s: hld up bhd ldng gp: effrt whn carried lft and bmpd over 2f out: sn struggling* 6/1[2]
5351 7 1/2 **Somerset Island (IRE)**[21] 1179 4-9-6 58 (p) AndrewMullen 6 32
(Michael Smith) *prom on outside: drvn along and wknd over 3f out* 5/4[1]
0250 8 3 1/4 **Ad Vitam (IRE)**[21] 1179 4-8-2 47 (tp) ClaireMurray(7) 7 14
(Micky Hammond) *s.i.s: racd wd in rr: struggling fr 1/2-way: nvr on terms* 20/1
00-3 9 15 **Jupiter Fidius**[10] 1384 5-8-12 57 GemmaTutty(7) 8
(Karen Tutty) *sn bhd on outside: struggling 1/2-way: sn btn: t.o* 7/1[3]

1m 42.35s (-1.35) **Going Correction** -0.20s/f (Stan) 9 Ran SP% **124.9**
Speed ratings (Par 101): **98,97,94,93,93 83,82,79,64**
toteswingers:1&2:£7.60, 1&3:£44.90, 2&3:£21.20 CSF £74.34 CT £2916.98 TOTE £16.10: £2.70, £1.70, £8.90; EX 43.00.
Owner O R Dukes **Bred** M J Wiley **Trained** Westow, N Yorks

FOCUS
An ordinary handicap in which seven sported headgear of some sort. There was a strong early pace on and most were done with 2f out. The winner basically ran to his best.
Orpen Wide(IRE) Official explanation: jockey said gelding hung right
Bold Diva Official explanation: jockey said mare suffered interference
Somerset Island(IRE) Official explanation: jockey said gelding never travelled
Ad Vitam(IRE) Official explanation: trainer's rep said gelding had a breathing problem

1584 32REDBINGO.COM H'CAP 7f (F)
8:10 (8:11) (Class 6) (0-65,63) 4-Y-O+ £1,704 (£503; £251) Stalls Low

Form RPR
6511 1 **Only Ten Per Cent (IRE)**[21] 1178 4-9-7 63 FrederikTylicki 3 79
(J R Jenkins) *hld up in tch: smooth hdwy to ld over 2f out: shkn up and qckndd clr fr over 1f out: edgd lft ins fnl f: easily* 4/7[1]
3531 2 4 1/2 **Bonnie Prince Blue**[14] 1283 9-9-1 60 (b) DaleSwift(3) 2 64
(Ian McInnes) *t.k.h: led 1f: chsd ldr: effrt and ev ch over 2f out: kpt on: no ch w wnr* 9/2[2]
5443 3 1 3/4 **Gracie's Gift (IRE)**[14] 1280 10-8-2 49 oh1 (v) DuilioDaSilva(5) 5 48
(Richard Guest) *chsd ldrs: effrt over 2f out: kpt on same pce over 1f out* 8/1[3]
-600 4 1 1/2 **Swinger**[14] 1283 4-8-8 50 (t) RobertWinston 1 45
(Scott Dixon) *chsd ldrs: drvn and led briefly 3f out: outpcd fnl 2f* 14/1
05- 5 4 1/2 **Adam De Beaulieu (USA)**[172] 7269 5-8-13 55 (t) PhillipMakin 4 38
(Ben Haslam) *hld up: drvn on outside over 3f out: struggling whn drifted lft over 2f out: nvr on terms* 10/1
06-6 6 2 1/4 **Drumpellier (IRE)**[10] 1383 5-8-2 49 oh4 (e[1]) NeilFarley(5) 6 26
(Simon West) *blindfold slow to remove and dwlt: t.k.h and led after 1f: hdd over 2f out: sn wknd* 25/1

1m 29.2s (-1.10) **Going Correction** -0.20s/f (Stan) 6 Ran SP% **112.6**
Speed ratings (Par 101): **98,92,90,89,84 81**
toteswingers:1&2:£1.10, 1&3:£1.30, 2&3:£2.70 CSF £3.53 TOTE £1.70: £1.10, £1.80; EX 3.10.
Owner B Silkman **Bred** Sandro Garavelli **Trained** Royston, Herts

FOCUS
A weak handicap that had a top-heavy look about it. The time was alright for the grade and the form is taken at something like face value. The winner is on a roll at present.
T/Plt: £351.00 to a £1 stake. Pool:£55,521.29 - 115.47 winning tickets T/Qpdt: £44.60 to a £1 stake. Pool:£6,112.99 - 101.41 winning tickets RY

[1528]WOLVERHAMPTON (A.W) (L-H)

Tuesday, April 24

OFFICIAL GOING: Standard

Wind: Fresh across Weather: Cloudy with sunny spells

1585 32RED.COM H'CAP 5f 20y(P)

2:20 (2:26) (Class 6) (0-60,60) 3-Y-O **£1,704** (£503; £251) **Stalls** Low

Form RPR

5-02 **1** **Betty Brook (IRE)**[50] 802 3-9-6 **59** RyanMoore 6 65
(Nick Littmoden) *hld up: hdwy over 1f out: rdn to ld wl ins fnl f: r.o* **4/1**[3]

050 **2** 1 1/4 **Ghazeer (IRE)**[24] 1138 3-9-1 **54** JoeFanning 2 55
(Derek Shaw) *led: hdd over 3f out: chsd ldr tl led again 2f out: shkn up over 1f out: edgd rt and hdd wl ins fnl f* **10/3**[2]

2425 **3** shd **Emma Jean (IRE)**[11] 1359 3-9-0 **53** (bt[1]) SilvestreDeSousa 9 54
(Frank Sheridan) *mid-div: pushed along 1/2-way: hdwy over 1f out: sn rdn and hung lft: r.o* **14/1**

00-0 **4** 1 1/4 **Kai**[20] 1182 3-9-1 **54** JamieSpencer 4 51
(Michael Bell) *sn pushed along in rr: reminder 1/2-way: r.o towards fin: nvr nrr* **7/4**[1]

-036 **5** nk **Jeremy Sue**[12] 1337 3-8-7 **46** oh1 (b) AndreaAtzeni 3 41
(Derek Haydn Jones) *chsd ldrs: rdn over 1f out: styd on* **14/1**

045 **6** nk **First Rebellion**[50] 802 3-8-0 **46** DarrenEgan(7) 5 40
(Tony Carroll) *chsd ldrs: rdn over 1f out: styd on* **14/1**

433 **7** nk **Miserere Mei (IRE)**[3] 1529 3-8-10 **52** (p) DeclanCannon(3) 8 45
(Richard Guest) *chsd ldrs: rdn and ev ch over 1f out: edgd rt and no ex ins fnl f* **15/2**

00-6 **8** 4 1/2 **Maltease Ah**[50] 802 3-8-8 **54** [1] DavidWarren(7) 1 31
(Andrew Reid) *chsd ldr tl led over 3f out: hdd 2f out: wknd fnl f* **66/1**

2-40 **9** 1 1/2 **Forever Janey**[53] 769 3-8-7 **46** oh1 JamesSullivan 7 18
(Paul Green) *s.i.s: outpcd* **50/1**

060- **10** hd **Cataract**[179] 7143 3-8-8 **47** (b) LukeMorris 10 18
(John Weymes) *s.i.s: outpcd* **28/1**

1m 2.59s (0.29) **Going Correction** +0.075s/f (Slow) **10** Ran SP% **118.1**

Speed ratings (Par 96): **100,98,97,95,95 94,94,87,84,84**

toteswingers:1&2:£4.40, 1&3:£6.30, 2&3:£8.70 CSF £17.86 CT £175.50 TOTE £6.70: £1.90, £1.20, £2.50; EX 24.90 Trifecta £91.90 Pool: £606.34 - 4.88 winning units..

Owner Mrs Emma Littmoden **Bred** Martin Francis Ltd **Trained** Newmarket, Suffolk

FOCUS

This moderate 3yo sprint handicap was run at a sound gallop and it suited those coming from off the pace. The winner built on her latest run for a small personal best, with the third setting the standard.

1586 £32 FREE AT 32RED.COM (S) STKS 7f 32y(P)

2:50 (2:55) (Class 6) 3-Y-O+ **£1,704** (£503; £251) **Stalls** High

Form RPR

4040 **1** **Bawaardi (IRE)**[23] 1156 6-9-8 **77** RichardEvans(3) 1 73
(David Evans) *chsd ldrs: rdn and nt clr run over 1f out: swtchd rt: r.o to ld wl ins fnl f* **7/4**[1]

3222 **2** 3/4 **Unlimited**[3] 1530 10-9-6 **70** NeilCallan 5 66
(Tony Carroll) *hld up: hdwy over 1f out: sn rdn: r.o to go 2nd post: nt rch wnr* **7/2**[3]

0110 **3** hd **Spin Again (IRE)**[15] 1263 7-9-11 **70** RichardKingscote 2 71
(Daniel Kubler) *led: rdn and hung lft over 1f out: hdd wl ins fnl f: lost 2nd post* **3/1**[2]

4056 **4** 3/4 **Finefrenzyrolling (IRE)**[15] 1248 4-8-12 **58** MichaelMetcalfe(3) 4 58
(Mrs K Burke) *hld up: hdwy over 1f out: n.m.r ins fnl f: r.o* **16/1**

000 **5** 1/2 **Eyes On**[14] 1283 4-9-1 **46** (bt) SilvestreDeSousa 3 57?
(Frank Sheridan) *chsd ldr: rdn over 1f out: styd on* **28/1**

0-20 **6** nse **Not My Choice (IRE)**[10] 1378 7-9-6 **66** (t) RyanMoore 6 62
(David C Griffiths) *sn chsng ldr: pushed along over 2f out: rdn over 1f out: styd on same pce ins fnl f* **5/1**

1m 29.87s (0.27) **Going Correction** +0.075s/f (Slow) **6** Ran SP% **109.6**

Speed ratings (Par 101): **101,100,99,99,98 98**

toteswingers:1&2:£2.00, 1&3:£1.80, 2&3:£1.70 CSF £7.72 TOTE £2.00: £1.10, £3.70; EX 6.00.There was no bid for the winner

Owner Exors of the late Mrs Sally Edwards **Bred** Millsec Limited **Trained** Pandy, Monmouths

FOCUS

This 7f seller was run at a steady pace and just over 2l separated the field passing the post. A muddling race with the form seemingly limited by the fifth.

1587 32RED H'CAP 7f 32y(P)

3:20 (3:27) (Class 4) (0-80,80) 4-Y-O+ **£4,204** (£1,251; £625; £312) **Stalls** High

Form RPR

-431 **1** **Indian Art (IRE)**[11] 1360 6-9-4 **77** JamesDoyle 12 84
(Sylvester Kirk) *hld up: hdwy over 1f out: r.o u.p to ld wl ins fnl f* **16/1**

-412 **2** nk **My Kingdom (IRE)**[15] 1254 6-9-5 **78** (t) JamieSpencer 7 84
(Ian Williams) *hld up: swtchd rt and hdwy over 1f out: sn rdn: r.o* **3/1**[1]

6326 **3** 1/2 **The Happy Hammer (IRE)**[10] 1378 6-8-8 **67** WilliamCarson 8 72
(Eugene Stanford) *hld up: hdwy over 1f out: rdn and swtchd lft ins fnl f: r.o* **14/1**

6555 **4** hd **Restless Bay (IRE)**[26] 1091 4-9-2 **75** ow1 (v) GeorgeBaker 4 79
(Reg Hollinshead) *hld up: swtchd lft and hdwy over 1f out: sn rdn: r.o* **5/1**[2]

0604 **5** 1/2 **All Right Now**[7] 1431 5-8-8 **67** AndreaAtzeni 6 70
(Derek Haydn Jones) *led: rdn and hung rt over 1f out: hdd wl ins fnl f* **13/2**[3]

4146 **6** nk **I Confess**[26] 1087 7-9-6 **79** (b) SilvestreDeSousa 5 81
(Geoffrey Harker) *chsd ldr 6f out: rdn over 2f out: ev ch ins fnl f: styd on same pce* **8/1**

0-16 **7** 1 **Amazing Star (IRE)**[11] 1354 7-9-7 **80** KierenFallon 3 80
(Declan Carroll) *s.i.s: hld up: hdwy over 1f out: sn rdn: styd on* **8/1**

0001 **8** 1/2 **Yankee Storm**[10] 1378 7-8-12 **71** (b) RyanMoore 9 69
(Michael Wigham) *a.p: rdn over 1f out: styng on same pce whn hmpd ins fnl f* **12/1**

16-0 **9** 1 1/2 **Al Muheer (IRE)**[23] 1156 7-9-4 **77** (b) JamesSullivan 2 71
(Ruth Carr) *plld hrd and prom: rdn over 1f out: styd on same pce whn hmpd wl ins fnl f* **20/1**

422- **10** 3 1/4 **Piddie's Power**[185] 7040 5-8-13 **75** SeanLevey(3) 1 60
(Ed McMahon) *racd keenly: trckd ldr 1f: remained handy: rdn over 1f out: wknd ins fnl f* **14/1**

00-3 **11** 1 **Julius Geezer (IRE)**[26] 1091 4-9-6 **79** RichardKingscote 10 62
(Tom Dascombe) *s.i.s: hdwy over 5f out: rdn over 2f out: wknd and eased fnl f* **8/1**

1m 29.06s (-0.54) **Going Correction** +0.075s/f (Slow) **11** Ran SP% **120.0**

Speed ratings (Par 105): **106,105,105,104,104 103,102,102,100,96 95**

toteswingers:1&2:£6.60, 1&3:£30.70, 2&3:£13.40 CSF £65.05 CT £718.24 TOTE £20.50: £5.60, £2.00, £5.60; EX 55.40 Trifecta £420.40 Part won. Pool: £568.16 - 0.82 winning units..

Owner R Hannon **Bred** Michael Woodlock And Seamus Kennedy **Trained** Upper Lambourn, Berks

■ Stewards' Enquiry : William Carson two-day ban: careless riding (May 8-9)

FOCUS

A competitive and open handicap, run at a strong pace. Plenty were still in with a chance entering the final furlong, the first two making their challenge widest of all in a thrilling finish. The winner's best form since he was a 3yo, with the third and fourth setting the standard.

1588 VISIT ATTHERACES.COM/PUNCHESTOWN H'CAP 2m 119y(P)

3:55 (4:00) (Class 6) (0-65,65) 4-Y-O+ **£1,704** (£503; £251) **Stalls** Low

Form RPR

015/ **1** **Fade To Grey (IRE)**[193] 1246 8-9-0 **53** (t) KierenFallon 8 63
(Shaun Lycett) *a.p: led over 2f out: rdn and hung rt fr over 1f out: hdd wl ins fnl f: rallied to ld post* **5/1**[2]

-025 **2** nk **Hallstatt (IRE)**[13] 1297 6-9-11 **64** (t) MichaelO'Connell 6 73
(John Mackie) *a.p: chsd wnr over 1f out: rdn to ld wl ins fnl f: hdd post* **7/1**[3]

0666 **3** 2 1/2 **Kavaloti (IRE)**[36] 963 8-9-12 **65** (b) RyanMoore 10 70
(Gary Moore) *s.i.s: hld up: hdwy u.p over 1f out: r.o* **15/2**

5531 **4** 1 3/4 **Cloudy Start**[11] 1361 6-9-6 **64** LeonnaMayor(5) 7 67
(Jamie Osborne) *hld up in tch: rdn over 2f out: styd on* **5/1**[2]

0112 **5** 6 **St Ignatius**[10] 1391 5-9-11 **64** DarryllHolland 3 58
(Alan Bailey) *hld up: rdn over 2f out: nvr trbld ldrs* **9/1**

1-53 **6** 3 1/4 **Hit The Switch**[12] 1338 6-9-10 **63** (p) SilvestreDeSousa 1 53
(Jennie Candlish) *set stdy pce tl qcknd over 5f out: rdn and hdd over 3f out: wknd wl over 1f out* **11/4**[1]

2214 **7** 3 **Corvette**[12] 1338 4-9-4 **61** LukeMorris 4 46
(Michael Appleby) *chsd ldr tl led over 3f out: rdn and hdd over 2f out: wknd over 1f out* **9/1**

656 **8** 3 **Godwit**[25] 1113 4-8-4 **47** WilliamCarson 9 28
(Eugene Stanford) *hld up: rdn and wknd over 2f out* **22/1**

3325 **9** 1/2 **Leyte Gulf (USA)**[11] 1361 9-9-6 **59** (p) LiamKeniry 2 40
(Chris Bealby) *chsd ldrs tl rdn and wknd over 2f out* **16/1**

3m 43.27s (1.47) **Going Correction** +0.075s/f (Slow)

WFA 4 from 5yo+ 4lb **9** Ran SP% **114.5**

Speed ratings (Par 101): **99,98,97,96,94 92,91,89,89**

toteswingers:1&2:£3.40, 1&3:£3.30, 2&3:£4.00 CSF £39.40 CT £259.56 TOTE £3.80: £1.20, £2.60, £2.90; EX 45.80 Trifecta £271.70 Pool: £973.12 - 2.65 winning units..

Owner Worcester Racing Club **Bred** Mount Coote Partnership **Trained** Clapton-on-the-Hill, Gloucs

FOCUS

This staying handicap was run at a steady pace with the field well strung out crossing the line. The winner was unexposed on the Flat and on a good mark compared with his jumps form. The form is rated around the second and third.

1589 PUNCHESTOWN FESTIVAL LIVE ON ATR SKY 415 MEDIAN AUCTION MAIDEN STKS 1m 1f 103y(P)

4:30 (4:36) (Class 6) 3-Y-O **£1,704** (£503; £251) **Stalls** Low

Form RPR

1 **Diamond Dame (IRE)** 3-8-12 **0** RyanMoore 2 66+
(Sir Michael Stoute) *hld up in tch: hung rt wl over 1f out: led 1f out: edgd lft: styd on wl* **15/8**[1]

20- **2** 2 **Hilali (IRE)**[186] 6994 3-9-3 **0** GeorgeBaker 1 67
(Gary Brown) *hld up: rdn over 1f out: r.o to go 2nd towards fin: nt trble wnr* **8/1**

552 **3** 3/4 **Green Mitas (ITY)**[12] 1340 3-9-3 **65** LukeMorris 5 65
(Frank Sheridan) *chsd ldrs: led over 1f out: sn rdn and hdd: styd on same pce ins fnl f: lost 2nd towards fin* **10/1**

45- **4** 1/2 **Mr Fong**[188] 6956 3-9-3 **0** MartinLane 8 64
(David Simcock) *led over 8f out: rdn and hdd over 2f out: styd on same pce ins fnl f* **9/4**[2]

-223 **5** 2 **Tenbridge**[61] 667 3-8-12 **69** (p) AndreaAtzeni 6 55
(Derek Haydn Jones) *led 1f: chsd ldr: led over 2f out: rdn and hdd over 1f out: no ex ins fnl f* **7/2**[3]

6 1 1/4 **Trulee Scrumptious** 3-8-7 **0** RosieJessop(5) 4 52?
(Peter Charalambous) *s.i.s hdwy over 5f out: pushed along over 2f out: nt clr run wl over 1f out: sn outpcd* **33/1**

2m 4.04s (2.34) **Going Correction** +0.075s/f (Slow) **6** Ran SP% **110.9**

Speed ratings (Par 96): **92,90,89,89,87 86**

toteswingers:1&2:£3.40, 1&3:£3.30, 2&3:£4.00 CSF £16.74 TOTE £2.10: £1.10, £3.20; EX 21.10 Trifecta £121.80 Pool: £1,276.26 - 7.75 winning units..

Owner Saeed Suhail **Bred** Rabbah Bloodstock Limited **Trained** Newmarket, Suffolk

FOCUS

A moderate auction maiden run at a steady pace. There is some doubt over what the bare form is worth, but the winner scored nicely on her racecourse debut and could improve considerably on this.

1590 32RED CASINO H'CAP 1m 1f 103y(P)

5:05 (5:11) (Class 6) (0-60,60) 3-Y-O **£1,704** (£503; £251) **Stalls** Low

Form RPR

463- **1** **Lady Arabella (IRE)**[153] 7514 3-9-7 **60** JamesDoyle 6 71
(Alastair Lidderdale) *hld up: pushed along over 3f out: hdwy over 2f out: rdn to ld over 1f out: edgd lft ins fnl f: r.o wl* **6/1**[2]

00-2 **2** 4 1/2 **Mexican Wave**[15] 1260 3-8-7 **46** oh1 HayleyTurner 7 47
(Michael Bell) *chsd ldrs: pushed along over 3f out: rdn and ev ch over 1f out: styd on same pce ins fnl f* **6/1**[2]

060- **3** nk **Lost Highway (IRE)**[181] 7101 3-9-6 **59** SilvestreDeSousa 8 62+
(Mark Johnston) *hld up: pushed along whn nt clr run over 2f out: swtchd rt and hdwy over 1f out: rdn and hung lft ins fnl f: styd on same pce* **11/10**[1]

000- **4** 3 1/2 **Mariannes**[125] 7837 3-8-8 **47** RyanMoore 10 40
(John Dunlop) *sn outpcd: r.o ins fnl f: nrst fin* **14/1**

-652 **5** 2 **Skyeron**[8] 1424 3-8-7 **46** oh1 LiamJones 1 35
(Mark Brisbourne) *chsd ldr tl led over 2f out: rdn and hdd over 1f out: wknd ins fnl f* **17/2**[3]

004 **6** 3 1/4 **Burning Passion**[64] 638 3-9-3 **56** PaddyAspell 4 38
(Michael Easterby) *prom: rdn over 2f out: nt clr run wl over 1f out: wknd fnl f* **10/1**

00-0 **7** 3 3/4 **Derek The Diamond**[14] 1270 3-8-8 **47** NeilChalmers 2 21
(Michael Appleby) *led: rdn over 3f out: hdd over 2f out: wknd over 1f out* **33/1**

-020 **8** *6* **Imperial Stargazer**[6] 1448 3 -9-3 **56** .....(v) MatthewDavies 5 18
(Mick Channon) *sn outpcd* **22/1**
1466 **9** *½* **Moment In The Sun**[8] 1424 3 -8-11 **57** .....(b) DarrenEgan(7) 9 18
(David Flood) *chsd ldrs tl rdn and wknd over 2f out* **12/1**
2m 1.95s (0.25) **Going Correction** +0.075s/f (Slow) **9**Ran SP% **117.5**
Speed ratings (Par 96): **101,97,96,93,91 88,85,80,79**
toteswingers:1&2:£4.30, 1&3:£3.00, 2&3:£3.90 CSF £42.54 CT £68.39 TOTE £8.90 : £1.90, £2.20, £1.10 ; EX 22.80 Trifecta £63.20 Pool: £1,150.19 - 13.45 winning units.
Owner The Arabella Partnership **Bred** Yeomanstown Stud **Trained** Lambourn, Berks

FOCUS
With three runners keen to lead, this handicap was run at a sound pace and it suited those ridden with restraint. The winner recorded a clear personal best with a step up from the runner-up.

1591 32REDPOKER.COM H'CAP 1m 4f 50y (P)
5:40 (5:40) (Class 6) (0-65,65) 3-Y-O **£1,704** (£503; £251) **Stalls** Low

Form RPR
500- **1** **Ukrainian (IRE)**[182] 7083 3 -9-7 **65** ..... SilvestreDeSousa 6 75+
(Mark Johnston) *mde all: shkn up over 1f out: clr fnl f: easily* **11/8**[1]
0361 **2** *4* **Aiaam Al Wafa (IRE)**[8] 1413 3 -9-2 **60** 6ex.....(p) LukeMorris 3 62
(Phil McEntee) *a.p: chsd wnr over 2f out: rdn over 1f out: styd on same pce* **16/1**
-501 **3** *1 ¾* **My New Angel (IRE)**[35] 973 3 -8-0 **51** oh1.....(be) DarrenEgan(7) 5 50
(Paul Green) *hld up: hdwy over 1f out: sn rdn: no ex ins fnl f* **14/1**
6-35 **4** *hd* **Cool Fantasy (IRE)**[15] 1267 3 -8-10 **54**.....(b) WilliamCarson 4 53
(Paul D'Arcy) *hld up: rdn over 2f out: hung lft fnl f: styd on same pce* **17/2**
2332 **5** *½* **Ctappers**[34] 983 3 -9-5 **63** ..... MatthewDavies 1 61
(Mick Channon) *chsd wnr tl rdn over 2f out: styd on same pce fr over 1f out* **5/1**[3]
666- **6** *10* **Altnaharra**[219] 6187 3 -8-11 **55** ..... KierenFallon 2 37
(Jim Goldie) *chsd ldrs: rdn over 2f out: wknd over 1f out* **5/2**[2]
2m 45.36s (4.26) **Going Correction** +0.075s/f (Slow) **6**Ran SP% **110.4**
Speed ratings (Par 96): **88,85,84,84,83 77**
toteswingers:1&2:£3.70, 1&3:£5.00, 2&3:£8.60 CSF £23.12 TOTE £2.20 : £1.10, £8.20 ; EX 19.50.
Owner Sheikh Majid Bin Mohammed al Maktoum **Bred** Mrs Fiona McStay **Trained** Middleham Moor, N Yorks

FOCUS
Little strength-in-depth in this 3yo handicap in which a couple of unexposed runners dominated the market. The winner made all in a tactical affair and he looks a nice type. The form is a little muddling.
Ukrainian(IRE) Official explanation: trainer's rep said, regarding apparent improvement in form, that this was the gelding's first run for six months and had strengthened and matured over the winter.
T/Jkpt: £93,959.80 to a £1 stake. Pool: £132,337.84. 1.00 winning tickets T/Plt: £66.80 to a £1 stake. Pool: £111,458.60. 1,217.13 winning tickets T/Qpdt: £27.60 to a £1 stake. Pool: £6,008.49. 160.58 w.tickets. CR

1592a- 1593a Foreign Racing (See Raceform Int.)

1292 CATTERICK (L-H)
Wednesday, April 25

OFFICIAL GOING: Good to soft (soft in places) changing to soft after race 3 (3:10)
Wind: Fresh, half behind Weather: wet and windy

1594 BHEST RACING TO SCHOOL (S) STKS 5f
2:05 (2:08) (Class 6) 2-Y-O **£1,704** (£503; £251) **Stalls** Low

Form RPR
62 **1** **Mad Jazz**[17] 1235 2 -8-6 **0** ..... BarryMcHugh 3 60
(Tony Coyle) *mde virtually all: kpt on wl fnl f* **7/1**
6225 **2** *1* **Perfect Words (IRE)**[7] 1437 2 -8-11 **0** ..... SamHitchcott 1 62
(Mick Channon) *chsd ldrs: wnt 2nd last 75yds: no ex* **2/1**[1]
52 **3** *3 ½* **Shop Til You Drop**[16] 1253 2 -8-6 **0** ..... PadraigBeggy 2 44
(David Evans) *w ldrs: wknd fnl 100yds* **5/2**[2]
4 *¾* **Saltaire Lass** 2 -8-6 **0** ..... DuranFentiman 6 41
(Paul Midgley) *s.s: kpt on fnl f* **10/1**
3 **5** *¾* **Red Koko (IRE)**[17] 1235 2 -8-6 **0** ..... PJMcDonald 4 39
(George Moore) *chsd ldrs: upsides over 2f out: wknd fnl f* **9/1**
4 **6** *nk* **Maggies Gem (IRE)**[17] 1235 2 -8-7 **0** ow1..... RussKennemore 5 39
(Paul Midgley) *chsd ldrs: drvn and outpcd after 2f: no threat after* **22/1**
0 **7** *24* **Amourous (IRE)**[23] 1164 2 -8-6 **0** ..... DavidAllan 7
(Tim Easterby) *swvd rt s: sn chsng ldrs: hung rt 2f out: sn lost pl: bhd whn eased: t.o* **6/1**[3]
1m 3.51s (3.71) **Going Correction** +0.50s/f (Yiel) **7**Ran SP% **112.1**
Speed ratings (Par 90): **90,88,82,81,80 79,41**
.The winner was bought in for 4,200gns. Perfect Words was claimed by \n \x\x Mrs Marjorie Fife for £5,000.
Owner Paul Inman & Tony Coyle **Bred** Usk Valley Stud **Trained** Norton, N Yorks

FOCUS
A weak event with one colt up against six fillies and all bar one of these had raced before. The form makes a bit of sense through the frustrating runner-up.

NOTEBOOK
Mad Jazz had already been comfortably beaten in two sellers, though she did have a couple of today's rivals behind her when second of four at Musselburgh last time. She saw her race out well after leading over a furlong from home, but doesn't appeal as the type to win anything better than this. She was retained for 4,200gns at the auction. (op 9-2 tchd 15-2)
Perfect Words (IRE) had had four previous tries already including when a beaten favourite on two occasions, but this drop in class appeared to give him a good chance of breaking his duck. He travelled well behind the leaders, but when asked for his effort the response was limited and the winner was always holding him. This result is yet another slap in the face for the form of the Brocklesby. (op 15-8 tchd 9-4)
Shop Til You Drop improved from her debut to finish runner-up to a previous winner in a Warwick seller last time and had every chance here with few apparent excuses. (tchd 11-4)
Saltaire Lass, out of a half-sister to a Group 3 winner and the only debutante in the field, made a little late progress after missing the break, but will still need to improve plenty in order to win a race. (op 16-1)
Amourous(IRE) again got restless in the stalls, as she did on her debut, and then saw plenty of daylight on the wide outside. (op 12-1)

1595 READ HAYLEY AT RACINGUK.COM EVERY FRIDAY MAIDEN STKS 7f
2:40 (2:41) (Class 5) 3-Y-O **£2,264** (£673; £336; £168) **Stalls** Centre

Form RPR
222- **1** **Trail Blaze (IRE)**[222] 6110 3 -9-3 **79** ..... PhillipMakin 1 79+
(Kevin Ryan) *mde all: drvn over 2f out: hld on wl clsng stages* **5/4**[1]
2 *1* **Liliargh (IRE)** 3 -8-12 **0** ..... PJMcDonald 5 71
(Ben Haslam) *sn chsng ldrs: styd on swtchd outside over 1f out: sn tk 3rd: styd on to take 2nd nr line* **50/1**
2620 **3** *nk* **Henry Bee**[46] 867 3 -9-3 **73** ..... TonyHamilton 6 75
(Richard Fahey) *chsd ldrs: upsides over 1f out: kpt on same pce last 100yds* **15/2**[3]
32-4 **4** *6* **Peter Anders**[27] 1086 3 -9-3 **72** ..... JoeFanning 10 59
(Mark Johnston) *chsd ldrs: chal over 2f out: wknd fnl f* **15/8**[2]
00- **5** *1 ¼* **Lean On Pete (IRE)**[196] 6805 3 -9-3 **0** ..... TomEaves 9 56+
(Ollie Pears) *s.i.s: bhd: hdwy 4f out: kpt on fnl 2f: nvr nr ldrs* **33/1**
0-4 **6** *1 ¼* **Hadrians Rule (IRE)**[14] 1296 3 -9-3 **0** ..... DavidAllan 3 53
(Tim Easterby) *trckd ldrs: t.k.h: effrt over 2f out: wknd appr fnl f* **9/1**
50- **7** *2 ½* **Twin Ivan (IRE)**[308] 3274 3 -8-12 **0** ..... DeanHeslop(5) 8 46
(Marjorie Fife) *s.i.s: bhd: kpt on fnl 2f: nvr a factor* **33/1**
0 **8** *2 ½* **Bollin Nancy**[16] 1250 3 -8-7 **0** ..... AdamCarter(5) 7 34
(Tim Easterby) *mid-div: outpcd over 3f out: nvr a factor after* **50/1**
9 *23* **Her Nibbs** 3 -8-12 **0** ..... TedDurcan 4
(James Bethell) *s.s: sn wl bhd: t.o after 2f* **33/1**
10 *41* **High Meadow Prince** 3 -9-0 **0** ..... DaleSwift(3) 2
(Ron Barr) *gave problems loading: s.s: sn wl bhd: t.o after 2f* **100/1**
1m 32.63s (5.63) **Going Correction** +0.775s/f (Yiel) **10**Ran SP% **114.7**
Speed ratings (Par 98): **98,96,96,89,88 86,83,81,54,7**
toteswingers:1&2:£17.20, 1&3:£3.00, 2&3:£29.90 CSF £83.90 TOTE £2.60 : £1.20, £12.10, £1.30; EX 63.30.
Owner Mr & Mrs Julian And Rosie Richer **Bred** Edmond Kent **Trained** Hambleton, N Yorks

FOCUS
An ordinary maiden. The winner set an above-average standard on his 2yo form and did not have to match that.

1596 CATTERICKBRIDGE.CO.UK H'CAP (DIV I) 7f
3:10 (3:12) (Class 6) (0-60,60) 3-Y-O **£2,045** (£603; £302) **Stalls** Centre

Form RPR
03-3 **1** **Art Dzeko**[13] 1337 3 -9-7 **60** ..... DavidAllan 10 65+
(Tim Easterby) *trckd ldrs: led 4f out: kpt on u.str.p fnl 2f* **11/4**[1]
-444 **2** *1 ½* **Son Of May**[71] 556 3 -8-13 **52** .....(b) TonyCulhane 3 53
(Jo Hughes) *s.i.s: reminders sn after s: hdwy over 3f out: wnt 2nd over 2f out: kpt on same pce fnl f* **17/2**
206- **3** *2 ½* **Becksies**[240] 5555 3 -8-7 **46** oh1..... RussKennemore 1 41
(Paul Midgley) *t.k.h: trckd ldrs: led over 3f out: wknd over 1f out: kpt on one pce* **25/1**
-000 **4** *2 ½* **Johnson's Cat (IRE)**[16] 1259 3 -8-3 **47** ..... DuilioDaSilva(5) 5 35
(Richard Guest) *hld up in rr: hdwy over 2f out: kpt on one pce* **11/2**[3]
53-0 **5** *3 ½* **Rock Canyon (IRE)**[17] 1241 3 -9-3 **59** ..... JulieBurke(3) 6 38
(Linda Perratt) *trckd ldrs: led briefly over 4f out: wknd over 1f out* **5/1**[2]
006- **6** *3* **Only A Round (IRE)**[164] 6274 3 -8-11 **50** ..... FrederikTylicki 9 21
(Micky Hammond) *led tl over 4f out: outpcd over 2f out: no threat after* **6/1**
0-56 **7** *1 ¼* **My Pearl (IRE)**[16] 1259 3 -8-13 **52** ..... PhillipMakin 2 20
(Kevin Ryan) *in rr: kpt on fnl 2f: nvr a factor* **15/2**
06-0 **8** *10* **Hopes Rebellion**[16] 1252 3 -8-11 **55** ..... NeilFarley(5) 4
(Declan Carroll) *mid-div: lost pl over 3f out: bhd fnl 2f* **40/1**
000- **9** *hd* **Time To Excel**[242] 5486 3 -8-13 **52** ..... TomEaves 7
(Michael Dods) *mid-div: lost pl over 3f out: bhd fnl 2f* **8/1**
000- **10** *24* **Ruskins View (IRE)**[294] 3728 3 -8-0 **46** oh1..... MatthewHopkins(7) 8
(Alan Berry) *s.i.s: sn trcking ldrs: lost pl over 3f out: wl bhd fnl 2f: t.o* **100/1**
1m 33.66s (6.66) **Going Correction** +0.775s/f (Yiel) **10**Ran SP% **113.7**
Speed ratings (Par 96): **92,90,87,84,80 77,75,64,64,36**
toteswingers:1&2:£4.00, 1&3:£6.40, 2&3:£11.80 CSF £26.00 CT £488.79 TOTE £2.60 : £1.10, £2.80, £6.90 ; EX 15.90.
Owner Middleham Park Racing LIX & Partners **Bred** Helier Stud **Trained** Great Habton, N Yorks
■ Stewards' Enquiry : David Allan two-day ban: used whip above permitted level (May 9-10)

FOCUS
A poor handicap contested by ten maidens. The winner did it nicely enough but the form could be very weak.

1597 RICHMOND CONDITIONS STKS 1m 3f 214y
3:45 (3:45) (Class 3) 3-Y-O **£6,411** (£1,919; £959; £479; £239) **Stalls** Low

Form RPR
11 **1** **Ed De Gas**[27] 1093 3 -8-12 **81** ..... ChrisCatlin 5 98
(Rae Guest) *trckd ldr: chal over 3f out: led 3f out: drvn clr over 1f out: eased last 50yds* **2/1**[2]
012 **2** *12* **Bordoni (USA)**[14] 1302 3 -9-4 **88** ..... JoeFanning 3 88
(Mark Johnston) *led: jnd 4f out: hdd 3f out: eased whn no ch w wnr last 75yds* **13/8**[1]
2-21 **3** *2 ¾* **Naseem Alyasmeen (IRE)**[7] 1519 3 -8-7 **67** ..... SamHitchcott 2 69
(Mick Channon) *trckd ldrs: t.k.h: effrt over 4f out: one pce: flattered* **9/4**[3]
2212 **4** *21* **Pelican Rock (IRE)**[12] 901 3 -8-12 **60** ..... DanielTudhope 1 41
(Andrew Crook) *hld up in rr: effrt over 4f out: wknd over 3f out: bhd whn eased over 1f out* **16/1**
0-0 **5** *32* **Actor (IRE)**[16] 1250 3 -8-12 **0** ..... JamesSullivan 4
(John Weymes) *s.i.s: sn chsng ldrs: drvn 6f out: lost tch over 4f out: sn t.o* **200/1**
2m 47.2s (8.30) **Going Correction** +0.775s/f (Yiel) **5**Ran SP% **108.6**
Speed ratings (Par 102): **103,95,93,79,57**
CSF £5.47 TOTE £3.70 : £1.30, £1.10 ; EX 6.30.
Owner R A Pegum **Bred** Canartam Ltd **Trained** Newmarket, Suffolk

FOCUS
A race that traditionally attracts a small field (no more than five runners since 2003), but an interesting contest nonetheless. The winning time was fractionally faster than the older handicappers in the following event. The winner continued his progress but it's hard to pin down quite what achieved here.

NOTEBOOK
Ed De Gas ◆ came into this unbeaten in two starts on Polytrack, but proved a revelation over a longer trip on this very different surface. Sent past the leader over 2f from home, he just pulled further and further clear and could hardly have been more impressive. It will be interesting to see where he goes next as he holds no big-race entries, but is starting to look very useful. (op 9-4 tchd 5-2 in a place)
Bordoni(USA) was another making his turf debut having also shown some decent form on Polytrack, though he still looked green last time. He set out to make all, but was easily picked off by the winner turning in and didn't appear to see it out. He is worth another chance on better ground. (op 11-8 tchd 15-8)
Naseem Alyasmeen (IRE)s stable had taken this five times in the previous six years (didn't have a runner in 2008) and unlike the two colts had nothing to prove with regards to the ground. She did have a bit to find with them at the weights, however, and she was in trouble with fully half a mile still to run. (op 11-4 tchd 2-1)
Pelican Rock (IRE) making his debut for the yard, has been running consistently well in moderate company on Fibresand this year, but this was a different task entirely. (op 12-1 tchd 18-1)

Actor(IRE) cost 100,000gns as a yearling, but has obviously had major problems. (op 100-1)

1598 GO RACING IN YORKSHIRE H'CAP 1m 3f 214y
4:15 (4:15) (Class 5) (0-70,71) 4-Y-0+ £2,264 (£673; £336; £168) Stalls Low

Form RPR
-100 1 **Light The City (IRE)**[22] [1175] 5-8-9 58 JamesSullivan 2 72+
(Ruth Carr) *trckd ldrs: led 2f out: sn drvn clr: heavily eased clsng stages* 12/1
0-00 2 6 **Not Til Monday (IRE)**[66] [521] 6-9-7 70 (v) FrederikTylicki 10 73
(J R Jenkins) *led: hdd over 2f out: kpt on same pce* 5/1[2]
524- 3 1 **Strong Knight**[143] [7357] 5-8-7 56 oh6 (p) DuranFentiman 1 57
(Tim Walford) *chsd ldrs: kpt on one pce fnl 2f* 10/1
56-0 4 3 **Bavarian Nordic (USA)**[14] [1297] 7-8-4 56 oh8 (v) AmyRyan(3) 9 52
(Richard Whitaker) *sn trcking ldrs: drvn over 3f out: one pce fnl 2f* 33/1
23-4 5 5 **Danceintothelight**[14] [1297] 5-8-12 61 KellyHarrison 14 49
(Micky Hammond) *mid-div: shkn up 7f out: sn chsng ldrs: wknd over 2f out* 7/2[1]
455- 6 shd **John Forbes**[18] [7772] 10-9-1 67 (p) PaulPickard(3) 3 55
(Brian Ellison) *sn drvn to r in midfield: outpcd over 3f out: kpt on fnl 2f: nvr a factor* 5/1[2]
23-0 7 4 1/2 **Deep Applause**[15] [1276] 4-8-11 61 (p) TomEaves 12 42
(Michael Dods) *hld up in rr: hdwy over 3f out: wknd over 2f out* 14/1
1-01 8 1 3/4 **Jack Dawkins (USA)**[8] [1429] 7-9-8 71 6ex AdrianNicholls 5 49
(David Nicholls) *trckd ldrs: led over 2f out: sn hdd and hung lft: wknd fnl f: eased nr fin* 6/1[3]
000- 9 2 **Lady Norlela**[197] [6775] 6-8-8 57 BarryMcHugh 6 32
(Brian Rothwell) *hld up in rr: nvr a factor* 25/1
500- 10 2 **Burns Night**[175] [7236] 6-9-6 69 JoeFanning 4 41
(Keith Dalgleish) *mid-div: effrt over 3f out: sn btn* 15/2
306- 11 12 **Stanley Rigby**[137] [7713] 6-9-4 70 LeeTopliss(3) 11 22
(Richard Fahey) *in rr: drvn over 3f out: sn bhd: eased clsng stages* 20/1

2m 47.26s (8.36) **Going Correction** +0.775s/f (Yiel)
WFA 4 from 5yo+ 1lb 11 Ran SP% **116.6**
Speed ratings (Par 103): **103,99,98,96,93 92,89,88,87,86 78**
toteswingers:1&2:£17.40, 1&3:£10.50, 2&3:£8.70 CSF £68.80 CT £632.32 TOTE £14.00: £4.20, £2.30, £3.10; EX 113.10.
Owner Atkins Legal Services **Bred** Rabbah Bloodstock Limited **Trained** Huby, N Yorks

FOCUS
This was a contest where it paid to race handily, and not many became involved. Improvement from the winner and the form has been taken at face value.
Jack Dawkins(USA) Official explanation: jockey said gelding hung left

1599 DINE AND VIEW AT CATTERICK RACES H'CAP 5f
4:45 (4:47) (Class 6) (0-65,65) 3-Y-O £2,045 (£603; £302) Stalls Low

Form RPR
0-51 1 **Laura's Bairn**[78] [455] 3-9-7 65 (v) FrederikTylicki 12 73
(J R Jenkins) *racd stands' side: sn chsng ldrs: styd on to ld nr fin* 9/1[3]
3026 2 nk **Lord Buffhead**[14] [1292] 3-8-3 52 DuilioDaSilva(5) 10 59
(Richard Guest) *chsd ldrs stands' side: led jst ins fnl f: edgd lft and hdd nr fin* 11/1
-033 3 2 1/4 **Celestial Dawn**[15] [1278] 3-8-11 55 PJMcDonald 6 54+
(John Weymes) *in rr: hdwy over 1f out: styd on ins fnl f* 11/1
0-35 4 1 1/2 **Economic Crisis (IRE)**[14] [1292] 3-8-10 54 PaulMulrennan 5 48+
(Alan Berry) *w ldrs: led over 2f out: hdd jst ins fnl f: wknd towards fin* 18/1
04-3 4 dht **Majestic Breeze (IRE)**[14] [1292] 3-8-7 51 oh1 BarryMcHugh 1 45+
(Brian Ellison) *w ldrs: kpt on same pce fnl 100yds: eased and lost outrt 4th nr line* 6/1[2]
0504 6 2 1/2 **Tuibama (IRE)**[14] [1292] 3-8-4 51 (b[1]) DeclanCannon(3) 2 36+
(Ben Haslam) *w ldrs: wknd fnl 150yds* 20/1
520- 7 2 1/4 **Just Like Heaven (IRE)**[194] [6827] 3-9-7 65 DavidAllan 3 41+
(Tim Easterby) *t.k.h: trckd ldrs: wknd over 1f out* 10/1
-652 8 1 **Wish Again (IRE)**[14] [1292] 3-9-5 63 (p) AdrianNicholls 4 36+
(David Nicholls) *chsd ldrs: wknd appr fnl f* 6/1[2]
04-0 9 1 1/4 **Elusive Bonus (IRE)**[16] [1252] 3-8-12 56 DanielTudhope 7 24+
(David O'Meara) *led: hdd over 2f out: sn btn* 10/1
02-2 10 1/2 **Cone Donkey (IRE)**[14] [1296] 3-9-6 64 TomEaves 11 31
(Bryan Smart) *racd towards stands' side: chsd ldr: wknd 2f out* 3/1[1]
4042 11 1 1/4 **Pressure Drop (IRE)**[12] [1353] 3-9-2 60 TonyCulhane 9 22+
(Jo Hughes) *racd towards centre: chsd ldrs: drvn over 2f out: lost pl over 1f out* 12/1

1m 3.59s (3.79) **Going Correction** +0.675s/f (Yiel) 11 Ran SP% **116.1**
Speed ratings (Par 96): **96,95,91,89,89 85,81,80,78,77 75**
toteswingers:1&2:£19.90, 1&3:£15.10, 2&3:£22.80 CSF £102.54 CT £1119.82 TOTE £11.70: £3.70, £3.80, £3.80; EX 110.80.
Owner Mark Goldstein **Bred** Greg Parsons **Trained** Royston, Herts
■ Stewards' Enquiry : Barry McHugh two-day ban: failed to take all reasonable and permissable measures to obtain best possible placing (May 9-10)

FOCUS
The form of this moderate sprint handicap can be taken with a pinch of salt, as the first two were part of a group of three who raced stands' side and they enjoyed a huge advantage. A small personal best from the winner.

1600 CATTERICKBRIDGE.CO.UK H'CAP (DIV II) 7f
5:15 (5:16) (Class 6) (0-60,60) 3-Y-O £2,045 (£603; £302) Stalls Centre

Form RPR
012- 1 **Regal Acclaim (IRE)**[211] [6424] 3-8-13 52 TedDurcan 2 60
(Tim Easterby) *mde virtually all: hld on gamely nr fin* 5/2[1]
-453 2 nk **Martha's Way**[33] [1012] 3-8-12 51 JamesSullivan 4 58
(Michael Easterby) *trckd ldrs: upsides over 2f out: no ex towards fin* 5/1[2]
00-2 3 4 1/2 **Rosie's Lady (IRE)**[11] [1386] 3-8-13 52 DanielTudhope 8 47
(David O'Meara) *mid-div: effrt and chsd 1st 2 over 2f out: kpt on same pce* 5/2[1]
4-06 4 4 1/2 **Sleepy Lucy**[16] [1260] 3-8-6 48 DeclanCannon(3) 6 32
(Richard Guest) *s.i.s: hdwy over 2f out: one pce* 14/1
1-00 5 3 **Mick Slates (IRE)**[12] [1359] 3-8-8 52 NeilFarley(5) 5 28
(Declan Carroll) *s.i.s: hdwy over 3f out: outpcd over 2f out: kpt on fnl f* 6/1[3]
000- 6 1 **Tallula (IRE)**[166] [7367] 3-8-7 46 oh1 KellyHarrison 10 19
(Micky Hammond) *tk fierce hold: w ldrs: hung rt and wd bnd 3f out: lost pl 2f out* 14/1
630- 7 3 3/4 **Brasingaman Espee**[243] [5454] 3-8-8 47 PJMcDonald 1 10
(George Moore) *in rr: nvr a factor* 20/1
0-06 8 37 **Tumbleowtashoes**[51] [801] 3-8-0 46 oh1 (t) BradleyBosley(7) 9
(John Ryan) *trckd ldrs: stdd after 1f: lost pl over 2f out: sn bhd: t.o whn eased ins fnl f* 100/1
024 9 27 **Chart**[28] [1072] 3-9-7 60 LeeNewman 3
(William Jarvis) *chsd ldrs: drvn over 3f out: sn lost pl: wl bhd whn eased over 1f out: t.o* 10/1

1m 33.44s (6.44) **Going Correction** +0.775s/f (Yiel) 9 Ran SP% **116.3**
Speed ratings (Par 96): **94,93,88,83,79 78,74,32,1**
toteswingers:1&2:£3.30, 1&3:£2.30, 2&3:£3.80 CSF £15.42 CT £34.06 TOTE £3.60: £1.90, £1.70, £1.10; EX 17.50.
Owner Mr And Mrs J D Cotton **Bred** Mrs H A Jellett **Trained** Great Habton, N Yorks
■ Stewards' Enquiry : Ted Durcan two-day ban: used whip in incorrect place (May 9-10)

FOCUS
Unlike in division one, a couple of previous winners took part in this leg. After what happened in the previous race, it was no surprise that the runners came stands' side in the home straight. Steps up from the first two.
Tallula(IRE) Official explanation: jockey said filly hung right-handed
Chart Official explanation: jockey said colt lost its action

1601 WE RACE AGAIN 8TH MAY APPRENTICE H'CAP 5f 212y
5:50 (5:51) (Class 6) (0-65,65) 4-Y-0+ £1,704 (£503; £251) Stalls Low

Form RPR
10-0 1 **Prince James**[14] [1298] 5-8-8 57 DavidSimmonson(5) 7 64
(Michael Easterby) *hld up towards rr: hdwy over 2f out: styd on wl to ld towards fin* 11/1
0-04 2 nk **Northern Bolt**[4] [1526] 7-9-7 65 (b) GeorgeChaloner 2 71
(Ian McInnes) *dwlt: in rr: reminders over 4f out: sn detached in last: hdwy towards far side 2f out: upsides last 50yds: no ex* 2/1[1]
2060 3 3/4 **Greenhead High**[4] [1526] 4-9-2 60 CDTimmons 5 63+
(David Nicholls) *led: hdd and no ex last 30yds* 6/1[3]
2-00 4 1 1/2 **Pulsatilla**[85] [370] 4-9-2 60 (b[1]) JustinNewman 10 58
(Bryan Smart) *rrd and rdr lost off side iron s: regained it and rr over 3f out: c stands' side and hdwy over 2f out: kpt on fnl f* 8/1
5000 5 nk **Forty Proof (IRE)**[4] [1528] 4-8-9 53 (v) DarylByrne 6 50
(David Evans) *in rr-div: hdwy over 2f out: kpt on fnl f* 10/1
4213 6 3/4 **Ace Of Spies (IRE)**[8] [1430] 7-9-2 63 NoelGarbutt(3) 1 57
(Conor Dore) *mid-div: outpcd over 4f out: kpt on fnl 2f: nvr a threat* 4/1[2]
40- 7 6 **Andrasta**[184] [7064] 7-8-0 51 oh1 MatthewHopkins(7) 3 24
(Alan Berry) *chsd ldrs: lost pl over 1f out* 33/1
4210 8 nk **Blueberry Fizz (IRE)**[28] [1070] 4-8-5 56 (v) BradleyBosley(7) 4 27
(John Ryan) *chsd ldrs: wknd over 1f out* 8/1
00-5 9 3/4 **Sophie's Beau (USA)**[113] [19] 5-8-2 51 oh5 (b) AliceHaynes(5) 9 20
(Michael Chapman) *w ldr: c stands' side over 2f out: wknd fnl f* 28/1

1m 20.99s (7.39) **Going Correction** +0.775s/f (Yiel) 9 Ran SP% **113.7**
Speed ratings (Par 101): **81,80,79,77,77 76,68,67,66**
toteswingers:1&2:£5.50, 1&3:£10.00, 2&3:£4.70 CSF £32.82 CT £148.67 TOTE £14.30: £3.00, £1.30, £3.00; EX 38.10.
Owner A Saha **Bred** A C M Spalding **Trained** Sheriff Hutton, N Yorks
■ Stewards' Enquiry : C D Timmons four-day ban: used whip above permitted level (May 9-12)

FOCUS
A moderate apprentice handicap in which the conditions played their part. The majority raced centre to stands' side in the straight but the principals ended up nearer the far rail. The leaders may have gone a little too hard early, as the first two home were the last pair early in the short straight. The winner was well treated compared with his AW mark.
Pulsatilla Official explanation: jockey said he lost a stirrup on leaving stalls
T/Plt: £175.20 to a £1 stake. Pool:£43,408.67 - 180.82 winning tickets T/Qpdt: £79.80 to a £1 stake. Pool:£3,820.73 - 35.42 winning tickets WG

EPSOM (L-H)
Wednesday, April 25

OFFICIAL GOING: Soft (heavy in places on derby course) changing to heavy after race 2 (2:50)
Rail dolled out unto 10yds from 1m to winning post, adding about 25yds to Derby course and distance.
Wind: Strong, across Weather: very heavy rain this morning, showers after

1602 INVESTEC SPECIALIST BANK H'CAP 5f
2:15 (2:17) (Class 3) (0-95,93) 4-Y-0+
£9,337 (£2,796; £1,398; £699; £349; £175) Stalls High

Form RPR
6200 1 **Cadeaux Pearl**[9] [1417] 4-8-11 83 (b) KierenFallon 8 92
(Scott Dixon) *sn bustled along and chsd ldrs: clr in ldng quartet ent fnl 2f: drvn to ld ins fnl f: styd on wl and forged ahd towards fin* 25/1
5110 2 1 **Taajub (IRE)**[25] [1141] 5-9-3 89 IanMongan 1 94
(Peter Crate) *broke fast and crossed over to chse ldrs but stl racing off stands' rail: clr in ldng quartet ent fnl 2f: ev ch 1f out: no ex and btn towards fin* 25/1
00-0 3 1 **Taurus Twins**[9] [1417] 6-8-10 82 (b) SilvestreDeSousa 5 84
(Richard Price) *broke fast: led and crossed to r against stands' rail: rdn over 1f out: drvn and hdd ins fnl f: no ex fnl 100yds* 14/1
053- 4 1/2 **Jamesway (IRE)**[249] [5268] 4-8-13 85 PaulHanagan 11 85+
(Richard Fahey) *taken down early: racd off the pce in midfield: hdwy over 1f out: styd on wl ins fnl f: gng on wl fin but unable to chal* 5/1[1]
001- 5 1 1/4 **Living It Large (FR)**[200] [6703] 5-9-3 89 JohnFahy 6 85
(Ed de Giles) *broke fast and crossed over to r nr stands' rail: chse ldr: clr in ldng quartet ent fnl 2f: rdn and outpcd over 1f out: wknd ent fnl f* 12/1
120- 6 1 1/4 **Bless You**[256] [5054] 4-8-11 83 DaneO'Neill 2 74
(Henry Candy) *racd off the pce in midfield: rdn 1/2-way: styd on fnl f: nvr trbld ldrs* 6/1[2]
0/5- 7 3/4 **Desert Phantom (USA)**[361] [1680] 6-9-4 90 JamieSpencer 4 78
(David Simcock) *in tch: effrt to chse ldng quartet jst over 2f out: no imp and btn ent fnl f: wknd* 8/1
64-3 8 1/2 **Perfect Pastime**[20] [1203] 4-8-8 80 MartinDwyer 10 67
(Jim Boyle) *racd off the pce in midfield: rdn 1/2-way: styd on fnl f: nvr trbld ldrs* 10/1
400- 9 2 **Fathom Five (IRE)**[193] [6865] 8-8-10 82 RyanMoore 15 61
(Gary Moore) *chsd ldrs: rdn 1/2-way: sn outpcd and btn 2f out: wknd fnl f* 7/1[3]
00-4 10 nk **Liberty Lady (IRE)**[14] [1316] 5-9-7 93 TomQueally 7 71
(Des Donovan) *racd off the pce in midfield: rdn 1/2-way: no prgress and nvr trbld ldrs* 20/1
6- 11 shd **Batchelors Star (IRE)**[199] [6733] 4-9-1 87 JamesDoyle 13 65
(Jim Boyle) *a in rr: rdn 1/2-way: styd on fnl f: nvr trbld ldrs* 12/1
1021 12 1 **Haadeeth**[20] [1204] 5-8-9 81 LukeMorris 12 55
(David Evans) *taken down early: a in rr: drvn and no prog over 2f out: n.d* 14/1

00-4 **13** *3* **Lost In Paris (IRE)**^{17} 1237 6-8-9 **81**..........................(p) TadhgO'Shea 14 44
(Tim Easterby) *a in rr: n.d* **10/1**

51-6 **14** *3/4* **Diamond Charlie (IRE)**^{60} 715 4-9-0 **86** ow1................ SebSanders 9 47
(Simon Dow) *stdd and swtchd sharply rt s: a bhd* **14/1**

57.45s (1.75) **Going Correction** +0.525s/f (Yiel) **14** Ran SP% **120.6**
Speed ratings (Par 107): **107,105,103,103,101 99,97,97,93,93 93,91,86,85**
toteswingers:1&2:£37.60, 1&3:£85.80, 2&3:£85.80 CSF £540.60 CT £8965.17 TOTE £39.40: £8.70, £9.90, £5.20; EX 849.80 TRIFECTA Not won..

Owner Paul J Dixon **Bred** Catridge Farm Stud Ltd **Trained** Babworth, Notts

■ Stewards' Enquiry : Silvestre De Sousa two-day ban: careless riding (May 9-10)

FOCUS

As usual for this C&D, the action unfolded towards the stands' rail, although a high draw wasn't essential. Those from off the pace struggled to get involved. The winner is rated around his best form.

NOTEBOOK

Cadeaux Pearl offered nothing at Windsor last time, but he had been much too free to post and he proved well suited by this proper speed track (has won at Catterick, another quick track), running as well as ever despite being 1lb wrong. He clearly handled the ground well, but is fine on a faster surface and the Dash, back over C&D on Derby day, is an obvious target. (tchd 33-1 in a place)

Taajub(IRE) ◆ was below form over 6f at Kempton on his previous start, but a high draw didn't help him that day, and he ran a fine race in defeat this time, despite again being unhelpfully drawn. He was caught a bit wider than ideal throughout, so his performance needs upgrading, and he could be a big player in the Dash.

Taurus Twins ◆ didn't shape too badly at Windsor on his reappearance, finishing ahead of Cadeaux Pearl, and he built on that effort despite being 2lb wrong. He had to do plenty of racing to grab the stands' rail, but kept on well. There should be more to come from him this year - he's long looked potentially decent. (tchd 16-1)

Jamesway(IRE) hasn't won since June 2010, but he was 3lb lower than when finishing close up in last year's Dash. Returning from a 249-day break, he would have been involved in the finish had he not been stuck behind a no-hoper when he should have been making his move. Official explanation: jockey said gelding hung right (tchd 9-2)

Living It Large(FR), resuming off 4lb higher than when winning at York last October, shaped like a horse in need of the run, fading after showing loads of speed. (tchd 14-1)

Bless You shaped encouragingly after a 256-day break as stall two meant she was caught wide throughout, and she didn't quite have the speed of some of these. (op 8-1)

Fathom Five(IRE) won this in 2009 and 2010 off marks in the low-90s, but he was well held on his debut for a new yard after 193 days off. (op 6-1)

Lost In Paris(IRE) Official explanation: jockey said gelding suffered interference in running

1603 INVESTEC GREAT METROPOLITAN H'CAP 1m 4f 10y

2:50 (2:53) (Class 3) (0-95,94) 4-Y-O+

£9,337 (£2,796; £1,398; £699; £349; £175) **Stalls** Centre

Form RPR

111- **1** **Aiken**^{277} 4316 4-9-3 **91**... WilliamBuick 2 105+
(John Gosden) *in tch: rdn and effrt 3f out: led over 1f out: sn edgd rt: clr ins fnl f: rdn out hands and heels fnl 100yds: a doing enough and holding on* **10/3**^{1}

1602 **2** *nk* **First Avenue**^{5} 1505 7-8-0 **80** oh1............................. CharlotteJenner$^{(7)}$ 1 91
(Laura Mongan) *hld up in rr: stl plenty to do and effrt wl off stands' rail over 1f out: chsd wnr and edgd rt ins fnl f: r.o wl to press wnr cl home* **14/1**

400- **3** *6* **Communicator**^{235} 5700 4-8-12 **86**................................ JimmyFortune 4 87
(Andrew Balding) *chsd ldr tl led and c to r against stands' rail over 3f out: rdn and hdd over 1f out: wknd ins fnl f* **9/2**^{2}

044- **4** *1 1/4* **Gosbeck**^{187} 6996 4-8-11 **85**.. DaneO'Neill 9 84
(Henry Candy) *in tch in last quartet: rdn and effrt to chse ldrs 2f out: no imp over 1f out: wknd ins fnl f* **15/2**

52-2 **5** *10* **Ithoughtitwasover (IRE)**^{11} 1374 4-9-6 **94**............. SilvestreDeSousa 3 77
(Mark Johnston) *chsd ldrs: rdn to chse ldr ent fnl 3f tl over 2f out: wknd over 1f out: fdd fnl f* **9/2**^{2}

24-4 **6** *7* **Romeo Montague**^{25} 1139 4-8-12 **86**................................ RyanMoore 5 58
(Ed Dunlop) *hld up in tch in last trio: hdwy over 4f out: rdn and struggling 3f out: sn wknd* **6/1**^{3}

40-0 **7** *8* **Unex Renoir**^{17} 1239 4-8-3 **80**...(p) KierenFox$^{(3)}$ 6 39
(Michael Attwater) *led: pushed along 5f out: rdn and hdd over 3f out: sn struggling: wknd wl over 2f out* **50/1**

330- **8** *nk* **Life And Soul (IRE)**^{250} 5250 5-9-2 **89**................................ NeilCallan 8 48
(Amanda Perrett) *t.k.h: hld up in tch: rdn over 3f out: wknd u.p over 2f out: wl bhd and eased ins fnl f* **9/1**

112- **9** *31* **Shesha Bear**^{213} 6376 7-8-7 **80** oh3............................(p) HayleyTurner 12
(Jonathan Portman) *hld up in last pair: rdn and lost tch 3f out: t.o and virtually p.u fr over 1f out* **11/1**

05-5 **10** *22* **Hung Parliament (FR)**^{32} 1035 4-9-4 **92**............... RichardKingscote 11
(Tom Dascombe) *chsd ldrs: hung rt over 5f out: lost pl and bhd over 3f out: t.o and virtually p.u fnl 2f* **33/1**

2m 52.66s (13.76) **Going Correction** +1.175s/f (Soft)
WFA 4 from 5yo+ 1lb **10** Ran SP% **115.4**
Speed ratings (Par 107): **101,100,96,95,89 84,79,79,58,43**
toteswingers:1&2:£11.70, 1&3:£4.60, 2&3:£13.80 CSF £51.74 CT £212.13 TOTE £3.60: £1.30, £5.10, £2.10; EX 62.70 Trifecta £672.30 Pool: £1,0256.70 - 1.13 winning units..

Owner George Strawbridge **Bred** George Strawbridge **Trained** Newmarket, Suffolk

FOCUS

This looks good form despite the desperate conditions, with the winner progressing, the runner-up well handicapped, and the third an interesting type. The winner was probably better than the bare form. They raced stands' side in the straight.

NOTEBOOK

Aiken only made his debut last June, but he won his last three starts of a four-race campaign, including on soft ground. Resuming off 11lb higher, he took a while to pick up but was always doing enough once in charge. There really should be more to come, although it remains to be seen how he'd cope with a fast surface. (op 11-4 tchd 5-2)

First Avenue was 1lb out of the handicap but still 2lb well-in following his close second over 2m on testing ground at Newbury. As usual, he travelled well and he made up significant ground in the closing stages, but it was noticeable he didn't pass the winner straight after the line, leaving the strong impression he was always held.

Communicator lost his way when last seen, but he returned off 2lb lower than when fourth in a hot running of the King George V Handicap at Royal Ascot on easy ground. Now a gelding and with a new trainer, he was well ridden to grab the stands' rail in the straight, but his finishing effort was a bit tame. There's obviously a good chance he needed this, however, and he could see his race out better next time. (op 5-1)

Gosbeck's record suggests this ground was softer than ideal, and she hadn't been seen for 187 days, so it was a promising return. (op 9-1 tchd 10-1)

Ithoughtitwasover(IRE) was seemingly unsuited by the ground and/or the track.

Life And Soul(IRE) Official explanation: jockey said gelding hung right

1604 INVESTEC DERBY TRIAL CONDITIONS 1m 2f 18y

3:20 (3:26) (Class 2) 3-Y-O

£31,125 (£9,320; £4,660; £2,330; £1,165; £585) **Stalls** Low

Form RPR

40-2 **1** **Goldoni (IRE)**^{24} 1160 3-8-13 86...................................... DavidProbert 5 99
(Andrew Balding) *led tl over 8f out: chsd ldr tl over 6f out: rdn and ev ch over 2f out: led narrowly 1f out: styd on wl and forged to ld fnl 75yds* **15/2**

10-2 **2** *1 3/4* **Mister Music**^{7} 1455 3-9-1 90... RyanMoore 6 97
(Richard Hannon) *led over 8f out: rdn and hdd over 3f out: led again wl over 2f out: battled on gamely u.p tl narrowly hdd 1f out: no ex and btn fnl 75yds* **6/1**

3-1 **3** *3 3/4* **Cameron Highland (IRE)**^{16} 1250 3-8-13 90...................... NeilCallan 4 88
(Roger Varian) *chsd ldrs: wnt 2nd over 6f out: led and racd against stands' rail over 3f out: sn rdn: hdd wl over 2f out: btn ent fnl f: wknd fnl 150yds* **9/4**^{1}

4 *2 3/4* **Thomasgainsborough (IRE)**^{14} 1327 3-9-1 90.................. JPO'Brien 3 84
(A P O'Brien, Ire) *hld up in tch in rr: hdwy on stands' rail 3f out: rdn and no imp whn edgd lft wl over 1f out: wknd ent fnl f* **11/4**^{2}

10-0 **5** *2 3/4* **Cravat**^{18} 1221 3-8-13 90... SilvestreDeSousa 2 77
(Mark Johnston) *nvr travelling wl: in tch in last pair: rdn and racd awkwardly on downhill run 4f out: edgd lft and wknd 2f out* **14/1**

415- **6** *2 3/4* **Unex Michelangelo (IRE)**^{155} 7508 3-8-13 99.............. WilliamBuick 1 71
(John Gosden) *t.k.h: hld up in tch: rdn and racing awkwardly on downhill run 4f out: wknd wl over 2f out: wl btn whn hung bdly lft over 1f out* **9/2**^{3}

2m 22.0s (12.30) **Going Correction** +1.175s/f (Soft) **6** Ran SP% **108.3**
Speed ratings (Par 104): **97,95,92,90,88 86**
toteswingers:1&2:£6.10, 1&3:£3.80, 2&3:£1.20 CSF £46.24 TOTE £8.80: £3.70, £2.50; EX 44.60.

Owner Mick and Janice Mariscotti **Bred** Marston Stud **Trained** Kingsclere, Hants

FOCUS

This is often contested by smart sorts, but so rarely has a bearing on the race for which it's supposed to serve as a trial. It was therefore good to see the prize fund had received a £20,000 boost, and the idea of granting the winner a 'wildcard' entry into the Derby was an exciting new initiative. However, allowing a gelding to run, and in this case win, defeated the object of the race. Again, they raced stands' side in the straight. The pace was muddling in the bad ground and the time was almost three seconds slower than the following City And Suburban Handicap, so the true worth of the form is unclear. Goldoni, though, has clearly improved.

NOTEBOOK

Goldoni(IRE) is quite well regarded by his trainer. He was beaten into second off 83 on his reappearance, but this was an improved performance, and clearly he appreciated the conditions. The Lingfield Derby Trial and the King Edward VII at Royal Ascot were mentioned as possible targets, and we should learn more about him next time. (op 7-1)

Mister Music, runner-up in the Feilden Stakes on his reappearance, ran another solid race, appearing to cope okay with the ground. He was conceding 2lb to the winner. (op 7-1 tchd 11-2)

Cameron Highland(IRE) won a Redcar maiden on easy ground on his reappearance, and his breeding suggested he might cope with these conditions, but perhaps the going was just too soft as he found little after appearing to travel well. (op 2-1)

Thomasgainsborough(IRE), beaten off 89 on his reappearance over 1m on Polytrack, was a bit keen early and didn't pick up for pressure. (op 5-2 tchd 9-4)

Cravat will be worth another chance under different conditions. (op 11-1)

Unex Michelangelo(IRE), returning from a five-month break, didn't seem to handle the track. (op 6-1)

1605 INVESTEC CITY AND SUBURBAN H'CAP 1m 2f 18y

3:55 (4:02) (Class 2) (0-105,100) 4-Y-O+

£24,900 (£7,456; £3,728; £1,864; £932; £468) **Stalls** Low

Form RPR

00U- **1** **Right Step**^{12} 7029 5-9-0 **90**.. JimCrowley 2 103
(Alan Jarvis) *hld up in rr: rdn and effrt over 2f out: gd hdwy over 1f out: str chal ins fnl f: led fnl 75yds: r.o wl* **14/1**

3040 **2** *1 1/2* **Sirvino**^{25} 1139 7-9-4 **97**.. HarryBentley$^{(3)}$ 9 107
(David Barron) *in tch: rdn and effrt over 2f out: chsd ldr 2f out: led ent fnl f: hdd ins fnl f: kpt on same pce* **16/1**

0-01 **3** *4 1/2* **Tres Coronas (IRE)**^{11} 1381 5-8-12 **88**........................ JamieSpencer 13 89
(David Barron) *stdd s: hld up in rr: nt clr run 3f out: rdn and hdwy towards centre over 1f out: r.o wl ins fnl f: snatched 3rd last stride: no ch w ldng pair* **8/1**

030- **4** *shd* **Ittirad (USA)**^{242} 5482 4-8-10 **86**.. NeilCallan 10 87
(Roger Varian) *mostly chsd ldr: rdn and unable qck over 2f out: styd on same pce u.p fnl 2f* **7/2**^{1}

14-3 **5** *3/4* **Ramona Chase**^{25} 1139 7-8-5 **86**..............................(t) MarkCoumbe$^{(5)}$ 7 85
(Michael Attwater) *in tch in midfield: rdn and unable qck over 3f out: hmpd and swtchd rt ent fnl 2f: no threat to ldrs but styd on wl fnl f* **14/1**

120- **6** *hd* **Halfsin (IRE)**^{235} 5700 4-9-8 **98**... AdamKirby 8 97
(Marco Botti) *led after 1f: rdn and fnd ex to go clr over 2f out: drvn and hdd ent fnl f: nt gng pce of ldng pair and btn fnl 150yds: lost 3 pls cl home* **9/1**

000- **7** *3* **Resurge (IRE)**^{172} 7297 7-9-3 **93**.............................. FergusSweeney 11 86
(Stuart Kittow) *hld up in rr: rdn and effrt whn hung lft ent fnl 2f: plugged on same pce after* **4/1**^{2}

04-0 **8** *1 1/4* **Good Boy Jackson**^{25} 1134 4-8-4 **80**...................... MickaelBarzalona 3 70
(Kevin Ryan) *in tch: rdn and unable qck 3f out: outpcd and btn 2f out: wknd wl over 1f out* **12/1**

00-3 **9** *2* **Ingleby Spirit**^{16} 1258 5-8-9 **85**....................................(v^{1}) PaulHanagan 14 71
(Richard Fahey) *in tch on outer: pushed along and nt travelling 6f out: rdn and outpcd over 3f out: n.d after* **16/1**

0-30 **10** *9* **Oceanway (USA)**^{60} 712 4-9-4 **94**........................... SilvestreDeSousa 1 62
(Mark Johnston) *in tch in midfield: rdn and effrt 3f out: wknd ent fnl 2f: wl btn over 1f out* **20/1**

321- **11** *14* **Dick Doughtywylie**^{214} 6324 4-9-0 **90**............................ WilliamBuick 4 30
(John Gosden) *led for 1f: rdn 4f out: wknd over 2f out: wl bhd and eased ins fnl f* **5/1**^{3}

56-6 **12** *1/2* **Askaud (IRE)**^{25} 1130 4-9-7 **97**..(p) IanMongan 5 36
(Scott Dixon) *chsd ldrs: rdn and struggling 3f out: sn wknd: wl bhd and eased ins fnl f* **20/1**

/005 **13** *46* **Fiery Lad (IRE)**^{62} 678 7-9-10 **100**.................................. KierenFallon 15
(Luca Cumani) *stdd s: a in last pl: niggled along and lost tch 6f out: sn t.o* **33/1**

2m 19.03s (9.33) **Going Correction** +1.175s/f (Soft) **13** Ran SP% **125.3**
Speed ratings (Par 109): **109,107,104,104,103 103,100,99,98,91 79,79,42**
toteswingers:1&2:£50.80, 1&3:£35.90, 2&3:£26.20 CSF £224.48 CT £1935.93 TOTE £18.20: £4.90, £6.60, £3.10; EX 281.90 TRIFECTA Not won..

Owner Allen B Pope & Jarvis Associates **Bred** Natton House Thoroughbreds & Mark Woodall **Trained** Twyford, Bucks

FOCUS
A good running of the City And Suburban despite the ground. This time the main action unfolded up the middle of the track. Decent form, with the winner back to something like his best.

NOTEBOOK
Right Step came into this only 1-21 on the Flat, but he'd won over hurdles recently and was 7lb lower than when second to Resurge over C&D on Oaks day last year. He took advantage in convincing fashion and looks as good as ever. (op 10-1)

Sirvino coped with conditions well enough to pull clear of the others, shaping a bit better than of late. (op 20-1)

Tres Coronas(IRE), up 4lb for winning on similar ground at Newcastle last time, just got going too late after finding a bit of trouble. (op 10-1 tchd 11-1)

Ittirad(USA), without the blinkers he had fitted when last seen in August, is now a gelding but his finishing effort wasn't as strong as had looked likely. There were a number of possible reasons, including the ground and racing more towards the inside of the track, while he might have needed the run, and in fairness this wasn't a bad performance. (op 5-1 tchd 6-1)

Ramona Chase was well held off 5lb higher than when third in this last year, but he would have been a bit closer with a clear run. (op 12-1 tchd 10-1)

Halfsin(IRE) sweated up and stayed more towards the inside than some. (op 8-1)

Resurge(IRE) wasn't at his best off 1lb lower than when second in this last year. (op 5-1)

Dick Doughtywylie Official explanation: jockey said gelding was unsuited by the heavy ground

1606 INVESTEC ASSET MANAGEMENT MAIDEN STKS — 1m 114y
4:30 (4:31) (Class 5) 3-4-Y-O — **£3,234** (£962; £481; £240) **Stalls** Low

Form — RPR

-32 **1** — **Valley Of Destiny**[16] [1257] 3-8-11 0 .... RyanMoore 1 — 81
(Richard Hannon) *mde all: rdn 3f out: styd on wl u.p and drew clr ins fnl f: rdn out* — **6/4**[1]

6-4 **2** *2½* **Cyrus Sod**[21] [1182] 3-8-11 0 .... TomMcLaughlin 5 — 76
(Ed Dunlop) *chsd ldrs: wnt 2nd 5f out tl hit rail ent fnl 3f: unable qck over 2f out: kpt on ins fnl f to go 2nd towards fin* — **14/1**

0-2 **3** *nk* **Sunpass**[16] [1250] 3-8-11 0 .... WilliamBuick 3 — 75
(John Gosden) *chsd ldrs: rdn and effrt 3f out: chsd wnr wl over 1f out: no ex jst ins fnl f: lost 2nd towards fin* — **10/3**[2]

66-2 **4** *3¾* **Benzanno (IRE)**[21] [1192] 3-8-11 73 .... DavidProbert 11 — 66
(Andrew Balding) *t.k.h: hld up in tch: rdn and effrt to chse wnr over 2f out tl wl over 1f out: edgd lft and wknd ent fnl f* — **6/1**[3]

46- **5** *½* **Brockwell**[182] [7101] 3-8-11 0 .... RichardKingscote 10 — 65
(Tom Dascombe) *s.i.s: in tch in last pair: hdwy 4f out: 5th and rdn ent fnl 2f: sn outpcd and btn: plugged on fnl f* — **8/1**

0- **6** *8* **Mr Fickle (IRE)**[181] [7126] 3-8-11 0 .... TomQueally 12 — 47
(Gary Moore) *bhd and pushed along after 2f out: rdn and struggling 4f out: n.d fnl 3f* — **66/1**

56 **7** *27* **Handy Chat (IRE)**[9] [1422] 3-8-11 0 .... MartinHarley 4
(Des Donovan) *chsd ldr tl 5f out: rdn and struggling 3f out: hung lft and wknd 2f out: t.o ins fnl f* — **50/1**

05- **8** *32* **Leitrim King (IRE)**[182] [7109] 3-8-11 0 .... ShaneKelly 8
(William Haggas) *in tch tl rdn and dropped to rr 4f out: lost tch 3f out: t.o fnl 2f* — **13/2**

1m 57.2s (11.10) **Going Correction** +1.175s/f (Soft) — 8 Ran SP% **111.9**
Speed ratings (Par 103): **97,94,94,91,90 83,59,31**
toteswingers:1&2:£5.40, 1&3:£2.30, 2&3:£8.80 CSF £24.10 TOTE £2.30: £1.10, £3.20, £1.10; EX 24.30 Trifecta £143.90 Pool: £1,469.15 - 7.55 winning units..
Owner W P Drew **Bred** J G Davis & Star Pointe Ltd **Trained** East Everleigh, Wilts

FOCUS
An ordinary maiden, and the runners were taken stands' side in the closing stages. The time was 0.55 seconds slower than the following Class 5 handicap. Not easy form to assess given the bad ground.

1607 INVESTEC INVESTMENT H'CAP — 1m 114y
5:00 (5:10) (Class 5) (0-75,75) 3-Y-O — **£3,234** (£962; £481; £240) **Stalls** Low

Form — RPR

50-5 **1** — **Jane Lachatte (IRE)**[68] [597] 3-8-8 **62** .... WilliamCarson 1 — 71
(Stuart Williams) *in tch in last trio: hdwy 4f out: rdn to ld ent fnl 3f: hung lft ent fnl f: continued edging lft but styd on wl to draw clr ins fnl f* — **14/1**

132- **2** *2¾* **My Sharona**[228] [5945] 3-9-3 **71** .... LiamKeniry 12 — 74
(Sylvester Kirk) *chsd ldr: rdn and pressing wnr over 2f out: stl ev ch whn carried lft ent fnl f: no ex and btn ins fnl f: battled on to hold 2nd* — **5/1**[2]

4230 **3** *½* **Attain**[14] [1312] 3-9-3 **71** .... JamesDoyle 3 — 73
(Julia Feilden) *chsd ldrs: rdn wl over 2f out: pressing ldrs u.p whn carried lft ent fnl f: no ex and btn fnl 150yds: kpt on same pce* — **8/1**

323- **4** *7* **Talk Of The North**[210] [6448] 3-8-13 **67** .... MichaelHills 7 — 53
(Hugo Palmer) *in tch: rdn: racing awkwardly and lost pl on downhill run over 4f out: outpcd and wl btn 3f out: rallied and hdwy into modest 4th over 1f out: no ch w ldrs* — **10/3**[1]

15 **5** *1¼* **Rockgoat (IRE)**[33] [1013] 3-9-5 **73** .... AdamKirby 9 — 56
(Marco Botti) *in tch: rdn and chsd ldrs over 3f out: 4th and wknd 2f out: sn wl btn* — **13/2**

-550 **6** *23* **King Of Wing (IRE)**[53] [787] 3-9-7 **75** .... (v) TomQueally 8
(Jim Boyle) *led tl rdn and hdd ent fnl 3f: wknd qckly over 2f out: wl bhd and eased ins fnl f* — **14/1**

543- **7** *7* **Piers Gaveston (IRE)**[225] [6019] 3-9-1 **69** .... JimmyFortune 6
(George Baker) *t.k.h and chsd ldrs early: stdd bk to rr after 2f: pushed along and nt travelling 6f out: lost tch over 3f out: t.o fnl 2f* — **7/1**

350- **8** *10* **Cape Rainbow**[187] [6994] 3-9-5 **73** .... IanMongan 4
(Mark Usher) *chsd ldrs: rdn along and lost pl over 4f out: lost tch over 3f out: t.o fnl 2f* — **11/2**[3]

1m 56.65s (10.55) **Going Correction** +1.175s/f (Soft) — 8 Ran SP% **105.4**
Speed ratings (Par 98): **100,97,97,90,89 69,63,54**
toteswingers:1&2:£9.60, 1&3:£16.00, 2&3:£7.90 CSF £68.74 CT £450.32 TOTE £14.00: £2.90, £2.00, £2.80; EX 50.80 TRIFECTA Not won..
Owner S P Tindall **Bred** Simon Tindall **Trained** Newmarket, Suffolk

FOCUS
A modest handicap and again they raced stands' side. The winner was much improved with the form taken at face value, despite the slight doubts given the state of the ground.

Jane Lachatte(IRE) Official explanation: trainer said, regarding apparent improvement in form, that the filly had run well on soft ground and was better suited by the step up in trip.

T/Jkpt: Not won. T/Plt: £5,764.30 to a £1 stake. Pool:£103,047.81 - 13.05 winning tickets T/Qpdt: £124.70 to a £1 stake. Pool:£7,474.63 - 44.35 winning tickets SP

1443 KEMPTON (A.W) (R-H)
Wednesday, April 25

OFFICIAL GOING: Standard
Wind: Fresh, half behind Weather: Heavy rain before meeting; overcast with showers

1608 WIN BIG WITH BETDAQ MULTIPLES CLASSIFIED STKS — 7f (P)
5:45 (5:45) (Class 6) 3-Y-O+ — **£1,617** (£481; £240; £120) **Stalls** Low

Form — RPR

241 **1** — **Rise To Glory (IRE)**[11] [1384] 4-9-8 55 .... RobertWinston 4 — 65
(Shaun Harris) *trckd ldrs disputing 6th: prog over 2f out: led over 1f out: pressed fnl f: styd on wl* — **9/2**[2]

2250 **2** *1* **Songbird Blues**[33] [1012] 3-8-9 52 .... DavidProbert 6 — 57
(Mark Usher) *hld up wl in rr: effrt and looking for room 3f out: prog on outer 2f out: rdn to chse wnr jst ins fnl f: styd on but a hld* — **13/2**[3]

6-10 **3** *2¾* **Ereka (IRE)**[36] [972] 4-9-8 53 .... LukeMorris 8 — 55
(John Best) *trckd ldng trio: prog to ld 2f out: hdd over 1f out: outpcd fnl f* — **8/1**

6005 **4** *1¼* **Custom House (IRE)**[28] [1070] 4-9-8 53 .... DaneO'Neill 1 — 52
(John E Long) *settled to trck ldrs in 5th: effrt on inner and cl enough 2f out: nt qckn over 1f out: one pce after* — **13/2**[3]

4210 **5** *1* **Flying Kitty**[28] [1067] 3-8-9 55 .... KieranO'Neill 5 — 44
(John Bridger) *hld up wl in rr: effrt on inner over 2f out: drvn and kpt on fr over 1f out: n.d* — **10/1**

065- **6** *½* **Lucifers Shadow (IRE)**[288] [3941] 3-8-6 55 .... SophieDoyle(3) 13 — 43
(Sylvester Kirk) *hld up wl in rr: shkn up 3f out: prog over 1f out: pushed along and kpt on fnl f* — **14/1**

5132 **7** *1* **The Bay Bandit**[14] [1309] 5-9-8 53 .... (e) JamieSpencer 2 — 45
(John Butler) *trckd ldng pair: cl enough and pushed along 2f out: nt qckn over 1f out: fdd* — **11/4**[1]

540- **8** *½* **Get The Trip**[162] [7421] 3-8-6 53 .... DominicFox(3) 3 — 39
(Anthony Carson) *hld up in midfield: effrt over 2f out: rdn and nt qckn over 1f out: fdd fnl f* — **20/1**

00-0 **9** *3¾* **Applaudere**[16] [1259] 3-8-9 46 .... FergusSweeney 7 — 28
(Jamie Osborne) *racd wd in rr: lost tch over 2f out: no ch after* — **33/1**

0-50 **10** *1¾* **Echo Of Thunder (IRE)**[55] [743] 3-8-9 48 .... KirstyMilczarek 11 — 24
(Nick Littmoden) *sn trckd ldr: led briefly jst over 2f out: wknd qckly fr over 1f out* — **40/1**

00-0 **11** *1* **The Young Master**[110] [56] 3-8-9 43 .... JohnFahy 12 — 21
(Neil Mulholland) *stdd fr wd draw and hld up last: no prog over 2f out: no ch after* — **66/1**

-000 **12** *7* **Gooseberry Bush**[28] [1074] 5-9-3 52 .... (p) LeonnaMayor(5) 10
(Gary Brown) *sn led and crossed fr wd draw: hdd jst over 2f out: wknd rapidly* — **33/1**

500- **13** *nk* **Mount St Mistress**[223] [6101] 3-8-9 54 .... KierenFallon 9
(George Baker) *racd wd in midfield and sn pushed along: wknd over 2f out* — **16/1**

1m 26.94s (0.94) **Going Correction** 0.0s/f (Stan)
WFA 3 from 4yo+ 13lb — 13 Ran SP% **118.8**
Speed ratings (Par 101): **94,92,89,88,87 86,85,84,80,78 77,69,69**
toteswingers: 1&2 £6.40, 1&3 £8.20, 2&3 £7.40 CSF £31.95 TOTE £4.20: £1.90, £2.10, £2.80; EX 32.80 Trifecta £239.70 Pool: £991.43 - 3.06 winning units..
Owner S A Harris **Bred** Bryan Ryan **Trained** Carburton, Notts

FOCUS
The pace was decent enough for this classified event and the form is straightforward for the grade.

1609 BACK OR LAY AT BETDAQ.COM FILLIES' H'CAP — 7f (P)
6:20 (6:20) (Class 5) (0-75,74) 4-Y-O+ — **£2,264** (£673; £336; £168) **Stalls** Low

Form — RPR

20-2 **1** — **Choral**[112] [33] 4-9-6 **73** .... RyanMoore 2 — 83
(Richard Hannon) *hld up in midfield: clsd on ldrs over 2f out: pushed firmly into ld over 1f out: rdn clr* — **7/2**[2]

0225 **2** *2* **Perfect Ch'I (IRE)**[11] [1378] 5-8-12 **65** .... JamesDoyle 1 — 70
(Ian Wood) *w ldr but restrained: led over 2f out and tried to kick on: hdd and nt qckn over 1f out: wl hld after* — **5/1**[3]

1012 **3** *1¼* **Qeethaara (USA)**[14] [1311] 8-9-5 **72** .... (p) LukeMorris 8 — 73
(Mark Brisbourne) *hld up in last trio: prog over 2f out: tried to press ldrs over 1f out: sn one pce* — **9/1**

313- **4** *1¼* **Ma Quillet**[305] [3390] 4-9-3 **70** .... DaneO'Neill 3 — 68
(Henry Candy) *t.k.h: hld up in last trio: effrt over 2f out: kpt on to take 4th ins fnl f: n.d* — **8/1**

220- **5** *2½* **Madame Kintyre**[196] [6801] 4-8-11 **64** ow1 .... JamesMillman 5 — 55
(Rod Millman) *t.k.h: narrow ldr to over 2f out: wknd over 1f out* — **16/1**

4054 **6** *4* **Avonrose**[34] [997] 5-9-7 **74** .... NeilCallan 7 — 54
(Derek Shaw) *t.k.h: cl up tl wknd 2f out* — **6/1**

00-0 **7** *1½* **Sonning Rose (IRE)**[24] [1156] 4-9-5 **72** .... MartinHarley 6 — 48
(Mick Channon) *hld up in last trio: rdn and no prog over 2f out: wl btn after* — **11/4**[1]

0534 **8** *8* **Cut The Cackle (IRE)**[21] [1193] 6-8-7 **60** oh1 .... (bt) WilliamCarson 4 — +
(Richard Guest) *plld hrd: hld up: v wd fr 5f out all way arnd bnd to 3f out: sn last and no ch: sddle slipped* — **16/1**

1m 25.77s (-0.23) **Going Correction** 0.0s/f (Stan) — 8 Ran SP% **112.7**
Speed ratings (Par 100): **101,98,97,95,93 88,86,77**
toteswingers: 1&2 £4.00, 1&3 £4.90, 2&3 £4.10 CSF £20.70 CT £142.50 TOTE £2.30: £1.30, £2.40, £2.20; EX 23.50 Trifecta £81.40 Pool: £1,023.48 - 9.30 winning units..
Owner Longview Stud & Bloodstock Ltd **Bred** Longview Stud & Bloodstock Ltd **Trained** East Everleigh, Wilts

FOCUS
An open-looking fillies' handicap, run at just an ordinary pace. The time wasn't bad and the winner is rated up a length.

Cut The Cackle(IRE) Official explanation: jockey said saddle slipped

1610 BETDAQ MOBILE APPS/BRITISH STALLION STUDS E B F MAIDEN FILLIES' STKS — 1m (P)
6:50 (6:52) (Class 5) 3-Y-O — **£3,557** (£1,058; £529; £264) **Stalls** Low

Form — RPR

2- **1** — **Dank**[222] [6128] 3-8-12 0 .... RyanMoore 11 — 87
(Sir Michael Stoute) *hld up in midfield tl quick prog on outer to press ldrs over 3f out: wnt 2nd 2f out: urged along to chal over 1f out: narrow ld ins fnl f: rdn out* — **5/4**[1]

\- **2** *nk* **Ihtifal** 3-8-12 0 .... (t) MickaelBarzalona 7 — 86
(Saeed Bin Suroor) *pressed ldr: led over 2f out: rdn and pressed over 1f out: narrowly hdd ins fnl f: styd on but a jst hld* — **10/1**[3]

2- **3** *4* **Disposition**[165] 7396 3-8-12 0 WilliamBuick 4 77
(John Gosden) *led at mod pce: hdd and nt qckn over 2f out: pushed along and outpcd by ldng pair fnl 2f* **11/4**[2]

3- **4** *1 ½* **La Pampita (IRE)**[211] 6432 3-8-12 0 JimCrowley 10 73
(William Knight) *dwlt: t.k.h: hld up wl in rr: 12th 3f out: pushed along and stdy prog fr 2f out: r.o to take 4th nr fin* **33/1**

5 *shd* **Khazeena** 3-8-12 0 PaulHanagan 9 73
(William Haggas) *hld up in midfield: outpcd by ldrs over 2f out: pushed along and styd on steadily fnl 2f: nt wout promise* **12/1**

6 *6* **Sun Seal** 3-8-12 0 DarryllHolland 3 59
(Hughie Morrison) *nt that wl away and rousted into midfield early: outpcd over 2f out: no ch after but kpt on fnl f* **50/1**

4 **7** *hd* **Black Mascara (IRE)**[16] 1256 3-8-12 0 PatDobbs 1 58
(Richard Hannon) *trckd ldng pair to over 2f out: sn outpcd: fdd over 1f out* **16/1**

0- **8** *2 ¾* **Mishhar (IRE)**[167] 7344 3-8-12 0 BrettDoyle 14 52
(Clive Brittain) *sn restrained to rr and racd wd: wdst of all bnd 3f out: rn green after but sme late prog* **66/1**

4 **9** *½* **Tatty**[28] 1068 3-8-12 0 JamesDoyle 6 50
(Ian Wood) *t.k.h: trckd ldrs: outpcd over 2f out: wknd over 1f out* **100/1**

10 *2 ½* **Ececheira** 3-8-12 0 NeilCallan 8 44
(Dean Ivory) *wl in tch tl outpcd over 2f out: sn wknd* **66/1**

11 *½* **Miss Socialite** 3-8-12 0 JamieSpencer 5 43
(Jeremy Gask) *dwlt: t.k.h: hld up wl in rr: outpcd over 2f out: wl btn after* **40/1**

12 *¾* **Little Miss Mayhem (IRE)** 3-8-9 0 AdamBeschizza(3) 2 41
(Philip McBride) *slowest away: a wl in rr: no ch over 2f out* **66/1**

3- **13** *7* **Sweet Ophelia**[198] 6744 3-8-12 0 FrankieDettori 13 25
(George Baker) *prom tl wknd qckly over 2f out: eased over 1f out* **10/1**[3]

14 *10* **Toppled (IRE)** 3-8-12 0 MartinDwyer 12
(Brian Meehan) *s.i.s: a in last pair: t.o* **33/1**

1m 40.69s (0.89) **Going Correction** 0.0s/f (Stan) **14 Ran SP% 118.6**
Speed ratings (Par 95): **95,94,90,89,89 83,82,80,79,77 76,75,68,58**
toteswingers: 1&2 £3.90, 1&3 £1.70, 2&3 £4.90 CSF £14.45 TOTE £2.60: £1.20, £2.80, £1.80; EX 15.80 Trifecta £49.70 Pool: £881.51 - 13.12 winning units..
Owner James Wigan **Bred** London Thoroughbred Services Ltd **Trained** Newmarket, Suffolk

FOCUS
The pace was modest, but in all probability this was a decent fillies' maiden, with two from top yards pulling clear of several promising types. The race should produce winners. Dank built on last year's debut form.

1611 BETDAQ CASINO GAMES H'CAP 1m (P)
7:25 (7:25) (Class 5) (0-75,75) 4-Y-0+ **£2,264** (£673; £336; £168) **Stalls Low**

Form RPR

4560 **1** **May's Boy**[11] 1378 4-8-2 63 (p) RachealKneller(7) 11 74
(Mark Usher) *racd wd: hld up towards rr: smooth prog on outer to ld over 1f out: shkn up and clr fnl f: readily* **8/1**

310- **2** *2 ¾* **Signora Frasi (IRE)**[139] 7671 7-8-8 62 FergusSweeney 12 67
(Tony Newcombe) *hld up in last: inclined to hang whn shuffled along fr 2f out: stdy prog after: shkn up and r.o fnl f to take 2nd last stride* **16/1**

1630 **3** *shd* **Rezwaan**[36] 967 5-9-0 68 (b) ShaneKelly 3 73
(Murty McGrath) *trckd ldrs: poised to chal over 2f out: chsd wnr over 1f out but marooned towards inner as wnr and others c wdr: nt qckn* **10/1**

100- **4** *nk* **Orpen'Arry (IRE)**[221] 6167 4-9-4 75 SeanLevey(3) 10 79
(Jimmy Fox) *hld up in last trio: effrt over 2f out: nt pce to threaten wnr but styd on fr over 1f out: nrly snatched 3rd* **16/1**

0-00 **5** *¾* **Dinner Date**[36] 967 10-8-6 63 RyanClark(3) 13 65
(Tom Keddy) *hld up in last trio: prog on outer over 2f out: rdn to chal for a pl 1f out: effrt flattened out* **20/1**

625- **6** *1* **Understory (USA)**[127] 7831 5-9-5 73 LukeMorris 7 73+
(Tim McCarthy) *disp ld tl led over 2f out: sn hung lft u.p: hdd & wknd over 1f out* **7/1**[3]

050- **7** *1* **Catchanova (IRE)**[32] 7447 5-9-3 71 NeilCallan 5 73+
(Eve Johnson Houghton) *hld up bhd ldrs: pushed along and effrt but nt gng as wl as wnr whn bdly hmpd wl over 1f out: renewed effrt fnl f: no ch and eased nr fin* **9/2**[1]

40-5 **8** *6* **Zing Wing**[14] 1311 4-9-1 69 JimmyFortune 4 53+
(Paul Cole) *trckd ldng pair: shkn up and effrt whn hmpd 2f out: nt rcvr and eased fnl f* **5/1**[2]

552- **9** *2 ¾* **Oetzi**[198] 6748 4-9-0 68 RyanMoore 9 46+
(Alan Jarvis) *racd wd: trckd ldrs: lost pl wl over 2f out: no room sn after and snatched up: eased* **9/2**[1]

00-0 **10** *1* **Hail Promenader (IRE)**[12] 1354 6-9-4 75 DominicFox(3) 1 50
(Anthony Carson) *hld up in rr: drvn and no prog over 2f out: wl btn after* **20/1**

2150 **11** *15* **Trip Switch**[76] 480 6-9-1 69 KierenFallon 2
(Paul Howling) *disp ld to over 2f out: wknd rapidly: t.o* **8/1**

1m 39.23s (-0.57) **Going Correction** 0.0s/f (Stan) **11 Ran SP% 118.1**
Speed ratings (Par 103): **102,99,99,98,98 97,96,90,87,86 71**
toteswingers: 1&2 £33.00, 1&3 £15.90, 2&3 £20.80 CSF £128.78 CT £1310.28 TOTE £12.50: £4.30, £8.40, £3.70; EX 190.20 TRIFECTA Not won..
Owner High Five Racing **Bred** John Richardson **Trained** Upper Lambourn, Berks
■ Stewards' Enquiry : Neil Callan two-day ban: careless riding (May 9-10)
Luke Morris four-day ban: careless riding (May 9-12)

FOCUS
The pace appeared decent in what was a modest handicap and those coming from off the pace were favoured. The winner's best form since his reappearance with the second to form.

1612 READ NICK LUCK IN THE RACING PLUS H'CAP 7f (P)
7:55 (7:55) (Class 4) (0-80,80) 3-Y-0 **£4,075** (£1,212; £606; £303) **Stalls Low**

Form RPR

51- **1** **Famous Poet (IRE)**[209] 6483 3-9-3 76 FrankieDettori 8 91+
(Saeed Bin Suroor) *trckd ldr: led wl over 1f out: pushed along and wl in command fnl f: eased nr fin* **10/3**[2]

31- **2** *1 ¾* **Lucky Henry**[203] 6629 3-9-6 79 AdamKirby 5 88+
(Clive Cox) *trckd ldng pair: brought to chal towards inner 2f out: chsd wnr over 1f out: styd on but no ch* **5/2**[1]

242- **3** *2 ¼* **Symphony Time (IRE)**[195] 6818 3-9-0 73 MartinDwyer 10 75
(Brian Meehan) *trckd ldrs: rdn over 2f out: hd high and nt qckn: styd on to take 3rd 1f out: no ch w ldng pair* **25/1**

122- **4** *1* **Dixie's Dream (IRE)**[199] 6724 3-9-4 77 RyanMoore 2 77+
(Richard Hannon) *hld up in last trio: pushed along over 2f out: gd prog on outer over 1f out: rdn and r.o to take 4th nr fin: did easily best of those hld up* **12/1**

60-5 **5** *½* **Red Larkspur (IRE)**[18] 1217 3-9-7 80 DaneO'Neill 3 78
(Roger Teal) *chsd ldrs: drvn and effrt 2f out: disp 3rd 1f out but outpcd: one pce after* **12/1**

31-6 **6** *2* **Holly Martins**[14] 1304 3-8-10 76 (t) NicoleNordblad(7) 1 69
(Hans Adielsson) *led at gd pce to wl over 1f out: steadily wknd* **12/1**

260- **7** *2 ¼* **Goldream**[182] 7095 3-9-5 78 KierenFallon 11 65+
(Luca Cumani) *hld up in midfield: pushed along over 2f out: no imp on ldrs over 1f out: fdd fnl f* **16/1**

51-5 **8** *nk* **Tinzapeas**[17] 1241 3-8-8 72 CharlesBishop(5) 4 58
(Mick Channon) *hld up in midfield: effrt over 2f out: no imp on ldrs over 1f out: fdd fnl f* **33/1**

051- **9** *2 ½* **Eraada**[267] 4632 3-9-0 73 PaulHanagan 6 52
(Mark Johnston) *nvr beyond midfield: pushed along on inner 1/2-way: nvr on terms* **10/1**

24-0 **10** *nk* **Tidy Affair (IRE)**[14] 1304 3-9-7 80 ShaneKelly 9 59
(Murty McGrath) *a towards rr: shkn up and no prog over 2f out* **33/1**

400- **11** *2 ¾* **Right Regal (IRE)**[187] 6983 3-9-2 75 MartinHarley 7 46
(Marco Botti) *t.k.h: trckd ldrs: rdn over 2f out: wknd over 1f out* **8/1**[3]

00-6 **12** *¾* **Jay Bee Blue**[25] 1138 3-8-10 72 SophieDoyle(3) 14 41
(J S Moore) *stdd s fr wd draw: hld up in last pair: nvr a factor* **66/1**

5P1- **13** *18* **Brimstone Hill (IRE)**[187] 6986 3-9-3 76 WilliamCarson 12
(Anthony Carson) *stdd s fr wd draw: a in last pair: t.o* **33/1**

1m 25.03s (-0.97) **Going Correction** 0.0s/f (Stan) **13 Ran SP% 115.0**
Speed ratings (Par 100): **105,103,100,99,98 96,93,93,90,90 87,86,65**
toteswingers: 1&2 £3.00, 1&3 £11.80, 2&3 £19.90 CSF £10.86 CT £173.51 TOTE £3.00: £2.20, £1.10, £7.70; EX 12.40 Trifecta £485.30 Part won. Pool: £655.84 - 0.30 winning units..
Owner Godolphin **Bred** Hadi Al Tajir **Trained** Newmarket, Suffolk

FOCUS
The two market leaders potentially looked ahead of the handicapper and duly drew clear. Few got into this from off the pace, but sound form none the less, with the time just 0.73secs above standard.

1613 READ HAYLEY AT RACINGUK.COM EVERY FRIDAY H'CAP 1m 4f (P)
8:25 (8:25) (Class 6) (0-65,62) 4-Y-0+ **£1,617** (£481; £240; £120) **Stalls Centre**

Form RPR

150- **1** **Passion Play**[173] 7264 4-9-6 62 JimCrowley 7 70
(William Knight) *mde all: wound up the pce fr over 3f out: edgd lft fr over 2f out: styd on wl to fend off rivals fnl f* **4/1**[1]

5032 **2** *1* **Royal Etiquette (IRE)**[36] 966 5-9-5 60 DaneO'Neill 3 66
(Lawney Hill) *hld up towards rr: rdn and prog over 2f out: disp 2nd fnl f: styd on but nvr able to chal seriously* **4/1**[1]

023- **3** *nk* **Reillys Daughter**[205] 6582 4-9-1 57 IanMongan 5 62
(Laura Mongan) *racd wd towards rr: pushed along over 3f out: looked to be struggling over 2f out: rallied sn after: styd on to dispute 2nd fnl f* **8/1**

-212 **4** *shd* **Trecase**[63] 651 5-8-7 55 (t) GeorgeDowning(7) 6 60
(Tony Carroll) *hld up in last: rdn and prog on outer fr 2f out: pressed for a pl fnl f: styd on* **11/2**[3]

000- **5** *hd* **Steely**[198] 6756 4-8-13 55 RyanMoore 8 60
(Gary Moore) *trckd wnr: rdn to chal and edgd lft over 2f out: nt qckn and hld over 1f out: lost pls ins fnl f* **5/1**[2]

6210 **6** *10* **Cantor**[26] 1106 4-9-2 58 (b) WilliamBuick 4 51
(Giles Bravery) *trckd ldng pair: drvn over 2f out: lost pl and wl btn over 1f out: eased* **11/2**[3]

30-3 **7** *6* **Entrance**[14] 1314 4-9-0 56 LukeMorris 1 35
(Julia Feilden) *hld up towards rr: gng wl enough 3f out: drvn and no prog 2f out: sn wknd: t.o* **8/1**

2/0 **8** *hd* **Sambulando (FR)**[15] 1282 9-9-5 60 JamesDoyle 2 39
(Frank Sheridan) *chsd ldng pair to over 2f out: wknd rapidly: t.o* **33/1**

2m 34.67s (0.17) **Going Correction** 0.0s/f (Stan)
WFA 4 from 5yo+ 1lb **8 Ran SP% 112.6**
Speed ratings (Par 101): **99,98,98,98,97 91,87,87**
toteswingers: 1&2 £1.30, 1&3 £8.80, 2&3 £7.20 CSF £19.26 CT £119.26 TOTE £4.50: £1.80, £1.50, £2.50; EX 21.90 Trifecta £323.00 Part won. Pool: £436.58 - 0.82 winning units..
Owner Mascalls Stud **Bred** Mascalls Stud **Trained** Patching, W Sussex

FOCUS
A modest middle-distance handicap. The winner made all and posted a personal best.

1614 MASCOT GRAND NATIONAL HERE 07.05.12 H'CAP 6f (P)
8:55 (8:55) (Class 5) (0-70,70) 4-Y-0+ **£2,264** (£673; £336; £168) **Stalls Low**

Form RPR

1 **1** **Mon Ami Jolie (USA)**[58] 720 4-9-3 69 SeanLevey(3) 8 82+
(Richard Hannon) *hld up in last trio: prog on inner over 2f out: sustained effrt and drvn to ld 1f out: styd on wl* **4/1**[1]

4231 **2** *1* **Twice Red**[14] 1305 4-8-10 64 RaulDaSilva(5) 4 74
(Mandy Rowland) *hld up in tch: sme prog over 2f out: swtchd sharply rt to ins rail wl over 1f out: drvn and styd on to take 2nd nr fin* **9/2**[2]

1211 **3** *¾* **Dorothy's Dancing (IRE)**[21] 1185 4-9-4 67 RyanMoore 1 75+
(Gary Moore) *t.k.h: trckd ldng pair: effrt to ld 2f out: sn rdn: hdd and no ex 1f out* **9/2**[2]

6-13 **4** *¾* **The Wee Chief (IRE)**[56] 735 6-9-6 69 KieranO'Neill 3 74
(Jimmy Fox) *hld up in tch: trckd ldrs over 2f out: hd high and nt qckn over 1f out: kpt on* **7/1**[3]

04-0 **5** *1 ½* **Homeboy (IRE)**[14] 1305 4-8-9 65 KatiaScallan(7) 6 65
(Marcus Tregoning) *trckd ldr to jst over 2f out: edgd lft after and steadily outpcd* **20/1**

0600 **6** *2* **Pick A Little**[16] 1254 4-9-4 70 RyanClark(3) 2 64
(Michael Blake) *led at gd pce to 2f out: steadily wknd* **25/1**

405- **7** *½* **Ever The Optimist (IRE)**[277] 4340 4-9-0 63 DaneO'Neill 5 55
(Tony Newcombe) *stdd s: hld up in last: pushed along and styd on fr over 1f out: nvr remotely involved* **14/1**

00-4 **8** *½* **Flashbang**[14] 1305 4-9-0 63 SilvestreDeSousa 11 54
(Paul Cole) *hld up in last trio: rdn and effrt over 2f out: no prog and btn over 1f out* **8/1**

1231 **9** *¾* **Waabel**[14] 1307 5-9-7 70 WilliamCarson 7 58
(Richard Guest) *t.k.h: trckd ldng pair to over 2f out: sn btn* **12/1**

4126 **10** *6* **Efistorm**[30] 1050 11-9-2 65 HayleyTurner 12 34
(Conor Dore) *racd v wd thrght: in trble fr 1/2-way: sn no ch* **16/1**

-302 **11** *2 ¾* **Amazon Twilight**[14] 1300 4-9-7 70 IanMongan 9 30
(Brett Johnson) *in tch to 1/2-way: struggling over 2f out: sn bhd* **9/1**

1m 11.82s (-1.28) **Going Correction** 0.0s/f (Stan) **11 Ran SP% 118.8**
Speed ratings (Par 103): **108,106,105,104,102 100,99,98,97,89 86**
toteswingers: 1&2 £5.10, 1&3 £4.00, 2&3 £5.10 CSF £21.96 CT £86.54 TOTE £5.60: £2.50, £2.20, £1.10; EX 24.50 Trifecta £82.50 Pool: £507.29 - 4.55 winning units..
Owner Andrew Tinkler **Bred** Haras La Madrugada S A **Trained** East Everleigh, Wilts

FOCUS
This looks good form for the level, with the right horses coming to the fore and the time being just 0.42secs over standard. There looks more to come from the winner.

Amazon Twilight Official explanation: jockey said filly hung left
T/Plt: £173.30 to a £1 stake. Pool: £81,398.62. 342.80 winning tickets. T/Qpdt: £54.50 to a £1 stake. Pool: £7,052.01. 95.72 winning tickets. JN

1435 BEVERLEY (R-H)

Thursday, April 26

1615 Meeting Abandoned - Waterlogged

BRIGHTON (L-H)

Thursday, April 26

OFFICIAL GOING: Good to soft (soft in places; 6.1)
All races run on inner line.
Wind: fresh, across Weather: dry and breezy

1622 GATWICKDIAMONDJOBS.COM H'CAP 5f 213y

4:35 (4:35) (Class 5) (0-70,74) 3-Y-O **£2,264** (£673; £336; £168) **Stalls** Low

Form RPR
516- **1** **Love Tale**[173] 7294 3-9-1 **64** FergusSweeney 3 71
(Mark Rimell) *in tch: effrt to chal 2f out: rdn to ld over 1f out: edgd rt but r.o strly ins fnl f* **8/1**[2]
0-21 **2** *1¾* **Mayo Lad (IRE)**[5] 1529 3-9-8 **74** 6ex SeanLevey(3) 7 75+
(Richard Hannon) *in tch: rdn and effrt whn nt clr run ent fnl f: swtchd rt jst ins fnl f: styd on to go 2nd nr fin: no threat to wnr* **5/6**[1]
64-3 **3** *nk* **Conowen**[69] 597 3-9-2 **68** HarryBentley(3) 5 68
(William Jarvis) *chsd ldr: rdn and ev ch 2f out tl unable qck and sltly hmpd jst ins fnl f: one pce fnl 100yds and lost 2nd nr fin* **10/1**[3]
5230 **4** *nk* **Diamond Marks (IRE)**[14] 1331 3-8-11 **60** JohnFahy 4 59
(John Gallagher) *stdd s: t.k.h: hld up in tch in rr: hdwy to chse ldrs jst over 1f out: rdn and styd on same pce ins fnl f* **8/1**[2]
04-2 **5** *3¾* **Christopher Chua (IRE)**[29] 1072 3-9-3 **69** AdamBeschizza(3) 8 56
(Simon Dow) *dwlt: sn rcvrd and led: rdn and hrd pressed ent fnl 2f: hdd over 1f out: btn whn sltly hmpd jst ins fnl f: wknd* **18/1**
65-1 **6** *1¾* **Ficelle (IRE)**[13] 1353 3-8-9 **65** DarrenEgan(7) 6 46
(Ronald Harris) *in tch: rdn and unable qck 2f out: outpcd and swtchd lft over 1f out: sn hung lft and no imp: wknd ins fnl f* **8/1**[2]
0332 **7** *4* **Arabian Flight**[8] 1444 3-8-11 **60** KieranO'Neill 9 29
(John Bridger) *t.k.h early: chsd ldrs: rdn and lost pl whn unbalanced ent fnl 2f: hung lft and wknd over 1f out* **10/1**[3]

1m 12.81s (2.61) **Going Correction** +0.40s/f (Good) 7 Ran SP% **111.3**
Speed ratings (Par 98): **98,95,95,94,89 87,82**
toteswingers:1&2:£2.60, 2&3:£2.30, 1&3:£8.00 CSF £14.37 CT £65.81 TOTE £13.20: £3.70, £1.50; EX 21.10 TRIFECTA Not won..
Owner Mark Rimell **Bred** Witney And Warren Enterprises Ltd **Trained** Leafield, Oxon

FOCUS
With the ground on the soft side, it was no surprise to see the runners all heading into the outer half of the course in the straight, but there was no advantage to being adjacent to the stands' rail. A number of these hadn't been overraced as juveniles, so several may have a little improvement in them, but this is modest form nonetheless. The winner is rated up 7lb.

1623 LIKE THISTLE BRIGHTON ON FACEBOOK MEDIAN AUCTION MAIDEN STKS 5f 59y

5:10 (5:10) (Class 5) 2-Y-O **£2,264** (£673; £336; £168) **Stalls** Low

Form RPR
1 **All On Red (IRE)** 2-8-12 0 StevieDonohoe 5 66
(Tobias B P Coles) *trckd ldng pair: swtchd lft and effrt ent fnl 2f: ev ch 1f out: led ins fnl f: r.o wl: readily* **12/1**
2 **2** *3* **Golac**[5] 1515 2-9-3 0 MartinHarley 1 60
(Mick Channon) *w ldr tl led after 1f: rdn 2f out: hrd pressed ent fnl f: hdd ins fnl f: wknd fnl 100yds* **8/11**[1]
3 *1¼* **Lady Phill** 2-8-9 0 KierenFox(3) 3 54+
(Bill Turner) *v.s.a: rn green and detached in last: rdn after 1f: no ch but styd on fnl f: gng on fin* **3/1**[2]
3 **4** *3½* **Reberty Lee**[16] 1284 2-9-3 0 TomQueally 4 43
(Noel Quinlan) *led for 1f: styd upsides ldrs: rdn wl over 1f out: btn ent fnl f: wknd ins fnl f* **9/2**[3]

1m 5.92s (3.62) **Going Correction** +0.40s/f (Good) 4 Ran SP% **108.8**
Speed ratings (Par 92): **87,82,80,74**
CSF £22.05 TOTE £13.10; EX 21.40 TRIFECTA Not won..
Owner Julian W H Broughton **Bred** Thomas Cahalan & Sophie Hayley **Trained** Newmarket, Suffolk

FOCUS
This wasn't competitive, but the debutante winner deserves credit for beating the well-backed favourite. The time was poor and this is modest form at best with a guessy opening level.

NOTEBOOK
All On Red(IRE), a half-sister to two winners up to 1m, was the outsider of four but she knew her job and won convincingly in the style of one who will have no problem staying further in due course. There was no fluke about this and she could win again if the ground remains soft. (op 8-1)
Golac, out quickly after showing promise when runner-up on his debut, filled the same position but yet again was comfortably beaten. It will be a weak maiden if he goes off favourite next time. (op Evens)
Lady Phill blew the start but began to show some ability in the last 200 yards. Her dam, who acted on soft, won her first three starts, and she is likely to do better with this experience behind her. (tchd 4-1)
Reberty Lee didn't run as well as he had on his debut, where there was also cut in the ground. The track may not have been ideal for him. (op 4-1 tchd 3-1)

1624 BRIGHTONCARBOOTSALE.CO.UK H'CAP 1m 1f 209y

5:40 (5:45) (Class 6) (0-60,60) 4-Y-O+ **£1,617** (£481; £240; £120) **Stalls** High

Form RPR
260- **1** **Lord Of The Storm**[169] 7333 4-8-8 **50** KierenFox(3) 3 62
(Bill Turner) *in tch in midfield: rdn and chsd ldr ent fnl 2f: ev ch and clr w rival 1f out: led fnl 100yds: styd on wl* **16/1**
5-32 **2** *1¾* **Byrd In Hand (IRE)**[15] 1310 5-9-1 **57** SeanLevey(3) 10 66
(John Bridger) *t.k.h: chsd ldrs: rdn to ld over 2f out: drvn and clr w wnr 1f out: hdd fnl 100yds: no ex* **9/2**[2]
00-3 **3** *3¼* **Tinkerbell Will**[37] 966 5-8-11 **50** RichardThomas 13 52
(John E Long) *chsd ldrs: rdn and chsd ldng pair 2f out: no ex and outpcd over 1f out: styd on same pce fnl f* **17/2**
1/5- **4** *½* **Finch Flyer (IRE)**[35] 6968 5-9-2 **55** (p) TomQueally 8 56
(Gary Moore) *hld up in tch towards rr: hdwy 2f out: drvn to chse ldrs jst over 1f out: no imp 1f out: wknd fnl 100yds* **7/1**
-003 **5** *1¼* **Heading To First**[79] 454 5-8-0 **46** oh1 (p) DarrenEgan(7) 2 45
(Paddy Butler) *hld up in tch towards rr: rdn and effrt wl over 1f out: no imp ent fnl f: plugged on same pce fnl f* **25/1**
50 **6** *shd* **Darsan (IRE)**[37] 974 4-9-0 **60** HarryPoulton(7) 11 58
(Phil McEntee) *hld up in tch: rdn and effrt against stands' rail over 2f out: swtchd lft ent fnl f: no imp* **25/1**
6-00 **7** *6* **Turbulent Priest**[75] 519 4-8-10 **49** ow3 (bt) JamieGoldstein 1 35
(Zoe Davison) *slowly away: rdn along and detached in last: styd towards inner rail st: styd on past btn horses fr over 1f out: n.d* **33/1**
040- **8** *4½* **Border Abby**[242] 5515 4-9-3 **56** ChrisCatlin 5 33
(Rae Guest) *t.k.h: hld up in tch in midfield: rdn and unable qck over 2f out: wknd over 1f out* **7/2**[1]
03-0 **9** *hd* **Notabadlad**[12] 1379 5-9-2 **58** AdamBeschizza(3) 12 35
(Simon Dow) *t.k.h: hld up in tch in rr: rdn and effrt over 2f out: no real prog: wknd wl over 1f out* **8/1**
6544 **10** *8* **Rosy Dawn**[36] 988 7-8-7 **46** oh1 MarcHalford 9 7
(Mark Hoad) *led tl rdn and hdd over 2f out: wknd 2f out: wl btn and eased ins fnl f* **18/1**
50-3 **11** *1½* **Starstuded (IRE)**[12] 1380 4-9-6 **59** DaneO'Neill 6 17
(Martyn Meade) *chsd ldrs: rdn and unable qck over 2f out: wknd 2f out: wl bhd and eased ins fnl f* **12/1**
13-6 **12** *19* **Royal Defence (IRE)**[16] 1286 6-9-7 **60** SebSanders 7
(Michael Quinn) *chsd ldr: ev ch and rdn 4f out: wknd over 2f out: wl bhd 1f out: eased fnl f: t.o* **11/2**[3]
10/0 **13** *42* **Lily Lily**[8] 1447 5-9-3 **59** (b) RyanClark(3) 15
(Natalie Lloyd-Beavis) *chsd ldrs tl rdn and lost pl over 5f out: t.o fnl 3f* **40/1**

2m 6.76s (3.16) **Going Correction** +0.40s/f (Good) **13** Ran SP% **121.8**
Speed ratings (Par 101): **103,101,99,98,97 97,92,89,88,82 81,66,32**
toteswingers:1&2:£17.20, 2&3:£9.00, 1&3:£24.70 CSF £85.45 CT £676.39 TOTE £22.80: £5.40, £1.50, £2.70; EX 115.30.
Owner Mrs M S Teversham **Bred** Mrs Monica Teversham **Trained** Sigwells, Somerset

FOCUS
This was a modest race, won by a runner who showed little last year. The form is rated around the runner-up.
Royal Defence(IRE) Official explanation: jockey said gelding hung left

1625 TAYLOR WIMPEY ROYAL ALEXANDRA QUARTER TAYLORWIMPEY.CO.UK CLASSIFIED STKS 7f 214y

6:15 (6:20) (Class 6) 3-Y-O+ **£1,617** (£481; £240; £120) **Stalls** Low

Form RPR
53-6 **1** **Ermyn Flyer**[41] 920 3-8-1 54 JemmaMarshall(5) 9 64
(Pat Phelan) *hld up in tch in midfield: rdn and effrt to ld over 1f out: r.o wl and drew clr fnl f* **9/2**[3]
6-50 **2** *4* **Cahala Dancer (IRE)**[12] 1379 4-9-1 55 MarkCoumbe(5) 14 59
(Roger Teal) *in tch on outer: rdn and hdwy 2f out: hung lft over 1f out: chsd wnr and continued to hang lft ins fnl f: no imp and outpcd fnl 100yds* **3/1**[1]
6-00 **3** *4½* **Clear Spring (IRE)**[36] 988 4-9-6 42 NickyMackay 6 49
(John Spearing) *in tch: effrt u.p 2f out: pressed ldrs and unable qck over 1f out: wknd fnl f* **16/1**
5504 **4** *1* **Waspy**[49] 832 3-8-6 43 (t) KieranO'Neill 10 42
(George Baker) *chsd ldr: rdn to ld over 2f out: hdd over 1f out: wknd ins fnl f* **16/1**
0400 **5** *¾* **Community (USA)**[30] 1052 4-9-6 55 KirstyMilczarek 12 45
(Phil McEntee) *in tch: effrt whn short of room and hmpd ent fnl 2f: lost pl: no ch after but kpt on ins fnl f* **17/2**
000- **6** *2* **Arbeejay**[239] 5625 3-7-13 20 (t) DarrenEgan(7) 2 36
(Bill Turner) *s.i.s: bhd: rdn over 2f out: styd on past btn horses fnl f: n.d* **40/1**
5330 **7** *1* **Emerald Royal**[15] 1310 4-9-6 50 (b) NeilCallan 13 41
(Eric Wheeler) *dwlt: hld up in tch: effrt 2f out: hung lft u.p over 1f out: wknd 1f out* **6/1**
051- **8** *2½* **Lightning Spirit**[182] 7119 4-9-6 53 (p) TomQueally 11 32
(Gary Moore) *chsd ldrs: rdn and unable qck whn jostling match w rival 2f out: wknd over 1f out* **10/3**[2]
0-00 **9** *nk* **Here Comes Jeanie**[64] 660 3-8-6 45 FrankieMcDonald 5 27
(Michael Madgwick) *broke wl and chsd ldrs early: grad stdd towards rr: rdn and no prog over 2f: sn wknd* **25/1**
0-00 **10** *7* **Litotes**[29] 1074 4-9-3 45 (v[1]) KierenFox(3) 8 15
(Michael Attwater) *led: styd towards centre 3f out: sn rdn and hdd: wknd 2f out: wl btn ins fnl f* **33/1**
\- **11** *9* **Mumbai Millionaire (IRE)**[217] 3-8-6 45 ow3 RyanClark(3) 4
(Brett Johnson) *racd keenly: chsd ldrs: hmpd and lost pl bnd 4f out: sn rdn and struggling: styd towards centre 3f out: sn bhd* **18/1**

1m 39.05s (3.05) **Going Correction** +0.40s/f (Good)
WFA 3 from 4yo+ 14lb 11 Ran SP% **117.3**
Speed ratings (Par 101): **100,96,91,90,89 87,86,84,83,76 67**
toteswingers:1&2:£4.20, 2&3:£9.60, 1&3:£11.60 CSF £18.00 TOTE £6.40: £2.30, £1.10, £5.10; EX 20.30 Trifecta £18.20 Pool: £719.31 - 3.59 winning units..
Owner Ermyn Lodge Stud **Bred** Ermyn Lodge Stud Limited **Trained** Epsom, Surrey

FOCUS
This was generally a low-grade race, but the winner does have minor potential at a modest level, although this wasn't a huge step forward on his best 2yo form. Most of the field came wide, as in the earlier races, but the leader into the straight stayed more towards the far side and finished well beaten.
Community(USA) Official explanation: trainer said filly finished distressed
Litotes Official explanation: jockey said filly ran too free

1626 J DAVIES BUILDING LTD SUPPORTS SUSSEX CRIMESTOPPERS H'CAP 7f 214y

6:50 (6:56) (Class 5) (0-70,70) 4-Y-O+ **£2,264** (£673; £336; £168) **Stalls** Low

Form RPR
3113 **1** **Prince Of Sorrento**[12] 1378 5-9-7 **70** StevieDonohoe 8 82
(Lee Carter) *prom: rdn to ld 2f out: hld hd awkwardly whn rdn: drew clr ins fnl f: r.o wl: eased cl home* **9/2**[1]
0026 **2** *3* **Hip Hip Hooray**[21] 1207 6-8-13 **62** FrankieMcDonald 12 67+
(Luke Dace) *stdd s: hld up in rr: effrt and nt clr run over 1f out: weaved through rivals ins fnl f: r.o wl ins fnl f: snatched 2nd last strides: no ch w wnr* **11/1**
0-23 **3** *nk* **Hereford Boy**[92] 301 8-9-7 **70** (v) NeilCallan 13 74
(Dean Ivory) *hld up in tch towards rr: sme hdwy 4f out: swtchd lft and drvn to chse wnr jst ins fnl f: no ex and outpcd fnl 100yds: lost 2nd last strides* **9/1**

0023 **4** 3/4 **Salient**[13] 1358 8-9-2 **68**........ KierenFox(3) 10 71
(Michael Attwater) *led: rdn over 2f out: hdd 2f out: styd pressing wnr tl unable qck 1f out: outpcd ins fnl f* **5/1**[2]

-002 **5** 1 1/2 **Ibiza Sunset (IRE)**[75] 531 4-9-4 **67**........ FergusSweeney 2 66+
(Brendan Powell) *stdd s: t.k.h: hld up in rr: rdn and effrt 2f out: swtchd lft ent fnl f: styd on: nvr trbld ldrs* **14/1**

0456 **6** 1/2 **Bold Ring**[15] 1311 6-8-10 **62**........ SophieDoyle(3) 7 60
(Eric Wheeler) *in tch in midfield: rdn and effrt wl over 2f out: unable qck and outpcd over 1f out: one pce after* **28/1**

-200 **7** *hd* **Northern Spy (USA)**[25] 1154 8-8-13 **62**........ SebSanders 9 60
(Simon Dow) *hld up in tch midfield: rdn and effrt to chse ldrs over 1f out: wknd ins fnl f* **10/1**

24-2 **8** 2 **Bedibyes**[34] 1009 4-8-1 **57**........ IanBurns(7) 3 50
(Richard Mitchell) *stdd s and flashing tail: hld up in rr: hdwy 2f out: rdn and chsd ldrs over 1f out: wknd fnl f* **17/2**

5630 **9** 4 1/2 **Shared Moment (IRE)**[27] 1108 6-8-0 **65**........ DarrenEgan(7) 11 48
(John Gallagher) *chsd ldrs: rdn and unable qck 2f out: wknd ent fnl f* **11/1**

400- **10** 1 **Isingy Red (FR)**[154] 7532 4-9-5 **68**........ TomQueally 1 48
(Jim Boyle) *racd keenly: chsd ldrs: rdn and unable qck over 1f out: btn 1f out: wknd* **7/1**[3]

-040 **11** 6 **Quite A Catch (IRE)**[13] 1358 4-9-4 **67**........(v) JimCrowley 5 34
(Jonathan Portman) *in tch: rdn and lost pl jst over 2f out: wl bhd fnl f* **12/1**

00-0 **12** 24 **High On The Hog (IRE)**[110] 91 4-9-7 **70**........ J-PGuillambert 6
(Paul Howling) *t.k.h: chsd ldrs tl lost pl qckly over 2f out: wl bhd and eased ins fnl f: t.o* **16/1**

1m 38.55s (2.55) **Going Correction** +0.40s/f (Good) 12 Ran SP% **117.3**
Speed ratings (Par 103): **103,100,99,98,97 96,96,94,90,89 83,59**
toteswingers:1&2:£11.10, 2&3:£17.90, 1&3:£6.80 CSF £53.44 CT £436.65 TOTE £5.80: £2.50, £3.50, £2.50; EX 67.40 Trifecta £397.20 Pool: £773.08 - 1.44 winning units..
Owner Exors of the Late John Akehurst **Bred** Mrs P Akhurst **Trained** Epsom, Surrey

FOCUS
This was typical Brighton fare, but competitive enough, and run at a good pace. The winner took his form to a new high.

1627 HILTON BRIGHTON METROPOLE SUPPORTS SUSSEX CRIMESTOPPERS H'CAP 6f 209y
7:25 (7:30) (Class 4) (0-85,82) 4-Y-O+ **£4,075** (£1,212; £606; £303) **Stalls** Low

Form RPR

6312 **1** **April Fool**[27] 1117 8-9-0 **82**........(b) DarrenEgan(7) 3 87
(Ronald Harris) *mde all: styd towards centre and racd alone fr 3f out: edgd lft u.p and kpt on wl ins fnl f* **11/4**[3]

250- **2** 3/4 **Midnight Feast**[210] 6478 4-9-2 **77**........ NeilCallan 4 80
(Eve Johnson Houghton) *hld up in 3rd: c to r towards stands' side 3f out: effrt u.p over 1f out: chsd wnr ins fnl f: kpt on* **7/2**

00-0 **3** 2 1/2 **Rigolleto (IRE)**[25] 1161 4-9-5 **80**........ MartinHarley 2 76
(Mick Channon) *chsd ldr: c to r towards stands' rail 3f out: drvn and unable qck 2f out: wknd ins fnl f* **5/2**[2]

414- **4** 3 1/4 **Flameoftheforest (IRE)**[174] 7262 5-9-6 **81**........(p) LiamKeniry 1 68
(Ed de Giles) *s.i.s: hld up in rr: c towards stands' side 3f out: rdn and effrt over 1f out: no prog: eased whn wl btn ins fnl f* **85/40**[1]

1m 25.57s (2.47) **Going Correction** +0.40s/f (Good) 4 Ran SP% **109.5**
Speed ratings (Par 105): **101,100,97,93**
CSF £11.94 TOTE £2.70; EX 8.80.
Owner S & A Mares **Bred** Miss B Swire **Trained** Earlswood, Monmouths
■ Stewards' Enquiry : Darren Egan two-day ban: used whip above permitted level (May 10-11)

FOCUS
There was a small field, but the quality and pace were fair enough. The winner raced alone and the form is hardly the most solid, but this form is taken at face value.

1628 READ RYAN MOORE EXCLUSIVELY ON BETFAIR H'CAP 6f 209y
7:55 (8:00) (Class 6) (0-60,60) 4-Y-O+ **£1,617** (£481; £240; £120) **Stalls** Low

Form RPR

2225 **1** **Katmai River (IRE)**[58] 729 5-9-6 **59**........(v) DavidProbert 3 69
(Mark Usher) *towards rr: pushed along and hdwy 4f out: styd towards inner fr 3f out: drvn and effrt to press ldrs 1f out: led ins fnl f: styd on wl* **11/4**[1]

0026 **2** 1 1/2 **Huzzah (IRE)**[15] 1305 7-9-4 **57**........ MichaelStainton 7 63
(Paul Howling) *chsd ldrs: styd on inner fr 3f out: rdn to ld 2f out: drvn and hdd ins fnl f: styd on same pce* **7/2**[2]

5300 **3** *nk* **Cristaliyev**[50] 818 4-9-1 **54**........(b) TomQueally 2 59
(Jim Boyle) *in tch in midfield: styd on inner fr 3f out: hdwy u.p over 1f out: swtchd rt 1f out: kpt on fnl f* **15/2**

264 **4** 1 1/2 **Basle**[9] 1428 5-9-6 **59**........(t) NeilCallan 13 60
(Gay Kelleway) *chsd ldrs: styd on inner fr 3f out: rdn and ev ch 2f out tl ins fnl f: no ex fnl 100yds: wknd cl home* **5/1**[3]

0-00 **5** 2 1/2 **Mucky Molly**[6] 1497 4-8-13 **52**........ KirstyMilczarek 6 46
(Olivia Maylam) *in tch in midfield: c towards centre 3f out: styng on whn hung lft over 1f out: kpt on ins fnl f* **28/1**

-000 **6** 1 1/4 **Inquisitress**[50] 822 8-8-8 **47**........ KieranO'Neill 4 38
(John Bridger) *s.i.s: hld up in tch in rr: c towards centre 3f out: effrt and stmbld 2f out: hdwy over 1f out: styd on same pce fnl f* **16/1**

5-60 **7** 1 1/2 **Danceyourselfdizzy (IRE)**[15] 1310 4-8-7 **46** oh1........(p) ChrisCatlin 11 33
(Phil McEntee) *towards rr: c centre 3f out: sme hdwy u.p and edgd lft over 1f out: kpt on but no threat to ldrs* **8/1**

0444 **8** 1 **Toms River Tess (IRE)**[22] 1183 4-8-10 **49** oh1 ow3. JamieGoldstein 12 33
(Zoe Davison) *in tch in midfield: c towards stands' rail 3f out: rdn and effrt 2f out: wknd over 1f out* **33/1**

0-00 **9** *hd* **Cuthbert (IRE)**[31] 1050 5-9-4 **60**........ KierenFox(3) 10 44
(Michael Attwater) *slowly away: bhd: styd on inner fr 3f out: sme hdwy u.p over 1f out: no prog ins fnl f: wknd fnl 100yds* **20/1**

0040 **10** 8 **Microlight**[40] 939 4-8-10 **49**........(b) RichardThomas 9
(John E Long) *chsd ldrs: c centre 3f out: sn rdn: wknd wl over 1f out: wl btn and eased ins fnl f* **20/1**

2026 **11** 6 **Little Perisher**[40] 938 5-8-11 **50** ow1........(p) J-PGuillambert 1
(Paul Howling) *led: c to r nr stands' rail 3f out: hdd 2f out: sn wknd: wl btn and eased fnl f* **16/1**

05 **12** 3 **Mi Regalo**[36] 986 4-8-6 **48** oh1 ow2........(b) RyanClark(3) 8
(Phil McEntee) *chsd ldr: c towards centre 3f out: sn struggling: wknd ent fnl 2f: wl bhd and eased ins fnl f* **25/1**

1m 26.32s (3.22) **Going Correction** +0.40s/f (Good) 12 Ran SP% **120.0**
Speed ratings (Par 101): **97,95,94,93,90 88,87,86,85,76 69,66**
toteswingers:1&2:£2.40, 2&3:£6.70, 1&3:£4.80 CSF £11.20 CT £66.07 TOTE £3.60: £1.50, £1.80, £2.00; EX 12.40 Trifecta £24.10 Pool: £919.78 - 28.22 winning units..
Owner M D I Usher **Bred** Mrs S M Roy **Trained** Upper Lambourn, Berks
■ Stewards' Enquiry : Michael Stainton two-day ban: used whip above permitted level (May 10-11)
Kieren Fox two-day ban: used whip above permitted level (May 10-11)

FOCUS
There were some modest performers on show here, but they went a good gallop and contributed to a competitive race in the last 2f. The finish was fought out by runners who stayed on the far side, with those who came wide being well beaten. The winner is rated to last year's turf best.
Inquisitress Official explanation: jockey said mare stumbled approaching 2f out
T/Plt: £2,454.20 to a £1 stake. Pool of £67,744.83 - 20.15 winning tickets. T/Qpdt: £28.90 to a £1 stake. Pool of £8,580.37 - 219.10 winning tickets. SP

1585 WOLVERHAMPTON (A.W) (L-H)
Thursday, April 26

OFFICIAL GOING: Standard
Wind: Fresh behind Weather: Overcast

1629 GRADUS LAFITE MAIDEN AUCTION STKS 5f 20y(P)
1:50 (1:50) (Class 5) 2-Y-O **£2,264** (£673; £336; £168) **Stalls** Low

Form RPR

1 **Madam Mojito (USA)** 2-8-11 0........ MichaelO'Connell 6 69+
(John Quinn) *prom: hung rt and pushed along 1/2-way: rdn to ld wl ins fnl f* **5/2**[2]

2 *nk* **Annaley My Darling (IRE)** 2-8-11 0........ TonyCulhane 3 68+
(Jo Hughes) *led: shkn up over 1f out: rdn and hdd wl ins fnl f* **15/8**[1]

234 **3** 2 1/4 **Suivez L'Argent**[14] 1330 2-8-4 0........ LukeMorris 2 53
(Joseph Tuite) *chsd ldr: rdn over 1f out: styd on same pce ins fnl f* **8/1**

5 **4** 1/2 **Until It Sleeps**[12] 1388 2-8-4 0........ TadhgO'Shea 4 51
(Alan McCabe) *hld up in tch: rdn over 1f out: styd on same pce ins fnl f* **10/3**[3]

65 **5** 2 **Sally Bruce**[16] 1284 2-7-13 0 ow2........ JenniferFerguson(7) 7 46
(Olivia Maylam) *s.i.s: hld up: rdn over 1f out: nvr trbld ldrs* **33/1**

4 **6** 3/4 **Black Eider**[17] 1253 2-8-4 0........ WilliamCarson 5 41
(John Spearing) *chsd ldrs: rdn over 1f out: no ex ins fnl f* **12/1**

1m 4.59s (2.29) **Going Correction** +0.10s/f (Slow) 6 Ran SP% **108.2**
Speed ratings (Par 92): **85,84,80,80,76 75**
toteswingers:1&2:£1.90, 2&3:£3.00, 1&3:£2.50 CSF £7.00 TOTE £2.80: £1.40, £1.30; EX 8.30.
Owner Ross Harmon **Bred** John Tl Jones III & W S Farish **Trained** Settrington, N Yorks

FOCUS
Four of these had previous experience, but the finish was fought out by the two newcomers.

NOTEBOOK
Madam Mojito(USA), a $25,000 filly out of a half-sister to eight winners, including the Lowther/Prince Margaret winner Enthused, didn't look like taking this for a long way (slapped down the shoulder at halfway), but she took off once in line for home and finished strongly to mug the favourite near the line. She is in the Weatherbys Super Sprint and her stable is now 2-2 with its juveniles this season. (tchd 9-4)
Annaley My Darling(IRE), a 15,500euros filly out of a winning sprinter, was the subject of sustained market support throughout the day and certainly knew her job, breaking well and looking likely to make all, but she was unfortunate to be mown down by her fellow debutante. She can win an early season maiden, though that won't be much comfort to those who lumped on her here. (op 9-4 tchd 5-2)
Suivez L'Argent had already shown some ability in plating company on turf, but she was firmly put in her place by a couple of unexposed rivals here and has little in the way of scope. (op 7-1)
Until It Sleeps showed ability in a C&D maiden on her debut 12 days earlier and travelled well behind the leaders for a long way here, but didn't find a lot off the bridle. (op 7-2 tchd 3-1)

1630 FOLLOW US ON TWITTER @WOLVESRACES (S) STKS 5f 216y(P)
2:20 (2:20) (Class 6) 3-Y-O+ **£1,704** (£503; £251) **Stalls** Low

Form RPR

6000 **1** **Red Cape (FR)**[7] 1476 9-9-5 80........(b) JamesSullivan 2 81
(Ruth Carr) *mde all: set stdy pce tl qcknd 2f out: shkn up and c clr fnl f: comf* **11/8**[1]

2550 **2** 4 1/2 **Whipphound**[7] 1481 4-9-5 64........ ShaneKelly 6 67
(Mark Brisbourne) *chsd wnr: rdn over 1f out: styd on same pce fnl f* **7/2**[3]

2115 **3** *nk* **Steelcut**[15] 1300 8-9-6 69........(p) MatthewCosham(5) 3 72
(David Evans) *chsd ldrs: rdn over 1f out: styd on same pce* **5/2**[2]

6052 **4** 3 1/4 **Chjimes (IRE)**[15] 1307 8-9-6 63........(b) DavidKenny(5) 1 61
(Conor Dore) *hld up in tch: rdn over 2f out: nvr trbld ldrs* **16/1**

100 **5** 4 **Sabys Gem (IRE)**[6] 1497 4-9-11 51........(b) LukeMorris 7 48
(Michael Wigham) *s.s: a in last pl* **11/1**

1m 15.26s (0.26) **Going Correction** +0.10s/f (Slow) 5 Ran SP% **107.1**
Speed ratings (Par 101): **102,96,95,91,85**
CSF £6.08 TOTE £1.70: £1.30, £2.00; EX 6.10.There was no bid for the winner.
Owner Middleham Park Racing LVI **Bred** Gilles And Mrs Forien **Trained** Huby, N Yorks

FOCUS
As straightforward a seller as you are ever likely to get with the five runners never changing their positions throughout the race and they finished just as adjusted official ratings suggested they should.

1631 DOWNLOAD OUR IPHONE APP H'CAP 1m 5f 194y(P)
2:50 (2:50) (Class 6) (0-60,60) 4-Y-O+ **£1,704** (£503; £251) **Stalls** Low

Form RPR

U **1** **Liberty Love (IRE)**[56] 741 7-8-7 **46** oh1........(bt) WilliamCarson 8 57+
(Shaun Harley, Ire) *hld up: hdwy over 2f out: rdn to ld ins fnl f: styd on* **5/1**[2]

0-53 **2** 2 1/4 **Needwood Park**[28] 1092 4-8-11 **52**........(p) MartinDwyer 5 60
(Ray Craggs) *led: rdn over 1f out: hdd and unable qck ins fnl f* **6/1**[3]

1130 **3** 1 **Celtic Charlie (FR)**[22] 1184 7-8-13 **52**........ IanMongan 2 59
(Pat Phelan) *s.i.s: sn prom: rdn over 1f out: styd on same pce ins fnl f* **7/1**

0662 **4** 2 1/4 **Delagoa Bay (IRE)**[22] 1189 4-8-6 **47**........ LukeMorris 1 50
(Sylvester Kirk) *hld up: hdwy u.p over 1f out: nt trble ldrs* **15/2**

00-0 **5** 1 1/4 **Media Stars**[17] 1251 7-8-12 **58**........ MatthewHopkins(7) 3 60
(Robert Johnson) *hld up: rdn over 1f out: r.o ins fnl f: nvr nrr* **100/1**

1504 **6** 1 1/2 **Black Iceman**[5] 1534 4-8-13 **57**........ SimonPearce(3) 6 57
(Lydia Pearce) *prom: rdn over 2f out: wknd ins fnl f* **8/1**

0212 **7** 3 **Asterales**[38] 961 5-9-0 **53**........ JamieMackay 7 48
(Willie Musson) *hld up: rdn over 2f out: wknd over 1f out* **7/1**

0-05 **8** *nse* **Dubara Reef (IRE)**[16] 1272 5-8-7 **46** oh1........(p) JamesSullivan 4 41
(Paul Green) *chsd ldrs: rdn over 3f out: wknd over 2f out* **20/1**

152- **9** 12 **Tigerino (IRE)**[181] 7145 4-8-11 **52**........ KierenFallon 9 31
(Chris Fairhurst) *hld up: racd keenly: hdwy 10f out: rdn whn hmpd 2f out: sn wknd* **9/2**[1]

0151 **10** 10 **Carnac (IRE)**[9] 1433 6-9-7 **60**........(p) ShaneKelly 11 25
(Alan McCabe) *chsd ldr after 2f: pushed along over 6f out: wknd over 3f out: t.o* **6/1**[3]

3m 5.4s (-0.60) **Going Correction** +0.10s/f (Slow)
WFA 4 from 5yo+ 2lb 10 Ran SP% **117.0**
Speed ratings (Par 101): **105,103,103,101,101 100,98,98,91,85**

CSF £35.27 CT £211.79 TOTE £6.30: £1.90, £2.60, £3.70; EX 38.20 Trifecta £509.80 Part won. Pool: £689.03 - 0.10 winning units..
Owner Cut Backs Partnership **Bred** C M R Farms **Trained** Letterkenny, Co Donegal
FOCUS
A moderate staying handicap and they didn't go much of a pace.

1632 PUNCHESTOWN FESTIVAL LIVE ON ATR VIRGIN 534 CLAIMING STKS 1m 4f 50y(P)
3:20 (3:20) (Class 6) 4-Y-0+ **£1,704** (£503; £251) **Stalls** Low

Form RPR
2312 **1** **Country Road (IRE)**[50] 824 6-8-8 **78**.......(p) LukeMorris 5 72
(Michael Appleby) *led over 10f out: hdd 8f out: chsd ldr tl led again over 3f out: rdn and hung lft fr over 1f out: all out* **5/4**[1]
2111 **2** *nk* **Overrule (USA)**[23] 1174 8-9-1 **76**.......(p) KierenFallon 1 79
(Jason Ward) *led: hdd over 10f out: chsd ldrs: pushed along 3f out: rdn over 1f out: ev ch ins fnl f: styd on* **15/2**[3]
3233 **3** *2 ¾* **Ahlawy (IRE)**[5] 1530 9-8-10 **68**.......(t) JamesDoyle 3 70
(Frank Sheridan) *hld up: rdn over 2f out: r.o ins fnl f: nt trble ldrs* **12/1**
-121 **4** *¾* **Stand Guard**[14] 1339 8-9-1 **78**....... ShaneKelly 4 73
(John Butler) *prom: hung rt over 4f out: sn lost pl: hdwy u.p over 1f out: nt rch ldrs* **15/8**[2]
50-0 **5** *8* **Sir Boss (IRE)**[102] 187 7-9-1 **80**....... MatthewCosham(5) 2 69
(Michael Mullineaux) *hld up: hdwy 4f out: rdn and wknd over 1f out* **15/2**[3]
6 *57* **Beat The Ref**[52] 4-8-9 **0**....... WilliamCarson 6
(Ronald Harris) *s.s: racd keenly: hdwy to ld 8f out: hung rt 7f out: hdd & wknd over 3f out: t.o* **66/1**
2m 40.84s (-0.26) **Going Correction** +0.10s/f (Slow)
WFA 4 from 6yo+ 1lb **6** Ran SP% **111.9**
Speed ratings (Par 101): **104,103,101,101,96 58**
toteswingers:1&2:£2.10, 2&3:£3.70, 1&3:£3.00 CSF £11.38 TOTE £1.70: £1.10, £3.00; EX 10.10.Country Road was claimed by A J Liddordale for £3000.
Owner S Hussain & P O'Neill **Bred** Brittas House Stud & Lynch Bages & Samac **Trained** Danethorpe, Notts
FOCUS
Just the six runners, but they had 18 previous course wins between them.
Stand Guard Official explanation: jockey said gelding hung right-handed in back straight
Beat The Ref Official explanation: jockey said gelding ran too freely

1633 BEAUFLOR MASSIF' H'CAP 1m 141y(P)
3:55 (3:56) (Class 4) (0-85,83) 4-Y-0+ **£4,075** (£1,212; £606; £303) **Stalls** Low

Form RPR
1214 **1** **Patriotic (IRE)**[17] 1262 4-8-12 **79**....... RaulDaSilva(5) 5 87
(Chris Dwyer) *trckd ldrs: racd keenly: rdn to ld 1f out: edgd lft: r.o* **9/4**[1]
66-2 **2** *1 ¼* **Angelic Upstart (IRE)**[14] 1342 4-8-13 **75**....... JimmyFortune 1 80
(Andrew Balding) *led: shkn up and hdd 1f out: styd on same pce* **11/4**[3]
66-1 **3** *½* **Aldedash (USA)**[12] 1391 4-8-12 **74**....... KierenFallon 4 78
(James Fanshawe) *chsd ldrs: rdn over 1f out: styd on* **5/2**[2]
2604 **4** *shd* **Mullins Way (USA)**[17] 1249 4-9-7 **83**.......(v[1]) TonyCulhane 6 87
(Jo Hughes) *hld up: rdn and r.o ins fnl f: nt rch ldrs* **11/2**
-534 **5** *3 ½* **Jake The Snake (IRE)**[9] 1430 11-9-4 **80**....... WilliamCarson 2 76
(Richard Guest) *hld up: rdn over 1f out: nt trble ldrs* **33/1**
000- **6** *6* **Breakheart (IRE)**[188] 6989 5-9-0 **76**....... MichaelStainton 3 58
(Paul Howling) *chsd ldr tl rdn over 1f out: wknd ins fnl f* **16/1**
1m 50.43s (-0.07) **Going Correction** +0.10s/f (Slow) **6** Ran SP% **110.2**
Speed ratings (Par 105): **104,102,102,102,99 93**
toteswingers:1&2:£1.60, 2&3:£1.50, 1&3:£1.80 CSF £8.43 TOTE £2.90: £1.30, £2.90; EX 9.50.
Owner M M Foulger **Bred** Darley **Trained** Six Mile Bottom, Cambs
FOCUS
A decent handicap, though they didn't appear to go that quick.

1634 ENJOY THE PUNTERS PACKAGE GROUP OFFER H'CAP (DIV I) 1m 141y(P)
4:30 (4:30) (Class 6) (0-60,60) 4-Y-0+ **£1,704** (£503; £251) **Stalls** Low

Form RPR
05-2 **1** **Goldstorm**[28] 1096 4-8-9 **48**....... RussKennemore 5 57+
(Brian Baugh) *hld up: nt clr run over 2f out: hdwy over 1f out: rdn to ld ins fnl f: r.o* **13/2**[2]
223 **2** *1 ¾* **Resplendent Alpha**[3] 1562 8-9-1 **59**.......(p) LeonnaMayor(5) 10 64
(Alastair Lidderdale) *s.i.s: hld up and bhd: hdwy and hung lft fr over 1f out: r.o* **7/1**[3]
0400 **3** *3 ¾* **Gambatte**[28] 1088 5-8-4 **46** oh1....... RyanPowell(3) 3 42
(Tony Carroll) *hld up: hdwy over 2f out: rdn over 1f out: styd on same pce fnl f* **40/1**
4556 **4** *nse* **Aggbag**[13] 1360 8-8-1 **47** oh1 ow1.......(p) RichardOliver(7) 7 43
(Michael Appleby) *chsd ldrs: rdn over 2f out: styd on same pce fnl f* **33/1**
0-00 **5** *hd* **Sky Diamond (IRE)**[76] 490 4-9-3 **56**.......(b) FrederikTylicki 1 52
(John Mackie) *led: rdn over 1f out: hdd and no ex ins fnl f* **4/1**[1]
2302 **6** *nk* **Cairanne**[10] 1423 4-8-2 **46** oh1....... RaulDaSilva(5) 6 41
(Tom Keddy) *s.i.s: hld up and bhd: nt clr run over 2f out: r.o ins fnl f: nt rch ldrs* **13/2**[2]
1050 **7** *1* **Stamp Duty (IRE)**[5] 1528 4-8-11 **57**....... JacobButterfield(7) 8 50
(Suzzanne France) *hld up: rdn over 2f out: styd on fr over 1f out: nvr trbld ldrs* **16/1**
0336 **8** *nk* **Karate (IRE)**[8] 1447 4-8-11 **57**.......(t) NicoleNordblad(7) 11 49
(Hans Adielsson) *chsd ldr: rdn over 2f out: hung lft over 1f out: wknd ins fnl f* **15/2**
0-05 **9** *2 ¼* **Bertie Blu Boy**[23] 1179 4-8-11 **50**....... JamesSullivan 12 37
(Paul Green) *chsd ldrs: rdn over 2f out: wknd over 1f out* **16/1**
0364 **10** *hd* **The Which Doctor**[28] 1088 7-9-3 **56**.......(e) WilliamCarson 2 48
(Richard Guest) *prom: rdn over 2f out: hmpd and eased over 1f out* **15/2**
1430 **11** *1 ¼* **Cwmni**[10] 1425 6-8-13 **52**....... LukeMorris 4 36
(Bryn Palling) *prom: pushed along 1/2-way: sn lost pl: looked hld whn hmpd 1f out* **12/1**
0060 **12** *23* **Justcallmehandsome**[22] 1191 10-9-0 **60**.......(v) JoshBaudains(7) 9
(Dominic Ffrench Davis) *hld up: rdn and wknd over 2f out: t.o* **14/1**
1m 50.92s (0.42) **Going Correction** +0.10s/f (Slow) **12** Ran SP% **114.2**
Speed ratings (Par 101): **102,100,97,97,96 96,95,95,93,93 92,71**
toteswingers:1&2:£5.20, 2&3:£34.60, 1&3:£55.50 CSF £49.52 CT £1692.00 TOTE £9.30: £3.10, £2.50, £15.60; EX 46.30 TRIFECTA Not won..
Owner Magnate Racing **Bred** Andrew Bailey **Trained** Audley, Staffs
■ Stewards' Enquiry : Richard Oliver one-day ban: carless riding (May 10)
William Carson caution: failed to take all reasonable and permissable measures to obtain best possible placing.
FOCUS
A moderate handicap.
Resplendent Alpha Official explanation: jockey said gelding hung left in home straight
Gambatte Official explanation: jockey said mare was denied a clear run

1635 ENJOY THE PUNTERS PACKAGE GROUP OFFER H'CAP (DIV II) 1m 141y(P)
5:00 (5:00) (Class 6) (0-60,60) 4-Y-0+ **£1,704** (£503; £251) **Stalls** Low

Form RPR
5355 **1** **Land Hawk (IRE)**[31] 1047 6-9-0 **56**....... SimonPearce(3) 7 65
(Lydia Pearce) *hld up: hdwy over 2f out: rdn to ld wl ins fnl f* **6/1**[2]
0-11 **2** *nk* **Russian Storm**[15] 1309 4-9-4 **57**....... IanMongan 3 65
(Pat Phelan) *trckd ldrs: led over 1f out: rdn and hdd wl ins fnl f* **13/8**[1]
4420 **3** *1 ¾* **Bygones For Coins (IRE)**[18] 1242 4-8-4 **50**....... MatthewHopkins(7) 4 54
(Robert Johnson) *mid-div: hdwy over 2f out: rdn over 1f out: styng on whn rdr dropped whip ins fnl f* **20/1**
3005 **4** *1* **Harvest Mist (IRE)**[10] 1423 4-8-7 **46**....... TadhgO'Shea 1 48
(Shaun Lycett) *hld up: edgd lft and r.o ins fnl f: nt rch ldrs* **14/1**
6-50 **5** *¾* **Downtown Boy (IRE)**[23] 1179 4-8-9 **48**....... MartinDwyer 9 48
(Ray Craggs) *chsd ldr: rdn over 2f out: ev ch over 1f out: styd on same pce ins fnl f* **20/1**
54-6 **6** *nk* **Flying Phoenix**[22] 1189 4-9-3 **56**....... KellyHarrison 5 56
(Dai Burchell) *mid-div: hdwy over 5f out: rdn over 2f out: styd on same pce ins fnl f* **8/1**
0-00 **7** *¾* **Rasteau (IRE)**[10] 1425 4-8-2 **46** oh1....... RaulDaSilva(5) 11 44
(Tom Keddy) *s.i.s: hld up: styd on ins fnl f: nvr nrr* **22/1**
44-0 **8** *nse* **Wishformore (IRE)**[92] 299 5-9-1 **57**.......(p) RyanPowell(3) 6 55
(J S Moore) *prom: rdn over 2f out: no ex ins fnl f* **10/1**
4301 **9** *1* **Fault**[15] 1310 6-9-0 **53**....... BrettDoyle 10 48
(Alastair Lidderdale) *led: edgd rt wl over 1f out: sn rdn and hdd: no ex fnl f* **10/1**
-340 **10** *9* **Forward Feline (IRE)**[22] 1191 6-9-7 **60**....... LukeMorris 2 35
(Bryn Palling) *hld up: rdn over 2f out: wknd sn after* **15/2**[3]
0/00 **11** *6* **Lady Brickhouse**[23] 1178 5-8-7 **46** oh1....... WilliamCarson 8
(Michael Squance) *chsd ldrs: rdn over 2f out: wknd over 1f out* **50/1**
1m 50.65s (0.15) **Going Correction** +0.10s/f (Slow) **11** Ran SP% **115.9**
Speed ratings (Par 101): **103,102,101,100,99 99,98,98,97,89 84**
toteswingers:1&2:£3.60, 2&3:£13.00, 1&3:£23.10 CSF £15.02 CT £185.37 TOTE £6.50: £2.30, £1.20, £6.40; EX 21.20 Trifecta £509.30 Part won. Pool: £688.28 - 0.92 winning units..
Owner S & M Supplies (Aylsham) Ltd **Bred** Sean O'Loughlin **Trained** Newmarket, Suffolk
FOCUS
The winning time was 0.27 seconds faster than the first division.

1636 ATTHERACES.COM EXCLUSIVE BARRY GERAGHTY BLOG APPRENTICE H'CAP 1m 141y(P)
5:35 (7:11) (Class 5) (0-75,75) 4-Y-0+ **£2,264** (£673; £336; £168) **Stalls** Low

Form RPR
0044 **1** **Goal (IRE)**[59] 722 4-8-8 **65**.......(t) DannyBrock(3) 2 72
(Richard Guest) *chsd ldrs: led over 7f out: rdn and hdd over 1f out: n.m.r sn after: rallied to ld post* **12/1**
10-2 **2** *nk* **Jack's Revenge (IRE)**[41] 922 4-9-3 **71**.......(vt) DavidKenny 8 77
(George Baker) *trckd ldrs: led over 1f out: sn rdn and hung lft: hdd post* **9/2**[3]
-234 **3** *2 ¼* **Hierarch (IRE)**[55] 760 5-8-4 **63**....... AliceHaynes(5) 3 64+
(David Simcock) *hld up in tch: nt clr run over 2f out: swtchd lft and no room over 1f out: swtchd rt and r.o ins fnl f: wnt 3rd post: nvr able to chal* **4/1**[2]
-350 **4** *hd* **Elijah Pepper (USA)**[17] 1249 7-9-7 **75**....... LMcNiff 1 75
(David Barron) *chsd ldrs: rdn over 3f out: styd on same pce ins fnl f: lost 3rd nr fin* **3/1**[1]
550- **5** *nk* **Only You Maggie (IRE)**[183] 7112 5-8-8 **62**....... MatthewLawson 7 62
(Gary Harrison) *hld up: pushed along over 3f out: hdwy u.p over 2f out: styd on* **25/1**
1425 **6** *½* **Prohibition (IRE)**[5] 1533 6-8-7 **61**.......(p) AmyScott 6 60+
(Alastair Lidderdale) *hld up: r.o ins fnl f: nvr nrr* **9/1**
5201 **7** *¾* **Just Five (IRE)**[22] 1191 6-8-13 **67**.......(v) RaulDaSilva 5 64
(John Weymes) *led 1f: chsd ldr tl rdn over 2f out: no ex fnl f* **11/2**
-325 **8** *½* **Beetuna (IRE)**[57] 736 7-8-8 **62**....... JamesRogers 9 58
(Daniel Mark Loughnane) *hld up: rdn over 1f out: n.d* **16/1**
-605 **9** *1 ½* **Scribe (IRE)**[28] 1094 4-8-7 **61**....... MatthewCosham 4 53
(David Evans) *hld up: a in rr* **7/1**
1m 53.3s (2.80) **Going Correction** +0.10s/f (Slow) **9** Ran SP% **118.5**
Speed ratings (Par 103): **91,90,88,88,88 87,87,86,85**
toteswingers:1&2:£9.30, 2&3:£5.00, 1&3:£11.10 CSF £66.97 CT £262.44 TOTE £18.30: £5.50, £2.10, £1.10; EX 68.30 Trifecta £231.10 Pool: £971.32 - 3.11 winning units..
Owner Willie McKay **Bred** A M F Persse **Trained** Stainforth, S Yorks
FOCUS
An ordinary apprentice handicap and they went no pace early, which didn't help a few. The winning time was by some way the slowest of the four races over the trip on the card.
T/Plt: £98.80 to a £1 stake. Pool of £71,030.99 - 524.48 winning tickets. T/Qpdt: £32.60 to a £1 stake. Pool of £5,365.85 - 121.76 winning tickets. CR

1154 DONCASTER (L-H)
Friday, April 27
OFFICIAL GOING: Heavy (soft in places; 5.0)
Wind: moderate behind Weather: Overcast and showers

1637 ZESTBARANDGRILL.COM MAIDEN FILLIES' STKS 6f
2:10 (2:10) (Class 5) 3-Y-0+ **£2,264** (£673; £336; £168) **Stalls** High

Form RPR
6 **1** **Pretty Primo (IRE)**[14] 1357 3-8-12 **0**....... KieranO'Neill 10 79+
(Richard Hannon) *mde most: racd nr stands' rail for 2f: grad swtchd lft to centre: jnd 2f out and sn rdn along: kpt on wl ins fnl f* **7/2**[2]
22- **2** *1 ½* **Shaleek**[200] 6758 3-8-12 **0**....... FrankieDettori 2 74
(Roger Varian) *prom: effrt to chal 2f out: rdn over 1f out and ev ch tl drvn and one pce wl ins fnl f* **11/10**[1]
3 *hd* **Catwalk (IRE)** 3-8-12 **0**....... KierenFallon 5 73+
(James Fanshawe) *in tch: pushed along and green over 2f out: hdwy over 1f out: styd on wl fnl f: nrst fin* **5/1**[3]
0-2 **4** *7* **Silver Lace (IRE)**[17] 1285 3-8-12 **0**....... TedDurcan 4 51+
(Chris Wall) *trckd ldrs: effrt over 2f out: sn rdn to chse ldng pair: wknd appr fnl f* **13/2**
4-6 **5** *3 ¼* **Whatsofunny (IRE)**[13] 1376 3-8-12 **0**....... JackMitchell 9 41
(Roger Varian) *wnt lft s: chsd ldrs: rdn along wl over 2f out: sn btn* **20/1**
0 **6** *1 ½* **Irish Girls Spirit (IRE)**[17] 1274 3-8-12 **0**....... MickyFenton 3 36
(Paul Midgley) *cl up: rdn along over 2f out: sn wknd* **100/1**
00- **7** *1 ½* **Oops Caroline (IRE)**[189] 6984 3-8-9 **0**....... DeclanCannon(3) 1 31
(David O'Meara) *chsd ldrs: rdn along wl over 2f out: sn wknd* **25/1**

8 9 **Saltire Blue** 3-8-12 0 ..... WilliamCarson 6
(William Jarvis) *dwlt: a in rr* **50/1**

1m 17.05s (3.45) **Going Correction** +0.45s/f (Yiel) **8** Ran SP% **111.4**
Speed ratings (Par 100): **95,93,92,83,79 77,75,63**
CSF £7.28 TOTE £4.40: £1.90, £1.20, £1.10; EX 8.80.
Owner Andrew Tinkler **Bred** Laundry Cottage Stud Farm **Trained** East Everleigh, Wilts

FOCUS
40mm rain over the previous three days including 25mm inr the last 24 hours resulted in ground described as soft. An ordinary 3yo maiden fillies' sprint, best rated around the runner-up. They set off in two groups of four but converged into one group towards the centre soon after halfway.

1638 ATTEYS SOLICITORS FILLIES' H'CAP 6f
2:45 (2:45) (Class 5) (0-70,70) 4-Y-0+ **£2,264** (£673; £336; £168) **Stalls** High

Form RPR

3442 **1** **Dancing Welcome**[7] 1497 6-8-7 **56** oh1 ..... (h) HayleyTurner 3 67
(Milton Bradley) *trckd ldrs: hdwy to ld 2f out and sn rdn: drvn ent fnl f: styd on wl* **5/2**[1]

0-05 **2** *3/4* **Shes Rosie**[18] 1246 4-8-12 **68** ..... DarrenEgan(7) 8 77
(John O'Shea) *cl up: pushed along and outpcd over 2f out: sn rdn and styd on wl ins fnl f* **8/1**

60-3 **3** *nk* **Red Roar (IRE)**[18] 1246 5-8-13 **65** ..... JulieBurke(3) 7 73
(Alan Berry) *prom: effrt to chal 2f out: sn rdn and ev ch tl one pce ins fnl f* **11/1**

-001 **4** *1* **Mata Hari Blue**[8] 1480 6-9-5 **68** ..... (t) RussKennemore 10 72
(John Holt) *chsd ldrs: hdwy and cl up over 2f out: sn rdn and ev ch tl one pce ent fnl f* **9/2**[2]

2-20 **5** *2 1/4* **Bailadeira**[13] 1383 4-8-9 **58** ..... JamesSullivan 6 55
(Tim Etherington) *hld up: hdwy wl over 2f out: rdn to chse ldrs over 1f out: sn chal and ev ch tl drvn and wknd ins fnl f* **14/1**

01-0 **6** *1 3/4* **Hoppy's Flyer (FR)**[18] 1251 4-9-2 **65** ..... MickyFenton 14 57
(Paul Midgley) *in rr: hdwy 2f out: sn rdn and kpt on: nvr rchd ldrs* **22/1**

4131 **7** *nk* **Mother Jones**[23] 1187 4-9-0 **68** ..... MatthewCosham(5) 2 59
(David Evans) *chsd ldrs: rdn along 2f out: sn drvn and no imp* **9/1**

5340 **8** *1 1/2* **Cut The Cackle (IRE)**[2] 1609 6-8-10 **59** ..... (bt) WilliamCarson 5 45
(Richard Guest) *nvr bttr than midfield* **33/1**

020- **9** *1* **Vizean (IRE)**[182] 7141 4-8-13 **67** ..... JustinNewman(5) 12 50
(John Mackie) *led: rdn along over 2f out: sn hdd and grad wknd* **13/2**[3]

3050 **10** *1* **Saktoon (USA)**[16] 1309 4-8-7 **56** oh5 ..... (v) JoeFanning 11 35
(Derek Shaw) *wnt lft s: a towards rr* **25/1**

060- **11** *1* **My Own Way Home**[206] 6604 4-8-13 **62** ..... PadraigBeggy 1 38
(David Evans) *a in rr* **33/1**

350- **12** *nk* **Needy McCredie**[199] 6779 6-8-12 **61** ..... PJMcDonald 9 36
(James Turner) *sltly hmpd s and towards rr: sme hdwy over 2f out: sn rdn along and n.d* **16/1**

000- **13** *32* **Questionnaire (IRE)**[194] 6895 4-9-7 **70** ..... (t) LukeMorris 13
(Nicky Vaughan) *racd alone stands' rail: cl up tl rdn and wknd 1/2-way: sn bhd and eased* **22/1**

1m 16.95s (3.35) **Going Correction** +0.45s/f (Yiel) **13** Ran SP% **120.5**
Speed ratings (Par 100): **95,94,93,92,89 86,86,84,83,81 80,80,37**
toteswingers:1&2:£10.40, 2&3:£8.30, 1&3:£7.00 CSF £21.17 CT £189.43 TOTE £3.80: £1.80, £3.40, £3.00; EX 26.60.
Owner J M Bradley **Bred** The Hon Mrs E J Wills **Trained** Sedbury, Gloucs

FOCUS
A modest fillies' sprint handicap but fair form for a race of its type with the winner and fourth both well in. They raced in one group towards the centre apart from one other, who finished well beaten.
Questionnaire(IRE) Official explanation: jockey said filly lost its action

1639 KAT COMMUNICATIONS KNOWLEDGE ABOUT TELECOMS H'CAP 5f
3:20 (3:21) (Class 3) (0-90,87) 3-Y-0 **£6,792** (£2,021; £1,010; £505) **Stalls** High

Form RPR

1- **1** **Pearl Secret**[203] 6673 3-9-5 **85** ..... JamieSpencer 1 102+
(David Barron) *stdd s and hld up in rr: hdwy 1/2-way: led appr fnl f: sn qcknd clr: easily* **8/13**[1]

23-6 **2** *4 1/2* **Lupo D'Oro (IRE)**[16] 1317 3-8-11 **77** ..... LukeMorris 4 77
(John Best) *prom: rdn to ld wl over 1f out: drvn and hdd appr fnl f: kpt on: no ch w wnr* **8/1**[3]

22-0 **3** *2 3/4* **See Clearly**[17] 1271 3-8-10 **76** ..... DavidAllan 3 63
(Tim Easterby) *chsd ldrs: rdn along and outpcd bef 1/2-way: kpt on u.p fr wl over 1f out: tk mod 3rd nr fin* **9/1**

00-4 **4** *3/4* **Electric Qatar**[44] 892 3-9-3 **83** ..... KierenFallon 6 67
(Tom Dascombe) *wnt lft s: led: pushed along 1/2-way: rdn over 2f out: hdd wl over 1f out: sn wknd* **13/2**[2]

000- **5** *6* **Cockney Fire**[188] 7019 3-9-0 **80** ..... PadraigBeggy 2 43
(David Evans) *chsd ldrs: rdn along wl over 2f out: sn wknd* **22/1**

310- **6** *3 1/4* **Powerful Wind (IRE)**[224] 6114 3-9-0 **87** ..... (t) DarrenEgan(7) 5 38
(Ronald Harris) *sltly hmpd s: sn prom: cl up 1/2-way: sn rdn and wknd over 2f out* **10/1**

1m 0.95s (0.45) **Going Correction** +0.45s/f (Yiel) **6** Ran SP% **109.8**
Speed ratings (Par 102): **114,106,102,101,91 86**
CSF £5.87 TOTE £1.70: £1.20, £2.50; EX 7.30.
Owner Pearl Bloodstock Ltd **Bred** Whitsbury Manor Stud & Pigeon House Stud **Trained** Maunby, N Yorks

NOTEBOOK
Pearl Secret ◆, who had three subsequent winners behind him and made a big impression when making a winning debut at York in October, was asked to make his handicap debut from a mark of 85. Backed as if defeat was out of the question and striking in appearance, he was ridden with bags of confidence. Sweeping to the front, he went clear in effortless fashion and looks at least Listed class already. He will need another outing if he is to take his chance in the valuable Class 2 0-105 Bond Tyres 3yo Trophy at York in June. (op 4-5)
Lupo D'Oro(IRE), placed seven times at two including when chasing home Pearl Secret at York, had an 8lb pull but it was nowhere near enough. Still a maiden, that elusive first win will surely come his way. (op 7-1)
See Clearly, a tough juvenile, snatched third place money. She likes the mud but all her best form has been shown in blinkers, which she was without here. (op 15-2)
Electric Qatar, 1-3 when only fourth in maiden company at Kempton, has been gelded since. He showed good form when tenth in the Super Sprint at Newbury (RPR 87) but he is turning into something of a major disappointment. (op 6-1 tchd 7-1)
Powerful Wind(IRE), a winner four times at two, resumed from a career-high mark. Fitted with a tongue tie for the first-time, he will struggle in handicap company until his rating comes down several pounds. (tchd 9-1)

1640 FREE BETS WITH FREEBETS.CO.UK H'CAP 2m 110y
3:55 (3:57) (Class 4) (0-85,85) 4-Y-0+ **£4,204** (£1,251; £625; £312) **Stalls** Low

Form RPR

/64- **1** **Secret Tune**[41] 6171 8-9-2 **75** ..... (t) DaneO'Neill 2 84
(Charlie Longsdon) *trckd ldrs: hdwy over 3f out: slt ld 2f out and sn rdn: drvn fnl f: styd on wl towards fin* **5/1**[3]

40-0 **2** *nk* **Lady Amakhala**[16] 1295 4-8-12 **75** ..... AndrewMullen 9 83
(George Moore) *a.p: cl up 6f out: rdn to take slt ld 3f out: sn jnd and hdd 2f out: cl up and ev ch tl drvn and no ex last 75yds* **8/1**

42-4 **3** *2 3/4* **Sohcahtoa (IRE)**[16] 1295 6-8-8 **72** ..... LMcNiff(5) 4 77
(David Barron) *hld up in rr: stdy hdwy over 6f out: trckd ldrs 3f out: rdn to chse ldng pair 2f out: sn drvn and no imp ins fnl f* **11/4**[1]

-443 **4** *7* **Bedouin Bay**[17] 1282 5-8-12 **71** ..... (p) MartinHarley 7 68
(Alan McCabe) *set stdy pce: pushed along 4f out: rdn over 3f out: sn hdd and grad wknd* **5/1**[3]

030- **5** *3/4* **Rosewin (IRE)**[157] 6171 6-9-9 **82** ..... MichaelO'Connell 3 78
(Ollie Pears) *s.i.s: plld hrd in rr: hdwy on outer 3f out: rdn 2f out: sn no imp* **22/1**

0-21 **6** *nk* **Boss's Destination**[17] 1282 5-9-12 **85** ..... PJMcDonald 5 81
(Alan Swinbank) *trckd ldr: effrt over 3f out: sn rdn along and wknd* **4/1**[2]

0362 **7** *33* **Russian George (IRE)**[29] 1085 6-9-2 **75** ..... (tp) JamieSpencer 8 35
(Steve Gollings) *hld up in tch: hdwy 4f out: rdn along 3f out: sn wknd and eased fr wl over 1f out* **14/1**

114- **8** *15* **Damascus Symphony**[186] 7062 4-8-4 **67** ..... WilliamCarson 1
(James Bethell) *reluctant to go to s: a in rr: rdn along 4f out: sn wknd and bhd* **10/1**

3m 58.11s (17.71) **Going Correction** +0.85s/f (Soft)
WFA 4 from 5yo+ 4lb **8** Ran SP% **111.2**
Speed ratings (Par 105): **92,91,90,87,86 86,71,64**
toteswingers:1&2:£13.10, 2&3:£5.80, 1&3:£5.90 CSF £41.58 CT £126.42 TOTE £5.80: £1.60, £3.00, £1.30; EX 64.20.
Owner R Davies **Bred** Juddmonte Farms Ltd **Trained** Over Norton, Oxon

FOCUS
A competitive 67-85 stayers' handicap. The pace was understandably just steady until the final three quarters of a mile and they raced in one group towards the centre in the home straight. The winner's best Flat form since he was a 3yo.

1641 FREE BETTING WITH FREEBETS.CO.UK H'CAP 1m 2f 60y
4:30 (4:30) (Class 4) (0-80,80) 3-Y-0 **£4,204** (£1,251; £625; £312) **Stalls** Low

Form RPR

12-4 **1** **Spirit Of The Law (IRE)**[23] 1190 3-8-12 **71** ..... HayleyTurner 13 84
(Ed Dunlop) *trckd ldr: effrt 2f out: rdn over 1f out: styd on u.p ins fnl f to ld nr fin* **14/1**

331- **2** *nk* **Beyond Conceit (IRE)**[196] 6825 3-9-7 **80** ..... JamieSpencer 6 92
(Tom Tate) *led: rdn wl over 1f out: drvn and hung persistently rt ins fnl f: hdd and no ex nr fin* **9/2**[2]

46-2 **3** *2 1/4* **Rocktherunway (IRE)**[9] 1440 3-9-0 **73** ..... TomEaves 2 81+
(Michael Dods) *hld up towards rr: pushed along 4f out: rdn and gd hdwy wl over 1f out: swtchd lft ent fnl f: kpt on* **9/2**[2]

13-2 **4** *5* **Ahzeemah (IRE)**[8] 1473 3-9-7 **80** ..... (p) FrankieDettori 8 79
(Saeed Bin Suroor) *trckd ldng pair: effrt over 2f out: rdn wl over 1f out: drvn appr fnl f and grad wknd* **5/2**[1]

1-40 **5** *1 1/4* **Maybeagrey**[25] 1167 3-8-8 **67** ..... DavidAllan 5 63
(Tim Easterby) *dwlt and towards rr: hdwy 2f out: sn rdn and styd on ins fnl f: nt rch ldrs* **50/1**

22-1 **6** *3 3/4* **Verse Of Love**[18] 1257 3-8-12 **76** ..... MatthewCosham(5) 11 65
(David Evans) *trckd ldrs: hdwy on outer 1/2-way: rdn along wl over 2f out: grad wknd* **14/1**

026- **7** *7* **Scrupul (IRE)**[178] 7209 3-9-3 **76** ..... KierenFallon 1 52
(Luca Cumani) *in tch: hdwy over 4f out: rdn along over 3f out: sn wknd* **14/1**

1 **8** *shd* **Ogaritmo**[60] 723 3-9-1 **74** ..... AdamKirby 9 50
(Marco Botti) *trckd ldrs: hdwy over 4f out: effrt 3f out: sn rdn and wknd 2f out* **9/1**

655- **9** *3* **Counsel (IRE)**[185] 7082 3-9-1 **74** ..... RichardMullen 10 44
(Sir Michael Stoute) *hld up towards rr: sme hdwy over 4f out: rdn along 3f out: n.d* **13/2**[3]

1222 **10** *8* **Flying Pickets (IRE)**[31] 1058 3-8-12 **71** ..... (be) MartinHarley 7 26
(Alan McCabe) *a towards rr* **33/1**

2m 17.72s (8.32) **Going Correction** +0.85s/f (Soft) **10** Ran SP% **113.2**
Speed ratings (Par 100): **100,99,97,93,92 89,84,84,81,75**
CSF £73.76 CT £332.87 TOTE £15.20: £3.30, £2.20, £1.10; EX 86.60.
Owner R J Arculli **Bred** Georgestown Stud **Trained** Newmarket, Suffolk
■ Stewards' Enquiry : Jamie Spencer caution: careless riding.

FOCUS
A competitive 67-80 3yo handicap on paper, but the ground did for plenty. The pace was steady until the final half-mile and the first pair raced 1-2, so perhaps this was not as good as it looks at face value.
Counsel(IRE) Official explanation: trainer's rep said gelding was unsuited by the heavy (soft in places) ground

1642 FREEBETS.CO.UK H'CAP (DIV I) 5f
5:00 (5:00) (Class 4) (0-85,85) 4-Y-0+ **£4,204** (£1,251; £625; £312) **Stalls** High

Form RPR

15-5 **1** **Pearl Blue (IRE)**[11] 1417 4-9-4 **82** ..... GeorgeBaker 7 92+
(Chris Wall) *trckd ldrs: effrt over 1f out: swtchd rt and rdn ent fnl f: qcknd wl to ld last 50yds* **4/1**[1]

-206 **2** *1/2* **West Coast Dream**[50] 835 5-9-5 **83** ..... TomEaves 15 91
(Roy Brotherton) *prom on wd outside: effrt and cl up wl over 1f out: rdn to chal ent fnl f and ev ch tl nt qckn last 50yds* **14/1**

250- **3** *3/4* **Bedloe's Island (IRE)**[273] 4516 7-8-12 **76** ..... JamesSullivan 12 81
(Neville Bycroft) *prom: hdwy to ld wl over 1f out and sn rdn: drvn ent fnl f: hdd and no ex last 50yds* **16/1**

36 **4** *1 1/4* **Head Space (IRE)**[14] 1362 4-9-1 **79** ..... PJMcDonald 11 80
(Ruth Carr) *in tch: hdwy over 1f out: sn rdn and styd on fnl f: nrst fin* **14/1**

23-1 **5** *3/4* **Bouncy Bouncy (IRE)**[17] 1290 5-8-10 **74** ..... (t) HayleyTurner 3 72+
(Michael Bell) *dwlt and towards rr: hdwy 1/2-way: swtchd rt and rdn wl over 1f out: styd on ins fnl f: nrst fin* **15/2**[3]

000- **6** *3/4* **Noodles Blue Boy**[169] 7355 6-9-1 **79** ..... TonyHamilton 2 74
(Ollie Pears) *cl up: rdn wl over 1f out: ev ch tl drvn and grad wknd ins fnl f* **33/1**

21-5 **7** 3/4 **Sleepy Blue Ocean**[117] 3 6-8-8 **72**............................(p) LukeMorris 1 65
(John Balding) *prom: rdn along wl over 1f out: grad wknd ins fnl f* **18/1**

0-53 **8** *nse* **Haajes**[19] 1236 8-9-4 **82**.. MickyFenton 6 75
(Paul Midgley) *chsd ldrs: rdn along wl over 1f out: edgd rt and sn one pce* **10/1**

64-1 **9** *shd* **Mayoman (IRE)**[19] 1237 7-9-4 **82**.................................... KierenFallon 13 74
(David O'Meara) *hld up towards rr: effrt and sme hdwy wl over 1f out: rdn: edgd lft and no imp fr over 1f out* **13/2**[2]

02-1 **10** 1/2 **Go Go Green (IRE)**[19] 1236 6-8-13 **77**.............................. GrahamLee 4 67
(Jim Goldie) *chsd ldrs: rdn along wl over 1f out: grad wknd* **16/1**

200- **11** *nk* **Tyfos**[216] 6331 7-9-7 **85**.. TomMcLaughlin 5 74
(Brian Baugh) *led: rdn along over 2f out: hdd wl over 1f out and sn wknd* **40/1**

13-1 **12** 3/4 **Rafaaf (IRE)**[4] 1564 4-8-12 **79** 6ex............................. AdamBeschizza(3) 8 66
(Robert Eddery) *a towards rr* **4/1**[1]

006- **13** *nk* **Rocket Rob (IRE)**[163] 7428 6-8-11 **75**......................... StevieDonohoe 17 61
(Willie Musson) *a towards rr* **18/1**

030- **14** 4 1/2 **The Nifty Fox**[193] 6917 8-8-11 **75**....................................... DavidAllan 14 44
(Tim Easterby) *dwlt: a in rr* **16/1**

1m 2.1s (1.60) **Going Correction** +0.45s/f (Yiel) **14** Ran SP% **121.1**
Speed ratings (Par 105): **105,104,103,101,99 98,97,97,97,96 95,94,94,87**
toteswingers:1&2:£18.30, 2&3:£50.40, 1&3:£20.10 CSF £63.43 CT £851.73 TOTE £4.90: £2.30, £4.60, £6.80; EX 86.50.
Owner Archangels 2 **Bred** L Queally **Trained** Newmarket, Suffolk

FOCUS
Division 1 of a highly competitive sprint handicap. It was the slowest of the three C&D times and the first four were always prominent, but there was still plenty to like about the winner.

1643 FREEBETS.CO.UK H'CAP (DIV II) 5f
5:35 (5:35) (Class 4) (0-85,84) 4-Y-0+ **£4,204** (£1,251; £625; £312) **Stalls** High

Form RPR

463- **1** **Long Awaited (IRE)**[244] 5484 4-9-5 **82**.................... GrahamGibbons 13 91+
(David Barron) *trckd ldrs: smooth hdwy and cl up wl over 1f out: led ent fnl f: rdn out* **4/1**[1]

-130 **2** 3/4 **Even Stevens**[34] 1033 4-9-0 **77**..................................... RobertWinston 2 83
(Scott Dixon) *chsd ldrs on outer: hdwy over 1f out: sn rdn styd on wl ins fnl f* **11/1**

045- **3** 3/4 **Flash City (ITY)**[160] 7487 4-9-5 **82**....................................(v) TomEaves 4 85
(Bryan Smart) *sn led: rdn along wl over 1f out: hdd ent fnl f: sn drvn and kpt on same pce* **16/1**

0402 **4** *shd* **Fair Passion**[14] 1362 5-8-7 **70** oh3.................................... JoeFanning 14 73
(Derek Shaw) *hld up towards rr: hdwy 2f out: rdn over 1f out: styd on fnl f: nrst fin* **10/1**

/26- **5** *hd* **Jack Luey**[321] 2938 5-8-12 **75**.. FrederikTylicki 16 77
(Lawrence Mullaney) *towards rr: hdwy wl over 1f out: sn rdn and styd on fnl f: nrst fin* **9/1**

5006 **6** *nse* **Captain Scooby**[8] 1478 6-8-9 **77**.............................. DuilioDaSilva(5) 10 79
(Richard Guest) *towards rr: hdwy whn nt clr run 2f out: sn swtchd rt and rdn: styd on wl fnl f: nrst fin* **6/1**[2]

-212 **7** *nse* **Master Of Disguise**[74] 545 6-8-9 **75**.....................(t) HarryBentley(3) 12 77
(Brian Baugh) *in tch: rdn along wl over 1f out: drvn and kpt on fnl f: nrst fin* **6/1**[2]

34/0 **8** *nk* **Ertikaan**[8] 1476 5-8-13 **83**.. DarrenEgan(7) 3 84
(Ronald Harris) *prom: cl up 2f out: sn rdn and ev ch tl drvn and wknd fnl f* **10/1**

516- **9** 1 1/4 **Another Wise Kid (IRE)**[193] 6917 4-9-7 **84**.................... MickyFenton 5 80
(Paul Midgley) *prom: rdn along wl over 1f out: grad wknd* **12/1**

040- **10** 2 **Green Park (IRE)**[193] 6913 9-8-11 **79**.............................. NeilFarley(5) 11 68
(Declan Carroll) *prom: rdn along 1/2-way: sn one pce* **16/1**

00-3 **11** 5 **Solemn**[11] 1417 7-9-5 **82**...(b) DaneO'Neill 7 53
(Milton Bradley) *a in rr* **7/1**[3]

/00- **12** 1/2 **Jameela Girl**[169] 7356 4-9-1 **78**.. PatCosgrave 8 47
(Robert Cowell) *chsd ldrs: rdn wl over 1f out: sn wknd* **33/1**

604- **13** 3 1/2 **Deliberation (IRE)**[128] 7840 4-8-12 **75**.......................... RoystonFfrench 6 32
(Mark Buckley) *prom: rdn along bef 1/2-way: sn wknd and bhd* **25/1**

1m 2.02s (1.52) **Going Correction** +0.45s/f (Yiel) **13** Ran SP% **123.8**
Speed ratings (Par 105): **105,103,102,102,102 102,101,101,99,96 88,87,81**
toteswingers:1&2:£12.90, 2&3:£33.30, 1&3:£14.40 CSF £50.97 CT £678.09 TOTE £4.60: £1.60, £4.20, £5.50; EX 60.20.
Owner Peter Jones **Bred** Mrs C Regalado-Gonzalez **Trained** Maunby, N Yorks

FOCUS
A competitive handicap run slightly quicker than division 1, and there was a bunch finish. There could be more to come from the winner.
Solemn Official explanation: jockey said gelding lost its action
T/Jkpt: Not won. T/Plt: £49.60 to a £1 stake. Pool of £96,204.28 - 1,413.18 winning tickets. T/Qpdt: £19.50 to a £1 stake. Pool of £5,318.07 - 201.22 winning tickets. JR

SANDOWN (R-H)
Friday, April 27

OFFICIAL GOING: Heavy (4.7)
Wind: Moderate, half against Weather: Overcast with showers, becoming brighter

1644 BET365 H'CAP 5f 6y
1:15 (1:15) (Class 2) (0-105,99) 3-Y-0
£12,450 (£3,728; £1,864; £932; £466; £234) **Stalls** Low

Form RPR

10-0 **1** **Ballesteros**[9] 1457 3-9-1 **93**... RyanMoore 6 102+
(Brian Meehan) *taken to post v early: wnt lft s: hld up: last tl prog 1/2-way: chsd clr ldr over 1f out: sn clsd: rdn to ld last 150yds: all out to hold on* **7/2**[2]

60-1 **2** *nk* **Bear Behind (IRE)**[20] 1219 3-9-7 **99**........................ RichardKingscote 4 107
(Tom Dascombe) *fast away: led and grabbed far rail: rdn at least 2 l clr over 1f out: hdd last 150yds: fought on wl: jst hld* **4/1**[3]

00-0 **3** 11 **Church Music (IRE)**[20] 1217 3-8-10 **88** ow1.................. DarrylHolland 2 56
(Michael Scudamore) *sn pushed along in 5th: no prog 2f out: kpt on ins fnl f to take remote 3rd nr fin* **20/1**

4-41 **4** 1 **Wicked Wench**[38] 977 3-8-2 **80** oh4...................... SilvestreDeSousa 1 45
(Jo Hughes) *chsd ldr: rdn 2f out: lost 2nd and btn over 1f out: wknd and lost remote 3rd nr fin* **11/1**

300- **5** 7 **Mister Musicmaster**[223] 6166 3-8-7 **85**........................ AndreaAtzeni 3 25
(Rod Millman) *chsd ldng pair to wl over 1f out: wknd* **14/1**

11- **6** 9 **Rafeej**[175] 7261 3-8-9 **87**.. PaulHanagan 5
(Mark Johnston) *racd on outer: chsd ldrs in 4th: struggling 1/2-way: sn last and wl btn* **6/5**[1]

1m 6.81s (5.21) **Going Correction** +1.15s/f (Soft) **6** Ran SP% **107.4**
Speed ratings (Par 104): **104,103,85,84,73 58**
CSF £16.07 TOTE £4.00: £1.50, £2.40; EX 16.20.
Owner Mrs P Good **Bred** Exors Of The Late J R Good **Trained** Manton, Wilts

FOCUS
There was 4mm of rain during the morning on top of ground already heavy from over an inch of rain this week. Ryan Moore described the ground as the worst he's ridden on at Sandown. This is often a decent handicap - last year's winner Night Carnation won a C&D Group 3 later in the season - but perhaps this wasn't the strongest renewal. The first two were the only ones to really handle conditions and they finished well clear. The winner may need similar conditions to match this figure.

NOTEBOOK
Ballesteros had previous winning form in heavy ground, taking a nursery at Haydock last October off 5lb lower, and he was sharper for his down-the-field reappearance at the Craven meeting. Dropped in from the outside stall, he came through to lead inside the last then was brave to hold the rally of the runner-up, a much bigger individual than him. The drop back to 5f suited this game gelding, who went early to post. (op 4-1)
Bear Behind(IRE) was put up 2lb after finishing first at Musselburgh recently, a race the stewards took off him. The topweight broke smartly to grab the rail, and fought back after the winner had headed him inside the last. This was a decent effort in the ground and he gives the impression that there is better still to come from him. (op 7-2)
Church Music(IRE) grabbed a well-beaten third close home and might have been a little closer had he not momentarily been forced to check on the fence. All his previous runs on turf, most of which were for Kevin Ryan, were on good ground. (tchd 22-1)
Wicked Wench, a dual Southwell winner, had not run on turf since her debut and was racing from 4lb out of the weights. She paid in the end for chasing the pace. (op 14-1)
Mister Musicmaster, gelded since last year, was found out off a 17lb higher mark than when winning on soft ground here last July. He had been on his toes in the preliminaries. (op 16-1)
Rafeej, unbeaten in two in his first season and a Group 1 Diamond Jubilee Stakes entry, was most disappointing. His second win came in bad ground at Ffos Las, but he hinted that day he'd prefer a better surface and he appeared not to handle the conditions here at all, floundering and being beaten at halfway. He's worth excusing this. Paul Hanagan reported that the colt was never travelling. Official explanation: jockey said colt never travelled (op Evens tchd 10-11)

1645 BET365.COM ESHER CUP (H'CAP) 1m 14y
1:50 (1:51) (Class 2) (0-100,96) 3-Y-0
£12,450 (£3,728; £1,864; £932; £466; £234) **Stalls** Low

Form RPR

56-1 **1** **Grey Mirage**[29] 1086 3-8-7 **82** oh1............................ SilvestreDeSousa 1 92
(Marco Botti) *mde all: mod pce tl drew 4 l clr 1/2-way: c bk 2f out: rdr saved enough and kpt on wl whn pressed: asserted fnl f: gng away fin* **6/1**[3]

42-1 **2** 4 **Kid Suitor (IRE)**[16] 1304 3-8-10 **85**.................................... RyanMoore 2 86+
(Richard Hannon) *trckd wnr: clsd to chal 2f out: rdn over 1f out: fended off fnl f: tired last 100yds* **5/2**[1]

120- **3** 1 **Graphic (IRE)**[188] 7026 3-9-4 **96**... SeanLevey(3) 4 94
(Richard Hannon) *hld up in last pair: shkn up and prog to go 3rd over 1f out: no imp tl clsd on tiring runner-up nr fin* **17/2**

21- **4** 1 **Grandeur (IRE)**[255] 5133 3-8-13 **88**................................. WilliamBuick 5 84
(Jeremy Noseda) *trckd ldng pair: shkn up and nt qckn over 2f out: wl btn over 1f out: plugged on nr fin* **3/1**[2]

104- **5** 4 1/2 **Otto The Great**[199] 6766 3-8-12 **87**..................................... ShaneKelly 6 73
(Peter Chapple-Hyam) *hld up in last pair: effrt on outer over 2f out: sn no prog and btn* **12/1**

31- **6** 8 **Trader Jack**[175] 7257 3-9-1 **90**.. JamesDoyle 3 57
(Roger Charlton) *trckd ldng pair: shkn up over 2f out: sn btn: wknd fnl f* **3/1**[2]

1m 54.3s (11.00) **Going Correction** +1.475s/f (Soft) **6** Ran SP% **111.1**
Speed ratings (Par 104): **104,100,99,98,93 85**
toteswingers:1&2:£2.10, 2&3:£3.70, 1&3:£4.70 CSF £20.88 TOTE £8.00: £3.30, £1.10; EX 15.10.
Owner Scuderia Vittadini Srl **Bred** Grundy Bloodstock Srl **Trained** Newmarket, Suffolk

FOCUS
The Esher Cup is not the race it once was, but this was still a decent handicap despite another small field. The runners remained on the far side once into the straight. There are the usual doubts over the form given the state of the ground, but the race has been rated on the positive side, with a sizeable step up from the winner.

NOTEBOOK
Grey Mirage ◆, a front-running winner of a Kempton maiden on his reappearance, repeated the tactics here, quickening to go several lengths clear turning in. The runner-up issued a challenge but he saw him off grittily and was pulling away again late on. This win came off 82, from a pound out of the weights, but he looks well up to something better and it would be no surprise to see this half-brother to dual Italian Group 1 mile winner Distant Way tackling a Listed race before long. (op 5-1)
Kid Suitor(IRE), like the winner, had race fitness on his side, having been successful off 5lb lower at Kempton. One of two runners for a stable which won this in 2005 and 2008, he chased the winner all the way and was perhaps only a neck down from the two pole to the one, but his stride shortened markedly from there. He had plenty in his favour here, including his ability to handle the ground, so it may be unwise to expect too much improvement. (op 9-4 tchd 11-4 in places)
Graphic(IRE), a stablemate of the runner-up, had some useful form at two but was more exposed than most of these. He improved along the rail from the rear but never seriously threatened the first pair. This was his first taste of a soft surface. (op 12-1)
Grandeur(IRE) has been gelded since beating a subsequent dual winner in a Brighton maiden last August. Upped in trip for this return, the grey briefly promised to close and was not knocked about when held. He should improve considerably on this. (op 9-2 tchd 5-1)
Otto The Great, trained at two by Walter Swinburn, tried to mount an effort out wide and could never get into it. The ground would have been completely new to him and he had his stamina to prove too. (op 16-1)
Trader Jack was a little keen early on and ran as if this reappearance was needed. He won in bad ground last back-end, but another winner at that Ffos Las meeting, Rafeej, was an earlier flop on this card. (op 5-2 tchd 9-4)

1646 BET365 MILE (GROUP 2) 1m 14y
2:20 (2:24) (Class 1) 4-Y-0+
£45,368 (£17,200; £8,608; £4,288; £2,152; £1,080) **Stalls** Low

Form RPR

31-1 **1** **Penitent**[26] 1158 6-9-0 108... DanielTudhope 1 116
(David O'Meara) *trckd ldr to over 6f out: styd handy: chsd ldr 1/2-way: led 2f out: rdn and gd battle after: grad asserted fnl f* **5/1**[3]

3-31 **2** 1 3/4 **Questioning (IRE)**[8] 1471 4-9-0 107..............................(p) WilliamBuick 3 112
(John Gosden) *hld up initially but trckd ldr over 6f out: led main gp to centre in st and led 3f out: hdd 2f out: kpt on wl but hld fnl f* **5/1**[3]

234- **3** *8* **Famous Name**[12] 1402 7-9-0 116 .... PatSmullen 6 94
(D K Weld, Ire) *racd wd 1st 3f: hld up: chsd ldng pair over 2f out: rdn and no imp wl over 1f out: no ch after* **15/8**[1]

44-0 **4** *8* **Dubawi Gold**[48] 879 4-9-0 117 .... JohnnyMurtagh 5 81
(Richard Hannon) *racd wd 1st 3f: sn hld up in last: effrt 3f out: shkn up and no rspnse over 2f out: eased over 1f out* **5/2**[2]

030- **5** *1 1/4* **Libranno**[174] 7298 4-9-0 112 .... RyanMoore 7 72
(Richard Hannon) *racd wd 1st 3f: prom: lost pl over 3f out: toiling in last pair over 2f out* **8/1**

-066 **6** *6* **Cochabamba (IRE)**[20] 1213 4-8-11 88 .... SilvestreDeSousa 2 56
(Roger Teal) *led: styd alone far side in st: hdd 3f out: sn btn* **100/1**

1m 52.58s (9.28) **Going Correction** +1.475s/f (Soft) **6** Ran SP% **108.8**
Speed ratings (Par 115): **112,110,102,94,93 87**
toteswingers:1&2:£3.10, 2&3:£2.50, 1&3:£2.10 CSF £27.48 TOTE £6.50: £2.80, £2.80; EX 20.20.
Owner Middleham Park Racing XVII **Bred** Cheveley Park Stud Ltd **Trained** Nawton, N Yorks

FOCUS
A fair edition of this Group 2 on paper, but not form to be taken too literally given the state of the ground, with only a couple really giving their running. Penitent has been rated to his old best. Three of the field ran wide down the back and all bar the leader raced up the centre of the track once into the straight, although the first two drifted back towards the rail late on. The time was the best part of two seconds quicker than the Esher Cup.

NOTEBOOK
Penitent beat Questioning in the Listed Doncaster Mile at the beginning of the season and confirmed his narrow superiority over that horse on the same terms. Showing ahead at the two pole, he hung to his right but battled on well to maintain his advantage. Well at home in soft conditions, he has made a fine start for his new connections but may not be that easy to place successfully now. (op 9-2 tchd 11-2)
Questioning(IRE) has taken the Group 3 Earl Of Sefton Stakes at Newmarket since being beaten by today's winner at Doncaster and he ran well here, sticking on in brave style but just held in the final furlong. Probably still improving, he'll likely be suited by going back over a little further. (op 9-2)
Famous Name was up against it on the trends, as there had been no Irish-trained winner of this race nor one as old as him. He was fit from a Leopardstown Listed victory and proven in testing ground, but failed to land a blow at the first two and wasn't at his best. He has failed to win in 13 tries above Group 3 level now, but has been placed in nine of those races. This was his first run in Britain. (op 2-1 tchd 7-4)
Dubawi Gold's trainer had won six of the past eight runnings of this event and was unrepresented in the other two years. This colt was back from an abortive trip to Meydan but was a dual Guineas runner-up last season and a winner when last at this level at Goodwood in August, for which he just avoided a penalty. Held up at the back and racing a little keenly, he was able to make only minor progress in the straight and was a good way below his best. He can be forgiven this, with the bad ground an obvious factor, but perhaps hasn't won the races he ought to have with his ability. He is in the Lockinge, but the stable's chief hope there appears to be Strong Suit. (tchd 11-4)
Libranno, the Hannon second string, dropped away tamely, but the mile on this ground surely stretched a horse who made the frame in the July Cup last summer. (tchd 9-1)
Cochabamba(IRE) faced a stiff task back on turf and found herself marooned on the inside after leading into the straight.

1647 BET365.COM H'CAP 1m 2f 7y
2:55 (2:55) (Class 3) (0-90,85) 3-Y-O
£6,847 (£2,050; £1,025; £512; £256; £128) **Stalls** Low

Form RPR

53-1 **1** **Samba King**[18] 1265 3-9-6 84 .... MickaelBarzalona 8 96
(Mahmood Al Zarooni) *mde all: led field in centre of crse in st: pushed along and asserted 2f out: rdn out fnl f* **11/2**[3]

1- **2** *4* **Little Dutch Girl**[242] 5537 3-8-10 74 .... (b) JohnFahy 1 78
(Clive Cox) *s.i.s and urged along to rch midfield: travelled bttr after: effrt 3f out: rdn to chse wnr over 1f out: styd on but nvr able to chal* **12/1**

013- **3** *4 1/2* **Daneking**[196] 6829 3-8-13 77 .... WilliamBuick 7 72+
(John Gosden) *prom: chsd wnr 4f out to 3f out: sn shkn up and nt qckn: kpt on to take 3rd 1f out* **4/1**[1]

22-3 **4** *4 1/2* **Clare Island Boy (IRE)**[8] 1473 3-9-4 85 .... SeanLevey(3) 5 71
(Richard Hannon) *chsd wnr to 4f out: sn rdn: wnt 2nd again 3f out to over 1f out: wknd: fin tired* **9/2**[2]

10- **5** *nk* **Oojooba**[181] 7169 3-9-4 82 .... AndreaAtzeni 2 67+
(Roger Varian) *hld up in tch: clsd on ldrs 3f out: rdn over 2f out: wknd quite qckly over 1f out* **4/1**[1]

523- **6** *10* **Strident Force**[216] 6334 3-9-0 78 .... RyanMoore 4 43
(Sir Michael Stoute) *hld up and sn last: shkn up and no prog 3f out: no ch after: rdn into 6th last strides* **11/2**[3]

6-1 **7** *shd* **Arch Of Colours**[91] 331 3-8-12 76 .... SilvestreDeSousa 9 41
(Mark Johnston) *prom early: sn dropped to last trio: pushed along 1/2-way: lost tch w ldrs over 2f out* **14/1**

20-5 **8** *13* **Tingo In The Tale (IRE)**[16] 1304 3-9-0 78 .... JamesDoyle 3 17
(David Arbuthnot) *hld up in last trio: gng wl enough over 3f out: rdn wl over 2f out and wknd: t.o* **15/2**

2m 24.78s (14.28) **Going Correction** +1.475s/f (Soft) **8** Ran SP% **115.1**
Speed ratings (Par 102): **101,97,94,90,90 82,82,71**
toteswingers:1&2:£11.10, 2&3:£6.60, 1&3:£3.40 CSF £67.98 CT £292.31 TOTE £6.10: £2.10, £2.60, £1.70; EX 78.40 Trifecta £136.60 Pool: £1089.33 - 5.90 winning units..
Owner Godolphin **Bred** Darley **Trained** Newmarket, Suffolk

FOCUS
Recent winners of this good handicap include Silkwood and Hazyview, both of whom went on to win Group races, plus King George V Handicap scorers Linas Selection and Colony. Four-time Group 1 winner Conduit was third in Colony's year. The pace was steady and the runners all came down the centre in the home straight. Improvement from the first two, but doubts over the form because of the ground.

NOTEBOOK
Samba King may well prove another useful winner to come out of this event, the scopey gelding following up his Yarmouth maiden win with another taking effort from the front. Maturing all the time, and well at home in these conditions, this tough sort should have further improvement in him and may even get 1m4f if required. It remains to be seen if he'll act on better ground. (op 4-1 tchd 6-1)
Little Dutch Girlwas slowly away, as she had been when winning her maiden at Chepstow last August. Again in blinkers, she came through to look the main threat to the winner in the straight but was second best through the final furlong. She gives the impression she will improve over a longer trip. (op 11-1)
Daneking, who still holds a Derby entry, travelled quite well but could only stick on at the same pace when let down. Beaten on heavy going on his final run at two, when he raced too freely, he will be suited by a return to better ground. (op 9-2)
Clare Island Boy(IRE), third to Main Sequence off this mark in a handicap at the Craven meeting, was officially 3lb well-in here but could not take advantage, finding only the one pace after coming under pressure early in the home straight. He will not necessarily be handicapped out of things off his new mark. (tchd 4-1 and 5-1)
Oojooba was not disgraced for all that she didn't get home in the conditions, but has yet to build on her debut win last September. (op 9-2 tchd 5-1)
Strident Force made no impact on this handicap bow and first start since being gelded. He could merit another chance on better ground. (op 8-1)
Arch Of Colours, a maiden winner on Polytrack when last seen three months previously, was the first in trouble. (op 12-1 tchd 10-1)
Tingo In The Tale(IRE), a soft-ground winner last season, was another who failed to act in the conditions. (op 8-1 tchd 6-1)

1648 CASINO AT BET365.COM CONDITIONS STKS 1m 14y
3:30 (3:30) (Class 3) 3-Y-O **£6,847Stalls** Low

Form RPR

21- **1** **Rewarded**[185] 7080 3-9-2 0 .... KirstyMilczarek 3
(James Toller) *walked over*

ms (-103.30) **1** Ran

Owner P C J Dalby & R D Schuster **Bred** Edward David Kessly **Trained** Newmarket, Suffolk

FOCUS
A walkover for Rewarded after Starboard and Poole Harbour were taken out because of the ground. The 'winner' is well regarded by his trainer. It was Kirsty Milczarek's first winner since her BHA ban was overturned.

1649 NORDOFF ROBBINS WILLIE ROBERTSON MEMORIAL MAIDEN FILLIES' STKS 1m 2f 7y
4:05 (4:08) (Class 4) 3-Y-O **£6,225** (£1,864; £932; £466; £233) **Stalls** Low

Form RPR

4- **1** **Morant Bay (IRE)**[177] 7233 3-9-0 0 .... TomQueally 2 79
(Sir Henry Cecil) *cl up: led jst over 2f out: sn asserted: coaxed along fr over 1f out tl rdn to hold on last 75yds* **7/4**[1]

2 *1/2* **Lascaux** 3-9-0 0 .... WilliamBuick 4 78
(John Gosden) *trckd ldr: led briefly over 2f out: sn outpcd by wnr: rallied fnl f: clsng at fin* **3/1**[2]

04- **3** *2 3/4* **Virginia Gallica (IRE)**[169] 7343 3-9-0 0 .... SebSanders 3 72
(J W Hills) *in tch: shkn up 3f out: sn outpcd: wnt 3rd over 1f out: kpt on but nvr able to chal* **9/2**[3]

3- **4** *3* **Caitlin**[188] 7025 3-9-0 0 .... JimmyFortune 5 66
(Andrew Balding) *led: steered v wd crse at modest pce: tried to qckn 3f out: hdd over 2f out: sn outpcd and btn* **3/1**[2]

0- **5** *9* **Bondi Mist (IRE)**[188] 7025 3-9-0 0 .... MickaelBarzalona 1 54
(Jonathan Portman) *hld up in tch: shkn up 3f out: sn no prog: wknd and eased ins fnl f* **20/1**

2m 30.27s (19.77) **Going Correction** +1.475s/f (Soft) **5** Ran SP% **109.3**
Speed ratings (Par 97): **79,78,76,74,66**
CSF £7.15 TOTE £2.70: £1.80, £2.50; EX 7.30.
Owner N Martin **Bred** Old Carhue & Grange Bloodstock **Trained** Newmarket, Suffolk

FOCUS
An interesting fillies' maiden. Multiple Group 1 scorer Dar Re Mi won this in 2008 and the following year's winner Star Ruby was second in the Musidora next time. Going back 20 years, triple Classic heroine User Friendly made a successful debut in this event. They went a steady pace and the time was more than five seconds slower than the earlier handicap. They raced far side down the back and once more came down the centre of the track in the home straight. The form is rated toawards the bottom end of the race averages.
T/Plt: £52.00 to a £1 stake. Pool of £75,750.14 - 1,061.48 winning tickets. T/Qpdt: £8.50 to a £1 stake. Pool of £4,878.77 - 424.48 winning tickets. JN

1637 DONCASTER (L-H)
Saturday, April 28

OFFICIAL GOING: Soft (6.4)
Wind: fresh behind Weather: cloudy, odd shower

1650 AJA LADY RIDERS' H'CAP (LADY AMATEUR RIDERS) 7f
5:05 (5:06) (Class 4) (0-80,79) 4-Y-O+ **£4,991** (£1,548; £773; £387) **Stalls** High

Form RPR

40-2 **1** **No Poppy (IRE)**[17] 1294 4-9-9 72 .... MissHayleyMoore(5) 4 81+
(Tim Easterby) *hld up in tch: hdwy to chse ldr 2f out: led jst ins fnl f: idled fnl 100yds: jst hld on* **6/1**[3]

6005 **2** *nk* **Levitate**[9] 1478 4-10-3 75 .... (v) MissZoeLilly 1 83
(Alan McCabe) *hld up in tch: pushed along over 3f out: hdwy over 1f out: kpt on wl: wnt 2nd fnl 100yds: nt quite rch wnr* **17/2**

6P-0 **3** *2 1/4* **Eastern Hills**[4] 1581 7-10-2 79 .... (p) MissDLenge(5) 3 81
(Alan McCabe) *racd keenly: prom: led over 2f out: sn rdn: hdd jst ins fnl f: no ex and lost 2nd fnl 100yds* **16/1**

06-0 **4** *1* **Illustrious Prince (IRE)**[27] 1161 5-9-13 78 .... MissCLWhitehead(7) 12 78
(Declan Carroll) *led: hdd over 2f out: plugged on* **25/1**

41-0 **5** *1 1/2* **Ted's Brother (IRE)**[15] 1354 4-10-3 75 .... MissSBrotherton 14 71
(Richard Guest) *hld up in tch: rdn over 2f out: no imp initially: kpt on ins fnl f: nvr threatened ldrs* **13/8**[1]

360- **6** *9* **Sea Salt**[200] 6779 9-9-5 68 .... MissVBarr(5) 2 40
(Ron Barr) *prom towards centre: hung lft towards far side 3f out: wknd over 1f out* **14/1**

343- **7** *hd* **Drakes Drum**[171] 7334 4-9-8 69 .... MissRachelKing(3) 9 41
(Clive Cox) *chsd ldrs: wknd over 1f out* **7/2**[2]

0124 **8** *3* **Flag Of Glory**[23] 1207 5-9-0 65 oh2 .... MissMEdden(7) 8 29
(Peter Hiatt) *chsd ldrs: lost pl wl over 3f out: sn btn* **16/1**

10-1 **9** *7* **Caldermud (IRE)**[19] 1263 5-9-11 69 .... (t) MissEJJones 6 15
(Olivia Maylam) *hld up in tch: rdn over 2f out: sn wknd* **14/1**

0454 **10** *13* **Dickie Le Davoir**[9] 1476 8-9-10 75 .... (p) MrsAGuest(7) 10
(Richard Guest) *slowly away: a wl bhd* **12/1**

1m 30.75s (4.45) **Going Correction** +0.525s/f (Yiel) **10** Ran SP% **121.8**
Speed ratings (Par 105): **95,94,92,90,89 78,78,75,67,52**
toteswingers:1&2:£7.50, 2&3:£18.30, 1&3:£16.40 CSF £58.78 CT £582.87 TOTE £7.30: £1.90, £2.90, £5.00; EX 73.30.
Owner Exors Of The Late Mrs P M Easterby **Bred** Michael O'Mahony **Trained** Great Habton, N Yorks
■ Stewards' Enquiry : Miss C L Whitehead four-day ban: used whip above permitted level (tbn)
Miss Zoe Lilly four-day ban: used whip above permitted level (tbn)

FOCUS
A typically modest race of its type. The winner had been given a chance by the handiacpper and is rated a length off her 3yo best. The main action was centre to stands' side from halfway.

1651 CROWNHOTEL-BAWTRY.COM MAIDEN STKS 5f
5:35 (5:36) (Class 5) 2-Y-O **£2,911** (£866; £432; £216) **Stalls** High

Form RPR

1 **Cumbrian Craic** 2-9-3 0 .... DavidAllan 4 76
(Tim Easterby) *prom: led after 1f: pushed clr over 1f out: kpt on: easily* **11/4**[2]

2 6 **Barracuda Boy (IRE)** 2-9-3 0 .... RichardKingscote 2 54+
(Tom Dascombe) *in tch: sltly bmpd over 3f out: sn outpcd and lost pl: hdwy over 1f out: kpt on to go 2nd ins fnl f: no ch w wnr* **6/5**[1]

3 2 **Blue Clumber** 2-8-12 0 .... RobbieFitzpatrick 5 42
(Shaun Harris) *led for 1f: chsd ldr: rdn and outpcd over 2f out: kpt on one pce ins fnl f* **7/1**

0 4 3 ½ **Only For You**[10] 1437 2-8-12 0 .... GrahamGibbons 3 30
(Alan Brown) *chsd ldr: rdn 2f out: wknd and lost 2 pls ins fnl f* **16/1**

F **Silver Fawn (IRE)** 2-9-3 0 .... PJMcDonald 1
(John Weymes) *s.i.s: sn pushed along towards rr: bhd over 2f out: hit rail and fell ins fnl f* **4/1**[3]

1m 3.96s (3.46) **Going Correction** +0.525s/f (Yiel) 5 Ran SP% **110.5**
Speed ratings (Par 92): **93,83,80,74,**
CSF £6.52 TOTE £2.90: £1.10, £1.60; EX 6.90.
Owner Mrs Jennifer E Pallister **Bred** Habton Farms **Trained** Great Habton, N Yorks

FOCUS
An easy success for the debut winner in this moderate juvenile maiden, and it's likely the opposition was weak. It's difficult form to rate.

NOTEBOOK
Cumbrian Craic took this race apart from the halfway stage and ran out a taking debut winner, handing his yard a quick-fire double in the process. From a family his trainer knows all about, he was professional from the gates and looked right at home on the deep surface. His dam won over this trip at two and it will be interesting to see where he's pitched in next. (tchd 5-2 and 3-1)
Barracuda Boy(IRE), a £68,000 purchase, looked to have to most scope of these and was popular to make a winning start to his career. He lost the race early on as he ran distinctly green more towards the centre of the track and the bird had flown by the time he picked up. This takes his stable's 2-y-o record so far this year to 0-14. (op 5-4 tchd 6-4 and 11-10)
Blue Clumber should come on a deal for this debut experience, but looked to want an extra furlong already. (op 17-2 tchd 13-2)
Only For You was comfortably held, but this was an improvement on his debut level ten days earlier. (op 14-1 tchd 12-1)
Silver Fawn(IRE) was well beaten off prior to coming down and it remains to be seen which way he goes from this. (op 9-2 tchd 5-1 and 7-2)

1652 ZINIZ OF BAWTRY FILLIES' H'CAP — 1m (S)
6:05 (6:07) (Class 4) (0-80,80) 4-Y-O+ **£5,175** (£1,540; £769; £384) **Stalls** High

Form RPR

000- 1 **She's A Character**[217] 6330 5-9-3 **76** .... PaulHanagan 9 84
(Richard Fahey) *midfield: rdn and hdwy over 2f out: led ins fnl f: kpt on wl* **8/1**

06-0 2 1 ½ **Bella Noir**[7] 1520 5-8-8 **70** ....(p) MichaelMetcalfe(3) 1 75
(Mrs K Burke) *midfield: hdwy over 3f out: rdn to ld narrowly over 2f out: hdd ins fnl f: kpt on* **5/1**[2]

-025 3 1 ¾ **Junket**[19] 1266 5-8-10 **72** .... SeanLevey(3) 13 73
(Dr Jon Scargill) *chsd ldrs: led over 3f out: rdn whn hdd over 2f out: remained w ev ch tl no ex ins fnl f* **7/1**[3]

2-53 4 ½ **Painted Tail (IRE)**[12] 1423 5-8-8 **67** oh1 ow1 .... PaulMulrennan 10 66
(Alan Swinbank) *led: hdd over 3f out: sn outpcd: styd on again fr over 1f out* **16/1**

-034 5 4 **Climaxfortackle (IRE)**[10] 1439 4-8-7 **66** oh2 .... NickyMackay 5 56
(Derek Shaw) *s.i.s: hld up: hdwy over 3f out: chsd ldrs 2f out: wknd ins fnl f* **14/1**

10-0 6 1 **Imaginary World (IRE)**[28] 1133 4-9-5 **78** ....(be) ShaneKelly 11 66
(Alan McCabe) *hld up: pushed along and hdwy to chse ldrs over 2f out: wknd ins fnl f* **16/1**

10-1 7 ¾ **Smart Step**[10] 1439 4-8-11 **70** .... SilvestreDeSousa 4 56
(Mark Johnston) *midfield: pushed along over 3f out: sn no imp* **3/1**[1]

03-0 8 ¾ **Lizzie (IRE)**[17] 1293 4-8-7 **66** oh1 ....(b) DavidAllan 8 50
(Tim Easterby) *hld up: pushed along 4f out: nvr threatened* **14/1**

010- 9 2 **Amoya (GER)**[190] 6996 5-9-0 **76** ....(t) AdamBeschizza(3) 3 56
(Philip McBride) *midfield: rdn over 3f out: wknd over 2f out* **20/1**

60-1 10 1 ¼ **Ssafa**[17] 1311 4-8-13 **72** .... SebSanders 7 49
(J W Hills) *chsd ldrs: rdn over 3f out: wknd over 1f out* **14/1**

002- 11 1 ¾ **Song Of The Siren**[239] 5676 4-9-1 **74** .... DanielTudhope 6 47
(David O'Meara) *hld up in midfield: rdn over 3f out: sn btn* **20/1**

220- 12 11 **Hurricane Lady (IRE)**[232] 5892 4-9-7 **80** .... GrahamGibbons 2 28
(Mike Murphy) *prom: pushed along and lost pl over 3f out: sn btn: eased over 1f out* **7/1**[3]

400- 13 31 **Cloud Illusions (USA)**[154] 7558 4-9-1 **74** ....[1] RichardKingscote 12
(Heather Main) *in tch: wknd qckly over 3f out* **12/1**

1m 43.04s (3.74) **Going Correction** +0.525s/f (Yiel) 13 Ran SP% **124.9**
Speed ratings (Par 102): **102,100,98,98,94 93,92,91,89,88 86,75,44**
CSF £48.47 CT £303.97 TOTE £9.20: £2.70, £2.50, £3.30; EX 63.60.
Owner Aykroyd And Sons Ltd **Bred** Genesis Green & Deerpark Stud **Trained** Musley Bank, N Yorks

FOCUS
This fillies' handicap looked wide open and was sound run. They kept mid-track and few landed a serious blow on the taxing surface. The winner is rated to last year's best

1653 CHINA ROSE OF BAWTRY H'CAP — 1m (S)
6:40 (6:41) (Class 3) (0-90,87) 3-Y-O **£8,409** (£2,502; £1,250; £625) **Stalls** High

Form RPR

20-2 1 **Nameitwhatyoulike**[26] 1167 3-8-12 **78** .... PaulMulrennan 10 87
(Michael Easterby) *mde all: rdn clr over 1f out: drvn out ins fnl f* **16/1**

140- 2 1 **Sovereign Debt (IRE)**[210] 6527 3-9-7 **87** .... HayleyTurner 5 94
(Michael Bell) *hld up: pushed along and hdwy over 2f out: chsd wnr over 1f out: kpt on* **15/2**

631- 3 2 ½ **Farang Kondiew**[226] 6075 3-8-11 **77** .... GrahamGibbons 13 78
(Declan Carroll) *in tch: rdn 3f out: kpt on one pce* **4/1**[1]

0-00 4 7 **Zakreet**[9] 1477 3-9-2 **82** .... JamesDoyle 2 67
(Kevin Ryan) *prom: rdn over 3f out: wknd over 1f out* **20/1**

16-2 5 ¾ **Bank On Me**[17] 1304 3-9-2 **82** ....(t) ShaneKelly 3 65
(Philip McBride) *chsd ldrs: rdn over 3f out: wknd over 1f out* **7/1**[3]

105- 6 2 ¼ **Quick Bite (IRE)**[189] 7021 3-9-0 **80** .... LukeMorris 12 58
(Hugo Palmer) *s.i.s: hld up: pushed along over 3f out: sn no imp* **6/1**[2]

112- 7 5 **Nemushka**[217] 6340 3-9-1 **81** .... PaulHanagan 4 48
(Richard Fahey) *dwlt: hld up: pushed along over 3f out: nvr threatened* **4/1**[1]

311- 8 ½ **Asifa (IRE)**[169] 7358 3-9-5 **85** ....(p) SilvestreDeSousa 8 51
(Saeed Bin Suroor) *midfield: pushed along over 3f out: wknd over 2f out* **7/1**[3]

41-0 9 16 **Choisan (IRE)**[9] 1477 3-8-12 **78** .... DavidAllan 7
(Tim Easterby) *trckd ldrs: wknd over 2f out* **12/1**

14-0 10 11 **Basantee**[21] 1217 3-8-11 **77** .... RichardKingscote 1
(Tom Dascombe) *hld up: rdn over 4f out: wknd over 3f out* **40/1**

-331 11 4 ½ **Three Bards (IRE)**[74] 552 3-8-13 **79** .... FrannyNorton 14
(Mark Johnston) *chsd ldrs: lost pl over 4f out: sn wknd* **16/1**

1m 42.9s (3.60) **Going Correction** +0.525s/f (Yiel) 11 Ran SP% **117.7**
Speed ratings (Par 102): **103,102,99,92,91 89,84,84,68,57 52**
toteswingers:1&2:£12.10, 2&3:£6.20, 1&3:£17.10 CSF £131.24 CT £592.15 TOTE £23.30: £5.00, £3.10, £2.20; EX 178.10.
Owner S Bowett, S Hollings & S Hull **Bred** A E Smith And Co **Trained** Sheriff Hutton, N Yorks

FOCUS
This was an interesting 3-y-o handicap, but underfoot conditions played a big part in proceedings and it paid to race handily, so the form is somewhat suspect. The winner's personal best doesn't look a fluke.

NOTEBOOK
Nameitwhatyoulike went down narrowly when second on his comeback at Redcar 26 days previously and gained compensation by readily going one better on this contrasting surface. He was 3lb higher and looked fairly exposed, but had obviously benefited for his seasonal debut. The ground was clearly also to his liking, but many failed to handle it and he could be a touch flattered. (op 14-1)
Sovereign Debt(IRE), a dual winner at two, did best of those coming from off the pace and posted a very pleasing seasonal return. The longer trip suited and he deserves to go one better again. (op 12-1)
Farang Kondiew ◆ was a comfortable maiden winner on easy ground when last seen in 2011. He took time to settle, but caught the eye moving nicely around halfway. It was clear shortly after that he was too far out of his ground, though, and a more positive ride would have probably suited. He's a lovely, big horse and is definitely one to follow this season. (op 7-2)
Zakreet had his chance and this was a lot more like it again from him. (op 16-1)
Bank On Me struggled to land a serious blow on this ground and is worth another chance. (op 11-1)
Quick Bite(IRE), who likes this sort of ground, left the definite impression she would benefit for this comeback outing. (op 8-1)
Nemushka is well regarded and impressed in three outings at two. She was again slow to break on this 3-y-o debut, however, and it was clear from halfway she was all at sea on the ground. She must be handed another chance on better ground, but evidently has some quirks. Official explanation: jockey said filly never travelled (tchd 9-2)
Asifa(IRE), bidding for a hat-trick on this seasonal debut, looked uneasy on the ground. (op 8-1)
Basantee Official explanation: jockey said filly never travelled

1654 ROBINSONSOFBAWTRY.COM H'CAP — 1m 2f 60y
7:10 (7:10) (Class 3) (0-95,93) 4-Y-O+ **£8,409** (£2,502; £1,250; £625) **Stalls** Low

Form RPR

001- 1 **War Poet**[123] 5729 5-9-0 **86** .... DanielTudhope 10 98
(David O'Meara) *hld up: smooth hdwy 3f out: led 2f out: sn pushed clr: edgd lft ins fnl f: kpt on* **20/1**

4/ 2 1 ½ **King's Warrior (FR)**[282] 5-9-2 **88** .... SilvestreDeSousa 9 96
(Peter Chapple-Hyam) *midfield: gd hdwy 3f out: chal 2f out: sn rdn: kpt on but a hld by wnr* **16/1**

340- 3 2 ½ **Little Rocky**[245] 5483 4-9-1 **87** .... PaulHanagan 6 90
(David Simcock) *in tch: rdn and hdwy over 2f out: kpt on* **9/2**[2]

313- 4 ½ **High Jinx (IRE)**[245] 5482 4-9-7 **93** .... MartinLane 7 95+
(James Fanshawe) *trckd ldrs: rdn over 3f out: sn outpcd: styd on wl fnl f* **9/4**[1]

126- 5 ½ **Scrapper Smith (IRE)**[175] 7297 6-8-13 **90** .... GarryWhillans(5) 14 91
(Alistair Whillans) *hld up: rdn and hdwy over 2f out: kpt on one pce* **12/1**

003- 6 2 ¼ **Bolivia (GER)**[150] 7584 6-9-2 **88** .... LukeMorris 3 85
(Lucy Wadham) *led: rdn whn hdd over 3f out: wknd over 1f out* **25/1**

25-1 7 2 **Mirrored**[18] 1273 6-9-4 **90** .... DuranFentiman 5 83
(Tim Easterby) *hld up: rdn over 2f out: sn no imp* **7/1**[3]

0300 8 3 ¼ **Reve De Nuit (USA)**[18] 1273 6-8-10 **82** .... ShaneKelly 8 69
(Alan McCabe) *midfield: rdn over 3f out: sn wknd* **33/1**

/10- 9 1 ¾ **Purification (IRE)**[317] 3069 4-9-2 **88** .... RobertHavlin 12 72
(John Gosden) *trckd ldrs: rdn over 3f out: wknd 2f out* **8/1**

25-6 10 7 **Beaumont's Party (IRE)**[18] 1273 5-9-6 **92** .... DavidProbert 11 62
(Chris Grant) *hld up in midfield: rdn over 3f out: sn btn* **20/1**

404- 11 3 ¼ **Sergeant Ablett (IRE)**[203] 6704 4-9-1 **87** .... PaulMulrennan 4 51
(James Given) *led narrowly: hdd over 3f out: sn wknd* **14/1**

53-3 12 17 **Northside Prince (IRE)**[18] 1273 6-9-4 **90** .... GrahamGibbons 15 22
(Alan Swinbank) *in tch tl wknd qckly over 3f out* **9/1**

2m 13.49s (4.09) **Going Correction** +0.60s/f (Yiel) 12 Ran SP% **119.1**
Speed ratings (Par 107): **107,105,103,103,103 101,99,97,95,90 87,73**
toteswingers:1&2:£37.70, 2&3:£6.90, 1&3:£21.70 CSF £295.04 CT £1703.36 TOTE £25.20: £5.90, £3.20, £1.60; EX 178.60.
Owner M Kirby **Bred** Darley **Trained** Nawton, N Yorks

FOCUS
A fair handicap and the ground played a part, but the form makes a fair bit of sense at face value. The winner resumed his Flat progress.

NOTEBOOK
War Poet cruised through the race and soon put it to bed when asked for his effort. He failed to score in three outings over hurdles in the winter, but had won his last outing in this sphere and looks a fast-improving performer for his burgeoning stable. He's now due a hike in the handicap, but this was the softest ground he has won on to date and he looks well worth his place in something more valuable now. (op 16-1)
King's Warrior(FR) ◆ attracted some support on this return to Britain following a spell in France and he turned in a promising effort. He couldn't quicken like the winner, but was a clear second-best and clearly has races in him. (tchd 9-1)
Little Rocky, solid in the betting for his comeback, needs this sort of ground and ran a nice race in defeat. He ought to come on nicely. (op 11-2)
High Jinx(IRE) won his maiden over C&D last year and was very well backed for his return. The top weight didn't seem too happy once asked to close up, however, and ultimately looked to need the run. (op 5-2)
Northside Prince(IRE) Official explanation: trainer said gelding was unsuited by the soft ground

1655 FINE & COUNTRY - BAWTRYS PREMIER AGENT MAIDEN STKS — 1m 4f
7:40 (7:41) (Class 5) 3-Y-O+ **£2,911** (£866; £432; £216) **Stalls** Low

Form RPR

5 1 **Suraj**[10] 1456 3-8-7 0 .... HayleyTurner 4 90+
(Michael Bell) *in tch: rdn and briefly outpcd over 3f out: hdwy to ld over 1f out: sn clr: easily* **1/1**[1]

04- 2 11 **Queen's Estate (GER)**[187] 7060 3-8-7 0 .... SilvestreDeSousa 10 72
(Mark Johnston) *led: rdn over 3f out: hdd over 1f out: sn no match wnr* **10/1**

42 3 1 ¼ **Torero**[21] 1223 3-8-7 0 .... PaulHanagan 7 70
(Kevin Ryan) *racd keenly in midfield: pushed along and outpcd over 3f out: kpt on fr over 1f out* **7/1**

02 4 8 **Falkland (IRE)**[12] 1415 3-8-7 0 ....(p) RobertHavlin 9 58
(John Gosden) *trckd ldr: chal on bit 3f out: rdn 2f out: wknd qckly appr fnl f* **4/1**[2]

5 1 ¼ **Omid**[162] 4-9-12 0 ....(t) LukeMorris 2 58
(Nicky Vaughan) *hld up: pushed along over 4f out: no imp* **20/1**
00- **6** *nk* **Searing Heat (USA)**[321] 2956 4-9-12 0 .... IanMongan 8 57
(Sir Henry Cecil) *trckd ldrs: pushed along over 3f out: sn wknd* **11/2**[3]
7 2 ¼ **Moonshine Ruby**[19] 6-9-8 0 .... DavidAllan 5 49
(Peter Hiatt) *dwlt: hld up: a in rr* **50/1**
3 **8** 3 ¼ **Faraway Land (USA)**[57] 762 4-9-4 0 .... AdamBeschizza(3) 1 43
(Julia Feilden) *hld up: a in rr* **33/1**
0-0 **9** *24* **Red Alex**[18] 1270 3-8-7 0 .... PaulMulrennan 3
(James Given) *midfield: wknd over 3f out: eased* **50/1**

2m 43.65s (8.75) **Going Correction** +0.60s/f (Yiel)
WFA 3 from 4yo 20lb 4 from 6yo 1lb **9** Ran SP% **118.6**
Speed ratings (Par 103): **94,86,85,80,79 79,77,75,59**
toteswingers:1&2:£3.90, 2&3:£4.40, 1&3:£3.20 CSF £12.61 TOTE £2.20: £1.30, £2.70, £2.40; EX 12.70.
Owner Lady Bamford **Bred** Lady Bamford **Trained** Newmarket, Suffolk

FOCUS
A commanding win for the promising Suraj, but there was questionable depth to this race. The form is rated loosely around the third.
Queen's Estate(GER) ◆ Official explanation: jockey said colt hung badly right
Torero Official explanation: jockey said gelding hung badly right

1656 INNOVATION AND COCO ICE OF BAWTRY FILLIES' H'CAP 1m 2f 60y
8:10 (8:10) (Class 4) (0-85,85) 4-Y-0+ **£5,175** (£1,540; £769; £384) **Stalls** Low

Form RPR
116- **1** **Dragonera**[198] 6822 4-9-5 **83** .... PaulHanagan 7 92
(Ed Dunlop) *in tch: rdn to chal over 2f out: led appr fnl f: drvn and kpt on* **9/1**
310- **2** *nk* **Battery Power**[202] 6729 4-8-10 **74** .... SilvestreDeSousa 1 82+
(Mark H Tompkins) *hld up in rr: rdn over 3f out: stl only 5th over 1f out: r.o strly ins fnl f: jst failed* **12/1**
040- **3** 4 ½ **Lady Chaparral**[189] 7022 5-9-5 **83** .... PaulMulrennan 6 83
(Michael Dods) *led: rdn whn hdd appr fnl f: wknd fnl 100yds* **9/2**[3]
61-1 **4** 2 ¼ **Night And Dance (IRE)**[8] 1491 4-9-4 **82** .... JohnFahy 4 78
(Clive Cox) *hld up in tch: rdn and sme hdwy over 2f out: one pce over 1f out* **5/2**[1]
2042 **5** 1 ¾ **Maven**[10] 1439 4-8-7 **71** .... DavidAllan 2 63
(Tim Easterby) *midfield: rdn over 3f out: sn no imp* **11/2**
-121 **6** *6* **Sail Home**[64] 689 5-8-4 **71** .... AdamBeschizza(3) 8 52
(Julia Feilden) *trckd ldrs: rdn over 3f out: sn wknd* **16/1**
60-1 **7** 4 ½ **Miss Aix**[19] 1258 4-9-7 **85** .... HayleyTurner 5 57
(Michael Bell) *trckd ldr: rdn over 4f out: sn wknd* **11/4**[2]

2m 17.85s (8.45) **Going Correction** +0.60s/f (Yiel) **7** Ran SP% **112.4**
Speed ratings (Par 102): **90,89,86,84,82 78,74**
toteswingers:1&2:£17.20, 2&3:£5.30, 1&3:£5.90 CSF £101.00 CT £547.68 TOTE £9.30: £5.10, £3.00; EX 154.90.
Owner J Weatherby, Champneys **Bred** Preston Lodge Stud **Trained** Newmarket, Suffolk

FOCUS
A fair fillies' handicap, run at an average pace. They came stands' side again in the home straight and the first pair were clear at the finish. The winner resumed last year's progress but the time was slow compared with the earlier handicap.
Night And Dance(IRE) Official explanation: trainer's rep said filly was unsuited by the soft ground
Miss Aix Official explanation: jockey said filly never picked up when asked to quicken
T/Jkpt: Not won. T/Plt: £431.00 to a £1 stake. Pool of £80,485.88 - 136.32 winning tickets. T/Qpdt: £44.70 to a £1 stake. Pool of £7,565.52 - 125.15 winning tickets. AS

HAYDOCK (L-H)
Saturday, April 28

OFFICIAL GOING: Soft (6.7)
All races on inner home straight and distances on round course reduced by 5yds.
Wind: Fresh, half-behind Weather: Overcast

1657 CONCOURSE PHARMACY 25TH ANNIVERSARY H'CAP 1m 2f 95y
5:55 (5:57) (Class 4) (0-80,80) 4-Y-0+ **£5,175** (£1,540; £769; £384) **Stalls** High

Form RPR
504- **1** **The Galloping Shoe**[168] 7215 7-8-10 **69** .... JimCrowley 10 86
(Alistair Whillans) *stdd s: hld up in rr: swtchd rt and hdwy 2f out: r.o and edgd lft ins fnl f: led towards fin* **7/1**[3]
01-1 **2** *hd* **Media Hype**[18] 1275 5-9-7 **80** .... PhillipMakin 7 97+
(Mrs K Burke) *hld up: smooth hdwy over 3f out: led wl over 1f out: sn hung lft: pressed wl ins fnl f: hdd towards fin* **7/4**[1]
256- **3** 1 ½ **Number Theory**[201] 6749 4-9-3 **76** .... RussKennemore 4 90
(John Holt) *hld up: hdwy over 3f out: swtchd lft to chse ldrs and rdn over 2f out: chalng fr over 1f out carried lft ins fnl f: kpt on same pce fnl 75yds* **7/1**[3]
5213 **4** *3* **Knowe Head (NZ)**[28] 1133 5-9-0 **73** .... LiamJones 1 81
(James Unett) *towards rr: hdwy into midfield 6f out: effrt to chse ldrs wl over 1f out: fdd fnl 75yds* **10/1**
-002 **5** 1 ½ **Amazing Blue Sky**[7] 1525 6-8-13 **72** .... JamesSullivan 9 77
(Ruth Carr) *sn led: rdn and hdd over 2f out: outpcd over 1f out: kpt on ins fnl f but no imp* **5/1**[2]
450- **6** *8* **Fourth Generation (IRE)**[334] 2544 5-9-1 **74** .... RobertWinston 8 64
(Alan Swinbank) *racd wd on bk st: prom: led over 2f out: sn rdn: hdd wl over 1f out: sn wknd: eased whn btn ins fnl f* **20/1**
3220 **7** *8* **Follow The Flag (IRE)**[7] 1513 8-8-6 **72** ....(be) NoraLooby(7) 3 47
(Alan McCabe) *racd keenly: sn dropped in midfield: rdn over 3f out: wknd over 2f out* **20/1**
00-0 **8** ¾ **Oratory (IRE)**[27] 1156 6-9-3 **76** .... PatCosgrave 11 50
(Keith Dalgleish) *racd wd on bk st: chsd ldrs: rdn over 2f out: wknd wl over 1f out* **12/1**
531- **9** *2* **One Pursuit (IRE)**[279] 4364 4-9-3 **76** .... AdrianNicholls 6 46
(David Nicholls) *racd keenly: led early: prom: pushed along over 3f out: wknd over 2f out* **16/1**
60-6 **10** *5* **Magic Echo**[14] 1382 8-8-8 **67** .... TomEaves 2 27
(George Foster) *in tch: chsd ldrs 6f out: lost pl 4f out: bhd over 2f out* **66/1**
112- **11** *1* **Tenhoo**[323] 2892 6-8-12 **76** .... NathanAllison(5) 5 34
(Eric Alston) *hld up: u.p over 3f out: wl bhd fnl 2f* **16/1**

2m 15.81s (0.31) **Going Correction** +0.125s/f (Good) **11** Ran SP% **117.6**
Speed ratings (Par 105): **105,104,103,101,100 93,87,86,85,81 80**
toteswingers:1&2:£4.70, 2&3:£5.30, 1&3:£9.70 CSF £19.13 CT £91.91 TOTE £9.80: £2.60, £1.40, £2.10; EX 32.40 Trifecta £274.80 Pool: £601.78 - 1.62 winning units..
Owner R Cabrey W Orr C Spark **Bred** Wood Hall Stud Limited **Trained** Newmill-On-Slitrig, Borders
■ Stewards' Enquiry : Phillip Makin three-day ban: careless riding (May 12, 14-15)

FOCUS
All races took place on the inner home straight, meaning distances beyond 5f were reduced by 5 yards. The ground was not riding as bad as it looked. A fair handicap in which the gallop was a reasonable one in the conditions. The winner was on a good mark and this was still 10lb off his best.

1658 MADNESS IN CONCERT ON 6TH JULY H'CAP 5f
6:25 (6:28) (Class 4) (0-85,80) 3-Y-0 **£5,175** (£1,540; £769; £384) **Stalls** Centre

Form RPR
0-01 **1** **Rusty Rocket (IRE)**[17] 1317 3-9-2 **75** .... JoeFanning 4 83
(Paul Green) *chsd ldr: rdn over 2f out: r.o ins fnl f to ld towards fin* **7/1**
612- **2** *nk* **Master Bond**[175] 7294 3-9-3 **76** .... TomEaves 3 83
(Bryan Smart) *led: rdn and edgd rt fractionally over 1f out: worn down towards fin* **3/1**[2]
435- **3** 1 ½ **Chooseday (IRE)**[197] 6827 3-9-7 **80** .... PhillipMakin 9 82
(Kevin Ryan) *sluggish s: in rr: hung lft fr 2f out: hdwy to chse ldrs over 1f out: kpt on ins fnl f but nt pce of front pair* **4/1**[3]
4-30 **4** *1* **Beau Mistral (IRE)**[17] 1322 3-8-6 **70** .... MatthewLawson(5) 5 68
(Paul Green) *chsd ldrs: rdn and nt qckn over 1f out: kpt on same pce ins fnl f* **14/1**
15-0 **5** ½ **Indian Tinker**[10] 1457 3-9-7 **80** .... JimCrowley 7 77
(Robert Cowell) *hld up: rdn 2f out: effrt to chse ldrs and hung lft over 1f out: one pce wl ins fnl f* **10/1**
00-6 **6** *5* **Kyanight (IRE)**[8] 1493 3-8-12 **71** .... PatCosgrave 1 50
(Clive Cox) *s.i.s: in tch: rdn over 1f out: sn wknd* **14/1**
05-5 **7** ¾ **Mitchum**[18] 1271 3-9-0 **78** .... DeanHeslop(5) 6 54
(David Barron) *chsd ldrs: rdn 2f out: wknd over 1f out* **9/4**[1]

1m 3.48s (2.68) **Going Correction** +0.575s/f (Yiel) **7** Ran SP% **110.7**
Speed ratings (Par 100): **101,100,98,96,95 87,86**
toteswingers:1&2:£4.10, 2&3:£3.40, 1&3:£4.00 CSF £26.41 CT £90.58 TOTE £6.40: £2.60, £2.60; EX 21.70 Trifecta £50.80 Pool: £578.74 - 8.43 winning units..
Owner Seven Stars Racing **Bred** Mike Hyde **Trained** Lydiate, Merseyside

FOCUS
A fair handicap run but, although the gallop was a decent one, the winner and runner-up filled the first two places throughout. The winner continued his progress and the fourth helps set the level.
Chooseday(IRE) Official explanation: jockey said gelding hung left-handed

1659 HAYDOCK PARK RAILS AND RING BOOKMAKERS H'CAP 1m
6:55 (6:55) (Class 5) (0-70,68) 4-Y-0+ **£2,911** (£866; £432; £216) **Stalls** Low

Form RPR
-431 **1** **Thackeray**[18] 1276 5-9-1 **62** .... KellyHarrison 8 75
(Chris Fairhurst) *hld up in rr: rdn and hdwy 2f out: edgd lft and r.o to ld wl ins fnl f: wl on top at fin* **7/1**
2-40 **2** *2* **Hayek**[7] 1520 5-8-9 **61** ....(b) AdamCarter(5) 9 70
(Tim Easterby) *s.i.s: hld up: impr into midfield after 2f: wnt 2nd over 2f out: led wl over 1f out: edgd lft ins fnl f: sn hdd: no ex towards fin* **16/1**
02-3 **3** *nk* **Tilsworth Glenboy**[19] 1262 5-9-7 **68** .... FrederikTylicki 13 76
(J R Jenkins) *hld up: hdwy over 2f out: rdn over 1f out: unable to go w wnr ins fnl f: styd on towards fin* **9/2**[2]
060- **4** 3 ½ **Spavento (IRE)**[182] 7159 6-8-10 **57** .... PatCosgrave 11 57
(Eric Alston) *broke wl: led early: chsd ldrs: outpcd over 3f out: rallied to chse ldrs again over 1f out: one pce fnl 100yds* **12/1**
00-0 **5** *shd* **Indian Giver**[18] 1283 4-8-2 **54** .... RaulDaSilva(5) 10 54
(Hugh McWilliams) *hld up: pushed along 4f out: effrt over 2f out: no imp on ldrs: styd on towards fin* **50/1**
-300 **6** *hd* **Dr Red Eye**[15] 1358 4-9-7 **68** .... RobertWinston 6 67
(Scott Dixon) *chsd ldrs: rdn over 1f out: kpt on same pce fr over 1f out* **5/1**[3]
1144 **7** ¾ **Dashing Eddie (IRE)**[86] 384 4-9-6 **67** ....(p) PhillipMakin 5 65
(Kevin Ryan) *chsd ldrs: rdn over 2f out: kpt on same pce fr over 1f out* **16/1**
-360 **8** 3 ¾ **Tanforan**[43] 929 10-8-7 **54** .... JoeFanning 1 43
(Brian Baugh) *hld up: sme hdwy 3f out: no imp on ldrs: wl btn wl ins fnl f* **22/1**
3041 **9** 1 ¼ **Bold Marc (IRE)**[4] 1578 10-9-0 **68** .... ConorHarrison(7) 14 54
(Mrs K Burke) *w ldr setting str gallop: led over 3f out: hdd wl over 1f out: wknd appr fnl f* **7/2**[1]
00-0 **10** 1 ¼ **Talent Scout (IRE)**[7] 1527 6-9-4 **65** .... JamesSullivan 12 48
(Tim Walford) *hld up early: chsd ldrs over 4f out: wknd 2f out* **40/1**
2616 **11** *4* **McCool Bannanas**[14] 1391 4-9-7 **68** .... LiamJones 4 42
(James Unett) *in rr: pushed along over 2f out: nvr a threat* **16/1**
5542 **12** *6* **Striker Torres (IRE)**[18] 1276 6-9-7 **68** ....(b[1]) TomEaves 2 28
(Ian McInnes) *midfield: pushed along over 3f out: sn wknd* **14/1**
50-0 **13** 3 ¼ **Cara's Request (AUS)**[18] 1269 7-9-6 **67** .... AdrianNicholls 7 20
(David Nicholls) *sn led at str gallop: hdd over 3f out: wknd over 2f out* **16/1**

1m 45.8s (2.10) **Going Correction** +0.45s/f (Yiel) **13** Ran SP% **116.2**
Speed ratings (Par 103): **103,101,100,97,97 96,96,92,91,89 85,79,76**
toteswingers:1&2:£14.80, 2&3:£13.10, 1&3:£7.60 CSF £108.58 CT £560.69 TOTE £7.30: £2.10, £5.10, £1.80; EX 129.80 Trifecta £453.90 Part won. Pool: £613.39 - 0.41 winning units..
Owner Mrs C A Arnold **Bred** Mrs R D Peacock **Trained** Middleham Moor, N Yorks

FOCUS
Exposed performers in a modest handicap. The gallop was soon sound and the two forcing the pace not surprisingly didn't get home. Another step up from the winner with the second close to his best.

1660 MAYOR'S APPEAL FOR DEMENTIA IN ST HELENS MAIDEN FILLIES' STKS 1m
7:25 (7:27) (Class 5) 3-Y-0+ **£2,911** (£866; £432; £216) **Stalls** Low

Form RPR
234- **1** **Magic Destiny**[225] 6110 3-9-0 70 .... MartinHarley 5 70
(Mrs K Burke) *hld up travelling wl: hdwy and brought to nr-side rail 3f out: led 2f out: edgd lft ins fnl f: r.o and a in control* **8/15**[1]
2 ¾ **Emily Carr (IRE)** 3-9-0 0 .... JoeFanning 7 68
(Mark Johnston) *racd keenly: prom: chsd ldr after 2f: led over 2f out: sn rdn and hdd: nt qckn over 1f out: kpt on ins fnl f but a hld* **11/4**[2]
645/ **3** *10* **Hold The Star**[829] 235 6-9-9 50 .... AnnStokell(5) 2 49
(Ann Stokell) *racd keenly: hld up early: impr to chse ldrs 5f out: outpcd and no ch fr over 1f out* **100/1**
0- **4** *7* **Last Supper**[213] 6449 3-9-0 0 .... TomEaves 3 29
(James Bethell) *s.i.s: hdwy to ld after nrly 1f: veered lft and hdd wl over 2f out: wknd over 1f out* **25/1**
306- **5** *8* **Landaho**[215] 6413 3-8-13 47 ow2 .... GaryBartley(3) 6 13
(Hugh McWilliams) *led for nrly 1f: remained handy: rdn and wknd over 2f out* **100/1**

6 1 ½ **Light From Hades** 3-9-0 0 .... JamesSullivan 4
(Tim Easterby) *racd keenly: hld up: toiling fnl 2f* **7/1**[3]

300- 7 3 **Goal Hanger**[248] 5374 3-8-9 62 .... RaulDaSilva(5) 1
(William Kinsey) *s.i.s: hld up: rdn 3f out: sn btn* **16/1**

1m 48.33s (4.63) **Going Correction** +0.45s/f (Yiel) 7 Ran SP% **116.1**
WFA 3 from 6yo 14lb
Speed ratings (Par 100): **90,89,79,72,64 62,59**
toteswingers:1&2:£1.20, 2&3:£17.90, 1&3:£4.70 CSF £2.36 TOTE £1.60: £1.10, £2.20; EX 2.90.
Owner Ray Bailey **Bred** Ray Bailey **Trained** Middleham Moor, N Yorks

FOCUS
Fair form from the principals but an uncompetitive maiden in which the first two pulled clear of the 50-rated third. It's doubtful the winner had to improve on her 2yo form. The gallop was soon fair.

1661 STEPS 21ST JULY H'CAP 1m
7:55 (7:56) (Class 5) (0-75,74) 3-Y-O **£2,911** (£866; £432; £216) **Stalls** Low

Form RPR

501- 1 **Twelve Strings (IRE)**[194] 6911 3-9-3 70 .... KirstyMilczarek 6 78
(Luca Cumani) *midfield: hdwy 3f out: rdn to ld narrowly wl over 1f out: gamely doing enough towards fin* **4/1**[2]

04-6 2 hd **Take Two**[27] 1155 3-8-12 65 .... RussKennemore 1 72
(John O'Shea) *s.i.s: hld up in rr: rdn and hdwy over 2f out: str chal wl ins fnl f: r.o* **17/2**

00-4 3 ½ **Chester Aristocrat**[27] 1155 3-9-1 68 .... PatCosgrave 10 74
(Eric Alston) *hld up: hdwy 2f out: str chal and upsides ins fnl f: nt qckn towards fin* **11/2**

1 4 1 ½ **Warfare**[57] 770 3-9-7 74 .... PhillipMakin 2 77+
(Kevin Ryan) *chsd ldrs: rdn and ev ch over 1f out: styd on same pce ins fnl f* **5/1**[3]

30-0 5 3 ¾ **It's A Privilege**[17] 1322 3-9-7 74 .... JimCrowley 8 68
(Ralph Beckett) *hld up: pushed along over 2f out: effrt over 1f out: no imp on ldrs* **13/2**

22-1 6 2 **Enery (IRE)**[75] 547 3-9-7 74 .... JoeFanning 3 63
(Mark Johnston) *led: rdn 2f out: hdd wl over 1f out: wknd ent fnl f* **7/2**[1]

600- 7 4 ½ **Kieron's Rock (IRE)**[187] 7051 3-8-10 63 .... GrahamLee 5 42
(Jedd O'Keeffe) *racd keenly: chsd ldr tl over 2f out: sn wknd: hung lft whn btn over 1f out* **22/1**

0-10 8 4 **Wolf Spirit (IRE)**[10] 1440 3-9-0 67 .... JamesSullivan 9 37
(Ruth Carr) *chsd ldrs: lost pl over 3f out: wl bhd over 1f out* **13/2**

1m 48.88s (5.18) **Going Correction** +0.45s/f (Yiel) 8 Ran SP% **115.8**
Speed ratings (Par 98): **88,87,87,85,82 80,75,71**
CSF £37.98 CT £189.13 TOTE £5.60: £2.00, £3.10, £1.50; EX 45.10 Trifecta £428.80 Part won. Pool: £579.58 - 0.51 winning units..
Owner S Stuckey **Bred** John & Anne-Marie O'Connor **Trained** Newmarket, Suffolk

FOCUS
A couple of unexposed sorts in a fair handicap. There are one or two doubts over the form, which looks ordinary for the grade. The field came to the stands' side early in the straight and, although the gallop was a steady one, this race could throw up a few winners.

1662 TURFTV.CO.UK MAIDEN STKS 1m 3f 200y
8:25 (8:25) (Class 5) 3-Y-O+ **£2,911** (£866; £432; £216) **Stalls** Centre

Form RPR

42-0 1 **Sir Graham Wade (IRE)**[28] 1132 3-8-8 79 .... JoeFanning 8 77
(Mark Johnston) *prom after 2f: lost pl 3f out: rallied over 1f out: led narrowly wl ins fnl f: r.o* **7/4**[2]

2 nk **Right To Rule (IRE)** 3-8-8 0 .... LiamJones 2 76
(William Haggas) *in tch: swtchd lft and effrt over 2f out: led briefly ins fnl f: r.o and continued to chal: hld fnl strides* **7/2**[3]

22 3 1 **Gabrial The Hero (USA)**[71] 595 3-8-8 0 .... JimCrowley 4 74
(David Simcock) *led: rdn over 2f out: hdd ins fnl f: styd on same pce towards fin* **6/4**[1]

0/ 4 ½ **Hawkeshead**[686] 2974 5-10-0 0 .... MichaelO'Connell 1 75
(Ian Williams) *hld up: hdwy 4f out: effrt whn hung lft over 1f out: kpt on ins fnl f but nt quite gng pce of ldrs* **16/1**

5 1 ¼ **Regal Swain (IRE)**[133] 4-9-13 0 .... RobertWinston 3 73
(Alan Swinbank) *hld up in tch: clsd over 4f out: rdn over 2f out: ch wl over 1f out: one pce fnl 100yds* **12/1**

0- 6 17 **Kings Apollo**[176] 7257 3-8-5 0 .... SimonPearce(3) 6 44
(Tom Symonds) *hld up in rr: pushed along 4f out: outpcd and lft bhd fnl 2f* **33/1**

000/ 7 22 **Mark Carmers**[637] 4584 5-10-0 40 .... TomEaves 5
(George Foster) *plld hrd: prom: rn wd early on bk st: lost pl 6f out: bhd fnl 5f* **100/1**

000/ 8 9 **Beaux Yeux**[904] 7270 6-9-4 43 .... AnnStokell(5) 7
(Ann Stokell) *racd keenly: sn prom: wknd 4f out* **50/1**

2m 39.31s (5.51) **Going Correction** +0.45s/f (Yiel) 8 Ran SP% **118.1**
WFA 3 from 4yo 20lb 4 from 5yo+ 1lb
Speed ratings (Par 103): **100,99,99,98,97 86,71,65**
toteswingers:1&2:£2.10, 2&3:£1.90, 1&3:£1.60 CSF £8.72 TOTE £2.70: £1.10, £1.20, £1.10; EX 8.30 Trifecta £18.90 Pool: £596.88 - 23.28 winning units..
Owner Paul Dean **Bred** P D Savill **Trained** Middleham Moor, N Yorks

FOCUS
Last year's renewal threw up subsequent King George winner Nathaniel and this race has also thrown up smart sorts in Spice Route (2007) and Bay Story (2005) but five of these finished in close proximity on the back of a modest gallop and the bare form of this is no better than fair. The winner did not need to match his 2yo best.
T/Plt: £40.80 to a £1 stake. Pool of £69439.13 - 1241.90 winning tickets. T/Qpdt: £7.10 to a £1 stake. Pool of £5199.30 - 540.95 winning tickets. DO

1352 LEICESTER (R-H)
Saturday, April 28
1663 Meeting Abandoned - waterlogged

1474 RIPON (R-H)
Saturday, April 28

OFFICIAL GOING: Soft (heavy in places; 6.2)
Rail on bend from 8f to home straight moved out 4m adding 12yds to races on round course.
Wind: fresh, half-against Weather: Overcast

1670 BETFRED GOALS GALORE H'CAP 1m
2:20 (2:22) (Class 3) (0-90,90) 4-Y-O+
£8,092 (£2,423; £1,211; £605; £302; £152) **Stalls** Low

Form RPR

0-63 1 **Memory Cloth**[11] 1431 5-8-13 82 .... KierenFallon 4 97
(Brian Ellison) *trckd ldrs: led over 2f out: rdn and edgd rt over 1f out: styd on strly fnl f* **13/2**[1]

01-0 2 3 ¼ **Silvery Moon (IRE)**[27] 1156 5-8-13 82 .... DavidAllan 10 89
(Tim Easterby) *t.k.h early: trckd ldrs: effrt and chsd wnr over 1f out: kpt on fnl f: nt pce to chal* **9/1**

4-60 3 2 ¼ **Moheebb (IRE)**[19] 1249 8-8-7 76 ....(v[1]) LukeMorris 5 78
(Ruth Carr) *in tch: rdn over 2f out: effrt over 1f out: kpt on fnl f: no imp* **12/1**

0-00 4 1 ½ **Jonny Lesters Hair (IRE)**[14] 1381 7-8-13 82 .... DuranFentiman 8 81
(Tim Easterby) *led to over 2f out: rdn and nt qckn over 1f out* **8/1**[3]

5403 5 1 **Dubai Dynamo**[7] 1522 7-9-5 88 .... PJMcDonald 3 84+
(Ruth Carr) *hld up in tch: pushed along whn n.m.r briefly over 2f out: effrt over 1f out: kpt on: nvr able to chal* **8/1**[3]

60-6 6 nk **Toto Skyllachy**[118] 5 7-8-12 81 .... DanielTudhope 16 77+
(David O'Meara) *in tch on outside: effrt over 2f out: no ex appr fnl f* **11/1**

40-1 7 nk **The Osteopath (IRE)**[7] 1520 9-8-9 78 .... PaulMulrennan 6 73+
(John Davies) *hld up on ins: effrt whn no room fr over 2f out: nt rcvr* **7/1**[2]

-160 8 2 **Amazing Star (IRE)**[4] 1587 7-8-11 80 .... GrahamGibbons 15 70+
(Declan Carroll) *s.i.s: bhd: effrt whn nt clr run 2f out: kpt on: nvr able to chal* **20/1**

36-0 9 1 ¼ **Silenceofthewind (USA)**[38] 987 5-8-10 79 .... MartinHarley 12 66
(Mrs K Burke) *plld hrd in midfield: rdn over 3f out: outpcd fnl 2f* **25/1**

164- 10 2 ¾ **The Mellor Fella**[292] 3904 4-8-13 82 .... PaulHanagan 1 63
(Richard Fahey) *in tch: pushed along 3f out: wknd over 1f out* **20/1**

3- 11 hd **Deire Na Sli (IRE)**[195] 6899 4-9-7 90 .... JamesDoyle 7 71
(Martyn Meade) *bhd: drvn along fr 3f out: nvr on terms* **25/1**

005- 12 1 ¾ **Daring Dream (GER)**[182] 7161 7-8-7 76 .... JamesSullivan 2 53
(Jim Goldie) *hld up ins: rdn over 3f out: btn fnl 2f* **40/1**

020- 13 ¾ **Pass Muster**[36] 6708 5-9-0 83 .... TomEaves 9 58
(Ollie Pears) *hld up: drvn and outpcd over 2f out: sn btn* **33/1**

100- 14 5 **City Of The Kings (IRE)**[204] 6672 7-9-4 87 .... GrahamLee 17 50
(Ollie Pears) *s.i.s: bhd: rdn over 3f out: nvr on terms* **33/1**

0-01 15 ½ **Solar Spirit (IRE)**[17] 1293 7-8-11 80 .... RobertWinston 13 42
(Tracy Waggott) *t.k.h: hld up on outside: hdwy over 2f out: edgd rt and wknd over 1f out* **18/1**

20-6 16 47 **Dolphin Rock**[19] 1249 5-9-0 83 .... LeeNewman 11
(David Barron) *hld up: rdn 3f out: sn wknd: t.o* **7/1**[2]

550- 17 1 ½ **Paramour**[218] 6302 5-9-1 84 .... AdrianNicholls 14
(David Nicholls) *cl up tl rdn and wknd over 2f out* **16/1**

1m 47.26s (5.86) **Going Correction** +0.925s/f (Soft) 17 Ran SP% **123.3**
Speed ratings (Par 107): **107,103,101,100,99 98,98,96,95,92 92,90,89,84,84 37,35**
Tote Swingers: 1&2 £9.70, 1&3 £31.10, 2&3 £40.00 CSF £57.74 CT £702.65 TOTE £7.10: £2.20, £2.80, £4.20, £2.40; EX 70.50 Trifecta £698.50 Part won. Pool of £943.97 - 0.30 winning units..
Owner Racing Management & Training Ltd **Bred** Darley **Trained** Norton, N Yorks

FOCUS
Quite a useful handicap run at a reasonable gallop in the conditions but as so often round here few got into contention from behind. The winner was on a good mark on his best French form.

NOTEBOOK
Memory Cloth ◆ might have been an uneasy favourite and tricky to load but once he moved to the front with around 2f to run his supporters had little cause to worry and he passed the post leaving the impression he could have pulled out a deal more if needed. A winner on soft when trained in France, these conditions clearly suit him well and he'll stay further if given the chance. (op 9-2)
Silvery Moon(IRE) has a noticeably round action and perhaps not coincidentally relishes this sort of ground. Never far away, he saw his race out well and was unfortunate to bump into one so well handicapped on the day as the winner. (op 10-1)
Moheebb(IRE) isn't easy to predict at the best of times and hadn't shown much this season, so it's hard to know if he'll build on this more encouraging effort tried in a visor instead of his usual blinkers. He didn't travel through the race like a well-handicapped horse, only getting third near the line and not shaping as well as some others. (op 14-1 tchd 16-1)
Jonny Lesters Hair(IRE), who went to post very early, had been running well this season and has a good record here so it wasn't surprising that ran well making the running as usual. It might be that he lacks the pace to be fully effective at a bare 1m these days, even under conditions as testing as these.
Dubai Dynamo travelled well until the winner went on but didn't find quite what was expected. (op 17-2)
Toto Skyllachy ◆ looked sure to play a part in the finish when looming upsides the winner 2f out but left the impression this first run since New Year's Day was needed. He probably needed this and is worth looking out for next time. (op 14-1 tchd 10-1)
The Osteopath(IRE) ◆ was unlucky not to finish much closer. He never got a run kept to the inside and wasn't given a hard time, passing the post virtually on the bridle. He looks well handicapped still and can gain consolation before long so long as the ground doesn't dry up. Official explanation: jockey said gelding was denied a clear run (op 8-1)
Amazing Star(IRE) left the impression he's still in form, staying on despite a troubled run having been set a lot to do in a higher grade than usual.
Dolphin Rock is normally reliable and clearly wasn't right, eased right off. Official explanation: trainer had no explanation for the poor form shown (op 8-1)

1671 STOWE FAMILY LAW LLP MAIDEN AUCTION FILLIES' STKS 5f
2:55 (2:56) (Class 5) 2-Y-O **£2,911** (£866; £432; £216) **Stalls** Low

Form RPR

1 **Lucies Diamond (IRE)** 2-8-8 0 .... TomEaves 3 67
(Michael Dods) *hld up in tch: hdwy and ev ch ins fnl f: kpt on to ld cl home* **16/1**

2 shd **Throwing Roses** 2-8-4 0 .... JamesSullivan 1 63
(Ollie Pears) *w ldrs: rdn 2f out: led ins fnl f: kpt on: hdd cl home* **25/1**

3 ½ **Sylvia Pankhurst (IRE)** 2-8-4 0 .... AdrianNicholls 4 61
(David C Griffiths) *sn outpcd: hdwy 1/2-way: rdn and kpt on wl fnl f: nrst fin* **22/1**

	4	1	**La Sylphe** 2-8-4 0 LeeNewman 5	57
			(David Barron) *slt ld tl edgd lft and hdd ins fnl f: kpt on same pce* **7/1**3	
3	5	1 3/4	**Twilight Pearl**10 1435 2-8-6 0 DavidAllan 7	53
			(Tim Easterby) *disp ld to over 1f out: sn rdn: no ex ins fnl f* **5/2**2	
4	6	*shd*	**Someone's Darling**21 1218 2-8-4 0 PaulHanagan 8	51+
			(Jim Goldie) *w ldrs: rdn 1/2-way: nt qckn fnl f* **2/1**1	
	7	8	**Starbotton** 2-8-8 0 GrahamGibbons 10	26
			(James Bethell) *s.i.s: bhd and detached: sme late hdwy: nvr on terms* **10/1**	
	8	1	**Another Ponty** 2-8-10 0 DuranFentiman 9	24
			(Tim Easterby) *bhd and rn green: hdwy 1/2-way: wknd over 1f out* **18/1**	
	9	7	**Lady Of Seville (IRE)** 2-8-10 0 MickyFenton 6	
			(Tom Tate) *cl up: rn green and outpcd after 2f: hung lft and sn struggling* **7/1**3	

1m 6.25s (5.55) **Going Correction** +0.925s/f (Soft) **9** Ran SP% **115.3**
Speed ratings (Par 89): **92,91,91,89,86 86,73,72,60**
Tote Swingers: 1&2 £30.30, 1&3 £17.10, 2&3 £21.50 CSF £341.38 TOTE £12.10: £2.80, £6.10, £4.50; EX 206.10.
Owner Business Development Consultants Limited **Bred** Chris Glynn **Trained** Denton, Co Durham

FOCUS
The stalls unusually were on the far rail. A maiden auction in which there was very little between most of the runners at any point despite varying degrees of inexperience and almost certainly very modest form. The time was slow too.

NOTEBOOK
Lucies Diamond(IRE), a cheap buy with winners at a variety of trips in her pedigree, travelled well in behind and looked the most likely winner from some way out so long as she got a clear run only to make harder work of it than it seemed. She might be open to progress on better ground, but doesn't appeal as likely to follow up in novice company. (tchd 20-1)
Throwing Roses, who is out of a mare that won at 1m4f, looks nothing if not game, always in the front rank and only just run out of it having finally nosed in front briefly late on. The soft ground might have helped her here. (op 16-1)
Sylvia Pankhurst(IRE) comes from a yard not associated with juvenile runners but might have made a winning debut with another few yards to travel having taken time to realise what was required. She didn't get a clear run late on, either, and is entitled to improve. (op 14-1 tchd 25-1)
La Sylphe shaped quite well after taking time to settle but looked green off the bridle, drifting left and taking several others with her. Her dam was a winner on Fibresand and she'd be worth a second look in a similar event next time with this experience behind her if taken to Southwell. (tchd 13-2 and 15-2)
Twilight Pearl was hampered late on but was slightly disappointing given that experience usually counts for a great deal under these conditions. (op 7-2)
Someone's Darling was hampered late on but like Twilight Pearl was slightly disappointing given that experience usually counts for a great deal under these conditions. (tchd 15-8 and 9-4)
Lady Of Seville(IRE), who is out of a half-sister to the good sprinter Captain Rio, might have been affected by getting squeezed out after the field had gone 2f as she dropped away and tended to hang to her left. Official explanation: jockey said filly hung left-handed (op 6-1 tchd 11-2 and 15-2)

1672 BETFRED "THE BONUS KING" H'CAP 2m
3:30 (3:30) (Class 2) (0-105,103) 4-Y-0+

£12,450 (£3,728; £1,864; £932; £466; £234) **Stalls** Low

Form				RPR
11-2	1		**Gulf Of Naples (IRE)**21 1214 4-9-3 **98** SilvestreDeSousa 8	108+
			(Mark Johnston) *mde virtually all: drvn over 3f out: clr over 1f out: readily* **8/11**1	
2223	2	5	**Halla San**21 1214 10-8-8 **85** PaulHanagan 6	86
			(Richard Fahey) *chsd ldrs: edgd rt over 1f out: kpt on: no imp* **7/1**3	
-000	3	1 1/2	**Montaff**21 1214 6-9-6 **97** SamHitchcott 1	96
			(Mick Channon) *hld up: effrt over 4f out: hdwy over 2f out: nt clr run and swtchd lft over 1f out: kpt on same pce* **4/1**2	
45-0	4	3 1/4	**Address Unknown**17 1318 5-9-6 **97** StevieDonohoe 5	92
			(Ian Williams) *chsd ldrs: outpcd over 3f out: kpt on ins fnl f* **22/1**	
400-	5	*nk*	**My Arch**112 6690 10-8-9 **86** GrahamLee 4	81
			(Ollie Pears) *chsd ldrs: outpcd over 3f out: kpt on ins fnl f* **8/1**	
40-6	6	8	**Hawk Mountain (UAE)**21 1214 7-8-10 **87** MichaelO'Connell 2	72
			(John Quinn) *trckd ldrs: lost pl over 6f out: bhd fnl 3f* **16/1**	

3m 48.51s (16.71) **Going Correction** +0.925s/f (Soft)
WFA 4 from 5yo+ 4lb **6** Ran SP% **111.7**
Speed ratings (Par 109): **95,92,91,90,89 85**
Tote Swingers: 1&2 £1.40, 1&3 £1.70, 2&3 £1.80 CSF £6.47 CT £12.23 TOTE £1.60: £1.10, £3.30; EX 4.10 Trifecta £14.40 Pool: £974.06 - 49.99 winning units..
Owner Sheikh Hamdan Bin Mohammed Al Maktoum **Bred** Stone Ridge Farm **Trained** Middleham Moor, N Yorks

FOCUS
A poor turnout for the prize on offer in what was virtually a re-run of the Queen' Prize at Kempton earlier this month. That form was upheld in a race the winner was able to dictate. He contunued to progress, and the form was rated around the runner-up.

NOTEBOOK
Gulf Of Naples(IRE) ◆ had been put 8lb for finishing clear of the rest when second in the Queen's Prize but this lightly-raced, progressive stayer is only going one way and bar a few brief moments early in the straight when he looked rather uncoordinated, he always had things well under control. Entries in the Yorkshire Cup and Gold Cup suggest he's considered a high-class stayer in the making in which case he'll make plenty of appeal under a 3lb penalty in the Chester Cup next month. (op 10-11)
Halla San ran creditably and is probably capable of ending his long losing run in weaker grade than this now he figures on a more realistic mark, but he's always going to be vulnerable up at this level taking on more progressive types. (op 13-2)
Montaff, who won this race in 2011, showed more than he had been doing in Dubai and in one spin on Polytrack earlier this year but even so he never threatened and looks some way removed right now from the horse that finished second in the Henry II Stakes last year. (op 6-1)
Address Unknown shaped a bit better than the result suggests once again without the headgear he wore in Ireland, looking a danger briefly early in the straight before fading. The trip under these conditions looked too far for him. (op 16-1)
My Arch was a disappointment under conditions he usually relishes. He possibly needed this first run since January. (op 15-2)
Hawk Mountain(UAE) almost certainly needs faster ground than this (op 9-1)

1673 BETFRED BONUS BINGO (S) STKS 1m 1f 170y
4:05 (4:05) (Class 6) 3-4-Y-0 **£2,264** (£673; £336; £168) **Stalls** Low

Form				RPR
-330	1		**Ollon (USA)**26 1172 4-9-7 58 MichaelMetcalfe(3) 3	67
			(Mrs K Burke) *hld up: chsd ldrs 7f out: led over 4f out: clr 2f out: easily* **5/4**1	
00-0	2	7	**Srimenanti**14 1382 4-9-5 50 (p) MickyFenton 2	45
			(Brian Rothwell) *hld up: effrt over 4f out: hung rt and wnt 2nd over 1f out: no ch w wnr* **9/2**3	
000-	3	7	**Red Mercury (IRE)**129 6461 4-9-10 58 GrahamLee 1	36
			(Ollie Pears) *prom: pushed along 7f out: wknd fnl f* **2/1**2	
06-4	4	4 1/2	**April Leyf (IRE)**18 1287 3-7-13 35 DeclanCannon(3) 8	18
			(Mark Brisbourne) *trckd ldrs: chal 4f out: drvn over 2f out: wknd over 1f out* **18/1**	
000-	5	82	**Mrs Awkward**169 7367 3-8-2 20 DuranFentiman 5	
			(Mark Brisbourne) *led: hdd over 4f out: lost pl over 3f out: sn bhd: t.o* **12/1**	

2m 17.92s (12.52) **Going Correction** +0.925s/f (Soft)
WFA 3 from 4yo 17lb **5** Ran SP% **108.9**
Speed ratings (Par 101): **86,80,74,71,5**
CSF £7.10 TOTE £2.20: £1.30, £2.20; EX 5.90.No bid for the winner.
Owner Keep Racing **Bred** William Patterson & James Glenn **Trained** Middleham Moor, N Yorks
■ Stewards' Enquiry : Duran Fentiman one-day ban: careless riding (May 12)

FOCUS
Six non runners rendered this a very uncompetitive seller and it's not form worth dwelling on. The winner is rated in line with last year's form.

1674 BETFRED MOBILE SPORTS CONDITIONS STKS 1m 4f 10y
4:40 (4:42) (Class 3) 4-Y-0+ **£8,092** (£2,423; £1,211; £605) **Stalls** Low

Form				RPR
360-	1		**Dawn Twister (GER)**168 7406 5-8-9 105 LukeMorris 1	101+
			(Lucy Wadham) *sn w ldr: led 7f out: drvn and styd on wl to draw clr over 1f out: eased towards fin* **2/1**2	
154-	2	3	**Troopingthecolour**253 5250 6-8-9 89 (t) TonyHamilton 2	92
			(Steve Gollings) *trckd ldrs: effrt and chal 4f out: edgd lft 2f out: kpt on same pce: no ch w wnr* **6/1**3	
10-1	3	18	**Midsummer Sun**14 1374 4-8-12 102 IanMongan 3	86
			(Sir Henry Cecil) *rrd over and fell at s: t.k.h and led early: hdwy to chal 4f out: hung lft: edgd rt and lost pl over 1f out* **8/11**1	
365/	4	23	**Steuben (GER)**692 2806 6-8-9 100 MickyFenton 5	
			(Barney Curley) *t.k.h: sn led: hdd 7f out: hung rt over 3f out: sn lost pl and bhd: t.o* **18/1**	

2m 49.87s (13.17) **Going Correction** +0.925s/f (Soft)
WFA 4 from 5yo+ 1lb **4** Ran SP% **110.8**
Speed ratings (Par 107): **93,91,79,63**
CSF £12.68 TOTE £2.50; EX 12.20.
Owner Ron Davies **Bred** Siftung Gestut Fahrhof **Trained** Newmarket, Suffolk

FOCUS
A bizarre minor event that featured two German imports making their British debuts and the stallion Monsun providing three of the four runners. The pace was very steady and the form is probably as misleading as it is limited.

NOTEBOOK
Dawn Twister(GER) won easing down but it would be wrong to say he was impressive and connections might feel in hindsight they rather got away with this one under a ride that didn't make the most of his undoubted stamina. Last year's Deutches St Leger third is clearly better than this effort makes him look, but whether he's up to winning in Listed company over here or worth his official rating of 105 remains to be seen. (op 3-1)
Troopingthecolour had a very stiff task at the weights but he's probably as good as he was last season judged on this effort. His proximity to a 105-rated rival shouldn't be taken at face value and the steady pace helped him see out the trip. (tchd 15-2)
Midsummer Sun had won impressively on his reappearance but he had been well beaten the only time he had tried soft ground before, albeit in Group 3 company. He was allowed to take part despite rearing over at the start and perhaps that experience allied to the conditions affected him as he was beaten quickly once the race started in earnest, hanging right. It's been all or nothing with him so far but it bears repeating that he looked on his reappearance as if he has a good race in him. Official explanation: jockey said colt hung left-handed in straight (op 4-6 tchd 4-5)
Steuben(GER), the second of the German imports, was having his first run since 2010 and pulled far too hard before dropping right out. Only his trainer knows what the plan with him is but it almost certainly entails getting his handicap mark down first. (op 12-1 tchd 20-1)

1675 BETFRED MOBILE CASINO H'CAP 5f
5:10 (5:14) (Class 5) (0-75,74) 4-Y-0+ **£2,911** (£866; £432; £216) **Stalls** Low

Form				RPR
40-6	1		**Mandalay King (IRE)**9 1476 7-9-4 **74** JulieBurke(3) 10	83
			(Marjorie Fife) *hld up: pushed along on outside over 2f out: edgd rt and hdwy to ld wl ins fnl f: rdn out* **12/1**	
1126	2	1	**Boucher Garcon (IRE)**7 1516 4-8-6 **64** NeilFarley(5) 6	69
			(Declan Carroll) *led: rdn 2f out: hdd wl ins fnl f: kpt on same pce* **5/2**2	
65-0	3	1	**Boundaries**20 1236 4-9-7 **74** (e1) DuranFentiman 1	76
			(Tim Easterby) *wnt lft s: trckd ldrs: drvn along 1/2-way: kpt on same pce ins fnl f* **13/2**	
20-4	4	3/4	**Just For Mary**9 1480 8-9-2 **69** (be) PadraigBeggy 11	68
			(Daniel Mark Loughnane) *s.i.s: bhd and pushed along: hdwy fnl f: kpt on towards fin* **5/1**3	
1612	5	*nk*	**Shawkantango**7 1516 5-9-5 **72** (v) GrahamLee 7	70
			(Derek Shaw) *trckd ldrs: drvn along fr 1/2-way: nt qckn fnl f* **9/4**1	
6-33	6	1 1/4	**Highland Warrior**9 1480 13-8-13 **66** MickyFenton 3	60+
			(Paul Midgley) *hld up in tch: effrt and rdn over 1f out: sn no imp* **8/1**	
34-5	7	*nk*	**Liberty Ship**18 1290 7-9-2 **69** RoystonFfrench 9	61
			(Mark Buckley) *in tch: rdn and hdwy over 1f out: wknd ins fnl f* **12/1**	

1m 4.86s (4.16) **Going Correction** +0.925s/f (Soft) **7** Ran SP% **115.8**
Speed ratings (Par 103): **103,101,99,98,98 96,95**
Tote Swingers: 1&2 £6.80, 1&3 £7.20, 2&3 £3.00 CSF £43.33 CT £218.69 TOTE £20.50: £7.60, £1.40; EX 73.20.
Owner R W Fife **Bred** Forenaghts Stud And Dermot Cantillon **Trained** Stillington, N Yorks

FOCUS
A run-of-the-mill sprint handicap in which the runners once again raced towards the far rail. The winner was better than ever last year and is rated in line with that.

1676 BETFRED DOUBLE DELIGHT MAIDEN STKS 1m 1f 170y
5:45 (5:47) (Class 5) 3-Y-0 **£2,911** (£866; £432; £216) **Stalls** Low

Form				RPR
223-	1		**Blades Lad**204 6675 3-9-3 74 TonyHamilton 6	75
			(Richard Fahey) *mde all: hrd pressed and rdn fr over 2f out: edgd lft ent fnl f: hld on wl fnl f* **10/3**3	
2-	2	3/4	**Fortieth And Fifth (IRE)**136 7751 3-9-3 0 StevieDonohoe 2	73
			(Michael Bell) *dwlt: sn cl up: hdwy to chal over 2f out: kpt on u.p fnl f: hld nr fin* **7/4**1	
0-	3	15	**Madam Lilibet (IRE)**179 7210 3-8-12 0 PaddyAspell 1	37
			(Sharon Watt) *t.k.h: in tch: rdn and outpcd over 3f out: plugged on fnl 2f: no ch w first two* **50/1**	
	4	1	**Stormbound (IRE)** 3-8-12 0 DuilioDaSilva(5) 4	40
			(Paul Cole) *hld up in tch: effrt on outside 3f out: wknd wl over 1f out* **7/2**	
	5	5	**Ukrainian Princess** 3-8-12 0 IanMongan 7	24
			(Sir Henry Cecil) *dwlt: t.k.h: chsd wnr after 2f: rdn 3f out: wandered and wknd over 2f out* **3/1**2	

0- **6** *11* **Border Hill Jack**[187] 7060 3-9-3 0 LeeNewman 5
(Robin Bastiman) *unruly bef s: missed break: bhd: struggling over 4f out: sn lost tch: t.o* **25/1**

2m 17.35s (11.95) **Going Correction** +0.925s/f (Soft) **6** Ran SP% **112.5**
Speed ratings (Par 98): **89,88,76,75,71 62**
Tote Swingers: 1&2 £1.70, 1&3 £8.10, 2&3 £8.70 CSF £9.66 TOTE £4.60: £2.60, £2.10; EX 7.60.
Owner Crown Select **Bred** David Holgate **Trained** Musley Bank, N Yorks

FOCUS
No more than a fair maiden in all probability, for all that the first two pulled well clear at the end of a steadily-run race. The winner improved 7lb on his 2yo form.
T/Plt: £1,770.10 to a £1 stake. Pool of £83,704.49 - 34.52 winning tickets. T/Qpdt: £73.00 to a £1 stake. Pool of £6,350.85 - 64.30 winning tickets. RY

1644 SANDOWN (R-H)
Saturday, April 28

OFFICIAL GOING: Jumps courses - soft (good to soft in places); flat course - heavy (4.6)
Mixed meeting. The first flight of hurdles in the back straight was omitted due to bad ground.
Wind: fresh, half behind Weather: rain

1677 BET365 GORDON RICHARDS STKS (GROUP 3) 1m 2f 7y
3:45 (3:47) (Class 1) 4-Y-0+
£31,190 (£11,825; £5,918; £2,948; £1,479; £742) Stalls Low

Form RPR
421- **1** **Colombian (IRE)**[175] 7313 4-9-0 115 WilliamBuick 2 117
(John Gosden) *chsd ldr: rdn to chal over 2f out: sustained duel w ldr tl led jst ins fnl f: tired and edgd rt: plugged on gamely u.p* **10/3**[3]

13-6 **2** *3* **Poet**[20] 1245 7-9-0 113 RyanMoore 4 111
(Clive Cox) *led and urged along: rdn and hrd pressed over 2f out: sustained duel w wnr tl hdd jst ins fnl f: swtchd lft and no ex fnl 100yds: fin tired* **15/8**[2]

10-2 **3** *6* **Twice Over**[9] 1471 7-9-0 125 TomQueally 5 99
(Sir Henry Cecil) *pushed along early: chsd ldng pair 7f out: rdn and effrt ent fnl 2f: no prog and btn ent fnl f: tired ins fnl f* **6/4**[1]

4005 **4** *30* **Sos Brillante (CHI)**[11] 1431 7-8-11 76 MarkCoumbe 6 36
(Terry Clement) *stdd s: bhd: lost tch 4f out: wl btn after: wnt poor 4th wl over 1f out* **200/1**

2000 **5** *10* **Lyssio (GER)**[35] 1034 5-9-0 96 J-PGuillambert 1 19
(Michael Attwater) *chsd ldng pair tl 7f out: rdn 6f out: lost tch 4f out: t.o* **50/1**

140- **6** *7* **World Domination (USA)**[316] 3105 4-9-0 101 JamieSpencer 7
(Sir Henry Cecil) *hld up in last pair: hdwy to chse ldng trio 5f out: rdn and no hdwy 4f out: t.o and eased ins fnl f* **9/1**

2m 24.6s (14.10) **Going Correction** +1.35s/f (Soft) **6** Ran SP% **110.3**
Speed ratings (Par 113): **97,94,89,65,57 52**
Tote Swingers: 1&2 £1.90, 2&3 £1.20 CSF £9.66 TOTE £4.00: £2.20, £1.20; EX 7.40 Trifecta £14.00 Pool: £1860.45 - 98.25 winning units..
Owner H R H Princess Haya Of Jordan **Bred** Smythson **Trained** Newmarket, Suffolk

FOCUS
High-class performers such as Red Rocks, Ask and Tartan Bearer had won this race in recent years, but this renewal was badly hit with four-non runners and only four of the remaining six truly counted. However, the contest will be mainly remembered for how tired the horses became in the last quarter-mile and you won't often see the runners in a Group 3 Flat race finish more leg-weary than this. The winning time was a massive 17.6 seconds outside standard and the last 2f was hand-timed at around 34 seconds.

NOTEBOOK
Colombian(IRE) was having his first start since November, but was unlikely to be bothered by the ground having ended last season with victory in the French Provinces on going described as 'very soft'. Always stalking the leader, it took him a good while and plenty of stoking to get the better of his rival, but he stuck at it and won this on account of finishing off his race less slowly than the others. He is a consistent performer who should enjoy further success, but may need a bit of time to get over this war of attrition. (op 4-1)
Poet finished well beaten on his Longchamp reappearance, but that effort blew the cobwebs away and he relishes these conditions. His jockey, who has such a fine recent record in this race, quickly had him out in front though he had to keep niggling away at him to keep him interested. Sticking close to the inside rail after turning in, there was one stage when it looked as though he might have kept enough in reserve to hold off the runner-up, but he was eventually worn down and was well held when his rival hung across him half a furlong out. (tchd 7-4 and 2-1 in places)
Twice Over was expected to need the run on his reappearance when beaten by Questioning (runner-up in the Group 2 here the previous day) in the Earl Of Sefton, but despite being the one to beat on official ratings (upwards of 10lb in hand), his ability to handle conditions as testing as these was unproven, as his trainer pointed out. His rider wasn't happy with him over 3f from home and his efforts to get on terms with the front pair came to nothing, but it would be wrong to write him off on account of this defeat under such desperate conditions. (op 7-4)
World Domination(USA) dropped right out and didn't even manage to beat the two big outsiders. He hadn't been seen since suffering an injury in the King Edward VII at Royal Ascot last June and although he had reportedly been working well recently, he obviously still has a lot to prove. (op 15-2 tchd 7-1)

1678 BET365 CLASSIC TRIAL (GROUP 3) 1m 2f 7y
4:15 (4:16) (Class 1) 3-Y-0 £31,190 (£11,825; £5,918; £2,948) Stalls Low

Form RPR
1 **Imperial Monarch (IRE)**[231] 5956 3-9-0 0 JPO'Brien 1 116+
(A P O'Brien, Ire) *led for 1f: chsd ldr tl swtchd to r against outer rail fr 7f out: dropped to last 6f out: rdn and effrt 2f out: chsd ldr 1f out: styd on wl to ld fnl 75yds* **11/8**[1]

1- **2** *1 3/4* **Thought Worthy (USA)**[200] 6774 3-9-0 88 WilliamBuick 2 112
(John Gosden) *led after 1f: rdn and fnd ex ent fnl 2f: forged ahd over 1f out: hdd and no ex fnl 75yds* **9/2**

13-1 **3** *9* **Rougemont (IRE)**[9] 1468 3-9-0 105 RyanMoore 4 95
(Richard Hannon) *nudged along in rr early: hdwy to chse ldr 6f out: rdn and pressed ldr ent fnl 2f: no ex over 1f out and btn 1f out: wknd ins fnl f* **11/4**[2]

43-1 **4** *31* **Stipulate**[10] 1455 3-9-0 103 TomQueally 3 36
(Sir Henry Cecil) *chsd ldrs: rdn and effrt over 2f out: no prog and btn wl over 1f out: eased ins fnl f: t.o* **7/2**[3]

2m 27.86s (17.36) **Going Correction** +1.35s/f (Soft) **4** Ran SP% **109.2**
Speed ratings (Par 108): **84,82,75,50**
CSF £7.64 TOTE £2.10; EX 6.20.
Owner Mrs John Magnier & Michael Tabor & Derrick Smith **Bred** David Magnier And Cobra Bloodstock **Trained** Ballydoyle, Co Tipperary

FOCUS
Not since 1986 has this race been won by the subsequent Derby winner, though Benny The Dip finished second in 1997 before going on to Epsom glory. Recent winners have hardly set the world alight and with just four runners this year (the smallest field since 2002) racing on very testing ground, one could be forgiven for questioning how much significance this year's renewal of the trial will have. However, there is a real possibility that this was won by a very nice horse and it was certainly an extraordinary spectacle.

NOTEBOOK
Imperial Monarch(IRE) ◆ went so wide in the back straight that he almost ended up on the road taken by the service vehicles. He also stuck to the outside rail on the home bend, thereby conceding a lot of ground, but it meant that he alone took the traditional soft-ground route up the home straight and it paid off, if only narrowly. This performance is impossible to gauge, as he was almost certainly racing on quicker ground, but he had a couple of subsequent winners behind when winning a Curragh maiden on soft ground on his sole appearance last year, so he has done everything asked of him and it seems very likely that he will be winning much bigger prizes than this. His pedigree suggests he will relish the Derby trip and he was cut to a general 16-1 shot for Epsom with most firms. (op 13-8 tchd 5-4)
Thought Worthy(USA), the only other of the quartet entered for the Derby along with the winner, landed a Newcastle soft-ground maiden on his debut last October and that form looks strong with the three who chased him home all winning their next starts. He was soon bowling along in front here and managed to hold off the pair who stayed with him towards the inside of the track after turning in, but the winner on the opposite flank was too strong for him late on. Being a brother to the St Leger winner Lucarno suggests that he will stay 1m4f without any problem, but although he should be up to winning at Group level it's hard to see him reversing form with Imperial Monarch should they meet again. (tchd 5-1)
Rougemont(IRE) was put up 20lb after winning the £250,000 Tattersalls Millions 3-Y-O Trophy at Newmarket nine days earlier so, with his fitness assured, he had every right for a shot at race like this, but he struggled to go past the runner-up in the home straight and didn't appear to see out the trip in the ground. He may not be the easiest to place now. (tchd 3-1)
Stipulate ran out an impressive winner of the Feilden Stakes at Newmarket ten days earlier, but had never raced on ground softer than good and dropped right out in the latter stages. It's probably best to put a line through this. (op 3-1 tchd 4-1)

1679 POKER AT BET365.COM H'CAP 1m 14y
4:50 (4:51) (Class 2) (0-105,100) 4-Y-0+ £12,450 (£3,728; £1,864; £932) Stalls Low

Form RPR
32-0 **1** **Weapon Of Choice (IRE)**[28] 1128 4-8-10 89 TomQueally 1 96
(Stuart Kittow) *sn led: rdn 3f out: drvn and hdd over 1f out: over 1 l down and looked hld whn edgd rt ins fnl f: rallied gamely to ld again towards fin* **15/8**[1]

005- **2** *½* **Sam Sharp (USA)**[145] 7339 6-8-4 83 WilliamCarson 4 89
(Ian Williams) *hld up in tch: rdn and effrt to chal 3f out: drvn to ld over 1f out: looked wnr ins fnl f: edgd lft and tiring fnl 100yds: hdd and no ex towards fin* **7/2**[2]

-026 **3** *19* **Mawaakef (IRE)**[17] 1321 4-8-5 84 MartinDwyer 8 46
(J R Jenkins) *t.k.h: hld up in tch: rdn and effrt 3f out: no ex 2f out and btn over 1f out: eased fnl 150yds* **15/8**[1]

15-0 **4** *35* **Bronze Prince**[14] 1373 5-9-0 93 J-PGuillambert 6
(Michael Attwater) *t.k.h: led briefly: stdd bk to rr 6f out: rdn and effrt 3f out: sn edgd rt and no hdwy: wl btn and eased fr over 1f out: t.o* **9/2**[3]

1m 56.66s (13.36) **Going Correction** +1.35s/f (Soft) **4** Ran SP% **110.0**
Speed ratings (Par 109): **87,86,67,32**
CSF £8.59 TOTE £2.50; EX 7.00.
Owner Chris & David Stam **Bred** Stone Ridge Farm **Trained** Blackborough, Devon

FOCUS
Much of the interest in this race was lost with half the declared eight runners missing, primarily the likely hot favourite Farhh, on account of the ground. The remaining quartet came up the centre of the track in the straight.

NOTEBOOK
Weapon Of Choice(IRE), ninth in the Spring Mile on his reappearance and on his debut for the yard, handles soft ground and attempted to make all, but looked cooked when the runner-up headed him a furlong out, but he was given another opportunity when his rival started to idle and, once switched, managed to rally and gain an unlikely victory. This was a fair effort off 7lb higher than when last successful, but the form may not be reliable. (tchd 7-4 and 2-1)
Sam Sharp(USA) hadn't been seen since a modest effort on his hurdles debut in December, but he does have a fine record following lengthy absences. Everything appeared to be going perfectly for him when was sent to the front over a furlong out (£12,884 was matched at 1.01 on Betfair), but he did little in front and grabbed defeat from the jaws of victory. He has won over 1m2f on soft ground, so stamina shouldn't have been an issue.
Mawaakef(IRE) attracted market support, but got very tired over the last furlong or so and is still without a win since his second start at two. (op 11-4)
Bronze Prince is yet to prove he stays 1m under any conditions, let alone in these, and he could barely raise a gallop inside the last 2f. He is better than this. (op 10-3 tchd 3-1)

1680 CASINO AT BET365.COM FLAT V JUMP JOCKEYS H'CAP 1m 14y
5:20 (5:24) (Class 4) (0-80,80) 4-Y-0+ £6,469 (£1,925; £962; £481) Stalls Low

Form RPR
121- **1** **Silken Thoughts**[247] 5407 4-11-1 77 AidanColeman 14 91
(John Berry) *racd wdst: chsd ldr tl 4f out: wnt 2nd again over 2f out: led over 1f out: sn clr and in command: rdn out ins fnl f* **8/1**

56-1 **2** *4* **Barwick**[19] 1262 4-11-0 76 WilliamBuick 7 81+
(Mark H Tompkins) *s.i.s: hld up wl off the pce in last trio: rdn and hdwy over 2f out: chsd clr wnr ins fnl f: styd on wl but nvr gng to rch wnr* **3/1**[1]

44-1 **3** *5* **Snow Trooper**[29] 1108 4-10-10 72 DaneO'Neill 6 65
(Dean Ivory) *racd wl off the pce in midfield: rdn and hdwy over 2f out: wnt modest 4th over 1f out: kpt on to go 3rd ins fnl f: no threat to wnr* **10/1**

000- **4** *3 ½* **Spa's Dancer (IRE)**[192] 6949 5-11-4 80 PaddyBrennan 12 65
(Ed de Giles) *led: rdn and hdd over 1f out: sn brushed aside by wnr: ducked lft ins fnl f and lost 2 pls fnl 150yds* **13/2**[2]

10-0 **5** *12* **European Dream (IRE)**[19] 1249 9-11-4 80 (p) DarylJacob 9 38
(Richard Guest) *stdd s: hld up in rr: rdn and hdwy over 2f out: modest 6th over 1f out: nvr trbld ldrs* **7/1**[3]

630- **6** *7* **Flipping**[171] 7339 5-11-1 77 RichardJohnson 11 19
(Eric Alston) *t.k.h: chsd ldng pair tl wnt 2nd 4f out tl over 2f out: wknd 2f out* **8/1**

50-0 **7** *15* **Cocohatchee**[38] 987 4-10-8 70 (p) FergusSweeney 3
(Pat Phelan) *hld up wl off the pce in rr: rdn and wl btn 3f out: no ch but styd on past btn horses fr over 1f out: t.o* **33/1**

25-4 **8** *4 ½* **Whitby Jet (IRE)**[16] 1342 4-10-12 74 TomQueally 5
(Ed Vaughan) *racd off the pce in midfield: rdn and effrt over 2f out: sn edgd rt and no hdwy: wl btn fnl 2f: t.o* **12/1**

00-0 **9** *4 ½* **Da Ponte**[29] 1117 4-10-10 72 PatDobbs 8
(Michael Scudamore) *chsd ldrs for 2f: rdn and wknd over 2f out: wl btn fnl 2f: t.o* **40/1**

16 **10** *69* **Mafi (IRE)**[38] 987 4-10-11 **73** DenisO'Regan 2
(Mark Hoad) *midfield: rdn and struggling 4f out: wl bhd fnl 3f: t.o and virtually p.u fnl f* **33/1**
5305 **11** *20* **Tartan Trip**[30] 1087 5-11-2 **78** JimmyFortune 10
(Andrew Balding) *chsd ldng trio: rdn and no hdwy 3f out: sn wknd: t.o and virtually p.u fnl f* **13/2**[2]
11-0 **12** *32* **Ancient Greece**[30] 1087 5-11-0 **76** (t) JasonMaguire 4
(George Baker) *midfield but sn niggled along: rdn 3f out: sn struggling and wknd: t.o and virtually p.u fnl f* **8/1**

1m 53.06s (9.76) **Going Correction** +1.35s/f (Soft) 12 Ran SP% **122.6**
Speed ratings (Par 105): **105,101,96,92,80 73,58,54,49, ,**
Tote Swingers: 1&2 £8.50, 1&3 £10.50, 2&3 £8.00 CSF £32.90 CT £253.80 TOTE £8.10: £3.10, £1.50, £3.10; EX 44.50 Trifecta £78.30 Pool: £1781.63 - 16.83 winning units..
Owner The Renewal Partnership **Bred** Burton Agnes Stud Co Ltd **Trained** Newmarket, Suffolk

FOCUS
A competitive line-up for this annual challenge, but the ground sorted them out and few ever got into it with three of the jump jockeys, including the winner and fourth, making sure there was no messing about. The runners raced much wider than in the previous contest and the time was 3.6 seconds faster.
T/Plt: £349.10 to a £1 stake. Pool of £197,556.20 - 412.99 winning tickets. T/Qpdt: £36.60 to a £1 stake. Pool of £11,931.09 - 240.87 winning tickets. SP

1681 - 1694a (Foreign Racing) - See Raceform Interactive

1569 LONGCHAMP (R-H)
Sunday, April 29

OFFICIAL GOING: Turf: heavy

1695a PRIX VANTEAUX (GROUP 3) (3YO FILLIES) (TURF) 1m 1f 55y
1:30 (12:00) 3-Y-O £33,333 (£13,333; £10,000; £6,666; £3,333)

RPR
1 **Trois Lunes (FR)**[43] 952 3-9-0 0 Francois-XavierBertras 1 104
(F Rohaut, France) *settled in 3rd cl bhd ldrs: rdn over 1 1/2f out: chal for ld ent fnl f: r.o wl to ld 1f out: chal 100yds out: hld on wl fnl 50yds* **9/2**[3]
2 *nk* **Sagawara**[187] 3-9-0 0 Christophe-PatriceLemaire 3 104
(A De Royer-Dupre, France) *settled in 4th: u.p over 1 1/2f out: r.o wl fnl f to go 2nd 150yds out: chal for ld ins fnl f but a being hld* **5/2**[1]
3 *2 ½* **Prima Noa (FR)**[31] 3-9-0 0 ThierryThulliez 7 99
(J Van Handenhove, France) *settled in rr of field: hrd rdn 1 1/2f out: r.o wl fnl f to go 3rd 50yds out* **25/1**
4 *nk* **Rock Me Baby**[33] 1059 3-9-0 0 OlivierPeslier 2 98
(X Thomas-Demeaulte, France) *sn led: chal 2f out: hdd over 1 1/2f out: rallied 1f out: r.o wl: hdd for 3rd 50yds out* **9/1**
5 *2 ½* **Preferential**[24] 3-9-0 0 StephanePasquier 5 93
(Mme C Head-Maarek, France) *settled in cl 2nd on outside of ldr: rdn 2f out: led briefly over 1 1/2f out but but sn hdd: no ex u.p fr 1f out: fdd* **5/2**[1]
6 *7* **Keegsquaw (IRE)**[21] 1243 3-9-0 0 MickaelBarzalona 4 79
(A Fabre, France) *s.i.s: rdn to go 5th after 1f: u.p early in st: cl up bhd ldrs over 1 1/2f out: rdn but no ex: fdd fnl f* **7/2**[2]
7 *dist* **Queen Bubble (IRE)**[21] 1243 3-9-0 0 (p) ChristopheSoumillon 6
(Y De Nicolay, France) *settled in 6th: rdn but no ex in st: wknd qckly: t.o* **14/1**

2m 1.8s (6.50) **Going Correction** +0.875s/f (Soft) 7 Ran SP% **118.1**
Speed ratings: **106,105,103,103,101 94,**
WIN (incl. 1 euro stake): 6.30. PLACES: 2.50, 2.40. SF: 22.70.
Owner Scea Haras De Saint Pair **Bred** Scea Haras De Saint Pair **Trained** Sauvagnon, France

NOTEBOOK
Trois Lunes(FR) is clearly well suited by this sort of ground. Her aim is the Prix de Diane.
Sagawara wants further and better ground, according to her trainer. She could go straight to the Prix Saint-Alary.

1696a PRIX GANAY (GROUP 1) (4YO+) (TURF) 1m 2f 110y
2:40 (12:00) 4-Y-O+ £142,850 (£57,150; £28,575; £14,275; £7,150)

RPR
1 **Cirrus Des Aigles (FR)**[29] 1149 6-9-2 0 OlivierPeslier 4 130+
(Mme C Barande-Barbe, France) *2nd early: sent to ld after 100yds: sn established clr ld: qcknd in st to go wl clr: rdn out hands and heels: easily* **8/13**[1]
2 *8* **Giofra**[21] 1245 4-8-13 0 MaximeGuyon 1 111+
(A De Royer-Dupre, France) *led for 100yds then settled in 2nd: chsd ldr in st: chal for 2nd 1 1/2f out: rallied to go clr 2nd in fnl f: no ch w wnr* **4/1**[2]
3 *2* **Reliable Man**[210] 6567 4-9-2 0 GeraldMosse 2 111+
(A De Royer-Dupre, France) *settled in 4th on inner: rdn early in st: chal for 2nd 1 1/2f out: no ex ins fnl f: r.o* **4/1**[2]
4 *8* **Wigmore Hall (IRE)**[29] 1148 5-9-2 0 HayleyTurner 6 95+
(Michael Bell) *settled in rr: slipped through early in st to go 4th over 1 1/2f out: styd on: no threat to first three* **16/1**[3]
5 *2 ½* **Saga Dream (FR)**[21] 1245 6-9-2 0 ThierryJarnet 3 90+
(F Lemercier, France) *settled in 4th: rdn early in st: nt qckn: fdd fr 1 1/2f out* **50/1**
6 *20* **Pagera (FR)**[33] 4-8-13 0 ChristopheSoumillon 5 48+
(H-A Pantall, France) *settled in 3rd: rdn bef st: u.p but no ex: wknd fnl 1 1/2f* **66/1**

2m 18.9s (8.70) **Going Correction** +1.225s/f (Soft) 6 Ran SP% **111.3**
Speed ratings: **117,111,109,103,102 87**
WIN (incl. 1 euro stake): 1.70. PLACES: 1.10, 1.40. SF: 3.00.
Owner Jean-Claude-Alain Dupouy **Bred** M Yvon Lelimouzin & M Benoit Deschamps **Trained** France

FOCUS
The six runners had to contend with heavy ground for the first Group 1 of the European season.

NOTEBOOK
Cirrus Des Aigles(FR) could manage only third behind Planteur in a stronger renewal of this race last year. He didn't stop improving last season, though, and came here on the back of winning the Sheema Classic at Meydan. Settled in front, he was kicked on turning into the straight and kept going further clear, never looking in any danger. Despite handling quicker ground, he revels in these conditions and looks to be still be improving as a 6yo. He has lots of options and connections aren't running shy of taking on Frankel.
Giofra was no match for the winner but still did well to hold on for second after looking likely to be run down in the closing stages. She made her mark in Group company when winning the Prix D'Harcourt here three weeks ago and this was a creditable enough effort to think this lightly raced filly can land a Group 1 back against her own sex, with a return to better ground in her favour.
Reliable Man tired in the final furlong on his seasonal reappearance. He disappointed in the Arc at the end of a busy classic season, but seems to have trained on and will have all the top middle-distance races in Europe as his objective.
Wigmore Hall(IRE) was unsuited by the ground and muddling early gallop, however he has been well beaten now on all three starts in Group 1 company in Europe and will find more realistic winning opportunities when returning to North America.

1697a PRIX DE BARBEVILLE (GROUP 3) (4YO+) (TURF) 1m 7f 110y
3:10 (12:00) 4-Y-O+ £33,333 (£13,333; £10,000; £6,666; £3,333)

RPR
1 **Usuelo (FR)**[25] 4-8-9 0 AntoineHamelin 6 110
(J-L Guillochon, France) *led: hdd at 1/2-way: racd in cl 3rd bef st: rdn 2f out: qcknd wl to ld over 1f out: r.o wl: wnt clr: easily* **16/1**
2 *1 ¾* **Prairie Star (FR)**[20] 1268 4-9-3 0 ChristopheSoumillon 4 116+
(E Lellouche, France) *settled in 6th: proged to 4th bef st: r.o wl fr 2f out: wnt 2nd 1 1/2f out: chsd ldr wout threatening: styd on wl* **9/2**
3 *¾* **Tac De Boistron (FR)**[20] 1268 5-9-1 0 FranckBlondel 3 109+
(A Lyon, France) *settled in 4th: proged over 2f out: r.o wl fnl 1 1/2f to go 3rd 1f out: styd on* **2/1**[1]
4 *3* **Brigantin (USA)**[20] 1268 5-9-5 0 Pierre-CharlesBoudot 1 110
(A Fabre, France) *settled in 5th on ins rail: u.p early in st: styd on wl fnl f to go 4th 100yds out* **4/1**[3]
5 *¾* **Ivory Land (FR)**[20] 1268 5-9-3 0 StephanePasquier 5 107
(A De Royer-Dupre, France) *settled towards rr: proged to 3rd at 1/2-way: wnt 2nd early in st: led briefly over 1 1/2f out: hdd by eventual wnr over 1f out: fdd ins fnl f* **10/3**[2]
6 *8* **Tidespring (IRE)**[16] 4-8-6 0 MaximeGuyon 7 90
(H-A Pantall, France) *settled in rr: rdn to improve bef st: nt qckn: styd on* **16/1**
7 *18* **Softsong (FR)**[20] 1268 4-8-9 0 RonanThomas 2 71
(R Chotard, France) *settled in 2nd: sent to ld at 1/2-way: led into st: hdd over 1 1/2f out: nt qckn u.p: wknd qckly* **25/1**
8 *dist* **Balaythous (FR)**[40] 980 6-9-1 0 FlavienPrat 8
(Mlle B Renk, France) *s.i.s: hrd rdn on outside bef st: no ex: wknd qckly* **12/1**

3m 42.2s (20.70) **Going Correction** +1.225s/f (Soft)
WFA 4 from 5yo+ 3lb 8 Ran SP% **117.9**
Speed ratings: **97,96,95,94,93 89,80,**
WIN (incl. 1 euro stake): 10.40 PLACES: 2.20, 1.90, 1.40. DF: 32.30. SF: 95.10.
Owner Jean-Luc Guillochon **Bred** J & Mme Mc Duvaldestin **Trained** France

NOTEBOOK
Usuelo(FR) sprang something of a shock against some of France's more established stayers, after his young jockey plotted a daring route up the inside. He'll now follow the logical programme for the stayers in France.

1409 CAPANNELLE (R-H)
Sunday, April 29

OFFICIAL GOING: Turf: good

1698a PREMIO PARIOLI (GROUP 3) (3YO COLTS) (TURF) 1m
3:20 (12:00) 3-Y-O £41,666 (£18,333; £10,000; £5,000)

RPR
1 **Malossol (USA)**[21] 3-9-2 0 FabioBranca 10 105
(G Botti, Italy) *hld up in last: rdn and outpcd in rr of main pack over 2f out: styd on strly u.p fr over 1f out: r.o to chal wl ins fnl f: led last strides* **89/10**
2 *shd* **Vedelago (IRE)**[203] 6740 3-9-2 0 MircoDemuro 7 105
(L Polito, Italy) *hld up in last pair: stdy prog on outer fr over 3f out: rdn to chal 2f out: sn led: kpt on ins fnl f: hdd last strides* **9/5**[2]
3 *2 ¼* **Farraaj (IRE)**[176] 7301 3-9-2 0 NeilCallan 8 100
(Roger Varian) *trckd ldr on outer: shkn up to chal over 2f out: rdn and kpt on wl for 3rd fr over 1 1/2f out: nt pce of front pair* **8/5**[1]
4 *nk* **Moustache (IRE)**[35] 3-9-2 0 CColombi 4 99
(D Grilli, Italy) *midfield: rdn to try and chal over 2f out: kpt on one pce u.p ins fnl f* **83/10**
5 *2 ½* **Art Of Dreams (FR)**[203] 3-9-2 0 CristianDemuro 2 93
(B Grizzetti, Italy) *midfield on inner: rdn over 3f out: kpt on one pce fr over 1 1/2f out* **53/1**
6 *7* **Facoltoso**[35] 3-9-2 0 StefanoLandi 6 77
(R Biondi, Italy) *led: stl gng wl whn chal jst over 2f out: rdn and hdd sn after: kpt on u.p tl no ex ins fnl f: eased fnl 100yds* **40/1**
7 *2* **Rockinante (FR)**[24] 1208 3-9-2 0 PatDobbs 3 73
(Richard Hannon) *trckd ldr on inner: rdn 2 1/2f out: wknd fr over 1f out: eased whn btn* **5/2**[3]
8 *2* **Saint Bernard** 3-9-2 0 SSulas 5 68
(D Camuffo, Italy) *midfield: rdn to try and improve over 2f out: no prog and fdd fr over 1f out: qckly eased whn btn* **59/1**
9 *4* **Rivertime (ITY)**[21] 3-9-2 0 CFiocchi 1 59
(R Menichetti, Italy) *midfield on inner: rdn to maintain position over 3f out: no ex over 2f out: qckly wknd and eased* **50/1**
10 *dist* **Lui E La Luna**[35] 3-9-2 0 DarioVargiu 9
(B Grizzetti, Italy) *midfield on outer: rdn 4f out: wknd over 3f out: eased: t.o* **125/10**

1m 38.5s (-1.30) 10 Ran SP% **138.9**
WIN (incl. 1 euro stake): 9.89. PLACES: 1.83, 1.33, 1.31. DF: 14.56.
Owner Selim Blanga Moghrabi & Ste B&B Botti **Bred** E Seltzer, R Anderson & K Goodman **Trained** Italy

FOCUS
This is the Italian 2000 Guineas.

NOTEBOOK
Malossol(USA) came from well off the pace to collar Vedelago inside the final 25 yards. He had broken broke his duck in a San Siro Listed race earlier this month, having been placed four times in France, where he had been based in the satellite yard run by Giuseppe Botti's son and assistant, Alessandro. He could go for the French Guineas.
Farraaj(IRE) was unsuited by the steady pace and would not really settle. He led very briefly and kept on at the same pace.
Rockinante(FR), another unsuited by the steady pace, was allowed to coast home once he was beaten entering the final furlong.

1699a PREMIO REGINA ELENA (GROUP 3) (3YO FILLIES) (TURF) 1m
4:35 (12:00) 3-Y-O £41,666 (£18,333; £10,000; £5,000)

RPR
1 **Cherry Collect (IRE)**[175] 3-8-11 0 FabioBranca 10 98
(S Botti, Italy) *settled in midfield: rdn to improve over 2f out: r.o strly to chal wl ins fnl f: led last strides* **43/20**[2]

2 *nk* **Last Night Show (ITY)**[21] 3-8-11 0.............................. MircoDemuro 13 97
(S Botti, Italy) *got across fr wd draw to ld: rdn to extend advantage 2 1/2f out: stl more than 2 l clr over 1f out: kpt on but diminishing advantage thrght fnl f: hdd last strides* **17/5**[3]

3 *2* **Icebreaking (IRE)**[35] 3-8-11 0..................................... CristianDemuro 5 92
(L Riccardi, Italy) *midfield: rdn to improve 2 1/2f out: r.o to go 3rd ins fnl f* **36/5**

4 *1 1/2* **Etoile D'Argent (ITY)**[35] 3-8-11 0.. CFiocchi 4 89
(G Mosconi, Italy) *midfield on inner: rdn and ev ch over 2f out: kpt on one pce ins fnl 1 1/2f* **191/10**

5 *2* **Fata Romana (IRE)**[175] 3-8-11 0.. GMarcelli 12 84
(L Riccardi, Italy) *hld up towards rr: rdn to improve over 3f out: outpcd over 2f out: rallied u.p and r.o to take 5th cl home* **46/1**

6 *hd* **Cool Wave**[180] 7219 3-8-11 0.. StefanoLandi 2 84
(B Grizzetti, Italy) *trckd ldr in clr 2nd: rdn over 2 1/2f out: kpt on one pce tl no ex and fdd wl ins fnl f: lost 5th cl home* **28/1**

7 *3/4* **Chellalla**[35] 3-8-11 0.. MarcoMonteriso 3 82
(L Polito, Italy) *dwlt: sn rcvrd and settled in midfield on inner: rdn and outpcd over 2f out: kpt on ins fnl 1 1/2f* **40/1**

8 *nk* **Alsindi (IRE)**[66] 680 3-8-11 0.. NeilCallan 9 81
(Clive Brittain) *trckd ldr in 3rd: rdn to try and chal over 2f out: no ex and btn over 1f out: fdd ins fnl f* **6/4**[1]

9 *1* **Sabbygo (IRE)** 3-8-11 0.. SDiana 14 79
(Valentina Matrullo, Italy) *hld up in last pair on outer: rdn 3f out: kpt on ins fnl 2f: nvr a factor* **32/5**

10 *1 1/2* **Naxos Beach (IRE)**[49] 3-8-11 0.................................. RoystonFfrench 6 76
(A Di Dio, Italy) *slow to stride: rdn to rcvr: settled in midfield on outer: rdn over 3f out: no ex and btn over 1 1/2f out: plugged on* **32/5**

11 *1 1/2* **Dark Ray (IRE)**[196] 6904 3-8-11 0.. GBietolini 11 72
(L Riccardi, Italy) *hld up in last pair on inner: rdn and sme prog over 2f out: no ex over 1f out: wknd ins fnl f* **36/5**

12 *nk* **Killachy Loose**[21] 3-8-11 0.. DarioVargiu 8 72
(B Grizzetti, Italy) *prom on outer: rdn to try and chal over 2f out: wkng whn short of room 1 1/2f out: coasted home ins fnl f*

13 *2* **Floral Art (IRE)** 3-8-11 0... SSulas 7 67
(D Camuffo, Italy) *hld up towards rr: rdn over 3f out: outpcd over 2f out: no ex and heavily eased ins fnl f* **99/1**

1m 38.0s (-1.80) **13** Ran SP% **159.9**
WIN (incl. 1 euro stake): 3.15. PLACES: 1.48, 1.88, 3.17. DF: 6.17.
Owner Effevi **Bred** Razza Del Velino **Trained** Italy

FOCUS
A 1-2 for Stefano Botti in this Italian 1000 Guineas.

NOTEBOOK
Cherry Collect(IRE) collared her stablemate close home to win in good style. She is widely regarded as the best three-year-old filly in Italy.
Alsindi(IRE) was beaten over one and a half furlongs out.

COLOGNE (R-H)
Sunday, April 29

OFFICIAL GOING: Turf: soft

1700a GERLING-PREIS (GROUP 2) (4YO+) (TURF) 1m 4f
4:15 (12:00) 4-Y-O+
£33,333 (£12,916; £5,416; £3,333; £2,083; £1,250)

RPR

1 **Atempo (GER)**[20] 4-9-0 0.. ADeVries 2 113
(J Hirschberger, Germany) *chsd ldr first 2f: sn settled in 4th: hrd rdn 2 1/2f out: styd on u.p to ld 175yds out: r.o* **14/5**[2]

2 *1* **Silvaner (GER)**[20] 4-9-0 0.. THellier 3 111
(P Schiergen, Germany) *settled in 5th on rail: scrubbed along ent fnl 2f: 5th and hrd rdn over 1f out: styd on fnl 150yds to take 2nd cl home: nt rch wnr* **102/10**

3 *1* **Sir Lando**[231] 5984 5-9-0 0.. FJohansson 1 108
(Wido Neuroth, Norway) *trckd ldr on rail in share of 2nd: relegated to 3rd but cl up 1/2-way: rdn and qcknd to chal ldr on outside ins fnl 2f: led briefly 1f out: sn hdd and kpt on at one pce u.p fnl f* **11/1**

4 *nse* **Earl Of Tinsdal (GER)**[217] 6396 4-9-6 0.................................. EPedroza 6 115
(A Wohler, Germany) *sn trcking ldr on outside of Sir Lando: wnt clr 2nd 1/2-way: pressed ldr on outside 3 1/2f out: outpcd briefly 2f out: 3rd and hrd rdn over 1f out: led briefly ins fnl f: hdd 175yds out: kpt on at one pce* **6/5**[1]

5 *3/4* **Saltas (GER)**[204] 6710 4-9-0 0... AStarke 5 108
(P Schiergen, Germany) *hld up towards rr: 5th and rdn 3f out: kpt on fnl f: nt pce to chal* **42/10**[3]

6 *3/4* **Mighty Mouse (GER)**[20] 4-9-0 0.................................... StefanieHofer 4 107
(P Vovcenko, Germany) *led: qcknd whn pressed over 3f out: hdd 1f out: no ex* **7/1**

7 *1* **Lindenthaler (GER)**[175] 7324 4-9-0 0..................................... FilipMinarik 8 105
(P Schiergen, Germany) *hld up in last: 6th and hrd rdn 2f out: nt pce to chal fnl 1 1/2f* **219/10**

8 *dist* **Fair Boss (IRE)**[20] 4-9-0 0.. DPorcu 7
(W Hickst, Germany) *a towards rr: c wd fnl bnd over 3f out: rdn and no imp fr 2f out: t.o* **161/10**

2m 30.91s (-1.99)
WFA 4 from 5yo 1lb **8** Ran SP% **131.0**
WIN (incl. 10 euro stake): 38. PLACES: 16, 24, 28. SF: 441.
Owner Gestut Schlenderhan **Bred** Gestut Schlenderhan **Trained** Germany
■ Part of a four-timer on the day for the owner, trainer and jockey.

FOCUS
Part of a four-timer on the day for the owner, trainer and jockey.

NOTEBOOK
Atempo(GER) was having only the fourth race of his life but scored in convincing fashion. He came there full of running on the outside and swept into the lead as they entered the final furlong. He will probably go next for the Gran Premio di Milano.

1701 - (Foreign Racing) - See Raceform Interactive

1608 KEMPTON (A.W) (R-H)
Monday, April 30

OFFICIAL GOING: Standard
Wind: Strong, half behind Weather: Fine

1702 OLLY MURS AT KEMPTON PARK 17.08.2012 H'CAP 1m (P)
2:15 (2:15) (Class 6) (0-60,59) 4-Y-O+ **£1,617** (£481; £240; £120) **Stalls** Low

Form RPR

0200 **1** **Gallantry**[12] 1447 10-9-5 **57**.. TomMcLaughlin 4 65
(Paul Howling) *pressed ldr after 100yds: led over 2f out and set sail for home: hld on wl nr fin* **25/1**

3360 **2** *1/2* **Karate (IRE)**[1] 1034 4-8-12 **67**........................... (t) NicoleNordblad(7) 7 64+
(Hans Adielsson) *t.k.h: hld up in midfield on inner: prog over 2f out: chsd wnr over 1f out: grad clsd: a jst hld* **9/1**

00-0 **3** *2 1/2* **Matavia Bay (IRE)**[16] 1379 4-9-6 **58**................................ KierenFallon 9 59
(Alan Jarvis) *trckd ldng pair: rdn over 2f out: nt qckn wl over 1f out: kpt on same pce after* **6/1**

6004 **4** *hd* **Sergeant Troy (IRE)**[11] 1487 4-9-4 **56**.......................(t) PatCosgrave 11 57
(George Baker) *chsd ldrs disputing 5th: rdn over 3f out: nt qckn and struggling over 2f out: kpt on again fr over 1f out to press for 3rd nr fin* **9/2**[2]

046- **5** *1* **Alexs Rainbow (USA)**[356] 1986 4-9-7 **59**......................... WilliamCarson 12 57+
(Peter Hiatt) *hld up and sn in last pair: pushed along on inner fr over 2f out: styd on steadily to take 5th nr fin: nvr nr ldrs* **40/1**

00-5 **6** *1* **Prince Of Passion (CAN)**[12] 1447 4-9-6 **58**............................ NeilCallan 2 54
(Derek Shaw) *t.k.h: trckd ldng pair: disp 2nd briefly wl over 1f out: fdd fnl f* **11/2**[3]

4100 **7** *1/2* **Having A Ball**[32] 1088 8-9-4 **56**... ChrisCatlin 13 51
(Jonathan Portman) *racd wd: hld up in last trio: drvn and no prog wl over 2f out: styd on fr over 1f out: nrst fin* **20/1**

2046 **8** *hd* **Querido (GER)**[19] 1310 8-9-0 **55**...........................(t) RobertLButler(3) 1 50
(Paddy Butler) *led after 100yds to over 2f out: wknd over 1f out* **20/1**

306- **9** *3/4* **Fitz**[134] 7810 6-9-1 **58**... LeeNewnes(5) 8 51
(Matthew Salaman) *hld up in midfield disputing 7th: lost pl over 2f out and pushed along: kpt on u.p fr over 1f out: n.d* **14/1**

43-6 **10** *3/4* **Luisa Tetrazzini (IRE)**[33] 1070 6-8-8 **51**..................... MarkCoumbe(5) 6 42
(Terry Clement) *rel to r and lft many l: ct up after 2f: drvn and effrt on inner over 2f out: no prog over 1f out* **33/1**

-310 **11** *shd* **Holyfield Warrior (IRE)**[38] 1009 8-8-10 **51**..................... KierenFox(3) 5 42
(Michael Attwater) *hld up in rr: prog into midfield 2f out: no imp on ldrs over 1f out: fdd* **16/1**

0055 **12** *hd* **Captainrisk (IRE)**[21] 1263 6-9-3 **55**...............................(v) IanMongan 14 45
(Christine Dunnett) *wl in rr: drvn in last pair 3f out: no ch after: plugged on late* **25/1**

/5-0 **13** *3 1/4* **Vantaa (IRE)**[45] 926 4-9-1 **53**... MartinHarley 3 36
(Mrs K Burke) *chsd ldrs disputing 5th: rdn fr 1/2-way: wknd u.p 2f out* **7/2**[1]

600 **14** *5* **Irie Ute**[21] 1263 4-9-1 **56**.. SophieDoyle(3) 10 27
(Sylvester Kirk) *fastest away and led 100yds: sn restrained into midfield on outer: rdn and wknd over 2f out* **16/1**

1m 40.96s (1.16) **Going Correction** -0.025s/f (Stan) **14** Ran SP% **121.1**
Speed ratings (Par 101): **93,92,90,89,88 87,87,87,86,85 85,85,82,77**
toteswingers: 1&2 £42.30, 1&3 £26.80, 2&3 £10.00. CSF £221.10 CT £1549.48 TOTE £34.50: £7.90, £2.70, £3.30; EX 198.40 Trifecta £439.10 Part won. Pool: £593.44 - 0.10 winning units..
Owner J Wright D Patrick P D Woodward **Bred** Cheveley Park Stud Ltd **Trained** Lee-On-The-Solent, Hants

FOCUS
They went a steady pace and those handy were favoured. Muddling form, rated around the runner-up to his winter best.

1703 BETFAIR SUPPORTING GRASSROOTS RACING MAIDEN STKS (DIV I) 1m (P)
2:45 (2:47) (Class 5) 3-Y-O+ **£2,264** (£673; £336; £168) **Stalls** Low

Form RPR

2- **1** **Hurricane In Dubai (IRE)**[159] 7521 3-9-0 0.................... EddieAhern 12 78
(Denis Coakley) *mde virtually all: skipped clr over 2f out: rdn over 1f out: hld on to dwindling ld fin* **7/1**[3]

5-5 **2** *nk* **Daliance (IRE)**[21] 1250 3-9-0 0...................................... RichardKingscote 11 77+
(Tom Dascombe) *hld up towards rr: prog over 2f out: rdn to chse clr wnr over 1f out: styd on wl and clsng qckly at fin* **5/1**[2]

3 *1 3/4* **Raheeba** 3-8-9 0.. SilvestreDeSousa 3 68
(Mark Johnston) *chsd ldng pair: rdn over 2f out: hung bdly lft after and ended against nr side rail: styd on same pce* **14/1**

4 *3/4* **Cactus Valley (IRE)** 3-9-0 0.. JamesDoyle 4 71+
(Roger Charlton) *chsd ldrs in 6th: rdn and rn green over 3f out: prog over 2f out to dispute 3rd over 1f out: kpt on* **25/1**

00- **5** *1/2* **District Attorney (IRE)**[185] 7134 3-9-0 0.......................... MichaelHills 9 70+
(William Haggas) *wl in tch in 7th: effrt on inner over 2f out: shkn up and styd on same pce fr over 1f out* **14/1**

34 **6** *nk* **Mutafaakir (IRE)**[12] 1450 3-9-0 0...............................(tp) PaulHanagan 13 69
(John Gosden) *hld up towards rr and off the pce: sme prog 3f out: shkn up and nt on terms 2f out: kpt on: nvr able to threaten* **5/4**[1]

6- **7** *3 3/4* **Tin Pan Alley**[347] 2231 4-10-0 0.. AmirQuinn 5 64
(Giles Bravery) *w wnr to 3f out: lft bhd sn after: lost 2nd and wknd over 1f out* **66/1**

3/ **8** *1 1/2* **Rulbin Realta**[487] 8021 5-9-9 0... IanMongan 2 56?
(Pat Phelan) *chsd ldng pair: drvn and stl in tch 2f out: wknd qckly over 1f out* **50/1**

9 *1* **Carthaginian (IRE)** 3-9-0 0... HayleyTurner 1 54+
(Ed Dunlop) *chsd ldrs in 6th: pushed along and rn green over 3f out: wknd qckly over 1f out* **10/1**

00- **10** *1 1/4* **Kaiser Wilhelm (IRE)**[222] 6245 3-9-0 0............................ ChrisCatlin 14 51+
(Paul Cole) *allowed to be v s.i.s and sn hld up in last: pushed along over 2f out: kpt on steadily: capable of bttr* **50/1**

11 *3/4* **Sabre Tooth (IRE)** 3-9-0 0.......................................(t) RyanMoore 8 49+
(Sir Michael Stoute) *slowly away: rn v green in last pair: drvn 3f out and looked likely tailing off: fnlly styd on fr over 1f out* **12/1**

50- **12** *4* **Mokbil (IRE)**[186] 7126 3-9-0 0...................................... TadhgO'Shea 6 40
(Roger Varian) *a in rr: looked awkward whn rdn wl over 2f out: nvr a factor* **20/1**

13 *1 1/2* **Tai Amour** 4-9-2 0... GeorgeanBuckell(7) 10 35
(Terry Clement) *chsd ldrs on outer: urged along 1/2-way: bmpd along vigorously and wknd 2f out* **100/1**

14 *6* **Albonny (IRE)** 3-9-0 0 KierenFallon 7 22
(Alan Jarvis) *slowest away: rn green and a wl in rr: t.o* **50/1**

1m 39.84s (0.04) **Going Correction** -0.025s/f (Stan)
WFA 3 from 4yo+ 14lb 14 Ran SP% **120.7**
Speed ratings (Par 103): **98,97,95,95,94 94,90,89,88,86 86,82,80,74**
toteswingers: 1&2 £5.10, 1&3 £10.60, 2&3 £15.50. CSF £40.15 TOTE £7.50: £2.00, £2.80, £5.40; EX 51.40 Trifecta £629.40 Pool: £1,046.20 - 1.23 winning units..
Owner John O'Riordan **Bred** M Ryan **Trained** West Ilsley, Berks

FOCUS
The pace was steady and the time was 1.15 seconds slower than the second leg. The form may not prove too reliable but has been taken at face value.
Raheeba Official explanation: jockey said filly hung left

1704 BETFAIR SUPPORTING GRASSROOTS RACING MAIDEN STKS (DIV II) 1m (P)
3:15 (3:17) (Class 5) 3-Y-0+ **£2,264** (£673; £336; £168) **Stalls** Low

Form RPR

1 **Mississippi**[218] 6387 3-9-0 0 MartinDwyer 3 88+
(Brian Meehan) *sn led: mde rest: drew away fr over 2f out: pushed along over 1f out: eased last 50yds* **10/3**[2]

0- 2 *3 ½* **Eagle Power (IRE)**[188] 7082 3-9-0 0 KierenFallon 6 77+
(James Fanshawe) *hld up in 8th: n.m.r 6f out: taken to outer and pushed along over 2f out: prog and reminder over 1f out: styd on wl to take 2nd last strides* **15/2**

0- 3 *nk* **Al Baidaa**[184] 7165 3-8-9 0 NeilCallan 9 71
(Roger Varian) *t.k.h: trckd ldng pair: chsd wnr wl over 2f out: no imp: lost 2nd last strides* **12/1**

2- 4 *1 ¼* **Pacific Heights (IRE)**[177] 7292 3-9-0 0 ShaneKelly 14 73
(Tim Pitt) *prom: rdn and nt qckn over 2f out: no ch w wnr after: kpt on* **7/1**

04- 5 *2 ¼* **Nassau Storm**[173] 7330 3-9-0 0 JimCrowley 1 68
(William Knight) *prom: n.m.r on inner after 2f: effrt to dispute 2nd over 2f out: fdd fnl f* **20/1**

6 *3 ¼* **Gold Edition** 3-9-0 0 JimmyFortune 13 60+
(Jeremy Noseda) *towards rr: wl off the pce over 2f out: drifted rt and effrt sn after: kpt on: n.d* **9/4**[1]

7 *½* **Class Win** 3-9-0 0 RyanMoore 10 59
(Sir Michael Stoute) *pressed wnr to 3f out: sn rdn and lost 2nd: grad fdd* **16/1**

8 *4 ½* **Bryer (IRE)** 3-9-0 0 SilvestreDeSousa 2 48+
(Mark Johnston) *wl in rr: pushed along over 3f out: rchd midfield but no ch whn crowded 2f out: plugged on* **13/2**[3]

9 *2 ½* **Nimble Thimble (USA)** 3-8-9 0 JamesDoyle 11 37+
(Roger Charlton) *settled wl in rr: pushed along in last and wl bhd 3f out: sme late prog* **25/1**

10 *4 ½* **Perfect Outlook** 4-9-9 0 PatCosgrave 4 30
(Jeremy Gask) *a in rr: wl bhd fr over 2f out* **100/1**

11 *nk* **American Bling (USA)** 3-9-0 0 AmirQuinn 5 31
(Gary Moore) *chsd ldrs: lft bhd fr over 3f out: wknd over 2f out* **100/1**

12 *8* **Mikdaar (IRE)** 3-9-0 0 PaulHanagan 7
(Ed Dunlop) *a wl in rr: no ch fr 3f out: t.o* **16/1**

0- 13 *1 ¾* **Ryedale Lass**[252] 5327 4-9-2 0 JacobMoore(7) 8
(Joseph Tuite) *a in rr: struggling bef 1/2-way: t.o* **100/1**

14 *14* **High Ball Roller**[37] 4-10-0 0 (t) LukeMorris 12
(Nicky Vaughan) *in tch on outer to 1/2-way: sn wknd: wl t.o* **100/1**

1m 38.69s (-1.11) **Going Correction** -0.025s/f (Stan)
WFA 3 from 4yo 14lb 14 Ran SP% **123.5**
Speed ratings (Par 103): **104,100,100,98,96 93,92,88,85,81 81,73,71,57**
toteswingers: 1&2 £5.70, 1&3 £9.90, 2&3 £16.70. CSF £28.51 TOTE £4.80: £2.10, £2.30, £3.70; EX 26.30 Trifecta £243.70 Pool: £833.28 - 2.53 winning units..
Owner Sir Robert Ogden **Bred** New England Stud & P J & P M Vela **Trained** Manton, Wilts
■ Stewards' Enquiry : Jimmy Fortune one-day ban: careless riding (May 14)

FOCUS
The time was much the quickest of three races at the trip, including 1.15 seconds faster than the first division. The winner was another successful front runner but it's doubtful he was flattered.

1705 BETFAIR SUPPORTING GRASSROOTS RACING MAIDEN FILLIES' STKS 6f (P)
3:45 (3:46) (Class 5) 3-Y-0 **£2,264** (£673; £336; £168) **Stalls** Low

Form RPR

0 1 **Furbelow**[11] 1472 3-9-0 0 JimmyFortune 9 78+
(Jeremy Noseda) *mde all: set v stdy pce to 1/2-way: stretched away fr over 2f out: in n.d whn edgd lft fnl f* **1/1**[1]

0- 2 *4 ½* **Miss Noble**[378] 1441 3-8-11 0 HarryBentley(3) 7 63
(Stuart Williams) *trckd ldrs: rdn to chse wnr 2f out: styd on but no imp* **50/1**

42 3 *2* **Catflap (IRE)**[16] 1376 3-9-0 0 NickyMackay 4 57
(Derek Haydn Jones) *t.k.h: trckd ldng pair: effrt to dispute 2nd 2f out: kpt on same pce after* **11/2**[2]

0- 4 *1* **Cynthia Calhoun**[204] 6725 3-9-0 0 JohnFahy 11 54
(Clive Cox) *t.k.h: trckd ldrs in 5th: shkn up and effrt over 2f out: styd on same pce* **9/1**[3]

- 5 *hd* **Gull Rock** 3-9-0 0 DaneO'Neill 12 53+
(Henry Candy) *slowest away: t.k.h: rchd midfield on outer over 3f out: outpcd over 2f out: styd on fnl f* **11/1**

0 6 *1* **Mystical Witch**[16] 1376 3-9-0 0 TomMcLaughlin 10 50?
(Christine Dunnett) *chsd wnr to 2f out: steadily fdd* **100/1**

6-4 7 *nk* **Allegra Byron**[10] 1492 3-9-0 0 LukeMorris 2 49
(Jonathan Portman) *hld up in midfield on inner: outpcd over 2f out: shkn up and styd on same pce fr over 1f out* **25/1**

8 *½* **Charity Box** 3-9-0 0 TedDurcan 6 47+
(Chris Wall) *dwlt: t.k.h: hld up in last trio: wl adrift 2f out: sme quite taking late prog* **16/1**

9 *3 ¾* **Litmus (USA)** 3-9-0 0 MichaelHills 8 35+
(Charles Hills) *hld up in rr: outpcd fr 1/2-way: no ch after* **10/1**

0 10 *1 ¾* **Perfect Policy**[26] 1182 3-9-0 0 JimCrowley 5 30
(Ralph Beckett) *nvr on terms w ldrs: pushed along 1/2-way: sn btn* **20/1**

5- 11 *¾* **Tenderly Place**[189] 7056 3-9-0 0 ShaneKelly 3 27
(William Knight) *hld up in last trio: nudged along and no prog 2f out: wknd* **12/1**

12 *3* **Mayo Miss** 3-9-0 0 HayleyTurner 1 18
(Tony Carroll) *sn last: nvr a factor* **50/1**

1m 14.09s (0.99) **Going Correction** -0.025s/f (Stan) 12 Ran SP% **119.9**
Speed ratings (Par 95): **92,86,83,82,81 80,80,79,74,72 71,67**
toteswingers: 1&2 £28.10, 1&3 £2.50, 2&3 £45.40. CSF £89.48 TOTE £2.20: £1.20, £12.40, £1.60; EX 90.30 Trifecta £493.20 Pool: £1,099.76 - 1.65 winning units..
Owner Cheveley Park Stud **Bred** Cheveley Park Stud Ltd **Trained** Newmarket, Suffolk

FOCUS
Muddling form with the time was 1.33 seconds slower than the later Class 6 for 3yos. Modest form overall, except the winner. There are a few doubts over the bare form.

1706 BETFAIR H'CAP 1m 3f (P)
4:15 (4:23) (Class 5) (0-75,75) 4-Y-0+ **£2,264** (£673; £336; £168) **Stalls** Low

Form RPR

1-50 1 **Refractor (IRE)**[21] 1258 4-9-7 **75** MartinLane 6 85+
(James Fanshawe) *uns rdr gng to s and evaded capture for several minutes: hld up in 6th: smooth prog over 2f out: led jst over 1f out: urged along and hld on* **8/1**

000- 2 *1 ¼* **Mafeteng**[164] 7453 4-8-8 **62** TedDurcan 11 70
(John Dunlop) *chsd ldr to 1/2-way and again wl over 2f out to wl over 1f out w hd to one side: followed wnr through and 2nd again ins fnl f: nt qckn* **25/1**

60-3 3 *2* **Laughing Jack**[32] 1094 4-9-0 **75** GeorgeDowning(7) 12 79+
(Tony Carroll) *reluctant to enter stalls: stdd s: hld up in last: stl there over 2f out: sme prog on outer but only 8th jst over 1f out: r.o strly to take 3rd last strides* **12/1**

1630 4 *½* **Shirataki (IRE)**[14] 1418 4-8-13 **67** ChrisCatlin 10 71
(Peter Hiatt) *led: kicked on 4f out: hdd jst over 1f out: fdd ins fnl f* **12/1**

0215 5 *½* **Isdaal**[31] 1106 5-8-9 **63** ShaneKelly 5 66
(Kevin Morgan) *hld up towards rr: prog on inner over 2f out: kpt on same pce fr over 1f out* **10/1**

-640 6 *3* **Brouhaha**[21] 1258 8-9-7 **75** RichardKingscote 8 72
(Tom Dascombe) *hld up in 8th: effrt wl over 2f out: drvn and hanging over 1f out: no imp on ldrs* **12/1**

155- 7 *¾* **Golden Waters**[210] 6592 5-9-4 **72** TomQueally 9 68
(Eve Johnson Houghton) *trckd ldrs: drvn in 4th over 2f out: tail whirling and nt qckn: fdd over 1f out* **14/1**

26-0 8 *1 ¼* **Beat Route**[14] 1418 5-9-2 **70** JohnFahy 1 64
(Michael Attwater) *trckd ldrs: cl up and rdn over 2f out: wknd over 1f out* **5/1**[2]

06-6 9 *2 ¾* **If You Whisper (IRE)**[79] 535 4-8-11 **65** MickyFenton 7 54
(Mike Murphy) *stdd s: plld hrd and hld up in last trio: hanging whn asked for effrt over 2f out: no prog* **11/1**

063- 10 *¾* **Danehill Dante (IRE)**[192] 6997 4-9-4 **72** FergusSweeney 4 59
(Alan King) *a in last trio: rdn and struggling 4f out* **11/2**[3]

3315 11 *25* **Archelao (IRE)**[7] 1566 4-9-4 **72** AmirQuinn 3 14
(Richard Rowe) *trckd ldng pair: wnt 2nd 1/2-way to wl over 2f out: wknd rapidly: t.o* **14/1**

411- 12 *¾* **Librettela**[196] 6923 4-9-0 **68** KierenFallon 2
(Alan Jarvis) *rn in snatches in midfield: wknd over 2f out: eased and t.o* **9/2**[1]

2m 19.65s (-2.25) **Going Correction** -0.025s/f (Stan) 12 Ran SP% **119.0**
Speed ratings (Par 103): **107,106,104,104,103 101,101,100,98,97 79,79**
toteswingers: 1&2 £60.90, 1&3 £21.60, 2&3 £65.00. CSF £190.75 CT £2383.74 TOTE £11.40: £3.50, £11.10, £4.50; EX 344.20 TRIFECTA Not won..
Owner Mr & Mrs W J Williams **Bred** B Dolan **Trained** Newmarket, Suffolk
■ Stewards' Enquiry : Martin Lane four-day ban: used whip in incorrect place (May 14-17)

FOCUS
An ordinary handicap run at what appeared a modest pace. The first two were among the least exposed, and a personal best from the winner.

1707 MASCOT GRAND NATIONAL 07.05.12 H'CAP 1m 3f (P)
4:45 (4:51) (Class 5) (0-75,75) 3-Y-0 **£2,264** (£673; £336; £168) **Stalls** Low

Form RPR

31-4 1 **Flying Trader (USA)**[19] 1302 3-9-3 **71** LukeMorris 8 81
(Jane Chapple-Hyam) *trckd ldrs and slotted in fr wd draw after 4f: urged along briefly 4f out: stoked up and c between rivals 2f out: led over 1f out: drvn clr* **15/2**[3]

662- 2 *2 ½* **Spanish Wedding**[132] 7835 3-9-7 **75** AndreaAtzeni 5 80
(Marco Botti) *trckd ldrs: tried to mount a chal over 2f out but sn rdn and nt qckn: styd on fnl f to take 2nd last strides* **5/2**[1]

-325 3 *½* **Dartford (USA)**[19] 1312 3-9-6 **74** RobertHavlin 4 78
(John Gosden) *dismntd at s tl jst bef ent stalls: led: drvn over 2f out: hdd and one pce over 1f out* **8/1**

2-43 4 *1* **Dynastic**[33] 1065 3-9-4 **75** SeanLevey(3) 10 77
(Richard Hannon) *t.k.h in rr: squeezed for room after 2f: prog on inner over 2f out: clsd on ldrs over 1f out: nt qckn after* **16/1**

02-4 5 *1 ¾* **Harry Buckle**[20] 1288 3-9-0 **68** KierenFallon 12 67+
(Philip McBride) *forced v wd on bnd after 2f: rchd midfield bef 1/2-way: drvn over 2f out: tried to cl on ldrs over 1f out: effrt petered out fnl f* **7/1**[2]

-123 6 *1 ¾* **Beauchamp Castle**[26] 1190 3-8-9 **70** (t) NicoleNordblad(7) 2 66
(Hans Adielsson) *hld up in rr: appeared gng strly in midfield over 2f out: reminder and no prog: hld together after* **15/2**[3]

14-2 7 *½* **Titus Star (IRE)**[39] 994 3-9-4 **72** LiamKeniry 6 67
(J S Moore) *trckd ldr: drvn to chal over 2f out: sn nt qckn: wknd fnl f* **25/1**

030- 8 *¾* **Dollar Bill**[232] 5967 3-9-5 **73** (p) JimmyFortune 3 67
(Andrew Balding) *hld up in rr: shkn up and no prog over 3f out: sme hdwy 2f out: nvr on terms* **20/1**

-314 9 *shd* **Bramshill Lass**[68] 656 3-9-4 **72** JimCrowley 1 66
(Amanda Perrett) *prom: wnt 3rd over 4f out: drvn to chal over 2f out: wknd rapidly jst over 1f out* **25/1**

401- 10 *¾* **Welsh Nayber**[203] 6760 3-8-11 **65** NeilCallan 7 57
(Amanda Perrett) *chsd ldng pair to over 4f out: sn lost pl u.p* **25/1**

10-3 11 *1 ½* **Bounty Seeker (USA)**[32] 1093 3-9-6 **74** SilvestreDeSousa 11 64
(Mark Johnston) *wd bnd after 2f: nvr beyond midfield: nt gng wl fr 1/2-way: dropped to rr and wl btn over 2f out* **8/1**

050- 12 *7* **Romantic (IRE)**[188] 7083 3-9-4 **72** (b[1]) TomQueally 9 49
(Sir Henry Cecil) *hld up in last pair: bmpd after 2f: gng wl enough 4f out: rdn and wknd qckly over 2f out* **10/1**

2m 20.11s (-1.79) **Going Correction** -0.025s/f (Stan) 12 Ran SP% **118.1**
Speed ratings (Par 98): **105,103,102,102,100 99,99,98,98,98 96,91**
toteswingers: 1&2 £6.70, 1&3 £15.20, 2&3 £7.00. CSF £25.01 CT £153.25 TOTE £9.30: £3.40, £1.90, £3.30; EX 33.00 Trifecta £329.90 Pool: £766.83 - 1.72 winning units..
Owner Greg Secker - Unlimited Racing **Bred** Hot Pepper Farm **Trained** Dalham, Suffolk

FOCUS
A fair handicap. The time was 0.46 seconds slower than the preceding Class 5 contest for older horses. The form looks pretty sound.

Romantic(IRE) Official explanation: jockey said gelding suffered interference in running

1708 BETFAIR.COM H'CAP 7f (P)
5:15 (5:16) (Class 4) (0-85,85) 4-Y-0+ £4,075 (£1,212; £606; £303) Stalls Low

Form RPR

130- 1 **Esprit De Midas**[219] 6331 6-9-4 82 ShaneKelly 5 89
(Dean Ivory) *hld up in midfield: stdy prog 2f out: clsd w pack over 1f out: drvn ahd last 50yds: won on the nod* 9/1

60-5 2 nse **Kakapuka**[61] 733 5-9-1 79 LukeMorris 14 86
(Anabel K Murphy) *t.k.h: racd wd first 2f: prom: drvn over 2f out: clsd w pack over 1f out: chal last 100yds: pipped on the post* 50/1

004/ 3 nk **Cape Rock**[596] 5997 7-9-3 81 [1] DarryllHolland 11 87
(William Knight) *t.k.h: trckd ldrs: drvn over 2f out: clsd w pack over 1f out: upsides 75yds out: nt qckn* 25/1

4-11 4 nk **Ducal**[33] 1066 4-9-5 83 JohnFahy 3 88+
(Mike Murphy) *hld up in rr: drvn on outer over 2f out: clsd to chal ldrs last 75yds: nt qckn fnl strides* 3/1[1]

0-40 5 shd **Intercept (IRE)**[17] 1354 4-9-2 80 [1] RobertHavlin 2 85
(John Gosden) *led: drew at least 4 l clr 1/2-way: c bk to field over 1f out: hdd and no ex last 50yds* 9/2[2]

0416 6 1 **Street Power (USA)**[33] 1066 7-8-9 78 RaulDaSilva(5) 7 80+
(Jeremy Gask) *t.k.h: hld up in last pair: brought wd and drvn 2f out: clsd on ldrs 1f out: nt qckn after* 12/1

130- 7 3/4 **Sea Soldier (IRE)**[236] 5830 4-9-6 84 JimmyFortune 13 86
(Andrew Balding) *chsd ldr who wnt clr at 1/2-way: clsd w pack fr over 1f out: lost 2nd last 150yds: no room sn after and eased* 7/1

3101 8 3/4 **Aldermoor (USA)**[65] 710 6-8-13 77 NickyMackay 10 75
(Stuart Williams) *hld up in midfield: in tch fr 2f out but nt pce to threaten clly-bunched pack fnl f* 25/1

11/2 9 1 **Dubarshi**[33] 1066 4-9-6 84 DaneO'Neill 1 80
(Jo Crowley) *hld up towards rr on inner: effrt over 2f out: nt qckn over 1f out: no hdwy after* 5/1[3]

151- 10 2 1/4 **The Guru Of Gloom (IRE)**[231] 6003 4-9-3 81 MartinDwyer 9 70
(William Muir) *hld up in rr: shkn up and no prog over 2f out: n.d after* 16/1

211- 11 3 **Konstantin (IRE)**[244] 5581 4-9-1 79 HayleyTurner 6 60
(Marcus Tregoning) *prom in chsng gp: rdn over 2f out: wknd over 1f out* 9/1

2010 12 10 **Titan Triumph**[37] 1035 8-9-4 82 (t) JimCrowley 12 36
(William Knight) *t.k.h: hld up in last pair: wknd over 2f out: eased* 40/1

1m 25.13s (-0.87) **Going Correction** -0.025s/f (Stan) 12 Ran SP% 118.0
Speed ratings (Par 105): **103,102,102,102,102 101,100,99,98,95 92,80**
toteswingers: 1&2 £35.70, 1&3 £32.60, 2&3 £43.70. CSF £404.71 CT £10450.96 TOTE £15.90: £3.30, £11.80, £7.00; EX 381.10 TRIFECTA Not won..
Owner Geoff Copp **Bred** Jeremy Green And Sons **Trained** Radlett, Herts

FOCUS
A good, competitive handicap, but the gallop was modest until Intercept gradually opened up a clear lead. Ordinary form for the grade.

1709 BOOK KEMPTON TICKETS ON 0844 579 3008 CLASSIFIED STKS 6f (P)
5:45 (5:45) (Class 6) 3-Y-O £1,617 (£481; £240; £120) Stalls Low

Form RPR

34-5 1 **Wiltshire Life (IRE)**[16] 1389 3-8-9 64 (p) RaulDaSilva(5) 10 70
(Jeremy Gask) *fast away fr wd draw: mde all: pressed 2f out: fnd ex to assert over 1f out: a holding on after* 20/1

1-5 2 1 **Dancheur (IRE)**[21] 1252 3-9-0 63 MartinHarley 6 67+
(Mrs K Burke) *stdd s: t.k.h and hld up in last pair: rdn over 2f out: nt qckn and sn outpcd: styd on fr over 1f out: tk 2nd last 50yds* 15/8[1]

-034 3 1/2 **Glennten**[26] 1192 3-9-0 65 LiamKeniry 9 65
(Sylvester Kirk) *trckd ldng pair: tried to chal jst over 2f out: nt qckn and hld after: wnt 2nd briefly last 100yds: kpt on* 14/1

20-4 4 1 **Subtle Knife**[25] 1201 3-8-11 65 RyanPowell(3) 11 62
(Giles Bravery) *racd wd towards rr: hanging and struggling over 2f out: styd on fr over 1f out: nrst fin* 40/1

510 5 1 1/2 **Cats Eyes**[70] 637 3-9-0 63 ShaneKelly 3 57
(Robert Cowell) *trckd wnr: chal jst over 2f out: nt qckn and hld over 1f out: wknd fnl f* 7/1

512- 6 3 1/2 **Intomist (IRE)**[134] 7808 3-8-9 64 NathanAlison(5) 1 46
(Jim Boyle) *hld up in last: sme prog jst over 2f out: no imp on ldrs over 1f out: fdd* 5/1[3]

641- 7 2 **I See You**[164] 7452 3-9-0 65 LukeMorris 8 39
(Peter Makin) *plld hrd: hld up bhd ldrs: nt qckn over 2f out: wknd over 1f out* 4/1[2]

1555 8 6 **Thorpe Bay**[11] 1482 3-8-9 65 (b) DavidKenny(5) 2 20
(Conor Dore) *t.k.h: hld up bhd ldrs: nt qckn over 2f out: wknd over 1f out* 40/1

50-5 9 2 1/2 **Star Kingdom (IRE)**[18] 1331 3-9-0 65 JimCrowley 5 12
(Robert Mills) *t.k.h: hld up bhd ldrs: outpcd over 2f out: sn wknd* 9/1

1m 12.77s (-0.33) **Going Correction** -0.025s/f (Stan) 9 Ran SP% 110.3
Speed ratings (Par 96): **101,99,99,97,95 91,88,80,77**
toteswingers: 1&2 £9.60, 1&3 £8.40, 2&3 £7.10. CSF £53.93 TOTE £24.40: £6.30, £1.50, £3.00; EX 72.60 Trifecta £676.30 Pool: £1,133.42 - 1.24 winning units..
Owner Mark Allen **Bred** Yeomanstown Stud **Trained** Sutton Veny, Wilts

FOCUS
Modest form, and again the pace held up well. The form is rated loosely around the third.
Thorpe Bay Official explanation: jockey said gelding lost its action
T/Jkpt: Not won. T/Plt: £184.70 to a £1 stake. Pool: £106,484.36. 420.72 winning tickets. T/Qpdt: £37.70 to a £1 stake. Pool: £10,252.69. 201.16 winning tickets. JN

1563 WINDSOR (R-H)
Monday, April 30
1710 Meeting Abandoned - Waterlogged

1629 WOLVERHAMPTON (A.W) (L-H)
Monday, April 30

OFFICIAL GOING: Standard
Wind: Fresh half-against Weather: Cloudy with sunny spells

1716 32RED.COM MEDIAN AUCTION MAIDEN STKS 1m 141y(P)
5:55 (5:55) (Class 5) 3-5-Y-O £2,264 (£673; £336; £168) Stalls Low

Form RPR

3 1 **Fluctuate (USA)**[11] 1467 3-8-12 0 WilliamBuick 6 90+
(John Gosden) *mde virtually all: shkn up over 1f out: clr fnl f: eased nr fin* 1/8[1]

55- 2 6 **Idyllic Star (IRE)**[252] 5320 3-8-7 0 DavidProbert 5 71
(J S Moore) *chsd wnr: rdn over 1f out: sn edgd lft and styd on same pce* 14/1[2]

3 9 **Temuco (IRE)**[129] 7862 3-8-12 62 RichardThomas 8 55
(David Evans) *chsd ldrs: rdn over 2f out: wknd over 1f out* 125/1

0-4 4 8 **Bridgehampton**[13] 1427 3-8-12 0 JamieSpencer 2 37+
(Michael Bell) *hld up: shkn up over 3f out: nvr nr to chal* 33/1

3-5 5 2 1/2 **Mighty Motive**[20] 1270 3-8-12 0 MichaelO'Connell 1 31+
(John Mackie) *hld up: racd keenly: nvr nr to chal* 20/1[3]

6 2 3/4 **Voodoo (IRE)** 3-8-12 0 WilliamCarson 4 25
(Daniel Mark Loughnane) *chsd ldrs tl rdn and wknd over 2f out* 66/1

5 7 1 1/4 **July Specialists**[13] 1427 3-8-4 0 DeclanCannon(3) 7 17
(Richard Guest) *s.i.s: hld up: drvn along over 3f out: nvr on terms* 300/1

0 8 1 1/2 **Gravie**[14] 1422 4-9-8 0 RussKennemore 3
(Brian Baugh) *prom: rdn over 3f out: wknd over 2f out* 400/1

9 2 3/4 **Polly Pease** 3-8-8 0 ow1 MichaelStainton 9
(Nikki Evans) *s.i.s: hdwy over 6f out: rdn and wknd over 2f out* 100/1

0 10 5 **Craniac**[14] 1420 5-9-13 0 (t) LiamJones 10
(Frank Sheridan) *s.i.s: a in rr: bhd fnl 3f: t.o* 125/1

1m 50.27s (-0.23) **Going Correction** -0.10s/f (Stan)
WFA 3 from 4yo+ 15lb 10 Ran SP% 107.9
Speed ratings (Par 103): **97,91,83,76,74 71,70,69,67,62**
toteswingers: 1&2 £2.00, 1&3 £10.40, 2&3 £8.30. CSF £1.55 TOTE £1.10: £1.02, £1.50, £14.20; EX 2.70.
Owner Magnolia Racing Cliveden Stud Ms R Hood **Bred** Cliveden Stud Ltd **Trained** Newmarket, Suffolk

FOCUS
As the betting suggested, this was a very one-sided maiden. The gallop was and ordinary one and the ready winner came down the centre in the straight. The easy winner was the first to test the Wood Ditton form. The race is rated loosely around the second.

1717 FOLLOW US ON TWITTER @WOLVESRACES H'CAP 1m 141y(P)
6:25 (6:25) (Class 6) (0-55,55) 4-Y-0+ £1,704 (£503; £251) Stalls Low

Form RPR

00-0 1 **Footstepsofspring (FR)**[76] 551 5-8-13 52 TonyCulhane 4 63
(Willie Musson) *a.p: rdn over 3f out: swtchd rt over 1f out: styd on u.p to ld wl ins fnl f* 11/2[2]

5-21 2 1 **Goldstorm**[4] 1634 4-9-1 54 6ex RussKennemore 12 63+
(Brian Baugh) *s.i.s: hld up: hdwy and nt clr run over 1f out: hmpd ins fnl f: r.o wl* 7/4[1]

6/06 3 nk **Wind Star**[32] 1092 9-9-2 55 (p) KirstyMilczarek 10 63
(Brendan Powell) *chsd ldrs: led over 1f out: rdn and hdd wl ins fnl f* 20/1

-5F0 4 2 **American Lover (FR)**[12] 1439 5-8-10 49 PaddyAspell 1 52
(John Wainwright) *hld up: hdwy over 1f out: sn rdn and edgd lft: styd on* 16/1

4653 5 nk **Join Up**[19] 1309 6-8-7 53 RachealKneller(7) 7 56
(Mark Brisbourne) *a.p: rdn over 2f out: styd on* 8/1[3]

453 6 2 **Lean Machine**[14] 1425 5-8-11 50 (p) WilliamCarson 6 48
(Ronald Harris) *racd keenly: sn led: rdn over 2f out: hdd over 1f out: no ex ins fnl f* 8/1[3]

0-00 7 3 1/4 **Nicholas Pocock (IRE)**[14] 1425 6-9-2 55 FrederikTylicki 5 46
(Ian McInnes) *hld up: styd on ins fnl f: nvr nrr* 28/1

20-0 8 1 1/4 **Deslaya (IRE)**[98] 274 4-8-12 51 MichaelO'Connell 2 39
(Linda Stubbs) *prom: rdn over 2f out: hmpd and wknd ins fnl f* 40/1

-004 9 2 1/2 **Hackett (IRE)**[9] 1530 4-8-13 52 (b) WilliamBuick 9 34
(Shaun Lycett) *hld up: bhd and rdn over 3f out: n.d* 20/1

400 10 2 **Mad Ginger Alice**[25] 1207 4-8-11 55 LauraPike(5) 13 32
(Olivia Maylam) *chsd ldr 7f out: rdn over 2f out: wknd over 1f out* 40/1

-000 11 3 **Strong Vigilance (IRE)**[53] 843 5-9-1 54 JamieSpencer 11 25
(Michael Bell) *s.i.s: sn drvn along to go prom: lost pl and reminders over 6f out: hrd drvn over 3f out: wknd over 2f out* 11/2[2]

4-00 P **Takhreej (IRE)**[30] 1052 4-9-0 53 JamesDoyle 8
(Paul Rich) *sn pushed along in rr: p.u wl over 5f out: fatally injured* 33/1

1m 49.92s (-0.58) **Going Correction** -0.10s/f (Stan) 12 Ran SP% 116.0
Speed ratings (Par 101): **98,97,96,95,94 93,90,89,86,85 82,**
toteswingers: 1&2 £4.30, 1&3 £31.60, 2&3 £11.10. CSF £13.80 CT £178.79 TOTE £7.20: £2.10, £1.40, £7.30; EX 22.70.
Owner Le Printemps Partnership **Bred** S R L Unitrade **Trained** Newmarket, Suffolk
■ Stewards' Enquiry : Michael O'Connell three-day ban: careless riding (May 14-16)

FOCUS
A moderate handicap run at just an ordinary gallop, and rather muddling. The winner came down the centre in the straight. The form could be rated a little higher.
Strong Vigilance(IRE) Official explanation: jockey said gelding was reluctant to race

1718 32RED CASINO CLAIMING STKS 1m 1f 103y(P)
6:55 (6:55) (Class 6) 4-Y-0+ £1,704 (£503; £251) Stalls Low

Form RPR

1203 1 **Standpoint**[18] 1341 6-8-8 82 (p) JackDuern(7) 2 70
(Reg Hollinshead) *led: hdd 8f out: chsd ldr tl led again over 2f out: rdn clr fr over 1f out* 8/15[1]

3124 2 2 1/4 **Daniel Thomas (IRE)**[31] 1105 10-8-9 70 (tp) WilliamCarson 5 59
(Richard Guest) *s.i.s: sn prom: chsd wnr over 2f out: rdn over 1f out: styd on* 9/2[2]

0-50 3 1/2 **Scamperdale**[41] 971 10-9-3 72 (p) TonyCulhane 6 66
(Brian Baugh) *hld up and bhd: hdwy over 2f out: rdn over 1f out: styd on* 11/1

2333 4 hd **Ahlawy (IRE)**[4] 1632 9-8-7 68 (t) LiamJones 7 56
(Frank Sheridan) *hld up: hdwy over 2f out: rdn over 1f out: r.o* 13/2[3]

4 dht **M'Lady Eliza**[697] 7-8-6 0 RichardThomas 1 55?
(David Evans) *hld up: swtchd rt over 1f out: rdn: hung lft and r.o ins fnl f: nt rch ldrs* 66/1

00-4 **6** 3 **Guga (IRE)**18 1339 6-8-7 52 (b) FrannyNorton 4 50
(John Mackie) *led 8f out: rdn and hdd over 2f out: wknd fnl f* **40/1**
00 **7** 29 **Miss Tooty Fruiti (IRE)**77 546 4-8-1 0 JakePayne(7) 3
(Bill Turner) *chsd ldrs: rdn over 3f out: wknd over 2f out: t.o* **150/1**
1m 59.48s (-2.22) **Going Correction** -0.10s/f (Stan) **7** Ran SP% **109.7**
Speed ratings (Par 101): **105,103,102,102,102 99,73**
toteswingers: 1&2 £1.20, 1&3 £2.10, 2&3 £3.20. CSF £2.91 TOTE £1.90: £1.30, £1.90; EX 3.30.Standpoint was claimed by Conor Dore for £9,000.
Owner Moores Metals Ltd **Bred** Juddmonte Farms Ltd **Trained** Upper Longdon, Staffs
FOCUS
A reasonable claimer run at just an ordinary gallop. The winner raced centre-to-far-side in the straight. Dubious form, rated negatively.

1719 £32 FREE AT 32RED.COM H'CAP 1m 4f 50y(P)
7:25 (7:25) (Class 5) (0-70,70) 4-Y-O+ **£2,264** (£673; £336; £168) **Stalls** Low

Form RPR
1 **Wicked Spirit (IRE)**178 7279 4-9-2 66 JoeFanning 7 73
(Mark Johnston) *mde all: shkn up over 1f out: r.o wl: eased nr fin* **7/2**2
2325 **2** 1 **Shabak Hom (IRE)**18 601 5-9-7 70 JamesDoyle 1 75
(David Evans) *hld up: hdwy over 2f out: rdn to chse wnr over 1f out: styd on* **17/2**
346- **3** 3/4 **Tropical Bachelor (IRE)**226 6157 6-9-0 63 FrederikTylicki 4 67
(Richard Ford) *chsd ldrs: rdn over 2f out: edgd lft over 1f out: styd on* **16/1**
5242 **4** 1 **Edgeworth (IRE)**29 1154 6-9-7 70 JamieSpencer 5 72
(David Bridgwater) *hld up in tch: nt clr run and lost pl over 2f out: hdwy and hmpd over 1f out: styd on: nvr able to chal* **3/1**1
00-1 **5** 3/4 **Saint Thomas (IRE)**44 944 5-9-1 64 MichaelO'Connell 3 65
(John Mackie) *hld up: rdn over 1f out: nt trble ldrs* **9/2**3
2510 **6** nk **Spartan King (IRE)**26 1191 4-8-7 57 MartinLane 9 58
(Ian Williams) *s.s: hld up: rdn over 1f out: nvr trbld ldrs* **12/1**
4-44 **7** shd **Mecox Bay (IRE)**31 1112 5-8-7 56 oh7 FrannyNorton 2 56
(Jennie Candlish) *prom: nt clr run and lost pl over 2f out: rallied and edgd rt over 1f out: no ex ins fnl f* **16/1**
5221 **8** 4 1/2 **Dazzling Valentine**11 1485 4-9-4 68 LiamJones 6 61
(Alan Bailey) *prom: chsd wnr over 3f out: rdn over 2f out: wknd fnl f* **5/1**
/00- **R** **That'll Do Nicely (IRE)**193 2734 9-9-2 65 GrahamLee 8
(Nicky Richards) *ref to r* **28/1**
2m 42.61s (1.51) **Going Correction** -0.10s/f (Stan)
WFA 4 from 5yo+ 1lb **9** Ran SP% **115.5**
Speed ratings (Par 103): **90,89,88,88,87 87,87,84,**
toteswingers: 1&2 £5.40, 1&3 £2.60, 2&3 £9.80. CSF £33.30 CT £419.84 TOTE £2.70: £1.10, £4.00, £7.80; EX 43.30.
Owner Mrs Joan Keaney **Bred** Mrs Joan Keaney **Trained** Middleham Moor, N Yorks
FOCUS
A modest handicap in which the gallop was a steady one to the home turn. The winner came down the centre in the straight. The winner had the run of the race and is rated back to his early Irish form.
Edgeworth(IRE) Official explanation: jockey said gelding was denied a clear run

1720 BOOK TICKETS ONLINE AT WOLVERHAMPTON-RACECOURSE.CO.UK CLAIMING STKS 5f 20y(P)
7:55 (7:55) (Class 6) 3-Y-O+ **£1,704** (£503; £251) **Stalls** Low

Form RPR
-221 **1** **Lesley's Choice**11 1483 6-9-10 67 (b) JamesDoyle 4 86
(Paul Rich) *mde all: rdn and edgd rt over 1f out: styd on* **8/1**
0001 **2** 1 1/2 **Red Cape (FR)**4 1630 9-9-6 80 (b) JamesSullivan 5 77
(Ruth Carr) *chsd wnr: rdn and edgd rt over 1f out: styd on same pce ins fnl f* **7/4**2
4120 **3** 1 3/4 **Black Baccara**26 1187 5-9-0 71 (be) RyanClark(3) 2 67
(Phil McEntee) *a.p: rdn to go 3rd ins fnl f: styd on same pce* **16/1**
1153 **4** 1/2 **Steelcut**4 1630 8-9-0 69 (p) MatthewCosham(5) 1 68
(David Evans) *chsd ldrs: rdn over 1f out: no ex ins fnl f* **6/1**3
/312 **5** 1 1/2 **Brenin Taran**38 1015 6-9-12 82 MartinLane 6 69
(David Simcock) *hld up in tch: hung rt 1/2-way: rdn and hung lft over 1f out: wknd ins fnl f* **13/8**1
50 **6** 6 **Mi Regalo**4 1628 4-9-5 43 (be) KirstyMilczarek 3 41
(Phil McEntee) *dwlt: outpcd* **150/1**
1m 1.13s (-1.17) **Going Correction** -0.10s/f (Stan) **6** Ran SP% **106.4**
Speed ratings (Par 101): **105,102,99,99,96 87**
toteswingers: 1&2 £2.60, 1&3 £6.30, 2&3 £2.80. CSF £20.19 TOTE £7.70: £2.80, £2.00; EX 25.10.
Owner L M Power **Bred** B C Allen **Trained** Newport, Gwent
FOCUS
A fair claimer run at a reasonable gallop. The winner came down the centre and is rated in line with his best form since his 2009 peak.
Brenin Taran Official explanation: trainer's rep said gelding finished lame

1721 32RED H'CAP 5f 216y(P)
8:25 (8:26) (Class 4) (0-80,80) 3-Y-O **£4,204** (£1,251; £625; £312) **Stalls** Low

Form RPR
4-21 **1** **Bartolomeu**16 1377 3-9-7 80 PatCosgrave 3 92
(Marco Botti) *sn chsng ldrs: led over 1f out: rdn clr* **3/1**2
034- **2** 3 **Uprise**215 6463 3-9-0 73 WilliamBuick 4 76+
(Sir Michael Stoute) *s.i.s: hld up: running on whn n.m.r ins fnl f: wnt 2nd nr fin: no ch w wnr* **2/1**1
2322 **3** hd **Homeward Strut**9 1529 3-8-8 67 (b) AndreaAtzeni 1 69
(Frank Sheridan) *prom: rdn to chse wnr ins fnl f: styd on same pce: lost 2nd nr fin* **16/1**
566- **4** 3/4 **Al's Memory (IRE)**178 7259 3-8-10 74 MatthewCosham(5) 10 74
(David Evans) *mid-div: swtchd lft 4f out: rdn 1/2-way: hdwy over 2f out: sn outpcd: swtchd rt and rallied over 1f out: styd on* **50/1**
2615 **5** 1 1/2 **Ghost Train (IRE)**21 1264 3-8-11 70 JoeFanning 13 65
(Mark Johnston) *prom: rdn over 2f out: edgd lft over 1f out: styd on same pce* **12/1**
01-0 **6** 1/2 **Jinker Noble**20 1271 3-9-7 80 JohnFahy 8 73
(Clive Cox) *led: rdn and hdd over 1f out: no ex ins fnl f* **6/1**3
-156 **7** 1/2 **Dubai Sunshine (IRE)**21 1264 3-9-6 79 JamieSpencer 6 71
(Michael Bell) *hld up: rdn over 1f out: styd on ins fnl f: nvr nrr* **14/1**
251- **8** nk **Kyleakin Lass**123 7905 3-9-5 78 JamesDoyle 11 69
(Ian Wood) *chsd ldrs: rdn over 2f out: wknd fnl f* **20/1**
040- **9** 1/2 **West Leake Hare (IRE)**210 6573 3-9-3 76 WilliamCarson 2 65
(Charles Hills) *mid-div: hmpd wl over 3f out: nvr on terms* **16/1**
15-6 **10** 3/4 **Blodwen Abbey**33 1063 3-8-13 72 LiamJones 9 61
(James Unett) *s.i.s: a in rr* **40/1**
40-3 **11** 1 **Barolo Top (IRE)**26 1181 3-8-13 72 SamHitchcott 12 55
(K F Clutterbuck) *s.i.s: a in rr* **100/1**
3342 **12** nk **Adranian (IRE)**47 897 3-9-5 78 (v) DavidProbert 7 60
(David C Griffiths) *chsd ldr: ev ch over 2f out: sn rdn: wknd fnl f* **12/1**
60-5 **13** shd **Monnoyer**101 230 3-9-4 77 PhillipMakin 5 59
(Scott Dixon) *hld up: rdn 1/2-way: wknd over 2f out* **33/1**
1m 13.6s (-1.40) **Going Correction** -0.10s/f (Stan) **13** Ran SP% **119.5**
Speed ratings (Par 100): **105,101,100,99,97 97,96,96,95,94 93,92,92**
toteswingers: 1&2 £3.10, 1&3 £10.50, 2&3 £7.80. CSF £8.94 CT £82.58 TOTE £3.30: £1.20, £1.40, £2.50; EX 12.60.
Owner H E Sheikh Sultan Bin Khalifa Al Nahyan **Bred** Sheikh Sultan Bin Khalifa Al Nayhan **Trained** Newmarket, Suffolk
■ Stewards' Enquiry : Matthew Cosham one-day ban: careless riding (May 14)
FOCUS
A couple of unexposed sorts in a fair handicap and a race that could throw up a few winners. The gallop was a fair one and the winner edged towards the far rail late on. Sound form set around the third and fourth.
Blodwen Abbey Official explanation: jockey said filly was denied a clear run

1722 32REDPOKER.COM H'CAP 7f 32y(P)
8:55 (8:56) (Class 6) (0-60,60) 4-Y-O+ **£1,704** (£503; £251) **Stalls** High

Form RPR
-042 **1** **Loyal N Trusted**12 1447 4-9-4 57 (p) JamesDoyle 3 67
(Richard Price) *a.p: swtchd rt 1f out: rdn to ld wl ins fnl f: r.o* **7/2**1
-000 **2** 1 **Kielty's Folly**12 1447 8-9-4 57 (p) FrederikTylicki 5 64
(Brian Baugh) *mid-div: hdwy over 2f out: led ins fnl f: sn rdn and hdd: styd on* **5/1**2
000- **3** 2 **Coastal Passage**123 7911 4-8-11 50 WilliamCarson 6 52
(Richard Guest) *hld up: rdn over 1f out: edgd lft and r.o ins fnl f: wnt 3rd post: nt rch ldrs* **12/1**
-520 **4** nk **Sottovoce**54 828 4-9-7 60 JamieSpencer 8 61
(Simon Dow) *a.p: rdn over 2f out: ev ch ins fnl f: styd on same pce* **11/2**3
-303 **5** 1/2 **Fortunate Bid (IRE)**11 1487 6-9-5 58 (p) MichaelO'Connell 12 57+
(Linda Stubbs) *s.i.s: hld up: nt clr run over 1f out: r.o ins fnl f: nvr nrr* **13/2**
200- **6** 3/4 **Yungaburra (IRE)**131 7844 8-9-4 57 (t) DavidProbert 7 54
(David C Griffiths) *led: rdn over 1f out: hdd and no ex ins fnl f* **25/1**
-656 **7** 3/4 **Bold Diva**6 1583 7-8-13 52 (v) GrahamLee 11 47
(Tony Carroll) *hld up: hdwy u.p over 1f out: styd on: nt trble ldrs* **16/1**
5345 **8** 3/4 **Jonnie Skull (IRE)**13 1433 6-8-9 55 (vt) DannyBrock(7) 4 48
(Phil McEntee) *prom: rdn over 1f out: no ex fnl f* **6/1**
00-0 **9** nse **Scommettitrice (IRE)**10 1497 4-8-10 49 AndreaAtzeni 10 42
(David Evans) *hld up: rdn over 2f out: nvr trbld ldrs* **25/1**
00-0 **10** 2 3/4 **Bilko Pak (IRE)**19 1306 4-9-3 56 (p) KirstyMilczarek 9 42
(Brendan Powell) *s.s: rdn and swtchd rt over 1f out: n.d* **12/1**
50-6 **11** 12 **Daddyow**20 1278 4-9-7 60 (b1) SamHitchcott 1 13
(Tim Vaughan) *chsd ldrs: rdn over 2f out: wknd over 1f out* **25/1**
1m 28.55s (-1.05) **Going Correction** -0.10s/f (Stan) **11** Ran SP% **114.7**
Speed ratings (Par 101): **102,100,98,98,97 96,95,95,95,91 78**
toteswingers: 1&2 £4.70, 1&3 £6.10, 2&3 £9.50. CSF £19.30 CT £183.55 TOTE £3.70: £1.40, £2.60, £5.60; EX 19.60.
Owner The Net Partnership & G Robinson **Bred** Mountgrange Stud Ltd **Trained** Ullingswick, H'fords
FOCUS
A moderate handicap run at a reasonable gallop. The winner came down the centre in the straight. Straightforward form, the winner back to his early best.
Daddyow Official explanation: jockey said gelding hung left-handed
T/Plt: £33.00 to a £1 stake. Pool: £103,767.73. 2,288.55 winning tickets. T/Qpdt: £32.40 to a £1 stake. Pool: £8,388.55. 191.30 winning tickets. CR

1702 KEMPTON (A.W) (R-H)
Tuesday, May 1

OFFICIAL GOING: Standard
Wind: Virtually nil Weather: Sunny early

1723 BETFAIR MEDIAN AUCTION MAIDEN STKS 6f (P)
6:05 (6:06) (Class 5) 3-5-Y-O **£2,264** (£673; £336; £168) **Stalls** Low

Form RPR
222- **1** **Gabriel's Lad (IRE)**173 7345 3-9-0 74 EddieAhern 1 87+
(Denis Coakley) *t.k.h: trckd ldrs: wnt 2nd ins fnl 3f: led ins fnl 2f: c clr fnl f: easily* **6/1**
423- **2** 2 1/2 **Sir Fredlot (IRE)**238 5812 3-9-0 78 DarryllHolland 4 79
(Charles Hills) *chsd ldrs: rdn over 2f out: styd on to chse wnr 1f out but nvr any ch* **2/1**1
23-3 **3** 3 **School Fees**19 1331 3-8-9 75 DaneO'Neill 12 64
(Henry Candy) *sn chsng ldr: rdn 3f out and dropped to 3rd: styd on same pce u.p fnl 2f* **7/2**2
532- **4** 1/2 **Backtrade (IRE)**251 5385 3-9-0 76 DavidProbert 8 68
(Andrew Balding) *sn led: rdn 3f out: hdd ins fnl 2f: wknd ins fnl f* **11/2**3
34 **5** 1/2 **Compton Prince**42 969 3-9-0 0 AdamKirby 6 66
(Clive Cox) *in tch: drvn along 2f out: kpt on fnl f: nt rch ldrs* **10/1**
332- **6** 2 **Khaleejiya (IRE)**216 6449 3-8-9 73 SilvestreDeSousa 11 55
(James Tate) *s.i.s: in rr: drvn along over 2f out: kpt on fnl f: nvr a threat* **16/1**
63 **7** 3/4 **Langley Vale**17 1376 3-9-0 0 SebSanders 9 57
(Roger Teal) *wnt lft s: s.i.s: in rr: c to outside 2f out: styd on fnl f* **20/1**
2- **8** hd **Silkee Supreme**285 4229 3-9-0 0 RyanMoore 3 57
(Richard Hannon) *s.i.s: in rr: c to outside over 2f out: styd on fnl f* **12/1**
9 hd **Snowy Valley** 3-8-9 0 RaulDaSilva(5) 10 56?
(Simon Earle) *s.i.s: in rr: sme prog fr over 1f out* **125/1**
40 **10** 5 **Exkaliber**17 1376 3-9-0 0 IanMongan 5 40
(Jeremy Gask) *chsd ldrs over 3f* **80/1**
0 **11** 2 3/4 **Indian Moon**12 1472 3-8-10 0 ow1 StevieDonohoe 7 27
(Tobias B P Coles) *chsd ldrs over 3f* **66/1**
12 1 3/4 **Starlight Secret** 3-9-0 0 J-PGuillambert 2 26
(Simon Earle) *s.i.s: in rr: rdn: green and sme hdwy on ins fr 3f out: wknd over 2f out* **125/1**
1m 12.42s (-0.68) **Going Correction** -0.075s/f (Stan) **12** Ran SP% **117.0**
Speed ratings (Par 103): **101,97,93,93,92 89,88,88,88,81 77,75**
toteswingers:1&2:£3.50, 2&3:£1.70, 1&3:£4.50 CSF £17.81 TOTE £4.90: £1.10, £1.40, £2.10; EX 29.00 Trifecta £78.90 Pool £994.41 - 9.32 winning units..
Owner Killoran Ennis Conway **Bred** Yeomanstown Stud **Trained** West Ilsley, Berks

FOCUS
An interesting 3yo maiden, run at a steady pace. The principals were all exposed to some degree and the first pair set the standard.

1724 BETFAIR.COM MEDIAN AUCTION MAIDEN STKS 1m 4f (P)
6:35 (6:38) (Class 5) 3-4-Y-O £2,264 (£673; £336; £168) Stalls Centre

Form RPR
2- 1 **Grandiloquent**[196] 6928 3-8-9 0 RyanMoore 6 82+
(Sir Michael Stoute) *mde all: drvn along ins fnl 3f: edgd rt and rn green wl over 2f out: styd on wl fnl f* **8/13**[1]
0- 2 2 **Tempest Fugit (IRE)**[196] 6933 3-8-4 0 NickyMackay 3 73+
(John Gosden) *hld up towards rr: hdwy 4f out: wnt 3rd over 2f out: chsd wnr over 1f out: sn drvn: rn green and edgd rt: kpt on but a readily hld* **7/2**[2]
60- 3 7 **Muhamee (IRE)**[171] 7398 3-8-9 0 MickaelBarzalona 1 70
(Saeed Bin Suroor) *chsd ldrs: drvn along fr 7f out: chsd wnr 3f out but no imp: wknd and lost 2nd over 1f out* **13/2**[3]
0 4 13 **Eanans Bay (IRE)**[21] 1270 3-8-9 0 EddieAhern 7 46+
(Mark H Tompkins) *in rr: mod prog ins fnl 2f* **66/1**
0-0 5 1 **Lady Burlesque (IRE)**[26] 1206 3-8-4 0 DavidProbert 5 40
(Mick Channon) *chsd ldrs: rdn 4f out: wknd 3f out* **50/1**
6 8 **Bridge That Gap** 4-10-0 0 DaneO'Neill 2 32
(Roger Ingram) *s.i.s: a in rr* **100/1**
-6 7 1 **Call Me April**[20] 1301 4-9-9 0 TomMcLaughlin 8 25
(Karen George) *chsd wnr to 3f out: sn wknd* **25/1**

2m 32.71s (-1.79) **Going Correction** -0.075s/f (Stan)
WFA 3 from 4yo 19lb 7 Ran SP% **105.8**
Speed ratings (Par 103): **102,100,96,87,86 81,80**
toteswingers:1&2:£1.20, 2&3:£2.10, 1&3:£1.20 CSF £2.41 TOTE £1.50: £1.10, £1.30; EX 2.70 Trifecta £5.10 pool £562.28 - 80.19 winning units..
Owner K Abdulla **Bred** Juddmonte Farms Ltd **Trained** Newmarket, Suffolk

FOCUS
With Palus San Marco withdrawn after refusing to enter the stalls, this looked a good opportunity for Derby entry Grandiloquent, who made no mistake. The winner set a fair pace and built on his 2yo debut.

1725 MASCOT GRAND NATIONAL 07.05.12 H'CAP 7f (P)
7:05 (7:05) (Class 6) (0-60,60) 3-Y-O £1,617 (£481; £240; £120) Stalls Low

Form RPR
010- 1 **Atlantis Crossing (IRE)**[172] 7358 3-9-3 57 PatCosgrave 10 69
(Jim Boyle) *in rr: hdwy over 2f out: led over 1f out: drvn out* **12/1**
5000 2 2 ½ **Marinus (IRE)**[20] 1320 3-9-6 60 RichardHughes 9 65
(Sylvester Kirk) *trckd ldrs: wnt 2nd over 2f out: chsd wnr appr fnl f: kpt on same pce* **11/2**[2]
600- 3 1 ½ **Mitch Rapp (USA)**[235] 5891 3-9-6 60 RyanMoore 5 61
(Harry Dunlop) *in tch: hdwy over 2f out: chsd ldng duo whn edging rt ins fnl f: nt pce to chal* **5/2**[1]
4144 4 3 ½ **Umph (IRE)**[15] 1419 3-9-5 59 (b) SilvestreDeSousa 4 51
(David Evans) *led: sn clr: rdn 3f out: hdd & wknd over 1f out* **6/1**[3]
-232 5 2 ¼ **Illustrious Lad (IRE)**[95] 322 3-9-6 60 TomQueally 3 45
(Jim Boyle) *chsd ldrs: rdn over 2f out: wknd over 1f out* **13/2**
000- 6 2 ¾ **Dana's Present**[215] 6489 3-9-4 58 LiamKeniry 11 36
(George Baker) *t.k.h in rr: drvn over 2f out: mod prog fnl f* **33/1**
30-0 7 3 ½ **Kylin**[18] 1359 3-9-4 58 IanMongan 7 27
(Olivia Maylam) *mid-div: drvn and no prog fr over 3f out* **33/1**
3320 8 3 ¾ **Arabian Flight**[5] 1622 3-9-3 60 SeanLevey(3) 13 18
(John Bridger) *slowly away: swtchd rt to rails after s: sme late hdwy* **11/1**
505 9 shd **Hugenot (IRE)**[22] 1260 3-9-3 57 StevieDonohoe 6 15
(Tobias B P Coles) *towards rr most of way* **16/1**
000- 10 nse **Johnny Splash (IRE)**[159] 7526 3-8-12 57 (v[1]) MarkCoumbe(5) 14 15
(Roger Teal) *a towards rr* **20/1**
2550 11 7 **Tectonic (IRE)**[34] 1062 3-9-3 57 (p) GeorgeBaker 8
(Chris Dwyer) *carried hd awkwardly thrght: chsd ldr tl wknd wl over 2f out* **10/1**
5-50 12 4 ½ **Thecornishcowboy**[10] 1517 3-9-2 56 (vt) KirstyMilczarek 2
(John Ryan) *chsd ldrs over 3f* **14/1**

1m 25.63s (-0.37) **Going Correction** -0.075s/f (Stan) 12 Ran SP% **119.9**
Speed ratings (Par 97): **99,96,94,90,87 84,80,76,76,76 68,63**
toteswingers:1&2:£18.30, 2&3:£3.90, 1&3:£28.00 CSF £76.07 CT £224.34 TOTE £25.50: £8.50, £3.10, £1.10; EX 135.40 TRIFECTA Not won..
Owner The 'In Recovery' Partnership **Bred** J K Thoroughbreds & P Doyle Bloodstock **Trained** Epsom, Surrey

FOCUS
Only a modest 7f handicap but it was run at a furious pace. The time was good, and it was a personal best from the winner.
Hugenot(IRE) Official explanation: jockey said gelding did not face the kickback
Thecornishcowboy Official explanation: jockey said gelding never travelled

1726 BETFAIR IPHONE & ANDROID APP H'CAP 1m 4f (P)
7:35 (7:36) (Class 6) (0-60,60) 3-Y-O £1,617 (£481; £240; £120) Stalls Centre

Form RPR
00-3 1 **Like Clockwork**[18] 1355 3-9-3 56 EddieAhern 5 62
(Mark H Tompkins) *chsd ldrs: rdn and hung rt fr ins fnl 2f: led 1f out: pushed out fnl 120yds* **8/1**
05-5 2 1 **Fleur De La Vie (IRE)**[20] 1319 3-9-5 58 JimCrowley 11 63+
(Ralph Beckett) *in rr: hdwy on ins over 2f out: styd on wl fnl f to take 2nd clsng stages but no imp on wnr* **8/1**
31-2 3 ½ **Better Be Mine (IRE)**[20] 1303 3-9-1 54 RyanMoore 4 58
(John Dunlop) *in tch: hdwy over 2f out: chal over 1f out and sn chsng wnr but no imp: lost 2nd clsng stages* **3/1**[1]
00-6 4 1 ¼ **Micquus (IRE)**[15] 1415 3-8-11 50 (v[1]) JimmyFortune 8 52
(Andrew Balding) *in rr: drvn and hdwy fr 2f out: kpt on fnl f but nt rch ldrs* **16/1**
-531 5 hd **Midnight Sequel**[20] 1303 3-8-10 49 KierenFallon 6 51
(Michael Blake) *chsd ldr: drvn to chal fr 2f out tl led briefly over 1f out: sn hdd: wknd fnl 120yds* **10/1**
-400 6 5 **Ice Loch**[10] 1517 3-8-8 47 (b) HayleyTurner 7 41
(Michael Blanshard) *in rr: effrt and n.m.r over 2f out: mod prog fnl f* **50/1**
5-05 7 1 **Dark Celt (IRE)**[20] 1303 3-8-7 46 RobertHavlin 10 38
(Tim Pitt) *stdd in rr: plld hrd tl rapid hdwy on outside to ld over 5f out: drvn and jnd over 1f out: wknd fnl f* **12/1**
-006 8 1 ¼ **Johanna Fosie (IRE)**[20] 1303 3-9-0 53 MartinHarley 13 43
(Mick Channon) *led tl hdd over 5f out: rdn 3f out: wknd ins fnl 2f* **33/1**
0-25 9 ¾ **Courtesy Call (IRE)**[34] 1062 3-9-7 60 SilvestreDeSousa 2 49
(Mark Johnston) *chsd ldrs: rdn fr over 4f out: wknd ins fnl 2f* **5/1**[3]
00-0 10 2 ¾ **Brundon**[15] 1414 3-9-7 60 DaneO'Neill 12 44
(Henry Candy) *chsd ldrs: rdn over 3f out: wknd 2f out* **9/2**[2]
4635 11 12 **Nic Nok**[36] 1045 3-8-5 49 RaulDaSilva(5) 3 14
(Harry Dunlop) *in rr: hung lft and no ch fr over 2f out* **16/1**
002- 12 ¾ **Cato Minor**[218] 6399 3-9-3 56 (b) DavidProbert 9 20
(Amanda Perrett) *chsd ldrs: rdn over 3f out: wknd over 2f out* **25/1**

2m 36.77s (2.27) **Going Correction** -0.075s/f (Stan) 12 Ran SP% **119.4**
Speed ratings (Par 97): **89,88,88,87,87 83,83,82,81,79 71,71**
toteswingers:1&2:£8.00, 2&3:£5.40, 1&3:£3.90 CSF £70.02 CT £238.93 TOTE £8.20: £1.60, £3.70, £2.00; EX 82.50 Trifecta £252.90 Pool £605.10 - 1.77 winning units..
Owner Dullingham Park **Bred** Dullingham Park **Trained** Newmarket, Suffolk

FOCUS
A modest if competitive 3yo handicap, run only at a pedestrian gallop. The level is set around the third and fifth.
Nic Nok Official explanation: jockey said colt hung left

1727 BETFAIR H'CAP 6f (P)
8:05 (8:05) (Class 4) (0-85,85) 4-Y-O+ £4,075 (£1,212; £606; £303) Stalls Low

Form RPR
2664 1 **Sulis Minerva (IRE)**[15] 1417 5-8-11 80 RaulDaSilva(5) 4 95
(Jeremy Gask) *trckd ldrs: wnt 2nd ins fnl 2f: led wl over 1f out: pushed along ins fnl f: comf* **8/1**[3]
3030 2 3 **Hatta Stream (IRE)**[21] 1289 6-8-11 78 SimonPearce(3) 5 83
(Lydia Pearce) *in rr: hdwy on ins fr 2f out: styd on wl to chse wnr fnl 120yds but no imp* **25/1**
3014 3 1 **Lastkingofscotland (IRE)**[33] 1091 6-8-11 75 (b) HayleyTurner 2 77+
(Conor Dore) *towards rr: pushed along fr 2f out: styd on strly fnl f: fin wl to take 3rd last strides: nt rch ldng duo* **11/1**
20-0 4 shd **We Have A Dream**[31] 1141 7-9-7 85 MartinDwyer 3 86
(William Muir) *led: rdn over 2f out: sn hrd pressed: hdd wl over 1f out: wknd fnl 120yds: ct for 3rd last strides* **16/1**
2-06 5 1 ¾ **Jack My Boy (IRE)**[21] 1289 5-9-0 78 (v) SilvestreDeSousa 8 74
(David Evans) *in rr: pushed along over 2f out: styd on clsng stages: nt rch ldrs* **10/1**
420- 6 shd **Silenzio**[145] 7675 4-9-0 78 RichardHughes 11 74
(Richard Hannon) *in rr: pushed along over 2f out: styd on fnl f: nt pce to rch ldrs* **14/1**
44-0 7 1 **Sutton Veny (IRE)**[15] 1417 6-9-7 85 RyanMoore 10 77
(Jeremy Gask) *chsd ldrs: drvn to chal 2f out: wknd fnl f* **5/1**[2]
1222 8 ¾ **Hinton Admiral**[27] 1181 8-8-11 75 TomQueally 6 65
(Conor Dore) *s.i.s: in rr: sme late hdwy* **16/1**
5313 9 1 ¼ **Last Sovereign**[40] 997 8-8-13 80 (b) DaleSwift(3) 9 66
(Ollie Pears) *racd on outer: chsd ldrs: wknd 2f out* **16/1**
622- 10 nse **Regal Approval**[215] 6478 4-9-0 78 PatCosgrave 1 64
(Jim Boyle) *mid-div and rdn over 3f out: in tch u.p 2f out: sn btn* **14/1**
0-00 11 1 **Button Moon (IRE)**[11] 1494 4-9-2 80 (p) JamesDoyle 7 63
(Ian Wood) *in tch: drvn to chse ldrs over 2f out: wknd qckly ins fnl f* **25/1**
134- 12 3 ¼ **Ganas (IRE)**[225] 6217 4-9-7 85 AdamKirby 12 57+
(Clive Cox) *sddle slipped; chsd ldrs: rdn over 2f out: wknd over 1f out* **9/4**[1]

1m 11.71s (-1.39) **Going Correction** -0.075s/f (Stan) 12 Ran SP% **114.6**
Speed ratings (Par 105): **106,102,100,100,98 98,96,95,94,94 92,88**
toteswingers:1&2:£52.60, 2&3:£24.00, 1&3:£12.80 CSF £183.89 CT £2170.53 TOTE £8.60: £2.70, £11.20, £3.20; EX 117.20 TRIFECTA Not won..
Owner Richard L Page **Bred** Kevin Blake **Trained** Sutton Veny, Wilts

FOCUS
A competitive sprint handicap, run at a fair pace. The winner resumed her progress, with the next two setting the standard.
Ganas(IRE) Official explanation: jockey said saddle slipped

1728 BETFAIR SUPPORTING GRASSROOTS RACING H'CAP 1m (P)
8:35 (8:36) (Class 5) (0-70,70) 3-Y-O £2,264 (£673; £336; £168) Stalls Low

Form RPR
63-1 1 **Tigers Tale (IRE)**[20] 1313 3-9-4 67 (v) JamesDoyle 4 74
(Roger Teal) *trckd ldr: led ins fnl 2f: drvn and qcknd whn chal ins fnl f: styd on strly clsng stages* **9/2**[2]
026- 2 1 ¼ **Good Luck Charm**[133] 7835 3-9-4 67 RyanMoore 12 71
(Gary Moore) *in rr: hdwy on outside fr 2f out: styd on wl fnl f to take 2nd last strides but nt rch wnr* **16/1**
06-5 3 hd **Darrow (IRE)**[21] 1288 3-9-5 68 ShaneKelly 7 72
(William Knight) *in tch: hdwy over 2f out: chsd wnr wl over 1f out: chal ins fnl f: outpcd fnl 120yds and lost 2nd last strides* **10/1**
2-16 4 1 **Manomine**[27] 1190 3-9-4 67 BrettDoyle 3 68
(Clive Brittain) *chsd ldrs: rdn 2f out: one pce fnl f* **14/1**
224- 5 ½ **Inniscastle Boy**[167] 7436 3-9-4 67 MartinDwyer 6 67
(William Muir) *chsd ldrs: rdn over 2f out: styd on same pce ins fnl f* **16/1**
50-4 6 2 ¾ **Rogue Reporter (IRE)**[41] 982 3-9-6 69 WilliamCarson 1 63
(Stuart Williams) *s.i.s: in rr: hdwy 3f out: rdn and styd on same pce fnl 2f* **8/1**
516- 7 ¾ **Netley Marsh**[305] 3595 3-9-7 70 RichardHughes 8 64
(Richard Hannon) *in rr: pushed along over 2f out: styng on whn n.m.r over 1f out: no prog after* **7/2**[1]
025- 8 hd **Rocky Reef**[172] 7358 3-9-3 66 (v[1]) JimmyFortune 9 58
(Andrew Balding) *s.i.s: in rr: hdwy towards outside fr 2f out: nvr gng pce to get into contenton* **22/1**
020- 9 ½ **Long Lost Love**[228] 6132 3-9-5 68 SilvestreDeSousa 11 58
(Mark Johnston) *sn led: hdd ins fnl 2f: wknd fnl f* **12/1**
665- 10 1 **Arabic**[202] 6792 3-9-2 65 KierenFallon 14 57
(James Fanshawe) *chsd ldrs: rdn 2f out: btn whn hmpd over 1f out* **7/1**[3]
343- 11 1 ½ **Zammy**[208] 6652 3-9-3 66 DarryllHolland 2 51
(Michael Wigham) *outpcd most of way* **40/1**
00-2 12 hd **Uncle Roger (IRE)**[20] 1322 3-9-5 68 NeilCallan 10 52
(Eve Johnson Houghton) *chsd ldrs tl wknd over 2f out* **14/1**
5-06 13 1 **Musically**[21] 1288 3-9-1 64 MartinHarley 13 46
(Mick Channon) *chsd ldrs: wknd over 2f out* **66/1**
1-04 U **Tweet Lady**[10] 1531 3-9-5 68 JamesMillman 5
(Rod Millman) *stmbld sn after s and uns rdr* **16/1**

1m 39.44s (-0.36) **Going Correction** -0.075s/f (Stan) 14 Ran SP% **120.1**
Speed ratings (Par 99): **98,96,96,95,95 92,91,91,90,89 88,88,87,**
toteswingers:1&2:£22.10, 2&3:£37.00, 1&3:£9.70 CSF £73.52 CT £714.53 TOTE £4.80: £1.40, £7.10, £5.30; EX 87.30 TRIFECTA Not won..
Owner B Kitcherside & Big Cat Partnership **Bred** Butlersgrove Stud **Trained** Ashtead, Surrey

FOCUS
Some interesting runners took their chance in this 3yo handicap. The time was reasonable and the winner took another step forward.

1729 "WIN A FREE STOVE WITH MORSTOVES" H'CAP (LONDON MILE QUALIFIER) 1m (P)
9:05 (9:10) (Class 5) (0-75,74) 4-Y-O+ £2,264 (£673; £336; £168) Stalls Low

Form RPR
/1-0 **1** **Scottish Star**[22] 1262 4-9-5 **72** LukeMorris 10 80
(James Eustace) *in rr: rdn over 3f out: hdwy 2f out: styd on wl fnl 120yds to ld last stride* **5/1**[2]
155- **2** *hd* **Good Authority (IRE)**[159] 7532 5-9-6 **73** DarryllHolland 6 80+
(Karen George) *hmpd and dropped to rr sn after s: hdwy on ins fr 3f out: drvn to ld over 1f out: hdd last stride* **7/1**[3]
026- **3** *nk* **Officer In Command (USA)**[171] 968 6-9-3 **70** JamesDoyle 4 76
(Paul Rich) *in rr: gd hdwy over 1f out: str run Ins fnl t to chal fnl 50yds: no ex last strides* **16/1**
-144 **4** *hd* **Zaheeb**[22] 1262 4-8-12 **65** WilliamCarson 1 71+
(Dave Morris) *chsd ldrs: led after 3f: rdn over 2f out: hdd over 1f out: styd on but nt pce of ldng trio clsng stages* **5/1**[2]
6-00 **5** *3 ¾* **Al Aqabah (IRE)**[90] 378 7-9-0 **70** (b) AdamBeschizza(3) 9 67
(Brian Gubby) *in rr but in tch: drvn and styd on fr over 1f out: kpt on clsng stages: nvr a threat* **10/1**
14-2 **6** *shd* **Methayel (IRE)**[46] 919 4-9-3 **70** RyanMoore 2 67
(Clive Brittain) *chsd ldrs: rdn over 2f out: wknd fnl f* **5/2**[1]
0465 **7** *nk* **Edgewater (IRE)**[27] 1186 5-9-3 **70** (v) StevieDonohoe 8 66
(Lee Carter) *sn slt ld: hdd after 3f: wknd wl over 1f out* **12/1**
-005 **8** *2* **West Leake (IRE)**[20] 1305 6-8-10 **63** LiamKeniry 7 55
(Paul Burgoyne) *chsd ldrs: rdn 3f out: wknd ins fnl 2f* **12/1**
6-05 **9** *5* **Abriachan**[36] 1051 5-8-10 **63** MartinHarley 11 43
(Noel Quinlan) *chsd ldrs 5f* **22/1**
0-02 **10** *¾* **L'Hirondelle (IRE)**[17] 1378 8-9-2 **69** (p) NeilCallan 12 47
(Michael Attwater) *drvn to dispute ld early: t.k.h: wknd fr 3f out* **12/1**

1m 38.8s (-1.00) **Going Correction** -0.075s/f (Stan) 10 Ran SP% **116.8**
Speed ratings (Par 103): **102,101,101,101,97 97,97,95,90,89**
toteswingers:1&2:£7.60, 2&3:£21.20, 1&3:£19.30 CSF £40.02 CT £534.11 TOTE £4.80: £1.50, £3.40, £5.60; EX 47.90 Trifecta £540.80 Part won. Pool £730.87 - 0.62 winning units..
Owner J C Smith **Bred** Mrs J McCreery **Trained** Newmarket, Suffolk

FOCUS
A fairly competitive, if modest handicap, but it was strong run. It produced a blanket finish and the first three came from the rear.
T/Jkpt: Not won. T/Plt: £143.70 to a £1 stake. Pool £96,301.73 - 489.13 winning units T/Qpdt: £87.00 to a £1 stake. Pool £5,459.49 - 46.40 winning units ST

1373 LINGFIELD (L-H)
Tuesday, May 1

OFFICIAL GOING: Standard
Wind: Medium, half behind Weather: dry after morning rain

1730 LINGFIELDPARK.CO.UK H'CAP 6f (P)
2:00 (2:00) (Class 5) (0-75,74) 3-Y-O £2,385 (£704; £352) Stalls Low

Form RPR
-224 **1** **Willies Wonder (IRE)**[8] 1560 3-9-5 72 MichaelHills 3 82
(Charles Hills) *chsd ldr: rdn and effrt to ld 1f out: in command and r.o wl fnl 150yds: rdn out* **7/2**[2]
236 **2** *2 ¼* **Trail Of Tears (IRE)**[21] 1274 3-8-13 66 (p) WilliamBuick 4 69
(John Gosden) *chsd ldrs: rdn and unable qck whn edgd rt bnd wl over 1f out: styd on u.p ins fnl f: no threat to wnr* **8/1**
1-50 **3** *1 ¼* **Lady Gibraltar**[13] 1449 3-9-7 74 (v) JimCrowley 7 73
(Alan Jarvis) *led: rdn over 1f out: hdd 1f out: no ex and wknd fnl 100yds* **9/1**
5-1 **4** *½* **Khubala (IRE)**[17] 1376 3-9-5 72 RyanMoore 5 69
(Ed Dunlop) *s.i.s and short of room s: bhd: rdn and effrt 2f out: no threat to wnr but styd on ins fnl f: rdr looking down and nt pushed towards fin* **6/4**[1]
64-4 **5** *2 ½* **Amphora**[13] 1449 3-9-3 70 JimmyFortune 1 59
(Andrew Balding) *t.k.h early: chsd ldrs: rdn and unable qck ent fnl 2f: drvn and wknd 1f out* **4/1**[3]
-604 **6** *½* **Darnathean**[53] 865 3-9-4 71 (b) WilliamCarson 2 59
(Paul D'Arcy) *taken down early: bhd: rdn and struggling wl over 2f out: wl btn fnl 2f* **25/1**
000- **7** *13* **Marah Music**[159] 7530 3-8-12 65 (b[1]) TomQueally 6
(Peter Makin) *wnt lft s: racd on outer in last trio: rdn and struggling over 2f out: lost tch wl over 1f out* **12/1**

1m 10.69s (-1.21) **Going Correction** -0.075s/f (Stan) 7 Ran SP% **114.9**
Speed ratings (Par 99): **105,102,100,99,96 95,78**
toteswingers:1&2:£3.80, 2&3:£4.10, 1&3:£6.80 CSF £31.13 TOTE £3.90: £1.50, £4.70; EX 32.20.
Owner John C Grant, Ray Harper, B W Hills **Bred** Rathbarry Stud **Trained** Lambourn, Berks

FOCUS
A modest 3yo handicap run in a good time for the age/grade. The winner produced improved form.
Khubala(IRE) Official explanation: jockey said colt moved poorly and hung left in straight
Amphora Official explanation: jockey said filly failed to handle the first bend
Darnathean Official explanation: jockey said saddle slipped

1731 BETFRED MOBILE SPORTS CLAIMING STKS 7f (P)
2:30 (2:30) (Class 6) 3-Y-O £1,704 (£503; £251) Stalls Low

Form RPR
2361 **1** **One More Roman (IRE)**[18] 1359 3-8-10 62 ow1 (bt) NeilCallan 4 65
(Gay Kelleway) *hld up in tch: rdn and effrt on inner 2f out: swtchd rt 1f out: drvn to ld fnl 75yds: r.o strly* **11/4**[1]
-400 **2** *1 ¾* **King's Future**[22] 1259 3-8-8 58 KierenFox(3) 1 61
(Lee Carter) *led: rdn and edgd rt bnd 2f out: hdd wl over 1f out: stl ev ch tl nt pce of wnr fnl 75yds* **14/1**
433- **3** *hd* **Dark Ages (IRE)**[194] 6975 3-8-5 65 ow1 (t) MickaelBarzalona 2 55
(George Baker) *t.k.h early: chsd ldrs: rdn and led on inner wl over 1f out: hrd drvn ent fnl f: hdd and outpcd fnl 75yds* **11/4**[1]
-323 **4** *2 ½* **Masters Club**[15] 1413 3-8-11 66 KirstyMilczarek 8 54
(John Ryan) *chsd ldr tl rdn and unable qck 2f out: plugged on same pce u.p fr over 1f out* **3/1**[2]
26-3 **5** *shd* **Chorister Sport (IRE)**[103] 214 3-9-0 67 HarryBentley(3) 7 62
(William Jarvis) *chsd ldrs: rdn over 1f out: hmpd and snatched up 1f out: nt rcvr and styd on same pce fnl f* **13/2**[3]
6244 **6** *1 ¾* **Maria Montez**[19] 1337 3-8-4 57 SilvestreDeSousa 5 42
(J W Hills) *plld hrd early: hld up in tch in rr: hmpd after 1f: rdn and effrt on inner wl over 1f out: no imp* **15/2**
0-5 **7** *16* **Trove (IRE)**[15] 1413 3-8-9 0 (p) WilliamCarson 3
(Mark Hoad) *stdd s: t.k.h: hung rt thrght: in tch: swtchd rt over 5f out: rdn over 2f out: hung bdly rt and lost tch bnd 2f out* **33/1**

1m 25.19s (0.39) **Going Correction** -0.075s/f (Stan) 7 Ran SP% **113.0**
Speed ratings (Par 97): **94,92,91,88,88 86,68**
toteswingers:1&2:£6.70, 2&3:£6.50, 1&3:£1.70 CSF £39.15 TOTE £7.30: £3.40, £9.30; EX 47.80 Trifecta £359.00 Pool £591.88 - 1.22 winning units..
Owner Miss Gay Kelleway **Bred** Mrs Fitriani Hay **Trained** Exning, Suffolk
■ Stewards' Enquiry : Harry Bentley two-day ban: careless riding (May 15-16)

FOCUS
A modest claimer. Unconvincing form, rated around the runner-up.
Chorister Sport(IRE) Official explanation: jockey said colt was denied a clear run
Trove(IRE) Official explanation: jockey said gelding ran too free

1732 LINGFIELD PARK OWNERS CLUB (S) STKS 1m 4f (P)
3:00 (3:00) (Class 6) 4-Y-O+ £1,704 (£503; £251) Stalls Low

Form RPR
1223 **1** **Eagle Nebula**[55] 824 8-9-8 68 IanMongan 4 72
(Brett Johnson) *t.k.h: chsd ldr tl rdn to ld 2f out: clr 1f out: styd on: rdn out* **10/3**[2]
6300 **2** *1* **Oneiric**[15] 1418 4-8-6 58 MarkCoumbe(5) 1 59
(Brett Johnson) *dwlt: chsd ldrs: rdn jst over 2f out: chsd wnr ins fnl f: styd on wl* **9/1**
1-13 **3** *3 ¼* **Irons On Fire (USA)**[102] 222 4-9-8 68 (p) KierenFallon 2 65
(George Baker) *led at stdy gallop: grad qcknd fr 5f out: rdn and hdd 2f out: unable qck over 1f out: wknd fnl 75yds* **7/2**[3]
30 **4** *2* **Total Obsession**[20] 1301 5-8-11 0 WilliamCarson 3 51?
(Mark Hoad) *stdd s: hld up on rr: rdn over 2f out: no ch w wnr but styd on ins fnl f* **150/1**
-102 **5** *3 ¾* **Kiss A Prince**[34] 1071 6-9-8 75 (b) ShaneKelly 5 56
(Dean Ivory) *t.k.h: chsd ldrs: rdn and struggling over 2f out: rn wd bnd 2f out: sn btn* **10/11**[1]

2m 41.12s (8.12) **Going Correction** -0.075s/f (Stan) 5 Ran SP% **108.3**
Speed ratings (Par 101): **69,68,66,64,62**
CSF £28.09 TOTE £1.80: £1.02, £4.70; EX 30.80.Irons On Fire was claimed by L. A. Carter for £6,000. There was no bid for the winner.
Owner Tann Racing **Bred** Juddmonte Farms Ltd **Trained** Epsom, Surrey
■ Stewards' Enquiry : Mark Coumbe two-day ban: used whip above permitted level (May 15-16)

FOCUS
A moderate seller and the early stages were run at a dawdle. Dubious form, rated around the winner.
Kiss A Prince Official explanation: trainer had no explanation for the poor form shown

1733 BETFRED GOALS GALORE FILLIES' H'CAP 7f (P)
3:30 (3:30) (Class 5) (0-70,70) 3-Y-O £2,385 (£704; £352) Stalls Low

Form RPR
3-16 **1** **Boudoir (IRE)**[10] 1531 3-9-3 **69** SeanLevey(3) 10 76
(Richard Hannon) *mde all: rdn and qcknd clr over 1f out: edgd rt but kpt on wl u.p fnl f* **9/1**
000- **2** *¾* **Saratoga Slew (IRE)**[220] 6329 3-9-7 **70** AdamKirby 2 75
(Marco Botti) *t.k.h early: chsd ldrs: rdn to chse clr wnr over 1f out: kpt on u.p and pressing wnr whn carried rt ins fnl f: one pce towards fin* **5/2**[1]
230- **3** *1 ¼* **Fine Painting (IRE)**[195] 6946 3-9-7 **70** RyanMoore 5 71+
(Gary Moore) *bhd: hdwy between horses jst over 1f out: r.o wl to go 3rd wl ins fnl f: nt rch ldrs* **14/1**
300- **4** *2* **City Dazzler (IRE)**[195] 6950 3-9-4 **67** RichardHughes 1 63
(Richard Hannon) *in tch in midfield: effrt u.p on inner wl over 1f out: styd on same pce fr over 1f out* **12/1**
00-1 **5** *½* **Jamhara**[15] 1420 3-8-13 **62** NeilCallan 11 57
(Clive Brittain) *restless in stalls: chsd ldr after 2f: rdn and unable qck bnd 2f out: one pce fr over 1f out* **15/2**[3]
50-4 **6** *¾* **Esprit Danseur**[13] 1445 3-9-3 **66** PatCosgrave 3 59
(Jim Boyle) *s.i.s: hld up in tch in last quartet: swtchd rt and hdwy 2f out: kpt on ins fnl f: nvr trbld ldrs* **20/1**
34-1 **7** *1* **Poker Hospital**[15] 1419 3-9-2 **70** (p) RaulDaSilva(5) 7 60
(John Stimpson) *t.k.h: chsd ldrs: rdn and unable qck wl over 1f out: styd on same pce and no threat to ldrs fr over 1f out* **10/1**
555- **8** *½* **Winter Dress**[173] 7343 3-9-3 **66** MartinDwyer 9 55
(Roger Teal) *s.i.s: niggled along in rr: hdwy and hmpd 1f out: styd on ins fnl f: n.d* **8/1**
635- **9** *2 ½* **Ida Inkley (IRE)**[325] 2919 3-8-13 **62** LeeNewman 6 44
(Jonathan Portman) *chsd ldr for 2f: styd prom: rdn over 2f out: wknd wl over 1f out* **100/1**
052- **10** *½* **Possibly**[285] 4250 3-8-11 **60** WilliamBuick 4 40
(Peter Chapple-Hyam) *in tch in midfield: switching rt to outer over 2f out: sltly hmpd sn after: wd and lost pl bnd 2f out: n.d after* **7/1**[2]
611- **11** *nk* **Elegant Flight**[160] 7514 3-9-4 **67** JimCrowley 12 47
(Alan Jarvis) *hld up in tch towards rr: hdwy on outside 3f out: lost pl bnd 2f out: n.d after* **11/1**
3-50 **12** *¾* **Shamardeliah (IRE)**[29] 1167 3-9-4 **67** (b[1]) KierenFallon 8 45
(James Tate) *chsd ldrs: rdn and unable qck ent fnl 2f: wknd over 1f out: fdd fnl f* **14/1**

1m 24.85s (0.05) **Going Correction** -0.075s/f (Stan) 12 Ran SP% **118.1**
Speed ratings (Par 96): **96,95,93,91,90 90,88,88,85,84 84,83**
toteswingers:1&2:£10.70, 2&3:£14.10, 1&3:£28.60 CSF £31.50 CT £326.84 TOTE £13.70: £3.90, £1.10, £5.70; EX 48.80 Trifecta £443.00 Part won. Pool £598.77 - 0.62 winning units..
Owner Highclere Thoroughbred Racing - Leonie **Bred** Airlie Stud **Trained** East Everleigh, Wilts
■ Stewards' Enquiry : Raul Da Silva three-day ban: careless riding (May 15-17)

FOCUS
A modest fillies' handicap, but quite a competitive event. The form is taken at something like face value.

1734 BETFRED MOBILE CASINO H'CAP (DIV I) 6f (P)
4:00 (4:00) (Class 6) (0-65,65) 4-Y-O+ £1,704 (£503; £251) Stalls Low

Form RPR
53-4 **1** **Proper Charlie**[17] 1378 4-9-7 **65** JimCrowley 4 72+
(William Knight) *broke fast and swtchd lft to inner rail: chsd ldr: swtchd rt and effrt over 1f out: drvn ahd ins fnl f: all out* **9/4**[1]
26-0 **2** *nk* **Amber Heights**[115] 87 4-9-0 **58** DaneO'Neill 1 64+
(Henry Candy) *hld up in tch in midfield: nt clr run jst over 1f out tl ins fnl f: swtchd lft and str run fnl 100yds: nt quite rch wnr* **3/1**[2]
0000 **3** *½* **Baby Dottie**[27] 1185 5-8-13 **57** IanMongan 9 61
(Pat Phelan) *chsd ldrs: rdn over 1f out: ev ch ins fnl f: kpt on* **5/1**[3]

35-0 **4** *nse* **Volito**[22] 1254 6-9-5 **63**.................................... RichardHughes 7 67
(Anabel K Murphy) *in tch in last trio: effrt on outer over 1f out: kpt on wl u.p ins fnl f* **15/2**

4220 **5** *nk* **Catalinas Diamond (IRE)**[20] 1305 4-9-5 **63**.................(t) RobertHavlin 3 66
(Pat Murphy) *stdd s: in tch in rr: hdwy on inner ent fnl f: styd on wl fnl 100yds: nt rch ldrs* **8/1**

553- **6** *hd* **Itum**[131] 7853 5-8-5 **52**.. DominicFox(3) 6 55
(Christine Dunnett) *led: rdn wl over 1f out: hdd jst ins fnl f: no ex fnl 75yds* **33/1**

5505 **7** *½* **Dvinsky (USA)**[20] 1306 11-9-4 **62**.............................(b) TomMcLaughlin 5 63
(Paul Howling) *rdn along leaving stalls: sn chsng ldr tl rdn and unable qck 2f out: styd on same pce u.p fnl f* **14/1**

5353 **8** *1 ¾* **Rightcar**[12] 1483 5-8-12 **56**.. RobbieFitzpatrick 8 51
(Peter Grayson) *hld up in tch: rdn and effrt whn n.m.r jst over 1f out: one pce and no hdwy fnl f* **14/1**

/0-0 **9** *1 ¼* **Speedyfix**[21] 1290 5-9-2 **60**..(v) WilliamCarson 2 51
(Christine Dunnett) *stdd after s: a in rr: no prog u.p over 1f out* **66/1**

1m 11.59s (-0.31) **Going Correction** -0.075s/f (Stan) **9** Ran SP% **113.1**
Speed ratings (Par 101): **99,98,97,97,97 97,96,94,92**
toteswingers:1&2:£3.00, 2&3:£4.90, 1&3:£4.10 CSF £8.73 CT £28.96 TOTE £3.60: £1.40, £1.80, £2.40; EX 7.60 Trifecta £60.40 Pool £587.81 - 7.20 winning units..
Owner Peter Oakley & Charles Whittaker **Bred** P And Mrs A G Venner **Trained** Patching, W Sussex

FOCUS
A moderate handicap and the principals finished in a heap. The winner built on his reappearance promise.

1735 BETFRED MOBILE CASINO H'CAP (DIV II) — 6f (P)
4:30 (4:31) (Class 6) (0-65,65) 4-Y-0+ **£1,704** (£503; £125; £125) **Stalls** Low

Form RPR

0524 **1** **Chjimes (IRE)**[5] 1630 8-9-5 **63**.......................................(b) HayleyTurner 7 71
(Conor Dore) *racd keenly: w ldr tl led after 1f: mde rest: rdn clr 2f out: in command fnl f: rdn out* **3/1**[2]

440- **2** *1 ¼* **Tenavon**[196] 6940 4-9-0 **58**... ShaneKelly 10 62+
(William Knight) *restless in stalls: s.i.s: rr: hdwy 1/2-way: drvn over 1f out: chsd wnr ins fnl f: styd on but no threat to wnr* **7/2**[3]

6230 **3** *½* **Avonvalley**[17] 1387 5-8-10 **54**..................................... RobbieFitzpatrick 6 56
(Peter Grayson) *in tch: rdn and outpcd over 2f out: rallied over 1f out: kpt on same pce fnl f* **8/1**

45-4 **3** *dht* **Danzoe (IRE)**[21] 1290 5-9-5 **63**...................................... WilliamCarson 2 65
(Christine Dunnett) *led for 1f: chsd wnr tl over 2f out: drvn and unable qck 2f out: no threat to wnr and styd on same pce fnl f* **11/4**[1]

0006 **5** *3 ¼* **Loyal Royal (IRE)**[10] 1528 9-9-0 **58**.................................(bt) DaneO'Neill 8 50
(Milton Bradley) *t.k.h: chsd ldrs: wnt 2nd over 2f out: drvn and unable qck wl over 1f out: wknd ins fnl f* **9/1**

-106 **6** *3* **Super Duplex**[20] 1306 5-9-7 **65**.. IanMongan 4 47
(Pat Phelan) *s.i.s: niggled along in rr and nvr gng wl: swtchd to outer 4f out: n.d* **5/1**

1m 11.83s (-0.07) **Going Correction** -0.075s/f (Stan) **6** Ran SP% **111.7**
Speed ratings (Par 101): **97,95,94,94,90 86**
TRICAST: £14.98 (Danzoe), £35.95 (Avonvalley); TRIFECTA: £9.90 (D), £11.30 (A); toteswingers:1&2:£3.10, 2&3:£1.10 (D), 2&3:£1.70 (A), 1&3:£1.20 (D), 1&3:£1.60 (A) CSF £13.67 TOTE £5.10: £2.00, £1.70; EX 12.90.
Owner Mrs Louise Marsh **Bred** Morgan O'Flaherty **Trained** Hubbert's Bridge, Lincs

FOCUS
This division was hit by four non-runners and the winning time was 0.24 seconds slower then the first leg. Modest form.

1736 BRITISH STALLION STUDS SUPPORTING BRITISH RACING EBF MAIDEN FILLIES' STKS — 7f (P)
5:00 (5:02) (Class 5) 3-Y-0 **£3,557** (£1,058; £529; £264) **Stalls** Low

Form RPR

35- **1** **Dance Company**[262] 5048 3-9-0 0.. JimCrowley 1 84
(William Knight) *chsd ldrs: rdn to chse ldr wl over 1f out: drvn ahd ins fnl f: sn clr and styd on wl* **11/1**

0 **2** *3 ¼* **Sputnik Sweetheart**[11] 1501 3-9-0 0..................................... RichardHughes 8 75
(Richard Hannon) *wnt freely to post: led: rdn and wnt clr 2f out: drvn and hdd ins fnl f: sn btn but kpt on for clr 2nd* **7/1**[3]

0- **3** *3 ¼* **Grey Seal (IRE)**[204] 6758 3-9-0 0...[1] KierenFallon 5 66
(James Fanshawe) *s.i.s and swtchd lft s: towards rr: effrt and nt clr run over 2f out: hdwy over 1f out: styd on wl to go 3rd ins fnl f: nvr trbld ldrs* **20/1**

6 **4** *1 ½* **Aarti (IRE)**[12] 1472 3-9-0 0.. LiamJones 6 62+
(William Haggas) *in tch in midfield: rdn and outpcd 3f out: rallied and swtchd rt ent fnl f: styd on past btn horses: no ch w ldrs* **4/1**[1]

2 **5** *1 ¼* **Piece Of Cake**[97] 298 3-9-0 0.. MichaelHills 10 59
(Charles Hills) *hld up towards rr: hdwy on outer to chse ldrs over 2f out: unable qck 2f out: wknd over 1f out* **8/1**

6 *1 ½* **Game All (IRE)** 3-9-0 0... MartinDwyer 12 55
(Hugo Palmer) *t.k.h: chsd ldrs: wnt 2nd 4f out tl 2f out: sn outpcd by ldng pair: wknd fnl f* **25/1**

6-2 **7** *nk* **Sareeah (IRE)**[15] 1422 3-9-0 0.. JimmyFortune 7 54
(Clive Brittain) *in tch in midfield: rdn and outpcd over 2f out: no ch and plugged on one pce fr over 1f out* **10/1**

0-6 **8** *½* **Looks Like Rain**[22] 1256 3-9-0 0.. ShaneKelly 13 53
(Michael Bell) *hld up in last quartet: pushed and outpcd over 2f out: no ch but plugged on ins fnl f* **100/1**

0-0 **9** *hd* **Desert Red (IRE)**[22] 1261 3-9-0 0...................................... HayleyTurner 14 52
(Michael Bell) *s.i.s: hld up in last quartet: outpcd over 2f out: nvr trbld ldrs* **33/1**

0 **10** *hd* **Manaar (USA)**[11] 1501 3-9-0 0... PaulHanagan 4 52
(John Gosden) *in tch: lost pl and rdn over 2f out: no ch w ldrs fnl 2f* **8/1**

0- **11** *½* **Muzdaan (IRE)**[185] 7164 3-9-0 0... NeilCallan 9 50
(Roger Varian) *chsd ldrs: rdn and unable qck 2f out: wknd over 1f out: fdd fnl f* **10/1**

-0 **12** *1 ¾* **Central Line (USA)**[12] 1472 3-9-0 0.................................... FrankieDettori 3 46
(Mahmood Al Zarooni) *in tch in midfield: rdn and no rspnse over 3f out: wknd u.p wl over 1f out* **5/1**[2]

5-4 **13** *4 ½* **Negin**[18] 1357 3-9-0 0.. WilliamBuick 11 33
(Ed Dunlop) *chsd ldr for 2f: styd handy: rdn and racd awkwardly wl over 1f out: sn wknd* **15/2**

14 *15* **Anniesuella (IRE)** 3-9-0 0... NeilChalmers 2
(Martin Bosley) *s.i.s: rn green: dropped to rr 4f out: wl bhd fnl 2f: t.o* **200/1**

1m 24.09s (-0.71) **Going Correction** -0.075s/f (Stan) **14** Ran SP% **122.7**
Speed ratings (Par 96): **101,97,93,91,90 88,88,87,87,87 86,84,79,62**
toteswingers:1&2:£16.40, 2&3:£44.30, 1&3:£52.50 CSF £84.60 TOTE £16.10: £4.40, £2.70, £9.70; EX 152.00 TRIFECTA Not won..
Owner Mrs P G M Jamison **Bred** David Jamison Bloodstock **Trained** Patching, W Sussex

FOCUS
An interesting maiden even though only the front pair mattered down the home straight. The time was reasonable and the winner posted a personal best.
Anniesuella(IRE) Official explanation: jockey said filly hung left

1737 MIRROR PUNTERS CLUB MEDIAN AUCTION MAIDEN STKS — 1m (P)
5:30 (5:32) (Class 6) 3-Y-0 **£1,704** (£503; £251) **Stalls** High

Form RPR

3- **1** **The Nile**[263] 4995 3-9-3 0.. WilliamBuick 3 98+
(John Gosden) *w ldr tl led 5f out: asserted 2f out: wl clr ins fnl f: eased towards fin* **1/2**[1]

32-2 **2** *11* **Zaeem**[22] 1265 3-9-3 78.. FrankieDettori 8 69
(Mahmood Al Zarooni) *led tl 5f out: styd upsides wnr and clr of field tl rdn and btn wl over 1f out: wl btn and fdd fnl f: a holding on to 2nd* **3/1**[2]

06- **3** *¾* **Exning Halt**[188] 7109 3-9-3 0.. MartinDwyer 12 67+
(James Fanshawe) *hld up wl off the pce in rr: stdy prog fr 3f out: styd on fnl f: no ch w wnr but clsng on 2nd fnl 100yds* **25/1**

4 *1 ¼* **Bajan Story** 3-9-3 0... NeilCallan 6 64
(Michael Blanshard) *racd wl off the pce in midfield: rdn 4f out: no ch but kpt on fnl f* **66/1**

6- **5** *3 ¼* **Autumn Fire**[179] 7258 3-8-12 0.. JimmyFortune 5 51
(Andrew Balding) *chsd ldng pair but nvr on terms: 3rd and wl btn 2f out: wknd* **20/1**

0- **6** *3 ¾* **Sea Fever (IRE)**[189] 7080 3-9-3 0...................................... KierenFallon 11 47+
(Luca Cumani) *t.k.h: hld up wl off the pce in rr: sme hdwy fnl 2f: n.d* **12/1**[3]

0-0 **7** *2* **Absolutely Me (IRE)**[22] 1257 3-8-12 0................................ LiamKeniry 9 37
(Dominic Ffrench Davis) *chsd ldng trio but nvr on terms: rdn over 4f out: wknd over 2f out* **66/1**

8 *7* **Red Mystique (IRE)** 3-9-3 0.. PaulHanagan 1 26
(Ed Dunlop) *s.i.s: rdn along and rn green thrght: a bhd* **20/1**

9 *1 ¾* **Inundate (USA)** 3-9-3 0.. MichaelHills 4 21
(Charles Hills) *s.i.s: a bhd* **12/1**[3]

0-4 **10** *nk* **Indian Blossom**[27] 1180 3-8-12 0..................................... JohnFahy 10 16
(Harry Dunlop) *nvr on terms: struggling u.p towards rr wl over 3f out: wl bhd over 2f out* **40/1**

11 *50* **Flag Is Up** 3-8-12 0.. MarkCoumbe(5) 2
(Brett Johnson) *racd off the pce in midfield: rdn over 4f out: wl t.o fnl 2f* **66/1**

1m 37.03s (-1.17) **Going Correction** -0.075s/f (Stan) **11** Ran SP% **127.3**
Speed ratings (Par 97): **102,91,90,89,85 82,80,73,71,70 20**
toteswingers:1&2:£1.40, 2&3:£10.40, 1&3:£4.30 CSF £2.29 TOTE £1.90: £1.10, £1.50, £8.70; EX 2.60 Trifecta £30.70 Pool £1,115.24 - 26.87 winning units..
Owner K Abdulla **Bred** Juddmonte Farms Ltd **Trained** Newmarket, Suffolk

FOCUS
An uncompetitive maiden, very few ever got into it, and they finished well strung out. The winner was impressive and has clear Group-race potential.
T/Plt: £864.30 to a £1 stake. Pool:£64,837.88 - 54.76 winning tickets T/Qpdt: £39.60 to a £1 stake. Pool:£5,816.95 - 108.65 winning tickets SP

1284 YARMOUTH (L-H)
Tuesday, May 1

OFFICIAL GOING: Heavy (5.2)
Outside of back straight and top bend dolled in 4metres.
Wind: Light across Weather: Overcast

1738 VISITENGLAND.COM MAIDEN AUCTION STKS — 5f 43y
2:10 (2:11) (Class 5) 2-Y-0 **£2,264** (£673; £336; £168) **Stalls** Centre

Form RPR

425 **1** **Just Past Andover (IRE)**[11] 1495 2-8-4 0.......................... JakePayne(7) 4 80+
(Bill Turner) *racd alone on stands' side: mde all: plld hrd: shkn up and c clr fnl f: easily* **13/8**[1]

5 **2** *9* **Otto The First**[20] 1308 2-8-12 0.. LukeMorris 2 46
(John Best) *racd centre: led that gp: edgd rt fr 1/2-way: rdn over 1f out: wknd fnl f* **9/4**[2]

3 *1 ¼* **Simply Dreaming** 2-8-4 0... MartinLane 6 33
(Michael Squance) *s.s: racd centre: hdwy 1/2-way: wknd fnl f* **15/2**

34 **4** *3* **Reberty Lee**[5] 1623 2-8-10 0 ow1...................................... MircoDemuro 5 28
(Noel Quinlan) *chsd ldrs in centre: rdn 1/2-way: edgd rt: wknd over 1f out* **9/2**[3]

5 *9* **Grapes Hill** 2-8-3 0 ow1... AdamBeschizza(3) 1
(Mark Rimmer) *s.i.s: racd centre and sn prom: rdn 1/2-way: wknd 2f out* **17/2**

1m 10.63s (7.93) **Going Correction** +1.325s/f (Soft) **5** Ran SP% **109.3**
Speed ratings (Par 93): **89,74,72,67,53**
CSF £5.45 TOTE £2.40: £1.10, £1.90; EX 5.50.
Owner Wackey Racers Harefield **Bred** Mrs M Marnane **Trained** Sigwells, Somerset

FOCUS
One-way traffic here with the easy winner coming up the stands' rail. He built on his Musselburgh effort and this rating may underestimate him, but the opposition was weak.

NOTEBOOK
Just Past Andover(IRE) was sent straight to the nearside rail and soon had this field in trouble, coming home pleasingly clear of his four opponents in a straightforward manner. This colt by Amadeus Wolf was the form choice in the field on account of his first two displays, particularly a good second at Musselburgh (RPR 72) on his penultimate start in a race working out well, and he looks to have built on that effort here having gone off too fast when favourite at Bath last month. Obviously, he handled this heavy ground well, but like most young horses at this stage of their careers he would prefer a better surface and should have more to offer. (op 2-1 tchd 9-4)
Otto The First looked well on the back of a respectable debut display and was fancied to build on that Lingfield effort last month. He set about the task of chasing the front-running winner down the middle of the track but could never get to grips with him. (op 5-2)
Simply Dreaming was making her debut on very testing ground and stayed on into third in a manner which suggested she will do better over further in time. (op 8-1 tchd 7-1)
Reberty Lee needs better ground. (op 11-4)
Grapes Hill showed next to nothing after a sluggish start. (op 14-1 tchd 8-1)

1739 WEATHERBYS BANK MEDIAN AUCTION MAIDEN STKS — 5f 43y
2:40 (2:40) (Class 6) 3-Y-0 **£1,617** (£481; £240; £120) **Stalls** Centre

Form RPR

4 **1** **Jocasta Dawn**[17] 1376 3-8-12 0....................................... FergusSweeney 5 76
(Henry Candy) *racd stands' side: chsd ldrs: rdn to ld wl ins fnl f: r.o* **5/1**[3]

5 **2** *2* **Sir Maximilian (IRE)**[15] 1420 3-9-3 0................................ JamieSpencer 8 74
(Ed Dunlop) *sn led on stands' side: shkn up and hdd wl ins fnl f: styd on same pce* **7/2**[2]

3-62 **3** *2* **Lupo D'Oro (IRE)**[4] [1639] 3-9-3 77.. LukeMorris 3 67
(John Best) *racd towards centre: chsd wnr: edgd rt 1/2-way: rdn over 1f out: no ex ins fnl f* **4/5**[1]

00 **4** *2 3/4* **Seventeen Seventy**[13] [1450] 3-9-3 0.............................. MircoDemuro 4 57
(Alan Coogan) *racd towards centre: in rr and pushed along 3f out: hung lft 1/2-way: rdn over 1f out: n.d* **200/1**

3 **5** *1 1/2* **Kashmiri Star**[21] [1285] 3-8-12 0.. FrannyNorton 2 47
(Michael Quinn) *racd towards centre: prom: rdn 1/2-way: sn outpcd* **16/1**

6 *2 3/4* **Jermatt** 3-9-3 0.. FrederikTylicki 1 42
(J R Jenkins) *s.i.s: racd towards centre: a in rr* **11/1**

0- **7** *2* **Azamara Star**[209] [6620] 3-8-12 0.. MartinLane 7 30
(Derek Shaw) *chsd ldrs on stands' side: rdn 1/2-way: wknd wl over 1f out* **125/1**

1m 8.55s (5.85) **Going Correction** +1.325s/f (Soft) **7** Ran SP% **110.0**
Speed ratings (Par 97): **106,102,99,95,92 88,85**
toteswingers:1&2:£1.90, 2&3:£1.70, 1&3:£1.90 CSF £20.97 TOTE £5.20: £2.40, £2.00, EX 23.70.
Owner Mrs David Blackburn & M Blackburn **Bred** Mrs M J Blackburn **Trained** Kingston Warren, Oxon

FOCUS
Straightforward enough maiden form, but not rated too positively due to the ground.
Kashmiri Star Official explanation: jockey said filly hung right

1740 D O'KANE FINANCIAL SERVICES H'CAP 1m 3y
3:10 (3:11) (Class 6) (0-60,60) 3-Y-O **£1,617** (£481; £240; £120) **Stalls** Centre

Form RPR

605- **1** **Northern Territory (IRE)**[196] [6937] 3-9-5 **58**.................... JamieSpencer 8 66
(Jim Boyle) *hld up: swtchd lft and hdwy over 3f out: rdn to ld and hung rt over 2f out: styd on u.p* **17/2**

-634 **2** *3* **Vexillum (IRE)**[10] [1517] 3-9-6 **59**.. SamHitchcott 3 60
(Mick Channon) *hld up: hdwy over 2f out: sn chsng wnr: rdn over 1f out: styd on same pce ins fnl f* **6/1**[2]

0-31 **3** *10* **Smart Affair**[48] [901] 3-8-6 **52**.. NatashaEaton(7) 4 30
(Alan Bailey) *mid-div: hdwy u.p over 2f out: wknd fnl f* **8/1**

-005 **4** *2 3/4* **Rainbow Riches (IRE)**[39] [1010] 3-8-6 **48**..................... RyanPowell(3) 10 20
(Roger Curtis) *chsd ldrs: rdn over 2f out: wknd over 1f out* **66/1**

3530 **5** *10* **Angel Cake (IRE)**[46] [923] 3-8-4 **50**.............................(p) DannyBrock(7) 6
(Phil McEntee) *chsd ldrs: rdn whn hmpd over 2f out: wknd wl over 1f out* **28/1**

046- **6** *18* **Fen Flyer**[229] [6101] 3-8-7 **46** oh1.. MartinLane 7
(Chris Dwyer) *hld up: wknd over 2f out: t.o* **50/1**

006- **7** *2 1/4* **Tigertoo (IRE)**[206] [6697] 3-9-2 **58**.. RyanClark(3) 5
(Stuart Williams) *led: rdn and hdd 3f out: wknd over 2f out: t.o* **10/1**

02-0 **8** *3 1/4* **Shredding (IRE)**[10] [1519] 3-8-11 **50**............................(b) RoystonFfrench 9
(Ed Vaughan) *chsd ldr tl led 3f out: rdn and hdd whn hmpd over 2f out: sn wknd: t.o* **25/1**

000- **9** *11* **Teacher (IRE)**[195] [6951] 3-8-4 **46** oh1......................... AdamBeschizza(3) 13
(William Haggas) *hld up in tch: pushed along whn hmpd over 2f out: sn wknd: t.o* **6/4**[1]

40-3 **10** *76* **Coach Montana (IRE)**[22] [1260] 3-9-1 **54**........................... LukeMorris 1
(Jane Chapple-Hyam) *racd alone centre: sn drvn along and off the pce: wknd and eased 1/2-way: t.o* **13/2**[3]

00-0 **11** *4* **Jenndale**[34] [1062] 3-8-7 **46** oh1.. JamieMackay 11
(Chris Dwyer) *s.i.s: a in rr: t.o fnl 5f* **100/1**

565 **12** *76* **Ruby Glass (IRE)**[15] [1422] 3-9-7 **60**...........................(b) RobertWinston 2
(Brian Meehan) *hld up in tch: rdn and wknd wl over 3f out: eased: t.o* **16/1**

1m 52.84s (12.24) **Going Correction** +1.325s/f (Soft) **12** Ran SP% **116.0**
Speed ratings (Par 97): **91,88,78,75,65 47,45,41,30, ,**
toteswingers:1&2:£6.40, 2&3:£7.30, 1&3:£14.20 CSF £55.54 CT £431.96 TOTE £8.60: £2.10, £1.90, £2.30; EX 81.10.
Owner Poppinghole Racing Partnership **Bred** J P Lim,K Marsden & South Hatch Racing **Trained** Epsom, Surrey

FOCUS
A weak 3-y-o handicap in which few landed a blow and they finished well strung out. A step forward from the winner.
Northern Territory(IRE) Official explanation: trainer's rep said, regarding apparent improvement in form, that the colt had benefited from strengthening up over the winter and the heavy ground.
Teacher(IRE) Official explanation: trainer said gelding was unsuited by the heavy ground
Coach Montana(IRE) Official explanation: jockey said gelding had no more to give
Ruby Glass(IRE) Official explanation: trainer's rep said gelding was unsuited by the heavy ground

1741 WEATHERBYS BLOODSTOCK INSURANCE H'CAP 7f 3y
3:40 (3:40) (Class 3) (0-95,93) 4-Y-0+ **£6,490** (£1,942; £971; £486; £242) **Stalls** Centre

Form RPR

0263 **1** **Mawaakef (IRE)**[3] [1679] 4-8-12 **84**................................. FrederikTylicki 6 90
(J R Jenkins) *mde all: rdn over 1f out: r.o: eased nr fin* **5/2**[2]

0-03 **2** *1 1/2* **Rigolleto (IRE)**[5] [1627] 4-8-8 **80**.. SamHitchcott 2 82
(Mick Channon) *chsd wnr: rdn over 1f out: styd on same pce ins fnl f* **6/1**[3]

500- **3** *3* **Al Khaleej (IRE)**[213] [6521] 8-9-7 **93**..................................... MartinLane 3 87
(David Simcock) *s.s: hld up: hdwy over 1f out: styd on same pce fnl f* **8/1**

3-14 **4** *1 1/2* **Triple Charm**[31] [1141] 4-8-12 **84**..................................(p) JamieSpencer 4 74
(Jeremy Noseda) *prom: rdn over 1f out: no ex fnl f* **15/8**[1]

00-0 **5** *7* **Space Station**[17] [1373] 6-8-7 **84**....................................(b) DavidKenny(5) 5 56
(Simon Dow) *chsd ldrs: rdn over 1f out: wknd fnl f* **7/1**

300- **6** *14* **Noble Citizen (USA)**[199] [6862] 7-9-1 **92**........................(be) LauraPike(5) 1 28
(David Simcock) *hld up: wknd over 2f out* **11/1**

1m 35.94s (9.34) **Going Correction** +1.325s/f (Soft) **6** Ran SP% **109.6**
Speed ratings (Par 107): **99,97,93,92,84 68**
toteswingers:1&2:£3.40, 2&3:£6.40, 1&3:£3.10 CSF £16.56 TOTE £3.50: £2.40, £4.40; EX 21.30.
Owner The Three Honest Men **Bred** J Egan, J Corcoran And J Judd **Trained** Royston, Herts

FOCUS
A fair handicap, but suspect form with the winner dominating on the stands' rail, and a slow time.

NOTEBOOK
Mawaakef(IRE) had placed in Group company as a juvenile, but his best effort for this new yard up until now had been a second off this mark of 84 over 1m on Fibresand at Southwell in February. He failed to run any sort of race over 1m on heavy ground at Sandown the previous Saturday, but made all up the nearside rail here for a clear-cut success in the manner of a horse who has much more to offer in handicap company. (op 7-2)
Rigolleto(IRE) ran third off this mark of 80 over 7f on good to soft ground at Brighton recently and appears to have run to a similar level on this occasion. (op 13-2 tchd 8-1)
Al Khaleej(IRE) was returning from a seven-month break on ground plenty soft enough for him and stayed on into third after a slow start. This was a pleasing enough introduction to the new season. (op 7-1 tchd 6-1)
Triple Charm ran well off this mark of 84 over 6f at Kempton in March and was prominent here until not finding much inside the final furlong. A drop in trip to 6f may suit on this type of ground, but it could also be that she's happiest on Polytrack. Official explanation: trainer's rep said filly was unsuited by the heavy ground (op 7-4 tchd 13-8 and 2-1)

1742 WEDDINGS AT GREAT YARMOUTH RACECOURSE FILLIES' H'CAP 7f 3y
4:10 (4:10) (Class 5) (0-70,67) 4-Y-0+ **£2,264** (£673; £336; £168) **Stalls** Centre

Form RPR

16-2 **1** **Viking Rose (IRE)**[22] [1263] 4-9-7 **67**..................................... LukeMorris 6 76
(James Eustace) *chsd ldr tl led over 1f out: drvn out* **13/8**[1]

-032 **2** *1/2* **Caramelita**[27] [1193] 5-8-13 **59**..(v) FrederikTylicki 4 67
(J R Jenkins) *hld up in tch: plld hrd: chsd wnr over 1f out: sn rdn: styd on* **11/4**[2]

441- **3** *10* **Dixie Gwalia**[196] [6940] 4-8-9 **55**.. MartinLane 1 37
(David Simcock) *hld up: hdwy u.p over 1f out: wknd fnl f* **3/1**[3]

04-0 **4** *6* **Five Hearts**[21] [1269] 4-8-8 **54**.. TedDurcan 3 20
(Mark H Tompkins) *trckd ldrs: plld hrd: rdn over 2f out: hung lft and wknd over 1f out* **15/2**

5-50 **5** *1/2* **Endaxi Mana Mou**[10] [1534] 4-8-2 **53** oh7........................ RosieJessop(5) 2 18
(Peter Charalambous) *led: clr 4f out: pushed along and hdd over 1f out: sn wknd* **16/1**

050 **6** *9* **Bright Girl (IRE)**[10] [1532] 4-8-0 **53** oh8..........................(b) NoelGarbutt(7) 7
(Mark Rimmer) *prom: rdn 1/2-way: wknd over 2f out* **66/1**

1m 35.76s (9.16) **Going Correction** +1.325s/f (Soft) **6** Ran SP% **108.9**
Speed ratings (Par 100): **100,99,88,81,80 70**
toteswingers:1&2:£1.60, 2&3:£1.90, 1&3:£1.70 CSF £5.90 TOTE £2.10: £2.10, £1.10; EX 5.00.
Owner J C Smith **Bred** Littleton Stud **Trained** Newmarket, Suffolk

FOCUS
A moderate fillies' handicap and another race where the main action came on the stands' rail as two pulled well clear. The winner is a gradual improver.

1743 HAVENHOLIDAYHOMES.CO.UK H'CAP 1m 1f
4:40 (4:41) (Class 5) (0-70,69) 4-Y-0+ **£2,264** (£673; £336; £168) **Stalls** Low

Form RPR

2-33 **1** **Tilsworth Glenboy**[3] [1659] 5-9-6 **68**.................................. FrederikTylicki 1 83+
(J R Jenkins) *hld up: hdwy over 1f out: led ins fnl f: rdn clr* **7/4**[1]

10-6 **2** *4 1/2* **Lieutenant Kojak**[32] [1114] 4-9-5 **67**................................. RobertWinston 6 72
(Peter Charalambous) *chsd ldr tl led over 2f out: rdn over 1f out: hdd and unable qck ins fnl f* **6/1**[3]

000- **3** *5* **Osgood**[35] [7236] 5-9-7 **69**.. SamHitchcott 3 63
(Mick Channon) *chsd ldrs: rdn over 2f out: sn ev ch: no ex ins fnl f* **13/2**

1450 **4** *6* **Nolecce**[14] [1432] 5-8-11 **62**...(p) DeclanCannon(3) 8 43
(Richard Guest) *hld up: rdn over 3f out: hdwy over 2f out: wknd fnl f* **11/1**

2220 **5** *17* **Zenarinda**[33] [1094] 5-9-4 **66**.. TedDurcan 9
(Mark H Tompkins) *hld up in tch: pushed along and hung lft over 3f out: wknd wl over 1f out: eased: t.o* **7/1**

221- **6** *10* **Double Trouble**[151] [7609] 4-8-12 **65**.......................(b[1]) AntiocoMurgia(5) 4
(Marco Botti) *led: rdn and hdd over 2f out: sn wknd and eased: t.o* **9/2**[2]

R00- **7** *33* **Negotiation (IRE)**[194] [6969] 6-9-1 **63**................................. FrannyNorton 7
(Michael Quinn) *rel to r: sn t.o* **33/1**

35-0 **8** *13* **Vertibes**[22] [1261] 4-9-0 **62**... MartinLane 2
(Marcus Tregoning) *in rr and pushed along over 6f out: wknd over 4f out: eased: t.o* **18/1**

2m 5.84s (10.04) **Going Correction** +1.20s/f (Soft) **8** Ran SP% **111.2**
Speed ratings (Par 103): **103,99,94,89,74 65,35,24**
toteswingers:1&2:£3.50, 2&3:£6.70, 1&3:£3.90 CSF £11.76 CT £52.24 TOTE £3.00: £1.50, £2.00, £1.10; EX 12.50.
Owner M Ng **Bred** Michael Ng **Trained** Royston, Herts

FOCUS
An ordinary handicap and they finished well strung out on bad ground. It's doubtful if the winner improved.

1744 PLEASUREWOOD HILLS THEME PARK H'CAP 1m 3f 101y
5:10 (5:11) (Class 6) (0-55,55) 4-Y-0+ **£1,617** (£481; £240; £120) **Stalls** Low

Form RPR

2556 **1** **Satwa Ballerina**[46] [767] 4-8-7 **49**...........................(b) AdamBeschizza(3) 2 54
(Mark Rimmer) *s.i.s: hld up: rdn over 4f out: hdwy over 2f out: led over 1f out: styd on wl* **14/1**

2421 **2** *2 1/2* **Dunaskin (IRE)**[7] [1580] 12-8-9 **51** 6ex.....................(b) DeclanCannon(3) 1 52
(Richard Guest) *chsd ldrs: rdn over 3f out: led 2f out: hung rt and hdd over 1f out: no ex fnl f* **4/1**[3]

6321 **3** *15* **So Is She (IRE)**[15] [1425] 4-8-6 **52**...........................(be) NatashaEaton(7) 4 27
(Alan Bailey) *chsd ldrs: led 3f out: rdn: hung rt and hdd 2f out: wknd over 1f out* **3/1**[2]

045 **4** *6* **Sweet Vera**[17] [1385] 7-8-11 **50**...................................(b[1]) RobertWinston 10 15
(Shaun Harris) *prom tl rdn and wknd over 3f out* **12/1**

03-6 **5** *15* **Famagusta**[32] [1112] 5-8-2 **46** oh1..................................(v) RosieJessop(5) 5
(Peter Charalambous) *trckd ldrs: racd keenly: lost pl 7f out: bhd fnl 5f: t.o* **3/1**[2]

0556 **6** *12* **If What And Maybe**[17] [1379] 4-9-2 **55**...........................(v) MichaelO'Connell 3
(John Ryan) *led: rdn and hdd 3f out: wknd over 2f out: t.o* **5/2**[1]

2m 49.48s (20.78) **Going Correction** +1.20s/f (Soft) **6** Ran SP% **112.9**
Speed ratings (Par 101): **72,70,59,54,44 35**
toteswingers:1&2:£5.50, 2&3:£1.90, 1&3:£6.70 CSF £68.40 CT £215.49 TOTE £21.40: £7.00, £1.90; EX 74.00.
Owner M E Rimmer **Bred** Jean Van Gysel **Trained** Newmarket, Suffolk

FOCUS
A weak handicap, run at a decent pace. The ground was a huge factor and this is not form to take too positively.
T/Plt: £87.70 to a £1 stake. Pool:£58,920.89 - 490.23 winning tickets T/Qpdt: £15.10 to a £1 stake. Pool:£3,994.28 - 195.45 winning tickets CR

MUNICH (L-H)

Tuesday, May 1

OFFICIAL GOING: Turf: good

1745a SILBERNE PEITSCHE (GROUP 3) (3YO+) (TURF) 6f 110y

4:00 (12:00) 3-Y-O+

£26,666 (£9,166; £4,583; £2,500; £1,666; £1,250)

RPR

1 **Smooth Operator (GER)**[32] 1126 6-9-6 0..................(b) StefanieHofer 2 100
(Mario Hofer, Germany) *trckd ldrs on inner: smooth hdwy to ld on turn into st: rdn and strly pressed 2f out: kpt on wl u.p to maintain advantage ins fnl 1 1/2f: rapidly diminishing advantage cl home but a doing enough* **53/10**[3]

2 *nk* **Walero (GER)**[32] 1126 6-9-6 0.. KClijmans 4 105
(Uwe Ostmann, Germany) *hld up in last trio on outer: swtchd ins and rdn to improve into midfield over 2f out: r.o to go 2nd ins fnl f: clsng rapidly on wnr fnl 50yds: jst failed* **99/10**

3 *nk* **Exciting Life (IRE)**[178] 7311 4-9-6 0.. AStarke 7 104
(P Schiergen, Germany) *midfield: rdn to improve on turn into st: sustained chal thrght fnl 1 1/2f but nvr quite on terms: kpt on wl for 3rd cl home* **14/5**[2]

4 *nk* **Nordic Truce (USA)**[290] 5-9-6 0.. DavyBonilla 3 103
(P Schiergen, Germany) *hld up in last pair on inner: stdy prog on rail fr over 2f out: stl gng wl bhd ldrs whn short of room over 1f out: had to wait for gap tl wl ins fnl f: r.o once in the clr: unlucky* **8/1**

5 *4* **Birthday Lion (GER)**[182] 7221 7-9-6 0.. GHind 6 92
(U Stoltefuss, Germany) *broke sharply fr wd draw to dispute ld: hdd and rdn over 2f out: no ex over 1f out: fdd* **157/10**

6 *hd* **Aslana (IRE)**[226] 5-9-3 0.. FilipMinarik 5 88
(P Schiergen, Germany) *hld up in last: prog to trck ldrs over 2f out: rdn and outpcd over 1f out: kpt on under v tender handling ins fnl f: should have been 5th* **8/1**

7 *4* **Stand My Ground (IRE)**[52] 880 5-9-6 0......................... FJohansson 1 80
(Mme Pia Brandt, France) *disp ld: briefly led on home turn: sn hdd: rdn and no rspnse over 1 1/2f out: wknd* **11/5**[1]

8 *½* **Konig Concorde (GER)**[145] 7678 7-9-6 0.......................... KKerekes 8 78
(C Sprengel, Germany) *trckd ldrs on outer: lost pl on turn into st: rdn and no ex fr over 1 1/2f out: eased ins fnl f* **57/10**

1m 16.19s (-3.81) **8** Ran SP% **125.7**
WIN (incl. 10 euro stake): 63. PLACES: 17, 21, 16. SF: 406.
Owner Gerd Zimmermann **Bred** Mario Hofer **Trained** Germany

1434 SAINT-CLOUD (L-H)

Tuesday, May 1

OFFICIAL GOING: Turf: very soft

1746a PRIX DU MUGUET (GROUP 2) (4YO+) (TURF) 1m

2:20 (12:00) 4-Y-O+ **£61,750** (£23,833; £11,375; £7,583; £3,791)

RPR

1 **Zinabaa (FR)**[30] 1163 7-8-11 0.................................. YannickLetondeur 8 117
(M Mace, France) *hld up at rr of field: swtchd to outside over 2f out: qcknd wl to chal 1f out: disp ld 150yds out: r.o wl to ld 100yds out: comf* **7/5**[1]

2 *nk* **No Risk At All (FR)**[30] 1163 5-8-11 0......................... IoritzMendizabal 5 116
(J-P Gallorini, France) *settled in 4th on outside: relegated to 5th ent st: rdn and qcknd wl over 1 1/2f out: disp ld w eventual wnr fr 1f out: hdd 100yds out: r.o wl* **58/10**[3]

3 *1 ¾* **Evaporation (FR)**[30] 1163 5-8-8 0...................................... OlivierPeslier 1 109
(C Laffon-Parias, France) *settled in 4th on inner rail: wnt 3rd early in st: unable to find opening over 1 1/2f out: had to be stdd: relegated to rr of field: swtchd away fr rail over 1f out: fnd split and qcknd wl to get up for 3rd fnl 50yds* **14/5**[2]

4 *hd* **Shamalgan (FR)**[31] 1143 5-9-1 0................................. GregoryBenoist 3 116
(X Nakkachdji, France) *hld up towards rr: patiently rdn tl 2 1/2f out: short of room to make chal 2f out: fin wl whn in clr fnl f to go 4th cl home* **12/1**

5 *¾* **Ch'Tio Bilote (FR)**[36] 4-8-11 0........................... ChristopheSoumillon 4 110
(J-P Gallorini, France) *settled in 3rd: relegated to 4th bef st: qcknd wl u.p 2f out: r.o wl: led briefly 1 1/2f out: sn hdd: no ex ins fnl f* **6/1**

6 *4* **Blue Soave (FR)**[23] 4-8-11 0.. GeraldMosse 2 101
(F Chappet, France) *settled in 2nd on ins: sent to ld over 3f out: rdn and r.o wl in st: hdd 1f out and sn fdd: nt hrd rdn whn ch gone* **26/1**

7 *5* **Private Jet (FR)**[27] 4-8-11 0....................................(p) MaximeGuyon 6 89
(H-A Pantall, France) *led fr s: hdd over 3f out: rdn and r.o in st: wknd 1 1/2f out: eased fnl f* **10/1**

1m 39.8s (-7.70) **7** Ran SP% **117.5**
WIN (incl. 1 euro stake): 2.40. PLACES: 1.30, 1.50, 1.30. DF: 7.00. SF: 9.30.
Owner Ecurie Victoria Dreams **Bred** Mlle V Dubois, J Dubois & E Dubois **Trained** France

NOTEBOOK
Zinabaa(FR), who was unlucky in running in the Prix Edmond Blanc on his return, had the ground in his favour and gained due reward. Another rise in class for the Prix d'Ispahan is now likely.

1723 KEMPTON (A.W) (R-H)

Wednesday, May 2

OFFICIAL GOING: Standard
Wind: Moderate ahead Weather: Cloudy

1747 BET AT BLUESQUARE.COM CONDITIONS STKS 5f (P)

2:00 (2:03) (Class 4) 2-Y-O **£4,046** (£1,211; £605; £302) **Stalls** Low

Form RPR

41 1 **Lyric Ace (IRE)**[19] 1352 2-8-11 0.................................. RichardHughes 3 94+
(Richard Hannon) *mde all: shkn up and qcknd fnl f: easily* **4/7**[1]

01 2 *1 ¾* **Chilworth Icon**[12] 1495 2-8-11 0...................................... MartinHarley 5 87
(Mick Channon) *s.i.s: racd in 4th but sn in tch: hdwy 2f out: drvn over 1f out: chsd wnr ins fnl f but easily outpcd* **10/1**[3]

1 3 *1 ½* **Baddilini**[16] 1411 2-9-1 0... GeorgeBaker 4 85
(Alan Bailey) *racd in 3rd tl chsd wnr over 3f out: rdn ins fnl 2f and no imp: outpcd into 3rd ins fnl f* **2/1**[2]

1 4 *1 ¾* **Mossgo (IRE)**[22] 1284 2-8-11 0... RyanMoore 2 75
(John Best) *reluctant to enter stalls: chsd wnr tl over 3f out: rdn ins fnl 2f: wknd fnl 120yds* **14/1**

59.67s (-0.83) **Going Correction** -0.175s/f (Stan) **4** Ran SP% **112.7**
Speed ratings (Par 95): **99,96,93,91**
CSF £7.34 TOTE £1.70; EX 6.60.
Owner Byerley Thoroughbred Racing **Bred** Rathasker Stud **Trained** East Everleigh, Wilts

FOCUS
This meeting had been due to take place at Ascot, but was rearranged due to waterlogging at the Berkshire track. Speed from the gate made the difference here. The time was decent and the form makes sense, with the winner building on his Leicester form.

NOTEBOOK
Lyric Ace(IRE) got a flyer, settled well on the lead and only had to be pushed out to score comfortably. Entered in the Group 1 Phoenix Stakes, he's a good, sharp 2yo, and all roads during the early part of the season will no doubt lead to the Norfolk Stakes. (op 8-13 tchd 4-6 and 4-5 in a place)
Chilworth Icon lost his chance at the start. By far the slowest away and detached in last early, he finished best of all, but there was just too much ground to make up on the winner. He should appreciate another furlong. (tchd 9-1)
Baddilini didn't run badly considering he had to give 4lb all round. (op 5-2 tchd 3-1)
Mossgo(IRE) was a little keener than ideal and weakened in the latter stages. (op 12-1)

1748 BET ON YOUR MOBILE AT BLUE SQUARE EBF CONDITIONS STKS (FILLIES) 1m (P)

2:35 (2:35) (Class 4) 3-Y-O **£4,357** (£1,304; £652; £326; £163) **Stalls** Low

Form RPR

125- 1 **Fallen For You**[222] 6299 3-8-12 110................................. RyanMoore 5 94+
(John Gosden) *s.i.s: sn rcvrd and trckd ldr after 1f: led after 2f: a travelling wl: increased pce fr over 2f out and c clr: easily* **1/5**[1]

314- 2 *3 ¼* **Gifted Girl (IRE)**[186] 7169 3-8-12 90.................................. NeilCallan 3 86
(Paul Cole) *t.k.h and led 2f: styd trcking wnr: drvn over 2f out: no imp: hung lft fnl f but hld on wl for 2nd* **7/1**[2]

140- 3 *1* **My Queenie (IRE)**[193] 7028 3-8-12 85......................... RichardHughes 2 84
(Richard Hannon) *racd in 5th tl hdwy to take 3rd over 1f out: pushed along and kpt on same pce ins fnl f* **12/1**[3]

4 4 *6* **Light Zabeel (USA)**[12] 1501 3-8-12 0............................ MartinHarley 4 70
(Mick Channon) *chsd ldrs in 3rd: rdn over 2f out: wknd and lost 3rd over 1f out* **20/1**

4-22 5 *5* **Nevaeh**[40] 1016 3-8-12 70.. DavidProbert 1 58
(Pat Eddery) *racd in 4th: rdn over 3f out: wknd wl over 2f out* **33/1**

1m 37.61s (-2.19) **Going Correction** -0.175s/f (Stan) **5** Ran SP% **111.2**
Speed ratings (Par 98): **103,99,98,92,87**
CSF £2.29 TOTE £1.10: £1.02, £2.30; EX 1.80.
Owner Normandie Stud Ltd **Bred** Normandie Stud Ltd **Trained** Newmarket, Suffolk

FOCUS
This looked an easy assignment for the favourite who did not need to match her 2yo best in this weak renewal.

1749 GET YOUR BET ON AT BLUE SQUARE PARADISE STKS (LISTED RACE) 1m (P)

3:10 (3:10) (Class 1) 4-Y-O+

£11,342 (£4,300; £2,152; £1,072; £538; £270) **Stalls** Low

Form RPR

500- 1 **Sri Putra**[200] 6861 6-9-0 114... NeilCallan 5 116
(Roger Varian) *in rr but in tch: rdn over 2f out: sn edgd lft: c to outside and gd hdwy over 1f out: drvn to ld ins fnl f: hld on all out* **11/2**[3]

6/0- 2 *nse* **Saamidd**[368] 1686 4-9-0 110.................................(t) FrankieDettori 1 116
(Saeed Bin Suroor) *s.i.s: hld up in rr: pushed lft and hdwy 2f out: c wd to r on stands' side over 1f out: str run fnl f: clsng on wnr nr fin: jst failed* **11/4**[1]

40-5 3 *2* **Side Glance**[31] 1158 5-9-0 115.. JimmyFortune 7 111
(Andrew Balding) *in tch: hdwy over 2f out: drvn to chal ins fnl f: outpcd by ldng duo fnl 120yds* **11/4**[1]

001- 4 *3* **King Torus (IRE)**[182] 7234 4-9-3 108.......................... RichardHughes 3 107
(Richard Hannon) *chsd ldrs: drvn to ld wl over 1f out: hdd ins fnl f: wknd fnl 120yds* **8/1**

212- 5 *1* **Skilful**[193] 7023 4-9-0 105.. RobertHavlin 6 102+
(John Gosden) *trckd ldrs: led over 4f out: hdd wl over 1f out: wknd ins fnl f* **4/1**[2]

25 6 *½* **Scarf (AUS)**[62] 757 5-9-0 107................................... SilvestreDeSousa 2 101+
(Saeed Bin Suroor) *led tl hdd over 4f out: styd chsng ldrs 2f out: wknd ins fnl f* **14/1**

10/5 7 *3 ¼* **Titus Mills (IRE)**[13] 1471 4-9-0 103.................................. MartinDwyer 4 93
(Brian Meehan) *chsd ldrs: outpcd 4f out: rallied over 2f out: wknd appr fnl f* **16/1**

1m 36.01s (-3.79) **Going Correction** -0.175s/f (Stan) **7** Ran SP% **112.4**
Speed ratings: **111,110,108,105,104 104,101**
toteswingers:1&2:£1.10, 1&3:£3.20, 2&3:£3.00 CSF £20.25 TOTE £7.10: £3.20, £1.10; EX 27.70.
Owner H R H Sultan Ahmad Shah **Bred** Glebe Stud And Partners **Trained** Newmarket, Suffolk
■ Stewards' Enquiry : Neil Callan caution; careless riding

FOCUS
The early pace was solid and the first two came from well behind. A decent standard for the grade.

NOTEBOOK
Sri Putra normally races over further than this, but at a higher level. The good gallop helped bring his stamina into play and this proved an ideal reappearance. He's not really up to winning at the top level on these shores, but might find more success abroad, and an Italian Group 1 next Sunday is apparently on the agenda next. (op 6-1 tchd 5-1)
Saamidd hadn't been seen since finishing tailed off in last year's Guineas, but he was a good 2yo (won Champagne Stakes) and this was a most promising return to action. Just like the winner he benefited from being held up off the decent gallop, and with his rider not being too hard on him, he should come on for this return. He's in the Lockinge and Queen Anne, and it'll be interesting to see if he takes up one of those engagements. (op 3-1)
Side Glance, who won this last year at Ascot, had a nice run through the race and no excuses. Perhaps this surface didn't suit him quite as well as fast turf. (tchd 5-2)
King Torus(IRE) faced no easy task giving 3lb all round, and he also raced closer to the pace than ideal given the gallop the leaders set. (op 9-1 tchd 10-1)
Skilful, at his best from the front, was taken wide of the rest early before crossing over and disputing it with Scarf. The pair ended up going too fast and setting things up for the closers. (op 9-2)

Titus Mills(IRE) showed he retains ability on his reappearance, but this was a step backwards. (op 20-1)

1750 BLUE SQUARE LEVY BOARD SAGARO STKS (GROUP 3) 2m (P)
3:45 (3:45) (Class 1) 4-Y-0+

£22,684 (£8,600; £4,304; £2,144; £1,076; £540) Stalls Low

Form				RPR
133-	1		**Colour Vision (FR)**[200] 6857 4-8-12 110 ... FrankieDettori 4 *(Saeed Bin Suroor) s.i.s: hld up in rr tl rapid hdwy to ld jst ins fnl f: edgd rt to far rail fnl f: r.o strly* **9/2**	121+
323-	2	1 ½	**Red Cadeaux**[143] 7729 6-9-1 115 ... RyanMoore 3 *(Ed Dunlop) towards rr but in tch: hdwy fr 3f out: drvn and qcknd to chse wnr ins fnl 2f: sn outpcd but kpt on wl for clr 2nd* **10/3**[3]	117
01-1	3	9	**Thimaar (USA)**[25] 1214 4-8-12 103 ... PaulHanagan 6 *(John Gosden) trckd ldr 4f: styd chsng ldrs: drvn along 4f out: trckd ldr over 3f out: led 2f out but sn hdd and btn* **5/2**[1]	106
31-0	4	5	**Barbican**[32] 1144 4-8-12 110 ... DarryllHolland 2 *(Alan Bailey) in tch: drvn to chse ldrs 3f out: wknd over 2f out* **3/1**[2]	100
-601	5	1 ¼	**Electrolyser (IRE)**[21] 1318 7-9-1 109 ... AdamKirby 1 *(Clive Cox) led tl hdd 2f out: wknd qckly* **14/1**	99
53-5	6	4	**Solar Sky**[21] 1318 4-8-12 103 ... TomQueally 5 *(Sir Henry Cecil) trckd ldr after 4f tl over 3f out: btn sn after* **10/1**	94

3m 21.5s (-8.60) **Going Correction** -0.175s/f (Stan) course record
WFA 4 from 6yo+ 3lb 6 Ran SP% **110.6**
Speed ratings: **114,113,108,106,105 103**
toteswingers:1&2:£2.90, 1&3:£1.90, 2&3:£2.10 CSF £19.08 TOTE £4.10: £1.40, £2.30; EX 23.70.
Owner Godolphin **Bred** Capricorn Stud **Trained** Newmarket, Suffolk

FOCUS

They went a solid gallop in this Group 3 race and that resulted in just under three seconds being taken off the track record, previously held by Thimaar. The form looks reliable for the grade, with the second and third close to their marks. Colour Vision looks a player in the top staying races.

NOTEBOOK

Colour Vision(FR) ♦, following on from the likes of Fox Hunt, Monterosso and Capponi, looks like another former Mark Johnston-trained runner who is likely to prove a smart performer for Godolphin. The gelding was detached in last through the early part of the race but by the time they turned into the straight he was travelling kindly at the back of the field. He quickened up smartly between horses when asked and, although he hung right once in the clear, he was well on top inside the last and Dettori was able to ease him down close home. He was thought likely to need the run, but looks an improved performer and his sights will have to be raised now. The Henry II might be his next race, before a tilt at the Gold Cup, for which he earned quotes of between 8-1 and 10-1 across the board, which now puts him ahead of Opinion Poll in the betting. (op 5-1)

Red Cadeaux set the standard on his performances in the Melbourne Cup and Hong Kong late last year, but his trainer had suggested he would benefit from this reappearance. Time may tell it was a good effort trying to give 3lb to the winner, and he did finish well clear of the rest, so connections can be satisfied, and apparently the Yorkshire Cup will be up next, before a summer break and another tilt at the Melbourne Cup. (op 7-2 tchd 3-1)

Thimaar(USA) was sent off favourite despite having only won a handicap off 93 last time. The switch of venue for this race was clearly in his favour, but having raced nearer the pace than the first two he was firmly put in his place in the straight. He can do better still, but probably wouldn't want soft ground back on turf. (op 9-4)

Barbican, easily forgiven his run in the Dubai Gold Cup, was a shade disappointing. It's possible that his win in a steadily run 1m6f race at Ascot made him look more of a stayer than he really is. (op 7-2)

Electrolyser(IRE), who stole a Listed race from the front on his reappearance, couldn't repeat the trick in this higher grade as he set too strong a gallop and paid the price in the straight. (op 12-1 tchd 10-1)

Solar Sky, who kept the leader company, fell in a hole with over 2f to run. (op 8-1)

1751 BLLUESQUARE.COM ASCOT.CO.UK PAVILION STKS (LISTED RACE) 6f (P)
4:20 (4:23) (Class 1) 3-Y-0

£11,342 (£4,300; £2,152; £1,072; £538; £270) Stalls Low

Form				RPR
1-11	1		**Gusto**[16] 1426 3-9-0 110 ... RichardHughes 1 *(Richard Hannon) wnt lft s: sn narrow ldr: hdd over 4f out: styd trcking ldr: chal ins fnl 2f: chsd ldr over 1f out: drvn and qcknd to ld fnl 120yds: readily* **6/4**[1]	112
-302	2	¾	**Bannock (IRE)**[14] 1453 3-9-0 109 ... SilvestreDeSousa 10 *(Mark Johnston) trckd ldrs: drvn to ld ins fnl 2f: jnd ins fnl f: hdd and outpcd fnl 120yds* **17/2**	109
320-	3	¾	**Burwaaz**[207] 6688 3-8-11 109 ... PaulHanagan 7 *(Ed Dunlop) in rr but in tch: hdwy and nt clr run ins fnl 2f: drvn and qcknd ins fnl f: gng on clsng stages: bit slipped through* **4/1**[2]	104+
00-6	4	hd	**West Leake Diman (IRE)**[14] 1453 3-8-11 105 ... FrankieDettori 3 *(Charles Hills) chsd ldrs: drvn over 2f out: kpt on fnl f: nt qckn fnl 120yds* **16/1**	103
00-0	5	¾	**B Fifty Two (IRE)**[14] 1453 3-8-11 105 ... SebSanders 9 *(J W Hills) chsd ldrs: edgd rt ins fnl 2f: rdn and kpt on fnl f but nvr gng pce to chal* **16/1**	101
2144	6	¾	**Pale Orchid (IRE)**[12] 1494 3-8-6 91 ... MircoDemuro 6 *(David Evans) chsd ldrs: rdn ins fnl 2f: kpt on but nvr gng pce to chal* **20/1**	94
114-	7	¾	**Bayleyf (IRE)**[242] 5715 3-8-11 101 ... GrahamGibbons 2 *(John Best) bmpd s: chsd ldr: slt ld fr over 4f out: hdd ins fnl 2f: wknd u.p fnl 120yds* **20/1**	96
120-	8	hd	**Samminder (IRE)**[207] 6688 3-8-11 98 ... RyanMoore 4 *(Peter Chapple-Hyam) hld up in rr: hdwy whn nt clr run wl over 1f out: no daylight after and fin on bridle* **11/2**[3]	96+
0-02	9	½	**Big Note (IRE)**[19] 1356 3-8-11 94 ... JimmyFortune 5 *(Andrew Balding) t.k.h in rr: rdn over 2f out: sme late prog* **33/1**	94
14-1	10	nse	**Accession (IRE)**[19] 1356 3-8-11 96 ... AdamKirby 8 *(Clive Cox) t.k.h in rr: rdn and sme hdwy on ins over 2f out: nvr rchd ldrs: wknd ins fnl f* **16/1**	94

1m 11.84s (-1.26) **Going Correction** -0.175s/f (Stan) 10 Ran SP% **116.0**
Speed ratings: **101,100,99,98,97 96,95,95,94,94**
toteswingers:1&2:£3.50, 1&3:£2.80, 2&3:£4.60 CSF £14.58 TOTE £2.10: £1.10, £3.50, £1.70; EX 10.40.
Owner Highclere Thoroughbred Racing-Rock Sand **Bred** New England, Mount Coote & P Barrett **Trained** East Everleigh, Wilts

FOCUS

A bit of a messy race with a bunhc finish, and it paid to race quite handily. Another small step forward from the winner and the form makes sense at face value.

NOTEBOOK

Gusto, back on a surface he's very comfortable on, broke well and held a good position on the rail throughout. With the pace not breakneck, Hughes was able to hold him together and save something for the finish, while those in behind got into all sorts of trouble. The form might be muddling but he's progressive - this was his fifth win on the bounce - and he might have more to offer back over 7f. The Jersey is the plan. (op 15-8)

Bannock(IRE) did well considering he was drawn on the wide outside and travelled further than the winner. He briefly hit the front before being seen off by the rallying Gusto, and posted a solid effort all things considered. (op 8-1 tchd 6-1)

Burwaaz ♦ had little go right for him as he was keen early off the ordinary gallop, got caught on heels as he was looking for ground to challenge in the straight, and found the line coming too soon as he finished strongly. The bit slipped through his mouth apparently, which wouldn't have helped either, and he's likely to be a different proposition back on a straight track. A drop back to 5f won't be a problem and he remains a smart prospect. Official explanation: jockey said colt's bit pulled through (op 10-3)

West Leake Diman(IRE) had a nice trip, tracking the winner on the rail, and ran as well as could be expected back sprinting. (tchd 20-1)

B Fifty Two(IRE) also looked better over this shorter distance. Official explanation: trainer said gelding was struck into behind. (op 20-1)

Pale Orchid(IRE) ran a sound race considering she had a bit to do at the weights. (op 16-1)

Bayleyf(IRE) benefited from racing prominently in a race where those held up were at a disadvantage, but he was a bit keener than ideal, and that probably cost him to some extent. (op 25-1)

Samminder(IRE) ♦ finished full of running having been denied racing room all the way up the straight. It goes without saying that his finishing position doesn't do him justice, and perhaps a handicap can be found for him off his current mark of 98 before he steps up in class again. Official explanation: jockey said colt was denied a clear run. (op 15-2 tchd 8-1)

1752 FOLLOW US ON TWITTER @BLUESQ H'CAP 1m (P)
4:55 (4:55) (Class 4) (0-85,90) 4-Y-0+ £4,204 (£1,251; £625; £312) Stalls Low

Form				RPR
40-3	1		**Great Shot**[20] 1342 4-8-8 72 ... JamesDoyle 10 *(Sylvester Kirk) sn led: pushed along 2f out: qcknd u.p fnl f: in command clsng stages* **11/1**	82
40-0	2	1	**Benandonner (USA)**[16] 1416 9-9-6 84 ... NeilCallan 8 *(Mike Murphy) in tch: chsd ldrs and rdn 2f out: kpt on fnl f to take 2nd last strides: nt rch wnr* **14/1**	92
56-2	3	nk	**Ree's Rascal (IRE)**[16] 1416 4-9-1 79 ... PatCosgrave 5 *(Jim Boyle) chsd ldrs: rdn to chse wnr 1f out: no imp ins fnl f: ct for 2nd last strides* **7/1**[2]	86
3124	4	nse	**Reachforthebucks**[11] 1513 4-9-6 84 ... AdamKirby 7 *(Jane Chapple-Hyam) in rr: rdn over 2f out: hdwy over 1f out: styd on ins fnl f: gng on cl home but no imp on wnr* **5/2**[1]	91+
2006	5	1 ¼	**Veroon (IRE)**[32] 1133 6-9-0 78 ... (p) PaulMulrennan 4 *(James Given) in tch: hdwy 2f out: chsd wnr over 1f out: wknd clsng stages* **8/1**[3]	82
0-04	6	1	**Yes Chef**[23] 1258 5-9-0 78 ... JamesMillman 2 *(Rod Millman) in rr: hdwy over 2f out: kpt on fnl f but nvr gng pce to chal* **12/1**	80+
12-1	7	1 ¼	**Push Me (IRE)**[74] 626 5-8-13 77 ... MichaelO'Connell 3 *(Jamie Poulton) in tch: chsd ldrs 2f out: wknd ins fnl f* **12/1**	76
050-	8	¾	**Nice Style (IRE)**[161] 7523 7-9-7 90 ... (tp) RaulDaSilva[(5)] 9 *(Jeremy Gask) s.i.s: in rr: hdwy 4f out: rdn and outpcd 2f out: styd on again cl home* **14/1**	87
10-0	9	¾	**George Baker (IRE)**[31] 1161 5-9-0 78 ... FrankieDettori 11 *(George Baker) in rr: sme hdwy 2f out: wknd: nvr rchd ldrs and sn btn* **10/1**	73
00-0	10	1	**Uncle Fred**[16] 1416 7-9-0 78 ... DavidProbert 1 *(Patrick Chamings) s.i.s: in rr: sme hdwy 2f out: nvr rchd ldrs and wknd fnl f* **9/1**	71
-030	11	nse	**First Post (IRE)**[32] 1128 5-9-6 84 ... (p) DaneO'Neill 14 *(Derek Haydn Jones) chsd ldr: rdn over 2f out: wknd sn after* **14/1**	77
000-	12	1	**Rougette**[179] 7296 4-9-4 82 ... MichaelHills 6 *(Charles Hills) chsd ldrs: rdn over 2f out: sn btn* **16/1**	73

1m 38.45s (-1.35) **Going Correction** -0.175s/f (Stan) 12 Ran SP% **120.9**
Speed ratings (Par 105): **99,98,97,97,96 95,94,93,92,91 91,90**
CSF £158.62 CT £1186.12 TOTE £19.20: £5.20, £8.10, £4.00; EX 305.60.
Owner J C Smith **Bred** Littleton Stud **Trained** Upper Lambourn, Berks

FOCUS

This looked pretty competitive but it was dominated from the front. The time was ordinary and the form is taken at face value.

First Post(IRE) Official explanation: jockey said gelding hung left.

Rougette Official explanation: jockey said filly lost her action.

T/Plt: £42.00 to a £1 stake. Pool:£75,034.29 - 1,303.08 winning tickets T/Qpdt: £22.10 to a £1 stake. Pool:£4,395.07 - 146.76 winning tickets ST

1556 PONTEFRACT (L-H)
Wednesday, May 2

OFFICIAL GOING: Heavy (soft in places; 6.4)

Wind: Light across Weather: Fine and dry

1753 WILLIAMHILL.COM/BRITISH STALLION STUDS EBF MAIDEN STKS 5f
2:20 (2:21) (Class 4) 2-Y-0 £4,398 (£1,309; £654; £327) Stalls Low

Form				RPR
	1		**Lastchancelucas** 2-8-10 0 ... JasonHart[(7)] 3 *(Declan Carroll) chsd ldrs on inner: hdwy 2f out: rdn over 1f out: styd on to ld ins fnl f: kpt on strly* **100/1**	85
3	2	1 ½	**Polski Max**[25] 1218 2-9-3 0 ... TonyHamilton 8 *(Richard Fahey) cl up: led wl over 1f out: rdn and edgd rt ent fnl f: sn drvn: hung rt and hdd: kpt on same pce* **5/2**[1]	80
	3	2	**Steer By The Stars (IRE)** 2-8-12 0 ... JoeFanning 7 *(Mark Johnston) chsd ldrs: rdn to chal wl over 1f out: ev ch whn edgd rt ent fnl f: sn swtchd lft and kpt on same pce* **5/1**[3]	67+
42	4	3 ¼	**Hillbilly Boy (IRE)**[14] 1435 2-8-12 0 ... DuilioDaSilva[(5)] 5 *(Bill Turner) chsd ldrs: pushed along and sltly outpcd over 2f out: sn rdn: kpt on u.p fnl f: nrst fin* **3/1**[2]	61
	5	2 ½	**Forray** 2-9-3 0 ... RichardMullen 10 *(Ed McMahon) racd wd: led: rdn along 2f out: sn hdd & wknd over 1f out* **5/1**[3]	54+
3	6	2	**Inchy Coo**[14] 1437 2-8-12 0 ... DavidAllan 2 *(Tim Easterby) in tch: rdn along over 2f out: sn one pce* **8/1**	40
	7	2 ½	**Roland** 2-9-3 0 ... PhillipMakin 1 *(Kevin Ryan) s.i.s: a in rr* **25/1**	39+

	8	3 1/4	**Mash Potato (IRE)** 2-9-3 0 ... TomEaves 6	24
			(Michael Dods) *s.i.s: a in rr* **16/1**	
	9	1 3/4	**Fat Gary** 2-9-3 0 ... RichardKingscote 9	18
			(Tom Dascombe) *s.i.s: a in rr* **16/1**	
6	10	nk	**Royal Jenray**[13] 1474 2-9-3 0 ... GrahamLee 4	16
			(Jedd O'Keeffe) *chsd ldrs: rdn along 1/2-way: sn wknd* **100/1**	

1m 7.36s (4.06) **Going Correction** +0.70s/f (Yiel) **10** Ran SP% **115.6**
Speed ratings (Par 95): **95,92,89,84,80 77,73,67,65,64**
toteswingers:1&2:£23.00, 1&3:£38.70, 2&3:£3.50 CSF £338.09 TOTE £68.30: £10.00, £1.70, £1.60; EX 788.10 TRIFECTA Not won..

Owner C H Stephenson & Partners **Bred** C H Stephenson **Trained** Sledmere, E Yorks

FOCUS
This is muddling form as the winner was the only one of the principals who raced towards the inside rail from the off - the others were positioned up the middle. The action unfolded far side for the remainder of the card. The form is rated around the runner-up.

NOTEBOOK
Lastchancelucas had already been gelded and made no appeal on breeding, but he defied his big odds to make a winning start, quite possibly helped by racing on the best ground. It remains to be seen whether he can build on this, especially on a faster surface.

Polski Max, a beaten favourite on his debut at Musselburgh, was probably racing on the wrong part of the track and can be given another chance. (tchd 11-4)

Steer By The Stars(IRE), a 50,000euros out of a 1m winner, looked fit. She probably only ran to a modest level but should find a race. (op 9-2)

Hillbilly Boy(IRE) was well below the level he appeared to run to when second at Beverley on his previous start. That form took a real knock as the fourth-placed finisher from Beverley, Inchy Coo, was also well beaten. (op 4-1)

Forray, a 31,000gns half-brother to a 5f juvenile winner in Italy, seemed to know his job well enough as he showed plenty of early speed up the middle of the track, but he gradually faded. He went widest of all, which seemingly didn't help, and he might not have appreciated such bad ground. (tchd 4-1)

1754 TOTEPOOL SUPPORTS THE NRC/BRITISH STALLION STUDS EBF MAIDEN STKS 1m 2f 6y
2:55 (2:58) (Class 5) 3-Y-O **£3,749** (£1,107; £553) **Stalls** Low

Form				RPR
44-	1		**Commitment**[190] 7082 3-9-3 0 ... KierenFallon 2	83+
			(Luca Cumani) *trckd ldng pair: hdwy 2f out: rdn to chal ent fnl f: styd on to ld last 100yds* **2/1**[2]	
00-	2	1 1/2	**Finity Run (GER)**[249] 5464 3-8-12 0 ... JoeFanning 1	74
			(Mark Johnston) *set stdy pce: qcknd over 3f out: rdn wl over 1f out: hdd and no ex last 100yds* **16/1**	
	3	nk	**Swnymor (IRE)** 3-9-3 0 ... LiamJones 7	79+
			(William Haggas) *trckd ldrs: hdwy on outer 3f out: rdn to chal over 1f out: ev ch whn green and edgd lft ins fnl f: kpt on same pce* **12/1**	
0-	4	1 1/4	**Cayuga**[222] 6300 3-9-3 0 ... RichardMullen 4	76+
			(Sir Michael Stoute) *wnt rt s: hld up: hdwy 2f out: rdn to chse ldrs over 1f out: green and one pce fnl f* **3/1**[3]	
0-	5	10	**Plastiki**[231] 6064 3-9-3 0 ... TomEaves 6	56+
			(Sir Michael Stoute) *sltly hmpd s: hld up: a in rr* **20/1**	
000-	6	6	**Isolde's Return**[221] 6345 3-8-12 30 ... AndrewMullen 3	39?
			(George Moore) *wnt rt s: cl up: rdn along over 2f out: sn wknd* **200/1**	
3	7	26	**Kashgar**[23] 1265 3-9-3 0 ... HayleyTurner 5	
			(Michael Bell) *unruly stalls: dwlt and hmpd s: in rr tl sme hdwy over 4f out: rdn along over 3f out: sn btn and bhd whn eased fnl f* **5/4**[1]	

2m 23.09s (9.39) **Going Correction** +0.70s/f (Yiel) **7** Ran SP% **121.6**
Speed ratings (Par 99): **90,88,88,87,79 74,53**
toteswingers:1&2:£6.90, 1&3:£2.70, 2&3:£9.00 CSF £35.35 TOTE £2.30: £1.10, £5.20; EX 33.80.

Owner Highclere Racing-Diamond Jubilee **Bred** Cheveley Park Stud Ltd **Trained** Newmarket, Suffolk

FOCUS
An ordinary maiden (time much the slowest of three races at the trip), but an interesting winner. The ground was bad and the time slow. The race has been rated around the race averages.

Kashgar Official explanation: jockey said colt got upset in stalls.

1755 BETFRED SUPPORTS THE NRC H'CAP 1m 4y
3:30 (3:30) (Class 5) (0-75,79) 4-Y-O+ **£2,385** (£704; £352) **Stalls** Low

Form				RPR
0-33	1		**Wiseman's Diamond (USA)**[22] 1269 7-8-8 62 ...(b) MickyFenton 1	70
			(Paul Midgley) *t.k.h: mde all: rdn clr over 1f out: kpt on strly* **10/1**	
52/2	2	2 1/2	**Edmaaj (IRE)**[9] 1561 4-9-3 71 ... DanielTudhope 4	73+
			(David O'Meara) *hld up towards rr: effrt 3f out: swtchd rt over 2f out: rdn to chse ldrs over 1f out: edgd lft and kpt on fnl f: nt rch wnr* **6/4**[1]	
03-0	3	nk	**Fazza**[23] 1249 5-9-2 75 ... ShaneBKelly(5) 2	77
			(Edwin Tuer) *trckd wnr: effrt over 2f out and sn rdn: drvn appr fnl f and kpt on same pce* **9/2**[2]	
3032	4	1/2	**Georgebernardshaw (IRE)**[11] 1527 7-8-8 62 ... KellyHarrison 8	62
			(Richard Guest) *hld up: hdwy 3f out: rdn to chse ldrs wl over 1f out: no imp fnl f* **15/2**	
/01-	5	3 3/4	**Betteras Bertie**[283] 4367 9-8-10 64 ...(p) BarryMcHugh 5	56
			(Tony Coyle) *t.k.h: chsd ldng pair: rdn along on inner over 2f out: wknd wl over 1f out* **28/1**	
2526	6	3 3/4	**Conducting**[23] 1266 4-9-1 69 ...(p) RobertWinston 3	52
			(Gay Kelleway) *trckd ldrs: effrt 3f out: rdn over 2f out: sn wknd* **9/1**	
1011	7	3/4	**Flying Applause**[9] 1561 7-9-8 79 6ex ...(bt) LeeTopliss(3) 7	60
			(Roy Bowring) *dwlt: sn chsng ldrs: rdn along wl over 2f out: sn wknd* **6/1**[3]	
0000	8	6	**Final Drive (IRE)**[11] 1513 6-9-5 73 ...(t) LiamKeniry 6	41
			(John Butler) *hld up: a in rr* **33/1**	
/06-	9	8	**Benidorm**[212] 6578 4-8-4 61 oh4 ... DeclanCannon(3) 9	
			(John Wainwright) *hld up: a in rr* **50/1**	

1m 50.32s (4.42) **Going Correction** +0.70s/f (Yiel) **9** Ran SP% **111.7**
Speed ratings (Par 103): **105,102,102,101,97 94,93,87,79**
toteswingers:1&2:£3.70, 1&3:£10.50, 2&3:£3.50 CSF £24.27 CT £77.17 TOTE £10.60: £2.50, £1.20, £1.70; EX 19.80 Trifecta £124.40 Pool £722.99 - 4.30 winning units..

Owner D I Perry **Bred** Hatta Bloodstock International **Trained** Westow, N Yorks

FOCUS
A modest handicap. The winner, who made all, is rated a bit closer to his old best.

Flying Applause Official explanation: jockey said gelding hung left through.

1756 LADBROKES.COM FILLIES' H'CAP 1m 2f 6y
4:05 (4:05) (Class 3) (0-90,86) 3-Y-O+ **£7,470** (£2,236; £1,118; £559; £279; £140) **Stalls** Low

Form				RPR
116-	1		**Easy Terms**[228] 6172 5-9-13 85 ... JamesSullivan 1	96
			(Edwin Tuer) *hld up in rr: hdwy 3f out: n.m.r 2f out: rdn to chal ent fnl f: sn led and styd on wl* **12/1**	
3112	2	1 3/4	**Cape Safari (IRE)**[14] 1442 3-8-5 78 ...(p) HayleyTurner 8	84
			(James Tate) *trckd ldng pair: hdwy 3f out: chal 2f out: rdn to ld over 1f out: drvn and hdd ins fnl f: kpt on same pce* **15/2**	
2C C	3	1 1/4	**Rio's Rosanna (IRE)**[21] 1295 5-9-5 77 ... RussKennemore 2	81
			(Richard Whitaker) *trckd ldrs: hdwy over 2f out: rdn to chse ldrs over 1f out: kpt on same pce* **3/1**[1]	
41-	4	4 1/2	**Swingland**[246] 5583 3-8-11 84 ... PhillipMakin 6	78
			(Paul Cole) *in tch: hdwy on outer to chse ldrs 4f out: rdn along over 2f out: sn one pce* **9/2**[2]	
410-	5	3 1/4	**El Torbellino (IRE)**[221] 6330 4-9-12 84 ... DanielTudhope 3	72
			(David O'Meara) *led: rdn along and hdd 2f out: sn wknd* **6/1**[3]	
60-4	6	2	**Rythmic**[89] 398 3-8-3 76 ... JoeFanning 4	59
			(Mark Johnston) *cl up on inner: rdn to ld briefly 2f out: hdd over 1f out and wknd qckly* **8/1**	
000-	7	3	**Antigua Sunrise (IRE)**[180] 7272 6-9-0 79 ... LauraBarry(7) 5	57
			(Richard Fahey) *chsd ldrs: rdn along over 4f out: sn wknd* **6/1**[3]	
00-1	8	61	**Cala Santanyi**[21] 1314 4-9-4 76 ... LukeMorris 7	
			(Gerard Butler) *hld up in rr: sme hdwy over 4f out: rdn along and wknd qckly wl over 2f out: sn bhd and eased* **11/1**	

2m 20.89s (7.19) **Going Correction** +0.70s/f (Yiel)
WFA 3 from 4yo+ 15lb **8** Ran SP% **110.7**
Speed ratings (Par 104): **99,97,96,92,90 88,86,37**
toteswingers:1&2:£9.40, 1&3:£4.80, 2&3:£2.90 CSF £91.27 CT £326.53 TOTE £12.30: £2.70, £2.10, £1.10; EX 97.10 Trifecta £397.60 Part won. Pool £537.31 - 0.92 winning units..

Owner E Tuer **Bred** T E Pocock **Trained** Birkby, N Yorks

FOCUS
A fair fillies' handicap run in a modest time. The form is rated around the second and third.

NOTEBOOK
Easy Terms ◆ resumed her progression with a likeable performance - she did this cosily and looked to have more in hand than the margin suggested. The winner landed four in a row last season, but was below form when last seen, perhaps being over the top and/or not appreciating quick ground. On this evidence there's more to come. (op 16-1)

Cape Safari(IRE), dropped in trip, ran her race but just ran into an improver. (op 8-1)

Rio's Rosanna(IRE) gained her only win so far on good to firm ground and she was well held this time. (op 4-1)

Swingland looked a good prospect when winning a 1m maiden at Goodwood last year, and then missed intended engagements in the Fillies' Mile and a Listed race. She's in the Oaks, confirming she's well regarded, but she ran to just a fair level on this return. Presumably she needed the run and perhaps the ground was too testing. (op 7-2)

El Torbellino(IRE) has won on soft ground but she was well held after 221 days off. (op 8-1)

Cala Santanyi Official explanation: trainers representative said filly was unsuited by ground.

1757 BETVICTOR H'CAP 1m 2f 6y
4:40 (4:40) (Class 5) (0-75,75) 3-Y-O **£2,385** (£704; £352) **Stalls** Low

Form				RPR
-323	1		**Eshaab (USA)**[13] 1484 3-9-7 75 ... TadhgO'Shea 1	80
			(Ed Dunlop) *in tch: hdwy to trck ldng pair over 2f out: effrt over 1f out: rdn to ld jst ins fnl f: kpt on* **7/2**[1]	
04-3	2	1/2	**Only Orsenfoolsies**[14] 1441 3-8-7 61 oh1 ... TomEaves 2	65
			(Micky Hammond) *in tch: hdwy to chse ldrs 3f out: rdn wl over 1f out: styd on strly fnl f* **9/1**	
51	3	3/4	**Danube River**[33] 1107 3-9-4 72 ... JoeFanning 7	75
			(Mark Johnston) *led: rdn along 2f out: drvn and hdd jst ins fnl f: kpt on same pce* **4/1**[2]	
4543	4	8	**Bapak Pintar**[11] 1519 3-8-11 65 ... PhillipMakin 5	52
			(Kevin Ryan) *chsd ldr: rdn along over 2f out: drvn and wknd wl over 1f out* **4/1**[2]	
1321	5	20	**Zain Princess (IRE)**[13] 1486 3-9-4 72 ... NickyMackay 4	19
			(Gerard Butler) *hld up in rr: sme hdwy 4f out: rdn along 3f out: nvr a factor* **7/2**[1]	
020-	6	52	**Bollin Tommy**[242] 5727 3-8-11 65 ... DavidAllan 3	
			(Tim Easterby) *chsd ldrs: rdn along 1/2-way: sn lost pl and bhd whn eased fnl 2f* **7/1**[3]	
003-	7	5	**Eastlands Lad (IRE)**[173] 7368 3-8-10 64 ... FrederikTylicki 6	
			(Micky Hammond) *a in rr: rdn along 4f out: sn outpcd and bhd whn eased fnl 2f* **14/1**	

2m 19.76s (6.06) **Going Correction** +0.70s/f (Yiel) **7** Ran SP% **113.6**
Speed ratings (Par 99): **103,102,102,95,79 38,34**
toteswingers:1&2:£5.10, 1&3:£3.10, 2&3:£3.70 CSF £34.24 TOTE £4.20: £1.90, £4.70; EX 33.60.

Owner Hamdan Al Maktoum **Bred** Shadwell Farm LLC **Trained** Newmarket, Suffolk

FOCUS
The time was quicker than the earlier two races at this trip, but the ground would have drying out. An ordinary handicap with an improved effort from the winner.

Zain Princess(IRE) Official explanation: trainers representative said filly was unsuited by ground.

1758 CORAL.CO.UK H'CAP 6f
5:15 (5:15) (Class 5) (0-75,75) 3-Y-O **£2,385** (£704; £352) **Stalls** Low

Form				RPR
1122	1		**Gabrial's Bounty (IRE)**[33] 1109 3-9-7 75 ... FrannyNorton 7	85
			(Mick Channon) *trckd ldrs: hdwy 2f out: rdn to chse ldr appr fnl f: styd on to ld last 100yds* **9/2**[2]	
003-	2	1 1/4	**Dora's Sister (IRE)**[200] 6866 3-8-7 61 ... TomEaves 8	67
			(John Quinn) *hld up: hdwy over 2f out: swtchd rt and rdn to chse ldrs appr fnl f: kpt on wl to take 2nd nr fin* **9/2**[2]	
113-	3	1/2	**Whisky Bravo**[127] 7881 3-9-7 75 ... MichaelStainton 2	79
			(David Brown) *cl up on inner: led 1/2-way: rdn clr over 1f out: wknd and hdd last 100yds* **9/2**[2]	
40-3	4	2	**On The Hoof**[11] 1521 3-9-1 69 ... JamesSullivan 6	67+
			(Michael Easterby) *hld up towards rr: hdwy on outer 2f out: rdn over 1f out: kpt on fnl f: nrst fin* **10/3**[1]	
420-	5	1 1/2	**Citybell (IRE)**[256] 5286 3-8-7 61 ... BarryMcHugh 3	54
			(Richard Fahey) *t.k.h and sltly hmpd s: hld up in rr: hdwy over 2f out: swtchd rt and rdn to chse ldrs over 1f out: sn no imp* **8/1**	
3-50	6	1 3/4	**Ambitious Icarus**[61] 769 3-8-4 61 ... DeclanCannon(3) 4	48
			(Richard Guest) *chsd ldrs: rdn along over 2f out: wkng whn n.m.r and hmpd over 1f out: bhd after* **28/1**	

665- **7** 3/4 **Magic Bounty**[264] 5005 3 -8-8**62**.. DavidAllan 1 47
(Tim Easterby) *chsd ldrs on inner: rdn along wl over 2f out: sn wknd* **6/1**[3]
40-6 **8** 3/4 **Al Shaqab (IRE)**[9] 1176 3 -9-6**74**.................................... PhillipMakin 5 56
(Kevin Ryan) *led to 1/2-way: cl up: rdn 2f out and sn wknd* **16/1**
1m 21.98s (5.08)**Going Correction** +0.70s/f (Yiel) **8**Ran SP% **112.4**
Speed ratings (Par 99): **94,92,91,89,87 84,83,82**
toteswingers:1&2:£3.60, 1&3:£2.70, 2&3:£5.30 CSF £24.10 CT £94.63 TOTE £6.80 : £2.30, £3.50, £1.70 ; EX 22.50 Trifecta £73.40 Pool £640.15 - 6.45 winning units.
Owner Dr Marwan Koukash **Bred** D And Mrs D Veitch **Trained** West Ilsley, Berks
■ Stewards' Enquiry : Barry McHugh two-day ban; careless rising (16-17th May)

FOCUS
A reasonable sprint handicap for the class, and straightforward form.
T/Plt: £124.90 to a £1 stake.. Pool:£59,033.56 - 344.77 winning tickets T/Qpdt: £21.20 to a £1 stake. Pool:£4,355.69 - 152.00 winning tickets. JR 1759a -1765a Foreing Racing (See RI)

1171 CHANTILLY (R-H)
Monday, April 30

OFFICIAL GOING: Turf: very soft

1766a PRIX ALLEZ FRANCE (GROUP 3) (4YO+ FILLIES & MARES) (TURF) 1m 2f
3:00 (12:00) 4-Y-O+ **£33,333** (£13,333; £10,000 ; £6,666 ; £3,333)

RPR
1 **Aquamarine (JPN)**[22] 4 -8-70.. ThomasHuet 5 109
(M Delzangles, France) *settled in 3rd on outside: rdn over 1 1/2f out: r.o wl u.p ent fnl f: led 100yds out: r.o wl to hold off chal of eventual runner-up* **22/1**
2 3/4 **Haya Landa (FR)**[34] 4 -8-90.. ThierryThulliez 3 109
(Mme L Audon, France) *settled in midfield: patiently rdn bhd ldrs 1 1/2f out: qcknd wl 1f out: r.o strly fnl 100yds: wnt 2nd 25yds out: r.o wl* **44/5**
3 *hd* **Shareta (IRE)**[155] 7563 4 -9-00.......... Christophe-PatriceLemaire 4 114
(A De Royer-Dupre, France) *led: stl in front 2f out: rdn 1 1/2f out: r.o wl: chal 150yds out: hdd 100yds out: r.o wl: lost 2nd 25yds out* **1/1**[1]
4 *2* **Dream Peace (IRE)**[97] 6909 4 -9-20.......................... GeraldMosse 9 112
(Robert Collet, France) *in rr: qcknd wl u.p 1 1/2f out: r.o wl fnl f: clst at fin* **63/10**[2]
5 *1 3/4* **Navarra Queen**[204] 6739 4 -9-00.. AStarke 7 106
(P Schiergen, Germany) *settled in 2nd on outside of ldr: rdn to chal for ld over 1 1/2f out: no ex: styd on one pce fnl f* **28/1**
6 *1 3/4* **Skallet (FR)**[171] 7386 4 -8-90.................................(b) StephanePasquier 8 98
(S Wattel, France) *settled in rr: u.p early in st: styd on u.p fnl f* **13/1**
7 *2* **Miss Lago (IRE)**[90] 7049 4 -8-90................................ GregoryBenoist 2 94
(E Lellouche, France) *settled in midfield: rdn over 1 1/2f out: no ex: styd on one pce fnl f* **44/5**
8 *1* **Andromeda Galaxy (FR)**[188] 7090 4 -8-90........ ChristopheSoumillon 6 92
(E Lellouche, France) *settled in midfield on outside: rdn over 1 1/2f out: nt qckn fnl f: nt hrd rdn fnl 100yds* **7/1**[3]
9 *dist* **Street Secret (USA)**[24] 4 -8-70.. MaximeGuyon 1
(Mme Pia Brandt, France) *settled in 3rd on ins: u.p early in st: no ex: wknd qckly 1 1/2f out: eased fnl f* **17/1**
2m 10.1s (5.30) **9**Ran SP% **117.1**
WIN (incl. 1 euro stake): 5.90 (Aquamarine coupled with Andromeda Galaxy). PLACES: 3.30, 2.20, 1.20. DF: 37.00. SF: 159.10 .
Owner Ecurie Wildenstein **Bred** Dayton Investments Limited **Trained** France

NOTEBOOK
Aquamarine(JPN) had the benefit of a previous outing, had the ground in her favour and was receiving 7lb from the favourite. She got the job done well and might go for the Prix Corrida next.
Shareta(IRE) comes out of the race as the best filly, as she was conceding 7lb to the winner and 5lb to the runner-up. Considering the ground was very testing and she was racing over a distance short of her best it was a good effort on her return, and she could reoppse the winner in the Prix Corrida, or possibly go to the Grand Prix de Saint-Cloud next.

1622 BRIGHTON (L-H)
Thursday, May 3

OFFICIAL GOING: Good to soft (soft in places) changing to soft (good to soft in places) after race 1 (5.05)
All races run inner line.
Wind: Virtually nil Weather: dull and murky

1767 BRITISH STALLION STUDS SUPPORTING BRITISH RACING E B F MAIDEN STKS 5f 59y
5:05 (5:05) (Class 5) 2-Y-O **£3,169** (£943; £471 ; £235) **Stalls Low**

Form RPR
0 **1** **Heavy Metal**[33] 1131 2 -9-30.. MircoDemuro 1 83+
(Mark Johnston) *mde all: rdn wl over 1f out: styd on wl fnl f: rdn out* **7/4**[1]
3 **2** *1* **Lady Phill**[7] 1623 2 -8-90.. KierenFox(3) 6 74
(Bill Turner) *chsd ldrs: c to stands' rail 3f out: chsd ldr over 2f out: rdn and pressing wnr over 1f out: styd on same pce fnl 100yds* **11/2**
3 **3** *5* **Fiducia**[22] 1308 2 -8-120.. SebSanders 3 56
(Simon Dow) *stdd s: t.k.h: hld up in tch: c to stands' rail 3f out: rdn and effrt to chse ldng pair wl over 1f out: wknd ins fnl f* **9/2**[3]
4 *nk* **Must Be Me** 2 -8-120.. FergusSweeney 5 55
(Eve Johnson Houghton) *in tch: c to stands' side 3f out: rdn and outpcd whn rn green wl over 1f out: wl hld but kpt on fnl f* **9/1**
3 **5** *2 1/4* **Ladweb**[21] 1330 2 -9-30.. IanMongan 2 52
(John Gallagher) *t.k.h: chsd ldrs: styd against ins rail 3f out: rdn and struggling ent fnl 2f: wl btn 1f out* **33/1**
6 *14* **Captain Blue** 2 -8-100.. RyanWhile(7) 7
(Bill Turner) *v.s.a: a bhd: c centre 3f out: nvr on terms* **14/1**
22 **7** *46* **Golac**[7] 1623 2 -9-30.. MartinHarley 4
(Mick Channon) *chsd ldr: c to stands' side 3f out: rdn and lost pl over 2f out: lost tch wl over 1f out: virtually p.u fnl f: t.o* **7/2**[2]
1m 4.62s (2.32)**Going Correction** +0.30s/f (Good) **7**Ran SP% **111.8**
Speed ratings (Par 93): **93,91,83,82,79 56,**
Tote Swingers:1&2:£2.20, 2&3:£5.70, 1&3:£2.30 CSF £11.27 TOTE £2.70 : £2.20, £2.60 ; EX 16.70.
Owner Sheikh Hamdan Bin Mohammed Al Maktoum **Bred** Darley **Trained** Middleham Moor, N Yorks
■ Mirco Demuro's first winner since basing himself in Britain.

FOCUS
All bar one of the runners came across to the stands' side in what was a fairly ordinary juvenile contest.

NOTEBOOK
Heavy Metal ◆, entered in the Group 1 Phoenix Stakes, should leave the bare form behind in time. Unable to do himself justice in the Brocklesby on debut, he won despite both track and ground appearing far from ideal, and looks to possess the scope to progress quite a bit, especially when faced with an extra furlong. He's one of two juveniles from the yard entered in next week's Lily Agnes at Chester. (op 2-1 tchd 13-8)
Lady Phill stepped up quite a bit on last week's debut third at the course, pulling clear of the third and looking sure to find easier opportunities against her own sex. (tchd 13-2)
Fiducia was unable to build on a promising debut switching to turf, but is worth another chance on drier ground. (op 5-1)
Must Be Me, a half-sister to 5f 2yo winner Roodle, out of a 5f-winning dam, looked in need of the experience and should benefit from racing on a more conventional track. (op 8-1 tchd 15-2 and 10-1)
Ladweb's gamble to stay far side didn't pay off. (op 25-1)
Captain Blue, a half-brother to four maidens, including one placed as a hurdler, had no chance following a very slow start. (op 16-1)
Golac, who had run well on soft ground on debut, finished ahead of Lady Phill last week and something clearly went amiss. Official explanation: vet said colt struck into itself

1768 CHECK BETFAIR BEFORE YOU BET H'CAP 6f 209y
5:40 (5:40) (Class 6) (0-55,54) 4-Y-O+ **£1,617** (£481; £240 ; £120) **Stalls Low**

Form RPR
0054 **1** **Custom House (IRE)**[9] 1608 4 -9-1**53**................................ DaneO'Neill 1 62
(John E Long) *chsd ldrs: drvn and pressed ldrs over 1f out: led jst ins fnl f: hdd fnl 100yds: kpt on u.p to ld again last stride* **15/2**[3]
0006 **2** *shd* **Inquisitress**[7] 1628 8 -8-9**47**.. JamieGoldstein 6 56
(John Bridger) *towards rr: rdn and hdwy wl over 1f out: drvn and ev ch jst ins fnl f: led fnl 100yds: kpt on tl hdd last stride* **12/1**
0-04 **3** *2* **Silvee**[117] 91 5 -8-12**53**... SeanLevey(3) 4 57
(John Bridger) *in tch in midfield: rdn and effrt wl over 1f out: drvn and ev ch ins fnl f: wknd fnl 75yds* **13/2**[2]
3003 **4** *1* **Cristaliyev**[7] 1628 4 -9-2**54**..(b) PatCosgrave 11 55
(Jim Boyle) *chsd ldrs: rdn wl over 1f out: edgd rt 1f out: styd on same pce ins fnl f* **9/2**[1]
0-00 **5** *3 3/4* **Simple Rhythm**[98] 312 6 -8-3**48**.......................................(p) RyanTate(7) 9 39
(John Ryan) *chsd ldr tl led 2f out: rdn and hung lft fr wl over 1f out: hdd jst ins fnl f: wknd fnl 100yds* **40/1**
0652 **6** *1* **Alpha Tauri (USA)**[61] 884 6 -9-0**52**..........................(t) WilliamCarson 8 41
(Richard Guest) *led tl hdd 2f out: sn rdn: wknd ent fnl f* **8/1**
-606 **7** *1/2* **Doctor Hilary**[24] 1263 10 -9-1**53**....................................(v) ChrisCatlin 3 41
(Mark Hoad) *in tch: styd on ins fnl 3f: drvn and hdwy over 1f out: no ex jst ins fnl f wknd fnl 100yds* **14/1**
0-00 **8** *2 3/4* **Avon Light**[47] 938 4 -8-8**46**.......................................(p) RussKennemore 12 26
(Milton Bradley) *chsd ldrs: rdn and unable qck over 2f out: wknd over 1f out* **14/1**
-000 **9** *2 1/4* **Litotes**[7] 1625 4 -8-4**45**...(v) KierenFox(3) 14 20
(Michael Attwater) *chsd ldrs: rdn and struggling over 2f out: wknd over 1f out* **40/1**
-040 **10** *1 3/4* **Hand Painted**[61] 781 6 -8-12**50**.......................................(p) LiamKeniry 7 20
(Anthony Middleton) *towards rr: styd against ins rail 3f out: hdwy u.p over 1f out: no imp 1f out: eased whn wl hld ins fnl f* **20/1**
3-60 **11** *1* **Luisa Tetrazzini (IRE)**[9] 1702 6 -8-8**51**.................(b) MarkCoumbe(5) 16 18
(Terry Clement) *chsd ldrs tl lost pl u.p over 2f out: bhd and hung lft over 1f out* **10/1**
-400 **12** *3/4* **Whitstable Native**[14] 1487 4 -9-0**52**................................ MartinHarley 5 17
(Joseph Tuite) *s.i.s: a bhd: styd against ins rail 3f out: n.d* **10/1**
5002 **13** *1 3/4* **Jemimaville (IRE)**[43] 985 5 -8-8**46**...................................(v) LiamJones 2 7
(Giles Bravery) *hld up towards rr: rdn and btn 2f out: wl bhd and hung lft over 1f out* **20/1**
50-3 **14** *1 1/4* **Yakama (IRE)**[24] 1263 7 -9-2**54**..........................(p) TomMcLaughlin 13 12
(Christine Dunnett) *a towards rr: rdn and btn over 2f out: wl bhd fnl f* **17/2**
1m 27.04s (3.94)**Going Correction** +0.575s/f (Yiel) **14**Ran SP% **118.5**
Speed ratings (Par 101): **100,99,97,96,92 91,90,87,84,82 81,80,78,77**
Tote Swingers:1&2:£26.30, 2&3:£23.10, 1&3:£7.50 CSF £88.65 CT £618.34 TOTE £11.40 : £3.60, £4.20 , £2.60 ; EX 150.80 Trifecta £175.10 Part won. Pool £236.64 - 0.20 winning units.
Owner B C Oakley & H Robin Heffer **Bred** John O'Brien **Trained** Caterham, Surrey

FOCUS
They were spread all across the track in this, but unsurprisingly the first two fought it out near the stands' rail. The winner is rated tin line with his winter AW form.

1769 READ RYAN MOORE EXCLUSIVELY ON BETFAIR H'CAP 6f 209y
6:10 (6:10) (Class 5) (0-75,75) 4-Y-O+ **£2,264** (£673; £336 ; £168) **Stalls Low**

Form RPR
2251 **1** **Katmai River (IRE)**[7] 1628 5 -8-11**65** 6ex.....................(v) DavidProbert 2 73
(Mark Usher) *in tch in midfield and sn pushed along: hdwy u.p to ld over 1f out: styd on wl* **3/1**[1]
555- **2** *1 1/2* **Bunce (IRE)**[294] 4006 4 -9-7**75**.. GeorgeBaker 9 79
(Paul Fitzsimons) *in tch in midfield: rdn and effrt to press wnr over 1f out: no ex and one pce fnl 100yds* **6/1**[3]
-233 **3** *1 1/4* **Hereford Boy**[7] 1626 8 -9-2**70**..(v) LukeMorris 6 71
(Dean Ivory) *racd in last quartet: rdn along 3f out: nt clr run wl over 1f out: hdwy u.p to chse ldng pair 1f out: kpt on but nvr able to chal* **9/2**[2]
0-04 **4** *6* **Smoky Cloud (IRE)**[6] 598 5 -8-13**67**.............................. DaneO'Neill 8 52
(Tony Newcombe) *led: rdn over 2f out: hdd over 1f out: btn ent fnl f. wknd* **9/1**
6-60 **5** *2* **Arctic Mirage**[22] 1305 4 -8-7**61** oh1.............................. FergusSweeney 3 41
(Michael Blanshard) *racd in last quartet: rdn 3f out: sme hdwy over 1f out: no prog and wl hld fnl f* **6/1**[3]
0-50 **6** *2* **Zing Wing**[8] 1611 4 -9-1**69**..(b1) ChrisCatlin 4 44
(Paul Cole) *racd keenly: chsd ldr tl wl over 1f out: wknd ent fnl f* **10/1**
3300 **7** *1 3/4* **Tiradito (USA)**[42] 991 5 -8-13**72**..................................(p) MarkCoumbe(5) 1 42
(Michael Attwater) *awkward leaving stalls: racd in last quartet: rdn and effrt 3f out: wknd over 1f out* **16/1**
-000 **8** *1* **Highland Harvest**[22] 1307 8 -8-7**61** oh1.............................. MartinLane 7 29
(Jamie Poulton) *hld up in rr: rdn over 2f out: no prog 2f out: wknd over 1f out* **18/1**
0441 **9** *1 1/4* **Goal (IRE)**[7] 1636 4 -9-2**70**..(t) WilliamCarson 5 34
(Richard Guest) *chsd ldrs tl wknd over 1f out: b.b.v* **8/1**
1m 26.44s (3.34)**Going Correction** +0.575s/f (Yiel) **9**Ran SP% **113.1**
Speed ratings (Par 103): **103,101,99,93,90 88,86,85,83**
Tote Swingers:1&2:£4.20, 2&3:£5.90, 1&3:£3.30 CSF £20.52 CT £78.75 TOTE £2.70 : £1.10, £4.10, £1.10 ; EX 20.70 Trifecta £99.70 Pool £641.68 - 4.76 winning units.
Owner M D I Usher **Bred** Mrs S M Roy **Trained** Upper Lambourn, Berks

FOCUS
Modest form for the grade with the front three clear. The winner is rated to his old best.
Goal(IRE) Official explanation: trainer's rep said gelding bled from the nose

1770 BETFAIR DON'T SETTLE FOR LESS H'CAP — 1m 3f 196y
6:40 (6:40) (Class 6) (0-60,59) 4-Y-0+ — **£1,617** (£481; £240; £120) Stalls High

Form — RPR

40-3 **1** **King's Road**[16] 1433 7-9-5 **57**.....(t) GeorgeBaker 4 62
(Anabel K Murphy) *in tch: hdwy and chsng ldrs whn lft 3rd 3f out: rdn to ld over 1f out: styd on wl fnl f* **9/2**[2]

0035 **2** *1* **Heading To First**[7] 1624 5-8-7 **45**.....(p) KirstyMilczarek 7 48
(Paddy Butler) *chsd ldrs: rdn to ld 2f out: hdd over 1f out: kpt on same pce u.p fnl f* **7/1**

-000 **3** *2 ½* **Turbulent Priest**[7] 1624 4-8-10 **48** ow2.....(b) JamieGoldstein 2 46
(Zoe Davison) *hld up in last pair: rdn and effrt 3f out: chsd ldng pair u.p ent fnl f: kpt on* **20/1**

300/ **4** *3 ¼* **Mossmann Gorge**[38] 3028 10-8-7 **45**.....(p) ChrisCatlin 1 39
(Anthony Middleton) *hld up in rr: rdn and hmpd 3f out: styd on past btn horses fnl f* **7/1**

00-0 **5** *1 ½* **Barbirolli**[38] 1047 10-8-4 **45**..... AdamBeschizza[(3)] 3 37
(William Stone) *in tch: rdn and effrt over 3f out: no imp and no threat to ldrs fnl f* **16/1**

-013 **6** *12* **Spiritual Art**[42] 992 6-9-5 **57**.....(b) TomMcLaughlin 8 30
(Luke Dace) *led tl hdd and rdn 2f out: wknd u.p over 1f out: fdd fnl f* **9/2**[2]

02-0 **7** *11* **Suhailah**[50] 895 6-8-4 **45**.....(p) KierenFox[(3)] 6
(Michael Attwater) *chsd ldr: lost pl 4f out: wl bhd 1f out: eased ins fnl f* **16/1**

1032 **8** *9* **Visions Of Johanna (USA)**[12] 1534 7-9-7 **59**..... WilliamCarson 9
(Richard Guest) *hld up in rr: hdwy into midfield 4f out: styd against ins rail and effrt 3f out: wl btn 1f out: eased fnl f: t.o* **5/1**[3]

3431 **F** **Prince Blue**[38] 1047 5-9-6 **58**..... RichardThomas 5
(John E Long) *chsd ldrs: 3rd and rdn whn lost action and fell 3f out: fatally injured* **4/1**[1]

2m 42.85s (10.15) **Going Correction** +0.575s/f (Yiel) — **9** Ran SP% **114.6**
Speed ratings (Par 101): **89,88,86,84,83 75,68,62,**
Tote Swingers:1&2:£4.90, 2&3:£17.40, 1&3:£28.70 CSF £35.62 CT £567.87 TOTE £6.20: £2.60, £2.00, £9.20; EX 31.50 TRIFECTA Not won..
Owner Mrs Anabel K Murphy **Bred** Mrs M Rogers **Trained** Wilmcote, Warwicks
■ Stewards' Enquiry : Jamie Goldstein three-day ban: weighed in 2lb heavy (May 17-18)

FOCUS
Visibility had worsened by this stage. This concerned only the front pair in the final 2f. Weak form, and it's doubtful the winner had to improve.
Mossmann Gorge Official explanation: jockey said gelding was hampered by faller
Suhailah Official explanation: trainer said mare was unsuited by the track

1771 BETFAIR BRINGS YOU BETTER VALUE H'CAP — 1m 1f 209y
7:10 (7:10) (Class 6) (0-65,65) 4-Y-0+ — **£1,617** (£481; £240; £120) Stalls High

Form — RPR

-322 **1** **Byrd In Hand (IRE)**[7] 1624 5-8-10 **57**..... SeanLevey[(3)] 1 68
(John Bridger) *t.k.h: chsd ldrs: led over 2f out: rdn and drew clr w chalr wl over 1f out: hdd 1f out: led again wl ins fnl f: styd on wl* **7/4**[1]

60-1 **2** *¾* **Lord Of The Storm**[7] 1624 4-8-9 **56** 6ex..... KierenFox[(3)] 3 65
(Bill Turner) *in tch: rdn and effrt over 2f out: chal and wnt clr w wnr wl over 1f out: led narrowly 1f out: hdd and one pce wl ins fnl f* **9/4**[2]

00 **3** *7* **Eurhythmic (IRE)**[55] 786 5-9-2 **60**..... GeorgeBaker 2 55
(Jim Old) *hld up in tch: rdn and effrt over 2f out: outpcd by ldng pair wl over 1f out: styd on to go 3rd ins fnl f: no threat to ldrs* **7/1**[3]

-050 **4** *2 ¾* **Thank You Joy**[30] 1179 4-9-2 **60**.....(v) DavidProbert 5 50
(J R Jenkins) *t.k.h: hld up in tch: rdn and effrt 3f out: chsd ldng pair wl over 1f out: outpcd and wl btn 1f out: wknd* **9/1**

100- **5** *2* **Phluke**[162] 7522 11-9-7 **65**..... FergusSweeney 7 51
(Eve Johnson Houghton) *led tl over 2f out: sn rdn and struggling: wknd wl over 1f out* **16/1**

000- **6** *3 ¾* **Fonterutoli (IRE)**[257] 5281 5-9-1 **59**..... RobertHavlin 4 37
(Roger Ingram) *v.s.a: sn rcvrd and hld up in rr: rdn and effrt over 2f out: no prog 2f out: wl btn ent fnl f* **20/1**

44-0 **7** *2 ¾* **Disturbia (IRE)**[12] 1534 4-8-7 **51** oh5..... KirstyMilczarek 9 24
(Olivia Maylam) *hld up in tch: rdn and effrt over 2f out: wknd wl over 1f out* **20/1**

5333 **8** *5* **Mcconnell (USA)**[9] 1578 7-9-4 **62**.....(b) MartinHarley 8 25
(Richard Guest) *plld hrd: hld up in tch in rr: rdn jst over 2f out: sn wknd* **12/1**

-000 **9** *26* **Give Or Take**[24] 1266 4-8-4 **51** oh6.....(tp) DominicFox[(3)] 6
(Christine Dunnett) *chsd ldrs tl over 2f out: sn bhd: t.o fnl f* **80/1**

2m 9.82s (6.22) **Going Correction** +0.575s/f (Yiel) — **9** Ran SP% **114.0**
Speed ratings (Par 101): **98,97,91,89,88 85,82,78,58**
Tote Swingers:1&2:£1.70, 2&3:£3.50, 1&3:£2.00 CSF £5.49 CT £20.01 TOTE £3.10: £1.10, £1.60, £2.90; EX 5.30 Trifecta £23.50 Pool £552.02 - 17.33 winning units..
Owner Bird In Hand (Hailey) Racing Partnership **Bred** Bricklow Ltd **Trained** Liphook, Hants

FOCUS
First and second in a C&D handicap last week, Lord Of The Storm and Byrd In Hand again dominated, although this time it was the last-named who came out on top from 6lb better terms. Limited form.

1772 BETTER PRICES ON BETFAIR MOBILE H'CAP — 7f 214y
7:40 (7:40) (Class 5) (0-70,69) 4-Y-0+ — **£2,264** (£673; £336; £168) Stalls Low

Form — RPR

50-6 **1** **Bloodsweatandtears**[20] 1358 4-9-7 **69**..... SebSanders 9 81
(William Knight) *mde all: rdn 2f out: awkward hd carriage and edgd lft 1f out: styd on wl and asserted ins fnl f: eased cl home* **15/8**[1]

-052 **2** *2 ½* **Brown Pete (IRE)**[30] 1179 4-8-7 **55**..... WilliamCarson 3 60
(Richard Guest) *t.k.h: hld up in tch: rdn and chal wl over 1f out: drvn ent fnl f: no ex and btn fnl 100yds* **11/2**[3]

336 **3** *1 ½* **Jumeirah Liberty**[50] 894 4-8-13 **61**..... JamieGoldstein 8 63
(Zoe Davison) *chsd ldrs: wnt 2nd 5f out: drvn to press wnr 2f out: unable qck u.p wl over 1f out: styd on same pce fnl f* **20/1**

054- **4** *5* **Budley**[309] 3513 4-9-6 **68**..... AmirQuinn 4 58
(Bill Turner) *in tch: rdn and outpcd over 2f out: no threat to ldrs and plugged on same pce fnl f* **12/1**

3051 **5** *2 ¾* **Saucy Buck (IRE)**[35] 1088 4-8-13 **61**..... MichaelO'Connell 7 45
(Jamie Poulton) *chsd ldr tl 1/2-way: rdn and struggling over 2f out: wknd over 1f out* **6/1**

0262 **6** *10* **Hip Hip Hooray**[7] 1626 6-9-0 **62**..... IanMongan 2 50
(Luke Dace) *in tch in last pair: rdn and effrt over 2f out: no hdwy: wl btn and eased ins fnl f* **2/1**[2]

1m 41.52s (5.52) **Going Correction** +0.575s/f (Yiel) — **6** Ran SP% **110.2**
Speed ratings (Par 103): **95,92,91,86,83 73**
Tote Swingers:1&2:£1.80, 2&3:£7.60, 1&3:£7.10 CSF £12.05 CT £139.53 TOTE £1.90: £1.10, £3.20; EX 10.10 Trifecta £134.90 Pool £404.74 - 2.22 winning units..
Owner Canisbay Bloodstock **Bred** Oakhill Stud **Trained** Patching, W Sussex

FOCUS
A weak handicap for the grade. The winner is rated back to something like his best.
Hip Hip Hooray Official explanation: trainer said mare was unsuited by the soft (good to soft places) ground

1773 TIMEFORM.BETFAIR.COM H'CAP — 5f 59y
8:10 (8:10) (Class 5) (0-70,70) 4-Y-0+ — **£2,264** (£673; £336; £168) Stalls Low

Form — RPR

0045 **1** **Welsh Inlet (IRE)**[12] 1528 4-8-12 **64**..... SeanLevey[(3)] 5 72
(John Bridger) *pressed ldr: rdn and ev ch over 1f out: led fnl 100yds: styd on wl: rdn out* **4/1**

2310 **2** *¾* **Waabel**[8] 1614 5-9-4 **67**.....(t) MartinHarley 6 72
(Richard Guest) *led: rdn 1/2-way: hrd pressed wl over 1f out: battled on gamely u.p tl hdd and no ex fnl 100yds* **10/3**[3]

00-0 **3** *2* **Alpha Delta Whisky**[17] 1417 4-9-7 **70**..... IanMongan 3 68
(John Gallagher) *trckd ldrs: rdn 2f out: ev ch and drvn over 1f out: unable qck ent fnl f: wknd fnl 100yds* **5/2**[1]

0546 **4** *2* **Speak The Truth (IRE)**[22] 1307 6-9-4 **67**.....(p) PatCosgrave 7 58
(Jim Boyle) *chsd ldrs: effrt u.p 2f out: unable qck over 1f out: edgd lft and wknd jst ins fnl f* **8/1**

103- **5** *1 ¾* **Colourbearer (IRE)**[175] 7356 5-9-4 **67**.....(t) RussKennemore 2 52
(Milton Bradley) *hld up wl in tch in rr: rdn and effrt towards centre 2f out: drvn and unable qck over 1f out: wknd fnl 150yds* **3/1**[2]

1m 4.97s (2.67) **Going Correction** +0.575s/f (Yiel) — **5** Ran SP% **107.8**
Speed ratings (Par 103): **101,99,96,93,90**
CSF £16.49 TOTE £7.90: £2.70, £1.40; EX 16.50 Trifecta £55.80 Pool £376.12 - 4.98 winning units..
Owner J J Bridger **Bred** Patrick Gleeson **Trained** Liphook, Hants

FOCUS
A low-grade sprint handicap, run on the worst of the ground. The winner is rated back to her best.
T/Plt: £160.60 to a £1 stake. Pool £77,004.26. 349.83 winning tickets T/Qpdt: £19.40 to a £1 stake. Pool £9,668.92. 367.30 winning tickets SP

1330 FOLKESTONE (R-H)
Thursday, May 3
1774 Meeting Abandoned - waterlogged

1352 LEICESTER (R-H)
Thursday, May 3
1781 Meeting Abandoned - waterlogged

1730 LINGFIELD (L-H)
Thursday, May 3
OFFICIAL GOING: Standard
Wind: Almost nil Weather: Overcast and drizzly

1787 TOTEPLACEPOT LADY RIDERS' H'CAP (FOR LADY AMATEUR RIDERS) — 5f (P)
2:10 (2:11) (Class 6) (0-60,57) 4-Y-0+ — **£1,646** (£506; £253) Stalls High

Form — RPR

500- **1** **Instructress**[169] 7429 4-9-7 48..... MissAliceMills[(5)] 6 58
(Robert Cowell) *prom: rdn to ld ins fnl f: r.o wl* **16/1**

0-40 **2** *3* **Papageno**[113] 118 5-9-2 45..... MissKMargarson[(7)] 4 44
(J R Jenkins) *led: rdn and hdd ins fnl f: one pce* **12/1**

6330 **3** *nse* **Sherjawy (IRE)**[14] 1483 8-10-2 57.....(b) MissHayleyMoore[(5)] 1 56+
(Zoe Davison) *chsd ldrs: lost pl 3f out: rallied over 1f out: styd on* **10/1**

1420 **4** *1 ½* **Do More Business (IRE)**[44] 972 5-10-1 54..... MissCWalton[(3)] 7 47+
(Alison Batchelor) *bhd tl r.o fr over 1f out: nvr nrr* **3/1**[2]

4303 **5** *hd* **Pharoh Jake**[29] 1183 4-9-11 47..... MissEJJones 8 40
(John Bridger) *in tch: effrt and disp 3rd 2f out: one pce* **10/1**

6653 **6** *1 ¾* **Slatey Hen (IRE)**[12] 1528 4-10-3 53.....(p) MissZoeLilly 5 39
(Richard Guest) *a abt same pl: nvr trbld ldrs* **10/3**[3]

500- **7** *1 ½* **Prophet In A Dream**[24] 6929 4-9-13 54..... MissMBryant[(5)] 9 35
(Paddy Butler) *s.s: wl bhd most of way: nvr nr ldrs* **40/1**

1006 **8** *8* **Tenancy (IRE)**[23] 1283 8-10-0 50.....(b) MrsAdeleMulrennan 3
(Shaun Harris) *prom tl wknd over 2f out* **17/2**

200/ **P** **First Order**[612] 5599 11-10-2 55.....(v) MissRachelKing[(3)] 2
(Ann Stokell) *chsd ldrs: disputing 3rd whn broke down and p.u over 1f out* **33/1**

59.47s (0.67) **Going Correction** -0.05s/f (Stan) — **9** Ran SP% **113.3**
Speed ratings (Par 101): **92,87,87,84,84 81,79,66,**
Tote Swingers:1&2:£20.60, 2&3:£7.00, 1&3:£8.80 CSF £187.46 CT £693.91 TOTE £27.80: £5.20, £3.40, £1.30; EX 153.90.
Owner Bottisham Heath Stud **Bred** Bottisham Heath Stud **Trained** Six Mile Bottom, Cambs

FOCUS
This replacement fixture for washed-out Folkestone opened with a lowly 5f handicap. The gallop was perfectly respectable and so was the winning time of around two seconds outside standard. Few got involved and the first pair were always 1-2. The winner's best form since she was a 2yo.
Slatey Hen(IRE) Official explanation: jockey said fill was slowly away

1788 TOTEQUICKPICK FILLIES' H'CAP — 6f (P)
2:40 (2:40) (Class 5) (0-70,69) 4-Y-0+ — **£2,385** (£704; £352) Stalls Low

Form — RPR

0-40 **1** **Flashbang**[8] 1614 4-8-12 60.....(b[1]) SilvestreDeSousa 2 76
(Paul Cole) *sn led: qcknd clr 3f out: comf* **4/1**[2]

431 **2** *2 ¾* **Big Wave (IRE)**[23] 1285 4-9-2 64..... RichardHughes 3 72
(Jane Chapple-Hyam) *chsd ldng pair: wnt 2nd over 1f out: no ch w wnr* **13/8**[1]

0214 **3** 1 1/4 **Lady Mango (IRE)**[44] 972 4-8-11 59................................ LukeMorris 6 63
(Ronald Harris) *outpcd in rr: sme hdwy and hrd rdn over 1f out: nt rch ldrs* **5/1**[3]

6462 **4** 1/2 **Anjomarba (IRE)**[19] 1387 5-8-7 55................................ HayleyTurner 1 57
(Conor Dore) *broke wl: chsd wnr tl no ex over 1f out* **8/1**

2252 **5** nk **Perfect Ch'l (IRE)**[8] 1609 5-9-3 65................................ JamesDoyle 5 66
(Ian Wood) *pushed along towards rr: rdn 3f out: mod effrt on outer ent st: no imp* **11/2**

13-3 **6** 7 **Bobby's Doll**[16] 1428 5-9-0 69................................ HarryPoulton(7) 4 48
(Terry Clement) *sn towards rr: lost tch 3f out* **18/1**

1m 10.85s (-1.05) **Going Correction** -0.05s/f (Stan) 6 Ran SP% **106.5**
Speed ratings (Par 100): **105,101,99,99,98 89**
Tote Swingers:1&2:£2.10, 2&3:£2.10, 1&3:£2.00 CSF £9.79 TOTE £3.60: £2.00, £1.50; EX 13.00.
Owner A H Robinson **Bred** D J Weston **Trained** Whatcombe, Oxon
■ Stewards' Enquiry : Richard Hughes one-day ban: careless riding (May 17)

FOCUS
A low-class small-field 6f handicap for older fillies run at a decent galllop and the winning time of under a second outside standard looks very respectable for the grade. The winner was back to form in the blinkers.

1789 MIRROR PUNTERS CLUB CLAIMING STKS 6f (P)
3:10 (3:10) (Class 6) 3-Y-O+ **£1,704** (£503; £251) **Stalls** Low

Form RPR

021- **1** **Aye Aye Digby (IRE)**[161] 7529 7-9-10 85................................ GeorgeBaker 6 91
(Patrick Chamings) *mde all: qcknd clr 1f out: easily* **1/1**[1]

1400 **2** 4 1/2 **Diamond Vine (IRE)**[24] 1254 4-9-8 70................................(p) LukeMorris 2 75
(Ronald Harris) *sn disputing 2nd: rdn to press wnr 2f out: outpcd and btn 1f out* **6/1**

0020 **3** 1 **Ghostwing**[10] 1564 5-9-7 78................................(b) FergusSweeney 3 71
(James Evans) *hld up in 4th: effrt 2f out: hd high and no imp* **7/2**[2]

1-35 **4** 3 3/4 **Le King Beau (USA)**[106] 201 3-8-7 69................................ SeanLevey(3) 1 55
(John Bridger) *disp 2nd tl wknd qckly over 1f out* **9/2**[3]

0-00 **5** 5 **Bilko Pak (IRE)**[3] 1722 4-9-1 56................................(v) KirstyMilczarek 5 37
(Brendan Powell) *missed break and lost 10 l: stl last but in tch after 2f: outpcd and lft bhd 2f out* **33/1**

1m 11.36s (-0.54) **Going Correction** -0.05s/f (Stan)
WFA 3 from 4yo+ 10lb 5 Ran SP% **107.6**
Speed ratings (Par 101): **101,95,93,88,82**
CSF £7.09 TOTE £2.40: £1.90, £2.10; EX 5.40.
Owner Trolley Action **Bred** G J King **Trained** Baughurst, Hants

FOCUS
An average small-field claimer run at a decent gallop and in a respectable time for the grade. The winner's best form for around two years.
Bilko Pak(IRE) Official explanation: jockey said gelding planted at start.

1790 TOTEPOOL H'CAP 7f (P)
3:40 (3:40) (Class 5) (0-80,80) 3-Y-O **£4,851** (£1,443; £721; £360) **Stalls** Low

Form RPR

06-6 **1** **Xinbama (IRE)**[22] 1313 3-8-11 70 ow1................................ SebSanders 5 78
(J W Hills) *hld up towards rr: gd hdwy over 1f out: r.o to ld fnl 30yds* **9/1**

120- **2** 1 1/4 **Ziefhd**[222] 6340 3-9-7 80................................ JimmyFortune 8 85
(Paul Cole) *led: rdn and narrowly hdd ent fnl f: kpt on* **10/1**

5-14 **3** nse **Incendiary (IRE)**[34] 1109 3-8-9 75................................ NoelGarbutt(7) 2 80
(Hugo Palmer) *hld up in midfield: hdwy to take slt ld ent fnl f: kpt on u.p: hdd fnl 30yds* **6/1**

50-1 **4** 1 1/4 **Jumeirah Palm Star**[41] 1004 3-8-12 74................................ SeanLevey(3) 6 75
(Richard Hannon) *chsd ldrs: rdn and one pce fnl 2f* **15/2**

1- **5** 2 3/4 **Ihtiraam (IRE)**[206] 6758 3-9-5 78................................ FrankieDettori 9 72
(Saeed Bin Suroor) *hld up towards rr on outer: drvn along 2f out: sme late hdwy* **11/4**[1]

3234 **6** shd **Masters Club**[2] 1731 3-8-4 66................................ RyanPowell(3) 1 60
(John Ryan) *sn prom: drvn to chal over 1f out: sn wknd* **25/1**

020- **7** 1 1/2 **Arctic Stryker**[224] 6281 3-8-11 70................................ LukeMorris 4 60
(John Best) *hld up in last: rdn over 2f out: mod hdwy on inner ent st: no imp* **50/1**

3120 **8** 1/2 **Lionrock (FR)**[15] 1441 3-8-11 70................................ SilvestreDeSousa 7 58
(Mark Johnston) *in tch: effrt on outer and wnt wd fnl bnd: hrd rdn and wknd* **4/1**[2]

011- **9** 1 1/4 **Beach Candy (IRE)**[199] 6921 3-9-3 76................................ RichardHughes 3 61
(Richard Hannon) *pressed ldr: edgd rt 3f out: wd and wknd qckly ent st* **9/2**[3]

1m 24.27s (-0.53) **Going Correction** -0.05s/f (Stan) 9 Ran SP% **115.8**
Speed ratings (Par 99): **101,99,99,98,94 94,93,92,91**
Tote Swingers:1&2:£13.70, 2&3:£9.30, 1&3:£10.50 CSF £94.72 CT £588.32 TOTE £16.40: £3.70, £2.20, £2.20; EX 96.50.
Owner Tony Waspe Partnership **Bred** P Heffernan **Trained** Upper Lambourn, Berks

FOCUS
An interesting 7f handicap for 3yos which was the feature on the card. It looked competitive beforehand and so it proved. They went a solid gallop which is normal at this speed-orientated track. The form looks pretty solid too.
Beach Candy(IRE) Official explanation: jockey said filly hung badly right.

1791 SUMMER EVENINGS AT LINGFIELD PARK H'CAP 2m (P)
4:10 (4:10) (Class 6) (0-60,59) 4-Y-O+ **£1,704** (£503; £251) **Stalls** Low

Form RPR

4326 **1** **Talbot Green**[20] 1361 4-9-3 58................................ MartinDwyer 5 65
(William Muir) *mde all: set weak pce: qcknd over 2f out: a in control: comf* **9/4**[1]

-504 **2** 2 3/4 **Galiotto (IRE)**[29] 1184 6-9-7 59................................(v) GeorgeBaker 4 63
(Gary Moore) *trckd ldng pair: wnt 2nd 2f out: no ch w wnr fnl f* **9/4**[1]

3002 **3** 3 1/4 **Oneiric**[2] 1732 4-8-12 58................................ MarkCoumbe(5) 1 58
(Brett Johnson) *s.s: t.k.h in rr: in tch 5f out: outpcd 3f out: styd on again fr over 1f out* **4/1**[2]

324/ **4** 3/4 **Il Portico**[530] 5923 5-8-13 51................................ RichardHughes 3 50
(Gary Moore) *in tch: effrt 2f out: no imp* **13/2**

06 **5** 1 **Darsan (IRE)**[7] 1624 4-9-2 57................................ SilvestreDeSousa 6 55
(Phil McEntee) *t.k.h: trckd ldr tl outpcd 2f out: sn btn* **6/1**[3]

000- **6** 10 **Lady Valtas**[47] 6032 4-8-5 46 ow1................................ RoystonFfrench 2 32
(Robin Dickin) *in tch tl drvn along and wknd over 3f out* **66/1**

3m 26.55s (0.85) **Going Correction** -0.05s/f (Stan)
WFA 4 from 5yo+ 3lb 6 Ran SP% **110.7**
Speed ratings (Par 101): **95,93,92,91,91 86**
Tote Swingers:1&2:£1.50, 2&3:£2.40, 1&3:£2.40 CSF £7.19 TOTE £3.40: £1.90, £1.80; EX 6.50.
Owner Claridge, Quaintance, Egan & Mercer **Bred** Usk Valley Stud **Trained** Lambourn, Berks

FOCUS
A lowly small-field 2m handicap for older horses run at a sedate-looking gallop. The winner made all and it's doubtful whether he improved.

1792 BET TOTEPOOL ON ALL UK RACING H'CAP 1m 2f (P)
4:40 (4:40) (Class 5) (0-75,73) 4-Y-O+ **£2,385** (£704; £352) **Stalls** Low

Form RPR

25-6 **1** **Understory (USA)**[8] 1611 5-9-5 71................................ HayleyTurner 9 79
(Tim McCarthy) *mde all: rdn and hld on wl fnl 2f* **7/1**

160 **2** 1 3/4 **Mafi (IRE)**[5] 1680 4-9-4 70................................ RobertHavlin 3 75
(Mark Hoad) *prom: chsd wnr over 2f out tl over 1f out: kpt on same pce* **13/2**[3]

10-4 **3** 1/2 **Midas Moment**[22] 1311 4-9-7 73................................ MartinDwyer 5 77
(William Muir) *plld hrd: in tch: drvn to press wnr over 1f out: one pce* **12/1**

300- **4** 1 1/2 **New River (IRE)**[272] 4763 4-9-5 71................................ RichardHughes 6 72+
(Richard Hannon) *s.i.s: hld up in rr: rdn 3f out: hdwy on inner over 1f out: nt qckn fnl f* **11/4**[1]

4343 **5** nk **Lisahane Bog**[38] 1051 5-9-2 68................................(p) NeilCallan 2 68
(Peter Hedger) *towards rr: rdn and sme hdwy 2f out: styd on same pce* **8/1**

-203 **6** 1 **Silver Alliance**[24] 1266 4-9-4 70................................ LukeMorris 10 68
(Julia Feilden) *t.k.h: prom tl hrd rdn and wknd jst over 1f out* **9/1**

/5-0 **7** hd **Sedgwick**[32] 1154 10-8-13 65................................ SilvestreDeSousa 4 63
(Shaun Harris) *bhd: rdn over 2f out: nvr rchd ldrs* **16/1**

14-3 **8** 6 **Yourinthewill (USA)**[110] 176 4-9-4 70................................ AndreaAtzeni 7 56
(Daniel Mark Loughnane) *in tch tl wknd over 2f out* **5/1**[2]

0/5- **9** 1/2 **Crimson Monarch (USA)**[480] 104 8-8-0 59 oh7................................ NoelGarbutt(7) 8 44
(Peter Hiatt) *rdn over 4f out: a bhd* **50/1**

1/0- **10** 12 **Honest Strike (USA)**[196] 6976 5-9-3 69................................ JimmyFortune 11 30
(Daniel Mark Loughnane) *prom: chsd wnr after 3f tl wknd over 2f out* **12/1**

000- **P** **South Cape**[235] 5969 9-9-2 68................................ GeorgeBaker 1
(Gary Moore) *mid-div: losing pl whn p.u 3f out: dismntd* **14/1**

2m 5.38s (-1.22) **Going Correction** -0.05s/f (Stan) 11 Ran SP% **120.2**
Speed ratings (Par 103): **102,100,100,99,98 97,97,93,92,83**
Tote Swingers:1&2:£9.20, 2&3:£17.30, 1&3:£11.00 CSF £53.26 CT £547.33 TOTE £10.60: £3.10, £3.10, £5.10; EX 50.50.
Owner The Bordeaux Fine Wines Racing Club **Bred** Darley **Trained** Godstone, Surrey

FOCUS
An average 1m2f handicap for older horses and for the second consecutive race they went a modest gallop. The winner, who made all, sets the standard.
South Cape Official explanation: vet reported gelding was distressed post race.

1793 CYPRIUM BAR AT MARRIOTT LINGFIELD MEDIAN AUCTION MAIDEN STKS 1m 2f (P)
5:10 (5:10) (Class 6) 3-4-Y-O **£1,704** (£503; £251) **Stalls** Low

Form RPR

2-30 **1** **Hefner (IRE)**[14] 1473 3-8-11 81................................ RichardHughes 5 73+
(Richard Hannon) *trckd ldr: led and qcknd over 2f out: drvn to hold on fnl f* **11/8**[1]

5- **2** 1/2 **Handsome Ransom**[231] 6100 3-8-11 0................................ NickyMackay 7 72+
(John Gosden) *hld up in 6th: hdwy over 2f out: drvn to chal ins fnl f: jst hld* **13/8**[2]

0- **3** 2 **Edraaq**[218] 6463 3-8-11 0................................ TadhgO'Shea 4 68+
(Brian Meehan) *chsd ldrs: rdn and one pce fnl 2f* **15/2**

05-0 **4** 1/2 **Thecornishcockney**[10] 1567 3-8-11 63................................ MichaelO'Connell 1 67
(John Ryan) *chsd ldrs: effrt 2f out: one pce appr fnl f* **33/1**

5 8 **Broadway Babe (IRE)** 3-8-6 0................................ SilvestreDeSousa 8 46
(Harry Dunlop) *s.i.s: plld hrd in rr: shkn up 2f out: nvr trbld ldrs* **28/1**

6 1 1/2 **Sporting Gold (IRE)** 3-8-11 0................................ NeilCallan 3 48
(Roger Varian) *in tch: rdn 3f out: wknd 2f out* **7/1**[3]

-0 **7** 2 1/4 **Play Tiger (FR)**[12] 1518 3-8-11 0................................ MartinDwyer 6 44
(David Simcock) *s.i.s: hld up in rr: effrt whn hmpd 2f out: n.d after* **66/1**

4- **8** 22 **Elmora**[209] 6663 3-8-3 0................................ SophieDoyle(3) 2
(Sylvester Kirk) *racd freely and heavily restrained in front: led tl over 2f out: wkng whn bmpd on fnl bnd* **25/1**

2m 4.88s (-1.72) **Going Correction** -0.05s/f (Stan) 8 Ran SP% **116.2**
Speed ratings (Par 101): **104,103,102,101,95 94,92,74**
Tote Swingers:1&2:£1.40, 2&3:£2.60, 1&3:£2.90 CSF £3.79 TOTE £2.70: £1.20, £1.10, £1.90; EX 4.00.
Owner Mrs J Wood **Bred** Denis A McCarthy **Trained** East Everleigh, Wilts
■ Stewards' Enquiry : Michael O'Connell two-day ban: careless riding (May 17-18)

FOCUS
An interesting median auction maiden stakes open to older horses, but contested entirely by 3yos. It was steadily run and the winner did not need to match his best.
Elmora Official explanation: jockey said filly suffered interference in running.
T/Plt: £146.60 to a £1 stake. Pool £65,521.48. 326.26 winning tickets T/Qpdt: £34.60 to a £1 stake. Pool £4,571.72. 97.66 winning tickets LM

1235 MUSSELBURGH (R-H)
Thursday, May 3

OFFICIAL GOING: Good to soft (good in places; 6.3)
Bottom bend moved out 2metres.
Wind: Virtually nil Weather: Fine and dry

1794 RANDOLPH HILL H'CAP (FOR AMATEUR RIDERS) 2m
2:00 (2:00) (Class 6) (0-60,60) 4-Y-O+ **£1,871** (£580; £290; £145) **Stalls** High

Form RPR

350- **1** **Talk Of Saafend (IRE)**[26] 7113 7-9-12 **51**................................ MissRobynGray(7) 3 59
(Dianne Sayer) *sn led at stdy pce: qcknd over 3f out: rdn 2f out: hung lft ins fnl f: kpt on wl* **14/1**

030- **2** 2 **Spruzzo**[199] 6915 6-10-10 **56**................................ MissSBrotherton 4 62
(Chris Fairhurst) *cl up: effrt 3f out: rdn 2f out and ev ch tl one pce ent fnl f* **4/1**[1]

30-4 **3** 1 3/4 **Dechiper (IRE)**[24] 1247 10-10-0 **46**................................(p) MrSWalker 2 50
(Robert Johnson) *trckd ldrs on inner: effrt and sltly outpcd wl over 2f out: sn rdn and kpt on fnl f* **8/1**

545- **4** 1 1/4 **Tower**[18] 2060 5-10-3 **54**................................(be) StevenFox(5) 10 56
(Chris Grant) *trckd ldrs: hdwy 3f out: rdn 2f out and ev ch tl wknd appr fnl f* **20/1**

0/2- **5** hd **Toshi (USA)**[13] 4499 10-9-8 **47**................................ MissElrving(7) 6 49
(Jim Goldie) *hld up in rr: hdwy 5f out: effrt on outer wl over 2f out: rdn to chse ldrs wl over 1f out: sn one pce* **11/2**[2]

4-00 **6** 3¾ **Munaawib**[16] 1432 4-9-6 **46** .... MrARawlinson(5) 12 43
(David C Griffiths) *hld up in midfield: hdwy over 4f out: chsd ldrs 3f out: rdn along over 2f out: drvn and one pce fr over 1f out* **22/1**

400/ **7** ½ **Ruff Diamond (USA)**[31] 3143 7-10-9 **60** .... MrGRSmith(5) 5 57
(David Thompson) *hld up: sme hdwy 3f out: sn rdn and no imp fnl 2f* **16/1**

4U54 **8** ¾ **Colliers Castle (IRE)**[20] 1361 6-9-9 **48** .... MrCEllingham(7) 11 44
(Lisa Williamson) *trckd ldrs: hdwy 4f out: rdn over 2f out: grad wknd* **6/1**[3]

-105 **9** ½ **Lil Ella (IRE)**[25] 1240 5-10-7 **58** .... MrsFreyaBrewer(5) 9 53
(Patrick Holmes) *hld up: a in rr* **15/2**

100/ **10** 2½ **Calculaite**[167] 5940 11-10-8 **59** .... MissNStead(5) 8 51
(Richard Ford) *hld up in rr: sme hdwy 3f out: rdn over 2f out: n.d* **25/1**

2-42 **11** ½ **Polly Holder (IRE)**[37] 1057 4-10-2 **58** ....(p) MrsRWilson(7) 7 50
(Paul D'Arcy) *trckd ldrs: pushed along over 5f out: rdn along 4f out: sn wknd* **11/2**[2]

3m 49.18s (15.68) **Going Correction** +0.60s/f (Yiel)
WFA 4 from 5yo+ 3lb **11** Ran SP% **113.4**
Speed ratings (Par 101): **84,83,82,81,81 79,79,78,78,77 77**
Tote Swingers:1&2:£14.10, 2&3:£6.90, 1&3:£10.20 CSF £65.01 CT £485.08 TOTE £17.30: £3.90, £1.60, £2.50; EX 92.80 Trifecta £275.00 Pool £371.64 - 1 winning unit..
Owner Dennis J Coppola **Bred** Michael Dalton **Trained** Hackthorpe, Cumbria
■ Robyn Gray's first winner under rules.
■ Stewards' Enquiry : Mr A Rawlinson one-day ban: careless riding (tbn)

FOCUS
The going was officially described as good to soft, good in places but was expected to ride a bit sticky. The form for this amateur riders' staying handicap can be taken with a large pinch of salt as they crawled until reaching the home straight and those at the head of affairs enjoyed a massive advantage. The form is rated around the first two to last year's form.
Polly Holder(IRE) Official explanation: jockey said filly ran too free.

1795 BRYNDLEY DAVIES WORKING FROM HOME MAIDEN AUCTION STKS 5f
2:30 (2:32) (Class 6) 2-Y-O **£1,940** (£577; £288; £144) **Stalls** High

Form RPR

4 **1** **Jubilee Games**[15] 1437 2-8-11 0 .... PaulHanagan 6 65+
(Richard Fahey) *trckd ldrs: swtchd rt and hdwy to chal over 1f out: rdn to ld appr fnl f: kpt on* **13/8**[1]

2 1½ **Dil Laney (IRE)** 2-8-13 0 .... DanielTudhope 2 62
(David O'Meara) *cl up: rdn to ld briefly whn rn green and hung lft over 1f out: sn hdd: kpt on fnl f* **15/2**

3 **3** 2¼ **Sylvia Pankhurst (IRE)**[5] 1671 2-8-4 0 .... AdrianNicholls 1 45
(David C Griffiths) *chsd ldrs: hdwy on outer to chal over 1f out: sn rdn and ev ch tl one pce ins fnl f* **2/1**[2]

0 **4** 2½ **Miss Penny Arcade**[15] 1437 2-8-6 0 .... JoeFanning 4 38+
(Keith Dalgleish) *wnt rt s: sn led: rdn along 2f out: hdd over 1f out and sn wknd* **11/2**[3]

0 **5** ½ **Moss The Boss (IRE)**[15] 1435 2-8-9 0 .... MickyFenton 3 39
(Paul Midgley) *sltly hmpd s: a in rr* **50/1**

6 2½ **Pastoral Prey** 2-8-9 0 .... LeeNewman 5 30
(George Foster) *dwlt: sn trcking ldrs on inner: effrt and nt clr run 2f out: swtchd rt and rdn over 1f out: no hdwy* **9/1**

1m 2.86s (2.46) **Going Correction** +0.175s/f (Good) **6** Ran SP% **110.5**
Speed ratings (Par 91): **87,84,81,77,76 72**
Tote Swingers:1&2:£2.30, 2&3:£2.30, 1&3:£1.70 CSF £13.83 TOTE £2.10: £1.70, £4.00; EX 13.70.
Owner Lets Go Racing 1 **Bred** P And Mrs A G Venner **Trained** Musley Bank, N Yorks
■ Stewards' Enquiry : Paul Hanagan two-day ban: careless riding (May 17-18)

FOCUS
Probably only a modest maiden, and no recent race averages to work on. The first two may do better.

NOTEBOOK
Jubilee Games had finished a fair fourth on his Beverley debut and stepped up on that here despite giving plenty of trouble before the start. He quickened up nicely when the gaps appeared and should continue to progress. (op 15-8 tchd 2-1 in places)
Dil Laney(IRE) ◆, who hit the front for a few strides over a furlong out before hanging all over the place, is the one to take from the race. The fact that he still kept on well for second despite that suggests that this 11,000euros gelding out of a half sister to two winners at up to 1m2f has a future. (op 8-1 tchd 7-1)
Sylvia Pankhurst(IRE) only went down narrowly when third on her Ripon debut five days earlier and had every chance on the wide outside here. This wasn't a step forward, though in her defence this race may have come soon enough. (op 6-4)
Miss Penny Arcade finished around 6l behind Jubilee Games on her Beverley debut and fared little better here after having made much of the early running. (op 6-1)
Moss The Boss(IRE), a well beaten last of ten on his Beverley debut, looked held when getting hampered by the winner over a furlong out. (op 66-1)
Pastoral Prey, a 2,500GBP half-brother to a 1m4f winner, was perhaps not surprisingly always struggling to go the pace after missing the break. (op 12-1 tchd 17-2)

1796 DM HALL H'CAP 1m
3:00 (3:01) (Class 5) (0-70,70) 3-Y-O+ **£3,234** (£962; £481; £240) **Stalls** Low

Form RPR

00-0 **1** **Northern Fling**[12] 1520 8-9-8 **70** .... GrahamLee 9 79
(Jim Goldie) *hld up: pushed along briefly 3f out: hdwy on bit to trck ldrs 2f out: swtchd rt and rdn to chal ins fnl f: carried hd high and edgd lft: led last 100yds* **20/1**

0-25 **2** 1 **Save The Bees**[12] 1520 4-9-1 **70** .... JasonHart(7) 6 77
(Declan Carroll) *a.p: effrt 2f out: rdn over 1f out: sn ev ch: kpt on* **9/2**[2]

32-1 **3** hd **Le Chat D'Or**[24] 1251 4-9-5 **67** ....(t) PaulMulrennan 8 74
(Michael Dods) *midfield: hdwy on outer wl over 2f out: rdn over 1f out: ev ch ins fnl f: nt qckn towards fin* **11/4**[1]

1144 **4** 1 **Cyflymder (IRE)**[19] 1384 6-9-3 **65** .... AdrianNicholls 3 69
(David C Griffiths) *sn led: rdn along over 2f out: drvn over 1f out: hdd & wknd last 100yds* **14/1**

1160 **5** 2¼ **Copperwood**[22] 1293 7-9-4 **66** .... JoeFanning 10 65
(Mark Johnston) *t.k.h: cl up: chal 3f out: rdn along 2f out: wknd appr fnl f* **12/1**

05-5 **6** ½ **Muftarres (IRE)**[69] 692 7-9-3 **65** .... MickyFenton 5 63
(Paul Midgley) *hld up: hdwy wl over 2f out: rdn to chse ldrs over 1f out: one pce fnl f* **10/1**

100- **7** 1 **Sabratha (IRE)**[184] 7213 4-9-6 **68** .... PhillipMakin 12 64
(Linda Perratt) *hld up towards rr: hdwy wl over 2f out: rdn wl over 1f out: sn no imp* **33/1**

26P- **8** ½ **Mangham (IRE)**[243] 5721 7-9-2 **64** .... LeeNewman 11 58
(George Foster) *dwlt and towards rr: hdwy 3f out: chsd ldrs 2f out: sn rdn and no imp* **33/1**

64-0 **9** ¾ **Hail Bold Chief (USA)**[33] 1134 5-9-1 **68** .... GarryWhillans(5) 1 61
(Alan Swinbank) *trckd ldrs: effrt 3f out: rdn 2f out: grad wknd* **12/1**

00-0 **10** 7 **Coax**[69] 692 4-9-3 **65** .... DanielTudhope 2 42
(Patrick Holmes) *hld up towards rr: hdwy on inner and in tch 3f out: rdn over 2f out and sn wknd* **25/1**

00-1 **11** 1½ **Nadeen (IRE)**[26] 1224 5-9-5 **67** .... AndrewMullen 4 40
(Michael Smith) *v.s.a and lost many l s: a bhd* **13/2**[3]

253- **12** 6 **Strong Man**[201] 6869 4-9-3 **65** .... JamesSullivan 7 24
(Michael Easterby) *a in rr* **13/2**[3]

1m 44.82s (3.62) **Going Correction** +0.60s/f (Yiel) **12** Ran SP% **117.1**
Speed ratings (Par 103): **105,104,103,102,100 100,99,98,97,90 89,83**
Tote Swingers:1&2:£23.30, 2&3:£3.10, 1&3:£16.20 CSF £103.18 CT £331.33 TOTE £33.30: £8.50, £1.90, £1.10; EX 170.30 TRIFECTA Not won..
Owner Paul Moulton **Bred** Lady Juliet Tadgell **Trained** Uplawmoor, E Renfrews
■ Graham Lee's first winner since switching to the Flat.
■ Stewards' Enquiry : Adrian Nicholls two-day ban: used whip above the permitted level (May 17-18)

FOCUS
An ordinary handicap and another race in which most of the principals, the winner apart, raced handily. The race was sound run and the winner is rated to last summer's form.
Northern Fling ◆ Official explanation: trainer had no explanation for the apparent improvement in form
Nadeen(IRE) Official explanation: jockey said gelding was reluctant to race.

1797 BYFORD DOLPHIN H'CAP 1m 4f 100y
3:30 (3:30) (Class 5) (0-75,75) 4-Y-O+ **£3,234** (£962; £481; £240) **Stalls** Low

Form RPR

056- **1** **Bradbury (IRE)**[21] 6191 4-8-13 **67** ....(p) GrahamGibbons 3 74
(James Bethell) *in tch on inner: hdwy 3f out: trckd ldrs 2f out: swtchd lft and rdn jst over 1f out: styd on wl to ld last 100yds* **9/1**

020- **2** 1¼ **Spirit Of A Nation (IRE)**[68] 6151 7-9-7 **75** .... PaddyAspell 11 80
(James Moffatt) *hld up in rr: swtchd lft and gd hdwy on outer 2f out: rdn over 1f out: styd on strly fnl f* **25/1**

21-U **3** nk **Law To Himself (IRE)**[10] 1561 5-9-2 **70** .... RobertWinston 8 75
(Alan Swinbank) *in tch: hdwy 3f out: chal 2f out: sn rdn and hung rt: led jst over 1f out: hdd and one pce last 100yds* **6/1**[2]

051/ **4** ½ **Silk Drum (IRE)**[12] 2109 7-8-13 **70** .... LeeTopliss(3) 12 75
(Dianne Sayer) *hld up towards rr: hdwy on inner over 2f out: nt clr run and swtchd lft jst over 1f out: n.m.r and hmpd jst ins fnl f: kpt on* **9/1**

405- **5** 5 **Hawdyerwheesht**[243] 5723 4-8-13 **67** .... GrahamLee 4 63
(Jim Goldie) *trckd ldrs: rdn and outpcd 2f out: styd on fnl f* **11/1**

200- **6** 2¼ **Cadore (IRE)**[30] 6918 4-9-5 **73** .... JoeFanning 10 66
(Lucinda Russell) *hld up in rr: hdwy 3f out: rdn to chse ldrs 2f out: sn drvn and one pce* **22/1**

3312 **7** 2¼ **Chookie Hamilton**[34] 1114 8-9-2 **75** .... JustinNewman(5) 7 64
(Ian Semple) *hld up in rr: hdwy whn nt clr run 2f out: sn rdn and n.d* **8/1**

40-3 **8** ½ **Sangar**[15] 1439 4-9-0 **68** .... PaulHanagan 1 56
(Ollie Pears) *cl up on inner whn n.m.r after 1f and t.k.h after: trckd ldng pair: effrt 3f out: disp ld 2f out: rdn over 1f out and ev ch tl wknd qckly jst ins fnl f* **11/4**[1]

-604 **9** 1½ **Pertemps Networks**[34] 1114 8-9-6 **74** .... JamesSullivan 6 60
(Michael Easterby) *led 1f: cl up tl led again 1/2-way: rdn along 3f out: wkng whn n.m.r and hmpd over 2f out* **12/1**

2-01 **10** 1½ **Tapis Libre**[10] 1562 4-8-6 **67** .... DavidSimmonson(7) 9 51
(Michael Easterby) *chsd ldrs on outer: rdn along 3f out: wknd over 2f out* **13/2**[3]

20-0 **11** 24 **Sally Friday (IRE)**[22] 1295 4-9-2 **70** .... TonyHamilton 2 16
(Edwin Tuer) *cl up: led after 1f: hdd 1/2-way: cl up tl rdn along 3f out and sn wknd* **16/1**

2m 51.81s (9.81) **Going Correction** +0.60s/f (Yiel) **11** Ran SP% **115.5**
Speed ratings (Par 103): **91,90,89,89,86 84,83,82,81,80 64**
Tote Swingers:1&2:£28.20, 2&3:£21.80, 1&3:£9.30 CSF £206.23 CT £1453.84 TOTE £10.00: £2.70, £9.00, £2.50; EX 337.90 TRIFECTA Not won..
Owner Clarendon Thoroughbred Racing **Bred** Pat Harnett **Trained** Middleham Moor, N Yorks

FOCUS
A modest handicap, but a fair pace thanks to a contested lead between Pertemps Networks and Sally Friday which suited those that came from behind. The time was slow, however. A personal best from the winner back on the Flat.
Chookie Hamilton Official explanation: jockey said gelding was denied a clear run.
Sangar Official explanation: trainer said filly failed to stay the trip.

1798 DICKSON MINTO W.S. H'CAP 7f 30y
4:00 (4:01) (Class 5) (0-75,73) 3-Y-O **£2,587** (£770; £384; £192) **Stalls** Low

Form RPR

2-12 **1** **Half A Billion (IRE)**[30] 1176 3-9-4 **73** .... LeeTopliss(3) 3 80
(Michael Dods) *mde all: rdn 2f out: drvn and edgd lft ent fnl f: drvn out* **11/2**[3]

120 **2** ¾ **Alkadi (IRE)**[19] 1392 3-9-6 **72** .... JoeFanning 7 77
(Mark Johnston) *a cl up: effrt to chal over 2f out: sn rdn and ev ch tl drvn and one pce wl ins fnl f* **4/1**[1]

32-1 **3** 1¾ **Joshua The First**[25] 1241 3-9-7 **73** .... PaulMulrennan 5 73
(Keith Dalgleish) *trckd ldrs: smooth hdwy over 2f out: rdn over 1f out: kpt on same pce fnl f* **9/2**[2]

432 **4** 1¾ **Outlaw Torn (IRE)**[9] 1582 3-7-13 **54** oh1 ....(e) DeclanCannon(3) 10 50
(Richard Guest) *in tch: hdwy to chse ldrs over 2f out: sn rdn and one pce* **12/1**

63-4 **5** 1¼ **Hi There (IRE)**[15] 1441 3-8-10 **62** .... PaulHanagan 6 54+
(Richard Fahey) *dwlt: in tch whn n.m.r on inner bnd after 2f: hdwy over 2f out: sn rdn and no imp* **13/2**

160- **6** 2¼ **Irrational**[213] 6573 3-8-11 **63** .... TomEaves 2 49
(Bryan Smart) *dwlt: sn chsng ldrs on inner: rdn along 3f out: drvn 2f out and sn btn* **18/1**

1- **7** 4½ **La Salida**[315] 3302 3-9-3 **69** .... LeeNewman 4 43
(David Barron) *in tch: rdn along on inner wl over 2f out: sn btn* **9/2**[2]

5-06 **8** 5 **The Blue Banana (IRE)**[14] 1477 3-9-7 **73** .... TonyHamilton 9 33
(Edwin Tuer) *dwlt and sn rdn along: a in rr: bhd fr 1/2-way* **6/1**

500- **9** shd **Balti's Sister (IRE)**[204] 6806 3-8-3 **55** .... JamesSullivan 8 15
(Michael Easterby) *chsd ldng pair on outer: rdn along 3f out: sn wknd* **33/1**

1m 33.04s (4.04) **Going Correction** +0.60s/f (Yiel) **9** Ran SP% **115.3**
Speed ratings (Par 99): **100,99,97,95,93 91,86,80,80**
Tote Swingers:1&2:£4.60, 2&3:£3.80, 1&3:£5.10 CSF £27.72 CT £108.12 TOTE £6.90: £2.30, £1.10, £2.40; EX 28.50 Trifecta £261.00 Pool £606.74 - 1.72 winning units..
Owner I Galletley, B Stenson, M Dods **Bred** Mount Coote Stud **Trained** Denton, Co Durham

FOCUS
Probably not a bad little 3yo handicap of its type although the front pair held those positions throughout. A small personal best from the winner, and the second reversed C&D latest with the third.

1799 SCOTTISH RACING H'CAP (DIV I) 7f 30y
4:30 (4:31) (Class 6) (0-60,61) 4-Y-0+ £1,940 (£577; £288; £144) Stalls Low

Form RPR
600- 1 **Cannon Bolt (IRE)**[196] 6982 4-9-0 50.....(b) LeeNewman 1 63
(Robin Bastiman) *qckly away and sn clr: rdn wl over 1f out: styd on strly* 11/1
4433 2 7 **Gracie's Gift (IRE)**[9] 1584 10-8-9 48.....(v) DeclanCannon(3) 4 42
(Richard Guest) *chsd ldng pair: rdn along 3f out: sltly outpcd over 2f out: sn swtchd rt and styd on fnl f: no ch w wnr* 15/2[3]
-505 3 2 ¾ **Ra Junior (USA)**[15] 1436 6-9-6 56..... MickyFenton 8 43
(Paul Midgley) *hld up: hdwy on outer wl over 2f out: sn rdn and styd on fnl f: nrst fin* 7/2[1]
030- 4 1 **Social Rhythm**[173] 7399 8-9-7 57..... PaulMulrennan 11 41
(Alistair Whillans) *hld up: hdwy 3f out: rdn wl over 2f out: drvn and kpt on same pce fnl f* 10/1
00-0 5 ¾ **Mr Khan**[25] 1238 4-8-13 49..... PhillipMakin 3 31
(Linda Perratt) *chsd wnr: rdn along over 2f out: sn edgd lft and wknd appr fnl f* 28/1
00-3 6 5 **Monel**[26] 1224 4-9-5 55..... GrahamLee 7 23
(Jim Goldie) *hld up in rr: rdn along 3f out: nvr a factor* 4/1[2]
2411 7 10 **Rise To Glory (IRE)**[8] 1608 4-9-11 61 6ex..... RobertWinston 5
(Shaun Harris) *hld up: hdwy on inner 3f out: sn rdn to chse ldrs 2f out: drvn and wknd over 1f out* 7/2[1]
5205 8 1 ¾ **Meydan Style (USA)**[43] 988 6-8-9 45.....(p) TonyHamilton 9
(Richard Ford) *a in rr: bhd fnl 3f* 12/1
00-0 9 17 **Chambers (IRE)**[119] 46 6-9-0 50..... FrederikTylicki 2
(Richard Ford) *chsd ldrs: rdn along 1/2-way: sn wknd* 12/1

1m 32.86s (3.86) **Going Correction** +0.60s/f (Yiel) 9 Ran SP% 112.5
Speed ratings (Par 101): **101,93,89,88,87 82,70,68,49**
Tote Swingers:1&2:£12.50, 2&3:£5.90, 1&3:£8.90 CSF £87.61 CT £351.52 TOTE £15.00: £4.80, £2.30, £2.90; EX 85.40 Trifecta £456.10 Part won. Pool £616.45 - 0.41 winning units..
Owner Robin Bastiman **Bred** Joseph G Reid **Trained** Cowthorpe, N Yorks

FOCUS
A moderate handicap and a one-sided contest. The winner has clearly improved, but was another winner to race prominently on the card. It was the pick of the C&D times and the form could be rated higher on face value.
Rise To Glory(IRE) Official explanation: jockey said colt lost its action.

1800 TURFTV H'CAP 5f
5:00 (5:00) (Class 6) (0-65,65) 4-Y-0+ £1,940 (£577; £288; £144) Stalls High

Form RPR
5-62 1 **Mercers Row**[25] 1242 5-9-5 63..... DanielTudhope 7 80
(Noel Wilson) *hld up in rr: nt clr run on inner and swtchd rt wl over 1f out: sn rdn and str run ent fnl f: led last 50yds* 7/2[2]
-204 2 ½ **Silvanus (IRE)**[22] 1300 7-9-6 64..... PaulHanagan 1 79
(Paul Midgley) *trckd ldrs: hdwy 2f out: chal over 1f out: rdn to ld briefly ins fnl f: hdd and nt qckn last 50yds* 15/2
3445 3 ¾ **Sandwith**[25] 1242 9-8-11 55.....(p) LeeNewman 8 68
(George Foster) *slt ld: rdn and edgd lft over 1f out: drvn and hdd ins fnl f: kpt on same pce* 14/1
1262 4 5 **Boucher Garcon (IRE)**[5] 1675 4-9-1 64..... NeilFarley(5) 3 59
(Declan Carroll) *cl up on outer: disp ld 1/2-way: rdn 2f out: wknd over 1f out* 15/8[1]
405- 5 1 ½ **Saxonette**[228] 6190 4-9-2 60..... PhillipMakin 10 49
(Linda Perratt) *cl up: rdn along 2f out: grad wknd over 1f out* 33/1
-020 6 shd **Tom Sawyer**[42] 996 4-9-4 62.....(v) PaulMulrennan 9 51
(Julie Camacho) *hld up towards rr: swtchd rt and hdwy whn sltly hmpd over 1f out: sn rdn and no imp* 17/2
5/5- 7 1 ¼ **Glenlini**[290] 4144 6-9-0 58..... GrahamLee 5 42
(Jim Goldie) *hld up towards rr: sme hdwy 2f out: sn rdn and n.d* 12/1
53-4 8 nse **Missile Attack (IRE)**[19] 1389 4-9-2 60..... TomEaves 2 44
(Ian Semple) *chsd ldrs: rdn along 2f out: sn wknd* 16/1
000- 9 2 **Distant Sun (USA)**[181] 7265 8-8-8 57..... ShaneBKelly(5) 4 34
(Linda Perratt) *n.d* 33/1
12-0 10 ¾ **Mecca's Team**[24] 1246 4-9-4 65..... LeeTopliss(3) 11 39
(Michael Dods) *cl up on rail: rdn along 1/2-way: sn wknd* 6/1[3]

1m 1.09s (0.69) **Going Correction** +0.175s/f (Good) 10 Ran SP% 119.7
Speed ratings (Par 101): **101,100,99,91,88 88,86,86,83,81**
Tote Swingers:1&2:£6.80, 2&3:£12.40, 1&3:£11.30 CSF £31.03 CT £336.72 TOTE £3.40: £1.50, £3.00, £5.30; EX 35.10 Trifecta £340.20 Pool £933.42 - 2.03 winning units..
Owner Mrs J A Smith & K Fitzsimons **Bred** Heather Raw **Trained** Middleham, N Yorks

FOCUS
A moderate sprint handicap, but they went a good pace. The winner built on his good C&D second, and the runner-up is a decent guide. The first three were clear.

1801 SCOTTISH RACING H'CAP (DIV II) 7f 30y
5:35 (5:36) (Class 6) (0-60,60) 4-Y-0+ £1,940 (£577; £288; £144) Stalls Low

Form RPR
1210 1 **Garstang**[43] 987 9-9-3 56..... FrederikTylicki 8 66
(Richard Ford) *towards rr: hdwy over 2f out: rdn to chse ldr over 1f out: sn edgd rt: drvn and styd on to ld wl ins fnl f* 9/4[1]
000- 2 ½ **Circuitous**[146] 7690 4-9-3 56.....(b) JoeFanning 2 65
(Keith Dalgleish) *led: rdn 2f out: drvn over 1f out: hdd and no ex wl ins fnl f* 14/1
0400 3 2 ½ **Crocodile Bay (IRE)**[23] 1283 9-8-7 49.....(p) DeclanCannon(3) 5 51
(Richard Guest) *midfield: pushed along 3f out: rdn wl over 1f out: kpt on fnl f* 14/1
040- 4 3 **Shunkawakhan (IRE)**[173] 7399 9-8-7 46 oh1..... JamesSullivan 9 40
(Linda Perratt) *in rr: hdwy on wd outside over 2f out: sn rdn and styd on fnl f: nrst fin* 33/1
40-0 5 ¾ **Abernethy (IRE)**[25] 1240 4-8-4 46 oh1.....(t) JulieBurke(3) 6 38
(Linda Perratt) *dwlt and bhd: hdwy 1/2-way: rdn to chse ldrs wl over 1f out: sn one pce* 18/1
0000 6 hd **Kwik Time**[12] 1526 4-8-7 46 oh1.....(b) LeeNewman 1 38
(Robin Bastiman) *chsd ldrs on inner: rdn along wl over 2f out: grad wknd fr wl over 1f out* 20/1
-640 7 1 ¼ **See The Storm**[41] 1014 4-8-9 48..... PaulHanagan 7 36
(Lisa Williamson) *chsd ldrs: rdn along wl over 2f out: grad wknd* 13/2[2]
000- 8 ½ **Whats For Pudding (IRE)**[167] 7459 4-8-10 54..... NeilFarley(5) 10 41
(Declan Carroll) *sn pushed along in rr: hdwy on inner over 2f out: n.m.r and swtchd lft over 1f out: nt clr run ins fnl f: nvr a factor* 8/1[3]
-004 9 ½ **Amno Dancer (IRE)**[19] 1387 5-8-11 50.....(p) TomEaves 4 36
(Ian Semple) *prom: effrt to chal 3f out: rdn over 2f out and sn wknd* 13/2[2]

1m 33.4s (4.40) **Going Correction** +0.60s/f (Yiel) 9 Ran SP% 94.8
Speed ratings (Par 101): **98,97,94,91,90 90,88,88,87**
Tote Swingers:1&2:£6.20, 2&3:£14.30, 1&3:£6.40 CSF £23.49 CT £176.58 TOTE £2.70: £1.30, £2.30, £3.40; EX 26.40 Trifecta £337.80 Pool £461.11 - 1.01 winning units..
Owner The Foulrice Twenty **Bred** Mrs S E Barclay **Trained** Garstang, Lancs

FOCUS
Much of the interest in this race was removed when Dunseverick, who had been a market mover during the day, was withdrawn at the start with his rider Tony Culhane having injured a foot (7/2, deduct 20p in the £ under R4). The winning time was 0.54 seconds slower than the first division, and this looked the weaker race. The winner carried over his recent AW form.
Whats For Pudding(IRE) Official explanation: jockey said filly was denied a clear run.
T/Jkpt: Not won. T/Plt: £247.00 to a £1 stake. Pool £74,886.17. 221.31 winning tickets T/Qpdt: £67.20 to a £1 stake. Pool £5,189.96. 57.10 winning tickets JR

1802 - 1809a (Foreign Racing) - See Raceform Interactive

CHEPSTOW (L-H)
Friday, May 4
1810 Meeting Abandoned - waterlogged

1794 MUSSELBURGH (R-H)
Friday, May 4

OFFICIAL GOING: Good to soft (good in places; 5.9)
Bottom bend moved out 2metres.
Wind: Moderate across Weather: overcast and showers

1817 "WEE BOAB'S 21ST" BIRTHDAY BASH H'CAP 5f
2:00 (2:00) (Class 6) (0-65,64) 3-Y-0 £1,940 (£577; £288; £144) Stalls High

Form RPR
0262 1 **Lord Buffhead**[9] 1599 3-8-9 52..... WilliamCarson 2 62
(Richard Guest) *in tch: hdwy 2f out: rdn to chse ldr over 1f out: styd on wl to ld on line* 9/2[3]
-531 2 nse **Wild Sauce**[77] 599 3-9-5 62.....(b) TomEaves 10 72
(Bryan Smart) *led: rdn over 1f out: drvn ins fnl f: hdd on line* 4/1[2]
4-42 3 1 ¼ **Phoenix Clubs (IRE)**[25] 1252 3-9-7 64..... BarryMcHugh 7 70
(Paul Midgley) *towards rr: hdwy 2f out: n.m.r and swtchd rt over 1f out: sn rdn and kpt on* 5/2[1]
600- 4 5 **Madam Bonny (IRE)**[232] 6075 3-8-2 45..... JamesSullivan 6 33
(Jim Goldie) *in tch: pushed along and outpcd 1/2-way: hdwy over 1f out: styng on whn hmpd ent fnl f: kpt on* 33/1
305- 5 1 **Red Shadow**[184] 7231 3-8-6 56..... JoshBaudains(7) 3 40
(Alan Brown) *prom: rdn along wl over 1f out: sn wknd: hung bdly lft fnl f* 9/1
5046 6 1 ¾ **Tuibama (IRE)**[9] 1599 3-8-4 52 ow1..... ShaneBKelly(5) 1 30
(Tracy Waggott) *prom on outer: rdn along over 2f out: sn wknd* 10/1
6006 7 shd **Windygoul Lad**[26] 1238 3-9-1 58..... AndrewMullen 8 42
(Keith Dalgleish) *a towards rr* 11/1
04-5 8 1 ¼ **Gran Canaria Queen**[26] 1238 3-8-11 54..... TonyHamilton 5 27
(Ian Semple) *chsd ldrs: rdn along 2f out: sn wknd: hmpd ent fnl f* 6/1
400- 9 5 **Angel Kiss (IRE)**[216] 6532 3-7-9 45..... ShirleyTeasdale(7) 4
(Colin Teague) *a in rr* 50/1

1m 0.9s (0.50) **Going Correction** +0.025s/f (Good) 9 Ran SP% 113.4
Speed ratings (Par 97): **97,96,94,86,85 82,82,80,72**
toteswingers:1&2:£4.10, 1&3:£2.80, 2&3:£2.50 CSF £22.39 CT £53.78 TOTE £5.10: £2.00, £1.70, £1.50; EX 21.70.
Owner Future Racing (Notts) Limited **Bred** T K & Mrs P A Knox **Trained** Stainforth, S Yorks

FOCUS
The bottom bend had been moved out two metres. After riding in the opener, James Sullivan said: "The ground is more or less the same as yesterday - just on the slow side of good." A moderate sprint handicap. They raced stands' side, but the rail wasn't essential. The time was decent for the age and grade and the form is sound.

1818 E B F STRIDES AHEAD AT RZ GROUP MAIDEN STKS 5f
2:30 (2:31) (Class 4) 2-Y-O £5,175 (£1,540; £769; £384) Stalls High

Form RPR
1 **Tatlisu (IRE)** 2-9-3 0..... PaulHanagan 8 80+
(Richard Fahey) *dwlt: midfield and pushed along 1/2-way: hdwy wl over 1f out: rdn ent fnl f: styd on strly to ld last 40yds* 4/1[3]
2 ¾ **Boxing Shadows** 2-9-3 0..... TomEaves 3 77+
(Bryan Smart) *in tch: smooth hdwy on outer 2f out: led over 1f out: rdn and hung lft ins fnl f: hdd last 40yds* 7/1
3 nse **Hototo** 2-9-3 0..... PhillipMakin 10 83+
(Kevin Ryan) *hmpd after 1f and bhd: hdwy 2f out: effrt and nt clr run over 1f out: swtchd rt ent fnl f and styd on strly* 12/1
4 nk **Blue Lotus (IRE)** 2-9-3 0..... DavidAllan 7 77+
(Tim Easterby) *trckd ldrs: effrt and nt clr run over 1f out: swtchd rt and rdn ins fnl f: kpt on* 18/1
5 1 **Baker's Pursuit** 2-8-12 0..... GrahamLee 11 67
(Jim Goldie) *towards rr: hdwy 2f out: kpt on fnl f: nrst fin* 33/1
6 2 ¾ **Finaz** 2-9-3 0..... PatCosgrave 9 63+
(Keith Dalgleish) *green and hung lft in rr after 1f: sn pushed along and outpcd: hdwy wl over 1f out: styng on whn hmpd ent fnl f: nvr nr ldrs* 7/2[2]
7 nse **Limit Up** 2-9-3 0..... JoeFanning 6 62
(Mark Johnston) *led: pushed along over 2f out: sn rdn and hdd: wknd over 1f out* 15/8[1]
8 1 ¾ **Capo Rosso (IRE)** 2-9-3 0..... RichardKingscote 5 56
(Tom Dascombe) *wnt rt s: cl up: rdn to ld briefly wl over 1f out: sn hdd & wknd* 16/1
9 4 **I'Ve No Money (IRE)** 2-9-3 0..... AndrewMullen 2 42
(David C Griffiths) *chsd ldng pair: rdn 2f out: hmpd and wknd ent fnl f* 40/1
10 2 **Stand N Applaude** 2-9-3 0..... AdrianNicholls 4 38+
(David Nicholls) *sltly hmpd s: a towards rr* 33/1

1m 2.73s (2.33) **Going Correction** +0.025s/f (Good) 10 Ran SP% 116.7
Speed ratings (Par 95): **82,80,80,80,78 74,74,71,64,61**
toteswingers:1&2:£5.80, 1&3:£8.80, 2&3:£9.40 CSF £31.66 TOTE £4.40: £1.20, £2.50, £2.90; EX 35.60.
Owner Middleham Park Racing LIV **Bred** J C And Rocal Bloodstock **Trained** Musley Bank, N Yorks

FOCUS
A field full of newcomers and it was a rough race, so the bare form is likely to prove unreliable. However winners should emerge from this.

NOTEBOOK

Tatlisu(IRE), an April foal, is a half-brother to a maiden and his dam was 0-16, but he proved good enough to make a successful start. His chance was helped by others finding trouble, but he should make a useful type.

Boxing Shadows, a £20,000 January foal, showed plenty of ability on this racecourse debut. (tchd 15-2)

Hototo ◆'s sales price increased from 4,500gns as a foal to £22,000 as a yearling, and he's out of a useful French middle-distance winner. He's even better than he showed as he dropped back to last when hampered against the stands' rail early on, and then had to wait for a run when trying to stay on. (op 16-1)

Blue Lotus(IRE) ◆, a 12,000euros purchase, has already been gelded but he may have made a winning debut had he not been continually denied a clear run in the closing stages.

Baker's Pursuit ◆, a £10,500 half-sister to multiple sprint winner Pick A Little, out of a 1m winner in the US, was the only filly in the line-up. She was doing her best work at the finish after getting behind.

Finaz, a half-brother to Joshua The First, who took an age to get off the mark for this stable (won here over 7f), ran as though he'll come on a good deal for the experience. (op 9-2)

Limit Up, a 78,000gns buy, faded after showing speed. His starting price suggests much better was expected. (op 2-1)

Stand N Applaude Official explanation: jockey said colt hung left throughout

1819 SEMICHEM.CO.UK H'CAP — 1m 1f

3:00 (3:01) (Class 3) (0-90,85) 3-Y-O — **£7,762** (£2,310; £1,154; £577) **Stalls** Low

Form — RPR

21 **1** **Prussian**[101] 279 3-9-0 **78** .... JoeFanning 8 — 93
(Mark Johnston) *trckd ldr: hdwy to ld wl over 2f out: rdn and qcknd over 1f out: styd on wl* **3/1**[1]

22-1 **2** *2* **Silver Blaze**[17] 1427 3-9-7 **85** .... RobertWinston 5 — 95
(Alan Swinbank) *hld up in rr: hdwy over 2f out: rdn to chse ldrs over 1f out: kpt on same pce fnl f* **6/1**

1 **3** *shd* **Clayton**[45] 974 3-9-7 **85** .... PhillipMakin 1 — 95
(Kevin Ryan) *dwlt: hld up in rr: hdwy on wd outside wl over 2f out: rdn to chse ldrs over 1f out: drvn ins fnl f: kpt on same pce* **7/2**[3]

26-4 **4** *2 1/4* **Act Your Shoe Size**[16] 1440 3-8-12 **76** .... DavidAllan 6 — 81
(Keith Dalgleish) *chsd ldrs: rdn along over 2f out: drvn wl over 1f out: kpt on same pce fnl f* **16/1**

40-3 **5** *1 1/2* **Satanic Beat (IRE)**[15] 1477 3-8-13 **77** .... TonyHamilton 2 — 79
(Jedd O'Keeffe) *chsd ldng pair: rdn along over 2f out: drvn wl over 1f out: grad wknd* **10/3**[2]

001- **6** *9* **Border Revia (IRE)**[223] 6344 3-8-13 **77** .... PaulHanagan 4 — 59
(Richard Fahey) *hld up: a towards rr* **8/1**

33-0 **7** *9* **Sound Advice**[15] 1473 3-9-4 **82** ....(b[1]) PatCosgrave 7 — 44
(Keith Dalgleish) *led: rdn along 3f out: sn hdd & wknd* **10/1**

2322 **8** *40* **Imtithal (IRE)**[29] 1206 3-8-8 **72** .... TomEaves 3 —
(James Tate) *chsd ldrs on inner: rdn along 3f out: sn wknd* **16/1**

1m 58.41s (4.51) **Going Correction** +0.575s/f (Yiel) — **8** Ran SP% **116.6**

Speed ratings (Par 103): **102,100,100,98,96 88,80,45**

toteswingers:1&2:£5.70, 1&3:£2.80, 2&3:£3.80 CSF £21.92 CT £66.01 TOTE £3.60: £1.10, £1.90, £1.80; EX 22.30.

Owner Sheikh Hamdan Bin Mohammed Al Maktoum **Bred** Darley **Trained** Middleham Moor, N Yorks

FOCUS

A reasonable race - the first three had all won maidens on their previous starts. They all stepped up on their previous wins, with the fourth setting the standard.

NOTEBOOK

Prussian had been absent since winning a 1m Polytrack maiden in January, but she's done well for her time off. She was helped by being more forwardly placed than the runner-up and third, plus racing on the far rail late on may have been advantageous, but there was still much to like about how well she stuck on, despite looking a bit green. There should be more to come. (op 7-2 tchd 4-1 in a place)

Silver Blaze, who made a winning reappearance over 1m on Fibresand, got a bit further back than ideal on this relative speed track but kept on well. He should stay further and might prefer a more galloping course. (op 5-1 tchd 13-2 and 7-1 in a place)

Clayton, a debut winner over 1m on the Southwell Fibresand in March, still looked green as he missed the break and ended up too far back. He kept on well and should have learnt plenty. (tchd 10-3 and 4-1)

Act Your Shoe Size didn't get the best of runs through but was basically well held. (op 25-1)

Satanic Beat(IRE) didn't prove his stamina. (op 9-2 tchd 3-1)

Sound Advice Official explanation: jockey said colt hung both ways throughout

1820 CORE (OIL AND GAS) LTD H'CAP — 1m 1f

3:30 (3:30) (Class 4) (0-85,85) 4-Y-O+ — **£5,175** (£1,540; £769; £384) **Stalls** Low

Form — RPR

525- **1** **Staff Sergeant**[216] 6533 5-8-13 **77** .... GrahamLee 3 — 86
(Jim Goldie) *mde all: rdn wl over 1f out: styd on wl fnl f* **11/2**[2]

035- **2** *1 3/4* **Lucky Windmill**[195] 7022 5-8-12 **76** .... RobertWinston 4 — 81
(Alan Swinbank) *trckd ldrs on inner: hdwy wl over 1f out: swtchd lft and rdn ent fnl f: kpt on* **14/1**

0-40 **3** *2* **Oriental Scot**[13] 1510 5-9-5 **83** .... WilliamCarson 12 — 84+
(William Jarvis) *hld up in midfield: hdwy on wd outside wl over 2f out: rdn to chse ldrs over 1f out: drvn and no imp fnl f* **8/1**[3]

30-6 **4** *2* **Judicious**[34] 1134 5-9-1 **79** .... JoeFanning 7 — 75
(Keith Dalgleish) *trckd wnr: effrt to chal over 2f out: sn rdn and ev ch tl drvn and one pce appr fnl f* **13/5**[1]

45-3 **5** *3/4* **Borug (USA)**[18] 1416 4-9-7 **85** .... PaulHanagan 1 — 80+
(James Tate) *in tch on inner: hdwy 3f out: swtchd lft over 2f out: rdn to chse ldrs wl over 1f out: wknd fnl f* **11/2**[2]

412- **6** *1* **Muffin McLeay (IRE)**[260] 5205 4-9-4 **82** .... LeeNewman 2 — 75+
(David Barron) *hld up in midfield: hdwy over 2f out: rdn along wl over 1f out and sn no imp* **11/2**[2]

325- **7** *3/4* **My Single Malt (IRE)**[240] 5820 4-9-0 **78** .... DanielTudhope 6 — 69
(Julie Camacho) *chsd ldrs: rdn along over 2f out: grad wknd* **28/1**

6044 **8** *nk* **Mullins Way (USA)**[8] 1633 4-9-5 **83** ....(v) TonyCulhane 11 — 74
(Jo Hughes) *prom: rdn along over 2f out: grad wknd appr fnl f* **10/1**

6-00 **9** *3 1/4* **Collateral Damage (IRE)**[25] 1249 9-8-11 **75** ....(t) DavidAllan 5 — 58
(Tim Easterby) *dwlt: a towards rr* **12/1**

411- **10** *nk* **Botham (USA)**[221] 6417 8-8-8 **72** .... JamesSullivan 9 — 54
(Jim Goldie) *hld up: a in rr* **25/1**

066- **11** *3* **Euston Square**[209] 6708 6-9-0 **78** .... TomEaves 10 — 54
(Alistair Whillans) *dwlt: a in rr* **25/1**

1m 57.48s (3.58) **Going Correction** +0.575s/f (Yiel) — **11** Ran SP% **119.6**

Speed ratings (Par 105): **107,105,103,101,101 100,99,99,96,96 93**

toteswingers:1&2:£18.30, 2&3:£24.10, 1&3:£8.70 CSF £78.92 CT £633.47 TOTE £6.50: £2.20, £3.20, £2.40; EX 106.80.

Owner J S Morrison **Bred** Darley **Trained** Uplawmoor, E Renfrews

FOCUS

The form, rated around the first two, is modest and wants to treating with caution. Another front-running winner.

1821 DAIKIN D1 INSTALLER H'CAP — 7f 30y

4:00 (4:02) (Class 3) (0-90,90) 4-Y-O+ — **£6,469** (£1,925; £962; £481) **Stalls** Low

Form — RPR

24-1 **1** **Powerful Presence (IRE)**[17] 1431 6-9-1 **81** .... DanielTudhope 9 — 93
(David O'Meara) *trckd ldng pair: smooth hdwy to ld wl over 2f out: rdn clr wl over 1f out: kpt on strly fnl f* **9/2**[2]

24-0 **2** *1 1/2* **Honeymead (IRE)**[20] 1373 4-9-5 **85** .... PaulHanagan 12 — 93
(Richard Fahey) *trckd ldrs: hdwy over 2f out: rdn over 1f out: drvn to chse wnr ins fnl f: no imp* **9/1**

0-06 **3** *1 1/2* **Capaill Liath (IRE)**[13] 1510 4-9-4 **87** ....(p) JulieBurke(3) 10 — 91
(Kevin Ryan) *towards rr: hdwy on wd outside over 2f out: sn rdn and styd on fnl f: nrst fin* **8/1**

0-05 **4** *1* **Imperial Djay (IRE)**[13] 1522 7-9-7 **87** .... JamesSullivan 8 — 88+
(Ruth Carr) *dwlt and bhd: hdwy 3f out: rdn over 2f out: kpt on: nrst fin* **14/1**

0-02 **5** *2 1/2* **Celtic Sultan (IRE)**[33] 1156 8-9-4 **84** .... MickyFenton 6 — 78
(Paul Midgley) *in tch: hdwy to chse ldrs 3f out: rdn over 2f out: drvn and one pce appr fnl f* **16/1**

30-2 **6** *4 1/2* **Naabegha**[20] 1373 5-9-7 **87** .... PhillipMakin 1 — 69
(Ed de Giles) *midfield: hdwy and in tch 1/2-way: rdn over 2f out: n.d* **4/1**[1]

5-25 **7** *1 1/4* **Santefisio**[83] 527 6-9-7 **87** ....(p) PatCosgrave 5 — 66
(Keith Dalgleish) *nvr nr ldrs* **16/1**

06-0 **8** *nse* **Elusive Prince**[33] 1157 4-9-10 **90** ....(v) LeeNewman 4 — 69
(David Barron) *chsd ldrs: rdn along 3f out: sn btn* **20/1**

00-0 **9** *3* **Snow Bay**[34] 1128 6-9-7 **87** .... AndrewMullen 2 — 58
(David Nicholls) *led: rdn along 3f out: sn hdd & wknd* **7/1**

4-00 **10** *13* **Oil Strike**[27] 1220 5-9-4 **84** .... PaddyAspell 3 —
(Michael Easterby) *cl up: rdn along 3f out: sn wknd* **33/1**

0-14 **11** *25* **Karaka Jack**[13] 1510 5-9-5 **85** .... AdrianNicholls 7 —
(David Nicholls) *a in rr: bhd fnl 2f* **6/1**[3]

0-60 **12** *1/2* **Reignier**[46] 962 5-9-4 **87** .... MichaelMetcalfe(3) 11 —
(Mrs K Burke) *midfield: rdn along 1/2-way: sn wknd and bhd fnl 2f* **18/1**

1m 31.63s (2.63) **Going Correction** +0.575s/f (Yiel) — **12** Ran SP% **117.5**

Speed ratings (Par 107): **107,105,103,102,99 94,93,92,89,74 46,45**

toteswingers:1&2:£5.40, 1&3:£6.10, 2&3:£10.30 CSF £44.44 CT £255.80 TOTE £5.00: £2.30, £3.40, £3.30; EX 50.70.

Owner The Lawton Bamforth Partnership **Bred** Corduff Stud **Trained** Nawton, N Yorks

FOCUS

Probably just an ordinary handicap for the grade. The first two were always well placed and the winner confirmed his recent improvement.

NOTEBOOK

Powerful Presence(IRE) was another winner who had the far rail in the final couple of furlongs, although he looked to take this on merit. He was defying a mark 2lb higher than when winning on Fibresand on his reappearance. (op 4-1 tchd 7-2)

Honeymead(IRE) improved on the form she showed at Lingfield on her reappearance and had no obvious excuse.

Capaill Liath(IRE) got behind and came under pressure a fair way out, but he kept on. A return to 1m might suit. (op 17-2 tchd 9-1)

Imperial Djay(IRE) got going much too late after a sluggish start.

Celtic Sultan(IRE), up 2lb, didn't build on his Doncaster second. (op 14-1)

Naabegha found disappointingly little for pressure and didn't build on a promising reappearance. (op 5-1)

Karaka Jack Official explanation: trainer's rep said gelding finished distressed

1822 AU REVOIR COLIN SHAND H'CAP — 1m 6f

4:30 (4:30) (Class 5) (0-70,69) 4-Y-O+ — **£3,881** (£1,155; £577; £288) **Stalls** Centre

Form — RPR

32-0 **1** **La Bacouetteuse (FR)**[27] 1222 7-9-2 **61** ....(p) DavidAllan 11 — 71
(Iain Jardine) *bhd and pushed along: stdy hdwy 3f out: rdn to ld over 1f out: edgd rt ins fnl f: drvn out: jst hld on* **14/1**

6/2- **2** *shd* **Categorical**[69] 6838 9-8-11 **61** .... ShaneBKelly(5) 8 — 70
(Keith Reveley) *dwlt and hld up in rr: hdwy 3f out: rdn to chse ldrs over 1f out: styd on to chal ins fnl f: ev ch tl no ex nr line* **12/1**

1001 **3** *6* **Light The City (IRE)**[9] 1598 5-9-5 **64** 6ex .... JamesSullivan 2 — 65+
(Ruth Carr) *trckd ldng pair: hdwy to ld wl over 2f out: rdn and hdd over 1f out: sn swtchd lft and drvn: kpt on same pce* **9/2**[2]

23-3 **4** *6* **Pokfulham (IRE)**[20] 1382 6-9-6 **65** ....(v) GrahamLee 6 — 58
(Jim Goldie) *in rr and sn pushed along: hdwy 3f out: rdn 2f out: styd on fnl f: nrst fin* **17/2**

50-0 **5** *3/4* **Silver Tigress**[20] 1382 4-8-9 **55** .... AndrewMullen 10 — 47
(George Moore) *midfield: hdwy 4f out: rdn over 2f out: kpt on same pce* **22/1**

0-15 **6** *13* **Maid Of Meft**[22] 1338 5-9-6 **65** .... JoeFanning 5 — 38
(Keith Dalgleish) *trckd ldrs: hdwy 3f out: rdn along over 2f out: grad wknd* **9/1**

12-0 **7** *3/4* **Vittachi**[20] 1382 5-8-12 **62** .... GarryWhillans(5) 9 — 34
(Alistair Whillans) *hld up: a in rr* **25/1**

33-1 **8** *2 3/4* **Ad Value (IRE)**[26] 1240 4-9-2 **62** .... RobertWinston 1 — 30
(Alan Swinbank) *hld up in tch: hdwy to chse ldrs 4f out: rdn along over 2f out: sn drvn and wknd* **7/2**[1]

02-3 **9** *6* **Mohawk Ridge**[23] 1297 6-9-7 **69** ....(p) LeeTopliss(3) 3 — 29
(Michael Dods) *led: rdn along over 3f out: hdd wl over 2f out and sn wknd* **5/1**[3]

636- **10** *2 1/2* **Madamlily (IRE)**[183] 4719 6-9-8 **67** .... TomEaves 7 — 24
(John Quinn) *chsd ldrs: rdn along 4f out: sn wknd* **15/2**

0-05 **11** *14* **Grey Command (USA)**[13] 1525 7-9-7 **66** .... PaulHanagan 12 —
(Mel Brittain) *chsd ldrs: rdn along over 3f out: sn wknd* **25/1**

0-20 **12** *10* **Goodness**[13] 1525 4-9-9 **69** ....(t) DanielTudhope 4 —
(David O'Meara) *cl up: rdn along over 5f out: wknd over 3f out* **12/1**

3m 13.11s (7.81) **Going Correction** +0.575s/f (Yiel)

WFA 4 from 5yo+ 1lb — **12** Ran SP% **123.5**

Speed ratings (Par 103): **100,99,96,93,92 85,84,83,79,78 70,64**

CSF £174.03 CT £887.70 TOTE £20.40: £5.60, £4.60, £1.30; EX 174.90.

Owner Miss S A Booth **Bred** Sarl Classic Breeding & Maria R Mendes **Trained** Bonchester Bridge, Borders

■ Stewards' Enquiry : Andrew Mullen two-day ban: careless riding (May 18,20)

FOCUS
An ordinary handicap run at what looked an overly strong pace. The first two came from the rear and the form is set around the second.

1823 SCOTTISH RACING BEST BET APPRENTICE H'CAP 7f 30y
5:00 (5:04) (Class 6) (0-65,65) 4-Y-0+ **£1,940** (£577; £288; £144) **Stalls** Low

Form RPR
-060 **1** **Lindoro**[31] 1178 7-9-2 **60** AmyRyan 11 75
(Brian Ellison) *midfield: smooth hdwy to trck ldrs 3f out: led 2f out: rdn and edgd lft ins fnl f: styd on* **6/1**[3]
1444 **2** *4* **Cyflymder (IRE)**[1] 1796 6-9-2 **65** DarylByrne(5) 2 69
(David C Griffiths) *sn chsng ldng pair: hdwy over 2f out: and sn rdn: drvn to chse wnr ins fnl f: no imp* **4/1**[2]
0-02 **3** *6* **Hellbender (IRE)**[20] 1384 6-9-0 **61** LMcNiff(3) 9 49
(George Foster) *chsd ldrs on outer: hdwy over 2f out: sn rdn and one pce* **14/1**
05-0 **4** *1 1/4* **Alluring Star**[20] 1384 4-9-2 **60** LeeTopliss 7 45
(Michael Easterby) *chsd ldrs: rdn along 3f out: drvn 2f out: plugged on one pce* **8/1**
6040 **5** *shd* **Best Trip (IRE)**[65] 735 5-8-11 **55** PaulPickard 1 39
(Brian Ellison) *cl up: led 3f out: rdn and hdd 2f out: sn drvn and wknd over 1f out* **11/4**[1]
-004 **6** *5* **Pulsatilla**[9] 1601 4-8-11 **60** (b) JustinNewman(5) 6 31
(Bryan Smart) *a towards rr* **10/1**
302/ **7** *3/4* **Turning Circle**[521] 7645 6-8-13 **60** NeilFarley(3) 10 29
(Mel Brittain) *nvr nr ldrs* **14/1**
5444 **8** *1 3/4* **Indian Arrow**[13] 1528 4-8-11 **55** MichaelO'Connell 4 19
(John Quinn) *chsd ldrs: rdn 3f out: sn wknd* **10/1**
-040 **9** *4 1/2* **Mark Anthony (IRE)**[13] 1526 5-8-11 **58** (p) DeanHeslop(3) 5
(Shaun Harris) *led: rdn along and hdd 3f out: sn wknd* **20/1**
60-0 **10** *1* **Cosmic Moon**[16] 1439 4-8-13 **60** ShaneBKelly(3) 3
(Richard Fahey) *a in rr* **8/1**

1m 32.13s (3.13) **Going Correction** +0.575s/f (Yiel) **10** Ran SP% **119.5**
Speed ratings (Par 101): **105,100,93,92,92 86,85,83,78,77**
CSF £31.06 CT £335.16 TOTE £6.80: £2.40, £2.00, £3.90; EX 35.20.
Owner Brian Ellison **Bred** Pigeon House Stud **Trained** Norton, N Yorks

FOCUS
The pace was much too strong in this moderate handicap. The winner is rated back to form on his first start for a new yard.
Cosmic Moon Official explanation: jockey said filly never travelled
T/Jkpt: Not won. T/Plt: £205.90 to a £1 stake. Pool:£85,251.94 - 302.11 winning tickets T/Qpdt: £101.20 to a £1 stake. Pool:£6,469.46 - 47.30 winning tickets JR

1716 WOLVERHAMPTON (A.W) (L-H)
Friday, May 4

OFFICIAL GOING: Standard
Wind: Light half-against Weather: Overcast

1824 WOLVERHAMPTON-RACECOURSE.CO.UK MAIDEN STKS (DIV I) 7f 32y(P)
2:10 (3:48) (Class 5) 3-Y-0+ **£2,264** (£673; £336; £168) **Stalls** High

Form RPR
0 **1** **Hometown Glory**[16] 1450 3-9-1 0 ShaneKelly 10 79+
(Brian Meehan) *hld up in tch: shkn up over 1f: edgd lft and r.o to ld wl ins fnl f* **7/4**[1]
04- **2** *1 1/4* **Levi Draper**[290] 4184 3-9-1 0 JackMitchell 7 76
(James Fanshawe) *hld up: r.o ins fnl f: wnt 2nd post: nt rch wnr* **40/1**
5/4- **3** *hd* **Al Janadeirya**[365] 1836 4-9-8 0 WilliamBuick 1 74
(Peter Chapple-Hyam) *led: clr over 1f out: rdn and hdd wl ins fnl f: lost 2nd post* **7/1**
22-5 **4** *3/4* **Discression**[25] 1257 3-9-1 80 PaulMulrennan 3 73
(Kevin Ryan) *chsd ldrs: edgd lft over 2f out: sn rdn: styd on same pce fnl f* **5/1**[3]
2- **5** *nse* **My Body Is A Cage (IRE)**[274] 4726 3-8-10 0 MartinDwyer 9 68
(Jeremy Noseda) *s.s: hld up: r.o ins fnl f: nvr trbld ldrs* **10/1**
503- **6** *1 1/4* **Strada Facendo (USA)**[196] 6983 3-9-1 78 KierenFallon 11 69
(Luca Cumani) *chsd ldrs: pushed along and hung rt wl over 1f out: no ex ins fnl f* **3/1**[2]
6U0- **7** *8* **Blue Tiger**[234] 6025 3-9-1 0 MickaelBarzalona 4 55
(Saeed Bin Suroor) *s.i.s: sn prom: pushed along whn hmpd over 2f out: n.m.r wl over 1f out: wknd and eased fnl f* **8/1**
04- **8** *1/2* **Sir Dylan**[160] 7559 3-9-1 0 LukeMorris 8 47
(Ronald Harris) *sn chsng ldr: rdn over 2f out: wknd over 1f out* **40/1**
6 **9** *3 1/4* **Khamseen**[30] 1192 5-9-8 0 DavidKenny(5) 5 42
(Karen George) *s.i.s: hld up: racd keenly: wknd over 2f out* **250/1**
0 **10** *31* **Buds Bruvver**[25] 1257 3-9-1 0 J-PGuillambert 2
(Brian Baugh) *mid-div: sn pushed along: wknd 3f out: t.o* **250/1**

1m 28.94s (-0.66) **Going Correction** -0.025s/f (Stan)
WFA 3 from 4yo+ 12lb **10** Ran SP% **116.4**
Speed ratings (Par 103): **102,100,100,99,99 98,88,88,84,49**
toteswingers:1&2:£7.80, 1&3:£4.10, 2&3:£16.90 CSF £81.91 TOTE £2.90: £1.10, £10.10, £2.00; EX 64.80 Trifecta £462.20 Part won. Pool £624.64 - 0.10 winning unit..
Owner Mascalls Stud **Bred** Mascalls Stud **Trained** Manton, Wilts

FOCUS
The first division of an average 7f maiden for 3yos and upwards. They went a genuine gallop and the winning time was around two seconds outside standard, but slower than division two. Probably an above-average maiden for the track.
My Body Is A Cage(IRE) Official explanation: jockey said filly was slowly away

1825 WOLVERHAMPTON-RACECOURSE.CO.UK MAIDEN STKS (DIV II) 7f 32y(P)
2:40 (3:48) (Class 5) 3-Y-0+ **£2,264** (£673; £336; £168) **Stalls** High

Form RPR
242- **1** **Sholaan (IRE)**[219] 6448 3-9-1 85 LiamJones 1 99+
(William Haggas) *mde all: clr over 1f out: shkn up and hung lft ins fnl f: sn hung rt: styd on* **6/4**[1]
025- **2** *2 1/2* **Curzon Line**[191] 7095 3-9-1 78 MickaelBarzalona 3 92
(Mahmood Al Zarooni) *a.p: chsd wnr over 1f out: rdn and edgd lft ins fnl f: styd on* **7/2**[3]
623- **3** *2 3/4* **Mizwaaj (IRE)**[216] 6525 3-9-1 79 SilvestreDeSousa 11 85
(Saeed Bin Suroor) *hld up in tch: racd keenly: rdn over 1f out: styd on: nt trbld ldrs* **85/40**[2]
4 *nk* **Dutch Supreme** 3-9-1 0 TedDurcan 5 84+
(David Lanigan) *hld up: nt clr run over 1f out: r.o ins fnl f: nrst fin* **16/1**
23-3 **5** *6* **Tortoni (IRE)**[11] 1560 3-9-1 75 PaulMulrennan 8 68
(Kevin Ryan) *prom: rdn over 2f out: wknd over 1f out* **12/1**
45/3 **6** *1* **Hold The Star**[6] 1660 6-9-3 50 AnnStokell(5) 9 64
(Ann Stokell) *chsd wnr tl rdn and wknd over 1f out* **66/1**
7 *2 3/4* **Standing Strong (IRE)** 4-9-13 0 StevieDonohoe 2 65
(Robert Mills) *prom: rdn over 2f out: wknd over 1f out* **33/1**
8 *15* **Pass The Time** 3-8-10 0 LiamKeniry 6
(Neil Mulholland) *dwlt: a in rr: bhd fnl 3f: t.o* **100/1**
50 **9** *3/4* **July Specialists**[4] 1716 3-8-7 0 DeclanCannon(3) 4
(Richard Guest) *a in rr: bhd fnl 3f: t.o* **100/1**
0-0 **10** *8* **Fireball Express**[120] 41 4-9-13 0 RussKennemore 7
(Brian Baugh) *a in rr: bhd fnl 3f: t.o* **200/1**

1m 27.64s (-1.96) **Going Correction** -0.025s/f (Stan)
WFA 3 from 4yo+ 12lb **10** Ran SP% **114.7**
Speed ratings (Par 103): **110,107,104,103,96 95,92,75,74,65**
toteswingers:1&2:£2.40, 1&3:£2.50, 2&3:£1.90 CSF £6.97 TOTE £2.20: £1.10, £1.10, £1.10; EX 7.60 Trifecta £9.80 Pool £949.63 - 71.56 winning unit..
Owner Sheikh Ahmed Al Maktoum **Bred** Kilnamoragh Stud **Trained** Newmarket, Suffolk

FOCUS
The second division of a slightly above average 7f maiden for 3yos and upwards. The winning time was significantly better than the first division and this is good maiden form for the track.

1826 CONNIE GLEESON BIRTHDAY (S) STKS 7f 32y(P)
3:10 (3:48) (Class 6) 3-Y-0 **£1,704** (£503; £251) **Stalls** High

Form RPR
2333 **1** **First Bid**[21] 1353 3-8-12 63 (b) PaulMulrennan 6 69
(James Given) *chsd ldrs: led over 1f out: rdn out* **9/2**[3]
4253 **2** *2 3/4* **Emma Jean (IRE)**[10] 1585 3-8-7 53 (bt) MircoDemuro 8 57
(Frank Sheridan) *hld up: hdwy over 2f out: rdn to chse wnr fnl f: styd on* **9/2**[3]
425- **3** *2 3/4* **Mad For Fun (IRE)**[255] 5342 3-8-7 50 RussKennemore 11 50
(Paul Midgley) *hld up: hdwy over 2f out: rdn over 1f out: edgd lft and styd on same pce ins fnl f* **16/1**
0-24 **4** *2 3/4* **Dansili Dutch (IRE)**[38] 1058 3-8-7 60 GrahamGibbons 9 42
(David Barron) *mid-div: pushed along 1/2-way: rdn and outpcd over 2f out: n.d after* **7/2**[1]
0-20 **5** *2* **Tooley Woods (IRE)**[24] 1274 3-8-4 65 (b[1]) RyanPowell(3) 3 37
(George Margarson) *prom: rdn over 2f out: wknd over 1f out* **4/1**[2]
-300 **6** *1 3/4* **Armiger**[25] 1260 3-8-12 52 (b[1]) MartinDwyer 4 37
(William Muir) *w ldr tl led over 2f out: rdn and hdd over 1f out: sn hung lft: wknd fnl f* **25/1**
7 *4 1/2* **One Bid Too Many (USA)** 3-8-7 0 LiamJones 7 20+
(Alan Bailey) *in rr and pushed along over 5f out: nvr nrr* **11/2**
0 **8** *3/4* **Felona E Serona**[21] 1357 3-8-7 0 KirstyMilczarek 2 18
(Laura Young) *led early: remained handy: rdn over 2f out: wknd over 1f out* **100/1**
0-06 **9** *1/2* **Hatha Zain (IRE)**[57] 840 3-8-12 37 (b[1]) DaneO'Neill 10 22
(Milton Bradley) *led over 6f out: rdn and hdd over 2f out: wknd over 1f out* **40/1**
10 *1 3/4* **Steady Nelly** 3-8-7 0 (t) LukeMorris 5
(Frank Sheridan) *s.s: a in rr: hung rt and wknd 1/2-way* **12/1**

1m 29.89s (0.29) **Going Correction** -0.025s/f (Stan) **10** Ran SP% **114.8**
Speed ratings (Par 97): **97,93,90,87,85 83,78,77,76,74**
toteswingers:1&2:£4.40, 1&3:£13.10, 2&3:£22.40 CSF £24.37 TOTE £5.80: £2.30, £2.00, £4.30; EX 27.20 Trifecta £382.80 Part won. Pool £517.42 - 0.60 winning unit..The winner was bought in for 3,750gns. One Bid Too Many was claimed by Mr Chris Hamilton for £6,000.
Owner Peter Swann **Bred** J W Ford **Trained** Willoughton, Lincs

FOCUS
A modest selling stakes confined to 3yos. Straightforward form.
Tooley Woods(IRE) Official explanation: jockey said filly hung right throughout
Steady Nelly Official explanation: jockey said filly was slowly away and hung right-handed

1827 LIKE US ON FACEBOOK WOLVERHAMPTON RACECOURSE H'CAP 5f 216y(P)
3:40 (3:48) (Class 5) (0-75,75) 4-Y-0+ **£2,264** (£673; £336; £168) **Stalls** Low

Form RPR
-304 **1** **Showboating (IRE)**[69] 713 4-9-1 **69** (tp) MartinHarley 8 80
(Alan McCabe) *hld up: hdwy and hmpd over 1f out: r.o to ld post* **12/1**
-346 **2** *hd* **Bond Fastrac**[31] 1177 5-9-1 **72** DaleSwift(3) 3 82
(Geoffrey Oldroyd) *mid-div: hdwy 2f out: nt clr run and swtchd rt over 1f out: rdn to ld ins fnl f: hdd post* **12/1**
5554 **3** *2 3/4* **Restless Bay (IRE)**[10] 1587 4-9-6 **74** (e) GeorgeBaker 5 81+
(Reg Hollinshead) *s.i.s: hld up: nt clr run over 1f out: n.m.r and r.o ins fnl f: wnt 3rd post: nrst fin* **4/1**[1]
302- **4** *nk* **Crew Cut (IRE)**[155] 7595 4-9-0 **73** RaulDaSilva(5) 2 73
(Jeremy Gask) *chsd ldrs: pushed along over 2f out: hmpd over 1f out: edgd lft and styd on same pce ins fnl f: lost 3rd post* **4/1**[1]
6-11 **5** *2* **Howyadoingnotsobad (IRE)**[23] 1300 4-8-12 **71** DavidKenny(5) 7 65+
(Karen George) *led: rdn over 1f out: hdd and no ex ins fnl f* **8/1**
22-0 **6** *2 3/4* **Piddie's Power**[10] 1587 5-9-4 **75** SeanLevey(3) 12 60+
(Ed McMahon) *s.i.s: hld up: hdwy and hmpd over 1f out: eased* **20/1**
06-3 **7** *shd* **Mawjoodah**[30] 1193 4-9-0 **68** KierenFallon 4 57+
(Brian Ellison) *mid-div: rdn over 2f out: hdwy sn after: hmpd over 1f out: eased ins fnl f* **7/1**[3]
/0-1 **8** *3 3/4* **Enjoyment**[13] 1528 5-8-13 **67** IPoullis 11 40
(Alan McCabe) *chsd ldr: rdn and ev ch over 1f out: wknd fnl f* **20/1**
10-4 **9** *4* **Timeless Elegance (IRE)**[23] 1293 5-9-6 **74** GrahamGibbons 6 34
(David Barron) *chsd ldrs: rdn over 2f out: wknd over 1f out* **11/2**[2]
5116 **10** *1 1/2* **Imprimis Tagula (IRE)**[51] 899 8-9-0 **75** (v) NatashaEaton(7) 1 30
(Alan Bailey) *a in rr: bhd fnl 3f* **20/1**
100- **11** *1 1/2* **Comptonspirit**[200] 6913 8-9-6 **74** J-PGuillambert 9 24
(Brian Baugh) *prom: rdn over 2f out: wknd wl over 1f out* **50/1**
-516 **12** *10* **Zip Lock (IRE)**[65] 735 6-9-4 **72** KirstyMilczarek 10
(Olivia Maylam) *mid-div: wknd over 2f out* **16/1**
00-0 **13** *1/2* **Questionnaire (IRE)**[7] 1638 4-8-10 **67** DeclanCannon(3) 13
(Nicky Vaughan) *prom tl hung rt and wknd over 2f out* **100/1**

1m 14.36s (-0.64) **Going Correction** -0.025s/f (Stan) **13** Ran SP% **117.5**
Speed ratings (Par 103): **103,102,99,98,96 92,92,87,81,79 77,64,63**
toteswingers:1&2:£30.60, 1&3:£6.70, 2&3:£7.20 CSF £136.00 CT £684.36 TOTE £17.20: £4.50, £2.60, £1.70; EX 148.80 TRIFECTA Not won..
Owner Mr & Mrs L Cooke A Pierce A McCabe **Bred** Crone Stud Farms Ltd **Trained** Averham Park, Notts
■ Stewards' Enquiry : Dale Swift five-day ban: careless riding (May 18-22)

FOCUS
An average sprint handicap for older horses. It was strong run, but quite a messy race. The winner's best run since September over C&D.

Zip Lock(IRE) Official explanation: jockey said gelding lost both front shoes

1828 DOWNLOAD OUR IPHONE APP H'CAP 5f 20y(P)
4:10 (4:10) (Class 4) (0-85,85) 4-Y-0+ **£4,204** (£1,251; £625; £312) **Stalls** Low

Form RPR
0-40 **1** **Titus Gent**[99] 311 7-8-10 **79**.. RaulDaSilva(5) 6 87
(Jeremy Gask) *trckd ldrs: rdn to ld wl ins fnl f: r.o* **14/1**
2060 **2** *3/4* **Desert Strike**[11] 1564 6-9-2 **80**..................................(p) KierenFallon 7 85
(Charles Hills) *hld up: hdwy over 1f out: r.o wl: wnt 2nd post: nt rch wnr* **15/2**[3]
3110 **3** *nk* **Island Legend (IRE)**[21] 1362 6-9-7 **85**...........................(p) DaneO'Neill 9 89
(Milton Bradley) *led: hung lft over 1f out: rdn and hdd wl ins fnl f* **12/1**
6614 **4** *1/2* **Rylee Mooch**[47] 1016 4 [illegible] **73**...............................(e) DeclanCannon(3) 11 74
(Richard Guest) *prom: drvn along 1/2-way: edgd lft ins fnl f: r.o* **16/1**
-355 **5** *1/2* **Courageous (IRE)**[16] 1438 6-9-7 **85**...........................(t) DarryllHolland 4 85
(Kevin Ryan) *hld up: hdwy 2f out: rdn over 1f out: r.o* **3/1**[1]
131- **6** *1 1/2* **Beauty Pageant (IRE)**[223] 6350 5-9-4 **82**.................... RichardMullen 2 77
(Ed McMahon) *chsd ldrs: rdn over 1f out: no ex ins fnl f* **4/1**[2]
20-2 **7** *nse* **Speightowns Kid (USA)**[30] 1187 4-8-10 **74**................... WilliamBuick 3 69
(Matthew Salaman) *chsd ldrs: outpcd wl over 3f out: nt clr run over 1f out: r.o towards fin* **3/1**[1]
125- **8** *1* **Baby Queen (IRE)**[281] 4475 6-8-11 **75** ow1................ J-PGuillambert 5 66
(Brian Baugh) *chsd ldr: rdn over 1f out: wknd ins fnl f* **25/1**
60-0 **9** *nk* **Lady Royale**[15] 1476 4-9-0 **81**..................................(p) DaleSwift(3) 10 71
(Geoffrey Oldroyd) *sn pushed along and a in rr* **22/1**
415 **10** *2 1/2* **Absa Lutte (IRE)**[39] 1049 9-8-7 **71**.................................... LiamJones 1 52
(Michael Mullineaux) *hld up: rdn over 1f out: a in rr* **25/1**
0/6- **11** *16* **Nickel Silver**[478] 125 7-9-3 **81**..................................(v) PaulMulrennan 8
(Bryan Smart) *hmpd s: a in rr: bhd fr 1/2-way* **25/1**

1m 1.4s (-0.90) **Going Correction** -0.025s/f (Stan) **11** Ran **SP% 117.9**
Speed ratings (Par 105): **106,104,104,103,102 100,100,98,98,94 68**
toteswingers:1&2:£14.40, 1&3:£17.20, 2&3:£13.60 CSF £109.37 CT £1295.07 TOTE £15.40: £4.40, £4.30, £1.50; EX 85.90 Trifecta £540.10 Part won. Pool £565.91 - 0.10 winning unit..
Owner Tony Bloom **Bred** Heather Raw **Trained** Sutton Veny, Wilts
■ Stewards' Enquiry : Declan Cannon two-day ban: used whip above permitted level (May 18,20)

FOCUS
This competitive 5f handicap for older horses was the feature on the card. They went a solid gallop and the winning time was just over one second above standard. Ordinary form.
Titus Gent Official explanation: trainer said, regarding apparent improvement in form, that the gelding had a bad draw last time and had freshened up.
Nickel Silver Official explanation: jockey said gelding reared as stalls opened and was slowly away

1829 WORLD HORSE WELFARE CELEBRATES 85 YEARS H'CAP 1m 4f 50y(P)
4:40 (4:40) (Class 6) (0-65,65) 4-Y-0+ **£1,704** (£503; £251) **Stalls** Low

Form RPR
1 **1** **Teak (IRE)**[13] 1534 5-9-0 **61**.. RyanClark(3) 6 71
(Ian Williams) *mid-div: hdwy over 5f out: chsd ldr over 3f out: rdn to ld wl ins fnl f: styd on* **2/1**[1]
0- **2** *nk* **Landesherr (GER)**[174] 954 5-9-2 **60**...........................(t) IanMongan 2 69
(Steve Gollings) *chsd ldr tl lft in ld over 5f out: rdn and hdd wl ins fnl f* **18/1**
0-02 **3** *1/2* **Hurakan (IRE)**[13] 1533 6-9-7 **65**.. JamesDoyle 3 73
(Richard Price) *mid-div: hdwy over 3f out: rdn and swtchd lft over 1f out: r.o* **7/2**[3]
3-36 **4** *1 1/4* **White Deer (USA)**[23] 1297 8-8-11 **55**.....................(p) SilvestreDeSousa 9 61
(Geoffrey Harker) *hld up: hdwy over 1f out: rdn and hung lft ins fnl f: r.o* **9/1**
32-1 **5** *9* **Ishikawa (IRE)**[13] 1533 4-9-6 **64**.................................. FergusSweeney 7 56
(Alan King) *hld up: rdn over 3f out: hdwy over 2f out: wknd over 1f out* **11/4**[2]
1125 **6** *9* **St Ignatius**[10] 1588 5-9-6 **64**.. DarryllHolland 10 42
(Alan Bailey) *hld up: rdn and wknd wl over 2f out* **11/1**
000- **7** *2 1/4* **Hurricane Thomas (IRE)**[191] 7112 8-8-0 **51** oh6........ GemmaTutty(7) 8 25
(Karen Tutty) *chsd ldrs tl wknd over 2f out* **66/1**
0-05 **8** *13* **Media Stars**[8] 1631 7-9-0 **58**.. KierenFallon 4 11
(Robert Johnson) *s.i.s: hld up: wknd wl over 2f out* **20/1**
431/ **9** *3/4* **Kissing Clara (IRE)**[218] 7271 4-9-7 **65**...........................(t) LukeMorris 5 17
(Alison Thorpe) *prom: rdn over 3f out: wknd over 2f out* **33/1**
000/ **P** **Gilded Youth**[44] 6546 8-8-8 **52** oh6 ow1...................... RussKennemore 1
(David Lewis) *led tl p.u over 5f out* **150/1**

2m 39.98s (-1.12) **Going Correction** -0.025s/f (Stan) **10** Ran **SP% 115.7**
Speed ratings (Par 101): **102,101,101,100,94 88,87,78,77,**
toteswingers:1&2:£7.10, 1&3:£2.90, 2&3:£12.10 CSF £39.34 CT £121.62 TOTE £4.50: £1.70, £5.10, £2.10; EX 48.50 Trifecta £168.50 Pool £888.46 - 3.90 winning unit..
Owner Farranamanagh **Bred** Michael Morrissey **Trained** Portway, Worcs
■ Stewards' Enquiry : Ryan Clark four-day ban: used whip above permitted level (May 18,20-22)

FOCUS
A modest middle-distance handicap for older horses. The first four finished clear and the third sets the standard.

1830 KEATING CHAMBERS H'CAP 1m 141y(P)
5:10 (5:10) (Class 6) (0-65,65) 4-Y-0+ **£1,704** (£503; £251) **Stalls** Low

Form RPR
00-0 **1** **Cono Zur (FR)**[24] 1276 5-9-4 **65**.. DaleSwift(3) 13 74
(Ruth Carr) *mde all: rdn over 1f out: styd on* **10/1**
0-12 **2** *1/2* **Douze Points (IRE)**[30] 1191 6-9-5 **63**.................................. AdamKirby 5 71+
(John Butler) *hld up: nt clr run wl over 1f out: hdwy sn after: rdn to go 2nd wl ins fnl f: nt rch wnr* **13/8**[1]
10-6 **3** *1 1/2* **Monashee Rock (IRE)**[100] 293 7-8-10 **54**.......................... LiamKeniry 1 58
(Patrick Chamings) *hld up: hdwy over 1f out: n.m.r ins fnl f: r.o* **16/1**
5545 **4** *nk* **Pitkin**[19] 1154 4-9-1 **59**.. PaulMulrennan 9 63
(Michael Easterby) *prom: rdn over 1f out: edgd lft: styd on same pce ins fnl f* **6/1**[2]
3/00 **5** *3/4* **Jalors (IRE)**[20] 1378 4-9-6 **64**.. LukeMorris 2 66
(Ronald Harris) *prom: rdn over 3f out: hung lft ins fnl f: styd on same pce* **13/2**[3]
000- **6** *1* **Bold Cross (IRE)**[214] 6583 9-9-0 **63**............................ MatthewCosham(5) 8 63
(Edward Bevan) *s.i.s: hld up: rdn over 2f out: r.o ins fnl f* **20/1**
6213 **7** *nk* **Piccolo Express**[43] 1002 6-9-5 **63**.................................. RussKennemore 3 62
(Brian Baugh) *s.i.s: hld up: rdn over 1f out: r.o ins fnl f: nvr trbld ldrs* **15/2**
0006 **8** *nse* **Portrush Storm**[50] 906 7-8-7 **51** oh6.............................. MircoDemuro 4 50?
(Ray Peacock) *chsd wnr tl rdn over 1f out: no ex wl ins fnl f* **100/1**
0-61 **9** *1 1/2* **Mr Chocolate Drop (IRE)**[16] 1447 8-8-12 **61**..........(t) RaulDaSilva(5) 10 62+
(Mandy Rowland) *hld up: hdwy over 2f out: nt clr run wl over 1f out: looked hld whn hmpd ins fnl f* **8/1**
503- **10** *1/2* **Generous Genella**[312] 3457 4-8-4 **51** oh1.............. AdamBeschizza(3) 6 45
(Julia Feilden) *chsd ldrs: rdn over 2f out: wknd over 1f out* **20/1**
50-5 **11** *2 1/4* **Only You Maggie (IRE)**[8] 1636 5-8-13 **62**........(v) MatthewLawson(5) 11 51
(Gary Harrison) *s.i.s: hdwy 1/2-way: rdn and wknd over 2f out* **20/1**

1m 50.42s (-0.08) **Going Correction** -0.025s/f (Stan) **11** Ran **SP% 118.8**
Speed ratings (Par 101): **99,98,97,96,96 95,95,95,93,93 91**
toteswingers:1&2:£5.20, 1&3:£22.80, 2&3:£11.70 CSF £25.73 CT £278.71 TOTE £14.40: £3.90, £1.20, £5.40; EX 40.20 Trifecta £407.40 Pool £682.69 - 1.24 winning unit..
Owner Ruth Carr Racing **Bred** Jean-Pierre-Joseph Dubois **Trained** Huby, N Yorks

FOCUS
A modest extended 1m handicap for older horses. The winner made the most of an easy lead in a steadily run race, and the form is rated cautiously.

1831 FOLLOW US ON TWITTER @WOLVESRACES APPRENTICE H'CAP1f 103y(P)
5:40 (5:40) (Class 6) (0-55,53) 4-Y-0+ **£1,704** (£503; £251) **Stalls** Low

Form RPR
2355 **1** **Harare**[10] 1580 11-8-7 **49**..(v) GemmaTutty(5) 5 60
(Karen Tutty) *mid-div: hdwy over 2f out: led over 1f out: r.o wl* **25/1**
2605 **2** *5* **Diamond Twister (USA)**[23] 1299 6-8-8 **45**.....................(t) LauraBarry 10 46
(Lisa Williamson) *chsd ldr tl led over 2f out: rdn and hdd over 1f out: styd on same pce* **25/1**
3213 **3** *hd* **So Is She (IRE)**[3] 1744 4-9-1 **52**..................................(be) IanBurns 1 52
(Alan Bailey) *chsd ldrs: rdn and ev ch over 1f out: styd on same pce* **5/1**[2]
6520 **4** *1 1/2* **Avon Supreme**[36] 1095 4-8-10 **52**.............................. JacobMoore(3) 3 49
(Gay Kelleway) *hld up in tch: rdn over 1f out: no ex ins fnl f* **20/1**
0023 **5** *1* **Lytham (IRE)**[44] 984 11-9-1 **52**.......................... WilliamTwiston-Davies 12 47
(Tony Carroll) *hld up: hdwy over 2f out: rdn and edgd lft over 1f out: no ex* **12/1**
260- **6** *1* **Politbureau**[213] 6613 5-9-1 **52**..................................(b[1]) DavidSimmonson 11 45
(Michael Easterby) *led: rdn and hdd over 2f out: wknd fnl f* **9/1**
436- **7** *4* **Byron Bear (IRE)**[233] 6049 4-8-13 **53**.............................. NedCurtis(3) 9 37
(Paul Midgley) *hld up: hdwy over 1f out: wknd fnl f* **14/1**
4203 **8** *hd* **Bygones For Coins (IRE)**[8] 1635 4-8-6 **50**.......... MatthewHopkins(7) 2 34
(Robert Johnson) *hld up: racd keenly: hdwy over 2f out: wknd over 1f out* **9/2**[1]
0-05 **9** *nk* **Lucas Pitt**[107] 200 5-8-8 **45**.. NoelGarbutt 6 28
(Michael Scudamore) *prom: lost pl over 6f out: n.d after* **11/2**[3]
20-5 **10** *1* **Naledi**[18] 1425 8-8-8 **48**.. JacobButterfield(3) 4 29
(Richard Price) *prom: racd keenly: rdn and wknd over 1f out* **10/1**
0500 **11** *4* **Hilbre Court (USA)**[57] 843 7-8-11 **48**.............................. JasonHart 13 21
(Brian Baugh) *hld up: pushed along 1/2-way: lost tch fr over 2f out* **16/1**
5002 **12** *2 3/4* **Harrys Yer Man**[18] 1425 8-9-2 **53**.................................. ConorHarrison 8 20
(Mark Brisbourne) *hld up: hdwy on outer over 2f out: sn wknd* **11/2**[3]

2m 1.76s (0.06) **Going Correction** -0.025s/f (Stan) **12** Ran **SP% 117.4**
Speed ratings (Par 101): **98,93,93,92,91 90,86,86,86,85 81,79**
toteswingers:1&2:£40.40, 1&3:£24.60, 2&3:£17.60 CSF £528.48 CT £3604.60 TOTE £36.30: £6.20, £7.00, £2.10; EX 492.90 TRIFECTA Not won..
Owner Thoroughbred Homes Ltd **Bred** Limestone Stud **Trained** Osmotherley, N Yorks

FOCUS
A lowly extended 1m1f handicap for older horses and restricted to apprentice jockeys. The winner is rated back to last year's best.
T/Plt: £143.40 to a £1 stake. Pool:£95,574.87 - 486.41 winning tickets T/Qpdt: £64.00 to a £1 stake. Pool:£6,865.23 - 79.30 winning tickets CR

1759 DUNDALK (A.W) (L-H)
Friday, May 4

OFFICIAL GOING: Standard

1832a IRISH STALLION FARMS EUROPEAN BREEDERS FUND 2YO MEDIAN AUCTION MAIDEN 5f (P)
6:05 (6:05) 2-Y-0 **£7,187** (£1,666; £729; £416)

RPR
1 **Tennessee Wildcat (IRE)** 2-9-5 .... GaryCarroll 1 82+
(G M Lyons, Ire) *dwlt: settled bhd ldrs: 7th 1/2-way: rdn into 4th 1 1/2f out: led 1f out: kpt on fnl f: drifted lft u.p* **13/2**
2 *1 3/4* **Versilia Gal (IRE)**[23] 1323 2-9-0 .... PatSmullen 7 72
(Patrick Martin, Ire) *disp early: sn chsd ldrs in 3rd: pushed along 2f out: rdn to chal 1f out: no ex in 2nd ins fnl f: hmpd fnl 100yds* **9/2**[2]
3 *hd* **Almanack** 2-9-5 .... WayneLordan 8 75+
(T Stack, Ire) *chsd ldrs and wd: 6th 1/2-way: rdn into 5th 1f out: kpt on fnl f* **11/4**[1]
4 *1 1/2* **Marshland**[13] 1515 2-9-5 .... FranBerry 4 70
(Mark Johnston) *sn prom and disp: rdn in 2nd 1 1/2f out: no ex ins fnl f* **11/4**[1]
5 *1/2* **Fairy Path (IRE)**[5] 1687 2-9-0 .... NGMcCullagh 3 63
(P J Prendergast, Ire) *sn led and disp: rdn 2f out: hdd 1f out: no ex fnl f* **25/1**
6 *1 3/4* **Wholelotofrosie (IRE)** 2-9-0 .... ShaneFoley 5 57+
(K J Condon, Ire) *s.i.s and in rr: pushed along 2f out: kpt on one pce fr over 1f out* **25/1**
7 *1* **Einsteins Folly (IRE)**[23] 1323 2-9-5 ....(p) KevinManning 2 58
(J S Bolger, Ire) *chsd ldrs: 4th 1/2-way: rdn and no ex under 2f out* **5/1**[3]
8 *2* **Granny On Fire (IRE)**[27] 1227 2-9-0 .... WJLee 6 46
(Michael Mulvany, Ire) *chsd ldrs: 5th 1/2-way: rdn and no ex over 2f out* **20/1**

59.22s (59.22) **8** Ran **SP% 114.0**
CSF £34.49 TOTE £5.50: £3.80, £1.40, £1.02; DF 36.30.
Owner Sean Jones **Bred** M Duffy **Trained** Dunsany, Co. Meath

FOCUS
An above-average maiden and one that is likely to produce plenty of winners. It's been rated around the time and the second to her fluid early-season figures.

NOTEBOOK
Tennessee Wildcat(IRE), a newcomer by Kheleyf, dwelt when the gates opened and forfeited his plum position on the rail. He seemed to have plenty on his plate turning for home with just the slow-starting Wholelotofrosie behind, but showed a smart of foot to challenge passing the furlong pole. He quickened and won with a bit in hand despite drifting across to the rail, slightly hampering the runner-up. He should improve for the experience and looks Group class in the making. (op 9/2)
Versilia Gal(IRE) gives the form a solid look. She had been placed in two maidens and seemed to run her race here. Always in a handy position, she kept on well when challenged and should be good enough to open her account before too long.
Almanack, only his trainer's second 2yo runner this season, holds an entry in the Phoenix Stakes and is obviously well thought of. Drawn widest of all in stall eight, he was never able to get any cover and came down the wide outside in the home straight. He travelled as well as anything to the furlong pole but couldn't match the winner close home. He certainly has ability. (op 3/1)

Marshland's debut effort wasn't anything to write home about (beaten 9l into fourth at Nottingham), so it was surprising to see him go off joint-favourite here. He knew his job and was soon helping to force the pace but folded pretty tamely inside the final furlong. Chances are this is as good as he is. (op 5/2)
Fairy Path(IRE) was well beaten on her debut at Navan and had no answers inside the final furlong here when headed. Still, this represented an improved showing and handicapping will be her game. (op 20/1)
Wholelotofrosie(IRE) is one to note. Slowest away, she was in danger of getting tailed off before turning into the straight but kept on in eyecatching fashion under tender handling. She will know much more next time.
Einsteins Folly(IRE) was one of the first to be asked for maximum effort and the response was disappointing. He may want further but looks only average at this stage. (op 4/1)

1834a IRADIO IWORK (C&G) 3YO MAIDEN 7f (P)
7:05 (7:07) 3-Y-O £5,750 (£1,333; £583; £333)

RPR
1 **Van Ellis**[10] 1452 3-9-5 ... FranBerry 10 91+
(Mark Johnston) *mde all: rdn clr over 1f out: kpt on strly: comf* **1/3**[1]
2 1 3/4 **That Boy David**[21] 1369 3-9-5 ... JohnnyMurtagh 2 86+
(G M Lyons, Ire) *chsd ldr in 2nd: rdn 2f out: no imp 1f out: kpt on same pce fnl f* **9/2**[2]
3 5 1/2 **Flying Doha (IRE)** 3-9-5 ... WayneLordan 4 71
(David Wachman, Ire) *chsd ldrs: 5th 1/2-way: rdn in 4th 2f out: no imp in 3rd 1f out: kpt on same pce* **10/1**[3]
4 4 3/4 **Aidan (IRE)**[13] 1539 3-9-0 ... SamJames(5) 8 58
(John Geoghegan, Ire) *mid-div: rdn into 6th and no imp 2f out: kpt on one pce fr over 1f out* **25/1**
5 3/4 **Treasure The Ridge (IRE)**[21] 1368 3-9-5 ... PatSmullen 6 56
(D K Weld, Ire) *mid-div: 6th 1/2-way: rdn and no imp 2f out: kpt on one pce* **14/1**
6 hd **Bensoon**[21] 1369 3-9-5 ... ShaneFoley 3 55
(M Halford, Ire) *towards rr for most: nvr a factor* **25/1**
7 nse **The Lost Legion (IRE)**[36] 1100 3-9-5 ... MichaelHussey 1 55
(John Patrick Shanahan, Ire) *chsd ldrs: 3rd 1/2-way: rdn over 2f out: no ex over 1f out* **20/1**
8 1 3/4 **Heroic Endeavour (IRE)**[198] 6963 3-9-5 ... KevinManning 5 51
(Mrs John Harrington, Ire) *chsd ldrs: 4th 1/2-way: rdn in 5th 2f out: no ex over 1f out* **33/1**
9 6 **Luaimneach**[112] 164 3-9-5 49... FergalLynch 7 34
(Liam McAteer, Ire) *a towards rr* **33/1**

1m 22.98s (82.98) 9 Ran SP% 127.3
CSF £2.46 TOTE £1.20: £1.02, £1.20, £1.60; DF 2.20.
Owner Sheikh Hamdan Bin Mohammed Al Maktoum **Bred** D A Yardy **Trained** Middleham Moor, N Yorks

FOCUS
This was won by a promising sort who could be anything. The first two pulled nicely clear and the race has been rated based on the time compared to the handicap over this C&D later on the card.

NOTEBOOK
Van Ellis was entitled to win this and he obliged with the minimum of fuss. It wasn't surprising to see him sent straight to the front and he got into a nice rhythm at the head of affairs. The tempo was gradually increased and passing the 2f pole the result was a foregone conclusion. He didn't go away from the runner-up the way some might have expected but won nicely and could have a bright future. (op 2/5)
That Boy David ◆ broke well and certainly wasn't aided when the winner cut across to the rail after a furlong. He proceeded to track that rival and, while he never looked like causing an upset, he stuck to the task well and was gaining ground at the finish. Winning a maiden, perhaps over 1m, should be a formality. (op 4/1)
Flying Doha(IRE) travelled well to the 2f pole, suggesting he has ability. He wasn't knocked about in the closing stages and is sure to come on a ton for the run. (op 8/1)
Aidan(IRE) performed better than his 100-1 starting price suggested at Naas last time and ran to a similar level here.
Treasure The Ridge(IRE) was never in contention at any stage but will be of interest now that he has acquired a handicap mark. He's probably better than he's shown so far.
Bensoon Official explanation: jockey said gelding ran short of room for five or six strides at the furlong pole and was unable to quicken up thereafter
Luaimneach Official explanation: jockey said gelding lost its action

1833 - 1838a (Foreign Racing) - See Raceform Interactive

CHURCHILL DOWNS (L-H)
Friday, May 4

OFFICIAL GOING: Dirt: fast; turf: firm

1839a LA TROIENNE STKS (GRADE 2) (4YO+ FILLIES & MARES) (DIRT) 1m 110y(D)
6:26 (6:27) 4-Y-O+
£128,184 (£41,349; £20,674; £10,337; £6,201; £2,109)

RPR
1 **Juanita (USA)**[48] 957 4-8-6 0... RADominguez 5 112+
(Michael J Maker, U.S.A) **167/10**
2 2 **St John's River (USA)**[258] 4-8-6 0... RosieNapravnik 2 107+
(Andrew Leggio Jr, U.S.A) **61/10**[2]
3 1 **Plum Pretty (USA)**[20] 4-8-11 0... RBejarano 4 110
(Bob Baffert, U.S.A) **2/5**[1]
4 5 **Absinthe Minded (USA)**[20] 5-8-8 0... MESmith 6 97
(D Wayne Lukas, U.S.A) **36/5**[3]
5 1/2 **Afleeting Lady (USA)**[162] 5-8-6 0...(b) JLCastanon 1 94
(Dale Romans, U.S.A) **11/1**
6 8 1/2 **Maristar (USA)**[181] 5-8-6 0... JamesGraham 7 77
(Gerard Butler) *dwlt: settled towards rr: rdn and no imp fr over 2f out: sn wl btn* **191/10**
7 1/2 **Love Theway Youare (USA)**[48] 4-8-6 0... JRosario 3 76
(Myung Kwon Cho, U.S.A) **197/10**

1m 42.82s (-1.55) 7 Ran SP% 121.5
PARI-MUTUEL (all including $2 stakes): WIN 35.40; PLACE (1-2) 13.20, 7.00; SHOW (1-2-3) 5.00, 3.20, 2.10; SF 228.60.
Owner William S & Graydon Patterson **Bred** Padua Stables **Trained** USA

1650 # DONCASTER (L-H)
Saturday, May 5

OFFICIAL GOING: Good to soft (good in places; 7.3)
Wind: Light behind Weather: Cloudy

1841 CROWNHOTEL-BAWTRY.COM APPRENTICE H'CAP 1m 2f 60y
5:50 (5:50) (Class 4) (0-85,85) 4-Y-0+ £5,175 (£1,540; £769; £384) Stalls Low

Form RPR
-020 1 **Calaf**[21] 1381 4-9-1 79... GeorgeChaloner 2 89
(Richard Fahey) *trckd ldrs: smooth hdwy 4f out: trckd ldr over 2f out: rdn to chal whn hit in face by opponent's whip 1 1/2f out: led jst ins fnl f: styd on* **4/1**[2]
621- 2 1 1/2 **Figaro**[213] 6633 4-8-13 80... WilliamTwiston-Davies(3) 6 86
(William Haggas) *led: rdn along 2f out: sn edgd rt: drvn and hdd jst ins fnl f: one pce* **2/1**[1]
-441 3 1 **Veiled Applause**[14] 1525 9-8-7 76... KevinLundie(5) 4 80
(John Quinn) *hld up in rr: hdwy over 3f out and sn pushed along: rdn to chse ldng pair over 1f out: sn swtchd lft and kpt on same pce* **6/1**
2200 4 12 **Follow The Flag (IRE)**[7] 1657 8-8-7 71 oh1...(be) NoraLooby 3 52
(Alan McCabe) *trckd ldr: pushed along 3f out: rdn over 2f out: sn one pce* **20/1**
0013 5 shd **West End Lad**[21] 1381 9-9-7 85...(b) CDTimmons 5 66
(Roy Bowring) *trckd ldr: pushed along 4f out: rdn 3f out: sn wknd* **9/2**[3]
11-2 6 9 **Glass Mountain (IRE)**[26] 1266 4-8-9 76... NoelGarbutt(3) 1 40
(James Fanshawe) *trckd ldrs: hdwy 3f out: rdn along 2f out: sn btn* **4/1**[2]

2m 11.1s (1.70) **Going Correction** +0.30s/f (Good) 6 Ran SP% 110.6
Speed ratings (Par 105): **105,103,103,93,93 86**
Tote Swingers: 1&2 £3.00, 1&3 £6.50, 2&3 £3.20 CSF £12.05 TOTE £4.40: £2.10, £1.40; EX 14.40.
Owner Dr Marwan Koukash **Bred** Norcroft Park Stud **Trained** Musley Bank, N Yorks

FOCUS
Only six runners but four came here in good form and another looked open to progress on his reappearance so the form among the principals looks solid enough. The gallop increased in the straight and the form looks reasonable, rated around the first three.

1842 POLYPIPE MAIDEN STKS 5f
6:25 (6:25) (Class 5) 2-Y-O £2,911 (£866; £432; £216) Stalls High

Form RPR
3 1 **Yes Two**[24] 1315 2-9-3 0... JamesMillman 6 82
(Rod Millman) *mde all: rdn wl over 1f out: sn jnd and drvn ins fnl f: kpt on gamely* **16/1**
3 2 3/4 **Dust Whirl**[15] 1499 2-9-0 0... SeanLevey(3) 2 79
(Richard Hannon) *a.p: cl up 2f out: effrt to chal wl over 1f out and ev ch tl drvn and one pce wl ins fnl f* **5/2**[1]
5 3 nk **Top Boy**[14] 1515 2-9-0 0... DaleSwift(3) 10 78+
(Derek Shaw) *t.k.h: hld up towards rr: gd hdwy 2f out: n.m.r and swtchd rt over 1f out: chsd ldrs and swtchd lft and rdn ent fnl f: styd on strly towards fin* **20/1**
3 4 1 3/4 **Regal Dan (IRE)**[19] 1411 2-9-3 0... MichaelHills 11 72+
(Charles Hills) *s.i.s and towards rr: stdy hdwy after 2f and sn chsng ldrs: rdn along and ev ch over 1f out: wknd ins fnl f* **7/2**[2]
5 nk **This Is Nice (IRE)** 2-8-12 0... RichardKingscote 4 66
(Tom Dascombe) *midfield: hdwy on outer wl over 1f out: sn rdn and kpt on fnl f* **16/1**
6 1 **Bispham Green** 2-9-3 0... DavidNolan 9 67+
(Richard Fahey) *chsd ldrs: rdn along whn sltly hmpd wl over 1f out: sn one pce* **13/2**[3]
7 1 3/4 **Hitherto** 2-9-3 0... GrahamGibbons 3 61
(David Barron) *s.i.s and bhd tl styd on appr fnl f* **25/1**
8 hd **Unassailable** 2-9-3 0... PhillipMakin 8 60
(Kevin Ryan) *trckd ldrs: hdwy 2f out: sn rdn and edgd lft over 1f out: wknd* **14/1**
9 2 3/4 **Team Challenge** 2-9-3 0... DavidAllan 1 50
(Tim Easterby) *unruly and loose in paddock: dwlt and in rr: sme hdwy on wd outside wl over 1f out: n.d* **50/1**
10 nk **Bronte Belle** 2-8-12 0... TomEaves 5 44
(Jedd O'Keeffe) *prom: rdn along over 2f out: sn wknd* **50/1**
2 11 2 **Ouzinkie (IRE)**[19] 1411 2-9-3 0... SamHitchcott 12 42
(Mick Channon) *chsd ldrs: rdn along over 2f out: sn drvn and wknd wl over 1f out* **7/2**[2]

1m 1.02s (0.52) **Going Correction** +0.15s/f (Good) 11 Ran SP% 117.3
Speed ratings (Par 93): **101,99,99,96,96 94,91,91,86,86 83**
Tote Swingers: 1&2 £10.50, 1&3 £24.60, 2&3 £15.50 CSF £54.27 TOTE £23.70: £4.90, £1.10, £4.10; EX 93.60 TRIFECTA Not won..
Owner Mustajed Partnership **Bred** Bearstone Stud **Trained** Kentisbeare, Devon

FOCUS
Probably at least a fair maiden (it was won by subsequent Chesham Stakes winner Zaidan in 2010) in which those with experience came to the fore. The runners raced middle to stands' side. The runner-up looks a sensible guide to the level.

NOTEBOOK
Yes Two looked to have a bit to find on form but he'd clearly learnt plenty from his debut, being much sharper through the early the stages on this occasion, and showed a gritty attitude after looking for a while as if he might get overhauled by the runner-up. His half-brother Josh was a useful juvenile and he's entitled to improve again, not least at 6f.
Dust Whirl possibly didn't quite run up to the form of his Newbury debut but he once again showed plenty of speed and is such a good-moving colt that he's likely to be a different proposition on faster ground. (tchd 11-4)
Top Boy ◆ is quite an expensive purchase for one from his yard but he ran promisingly considering he took quite a grip early on and then looked inexperienced off the bridle before coming home strongly. He looks to have some substance about him and seems certain to improve again and win a race. The progeny of his sire have a good record on Fibresand, so it would be no surprise if his trainer looks for a race there. (op 22-1 tchd 25-1)
Regal Dan(IRE) reversed Windsor form with Ouzinkie but didn't do himself any favours with a slow start and would probably have finished closer to had he not made his ground so quickly through the middle part of the race. He can do better again. (tchd 3-1)
This Is Nice(IRE), one of two fillies in the field, stayed on without threatening and promises to do better over further as her pedigree suggests.
Bispham Green, a son of Green Desert out of a fast mare, showed up well until lack of condition seemed to tell. There's every likelihood too given his sire that he's another who'll do better on faster ground. (tchd 6-1 and 7-1)
Hitherto, a gelded son of Bertolini, started to get the hang of things late on and should do better over 6f. (tchd 20-1)
Unassailable, by Bahamian Bounty and the late foal of a 7f winner, ran around off the bridle after showing up to the furlong pole and might need a bit more time. (tchd 16-1)

Team Challenge, who has already been gelded, got loose in the paddock and took a fall but escaped unharmed. He was always behind. (op 66-1 tchd 40-1)
Ouzinkie(IRE) should have been thereabouts on his debut form but was never travelling as well as he had then and perhaps this softer ground wasn't in his favour. Official explanation: trainer's rep said he had no explanation for the poor form shown (op 5-1)

1843 SHEFFIELD INSULATIONS MAIDEN STKS 6f
6:55 (6:58) (Class 5) 3-4-Y-O **£2,911** (£866; £432; £216) **Stalls** High

Form RPR
0- **1** **Shahzan (IRE)**[357] 2103 4-9-12 0 AndreaAtzeni 4 94+
(Roger Varian) *trckd ldrs: hdwy over 2f out: rdn to chal over 1f out: styd on to ld ins fnl f* **7/2**[2]
2 ½ **Miliika** 3-8-11 0 WilliamCarson 17 84+
(Rae Guest) *hld up in rr: gd hdwy on wd outside over 2f out: rdn to chse ldrs and hung bdly lft over 1f out: bmpd and led appr fnl f: hdd insd fnl f: no ex* **16/1**
02-0 **3** 5 **Out Do**[17] 1452 3-9-2 84 KierenFallon 7 73
(Luca Cumani) *trckd ldrs: smooth hdwy to ld wl over 2f out: rdn: edgd rt and bmpd jst over 1f out: sn hdd and one pce* **11/10**[1]
4 2 ¼ **Art Form** 3-8-8 0 (t) SeanLevey(3) 1 61
(Alan McCabe) *hld up in tch: hdwy 2f out: sn rdn and kpt on fnl f: nrst fin* **66/1**
5 **5** 1 ¼ **Radioactive**[15] 1501 3-8-11 0 RichardKingscote 2 57
(Ralph Beckett) *slt ld: rdn along and hdd wl over 2f out: grad wknd* **5/1**[3]
0 **6** shd **Taizong (IRE)**[12] 1560 3-8-13 0 RyanClark(3) 9 62
(Ian Williams) *bolted to s: cl up: rdn along over 2f out: grad wknd* **20/1**
7 2 **Ptolemy** 3-9-2 0 GrahamGibbons 10 55
(David Barron) *s.i.s and towards rr: hdwy over 2f out: sn rdn and edgd lft: nvr nr ldrs* **25/1**
00- **8** 1 ¼ **Watanee**[220] 6449 3-8-11 0 BrettDoyle 3 46
(Clive Brittain) *prom: rdn along wl over 2f out: grad wknd* **40/1**
9 1 ½ **College Doll** 3-8-8 0 DominicFox(3) 12 41
(Christine Dunnett) *in rr: pushed along and hdwy 1/2-way: rdn over 2f out: kpt on: nvr nr ldrs* **200/1**
65 **10** nk **Give Us A Belle (IRE)**[25] 1285 3-9-2 0 TomMcLaughlin 11 46
(Christine Dunnett) *nvr bttr than midfield* **150/1**
11 1 **Hurricane Max (IRE)** 3-8-13 0 DaleSwift(3) 6 42
(Chris Fairhurst) *s.i.s: a in rr* **66/1**
0- **12** hd **Sapphire Seeker**[252] 5480 3-9-2 0 DaneO'Neill 5 42
(Des Donovan) *t.k.h: chsd ldrs: pushed along 1/2-way: sn rdn and wknd* **200/1**
2-0 **13** nk **Hannibal Hayes (USA)**[46] 969 3-9-2 0 RoystonFfrench 16 41
(Jeremy Noseda) *nvr nr ldrs* **12/1**
0-6 **14** hd **Joy To The World (IRE)**[24] 1296 3-8-11 0 PhillipMakin 15 35
(Paul Cole) *in tch: rdn along over 2f out: grad wknd* **33/1**
15 3 ¾ **Jerry Ellen (IRE)** 3-9-2 0 DuranFentiman 8 28
(Tim Easterby) *a in rr* **50/1**
16 4 **Kapunda** 4-9-12 0 TomEaves 18
(Jedd O'Keeffe) *a towards rr* **100/1**
4-0 **17** 6 **Cried For You (IRE)**[14] 1521 3-8-11 0 DavidAllan 13
(Tim Easterby) *in tch: rdn along 1/2-way: sn wknd* **40/1**
06 **18** 2 ½ **Irish Girls Spirit (IRE)**[8] 1637 3-8-11 0 MickyFenton 14
(Paul Midgley) *a towards rr* **100/1**

1m 13.01s (-0.59) **Going Correction** +0.15s/f (Good)
WFA 3 from 4yo 10lb **18** Ran SP% **125.1**
Speed ratings (Par 103): **109,108,101,98,97 96,94,92,90,90 88,88,88,87,82 77,69,66**
Tote Swingers: 1&2 £8.50, 1&3 £1.40, 2&3 £9.20 CSF £55.12 TOTE £5.50: £1.90, £4.00, £1.20; EX 70.20 Trifecta £123.50 Pool: £368.98 - 2.21 winning units..
Owner H R H Sultan Ahmad Shah **Bred** J Hanly, A Stroud And T Stewart **Trained** Newmarket, Suffolk

FOCUS
A big field but little strength in depth on the day as the market suggested, though the winner looks destined for better things and some of those behind seem likely to do better in handicaps in time. The runners stayed in the middle of the track. The first two can rate higher with the fourth to eighth ultimately setting the level.

1844 FREEBETS.CO.UK H'CAP 6f
7:25 (7:29) (Class 3) (0-90,90) 4-Y-0+ **£8,409** (£2,502; £1,250; £625) **Stalls** High

Form RPR
20-6 **1** **Farlow (IRE)**[35] 1141 4-9-0 86 HarryBentley(3) 19 94
(Ralph Beckett) *a.p: effrt 2f out: rdn to ld ent fnl f: kpt on wl* **12/1**
106- **2** ½ **Summerinthecity (IRE)**[168] 7489 5-9-5 88 LiamKeniry 15 94
(Ed de Giles) *trckd ldrs: hdwy 2f out: sn rdn and ev ch ins fnl f: no ex towards fin* **33/1**
2-00 **3** ½ **Beckermet (IRE)**[16] 1478 10-8-11 83 DaleSwift(3) 20 88
(Ruth Carr) *a.p: effrt 2f out: rdn over 1f out and ev ch tl nt qckn wl ins fnl f* **40/1**
0-44 **4** hd **Azrael**[21] 1373 4-8-12 84 SeanLevey(3) 17 88
(Alan McCabe) *a.p: effrt 2f out: rdn over 1f out and ev ch tl nt qckn ins fnl f* **16/1**
0-33 **5** nse **Tajneed (IRE)**[12] 1558 9-9-0 90 ShirleyTeasdale(7) 18 94
(David Nicholls) *a.p: effrt wl over 1f out: sn rdn and kpt on fnl f* **14/1**
0553 **6** ½ **Baby Strange**[17] 1438 8-9-3 86 TomEaves 7 88+
(Derek Shaw) *hld up in midfield: hdwy over 2f out: swtchd lft and rdn over 1f out: kpt on ins fnl f: nrst fin* **14/1**
-041 **7** shd **Thunderball**[16] 1476 6-9-7 90 (b) KierenFallon 8 92
(Scott Dixon) *chsd ldrs: rdn 2f out: kpt on u.p fnl f* **14/1**
130- **8** nse **L'Ami Louis (IRE)**[301] 3841 4-9-0 83 DaneO'Neill 16 85
(Henry Candy) *racd nr stands' rail: led: rdn wl over 1f out: drvn and hdd ent fnl f: grad wknd* **11/1**
46-0 **9** ¾ **Johannes (IRE)**[34] 1157 9-9-3 86 DavidNolan 12 86+
(Richard Fahey) *hld up in midfield: hdwy 2f out: sn rdn and kpt on fnl f: nrst fin* **18/1**
0-00 **10** ½ **Sunraider (IRE)**[17] 1438 5-9-2 85 MickyFenton 9 83
(Paul Midgley) *cl up: rdn along wl over 1f out: drvn ent fnl f: wknd towards fin* **33/1**
001- **11** ½ **Loki's Revenge**[208] 6762 4-9-0 83 (b) WilliamCarson 1 79
(William Jarvis) *wnt lft s: in tch on wd outside: rdn along over 2f out: kpt on same pce appr fnl f* **33/1**
3-01 **12** 2 **Fast Shot**[16] 1478 4-9-4 87 DavidAllan 10 77
(Tim Easterby) *midfield: hdwy 2f out: sn rdn and no imp appr fnl f* **9/1**[3]
-253 **13** hd **Layla's Hero (IRE)**[22] 1354 5-9-4 87 (p) FrannyNorton 11 76
(John Quinn) *towards rr: sme hdwy over 2f out: nvr a factor* **15/2**[2]
1/0- **13** dht **Pearl Ice**[203] 6862 4-9-6 89 GrahamGibbons 2 78
(David Barron) *prom: pushed along whn n.m.r over 2f out: sn rdn and wknd* **3/1**[1]
0-1U **15** 1 **Arganil (USA)**[27] 1236 7-9-4 87 (p) PhillipMakin 14 73
(Kevin Ryan) *dwlt: a towards rr* **20/1**
04-4 **16** 1 ¼ **Misplaced Fortune**[16] 1478 7-8-9 85 DanielleMooney(7) 4 67
(Nigel Tinkler) *a towards rr* **33/1**
003- **17** 4 ½ **Ballista (IRE)**[193] 7076 4-9-4 87 RichardKingscote 13 55
(Tom Dascombe) *dwlt: a in rr* **28/1**
300- **18** 3 **Oneladyowner**[218] 6500 4-9-2 85 EddieAhern 5 43
(David Brown) *midfield: sme hdwy over 2f out: sn rdn and wknd* **14/1**
0-00 **19** ¾ **Marine Commando**[17] 1438 4-9-0 90 GeorgeChaloner(7) 6 46
(Richard Fahey) *v.s.a and lost many l s: a bhd* **50/1**
000- **20** 2 **Ginger Ted (IRE)**[196] 7018 5-9-2 85 (p) TomMcLaughlin 3 34
(Stuart Williams) *midfield: rdn along 1/2-way: sn wknd* **28/1**

1m 13.44s (-0.16) **Going Correction** +0.15s/f (Good) **20** Ran SP% **128.4**
Speed ratings (Par 107): **107,106,105,105,105 104,104,104,103,102 102,99,99,99,97 96,90,86,85,82**
Tote Swingers: 1&2 £162.30, 1&3 £42.10, 2&3 £204.50 CSF £382.27 CT £7203.86 TOTE £15.40: £3.70, £14.00, £6.30, £4.80; EX 650.70 TRIFECTA Not won..
Owner Lawrence, Deal & Carolyn Thornton **Bred** Patrick J Monahan **Trained** Kimpton, Hants

FOCUS
Quite a useful handicap dominated by the smaller stand-side group whose riders showed no sign of dithering and were soon clear. The pace was good but the time was slower than the preceding maiden, and the form is rated at face value.

NOTEBOOK
Farlow(IRE) possibly hadn't been himself at Kempton on his comeback as he resumed the progress he was showing for the most part last year with a gritty display. For all he was helped by an ideal position through the race and didn't obviously have much in hand he still hasn't had much racing and remains open to more improvement, and this run has also shown he can handle softish ground. (op 10-1)
Summerinthecity(IRE) won over this C&D as a juvenile, since when he has scored twice. He looks as good as ever on this evidence, though like the winner had a near-perfect trip through the race.
Beckermet(IRE) was another to race close to the strong pace and, though he's a fair bit higher in the weights now than when winning in the autumn, he's still well treated on old form and his yard are starting to hit form. He seems sure to run well again next time, not least if stepped back up to 7f.
Azrael continued his good run of form this year down at this trip for the first time but if anything he left the impression he just found it slightly on the sharp side. He looks well handicapped now and will be interesting back at 7f. (op 20-1)
Tajneed(IRE) is another on a decent mark after a recent defeat in a claimer and showed he's on the back number with a decent effort always thereabouts. He's worth looking out for if running at Ripon soon and the ground is still on the soft side. (op 11-1)
Baby Strange ◆ ran really well considering he needs a much stronger pace than he had in his group and was poorly placed at halfway. He looks ready to strike when things fall more in his favour. (op 12-1)
Thunderball was always close to the head of the far-side runners and had more chance than most in that group to show his form.
L'Ami Louis(IRE) ◆ showed plenty of pace under the stand rail and this first run since last July will have blown away the cobwebs. Still lightly raced and in very good hands, his best form has come on faster ground and he left the impression he has a decent sprint in him this year. (tchd 10-1)
Pearl Ice started favourite on her first run since leaving Sir Mark Prescott but probably shouldn't be judged on this as she didn't seem to handle the softish ground. (op 4-1)
Misplaced Fortune ran better than the result suggests in the far-side group, getting too far behind in a race not run at a strong enough gallop and not given a hard time.
Marine Commando Official explanation: jockey said gelding missed the break

1845 FIRSTSECURITY.CO.UK CONDITIONS STKS 7f
8:00 (8:00) (Class 3) 3-Y-O **£8,092** (£2,423; £1,211; £605) **Stalls** High

Form RPR
1 **1** **Sentaril**[15] 1501 3-8-10 0 ow1 JohnnyMurtagh 5 108+
(William Haggas) *t.k.h: trckd ldng pair: hdwy to ld wl over 1f out: sn pushed clr: easily* **1/5**[1]
230- **2** 5 **Silverheels (IRE)**[186] 7220 3-8-12 103 HayleyTurner 3 95
(Paul Cole) *hld up in rr: hdwy over 2f out: rdn to chse wnr over 1f out: sn no imp* **6/1**[2]
62-0 **3** 13 **Semayyel (IRE)**[28] 1215 3-8-9 97 BrettDoyle 4 57+
(Clive Brittain) *led 2f: cl up: rdn along over 2f out: outpcd fr wl over 1f out* **20/1**[3]
64-6 **4** 3 ½ **Red Seventy**[28] 1216 3-8-13 95 SeanLevey(3) 2 54
(Richard Hannon) *cl up: led after 2f: rdn along over 2f out: hdd wl over 1f out: wknd qckly and heavily eased* **20/1**[3]

1m 27.22s (0.92) **Going Correction** +0.15s/f (Good) **4** Ran SP% **107.1**
Speed ratings (Par 103): **100,94,79,75**
CSF £1.77 TOTE £1.20; EX 1.40.
Owner Lael Stable **Bred** Lael Stables **Trained** Newmarket, Suffolk

FOCUS
Only four runners but an intriguing minor event nonetheless and a bloodless victory for a filly who has probably shown a useful level of form here and still looks set for much better things. The pace wasn't strong.

NOTEBOOK
Sentaril could hardly have been more impressive at Newbury and, though she wasn't quite so dazzling here, she didn't need to be despite still achieving much more from a form perspective in what developed into something of a tactical affair. Still a bit keen early, she put the race to bed quickly once give the office and proved much too good for the useful Silverheels. She's not short of speed and given her pedigree might not be quite so effective at 1m, so something like the Listed Eternal Stakes at Warwick next month would prove right up her street, but her connections are probably right to have aspirations higher than that, with the Jersey Stakes being considered. (op 1-4)
Silverheels(IRE) loomed up looking threatening with 2f to run but she was quickly put in her place by the winner. She was on the fringe of Pattern company last year and this run suggests she might continue to come up short at that level. (tchd 11-2)
Semayyel(IRE), who has form on ground this soft, was quickly brushed aside inside the 2f marker but despite being eased still got back up for third. (op 12-1)
Red Seventy looked to go wrong and was eased. Official explanation: jockey said colt hung badly right

1846 ATTHERACES.COM EXCLUSIVE WILLIAM BUICK BLOG H'CAP 1m 6f 132y
8:30 (8:30) (Class 4) (0-85,84) 4-Y-0+ **£5,175** (£1,540; £769; £384) **Stalls** Low

Form RPR
023- **1** **Royal Swain (IRE)**[142] 7772 6-9-1 75 RobertWinston 4 82
(Alan Swinbank) *in tch: hdwy 4f out: rdn to chse ldr 2f out: drvn to chal over 1f out: styd on to ld ins fnl f* **10/1**
23-0 **2** 1 **Odin's Raven (IRE)**[25] 1275 7-8-11 74 PaulPickard(3) 3 80
(Brian Ellison) *hld up in rr: hdwy 3f out: rdn to chse ldrs 2f out: drvn and kpt on ins fnl f: nrst fin* **12/1**

2-43 **3** *nk* **Sohcahtoa (IRE)**[8] 1640 6-8-7 **72** .... LMcNiff(5) 12 78
(David Barron) *trckd ldng pair: smooth hdwy to ld 3f out: rdn 2f out: drvn and edgd lft ent fnl f: sn hdd and kpt on same pce* **9/2**[2]

04-1 **4** *2 ½* **Golden Future**[24] 1297 9-8-2 **69** .... FrancescaWoliter(7) 6 71
(Peter Niven) *hld up in tch: hdwy over 3f out: rdn 2f out and sn no imp* **16/1**

264- **5** *4* **Jivry**[237] 5963 5-9-7 **81** .... GrahamLee 8 78
(Anthony Honeyball) *hld up towards rr: hdwy over 3f out: rdn along over 2f out: plugged on same pce:* **7/2**[1]

004/ **6** *4 ½* **General Ting (IRE)**[55] 6822 7-8-9 **69** ....(t) EddieAhern 11 60
(Lucy Wadham) *in tch on outer: rdn along over 3f out: sn drvn and wknd* **10/1**

1112 **7** *½* **Overrule (USA)**[9] 1632 8-9-2 **76** .... MichaelStainton 5 67
(Jason Ward) *dwlt and in rr: sme hdwy fr over 2f out: nvr a factor* **33/1**

3-22 **8** *¾* **Pittodrie Star (IRE)**[19] 1421 5-9-7 **81** .... DanielTudhope 9 71
(David O'Meara) *trckd ldrs: hdwy over 4f out: rdn along 3f out: sn wknd* **6/1**[3]

00-5 **9** *½* **Sherman McCoy**[39] 1056 6-9-7 **81** .... JamesMillman 7 70
(Rod Millman) *chsd ldrs: rdn along over 4f out: sn wknd* **16/1**

-353 **10** *7* **Wild Desert (FR)**[19] 1421 7-9-10 **84** .... DaneO'Neill 1 64
(Charlie Longsdon) *trckd ldr: hdwy and cl up 5f out: rdn along 3f out: wknd over 2f out* **14/1**

520- **11** *3 ¼* **Royal Trooper (IRE)**[197] 6988 6-9-8 **82** .... PaulMulrennan 10 58
(James Given) *hld up: a towards rr* **9/1**

130- **12** *nk* **Wells Lyrical (IRE)**[301] 3851 7-9-6 **80** .... TomEaves 2 55
(Bryan Smart) *led: rdn along 4f out: hdd 3f out: sn wknd* **16/1**

3m 12.53s (5.13) **Going Correction** +0.30s/f (Good) **12** Ran SP% **117.8**
Speed ratings (Par 105): **98,97,97,95,93 91,91,90,90,86 85,84**
CSF £123.54 CT £620.82 TOTE £14.00: £3.10, £2.50, £1.80; EX 97.40 Trifecta £216.40 Pool: £438.79 - 1.50 winning units..
Owner Andrew Sparks **Bred** Patrick Cummins **Trained** Melsonby, N Yorks

FOCUS
An open handicap in which the pace was fair initially but picked up far enough out for it to be a reasonable test at the trip. The form is ordinary, with the first three helping to set the level.
Overrule(USA) Official explanation: jockey said gelding reared coming out of stalls
T/Plt: £116.10 to a £1 stake. Pool: £85,784.31 - 538.99 winning tickets. T/Qpdt: £51.40 to a £1 stake. Pool: £6,38.79 - 86.82 winning tickets. JR

GOODWOOD (R-H)

Saturday, May 5

OFFICIAL GOING: Soft (6.3)
First 2f of mile course dolled out 15yds.
Wind: Moderate, across (towards stands) Weather: Overcast, cold

1847 BETFRED GOALS GALORE EBF MAIDEN STKS 5f
1:40 (1:40) (Class 5) 2-Y-O **£3,557** (£1,058; £529; £264) **Stalls** High

Form RPR

1 **Mrs Brown's Boy** 2-8-10 0 .... DarrenEgan(7) 2 80+
(Ronald Harris) *dwlt and swvd rt s: steadily rcvrd on outer: prog to go 2nd 2f out: pushed into ld jst ins fnl f: styd on wl* **14/1**

0 **2** *3* **Fletcher Christian**[19] 1411 2-9-3 0 .... NeilCallan 3 69
(John Gallagher) *led against nr side rail: shkn up over 1f out: hdd and one pce jst ins fnl f* **11/2**[3]

3 *8* **Strong Conviction** 2-9-3 0 .... ChrisCatlin 4 40+
(Mick Channon) *dwlt and sltly squeezed s: sn pushed along in last: wl bhd over 1f out: kpt on late to take modest 3rd nr fin* **11/4**[2]

4 *hd* **Jimmy Elder** 2-9-3 0 .... PatDobbs 1 40
(Richard Hannon) *mostly chsd ldng pair: rdn and steadily wknd over 1f out: lost modest 3rd nr fin* **2/1**[1]

0 **5** *6* **Hats Off**[28] 1211 2-9-3 0 .... LukeMorris 5 18
(John Best) *pressed ldr: rdn to chal 1/2-way: lost 2nd and wknd qckly 2f out* **11/4**[2]

1m 3.45s (3.25) **Going Correction** +0.75s/f (Yiel) **5** Ran SP% **108.7**
Speed ratings (Par 93): **89,84,71,71,61**
CSF £78.97 TOTE £11.20: £2.70, £3.20; EX 61.30.
Owner Anisska Racing Limited **Bred** Peter Winkworth **Trained** Earlswood, Monmouths

FOCUS
Probably just a modest contest, run in bad ground, but the winner was quite impressive.

NOTEBOOK
Mrs Brown's Boy, a £5,000 half-brother to 7f winner Loving Thought, caught the eye before the off considering his size but looked to have blown his chance when veering right leaving the stalls. However, under another good ride by Darren Egan, who didn't panic, the horse showed plenty of speed when in touch and won convincingly. It could be that he handled the ground much better than his rivals, but there's no doubting he should come on for this and should be respected in better company. (op 12-1)
Fletcher Christian, who beat only one rival at Windsor last month, showed good speed to get across to the stands' rail and was a clear second. His dam has produced winners already, and there's every chance he'll enhance her record. (op 6-1)
Strong Conviction, a half-brother to Rileyskeepingfaith, who did well for this trainer, seemed certain to finish last at halfway, but kept on to pass a couple of rivals in the final furlong, albeit one that was being eased. (op 10-3)
Jimmy Elder only reached his second birthday recently so can be expected to improve mentally for this, which he will need to if making any impact next time. (op 13-8 tchd 9-4 in a place)
Hats Off doesn't look like winning any time soon, although he may not have liked underfoot conditions. (op 3-1 tchd 5-2)

1848 BETFRED THE BONUS KING EBF DAISY WARWICK STKS (LISTED RACE) (F&M) 1m 4f
2:15 (2:26) (Class 1) 4-Y-O+ **£20,720** (£7,836; £3,916; £1,956) **Stalls** High

Form RPR

220- **1** **Vita Nova (IRE)**[203] 6859 5-8-12 115 .... IanMongan 5 109
(Sir Henry Cecil) *hld up in midfield: shkn up over 3f out: chsd ldr over 2f out: rdn and styd on to ld ins fnl f: grad asserted* **4/9**[1]

055- **2** *1 ¾* **Shimmering Surf (IRE)**[252] 5493 5-8-12 94 .... NeilCallan 8 106
(Roger Varian) *mostly trckd ldr: led 4f out against nr side rail: drvn over 1f out: hdd ins fnl f: styd on* **16/1**

420- **3** *8* **Creme Anglaise**[231] 6172 4-8-12 91 .... StevieDonohoe 7 93
(Michael Bell) *hld up in last pair: prog 3f out: chsd ldng pair 2f out: steadily lft bhd after* **33/1**

54-6 **4** *2 ¾* **Twin Soul (IRE)**[21] 1374 4-8-12 93 .... DavidProbert 1 88
(Andrew Balding) *hld up in tch: rdn and effrt over 3f out: no imp 2f out: steadily fdd* **20/1**

03-6 **5** *nk* **Bolivia (GER)**[7] 1654 6-8-12 86 .... PatDobbs 9 88
(Lucy Wadham) *prom: rdn and cl up disputing 2nd wl over 2f out: wknd over 1f out* **40/1**

553- **6** *6* **Western Pearl**[158] 7580 5-8-12 100 .... AdamKirby 4 78
(William Knight) *in tch: rdn and effrt over 3f out: no prog over 2f out: sn wknd* **10/1**[3]

210- **7** *50* **Qushchi**[191] 7129 4-8-12 96 .... DarryllHolland 3
(William Jarvis) *led: rdn and hdd 4f out: wknd rapidly over 2f out: virtually p.u fnl f* **14/1**

430- **8** *28* **Polygon (USA)**[241] 5839 4-8-12 102 .... NickyMackay 2
(John Gosden) *prom: rdn 5f out: wknd rapidly over 3f out: t.o and virtually p.u fnl 2f* **10/1**[3]

040- **9** *3 ½* **Tameen**[158] 7580 4-8-12 100 .... LukeMorris 6
(Ed Dunlop) *hld up in last pair: plld way through to go 2nd after 4f: sn hanging and jockey looking down: styd handy tl wknd rapidly over 3f out: virtually p.u: bit slipped through* **7/1**[2]

2m 50.46s (12.06) **Going Correction** +0.875s/f (Soft) **9** Ran SP% **122.6**
Speed ratings (Par 111): **94,92,87,85,85 81,48,29,27**
toteswingers:1&2:£2.50, 1&3:£7.10, 2&3:£13.80 CSF £10.97 TOTE £1.40: £1.10, £3.50, £7.30; EX 12.90 Trifecta £238.40 Pool £1,282.46 - 3.98 winning unit..
Owner H E Sheikh Sultan Bin Khalifa Al Nahyan **Bred** Paget Bloodstock **Trained** Newmarket, Suffolk

■ Stewards' Enquiry : Stevie Donohoe two-day ban: careless riding (May 20-21)

FOCUS
One of these stuck out on official figures and was heavily backed to make a successful seasonal debut. The start was delayed for over ten minutes while the favourite was reshod. She was 10lb off her best, with the second back to her 3yo best.

NOTEBOOK
Vita Nova(IRE) finished runner-up three times in good company last year, notably in the Lancashire Oaks at Haydock (saddle slipped, appeared unlucky) and the Yorkshire equivalent, where she was beaten by Guineas/Irish Oaks winner Blue Bunting. This looked an ideal opportunity to kick off her season with a success, but she made really hard work of getting the better of a horse rated 94. She is capable of much better, and will need to up her game when raised to Group level again. (op 1-2 tchd 2-5)
Shimmering Surf(IRE), formerly trained by Peter Winkworth, who still owns her, had run well over a range of trips during her career and put up what must have been close to, if not, a career-best effort here on ground she wasn't proven in. (op 14-1)
Creme Anglaise needed to find improvement from the previous year to get involved here, and although she was third, gaining some valuable black type, she didn't really pose a serious threat from the 1f marker. The interference she suffered about 3f from home probably made little difference to her placing.
Qushchi Official explanation: trainer said filly was unsuited by the soft ground
Polygon(USA) was disappointing on soft ground at Saint-Cloud on her final start of last season and again here, so presumably she doesn't act in that ground considering this performance. Official explanation: trainer said filly was unsuited by the soft ground (tchd 9-1)
Tameen looked useful on a couple of occasions during 2011 when easily winning a C&D handicap and finishing second in a Listed contest at Doncaster. She'd been sold out of John Dunlop's yard since her final outing but pulled her way towards the head of affairs after being held up, then went wide of her rivals when there before finding little once in the straight. Official explanation: jockey said bit slipped through filly's mouth (op 8-1)

1849 BETFRED THE BONUS KING BINGO STKS (H'CAP) 5f
2:50 (2:53) (Class 3) (0-95,93) 4-Y-O+ **£9,703** (£2,887; £1,443; £721) **Stalls** High

Form RPR

00-3 **1** **Lui Rei (ITY)**[15] 1498 6-9-6 **92** .... AdamKirby 5 101
(Robert Cowell) *trckd ldrs: plld out and effrt 2f out: led over 1f out: drvn and styd on wl* **7/2**[2]

054- **2** *1 ½* **Judge 'n Jury**[196] 7018 8-8-8 **87** ....(t) DarrenEgan(7) 4 91
(Ronald Harris) *mde most: jnd 2f out: hanging rt after: hdd over 1f out: kpt on* **9/2**[3]

001- **3** *shd* **Steps (IRE)**[196] 7018 4-9-6 **92** .... NeilCallan 3 95
(Roger Varian) *pressed ldr: upsides fr 2f out: leaned into whn trying to chse wnr fnl f: lost 2nd post* **10/3**[1]

0-30 **4** *½* **Tagula Night (IRE)**[17] 1438 6-9-2 **88** ....(b[1]) TedDurcan 2 89
(Dean Ivory) *hld up bhd ldrs: effrt 2f out: kpt on fr over 1f out: nvr quite gng pce to chal* **7/1**

000- **5** *3 ¼* **Rowe Park**[217] 6522 9-9-2 **88** .... IanMongan 7 78
(Linda Jewell) *dwlt: mostly in last: plld out wd 2f out: no real prog* **25/1**

5013 **6** *nk* **Sugar Beet**[15] 1494 4-9-7 **93** .... LukeMorris 6 82
(Ronald Harris) *racd alone against nr side rail: nvr quite on terms w ldrs: rdn 1/2-way: fdd over 1f out* **11/2**

/5-0 **7** *1* **Desert Phantom (USA)**[10] 1602 6-9-3 **89** .... MartinLane 1 74
(David Simcock) *chsd ldrs: rdn bef 1/2-way: wknd over 1f out* **9/2**[3]

1m 1.16s (0.96) **Going Correction** +0.75s/f (Yiel) **7** Ran SP% **113.4**
Speed ratings (Par 107): **107,104,104,103,98 97,96**
toteswingers:1&2:£2.60, 1&3:£4.60, 2&3:£3.00 CSF £19.19 CT £55.50 TOTE £4.60: £2.20, £2.90; EX 12.30.
Owner Rei Of Sunshine Partnership **Bred** Az Ag Antezzate Srl **Trained** Six Mile Bottom, Cambs

FOCUS
This was a strange race in some respects because the leading pair took a bit of a hold but still had enough in the locker to finish in the places. The form is straightforward enough.

NOTEBOOK
Lui Rei(ITY) ran well from out of the weights at Newbury on his comeback especially after being left at the start, and came on for that to take this nicely. He has an entry in the Epsom Dash, so one would imagine he'll head there considering he showed he can handle the track last year. (tchd 3-1)
Judge 'n Jury has only won twice from plenty of attempts since October 2008, but started his season off with another sound effort. His consistency affords him no respite from the handicapper. (tchd 5-1)
Steps(IRE), who was in front of Judge 'n Jury when they both last ran, helped to share the lead and kept on in fair style, while the runner-up leaned on to him, once asked to lengthen. (op 4-1)
Tagula Night(IRE) had gained all of his wins in headgear but new connections hadn't tried them until fitting blinkers (first time) in this. A two time 6f winner at the course, he couldn't quite get on terms, looking in need of that extra distance. (op 13-2 tchd 15-2)
Rowe Park had run plenty of decent races here since 2007, including in Group company, but never played a part. (tchd 28-1)
Sugar Beet, who'd won on her only previous start over C&D, came into this in great heart, but her handicap mark had gone up accordingly and she only found the one pace under pressure. (op 9-2)

Desert Phantom(USA), fifth in this last year off an official mark of 92, was fairly handicapped on his best efforts but made no show in this. (op 11-2 tchd 6-1)

1850 BETFRED MOBILE SPORTS STKS (H'CAP) 1m 6f

3:30 (3:30) (Class 2) (0-105,96) 4-Y-0+ **£16,172** (£4,812; £2,405; £1,202) **Stalls** High

Form RPR

-051 **1** **Lifetime (IRE)**[21] 1382 4-7-7 **73**.................................... DarrenEgan(7) 1 81
(Brian Ellison) *t.k.h: hld up in 4th: lost pl 6f out: last and rdn over 4f out: rallied against rail 2f out: squeezed through to ld jst ins fnl f: drvn and kpt on wl* **3/1**[1]

331- **2** ½ **Spice Fair**[191] 7120 5-8-13 **85**.................................... NeilCallan 7 92
(Mark Usher) *hld up in last pair: prog over 4f out: trckd ldrs gng strly but nowhere to go fr over 2f out and swtchd more than once: got through jst over 1f out: drvn to join wnr 100yds out: nt qckn* **11/2**[3]

056- **3** 2 ¾ **Very Good Day (FR)**[273] 4806 5-8-13 **85**.................................... ChrisCatlin 8 88
(Mick Channon) *hld up in last: prog over 3f out to press ldr over 2f out: led over 1f out: hdd and no ex jst ins fnl f* **6/1**

2-02 **4** 3 ¾ **Taikoo**[25] 1282 7-8-13 **85**.................................... DarryllHolland 6 83
(Hughie Morrison) *led at brisk pce: 10 l clr 1/2-way: c bk to rivals over 4f out: drvn and hdd over 1f out: wknd* **9/2**[2]

330- **5** ¾ **Woolfall Treasure**[70] 7226 7-9-10 **96**....................(v) GeorgeBaker 3 93
(Gary Moore) *prom in chsng gp: lost pl 6f out: pushed along 4f out: prog on outer over 2f out: tried to chal over 1f out: nt qckn then wknd fnl f* **14/1**

/21- **6** 10 **No Heretic**[348] 2360 4-8-10 **83**.................................... MartinLane 4 66
(David Simcock) *sn restrained bhd ldrs: effrt gng strly over 3f out but lost pl: wknd over 2f out* **6/1**

224- **7** 12 **Four Nations (USA)**[237] 5966 4-8-7 **80**.................................... LukeMorris 2 46
(Amanda Perrett) *mostly chsd clr ldr to over 2f out: wknd rapidly* **9/2**[2]

3m 16.48s (12.88) **Going Correction** +0.875s/f (Soft)
WFA 4 from 5yo+ 1lb **7 Ran SP% 112.0**
Speed ratings (Par 109): **98,97,96,94,93 87,81**
toteswingers:1&2:£1.30, 1&3:£5.30, 2&3:£1.50 CSF £18.84 CT £90.33 TOTE £4.10: £2.10, £3.00; EX 20.40 Trifecta £62.90 Pool £636.93 - 7.49 winning unit..
Owner Koo's Racing Club **Bred** Lynn Lodge Stud And Foxtale Farm **Trained** Norton, N Yorks
■ Stewards' Enquiry : Darren Egan four-day ban: used whip above permittedlevel (May 20-23)

FOCUS
A useful contest run at a decent pace for the conditions. The winner got first run on the second but the form is taken at face value.

NOTEBOOK
Lifetime(IRE) caught the eye off a low weight up in trip on the Flat, and got a dream run up the rail in the final stages to grind out success. One would imagine connections will want to get the horse out as quickly as possible, because the handicapper is sure to sent him up the weights for this. (op 4-1)
Spice Fair, who made a winning reappearance here last term, found his final effort hindered by getting stuck in a pocket when his jockey was looking to get out. However, all things considered, he was in the clear early enough and probably the weight concession to Lifetime was more to blame for defeat. (tchd 5-1)
Very Good Day(FR) is fairly treated if getting his career back on track and didn't shape too badly after holding every chance. (op 7-1)
Taikoo had a clear advantage at around halfway, and looked sure to be difficult to reel back in, but his lead was eroded quickly heading to the 3f, and he didn't find an extra gear. (op 4-1)
Woolfall Treasure looked seriously one-paced in the latter stages, but is still not below his highest-winning mark. He also wants quicker ground. (op 12-1)
No Heretic ◆, off for almost a year, showed progressive form in maidens for Paul Cole before a victory at Leicester last May over 1m4f - he was dismounted after the line there, and the jockey reported that the colt had banged himself. Up in trip on his debut for David Simcock, he pulled hard early and didn't have much left at the end, but the horse is built like a tank and will surely have more to come. (op 9-2)
Four Nations(USA) looked of obvious interest due to his previous form at the course but was a major disappointment for no obvious reason. (op 5-1)

1851 MOBILE CASINO BRITISH STALLION STUDS EBF CONQUEROR STKS (LISTED RACE) (F&M) 1m

4:05 (4:05) (Class 1) 3-Y-0+

£19,848 (£7,525; £3,766; £1,876; £941; £472) **Stalls** Low

Form RPR

/20- **1** **Boastful (IRE)**[159] 4-9-7 87.................................... NeilCallan 1 104
(Mrs K Burke) *plld hrd early: trckd ldng pair: moved up smoothly over 2f out: led over 1f out: hung rt and rdn fnl f: a in command* **20/1**

333- **2** 1 ½ **Winter's Night (IRE)**[288] 4265 4-9-7 98.................................... AdamKirby 2 101
(Clive Cox) *hld up in 5th: rdn on outer over 2f out: styd on to take 2nd fnl f: unable to chal* **7/2**[3]

51-4 **3** 1 ½ **Raasekha**[28] 1213 4-9-7 94.................................... TadhgO'Shea 5 98
(Charles Hills) *led: rdn and hdd over 1f out: kpt on one pce after* **16/1**

554- **4** nse **Barefoot Lady (IRE)**[245] 5745 4-9-7 108.................................... TonyHamilton 7 97
(Richard Fahey) *trckd ldr: rdn to ld against nr side rail over 2f out: hdd and one pce over 1f out* **7/4**[1]

21-1 **5** ¾ **Neutrafa (IRE)**[24] 1321 4-9-7 93.................................... GeorgeBaker 3 96
(John Mackie) *hld up in last: sme prog over 2f out: cl enough over 1f out: hanging and nt qckn after* **9/4**[2]

3-31 **6** 5 **Esentepe (IRE)**[17] 1454 3-8-13 100.................................... PatDobbs 4 89
(Richard Hannon) *trckd ldrs in 4th: rdn over 2f out: wknd over 1f out* **7/1**

1m 45.49s (5.59) **Going Correction** +0.875s/f (Soft)
WFA 3 from 4yo+ 13lb **6 Ran SP% 112.5**
Speed ratings (Par 111): **107,105,104,103,103 98**
toteswingers:1&2:£4.60, 1&3:£17.30, 2&3:£6.40 CSF £87.61 TOTE £22.90: £4.80, £2.30; EX 202.80.
Owner Mrs Louise Quinn **Bred** Kevin Quinn **Trained** Middleham Moor, N Yorks

FOCUS
An interesting contest but the winner was difficult to find before the off. Muddling fillies' Listed form, with a clear personal best from the winner.

NOTEBOOK
Boastful(IRE) ◆, a half-sister to Lesson In Humility, who did so well for this stable in the past, had joined these connections for 40,000gns in February and seemed a most unlikely winner of this considering she was noticeably keen for much of the early parts. However, she still found plenty when required and took this nicely. Most of her recent form in France had come between 4f 110yds and 6f, but she saw the 1m out okay and is an interesting sort. (op 16-1)
Winter's Night(IRE), who'd taken a 6f event on her only previous start at the track, won first time up in 2011 but never quite looked like repeating the feat this year after needing to be pushed along heading into the home straight. (op 6-1)
Raasekha, who has a couple of Group 2 entries, shaped well in a Listed contest at Kempton last time and was unexposed, but she was soundly held after holding the lead. (op 12-1)
Barefoot Lady(IRE) raced exclusively in Pattern company last season, winning the Nell Gwyn at Newmarket on reappearance and generally acquitting herself well afterwards, including in the 1,000 Guineas, Musidora and Coronation Stakes at Royal Ascot. Things looked promising as she came into contention up the stands' rail, but she didn't find a great deal and ran miles below what she was capable of on better ground. (op 11-8)
Neutrafa(IRE) made a winning comeback in a handicap at Nottingham, scoring with plenty to spare, so rightfully took her chance at this level. She closed up to look dangerous but couldn't sustain her run. (op 3-1)
Esentepe(IRE), who took the Nell Gwyn this year, appeared vulnerable under a penalty against her elders, and that proved to be the case. It was still a moderate effort compared to the balance of her form. (op 5-1)

1852 BETFRED.COM MEDIAN AUCTION MAIDEN STKS 7f

4:40 (4:41) (Class 5) 3-Y-0 **£3,234** (£962; £481; £240) **Stalls** Low

Form RPR

224- **1** **Balady (IRE)**[189] 7164 3-8-12 79.................................... TadhgO'Shea 4 78
(John Dunlop) *mde all: 3 l clr 1/2-way: shkn up and stl clr over 1f out: rdn out fnl f: nvr seriously threatened* **3/1**[2]

0- **2** 1 ¼ **Sir Mike**[252] 5479 3-9-3 0.................................... AdamKirby 3 80
(Amanda Perrett) *in tch: rdn 3f out: responded to press and styd on to take 2nd 1f out: nvr really able to threaten wnr* **10/1**

3 3 ½ **Unex Annigoni (IRE)** 3-9-3 0.................................... NickyMackay 8 71
(John Gosden) *racd wd early: wl in tch: chsd wnr 3f out: no imp and lost 2nd 1f out: pushed along and one pce* **6/1**

4 **4** 6 **Anya**[16] 1472 3-8-12 0.................................... J-PGuillambert 2 50
(Ed Walker) *rrd s: pushed along in last after 2f: bhd over 2f out: kpt on fr over 1f out* **9/2**[3]

00- **5** 1 ½ **Coup De Grace (IRE)**[220] 6455 3-9-3 0.................................... DarryllHolland 5 51
(Amanda Perrett) *mostly chsd wnr to 3f out: steadily wknd* **20/1**

25-5 **6** 4 ½ **Poole Harbour (IRE)**[17] 1450 3-9-3 83.................................... PatDobbs 7 40
(Richard Hannon) *hld up in last pair: effrt over 2f out: sn rdn and no imp: wknd over 1f out* **5/2**[1]

3 **7** 21 **Charles Tyrwhitt**[26] 1256 3-9-3 0.................................... TedDurcan 1
(George Baker) *in tch: rdn 3f out: sn wknd: t.o* **7/1**

1m 32.45s (5.45) **Going Correction** +0.875s/f (Soft) **7 Ran SP% 112.4**
Speed ratings (Par 99): **103,101,97,90,89 83,59**
toteswingers:1&2:£4.30, 1&3:£4.80, 2&3:£42.60 CSF £30.82 TOTE £3.80: £1.60, £4.30; EX 31.90.
Owner Hamdan Al Maktoum **Bred** Shadwell Estate Company Limited **Trained** Arundel, W Sussex

FOCUS
Quite an open-looking maiden, but ordinary form. The winner was the form pick and is rated close to form.
Charles Tyrwhitt Official explanation: trainer's rep said colt was unsuited by the soft ground

1853 COLLECT TOTEPOOL BETS AT BETFRED SHOPS STKS (H'CAP) 1m 1f 192y

5:15 (5:16) (Class 5) (0-70,70) 3-Y-0 **£3,234** (£962; £481; £240) **Stalls** Low

Form RPR

1551 **1** **Whipcrackaway (IRE)**[24] 1319 3-9-4 **67**.................................... NeilCallan 6 82
(Peter Hedger) *hld up in midfield disputing 8th: prog over 2f out: sn rdn: wnt 2nd jst over 1f out: drvn to ld last 150yds: forged clr* **9/2**[1]

06-2 **2** 3 ¾ **Nicholascopernicus (IRE)**[24] 1319 3-9-3 **66**............ J-PGuillambert 13 73
(Ed Walker) *sn prom: led over 3f out: kpt on wl whn pressed: hdd and outpcd last 150yds* **5/1**[2]

0-42 **3** 6 **Play Street**[79] 573 3-9-0 **63**.................................... NickyMackay 11 58
(Jonathan Portman) *hld up in midfield disputing 6th: effrt 3f out: rdn over 2f out: kpt on fr over 1f out to snatch 3rd last stride* **25/1**

52-5 **4** nse **Joyful Spirit (IRE)**[24] 1320 3-8-12 **61**.................................... TedDurcan 5 56+
(John Dunlop) *hld up in midfield disputing 6th: smooth prog fr 3f out: pressed ldr wl over 1f out: lost 2nd jst over 1f out: wknd fnl f: lost 3rd last stride* **6/1**[3]

350- **5** 3 ¼ **Byron Blue (IRE)**[206] 6807 3-9-5 **68**.................................... GeorgeBaker 7 56
(Jamie Osborne) *dwlt: hld up in last: wl bhd 1/2-way: jst pushed along and styd on steadily fnl 3f: nrst fin* **6/1**[3]

3-61 **6** ¾ **Ermyn Flyer**[9] 1625 3-8-6 **60**.................................... JemmaMarshall(5) 4 47
(Pat Phelan) *prom: pressed ldr 3f out to wl over 1f out: sn wknd* **9/1**

6106 **7** 3 **Captain Cardington (IRE)**[24] 1320 3-9-2 **65**..................(v) ChrisCatlin 9 46
(Mick Channon) *wl in rr: detached in last trio over 4f out: sme prog u.p fr 3f out: no ch* **20/1**

00-6 **8** 8 **Wreaths Of Empire (IRE)**[14] 1506 3-9-5 **68**.................... PatDobbs 14 33
(Richard Hannon) *hld up in midfield disputing 8th: rdn wl over 2f out and no prog: wknd over 1f out* **9/1**

025- **9** 1 ½ **Dont Take Me Alive**[222] 6399 3-9-6 **69**.................................... AdamKirby 12 31
(Clive Cox) *towards rr: rdn sn after 1/2-way: sme prog u.p to take 6th over 1f out but no ch: wknd fnl f* **16/1**

00-4 **10** 19 **Madame St Clair (IRE)**[16] 1486 3-9-2 **65**..................(b[1]) TadhgO'Shea 2
(Brian Meehan) *prom: cl enough 3f out: wknd rapidly over 2f out: t.o* **14/1**

64-0 **11** 2 **Renegotiate**[24] 1320 3-9-1 **64**....................................(v) DavidProbert 10
(Andrew Balding) *mostly pressed ldr: led jst over 4f out to over 3f out: sn wknd: t.o* **12/1**

044- **12** 66 **Autarch (USA)**[192] 7109 3-9-7 **70**.................................... DarryllHolland 8
(Amanda Perrett) *sn won battle for ld and set gd pce: hdd jst over 4f out: sn wknd rapidly: wl t.o* **14/1**

405- **13** 24 **Silent Energy (IRE)**[136] 7849 3-8-11 **60**.................................... LukeMorris 3
(Ronald Harris) *nvr gng: sn drvn in rr: wl t.o* **33/1**

2m 17.88s (9.78) **Going Correction** +0.875s/f (Soft) **13 Ran SP% 121.9**
Speed ratings (Par 99): **95,92,87,87,84 83,81,75,73,58 57,4,**
toteswingers:1&2:£2.50, 1&3:£12.20, 2&3:£16.20 CSF £26.25 CT £520.14 TOTE £5.70: £1.80, £2.30, £12.40; EX 15.80.
Owner P R Hedger **Bred** Kilfrush Stud **Trained** Dogmersfield, Hampshire

FOCUS
This is usually an informative 3yo handicap for the grade with a few improvers, but the ground sorted them out. A recent result at Nottingham proved the key here.
Byron Blue(IRE) Official explanation: jockey said colt was denied a clear run
Autarch(USA) Official explanation: trainer said gelding was unsuited by the soft ground
T/Plt: £2,273.60 to a £1 stake. Pool:£69,298.81 - 22.25 winning tickets T/Qpdt: £115.20 to a £1 stake. Pool:£5,935.29 - 38.10 winning tickets JN

[1466] NEWMARKET (R-H)

Saturday, May 5

OFFICIAL GOING: Good to soft (overall 7.1; stands' side 7.0; centre 7.1; far side 7.2)

Stands' side course used. Stalls stands' side except 2000 Guineas centre and 1m4f far side. Rail repositioning increased 1m4f races by 12m.

Wind: fresh, half behind Weather: dry, overcast

1854 MAKFI SUFFOLK STKS (H'CAP) 1m 1f

2:00 (2:00) (Class 2) 3-Y-0+

£27,390 (£8,201; £4,100; £2,050; £1,025; £514) **Stalls** High

Form RPR

202- **1** **Tullius (IRE)**[215] 6574 4-8-12 **92**........ JimmyFortune 4 107
(Andrew Balding) *hld up wl in tch towards rr: hdwy 3f out: rdn and qcknd to ld 2f out: kpt on wl u.p fnl f: rdn out* **12/1**

-631 **2** ¾ **Memory Cloth**[7] 1670 5-8-10 **90**........ BarryMcHugh 7 103
(Brian Ellison) *hld up wl in tch: effrt 3f out: rdn and effrt to chse wnr over 1f out: pressed wnr thrght fnl f: kpt on wl but a hld* **6/1**[2]

0-32 **3** 5 **Fury**[14] 1510 4-9-10 **104**........ KierenFallon 8 106
(William Haggas) *dwlt: sn in tch in midfield: pushed along and effrt wl over 2f out: hdwy to chse ldng pair ent fnl f: drvn and no imp fnl 150yds* **4/1**[1]

00-0 **4** 3 ¾ **Fattsota**[35] 1139 4-8-11 **91**........ MircoDemuro 13 85
(Marco Botti) *t.k.h: pressed ldr tl led after 1f: hdd and rdn over 2f out: no ex wl over 1f out: 5th and wl hld 1f out: plugged on* **16/1**

20-3 **5** ¾ **Graphic (IRE)**[8] 1645 3-8-2 **96**........ KieranO'Neill 6 86+
(Richard Hannon) *chsd ldrs: rdn to ld over 2f out: sn hdd and nt gng pce of wnr wl over 1f out: 4th and btn ent fnl f: plugged on* **20/1**

460- **6** nk **Pleasant Day (IRE)**[203] 6862 5-8-7 **87**........ PaulHanagan 2 78
(Richard Fahey) *hld up wl in tch towards rr: rdn and effrt wl over 1f out: hdwy 2f out: 6th and no imp over 1f out: wknd fnl f* **16/1**

023- **7** 3 **Proponent (IRE)**[224] 6339 8-9-9 **103**........ JamesDoyle 1 88
(Roger Charlton) *in tch in midfield: rdn and effrt 3f out: unable qck and outpcd over 2f out: plugged on but no threat to ldrs fnl 2f* **14/1**

125- **8** nk **Danadana (IRE)**[324] 3069 4-8-6 **86**........ HayleyTurner 9 70
(Luca Cumani) *t.k.h: chsd ldrs: hdwy and ev ch 3f out: sn rdn and unable qck: wknd over 1f out* **8/1**

006- **9** ½ **Spanish Duke (IRE)**[250] 5544 5-9-6 **100**........ RyanMoore 11 83
(John Dunlop) *stdd s: t.k.h: hld up wl in tch in rr: rdn and no hdwy wl over 2f out: wl btn fnl 2f* **10/1**

21-0 **10** ½ **Dick Doughtywylie**[10] 1605 4-8-9 **89**........ WilliamBuick 14 71
(John Gosden) *led for 1f: styd pressing ldrs: ev ch and rdn 3f out: wknd wl over 1f out* **12/1**

2050 **11** 3 ¾ **Licence To Till (USA)**[25] 1273 5-8-4 **84**........ JoeFanning 15 58
(Mark Johnston) *in tch: rdn and unable qck ent fnl 3f: sn struggling and wknd 2f out: bhd fnl f* **20/1**

6-60 **12** 3 **Askaud (IRE)**[10] 1605 4-9-1 **95**........(p) TomQueally 16 62
(Scott Dixon) *hld up in tch towards rr: rdn and unable qck over 2f out: wkng and bhd whn sltly hmpd wl over 1f out* **33/1**

5530 **13** 9 **Mia's Boy**[35] 1130 8-9-3 **97**........ AndreaAtzeni 12 44
(Chris Dwyer) *hld up in tch towards rr: rdn and short-lived effrt wl over 2f out: sn btn: bhd and eased ins fnl f* **33/1**

20-3 **14** 2 ½ **Circumvent**[42] 1034 5-9-6 **100**........ ChristopheSoumillon 3 42
(Paul Cole) *chsd ldrs: rdn and struggling ent fnl 3f: wknd over 2f out: bhd and eased fnl f: t.o* **7/1**[3]

22-0 **15** ¾ **Las Verglas Star (IRE)**[25] 1273 4-8-8 **88**........ PatrickMathers 10 28
(Richard Fahey) *t.k.h: hld up in tch: rdn and unable qck 3f out: wknd 2f out: bhd and eased fnl f: t.o* **33/1**

1m 55.36s (3.66) **Going Correction** +0.65s/f (Yiel)
WFA 3 from 4yo+ 14lb **15** Ran SP% **119.2**
Speed ratings (Par 109): **109,108,103,100,99 99,96,96,96,95 92,89,81,79,78**
toteswingers:1&2:£17.00, 1&3:£12.30, 2&3:£3.90 CSF £75.53 CT £341.39 TOTE £15.30: £4.70, £2.30, £2.10; EX 106.10 Trifecta £503.00 Pool £2,467.41 - 3.63 winning unit..
Owner Kennet Valley Thoroughbreds VI **Bred** Sc Archi Romani **Trained** Kingsclere, Hants

FOCUS

Stands' side course used. Stalls stands' side except 2000 Guineas centre and 1m4f far side. Rail repositioning increased 1m4f races by 12m. There was 33 meters of fresh ground that hadn't been used since last October, but the time of this opener suggested the going was softer than the official description - it was the third slowest of 52 races over this trip since 2005. Conditions were, however, expected to dry out throughout the day. Despite the stalls being on the stands' side, the action unfolded towards the centre of the track. The sectionals showed the pace was even more or less throughout - the second furlong through to the eighth furlong were all run in 12-odd seconds, before the runners tired inside the last. The front two pulled clear of the third, who in turn drew away from the remainder, so pretty solid form, although plenty of these didn't appreciate such soft ground. The winner may not have stopped improving yet.

NOTEBOOK

Tullius(IRE) had only raced ten times for Peter Winkworth and he showed he's still improving on his debut for a new yard after 215 days off. He displayed a good attitude, despite carrying his head high, and it's possible he'll now be saved for the Royal Hunt Cup. Quicker ground doesn't bother him. (tchd 14-1)

Memory Cloth was up 8lb for a convincing win over 16 rivals at Ripon (1m, soft), and he improved again. He had to wait for a run after travelling enthusiastically, but was beaten on merit. Clearly this ground really suits. (op 11-2, tchd 5-1 in places)

Fury is a frustrating horse, and not one to be following, but in fairness he was finishing placed in a big handicap for the third time this season, and was 5lb higher than when a close second in the Spring Cup. He could now for a Listed handicap at York. (op 9-2 tchd 5-1)

Fattsota helped set the even fractions (credit to Mirco Demuro), so it was no surprise he kept on. (tchd 14-1)

Graphic(IRE), the only 3yo in the line-up, went well for a long way before getting tired. There should be more to come, probably back over shorter, and maybe on slightly better ground. (op 25-1)

Proponent(IRE) was off a career-high mark for his reappearance, being fully 13lb higher than when taking this in 2008 (and 8lb higher than when second last year), and he wants better ground. (op 12-1 tchd 16-1)

Danadana(IRE) hadn't been seen for 324 days, so was entitled to need it. (tchd 9-1)

Circumvent, third in the Winter Derby on his previous start, was eased as though something was amiss. (tchd 6-1)

1855 QATAR BLOODSTOCK JOCKEY CLUB STKS (GROUP 2) 1m 4f

2:30 (2:33) (Class 1) 4-Y-0+

£56,710 (£21,500; £10,760; £5,360; £2,690; £1,350) **Stalls** Low

Form RPR

222- **1** **Al Kazeem**[196] 7027 4-8-12 112........ JamesDoyle 1 121
(Roger Charlton) *hld up in last trio: hdwy to chse ldng pair over 4f out: chal and wnt clr w runner-up wl over 1f out: rdn to ld over 1f out: in command whn hung lft ins fnl f: r.o strly* **15/2**

115- **2** 4 ½ **Quest For Peace (IRE)**[202] 6910 4-8-12 114........ KierenFallon 6 114
(Luca Cumani) *led for 1f: t.k.h and chsd ldr after: rdn to ld over 2f out: clr w wnr wl over 1f out: hdd and nt pce of wnr over 1f out: no ch w wnr but hld on for 2nd fnl f* **12/1**

111- **3** 1 ¼ **Dunaden (FR)**[146] 7729 6-9-3 0........ JohnnyMurtagh 2 117
(M Delzangles, France) *t.k.h: hld up in midfield: grad stdd bk and in last trio 1/2-way: rdn and outpcd 3f out: 7th and looked wl btn over 1f out: hdwy ent fnl f: styd on but no ch w wnr* **9/2**[2]

126- **4** 2 ¼ **Meandre (FR)**[216] 6567 4-8-12 122........ MaximeGuyon 7 108
(A Fabre, France) *t.k.h: chsd ldrs: rdn 3f out: sn outpcd and no threat to ldrs over 1f out: styd on ins fnl f* **11/8**[1]

06-4 **5** 1 ½ **Blue Bajan (IRE)**[24] 1318 10-8-12 109........ DanielTudhope 3 106
(David O'Meara) *stdd s: hld up in rr: rdn and effrt 3f out: drvn and styd on same pce fr over 1f out: nvr trbld ldrs* **25/1**

122- **6** 1 ½ **Fiorente (IRE)**[284] 4411 4-8-12 108........ RyanMoore 4 104
(Sir Michael Stoute) *hld in last trio: rdn and effrt 3f out: drvn and one pce wl over 1f out: wknd ins fnl f* **13/2**[3]

110- **7** 6 **Masked Marvel**[216] 6567 4-9-3 121........ WilliamBuick 8 99
(John Gosden) *led after 1f and set stdy gallop: qcknd over 4f out: hdd and rdn over 2f out: 3rd and outpcd whn edgd lft wl over 1f out: wknd over 1f out: bhd and eased towards fin* **9/1**

131- **8** 10 **Sadeek's Song (USA)**[194] 7053 4-8-12 103........ FrankieDettori 5 78
(Mahmood Al Zarooni) *stdd s: sn chsng ldrs: rdn and unable qck 4f out: drvn and lost pl 3f out: bhd fnl 2f: eased ins fnl f* **14/1**

2m 39.66s (7.66) **Going Correction** +0.775s/f (Yiel) **8** Ran SP% **113.6**
Speed ratings (Par 115): **105,102,101,99,98 97,93,87**
toteswingers:1&2:£7.60, 1&3:£5.50, 2&3:£8.20 CSF £89.56 TOTE £9.70: £2.40, £3.80, £1.50; EX 88.70 Trifecta £812.00 Pool £11,259.18 - 10.26 winning unit..
Owner D J Deer **Bred** D J And Mrs Deer **Trained** Beckhampton, Wilts

FOCUS

The strongest edition of this race for a while, with last season's Grand Prix de Paris, St Leger, and Melbourne Cup winners all featuring. The early pace was slow, however, and a number of the runners failed to run up to their best as a result of the ground, making it form to be slightly wary of. The winner could be rated higher at face value.

NOTEBOOK

Al Kazeem handled the ground better than most and ran out an emphatic winner. Runner-up on all three tries at Group level last season, the son of Dubawi, who had been due to run at Sandown the previous weekend, has clearly progressed from three to four and travelled up ominously well before stretching right away from his field. He's entitled to take his chance at the top level now, with the Coronation Cup the obvious next step. (op 10-1 tchd 11-1)

Quest For Peace(IRE) won the Group 3 Cumberland Lodge Stakes on his debut for Luca Cumani last season (ex-Aidan O'Brien), and he too looks to have taken a step forward over the winter. Although unable to match the winner, he always seemed likely to hold second and it would be no surprise to see him head abroad at some point this season. The Coronation Cup is the immediate target, though. (op 8-1)

Dunaden(FR), last year's Melbourne Cup winner, won the Group 1 Hong Kong Vase over this trip subsequently and was conceding 5lb to all bar one. He came in for support, though, and ran a really good race considering the lack of early pace would have inconvenienced him. He should prove a solid Group 1 performer this season, with his trainer hoping he can develop into an Arc contender later in the year. (op 7-1)

Meandre(FR), last year's Arc sixth, was disappointing on the face of it, but his peak effort last season, when winning the Grand Prix de Paris, came on a much faster surface and he did himself few favours by proving very keen early. He should leave this form behind as the season progresses. (op 13-8, tchd 7-4 in places)

Blue Bajan(IRE) ran well considering the lack of pace as this trip is a bare minimum for him. (op 28-1 tchd 33-1)

Fiorente(IRE), runner-up in last season's King Edward VII, was having only the fifth start of his career and briefly threatened to make a challenge, but had to switch inside and faded soon after. Clearly in need of the run, he'd been withdrawn from his intended reappearance at Newbury due to soft ground, so faster conditions will suit in future, and he should leave this form well behind. (op 11-2 tchd 5-1)

Masked Marvel, shouldering a 5lb penalty, had the run of the race and obviously stays further, so it was disappointing to see him fade the way he did. His trainer had warned he'd come on for the run, however, and he's another whom faster ground suits best. (op 7-1 tchd 10-1)

Sadeek's Song(USA) was up markedly in grade for this seasonal reappearance and found himself quickly beaten when the tempo increased. There were doubts over the suitability of the ground, though, and he should show this running to be wrong. (op 12-1)

1856 QIPCO 2000 GUINEAS STKS (204TH RUNNING) (BRITISH CHAMPIONS SERIES) (GROUP 1) (C&F) 1m

3:10 (3:13) (Class 1) 3-Y-0

£213,513 (£80,947; £40,511; £20,180; £10,127; £5,082) **Stalls** Centre

Form RPR

1- **1** **Camelot**[196] 7020 3-9-0 119........ JPO'Brien 12 122+
(A P O'Brien, Ire) *racd stands' side: hld up in rr: stl plenty to do and effrt ent fnl 2f: rdn to chse ldrs and swtchd rt jst over 1f out: led ins fnl f: sn hrd pressed and drvn: fnd ex and styd on wl cl home* **15/8**[1]

21-1 **2** nk **French Fifteen (FR)**[30] 1208 3-9-0 115........ OlivierPeslier 16 121
(N Clement, France) *racd stands' side: hld up towards rr: effrt and hdwy 2f out: drvn and chal ins fnl f: sustained effrt tl no ex and btn towards fin: 2nd of 14 in gp* **12/1**

3 **3** 2 ¼ **Hermival (IRE)**[30] 1208 3-9-0 111........ GregoryBenoist 4 116
(M Delzangles, France) *racd far side: in tch overall: effrt ent fnl 2f: led far side and pressing overall ldrs over 1f out: no ex and one pce ins fnl f: 1st of 4 in gp* **16/1**

15-1 **4** 1 ¼ **Trumpet Major (IRE)**[16] 1470 3-9-0 116........ RichardHughes 18 113
(Richard Hannon) *racd on stands' side: chsd ldrs tl led 3f out: rdn ent fnl 2f: hdd wl over 1f out: led again over 1f out tl hdd ins fnl f: wknd fnl 100yds: 3rd of 14 in gp* **8/1**[3]

51-5 **5** nse **Coupe De Ville (IRE)**[16] 1468 3-9-0 105........ PaulHanagan 3 113
(Richard Hannon) *racd far side: hld up towards rr overall: rdn and effrt 2f out: styd on same pce u.p fnl f: 2nd of 4 in gp* **66/1**

313- **6** *2 1/4* **Fencing (USA)**[196] 7020 3-9-0 111 .... WilliamBuick 15 108
(John Gosden) *racd stands' side: chsd ldrs: rdn and effrt ent fnl 2f: unable qck and drvn wl over 1f out: wknd ent fnl f: 4th of 14 in gp* **25/1**

12-4 **7** *1/2* **Ptolemaic**[16] 1470 3-9-0 96 .... (v) TomEaves 1 106
(Bryan Smart) *racd far side: in tch in midfield overall: rdn over 2f out and outpcd 2f out: kpt on u.p fnl f: no threat to ldrs: 3rd of 4 in gp* **250/1**

21-2 **8** *1 1/2* **Abtaal (USA)**[30] 1208 3-9-0 114 .... ChristopheSoumillon 2 103
(J-C Rouget, France) *racd far side: led far side gp and handy overall: rdn over 2f out: drvn and no ex over 1f out: wknd ins fnl f: last of 4 in gp* **7/1**[2]

50-1 **9** *nk* **Caspar Netscher**[14] 1509 3-9-0 114 .... ShaneKelly 5 102
(Alan McCabe) *racd in centre trio: in tch: effrt to press ldrs whn gp merged w stands' side 3f out: drvn to ld wl over 1f out tl over 1f out: btn 1f out: wknd ins fnl f: 5th of 14 in gp* **22/1**

02-4 **10** *3/4* **Redact (IRE)**[17] 1453 3-9-0 109 .... JimCrowley 13 101
(Richard Hannon) *racd stands' side: in tch: rdn and unable qck over 2f out: wknd over 1f out: 6th of 14 in gp* **150/1**

20-5 **11** *1/2* **Red Duke (USA)**[35] 1145 3-9-0 112 .... TomQueally 10 99
(John Quinn) *racd stands' side: in tch in midfield: rdn and effrt ent fnl 2f: drvn and no imp wl over 1f out: wknd jst over 1f out: 7th of 14 in gp* **66/1**

12- **12** *1/2* **Born To Sea (IRE)**[188] 7185 3-9-0 107 .... JohnnyMurtagh 14 98
(John M Oxx, Ire) *racd stands' side: t.k.h: chsd ldrs: rdn over 2f out: sn struggling: wknd wl over 1f out: 8th of 14 in gp* **10/1**

22-2 **13** *3/4* **Boomerang Bob (IRE)**[14] 1509 3-9-0 112 .... SebSanders 8 97
(J W Hills) *racd stands' side hld up in rr: rdn and effrt jst over 2f out: no imp: nvr trbld ldrs: 9th of 14 in gp* **40/1**

362- **14** *1 1/2* **Saigon**[196] 7026 3-9-0 110 .... RobertHavlin 7 93
(James Toller) *racd in centre trio tl merged w stands' side 3f out: hld up towards rr overall: rdn and hdwy over 2f out: drvn and wknd over 1f out: 10th of 14 in gp* **66/1**

14-3 **15** *1/2* **Bronterre**[14] 1509 3-9-0 114 .... JamieSpencer 11 92
(Richard Hannon) *racd stands' side: stdd s: hld up in rr: rdn and effrt 3f out: no imp: n.d: 11th of 14 in gp* **28/1**

1- **16** *6* **Top Offer**[267] 4996 3-9-0 0 .... JamesDoyle 9 78+
(Roger Charlton) *racd stands' side: in tch: rdn and effrt over 2f out: wknd wl over 1f out: bhd and eased ins fnl f: 12th of 14 in gp* **14/1**

212- **17** *18* **Power**[210] 6689 3-9-0 117 .... RyanMoore 17
(A P O'Brien, Ire) *racd stands' side: towards rr: rdn and effrt over 2f out: hung rt and no hdwy wl over 1f out: bhd and eased ins fnl f: t.o: 13th of 14 in gp* **7/1**[2]

05-1 **18** *1 1/4* **Talwar (IRE)**[21] 1375 3-9-0 107 .... FrankieDettori 6
(Jeremy Noseda) *racd in centre trio: overall ldr tl over 3f out: sn wknd and btn whn gps merged 3f out: wl bhd and eased fnl f: t.o: 14th of 14 in gp* **50/1**

1m 42.46s (3.86) **Going Correction** +0.775s/f (Yiel) **18** Ran SP% **121.8**
Speed ratings (Par 113): **111,110,108,107,107 104,104,102,102,101 101,100,100,98,98 92,74,72**
toteswingers:1&2:£7.70, 1&3:£15.70, 2&3:£16.40 CSF £23.53 CT £303.89 TOTE £3.00: £1.90, £2.70, £3.50; EX 36.20 Trifecta £288.80 Pool £18,576.18 - 47.59 winning unit..
Owner Derrick Smith & Mrs John Magnier & Michael Tabor **Bred** Sheikh Abdulla Bin Isa Al-Khalifa **Trained** Ballydoyle, Co Tipperary

FOCUS
The splits for each furlong were as follows: 15.24 (from a standing start), 12.12, 12.25, 12.39, 12.60, 12.18, 12.53 and finally 13.16. So while the pace slowed just a touch at around halfway, it was essentially an even gallop. The final time confirmed the ground was really soft with this the 11th slowest of 211 races to be run over C&D since 2005. There were three separate groups early on, before the main action unfolded middle to stands' side. However, the four runners who stayed towards the far rail all finished in the first eight, including a couple at massive prices, suggesting they may have been on the best ground. As such, it makes sense to treat this as two separate races. Only time will show the true worth of the form but, leaving the four who raced next to the far rail aside, the form of the main group looks solid enough as the highly promising Camelot just denied a Prix Djebel winner, with the pair clear of a horse who had defied a penalty in the Craven, albeit that one was a bit below his best. Next home was Fencing (Camelot more than doubled his superiority over that rival from their meeting in the Racing Post Trophy), and then came the Greenham winner. The bare form is average for the race but Camelot is clearly capable of better over further.

NOTEBOOK
Camelot ◆ became the first horse to do the Racing Post Trophy/2000 Guineas double since High Top in 1972, his rider's brave decision to challenge between horses probably making the difference between victory and defeat. The horse had to be game to see off the runner-up's strong challenge, and is more straightforward than many of his late sire's progeny. While the soft ground put the emphasis on stamina, undoubtedly helping a horse who is bred for middle-distances, he had the quickest sectional in the sixth and seventh furlongs, and certainly didn't just outstay his rivals. He won't need this ground when going up in distance (already won twice on good), and should be hard to beat in the Derby. A top-price of 5-4 is justified. (tchd 2-1 and 5-2 in a place)
French Fifteen(FR) is a tough, progressive colt who had conditions to suit, but he has a little way to go if he's to make a genuinely top-class miler considering he was denied by a rival who is likely to need further. (op 16-1, tchd 17-1 in a place)
Hermival(IRE) had a similar profile to 2010 winner Makfi, including the same sire and trainer. Unlike his erstwhile stablemate, this one didn't win the Prix Djebel, but he received the same RPR of 110. It's doubtful, however, that he stepped forward as expected as the form of the quartet who raced far side looks ordinary by the standards of this race. (op 20-1)
Trumpet Major(IRE) ◆ is not considered a soft ground horse (flopped on testing going in last year's Solario), so it's no surprise he was below form (final time was just over five seconds slower than when he won the Craven over C&D) and he probably did well to finish so close. (op 9-1, tchd 10-1 in places)
Coupe De Ville(IRE) was second of those who raced far side. He found 1m2f too far on his comeback and this was obviously better, but until he proves otherwise his proximity suggests the far side may have been favoured.
Fencing(USA) handled the ground but got tired, having missed his prep. He's a longer-term project than some of these. (tchd 33-1)
Ptolemaic's finishing position adds weight to the idea the far side was the best ground.
Abtaal(USA) didn't go on as expected from his second-place finish (split French Fifteen and Hermival) in the Prix Djebel. He's probably had enough of racing on soft ground and could be a different proposition on a faster surface, but he does need to bounce back. (op 15-2 tchd 8-1)
Caspar Netscher wasn't helped by racing with only two other horses (both finished well beaten) up the middle of the track early on, and was keen. He should do better back over shorter on a quicker surface. (tchd 20-1 and 25-1)
Redact(IRE) didn't prove his stamina but still ran creditably.
Red Duke(USA) ◆ can be given another chance. He's had a number of excuses since last showing his best form, and this time the soft ground was no use. It wouldn't surprise to see him win a big race at a price when back on a decent surface and getting a strong pace. He's in the Irish Guineas.
Born To Sea(IRE) is a half-brother to Galileo and Sea The Stars among others, but he lacks the scope and stamina of those types. He was much too keen. Official explanation: jockey said colt ran too keen (tchd 9-1)
Bronterre can be given another chance on better ground. (tchd 33-1 in places)
Top Offer had missed his intended prep in the Greenham on account of testing conditions, and this inexperienced colt can be given another chance. (op 12-1, tchd 16-1 in places)
Power reportedly met with a setback over the winter. It wasn't thought to be serious, but he ran no race at all on this comeback. Official explanation: trainer said colt was unsuited by the good to soft ground (op 8-1)

1857 PEARL BLOODSTOCK PALACE HOUSE STKS (GROUP 3) 5f
3:45 (3:48) (Class 1) 3-Y-0+

£31,190 (£11,825; £5,918; £2,948; £1,479; £742) **Stalls** High

Form RPR

2-31 **1** **Mayson**[16] 1469 4-9-0 110 .... PaulHanagan 2 114
(Richard Fahey) *taken down early: hld up in midfield: hdwy on far side of field 2f out: rdn to ld jst ins fnl f: r.o wl and in command fnl 100yds: rdn out* **7/2**[1]

200- **2** *3/4* **Definightly**[163] 7534 6-9-0 107 .... (b) RyanMoore 4 111
(Roger Charlton) *chsd ldr tl rdn to ld over 1f out: hrd pressed and drvn 1f out: sn hdd and styd on same pce fnl 150yds* **16/1**

22-6 **3** *shd* **Elusivity (IRE)**[16] 1469 4-9-0 95 .... FrankieDettori 6 111
(Brian Meehan) *in tch in midfield: rdn and effrt wl over 1f out: pressed ldrs and drvn 1f out: kpt on same pce ins fnl f* **12/1**

1-22 **4** *3/4* **Spirit Quartz (IRE)**[14] 1538 4-9-0 106 .... JimCrowley 10 108
(Robert Cowell) *hld up towards rr: hdwy and swtchd lft over 1f out: kpt on wl u.p fnl f* **33/1**

56-5 **5** *1/2* **Night Carnation**[15] 1494 4-8-11 106 .... JimmyFortune 18 104+
(Andrew Balding) *in tch: rdn and effrt jst over 2f out: hdwy ent fnl f: kpt on fnl 100yds: nt rch ldrs* **9/1**

13-2 **6** *shd* **Caledonia Lady**[15] 1494 3-8-2 104 .... JoeFanning 15 99+
(Jo Hughes) *s.i.s: sn outpcd in rr: hdwy but stl in rr whn nt clr run 2f out: hdwy over 1f out: r.o wl ins fnl f: nt rch ldrs* **12/1**

141- **7** *1 3/4* **Eton Rifles (IRE)**[163] 7534 7-9-0 111 .... WilliamCarson 16 101
(Stuart Williams) *in tch: rdn and effrt over 1f out: drvn and styd on same pce ins fnl f* **8/1**[3]

241- **7** *dht* **Move In Time**[217] 6522 4-9-0 102 .... TomEaves 3 101
(Bryan Smart) *chsd ldrs: rdn and unable qck jst over 1f out: styd on same pce ins fnl f* **16/1**

2350 **9** *1/2* **Inxile (IRE)**[35] 1147 7-9-0 113 .... (p) AdrianNicholls 5 99
(David Nicholls) *taken down early: led tl rdn and hdd over 1f out: wknd jst ins fnl f: eased cl home* **25/1**

23-2 **10** *1 1/4* **Hamish McGonagall**[28] 1219 7-9-0 114 .... DavidAllan 9 95
(Tim Easterby) *chsd ldrs: rdn and grad lost pl 1/2-way: bhd wl over 1f out: no threat to ldrs but kpt on again ins fnl f* **11/1**

60-U **11** *3 1/2* **Astrophysical Jet**[15] 1494 5-8-11 97 .... ShaneKelly 8 81
(Ed McMahon) *chsd ldrs: rdn and unable qck ent fnl 2f: wkng whn sltly hmpd over 1f out: wl hld 1f out* **33/1**

410/ **12** *2 1/4* **Temple Meads**[582] 6531 4-9-0 113 .... RichardMullen 1 77
(Ed McMahon) *s.i.s: bhd early: clsd and wl in tch 1/2-way: rdn: edgd lft and wknd over 1f out* **14/1**

111- **13** *6* **Stepper Point**[190] 7155 3-8-5 108 .... MartinDwyer 11 54
(William Muir) *in tch: rdn and unable qck 1/2-way: wknd u.p over 1f out: bhd ins fnl f* **25/1**

00-2 **14** *nk* **Foxy Music**[24] 1316 8-9-0 90 .... PatCosgrave 17 57
(Eric Alston) *restless in stalls: dwlt: a towards rr: hung rt 1/2-way: wknd wl over 1f out: bhd fnl f* **100/1**

30-1 **15** *shd* **Jonny Mudball**[24] 1316 6-9-0 105 .... (t) SebSanders 12 56
(Tom Dascombe) *chsd ldrs: rdn and struggling 1/2-way: wknd wl over 1f out: bhd fnl f* **16/1**

0-00 **16** *1* **Margot Did (IRE)**[35] 1146 4-8-11 114 .... (t) HayleyTurner 13 50
(Michael Bell) *sn rdn along and outpcd in rr: clsd 1/2-way: wknd wl over 1f out: bhd fnl f* **6/1**[2]

1m 1.42s (2.32) **Going Correction** +0.775s/f (Yiel)
WFA 3 from 4yo+ 9lb **16** Ran SP% **120.2**
Speed ratings (Par 113): **112,110,110,109,108 108,105,105,104,102 97,93,84,83,83 81**
toteswingers:1&2:£11.10, 1&3:£5.90, 2&3:£19.50 CSF £58.24 TOTE £4.30: £1.70, £5.90, £4.10; EX 39.60 Trifecta £780.00 Pool £52,453.25 - 49.76 winning unit..
Owner David W Armstrong **Bred** Highfield Farm Llp **Trained** Musley Bank, N Yorks
■ Stewards' Enquiry : Jim Crowley two-day ban: careless riding (May 20-21)

FOCUS
Often a hotly contested Group 3 sprint, no different this time round, and those who raced more down the centre of the track from the low stalls came out on top. Mayson has clearly improved this year.

NOTEBOOK
Mayson, who'd been well placed when winning the 6f Abernant Stakes at the course over two weeks earlier, was on the outside of the entire field this time, but picked up best of all and saw it out strongly, confirming himself a highly progressive sprinter. He's got a way to go before he could be considering for sprinting honours at the top level, but will bid to take the next step in the Duke Of York. (op 9-2)
Definightly is well at home in soft ground and he appeared to run to his best on this seasonal reappearance, being well placed throughout and holding every chance. This was his first try at 5f and the fact he coped well should open up more options. (op 11-1 tchd 10-1)
Elusivity(IRE) travelled well and got much closer to the winner than he had done two weeks earlier, moving through comfortably before proving unable to quicken sufficiently once switched. He remains capable of further progress and should be suited by a return to 6f. (tchd 11-1)
Spirit Quartz(IRE) did best of those challenging more towards the stands' side, staying on to run another solid race.
Night Carnation, disappointing in a Listed race at Bath on her reappearance, is ideally suited by faster ground, but still returned to something like her best, running on well having ended up nearest the stands' rail and reversing last-time-out form with Caledonia Lady. (op 12-1)
Caledonia Lady fared best of the two 3yos and would have finished closer with a better trip. (tchd 14-1)
Eton Rifles(IRE), for whom this trip is probably on the sharp side, looked as though the run would do him good.
Inxile(IRE) showed early speed before struggling late. (op 20-1)
Temple Meads, returning from a long absence, never got into it but can improve. (op 11-1)
Stepper Point, the other 3yo, ended last season on a high and he can probably better this form when his yard really gets going. (op 16-1)
Jonny Mudball Official explanation: jockey said gelding hung left
Margot Did(IRE) offered little in a first-time tongue-tie and is now left with a bit to prove. (op 15-2)

1858 AL RAYAN H'CAP 6f
4:20 (4:28) (Class 2) (0-100,99) 3-Y-O **£12,938** (£3,850; £1,924; £962) **Stalls** High

Form RPR

12-5 **1** **Red Quartet (IRE)**[15] 1500 3-8-3 **81** .... AndreaAtzeni 3 90
(Robert Eddery) *in tch: jnd ldrs on bit wl over 1f out: rdn to ld and edgd lft over 1f out: hld on wl fnl f* **12/1**

112- **2** *hd* **Mince**[204] 6827 3-8-4 **85** .... HarryBentley(3) 4 93
(Roger Charlton) *hld up towards rr: hdwy and n.m.r wl over 1f out: swtchd rt and chsd ldrs over 1f out: str chal fnl f: r.o but a jst hld* **5/1**[1]

213- **3** 2 **Democretes**[231] 6166 3-8-9 **87** RichardHughes 1 89
(Richard Hannon) *hld up in rr: hdwy and switching lft fr over 1f out: wnt between horses and styd on wl fnl f: nt rch ldrs* **8/1**[3]

21-2 **4** 3/4 **Personal Touch**[24] 1317 3-8-4 **82** oh4 ow2 PatrickMathers 15 82
(Richard Fahey) *pressed ldr tl drvn to ld wl over 1f out: sn hdd: styd on same pce fnl f* **20/1**

21-4 **5** 1/2 **Hurry Up George**[51] 914 3-9-7 **99** JimCrowley 10 97
(Ralph Beckett) *hld up in midfield: hdwy to chse ldrs and rdn jst over 1f out: fnd little and styd on same pce ins fnl f* **28/1**

4542 **6** 1 **I'll Be Good**[14] 1524 3-8-5 **83** MickaelBarzalona 2 78
(Robert Johnson) *in tch: drvn to press ldrs over 1f out: no ex 1f out: wknd fnl 100yds* **20/1**

3-00 **7** nk **Parc De Launay**[14] 1524 3-8-6 **84** AdrianNicholls 6 78
(Tom Tate) *t.k.h: chsd ldrs: rdn and effrt wl over 1f out: no ex and one pce fnl f* **33/1**

14- **8** nk **Ultrasonic (USA)**[196] 7028 3-9-1 **93** RyanMoore 21 86+
(Sir Michael Stoute) *stdd s: t.k.h: hld up in rr: hdwy over 2f out: chsng ldrs and rdn over 1f out: wknd ins fnl f* **14/1**

2311 **9** 3/4 **Heartsong (IRE)**[14] 1514 3-8-7 **85** JohnFahy 8 75
(John Gallagher) *pressed ldrs: rdn and ev ch wl over 1f out: wknd u.p ins fnl f* **25/1**

1-0 **10** 1/2 **Muaamara**[17] 1454 3-8-11 **89** MartinHarley 17 78+
(Mick Channon) *in tch: jnd ldrs on bit wl over 1f out: rdn and fnd little over 1f out: wknd ins fnl f* **25/1**

6-16 **11** 1 1/4 **Muarrab**[17] 1452 3-8-5 **83** PaulHanagan 5 68+
(Ed Dunlop) *in tch: rdn and effrt to chse ldrs wl over 1f out: wknd ins fnl f* **12/1**

05-5 **12** 1/2 **Alejandro (IRE)**[17] 1457 3-8-9 **94** LauraBarry(7) 9 77
(Richard Fahey) *led tl rdn and hdd over 1f out: wknd ins fnl f* **16/1**

1-02 **13** 2 1/4 **Mezzotint (IRE)**[17] 1449 3-8-8 **86** PatCosgrave 11 62
(Marco Botti) *in tch: effrt u.p 2f out: drvn and wknd ent fnl f* **16/1**

303- **14** 1 1/2 **Fulbright**[196] 7021 3-9-2 **94** JoeFanning 20 65
(Mark Johnston) *in tch in midfield: rdn and struggling over 2f out: wknd wl over 1f out* **20/1**

60-2 **15** nse **Sans Loi (IRE)**[17] 1457 3-8-7 **85** MartinDwyer 18 56+
(Alan McCabe) *t.k.h: hld up in rr: effrt and hmpd ent fnl 2f: n.d* **8/1**[3]

014- **16** 1 1/4 **Tioman Legend**[348] 2367 3-9-2 **94** JamieSpencer 12 61+
(Roger Charlton) *stdd s: t.k.h: rdn and no prog over 2f out: no ch whn hung rt over 1f out* **25/1**

21-4 **17** 3 **Right Result (IRE)**[25] 1271 3-8-2 **80** MircoDemuro 14 38
(James Bethell) *in tch in midfield: rdn and struggling ent fnl 2f: wknd wl over 1f out* **12/1**

155- **18** 8 **Al Khan (IRE)**[238] 5926 3-9-1 **93** WilliamBuick 7 25+
(Peter Chapple-Hyam) *hld up in rr: effrt but stl plenty to do whn hmpd ent fnl 2f: no ch after* **7/1**[2]

210- **19** 11 **Princess Of Orange**[231] 6146 3-8-7 **85** WilliamCarson 19
(Rae Guest) *t.k.h: hld up in rr: lost tch over 2f out: t.o* **33/1**

1m 16.03s (3.83) **Going Correction** +0.775s/f (Yiel) **19** Ran SP% **128.1**
Speed ratings (Par 105): **105,104,102,101,100 99,98,98,97,96 94,94,91,89,89 87,83,72,58**
toteswingers:1&2:£11.50, 1&3:£93.50, 2&3:£15.30 CSF £62.66 CT £391.68 TOTE £9.00: £3.10, £1.90, £2.60, £5.70; EX 53.20 Trifecta £62.40 Pool £4,557.65 - 54.02 winning unit..
Owner Anderson, Donaldson, Keane & Rayment **Bred** Mrs Brid Cosgrove **Trained** Newmarket, Suffolk

■ Stewards' Enquiry : Andrea Atzeni two-day ban: used whip above permitted level (May 20-21)
Patrick Mathers six-day ban: weighed in 2lb heavy (May 19-24)

FOCUS
A strong 3yo sprint handicap, and the field raced up the middle of the track. Despite the ground this is form to be fairly positive about. The winner resumed his progress.

NOTEBOOK
Red Quartet(IRE) was unsuited by being held up off a slow pace over 7f on his return, and this was more like it. He wandered a bit under pressure, suggesting he still has learning to do, and he should progress to a decent level. (op 14-1 tchd 11-1 and 16-1 in a place)
Mince ◆ was 9lb higher than when a close second on her final start of a promising juvenile campaign, but the winner that day, Ballesteros, had recently won again off 5lb higher. She had to wait for an opening, allowing Red Quartet first run, and then took a while to get organised, and it probably cost her. This likeable type can continue her progression towards pattern company. (op 11-2 tchd 6-1)
Democretes, returning from 231 days off, didn't have the pace of the front two and ended up having to be switched, before running on nicely but too late. He can build on this. (op 14-1)
Personal Touch ran a big race from 4lb out of the handicap. The Stewards held an enquiry following a report from the Clerk of the Scales that Patrick Mathers had weighed in 2lb or more than the weight at which he weighed out, and the rider, found in breach of Rule (B)67.4.3, was suspended for six days. (op 16-1 tchd 25-1)
Hurry Up George might not have found as much as expected, but this was still a decent effort under top weight on his first turf start. (op 25-1)
I'll Be Good did well to finish so close considering he was too keen without cover.
Ultrasonic(USA) was going on okay at the finish and should build on this first run for 196 days.
Muaamara travelled into the race suggesting she's a filly with plenty of ability, but her finishing kick was tame. (op 20-1 tchd 14-1)
Muarrab was another who found disappointingly little. (op 14-1 tchd 16-1)
Sans Loi(IRE) was attended by the farrier before the off, and this ground was probably softer than ideal, so he can be given another chance. (op 10-1)
Tioman Legend Official explanation: jockey said gelding ran too free
Al Khan(IRE) just didn't pick up and was presumably unsuited by the ground. (op 13-2 tchd 15-2)

1859 QATAR RACING NEWMARKET STKS (LISTED RACE) (C&G) 1m 2f
4:55 (4:59) (Class 1) 3-Y-O **£22,684** (£8,600; £4,304; £2,144; £1,076) **Stalls** High

Form RPR

2-1 **1** **Noble Mission**[14] 1506 3-8-12 0 TomQueally 7 110+
(Sir Henry Cecil) *stdd s: t.k.h: hld up in 4th: clsd and swtchd rt over 2f out: drvn to chse ldr jst ins fnl f: led wl ins fnl f: kpt on wl* **7/4**[1]

1 **2** nk **Mariner's Cross (IRE)**[16] 1467 3-8-12 0 FrankieDettori 3 106
(Mahmood Al Zarooni) *chsd ldr: jnd ldr gng wl over 2f out: rdn and qcknd to ld over 1f out: drvn fnl f: hdd wl ins fnl f: kpt on gamely* **9/4**[2]

3 1/2 **Michelangelo** 3-8-12 0 WilliamBuick 1 105
(John Gosden) *chsd ldng pair: rdn wl over 1f out: drvn and chsd ldr briefly 1f out: kpt on wl but unable qck fnl 100yds* **15/2**

3- **4** 5 **Stencive**[197] 6994 3-8-12 0 JohnnyMurtagh 4 95+
(William Haggas) *hld up in last pl: clsd over 2f out: nt clr run and swtchd rt ent fnl f: sn drvn and outpcd* **4/1**[3]

0-22 **5** 4 1/2 **Mister Music**[10] 1604 3-8-12 98 RichardHughes 2 86
(Richard Hannon) *led: rdn and qcknd over 2f out: hdd over 1f out: btn 1f out: wknd fnl f* **17/2**

2m 11.45s (5.65) **Going Correction** +0.775s/f (Yiel) **5** Ran SP% **109.4**
Speed ratings (Par 107): **108,107,107,103,99**
CSF £5.88 TOTE £2.30: £1.50, £2.10; EX 3.20.
Owner K Abdulla **Bred** Juddmonte Farms Ltd **Trained** Newmarket, Suffolk

FOCUS
Muddling form, with the pace being very steady and it developing into something of a sprint. Still, a trio of clearly very useful types drew clear. The form is rated around the race averages, with improvement from the first two.

NOTEBOOK
Noble Mission impressed with the manner of his Newbury maiden victory (wore a first-time hood), and he did quite well to follow up with Mariner's Cross having gained first run on him. This wasn't a true test at the distance, but he shapes like a horse who may stay 1m4f and deserves to take his chance in a Derby trial. (op 6-4 tchd 11-8)

Mariner's Cross(IRE) won what is already looking a stronger Wood Ditton than usual on last month's debut and he moved smoothly in behind the early leader on this step up to 1m2f. He looked the likely winner 2f out, but couldn't get away from them and was worn down close home, ending up on the stands' rail. There's plenty of stamina in his family and he can improve again. (op 2-1, tchd 15-8 in places)

Michelangelo, a son of Galileo, from a good family, who is entered in both the Derby and King Edward VII, put up a big performance on his debut. His inexperience may have ultimately made the difference and he should have little trouble winning a maiden before stepping back up in grade, possibly at Royal Ascot. (op 12-1)

Stencive attracted support and fared better than the bare result, becoming outpaced after his path was blocked. Faster ground ought to suit this half-brother to Joshua Tree, as should a truer test of stamina, and winning a maiden should prove a formality. (op 11-2)

Mister Music took them along until being readily outclassed. He isn't going to be easy to place from now on. (op 15-2 tchd 7-1)

1860 QIPCO SUPPORTS RACING WELFARE H'CAP 1m
5:30 (5:31) (Class 2) (0-105,92) 3-Y-O **£12,938** (£3,850; £1,924; £962) **Stalls** High

Form RPR

21-1 **1** **Rewarded**[8] 1648 3-8-12 **83** KirstyMilczarek 8 95+
(James Toller) *t.k.h: chsd ldr: rdn and outpcd over 1f out: rallied fnl f: styd on wl to ld on post* **10/3**[1]

16- **2** nse **Archbishop (USA)**[262] 5181 3-9-3 **88** MartinDwyer 3 99+
(Brian Meehan) *led: rdn and wnt clr over 1f out: edgd lft ent fnl f: hrd pressed wl ins fnl f: hdd on post* **7/2**[2]

113- **3** 2 1/2 **Frog Hollow**[175] 7390 3-9-5 **90** JimCrowley 10 96+
(Ralph Beckett) *stdd s: hld up in rr: rdn and effrt wl over 1f out: kpt on u.p fnl f* **6/1**[3]

1-12 **4** nk **Mr Red Clubs (IRE)**[112] 180 3-9-6 **91** ShaneKelly 4 96
(Tim Pitt) *t.k.h: in tch: rdn and effrt to chse ldng pair over 1f out: kpt on same pce fnl f* **25/1**

13-3 **5** 3 1/4 **Hadaj**[28] 1217 3-9-7 **92** TomQueally 1 90
(Clive Brittain) *hld up in tch towards rr: rdn and hdwy wl over 1f out: drvn and no imp ent fnl f: wknd fnl 100yds* **14/1**

01-6 **6** 4 **Campanology**[16] 1470 3-9-5 **90** RichardHughes 9 78
(Richard Hannon) *racd along towards stands' rail: in tch: rdn and pressing ldrs wl over 1f out: wknd ent fnl f: eased whn wl btn ins fnl f* **8/1**

210- **7** 1 1/4 **Ghost Protocol (IRE)**[226] 6270 3-9-5 **90** JamieSpencer 5 75
(David Simcock) *stdd s: hld up in rr: rdn and little rspnse over 2f out: swtchd lft 2f out: n.d after* **20/1**

133- **8** hd **Devdas (IRE)**[197] 6986 3-8-10 **81** JohnFahy 6 66
(Clive Cox) *t.k.h: hld up in midfield: rdn and effrt wl over 1f out: wknd ent fnl f* **9/1**

23-1 **9** 1/2 **Fourth Of June (IRE)**[26] 1264 3-8-9 **80** RyanMoore 7 64
(Ed Dunlop) *t.k.h: chsd ldrs: rdn and unable qck wl over 1f out: wknd jst over 1f out* **17/2**

524- **10** 9 **Elkhart (IRE)**[252] 5487 3-9-3 **88** JoeFanning 2 51
(Mark Johnston) *chsd ldrs: rdn and unable qck 2f out: sn wknd: bhd and eased ins fnl f* **16/1**

4-00 **11** 10 **Ghostwriting (USA)**[16] 1477 3-9-2 **87** WilliamBuick 11 27
(John Gosden) *hld up in last trio: rdn and effrt ent fnl 2f: sn wknd: wl bhd and eased ins fnl f* **20/1**

1m 43.91s (5.31) **Going Correction** +0.775s/f (Yiel) **11** Ran SP% **117.1**
Speed ratings (Par 105): **104,103,101,101,97 93,92,92,91,82 72**
toteswingers:1&2:£2.60, 1&3:£4.90, 2&3:£5.70 CSF £14.45 CT £68.27 TOTE £3.70: £1.80, £1.60, £2.00; EX 13.00 Trifecta £58.40 Pool £3,088.39 - 39.08 winning unit..

Owner P C J Dalby & R D Schuster **Bred** Edward David Kessly **Trained** Newmarket, Suffolk

■ Stewards' Enquiry : Kirsty Milczarek seven-day ban: used whip above permitted level (May 19-25)

FOCUS
A good-quality 3yo handicap that saw the pair at the head of the market draw a little way clear. The form is rated around the fourth.

NOTEBOOK
Rewarded, who holds a St James's Palace Stakes entry, enjoyed a walkover at Sandown the week before. He looked to be making his handicap debut from a lenient mark and benefited from the runner-up failing to run straight, producing a strong finish to just shade the verdict. A bit of cut is clearly no bother to the son of Motivator, who looks to need 1m2f, but he's no Group 1 performer, and handicaps remain the best option for now. (op 3-1, tchd 7-2 in places and 11-4 in a place)

Archbishop(USA), off since fading disappointingly in last season's 7f Acomb Stakes, travelled best in front and looked the winner when kicking on, but he wandered left and was ultimately nabbed. This is probably as far as he wants to go and better ground will help also, but he'll be asked to race off a mark in the 90s next time. (op 4-1)

Frog Hollow came from further back than the front pair and should improve, as his trainer expected him to. There's probably a decent handicap in him. (tchd 7-1)

Mr Red Clubs(IRE), in fine form on the AW, winning five of his last seven, performed better than expected on this turf debut and will probably benefit from a more forward ride next time. (op 33-1)

Hadaj didn't get home on the soft ground and probably needs to come down a few pounds in the weights. (op 12-1)

Campanology raced alone on the stands' rail and didn't get home having been on terms for much of the way.

Ghost Protocol(IRE) seemed to find this mark beyond him on this handicap debut. (op 25-1)

Fourth Of June(IRE) found the combination of a rise in grade and step up to 1m beyond him. (op 10-1 tchd 11-1)

T/Jkpt: Not won. T/Plt: £84.80 to a £1 stake. Pool:£236,342.33 - 2,032.48 winning tickets T/Qpdt: £11.10 to a £1 stake. Pool:£11,888.18 - 792.32 winning tickets SP

1520 **THIRSK (L-H)**

Saturday, May 5

OFFICIAL GOING: Good to soft (good in places; 7.7)

Both bends railed out 3-4 metres from inner line.

Wind: fresh half against Weather: Cloudy

1861 BET TOTESCOOP6 TEXT TOTE TO 89660 MAIDEN AUCTION STKS 5f

2:10 (2:10) (Class 5) 2-Y-O £3,234 (£962; £481; £240) Stalls High

Form RPR

35 1 **Mayfield Girl (IRE)**17 1435 2-8-12 0 RobertWinston 7 68
(Mel Brittain) *mde all: drvn and hung lft over 1f out: kpt on* **3/1**1

0 2 1 1/4 **Mount Seymour (IRE)**17 1437 2-9-0 0 DeclanCannon(3) 6 69
(Nigel Tinkler) *in tch: rdn over 2f out: hdwy to chse wnr ins fnl f: kpt on* **33/1**

3 nk **Peep N Creep (IRE)** 2-8-12 0 GrahamGibbons 4 62+
(Tim Easterby) *chsd ldrs: rdn over 2f out: kpt on* **17/2**

4 2 **Hiddon Coin (IRE)** 2-9-3 0 EddieAhern 1 60+
(David O'Meara) *briefly loose befhand: wnt lft s: sn outpcd in rr: swtchd rt to rail over 1f out: kpt on fnl f: nrst fin* **7/2**2

5 1/2 **Shrimper Roo** 2-9-3 0 DuranFentiman 5 58
(Tim Easterby) *w ldr: rdn over 1f out: wknd ins fnl f* **9/2**3

6 nk **Brazilian Clown (IRE)** 2-9-3 0 RichardKingscote 8 57
(Tom Dascombe) *s.i.s: hld up: pushed along over 2f out: sme hdwy over 1f out: one pce fnl f* **7/2**2

7 1 **Taxiformissbyron** 2-8-12 0 PaulMulrennan 2 49+
(Ollie Pears) *hld up in tch: pushed along over 2f out: sn one pce* **8/1**

8 24 **Elusive Shadow** 2-8-12 0 FrannyNorton 3
(Alan Brown) *dwlt: hld up: sn pushed along: wknd over 1f out: eased down* **33/1**

1m 4.56s (4.96) **Going Correction** +0.675s/f (Yiel) 8 Ran SP% **115.1**

Speed ratings (Par 93): **87,85,84,81,80 80,78,40**

Tote Swingers: 1&2 £7.30, 1&3 £4.60, 2&3 £7.70 CSF £95.47 TOTE £3.60: £1.10, £4.60, £2.20; EX 70.60.

Owner Mel Brittain **Bred** Mark Commins **Trained** Warthill, N Yorks

FOCUS

Both bends railed out 3-4 metres from inner line. Just 1mm of rain over the previous 24 hours. A cold day with a brisk headwind in the home straight. The ground was described as nearly good, just on the easy side after the opening juvenile contest. Probably a very ordinary maiden auction event with less than six lengths between the first seven and the time moderate. the winner is rated roughly to her Brocklesby form.

NOTEBOOK

Mayfield Girl(IRE), third in the Brocklesby, started slowly and raced wide at Beverley next time. With the rail to race against, she hung violently left and the bit pulled through her mouth. Even so, she did enough in the end. (tchd 10-3)

Mount Seymour(IRE), another with the benefit of a previous outing, came home in good style after a sluggish start. He should improve again. (op 40-1)

Peep N Creep(IRE) was another putting in solid work at the line and this will have taught her plenty.

Hiddon Coin(IRE) was very green and unseated his rider leaving the paddock. With nothing on his outside he dived left leaving the stalls. Unable to go the pace, when making his way towards the stands' side rail he came home in great style. This should have opened his eyes. (tchd 3-1)

Shrimper Roo, fitted with a rope halter, matched strides with the winner but weakened noticeably late on. He should improve and find a race soon. (op 4-1)

Brazilian Clown(IRE), noisy in the paddock, never landed a blow but is another who will come on for the experience. (op 11-2)

Taxiformissbyron looked to be carrying plenty of condition first time and there will be better to come in time. (op 15-2)

1862 FREE RACING POST FORM AT TOTEPOOL.COM CLASSIFIED STKS 6f

2:40 (2:40) (Class 5) 3-Y-O £3,234 (£962; £481; £240) Stalls High

Form RPR

16 1 **Fairway To Heaven (IRE)**87 471 3-9-0 75 RobertWinston 6 89
(Michael Wigham) *dwlt: hld up: angled lft to outer and smooth hdwy over 1f out: led 1f out: edgd rt: kpt on wl: comf* **17/2**

6203 2 3 1/2 **Henry Bee**10 1595 3-8-11 73 LeeTopliss(3) 2 78
(Richard Fahey) *hld up in tch: pushed along 3f out: hdwy 2f out: led over 1f out: edgd lft: sn hdd: kpt on: no ch w wnr* **6/1**

203- 3 1/2 **Show Flower**246 5689 3-9-0 74 SamHitchcott 4 76
(Mick Channon) *hld up in tch: gng wl whn short of room 2f out tl over 1f out: kpt on* **8/1**

421- 4 8 **Dark Falcon (IRE)**135 7855 3-9-0 72 EddieAhern 3 51
(James Tate) *prom: pushed along over 3f out: remained w ev ch tl wknd appr fnl f* **9/2**3

021- 5 1 1/2 **Lollina Paulina**199 6946 3-9-0 74 PhillipMakin 8 46
(Kevin Ryan) *trckd ldrs: short of room 2f out and again appr fnl f: no ch after* **7/2**2

31-3 6 3/4 **Sky Crossing**17 1449 3-9-0 75 PaulMulrennan 5 44
(James Given) *led: rdn whn hdd over 1f out: wknd* **3/1**1

150- 7 shd **Fortrose Academy (IRE)**131 7875 3-9-0 75 LiamKeniry 7 43
(Andrew Balding) *prom: lost pl 2f out: sn wknd* **8/1**

000- 8 12 **Nearly A Gift (IRE)**203 6864 3-9-0 74 DuranFentiman 1
(Tim Easterby) *trckd ldrs towards outer: wknd qckly appr fnl f* **20/1**

1m 16.58s (3.88) **Going Correction** +0.675s/f (Yiel) 8 Ran SP% **117.2**

Speed ratings (Par 99): **101,96,95,85,83 82,81,65**

Tote Swingers: 1&2 £27.00, 1&3 £3.90, 2&3 £9.00 CSF £59.73 TOTE £15.30: £4.10, £2.10, £3.10; EX 49.10.

Owner Palatinate Thoroughbred Racing Limited **Bred** J Cullinan **Trained** Newmarket, Suffolk

■ Stewards' Enquiry : Robert Winston caution: careless riding.

FOCUS

A tight knit 3-y-o classified stakes with just 3lb between the eight runners on official ratings but in the end the first three finished clear. The form is not rated too positively.

1863 FOLLOW TOTEPOOL ON FACEBOOK AND TWITTER H'CAP 7f

3:20 (3:23) (Class 4) (0-85,85) 4-Y-O+ £5,336 (£1,588; £793; £396) Stalls Low

Form RPR

065- 1 **Orpsie Boy (IRE)**193 7074 9-9-0 81 DaleSwift(3) 8 92
(Ruth Carr) *t.k.h early: sn restrained into midfield: rdn and hdwy over 1f out: kpt on wl: led towards fin* **16/1**

-450 2 3/4 **Klynch**18 1431 6-9-0 78 (b) JamesSullivan 6 87
(Ruth Carr) *led: rdn 2f out: kpt on: edgd rt ins fnl f: hdd towards fin* **14/1**

050- 3 2 1/2 **Mon Brav**193 7076 5-9-2 83 PaulPickard(3) 3 85
(Brian Ellison) *in tch towards inner: rdn over 2f out: kpt on* **16/1**

1600 4 1 1/4 **Amazing Star (IRE)**7 1670 7-9-1 79 GrahamGibbons 7 78
(Declan Carroll) *dwlt: hld up in tch: pushed along over 4f out: hdwy over 1f out: kpt on fnl f* **10/1**

00-3 5 shd **Defence Council (IRE)**34 1161 4-9-2 80 RobertWinston 2 79
(Mel Brittain) *trckd ldr: rdn and ev ch 2f out: no ex fnl f* **9/1**

0-10 6 shd **The Osteopath (IRE)**7 1670 9-9-0 78 PaddyAspell 9 76+
(John Davies) *midfield: stmbld over 5f out: short of room 2f out: sn rdn: kpt on fnl f* **9/2**1

6-00 7 1 1/4 **Silenceofthewind (USA)**7 1670 5-8-9 76 MichaelMetcalfe(3) 5 71
(Mrs K Burke) *in tch: rdn over 1f out: sn one pce: hung rt ins fnl f* **9/1**

00-3 8 1/2 **Blues Jazz**26 1249 6-8-11 80 GarryWhillans(5) 12 74
(Ian Semple) *trckd ldr: pushed along and outpcd over 2f out: no imp fr over 1f out* **8/1**3

000- 9 1/2 **Kalk Bay (IRE)**203 6862 5-9-0 85 (t) DavidSimmonson(7) 11 77
(Michael Easterby) *hld up: sme hdwy over 1f out: kpt on: nvr threatened ldrs* **33/1**

1-06 10 2 1/2 **Sam Nombulist**14 1522 4-8-13 80 (v) AmyRyan(3) 10 66
(Richard Whitaker) *in tch: rdn over 2f out: sn no imp* **5/1**2

000- 11 6 **Namwahjobo (IRE)**189 7171 4-8-13 77 GrahamLee 4 46
(Jim Goldie) *dwlt: hld up: rdn over 3f out: wknd over 1f out* **8/1**3

00-1 12 2 **Mujaadel (USA)**34 1161 7-9-1 79 (p) AndrewMullen 14 43
(David Nicholls) *chsd ldrs: wknd 2f out* **14/1**

06-0 13 3/4 **Point North (IRE)**14 1522 5-9-4 82 (t) PaulMulrennan 13 44
(John Balding) *hld up: hmpd over 5f out: hdwy on outer over 3f out: wknd over 1f out* **14/1**

005/ 14 7 **Day Of The Eagle (IRE)**637 4843 6-9-7 85 DavidNolan 1 28
(Michael Easterby) *s.i.s: hld up: a towards rr* **25/1**

1m 30.95s (3.75) **Going Correction** +0.675s/f (Yiel) 14 Ran SP% **124.7**

Speed ratings (Par 105): **105,104,101,99,99 99,98,97,97,94 87,85,84,76**

Tote Swingers: 1&2 £14.00, 1&3 £34.40 CSF £231.40 CT £3642.99 TOTE £22.40: £5.10, £5.30, £4.60; EX 110.80.

Owner Miss Vanessa Church **Bred** Minch Bloodstock **Trained** Huby, N Yorks

■ Stewards' Enquiry : Paul Pickard four-day ban: used whip above permitted level (May 20-23)

FOCUS

A 76-85 handicap run at just a steady pace to past halfway. The form looks sound though and potentially better than rated.

The Osteopath(IRE) Official explanation: jockey said gelding clipped heels approaching bend leaving back straight

Sam Nombulist Official explanation: trainer's rep said gelding was struck into behind

1864 READ LATEST TOTESCOOP6 NEWS AT TOTEPOOL.COM MAIDEN STKS 7f

3:55 (3:55) (Class 4) 3-Y-O £5,336 (£1,588; £793; £396) Stalls Low

Form RPR

3- 1 **Dos Amigos (IRE)**186 7209 3-9-3 0 PaulMulrennan 11 77+
(Michael Dods) *in tch: pushed along and hdwy 3f out: led 2f out: sn rdn: kpt on wl* **4/1**2

2 3/4 **Keyaadi** 3-9-3 0 JackMitchell 3 75+
(Roger Varian) *in tch: swtchd rt over 2f out: sn hdwy to chal: kpt on but a jst hld fnl f* **7/2**1

5- 3 nk **All Or Nothin (IRE)**329 2936 3-9-3 0 MichaelO'Connell 13 74
(John Quinn) *racd keenly in midfield: rdn over 2f out: hdwy to chse wnr over 1f out: kpt on* **9/2**3

0 4 3 3/4 **Warrick Brown**14 1521 3-9-3 0 DuranFentiman 4 64
(Tim Easterby) *trckd ldrs: rdn over 2f out: no ex fnl f* **66/1**

5 nk **Star Deal (IRE)** 3-8-12 0 GarryWhillans(5) 7 63+
(Alan Swinbank) *midfield: pushed along over 2f out: kpt on fnl f* **28/1**

0-4 6 4 1/2 **Young Freddie (IRE)**53 885 3-9-3 0 RoystonFfrench 6 51
(Bryan Smart) *prom: rdn to ld over 2f out: sn hdd: wknd fnl f* **10/1**

4- 7 2 **Sabore**276 4675 3-8-7 0 ShaneBKelly(5) 5 41
(Richard Fahey) *in tch: pushed along whn hmpd over 2f out: kpt on: nvr threatened* **18/1**

00 8 1/2 **Icewan**16 1479 3-9-3 0 MickyFenton 8 44
(Paul Midgley) *slowly away: sn pushed along towards rr: bhd tl sme late hdwy* **66/1**

30- 9 4 **Shotley Music**260 5254 3-9-3 0 JamesSullivan 14 33
(Neville Bycroft) *sn pushed along towards rr: nvr threatened* **14/1**

10 shd **Judy Teen** 3-8-12 0 GrahamGibbons 9 28
(Tim Easterby) *s.i.s: hld up: pushed along and hdwy over 2f out: wknd over 1f out* **20/1**

03 11 8 **Dream Prospector**66 737 3-9-3 0 EddieAhern 1 12
(James Tate) *led: rdn whn hdd over 2f out: sn wknd* **4/1**2

00 12 1 **Bollin Nancy**10 1595 3-8-7 0 AdamCarter(5) 2
(Tim Easterby) *sn outpcd towards rr: a bhd* **66/1**

0 13 22 **Lothair (IRE)**16 1479 3-9-3 0 RobertWinston 12
(Alan Swinbank) *t.k.h: in tch towards outer: wnt prom over 3f out: wknd qckly 2f out* **16/1**

1m 32.57s (5.37) **Going Correction** +0.675s/f (Yiel) 13 Ran SP% **120.0**

Speed ratings (Par 101): **96,95,94,90,90 85,82,82,77,77 68,67,42**

Tote Swingers: 1&2 £7.10, 1&3 £5.80, 2&3 £4.20 CSF £17.75 TOTE £4.30: £2.10, £1.90, £1.40; EX 20.90.

Owner Doug Graham,Roger Stokell,Michael Dods **Bred** Rathasker Stud **Trained** Denton, Co Durham

FOCUS

Plenty of dead wood in this modest 7f maiden race but in the end the cream rose to the top. The form is rated around the averages and time, so the level is a bit fluid.

Young Freddie(IRE) Official explanation: jockey said gelding hung right

Dream Prospector Official explanation: jockey sasid gelding hung right round bend and had no more to give

Lothair(IRE) Official explanation: jockey said gelding ran too free

1865 TOTEPOOL.COM THIRSK HUNT CUP (H'CAP) 1m

4:30 (4:31) (Class 2) (0-100,100) 4-Y-O+ £13,099 (£3,898; £1,948; £974) Stalls Low

Form RPR

1/1- 1 **Farhh**189 7168 4-9-2 100 AntiocoMurgia(5) 10 118+
(Saeed Bin Suroor) *dwlt: midfield: gd hdwy over 2f out: led 2f out: sn qcknd clr: v impressive* **5/4**1

00-4 2 6 **Osteopathic Remedy (IRE)**12 1558 8-8-12 91 PhillipMakin 18 95
(Michael Dods) *racd keenly in tch: rdn over 2f out: kpt on: no ch w wnr* **12/1**

4035 3 nk **Dubai Dynamo**7 1670 7-8-8 87 JamesSullivan 12 90+
(Ruth Carr) *hld up in tch: hdwy over 2f out: sn rdn: kpt on* **16/1**

2-02 4 2 1/4 **Kay Gee Be (IRE)**23 1341 8-8-3 87 ShaneBKelly(5) 14 85
(Richard Fahey) *trckd ldrs: rdn over 2f out: kpt on* **20/1**

0-02 5 1/2 **Kiwi Bay**14 1522 7-8-10 89 PaulMulrennan 7 86
(Michael Dods) *trckd ldrs: rdn over 2f out: kpt on one pce* **16/1**

26-6 **6** *1 1/2* **Extraterrestrial**28 1212 8-8-9 **91** LeeTopliss(3) 11 85+
(Richard Fahey) *hld up in rr: hdwy over 1f out: kpt on fnl f: nrst fin* **10/1**3
4-30 **7** *1 1/4* **Mont Ras (IRE)**14 1510 5-8-9 **88** GrahamGibbons 17 79
(David O'Meara) *prom: rdn to ld over 2f out: hdd 2f out: grad wknd* **8/1**2
00-2 **8** *shd* **Advanced**34 1157 9-8-13 **95** AmyRyan(3) 1 85
(Kevin Ryan) *mdfield: rdn over 2f out: sn no imp* **16/1**
3300 **9** *1 1/2* **Clockmaker (IRE)**12 1558 6-8-11 **90** DuranFentiman 8 77
(Tim Easterby) *led: rdn whn hdd over 2f out: wknd over 1f out* **40/1**
052- **10** *1* **Space War**197 6989 5-8-8 **87** PaddyAspell 5 72
(Michael Easterby) *hld up in midfield: rdn over 2f out: sn no imp* **20/1**
23-0 **11** *2 1/2* **Stevie Thunder**35 1130 7-8-13 **95** RyanClark(3) 2 74
(Ian Williams) *hld up: pushed along over 3f out: nvr threatened* **12/1**
60-3 **12** *1 1/4* **Wannabe King**16 1475 6-8-11 **90** (v) RobertWinston 13 66
(Geoffrey Harker) *swtchd lft s: hld up in rr towards inner: short of room over 2f out tl over 1f out: no ch after* **16/1**
06-0 **13** *1 1/4* **Hot Rod Mamma (IRE)**14 1522 5-8-10 **89** GrahamLee 15 62
(Dianne Sayer) *hld up: a towards rr* **40/1**
2604 **14** *3 3/4* **Kingscroft (IRE)**14 1522 4-8-8 **87** FrannyNorton 9 52
(Mark Johnston) *midfield: rdn over 2f out: wknd over 1f out* **28/1**
01-0 **15** *1 1/4* **Don't Call Me (IRE)**35 1130 5-8-9 **95** ShirleyTeasdale(7) 6 57
(David Nicholls) *midfield: wknd over 2f out* **20/1**
620- **16** *6* **Majestic Dream (IRE)**199 6949 4-8-7 **86** oh2 SamHitchcott 3 34
(Michael Easterby) *in tch on inner: wknd over 2f out* **25/1**

1m 42.52s (2.42) **Going Correction** +0.675s/f (Yiel) **16** Ran SP% **130.0**
Speed ratings (Par 109): **114,108,107,105,104 103,102,102,100,99 97,95,94,90,89 83**
Tote Swingers: 1&2 £5.70, 1&3 £7.90, 2&3 £18.30 CSF £16.52 CT £199.96 TOTE £1.90: £1.20, £2.40, £2.80, £5.60; EX 22.90.
Owner Godolphin **Bred** Darley **Trained** Newmarket, Suffolk

FOCUS
Traditionally a very strong mile handicap but this time the field was torn apart by the unbeaten Farhh, a Group horse running in a handicap if ever there was one. The runner-up is rated close to his best and sets the level.

NOTEBOOK
Farhh ◆, already rated 100, had won a maiden at Newmarket at two and a handicap there last October from a mark of 90. A grand, big son of Pivotal, he went round in cruise control and only needed a shake of the reins to shoot clear. He holds Group 1 entries and is clearly a horse of outstanding potential. (op 11-8)
Osteopathic Remedy(IRE), who took this two years ago from a 5lb lower mark, had the worst of the draw. He is right back to his best.
Dubai Dynamo is slipping down the ratings and is now just 2lb higher than his last win at Ripon a year ago. His stable has struck a rich vein of form. (op 14-1)
Kay Gee Be(IRE), runner-up in a claimer on the all-weather, is another who looks back on song.
Kiwi Bay, back up in trip, was very keen. In the circumstances he ran with credit and his last three victories have been recorded at Redcar. (tchd 18-1)
Extraterrestrial, who took this back in 2008, showed that even at eight he is no back-number. These big field handicaps suit him ideally. (tchd 9-1)
Mont Ras(IRE), drawn one off the outside, probably did too much too soon. (op 10-1)
Advanced clearly stays a mile but the old boy is more effective over shorter. (tchd 20-1)

1866 BET TOTEPOOL TEXT TOTE TO 89660 MAIDEN STKS (DIV I) 1m 4f
5:05 (5:06) (Class 5) 3-Y-0+ **£3,234** (£962; £481; £240) **Stalls** Low

Form RPR
0- **1** **Countess Ferrama**197 6984 3-8-4 0 KellyHarrison 8 77+
(William Haggas) *trckd ldr: pushed along and briefly outpcd over 2f out: rdn and kpt on fr over 1f out: led fnl 100yds* **18/1**
6-23 **2** *1 1/2* **Rocktherunway (IRE)**8 1641 3-8-9 78 PaulMulrennan 4 80
(Michael Dods) *led for 1f: trckd ldr: rdn over 2f out: kpt on: wnt 2nd towards fin* **1/1**1
0-0 **3** *1* **Rainbow Gold**17 1456 3-8-9 0 FrannyNorton 12 78
(Mark Johnston) *led after 1f: pushed along over 2f out: drvn ins fnl f: hdd fnl 100yds: no ex* **8/1**
0 **4** *3 1/2* **Entihaa**21 1385 4-10-0 0 RobertWinston 3 75
(Alan Swinbank) *in tch: rdn and hdwy to chse ldrs over 2f out: no ex fnl f* **100/1**
5 *hd* **Noble Alan (GER)**175 9-10-0 0 GrahamLee 7 74+
(Nicky Richards) *v.s.a: hld up in rr: pushed along and hdwy over 2f out: kpt on: nrst fin* **13/2**3
0 **6** *2* **Aegaeus**19 1414 3-8-9 0 TomMcLaughlin 10 69
(Ed Dunlop) *midfield: pushed along and hdwy over 2f out: briefly chsd ldr: one pce over 1f out: eased fnl 75yds* **25/1**
4- **7** *1 3/4* **Incitement**357 2097 4-10-0 0 EddieAhern 2 68
(Andrew Crook) *in tch: pushed along over 3f out: sn one pce: eased fnl 75yds* **11/1**
5 **8** *14* **Omid**7 1655 4-10-0 0 (t) MickyFenton 11 46
(Nicky Vaughan) *midfield: pushed along over 3f out: sn wknd* **28/1**
50- **9** *9* **Sirious Oss**197 6983 3-8-9 0 JamesSullivan 9 30
(Michael Easterby) *hld up: nvr threatened* **28/1**
10 *34* **Flaming Telepath** 4-9-6 0 DominicFox(3) 5
(Christine Dunnett) *v.s.a: veered lft leaving stall: hld up in rr: a wl bhd* **100/1**
3- **11** *7* **Haman (CAN)**278 4617 4-10-0 0 AhmedAjtebi 1
(Mahmood Al Zarooni) *trckd ldr: wknd qckly over 2f out: eased* **5/1**2
0 **12** *40* **On Command (IRE)**16 1484 4-10-0 0 LiamKeniry 6
(Don Cantillon) *hld up: pushed along over 4f out: sn wknd: t.o* **40/1**

2m 46.99s (10.79) **Going Correction** +0.675s/f (Yiel)
WFA 3 from 4yo+ 19lb **12** Ran SP% **119.9**
Speed ratings (Par 103): **91,90,89,87,86 85,84,75,69,46 41,15**
Tote Swingers: 1&2 £6.40, 1&3 £8.20, 2&3 £3.10 CSF £35.73 TOTE £25.70: £5.10, £1.10, £2.60; EX 55.40.
Owner B Kantor & M Jooste **Bred** Cliveden Stud Ltd **Trained** Newmarket, Suffolk
■ Stewards' Enquiry : Paul Mulrennan four-day ban: used whip above permitted level (May 20-23)

FOCUS
A modest maiden run at a very steady pace until the final 3f. Very little to choose between the first seven home 2f out. The runner-up rated to recent form is the best guide.
Haman(CAN) Official explanation: trainer's rep said colt was unsuited by the good to soft (good in places) ground

1867 BET TOTEPOOL TEXT TOTE TO 89660 MAIDEN STKS (DIV II) 1m 4f
5:35 (5:36) (Class 5) 3-Y-0+ **£3,234** (£962; £481; £240) **Stalls** Low

Form RPR
3 **1** **Yazdi (IRE)**17 1456 3-8-9 0 RobertWinston 3 81+
(Brian Meehan) *trckd ldr: pushed along to ld 2f out: sn clr: eased nr fin* **2/5**1
5 **2** *7* **Regal Swain (IRE)**7 1662 4-9-9 0 GarryWhillans(5) 8 69
(Alan Swinbank) *in tch: hdwy over 4f out: led 3f out: hdd 2f out: sn no match wnr* **20/1**
44 **3** *2 1/4* **Polurrian (IRE)**18 1429 5-9-11 0 DeclanCannon(3) 7 65+
(David O'Meara) *hld up: pushed along and hdwy over 2f out: hung lft over 1f out: kpt on fnl f: nrst fin* **50/1**
0 **4** *nk* **Seventh Sign**14 1506 3-8-6 0 AdamBeschizza(3) 12 63+
(William Haggas) *dwlt: hld up: pushed along over 3f out: hdwy over 1f out: kpt on fnl f: nrst fin* **12/1**
5 *1/2* **Cape Explorer** 3-8-9 0 EddieAhern 1 62+
(James Tate) *racd keenly: sn led: wnt wd on bnd after 2f: hdd 3f out: sn one pce in 3rd: wknd and lost 2 pls fnl 100yds* **10/1**3
6- **6** *3* **Guardi (IRE)**220 6447 3-8-9 0 AhmedAjtebi 2 60
(Mahmood Al Zarooni) *midfield: rdn over 2f out: sn one pce: hung lft fr over 1f out: eased fnl 50yds* **11/1**
0-6 **7** *1 1/2* **Kings Apollo**7 1662 3-8-6 0 SimonPearce(3) 5 55
(Tom Symonds) *prom: pushed along and lost pl over 4f out: rdn and outpcd over 3f out: plugged on again fr over 1f out* **100/1**
6 **8** *hd* **Cruachan (IRE)**21 1305 3-8-9 0 PaulMulrennan 4 54
(Ian Semple) *midfield: pushed along over 2f out: one pce* **100/1**
0/0- **9** *4* **Sposalizio (IRE)**59 7774 5-10-0 45 (v1) RobbieFitzpatrick 6 50
(Colin Teague) *trckd ldrs: rdn over 3f out: sn wknd* **100/1**
10 *1 1/4* **Isabelle B (IRE)**80 5-9-2 0 BTTreanor(7) 9 43
(Nicky Richards) *dwlt: hld up: pushed along over 4f out: sn btn* **66/1**
11 *34* **King Of The Night (GER)**168 8-9-11 0 LeeTopliss(3) 11
(Richard Fahey) *s.i.s: hld up in rr: rdn over 3f out: sn no imp: eased over 1f out* **7/1**2

2m 47.19s (10.99) **Going Correction** +0.675s/f (Yiel)
WFA 3 from 4yo+ 19lb **11** Ran SP% **120.2**
Speed ratings (Par 103): **90,85,83,83,83 81,80,80,77,76 54**
Tote Swingers: 1&2 £2.80, 1&3 £9.60, 2&3 £23.00 CSF £17.20 TOTE £1.40: £1.02, £4.30, £13.30; EX 13.20.
Owner Iraj Parvizi **Bred** Yeguada De Milagro & Balmerino B/Stock **Trained** Manton, Wilts

FOCUS
No strength in depth in this very ordinary maiden but in the end a wide margin eased down winner of some potential. The form is a bit fluid with the runner-up the best guide.
Polurrian(IRE) Official explanation: jockey said gelding hung left

1868 TOTEPOOL MOBILE TEXT TOTE TO 89660 H'CAP 5f
6:05 (6:07) (Class 4) (0-80,80) 4-Y-0+ **£5,336** (£1,588; £793; £396) **Stalls** High

Form RPR
00-6 **1** **Noodles Blue Boy**8 1642 6-9-4 **77** PaddyAspell 16 89
(Ollie Pears) *racd towards stands' rail: w ldr: rdn to ld appr fnl f: kpt on* **11/2**2
63-2 **2** *1/2* **Trade Secret**16 1478 5-9-2 **75** RobertWinston 18 85
(Mel Brittain) *awkward s: hld up: rdn and hdwy over 2f out: chsd wnr appr fnl f: drvn and kpt on wl: jst hld* **4/1**1
246- **3** *1 1/4* **Lenny Bee**136 7847 6-9-2 **80** (t) JustinNewman(5) 14 86
(Deborah Sanderson) *prom: rdn over 2f out: kpt on* **16/1**
05-5 **4** *1 1/4* **Bronze Beau**27 1237 5-9-6 **79** (t) JamesSullivan 2 80
(Linda Stubbs) *racd wd: overall ldr: rdn and edgd rt over 1f out: hdd appr fnl f: no ex* **20/1**
060- **5** *nk* **Rasaman (IRE)**203 6865 8-9-5 **78** GrahamLee 7 78
(Jim Goldie) *rrd s: hld up: pushed along and hdwy over 1f out: kpt on: nrst fin* **16/1**
0-30 **6** *nk* **Waking Warrior**16 1478 4-8-13 **77** (t) AliceCartwright(5) 5 76
(Kevin Ryan) *racd wd: w ldr: rdn and edgd lft over 1f out: one pce fnl f* **18/1**
6521 **7** *nse* **Dispol Grand (IRE)**14 1516 6-8-9 **68** RussKennemore 1 67
(Paul Midgley) *racd wd: chsd ldr: rdn over 2f out: kpt on one pce* **10/1**
0-61 **8** *3/4* **Mandalay King (IRE)**7 1675 7-9-2 **78** JulieBurke(3) 4 74
(Marjorie Fife) *s.i.s: sn outpcd towards rr: hdwy over 1f out: kpt on fnl f: nrst fin* **10/1**
1-50 **9** *nk* **Sleepy Blue Ocean**8 1642 6-8-8 **70** (p) SimonPearce(3) 8 65
(John Balding) *chsd ldrs: rdn over 2f out: one pce* **16/1**
40-0 **10** *shd* **Green Park (IRE)**8 1643 9-8-13 **77** NeilFarley(5) 17 72
(Declan Carroll) *chsd ldrs: rdn over 2f out: one pce* **20/1**
420- **11** *2* **Ryedane (IRE)**127 7928 10-8-1 **67** (b) RachelRichardson(7) 13 55
(Tim Easterby) *dwlt: hld up: bhd tl sme late hdwy* **50/1**
444- **12** *hd* **Select Committee**217 6537 7-8-13 **72** MichaelO'Connell 9 59
(John Quinn) *prom towards centre: wknd fnl f* **20/1**
4024 **13** *3/4* **Fair Passion**8 1643 5-8-8 **70** LeeTopliss(3) 15 54
(Derek Shaw) *in tch: rdn over 1f out: wknd ins fnl f* **7/1**3
000- **14** *1/2* **Indian Trail**210 6703 12-9-7 **80** (v) PaulQuinn 12 62
(David Nicholls) *hld up in midfield: rdn over 2f out: wknd ins fnl f* **28/1**
210- **15** *1* **Pelmanism**203 6865 5-9-4 **80** PaulPickard(3) 11 59
(Brian Ellison) *a outpcd towards rr* **12/1**
-064 **16** *1* **Ingleby Star (IRE)**27 1236 7-9-4 **77** (p) LeeNewman 3 52
(Ian McInnes) *racd wd: chsd ldrs: wknd over 1f out* **25/1**
30-0 **17** *3 1/4* **The Nifty Fox**8 1642 8-8-13 **72** PaulMulrennan 6 35
(Tim Easterby) *chsd ldrs towards centre: wknd over 1f out* **16/1**

1m 2.2s (2.60) **Going Correction** +0.675s/f (Yiel) **17** Ran SP% **126.1**
Speed ratings (Par 105): **106,105,103,101,100 100,100,98,98,98 95,94,93,92,91 89,84**
Tote Swingers: 1&2 £4.00, 1&3 £17.10, 2&3 £13.90 CSF £25.51 CT £280.56 TOTE £6.60: £1.60, £1.40, £4.00, £6.20; EX 26.50.
Owner Keith Taylor & Keith West **Bred** Fifehead Farms M C Denning **Trained** Norton, N Yorks
■ Stewards' Enquiry : Robert Winston four-day ban: used whip above permitted level (May 20-23)

FOCUS
A big field for this modest sprint handicap. The six lowest drawn horses tended to race isolated towards the far side but in the end the high numbers dominated. The winner is rated close to his best backed up by the third.
Fair Passion Official explanation: jockey said mare hung left
T/Plt: £330.90 to a £1 stake. Pool:£58,554.66 - 129.15 winning tickets T/Qpdt: £100.00 to a £1 stake. Pool:£3,570.76 - 26.40 winning tickets AS

1746 SAINT-CLOUD (L-H)
Saturday, May 5

OFFICIAL GOING: Turf: very soft changing to heavy after race 4 (5.20)

1869a PRIX GREFFULHE (GROUP 2) (3YO COLTS & FILLIES) (TURF) 1m 2f
4:50 (12:00) 3-Y-0 **£61,750** (£23,833; £11,375; £7,583; £3,791)

RPR
1 **Kesampour (FR)**34 1162 3-9-2 0 Christophe-PatriceLemaire 6 110+
(M Delzangles, France) *settled in 2nd bhd pcemaker: rdn to chal 2f out: led 1 1/2f out: r.o wl fnl f: hld on wl fnl 50yds* **7/10**1

2 *hd* **Albion**[16] 3 -9-20.............. Pierre-CharlesBoudot 2 110
(A Fabre, France) *settled in 4th on ins: rdn to go 2nd over 1 1/2f out: r.o wl fnl f: nt quite rch ldr* **9/1**

3 *1/2* **Eldandy (IRE)**[19] 3 -9-20.............. AnthonyCrastus 4 109
(C Laffon-Parias, France) *hld up towards rr: gd prog 2f out: r.o wl towards outside fnl f: got up for 3rd fnl strides* **15/2**

4 *shd* **Saonois (FR)**[27] 1244 3 -9-20.............. AntoineHamelin 3 108
(J-P Gauvin, France) *settled in 3rd on outer: r.o wl fr over 1 1/2f out: lost 3rd fnl strides* **33/10**[2]

5 *1* **First Date**[23] 3 -9-20.............. ThierryThulliez 1 106
(P Bary, France) *settled in 5th: relegated to rr early in st: had to be swtchd to outside to make run over 1 1/2f out: r.o wl fnl f wout threatening ldrs* **7/1**[3]

6 *10* **Shalamzar (FR)**[207] 3 -9-20.............. ThomasHuet 5 86
(M Delzangles, France) *rdn to ld after 100yds: set gd pce: hdd 1 1/2f out: wknd fnl f: eased* **23/1**

2m 9.4s (-6.60) **6**Ran SP% **120.5**
WIN (incl. 1 euro stake): 1.70 (Kesampour coupled with Shalamzar). PLACES: 1.30, 2.60. SF: 7.70.
Owner H H Aga Khan **Bred** Aga Khan **Trained** France 1870a-1871a, 1873a-1874a (See RI)

1839 CHURCHILL DOWNS (L-H)
Saturday, May 5

OFFICIAL GOING: Dirt: fast; turf: good

1872a KENTUCKY DERBY PRESENTED BY YUM! BRANDS (GRADE 1) (3YO) (DIRT) 1m 2f (D)
11:24 (11:31) 3-Y-O **£941,677** (£258,064; £129,032 ; £64,516 ; £38,709)

RPR

1 **I'll Have Another (USA)**[28] 1234 3 -9-00.............. MGutierrez 19 126
(Doug O'Neill, U.S.A) **153/10**

2 *1 1/2* **Bodemeister (USA)**[21] 1396 3 -9-00.............. MESmith 6 125+
(Bob Baffert, U.S.A) **42/10**[1]

3 *nk* **Dullahan (USA)**[21] 1395 3 -9-00.............. KDesormeaux 5 122
(Dale Romans, U.S.A) **121/10**

4 *3/4* **Went The Day Well (USA)**[43] 3 -9-00..............(b[1]) JRVelazquez 13 121+
(H Graham Motion, U.S.A) **31/1**

5 *1/2* **Creative Cause (USA)**[28] 1234 3 -9-00.............. JRosario 8 120
(Mike Harrington, U.S.A) **119/10**

6 *4* **Liaison (USA)**[28] 1234 3 -9-00..............(b) MGarcia 20 112
(Bob Baffert, U.S.A) **56/1**

7 *1/2* **Union Rags (USA)**[35] 1151 3 -9-00.............. JRLeparoux 4 111
(Michael Matz, U.S.A) **51/10**[2]

8 *3/4* **Rousing Sermon (USA)**[34] 3 -9-00..............(b) JLezcano 7 109
(Jerry Hollendorfer, U.S.A) **41/1**

9 *2* **Hansen (USA)**[21] 1395 3 -9-00.............. RADominguez 14 105+
(Michael J Maker, U.S.A) **131/10**

10 *1 1/4* **Daddy Nose Best (USA)**[40] 3 -9-00.............. GKGomez 10 103
(Steven Asmussen, U.S.A) **14/1**

11 *1/2* **Optimizer (USA)**[21] 1396 3 -9-00.............. JKCourt 2 102
(D Wayne Lukas, U.S.A) **42/1**

12 *7 1/4* **Alpha (USA)**[28] 1232 3 -9-00.............. RMaragh 11 87
(Kiaran McLaughlin, U.S.A) **196/10**

13 *3/4* **El Padrino (USA)**[35] 1151 3 -9-00.............. RBejarano 16 86
(Todd Pletcher, U.S.A) **29/1**

14 *3 1/2* **Done Talking (USA)**[28] 3 -9-00.............. SheldonRussell 17 79
(Hamilton Smith, U.S.A) **39/1**

15 *1 1/4* **Sabercat (USA)**[21] 1396 3 -9-00.............. CNakatani 18 76
(Steven Asmussen, U.S.A) **38/1**

16 *5 1/4* **Gemologist (USA)**[28] 1232 3 -9-00.............. JJCastellano 15 66
(Todd Pletcher, U.S.A) **43/5**[3]

17 *1 1/2* **Trinniberg (USA)**[28] 3 -9-00.............. WMartinez 9 63+
(Bisnath Parboo, U.S.A) **45/1**

18 *3* **Prospective (USA)**[21] 1395 3 -9-00..............(b) LContreras 12 57
(Mark Casse, Canada) **58/1**

19 *15 1/2* **Take Charge Indy (USA)**[35] 1151 3 -9-00..............(b) CHBorel 3 26
(Patrick Byrne, U.S.A) **119/10**

P **Daddy Long Legs (USA)**[35] 1145 3 -9-00.............. CO'Donoghue 1
(A P O'Brien, Ire) **26/1**

2m 1.83s (0.64) **20**Ran SP% **119.5**
PARI-MUTUEL (all including $2 stakes): WIN 32.60; PLACE (1-2) 13.80, 6.20; SHOW (1-2-3) 9.00, 5.60, 7.20; SF 306.60 .
Owner Reddam Racing Llc **Bred** Harvey Clarke **Trained** USA

FOCUS
The best horse on the day finished second as Bodemeister was asked to set an unsustainable pace. Bob Baffert's runner clocked the following sectionals: 22.32, 45.39 (fifth-fastest in Derby history), 1.09.80 (fourth-fastest in Derby history), and 1.35.19.

NOTEBOOK
I'll Have Another (USA) has to be considered second best, but he's an improving colt and is not to be underestimated. His two trial wins were nothing special, the latter gained narrowly in the Santa Anita Derby, but he evidently hasn't stopped progressing. He might lack the raw talent of Bodemeister, but there may well be more to come and it's certainly not out of the question he can claim the second leg of the Triple Crown, the Preakness on May 19.
Bodemeister(USA) seemingly got carried away with the speed of the track, and was perhaps wary that his mount's impressive trial win came from the front, but it was an inexcusable error of judgement. Bodemeister will obviously hold outstanding claims if taking his chance in the Preakness, but there's just a nagging worry that his exertions will take their toll at some point. This came just three weeks after a huge performance in the Arkansas Derby, and he had been trained hard. Plus he doesn't have the foundation of a juvenile campaign (was bidding to become the first horse since 1882 to take this without racing it at two), although clearly that's not what cost him.
Dullahan(USA) got the strong pace he needed and closed well. He was forced wide with his challenge, but can have no excuse.
Went The Day Well (USA) represented the same connections as last year's winner Animal Kingdom, and he'd won the same prep, the Spiral Stakes. Fitted with blinkers for the first time, he ran on strongly from well back, but much too late, and he should have learnt plenty.
Creative Cause (USA) was just denied by I'll Have Another in the Santa Anita Derby. He didn't improve as much as his old rival, but still ran with credit.
Union Rags (USA) missed the break and found a whole heap of trouble. He probably did well to get so close and will doubtless be popular again if lining up in the Preakness.
Hansen(USA) was worked up beforehand and was too keen in the race. The occasion got to him.
Gemologist(USA) came into this 5-5, including two course wins, but he was bitterly disappointing. He was beaten going down the back straight.
Daddy Long Legs (USA) was just about best out of the stalls, so the inside draw wasn't the issue it might have been, but he was struggling to keep up going down the back straight and soon dropped away. It's hoped he returned sound.

HAMILTON (R-H)
Sunday, May 6

OFFICIAL GOING: Good to soft (good in places; 7.2)
Races on round course run over approximately 25yds further than advertised.
Wind: Slight, across Weather: Cloudy, bright

1875 BET WITH TOTEPOOL ON THE GUINEAS H'CAP 6f 5y
2:15 (2:16) (Class 5) (0-70,70) 4-Y-0+ **£3,234** (£962; £481 ; £240) **Stalls** High

Form RPR

2-1 **1** **Alive And Kicking**[25] 1296 4 -9-470.............. AmyRyan[(3)] 1 83
(James Bethell) *t.k.h: mde all: rdn and clr over 1f out: hld on wl fnl f* **11/4**[1]

000- **2** *3/4* **Breezolini**[191] 7141 4 -9-265.............. RobertWinston 10 75
(Geoffrey Harker) *sn bhd: rdn and hdwy over 1f out: chsd wnr ins fnl f: clsng at fin* **8/1**

00-5 **3** *3* **Crimson Knot (IRE)**[28] 1236 4 -8-1369.............. MatthewHopkins[(7)] 11 70
(Alan Berry) *midfield: hung rt thrght: hdwy to chse wnr over 1f out: drifted rt: kpt on same pce fnl f* **16/1**

50-0 **4** *2 3/4* **Needy McCredie**[9] 1638 6 -8-1059.............. PaddyAspell 4 51
(James Turner) *s.i.s: hld up: rdn and hdwy over 1f out: kpt on fnl f: nrst fin* **14/1**

50-0 **5** *1 1/4* **Insolenceofoffice (IRE)**[25] 1293 4 -8-761..............(p) LMcNiff[(5)] 8 49
(Richard Ford) *prom: rdn over 2f out: edgd rt and no ex over 1f out* **11/1**

2226 **6** *1/2* **Argentine (IRE)**[28] 1237 8 -9-063..............(b) DanielTudhope 3 49
(Ian Semple) *s.i.s: sn prom: rdn and wknd over 1f out* **12/1**

02-0 **7** *2 3/4* **Brave Dream**[27] 1254 4 -9-265.............. PhillipMakin 6 43
(Kevin Ryan) *hld up in midfield: effrt and shkn up over 2f out: wknd over 1f out* **17/2**

-310 **8** *3/4* **Khandaq (USA)**[83] 548 5 -9-568.............. PaulMulrennan 9 43
(Keith Dalgleish) *missed break: bhd: hdwy on outside over 2f out: wknd over 1f out* **7/1**[3]

501- **9** *1/2* **Henry Morgan**[195] 7064 5 -9-366.............. TomEaves 2 40
(Bryan Smart) *pressed wnr tl rdn and wknd over 1f out* **11/2**[2]

346- **10** *3 1/2* **Tadalavil**[193] 7104 7 -8-1261.............. MartinLane 7 23
(Linda Perratt) *prom: rdn and struggling over 2f out: sn btn* **9/1**

1m 12.68s (0.48) **Going Correction** +0.175s/f (Good) **10**Ran SP% **114.8**
Speed ratings (Par 103): **103,102,98,94,92 92,88,87,86,82**
toteswingers: 1&2 £4.50, 1&3 £11.60, 2&3 £30.40 CSF £24.49 CT £301.69 TOTE £2.70 : £1.30 , £3.10, £5.30 ; EX 32.80 .
Owner M J Dawson **Bred** M J Dawson **Trained** Middleham Moor, N Yorks

FOCUS
Races on Round course run over approximately 25yds further than advertised. A first race run in a time just under three seconds above standard on ground described offically as good to soft, good in places. Modest form but a step up from the winner.
Argentine(IRE) Official explanation: jockey said gelding hung right
Brave Dream Official explanation: trainer said gelding finished distressed

1876 CANCER RESEARCH UK CLAIMING STKS 6f 5y
2:45 (2:45) (Class 6) 4-6-Y-0 **£2,385** (£704; £352) **Stalls** High

Form RPR

0-00 **1** **Qubuh (IRE)**[15] 1526 4 -8-1064.............. MichaelO'Connell 1 69
(Linda Stubbs) *chsd ldng gp: hdwy on outside to ld over 1f out: hdd briefly ins fnl f: hld on gamely towards fin* **17/2**

0000 **2** *hd* **Frequency**[44] 1007 5 -9-572..............(b) PaulMulrennan 3 77
(Keith Dalgleish) *trckd ldrs gng wl: shkn up and hdwy to ld briefly ins fnl f: kpt on: hld nr fin* **8/1**[3]

05-0 **3** *1* **Ursula (IRE)**[25] 1294 6 -8-772.............. RobertWinston 5 62
(Mrs K Burke) *hld up: hdwy on outside over 1f out: rdn and ev ch ins fnl f: kpt on same pce towards fin* **15/8**[2]

54-0 **4** *4* **Saucy Brown (IRE)**[7] 1478 6 -9-381.............. AdrianNicholls 4 59
(David Nicholls) *t.k.h: cl up: rdn to ld briefly over 1f out: sn hdd: wknd ins fnl f* **5/4**[1]

0-05 **5** *7* **Mr Khan**[3] 1799 4 -8-649.............. JulieBurke[(3)] 6 29
(Linda Perratt) *pressed ldr: rdn and led over 2f out to over 1f out: sn wknd* **25/1**

30-0 **6** *4* **Hardrock Diamond**[22] 1383 4 -8-746.............. DuranFentiman 2 14
(Ian Semple) *s.i.s: hld up: hdwy over 2f out: rdn and wknd wl over 1f out* **50/1**

0040 **7** *2* **Amno Dancer (IRE)**[3] 1801 5 -8-850.............. TomEaves 7 9
(Ian Semple) *led to over 2f out: sn drvn and wknd* **18/1**

1m 13.18s (0.98) **Going Correction** +0.175s/f (Good) **7**Ran SP% **111.9**
Speed ratings: **100,99,98,93,83 78,75**
toteswingers: 1&2 £3.80, 1&3 £2.60, 2&3 £2.50 CSF £68.98 TOTE £8.60 : £3.10 , £4.70 ; EX 68.50.
Owner D M Smith **Bred** Irish National Stud **Trained** Norton, N Yorks

FOCUS
Fair efforts from the leading trio who came clear. The winner is the best guide and there is a chance the form is worth a little more, although the time does not back that up.

1877 TOTEPOOL TANGERINE TREES CONDITIONS STKS 5f 4y
3:25 (3:26) (Class 3) 3-Y-0 **£9,056** (£2,695; £1,346 ; £673) **Stalls** High

Form RPR

53-0 **1** **Dam Beautiful**[18] 1457 3 -8-691.............. AmyRyan[(3)] 1 99
(Kevin Ryan) *carried rt s: chsd ldng gp: gd hdwy to ld over 1f out: edgd rt: kpt on strly fnl f* **13/2**

104- **2** *2 1/2* **Stonefield Flyer**[218] 6518 3 -9-0103.............. PaulMulrennan 2 95
(Keith Dalgleish) *w ldrs: rdn over 1f out: kpt on fnl f: nt pce of wnr* **85/40**[2]

01-1 **3** *3 3/4* **Free Zone**[15] 1524 3 -9-294 ow2.............. TomEaves 3 82
(Bryan Smart) *mde most to over 1f out: sn rdn and outpcd* **13/8**[1]

526- **4** *2 1/4* **Vocational (USA)**[240] 5882 3 -9-0104.............. FrannyNorton 5 73
(Mark Johnston) *chsd ldrs: shkn up and wknd over 1f out* **7/2**[3]

40-3 **5** *4* **Luv U Forever**[23] 1356 3 -8-290.............. JoshBaudains[(7)] 4 54
(Jo Hughes) *w ldrs: rdn over 2f out: wknd over 1f out* **20/1**

1m 0.67s (0.67) **Going Correction** +0.175s/f (Good) **5**Ran SP% **110.4**
Speed ratings (Par 103): **101,97,91,87,81**
CSF £20.67 TOTE £7.00 : £2.40 , £2.30 ; EX 23.20 .
Owner Mrs Lisa Dartnell **Bred** Lady Lonsdale **Trained** Hambleton, N Yorks

FOCUS
A useful conditions event but not the most solid form. There was a smallish field but a few of these like to go on and there was no shortage of pace, setting it up for the winner to some extent.

NOTEBOOK

Dam Beautiful hadn't cut much ice in a competitive Newmarket handicap on her return but got firmly back on track here with a very useful effort, taken off her feet a bit early but coming through as the leaders faltered. Things did drop right here but she's lightly raced enough to suggest we may not have seen the best of her yet, the filly and mares' Listed sprint at Ayr next month is just one obvious target. (op 6-1 tchd 7-1)

Stonefield Flyer was one of the best sprint juveniles of last season and all his speed remains intact judged on this, as he travelled strongly for a long way, faring easily best of the pacesetters. Just as effective on quicker surface, he's a likely sort for something like the 5f Scurry Stakes at Sandown next month. (op 11-4 tchd 2-1)

Free Zone had been impressive on his reappearance at Thirsk but failed to reproduce that form here, taken on for the lead this time and having nothing left in the closing stages. (tchd 6-4 and 7-4)

Vocational(USA) was very useful at her best last year, finishing second in the Group 3 Sirenia, but wasn't anywhere near that level on her return, never appearing to be going with that much fluency on softer going than she tackled last year. (tchd 10-3 and 4-1)

Luv U Forever had a fair bit on at the weights but was well below par in any case. Official explanation: trainer said filly was unsuited by the good to soft (good in places) ground (op 16-1)

1878 SCOTTISH RACING MAIDEN STKS — 1m 65y

4:00 (4:07) (Class 5) 3-5-Y-O — **£3,234** (£962; £481; £240) **Stalls** Low

Form — RPR

0 **1** **Sheikhzayedroad**[17] 1467 3-9-1 0 ... MartinLane 7 — 76+
(David Simcock) *s.i.s: hld up: hdwy and swtchd lft 2f out: styd on wl fnl f: led towards fin* **9/4**[1]

06- **2** *shd* **Warcrown (IRE)**[251] 5548 3-8-12 0 ... LeeTopliss(3) 5 — 75+
(Richard Fahey) *trckd ldr: led over 2f out: rdn and edgd lft fnl f: kpt on wl: hdd nr fin* **9/2**

2-0 **3** *6* **Shuja (USA)**[18] 1456 3-9-1 0 ... PhillipMakin 9 — 61
(Saeed Bin Suroor) *in tch: effrt and pushed along fr over 2f out: outpcd fnl f* **3/1**[3]

4 **4** *hd* **Border Bandit (USA)**[27] 1250 4-10-0 0 ... PaddyAspell 2 — 64
(Tracy Waggott) *in tch: effrt and pushed along over 2f out: no imp fr over 1f out* **33/1**

2 **5** *¾* **Emily Carr (IRE)**[8] 1660 3-8-10 0 ... FrannyNorton 4 — 54
(Mark Johnston) *led: rdn and hdd over 2f out: wknd fnl f* **11/4**[2]

0- **6** *2 ¼* **Running Reef (IRE)**[198] 6983 3-9-1 0 ... TomEaves 3 — 54
(Tracy Waggott) *t.k.h: trckd ldrs tl rdn and wknd over 1f out* **80/1**

7 *6* **In The Crowd (IRE)** 3-9-1 0 ... RobertWinston 8 — 40+
(Alan Swinbank) *loose in preliminaries and galloped rdrless for 3f: hld up: hdwy on outside over 2f out: rdn and wknd over 1f out* **14/1**

5 **8** *1 ½* **Hurricane Rita (IRE)**[22] 1380 4-9-9 0 ... PaulMulrennan 6 — 35
(Alan Swinbank) *hld up: shkn up over 2f out: sn outpcd* **40/1**

0 **9** *3 ½* **Hulwa (USA)**[27] 1250 3-8-5 0 ... ShaneBKelly(5) 10 — 24
(Tracy Waggott) *trckd ldrs tl rdn and wknd fr 3f out* **100/1**

10 *¾* **Pioneer Boy (USA)** 3-8-10 0 ... GarryWhillans(5) 1 — 27
(Alan Swinbank) *dwlt: sn midfield: struggling over 3f out: sn wknd* **40/1**

1m 51.27s (2.87) **Going Correction** +0.45s/f (Yiel)
WFA 3 from 4yo 13lb — **10** Ran SP% **117.3**
Speed ratings (Par 103): **103,102,96,96,95 93,87,86,82,81**
toteswingers: 1&2 £3.10, 1&3 £2.30, 2&3 £3.90 CSF £12.71 TOTE £2.60: £1.10, £1.80, £1.60; EX 15.30.
Owner Mohammed Jaber **Bred** Rabbah Bloodstock Limited **Trained** Newmarket, Suffolk
■ Stewards' Enquiry : Martin Lane one-day ban: careless riding (May 20)

FOCUS

Form to view reasonably, at least from the leading pair, who came well clear in the end. The first two are improvers but the form is limited by the fourth and sixth to some extent.

1879 CARIBBEAN NIGHT ON FRIDAY H'CAP — 1m 65y

4:35 (4:37) (Class 5) (0-70,70) 4-Y-0+ — **£3,234** (£962; £481; £240) **Stalls** Low

Form — RPR

60-4 **1** **Spavento (IRE)**[8] 1659 6-8-8 57 ... DavidAllan 6 — 67
(Eric Alston) *hld up towards rr: stdy hdwy over 2f out: effrt and rdn over 1f out: styd on wl fnl f to ld cl home* **9/2**[3]

021- **2** *shd* **Royal Straight**[193] 7099 7-8-10 62 ... (t) JulieBurke(3) 7 — 72
(Linda Perratt) *s.i.s: hld up: gd hdwy on outside to ld appr fnl f: edgd rt: kpt on fnl f: hdd cl home* **18/1**

1605 **3** *3 ¾* **Copperwood**[3] 1796 7-9-3 66 ... FrannyNorton 4 — 67
(Mark Johnston) *trckd ldrs: effrt and rdn over 2f out: kpt on same pce appr fnl f* **13/2**

0324 **4** *1* **Georgebernardshaw (IRE)**[4] 1755 7-8-13 62 ... KellyHarrison 2 — 61
(Richard Guest) *led: rdn and hdd appr fnl f: sn one pce* **7/2**[1]

1440 **5** *1* **Dashing Eddie (IRE)**[8] 1659 4-9-1 64 ... (p) PhillipMakin 9 — 61
(Kevin Ryan) *trckd ldrs: rdn over 2f out: outpcd wl over 1f out: kpt on fnl f* **8/1**

656- **6** *4 ½* **Honest Deal**[251] 5560 4-9-7 70 ... RobertWinston 5 — 56
(Alan Swinbank) *t.k.h: in tch: effrt over 2f out: rdn and wknd over 1f out* **4/1**[2]

40-6 **7** *1 ¼* **Spey Song (IRE)**[18] 1439 4-9-4 67 ... TomEaves 10 — 51
(James Bethell) *hld up: rdn and edgd rt over 2f out: sn no imp* **14/1**

552- **8** *hd* **Avison (IRE)**[190] 7158 4-8-10 62 ... LeeTopliss(3) 8 — 45
(Richard Fahey) *t.k.h: in tch: rdn and outpcd over 2f out: edgd rt and n.d after* **9/1**

230- **9** *4* **Glenluji**[246] 5721 7-8-9 58 ... GrahamLee 3 — 32
(Jim Goldie) *hld up: drvn over 2f out: sn wknd* **14/1**

040- **10** *2* **Retreat Content (IRE)**[156] 7604 4-9-0 63 ... PaulMulrennan 1 — 32
(Linda Perratt) *trckd ldrs tl rdn and wknd 2f out* **25/1**

1m 50.92s (2.52) **Going Correction** +0.45s/f (Yiel) — **10** Ran SP% **117.3**
Speed ratings (Par 103): **105,104,101,100,99 94,93,93,89,87**
toteswingers: 1&2 £10.90, 1&3 £8.00, 2&3 £21.10 CSF £82.01 CT £528.75 TOTE £6.00: £2.00, £5.00, £3.10; EX 70.00.
Owner Whitehills Racing Syndicate **Bred** E Prosser, J Singh, & N & E Kent **Trained** Longton, Lancs

FOCUS

Just a run-of-the-mill contest, although the leading pair deserve a bit of credit for pulling clear. The third, close to his latest form, looks the best guide.

1880 TOTEPOOL.COM BUTTONHOOK H'CAP — 1m 5f 9y

5:10 (5:11) (Class 3) (0-90,85) 4-Y-0+ — **£9,056** (£2,695; £1,346; £673) **Stalls** Low

Form — RPR

20-5 **1** **Persian Peril**[28] 1239 8-9-5 83 ... RobertWinston 5 — 91
(Alan Swinbank) *stdd s: hld up: rdn over 2f out: hdwy on outside to ld over 1f out: kpt on wl fnl f* **12/1**

142- **2** *2 ¾* **Getabuzz**[231] 6191 4-9-0 78 ... DavidAllan 8 — 82+
(Tim Easterby) *hld up in tch: smooth hdwy to ld over 2f out: hdd over 1f out: rdn and kpt on same pce fnl f* **5/1**

000/ **3** *½* **Outrageous Request**[15] 6516 6-8-8 75 ... JulieBurke(3) 6 — 78
(Lucinda Russell) *led: rdn and hdd over 2f out: rallied: kpt on same pce over 1f out* **18/1**

133- **4** *½* **Jonny Delta**[205] 6832 5-8-11 75 ... GrahamLee 7 — 77
(Jim Goldie) *hld up: stdy hdwy over 3f out: rdn over 2f out: no imp tl styd on fnl f: nvr able to chal* **4/1**[2]

324- **5** *¾* **Hong Kong Island (IRE)**[227] 6277 5-9-2 85 ... ShaneBKelly(5) 1 — 86
(Micky Hammond) *t.k.h: prom: rdn over 2f out: wknd over 1f out* **9/2**[3]

20-2 **6** *6* **Spirit Of A Nation (IRE)**[3] 1797 7-8-11 75 ... PaddyAspell 4 — 67
(James Moffatt) *in tch: drvn and outpcd over 3f out: n.d after* **8/1**

6-45 **7** *6* **Jeu De Vivre (IRE)**[26] 1282 4-9-2 80 ... FrannyNorton 3 — 63
(Mark Johnston) *cl up tl rdn and wknd over 2f out* **3/1**[1]

/60- **8** *4 ½* **Marhaba Malyoon (IRE)**[337] 2715 4-9-0 78 ... MartinLane 2 — 55
(David Simcock) *hld up: stdy hdwy and prom 1/2-way: wknd over 2f out* **12/1**

4/6- **9** *11* **Proud Times (USA)**[90] 1470 6-8-13 82 ... GarryWhillans(5) 9 — 42
(Alan Swinbank) *in tch: drvn and outpcd over 4f out: sn struggling: n.d after* **25/1**

2m 57.2s (3.30) **Going Correction** +0.45s/f (Yiel) — **9** Ran SP% **115.5**
Speed ratings (Par 107): **107,105,105,104,104 100,96,94,87**
toteswingers: 1&2 £8.80, 1&3 £18.20, 2&3 £15.80 CSF £70.86 CT £1086.32 TOTE £16.70: £4.30, £2.30, £5.10; EX 93.40.
Owner Mrs J Porter **Bred** Mrs P Lewis **Trained** Melsonby, N Yorks

FOCUS

A fairly useful handicap. The gallop was no better than modest to past halfway and the form, although straightforward, looks pretty ordinary.

NOTEBOOK

Persian Peril was clearly sharper for last month's reappearance and is evidently better than ever, this much the highest handicap mark he's ever defied, coming clear inside the last. A rise in the weights may find him out, though. (op 10-1)

Getabuzz is still fairly lightly raced and this reappearance definitely promised more to come this year, travelling strongly to the front before lack of race sharpness perhaps just found him out in the end. He's definitely the one to take out of the race.

Outrageous Request, fit from hurdling, was a fair handicapper on the Flat back in 2010 and retains all that ability judged on this, though he had the run of things from the front and needs no excuses.

Jonny Delta is still fairly lightly raced and leaves the impression he has a better performance in him at some stage, this a pretty encouraging return to action, keeping on steadily having travelled well for a long way under restraint. A well-run race at around this sort of trip will probably see him in his best light. (op 9-2, tchd 5-1 in a place)

Hong Kong Island(IRE) made a perfectly respectable reappearance but chances are he needs to come down a little in the weights, and his consistency doesn't really allow that to happen. (tchd 5-1)

Spirit Of A Nation(IRE) presumably just found this coming a little quick after Musselburgh and is better judged on that effort.

Jeu De Vivre(IRE) had a good record here last season so this run was all the more disappointing. Official explanation: trainer had no explanation for the poor form shown (op 4-1)

Marhaba Malyoon(IRE), last seen running in the Epsom Derby, still looked to have a bit of potential back at this more realistic level but it's hard to derive much encouragement out of this. (op 9-1)

1881 RACING UK ON SKY 432 H'CAP — 5f 4y

5:45 (5:48) (Class 6) (0-60,59) 4-Y-0+ — **£2,385** (£704; £352) **Stalls** High

Form — RPR

40-0 **1** **Dotty Darroch**[22] 1383 4-8-12 50 ... DanielTudhope 3 — 58
(Robin Bastiman) *prom: rdn 1/2-way: hdwy to ld over 1f out: hld on wl fnl f* **7/1**

60-6 **2** *¾* **Here Now And Why (IRE)**[28] 1242 5-9-4 56 ... (p) RobertWinston 12 — 61
(Ian Semple) *t.k.h: prom: effrt and rdn ent fnl f: kpt on to take 2nd nr fin* **11/4**[1]

050- **3** *shd* **Lady Del Sol**[187] 7216 4-9-1 58 ... DeanHeslop(5) 11 — 63
(Marjorie Fife) *prom: drvn 1/2-way: chsd wnr over 1f out: hld and lost 2nd cl home* **6/1**[3]

-053 **4** *1* **Sally's Swansong**[22] 1383 6-8-12 50 ... DavidAllan 1 — 51
(Eric Alston) *midfield on outside: rdn 1/2-way: effrt and cl up over 1f out: kpt on same pce ins fnl f* **9/2**[2]

06- **5** *2* **Lees Anthem**[224] 6386 5-9-2 54 ... PaddyAspell 13 — 48
(Colin Teague) *hld up: hdwy 1/2-way: rdn and kpt on same pce fnl f* **16/1**

0-00 **6** *hd* **Pivotal Prospect**[27] 1248 4-8-4 47 ow2 ... ShaneBKelly(5) 6 — 40
(Tracy Waggott) *bhd: rdn and hdwy over 1f out: kpt on same pce ins fnl f* **25/1**

136- **7** *¾* **Pinball (IRE)**[263] 5175 6-8-13 54 ... (p) AmyRyan(3) 14 — 44
(Lisa Williamson) *hld up bhd ldng gp: effrt and rdn over 1f out: kpt on fnl f: nt pce to chal* **12/1**

6-66 **8** *shd* **Drumpellier (IRE)**[12] 1584 5-8-2 45 ... (e) NeilFarley(5) 8 — 35
(Simon West) *in tch: drvn 1/2-way: outpcd over 1f out* **25/1**

260- **9** *¾* **Weetentherty**[177] 7371 5-9-0 52 ... PhillipMakin 9 — 39+
(Linda Perratt) *s.i.s: bhd: effrt and pushed along over 1f out: n.m.r briefly ins fnl f: n.d* **20/1**

005- **10** *½* **Face East (USA)**[292] 4172 4-8-0 45 ... MatthewHopkins(7) 5 — 31
(Alan Berry) *bhd: hdwy on outside over 1f out: rdn and hung rt: sn n.d* **66/1**

425- **11** *1* **Cayman Fox**[184] 7266 7-9-7 59 ... PaulMulrennan 2 — 41
(Linda Perratt) *swtchd lft s: led to over 1f out: sn btn* **11/1**

6426 **12** *¾* **Hambleton**[24] 1343 5-8-12 50 ... (p) TomEaves 10 — 29
(Bryan Smart) *in tch: drvn 1/2-way: wknd wl over 1f out* **10/1**

000 **13** *½* **Green Warrior**[28] 1242 4-9-1 56 ... (e) DeclanCannon(3) 4 — 33
(Richard Guest) *taken early to post: prom tl rdn and wknd wl over 1f out* **33/1**

000 **14** *4 ½* **Diggers Daydream (IRE)**[20] 1422 4-8-4 45 ... RossAtkinson(3) 7 — 6
(Lisa Williamson) *in tch to 1/2-way: sn rdn and wknd* **100/1**

1m 1.05s (1.05) **Going Correction** +0.175s/f (Good) — **14** Ran SP% **120.5**
Speed ratings (Par 101): **98,96,96,95,91 91,90,90,88,88 86,85,84,77**
toteswingers: 1&2 £7.40, 1&3 £10.70, 2&3 £5.10 CSF £24.78 CT £129.62 TOTE £9.10: £3.20, £1.50, £3.00; EX 37.10.
Owner The McMaster Springford Partnership **Bred** Ptarmigan Bloodstock Ltd **Trained** Cowthorpe, N Yorks

FOCUS

A low-grade sprint. They raced centre to stands' side and no part of the track seemed to offer an advantage, the winner out towards the middle but the second and third more towards the rail. The fourth is the best guide to the level.

Pinball(IRE) Official explanation: jockey said mare was denied a clear run

Weetentherty Official explanation: jockey said gelding was denied a clear run

T/Plt: £1,039.10 to a £1 stake. Pool: £56,012.96. 39.35 winning tickets. T/Qpdt: £43.10 to a £1 stake. Pool: £4,771.04. 81.80 winning tickets. RY

[1854]NEWMARKET (R-H)

Sunday, May 6

OFFICIAL GOING: Good to soft (stands' side 7.3; centre 7.3; far side 7.4) changing to soft after race 5 (4.25)

Stands' side course used. Stalls stands' side except 1000 Guineas centre and 1m4f far side. Rail repositioning increased 1m4f races by 12m.

Wind: Light, half behind Weather: Overcast

1882 QIPCO SUPPORTING BRITISH RACING STKS (H'CAP) 1m 4f

2:05 (2:10) (Class 2) (0-105,101) 4-Y-O+

£24,900 (£7,456; £3,728; £1,864; £932; £468) **Stalls** Low

Form RPR

2-25 **1** **Ithoughtitwasover (IRE)**[11] 1603 4-9-0 **91** .... KierenFallon 10 99+
(Mark Johnston) *chsd ldrs: rdn and effrt to ld over 2f out: styd on wl fnl f: hung lft towards fin* **10/1**

531/ **2** *¾* **Local Hero (GER)**[15] 7282 5-8-7 **84** ....(p) DarryllHolland 8 91+
(Steve Gollings) *hld up in tch: rdn and effrt ent fnl 2f: styng on whn nt clr run and swtchd rt ins fnl f: r.o strly fnl 100yds: nt quite rch wnr* **5/1**[1]

0/5- **3** *½* **Caucus**[346] 2438 5-9-9 **100** .... WilliamBuick 9 106
(John Gosden) *chsd ldrs: rdn and effrt wl over 2f out: chsd wnr 2f out: styd on same pce ins fnl f: lost 2nd towards fin* **11/1**

141- **4** *½* **Sandusky**[228] 6248 4-8-11 **88** .... MickaelBarzalona 15 93+
(Mahmood Al Zarooni) *stdd s: t.k.h: hld up in tch in rr: rdn and hdwy 3f out: drvn and chsng ldrs ent fnl f: wnt 2nd and edgd lft fnl 150yds tl no ex and lost 2 pls towards fin* **8/1**

321- **5** *2* **Franciscan**[215] 6607 4-8-10 **87** .... JamieSpencer 14 89
(Luca Cumani) *in tch: rdn and effrt to press ldrs ent fnl 2f: unable qck 1f out: one pce fnl f* **14/1**

614- **6** *1 ¾* **Mountain Range (IRE)**[165] 7523 4-8-10 **87** .... EddieAhern 16 86
(John Dunlop) *hld up in tch towards rr: rdn and effrt ent fnl 2f: hdwy and edgd rt over 1f out: kpt on wl fnl f: nt rch ldrs* **16/1**

0/0- **7** *nse* **Bernie The Bolt (IRE)**[211] 6690 6-9-3 **94** .... PatCosgrave 12 93
(Andrew Balding) *t.k.h: hld up in tch in rr: rdn and hdwy over 1f out: styd on fnl f: nt rch ldrs* **33/1**

111- **8** *2* **Anatolian**[225] 6342 4-9-6 **97** .... FrankieDettori 4 93
(Mahmood Al Zarooni) *chsd ldrs: rdn and pressed ldrs wl over 2f out: unable qck u.p over 1f out: wknd fnl 150yds* **13/2**[2]

400- **9** *½* **Rock A Doodle Doo (IRE)**[274] 4778 5-9-3 **94** .... MartinDwyer 7 89+
(William Jarvis) *hld up in tch in midfield: rdn and unable qck 3f out: rallying and edging rt over 1f out: keeping on but no threat to ldrs whn nt clr run ins fnl f: nt pushed after* **7/1**[3]

60-0 **10** *nk* **Bridle Belle**[22] 1374 4-8-8 **85** .... PaulHanagan 13 80+
(Richard Fahey) *t.k.h: hld up in tch: rdn and effrt ent fnl 2f: keeping on same pce and btn whn sltly hmpd 1f out: plugged on fnl f* **20/1**

1615 **11** *4 ½* **Tappanappa (IRE)**[35] 1159 5-8-11 **88** ....(v) DavidProbert 1 75
(Andrew Balding) *stdd s: hld up in tch towards rr: rdn and hdwy 3f out: chsng ldrs and drvn over 1f out: no ex and struggling whn pushed rt 1f out: fdd fnl f* **25/1**

46-3 **12** *2 ½* **Hurricane Higgins (IRE)**[36] 1137 4-9-9 **100** .... JoeFanning 5 86
(Mark Johnston) *chsd ldr: rdn to ld 3f out: sn hdd: wkng u.p whn squeezed for room and snatched up 1f out: wl btn after* **12/1**

4-12 **13** *17* **Colinca's Lad (IRE)**[13] 1566 10-7-8 **76** ow1 .... RosieJessop(5) 6 32
(Peter Charalambous) *t.k.h: chsd ldrs tl rdn and wknd 2f out: t.o fnl f* **20/1**

13/4 **14** *9* **Eye Of The Tiger (GER)**[15] 1507 7-9-10 **101** .... TomQueally 11 43
(Barney Curley) *racd wd: led tl hdd and rdn 3f out: sn dropped out and bhd: t.o and eased fnl f* **66/1**

10-1 **15** *nk* **Charles Camoin (IRE)**[36] 1139 4-9-4 **95** .... JimmyFortune 3 36
(Sylvester Kirk) *t.k.h: chsd ldrs: rdn 3f out: losing pl and towards rr whn hmpd ent fnl 2f: t.o and eased fnl f* **10/1**

2m 40.51s (8.51) **Going Correction** +0.55s/f (Yiel) **15 Ran SP% 118.2**

Speed ratings (Par 109): **93,92,92,91,90 89,89,87,87,87 84,82,71,65,65**

toteswingers: 1&2 £11.30, 1&3 £19.60, 2&3 £12.60 CSF £53.97 CT £570.35 TOTE £11.80: £3.30, £2.00, £3.90; EX 68.00 Trifecta £507.30 Pool: £2,283.23 - 3.33 winning units..

Owner Crone Stud Farms Ltd **Bred** Stonethorn Stud Farms Ltd **Trained** Middleham Moor, N Yorks

FOCUS

The ground remained good to soft on the Rowley Mile, as it was dry overnight and the overall going stick at 10am came in at 7.4 as against 7.1 the previous afternoon. Michael Prosser expected the course to ride faster, but felt the slowest part was the stands' rail. However, both Frankie Dettori and Darryll Holland said after the opener it was "dead" (their mounts raced centre to far-side). This race had been dominated by four and 5yos in recent years, and the 2011 winner Times Up developed into a Group-placed stayer. The early pace was even but ordinary, and quickened around 5f from home. The form is rated at face value around the principals.

NOTEBOOK

Ithoughtitwasover(IRE) ran poorly on testing ground at Epsom 11 days previously, but found this going much easier to handle and won despite hanging towards the stands' side in the final stages. It was a good effort but the rider gets plenty of credit for having his mount well-placed to attack. A trip to Royal Ascot for something like the Duke Of Edinburgh (Mark Johnston has won that three times since 2000, all of them 4-y-os) could be on the agenda in the summer. (op 11-1 tchd 9-1)

Local Hero(GER) ◆ looked really interesting returned to the Flat after some excellent performances over hurdles. He got locked behind a wall of horses here before hitting a flat spot, but then ran on strongly inside the final furlong. A more strongly run contest will suit and he can be counted unlucky in this. (op 11-2)

Caucus ran only once last season, a respectable fifth in the Group 2 Henry II Stakes (2m) in May. Subsequently gelded, he made a pleasing return and will no doubt be suited by further in due course. (op 9-1)

Sandusky ◆, off since late September, was one of the least exposed of these and his run can be marked up, as he sat out the back for much of the contest before coming with a strong bid wide of rivals. Giving up ground early probably told in the final stages and he remains one to be interested in. (op 7-1)

Franciscan was 7lb higher than his previous start, a win at Leicester last October on quick ground, and made a satisfactory comeback after sitting upsides the third for much of the race. (tchd 12-1 and 16-1 in a place)

Mountain Range(IRE) stayed on to post solid performances and maintained his consistent profile.

Bernie The Bolt(IRE), was another to run a solid race, especially as this trip is too short for him. (op 50-1)

Anatolian, who holds a Yorkshire Cup entry, was always well placed here but found nothing for pressure inside the 3f marker and tended to roll about a bit. One would imagine a step up in trip will be tried sooner rather than later. (op 11-2 tchd 5-1)

Rock A Doodle Doo(IRE), gelded since his last outing, was just making ground into a promising position when hampered at least once and lost valuable momentum in the process. With a clear passage, he'd probably have been in the places. (op 10-1)

1883 QATAR BLOODSTOCK DAHLIA STKS (GROUP 3) (F&M) 1m 1f

2:35 (2:41) (Class 1) 4-Y-O+

£31,190 (£11,825; £5,918; £2,948; £1,479; £742) **Stalls** High

Form RPR

131- **1** **Izzi Top**[194] 7090 4-9-1 110 .... WilliamBuick 2 110+
(John Gosden) *t.k.h: chsd ldr: rdn and ev ch over 1f out: drvn ahd jst ins fnl f: r.o wl: drvn out* **3/1**[2]

30-1 **2** *1 ¼* **Captivator**[29] 1213 5-8-12 105 .... KierenFallon 1 104+
(James Fanshawe) *t.k.h: hld up in last trio: rdn and effrt 2f out: chsd ldng pair over 1f out: drvn and chsd wnr fnl 100yds: kpt on* **6/1**[3]

210- **3** *½* **Primevere (IRE)**[252] 5523 4-8-12 105 .... HayleyTurner 3 103
(Roger Charlton) *t.k.h: chsd ldr tl led over 6f out: stl set stdy gallop tl rdn and qcknd 2f out: drvn and hdd jst ins fnl f: one pce fnl 100yds* **10/1**

320- **4** *4 ½* **Timepiece**[225] 6338 5-8-12 114 .... TomQueally 4 93
(Sir Henry Cecil) *t.k.h: hld up in tch in last trio: rdn and effrt 2f out: no ex u.p: wknd jst ins fnl f* **15/8**[1]

0054 **5** *¾* **Sos Brillante (CHI)**[8] 1677 7-8-12 74 .... MarkCoumbe 5 91?
(Terry Clement) *t.k.h: hld up in tch: rdn and immediately outpcd whn gallop qcknd 2f out: no threat to ldrs but kpt on again fnl f* **250/1**

13-2 **6** *¾* **Law Of The Range**[29] 1213 5-8-12 104 .... AdamKirby 6 90
(Marco Botti) *broke fast: set v stdy gallop tl over 6f out: chsd ldng pair after: rdn and outpcd 2f out: wknd jst over 1f out* **6/1**[3]

/11- **7** *12* **Khawlah (IRE)**[407] 998 4-8-12 110 .... FrankieDettori 7 63
(Saeed Bin Suroor) *t.k.h: hld up in last trio: stuck on rail bhd a wall of horses and rdn jst over 2f out: no rspnse and unbalanced on downhill run over 1f out: sn wl btn* **13/2**

1m 56.38s (4.68) **Going Correction** +0.55s/f (Yiel) **7 Ran SP% 111.2**

Speed ratings (Par 113): **101,99,99,95,94 94,83**

toteswingers: 1&2 £3.80, 1&3 £5.50, 2&3 £8.60 CSF £19.89 TOTE £3.90: £2.00, £3.10; EX 25.00.

Owner Helena Springfield Ltd **Bred** Meon Valley Stud **Trained** Newmarket, Suffolk

FOCUS

This Group 3 for older fillies and mares has been won by some solid Group performers, although Echelon was the only recent winner to have subsequently scored at the top level. However, this year's running included Timepiece, who won the Group 1 Falmouth Stakes in 2011 and was making her seasonal reappearance. With the steady early gallop and the proximity of the fifth there are doubts over the form, which is best rated around the first two for now.

NOTEBOOK

Izzi Top ◆, never out of the first three in six previous runs (although subsequently disqualified once), was a Group 3 winner last season but also narrowly got beaten by Oaks winner Dancing Rain at Newbury before finishing third to the same filly at Epsom. Carrying a penalty here, she was always in the right place as the race was run but was pretty keen in the early stages. However, she stays further than this and dug deep when asked to keep on strongly up the hill. She looks on the upgrade and the Middleton Stakes at York looks a possible next target. (op 7-2 tchd 11-4 and 4-1 in a place)

Captivator ◆, a useful handicapper at around this trip last season when improved by the fitting of a hood, improved again to beat Law Of The Range in a Listed race on her reappearance on Kempton's Polytrack. Held up early, she had to make ground as the pace was quickening in front of her and, although she got close enough to make a challenge, she could not sustain the effort up the hill. She can be given extra credit in the circumstances and should be able to win a Group race this season. (op 9-1 tchd 10-1)

Primevere(IRE) finished half a length behind today's winner in the Pretty Polly at this meeting last year and was 3lb better off here. Quietly progressive in Listed company until disappointing at the Curragh on her last start, her rider sensibly went on when the early pace was too steady and the filly stuck on well once headed to gain her first placing at this level. She is another who still looks to be going the right way. (tchd 9-1 and 11-1)

Timepiece, easy in the market, was held up on the outside of the field early, when the pace was pretty steady, but appeared to have every chance before failing to pick up running down the hill. She took a while to hit top form last season so can be expected to do better later on. (op 6-4 tchd 2-1)

Sos Brillante(CHI), an ex-Chilean and Godolphin mare who looked well out of her depth at this level, unexpectedly earned some decent prizemoney. It is to be hoped the handicapper does not take this performance at face value. (op 200-1)

Law Of The Range, a consistent mare who was narrowly beaten by today's runner-up on her reappearance and AW debut, set the pedestrian early pace before taking a lead from the third and had her chance, but still has to prove she truly stays beyond 1m. (op 13-2 tchd 11-2)

Khawlah(IRE), lightly raced and with a good strike-rate, had not been seen since completing the UAE Oaks and Derby double at Meydan in March 2011. Held up at the back, she was under pressure and going nowhere over 2f out before appearing to lose her action running into the Dip; this was later confirmed by her jockey. She has clearly not been easy to train and has to prove she retains her ability. Official explanation: jockey said filly lost its action (op 7-1 tchd 6-1)

1884 QIPCO 1000 GUINEAS STKS (BRITISH CHAMPIONS SERIES) (GROUP 1) (FILLIES) 1m

3:15 (3:43) (Class 1) 3-Y-O

£213,513 (£80,947; £40,511; £20,180; £10,127; £5,082) **Stalls** Centre

Form RPR

0-01 **1** **Homecoming Queen (IRE)**[21] 1403 3-9-0 106 .... RyanMoore 2 117
(A P O'Brien, Ire) *mde all: clr thrght: rdn and qcknd wl clr 2f out: in n.d and edgd rt fnl f: kpt up to work and styd on strly: impressive* **25/1**

1-4 **2** *9* **Starscope**[18] 1454 3-9-0 98 .... JimmyFortune 7 96+
(John Gosden) *hld up towards rr: rdn and hdwy over 2f out: drvn and styd on fr over 1f out: wnt 2nd ins fnl f: no ch w wnr* **33/1**

111- **3** *1* **Maybe (IRE)**[252] 5525 3-9-0 116 .... JPO'Brien 9 94
(A P O'Brien, Ire) *in tch: rdn and outpcd by wnr 2f out: no ch w wnr after but kpt on u.p fnl f* **13/8**[1]

1- **4** *¾* **The Fugue**[190] 7165 3-9-0 0 .... WilliamBuick 12 92+
(John Gosden) *hld up towards rr: rdn and hdwy ent fnl 2f: no ch w wnr but kpt on u.p fnl f* **22/1**

213- **5** *¾* **La Collina (IRE)**[252] 5525 3-9-0 114 .... DeclanMcDonogh 8 91
(Kevin Prendergast, Ire) *in tch in midfield: rdn 1/2-way: struggling and outpcd wl over 2f out: no ch w wnr but rallied 1f out: kpt on fnl f* **25/1**

6 *shd* **Alla Speranza**[182] 7320 3-9-0 101 .... KevinManning 1 90+
(J S Bolger, Ire) *chsd ldrs: rdn to chse ldr but immediately outpcd 2f out: no imp and wl hld after: wknd ins fnl f* **28/1**

26-3 **7** *½* **Lily's Angel (IRE)**[18] 1454 3-9-0 98 .... PaulHanagan 15 89
(Richard Fahey) *in tch in midfield: rdn 3f out: outpcd by wnr and btn 2f out: wl hld but kpt on u.p fnl f* **50/1**

211 **8** *shd* **Laugh Out Loud**[29] 1215 3-9-0 96 GeraldMosse 18 89+
(Mick Channon) *stdd s: t.k.h: hld up towards rr: hdwy 1/2-way: effrt but outpcd by wnr 2f out: wl hld and plugged on same pce u.p fr over 1f out* **50/1**

31-2 **9** *nk* **Nayarra (IRE)**[18] 1454 3-9-0 106 MartinDwyer 17 88
(Mick Channon) *chsd ldr tl 3f out: sn rdn and outpcd ent fnl 2f: wl btn but stl pressing for placings 1f out: wknd towards fin* **50/1**

25-6 **10** *2 1/4* **Sunday Times**[18] 1454 3-9-0 107 JamieSpencer 4 83
(Peter Chapple-Hyam) *stdd s: hld up in rr: hdwy 5f out: rdn and outpcd 2f out: no ch w wnr after: wknd ins fnl f* **100/1**

21- **11** *6* **Diala (IRE)**[200] 6950 3-9-0 90 EddieAhern 13 69+
(William Haggas) *hld up in tch: rdn and sltly hmpd wl over 3f out: sn struggling: bhd fnl 2f* **14/1**

22-1 **12** *1/2* **Mashoora (IRE)**[31] 1209 3-9-0 105 ChristopheSoumillon 3 68+
(J-C Rouget, France) *hld up in midfield: stl travelling wl over 2f out: rdn and no prog wl over 1f out: wknd ent fnl f* **13/2**[2]

311- **13** *3 1/2* **Lightening Pearl (IRE)**[225] 6337 3-9-0 111 JohnnyMurtagh 5 60+
(G M Lyons, Ire) *chsd ldrs: wnt 2nd 3f out tl 2f out: sn outpcd and btn: fdd 1f out: eased ins fnl f* **20/1**

23-2 **14** *9* **Radio Gaga**[15] 1508 3-9-0 98 RichardMullen 16 39
(Ed McMahon) *in tch: rdn and struggling 1/2-way: bhd fnl 2f* **100/1**

11 **15** *14* **Moonstone Magic**[15] 1508 3-9-0 106 JimCrowley 6
(Ralph Beckett) *hld up towards rr: hmpd over 6f out: rdn and btn over 3f out: bhd fnl 2f: eased fr over 1f out: t.o* **13/2**[2]

11- **16** *44* **Discourse (USA)**[274] 4803 3-9-0 109 MickaelBarzalona 11
(Mahmood Al Zarooni) *hmpd sn after s: hld up in rr: rdn over 3f out: sn btn: wl t.o and virtually p.u fnl f* **10/1**

111- **D** *7* **Lyric Of Light**[226] 6299 3-9-0 112 FrankieDettori 10
(Mahmood Al Zarooni) *in tch in midfield: rdn and lost pl 1/2-way: bhd fnl 3f: virtually p.u fr wl over 1f out* **8/1**[3]

1m 40.45s (1.85) **Going Correction** +0.55s/f (Yiel) **17** Ran SP% **122.7**
Speed ratings (Par 110): **112,103,102,101,100 100,99,99,99,97 91,90,87,78,64 20,13**
toteswingers: 1&2 £99.80, 1&3 £13.10, 2&3 £18.40 CSF £658.57 CT £2185.33 TOTE £25.20: £6.00, £9.90, £1.30; EX 724.50 Trifecta £6909.30 Pool: £11,391.08 - 1.22 winning units..
Owner Mrs John Magnier & Michael Tabor & Derrick Smith **Bred** Tower Bloodstock **Trained** Ballydoyle, Co Tipperary

FOCUS
This looked a decent renewal of the first fillies' Classic, with five of them coming into it unbeaten. However, not many could have predicted the way the race would play out. There was a lengthy delay to the start when Gray Pearl got herself wedged underneath the stalls when almost all the runners had been loaded. The stalls were emptied and the remainder stood behind the stalls for some 25 minutes. Sadly Gray Pearl had to be put down. Interestingly, the first two home hadn't gone into their berths when the incident occurred. In the circumstances and given the ground, the form is rated cautiously despite the winning margin

NOTEBOOK
Homecoming Queen(IRE) ◆ set some really strong fractions and gave the impression she'd tee the race up for something behind. Ryan Moore was relentless in making his mount go forward and it soon became apparent that nothing was going to catch what had looked the stable's second string. She is exceptionally well bred, being a half-sister to the top class Dylan Thomas and the unbeaten Queen's Logic (who would have started for the favourite for the 2002 renewal of this race) among others, so from that perspective the information was all there. That said, she'd taken eight races to get off the mark as a juvenile and didn't give the obvious impression she'd be following in her siblings footsteps. One can only rate the performance positively until it is proven otherwise, but she is small in stature and one wonders if she'll maintain her form throughout a long season, considering this was her third outing of 2012. The jockey felt the filly will get further. (op 20-1 tchd 16-1)
Starscope tended to wander here when the field started to make some in-roads on the leader but stayed on nicely to claim second. There must be a slight suspicion that she isn't a completely straightforward ride, talented though she is, but this was her first big test and may come on for it mentally. She's certainly in the right hands to have a big season. (op 28-1)
Maybe(IRE) ◆ was a perfect 5-5 in 2011, finishing with a Group 1 success in the Moyglare Stud Stakes at the Curragh. Everything about her suggested the 1m trip wouldn't cause her any particular problems and she moved nicely in the chasing group while others needed motivating. Things looked perfectly set up for her but, like all those beaten, she didn't find that extra gear and couldn't close the gap down. She is undoubtedly better than this, something backed up by the way she travelled, and can readily be given another chance wherever connections send her next. (op 6-4 tchd 11-8, 2-1 and 15-8 in places)
The Fugue won a 7f maiden here, in which she and the runner-up pulled clear, so was an intriguing runner from a top stable. Seemingly the choice of stable jockey William Buick, she got behind before making ground past rivals when they came to the end of their tether. Bred to be better over further, she appeared to run a decent trial for the Oaks but was struck into behind and John Gosden is going to monitor the situation with that injury before making plans, so bets for Epsom should be put on hold until positive news is known. (op 20-1 tchd 25-1)
La Collina(IRE) ◆, a Group 1 winner, seemed to be going nowhere over 3f and also looked tightened for room at one point, but she found a bit extra when pulled out and kept on into a decent fifth. Her big victory came over 6f, but she has the potential to stay at least 1m2f on pedigree and is definitely worth a try over further. (op 22-1)
Alla Speranza was always prominent here but didn't quicken and lost a couple of places inside the final furlong. Her pedigree suggests she might get the Oaks trip. (op 25-1)
Lily's Angel(IRE) ran okay and had no excuses.
Laugh Out Loud ◆ tended to pull hard off the gallop on her first start on turf, and is definitely heading in the right direction. (op 40-1)
Nayarra(IRE), an Italian Group 1 winner, has developed in a solid performer and will make her presence felt in lesser Pattern company. (tchd 66-1)
Sunday Times never looked like taking this at any stage but made some nice progress from the back.
Diala(IRE) had become an interesting outsider in recent weeks but wasn't good enough to get involved. (tchd 18-1)
Mashoora(IRE) took the Group 3 Prix Imprudence in impressive style on her previous outing, when value for much more than the winning distance, and Christophe Soumillon looked keen to track Maybe while the winner got on with things in front. His mount's response off the bridle was disappointing but she may not have handled the undulations. (op 12-1)
Lightening Pearl(IRE), who got agitated before the off, which isn't like her, showed speed early before weakening. She'll surely be better over shorter but her dam didn't go on at three, so they'll be a slight worry about that potential issue until posting a solid effort. (op 22-1 tchd 25-1)
Radio Gaga was not good enough and dropped out. (tchd 66-1)
Moonstone Magic got hampered in the early stages while in rear, and was never really going from that point. This was a huge jump in class but still looked a disappointing effort. The trainer later reported that the filly did cough afterwards, so was given a tracheal wash, and the rider reported that she felt flat in the race, so she probably deserves another chance when the ground is in her favour. (op 8-1)
Discourse(USA) got badly hampered soon after start and showed little, although her jockey eased off in the final stages. (op 12-1 tchd 14-1)
Lyric Of Light ran miles below expectations but Frankie Dettori reported afterwards the ground went again his filly. Official explanation: jockey said filly was unsuited by the good to soft ground (op 9-1 tchd 10-1 in a place)

1885 QATAR RACING H'CAP 6f
3:50 (4:20) (Class 2) 4-Y-0+
£27,390 (£8,201; £4,100; £2,050; £1,025; £514) **Stalls** High

Form RPR

41-2 **1** **Maarek**[15] 1540 5-9-8 **102** JPO'Brien 24 114
(David Peter Nagle, Ire) *racd stands' side: hld up in rr: swtchd rt and hdwy over 1f out: hdwy to ld gp and chsd overall ldrs ins fnl f: r.o wl to ld cl home* **12/1**[3]

4-10 **2** *nk* **Shropshire (IRE)**[13] 1558 4-8-5 **90** MatthewLawson(5) 2 101
(Charles Hills) *racd far side: in tch: rdn and effrt to ld overall 1f out: kpt on wl tl hdd and no ex cl home: 1st of 13 in gp* **25/1**

0001 **3** *1 1/4* **Colonel Mak**[35] 1157 5-9-10 **104** LeeNewman 3 111
(David Barron) *racd far side: chsd ldr: ev ch and rdn 2f out: overall ldr over 1f out tl 1f out: no ex fnl 100yds: 2nd of 13 in gp* **33/1**

0-45 **4** *1/2* **Parisian Pyramid (IRE)**[13] 1558 6-8-11 **91** JamieSpencer 22 96
(Kevin Ryan) *racd stands' side: led gp and prom overall: ev ch and edgd lft ent fnl f: edgd rt u.p and one pce fnl 150yds: 2nd of 11 in gp* **9/1**[2]

2213 **5** *3/4* **Alben Star (IRE)**[36] 1140 4-9-4 **98** PaulHanagan 21 101
(Richard Fahey) *racd stands' side: in tch: effrt u.p over 1f out: chsd ldrs and drvn ins fnl f: kpt on same pce: 3rd of 11 in gp* **9/1**[2]

26-1 **6** *1/2* **Seal Rock**[13] 1558 4-9-5 **99** DaneO'Neill 1 100
(Henry Candy) *racd far side: in tch: effrt u.p over 1f out: kpt on same pce ins fnl f: 3rd of 13 in gp* **6/1**[1]

03-3 **7** *1/2* **The Confessor**[22] 1373 5-8-10 **90** JohnnyMurtagh 7 90
(Henry Candy) *racd far side: chsd ldrs: rdn and pressing ldrs wl over 1f out: no ex 1f out: wknd fnl 100yds: 4th of 13 in gp* **6/1**[1]

0-12 **8** *3/4* **Mirza**[13] 1558 5-9-4 **98** DavidProbert 18 95
(Rae Guest) *racd stands' side: in tch: rdn and effrt 2f out: sme hdwy ent fnl f: styd on same pced ins fnl f: 4th of 11 in gp* **14/1**

00-0 **9** *shd* **Waffle (IRE)**[36] 1129 6-9-6 **100** GrahamGibbons 25 97+
(David Barron) *racd stands' side: in tch: rdn and unable qck over 1f out: styd on same pce fnl f: 5th of 11 in gp* **14/1**

024- **9** *dht* **Irish Heartbeat (IRE)**[263] 5180 7-8-10 **90** BarryMcHugh 10 87
(Richard Fahey) *racd far side: chsd ldrs: unable qck u.p over 1f out: wknd ins fnl f: 5th of 13 in gp* **20/1**

00-1 **11** *shd* **Jarrow (IRE)**[38] 1091 5-7-9 **82** ShirleyTeasdale(7) 16 79
(David Nicholls) *racd stands' side: in tch: swtchd lft and poised to chal whn pushed lft and bmpd rival ent fnl f: swtchd rt and kpt on ins fnl f: 6th of 11 in gp* **20/1**

04-0 **12** *nse* **Valery Borzov (IRE)**[18] 1438 8-8-12 **92** (v) TonyHamilton 5 89
(Richard Fahey) *racd far side: in tch: effrt u.p over 1f out: no imp and no threat to ldrs fnl f:6th of 13 in gp* **66/1**

530- **13** *3/4* **Fathsta (IRE)**[232] 6145 7-8-10 **90** MartinDwyer 14 84
(David Simcock) *racd far side: hld up in rr: hdwy u.p over 1f out: kpt on: nvr trbld ldrs: 7th of 13 in gp* **33/1**

00-4 **14** *3/4* **Cheveton**[16] 1498 8-8-8 **91** DaleSwift(3) 12 83
(Richard Price) *racd far side: chsd ldrs: rdn and unable qck wl over 1f out: wknd ins fnl f: 8th of 13 in gp* **22/1**

510- **15** *1/2* **Bertiewhittle**[232] 6145 4-8-11 **91** WilliamCarson 19 81+
(David Barron) *racd stands' side: hld up in rr: swtchd lft 1/2-way: effrt against stands' rail whn nt clr run and bdly hmpd ent fnl f: swtchd rt and styd on fnl 100yds: no ch: 7th of 11 in gp* **16/1**

13-2 **16** *hd* **Doc Hay (USA)**[18] 1438 5-8-13 **93** JoeFanning 20 83
(Keith Dalgleish) *racd stands' side: hld up towards rr: rdn and effrt over 1f out: edgd rt and no imp whn nt clr run ins fnl f: 8th of 11 in gp* **16/1**

030- **17** *shd* **King Of Eden (IRE)**[190] 7171 6-8-2 **82** AndrewMullen 9 71
(Eric Alston) *racd far side: hld up towards rr: effrt u.p over 1f out: edgd rt and kpt on fnl f: nvr trbld ldrs: 9th of 13 in gp* **50/1**

60-2 **18** *3/4* **Bathwick Bear (IRE)**[27] 1255 4-8-10 **90** NeilCallan 17 77
(David Evans) *racd stands' side: pressed ldr: rdn and unable qck over 1f out: wknd jst ins fnl f: eased fnl 75yds: 9th of 11 in gp* **33/1**

-032 **19** *1 1/4* **Escape To Glory (USA)**[20] 1417 4-8-4 **84** HayleyTurner 27 67+
(Mikael Magnusson) *racd stands' side: hld up in tch: effrt and poised to chal whn squeezed for room and bdly hmpd ent fnl f: nt rcvr: 10th of 11 in gp* **18/1**

50-0 **20** *2 3/4* **Damika (IRE)**[35] 1157 9-8-7 **87** MichaelStainton 15 61
(David Brown) *racd far side: a towards rr: rdn and struggling 2f out: wknd over 1f out: 10th of 13 in gp* **33/1**

500- **21** *1/2* **Victorian Bounty**[138] 7832 7-8-2 **82** AndreaAtzeni 11 54
(Tony Newcombe) *racd far side: chsd ldrs tl rdn and wknd over 1f out: 11th of 13 in gp* **100/1**

00-0 **22** *1/2* **Victoire De Lyphar (IRE)**[13] 1558 5-9-1 **95** KierenFallon 23 66
(David Nicholls) *racd stands' side: in tch: rdn and struggling wl over 1f out: wknd over 1f out: bhd and eased ins fnl f: 11th of 11 in gp* **25/1**

100- **23** *5* **Dungannon**[232] 6147 5-9-4 **98** JimmyFortune 8 53+
(Andrew Balding) *racd far side: in tch: rdn and unable qck wl over 1f out: wknd 1f out: 12th of 13 in gp* **25/1**

1441 **24** *8* **Piscean (USA)**[48] 962 7-8-5 **85** MickaelBarzalona 4 14
(Tom Keddy) *racd far side: a in rr: lost tch over 1f out: eased ins fnl f: 13th of 13 in gp* **25/1**

1m 14.03s (1.83) **Going Correction** +0.55s/f (Yiel) **24** Ran SP% **132.1**
Speed ratings (Par 109): **109,108,106,106,105 104,103,102,102,102 102,102,101,100,99 99,99,98,96,93 92,91,85,74**
toteswingers: 1&2 Not won, 1&3 £84.30, 2&3 £136.70 CSF £292.69 CT £9424.06 TOTE £10.60: £2.70, £5.50, £9.10, £3.60; EX 717.10 Trifecta £1924.60 Part won. Pool: £2,600.88 - 0.10 winning units..
Owner Lisbunny Syndicate **Bred** New England Stud & P J & P M Vela **Trained** Fethard, Co Tipperary
■ Stewards' Enquiry : Jamie Spencer three-day ban: careless riding (May 20-22)

FOCUS
A high-class, ultra-competitive sprint handicap in which the large field split into two groups, but there appeared no advantage as the first pair raced on opposite sides of the track. It had been raining for about half an hour before this race, which may have made the ground easier to get though, and the time was 4.03 secs outside the standard. The placed horses help set the level to the best of their recent form.

NOTEBOOK
Maarek ◆, a progressive Irish-trained sprinter, was 13lb higher than when winning last September but had scored off 5lb lower than this last time and likes soft ground. Held up at the rear of the nearside group, he was able to avoid the scrimmaging that took place in front of him running into the Dip and powered up the hill to get to the front near the finish. He appears better than ever this year and looks worth his chance in Pattern company, given his favoured conditions. (op 14-1)

Shropshire(IRE) ◆ had finished some way behind Seal Rock on soft at Pontefract, but handles conditions and came through to win his race on the far side, only to be caught by the strong-finishing winner on the opposite flank. He should be capable of gaining compensation on this evidence.
Colonel Mak bounced back for a return to turf last time by winning a similar race to this at Doncaster off 6lb lower. Suited by cut in the ground, he showed up throughout and stuck to his guns under pressure. He is clearly in good heart at the moment.
Parisian Pyramid(IRE) hasn't won for a long time but is well suited by the trip and ground, and had run well behind Seal Rock on his latest start, having come towards the stands' side at Pontefract (first home on that side). He led the nearside group for a long way here but drifted left running into the Dip and could not pick up from that point. He usually runs well at York so can be expected to take his chance at the Dante meeting next, but is also one to bear in mind if sent down to Goodwood, where he has scored twice in the past. (op 10-1 tchd 11-1)
Alben Star(IRE) had won two of three starts on turf in 2010, both on a sound surface; and had been progressive on Polytrack this year after a long absence. Although 6lb above his last winning mark, he ran creditably and proved he could handle soft ground. (tchd 10-1 in place)
Seal Rock headed the market and showed up well before being run out of it up the hill. He had won his first two starts last season on fast ground but scored on his reappearance on soft this time around from Mirza and several others in this contest. He appeared to have his chance but could not pick up under pressure. (tchd 11-2)
The Confessor, joint market leader with his stable companion, had shown most of his form at 7f but had won at this trip and is suited by cut in the ground. He was well backed and given a positive ride, but was unable to respond when taken on. (op 15-2 tchd 8-1)
Mirza closely matched with Seal Rock on Pontefract form, is well suited by soft ground and ran reasonably, having had to race more towards the centre than most in the nearside group.
Irish Heartbeat(IRE) ◆ is versatile as regards trip and is well suited by good or softer ground. Winless last season and making his first start since August, he was another to perform encouragingly and is one to keep an eye on while there is ease in the ground. (op 18-1)
Jarrow(IRE) travelled well and was challenging when carried across to the nearside rail by Parisian Pyramid running into the Dip, which caused him to hamper Escape To Glory and in turn Bertiewhittle against the fence.
Valery Borzov(IRE), another versatile sprinter who is well suited by cut in the ground, had the visor back on for the first time in a while and showed the benefit of the headgear. (tchd 50-1)
Bertiewhittle was held up but was running on when caught up in the shemozzle towards the stands' rail, ending any chance he may have had.
Escape To Glory(USA) was beginning a run up the nearside rail when badly hampered, effectively ending any chance he may have had. (op 16-1)

1886 MAKFI FUTURE STARS MAIDEN STKS — 5f

4:25 (4:50) (Class 4) 2-Y-O — **£6,469** (£1,925; £962; £481) **Stalls** High

Form — RPR

1 — **New Pearl (IRE)** 2-9-3 0 — JohnnyMurtagh 9 — 89+
(David Brown) *mde all: hrd pressed and rdn over 1f out: fnd ex and r.o strly ins fnl f: impressive* — **7/2[2]**

2 — 4 1/2 — **Emirates Echo** 2-9-3 0 — JamieSpencer 5 — 73+
(David Simcock) *in tch: effrt to chse ldng pair 2f out: rdn and pressing ldrs over 1f out: nt pce of wnr and wl btn ins fnl f: kpt on to go 2nd fnl 100yds* — **15/2**

3 — 3/4 — **Gold Hunter (IRE)** 2-9-3 0 — FrankieDettori 6 — 70+
(Saeed Bin Suroor) *chsd ldrs: wnt 2nd 1/2-way: rdn and ev ch over 1f out: nt pce of wnr and btn jst ins fnl f: wknd and lost 2nd fnl 100yds* — **9/2[3]**

4 — nse — **Mysterial** 2-9-3 0 — RyanMoore 12 — 70+
(Richard Hannon) *towards rr: rdn along 1/2-way: hdwy ent fnl f: r.o and swtchd rt fnl 100yds: no ch w wnr but gng on wl fin* — **3/1[1]**

5 — 1/2 — **Kimberella** 2-9-3 0 — HayleyTurner 11 — 68+
(Michael Bell) *chsd ldrs: rdn: edgd rt and outpcd wl over 1f out: no ch w wnr but rallied and kpt on ins fnl f* — **8/1**

6 — 2 — **Bentleysoysterboy (IRE)** 2-9-3 0 — NickyMackay 2 — 63+
(David Elsworth) *s.i.s: bhd and rn green: wnt rt and hdwy ent fnl 2f: no prog and btn over 1f out: wknd fnl f* — **20/1**

7 — 5 — **Harrogate Fair** 2-9-3 0 — AndreaAtzeni 10 — 43
(Michael Squance) *s.i.s: sn rcvrd and in tch in midfield: rdn and struggling ent fnl 2f: wknd over 1f out* — **50/1**

8 — 1 — **True Spirit** 2-9-3 0 — PaulHanagan 3 — 39
(Paul D'Arcy) *in tch in midfield: rdn and struggling 1/2-way: wknd 2f out* — **16/1**

9 — 3 1/2 — **Prince Of Prophets (IRE)** 2-9-3 0 — WilliamCarson 13 — 27
(Stuart Williams) *stdd s: in tch in midfield: rdn ent fnl 2f: wknd over 1f out: bhd fnl f* — **100/1**

10 — 2 1/2 — **Cuisine (IRE)** 2-9-3 0 — JimmyFortune 4 — 18
(Andrew Balding) *towards rr: struggling 1/2-way: bhd fnl 2f* — **17/2**

11 — 8 — **Ocean Applause** 2-9-3 0 — KierenFallon 1
(John Ryan) *wnt rt s: alway rr: wl bhd fnl 2f* — **20/1**

12 — 4 1/2 — **Shearian** 2-9-3 0 — AhmedAjtebi 7
(Brian Meehan) *chsd wnr tl 1/2-way: grad lost pl: wl bhd and eased ins fnl f: t.o* — **28/1**

1m 3.22s (4.12) **Going Correction** +0.55s/f (Yiel) — 12 Ran SP% **120.6**
Speed ratings (Par 95): **89,81,80,80,79 76,68,66,61,57 44,37**
toteswingers: 1&2 £16.90, 1&3 £5.30, 2&3 £6.40 CSF £28.75 TOTE £4.70: £2.00, £2.70, £2.20; EX 56.10 Trifecta £794.70 Pool: £1,310.23 - 1.22 winning units..
Owner Pearl Bloodstock Ltd **Bred** New Deal Partnership **Trained** Averham Park, Notts

FOCUS
This has always been a well-above average juvenile contest down the years, contested by plenty of horses that go on to better things. Sometimes the winner isn't the one to concentrate on as Henrythenavigator, Conquest and Radiohead were all beaten before going on to Group success at two.

NOTEBOOK
New Pearl(IRE) ◆ is trained by a man who knows how to handle an exciting juvenile after his exploits with Frederick Engels in 2011. A brother to Alrasm, who was a close second on his 2-y-o debut before making up into useful sort over further, Johnny Murtagh's mount clearly knew his job, jumped quickly and bagged the stands' rail. He readily fended off anything that tried to get to him, quickening the tempo at the 2f pole, and firmly put himself in the picture for the Coventry Stakes at Royal Ascot. Connections feel he'll handle better ground, and the horse may have another run before heading to the Berkshire track. (tchd 4-1)
Emirates Echo, a 26,000gns yearling whose dam won on her racecourse debut at the July course over 7f, doesn't have the physical scope of a few around him but he showed good pace and is a sure-fire maiden winner. (tchd 8-1)
Gold Hunter(IRE), a 220,000gns purchase as a yearling, whose winning relatives include the mud-loving Zafisio, looks to have plenty of substance and made a pleasing debut. (op 5-1)
Mysterial ◆, whose dam is an unraced half-sister to ten winners, including some useful sorts, represented a stable who'd won this race with debutants in 2002, 2003 and 2006. Costing 150,000gns at the sales, he took a little while to get going, although he was never going that badly, and flew home to almost snatch third. (tchd 11-4 and 7-2)
Kimberella is related to plenty of winners, most notably brother Arabian Gleam, a three-time Group 2 winner at 7f, and ran well without being given a hard time when it was obvious he couldn't win.
Bentleysoysterboy(IRE) ◆, who cost 27,000gns as a yearling, was arguably the eyecatcher of the race considering he didn't seem to handle the track at all when placed under pressure. He looks to have size about him and can be expected to come on for this. (op 22-1)
Cuisine(IRE), whose dam won on her 2-y-o debut and is a half-sister to Group 1 winner Zahrat Dubai, appeared to run well below market expectations. (op 12-1)

1887 TWEENHILLS PRETTY POLLY STKS (LISTED RACE) (FILLIES) — 1m 2f

5:00 (5:27) (Class 1) 3-Y-O — **£22,684** (£8,600; £4,304; £2,144; £1,076; £540) **Stalls** High

Form — RPR

1- — 1 — **Kailani**[201] 6933 3-8-12 82 — MickaelBarzalona 2 — 107+
(Mahmood Al Zarooni) *stdd s: hld up in last pair: hdwy towards far side over 2f out: rdn to ld 2f out: clr over 1f out: r.o wl: comf* — **6/1**

312- — 2 — 7 — **Hazel Lavery (IRE)**[218] 6526 3-9-1 95 — MichaelHills 6 — 96
(Charles Hills) *in tch in midfield: rdn and effrt to press ldrs 2f out: outpcd by wnr and btn over 1f out: wnt 2nd ent fnl f: plugged on* — **4/1[2]**

1- — 3 — 3 1/4 — **Lacily (USA)**[198] 6984 3-8-12 79 — FrankieDettori 10 — 86+
(Mahmood Al Zarooni) *led and sn clr: hdd 2f out: sn rdn and outpcd over 1f out: 3rd and wl btn 1f out: wknd ins fnl f* — **5/1[3]**

545- — 4 — 1 — **Salford Art (IRE)**[202] 6914 3-9-0 99 ow2 — JohnnyMurtagh 8 — 84
(David Elsworth) *chsd ldr tl 2f out: sn outpcd u.p: wknd and wl btn 4th 1f out* — **10/1**

4- — 5 — 4 — **Miracle Maid**[197] 7025 3-8-12 0 — AdamKirby 3 — 76+
(Clive Cox) *hld up in last quartet: clsd and in tch 3f out: rdn and outpcd 2f out: sn wknd* — **16/1**

16-0 — 6 — 1 3/4 — **What's Up (IRE)**[18] 1454 3-8-12 91 — JamieSpencer 7 — 73
(Kevin Ryan) *stdd s: hld up in rr: rdn and hdwy 3f out: wknd wl over 1f out: bhd fnl f* — **20/1**

5-4 — 7 — 1/2 — **Petaluma**[15] 1512 3-8-12 0 — MartinHarley 5 — 72
(Mick Channon) *hld up in last quartet: clsd and in tch 3f out: rdn and struggling ent fnl 2f: sn wknd* — **33/1**

5-53 — 8 — 10 — **Arsaadi (IRE)**[17] 1468 3-8-12 92 — AhmedAjtebi 1 — 52
(William Haggas) *racd away fr rivals against far side rail: in tch: rdn and edgd rt fr over 2f out: wknd 2f out: wl bhd and eased ins fnl f* — **5/2[1]**

5-1 — 9 — 8 — **Bon Allumage**[23] 1363 3-8-12 78 — TomQueally 4 — 36
(Sir Henry Cecil) *in tch in midfield: rdn and struggling 3f out: wknd over 2f out: t.o and eased fnl f* — **10/1**

32 — 10 — 6 — **Red Hand (USA)**[16] 1503 3-8-12 0 — WilliamBuick 11 — 24
(John Gosden) *t.k.h: chsd ldrs tl wknd over 2f out: wl bhd and eased fnl f: t.o* — **10/1**

2m 9.75s (3.95) **Going Correction** +0.55s/f (Yiel) — **10** Ran SP% **120.4**
Speed ratings (Par 104): **106,100,97,97,93 92,92,84,77,72**
toteswingers: 1&2 £7.30, 1&3 £6.30, 2&3 £5.20 CSF £31.32 TOTE £7.70: £2.90, £2.00, £2.10; EX 46.40 Trifecta £189.40 Pool: £1,745.55 - 6.82 winning units..
Owner Godolphin **Bred** Darley **Trained** Newmarket, Suffolk

FOCUS
The ground was changed to soft before this race. The best recent winner of this Oaks trial was the brilliant multiple Group 1 scorer Ouija Board and, although this year's line-up did not include any filly officially rated in three figures, many of them were lightly raced or unexposed and with potential on breeding. The time was 2.06secs faster than the closing handicap.

NOTEBOOK
Kailani ◆ is a daughter of the 1000 Guineas and Oaks winner Kazzia, and came into this having won her only previous start. Held up at the back, she cruised up to join issue well over 2f out and, once in front, drew clear under hands and heels riding. At the time of writing she is not in the Oaks but is likely to be supplemented in an attempt to emulate her dam. Her pedigree leaves no doubt that she will stay, and she also traces to another Oaks winner through her dam's sire. She is priced at between 6-1 and 12-1 for that race, and looks a sound each-way bet at the latter price.
Hazel Lavery(IRE) had some sound form last season, including on easy ground. Stepping up 3f in trip, she was being niggled along at about halfway but picked up in the closing stages, despite having no chance with the winner. She can probably win a Pattern race and connections were encouraged enough to still have the Oaks on the agenda. They also believe she will prefer better ground. (op 9-2)
Lacily(USA), like her stable companion the daughter of an Oaks winner, in her case the Irish Oaks heroine Lailani, was also the winner of her sole juvenile start. She made the running up the centre and stuck to her task, but could not respond when her stablemate challenged. Her rider believes the ground did not suit her and better can be expected. (op 4-1 tchd 11-2)
Salford Art(IRE), who had the highest official rating based on her fourth in the Fillies' Mile, ran reasonably considering the best of her previous efforts had been on a sound surface. (op 8-1)
Miracle Maid had made an encouraging debut at Newbury last back-end and stayed on in the closing stages without looking to really handle the ground. She should be able to win races on a sounder surface.
Arsaadi(IRE) was sent off favourite having run well in a sales race here last month and with previous form on soft ground. She showed up early but was struggling fully 3f from home and was eventually eased. (op 4-1 tchd 9-4)

1888 AL RAYAN H'CAP — 1m 2f

5:35 (5:58) (Class 2) (0-100,93) 3-Y-O — **£12,450** (£3,728; £1,864; £932; £466; £234) **Stalls** High

Form — RPR

31-1 — 1 — **Sparkling Portrait**[18] 1440 3-8-13 **85** — TonyHamilton 1 — 98
(Richard Fahey) *hld up towards rr: hdwy 3f out: rdn and ev ch wl over 1f out: led over 1f out: kpt on wl u.p fnl f* — **4/1[2]**

61- — 2 — 3/4 — **Deia Sunrise (IRE)**[221] 6447 3-8-7 **79** — WilliamBuick 4 — 90
(John Gosden) *stdd s: hld up in tch: effrt 3f out: rdn to ld wl over 1f out: sn hdd: battled on gamely and pressing wnr thrght fnl f: a jst hld* — **5/1**

12- — 3 — 1 1/2 — **Open Water (FR)**[200] 6957 3-8-10 **82** — JimmyFortune 8 — 90
(Andrew Balding) *led: rdn and hdd wl over 1f out: no ex 1f out: styd on same pce fnl f* — **7/1**

052- — 4 — 3 3/4 — **Mubaraza (IRE)**[200] 6954 3-8-10 **82** — PaulHanagan 6 — 83
(John Dunlop) *bmpd s: sn rcvrd and chsng ldrs: rdn and ev ch ent fnl 2f: wknd ent fnl f* — **9/2[3]**

32-6 — 5 — 4 — **Ocean Tempest**[13] 1565 3-8-6 **78** — KirstyMilczarek 9 — 71
(John Ryan) *stdd s: hld up in rr: rdn and effrt wl over 2f out: no prog wl over 1f out: 5th and wl btn 1f out* — **40/1**

001- — 6 — 1 — **Jupiter Storm**[199] 6970 3-8-11 **83** — RyanMoore 5 — 74
(Gary Moore) *stdd and wnt lft s: hld up in rr: rdn and effrt wl over 2f out: no prog and wl btn over 1f out* — **11/1**

3-11 — 7 — 14 — **Samba King**[9] 1647 3-9-7 **93** — MickaelBarzalona 10 — 56
(Mahmood Al Zarooni) *stdd s: hld up in rr: swtchd lft to r against stands' rail after 2f: clsd and in tch 1/2-way: wknd 2f out: wl bhd and eased fnl f* — **7/2[1]**

1 — 8 — 2 — **Good Of Luck**[93] 399 3-8-10 **82** — MartinHarley 2 — 41
(Mick Channon) *hld up in rr: rdn and struggling 3f out: bhd wl over 1f out* — **11/1**

51- **9** *shd* **Nelson's Bay**[229] 6230 3-8-10 **82**.. ShaneKelly 11 40
(Brian Meehan) *chsd ldr tl 4f out: rdn and wknd over 2f out: wl bhd and eased fnl f* **33/1**

0-05 **10** *2* **Cravat**[11] 1604 3-9-2 **88**.. JoeFanning 7 42
(Mark Johnston) *chsd ldrs tl rdn and wknd over 2f out: wl bhd over 1f out: eased fnl f* **25/1**

2m 11.81s (6.01) **Going Correction** +0.55s/f (Yiel) **10** Ran SP% **115.5**
Speed ratings (Par 105): **97,96,95,92,89 88,77,75,75,73**
toteswingers: 1&2 £4.10, 1&3:£5.00, 2&3 £7.60 CSF £23.64 CT £135.35 TOTE £4.80: £1.90, £2.40, £2.40; EX 31.40 Trifecta £150.40 Pool: £1,774.44 - 8.73 winning units..
Owner Mike Browne **Bred** Dukes Stud & Overbury Stallions Ltd **Trained** Musley Bank, N Yorks

FOCUS
Another good-class, competitive handicap which included several unexposed sorts and a couple of progressive types. The majority of the field raced up the centre for most of the way and the time was 2.06secs slower than the preceding fillies' Listed race.

NOTEBOOK
Sparkling Portrait ◆ has progressed quickly since bolting up in a Fibresand maiden just before Christmas. He showed a good attitude to take a Beverley handicap on his reappearance and displayed similar qualities to win this better race off a 7lb higher mark. There is no reason to think he cannot continue his winning run, even after re-assessment. (op 5-1 tchd 7-2)
Deia Sunrise(IRE) ◆ progressed from his debut to score on his second start and stepped up again here, only losing out to a more experienced and fitter rival. He looks capable of building on this and should gain compensation before long.
Open Water(FR) made the running and stuck to his guns once headed, not being beaten far at the finish. He is a likeable type and can be expected to win decent races this season. (op 6-1)
Mubaraza(IRE), a maiden who was making his handicap debut, was ridden a fair way from home but kept staying on and his breeding suggests a longer trip and better ground will be in his favour.
Ocean Tempest tracked the pace throughout but could not pick up. All his best form has been on better ground or Polytrack but he has yet to prove he stays this far.
Jupiter Storm, whose success last season was gained on fast going, was lit up by being bumped leaving the stalls but ran on towards the finish having been held up. Better can be expected in future. (op 10-1 tchd 12-1)
Samba King, who had made all when scoring twice last month, was switched to the stands' side to race alone. However, he was never able to get to the head of affairs and eventually finished well beaten. (op 4-1)
Nelson's Bay, another whose previous win was on fast ground, probably ran too free in the conditions and didn't get home. (tchd 28-1)
T/Jkpt: Not won. T/Plt: £348.70 to a £1 stake. Pool: £216,837.28. 453.88 winning tickets. T/Qpdt: £35.50 to a £1 stake. Pool: £11,349.78. 236.37 winning tickets. SP

SALISBURY (R-H)

Sunday, May 6

OFFICIAL GOING: Good to soft (soft in places; 7.1)
Ground between 7f and 2f railed off on stands' side.
Wind: Virtually nil Weather: Cloudy with sunny periods

1889 BETFRED MOBILE MAIDEN STKS 6f
1:50 (1:53) (Class 5) 3-Y-O+ **£2,911** (£866; £432; £216) **Stalls** Low

Form RPR

520- **1** **Fort Bastion (IRE)**[217] 6565 3-9-0 106........................ RichardHughes 10 103
(Richard Hannon) *trckd ldrs: led 2f out: sn drew wl clr: easily* **1/8**[1]

2 *12* **Zhiggy's Stardust** 3-9-0 0........................ FergusSweeney 8 65
(Henry Candy) *led tl rdn 2f out: sn no ch w wnr: kpt on same pce* **8/1**[2]

5-2 **3** *1 ½* **Captain Kendall (IRE)**[16] 1492 3-8-9 0................ MatthewCosham(5) 6 60
(David Evans) *trckd ldrs: rdn 3f out: kpt on same pce fnl 2f* **11/1**

0 **4** *1 ¾* **Petrarchan**[20] 1420 4-9-10 0........................(t) LukeMorris 5 57
(Milton Bradley) *mid-div: rdn over 2f out: no imp tl kpt on ins fnl f* **100/1**

00- **5** *2 ¼* **Infinite Jest**[179] 7330 3-9-0 0........................ SebSanders 2 47
(J W Hills) *trckd ldrs: rdn over 2f out: fdd ent fnl f* **18/1**

35 **6** *1 ½* **Choice Words (USA)**[36] 1138 4-9-10 0........................ SamHitchcott 4 45
(Emma Lavelle) *prom: rdn over 2f out: wknd ent fnl f* **14/1**

7 *hd* **Oceana Dreamer (IRE)** 3-9-0 0........................ LiamKeniry 3 42
(Andrew Balding) *mid-div: rdn over 3f out: nvr gng pce to get involved* **10/1**[3]

6 **8** *2* **Temple Road (IRE)**[20] 1420 4-9-10 0........................ RussKennemore 1 38
(Milton Bradley) *hld up: hdwy over 2f out: sn rdn: wkng whn stmbld ins fnl f* **100/1**

60 **9** *¾* **Smarty Time**[25] 1301 5-9-2 0........................ SeanLevey(3) 7 31
(John Bridger) *wnt bdly lft s nrly unseating rdr: did keep on fnl f but a bhd* **80/1**

0- **10** *2* **Top Design**[312] 3513 4-9-10 0........................ TomMcLaughlin 9 30
(Karen George) *prom: rdn over 2f out: wknd over 1f out* **100/1**

1m 15.48s (0.68) **Going Correction** +0.275s/f (Good)
WFA 3 from 4yo+ 10lb **10** Ran SP% **133.6**
Speed ratings (Par 103): **106,90,88,85,82 80,80,77,76,74**
toteswingers: 1&2 £2.00, 1&3 £2.40, 2&3 £3.80 CSF £3.46 TOTE £1.10: £1.02, £1.80, £2.30; EX 4.60.
Owner Sir Robert Ogden **Bred** L White & D McGregor **Trained** East Everleigh, Wilts

FOCUS
Ground between 7f and 2f railed off on stands' side. After a dry night the going was officially described as soft, good to soft in places, and the opener provided an easy opportunity for a 106-rated maiden to land his first career success. The third is rated to his latest Bath form.
Captain Kendall(IRE) Official explanation: jockey said gelding jumped right out of stalls
Temple Road(IRE) Official explanation: jockey said gelding stunmbled about 1f out
Smarty Time Official explanation: jockey said mare swerved violently left after stalls opened

1890 BETFRED "CITY BOWL" H'CAP 1m 6f 21y
2:20 (2:21) (Class 3) (0-90,90) 4-Y-O+
£12,450 (£3,728; £1,864; £932; £466; £234)

Form RPR

310- **1** **Rockfella**[234] 6103 6-8-12 **78**........................ TadhgO'Shea 1 86
(Denis Coakley) *led after 1f: rdn whn hrd pressed over 2f out: styd on gamely fnl f: drvn out* **12/1**

/41- **2** *nk* **Albert Bridge**[233] 6130 4-8-9 **79**........................ HarryBentley(3) 9 86
(Ralph Beckett) *hld up: hdwy over 4f out: rdn to chal over 2f out: ev ch thrght fnl f: hld nring fin* **7/2**[2]

1/3- **3** *6* **Hawridge Star (IRE)**[360] 2034 10-8-10 **76**........................ LiamKeniry 2 75
(Stuart Kittow) *hld up: hdwy over 3f out: rdn to chse ldng pair over 2f out: styd on same pce* **10/1**

365- **4** *1* **Mattoral**[9] 5407 4-8-4 **71** oh1........................(v) LiamJones 10 69
(Chris Gordon) *mid-div: rdn over 3f out: styd on same pce: nvr threatened ldrs* **11/1**

213/ **5** *5* **Mezzanisi (IRE)**[64] 3620 7-9-5 **85**........................ LukeMorris 6 76
(Peter Bowen) *rear wd: hld up: looked nt to be travelling and hanging lft over 5f out: sn rdn: styd on same pce fnl 3f* **20/1**

600/ **6** *2* **Princely Hero (IRE)**[16] 1388 8-8-6 **72** oh1 ow1..........(t) SamHitchcott 3 60
(Chris Gordon) *trckd ldrs: rdn 3f out: fdd fnl f* **80/1**

7 *1 ½* **Enfant De Lune (FR)**[15] 3291 8-9-2 **82**........................(t) SebSanders 4 68
(David Pipe) *trckd ldrs: rdn to chse wnr over 3f out tl over 2f out: fdd over 1f out* **13/2**[3]

510- **8** *9* **Samsons Son**[183] 7297 8-9-10 **90**........................ FergusSweeney 8 63
(Alan King) *mid-div: effrt over 2f out: wknd over 1f out* **16/1**

2-66 **9** *24* **O Ma Lad (IRE)**[16] 1505 4-8-4 **74**........................ SophieDoyle(3) 5
(Sylvester Kirk) *trckd ldrs: rdn over 3f out: sn wknd* **16/1**

1100 **10** *¾* **Storm Hawk (IRE)**[18] 1446 5-8-11 **80**........................(b) KierenFox(3) 11
(Pat Eddery) *led for 1f: chsd wnr tl over 3f out: sn wknd* **40/1**

51 3 **11** *7* **Royal Peculiar**[22] 1374 4-9-7 **88**........................ IanMongan 7
(Sir Henry Cecil) *trckd ldrs: rdn 3f out: wknd wl over 1f out: eased whn btn* **7/4**[1]

3m 9.82s (2.42) **Going Correction** +0.05s/f (Good)
WFA 4 from 5yo+ 1lb **11** Ran SP% **117.2**
Speed ratings (Par 107): **95,94,91,90,87 86,85,80,67,66 62**
toteswingers: 1&2 £9.30, 1&3 £23.00, 2&3 £5.30 CSF £52.95 CT £447.07 TOTE £19.10: £5.10, £1.60, £1.90; EX 63.80 Trifecta £307.30.
Owner Keeper's 12 **Bred** Ascagnano S P A **Trained** West Ilsley, Berks

FOCUS
A competitive staying handicap run at a good gallop, as usual for this race there were no stalls. Not the strongest form.

NOTEBOOK
Rockfella is a tough front-runner and he made most on his return from 234 days off. He benefitted from a good ride and had most of the field in trouble when quickening the pace entering the straight, before holding off his main challenger in determined style. He's open to improvement over this trip and can continue to give a good account, especially when likely to get his own way in front. (tchd 14-1)
Albert Bridge was the only runner to offer any serious challenge, but found the winner too tough close home. He had improved for a step up in trip when scoring on his handicap debut at Newbury last autumn, and this was a fine effort off a 4lb higher mark, back after a 233-day layoff. He relished this further step up in trip, and given that he's only lightly raced he looks open to further improvement. (op 4-1 tchd 9-2)
Hawridge Star(IRE) had only run once since winning over 2m at Newmarket in 2010, but has run well fresh in the past and did so again, returning from 360 days off. (op 11-1)
Mattoral had been running over hurdles and was up in trip on his return to the Flat. He passed several tiring rivals in the straight, suggesting he got the trip. (op 16-1 tchd 18-1)
Mezzanisi(IRE) Official explanation: jockey said gelding hung left throughout
O Ma Lad(IRE) Official explanation: jockey said gelding suffered interference in running
Royal Peculiar, who had an Ascot Gold Cup and Yorkshire Cup entry, was disappointing. Sent off the warm 7-4 favourite, he travelled okay before making his challenge in the straight, but he couldn't pick up on the softest ground he had encountered in his four starts to date. (op 13-8 tchd 6-4)

1891 BETFRED "THE BONUS KING" FILLIES' CONDITIONS STKS 5f
2:55 (2:58) (Class 3) 2-Y-O **£7,439** (£2,213; £1,106; £553) **Stalls** Low

Form RPR

1 **1** **Judy In Disguise**[31] 1202 2-8-5 0........................ RyanWhile(7) 7 89+
(Bill Turner) *disp ld tl clr ldr over 2f out: kpt on wl fnl f: readily* **12/1**

1 **2** *3* **All On Red (IRE)**[10] 1623 2-8-9 0........................ StevieDonohoe 5 75
(Tobias B P Coles) *s.i.s: outpcd in last pair: hdwy wl over 1f out: kpt on to go 2nd ins fnl f: no ch w wnr* **16/1**

3 *1 ¼* **Rio's Pearl** 2-8-3 0........................ HarryBentley(3) 3 68+
(Ralph Beckett) *chsd ldrs: rdn wl over 2f out: kpt on but nt pce to chal* **10/1**[3]

0113 **4** *2 ¼* **Dreamy Ciara**[18] 1451 2-8-7 0........................ MatthewCosham(5) 2 65
(David Evans) *disp ld tl rdn over 2f out: sn one pce* **25/1**

21 **5** *1* **Effie B**[15] 1515 2-8-12 0........................ ChrisCatlin 6 62
(Mick Channon) *chsd ldrs: rdn 2f out: nt pce to chal: fdd fnl f* **9/2**[2]

04 **6** *14* **Cherryred Girl (IRE)**[34] 1165 2-8-9 0........................ LiamKeniry 1
(J S Moore) *chsd ldrs: rdn 3f out: wknd wl over 1f out* **100/1**

1 **7** *22* **Tassel**[17] 1466 2-8-12 0........................ RichardHughes 8
(Richard Hannon) *s.i.s: nvr travelling: a last: eased whn wl btn 2f out* **2/5**[1]

1m 2.08s (1.08) **Going Correction** +0.275s/f (Good) **7** Ran SP% **117.1**
Speed ratings (Par 94): **102,97,95,91,90 67,32**
toteswingers: 1&2 £8.30, 1&3 £3.40, 2&3 £7.30 CSF £176.30 TOTE £14.40: £4.20, £4.70; EX 81.60.
Owner Mrs Tracy Turner **Bred** Mrs Hugh Maitland-Jones **Trained** Sigwells, Somerset

FOCUS
Much of the interest was lost in this conditions event when it was clear the favourite was struggling from an early stage, but the winner did it nicely. The race averages are quite solid and the time was decent, so this race might be better than rated.

NOTEBOOK
Judy In Disguise looked good when winning on her debut on faster ground, and made it 2-2 with another polished performance. She raced enthusiastically down the centre of the track, and showed a smart turn of foot to pull clear of her rivals.
All On Red(IRE), the outsider of four when scoring on her debut, couldn't go the early pace and was detached. She eventually picked up really well when making her challenge against the far rail, but proved no match for the winner. (op 10-1)
Rio's Pearl, a 50,000GBP sister to Agony And Ecstacy and half-sister to several winners, made a promising debut. She knew her job and was challenging for the lead entering the final furlong, but couldn't match the pace of the front two. She can only benefit from the experience and looks capable of winning her maiden. (op 8-1 tchd 11-1)
Dreamy Ciara was one-paced. (op 16-1)
Effie B, who improved from her debut when easily winning a soft-ground maiden at Nottingham, but has something to prove now. (op 4-1)
Tassel made a good impression when winning on her debut at Newmarket and is held in high regard, while her trainer has a good record in this race having won it in the past with the classy juveniles Presto Vento, Gilded and Cake. She was backed as though defeat was out of the question but she was never travelling and got out paced at an early stage, before being eased with a furlong to go. Official explanation: vet said filly was lame behind (op 4-5)

1892 BETFRED GOALS GALORE H'CAP 1m 1f 198y
3:35 (3:37) (Class 4) (0-85,84) 3-Y-O **£5,175** (£1,540; £769; £384) **Stalls** Low

Form RPR

03-1 **1** **Expense Claim (IRE)**[25] 1301 3-9-2 **79**........................ LiamKeniry 4 88+
(Andrew Balding) *trckd ldr: led over 2f out: sn rdn: hld on wl whn pressed fnl f: rdn out* **9/2**[2]

00-3 **2** *nk* **Perfect Delight**[13] 1565 3-9-2 **79**........................ JohnFahy 5 87
(Clive Cox) *trckd ldrs: effrt over 2f out: chal over 1f out: ev ch fnl f: kpt on but no ex nring fin* **5/1**[3]

006- **3** *3* **Cades Reef (IRE)**[240] 5891 3-8-5 **71** .... SimonPearce(3) 6 73
(Andrew Balding) *hld up: hdwy whn nt clr run 2f out: swtchd lft and rdn sn after: styd on* **10/1**

41-0 **4** *2 1/4* **Handsome Man (IRE)**[17] 1468 3-9-2 **79** .... TedDurcan 2 77
(Saeed Bin Suroor) *mid-div: hdwy 3f out: sn rdn to chse ldrs: styd on same pce tl no ex ins fnl f* **8/1**

1-66 **5** *6* **Holly Martins**[11] 1612 3-8-4 **74** ....(t) NicoleNordblad(7) 1 60
(Hans Adielsson) *trckd ldrs: rdn 3f out: wknd over 1f out* **16/1**

0-12 **6** *1/2* **Sheila's Buddy**[25] 1320 3-8-9 **72** .... TadhgO'Shea 8 57
(J S Moore) *hld up: hdwy 3f out: sn rdn: wknd over 1f out* **8/1**

00-4 **7** *7* **Jack Who's He (IRE)**[13] 1565 3-9-2 **84** ....(p) MatthewCosham(5) 7 55
(David Evans) *mid-div: rdn 3f out: wknd over 1f out* **6/1**

321- **8** *3 3/4* **Rebel Song (IRE)**[176] 7398 3-9-1 **78** .... RichardHughes 3 41
(Mahmood Al Zarooni) *set decent pce: rdn and hdd over 2f out: sn btn* **9/4**[1]

1-32 **9** *7* **Island Melody (IRE)**[83] 547 3-8-8 **71** .... LukeMorris 9 20
(J S Moore) *s.i.s: struggling over 4f out: a towards rr: wknd 2f out* **20/1**

2m 9.92s (0.02) **Going Correction** +0.05s/f (Good) **9** Ran SP% **121.9**
Speed ratings (Par 101): **101,100,98,96,91 91,85,82,77**
toteswingers: 1&2 £6.00, 1&3 £11.60, 2&3 £11.70 CSF £28.99 CT £220.33 TOTE £6.50: £2.50, £1.40, £2.90; EX 34.20.
Owner Another Bottle Racing 2 **Bred** Glending Bloodstock **Trained** Kingsclere, Hants

FOCUS
An open and competitive 3yo handicap . The pace was muddling but the first two finished nicely clear and the form should stand up, with the runner-up the key to the level.
Jack Who's He(IRE) Official explanation: jockey said geldingdid not handle the bend

1893 BETFRED "DOUBLE DELIGHT" EBF MAIDEN STKS 1m 4f
4:10 (4:12) (Class 5) 3-Y-O **£4,204** (£1,251; £625; £312) **Stalls** Low

Form RPR

0- **1** **Estimate (IRE)**[243] 5807 3-8-12 0 .... PatDobbs 2 86
(Sir Michael Stoute) *mid-div: hdwy over 3f out: rdn to ld wl over 1f out: styd on strly: comf* **12/1**

44- **2** *2 3/4* **Mysterious Man (IRE)**[208] 6771 3-9-3 0 .... LiamKeniry 8 87
(Andrew Balding) *led: rdn and hung lft whn hdd wl over 1f out: styd on but sn hld by wnr* **3/1**[1]

3 *4* **New Youmzain (FR)** 3-9-3 0 .... SamHitchcott 9 81
(Mick Channon) *hld up towards rr: rdn over 3f out: styd on to go 3rd ins fnl f: nvr threatened ldrs* **25/1**

36- **4** *1/2* **Corsetry (USA)**[225] 6329 3-8-12 0 .... IanMongan 6 75
(Sir Henry Cecil) *trckd ldrs: jnd ldr 5f out tl rdn 3f out: styd on same pce fnl f* **15/2**

2 **5** *hd* **Right To Rule (IRE)**[8] 1662 3-9-3 0 .... LiamJones 12 79
(William Haggas) *trckd ldrs: rdn over 2f out: styd on same pce fnl f* **5/1**[3]

6 **6** *3 3/4* **Sign Manual**[15] 1511 3-9-3 0 .... LukeMorris 1 73
(Michael Bell) *sn trcking ldrs: effrt 3f out: one pce fnl 2f* **25/1**

32 **7** *3 3/4* **Kudoz**[26] 1270 3-9-3 0 .... JohnFahy 10 67
(Clive Cox) *mid-div: hdwy 4f out: sn rdn: wknd ent fnl f* **8/1**

3 **8** *1* **Synchronicity (IRE)**[15] 1511 3-9-3 0 .... RichardHughes 4 66
(Richard Hannon) *sn prom: chsng ldrs whn reminders over 5f out: rdn 3f out: wknd fnl f* **7/2**[2]

5 **9** *18* **Caphene**[16] 1503 3-8-12 0 .... TedDurcan 3 32
(John Dunlop) *mid-div tl over 4f out: t.o* **9/1**

0- **10** *22* **Lord Nandi**[169] 7493 3-9-3 0 .... GeorgeBaker 11
(Sir Henry Cecil) *trckd ldrs tl rdn and lost pl over 4f out: sn bhd: eased over 1f out: t.o* **12/1**

00 **11** *5* **Brave Kiss**[20] 1415 3-8-12 0 .... FergusSweeney 5
(Mark Gillard) *wknd 2f out: a towards rr: t.o* **150/1**

12 *8* **Hendry Trigger** 3-9-3 0 .... RussKennemore 7
(Milton Bradley) *s.i.s: a last: wknd 2f out: t.o* **150/1**

2m 39.97s (1.97) **Going Correction** +0.05s/f (Good) **12** Ran SP% **121.2**
Speed ratings (Par 99): **95,93,90,90,90 87,85,84,72,57 54,49**
toteswingers: 1&2 £9.10, 1&3 £7.10, 2&3 £22.20 CSF £48.33 TOTE £16.00: £3.00, £2.00, £4.80; EX 93.70.
Owner The Queen **Bred** His Highness The Aga Khan's Studs S C **Trained** Newmarket, Suffolk

FOCUS
This looked a strong maiden with several unexposed runners having already hinted that they were capable of better. The pace was modest which favoured those ridden prominently and the winner was impressive. The form is best rated around the fourth, fifth and sixth.
Brave Kiss Official explanation: jockey said filly lost its action 2f out

1894 BETFRED MOBILE CASINO H'CAP 6f 212y
4:45 (4:47) (Class 3) (0-95,85) 3-Y-O **£8,409** (£2,502; £1,250; £625) **Stalls** Low

Form RPR

100- **1** **Apostle (IRE)**[262] 5216 3-9-7 **85** .... LukeMorris 8 94
(Michael Bell) *in tch: pushed along over 4f out: rdn over 3f out: led jst over 2f out: styd on u.str.p fnl f: on top at fin* **11/2**[3]

144- **2** *3/4* **Three Am Tour (IRE)**[193] 7095 3-9-6 **84** .... RichardHughes 4 91
(Richard Hannon) *trckd ldrs: drew upsides wnr over 1f out: rdn jst ins fnl f: nt qckn: hld nring fin* **9/2**[2]

010- **3** *8* **Lunar Deity**[263] 5184 3-9-4 **82** .... JohnFahy 6 68
(Eve Johnson Houghton) *trckd ldrs: rdn to ld briefly over 2f out: fdd ins fnl f* **10/1**

36-5 **4** *1 1/4* **Emperor Vespasian**[16] 1492 3-8-10 **74** .... LiamKeniry 2 57
(Andrew Balding) *prom: rdn 3f out: sn one pce: fdd ins fnl f* **11/1**

46-0 **5** *6* **Shamrocked (IRE)**[29] 1221 3-9-2 **80** .... SamHitchcott 1 47
(Mick Channon) *led tl rdn over 2f out: wknd ent fnl f* **14/1**

150- **6** *5* **Alice's Dancer (IRE)**[191] 7135 3-8-12 **79** .... SeanLevey(3) 5 33
(William Muir) *racd keenly: prom tl rdn over 2f out: wknd over 1f out* **12/1**

14-3 **7** *31* **Gabrial's Gift (IRE)**[36] 1142 3-8-13 **77** .... ChrisCatlin 3
(David Simcock) *rrd leaving stalls: last: rdn in last but in tch whn bdly hmpd over 2f out: eased whn no ch after* **9/2**[2]

21-1 **U** **Haaf A Sixpence**[22] 1392 3-8-12 **79** .... HarryBentley(3) 7
(Ralph Beckett) *trckd ldrs: being pushed along whn short of room: clipped heels: stmbld v bdly and uns rdr over 2f out* **15/8**[1]

1m 30.69s (2.09) **Going Correction** +0.275s/f (Good) **8** Ran SP% **118.3**
Speed ratings (Par 103): **99,98,89,87,80 75,39,**
toteswingers: 1&2 £11.00, 1&3 £3.80, 2&3 £6.80 CSF £31.55 CT £246.28 TOTE £5.90: £2.20, £1.90, £2.80; EX 37.00.
Owner Highclere Thoroughbred Racing - Jackson **Bred** Mrs Eleanor Kent **Trained** Newmarket, Suffolk

FOCUS
A modest 3-y-o handicap run at an average pace, the first two pulled well clear of the rest. With the favourite unseating and the third and fourth not solid guides there are doubts over the form.

NOTEBOOK
Apostle(IRE) didn't build on his maiden win in two subsequent runs and had shown a tendency to start slowly. He got off on terms this time, and although he came under early pressure he found plenty on his first start over 7f. (tchd 6-1)
Three Am Tour(IRE) was travelling better than anything between the last 2f but was outbattled by a determined winner. She was progressive at two, and this was a good effort on his return from 193 days off.
Lunar Deity, who lowered the 2-y-o course record at Ffos Las when winning her maiden, had something to prove on her seasonal debut after disappointing on her final start at two. She could only plug on for third and may appreciate a sounder surface. (op 8-1)
Emperor Vespasian hasn't progressed since finishing third in a decent novice event over C&D last season. (op 12-1)
Alice's Dancer(IRE) suffered interference when Haaf A Sixpence came down and he was eased. He was under pressure at the time but it was too far out to have completely written him off. This run can be ignored. (op 11-1)
Gabrial's Gift(IRE) suffered interference when Haaf A Sixpence came down and he was eased. He was under pressure at the time but it was too far out to have completely written him off. This run can be ignored. Official explanation: jockey said colt was hampered by a faller (op 4-1)
Haaf A Sixpence was a well-backed favourite on his turf debut, but clipped heels shortly after the 3f pole and came down. (op 11-4)

1895 BETFRED BONUS KING BINGO LADY RIDERS' H'CAP (FOR LADY AMATEUR RIDERS) 6f 212y
5:20 (5:21) (Class 6) (0-65,64) 4-Y-0+ **£1,996** (£619; £309; £154) **Stalls** Low

Form RPR

0460 **1** **Querido (GER)**[6] 1702 8-9-8 **56** ow1 ....(tp) MissMBryant(5) 4 64
(Paddy Butler) *mid-div: hdwy over 2f out: rdn to ld ent fnl f: kpt on* **16/1**

046- **2** *3/4* **The Name Is Frank**[170] 7462 7-10-7 **64** .... MissEJJones 5 70
(Mark Gillard) *wnt to s early: led: rdn and edgd lft over 1f out: hdd ent fnl f: kpt on* **16/1**

0060 **3** *nk* **Rapid Water**[15] 1528 6-9-13 **59** .... MissRachelKing(3) 7 64
(Pat Eddery) *trckd ldrs: rdn 2f out: ev ch ent fnl f: kpt on* **8/1**

-605 **4** *hd* **Arctic Mirage**[3] 1769 4-9-12 **60** .... MissHayleyMoore(5) 11 64
(Michael Blanshard) *mid-div: hdwy over 2f out: sn rdn: kpt on ins fnl f* **9/2**[2]

-043 **5** *3 3/4* **Silvee**[3] 1768 5-9-10 **53** .... MissSBrotherton 2 47
(John Bridger) *trckd ldr: rdn over 2f out: fdd ins fnl f* **11/4**[1]

0062 **6** *3/4* **Inquisitress**[3] 1768 8-9-2 **50** oh5 .... MissNDumelow(5) 10 42
(John Bridger) *s.i.s: in rr: swtchd rt 4f out: styd on but nvr threatened ldrs* **11/2**[3]

232 **7** *2 1/4* **Resplendent Alpha**[10] 1634 8-10-0 **57** ....(p) MissZoeLilly 3 43
(Alastair Lidderdale) *hld up: racd alone on stands' side fr 3f out: rdn over 2f out: nvr any imp* **6/1**

0600 **8** *nse* **Justcallmehandsome**[10] 1634 10-9-2 **50** ....(v) MissCBoxall(5) 6 36
(Dominic Ffrench Davis) *trckd ldrs: effrt 3f out: fdd ins fnl f* **25/1**

4256 **9** *1 1/4* **Prohibition (IRE)**[10] 1636 6-9-10 **60** ....(p) MissKMargarson(7) 8 43
(Alastair Lidderdale) *s.i.s: towards rr: effrt over 2f out: wknd ent fnl f* **8/1**

60-0 **10** *8* **Green Pearl (IRE)**[109] 198 4-9-4 **54** ow1....(t) MissLindseyMetcalfe(7) 1 15
(Ralph Beckett) *mid-div: rdn over 2f out: wknd ent fnl f* **14/1**

1m 32.22s (3.62) **Going Correction** +0.275s/f (Good) **10** Ran SP% **119.0**
Speed ratings (Par 101): **90,89,88,88,84 83,80,80,79,70**
toteswingers: 1&2 £47.70, 1&3 £29.70, 2&3 £27.40 CSF £249.49 CT £2204.44 TOTE £24.90: £6.20, £3.20, £3.20; EX 237.70.
Owner Homewoodgate Racing Club **Bred** Gestut Brummerhof **Trained** East Chiltington, E Sussex
■ Stewards' Enquiry : Miss E J Jones two-day ban: used whip above permitted level (tbn)

FOCUS
This modest handicap for lady riders was run at a steady pace, and it produced a close finish with several still in with a chance at the furlong-marker. The form is weak but reasonably sound rated around the placed horses.
T/Plt: £2,366.90 to a £1 stake. Pool: £58,848.70. 18.15 winning tickets. T/Qpdt: £561.40 to a £1 stake. Pool: £3,679.71. 4.85 winning tickets. TM

1896 - 1899a (Foreign Racing) - See Raceform Interactive

FRANKFURT (L-H)
Sunday, May 6

OFFICIAL GOING: Turf: good to soft

1900a FRUHJAHRS-PREIS DES BANKHAUSES METZLER - STADTRAT ALBERT VON METZLER-RENNEN (GROUP 3) (3YO) (TURF) 1m 2f
4:05 (4:10) 3-Y-0
£26,666 (£9,166; £4,583; £2,500; £1,666; £1,250)

RPR

1 **Novellist (IRE)**[28] 3-9-2 0 .... EPedroza 5 112
(A Wohler, Germany) *hld up in last pair: impr on outer to chal on turn into st: rdn to ld over 1 1/2f out: hung lft u.p: bounded clr ins fnl f: impressive* **11/10**[1]

2 *6* **All Shamar**[166] 7508 3-9-2 0 .... ADeVries 2 100
(W Hickst, Germany) *towards rr on inner: gd prog to chal on turn into st: rdn and outpcd by eventual wnr over 1f out: kpt on wl for 2nd ins fnl f: no ch w wnr* **11/5**[2]

3 *nk* **Mano Diao** 3-9-2 0 .... OlivierPeslier 7 99
(Mario Hofer, Germany) *hld up in last: rdn to improve on turn into st: wnt 3rd over 1f out: kpt on one pce ins fnl f* **7/2**[3]

4 *6* **Pakal (GER)**[14] 1553 3-9-2 0 .... KKerekes 3 87
(W Figge, Germany) *midfield on inner: rdn and outpcd over 1 1/2f out: plugged on to go 4th ins fnl f* **51/10**

5 *3* **Chattleya (FR)**[44] 3-8-13 0 .... JulienAuge 1 78
(S Smrczek, Germany) *disp ld early: reigned bk to trck ldr after 3f: regained advantage over 3f out: rdn and hdd over 1 1/2f out: no ex and fdd ins fnl f* **136/10**

6 *9* **Baltic Rock (IRE)**[280] 3-9-2 0 ....(b) MrDennisSchiergen 4 63
(P Schiergen, Germany) *midfield on outer: rdn to try and chal on turn into st: awkward u.p and wknd over 1 1/2f out: eased ins fnl f* **213/10**

7 *14* **The Dude (FR)**[8] 3-9-2 0 ....(b) StefanieHofer 6 35
(Mario Hofer, Germany) *disp ld early: sn led: hdd over 3f out: no ex and wknd fr over 2f out: eased ins fnl f: t.o* **33/1**

2m 11.27s (2.70) **7** Ran SP% **131.8**
WIN (incl. 10 euro stake): 21. PLACES: 11, 12, 13. SF: 47.
Owner Dr Christoph Berglar **Bred** Christoph Berglar **Trained** Germany

HOPPEGARTEN (R-H)

Sunday, May 6

OFFICIAL GOING: Turf: good

1901a OLEANDER-RENNEN - PREIS DER DEUTSCHEN BESITZER UND ZUCHTER (GROUP 3) (4YO+) (TURF) 2m

3:15 (12:00) 4-Y-0+

£26,666 (£9,166; £4,583; £2,500; £1,666; £1,250)

RPR

1 **Altano (GER)**^{197} 7045 6-9-2 0 RJuracek 3 114
(A Wohler, Germany) *midfield on outer: rdn and outpcd over 2 1/2f out: began to improve fr over 1 1/2f out: styd on strly ins fnl f to ld post* **13/2**

2 *nk* **Tres Rock Danon (FR)**^{27} 1268 6-9-2 0 APietsch 5 113
(W Hickst, Germany) *led: set stdy pce: hdd over 3 1/2f out: rdn over 2f out: regained ld ins fnl f: kpt on: hdd post* **31/10^{2}**

3 *2* **Earlsalsa (GER)**^{172} 8-8-11 0 FilipMinarik 7 106
(C Von Der Recke, Germany) *w.w towards rr: prog through field to ld over 3 1/2f out: rdn to maintain advantage on turn into st: kpt on tl no ex and hdd wl ins fnl f: lost 2nd ins fnl 75yds* **74/10**

4 *2* **Lacateno**^{27} 1268 5-9-2 0 JohanVictoire 9 107
(W Hickst, Germany) *trckd ldr in 2nd: dropped to 3rd and rdn over 2 1/2f out: outpcd over 1 1/2f out: kpt on to go 4th ins fnl 100yds* **56/10**

5 *1/2* **Flamingo Fantasy (GER)**^{224} 6396 7-8-11 0 AStarke 6 103
(S Smrczek, Germany) *midfield: rdn to try and improve over 2 1/2f out: kpt on one pce ins fnl 1 1/2f: lost 4th ins fnl 100yds* **41/10^{3}**

6 *2 1/2* **Kings Messenger (GER)**^{27} 1268 5-8-11 0 JBojko 2 101
(A Wohler, Germany) *midfield on inner: rdn to try and chal over 2f out: wnt 2nd over 1 1/2f out: kpt on tl no ex and wknd jst ins fnl f* **27/10^{1}**

7 *9* **Greek Wedding (IRE)**^{27} 5-8-10 0 ow2 KPattinson 4 90
(Petr Juranek, Czech Republic) *hld up in last: rdn to try and improve over 2 1/2f out: bdly outpcd over 2f out: plugged on ins fnl 1 1/2f* **25/1**

8 *6* **Caudillo (GER)**^{27} 1268 9-9-0 0 DPorcu 8 87
(Dr A Bolte, Germany) *prom on outer: dropped towards rr over 3 1/2f out: rdn to try and improve 2 1/2f out: no ex and btn over 1 1/2f out: eased ins fnl f* **168/10**

9 *7* **Aviator (GER)**^{231} 6200 4-8-11 0 NRichter 1 79
(P Harley, Germany) *towards rr on inner: plld hrd: dropped to last and reminders over 3 1/2f out: rdn and effrt to improve over 2 1/2f out: no ex and btn 1 1/2f out: wknd: eased ins fnl f* **112/10**

3m 36.8s (216.80)
WFA 4 from 5yo+ 3lb **9** Ran SP% **129.1**
WIN (incl. 10 euro stake): 75. PLACES: 22, 21, 26. SF: 515.
Owner Frau Dr I Hornig **Bred** Gestut Hof Ittlingen **Trained** Germany

1701 SHA TIN (R-H)

Sunday, May 6

OFFICIAL GOING: Turf: good

1902a BMW CHAMPIONS MILE (GROUP 1) (3YO+) (TURF) 1m

9:35 (12:00) 3-Y-0+

£568,578 (£219,451; £99,750; £56,525; £33,250; £19,950)

RPR

1 **Xtension (IRE)**^{36} 1148 5-9-0 0 JamesMcDonald 8 122
(J Moore, Hong Kong) *prom on inner: rdn to improve over 2f out: looking for room over 1 1/2f out: swtchd out and r.o to chal ins fnl f: led ins fnl 50yds: kpt on* **179/10**

2 *1/2* **Glorious Days (AUS)**^{35} 5-9-0 0 FCoetzee 6 121
(J Size, Hong Kong) *midfield: rdn 2 1/2f out: gd prog fr over 1 1/2f out: r.o to chal ins fnl f: wnt 2nd ins fnl 50yds: hld by wnr cl home* **56/10^{3}**

3 *1/2* **Lucky Nine (IRE)**^{36} 1147 5-9-0 0 BrettPrebble 14 120
(C Fownes, Hong Kong) *got across fr wd draw to trck ldr on outer: rdn to chal 2f out: kpt on wl u.p thrght fnl 1 1/2f: stl ev ch tl no ex and dropped to 3rd ins fnl 50yds* **11/1**

4 *nk* **Ambitious Dragon (NZ)**^{36} 1148 6-9-0 0 (b) DouglasWhyte 4 119
(A T Millard, Hong Kong) *hld up in last quartet on inner: rdn to improve over 2f out: r.o ins fnl 1 1/2f: wnt 4th ins fnl 50yds* **37/10^{2}**

5 *shd* **Able One (NZ)**^{35} 10-9-0 0 JeffLloyd 9 119
(J Moore, Hong Kong) *led: set stdy pce: strly pressed and rdn over 1 1/2f out: kpt on tl no ex and hdd ins fnl 100yds: dropped to 5th cl home* **22/1**

6 *1 1/4* **African Story**^{36} 1143 5-9-0 0 SilvestreDeSousa 10 116
(Saeed Bin Suroor) *trckd ldng gp: rdn to try and improve on turn into st: kpt on one pce fr over 1 1/2f out* **13/1**

7 *1/2* **Musir (AUS)**^{36} 1148 6-9-0 0 KShea 12 115
(M F De Kock, South Africa) *midfield: rdn to try and chal over 2f out: kpt on one pce ins fnl 1 1/2f* **60/1**

8 *1/2* **Admiration (AUS)**^{35} 5-9-0 0 WCMarwing 5 114
(J Moore, Hong Kong) *hld up in last trio: rdn to improve 2 1/2f out: swtchd to outer and kpt on fr over 1 1/2f out: nt pce to chal* **16/1**

9 *3/4* **Sunny King (IRE)**^{35} 9-9-0 0 TimothyClark 3 112
(J Moore, Hong Kong) *hld up in last: swtchd to outer and rdn to improve on turn into st: kpt on one pce ins fnl 1 1/2f: nvr able to chal* **98/1**

10 *nk* **Cityscape**^{36} 1148 6-9-0 0 JamesDoyle 7 111
(Roger Charlton) *slow to stride: qckly rcvrd and settled in midfield: rdn to try and improve on turn into st: short of room 2f out: swtchd ins and looking for room 1 1/2f out: kpt on one pce once in the clr: nt given hrd time whn ch had gon* **6/5^{1}**

11 *1* **King's Rose (NZ)**^{29} 5-8-10 0 LukeNolen 11 105
(Peter G Moody, Australia) *prom on outer: rdn to chal over 2f out: no ex and fdd ins fnl 1 1/2f* **56/1**

12 *1/2* **Beauty Flash (NZ)**^{35} 7-9-0 0 (t) MatthewChadwick 1 108
(A S Cruz, Hong Kong) *midfield on inner: rdn 2 1/2f out: outpcd over 1 1/2f out: fdd* **115/1**

13 *3/4* **Fair Trade (AUS)**^{7} 7-9-0 0 ODoleuze 13 106
(C Fownes, Hong Kong) *hld up towards rr in early stages: t.k.h: prog in to midfield over 4f out: rdn to try and chal on turn into st: no ex and btn 1 1/2f out: wknd* **45/1**

14 *3/4* **Destined For Glory (IRE)**^{35} 5-9-0 0 (t) TyeAngland 2 104
(J Moore, Hong Kong) *hld up in last pair on inner: swtchd out and rdn to try and improve on turn into st: outpcd and dropped to last over 1 1/2f out: no ex and btn over 1f out* **60/1**

1m 35.23s (0.53) **14** Ran SP% **122.0**
PARI-MUTUEL (all including HK$10 stake): WIN 188.50; PLACE 41.50, 17.00, 30.50; DF 408.00.
Owner Mr & Mrs Steven Lo Kit Sing **Bred** Paul McCartan **Trained** Hong Kong

FOCUS
They went only an even tempo and the home team filled the first five places. The winner has been rated to his mark.

NOTEBOOK
Xtension(IRE) followed up his victory last year in straightforward fashion. He sat third on the rail until being switched to come with his challenge between rivals 1 1/2f out, displaying a smart turn of foot to quickly assert. He ran only a fair race stepped up to 1m2f, when behind Cityscape in the Dubai Duty Free on his last start, and this confirms that 1m is his trip, even if conditions were very much in his favour here.
Glorious Days(AUS) has plenty of speed having done most of his winning over 7f. In rear early, he came with a withering run in the straight and was upsides the winner with 1f to run. He had to use up plenty of energy to get to that point and couldn't quite go on when the winner quickened. This still rates a personal best and he is a horse going the right way.
Lucky Nine(IRE), another to come here on the back of a run in Meydan (finished 3rd in the Golden Shaheen), was trying 1m for the first time since finishing runner-up in this last year. He can have no excuses having been perfectly positioned throughout.
Ambitious Dragon(NZ) put up a big effort considering he was last turning into the straight. He did get a clear run up the inside, but he's a strong stayer at this trip (won the Hong Kong Gold Cup over 1m2f here in February) and would have been suited by a truer gallop.
African Story was unable to continue his winning run from the Godolphin Mile at Meydan. He's well suited to the Tapeta surface over there, however his best form in France was with cut in the ground so it may be too soon to write him off as a synthetics specialist.
Cityscape surprised most people with a facile success in the Duty Free, where he had both Xtension and Ambitious Dragon behind. He had a favourable trip that day, which certainly wasn't the case here. Slowly away, he got caught on the heels of Fair Trade when trying to make his run and, when out in the clear, was never going to be able to pick up the front five. He's a solid Group 1 performer without being the superstar many hailed him as after Meydan.

1491 BATH (L-H)

Monday, May 7

OFFICIAL GOING: Soft (5.5)
Wind: Fairly strong against. Weather: overcast

1903 ALL MAKES & MODELS MEDIAN AUCTION MAIDEN STKS 5f 11y

2:10 (2:12) (Class 6) 2-Y-O **£1,617** (£481; £240; £120) **Stalls** Centre

Form RPR

4 1 **Sign Of The Zodiac (IRE)**^{17} 1499 2-9-3 0 PatDobbs 2 85+
(Richard Hannon) *uns rdr and cantered loose to s: mde all: rdn 2f out: hrd pressed thrght fnl f: kpt on wl* **11/10^{1}**

424 2 *1/2* **Hillbilly Boy (IRE)**^{5} 1753 2-8-10 0 RyanWhile$^{(7)}$ 5 83+
(Bill Turner) *prom: rdn 2f out: ev ch fnl f: kpt on but no ex towards fin* **15/8^{2}**

0 3 *7* **Majestic Jess (IRE)**^{30} 1218 2-9-3 0 LiamKeniry 6 58+
(Tom Dascombe) *prom for 2f: sn rdn to chse ldrs: kpt on same pce fnl f* **11/1**

4 *1/2* **Spray Tan** 2-8-12 0 KirstyMilczarek 7 51
(Tony Carroll) *trckd ldrs: rdn over 2f out: kpt on same pce fnl f* **33/1**

5 *1/2* **Unidexter (IRE)** 2-9-3 0 MartinHarley 8 54
(Mick Channon) *outpcd in rr early: hdwy after 2f: sn rdn: kpt on same pce fnl f* **7/1^{3}**

0 6 *2 1/4* **Icanboogie**^{17} 1495 2-9-3 0 DarryllHolland 1 46
(Karen George) *trckd ldrs: rdn 2f out: fdd ins fnl f* **50/1**

7 *5* **Kwanto** 2-8-12 0 TomMcLaughlin 3 23
(Malcolm Saunders) *dwlt: racd green: a in rr* **20/1**

8 *1* **Gowertonian (IRE)** 2-8-10 0 DarrenEgan$^{(7)}$ 4 25
(Ronald Harris) *s.i.s: outpcd in rr early: wknd over 1f out* **33/1**

1m 5.15s (2.65) **Going Correction** +0.325s/f (Good) **8** Ran SP% **115.8**
Speed ratings (Par 91): **91,90,79,78,77 73,65,64**
toteswingers:1&2:£1.20, 2&3:£4.00, 1&3:£3.80 CSF £3.23 TOTE £2.00: £1.20, £1.20, £2.80; EX 3.60.
Owner Mrs J Wood **Bred** James Doyle **Trained** East Everleigh, Wilts

FOCUS
A low-class 5f median auction maiden stakes for juveniles. They went a decent gallop and the winning time was about 4 secs outside standard. The jockeys reported that the ground was consistent with an official going description of soft. The first two pulled clear and are rated small improvers.

NOTEBOOK
Sign Of The Zodiac(IRE) reportedly looked well in the paddock, but had two handlers, and was on his toes. He dumped Pat Dobbs out of the saddle going down, and effectively took himself to the start, before being caught. He showed no ill-effects in the race itself, winning a shade cosily after racing prominently and travelling well over 1f out. He was dropping two grades in class here after a fine debut fourth under similar conditions at Newbury last month. He is a half-brother to several winners, including this year's Lincoln winner Brae Hill, who also won over 5f as a 2yo, he looks capable of further juvenile success, possibly over 6f/7f, but may need some cut in the ground. (op 4-5 tchd 8-11)
Hillbilly Boy(IRE) raced prominently throughout and produced a game display in second. He was beaten a neck under similar conditions at Beverley on his penultimate start in April (RPR 78) and looks to have returned to somewhere near that level. (op 11-4)
Majestic Jess(IRE) went the right way from his modest debut at Musselburgh last month. (op 12-1)
Spray Tan caught the eye in the paddock and this was a fair debut effort. (op 40-1)

1904 BATH CHRONICLE (S) STKS 5f 11y

2:40 (2:42) (Class 6) 2-Y-O **£1,704** (£503; £251) **Stalls** Centre

Form RPR

1 **Studfarmer** 2-8-11 0 PadraigBeggy 4 60+
(David Evans) *chsd ldrs: led 2f out: sn rdn: kpt on wl* **10/3^{2}**

5 2 *1 3/4* **Silicon Valley**^{28} 1253 2-8-6 0 ChrisCatlin 2 49+
(Dominic Ffrench Davis) *disp ld tl rdn over 2f out: kpt on to regain 2nd ins fnl f* **12/1**

6 3 *5* **Captain Blue**^{4} 1767 2-8-4 0 RyanWhile$^{(7)}$ 1 36
(Bill Turner) *chsd ldrs: rdn over 3f out: nvr gng pce to threaten* **4/1^{3}**

220 4 *2 1/4* **Golac**^{4} 1767 2-8-11 0 SamHitchcott 3 28
(Mick Channon) *disp ld tl rdn and hdd 2f out: wknd ins fnl f* **5/2^{1}**

5 1 ½ **Symphony Of Dreams** 2-8-3 0 .... RyanPowell(3) 6 17
(Dai Burchell) *s.i.s: chsd ldrs: rdn 3f out: wknd ent fnl f* **16/1**

1m 6.6s (4.10) **Going Correction** +0.325s/f (Good) **5** Ran SP% **85.2**

Speed ratings (Par 91): **80,77,69,65,63**

CSF £20.69 TOTE £4.70: £2.70, £4.50; EX 20.40.The winner was bought in for 5,200gns.

Owner W T Whittle & R Kent **Bred** W T Whittle And Mickley Stud Ltd **Trained** Pandy, Monmouths

■ Eloquent Star (3/1F)was withdrawn after refusing to go in the stalls. Deduct 25p in the £ under R4.

■ Stewards' Enquiry : Ryan While four-day ban: used whip above permitted level (May 21-24)

FOCUS

A 5f selling stakes for juveniles. There was a contested pace and the time was respectable for the grade on soft ground. The race averages help with the form.

NOTEBOOK

Studfarmer was one of two horses due to represent David Evans, who has now won this race three times in the last four years, but his Eloquent Star was intractable at the stalls and had to be withdrawn. The winner is a sturdy individual out of a dual 2yo sprint winner and was on his toes in the paddock. He was sent off a not unconsidered 100-30 in the market and this was a good effort on his debut over a trip that clearly suits. This colt by Multiplex (son of Danehill) should have more to offer on this evidence, even on better ground, and should get further on breeding. He was bought back in for 5,200 guineas in the subsequent auction. (op 4-1 tchd 3-1)

Silicon Valley was initially prominent, before getting shuffled back. She stayed on well into second at the end and can do better with a more even gallop over a longer trip. (op 14-1)

Captain Blue looked on good terms with himself beforehand, but didn't handle the turn and did well to get back on an even keel. He stayed on into third and stepped up significantly on his debut at Brighton this month. (op 5-1 tchd 11-2)

Golac raced prominently until finding disappointingly little on the run for home. (op 2-1 tchd 11-4)

1905 EMRYS PRICE JONES IS 80 H'CAP — 2m 1f 34y

3:10 (3:11) (Class 4) (0-85,85) 4-Y-0+ **£4,075** (£1,212; £606; £303) **Stalls** Centre

Form RPR

-352 **1** **Salontyre (GER)**[17] [1496] 6-8-6 **67** ....(p) ChrisCatlin 5 71
(Bernard Llewellyn) *trckd ldrs: pushed along over 6f out: rdn wl over 2f out: chal ent fnl f: styd on wl to ld fnl 75yds* **4/1**[3]

00-0 **2** ½ **L Frank Baum (IRE)**[17] [1505] 5-9-1 **76** .... LiamKeniry 4 79
(Bernard Llewellyn) *little slowly away: sn pushed along to join ldr: rdn over 2f out: ev ch thrght fnl f: styd on* **8/1**

-331 **3** ¾ **Gilded Age**[17] [1505] 6-8-11 **72** ....(tp) SamHitchcott 7 75
(Chris Gordon) *led: rdn and hrd pressed fr over 2f out: styd on but no ex whn hdd fnl 75yds* **7/1**

5-33 **4** *hd* **Captain Sharpe**[19] [968] 4-7-13 **66** oh3......................(p) RyanPowell(3) 2 68
(Bernard Llewellyn) *hld up: hdwy wl over 2f out: sn rdn: styd on ins fnl f: nvr quite getting there* **5/2**[1]

00-5 **5** 3 **My Arch**[9] [1672] 10-9-9 **84** .... FrannyNorton 6 83
(Ollie Pears) *hld up bhd ldrs: effrt over 2f out: one pce fnl f* **7/2**[2]

12-0 **6** 12 **Saborido (USA)**[16] [1513] 6-9-7 **82** .... PatDobbs 1 66
(Amanda Perrett) *trckd ldrs: rdn 3f out: wknd fnl f* **6/1**

4m 4.9s (13.00) **Going Correction** +0.80s/f (Soft)

WFA 4 from 5yo+ 3lb **6** Ran SP% **108.7**

Speed ratings (Par 105): **101,100,100,100,98 93**

toteswingers: 1&2:£6.10, 2&3:£8.30, 1&3:£1.70 CSF £31.67 TOTE £6.20: £2.60, £5.00; EX 29.30.

Owner Alex James **Bred** Gestut Wittekindshof **Trained** Fochriw, Caerphilly

FOCUS

An interesting staying handicap for older horses which was the feature on this card. They went a sensible gallop, considering the marathon trip on soft ground. The winning time was around 25 seconds slower than standard. The form may not be the most solid but has been taken at face value for now.

1906 LEANNE SPERRINGS CLASSIFIED STKS — 1m 5y

3:45 (3:45) (Class 5) 3-Y-0 **£2,385** (£704; £352) **Stalls** Low

Form RPR

4-62 **1** **Take Two**[9] [1661] 3-9-0 67 .... ChrisCatlin 6 75+
(John O'Shea) *hld up: rdn and hdwy over 2f out: led jst over 1f out: edgd lft: styd on wl: rdn out* **4/1**[2]

024- **2** 1 ½ **Shot In The Dark (IRE)**[174] [7422] 3-9-0 69 .... LiamKeniry 4 71
(Andrew Balding) *trckd ldr: rdn and ev ch over 1f out: short of room briefly ent fnl f: styd on* **6/1**[3]

4212 **3** ¾ **Emman Bee (IRE)**[16] [1517] 3-8-7 70 .... DarrenEgan(7) 9 69
(John Gallagher) *s.i.s: sn in tch: rdn 2f out: ev ch jst over 1f out: styd on same pce* **13/8**[1]

00-4 **4** 2 ¾ **City Dazzler (IRE)**[6] [1733] 3-9-0 67 .... PatDobbs 3 63
(Richard Hannon) *led: rdn 2f out: hdd jst over 1f out: no ex* **7/1**

2-30 **5** ¾ **Altona (IRE)**[33] [1190] 3-9-0 70 .... MartinHarley 1 61
(Mick Channon) *trckd ldr: rdn over 2f out: sn one pce* **8/1**

54-0 **6** 3 ½ **News Show**[16] [1532] 3-8-9 67 .... LauraPike(5) 5 53
(David Simcock) *slowly away: last: rdn over 3f out: nvr any imp on ldrs* **16/1**

531- **7** 5 **Chrissycross (IRE)**[149] [7708] 3-9-0 70 ....(b) JackMitchell 2 42
(Roger Teal) *in tch whn short of room and snatched up after 2f: in last trio: rdn 4f out: nvr any imp* **10/1**

40-4 **8** 8 **Tallevu (IRE)**[19] [1442] 3-9-0 70 ....(b[1]) DarryllHolland 7 23
(Tom Dascombe) *in tch: pushed along 5f out: rdn 3f out: wknd over 1f out* **33/1**

1m 46.43s (5.63) **Going Correction** +0.80s/f (Soft) **8** Ran SP% **113.9**

Speed ratings (Par 99): **103,101,100,98,97 93,88,80**

toteswingers: 1&2:£4.10, 2&3:£3.00, 1&3:£2.50 CSF £27.87 TOTE £5.50: £2.40, £2.70, £1.50; EX 23.20.

Owner S P Bloodstock **Bred** Steven & Petra Wallace **Trained** Elton, Gloucs

FOCUS

An average 1m classified stakes. The pace was solid on soft ground and the winning time of around 7secs outside standard appears respectable. A tight race on the fuigures and the winner continued his progress.

1907 WESTERN DAILY PRESS H'CAP (DIV I) — 1m 5y

4:15 (4:15) (Class 6) (0-55,55) 4-Y-0+ **£2,264** (£673; £336; £168) **Stalls** Low

Form RPR

0-04 **1** **Titan Diamond (IRE)**[39] [1096] 4-8-0 **46** oh1 .... RachealKneller(7) 11 53
(Mark Usher) *chsd ldrs: sltly hmpd 2f out: rdn to chal ent fnl f: styd on wl to ld fnl 40yds* **7/1**

-502 **2** *nk* **Cahala Dancer (IRE)**[11] [1625] 4-8-9 **53** .... MarkCoumbe(5) 9 59+
(Roger Teal) *mid-div: gd hdwy to ld 2f out: sn rdn and edgd lft: kpt on whn pressed ins fnl f: no ex whn hdd fnl 40yds* **11/4**[1]

2630 **3** 2 **Monsieur Pontaven**[30] [1224] 5-8-12 **51** ow1 .... DarryllHolland 7 53
(Robin Bastiman) *hld up towards rr: hdwy over 2f out: sn rdn to chse ldrs: styd on* **5/1**[2]

343 **4** *nk* **Prince Namid**[69] [729] 10-8-8 **54** .... DarrenEgan(7) 1 55
(Jonathen de Giles) *hld up towards rr: hdwy on inner fr 4f out: rdn to chse ldrs over 2f out: styd on same pce fnl f* **10/1**

0-60 **5** *hd* **Glens Wobbly**[38] [1106] 4-8-1 **47** .... KatiaScallan(7) 2 48
(Jonathan Geake) *in tch: rdn over 2f out: styd on same pce* **33/1**

4-66 **6** *nk* **Flying Phoenix**[11] [1635] 4-8-12 **54** .... RyanPowell(3) 13 54
(Dai Burchell) *in tch: rdn over 2f out: styd on same pce fnl f* **13/2**[3]

0005 **7** 1 ½ **Eyes On**[13] [1586] 4-8-9 **48** ....(bt) MircoDemuro 10 44
(Frank Sheridan) *disp ld tl rdn and hdd 2f out: styng on at same pce whn short of room ins fnl f* **14/1**

-000 **8** 4 **Avon Light**[4] [1768] 4-8-8 **47** ow1 ....(b[1]) LiamKeniry 4 34
(Milton Bradley) *in tch: rdn 3f out: wknd ent fnl f* **14/1**

400/ **9** 6 **King Of Cadeaux (IRE)**[1161] [746] 7-8-7 **46** oh1 .... ChrisCatlin 3 19
(Mikael Magnusson) *disp ld tl rdn and hdd over 2f out: wknd over 1f out* **14/1**

500- **10** 1 ¼ **Aaranyow (IRE)**[207] [6816] 4-8-11 **50** .... MartinHarley 5 21
(Bryn Palling) *mid-div: rdn over 2f out: wknd over 1f out* **33/1**

3-00 **11** 7 **Hollie**[67] [740] 4-8-5 **47** .... SimonPearce(3) 8
(Peter Makin) *s.i.s: a in rr* **20/1**

43-0 **12** 37 **Tigerbill**[21] [1425] 4-8-9 **53** ....(t) RaulDaSilva(5) 12
(Nicky Vaughan) *chsd ldrs tl wknd over 2f out* **9/1**

60/0 **13** *nk* **Komreyev Star**[97] [370] 10-8-8 **47** oh1 ow1 ....(p) SamHitchcott 6
(Ray Peacock) *mid-div tl 3f out* **66/1**

1m 46.87s (6.07) **Going Correction** +0.80s/f (Soft) **13** Ran SP% **120.4**

Speed ratings (Par 101): **101,100,98,98,98 97,96,92,86,85 78,41,40**

toteswingers: 1&2:£4.40, 2&3:£4.40, 1&3:£9.20 CSF £25.80 CT £108.80 TOTE £11.40: £2.90, £1.20, £2.00; EX 24.50.

Owner M D I Usher **Bred** Ballyhane Stud **Trained** Upper Lambourn, Berks

■ Stewards' Enquiry : Ryan Powell four-day ban: used whip above permitted level (May 21-24)

Mark Coumbe two-day ban: used whip above permitted level (May 21-22)

FOCUS

The first division of a lowly 1m handicap for older horses, run in a similar time to division II. They went a decent gallop on soft ground. The winner is rated in line with his AW form.

1908 WESTERN DAILY PRESS H'CAP (DIV II) — 1m 5y

4:45 (4:45) (Class 6) (0-55,55) 4-Y-0+ **£2,264** (£673; £336; £168) **Stalls** Low

Form RPR

6535 **1** **Join Up**[7] [1717] 6-8-9 **48** .... TomMcLaughlin 8 59
(Mark Brisbourne) *trckd ldrs: led over 2f out: sn rdn: kpt on wl whn chal ins fnl f: drvn out* **8/1**

66-4 **2** *nk* **Kyllachykov (IRE)**[13] [1583] 4-8-7 **46** oh1 .... MircoDemuro 13 56
(Robin Bastiman) *mid-div: hdwy over 2f out: sn rdn to chse wnr: chal ins fnl f: hld nring fin* **4/1**[1]

51-0 **3** ½ **Hamilton Hill**[14] [968] 5-8-13 **52** .... KellyHarrison 10 61+
(Dai Burchell) *hld up towards rr: rdn and hdwy fr 2f out: wnt 3rd ins fnl f: styd on wl* **12/1**

456 **4** 2 **Teen Ager (FR)**[39] [1088] 8-8-2 **46** oh1 .... RaulDaSilva(5) 4 51
(Paul Burgoyne) *t.k.h in mid-div: hdwy over 2f out: sn rdn: kpt on same pce fnl f* **9/1**

036- **5** 3 **Corrib (IRE)**[131] [7892] 9-8-10 **54** ....(p) DavidKenny(5) 12 52
(Bryn Palling) *mid-div: rdn and hdwy on outer fr 2f out: styd on same pce fnl f* **20/1**

60-0 **6** 1 ¼ **Perfect Honour (IRE)**[23] [1387] 6-8-5 **47** .... KierenFox(3) 2 42
(Des Donovan) *hld up towards rr: rdn and stdy prog fr over 2f out: styd on: nvr trbld ldrs* **14/1**

-430 **7** 2 **Kyllachy Storm**[17] [1497] 8-9-2 **55** .... SamHitchcott 11 45
(Ron Hodges) *racd freely: prom: led 6f out: rdn and hdd over 2f out: fdd fnl f* **12/1**

4536 **8** 2 ¼ **Lean Machine**[7] [1717] 5-8-4 **50** ....(p) DarrenEgan(7) 5 35
(Ronald Harris) *mid-div: rdn and hdwy over 2f out: wknd fnl f* **11/2**[3]

000- **9** 4 **Belle Park**[147] [7741] 5-9-1 **54** .... DarryllHolland 6 30
(Karen George) *awkward leaving stalls: trckd ldrs: rdn over 2f out: wknd over 1f out* **12/1**

60/0 **10** 7 **Our Georgie Girl**[48] [966] 5-8-7 **46** oh1 .... ChrisCatlin 9
(Rod Millman) *led tl 6f out: chsd ldr tl wknd over 2f out* **40/1**

36-5 **11** *nk* **Excellent Vision**[119] [104] 5-9-0 **53** ....(t) LiamKeniry 3
(Milton Bradley) *hld up towards rr: rdn over 2f out: nvr any imp* **16/1**

43/6 **P** **Second To Nun (IRE)**[38] [1106] 6-8-7 **46** .... KirstyMilczarek 7
(Michael Blanshard) *bhd whn lost action and p.u after 2f* **9/2**[2]

1m 46.81s (6.01) **Going Correction** +0.80s/f (Soft) **12** Ran SP% **117.5**

Speed ratings (Par 101): **101,100,100,98,95 93,91,89,85,78 78,**

toteswingers: 1&2:£4.00, 2&3:£16.30, 1&3:£16.20 CSF £39.57 CT £394.19 TOTE £9.20: £3.60, £2.20, £5.20; EX 41.60.

Owner P R Kirk **Bred** A S Reid **Trained** Great Ness, Shropshire

FOCUS

The second division of a lowly 1m handicap for older horses. They went a decent gallop on the soft ground. The winning time was very marginally better than the first division and the form is of a similar standard. The winner is rated in line with his recent AW form.

Kyllachy Storm Official explanation: jockey said gelding ran too free

Belle Park Official explanation: jockey said mare jumped awkwardly from the stalls

1909 "THISISBATH" CHRONICLE FILLIES' H'CAP — 1m 5y

5:15 (5:15) (Class 5) (0-75,75) 4-Y-0+ **£2,385** (£704; £352) **Stalls** Low

Form RPR

000- **1** **Miss Bootylishes**[211] [6727] 7-9-2 **75** .... DavidKenny(5) 1 82
(Paul Burgoyne) *trckd ldrs: led over 2f out: sn rdn: in command fnl f: eased nr fin* **6/1**[2]

-142 **2** 1 **Tidal Run**[17] [1491] 4-9-2 **70** .... MatthewDavies 4 74
(Mick Channon) *w ldr for 3f: trckd ldrs: rdn over 2f out: sn chsng wnr: no ex ins fnl f* **15/8**[1]

-505 **3** 1 ¾ **Pandorica**[18] [1485] 4-8-11 **65** .... LiamKeniry 3 65
(Bernard Llewellyn) *led for 3f: trckd ldr: rdn over 3f out: styd on same pce fnl 2f* **15/8**[1]

0-6 **4** ½ **Lisselan Pleasure (USA)**[18] [1485] 5-8-5 **62** .... RyanPowell(3) 2 61
(Bernard Llewellyn) *s.i.s: trckd ldrs: rdn over 2f out: nt pce to chal: drifted rt ent fnl f* **8/1**[3]

6300 **5** 4 **Shared Moment (IRE)**[11] [1626] 6-8-9 **63** ....(b) ChrisCatlin 5 52
(John Gallagher) *trckd ldrs: led after 3f: rdn and hdd over 2f out: sn hld* **6/1**[2]

1m 48.58s (7.78) **Going Correction** +0.80s/f (Soft) **5** Ran SP% **109.2**

Speed ratings (Par 100): **93,92,90,89,85**

CSF £17.40 TOTE £10.00: £4.70, £1.10; EX 16.00.

Owner Mrs Helen Adams **Bred** T P Young And D Hanson **Trained** Shepton Montague, Somerset

FOCUS
The gallop was not overly-strong in the early stages. The winning time was a fair bit slower than the previous three races over this trip and this is weak, muddling form.

1910 BUBBLE CHRISTMAS PARTIES H'CAP 5f 11y
5:45 (5:45) (Class 6) (0-60,60) 4-Y-O+ **£1,704** (£503; £251) **Stalls** Centre

Form RPR
-005 **1** **Namir (IRE)**[48] 979 10-9-2 **55**.....(vt) DarryllHolland 3 63
(James Evans) *mid-div: nt clr run over 2f out: swtchd lft and sn rdn: r.o wl ent fnl f: led narrowly fnl 120yds: hld on* **28/1**
0/00 **2** *hd* **Yanza**[25] 1343 6-8-4 **48**..... LauraPike(5) 14 55
(Pam Ford) *mid-div: hdwy over 2f out: sn rdn: led narrowly over 1f out: edgd lft: narrowly hdd fnl 120yds: kpt on* **28/1**
20-0 **3** *shd* **My Meteor**[17] 1497 5-9-6 **59**..... ChrisCatlin 9 66
(Tony Newcombe) *towards rr: hdwy over 2f out: sn rdn: str chal ins fnl f: kpt on* **3/1**[1]
50-4 **4** *shd* **Ginzan**[18] 1483 4-9-7 **60**..... TomMcLaughlin 2 67
(Malcolm Saunders) *chsd ldrs: rdn over 2f out: bmpd over 1f out: rdr had whip hit out of hand sn after: str chal thrght fnl f: kpt on* **7/2**[2]
3324 **5** *1 3/4* **Amazing Win (IRE)**[17] 1497 4-9-3 **56**..... SamHitchcott 10 56
(Mick Channon) *trckd ldrs: rdn over 2f out: kpt on same pce fnl f* **4/1**[3]
3044 **6** *6* **Metropolitan Chief**[26] 1306 8-8-2 **46**..... RaulDaSilva(5) 4 25
(Paul Burgoyne) *prom: rdn to ld over 2f out: hdd whn hmpd over 1f out: fdd fnl 120yds* **10/1**
350- **7** *1 1/2* **Festival Dance**[224] 6403 4-9-7 **60**..... MatthewDavies 1 33
(Ron Hodges) *s.i.s: towards rr: hdwy whn nt clr run over 2f out: sn rdn: fdd fnl f* **22/1**
5430 **8** *1/2* **Decider (USA)**[17] 1497 9-8-6 **52**.....(b) DarrenEgan(7) 12 23
(Ronald Harris) *wnt to s early: trckd ldrs: rdn over 2f out: wknd jst over 1f out* **10/1**
4600 **9** *1* **Spic 'n Span**[18] 1483 7-8-7 **46**.....(b) KirstyMilczarek 11 14
(Ronald Harris) *wnt to s early: little s.i.s: sn led: rdn and hdd over 2f out: short of room ent fnl f: fdd* **11/1**
0-00 **10** *2* **Haafhd Decent (IRE)**[17] 1497 4-8-5 **47**..... NataliaGemelova(3) 8
(Dai Williams) *rdn over 2f out: nvr bttr than mid-div* **66/1**
4300 **11** *1 1/2* **Cape Of Storms**[18] 1481 9-9-0 **53**.....(b) LiamKeniry 6
(Roy Brotherton) *prom for 2f: sn rdn to chse ldrs: wknd over 1f out* **12/1**
650- **12** *4 1/2* **Greyemkay**[204] 6889 4-8-4 **48** ow2..... DavidKenny(5) 7
(Richard Price) *awkward leaving stalls: a towards rr* **14/1**

1m 5.18s (2.68) **Going Correction** +0.575s/f (Yiel) **12** Ran SP% **120.8**
Speed ratings (Par 101): **101,100,100,100,97 87,85,84,83,79 77,70**
toteswingers: 1&2:£51.70, 2&3:£27.70, 1&3:£25.50 CSF £644.89 CT £3080.65 TOTE £22.70: £5.40, £13.10, £1.10; EX 308.00.
Owner Shakespeare Racing **Bred** B Kennedy **Trained** Broadwas, Worcs

FOCUS
A modest 5f handicap for older horses, rated around the third and fourth. The gallop looked pretty strong on soft ground.
Greyemkay Official explanation: jockey said gelding never travelled
T/Plt: £209.70 to a £1 stake. Pool £67,074.17. 233.48 winning units T/Qpdt: £10.70 to a £1 stake. Pool £4,867.04. 336.44 winning units TM

1435 BEVERLEY (R-H)
Monday, May 7

OFFICIAL GOING: Good to soft (good in places; 6.4)
Wind: Light half behind Weather: Cloudy

1911 TURFTV MEDIAN AUCTION MAIDEN STKS 5f
2:25 (2:25) (Class 6) 2-Y-O **£1,681** (£500; £250; £125) **Stalls** Low

Form RPR
1 **Indian Jade** 2-9-3 0..... PhillipMakin 4 77+
(Kevin Ryan) *trckd ldrs: effrt over 1f out: sn rdn and hdwy to ld ins fnl f: edgd rt and kpt on wl* **9/4**[2]
3 **2** *1 1/2* **Fly Fisher (IRE)**[18] 1474 2-9-3 0..... TonyHamilton 2 70
(Richard Fahey) *trckd ldrs: hdwy on inner 2f out: rdn to ld briefly ent fnl f: sn hdd and kpt on same pce* **2/1**[1]
3 *1/2* **Faithfilly (IRE)** 2-8-12 0..... J-PGuillambert 7 63+
(Ed Walker) *hld up in tch: hdwy on inner 2f out: rdn to chse ldrs over 1f out: kpt on* **9/1**
4 *1/2* **Top Notch Tonto (IRE)** 2-9-3 0..... PatrickMathers 9 66+
(Ian McInnes) *towards rr: hdwy on outer wl over 1f out: sn rdn and styd on fnl f: nrest at fin* **100/1**
6 **5** *2 3/4* **Mace The Ace**[14] 1556 2-8-12 0..... AndrewMullen 1 52
(David C Griffiths) *cl up: rdn to ld over 1f out: hdd ent fnl f: sn wknd* **20/1**
6 *3/4* **Space Artist (IRE)** 2-9-3 0..... RoystonFfrench 5 54
(Bryan Smart) *sltly hmpd s and towards rr: hdwy 2f out: sn rdn and kpt on: nrst fin* **13/2**[3]
7 *3 1/4* **Relight My Fire** 2-9-3 0..... DavidAllan 3 42
(Tim Easterby) *s.i.s: a in rr* **16/1**
26 **8** *8* **Stripped Bear (IRE)**[23] 1388 2-8-9 0..... RossAtkinson(3) 8
(Tom Dascombe) *led: rdn along 2f out: drvn and hdd over 1f out: sn wknd* **11/1**
9 *5* **Cosmic Dream** 2-9-3 0..... RobertWinston 6
(Deborah Sanderson) *chsd ldng pair: rdn along 2f out: sn wknd* **20/1**
10 *3 1/4* **Clock On Tom** 2-8-10 0..... DavidSimmonson(7) 10
(Michael Easterby) *hmpd s: a bhd* **20/1**
11 *5* **Lady Ibrox** 2-8-12 0..... GrahamGibbons 11
(Alan Brown) *prom: rdn along over 2f out: wknd wl over 1 1/2f out* **33/1**

1m 6.69s (3.19) **Going Correction** +0.30s/f (Good) **11** Ran SP% **119.9**
Speed ratings (Par 91): **86,83,82,82,77 76,71,58,50,45 37**
toteswingers:1&2:£1.20, 2&3:£7.00, 1&3:£11.00 CSF £6.74 TOTE £3.20: £1.10, £1.60, £2.80; EX 8.30.
Owner Michael Beaumont **Bred** Hillwood Thoroughbred Breeding Ltd **Trained** Hambleton, N Yorks

FOCUS
A modest juvenile maiden. The winner did this well and the runner-up and the time set the level of the form.

NOTEBOOK
Indian Jade ◆, quite a big, well-made son of Sleeping Indian, has a high knee action. Pulled wide for a run, he really knuckled down and in the end won going away. He looks a decent prospect. (op 2-1)
Fly Fisher(IRE), who showed promise when third behind a Kevin Ryan-trained winner first time at Ripon, showed ahead entering the final furlong but in the end found the winner too strong. He will surely find a race. (op 3-1)
Faithfilly(IRE), a 25,000gns yearling, made a highly pleasing debut staying on nicely from midfield. She will be sharper next time. (op 12-1)
Top Notch Tonto(IRE), from a stable not generally associated with first-time-out 2yo winners, cost just 3,000euros. After going sideways at the start he stayed on in resolute fashion. He will be suited by a step up to 6f. (op 66-1)
Mace The Ace, having her second start, showed bags of toe and will be suited by a less-demanding track. (op 16-1)
Clock On Tom Official explanation: jockey said gelding suffered interference shortly after start

1912 MAYDAY RACEDAY STKS (H'CAP) 5f
2:55 (2:56) (Class 5) (0-75,73) 3-Y-O **£2,296** (£683; £341; £170) **Stalls** Low

Form RPR
0210 **1** **Towbee**[16] 1529 3-9-1 **67**..... JamesSullivan 1 83
(Michael Easterby) *prom on inner: led over 2f out: rdn clr appr fnl f: kpt on wl* **2/1**[1]
12-0 **2** *3 1/2* **Ashpan Sam**[26] 1317 3-9-7 **73**..... RobertWinston 4 76
(John Spearing) *dwlt: sn chsng ldrs: rdn 2f out: kpt on to chse wnr fnl f: no imp* **11/2**[2]
06-3 **3** *5* **Middleton Flyer (IRE)**[16] 1514 3-9-1 **67**..... RussKennemore 3 52
(Paul Midgley) *led: rdn along 1/2-way: sn hdd and drvn: kpt on same pce* **8/1**
043- **4** *nk* **Love Island**[170] 7482 3-8-11 **66**..... AmyRyan(3) 7 50
(Richard Whitaker) *chsd ldrs: rdn along 2f out: sn one pce* **12/1**
611U **5** *1/2* **Gin Twist**[17] 1494 3-9-2 **71**.....(b) RossAtkinson(3) 8 53
(Tom Dascombe) *dwlt and hmpd s: sn pushed along in rr: rdn and hdwy 2f out: kpt on u.p fnl f: nrest at fin* **12/1**
03-5 **6** *3* **Blue Shoes (IRE)**[19] 1441 3-8-12 **64**..... DavidAllan 6 35
(Tim Easterby) *chsd ldrs: rdn along over 2f out: sn wknd* **6/1**[3]
40-2 **7** *1 1/4* **Kyllachy Dancer**[23] 1389 3-8-9 **61**..... MichaelO'Connell 10 28
(John Quinn) *in tch on outer: rdn along bef 1/2-way: sn outpcd* **10/1**
21-2 **8** *nk* **First Fast Now (IRE)**[16] 1514 3-8-9 **64**..... DeclanCannon(3) 5 30
(Nigel Tinkler) *in tch: rdn along 1/2-way: sn wknd* **15/2**
100- **9** *3 3/4* **Kylesku (IRE)**[258] 5348 3-8-13 **72**..... KevinStott(7) 9 24
(Kevin Ryan) *sltly hmpd s: a in rr* **20/1**
2050 **10** *nse* **Dawn Lightning**[67] 749 3-8-11 **63**.....(p) AndrewMullen 2 15
(Alan McCabe) *chsd ldrs: rdn along 1/2-way: sn wknd* **33/1**

1m 5.08s (1.58) **Going Correction** +0.30s/f (Good) **10** Ran SP% **118.1**
Speed ratings (Par 99): **99,93,85,84,84 79,77,76,70,70**
toteswingers:1&2:£3.50, 2&3:£7.10, 1&3:£2.10 CSF £12.92 CT £73.84 TOTE £4.60: £2.00, £2.60, £2.60; EX 16.10.
Owner Mrs A Jarvis **Bred** Mrs A Jarvis **Trained** Sheriff Hutton, N Yorks

FOCUS
A moderate 3yo sprint handicap. The first three were well drawn and always prominent and the winner took another step forward.
Blue Shoes(IRE) Official explanation: jockey said bit slipped through filly's mouth
First Fast Now(IRE) Official explanation: jockey said filly hung left throughout

1913 WESTWOOD H'CAP 1m 1f 207y
3:25 (3:26) (Class 4) (0-80,77) 4-Y-O+ **£4,140** (£1,232; £615; £307) **Stalls** Low

Form RPR
0025 **1** **Amazing Blue Sky**[9] 1657 6-9-2 **72**..... JamesSullivan 1 84
(Ruth Carr) *mde all: rdn 2f out: drvn ins fnl f and kpt on strly* **7/2**[1]
1-50 **2** *3 1/4* **Brockfield**[14] 1561 6-8-12 **68**..... DavidAllan 10 74
(Mel Brittain) *trckd ldrs: hdwy 3f out: rdn to chse wnr over 1f out: drvn and edgd rt jst ins fnl f: sn no imp* **7/1**[3]
00-6 **3** *1 1/4* **Tribal Myth (IRE)**[37] 1135 5-8-4 **67**..... PaulMcGiff(7) 2 70
(Kevin Ryan) *trckd ldng pair: hdwy 3f out: rdn 2f out and sn swtchd lft: kpt on same pce appr fnl f* **12/1**
0-10 **4** *4 1/2* **Smart Step**[9] 1652 4-9-0 **70**..... JoeFanning 4 64
(Mark Johnston) *trckd wnr: effrt 3f out: sn rdn: drvn wl over 1f out and grad wknd* **5/1**[2]
0-33 **5** *1/2* **Doctor Zhivago**[20] 1429 5-8-13 **72**..... DaleSwift(3) 8 65
(Ian McInnes) *hld up towards rr: hdwy 3f out: rdn over 2f out: kpt on u.p fnl f: n.d* **8/1**
01-0 **6** *2* **Count Bertoni (IRE)**[36] 1156 5-9-7 **77**..... DanielTudhope 3 66
(David O'Meara) *in tch: hdwy over 3f out: rdn over 2f out: sn no imp* **12/1**
0-02 **7** *4* **Ailsa Craig (IRE)**[23] 1381 6-9-5 **75**..... TonyHamilton 12 56
(Edwin Tuer) *in tch: effrt over 3f out: sn rdn along: btn 2f out* **7/2**[1]
00-5 **8** *4 1/2* **Maybeme**[19] 1439 6-8-1 **64** oh6 ow1..... TerenceFury(7) 9 36
(Neville Bycroft) *stdd s: hld up: a bhd* **20/1**
40-0 **9** *6* **Souter Point (USA)**[37] 1134 6-9-5 **75**..... PhillipMakin 7 35
(Peter Salmon) *a in rr* **18/1**
0/0- **10** *3* **Shaloo Diamond**[328] 3023 7-8-12 **68**..... RussKennemore 5 22
(Richard Whitaker) *t.k.h: hld up: a in rr* **16/1**
0450 **11** *7* **Yorksters Prince (IRE)**[27] 1276 5-8-11 **67**.....(b) BarryMcHugh 11
(Tony Coyle) *hld up: a in rr* **25/1**

2m 9.47s (2.47) **Going Correction** +0.375s/f (Good) **11** Ran SP% **119.9**
Speed ratings (Par 105): **105,102,101,97,97 95,92,89,84,81 76**
toteswingers:1&2:£8.90, 2&3:£26.30, 1&3:£6.70 CSF £28.80 CT £270.51 TOTE £4.80: £2.10, £1.70, £3.50; EX 31.90.
Owner Graham Scruton **Bred** Hong Kong Breeders Club **Trained** Huby, N Yorks

FOCUS
An open handicap and it paid to race prominently. The form makes sense among the first four, who were the only ones who counted.

1914 PETWISE ZOO IN THE COURSE ENCLOSURE H'CAP 1m 100y
4:00 (4:00) (Class 4) (0-85,83) 4-Y-O+ **£4,204** (£1,251; £625; £312) **Stalls** Low

Form RPR
0-66 **1** **Toto Skyllachy**[9] 1670 7-9-4 **80**..... DanielTudhope 9 90
(David O'Meara) *trckd ldng pair: cl up 1/2-way: led 3f out: rdn clr over 1f out: edgd rt jst ins fnl f: drvn out* **4/1**[1]
420- **2** *nk* **Carragold**[144] 7771 6-8-8 **70**..... DuranFentiman 12 79
(Mel Brittain) *prom: led after 1 1/2f: hdd 3f out: rdn 2f out: rallied and styd on wl fnl f: jst hld* **12/1**
-603 **3** *2 3/4* **Moheebb (IRE)**[9] 1670 8-8-13 **75**.....(v) JamesSullivan 6 78
(Ruth Carr) *midfield: hdwy wl over 2f out: rdn to chse ldng pair over 1f out: kpt on same pce* **4/1**[1]
-000 **4** *3 3/4* **Collateral Damage (IRE)**[3] 1820 9-8-13 **75**.....(t) DavidAllan 8 69+
(Tim Easterby) *hld up in rr: hdwy 3f out: rdn 2f out: styd on fnl f: nrest at fin* **11/1**
100- **5** *1/2* **I'm Super Too (IRE)**[227] 6290 5-9-2 **83**..... GarryWhillans(5) 7 76
(Alan Swinbank) *chsd ldrs: rdn over 2f out: sn drvn and one pce* **16/1**
20-0 **6** *2* **Pass Muster**[9] 1670 5-9-6 **82**..... TonyHamilton 3 71
(Ollie Pears) *hld up: hdwy over 3f out: sn rdn and no imp* **9/1**
-002 **7** *1 3/4* **Arabian Spirit**[13] 1578 7-8-13 **80**..... ShaneBKelly(5) 5 65
(Richard Fahey) *chsd ldrs on inner: rdn along over 3f out: wknd over 2f out* **8/1**[3]

0-05 **8** *nk* **European Dream (IRE)**[9] 1680 9-9-2 **78**..................(p) WilliamCarson 4 62
(Richard Guest) *hld up: a in rr* **14/1**

2-04 **9** *2* **Icy Blue**[14] 1561 4-8-7 **72**.. AmyRyan(3) 10 51
(Richard Whitaker) *in tch: hdwy on outer 1/2-way: rdn to chse ldrs 3f out: sn btn* **7/1**[2]

00-0 **10** *3 ¾* **Quite Sparky**[28] 1249 5-9-4 **80**..(v) GrahamLee 2 51
(Mike Sowersby) *midfield: rdn along 3f out: sn wknd* **28/1**

-640 **11** *4 ½* **Gritstone**[37] 1133 5-8-11 **76**.. LeeTopliss(3) 1 36
(Richard Fahey) *led 1 1/2f: prom: rdn along 3f out and sn wknd* **7/1**[2]

1m 49.87s (2.27) **Going Correction** +0.375s/f (Good) **11** Ran SP% **118.1**
Speed ratings (Par 105): **103,102,99,96,95 93,91,91,89,85 81**
toteswingers:1&2:£16.50, 2&3:£30.40, 1&3:£2.30 CSF £54.77 CT £210.32 TOTE £7.50: £2.50, £4.20, £1.10; EX 75.10.
Owner Richard Walker **Bred** Mrs G Slater **Trained** Nawton, N Yorks

FOCUS
A modest handicap where racing handy was again an advantage. The winner is rated back to his best.
Gritstone Official explanation: jockey said gelding lost its action

1915 PICNIC, PUNTERS AND POSH PACKAGES H'CAP — 1m 4f 16y
4:30 (4:30) (Class 5) (0-70,66) 3-Y-O — **£2,420** (£714; £357) **Stalls** Low

Form — RPR

50-2 **1** **Party Line**[24] 1355 3-9-7 **66**.. JoeFanning 8 76+
(Mark Johnston) *in tch: hdwy 4f out: chsd ldr wl over 2f out: rdn to ld over 1f out: drvn ins fnl f: jst hld on* **9/4**[1]

5-45 **2** *shd* **Minnie Diva (IRE)**[27] 1281 3-9-0 **59**.................................... GrahamLee 2 68
(Kevin Ryan) *led: clr 1/2-way: rdn along over 2f out: hdd over 1f out: drvn and rallied ins fnl f: jst hld* **20/1**

63-3 **3** *2 ½* **Neil's Pride**[26] 1320 3-8-11 **56**...................................... TonyHamilton 1 61
(Richard Fahey) *in tch: hdwy 3f out: rdn over 2f out: styd on appr fnl f: nrest at fin* **10/3**[2]

6536 **4** *8* **Dilizan (IRE)**[26] 1322 3-9-4 **63**.. BarryMcHugh 3 55
(Brian Ellison) *hld up towards rr: hdwy 3f out: rdn to chse ldrs 2f out: sn drvn and no imp* **9/2**[3]

-405 **5** *10* **Maybeagrey**[10] 1641 3-9-6 **65**.. DavidAllan 5 41
(Tim Easterby) *hld up towards rr: hdwy over 3f out: rdn to chse ldrs over 2f out: sn drvn and wknd* **8/1**

655- **6** *17* **Miss Ella Jade**[149] 7708 3-8-7 **55**.................................... AmyRyan(3) 10
(Richard Whitaker) *hld up in rr: hdwy on outer over 3f out: in tch and rdn over 2f out: sn wknd* **40/1**

00-0 **7** *21* **Fine Kingdom**[26] 1319 3-8-10 **55**................................(p) PaulMulrennan 4
(Michael Dods) *chsd ldrs: rdn along 5f out: sn wknd: bhd whn eased fnl 2f* **25/1**

6-13 **8** *10* **Palmyra (IRE)**[75] 656 3-9-3 **62**...................................... StevieDonohoe 9
(David Simcock) *hld up: a in rr* **14/1**

00-0 **9** *18* **Gabrial's Layla (IRE)**[21] 1424 3-8-5 **50**...................... RoystonFfrench 6
(Mark Johnston) *sn chsng ldr: rdn along 4f out: sn wknd and bhd whn eased fnl 2f* **25/1**

60-3 **10** *6* **Lost Highway (IRE)**[13] 1590 3-9-0 **59**............................ AdrianNicholls 7
(Mark Johnston) *chsd ldr 2f: prom tl chsd ldr again 1/2-way: rdn along over 3f out: sn wknd and bhd whn eased fnl 2f* **15/2**

2m 44.78s (4.98) **Going Correction** +0.375s/f (Good) **10** Ran SP% **116.5**
Speed ratings (Par 99): **98,97,96,90,84 72,58,52,40,36**
toteswingers:1&2:£29.50, 2&3:£12.20, 1&3:£2.40 CSF £54.12 CT £151.16 TOTE £4.30: £3.10, £6.60, £1.02; EX 41.40.
Owner S R Counsell **Bred** Highclere Stud And Balmerino Bloodstock **Trained** Middleham Moor, N Yorks

FOCUS
A strongly run 3-y-o handicap and they finished well strung out. It looks form to be fairly positive about.
Palmyra(IRE) Official explanation: trainer's rep said filly was unsuited by the good to soft (good in places) ground

1916 WHITE RABBIT H'CAP (DIV I) — 7f 100y
5:00 (5:01) (Class 6) (0-65,66) 3-Y-O — **£1,681** (£500; £250; £125) **Stalls** Low

Form — RPR

303- **1** **Lolita Lebron (IRE)**[192] 7140 3-9-7 **65**............................ RobertWinston 3 73
(Lawrence Mullaney) *trckd ldrs on inner: effrt whn nt clr run 2f out: sn swtchd lft and rdn to ld over 1f out: drvn out* **6/1**[3]

-005 **2** *1 ¼* **Mick Slates (IRE)**[12] 1600 3-8-7 **51** oh1...................... GrahamGibbons 7 56
(Declan Carroll) *sltly hmpd s: sn prom: effrt over 2f out: sn rdn and ev ch tl drvn and one pce ins fnl f* **11/2**[2]

00-0 **3** *1 ¼* **More Bottle (IRE)**[16] 1519 3-8-7 **51** oh4........................ AndrewMullen 8 54
(Tom Tate) *trckd ldrs: effrt whn nt clr run on inner over 1f out: sn swtchd lft and rdn: styd on ins fnl f* **33/1**

00-0 **4** *½* **Balti's Sister (IRE)**[4] 1798 3-8-11 **55**............................ JamesSullivan 5 56+
(Michael Easterby) *midfield whn hmpd and lost pl after 1f: bhd: hdwy on wd outside over 2f out: rdn to chse ldrs over 1f out: drvn and one pce ins fnl f* **10/1**

10-6 **5** *2* **Lady Advocate (IRE)**[23] 1386 3-8-13 **57**........................(b) DavidAllan 10 53
(Tim Easterby) *led: rdn 2f out: drvn and hdd over 1f out: wknd* **16/1**

00-0 **6** *1 ¾* **Oops Caroline (IRE)**[10] 1637 3-8-11 **55**...................... DanielTudhope 4 46
(David O'Meara) *midfield: effrt 3f out: rdn over 2f out: no hdwy* **14/1**

0004 **7** *6* **Johnson's Cat (IRE)**[12] 1596 3-8-7 **51** oh6.............(e[1]) WilliamCarson 1 27
(Richard Guest) *hld up in rr: hdwy on outer wl over 2f out: sn rdn and nvr nr ldrs* **10/1**

060- **8** *4 ½* **Siberian Belle (IRE)**[196] 7051 3-8-7 **51** oh1................ BarryMcHugh 11 16
(Richard Fahey) *midfield: rdn along 1/2-way: sn wknd* **8/1**

040- **9** *1 ½* **Louis Hull**[298] 4019 3-8-11 **60**...................................... JustinNewman(5) 2 21
(Deborah Sanderson) *a in rr* **8/1**

05-0 **10** *5* **Kathleensluckylad (IRE)**[25] 1337 3-9-0 **58**.................... PhillipMakin 6
(Kevin Ryan) *t.k.h: cl up: rdn along 3f out: hung rt and drvn 2f out: sn wknd* **9/2**[1]

540- **11** *22* **Yes It's The Boy (USA)**[194] 7094 3-9-1 **66** ow1..... MichaelJMurphy(7) 9
(Ed Walker) *a in rr: sddle slipped 1/2-way* **6/1**[3]

1m 37.73s (3.93) **Going Correction** +0.375s/f (Good) **11** Ran SP% **118.0**
Speed ratings (Par 97): **92,90,89,88,86 84,77,72,70,64 39**
toteswingers:1&2:£5.10, 2&3:£27.00, 1&3:£27.00 CSF £39.17 CT £1033.44 TOTE £9.80: £3.90, £1.50, £15.00; EX 45.70.
Owner Ian Buckley **Bred** Epona Bloodstock Ltd **Trained** Great Habton, N Yorks

FOCUS
An ordinary 3-y-o handicap and another for prominent runners. The time was reasonable and the form is rated around the best view of the winner's nursery form.
Lady Advocate(IRE) Official explanation: jockey said filly hung right throughout
Yes It's The Boy(USA) Official explanation: jockey said saddle slipped

1917 YORKSHIRE RACING SUMMER FESTIVAL IN JULY H'CAP — 7f 100y
5:30 (5:31) (Class 5) (0-75,75) 4-Y-O+ — **£2,296** (£683; £341; £170) **Stalls** Low

Form — RPR

6-00 **1** **Al Muheer (IRE)**[13] 1587 7-9-7 **75**..........................(b) JamesSullivan 13 84
(Ruth Carr) *hld up towards rr: hdwy wl over 2f out: rdn to chse ldrs over 1f out: styd on wl to ld last 50yds* **12/1**

06-3 **2** *1* **Cottam Donny**[37] 1135 4-8-7 **61**.. DavidAllan 1 68
(Mel Brittain) *led: rdn along 2f out: drvn over 1f out: hdd and no ex last 50yds* **11/2**[1]

41-0 **3** *¾* **Ventura Sands (IRE)**[24] 1354 4-9-3 **71**........................ TonyHamilton 2 76
(Richard Fahey) *trckd ldng pair on inner: effrt 2f out: sn rdn and ev ch tl drvn and one pce ins fnl f* **8/1**

003- **4** *¾* **Fieldgunner Kirkup (GER)**[188] 7213 4-9-4 **72**......... GrahamGibbons 8 75
(David Barron) *hld up: hdwy on inner wl over 2f out: effrt and nt clr run over 1f out: sn rdn and kpt on towards fin* **9/1**

630- **5** *1 ½* **Summer Dancer (IRE)**[191] 7176 8-8-13 **67**.................. MickyFenton 10 66
(Paul Midgley) *hmpd s and bhd: hdwy over 2f out: rdn over 1f out: styd on fnl f: nrest at fin* **20/1**

6404 **6** *1 ½* **Piceno (IRE)**[16] 1520 4-9-0 **68**..(p) PhillipMakin 9 64
(Scott Dixon) *midfield: hdwy over 2f out: sn rdn and no imp appr fnl f* **8/1**

050- **7** *2 ¾* **Shadowtime**[235] 6093 7-9-4 **72**.. RobertWinston 3 61
(Tracy Waggott) *trckd ldrs: hdwy and cl up over 3f out: rdn to chal 2f out and ev ch tl drvn and wknd ent fnl f* **10/1**

U6-1 **8** *1 ¾* **Just The Tonic**[16] 1527 5-9-3 **74**.. JulieBurke(3) 5 58
(Marjorie Fife) *hld up in rr: sme hdwy wl over 2f out: sn rdn and nvr a factor* **13/2**[3]

00-3 **9** *2 ¼* **Smalljohn**[51] 942 6-9-1 **69**..(v) RoystonFfrench 4 48
(Bryan Smart) *cl up: rdn over 2f out: drvn and wkng whn n.m.r over 1f out* **16/1**

0-50 **10** *hd* **Maggie Mey (IRE)**[16] 1520 4-8-11 **65**........................ RussKennemore 7 43
(Paul Midgley) *prom: rdn 3f out: grad wknd fnl 2f* **16/1**

2554 **11** *hd* **River Ardeche**[19] 1436 7-8-12 **66**...................................... JoeFanning 14 44
(Tracy Waggott) *chsd ldrs: rdn along 3f out: sn wknd* **16/1**

51-5 **12** *nk* **Watts Up Son**[14] 1561 4-8-9 **70**.......................................(vt[1]) JasonHart(7) 11 47
(Declan Carroll) *awkward and almost uns rdr s: sn pushed along to chse ldrs on outer: wd bnd at 1/2-way: sn rdn and btn* **6/1**[2]

-042 **13** *1 ¼* **Northern Bolt**[12] 1601 7-9-1 **69**................................(b) PatrickMathers 6 43
(Ian McInnes) *a in rr* **20/1**

000- **14** *4 ½* **Last Destination (IRE)**[198] 7024 4-8-3 **64**........... DanielleMooney(7) 12 27
(Nigel Tinkler) *a in rr* **80/1**

1m 36.48s (2.68) **Going Correction** +0.375s/f (Good) **14** Ran SP% **120.4**
Speed ratings (Par 103): **99,97,97,96,94 92,89,87,85,84 84,84,82,77**
toteswingers:1&2:£8.10, 2&3:£7.20, 1&3:£13.50 CSF £75.10 CT £588.29 TOTE £14.30: £4.10, £1.10, £2.90; EX 66.60.
Owner Sprint King Racing (Antigua Cavaliers) **Bred** Foursome Thoroughbreds **Trained** Huby, N Yorks
■ Stewards' Enquiry : James Sullivan two-day ban: used whip above permitted level (May 21-22)

FOCUS
A decent pace on here and it proved one for the hold-up horses. The form looks sound.
Maggie Mey(IRE) Official explanation: jockey said filly hung left throughout
Watts Up Son Official explanation: jockey said gelding hung right throughout

1918 WHITE RABBIT H'CAP (DIV II) — 7f 100y
6:00 (6:00) (Class 6) (0-65,65) 3-Y-O — **£1,681** (£500; £250; £125) **Stalls** Low

Form — RPR

24-4 **1** **Dubious Escapade (IRE)**[24] 1364 3-9-5 **63**...................... GrahamLee 8 74
(Ann Duffield) *trckd ldng pair: cl up 1/2-way: chal 2f out: led over 1f out: rdn and styd on wl fnl f* **9/2**[2]

64-6 **2** *2 ¼* **Gulf Storm (IRE)**[118] 112 3-8-11 **55**..........................(t) RoystonFfrench 3 60
(Bryan Smart) *cl up: led after 2f: rdn along and jnd 2f out: hdd over 1f out: drvn and kpt on fnl f* **7/1**

14-5 **3** *4* **Red Tyke (IRE)**[23] 1386 3-8-7 **51** oh1.......................... MichaelO'Connell 2 46
(John Quinn) *led 2f: cl up: rdn along 2f out: drvn over 1f out and grad wknd* **11/2**

U53- **4** *2 ½* **Be Calm**[213] 6667 3-8-5 **56**.. DavidSimmonson(7) 4 45
(Michael Easterby) *midfield: hdwy to chse ldrs 3f out: swtchd rt to inner 2f out: sn rdn and one pce* **5/1**[3]

00-4 **5** *2* **Divine Success (IRE)**[28] 1259 3-8-8 **55**.............................. LeeTopliss(3) 1 39+
(Richard Fahey) *in rr: sme hdwy over 2f out: sn rdn and n.d* **7/2**[1]

53-6 **6** *½* **Millymonkin**[45] 1016 3-9-7 **65**.. PaddyAspell 6 48
(Michael Easterby) *hmpd s and bhd: hdwy on outer 1/2-way: rdn and wknd over 2f out* **12/1**

-064 **7** *2 ½* **Sleepy Lucy**[12] 1600 3-8-4 **51** oh5............................ DeclanCannon(3) 7 27
(Richard Guest) *wnt rt s: a towards rr* **16/1**

5013 **8** *1* **My New Angel (IRE)**[13] 1591 3-8-7 **51** oh1..................(be) JoeFanning 5 25
(Paul Green) *wnt lft s: a in rr* **9/1**

600- **9** *16* **Trioomph**[186] 7248 3-9-0 **58**.. PaulMulrennan 10
(James Given) *chsd ldrs: rdn along 3f out: sn wknd* **14/1**

1m 37.47s (3.67) **Going Correction** +0.375s/f (Good) **9** Ran SP% **115.2**
Speed ratings (Par 97): **94,91,86,84,81 81,78,77,58**
toteswingers:1&2:£3.40, 2&3:£8.90, 1&3:£13.40 CSF £35.85 CT £177.54 TOTE £7.00: £2.90, £2.80, £1.20; EX 45.10.
Owner Les Stirling **Bred** Ballygallon Stud Limited **Trained** Constable Burton, N Yorks

FOCUS
The second division of the 7.5f handicap and another weak affair, but slightly faster than division I. Front runners dominated and the winner showed improvement.
T/Jkpt: £7,498.30 to a £1 stake. Pool:£68,646.42 - 6.50 winning units. T/Plt: £42.90 to a £1 stake. Pool:£75,890.22 - 1,288.67 winning units. T/Qpdt: £20.60 to a £1 stake. Pool:£4,351.15 - 156.30 winning units. JR

1747 KEMPTON (A.W) (R-H)
Monday, May 7

OFFICIAL GOING: Standard
Wind: Almost nil Weather: ovsercast

1919 BET AT BLUESQUARE.COM H'CAP — 1m 2f (P)
2:15 (2:15) (Class 6) (0-65,65) 4-Y-O+ — **£1,617** (£481; £240; £120) **Stalls** Low

Form — RPR

001- **1** **Rockweiller**[194] 7113 5-9-3 **61**..(v) JamieSpencer 1 70
(Steve Gollings) *led tl hdd after 1f: remained cl up: rdn over 2f out: pressed ldrs 1f out: drvn to assert cl home* **10/1**

3322 **2** ½ **Laser Blazer**[47] 984 4-8-10 **54**..........(p) RichardKingscote 10 62
(Jeremy Gask) *t.k.h to post and in r: cl up: pushed along 2f out: drvn and duelled for ld 1f out: hdd and no ex cl home* **5/1**[2]

0-40 **3** 1 **Iguacu**[16] 1534 8-8-8 **52**.......... SilvestreDeSousa 4 58
(Richard Price) *in tch: rdn and hdwy on inner over 2f out: drvn and pressed duelling ldrs 1f out: no ex fnl 75yds* **20/1**

-203 **4** 1¾ **Regal Rave (USA)**[23] 1379 5-8-7 **51**..........(v) JohnFahy 14 54+
(Peter Hedger) *slowly away and dropped out in rr: pushed along over 2f out: swtchd to outer and drvn over 1f out: kpt on nicely ins fnl f* **11/1**

4231 **5** hd **Penbryn (USA)**[23] 1379 5-9-4 **62**..........(v) GeorgeBaker 6 64
(Nick Littmoden) *hld up: t.k.h: urged along over 2f out: rdn over 1f out: no immediate rspnse: one pce fnl 100yds* **4/1**[1]

-030 **6** ¾ **Gower Rules (IRE)**[16] 1534 4-9-0 **58**.......... KieranO'Neill 5 59
(John Bridger) *led after 1f: rdn and hdd 2f out: railled u.p to press ldrs over 1f out: no ex ins fnl f* **17/2**

-005 **7** nk **Dinner Date**[12] 1611 10-9-0 **61**.......... RyanClark(3) 9 61
(Tom Keddy) *hld up: rdn 2f out: drvn and no impact on ldrs 1f out: kpt on one pce* **16/1**

310- **8** ½ **Rajnagan (IRE)**[171] 5015 8-9-6 **64**..........(t) WilliamBuick 13 63
(Paul Webber) *cl up: pushed along over 2f out: led 2f out: hdd over 1f out: wknd fnl f* **8/1**[3]

5330 **9** 1 **Potentiale (IRE)**[37] 1135 8-9-4 **62**..........(v) SebSanders 12 59
(J W Hills) *in rr: urged along 3f out: rdn and outpcd 2f out: plugged on but no real imp ins fnl f* **9/1**

010- **10** shd **Secret Era**[220] 6507 5-9-4 **62**.......... MartinDwyer 3 59
(William Muir) *s.i.s: in rr: pushed along 4f out: drvn and one pce 2f out: nvr a threat* **25/1**

3046 **11** ¾ **Mister Green (FR)**[21] 1421 6-9-7 **65**..........(bt) JamesDoyle 7 60
(David Flood) *in tch: hdwy to chse ldrs 3f out: rdn and little rspnse 2f out: btn and no ex fnl f* **12/1**

6-05 **12** 1½ **Rainsborough**[23] 1379 5-8-2 **51** oh1..........(p) AmyScott(5) 2 43
(Peter Hedger) *in rr: pushed along over 2f out: fnd little and sn btn* **16/1**

0454 **13** 11 **Sweet Vera**[6] 1744 7-8-7 **51** oh1.......... HayleyTurner 8 21
(Shaun Harris) *a in rr: rdn after 2f: drvn and struggling 4f out: wl btn fnl 2f* **50/1**

500- **14** 10 **Emperor Of Rome (IRE)**[203] 6916 4-9-5 **63**.......... TomEaves 11 13
(Tim Fitzgerald) *bkward: in tch and t.k.h: drvn and lost pl rapidly 3f out: sn no ch* **40/1**

2m 5.9s (-2.10) **Going Correction** -0.15s/f (Stan) **14** Ran SP% **118.2**
Speed ratings (Par 101): **102,101,100,99,99 98,98,98,97,97 96,95,86,78**
toteswingers:1&2:£11.40, 2&3:£26.60, 1&3:£64.80 CSF £56.06 CT £996.21 TOTE £9.00: £3.40, £2.60, £5.70; EX 52.40 TRIFECTA Not won..
Owner P Whinham **Bred** Exors Of The Late Mrs E A Hankinson **Trained** Scamblesby, Lincs

FOCUS
A modest handicap with a solid pace set by confirmed front-runner Gower Rules. Straightforward form.

1920 BET ON YOUR MOBILE AT BLUE SQUARE E B F MAIDEN STKS 5f (P)
2:45 (2:45) (Class 5) 2-Y-O **£3,299** (£981; £490; £245) **Stalls** Low

Form RPR

24 **1** **Ceiling Kitty**[19] 1435 2-8-12 0.......... RichardKingscote 2 75+
(Tom Dascombe) *chsd ldr: rdn and hmpd over 1f out: swtchd ins and regained momentum 1f out: kpt on wl to ld fnl 100yds* **5/2**[2]

3 **2** ½ **Citius (IRE)**[17] 1495 2-9-3 0.......... RichardHughes 3 78
(Richard Hannon) *sn led: pushed along over 1f out and drifted lft: hrd rdn and continued to drift lft: hmpd rivals ins fnl f: hdd fnl 100yds and btn* **4/6**[1]

3 ½ **Jubilee Brig** 2-9-3 0.......... TomQueally 5 77
(Gary Moore) *in tch: rdn over 1f out and hmpd: drvn and carried lft thrght fnl f: no ex and hld cl home* **14/1**

4 6 **Composed** 2-9-3 0.......... SilvestreDeSousa 4 55
(Paul Cole) *in rr: drvn along and sn running green: wl btn 2f out* **8/1**[3]

5 1¼ **Rioja Day (IRE)** 2-9-3 0.......... SebSanders 1 50
(J W Hills) *hld up: rdn and lost pl 2f out: sn dropped away* **22/1**

1m 0.92s (0.42) **Going Correction** -0.15s/f (Stan) **5** Ran SP% **110.7**
Speed ratings (Par 93): **90,89,88,78,76**
CSF £4.59 TOTE £2.70: £2.20, £1.10; EX 5.10.
Owner A Black & The Master Bettors **Bred** A Black **Trained** Malpas, Cheshire

FOCUS
An ordinary juvenile maiden, but a rough race. The time suggests the front two may not have improved and the form has been rated a little negatively.

NOTEBOOK
Ceiling Kitty was disappointing at Beverley following her promising debut in a race over this C&D that is working out well, but appreciated the return to this venue. Despite getting hampered by the leader over a furlong out, she had time to switch inside her errant rival and was able to deliver a sustained effort, despite having lost a shoe at some point. (op 11-4)
Citius(IRE) had shown plenty of promise on his Bath debut and should have won this. Soon in front, he looked to be in control when appearing to hesitate as a couple of birds flew across the track over a furlong out. From that point he hung badly away to his left, hampering the winner and third, and basically threw it away. He can gain compensation soon, but seems likely to improve for further in due course. (op 8-11)
Jubilee Brig ◆, a 40,000GBP 2yo and half-brother to a winner at up to 7f, ran a blinder against a pair of experienced rivals, especially as he was repeatedly hampered from over a furlong out and could never run in a straight line. This gives his connections something to build on. (op 16-1)

1921 BLUE SQUARE H'CAP 5f (P)
3:15 (3:15) (Class 4) (0-85,85) 3-Y-O **£4,075** (£1,212; £606; £303) **Stalls** Low

Form RPR

241- **1** **Exceedance**[189] 7194 3-9-1 **79**.......... TomEaves 5 97
(Bryan Smart) *broke sharply: mde all: blitzed clr wl over 1f out: in n.d but kpt up to work ins fnl f* **7/1**

210- **2** 5 **Place In My Heart**[219] 6535 3-9-7 **85**.......... JamieSpencer 6 85
(George Baker) *wnt lft s: t.k.h: in tch: pushed along 2f out: kpt on one pce and tk 2nd cl home: no hope of catching wnr* **9/2**[1]

55-1 **3** hd **Charlotte Rosina**[21] 1412 3-9-2 **80**.......... SebSanders 1 79
(Roger Teal) *chsd wnr: drvn and no imp on clr wnr: wknd and lost 2nd cl home* **13/2**[3]

24- **4** 1 **Supreme Quest**[352] 2309 3-9-4 **82**.......... JamesDoyle 4 77+
(Roger Charlton) *slowly away: hmpd shortly after s: in rr: rdn over 2f out: swtchd to outer and kpt on over 1f out: r.o wl and pressed for pls ins fnl f: should improve* **9/2**[1]

-323 **5** nk **Waseem Faris (IRE)**[16] 1524 3-9-3 **81**.......... TonyCulhane 3 75
(Mick Channon) *hmpd s: in tch: pushed along over 2f out: drvn and duelled for pls tl no ex and wknd fnl 100yds* **5/1**[2]

00-0 **6** 3½ **Airborne Again (IRE)**[26] 1317 3-9-2 **80**.......... EddieAhern 9 62
(Harry Dunlop) *sltly hmpd s: rn wd in rr: rdn 2f out: one pce and sn no imp* **25/1**

0-44 **7** 2¼ **Electric Qatar**[10] 1639 3-9-2 **80**..........(b[1]) RichardKingscote 2 54
(Tom Dascombe) *in tch: rdn and rn wd ent st 2f out: sn wknd and btn* **15/2**

11-0 **8** 1¾ **Beach Candy (IRE)**[4] 1790 3-8-12 **76**.......... RichardHughes 8 43
(Richard Hannon) *wnt lft s: sn veered rt and hmpd rivals and almost unrideable: pushed along 2f out: sn btn and eased* **13/2**[3]

14-0 **9** 2 **Marygold**[19] 1457 3-9-2 **80**.......... HayleyTurner 7 40
(Lee Carter) *a in rr: drvn and btn over 2f out* **20/1**

58.33s (-2.17) **Going Correction** -0.15s/f (Stan) **9** Ran SP% **112.6**
Speed ratings (Par 101): **111,103,102,101,100 95,91,88,85**
toteswingers: 1&2:£2.40, 2&3:£1.50, 1&3:£2.60 CSF £37.34 CT £214.87 TOTE £6.70: £2.60, £2.30, £2.10; EX 23.20 Trifecta £26.20 Pool £291.81 - 8.23 winning units..
Owner Andrew Tinkler **Bred** A S Denniff **Trained** Hambleton, N Yorks

FOCUS
This looked a competitive sprint handicap beforehand, but it became a one-horse rout and the winner knocked 0.17 seconds off the 5f course record. The form is taken at face value and this was a very useful performance, but there is a bit of doubt whether he can repeat it.
Beach Candy(IRE) Official explanation: jockey said filly hung badly right

1922 GET YOUR BET ON AT BLUE SQUARE MAIDEN STKS (DIV I) 1m (P)
3:50 (3:51) (Class 4) 3-Y-O **£4,075** (£1,212; £606; £303) **Stalls** Low

Form RPR

0 **1** **Mawasem**[18] 1467 3-9-3 0.......... PaulHanagan 12 93+
(Sir Michael Stoute) *cl up: rdn and hdwy to press ldrs over 1f out: drvn and kpt on wl to ld fnl 100yds* **7/4**[1]

2 **2** ¾ **Nine Realms**[19] 1450 3-9-3 0.......... LiamJones 2 91+
(William Haggas) *cl up: pushed along to chse ldr 2f out: ev ch and drvn 1f out: kpt on and tk 2nd cl home* **7/2**[2]

-2 **3** ½ **Ihtifal**[12] 1610 3-8-12 0..........(t) MickaelBarzalona 3 85
(Saeed Bin Suroor) *mounted outside paddock: wore earplugs: t.k.h: sn led: rdn and qcknd clr over 1f out: drvn and shifted lft ins fnl f and strly pressed: hdd fnl 100yds and lost 2 pls* **7/2**[2]

3-0 **4** 3 **Qaadira (USA)**[18] 1472 3-8-12 0.......... TadhgO'Shea 5 78+
(John Gosden) *t.k.h in midfield: swtchd to outer and rdn 2f out: carried hd high u.p but kpt on wl to go 4th fnl f* **33/1**

4 **5** 2¾ **Stormbound (IRE)**[9] 1676 3-8-12 0.......... DuilioDaSilva(5) 10 76
(Paul Cole) *t.k.h in rr: hdwy over 4f out: last of 8 w a ch 3f out: drvn and kpt on wout threatening ldrs* **100/1**

0 **6** 7 **Bitter Harvest**[16] 1512 3-9-3 0.......... HayleyTurner 8 60+
(Michael Bell) *midfield: pushed along 3f out: outpcd fnl 2f: swtchd ins and plugged on one pce fnl f* **12/1**

7 1½ **Geeaitch** 3-9-0 0.......... DominicFox(3) 1 56
(Anthony Carson) *cl up: lost pl 3f out: drvn and wknd fnl 2f* **100/1**

40- **8** nk **Maistro (IRE)**[193] 7126 3-9-0 0.......... PatrickHills(3) 7 55+
(Luca Cumani) *slowly away and a in rr: wl bhd whn rdn 3f out: sn no hope of catching ldrs* **25/1**

0- **9** ½ **Alvitude (USA)**[297] 4053 3-9-3 0.......... JamesDoyle 13 54+
(Roger Charlton) *in rr and pushed along 3f out: no ch fnl 2f* **20/1**

-6 **10** 1½ **Straight Shot (IRE)**[18] 1467 3-9-3 0..........(t) MartinDwyer 6 50
(Brian Meehan) *cl up: rdn 2f out: pressed ldrs briefly over 1f out: drvn and grad wknd fnl f* **9/1**[3]

11 2 **Sir Lexington (IRE)** 3-9-0 0.......... SeanLevey(3) 9 46
(Richard Hannon) *in rr: pushed along 3f out: toiling fnl 2f and btn* **33/1**

4- **12** 12 **Whispering Warrior (IRE)**[130] 7906 3-9-3 0.......... JamieSpencer 4 17
(Jeremy Noseda) *nvr beyond midfield: pushed along 3f out: one pce and no imp* **16/1**

13 ¾ **Opus (IRE)** 3-9-3 0..........(t) TomQueally 14 15
(Amanda Perrett) *in rr: struggling whn short of room over 3f out: sn btn* **66/1**

14 5 **Hoonose** 3-9-0 0..........(tp) HarryBentley(3) 11
(William Knight) *midfield and pushed along thrght: lost pl 4f out: sn toiling* **66/1**

1m 37.81s (-1.99) **Going Correction** -0.15s/f (Stan) **14** Ran SP% **123.8**
Speed ratings (Par 101): **103,102,101,98,96 89,87,87,86,85 83,71,70,65**
toteswingers: 1&2:£3.10, 2&3:£3.60, 1&3:£2.70 CSF £7.38 TOTE £2.40: £1.10, £2.20, £2.40; EX 8.90 Trifecta £17.20 Pool £529.52 - 22.78 winning units..
Owner Hamdan Al Maktoum **Bred** Ballygallon Stud Limited **Trained** Newmarket, Suffolk

FOCUS
A big field for this maiden, but they finished very well spread out and the first five pulled clear of the rest. It was the best of the C&D times, and the winner built on his debut promise.
Maistro(IRE) Official explanation: jockey said colt was slowly away
Alvitude(USA) Official explanation: jockey said, regarding running and riding, that his orders were to drop in if he missed the break and then finish in the best possible position, he felt the race got away with him and he had to take off heels approaching 3f mark and suffered slight interference at the 2f mark, he switched right and rode out hands and heels; trainer said the gelding had a split pastern last year and had not been in training long and felt it needed further.

1923 GET YOUR BET ON AT BLUE SQUARE MAIDEN STKS (DIV II) 1m (P)
4:20 (4:23) (Class 4) 3-Y-O **£4,075** (£1,212; £606; £303) **Stalls** Low

Form RPR

4- **1** **Kahruman (USA)**[208] 6805 3-9-3 0.......... PaulHanagan 4 92+
(William Haggas) *mde all: pushed along and drew clr w one rival 2f out: drvn to assert ins fnl f* **8/1**[3]

4 **2** 2¾ **Hill Street (IRE)**[18] 1467 3-9-3 0.......... WilliamBuick 13 85+
(John Gosden) *midfield: rushed up on outer to press ldr after 3f: effrt and qcknd clr w rival 2f out: drvn and unable to cl on wnr ins fnl f* **4/5**[1]

44- **3** 5 **Muntasir (IRE)**[235] 6100 3-9-3 0.......... FrankieDettori 10 73
(Saeed Bin Suroor) *cl up: rdn and outpcd 3f out: swtchd rt 2f out and drvn: kpt on to take 3rd cl home* **3/1**[2]

4 shd **Chigun** 3-8-12 0.......... TomQueally 9 68
(Sir Henry Cecil) *cl up: pushed along and unable qck w ldng pair 2f out: duelled for 3rd ins fnl f* **20/1**

0 **5** 2 **Sabre Tooth (IRE)**[7] 1703 3-9-3 0..........(t) RichardMullen 7 68
(Sir Michael Stoute) *in tch: rdn and outpcd 3f out: drvn and no imp fnl f* **33/1**

6 ½ **Cool Sky** 3-9-0 0.......... HarryBentley(3) 5 67
(William Knight) *prom: rdn 3f out: drifted lft u.p 2f out: sn no imp on ldng pair and duelled for 3rd tl wknd ins fnl f* **100/1**

0 **7** 2½ **Morlotti**[18] 1467 3-9-0 0.......... PatrickHills(3) 12 61+
(Luca Cumani) *midfield: urged along and rn green 3f out: kpt on wout threatening plcd horses* **100/1**

6- **8** *1 1/4* **Tafawuk (USA)**[235] 6100 3-9-3 0 .... TadhgO'Shea 11 58+
(Roger Varian) *hld up: pushed along 3f out: btn whn hmpd 2f out: kpt on one pce* **16/1**

8 *dht* **Bedazzled** 3-8-12 0 .... EddieAhern 2 53+
(James Fanshawe) *in rr: pushed along 4f out: wknd and btn wl over 2f out* **14/1**

10 *3 1/4* **Iron Butterfly** 3-8-12 0 .... HayleyTurner 8 45
(James Eustace) *hld up and bhd: rdn and no imp fnl 3f* **50/1**

0 **11** *1 1/2* **Guiletta (IRE)**[121] 84 3-8-12 0 .... SebSanders 6 41
(Rae Guest) *a in rr: drvn and stopped qckly 3f out* **50/1**

-0 **12** *3/4* **Capitol Gain (IRE)**[18] 1467 3-9-3 0 .... MartinDwyer 14 45
(Brian Meehan) *slowly away: in rr: rdn over 3f out: no imp fnl 2f* **25/1**

0 **13** *14* **Razzle Dazzle 'Em**[37] 1132 3-9-3 0 .... SilvestreDeSousa 1 11
(Shaun Harris) *midfield on inner: drvn and lost pl 3f out: sn bhd* **100/1**

1m 38.65s (-1.15) **Going Correction** -0.15s/f (Stan) 13 Ran SP% 122.7
Speed ratings (Par 101): **99,96,91,91,89 88,86,84,84,81 80,79,65**
toteswingers: 1&2:£2.20, 2&3:£1.40, 1&3:£3.40 CSF £14.57 TOTE £5.80: £1.40, £1.10, £1.70; EX 20.80 Trifecta £91.90 Pool £1,214.61 - 9.77 winning units..
Owner Hamdan Al Maktoum **Bred** Shadwell Farm LLC **Trained** Newmarket, Suffolk

FOCUS
Again they finished well spread out and the front pair pulled clear. The winning time was 0.89 seconds slower than the first division and the form is of a similar standard. A number of thses should do better in time.
Tafawuk(USA) ◆ Official explanation: jockey said gelding was denied a clear run

1924 BLUESQUARE.COM JUBILEE H'CAP (LONDON MILE QUALIFIER) 1m (P)
4:50 (4:51) (Class 3) (0-90,90) 4-Y-O+
£6,411 (£1,919; £959; £479; £239; £120) **Stalls** Low

Form RPR

20-0 **1** **Cruiser**[16] 1510 4-9-0 **83** .... MartinDwyer 11 90
(William Muir) *cl up: pushed along 3f out: rdn and led over 1f out: hrd drvn and kpt finding for press: all out* **28/1**

1/1- **2** *nk* **Terdaad (IRE)**[271] 4914 4-9-7 **90** .... (p) FrankieDettori 10 96+
(Saeed Bin Suroor) *in tch: urged along 3f out: swtchd outside and drvn along 2f out: kpt on wl 1f out: fin strly: jst failed* **7/2**[1]

160- **3** *hd* **Indian Jack (IRE)**[191] 7168 4-9-5 **88** .... MickaelBarzalona 12 94
(Luca Cumani) *slowly away: hdwy 3f out: drvn along and effrt 2f out: pressed ldrs 1f out: kpt on cl home* **7/1**[3]

-111 **4** *3/4* **Forceful Appeal (USA)**[65] 785 4-9-5 **88** .... HayleyTurner 6 92
(Simon Dow) *cl up: rdn along 2f out: ev ch whn drvn 1f out: no ex fnl 75yds* **9/1**

100- **5** *hd* **Directorship**[191] 7168 6-9-7 **90** .... GeorgeBaker 2 94+
(Patrick Chamings) *hld up: short of room after 2f: pushed along 2f out: rdn and kpt on one pce ins fnl f* **16/1**

005- **6** *3/4* **Loving Spirit**[191] 7166 4-9-7 **90** .... RobertHavlin 1 92+
(James Toller) *in rr: drvn along 3f out: hdwy and hmpd over 1f out: nt rcvr* **14/1**

13-0 **7** *nk* **Perfect Cracker**[37] 1128 4-9-5 **88** .... AdamKirby 4 89
(Clive Cox) *cl up: pushed along 3f out: drvn along and ev ch 1f out sn pressed ldrs tl wknd ins fnl f* **10/1**

040- **8** *1/2* **Tropical Beat**[284] 4467 4-9-2 **85** .... WilliamBuick 14 85+
(John Gosden) *t.k.h in rr: drvn and no imp 2f out* **11/1**

116- **9** *1/2* **Camberley Two**[199] 6989 4-9-2 **85** .... JamesDoyle 7 84
(Roger Charlton) *in rr: rdn and outpcd over 2f out: plugged on one pce fnl f* **12/1**

/U0- **10** *1 1/2* **Unex El Greco**[275] 4802 4-9-5 **88** .... SilvestreDeSousa 13 84+
(John Gosden) *v.s.a: in rr: rdn 2f out: hdwy on ins whn nt clr run ins fnl 2f: unable to rcvr and eased* **25/1**

2160 **11** *1/2* **Shifting Star (IRE)**[65] 785 7-9-1 **87** .... SeanLevey(3) 5 81
(John Bridger) *cl up: drvn along and pressed ldr 2f out: wknd fnl f* **50/1**

50-1 **12** *4 1/2* **Ashva (USA)**[39] 1087 4-9-3 **86** .... TomEaves 9 70
(Michael Dods) *in rr: dropped to last and rdn 2f out: sn no imp* **11/2**[2]

36-5 **13** *2 3/4* **Chapter And Verse (IRE)**[30] 1212 6-9-6 **89** .... TonyCulhane 3 67
(Mike Murphy) *midfield: hmpd after 2f rousted along to rcvr: hdwy 4f out: drvn and wknd over 2f out* **12/1**

1151 **14** *2 3/4* **Munsarim (IRE)**[25] 1341 5-9-3 **86** .... (b) PaulHanagan 8 57
(Richard Fahey) *led: qcknd clr 2f out: drvn and wknd over 1f out: sn btn* **20/1**

1m 38.06s (-1.74) **Going Correction** -0.15s/f (Stan) 14 Ran SP% 119.5
Speed ratings (Par 107): **102,101,101,100,100 99,99,99,98,97 96,92,89,86**
toteswingers: 1&2:£15.40, 2&3:£4.60, 1&3:£42.60 CSF £119.39 CT £623.73 TOTE £44.30: £8.60, £1.20, £1.80; EX 123.90 Trifecta £476.60 Part won. Pool £644.07 - 0.10 winning units..
Owner C L A Edginton **Bred** The Hill Stud **Trained** Lambourn, Berks
■ Stewards' Enquiry : Robert Havlin one-day ban: careless riding (May 21)

FOCUS
A good, competitive handicap, but a bunch finish and the form may not prove that solid. The winner made the most of a good position.

NOTEBOOK
Cruiser came into this 1-17 and was making his AW debut, but he represented last year's winning stable and some of his turf form last year gave him a good chance. He was under pressure in a handy position on the home bend, but stuck at it and, having hit the front over a furlong from home, managed to hold on all-out. Official explanation: trainer said, regarding apparent improvement in form, that the gelding was better suited by the faster surface. (op 40-1)
Terdaad(IRE) was returning from another lengthy layoff, but there was no doubt over his ability to produce the goods fresh. The problem for him here was that he took too long on picking up when asked and the line was always going to just beat him. His rider reported that the gelding ran too free. Official explanation: jockey said gelding ran too free
Indian Jack(IRE), 3-4 here coming into this, was making his debut for the yard after 191 days off, but he won first time out last year so fitness shouldn't have been an issue. However, a slow break and then seeing plenty of daylight on the wide outside certainly didn't help and under the circumstances he did well to finish so close after holding every chance. (tchd 13-2)
Forceful Appeal(USA), bidding for a four-timer off a 5lb higher mark after three wins at Lingfield, travelled well behind the leaders and had every chance. The different orientation didn't seem to be a problem and, as he only made his debut less than a year ago, it would be dangerous to assume he is held off this sort of mark. (tchd 10-1)
Directorship ◆, making his AW debut on his 23rd start after 191 days off, met trouble in the back straight and didn't seem to enjoy the clearest of runs in the home straight as well, so this was an even better performance than it looked. He is one to watch. Official explanation: jockey said gelding suffered interference in running (op 20-1)
Loving Spirit was held up right out the back early, but made steady late progress in the home straight without being by any means knocked about. He did run into the back of the weakening Chapter And Verse over a furlong out as he tried for a run up the rail, but passed the line full of running. Making his AW debut after 191 days off and gelded in the meantime, he finished ninth behind Frankel in last year's 2000 Guineas so is obviously thought a bit of and he can surely win a nice handicap at some point this year. (op 16-1)
Perfect Cracker was successful in his last two visits here in December, but was 13lb higher than for the last of those and having moved into a challenging position over 2f from out, didn't seem to get home. (op 9-1 tchd 11-1)
Tropical Beat, gelded since last seen ten months ago, pulled hard near the back of the field and held his head up when asked for an effort after turning in. He did finish well, but much too late. (op 14-1 tchd 10-1)

1925 FOLLOW US ON TWITTER @BLUESQ H'CAP 2m (P)
5:20 (5:22) (Class 5) (0-75,74) 4-Y-O+ **£2,264** (£673; £336; £168) **Stalls** Low

Form RPR

15/1 **1** **Fade To Grey (IRE)**[13] 1588 8-8-7 **57** .... (t) SilvestreDeSousa 9 70
(Shaun Lycett) *in rr: nudged along thrght and nt travel wl: drvn and reminders 5f out: hdwy to chse ldng pair 3f out: styd on wl to ld cl home: comf* **5/2**[1]

30-1 **2** *1* **Veloce (IRE)**[45] 1011 4-9-0 **67** .... FrannyNorton 5 79
(Ian Williams) *cl up: hdwy 3f out: pressed ldr 2f out: battled on wl over 1f out and ev ch: no ex cl home* **5/2**[1]

5243 **3** *3/4* **Jamarjo (IRE)**[27] 1286 5-9-2 **66** .... MickaelBarzalona 1 77
(Steve Gollings) *midfield: rushed up to ld 4f out: drvn along over 2f out: kpt finding for press tl hdd and lost 2 pls fnl 100yds* **6/1**[2]

300 **4** *16* **Maison Brillet (IRE)**[21] 1418 5-9-3 **67** .... (p) RobertHavlin 4 59
(Clive Drew) *midfield: rdn along 4f out: grad wknd fnl 3f* **25/1**

12-0 **5** *9* **Kadouchski (FR)**[49] 963 8-8-3 **60** .... HannahNunn(7) 10 41
(John Berry) *hld up wl in rr: plenty to do and had only one rival bhd 4f out: pushed along but nvr any hope of catching ldrs fnl 3f* **20/1**

/2-2 **6** *8* **Ambrose Princess (IRE)**[17] 1272 7-9-10 **74** .... (p) JamieGoldstein 7 45
(Michael Scudamore) *hld up: rdn and reminders 6f out: struggling fnl 4f* **11/1**

046- **7** *8* **Callisto Moon**[30] 5273 8-9-3 **67** .... (p) SebSanders 6 29
(Jo Hughes) *in tch: pressed ldr 7f out tl drvn and wknd 3f out* **14/1**

021- **8** *21* **Rose Of Sarratt (IRE)**[188] 7212 4-8-13 **66** .... PaulHanagan 8
(Rae Guest) *hld up: urged along 5f out: struggling fnl 3f* **13/2**[3]

3 **9** *29* **Gay Sloane (IRE)**[25] 1339 8-9-1 **65** .... (b) HayleyTurner 3
(John Coombe) *led: drvn and hdd 4f out: stopped qckly and sn btn* **20/1**

3m 25.2s (-4.90) **Going Correction** -0.15s/f (Stan)
WFA 4 from 5yo+ 3lb 9 Ran SP% 113.1
Speed ratings (Par 103): **106,105,105,97,92 88,84,74,59**
toteswingers: 1&2:£1.90, 2&3:£3.20, 1&3:£3.70 CSF £8.93 CT £31.72 TOTE £3.40: £1.70, £1.30, £1.70; EX 8.90 Trifecta £58.50 Pool £789.01 - 9.97 winning units..
Owner Worcester Racing Club **Bred** Mount Coote Partnership **Trained** Clapton-on-the-Hill, Gloucs

FOCUS
An ordinary staying handicap, but the pace seemed decent and they finished well spread out. A fairly positive view has been taken of the form.
Ambrose Princess(IRE) Official explanation: jockey said mare never travelled

1926 BET AND WATCH AT BLUESQUARE.COM FILLIES' H'CAP 6f (P)
5:50 (5:50) (Class 4) (0-85,84) 4-Y-O+ **£4,075** (£1,212; £606; £303) **Stalls** Low

Form RPR

1-13 **1** **Haamaat (IRE)**[40] 1066 4-9-5 **82** .... PaulHanagan 6 91+
(William Haggas) *t.k.h in rr: swtchd outside and rdn over 1f out: kpt on wl to ld fnl 100yds: won gng away* **10/11**[1]

310- **2** *3/4* **Camache Queen (IRE)**[185] 7262 4-9-2 **79** .... EddieAhern 5 85
(Denis Coakley) *hld up: pushed along and hdwy over 2f out: ev ch and drvn 1f out: wnt 2nd cl home* **8/1**

4-3 **3** *hd* **Jedward (IRE)**[18] 1476 5-9-2 **79** .... FrannyNorton 2 84
(Richard Fahey) *hmpd s: midfield: drvn along 2f out: led 1f out: hdd fnl 100yds: lost 2nd cl home* **5/1**[2]

25-1 **4** *2 1/4* **Ray Of Joy**[27] 1289 6-9-7 **84** .... TomQueally 4 85+
(J R Jenkins) *hld up: hdwy over 2f out: ev ch whn rdn and hmpd over 1f out: nt rcvr and plugged on fnl 100yds* **6/1**[3]

114- **5** *1/2* **Fair Value (IRE)**[228] 6272 4-9-7 **84** .... SebSanders 3 80
(Simon Dow) *chsd ldr tl led 3f out: drvn and hdd 1f out: wknd fnl f* **6/1**[3]

310- **6** *2 1/4* **Yurituni**[235] 6094 5-9-4 **81** .... (v) SilvestreDeSousa 1 70
(Eve Johnson Houghton) *awkward leaving stalls: led: pushed along and hdd 3f out: remained pressing ldrs tl wknd ins fnl f* **33/1**

1m 11.71s (-1.39) **Going Correction** -0.15s/f (Stan) 6 Ran SP% 111.7
Speed ratings (Par 102): **103,102,101,98,98 95**
toteswingers: 1&2:£2.50, 2&3:£5.30, 1&3:£2.50 CSF £8.93 TOTE £1.90: £1.20, £3.00; EX 8.60.
Owner Hamdan Al Maktoum **Bred** Hunscote House Farm Stud **Trained** Newmarket, Suffolk

FOCUS
Quite a rough race for this fillies' handicap despite only six runners. They went a fair pace with Fair Value and Yurituni duelling for the advantage for much of the way, but it didn't appear to help either with their chances. The second and third set the standard.
Ray Of Joy Official explanation: jockey said mare suffered interference in runing
T/Plt: £12.60 to a £1 stake. Pool £61,175.42. 3,530.70 winning tickets T/Qpdt: £3.30 to a £1 stake. Pool £3,494.96. 778.47 winning tickets CS

1253 WARWICK (L-H)
Monday, May 7

1927 Meeting Abandoned - waterlogged

1563 WINDSOR (R-H)
Monday, May 7

OFFICIAL GOING: Soft (5.6)
Str. dolled out 8yds from 6f to intersection and full width thereafter. Top bend dolled out 7yds adding 27yds to races of a mile and over.
Wind: Moderate across Weather: Overcast

1934 DAVISBAKERYCARIBBEAN.COM APPRENTICE TRAINING SERIES H'CAP PART OF EXCELLENCE INITIATIVE) 6f
2:30 (2:31) (Class 6) (0-65,64) 4-Y-O+ **£1,617** (£481; £240; £120) **Stalls** Low

Form RPR

0-64 **1** **Gracie's Games**[16] 1516 6-8-5 **53** .... (v) JacobButterfield(5) 8 65
(Richard Price) *chsd ldrs: led over 2f out: drvn and jnd ins fnl f: kpt on wl clsng stages* **11/2**[3]

4421 **2** *1/2* **Dancing Welcome**[10] 1638 6-9-2 **62** .... (b) IanBurns(3) 1 72
(Milton Bradley) *chsd ldrs: racd towards stands' side tl hung lft fr 2f out: drvn to press wnr ins fnl f: outpcd clsng stages* **11/4**[1]

3106 **3** 2 ¾ **Strictly Pink (IRE)**[18] 1481 4-9-7 **64**................................ NatashaEaton 2 66
(Alan Bailey) *chsd ldrs: wnt 2nd ins fnl 2f: no imp on wnr sn after: wknd ins fnl f* **6/1**

5-20 **4** 3 **Arachnophobia (IRE)**[74] 670 6-8-9 **59**...................(v) KirstenSmith(7) 9 51
(Martin Bosley) *pressed ldrs: slt ld over 3f out: hdd over 2f out: sn hung rt: wknd fnl f* **20/1**

-005 **5** 1 **Mucky Molly**[11] 1628 4-8-2 **50**................................ JenniferFerguson(5) 7 39
(Olivia Maylam) *chsd ldrs: chal over 3f out to 2f out: wknd fnl f* **20/1**

41-3 **6** 1 **Dixie Gwalia**[6] 1742 4-8-5 **55**................................ SiobhanMiller(7) 6 41
(David Simcock) *in rr: sme prog 1/2-way: nvr rchd ldrs: wknd fnl f* **15/2**

6300 **7** 3 **Mack's Sister**[26] 1305 5-8-11 **54**......................................(p) DannyBrock 5 30
(Dean Ivory) *s.i.s: rdn 1/2-way: outpcd most of way* **12/1**

2211 **8** 2 **Punching**[20] 1430 8-9-0 **57**.. JakePayne 4 27
(Conor Dore) *slt ld tl hdd over 3f out: wknd fr 2f out* **9/2**[2]

6-54 **9** nse **Griffin Point (IRE)**[90] 456 5-9-1 **61**......................... NicoleNordblad(3) 3 30
(William Muir) *outpcd most of way* **14/1**

050- **10** 4 **Pose (IRE)**[144] 7764 5-8-8 **58**......................................(t) DanielCremin(7) 10 15
(Roger Ingram) *in rr: hdwy over 3f out: chsng ldrs whn wnt lft to r alone towards far side sn after: wknd 2f out* **18/1**

1m 18.2s (5.20) **Going Correction** +0.80s/f (Soft) **10** Ran SP% **115.4**
Speed ratings (Par 101): **97,96,92,88,87 86,82,79,79,73**
toteswingers:1&2:£4.00, 2&3:£3.40, 1&3:£5.60 CSF £20.74 CT £93.89 TOTE £5.50: £1.90, £1.50, £2.30; EX 18.10.
Owner David Prosser & Keith Warrington **Bred** David Prosser & Keith Warrington **Trained** Ullingswick, H'fords

■ Stewards' Enquiry : Ian Burns 7-day ban: used whip in the forehand (dates tbn)
Jacob Butterfield 16-day ban: used whip excessively above permitted level (tbn)

FOCUS
The straight was dolled out eight yards from 6f to the intersection, and was at full width thereafter. The top bend was dolled seven yards from the normal inner configuration, adding 27 yards to race distances at 1m-plus. They were spread out across the track in the straight and the main action unfolded up the centre. The winner is rated back to her best. The first two riders both broke the whip rules for this series.

1935 DAVISBAKERYCARIBBEAN.COM H'CAP (DIV I) 6f
3:00 (3:01) (Class 4) (0-80,80) 4-Y-0+ **£4,204** (£1,251; £625; £312) **Stalls** Low

Form RPR

0006 **1** **Seek The Fair Land**[23] 1373 6-9-5 **78**.........................(b) JimmyFortune 4 90
(Jim Boyle) *trckd ldrs: grabbed far rail and led appr fnl 2f: pushed out fnl f: comf* **6/1**[3]

05-6 **2** 1 ¼ **Emiratesdotcom**[14] 1564 6-9-1 **74**...................................... RyanMoore 6 82
(Milton Bradley) *in tch: hdwy over 2f out: chsd wnr appr fnl f: kpt on u.p but readily hld* **4/1**[2]

0-00 **3** 1 ½ **Cocohatchee**[9] 1680 4-8-8 **67**...(p) TedDurcan 9 70
(Pat Phelan) *s.i.s: towards rr: hdwy on far rail over 2f out: sn drvn and hanging lft: styd on to take one pce 3rd ins fnl f* **15/2**

400- **4** ¾ **Cardinal**[158] 7596 7-8-9 **68**.. ShaneKelly 8 69
(Robert Cowell) *in rr: hdwy fr 2f out: chsd ldrs and styd on one pce ins fnl f* **6/1**[3]

0-45 **5** 3 ½ **Beat The Bell**[20] 1430 7-9-4 **77**.................................... FergusSweeney 3 67
(Jamie Osborne) *sn led: hdd appr fnl 2f: wknd appr fnl f* **11/1**

020- **6** 2 ¾ **Rash Judgement**[191] 7171 7-9-3 **76**.................................. IanMongan 10 57
(Stuart Kittow) *t.k.h: towards rr: rdn and no imp fnl 2f* **3/1**[1]

315- **7** ½ **Emkanaat**[230] 6239 4-9-7 **80**.. NeilCallan 1 59
(Roger Varian) *chsd ldrs: wknd ins fnl 2f* **6/1**[3]

2-15 **8** 17 **Aqua Ardens (GER)**[66] 765 4-9-2 **75**............................... PatCosgrave 5
(George Baker) *chsd ldr 3f: wknd fr 1/2-way: eased whn no ch fnl 2f* **20/1**

1m 16.93s (3.93) **Going Correction** +0.80s/f (Soft) **8** Ran SP% **112.7**
Speed ratings (Par 105): **105,103,101,100,95 92,91,68**
toteswingers:1&2:£4.40, 2&3:£6.10, 1&3:£5.10 CSF £29.29 CT £181.91 TOTE £7.10: £1.70, £1.90, £2.40; EX 28.00.
Owner Chris Watkins And David N Reynolds **Bred** Raimon Bloodstock **Trained** Epsom, Surrey

FOCUS
The time was 0.76 seconds quicker than the second division. They raced far side and the winner had the rail in the closing stages. It could be above average form for the grade, with the winner on a good mark compared with his AW form.

1936 DAVISBAKERYCARIBBEAN.COM H'CAP (DIV II) 6f
3:30 (3:30) (Class 4) (0-80,79) 4-Y-0+ **£4,204** (£1,251; £625; £312) **Stalls** Low

Form RPR

15-2 **1** **Highland Colori (IRE)**[14] 1564 4-9-3 **75**.......................... DavidProbert 7 84
(Andrew Balding) *chsd ldrs: drvn to chal appr fnl f tl def advantage fnl 120yds: kpt on wl u.p* **7/2**[1]

46-3 **2** hd **Midnight Rider (IRE)**[14] 1564 4-9-3 **75**............................ TedDurcan 10 83
(Chris Wall) *towards rr but in tch: hdwy on ins over 2f out: drvn to chal appr fnl f tl outpcd by wnr fnl 120yds* **11/2**

50-2 **3** 1 ¼ **Midnight Feast**[11] 1627 4-9-4 **76**... NeilCallan 3 80
(Eve Johnson Houghton) *chsd ldrs: led over 1f out: sn jnd: wknd into 3rd fnl 150yds* **5/1**[3]

6-00 **4** 1 ¼ **Kings 'n Dreams**[14] 1564 5-8-12 **70**................................(b) JimCrowley 6 70
(Dean Ivory) *s.i.s: t.k.h in rr: hdwy and rdn over 1f out: styd on clsng stages but nvr a threat* **16/1**

600- **5** nk **Picabo (IRE)**[213] 6665 4-9-2 **74**... DaneO'Neill 2 73
(Henry Candy) *in tch: hdwy to chse ldrs 2f out: one pce fnl f* **15/2**

100- **6** 1 **George Thisby**[196] 7057 6-8-9 **67**.................................. FergusSweeney 1 63
(Rod Millman) *sn pressing ldr: stl ev ch 2f out: wknd ins fnl f* **20/1**

4-30 **7** 1 ¾ **Perfect Pastime**[12] 1602 4-9-7 **79**................................(v[1]) PatCosgrave 4 69
(Jim Boyle) *in rr but in tch: hdwy 2f out: nvr gng pce to rch ldrs and one pce fr over 1f out* **9/1**

305- **8** 3 **Macdillon**[185] 7262 6-9-5 **77**... IanMongan 9 58
(Stuart Kittow) *in rr: hdwy on ins over 2f out: nvr gng pce to rch ldrs: wknd fnl f* **4/1**[2]

0315 **9** hd **Night Trade (IRE)**[86] 526 5-9-3 **78**.......................... CPGeoghegan(3) 8 58
(Ronald Harris) *rrd s: chsd ldrs: led on far rail over 2f out: hdd over 1f out: sn btn* **25/1**

000- **10** 11 **Bassett Road (IRE)**[179] 7348 4-8-10 **68**......................... JamieMackay 5 13
(Willie Musson) *sn slt ld: hdd over 2f out: wkng whn hmpd ins fnl 2f* **22/1**

1m 17.69s (4.69) **Going Correction** +0.80s/f (Soft) **10** Ran SP% **114.9**
Speed ratings (Par 105): **100,99,98,96,96 94,92,88,88,73**
toteswingers:1&2:£2.20, 2&3:£3.10, 1&3:£3.70 CSF £21.75 CT £96.96 TOTE £3.80: £1.90, £2.20, £2.20; EX 14.20.
Owner Evan M Sutherland **Bred** Rathbarry Stud **Trained** Kingsclere, Hants

FOCUS
A slower time than the first division, but the form looks fair with the first two close to their lates C&D form. Again, they raced far side.

Macdillon Official explanation: jockey said gelding ran too freely

1937 DAVISBAKERYCARIBBEAN.COM MEDIAN AUCTION MAIDEN STKS 1m 67y
4:05 (4:05) (Class 5) 3-4-Y-0 **£2,264** (£673; £336; £168) **Stalls** Low

Form RPR

32-0 **1** **Flaxen Flare (IRE)**[19] 1450 3-9-1 **80**................................ JimmyFortune 6 81+
(Andrew Balding) *sn led: jnd fr ins fnl 4f and drvn whn strly chal fr over 2f out: asserted over 1f out: styd on wl u.p fnl f* **2/1**[2]

54- **2** 1 **Al Wajba (USA)**[193] 7125 3-8-7 0........................... AdamBeschizza(3) 10 73+
(William Haggas) *in rr: pushed along and hdwy fr 2f out: edgd rt over 1f out: styd on to go 2nd fnl 120yds: fin wl but nt rch wnr* **16/1**

50- **3** 4 ½ **Acer Diamonds (IRE)**[317] 3401 3-9-1 0............................. JimCrowley 9 68
(Julia Feilden) *chsd wnr: chal fr ins fnl 4f and stl upsides u.p 2f out one pce over 1f out: wknd and lost 2nd fnl 120yds* **8/1**

0-5 **4** 1 ¾ **Bondi Mist (IRE)**[10] 1649 3-8-10 0.................................... LeeNewman 1 59
(Jonathan Portman) *chsd ldrs: rdn along and one pce fr over 3f out: kpt on again clsng stages* **66/1**

5 1 **Upper Grosvenor** 3-9-1 0.. NeilCallan 4 62+
(Roger Varian) *t.k.h and sn chsng ldrs: rdn over 2f out: green: hung lft and wknd appr fnl f* **15/8**[1]

6 3 **On Stage** 3-8-10 0.. FergusSweeney 5 50
(Stuart Kittow) *s.i.s: in rr: pushed along over 2f out: sme prog fnl f* **20/1**

0 **7** 1 ¾ **Fly On By**[16] 1506 3-9-1 0.. DaneO'Neill 2 51
(Henry Candy) *slowly away: in rr: rdn over 3f out and sme prog: nvr rchd ldrs: wknd fr 2f out* **40/1**

0 **8** 1 ½ **Class Win**[7] 1704 3-9-1 0... RyanMoore 8 47
(Sir Michael Stoute) *t.k.h: stdd in rr after 2f: rdn and no prog 4f out: no ch after* **9/2**[3]

0-0 **9** ½ **Ryedale Lass**[7] 1704 4-9-2 0... JacobMoore(7) 3 44
(Joseph Tuite) *chsd ldrs 5f* **200/1**

1m 50.7s (6.00) **Going Correction** +0.70s/f (Yiel)
WFA 3 from 4yo 13lb **9** Ran SP% **112.5**
Speed ratings (Par 103): **98,97,92,90,89 86,85,83,83**
toteswingers:1&2:£4.60, 2&3:£7.40, 1&3:£3.30 CSF £30.67 TOTE £2.90: £1.10, £2.70, £2.00; EX 25.10.
Owner Kennet Valley Thoroughbreds VIII **Bred** Denis And Mrs Teresa Bergin **Trained** Kingsclere, Hants

FOCUS
An ordinary maiden, run in a time 1.17 seconds slower than the later handicap. They raced far side in the straight. The winner did not need to match his 2yo best.

1938 SKYBET MOBILE FOR IPHONE & ANDROID H'CAP 1m 67y
4:35 (4:35) (Class 3) (0-90,84) 3-Y-0 **£6,792** (£2,021; £1,010; £505) **Stalls** Low

Form RPR

221- **1** **Takeitfromalady (IRE)**[185] 7259 3-8-12 **75**...................(b) JimCrowley 1 86
(Ralph Beckett) *trckd ldrs: wnt 2nd appr fnl f: drvn to chal fnl 120yds: pushed out and a jst doing enough last strides* **15/2**

221- **2** shd **Fire Ship**[210] 6757 3-9-0 **77**.. ShaneKelly 2 88
(William Knight) *wnt lft s: led: hrd pressed fr over 3f out tl asserted again ins fnl 2f: sn u.p: jnd fnl 120yds: hdd last strides* **4/1**[2]

-321 **3** 2 **Valley Of Destiny**[12] 1606 3-9-2 **79**........................... RichardHughes 3 85
(Richard Hannon) *bmpd s: sn chsng ldr: dropped to cl 3rd over 3f out: wnt 2nd again and hrd drvn ins fnl 2f: wknd into 3rd fnl f* **11/2**

42-2 **4** nk **Debating Society (IRE)**[28] 1261 3-8-13 **76**...................... RyanMoore 5 81
(Sir Michael Stoute) *in rr but in tch: drvn over 2f out: styd on fnl f but no imp on ldrs* **5/1**[3]

1 **5** 4 **Falcon In Flight**[28] 1261 3-9-7 **84**.................................. JimmyFortune 6 80
(Jeremy Noseda) *chsd ldrs: rdn to chal fr over 3f out tl wknd fr 2f out* **11/8**[1]

05-1 **6** ½ **Moment In Time (IRE)**[33] 1180 3-8-10 **73**.......................... MartinLane 4 68
(David Simcock) *rdn 3f out: a towards rr* **20/1**

1m 49.53s (4.83) **Going Correction** +0.70s/f (Yiel) **6** Ran SP% **110.7**
Speed ratings (Par 103): **103,102,100,100,96 96**
toteswingers:1&2:£3.60, 2&3:£3.10, 1&3:£3.90 CSF £35.77 TOTE £9.30: £3.20, £2.30; EX 37.80.
Owner R Roberts **Bred** Sean Collins **Trained** Kimpton, Hants

FOCUS
A decent 3yo handicap run in a time 1.17 seconds quicker than the earlier maiden, and once again the runners raced towards the far rail. A step up from the winner and the form overall seems sound enough.

NOTEBOOK
Takeitfromalady(IRE) won a heavy-ground nursery when last seen in November (when fitted with blinkers for the first time), so clearly didn't mind these conditions and defied a 5lb higher mark. He's already shown form on a faster surface and there might be more to come. (op 8-1)
Fire Ship, a C&D winner when last seen in October, is versatile ground-wise and ran well off 6lb higher. He was making his debut for a new yard. (op 9-2)
Valley Of Destiny won a maiden on heavy ground last time, but he struggled on this switch to handicap company. (op 4-1)
Debating Society(IRE) didn't improve as expected on this switch to handicap company. He probably wants better ground, and maybe a longer trip. (op 6-1)
Falcon In Flight really impressed when making a winning debut under similar conditions at Yarmouth, thrashing Debating Society, and she now holds Group-race entries, but she was bitterly disappointing this time. (op 6-4 tchd 11-10)

1939 DAVIS WEST INDIAN BAKERY H'CAP 1m 2f 7y
5:05 (5:05) (Class 4) (0-85,83) 4-Y-0+ **£4,851** (£1,443; £721; £360) **Stalls** Centre

Form RPR

260- **1** **Aldwick Bay (IRE)**[234] 6130 4-9-3 **79**......................... RichardHughes 10 90
(Richard Hannon) *hld up in rr: hdwy 4f out: drvn to chse ldr whn n.m.r on far rail over 1f out: led sn after: drvn clr fnl 150yds* **13/2**

4310 **2** 1 ¼ **Copper Canyon**[29] 1239 4-9-5 **81**................................. DavidProbert 11 88
(J S Moore) *s.i.s: in rr: rdn 3f out: hdwy over 2f out: chsd wnr ins fnl f but no imp* **16/1**

300- **3** 3 ¾ **Chain Of Events**[217] 6592 5-8-10 **72**................................. JimCrowley 8 71
(Sarah Humphrey) *chsd ldrs: rdn to ld over 2f out: edgd lft over 1f out: hdd sn after: no imp on wnr: lost 2nd ins fnl f* **9/1**

5233 **4** 4 ½ **Big Creek (IRE)**[33] 1186 5-9-4 **80**.................................... RyanMoore 9 70
(Jeremy Noseda) *chsd ldrs: rdn and outpcd over 3f out: mod prog fr over 1f out* **11/4**[1]

1325 **5** 1 ½ **Uphold**[52] 928 5-9-7 **83**..(vt) NeilCallan 4 70
(Gay Kelleway) *led: styd alone stands' side over 3f out and upsides w main gp tl wknd ins fnl 2f* **11/1**

504- **6** shd **Ken's Girl**[187] 7236 8-8-12 **74**.. FergusSweeney 6 61
(Stuart Kittow) *chsd ldr: led main gp over 3f out: hdd over 2f out: sn btn* **7/2**[2]

-000 7 nk **Epsom Salts**[19] 1446 7-8-11 **73** ShaneKelly 3 59
(Pat Phelan) *slowly away: in rr: rdn over 3f out: mod prog fnl f* **20/1**
302- 8 ½ **Looking On**[209] 6773 4-8-13 **75** DaneO'Neill 2 60
(Henry Candy) *chsd ldrs: rdn 3f out: wknd 2f out* **5/1**[3]
400/ 9 3 ½ **Minneapolis**[20] 3102 7-9-4 **80** IanMongan 5 58
(Alison Batchelor) *chsd ldrs to 3f out: wknd over 2f out* **25/1**
200- 10 7 **Jacobs Son**[239] 5966 4-8-8 **77** DanielCremin(7) 1 41
(Robert Mills) *bhd most of way* **33/1**

2m 15.07s (6.37) **Going Correction** +0.70s/f (Yiel) **10** Ran SP% **114.7**
Speed ratings (Par 105): **102,101,98,94,93 93,92,92,89,84**
toteswingers:1&2:£4.00, 2&3:£16.30, 1&3:£16.20 CSF £98.67 CT £934.15 TOTE £8.30: £2.60, £4.10, £3.40; EX 139.80.
Owner Mrs Ann Williams **Bred** Ailesbury Bloodstock **Trained** East Everleigh, Wilts

FOCUS
A fair handicap, but not rated as positively as it may have been. The winner may build on this.

1940 GO ONLINE @ DAVISBAKERYCARIBBEAN.COM H'CAP 1m 3f 135y
5:35 (5:36) (Class 4) (0-85,85) 4-Y-0+ £4,851 (£1,443; £721; £360) Stalls Centre

Form RPR
306- 1 **Quiz Mistress**[145] 7753 4-8-12 **76** RyanMoore 5 92
(Hughie Morrison) *s.i.s: in rr: hdwy 3f out: drvn and styd on to chse ldr over 1f out: styd on to ld fnl 120yds: won gng away* **10/1**
54-0 2 2 **Roberto Pegasus (USA)**[17] 1505 6-8-11 **75** ow1 DaneO'Neill 9 88
(Pat Phelan) *trckd ldr: chal over 3f out: sn led: rdn 2f out: styd on fnl f: hdd and outpcd fnl 120yds* **11/2**[3]
0-1 3 3 **Kuda Huraa (IRE)**[18] 1484 4-9-1 **79** JamieSpencer 10 87
(Roger Varian) *led: jnd over 3f out: sn hdd: styd pressing ldr to 2f out: lost 2nd over 1f out: sn btn* **4/1**[2]
000- 4 4 ½ **Kathleen Frances**[192] 7136 5-8-13 **77** TedDurcan 3 77
(Mark H Tompkins) *in rr: pushed along and hdwy over 3f out: chsd ldrs over 2f out: no imp and wknd fnl f* **8/1**
22-0 5 2 **Persian Herald**[28] 960 4-8-8 **72** RichardMullen 7 69
(William Muir) *in rr: rdn and sme hdwy over 3f out: styd on same pce* **33/1**
34-4 6 1 **Achalas (IRE)**[14] 1566 4-8-12 **76** NeilCallan 8 71
(Heather Main) *in tch: hdwy to chse ldrs 5f out: rdn fr 4f out: wknd fr 2f out* **16/1**
250- 7 14 **Devoted (IRE)**[210] 6749 4-8-11 **75** JimCrowley 1 46
(Ralph Beckett) *in tch: drvn to chal 4f out: hung lft and wknd over 2f out* **15/2**
231- 8 9 **Lily In Pink**[245] 5782 4-8-12 **76** LeeNewman 11 32
(Jonathan Portman) *chsd ldrs: rdn over 3f out: wknd over 2f out* **16/1**
40-1 9 8 **Kleitomachos (IRE)**[14] 1566 4-8-13 **77** IanMongan 4 19
(Stuart Kittow) *in rr: sme hdwy 5f out: chsd ldrs 4f out: wknd 3f out* **9/4**[1]
0/ 10 18 **Balerina (FR)**[68] 952 5-9-7 **85** FergusSweeney 6
(Alan King) *chsd ldrs: rdn and btn 4f out: eased whn no ch* **25/1**

2m 36.29s (6.79) **Going Correction** +0.70s/f (Yiel) **10** Ran SP% **116.7**
Speed ratings (Par 105): **105,103,101,98,97 96,87,81,76,64**
toteswingers:1&2:£12.00, 2&3:£5.50, 1&3:£11.10 CSF £64.19 CT £260.25 TOTE £11.90: £3.40, £2.30, £2.20; EX 88.60.
Owner The Fairy Story Partnership **Bred** Deepwood Farm Stud **Trained** East Ilsley, Berks

FOCUS
This looked a reasonable race, and yet again events unfolded on the far side in the straight. The form seems sound enough.
Kleitomachos(IRE) Official explanation: trainer had no explanation for the form shown

1941 SKYBET.COM H'CAP 5f 10y
6:05 (6:09) (Class 5) (0-70,69) 3-Y-0 £2,264 (£673; £336; £168) Stalls Low

Form RPR
660- 1 **Tioman Pearl**[184] 7292 3-9-7 **69** NeilCallan 5 87+
(Roger Varian) *trckd ldrs: led over 2f out: c clr fnl f: heavily eased clsng stages* **6/4**[1]
510- 2 5 **Courtland Avenue (IRE)**[219] 6524 3-9-7 **69** LeeNewman 6 63
(Jonathan Portman) *in tch: rdn and outpcd 1/2-way: styd on wl fnl f to take 2nd fnl 75yds: nvr any ch w heavily eased wnr* **8/1**
-423 3 2 ½ **Chicarito**[17] 1492 3-8-11 **59** (v[1]) MartinLane 2 44
(John Gallagher) *led tl hdd over 2f out: styd on same pce for wl-hld 3rd fnl f* **11/4**[2]
20-1 4 ½ **Pucon**[108] 219 3-9-5 **67** DaneO'Neill 4 50
(Roger Teal) *chsd ldr: chal over 2f out: chsd wnr sn after but no ch: lost 2 pls fnl 75yds* **6/1**
10-0 5 1 **Subtle Embrace (IRE)**[26] 1313 3-9-2 **64** JimCrowley 7 44
(Harry Dunlop) *in rr and sn outpcd: styd on wl clsng stages but nvr any ch* **11/1**
101 6 nk **Russian Bullet**[19] 1444 3-9-3 **65** FergusSweeney 1 44
(Jamie Osborne) *stdd s: in rr: hdwy 2f out: nvr quite rchd ldrs and wknd fnl f* **9/2**[3]

1m 3.98s (3.68) **Going Correction** +0.80s/f (Soft) **6** Ran SP% **118.6**
Speed ratings (Par 99): **102,94,90,89,87 87**
toteswingers:1&2:£3.00, 2&3:£5.90, 1&3:£2.00 CSF £15.48 TOTE £2.40: £1.60, £4.60; EX 17.00.
Owner H R H Sultan Ahmad Shah **Bred** Mrs Mary Taylor And James F Taylor **Trained** Newmarket, Suffolk
■ Copp The Lott (8/1) was withdrawn after breaking out of the stalls. Deduct 10p in the £ under R4. New market formed.

FOCUS
They raced far side. Probably just an ordinary handicap, but an impressive performance from Tioman Pearl. He showed big improvement, butr it;s hard to knowe exactly what he achieved.
Tioman Pearl Official explanation: trainer's rep said, regarding apparent improvement in form, that the colt had strengthened up over the winter and was suited by the drop back to 5f.
T/Plt: £260.00 to a £1 stake. Pool:£87,293.56 - 245.06 winning units. T/Qpdt: £34.00 to a £1 stake. Pool:£4,889.74 - 106.32 winning units. ST

1942 - (Foreign Racing) - See Raceform Interactive

1545 CURRAGH (R-H)
Monday, May 7

OFFICIAL GOING: Straight course - soft changing to soft to heavy after race 2 (2.50); round course - soft
Races on far side of straight, approximately 40m off stands' side rail.

1943a DYLAN THOMAS EUROPEAN BREEDERS FUND TETRARCH STKS (LISTED RACE) 7f
2:50 (2:50) 3-Y-0 £27,083 (£7,916; £3,750; £1,250)

RPR
1 **Takar (IRE)**[183] 7317 3-9-3 (t) JohnnyMurtagh 1 109+
(John M Oxx, Ire) *trckd ldrs in 4th: poised to chal fr 2f out: swtchd rt early fnl f and qcknd to ld fnl 100yds: comf* **5/4**[1]
2 1 ¼ **Coolnagree (IRE)**[15] 1548 3-9-0 95 WayneLordan 4 101
(W McCreery, Ire) *trckd ldrs in 3rd racing keenly: poised to chal fr 2f out: rdn and swtchd lft ins fnl f: kpt on u.p on stands' side rail* **7/2**[3]
3 nk **Triumphant (IRE)**[304] 3835 3-9-3 92 (b[1]) JPO'Brien 2 103
(A P O'Brien, Ire) *trckd ldr in 2nd: rdn to chal over 1f out: led briefly ins fnl f: hdd and no imp on wnr fnl 100yds* **9/4**[2]
4 1 ¾ **Janey Muddles (IRE)**[5] 1760 3-9-0 97 KevinManning 3 95
(J S Bolger, Ire) *settled in rr: hdwy on outer to go 3rd over 2f out: rdn to chal over 1f out: hdd and no ex ins fnl f* **8/1**
5 3 ¼ **Quote Of The Day (IRE)**[183] 7320 3-9-3 93 (t) ShaneFoley 5 90
(Edward Lynam, Ire) *led: strly pressed and jnd over 1f out: hdd u.p fnl f and no ex* **16/1**

1m 34.77s (3.97) **Going Correction** +0.55s/f (Yiel) **5** Ran SP% **114.4**
Speed ratings: **99,97,97,95,91**
CSF £6.36 TOTE £1.50: £1.10, £1.50; DF 4.80.
Owner H H Aga Khan **Bred** His Highness The Aga Khan's Studs S C **Trained** Currabeg, Co Kildare
■ Stewards' Enquiry : J P O'Brien severe caution: excessive use of whip

FOCUS
A good performance by the winner but the time was ordinary.

NOTEBOOK
Takar(IRE) ◆ looked a colt of some potential when he won his maiden by a wide margin at Leopardstown last term and he underlined that impression again. Held up at the tail of the quintet, his rider oozed confidence as he bided his time but once he switched the Oratorio colt right and asked him to quicken the response was certainly eye-catching. He'll step up to 1m in the Irish 2,000 Guineas next and, given that he was held up before this, improvement should be forthcoming. He looks a nice prospect for the Oxx team. (op 1/1 tchd 6/4)
Coolnagree(IRE), narrowly defeated in Listed company over this C&D, had won twice in similar conditions and she ran well again. In contrast to the winner, she had the benefit of a couple previous runs this season but had no answer when the favourite seized the initiative inside the final furlong. (op 4/1)
Triumphant(IRE) had a similar profile to Takar having also won on his second start as a juvenile. Blinkered for the first time and having his first outing since July, he tracked the long-time leader and led briefly as the race unfolded. The lack of a recent run probably told in the end and he should be sharper with this seasonal comeback outing behind him. (op 4/1 tchd 2/1)
Janey Muddles(IRE) already had three runs behind her this season. She was pushed along to close passing the 2f pole but was soon struggling to maintain her momentum entering the final furlong in this testing ground. (op 6/1)
Quote Of The Day(IRE) had made the running when he disappointed in the Eyrefield Stakes last back-end. The runaway Navan maiden winner over 1m previously brought them along again until he gave way entering the final furlong. (op 12/1)

1944a CANFORD CLIFFS EUROPEAN BREEDERS FUND ATHASI STKS (GROUP 3) (F&M) 7f
3:20 (3:20) 3-Y-0+ £39,270 (£11,479; £5,437; £1,812)

RPR
1 **Gossamer Seed (IRE)**[185] 7277 4-9-9 93 (t) ShaneFoley 5 108+
(John Joseph Murphy, Ire) *trckd ldrs: 3rd 1/2-way: hdwy to ld under 2f out: sn drvn clr and styd on wl fnl f* **9/1**
2 4 ¾ **Bulbul (IRE)**[22] 1403 3-8-11 98 DeclanMcDonogh 4 91
(Kevin Prendergast, Ire) *rrd and s.i.s: sn in tch: 4th 2f out: rdn in 3rd over 1f out and sn no ch w wnr: kpt on same pce* **5/4**[1]
3 2 ¼ **Ishvana (IRE)**[5] 1760 3-8-11 96 SeamieHeffernan 2 87
(A P O'Brien, Ire) *prom and trckd ldr in 2nd: rdn to ld briefly over 2f out: no ch w wnr fr over 1f out and dropped to 3rd ins fnl f* **11/8**[2]
4 12 **An Ghalanta (IRE)**[30] 1226 3-8-11 98 (t) KevinManning 3 53
(J S Bolger, Ire) *led: strly pressed and hdd over 2f out: no ex in 4th over 1f out: wknd* **6/1**[3]
5 11 **My Fere Lady (USA)**[8] 1688 3-8-11 RoryCleary 1 23
(J S Bolger, Ire) *chsd ldrs: 4th 1/2-way and sn rdn: no ex over 2f out and wknd* **50/1**

1m 34.13s (3.33) **Going Correction** +0.55s/f (Yiel)
WFA 3 from 4yo 12lb **5** Ran SP% **112.8**
Speed ratings: **103,97,95,81,68**
CSF £21.54 TOTE £15.40: £5.40, £1.70; DF 34.30.
Owner O Finetto **Bred** P Byrne **Trained** Upton, Co. Cork

FOCUS
The winning time was slower than the maiden.

NOTEBOOK
Gossamer Seed(IRE), the sole 4yo in the small field, obliged. The manner of her win was certainly impressive, too, after she travelled well before kicking for home under 2f out. Connections expressed their concern afterwards about conceding weight all round under the race conditions, but once she went on the outcome was never in doubt and she clearly relished this testing surface. (op 7/1)
Bulbul(IRE) was well backed to build on her seasonal debut in the 1,000 Guineas Trial won by Saturday's Newmarket heroine Homecoming Queen. She was held up before been asked to close after halfway but she struggled to pick up enough to make the winner work and this was a disappointing effort from the Etihad Airways Irish 1,000 Guineas entry. (op 6/4 tchd 1/1)
Ishvana(IRE) tracked the leader before moving to the front just over 2f out but the 7f Dundalk AW winner was soon going nowhere on this ground and faded out of contention. (op 6/4 tchd 2/1)
An Ghalanta(IRE) finished out of the money just once in ten starts last season, winning twice over the minimum trip in the process. Her comeback run at Cork was no refection of her consistency last season over a furlong shorter and tackling this trip for the first time she dropped away after making the early running. (op 9/2)

My Fere Lady(USA), who like the runner-up is also among the entries for the Irish 1,000 Guineas, never got in a blow when the tempo increased after halfway. (op 33/1)

1946a HIGH CHAPARRAL EUROPEAN BREEDERS FUND MOORESBRIDGE STKS (GROUP 3) 1m 2f
4:25 (4:27) 4-Y-0+ **£39,270** (£11,479; £5,437; £1,812)

			RPR
1		**Windsor Palace (IRE)**[15] 1549 7-9-3 99.....................(b) CO'Donoghue 3 (A P O'Brien, Ire) *trckd ldr in 2nd and clr of remainder fr bef 1/2-way: chal in st and led under 2f out: kpt on u.p* **66/1**	107?
2	1	**St Nicholas Abbey (IRE)**[37] 1149 5-9-8 124........................ JPO'Brien 1 (A P O'Brien, Ire) *settled in 3rd: 10 l off pce 1/2-way: dropped to mod 4th early st: rdn over 1f out and kpt on wl ins fnl f: nt rch wnr* **2/5**[1]	110+
3	1 ½	**Sharestan (IRE)**[22] 1402 4-9-3 108.............................. JohnnyMurtagh 7 (John M Oxx, Ire) *settled in 4th: abt 10 l off pce 1/2-way: smo hdwy to go 3rd early st: sn rdn and kpt on u.p fnl f* **5/2**[2]	102+
4	2 ¼	**Robin Hood (IRE)**[8] 1694 4-9-3 98.........................(b) SeamieHeffernan 4 (A P O'Brien, Ire) *led: strly pressed and hdd 1 1/2f out: no ex ins fnl f and dropped to 4th* **33/1**	98
5	3 ½	**Parkers Mill (IRE)**[43] 1043 4-9-3 97................................ WayneLordan 6 (T Stack, Ire) *chsd clr ldrs: mod 6th 1/2-way: nvr a factor: kpt on one pce in 5th fr 2f out* **25/1**[3]	91+
6	7 ½	**Bob Le Beau (IRE)**[220] 6514 5-9-3 107................................ FranBerry 5 (Mrs John Harrington, Ire) *chsd clr ldrs: mod 5th 1/2-way: nvr a factor: no ex in 6th under 2f out* **25/1**[3]	76+
7	15	**Elusive Ridge (IRE)**[22] 1402 6-9-3 97................................ PatSmullen 2 (H Rogers, Ire) *a in rr: nvr a factor* **66/1**	46+

2m 19.41s (5.11) **Going Correction** +0.725s/f (Yiel) 7 Ran SP% **113.6**
Speed ratings: **108,107,106,104,101 95,83**
CSF £96.42 TOTE £38.50: £10.40, £1.10; DF 90.80.
Owner Derrick Smith **Bred** King Bloodstock **Trained** Ballydoyle, Co Tipperary

FOCUS
A shock result and dubious form, as the winner was allowed a lengthy lead.

NOTEBOOK
Windsor Palace(IRE) finished four lengths behind new addition to Ballydoyle, Excelebration, on his second start back this term and clearly stepped up again here. His stablemate Robin Hood set a good clip and when the winner took over a furlong and a half down he stuck to his task well on this favourable surface. (op 50/1)
St Nicholas Abbey(IRE) started a warm favourite. While this trip was probably on the short side for the dual Group 1 winner, the prevailing conditions should have brought his stamina in to play. Left with plenty to do when they straightened for home, he stayed on in the closing stages with his trainer at pains to say afterwards he wasn't going to have a hard race in this ground. The form of his Dubai Sheema Classic runner-up effort was paid a handsome compliment when Cirrus Des Aigles followed up in impressive fashion in the Prix Ganay and on paper this should have been a straightforward task returning from a break since his trip to the Emirates. Aidan O'Brien was asked to explain the situation to the stewards afterwards in a running and riding enquiry. He told them he was training the dual Group 1 winner with the Coronation Cup in mind and this ground was against him. He was beaten in the Alleged Stakes last year in similar ground before winning the Ormonde at Chester. Official explanation: jockey said, regarding running and riding, that instructions were to get his mount to switch off, get him settled and make the best of his way home; he said his mount hated the ground and he was never happy with the way the horse travelled; he said he tried to get his mount to creep into the race and he held onto him as long as possible to make sure he got home on the ground; he felt that if the horse had come off the bridle earlier in the straight he would not have finished out his race as well as he did; the trainer confirmed the instructions and outlined how his charge had been to Dubai earlier in the year followed by a little break afterwards; he said that he trained the horse since then with a view to running today on route to the Coronation Cup; he explained how his charge had been beaten in this corresponding race last year on soft ground, and that it had shown a preference for better ground in the past; he stated that if his rider went after the pacemakers earlier in the race, he would have been out on his head and it would not have lasted home. (op 2/5 tchd 4/9)
Sharestan(IRE), a shade unlucky not to get the better of Famous Name over 2f shorter at Leopardstown, was stepping back up in trip and was expected to run well. The Irish Lincoln winner has improved considerably this term and seems versatile in terms of ground but, like the runner-up, never looked like getting there, with his rider admitting afterwards he "probably didn't get home".
Robin Hood(IRE), one of three Ballydoyle runners, set a decent clip up front before the winner went on, and this was a respectable effort from the dual winner, who was fit from three previous outings this term. (op 25/1)
Bob Le Beau(IRE) chased home So You Think in this race last year but the lack of a run since last September was clearly evident on this unfavourable surface. (op 22/1 tchd 20/1)

1947 - 1948a (Foreign Racing) - See Raceform Interactive

1594 CATTERICK (L-H)
Tuesday, May 8

OFFICIAL GOING: Good to soft (7.2)
Wind: moderate 1/2 against Weather: mainly fine

1949 FOLLOW US ON TWITTER @CATTERICKRACES MAIDEN AUCTION STKS 5f
6:10 (6:10) (Class 6) 2-Y-O **£2,045** (£603; £302) **Stalls** Low

Form				RPR
0	1		**Dream Vale (IRE)**[20] 1435 2-8-4 0................................ DuranFentiman 5 (Tim Easterby) *chsd ldrs: hmpd after 1f: led over 1f out: drvn clr* **25/1**	73
2	2	7	**Throwing Roses**[10] 1671 2-8-4 0................................ JamesSullivan 1 (Ollie Pears) *led: drvn over 2f out: hdd over 1f out: edgd rt: kpt on same pce* **1/1**[1]	48
	3	1 ¾	**Pixilated** 2-8-8 0................................ DannyBrock(7) 7 (Gay Kelleway) *swvd rt s: sn chsng ldrs: kpt on same pce fnl f* **11/2**[3]	53
	4	1 ¾	**Lucy Bee** 2-8-6 0................................ AdrianNicholls 6 (Keith Dalgleish) *sn drvn along: rn green: edgd rt over 2f out: styd on ins fnl f* **5/1**[2]	37+
0	5	3 ¼	**Sound Affects**[19] 1474 2-8-6 0................................ SilvestreDeSousa 4 (Alan Brown) *w ldr: wknd ins fnl f* **33/1**	26
54	6	1 ¼	**Until It Sleeps**[12] 1629 2-8-4 0................................ AndrewMullen 3 (Alan McCabe) *s.i.s: edgd rt and bmpd after 1f: reminders over 2f out: wknd over 1f out* **13/2**	19
	7	22	**Nors The Panic** 2-8-12 0................................ DeclanCannon(3) 2 (Richard Guest) *in tch: drvn over 2f out: lost pl over 1f out: sn bhd: t.o* **12/1**	

1m 3.56s (3.76) **Going Correction** +0.525s/f (Yiel) 7 Ran SP% **109.9**
Speed ratings (Par 91): **90,78,76,73,68 66,30**
toteswingers:1&2:£5.90, 2&3:£1.80, 1&3:£15.20 CSF £47.21 TOTE £39.80: £10.40, £1.50; EX 65.50.
Owner Habton Farms **Bred** Jaykayeen Breeding **Trained** Great Habton, N Yorks

FOCUS
This looked a weak juvenile maiden.

NOTEBOOK
Dream Vale(IRE) left behind a poor debut performance and was much the best. She was getting weight from a few of her rivals, and she's set to face tougher company in future, but she shaped like a filly of fair ability. (op 22-1)
Throwing Roses was beaten just a short-head on her debut at Ripon, but the ground wasn't quite as testing here, and that failed to suit a filly who's out of a 1m4f winner. (tchd 5-6 and 11-10)
Pixilated, a £10,000 April foal, is a brother to a dual 5f-winning juvenile (on Polytrack) and he travelled like a horse with a reasonable amount of ability. There should be better to come. (op 7-1 tchd 5-1)
Lucy Bee, a February foal half-sister to a few winners, struggled throughout. She briefly looked a threat early in the straight, but was basically never going the required pace. (op 11-2 tchd 6-1)

1950 RACING AGAIN ON FRIDAY 25TH MAY CLAIMING STKS 1m 3f 214y
6:40 (6:40) (Class 6) 4-Y-0+ **£1,704** (£503; £251) **Stalls** Low

Form				RPR
0110	1		**Flying Applause**[6] 1755 7-9-0 80................................(bt) LeeTopliss(3) 7 (Roy Bowring) *led rdrless to s: s.i.s: t.k.h: hdwy to trck ldrs after 2f: wnt cl 2nd 3f out: led over 1f out: bmpd nr line: all out* **11/4**[2]	74
555-	2	nse	**Eijaaz (IRE)**[189] 7215 11-8-7 59................................(p) SilvestreDeSousa 2 (Geoffrey Harker) *in rr and sn pushed along: hdwy 7f out: drvn to chse ldrs over 3f out: poised to chal over 1f out: upsides ins fnl f: hung lft: jst hld* **7/2**[3]	64
104-	3	4	**Dontpaytheferryman (USA)**[31] 7241 7-9-4 75............ PaulPickard(3) 8 (Brian Ellison) *chsd ldrs: drvn over 6f out: kpt on one pce to take 3rd last 75yds* **9/4**[1]	72
600-	4	2 ¼	**Dimashq**[226] 6379 10-8-2 45................................ DuranFentiman 4 (Paul Midgley) *led 1f: trckd ldrs: led 3f out: hdd over 1f out: wknd fnl 75yds* **33/1**	49
6	5	9	**Lucky For Some**[20] 1436 5-7-13 0................................ JulieBurke(3) 6 (Marjorie Fife) *chsd ldrs: drvn over 6f out: outpcd and lost pl 5f out: no threat after* **25/1**	35
30-0	6	49	**Labroc (IRE)**[24] 1384 4-8-9 52................................ RobertWinston 1 (Alan Swinbank) *in rr: bhd and drvn after 4f: hung bdly lft: t.o 5f out* **12/1**	
6664	7	8	**Hidden Glory**[15] 1562 5-8-13 69................................(b) PaulMulrennan 5 (James Given) *led after 1f: hdd 3f out: sn lost pl: bhd whn eased 1f out: t.o* **9/2**	

2m 46.64s (7.74) **Going Correction** +0.45s/f (Yiel) 7 Ran SP% **112.3**
Speed ratings (Par 101): **92,91,89,87,81 49,43**
CSF £12.34 TOTE £6.00: £3.50, £3.20; EX 13.90 Trifecta £26.70 Pool: £613.43 - 16.98 winning units..
Owner K Nicholls **Bred** G H Beeby And Viscount Marchwood **Trained** Edwinstowe, Notts

FOCUS
The pace looked too strong, thanks to Hidden Glory (awkward around the final bend), and this set up for a couple of horses who were off the speed through the early stages. Modest claiming form and the winner did not need to match his recent 1m wins.
Labroc(IRE) Official explanation: jockey said gelding hung left throughout
Hidden Glory Official explanation: trainer's rep said gelding was unsuited by making the running

1951 YORKSHIRE-OUTDOORS.CO.UK H'CAP 7f
7:10 (7:12) (Class 4) (0-80,80) 4-Y-0+ **£4,075** (£1,212; £606; £303) **Stalls** Centre

Form				RPR
011-	1		**Green Howard**[189] 7213 4-9-6 79................................ DanielTudhope 10 (Robin Bastiman) *trckd ldrs: smooth hdwy over 2f out: r.o to ld last 100yds* **8/1**	92+
0052	2	½	**Levitate**[10] 1650 4-9-6 79................................(v) IPoullis 7 (Alan McCabe) *chsd ldrs: wnt cl 2nd over 2f out: no ex in clsng stages* **14/1**	88
-010	3	¾	**Solar Spirit (IRE)**[10] 1670 7-9-7 80................................ RobertWinston 3 (Tracy Waggott) *t.k.h: trckd ldrs: stdd into rr after 2f: hdwy over 2f out: chsng ldrs whn nt clr run over 1f out: swtchd rt ins fnl f: r.o* **10/1**	87
210-	4	2 ¼	**Mingun Bell (USA)**[192] 7171 5-9-5 78................................ LiamKeniry 4 (Ed de Giles) *hld up: hdwy over 2f out: kpt on ins fnl f* **16/1**	79
4502	5	nk	**Klynch**[3] 1863 6-9-5 78................................(b) JamesSullivan 6 (Ruth Carr) *trckd ldrs: led over 2f out: hdd last 100yds: fdd* **4/1**[2]	78
0-1	6	2 ¾	**President Lincoln (USA)**[30] 1238 4-9-6 79............. GrahamGibbons 1 (Declan Carroll) *s.i.s: in rr: kpt on fnl 2f: nvr a factor* **10/1**	72
04-2	7	½	**Madam Macie (IRE)**[27] 1293 5-9-7 80.................... SilvestreDeSousa 5 (David O'Meara) *chsd ldrs: drvn over 3f out: wknd ins fnl f: eased nr fin* **5/2**[1]	75
60-0	8	1 ½	**Gala Casino Star (IRE)**[28] 1275 7-8-6 72.............(p) JordanNason(7) 11 (Geoffrey Harker) *sn in rr: kpt on fnl 2f: nvr a factor* **50/1**	59
221-	9	12	**Chookie Royale**[201] 6980 4-9-5 78................................(p) JoeFanning 8 (Keith Dalgleish) *s.i.s: bhd fnl 2f* **7/1**[3]	33
600-	10	5	**Dhhamaan (IRE)**[192] 7175 7-8-8 67................................(b) PaulMulrennan 9 (Ruth Carr) *led: hdd over 2f out: lost pl over 1f out: sn bhd* **25/1**	8
0-06	11	hd	**Rio Cobolo (IRE)**[27] 1293 6-8-13 72................................ AdrianNicholls 2 (David Nicholls) *chsd ldrs: lost pl 2f out: sn bhd* **28/1**	13

1m 29.11s (2.11) **Going Correction** +0.45s/f (Yiel) 11 Ran SP% **112.2**
Speed ratings (Par 105): **105,104,103,101,100 97,96,95,81,75 75**
toteswingers:1&2:£37.70, 2&3:£22.60, 1&3:£15.90 CSF £106.20 CT £1147.26 TOTE £9.40: £3.20, £4.50, £3.20; EX 141.80 Trifecta £537.50 Part won. Pool: £726.45 - 0.62 winning units..
Owner Ms M Austerfield **Bred** Miss A J Rawding & P M Crane **Trained** Cowthorpe, N Yorks
■ Stewards' Enquiry : I Poullis two-day ban: used whip above permitted level (May 22-23)

FOCUS
A fair handicap for the grade. The winner stepped up on his progressive 3yo form and there may be more to come. The next two set a sound standard.

1952 GO RACING IN YORKSHIRE H'CAP 1m 7f 177y
7:40 (7:40) (Class 6) (0-65,65) 4-Y-0+ **£2,045** (£603; £302) **Stalls** Centre

Form				RPR
5/21	1		**Ministerofinterior**[18] 1496 7-9-6 61................................(tp) GrahamLee 12 (Richard Ford) *mid-div: hdwy to trck ldrs over 7f out: led over 2f out: hld on wl in clsng stages* **9/2**[2]	77
040-	2	¾	**Pocket Too**[11] 1959 9-8-9 50................................(p) JoeFanning 8 (Victor Dartnall) *trckd ldrs: hrd drvn over 5f out: upsides 2f out: no ex last 50yds* **12/5**[1]	65
-050	3	9	**Dubara Reef (IRE)**[12] 1631 5-8-11 52.................(p) SilvestreDeSousa 10 (Paul Green) *led early: chsd ldrs: led over 4f out: hdd over 2f out: one pce* **10/1**	56
6322	4	1	**Three White Socks (IRE)**[35] 1175 5-9-6 61................. BarryMcHugh 1 (Brian Ellison) *hld up in rr: drvn over 3f out: kpt on fnl 2f: nvr a threat* **7/1**[3]	64
53-2	5	2 ½	**Dan's Heir**[29] 1247 10-8-8 52................................ DominicFox(3) 9 (Wilf Storey) *hld up in rr: hdwy 7f out: one pce fnl 3f* **16/1**	52
335-	6	3 ¼	**Shirls Son Sam**[206] 6870 4-8-7 51................................ KellyHarrison 5 (Chris Fairhurst) *s.i.s: in rr: t.k.h and sme hdwy 6f out: one pce fnl 3f* **20/1**	47

14-0 **7** ¾ **Damascus Symphony**[11] 1640 4-9-7 **65**.................. GrahamGibbons 14 60
(James Bethell) *s.s: hdwy after 3f: chsng ldrs 4f out: wknd over 1f out* **22/1**

23-2 **8** 1¼ **Hi Dancer**[27] 1297 9-9-0 **55**.. PhillipMakin 6 48
(Ben Haslam) *mid-div: hdwy to trck ldrs over 7f out: drvn over 4f out: wknd 2f out* **9/2**[2]

36-6 **9** 10 **Seawood**[77] 644 6-8-6 **47**... RoystonFfrench 13 28
(Roy Bowring) *chsd ldrs: lost pl over 1f out* **50/1**

24-3 **10** ½ **Strong Knight**[13] 1598 5-8-13 **54**..............................(p) DuranFentiman 3 35
(Tim Walford) *t.k.h in mid-div: lost pl over 4f out: hdwy over 2f out: hung lft and wknd over 1f out* **12/1**

00-0 **11** 13 **Tarantella Lady**[28] 1272 4-9-5 **63**..............................(v[1]) AndrewMullen 4 28
(George Moore) *sn led: hdd over 4f out: lost pl over 2f out: sn bhd* **33/1**

0-02 **12** 3 **Srimenanti**[10] 1673 4-8-1 **48**...(p) JulieBurke(3) 2
(Brian Rothwell) *chsd ldrs: drvn over 7f out: lost pl 4f out: wl bhd fnl 2f* **100/1**

3m 39.87s (7.87) **Going Correction** +0.45s/f (Yiel)
WFA 4 from 5yo+ 3lb **12** Ran SP% **115.9**
Speed ratings (Par 101): **98,97,93,92,91 89,89,88,83,83 77,75**
toteswingers:1&2:£5.40, 2&3:£8.40, 1&3:£13.40 CSF £14.45 CT £102.21 TOTE £7.60: £2.20, £1.10, £3.40; EX 17.20 Trifecta £210.50 Part won. Pool: £284.58 - 0.62 winning units..
Owner D E Simpson & R Farrington-Kirkham **Bred** Deerfield Farm **Trained** Garstang, Lancs

FOCUS
A moderate staying handicap with little depth, but a couple of bang-in form runners pulled well clear. Both were on good marks compared with their jumps form.
Hi Dancer Official explanation: trainer had no explanation for the poor form shown
Strong Knight Official explanation: jockey said gelding hung left

1953 CATTERICKBRIDGE.CO.UK MAIDEN STKS 7f
8:10 (8:11) (Class 5) 3-Y-O+ **£2,264** (£673; £336; £168) **Stalls** Centre

Form RPR

1 **Prophesy (IRE)**[272] 4934 3-9-0 77............................... GrahamGibbons 6 76+
(Declan Carroll) *trckd ldrs: wnt 2nd over 3f out: led on bit 2f out: sn nudged clr: easily* **4/5**[1]

40 **2** 3 **Pursuit of Passion**[17] 1521 4-9-4 0................................ LeeTopliss(3) 8 64
(Richard Fahey) *sn drvn along in rr: hdwy over 3f out: wnt 2nd 1f out: no ch w wnr whn rdr dropped whip in clsng stages* **8/1**[2]

3 ¾ **Fleurtille** 3-8-10 0 ow1.. PaddyAspell 5 59
(Ray Craggs) *s.v.s: in rr: hdwy on outside over 2f out: kpt on to take 3rd 1f out* **66/1**

4 1½ **Fame Again**[35] 4-9-12 0... JamesSullivan 3 63
(Michael Easterby) *s.s: drvn over 3f out: hdwy and swtchd ins over 1f out: kpt on* **28/1**

66- **5** 3½ **Gibraltar Road**[224] 6425 3-9-0 0................................ MichaelO'Connell 4 50
(John Quinn) *t.k.h: led 1f: chsd ldrs: wknd fnl f* **8/1**[2]

4 **6** 2 **Brother Superior**[36] 1166 3-9-0 0................................ DuranFentiman 9 44
(Tim Easterby) *chsd ldrs: drvn 4f out: wknd appr fnl f* **17/2**[3]

00- **7** 2¾ **Niceonemyson**[189] 7209 3-9-0 0.. TomEaves 1 37
(Christopher Wilson) *in tch: outpcd 3f out: no threat whn edgd rt over 1f out* **50/1**

005- **8** nk **Phair Winter**[246] 5789 4-9-7 45.............................. SilvestreDeSousa 7 35
(Alan Brown) *led after 1f: hdd 2f out: wknd fnl f: eased nr fin* **11/1**

- **9** 10 **Lord Gaga (IRE)** 3-9-0 0.. AdrianNicholls 2
(David Nicholls) *mid-div: drvn and lost pl over 5f out: bhd fnl 3f* **11/1**

1m 32.0s (5.00) **Going Correction** +0.45s/f (Yiel)
WFA 3 from 4yo 12lb **9** Ran SP% **111.9**
Speed ratings (Par 103): **89,85,84,83,79 76,73,73,61**
toteswingers:1&2:£1.80, 2&3:£39.70, 1&3:£11.20 CSF £7.25 TOTE £1.80: £1.10, £1.90, £15.20; EX 7.30 Trifecta £161.40 Pool: £713.33 - 3.27 winning units..
Owner M Stewart **Bred** King Bloodstock And R Scarborough **Trained** Sledmere, E Yorks

FOCUS
A weak and uncompetitive maiden run relatively slowly and won easily by Prophesy, who is rated in line with his 2yo form.

1954 DON'T MISS JUBILEE SATURDAY 2ND JUNE H'CAP 5f
8:40 (8:40) (Class 5) (0-70,69) 4-Y-O+ **£2,385** (£704; £352) **Stalls** Low

Form RPR

50-0 **1** **Nomoreblondes**[29] 1246 8-8-13 **68**...............................(v) NedCurtis(7) 8 79
(Paul Midgley) *mde all: jst hld on* **22/1**

2111 **2** shd **First In Command (IRE)**[42] 1054 7-9-7 **69**.....................(t) ShaneKelly 5 80
(Daniel Mark Loughnane) *chsd ldrs: hrd rdn and styd on ins fnl f: jst failed* **4/1**[2]

343- **3** ¾ **Diamond Blue**[237] 6044 4-9-3 **68**.. AmyRyan(3) 3 76
(Richard Whitaker) *trckd ldrs: chal over 1f out: no ex last 50yds* **11/4**[1]

5-04 **4** 2¼ **Ever Roses**[27] 1298 4-8-11 **59**..................................(v) MichaelO'Connell 1 59
(Paul Midgley) *chsd ldrs: outpcd and lost pl over 2f out: hdwy over 1f out: kpt on one pce* **8/1**

000- **5** 1¾ **On The High Tops (IRE)**[165] 7535 4-9-5 **67**................ JamesSullivan 9 61
(Ruth Carr) *trckd ldrs: effrt over 1f out: kpt on same pce* **7/1**

100- **6** 1 **Ingenti**[196] 7079 4-8-7 **55** oh1.. TomEaves 7 45
(Christopher Wilson) *stdd s: hld up: hdwy on outside and hmpd over 1f out: nvr nr ldrs* **33/1**

0-01 **7** 3 **Prince James**[13] 1601 5-9-0 **62**... PaddyAspell 6 41
(Michael Easterby) *in rr: hung lft over 1f out: nvr a factor* **16/1**

5465 **8** ½ **No Mean Trick (USA)**[34] 1187 6-8-11 **59**....................... MickyFenton 11 36
(Paul Midgley) *chsd ldrs on outer: hung rt and lost pl over 1f out* **9/1**

03-0 **9** ½ **Cross Of Lorraine (IRE)**[27] 1298 9-9-1 **63**..............(b) TonyHamilton 10 39
(Chris Grant) *chsd ldrs: lost pl over 2f out* **20/1**

4U05 **10** 6 **Lucky Dan (IRE)**[27] 1298 6-9-2 **64**.........................(v[1]) SilvestreDeSousa 2 18
(Paul Green) *chsd ldrs: rdn and outpcd over 2f out: eased ins fnl f* **6/1**[3]

1m 1.99s (2.19) **Going Correction** +0.525s/f (Yiel) **10** Ran SP% **112.5**
Speed ratings (Par 103): **103,102,101,98,95 93,88,88,87,77**
toteswingers:1&2:£11.90, 2&3:£3.80, 1&3:£10.90 CSF £102.38 CT £324.53 TOTE £28.70: £6.80, £2.00, £1.40; EX 164.10 Trifecta £587.20 Part won. Pool: £793.57 - 0.50 winning units..
Owner Anthony D Copley **Bred** P John And Redmyre Bloodstock **Trained** Westow, N Yorks

FOCUS
A modest sprint handicap, and they raced up the middle of the track. The time was decent and there are grounds for thinking the fron three are slightly ahead of their marks.
No Mean Trick(USA) Official explanation: jockey said gelding hung right throughout
T/Jkpt: Not won. T/Plt: £68.10 to a £1 stake. Pool of £69399.35- 743.01 winning tickets. T/Qpdt: £25.70 to a £1 stake. Pool of £6199.99- 177.90 winning tickets. WG

1578 SOUTHWELL (L-H)
Tuesday, May 8

OFFICIAL GOING: Standard
Replacement meeting for the abandoned Newcastle fixture.
Wind: Fresh, across Weather: Cloudy, bright

1955 E B F 32RED MEDIAN AUCTION MAIDEN STKS 5f (F)
2:15 (2:15) (Class 5) 2-Y-O **£3,040** (£904; £452; £226) **Stalls** High

Form RPR

36 **1** **Mosstang (IRE)**[25] 1352 2-9-3 0.................................... StevieDonohoe 2 72
(Robert Mills) *mde all: shkn up over 1f out: rdn clr ins fnl f: eased nr fin* **6/5**[1]

2 4 **Ryedale Valley** 2-9-3 0... DavidAllan 4 57
(Tim Easterby) *chsd wnr thrght: rdn after 2f: kpt on same pce appr fnl f* **5/1**[3]

3 ½ **Ace Pearl (USA)** 2-9-3 0.. MichaelStainton 5 55+
(David Brown) *dwlt: sn chsng ldrs: drvn along and effrt 1/2-way: no imp fr over 1f out* **5/4**[2]

4 9 **Baraboy (IRE)** 2-9-3 0.. DuranFentiman 3 22
(Tim Easterby) *prom: hung lft thrght: rdn along and struggling 1/2-way: sn btn* **8/1**

59.33s (-0.37) **Going Correction** -0.225s/f (Stan) **4** Ran SP% **117.7**
Speed ratings (Par 93): **93,86,85,71**
CSF £7.98 TOTE £3.00; EX 8.40.
Owner Pinehurst Racing & Mrs B B Mills **Bred** Ringfort Stud Ltd **Trained** Headley, Surrey

FOCUS
A weak juvenile maiden.

NOTEBOOK
Mosstang(IRE) was the only runner here with previous experience and that counted for plenty as he made it third time lucky, handing his yard a welcome winner in the process. He got bogged down on bad ground at Leicester last time (reportedly coughed), but was placed in a good event on his debut at Kempton the time before and this was a return to that sort of decent form. He has scope and is open to improvement, so a step into novice company should tell us more about his true potential. (op 13-8)
Ryedale Valley knew his job pretty much and pressed the winner at the furlong marker. His lack of fitness told soon after and it was a pleasing introduction from this nicely bred colt. (op 9-2)
Ace Pearl(USA), whose connections sent out an impressive debut winner at Newmarket last weekend, proved popular in the betting. He was always playing catch-up after a tardy start and ultimately the outing was needed. He reportedly hasn't been in the yard that long and ought to come on plenty. (op 11-8 tchd 6-4)
Baraboy(IRE) is a stablemate of the runner-up and his trainer's second string. He proved far too green, but is half-brother to four juvenile winners and so improvement will be on the cards as he gets more streetwise. (op 6-1)

1956 32RED.COM H'CAP 1m 4f (F)
2:45 (2:45) (Class 5) (0-70,70) 4-Y-O+ **£2,264** (£673; £336; £168) **Stalls** Low

Form RPR

2320 **1** **Resplendent Alpha**[2] 1895 8-8-5 59.......................... LeonnaMayor(5) 3 66
(Alastair Lidderdale) *stdd s: t.k.h in tch on ins: nt clr run briefly over 3f out: hdwy to ld appr fnl f: edgd rt and kpt on wl towards fin* **7/2**[3]

32-6 **2** ½ **Lakeman (IRE)**[14] 1578 6-8-10 59.............................(be) BarryMcHugh 5 65
(Brian Ellison) *trckd ldrs: hdwy to ld over 3f out: rdn and hdd appr fnl f: kpt on: hld nr fin* **5/1**

6201 **3** 4½ **Kingaroo (IRE)**[21] 1432 6-8-7 56.. WilliamBuick 1 55
(Garry Woodward) *led 2f: chsd ldr: rdn and ev ch over 3f out to wl over 1f out: outpcd appr fnl f* **6/4**[1]

4-30 **4** 8 **Yourinthewill (USA)**[5] 1792 4-9-7 70........................... PadraigBeggy 2 56
(Daniel Mark Loughnane) *prom: drvn and outpcd 3f out: n.d after* **11/4**[2]

300/ **5** 7 **Apache Dawn**[45] 4170 8-8-2 56 oh11.............................(t) RaulDaSilva(5) 6 31
(Aytach Sadik) *w ldr: led after 2f to over 3f out: sn rdn: wknd over 2f out* **25/1**

53-0 **6** 19 **Trachonitis (IRE)**[91] 460 8-9-4 67.. ShaneKelly 4
(J R Jenkins) *hld up: struggling over 3f out: sn btn: t.o* **4/1**

2m 39.51s (-1.49) **Going Correction** -0.125s/f (Stan) **6** Ran SP% **129.4**
Speed ratings (Par 103): **99,98,95,90,85 73**
toteswingers:1&2:£4.80, 2&3:£1.60, 1&3:£3.40 CSF £24.54 TOTE £7.00: £2.30, £2.80; EX 39.80.
Owner Chris Beek Racing **Bred** Sunley Stud **Trained** Lambourn, Berks
■ Stewards' Enquiry : Barry McHugh two-day ban: used whip above permitted level (May 22-23)

FOCUS
A weak handicap, run at a decent pace. The favourite disappointed and the winner is rated in line with recent form.

1957 £32 BONUS AT 32RED.COM MAIDEN FILLIES' STKS 1m 3f (F)
3:15 (3:15) (Class 5) 3-Y-O+ **£2,264** (£673; £336) **Stalls** Low

Form RPR

2- **1** **Tajriba (IRE)**[180] 7343 3-8-8 0................................ SilvestreDeSousa 3 82
(Saeed Bin Suroor) *dwlt: t.k.h and led at stdy gallop after 1f: shkn up and rn green over 2f out: kpt on wl: comf* **6/4**[2]

2 **2** 2¼ **Lascaux**[11] 1649 3-8-8 0.. WilliamBuick 1 78
(John Gosden) *led 1f: trckd wnr: effrt and rdn over 2f out: one pce whn hung lft appr fnl f* **1/2**[1]

00/0 **3** 59 **Beaux Yeux**[10] 1662 6-9-6 45.. AnnStokell(5) 4
(Ann Stokell) *chsd ldrs to 1/2-way: sn rdn and struggling: t.o* **66/1**[3]

2m 26.47s (-1.53) **Going Correction** -0.125s/f (Stan)
WFA 3 from 6yo 17lb **3** Ran SP% **108.2**
Speed ratings (Par 100): **100,98,55**
CSF £2.71 TOTE £1.80; EX 2.50.
Owner Godolphin **Bred** Mrs C L Weld **Trained** Newmarket, Suffolk

FOCUS
A slowly run maiden and there are doubts over whether the form can be taken at face value.

1958 32RED CASINO H'CAP 7f (F)
3:45 (3:45) (Class 5) (0-75,74) 4-Y-O+ **£2,264** (£673; £336; £168) **Stalls** Low

Form RPR

6526 **1** **Alpha Tauri (USA)**[5] 1768 6-9-0 67..............................(t) MartinHarley 7 84
(Richard Guest) *mde all: qcknd clr 1/2-way: shkn up and kpt on strly fr 2f out: unchal* **7/1**[2]

4130 **2** 6 **Beachwood Bay**[24] 1384 4-8-4 64............................... JoshBaudains(7) 11 65
(Jo Hughes) *chsd wnr thrght: effrt over 2f out: drifted lft and no imp fr over 1f out* **7/1**[2]

256- **3** 3 1/4 **Hakuna Matata**[7] 3399 5-9-5 72 BarryMcHugh 3 64
(Brian Ellison) *dwlt: bhd and sn drvn along: hdwy against ins rail 2f out: kpt on: nvr able to chal* **16/1**

3000 **4** 1 **Joe Le Taxi (IRE)**[29] 1263 4-8-7 60 JoeFanning 8 49
(Mark Johnston) *hld up: rdn wl over 3f out: kpt on fr 2f out: nvr rchd ldrs* **11/1**

2060 **5** 3/4 **Legal Legacy**[26] 1342 6-9-7 74 (e[1]) WilliamBuick 9 61
(David C Griffiths) *s.i.s: bhd and pushed along: edgd lft and kpt on fr 2f out: nvr rchd ldrs* **9/1**[3]

5111 **6** 3/4 **Only Ten Per Cent (IRE)**[14] 1584 4-9-5 72 DarryllHolland 4 57
(J R Jenkins) *hld up in tch: rdn over 3f out: no imp fr 2f out* **6/4**[1]

-204 **7** nse **Nezami (IRE)**[17] 1527 7-9-1 68 MickyFenton 1 53
(Paul Midgley) *dwlt: hld up: stdy hdwy over 4f out: rdn and struggling over 2f out* **9/1**[3]

0105 **8** 2 3/4 **Mazovian (USA)**[14] 1581 4-9-5 72 RobbieFitzpatrick 10 50
(Michael Chapman) *midfield: drvn along over 3f out: wknd over 2f out* **14/1**

3524 **9** 1/2 **Elhamri**[14] 1581 8-9-0 67 KirstyMilczarek 6 43
(Conor Dore) *chsd ldrs tl rdn and wknd over 2f out* **14/1**

2136 **10** 2 3/4 **Ace Of Spies (IRE)**[13] 1601 7-9-0 67 HayleyTurner 5 36
(Conor Dore) *prom: drvn 1/2-way: wknd fnl 2f* **12/1**

500- **11** 5 **Conry (IRE)**[192] 7176 6-8-12 65 ShaneKelly 2 20
(Daniel Mark Loughnane) *hld up on ins: struggling over 3f out: sn btn* **25/1**

1m 27.17s (-3.13) **Going Correction** -0.125s/f (Stan) 11 Ran SP% 124.1
Speed ratings (Par 103): **112,105,101,100,99 98,98,95,94,91 85**
toteswingers:1&2:£7.60, 2&3:£19.70, 1&3:£14.60 CSF £58.63 CT £789.78 TOTE £11.60: £3.70, £2.30, £4.10; EX 71.10 Trifecta £506.90 Part won. Pool of £685.11 - 0.10 winning units..
Owner Willie McKay **Bred** Flaxman Holdings Ltd **Trained** Stainforth, S Yorks

FOCUS
A moderate handicap and a taking win for C&D specialist Alpha Tauri, in a time inside standard. He's rated back to his old best.
Legal Legacy Official explanation: jockey said gelding missed the break
Only Ten Per Cent(IRE) ◆ Official explanation: trainer had no explanation for the poor form shown

1959 32REDPOKER.COM H'CAP 1m (F)
4:15 (4:15) (Class 5) (0-70,70) 3-Y-O **£2,264** (£673; £336; £168) **Stalls** Low

Form RPR
2-44 **1** **Peter Anders**[13] 1595 3-9-7 70 JoeFanning 2 78
(Mark Johnston) *trckd ldrs: rdn over 2f out: hdwy to ld appr fnl f: rdn and hld on wl* **15/8**[2]

-020 **2** nk **Feeling Good**[19] 1479 3-9-7 70 BarryMcHugh 5 77
(Brian Ellison) *led: rdn 2f out: hdd appr fnl f: rallied: hld nr fin* **6/5**[1]

04-6 **3** 9 **Sygnature**[36] 1167 3-9-5 68 WilliamBuick 4 54
(Alan Swinbank) *t.k.h: trckd ldrs: drvn and outpcd 2f out: sn n.d* **3/1**[3]

426- **4** 5 **Sweet Grace**[131] 7915 3-8-9 58 MichaelStainton 1 33
(David Brown) *disp ld to 2f out: sn rdn and wknd* **12/1**

1m 42.3s (-1.40) **Going Correction** -0.125s/f (Stan) 4 Ran SP% 112.9
Speed ratings (Par 99): **102,101,92,87**
CSF £4.78 TOTE £3.80; EX 5.50.
Owner Newsells Park Stud **Bred** Newsells Park Stud **Trained** Middleham Moor, N Yorks

FOCUS
An ordinary 3-y-o handicap. It was run at a sound pace and the first pair came nicely clear. Only they showed their form, but they've been given some credit for pulling away.

1960 32REDBINGO.COM H'CAP 6f (F)
4:45 (4:45) (Class 5) (0-70,69) 3-Y-O **£2,264** (£673; £336; £168) **Stalls** Low

Form RPR
3-31 **1** **Art Dzeko**[13] 1596 3-9-3 65 DavidAllan 6 72+
(Tim Easterby) *cl up: led gng wl over 2f out: rdn and hung rt over 1f out: drvn out ins fnl f* **8/11**[1]

-304 **2** 1 1/4 **Beau Mistral (IRE)**[10] 1658 3-9-2 69 MatthewLawson(5) 3 72
(Paul Green) *prom: rdn and outpcd wl over 2f out: rallied and hung lft wl over 1f out: chsd wnr ins fnl f: kpt on* **8/1**

0-04 **3** shd **Travis County (IRE)**[14] 1582 3-9-5 67 BarryMcHugh 7 70
(Brian Ellison) *s.i.s: in tch on outside: effrt over 2f out: chsd wnr over 1f out to ins fnl f: kpt on* **5/1**[2]

0333 **4** 6 **Celestial Dawn**[13] 1599 3-8-2 55 RaulDaSilva(5) 4 39
(John Weymes) *led tl rdn and hdd over 2f out: rallied: wknd ent fnl f* **6/1**

2-20 **5** 17 **Cone Donkey (IRE)**[13] 1599 3-9-1 63 TomEaves 1
(Bryan Smart) *disp ld to over 2f out: sn rdn and struggling: t.o* **11/2**[3]

1m 15.68s (-0.82) **Going Correction** -0.125s/f (Stan) 5 Ran SP% 115.4
Speed ratings (Par 99): **100,98,98,90,67**
CSF £7.90 TOTE £1.90: £1.70, £2.40; EX 9.50.
Owner Middleham Park Racing LIX & Partners **Bred** Helier Stud **Trained** Great Habton, N Yorks

FOCUS
A modest 3-y-o sprint handicap. The winner is on the up but the form is rated a bit cautiously.

1961 32REDBET.COM H'CAP 7f (F)
5:15 (5:15) (Class 6) (0-60,60) 4-Y-O+ **£1,617** (£481; £240; £120) **Stalls** Low

Form RPR
0601 **1** **Lindoro**[4] 1823 7-8-12 51 BarryMcHugh 2 70
(Brian Ellison) *chsd clr ldr: hdwy over 2f out: rdn to ld over 1f out: sn clr* **10/11**[1]

5312 **2** 4 **Bonnie Prince Blue**[14] 1584 9-9-4 60 (b) DaleSwift(3) 12 68
(Ian McInnes) *bhd: struggling 1/2-way: gd hdwy on outside over 1f out: chsd (clr) wnr ins fnl f: no imp* **6/1**[2]

4-00 **3** 1 3/4 **This Ones For Eddy**[19] 1487 7-9-5 58 MartinLane 7 61
(John Balding) *dwlt: bhd and pushed along: styd on fr 2f out: nrst fin* **14/1**

400/ **4** 1 **Amber Moon**[763] 1142 7-8-4 46 oh1 (b) AdamBeschizza(3) 10 47
(Ann Stokell) *cl up: rdn 3f out: kpt on same pce fr 2f out* **100/1**

00-3 **5** 1 1/4 **Coastal Passage**[8] 1722 4-8-11 50 MartinHarley 5 47
(Richard Guest) *in tch: drvn over 3f out: edgd lft and no imp fnl 2f* **8/1**[3]

000- **6** 1 1/2 **Queen's Choice (IRE)**[186] 7270 4-8-7 46 oh1 (t) KirstyMilczarek 11 39
(Anabel K Murphy) *missed break: bhd and drvn along: kpt on fnl f: nvr on terms* **50/1**

-050 **7** 3/4 **Bertie Blu Boy**[12] 1634 4-8-4 48 ow1 MatthewLawson(5) 4 39
(Paul Green) *sn pushed along in midfield: outpcd 3f out: sn n.d* **20/1**

-000 **8** nk **Hab Reeh**[35] 1179 4-8-8 47 oh1 ow1 (bt) TomEaves 6 37
(Ruth Carr) *plld hrd: led and sn clr: rdn over 2f out: hdd over 1f out: wknd ins fnl f* **25/1**

054- **9** 6 **Wotatomboy**[171] 7484 6-8-10 49 RussKennemore 3 23
(Richard Whitaker) *hld up in tch: drvn over 3f out: wknd fr 2f out* **50/1**

4110 **10** 20 **Rise To Glory (IRE)**[5] 1799 4-9-5 58 RobbieFitzpatrick 1
(Shaun Harris) *in tch on ins: struggling over 3f out: lost tch fr 2f out* **9/1**

1m 29.78s (-0.52) **Going Correction** -0.125s/f (Stan) 10 Ran SP% 108.0
Speed ratings (Par 101): **97,92,90,89,87 86,85,84,78,55**
toteswingers:1&2:£2.60, 2&3:£11.30, 1&3:£3.80 CSF £5.09 CT £36.68 TOTE £2.20: £1.50, £1.02, £5.40; EX 6.10 Trifecta £21.80.
Owner Brian Ellison **Bred** Pigeon House Stud **Trained** Norton, N Yorks
■ Cheers Buddy (10/1) was withdrawn after becoming upset in the stalls (R4 applies, deduct 5p in the £.)

FOCUS
The pace rather collapsed. This was all about the very well-handicapped winner, who's possibly better than the bare form and didn't need to match his turf latest. The runner-up sets the level.
T/Plt: £306.40 to a £1 stake. Pool of £62,921.24 - 149.90 winning tickets. T/Qpdt: £48.80 to a £1 stake. Pool of £3,826.03 - 57.90 winning tickets. RY

1380 NEWCASTLE (L-H)
Tuesday, May 8

1962 Meeting Abandoned - Waterlogged
Meeting replaced by Southwell

1969 - 1970a (Foreign Racing) - See Raceform Interactive

1809 LONGCHAMP (R-H)
Tuesday, May 8

OFFICIAL GOING: Turf: very soft

1971a PRIX D'HEDOUVILLE (GROUP 3) (4YO+) (TURF) 1m 4f
2:50 (12:00) 4-Y-O+ **£33,333** (£13,333; £10,000; £6,666; £3,333)

RPR
1 **Allied Powers (IRE)**[17] 1507 7-8-11 0 IoritzMendizabal 6 110
(Michael Bell) *settled in 3rd: rdn over 1 1/2f out: r.o wl ent fnl f: chsd ldr u.p: got up fnl strides* **6/1**[2]

2 3 **Solemia (IRE)**[19] 1490 4-8-8 0 OlivierPeslier 5 102
(C Laffon-Parias, France) *racd in midfield under restraint: clsd on ldrs 1 1/2f out: swtchd towards rail 1f out: short of room to chal whn ldr edgd towards rail: had to be stdd and lost ch: r.o fnl f: fin 3rd: promoted to 2nd* **10/11**[1]

3 hd **Molly Malone (FR)**[25] 4-8-6 0 GregoryBenoist 4 100
(M Delzangles, France) *settled in 2nd: rdn to ld 2f out: r.o wl: edgd towards rail 1f out: r.o wl fnl f: hdd fnl strides: fin 2nd: disqualified and plcd 3rd* **9/1**

4 2 1/2 **Dance Moves**[21] 4-8-9 0 MaximeGuyon 3 99
(A Fabre, France) *settled in midfield: rdn 2f out: r.o fnl f wout threatening ldrs* **13/2**[3]

5 hd **Winter Dream (IRE)**[12] 8-8-9 0 GeraldMosse 1 98
(Robert Collet, France) *hld up towards rr: rdn early in st: no ex: styd on one pce fnl 1 1/2f* **12/1**

6 3/4 **Starlish (IRE)**[49] 980 7-8-10 0 ow1 ChristopheSoumillon 8 98
(E Lellouche, France) *led fr s: stl in front ent st: rdn and hdd 2f out: styd on one pce fnl f* **13/2**[3]

7 1/2 **Fannon Blue (ITY)**[33] 5-8-9 0 (b) ThierryThulliez 2 96
(Mme C Barande-Barbe, France) *a in rr: styd on fnl f* **18/1**

2m 45.1s (14.70) 7 Ran SP% 116.3
WIN (incl. 1 euro stake): 8.90. PLACES: 1.90, 1.20, 1.70. SF: 20.10.
Owner David Fish And Edward Ware **Bred** Saad Bin Mishrif **Trained** Newmarket, Suffolk

NOTEBOOK
Allied Powers(IRE) may have been fortunate that the favourite endured a luckless run, but nevertheless, he is a capable performer at this level when conditions suit - in 11 starts on soft or heavy ground he's won four times and only finished out of the places on three occasions. He followed up in the Grand Prix de Chantilly after winning this race two years ago, and the plan is to attempt to repeat that feat.
Solemia(IRE), impressive in Listed company last time out, was sent off a short-priced favourite to take this rise in class in her stride, and she was arguably unlucky not to score. Held up off a steady early pace, she was cut off in her run when switched to the inside and finished full of running. This is easily excused.

CHESTER (L-H)
Wednesday, May 9

OFFICIAL GOING: Soft (good to soft in places) changing to soft after race 1 (1.35)

1972 MANOR HOUSE STABLES LILY AGNES CONDITIONS STKS 5f 16y
1:35 (1:42) (Class 2) 2-Y-O
£9,960 (£2,982; £1,491; £745; £372; £187) **Stalls** Low

Form RPR
22 **1** **All Fur Coat**[20] 1466 2-8-7 0 FrannyNorton 4 84+
(Jo Hughes) *mde all: rdn over 1f out: r.o wl fnl f* **9/2**[3]

4251 **2** 2 3/4 **Just Past Andover (IRE)**[8] 1738 2-8-12 0 KierenFallon 2 79
(Bill Turner) *chsd wnr thrght: rdn 2f out: no imp fnl f* **11/4**[1]

13 **3** 1 1/4 **Baddilini**[7] 1747 2-9-1 0 RyanMoore 8 77+
(Alan Bailey) *midfield: hdwy ins fnl f: r.o towards fin* **5/1**

1 **4** 1 **Tharawal Lady (IRE)**[21] 1437 2-8-7 0 TomEaves 1 66
(John Quinn) *dwlt: chsd ldrs: rdn over 1f out: no ex wl ins fnl f* **10/3**[2]

3 **5** 1 1/4 **Blue Clumber**[11] 1651 2-8-7 0 GrahamGibbons 11 61
(Shaun Harris) *racd keenly: chsd ldrs: lost pl 1/2-way: n.d after* **150/1**

6 **6** nk **Brazilian Clown (IRE)**[4] 1861 2-8-12 0 RussKennemore 3 65
(Tom Dascombe) *hld up: swtchd rt and rdn over 1f out: no imp* **16/1**

7 1 **Deauville Prince (FR)** 2-8-12 0 JimCrowley 6 61+
(Tom Dascombe) *a bhd: rdn 2f out: nvr on terms* **9/1**

8 1 1/4 **Pippy** 2-8-12 0 RichardKingscote 5 57+
(Tom Dascombe) *rn green: a bhd* **9/1**

1m 3.52s (2.52) **Going Correction** +0.475s/f (Yiel) 8 Ran SP% 111.1
Speed ratings (Par 99): **98,93,91,90,88 87,85,83**
toteswingers:1&2:£3.60, 2&3:£2.90, 1&3:£3.40 CSF £16.27 TOTE £5.60: £1.80, £1.40, £1.30; EX 17.30 Trifecta £55.10 Pool: £1082.12 - 14.53 winning units..
Owner R Kent **Bred** Platt Promotions Ltd **Trained** Lambourn. Berks
■ Dreamy Ciara was withdrawn (25/1, ref to ent stalls).

FOCUS
This race has a mixed history of producing horses that go on to do better at a higher level, but last year's winner Lily's Angel has certainly proved to be one of the best in recent times. Julius Geezer, who won in 2010, is still seeking his next success. The winner's time compared favourably with the races for older horse on the card over the same trip, but it must be remembered this was the first race of the meeting and the ground deteriorated through the card. This looked a fairly weak renewal.

NOTEBOOK
All Fur Coat broke really quickly and never saw another rival. She appears to handle both good and soft ground really well, so will have something to prove on a quick surface during the summer. Either the Albany Stakes or the Queen Mary at Royal Ascot are obvious targets in the short-term. (op 7-2 tchd 5-1)

Just Past Andover(IRE) didn't get away as quickly as the winner, and pulled for a few strides in behind, but had every chance to get past and couldn't. That said, he's still an above-average sort for the time of year. (op 7-2 tchd 5-2)

Baddilini, conceding weight all round, floundered in the ground a bit from his wide draw before keeping on strongly into a place. (tchd 9-2)

Tharawal Lady(IRE) created a pleasing impression on her debut when winning at Beverley after reportedly showing plenty at home, but faded in the home straight here and lost out on third in the final 50 yards. (op 11-4 tchd 7-2)

Blue Clumber ran very much as the market expected her to. (op 125-1)

Brazilian Clown(IRE), making a quick reappearance, has a bit of size about him and didn't look particularly happy on the bend.

Deauville Prince(FR), whose price rose to £30,000 as a 2yo, didn't show any immediate promise but wasn't given a hard time in the home straight. (op 16-1)

Pippy, Wayne and Coleen Rooney's first runner, and a half-brother to three sprint winners, was green and got baulked early on. This effort can be completely ignored. (op 11-1 tchd 12-1)

1973 WEATHERBYS BANK CHESHIRE OAKS (FOR THE ROBERT SANGSTER MEMORIAL CUP) (LISTED RACE) (FILLIES) 1m 3f 79y

2:05 (2:10) (Class 1) 3-Y-O

£19,848 (£7,525; £3,766; £1,876; £941; £472) **Stalls** Low

Form			Horse	Jockey	RPR
1323	**1**		**Good Morning Star (IRE)**[21] 1442 3-8-12 74 (Mark Johnston) *hld up: rdn and hdwy 3f out: styd on ins fnl f to ld post* **50/1**	FrannyNorton 6	90
	2	*shd*	**Betterbetterbetter (IRE)**[21] 1462 3-8-12 0 (A P O'Brien, Ire) *sn chsng ldr: moved upsides 2f out: led and edgd lft over 1f out: ct post* **2/1**[1]	JPO'Brien 2	89
21-	**3**	*1 ¾*	**Cubanita**[189] 7233 3-8-12 80 (Ralph Beckett) *s.i.s: sn in tch: hung rt fr over 2f out: effrt over 1f out: kpt on u.p ins fnl f* **5/2**[2]	JimCrowley 1	86
46-2	**4**	*hd*	**Everlong**[19] 1502 3-8-12 89 (Peter Chapple-Hyam) *racd keenly: led: rdn and hdd over 1f out: styd on same pce ins fnl f* **9/1**	JamieSpencer 8	86
2-23	**5**	*nk*	**Safarjal (IRE)**[19] 1503 3-8-12 77 (Charles Hills) *dwlt: in rr: hdwy over 2f out: r.o ins fnl f: nrest at fin* **20/1**	PaulHanagan 9	85+
311	**6**	*1 ½*	**Cockney Sparrow**[21] 1442 3-8-12 81 (Peter Chapple-Hyam) *hld up: pushed along over 2f out: sme hdwy u.p over 1f out: no imp on ldrs ins fnl f* **25/1**	CO'Donoghue 12	83
2-	**7**	*16*	**Absolute Crackers (IRE)**[32] 1229 3-8-12 0 (Mrs John Harrington, Ire) *in tch: lost pl after 3f: hdwy over 5f out: rdn over 3f out: wknd over 2f out* **11/2**[3]	FranBerry 11	55
3-1	**8**	*1 ¾*	**Inchina**[19] 1503 3-8-12 80 (Roger Charlton) *midfield: rdn and wknd over 3f out* **11/1**	JamesDoyle 4	52
61-	**9**	*18*	**Dreams Of Fire (USA)**[195] 7118 3-8-12 78 (Sir Michael Stoute) *racd keenly: prom tl wknd qckly over 3f out: t.o* **14/1**	RyanMoore 10	21

2m 31.87s (7.07) **Going Correction** +0.60s/f (Yiel) 9 Ran SP% 112.9
Speed ratings (Par 104): **98,97,96,96,96 95,83,82,69**
toteswingers:1&2:£11.70, 2&3:£2.20, 1&3:£22.00 CSF £144.14 TOTE £65.70: £6.10, £1.20, £1.60; EX 155.00 Trifecta £575.50 Pool: £1244.35 - 1.60 winning units..

Owner Dr Marwan Koukash **Bred** Wardstown Stud Ltd **Trained** Middleham Moor, N Yorks

■ Stewards' Enquiry : J P O'Brien four-day ban; used whip above permitted level (23rd-26th May)

Franny Norton two-day ban; used whip above permitted level (23rd-24th May)

FOCUS
In the previous five years, this race has thrown up a winner (Light Shift) and a runner-up (Wonder Of Wonders last year) in the Epsom Oaks, but it's extremely difficult to believe we saw a winner or placed horse in that Classic here unless there is some dramatic improvement in the interim. In fact the form was barely up to the grade, and a below-average renewal. It turned into something of a sprint and the jockeys on the first two both received whip bans for use above the permitted level.

NOTEBOOK
Good Morning Star(IRE) was behind Cockney Sparrow last time at Beverley but reversed that piece of form in comprehensive style in similar ground. Beaten in three 0-75 handicaps after winning one on her first try in them, seemingly she only ran because the owner had no other suitable horse for the race - he even indicated afterwards that he had been looking for a claimer for her - but she may head for the Ribblesdale next. Long-term, he will probably keep her to breed from. (op 40-1)

Betterbetterbetter(IRE), related to six winners including Irish 1,000 Guineas winner Yesterday, Moyglare Stud winner Quarter Moon and 1m2f winner All My Loving, all of which placed in the Oaks, was ridden close to the lead, got to the front at what looked the right time before not going away. She appeared to doss while at the head of affairs but did respond when the winner came upsides, albeit too late. She has a lot of size about her and should have some more improvement left in her. (tchd 9-4 and 5-2 in a place)

Cubanita, whose Salisbury debut effort was a second to Derby hopeful Bonfire, had been off since winning a 1m Nottingham maiden the previous November but the trainer said before the off he felt his filly had done well over the winter. However, she didn't give the impression she was in love with the track and did well to get into an honourable third and earn black type. (op 3-1 tchd 9-4)

Everlong stopped fairly quickly under pressure after holding the lead, but is worth another chance on better ground (op 11-1)

Safarjal(IRE) ran nicely when a hood was placed on last time behind Inchina, and plugged on into fifth, reversing the form with the Roger Charlton filly. (op 16-1)

Cockney Sparrow will prove to be better than she showed here and is readily given another chance. (op 22-1 tchd 20-1)

Absolute Crackers(IRE) didn't act on the course - her rider reported that the filly hung right-handed. Official explanation: jockey said filly hung right-handed. (op 6-1 tchd 5-1)

Inchina looked to get outpaced when the tempo increased. (op 8-1)

Dreams Of Fire(USA), a half-sister to Kris Kin, won her maiden on the AW on her final start as a juvenile, so is another who'll probably leave this effort well behind on faster ground. (tchd 16-1)

1974 STANJAMES.COM CHESTER CUP (HERITAGE H'CAP) 2m 2f 147y

2:35 (2:39) (Class 2) 4-Y-0+

£62,250 (£18,640; £9,320; £4,660; £2,330; £1,170)

Form			Horse	Jockey	RPR
00U-	**1**		**Ile De Re (FR)**[60] 7297 6-8-11 93 (Donald McCain) *midfield: hdwy over 4f out: wnt 2nd over 3f out: rdn to ld over 1f out: styd on wl* **10/1**[3]	JimCrowley 13	103
160-	**2**	*1 ¾*	**Overturn (IRE)**[57] 4469 8-9-10 106 (Donald McCain) *led: swtchd off rail over 6f out: rdn over 2f out: hdd over 1f out: kpt on u.p ins fnl f* **7/1**[2]	EddieAhern 8	114
1-21	**3**	*5*	**Gulf Of Naples (IRE)**[11] 1672 4-9-1 101 3ex (Mark Johnston) *racd keenly: chsd ldrs: wnt 2nd briefly over 3f out: rdn over 2f out: styd on same pce ins fnl f* **11/2**[1]	FrannyNorton 19	104
6-16	**4**	*13*	**Eternal Heart (IRE)**[28] 1318 4-9-3 103 (Mark Johnston) *hld up: rdn over 5f out: hdwy over 3f out: styd on fnl 2f: nvr trbld ldrs* **14/1**	JoeFanning 5	91
0/0-	**5**	*2 ½*	**Harrison's Cave**[24] 1406 4-8-8 94 (A P O'Brien, Ire) *hld up in rr: hdwy over 4f out: swtchd rt over 3f out: kpt on fnl 2f: nvr trbld ldrs* **11/2**[1]	RyanMoore 15	79+
20-0	**6**	*11*	**Kiama Bay (IRE)**[32] 1214 6-9-1 97 (John Quinn) *in tch: rdn over 5f out: wknd over 3f out* **16/1**	TomEaves 9	70
010-	**7**	*1*	**Dazinski**[214] 6690 6-8-7 89 (Mark H Tompkins) *chsd ldrs tl rdn and wknd over 3f out* **16/1**	PaulMulrennan 1	61
211-	**8**	*27*	**Never Can Tell (IRE)**[214] 6690 5-9-0 96 (Jamie Osborne) *chsd ldr tl over 3f out: wknd over 2f out* **11/1**	FrankieDettori 6	39
003-	**9**	*10*	**Merchant Of Dubai**[141] 7297 7-8-12 94 (Jim Goldie) *hld up: struggling over 5f out: t.o* **20/1**	GrahamLee 10	26
1-04	**10**	*½*	**Barbican**[7] 1750 4-9-10 110 (Alan Bailey) *in tch: rdn and wknd over 3f out: t.o* **20/1**	DarryllHolland 7	41
/3-1	**11**	*23*	**Shubaat**[31] 1239 5-8-4 89 (Roger Varian) *hld up: struggling over 5f out: t.o* **11/2**[1]	DominicFox(3) 3	
5-04	**12**	*2 ½*	**Address Unknown**[11] 1672 5-9-1 97 (v[1]) (Ian Williams) *midfield: rdn and wknd over 5f out: t.o* **40/1**	StevieDonohoe 14	
254-	**13**	*50*	**Tominator**[243] 5883 5-9-1 100 (Reg Hollinshead) *hld up: struggling over 5f out: t.o* **12/1**	PaulPickard(3) 2	
00-	**14**	*12*	**Mystery Star (IRE)**[214] 6690 7-8-12 94 (Mark H Tompkins) *midfield: rdn over 5f out: sn wknd: t.o* **33/1**	PaulHanagan 18	
304-	**15**	*61*	**Ajaan**[249] 5705 8-9-2 98 (b) (Sir Henry Cecil) *midfield: rdn and wknd wl over 7f out: t.o* **20/1**	TomQueally 17	
220-	**P**		**Kazbow (IRE)**[214] 6690 6-8-11 93 (Chris Grant) *hld up: struggling wl over 7f out: sn p.u* **50/1**	KierenFallon 11	

4m 10.2s (5.40) **Going Correction** +0.60s/f (Yiel)
WFA 4 from 5yo+ 4lb 16 Ran SP% **123.8**
Speed ratings (Par 109): **112,111,109,103,102 98,97,86,82,81 72,71,50,44,19**
toteswingers:1&2:£24.00, 2&3:£7.70, 1&3:£12.50 CSF £72.78 CT £436.76 TOTE £11.70: £3.80, £2.50, £1.10, £3.40; EX 139.00 Trifecta £1000.80 Pool: £3516.35 - 2.60 winning units..

Owner D Mead **Bred** R Moser & Haras De S A Aga Khan Scea **Trained** Cholmondeley, Cheshire

FOCUS
This famous old staying handicap has often proved a fruitful target for horses better known as hurdlers, with such as dual winners Top Cees and Sea Pigeon, Triumph Hurdle winner Attivo and Champion Hurdle runner-up Major Rose all proving successful. Added to that the last two renewals had fallen to Mamlook and Overturn, and the trend continued here. Despite the long distance a low draw has often proved important, although horses drawn very high have also been successful. Due to the soft ground the race was started by flag, and two of the first three were drawn in double figures. However the horses didn't line up as per their draws. The pace was pretty solid in the conditions and the runners finished strung out like the finish of a steeplechase, most appropriate as the first two were both trained by leading jumps trainer Donald McCain. A 4lb personal best from Ile De Re, and a smart effort from Overturn.

NOTEBOOK
Ile De Re(FR), twice a winner over hurdles for Ian Williams, was last seen finishing down the field in the Imperial Cup. However, he had previously proved he was a Listed-class stayer on the Flat and was well backed in the morning. Given a confident ride, it was clear half a mile out he was the main danger to his stable companion. He stayed on strongly in the straight and could now contest races such as the Ascot Stakes or Northumberland Plate, although he will probably not want the ground too quick. (op 11-1 tchd 12-1)

Overturn(IRE), bidding to repeat last year's success off a 7lb higher mark, got to the front and gained a comparatively uncontested lead for over a circuit. However, he was taken on by Never Can Tell about 6f out and probably ended up racing in earnest too soon, leaving him with nothing in reserve when challenged by his stable companion. He would also have preferred better ground and lost no caste in defeat. (op 8-1 tchd 9-1)

Gulf Of Naples(IRE), who did not make his debut until late July last year, has progressed well since being upped in trip. He had proved himself on soft ground but had to be made plenty of use of to gain a good early pitch from his outside draw. He deserves extra credit for staying in contention throughout and looks sure to pick up a good handicap on the way to becoming a Pattern-class performer. (op 5-1)

Eternal Heart(IRE), a stable companion of the third, is usually a prominent racer but missed the break slightly from the flag start and then was short of room early, forcing him to adopt different tactics. He stayed on steadily in the closing stages and will be a different proposition when things go his way. (op 16-1)

Harrison's Cave, a progressive sort last season, was deliberately held up from his high draw over this longer trip. He was another to run on late and looks worth another try in this sort of contest when the ground is soft. (op 13-2)

Kiama Bay(IRE), trying his longest trip to-date, tracked the pace but came under pressure a good 6f from home and stuck to his task pretty well considering. (op 20-1)

Dazinski got a good pitch just off the pace, but his best from has been on a sound surface and he tired in the ground through the latter stages. (op 28-1)

Never Can Tell(IRE), a dual winner here and successful in last season's Cesarewitch, had a decent draw and was ridden positively. Her rider tried to get past the runner-up fully 6f out but was beaten off and dropped away before the straight, being eased considerably. She will be a different proposition back on a sound surface. Frankie Dettori subsequently reported that the mare tired in the soft ground. Official explanation: jockey said mare tired in soft ground. (op 9-1, tchd 12-1 in a place)

Barbican, progressive at middle-distances last season, had raced over 2m twice recently without making much impact. He tracked the pace but did not appear to get home on the softest ground he has yet encountered. The trainer reported that the gelding was unsuited by the soft ground. Official explanation: trainer said gelding was unsuited by soft ground. (op 25-1)

Shubaat, a lightly raced but progressive 5yo, did not get the best of starts from his good draw and found himself out the back and posted wide for much of the race, not really handling the bends. Dominic Fox reported that the gelding was never travelling and this effort can be ignored. Official explanation: jockey said gelding was never travelling. (op 9-2, tchd 6-1 in a place)

Kazbow(IRE) Official explanation: trainer said gelding had a breathing problem.

1975 STELLAR GROUP H'CAP 5f 16y
3:05 (3:11) (Class 2) (0-105,100) 4-Y-0+ £14,007 (£4,243; £2,121; £1,062; £528) **Stalls** Low

Form RPR

0-06 **1** **Confessional**[19] 1498 5-9-2 **95**....................(be) PaulMulrennan 2 105
(Tim Easterby) *chsd ldrs: nt clr run 2f out: wnt 2nd over 1f out: r.o to ld wl ins fnl f: in command at fin* **5/1**[2]

0-20 **2** ¾ **Foxy Music**[4] 1857 8-8-11 **90**.................... GrahamGibbons 7 97
(Eric Alston) *hung rt thrght: led: rdn over 1f out: hdd wl ins fnl f: kpt on but hld cl home* **9/1**

0-01 **3** 1 ½ **Arctic Feeling (IRE)**[26] 1362 4-8-2 **88**.................... LauraBarry(7) 9 90
(Richard Fahey) *chsd ldrs: rdn and nt qckn over 1f out: r.o ins fnl f* **14/1**

600- **4** nk **Lexi's Hero (IRE)**[214] 6706 4-9-7 **100**....................(p) JamieSpencer 5 101
(Kevin Ryan) *a.p: rdn over 1f out: edgd rt ins fnl f: nt qckn* **5/1**[2]

000- **5** 1 ¼ **Doctor Parkes**[214] 6706 6-8-13 **92**.................... PaulHanagan 11 88+
(Eric Alston) *midfield: rdn over 1f out: styd on ins fnl f: nt gng pce to trble ldrs* **20/1**

00-3 **6** shd **Tax Free (IRE)**[28] 1316 10-9-1 **94**.................... AdrianNicholls 1 90
(David Nicholls) *midfield: sn rdn along: styd on ins fnl f: one pce fnl 100yds: nt pce to trble ldrs* **13/2**[3]

20-5 **7** ½ **Fitz Flyer (IRE)**[38] 1157 6-8-7 **93**.................... ShirleyTeasdale(7) 10 87
(David Nicholls) *prom: pushed along 2f out: no ex fnl 100yds* **20/1**

01-5 **8** ½ **Living It Large (FR)**[14] 1602 5-8-10 **89**.................... JohnFahy 15 81
(Ed de Giles) *midfield: rdn over 1f out: nvr able to chal* **20/1**

0-20 **9** nk **Bathwick Bear (IRE)**[3] 1885 4-8-11 **90**.................... PadraigBeggy 12 81
(David Evans) *midfield: rdn over 1f out: kpt on u.p ins fnl f: nvr able to chal* **16/1**

022- **10** ¾ **Dickie's Lad (IRE)**[145] 7790 4-9-1 **94**....................(t) PhillipMakin 3 82+
(Kevin Ryan) *bdly hmpd s and again after abt 100yds: bhd: nvr able to rcvr* **9/2**[1]

00-0 **11** ¾ **Star Rover (IRE)**[38] 1157 5-8-7 **86**....................(v) AndreaAtzeni 6 72
(David Evans) *midfield: rdn and lost pl 2f out: nvr a threat* **12/1**

0-42 **12** ¾ **Blue Jack**[19] 1498 7-9-1 **94**....................(v) RichardKingscote 14 77
(Tom Dascombe) *missed break: a bhd: nvr on terms* **16/1**

600- **13** ¾ **Partner (IRE)**[269] 5086 6-8-9 **88**....................(b) FrannyNorton 13 68
(Kevin Ryan) *swtchd lft s: a bhd* **25/1**

0220 **14** 7 **Falasteen (IRE)**[88] 525 5-8-11 **90**....................(b) KierenFallon 4 45
(Kevin Ryan) *awkward leaving stalls: racd keenly: a bhd* **16/1**

1m 3.39s (2.39) **Going Correction** +0.725s/f (Yiel) **14 Ran SP% 125.0**
Speed ratings (Par 109): **109,107,105,104,102 102,101,101,100,99 98,97,95,84**
toteswingers:1&2:£8.60, 2&3:£30.80, 1&3:£20.40 CSF £48.60 CT £626.04 TOTE £6.40: £1.90, £3.20, £5.90; EX 57.00 Trifecta £1110.90 Part won. Pool: £1501.34 - 0.50 winning units..
Owner T G & Mrs M E Holdcroft **Bred** Bearstone Stud **Trained** Great Habton, N Yorks

FOCUS
This big-field sprint for mainly smart handicappers was always likely to be run at a strong pace considering some potential front-runners were in low stalls. The form is sound enough among the principals but a number didn't show their form.

NOTEBOOK
Confessional, who handles ease in the ground, settled in just behind from a low draw and, after snatching up for a few strides turning in, stayed on to gain a first victory since September 2010, which came off a mark of 88. He rarely runs badly but will always be up against it when faced with a less-exposed sort. (tchd 11-2)
Foxy Music, out of his depth in the Group 3 Palace House the previous weekend, had plenty of form around here and likes ease in the going. He flew out of stall seven and set a decent gallop despite hanging, but couldn't quite hold on in the final 50 yards. He'll always be one to fear around here, especially on his favoured ground.
Arctic Feeling(IRE), who beat subsequent Group 1 winner Krypton Factor as a 2yo, had slipped down the weights before returning to winning ways off a 4lb lower mark than this at Kempton on his latest start. Another never far away, he kept on to finish third. (op 16-1 tchd 20-1)
Lexi's Hero(IRE), who can go well fresh, showed good pace but didn't quite see it out. He's still above his highest winning mark. (op 6-1)
Doctor Parkes, who'd won first-time up on two of the last three seasons, took this last year off 89 but was never able to quite get on terms here, although he did just enough to hold off the sixth. (op 25-1)
Tax Free(IRE), who is without a handicap victory since 2005, made late headway. (op 7-1 tchd 8-1)
Dickie's Lad(IRE), off since narrowly beaten (winner and third both since won) at Dundalk in December, had done well over the winter according to his trainer and can be rated better than he showed in this, as he was hampered when squeezed up just after leaving the stalls, and then again after another 20-30 yards, the second time was worse than the first. (op 6-1)

1976 GL EVENTS OWEN BROWN MAIDEN STKS 1m 2f 75y
3:40 (3:40) (Class 4) 3-Y-O £6,469 (£1,925; £962; £481)

Form RPR

1 **Father Of Science (IRE)**[10] 1691 3-9-3 0.................... JPO'Brien 11 88+
(A P O'Brien, Ire) *chsd ldrs: wnt 2nd over 2f out: led over 1f out: r.o wl and in command ins fnl f* **5/2**[1]

-4 **2** 2 ¾ **Star For Life (USA)**[60] 869 3-9-3 0....................(p) RyanMoore 7 83
(Mikael Magnusson) *hld up: hdwy into midfield over 3f out: rdn and prog over 1f out: fin wl to take 2nd cl home* **25/1**

432 **3** nk **Fleeting Image**[18] 1532 3-8-5 78.................... NatashaEaton(7) 2 77
(Alan Bailey) *chsd ldr: led over 3f out: rdn and hdd over 1f out: no ex wl ins fnl f: lost 2nd cl home* **8/1**

40-2 **4** 1 ½ **Star Date (IRE)**[38] 1155 3-9-3 78.................... DaneO'Neill 9 79
(Gerard Butler) *in tch: effrt 3f out: rdn whn chsng ldrs over 1f out: styd on same pce ins fnl f* **13/2**

54- **5** 4 **Linkable**[215] 6675 3-9-3 0.................... MichaelHills 5 72
(Charles Hills) *chsd ldrs: effrt over 2f out: one pce ins fnl f* **9/2**[2]

5 **6** 2 **On My Own (TUR)**[18] 1506 3-9-3 0.................... RichardMullen 4 68
(Marcus Tregoning) *midfield: hdwy whn nt clr run over 2f out: rdn over 1f out: one pce ins fnl f* **12/1**

600 **7** 1 ½ **Hyson**[91] 475 3-9-3 69.................... RussKennemore 14 65
(Reg Hollinshead) *bhd: u.p 3f out: kpt on modly ins fnl f: nvr a threat* **100/1**

2224 **8** nk **Devote Myself (IRE)**[46] 1031 3-8-12 70.................... PadraigBeggy 3 59
(David Evans) *in tch: rdn over 3f out: lost pl over 2f out: wknd over 1f out* **25/1**

0- **9** 5 **King Of Paradise (IRE)**[263] 5269 3-9-3 0.................... GrahamGibbons 6 55
(Eric Alston) *led: hdd over 3f out: rdn and wknd over 1f out* **100/1**

0 **10** 2 ¾ **Almost Gemini (IRE)**[16] 1567 3-9-3 0.................... JamieSpencer 1 50
(Roger Varian) *a bhd: sn u.p: nvr on terms* **16/1**

60 **11** 1 **Ultimate Destiny**[28] 1312 3-9-3 0.................... JimCrowley 12 48
(Ralph Beckett) *hld up: struggling 5f out: nvr on terms* **40/1**

422- **12** 11 **Badea**[279] 4714 3-9-3 78.................... FrankieDettori 8 27
(Richard Fahey) *midfield: wknd over 3f out: sn eased whn wl btn* **11/2**[3]

00-2 **13** 1 ¼ **Finity Run (GER)**[7] 1754 3-8-12 0.................... JoeFanning 10 19
(Mark Johnston) *midfield early: niggled along over 6f out: bhd fnl 4f* **11/1**

2m 17.4s (6.20) **Going Correction** +0.725s/f (Yiel) **13 Ran SP% 120.6**
Speed ratings (Par 101): **104,101,101,100,97 95,94,94,90,87 87,78,77**
toteswingers:1&2:£15.90, 2&3:£26.90, 1&3:£7.00 CSF £78.35 TOTE £3.10: £2.00, £6.40, £2.90; EX 72.90 Trifecta £661.00 Part won. Pool: £893.37 - 0.50 winning units..
Owner Mrs John Magnier & Michael Tabor & Derrick Smith **Bred** Tower Bloodstock **Trained** Ballydoyle, Co Tipperary
■ Stewards' Enquiry : Natasha Eaton seven-day ban; used whip above permitted level (23rd-26th, 28th-30th May).

FOCUS
A flag start was used for this maiden. With horses like Mountain High and Harbinger taking this in the previous seven years, both subsequent Group 1 winners, plus Colombian, who went on to finish fourth in the French Derby on his next outing, Father Of Science is one to watch out for during the coming season. Other than him the form is only fair, with the third to sixth all close to their pre-race marks.
Fleeting Image ◆ Official explanation: seven-day ban; used whip above permitted level (
On My Own(TUR) ◆ Official explanation: jockey said colt was denied a clear run.
Badea Official explanation: trainers representative reported gelding was unsuited by soft ground.

1977 IRISH THOROUGHBRED MARKETING CONDITIONS STKS 5f 16y
4:15 (4:15) (Class 3) 3-Y-O+ £9,056 (£2,695; £1,346; £673) **Stalls** Low

Form RPR

320- **1** **Duchess Dora (IRE)**[245] 5827 5-8-13 102.................... TomQueally 6 102
(John Quinn) *racd off the pce: effrt wl over 1f out: hdwy ins fnl f: r.o to ld cl home* **9/4**[1]

0-05 **2** ¾ **Borderlescott**[32] 1219 10-9-4 105.................... DanielTudhope 7 105
(Robin Bastiman) *in tch: effrt over 1f out: led ins fnl furlng: hdd cl home* **13/2**

40-4 **3** 1 ¼ **Shoshoni Wind**[32] 1219 4-8-13 95.................... PhillipMakin 11 95
(Kevin Ryan) *a.p: rdn and nt qckn over 1f out: kpt on ins fnl f: nt quite gng pce of first two* **9/1**

10-6 **4** ¾ **Noble Storm (USA)**[46] 1033 6-9-11 108.................... GrahamGibbons 3 104
(Ed McMahon) *led: rdn over 1f out: hdd ins fnl f: no ex fnl 75yds* **7/2**[3]

1150 **5** 2 **Addictive Dream (IRE)**[39] 1146 5-9-4 112.................... AdrianNicholls 1 90+
(David Nicholls) *s.i.s: sn hmpd: racd in rr: nt clr run over 1f out: kpt on ins fnl f: nt gng pce of ldrs* **3/1**[2]

36-4 **6** 1 ¾ **Bubbly Ballerina**[78] 645 3-8-4 84.................... FrannyNorton 5 83+
(Alan Bailey) *chsd ldrs: effrt on inner over 1f out: styng on whn n.m.r and snatched up ins fnl f: nt rcvr* **20/1**

05/- **7** 3 **Nosedive**[620] 5512 5-9-4 94.................... KierenFallon 2 73
(David Nicholls) *in tch: u.p over 1f out: wl btn ins fnl f* **16/1**

1m 4.1s (3.10) **Going Correction** +0.85s/f (Soft)
WFA 3 from 4yo+ 9lb **7 Ran SP% 112.0**
Speed ratings (Par 107): **109,107,105,104,101 98,93**
toteswingers:1&2:£4.10, 2&3:£7.70, 1&3:£5.40 CSF £16.65 TOTE £3.60: £1.60, £3.00; EX 17.90 Trifecta £199.60 Pool: £1111.59 - 4.12 winning units..
Owner The Clay Family **Bred** Glending Bloodstock **Trained** Settrington, N Yorks
■ Stewards' Enquiry : Graham Gibbons two-day ban; careless riding (23rd, 24th May)

FOCUS
The withdrawal of quite a few runners, including Dinkum Diamond, did weaken this contest a bit, although it still remained competitive. It was the slowest of the three C&D times, understandably on worsening ground, and the form is straightforward enough.

NOTEBOOK
Duchess Dora(IRE), who made a successful reappearance two seasons previously, wasn't hurried by her rider early before being produced towards the middle of the course to get up close to the line. She shapes as though she'll get 6f but all of her seven victories have come over about a furlong shorter. The trainer is hopeful of getting at least a Listed victory into the mare, and she might head to the Investec Dash. (op 3-1)
Borderlescott goes really well here, and has a fairly good record when ridden by a new jockey. He showed plenty of sparkle and, while his Group-winning days might be behind him, a race of this nature is still within his capabilities judged on this. (op 15-2 tchd 8-1)
Shoshoni Wind posted a solid effort against higher-rated rivals, and did as well as could have been expected at the weights. (op 12-1)
Noble Storm(USA) did too much in front when below form on his reappearance in March and again here. Although he has won in soft, he'll be far more interesting if continuing to race like this on a fast turf surface. (op 3-1)
Addictive Dream(IRE) wasn't quickly into stride on his return to Britain, after showing good form in Dubai, but had at least two tries to get through in the home straight and found the way blocked both times. Ideally, he wants a quicker surface but one got the impression he wouldn't have been too far away with a clear passage. (tchd 11-4 and 54-1 in a place)
Bubbly Ballerina, back on turf, was keeping on really well up the inside rail when hampered by Noble Storm. She is a good few lengths better than her finishing position suggests. (op 16-1)

1978 MERSEYRAIL DAY SAVER TICKET H'CAP 1m 4f 66y
4:45 (4:47) (Class 3) (0-95,88) 3-Y-O £9,056 (£2,695; £1,346; £673) **Stalls** Low

Form RPR

4-1 **1** **Rosslyn Castle**[23] 1414 3-9-6 **87**.................... JamesDoyle 12 98+
(Roger Charlton) *dwlt: hld up in last pl: hdwy over 3f out: led over 1f out: r.o wl to stretch clr ins fnl f* **7/1**[3]

5-1 **2** 3 ¼ **Gabrial The Great (IRE)**[25] 1385 3-9-1 **82**.................... JamieSpencer 8 88+
(Michael Bell) *hld up: hdwy on outer 4f out: chalng over 1f out: unable to go w wnr ins fnl f* **7/2**[2]

15-6 **3** 1 **Martin Chuzzlewit (IRE)**[20] 1473 3-9-7 **88**.................... RyanMoore 11 92
(Sir Michael Stoute) *led for 1f: remained prom: regained ld jst over 2f out: hdd over 1f out: kpt on u.p but hld ins fnl f* **15/2**

12-5 **4** 1 ¾ **Montaser (IRE)**[38] 1160 3-8-13 **80**.................... FrankieDettori 2 81+
(David Simcock) *chsd ldrs: bmpd over 2f out: sn rdn: ev ch over 1f out: one pce ins fnl f* **11/4**[1]

34-1 **5** ½ **Juno The Muffinman (IRE)**[43] 1055 3-8-8 **75**....................(b[1]) KierenFallon 4 76
(Tom Dascombe) *racd keenly: led after 1f: hdd jst over 2f out: no ex 1f out* **16/1**

03-1 **6** 1 **Rapid Heat Lad (IRE)**[74] 709 3-8-7 **74** ow1.................... GrahamGibbons 10 73
(Reg Hollinshead) *midfield: lost pl over 4f out: kpt on u.p over 1f out: nvr able to trble ldrs* **33/1**

1 **7** nk **Bob's World**[40] 1113 3-8-13 **80**.................... FrannyNorton 5 79+
(Jennie Candlish) *hld up: swtchd rt over 1f out: nvr on terms w ldrs* **16/1**

21- **8** 6 **Third Half**[180] 7367 3-8-10 **77**.................... RichardKingscote 1 66
(Tom Dascombe) *midfield: rdn 3f out: wknd 2f out* **10/1**

21-3 **9** 20 **Cherry Street**[28] 1302 3-9-3 **84**.................... JimmyFortune 6 42
(Andrew Balding) *chsd ldrs tl rdn and wknd over 2f out: eased whn wl btn ins fnl f* **9/1**

0122 **10** 15 **Bordoni (USA)**[14] 1597 3-9-7 **88**.................... JoeFanning 3 23
(Mark Johnston) *chsd ldrs tl rdn and wknd over 3f out* **11/1**

31-0 **11** *37* **Sir Trevor (IRE)**[21] 1440 3-8-5 **75**................................ RossAtkinson(3) 9
(Tom Dascombe) *hld up: hdwy over 4f out: rdn and wknd over 3f out: t.o*
66/1

2m 49.26s (10.76) **Going Correction** +0.85s/f (Soft) **11** Ran SP% **116.8**
Speed ratings (Par 103): **98,95,95,94,93 93,92,88,75,65 40**
toteswingers:1&2:£4.40, 2&3:£5.80, 1&3:£7.90 CSF £31.43 CT £191.87 TOTE £8.40: £2.90, £2.10, £2.30; EX 23.60 Trifecta £153.00 Pool: £1251.68 - 6.05 winning units..
Owner Lady Rothschild **Bred** Carwell Equities Ltd **Trained** Beckhampton, Wilts

FOCUS

Subsequent Group horses such as Brown Panther (2011) and Allied Powers (2008) have taken this, so the future looks bright for the winner, who improved again. Good form, despite it being run on the worst of the ground.

NOTEBOOK

Rosslyn Castle ♦ finished strongly when landing a 1m2f Windsor maiden last month and again here after being dropped out the back. He is not the biggest but this was a visually very impressive performance and his entry in the Group 2 King Edward VII Stakes at Royal Ascot is definitely justified. It's difficult to believe that he won't have a victory in Pattern company before the end of the year. (op 11-2)

Gabrial The Great(IRE) ♦, who's in the Derby, moved like a smart sort here. His jockey seemed keen not to hit the front too early, but when they did reach the front, the winner was hitting top gear and swept past. A lovely big type, he is a serious prospect if maintaining his progress and could still make an impact at handicap level if not harshly treated for this. (op 9-2)

Martin Chuzzlewit(IRE) ran below expectations at Newmarket on his reappearance upped to 1m2f, but did better here over further again after racing prominently. The handicapper appears to have him about right, so much depends whether he has more to offer on faster ground. (op 8-1, tchd 9-1 in a place)

Montaser(IRE) was still travelling okay when hemmed in by Gabrial The Great turning in, which was enough to stop his momentum. He can be given another chance, especially on better going. (op 7-2, tchd 4-1 in a place)

Juno The Muffinman(IRE), with headgear applied for the first time, had his own way out in front and didn't get home after being a bit keen. (op 12-1)

Bob's World ♦, the 20-1 winner of a 1m4f Wolverhampton maiden in March that has worked out nicely, is much better than his final position considering he got stopped a few times when the race took shape. (op 11-1)

Third Half gave the impression he wasn't in love with the underfoot conditions, and is another who'll be better judged on faster ground. (op 14-1)

T/Jkpt: Not won. T/Plt: £110.00 to a £1 stake. Pool of £162,357.56 - 1,076.72 winning tickets. T/Qpdt: £52.20 to a £1 stake. Pool of £8,696.12 123.27 winning tickets DO

1919 KEMPTON (A.W) (R-H)

Wednesday, May 9

OFFICIAL GOING: Standard

Wind: Fresh, half behind Weather: Overcast, drizzly

1979 WIN BIG WITH BETDAQ MULTIPLES H'CAP 1m (P)

5:50 (8:12) (Class 6) (0-60,60) 3-Y-O **£1,617** (£481; £240; £120) **Stalls** Low

Form RPR

4660 **1** **Moment In The Sun**[15] 1590 3-9-4 **57**...................(b) MickaelBarzalona 9 63
(David Flood) *hld up in midfield: t.k.h fr 1/2-way: prog over 2f out: shkn up to ld 1f out: cajoled along to hold on nr fin* **16/1**

0-50 **2** *½* **Song Of Joy (IRE)**[30] 1260 3-9-4 **57**.. AdamKirby 12 62
(Paul D'Arcy) *hld up in last trio: prog over 2f out: hrd rdn over 1f out: wnt 2nd ins fnl f: clsd on wnr fin* **20/1**

163 **3** *1 ½* **Sudden Wish (IRE)**[44] 1046 3-9-2 **55**............................ NickyMackay 7 57
(Alan Bailey) *hld up towards rr: prog on inner over 2f out: drvn over 1f out: styd on but nvr gng pce to chal* **5/2**[1]

06-6 **4** *¾* **Titus Bolt (IRE)**[26] 1359 3-9-6 **59**....................................... PatCosgrave 3 59
(Jim Boyle) *prom: rdn to dispute 2nd over 2f out: nt qckn wl over 1f out: styd on* **10/3**[2]

0-53 **5** *1 ¼* **Compton Target (IRE)**[21] 1445 3-9-0 **60**..............(t) NicoleNordblad(7) 2 57
(Hans Adielsson) *t.k.h: led after 1f: rdn 2f out: hdd and fdd 1f out* **8/1**

00-4 **6** *1* **Represent (IRE)**[26] 1365 3-9-2 **60**........................... CharlesBishop(5) 1 55
(Mick Channon) *led 1f: chsd ldr: rdn over 2f out: upsides jst over 1f out: wknd ins fnl f* **9/1**

2-44 **7** *2 ½* **Speedi Mouse**[92] 466 3-9-7 **60**................................. RichardHughes 11 49
(Philip McBride) *hld up and sn in last: rdn and sme prog on outer 2f out: rchd 7th 1f out but no ch w ldrs: eased last 100yds* **14/1**

40-6 **8** *1 ½* **Saint Irene**[20] 1486 3-9-7 **60**... FergusSweeney 4 45
(Michael Blanshard) *t.k.h: hld up in midfield: rdn and no prog over 2f out: wl btn over 1f out* **20/1**

260- **9** *hd* **Shomberg**[197] 7080 3-9-7 **60**....................................... SebSanders 10 45
(Mark H Tompkins) *racd wd: in tch: rdn and no prog over 2f out: wl btn over 1f out* **11/2**[3]

060- **10** *2 ¼* **Tazweed (IRE)**[168] 7521 3-8-12 **58**.................... JeanVanOvermeire(7) 13 38
(Roger Varian) *racd wd: prom tl pushed along and wknd over 2f out* **14/1**

005- **11** *8* **Retromania (IRE)**[196] 7094 3-9-6 **59**.................................. BrettDoyle 8 20
(John Best) *dwlt: a in last trio: rdn and struggling 3f out* **33/1**

560 **12** *21* **Handy Chat (IRE)**[14] 1606 3-9-1 **57**..........................(p) PatrickHills(3) 14
(Des Donovan) *prom tl wknd rapidly 3f out: t.o* **66/1**

1m 40.76s (0.96) **Going Correction** -0.125s/f (Stan) **12** Ran SP% **121.3**
Speed ratings (Par 97): **90,89,88,87,86 85,82,81,80,78 70,49**
toteswingers:1&2:£23.50, 2&3:£12.60, 1&3:£10.60 CSF £306.79 CT £1096.37 TOTE £14.60: £6.00, £8.00, £1.10; EX 242.90 Trifecta £361.00 Pool: £492.75 - 1.01 winning units..
Owner Flood Family Racing Limited **Bred** Foursome Thoroughbreds **Trained** Exning, Suffolk

FOCUS

This was little better than selling standard, but the in-form third sets a fair standard for the grade. The pace was ordinary.

1980 BACK OR LAY BETDAQ.COM FILLIES' H'CAP 1m (P)

6:20 (8:12) (Class 5) (0-70,70) 4-Y-O+ **£2,264** (£673; £336; £168) **Stalls** Low

Form RPR

12-1 **1** **Love Your Looks**[23] 1423 4-9-7 **70**................................ TonyCulhane 3 84+
(Mike Murphy) *sn trckd ldr: led wl over 2f out and sn pushed clr: urged along and styd on fr over 1f out: unchal* **13/8**[1]

100- **2** *5* **Pearl Opera**[189] 7228 4-8-9 **58**...................................... TadhgO'Shea 4 60
(Denis Coakley) *hld up in tch: effrt over 2f out: disp 2nd fr over 1f out: no imp on wnr* **13/2**

106- **3** *nk* **Ashkalara**[206] 6888 5-8-12 **61**... IanMongan 6 62
(Stuart Howe) *t.k.h early: rdn in 5th sn after 1/2-way and struggling: kpt on fr over 1f out to take 3rd last stride* **15/2**

10-2 **4** *shd* **Signora Frasi (IRE)**[14] 1611 7-8-13 **62**....................... FergusSweeney 5 63
(Tony Newcombe) *restrained into last: prog over 2f out: rdn to dispute 2nd over 1f out: no imp and lost in battle for pls nr fin* **11/2**

500- **5** *8* **Sasheen**[133] 7895 5-8-10 **64**..(p) RaulDaSilva(5) 1 46
(Jeremy Gask) *led to wl over 2f out: lost 2nd and wknd qckly over 1f out* **9/2**[2]

4165 **6** *21* **Inpursuitoffreedom**[26] 1358 5-9-3 **66**.......................(v) RichardHughes 7
(Philip McBride) *sweating: prom tl wknd rapidly over 2f out: t.o* **5/1**[3]

1m 38.88s (-0.92) **Going Correction** -0.125s/f (Stan) **6** Ran SP% **113.4**
Speed ratings (Par 100): **99,94,93,93,85 64**
toteswingers:1&2:£2.70, 2&3:£8.30, 1&3:£3.30 CSF £13.01 CT £60.74 TOTE £3.10: £1.90, £1.10; EX 16.40 Trifecta £113.90 Pool: £423.32 - 2.75 winning units..
Owner M Murphy **Bred** Ellis Stud And Bellow Hill Stud **Trained** Westoning, Beds

FOCUS

This was a fair-to-middling race for the surface, but the winner will have to take a step up in grade when re-handicapped. There are doubts over the form, with the second the best guide.

Inpursuitoffreedom Official explanation: jockey said mare lost her action.

1981 BETDAQ MOBILE APPS MEDIAN AUCTION MAIDEN STKS 1m 3f (P)

6:55 (8:12) (Class 5) 3-5-Y-O **£2,264** (£673; £336; £168) **Stalls** Low

Form RPR

25-5 **1** **Ballyheigue (IRE)**[18] 1518 3-8-11 71..............................(b[1]) ShaneKelly 2 78
(Brian Meehan) *kpt away fr rest at s: mde all and set str pce: breather 1/2-way: kicked on again over 3f out: wandered u.p fnl 2f: hrd pressed fr over 1f out: hld on gamely* **13/2**

4 **2** *hd* **Savida (IRE)**[23] 1415 3-8-6 0.. DavidProbert 8 73
(Sir Michael Stoute) *prom: chsd wnr 1/2-way: drvn over 2f out: clsd to chal over 1f out: upsides ins fnl f: could nt go past nr fin* **11/2**[2]

2-33 **3** *10* **Viola Da Gamba (IRE)**[35] 1180 3-8-3 67............... HarryBentley(3) 1 55
(William Knight) *prom: chsd wnr after 3f to 1/2-way: rdn over 3f out: lft bhd fr 2f out* **6/1**[3]

32 **4** *1 ½* **Mister Fizz**[86] 546 4-9-9 0.. MatthewCosham(5) 6 58
(Edward Bevan) *nt gng wl in rr and pushed along: sme prog 1/2-way: drvn over 3f out: kpt on one pce to take 4th fnl f* **6/1**[3]

03-4 **5** *2 ½* **Totom Chief**[28] 1301 3-8-11 70.......................... JamieGoldstein 13 52
(Gay Kelleway) *chsd ldrs: rdn in 5th over 3f out: effrt u.p over 2f out: fdd fnl f* **8/1**

3 **6** *½* **Plus Fours (USA)**[51] 959 3-8-11 0...........................(p) RichardHughes 5 52
(Amanda Perrett) *chsd wnr 3f: drvn in 4th over 3f out: no imp 2f out: fdd* **7/2**[1]

04 **7** *nk* **Eanans Bay (IRE)**[8] 1724 3-8-11 0.................................. SebSanders 12 53
(Mark H Tompkins) *settled towards rr: pushed along over 3f out: no ch but keeping on steadily to join battle for 4th whn squeezed out 1f out* **33/1**

0 **8** *2 ¼* **Imperial Ruby**[18] 1511 3-8-11 0.................................. SamHitchcott 11 47
(Mick Channon) *dwlt: wl in rr: effrt over 4f out: rdn to latch on to chsng pce 2f out: wknd fnl f* **33/1**

6 **9** *6* **Trulee Scrumptious**[15] 1589 3-8-1 0......................... RosieJessop(5) 10 31
(Peter Charalambous) *a wl in rr: no ch over 2f out* **33/1**

10 *3 ¼* **Black Motive** 3-8-12 0 ow1.. StevieDonohoe 14 31
(Michael Bell) *rel to r and lft 15 l: ct up at bk of field after 4f: wknd 3f out* **16/1**

11 *3 ½* **Missus Mills (IRE)** 3-8-6 0...................................... MickaelBarzalona 4 19
(George Baker) *in tch in midfield: rdn in 6th over 3f out: no prog on inner 2f out: wknd rapidly and eased* **16/1**

0-30 **12** *8* **Leading Star**[48] 993 3-8-3 45... RyanPowell(3) 9
(Michael Madgwick) *hld up: sltly impeded after 2f: a wl in rr: t.o* **66/1**

/0- **P** **Balesteem**[251] 5639 5-10-0 0... IanMongan 3
(Clifford Lines) *hld up in midfield: lost action and p.u over 7f out* **14/1**

2m 19.25s (-2.65) **Going Correction** -0.125s/f (Stan)
WFA 3 from 4yo+ 17lb **13** Ran SP% **119.4**
Speed ratings (Par 103): **104,103,96,95,93 93,93,91,87,84 82,76,**
toteswingers:1&2:£12.60, 2&3:£6.00, 1&3:£5.50 CSF £41.03 TOTE £8.70: £3.00, £2.10, £3.10; EX 60.10 Trifecta £274.90 Pool: £460.78 - 1.24 winning units..
Owner A Bengough,P O'Sullivan,KWB Bloodstock **Bred** Gerry Flannery Developments **Trained** Manton, Wilts

FOCUS

The winner made all, but the pace was fair enough in a maiden which should turn out some future winners when they are running over their best distances. The first two came clear and the form could be worth more at face value.

Balesteem Official explanation: vet said gelding pulled up lame

1982 BETDAQ CASINO GAMES H'CAP 1m 3f (P)

7:30 (8:12) (Class 6) (0-65,65) 3-Y-O **£1,617** (£481; £240; £120) **Stalls** Low

Form RPR

00-3 **1** **Hector's Chance**[28] 1301 3-9-2 **60**.............................. RichardHughes 3 67
(Heather Main) *prom: chsd ldr over 3f out: drvn to cl 2f out: led ent fnl f: styd on wl* **11/1**

0-01 **2** *2* **Daring Damsel (IRE)**[21] 1443 3-9-7 **65**..................(b) StevieDonohoe 12 68
(Paul Cole) *led: kicked on 4f out: hrd pressed over 1f out: hdd ent fnl f: jst hld on for 2nd* **20/1**

00-0 **3** *nk* **Silver Samba**[28] 1312 3-9-3 **61**....................................... DavidProbert 4 63+
(Andrew Balding) *hld up in midfield: gng bttr than many over 3f out: shkn up and prog whn nt clr run wl over 1f out: r.o ins fnl f: nrly snatched 2nd* **8/1**

25-0 **4** *shd* **Dovils Date**[16] 1568 3-9-4 **62**.. JamesMillman 5 64
(Rod Millman) *s.s: wl in rr: plld out and effrt over 2f out: gd prog over 1f out: r.o and nrly snatched 2nd* **25/1**

0-25 **5** *1 ¾* **Lady Romanza (IRE)**[16] 1568 3-9-0 **63**................ JemmaMarshall(5) 10 62
(Brendan Powell) *chsd ldr 3f: styd handy: rdn over 3f out: wnt 3rd over 1f out on inner: no imp and lost pl last 100yds* **33/1**

-053 **6** *1 ½* **Corn Maiden**[30] 1267 3-8-2 **53**....................................... LewisWalsh(7) 6 49
(Phil McEntee) *chsd ldr after 3f tl after 5f: urged along over 2f out: fdd fnl f* **50/1**

-642 **7** *hd* **Kelpie Blitz (IRE)**[29] 1288 3-9-6 **64**.............................. GeorgeBaker 11 60
(Seamus Durack) *hld up towards rr: effrt gng bttr than most 3f out: prog to dispute 3rd over 1f out but no imp: fdd ins fnl f* **9/2**[2]

-313 **8** *1 ¾* **Smart Affair**[8] 1740 3-8-8 **52**.. LiamJones 8 45
(Alan Bailey) *sn in last and nt gng that wl: urged along on outer 4f out: racd awkwardly but passed wkng rivals fnl 2f* **20/1**

0-42 **9** *1* **Rocco Breeze (IRE)**[21] 1448 3-8-2 **51**............................ RaulDaSilva(5) 9 42
(Philip McBride) *prom on inner: rdn over 3f out: steadily fdd fr over 2f out* **10/1**

0441 **10** *½* **Foster's Road**[42] 1062 3-9-4 **62**...................................... MartinHarley 1 52
(Mick Channon) *hld up in rr: shkn up 3f out: jst pushed along fnl 2f and nvr involved* **8/1**

0632 **11** *1 ½* **Chankillo**[30] 1267 3-9-5 **63**.. SebSanders 2 51
(Mark H Tompkins) *hld up in last pair: stl there 3f out: jst pushed along after: nvr remotely involved* **8/1**

066 **12** *2 ¾* **Arctic Galaxy (CAN)**[16] 1567 3-9-7 **65** .... WilliamBuick 14 48
(John Gosden) *s.i.s: racd wd towards rr: sme prog on outer over 3f out: rdn and btn over 2f out: fdd* **4/1**[1]

656- **13** *nk* **Zamarelle**[240] 6000 3-9-2 **63** .... HarryBentley(3) 7 45
(Roger Charlton) *wl in tch in midfield: rdn over 3f out: wknd over 2f out* **6/1**[3]

0-20 **14** *7* **Always Ends Well (IRE)**[20] 1486 3-9-4 **62** .... MircoDemuro 13 31
(Mark Johnston) *racd wd: prog to chse ldr after 5f to over 3f out: wknd v rapidly over 1f out* **20/1**

2m 20.96s (-0.94) **Going Correction** -0.125s/f (Stan) **14** Ran SP% **126.3**
Speed ratings (Par 97): **98,96,96,96,94 93,93,92,91,91 90,88,88,82**
toteswingers:1&2:£111.60, 2&3:£104.00, 1&3:£25.60 CSF £224.75 CT £1880.39 TOTE £15.00: £3.80, £5.40, £1.30; EX 386.90 Trifecta £404.20 Part won. Pool: £546.26 - 0.62 winning units..
Owner M Scott Russell **Bred** Wickham Stud **Trained** Kingston Lisle, Oxon

FOCUS
There was a solid gallop for this modest but interesting handicap in which potential improvers finished first, third and fourth. The form is only ordinary, however.

1983 RACING PLUS SPONSORS OF MILLWALL F.C. H'CAP 6f (P)
8:00 (8:12) (Class 4) (0-85,83) 3-Y-O **£4,528** (£1,010; £1,010; £336) **Stalls** Low

Form RPR
01- **1** **Priceless Jewel**[201] 6992 3-9-5 **81** .... GeorgeBaker 5 91+
(Roger Charlton) *hld up in rr: stdy prog over 2f out: produced w wl-timed run to ld last 100yds: readily* **3/1**[3]

341- **2** *½* **Safari Sunseeker (IRE)**[130] 7938 3-9-0 **76** .... JimCrowley 1 84
(William Knight) *chsd ldr 1f: styd prom: rdn to ld over 1f out: hung lft fnl f: hdd last 100yds* **14/1**

1-36 **2** *dht* **Galician**[32] 1217 3-9-0 **76** .... MircoDemuro 9 84
(Mark Johnston) *trckd ldrs on outer: urged along 2f out: brought to chal fnl f: nt qckn* **8/1**

34-2 **4** *3* **Uprise**[9] 1721 3-8-11 **73** .... WilliamBuick 4 72
(Sir Michael Stoute) *trckd ldrs: rdn and nt qckn over 2f out: one pce and no threat to ldrs over 1f out* **11/4**[2]

3420 **5** *nse* **Adranian (IRE)**[9] 1721 3-9-2 **78** ....(v) MartinDwyer 7 77
(David C Griffiths) *awkward s: chsd ldr after 1f: rdn to chal 2f out: nt qckn and hld whn bdly bmpd last 150yds* **33/1**

31-0 **6** *hd* **Sheikh The Reins (IRE)**[16] 1565 3-9-3 **79** .... LiamJones 6 77
(John Best) *led: rdn and hdd over 1f out: hld whn hmpd last 150yds* **25/1**

10-1 **7** *¾* **Larwood (IRE)**[21] 1445 3-9-3 **79** .... DaneO'Neill 2 75
(Henry Candy) *t.k.h: hld up in rr: rdn over 2f out: racd awkwardly and no imp on ldrs* **2/1**[1]

00-5 **8** *¾* **Mister Musicmaster**[12] 1644 3-9-7 **83** .... JamesMillman 3 76
(Rod Millman) *sn pushed along and mostly last: racd awkwardly but plugged on fnl f: nvr a threat* **50/1**

21-5 **9** *8* **Gabbiano**[19] 1493 3-9-4 **80** .... TonyCulhane 8 48
(Jeremy Gask) *plld hrd: racd wd: in tch tl wknd qckly 2f out* **16/1**

1m 12.25s (-0.85) **Going Correction** -0.125s/f (Stan) **9** Ran SP% **117.4**
Speed ratings (Par 101): **100,99,99,95,95 95,94,93,82**toteswingers:1&G £6.90, 1&SS £7.40, G&SS £5.30.PL: Galician £1.10 Safari Sunseeker £2.20 EX: Priceless Jewel/Galician £19.30 Priceless Jewel/ Safari Sunseeker £24.80 CSF: PJ/G £13.60 PJ/SS £21.77 TRI: PJ/G/SS £148.14 PJ/SS/G £156.23 TOTE £6.30: £1.90, £0.27, £Owner, £B E NielsenBred Bjorn E Nielsen Trifecta £Trained Beckhampton, Wilts.

FOCUS
A decent race for the money, with some useful second-season types contesting it. The winner improved on his maiden win.
Gabbiano Official explanation: jockey said gelding ran too freely.

1984 SKYSPORTS.COM H'CAP 1m 4f (P)
8:30 (8:30) (Class 6) (0-65,65) 4-Y-O+ **£1,617** (£481; £240; £120) **Stalls** Centre

Form RPR
-010 **1** **Whodathought (IRE)**[56] 891 4-9-6 **64** ....(b) AdamKirby 8 73
(Paul Rich) *wl in rr: pushed along briefly after 3f: rdn fr 4f out: prog u.p over 2f out: chsd ldr over 1f out: clsd to ld last 100yds: sn clr* **8/1**[3]

4600 **2** *1 ¾* **Bennelong**[76] 672 6-9-7 **65** .... AmirQuinn 2 71+
(Richard Rowe) *trckd ldrs: smooth prog to ld over 2f out: 2 l clr w rdr looking arnd over 1f out: drvn frntically and hdd last 100yds: nt qckn* **10/1**

2-42 **3** *nk* **Shy**[27] 1339 7-9-2 **60** ....(b) JamesMillman 6 66
(Rod Millman) *settled in midfield: pushed along over 4f out: lost pl steadily and in last trio 3f out: rdn and gd prog over 1f out: r.o and nrly snatched 2nd* **12/1**

0-65 **4** *3 ¾* **Minstrel Lad**[28] 1301 4-8-6 **53** .... SimonPearce(3) 1 53+
(Lydia Pearce) *hld up in last trio: prog on inner whn n.m.r at least twice arnd 2f out: styd on but nt gng pce to threaten ldrs* **25/1**

3602 **5** *1 ¼* **Karate (IRE)**[9] 1702 4-8-4 **55** ....(t) NicoleNordblad(7) 14 53
(Hans Adielsson) *dropped in fr wd draw and hld up in last: effrt on outer over 2f out: styd on but nvr a threat* **14/1**

01-2 **6** *¾* **Grandad Mac**[29] 1286 4-9-3 **61** .... RichardHughes 10 58
(Jane Chapple-Hyam) *pressed ldrs: rdn over 3f out: chal and upsides over 2f out: chsd ldr to over 1f out: wknd and eased* **11/4**[1]

2-00 **7** *3* **Edgware Road**[50] 818 4-9-3 **64** .... SophieDoyle(3) 3 56
(Paul Rich) *disp ld 2f: styd prom: lost pl over 2f out: steadily fdd* **8/1**[3]

1122 **8** *shd* **Holden Eagle**[27] 1338 7-9-0 **65** .... IanBurns(7) 11 57
(Tony Newcombe) *rapid prog on outer to ld after 2f: urged along and hdd over 2f out: wknd and edgd rt over 1f out* **7/1**[2]

-604 **9** *2* **Bashama**[23] 1423 4-8-12 **56** .... DavidProbert 5 44
(Nikki Evans) *a in rr and nt gng wl early: effrt u.p over 2f out: nvr a factor* **25/1**

0306 **10** *2 ¾* **Gower Rules (IRE)**[2] 1919 4-9-0 **58** .... KieranO'Neill 4 42
(John Bridger) *disp ld for 2f: pressed new ldr tl over 2f out: wknd* **8/1**[3]

006- **11** *7* **Camera Shy (IRE)**[175] 7441 8-9-2 **60** .... PatCosgrave 9 33
(Kevin Morgan) *settled in midfield: prog on outer over 4f out to press ldrs over 3f out: upsides over 2f out: wknd rapidly over 1f out* **12/1**

-203 **12** *1* **Musashi (IRE)**[48] 915 7-8-10 **54** ....(b) JimCrowley 13 25
(Laura Mongan) *a towards rr: struggling u.p over 2f out: sltly checked over 1f out: wknd* **20/1**

6106 **13** *36* **Sumani (FR)**[34] 1205 6-9-4 **62** .... SebSanders 12
(Simon Dow) *chsd ldrs on outer: rdn over 4f out: wknd rapidly over 3f out: t.o* **11/1**

2m 32.72s (-1.78) **Going Correction** -0.125s/f (Stan) **13** Ran SP% **124.4**
Speed ratings (Par 101): **100,98,98,96,95 94,92,92,91,89 84,84,60**
toteswingers:1&2:£21.90, 2&3:£19.00, 1&3:£19.50 CSF £87.07 CT £968.30 TOTE £5.20: £1.30, £6.50, £4.50; EX 158.30 TRIFECTA Not won..
Owner L M Power **Bred** Meadowlands Stud **Trained** Newport, Gwent

FOCUS
This was routine Polytrack fare, run at a medium gallop. The pace rather collapsed and four of the first five came from the back.

1985 SKYSPORTS.COM RACING CLASSIFIED STKS 7f (P)
9:00 (9:01) (Class 5) 3-Y-O **£2,264** (£673; £336; £168) **Stalls** Low

Form RPR
234- **1** **Obliteright (IRE)**[175] 7431 3-9-0 **75** .... JimCrowley 1 89+
(William Knight) *trckd ldng pair: led on inner over 1f out and sn qcknd clr: eased last 100yds: impressive* **13/2**

-212 **2** *4 ½* **Mayo Lad (IRE)**[13] 1622 3-9-0 **75** .... RichardHughes 3 75
(Richard Hannon) *hld up bhd ldrs: sltly impeded after 1f: effrt 2f out: drvn and styd on to take 2nd last 150yds: no ch w wnr* **3/1**[1]

40-3 **3** *¾* **Sandbetweenourtoes (IRE)**[25] 1377 3-9-0 **75** .... ShaneKelly 0 73
(Brian Meehan) *led: rdn and hdd over 1f out: no ch w wnr: one pce and lost 2nd last 150yds* **4/1**[2]

026- **4** *1 ¾* **Amy Dorrit**[181] 7343 3-9-0 **75** .... WilliamBuick 2 67
(John Gosden) *trckd ldrs: rdn and outpcd fr 2f out: kpt on same pce after* **10/1**

10-3 **5** *¾* **Serene Oasis (IRE)**[23] 1412 3-8-9 **75** .... CharlesBishop(5) 9 65
(Mick Channon) *trckd ldrs: drvn and outpcd fr 2f out: one pce after* **33/1**

14- **6** *½* **Relentless Harry (IRE)**[219] 6590 3-9-0 **75** ....(t) MickaelBarzalona 4 63
(George Baker) *plld hrd and hld up in last trio: rdn over 2f out: kpt on ins fnl f: no ch* **8/1**

1 **7** *nk* **Perfect Fantasy (IRE)**[69] 742 3-9-0 **72** .... JohnFahy 6 62
(Clive Cox) *reluctant to enter stalls: dwlt: hld up in last: drvn and sme prog 2f out: no hdwy fnl f* **7/1**

1- **8** *4* **Slewtoo**[140] 7838 3-9-0 **72** .... AdamKirby 12 49
(Marco Botti) *stdd s fr wd draw: hld up in last trio: drvn and no prog 2f out: wknd over 1f out* **6/1**[3]

323- **9** *2 ½* **Daunt (IRE)**[244] 5840 3-8-11 **73** .... SeanLevey(3) 10 41+
(Richard Hannon) *plld hrd and sn w ldr: wknd rapidly 2f out* **12/1**

02-6 **10** *11* **Toffee Tart**[21] 1449 3-9-0 **75** .... SebSanders 7
(J W Hills) *racd wd: in tch: wknd rapidly sn after 1/2-way: t.o* **25/1**

1m 24.69s (-1.31) **Going Correction** -0.125s/f (Stan) **10** Ran SP% **119.8**
Speed ratings (Par 99): **102,96,96,94,93 92,92,87,84,72**
toteswingers:1&2:£7.30, 2&3:£3.30, 1&3:£6.40 CSF £27.09 TOTE £3.20: £1.10, £1.90, £2.20; EX 28.50 Trifecta £189.90 Pool: £900.88 - 3.51 winning units..
Owner The Oil Men Partnership **Bred** Lodge Park Stud **Trained** Patching, W Sussex

FOCUS
This wasn't a bad race, with some potential improvers in the line-up, so it was a particularly good effort from the winner.
Daunt(IRE) Official explanation: jockey said colt ran too freely.
T/Plt: £777.70 to a £1 stake. Pool of £63,286.04 - 59.40 winning tickets. T/Qpdt: £136.70 to a £1 stake. Pool of £5,619.08 - 30.40 winning tickets. JN

1955 SOUTHWELL (L-H)
Wednesday, May 9

OFFICIAL GOING: Standard
Wind: Virtually nil Weather: Cloudy

1986 WORLD HORSE WELFARE CELEBRATES 85 YEARS MAIDEN STKS 5f (F)
1:55 (1:55) (Class 5) 3-Y-O+ **£2,385** (£704; £352) **Stalls** High

Form RPR
50-0 **1** **Orders From Rome (IRE)**[21] 1452 3-8-10 **80** .... AmyScott(5) 5 71
(Eve Johnson Houghton) *trckd ldrs: hdwy 1/2-way and sn cl up: rdn to ld and hung lft ent fnl f: kpt on* **1/1**[1]

566 **2** *1* **Demora**[25] 1389 3-8-10 **52** .... NeilChalmers 6 63
(Michael Appleby) *cl up: led over 2f out: rdn wl over 1f out: hdd ent fnl f: kpt on same pce* **28/1**

2362 **3** *1 ½* **Trail Of Tears (IRE)**[8] 1730 3-8-10 **66** ....(p) RobertHavlin 9 57
(John Gosden) *racd nr stands' rail: a.p: rdn along wl over 1f out: kpt on same pce* **5/2**[2]

60 **4** *1* **Noble Bounty**[18] 1521 3-8-12 **0** .... JulieBurke(3) 3 59
(Kevin Ryan) *cl up on outer: pushed along over 2f out: rdn wl over 1f out: sn one pce* **20/1**

-354 **5** *1 ¼* **Economic Crisis (IRE)**[14] 1599 3-8-3 **53** .... MatthewHopkins(7) 4 49
(Alan Berry) *dwlt and in rr: hdwy 2f out: sn rdn and kpt on fnl f: nrest at fin* **12/1**

53-6 **6** *¾* **Itum**[8] 1734 5-9-10 **52** .... TomMcLaughlin 8 55
(Christine Dunnett) *slt ld: rdn along 1/2-way: hdd over 2f out: grad wknd fr over 1f out* **9/1**[3]

0 **7** *2 ¼* **Beaurepaire Kid**[16] 1560 3-9-1 **0** .... LeeNewman 2 43
(David Barron) *chsd ldrs: rdn along over 2f out: sn wknd* **10/1**

0-0 **8** *2 ¼* **Azamara Star**[8] 1739 3-8-10 **0** .... MartinLane 1 30
(Derek Shaw) *dwlt: a in rr* **100/1**

1m 0.45s (0.75) **Going Correction** +0.125s/f (Slow)
WFA 3 from 4yo+ 9lb **8** Ran SP% **114.6**
Speed ratings (Par 103): **99,97,95,93,91 90,86,83**
toteswingers:1&2:£8.00, 2&3:£16.50, 1&3:£1.10 CSF £38.13 TOTE £1.50: £1.10, £5.20, £1.10; EX 38.20.
Owner G C Stevens **Bred** Bgd Breeders **Trained** Blewbury, Oxon
■ Stewards' Enquiry : Amy Scott two-day ban; used whip above permitted level (23rd-24th May)

FOCUS
Little to get excited about in this maiden with a predictable result.

1987 MIRROR PUNTERS CLUB H'CAP 6f (F)
2:25 (2:26) (Class 6) (0-55,55) 4-Y-O+ **£1,704** (£503; £251) **Stalls** Low

Form RPR
00-0 **1** **Mary's Pet**[28] 1306 5-8-12 **54** ....(p) KierenFox(3) 10 67
(Lee Carter) *mde virtually all: rdn clr wl over 2f out: kpt on* **14/1**

4332 **2** *2 ¼* **Gracie's Gift (IRE)**[6] 1799 10-8-5 **47** ....(v) DeclanCannon(3) 5 53
(Richard Guest) *trckd ldrs: hdwy 1/2-way: chsd wnr 2f out: sn rdn and no imp fnl f* **4/1**[1]

6036 **3** *1* **Bookiesindex Boy**[28] 1300 8-9-2 **55** .... HayleyTurner 7 58
(J R Jenkins) *trckd ldrs: hdwy 2f out: sn rdn and kpt on same pce fnl f* **11/2**[2]

2302 **4** *hd* **Flow Chart (IRE)**[29] 1283 5-8-8 **47** .... RobbieFitzpatrick 3 49
(Peter Grayson) *chsd ldrs: hdwy over 2f out: rdn to chse ldng pair wl over 1f out: sn hrd drvn and one pce* **11/2**[2]

3-06 **5** *6* **Charles Parnell (IRE)**[22] 1430 9-8-11 **50** ....(p) MichaelStainton 9 33
(Simon Griffiths) *s.i.s and in rr: hdwy over 2f out: sn rdn and edgd lft: kpt on fnl f: nrest at fin* **25/1**

3/0- **6** *1 1/2* **Red Rhythm**^{341} 2670 5-8-13 **55**.. DaleSwift$^{(3)}$ 8 33
(Micky Hammond) *towards rr: hdwy into midfield 1/2-way: rdn over 2f out: n.d* **13/2**^{3}

0260 **7** *3 3/4* **Little Perisher**^{13} 1628 5-8-5 **49**.............................(p) LeonnaMayor$^{(5)}$ 11 15
(Paul Howling) *dwlt: in rr and swtchd to outer: bhd 1/2-way: styd on fnl 2f: nvr a factor* **9/1**

000/ **8** *2* **Pawan (IRE)**^{545} 7405 12-8-11 **55**...............................(be) AnnStokell$^{(5)}$ 14 15
(Ann Stokell) *s.i.s: a in rr* **33/1**

0300 **9** *nk* **Cheyenne Red (IRE)**^{25} 1383 6-8-11 **50**....................(p) TonyHamilton 2 9
(Michael Herrington) *cl up on inner: rdn along 1/2-way: wknd over 2f out* **8/1**

340- **10** *1 3/4* **Avec Moi**^{218} 6610 5-8-7 **46** oh1...............................(p) KirstyMilczarek 13
(Christine Dunnett) *a in rr* **28/1**

006- **11** *3/4* **Stella Marris**^{208} 6839 5-8-4 **46** oh1.............................(p) JulieBurke$^{(3)}$ 12
(Christopher Wilson) *chsd ldrs: rdn along 1/2-way: sn wknd* **50/1**

6500 **12** *14* **Bird Dog**^{55} 910 6-8-2 **48**...(v) DannyBrock$^{(7)}$ 1
(Phil McEntee) *dwlt: a in rr* **9/1**

4-00 **13** *25* **Finn's Rainbow**^{49} 985 4-8-5 **49**.............................(b^{1}) RaulDaSilva$^{(5)}$ 6
(John Weymes) *disp ld: rdn along 1/2-way: sn wknd* **20/1**

1m 14.84s (-1.66) **Going Correction** -0.075s/f (Stan) 13 Ran SP% **118.8**
Speed ratings (Par 101): **108,105,103,103,95 93,88,85,85,83 82,63,30**
toteswingers:1&2:£15.30, 2&3:£3.40, 1&3:£26.20 CSF £65.09 CT £356.41 TOTE £19.90: £5.10, £1.10, £2.70; EX 115.20.

Owner Mrs I Marshall **Bred** Green Pastures Farm **Trained** Epsom, Surrey

■ Stewards' Enquiry : Robbie Fitzpatrick twenty-day ban; used whip above permitted level and did not give mount time to respond (23rd-26th May, 28th May-9th June, 11th-13th June)
Kieren Fox four day ban; used whip above permitted level (23rd-26th May)

FOCUS
A rock-bottom 0-55 sprint handicap in which the first four came right away.

Mary's Pet Official explanation: trainer said regarding mares apparent improvement in form that the drop in class had enabled her to dominate.

1988 BETFRED MOBILE SPORTS H'CAP 1m (F)
2:55 (2:55) (Class 6) (0-65,65) 4-Y-0+ **£1,704** (£503; £251) **Stalls** Low

Form RPR

5000 **1** **Hilbre Court (USA)**^{5} 1831 7-8-7 **51** oh3...............(v^{1}) DuranFentiman 12 59
(Brian Baugh) *prom: led after 3f: rdn over 2f out: drvn over 1f out: hld on gamely towards fin* **22/1**

-065 **2** *1* **Hits Only Jude (IRE)**^{15} 1583 9-8-7 **56**......................(v) NeilFarley$^{(5)}$ 13 62
(Declan Carroll) *racd wd: reminders after s: sn pushed along to chse ldrs after 2f: rdn wl over 3f out: drvn thrght fnl 2f: styd on ins fnl f: nt rch wnr* **10/1**

0100 **3** *1 1/2* **Putin (IRE)**^{36} 1179 4-8-3 **52** oh3 ow1..................(be) LeonnaMayor$^{(5)}$ 10 54
(Phil McEntee) *led 3f: cl up: rdn over 2f out: drvn and one pce fnl f* **22/1**

-060 **4** *3 3/4* **Sartingo (IRE)**^{18} 1525 5-9-6 **64**.................................... RobertWinston 4 58
(Alan Swinbank) *chsd ldng pair: rdn along and swtchd rt 3f out: drvn 2f out: sn edgd lft and wknd* **9/2**^{2}

0564 **5** *hd* **Sofias Number One (USA)**^{76} 671 4-8-11 **55**.....(b) RoystonFfrench 8 48
(Roy Bowring) *dwlt: sn in midfield: hdwy 3f out: rdn wl over 2f out: kpt on: nt rch ldrs* **14/1**

-610 **6** *1* **Mr Chocolate Drop (IRE)**^{5} 1830 8-8-12 **61**.............(t) RaulDaSilva$^{(5)}$ 9 52
(Mandy Rowland) *chsd ldrs: rdn along over 2f out: drvn over 1f out: sn no imp* **10/1**

5343 **7** *1 1/2* **General Tufto**^{43} 1052 7-9-1 **59**..............................(b) RobbieFitzpatrick 1 46
(Charles Smith) *in rr and sn pushed along: hdwy on inner 3f out: sn rdn and plugged on: nvr nr ldrs* **9/1**^{3}

3250 **8** *1 1/2* **Beetuna (IRE)**^{13} 1636 7-8-12 **61**................................. MarkCoumbe$^{(5)}$ 7 45
(Daniel Mark Loughnane) *stdd s and hld up in rr: hdwy and wd st: rdn along over 2f out: nvr nr ldrs* **14/1**

50/0 **9** *nk* **Yas Marina (USA)**^{28} 1296 4-8-5 **52**.......................... DeclanCannon$^{(3)}$ 2 35
(David O'Meara) *dwlt: sn in tch: rdn along over 3f out: sn wknd* **7/2**^{1}

-534 **10** *4* **Painted Tail (IRE)**^{11} 1652 5-9-2 **65**......................... GarryWhillans$^{(5)}$ 3 39
(Alan Swinbank) *a in rr* **7/2**^{1}

0/00 **11** *10* **Lily Lily**^{13} 1624 5-8-8 **52** ow1...(b) RobertHavlin 5
(Natalie Lloyd-Beavis) *in tch: rdn along wl over 3f out: sn wknd* **66/1**

000- **12** *25* **Striking Priorite**^{196} 7098 4-8-9 **53**.............................. TonyHamilton 11
(Tim Fitzgerald) *prom: rdn along 1/2-way: sn wknd* **66/1**

10/ **13** *25* **Patronne**^{1174} 620 6-8-7 **51** oh1.................................(v^{1}) KirstyMilczarek 6
(Ann Stokell) *prom: rdn along over 4f out: sn wknd* **80/1**

1m 42.15s (-1.55) **Going Correction** -0.075s/f (Stan) 13 Ran SP% **117.1**
Speed ratings (Par 101): **104,103,101,97,97 96,95,93,93,89 79,54,29**
toteswingers:1&2:£26.40, 2&3:£32.30, 1&3:£46.50 CSF £216.84 CT £2878.87 TOTE £22.30: £5.10, £3.60, £7.80; EX 251.60.

Owner Saddle Up Racing **Bred** Richard Nip & Omar Trevino **Trained** Audley, Staffs

■ Stewards' Enquiry : Neil Farley fifteen-day ban; used whip above permitted level (23rd-26th May, 28th May-7th June)

FOCUS
This was only a little better than the preceding event, but again those that raced at the head of affairs enjoyed a significant edge.

Hilbre Court(USA) Official explanation: trainer said regarding apparent improvement in form that his stable is coming into form.

Painted Tail(IRE) Official explanation: jockey said mare was never travelling.

1989 BETFRED MOBILE LOTTOS MEDIAN AUCTION MAIDEN STKS 7f (F)
3:30 (3:31) (Class 6) 3-4-Y-0 **£1,704** (£503; £251) **Stalls** Low

Form RPR

2- **1** **Vivid Blue**^{194} 7132 3-8-4 0.. LiamJones 7 69+
(William Haggas) *mde all: pushed clr wl over 1f out: rdn ins fnl f: kpt on* **2/5**^{1}

2 *2 1/2* **Queen Cassiopeia** 3-8-4 0.. HayleyTurner 2 63
(J R Jenkins) *towards rr: hdwy over 2f out: rdn to chse ldrs wl over 1f out: kpt on ins fnl f: nrst fin* **14/1**

2463 **3** *1 3/4* **Lord Paget**^{40} 1111 3-8-2 64...................................(p) JackDuern$^{(7)}$ 6 63
(Reg Hollinshead) *prom: effrt 3f out: sn rdn and one pce fr wl over 1f out* **10/1**^{3}

60- **4** *3 3/4* **Emperors Waltz (IRE)**^{211} 6771 3-8-4 0.......................... ChrisCatlin 8 48
(Rae Guest) *towards rr: hdwy on outer over 2f out: rdn wl over 1f out: kpt on fnl f: nrst fin* **25/1**

53 **5** *2 1/2* **Ty Gwr**^{22} 1427 3-8-9 0.. MartinLane 5 46
(David Simcock) *dwlt: sn in tch: hdwy to chse ldng pair over 2f out: rdn wl over 1f out: grad wknd* **4/1**^{2}

00-0 **6** *3 1/4* **Passing Moment**^{90} 483 4-9-2 42.................................. J-PGuillambert 9 36
(Brian Baugh) *chsd ldrs: rdn along over 3f out: sn wknd* **100/1**

0 **7** *shd* **Little Bucks**^{23} 1422 3-8-9 0.. AndrewMullen 3 37
(Alan McCabe) *prom: rdn along 1/2-way: sn wknd* **40/1**

000- **8** *5* **Grippa**^{234} 6187 3-8-9 45... MichaelStainton 1 24
(David Brown) *prom on inner: rdn along 1/2-way: sn wknd* **50/1**

9 *3/4* **Shakespeare Dancer** 3-8-1 0.................................... SimonPearce$^{(3)}$ 10 17
(James Evans) *dwlt: green and a bhd* **33/1**

1m 30.71s (0.41) **Going Correction** -0.075s/f (Stan)
WFA 3 from 4yo 12lb 9 Ran SP% **119.4**
Speed ratings (Par 101): **94,91,89,84,82 78,78,72,71**
toteswingers:1&2:£3.90, 2&3:£6.50, 1&3:£1.40 CSF £8.10 TOTE £1.80: £1.10, £4.40, £1.10; EX 9.20.

Owner Mrs F Woodd & Mrs Julia Scott **Bred** Glebe Stud And Mrs F Woodd **Trained** Newmarket, Suffolk

FOCUS
A one-sided maiden.

1990 BETFRED GOALS GALORE FILLIES' H'CAP 5f (F)
4:00 (4:01) (Class 4) (0-80,80) 4-Y-0+ **£4,075** (£1,212; £606; £303) **Stalls** High

Form RPR

5013 **1** **Gorgeous Goblin (IRE)**^{15} 1581 5-8-12 **71**...............(t) KirstyMilczarek 3 82
(David C Griffiths) *trckd ldrs: smooth hdwy wl over 1f out: chal ent fnl f: sn rdn: led last 100yds: kpt on wl* **11/4**^{1}

3-15 **2** *hd* **Bouncy Bouncy (IRE)**^{12} 1642 5-9-0 **73**.......................(t) HayleyTurner 7 83
(Michael Bell) *trckd ldrs: hdwy to ld over 1f out: sn jnd and rdn: hdd last 100yds: no ex towards fin* **10/3**^{3}

0240 **3** *6* **Fair Passion**^{4} 1868 5-9-4 **80**... DaleSwift$^{(3)}$ 2 68+
(Derek Shaw) *s.i.s and bhd: swtchd rt and hdwy wl over 1f out: kpt on to take 3rd ins fnl f* **3/1**^{2}

-205 **4** *2 1/4* **Bailadeira**^{12} 1638 4-8-7 **66** oh5....................................... JamesSullivan 8 46
(Tim Etherington) *prom: hdwy to ld 2f out: sn rdn and hdd over 1f out: wknd* **10/1**

00-0 **5** *2* **Jameela Girl**^{12} 1643 4-8-13 **72**... MartinLane 1 45
(Robert Cowell) *dwlt and towards rr: hdwy on outer 2f out: sn rdn and btn* **10/1**

563- **6** *6* **Wicked Wilma (IRE)**^{228} 6348 8-8-7 **73**................. MatthewHopkins$^{(7)}$ 6 25
(Alan Berry) *led 2f: rdn along 1/2-way: grad wknd* **20/1**

0-10 **7** *3 1/4* **Enjoyment**^{5} 1827 5-8-8 **67**.. IPoullis 4
(Alan McCabe) *cl up: led after 2f: sn rdn: hdd 2f out and sn wknd* **6/1**

59.21s (-0.49) **Going Correction** +0.125s/f (Slow) 7 Ran SP% **112.0**
Speed ratings (Par 102): **108,107,98,94,91 81,76**
toteswingers:1&2:£2.20, 2&3:£2.70, 1&3:£2.00 CSF £11.66 CT £27.50 TOTE £4.40: £2.10, £2.60; EX 7.80.

Owner K Humphries & Sons Roofing Contractors **Bred** S & L Humphries **Trained** Bawtry, S Yorks

FOCUS
A fair fillies' sprint handicap in which the front pair pulled clear.

Enjoyment Official explanation: trainer said mare bled from nose.

1991 BETFRED BONUS KING BINGO H'CAP 1m 6f (F)
4:35 (4:36) (Class 5) (0-75,72) 4-Y-0+ **£2,264** (£673; £336; £168) **Stalls** Low

Form RPR

/5-4 **1** **Rory Boy (USA)**^{25} 673 7-9-0 **61**.........................(v^{1}) MichaelStainton 5 77
(Graeme McPherson) *trckd ldr: cl up 1/2-way: led 4f out: rdn clr wl over 2f out: kpt on strly* **9/2**^{3}

06/ **2** *16* **Dorset Square (IRE)**^{46} 6966 8-9-10 **71**.......................(t) ChrisCatlin 1 65
(Sarah Humphrey) *trckd ldrs: cl up 4f out: sn pushed along: rdn to chse wnr wl over 2f out: sn drvn and kpt on: no ch w wnr* **17/2**

1510 **3** *5* **Carnac (IRE)**^{13} 1631 6-8-12 **66**.................................(p) NoraLooby$^{(7)}$ 2 53
(Alan McCabe) *trckd ldrs: effrt 4f out: rdn 3f out and sn one pce* **5/2**^{2}

1 **4** *19* **Wicked Spirit (IRE)**^{9} 1719 4-9-5 **72** 6ex........................ DarylByrne$^{(5)}$ 4 32
(Mark Johnston) *slt ld: jnd 1/2-way: pushed along and hdd 4f out: sn rdn and wknd qckly 3f out* **6/5**^{1}

0-00 **5** *28* **Rajeh (IRE)**^{23} 1421 9-9-8 **69**.. RobbieFitzpatrick 3
(Peter Grayson) *trckd ldrs: pushed along over 5f out: sn outpcd and bhd* **20/1**

3m 7.15s (-1.15) **Going Correction** -0.075s/f (Stan)
WFA 4 from 6yo+ 1lb 5 Ran SP% **107.5**
Speed ratings (Par 103): **100,90,88,77,61**
toteswingers: CSF £35.12 TOTE £4.70: £1.90, £2.10; EX 28.30.

Owner Peter Randall **Bred** John Kerber And Iveta Kerber **Trained** Upper Oddington, Gloucs

■ Stewards' Enquiry : Nora Looby caution; entered wrong stall.

FOCUS
A modest staying handicap, but despite the pace looking ordinary they finished well spread out.

1992 FIND US ON FACEBOOK SOUTHWELL RACECOURSE H'CAP 1m 3f (F)
5:05 (5:05) (Class 5) (0-70,70) 3-Y-O **£2,264** (£673; £336; £168) **Stalls** Low

Form RPR

-500 **1** **Run Of The Day**^{28} 1319 3-8-2 **56** oh4.............................. AmyScott$^{(5)}$ 5 59
(Eve Johnson Houghton) *trckd ldrs: hdwy over 3f out: rdn to chse ldr over 1f out: hung lft jst ins fnl f: styd on to ld last 20yds* **18/1**

05-3 **2** *1 1/4* **Landown Littlerock**^{20} 1486 3-8-5 **61**............................... JackDuern$^{(7)}$ 4 62
(Reg Hollinshead) *trckd ldrs: hdwy 4f out: led wl over 2f out: rdn wl over 1f out: drvn and edgd rt ins fnl f: hdd and no ex last 20yds* **15/8**^{1}

-151 **3** *5* **Quiet Appeal (IRE)**^{21} 1448 3-8-6 **60**.............................. DarylByrne$^{(5)}$ 7 52
(Mark Johnston) *led: rdn along 4f out: hdd 3f out: drvn and wknd wl over 1f out* **10/3**^{3}

423 **4** *3/4* **Torero**^{11} 1655 3-9-7 **70**.. TonyHamilton 3 60
(Kevin Ryan) *cl up on inner: rdn along 4f out: sn outpcd and bhd whn hung bdly rt 2f out* **2/1**^{2}

002- **5** *19* **Istan Star (USA)**^{212} 6760 3-8-7 **56** oh2......................... RoystonFfrench 1
(Julie Camacho) *a in rr: outpcd and bhd fr 4f out* **6/1**

2m 27.93s (-0.07) **Going Correction** -0.075s/f (Stan) 5 Ran SP% **110.7**
Speed ratings (Par 99): **97,96,92,91,78**
CSF £52.20 TOTE £32.80: £15.40, £1.90; EX 60.00.

Owner Mrs R F Johnson Houghton **Bred** Mrs R F Johnson Houghton **Trained** Blewbury, Oxon

FOCUS
A modest handicap and quite an odd race.

Run Of The Day Official explanation: trainer said regarding apparent improvement in form that she had no explination other that it was the fillies first run on fibresand.

Istan Star(USA) Official explanation: trainer said gelding did not face kickback.

T/Plt: £136.70 to a £1 stake. Pool of £53,342.43 - 284.83 winning tickets. T/Qpdt: £62.30 to a £1 stake. Pool of £3,811.34 45.26 winning tickets JR

1972 CHESTER (L-H)

Thursday, May 10

OFFICIAL GOING: Soft (heavy in places; 5.1)

Rail between 6f and 1.5f moved out 3yds inc. race distances as follows: 1m 2f 89y +14y, 1m 4f 86y +20y, 7f 135y +13y, 5f 26y +10y, 6f 31y +13y.

Wind: Fresh, half-behind Weather: Overcast

1993 M&S MONEY H'CAP — 1m 2f 75y

1:35 (1:42) (Class 2) (0-105,101) 4**£14,177** (£4,243; £2,121; £1,062; £528)

Form — RPR

222- **1** **Absinthe (IRE)**41 [6803] 6-8-11 **91**.....(t) GrahamLee 6 — 99
(Donald McCain) *led for 2f: remained prom: regained ld over 1f out: styd on wl and in control ins fnl f* **10/3**2

4/2 **2** *1 ½* **King's Warrior (FR)**12 [1654] 5-8-12 **92**..... RyanMoore 1 — 97
(Peter Chapple-Hyam) *hld up in rr: hdwy 2f out: rdn and c wd ent st wl over 1f out: wnt 2nd fnl 150yds: styd on towards fin wout troubling wnr* **5/2**1

-300 **3** *2 ¼* **Oceanway (USA)**15 [1605] 4-8-13 **93**..... JoeFanning 10 — 94
(Mark Johnston) *in tch: trckd ldrs after 2f: wnt cl 2nd 6f out: led wl over 2f out: rdn and hdd over 1f out: lost 2nd fnl 150yds: no ex towards fin* **16/1**

6-5 **4** *3 ¾* **Robemaker**29 [1321] 4-8-11 **91**..... WilliamBuick 3 — 85
(John Gosden) *chsd ldrs: effrt over 3f out: ev ch wl over 1f out: sn edgd rt u.p ent st: one pce ins fnl f* **5/2**1

-300 **5** *3 ¾* **The Bells O Peover**26 [1374] 4-8-6 **86**.....(b) FrannyNorton 9 — 73
(Mark Johnston) *racd keenly: chsd ldr: led after 2f: hdd wl over 2f out: wknd wl over 1f out* **11/1**

-310 **6** *2 ¾* **Call To Reason (IRE)**29 [1321] 5-8-6 **86**..... MickaelBarzalona 8 — 67
(Ian Williams) *racd keenly: hld up: effrt on outer over 3f out: outpcd and lost pl 2f out: bhd after* **13/2**3

2m 19.8s (8.60) **Going Correction** +1.00s/f (Soft) **6** Ran SP% **107.8**
Speed ratings (Par 109): **105,103,102,99,96 93**
toteswingers:1&2:£1.70, 2&3:£3.40, 1&3:£3.90 CSF £11.05 CT £93.98 TOTE £4.50: £2.00, £1.60; EX 11.40 Trifecta £127.90 Pool: £1279.89 - 7.40 winning units..
Owner Mr & Mrs Paul Rooney **Bred** Moyglare Stud Farm Ltd **Trained** Cholmondeley, Cheshire

FOCUS

There was 5mm of rain up to 6.30pm on Wednesday and a further 12mm overnight, so the ground was described as soft, heavy in places. The rail between the 6f and 1.5f point had been moved by 3yds for the second day, so all the race distances increased from between 13yds to 20yds. The three 1m2f races were started without stalls. A very decent handicap started proceedings and the pace set by the leader was understandably modest. The form is rated around the first two, with possible improvement from the winner.

NOTEBOOK

Absinthe(IRE) had been showing good form over hurdles since joining Donald McCain, winning his most recent outing by 13l at Wetherby in a first-time tongue-tie. Settled just in behind the leader by Graham Lee (having only his second ride at the course), he had plenty to offer turning in and won in good style. He might have a bit more scope to win a valuable handicap on the Flat. (op 11-4 tchd 7-2)

King's Warrior(FR) shaped pleasingly on his first run for Peter Chapple-Hyam after a spell in France, and he did so again. He was forced wide off the final bend by the fourth, which can't have helped. (op 9-4 tchd 2-1)

Oceanway(USA), who won on her only previous start here over C&D, came into this off a poor effort at Epsom on heavy ground so this was a bit better. (op 12-1)

Robemaker is well above the mark he won his only race off, but hadn't dropped in the weights due to some consistent efforts. Trying this trip for the first time, he didn't get home in the conditions after racing a bit keenly in behind. (op 7-2)

The Bells O Peover was easily brushed aside after making most of the running. A drop in the weights for this would put him close to a dangerous mark. (op 10-1 tchd 9-1)

Call To Reason(IRE), trying the trip for the first time, was caught wide on the final bend and never got involved. (op 15-2 tchd 8-1)

1994 BETFAIR HUXLEY STKS (FOR THE TRADESMAN'S CUP) (GROUP 3) — 1m 2f 75y

2:05 (2:07) (Class 1) 4-Y-O+

£31,190 (£11,825; £5,918; £2,948; £1,479; £742)

Form — RPR

-365 **1** **Marcret (ITY)**68 [792] 5-9-0 0.....1 RyanMoore 5 — 110
(Marco Botti) *racd keenly: a.p: rdn to ld over 1f out: edgd rt to stands' rail ins fnl f: r.o and a doing enough towards fin* **13/2**3

5-00 **2** *½* **Myplacelater**29 [1318] 5-8-11 98..... FrannyNorton 6 — 106
(Richard Fahey) *hld up: rdn and hdwy over 1f out: styd on to take 2nd in clsng stages: clsd on wnr at fin* **20/1**

-644 **3** *1 ¼* **Wigmore Hall (IRE)**11 [1696] 5-9-7 114..... JamieSpencer 2 — 114
(Michael Bell) *trckd ldrs: rdn over 1f out: c to chal between runners wl ins fnl f: nt qckn* **15/2**

-312 **4** *shd* **Questioning (IRE)**13 [1646] 4-9-3 114.....(p) WilliamBuick 1 — 109
(John Gosden) *led: rdn and hdd over 1f out: stl ev ch ins fnl f: no ex towards fin* **9/4**1

-546 **5** *6* **Glen's Diamond**70 [759] 4-9-0 0..... TonyHamilton 4 — 95
(Richard Fahey) *in tch: rdn over 2f out: sn wknd* **17/2**

611- **6** *1 ¾* **Hunter's Light (IRE)**180 [7391] 4-9-0 110..... FrankieDettori 8 — 92
(Saeed Bin Suroor) *hld up in rr: effrt 2f out: rdn and unable to pick-up over 1f out: wknd ins fnl f* **5/2**2

15-0 **7** *26* **Prince Siegfried (FR)**21 [1471] 6-9-0 112..... MickaelBarzalona 9 — 42
(Saeed Bin Suroor) *in tch: sn prom on outer: niggled along 4f out: wknd over 2f out: eased whn wl btn ins fnl f* **10/1**

2m 19.3s (8.10) **Going Correction** +1.00s/f (Soft) **7** Ran SP% **108.8**
Speed ratings (Par 113): **107,106,105,105,100 99,78**
toteswingers:1&2:£13.00, 2&3:£13.40, 1&3:£5.70 CSF £103.36 TOTE £7.80: £3.00, £7.10; EX 64.40 Trifecta £512.00 Pool: £1224.78 - 1.77 winning units..
Owner Dr Marwan Koukash **Bred** Az Ag Antezzate Srl **Trained** Newmarket, Suffolk
■ Stewards' Enquiry : Franny Norton two-day ban: used whip above permitted level (May 25-26)

FOCUS

Some decent horses for the level were on show, but the underfoot conditions mean the form needs to be treated with caution. It was interesting to note the field jumped off towards the centre of the course without the use of stalls, and they pretty much stayed on that route throughout. The ex-Italian winner continues to progress, but there are doubts over the form.

NOTEBOOK

Marcret(ITY), tried in a hood for the first time, was having his first run in the colours of Dr Marwan Koukash after being purchased the previous week, and seemed certain to handle the ground judged on his form in Italy, where he'd secured ten victories. By the same sire as Godolphin's ultra-tough miler/1m2f winner Ramonti, he showed a likable attitude when asked to lengthen, despite edging across to the stands' rail. This was the immediate plan so nothing definite has been decided about the horse's next outing. (op 6-1 tchd 7-1)

Myplacelater, dropped in trip in a bid to end a losing run dating back to 2010, had to wait for run but finished strongly once in the clear. (op 16-1)

Wigmore Hall(IRE) had a 7lb penalty and was racing on ground his record suggested was softer than ideal, so this was a good performance in defeat. (op 12-1)

Questioning(IRE) has returned an improved horse as a 4yo with cheekpieces on, and he probably ran somewhere close to his best. This trip may have stretched him just a bit. (tchd 2-1 and 5-2 in a place)

Glen's Diamond, the previous year's Dee Stakes winner, had run three fair races at Meydan over further than this, the last two coming over 1m6f, and got left behind when the pace increased. A return to further will no doubt help. (op 9-1)

Hunter's Light(IRE) finished last season really well with a couple of Listed victories, including one on soft ground. Having his first outing since mid-November, he wasn't best placed considering the way the contest developed and can be given another chance in less-demanding conditions. (op 9-4)

Prince Siegfried(FR) is a solid performer at Listed/Group 3 level, but this was poor. However, his effort can be forgiven to some extent as his jockey doesn't yet seem to know how to ride this unique course, going wide at the wrong time on his mount. (op 11-1)

1995 MBNA CHESTER VASE (GROUP 3) (C&G) — 1m 4f 66y

2:35 (2:35) (Class 1) 3-Y-O **£31,190** (£11,825; £5,918; £2,948; £1,479) **Stalls** Low

Form — RPR

2142 **1** **Mickdaam (IRE)**21 [1468] 3-8-12 104..... TonyHamilton 5 — 112
(Richard Fahey) *hld up: tk cl order to go prom on outer 7f out: chalng 3 out: led wl over 1f out: sn rdn and hung lft: styd on for press: all out towards fin: jst hld on* **8/1**

3-1 **2** *nse* **Model Pupil**22 [1456] 3-8-12 0..... MichaelHills 1 — 112+
(Charles Hills) *hld up: pushed along and outpcd over 2f out: rdn over 1f out: styd on ins fnl f: clsd towards fin: rdr's foot slipped through rt iron at line: jst failed* **6/1**3

2 **3** *1 ½* **Call To Battle (IRE)**25 [1404] 3-8-12 0..... JohnnyMurtagh 2 — 110
(John M Oxx, Ire) *chsd ldr: chalng fr 3f out: rdn whn carried lft sltly over 1f out: kpt on same pce fnl 50yds* **2/1**2

31-5 **4** *4 ½* **David Livingston (IRE)**25 [1404] 3-9-2 0..... JPO'Brien 4 — 106
(A P O'Brien, Ire) *led: pressed fr 3f out: rdn and hdd wl over 1f out: sn carried lft sltly: wknd ins fnl f* **6/4**1

21 **5** *1 ¼* **Minimise Risk**19 [1511] 3-8-12 92..... JamieSpencer 3 — 100
(Andrew Balding) *trckd ldrs: dropped to rr wl over 7f out: pushed along and outpcd over 2f out: hung lft over 1f out: wl btn ins fnl f* **8/1**

2m 50.01s (11.51) **Going Correction** +1.00s/f (Soft) **5** Ran SP% **109.8**
Speed ratings (Par 109): **101,100,99,96,96**
CSF £49.76 TOTE £7.90: £2.70, £2.70; EX 27.20.
Owner Sheikh Mohammed Bin Khalifa Al Maktoum **Bred** Victor Stud Bloodstock Ltd **Trained** Musley Bank, N Yorks

FOCUS

Although no horse has won the Chester Vase and gone on to win the Derby since Shergar in 1981, the race has produced some top-class performers in the meantime with last year's winner Treasure Beach taking the Irish Derby and runner-up Nathaniel landing the King George. The pace was by no means strong, which was sensible in the conditions.

NOTEBOOK

Mickdaam(IRE) went close to winning a valuable sales race at Newmarket on his return to this yard following a successful spell in Dubai, but the winner was then well held behind the O'Brien-trained Imperial Monarch at Sandown, whilst this testing ground was a complete unknown. As things turned out he handled the conditions well, and taking a wider route than his rivals was probably a shrewd move. Forced to the front on the wide outside turning in, he did hang about a bit once into the straight, but kept on finding and had established enough of an advantage to hold off the runner-up by the skin of his teeth. He was generally quoted at 33-1 for the Derby immediately afterwards, but doesn't appeal as a likely winner of the Epsom classic. (op 13-2)

Model Pupil, the only one of these not entered in the Derby, is the one to take from the race. Narrow winner of a Newmarket maiden on his reappearance last month (form working out well), he hadn't raced on ground like this before and was just about the first of the quintet off the bridle, but once angled out for an effort over a furlong out he finished with a rattle and failed by the narrowest margin. This track almost certainly didn't play to his strengths and there is much more to come.

Call To Battle(IRE) had David Livingston over 3l behind him in the Ballysax last month and both juvenile wins came on soft ground. Having stalked the leader throughout, he had every chance inside the last 3f and was slightly hampered by the winner over a furlong out, but lack of a finishing kick was his main undoing. He looks a real galloper and may benefit from an even greater test of stamina. (op 9-4)

David Livingston(IRE), from a stable looking to win this race for the fourth time in six years, had winning form on heavy ground from last year and was soon bowling along in an uncontested lead, but the distress signals were being sent out when he was pressed over 2f out and he eventually dropped away pretty tamely. (op 7-4 tchd 15-8 in a place)

Minimise Risk had much more on his plate than when narrowly winning a soft-ground maiden at Newbury last month. Off the bridle over 2f from home, he started to hang about badly in the home straight and didn't seem to enjoy himself at all. (op 9-1 tchd 7-1)

1996 BOODLES DIAMOND ETERNITY H'CAP — 7f 122y

3:05 (3:05) (Class 2) (0-100,96) 3-**£14,177** (£4,243; £2,121; £1,062; £528) **Stalls** Low

Form — RPR

220- **1** **Arnold Lane (IRE)**215 [6688] 3-9-5 **94**..... SamHitchcott 1 — 103
(Mick Channon) *chsd ldrs: carried lft sltly whn chalng over 1f out: styd on to ld towards fin* **9/1**

10-0 **2** *nk* **Gabrial (IRE)**33 [1221] 3-9-0 **89**..... JamieSpencer 3 — 97
(Richard Fahey) *racd keenly: hld up: hdwy 3f out: rdn to ld and hung lft over 1f out: hung rt wl ins fnl f: hdd towards fin* **2/1**1

3150 **3** *½* **Switzerland (IRE)**22 [1452] 3-9-5 **94**..... JoeFanning 7 — 101
(Mark Johnston) *hld up: hdwy 2f out: chalng fr over 1f out: nt qckn towards fin* **8/1**

22-1 **4** *1 ¾* **Glen Moss (IRE)**40 [1138] 3-8-7 **87**..... MatthewLawson(5) 6 — 90
(Charles Hills) *racd keenly: chsd ldr: w ldr over 3f out: led 2f out: hdd and carried sltly lft over 1f out: kpt on same pce fnl 100yds* **4/1**2

16- **5** *4 ½* **Seanie (IRE)**33 [1225] 3-9-7 **96**..... RyanMoore 9 — 87+
(David Marnane, Ire) *rrd sed and missed break: bhd: pushed along 3f out: rdn and hdwy to chse ldrs over 1f out but no imp: eased whn wl btn fnl 75yds* **5/1**3

-060 **6** *7* **Boris Grigoriev (IRE)**30 [1271] 3-8-10 **92**..... DavidSimmonson(7) 5 — 66
(Michael Easterby) *racd keenly: led: jnd over 3f out: hdd 2f out: wknd over 1f out* **22/1**

04-2 **7** *20* **Evervescent (IRE)**33 [1221] 3-9-0 **89**.....(p) GrahamGibbons 2 — 13
(J S Moore) *chsd ldrs: rdn over 2f out: sn wknd* **5/1**3

1m 40.14s (6.34) **Going Correction** +1.00s/f (Soft) **7** Ran SP% **112.1**
Speed ratings (Par 105): **108,107,107,105,100 93,73**
toteswingers:1&2:£4.10, 2&3:£4.90, 1&3:£8.30 CSF £26.38 CT £150.81 TOTE £10.00: £2.70, £1.60; EX 31.30 Trifecta £152.20 Pool: £1798.30 - 8.74 winning units..
Owner Nick & Olga Dhandsa & John & Zoe Webster **Bred** Lynn Lodge Stud **Trained** West Ilsley, Berks

FOCUS
A decent handicap which looked sound run, and a fairly positive view is taken over the form. The winner is rated in line with his penultimate run.

NOTEBOOK
Arnold Lane(IRE) was last seen finishing out the back in the Middle Park and was racing beyond 6f for the first time on this reappearance, though he did run well on his only previous try on soft ground. He was always travelling well behind the leaders, but didn't see a lot of daylight and things got tight for him entering the last furlong as he was delivered with his challenge, but the runner-up's antics in the closing stages gave him one more chance and he took full advantage. He saw the trip out well in the conditions and can go on from here. (tchd 10-1)
Gabrial(IRE), the only previous course winner in the line-up (landed the 2yo maiden on this card last year), finished behind a couple of these on his return from 298 days off at Musselburgh last month, but met trouble in running that day. He wasn't going to meet trouble the way he was ridden here, taking a wide route throughout, and looked to have been produced with a race-winning effort inside the last furlong, but once there he started to hang about the track and threw it away. (op 15-8 tchd 7-4)
Switzerland(IRE) had disappointed since returning to turf following his Polytrack successes earlier in the year and had never been on ground this soft, but this was more like it and he had every chance after getting a nice run through on the inside after turning in.
Glen Moss(IRE), making his handicap debut after beating a dual subsequent winner on his Kempton return, was always up there but he was keen enough in the early stages considering the conditions and that may have cost him in the closing stages. (op 11-2)
Seanie(IRE), an Irish challenger back up to a more suitable trip and a winner in testing conditions, gave away a lot of ground at the start and you can't afford to do that here. Official explanation: jockey said gelding was slowly away
Boris Grigoriev(IRE), placed in Pattern company for Aidan O'Brien last year including with cut in the ground, had only shown limited promise in three starts for his new yard and didn't stay in his only previous try over a similar trip. Given a positive ride, he was free early and didn't see this out either. (op 20-1)
Evervescent(IRE) was up another 4lb following last month's narrow defeat on his Musselburgh reappearance (two of these behind), but he dropped right out inside the last 2f and this was too bad to be true.

1997 EQUESTRIANARTUK.COM E B F MAIDEN STKS 5f 16y
3:40 (3:41) (Class 3) 2-Y-O **£7,762** (£2,310; £1,154; £577) **Stalls** Low

Form				RPR
0	**1**		**Fat Gary**[8] 1753 2-9-3 0 ... JamesDoyle 4 (Tom Dascombe) *w ldr: rdn to ld 1f out: sn edgd lft: edgd rt wl ins fnl f: hld on wl at fin* **12/1**	81+
	2	*shd*	**Mandy Lexi (IRE)** 2-8-12 0 ... RichardMullen 7 (Bryan Smart) *trckd ldrs: pushed along 2f out: styd on to take 2nd and hung rt wl ins fnl f: clsd towards fin* **8/1**	75
	3	*3*	**Trinityelitedotcom (IRE)** 2-9-3 0 ... RichardKingscote 1 (Tom Dascombe) *led: rdn and hdd 1f out: no ex fnl 75yds* **6/1**	70+
	4	*nk*	**Party Royal** 2-9-3 0 ... JoeFanning 9 (Mark Johnston) *midfield: effrt 1/2-way: styd on ins fnl f: gng on at fin: nt gng pce to trble ldrs* **5/1**[3]	69+
	5	*5*	**Tommy's Secret** 2-9-3 0 ... JimmyFortune 3 (Jane Chapple-Hyam) *dwlt: bhd and pushed along: styd on ins fnl f: nvr able to trble ldrs* **8/1**	51+
03	**6**	*3 1/2*	**Majestic Jess (IRE)**[3] 1903 2-9-0 0 ... RossAtkinson(3) 10 (Tom Dascombe) *dwlt: sn in tch on outer: pushed along 1/2-way: sn wknd* **25/1**	38
	7	*9*	**Tomway** 2-9-3 0 ... RobertWinston 11 (Tom Dascombe) *dwlt: sn pushed along and bhd: nvr on terms* **25/1**	6
2	**8**	*1*	**Annaley My Darling (IRE)**[14] 1629 2-8-12 0 ... TonyCulhane 5 (Jo Hughes) *trckd ldrs tl rdn and wknd 1/2-way* **11/4**[1]	
3	**9**	*41*	**Lexi The Princess (IRE)**[26] 1388 2-8-12 0 ... FrannyNorton 8 (Kevin Ryan) *dwlt and veered bdly rt s: a wl bhd: t.o* **4/1**[2]	

1m 6.94s (5.94) **Going Correction** +1.00s/f (Soft) **9** Ran SP% **115.2**
Speed ratings (Par 97): **92,91,87,86,78 72,58,56,**
toteswingers:1&2:£10.40, 2&3:£8.30, 1&3:£13.30 CSF £103.45 TOTE £9.40: £2.40, £3.00, £2.20; EX 119.70 Trifecta £1022.70 Part won. Pool: £1382.11 - 0.30 winning units..
Owner Fat Gary Sports **Bred** J M Beever **Trained** Malpas, Cheshire

FOCUS
An ordinary maiden and the conditions told on a few. The winner left his debut form behind and the race is rated in line with the race averages.

NOTEBOOK
Fat Gary, a 34,000euros colt, was always behind on his Pontefract debut when he appeared to have his mind on other things, but there is plenty of stamina on the dam's side of his pedigree and that would have been a help in these conditions. Always handy before being ridden to the front inside the last, he got first run on the runner-up and just managed to hold on with nothing to spare. He looks the type who needs plenty of assistance from the saddle and he got that here. (op 10-1)
Mandy Lexi(IRE), a 17,000GBP 2yo, was always close to the pace and when finally finding her stride very nearly made a winning debut. Her pedigree looks a mix of speed and stamina and there should be a race or two in her. (op 15-2)
Trinityelitedotcom(IRE), a 30,000GBP 2yo out of a half-sister to six winners, was the choice of Richard Kingscote over his three stablemates despite being withdrawn from the previous day's Lily Agnes on account of the ground. Soon in front from the plum draw, he was given little peace by the winner the whole way and was eventually worn down. He should win races on better ground. (op 13-2)
Party Royal, a 30,000gns colt out of a winner at up to 1m2f, seemed to find this sharp enough even in these conditions and didn't get going until it was too late. He should improve for another furlong. (op 6-1 tchd 13-2 and 7-1 in a place)
Tommy's Secret, retained for just 1,000GBP as a yearling, is a half-brother to a 7f juvenile winner. He seemed more likely to finish tailed off for most of the way, but showed some ability as the race progressed and it worth keeping an eye on. (tchd 7-1)
Annaley My Darling(IRE) seemed to know her job when narrowly beaten on her Wolverhampton debut, but didn't seem to handle these very different conditions and was on the retreat a fair way out. (op 3-1 tchd 10-3 in a place)
Lexi The Princess(IRE) looked in need of the experience when an encouraging third on her Wolverhampton debut last month, but didn't learn from that and was virtually unrideable soon after leaving the stalls. Official explanation: jockey said filly yung badly right at start (tchd 9-2)

1998 INVESTEC STRUCTURED PRODUCTS H'CAP 6f 18y
4:15 (4:16) (Class 3) (0-90,88) 3-Y-O **£9,056** (£2,695; £1,346; £673) **Stalls** Low

Form				RPR
21	**1**		**Jack Dexter**[19] 1521 3-8-11 **78** ... GrahamLee 8 (Jim Goldie) *midfield: hdwy over 1f out: carried rt ins fnl f: sn led: r.o* **9/2**[2]	85+
1221	**2**	*nk*	**Gabrial's Bounty (IRE)**[8] 1758 3-9-0 **81** 6ex ... FrannyNorton 9 (Mick Channon) *a handy: effrt 2f out: rdn over 1f out: edgd rt ins fnl f: sn chalng: r.o for press* **8/1**	87
1-24	**3**	*nse*	**Personal Touch**[5] 1858 3-8-9 **76** ... TonyHamilton 7 (Richard Fahey) *chsd ldr: rdn to ld over 1f out: sn hung lft: hdd wl ins fnl f: r.o: hld fnl strides* **3/1**[1]	82
251-	**4**	*nk*	**Kimbali (IRE)**[227] 6413 3-9-1 **82** ... SamHitchcott 10 (Richard Fahey) *hld up: pushed along over 2f out: hdwy over 1f out: r.o ins fnl f: chalng cl home* **6/1**[3]	87
-011	**5**	*1 1/2*	**Rusty Rocket (IRE)**[12] 1658 3-8-13 **80** ... RyanMoore 13 (Paul Green) *bhd: swtchd rt and hdwy over 1f out: styd on ins fnl f: nrst fin* **14/1**	80+
01-	**6**	*hd*	**Intransigent**[181] 7359 3-9-7 **88** ... JimmyFortune 12 (Andrew Balding) *racd on wd outside: hld up: hdwy 2f out: effrt and hung lft over 1f out: carried rt whn chsng ldrs ins fnl f: one pce fnl 100yds* **20/1**	88+
521-	**7**	*3 1/2*	**Decision By One**[167] 7540 3-9-0 **81** ... (t) RichardKingscote 5 (Tom Dascombe) *fractious in stalls: led: rdn and hdd over 1f out: wknd fnl 150yds* **14/1**	69
060-	**8**	*nk*	**Hamza (IRE)**[266] 5216 3-9-5 **86** ... PhillipMakin 11 (Kevin Ryan) *squeezed out jst after s: a bhd and nvr gng wl: kpt on modly ins fnl f: nvr a threat* **40/1**	73
13-3	**9**	*4*	**Whisky Bravo**[8] 1758 3-8-8 **75** ... RichardMullen 2 (David Brown) *prom: rdn over 2f out: wknd ins fnl f: eased whn btn fnl 100yds* **6/1**[3]	50
32-1	**10**	*9*	**Marford Missile (IRE)**[57] 897 3-8-13 **80** ... JamesDoyle 6 (Tom Dascombe) *flashed tail sn after s: hld up: pushed along over 2f out: wknd over 1f out: eased whn wl btn ins fnl f* **12/1**	26
612-	**11**	*11*	**Profile Star (IRE)**[132] 7918 3-8-11 **78** ... GrahamGibbons 4 (David Barron) *chsd ldrs tl rdn and wknd over 1f out* **16/1**	

1m 20.78s (6.98) **Going Correction** +1.00s/f (Soft) **11** Ran SP% **117.0**
Speed ratings (Par 103): **93,92,92,92,90 89,85,84,79,67 52**
toteswingers:1&2:£8.50, 2&3:£5.90, 1&3:£4.20 CSF £40.26 CT £125.30 TOTE £3.80: £1.20, £2.50, £2.00; EX 40.00 Trifecta £160.70 Pool: £1869.78 - 8.61 winning units..
Owner Jim Goldie Racing Club **Bred** Jim Goldie **Trained** Uplawmoor, E Renfrews

FOCUS
This was quite a rough race, but despite the narrow margins separating the principals at the line this looks form to take a positive view about. The first six are all progressive types.

NOTEBOOK
Jack Dexter was one of the least exposed runners in the field and was making his handicap debut after winning a soft-ground Thirsk maiden. He didn't see much daylight at various stages and took quite a hefty bump entering the last furlong, but still managed to put in a sustained effort and can be considered better than the winning margin. He should continue to improve and looks a sprinter to keep onside. (op 7-2)
Gabrial's Bounty(IRE) has been in great form this year and was carrying a 6lb penalty for his success in heavy ground at Pontefract eight days earlier. He was being ridden along in a handy position over 2f out, but gave his all and was only just run out of it. He may go up again for this, but can't be written off in his current mood. (op 15-2)
Personal Touch was 6lb wrong (including 2lb overweight) when fourth of 19 in a hotter handicap at Newmarket five days earlier and was officially 5lb well in here. He was always handy before hitting the front inside the last, but then hung to the inside rail and was run out of it. This was another smart effort, but his imminent rise will make things a bit harder. (op 10-3 tchd 4-1 in a place and 7-2 in places)
Kimbali(IRE), last seen winning on soft ground at Hamilton last September, was 4lb higher for this return having been gelded in the meantime. He came from further back than the three ahead of him and didn't enjoy much room turning in, but he came home in style to finish right alongside the placed horses. This should set him up nicely for the coming season. (op 13-2)
Rusty Rocket(IRE) was up another 5lb in his bid for a hat-trick after two wins at 5f, but he scored over 7f at two and is proven on soft ground. Having been dropped right out from the outside stall, he gave himself a mountain to climb so can be given plenty of credit for finishing where he did. (op 12-1)
Intransigent, last seen winning a 5f Lingfield Polytrack maiden in November, gave away plenty of ground by racing wide of his rivals and still looked green in the home straight, so he is another who earned himself credit on just this third start. (tchd 25-1)
Decision By One was making his turf debut having not been seen since winning a Wolverhampton maiden in November (form working out well). He made the running to a furlong from home and can be expected to last longer next time, possibly on better ground. (op 16-1)
Hamza(IRE), gelded since last seen nine months ago, won first time out at two but had never run on ground like this. Considering he met trouble after the start and found himself at the back of the field, he ran better here than it may have seemed.

1999 CHESHIRE OAKS H'CAP 1m 2f 75y
4:45 (4:45) (Class 3) (0-90,90) 4-Y-O+ **£9,056** (£2,695; £1,346; £673)

Form				RPR
00-0	**1**		**Resurge (IRE)**[15] 1605 7-9-6 **89** ... AdamKirby 8 (Stuart Kittow) *hld up in rr: pushed along over 3f out: hdwy on outer over 2f out: led narrowly wl over 1f out but jnd and strly pressed: sltly hdd 75yds out: battled gamely to prevail on the nod* **8/1**[3]	100
01-1	**2**	*shd*	**Stand To Reason (IRE)**[19] 1513 4-9-7 **90** ... RyanMoore 6 (Mikael Magnusson) *trckd ldrs: effrt 2f out: upsides and str chal fr over 1f out: nosed ahd 75yds out: hdd post* **6/4**[1]	101
0201	**3**	*13*	**Calaf**[5] 1841 4-8-10 **79** ... TonyHamilton 5 (Richard Fahey) *hld up: rdn 2f out: hdwy over 1f out: kpt on u.p to take 3rd wl ins fnl f: no ch w front pair* **2/1**[2]	65
1-	**4**	*1 1/2*	**Elizabeth Coffee (IRE)**[90] 507 4-8-8 **77** ... FrannyNorton 2 (Ian Williams) *racd keenly: led early: remained prom: chalng 2f out: outpcd by ldrs over 1f out: sn no ch: plugged on at one pce after* **12/1**	60
00-5	**5**	*2 1/2*	**Silver Grey (IRE)**[26] 1381 5-8-11 **80** ... (p) JamesDoyle 3 (Martyn Meade) *in tch: rdn over 2f out: one pce over 1f out and no ch w ldrs: eased whn wl btn fnl 75yds* **9/1**	59
004-	**6**	*nk*	**Early Applause**[59] 6922 4-8-9 **78** ... RobertWinston 9 (Charles Hills) *sn led: hdd wl over 1f out: sn wknd: eased whn wl btn fnl 100yds* **20/1**	56
510-	**7**	*14*	**Cool Macavity (IRE)**[287] 4467 4-9-1 **84** ... [1] MichaelHills 7 (Charles Hills) *racd keenly: hld up: hdwy on outer over 3f out: wknd over 2f out: eased whn wl btn over 1f out* **14/1**	35

2m 19.3s (8.10) **Going Correction** +1.00s/f (Soft) **7** Ran SP% **113.6**
Speed ratings (Par 107): **107,106,96,95,93 93,81**
toteswingers:1&2:£3.30, 2&3:£1.70, 1&3:£4.10 CSF £20.24 CT £33.49 TOTE £10.30: £4.20, £1.40; EX 25.10 Trifecta £63.90 Pool: £1675.61 - 19.40 winning units..
Owner Chris & David Stam **Bred** Sweetmans Bloodstock **Trained** Blackborough, Devon

FOCUS
They went a good pace in this and the first two pulled miles clear of the rest. The winner's rating could be a little out either way.

NOTEBOOK
Resurge(IRE) has gone well fresh in the past and handles soft ground, so might have been expected to have run better at his beloved Epsom last month, but another 4lb drop since then meant he was 8lb lower than when winning at the Surrey track last June. He was held up early, but a wide sweeping move over 2f from home took him to the front and from then on it came down to pure guts in his protracted battle with the runner-up. Even after a rise for this success he may still be dangerously well handicapped if bidding to follow up in the same Epsom handicap next month.

Stand To Reason(IRE), bidding for a hat-trick after two wins on soft ground, was 8lb higher than when defying a nine-month absence at Newbury last month. He responded gamely when the winner was delivered on his outside turning for home, but his streetwise opponent (who was having his 39th start whilst he was only having his sixth) just had his head in front where it mattered. He is likely to go up again for this, but still seems to be progressing and should win another decent prize or two this season. (op 11-8)
Calaf was 6lb well in having escaped a penalty for his success in a Doncaster apprentice event five days earlier and he has winning form over C&D, but he merely plugged on for a remote third and things are soon going to get that much harder. (op 11-4)
Elizabeth Coffee(IRE) was making her debut for the yard (picked up for 11,000euros) after a three-month absence having shown good form for Mick Halford at Dundalk during the winter, but didn't get home in the ground. (op 10-1)
Silver Grey(IRE) was just about the first beaten and is now 2-26. (op 8-1)
Early Applause, twice unplaced over hurdles since last seen on the Flat in October, was responsible for the solid pace but fell in a hole over a furlong from home. Official explanation: trainer's rep said gelding was unsuited by the soft (heavy in places) ground (op 25-1)
Cool Macavity(IRE) hadn't been seen in ten months and failed to settle in the first-time hood.
T/Jkpt: Not won. T/Plt: £536.60 to a £1 stake. Pool of £189,604.36 - 257.90 winning tickets.
T/Qpdt: £48.00 to a £1 stake. Pool of £12,202.84 - 187.90 winning tickets. DO

1847 GOODWOOD (R-H)
Thursday, May 10

2000 Meeting Abandoned - waterlogged

1738 YARMOUTH (L-H)
Thursday, May 10

OFFICIAL GOING: Heavy (4.3)
Top bend and back straight dolled in 4m.
Wind: Medium, half-against Weather: light rain

2008 BRITISH STALLION STUDS SUPPORTING BRITISH RACING E B F MAIDEN FILLIES' STKS — 1m 3f 101y
5:20 (5:20) (Class 5) 3-Y-O+ — **£3,557** (£1,058; £529; £264) **Stalls** Centre

Form — RPR
5- **1** **Great Heavens**229 6329 3-8-8 0 ... RobertHavlin 5 — 92+
(John Gosden) *w ldr tl led 6f out: shkn up and readily asserted over 1f out: pushed out fnl f: comf* **1/1**1
2 *3* **Monshak (IRE)** 3-8-8 0 ... ChrisCatlin 2 — 85
(Sir Michael Stoute) *rn green: chsd ldrs: rdn along briefly to chse ldng pair 6f out: pressed wnr travelling okay 3f out: rdn and unable qck 2f out: one pce after* **13/2**3
0 **3** *26* **Amaraja (GER)**20 1502 3-8-9 0 ow1 ... EddieAhern 6 — 45
(Sir Henry Cecil) *led tl 6f out: styd upsides wnr tl rdn and unable qck over 2f out: wknd 2f out: wl btn and eased ins fnl f* **2/1**2
4 *14* **Jorum** 3-8-8 0 ... PaulMulrennan 4 — 21
(Sir Henry Cecil) *dwlt: rn green and rdn along early: hdwy to chse ldng pair 9f out tl 6f out: sn rdn and struggling: lost tch 3f out: t.o* **16/1**
50 **5** *50* **Plumbago Blue**19 1532 3-8-5 0 ... AdamBeschizza(3) 3
(Marco Botti) *in tch: rdn and struggling 6f out: lost tch 4f out: wl t.o fnl 3f* **14/1**

2m 41.48s (12.78) **Going Correction** +1.275s/f (Soft) — **5** Ran SP% **109.2**
Speed ratings (Par 100): **104,101,82,72,36**
CSF £7.91 TOTE £2.10: £1.60, £2.00; EX 6.40.
Owner Lady Rothschild **Bred** Kincorth Investments Inc **Trained** Newmarket, Suffolk

FOCUS
An average maiden fillies' stakes. They went a sensible gallop on heavy ground and the winning time was around 18 seconds outside standard. They fionished well strung out behind the potentiall smart winner. The form is rated around the race averages and the time.

2009 INJURED JOCKEYS FUND H'CAP — 1m 3f 101y
5:55 (5:55) (Class 6) (0-60,63) 4-Y-O+ — **£1,617** (£481; £240; £120) **Stalls** Centre

Form — RPR
065 **1** **Darsan (IRE)**7 1791 4-9-4 57 ... ChrisCatlin 1 — 69
(Phil McEntee) *led for 1f: chsd ldrs after and clr of field: led over 4f out and sn clr: drvn over 1f out: tiring but in n.d ins fnl f: rdn out* **10/1**
543- **2** *8* **Cuckoo Rock (IRE)**70 6438 5-9-7 60 ... LeeNewman 6 — 59
(Jonathan Portman) *chsd clr ldng pair tl 7f out: sn rdn: hdwy to chse clr wnr over 3f out: no imp: jinked rt ins fnl f: kpt on but no ch w wnr* **5/1**
0413 **3** *15* **Khun John (IRE)**19 1534 9-9-6 59 ... StevieDonohoe 5 — 34
(Willie Musson) *hld up off the pce in midfield: rdn and effrt to go 4th 3f out: no imp on wnr: plugged on fnl f and snatched modest 3rd cl home* **10/3**1
0-31 **4** *nk* **King's Road**7 1770 7-9-10 63 6ex ... (t) GeorgeBaker 2 — 38
(Anabel K Murphy) *hld up off the pce in last trio: hdwy to go 3rd over 3f out: rdn over 2f out: fnd nil and sn wl btn: tired fnl f and lost 3rd cl home* **7/2**2
05-5 **5** *6* **Dzesmin (POL)**26 1382 10-9-4 60 ... (p) DeclanCannon(3) 4 — 25
(Richard Guest) *hld up in rr: rdn and effrt to go modest 5th 3f out: no imp and wl btn after* **4/1**3
3-60 **6** *4* **Royal Defence (IRE)**14 1624 6-9-0 58 ... LauraPike(5) 8 — 17
(Michael Quinn) *chsd clr ldng pair: rdn over 5f out: wknd and bhd 3f out: t.o fnl f* **18/1**
0320 **7** *77* **Visions Of Johanna (USA)**7 1770 7-9-6 59 ... WilliamCarson 7
(Richard Guest) *dwlt: rdn along early and hdwy to ld after 1f: sn clr: rdn and hdd over 4f out: sn wknd: wl t.o and virtually p.u fnl 2f* **14/1**
-000 **8** *6* **Rasteau (IRE)**14 1635 4-8-0 46 oh1 ... (p) DannyBrock(7) 3
(Tom Keddy) *bhd: hdwy into midfield but stl wl off the pce 8f out: lost tch over 3f out: wl t.o and virtually p.u fnl 2f* **12/1**

2m 42.55s (13.85) **Going Correction** +1.275s/f (Soft) — **8** Ran SP% **110.7**
Speed ratings (Par 101): **100,94,83,83,78 75,19,15**
Tote Swingers:1&2:£10.00, 2&3:£4.40, 1&3:£6.90 CSF £55.28 CT £194.25 TOTE £11.50: £2.80, £1.80, £1.40; EX 106.20 TRIFECTA Not won..
Owner Eventmaker Racehorses **Bred** P J B O Callaghan **Trained** Newmarket, Suffolk

FOCUS
A lowly extended 1m3f handicap for older horses. This looked a proper test on heavy ground. The winning time was about a second slower than the useful filly in the first race managed over the same C&D. Some doubt about what the winner achieved, but it has to rate a personal best.

2010 RACING WELFARE H'CAP — 6f 3y
6:25 (6:27) (Class 6) (0-60,59) 3-Y-O — **£1,617** (£481; £240; £120) **Stalls** Centre

Form — RPR
000- **1** **Dream Walker (FR)**274 4899 3-8-12 50 ... PatrickMathers 2 — 68+
(Ian McInnes) *in tch: rdn and effrt ent fnl 2f: led over 1f out: styd on strly and drew clr fnl f: readily* **25/1**
5443 **2** *6* **Auntie Kathryn (IRE)**43 1067 3-8-7 45 ... PaulHanagan 14 — 45
(Stuart Williams) *hld up towards rr: rdn and hdwy jst over 2f out: wnt 3rd and swtchd lft 1f out: no ch w wnr but kpt on to go 2nd fnl 50yds* **13/2**
00-1 **3** *1* **Oneniteinheaven (IRE)**29 1292 3-9-7 59 ... MichaelO'Connell 12 — 56
(Jane Chapple-Hyam) *chsd ldr: rdn and chsd wnr over 1f out: unable qck and btn fnl 150yds: wknd and lost 2nd fnl 50yds* **9/1**
550 **4** *6* **Russian Rumba (IRE)**27 1357 3-9-2 54 ... LeeNewman 15 — 33
(Jonathan Portman) *in tch: rdn and effrt to chse ldrs ent fnl 2f: btn 1f out: wknd fnl f* **18/1**
000- **5** *2* **Enthrall (IRE)**182 7344 3-8-9 47 ... EddieAhern 1 — 20
(Denis Coakley) *in tch: rdn and fnd little over 1f out: sn btn: wknd fnl f* **4/1**1
500- **6** *3 1/4* **Sarah Berry**168 7530 3-9-3 55 ... DarryllHolland 7 — 18
(Chris Dwyer) *hld up in tch: rdn and effrt over 2f out: no imp: wknd and wl btn 1f out* **33/1**
000- **7** *1 1/2* **Ooi Long**189 7242 3-8-5 46 ... AdamBeschizza(3) 10
(Mark Rimmer) *led tl rdn and hdd over 1f out: sn btn: fdd fnl f* **33/1**
00-6 **8** *3/4* **Lucky Mark (IRE)**17 1560 3-9-2 57 ... DaleSwift(3) 8
(Deborah Sanderson) *chsd ldrs: rdn and struggling over 2f out: wknd u.p over 1f out: fdd fnl f* **13/2**
-500 **9** *3/4* **Thecornishcowboy**9 1725 3-9-4 56 ... (p) JackMitchell 9
(John Ryan) *a towards rr: bhd and struggling u.p: no ch fnl 2f* **25/1**
-424 **10** *1/2* **Pearls From Sydney**30 1278 3-9-4 56 ... StevieDonohoe 6
(Paul Cole) *in tch and looked to be travelling wl: rdn and fnd nil ent fnl 2f: sn btn: fdd over 1f out* **22/1**
-035 **11** *25* **Stormin Gordon (IRE)**43 1067 3-8-1 46 ... (p) IanBurns(7) 13
(Noel Quinlan) *in tch towards rr: rdn and struggling whn edgd lft 1/2-way: sn wl bhd: t.o and eased fnl f* **33/1**
0-04 **12** *12* **Kai**16 1585 3-9-2 54 ... HayleyTurner 5
(Michael Bell) *dwlt: a towards rr: lost tch over 2f out: t.o and eased fnl f* **9/2**2
0040 **13** *3* **Johnson's Cat (IRE)**3 1916 3-8-7 45 ... (e) WilliamCarson 4
(Richard Guest) *racd alone towards far side for over 1f: grad c bk towards centre and rejnd field 1/2-way: rdn along thrght: midfield tl wknd 1/2-way: t.o and eased fnl f* **6/1**3

1m 21.44s (7.04) **Going Correction** +1.275s/f (Soft) — **13** Ran SP% **115.3**
Speed ratings (Par 97): **104,96,94,86,84 79,77,76,75,75 41,25,21**
Tote Swingers:1&2:£26.20, 2&3:£6.90, 1&3:£42.80 CSF £163.79 CT £1632.29 TOTE £47.40: £9.80, £2.70, £3.30; EX 315.10 TRIFECTA Not won..
Owner Keith Brown **Bred** John Berry **Trained** Catwick, E Yorks

FOCUS
A low-class 6f handicap confined to 3yos. They went a solid gallop up the nearside rail and the winning time of about ten seconds outside standard looks very respectable for this grade on heavy ground. The winner had shown little previously and there are some doubts over the form.
Dream Walker(FR) Official explanation: trainer said, regarding apparent improvement in form, that the gelding had strengthened up since last year and possibly benefited from the heavy ground.
Auntie Kathryn(IRE) Official explanation: jockey said filly was denied a clear run
Russian Rumba(IRE) Official explanation: trainer said filly was unsuited by the heavy ground
Kai Official explanation: trainer's rep had no explanation for the poor form shown

2011 DAVID BROOKS MEMORIAL H'CAP — 1m 3y
6:55 (6:55) (Class 4) (0-80,78) 4-Y-O+ — **£4,075** (£1,212; £606; £303) **Stalls** Centre

Form — RPR
1131 **1** **Prince Of Sorrento**14 1626 5-9-4 75 ... StevieDonohoe 2 — 91
(Lee Carter) *chsd ldr tl led over 4f out: gng best 3f out: rdn and clr ent fnl 2f: styd on strly and drew wl clr fnl f* **7/2**2
-050 **2** *7* **European Dream (IRE)**3 1914 9-9-4 78 ... (p) DeclanCannon(3) 8 — 79
(Richard Guest) *hld up in tch in last pair: hdwy to trck ldrs 1/2-way: rdn to chse wnr over 2f out: sn drvn: no ex and btn over 1f out* **13/2**3
00-2 **3** *7* **Batgirl**31 1262 5-9-3 74 ... TomMcLaughlin 6 — 61
(John Berry) *hld up in last pair: hdwy to trck ldrs 1/2-way: 3rd and rdn over 2f out: edgd lft and btn wl over 1f out: wknd fnl f* **15/2**
0/1- **4** *8* **Jawhar (IRE)**248 5792 4-9-6 77 ... PaulHanagan 5 — 47
(William Haggas) *chsd ldrs: wnt 2nd over 4f out tl over 2f out: wknd over 1f out* **10/11**1
5266 **5** *24* **Conducting**8 1755 4-8-5 69 ... DannyBrock(7) 4
(Gay Kelleway) *in tch: rdn and struggling over 3f out: lost tch over 2f out: t.o and eased fnl f* **16/1**
3000 **6** *61* **On The Cusp (IRE)**17 1561 5-8-9 66 ... (p) WilliamCarson 1
(Richard Guest) *led tl over 4f out: sn lost pl and bhd: wl t.o and eased fnl 2f* **28/1**

1m 49.72s (9.12) **Going Correction** +1.275s/f (Soft) — **6** Ran SP% **109.0**
Speed ratings (Par 105): **105,98,91,83,59**
Tote Swingers:1&2:£2.50, 2&3:£4.60, 1&3:£1.60 CSF £23.94 CT £141.94 TOTE £3.90: £2.20, £3.00; EX 24.70 Trifecta £58.20 Pool 366.00 - 4.65 winning units..
Owner Bill Hinge & John Searchfield **Bred** Mrs P Akhurst **Trained** Epsom, Surrey

FOCUS
An average 1m handicap for older horses. They went a solid gallop on heavy ground and the winning time of nearly 13 seconds slower than standard is respectable. Only the winner really showed his form, but it's hard to take this too literally.
Jawhar(IRE) Official explanation: trainer's rep said gelding was unsuited by the heavy ground

2012 HAMMOND SUBARU FILLIES' H'CAP — 6f 3y
7:25 (7:25) (Class 5) (0-75,74) 4-Y-O+ — **£2,264** (£673; £336; £168) **Stalls** Centre

Form — RPR
24-4 **1** **Interakt**17 1564 5-9-2 72 ... HarryBentley(3) 6 — 81
(Joseph Tuite) *chsd ldrs: rdn and effrt to chal over 1f out: led 1f out: kpt on wl and in command after: rdn out* **7/2**2
0322 **2** *1 1/2* **Caramelita**9 1742 5-8-7 60 oh1 ... (v) PaulHanagan 2 — 64
(J R Jenkins) *chsd ldr: rdn to ld wl over 1f out: hdd and unable qck 1f out: styd on same pce fnl f* **3/1**1
644 **3** *1/2* **Basle**14 1628 5-8-7 60 oh3 ... (t) ChrisCatlin 1 — 62
(Gay Kelleway) *chsd ldrs: rdn and effrt to press ldrs wl over 1f out: drvn and styd on same pce fnl f* **9/1**

-052 **4** *3 ¾* **Shes Rosie**[13] 1638 4 -9-3**70** HayleyTurner 7 60
(John O'Shea) *dwlt and rdn along leaving stalls: rdn 1/2-way: chsd ldng trio over 1f out: no imp* **3/1**[1]

045- **5** *6* **Clumber Place**[198] 7076 6 -9-0**67** PaulMulrennan 4 38
(James Given) *hmpd and lost pl sn after s: a bhd and nt travelling wl after: rdn over 4f out: wknd 2f out* **5/1**[3]

-401 **6** *20* **Flashbang**[7] 1788 4 -8-13**66** 6ex (b) StevieDonohoe 3
(Paul Cole) *led and swtchd rt after s: rdn and hdd wl over 1f out: sn drvn and btn: fdd 1f out: eased fnl 100yds* **15/2**

1m 21.23s (6.83)**Going Correction** +1.275s/f (Soft) **6**Ran SP% **110.7**
Speed ratings (Par 100): **105,103,102,97,89 62**
Tote Swingers:1&2:£2.10, 2&3:£3.60, 1&3:£6.80 CSF £13.92 TOTE £3.70 : £2.10 , £2.20 ; EX 10.60.
Owner Heart Of The South Racing **Bred** P C Hunt **Trained** Great Shefford, Berks
■ Stewards' Enquiry : Stevie Donohoe one-day ban: careless riding (May 24)

FOCUS
An average 6f fillies' handicap for 4yo+. They went a strong pace on heavy ground. The winner picked up her 2011 progress and the next two were close to their marks.
Shes Rosie Official explanation: jockey said filly put its head down just before gates opened making it difficult to remove blindfold.
Flashbang Official explanation: trainer's rep said filly was unsuited by the heavy ground

2013 CONFERENCES AT GREAT YARMOUTH RACECOURSE H'CAP 1m 2f 21y
7:55 (7:55) (Class 6) (0-55,55) 4-Y-0+ **£1,617** (£481; £240 ; £120) **Stalls** Low

Form RPR
3026 **1** **Cairanne**[14] 1634 4 -8-8**50** RyanClark(3) 3 61
(Tom Keddy) *taken down early: chsd ldr tl led 5f out: rdn wl clr 3f out: idled and drvn ent fnl f: kpt on* **6/1**

/550 **2** *5* **Director's Dream (IRE)**[31] 1263 4 -8-11**53** AdamBeschizza(3) 1 54
(Mark Rimmer) *in tch in last trio: rdn and struggling over 4f out: 6th and looked wl hld 3f out: swtchd lft and hdwy over 2f out: chsd wnr 1f out: kpt on but nvr able to chal* **5/1**[3]

-000 **3** *10* **Nicholas Pocock (IRE)**[10] 1717 6 -8-13**55** (p) DaleSwift(3) 6 36
(Ian McInnes) *in tch in midfield: rdn 5f out: chsd clr wnr 3f out: no imp: lost 2nd 1f out: wknd fnl f* **8/1**

5204 **4** *3 ¾* **Avon Supreme**[6] 1831 4 -8-13**52** ChrisCatlin 8 26
(Gay Kelleway) *hld up in last pair: pushed along and effrt 4f out: rdn 3f out: 4th and wl btn fnl 2f* **7/2**[1]

001/ **5** *9* **Pindar (GER)**[1522] 6152 8 -8-9**48** MickyFenton 4
(Barney Curley) *stdd s: t.k.h: hld up in rr: hdwy 3f out: sn rdn and no hdwy: wl btn fnl 2f* **4/1**[2]

640- **6** *29* **Crabbies Gold (IRE)**[261] 5352 4 -8-11**50** (p) PaulMulrennan 7
(Lisa Williamson) *in tch: chsd ldrs 5f out: sn rdn and struggling: t.o fnl 2f* **9/1**

-600 **7** *2 ¼* **Danceyourselfdizzy (IRE)**[14] 1628 4 -8-7**46** oh1 (p) KirstyMilczarek 2
(Phil McEntee) *led tl over 4f out: sn rdn: wknd 3f out: wl bhd fnl 2f: t.o* **5/1**[3]

0000 **8** *7* **Give Or Take**[7] 1771 4 -8-4**46** oh1 (tp) DominicFox(3) 5
(Christine Dunnett) *chsd ldrs: reminder 7f out: drvn and lost pl 4f out: t.o over 2f out* **50/1**

2m 22.85s (12.35)**Going Correction** +1.275s/f (Soft) **8**Ran SP% **112.9**
Speed ratings (Par 101): **101,97,89,86,78 55,53,48**
Tote Swingers:1&2:£6.40, 2&3:£7.20, 1&3:£8.30 CSF £34.97 CT £239.46 TOTE £7.50 : £3.40 , £1.60, £3.50 ; EX 35.00 Trifecta £187.60 Pool 562.80 - 2.22 winning units.
Owner Howard Fielding **Bred** Lady Jennifer Green And John Eyre **Trained** Newmarket, Suffolk

FOCUS
A lowly 1m2f handicap for older horses. They went a sensible gallop on heavy ground and finished strung out. There are doubts over the form, which has been rated around the winner.
Pindar(GER) Official explanation: jockey said gelding hung left

2014 HOLIDAY ON THE NORFOLK BROADS H'CAP 1m 2f 21y
8:25 (8:26) (Class 6) (0-65,65) 3-Y-0 **£1,617** (£481; £240 ; £120) **Stalls** Low

Form RPR
00-3 **1** **Kozmina Bay**[22] 1443 3 -8-11**55** LeeNewman 2 60
(Jonathan Portman) *pressed ldr: rdn and ev ch 3f out: led narrowly over 1f out: kpt on gamely fnl f: rdn out* **11/4**[2]

000- **2** *nk* **Hardy Plume**[159] 7627 3 -8-8**52** oh2 ow1 EddieAhern 8 56
(Denis Coakley) *sn led: rdn 3f out: clr w wnr whn narrowly hdd over 1f out: battled on gamely tl no ex fnl 100yds* **13/8**[1]

063 **3** *12* **Lyrical Gangster (IRE)**[72] 731 3 -9-4**62** RobertHavlin 5 42
(Peter Chapple-Hyam) *hld up in tch: rdn and effrt 3f out: sn struggling: outpcd and btn 2f out: plugged on to go modest 3rd ins fnl f* **13/2**

00-6 **4** *2 ¾* **La Confession**[22] 1448 3 -8-7**51** oh1 ChrisCatlin 6 26
(Rae Guest) *stdd s: hld up in rr: rdn and effrt 3f out: sn struggling: wknd 2f out* **9/2**[3]

055- **5** *1 ¼* **Arrow Lake (FR)**[216] 6662 3 -9-7**65** WilliamCarson 4 37
(Noel Quinlan) *hld up in tch: hdwy to press ldrs 4f out: rdn and unable qck over 2f out: drvn and wknd 2f out* **13/2**

2m 29.32s (18.82)**Going Correction** +1.275s/f (Soft) **5**Ran SP% **109.6**
Speed ratings (Par 97): **75,74,65,62,61**
CSF £7.58 TOTE £7.30 : £2.50 , £1.10 ; EX 6.70 Trifecta £37.50 Pool 508.28 - 10.02 winning units..
Owner P A Deal **Bred** Hermes Services Ltd **Trained** Compton, Berks

FOCUS
A weak handicap confined to 3yos. They went a conservative gallop on heavy ground and the time was relativly slow. The first pair came clear and were unexposed, but this is not form to be too positive about.
T/Plt: £113.90 to a £1 stake. Pool £64,874.74. 415.55 winning tickets T/Qpdt: £42.50 to a £1 stake. Pool £5,726.87. 99.59 winning tickets SP

2015a - 2018a - (Foreign Racing) - See Raceform Interactive

ASCOT (R-H)
Friday, May 11

OFFICIAL GOING: Soft (6.1)
Wind: Moderate across Weather: Sunny spells early

2019 2 MILLION ATR VIEWERS MAIDEN FILLIES' STKS (DIV I) 5f
5:25 (5:26) (Class 4) 2-Y-0 **£5,175** (£1,540; £769 ; £384) **Stalls** Centre

Form RPR
0 **1** **Premier Steps (IRE)**[21] 1499 2 -9-0**0** RichardKingscote 4 73
(Tom Dascombe) *mde all: shkn up 2f out: styd on strly thrght fnl f* **15/8**[1]

2 *1* **Equitania** 2 -9-0**0** RichardHughes 5 70
(Richard Hannon) *disp 2nd tl chsd wnr ins fnl 2f: drvn and qcknd fnl f but a hld* **2/1**[2]

3 *½* **Symboline** 2 -9-0**0** MartinHarley 3 68+
(Mick Channon) *trckd ldrs in 4th: drvn and hdwy to take 3rd over 1f out: kpt on fnl 120yds but a jst hld by ldng duo* **11/1**

46 **4** *2 ½* **Someone's Darling**[13] 1671 2 -9-0**0** LiamKeniry 1 59
(Jim Goldie) *wnt rt s: in rr but in tch: pushed along 2f out: styd on to take 4th fnl 120yds* **7/1**

5 *3 ½* **Clock Opera (IRE)** 2 -9-0**0** NeilCallan 2 46
(Mrs K Burke) *disp 2nd tl ins fnl 2f: wknd over 1f out* **7/2**[3]

1m 5.8s (5.30)**Going Correction** +0.75s/f (Yiel) **5**Ran SP% **111.2**
Speed ratings (Par 92): **93,91,90,86,81**
CSF £6.05 TOTE £2.90 : £1.80 , £1.80 ; EX 5.00 .
Owner Attenborough Bellman Ingram Lowe **Bred** Manister House Stud **Trained** Malpas, Cheshire

FOCUS
All races were up the straight, as the round course was waterlogged. The five runners in this fillies' maiden raced up the far side of the track, with the front two in the market asserting inside the final furlong. Just fair form, but the time was not bad. The winner is rated up 10lb.

NOTEBOOK
Premier Steps (IRE) had run well on her debut in a 5f Newbury maiden on soft ground and had clearly benefited from that experience. Quickly out of the stalls she was able to dictate a steady pace and, while briefly looking in trouble a furlong out, battled on well to the line. She was the third juvenile winner from the yard this week and can improve again once the ground improves. (op 2-1)

Equitania, weak in the market, was the real eye-catcher of the race. She travelled beautifully throughout and looked to be coming to win her race under a typically confident Richard Hughes, but was outbattled by her more experienced rival. The yard's juveniles have tended to need their first run this season and this Totepool Two-Year-Old Trophy entry looks above average. (op 9-4 tchd 5-2)

Symboline, who is bred to be speedy, ran an encouraging race for a yard whose 2yos generally improve for experience. (op 12-1 tchd 10-1)

Someone's Darling showed much improved form on her third start, staying on well over an inadequate trip, and is now qualified for handicaps. (op 6-1)

Clock Opera (IRE) hailing from last year's winning stable, travelled nicely into the race before weakening late on, suggesting she did not act on the testing ground. (tchd 10-3)

2020 2 MILLION ATR VIEWERS MAIDEN FILLIES' STKS (DIV II) 5f
6:00 (6:00) (Class 4) 2-Y-0 **£5,175** (£1,540; £769 ; £384) **Stalls** Centre

Form RPR
3 **1** **Graphic Guest**[22] 1466 2 -9-0**0** MartinHarley 2 76+
(Mick Channon) *s.i.s: sn rcvrd to dispute 2nd: chal over 1f out: drvn to ld ins fnl f: edgd rt and kpt on wl clsng stages* **1/1**[1]

3 **2** *1 ¼* **Steer By The Stars (IRE)** 1753 2 -9-0**0** SilvestreDeSousa 1 72
(Mark Johnston) *led after 1f: drvn along 2f out: jnd over 1f out: hdd ins fnl f: hld whn sltly crossed and edgd lft nr fin* **15/8**[2]

3 *1 ½* **Surely Speightful (USA)** 2 -9-0**0** JamieSpencer 3 66+
(Kevin Ryan) *led 1f: disp 2nd to 2f out: drvn and one pce fr over 1f out* **15/2**[3]

4 *1 ½* **Malilla (IRE)** 2 -9-0**0** AdamKirby 4 61
(Clive Cox) *t.k.h early: chsd ldrs: drvn 2f out swtchd rt over 1f out: kpt on same pce* **8/1**

1m 5.37s (4.87)**Going Correction** +0.75s/f (Yiel) **4**Ran SP% **107.7**
Speed ratings (Par 92): **96,94,91,89**
CSF £3.10 TOTE £2.10 ; EX 2.70 .
Owner John Guest Racing **Bred** Barry Taylor **Trained** West Ilsley, Berks

FOCUS
Unlike the first Division of this fillies' maiden, the four runners raced more towards the centre of the track, with the two experienced fillies drawing clear towards the line. Not easy form to assess, but the winner is likely to do considerably better off a proper pace.

NOTEBOOK
Graphic Guest had created a decent impression when third in a competitive Newmarket maiden (runner-up won the Lily Agnes Stakes at Chester on Wednesday) and she won cleverly enough. Again not the quickest away from the gates, she cruised into contention a furlong out, to win going away. She will be better in a bigger field, off a quicker pace, and looks a nice type. (op 10-11 tchd 5-6)

Steer By The Stars (IRE) had handled testing conditions when third at Pontefract on her debut and ran another sound race here. Without the scope of the winner, she can land a small maiden. (op 2-1 tchd 9-4)

Surely Speightful (USA) showed bright pace to lead early, but could not quicken with the principals on ground that did not suit. She stayed on well and will improve for this. (op 8-1)

Malilla(IRE) was driven some way from home, but stayed on nicely, suggesting this 5f trip was on the short side. (op 17-2 tchd 7-1)

2021 1.3 MILLION ATTHERACES.COM USERS H'CAP 1m (S)
6:35 (6:36) (Class 4) (0-85,82) 3-Y-0 **£5,175** (£1,540; £769 ; £384) **Stalls** Centre

Form RPR
14 **1** **Warfare**[13] 1661 3 -8-13**74** JamieSpencer 6 86+
(Kevin Ryan) *stdd s: hld up: hdwy and nt clr run ins fnl 2f: swtchd lft over 1f out: str run to chse ldr ins fnl f: led fnl 120yds: readily* **9/2**[3]

6-64 **2** *1 ½* **Tight Lipped (IRE)**[12] 1264 3 -8-11**72** RichardHughes 9 78
(James Eustace) *trckd ldrs: drvn 2f out: led over 1f out: hdd and outpcd fnl 120yds but styd clr of 3rd* **9/1**

16-61 **3** *4 ½* **Fennell Bay (IRE)**[17] 1582 3 -8-11**72** SilvestreDeSousa 1 68
(Mark Johnston) *disp cl 2nd tl chal 3f out: slt ld ins fnl 2f: hdd over 1f out: wknd fnl 150yds* **4/1**[2]

610- **4** *2 ¼* **Halling Dancer**[198] 7095 3 -9-3**78** DarryllHolland 8 68
(Lee Carter) *chsd ldrs: rdn over 2f out: wknd appr fnl f* **9/1**

10- **5** *nk* **Now My Sun**[268] 5181 3 -8-11**72** MartinHarley 4 62
(Mrs K Burke) *sn led: jnd 3f out: hdd ins fnl 2f: wknd fnl f* **4/1**[2]

1-62 **6** *13* **Presburg (IRE)**[18] 1565 3 -9-7**82** LiamKeniry 3 42
(Joseph Tuite) *disp 2nd: ev ch 3f out: sn rdn: btn whn sltly hmpd ins fnl 2f: eased fnl f* **7/2**[1]

2-23 **7** *21* **Beau Duke (IRE)**[25] 1422 3 -8-11**72** (v) DavidProbert 2
(Andrew Balding) *t.k.h in rr but in tch: rdn 3f out: wknd over 2f out: eased fnl f* **7/1**

1m 48.33s (7.53)**Going Correction** +0.95s/f (Soft) **7**Ran SP% **112.9**
Speed ratings (Par 101): **99,97,93,90,90 77,56**
toteswingers: 1&2 £6.90, 1&3 £2.00, 2&3 £7.70. CSF £41.88 CT £173.03 TOTE £4.30 : £2.40 , £3.60; EX 36.10 Trifecta £165.00 Pool: £452.31 - 2.02 winning units. .
Owner Guy Reed **Bred** G Reed **Trained** Hambleton, N Yorks

FOCUS
This 1m handicap looked competitive beforehand but the field were well strung out crossing the line, despite the steady early pace. A pretty ordinary race for the track and grade, but the winner impressed and there should be more to come.

2022 AT THE RACES H'CAP 7f
7:10 (7:11) (Class 2) (0-105,99) 3-Y-O **£12,938** (£3,850; £1,924; £962) **Stalls** Centre

Form RPR
40-2 **1** **Sovereign Debt (IRE)**^{13} [1653] 3-8-12 **90**...................... JamieSpencer 7 108+
(Michael Bell) *stdd s: hld up in rr: stdy hdwy over 2f out: led over 1f out: sn qcknd clr: v easily* **11/4^{1}**
5-1 **2** *3 1/2* **Perfect Step (IRE)**^{22} [1472] 3-8-10 **88**................................ NeilCallan 11 94+
(Roger Varian) *chsd ldrs: led 2f out: riddn and hdd over 1f out: sn no ch w easy wnr but kpt on for clr 2nd* **10/3^{2}**
16-3 **3** *4 1/2* **Tidentimo (USA)**^{23} [1462] 3-9-1 **93**................................... MartnHarley 6 87
(Mick Channon) *in rr but in tch: drvn and hdwy over 2f out: chsd ldng duo over 1f out but nvr any ch* **8/1**
21-5 **4** *1/2* **Lord Ofthe Shadows (IRE)**^{34} [1216] 3-9-6 **98**........... RichardHughes 9 91
(Richard Hannon) *towards rr but in tch: hdwy to chse ldrs 2f out: sn rdn and one pce* **8/1**
12- **5** *7* **Abishena (IRE)**^{195} [7169] 3-9-1 **93**............................ SilvestreDeSousa 5 68
(Mark Johnston) *chsd ldrs: rdn 3f out: ev ch u.p 2f out: wknd sn after* **4/1^{3}**
40-0 **6** *2 1/2* **Worthington (IRE)**^{31} [1271] 3-8-7 **85**......................... PatrickMathers 2 53
(Richard Fahey) *wnt rt s: sn upsides: rdn 3f out: stl ev ch 2f out: sn wknd* **28/1**
040- **7** *1* **Moon Pearl (USA)**^{216} [6692] 3-9-7 **99**................................ JimCrowley 8 65
(Ralph Beckett) *chsd ldrs: rdn over 2f out: sn btn* **10/1**
50-6 **8** *3 1/2* **Crown Dependency (IRE)**^{48} [1032] 3-9-4 **99**................ SeanLevey$^{(3)}$ 4 56
(Richard Hannon) *towards rr: drvn over 3f out: nvr rchd ldrs and wknd 2f out* **16/1**
1-4 **9** *1 1/2* **Spykes Bay (USA)**^{27} [1375] 3-8-3 **81** oh2 ow1.................... ChrisCatlin 3 34
(Mrs K Burke) *sn led: rdn 3f out: hdd & wknd 2f out* **20/1**
1m 33.5s (5.90) **Going Correction** +0.95s/f (Soft) **9** Ran SP% **115.2**
Speed ratings (Par 105): **102,98,92,92,84 81,80,76,74**
toteswingers: 1&2 £2.60, 1&3 £3.10, 2&3 £6.60. CSF £11.88 CT £64.36 TOTE £3.10: £1.50, £1.70, £1.90; EX 10.60 Trifecta £42.90 Pool: £799.34 - 13.77 winning units..
Owner Lawrie Inman **Bred** Yeomanstown Stud **Trained** Newmarket, Suffolk

FOCUS
The nine-strong field angled towards the stands rail early. The race was run at a steady pace but again they were well strung out crossing the line. A decent 3yo handicap. The first two finished clear and the form is taken at face value. The winner is valuable for further.

NOTEBOOK
Sovereign Debt(IRE) showed he handled soft ground when runner-up at Doncaster on his seasonal debut and clearly benefited from that outing, as he ran out a most impressive winner, under a typically confident Jamie Spencer ride. Rated 90 before this success, he looks capable of performing in better grades than this, especially with give underfoot. (op 10-3)
Perfect Step(IRE) ran a fine race on only her third career start, travelling well throughout and pulling clear of the third. She is still open to any amount of improvement. (op 4-1)
Tidentime(USA), who finished 3rd in the 6f Tattersalls Millions 3-Y-O Sprint in April, travelled well but was unable to quicken in this ground. He looks a nice enough type when the ground firms up. (op 6-1)
Lord Ofthe Shadows(IRE) was another who travelled well into the race, but could not quicken on this testing ground. (tchd 13-2)
Abishena(IRE) did not enjoy her first run on testing ground and was not helped by having to race wide. (op 9-2)
Moon Pearl(USA) did not enjoy the ground and was driven a long way out. (op 9-1)
Crown Dependency(IRE) did not settle early, but ran another disappointing race and does not look to be enjoying his racing at present. (tchd 20-1)

2023 EXCLUSIVE WILLIAM BUICK BLOG ON ATTHERACES.COM H'CAP (DIV I) 6f
7:45 (7:45) (Class 3) (0-95,94) 4-Y-0+ **£7,115** (£2,117; £1,058; £529) **Stalls** Centre

Form RPR
0410 **1** **Thunderball**^{6} [1844] 6-9-3 **90**...(p) TomQueally 3 98
(Scott Dixon) *chsd ldrs: rdn to ld over 1f out: drvn and styd on wl fnl f* **2/1^{1}**
50-2 **2** *1 1/4* **Gouray Girl (IRE)**^{28} [1354] 5-8-13 **86**.................................. DaneO'Neill 1 90
(Henry Candy) *hld up in rr in last pl tl hdwy over 2f out: nt clr run and swtchd lft over 1f out: styd on to chse wnr ins fnl f but no imp fnl 120yds* **9/4^{2}**
255- **3** *1 1/2* **Secret Witness**^{153} [7721] 6-9-7 **94**..................................(b) JamesDoyle 4 93
(Ronald Harris) *s.i.s: hld up towards rr: drvn 2f out: hdwy and rdn over 1f out: styd on to take one pce 3rd ins fnl f* **8/1**
226- **4** *2* **Kingsdine (IRE)**^{308} [3802] 5-8-12 **85**........................... TomMcLaughlin 5 78
(Malcolm Saunders) *led 1f: styd pressing ldr tl led again over 2f out: hdd over 1f out: wknd ins fnl f* **12/1**
4521 **5** *3/4* **Masai Moon**^{17} [1581] 8-8-9 **82**......................................(b) JamesMillman 6 72
(Rod Millman) *led after 1f: sn hrd pressed: narrowly hdd over 2f out: wkng whn hmpd over 1f out* **5/1^{3}**
6641 **6** *2 1/2* **Sulis Minerva (IRE)**^{10} [1727] 5-8-5 **83** 6ex..................... RaulDaSilva$^{(5)}$ 2 65
(Jeremy Gask) *t.k.h towards rr but in tch: hdwy 3f out: sn rdn and chsng ldrs but one pce whn hmpd over 1f out: sn btn* **7/1**
1m 18.92s (4.42) **Going Correction** +0.95s/f (Soft) **6** Ran SP% **112.1**
Speed ratings (Par 107): **107,105,103,100,99 96**
toteswingers: 1&2 £1.60, 1&3 £5.60, 2&3 £4.00. CSF £6.76 TOTE £3.40: £1.70, £1.70; EX 7.80.
Owner Paul J Dixon **Bred** Mrs Yvette Dixon **Trained** Babworth, Notts
■ Stewards' Enquiry : James Millman caution: careless riding.
Dane O'Neill two-day ban: careless riding (May 25-26)

FOCUS
This 6f handicap was run at a steady pace with the field well grouped a furlong out. Not the strongest form for the grade, with the winner rated to his best.

NOTEBOOK
Thunderball confirmed his liking for testing conditions with a hard fought success off his highest winning mark. He was ideally positioned throughout and saw it out gamely and has now won twice, and been placed three times, from six runs on soft ground. (op 5-2 tchd 11-4)
Gouray Girl(IRE), who ran well when runner-up over 7f last time, was unlucky here. Settled in rear she had to be switched when making her move and the lost momentum proved crucial. She would have been better suited by a quicker pace. (tchd 5-2)
Secret Witness, who has yet to win on anything softer than good, travelled well but was unable to quicken in the ground. (tchd 7-1)
Kingsdine(IRE), 18lb above his highest winning mark, ran well enough on his first start since July, over a trip shorter than ideal. (tchd 14-1)
Masai Moon was too keen early and understandably faded on ground softer than he wants. (op 9-2 tchd 4-1)
Sulis Minerva(IRE), 3lb higher than when successful at Kempton last week, was in trouble a long way from home and did not enjoy the soft ground. (op 6-1)

2024 EXCLUSIVE WILLIAM BUICK BLOG ON ATTHERACES.COM H'CAP (DIV II) 6f
8:20 (8:20) (Class 3) (0-95,94) 4-Y-0+ **£7,115** (£2,117; £1,058; £529) **Stalls** Centre

Form RPR
0-00 **1** **Masked Dance (IRE)**^{20} [1522] 5-8-10 **83**.........................(p) TomQueally 2 88
(Scott Dixon) *pressed ldr: rdn 2f out: chal ins fnl f: led fnl 150yds: kpt on wl* **5/1^{3}**
2103 **2** *3/4* **Chilli Green**^{53} [962] 5-9-0 **87**....................................(p) StevieDonohoe 4 90
(Lee Carter) *sn slt ld: rdn and jnd 2 out: strly chal ins fnl f: hdd and no ex fnl 150yds* **9/4^{1}**
000- **3** *2 1/2* **Swiss Franc**^{245} [5887] 7-9-7 **94**.. JamioSpenccr 5 09
(David Elsworth) *t.k.h: hld up in rr: rdn and hdwy 2f out: nvr gng pce to rch ldrs: hung rt and btn over 1f out but plugged on to take 3rd clsng stages* **11/4^{2}**
6-0 **4** *nk* **Batchelors Star (IRE)**^{16} [1602] 4-8-12 **85**........................ JamesDoyle 3 79
(Jim Boyle) *chsd ldrs: rdn over 2f out: edgd rt and btn over 1f out: wknd fnl f and lost 3rd clsng stages* **9/4^{1}**
6/2- **5** *16* **Matsunosuke**^{484} [137] 10-8-9 **82**...................................... MartinHarley 1 25
(Dr Richard Newland) *stdd s: t.k.h: sn chsng ldrs: wknd 2f out: eased whn no ch* **22/1**
1m 19.61s (5.11) **Going Correction** +0.95s/f (Soft) **5** Ran SP% **109.2**
Speed ratings (Par 107): **103,102,98,98,76**
CSF £16.28 TOTE £5.40: £1.70, £1.60; EX 18.20.
Owner Mrs S Morcombe **Bred** Canice Farrell Jnr **Trained** Babworth, Notts

FOCUS
An interesting handicap to conclude the card despite the small field size, it paid to race up with the pace.

NOTEBOOK
Masked Dance(IRE), 4lb lower than when winning at Newcastle last July, confirmed his liking for testing conditions with a hard fought success to give his handler a double on the card. Four of his five career wins have been over 7f and understandably he stayed on strongly over this 6f trip. He looks nicely handicapped, having shown a return to form, especially if the ground remains testing. Official explanation: trainer said, regarding apparent improvement in form, that the gelding was better suited by being able to race prominently and a straight course. (op 15-2 tchd 9-2)
Chilli Green, who is yet to win from seven starts on the turf, ran well but may have been flattered by this effort, as she benefited from the racing up with the pace. All her three career wins have come at Kempton. (op 3-1 tchd 7-2)
Swiss Franc, unproven on ground slower than good to soft, was too keen early on his first start for 245 days and did not pick up when asked. This should bring him on and he will appreciate quicker ground. (op 2-1)
Batchelors Star(IRE) hinted a step up to this trip would suit, when running over 5f last time. The 4yo looked dangerous 2f out, but wandered about under pressure and may be seen to better effect on a sounder surface. (op 2-1 tchd 15-8)
Matsunosuke, having his first run for Dr Richard Newland, is without a win since November 2010 and found this all too much, on his first start for 484 days. (op 25-1 tchd 20-1)
T/Plt: £71.30 to a £1 stake. Pool: £62,906.09 - 643.76 winning tickets. T/Qpdt: £21.60 to a £1 stake. Pool: £5,414.10 - 184.66 winning tickets. ST

1993 CHESTER (L-H)
Friday, May 11

OFFICIAL GOING: Soft (heavy in places; 5.4)
Rail moved out further 3yds fr. 6f to1.5f. Race distances inc. as follows: 7f 2y 7f 122y +24y, 1m2f 75 +26y, 1m5f 89y +44y, 5f 16y +20y, 1m4f 76y +38y.
Wind: Fairly strong, against Weather: Overcast

2025 FAT GARY SPORTS EARL GROSVENOR H'CAP 7f 122y
1:35 (1:35) (Class 2) (0-105,94) 4-Y-0+ **£15,752** (£4,715; £2,357; £1,180; £587) **Stalls** Low

Form RPR
-000 **1** **Pintura**^{20} [1510] 5-9-5 **92**... JamieSpencer 3 99
(David Simcock) *a.p: led over 1f out: wnt lft jst ins fnl f: r.o in driving fin: narrowly prevailed* **9/2^{3}**
00-0 **2** *shd* **Grissom (IRE)**^{18} [1558] 6-9-3 **90**.. DavidAllan 1 97
(Tim Easterby) *hld up: hdwy over 1f out: carried lft whn chalng jst ins fnl f: r.o and jst btn in driving fin* **9/1**
-054 **3** *shd* **Imperial Djay (IRE)**^{7} [1821] 7-8-11 **87**............................... DaleSwift$^{(3)}$ 6 94
(Ruth Carr) *stdd s: hld up: swtchd lft and hdwy 1f out: r.o and chalng in driving fin: jst btn* **10/1**
05-2 **4** *1 3/4* **Kyllachy Star**^{41} [1128] 6-9-4 **91**.. TonyHamilton 4 93
(Richard Fahey) *midfield: effrt 1f out: lugged lft and styd on ins fnl f: nt pce to chal* **4/1^{2}**
0353 **5** *nk* **Dubai Dynamo**^{6} [1865] 7-9-0 **87**.. JamesSullivan 2 89
(Ruth Carr) *trckd ldrs: lost pl 4f out: edgd rt whn chalng over 1f out: carried lft jst ins fnl f: no ex fnl 50yds* **7/2^{1}**
323- **6** *6* **Louis The Pious**^{224} [6500] 4-9-7 **94**................................... PhillipMakin 9 81
(Kevin Ryan) *in tch on outer: pushed along 2f out: rdn over 1f out: wknd ins fnl f* **8/1**
266- **7** *1 3/4* **Jamesie (IRE)**^{20} [1540] 4-9-4 **91**.. RyanMoore 7 73
(David Marnane, Ire) *racd keenly: prom: rdn over 1f out: wknd ins fnl f* **12/1**
0-00 **8** *3 1/4* **Light From Mars**^{41} [1130] 7-9-5 **92**.................................. FrannyNorton 5 66
(John Quinn) *sn led: rdn and hdd over 1f out: wknd jst ins fnl f* **14/1**
00-1 **9** *shd* **She's A Character**^{13} [1652] 5-8-8 **81**.............................. PaulHanagan 10 55
(Richard Fahey) *hld up: pushed along over 2f out: no imp u.p over 1f out: nvr a threat* **10/1**
1m 40.68s (6.88) **Going Correction** +1.10s/f (Soft) **9** Ran SP% **114.1**
Speed ratings (Par 109): **109,108,108,107,106 100,99,95,95**
Tote Swingers: 1&2 £8.40, 1&3 £10.50, 2&3 £20.40 CSF £43.80 CT £384.49 TOTE £6.30: £2.10, £3.10, £3.10; EX 45.00 Trifecta £424.80 Pool: £1,131.08 - 1.97 winning units..
Owner Dr Marwan Koukash **Bred** Dulverton Equine **Trained** Newmarket, Suffolk

FOCUS
Just 1mm of rain overnight and the ground was given as soft, heavy in places (GoingStick 5.1). The rail was out by a further 3yds from the 6f to the 1 1/2f point. Not as good a race as the rating band would have one believe, as the top-weight was rated 11lb lower than the ceiling. The early gallop, set by Light From Mars, wasn't hectic and it turned into a bit of a sprint from the turn in. The result was a three-way photo finish. Pretty straightforward form, the winner similar as to when runner-up last year.

NOTEBOOK
Pintura, one of three in the race representing owner Dr Marwan Koukash, was going one better than in this race last year, and had to survive a stewards' enquiry having given the runner-up a bump when quickening up a furlong out. He appreciates this sort of ground. (op 5-1)

Grissom(IRE) deserves credit because, unlike the winner who had a nice trip, he was asked to make up ground from the rear off the steady gallop. He also got squeezed up by the winner just inside the last so might have been a shade unlucky. (op 10-1 tchd 11-1)

Imperial Djay(IRE), who won at this meeting last year, is back on a winning mark and ran well considering he's probably more at home on a sounder surface and, like the runner-up, had to make ground up from the rear in a fairly steadily run contest. (op 11-1 tchd 12-1)

Kyllachy Star won this race last year and came here on the back of a good reappearance effort at Doncaster. Considering he was never travelling on this testing ground he didn't run at all badly. (op 3-1)

Dubai Dynamo is a consistent sort and, despite being a bit keen, again ran his race. He's done all his winning on turf on good ground or quicker. (op 9-2)

Louis The Pious, who did his winning over 6f last year, was the only one in the race making his seasonal reappearance. That lack of race-fitness seemed to find him out in the ground. (op 7-1 tchd 9-1 in a place)

Jamesie(IRE) was stepping up in distance and tackling softer ground, and he found the combination against him. (op 11-1)

2026 STOBART BARRISTERS DEE STKS (GROUP 3) (C&G) 1m 2f 75y

2:05 (2:05) (Class 1) 3-Y-O **£31,190** (£11,825; £5,918; £2,948) **Stalls** High

Form RPR

33- **1** **Astrology (IRE)**[216] 6692 3-8-12 108........................ JPO'Brien 4 115
(A P O'Brien, Ire) *mde all: kicked on 2f out: in command after: r.o wl to draw clr fnl f* **11/10**[1]

10-4 **2** *11* **Oxford Charley (USA)**[23] 1455 3-8-12 90........................ KierenFallon 3 94
(Mikael Magnusson) *s.i.s: hld up in 3rd pl: wnt 2nd over 4f out: tried to chal 3f out: wl outpcd by wnr fr 2f out: no ch after* **7/1**

1-1 **3** *5* **Kingsdesire (IRE)**[40] 1160 3-8-12 94........................(t) JamieSpencer 6 85
(Marco Botti) *hld up in last pl: wnt 3rd 4f out: rdn and outpcd over 2f out: wl adrift after* **10/3**[3]

5-2 **4** *4 ½* **Uriah Heep (FR)**[20] 1511 3-8-12 0........................ RyanMoore 5 76
(Sir Michael Stoute) *racd in 2nd pl tl over 4f out: sn pushed along and bhd: wl adrift after* **3/1**[2]

2m 21.57s (10.37) **Going Correction** +1.10s/f (Soft) **4** Ran SP% **108.2**
Speed ratings (Par 109): **102,93,89,85**
CSF £8.62 TOTE £1.40; EX 7.20.

Owner Derrick Smith **Bred** A-Mark Racing Et Al **Trained** Ballydoyle, Co Tipperary

FOCUS
We have to go back to 2003 and Kris Kin for the last winner of the Dee Stakes who followed up in the Derby, and with Bonfire a non-runner the race was robbed of its most interesting contender. Astrology had the run of things but was impressive all the same and the form is rated second only to Kris Kin in this race in the last ten years.

NOTEBOOK
Astrology(IRE) made every yard for an easy success. The winner was a shade disappointing on his final start at two in the Autumn Stakes, and looked in need of this outing beforehand, but he still had too much class for the others and kept up a strong gallop to see them off from the turn in. He probably doesn't need the ground this soft, but he clearly stays well and, with improvement almost guaranteed it won't be a surprise if he makes the line-up in one Derby or another. (op 5-4 tchd 11-8 in a place)

Oxford Charley(USA) tried to make a race of it from 3f out but was soon brushed aside. The ground wasn't really to his liking but he's a half-brother to Les Arcs, so there has to be a good chance he'll improve with age and experience. (op 15-2 tchd 13-2)

Kingsdesire(IRE) didn't seem to handle the ground at all and can be given another chance. (op 11-4)

Uriah Heep(FR), despite running well on soft at Newbury last time and being by Danehill Dancer, also failed to give his running on this tacky surface. (op 10-3)

2027 BOODLES DIAMOND ORMONDE STKS (GROUP 3) 1m 5f 89y

2:35 (2:36) (Class 1) 4-Y-O+ **£39,697** (£15,050; £7,532; £3,752) **Stalls** High

Form RPR

243- **1** **Memphis Tennessee (IRE)**[320] 3442 4-9-0 117.................. JPO'Brien 2 110+
(A P O'Brien, Ire) *led at stdy pce for nrly 5f: racd in 2nd pl tl dropped to 3rd 5f out: impr to go 2nd 2f out: led jst over 1f out: r.o ins fnl f: drew clr towards fin* **1/1**[1]

26-0 **2** *4* **Vivacious Vivienne (IRE)**[19] 1546 6-8-11 100............. JamieSpencer 3 101
(Donal Kinsella, Ire) *trckd ldrs: wnt 2nd 5f out: upsides and chalng 3f out: led over 2f out: rdn and hdd jst over 1f out: no ex and no ch fnl 100yds* **10/1**[3]

3 *1 ¼* **Calico Cat** 4-9-0 0........................ KatiaScallan 4 102?
(Alastair Lidderdale) *dwlt: in rr: pushed along over 5f out: toiling over 3f out: plugged on to take mod 3rd ins fnl f: nvr a threat* **66/1**

522- **4** *15* **Brown Panther**[244] 5928 4-9-0 116........................ KierenFallon 5 80
(Tom Dascombe) *on toes in paddock: plld hrd: chsd ldr: led after nrly 5f: pressed 3f out: hdd over 2f out: sn checked: wknd over 1f out: lost tch ins fnl f* **6/5**[2]

3m 8.73s (16.03) **Going Correction** +1.10s/f (Soft) **4** Ran SP% **106.0**
Speed ratings (Par 113): **94,91,90,81**
CSF £9.65 TOTE £1.50; EX 8.40.

Owner Mrs John Magnier & Michael Tabor & Derrick Smith **Bred** Kilfrush Stud **Trained** Ballydoyle, Co Tipperary

FOCUS
With Sea Moon a non-runner, this looked a match on paper, but the early gallop was pedestrian, Brown Panther disappointed, and with the newcomer finishing close up, the form looks pretty dubious. Memphis Tennessee did not need to match last year's best.

NOTEBOOK
Memphis Tennessee(IRE) just about set the standard on his fourth in the Derby and third in the Irish Derby, but he hadn't been seen since that last outing in June so was fully entitled to need this. Ridden with plenty of confidence by Joseph O'Brien, he got the job done easily enough without having to have a hard race. He should step forward from this, will appreciate getting back on a decent surface, and the Hardwicke Stakes looks the ideal target for him. That said, considering how well he ran at Epsom last year, it wouldn't be a surprise to see him turn up as part of a team from the stable in the Coronation Cup. (tchd 11-10, 6-5 in a place)

Vivacious Vivienne(IRE), for whom the ground was the question mark, handled it better than expected. That said, she's flattered by her proximity to the winner, who could have beaten her by further had he been asked. (tchd 8-1)

Calico Cat, a Darley cast-off, is a half-brother to Racing Post Trophy winner Ibn Khaldun out of the top-class soft-ground mare Gossamer. Ridden patiently out the back on his belated debut, he was detached from the rest with 3f to run, but kept plugging away, and was never nearer than at the finish. Indeed, he was second shortly after the line. This isn't form to take literally but he's clearly not short of ability, although he might need this sort of ground.

Brown Panther was edgy beforehand and keen early in the race. Pressing on heading out on the final circuit, he'd run his race by the time he was joined with half a mile to run. Clearly this wasn't his true form. Fallon said he felt the colt was flat and that it wasn't simply the ground, as he'd worked well in similar conditions in preparation for this race. Official explanation: trainer's rep had no explanation for the poor form shown (op 11-10)

2028 EDWARDSHOMES.CO.UK E B F H'CAP 5f 16y

3:05 (3:08) (Class 2) (0-105,104) 3£14,177 (£4,243; £2,121; £1,062; £528) **Stalls** Low

Form RPR

0-01 **1** **Ballesteros**[14] 1644 3-9-2 **99**........................ RyanMoore 3 109
(Brian Meehan) *midfield: hdwy over 1f out: r.o and brought to nr side ins fnl f: led fnl 110yds: in command towards fin* **11/8**[1]

12-1 **2** *2 ½* **Sonko (IRE)**[125] 86 3-8-2 **85** oh1........................(p) FrannyNorton 5 86
(Tim Pitt) *led: rdn over 1f out: hdd fnl 110yds: unable to go w wnr towards fin* **7/1**[3]

0-03 **3** *½* **Church Music (IRE)**[14] 1644 3-8-2 **85**........................(p) MircoDemuro 6 84
(Michael Scudamore) *midfield: hdwy over 1f out: styd on ins fnl f but nt quite pce to mount serious chal* **20/1**

1446 **4** *1* **Pale Orchid (IRE)**[9] 1751 3-8-8 **91**........................ PadraigBeggy 2 86
(David Evans) *chsd ldrs: rdn to 2nd over 1f out tl ins fnl f: kpt on same pce fnl 100yds* **7/1**[3]

3-01 **5** *1* **Dam Beautiful**[5] 1877 3-8-11 **97** 6ex........................ AmyRyan(3) 7 89
(Kevin Ryan) *hld up: hdwy over 1f out: rdn and kpt on ins fnl f: nt pce to trble ldrs* **4/1**[2]

-440 **6** *5* **Electric Qatar**[4] 1921 3-7-13 **85** oh5........................ DominicFox(3) 10 59
(Tom Dascombe) *led to post: edgey at s: missed break: bhd: rdn over 1f out: kpt on modly ins fnl f: nvr on terms w ldrs* **33/1**

6-46 **7** *6* **Bubbly Ballerina**[2] 1977 3-7-9 **85** oh1........................ NatashaEaton(7) 11 37
(Alan Bailey) *prom on outer: rdn and wknd over 1f out* **11/1**

10-6 **8** *15* **Powerful Wind (IRE)**[14] 1639 3-8-3 **86**........................ AndreaAtzeni 1
(Ronald Harris) *chsd ldr tl rdn over 1f out: sn wknd* **14/1**

25-5 **9** *3 ¾* **Last Bid**[20] 1524 3-8-11 **94**........................ DavidAllan 4
(Tim Easterby) *a outpcd and bhd: eased whn wl btn over 1f out* **14/1**

1m 6.0s (5.00) **Going Correction** +1.10s/f (Soft) **9** Ran SP% **116.5**
Speed ratings (Par 105): **104,100,99,97,96 88,78,54,48**
Tote Swingers: 1&2 £3.30, 1&3 £7.40, 2&3 £21.30 CSF £11.73 CT £135.27 TOTE £2.00: £1.10, £2.50, £4.30; EX 9.30 Trifecta £86.90 Pool: £1,567.12 - 13.34 winning units..

Owner Mrs P Good **Bred** Exors Of The Late J R Good **Trained** Manton, Wilts

FOCUS
This was run at a strong pace considering the conditions. This wasn't a strong race for the grade, but the winner is progressive in soft ground and the form has been rated at something like face value.

NOTEBOOK
Ballesteros ◆, who had looked a pattern-class performer in the making when scoring at Sandown last time, confirmed that impression here in a race run to suit. Clearly ground conditions are crucial to him (now 4-4 on good to soft or softer), but he has plenty of potential and it's not out of the question that he could be an Abbaye type by autumn time. (op 7-4 tchd 15-8 in a place)
Sonko(IRE) ◆ did really well to hang on for second having set such a good gallop throughout (closest pursuers Powerful Wind and Bubbly Ballerina finished well beaten). A sharp track suits her style of running and there will definitely be other days for her. (tchd 8-1)
Church Music(IRE), thumped 11 lengths by Ballesteros at Sandown last time, cut that deficit back to three lengths thanks to a combination of a sharper track and 9lb pull in the weights. (tchd 25-1)
Pale Orchid(IRE) looks handicapped right up to her best but she ran a solid race considering she raced closer to the pace than the winner, third, fifth and sixth. (tchd 13-2)
Dam Beautiful, a winner at Hamilton last time when the leaders went off too quick, once again got the pace scenario to suit, but on this sharper track she couldn't muster the pace to lay down a serious challenge. (op 9-2 tchd 5-1)
Electric Qatar, who hasn't lived up to the expectations connections held for him, faced a stiff task from 5lb out of the handicap, and his cause was made even more difficult when he missed the break quite badly.

2029 EDGE WORLDWIDE H'CAP 7f 2y

3:40 (3:40) (Class 4) (0-85,87) 4-Y-O+ **£6,469** (£1,925; £962; £481) **Stalls** Low

Form RPR

4140 **1** **Viva Ronaldo (IRE)**[40] 1156 6-9-6 **84**........................ PaulHanagan 2 94
(Richard Fahey) *in tch: effrt over 2f out: led jst over 1f out: r.o ins fnl f: won gng away* **11/2**[2]

00-4 **2** *2 ¾* **Spa's Dancer (IRE)**[13] 1680 5-9-2 **80**........................ KierenFallon 3 83
(Ed de Giles) *handy: chsd ldr over 4f out: led over 3f out: rdn and hdd jst over 1f out: kpt on u.p tl one pce and wl hld fnl 75yds* **7/2**[1]

65-1 **3** *nk* **Orpsie Boy (IRE)**[6] 1863 9-9-6 **87** 6ex........................ DaleSwift(3) 5 89
(Ruth Carr) *midfield: hdwy over 1f out: r.o to chse ldrs ins fnl f: nrst fin* **15/2**[3]

3121 **4** *¾* **April Fool**[15] 1627 8-9-2 **83**........................(b) CPGeoghegan(3) 1 83
(Ronald Harris) *led: hdd over 3f out: chsd ldr tl over 2f out: styd on same pce ins fnl f* **15/2**[3]

-001 **5** *nk* **Al Muheer (IRE)**[4] 1917 7-9-3 **81** 6ex........................(b) JamesSullivan 14 80+
(Ruth Carr) *wnt rt s: bhd: hdwy on outer over 1f out: styd on ins fnl f: nvr able to rch ldrs* **8/1**

20-5 **6** *10* **Corporal Maddox**[27] 1373 5-9-6 **84**........................ StevieDonohoe 8 57
(Jamie Osborne) *s.i.s: midfield travelling wl: hdwy to chse ldrs over 1f out: no imp over 1f out: wl btn ins fnl f* **8/1**

4262 **7** *4 ½* **Tamareen (IRE)**[97] 431 4-9-3 **81**........................ TonyHamilton 7 43
(Richard Fahey) *midfield: hdwy 2f out: nvr rchd ldrs: one pce ins fnl f* **14/1**

0-42 **8** *4 ½* **Mappin Time (IRE)**[17] 1581 4-9-4 **82**........................(p) JimmyFortune 9 32
(Tim Easterby) *in rr: hdwy on inner 2f out: one pce and no imp over 1f out: eased whn wl btn ins fnl f* **18/1**

55-1 **9** *8* **Kingswinford (IRE)**[36] 1203 6-9-3 **81**........................ PadraigBeggy 4 10
(David Evans) *in tch: pushed along 4f out: sn lost pl: n.d after* **10/1**

0-00 **10** *¾* **No Hubris (USA)**[18] 1558 5-9-6 **84**........................ AndrewMullen 13 11
(Ruth Carr) *wnt rt s: sn prom: pushed along and lost pl over 3f out: bhd over 2f out* **40/1**

460- **11** *1 ¼* **Barons Spy (IRE)**[207] 6920 11-9-4 **82**........................ FrannyNorton 11
(Richard Price) *in rr: hdwy into midfield over 2f out: no imp over 1f out: eased whn wl btn ins fnl f* **33/1**

440- **12** *shd* **Glenridding**[160] 7625 8-9-5 **83**........................ PaulMulrennan 12
(James Given) *prom: pushed along over 2f out: wknd wl over 1f out* **22/1**

300- **13** *7* **One Scoop Or Two**[230] 6326 6-9-6 **84**..................(p) GrahamGibbons 10
(Reg Hollinshead) *midfield early: bhd after 2f: eased whn wl btn over 1f out* **14/1**

1m 33.72s (7.22) **Going Correction** +1.175s/f (Soft) **13** Ran SP% **120.8**
Speed ratings (Par 105): **105,101,101,100,100 88,83,78,69,68 67,67,59**
Tote Swingers: 1&2 £4.20, 1&3 £6.40, 2&3 £4.90 CSF £24.80 CT £134.08 TOTE £6.60: £2.10, £1.40, £2.30; EX 20.40 Trifecta £91.70 Pool: £1,404.06 - 11.32 winning units..

Owner Aykroyd And Sons Ltd **Bred** Thomas Foy **Trained** Musley Bank, N Yorks

The Form Book Flat, Raceform Ltd, Compton, RG20 6NL

FOCUS
Once again there was a decent gallop on considering the tacky ground. The pace held up pretty well and the form is rated around the winner.
Corporal Maddox Official explanation: jockey said gelding lost its action
Barons Spy(IRE) Official explanation: jockey said gelding had no more to give
One Scoop Or Two Official explanation: jockey said gelding never travelled

2030 HIGHSTREETVOUCHERS.COM MAIDEN FILLIES' STKS 7f 2y
4:15 (4:16) (Class 4) 3-Y-O **£6,469** (£1,925; £962; £481) **Stalls** Low

Form RPR
0623 1 **Ozz**[27] 1389 3-9-0 61 (bt) MircoDemuro 2 67
(Frank Sheridan) *chsd ldrs: impr to go 2nd wl over 1f out: r.o and nosed ahd wl ins fnl f: kpt on and a doing enough cl home* **25/1**
0-4 2 *nk* **Last Supper**[13] 1660 3-9-0 0 GrahamGibbons 4 66
(James Bethell) *chsd ldr: led over 2f out: hdd narrowly wl ins fnl f: kpt on but hld* **28/1**
60-0 3 *5* **So Cheeky**[40] 1155 3-9-0 55 AndrewMullen 3 53
(Peter Salmon) *led: rdn and hdd over 2f out: one pce over 1f out: n.d to front pair ins fnl f* **33/1**
6- 4 *hd* **Yojojo (IRE)**[188] 7293 3-9-0 0 JimmyFortune 1 52
(Gay Kelleway) *hld up: hdwy over 1f out: hung lft ins fnl f: kpt on but no imp on ldrs* **9/1**[3]
5-22 5 *nk* **Lady Loch**[28] 1357 3-9-0 70 PaulHanagan 7 52
(Richard Fahey) *nvr travelling wl and bhd: wl adrift over 2f out: c wd ent st wl over 1f out: prog ins fnl f: styd on towards fin: nvr nrr* **15/8**[2]
5 6 *18* **Bunraku**[22] 1467 3-9-0 0 MichaelHills 8
(Charles Hills) *nvr travelling wl and a bhd: eased whn wl btn over 1f out* **11/8**[1]
4 7 *nse* **Diamondsinhereyes (IRE)**[91] 499 3-9-0 0 FrannyNorton 5
(Ed Vaughan) *chsd ldrs: effrt 2f out: wknd over 1f out* **12/1**
0 8 *1 1/2* **Shy Rosa (USA)**[22] 1472 3-9-0 0 KierenFallon 6
(Marcus Tregoning) *in tch: hdwy 3f out: effrt 2f out: no imp whn faltered 1f out: sn dropped away* **9/1**[3]
1m 35.75s (9.25) **Going Correction** +1.25s/f (Soft) 8 Ran SP% **114.8**
Speed ratings (Par 98): **97,96,90,90,90 69,69,68**
Tote Swingers: 1&2 £23.20, 1&3 £21.40, 2&3 £36.00 CSF £516.94 TOTE £60.60: £6.90, £7.20, £12.70; EX 401.50 Trifecta £878.90 Pool: £1,662.90 - 1.40 winning units..
Owner Arc Racing (North) **Bred** F Sheridan **Trained** Wolverhampton, W Midlands
FOCUS
With the first two in the betting disappointing this maiden didn't take much winning. Dubious, shaky form, some way off the usual standard for the track.
Bunraku Official explanation: jockey said filly never travelled

2031 GRAVITY GLOBAL INVESTMENTS H'CAP 1m 4f 66y
4:45 (4:46) (Class 4) (0-85,85) 4-Y-O+ **£6,469** (£1,925; £962; £481) **Stalls** Low

Form RPR
060- 1 **Mica Mika (IRE)**[136] 6155 4-8-13 77 PaulHanagan 4 89+
(Richard Fahey) *led for 1f: remained prom: led over 2f out: drew clr over 1f out: in command after: r.o wl: eased down cl home* **3/1**[2]
2 *2 1/4* **Luggers Hall (IRE)**[24] 4872 4-8-9 73 MircoDemuro 6 78
(Tony Carroll) *dwlt: sn bhd: rdn and hdwy over 3f out: wnt 2nd 1f out: styd on ins fnl f: nt trble wnr* **6/1**
44-0 3 *10* **Pintrada**[30] 1295 4-8-11 75 GrahamGibbons 1 65
(James Bethell) *led after 1f: hdd over 2f out: one pce u.p over 1f out: wl btn ins fnl f* **11/2**[3]
0-05 4 *3 1/4* **Sir Boss (IRE)**[15] 1632 7-8-10 74 (t) KierenFallon 2 59
(Michael Mullineaux) *s.i.s: midfield: pushed along 4f out: hdwy over 3f out: sn cl up: one pce over 1f out: wl btn ins fnl f* **6/1**
1256 5 *3* **St Ignatius**[7] 1829 5-8-0 71 oh7 (p) NatashaEaton(7) 7 51
(Alan Bailey) *prom: effrt on outer and ev ch over 3f out: wknd over 2f out* **25/1**
-330 6 *17* **English Summer**[34] 1214 5-9-7 85 FrannyNorton 3 39
(Mark Johnston) *chsd ldrs: rdn 3f out: wknd over 2f out* **5/2**[1]
22-0 7 *10* **Meetings Man (IRE)**[33] 1239 5-9-0 78 FrederikTylicki 8 16
(Micky Hammond) *hld up: toiling over 3f out: nvr a threat* **8/1**
2m 52.91s (14.41) **Going Correction** +1.325s/f (Soft) 7 Ran SP% **112.5**
Speed ratings (Par 105): **104,102,95,93,91 80,73**
Tote Swingers: 1&2 £2.70, 1&3 £3.40, 2&3 £4.70 CSF £20.41 CT £92.09 TOTE £3.20: £1.30, £3.40; EX 13.40 Trifecta £120.00 Pool: £936.39 - 5.77 winning units..
Owner Mrs Una Towell **Bred** Yeomanstown Stud **Trained** Musley Bank, N Yorks
FOCUS
This took plenty of getting. The first two finished clear and the winner is rated back to his best.
Sir Boss(IRE) Official explanation: trainer said gelding had a breathing problem
T/Plt: £5,565.50 to a £1 stake. Pool: £144,857.00 - 19.00 winning tickets. T/Qpdt: £243.00 to a £1 stake. Pool: £8540.00 - 26.00 winning tickets. DO

1875 HAMILTON (R-H)
Friday, May 11

OFFICIAL GOING: Soft (6.6)
Races on round course increased by 25yds.
Wind: Almost nil Weather: Overcast, raining

2032 FOLLOW @HAMILTONPARKRC ON TWITTER APPRENTICE H'CAP (ROUND ONE APPRENTICE SERIES) 5f 4y
6:05 (6:11) (Class 6) (0-65,65) 4-Y-O+ **£2,045** (£603; £302) **Stalls** Centre

Form RPR
4453 1 **Sandwith**[8] 1800 9-9-0 55 (p) GeorgeChaloner 10 65
(George Foster) *mde virtually all: rdn 1/2-way: edgd lft ins fnl f: kpt on wl* **5/1**
1312 2 *1/2* **Da'Quonde (IRE)**[24] 1428 4-9-5 65 PeterSword(5) 7 73
(Bryan Smart) *wnt sltly rt s: t.k.h in tch: effrt and edgd rt over 1f out: carried lft by wnr ins fnl f: swtchd rt and styd on towards fin* **15/8**[1]
-053 3 *1 1/4* **Cerejeira (IRE)**[33] 1242 4-8-11 55 (t) JasonHart(3) 5 59
(Eric Alston) *in tch: rdn 1/2-way: kpt on wl fnl f: tk 3rd cl home* **9/2**[3]
5-00 4 *shd* **Sharp Shoes**[30] 1298 5-9-2 60 (p) LauraBarry(3) 3 63
(Ann Duffield) *w wnr: rdn over 2f out: kpt on same pce fr over 1f out: lost 3rd cl home* **4/1**[2]
0-0 5 *4 1/2* **Andrasta**[16] 1601 7-8-1 49 MatthewHopkins(7) 6 36
(Alan Berry) *chsd ldrs: drvn along and outpcd 2f out: no imp fnl f* **33/1**
0600 6 *3* **Chosen One (IRE)**[20] 1516 7-8-6 50 ow1 DavidSimmonson(3) 2 26
(Ruth Carr) *prom: rdn 1/2-way: wknd over 1f out* **9/1**
505- 7 *5* **Miss Pronounce**[195] 7158 4-8-0 46 oh1 KevinLundie(5) 8
(Linda Perratt) *in tch: drvn and outpcd 1/2-way: sn btn* **66/1**
05-5 8 *15* **Saxonette**[8] 1800 4-9-0 60 RossSmith(5) 1
(Linda Perratt) *in tch on outside: struggling over 2f out: sn btn: eased whn no ch fnl f* **14/1**
1m 5.13s (5.13) **Going Correction** +1.075s/f (Soft) 8 Ran SP% **110.7**
Speed ratings (Par 101): **101,100,98,98,90 86,78,54**
toteswingers: 1&2 £2.40, 1&3 £2.20, 2&3 £1.90. CSF £13.81 CT £41.97 TOTE £8.30: £2.50, £1.70, £2.00; EX 14.40.
Owner Stoneypath Racing Club **Bred** R R Whitton **Trained** Haddington, East Lothian
FOCUS
A modest sprint handicap for apprentices in which the stalls were in the centre and the field raced there until drifting towards the stands' rail in the closing stages. Straightforward form amongst the placers.
Miss Pronounce Official explanation: jockey said filly hung left

2033 ALEX FERGUSSON H'CAP 1m 65y
6:40 (6:45) (Class 6) (0-65,64) 4-Y-O+ **£1,940** (£577; £288; £144) **Stalls** Low

Form RPR
0-05 1 **Indian Giver**[13] 1659 4-8-8 54 ow2 PaulPickard(3) 4 63
(Hugh McWilliams) *chsd ldrs: hdwy to ld over 2f out: edgd lft over 1f out: kpt on strly fnl f* **10/1**
0- 2 *2 3/4* **Tropenfeuer (FR)**[55] 1491 5-8-8 51 ow1 PaddyAspell 1 54
(James Moffatt) *in tch on ins: rdn over 3f out: rallied over 1f out: chsd wnr ins fnl f: kpt on: no imp* **33/1**
40-0 3 *6* **Retreat Content (IRE)**[5] 1879 4-9-6 63 GrahamLee 5 52
(Linda Perratt) *hld up: stdy hdwy over 2f out: swtchd lft over 1f out: kpt on fnl f: no ch w first two* **16/1**
3-00 4 *nk* **Deep Applause**[16] 1598 4-9-1 58 (p) TomEaves 2 46
(Michael Dods) *taken early to post: in tch on outside: hdwy and ev ch over 2f out: sn rdn and edgd rt: no ex over 1f out* **13/2**[3]
265- 5 *1 1/4* **Henrys Gift (IRE)**[195] 7159 4-8-11 54 BarryMcHugh 6 39
(Michael Dods) *led after 2f to 3f out: sn drvn: no ex over 1f out* **15/2**
21-2 6 *nk* **Royal Straight**[5] 1879 7-9-2 62 (t) JulieBurke(3) 7 47
(Linda Perratt) *missed break: hld up: stdy hdwy over 2f out: sn rdn: nvr able to chal* **11/4**[2]
1-26 7 *nk* **Beautiful Day**[20] 1520 4-9-7 64 PhillipMakin 3 48
(Kevin Ryan) *cl up: rdn and chsd wnr over 2f out to ins fnl f: sn btn* **13/8**[1]
30-6 8 *1/2* **Spread Boy (IRE)**[58] 903 5-8-1 51 oh2 ow1 MatthewHopkins(7) 9 34
(Alan Berry) *in tch: hdwy to ld briefly 3f out: sn rdn: wknd over 1f out* **50/1**
1m 58.65s (10.25) **Going Correction** +1.35s/f (Soft) 8 Ran SP% **109.7**
Speed ratings (Par 101): **102,99,93,92,91 91,91,90**
toteswingers: 1&2 not won, 1&3 £16.30, 2&3 £16.30. CSF £242.72 CT £4799.92 TOTE £12.40: £2.90, £11.20, £4.50; EX 469.30.
Owner J D Riches **Bred** M C Denning **Trained** Pilling, Lancs
FOCUS
A modest but competitive handicap and something of a surprise result, with the two females coming clear. Not the most solid of form.
Royal Straight Official explanation: trainer said gelding was unsuited by the soft ground
Beautiful Day Official explanation: jockey said gelding hung left

2034 WILLIAM HILL BRAVEHEART NIGHT NEXT WEEK CLAIMING STKS 1m 3f 16y
7:15 (7:20) (Class 6) 4-Y-O+ **£2,045** (£603; £302) **Stalls** Low

Form RPR
463- 1 **Bollin Dolly**[300] 4083 9-8-1 73 JulieBurke(3) 2 58
(James Moffatt) *t.k.h: trckd ldr: led gng wl over 2f out: sn rdn: kpt on strly to go clr fr over 1f out* **6/5**[1]
00-0 2 *4* **Stansonnit**[108] 287 4-8-9 60 AndrewElliott 5 56
(Alan Swinbank) *t.k.h: trckd ldrs: rdn and outpcd over 2f out: rallied to chse (clr) wnr ins fnl f: no imp* **11/2**[3]
0-05 3 *4* **Abernethy (IRE)**[8] 1801 4-8-6 42 (t) BarryMcHugh 1 46
(Linda Perratt) *hld up in tch: hdwy to chse wnr over 2f out: sn rdn and edgd rt: lost 2nd and wknd ins fnl f* **10/1**
4 *nk* **Santiago Boy**[107] 6-8-7 0 TomEaves 6 46
(Linda Perratt) *missed break: hld up: hdwy and prom over 4f out: rdn and wknd over 2f out* **12/1**
0-05 5 *9* **Sharp Sovereign (USA)**[24] 1432 6-8-8 64 PaulPickard(3) 3 34
(Ian McInnes) *led to over 2f out: sn rdn: wknd over 1f out* **9/4**[2]
2m 38.2s (12.60) **Going Correction** +1.35s/f (Soft) 5 Ran SP% **108.4**
Speed ratings (Par 101): **108,105,102,101,95**
toteswinger: 1&2 £4.30. CSF £7.91 TOTE £2.20: £1.80, £1.10; EX 7.30.
Owner D J Moffatt **Bred** Sir Neil And Lady Westbrook **Trained** Cartmel, Cumbria
FOCUS
The absence of hot morning favourite Just Lille meant that the winner looked set to dominate this uncompetitive claimer based on official ratings and that proved to be the case. Bollin Dolly did not need to be anywhere near her best.

2035 HAMILTON-PARK.CO.UK H'CAP 1m 1f 36y
7:50 (7:55) (Class 4) (0-80,80) 4-Y-O+ **£5,175** (£1,540; £769; £384) **Stalls** Low

Form RPR
50-6 1 **Fourth Generation (IRE)**[13] 1657 5-8-13 72 AndrewElliott 1 81
(Alan Swinbank) *prom: hdwy to ld over 2f out: sn rdn: hld on wl towards fin* **9/2**[3]
4-00 2 *nk* **Good Boy Jackson**[16] 1605 4-9-4 77 PhillipMakin 7 85
(Kevin Ryan) *trckd ldr: rdn and outpcd over 2f out: rallied over 1f out: chsd wnr wl ins fnl f: r.o* **5/2**[2]
10-5 3 *1 1/2* **Royal Opera**[48] 501 4-8-12 71 BarryMcHugh 6 76
(Brian Ellison) *led to over 2f out: sn drvn: rallied: kpt on same pce wl ins fnl f* **9/4**[1]
33-6 4 *7* **Petsas Pleasure**[32] 1251 6-8-7 66 oh3 TomEaves 2 56
(Ollie Pears) *hld up in tch: stdy hdwy and cl up over 3f out: outpcd over 2f out: n.d after* **16/1**
05-0 5 *1 1/4* **Daring Dream (GER)**[13] 1670 7-9-2 75 GrahamLee 3 62
(Jim Goldie) *hld up in tch: rdn and outpcd over 3f out: no imp fr 2f out* **9/1**
300- 6 *7* **Silver Rime (FR)**[195] 7161 7-9-4 80 JulieBurke(3) 4 51
(Linda Perratt) *missed break: hld up: outpcd over 4f out: sn n.d* **18/1**
0-00 7 *1/2* **Landaman (IRE)**[32] 1258 4-9-5 78 JoeFanning 5 48
(Mark Johnston) *trckd ldrs: hdwy and ev ch over 2f out: sn rdn: wknd over 1f out* **7/1**
2m 10.6s (10.90) **Going Correction** +1.35s/f (Soft) 7 Ran SP% **111.2**
Speed ratings (Par 105): **105,104,103,97,96 89,89**
toteswingers: 1&2 £4.50, 1&3 £3.70, 2&3 £3.40. CSF £15.24 TOTE £4.70: £2.50, £1.10; EX 16.90.
Owner B Boanson & M Wane **Bred** Mrs Christine Kelly **Trained** Melsonby, N Yorks
■ Stewards' Enquiry : Barry McHugh two-day ban: used whip above permitted level (May 25-26)
FOCUS
A tight contest for the feature race and it produced a good finish. The first three finished clear and the form looks sound.

Silver Rime(FR) Official explanation: jockey said she was slow to remove blindfold and gelding was slowly away

2036 BARRHEAD TRAVEL MAIDEN STKS 6f 5y
8:25 (8:32) (Class 5) 3-Y-O+ **£3,234** (£962; £481; £240) **Stalls** Centre

Form RPR
3-05 1 **Rock Canyon (IRE)**[16] 1596 3-9-3 56 JoeFanning 4 62
(Linda Perratt) *led 1f: cl up: rdn to ld over 1f out: kpt on wl fnl f* **10/1**[3]
2 1 1/4 **Legal Bond** 3-9-3 0 TomEaves 5 58
(Bryan Smart) *dwlt: t.k.h and sn cl up: rdn and rn green over 1f out: edgd rt and chsd wnr fnl f: r.o* **7/1**[2]
5-2 3 3 3/4 **Gowanharry (IRE)**[20] 1521 3-8-12 0 PhillipMakin 2 41
(Michael Dods) *t.k.h: trckd ldrs: effrt and rdn wl over 1f out: sn one pce* **30/100**[1]
4 1/2 **Way To Finish**[415] 6-9-13 0 PaddyAspell 6 47
(James Moffatt) *dwlt: t.k.h and led after 1f: hdd over 1f out: sn outpcd: plugged on ins fnl f* **25/1**
54 5 nk **Julier Pass (IRE)**[25] 1420 3-9-1 60 ow1 GaryBartley(3) 8 44
(Hugh McWilliams) *t.k.h: trckd ldrs: drvn and outpcd over 1f out: sn n.d* **16/1**
R00- 6 3/4 **Tinzo (IRE)**[227] 6428 4-9-6 40 MatthewHopkins(7) 3 44?
(Alan Berry) *dwlt: chsd ldng gp: rdn over 2f out: btn over 1f out* **100/1**
652- 7 5 **Great Nicanor (IRE)**[148] 7769 3-9-3 63 BarryMcHugh 1 25
(Ian Semple) *s.i.s: bhd: shortlived effrt over 2f out: sn btn* **16/1**
8 3/4 **Early Shirley** 3-8-12 0 GrahamLee 7 18
(Kevin Ryan) *missed break: outpcd and pushed along: sme hdwy over 2f out: sn btn* **12/1**

1m 18.13s (5.93) **Going Correction** +1.075s/f (Soft)
WFA 3 from 4yo+ 10lb 8 Ran SP% **122.8**
Speed ratings (Par 103): **103,101,96,95,95 94,87,86**
toteswingers: 1&2 £5.70, 1&3 £1.70, 2&3 £1.20. CSF £82.85 TOTE £6.80: £1.30, £3.00, £1.02; EX 58.60.
Owner Mrs Helen Perratt **Bred** Patrick J Connolly **Trained** East Kilbride, S Lanarks

FOCUS
Those with official ratings set a modest standard in this sprint maiden. The bare form is weak and shaky.
Rock Canyon(IRE) Official explanation: trainer said, regarding apparent improvement in form, that the gelding was better suited by the drop back to 6f over a straight course.
Gowanharry(IRE) Official explanation: trainer's rep said, regarding running, that the filly was unsuited by the soft ground

2037 TURFTV H'CAP 6f 5y
8:55 (9:00) (Class 5) (0-70,69) 4-Y-O+ **£3,408** (£1,006; £503) **Stalls** Centre

Form RPR
0-53 1 **Crimson Knot (IRE)**[5] 1875 4-9-0 **69** MatthewHopkins(7) 8 80
(Alan Berry) *mde all: rdn over 1f out: kpt on strly to go clr fnl f* **2/1**[2]
60-0 2 3 1/4 **Weetentherty**[5] 1881 5-8-4 **55** oh3 JulieBurke(3) 3 56
(Linda Perratt) *t.k.h: hld up in tch: stdy hdwy over 1f out: chsd (clr) wnr and carried hd high ins fnl f: no imp* **6/1**
000- 3 2 **North Central (USA)**[229] 6382 5-9-5 **67** (p) GrahamLee 6 62
(Jim Goldie) *t.k.h: chsd wnr: rdn over 2f out: lost 2nd and btn ins fnl f* **11/2**[3]
0/00 4 2 **Tagula Breeze (IRE)**[30] 1298 6-9-0 **62** BarryMcHugh 4 51
(Ian McInnes) *t.k.h: cl up: effrt over 1f out: outpcd ins fnl f* **12/1**
0400 5 1/2 **Amno Dancer (IRE)**[5] 1876 5-8-7 **55** oh5 TomEaves 9 43
(Ian Semple) *hld up bhd ldng gp: stdy hdwy 2f out: sn rdn: nvr able to chal* **16/1**
0420 6 2 1/2 **Northern Bolt**[4] 1917 7-9-4 **69** (b) PaulPickard(3) 5 49
(Ian McInnes) *missed break: bhd: hdwy to chse ldrs after 2f: rdn over 2f out: wandered and wknd over 1f out* **7/4**[1]

1m 18.51s (6.31) **Going Correction** +1.075s/f (Soft) 6 Ran SP% **112.9**
Speed ratings (Par 103): **100,95,93,90,89 86**
toteswingers: 1&2 £3.10, 1&3 £1.40, 2&3 £7.50. CSF £14.41 CT £55.64 TOTE £3.80: £1.70, £2.90; EX 20.10.
Owner William Burns **Bred** Iona Equine **Trained** Cockerham, Lancs

FOCUS
A modest sprint with three of non-runners and another pair racing from out of the weights. The time was slower than the preceding maiden. It's doubtful this took much winning and Crimson Knot is rated in line with last year's form.
T/Plt: £270.50 to a £1 stake. Pool: £51,457.97 - 138.85 winning tickets. T/Qpdt: £14.60 to a £1 stake. Pool: £3,834.92 - 194.20 winning tickets. RY

1787 LINGFIELD (L-H)
Friday, May 11

OFFICIAL GOING: Standard
Wind: Fresh, across (towards stands), 1st 6 races;half against, last 2 races
Weather: Fine

2038 BETFRED MOBILE LOTTO CLASSIFIED STKS 1m 2f (P)
1:45 (1:46) (Class 5) 3-Y-O **£2,385** (£704; £352) **Stalls** Low

Form RPR
62-4 1 **Ruscello (IRE)**[30] 1312 3-9-0 75 J-PGuillambert 6 77+
(Ed Walker) *hld up in last pair: prog on inner over 1f out: rdn and edgd rt ins fnl f: r.o to ld last 50yds: snugly* **9/2**[2]
354- 2 1/2 **Isthmus**[170] 7521 3-9-0 74 IanMongan 2 76
(Amanda Perrett) *mde most: kicked on 3f out: jnd jst over 1f out: hdd last 50yds: short of room fnl strides* **11/1**
044- 3 shd **Running Deer (IRE)**[203] 6984 3-9-0 71 TomQueally 1 76
(Sir Henry Cecil) *trckd ldrs: rdn and prog on inner over 1f out: jnd ldng pair fnl f: stl upsides whn bmpd 75yds out: kpt on* **4/1**[1]
41- 4 nse **Instrumentalist (IRE)**[158] 7634 3-9-0 75 HayleyTurner 4 76
(John Best) *racd wd: trckd ldng pair: wnt 2nd wl over 1f out and sn upsides: stl disputing ld 75yds out: nt qckn* **10/1**
01- 5 1 3/4 **Awesome Pearl (USA)**[205] 6945 3-8-11 75 HarryBentley(3) 5 72+
(Sir Mark Prescott Bt) *hld up in midfield: one of first to be rdn 3f out: tried to cl on ldrs 1f out: one pce* **5/1**[3]
-434 6 1 **Dynastic**[11] 1707 3-9-0 75 (b[1]) RichardHughes 8 70
(Richard Hannon) *hld up in last pair: rdn 3f out: sn struggling: tried to rally 1f out: one pce* **6/1**
1 7 3/4 **Diamond Dame (IRE)**[17] 1589 3-9-0 74 RichardMullen 7 69+
(Sir Michael Stoute) *hld up in last trio: prog on wd outside over 2f out: lost grnd bnd wl over 1f out: no imp on ldrs after* **7/1**
6-10 8 4 **Arch Of Colours**[14] 1647 3-9-0 75 SilvestreDeSousa 3 61
(Mark Johnston) *pressed ldr to wl over 1f out: wknd qckly* **8/1**

2m 5.59s (-1.01) **Going Correction** +0.025s/f (Slow) 8 Ran SP% **110.2**
Speed ratings (Par 99): **105,104,104,104,103 102,101,98**
Tote Swingers: 1&2 £10.70, 1&3 £2.80, 2&3 £8.70 CSF £48.03 TOTE £3.50: £1.50, £3.70, £2.10; EX 60.70.
Owner Laurence A Bellman **Bred** Ballymacoll Stud Farm Ltd **Trained** Newmarket, Suffolk

FOCUS
A typically competitive race of its type. The pace was fairly steady and that resulted in something of a dash for home, the front four being separated by under a length. Most of these were unexposed and the form could be rated higher.

2039 BRITISH STALLION STUDS SUPPORTING BRITISH RACING E B F MAIDEN STKS 5f (P)
2:15 (2:15) (Class 5) 2-Y-O **£3,169** (£943; £471; £235) **Stalls** High

Form RPR
32 1 **Lady Phill**[8] 1767 2-8-5 0 RyanWhile(7) 7 73+
(Bill Turner) *mde all: shkn up to assert over 1f out: styd on wl* **3/1**[2]
2 2 1/4 **Sutton Sid** 2-9-3 0 PatCosgrave 6 70+
(George Baker) *s.s: rdn to rcvr on outer: effrt 2f out: styd on fnl f to take 2nd last stride* **6/1**
3 shd **Opt Out** 2-9-3 0 SilvestreDeSousa 2 70
(Mark Johnston) *sn pushed along to chse ldng trio: effrt 2f out: styd on to chse wnr last 150yds: no imp: lost 2nd post* **2/1**[1]
4 1 1/2 **Augustinian** 2-9-3 0 RichardHughes 8 64
(Richard Hannon) *pressed wnr: rdn 2f out: nt qckn and hld over 1f out: wknd and lost pl last 150yds* **9/2**[3]
5 nk **Pairumani Prince (IRE)** 2-9-3 0 TomMcLaughlin 3 63
(Ed Dunlop) *dwlt: in tch in 6th: pushed along 2f out: kpt on same pce fr over 1f out: nvr able to threaten* **12/1**
6 1 **Birdie Queen** 2-8-12 0 HayleyTurner 5 54
(John Best) *chsd ldng pair: pushed along and nt qckn over 1f out: fdd fnl f* **14/1**
7 4 1/2 **Epsom Flyer** 2-9-3 0 IanMongan 4 43
(Pat Phelan) *dwlt: a same pl: nt on terms after 2f: no prog after* **14/1**
8 17 **Tough Question** 2-9-3 0 JamieGoldstein 1
(Michael Madgwick) *slowly away and swvd bdly lft: a t.o* **33/1**

59.35s (0.55) **Going Correction** +0.025s/f (Slow) 8 Ran SP% **114.8**
Speed ratings (Par 93): **96,92,92,89,89 87,80,53**
Tote Swingers: 1&2 £3.60, 1&3 £1.70, 2&3 £3.20 CSF £21.47 TOTE £4.90: £1.40, £1.50, £1.70; EX 24.70.
Owner Mrs M S Teversham **Bred** Mrs Monica Teversham **Trained** Sigwells, Somerset

FOCUS
An ordinary juvenile sprint maiden in which most were beaten after 2f. The winner was always in command and the bare form is ordinary.

NOTEBOOK
Lady Phill's previous experience told, the daughter of Avonbridge being quickly away and soon dominating. She readily asserted down the straight, her capable rider's 7lb claim being an added bonus, and she may be capable of picking up a minor novice event before going handicapping. (op 7-2)
Sutton Sid, a March foal whose dam was placed over 5f at two, was arguably the slowest away, but showed good mid-race speed and the way he finished suggests he may be able to win a standard maiden. (tchd 5-1 and 13-2)
Opt Out ◆, still a few days short of his second birthday, lacked the pace off the final bend, but he looked fairly professional and, as a half-brother to Sussex Stakes winner Court Masterpiece, he should get better. He can probably win next time. (op 5-2 tchd 11-4)
Augustinian, an April foal, is bred to want a stiffer test and he was left trailing late having shown some early pace. (op 4-1 tchd 7-2 and 5-1)
Pairumani Prince(IRE) ◆, a February foal, has a ton of stamina on the dam's side of his pedigree and he lacked the pace to get involved following a slow start, but did keep on and should relish an extra furlong. (tchd 14-1)
Birdie Queen has only just turned two and should improve for the experience/a stiffer test. (op 16-1)

2040 BETFRED "BONUS KING BINGO" H'CAP 5f (P)
2:45 (2:45) (Class 4) (0-85,85) 4-Y-O+ **£4,075** (£1,212; £606; £303) **Stalls** High

Form RPR
360- 1 **Kingsgate Choice (IRE)**[286] 4531 5-9-3 **81** LiamKeniry 6 94
(Ed de Giles) *mde all: stretched clr over 1f out: in n.d fnl f* **7/2**[2]
0602 2 2 1/4 **Desert Strike**[7] 1828 6-8-11 **80** (p) MatthewLawson(5) 2 85
(Charles Hills) *taken steadily to post: t.k.h: hld up in 4th: waited tl jst over 1f out: urged along and r.o to take 2nd wl ins fnl f: no ch w wnr* **5/1**[3]
1-60 3 nk **Diamond Charlie (IRE)**[16] 1602 4-9-7 **85** SebSanders 4 89
(Simon Dow) *hld up in last: taken wd and prog 2f out: hrd rdn over 1f out: disp 2nd ins fnl f: no ch w wnr* **3/1**[1]
00-0 4 1 3/4 **Fathom Five (IRE)**[16] 1602 8-9-2 **80** TomQueally 3 78
(Gary Moore) *chsd wnr: t.k.h after 2f: outpcd and rdn over 1f out: sn btn* **3/1**[1]
510- 5 3/4 **Best Be Careful (IRE)**[212] 6801 4-8-7 **71** HayleyTurner 5 66
(Mark Usher) *chsd ldng pair to over 2f out: pushed along in last over 1f out: n.d after* **7/2**[2]

58.39s (-0.41) **Going Correction** +0.025s/f (Slow) 5 Ran SP% **111.1**
Speed ratings (Par 105): **104,100,99,97,95**
CSF £20.30 TOTE £4.50: £1.60, £2.90; EX 20.90.
Owner T Gould **Bred** Michael Staunton **Trained** Ledbury, H'fords

FOCUS
Few had a chance to get into what was a fair sprint handicap. The winner is rated back to something like his 2011 best.

2041 BETFRED MOBILE SPORTS MAIDEN STKS (DIV I) 7f (P)
3:15 (3:16) (Class 5) 3-Y-O+ **£2,385** (£704; £352) **Stalls** Low

Form RPR
23-3 1 **Mizwaaj (IRE)**[7] 1825 3-9-0 79 FrankieDettori 10 88+
(Saeed Bin Suroor) *t.k.h: trckd ldng pair: rdn over 1f out: clsd to ld jst ins fnl f: r.o wl: readily* **7/2**[2]
02 2 1 3/4 **Sputnik Sweetheart**[10] 1736 3-8-9 0 RichardHughes 14 78
(Richard Hannon) *pressed ldr: rdn to ld wl over 1f out: hdd jst ins fnl f: r.o but outpcd* **9/2**[3]
0 3 1 **Standing Strong (IRE)**[7] 1825 4-9-12 0 RobertHavlin 6 84
(Robert Mills) *trckd ldrs disputing 5th: rdn over 1f out: r.o to take 3rd ins fnl f: fin wl* **33/1**
0 4 3 1/4 **Selfara**[21] 1501 3-8-9 0 JamesDoyle 2 67
(Roger Charlton) *trckd ldng pair: shkn up and outpcd fr 2f out: styd on again to take 4th nr fin* **3/1**[1]

5 *nk* **Register (IRE)** 3-9-0 0 DaneO'Neill 4 71
(William Muir) *trckd ldrs disputing 5th: outpcd wl over 1f out: squeezed out ent fnl f: styd on after* **66/1**

23 6 *shd* **Pashan Garh**[25] 1420 3-8-9 0 RaulDaSilva(5) 1 70
(Pat Eddery) *led to wl over 1f out: wknd fnl f* **9/1**

4- 7 *1* **Sondeduro**[296] 4213 3-9-0 0 FergusSweeney 5 68+
(Jamie Osborne) *a in midfield and mostly disputing 8th: outpcd and pushed along over 2f out: kpt on steadily fr over 1f out* **10/1**

8 *¾* **Muhdiq (USA)** 3-9-0 0 TadhgO'Shea 13 66
(Brian Meehan) *ponied to s: a abt same pl: outpcd by ldng gp fr 3f out: pushed along and kpt on fnl f* **16/1**

30 9 *½* **Red Ramesses (IRE)**[20] 1512 3-9-0 0 BrettDoyle 12 64
(John Best) *t.k.h: racd wd: chsd ldrs disputing 5th: outpcd 2f out: rdn and hung rt over 1f out: kpt on* **25/1**

10 *5* **Highly Skilled** 3-9-0 0 TomQueally 8 51
(Sir Henry Cecil) *slowest away: t.k.h and sn jnd those in rr: effrt on outer 1/2-way: no prog over 2f out* **10/1**

6 11 *2¼* **Pursue**[32] 1257 3-8-11 0 AdamBeschizza(3) 11 45
(William Haggas) *a in rr gp: pushed along and wl off the pce 3f out: no ch after* **12/1**

12 *1¾* **Tatting** 3-9-0 0 LiamKeniry 7 40
(Chris Dwyer) *hld up in rr: wl off the pce 3f out: pushed along and no ch after* **100/1**

3/0 13 *½* **Rulbin Realta**[11] 1703 5-9-2 0 JemmaMarshall(5) 9 38
(Pat Phelan) *restrained into last trio s: a bhd: struggling fr 1/2-way* **100/1**

0 14 *29* **Flag Is Up**[10] 1737 3-9-0 0 DavidProbert 3
(Brett Johnson) *nvr gng wl: a wl in rr: t.o* **200/1**

1m 23.63s (-1.17) **Going Correction** +0.025s/f (Slow)
WFA 3 from 4yo+ 12lb **14** Ran SP% **117.9**
Speed ratings (Par 103): **107,105,103,100,99 99,98,97,97,91 88,86,86,53**
Tote Swingers: 1&2 £50.00 CSF £18.70 TOTE £3.80: £1.20, £2.10, £7.60; EX 12.40.
Owner Godolphin **Bred** Darley **Trained** Newmarket, Suffolk

FOCUS
This looked the stronger of the two divisions and the time, which was 1.19secs quicker, seemed to confirm that impression. The form looks sound.
Highly Skilled Official explanation: jockey said colt was slowly away

2042 BETFRED MOBILE SPORTS MAIDEN STKS (DIV II) 7f (P)
3:50 (3:53) (Class 5) 3-Y-0+ **£2,385** (£704; £352) **Stalls** Low

Form RPR

1 **Dutch Old Master** 3-9-0 0 JamesDoyle 9 80
(Gary Moore) *t.k.h: trckd ldrs: shkn up and produced to take narrow ld ins fnl f: jst hld on* **9/1**

2-53 2 *nse* **Periphery (USA)**[23] 1450 3-9-0 83 (t) FrankieDettori 5 80
(Mahmood Al Zarooni) *pressed ldr: rdn to ld narrowly jst over 1f out: hdd ins fnl f: rallied nr fin: jst failed* **8/13[1]**

5 3 *shd* **Tharawal (IRE)**[37] 1182 3-9-0 0 MarcHalford 2 79
(Terry Clement) *t.k.h: trckd ldng pair: chal on inner and upsides 1f out: kpt on wl: jst hld* **33/1**

3- 4 *1* **Poisson D'Or**[274] 4968 3-8-9 0 ChrisCatlin 13 72+
(Rae Guest) *prog on outer after 2f to take 6th 1/2-way: last of those w ch after: swtchd ins and urged along over 1f out: styd on wl to take 4th nr fin then eased* **7/1[3]**

3- 5 *nk* **Byton**[263] 5323 3-8-9 0 DaneO'Neill 12 71+
(Henry Candy) *trckd ldng pair on outer: wdst of ldng gp bnd 2f out: sn rdn: styd on but nvr quite pce to chal* **6/1[2]**

60- 6 *1½* **Shatter (IRE)**[192] 7209 3-8-9 0 KellyHarrison 1 67
(William Haggas) *led to jst over 1f out: fdd ins fnl f* **20/1**

0-0 7 *2¾* **Mishhar (IRE)**[16] 1610 3-8-9 0 BrettDoyle 11 59
(Clive Brittain) *restrained into rr gp s and quite keen: wl off the pce 1/2-way: pushed along and kpt on quite encouragingly fr over 1f out* **50/1**

6-0 8 *2* **Royal Dutch**[32] 1256 3-9-0 0 TadhgO'Shea 4 59+
(Denis Coakley) *rrd s and bdly away: wl off the pce in rr gp: pushed along and kpt on fr 2f out on outer* **14/1**

00 9 *shd* **Saharan Air (IRE)**[43] 1086 3-9-0 0 LiamKeniry 7 59
(George Baker) *a in rr gp: wl off the pce fr 1/2-way and shoved along: nvr on terms* **100/1**

00- 10 *½* **Authoritarian**[197] 7118 3-8-9 0 KieranO'Neill 14 52+
(Richard Hannon) *sn stdd into rr gp: wl off the pce 1/2-way: pushed along and kpt on fr over 1f out* **50/1**

11 *3¾* **Beach Rhythm (USA)**[155] 5-9-9 0 AdamBeschizza(3) 8 51
(Jim Allen) *dwlt: a in rr gp: wl off the pce fr 1/2-way: no prog* **150/1**

12 *6* **Linton Hill (IRE)** 3-9-0 0 ShaneKelly 6 31
(Murty McGrath) *hld up in midfield: outpcd bef 1/2-way and sn dropped to rr: bhd over 1f out* **100/1**

0 13 *4* **Extremely Alert**[32] 1261 3-9-0 0 HayleyTurner 10 20
(Michael Bell) *dwlt: a in rr gp: wl off the pce fr 1/2-way: bhd fnl 2f* **25/1**

1m 24.82s (0.02) **Going Correction** +0.025s/f (Slow)
WFA 3 from 5yo 12lb **13** Ran SP% **123.5**
Speed ratings (Par 103): **100,99,99,98,98 96,93,91,91,90 86,79,74**
Tote Swingers: 1&2 £5.40, 1&3 £35.60, 2&3 £6.80 CSF £14.87 TOTE £9.60: £2.30, £1.10, £4.30; EX 20.60.
Owner R A Green **Bred** Mrs D M Solomon **Trained** Lower Beeding, W Sussex

FOCUS
Less depth than division one and the time was 1.19secs slower. Prominent runners dominated and there is a bit of doubt over the bare form.
Extremely Alert Official explanation: vet said colt lost a right-hind shoe

2043 PANTHERA LADIES DAY H'CAP (LADY AMATEUR RIDERS) 7f (P)
4:20 (4:20) (Class 5) (0-75,75) 4-Y-0+ **£2,305** (£709; £354) **Stalls** Low

Form RPR

1160 1 **Imprimis Tagula (IRE)**[7] 1827 8-10-0 75 (v) MissAlexOwen(7) 3 83
(Alan Bailey) *sn off the pce in midfield: no prog 2f out: r.o u.p fr over 1f out: clsd on tiring ldrs to ld nr fin* **12/1**

000- 2 *1* **Moody Tunes**[144] 7816 9-9-1 62 MissALMurphy(7) 8 67
(Tom Dascombe) *chsd ldrs: outpcd fr 3f out: styd on inner and clsd again fr over 1f out: styd on to take 2nd last strides: jst outpcd* **12/1**

12-0 3 *nk* **Comrade Bond**[31] 1289 4-9-9 70 MissNMcCaffrey(7) 9 74+
(Mark H Tompkins) *t.k.h: led: fended off chalr fr over 1f out: tired and swamped nr fin* **9/1**

000- 4 *¾* **Heezararity**[191] 7235 4-9-11 65 (t) MissSBrotherton 7 67
(David Evans) *unable to go the pce and sn in rr: wl off the pce 1/2-way: last 2f out: r.o fnl f: nrst fin* **5/1[2]**

43-0 5 *hd* **Drakes Drum**[13] 1650 4-9-11 68 (p) MissRachelKing(3) 4 70+
(Clive Cox) *plld hrd: trckd ldng pair: wnt 2nd 2f out: tried to chal fnl f: hld and lost pls nr fin* **9/2[1]**

1025 6 *nk* **Kiss A Prince**[10] 1732 6-10-0 75 MissECrossman(7) 1 76
(Dean Ivory) *s.s: wl off the pce in last trio as ldrs wnt off hrd: styd on fr over 1f out: no ex last 100yds* **9/1**

1240 7 *½* **Flag Of Glory**[13] 1650 5-9-2 63 MissMEdden(7) 5 63
(Peter Hiatt) *sn wl bhd in last: no prog over 2f out: styd on as ldrs tired fnl f: nrst fin* **12/1**

204- 8 *1½* **Greek Islands (IRE)**[184] 6796 4-10-3 71 MissEJJones 6 67
(Ed de Giles) *sn chsd ldng trio: brought wd bnd 2f out and tried to chal: wknd fnl f* **9/2[1]**

0025 9 *1* **Ibiza Sunset (IRE)**[15] 1626 4-9-4 65 ow3 MissSKerswell(7) 2 58
(Brendan Powell) *a off the pce towards rr: no prog fnl 2f* **11/2[3]**

006- 10 *4* **Guilded Warrior**[246] 5858 9-9-13 72 (p) MissMBryant(5) 10 54
(Paddy Butler) *pressed ldr to 2f out: wknd qckly* **20/1**

1m 24.93s (0.13) **Going Correction** +0.025s/f (Slow) **10** Ran SP% **116.3**
Speed ratings (Par 103): **100,98,98,97,97 97,96,94,93,89**
Tote Swingers: 1&2 £24.40 CSF £146.17 CT £1392.83 TOTE £15.60: £5.50, £3.20, £2.40; EX 176.50.
Owner Middleham Park Racing XLI & Alan Bailey **Bred** Glashare House Stud **Trained** Newmarket, Suffolk
■ Stewards' Enquiry : Miss Alex Owen two-day ban: used whip above permitted level (tbn)

FOCUS
A messy race and form to be wary of, with the leaders going too quick and the picture changing quickly in the final 50 yards, with several flying from the back. The winner is rated to form.

2044 HEART'S FEEL GOOD FRIDAY H'CAP 1m (P)
4:55 (4:56) (Class 5) (0-70,70) 4-Y-0+ **£2,385** (£704; £352) **Stalls** High

Form RPR

6303 1 **Rezwaan**[16] 1611 5-9-3 68 (be) ShaneKelly 5 76
(Murty McGrath) *trckd ldrs: effrt over 1f out: drvn to ld jst ins fnl f: styd on wl* **17/2**

26-3 2 *1¼* **Officer In Command (USA)**[10] 1729 6-9-5 70 (b) JamesDoyle 11 75
(Paul Rich) *appeared to try to break out of stalls early and then missed s completely: ct up after 2f and stdy prog to trck ldrs 2f out: drvn over 1f out: styd on to take 2nd last stride* **9/2[1]**

540- 3 *nse* **For What (USA)**[231] 6311 4-9-3 68 TedDurcan 1 73
(David Lanigan) *trckd ldrs on inner: rdn to chal 1f out: nt qckn last 100yds* **9/2[1]**

-020 4 *shd* **L'Hirondelle (IRE)**[10] 1729 8-9-4 69 (p[1]) J-PGuillambert 10 74
(Michael Attwater) *pressed ldr: rdn to ld jst over 1f out to jst ins fnl f: nt qckn* **16/1**

-516 5 *2¼* **Muhandis (IRE)**[76] 713 4-9-2 67 (v) ChrisCatlin 7 66
(Nick Littmoden) *t.k.h: hld up in tch: rdn and nt qckn over 1f out: styd on ins fnl f* **20/1**

-005 6 *nse* **Al Aqabah (IRE)**[10] 1729 7-9-2 70 (v[1]) AdamBeschizza(3) 4 69
(Brian Gubby) *trckd ldrs: lost pl sn after 1/2-way: drvn in last trio over 2f out: styd on again fnl f* **10/1**

3310 7 *½* **Marvo**[23] 1436 8-9-2 67 (b) EddieAhern 3 65+
(Mark H Tompkins) *hld up in rr: n.m.r over 3f out: gng wl enough 2f out: nt qckn over 1f out* **9/1**

0660 8 *1¼* **Opus Maximus (IRE)**[18] 1561 7-9-3 68 HayleyTurner 8 63+
(Conor Dore) *plld hrd: hld up last: stl there 2f out: effrt on inner over 1f out: nt clrest of runs but nvr gng pce to threaten* **8/1[3]**

0430 9 *½* **Satwa Laird**[29] 1342 6-9-2 70 HarryBentley(3) 9 64
(Conor Dore) *led: kicked on 3f out: hdd jst over 1f out: wknd qckly* **10/1**

5601 10 *½* **May's Boy**[16] 1611 4-8-12 68 (p) RachealKneller(5) 12 61
(Mark Usher) *racd wd: pressed ldrs: lost grnd bnd 2f out: steadily wknd* **6/1[2]**

624- 11 *4½* **Larkrise Star**[155] 7671 5-8-11 69 PaulBooth(7) 6 51
(Dean Ivory) *t.k.h: hld up in rr and racd v wd: no prog over 2f out: wknd* **14/1**

1m 37.86s (-0.34) **Going Correction** +0.025s/f (Slow) **11** Ran SP% **117.8**
Speed ratings (Par 103): **102,100,100,100,98 98,97,96,96,95 91**
Tote Swingers: 1&2 £10.10, 1&3 £3.40, 2&3 £5.90 CSF £46.65 CT £200.74 TOTE £10.40: £3.00, £1.10, £2.40; EX 36.80.
Owner Gallagher Equine Ltd **Bred** Shadwell Estate Company Limited **Trained** East Malling, Kent
■ Stewards' Enquiry : James Doyle two-day ban: careless riding (May 25-26)

FOCUS
A moderate handicap run at a fairly steady gallop early. Officer In Command would surely have won but for losing many lengths at the start. The winner basically matched his winter form.

2045 THAKEHAM HOMES WITH CUBITT & WEST H'CAP 7f (P)
5:30 (5:32) (Class 5) (0-70,70) 3-Y-O **£2,385** (£704; £352) **Stalls** Low

Form RPR

3331 1 **First Bid**[7] 1826 3-9-5 68 6ex (b) J-PGuillambert 1 72
(James Given) *led: rdn and hdd 2f out: sn ld again: hrd pressed fnl f: hld on* **14/1**

40-0 2 *½* **Foot Tapper**[29] 1331 3-9-0 63 SebSanders 9 65
(Chris Wall) *trckd ldrs: rdn over 2f out: responded to press to go 2nd ins fnl f: chal last 100yds: nt qckn* **10/1**

445- 3 *¾* **Lovage**[215] 6724 3-9-2 65 JamesDoyle 3 65+
(Roger Charlton) *pushed along in rr early: prog 3f out: looking for room over 1f out: rdn and styd on to take 3rd last strides* **9/2[2]**

20-0 4 *hd* **Arctic Stryker**[8] 1790 3-9-7 70 BrettDoyle 7 70
(John Best) *cl up on inner: rdn over 2f out: kpt on and stl cl up 1f out: nt qckn after* **50/1**

2444 5 *½* **Millibar (IRE)**[56] 917 3-9-5 68 (p) ChrisCatlin 2 66
(Nick Littmoden) *t.k.h: hld up towards rr: prog into midfield 2f out and n.m.r: tried to cl fnl f but nvr gng pce to threaten* **25/1**

30-3 6 *nk* **Fine Painting (IRE)**[10] 1733 3-9-7 70 FergusSweeney 4 68
(Gary Moore) *hld up bhd ldrs on outer: effrt 2f out: rdn and nt qckn over 1f out: kpt on* **5/1[3]**

03-3 7 *½* **Stepturn**[32] 1257 3-9-2 65 DaneO'Neill 8 61
(George Baker) *v free to post: w wnr: led briefly 2f out: stl 2nd 1f out: wknd last 100yds* **7/2[1]**

532- 8 *¾* **Flamborough Breeze**[155] 7672 3-9-7 70 RichardMullen 13 64
(Ed Vaughan) *dropped in fr wd draw and hld up last: prog on inner over 1f out: no real hdwy fnl f* **28/1**

6-53 9 *¾* **Darrow (IRE)**[10] 1728 3-9-5 68 ShaneKelly 11 60+
(William Knight) *dropped in fr wd draw and hld up in rr: looking for room 2f out: shkn up over 1f out: kpt on but nvr on terms* **9/2[2]**

0-60 10 *3* **Jay Bee Blue**[16] 1612 3-9-2 68 SophieDoyle(3) 6 52
(J S Moore) *t.k.h and hld up in rr: rdn over 2f out: no real prog* **33/1**

52-5 11 *1¼* **Ghalaa (IRE)**[39] 1167 3-9-2 65 TadhgO'Shea 10 46
(Mark Johnston) *pressed ldng pair: stl there over 1f out: wknd qckly* **9/1**

350- 12 *1¼* **Baltic Flyer (IRE)**[216] 6695 3-8-12 64 AdamBeschizza(3) 12 41
(Robert Eddery) *racd wd in midfield: wknd 2f out* **25/1**

10-0 **13** *1 ¾* **Red Mischief (IRE)**[23] 1449 3-9-7 **70**................................ EddieAhern 5 43
(Harry Dunlop) *a in rr: shkn up and no prog over 2f out on outer: sn bhd*
50/1

1m 25.4s (0.60) **Going Correction** +0.025s/f (Slow) 13 Ran SP% **119.0**
Speed ratings (Par 99): **97,96,95,95,94 94,93,93,92,88 87,85,83**
Tote Swingers: 1&2 £48.90, 1&3 £15.20, 2&3 £15.30 CSF £135.85 CT £761.79 TOTE £17.60: £4.90, £2.50, £3.40; EX 160.40.
Owner Peter Swann **Bred** J W Ford **Trained** Willoughton, Lincs

FOCUS
Not a bad race for the grade and it should produce winners. First Bid was another on the card to win from the front and this rates a personal best.
Lovage Official explanation: jockey said filly suffered interference in running
T/Plt: £117.40 to a £1 stake. Pool: £56,895.00 - 2,345.37 winning tickets. T/Qpdt: £16.20 to a £1 stake. Pool: £4,393.00 - 198.12 winning tickets. JN

1514 NOTTINGHAM (L-H)
Friday, May 11

OFFICIAL GOING: Soft (heavy in places; 5.4)
Races on outer course.
Wind: Fresh half-against Weather: Cloudy with sunny spells

2046 CALVERTS CARPETS YORK LTD APPRENTICE H'CAP 6f 15y
5:35 (5:45) (Class 6) (0-60,60) 4-Y-0+ **£1,940** (£577; £288; £144) **Stalls** High

Form RPR

1 **Hopes N Dreams (IRE)**[98] 412 4-9-2 **55**..................... GarryWhillans 5 69
(Tony Coyle) *a.p: rdn to ld over 1f out: edgd lft: styd on* **15/2**

010 **2** *2* **Fault**[15] 1635 6-8-11 **53**.. LeonnaMayor(3) 11 61
(Alastair Lidderdale) *chsd ldrs: rdn over 1f out: r.o to go 2nd nr fin: nt rch wnr* **6/1**3

-641 **3** *1 ¾* **Gracie's Games**[4] 1934 6-9-1 **59** 6ex...................(v) JacobButterfield(5) 2 61
(Richard Price) *s.i.s: hdwy over 3f out: nt clr run and swtchd lft over 2f out: chsd wnr over 1f out: no ex ins fnl f: lost 2nd nr fin* **5/2**1

0040 **4** *1 ¾* **Steel City Boy (IRE)**[20] 1516 9-9-2 **55**.................................... LMcNiff 8 52
(Garry Woodward) *led 2f: led again over 2f out: rdn and hdd over 1f out: no ex fnl f* **14/1**

0-10 **5** *6* **Avoncreek**[77] 690 8-8-6 **50**..(v) AliceHaynes(5) 9 28
(Brian Baugh) *hld up: hdwy over 2f out: rdn and wkng whn hung rt over 1f out* **16/1**

00-0 **6** *¾* **Cottam Stella**[27] 1383 4-8-7 **46**.. NeilFarley 4 21
(Mel Brittain) *sn pushed along in mid-div: n.d* **50/1**

0/00 **7** *1* **Whiteoak Lady (IRE)**[21] 1497 7-9-2 **55**..................... CharlesBishop 13 27
(John Spearing) *prom: rdn over 2f out: sn wknd: hung rt fr over 1f out* **11/1**

-364 **8** *4 ½* **Ace Master**[78] 670 4-9-1 **59**.................................. ShirleyTeasdale(5) 1 17
(Roy Bowring) *prom: rdn 1/2-way: wknd 2f out* **9/2**2

4-00 **9** *½* **Whiskey Junction**[32] 1263 8-9-2 **60**..................... MichaelJMurphy(5) 12 16
(Michael Quinn) *s.i.s: sn pushed along towards rr: wknd over 2f out* **10/1**

/540 **10** *4* **Dikanta**[29] 1343 4-8-8 **50**.. JakePayne(3) 15
(Robert Cowell) *s.i.s: sme hdwy over 3f out: wknd 2f out* **25/1**

-100 **11** *3 ¾* **Prigsnov Dancer (IRE)**[52] 979 7-8-4 **50**............... GarethEdwards(7) 7
(Garry Woodward) *w ldr tl led 4f out: rdn and hdd over 2f out: wknd wl over 1f out* **16/1**

5000 **12** *3* **Bird Dog**[2] 1987 6-8-1 **47** oh1 ow1........................(v) RobJFitzpatrick(7) 14
(Phil McEntee) *racd alone towards stands' side: in tch over 3f* **33/1**

1m 21.73s (6.83) **Going Correction** +0.95s/f (Soft) 12 Ran SP% **117.4**
Speed ratings (Par 101): **92,89,87,84,76 75,74,68,67,62 57,53**
toteswingers: 1&2 £9.20, 1&3 £4.60, 2&3 £5.00. CSF £50.72 CT £147.58 TOTE £8.90: £2.70, £2.90, £1.10; EX 60.50.
Owner Matt & Lauren Morgan **Bred** J & Mrs Brennan & Edward & Mrs O'Regan **Trained** Norton, N Yorks

FOCUS
Races on outer course. This looked a proper test at the trip and the time was over 9secs above standard. The main action unfolded up the middle. This was a really moderate contest with the runner-up the best guide.
Dikanta Official explanation: jockey said gelding hung left

2047 CALVERTS CARPETS YORK LTD MEDIAN AUCTION MAIDEN FILLIES' STKS 5f 13y
6:10 (6:24) (Class 5) 2-Y-0 **£2,264** (£673; £336; £168) **Stalls** Low

Form RPR

4 **1** **Ishi Honest**[18] 1563 2-9-0 0.. RyanMoore 7 72
(Mark Usher) *hmpd s: sn prom: outpcd 1/2-way: hdwy u.p over 1f out: edgd lft and r.o to ld towards fin* **13/2**

2 **2** *2 ¼* **Uncomplicated**[18] 1563 2-9-0 0.. PatCosgrave 6 64
(Jim Boyle) *wnt rt s: chsd ldrs: rdn to ld wl ins fnl f: hdd and no ex towards fin* **5/2**2

322 **3** *1 ¼* **Poetic Princess**[21] 1495 2-9-0 0...................................... TonyCulhane 3 59
(Jo Hughes) *led: hdd over 3f out: outpcd 1/2-way: r.o wl ins fnl f* **6/1**3

4 *1 ¼* **Betty Boo (IRE)** 2-9-0 0.. RobbieFitzpatrick 2 55
(Shaun Harris) *prom: rdn over 1f out: styd on same pce* **50/1**

4 **5** *½* **La Sylphe**[13] 1671 2-9-0 0.. WilliamCarson 9 53
(David Barron) *chsd ldrs: led and hung lft fr over 3f out: rdn and hdd over 1f out: styd on same pce* **10/1**

6 *nk* **Body And Soul (IRE)** 2-9-0 0.. DavidAllan 1 52+
(Tim Easterby) *wnt lft s: sn chsng ldrs: led over 1f out: hdd & wknd wl ins fnl f* **9/4**1

7 *3* **Ishigunnaeatit** 2-8-11 0.. MichaelMetcalfe(3) 5 41
(Mrs K Burke) *s.s: sn pushed along in rr: n.d* **9/1**

8 *2 ¼* **Dalhousie Lassie** 2-9-0 0... LiamJones 8 33
(James Unett) *dwlt: outpcd* **40/1**

9 *22* **Shirley's Pride** 2-9-0 0.. KirstyMilczarek 4
(John Holt) *w ldrs tl wknd wl over 1f out: eased: t.o* **33/1**

1m 6.32s (5.32) **Going Correction** +0.95s/f (Soft) 9 Ran SP% **113.4**
Speed ratings (Par 90): **95,91,89,87,86 86,81,77,42**
toteswingers: 1&2 £4.00, 1&3 £5.00, 2&3 £2.10. CSF £22.46 TOTE £8.50: £2.60, £1.40, £1.50; EX 22.50.
Owner High Five Racing **Bred** Miss A V Hill **Trained** Upper Lambourn, Berks

FOCUS
The leaders seemed to go too fast faced with this demanding test, and the bare form is suspect. They raced middle to stands' side, but off the rail. The form looks reasonably close to race averages.

NOTEBOOK
Ishi Honest improved on the form she showed when fourth on her debut at Windsor, helped by the leaders coming back to her. She'll need to prove she can run to this sort of level on better ground off a more even gallop. (op 6-1)
Uncomplicated had Ishi Honest 3l behind when beaten a short-head on her debut at Windsor and was 4lb better off, so it was disappointing she couldn't confirm form. However, while she clearly didn't go on from that initial experience, she may simply have gone off too fast. (op 7-2)
Poetic Princess ran on after getting outpaced. She's now been placed on all four of her starts but isn't progressing. (tchd 11-2)
Betty Boo(IRE), a half-sister to a couple of winners on testing ground between 6f-1m1f, including a decent sort, showed ability, even if she was helped by racing off the hot pace. She was best of the newcomers. (op 40-1)
La Sylphe's debut form is not working out and she couldn't sustain her bid after doing plenty early. William Carson reported the filly hung badly left. Official explanation: jockey said filly hung badly left (op 17-2)
Body And Soul(IRE) ◆ managed only sixth but shaped like much the best filly in the race. A 7,500GBP January foal, she was strongly supported in the market even though her trainer has a modest record with newcomers, and has plenty of size. She showed plenty of natural pace, despite running green (not helped by widest stall), and simply got tired having gone off too fast. There's significant improvement to come. (op 15-8 tchd 5-2)
Shirley's Pride's trainer reported the filly was unsuited by the ground. Official explanation: trainer said filly was unsuited by the soft (heavy in places) ground (op 40-1)

2048 CALVERTS CARPETS & FLOORING LTD H'CAP 1m 2f 50y
6:45 (6:55) (Class 6) (0-60,60) 4-Y-0+ **£1,940** (£577; £288; £144) **Stalls** Low

Form RPR

000- **1** **Ptolomeos**[42] 7885 9-8-2 **46** oh1.....................................(p) AmyScott(5) 1 60
(Sean Regan) *dwlt: hld up: hdwy over 3f out: led 2f out: sn pushed clr: eased ins fnl f* **33/1**

40-0 **2** *9* **Penderyn**[23] 1436 5-8-7 **46** oh1.. JohnFahy 6 43
(Charles Smith) *sn pushed along: chsd ldr after 1f: rdn over 3f out: ev ch 2f out: sn outpcd* **28/1**

/640 **3** *2* **Josie's Dream (IRE)**[30] 1310 4-8-10 **49**.......................... TonyCulhane 2 42
(Jo Hughes) *mid-div: rdn over 3f out: hdwy over 2f out: styd on same pce fr over 1f out* **20/1**

2013 **4** *shd* **Kingaroo (IRE)**[3] 1956 6-8-13 **52**.................................. KirstyMilczarek 9 45
(Garry Woodward) *led: rdn and hdd 2f out: styd on same pce* **10/1**

-620 **5** *1 ¾* **Market Puzzle (IRE)**[18] 1562 5-9-3 **56**...........................(p) RyanMoore 4 46
(Mark Brisbourne) *hld up: hdwy over 2f out: sn rdn: styd on same pce* **13/2**3

3301 **6** *8* **Ollon (USA)**[13] 1673 4-9-3 **59**................................ MichaelMetcalfe(3) 13 33
(Mrs K Burke) *chsd ldrs: rdn over 2f out: wknd wl over 1f out* **5/2**1

0504 **7** *3 ½* **Thank You Joy**[8] 1771 4-9-0 **60**.. NedCurtis(7) 8 28
(J R Jenkins) *hld up: rdn 1/2-way: nvr on terms* **16/1**

0652 **8** *¾* **Hits Only Jude (IRE)**[2] 1988 9-8-8 **52**..........................(v) NeilFarley(5) 12 18
(Declan Carroll) *prom: pushed along 1/2-way: rdn over 3f out: sn wknd* **5/1**2

00-0 **9** *6* **Lady Norlela**[16] 1598 6-9-1 **54**... PatCosgrave 7
(Brian Rothwell) *hld up: rdn over 3f out: n.d: t.o* **20/1**

600- **10** *2 ¼* **Stillington**[230] 6349 6-8-11 **50**................................ RobbieFitzpatrick 14
(Mel Brittain) *prom: rdn over 3f out: sn wknd: t.o* **22/1**

060- **11** *1 ¼* **Applaude**[178] 7426 7-8-7 **46** oh1................................(b) SamHitchcott 11
(Chris Bealby) *hld up: effrt over 3f out: sn wknd: t.o* **14/1**

056- **12** *nk* **Think**[153] 7712 5-8-11 **50**... PaulMulrennan 3
(Clive Mulhall) *chsd ldrs: rdn over 3f out: wknd over 2f out: t.o* **8/1**

20-0 **13** *31* **Marina Ballerina**[99] 389 4-8-11 **50**.............................. RoystonFfrench 15
(Roy Bowring) *sn pushed along in rr: bhd fr 1/2-way: t.o* **14/1**

2m 19.49s (7.79) **Going Correction** +0.95s/f (Soft) 13 Ran SP% **118.3**
Speed ratings (Par 101): **106,98,97,97,95 89,86,85,81,79 78,78,53**
toteswingers: 1&2 £70.00, 1&3 £73.40, 2&3 £75.80. CSF £721.93 CT £17327.73 TOTE £68.40: £19.50, £12.20, £9.20; EX 720.40.
Owner Mrs Connie Taylor **Bred** G Prodromou **Trained** West Witton, N Yorks

FOCUS
This was a really moderate race, run at a strong pace considering the conditions, and it was won with surprising ease. The winner is rated back to the best of his 2010 level but overall the form looks shaky.
Ptolomeos Official explanation: trainer said, regarding apparent improvement in form, that the gelding had freshened up after running over hurdles.
Marina Ballerina Official explanation: jockey said filly never travelled

2049 CALVERTS CARPETS YORK LTD H'CAP 1m 6f 15y
7:20 (7:30) (Class 5) (0-75,68) 3-Y-0 **£2,264** (£673; £336; £168) **Stalls** Low

Form RPR

0-46 **1** **Spanish Fork (IRE)**[18] 1568 3-9-2 **63**............................ SamHitchcott 6 68
(Mick Channon) *hld up: shkn up at various stages tl hdwy over 4f out: rdn over 2f out: styd on u.p to ld nr fin* **10/3**1

44-0 **2** *hd* **Bathwick Street**[20] 1519 3-8-6 **53**.................................. WilliamCarson 1 58
(David Evans) *chsd ldr 2f: remained handy: led wl over 3f out: rdn over 1f out: hdd nr fin* **4/1**3

500- **3** *2 ½* **Stickleback**[183] 7343 3-8-3 **50**...................................... KirstyMilczarek 2 51
(Harry Dunlop) *a.p: rdn and hung lft 2f out: hung rt over 1f out: hung lft ins fnl f: styd on same pce* **7/2**2

3113 **4** *18* **Spartilla**[31] 1281 3-9-1 **65**.. RyanPowell(3) 7 41
(Daniel O'Brien) *prom: chsd ldr after 2f: rdn over 2f out: wknd wl over 1f out* **10/3**1

34-6 **5** *7* **Our Ivor**[113] 217 3-8-3 **57**.. JackDuern(7) 4 23
(Michael Appleby) *s.i.s: hld up: hdwy over 4f out: wknd over 2f out* **9/1**

0-63 **6** *32* **Blue Pencil**[23] 1448 3-8-3 **50** oh4 ow1.................................... JohnFahy 3
(Roger Curtis) *led: hdd wl over 3f out: sn wknd and eased: t.o* **7/1**

3m 20.54s (14.24) **Going Correction** +0.95s/f (Soft) 6 Ran SP% **110.9**
Speed ratings (Par 99): **100,99,98,88,84 65**
toteswingers: 1&2 £4.10, 1&3 £3.40, 2&3 £4.00. CSF £16.38 TOTE £4.10: £1.90, £3.40; EX 13.30.
Owner R Bastian **Bred** Mike Channon Bloodstock Ltd **Trained** West Ilsley, Berks

FOCUS
A moderate contest in which few seemed likely to appreciate what was a really demanding test for 3-y-os. The form looks weak but the winner is progressing.
Spartilla Official explanation: jockey said colt hung left

2050 CALVERTS CARPETS YORK LTD MAIDEN FILLIES' STKS 1m 75y
7:55 (8:06) (Class 5) 3-Y-0 **£2,264** (£673; £336; £168) **Stalls** Centre

Form RPR

1 **Secret Quest** 3-9-0 0.. MickaelBarzalona 6 79
(James Fanshawe) *hld up: hdwy over 2f out: chsd ldr over 1f out: rdn to ld wl ins fnl f* **11/2**3

0- **2** *nk* **Cufflink**[142] 7838 3 -9-00 WilliamCarson 2 78
(Rae Guest) *hld up: plld hrd: hdwy over 3f out: led over 2f out: rdn and edgd lft over 1f out: hdd wl ins fnl f* **25/1**

2- **3** *4* **Medea (IRE)**[248] 5813 3 -9-00 RyanMoore 4 69
(Sir Michael Stoute) *led: rdn and hdd over 3f out: edgd lft 2f out: styd on same pce fr over 1f out* **5/6**[1]

4 *3 1/2* **Kunegunda** 3 -9-00 JackMitchell 12 61+
(James Fanshawe) *hld up: r.o ins fnl f: nvr nrr* **10/1**

50- **5** *1 1/2* **Chignon (IRE)**[161] 7599 3 -9-00 IanMongan 9 58
(Sir Henry Cecil) *plld hrd and prom: rdn over 2f out: wknd over 1f out* **12/1**

40 **6** *10* **Tatty**[16] 1610 3 -8-70 JackDuern(7) 10 35
(Ian Wood) *racd keenly: trckd ldr 2f: remained handy: led over 3f out: hdd over 2f out: wknd over 1f out* **66/1**

0 **7** *2* **Miss Socialite**[16] 1610 3 -9-00 PatCosgrave 3 30
(Jeremy Gask) *plld hrd and prom: wknd and eased over 1f out* **40/1**

8 *11* **Majestic South** 3 -9-00 SamHitchcott 11
(Mick Channon) *s.i.s: hld up: wknd 3f out: t.o* **25/1**

05- **9** *1 3/4* **Top Frock (IRE)**[95] 7164 3 -9-00 JohnFahy 5
(Clive Cox) *plld hrd and prom: trckd ldr 6f out tl rdn over 3f out: wknd over 2f out: t.o* **9/2**[2]

1m 56.29s (10.69)**Going Correction** +0.95s/f (Soft) **9**Ran SP% **116.5**
Speed ratings (Par 96): **84,83,79,76,74 64,62,51,49**
toteswingers: 1&2 £19.10, 1&3 £1.50, 2&3 £8.00. CSF £128.43 TOTE £7.30 : £2.00 , £7.00 , £1.10; EX 180.10 .
Owner Cheveley Park Stud **Bred** Cheveley Park Stud Ltd **Trained** Newmarket, Suffolk

FOCUS
An ordinary fillies' maiden run at a steady early pace and the form is rated cautiously given the ground.

2051 INKERMAN LONDON H'CAP (BETFAIR 10 FURLONG FLAT SERIES QUALIFIER) 1m 2f 50y
8:30 (8:35) (Class 5) (0-75,74) 4-Y-0+ **£3,234** (£962; £481 ; £240) **Stalls** Low

Form RPR

-331 **1** **Tilsworth Glenboy**[10] 1743 5 -9-974 6ex FrederikTylicki 3 86+
(J R Jenkins) *hld up: nt clr run over 2f out: hdwy over 1f out: r.o to ld wl ins fnl f* **11/4**[1]

040- **2** *1* **King Zeal (IRE)**[21] 6507 8 -9-469 (t) RoystonFfrench 9 77
(Barry Leavy) *chsd ldrs: rdn over 2f out: led over 1f out: hdd and unable qck wl ins fnl f* **9/1**[3]

5604 **3** *3/4* **The Lock Master (IRE)**[8] 1358 5 -8-765 JackDuern(7) 12 72
(Michael Appleby) *hld up: hdwy 1/2-way: chsd ldr over 2f out: led wl over 1f out: sn hdd: styd on same pce ins fnl f* **12/1**

4-64 **4** *6* **Highlife Dancer**[32] 1266 4 -9-070 CharlesBishop(5) 16 66
(Mick Channon) *chsd ldrs: rdn over 2f out: wknd ins fnl f* **16/1**

4504 **5** *1 3/4* **Nolecce**[10] 1743 5 -8-862 (p) DeclanCannon(3) 10 54
(Richard Guest) *prom: rdn over 2f out: sn hung lft: wknd fnl f* **28/1**

110- **6** *1 3/4* **My Mate Jake (IRE)**[92] 7215 4 -9-469 PaulMulrennan 13 58
(James Givon) *prom: rdn over 3f out: wknd fnl f* **14/1**

036- **7** *hd* **Lady of Burgundy**[165] 7570 6 -9-272 LeeNewnes(5) 7 61
(Mark Usher) *hld up: styd on fnl f: nvr trbld ldrs* **16/1**

3201 **8** *3/4* **Resplendent Alpha**[3] 1956 8 -8-763 6ex LeonnaMayor(5) 6 50
(Alastair Lidderdale) *s.i.s: hld up: r.o ins fnl f: nvr nrr* **12/1**

-230 **9** *1 1/2* **Mighty Clarets (IRE)**[10] 771 5 -8-1364 KirstyMilczarek 1 48
(Barry Leavy) *sn led: hdd over 8f out: remained handy tl rdn and wknd over 1f out* **20/1**

500- **10** *1 3/4* **Cobbs Quay**[244] 5938 4 -9-570 MickaelBarzalona 15 51
(Daniel Kubler) *chsd ldrs: led over 8f out: rdn over 2f out: hit rails wl over 1f out: sn hdd: wknd fnl f* **7/2**[2]

6350 **11** *9* **Menadati (USA)**[65] 826 4 -9-065 WilliamCarson 11 29
(Peter Hiatt) *hld up: rdn over 3f out: wknd over 2f out* **33/1**

466- **12** *shd* **Effigy**[221] 6592 8 -8-1268 AmyScott(5) 2 32
(Henry Candy) *hld up: effrt over 3f out: sn wknd* **18/1**

2004 **13** *4 1/2* **Follow The Flag (IRE)**[8] 1841 8 -9-570 (be) RyanMoore 8 25
(Alan McCabe) *mid-div: wknd over 3f out* **16/1**

00-6 **14** *46* **Searing Heat (USA)**[13] 1655 4 -9-267 IanMongan 5
(Sir Henry Cecil) *hld up in tch: wknd over 3f out: t.o* **12/1**

2m 20.42s (8.72)**Going Correction** +0.95s/f (Soft) **14**Ran SP% **122.7**
Speed ratings (Par 103): **103,102,101,96,95 94,93,93,92,90 83,83,79,42**
toteswingers: 1&2 £5.20, 1&3 £9.60, 2&3 £25.00. CSF £27.76 CT £267.24 TOTE £3.40 : £2.20, £3.10, £4.20 ; EX 32.00 .
Owner M Ng **Bred** Michael Ng **Trained** Royston, Herts
■ Stewards' Enquiry : Royston Ffrench two-day ban: used whip above permitted level (May 25-26)

FOCUS
A reasonable race for the grade run at a good pace.
Nolecce Official explanation: stewards noted that the gelding lost a cheek piece in running
T/Jkpt: Not won. T/Plt: £465.70 to a £1 stake. Pool: £61,053.51 - 95.69 winning tickets. T/Qpdt: £158.80 to a £1 stake. Pool: £36,40.08 - 16.96 winning tickets. CR

[1670]RIPON (R-H)
Friday, May 11
2052 Meeting Abandoned - waterlogged

[1766]CHANTILLY (R-H)
Friday, May 11
OFFICIAL GOING: Turf: soft; polytrack: standard

2064a PRIX DE GUICHE (GROUP 3) (3YO COLTS) (TURF) 1m 1f
2:20 (12:00) 3-Y-0 **£33,333** (£13,333; £10,000 ; £6,666 ; £3,333)

RPR

1 **Saint Baudolino (IRE)**[15] 3 -9-20 MaximeGuyon 2 114+
(A Fabre, France) *racd in 3rd on inner cl bhd ldrs: rdn 1 1/2f out: had to be stdd 1f out whn no split appeared between ldrs: hrd rdn to split ldrs and chal 25yds out: barged Xanadou in process: got up on line* **37/10**

2 *snk* **Sofast (FR)**[26] 1408 3 -9-20 OlivierPeslier 1 111
(F Head, France) *racd in 5th: qcknd wl on outside 1f out: chal 100yds out: led 50yds out: r.o strly: hdd fnl strides* **5/2**[2]

3 *nk* **Mandour (USA)**[36] 3 -9-20 Christophe-PatriceLemaire 4 111
(A De Royer-Dupre, France) *led fr s: set stdy pce: rdn 1 1/2f out: hdd 1f out: styd on wl fnl f* **2/1**[1]

4 *1 3/4* **Xanadou (IRE)**[45] 3 -9-20 ChristopheSoumillon 6 107
(J-C Rouget, France) *racd in 4th towards outside: rdn over 1f out: qcknd wl to ld 100yds out: hdd 50yds out: bmpd by eventual wnr ins fnl 25yds: nrly b.d: had to be snatched up and lost all momentum* **3/1**[3]

5 *2 1/2* **Silver Northern (FR)**[29] 3 -9-20 AlexisBadel 5 102
(D Chenu, France) *settled in 2nd outside ldr: rdn to ld 1f out: hdd 100yds out: no ex u.p: styd on wl* **32/1**

6 *5* **American Devil (FR)**[222] 6565 3 -9-20 StephanePasquier 3 91
(J Van Handenhove, France) *racd freely at rr of field: rdn 1 1/2f out: r.o to cl on ldrs: began to weaken 150yds out: dropped away* **14/1**

1m 57.8s (6.70) **6**Ran SP% **117.9**
WIN (incl. 1 euro stake): 4.70. PLACES: 2.10, 2.00. SF: 13.10 .
Owner Godolphin **Bred** Darley Stud Management Co Ltd **Trained** Chantilly, France

NOTEBOOK
Saint Baudolino (IRE) who was supplemented for this race, quickened best of all between horses to land a narrow success in this French Derby trial. By Pivotal out of a mare who won over 1m4f, he promises to stay the Jockey Club distance.
Sofast(FR), who was only narrowly denied, isn't sure to go to the Prix du Jockey Club. There's a lot of speed on the dam's side of his pedigree and his stamina for that longer distance would be in doubt. He might drop back to 1m instead.

2059a-2063a Foreign Racing (See RI)

[2019]ASCOT (R-H)
Saturday, May 12
OFFICIAL GOING: Straight course - soft changing to good to soft after race 6 (4.35); round course - heavy (soft in places) changing to soft after race 2 (2.20)
Rail positioned 4yds in from 1m4f start, inc. to 8yds at home bend before joining straight adding 16y to 1m 4f race and 19y to 2m race.
Wind: Virtually nil Weather: Sunny

2065 JOHN DOYLE MAIDEN STKS 5f
1:45 (1:45) (Class 3) 3-Y-0+ **£9,703** (£2,887; £1,443 ; £721) **Stalls** Centre

Form RPR

03-3 **1** **Show Flower**[7] 1862 3 -8-1274 MartinHarley 2 78
(Mick Channon) *trckd ldrs: wnt 2nd ins fnl 2f: drvn to ld jst ins fnl f: styd on strly clsng stages* **15/8**[1]

52 **2** *1 1/4* **Sir Maximilian (IRE)**[11] 1739 3 -9-30 RyanMoore 1 79
(Ed Dunlop) *sn led: drvn along 2f out: hdd jst ins fnl f: outpcd fnl 120yds* **11/4**[2]

5-44 **3** *2 3/4* **Tahnee Mara (IRE)**[21] 1514 3 -8-967 (p) AmyRyan(3) 5 64
(Kevin Ryan) *chsd ldr: rdn 2f out: sn one pce into 3rd and no ch w ldng duo fnl f* **11/1**

-225 **4** *1* **Nevaeh**[10] 1748 3 -8-970 (p) KierenFox(3) 7 60
(Pat Eddery) *prom tl outpcd after 2f: sn rdn: styd on fnl f but nt gng pce to rch ldrs* **12/1**

0 **5** *1/2* **Common Cents**[41] 1155 3 -8-100 DarrenEgan(7) 8 63
(Ronald Harris) *chsd ldrs: rdn 1/2-way: wknd fnl f* **28/1**

0-6 **6** *2* **Mr Fickle (IRE)**[7] 1606 3 -9-30 GeorgeBaker 4 56
(Gary Moore) *slowly away and bhd: pushed along 2f out: styd on wl fnl f: gng on clsng stages* **80/1**

0 **7** *1/2* **Rum Punch**[22] 1501 3 -8-120 JohnFahy 3 49
(Eve Johnson Houghton) *rrd stalls: sn prom: sn drvn: wknd ins fnl 2f* **16/1**

8 *1/2* **New Lease Of Life** 3 -9-30 GrahamLee 6 52
(Jim Goldie) *spd to 1/2-way* **7/1**[3]

0 **9** *4* **Ishi**[22] 1501 3 -8-120 JamesMillman 10 33
(Rod Millman) *racd stands' side: early spd: no ch fr 1/2-way* **40/1**

0-2 **10** *24* **Miss Noble**[12] 1705 3 -8-120 WilliamCarson 9
(Stuart Williams) *racd stands' side: no ch fr 1/2-way: eased fnl f* **10/1**

1m 3.04s (2.54)**Going Correction** +0.625s/f (Yiel) **10**Ran SP% **112.1**
Speed ratings (Par 107): **104,102,97,95,95 92,91,90,84,45**
toteswingers:1&2:£1.70, 1&3:£5.60, 2&3:£8.70 CSF £6.44 TOTE £2.80 : £1.20 , £1.60 , £3.10 ; EX 7.70 Trifecta £47.60 Pool: £1,097.63 - 17.05 winning units.
Owner Jaber Abdullah **Bred** Maywood Stud **Trained** West Ilsley, Berks
■ Stewards' Enquiry : Kieren Fox seven-day ban: used whip above permitted level (May 28-Jun 3)

FOCUS
The round course passed an early morning inspection and the ground there was given as heavy, soft in places (GoingStick 5.2), while on the straight track it was soft (GoingStick stands' side 6.1, centre 6.2, far side 6.1). The field for this ordinary maiden split into two groups, with the majority racing up the centre of the track. The pair who raced apart, nearer the stands' side (Ishi and Miss Noble) finished last and second-last. The winning rider described the ground as "dead". The form looks straightforward with the first two to form.

NOTEBOOK
Show Flower ran well in some good maidens last year, including when finishing in front of Elusive Kate on debut and when beaten 4l by Lyric Of Light, but she was often too keen for her own good, and bringing her back to the minimum trip on her second start this year proved a good move. She quickened up well when asked and should have more to offer over this trip. (op 9-4 tchd 7-4)
Sir Maximilian (IRE)again showed good speed throughout. He has the option of going down the handicapping route now, and better ground might bring about more improvement. (op 15-8)
Tahnee Mara (IRE)is pretty exposed now. (op 10-1 tchd 14-1)
Nevaeh was being niggled along from an early stage. The drop back to 5f just didn't work for her. (op 14-1)
Common Cents showed more than on his debut and might be of interest after one more run and being allocated a handicap mark. (op 25-1)
Rum Punch can be excused this effort as she reared badly as the stalls opened, possibly banging her head in the process. Official explanation: jockey said filly reared on leaving stalls (tchd 18-1)
Miss Noble Official explanation: trainer said filly was unsuited by the soft ground

2066 JOHN DOYLE BUCKHOUNDS STKS (LISTED RACE) 1m 4f
2:20 (2:20) (Class 1) 4-Y-0+ **£18,714** (£7,095; £3,550 ; £1,768 ; £887) **Stalls** Low

Form RPR

11-1 **1** **Aiken**[17] 1603 4 -8-1299 RyanMoore 2 116
(John Gosden) *trckd ldrs in 3rd: shkn up and qcknd to ld 2f out: sn pushed clr: v easily* **2/5**[1]

40-0 **2** *10* **Tameen**[7] 1848 4 -8-7100 HayleyTurner 1 96
(Ed Dunlop) *trckd ldr: chal fr 6f out tl rdn and slt ld over 2f out: sn hdd and no ch w wnr but kpt on wl for clr 2nd fnl 120yds* **12/1**[3]

60-1 **3** *1 1/2* **Dawn Twister (GER)**[14] 1674 5 -8-12105 IanMongan 5 99
(Lucy Wadham) *led: jnd fr 6f out: rdn 3f out: hdd over 2f out: styd on same pce for wl-hld 3rd fnl f* **10/3**[2]

4-64 **4** *1* **Twin Soul (IRE)**[7] 1848 4-8-8 87 ow1 .... DarryllHolland 3 93
(Andrew Balding) *steaded rr and racd in 5th: rdn and outpcd over 3f out: styd on u.p fr over 1f out to cl on wl hld 3rd clsng stages* **16/1**

0545 **5** *8* **Sos Brillante (CHI)**[6] 1883 7-8-7 74 .... MarkCoumbe 4 80
(Terry Clement) *racd in 4th: rdn and wknd 3f out* **50/1**

2m 40.12s (7.62) **Going Correction** +0.875s/f (Soft) **5** Ran SP% **110.0**
Speed ratings (Par 111): **109,102,101,100,95**
CSF £6.49 TOTE £1.40: £1.10, £4.20; EX 4.60.
Owner George Strawbridge **Bred** George Strawbridge **Trained** Newmarket, Suffolk

FOCUS
Rail movements added 16yds to the distance of both 1m4f races. Not a strong Listed race, but hard not be taken by the way the winner scored and the form is rated at something like face value.

NOTEBOOK
Aiken drew well clear in the straight. He was helped by the fact that his two main market rivals took each other on in front and that set things up nicely for him turning into the straight, but he galloped on strongly to the line and looks a highly progressive colt. Given his pedigree a bit of cut in the ground is always likely to suit him, and if the ground dries up it wouldn't be a surprise to see him pointed towards Group contests on the continent. (tchd 4-11 and 4-9 and 1-2 in places)
Tameen had an excuse on her reappearance at Goodwood as the bit slipped through her mouth. Wearing a different bit this time, she secured some valuable black type by keeping on for second, and might have finished a little closer to the winner had she been allowed the run of things in front rather than disputing it with Dawn Twister. (op 10-1)
Dawn Twister(GER) likes this sort of ground and made a winning debut for the stable at Ripon a fortnight earlier, but having looked likely to be allowed to dominate at his own pace, he was joined by Tameen, and the pair probably did each other no favours by beginning to race from some way out. (op 4-1)
Twin Soul(IRE) was keeping on at the finish, but this ground was probably too soft for her. (op 14-1)
Sos Brillante(CHI) was outclassed, and racing keenly over this longer trip didn't help matters either.

2067 BOVIS HOMES FILLIES' H'CAP 1m (S)
2:50 (2:50) (Class 2) 3-Y-O+ **£29,110** (£8,662; £4,329; £2,164) **Stalls** Centre

Form RPR

500- **1** **Making Eyes (IRE)**[196] 7168 4-9-2 84 .... IanMongan 12 96
(Hugo Palmer) *t.k.h: stdd towards rr: drvn and hdwy over 2f out: rdn to ld ins fnl f: hld on wl* **11/2**[2]

40-3 **2** *½* **My Queenie (IRE)**[10] 1748 3-8-4 85 .... HayleyTurner 9 93
(Richard Hannon) *in tch: hdwy over 2f out: drvn to chal 1f out: stl ev ch ins fnl f: no ex fnl 75yds* **10/1**

55-0 **3** *1 ½* **Russian Rave**[29] 1354 6-8-10 78 .... EddieAhern 8 86
(Jonathan Portman) *in rr: hdwy and nt much daylight ins fnl 2f: styd on wl fnl f to take 3rd clsng stages but no imp on ldng duo* **14/1**

02-1 **4** *nk* **Moone's My Name**[26] 1416 4-9-6 88 .... MartinLane 10 95
(Ralph Beckett) *stdd s: in rr: hdwy 2f out: styd on to chse ldng duo ins fnl f but no imp: lost 3rd clsng stages* **9/2**[1]

031- **5** *1 ¼* **Free Verse**[210] 6864 3-8-1 85 .... RyanPowell(3) 2 86
(Richard Hannon) *chsd ldrs: led appr 2f out: sn rdn: hdd ins fnl f: wknd fnl 120yds* **7/1**

00-2 **6** *½* **Certral**[31] 1321 4-8-4 79 .... DarrenEgan(7) 7 82
(Brian Ellison) *in tch: chsd ldrs and rdn 2f out: no ex fnl f* **6/1**[3]

0666 **7** *hd* **Cochabamba (IRE)**[15] 1646 4-9-6 88 .... GeorgeBaker 11 90
(Roger Teal) *sn led: rdn and hdd appr fnl 2f: rdn and bmpd over 1f out: edgd lft ins fnl f: kpt on again clsng stages* **20/1**

114- **8** *2* **Diverting**[196] 7168 4-9-1 86 .... HarryBentley(3) 6 84
(William Jarvis) *in tch: drvn and outpcd over 2f out: styng on whn bmpd ins fnl f: kpt on again clsng stages* **9/1**

310- **9** *6* **Shesastar**[248] 5830 4-9-4 86 .... RyanMoore 5 87
(David Barron) *chsd ldrs: edgd rt over 1f out wkng whn bmpd ins fnl f* **6/1**[3]

66-2 **10** *2* **Fork Handles**[42] 1139 4-9-10 92 .... MartinHarley 3 71
(Mick Channon) *in rr: hdwy 3f out wknd fr 2f out* **12/1**

0-21 **11** *16* **Chatterati (USA)**[72] 747 3-7-9 79 oh2 .... DominicFox(3) 1
(Mark Johnston) *chsd ldrs: rdn 3f out: wknd qckly over 2f out: eased fnl f* **20/1**

1m 44.72s (3.92) **Going Correction** +0.625s/f (Yiel)
WFA 3 from 4yo+ 13lb **11** Ran SP% **117.6**
Speed ratings (Par 96): **105,104,103,102,101 100,100,98,92,90 74**
toteswingers:1&2:£17.80, 1&3:£37.80, 2&3:£89.70 CSF £59.55 CT £723.25 TOTE £7.00: £2.30, £3.10, £5.60; EX 125.20 TRIFECTA Not won..
Owner Starter For Ten Partnership **Bred** F Dunne **Trained** Newmarket, Suffolk
■ Stewards' Enquiry : Ian Mongan four-day ban: used whip above permitted level (May 26,28-30)

FOCUS
A competitive fillies' handicap in which the first four came from off the pace. The form looks pretty sound with the third, fourth and fifth close to their marks.

NOTEBOOK
Making Eyes(IRE) bolted up first time up on soft ground last year and she was quietly backed from 8-1 in the morning to do likewise this time around. She got the solid gallop she requires and saw the trip out well, which is not surprising given she's won over as far as 1m3f in the past. Lightly raced, it'll be interesting to see if she holds her form a bit better than she did last year. (op 6-1 tchd 5-1)
My Queenie(IRE), who was running in a handicap for the first time, looked fairly weighted on the best of her form from last year. Doing best of the three 3-y-os in the line-up, she should be capable of winning something similar.
Russian Rave, for whom the trip was a bit of a concern, was staying on nicely at the finish and got it fine. The problem for her is that she is likely to keep bumping into better treated rivals. (tchd 16-1)
Moone's My Name kept on from the back of the field in a race run to suit, but all her previous form has been on good ground or quicker and this surface was probably slower than ideal. (op 4-1)
Free Verse, never far off the pace in a race run at a solid gallop, didn't quite get home. Judgement needs to be reserved on whether it was the longer trip or lack of a previous outing which told in the end, as the ground wasn't the problem. (op 8-1)
Certral ran a promising race on her reappearance so this was a shade disappointing considering her stable is in such good form. Her winning form is all on good to firm ground, though. (op 15-2 tchd 8-1)
Shesastar came there to have her chance but didn't see her race out. The trip seemed to stretch her. (op 7-1)

2068 BETFRED VICTORIA CUP (H'CAP) 7f
3:25 (3:27) (Class 2) 4-Y-O+
£52,912 (£15,844; £7,922; £3,961; £1,980; £994) **Stalls** Centre

Form RPR

0513 **1** **Global Village (IRE)**[21] 1510 7-8-5 88 .... TadhgO'Shea 2 100
(Brian Ellison) *chsd ldrs towards far side: drvn to ld jst ins fnl f: rdr dropped whip: drvn out* **9/1**[2]

001- **2** *¾* **Bonnie Brae**[189] 7295 5-8-13 96 .... RyanMoore 1 106
(David Elsworth) *in rr: hdwy towards far side over 2f out: styd on wl to chse wnr fnl 120yds but no imp* **11/1**

00-3 **3** *1 ¼* **King Of Jazz (IRE)**[41] 1157 4-9-0 97 .... HayleyTurner 5 104
(Michael Bell) *chsd ldrs towards far side: rdn and kpt on to chse wnr ins fnl f: no imp and one pce into 3rd fnl 120yds* **14/1**

00-1 **4** *½* **Brae Hill (IRE)**[42] 1130 6-9-2 99 .... TonyHamilton 8 104
(Richard Fahey) *led and racd towards far side: rdn and hdd 2f out: kpt on again clsng stages* **20/1**

121- **5** *¾* **Lightning Cloud (IRE)**[248] 5830 4-8-9 95 .... AmyRyan(3) 15 99+
(Kevin Ryan) *chsd ldrs towards centre of crse: styd on wl clsng stages but nvr quite gng pce of those racing towards far side* **14/1**

451- **6** *½* **Pastoral Player**[224] 6521 5-9-10 107 .... DarryllHolland 12 109
(Hughie Morrison) *racd towards far side: drvn and hdwy fr 2f out: styd on same pce ins fnl f* **11/1**

02-0 **7** *½* **Pravda Street**[21] 1522 7-8-3 86 .... JohnFahy 16 87
(Brian Ellison) *in tch towards centre of crse: styd on u.p fnl f: nt rch ldrs* **16/1**

306- **8** *½* **Imperial Guest**[210] 6862 6-8-10 96 .... AshleyHamblett(3) 6 96
(George Margarson) *chsd ldrs towards far side: rdn over 2f out: one pce fnl f* **28/1**

01-1 **9** *shd* **Tariq Too**[21] 1522 5-8-8 91 .... EddieAhern 4 90
(Amy Weaver) *racd towards far side: slt ld and rdn 2f out: hdd & wknd ins fnl f* **8/1**[1]

4- **10** *½* **Cool Marble (IRE)**[44] 5-7-11 85 .... RaulDaSilva(5) 3 83
(Jeremy Gask) *chsd ldrs far side: rdn over 2f out: wknd fnl f* **28/1**

004- **11** *nk* **Hawkeyethenoo (IRE)**[224] 6521 6-9-6 103 .... GrahamLee 19 100+
(Jim Goldie) *racd towards centre: in tch: rdn and sme hdwy over 1f out: nvr rchd ldrs and wknd fnl f* **12/1**

23-2 **12** *1* **New Leyf (IRE)**[42] 1141 6-8-7 90 ....(b) J-PGuillambert 23 85
(Ed Walker) *in rr and racd towards centre of crse: styd on u.p fnl f: nvr rchd ldrs* **33/1**

10-0 **13** *½* **Fantasy Gladiator**[35] 1212 6-8-0 83 ....(p) AndreaAtzeni 10 76
(Robert Cowell) *racd towards far side: rdn over 2f out: nvr gng pce to rch ldrs: lost cheekpiece in running* **40/1**

220- **14** *¾* **Excellent Guest**[294] 4314 5-8-12 95 .... IanMongan 22 86
(George Margarson) *racd towards centre crse: in tch: rdn and no prog fnl 2f* **12/1**

0-02 **15** *1 ½* **Benandonner (USA)**[10] 1752 9-8-1 84 .... MartinLane 9 72
(Mike Murphy) *chsd ldrs towards far side: rdn 3f out: wknd fr 2f out* **33/1**

630- **16** *1 ½* **White Frost (IRE)**[210] 6862 4-8-9 92 .... WilliamCarson 7 76
(Charles Hills) *chsd ldrs towards far side: wknd fr 2f out* **10/1**[3]

0-20 **17** *1 ½* **Advanced**[7] 1865 9-8-9 95 .... JulieBurke(3) 20 75
(Kevin Ryan) *pressed ldrs towards centre of crse over 4f* **33/1**

000 **18** *1 ¼* **Mabait**[86] 586 6-8-7 97 .... AliceHaynes(7) 13 73
(David Simcock) *in rr and racd towards far side: outpcd most of way* **33/1**

30-0 **19** *1* **Fathsta (IRE)**[6] 1885 7-8-7 90 .... MartinDwyer 14 64
(David Simcock) *outpcd fr 1/2-way* **12/1**

05-6 **20** *2 ¼* **Kakatosi**[129] 29 5-8-12 95 .... JimmyFortune 24 63
(Andrew Balding) *chsd ldrs towards centre of crse over 3f* **33/1**

6-00 **21** *nk* **Nasri**[19] 1558 6-8-5 95 .... DarrenEgan(7) 21 62
(David Nicholls) *bhd fr 1/2-way* **20/1**

0-05 **22** *1 ¾* **Space Station**[11] 1741 6-7-10 82 ....(b) DominicFox(3) 17 45
(Simon Dow) *bhd fr 1/2-way* **50/1**

104- **23** *1 ½* **Dhaular Dhar (IRE)**[132] 7719 10-7-7 83 .... NoelGarbutt(7) 11 42
(Jim Goldie) *bhd fr 1/2-way* **40/1**

-422 **24** *nk* **Rodrigo De Torres**[21] 1523 5-9-1 98 .... MartinHarley 18 56
(Mrs K Burke) *chsd ldrs to 1/2-way* **20/1**

1m 30.3s (2.70) **Going Correction** +0.625s/f (Yiel) **24** Ran SP% **131.9**
Speed ratings (Par 109): **109,108,106,106,105 104,104,103,103,102 102,101,100,99,98 96,94,93,92,89 89,87,85,85**
toteswingers:1&2:£28.10, 1&3:£37.50, 2&3:£50.50 CSF £91.39 CT £894.06 TOTE £10.00: £3.30, £2.60, £3.10, £4.90; EX 110.10 Trifecta £2335.00 Pool: £33,332.92 - 10.56 winning units..
Owner Jack Racing Melksham **Bred** Kilfrush Stud **Trained** Norton, N Yorks

FOCUS
The field split into two groups and the far-side bunch dominated at the finish, with the first three drawn in the bottom five boxes. The winner is progressive and the third and fourth set the standard.

NOTEBOOK
Global Village(IRE) ran a fine race when third in the Spring Cup last time out and, with the ground in his favour, a 2lb rise wasn't going to be a problem if he turned up here in the same form. The drop back from 1m to 7f was in his favour and, as it turned out, he was drawn on the right side. His stable can do little wrong at present. (op 10-1)
Bonnie Brae ◆ was an improving filly last back-end, and made a really pleasing return to action, just finding a race-fit rival too strong at the finish. Her trainer was quoted beforehand as expecting her to come on for this and, whether she sticks to handicaps or tries her hand in pattern company, there should be better to come from her.
King Of Jazz(IRE) was taken out of the Buckingham Palace Stakes last year on account of the soft ground, so considering the conditions he ran well, albeit from what turned out to be a good draw, and with the far rail to help. (tchd 16-1)
Brae Hill(IRE), the Lincoln winner, was fourth in this last year when given a hold-up ride on fast ground. Ridden from the front this time on soft, he replicated that finishing position, confirming himself once again an admirably versatile gelding. (op 16-1)
Lightning Cloud(IRE) ◆, progressive last year, winning five of his seven starts, doesn't look to have stopped improving over the winter. He was first home from the group that raced up the centre of the track, is seemingly a 7f specialist, and will be of serious interest if returning for the Buckingham Palace Stakes.
Pastoral Player put in some good late work on the far side and was far from disgraced off a mark of 107. He needs a strong pace so small-field Group races are no good to him, but he really is going to continue to be up against it in the top handicaps off this sort of mark. (tchd 10-1)
Pravda Street was badly hampered on his reappearance and had a nice pull at the weights with the winner that day, Tariq Too. Prominent throughout, he was second home from the group that raced up the centre, and this was a solid effort.
Imperial Guest has run well in each of his of his last four starts over this C&D without quite making the first five, and while he might come on for this reappearance run (has gone well fresh in the past), it looks like the handicapper just about has him at the moment. (op 33-1 tchd 25-1)
Tariq Too impressed on his reappearance at Thirsk but didn't see his race out in this stronger contest on this stiffer track. (tchd 10-1)
Cool Marble(IRE), who has run all over Europe for prevuious trainers, was debuting in Britain and ran respectably for his new trainer, albeit from the favoured group. (op 33-1)
Hawkeyethenoo(IRE), last year's winner, finished third from the group racing up the centre, which was a sound effort considering he was 7lb higher than last year and the ground was softer than ideal. (op 14-1)
Fantasy Gladiator Official explanation: stewards noted the gelding had accidentally lost a cheek piece in running.

White Frost(IRE), who won first time up last season, was disappointing. He has won on soft ground before and run well at this track in the past, so this is hard to explain. Perhaps he needed it more than expected. (op 12-1)

2069 MCGEE GROUP MAIDEN STKS 5f
4:00 (4:01) (Class 3) 2-Y-O £7,762 (£2,310; £1,154; £577) Stalls Centre

Form RPR

5 **1** **Cay Verde**[22] 1499 2-9-3 0 .... MartinHarley 11 94+
(Mick Channon) *chsd ldrs: drvn and qcknd to ld jst ins fnl f: r.o strly clsng stages* **11/2**

3 **2** *2 ½* **Hototo**[8] 1818 2-9-3 0 .... JimmyFortune 3 85
(Kevin Ryan) *chsd ldrs: chal ins fnl 2f: slt ld u.p over 1f out: hdd jst ins fnl f: kpt on same pce* **7/2**[2]

3 *1* **Janoub Nibras (IRE)** 2-9-3 0 .... RyanMoore 1 82
(Richard Hannon) *chsd ldrs: str chal and rdn fr over 1f out: one pce ins fnl f* **3/1**[1]

53 **4** *½* **Top Boy**[8] 1842 2-9-3 0 .... GeorgeBaker 2 80+
(Derek Shaw) *t.k.h: in tch: shkn up over 1f out: kpt on fnl f but nvr gng pce to press ldrs* **9/2**[3]

02 **5** *3 ½* **Marvelino**[35] 1211 2-9-3 0 .... TadhgO'Shea 5 67
(Pat Eddery) *chsd ldrs: rdn and outpcd 2f out: styd on again clsng stages* **9/1**

6 *1 ½* **Classic Art** 2-9-3 0 .... EddieAhern 8 62+
(Roger Teal) *s.i.s: green and in rr: pushed along over 2f out in last pl: styd on fnl f but nvr any ch* **33/1**

7 *hd* **Forbidden Fruit (IRE)** 2-9-3 0 .... MartinDwyer 4 61
(Brian Meehan) *outpcd early: sme prog fnl f* **16/1**

8 *1 ½* **Melodee Princess (IRE)** 2-8-5 0 .... DarrenEgan[(7)] 6 51
(Ronald Harris) *outpcd most of way* **33/1**

0 **9** *hd* **Limit Up**[8] 1818 2-9-3 0 .... IanMongan 10 55
(Mark Johnston) *led tl jnd ins fnl 2f: sn hdd: wknd qckly fnl f* **9/1**

10 *½* **The Manx Missile** 2-9-3 0 .... HayleyTurner 7 53
(Michael Bell) *t.k.h: chsd ldrs over 3f: sn wknd* **28/1**

1m 3.16s (2.66) **Going Correction** +0.625s/f (Yiel) **10** Ran SP% **116.0**
Speed ratings (Par 97): **103,99,97,96,91 88,88,85,85,84**
toteswingers:1&2:£4.70, 1&3:£5.60, 2&3:£1.20 CSF £24.51 TOTE £5.80: £2.20, £1.70, £1.80; EX 22.00 Trifecta £77.20 Pool: £1,931.74 - 18.49 winning units..
Owner Box 41 **Bred** Lady Whent **Trained** West Ilsley, Berks

FOCUS
As is often the case previous experience proved crucial here, and it was an impressive performance from the winner. The winner looks an improver with the fourth rated close to his debut form.

NOTEBOOK
Cay Verde ◆, who ran fifth in a decent Newbury maiden first time up, built on that here, travelling and quickening right away like a good horse, and recording a time only marginally slower than the currently 74-rated 3-y-o filly carrying 5lb less managed in the opening race. It's hard to know the true value of the form, but the runner-up got an RPR of 85 on his debut at Musselburgh, and the style of his success was eyecatching. He could be one for the Norfolk, perhaps after taking in a conditions event somewhere beforehand. (op 8-1)
Hototo, unlucky on his debut at Musselburgh, had no excuses this time, and was simply beaten for a turn of foot. He might have bumped into a smart rival, though, and he should still win his maiden. (op 9-2)
Janoub Nibras(IRE), who cost 105,000gns, ran a promising race on his debut against two good rivals who had the benefit of previous experience. He should take some beating next time out. (op 7-2, tchd 4-1 in a place)
Top Boy was a little keener than ideal, but his performance helps give the form a solid look. (op 4-1 tchd 7-2 and 5-1 in a place)
Marvelino, like the fourth, was a bit keen early, but he too gives some substance to the form. (op 15-2)
Classic Art was slowly away, green and detached in last for much of the race, but he was keeping on nicely at the finish and should come on for the outing. His pedigree suggests another furlong won't go amiss. (op 28-1)
Forbidden Fruit(IRE) didn't settle at all early so unsurprisingly weakened right out in the closing stages. A half-brother to six winners, he ought to do better next time. Official explanation: jockey said colt ran too freely (tchd 14-1)

2070 BETFRED THE BONUS KING H'CAP (DIV I) 6f
4:35 (4:35) (Class 4) (0-80,84) 4-Y-O+ £5,175 (£1,540; £769; £384) Stalls Centre

Form RPR

044- **1** **Moretta Blanche**[264] 5322 5-9-5 77 ....(t) JimCrowley 7 85
(Ralph Beckett) *s.i.s: in rr: rapid hdwy over 1f out: str run ins fnl f: fin wl to ld last strides* **8/1**

/0P- **2** *hd* **Slip Sliding Away (IRE)**[334] 3000 5-9-7 79 .... JohnFahy 4 86
(Peter Hedger) *s.i.s: in rr: hdwy over 1f out: drvn fnl f and led fnl 120yds: hdd last strides* **14/1**

60-2 **3** *shd* **Rothesay Chancer**[34] 1237 4-9-4 76 .... GrahamLee 13 83
(Jim Goldie) *hld up in rr: drvn and rapid hdwy fnl f str run clsng stages: nt quite get up* **8/1**

5-62 **4** *½* **Emiratesdotcom**[5] 1935 6-9-2 74 .... HayleyTurner 3 80
(Milton Bradley) *pressed ldrs: chal fr over 2f out and stl upsides fnl 120yds: no ex clsng stages* **6/1**[3]

0302 **5** *¾* **Hatta Stream (IRE)**[11] 1727 6-8-6 67 .... SimonPearce[(3)] 1 70
(Lydia Pearce) *pressed ldrs tl led appr fnl 2f: sn drvn: hdd fnl 120yds: sn wknd* **14/1**

0014 **6** *1 ¼* **Mata Hari Blue**[15] 1638 6-9-0 72 ....(t) KirstyMilczarek 6 72
(John Holt) *in tch: drvn and hdwy 2f out: kpt on fnl f but nvr gng pce to press ldrs* **10/1**

0061 **7** *nk* **Seek The Fair Land**[5] 1935 6-9-12 84 6ex ....(b) JimmyFortune 5 83
(Jim Boyle) *in tch: rdn over 2f out: effrt over 1f out: styd on same pce* **5/1**[2]

11 **8** *½* **Mon Ami Jolie (USA)**[17] 1614 4-9-3 75 .... RyanMoore 8 72
(Richard Hannon) *t.k.h: chsd ldrs: rdn over 2f out: wknd fnl f* **9/4**[1]

3150 **9** *¾* **Night Trade (IRE)**[5] 1936 5-8-13 78 .... DarrenEgan[(7)] 11 73
(Ronald Harris) *racd alone towards centre crse and outpcd: rdn over 2f out: kpt on clsng stages* **25/1**

-065 **10** *½* **Jack My Boy (IRE)**[11] 1727 5-9-4 76 ....(v) PadraigBeggy 9 69
(David Evans) *sn led: hdd appr fnl 2f: wknd appr fnl f* **16/1**

0230 **11** *nk* **Earlsmedic**[19] 1564 7-9-0 72 ....(v) SaleemGolam 12 65
(Stuart Williams) *in rr: pushed along and styd on same pce fr over 1f out* **33/1**

-005 **12** *7* **Local Singer (IRE)**[37] 1203 4-9-1 73 ....(t) J-PGuillambert 2 45
(Paul Howling) *t.k.h: chsd ldrs 4f: sn btn* **33/1**

1m 17.62s (3.12) **Going Correction** +0.625s/f (Yiel) **12** Ran SP% **122.0**
Speed ratings (Par 105): **104,103,103,102,101 100,99,99,98,97 97,87**
CSF £115.58 CT £949.68 TOTE £10.10: £3.20, £4.10, £2.80; EX 218.60 Trifecta £1582.60 Part won. Pool: £2,138.75 - 0.62 winning units..
Owner P K Gardner **Bred** Springcombe Park Stud **Trained** Kimpton, Hants

■ Stewards' Enquiry : Simon Pearce two-day ban: used whip above permitted level (May 26,28)
John Fahy two-day ban: used whip above permitted level (May 26,28)

FOCUS
A pretty open handicap, and there was a three-way photo-finish at the line. The form is ordinary with the third looking as good as ever.

2071 ALFRED FRANKS & BARTLETT SUNGLASSES H'CAP (DIV II OF THE 4.35PM) 6f
5:10 (5:10) (Class 4) (0-80,80) 4-Y-O+ £5,175 (£1,540; £769; £384) Stalls Centre

Form RPR

0236 **1** **Italian Tom (IRE)**[33] 1254 5-8-7 73 .... DarrenEgan[(7)] 9 84
(Ronald Harris) *in rr: hdwy over 1f out: hrd drvn and styd on wl fnl f: led last strides* **20/1**

4166 **2** *hd* **Street Power (USA)**[12] 1708 7-8-9 73 .... RaulDaSilva[(5)] 6 83
(Jeremy Gask) *in tch: drvn and hdwy over 1f out: edgd lft and r.o strly fnl 120yds: str chal to take 2nd last strides but nt quite rch wnr* **17/2**

16-0 **3** *hd* **Apollo D'Negro (IRE)**[41] 1161 4-9-0 73 ....(v) JohnFahy 7 82
(Clive Cox) *chsd ldrs: drvn to ld appr fnl f: hrd pressed fnl 120yds: hdd and lost two pls last strides* **9/1**

3264 **4** *1 ¾* **Kylladdie**[32] 1289 5-9-4 77 ....(b) RyanMoore 10 81
(Steve Gollings) *chsd ldrs: rdn over 1f out: kpt on ins fnl f but nvr gng pce to rch ldng trio* **15/2**

-134 **5** *shd* **The Wee Chief (IRE)**[17] 1614 6-8-10 69 .... KieranO'Neill 11 73
(Jimmy Fox) *in rr hdwy towards outside over 1f out: styng on whn pushed lft and one pce fnl 120yds* **14/1**

0-10 **6** *2* **Divine Call**[21] 1520 5-9-5 78 .... MartinLane 3 76
(Milton Bradley) *led tl hdd appr fnl f: wknd fnl 120yds* **11/1**

4-41 **7** *¾* **Interakt**[2] 2012 5-9-2 78 6ex .... HarryBentley[(3)] 8 74
(Joseph Tuite) *chsd ldr: rdn over 2f out: wknd 1f out* **5/1**[2]

55-2 **8** *nk* **Bunce (IRE)**[9] 1769 4-9-4 77 .... GeorgeBaker 12 72
(Paul Fitzsimons) *in rr: hdwy to cl on ldrs ins fnl 2f: nvr quite on terms and wknd fnl f* **9/2**[1]

06-0 **9** *nk* **Rocket Rob (IRE)**[15] 1642 6-8-13 72 .... StevieDonohoe 5 66
(Willie Musson) *hmpd sn after s and in rr: styd on clsng stages* **25/1**

-306 **10** *1* **Waking Warrior**[7] 1868 4-8-13 75 ....(tp) AmyRyan[(3)] 1 66
(Kevin Ryan) *t.k.h: chsd ldrs: rdn 2f out: sn wknd* **7/1**[3]

111- **11** *3* **Peace Seeker**[136] 7896 4-9-3 76 .... WilliamCarson 2 58
(Anthony Carson) *in rr: hdwy to chse ldrs 2f out: wknd sn after* **9/1**

1165 **12** *10* **Woolfall Sovereign (IRE)**[33] 1255 6-9-7 80 .... IanMongan 4 32
(George Margarson) *chsd ldrs: wknd appr fnl 2f* **16/1**

1m 17.36s (2.86) **Going Correction** +0.625s/f (Yiel) **12** Ran SP% **119.1**
Speed ratings (Par 105): **105,104,104,102,102 99,98,97,97,96 92,78**
toteswingers:1&2:£41.60, 1&3:£28.50, 2&3:£16.60 CSF £181.84 CT £1656.49 TOTE £30.90: £7.10, £3.60, £3.40; EX 391.00 Trifecta £1169.60 Pool: £2,634.29 - 1.66 winning units..
Owner S & A Mares **Bred** Tom Radley **Trained** Earlswood, Monmouths

FOCUS
The ground was changed to good to soft before this race, and it was the quicker of the two divisions by 0.26sec. The winner is rated to his old best backed up by the second.
Peace Seeker Official explanation: jockey said gelding suffered interference in running

2072 LEO BANCROFT SIGNATURE HAIRCARE H'CAP 1m 4f
5:40 (5:40) (Class 3) (0-95,93) 4-Y-O+ £8,409 (£2,502; £1,250; £625) Stalls Low

Form RPR

323- **1** **Grumeti**[30] 5968 4-8-11 83 .... JimmyFortune 1 94
(Alan King) *hld up in 4th: drvn and hdwy to take 3rd 3f out: styd on to chal 2f out: led sn after and swtchd rt to far rail wl over 1f out: kpt on strly* **6/4**[2]

31/2 **2** *1 ½* **Local Hero (GER)**[6] 1882 5-8-12 84 ....(p) DarryllHolland 6 92
(Steve Gollings) *trckd ldr tl led ins fnl 4f: rdn 3f out: jnd 2f out: sn hdd and dropped to 3rd: kpt on to chse wnr fnl 120yds but nvr any ch* **11/10**[1]

16-1 **3** *2 ¼* **Dragonera**[14] 1656 4-9-3 89 .... RyanMoore 2 94
(Ed Dunlop) *trckd ldrs in 3rd: rdn to chal over 2f out: hld whn hmpd wl over 1f out: wknd and lost 2nd fnl 120yds* **5/1**[3]

65/4 **4** *20* **Steuben (GER)**[14] 1674 6-9-7 93 .... GrahamLee 5 68
(Barney Curley) *led tl hdd ins fnl 4f: sn wknd* **33/1**

2m 42.82s (10.32) **Going Correction** +0.875s/f (Soft) **4** Ran SP% **107.2**
Speed ratings (Par 107): **100,99,97,84**
CSF £3.47 TOTE £2.40; EX 3.60.
Owner McNeill Family **Bred** Catridge Farm Stud Ltd **Trained** Barbury Castle, Wilts
■ Stewards' Enquiry : Jimmy Fortune two-day ban: careless riding (May 26,28)

FOCUS
Drying conditions caused the ground on the round course to be changed to soft. Despite the small field three interesting, progressive types lined up here. The form looks muddling but the form is taken at something like face value.

NOTEBOOK
Grumeti found most for pressure and stayed on strongest. Following on from a successful juvenile hurdling campaign he looks capable of improving further on the level, and his trainer is keen to keep going with him, eyeing up the Duke of Edinburgh Stakes as a potential target next month. Better ground won't be a problem. (op 15-8)
Local Hero(GER) rallied late to take second, but he had no chance with the winner. He might do better in a bigger field where he'll get a stronger pace to run at. (op 6-5 tchd 5-4)
Dragonera was hampered by the winner as that one hung right when going to the front, but it didn't make a huge amount of difference to the result. She might have bumped into a couple of well-handicapped rivals, though, and it might be an idea not to be too critical of her. (op 7-2)
Steuben(GER) made the early running but was beaten off before the turn into the straight. (op 22-1)
T/Plt: £99.70 to a £1 stake. Pool: £146.990.06 - 1,075.85 winning tickets. T/Qpdt: £92.50 to a £1 stake. Pool: £8,018.59 - 64.10 winning tickets. ST

[1657] HAYDOCK (L-H)
Saturday, May 12

OFFICIAL GOING: Hurdle course - soft (6.6); flat course - good to soft (soft in places; 6.8)
Hurdles: Bends out 6yds adding 42y to 2m hurdle and 63y to 3m hurdle. Flat: Races on inner home straight.
Wind: Light, against Weather: Fine

2073 BUCKLEY'S SILVER WEDDING ANNIVERSARY MAIDEN STKS 6f
2:35 (2:36) (Class 5) 2-Y-O £2,911 (£866; £432; £216) Stalls Centre

Form RPR

1 **Euxton Hall (IRE)** 2-9-3 0 .... PaulHanagan 2 89+
(Richard Fahey) *led for 1f: remained w ldr: regained ld 2f out: pushed along over 1f out: r.o and in command towards fin* **4/1**[3]

2	1 1/4	**Annunciation** 2-9-3 0 ... RichardHughes 4	85+
		(Richard Hannon) *trckd ldrs: rdn to chse wnr over 1f out: chal ins fnl f: no ex fnl 75yds* **7/2**[2]	
3	6	**Luhaif** 2-9-3 0 ... SamHitchcott 3	67
		(Mick Channon) *trckd ldrs: rdn over 2f out: one pce over 1f out: no ch w front two ins fnl f* **12/1**	
4	2 1/2	**Gold Beau (FR)** 2-9-3 0 ... MichaelO'Connell 8	60+
		(Linda Stubbs) *in rr: pushed along and outpcd 1/2-way: kpt on modly fnl f: nvr a threat* **20/1**	
2 5	1	**Barracuda Boy (IRE)**[14] 1651 2-9-3 0 ... TomEaves 5	57
		(Tom Dascombe) *w ldr: led after 1f: rdn and hdd 2f out: unable to go w wnr over 1f out: wknd ins fnl f* **15/8**[1]	
6	2	**Red Dragon (IRE)** 2-9-3 0 ... MichaelHills 1	51+
		(Charles Hills) *s.i.s: in rr: u.p over 1f out: nvr a threat* **13/2**	
7	6	**Oasis Cannes** 2-9-3 0 ... SebSanders 7	33+
		(Sir Mark Prescott Bt) *trckd ldrs: rdn over 2f out: wknd over 1f out* **10/1**	

1m 18.07s (4.27) **Going Correction** +0.80s/f (Soft) **7** Ran SP% **111.9**
Speed ratings (Par 93): **103,101,93,90,88 86,78**
toteswingers:1&2:£3.80, 2&3:£7.90, 1&3:£11.10 CSF £17.53 TOTE £4.90: £2.40, £3.00; EX 14.20 Trifecta £208.10 Pool: £309.38 - 1.10 winning units..
Owner David W Armstrong **Bred** B Scholer **Trained** Musley Bank, N Yorks

FOCUS
Mixed reports on the ground from the jockeys, with "soft", "dead" and "sticky" all mentioned. Only one had previous racecourse experience in this maiden, in which the runners raced down the centre. The first two came clear and look a couple of decent early juveniles. The time was fast relative to the older-horse conditions race.

NOTEBOOK
Euxton Hall(IRE) ◆ had no trouble laying up with the pace and his rider did not need to get anything like serious with him in the latter stages as he saw off the runner-up. An 80,000gns yearling out of a 6f winner in Germany, he holds Listed/sales race entries later in the season and looks an interesting prospect. Royal Ascot, presumably the Coventry Stakes, could be on the agenda. (tchd 7-2)
Annunciation, whose dam won over this trip at two, was the subject of good reports. After travelling up well he could not get by the winner, but he finished nicely clear of the rest and will surely land a similar race in the next few weeks. (op 4-1 tchd 9-2)
Luhaif shaped with promise, showing an action suited to easy ground, and is likely to improve for the outing. He holds an entry in the Group 1 Phoenix Stakes at the Curragh in August. (op 11-1)
Gold Beau(FR), already a gelding, was under pressure in rear not long past halfway but came through for fourth. This was a modest start but he should do better with time. (op 14-1)
Barracuda Boy(IRE), runner-up at Doncaster on his debut, albeit beaten 6l, had the benefit of previous experience and was soon in front. He faded in the latter stages and may not have seen out the extra furlong at this stage. (op 9-4)
Red Dragon(IRE), a 60,000gns yearling from the family of top sprinter Pipalong, missed the break and will definitely improve with the outing behind him. (op 11-2 tchd 7-1)
Oasis Cannes, Sir Mark Prescott's first runner on turf this year, ran green but might have finished a little closer had his rider not got into a tangle with his reins over a furlong out. (op 15-2)

2074 NETWORK HEALTHCARE CONDITIONS STKS 6f
3:05 (3:05) (Class 2) 3-Y-O+

£12,450 (£3,728; £1,864; £932; £466; £234) **Stalls** Centre

Form				RPR
210-	1		**Our Jonathan**[189] 7298 5-9-0 114 ... FrannyNorton 2	112
			(Kevin Ryan) *hld up: hdwy and hung lft over 1f out: led ins fnl f: r.o: in control towards fin* **15/8**[1]	
2400	2	3/4	**Regal Parade**[72] 756 8-9-0 105 ... AdrianNicholls 6	109
			(David Nicholls) *sn prom: rdn over 1f out: chalng ins fnl f: r.o: hld towards fin* **13/2**[3]	
150-	3	1	**Morache Music**[216] 6733 4-9-0 105 ... SebSanders 4	106
			(Peter Makin) *hld up: effrt to chse ldrs over 1f out: styd on u.p ins fnl f: nt quite gng pce to mount serious chal* **14/1**	
204-	4	shd	**Markab**[245] 5935 9-9-0 109 ... DaneO'Neill 5	106
			(Henry Candy) *led: rdn over 1f out: hdd ins fnl f: styd on u.p tl no ex fnl 50yds* **2/1**[2]	
0-50	5	3 1/2	**Medicean Man**[22] 1498 6-9-0 106 ...(p) PaulHanagan 1	94
			(Jeremy Gask) *in rr: pushed along over 1f out: one pce ins fnl f: nvr able to chal* **9/1**	
03-4	6	7	**Cheviot (USA)**[23] 1469 6-9-0 100 ...(p) TomEaves 3	72
			(Ian Semple) *prom tl rdn and wknd over 1f out* **11/1**	

1m 17.21s (3.41) **Going Correction** +0.80s/f (Soft) **6** Ran SP% **106.4**
Speed ratings (Par 109): **109,108,106,106,101 92**
toteswingers:1&2:£19.40, 1&3:£6.30, 2&3:£9.30 CSF £12.69 TOTE £2.60: £2.10, £3.90; EX 7.70.
Owner Dr Marwan Koukash **Bred** W G M Turner **Trained** Hambleton, N Yorks

FOCUS
Bated Breath beat Society Rock in this conditions event last year and this was another good renewal, but the pace was only steady until halfway and the time didn't compare favourably with the two-year-old maiden. It's doubtful the form is entirely solid and Our Jonathan did not need to match his Ayr Gold Cup form.

NOTEBOOK
Our Jonathan had 5lb in hand on official ratings. Last season's Ayr Gold Cup winner hung when coming with his run and ended up near the far rail, but still won with a bit to spare. He holds entries in a Group 3 at the Curragh at the end of the month and in the Diamond Jubilee Stakes, although the latter would perhaps be flying too high. His best form has come on soft ground. (op 9-4 tchd 7-4)
Regal Parade, one of two former winners of the Haydock Sprint Cup in opposition, stuck on quite well without matching the pace of the winner. He's reportedly had a wind operation since returning from Dubai, and this was a pleasing effort. (op 11-2)
Morache Music, gelded since his last run, represents a yard yet to have a winner this season. The easy ground was in his favour and connections will have been pleased with this reappearance, but he may not be too easy to place successfully this year. (op 12-1)
Markab, the 2010 Sprint Cup winner, made the running but was collared inside the final furlong. His second to Deacon Blues at Newbury last July reads well, but he was below that form in his other outings last season and has a little to prove now. (op 9-4 tchd 5-2)
Medicean Man seems best over a fast-run 5f at Ascot these days, and his head carriage was not very attractive. (op 7-1)
Cheviot(USA) had the worst chance at the weights but the way he dropped away was still disappointing. (op 8-1 tchd 12-1)

2075 NETWORK GROUP SPRING TROPHY STKS (LISTED RACE) 7f
4:15 (4:16) (Class 1) 3-Y-O+

£18,714 (£7,095; £3,550; £1,768; £887; £445) **Stalls** Low

Form				RPR
42-3	1		**Red Jazz (USA)**[42] 1143 5-9-7 112 ... MichaelHills 1	113
			(Charles Hills) *mde all: pushed along over 2f out: kpt on wl whn pressed ins fnl f: a doing enough towards fin* **15/8**[2]	
131-	2	nk	**Firebeam**[242] 6027 4-9-7 106 ... RichardHughes 4	112
			(William Haggas) *racd in 2nd pl: gng wl and upsides 3f out: rdn whn stl ev ch ins fnl f: nt qckn towards fin* **7/4**[1]	
202-	3	1 3/4	**Majestic Myles (IRE)**[176] 4-9-7 111 ... PaulHanagan 2	107
			(Richard Fahey) *racd keenly: chsd ldrs: effrt over 1f out: nvr able to chal front pair: styd on same pce: wl hld cl home* **11/2**[3]	
0-03	4	6	**Smarty Socks (IRE)**[21] 1523 8-9-7 101 ... DanielTudhope 3	91
			(David O'Meara) *hld up: rdn over 2f out: chsd ldrs over 1f out: one pce and no imp after* **14/1**	
256	5	1 3/4	**Scarf (AUS)**[10] 1749 5-9-7 105 ... SilvestreDeSousa 7	86
			(Saeed Bin Suroor) *plld hrd: hld up in rr: rdn over 2f out: edgd lft whn no imp over 1f out: nvr a threat* **14/1**	
35-6	6	26	**Beacon Lodge (IRE)**[20] 1549 7-9-7 112 ... AdrianNicholls 6	16
			(David Nicholls) *racd keenly: in tch: wknd qckly 2f out: eased whn wl btn fnl f: t.o* **10/1**	

1m 29.96s (-0.74) **Going Correction** +0.05s/f (Good) **6** Ran SP% **109.0**
Speed ratings (Par 111): **107,106,104,97,95 66**
toteswingers:1&2:£1.10, 2&3:£3.00, 1&3:£3.40 CSF £5.17 TOTE £3.10: £1.50, £1.10; EX 4.10.
Owner R J Arculli **Bred** William F Murphy & Annabel Murphy **Trained** Lambourn, Berks

FOCUS
A fair Listed race which looked tight on official figures. The pace was reasonable and the race only really concerned the first three. The runners raced down the centre once into the home straight. The form is rated around the winner.

NOTEBOOK
Red Jazz(USA) had contested Group 1 or 2 races on his last seven outings and this represented a drop in grade. Third on Tapeta in Dubai on his seasonal debut six weeks ago, he made all the running here and showed admirable grit in fending off the runner-up's sustained challenge. He is tough and smart and can pick up plenty more prize money this term. (op 6-4 tchd 2-1 in a place)
Firebeam progressed well in his first season and is clearly held in high regard as he holds an entry in the Group 1 Queen Anne Stakes at Royal Ascot. This tall gelding travelled very smoothly and looked set to ease to the front at one stage, but could not get past the winner, with whom he had 6lb to find on BHA figures. He didn't do much wrong - there was no repeat of the tail-swishing he showed on his last start at three - and he looks to have further improvement in him. (op 2-1 tchd 9-4)
Majestic Myles(IRE) could never quite get in a blow at the first two, but ran his race in third. This is his level and he should pay his way in similar races this year, perhaps on quicker ground. (op 13-2)
Smarty Socks(IRE), having his first run in Listed company at the age of eight, never looked like seriously troubling the principals. His best form has been shown on straight tracks in big-field handicaps. (op 12-1 tchd 16-1)
Scarf(AUS) was smart in Australia but has yet to click for his new connections. He was too keen here.
Beacon Lodge(IRE) won this race for Clive Cox in both 2009 and 2011, his last two wins in this country, but has now disappointed on both starts since joining David Nicholls. Again racing freely, he was eased down when beaten. (op 9-1)

2076 PERTEMPS H'CAP 1m
4:50 (4:51) (Class 3) (0-95,88) 3-Y-O **£8,409** (£2,502; £1,250; £625) **Stalls** Low

Form				RPR
22-1	1		**Trail Blaze (IRE)**[17] 1595 3-8-12 **79** ... MichaelHills 6	83
			(Kevin Ryan) *mde all: rdn over 1f out: hrd pressed ins fnl f: r.o gamely to prevail* **8/1**	
50-2	2	hd	**Dance The Rain**[23] 1477 3-9-0 **81** ... RoystonFfrench 3	84
			(Bryan Smart) *trckd ldrs: rdn 2f out: str chal ins fnl f: r.o: jst hld* **9/2**[3]	
11-4	3	1/2	**Mr Spiggott (IRE)**[23] 1477 3-9-2 **83** ... FrannyNorton 7	85
			(Mick Channon) *hld up in rr: rdn and hdwy to chse ldrs 2f out: styd on ins fnl f: nt quite pce of first two* **11/4**[1]	
6-44	4	1 1/2	**Act Your Shoe Size**[8] 1819 3-8-8 **75** ... SilvestreDeSousa 5	74
			(Keith Dalgleish) *prom: rdn and ev ch over 1f out: nt qckn ins fnl f: styd on same pce fnl 75yds* **11/1**	
42-5	5	11	**Bountiful Girl**[23] 1477 3-8-12 **79** ... PaulHanagan 2	52
			(Richard Fahey) *trckd ldrs: rdn over 2f out: sn wknd* **9/1**	
1-	6	4 1/2	**Assizes**[204] 6993 3-9-7 **88** ... JoeFanning 4	51
			(Mark Johnston) *hld up in rr: checked over 3f out: sn pushed along: no imp over 2f out: nvr a threat* **7/2**[2]	
2-34	7	3 1/4	**Clare Island Boy (IRE)**[15] 1647 3-9-7 **88** ... RichardHughes 1	43
			(Richard Hannon) *hld up: rdn 3f out: nvr on terms w ldrs: eased whn btn ins fnl f* **5/1**	

1m 44.29s (0.59) **Going Correction** +0.05s/f (Good) **7** Ran SP% **113.2**
Speed ratings (Par 103): **95,94,94,92,81 77,74**
totewingers:1&2:£3.10, 2&3:£3.30, 1&3:£4.80 CSF £42.49 CT £124.03 TOTE £9.10: £4.10, £3.60; EX 37.20 Trifecta £113.40 Pool: £616.24 - 4.02 winning units..
Owner Mr & Mrs Julian And Rosie Richer **Bred** Edmond Kent **Trained** Hambleton, N Yorks

FOCUS
A decent handicap run at a fair pace. The winner was possibly in the best place up front but was enitled to improve.

NOTEBOOK
Trail Blaze(IRE) got over from stall 6 to lead and was in no mood to give up his advantage, sticking his neck out in willing style when tackled. He has the right attitude and there may be more to come from him. (op 15-2)
Dance The Rain travelled nicely before delivering a sustained challenge down the outside in the straight, but the winner proved too tough. She had been put up 5lb for her reappearance second at Ripon, when she had two of these opponents behind, and should remain competitive off this sort of mark. (op 4-1 tchd 5-1)
Mr Spiggott(IRE) had been two places behind Dance The Rain at Ripon. Slowly away again, he kept staying on but edged towards the inside rail as he did so. It might be interesting to see how he handles a sound surface, something he hasn't encountered since his debut. (op 3-1 tchd 7-2 in a place)
Act Your Shoe Size ran her race with no apparent excuses. She is not getting much help from the handicapper. (op 14-1)
Bountiful Girl had been fifth in the Ripon race but ran a lacklustre race here. (tchd 17-2)
Assizes was disappointing, although he was slightly tightened up early in the home straight. Winner of his only start at two, he has been given Listed entries but will need to step up considerably on this. He may not have handled the ground and was also a little keen early on. (tchd 10-3 and 4-1)
Clare Island Boy(IRE) had a hard race in testing conditions at Sandown and he failed to pick up here. (tchd 11-2)

2077 NETWORK SALES & MARKETING H'CAP 1m 2f 95y
5:25 (5:25) (Class 4) (0-85,83) 4-Y-O+ **£5,175** (£1,540; £769; £384) **Stalls** High

Form				RPR
0500	1		**Licence To Till (USA)**[7] 1854 5-9-7 **83** ... JoeFanning 6	96
			(Mark Johnston) *mde all: rdn over 1f out: styd on wl to draw clr ins fnl f* **3/1**[2]	

212- **2** 3 ½ **Sugar Hiccup (IRE)**239 6130 4-8-11 73 FrannyNorton 5 79
(David Simcock) *a.p: pushed along over 3f out: rdn over 1f out: kpt on but no imp on wnr ins fnl f* 5/2[1]
220- **3** 3 **Jo'Burg (USA)**204 6989 8-9-5 81 SilvestreDeSousa 4 82
(David O'Meara) *hld up: pushed along over 3f out: effrt over 1f out: unable to go w wnr: one pce fnl 150yds* 10/3[3]
6406 **4** 1 ¾ **Brouhaha**12 1706 8-8-10 72 RoystonFfrench 7 69
(Tom Dascombe) *prom: pushed along over 2f out: wknd over 1f out* 7/1
006- **5** 5 **Braveheart Move (IRE)**203 7022 6-9-6 82 (p) SebSanders 1 70
(Geoffrey Harker) *hld up: pushed along over 3f out: no imp: wl btn over 1f out* 7/2

2m 15.04s (-0.46) **Going Correction** +0.05s/f (Good) **5** Ran SP% **111.4**
Speed ratings (Par 105): **105,102,99,98,94**
CSF £10.99 TOTE £3.60: £1.90, £2.40; EX 11.00.
Owner The Vine Accord **Bred** John Hettinger **Trained** Middleham Moor, N Yorks

FOCUS
There were doubts about all of these in this ordinary handicap. The winner was another to make all on the round course and the form is rated cautiously.
T/Jkpt: £28,543.10 to a £1 stake. Pool: £140,705.71 - 3.50 winning tickets. T/Plt: £263.80 to a £1 stake. Pool: £125,855.13 - 348.49 winning tickets. T/Qpdt: £18.00 to a £1 stake. Pool: £6,833.02 - 279.70 winning tickets. DO

2038 LINGFIELD (L-H)
Saturday, May 12

OFFICIAL GOING: Standard
Wind: light, half against Weather: dry and bright

2078 BETFRED MOBILE CHARTWELL FILLIES' STKS (GROUP 3) 7f (P)
2:10 (2:11) (Class 1) 3-Y-0+
£31,190 (£11,825; £5,918; £2,948; £1,479; £371) **Stalls** Low

Form RPR
322- **1** **Chachamaidee (IRE)**217 6687 5-9-3 113 TomQueally 5 104+
(Sir Henry Cecil) *stdd s: hld up in last pair: 10th and stl plenty to do whn swtchd lft 1f out: qcknd and str run to ld fnl 50yds: sn in command and gng away at fin* 9/4[1]
0145 **2** 1 ¼ **Night Lily (IRE)**35 1213 6-9-3 94 JimCrowley 8 101
(Paul D'Arcy) *chsd ldr: rdn to ld over 1f out: hrd drvn and kpt on wl fnl f tl hdd and nt pce of wnr fnl 50yds* 20/1
00 **3** 1 ¼ **Dysphonia (AUS)**63 876 6-9-3 112 (p) FrankieDettori 13 98+
(Saeed Bin Suroor) *stdd s: hld up in rr on outer: c wdst of all bnd 2f out: hdwy ent fnl f: r.o wl to go 3rd cl home* 16/1
0210 **4** nk **Libys Dream (IRE)**48 1041 4-9-3 95 RichardKingscote 4 97
(Tom Dascombe) *wnt rt s: chsd ldrs: rdn and effrt 2f out: pressed ldr and hrd drvn 1f out: no ex and btn fnl 100yds: lost 3rd cl home* 12/1
06-0 **5** ½ **Villeneuve**21 1508 3-8-5 87 NickyMackay 6 91
(William Muir) *in tch in midfield: hdwy u.p over 1f out: kpt on same pce and no imp fnl 150yds* 100/1
00-0 **6** ½ **Perfect Tribute**22 1494 4-9-3 100 AdamKirby 9 94+
(Clive Cox) *taken down early: t.k.h: hld up in midfield: n.m.r wl over 1f out: hdwy u.p over 1f out: kpt on fnl f but nvr threatened ldrs* 25/1
25-1 **6** dht **Fallen For You**10 1748 3-8-6 110 ow1 WilliamBuick 7 91+
(John Gosden) *hld up in tch in midfield: hit rail bnd ent fnl 2f: sn swtchd rt and n.m.r wl over 1f out: hdwy 1f out: kpt on but nvr threatened ldrs* 9/4[1]
100- **8** ½ **Theladyinquestion**224 6523 5-9-3 89 DavidProbert 12 93
(Andrew Balding) *stdd s: hld up in last trio: rdn and effrt on outer wl over 1f out: styd on fnl f: no threat to ldrs* 66/1
3-60 **9** nk **Marvada (IRE)**35 1226 4-9-3 103 ShaneFoley 2 92
(K J Condon, Ire) *chsd ldrs: rdn and unable qck ent fnl 2f: swtchd rt and no imp wl over 1f out: btn 1f out: n.m.r and eased towards fin* 10/1[3]
15-5 **10** hd **Best Terms**21 1508 3-8-5 115 KieranO'Neill 1 87
(Richard Hannon) *led: rdn ent fnl 2f: hdd and drvn over 1f out: no ex 1f out: wknd fnl 100yds* 7/1[2]
100- **11** 2 ½ **My Propeller (IRE)**224 6518 3-8-5 99 MartinDwyer 11 81
(Peter Chapple-Hyam) *t.k.h: hld up in tch in midfield: rdn and unable qck ent fnl 2f: wknd over 1f out* 33/1
13-0 **12** 8 **Fillionaire**21 1508 3-8-5 96 ChrisCatlin 3 59
(Mick Channon) *dwlt: a towards rr: rdn and struggling over 2f out: lost tch over 1f out* 33/1
050- **13** 5 **Mortitia**332 3034 4-9-3 92 MickaelBarzalona 10 50
(Brian Meehan) *chsd ldrs: rdn and struggling 2f out: wknd qckly over 1f out: bhd fnl f* 50/1

1m 23.3s (-1.50) **Going Correction** -0.075s/f (Stan)
WFA 3 from 4yo+ 12lb **13** Ran SP% **115.6**
Speed ratings: **105,103,102,101,101 100,100,100,99,99 96,87,81**
toteswingers:1&2:£9.70, 2&3:£29.50, 1&3:£9.90 CSF £55.19 TOTE £3.40: £1.20, £3.60, £4.60; EX 50.30 Trifecta £812.50 Part won. Pool: £1,098.02 - 0.70 winning units..
Owner R A H Evans **Bred** Cheval Court Stud **Trained** Newmarket, Suffolk

FOCUS
As on the previous day, this meeting was moved on to the Polytrack with the turf course unraceable. The change of surface makes comparisons with previous runnings of the three Pattern races on this card a little less relevant. Perfect Tribute won this as a 3-y-o last year, but the previous six runnings had all been won by older fillies and mares and, in a race run at a decent pace, the seniors held sway again this time.

NOTEBOOK
Chachamaidee(IRE) ◆ was returning from 217 days off, but has a fine record fresh and would have had a 4lb penalty to carry had last year's Glorious Goodwood success been three days later. This was her AW debut, but her sire has an 18% strike-rate here and she seemed to relish the surface. Not that she made things easy for herself, as she had plenty of ground to make up and not much room to play with turning in, but once in the clear she produced an amazing turn of foot to land the prize. This ultra-consistent mare should continue to enjoy plenty more success. (tchd 2-1)
Night Lily(IRE) is a five-time winner on Polytrack at 1m, but she had plenty on in this company. Under the circumstances she ran a blinder, making full use of her stamina under a positive ride and looking the most likely winner inside the last furlong until the winner engaged the afterburner. (tchd 18-1)
Dysphonia(AUS), a Listed winner in Australia, had disappointed in two runs at Meydan for Godolphin earlier this year, but this was much better. Her performance can be marked up too, as she soon found herself in stone last and was forced extremely wide on the home bend, but she finished to good effect. Her next start should be interesting. (tchd 14-1)
Libys Dream(IRE) was well held on an easy surface in Group 3 company at the Curragh last time and had plenty to find on official ratings, but she is a four-time winner on Polytrack including at Listed level. Never far away, she had every chance a furlong out before getting outpaced, but ran right up to her best. (tchd 10-1)
Villeneuve finished well beaten in the Fred Darling on her reappearance, but her sole win came on Polytrack and she came out best of the 3-y-os here. She had the lowest BHA mark of these and can find easier assignments.
Perfect Tribute, winner of this race last year, was faced with very different conditions this time with this being her AW debut. Her sire is 20% here, but she could only plug on late without offering a threat. (op 11-4)
Fallen For You, runner-up in the May Hill and fifth in the Fillies' Mile at two, did no more than she was entitled to when landing odds of 1-5 in a Kempton conditions event ten days ago, but she never got into this at all and there seemed no obvious excuse. (op 11-4)
Best Terms was one of the top juvenile fillies of last season, but her defeats in the Cheveley Park and Fred Darling on her reappearance were mainly down to her refusal to settle. She was keen enough early on here and wasn't given much peace up front by the runner-up, but she still faded pretty tamely late on. She may just be a sprinter, but she still needs to show that she has trained on. (op 11-2)

2079 BETFRED "THE BONUS KING" OAKS TRIAL STKS (LISTED RACE) (FILLIES) 1m 4f (P)
2:40 (2:41) (Class 1) 3-Y-0
£22,684 (£8,600; £4,304; £2,144; £1,076; £540) **Stalls** Low

Form RPR
1 **1** **Vow**22 1502 3-8-12 95 JohnnyMurtagh 8 109+
(William Haggas) *w ldr: qcknd clr w ldr 3f out: led 2f out: gng clr whn hung bdly rt over 1f out: in command whn wnt lft 1f out: edging bk rt and pushed out fnl f: easily* 11/10[1]
1- **2** 3 ¼ **Colima (IRE)**192 7232 3-8-12 0 JimCrowley 7 100+
(Ralph Beckett) *stdd s: hld up in last pair: rdn and effrt jst over 2f out: modest 4th but hdwy over 1f out: chsd clr wnr ins fnl f: kpt on but no imp* 5/1[2]
51- **3** 5 **Estrela**203 7025 3-8-12 0 JamesDoyle 2 92
(Roger Charlton) *led and set stdy gallop: rdn and qcknd clr w wnr 3f out: hdd 2f out: sn outpcd by wnr and wl hld 1f out: lost 2nd and wknd ins fnl f* 11/2[3]
1-21 **4** ¾ **Apothecary**38 1190 3-8-12 84 NickyMackay 9 91
(John Gosden) *in tch: rdn and chsd ldrs 2f out: outpcd and wl btn over 1f out: wknd fnl f* 8/1
1- **5** 3 ¼ **Zimira (IRE)**171 7520 3-8-12 0 FrankieDettori 6 86
(Ed Dunlop) *t.k.h: chsd ldrs tl grad stdd bk into last trio 8f out: rdn and effrt on outer 3f out: struggling u.p 2f out: sn wknd* 14/1
4- **6** 4 ½ **Dinvar Diva**249 5807 3-8-12 0 WilliamBuick 3 79
(John Gosden) *t.k.h: hld up in tch towards rr: rdn and struggling over 2f out: rn green and wknd bnd 2f out: bhd fnl f* 9/1
04- **7** 1 ¼ **Anabedweyah (IRE)**162 7599 3-8-12 0 NeilCallan 1 77
(Clive Brittain) *chsd ldrs: rdn and unable qck wl over 2f out: wknd 2f out: bhd fnl f* 50/1
3 **8** 5 **Secrets Away (IRE)**21 1518 3-8-12 0 AdamKirby 4 69
(Marco Botti) *t.k.h: chsd ldrs: rdn and unable qck wl over 2f out: wknd qckly 2f out: wl bhd fnl f* 25/1

2m 30.56s (-2.44) **Going Correction** -0.075s/f (Stan) **8** Ran SP% **113.3**
Speed ratings: **105,102,99,99,96 93,93,89**
toteswingers:1&2:£2.20, 2&3:£3.60, 1&3:£2.10 CSF £6.66 TOTE £2.10: £1.30, £1.70, £1.70; EX 7.10 Trifecta £16.50 Pool: £1,577.96 - 70.96 winning units..
Owner Highclere Thoroughbred Racing-Pocahontas **Bred** J B Haggas **Trained** Newmarket, Suffolk

FOCUS
This race hasn't been won by a subsequent Oaks winner since Ramruma in 1999, although Epsom heroine Look Here finished runner-up in this in 2008 and the 2009 winner Midday went on to run Sariska to a head in the fillies' classic. The value of this form could be questioned as they went no pace at all early and it developed into a sprint, helping those who raced handily. This is rarely a strong trial and the level is set around the standard for the race, although the winner can do better.

NOTEBOOK
Vow overcame greenness to make a winning debut in a 14-runner soft-ground maiden at Newbury last month. Always on the shoulder of the leader here, she again demonstrated signs of inexperience after taking up the running, hanging about all over the place in the home straight yet still proving far too good for this field. Bookmakers were divided over her Oaks prospects afterwards with prices ranging from between 5-1 and 10-1, but while she has all the ability in the world, she will need to come on again for the experience if she is to cope with the demands and hurly burly of Epsom. (op 5-4)
Colima(IRE) ◆ did it nicely when winning a 17-runner Nottingham maiden on her debut in November and her stable have a good record in this. However, she faced a tall order in trying to come from the back of the field in a slowly run race and by the time she had clicked into gear the winner had flown. It wouldn't be the biggest surprise to see her narrow the gap significantly in the Oaks, for which she was a top-price 25-1. (tchd 9-2)
Estrela won a 1m Newbury maiden nicely on her second start at two, though the form of that race hasn't really worked out. Despite enjoying the run of the race out in front on this reappearance, the feeling was that she didn't see out the trip. (op 6-1)
Apothecary's three previous runs had all been on Polytrack with two wins and a narrow defeat, but having given the wide outside away to no-one she was firmly put in her place. (op 7-1)
Zimira(IRE) made a winning debut in a 1m maiden here in November (subsequent winners behind) and her breeding suggested she would relish this extra 4f, but she found the rise in class too much for her. (op 12-1)
Dinvar Diva, not seen since finishing fourth behind the subsequent Nell Gwyn-winner Esentepe on her Leicester debut in September, looked the stable's first string but she never managed to land a blow. (tchd 10-1)
Anabedweyah(IRE) finished just behind a couple of subsequent winners when fourth in a 1m maiden here in December but, although she raced prominently for much of the way, this grade proved well beyond her. (op 33-1)
Secrets Away(IRE) showed ability when third of nine on her Nottingham debut last month (fifth has won since), but gave herself no chance by pulling too hard early. (op 20-1 tchd 28-1)

2080 BETFRED DERBY TRIAL STKS (GROUP 3) (C&G) 1m 4f (P)
3:10 (3:10) (Class 1) 3-Y-0
£34,026 (£12,900; £6,456; £3,216; £1,614; £810) **Stalls** Low

Form RPR
11-1 **1** **Main Sequence (USA)**23 1473 3-8-12 98 TedDurcan 4 113+
(David Lanigan) *stdd s: hld up in last pair: wl in tch but stuck bhd a wall of horses ent fnl 2f: swtchd lft and qcknd to chse ldr over 1f out: flashed tail u.p but chal 1f out: led ins fnl f: r.o wl* 3/1[2]
2-2 **2** ¾ **Shantaram**24 1456 3-8-12 0 WilliamBuick 2 111+
(John Gosden) *chsd ldrs: rdn to ld over 1f out: hrd pressed but drew clr w wnr 1f out: hdd and nt pce of wnr ins fnl f* 5/4[1]
211- **3** 6 **Cavaleiro (IRE)**239 6126 3-8-12 90 RichardMullen 3 101
(Marcus Tregoning) *wl in tch in midfield: rdn and unable qck 3f out: rallied on inner and pushed lft wl over 1f out: chsd ldng pair over 1f out: outpcd and btn 1f out: plugged on* 20/1
61-3 **4** 3 **Halling's Quest**22 1504 3-8-12 88 KierenFallon 5 96
(Hughie Morrison) *short of room and swtchd rt sn after s: hdwy to ld wl over 6f out and qcknd gallop: rdn and hdd over 1f out: sn outpcd and btn: wknd fnl f* 25/1

3-13 **5** *nk* **Rougemont (IRE)**[14] 1678 3-8-12 105 .... PatDobbs 6 96
(Richard Hannon) *in tch on outer: rdn and effrt to chse ldrs 3f out: outpcd and struggling whn hung lft and bmpd rival wl over 1f out: sn wknd* **13/2**[3]

0-21 **6** *1 ¾* **Goldoni (IRE)**[17] 1604 3-8-12 100 .... DavidProbert 8 93
(Andrew Balding) *t.k.h: mostly chsd ldr: rdn and ev ch 3f out: unable qck 2f out: struggling whn cannoned into wl over 1f out: sn wknd* **14/1**

111 **7** *nk* **Ed De Gas**[17] 1597 3-8-12 97 .... ChrisCatlin 7 92
(Rae Guest) *in tch in rr: rdn and in tch on outer over 2f out: struggling and wd bnd 2f out: wknd over 1f out* **7/1**

4-23 **8** *11* **Hazaz (IRE)**[24] 1453 3-8-12 96 .... NeilCallan 1 75
(Clive Brittain) *led tl wl over 6f out: chsd ldrs: rdn 3f out: struggling and losing pl whn hmpd wl over 1f out: sn wknd qckly wl bhd fnl f* **25/1**

2m 28.83s (-4.17) **Going Correction** -0.075s/f (Stan) 8 Ran SP% **114.4**
Speed ratings: **110,109,105,103,103 102,101,94**
toteswingers:1&2:£1.60, 1&3:£12.00, 2&3:£6.60 CSF £6.92 TOTE £5.30: £1.50, £1.20, £3.20; EX 9.10 Trifecta £84.90 Pool: £2,215.62 - 19.31 winning units..
Owner Niarchos Family **Bred** Flaxman Holdings Ltd **Trained** Upper Lambourn, Berks

FOCUS
High-Rise in 1998 was the last Derby winner to take this contest en-route and despite the different surface, this was the largest field for the race since 2001. The pace was more solid that in the fillies' trial and the time was 1.73 seconds faster. The front pair pulled clear and the front pair are rated as up to scratch for the race.

NOTEBOOK
Main Sequence(USA) came into this unbeaten in three starts on turf and was stepping up from handicap company, but he was given a very cool ride by Ted Durcan who held him up right out the back of the field before delivering him with a race-winning challenge against the inside rail a furlong from home. It was slightly unnerving to see him flash his tail as he hit the front, but you can't knock a perfect 4-4 record. He was cut to a top-priced 25-1 for the Derby, but he is also in the King Edward VII and that may be a more suitable race for him. (tchd 7-2)
Shantaram was beaten a nose in his first two starts including by the Chester Vase runner-up Model Pupil at Newmarket last month (form which gave him a little bit to find with Rougemont through Mickdaam) and his sire's 19% record here suggested that the surface would suit. Everything seemed to be going perfectly when a huge gap opened up for him turning in and he soon swept to the front, but the winner then arrived up his inside and seemed to want it that much more. He did pull well clear of the rest, but seems likely to return to maiden company next before a crack at the King Edward VII.. (op 7-4)
Cavaleiro(IRE) ◆ ended last season with wins at Chepstow and Newbury, but he had a bit to find on official ratings here. However, he stayed on again after getting outpaced inside the last half-mile and deserves credit as he was the only one of these lacking a recent run. (op 16-1)
Halling's Quest is proven on Fibresand, but had been well beaten in both turf starts. One of three helping force the pace starting out on the final circuit, he had little left once headed turning for home. Unfortunately he is not going to find many races for a horse with his rating back on Fibresand, so he may not be the easiest to place. (tchd 28-1)
Rougemont(IRE) got bogged down in the ground at Sandown last time, but his previous defeat of Mickdaam at Newmarket was boosted by the runner-up taking the Chester Vase. However, an effort racing towards the home turn came to little and he looked beaten when colliding with Goldoni over a furlong from home. He lacks the scope of a few of these. (tchd 7-1)
Goldoni(IRE) Official explanation: jockey said gelding suffered interference in running
Ed De Gas was up in class in a bid to maintain his unbeaten record after two wins on Polytrack and an easy success in a soft-ground conditions event at Catterick, but he never got into it and this may be as good as he is. (op 13-2)

2081 WEATHERBYS BLOODSTOCK INSURANCE CONDITIONS STKS 1m 2f (P)
3:45 (3:45) (Class 3) 4-Y-0+ **£8,409** (£2,502; £1,250; £625) **Stalls** Low

Form RPR

55- **1** **Retrieve (AUS)**[196] 7170 5-8-12 109 .... FrankieDettori 1 115+
(Saeed Bin Suroor) *t.k.h: hld up in tch: gng best jst over 2f out: effrt on inner wl over 1f out: qcknd to ld ent fnl f: rdn clr: comf* **10/3**[2]

0-30 **2** *4* **Circumvent**[7] 1854 5-8-12 104 .... NeilCallan 7 107
(Paul Cole) *dwlt: rdn along early: hdwy to ld over 8f out: drvn 2f out: hdd ent fnl f: nt pce of wnr and sn btn: wkng fnl 100yds but a holding 2nd* **12/1**

01-2 **3** *1 ¼* **Cai Shen (IRE)**[49] 1034 4-9-0 105 .... PatDobbs 6 106+
(Richard Hannon) *chsd ldrs: rdn wl over 2f out: outpcd and drvn wl over 1f out: no ch w wnr but kpt on again u.p fnl f* **3/1**[1]

046- **4** *¾* **Lost In The Moment (IRE)**[193] 7218 5-8-12 111 .(p) MickaelBarzalona 5 103
(Saeed Bin Suroor) *dwlt: in tch in rr: rdn over 3f out: drvn and outpcd wl over 1f out: no ch w wnr but kpt on again u.p ins fnl f* **6/1**

000- **5** *1 ½* **Kings Gambit (SAF)**[267] 5252 8-8-12 109 .... JamieSpencer 4 100
(Tom Tate) *broke fast: led tl over 8f out: rdn and unable qck ent fnl 2f: drvn and btn over 1f out: wknd ins fnl f* **7/1**

40-6 **6** *1* **World Domination (USA)**[14] 1677 4-8-12 95 .... TomQueally 2 98
(Sir Henry Cecil) *t.k.h: stdd after s: hld up in tch: rdn and no prog wl over 1f out: kpt on but no ch ins fnl f* **11/2**

314- **7** *9* **Beachfire**[308] 3876 5-8-12 107 ....(b) WilliamBuick 3 80
(John Gosden) *t.k.h: hld up in rr: rdn 4f out: drvn and struggling 3f out: wknd wl over 1f out: bhd and eased ins fnl f* **5/1**[3]

2m 3.17s (-3.43) **Going Correction** -0.075s/f (Stan) 7 Ran SP% **114.6**
Speed ratings (Par 107): **110,106,105,105,104 103,96**
toteswingers:1&2:£9.60, 2&3:£6.40, 1&3:£3.00 CSF £41.08 TOTE £4.30: £1.50, £6.00; EX 60.30.
Owner Godolphin **Bred** Darley **Trained** Newmarket, Suffolk

FOCUS
An interesting conditions event, but there was only one horse in it. The winner is rated near to his Australian form with the runner-up setting the standard.

NOTEBOOK
Retrieve(AUS) ◆, a dual Group 3 winner in Australia, had finished unplaced in his first two starts for Godolphin last October. However, it looked significant that Frankie Dettori had chosen to ride him and market support was another encouraging sign. He travelled like a winner throughout too and, once in front over a furlong out, powered right away. He looks capable of winning something better now that he seems to have come to himself. (op 7-2)
Circumvent ran terribly at Newmarket seven days earlier, but had previously finished just a head behind Cai Shen in the Winter Derby. His rider was keen to take him to the front after 2f and he stayed there until blown apart by the winner once in line for home. (op 11-1 tchd 14-1)
Cai Shen(IRE) proved his suitability for the surface when beaten just half a length by Premio Loco in the Winter Derby, but he lacked a finishing kick this time and may need a stronger pace to run at. (tchd 7-2)
Lost In The Moment(IRE), last seen finishing sixth in the Melbourne Cup, never landed a blow but is going to need a stiffer test than this. (tchd 11-2 and 13-2)
Kings Gambit(SAF) has a good record fresh so the 267-day absence wasn't a problem, but this was his AW debut and he was made to look one-paced after showing to the fore for a long way. (op 10-1)
World Domination(USA) looked a potential star this time last year, but despite having excuses for heavy defeats in his last two appearances he still had a major question mark against him and failed to answer it here. (tchd 4-1)
Beachfire, winner of his only previous start on Polytrack, hadn't been seen since finishing fourth in the John Smith's Cup at York last July and had been gelded in the meantime. Always out the back, he was under pressure and going nowhere a long way out. (op 11-2)

2082 BETFRED "STILL TREBLE ODDS ON LUCKY 15'S" H'CAP 1m (P)
4:20 (4:22) (Class 3) (0-95,95) 4-Y-0+ **£8,409** (£2,502; £1,250; £625) **Stalls** High

Form RPR

5-04 **1** **Bronze Prince**[14] 1679 5-9-5 93 .... JamieSpencer 8 102
(Michael Attwater) *racd keenly: mde all: drvn and wnt clr over 1f out: tiring fnl 100yds but a holding on: drvn out* **33/1**

631- **2** *¾* **Dimension**[225] 6495 4-9-7 95 .... KierenFallon 7 102+
(James Fanshawe) *in tch in last trio: rdn and effrt wl over 1f out: cannoned into and hmpd over 1f out: hdwy u.p 1f out: chsd wnr fnl 100yds: clsng qckly towards fin* **3/1**[1]

00-3 **3** *nk* **Stage Attraction (IRE)**[31] 1321 4-8-11 85 .... DavidProbert 3 92
(Andrew Balding) *in tch: rdn and effrt ent fnl 2f: r.o wl u.p ins fnl f: clsng on wnr towards fin* **12/1**

23-2 **4** *2 ¾* **Double Dealer**[35] 1212 4-9-4 92 .... FrankieDettori 4 92
(Mahmood Al Zarooni) *chsd ldrs: chsd wnr 6f out: rdn and nt pce of wnr over 1f out: btn ins fnl f: wknd fnl 100yds* **7/2**[2]

0450 **5** *nse* **Prince Of Burma (IRE)**[31] 1321 4-8-13 87 ....(b) JamesDoyle 5 90+
(Jeremy Gask) *dwlt: bhd: rdn and swtchd rt wl over 1f out: gng for impossible gap and cannoned into rival sn after: lost pl and btn 1f out: styd on fnl 100yds* **12/1**

002- **6** *1 ¾* **Roayh (USA)**[196] 7168 4-9-7 95 .... MickaelBarzalona 2 91
(Saeed Bin Suroor) *chsd wnr tl 6f out: drvn and struggling wl over 2f out: wknd u.p ent fnl f* **6/1**[3]

-000 **7** *1* **Lowther**[42] 1130 7-9-5 93 ....(b) AdamKirby 6 87
(Brett Johnson) *stdd after s: hld up in rr: effrt and wd bnd 2f out: no imp over 1f out: nvr trbld ldrs* **16/1**

11-5 **8** *1 ½* **Emilio Largo**[21] 1510 4-9-4 92 .... TomQueally 1 82
(Sir Henry Cecil) *in tch: short of room and hmpd over 6f out: rdn and effrt ent fnl 2f: wknd over 1f out* **3/1**[1]

2141 **9** *2 ¾* **Patriotic (IRE)**[16] 1633 4-8-10 84 .... NeilCallan 9 68
(Chris Dwyer) *in tch: rdn and unable qck whn edgd rt wl over 1f out: sn wknd: bhd and eased wl ins fnl f* **18/1**

1m 35.8s (-2.40) **Going Correction** -0.075s/f (Stan) 9 Ran SP% **116.0**
Speed ratings (Par 107): **109,108,107,105,105 103,102,100,98**
toteswingers:1&2:£11.10, 1&3:£29.70, 2&3:£9.40 CSF £131.05 CT £1308.20 TOTE £37.50: £6.10, £1.80, £2.60; EX 132.60.
Owner Canisbay Bloodstock **Bred** Coln Valley Stud **Trained** Epsom, Surrey
■ Stewards' Enquiry : Jamie Spencer caution: careless riding.
James Doyle three-day ban: careless riding (May 28-30)

FOCUS
A decent handicap, but very few ever got into it. The runner-up is rated to form and sets the level.

NOTEBOOK
Bronze Prince had excuses for his two performances since joining his current yard, getting hampered here and sinking in the bottomless ground at Sandown. He had also looked best over 7f before now, but he was given the most positive of rides and quickening from the front off the final bend won him the race. He was trying up towards the end, but the prize was safe by then and if you are going to get 1m anywhere, it's most likely to be here. (op 28-1)
Dimension, a winner on Polytrack on his reappearance last season, had been gelded since last seen when winning at Ascot in September. He stayed on well from off the pace late, despite getting a bump over a furlong out, only to find the winner had gone beyond recall. This was still a pleasing enough return. (op 11-4)
Stage Attraction(IRE), making his AW debut following his encouraging Nottingham return, was another to finish well having come off the bridle before the home turn. He may be worth a try over a bit further. (tchd 14-1)
Double Dealer didn't enjoy much luck in his last two starts, but had every chance here after travelling well. He didn't find as much off the bridle as had seemed likely and may not be totally straightforward. (tchd 10-3)
Prince Of Burma(IRE) ◆ remains 6lb higher than when winning over C&D in January, but can be given extra credit as he was staying on when getting badly hampered over a furlong from home. (op 16-1)
Roayh(USA), proven on Polytrack, was having his first start since finishing just ahead of Double Dealer at Newmarket in October having been gelded in the meantime. He was in trouble some way out, but was entitled to need it. (op 13-2 tchd 15-2)
Emilio Largo, a progressive sort last season and a decent fifth in the Newbury Spring Cup on his return, was making his AW debut. Although he became short of room when hampered by Roayh after 2f, it wasn't enough to explain this tame effort. (op 7-2 tchd 11-4)

2083 BETFRED MOBILE CASINO H'CAP 7f (P)
4:55 (4:56) (Class 4) (0-85,82) 4-Y-0+ **£5,175** (£1,540; £769; £384) **Stalls** Low

Form RPR

240- **1** **Ongoodform (IRE)**[206] 6949 5-9-3 78 .... NeilCallan 6 85
(Paul D'Arcy) *in tch: rdn and effrt to chal ent fnl f: kpt on wl fnl 100yds to ld last stride* **20/1**

6053 **2** *shd* **Copperwood**[6] 1879 7-9-1 76 .... KierenFallon 7 83
(Mark Johnston) *in tch: rdn and effrt to chal over 1f out: led 1f out: kpt on wl u.p tl hdd last stride* **13/2**[2]

1010 **3** *1* **Aldermoor (USA)**[12] 1708 6-8-13 77 .... RyanClark(3) 8 81
(Stuart Williams) *hld up in tch in last quartet: rdn and hdwy ent fnl f: drvn and swtchd rt fnl 100yds: r.o wl* **16/1**

-405 **4** *hd* **Intercept (IRE)**[12] 1708 4-9-5 80 .... WilliamBuick 1 84
(John Gosden) *chsd ldrs: rdn and effrt on inner over 1f out: rdn and nt qckn 1f out: styd on same pce fnl 100yds* **10/3**[1]

4200 **5** *½* **Dozy Joe**[45] 1066 4-9-6 81 .... JamesDoyle 9 83
(Ian Wood) *chsd ldrs: rdn and effrt over 1f out: drvn and kpt on same pce ins fnl f* **12/1**

0-52 **6** *hd* **Kakapuka**[12] 1708 5-9-6 81 .... MickaelBarzalona 10 83
(Anabel K Murphy) *chsd ldr: rdn and ev ch wl over 1f out tl ins fnl f: wknd towards fin* **12/1**

51-0 **7** *½* **The Guru Of Gloom (IRE)**[12] 1708 4-9-6 81 .... DavidProbert 14 82
(William Muir) *t.k.h: hld up in tch in midfield on outer: rdn over 1f out: kpt on ins fnl f: nt rch ldrs* **10/1**

2031 **8** *1* **Standpoint**[12] 1718 6-9-7 82 ....(p) FrankieDettori 3 80
(Conor Dore) *led: rdn wl over 1f out: drvn and hdd 1f out: wknd fnl 100yds* **11/1**

0-21 **9** *¾* **Choral**[17] 1609 4-9-3 78 .... PatDobbs 11 74
(Richard Hannon) *in tch in last quartet: nvr much room fr over 1f out: rdn and kpt on ins fnl f: nvr trbld ldrs* **10/1**

0143 **10** *2 ½* **Lastkingofscotland (IRE)**[11] 1727 6-9-0 75 ....(b) TomQueally 5 64
(Conor Dore) *in rr but in tch: niggled along sn after s: drvn and no imp over 2f out: nvr trbld ldrs* **7/1**[3]

00-0 **11** ¾ **Flynn's Boy**[29] 1354 4-9-2 77 .... ChrisCatlin 2 64
(Rae Guest) *in tch but a towards rr: rdn and struggling wl over 2f out: n.d* **9/1**

50-0 **12** 2 ¾ **Silverware (USA)**[41] 1161 4-9-2 77 .... TedDurcan 4 57
(Linda Stubbs) *in tch in midfield: rdn and unable qck ent fnl 2f: wknd over 1f out* **14/1**

1m 24.48s (-0.32) **Going Correction** -0.075s/f (Stan) 12 Ran SP% **118.1**
Speed ratings (Par 105): **98,97,96,96,95 95,95,94,93,90 89,86**
toteswingers:1&2:£22.80, 1&3:£33.30, 2&3:£27.70 CSF £144.49 CT £2153.86 TOTE £16.50: £3.30, £2.30, £3.00; EX 206.40.
Owner Dr J S Kinnear **Bred** Stephanie Hanly **Trained** Newmarket, Suffolk

FOCUS
A competitive handicap and several held a chance at some stage. The form is straightforward.
T/Plt: £189.70 to a £1 stake. Pool: £45,492.16 - 31.83 winning tickets. T/Qpdt: £101.70 to a £1 stake. Pool: £5,318.50 - 38.66 winning tickets. SP

2046 NOTTINGHAM (L-H)
Saturday, May 12

OFFICIAL GOING: Soft (6.0)
Wind: Virtually nil Weather: Cloudy with sunny periods

2084 MCARTHURGLEN EAST MIDLANDS DESIGNER OUTLET H'CAP (BETFAIR SPRINT FLAT SERIES QUALIFIER) 5f 13y
2:15 (2:16) (Class 5) (0-75,71) 4-Y-0+ **£3,234** (£962; £481; £240) **Stalls** High

Form RPR

5210 **1** **Dispol Grand (IRE)**[7] 1868 6-8-10 **67** .... NedCurtis(7) 4 79
(Paul Midgley) *trckd ldrs: hdwy 2f out: swtchd rt and effrt over 1f out: qcknd wl to ld ins fnl f: sn clr* **3/1**[1]

2624 **2** 3 **Boucher Garcon (IRE)**[9] 1800 4-8-8 **65** .... JasonHart(7) 6 66
(Declan Carroll) *led: rdn clr 2f out: edgd lft over 1f out: hdd and no ex ins fnl f* **6/1**[3]

440- **3** 1 ¾ **Whitecrest**[203] 7040 4-9-7 **71** .... PatCosgrave 10 66
(John Spearing) *in tch: hdwy to chse ldrs 2f out: rdn wl over 1f out: kpt on ins fnl f* **14/1**

060- **4** ½ **Cruise Tothelimit (IRE)**[166] 7566 4-8-12 **62** .... PaulMulrennan 7 55
(Ian Williams) *prom: chsd ldr 2f out: sn rdn and kpt on same pce* **5/1**[2]

150 **5** 1 ½ **Absa Lutte (IRE)**[8] 1828 9-9-6 **70** .... LiamJones 5 58
(Michael Mullineaux) *towards rr: hdwy 2f out: sn rdn and one pce* **33/1**

-344 **6** hd **Dancing Maite**[82] 639 7-9-4 **68** .... AmirQuinn 8 55
(Roy Bowring) *dwlt and in rr: swtchd rt and hdwy 1/2-way: rdn wl over 1f out: no imp fnl f* **17/2**

025- **7** 7 **Black Annis Bower**[200] 7073 4-9-6 **70** .... JamesSullivan 2 32
(Michael Eactorby) *in tch: rdn along 1/2-way: sn wknd* **7/1**

100- **8** ½ **Cape Royal**[166] 7567 12-9-3 **70** ....(tp) SeanLevey(3) 1 30
(Milton Bradley) *racd alone towards far rail: chsd ldrs: rdn along 1/2-way: sn outpcd* **25/1**

4005 **9** 3 ¼ **Sir Geoffrey (IRE)**[23] 1480 6-9-3 **67** ....(b) RobertWinston 9 15
(Scott Dixon) *prom: rdn along 1/2-way: sn wknd* **8/1**

6143 **10** 2 ¼ **Triple Dream**[37] 1204 7-9-7 **71** ....(tp) LiamKeniry 11 11
(Milton Bradley) *prom: rdn along 1/2-way: sn wknd* **17/2**

1m 3.43s (2.43) **Going Correction** +0.575s/f (Yiel) 10 Ran SP% **114.1**
Speed ratings (Par 103): **103,98,95,94,92 91,80,79,74,71**
toteswingers:1&2:£2.00, 2&3:£12.50, 1&3:£9.10 CSF £20.26 CT £220.42 TOTE £4.00: £1.50, £2.30, £3.00; EX 20.60.
Owner T W Midgley **Bred** Martyn J McEnery **Trained** Westow, N Yorks

FOCUS
Plenty of pace on in this moderate sprint handicap and the winner is rated back to his former best.

2085 BOX CLEVER DISPLAY MEDIAN AUCTION MAIDEN STKS 6f 15y
2:45 (2:47) (Class 5) 3-Y-0 **£2,911** (£866; £432; £216) **Stalls** High

Form RPR

22-4 **1** **Colbyor**[34] 1241 3-9-0 69 .... LeeTopliss(3) 7 69+
(Richard Fahey) *trckd ldrs: hdwy on outer 1/2-way: rdn to ld over 1f out: kpt on* **9/4**[1]

5-30 **2** 2 **Samba Night (IRE)**[24] 1445 3-9-3 64 .... GrahamGibbons 4 62
(James Eustace) *sn led: rdn along 2f out: hdd over 1f out: kpt on u.p fnl f* **11/1**

3 2 ¼ **If So** 3-8-12 0 .... JackMitchell 6 50+
(James Fanshawe) *in tch: hdwy 1/2-way: rdn to chse ldng pair over 1f out: no imp ins fnl f* **9/4**[1]

35 **4** ¾ **Kashmiri Star**[11] 1739 3-8-12 0 .... PatCosgrave 1 47
(Michael Quinn) *dwlt: sn prom: rdn along 2f out: grad wknd* **25/1**

-205 **5** 6 **Bountiful Catch**[21] 1517 3-9-3 51 .... MickyFenton 5 33
(Pam Sly) *prom: rdn along wl over 2f out: sn wknd* **11/1**

32-6 **6** 3 **Khaleejiya (IRE)**[11] 1723 3-8-12 72 .... RobertWinston 3 19
(James Tate) *towards rr: hdwy and in tch 1/2-way: rdn along over 2f out and sn wknd* **7/2**[2]

3- **7** 15 **Multi Bene**[211] 6842 3-9-0 0 .... RossAtkinson(3) 8
(Tom Dascombe) *a in rr: outpcd and bhd fr over 2f out* **8/1**[3]

0 **8** 41 **L'Ile Rousse**[33] 1261 3-8-12 0 ....(p) PaulMulrennan 2
(Chris Dwyer) *dwlt: a in rr: outpcd and bhd fr 1/2-way* **100/1**

1m 19.4s (4.50) **Going Correction** +0.575s/f (Yiel) 8 Ran SP% **116.4**
Speed ratings (Par 99): **93,90,87,86,78 74,54,**
toteswingers:1&2:£14.30, 2&3:£7.20, 1&3:£1.50 CSF £29.74 TOTE £2.20: £1.10, £2.00, £1.40; EX 23.00.
Owner E Bruce **Bred** Mr And Mrs E Bruce **Trained** Musley Bank, N Yorks

FOCUS
Little depth to this sprint maiden with the runner-up and fourth limiting the form.

2086 WEATHERBYS BLOODSTOCK INSURANCE H'CAP 1m 6f 15y
3:15 (3:15) (Class 4) (0-85,85) 4-Y-0+ **£5,175** (£1,540; £769; £384) **Stalls** Low

Form RPR

04/6 **1** **General Ting (IRE)**[7] 1846 7-8-4 **68** ow1 ....(t) AdamBeschizza(3) 5 73
(Lucy Wadham) *trckd ldng pair tl led after 4f: pushed along 3f out: rdn clr 2f out: drvn ins fnl f: jst hld on* **9/2**

65-4 **2** nse **Mattoral**[6] 1890 4-8-8 **70** ....(v) LiamJones 2 75
(Chris Gordon) *trckd ldrs: hdwy over 5f out: cl up 3f out: chsd wnr 2f out and sn rdn: edgd lft ent fnl f: drvn and styd on wl towards fin: jst failed* **3/1**[3]

36-6 **3** 6 **Korngold**[21] 1525 4-8-8 **70** .... MircoDemuro 1 67
(John Dunlop) *led after 1 1/2f: hdd after 4f: cl up: pushed along 4f out: rdn over 3f out: drvn over 2f out: wknd wl over 1f out* **15/8**[1]

2232 **4** 17 **Halla San**[14] 1672 10-9-7 **85** .... LeeTopliss(3) 3 65
(Richard Fahey) *led 1 1/2f: trckd ldng pair: pushed along 4f out: rdn 3f out: wknd over 2f out: eased appr fnl f* **2/1**[2]

3m 11.96s (5.66) **Going Correction** +0.575s/f (Yiel)
WFA 4 from 5yo+ 1lb 4 Ran SP% **111.3**
Speed ratings (Par 105): **106,105,102,92**
CSF £17.46 TOTE £8.20; EX 21.90.
Owner A T Partnership **Bred** R N Auld **Trained** Newmarket, Suffolk
■ Stewards' Enquiry : Adam Beschizza two-day ban: used whip down shoulder in the forehand (May 26,28)

FOCUS
The form of this is worth little, with neither Korngold or in particular Halla San running to their best. The pace was steady and the runner-up looks the best guide to the level.

2087 WEATHERBYS BLOODSTOCK INSURANCE KILVINGTON FILLIES' STKS (LISTED RACE) 6f 15y
3:50 (3:50) (Class 1) 3-Y-0+
£19,848 (£7,525; £3,766; £1,876; £941; £472) **Stalls** High

Form RPR

102- **1** **Swiss Dream**[233] 6272 4-9-3 99 .... LiamKeniry 3 106
(David Elsworth) *mde all: pushed along 2f out: rdn jst over 1f out: kpt on wl u.p fnl f* **7/1**

42-6 **2** 1 **Sioux Rising (IRE)**[22] 1494 6-9-3 97 .... LeeTopliss 10 103
(Richard Fahey) *prom on outer: effrt and edgd lft 2f out: rdn over 1f out: ev ch ins fnl f: sn drvn and no ex last 75yds* **8/1**

310- **3** nse **Ladies Are Forever**[210] 6858 4-9-3 108 .... RobertWinston 2 103
(Geoffrey Oldroyd) *hld up in tch: hdwy 2f out: rdn over 1f out: drvn to chal whn edgd rt ins fnl f: kpt on same pce towards fin* **11/4**[2]

15-0 **4** 4 **Roger Sez (IRE)**[21] 1508 3-8-13 107 ....(b) DavidAllan 9 93
(Tim Easterby) *in rr and pushed along after 2f: rdn and hdwy on wd outside wl over 1f out: kpt on fnl f: n.d* **9/1**

311- **5** 3 ¼ **Artistic Jewel (IRE)**[197] 7135 3-8-11 101 .... GrahamGibbons 6 80
(Ed McMahon) *t.k.h: trckd ldrs: cl up 1/2-way: rdn 2f out: wknd over 1f out* **5/2**[1]

100- **6** 7 **Pepper Lane**[231] 6347 5-9-3 102 .... PaulMulrennan 4 57
(David O'Meara) *cl up: rdn along wl over 2f out: wknd over 1f out* **9/2**[3]

0-40 **7** 14 **Liberty Lady (IRE)**[17] 1602 5-9-3 90 .... PatCosgrave 1
(Des Donovan) *in tch: chsd ldrs 1/2-way: sn rdn and wknd over 2f out: eased* **22/1**

1m 17.5s (2.60) **Going Correction** +0.575s/f (Yiel)
WFA 3 from 4yo+ 10lb 7 Ran SP% **111.4**
Speed ratings (Par 108): **105,103,103,98,93 84,65**
toteswingers:1&2:£13.50, 2&3:£3.80, 1&3:£3.40 CSF £56.63 TOTE £5.70: £2.60, £2.30; EX 49.00.
Owner Lordship Stud **Bred** Lordship Stud **Trained** Newmarket, Suffolk

FOCUS
Quite a competitive Listed sprint won by an improver with the runner-up rated to form in an ordinary race for the grade.

NOTEBOOK
Swiss Dream, despite not looking totally in love with the ground, was able to gain her second win at this level, battling well to make every yard. She looks to have progressed again from three to four and, as her trainer was expecting her to need this, it's likely there's more to come. She'll step into Group company now, with the Temple Stakes a probable target. (op 6-1 tchd 15-2)
Sioux Rising(IRE) is a useful sprinting mare who ran right up to her best in second, considering the ground would have been slower than ideal. All her wins have come at Pontefract. (tchd 15-2)
Ladies Are Forever handles soft ground and made a perfectly good reappearance. She should improve. (op 3-1 tchd 10-3)
Roger Sez(IRE) did best of the two 3-y-os, staying on late and showing her run in the Fred Darling to be all wrong. (op 7-1)
Artistic Jewel(IRE) was progressive as a juvenile, winning three of five starts, including one at this level, but she was keen and saw plenty of daylight on this reappearance, leading to a tame finishing effort. She should leave this form behind with the run behind her. (op 7-2)
Pepper Lane was a progressive handicapper last season and has a fine record fresh, so it was disappointing to see her so readily beaten off. (op 10-3)

2088 WEATHERBYS BANK H'CAP 1m 2f 50y
4:25 (4:26) (Class 3) (0-90,87) 3-Y-0 **£8,409** (£2,502; £1,250; £625) **Stalls** Low

Form RPR

51 **1** **Last Shadow**[21] 1518 3-8-11 **77** .... MircoDemuro 7 87
(William Muir) *hld up towards rr: hdwy over 3f out: rdn wl over 1f out: chsd clr ldr fnl f: styd on strly to ld last 50yds* **9/2**[3]

2-41 **2** 1 ½ **Spirit Of The Law (IRE)**[15] 1641 3-8-12 **78** .... TomMcLaughlin 1 85
(Ed Dunlop) *dwlt: sn in tch: hdwy on wd outside 3f out: rdn to ld wl over 1f out: drvn: edgd lft and wknd ins fnl f: hdd and no ex last 50yds* **5/2**[2]

-004 **3** 3 ½ **Zakreet**[14] 1653 3-8-13 **79** .... ShaneKelly 3 79
(Kevin Ryan) *set str pce: clr 1/2-way: pushed along 3f out: rdn and hung rt 2f out: sn hdd and kpt on same pce* **8/1**

11-0 **4** 1 ½ **Just Fabulous**[23] 1477 3-9-7 **87** .... AndrewMullen 6 84
(George Moore) *t.k.h: trckd ldng pair: hdwy to chse clr ldr 1/2-way: rdn along 3f out: drvn over 2f out: kpt on same pce* **12/1**

211 **5** 9 **Prussian**[8] 1819 3-9-5 **85** .... FrederikTylicki 5 64
(Mark Johnston) *chsd ldrs: pushed along over 4f out: rdn over 3f out: sn wknd* **9/4**[1]

115- **6** 6 **Night Flash (GER)**[157] 7653 3-8-8 **74** .... JamesSullivan 2 41
(James Given) *chsd ldrs: rdn along over 3f out: sn wknd* **22/1**

11-5 **7** 48 **Finbar**[23] 1473 3-9-1 **81** .... PaulMulrennan 4
(James Given) *chsd ldr to 1/2-way: sn rdn along: wknd qckly 3f out: sn bhd and eased fnl 2f* **15/2**

2m 16.74s (5.04) **Going Correction** +0.575s/f (Yiel) 7 Ran SP% **112.4**
Speed ratings (Par 103): **102,100,98,96,89 84,46**
toteswingers:1&2:£1.90, 2&3:£6.30, 1&3:£7.20 CSF £15.61 TOTE £7.20: £5.00, £2.80; EX 20.00.
Owner M J Caddy **Bred** Newsells Park Stud **Trained** Lambourn, Berks

FOCUS
The pace increased a long way out in this ordinary handicap and the picture changed dramatically late on, Spirit Of The Law, who had committed looking far the likeliest winner (touched 1.01 on Betfair), being claimed close home by Last Shadow. The fourth is rated to her best maiden form.

NOTEBOOK
Last Shadow was simply unable to keep up early in the straight but finished strongly under Mirco Demuro to win with a bit in hand. A fine big sort who clearly needs soft ground, the winner looks to be crying out for at least 1m4f and should have plenty more improving to do. (tchd 5-1)
Spirit Of The Law(IRE), up 7lb for his narrow Doncaster win on heavy ground, couldn't see it out in the ground having made what appeared to be a winning run. He was best on the day and looks capable of getting competitive in some decent handicaps this year. (op 11-4)
Zakreet didn't hang around on this step up in trip and ran easily his most promising race of the season so far. He likes soft ground and can win from this sort of mark. (op 9-1 tchd 15-2)

Just Fabulous kept going fairly well considering he was keen on this step up to 1m2f. (op 10-1)
Prussian failed to reproduce the form of last week's Musselburgh win, being beaten before the 7lb rise had a chance to take a toll. Perhaps the race came too soon. (op 5-2)
Night Flash(GER) has been doing his winning on the AW and appeared to fail to handle the ground. (op 16-1)
Finbar stopped very quickly returning to turf and probably failed to handle the ground. (op 11-2)

2089 PETRA'S HEN PARTY H'CAP — 1m 75y

5:00 (5:00) (Class 5) (0-75,75) 3-Y-0 — **£2,911** (£866; £432; £216) **Stalls** Centre

Form — RPR

3514 **1** **Masters Blazing**[21] 1519 3-8-12 **66** .... BrettDoyle 2 — 78+
(John Ryan) *trckd ldng pair on inner: hdwy to chse clr ldr wl over 2f out: led wl over 1f out and sn clr: eased towards fin* **7/2**[2]

14-3 **2** 4 ½ **The Noble Ord**[33] 1264 3-9-6 **74** .... LiamKeniry 10 — 71
(Sylvester Kirk) *dwlt and in rr: hdwy on inner over 3f out: rdn to chse ldng pair 2f out: drvn and styd on fnl f: tk 2nd towards fin* **7/2**[2]

135- **3** ¾ **Loyal Master (IRE)**[238] 6144 3-9-2 **75** ....(t) JustinNewman(5) 3 — 70
(Deborah Sanderson) *sn led: pushed clr 1/2-way: rdn 3f out: hdd jst ins fnl f: kpt on one pce: lost 2nd towards fin* **8/1**

650- **4** 1 ¼ **Double Cee**[211] 6846 3-8-7 **61** oh1........ PatrickMathers 4 — 53
(Richard Fahey) *chsd ldrs: pushed along and sltly outpcd over 3f out: sn rdn and kpt on u.p appr fnl f* **7/1**[3]

63-5 **5** 10 **Dutch Master**[19] 1565 3-9-5 **73** .... PatCosgrave 6 — 42
(Andrew Balding) *hld up towards rr: hdwy over 4f out: rdn along 3f out: sn btn* **3/1**[1]

40-3 **6** ½ **Pius Parker (IRE)**[33] 1259 3-8-7 **61** oh1........ LiamJones 8 — 29
(John Gallagher) *chsd ldr: rdn along over 3f out: wknd over 2f out* **10/1**

21-0 **7** 7 **Equity Card (FR)**[38] 1190 3-9-4 **72** .... FrederikTylicki 9 — 24
(Mark Johnston) *chsd ldrs: rdn along over 3f out: sn wknd* **8/1**

1m 51.91s (6.31) **Going Correction** +0.575s/f (Yiel) — **7** Ran SP% **113.3**
Speed ratings (Par 99): **91,86,85,84,74 74,67**
toteswingers:1&2:£3.50, 2&3:£4.50, 1&3:£3.90 CSF £15.83 CT £88.98 TOTE £4.80: £2.80, £4.70; EX 19.30.
Owner Gerry McGladery **Bred** D R Botterill **Trained** Newmarket, Suffolk

FOCUS
A few of these failed to handle the ground, so not form to get carried away with. The winner is improved for soft ground but the level is fluid.

2090 NOTTINGHAM RACECOURSE HOSPITALITY & SPONSORSHIP APPRENTICE TRAINING SERIES H'CAP (REI) — 1m 75y

5:30 (5:31) (Class 6) (0-60,58) 4-Y-0+ — **£2,070** (£616; £307; £153) **Stalls** Centre

Form — RPR

5351 **1** **Join Up**[5] 1908 6-9-2 **53** 6ex........ RachealKneller 9 — 64
(Mark Brisbourne) *hld up: hdwy on outer 1/2-way: chal 2f out: led wl over 1f out: sn rdn: edgd lft ins fnl f: kpt on* **7/2**[1]

5-04 **2** 1 ½ **Alluring Star**[8] 1823 4-9-4 **58** .... DavidSimmonson(3) 6 — 66
(Michael Easterby) *led 3f: cl up tl led again 3f out: rdn over 2f out: hdd wl over 1f out: kpt on same pce* **12/1**

0/02 **3** ½ **Woteva**[24] 1436 6-8-12 **56** ....(p) EvaMoscrop(7) 2 — 62
(Nigel Tinkler) *prom whn n.m.r and hmpd after 1f and again after 2f and sn lost pl: hdwy over 2f out: sn rdn and styd on fnl f: nrst fin* **4/1**[2]

-005 **4** 2 ¼ **Sky Diamond (IRE)**[16] 1634 4-9-3 **54** ....(b) GeorgeDowning 11 — 55
(John Mackie) *hld up: hdwy 1/2-way: chsd ldrs 2f out: sn rdn and kpt on same pce* **6/1**

4003 **5** 1 **Crocodile Bay (IRE)**[9] 1801 9-8-8 **48** ....(p) IanBurns(3) 1 — 47
(Richard Guest) *chsd ldrs: rdn along wl over 2f out: sn one pce* **14/1**

/0-0 **6** 2 ¼ **Centre Stage**[25] 1429 4-8-8 **45** .... JackDuern 5 — 39
(Michael Appleby) *bhd: hdwy on inner and in tch over 3f out: rdn wl over 2f out: sn no imp* **28/1**

000- **7** 1 ¾ **Femme Royale**[241] 6071 4-8-4 **46** ow1........ JacobButterfield(5) 7 — 36
(Richard Price) *in tch: lost pl over 4f out: wknd over 2f out* **25/1**

2310 **8** 13 **Caledonia Prince**[33] 1251 4-9-1 **55** ....(p) JoshBaudains(3) 10 — 15
(Jo Hughes) *prom: led after 3f: pushed along and hdd 3f out: sn rdn and wknd* **9/2**[3]

5662 **9** 1 ¾ **Myraid**[18] 1583 5-8-10 **50** ....(b) NedCurtis(3) 8
(Ruth Carr) *hld up: n.m.r and swtchd lft after 1f: hdwy 4f out: rdn over 3f out: sn wknd* **5/1**

1m 54.42s (8.82) **Going Correction** +0.575s/f (Yiel) — **9** Ran SP% **113.0**
Speed ratings (Par 101): **78,76,76,73,72 70,68,55,54**
toteswingers:1&2:£11.10, 2&3:£11.30, 1&3:£3.50 CSF £45.05 CT £173.51 TOTE £6.10: £2.10, £4.30, £1.50; EX 44.00.
Owner P R Kirk **Bred** A S Reid **Trained** Great Ness, Shropshire

FOCUS
A low-grade handicap run at a decent gallop early. The form is modest with the winner rated to his best effort since his AW win at the end of last year.
T/Plt: £1,043.30 to a £1 stake. Pool: £45,492.16 - 31.83 winning tickets. T/Qpdt: £174.50 to a £1 stake. Pool: £2,571.72 - 10.90 winning tickets. JR

1861 THIRSK (L-H)

Saturday, May 12

OFFICIAL GOING: Soft (good to soft in places; 7.8)
Wind: fresh 1/2 behind Weather: fine

2091 RACHEL ROBERTS WINS WITH THE YORKSHIRE POST H'CAP — 7f

6:15 (6:16) (Class 6) (0-55,60) 4-Y-0+ — **£2,587** (£770; £384; £192) **Stalls** Low

Form — RPR

50-0 **1** **It's A Mans World**[39] 1179 6-8-10 **50** .... PaulPickard(3) 7 — 59
(Kevin M Prendergast) *chsd ldrs: led over 1f out: edgd rt ins fnl f: drvn out* **40/1**

0-03 **2** 2 **Fama Mac**[21] 1526 5-8-13 **50** .... MichaelO'Connell 3 — 54
(Neville Bycroft) *chsd ldrs: chal over 2f out: swtchd lft ins fnl f: kpt on same pce* **5/2**[1]

00-0 **3** nk **Whats For Pudding (IRE)**[9] 1801 4-8-10 **52** .... NeilFarley(5) 6 — 55
(Declan Carroll) *drvn to chse ldrs: kpt on wl fnl f* **14/1**

400- **4** 1 **Fairy Mist (IRE)**[191] 7246 5-8-6 **50** ....(p) JasonHart(7) 5 — 50
(Brian Rothwell) *chsd ldrs: kpt on same pce fnl 2f* **25/1**

145/ **5** 1 ¼ **Shaker Style (USA)**[1062] 1063 6-9-4 **55** .... DavidNolan 4 — 52
(Martin Todhunter) *in rr: kpt on fnl 2f: nt rch ldrs* **66/1**

5F04 **6** 1 ½ **American Lover (FR)**[12] 1717 5-9-1 **52** .... PaddyAspell 2 — 45
(John Wainwright) *s.i.s: hdwy on inner whn nt clr run 2f out: kpt on fnl f* **20/1**

0500 **7** nk **Stamp Duty (IRE)**[16] 1634 4-9-1 **55** .... DaleSwift(3) 8 — 47
(Suzzanne France) *in rr: edgd rt 2f out: kpt on fnl f* **16/1**

6-20 **8** 4 **Sleights Boy (IRE)**[28] 1387 4-8-13 **53** ....(v) DeclanCannon(3) 10 — 35
(Ian McInnes) *chsd ldrs: wknd over 1f out* **20/1**

006- **9** shd **Gadobout Dancer**[299] 4143 5-9-2 **53** .... BarryMcHugh 12 — 35
(Tony Coyle) *in rr: hdwy on inner whn nt clr run 2f out: sn wknd* **16/1**

-043 **10** 3 ¼ **Red Scintilla**[33] 1248 5-8-8 **52** ....(p) DanielleMooney(7) 16 — 25
(Nigel Tinkler) *hld up in rr: hung lft and kpt on fnl 2f: nvr a factor* **16/1**

050- **11** 10 **Tombellini (IRE)**[50] 7064 5-8-10 **54** .... GemmaTutty(7) 1
(Noel Wilson) *led after 1f: hdd over 2f out: hung lft and lost pl over 1f out* **16/1**

00-1 **12** ½ **Cannon Bolt (IRE)**[9] 1799 4-9-9 **60** ....(b) LeeNewman 9
(Robin Bastiman) *w ldrs: wknd 2f out* **4/1**[2]

5-15 **13** 5 **Monte Cassino (IRE)**[79] 670 7-9-4 **55** .... TomEaves 14
(Bryan Smart) *a in rr* **20/1**

-530 **14** 2 ½ **Double Carpet (IRE)**[103] 359 9-9-4 **55** .... MickyFenton 11
(Garry Woodward) *led 1f: w ldrs: led over 2f out: hdd over 1f out: wknd: heavily eased last 100yds* **20/1**

-065 **15** 2 **Thrust Control (IRE)**[31] 1294 5-9-0 **51** .... RobertWinston 13
(Tracy Waggott) *prom: effrt over 2f out: sn wknd: eased fnl f* **12/1**[3]

10-4 **16** 7 **Fair Bunny**[28] 1383 5-8-13 **50** ....(b) GrahamGibbons 15
(Alan Brown) *dwlt: a in rr: eased towards fin* **12/1**[3]

1m 32.15s (4.95) **Going Correction** +0.725s/f (Yiel) — **16** Ran SP% **121.0**
Speed ratings (Par 101): **100,97,97,96,94 93,92,88,88,84 72,72,66,63,61 53**
toteswingers:1&2:£40.00, 2&3:£12.50, 1&3:£121.60 CSF £128.07 CT £1558.29 TOTE £84.90: £13.40, £1.02, £4.60, £8.00; EX 384.30 TRIFECTA Not won..
Owner K Blackstone **Bred** Cheveley Park Stud Ltd **Trained** Pockley, N Yorks
■ Stewards' Enquiry : Paul Pickard four-day ban: used whip above permitted level (May 26,28-30)

FOCUS
A low-grade 7f handicap, run at a strong pace in testing conditions and something an upset. The form is rated cautiously given the ground, the winner to his best since he was a 3yo.
Cannon Bolt(IRE) Official explanation: jockey said gelding was unable to dominate
Double Carpet(IRE) Official explanation: jockey said gelding moved poorly throughout

2092 THIRSK RACES IRISH DAY SATURDAY 19TH MAY (S) STKS — 6f

6:45 (6:46) (Class 6) 3-Y-0+ — **£2,587** (£770; £384; £192) **Stalls** High

Form — RPR

2-10 **1** **Go Go Green (IRE)**[15] 1642 6-9-11 75........ DanielTudhope 10 — 79
(Jim Goldie) *hld up in rr: hdwy over 2f out: chsd ldr over 1f out: styd on to ld last 50yds* **6/5**[1]

0-00 **2** ¾ **Green Park (IRE)**[7] 1868 9-9-1 75........(b) NeilFarley(5) 6 — 72
(Declan Carroll) *w ldrs: led 2f out: hdd and no ex wl ins fnl f* **3/1**[2]

0-04 **3** 4 **Needy McCredie**[6] 1875 6-9-1 59........ PaddyAspell 4 — 54
(James Turner) *unruly in stalls: rrd s: in rr: hdwy over 1f out: edgd rt 1f out: styd on to take 3rd last 100yds* **8/1**

20-0 **4** 2 ¼ **Ryedane (IRE)**[7] 1868 10-8-13 65........(b) RachelRichardson(7) 8 — 52
(Tim Easterby) *in rr: hdwy whn n.m.r 1f out: kpt on* **16/1**

-615 **5** 7 **Bertie Southstreet**[23] 1483 9-9-11 61........(b) MickyFenton 1 — 34
(Paul Midgley) *hld up in mid-div: effrt over 2f out: wknd over 1f out* **28/1**

3130 **6** ½ **Last Sovereign**[11] 1727 8-9-11 80........(b) MichaelO'Connell 2 — 33
(Ollie Pears) *hood removed v late: dwlt: drvn to chse ldrs after 2f: edgd rt to ld 2f out: hdd 2f out: wknd fnl f* **11/2**[3]

0-50 **7** 1 ¾ **Sophie's Beau (USA)**[17] 1601 5-9-6 46........(bt) RobbieFitzpatrick 9 — 22
(Michael Chapman) *chsd ldrs: wknd over 1f out* **100/1**

50 **8** 5 **Hurricane Rita (IRE)**[6] 1878 4-9-1 0........ RobertWinston 5
(Alan Swinbank) *sn outpcd and in rr: eased over 1f out* **28/1**

3003 **9** 1 ½ **Lady Nickandy (IRE)**[44] 1090 3-7-12 50........(v) GemmaTutty(7) 7
(Karen Tutty) *chsd ldrs: lost pl over 1f out* **40/1**

6000 **10** 3 ¾ **Vogarth**[18] 1578 8-8-13 39........(b) ShirleyTeasdale(7) 3
(Michael Chapman) *led 2f: lost pl 2f out* **200/1**

1m 16.03s (3.33) **Going Correction** +0.675s/f (Yiel)
WFA 3 from 4yo+ 10lb — **10** Ran SP% **113.7**
Speed ratings (Par 101): **104,103,97,94,85 84,82,75,73,68**
toteswingers:1&2:£1.10, 2&3:£6.00, 1&3:£2.90 CSF £4.43 TOTE £1.70: £1.02, £2.20, £3.30; EX 4.30 Trifecta £34.10 Pool: £532.67 - 11.53 winning units..No bid for the winner.
Owner Jim Goldie Racing Club **Bred** Edmond And Richard Kent **Trained** Uplawmoor, E Renfrews
■ Stewards' Enquiry : Daniel Tudhope two-day ban: used whip above permitted level (May 26,28)

FOCUS
A fair seller, dominated by the market principals. The form is rated around the winner to his Musselburgh form.

2093 GT GROUP H'CAP — 1m 4f

7:15 (7:15) (Class 4) (0-80,80) 4-Y-0+ — **£5,498** (£1,636; £817; £408) **Stalls** Low

Form — RPR

000- **1** **Yahrab (IRE)**[138] 3071 7-8-8 **67** .... GrahamGibbons 3 — 77
(Declan Carroll) *mid-div: hdwy over 3f out: chal over 2f out: led over 1f out: jst hld on* **28/1**

111- **2** hd **Lordofthehouse (IRE)**[232] 6294 4-9-5 **78** .... PaulHanagan 10 — 87+
(William Haggas) *s.i.s: hdwy after 4f: effrt over 3f out: sn chsng ldrs: rdn over 1f out: styd on towards fin: jst hld* **10/11**[1]

040- **3** 2 **Eltheeb**[253] 5686 5-9-7 **80** .... DanielTudhope 6 — 86+
(David O'Meara) *hld up towards rr: hdwy on inner whn nt clr run over 2f out: chsng ldrs over 1f out: kpt on same pce fnl 100yds* **16/1**

0425 **4** 1 **Maven**[14] 1656 4-8-11 **70** .... DavidAllan 8 — 74
(Tim Easterby) *t.k.h in mid-div: hdwy over 2f out: hung lft and kpt on same pce fnl f* **25/1**

0013 **5** 1 **Light The City (IRE)**[8] 1822 5-8-8 **67** .... JamesSullivan 7 — 70
(Ruth Carr) *trckd ldr: led 3f out: hdd over 1f out: wknd last 100yds* **8/1**[3]

3-02 **6** 1 ½ **Odin's Raven (IRE)**[7] 1846 7-9-2 **75** .... BarryMcHugh 9 — 75
(Brian Ellison) *in rr: drvn over 4f out: nt clr run and swtchd rt over 1f out: kpt on same pce* **17/2**

162- **7** 5 **Flying Power**[222] 6592 4-9-3 **76** .... PaddyAspell 1 — 68
(John Norton) *chsd ldrs: drvn over 1f out: fdd appr fnl f* **40/1**

340- **8** 4 ½ **Beat The Shower**[159] 7102 6-9-3 **76** .... RobertWinston 12 — 61
(Peter Niven) *hld up towards rr: sme hdwy over 2f out: wknd over 1f out* **11/1**

-502 **9** 4 ½ **Brockfield**[5] 1913 6-8-9 **68** .... DuranFentiman 4 — 46
(Mel Brittain) *led: qcknd pce 4f out: hdd 3f out: wknd over 1f out* **15/2**[2]

212- **10** 9 **Singzak**[201] 7062 4-9-1 **74** .... PaulMulrennan 11 — 38
(Michael Easterby) *swvd lft s: sn chsng ldrs: lost pl 2f out: sn bhd* **25/1**

144- **11** 5 **Fossgate**[251] 5761 11-9-1 **74** .... AndrewElliott 2 — 30
(James Bethell) *in rr: drvn over 4f out: bhd fnl 3f* **40/1**

3203 **12** 67 **Mazij**[43] 1114 4-9-2 **75** .... MickyFenton 5
(Peter Hiatt) *chsd ldrs: sn drvn along: lost pl over 2f out: sn bhd: t.o: virtually p.u* **33/1**

2m 45.33s (9.13) **Going Correction** +0.725s/f (Yiel) — **12** Ran SP% **119.0**
Speed ratings (Par 105): **98,97,96,95,95 94,90,87,84,78 75,30**
totewingers:1&2:£11.70, 2&3:£3.60, 1&3:£77.50 CSF £51.92 CT £475.10 TOTE £33.00: £7.20, £1.10, £4.70; EX 88.60 TRIFECTA Not won..

Owner Exors of the Late I D Woolfitt **Bred** Swettenham Stud **Trained** Sledmere, E Yorks

FOCUS

A fair handicap with a fine finish. The form is rated around the third to fifth.

Mazij Official explanation: jockey said filly lost its action

2094 CALVERTS CARPETS H'CAP 1m

7:45 (7:46) (Class 5) (0-75,75) 4-Y-O+ £2,943 (£875; £437; £218) Stalls Low

Form RPR

3-03 **1** **Fazza**[10] 1755 5-9-2 **75** ShaneBKelly(5) 8 89
(Edwin Tuer) *s.i.s: hdwy on ins over 2f out: swtchd rt over 1f out: r.o wl to ld last 75ds:* **9/2**[2]

-252 **2** 2 ½ **Save The Bees**[9] 1796 4-9-2 **70** GrahamGibbons 15 78
(Declan Carroll) *chsd ldrs: edgd lft 2f out: sn led: hdd and no ex ins fnl f* **5/2**[1]

610- **3** 3 ¼ **Elspeth's Boy (USA)**[182] 7397 5-8-13 **72** GarryWhillans(5) 9 73
(Philip Kirby) *in tch: hdwy over 2f out: hmpd over 1f out: kpt on same pce* **16/1**

4 2 **The Lodge Road (IRE)**[197] 7154 4-9-1 **69** PaulHanagan 11 65
(Martin Todhunter) *in rr: hdwy over 2f out: kpt on one pce* **14/1**

620- **5** 1 **Skyfire**[27] 6586 5-9-0 **68** MichaelStainton 16 62
(Nick Kent) *in rr: hdwy on outside over 2f out: kpt on fnl f* **16/1**

53-0 **6** 1 ¼ **Strong Man**[9] 1796 4-8-11 **65** (b[1]) PaulMulrennan 17 56
(Michael Easterby) *chsd ldrs: drvn 3f out: sn led: edgd rt and hdd over 1f out: sn fdd* **20/1**

020- **7** 1 ¾ **Triple Eight (IRE)**[145] 7823 4-9-6 **74** (p) MichaelO'Connell 3 61
(Philip Kirby) *mid-div: hdwy 3f out: keeping on one pce whn sltly hmpd over 1f out* **18/1**

01-5 **8** ½ **Betteras Bertie**[10] 1755 9-8-10 **64** (p) BarryMcHugh 12 50
(Tony Coyle) *s.s: in rr: hdwy over 2f out: nvr nr ldrs* **20/1**

-331 **9** 1 ¼ **Wiseman's Diamond (USA)**[10] 1755 7-9-0 **68** (b) MickyFenton 2 51
(Paul Midgley) *led: hdd over 2f out: sn hmpd: wknd fnl f* **17/2**

600- **10** 2 ½ **Rasselas (IRE)**[240] 6079 5-8-13 **67** AndrewMullen 1 44
(David Nicholls) *prom: wknd over 1f out* **16/1**

100- **11** 2 **Desert Vision**[192] 7237 8-9-5 **73** (t) JamesSullivan 5 46
(Michael Easterby) *in rr: nvr a factor* **33/1**

100/ **12** 8 **Loukoumi**[567] 7085 4-9-1 **69** TomEaves 13 23
(Tim Easterby) *in tch: lost pl over 1f out* **18/1**

30-6 **13** 6 **Flipping**[14] 1680 5-9-7 **75** DavidAllan 6 15
(Eric Alston) *chsd ldr: wknd wl over 1f out: bhd whn eased ins fnl f* **15/2**[3]

230- **14** *shd* **Ballinargh Girl (IRE)**[214] 6778 4-9-0 **75** MatthewHopkins(7) 18 15
(Danielle McCormick) *hld up in rr: bhd fnl 2f* **20/1**

40-0 **15** 34 **Touch Tone**[21] 1527 5-8-13 **67** DanielTudhope 14
(David Thompson) *mid-div: lost pl over 2f out: bhd whn eased over 1f out: t.o* **50/1**

1m 45.3s (5.20) **Going Correction** +0.725s/f (Yiel) **15** Ran SP% **123.1**

Speed ratings (Par 103): **103,100,97,95,94 93,91,90,89,87 85,77,71,70,36**

toteswingers:1&2:£2.90, 2&3:£11.70, 1&3:£18.20 CSF £15.04 CT £176.38 TOTE £3.90: £1.10, £1.80, £9.10; EX 17.50 Trifecta £231.80 Part won. Pool: £313.33 - 0.72 winning units..

Owner Ontoawinner **Bred** D R Tucker **Trained** Birkby, N Yorks

■ Stewards' Enquiry : Shane B Kelly one-day ban: careless riding (May 26)

FOCUS

A competitive if modest handicap. A personal best from the winner, who has a good record here.

2095 ABF SOLDIERS' CHARITY MAIDEN STKS 1m

8:15 (8:17) (Class 5) 3-Y-O+ £2,943 (£875; £437; £218) Stalls Low

Form RPR

1 **Exclusive Dancer** 3-8-8 0 TomEaves 12 68+
(George Moore) *s.s: in rr: hdwy on outside over 2f: styd on wl to ld nr fin* **33/1**

04 **2** 1 **Entihaa**[7] 1866 4-9-12 0 RobertWinston 1 74
(Alan Swinbank) *s.i.s: hdwy over 3f out: chal 2f out: led 100yds out: hdd and no ex towards fin* **8/1**

52 **3** *nk* **Regal Swain (IRE)**[7] 1867 4-9-7 0 GarryWhillans(5) 14 73
(Alan Swinbank) *chsd ldrs: led 2f out: hdd and no ex ins fnl f* **10/3**[2]

4 1 **Gladsome** 4-9-7 0 MichaelStainton 13 66
(Jason Ward) *w ldr: led over 2f out: sn hdd: kpt on same pce fnl f* **100/1**

4 **5** ½ **Fame Again**[4] 1953 4-9-12 0 PaddyAspell 2 70
(Michael Easterby) *mid-div: hdwy over 2f out: one pce last 100yds* **16/1**

0-0 **6** 1 ½ **Attwaal (IRE)**[19] 1567 3-8-13 0 JackMitchell 6 63+
(Roger Varian) *chsd ldrs: effrt on ins over 2f out: sn rdn one pce* **11/4**[1]

4- **7** 1 ¾ **Rex Romanorum (IRE)**[199] 7111 4-9-12 0 DanielTudhope 7 62
(Patrick Holmes) *chsd ldrs: one pce fnl 2f* **10/1**

053- **8** ½ **Crossley**[211] 6837 3-8-10 67 DaleSwift(3) 10 58
(Geoffrey Oldroyd) *chsd ldrs: one pce fnl 2f* **8/1**

530- **9** 1 **Jay Kay**[220] 6627 3-8-6 54 MatthewHopkins(7) 8 56
(Danielle McCormick) *towards rr: kpt on fnl 2f: nvr a factor* **33/1**

10 2 ½ **Certainly Elusive (IRE)** 3-8-13 0 (b[1]) JamesSullivan 9 50
(Alan Swinbank) *s.i.s: nvr a factor* **40/1**

0 **11** 5 **Her Nibbs**[17] 1595 3-8-8 0 AndrewElliott 4 34
(James Bethell) *prom: drvn and outpcd over 4f out: wknd over 1f out* **80/1**

12 12 **Alaskan Prince (IRE)**[213] 7-9-12 0 AndrewMullen 3
(Peter Salmon) *s.i.s: t.k.h: hdwy over 5f out: wknd over 1f out* **66/1**

0 **13** 3 **Highway Warrior**[46] 1053 3-8-8 0 ow3 PaulPickard(3) 11
(Kevin M Prendergast) *led: hdd over 2f out: sn wknd* **33/1**

14 21 **Pinot** 3-8-13 0 PaulHanagan 5
(Richard Fahey) *in rr: bhd fnl 5f: t.o 3f out* **6/1**[3]

1m 47.57s (7.47) **Going Correction** +0.725s/f (Yiel)

WFA 3 from 4yo+ 13lb **14** Ran SP% **116.2**

Speed ratings (Par 103): **91,90,89,88,88 86,84,84,83,80 75,63,60,39**

toteswingers:1&2:£53.00, 2&3:£9.30, 1&3:£18.00 CSF £264.94 TOTE £28.60: £10.40, £3.40, £2.30; EX 437.70 Trifecta £214.30 Pool: £235.29 - 1.40 winning units..

Owner David Parker **Bred** London Thoroughbred Services Ltd **Trained** Middleham Moor, N Yorks

FOCUS

Probably not the strongest of maiden races. The time was relatively slow and there are doubts over the bare form, which has been rated around the second and third.

2096 DICK PEACOCK SPRINT H'CAP 6f

8:45 (8:52) (Class 5) (0-75,78) 4-Y-O+ £2,943 (£875; £437; £218) Stalls High

Form RPR

03-6 **1** **Secret City (IRE)**[21] 1526 6-8-10 **64** (b) DanielTudhope 9 73
(Robin Bastiman) *uns rdr after leaving paddock and galloped full circ: rr-div: sn drvn along: hdwy over 2f out: led over 1f out: styd on wl* **25/1**

4206 **2** 2 ¼ **Northern Bolt**[1] 2037 7-9-1 **69** (b) PatrickMathers 6 71
(Ian McInnes) *slowly away: bhd and reminders after s: hdwy on wd outside over 1f out: edgd lft and styd on to chse wnr ins fnl f* **20/1**

26-5 **3** ¾ **Jack Luey**[15] 1643 5-9-7 **75** FrederikTylicki 7 75+
(Lawrence Mullaney) *led: hdd over 1f out: kpt on same pce* **13/2**[2]

3462 **4** 1 ¼ **Bond Fastrac**[8] 1827 5-9-6 **77** DaleSwift(3) 11 73
(Geoffrey Oldroyd) *dwlt: hld up in rr: hdwy 2f out: kpt on same pce fnl f* **9/1**

10-1 **5** 1 **Half A Crown (IRE)**[21] 1526 7-8-6 **67** HannahNunn(7) 2 60
(Peter Salmon) *trckd ldrs on outer: one pce appr fnl f* **10/1**

60-6 **6** 2 **Sea Salt**[14] 1650 9-8-8 **67** ShaneBKelly(5) 8 54
(Ron Barr) *chsd ldrs: edgd lft over 1f out: one pce* **25/1**

3-53 **7** 1 **Chosen Character (IRE)**[19] 1561 4-9-5 **73** (vt) RichardKingscote 4 57
(Tom Dascombe) *mid-div: effrt over 2f out: nvr nr ldrs* **8/1**[3]

61-6 **8** 1 ½ **Song Of Parkes**[33] 1246 5-9-4 **72** DavidAllan 12 52
(Eric Alston) *chsd ldrs: wknd fnl f* **12/1**

05-0 **9** 1 **Iceblast**[21] 1527 4-8-10 **64** PaulMulrennan 10 41
(Michael Easterby) *in rr: sme hdwy 2f out: nvr a factor* **12/1**

0-03 **10** 6 **Calypso Cay**[21] 1527 4-8-11 **65** AndrewMullen 3 24
(Peter Salmon) *w ldr: wknd 1f out* **33/1**

3-22 **11** *shd* **Trade Secret**[7] 1868 5-9-10 **78** RobertWinston 13 36+
(Mel Brittain) *rrd s: hld up: hdwy stands' side 3f out: chsng ldrs over 1f out: wknd and heavily eased jst ins fnl f* **13/8**[1]

3-00 **12** 2 **Lizzie (IRE)**[14] 1652 4-8-10 **64** (b) GrahamGibbons 5 16
(Tim Easterby) *swtchd rt s: towards rr: bhd fnl 2f* **14/1**

0-00 **13** 1 ½ **Another Citizen (IRE)**[23] 1478 4-8-11 **72** GaryMahon(7) 1 20
(Tim Easterby) *towards rr on outer: hung rt and lost pl over 1f out* **40/1**

1m 16.2s (3.50) **Going Correction** +0.675s/f (Yiel) **13** Ran SP% **121.5**

Speed ratings (Par 103): **103,100,99,97,96 93,92,90,88,80 80,77,75**

toteswingers:1&2:£38.60, 2&3:£75.80, 1&3:£43.90 CSF £439.12 CT £3618.11 TOTE £27.00: £6.80, £7.90, £3.40; EX 326.30 TRIFECTA Not won..

Owner Ms M Austerfield **Bred** Miss Karen Theobald **Trained** Cowthorpe, N Yorks

FOCUS

An ordinary handicap run at a strong pace. Improvement from the winner.

T/Plt: £180.40 to a £1 stake. Pool: £68,343.00 - 276.41 winning units. T/Qpdt: £49.20 to a £1 stake. Pool: £4,287.00 - 64.36 winning units. WG

2097 - 2099a (Foreign Racing) - See Raceform Interactive

1400 LEOPARDSTOWN (L-H)

Sunday, May 13

OFFICIAL GOING: Good to soft (soft in places)

2100a AMETHYST STKS (GROUP 3) 1m

2:45 (2:45) 3-Y-O+ £31,145 (£9,104; £4,312; £1,437)

RPR

1 **Famous Name**[16] 1646 7-9-12 115 PatSmullen 3 118+
(D K Weld, Ire) *trckd ldrs in 3rd: hdwy ent st and led 2f out: sn qckned clr and styd on wl: v easily* **1/5**[1]

2 4 ½ **Sweet Lightning**[407] 1094 7-9-9 (t) JohnnyMurtagh 4 104+
(Thomas Carmody, Ire) *settled in rr: hdwy ent st: wnt 2nd over 1f out but no ch w easy wnr: kpt on one pce* **11/2**[2]

3 4 ½ **Barack (IRE)**[28] 1402 6-9-9 103 (bt) BenCurtis 1 95
(Francis Ennis, Ire) *chsd ldrs in 4th: rdn in 3rd ent st: sn no ch w easy wnr and no ex fnl f* **12/1**[3]

4 6 **Ask Jack (USA)**[21] 1546 8-9-9 97 (p) ShaneFoley 5 80
(Joseph G Murphy, Ire) *sn led: drvn along ent st and hdd 2f out: sn no ex and wknd* **25/1**

5 4 ½ **Kargali (IRE)**[14] 1694 7-9-9 87 (bt[1]) KevinManning 2 69
(Luke Comer, Ire) *prom and trckd ldr in 2nd: rdn and dropped to rr ent st: no threat fr 2f out* **33/1**

1m 42.59s (1.39) **Going Correction** +0.525s/f (Yiel) **5** Ran SP% **113.2**

Speed ratings: **114,109,105,99,94**

CSF £1.99 TOTE £1.10: £1.02, £1.20; DF 1.50.

Owner K Abdulla **Bred** Juddmonte Farms Ltd **Trained** The Curragh, Co Kildare

FOCUS

Famous Name won this event for the third consecutive year and brought his score at the track to 11 wins, all of them at Group 3 or Listed level. The time was good compared with the 1,000 Guineas trial.

NOTEBOOK

Famous Name put the race to bed very quickly once hitting the front under 2f out. His career tally is now 16 wins and while he has never won at higher than this level he has been placed several times in Group 1 company. He was a well beaten third in the Group 2 bet365 Mile at Sandown on his previous start and trainer Dermot Weld is convinced that he was unsuited by the very heavy ground on that occasion. (op 2/9)

Sweet Lightning has had his problems and was making his Irish debut on his first start since winning the William Hill Lincoln over a year ago. This was his first venture at pattern level and considering his long absence he acquitted himself quite well. Held up in rear, he went third into the straight and kept on without making any impression on the winner. (op 11/2 tchd 6/1)

Barack(IRE), a Listed winner over the course and trip last year, had been beaten almost 12 lengths behind Famous Name on his reappearance here last month. He got a little closer on this occasion without posing a serious threat.

Ask Jack(USA) had plenty on his plate here and, after making the running until early in the straight, quickly dropped out of contention.

Kargali(IRE), without a win since landing the Group 3 Gladness Stakes at the Curragh over two years ago, was fitted with first-time blinkers and raced in second place until dropping out quickly on the final bend.

2101a DERRINSTOWN STUD 1,000 GUINEAS TRIAL (GROUP 3) (FILLIES) 1m

3:15 (3:16) 3-Y-O £33,854 (£9,895; £4,687; £1,562)

RPR

1 **Yellow Rosebud (IRE)**[224] 6564 3-9-0 108 PatSmullen 6 108+
(D K Weld, Ire) *settled in mid-div on inner: wnt 3rd early st: 2nd and chal over 1f out: led ins fnl f and drvn out to maintain advantage* **13/2**[3]

2 1 **Devotion (IRE)**[32] 1329 3-9-0 95 SeamieHeffernan 7 105+
(A P O'Brien, Ire) *in rr of mid-div: 8th 1/2-way: hdwy on outer early st to go 4th 1f out: kpt on ins fnl f wout rching wnr* **25/1**

3 *shd* **Coral Wave (IRE)**[231] 6389 3-9-0 109 DeclanMcDonogh 2 105
(P J Prendergast, Ire) *trckd ldrs racing keenly: 3rd 1/2-way: 2nd ent st: rdn in 3rd over 1f out: kpt on same pce wout troubling wnr* **5/1**[2]

4 ½ **Duntle (IRE)**[25] 1458 3-9-0 WJLee 1 104
(David Wachman, Ire) *prom and disp ld: led appr st: drvn along fr 2f out and hdd ins fnl f: no ex and dropped to 4th cl home* **4/1**[1]

5 ¾ **Remember Alexander**[28] 1403 3-9-0 105 ShaneFoley 5 102
(Mrs John Harrington, Ire) *trckd ldrs on inner: 5th 1/2-way: pushed along appr st: no imp fr 1f out: kpt on one pce* **15/2**

6 1 3/4 **Soon (IRE)**[7] 1896 3-9-0 99 ..... RyanMoore 4 98+
(A P O'Brien, Ire) *in rr: nvr a factor: kpt on one pce in st wout threatening* **8/1**

7 2 3/4 **Alla Speranza**[7] 1884 3-9-0 101 ..... KevinManning 8 92
(J S Bolger, Ire) *mid-div: 6th 1/2-way: 7th early st and no imp fr over 1f out* **5/1**[2]

8 1 3/4 **Rubina (IRE)**[28] 1403 3-9-0 104 ..... (t) JohnnyMurtagh 10 88
(John M Oxx, Ire) *settled towards rr: 6th and rdn early st: no ex fr over 1f out* **10/1**

9 15 **Ronan's Bay (USA)**[217] 6731 3-9-0 90 ..... RonanWhelan 9 53
(George J Kent, Ire) *chsd ldrs on outer: rdn along in 4th 1/2-way: no ex and dropped to rr ent st: eased whn btn fnl f* **20/1**

10 4 1/2 **Princess Sinead (IRE)**[49] 1041 3-9-0 105 ..... FranBerry 3 43
(Mrs John Harrington, Ire) *led or disp ld: hdd appr st: no ex u.p fr 2f out and wknd: eased whn btn ins fnl f* **5/1**[2]

1m 42.94s (1.74) **Going Correction** +0.525s/f (Yiel) **10** Ran SP% **123.9**
Speed ratings: **112,111,110,110,109 107,105,103,88,83**
CSF £161.56 TOTE £9.20: £3.10, £5.80, £2.30; DF 151.00.
Owner Dr R Lambe **Bred** Irish National Stud **Trained** The Curragh, Co Kildare

FOCUS
A decent trial run in a good time and it's been rated around the third and fourth.

NOTEBOOK
Yellow Rosebud(IRE) ◆ ran out a game winner and will now try to emulate her former stablemate, Bethrah, who won this trial and the Irish 1,000 Guineas two years ago. Held up, she began her run approaching the straight and hit the front under 1f out. She appeared to tire somewhat in the closing stages but was always doing enough to prevail. One of only three in the race without a previous run this season, she should come on for the race and on the evidence of this effort easy ground is not a problem. (op 11/2 tchd 7/1)
Devotion(IRE) produced her best performance to date. She had only one rival behind her turning for home before staying on quite well when switched to the outside. She should stay further and like so many of Ballydoyle's 3yo fillies who have plenty of racing done there is every chance that there will be better to come. (op 25/1 tchd 20/1)
Coral Wave(IRE), the only filly in the race with a Group race win to her credit - she beat the Qipco 1,000 Guineas winner Homecoming Queen by a neck in a 7f Group 3 event at the Curragh in September - was making her reappearance. She had suffered a setback earlier this year and her trainer reported she should come on considerably for this run. She was very keen early on before settling in third place and had every chance in the straight before finding no extra inside the final furlong. She is not entered for the Irish Guineas but has many options, including the Coronation Stakes and the Darley Irish Oaks. (op 4/1)
Duntle(IRE) was very much the unknown quantity as she stepped up considerably in class after her front-running, 18-length win at Dundalk last month. There was plenty of support for her and she coped quite well at this higher level, leading and disputing and only giving best under 1f out from where she kept on at the same pace. (op 11/2 tchd 6/1)
Remember Alexander was unable to make much impression when asked to raise her effort. (op 8/1)
Soon(IRE) had run her best race to date when runner-up in a 1m2f Listed event at Gowran Park a week previously. She was last into the straight here before staying on quite well in the closing stage and will appreciate going back up in distance. (op 8/1 tchd 9/1)

2102a DERRINSTOWN STUD DERBY TRIAL STKS (GROUP 2) 1m 2f
3:45 (3:45) 3-Y-O **£51,458** (£15,041; £7,125; £2,375)

RPR

1 **Light Heavy (IRE)**[28] 1404 3-9-3 109 ..... (tp) KevinManning 3 113+
(J S Bolger, Ire) *trckd ldr in 2nd: rdn to chal early st: led ins fnl f and kpt on u.p* **15/8**[2]

2 nk **Tower Rock (IRE)**[28] 1404 3-9-3 101 ..... SeamieHeffernan 1 112
(A P O'Brien, Ire) *led: strly pressed early st: hdd ins fnl f: kpt on u.p but nt match wnr* **9/1**[3]

3 7 1/2 **Wrote (IRE)**[43] 1145 3-9-6 115 ..... RyanMoore 2 104+
(A P O'Brien, Ire) *trckd ldrs in 3rd: rdn ent st and no imp on first 2 fr 2f out: no threat and kpt on one pce* **8/13**[1]

4 4 1/4 **Calgacus (IRE)**[9] 1836 3-9-3 77 ..... MichaelHussey 5 89
(Tracey Collins, Ire) *chsd ldrs: 4th fr 1/2-way: rdn ent st and sn no ex* **100/1**

5 3 3/4 **Hit The Jackpot (IRE)**[28] 1404 3-9-3 97 ..... (b) PatSmullen 4 84+
(D K Weld, Ire) *hld up in 4th and t.k.h: 5th fr 1/2-way: rdn and no imp ent st: no ex* **20/1**

2m 11.5s (3.30) **Going Correction** +0.525s/f (Yiel) **5** Ran SP% **112.5**
Speed ratings: **107,106,100,97,94**
CSF £17.74 TOTE £2.60: £1.40, £4.70; DF 13.30.
Owner Mrs J S Bolger **Bred** J S Bolger **Trained** Coolcullen, Co Carlow

FOCUS
As a trial for the Investec Derby this race offered no significant clues as the winner isn't entered.

NOTEBOOK
Light Heavy(IRE) showed himself to be a tough and genuine sort as he battled his way to a narrow victory having fought it out with Tower Rock over the last furlong and a half. Four lengths had separated the pair when they ran first and third respectively in the Group 3 Ballysax Stakes over the same course and trip last month and on that basis Tower Rock would appear to have made the greater progress, although winning trainer Jim Bolger believes the winner to be much better suited by drier ground than he encountered here. The Dubai Duty Free Irish Derby is now the target with Bolger dismissing any suggestion of the colt being supplemented for Epsom. (op 11/8)
Tower Rock(IRE) made the running and was asked to raise the tempo before the straight. He responded and kept on quite well although the winner had his measure towards the finish. (op 8/1 tchd 10/1)
Wrote(IRE) proved disappointing here and found little or nothing when asked to improve his position off the last bend. He is entered for the Derby but did nothing to advertise his claims. (op 10/11 tchd 4/7)
Calgacus(IRE) looked completely out of his depth and never posed a threat.
Hit The Jackpot(IRE) finished further behind the winner on this occasion than he had on two previous occasions. He will need to have his sights lowered. (op 16/1)

2103 - 2105a (Foreign Racing) - See Raceform Interactive

1698 CAPANNELLE (R-H)
Sunday, May 13

OFFICIAL GOING: Turf: good

2106a PREMIO PRESIDENTE DELLA REPUBBLICA GBI RACING (GROUP 1) (4YO+) (TURF) 1m 2f
4:30 (12:00) 4-Y-O+ **£79,166** (£34,833; £19,000; £9,500)

RPR

1 **Crackerjack King (IRE)**[35] 4-9-2 0 ..... FabioBranca 6 118+
(S Botti, Italy) *settled towards rr: gd hdwy over 2 1/2f out: sn chsng ldr: rdn and chal on outside over 1f out: led ent fnl f: sn clr: r.o wl* **8/5**[1]

2 2 1/2 **Afsare**[24] 1471 5-9-2 0 ..... KierenFallon 5 113
(Luca Cumani) *trckd ldrs: effrt on outside over 3 1/2f out: led appr 3f out: hdd ins fnl f: no ex* **41/10**[2]

3 2 1/2 **Quiza Quiza Quiza**[35] 6-8-13 0 ..... CristianDemuro 1 105+
(L Riccardi, Italy) *hld up towards rr: rdn and effrt on outside over 2f out: styd on u.p fnl f: nt pce to chal* **48/10**

4 1/2 **Waldpark (GER)**[34] 4-9-2 0 ..... EPedroza 4 107
(A Wohler, Germany) *prom on rail: on heels of ldrs and gng wl but hemmed in on rail 3f out: shuffled bk by wkng ldr and hmpd 2 1/2f out: swtchd outside and styd on u.p fnl 1 1/2f: nt rch ldrs* **9/2**[3]

5 5 **Theo Danon (GER)**[21] 4-9-2 0 ..... FilipMinarik 8 97
(P Schiergen, Germany) *trckd ldr on outside: 2nd 3 1/2f out: sn outpcd and lost pl: last over 1 1/2f out: styd on past btn horses fnl f* **27/1**

6 shd **Sri Putra**[11] 1749 6-9-2 0 ..... NeilCallan 3 97
(Roger Varian) *hld up towards rr: rdn and short-lived effrt on outside over 2f out: no real imp on ldrs* **41/10**[2]

7 3/4 **Saratoga Black (IRE)**[7] 5-9-2 0 ..... DarioVargiu 7 95
(B Grizzetti, Italy) *settled in midfield on outside of Afsare: 3rd and scrubbed along over 2f out: sn btn: eased fnl 150yds* **206/10**

8 1/2 **Estejo (GER)**[21] 1554 8-9-2 0 ..... MircoDemuro 2 94
(R Rohne, Germany) *led: scrubbed along and hdd appr 3f out: wknd on rail: eased ins fnl f* **74/10**

2m 1.3s (-2.00) **8** Ran SP% **133.2**
WIN (incl. 1 euro stake): 2.60. PLACES: 1.36, 1.69, 1.62..
Owner Effevi Snc Di Villa Felice & Co **Bred** Azienda Agricola Allevamento Deni **Trained** Italy

NOTEBOOK
Crackerjack King(IRE), winner of last year's Italian Derby, travelled smoothly into contention and ran out a good winner on his reappearance. He will now join Marco Botti and should not be underestimated when taking on stronger opposition.
Afsare kicked clear from 3f out but was worn down by the winner inside the last. He's a fair guide to the level of the form.
Sri Putra, a winner on the Polytrack on his reappearance, was disappointing, failing to pick up from the back of the field.

1700 COLOGNE (R-H)
Sunday, May 13

OFFICIAL GOING: Turf: good

2107a KARIN BARONIN VON ULLMANN - SCHWARZGOLD-RENNEN (GROUP 3) (3YO FILLIES) (TURF) 1m
4:00 (12:00) 3-Y-O
£26,666 (£9,166; £4,583; £2,500; £1,666; £1,250)

RPR

1 **Survey (GER)**[28] 3-9-2 0 ..... THellier 5 101
(Mario Hofer, Germany) *led: hdd 2f out: sn rdn: 2nd and edgd lft 1f out: rallied u.p on outside to regain ld cl home* **27/10**[1]

2 3/4 **Ilena (GER)** 3-9-2 0 ..... ADeVries 7 99
(Dr A Bolte, Germany) *settled towards rr: hdwy 2 1/2f out: chal between two ldrs 1f out: nvr quite put hd in front: r.o u.p: no ex cl home* **48/10**

3 nse **Paraisa**[196] 3-9-2 0 ..... JBojko 2 99
(A Wohler, Germany) *trckd ldr: hrd rdn and led 2f out: sn rdn on rail: hdd cl home* **29/10**[2]

4 1 1/4 **Molly Filia (GER)** 3-9-2 0 ..... FrederikTylicki 6 96
(Uwe Ostmann, Germany) *racd towards rr: 7th but in tch 3f out: scrubbed along ins fnl 2f: wnt 4th over 1f out: kpt on wout qckning* **81/10**

5 1 3/4 **Lady Of Budysin (GER)** 3-9-2 0 ..... AStarke 3 92
(Andreas Lowe, Germany) *settled in rr: last and adrift of main pack 2 1/2f out: styd on u.p ins fnl 2f: nvr on terms* **16/5**[3]

6 hd **Absolutly Me (FR)**[20] 1569 3-9-2 0 ..... Pierre-CharlesBoudot 1 92
(H-A Pantall, France) *hld up in midfield on rail: 4th and hrd rdn 1 1/2f out: wknd ins fnl f* **41/5**

7 7 **Liszar Jo (GER)** 3-9-2 0 ..... TomQueally 4 76
(Markus Klug, Germany) *racd in midfield: rdn and dropped away fr 1 1/2f out* **107/10**

8 5 **Enjoy The Life**[196] 3-9-2 0 ..... EFrank 8 64
(Mario Hofer, Germany) *chsd ldrs on outside: rdn and nt qckn 3f out: wknd fnl 2f* **156/10**

1m 39.22s (0.83) **8** Ran SP% **130.1**
WIN (incl. 10 euro stake): 37. PLACES: 13, 16, 13. SF: 342.
Owner Eckhard Sauren **Bred** R Lerner **Trained** Germany

1970 LONGCHAMP (R-H)
Sunday, May 13

OFFICIAL GOING: Turf: good to soft

2108a PRIX HOCQUART (GROUP 2) (3YO COLTS & FILLIES) (TURF) 1m 3f
1:30 (12:00) 3-Y-O **£61,750** (£23,833; £11,375; £7,583; £3,791)

RPR

1 **Top Trip**[42] 1162 3-9-2 0 ..... ThomasHuet 2 110
(F Doumen, France) *hld up in rr: last ent st: rdn 2f out: qcknd wl ent fnl f: r.o strly between horses fnl 50yds: led fnl 20yds* **16/1**

2 1/2 **Masterstroke (USA)**[31] 3-9-2 0 ..... MaximeGuyon 1 109
(A Fabre, France) *settled in 4th: hrd rdn 1 1/2f out: r.o wl fnl f to chal for ld 100yds out: shared 2nd tl hdd fnl 20yds: r.o wl* **5/6**[1]

3 nk **Sir Jade (FR)**[19] 1592 3-9-2 0 ..... ChristopheSoumillon 3 108
(J-M Capitte, France) *racd in 2nd: chal for ld 2f out: tk ld u.p 1 1/2f out: wandered off st line: r.o wl fnl f: shared ld tl hdd fnl 20yds: no ex and lost 2nd cl home* **16/1**

4 1 1/4 **Saint Loup (FR)**[35] 1244 3-9-2 0 ..... GregoryBenoist 5 106
(J-C Rouget, France) *racd in 3rd: rdn 2f out: r.o wl ent fnl f but nt pce to chal for ld: r.o fnl f* **8/1**

5 snk **Athens (IRE)**[14] 1693 3-9-2 0 ..... JPO'Brien 6 106?
(A P O'Brien, Ire) *led: set gd pce: 2 l clr ent st: sn u.p: hdd 1 1/2f out: styd on fnl f* **6/1**[3]

6 snk **Loi (IRE)**[20] 1570 3-9-2 0 OlivierPeslier 4 106
(J-M Beguigne, France) *hld up towards rr: rdn 2f out: nt pce to chal ldrs: styd on fnl f* **10/3**[2]

2m 18.33s (-1.57) **Going Correction** +0.175s/f (Good) **6** Ran SP% **114.8**
Speed ratings: **112,111,111,110,110 110**
WIN (incl. 1 euro stake): 12.20. PLACES: 2.90, 1.40. SF: 24.70.
Owner Joerg Vasicek **Bred** Kenilworth House Stud & Haras D'ecouves **Trained** Bouce, France

NOTEBOOK

Top Trip, second to subsequent Prix Greffulhe winner and possible Espom Derby contender Kesampour on his reappearance, quickened best between horses to score a shade more comfortably than the margin might suggest. He's earned his crack at the Prix du Jockey Club now, but more will be required there.

Masterstroke(USA) had every chance but lacked the winner's speed at the finish. He looks the type that might be better off going for the Grand Prix de Paris over 1m4f rather than the Jockey Club.

Sir Jade(FR) edged left under pressure in the straight, which left open a gap for the first two to take. He ran his race and is probably a fair guide to the level of the form.

Saint Loup(FR), only fourth when sent off at odds-on for the Group 2 Prix Noailles on his reappearance, was entitled to bounce back on this better ground, but he didn't really pick up for pressure and was again disappointing.

Athens(IRE) was able to go his own pace out in front and was simply outpaced when it came to quickening up for home in the straight. He wouldn't be one of his stable's best 3yo colts, but helps give Aidan O'Brien a line to the French form with a view to the Jockey Club.

2109a POULE D'ESSAI DES POULICHES (GROUP 1) (3YO FILLIES) (TURF) 1m

2:40 (12:00) 3-Y-0 **£214,275** (£85,725; £42,862; £21,412; £10,725)

RPR

1 **Beauty Parlour**[28] 1407 3-9-0 0 ChristopheSoumillon 7 115+
(E Lellouche, France) *midfield on outer: prog gng wl over 2f out: rdn to chal over 1 1/2f out: sn led: kpt on wl under hands and heels ins fnl f: comf* **8/13**[1]

2 1 **Up (IRE)**[28] 1403 3-9-0 0 JPO'Brien 14 113
(A P O'Brien, Ire) *hld up in last pair on outer: rdn to improve over 2f out: styd on strly ins fnl 1 1/2f: wnt 2nd ins fnl 150yds* **14/1**

3 1 3/4 **Topeka (IRE)**[38] 1209 3-9-0 0 IoritzMendizabal 11 109
(Robert Collet, France) *hld up in last on inner: stl last on turn into st: short of room and forced to wait for gap over 2f out: in the clr and rdn to improve 1 1/2f out: r.o strly to go 3rd wl ins fnl f* **20/1**

4 1/2 **After (IRE)**[28] 1403 3-9-0 0 CO'Donoghue 5 108
(A P O'Brien, Ire) *hld up towards rr on inner: swtchd out and rdn to improve over 1 1/2f out: r.o to take 4th fnl strides* **16/1**

5 nk **Fire Lily (IRE)**[28] 1403 3-9-0 0 WayneLordan 9 107
(David Wachman, Ire) *hld up towards rr on outer: stdy prog fr over 3f out: rdn over 2f out: r.o to go 2nd 1f out: no ex and fdd wl ins fnl f: ct for 4th fnl strides* **8/1**[3]

6 1 1/4 **Azeville (GER)**[16] 3-9-0 0 (p) Christophe-PatriceLemaire 12 104
(F Rohaut, France) *chsd ldrs on outer: rdn to chal 2f out: wnt 2nd over 1f out: no ex and fdd ins fnl f: dropped to 6th cl home* **40/1**

7 1 **Chica Loca (FR)**[194] 7220 3-9-0 0 Francois-XavierBertras 10 102
(M Figge, Germany) *hld up towards rr: rdn and outpcd over 2f out: relegated to last over 1 1/2f out: r.o wl u.p ins fnl f: wnt 7th post* **40/1**

8 snk **Petite Noblesse (FR)**[20] 1569 3-9-0 0 MaximeGuyon 4 101
(A Fabre, France) *midfield: t.k.h: rdn to maintain position over 3f out: outpcd over 1 1/2f out: kpt on under hands and heels ins fnl f: lost 7th post* **6/1**[2]

9 2 1/2 **Samitar**[25] 1452 3-9-0 0 OlivierPeslier 1 96
(Mick Channon) *broke wl to ld through first 3f: hdd and trckd runaway ldr on inner: rdn over 2f out: kpt on tl no ex and wknd ins fnl f* **20/1**

10 snk **Cheriearch (USA)**[35] 1243 3-9-0 0 GeraldMosse 6 95
(L A Urbano-Grajales, France) *sn trcking ldng pair: rdn to improve 2f out: brief effrt to chal 1 1/2f out: no ex and wknd rapidly ins fnl f: eased cl home* **33/1**

11 1 3/4 **Kendam (FR)**[28] 1407 3-9-0 0 MickaelBarzalona 13 91
(H-A Pantall, France) *s.i.s: pushed up to sit in midfield on inner: rdn to try and improve 2 1/2f out: outpcd and btn whn short of room and forced to check ins fnl f: qckly eased* **40/1**

12 nse **Miss Carmie (FR)**[28] 1407 3-9-0 0 ThierryJarnet 3 91
(Mlle S-V Tarrou, France) *prom on inner: rdn over 2f out: btn over 1f out: wknd* **50/1**

13 4 **Regatta (FR)**[57] 952 3-9-0 0 AnthonyCrastus 8 82
(E Lellouche, France) *trckd ldr on outer: led after 3f: opened up clr advantage over 3f out: rdn 2f out: sn hdd: wknd rapidly ins fnl f: eased* **66/1**

1m 37.15s (-1.25) **Going Correction** +0.175s/f (Good) **13** Ran SP% **123.1**
Speed ratings: **113,112,110,109,109 108,107,107,104,104 102,102,98**
WIN (incl. 1 euro stake): 1.60 (Beauty Parlour coupled with Regatta). PLACES: 1.10, 5.10, 2.80. DF: 20.00. SF: 20.40.
Owner Ecurie Wildenstein **Bred** Dayton Investments Ltd **Trained** Lamorlaye, France

FOCUS

Thanks to pacemaker Regatta and the Mick Channon-trained Samitar taking each other on after going 2f this was run at a strong gallop, and that suited those held up. It has been rated around the fifth, seventh and tenth.

NOTEBOOK

Beauty Parlour extended her winning run to four with a comfortable success. She's going to be suited by longer distances in future, is clearly the one to beat in the Prix de Diane, and further down the line the Arc, for which she's a best price 16-1 with a couple of firms, is likely to be on her agenda. Christophe Soumillon compared her to Zarkava after she won the Prix De La Grotte on her reappearance, and she still has plenty of untapped potential.

Up(IRE) gave the form of English 1000 Guineas winner Homecoming Queen a boost as she'd finished third to her in the Guineas Trial at Leopardstown last time out. From the worst draw out in stall 14, she was caught wider than ideal for much of the race, but finished off strongly from the back of the field, and this daughter of Galileo looks to be crying out for another couple of furlongs. She was clipped in to a best price of 25-1 for the Oaks, but perhaps a better option would be to return to France and take on the winner again in the Diane.

Topeka(IRE)'s trainer had warned that she would badly need her reappearance run in the Imprudence, and she duly improved a fair bit on that effort. While she benefited from being held up out the back in a strongly run race, she didn't get the clearest of runs, although the first two were finishing stronger than her at the finish. The Coronation Stakes, which her trainer won with Immortal Verse last year, looks a suitable target.

After(IRE), fifth in the Guineas Trial at Leopardstown, was another who finished well having been held up out the back. She saved ground on the rail for a long way, but her challenge in the straight was delayed as her rider attempted to angle her to the outside and get daylight. The longer trip suited her.

Fire Lily(IRE) finished in front of Up and After last time out, but she was another who got trapped a little wider than ideal, and her stamina ebbed away in the closing stages over this longer trip. Her dam won the Group 2 Prix du Gros-Chene over 5f and it'll be interesting if she has her attentions switched to sprinting now, as she could be useful in that sphere.

Azeville(GER) was caught wide from stall 12 early and had more use made of her than most who swept by her in the closing stages. Had she been ridden with more restraint she would have probably finished in front of some of those that finished ahead of her.

Chica Loca(FR), the only filly in the field making her seasonal reappearance, merely stayed on past beaten horses and was never a threat.

Petite Noblesse(FR) was the disappointment of the race. This was a big step up in class for her from a C&D conditions race, and she showed her relative lack of experience when a little slowly away from the stalls and then getting into a bit of trouble on the turn at halfway. Under pressure early in the straight, she just didn't pick up, and perhaps this was all too much at this stage of her career. She's bred to get further and could easily leave this form behind in time.

Samitar had far too much use made of her in taking on the pacemaker for the lead.

2110a POULE D'ESSAI DES POULAINS (GROUP 1) (3YO COLTS) (TURF) 1m

3:10 (12:00) 3-Y-0 **£214,275** (£85,725; £42,862; £21,412; £10,725)

RPR

1 **Lucayan (FR)**[16] 3-9-2 0 (p) StephanePasquier 5 114
(F Rohaut, France) *midfield on outer: rdn to improve over 2f out: r.o wl ins fnl 1 1/2f to ld last strides* **33/1**

2 snk **Veneto (FR)**[20] 3-9-2 0 ThierryThulliez 2 113
(B De Montzey, France) *led: allowed to dictate stdy pce: over 2 l clr and stl gng wl on turn into st: rdn to increase advantage 2f out: kpt on ins fnl 1 1/2f: hdd last strides* **50/1**

3 snk **Furner's Green (IRE)**[28] 1401 3-9-2 0 JPO'Brien 11 113+
(A P O'Brien, Ire) *hld up in last trio on inner: rdn to improve over 2f out: briefly ct on heels over 1 1/2f out: r.o really strly ins fnl f: wnt 3rd post* **5/1**[3]

4 nse **Amaron**[21] 1553 3-9-2 0 DavyBonilla 3 113
(Andreas Lowe, Germany) *chsd ldrs in 3rd on inner: rdn to improve fr over 2 1/2f out: r.o to chal wl ins fnl f: ct for 3rd post* **25/1**

5 snk **Gregorian (IRE)**[23] 1500 3-9-2 0 WilliamBuick 12 113
(John Gosden) *hld up in last quartet on outer: rdn to improve over 2f out: r.o ins fnl 1 1/2f: wnt 5th post* **25/1**

6 snk **Dabirsim (FR)**[28] 1408 3-9-2 0 ChristopheSoumillon 1 112
(C Ferland, France) *midfield on inner: t.k.h: short of room and forced to check 2f out: swtchd out and rdn to improve over 1 1/2f out: r.o to chal wl ins fnl f: no ex and lost 2 pls fnl 50yds* **6/5**[1]

7 3/4 **Coupe De Ville (IRE)**[8] 1856 3-9-2 0 RichardHughes 6 111
(Richard Hannon) *midfield on inner: rdn over 2f out: outpcd over 1 1/2f out: kpt on ins fnl f: wnt 7th ins fnl 50yds* **14/1**

8 3/4 **Beauvoir (IRE)**[35] 1244 3-9-2 0 Christophe-PatriceLemaire 7 109
(J-C Rouget, France) *prom on outer: rdn to improve 2 1/2f out: wnt 2nd 1 1/2f out: keeping on whn short of room and forced to check wl ins fnl f: nt rcvr and dropped to 8th cl home* **12/1**

9 nk **Dragon Pulse (IRE)**[28] 1408 3-9-2 0 GregoryBenoist 9 108
(M Delzangles, France) *hld up in last pair on outer: rdn to try and improve over 2f out: outpcd over 1f out: plugged on ins fnl f: wnt 9th last strides: nvr able to chal* **3/1**[2]

10 snk **Nutello (USA)**[42] 3-9-2 0 OlivierPeslier 8 108
(C Laffon-Parias, France) *midfield: rdn over 2f out: kpt on tl no ex and fdd ins fnl f: ct for 9th last strides* **16/1**

11 6 **Telwaar**[25] 1453 3-9-2 0 GeraldMosse 10 94
(Peter Chapple-Hyam) *hld up in last: rdn and stl in rr 2f out: no prog and sn btn: eased ins fnl f* **33/1**

12 8 **Vault (IRE)**[28] 1401 3-9-2 0 (b) CO'Donoghue 4 76
(A P O'Brien, Ire) *trckd ldr on outer: rdn to try and chal on turn into st: no ex and wknd over 1 1/2f out: heavily eased ins fnl f* **66/1**

1m 37.11s (-1.29) **Going Correction** +0.175s/f (Good) **12** Ran SP% **124.4**
Speed ratings: **113,112,112,112,112 112,111,110,110,110 104,96**
WIN (incl. 1 euro stake): 28.00. PLACES: 5.80, 16.80, 5.90. DF: 333.30. SF: 681.60.
Owner A Mouknass & Pandora Stud LLC **Bred** J-P Colombu **Trained** Sauvagnon, France

FOCUS

A very messy race, impossible to rate positively given the bunch finish and pacemaker finishing second. Although the winning time was almost identical to that recorded by the fillies in the Pouliches, the leader went 0.45sec quicker for the first 600m, while the final 200m was covered in a time 0.34sec slower.

NOTEBOOK

Lucayan(FR), unlike some in the race, enjoyed a trouble-free passage down the outside and was just able to put his nose in front near the line. Winner of a Listed race at Toulouse last time out, he looked to have it to do in this company, but he was aided by some his rivals experiencing misfortune, and he took full advantage. His dam won at up to 1m4f so there's reason to believe he'll get further, and the Prix du Jockey Club is the logical next step, although the St James's Palace Stakes will no doubt also be considered.

Veneto(FR) had been leased by the owner of Dabirsim to run as a pacemaker for the keen-going favourite. Winner of a conditions race over this C&D last month, he's clearly an able performer in his own right (beaten a length by Dabirsim in the Group 1 Prix Jean-Luc Lagardere last back-end), but he couldn't quite last home having set sensible fractions.

Furner's Green(IRE), winner of the Guineas Trial at Leopardstown, was unlucky not to win as he was hampered and had his momentum checked by Dabirsim just as he was beginning to role 2f out. Finishing strongest of all, the line came too soon for him, but it was a good effort, and very saddening that he broke down soon after the line.

Amaron, a dual Group 3 winner in Germany, enjoyed a ground-saving trip throughout, leading the main pack behind the two pacemakers, and as such he had no excuses.

Gregorian(IRE) put up a noteworthy effort considering he only won a Newbury handicap off 88 last time out. Trapped wide from stall 12, Trakus data would no doubt have him having travelled further than anything else in the race, and there has further improvement in him. Perhaps the St James's Palace Stakes will come into consideration now.

Dabirsim(FR), despite having a pacemaker in the line-up, still didn't settle. Going for a run up the inside with 2f to run, he got hampered and cut off by Amaron. Regaining his momentum, he initially quickened up well before flattening out slightly and running out of room once again close home. No doubt Soumillon will get plenty of criticism, but the colt is not a straightforward ride, and the likelihood is that he's not a miler. He's a strong traveller with a turn of foot, but this trip just stretches him, and dropping back to sprinting (he's in the July Cup) could be the making of him.

Coupe De Ville(IRE), fifth in the English 2000 Guineas, tracked the favourite through on the rail and kept on well enough, but he just looks a little short of this class.

Beauvoir(IRE), who was dropping back from 1m2f, would have finished closer had he not run into the back of the weakening Veneto close home. Eased right off, his finishing position doesn't do him justice.

Dragon Pulse(IRE), who beat Dabirsim in the Prix de Fontainebleau on his reappearance, never got involved and was desperately disappointing. He was too keen through the early stages and could never land a blow from off the pace.

Nutello(USA) was taking a big step up in class and wasn't up to it, but a longer trip should suit him in future.

2112a PRIX DE SAINT-GEORGES (GROUP 3) (3YO+) (TURF) 5f (S)

4:15 (12:00) 3-Y-0+ **£33,333** (£13,333; £10,000; £6,666; £3,333)

RPR

1 **Beyond Desire**[23] 1494 5-8-13 0 .... JamieSpencer 11 112
(Roger Varian) *mde all: broke wl to get across fr wd draw: rdn to go over 2 l clr 2 1/2f out: kpt on wl ins fnl 1 1/2f: diminishing advantage thrght fnl f: strly pressed cl home: jst hld on all out* **10/1**

2 *shd* **Monsieur Joe (IRE)**[43] 1146 5-9-0 0 .... WilliamBuick 6 113
(Robert Cowell) *midfld: rdn to improve over 2 1/2f out: wnt 2nd over 1f out: r.o strly ins fnl f to chal cl home: jst failed* **7/1**

3 *1* **Calahorra (FR)**[27] 1426 3-8-4 0 .... ThierryJarnet 1 104
(C Baillet, France) *hld up towards rr on nr side rail: smooth prog into midfield over 2f out: rdn to go 3rd over 1f out: kpt on wout matching front pair ins fnl f* **25/1**

4 *1* **Huma Bird**[27] 1426 3-8-4 0 ow2 .... MickaelBarzalona 4 100
(H-A Pantall, France) *midfield on nr side rail: rdn to improve 2 1/2f out: outpcd by front trio ins fnl f: kpt on wl for 4th* **12/1**

5 *1* **Wizz Kid (IRE)**[211] 6858 4-9-5 0 .... GeraldMosse 7 107
(Robert Collet, France) *hld up towards rr on outer: rdn and outpcd 2 1/2f out: r.o to take 5th ins fnl f: nt pce to chal* **9/2[1]**

6 *1* **Zantenda**[28] 1407 3-8-8 0 ....(b[1]) OlivierPeslier 2 97
(F Head, France) *hld up in last pair on outer: rdn and outpcd over 2f out: r.o to go 6th ins fnl f: nrst fin* **5/1[2]**

7 *1* **Fred Lalloupet**[19] 1593 5-9-2 0 .... GregoryBenoist 8 97
(D Smaga, France) *midfield: rdn over 2f out: no ex over 1f out: fdd ins fnl f* **5/1[2]**

8 *2 1/2* **Mar Adentro (FR)**[64] 875 6-9-2 0 ....(p) ChristopheSoumillon 10 88
(R Chotard, France) *prom on outer: stl gng wl in bhd clr ldr over 2f out: rdn and no rspnse over 1f out: fdd ins fnl f* **6/1[3]**

9 *shd* **Malikayah (IRE)**[28] 1409 4-8-13 0 .... UmbertoRispoli 3 84
(D Camuffo, Italy) *hld up towards rr: rdn over 2 1/2f out: no ex and btn over 1f out: eased ins fnl f* **20/1**

10 *1* **Captain Chop (FR)**[19] 1593 4-9-0 0 ....(b) FlavienPrat 5 82
(D Guillemin, France) *hld up in last: rdn and outpcd 3f out: nvr a factor* **20/1**

0 **Sabratah**[44] 1126 4-8-10 0 .... FabriceVeron 9
(H-A Pantall, France) *chsd clr ldr: rdn 2 1/2f out: no ex and btn over 1 1/2f out: heavily eased and dropped to last ins fnl f* **6/1[3]**

57.03s (0.73) **Going Correction** +0.475s/f (Yiel)
WFA 3 from 4yo+ 9lb **11** Ran SP% **122.7**
Speed ratings: **113,112,111,109,108 106,104,100,100,99**
WIN (incl. 1 euro stake): 19.70. PLACES: 5.90, 2.60, 6.50. DF: 30.90. SF: 64.50.
Owner Clipper Logistics **Bred** Pinnacle Bloodstock **Trained** Newmarket, Suffolk

NOTEBOOK

Beyond Desire looked to have a tricky draw but she had conditions to suit, pinged the gates and made every yard, battling on well when strongly challenged by Monsieur Joe in the closing stages. She's a real speedster and a sharp or flat track is always likely to see her at her best. She's in the Temple Stakes, and that looks a suitable race for her.
Monsieur Joe(IRE) looked an improved performer in Dubai and this was a pleasing return to action in Europe. He only came up narrowly short and will surely break his Group race duck soon.
Calahorra(FR), who did best of the 3yos, had a good draw and picked up well from off the pace to take third. The drying ground might not have been in her favour.
Huma Bird posted a solid effort, but she did have the advantage of the rail throughout.
Wizz Kid(IRE) faced a stiff task on her reappearance conceding weight all round. Given a patient ride, she was staying on at the finish, and this ought to have blown the cobwebs away.
Zantenda, whose previous four starts had come over a mile, was an intriguing contender dropped back to the minimum trip with blinkers fitted for the first time, as there's plenty of speed in her pedigree. Worst away from the stalls, she lacked the early pace required, but she travelled strongly towards the rear and, under what looked something of an educational ride, was eating up the ground late without really being asked a serious question. She will be interesting over 6f on this evidence and certainly has the ability to make her mark at the sprinting game.

2111 - 2117a (Foreign Racing) - See Raceform Interactive

[1246]REDCAR (L-H)

Monday, May 14

OFFICIAL GOING: Soft (good to soft in places; 6.5)
Wind: Moderate across Weather: Cloudy with sunny periods

2118 HAMBLETON RACING SUPPORTS BARNEY'S CHALLENGE H'CAP 1m 1f

2:00 (2:00) (Class 5) (0-70,70) 3-Y-0 **£2,264** (£673; £336; £168) **Stalls** Low

Form RPR

-052 **1** **Priestley's Reward (IRE)**[28] 1413 3-9-4 **67** ....(v[1]) RobertWinston 4 77+
(Mrs K Burke) *trckd ldrs: smooth hdwy 4f out: cl up wl over 2f out: led on bit wl over 1f out: sn pushed clr: comf* **5/1[3]**

01- **2** *1 1/4* **Eastern Destiny**[273] 5104 3-9-2 **70** .... ShaneBKelly[(5)] 1 76
(Richard Fahey) *in tch: hdwy over 4f out effrt on inner and nt clr run 2f out: sn swtchd rt and rdn to chse wnr ent fnl f: kpt on* **9/2[2]**

56-0 **3** *1 1/4* **Remember Rocky**[23] 1519 3-8-7 **56** oh1 ....(p) SilvestreDeSousa 3 57
(Steve Gollings) *in tch: pushed along and lost pl 1/2-way: hdwy over 3f out: rdn to chse ldrs 2f out: kpt on same pce appr fnl f* **8/1**

0-43 **4** *8* **Chester Aristocrat**[16] 1661 3-9-6 **69** .... GrahamGibbons 8 52
(Eric Alston) *in tch: hdwy over 3f out: rdn along 2f out: sn one pce* **7/2[1]**

50-0 **5** *2 1/4* **Twin Ivan (IRE)**[19] 1595 3-8-6 **60** .... DeanHeslop[(5)] 5 38
(Marjorie Fife) *bhd: hdwy on wd outside 3f out: kpt on u.p fnl 2f: nvr nr ldrs* **40/1**

045 **6** *nk* **Adili (IRE)**[41] 1173 3-9-2 **68** .... PaulPickard[(3)] 12 46
(Brian Ellison) *hld up towards rr: hdwy wl over 2f out: sn rdn and kpt on fnl f: nvr nr ldrs* **16/1**

020- **7** *1 1/2* **Bedlam**[210] 6911 3-9-1 **64** ....(p) DavidAllan 2 38
(Tim Easterby) *chsd ldr: rdn along 4f out: wknd over 3f out* **16/1**

-100 **8** *1/2* **Wolf Spirit (IRE)**[16] 1661 3-9-1 **67** .... DaleSwift[(3)] 11 40
(Ruth Carr) *sn led: pushed along 3f out: rdn and hung lft jst over 2f out: sn hdd & wknd* **16/1**

65-5 **9** *1 3/4* **No Dominion (IRE)**[25] 1479 3-9-1 **64** .... PaulMulrennan 7 34
(James Given) *prom: effrt 3f out: rdn to ld briefly 2f out: sn hdd & wknd* **9/2[2]**

0046 **10** *10* **Burning Passion**[20] 1590 3-8-4 **56** oh3 .... JulieBurke[(3)] 6
(Michael Easterby) *a in rr* **50/1**

53-4 **11** *34* **Be Calm**[7] 1918 3-8-7 **56** .... PaddyAspell 10
(Michael Easterby) *dwlt: a in rr: lame* **16/1**

2m 0.39s (7.39) **Going Correction** +0.80s/f (Soft) **11** Ran SP% **114.3**
Speed ratings (Par 99): **99,97,96,89,87 87,86,85,84,75 44**
toteswingers:1&2:£4.40, 1&3:£11.90, 2&3:£6.50 CSF £26.90 CT £153.47 TOTE £6.90: £2.20, £1.50, £3.10; EX 33.70.
Owner P Dean & Mrs E Burke **Bred** Michael Mullins **Trained** Middleham Moor, N Yorks

FOCUS
A modest 3yo handicap with plenty stepping up in distance on their handicap bows.
Be Calm Official explanation: trainer's rep said filly finished lame

2119 BETFRED IS BACKING BARNEY H'CAP 7f

2:30 (2:30) (Class 4) (0-85,83) 3-Y-0+ **£4,075** (£1,212; £606; £303) **Stalls** Centre

Form RPR

0-21 **1** **No Poppy (IRE)**[16] 1650 4-9-2 **77** .... AdamCarter[(5)] 2 81
(Tim Easterby) *trckd ldrs: hdwy over 2f out: rdn to chal and edgd rt ent fnl f: drvn to ld last 75yds: gamely* **9/2[2]**

21-0 **2** *hd* **Little Jimmy Odsox (IRE)**[25] 1476 4-9-8 **78** .... DavidAllan 8 81
(Tim Easterby) *in tch: hdwy wl over 2f out: rdn to chse ldrs and n.m.r over 1f out: swtchd lft and drvn ent fnl f: sn ev ch: edgd lft and kpt on towards fin* **17/2**

-003 **3** *nse* **Beckermet (IRE)**[9] 1844 10-9-10 **83** .... DaleSwift[(3)] 7 86
(Ruth Carr) *cl up: led wl over 1f out: sn rdn: hdd last 75yds: no ex* **11/2[3]**

1500 **4** *hd* **Aquarian Spirit**[35] 1249 5-8-13 **76** .... GeorgeChaloner[(7)] 3 78
(Richard Fahey) *s.i.s and bhd: hdwy wl over 2f out: sn rdn along: styd on wl u.p fnl f* **12/1**

50-0 **5** *1 3/4* **Diman Waters (IRE)**[33] 1293 5-9-2 **72** .... GrahamGibbons 6 70
(Eric Alston) *led: rdn along over 2f out: hdd wl over 1f out: grad wknd* **16/1**

040- **6** *1 3/4* **Robert The Painter (IRE)**[219] 6704 4-9-9 **79** .... DanielTudhope 1 72
(David O'Meara) *hld up in tch: pushed along 3f out: rdn 2f out and sn no imp* **9/2[2]**

1-36 **7** *1* **Aerodynamic (IRE)**[43] 1156 5-9-6 **76** .... PaddyAspell 5 67
(Michael Easterby) *hld up: sme hdwy and in tch wl over 2f: sn rdn and btn wl over 1f out* **2/1[1]**

540- **8** *8* **Koo And The Gang (IRE)**[139] 7339 5-9-3 **76** .... PaulPickard[(3)] 4 46
(Brian Ellison) *chsd ldng pair: rdn along 3f out: sn wknd* **8/1**

1m 27.91s (3.41) **Going Correction** +0.375s/f (Good) **8** Ran SP% **120.3**
Speed ratings (Par 105): **95,94,94,94,92 90,89,80**
toteswingers:1&2:£4.40, 1&3:£3.90, 2&3:£4.70 CSF £44.27 CT £221.39 TOTE £5.70: £1.60, £2.50, £2.10; EX 19.90.
Owner Exors Of The Late Mrs P M Easterby **Bred** Michael O'Mahony **Trained** Great Habton, N Yorks

■ Stewards' Enquiry : Dale Swift four-day ban: used whip above the permitted level (May 28-31)

FOCUS
A tight 72-83 handicap with four horses flashing over the finishing line almost as one.

2120 GO RACING IN YORKSHIRE BACKS BARNEY CLAIMING STKS 6f

3:00 (3:05) (Class 6) 3-Y-O+ **£1,704** (£503; £251) **Stalls** Centre

Form RPR

-361 **1** **Zomerlust**[35] 1248 10-9-6 75 ....(v) MichaelO'Connell 3 73
(John Quinn) *led: pushed along and jnd over 2f out: rdn and hdd wl over 1f out: rallied to ld again ins fnl f: kpt on wl* **5/2[2]**

5-03 **2** *3/4* **Ursula (IRE)**[8] 1876 6-9-0 72 .... RobertWinston 6 64
(Mrs K Burke) *in tch: hdwy 1/2-way: jnd ldr over 2f out: led wl over 1f out: rdn and edgd lft jst ins fnl f: sn hdd and one pce* **3/1[3]**

5-06 **3** *3 1/4* **Baybshambles (IRE)**[25] 1480 8-9-3 55 .... DaleSwift[(3)] 5 60
(Ron Barr) *chsd ldrs: hdwy 2f out: sn rdn and kpt on same pce fnl f* **28/1**

442- **4** *1/2* **Mango Music**[262] 5442 9-8-12 77 ....(p) SilvestreDeSousa 1 50
(Geoffrey Harker) *hld up: smooth hdwy to trck ldng pair over 2f out: rdn over 1f out: sn btn* **7/4[1]**

-001 **5** *3* **Qubuh (IRE)**[8] 1876 4-9-7 64 .... TonyHamilton 2 50
(Linda Stubbs) *cl up: rdn along over 2f out: sn wknd* **6/1**

0-05 **6** *1 1/4* **Andrasta**[3] 2032 7-8-5 49 .... MatthewHopkins[(7)] 7 37
(Alan Berry) *prom: rdn along 1/2-way: sn wknd* **125/1**

1m 13.51s (1.71) **Going Correction** +0.375s/f (Good) **6** Ran SP% **108.5**
Speed ratings (Par 101): **103,102,97,97,93 91**
toteswingers:1&2:£1.80, 1&3:£6.40, 2&3:£5.50 CSF £9.64 TOTE £3.00: £1.20, £1.60; EX 8.60.Mango Music was claimed by David Thompson for £5,000.
Owner Mrs S Quinn **Bred** The Lavington Stud **Trained** Settrington, N Yorks

FOCUS
Some familiar old faces in this 6f claimer.

2121 REDCAR RACECOURSE SUPPORTS RACING WELFARE MAIDEN FILLIES' STKS 6f

3:30 (3:31) (Class 5) 3-Y-O+ **£2,264** (£673; £336; £168) **Stalls** Centre

Form RPR

1 **Isola Verde** 3-8-12 0 .... JackMitchell 8 71+
(James Fanshawe) *trckd ldrs: hdwy on outer 1/2-way: led over 1f out: pushed out* **11/2[2]**

56 **2** *2 1/4* **Elegant Girl (IRE)**[23] 1521 3-8-12 0 .... DavidAllan 7 62
(Tim Easterby) *prom: cl up 1/2-way: led wl over 2f out: rdn and hdd over 1f out: kpt on same pce fnl f* **8/1[3]**

22-2 **3** *1* **Shaleek**[17] 1637 3-8-12 76 .... NeilCallan 5 59
(Roger Varian) *in tch: pushed along to chse ldrs over 2f out: sn rdn: swtchd rt and drvn over 1f out: sn no imp* **2/11[1]**

4 *1 1/2* **Mon Duchess** 4-9-8 0 .... DuranFentiman 2 58?
(Lawrence Mullaney) *cl up: led briefly 1/2-way: sn hdd and rdn: kpt on same pce fr wl over 1f out* **25/1**

0 **5** *3 1/4* **Toodeloo**[34] 1274 3-8-12 0 .... PaulMulrennan 4 44
(Kevin Ryan) *in rr and green: pushed along and wl outpcd 1/2-way: sme hdwy fnl 2f:* **16/1**

6 *1 1/2* **Dolly Diva** 3-8-12 0 .... MickyFenton 3 39
(Paul Midgley) *s.i.s: a in rr* **20/1**

56-0 **7** *6* **Misshollygolightly**[81] 662 4-9-8 37 .... DanielTudhope 6 24
(Brian Baugh) *dwlt: a in rr* **33/1**

505- **8** *9* **Never In (IRE)**[230] 6425 3-8-5 45 .... MatthewHopkins[(7)] 1
(Alan Berry) *led: rdn along and hdd 1/2-way: sn wknd* **50/1**

1m 14.73s (2.93) **Going Correction** +0.375s/f (Good)
WFA 3 from 4yo 10lb **8** Ran SP% **130.5**
Speed ratings (Par 100): **95,92,90,88,84 82,74,62**
toteswingers:1&2:£1.90, 1&3:£1.10, 2&3:£1.60 CSF £50.74 TOTE £6.20: £1.30, £2.20, £1.02; EX 50.70.
Owner Jan and Peter Hopper **Bred** Jan & Peter Hopper **Trained** Newmarket, Suffolk

FOCUS
What looked the proverbial penalty kick for the long odds-on favourite in this fillies' maiden turned out otherwise.

2122 STAN JAMES IS SUPPORTING BARNEY'S CHALLENGE (S) STKS 5f
4:00 (4:00) (Class 6) 3-Y-0+ **£1,704** (£503; £251) **Stalls** Centre

Form RPR
200- **1** **Fol Hollow (IRE)**[200] [7116] 7-9-12 80 AdrianNicholls 2 73
(David Nicholls) *led: rdn along wl over 1f out: edgd rt ent fnl f: sn drvn and hdd last 75yds: rallied to ld again nr line* **5/2**[2]
-244 **2** *hd* **Angelo Poliziano**[40] [1187] 6-9-12 73 (p) DuranFentiman 6 72
(George Foster) *trckd wnr: hdwy 2f out: swtchd lft ent fnl f and sn rdn to chal: drvn to ld last 75yds: hdd and no ex nr line* **6/1**[3]
-006 **3** *2 ¾* **Pivotal Prospect**[8] [1881] 4-9-2 35 ShaneBKelly[(5)] 5 57
(Tracy Waggott) *dwlt and in rr: pushed along 1/2-way: rdn and hdwy wl over 1f out: kpt on same pce* **33/1**
2120 **4** *5* **Master Of Disguise**[17] [1643] 6-9-12 75 (t) PaulMulrennan 7 44
(Brian Baugh) *chsd ldng pair: rdn along over 2f out: btn wl over 1f out* **4/7**[1]

1m 0.58s (1.98) **Going Correction** +0.375s/f (Good) **4** Ran SP% **109.5**
Speed ratings (Par 101): **99,98,94,86**
CSF £15.20 TOTE £2.70; EX 11.20.There was no bid for the winner.
Owner Middleham Park Racing Iii **Bred** Dan O'Brien **Trained** Sessay, N Yorks

FOCUS
A depleted field for this 5f selling race.
Master Of Disguise Official explanation: jockey said gelding never travelled

2123 GR RACING IS BACKING BARNEY MEDIAN AUCTION MAIDEN STKS 5f
4:30 (4:30) (Class 6) 2-Y-0 **£1,704** (£503; £251) **Stalls** Centre

Form RPR
1 **Poppy Bond** 2-8-12 0 DuranFentiman 7 64+
(Chris Fairhurst) *wnt rt s and bhd: hdwy wl over 1f out: styd on strly ins fnl f to ld nr fin* **16/1**
2 *½* **Liber** 2-9-3 0 LukeMorris 3 67+
(Sir Mark Prescott Bt) *trckd ldrs: hdwy 2f out: rdn to chal ins fnl f: led briefly 50yds out: hdd nr line* **7/4**[1]
4 **3** *½* **Hellolini**[20] [1579] 2-8-12 0 RobertWinston 2 60
(Robin Bastiman) *led: rdn along wl over 1f out: drvn ent fnl f: hdd and no ex last 50yds* **20/1**
0 **4** *1* **Relight My Fire**[7] [1911] 2-9-3 0 DavidAllan 6 62
(Tim Easterby) *chsd ldrs: hdwy 2f out: sn rdn and one pce ins fnl f* **8/1**
0 **5** *2 ¼* **Roland**[12] [1753] 2-9-3 0 PaulMulrennan 5 54+
(Kevin Ryan) *prom: chsd ldng pair 2f out: sn rdn and wknd over 1f out* **8/1**
6 *3 ¾* **Moss Quito (IRE)** 2-9-3 0 DanielTudhope 4 40
(David O'Meara) *chsd ldr: cl up 1/2-way: rdn along 2f out: sn wknd* **15/2**[3]
02 **7** *¾* **Mount Seymour (IRE)**[9] [1861] 2-9-3 0 SilvestreDeSousa 1 38
(Nigel Tinkler) *hld up in rr: sme hdwy over 2f out: sn rdn and wknd over 1f out* **5/2**[2]

1m 1.2s (2.60) **Going Correction** +0.375s/f (Good) **7** Ran SP% **109.6**
Speed ratings (Par 91): **94,93,92,90,87 81,80**
toteswingers:1&2:£6.30, 1&3:£20.90, 2&3:£8.50 CSF £40.91 TOTE £15.80: £8.10, £1.40; EX 57.90.
Owner North Cheshire Trading & Storage Ltd **Bred** North Cheshire Trading And Storage Ltd **Trained** Middleham Moor, N Yorks

FOCUS
Probably a weak median auction 2yo maiden and an unlikely winner in the first half of the race. They finished in a heap in a slow time.

NOTEBOOK
Poppy Bond, from a family that has stood this yard in good stead over the years, looks weak at present. She gave them several lengths at the start but came from last to first with a strong run in the final furlong and a half. She looks sure to improve given more time. (op 14-1)
Liber, a good-bodied newcomer, is bred for speed. Green to post, he finally mastered the pacesetter only to be mugged near the line. He raced on the wide outside and the experience will not be lost on him. (op 9-4)
Hellolini, from a yard going great guns at present, was last of four on the all-weather at Southwell when making her debut in a novice event. She knew her job this time and was only worn down in the closing stages.
Relight My Fire had clearly learned from his debut and was putting in some good work at the line. He will improve again. (op 15-2)
Roland, a well-made type, looked to be still carrying plenty of condition. He too stepped up on his debut run and should improve again. (op 9-1)
Moss Quito(IRE) showed bags of toe before tiring and he will come on for this first run. (op 8-1)
Mount Seymour(IRE), who put up a RPR of 69 when runner-up second time at Thirsk, was most disappointing, never really figuring at any stage. (op 2-1)
T/Plt: £87.00 to a £1 stake. Pool:£60,020.30 - 503.26 winning tickets T/Qpdt: £24.80 to a £1 stake. Pool:£4,394.08 - 130.60 winning tickets JR

1934 WINDSOR (R-H)
Monday, May 14

OFFICIAL GOING: Soft (good to soft in places; 5.9)
Inner rail of Straight dolled out 8yds from 6f to the intersection. Top bend dolled out 7yds adding 27yds to races of a mile and over.
Wind: Light, behind Weather: Overcast becoming bright

2124 MIRROR PUNTERS CLUB MAIDEN FILLIES' STKS 5f 10y
5:40 (5:40) (Class 4) 2-Y-0 **£3,428** (£1,020; £509; £254) **Stalls** Centre

Form RPR
1 **Hairy Rocket** 2-9-0 0 RyanMoore 2 89+
(Richard Hannon) *w ldr: led 1/2-way and grabbed far rail sn after: shkn up over 1f out: drew clr* **6/1**
2 *5* **Miss Diva** 2-9-0 0 RichardHughes 5 71+
(Richard Hannon) *cl up: trckd ldng pair after 2f: reminder 1f out: chsd clr wnr ins fnl f: no imp and jst hld on for 2nd* **17/2**
3 *nse* **Fantacise** 2-9-0 0 MickaelBarzalona 4 71+
(Brian Meehan) *dwlt: pushed along firmly in 6th and nt on terms w ldrs: prog fr 1/2-way: styd on wl to take 3rd nr fin and nrly ct runner-up* **9/2**[2]
3 **4** *1* **Rio's Pearl**[8] [1891] 2-9-0 0 JimCrowley 1 67
(Ralph Beckett) *led to 1/2-way: pressed wnr to over 1f out: sn lft bhd: one pce and lost 2 pls ins fnl f* **6/4**[1]
6 **5** *3 ¼* **Edged Out**[24] [1499] 2-9-0 0 DavidProbert 7 56
(Bryn Palling) *cl up: steadily fdd fnl 2f* **5/1**[3]
6 *2 ½* **Faluka (IRE)** 2-9-0 0 (t) JimmyFortune 8 47
(Paul Cole) *rn green: sn bdly outpcd: virtually t.o 1/2-way: plugged on* **12/1**
7 *4* **Poetic Verse** 2-9-0 0 JamesMillman 6 32
(Rod Millman) *rn green and bdly outpcd in last pair: virtually t.o 1/2-way: penny dropped ins fnl f and fin w a flourish* **100/1**
8 *2 ¾* **Harleys Rocket** 2-9-0 0 KirstyMilczarek 3 22
(Brendan Powell) *t.k.h: cl up 2f: sn wknd* **33/1**

1m 1.88s (1.58) **Going Correction** +0.45s/f (Yiel) **8** Ran SP% **111.3**
Speed ratings (Par 92): **105,97,96,95,90 86,79,75**
toteswingers:1&2:£4.40, 1&3:£3.70, 2&3:£4.20 CSF £52.19 TOTE £6.60: £2.30, £1.70, £2.00; EX 24.00 Trifecta £206.70 Pool: £9,421.74 - 33.72 winning units..
Owner Rockcliffe Stud **Bred** Rockcliffe Stud **Trained** East Everleigh, Wilts

FOCUS
After a dry night the going was changed to soft, good to soft in places (from soft). The straight was dolled out eight yards from 6f to the intersection, and was full width thereafter. The top bend was dolled out seven yards from the normal inner configuration, adding 27 yards to race distances 1m and over. This opening maiden has been won by an above-average filly the last two years, 2011 Angels Will Fall and 2010 Rimth. The winner this time has been rated to the top end of the race averages.

NOTEBOOK
Hairy Rocket impressed with the style of victory. A daughter of Pivotal with a speedy pedigree, she tracked the leader and headed towards the far rail before pulling well clear of her rivals. She may now be targeted at the National Stakes at Sandown and could develop into a Royal Ascot filly. (tchd 11-2)
Miss Diva, a 23,000gns February foal is bred to be quick and made it a 1-2 for the yard. This was a promising debut although she proved no match for the winner. (op 8-1)
Fantacise is a half-sister to Royal Ascot winners Romantic Myth and Romantic Liason and was the subject of a positive mention in her trainer's Stable Tour. She was a bit fresh in the preliminaries and was slowly away but picked up well inside the final furlong, just failing to snatch second on the line. Another daughter of Pivotal, she handled the conditions well and shaped very much as though she would improve considerably for the experience. (op 7-2)
Rio's Pearl, who had made an encouraging debut when third at Salisbury, set a decent decent gallop but was one-paced late on. (op 2-1 tchd 9-4)
Edged Out didn't build on the promise she had shown when fifth in a race that has produced several winners on her debut. (op 9-2 tchd 7-2)
Faluka(IRE) wore a tongue-tie on her debut and was outpaced from an early stage. (op 11-1 tchd 10-1 and 14-1)

2125 DAVISBAKERYCARIBBEAN.COM MEDIAN AUCTION MAIDEN STKS 1m 2f 7y
6:10 (6:11) (Class 5) 3-5-Y-0 **£2,264** (£673; £336; £168) **Stalls** Centre

Form RPR
1 **Sir John Hawkwood (IRE)** 3-8-13 0 RyanMoore 2 92+
(Sir Michael Stoute) *settled in rr early: prog 1/2-way: clsng whn n.m.r over 2f out and swtchd lft: shkn up and r.o to ld over 1f out: sn clr* **5/1**[2]
03- **2** *5* **Bank Bonus**[224] [6588] 3-8-13 0 JimmyFortune 5 80+
(Andrew Balding) *cl up: led after 4f: rdn and tried to kick on over 3f out: hdd over 1f out: styd on but no ch w wnr* **10/11**[1]
3 *9* **Stock Hill Fair**[30] 4-10-0 0 FergusSweeney 3 62
(Brendan Powell) *sn prom: rdn 3f out: hanging lft over 2f out: sn lft bhd by front pair: plugged on to hold modest 3rd nr fin* **18/1**
4 **4** *nk* **Joe The Coat**[35] [1265] 3-8-13 0 TedDurcan 1 61
(Mark H Tompkins) *hld up in last early: pushed along and prog over 3f out: one pce but pressed for modest 3rd fnl f* **7/1**[3]
4 **5** *hd* **Sarmatian Knight (IRE)**[34] [1270] 3-8-10 0 RyanPowell[(3)] 8 61
(Ian Williams) *led 4f: styd prom: rdn and lft bhd by ldng pair fr 2f out* **25/1**
6 **6** *¾* **Sporting Gold (IRE)**[11] [1793] 3-8-13 0 TomQueally 4 60+
(Roger Varian) *in tch: dropped to rr over 3f out: pushed along and kpt on one pce after* **12/1**
0- **7** *3 ½* **Astra Hall**[173] [7521] 3-8-8 0 JimCrowley 10 48
(Ralph Beckett) *w ldrs: shkn up and lost pl over 2f out: steadily fdd* **14/1**
8 *9* **Scarborough Rock** 3-8-13 0 EddieAhern 7 35
(Tom Symonds) *t.k.h early: cl up: lost pl and shkn up 3f out: wknd* **66/1**
5- **9** *16* **Princely Sum (IRE)**[206] [6983] 3-8-13 0 (t) WilliamCarson 9
(Stuart Williams) *in tch tl wknd 4f out: t.o* **22/1**
10 *32* **Mellor** 3-8-13 0 ChrisCatlin 6
(Chris Wall) *rdn in last bef 1/2-way: wl t.o* **50/1**

2m 13.34s (4.64) **Going Correction** +0.50s/f (Yiel) **10** Ran SP% **112.8**
WFA 3 from 4yo 15lb
Speed ratings (Par 103): **101,97,89,89,89 88,86,78,66,40**
toteswingers:1&2:£1.70, 1&3:£18.80, 2&3:£4.80 CSF £9.22 TOTE £4.70: £1.20, £1.30, £2.20; EX 12.80 Trifecta £75.30 Pool: £6,415.11 - 63.03 winning units..
Owner Ballymacoll Stud **Bred** Ballymacoll Stud Farm Ltd **Trained** Newmarket, Suffolk

FOCUS
An interesting maiden which was run at an honest pace, the runners raced up the centre of the track before heading to the far rail. The first two, who pulled well clear, look above average.

2126 DAVISBAKERYCARIBBEAN.COM H'CAP 1m 2f 7y
6:40 (6:33) (Class 5) (0-75,73) 3-Y-0 **£2,264** (£673; £336; £168) **Stalls** Centre

Form RPR
506- **1** **Swift Cat**[194] [7222] 3-8-13 **65** JimCrowley 1 71
(John Best) *hld up in rr: prog far side over 2f out: drvn to chal over 1f out: led gp and overall ldr last 100yds: hld on* **33/1**
000- **2** *hd* **Burnham**[206] [6994] 3-8-10 **62** RobertHavlin 2 68
(Hughie Morrison) *trckd ldrs: prog far side 3f out: drvn to chal over 1f out: upsides ins fnl f: styd on: jst hld* **11/2**[3]
05-5 **3** *¾* **Drummond**[33] [1322] 3-9-5 **71** AdamKirby 6 75
(Clive Cox) *led: styd alone nr side in st: probably stl overall ldr tl wandered u.p ins fnl f: kpt on* **11/2**[3]
6-42 **4** *½* **Cyrus Sod**[19] [1606] 3-9-7 **73** RyanMoore 7 76
(Ed Dunlop) *trckd ldrs: rdn 4f out: pressed far side ldr over 2f out: led gp over 1f out: hdd and no ex ins fnl f* **3/1**[1]
26-2 **5** *10* **Good Luck Charm**[13] [1728] 3-9-3 **69** TomQueally 3 52
(Gary Moore) *hld up in last: prog over 4f out: grabbed far side rail in st and led gp 3f out to over 1f out: wknd* **10/1**
430- **6** *¾* **Buster Brown (IRE)**[206] [6986] 3-9-6 **72** JimmyFortune 8 54
(James Given) *pressed ldr: led main gp to far side in st: hdd & wknd 3f out* **9/2**[2]
16-0 **7** *6* **Netley Marsh**[13] [1728] 3-9-4 **70** RichardHughes 4 40
(Richard Hannon) *prom: shkn up 4f out: ploughed lone furrow down centre fnl 3f: sn bhd* **8/1**

05-1 **8** 2 1/2 **Northern Territory (IRE)**[13] 1740 3-8-12 **64**.................... PatCosgrave 5 29
(Jim Boyle) *t.k.h early: hld up in last trio: wknd 3f out: sn bhd* **11/2**[3]
2m 15.01s (6.31) **Going Correction** +0.50s/f (Yiel) **8** Ran SP% **112.5**
Speed ratings (Par 99): **94,93,93,92,84 84,79,77**
toteswingers:1&2:£5.30, 1&3:£7.50, 2&3:£6.50 CSF £197.26 CT £1165.64 TOTE £26.00: £5.40, £2.80, £2.60; EX 271.90 TRIFECTA Not won..
Owner SN Racing III **Bred** S Nunn **Trained** Hucking, Kent
■ Stewards' Enquiry : Adam Kirby two-day ban: used whip above permitted level (May 28-29)

FOCUS
An open 3yo handicap in which none of the runners had been tried over the trip. The majority of the field headed towards the far rail while Netley Marsh ran up the centre of the track and Drummond raced alone up the stands' rail. The pace was muddling and the 33/1 outsider came out on top.
Swift Cat Official explanation: trainer's rep said, regarding apparent improvement in form, that it had been gelded since its last run, had benefited from the longer distance and had settled.

2127 SKY BET STKS (LISTED RACE) (C&G) (REGISTERED AS THE ROYAL WINDSOR STAKES) 1m 67y
7:10 (7:10) (Class 1) 3-Y-0+ **£18,714** (£7,095; £3,550; £1,768; £887) **Stalls** Low

Form RPR
02-1 **1** **Tullius (IRE)**[9] 1854 4-9-2 99.. JimmyFortune 4 115+
(Andrew Balding) *hld up in 4th: prog to go 2nd 2f out: hrd rdn to cl over 1f out: sustained effrt to ld last 100yds* **5/2**[2]
12-5 **2** 1 1/4 **Skilful**[12] 1749 4-9-2 105.. WilliamBuick 5 112
(John Gosden) *led at gd pce: had nrest rivals in trble over 2f out: drvn fnl f: hdd and nt qckn last 100yds* **7/4**[1]
6312 **3** 5 **Memory Cloth**[9] 1854 5-9-2 95.. BarryMcHugh 2 101
(Brian Ellison) *mostly chsd ldr to 2f out: steadily lft bhd u.p* **3/1**[3]
01-4 **4** 3 **King Torus (IRE)**[12] 1749 4-9-6 108.. RichardHughes 1 98
(Richard Hannon) *trckd ldng pair: rdn 3f out: steadily wknd fnl 2f* **11/2**
04-0 **5** 2 3/4 **Albaqaa**[25] 1471 7-9-2 99.. PatCosgrave 3 87
(P J O'Gorman) *hld up in last pair: nt qckn over 2f out: rdn and wknd over 1f out* **22/1**
1m 46.42s (1.72) **Going Correction** +0.50s/f (Yiel) **5** Ran SP% **109.7**
Speed ratings (Par 111): **111,109,104,101,99**
CSF £7.24 TOTE £2.90: £1.50, £1.70; EX 8.40.
Owner Kennet Valley Thoroughbreds VI **Bred** Sc Archi Romani **Trained** Kingsclere, Hants
■ Stewards' Enquiry : Jimmy Fortune two-day ban: used whip above permitted level (May 29-30)

FOCUS
Only five runners lined up for this Listed race but the pace was good, with the first two home deserving credit for pulling nicely clear.

NOTEBOOK
Tullius(IRE) made it 2-2 for his new yard and built on his Newmarket handicap win with another improved performance. He carried his head a bit high but this was a decent effort in quickening past a strong front-runner and he's most progressive. He may take his chance in Group company now and step back up to a longer trip. (tchd 9-4)
Skilful had his chance compromised by getting into a speed duel when fifth on his return in a similar race at Kempton, but enjoyed an uncontested lead this time. Clearly happy in the conditions, he looked likely to score inside the final furlong but couldn't match the pace of the winner close home. This was still a good run and he's clearly at his best under front-running tactics. (op 2-1 tchd 9-4)
Memory Cloth had finished second to the winner last time at Newmarket and was 2lb worse off but couldn't reverse the placings. He wasn't disgraced in third and remains in form. (tchd 7-2)
King Torus(IRE), conceding 4lb to all his rivals, could only keep on one-paced. He has winning form on soft but he has scored four times on fast ground and he will probably be suited by the return to a sounder surface. (op 5-1 tchd 6-1)
Albaqaa travelled well in rear but couldn't compete when the pace quickened in the straight. (op 18-1 tchd 16-1)

2128 SIS LIVE H'CAP 1m 67y
7:40 (7:41) (Class 5) (0-70,70) 3-Y-0 **£2,264** (£673; £336; £168) **Stalls** Low

Form RPR
000- **1** **Golden Jubilee (USA)**[214] 6812 3-8-13 62................. RichardHughes 6 65
(Richard Hannon) *trckd ldrs: prog to go 2nd 2f out: led 1f out: rdn and sn asserted* **7/1**
0-05 **2** 1 1/4 **It's A Privilege**[16] 1661 3-9-7 70.. JimCrowley 7 70
(Ralph Beckett) *dwlt: sn w ldr: led 6f out: drvn 2f out: hdd 1f out: kpt on same pce* **5/1**[2]
300- **3** 1/2 **Derfenna Art (IRE)**[217] 6753 3-9-3 66..........................(t) GeorgeBaker 1 65
(Seamus Durack) *towards rr: rdn in last trio over 2f out: hanging but prog over 1f out: styd on wl to take 3rd and cl on runner-up fin* **20/1**
00-2 **4** 1 3/4 **White Flight**[40] 1180 3-9-2 65.. LeeNewman 10 60
(Jonathan Portman) *trckd ldrs: effrt over 2f out: drvn to dispute 2nd wl over 1f out: one pce after* **25/1**
10-0 **5** 1/2 **Wyndham Wave**[33] 1322 3-9-4 67.. JamesMillman 8 61
(Rod Millman) *hld up in last pair: pushed along over 2f out: prog over 1f out: styd on quite takingly fnl f: nrst fin* **14/1**
430- **6** 1 1/2 **Lady Percy (IRE)**[214] 6818 3-8-11 60.. DavidProbert 9 50
(Mark Usher) *led 2f: chsd ldr to 2f out: steadily fdd* **14/1**
310- **7** 1 3/4 **The New Black (IRE)**[202] 7081 3-9-2 65.. EddieAhern 3 51
(Gay Kelleway) *hld up in rr: prog into midfield 3f out gng wl: rdn and nt qckn 2f out: wknd fnl f* **33/1**
24-2 **8** hd **Shot In The Dark (IRE)**[7] 1906 3-9-6 69.. LiamKeniry 11 55
(Andrew Balding) *t.k.h early: trckd ldng pair: rdn over 2f out: wknd over 1f out* **9/4**[1]
000- **9** 2 1/4 **Whinging Willie (IRE)**[180] 7436 3-9-7 70.. RyanMoore 2 51
(Gary Moore) *trckd ldrs: shkn up over 2f out: wknd over 1f out: eased ins fnl f* **6/1**[3]
00-6 **10** 39 **Surrey Dream (IRE)**[23] 1512 3-9-4 67.. SebSanders 4
(Roger Teal) *s.i.s: in tch: rdn over 3f out: wknd over 2f out: t.o and eased* **6/1**[3]
1m 50.24s (5.54) **Going Correction** +0.50s/f (Yiel) **10** Ran SP% **113.4**
Speed ratings (Par 99): **92,90,90,88,88 86,84,84,82,43**
toteswingers:1&2:£5.50, 1&3:£18.70, 2&3:£24.60 CSF £39.64 CT £681.41 TOTE £7.00: £2.50, £1.80, £6.30; EX 40.20 Trifecta £798.00 Pool: £4,134.14 - 3.83 winning units..
Owner Mrs J K Powell **Bred** Dixiana Farms Llc **Trained** East Everleigh, Wilts

Golden Jubilee(USA) Official explanation: trainer said, regarding apparent improvement in form, that the colt had strengthened and matured over the winter.

2129 BUGLER DEVELOPMENTS 30TH ANNIVERSARY H'CAP 1m 3f 135y
8:10 (8:10) (Class 5) (0-75,75) 3-Y-0 **£2,264** (£673; £336; £168) **Stalls** Centre

Form RPR
00-4 **1** **Rye House (IRE)**[21] 1567 3-9-7 75.. RyanMoore 7 89+
(Sir Michael Stoute) *mde virtually all: set stdy pce to 4f out: drvn and jnd over 1f out: gd battle after: jst in front last strides* **11/4**[2]
06-1 **2** hd **Man Of Plenty**[28] 1415 3-9-6 74.. DaneO'Neill 1 87+
(John Dunlop) *hld up in tch: prog to go 2nd over 2f out: drvn to chal over 1f out: sustained battle after: jst hld fnl strides* **7/1**
1543 **3** 9 **Somemothersdohavem**[21] 1568 3-9-0 68......................(p) AdamKirby 2 66
(John Ryan) *t.k.h: pressed wnr: upsides over 3f out: lost 2nd over 2f out: steadily lft bhd* **12/1**
30-2 **4** nk **Wayne Manor (IRE)**[21] 1568 3-8-11 65.. JimCrowley 5 62
(Ralph Beckett) *t.k.h early: cl up: rdn over 3f out: sn struggling: plugged on fnl f to press for 3rd nr fin* **7/2**[3]
06-3 **5** 5 **Cades Reef (IRE)**[8] 1892 3-9-3 71.. JimmyFortune 9 60
(Andrew Balding) *hld up in last pair: rdn over 3f out: limited prog over 2f out: sn wl btn* **2/1**[1]
6214 **6** 6 **Excellent News (IRE)**[30] 1390 3-8-12 66.. SebSanders 3 45
(J W Hills) *hld up in last pair: rdn over 3f out: no imp on ldrs 2f out: wknd qckly* **25/1**
00-0 **7** 17 **Polydamos**[39] 1206 3-9-2 70.. EddieAhern 8 20
(Harry Dunlop) *prom after 4f: wknd over 3f out: t.o* **20/1**
2m 37.06s (7.56) **Going Correction** +0.50s/f (Yiel) **7** Ran SP% **111.0**
Speed ratings (Par 99): **94,93,87,87,84 80,69**
toteswingers:1&2:£3.40, 1&3:£3.90, 2&3:£3.70 CSF £20.68 CT £186.70 TOTE £3.60: £1.50, £2.50; EX 12.60 Trifecta £51.80 Pool: £633.01 - 9.03 winning units..
Owner Philip Newton **Bred** Philip Newton **Trained** Newmarket, Suffolk

FOCUS
An ordinary 3yo handicap but the first two pulled well clear, the winner providing Ryan Moore with a treble on the card and Sir Michael Stoute with a double.
T/Jkpt: Not won. T/Plt: £173.70 to a £1 stake. Pool:£83,891.98 - 352.47 winning tickets T/Qpdt: £47.20 to a £1 stake. Pool:£7,427.46 - 116.28 winning tickets JN

1824 WOLVERHAMPTON (A.W) (L-H)
Monday, May 14

OFFICIAL GOING: Standard
Wind: Fresh behind Weather: Cloudy with sunny spells

2130 LADBROKES CASINO H'CAP (DIV I) 7f 32y(P)
1:45 (1:46) (Class 6) (0-60,60) 3-Y-0 **£1,704** (£503; £251) **Stalls** High

Form RPR
2532 **1** **Emma Jean (IRE)**[10] 1826 3-9-1 54..........................(bt) MircoDemuro 11 57
(Frank Sheridan) *hdwy over 5f out: led 1f out: pushed out* **9/2**[2]
06-0 **2** hd **Artful Lady (IRE)**[35] 1259 3-8-6 48.. RyanPowell(3) 7 50+
(George Margarson) *prom: lost pl 1/2-way: edgd lft over 2f out: hdwy over 1f out: r.o* **12/1**
000- **3** 1/2 **Men Don't Cry (IRE)**[251] 5801 3-9-7 60.. LiamKeniry 10 61
(Ed de Giles) *chsd ldrs: rdn over 1f out: sn ev ch: r.o* **8/1**[3]
06-0 **4** nk **Purley Queen (IRE)**[30] 1392 3-9-6 59.. JamesDoyle 2 59
(Sylvester Kirk) *led: hdd over 4f out: rdn and ev ch over 1f out: styd on* **4/1**[1]
600 **5** 1/2 **Big Sylv (IRE)**[28] 1420 3-8-12 51.. LiamJones 12 50
(James Unett) *chsd ldr: led over 4f out: pushed along over 2f out: hdd 1f out: styd on same pce* **16/1**
00-0 **6** 2 1/4 **Pendle Lady (IRE)**[23] 1529 3-9-4 57.. TomMcLaughlin 6 50
(Mark Brisbourne) *plld hrd and prom: hmpd 6f out: sn lost pl: pushed along 1/2-way: r.o ins fnl f: nt rch ldrs* **14/1**
0-00 **7** nk **Gone By Sunrise**[75] 734 3-8-10 49..........................(t) JoeFanning 8 41
(Derek Shaw) *hld up: hdwy over 2f out: styd on* **11/1**
0-00 **8** 3/4 **Applaudere**[19] 1608 3-8-2 46..........................(b[1]) LeonnaMayor(5) 5 36
(Jamie Osborne) *hld up: hdwy over 4f out: rdn over 1f out: no ex fnl f* **20/1**
505- **9** 1 1/2 **Dazzlin Bluebell (IRE)**[234] 6293 3-8-13 52.. GrahamLee 3 38
(Tim Easterby) *hld up: rdn over 1f out: n.d* **9/2**[2]
4060 **10** hd **Auntie Joy**[26] 1441 3-9-3 56..........................(v[1]) JamesSullivan 1 41
(Michael Easterby) *chsd ldrs: rdn whn hmpd over 2f out: sn wknd* **12/1**
11 3 1/2 **Nickeys On Time (IRE)**[47] 1079 3-8-9 53................. MarkCoumbe(5) 4 29
(Daniel Mark Loughnane) *s.s: a in rr* **14/1**
1m 31.54s (1.94) **Going Correction** 0.0s/f (Stan) **11** Ran SP% **115.2**
Speed ratings (Par 97): **88,87,87,86,86 83,83,82,80,80 76**
toteswingers:1&2:£7.60, 1&3:£4.30, 2&3:£17.20 CSF £56.29 CT £419.48 TOTE £3.80: £1.60, £3.20, £2.70; EX 61.80 TRIFECTA Not won..
Owner Arc Racing (North) **Bred** Honora Corridan And Mrs Mary Murphy **Trained** Wolverhampton, W Midlands
■ Stewards' Enquiry : Ryan Powell two-day ban: used whip above permitted level (May 28,tbn)

FOCUS
A poor handicap with ten of the 11 runners maidens coming into it and the first five finished in a heap.

2131 LADBROKES CASINO H'CAP (DIV II) 7f 32y(P)
2:15 (2:16) (Class 6) (0-60,60) 3-Y-0 **£1,704** (£503; £251) **Stalls** High

Form RPR
65-6 **1** **Lucifers Shadow (IRE)**[19] 1608 3-8-13 52.. JamesDoyle 11 62
(Sylvester Kirk) *chsd ldrs: led wl over 5f out: pushed clr 2f out: rdn and edgd rt ins fnl f: styd on* **15/2**
005- **2** 1 **Twenty One Choice (IRE)**[207] 6973 3-8-10 49.. LiamKeniry 9 56
(Ed de Giles) *hld up: hdwy over 1f out: r.o: nt rch wnr* **20/1**
00-5 **3** hd **Lean On Pete (IRE)**[19] 1595 3-9-7 60.. TomEaves 5 67
(Ollie Pears) *chsd ldrs: pushed along over 2f out: rdn over 1f out: r.o* **2/1**[1]
0 **4** 3 3/4 **Collectable**[40] 1182 3-8-11 50.. GrahamLee 1 47
(Jonathan Portman) *hld up: hdwy over 1f out: nt trble ldrs* **13/2**[2]
0-00 **5** 3/4 **Rano Pano (USA)**[23] 1517 3-8-8 47..........................(b[1]) BarryMcHugh 10 42
(Brian Ellison) *dwlt: sn pushed along in rr: styd on ins fnl f: nvr nrr* **9/1**
05-4 **6** 2 1/2 **Indiana Guest (IRE)**[34] 1285 3-9-3 56.. IanMongan 4 44
(George Margarson) *hld up: hdwy 3f out: rdn over 1f out: sn wknd* **15/2**
00-0 **7** 1/2 **Aubrietia**[30] 1376 3-8-7 46 oh1.. AndreaAtzeni 7 33
(Ed Vaughan) *chsd ldrs: rdn 1/2-way: wknd over 1f out* **50/1**
540- **8** 1 1/2 **New Romantic**[193] 7242 3-9-0 53..........................[1] FrederikTylicki 3 35
(Julie Camacho) *prom: rdn over 2f out: wknd over 1f out* **11/1**
50-0 **9** 2 1/2 **Champagne Valley**[30] 1386 3-8-13 52.. JoeFanning 6 28
(Sharon Watt) *led: hdd wl over 5f out: chsd ldr: rdn over 2f out: wknd over 1f out* **50/1**
040- **10** 2 1/4 **Zigazag (IRE)**[193] 7251 3-9-3 56..........................(t) PadraigBeggy 8 26
(David Evans) *hld up: rdn over 1f out: a in rr* **25/1**
005- **11** 7 **Best In Show**[296] 4339 3-9-4 57.. SebSanders 2
(J W Hills) *hld up: hdwy over 2f out: wknd wl over 1f out* **7/1**[3]
1m 29.76s (0.16) **Going Correction** 0.0s/f (Stan) **11** Ran SP% **113.6**
Speed ratings (Par 97): **99,97,97,93,92 89,89,87,84,81 73**
toteswingers:1&2:£21.40, 1&3:£5.00, 2&3:£10.40 CSF £146.26 CT £415.93 TOTE £8.70: £3.20, £6.00, £1.10; EX 150.10 TRIFECTA Not won..
Owner Dr John Wilson **Bred** J & M & E Doyle **Trained** Upper Lambourn, Berks

FOCUS
There were no previous winners at all in this division, but the winning time was 1.78 seconds faster than the first leg and the front three (who came clear) may still have a bit more to offer.
Lucifers Shadow(IRE) Official explanation: trainer said, regarding apparent improvement in form, that the gelding had come on for its first run of the season and benefited from a change in tactics.

2132 FIND US ON FACEBOOK WOLVERHAMPTON RACECOURSE CLAIMING STKS 5f 20y(P)
2:45 (2:45) (Class 6) 2-Y-O **£1,704** (£503; £251) **Stalls** Low

Form RPR
51 **1** **Caught Napping**[33] 1308 2-8-5 0 .... JakePayne(7) 3 64
(Bill Turner) *sn led: rdn and edgd lft fr over 1f out: styd on* **1/4**[1]
66 **2** *1 ¾* **Tiger Sunset (IRE)**[24] 1495 2-8-8 0 .... (p) LiamKeniry 2 54
(J S Moore) *chsd wnr: pushed along 1/2-way: rdn over 1f out: styd on same pce ins fnl f* **12/1**[3]
04 **3** *3* **Miss Penny Arcade**[11] 1795 2-8-2 0 .... FrannyNorton 1 38
(Keith Dalgleish) *chsd ldrs: sn pushed along: outpcd fr 1/2-way* **9/2**[2]
1m 3.3s (1.00) **Going Correction** 0.0s/f (Stan) **3** Ran SP% **105.9**
Speed ratings (Par 91): **92,89,84**
CSF £3.57 TOTE £1.20; EX 3.90.
Owner E A Brook **Bred** Whitson Bloodstock Limited **Trained** Sigwells, Somerset

FOCUS
Little to get excited about in this weak claimer and the order barely changed. The winner is rated just below his maiden victory.

NOTEBOOK
Caught Nappingwas proven on Polytrack having won a five-runner Lingfield maiden auction last month, and had little difficulty in , making just about all against two modest rivals, despite hanging to the inside rail late on. This told us nothing new about him.
Tiger Sunset(IRE) was tried in cheekpieces after showing nothing in his first two starts, but his efforts to get on terms with the red-hot favourite proved futile and he didn't achieve that much here. (op 16-1 tchd 20-1)
Miss Penny Arcade had shown early speed in her first two starts on turf, but couldn't do the same on this different surface and was always finding it hard to keep in touch with the other pair. (op 4-1)

2133 LADBROKES MOBILE CLAIMING STKS 5f 20y(P)
3:15 (3:15) (Class 6) 3-Y-0+ **£1,704** (£503; £251) **Stalls** Low

Form RPR
2211 **1** **Lesley's Choice**[14] 1720 6-9-6 77 .... (b) JamesDoyle 2 83
(Paul Rich) *mde all: rdn and edgd rt over 1f out: hung rt ins fnl f: styd on u.p* **13/8**[1]
1534 **2** *¾* **Steelcut**[14] 1720 8-8-10 67 .... (p) MatthewCosham(5) 3 75
(David Evans) *chsd ldrs: rdn over 1f out: chsd wnr ins fnl f: styd on* **12/1**
0012 **3** *1 ½* **Red Cape (FR)**[14] 1720 9-9-3 77 .... (b) JamesSullivan 6 72
(Ruth Carr) *chsd wnr: rdn and hmpd over 1f out: styd on same pce ins fnl f* **9/2**[3]
310 **4** *1 ¾* **Mother Jones**[17] 1638 4-8-12 68 .... (p) PadraigBeggy 5 61
(David Evans) *chsd ldrs: rdn over 1f out: styd on same pce* **8/1**
-1U0 **5** *nk* **Arganil (USA)**[9] 1844 7-9-7 94 .... BrianToomey(5) 4 74
(Kevin Ryan) *s.i.s: outpcd: hdwy over 1f out: nvr trbld ldrs* **7/4**[2]
3335 **6** *18* **Porthgwidden Beach (USA)**[47] 1061 4-8-11 45 .... (tp) LiamKeniry 1
(Anthony Middleton) *sn outpcd* **100/1**
7 *2 ¾* **Green Wave (ITY)** 3-8-5 0 .... (bt[1]) MircoDemuro 7
(Frank Sheridan) *dwlt: outpcd* **50/1**
1m 1.9s (-0.40) **Going Correction** 0.0s/f (Stan)
WFA 3 from 4yo+ 9lb **7** Ran SP% **114.4**
Speed ratings (Par 101): **103,101,99,96,96 67,62**
toteswingers:1&2:£4.80, 1&3:£2.60, 2&3:£5.30 CSF £21.90 TOTE £3.00: £2.10, £5.50; EX 25.20.Steelcut was claimed by Mark Buckley for £5,000.
Owner L M Power **Bred** B C Allen **Trained** Newport, Gwent

FOCUS
Almost a repeat of a similar claimer over C&D last month in which the 1-4-2 there finished 1-2-3 here.
Arganil(USA) Official explanation: jockey said gelding never travelled
Green Wave(ITY) Official explanation: jockey said filly was slowly into stride and hung right-handed throughout

2134 LADBROKES MOBILE H'CAP 1m 5f 194y(P)
3:45 (3:45) (Class 6) (0-65,64) 4-Y-0+ **£1,704** (£503; £251) **Stalls** Low

Form RPR
6624 **1** **Delagoa Bay (IRE)**[18] 1631 4-8-5 **46** .... MartinDwyer 7 60
(Sylvester Kirk) *chsd ldrs: led over 3f out: rdn clr fnl 2f* **13/2**
5106 **2** *6* **Spartan King (IRE)**[14] 1719 4-8-12 **56** .... RyanClark(3) 2 62
(Ian Williams) *dwlt: hld up: hdwy over 2f out: rdn to go 2nd fnl f: no ch w wnr* **9/2**[2]
-440 **3** *5* **Mecox Bay (IRE)**[14] 1719 5-8-9 **49** .... FrannyNorton 1 48
(Jennie Candlish) *hld up: hdwy over 4f out: chsd wnr over 3f out: rdn over 2f out: wknd fnl f* **17/2**
5314 **4** *hd* **Cloudy Start**[20] 1588 6-9-5 **64** .... LeonnaMayor(5) 9 62
(Jamie Osborne) *s.i.s: hld up: hdwy over 2f out: sn rdn: nvr trbld ldrs* **5/1**[3]
46-3 **5** *½* **Tropical Bachelor (IRE)**[14] 1719 6-9-8 **62** .... FrederikTylicki 3 60
(Richard Ford) *prom: lost pl over 6f out: n.d after: lame* **3/1**[1]
025- **6** *5* **Call Of Duty (IRE)**[189] 7112 7-9-4 **58** .... GrahamLee 6 49
(Dianne Sayer) *hld up: hdwy over 4f out: rdn and wknd over 1f out* **15/2**
0/0- **7** *1 ¼* **Party Palace**[400] 955 8-8-5 **45** .... LiamJones 5 34
(Stuart Howe) *prom: pushed along over 6f out: wknd over 2f out* **33/1**
02-0 **8** *37* **Arashi**[23] 1533 6-9-8 **62** .... (p) JoeFanning 4
(Derek Shaw) *chsd ldr tl led over 7f out: hdd & wknd over 3f out: t.o* **10/1**
60-0 **9** *13* **Jewelled Dagger (IRE)**[33] 1295 8-9-0 **59** .... GarryWhillans(5) 8
(Sharon Watt) *led: hdd over 7f out: wknd over 3f out: t.o* **50/1**
450- **10** *34* **Goodlukin Lucy**[51] 4971 5-9-6 **63** .... LeeTopliss(3) 10
(Dianne Sayer) *hld up: rdn over 6f out: wknd over 3f out: t.o* **14/1**
3m 3.58s (-2.42) **Going Correction** 0.0s/f (Stan)
WFA 4 from 5yo+ 1lb **10** Ran SP% **116.1**
Speed ratings (Par 101): **106,102,99,99,99 96,95,74,67,47**
toteswingers:1&2:£5.60, 1&3:£8.20, 2&3:£6.50 CSF £35.71 CT £252.51 TOTE £7.00: £1.90, £1.40, £2.60; EX 39.30 Trifecta £141.40 Pool: £904.29 - 4.73 winning units..
Owner Homebred Racing **Bred** J Ryan **Trained** Upper Lambourn, Berks

FOCUS
A moderate staying handicap, but they certainly went a decent pace with Jewelled Dagger and Arashi duelling in a clear advantage, much to their detriment.
Tropical Bachelor(IRE) Official explanation: vet said gelding finished lame

2135 MIRROR PUNTERS CLUB MAIDEN AUCTION FILLIES' STKS 5f 20y(P)
4:15 (4:15) (Class 5) 2-Y-O **£2,385** (£704; £352) **Stalls** Low

Form RPR
33 **1** **Sylvia Pankhurst (IRE)**[11] 1795 2-8-4 0 .... HayleyTurner 6 63+
(David C Griffiths) *sn pushed along and prom: led ins fnl f: r.o* **5/2**[1]
2 *2* **Cymeriad** 2-8-5 0 .... JamesSullivan 7 57+
(Michael Easterby) *s.s: outpcd: r.o ins fnl f: wnt 2nd post: nt rch wnr* **5/1**[2]
0 **3** *nk* **Emperor's Daughter**[44] 1131 2-8-5 0 .... FrannyNorton 2 56
(Tim Pitt) *led: rdn over 1f out: hdd and unable qck ins fnl f* **11/2**[3]
546 **4** *1* **Until It Sleeps**[6] 1949 2-8-1 0 .... DeclanCannon(3) 4 51
(Alan McCabe) *chsd ldrs: pushed along and hung rt 1/2-way: styd on same pce fnl f* **9/1**
4 **5** *1 ½* **Lucy Bee**[6] 1949 2-8-6 0 .... JoeFanning 1 48
(Keith Dalgleish) *w ldr: rdn and ev ch over 1f out: no ex ins fnl f* **5/2**[1]
6 *1 ¼* **Mission Bell** 2-7-13 0 .... RachealKneller(5) 5 41
(Mark Usher) *s.s: outpcd: nvr nrr* **14/1**
7 *½* **Mill End Dancer** 2-8-8 0 ow1 .... TomEaves 8 43
(Michael Easterby) *s.s: hld up: nvr trbld ldrs* **25/1**
1m 3.25s (0.95) **Going Correction** 0.0s/f (Stan) **7** Ran SP% **109.7**
Speed ratings (Par 90): **92,88,88,86,84 82,81**
toteswingers:1&2:£2.80, 1&3:£2.90, 2&3:£3.10 CSF £14.02 TOTE £3.10: £2.00, £3.70; EX 14.50 Trifecta £66.00 Pool: £756.76 - 8.48 winning units..
Owner Norton Common Farm Racing **Bred** T Cahalan & D Cahalan **Trained** Bawtry, S Yorks

FOCUS
A weak fillies' maiden run at a brisk early pace. The time was only marginally faster than the earlier three-runner juvenile claimer and this looks plating-class form.

NOTEBOOK
Sylvia Pankhurst(IRE) had shown plenty of ability on last month's Ripon debut and her next start five days later may have come too soon. Apart from briefly getting outpaced before halfway, she was always travelling best and picked up nicely once switched right over a furlong from home. She should continue to pay her way. (op 9-4 tchd 11-4)
Cymeriad, retained for 2,000GBP as a yearling, is out of a six-time winner from 5f to 1m. She raced green near the back of the field early, but showed ability as the race progressed and stayed on nicely into second. She fared much the best of the three newcomers and may prove to be the best of these long-term. (op 9-2 tchd 4-1)
Emperor's Daughter was never in the race when ninth of 12 in the Brocklesby, but was much more alert this time and she set the pace until the winner was unleashed inside the last. An ordinary early season maiden can come her way. (tchd 5-1)
Until It Sleeps had the benefit of previous experience when behind Lucy Bee at Catterick six days earlier and managed to turn that form around, but she lacked the pace to put in an effective challenge and has had a few chances now. (op 10-1)
Lucy Bee looked green when fourth of seven on her Catterick debut, but may have paid for trying to match strides with Emperor's Daughter in the early stages here. (op 3-1)

2136 LADBROKES FILLIES' H'CAP 1m 141y(P)
4:45 (4:45) (Class 5) (0-70,70) 3-Y-O **£2,264** (£673; £336; £168) **Stalls** Low

Form RPR
06-3 **1** **Supaheart**[48] 1053 3-9-2 **65** .... DarryllHolland 9 72+
(Hughie Morrison) *mde all: rdn and hung lft over 1f out: r.o: eased nr fin* **7/2**[2]
3136 **2** *1 ½* **Bint Alzain (IRE)**[30] 1392 3-9-2 **70** .... RaulDaSilva(5) 6 73
(Gerard Butler) *hld up in tch: racd keenly: rdn over 1f out: wnt 2nd ins fnl f: nt rch wnr* **9/2**[3]
50-0 **3** *½* **Silvas Romana (IRE)**[30] 1392 3-9-7 **70** .... TomMcLaughlin 12 72
(Mark Brisbourne) *a.p: chsd wnr over 2f out: rdn over 1f out: styd on* **66/1**
104- **4** *¾* **Travelling**[217] 6753 3-9-7 **70** .... MircoDemuro 4 70+
(Marco Botti) *hld up: hdwy over 3f out: rdn over 1f out: styd on* **11/4**[1]
06-0 **5** *nk* **Moody Dancer**[23] 1517 3-9-0 **63** .... MartinDwyer 10 63
(William Muir) *chsd wnr tl rdn over 2f out: styd on same pce fnl f* **20/1**
0-46 **6** *2 ¼* **Represent (IRE)**[5] 1979 3-8-11 **60** .... MartinHarley 1 54
(Mick Channon) *hld up: nt clr run over 2f out: hdwy over 1f out: nt trble ldrs* **16/1**
5-60 **7** *2 ½* **Blodwen Abbey**[14] 1721 3-9-7 **70** .... LiamJones 5 59
(James Unett) *s.s: hld up: plld hrd: n.d* **14/1**
22-5 **8** *nk* **Remix (IRE)**[109] 308 3-9-4 **67** .... SebSanders 2 55
(J W Hills) *hld up: nvr trbld ldrs* **12/1**
0-05 **9** *½* **Ocean Myth**[26] 1445 3-9-2 **65** .... GrahamLee 3 52
(Jonathan Portman) *hld up: a in rr* **33/1**
061- **10** *¾* **Choccywoccydoodah**[150] 7784 3-9-3 **66** .... JamesSullivan 8 51
(James Given) *plld hrd and prom: rdn over 2f out: wknd over 1f out* **20/1**
4-10 **11** *½* **Poker Hospital**[13] 1733 3-9-0 **70** .... (p) DarrenEgan(7) 11 54
(John Stimpson) *s.i.s: hld up: nvr on terms* **22/1**
006- **12** *8* **Silver Marizah (IRE)**[152] 7757 3-9-2 **65** .... GeorgeBaker 7 31
(Gary Moore) *prom: rdn over 2f out: wknd wl over 1f out* **17/2**
1m 51.2s (0.70) **Going Correction** 0.0s/f (Stan) **12** Ran SP% **116.1**
Speed ratings (Par 96): **96,94,94,93,93 91,89,88,88,87 87,80**
toteswingers:1&2:£4.60, 1&3:£25.90, 2&3:£52.00 CSF £17.68 CT £883.93 TOTE £4.60: £1.90, £2.10, £9.30; EX 18.70 Trifecta £383.80 Pool: £1,063.33 - 2.05 winning units..
Owner Sir Martyn Arbib **Bred** Arbib Bloodstock Partnership **Trained** East Ilsley, Berks
■ Stewards' Enquiry : Raul Da Silva two-day ban: careless riding (May 28,30)

FOCUS
A modest fillies' handicap in which it paid to be handy, but the winner can rate higher.

2137 DOWNLOAD OUR IPHONE APP AMATEUR RIDERS' H'CAP 1m 4f 50y(P)
5:15 (5:16) (Class 6) (0-55,55) 4-Y-0+ **£1,646** (£506; £253) **Stalls** Low

Form RPR
65-0 **1** **William's Way**[133] 9 10-10-8 **52** .... (tp) MrCMartin(3) 10 62+
(Ian Wood) *s.s: hld up: hdwy over 2f out: r.o to ld post* **14/1**
3406 **2** *hd* **Beneath**[56] 961 5-11-0 **55** .... (bt) MrSWalker 4 64
(Neil Mulholland) *hld up: hdwy over 3f out: led wl over 1f out: sn rdn: hdd post* **15/2**
-256 **3** *4* **Laconicos (IRE)**[101] 400 10-10-7 **55** .... (t) MissCScott(7) 3 58+
(William Stone) *mid-div: hdwy over 7f out: rdn over 1f out: styd on* **16/1**
2133 **4** *1* **So Is She (IRE)**[10] 1831 4-10-3 **51** .... (be) MissAlexOwen(7) 6 52
(Alan Bailey) *chsd ldr 4f: lost pl 7f out: rdn over 1f out: styd on ins fnl f* **13/2**[3]
-144 **5** *¾* **Mustajed**[69] 811 11-10-9 **55** .... (b) MrPMillman(5) 11 55
(Rod Millman) *prom: chsd ldr over 5f out: rdn to ld over 2f out: hdd wl over 1f out: no ex fnl f* **22/1**
2132 **6** *3* **Mayan Flight (IRE)**[59] 924 4-10-8 **52** .... MrMJJSmith(3) 2 47
(Tony Carroll) *mid-div: hdwy over 3f out: rdn and ev ch over 2f out: wknd over 1f out* **7/2**[2]
3060 **7** *2* **Merrjanah**[26] 1439 4-10-5 **53** .... MrAFrench(7) 12 45
(John Wainwright) *hld up: hdwy over 7f out: rdn over 2f out: sn wknd* **12/1**

20-0 **8** *1 1/4* **Alaghiraar (IRE)**66 367 8-10-9 **55**............................(v) MissNStead(5) 9 45
(Richard Ford) *led: rdn and hdd over 2f out: wknd over 1f out* **28/1**
060- **9** *2 3/4* **Commerce**32 7203 5-10-7 **55**......................................(p) MissSLewis(7) 8 41
(Dai Burchell) *hld up: nvr on terms* **25/1**
6-50 **10** *5* **Excellent Vision**7 1908 5-10-7 **53**.............................(t) MissHDavies(5) 5 31
(Milton Bradley) *s.s: hld up: a in rr* **16/1**
50-1 **11** *13* **Talk Of Saafend (IRE)**11 1794 7-10-7 **55**.................... MissNSayer(7) 7 12
(Dianne Sayer) *prom: chsd ldr 8f out tl over 5f out: wknd 3f out: t.o* **14/1**
005- **12** *16* **Cool Baranca (GER)**16 6833 6-10-9 **50**....................... MissECSayer 1
(Dianne Sayer) *s.s: sn pushed along and a in rr: t.o* **3/1**1

2m 42.5s (1.40) **Going Correction** 0.0s/f (Stan) 12 Ran SP% **116.8**
Speed ratings (Par 101): **95,94,92,91,91 89,87,86,85,81 73,62**
toteswingers:1&2:£24.90, 1&3:£32.70, 2&3:£21.40 CSF £110.82 CT £1707.51 TOTE £20.70: £5.20, £2.50, £6.50; EX 143.00 TRIFECTA Not won..
Owner Neardown Stables **Bred** Lewis Caterers **Trained** Upper Lambourn, Berks
■ Stewards' Enquiry : Miss H Davies five-day ban: used whip when out of contention (tbn)
Mr S Walker two-day ban: used whip above permitted level (tbn)

FOCUS
A moderate contest and a reminder of the dangers of assuming that a horse can transfer ability from one discipline to another.
Cool Baranca(GER) Official explanation: jockey said mare never travelled
T/Plt: £89.10 to a £1 stake. Pool:£61,391.33 - 502.48 winning tickets T/Qpdt: £17.90 to a £1 stake. Pool:£4,907.78 - 202.66 winning tickets CR

1911 BEVERLEY (R-H)

Tuesday, May 15

OFFICIAL GOING: Good (good to soft in places in home straight; 6.9)
GOOD (Good to soft in places home straight; 6.9)
Wind: Strong across Weather: Overcast

2138 TURFTV BETTING SHOP SERVICE MAIDEN STKS 5f
2:00 (2:00) (Class 5) 2-Y-0 **£2,420** (£714; £357) **Stalls** Low

Form RPR
4 **1** **Top Notch Tonto (IRE)**8 1911 2-9-3 0....................... PatrickMathers 7 77+
(Ian McInnes) *in tch: hdwy on outer 2f out: rdn to ld jst ins fnl f: kpt on wl* **17/2**3
2 *1 1/2* **Pearl Noir** 2-9-3 0... FrederikTylicki 11 71+
(Scott Dixon) *dwlt: sn in tch: hdwy to chse ldrs wl over 1f out: rdn and styd on ins fnl f: nrst fin* **16/1**
3 *1* **Fraserburgh (IRE)** 2-9-3 0.................................... SilvestreDeSousa 12 68+
(Mark Johnston) *prom: effrt wl over 1f out: sn rdn and kpt on same pce fnl f* **5/1**2
32 **4** *1/2* **Fly Fisher (IRE)**8 1911 2-9-3 0.................................... TonyHamilton 8 66
(Richard Fahey) *prom: hdwy and cl up 2f out: rdn to chal over 1f out and ev ch tl one pce ins fnl f* **5/1**2
3 **5** *2 3/4* **Crystal Cove**35 1277 2-9-3 0...................................... GrahamGibbons 9 56
(Tim Easterby) *led: rdn along wl over 1f out: hdd jst ins fnl f: grad wknd* **5/1**2
6 *3/4* **Strasbourg Place** 2-8-12 0....................................... AndrewMullen 13 48+
(Nigel Tinkler) *towards rr: hdwy 2f out: sn rdn and kpt on fnl f: nrst fin* **40/1**
7 *nk* **Chiming Hart** 2-8-12 0.. DuranFentiman 5 47+
(Tim Easterby) *dwlt and in rr: hdwy wl over 1f out: kpt on fnl f: nrst fin* **40/1**
8 *3/4* **Rat Catcher (IRE)** 2-9-3 0... DavidAllan 3 50+
(Tim Easterby) *chsd ldrs: rdn along over 2f out: sn wknd* **12/1**
9 *1/2* **El Molino Blanco** 2-8-12 0... JamesSullivan 6 43
(Michael Easterby) *s.i.s: a towards rr* **20/1**
0 **10** *shd* **Clock On Tom**8 1911 2-9-3 0.. PaddyAspell 4 47
(Michael Easterby) *chsd ldrs: rdn along 2f out: wknd over 1f out* **50/1**
11 *2* **Yorkshire Icon** 2-9-3 0.. PaulMulrennan 10 40+
(Ann Duffield) *dwlt: t.k.h and a towards rr* **17/2**3
12 *1* **Hashegotanymoney** 2-8-10 0.............................. DavidSimmonson(7) 2 37
(Michael Easterby) *a in rr* **40/1**
U **Panama Cat (USA)** 2-8-12 0....................................... JamieSpencer 1
(Kevin Ryan) *prom whn stmbld and uns rdr ins first f* **4/1**1

1m 7.61s (4.11) **Going Correction** +0.425s/f (Yiel) 13 Ran SP% **119.3**
Speed ratings (Par 93): **84,81,80,79,74 73,73,71,71,70 67,66,**
toteswingers: 1&2 £26.50, 1&3 £9.80, 2&3 £18.00. CSF £128.92 TOTE £10.50: £3.30, £6.80, £2.60; EX 160.40 Trifecta £388.10 Part won. Pool: £524.56 - 0.62 winning units..
Owner Keith Brown **Bred** Seamus Finucane **Trained** Catwick, E Yorks

FOCUS
This opener was run on ground described as being on the easy side. There was also a strong cross-wind for these juveniles to cope with. Fair form from the principals in this maiden, with the winner building on his debut effort.

NOTEBOOK
Top Notch Tonto(IRE) built on the promise of his recent C&D debut, staying on in the manner of one who'll be seen to even better effect when he gets the chance to tackle 6f plus. (op 8-1 tchd 10-1)
Pearl Noir produced a most promising debut, as he was clearly green before finishing with real purpose (also briefly tight for room inside the last). The stable's only other juvenile runner so far this season was a winner and this one will be adding to the tally before long. (tchd 14-1)
Fraserburgh(IRE), a Shamardal colt, showed clear ability on his debut and should go close at a similar level next time with anything like normal improvement, keeping on again after being slightly hampered approaching the final furlong. (tchd 9-2 and 11-2)
Fly Fisher(IRE) has a fair level of ability but there's no obvious indication he's going to be capable of much better, this probably in line with his two previous runs. (op 4-1)
Crystal Cove has plenty of speed and a sharper 5f will likely suit him better at this stage, fading after cutting out a lot of the running. (op 4-1)
Strasbourg Place hinted at ability amidst greenness, leaving the impression she'll be sharper with this initial experience behind her. (op 50-1)

2139 FANTASTIC PRIZES AT LUCKY IN LOVE (S) STKS 5f
2:30 (2:30) (Class 6) 3-Y-0 **£1,681** (£500; £250; £125) **Stalls** Low

Form RPR
00-6 **1** **Made In The Shade**36 1252 3-8-3 51............................... AmyRyan(3) 6 56
(Paul Midgley) *trckd ldrs: hdwy on outer and cl up 2f out: led over 1f out: rdn and edgd rt ins fnl f: kpt on* **5/1**
05-5 **2** *1/2* **Red Shadow**11 1817 3-8-6 54.................................. SilvestreDeSousa 2 54
(Alan Brown) *hld up: hdwy 2f out: swtchd rt and effrt appr fnl f: sn rdn and ch tl edgd lft and no ex towards fin* **5/2**1
06-4 **3** *1* **Brunswick Vale (IRE)**43 1169 3-8-6 39....................(b) DuranFentiman 9 51
(Paul Midgley) *in rr and sn rdn along: hdwy wl over 1f out: styd on u.p fnl f: nrst fin* **28/1**
3213 **4** *1 3/4* **El McGlynn (IRE)**26 1482 3-8-11 62..............................(v1) ChrisCatlin 10 49
(John O'Shea) *in tch: hdwy on outer to trck ldrs 2f out: rdn over 1f out: no imp* **6/1**
500- **5** *3 3/4* **Slenningford**224 6597 3-8-6 63....................................... JamesSullivan 5 31
(Ollie Pears) *cl up: rdn wl over 1f out: edgd rt and wknd ent fnl f* **3/1**2
-040 **6** *3/4* **Script**62 898 3-7-13 45.. MatthewHopkins(7) 7 28
(Alan Berry) *chsd ldrs: rdn along 2f out: sn one pce* **100/1**
060 **7** *1 1/2* **Tumbleowtashoes**20 1600 3-8-8 24...........................(t) RyanPowell(3) 8 28
(John Ryan) *a in rr* **100/1**
6520 **8** *4* **Wish Again (IRE)**20 1599 3-8-11 62........................(v1) AdrianNicholls 3 13
(David Nicholls) *cl up: led after 2f: rdn along wl over 1f out: sn hdd & wknd appr fnl f* **4/1**3
9 *2 3/4* **Kuraanda** 3-8-7 0 ow1.. PaddyAspell 4
(John Wainwright) *dwlt: a in rr* **33/1**
42-0 **10** *nk* **Italian Ice**124 135 3-8-7 41 ow1....................................... TomEaves 1
(Bryan Smart) *led 2f: rdn along over 2f out: sn wknd* **14/1**

1m 6.64s (3.14) **Going Correction** +0.425s/f (Yiel) 10 Ran SP% **119.6**
Speed ratings (Par 97): **91,90,88,85,79 78,76,69,65,64**
toteswingers: 1&2 £26.50, 1&3 £9.80, 2&3 £18.00. CSF £18.19 TOTE £5.90: £2.10, £1.20, £6.00; EX 19.10 Trifecta £512.30 Part won. Pool: £692.41 - 0.71 winning units..The winner was bought in for £5,200.
Owner Sandfield Racing **Bred** W B Imison **Trained** Westow, N Yorks

FOCUS
A moderate contest even by selling standards, the finish fought by a pair rated in the low-50s.

2140 ANNIE OXTOBY MEMORIAL H'CAP 5f
3:00 (3:00) (Class 5) (0-75,75) 4-Y-0+ **£2,296** (£683; £341; £170) **Stalls** Low

Form RPR
-621 **1** **Mercers Row**12 1800 5-9-1 **69**...................................... DanielTudhope 3 80
(Noel Wilson) *trckd ldrs: swtchd lft and hdwy 2f out: rdn to ld ins fnl f: drvn out* **11/4**2
44-0 **2** *3/4* **Select Committee**10 1868 7-9-3 **71**......................... MichaelO'Connell 5 79
(John Quinn) *towards rr: hdwy 2f out: swtchd rt and rdn over 1f out: styd on to chal ins fnl f and ev ch tl drvn and nt qckn nr fin* **10/1**
43-3 **3** *2 1/4* **Diamond Blue**7 1954 4-8-11 **68**.. AmyRyan(3) 1 68
(Richard Whitaker) *prom: cl up 2f out: rdn to ld briefly appr fnl f: hdd and drvn ins fnl f: one pce* **2/1**1
-336 **4** *3 1/2* **Highland Warrior**17 1675 13-8-11 **65**.............................. MickyFenton 2 52
(Paul Midgley) *towards rr: hdwy on inner wl over 1f out: rdn to chal ent fnl f: sn drvn and wknd* **14/1**
63-6 **5** *1/2* **Wicked Wilma (IRE)**6 1990 8-8-12 **73**.................. MatthewHopkins(7) 7 59
(Alan Berry) *led: rdn along 2f out: drvn and hdd 1f out: wknd* **20/1**
501- **6** *1/2* **We'll Deal Again**282 4820 5-8-13 **74**.................. DavidSimmonson(7) 11 58
(Michael Easterby) *wnt lft s: sn chsng ldrs on outer: rdn along 2f out: wknd over 1f out* **16/1**
6125 **7** *1 1/4* **Shawkantango**17 1675 5-9-0 **71**... DaleSwift(3) 8 50
(Derek Shaw) *wnt rt s and in rr: sme hdwy over 2f out: sn rdn and n.d* **13/2**3
0640 **8** *1 3/4* **Ingleby Star (IRE)**10 1868 7-9-4 **75**...........................(p) PaulPickard(3) 9 48
(Ian McInnes) *stmbld and dwlt s: sn chsng ldrs on outer: rdn along 2f out: sn wknd* **11/1**
030- **9** *4* **Lady Kildare (IRE)**206 7040 4-8-13 **67**............................. TonyHamilton 4 26
(Jedd O'Keeffe) *cl up: rdn along 1/2-way: sn wknd* **20/1**
4-50 **10** *10* **Liberty Ship**17 1675 7-8-13 **67**..................................... RoystonFfrench 6
(Mark Buckley) *a in rr* **16/1**

1m 5.17s (1.67) **Going Correction** +0.425s/f (Yiel) 10 Ran SP% **118.7**
Speed ratings (Par 103): **103,101,98,92,91 91,89,86,79,63**
toteswingers: 1&2 £6.70, 1&3 £2.10, 2&3 £5.70. CSF £31.37 CT £65.04 TOTE £4.70: £1.50, £2.70, £1.40; EX 36.50 Trifecta £66.40 Pool: £621.98 - 6.93 winning units..
Owner Mrs J A Smith & K Fitzsimons **Bred** Heather Raw **Trained** Middleham, N Yorks

FOCUS
A fair sprint which was run at a good pace, as in the previous races the action unfolded towards the centre.
Diamond Blue Official explanation: trainer's rep said filly lost a front shoe
Liberty Ship Official explanation: jockey said gelding lost its action

2141 BEVERLEY MIDDLE DISTANCE SERIES H'CAP 1m 4f 16y
3:30 (3:31) (Class 6) (0-60,60) 3-Y-0 **£2,587** (£770; £384; £192) **Stalls** Low

Form RPR
0-44 **1** **Bridgehampton**15 1716 3-8-13 **52**................................ JamieSpencer 10 69
(Michael Bell) *trckd ldrs: smooth hdwy over 3f out: chal over 2f out: led wl over 1f out: sn rdn clr and styd on* **3/1**1
66-5 **2** *4* **Cheviot Quest (IRE)**24 1519 3-9-4 **57**.............................. LeeNewman 3 67
(William Jarvis) *trckd ldrs: hdwy 3f: led over 2f out and sn rdn: hdd wl over 1f out: hung lft and one pce* **9/2**3
-250 **3** *7* **Courtesy Call (IRE)**14 1726 3-9-6 **59**...................... SilvestreDeSousa 7 58
(Mark Johnston) *hld up: hdwy on inner 4f out: rdn wl over 2f out: kpt on same pce* **8/1**
34-0 **4** *6* **Bursting Bubbles (IRE)**29 1424 3-9-2 **55**......................... RyanMoore 6 44
(Ed Dunlop) *in tch: rdn along and hdwy over 3f out: drvn over 2f out: n.d* **9/1**
50-5 **5** *3/4* **Flashman**32 1355 3-9-4 **60**.. LeeTopliss(3) 4 48
(Richard Fahey) *prom: rdn along to ld 3f out: sn hung lft and wd to stands' rail in st: sn hdd: drvn and wknd* **14/1**
0-04 **6** *1 3/4* **Mr Snoozy**31 1385 3-9-1 **54**.. GrahamGibbons 5 39
(Tim Walford) *midfield: rdn along over 4f out: n.d* **10/1**
50-4 **7** *1 1/2* **No Time To Cry**43 1170 3-9-3 **56**.................................... PaddyAspell 1 39
(Ann Duffield) *chsd ldrs: rdn along wl over 2f out: grad wknd* **20/1**
363- **8** *5* **Margo Channing**211 6911 3-9-1 **54**............................... FrederikTylicki 9 29
(Micky Hammond) *a towards rr* **4/1**2
66-6 **9** *1 1/2* **Altnaharra**21 1591 3-8-13 **52**.. GrahamLee 12 25
(Jim Goldie) *dwlt: a towards rr* **16/1**
0-00 **10** *5* **Fine Kingdom**8 1915 3-9-2 **55**......................................(bt1) TomEaves 8 20
(Michael Dods) *a in rr* **33/1**
00-0 **11** *3 1/4* **Maliha (IRE)**34 1320 3-9-4 **57**.................................... PaulMulrennan 11 16
(Kevin Ryan) *a towards rr* **22/1**
-050 **12** *12* **Henry George**27 1448 3-8-13 **52**.................................... FrannyNorton 2
(Mark Johnston) *led: rdn along over 4f out: hdd 3f out and sn wknd* **25/1**

2m 45.15s (5.35) **Going Correction** +0.325s/f (Good) 12 Ran SP% **121.8**
Speed ratings (Par 97): **95,92,87,83,83 82,81,77,76,73 71,63**
toteswingers: 1&2 £5.30, 1&3 £6.40, 2&3 £6.10. CSF £15.77 CT £101.56 TOTE £5.80: £1.70, £2.20, £2.20; EX 22.10 Trifecta £82.90 Pool: £710.29 - 6.34 winning units..
Owner M B Hawtin **Bred** The Kingwood Partnership **Trained** Newmarket, Suffolk

FOCUS
Probably not a great deal of depth to this middle-distance handicap.
Flashman Official explanation: jockey said gelding hung left in straight

No Time To Cry Official explanation: jockey said filly hung left throughout

2142 BEVERLEY RACECOURSE IS PERFECT FOR WEDDINGS H'CAP 1m 100y
4:00 (4:01) (Class 4) (0-85,86) 4-Y-O+ **£4,140** (£1,232; £615; £307) **Stalls** Low

Form RPR

20-2 **1** **Carragold**[8] 1914 6-8-8 **70** RobertWinston 4 82
(Mel Brittain) *prom: cl up 2f out: rdn to ld ent fnl f: sn edgd lft and kpt on wl* **11/4**[1]

-661 **2** *3 ¾* **Toto Skyllachy**[8] 1914 7-9-10 **86** 6ex DanielTudhope 1 89
(David O'Meara) *chsd ldr: hdwy to ld 2f out: sn rdn: drvn ent fnl f: sn hdd and one pce* **10/3**[2]

6033 **3** *1 ¼* **Moheebb (IRE)**[8] 1914 8-8-13 **75** (v) JamesSullivan 6 76
(Ruth Carr) *towards rr: hdwy 2f out: sn rdn and styd on fnl f: nrst fin* **5/1**[3]

0004 **4** *nk* **Collateral Damage (IRE)**[8] 1914 9-8-11 **73** (t) DavidAllan 8 73
(Tim Easterby) *dwlt and in rr: hdwy over 2f out: rdn wl over 1f out: styd on fnl f: nrst fin* **13/2**

21-0 **5** *3* **Change The Subject (USA)**[34] 1321 4-8-13 **75** AndrewMullen 2 68
(Peter Salmon) *chsd ldrs: rdn along over 2f out: drvn and no hdwy over 1f out* **20/1**

0-06 **6** *3 ¼* **Polish World (USA)**[38] 1220 8-9-7 **83** MickyFenton 7 68
(Paul Midgley) *led and sn clr: rdn along 3f out: hdd 2f out: wknd appr fnl f* **10/1**

12-1 **7** *½* **Abidhabidubai**[36] 1249 4-9-2 **78** TomEaves 5 62
(John Quinn) *in tch: rdn along 3f out: sn wknd* **5/1**[3]

002- **8** *½* **Gold Rules**[293] 4440 5-8-9 **71** PaddyAspell 3 54
(Michael Easterby) *hld up: a towards rr* **25/1**

1m 49.2s (1.60) **Going Correction** +0.325s/f (Good) **8 Ran SP% 114.1**
Speed ratings (Par 105): **105,101,100,99,96 93,92,92**
toteswingers: 1&2 £2.70, 1&3 £3.10, 2&3 £3.80. CSF £11.98 CT £42.59 TOTE £4.40: £1.70, £1.80, £2.30; EX 12.80 Trifecta £30.20 Pool: £806.60 - 19.73 winning units..
Owner Mel Brittain **Bred** Darley **Trained** Warthill, N Yorks

FOCUS
A fairly useful handicap, run at a good pace.
Abidhabidubai Official explanation: jockey said filly never travelled

2143 NOSEBAG CAFETERIA MAIDEN STKS 7f 100y
4:30 (4:35) (Class 5) 3-Y-O **£2,296** (£683; £341; £170) **Stalls** Low

Form RPR

0-34 **1** **On The Hoof**[13] 1758 3-9-3 69 PaulMulrennan 5 76
(Michael Easterby) *trckd ldrs: hdwy on inner 2f out: rdn to chal ent fnl f: styd on wl to ld last 50yds: jst hld on* **14/1**

6 **2** *nse* **Courage (IRE)**[27] 1450 3-9-3 0 RyanMoore 6 76+
(Sir Michael Stoute) *t.k.h early: hld up towards rr: hdwy on outer over 2f out: rdn over 1f out: str run ent fnl f: sn drvn: edgd rt and jst failed* **5/6**[1]

06-2 **3** *½* **Warcrown (IRE)**[9] 1878 3-9-0 0 LeeTopliss(3) 1 75
(Richard Fahey) *cl up: led after 1f: pushed along 2f out: rdn over 1f out: drvn and edgd rt whn hdd last 50yds: no ex* **9/4**[2]

00 **4** *2 ¾* **Haywain**[35] 1270 3-9-3 0 FrannyNorton 2 68
(Kevin Ryan) *led 1f: cl up: rdn along 2f out: drvn and ev ch ent fnl f: hld whn n.m.r towards fin* **66/1**

0- **5** *2* **Two Cities (IRE)**[158] 7702 3-9-3 0 GrahamLee 9 63
(Ann Duffield) *chsd ldrs: hdwy 3f out: rdn 2f out: drvn and wknd appr fnl f* **25/1**

6 **6** *2 ½* **Go On Gilbert**[26] 1479 3-9-3 0 PaddyAspell 7 57
(John Wainwright) *in rr tl styd on fnl 2f: n.d* **66/1**

00- **7** *¾* **Minty Jones**[197] 7197 3-9-3 0 SilvestreDeSousa 8 55
(Michael Mullineaux) *chsd ldrs: rdn along over 2f out: grad wknd* **100/1**

36- **8** *1* **Darling Grace**[210] 6934 3-8-12 0 LiamJones 3 47
(William Haggas) *chsd ldrs: rdn along over 2f out: drvn and wknd wl over 1f out* **8/1**[3]

9 *3* **Alpha Arion (IRE)** 3-9-3 0 DavidAllan 4 45
(Tim Easterby) *a in rr* **50/1**

06 **10** *8* **Bitter Harvest**[8] 1922 3-9-3 0 JamieSpencer 10 25
(Michael Bell) *a in rr* **14/1**

1m 36.32s (2.52) **Going Correction** +0.325s/f (Good) **10 Ran SP% 119.6**
Speed ratings (Par 99): **98,97,97,94,91 89,88,87,83,74**
toteswingers: 1&2 £4.30, 1&3 £4.40, 2&3 £1.50. CSF £26.85 TOTE £18.60: £3.60, £1.10, £1.30; EX 43.00 Trifecta £59.40 Pool: £1,216.99 - 59.40 winning units..
Owner A Chandler & L Westwood **Bred** Whitsbury Manor Stud & Pigeon House Stud **Trained** Sheriff Hutton, N Yorks
■ Stewards' Enquiry : Lee Topliss one-day ban: careless riding (May 29); two-day ban: used whip above permitted level (May 30-31)

FOCUS
Fair form in this maiden.

2144 BEST UK RACECOURSES ON TURFTV H'CAP 1m 1f 207y
5:00 (5:02) (Class 5) (0-70,73) 3-Y-O **£2,296** (£683; £341; £170) **Stalls** Low

Form RPR

4-53 **1** **Fisher**[35] 1270 3-8-13 **62** AdrianNicholls 3 70
(David Nicholls) *set stdy pce: qcknd clr over 3f out: rdn wl over 1f out: drvn and styd on wl fnl f* **25/1**

5-31 **2** *2 ½* **Mistress Of Rome**[24] 1517 3-9-6 **69** PaulMulrennan 4 72
(Michael Dods) *prom: effrt over 2f out: rdn to chse wnr over 1f out: sn drvn and no imp fnl f* **5/1**[1]

56-5 **3** *½* **Porcini**[32] 1363 3-9-7 **70** JamieSpencer 10 72+
(Philip McBride) *hld up towards rr: hdwy on outer over 2f out: rdn wl over 1f out: edgd rt and styd on fnl f: nrst fin* **7/1**[2]

50-6 **4** *1* **Spirit Na Heireann (IRE)**[34] 1319 3-9-0 **63** TonyHamilton 1 63
(Richard Fahey) *prom: chsd wnr 1/2-way: rdn over 2f out: drvn wl over 1f out: sn one pce* **8/1**[3]

-212 **5** *3 ½* **Quixote**[35] 1281 3-9-6 **69** RyanMoore 7 62
(Clive Brittain) *trckd ldrs on inner: n.m.r and swtchd lft over 2f out: rdn wl over 1f out: sn no imp* **5/1**[1]

552 **6** *nk* **Ma Kellys (IRE)**[27] 1441 3-8-10 **59** FrederikTylicki 8 51
(Micky Hammond) *chsd ldrs: rdn along over 2f out: sn one pce* **11/1**

-621 **7** *1* **Take Two**[8] 1906 3-9-10 **73** 6ex ChrisCatlin 11 63
(John O'Shea) *dwlt and t.k.h in rr: sme hdwy over 2f out: sn rdn and n.d* **5/1**[1]

530- **8** *nk* **Hurricane Emerald (IRE)**[211] 6911 3-9-5 **68** SilvestreDeSousa 12 58
(Mark Johnston) *in tch: rdn along 3f out: btn over 2f out* **14/1**

054- **9** *nk* **Dr Irv**[211] 6911 3-8-13 **62** MichaelO'Connell 13 51
(Kate Walton) *hld up in rr: sme hdwy on wd outside wl over 2f out: sn rdn and nvr a factor* **20/1**

300- **10** *1* **Blue Top**[211] 6911 3-8-12 **61** DuranFentiman 14 48
(Tim Walford) *in tch: hdwy to chse ldrs 3f out: rdn wl over 2f out: sn wknd* **33/1**

40-1 **11** *¾* **Dorry K (IRE)**[34] 1320 3-9-0 **68** DeanHeslop(5) 9 54
(David Barron) *s.i.s: a in rr* **8/1**[3]

5504 **12** *4 ½* **Roughlyn**[34] 1319 3-8-2 **56** AliceCartwright(5) 5 33
(Kevin Ryan) *a in rr* **12/1**

5650 **13** *35* **Ruby Glass (IRE)**[14] 1740 3-8-11 **60** (b) JamesSullivan 6
(Ruth Carr) *chsd ldrs: rdn along 3f out: sn wknd* **25/1**

2m 11.15s (4.15) **Going Correction** +0.325s/f (Good) **13 Ran SP% 122.8**
Speed ratings (Par 99): **96,94,93,92,90 89,88,88,88,87 87,83,55**
toteswingers: 1&2 £19.90, 1&3 £25.80, 2&3 £9.50. CSF £144.63 CT £1002.46 TOTE £34.00: £6.50, £2.30, £3.70; EX 203.10 TRIFECTA Not won..
Owner D W Barker **Bred** Highclere Stud **Trained** Sessay, N Yorks
■ Stewards' Enquiry : Adrian Nicholls two-day ban: used whip above permitted level (May 29-30)

FOCUS
Just a modest 3yo handicap. The winner was able to dictate and it definitely paid to race handily, with the performance of the third worth marking up slightly.
Take Two Official explanation: jockey said colt suffered interference at start
T/Plt: £52.30 to a £1 stake. Pool:£69,936.06 - 974.57 winning tickets. T/Qpdt: £3.20 to a £1 stake. Pool:£5,654.86 - 1,275.50 winning tickets. JR

1979 KEMPTON (A.W) (R-H)
Tuesday, May 15

OFFICIAL GOING: Standard
Wind: medium, half against Weather: showers

2145 KEMPTON.CO.UK MEDIAN AUCTION MAIDEN STKS 7f (P)
6:20 (8:06) (Class 6) 3-Y-O **£1,617** (£481; £240; £120) **Stalls** Low

Form RPR

04-5 **1** **Nassau Storm**[15] 1704 3-9-3 73 JimCrowley 7 78
(William Knight) *mde all: rdn ent fnl 2f: drvn fnl f: jst lasted: all out* **8/1**[3]

52 **2** *hd* **Cooler Climes**[41] 1182 3-9-3 0 LukeMorris 9 77
(Pat Eddery) *chsd wnr thrght: rdn and effrt ent fnl f: drvn and kpt on wl ins fnl f: steadily clsng on wnr fnl 100yds: nt quite get up* **7/2**[1]

23-6 **3** *1 ¼* **Strident Force**[18] 1647 3-9-3 76 KierenFallon 11 74
(Sir Michael Stoute) *t.k.h: hld up in tch: rdn and effrt ent fnl 2f: drvn over 1f out: kpt on u.p fnl f* **4/1**[2]

0 **4** *2 ¼* **Charity Box**[15] 1705 3-8-12 0 TedDurcan 6 63
(Chris Wall) *t.k.h: hld up in tch: rdn jst over 2f out: kpt on same pce fnl f* **12/1**

05- **5** *2 ½* **Monymusk**[297] 4330 3-9-3 0 NickyMackay 4 61+
(David Elsworth) *t.k.h: chsd ldrs: rdn and effrt 2f out: pressed ldrs over 1f out: fdd ins fnl f* **7/2**[1]

0 **6** *1 ¼* **Saltire Blue**[18] 1637 3-8-12 0 WilliamCarson 5 53+
(William Jarvis) *t.k.h: hld up in midfield: rdn 1/2-way: struggling and outpcd jst over 2f out: n.d after* **100/1**

4 **7** *½* **Ta Ajabb**[24] 1521 3-9-0 0 AdamBeschizza(3) 8 57
(William Haggas) *hld up in tch in midfield: rdn and unable qck over 3f out: outpcd ent fnl 2f: n.d after* **4/1**[2]

8 *½* **Wyebridge** 3-8-12 0 FergusSweeney 1 50
(Gary Moore) *in tch towards rr: rdn and struggling 1/2-way: plugged on fr over 1f out: no threat to ldrs* **100/1**

5- **9** *1 ¾* **Cha Ching (IRE)**[215] 6819 3-8-12 0 SebSanders 12 45
(J W Hills) *chsd ldrs: rdn and unable qck over 2f out: wknd wl over 1f out: fdd fnl f* **33/1**

10 *½* **Indigo Iris (IRE)** 3-9-3 0 RichardHughes 3 49
(Richard Hannon) *s.i.s: rdn along leaving stalls: clsd and in tch after 1f out: rdn and struggling over 2f out: sn btn* **18/1**

11 *19* **Boragh Waters (IRE)** 3-8-12 0 MartinDwyer 13
(Brian Meehan) *v.s.a: dashed up into midfield after 2f out: struggling and lost pl 1/2-way: hung lft and v wd bnd 3f out: sn lost tch* **100/1**

12 *35* **Crimson Cheer (USA)** 3-8-12 0 (t) ShaneKelly 2
(Brian Meehan) *bhd and struggling 1/2-way: t.o and eased fnl 2f* **40/1**

1m 25.61s (-0.39) **Going Correction** -0.10s/f (Stan) **12 Ran SP% 116.9**
Speed ratings (Par 97): **98,97,96,93,90 89,88,88,86,85 64,24**
toteswingers:1&2:£3.70, 2&3:£3.30, 1&3:£6.50 CSF £35.23 TOTE £8.90: £3.20, £1.70, £2.00; EX 48.70 Trifecta £370.60 Pool £606.11 - 1.21 winning units..
Owner The Oil Men Partnership **Bred** Glebe Stud & J F Dean **Trained** Patching, W Sussex

FOCUS
An ordinary maiden, and it proved hard to make up significant ground with the first two finishers in the front two more or less throughout.
Boragh Waters(IRE) Official explanation: jockey said filly hung left

2146 RACING UK H'CAP 6f (P)
6:50 (8:06) (Class 5) (0-70,70) 4-Y-O+ **£2,264** (£673; £336; £168) **Stalls** Low

Form RPR

1260 **1** **Efistorm**[20] 1614 11-9-1 **64** TomQueally 6 72
(Conor Dore) *in tch: rdn and effrt over 1f out: drvn to chal ins fnl f: led fnl 75yds: sn in command* **20/1**

6232 **2** *¾* **Riflessione**[26] 1480 6-8-11 **67** (b) DarrenEgan(7) 5 73
(Ronald Harris) *led: rdn and edgd rt u.p over 1f out: hdd and one pce fnl 75yds* **10/1**

1103 **3** *¾* **Spin Again (IRE)**[21] 1586 7-9-7 **70** MickaelBarzalona 2 77+
(Daniel Kubler) *in tch: rdn and effrt on inner to press ldr whn gap clsd and snatched up over 1f out: swtchd lft and kpt on ins fnl f* **5/1**[1]

3000 **4** *½* **With Hindsight (IRE)**[34] 1300 4-8-13 **67** DavidKenny(5) 4 69
(Michael Scudamore) *in tch towards rr: rdn and effrt wl over 1f out: nt clr run and swtchd rt 1f out: kpt on wl u.p ins fnl f* **40/1**

36-3 **5** *1 ½* **Links Drive Lady**[34] 1306 4-9-2 **65** (p) ShaneKelly 7 62
(Dean Ivory) *in tch: pushed along 1/2-way: drvn and kpt on same pce fnl f over 1f out* **6/1**[2]

6-30 **6** *nk* **Mawjoodah**[11] 1827 4-9-4 **67** BarryMcHugh 10 63
(Brian Ellison) *wnt lft and stdd s: sn swtchd rt and hld up in rr: rdn and effrt on inner 2f out: hdwy and swtchd lft 1f out: no imp fnl 100yds* **8/1**[3]

3-41 **7** *½* **Proper Charlie**[14] 1734 4-9-5 **68** JimCrowley 11 63
(William Knight) *stdd and swtchd rt s: hld up in rr: rdn and effrt 2f out: hdwy over 1f out: no imp ins fnl f* **6/1**[2]

5040 **8** *1* **Roodee Queen**[22] 1564 4-9-7 **70** DaneO'Neill 8 61
(Milton Bradley) *chsd ldr: rdn and unable qck wl over 1f out: lost 2nd ent fnl f: wknd fnl 150yds* **10/1**

6006 **9** *½* **Pick A Little**[20] 1614 4-9-2 **68** RyanClark(3) 3 58
(Michael Blake) *in tch towards rr: rdn and effrt wl over 1f out: styd on same pce and no imp 1f out* **10/1**

31-0 **10** *4 ½* **Sketchy Evidence (USA)**[129] 91 4-9-2 **65** LukeMorris 1 40
(John Best) *hld up in rr: rdn and no rspnse 2f out: sn wknd* **6/1**[2]

0000 **11** *4* **Sermons Mount (USA)**[36] 1254 6-9-1 **64**............................ JohnFahy 9 27
(Paul Howling) *j. shadow sn after s: a towards rr: rdn and no rspnse 2f out: wknd* **12/1**

1m 12.36s (-0.74) **Going Correction** -0.10s/f (Stan) **11** Ran SP% **112.8**
Speed ratings (Par 103): **100,99,98,97,95 94,94,92,92,86 80**
toteswingers:1&2:£25.60, 2&3:£9.50, 1&3:£29.10 CSF £198.65 CT £1158.91 TOTE £24.60: £4.90, £2.20, £2.00; EX 106.40 Trifecta £178.10 Pool £365.86 - 1.52 winning units..
Owner Sean J Murphy **Bred** E Duggan And D Churchman **Trained** Hubbert's Bridge, Lincs
■ Stewards' Enquiry : Darren Egan one-day ban: careless riding (May 29)

FOCUS
Like in the opening race, it proved hard to make up ground, and that's despite the pace appearing decent enough.
Riflessione Official explanation: jockey said gelding hung right

2147 KEMPTON FOR WEDDINGS MEDIAN AUCTION MAIDEN STKS 6f (P)
7:20 (8:06) (Class 5) 3-Y-O **£2,264** (£673; £336; £168) **Stalls** Low

Form RPR

4 **1** **Dutch Supreme**[11] 1825 3-9-3 0............................ TedDurcan 11 86+
(David Lanigan) *awkward leaving stalls: chsd ldrs: rdn and qcknd to ld 1f out: r.o strly* **15/8[2]**

23-2 **2** *2 1/4* **Sir Fredlot (IRE)**[14] 1723 3-9-3 78............................ MichaelHills 5 75
(Charles Hills) *chsd ldr: rdn to chal over 2f out: led narrowly 2f out: hdd 1f out: sn outpcd by wnr and btn: kpt on for 2nd* **5/4[1]**

52-0 **3** *nk* **Cheworee**[32] 1357 3-8-12 76............................ NickyMackay 10 69
(David Elsworth) *t.k.h: chsd ldrs: rdn and effrt wl over 1f out: ev ch 1f out: outpcd by wnr fnl 150yds: kpt on* **7/1[3]**

50-0 **4** *4* **Wrapped Up**[32] 1359 3-8-12 53............................ RichardHughes 2 56
(Heather Main) *led: hdd and rdn 2f out: wknd ins fnl f* **12/1**

0- **5** *hd* **Picture Dealer**[207] 6991 3-9-3 0............................ TomQueally 9 60+
(Gary Moore) *s.i.s: bhd: rdn 1/2-way: hdwy but stl plenty to do over 1f out: r.o strly ins fnl f: nvr trbld ldrs* **20/1**

000- **6** *2 1/2* **Seraphiel**[207] 6992 3-9-3 59............................ DaneO'Neill 1 52
(Chris Down) *hld up in midfield: rdn and outpcd ent fnl 2f: n.d fr wl over 1f out* **50/1**

7 *1/2* **Gladiatrix** 3-8-12 0............................ JamesMillman 4 46
(Rod Millman) *in tch: rdn 1/2-way: struggling over 2f out: sn wknd* **33/1**

000- **8** *hd* **Clapped**[192] 7292 3-9-3 0............................ JimCrowley 7 50
(Ed Vaughan) *s.i.s: a towards rr: modest late hdwy fnl f: n.d* **50/1**

0 **9** *4* **Starlight Secret**[14] 1723 3-9-3 0............................ FergusSweeney 6 37
(Simon Earle) *t.k.h: hld up in midfield: rdn and struggling over 2f out: sn wknd* **100/1**

10 *1/2* **Compton Crofter** 3-8-10 0............................(t) NicoleNordblad(7) 12 36
(Hans Adielsson) *hld up off the pce in last quartet: rdn and effrt on outer jst over 2f out: no prog whn hung rt over 1f out: n.d* **50/1**

11 *1 1/2* **Made Of More** 3-9-3 0............................ RobertHavlin 3 31
(Roger Ingram) *s.i.s: a bhd: hung lft whn rdn over 2f out: n.d* **50/1**

1m 12.45s (-0.65) **Going Correction** -0.10s/f (Stan) **11** Ran SP% **116.0**
Speed ratings (Par 99): **100,97,96,91,91 87,87,86,81,80 78**
toteswingers:1&2:£1.60, 2&3:£2.60, 1&3:£3.80 CSF £4.21 TOTE £3.10: £1.20, £1.10, £1.90; EX 4.70 Trifecta £20.60 Pool £912.88 - 32.71winning units..
Owner Trevor Benton **Bred** Mr & Mrs J Laws **Trained** Upper Lambourn, Berks

FOCUS
Not a strong race, but the winner looks useful.
Wrapped Up Official explanation: jockey said filly hung right

2148 BETFAIR MEDIAN AUCTION MAIDEN FILLIES' STKS 1m 3f (P)
7:50 (8:06) (Class 5) 3-Y-O **£2,264** (£673; £336; £168) **Stalls** Low

Form RPR

06- **1** **Dedication**[207] 6985 3-9-0 0............................ JamesDoyle 6 76
(Roger Charlton) *hld up in tch: hdwy to press ldr 5f out: rdn to chal and bmpd 2f out: led fnl 100yds: hld on cl home* **13/2[2]**

0-32 **2** *nse* **Perfect Delight**[9] 1892 3-9-0 79............................ JohnFahy 4 76
(Clive Cox) *chsd ldr tl 5f out: chsd ldrs: rdn and swtchd rt 2f out: ev ch but hanging lft fr over 1f out: led 1f out: hdd fnl 100yds: battled bk cl home: jst hld* **4/6[1]**

30-2 **3** *2 1/2* **Aliante**[49] 1055 3-9-0 69............................ JoeFanning 5 71
(Mark Johnston) *led: rdn and veered lft 2f out: hdd 1f out: wknd fnl 100yds* **10/1**

4 *4* **Moonglow** 3-9-0 0............................ WilliamBuick 1 64+
(John Gosden) *in tch: rdn 4f out: rn green and outpcd over 2f out: swtchd rt over 1f out: kpt on again ins fnl f* **8/1**

040- **5** *3/4* **Lily Potts**[187] 7343 3-9-0 70............................ DaneO'Neill 2 62
(Chris Down) *chsd ldrs: rdn and effrt over 2f out: unable qck and sltly hmpd ent fnl 2f: wknd over 1f out* **20/1**

6 *12* **Jaja De Jau** 3-9-0 0............................ JimCrowley 7 41
(Anthony Honeyball) *in tch towards rr: rdn 3f out: wknd over 2f out* **7/1[3]**

00 **7** *69* **Felona E Serona**[11] 1826 3-9-0 0............................ KirstyMilczarek 3
(Laura Young) *in tch in last trio: rdn 1/2-way: lost tch 5f out: sn wl t.o* **100/1**

0 **8** *82* **Let's Confer**[69] 816 3-9-0 0............................ J-PGuillambert 8
(Michael Attwater) *veered lft leaving stalls and virtually ref to r: eventually set off 3f bhd* **66/1**

2m 21.76s (-0.14) **Going Correction** -0.10s/f (Stan) **8** Ran SP% **113.3**
Speed ratings (Par 96): **96,95,94,91,90 81,31,**
toteswingers:1&2:£2.10, 2&3:£2.30, 1&3:£7.60 CSF £11.05 TOTE £7.50: £1.90, £1.02, £2.20; EX 13.70 Trifecta £55.30 Pool £563.32 - 7.53 winning units..
Owner K Abdulla **Bred** Juddmonte Farms Ltd **Trained** Beckhampton, Wilts

FOCUS
Perhaps not a race to be too positive about.

2149 BETFAIR SUPPORTING GRASSROOTS RACING FILLIES' H'CAP 1m 4f (P)
8:20 (8:21) (Class 5) (0-70,69) 4-Y-O+ **£2,264** (£673; £336; £168) **Stalls** Centre

Form RPR

2155 **1** **Isdaal**[15] 1706 5-8-6 61............................ DarrenEgan(7) 2 69+
(Kevin Morgan) *hld up in last trio: rdn and gd hdwy to ld over 1f out: r.o wl fnl f* **11/2**

1-54 **2** *1 3/4* **Moresweets 'n Lace**[34] 1314 5-9-7 69............................ RichardHughes 7 74
(Gary Moore) *stdd s: t.k.h: swtchd rt after 1f: hld up in midfield: hdwy to chse ldrs and n.m.r wl over 1f out: swtchd lft 1f out: chsd wnr ins fnl f: no imp* **8/1**

50-1 **3** *1/2* **Passion Play**[20] 1613 4-9-4 66............................ JimCrowley 3 70
(William Knight) *led: rdn over 2f out: hdd and drvn over 1f out: styd on same pce fnl f* **11/4[1]**

060- **4** *2* **On The Feather**[225] 6592 6-9-4 66............................ JamesMillman 1 67
(Rod Millman) *t.k.h: hld up in tch in last trio: rdn and effrt jst over 2f out: kpt on but no threat to ldrs fnl f* **13/2**

00-2 **5** *1/2* **Mafeteng**[15] 1706 4-9-2 64............................ TedDurcan 4 64
(John Dunlop) *chsd ldrs: rdn and effrt on inner jst over 2f out: drvn and unable qck: one pce and btn fnl f* **10/3[2]**

000- **6** *3/4* **Rather Cool**[215] 6823 4-8-7 55 oh5............................ KieranO'Neill 5 54
(John Bridger) *bhd: rdn 4f out: sme hdwy over 1f out: styd on same pce fnl f* **50/1**

14 **7** *11* **Wicked Spirit (IRE)**[6] 1991 4-9-7 69............................ JoeFanning 6 50
(Mark Johnston) *t.k.h: chsd ldr tl wl over 1f out: wknd qckly 1f out: eased fnl 100yds* **9/2[3]**

2m 34.38s (-0.12) **Going Correction** -0.10s/f (Stan) **7** Ran SP% **109.7**
Speed ratings (Par 100): **96,94,94,93,92 92,85**
toteswingers:1&2:£5.30, 2&3:£3.50, 1&3:£2.60 CSF £43.54 CT £134.43 TOTE £7.40: £2.70, £3.80; EX 52.60 Trifecta £336.50 Part won. Pool £454.76 - 0.72 winning units..
Owner Roemex Ltd **Bred** Shadwell Estate Company Limited **Trained** Gazeley, Suffolk

FOCUS
An ordinary fillies' handicap.

2150 KEMPTON FOR OUTDOOR EVENTS H'CAP 1m (P)
8:50 (8:53) (Class 4) (0-80,79) 3-Y-O **£4,075** (£1,212; £606; £303) **Stalls** Low

Form RPR

25-2 **1** **Curzon Line**[11] 1825 3-9-7 79............................ MickaelBarzalona 7 86
(Mahmood Al Zarooni) *dwlt: pushed along after 2f: rdn and gd hdwy ent fnl 2f: chal jst ins fnl f: r.o wl to ld fnl 50yds* **5/1[2]**

10 **2** *shd* **Basseterre (IRE)**[22] 1565 3-9-5 77............................ MichaelHills 4 84
(Charles Hills) *hld up in tch towards rr: rdn over 2f out: qcknd to ld 2f out: hrd pressed 1f out: battled on wl tl hdd and no ex fnl 50yds* **5/1[2]**

204- **3** *nk* **Dynamic Duo (IRE)**[239] 6216 3-9-3 75............................ RichardHughes 10 81
(Richard Hannon) *chsd ldrs: wnt 2nd 5f out: rdn and ev ch fr wl over 1f out: unable qck fnl 50yds* **16/1**

1 **4** *1 3/4* **Main Line**[29] 1422 3-9-7 79............................ TedDurcan 3 81+
(David Lanigan) *dwlt: sn in tch in midfield: lost pl and dropped to rr 1/2-way: stuck bhd field on inner over 2f out: switching lft and hdwy over 1f out: r.o wl fnl f: nt rch ldrs* **4/1[1]**

51-2 **5** *1* **Johnno**[31] 1392 3-9-6 78............................ SebSanders 9 78+
(J W Hills) *hld up in tch towards rr: swtchd lft and effrt 2f out: kpt on wl fnl f: nt rch ldrs* **6/1**

5141 **6** *3/4* **Masters Blazing**[3] 2089 3-8-10 68 6ex............................(p) BrettDoyle 2 66
(John Ryan) *chsd ldr for 3f: styd chsng ldrs: rdn and effrt to press ldrs wl over 1f out: no ex 1f out: wknd ins fnl f* **9/1**

220- **7** *4* **Siouxperhero (IRE)**[196] 7205 3-8-12 70............................ JimCrowley 5 59
(William Muir) *in tch towards rr: rdn and hdwy 2f out: no imp over 1f out: wknd fnl f* **25/1**

236- **8** *3* **Abhaath (USA)**[186] 7358 3-8-13 71............................ PaulHanagan 6 53
(Ed Dunlop) *t.k.h: chsd ldrs: rdn and effrt over 2f out: wknd ent fnl f* **16/1**

4-21 **9** *1* **Hamis Al Bin (IRE)**[54] 1001 3-9-6 78............................ JoeFanning 8 58
(Mark Johnston) *hld up in tch towards rr: rdn and effrt on outer over 2f out: no imp over 1f out: wknd fnl f* **11/2[3]**

4-00 **10** *8* **Tidy Affair (IRE)**[20] 1612 3-9-6 78............................ AdamKirby 1 39
(Murty McGrath) *led: rdn and hdd 2f out: wknd qckly over 1f out: fdd fnl f* **50/1**

225- **11** *3/4* **Tidal's Baby**[216] 6786 3-9-2 74............................ TomQueally 12 33
(Tony Carroll) *s.i.s: styd wd: hdwy to chse ldrs 5f out: wkng whn hmpd 2f out: sn bhd* **40/1**

1m 38.08s (-1.72) **Going Correction** -0.10s/f (Stan) **11** Ran SP% **113.0**
Speed ratings (Par 101): **104,103,103,101,100 100,96,93,92,84 83**
toteswingers:1&2:£5.50, 2&3:£16.40, 1&3:£12.00 CSF £28.46 CT £373.61 TOTE £6.20: £1.90, £2.00, £5.10; EX 31.30 Trifecta £156.40 Pool £753.35 - 3.56 winning units..
Owner Godolphin **Bred** Darley **Trained** Newmarket, Suffolk

FOCUS
The pace was a bit muddling, appearing quick early before slowing on the turn into the straight, but this race should produce some nice winners in the coming weeks.

2151 BETFAIR.COM RACING H'CAP (LONDON MILE QUALIFIER) 1m (P)
9:20 (9:21) (Class 4) (0-85,84) 4-Y-O+ **£4,075** (£1,212; £606; £303) **Stalls** Low

Form RPR

3400 **1** **Sinfonico (IRE)**[24] 1510 4-9-3 80............................ RichardHughes 5 89
(Richard Hannon) *hld up in midfield: swtchd lft and rdn 2f out: hdwy over 1f out: chal ins fnl f: drvn to ld wl ins fnl f: r.o wl* **4/1[1]**

0-00 **2** *nk* **Shavansky**[34] 1321 8-9-5 82............................ JamesMillman 12 90
(Rod Millman) *dwlt: t.k.h: hdwy into midfield 1/2-way: rdn and effrt on inner jst over 2f out: ev ch ins fnl f: r.o wl* **8/1[2]**

330- **3** *hd* **Rustic Deacon**[217] 6773 5-8-11 74............................ JamieMackay 1 82
(Willie Musson) *broke wl and led for 1f: t.k.h and hld up in bhd ldrs after: rdn and qcknd to ld jst over 1f out: drvn and battled on wl tl hdd and lost 2 pls wl ins fnl f* **16/1**

231- **4** *2 1/4* **Top Diktat**[207] 6997 4-9-3 80............................ KierenFallon 2 83
(Sir Michael Stoute) *in tch: rdn and effrt to chse ldrs 2f out: drvn and one pce fnl f: wl hld and eased towards fin* **4/1[1]**

-353 **5** *1* **Den's Gift (IRE)**[47] 1087 8-9-0 77............................(b) AdamKirby 13 78
(Clive Cox) *chsd ldr after 2f: rdn and ev ch ent fnl 2f: unable qck over 1f out: wknd ins fnl f* **10/1[3]**

3006 **6** *3/4* **Dr Red Eye**[17] 1659 4-8-12 75............................ TomQueally 7 74
(Scott Dixon) *led after 1f: rdn ent fnl 2f: hdd jst over 1f out: wknd ins fnl f* **8/1[2]**

201- **7** *1 1/2* **Uppercut**[204] 7050 4-9-5 82............................ FergusSweeney 14 77
(Stuart Kittow) *in tch on outer: rdn and unable qck 2f out: wknd ent fnl f* **20/1**

00- **8** *1/2* **Soweto Star (IRE)**[219] 6727 4-9-0 77............................ LukeMorris 4 71
(John Best) *chsd ldrs: rdn and unable qck over 2f out: wknd ent fnl f* **20/1**

150- **9** *nk* **Main Beach**[164] 7628 5-9-7 84............................(t) StevieDonohoe 11 78
(Tobias B P Coles) *s.i.s: hld up in last quartet: rdn and effrt on inner 2f out: no imp 1f out: wknd ins fnl f* **12/1**

00-4 **10** *1/2* **Orpen'Arry (IRE)**[20] 1611 4-8-8 74............................ SeanLevey(3) 10 66
(Jimmy Fox) *chsd ldrs: rdn and unable qck jst over 1f out: drvn and wknd jst over 1f out* **20/1**

60-0 **11** *1 3/4* **Aciano (IRE)**[29] 1416 4-9-0 77............................(v[1]) TedDurcan 8 65
(Brendan Powell) *in tch in midfield: struggling u.p over 2f out: wknd 2f out* **33/1**

2-50 **12** *1* **Musnad (USA)**[44] 1156 4-8-7 70 oh1............................ BarryMcHugh 6 56
(Brian Ellison) *stdd after s: a in rr: rdn and no imp over 2f out: n.d* **8/1[2]**

504- **13** *3/4* **My Son Max**[219] 6728 4-9-1 78............................ WilliamBuick 9 62
(P J O'Gorman) *t.k.h: hld up in last quartet: rdn and no prog jst over 2f out: n.d* **20/1**

0-00 **14** *1 1/4* **Hail Promenader (IRE)**[20] 1611 6-8-7 **70** oh2............. WilliamCarson 3 51
(Anthony Carson) *in tch: lost pl and pushed along 1/2-way: rdn and wknd jst over 2f out: bhd fnl f* **50/1**

1m 37.28s (-2.52) **Going Correction** -0.10s/f (Stan) **14** Ran SP% **119.9**
Speed ratings (Par 105): **108,107,107,105,104 103,102,101,101,100 98,97,97,95**
toteswingers:1&2:£11.80, 2&3:£35.10, 1&3:£29.70 CSF £31.61 CT £482.73 TOTE £4.20: £1.60, £3.20, £7.30; EX 45.70 TRIFECTA Not won..
Owner White Beech Farm **Bred** P Doyle Bloodstock & J K Thoroughbred **Trained** East Everleigh, Wilts

FOCUS
A fair, competitive handicap and the pace was good enough to set this up for the closers.
My Son Max Official explanation: jockey said gelding hung right
T/Jkpt: Not won. T/Plt: £115.40 to a £1 stake. Pool £80,663.47 - 510.07 winning units. T/Qpdt: £38.40 to a £1 stake. Pool £7,408.32 - 142.70 winning units. SP

[1869]SAINT-CLOUD (L-H)
Tuesday, May 15

OFFICIAL GOING: Turf: good

2156a PRIX CLEOPATRE (GROUP 3) (3YO FILLIES) (TURF) 1m 2f 110y
2:20 (12:00) 3-Y-O **£33,333** (£13,333; £10,000; £6,666; £3,333)

RPR

1 **Dalkala (USA)**[26] 3-8-9 0............................ Christophe-PatriceLemaire 4 112+
(A De Royer-Dupre, France) *settled in 3rd: travelled smoothly: chal for ld 2f out: led 1 1/2f out: sn wnt clr: r.o wl: nvr threatened: comf* **47/10[2]**

2 *4* **Poupee Flash (USA)**[29] 3-8-9 0.............................. StephanePasquier 3 103
(P Bary, France) *settled in 4th: rdn to chse ldrs fr 2 1/2f out: wnt 3rd 2f out: tk 2nd ent fnl f: styd on: no threat to wnr* **58/10[3]**

3 *3 1/2* **La Conquerante**[40] 3-8-10 0 ow1........................ ChristopheSoumillon 5 97
(J-C Rouget, France) *s.i.s: hld up in rr: u.p fr 1 1/2f out: r.o fnl f wout threatening ldrs: nrest at fin* **6/1**

4 *4* **Waldlerche**[28] 1434 3-9-0 0.. MaximeGuyon 2 93
(A Fabre, France) *led fr s: sn wl clr: wnt further clr ent st: u.p 2f out: hdd 1 1/2f out: fdd* **3/5[1]**

5 *3/4* **Brocottes (FR)**[28] 1434 3-8-9 0.................................... GregoryBenoist 1 87
(N Clement, France) *settled in 2nd: rdn to chse ldr ent st: no ex fr over 1 1/2f out: fdd* **11/1**

2m 13.7s (-5.90) **5** Ran SP% **117.4**
WIN (incl. 1 euro stake): 5.70. PLACES: 3.10, 2.80. SF: 23.70.
Owner H H Aga Khan **Bred** His Highness The Aga Khan Studs Sc **Trained** Chantilly, France

NOTEBOOK
Dalkala(USA) extended her unbeaten run to three with a comfortable four-length success on this step up to Group company, and will now head to the Prix de Diane as a major contender. She's the first foal of a 1m winner (inc at 2 and Group 3) from the family of Daylami and Dalakhani.

2157 - 2158a (Foreign Racing) - See Raceform Interactive

JAGERSRO (R-H)
Tuesday, May 15

OFFICIAL GOING: Dirt: standard

2159a LANWADES STUD JAGERSRO SPRINT (LISTED RACE) (3YO+) (DIRT) 6f (D)
6:31 (12:00) 3-Y-O+ **£28,089** (£9,363; £4,681; £2,808; £1,872)

RPR

1 **Alcohuaz (CHI)**[226] 6563 7-9-6 0....................................... FJohansson 2 106
(Lennart Reuterskiold Jr, Sweden) **30/100[1]**

2 *3* **Govinda (USA)**[169] 5-9-6 0... EPedroza 7 96
(A Wohler, Germany) **103/10**

3 *6* **Match Point (FR)**[219] 6741 6-9-3 0......................... Per-AndersGraberg 6 74
(Niels Petersen, Norway) **15/2[3]**

4 *3 1/2* **Fratellino**[45] 1129 5-9-6 0... MartinHarley 1 66
(Alan McCabe) *s.i.s and bhd early: detached in last and rdn over 3f out: sme late prog to go 4th ins fnl f: nvr a factor* **26/5[2]**

5 *2 1/2* **Reggae Dancer (IRE)**[935] 7006 5-9-6 0......................... RafaelSchistl 3 58
(Bent Olsen, Denmark) **136/10**

6 *1 1/2* **Panama Jack**[698] 3111 5-9-6 0................................(b) ValmirDeAzeredo 4 53
(Vanja Sandrup, Sweden) **171/10**

1m 11.3s (71.30)
WFA 3 from 5yo+ 10lb **6** Ran SP% **126.0**
PARI-MUTUEL (all including 1sek stake): WIN 1.31; PLACE 1.00, 1.03, 1.02; SF 6.21.
Owner Dr Omar Zawawi **Bred** Haras De Pirque (chile) **Trained** Sweden

2160a IKC RACING PRAMMS MEMORIAL (GROUP 3) (4YO+) (DIRT) 1m 143y(D)
8:03 (12:00) 4-Y-O+ **£65,543** (£23,408; £11,235; £7,490; £4,681)

RPR

1 **Premio Loco (USA)**[52] 1034 8-9-4 0.............................. GeorgeBaker 6 110
(Chris Wall) *sn trcking ldr in 2nd on outer: rdn to chal on turn into st: r.o to ld ins fnl f: pushed out* **6/5[1]**

2 *3/4* **Silver Ocean (USA)**[66] 876 4-9-4 0..................... Per-AndersGraberg 9 108
(Niels Petersen, Norway) *got across fr wd draw to ld bef first turn: rdn and strly pressed on turn into st: hdd ins fnl f: kpt on* **21/10[2]**

3 *1* **Empire Storm (GER)**[30] 1410 5-9-4 0................................... EPedroza 2 106
(A Wohler, Germany) *trckd ldr in 3rd on rail: rdn to try and chal on turn into st: outpcd by ldng duo ins fnl f: kpt on for clr 3rd cl home* **109/10**

4 *5* **Nova Valorem (IRE)**[44] 4-9-4 0.................................... FredericSpanu 1 95
(F Rohaut, France) *settled in midfield on rail: swtchd off rail and rdn to try and improve over 2 1/2f out: outpcd by ldng trio over 1f out: kpt on for wl hld 4th ins fnl f* **212/10**

5 *nse* **La Zona (IRE)**[184] 6-9-1 0... FJohansson 7 92
(Wido Neuroth, Norway) *hld up in last trio: stdy prog into midfield over 3f out: rdn and outpcd on turn into st: kpt on ins fnl f* **77/10**

6 *hd* **Luca Brasi (FR)**[229] 8-9-4 0.. ManuelMartinez 3 94
(Francisco Castro, Sweden) *hld up in last pair early: short of room and dropped to last on run to first turn: rdn to try and improve over 2f out: kpt on one pce ins fnl f* **73/10[3]**

7 *1 1/4* **Let'sgoforit (IRE)** 4-9-4 0.. ElioneChaves 8 92
(Bodil Hallencreutz, Sweden) *midfield on outer: rdn and outpcd over 1 1/2f out: no ex and fdd ins fnl f* **36/1**

8 *hd* **Highway (IRE)**[368] 9-9-4 0......................................(b) ValmirDeAzeredo 5 91
(Francisco Castro, Sweden) *broke wl to ld: taken bk and settled towards rr on run to first turn: rdn to improve over 1 1/2f out: kpt on tl no ex and fdd wl ins fnl f* **55/1**

9 *1 3/4* **Peas And Carrots (DEN)**[17] 9-9-4 0............................. RafaelSchistl 4 87
(Lennart Reuterskiold Jr, Sweden) *hld up in last pair on outer: rdn and outpcd over 2f out: no ex and dropped to last on turn into st: plugged on ins fnl f* **103/10**

1m 46.8s (106.80) **9** Ran SP% **127.5**
PARI-MUTUEL (all including 1sek stake): WIN 2.26; PLACE 1.23, 1.25, 1.71; SF 6.24.
Owner Bernard Westley **Bred** Kidder, Cole & Griggs **Trained** Newmarket, Suffolk

[1903]BATH (L-H)
Wednesday, May 16

OFFICIAL GOING: Good (7.7)
Wind: Moderate, ahead Weather: Sunny early

2161 PREMIER CONSERVATORY ROOFS FILLIES' H'CAP 1m 5y
5:40 (5:40) (Class 5) (0-75,81) 4-Y-O+ **£2,264** (£673; £336; £168) **Stalls** Low

Form RPR

1422 **1** **Tidal Run**[9] 1909 4-9-2 **70**... MatthewDavies 3 77
(Mick Channon) *broke wl: stdd in tch: drvn over 3f out: chal fr 2f out tl slt ld over 1f out: drvn and styd on wl fnl f and a doing enough* **9/4[1]**

526- **2** *nk* **Barathea Dancer (IRE)**[238] 6256 4-9-6 **74**......................... DaneO'Neill 8 80
(Roger Teal) *sn led: drvn and jnd 2f out: narrowly hdd over 1f out: kpt on u.p fnl f but a hld* **5/2[2]**

00-1 **3** *1 3/4* **Miss Bootylishes**[9] 1909 7-9-8 **81** 6ex.......................... DavidKenny(5) 6 83
(Paul Burgoyne) *towards rr but in tch: drvn along 3f out: hdwy and wnt 3rd 2f out: rdn dropped whip sn after: styd on same pce fnl f* **9/2[3]**

00-0 **4** *4 1/2* **Cloud Illusions (USA)**[18] 1652 4-9-2 **70**................. RichardKingscote 2 62
(Heather Main) *sn chsng ldr tl over 3f out: wknd ins fnl 2f* **17/2**

-030 **5** *3 3/4* **Ellielusive (IRE)**[70] 822 5-8-4 **61** oh16..................... DeclanCannon(3) 4 44
(Mark Brisbourne) *t.k.h: trckd ldrs: chsd ldr over 3f out: sn rdn: wknd 2f out* **33/1**

0610 **6** *8* **Marksbury**[27] 1487 5-8-7 **61** oh1... LiamJones 5 26
(Mark Brisbourne) *chsd ldrs: rdn over 4f out: wknd over 2f out* **9/1**

0123 **7** *1/2* **Qeethaara (USA)**[21] 1609 8-9-4 **72**.......................(p) TomMcLaughlin 7 35
(Mark Brisbourne) *rrd bef s: chsd ldrs: rdn over 3f out: wknd over 2f out* **9/1**

1m 44.71s (3.91) **Going Correction** +0.30s/f (Good) **7** Ran SP% **111.0**
Speed ratings (Par 100): **92,91,89,85,81 73,73**
toteswingers: 1&2 £1.30, 1&3 £2.30, 2&3 £2.60 CSF £7.60 CT £20.48 TOTE £2.90: £1.20, £2.20; EX 9.70 Trifecta £27.50 Pool: £276.26 - 7.42 winning units..
Owner M Channon **Bred** Barry Walters Farms **Trained** West Ilsley, Berks

FOCUS
Solid form for the grade.

2162 K2 CONSERVATORIES H'CAP 1m 5y
6:10 (6:11) (Class 6) (0-60,60) 3-Y-O **£1,617** (£481; £240; £120) **Stalls** Low

Form RPR

6525 **1** **Skyeron**[22] 1590 3-8-10 **49**... LiamJones 13 54
(Mark Brisbourne) *sn chsng ldr: drvn to ld over 1f out: styd on wl u.p fnl f* **14/1**

50-1 **2** *1* **Our Phylli Vera (IRE)**[37] 1259 3-9-7 **60**............................ LukeMorris 1 63
(Harry Dunlop) *in tch: hrd rdn and styd on fr 2f out: kpt on u.p fnl f to take 2nd cl home but no imp on wnr* **7/1[3]**

00-6 **3** *hd* **Choral Bee**[25] 1518 3-9-2 **55**.. DaneO'Neill 12 58
(Henry Candy) *chsd ldrs: rdn 2f out: disp 2nd u.p ins fnl f: no imp on wnr and dropped to 3rd cl home* **10/1**

2200 **4** *2* **Athletic**[36] 1288 3-9-4 **57**......................................(p) WilliamCarson 5 55
(Andrew Reid) *towards rr: n.m.r over 4f out hdwy on outside over 2f out: styd on u.p fnl f: nt rch ldrs* **25/1**

30-0 **5** *3/4* **Strictly Mine**[35] 1303 3-8-11 **50**........................... RichardKingscote 11 46
(Jonathan Portman) *sn led: rdn over 2f out: hdd over 1f out: disp 2nd ins fnl f: wknd fnl 120yds* **9/1**

000- **6** *1/2* **Isola Bella**[200] 7177 3-8-8 **47**... MartinHarley 14 42
(Jonathan Portman) *chsd ldrs: rdn over 2f out: styng on same pce whn rdr dropped whip ins fnl f* **25/1**

6342 **7** *nk* **Vexillum (IRE)**[15] 1740 3-9-6 **59**.................................. SamHitchcott 10 53
(Mick Channon) *towards rr: rdn over 2f out: styd on ins fnl f: kpt on clsng stages: nt rch ldrs* **4/1[1]**

4-60 **8** *3 1/2* **Rockme Cockney**[25] 1517 3-9-2 **60**....................... MatthewCosham(5) 3 46
(Jeremy Gask) *in tch: rdn 3f out: styd on same pce fr 2f out* **12/1**

006- **9** *nse* **Miss Granger**[222] 6662 3-8-9 **51**.................................... SophieDoyle(3) 15 37
(Ronald Harris) *towards rr: pushed along and hdwy towards outer fr 3f out: kpt on fnl f but nvr gng pce to rch ldrs* **50/1**

00-0 **10** *3/4* **Highly Likely (IRE)**[37] 1259 3-8-7 **46**.............................. DavidProbert 2 30
(John Dunlop) *towards rr: rdn 3f out: nvr gng pce to get beyond mid-div* **7/1[3]**

00-2 **11** *nk* **Hardy Plume**[6] 2014 3-8-10 **49**.. JohnFahy 9 33
(Denis Coakley) *chsd ldrs: rdn 3f out: wknd fr 2f out* **5/1[2]**

00-4 **12** *shd* **Mariannes**[22] 1590 3-8-8 **47**.. KieranO'Neill 8 31
(John Dunlop) *towards rr: sme hdwy over 2f out: nvr in contention* **14/1**

0-00 **13** *2* **Kylin**[15] 1725 3-9-1 **54**.. LiamKeniry 7 33
(Olivia Maylam) *chsd ldrs: rdn 3f out: wknd over 2f out* **40/1**

0-05 **14** *shd* **The Quarterjack**[78] 730 3-8-8 **50**............................... SimonPearce(3) 4 29
(Ron Hodges) *a towards rr* **40/1**

505 **15** *18* **Petersboden**[32] 1377 3-9-5 **58**.................................... FergusSweeney 6
(Michael Blanshard) *towards rr: sme hdwy over 3f out: sn wknd* **33/1**

006- **16** *11* **You Got The Love**[179] 7481 3-8-7 **46**.................(b) AdamBeschizza(3) 16
(Jeremy Gask) *s.i.s: towards rr: wd bnd 3f out and brief effrt: sn wknd* **33/1**

1m 44.93s (4.13) **Going Correction** +0.30s/f (Good) **16** Ran SP% **122.2**
Speed ratings (Par 97): **91,90,89,87,87 86,86,82,82,81 81,81,79,79,61 50**
toteswingers: 1&2 £17.30, 1&3 £19.90, 2&3 £14.40 CSF £102.58 CT £1091.86 TOTE £18.40: £3.30, £2.00, £2.10, £5.90; EX 161.30 TRIFECTA Not won..
Owner Mark Brisbourne **Bred** Manor Farm Stud (rutland) **Trained** Great Ness, Shropshire
■ Stewards' Enquiry : William Carson one-day ban: careless riding (May 30)

FOCUS
A low-grade handicap that little got into from off the pace.

2163 OAKLEY GREEN CONSERVATORIES MAIDEN AUCTION STKS 5f 11y
6:40 (6:45) (Class 6) 2-Y-O **£1,704** (£503; £251) **Stalls** Centre

Form RPR
1 **Rebel Magic** 2-8-6 0 ... KieranO'Neill 5 69+
(Richard Hannon) *s.i.s: sn rcvrd: hdwy over 2f out: chsd ldr 1f out: drvn and styd on strly fnl f to ld last strides* **5/1**[3]
2 2 shd **Lucky Beggar (IRE)**[28] 1451 2-9-3 0 ... MichaelHills 3 80
(Charles Hills) *led: drvn and kpt on fnl f: hdd last strides* **4/5**[1]
32 3 1 ¾ **Marchwood**[34] 1330 2-8-13 0 ... LiamKeniry 6 70
(J S Moore) *chsd ldr: rdn 2f out: lost 2nd 1f out: one pce ins fnl f* **4/1**[2]
4 6 **Lobelia** 2-8-6 0 ... MartinDwyer 1 41
(Brian Meehan) *chsd ldrs pushed along 3f out: wknd wl over 1f out* **14/1**
0 5 1 ¼ **Baltic Gin (IRE)**[26] 1495 2-8-8 0 ... DavidProbert 4 39
(Malcolm Saunders) *chsd ldrs: drvn over 2f out: wknd wl over 1f out* **25/1**
6 6 2 ¼ **Schottische**[42] 1188 2-8-6 0 ... LiamJones 8 29
(Derek Haydn Jones) *loose bef s: sn ct: drvn and wd 3f out: outpcd* **33/1**
7 1 **Honey Haven (IRE)** 2-8-6 0 ... LukeMorris 7 25
(Mark Brisbourne) *loose bef s: sn ct: rdn: green and bhd: kpt on clsng stages* **25/1**
8 nk **Devout (IRE)** 2-8-12 0 ... FergusSweeney 2 30
(Jamie Osborne) *sn outpcd* **12/1**

1m 4.22s (1.72) **Going Correction** +0.25s/f (Good) 8 Ran SP% **117.2**
Speed ratings (Par 91): **96,95,93,83,81 77,76,75**
toteswingers: 1&2 £1.80, 1&3 £3.70, 2&3 £2.10 CSF £9.49 TOTE £7.10: £1.70, £1.02, £1.20; EX 13.50 Trifecta £29.90 Pool: £385.52 - 9.53 winning units..
Owner Green Pastures Farm **Bred** Green Pastures Farm **Trained** East Everleigh, Wilts

FOCUS
A modest juvenile maiden but sound form for the level none the less. The first three were clear.

NOTEBOOK
Rebel Magic, whose dam was a 6f winner two, wasn't the best away, but proved strong in the second half of the race and should improve further with the experience behind her. (op 13-2)
Lucky Beggar(IRE), who missed Chester because of heavy ground, appeared the one to beat at this level and showed good speed, but could never get away from his field. Whether or not he wins a small maiden, his future lay in handicaps. (op 10-11)
Marchwood has run to a similar level on each of his three starts but shall remain vulnerable in maidens.
Lobelia is from a yard whose juvenile often improve for a run and her breeding suggests she'll need further than this in time. (op 12-1)

2164 BRITISH STALLION STUDS/PREMIER CONSERVATORY ROOFS E B F MAIDEN STKS 5f 161y
7:10 (7:11) (Class 5) 2-Y-O **£3,340** (£986; £493) **Stalls** Centre

Form RPR
1 **Sir Prancealot (IRE)** 2-9-3 0 ... DaneO'Neill 10 82+
(Richard Hannon) *t.k.h: led after 1f: shkn up and qcknd fnl f: readily* **2/1**[1]
3 2 2 **Strong Conviction**[11] 1847 2-9-3 0 ... MartinHarley 4 73
(Mick Channon) *chsd ldrs: rdn over 1f out: disp 2nd ins fnl f: chsd wnr and no imp fnl 120yds but styd on wl for 2nd* **5/2**[2]
3 ½ **Shahdaroba (IRE)** 2-9-3 0 ... JamesMillman 2 72+
(Rod Millman) *in tch: hdwy fr 3f out: drvn: hdwy and edgd rt ins fnl 2f: styd on to dispute 2nd ins fnl f: no imp on wnr and one pce into 3rd fnl 120yds* **25/1**
4 4 ¾ **Indian Affair**[26] 1495 2-9-3 0 ... RichardKingscote 6 69
(Milton Bradley) *led 1f: styd chsng wnr: rdn 2f out: stl disputing 2nd ins fnl f: outpcd fnl 120yds* **9/2**[3]
0 5 9 **Kwanto**[9] 1903 2-8-12 0 ... TomMcLaughlin 9 35
(Malcolm Saunders) *chsd ldrs: rdn and effrt whn pushed rt ins fnl 2f: wknd qckly fr 1f out* **50/1**
6 1 **Alexandrakollontai (IRE)** 2-8-12 0 ... LiamKeniry 1 31+
(J S Moore) *s.i.s: towards rr: sme hdwy on ins over 2f out whn n.m.r and green: drvn and styd on again ins fnl f* **40/1**
7 nk **Hardy Red (IRE)** 2-9-3 0 ... FergusSweeney 3 35+
(Jamie Osborne) *towards rr: hdwy on outside 2f out: pushed rt sn after and wknd over 1f out* **28/1**
8 3 ¾ **Khefyn (IRE)** 2-9-3 0 ... LukeMorris 8 23
(Ronald Harris) *s.i.s: towards rr: sme hdwy on ins over 2f out: sn pushed along and wknd* **12/1**
52 9 1 ¾ **Silicon Valley**[9] 1904 2-8-12 0 ... JohnFahy 7 12
(Dominic Ffrench Davis) *chsd ldrs: rdn 1/2-way: wknd ins fnl 2f* **16/1**
10 15 **Run It Twice (IRE)** 2-9-3 0 ... LiamJones 5
(Brian Meehan) *slowly away: sn rdn: v green and a wl bhd* **8/1**

1m 13.45s (2.25) **Going Correction** +0.25s/f (Good) 10 Ran SP% **116.5**
Speed ratings (Par 93): **95,92,91,90,78 77,76,71,69,49**
toteswingers: 1&2 £1.80, 1&3 £13.40, 2&3 £16.60 CSF £6.78 TOTE £2.30: £1.50, £1.20, £5.60; EX 8.10 Trifecta £150.60 Part won. Pool: £203.63 - 0.20 winning units..
Owner Andrew Tinkler **Bred** Dermot Cantillon And Forenaghts Stud **Trained** East Everleigh, Wilts

FOCUS
Not a bad juvenile maiden and a taking debut winner. He looks above average for the track.

NOTEBOOK
Sir Prancealot(IRE) ◆ created quite a good impression, clearly knowing his job and stretching right away. Related to numerous winners and out of a mare who won over 5f, he holds an entry in next year's Derby and one would expect to see him in a novice/conditions event next time. It would appear Royal Ascot is on his agenda. (tchd 15-8 and 9-4)
Strong Conviction improved on his debut effort and can find a race at a modest level, with 6f likely to suit. (op 3-1)
Shahdaroba(IRE), closely related to 6f 2yo winner Honours List, is from a yard whose runners often need a run so this goes down a really promising debut. Marked improvement should be forthcoming and he can win something similar.
Indian Affair improved slightly on his initial effort and should find an opening in nurseries later in the campaign. (op 6-1)
Kwanto showed more than she had on debut.
Hardy Red(IRE) travelled well before being forced wide when trying to challenge. (tchd 33-1)

2165 PREMIER CONSERVATORY ROOFS 12TH ANNIVERSARY H'CAP 5f 161y
7:40 (7:44) (Class 5) (0-70,70) 4-Y-O+ **£2,264** (£673; £336; £168) **Stalls** Centre

Form RPR
3001 1 **Valmina**[26] 1497 5-8-11 **67** ... (t) GeorgeDowning(7) 2 76
(Tony Carroll) *in rr: hdwy 1/2-way: squeezed through ins fnl 2f: chal over 1f out: sn led: drvn out hands and heels fnl 120yds* **7/1**[3]
1-14 2 1 **Cheers**[90] 574 4-9-0 **63** ... TravisBlock 15 69
(Oliver Sherwood) *in rr: hdwy and nt clr run ins fnl 2f: drvn and qcknd fnl f: chsd wnr fnl 200yds but hld clsng stages* **12/1**
5502 3 1 ¼ **Whipphound**[20] 1630 4-8-13 **62** ... TomMcLaughlin 11 64
(Mark Brisbourne) *chsd ldrs: rdn and n.m.r over 1f out: styd on to take 3rd fnl 50yds but nt pce of ldng duo* **10/1**
4002 4 ½ **Diamond Vine (IRE)**[13] 1789 4-9-7 **70** ... (p) LukeMorris 13 70
(Ronald Harris) *in tch 1/2-way: hdwy on outside fr 2f out: styd on to chse ldrs ins fnl f but no imp nr fin* **12/1**
2023 5 2 ½ **Going French (IRE)**[27] 1481 5-8-13 **62** ... (t) SamHitchcott 9 54
(Dai Burchell) *chsd ldrs: disp ld and rdn over 1f out: wknd fnl 120yds* **16/1**
5464 6 ¾ **Speak The Truth (IRE)**[13] 1773 6-9-2 **65** ... MatthewDavies 10 54
(Jim Boyle) *s.i.s: in rr: n.m.r 2f out and swtchd rt over 1f out: kpt on: nt rch ldrs* **20/1**
20-0 7 ½ **Seamus Shindig**[23] 1564 10-9-2 **70** ... AmyScott(5) 16 57
(Henry Candy) *s.i.s: in rr: nt clr run fr ins fnl 2f: styd on wl fnl f: nt rch ldrs* **13/2**[2]
03-5 8 3 ¼ **Colourbearer (IRE)**[13] 1773 5-9-1 **64** ... (t) LiamKeniry 8 40
(Milton Bradley) *chsd ldrs: rdn and pushed rt over 1f out: wknd ins fnl f* **16/1**
03/0 9 1 ¼ **Red Avalanche (IRE)**[133] 31 5-9-1 **64** ... DaneO'Neill 4 36
(Tony Newcombe) *in rr: n.m.r 2f out: styd on ins fnl f: nt rch ldrs* **12/1**
0524 10 1 ¾ **Shes Rosie**[6] 2012 4-9-7 **70** ... MartinHarley 6 36
(John O'Shea) *chsd ldrs: rdn 2f out: wknd fnl f: eased clsng stages* **6/1**[1]
23-0 11 1 ¼ **Oh My Days (IRE)**[35] 1306 4-8-11 **60** ... JohnFahy 14 22
(Clive Cox) *chsd ldrs: rdn and n.m.r over 1f out: wknd fnl f* **12/1**
51-5 12 1 ¾ **Jolly Ranch**[131] 59 6-8-13 **62** ... FergusSweeney 7 18
(Tony Newcombe) *led: rdn 2f out: hdd appr fnl f and sn wknd* **11/1**
060- 13 ½ **Superior Edge**[213] 6895 5-9-1 **64** ... DavidProbert 5 18
(Christopher Mason) *chsd ldrs: rdn and wknd ins fnl 2f* **25/1**
3600 14 1 **Novabridge**[35] 1305 4-8-9 **63** ... (b) DavidKenny(5) 12 14
(Neil Mulholland) *chsd ldrs over 3f* **20/1**
0120 15 4 ½ **Sole Danser (IRE)**[37] 1254 4-9-7 **70** ... RichardKingscote 17 5
(Milton Bradley) *reluctant to post: s.i.s: outpcd most of way* **11/1**
20-0 U **Llewellyn**[51] 1050 4-9-4 **67** ... PatCosgrave 1
(Jim Boyle) *rrd and uns rdr leaving stalls* **28/1**

1m 12.71s (1.51) **Going Correction** +0.25s/f (Good) 16 Ran SP% **125.2**
Speed ratings (Par 103): **99,97,96,95,92 91,90,86,84,82 80,78,77,76,70**
toteswingers: 1&2 £18.90, 1&3 £22.60, 2&3 £28.70 CSF £86.04 CT £891.78 TOTE £5.50: £1.20, £3.20, £2.40, £4.10; EX 100.90 Trifecta £277.80 Part won. Pool: £375.51 - 0.30 winning units..
Owner Mayden Stud **Bred** Mayden Stud, J A And D S Dewhurst **Trained** Cropthorne, Worcs

FOCUS
A typically competitive handicap sprint for the track.

2166 PREMIER CONSERVATORY ROOFS H'CAP 5f 11y
8:10 (8:10) (Class 5) (0-70,64) 3-Y-O **£2,385** (£704; £352) **Stalls** Centre

Form RPR
5105 1 **Cats Eyes**[16] 1709 3-9-5 **62** ... PatCosgrave 11 71
(Robert Cowell) *bmpd s chsd ldrs: wnt 2nd 2f out: rdn to ld appr fnl f: hrd rdn: hld on wl* **9/2**[3]
-126 2 1 **Welease Bwian (IRE)**[34] 1331 3-9-5 **62** ... (t) WilliamCarson 6 67
(Stuart Williams) *trckd ldrs: travelling wl appr fnl f: sn rdn to chse wnr: kpt on u.p but no imp fnl 120yds* **4/1**[2]
5-16 3 ¾ **Ficelle (IRE)**[20] 1622 3-9-6 **63** ... LukeMorris 8 65
(Ronald Harris) *bmpd s: in rr: hdwy on outside fr 2f out: wnt 3rd 1f out: styd on same pce u.p fnl 120yds* **6/1**
00-0 4 1 ¾ **Madame Feu**[32] 1376 3-9-1 **58** ... DaneO'Neill 3 54
(Henry Candy) *in tch: hdwy 1/2-way: sn rdn: styd on same pce fnl f* **14/1**
400 5 2 ½ **One Last Dream**[42] 1182 3-8-4 **50** oh5 ... SimonPearce(3) 1 37
(Ron Hodges) *chsd ldrs: rdn over 2f out: hmpd 3f out: sn rdn: wknd fr 2f out* **40/1**
0365 6 2 ¾ **Jeremy Sue**[22] 1585 3-8-2 **50** oh5 ... (b) AmyScott(5) 2 27
(Derek Haydn Jones) *in rr: sn pushed along: stl last appr fnl f: r.o wl clsng stages but nvr any ch* **16/1**
355- 7 ½ **Jawim**[213] 6890 3-8-11 **54** ... SamHitchcott 4 29
(Malcolm Saunders) *chsd ldrs: rdn 1/2-way: wknd wl over 1f out* **15/2**
4233 8 nse **Chicarito**[9] 1941 3-9-2 **59** ... (v) MartinDwyer 10 34
(John Gallagher) *wnt lft and rr after s: sn led: hdd over 1f out: wknd qckly* **9/4**[1]
-060 9 2 ½ **Hatha Zain (IRE)**[12] 1826 3-8-7 **50** oh5 ... (b) RichardKingscote 7 16
(Milton Bradley) *chsd ldr to 2f out: sn btn* **25/1**

1m 4.09s (1.59) **Going Correction** +0.25s/f (Good) 9 Ran SP% **113.8**
Speed ratings (Par 99): **97,95,94,91,87 83,82,82,78**
toteswingers: 1&2 £4.20, 1&3 £4.80, 2&3 £6.60 CSF £22.50 CT £108.12 TOTE £6.40: £2.20, £2.20, £2.40; EX 21.30 Trifecta £109.70 Part won. Pool: £148.26 - 0.20 winning units..
Owner Manor Farm Stud (rutland) **Bred** Manor Farm Stud & Mrs A J Ralli **Trained** Six Mile Bottom, Cambs

FOCUS
A modest 3-y-o sprint, but one that should produce winners at a similar level.

2167 INTERNATIONAL PLYWOOD LIMITED FILLIES' H'CAP 1m 5f 22y
8:40 (8:40) (Class 5) (0-70,69) 4-Y-O+ **£2,385** (£704; £352) **Stalls** High

Form RPR
113- 1 **Maydream**[230] 6476 5-8-11 **59** ... KieranO'Neill 7 68
(Jimmy Fox) *hld up in rr: gd hdwy fr 3f out: chsd ldr 1f out: sn led: hrd drvn whn chal fnl 100yds: kpt on wl and a jst doing enough* **7/2**[1]
065- 2 hd **Now What**[55] 6769 5-8-10 **58** ... RichardKingscote 9 67
(Jonathan Portman) *chsd ldrs: wnt 2nd 3f out: rdn 2f out: chsd ldr ins fnl f: kpt on u.p fnl 100yds but a jst hld* **8/1**[3]
-423 3 3 ¾ **Shy**[7] 1984 7-9-1 **63** ... (b) JamesMillman 5 66
(Rod Millman) *chsd ldrs: led 4f out: rdn over 2f out: hdd jst ins fnl f: sn outpcd by ldng duo: jst hld on for 3rd clsng stages* **5/1**[2]
10-5 4 shd **Shades Of Grey**[30] 1418 5-9-5 **67** ... JohnFahy 2 70
(Clive Cox) *in rr: hdwy over 2f out: styd on u.p fr over 1f out: clsd on 3rd nr fin but no ch w ldng duo* **7/2**[1]
5053 5 7 **Pandorica**[9] 1909 4-9-3 **65** ... LiamKeniry 1 58
(Bernard Llewellyn) *chsd ldrs: rdn fr 4f out: wknd over 1f out* **9/1**
125- 6 1 ½ **Aegean Destiny**[60] 7264 5-8-12 **63** ... DeclanCannon(3) 8 53
(John Mackie) *in tch: chsd ldrs and rdn 3f out: wknd ins fnl 2f* **8/1**[3]
56/6 7 2 ¼ **Valmari (IRE)**[12] 296 9-8-5 **56** ... SimonPearce(3) 6 43
(Tom Symonds) *sn drvn to ld: hdd 4f out: wknd wl over 2f out* **17/2**
8 2 **Squirrel Wood (IRE)**[239] 4-9-7 **69** ... GeorgeBaker 4 53
(Mary Hambro) *trckd ldrs: dosputed 2nd 3f out: wknd qckly 2f out* **11/1**

0-64 **9** *10* **Lisselan Pleasure (USA)**[9] 1909 5-9-0 **62**...................... DavidProbert 3 31
(Bernard Llewellyn) *t.k.h towards rr: hdwy 5f out: nvr rchd ldrs and wknd u.p over 2f out* **20/1**

2m 55.73s (3.73) **Going Correction** +0.30s/f (Good) **9** Ran SP% **117.0**
Speed ratings (Par 100): **100,99,97,97,93 92,90,89,83**
toteswingers: 1&2 £7.20, 1&3 £2.10, 2&3 £4.10 CSF £32.62 CT £140.66 TOTE £3.30: £1.40, £2.80, £1.50; EX 40.20 Trifecta £234.20 Pool: £512.71 - 1.62 winning units..
Owner The Dancing Partners **Bred** The Dancing Partners **Trained** Collingbourne Ducis, Wilts

FOCUS
A moderate fillies' handicap that was run at a good gallop.
T/Plt: £42.00 to a £1 stake. Pool: £64,235.61. 1,115.26 winning tickets. T/Qpdt: £8.00 to a £1 stake. Pool: £5,908.64. 545.38 winning tickets. ST

2078 LINGFIELD (L-H)
Wednesday, May 16

OFFICIAL GOING: Standard
Wind: Medium, across Weather: Cloudy, brighter spells

2168 BETFRED "DOUBLE DELIGHT" CLASSIFIED CLAIMING STKS 1m (P)
1:50 (1:50) (Class 6) 3-Y-O+ **£1,704** (£503; £251) **Stalls** High

Form RPR
0605 **1** **Legal Legacy**[8] 1958 6-9-3 74....................................... KirstyMilczarek 5 74
(David C Griffiths) *dwlt: hld up in tch in rr: rdn and hdwy over 1f out: rn wl to ld ins fnl f: gng away at fin* **5/2**[1]

3100 **2** *3/4* **Marvo**[5] 2044 8-9-4 67..(b) EddieAhern 6 73
(Mark H Tompkins) *t.k.h: hld up wl in tch: hdwy to press ldrs and stl travelling strly 2f out: drvn to ld ins fnl f: sn hdd and one pce* **8/1**

4644 **3** *1* **Aquilifer (IRE)**[29] 4-9-2 70....................................(t) MichaelMetcalfe(3) 3 72
(Mrs K Burke) *hld up wl in tch: trcking ldrs and travelling strly 2f out: rdn and effrt over 1f out: drvn and r.o ins fnl f* **11/2**[3]

4650 **4** *1/2* **Edgewater (IRE)**[15] 1729 5-8-12 68......................... JemmaMarshall(5) 4 69
(Lee Carter) *hld up in tch: rdn and hdwy on inner over 1f out: drvn and ev ch 1f out: no ex and one pce fnl 100yds* **6/1**

3102 **5** *1/2* **Spinning Ridge (IRE)**[33] 1360 7-9-5 73..........................(b) LukeMorris 8 70
(Ronald Harris) *t.k.h: sn chsng ldr: led on bit 2f out: rdn over 1f out: hdd ins fnl f: sn btn: wknd towards fin* **9/2**[2]

2220 **6** *2 1/4* **Hinton Admiral**[15] 1727 8-9-6 73..................................... HayleyTurner 1 65
(Conor Dore) *t.k.h: sn chsng ldrs: rdn and unable qck 2f out: wknd 1f out* **9/2**[2]

2030 **7** *1 3/4* **Musashi (IRE)**[7] 1984 7-9-1 54...[1] IanMongan 7 56
(Laura Mongan) *in tch in last pair: rdn over 4f out: struggling u.p 2f out: wknd over 1f out* **40/1**

0006 **8** *1* **On The Cusp (IRE)**[6] 2011 5-9-7 72.........................(bt) WilliamCarson 2 60
(Richard Guest) *racd keenly: led tl hdd 2f out: sn drvn: wknd over 1f out* **28/1**

1m 37.87s (-0.33) **Going Correction** -0.025s/f (Stan) **8** Ran SP% **111.6**
Speed ratings (Par 101): **100,99,98,97,97 95,93,92**
CSF £22.24 TOTE £2.90: £1.50, £1.40, £3.10; EX 23.70.The winner was claimed by Legal Legacy for Mr J Ryan £6,000.
Owner Eros Bloodstock **Bred** D Dowling **Trained** Bawtry, S Yorks
■ Stewards' Enquiry : Jemma Marshall two-day ban: used whip above permitted level (May 30-31)

FOCUS
A modest claiming event, run at a very steady pace.

2169 BETFRED "BONUS KING BINGO" (S) STKS 6f (P)
2:20 (2:20) (Class 6) 3-Y-O+ **£1,704** (£503; £251) **Stalls** Low

Form RPR
5345 **1** **Jake The Snake (IRE)**[20] 1633 11-9-6 77................. RobbieFitzpatrick 5 77
(Richard Guest) *awkward leaving stalls and urged along briefly: hld up in rr: rdn and hdwy over 1f out: rdn to ld fnl 100yds: r.o wl: comf* **9/4**[1]

0564 **2** *1 3/4* **Finefrenzyrolling (IRE)**[22] 1586 4-8-12 58.........(p) MichaelMetcalfe(3) 4 66
(Mrs K Burke) *chsd ldr: upsides ldr 3f out: rdn to ld wl over 1f out: hdd fnl 100yds: sn outpcd* **7/2**[2]

5241 **3** *4* **Chjimes (IRE)**[15] 1735 8-9-11 67..................................(b) HayleyTurner 6 63
(Conor Dore) *t.k.h: in tch: hdwy to join ldrs 3f out: rdn and unable qck over 1f out: outpcd by ldrs and wl hld fnl f* **9/4**[1]

5160 **4** *1* **Zip Lock (IRE)**[12] 1827 6-9-11 71................................... KirstyMilczarek 3 60
(Olivia Maylam) *t.k.h: in tch: rdn and effrt over 1f out: outpcd and btn fnl f* **7/2**[2]

005 **5** *2* **Simple Rhythm**[13] 1768 6-8-12 47...............................(p) RyanPowell(3) 1 44
(John Ryan) *racd keenly: led: rdn and hdd wl over 1f out: wknd ent fnl f* **33/1**[3]

1m 11.29s (-0.61) **Going Correction** -0.025s/f (Stan) **5** Ran SP% **108.9**
Speed ratings (Par 101): **103,100,95,94,91**
CSF £10.15 TOTE £5.30: £3.10, £5.50; EX 15.20.The winner was sold to Tony Carroll for 7,400gns.
Owner Willie McKay **Bred** J F Tuthill **Trained** Stainforth, S Yorks

FOCUS
Not a bad contest for this grade and it was won in decisive fashion by the veteran.

2170 BETFRED HOME OF THE BIG WINNERS H'CAP (DIV I) 7f (P)
2:50 (2:51) (Class 6) (0-60,60) 4-Y-O+ **£2,045** (£603; £302) **Stalls** Low

Form RPR
-103 **1** **Ereka (IRE)**[21] 1608 4-9-0 **53**.. LukeMorris 12 61
(John Best) *in tch: rdn and effrt 2f out: drvn and hdwy 1f out: r.o wl to ld towards fin: rdn out* **12/1**

5050 **2** *1/2* **Dvinsky (USA)**[15] 1734 11-9-7 **60**............................(b) TomMcLaughlin 5 67
(Paul Howling) *w ldr: led 2f out: drvn over 1f out: battled on wl u.p tl hdd and no ex towards fin* **25/1**

43-3 **3** *1/2* **Ymir**[35] 1310 6-9-2 **55**..(tp) J-PGuillambert 13 61
(Michael Attwater) *racd wd: led tl 2f out: stl ev ch and rdn over 1f out: styd on same pce ins fnl f* **10/1**[3]

0002 **4** *nk* **Kielty's Folly**[16] 1722 8-9-7 **60**.......................................(p) JackMitchell 2 65
(Brian Baugh) *rdn along leaving stalls: sn chsng ldrs: rdn and effrt over 1f out: kpt on u.p fnl f* **11/1**

0-63 **5** *nk* **Monashee Rock (IRE)**[12] 1830 7-9-1 **54**................................ LiamKeniry 9 58
(Patrick Chamings) *taken down early: in tch in midfield: rdn over 4f out: lost pl u.p 2f out: rallied 1f out: swtchd rt ins fnl f: styd on wl* **14/1**

1204 **6** *nk* **Royal Envoy (IRE)**[35] 1309 9-8-12 **51**................................. AmirQuinn 7 54
(Paul Howling) *chsd ldrs: rdn and effrt 2f out: stling chsng ldrs and keeping on whn nt clr run briefly ins fnl f: kpt on* **20/1**

40-2 **7** *3/4* **Tenavon**[15] 1735 4-9-6 **59**...[1] EddieAhern 6 60
(William Knight) *chsd ldrs: rdn and unable qck over 1f out: no ex and btn ins fnl f* **9/2**[1]

256- **8** *nk* **Louphole**[267] 5355 10-9-0 **58**...................................... RachealKneller(5) 8 58
(J R Jenkins) *stdd s and sn swtchd lft: hld up in last quartet: rdn and hdwy 1f out: swtchd rt ins fnl f: kpt on: nvr trbld ldrs* **16/1**

6-02 **9** *hd* **Amber Heights**[15] 1734 4-9-7 **60**..................................... JimmyFortune 11 60
(Henry Candy) *hld up in last quartet: effrt and wd bnd 2f out: styd on ins fnl f: nvr trbld ldrs* **6/1**[2]

3035 **10** *nse* **Fortunate Bid (IRE)**[16] 1722 6-9-5 **58**......................(p) RoystonFfrench 3 58
(Linda Stubbs) *t.k.h: hld up towards rr: rdn and effrt on inner over 1f out: kpt on fnl f: nvr trbld ldrs* **10/1**[3]

102 **11** *shd* **Fault**[5] 2046 6-9-0 **53**... BrettDoyle 14 52
(Alastair Lidderdale) *t.k.h early: hld up in midfield: rdn and outpcd jst over 2f out: rallied and kpt on ins fnl f: nvr trbld ldrs* **16/1**

4624 **12** *1/2* **Anjomarba (IRE)**[13] 1788 5-9-1 **54**................................... HayleyTurner 1 52
(Conor Dore) *in tch in midfield: rdn and struggling wl over 1f out: kpt on fnl f but no threat to ldrs* **12/1**

4-20 **13** *4* **Bedibyes**[20] 1626 4-9-3 **56**.. KirstyMilczarek 4 43
(Richard Mitchell) *dwlt: a bhd* **12/1**

46-5 **14** *7* **Alexs Rainbow (USA)**[16] 1702 4-9-6 **59**........................ WilliamCarson 10 27
(Peter Hiatt) *t.k.h: hld up towards rr: rdn and wknd over 2f out: wl bhd fnl f* **14/1**

1m 24.62s (-0.18) **Going Correction** -0.025s/f (Stan) **14** Ran SP% **115.8**
Speed ratings (Par 101): **100,99,98,98,98 97,96,96,96,96 96,95,91,83**
toteswingers: 1&2 £17.60, 1&3 £53.60, 2&3 £18.70 CSF £270.75 CT £3161.34 TOTE £15.90: £6.80, £6.40, £2.50; EX 272.30.
Owner Mrs A M Riney **Bred** Mrs A M Riney **Trained** Hucking, Kent

FOCUS
A low-grade if competitive handicap, run at a decent pace.
Royal Envoy(IRE) Official explanation: jockey said gelding was denied a clear run final half furlong
Bedibyes Official explanation: jockey said filly never travelled

2171 BETFRED HOME OF THE BIG WINNERS H'CAP (DIV II) 7f (P)
3:20 (3:20) (Class 6) (0-60,60) 4-Y-O+ **£2,045** (£603; £302) **Stalls** Low

Form RPR
2143 **1** **Lady Mango (IRE)**[13] 1788 4-9-6 **59**.................................. LukeMorris 6 70
(Ronald Harris) *in tch: rdn and effrt 2f out: swtchd rt and drvn to chal ent fnl f: led ins fnl f: hld on wl towards fin* **9/2**[1]

3400 **2** *hd* **Cut The Cackle (IRE)**[19] 1638 6-9-6 **59**..................(bt) WilliamCarson 5 69
(Richard Guest) *bmpd s: towards rr: rdn and effrt over 1f out: swtchd rt and gd hdwy 1f out: str chal ins fnl f: r.o but a jst hld* **16/1**

4204 **3** *1 1/4* **Do More Business (IRE)**[13] 1787 5-9-0 **53**...................... IanMongan 2 60
(Alison Batchelor) *in tch in midfield: edging out rt and effrt wl over 1f out: hdwy u.p to chse ldrs jst ins fnl f: no imp fnl 75yds* **8/1**

-655 **4** *1/2* **Gazboolou**[112] 293 8-9-0 **53**... EddieAhern 7 58
(Henry Candy) *midfield and niggled along early: rdn and effrt over 2f out: hdwy over 1f out and chsd ldrs 1f out: one pce fnl 100yds* **13/2**[2]

1253 **5** *1* **Warbond**[28] 1447 4-9-6 **59**... JamieGoldstein 10 62+
(Michael Madgwick) *s.i.s: towards rr: rdn over 2f out: hdwy u.p 1f out: swtchd rt and r.o wl ins fnl f: nt rch ldrs* **15/2**[3]

055- **6** *1 1/4* **For Life (IRE)**[138] 7919 10-9-4 **60**.......................... NataliaGemelova(3) 14 59
(John E Long) *taken down early: led and grad crossed towards inner: rdn wl over 1f out: hdd jst ins fnl f: wknd fnl 100yds* **20/1**

0550 **7** *1 1/4* **Captainrisk (IRE)**[16] 1702 6-9-1 **54**..............................(v) SebSanders 11 50
(Christine Dunnett) *chsd ldrs: rdn over 3f out: unable qck u.p 2f out: wknd jst ins fnl f* **16/1**

6054 **8** *shd* **Arctic Mirage**[10] 1895 4-9-7 **60**... LiamKeniry 13 56
(Michael Blanshard) *s.i.s and rdn along in rr: swtchd lft and hdwy on inner over 1f out: kpt on ins fnl f: nvr trbld ldrs* **12/1**

3450 **9** *3/4* **Jonnie Skull (IRE)**[16] 1722 6-9-1 **54**................................(vt) ChrisCatlin 3 48
(Phil McEntee) *chsd ldrs: rdn and unable qck ent fnl 2f: wknd 1f out* **16/1**

00-6 **10** *nk* **Yungaburra (IRE)**[16] 1722 8-9-2 **55**..........................(t) KirstyMilczarek 9 48
(David C Griffiths) *taken down early: pressed ldr: rdn and ev ch 2f out: stl ev ch 1f out: btn jst ins fnl f: fdd fnl 100yds* **16/1**

4-04 **11** *3/4* **Five Hearts**[15] 1742 4-8-12 **51**... TedDurcan 12 42
(Mark H Tompkins) *a towards rr: rdn and no imp whn hung lft wl over 1f out: nvr trbld ldrs* **20/1**

100- **12** *shd* **Lady On Top (IRE)**[238] 6253 4-8-13 **52**................................ AmirQuinn 4 42
(Nerys Dutfield) *in tch in midfield: rdn and unable qck ent fnl 2f: wknd ent fnl f: no ch whn swtchd rt wl ins fnl f* **33/1**

50-0 **13** *3/4* **Pose (IRE)**[9] 1934 5-9-5 **58**..(t) HayleyTurner 1 46
(Roger Ingram) *in tch: effrt u.p on inner over 1f out: wknd ent fnl f: fdd fnl f* **20/1**

0262 **14** *1 1/4* **Huzzah (IRE)**[20] 1628 7-9-5 **58**....................................... J-PGuillambert 8 43
(Paul Howling) *stdd s: t.k.h: hld up in rr: swtchd rt to outer after 1f: rdn and no rspnse 2f out: n.d* **13/2**[2]

1m 24.2s (-0.60) **Going Correction** -0.025s/f (Stan) **14** Ran SP% **116.2**
Speed ratings (Par 101): **102,101,100,99,98 97,95,95,94,94 93,93,92,91**
toteswingers: 1&2 £35.30, 1&3 £7.40, 2&3 £40.60 CSF £71.33 CT £561.49 TOTE £5.50: £1.80, £5.10, £2.70; EX 63.50.
Owner L Scadding & Mrs S Peachey-Scadding **Bred** Mount Coote Stud **Trained** Earlswood, Monmouths

FOCUS
The second division of this handicap appeared to be run at a stronger pace and it served up a good finish.
Huzzah(IRE) Official explanation: jockey said gelding ran too freely

2172 CYPRIUM BAR AT MARRIOTT LINGFIELD MEDIAN AUCTION MAIDEN STKS 1m (P)
3:55 (3:56) (Class 5) 3-5-Y-O **£2,726** (£805; £402) **Stalls** High

Form RPR
0 **1** **Roserrow**[27] 1467 3-9-0 0.. JimmyFortune 2 85+
(Andrew Balding) *t.k.h: pressed ldr: rdn and ev ch over 1f out: led ins fnl f: styd on wl and drew clr fnl 100yds* **12/1**

0-2 **2** *2 1/4* **Sir Mike**[11] 1852 3-9-0 0... IanMongan 1 80
(Amanda Perrett) *led: jnd 3f out: rdn ent fnl 2f: edgd rt u.p ins fnl f: hdd fnl 100yds: sn outpcd* **9/2**[2]

3-4 **3** *1/2* **La Pampita (IRE)**[21] 1610 3-8-9 0.. EddieAhern 12 74+
(William Knight) *t.k.h: hld up in tch: rdn and chsd ldrs over 1f out: swtchd rt 1f out: carried rt and one pce fnl 100yds* **13/2**[3]

2- **4** *2* **Tawaasul**[208] 6992 3-8-9 0.. TadhgO'Shea 10 69
(William Haggas) *in tch: hdwy to join ldrs 3f out: wdst of ldrs and unable qck bnd 2f out: drvn and no prog over 1f out: wknd 1f out* **5/6**[1]

2-0 **5** *1 3/4* **Silkee Supreme**[15] 1723 3-8-11 0.................................... SeanLevey(3) 8 70
(Richard Hannon) *t.k.h: hld up in tch: effrt u.p on inner over 1f out: wknd 1f out* **16/1**

6 2 ¾ **Scarlett Fever** 3-8-2 0 KatiaScallan(7) 5 58+
(Marcus Tregoning) *dwlt: racd in last trio: hdwy into modest 6th 2f out: kpt on but no imp* **25/1**

0-6 7 1 ¾ **Sea Fever (IRE)**[15] 1737 3-9-0 0 J-PGuillambert 6 59+
(Luca Cumani) *dwlt: hld up in rr: rdn over 2f out: modest late hdwy fnl f: n.d* **20/1**

0- 8 3 ¼ **Lady Ocarina**[284] 4804 3-8-9 0 TedDurcan 4 46
(John Dunlop) *s.i.s: hld up in last trio: rdn and struggling over 2f out: wknd 2f out* **50/1**

9 ¾ **Pont Menai** 3-9-0 0 JamieGoldstein 11 49
(J R Jenkins) *dwlt: sn in midfield: lost pl and rdn over 2f out: wknd 2f out* **66/1**

10 2 ¾ **Roman Around** 3-8-9 0 HayleyTurner 3 38
(William Knight) *rdn along early: chsd ldrs: rdn 4f out: wknd over 2f out* **33/1**

1m 37.73s (-0.47) **Going Correction** -0.025s/f (Stan) 10 Ran SP% **114.6**
Speed ratings (Par 103): **101,98,98,96,94 91,90,86,86,83**
CSF £60.81 TOTE £12.40: £3.20, £1.40, £1.10; EX 77.60.
Owner Sir Roger Buckley, Gerald Oury **Bred** Sir R J Buckley & G Oury **Trained** Kingsclere, Hants

2173 DORMANSLAND H'CAP 1m (P)
4:30 (4:30) (Class 5) (0-70,68) 4-Y-0+ **£2,385** (£704; £352) **Stalls** High

Form RPR

3-34 1 **Woolston Ferry (IRE)**[112] 301 6-9-5 66 JimmyFortune 2 77
(Henry Candy) *in tch: rdn and effrt 2f out: chsd ldr over 1f out: led ins fnl f: r.o wl: rdn out* **8/1**[3]

4442 2 2 **Cyflymder (IRE)**[12] 1823 6-9-4 65 HayleyTurner 11 72
(David C Griffiths) *chsd ldr tl led after 2f: rdn and fnd ex over 1f out: hdd ins fnl f: one pce* **4/1**[1]

5420 3 ¾ **Striker Torres (IRE)**[18] 1659 6-9-7 68 (v) GeorgeBaker 6 73
(Ian McInnes) *stdd s: hld up towards rr: hdwy on inner wl over 1f out: drvn and chsd ldng pair ent fnl f: one pce fnl f* **8/1**[3]

-351 4 4 ½ **Idol Deputy (FR)**[79] 725 6-9-0 66 RachealKneller(5) 7 61
(Mark Usher) *in tch towards rr: hdwy to chse ldrs: rdn and outpcd over 1f out: wknd ins fnl f* **9/2**[2]

00-0 5 ¾ **Isingy Red (FR)**[20] 1626 4-9-3 64 PatCosgrave 12 57
(Jim Boyle) *stdd s and grad dropped in bhd: rdn and hdwy whn swtchd lft over 1f out: sn no imp and wl hld fnl f* **16/1**

0234 6 hd **Salient**[20] 1626 8-9-7 68 J-PGuillambert 9 60
(Michael Attwater) *in tch in last pair: pushed along and hdwy on outer into midfield over 2f out: rdn and no prog over 1f out: wknd 1f out* **11/1**

2550 7 2 **Cativo Cavallino**[32] 1378 9-9-1 62 RichardThomas 5 50
(John E Long) *sn bustled along in midfield: rdn over 3f out: struggling and outpcd over 2f out: wl btn over 1f out* **14/1**

10-0 8 1 ¾ **Blue Deer (IRE)**[32] 1378 4-9-3 64 StevieDonohoe 8 48
(Lee Carter) *led for 2f: chsd ldrs after: rdn and struggling 2f out: wknd over 1f out: fdd fnl f* **10/1**

3150 9 nk **Archelao (IRE)**[16] 1706 4-9-7 68 AmirQuinn 4 51
(Richard Rowe) *stdd after s: hld up in rr: swtchd rt and rdn 2f out: nvr on terms* **20/1**

3130 10 3 ½ **Moral Issue**[36] 1269 4-9-7 68 (p) RoystonFfrench 10 43
(Ian McInnes) *chsd ldrs: rdn over 2f out: wknd wl over 1f out: fdd 1f out* **10/1**

461 11 4 **Catalyze**[49] 1069 4-9-4 65 (t) RobbieFitzpatrick 3 31
(Richard Guest) *in tch in midfiield: rdn and no prog wl over 1f out: sn wknd and bhd fnl f* **14/1**

2-01 12 ½ **Indian Violet (IRE)**[91] 568 6-9-2 63 JamieGoldstein 1 28
(Zoe Davison) *in tch: rdn and lost pl on inner over 2f out: bhd fnl f* **25/1**

1m 36.85s (-1.35) **Going Correction** -0.025s/f (Stan) 12 Ran SP% **114.7**
Speed ratings (Par 103): **105,103,102,97,97 96,94,93,92,89 85,84**
toteswingers: 1&2 £5.10, 1&3 £6.10, 2&3 £6.10 CSF £38.58 CT £270.38 TOTE £7.60: £2.70, £1.90, £2.50; EX 36.50.
Owner Ms L Burns **Bred** Tim Taylor **Trained** Kingston Warren, Oxon

FOCUS
A competitive mile handicap..
Archelao(IRE) Official explanation: jockey said gelding suffered interference in running
Catalyze Official explanation: jockey said gelding hung badly right
Indian Violet(IRE) Official explanation: jockey said gelding was denied a clear run

2174 TANDRIDGE H'CAP 1m 5f (P)
5:05 (5:05) (Class 4) (0-80,80) 4-Y-0+ **£4,204** (£1,251; £625; £312) **Stalls** Low

Form RPR

10-3 1 **Star Commander**[30] 1418 4-9-7 80 EddieAhern 7 89
(Mark H Tompkins) *mde all: qcknd 3f out: rdn and hrd pressed 2f out: edgd rt u.p fnl f: hld on wl: all out* **15/2**[3]

-521 2 shd **Sand Skier**[76] 745 5-8-10 76 NicoleNordblad(7) 10 85
(Hans Adielsson) *t.k.h: hld up in last trio: hdwy into midfield 10f out: rdn and hdwy to chal 2f out: wnt clr w wnr ent fnl f: carried rt but sustained chal fnl f: jst hld* **14/1**

561- 3 2 ¾ **Knightly Escapade**[220] 6729 4-9-4 77 IanMongan 3 82+
(John Dunlop) *t.k.h: hld up towards rr: hdwy over 2f out: rdn and effrt wl over 1f out: chsd ldng pair ins fnl f: no imp: eased cl home* **4/1**[1]

6002 4 ½ **Bennelong**[7] 1984 6-8-7 66 oh1 HayleyTurner 11 70
(Richard Rowe) *stdd s and dropped in bhd: hld up in rr: hdwy jst over 2f out: swtchd rt over 1f out: styd on wl fnl f* **11/1**

0-45 5 ½ **Saint Helena (IRE)**[28] 1446 4-9-1 74 TedDurcan 9 78
(Harry Dunlop) *chsd ldrs: rdn over 2f out: drvn and unable qck over 1f out: styd on same pce fnl f* **14/1**

16-2 6 nk **Iron Condor**[41] 1205 5-9-4 77 MickaelBarzalona 2 80
(James Eustace) *in tch: rdn and effrt on inner 2f out: drvn and chsd ldrs over 1f out: unable qck and btn jst ins fnl f: one pce* **15/2**[3]

51-0 7 1 ¾ **Hidden Valley**[26] 1505 4-8-13 72 (v) JimmyFortune 6 72
(Andrew Balding) *hld up towards rr: rdn and hdwy into midfield on outer over 2f out: no imp and styd on same pce fr over 1f out* **16/1**

-333 8 1 **Where's Susie**[57] 971 7-9-6 79 GeorgeBaker 4 78
(Michael Madgwick) *in tch in midfield: rdn and effrt over 2f out: drvn and no imp over 1f out* **8/1**

620- 9 nk **Tasfeya**[197] 7204 4-9-6 79 StevieDonohoe 5 77
(Lee Carter) *chsd ldrs tl rdn and unable qck over 2f out: wknd over 1f out* **14/1**

400- 10 ½ **Dubai Glory**[216] 6822 4-9-2 75 ChrisCatlin 12 73
(Sheena West) *chsd ldr tl unable qck and short of room ent fnl 2f: wknd over 1f out* **25/1**

-1 11 nk **Kangaroo Court (IRE)**[74] 355 8-9-3 76 DarryllHolland 1 73
(Emma Lavelle) *racd in last trio: rdn and outpcd whn gallop qcknd 3f out: no threat to ldrs after: edging rt and plugged on ins fnl f* **5/1**[2]

0-00 12 2 ¼ **Unex Renoir**[21] 1603 4-9-3 76 (p) J-PGuillambert 13 70
(Michael Attwater) *in tch: hdwy to press ldrs 4f out: rdn and ev ch 2f out: sn wknd* **25/1**

100- 13 9 **First Battalion (IRE)**[272] 5205 4-9-2 75 (b[1]) SebSanders 8 55
(Paul Rich) *t.k.h: hld up towards rr: rdn and struggling whn gallop qcknd 3f out: wknd wl over 1f out: bhd fnl f* **20/1**

2m 46.8s (0.80) **Going Correction** -0.025s/f (Stan) 13 Ran SP% **118.0**
Speed ratings (Par 105): **96,95,94,93,93 93,92,91,91,91 91,89,84**
toteswingers: 1&2 £17.00, 1&3 £8.00, 2&3 £13.60 CSF £103.64 CT £478.58 TOTE £8.60: £2.20, £3.30, £2.00; EX 109.00.
Owner John Brenchley **Bred** Mary-Ann Penfold **Trained** Newmarket, Suffolk
■ Stewards' Enquiry : Eddie Ahern two-day ban: careless riding (May 30-31)

FOCUS
A wide-open staying handicap.
Kangaroo Court(IRE) Official explanation: jockey said gelding was slowly away

2175 LINGFIELD MARRIOTT HOTEL & COUNTRY CLUB H'CAP 2m (P)
5:35 (5:36) (Class 6) (0-60,58) 4-Y-0+ **£2,045** (£603; £302) **Stalls** Low

Form RPR

040- 1 **Alfraamsey**[29] 7640 4-8-13 52 JimmyFortune 9 64+
(Sheena West) *mde all: gng best 2f out: rdn and readily fnd ex to go clr over 1f out: styd on wl* **5/1**[3]

560/ 2 5 **Tae Kwon Do (USA)**[229] 4946 6-8-8 45 (t) MickaelBarzalona 4 51+
(Tim Vaughan) *t.k.h: hld up in rr: hdwy on outer 3f out: 3rd and rdn 2f out: kpt on ins fnl f to go 2nd towards fin: no ch w wnr* **13/2**

1633 3 ½ **Waldsee (GER)**[33] 1361 7-9-7 58 SebSanders 11 63
(Paul Rich) *chsd ldrs: chsd wnr over 4f out: rdn over 2f out: readily brushed aside by wnr and btn over 1f out: plugged on same pce: lost 2nd towards fin* **4/1**[2]

2212 4 1 ¾ **Broughtons Bandit**[33] 1361 5-9-4 55 StevieDonohoe 5 58
(Willie Musson) *in tch in midfield: rdn and effrt to chse ldrs over 2f out: styd on same pce and no threat to wnr fr over 1f out* **5/2**[1]

23-3 5 ½ **Reillys Daughter**[21] 1613 4-9-4 57 IanMongan 1 59
(Laura Mongan) *hld up towards rr: swtchd to outer and rdn over 2f out: kpt on fnl f: no ch w wnr* **17/2**

024/ 6 nk **Little Carmela**[137] 190 8-9-6 57 EddieAhern 7 59
(Sarah Humphrey) *in tch in midfield: rdn and lost pl over 2f out: rallied and styd on fnl f: no ch w wnr* **14/1**

2-00 7 4 ½ **Suhailah**[13] 1770 6-8-12 49 J-PGuillambert 6 46
(Michael Attwater) *in tch in midfield: rdn and unable qck over 2f out: wknd wl over 1f out* **33/1**

/0-0 8 1 ¾ **Ray Diamond**[37] 558 7-8-5 45 (v) RyanPowell(3) 8 39
(Michael Madgwick) *chsd wnr tl 12f out: chsd ldrs after: rdn and struggling over 2f out: wknd wl over 1f out* **33/1**

304- 9 3 **Beauchamp Viking**[22] 598 8-8-8 45 (t) HayleyTurner 2 36
(Simon Burrough) *t.k.h: hld up in rr: rdn and no prog over 2f out: wknd 2f out: bhd fnl f* **25/1**

24/4 10 2 **Il Portico**[13] 1791 5-8-13 50 DarryllHolland 3 38
(Gary Moore) *hld up in tch towards rr: rdn and struggling on inner over 2f out: wknd 2f out* **10/1**

4300 11 11 **Spiritonthemount (USA)**[53] 395 7-8-8 45 (b) ChrisCatlin 10 20
(Peter Hiatt) *v.s.a and rdn along early: grad rcvrd and chsd wnr 12f out tl over 4f out: sn dropped out: bhd fnl 2f* **50/1**

3m 26.2s (0.50) **Going Correction** -0.025s/f (Stan)
WFA 4 from 5yo+ 2lb 11 Ran SP% **116.5**
Speed ratings (Par 101): **97,94,94,93,93 92,90,89,88,87 81**
toteswingers: 1&2 £6.40, 1&3 £4.70, 2&3 £7.10 CSF £35.83 CT £143.12 TOTE £4.10: £1.10, £3.00, £1.50; EX 41.70.
Owner Tapestry Partnership **Bred** G Hedley & Mike Channon Bloodstock Limited **Trained** Falmer, E Sussex

FOCUS
This developed into a tactical affair and, like the previous handicap on the card, it paid to be handy.
T/Plt: £282.40 to a £1 stake. Pool: £58,951.33. 152.37 winning tickets. T/Qpdt: £39.20 to a £1 stake. Pool: £4,469.33. 84.26 winning tickets. SP

YORK (L-H)
Wednesday, May 16

OFFICIAL GOING: Good (7.5)
Wind: Moderate, half against Weather: Fine

2176 INFINITY TYRES STKS (H'CAP) 1m 2f 88y
1:30 (1:31) (Class 2) (0-100,100) 4-Y-0+ **£12,938** (£3,850; £1,924; £962) **Stalls** Low

Form RPR

214- 1 **Gatewood**[297] 4355 4-8-7 86 WilliamBuick 5 95+
(John Gosden) *lw: in rr-div: hdwy over 3f out: wnt 2nd over 2f out: led over 1f out: edgd rt ins fnl f: styd on wl towards fin* **13/2**[2]

4-46 2 1 ½ **Romeo Montague**[21] 1603 4-8-7 86 oh1 JoeFanning 14 92
(Ed Dunlop) *in rr: hdwy over 3f out: n.m.r 2f out: styd on to chal ins fnl f: no ex clsng stages* **22/1**

0402 3 ¾ **Sirvino**[21] 1605 7-9-7 100 JamieSpencer 6 105
(David Barron) *mid-div: effrt 3f out: chsng ldrs over 1f out: keeping on same pce whn sltly hmpd ins fnl f* **10/1**

5-44 4 2 ¼ **Suits Me**[36] 1273 9-9-2 95 RichardHughes 7 96
(David Barron) *led: edgd rt and hdd over 1f out: kpt on same pce* **20/1**

5-10 5 1 **Mirrored**[18] 1654 6-8-10 89 DuranFentiman 10 88
(Tim Easterby) *trckd ldrs: t.k.h: kpt on same pce over 1f out* **18/1**

3-30 6 1 ½ **Northside Prince (IRE)**[18] 1654 6-8-10 89 RobertWinston 15 85
(Alan Swinbank) *in rr: kpt on fnl 3f: nvr nr to chal* **33/1**

20-0 7 ½ **Majestic Dream (IRE)**[11] 1865 4-8-7 86 oh3 JamesSullivan 13 81
(Michael Easterby) *in rr: hdwy 3f out: edgd lft: kpt on: nvr nr ldrs* **100/1**

221- 8 ½ **Area Fifty One**[224] 6632 4-8-8 87 PaulHanagan 11 81
(Richard Fahey) *lw: w ldr: c centre over 4f out: one pce fnl 2f* **10/1**

201- 9 nk **Kirthill (IRE)**[207] 7029 4-9-7 100 KierenFallon 9 93+
(Luca Cumani) *s.i.s: in rr: kpt on fnl 3f: nvr nr ldrs* **8/1**

0U-1 10 13 **Right Step**[21] 1605 5-9-4 97 JimCrowley 12 65
(Alan Jarvis) *lw: mid-div: effrt 4f out: sn chsng ldrs: wknd over 1f out: heavily eased last 100yds* **9/1**

52-0 11 14 **Space War**[11] 1865 5-8-8 87 PaulMulrennan 3 29
(Michael Easterby) *chsd ldrs: wknd 2f out: eased ins fnl f* **11/1**

10-0 **12** *9* **Labarinto**25 1510 4-9-4 **97** .... RyanMoore 1 21
(Sir Michael Stoute) *chsd ldrs: lost pl over 1f out: heavily eased ins fnl f* **15/2**3

25-2 **13** *30* **New Hampshire (USA)**27 1475 4-8-8 **90** .... LeeTopliss(3) 8
(Tony Coyle) *on toes: trckd ldrs: t.k.h: wknd 2f out: heavily eased: virtually p.u: t.o* **14/1**

/32- **P** **Flag Officer**340 2935 4-9-2 **95** .... FrankieDettori 16
(Saeed Bin Suroor) *missed break: racd v wd and sn heavily eased: p.u after 1f: lame bhd* **4/1**1

2m 11.23s (-1.27) **Going Correction** +0.10s/f (Good) **14** Ran SP% **117.7**
Speed ratings (Par 109): **109,107,107,105,104 103,103,102,102,91 80,73,49,**
toteswingers: 1&2 £27.80, 1&3 £13.50, 2&3 £35.00 CSF £146.71 CT £1420.54 TOTE £6.30: £3.10, £6.90, £3.80; EX 168.80 Trifecta £1208.40 Part won. Pool: £1,633.10 - 0.20 winning units..
Owner George Strawbridge **Bred** George Strawbridge **Trained** Newmarket, Suffolk
■ Stewards' Enquiry : William Buick caution: careless riding

FOCUS
The rail was on the traditional racing line. The winning time suggested the ground was on the slow side of good. Run at a good pace, thanks to Suits Me, this is likely to prove solid, reliable handicap form. The winner could turn out smart.

NOTEBOOK
Gatewood picked up a problem last year and wasn't seen after July, but he's a well-bred son of Galileo and, having had only three previous starts, was open to more improvement than anything else in the race. Held up out the back, the good gallop saw him travel well into contention and, although he showed some greenness once edging ahead, he found more when challenged and was pulling clear again at the line. There should be more to come from him, and it'll be no surprise if he gets 1m4f.
Romeo Montague isn't an easy horse to win with, but the good pace up front allowed him to cruise into contention. It wasn't a huge surprise to see him outbattled, though. (op 20-1)
Sirvino ran well in a race run to suit, but he's on a stiff mark and won't be given any assistance from the handicapper any time soon following this solid effort. (tchd 9-1)
Suits Me didn't hang about but he's a tough front-runner and still didn't go down easily. His current mark doesn't make things easy, as he's still 8lb higher than when last successful, but he did by far the best of those who raced prominently and might yet be able to win something similar. (op 25-1)
Mirrored has never run well here in the past, but thanks to the good gallop he was able to settle better than has sometimes been the case, and he put up a respectable effort. (op 20-1)
Northside Prince(IRE) was another who benefited from sitting out the back off a good pace. (tchd 50-1)
Area Fifty One, gelded since he last ran and debuting for Richard Fahey, had plenty of use made of him chasing the leader, and with his trainer having warned he would need the run, it was no surprise to see him drop out late on. This was a better performance than his finishing position might suggest and he's one to keep in mind next time granted a decent surface. (tchd 11-1)
Kirthill(IRE) had the race run to suit so perhaps he needed it. (tchd 17-2)
Right Step, who was second in this last year, had no excuse on the fitness front as he'd won at Epsom on his reappearance. Official explanation: trainer had no explanation for the poor form shown (op 8-1)
Labarinto, who wore earplugs for the first time but proved uncooperative before the start, paid for racing closer to the pace than was ideal. (op 8-1)
Flag Officer couldn't raise a gallop from the moment the stalls opened, and something was clearly amiss. Official explanation: jockey said, regarding running and riding, that although the gelding moved well going to start he felt wrong shortly after leaving stalls and pulled up; vet said gelding returned lame.

2177 WILLIAM BIRCH & SONS CONSTRUCTION STKS (H'CAP) 6f
2:00 (2:03) (Class 2) (0-105,100) 4-Y-O+ **£12,938** (£3,850; £1,924; £962) **Stalls** Centre

Form RPR

55-3 **1** **Secret Witness**5 2023 6-9-1 **94** .... (b) JamesDoyle 15 104
(Ronald Harris) *hld up towards rr: swtchd rt over 2f out: str run to ld ent fnl f: drvn out* **14/1**

5536 **2** *½* **Baby Strange**11 1844 8-8-6 **85** .... JoeFanning 6 93
(Derek Shaw) *hld up in rr: hdwy 1/2-way: swtchd lft and effrt 2f out: rdn over 1f out: styd on ins fnl f* **12/1**

-010 **3** *1 ¼* **Fast Shot**11 1844 4-8-8 **87** .... DavidAllan 18 91
(Tim Easterby) *lw: hld up: hdwy over 2f out: rdn over 1f out: chal ent fnl f: kpt on* **25/1**

0-00 **4** *shd* **Waffle (IRE)**10 1885 6-9-7 **100** .... GrahamGibbons 7 104
(David Barron) *in tch: hdwy 2f out: rdn to chse ldrs over 1f out: kpt on wl towards fin* **10/1**3

22-0 **5** *hd* **Dickie's Lad (IRE)**7 1975 4-9-1 **94** .... (t) GrahamLee 11 97
(Kevin Ryan) *led to 1/2-way: cl up: rdn over 1f out: one pce and hld whn n.m.r towards fin* **16/1**

10-6 **6** *¾* **Coolminx (IRE)**23 1558 5-8-10 **89** .... PaulHanagan 20 90
(Richard Fahey) *prom: rdn along and sltly outpcd 2f out: kpt on u.p fnl f* **16/1**

-335 **7** *1 ½* **Tajneed (IRE)**11 1844 9-8-4 **90** .... ShirleyTeasdale(7) 17 86
(David Nicholls) *chsd ldrs: rdn along wl over 1f out: kpt on same pce fnl f* **14/1**

0320 **8** *shd* **Escape To Glory (USA)**10 1885 4-8-5 **84** .... FrannyNorton 8 80
(Mikael Magnusson) *outpcd and bhd: rdn along 2f out: kpt on u.p fnl f: nrst fin* **10/1**3

320- **9** *½* **Kaldoun Kingdom (IRE)**208 6987 7-8-11 **97** .... LauraBarry(7) 4 91
(Richard Fahey) *prom: led 1/2-way: rdn wl over 1f out: hdd & wknd ent fnl f* **16/1**

34/ **10** *½* **Khawatim**347 4-9-2 **95** .... MickyFenton 1 88
(Paul Midgley) *in tch on outer: pushed along and hdwy over 2f out: sn rdn and no imp* **66/1**

000- **11** *1 ¼* **Medici Time**207 7018 7-8-6 **85** .... (v) TomEaves 16 74
(Tim Easterby) *dwlt and hld up in rr: hdwy 2f out: sn rdn and one pce* **50/1**

452- **12** *¾* **Barnet Fair**240 6217 4-8-11 **90** .... SilvestreDeSousa 10 76
(Richard Guest) *chsd ldrs: rdn along over 2f out: sn wknd* **12/1**

3-15 **13** *1 ½* **New Planet (IRE)**27 1469 4-9-7 **100** .... TomQueally 14 82
(John Quinn) *a in midfield* **12/1**

300- **14** *½* **Roker Park (IRE)**272 5218 7-8-10 **89** .... DanielTudhope 2 69
(David O'Meara) *dwlt: a in rr* **33/1**

310- **15** *2* **Instance**298 4332 4-8-12 **91** .... WilliamBuick 19 65
(Jeremy Noseda) *towards rr: rdn along and sme hdwy on wd outside fnl 2f: nvr a factor* **14/1**

4-00 **16** *½* **Valery Borzov (IRE)**10 1885 8-8-13 **92** .... (v) TonyHamilton 13 64
(Richard Fahey) *chsd ldrs: rdn along 1/2-way: sn wknd* **25/1**

-102 **17** *4* **Shropshire (IRE)**10 1885 4-8-6 **90** .... MatthewLawson(5) 12 49
(Charles Hills) *on toes: t.k.h: chsd ldrs: rdn along 1/2-way: sn lost pl and bhd* **8/1**2

000- **18** *3 ¾* **Love Delta (USA)**180 7468 5-8-10 **92** .... AmyRyan(3) 3 39
(Kevin Ryan) *ldrs: rdn along over 2f out: sn wknd* **50/1**

115- **19** *11* **York Glory (USA)**249 5927 4-9-3 **96** .... PhillipMakin 5
(Kevin Ryan) *hld up: hdwy and in tch 1/2-way: rdn over 2f out: sn wknd* **9/2**1

1m 13.28s (1.38) **Going Correction** +0.475s/f (Yiel) **19** Ran SP% **124.2**
Speed ratings (Par 109): **109,108,106,106,106 105,103,103,102,101 100,99,97,96,93 93,87,82,68**
toteswingers: 1&2:£42.40, 1&3:£65.30, 2&3:£58.40 CSF £163.68 CT £4249.37 TOTE £17.10: £3.30, £2.70, £5.70, £2.90; EX 224.00 Trifecta £1763.50 Part won. Pool: £2,383.18 - 0.60 winning units..
Owner Paul Moulton **Bred** Cheveley Park Stud Ltd **Trained** Earlswood, Monmouths

FOCUS
They raced up the middle, and the time was 0.32 seconds slower than the Duke of York. The unexposed potential improvers all underperformed and the form looks ordinary for the class. The winner matched his improved AW form from last year.

NOTEBOOK
Secret Witness had more in hand than the margin suggests. He quickly asserted once asked, but idled in front, not helped by the runner-up challenging away from him. While the winner wasn't obviously well handicapped, he is capable of smart form on his day and this was up there with his best efforts, again showing a liking for York (good second only other start here).
Baby Strange, better than he showed at Doncaster on his previous start when he had to make his move away from the main pace, again found himself challenging further away from the action than ideal. However, while this was a creditable performance, he was only able to get so close thanks to the winner idling. (op 11-1)
Fast Shot ran an honest race and posted a useful performance, but he just wasn't good enough. (op 28-1)
Waffle(IRE), 1lb wrong, travelled well, as is often the case, but his run flattened out. He only has a debut maiden win to his name. (op 14-1)
Dickie's Lad(IRE) ◆ gained his only win so far over this trip, but he travelled like a horse who will be comfortable back at 5f. This was only his second start of the campaign, and his first was a write-off, so he can yet do better. (op 14-1 tchd 18-1)
Coolminx(IRE) probably would have preferred softer ground.
Escape To Glory(USA) Official explanation: trainer said colt lost a front shoe
Barnet Fair looked a sprinter to keep on side this year, so it was a bit disappointing he didn't show more, but he was entitled to need the run.
Instance had won three of her previous five starts, but hadn't been seen since last July and was extremely weak in the market. She didn't show much, but it must count for something that she's being persevered with by a powerful yard.
Shropshire(IRE) was 5lb well in following his recent second at Newmarket, but he has now failed to run to form in four starts here. Official explanation: jockey said gelding never travelled (op 15-2)
York Glory(USA) was strong in the market despite reappearing without his usual blinkers, but something was presumably amiss. Official explanation: jockey said colt ran flat (op 11-2)

2178 TATTERSALLS MUSIDORA STKS (GROUP 3) (FILLIES) 1m 2f 88y
2:30 (2:31) (Class 1) 3-Y-O
£36,861 (£13,975; £6,994; £3,484; £1,748; £877) **Stalls** Low

Form RPR

1-4 **1** **The Fugue**10 1884 3-8-12 0 .... WilliamBuick 3 115+
(John Gosden) *lw: trckd ldrs: swtchd lft and led over 2f out: pushed clr ins fnl f: v readily* **15/8**2

2 **2** *4 ½* **Twirl (IRE)**52 1041 3-8-13 103 ow1 .... JPO'Brien 2 106
(A P O'Brien, Ire) *athletic: lw: led tl over 7f out: chal over 2f out: styd on same pce fnl f* **5/6**1

-316 **3** *3 ¾* **Esentepe (IRE)**11 1851 3-8-12 100 .... RichardHughes 6 98
(Richard Hannon) *lw: hld up in rr: hdwy 3f out: wnt 3rd over 1f out: no threat* **20/1**

45-4 **4** *hd* **Salford Art (IRE)**10 1887 3-8-12 99 .... RyanMoore 1 97
(David Elsworth) *warm: in rr: drvn over 3f out: chsng ldrs 2f out: sn outpcd and swtchd rt: styd on fnl f* **14/1**3

64-3 **5** *5* **Aniseed (IRE)**25 1532 3-8-12 76 .... KierenFallon 5 88
(William Haggas) *s.s: hdwy to ld over 7f out: hung lft and hdd over 2f out: wknd over 1f out* **33/1**

3231 **6** *nk* **Good Morning Star (IRE)**7 1973 3-8-12 74 .... FrannyNorton 4 87
(Mark Johnston) *trckd ldrs: effrt over 3f out: lost pl over 2f out* **20/1**

2m 11.36s (-1.14) **Going Correction** +0.10s/f (Good) **6** Ran SP% **108.5**
Speed ratings (Par 106): **108,104,101,101,97 97**
toteswingers: 1&2 £1.30, 1&3 £4.20, 2&3 £3.90 CSF £3.45 TOTE £2.30: £1.30, £1.10; EX 3.80.
Owner Lord Lloyd-Webber **Bred** Watership Down Stud **Trained** Newmarket, Suffolk

FOCUS
Compared with the opening handicap, they went a little slower early but finished faster. The winning time was just 0.13sec slower. This looked a two-horse race on paper and it developed as such. The Fugue rates one of the better winners of this race and has a strong chance in the Oaks on form. The form reads sound, with the second to fourth all close to their marks.

NOTEBOOK
The Fugue won in style having come to challenge Twirl going easily. She did get the run of the race as the Ballydoyle favourite was taken on in front by Aniseed, but there's no denying that she won with authority, is bred to handle a step up to 1m4f (dam was narrowly beaten in the Ribblesdale) and looks to be progressing with racing. The Oaks will be next - she was predictably shortened to a best price of 9-2 - and she'll go to Epsom with sound claims, but whether the form of this race is that strong is open to question. (op 2-1 tchd 9-4)
Twirl(IRE)'s place in the Ballydoyle pecking order is unknown, but she was strong in the market. That said, while she's a sister to Misty For Me, her previous form hadn't suggested she was anything special, and with Kissed and Maybe among the stable's options for the Oaks, it's likely they have stronger cards to play. A little keener than ideal early on, she was taken on for the lead, things didn't fall for her like the winner, and not for the first time she didn't impress with her head carriage in the closing stages. (op 4-5 tchd 8-11)
Esentepe(IRE) ran poorly at Goodwood last time and, while this was better up in distance back on a more favourable surface, she's nothing special and will continue to be vulnerable at this level.
Salford Art(IRE), who was well held on soft ground in the Pretty Polly on her reappearance, is a half-sister to a 2m winner, but she again failed to see out her race. She needs a drop in class. (op 16-1)
Aniseed(IRE) was a little slowly away from the stalls, but she pulled her way to the front to dispute things with the favourite. Leading them into the straight, she proved a sitting duck, but on everything we knew about her she faced a stiff task in this company. In any case, her trainer has a much stronger Oaks prospect in the shape of Lingfield trial winner Vow.
Good Morning Star(IRE), who recorded a shock win in the Cheshire Oaks a week earlier, finished well beaten on this quicker ground. It seems she needs it hock-deep to show her best. (tchd 16-1 and 22-1)

2179 DUKE OF YORK TOTEPOOL STKS (GROUP 2) 6f
3:00 (3:02) (Class 1) 3-Y-O+
£60,481 (£22,929; £11,475; £5,716; £2,868; £1,439) **Stalls** Centre

Form RPR

00-0 **1** **Tiddliwinks**27 1469 6-9-7 100 .... JamieSpencer 7 116
(Kevin Ryan) *hld up: hdwy on outer over 2f out: edgd rt and led over 1f out: all out* **25/1**

33-1 **2** *hd* **The Cheka (IRE)**[46] 1129 6-9-7 108..............(p) NeilCallan 12 115
(Eve Johnson Houghton) *sn chsng ldrs: kpt on wl ins fnl f: jst hld* **9/1**

600- **3** *nk* **Society Rock (IRE)**[157] 7730 5-9-7 117.............. KierenFallon 3 114
(James Fanshawe) *dwlt: hld up: hdwy 2f out: pushed rt over 1f out: n.m.r and styd on ins fnl f* **8/1**[3]

610- **4** *hd* **Bogart**[197] 7220 3-8-12 106.............. PhillipMakin 1 111
(Kevin Ryan) *w ldrs: led over 3f out: hung rt and hdd over 1f out: no ex last 75yds* **25/1**

163- **5** *3 ¾* **Hoof It**[256] 5707 5-9-7 118.............. RyanMoore 11 101
(Michael Easterby) *lw: in rr: hdwy over 1f out: edgd lft: kpt on: nvr nr ldrs* **2/1**[1]

6/10 **6** *hd* **Soul (AUS)**[46] 1147 5-9-7 113.............. FrankieDettori 5 101
(Saeed Bin Suroor) *lw: led over 1f: edgd rt over 1f out: one pce* **16/1**

11-4 **7** *1 ¾* **Restiadargent (FR)**[41] 1209 3-8-12 112.............. OlivierPeslier 9 93+
(H-A Pantall, France) *angular: hld up in rr: styd on fnl 2f: nt rch ldrs* **11/1**

604- **8** *1 ½* **Doncaster Rover (USA)**[180] 6-9-7 107.............. SilvestreDeSousa 8 90+
(David Brown) *in rr: sn pushed along: styng on whn nt clr run 1f out* **40/1**

411- **9** *3 ½* **Elnawin**[339] 2961 6-9-7 110.............. PatDobbs 10 79
(Richard Hannon) *trckd ldrs: wkng whn n.m.r 1f out* **33/1**

1-00 **10** *hd* **Sirius Prospect (USA)**[27] 1469 4-9-7 109.............. ShaneKelly 14 78
(Dean Ivory) *s.s: swtchd lft after s: kpt on fnl 2f: nvr a factor* **11/1**

3022 **11** *4 ½* **Bannock (IRE)**[14] 1751 3-8-12 109.............. JoeFanning 4 62
(Mark Johnston) *w ldrs: wknd over 1f out* **33/1**

30-5 **12** *23* **Libranno**[19] 1646 4-9-7 112.............. RichardHughes 6
(Richard Hannon) *chsd ldrs: lost pl 2f out: sn bhd and eased: t.o* **16/1**

-311 **13** *14* **Mayson**[11] 1857 4-9-7 110.............. PaulHanagan 2 +
(Richard Fahey) *upset in stalls: dwlt: sn chsng ldrs: lost pl 2f out: sn heavily eased: t.o* **7/2**[2]

1m 12.96s (1.06) **Going Correction** +0.475s/f (Yiel)
WFA 3 from 4yo+ 9lb **13** Ran SP% **121.1**
Speed ratings (Par 115): **111,110,110,110,105 104,102,100,95,95 89,58,40**
toteswingers: 1&2 £37.80, 1&3 £43.80, 2&3 £7.60 CSF £228.88 TOTE £34.20: £6.90, £3.20, £3.00; EX 427.00 Trifecta £2166.40 Part won. Pool: £2,927.59 - 0.60 winning units..
Owner Guy Reed **Bred** Guy Reed **Trained** Hambleton, N Yorks
■ Stewards' Enquiry : Jamie Spencer two-day ban: careless riding (May 30-31)

FOCUS
Often an ordinary race for the level and the form of this latest running looks particularly weak, albeit the winner's official mark of only 100 is misleading. He rates similar to his run in this last year, with the second to form. The time was 0.32 seconds quicker than the earlier Class 2 handicap. They raced up the middle through the early stages, but ended up towards the stands' rail.

NOTEBOOK
Tiddliwinks reportedly had the odd niggly problem during an inconsistent campaign last year, but he showed some smart form, notably when third in this race. He had excuses when well beaten at Newmarket on his reappearance (blindfold slow to be removed and found trouble), and stepped up considerably on this return to a track that clearly brings out the best in him. He's now heading for the Diamond Jubilee, but will have next to no chance if meeting a peak-form Black Caviar, whose Royal Ascot odds were trimmed following this race. (op 33-1)
The Cheka(IRE) won the Listed Cammidge Trophy when dropped back to this trip on his reappearance, and he probably ran to a similar level. He's also in the Diamond Jubilee, but significantly more will be required at Royal Ascot.
Society Rock(IRE), winner of last season's Golden Jubilee (known as the Diamond Jubilee this year), didn't produce his best after over five months off, but he should go on from this. He raced a bit too enthusiastically and didn't have much room when keeping on near the line. However, it's highly unlikely he'll successfully defend his Royal Ascot title, even though he saves his best for that course. (op 9-1 tchd 10-1)
Bogart ◆ showed smart juvenile form and ran a fine race on this return. He tanked along (without cover) in the manner of a horse who will be suited by a drop to 5f in due course, and did well to finish so close considering how much he must have taken out of himself. His trainer expects him to improve significantly for the run. Official explanation: jockey said colt hung right-handed (tchd 28-1 and 33-1 in a place)
Hoof It made a disappointing return, never travelling and failing to pick up for pressure. He was successful on his reappearance in the 6f handicap on this card 12 months ago, making this performance all the more off-putting. (op 9-4)
Soul(AUS), formerly trained in Australia and then Dubai, wasn't quite up to this level. (op 22-1 tchd 25-1)
Restiadargent(FR), a dual Group winner when trained in France and fourth in the Prix Imprudence on her return, got further back than ideal and never had a great deal of room. She can do better. (op 16-1)
Mayson, a Listed and Group 3 winner at Newmarket already this season, ruined his chance by getting upset at the start. Official explanation: jockey said colt became upset in stalls and never travelled (op 10-3)

2180 CONSTANT SECURITY STKS (H'CAP) 1m 4f
3:35 (3:36) (Class 4) (0-85,89) 4-Y-O+ **£7,762** (£2,310; £1,154; £577) **Stalls** Centre

Form RPR

153- **1** **Mulaqen**[298] 4316 4-9-6 84.............. PaulHanagan 2 99+
(Marcus Tregoning) *lw: trckd ldrs: hdwy and cl up 4f out: led wl over 2f out: sn rdn clr: comf* **8/1**[3]

60-1 **2** *2 ¼* **Mica Mika (IRE)**[5] 2031 4-9-0 83 6ex.............. ShaneBKelly(5) 6 90
(Richard Fahey) *lw: in tch: hdwy 4f out: chsd wnr wl over 1f out: sn rdn and kpt on: no imp* **7/1**[2]

315- **3** *1 ¾* **Eagle Rock (IRE)**[34] 7017 4-9-2 80.............. AndrewMullen 19 84
(Tom Tate) *hld up in midfield: pushed along and outpcd 4f out: hdwy over 2f out: sn rdn and styd on appr fnl f: nrst fin* **12/1**

200/ **4** *¾* **Swinging Hawk (GER)**[109] 6926 6-9-5 83.............. JamieSpencer 18 86
(Ian Williams) *hld up in rr: hdwy over 3f out: rdn 2f out: styd on wl fnl f: nrst fin* **33/1**

60-1 **5** *shd* **Aldwick Bay (IRE)**[9] 1939 4-9-7 85 6ex.............. RichardHughes 12 88
(Richard Hannon) *b.hind: hld up: hdwy over 4f out: chsd ldrs over 3f out: rdn 2f out and kpt on same pce* **16/1**

10-5 **6** *nk* **El Torbellino (IRE)**[14] 1756 4-9-4 82.............. DanielTudhope 4 84
(David O'Meara) *led 3f: cl up: led again over 3f out: sn rdn and hdd over 2f out: sn drvn and one pce* **28/1**

0-66 **7** *1 ¾* **Hawk Mountain (UAE)**[18] 1672 7-9-6 84.............. MichaelO'Connell 5 84
(John Quinn) *towards rr: stdy hdwy over 5f out: in tch 3f out: rdn to chse ldrs over 2f out: sn one pce* **20/1**

56-0 **8** *2* **Red Jade**[38] 1239 7-9-3 81.............. NeilCallan 7 77
(Mrs K Burke) *hld up: hdwy over 4f out: in tch over 2f out: sn rdn and no further prog* **10/1**

041- **9** *3 ¾* **Vasily**[216] 6810 4-9-4 82..............(t) AndreaAtzeni 14 72
(Robert Eddery) *cl up: led after 3f: rdn along over 4f out: hdd over 3f out and grad wknd* **8/1**[3]

1-5 **10** *3 ¾* **The Fun Crusher**[46] 1133 4-9-2 80.............. DavidAllan 17 64
(Tim Easterby) *lw: dwlt and swtchd lft s: towards rr: sme hdwy over 3f out: rdn along wl over 2f out: n.d* **4/1**[1]

550- **11** *3 ¾* **Granston (IRE)**[276] 5078 11-9-7 85.............. GrahamGibbons 11 63
(James Bethell) *chsd ldrs: rdn along over 3f out: wknd over 2f out* **25/1**

00-2 **12** *½* **Always The Lady**[25] 1513 4-9-5 83.............. AdamKirby 10 61
(Clive Cox) *a towards rr* **12/1**

03-0 **13** *3 ½* **King Kurt (IRE)**[32] 1381 4-9-4 82.............. PhillipMakin 20 54
(Kevin Ryan) *a towards rr* **20/1**

3/0- **14** *5* **Bollin Felix**[361] 2285 8-9-2 85.............. AdamCarter(5) 13 49
(Tim Easterby) *a towards rr* **66/1**

0-51 **15** *4* **Persian Peril**[10] 1880 8-9-11 89 6ex.............. RobertWinston 3 47
(Alan Swinbank) *in tch: t.k.h: hdwy on inner to chse ldrs 5f out: rdn along over 3f out: grad wknd* **20/1**

010- **16** *47* **Tartan Gigha (IRE)**[208] 6989 7-9-2 80.............. SilvestreDeSousa 16
(Geoffrey Harker) *a towards rr* **33/1**

-231 **17** *16* **Crunched**[88] 625 5-9-4 82..............(b) WilliamBuick 15
(Tim Pitt) *chsd ldrs on outer: rdn along 5f out: sn wknd* **25/1**

10-4 **18** *23* **Kyllachy Spirit**[42] 1186 4-9-5 83.............. ShaneKelly 8
(William Knight) *prom: rdn along over 3f out: sn wknd and bhd whn eased over 1f out* **33/1**

2m 34.38s (1.18) **Going Correction** +0.10s/f (Good) **18** Ran SP% **120.8**
Speed ratings (Par 105): **100,98,97,96,96 96,95,94,91,89 86,86,83,80,77 46,35,20**
toteswingers: 1&2 £10.50, 1&3 £22.30, 2&3 £22.50 CSF £48.18 CT £515.12 TOTE £7.50: £2.00, £2.00, £3.40, £5.20; EX 46.30 Trifecta £904.60 Pool: £1,503.63 - 1.20 winning units..
Owner Hamdan Al Maktoum **Bred** Stowell Hill Ltd **Trained** Lambourn, Berks

FOCUS
A good handicap, although the early pace looked modest. The action unfolded up the middle of the track. The winner was value for extra and the form looks solid.
Always The Lady Official explanation: jockey said filly never travelled
Persian Peril Official explanation: jockey said gelding ran too free
Crunched Official explanation: jockey said gelding lost its action

2181 RIPLEYCOLLECTION.COM E B F NOVICE STKS 5f
4:10 (4:11) (Class 3) 2-Y-O **£7,762** (£2,310; £1,154; £577) **Stalls** Centre

Form RPR

1 **1** **Lastchancelucas**[14] 1753 2-8-12 0.............. JasonHart(7) 1 86
(Declan Carroll) *lengthy: on toes: w ldr: led over 2f out: hld on wl* **8/1**

2 *½* **Hoofalong** 2-9-0 0.............. PaulMulrennan 5 79+
(Michael Easterby) *leggy: unf: dwlt: sn trcking ldrs: swtchd lft and chal over 1f out: no ex nr fin: will improve* **25/1**

1 **3** *2 ½* **Mrs Brown's Boy**[11] 1847 2-8-12 0.............. DarrenEgan(7) 2 75
(Ronald Harris) *tall: leggy: athletic: w ldrs: drvn over 2f out: kpt on same pce fnl f* **5/1**[3]

50 **4** *hd* **Lucky Lodge**[28] 1437 2-9-0 0.............. RobertWinston 4 69
(Mel Brittain) *leggy: on toes: led tl over 1f out: styd on same pce fnl f* **40/1**

1 **5** *2 ¼* **Tatlisu (IRE)**[12] 1818 2-9-5 0.............. PaulHanagan 3 72+
(Richard Fahey) *athletic: dwlt: repeatedly bucked sn after s: sn detached in last: hdwy 2f out: wandered ins fnl f: wknd towards fin* **9/4**[1]

2 **6** *1 ¼* **Botanic Garden**[27] 1474 2-9-0 0.............. RichardMullen 7 56
(David Brown) *unf: restless in stalls: in tch: outpcd over 2f out: hdwy and swtchd lft over 1f out: nt clr run and swtchd lft ins fnl f: nvr nr ldrs* **11/2**

32 **7** *1 ½* **Citius (IRE)**[9] 1920 2-9-0 0.............. RichardHughes 8 51
(Richard Hannon) *w'like: trckd ldrs: effrt over 1f out: sn wknd* **7/1**

1 **8** *2* **Cumbrian Craic**[18] 1651 2-9-5 0.............. DavidAllan 6 49
(Tim Easterby) *str: lw: chsd ldrs: wknd fnl f* **4/1**[2]

1m 1.71s (2.41) **Going Correction** +0.475s/f (Yiel) **8** Ran SP% **112.7**
Speed ratings (Par 97): **99,98,94,93,90 88,85,82**
toteswingers: 1&2 £14.30, 1&3 £8.00, 2&3 £19.80 CSF £168.55 TOTE £8.70: £2.70, £3.30, £2.10; EX 189.90 Trifecta £842.90 Pool: £2,004.94 - 1.76 winning units..
Owner C H Stephenson & Partners **Bred** C H Stephenson **Trained** Sledmere, E Yorks
■ Stewards' Enquiry : Jason Hart two-day ban: used whip above permitted level (May 30-31)

FOCUS
Perhaps not the strongest of novices but the winner proved his Pontefract victory was no fluke. The form is rated around the first two and the lower end of the race averages.

NOTEBOOK
Lastchancelucas may struggle to confirm the form in future, but he knew his job better than one or two here and followed up his shock Pontefract success, showing that win to be no fluke and himself to be not just a soft-ground colt. Showing plenty of speed on a track where it often holds up, he had just enough to hold on at the finish and his trainer believes he'll get another furlong, with the Woodcote a possible target. (op 15-2 tchd 10-1)
Hoofalong, the only runner in the line-up making his debut, missed the break and then raced keenly behind the speed. Switched to challenge, he ran green when asked to pick up and came up a little short. Like the winner a late-April foal, he'll come on plenty for this and it'll be a surprise if he doesn't reverse the form if the pair ever meet again.
Mrs Brown's Boy won what looked an ordinary maiden at Goodwood last time, so this was a step up. He should get another furlong in time. (op 11-2 tchd 13-2)
Lucky Lodge, who finished fifth in the Brocklesby on his debut, ran poorly on soft ground last time, but this was a return to form and clearly the Beverley run was the outlier. (op 33-1 tchd 50-1)
Tatlisu(IRE) jumped very awkwardly out of the stalls and lost several lengths before getting into stride. The fact he got as close at the finish suggests that had he broken on terms he'd have probably won. It's probably wise to write this off - he didn't do this on his debut - and he looks to have the raw ability to win something similar. (op 11-4)
Botanic Garden still looked green, but was keeping on at the finish and a maiden can come his way. (op 5-1 tchd 6-1)
Citius(IRE) had quite a bit on his plate judged on his two previous starts. He was eased down when all chance had gone. (op 6-1 tchd 8-1)
Cumbrian Craic was disappointing, but his debut win came on soft ground and conditions were quicker here. Perhaps he's ground-dependent. (op 7-2 tchd 3-1)

2182 MCARTHURGLEN'S YORK DESIGNER OUTLET STKS (H'CAP) 7f
4:45 (4:49) (Class 3) (0-90,88) 3-Y-O **£9,056** (£2,695; £1,346; £673) **Stalls** Low

Form RPR

31- **1** **Baccarat (IRE)**[152] 7783 3-8-8 75.............. PaulHanagan 14 88+
(Richard Fahey) *lw: chsd ldrs: chal over 1f out: led and edgd lft ins fnl f: hld on wl* **5/1**[1]

13-3 **2** *nk* **Van Der Art**[26] 1500 3-9-3 84.............. KierenFallon 11 96+
(Alan Jarvis) *lw: hmpd s: in rr: hdwy on inner over 3f out: edgd rt and chsd wnr ins fnl f: no ex towards fin* **10/1**

44-2 **3** *4* **Three Am Tour (IRE)**[10] 1894 3-9-3 84.............. RichardHughes 7 85
(Richard Hannon) *lw: hld up in mid-div: hdwy over 2f out: kpt on to take 3rd nr fin* **8/1**[3]

0-21 **4** *½* **Nameitwhatyoulike**[18] 1653 3-9-2 83.............. PaulMulrennan 9 83+
(Michael Easterby) *wnt rt s: led: hdd jst ins fnl f: kpt on same pce* **10/1**

01-2 **5** *1 ¾* **Tartiflette**[26] 1500 3-9-2 83.............. GrahamGibbons 12 78+
(Ed McMahon) *lw: hmpd s: hdwy over 3f out: kpt on: nvr nr to chal* **11/2**[2]

34-6 **6** *1 ¼* **Deepsand (IRE)**[28] 1440 3-8-11 78.............. DavidAllan 2 70
(Tim Easterby) *chsd ldrs: one pce fnl 2f* **10/1**

5-50 **7** *1* **Mitchum**[18] 1658 3-8-8 **75** LeeNewman 18 64
(David Barron) *mid-div: kpt on fnl 2f: nvr nr to chal* **66/1**
14-0 **8** *nk* **Ralphy Boy (IRE)**[36] 1271 3-9-7 **88** AdrianNicholls 8 76
(David Nicholls) *in rr: kpt on fnl 2f: nvr a factor* **50/1**
-000 **9** *1 3/4* **Parc De Launay**[11] 1858 3-9-1 **82** JamieSpencer 3 66
(Tom Tate) *chsd ldrs: fdd appr fnl f* **16/1**
1-34 **10** *hd* **Kinloch Castle**[35] 1304 3-9-4 **85** SilvestreDeSousa 4 68
(Mark Johnston) *chsd ldrs: one pce fnl 2f* **16/1**
141 **11** *2 1/2* **Warfare**[5] 2021 3-8-13 **80** 6ex PhillipMakin 16 56
(Kevin Ryan) *nvr bttr than mid-div* **12/1**
5-1 **12** *2 1/4* **Lady Macduff (IRE)**[55] 990 3-9-1 **82** JoeFanning 6 52
(Mark Johnston) *in tch: effrt over 2f out: wknd over 1f out* **25/1**
24-1 **13** *1/2* **Lisiere (IRE)**[36] 1274 3-8-13 **80** NeilCallan 10 49
(Mrs K Burke) *hmpd s: hdwy on outer 3f out: sn in tch: wknd over 1f out* **16/1**
251- **14** *1/2* **Intuition**[196] 7225 3-8-10 **77** RyanMoore 1 44
(Richard Hannon) *lw: a towards rr* **20/1**
56-1 **15** *hd* **Ardmay (IRE)**[28] 1441 3-8-7 **77** JulieBurke(3) 5 44
(Kevin Ryan) *chsd ldrs: lost pl over 1f out* **20/1**
51-6 **16** *3 1/2* **Byronic Hero**[36] 1271 3-8-10 **77** TonyHamilton 13 34
(Jedd O'Keeffe) *lw: wnt lft s: a in rr* **33/1**
21-2 **17** *6* **Grizzle**[37] 1264 3-9-3 **84** FrankieDettori 17 25
(Mahmood Al Zarooni) *dwlt: in rr: effrt on outside over 2f out: sn wknd: eased whn bhd ins fnl f* **9/1**

1m 26.27s (0.97) **Going Correction** +0.225s/f (Good) **17** Ran SP% **125.5**
Speed ratings (Par 103): **103,102,98,97,95 94,92,92,90,90 87,84,84,83,83 79,72**
toteswingers: 1&2 £15.10, 1&3 £8.40, 2&3 £18.80 CSF £51.18 CT £421.72 TOTE £5.30: £1.60, £2.50, £2.50, £2.80; EX 78.50 Trifecta £1411.40 Pool: £2,498.67 - 1.31 winning units..
Owner Sir Robert Ogden **Bred** Twelve Oaks Stud **Trained** Musley Bank, N Yorks

FOCUS
This looked a strong 3yo handicap, and the right sort of horses came to the fore, so it's likely to prove reliable. The winner produced a personal best.

NOTEBOOK
Baccarat(IRE) was caught wide from his draw in stall 14, but proved himself a well-handicapped horse with an all-out win over a reliable yardstick. This was just his third-ever start, he should get a mile, and there ought to be further improvement to come. (op 13-2 tchd 7-1)
Van Der Art, a consistent sort, wasn't best away but she kept on well for pressure and posted another solid effort in defeat. She'll creep up another few pounds in the handicap for this, but is versatile when it comes to ground and should continue to run well. (op 11-1 tchd 9-1)
Three Am Tour(IRE) travelled strongly through the race but, not for the first time, didn't find as much as had looked likely under pressure. She might be one for the in-running layers. (op 11-1)
Nameitwhatyoulike, who made all at Doncaster last time out, had no problem with the drop back to 7f and led for most of the way. He couldn't hold them all off in the closing stages, but it was still a sound effort off a 5lb higher mark. (op 8-1)
Tartiflette finished one place in front of Van Der Art at Newbury on her reappearance, but wasn't able to confirm that form on this quicker ground. She wasn't helped by being slightly hampered at the start and being caught a little wide. (op 9-2)
Deepsand(IRE), dropping back from 1m2f, raced in touch for much of the way but didn't see his race out. He looks a little high in the handicap. (op 12-1)
Mitchum did well to cross over from his wide draw and save ground more towards the inside, but he ran into the back of the weakening Parc de Launay just inside the final 2f, and proved one-paced once switched. He might do better back over sprint distances.
Ralphy Boy(IRE) didn't settle in rear early on, but ran on past several rivals in the closing stages. He might be better off in a strongly run sprint, and might be interesting dropped a pound or two.
Warfare might have found this race coming a bit soon following his Ascot win.
T/Jkpt: Not won. T/Plt: £3,044.20 to a £1 stake. Pool: £206,214.48. 49.45 winning tickets. T/Qpdt: £176.40 to a £1 stake. Pool: £12,133.47. 50.89 winning tickets. WG

2183 - (Foreign Racing) - See Raceform Interactive

1535 NAAS (L-H)
Wednesday, May 16

OFFICIAL GOING: Good to yielding

2184a FISHERY LANE 2YO RACE 6f
5:50 (5:51) 2-Y-O **£8,625** (£2,000; £875; £500)

RPR
1 **Dawn Approach (IRE)**[52] 1038 2-9-7 KevinManning 2 105+
(J S Bolger, Ire) *trckd ldr in 2nd: travelling best to ld under 2f out: sn asserted and clr fnl f: styd on wl: easily* **4/6**[1]
2 *5 1/2* **Canary Row (IRE)**[13] 1802 2-9-7 NGMcCullagh 1 85
(P J Prendergast, Ire) *led: rdn 1/2-way: strly pressed and hdd under 2f out: sn no ch w wnr and kpt on same pce u.p* **11/2**[3]
3 *2 1/2* **Tennessee Wildcat (IRE)**[12] 1832 2-9-5 GaryCarroll 6 75+
(G M Lyons, Ire) *trckd ldrs in 4th and t.k.h: carried rt under 2f out and sn hung bdly lft: 3rd and no ch w easy wnr whn dived rt ins fnl f* **10/1**
4 *6* **Spirit Of The Air (IRE)** 2-9-3 (t) ShaneFoley 5 55
(John Joseph Murphy, Ire) *chsd ldrs in 5th: rdn along 1/2-way: no threat fr 2f out: wnt mod 4th fnl f* **33/1**
5 *1 1/2* **Parliament Square (IRE)** 2-9-3 JPO'Brien 3 51+
(A P O'Brien, Ire) *trckd ldrs in 3rd: rdn and edgd rt under 2f out: sn carried lft: no ch w easy wnr in 4th over 1f: no ex* **3/1**[2]
6 *18* **Three Free Spirits (IRE)**[24] 1545 2-9-0 AndrewPThornton(3) 4
(S Donohoe, Ire) *a bhd: nvr a factor* **200/1**

1m 15.33s (2.13) **6** Ran SP% **112.9**
CSF £5.12 TOTE £1.50: £1.30, £1.30; DF 3.90.
Owner Mrs J S Bolger **Bred** J S Bolger **Trained** Coolcullen, Co Carlow

FOCUS
A smart performance from the winner who booked his Royal Ascot ticket.

NOTEBOOK
Dawn Approach(IRE) ◆ confirmed the promise of his debut win and booked his Royal Ascot ticket in the process with a smart performance. The extra furlong clearly suited and, having beaten Canary Row by one length at the Curragh, he put five and a half lengths between himself and that rival here. He travelled strongly on the pace and was clearly going the better when sent to the front under 2f out. He ran on well to go clear up the hill and will be aimed at either the Coventry Stakes or the Chesham Stakes. (op 4/7)
Canary Row(IRE) made the running. Ridden along at halfway, he was under pressure before the winner went on under 2f out and was always fighting a losing battle thereafter. (op 9/2)
Tennessee Wildcat(IRE) would have finished closer but for running all over the track inside the last 2f. He was carried right by Parliament Square under 2f out and then went left before hanging badly right under pressure inside the final furlong, much to the surprise of trainer Ger Lyons, who said that the colt showed no such wayward tendencies at home. (op 7/1)
Spirit Of The Air(IRE) was never able to get into serious contention. (op 25/1)
Parliament Square(IRE) got very upset in the stalls but was close up for almost 4f before edging right under pressure. He was slightly hampered when Tennessee Waltz drifted left soon afterwards but was beaten at the time. (op 9/2)
Three Free Spirits(IRE) got upset in the stalls and lost ground by swerving right when they opened. (op 100/1)

2187a IRISH STALLION FARMS EUROPEAN BREEDERS FUND BLUE WIND STKS (GROUP 3) (F&M) 1m 2f
7:20 (7:21) 3-Y-O+ **£41,979** (£12,270; £5,812; £1,937)

RPR
1 **Princess Highway (USA)**[49] 1075 3-8-9 PatSmullen 4 104+
(D K Weld, Ire) *trckd ldr in 2nd: hdwy to ld 2f out: rdn and kpt on wl fnl f* **7/2**[2]
2 *1* **Aaraas**[17] 1690 3-8-9 96 DeclanMcDonogh 2 102
(Kevin Prendergast, Ire) *trckd ldrs: 3rd ent st: 2nd 2f out and sn rdn: kpt on same pce u.p fnl f wout really troubling wnr* **12/1**
3 *1 3/4* **Was (IRE)**[283] 4830 3-8-9 SeamieHeffernan 1 99+
(A P O'Brien, Ire) *settled in 5th: sme hdwy into 3rd under 2f out: rdn and no imp fr 1f out: kpt on one pce* **7/2**[2]
4 *nk* **Cleofila (IRE)**[17] 1690 3-8-9 92 KevinManning 6 98
(J S Bolger, Ire) *trckd ldrs: 3rd 1/2-way: rdn in 4th ent st: no imp u.p over 1f out: kpt on one pce* **9/1**[3]
5 *shd* **Shebella (IRE)**[48] 1098 3-8-9 JohnnyMurtagh 5 98+
(John M Oxx, Ire) *settled in 6th: rdn 2f out and sn no imp: kpt on one pce fnl f* **3/1**[1]
6 *12* **Aloof (IRE)**[35] 1329 3-8-9 96 WJLee 3 74
(David Wachman, Ire) *sn led: hdd 2f out and sn no ex: eased whn btn fnl f* **3/1**[1]

2m 17.64s (2.04) **6** Ran SP% **112.1**
CSF £40.55 TOTE £5.90: £1.40, £5.60; DF 34.00.
Owner Moyglare Stud Farm **Bred** Moyglare Stud **Trained** The Curragh, Co Kildare

FOCUS
The winner goes for the Ribblesdale next. It's difficult to be too confident whether this form will work out.

NOTEBOOK
Princess Highway(USA) followed up her maiden win over the same trip at Leopardstown by landing this Group 3 event in good style. As had been the case at Leopardstown, she raced in second place and, after going to the front 2f out, she kept on well and was well on top in the closing stages. (op 9/4)
Aaraas had found Investec Oaks candidate Kissed eight and a half lengths too good for her over this trip at Navan last month. Always close up, she was driven along in third into the straight and kept on under pressure having gone second 2f out. The winner was always holding her in the closing stages. (op 11/1)
Was(IRE) ◆ had met with a setback early this season. Held up, she made headway into third under 2f out and kept on without making much impression. She is in the Investec Oaks and improvement is very much on the cards wherever she next appears. (op 11/4)
Cleofila(IRE) had finished third behind Kissed and Aaraas on her reappearance at Navan. Driven along in fourth turning for home, she was unable to get to the leaders but stuck to her task and stayed on. (op 8/1)
Shebella(IRE) was held up in rear and sat three lengths off the second-last horse until nearing the straight. She made some headway over 2f out and looked as if she might run in the first three before her effort petered out. (op 11/4 tchd 5/2)
Aloof(IRE) made the running until 2f out before dropping out and being eased when her chance had gone. Official explanation: jockey said filly ran free in the early stages and may not have liked today's ground (op 7/1)

2188 - 2192a (Foreign Racing) - See Raceform Interactive

1882 NEWMARKET (R-H)
Thursday, May 17

OFFICIAL GOING: Good to firm (good in places; 7.8)
Far side course used and stalls on far side.
Wind: Light, against Weather: Overcast

2193 HOMESTORE AND SAFEPAC MAIDEN AUCTION STKS 6f
5:20 (5:21) (Class 5) 2-Y-O **£3,234** (£962; £481; £240) **Stalls** Low

Form RPR
04 **1** **Fortinbrass (IRE)**[31] 1411 2-8-11 0 RichardKingscote 10 78
(Ralph Beckett) *led 1f: chsd ldrs: rdn to ld wl ins fnl f: r.o* **8/1**[3]
2 *1/2* **Rhamnus** 2-9-3 0 RichardHughes 12 83+
(Richard Hannon) *s.s: hld up: hdwy over 1f out: rdn and r.o ins fnl f: wnt 2nd nr fin: nt rch wnr* **4/1**[2]
3 *hd* **You're The Boss** 2-9-1 0 J-PGuillambert 2 80+
(Ed Walker) *mid-div: hdwy 1/2-way: shkn up and edgd lft over 1f out: rdn and r.o ins fnl f: wnt 3rd nr fin* **9/1**
4 **4** *3/4* **Excel Yourself (IRE)**[24] 1556 2-8-12 0 MartinDwyer 11 75
(James Tate) *led 5f out: rdn and hdd wl ins fnl f: styd on same pce* **8/1**[3]
5 *3/4* **Becky Lou (USA)** 2-8-12 0 WilliamBuick 13 72+
(Jeremy Noseda) *s.i.s: sn pushed along in rr: hdwy over 1f out: edgd rt ins fnl f: r.o: nrst fin* **16/1**
6 *nk* **Jontleman (IRE)** 2-8-9 0 MartinHarley 3 69+
(Mick Channon) *sn pushed along in rr: nt clr run over 2f out: r.o ins fnl f: nvr nrr* **11/1**
6 **7** *1 3/4* **Bentleysoysterboy (IRE)**[11] 1886 2-9-3 0 NickyMackay 6 71
(David Elsworth) *prom: shkn up over 1f out: no ex ins fnl f* **11/4**[1]
8 *3/4* **Grace Of Hearts** 2-8-4 0 PaoloSirigu 8 56+
(Robert Eddery) *plld hrd and prom: stdd and lost pl after 1f: nt clr run over 1f out: nvr trbld ldrs* **22/1**
9 *3* **Senafe** 2-8-4 0 LukeMorris 9 47
(Marco Botti) *mid-div: pushed along over 3f out: wknd over 2f out* **25/1**
10 *2 3/4* **Her Royal Empress** 2-8-8 0 LiamJones 7 43
(James Unett) *hdwy 4f out: rdn and wknd over 1f out* **33/1**
3 **11** *1/2* **Simply Dreaming**[16] 1738 2-8-4 0 KirstyMilczarek 4 37
(Michael Squance) *chsd ldrs over 4f* **50/1**
12 *nse* **Getaway Car** 2-8-13 0 NeilCallan 1 46
(Gerard Butler) *chsd ldrs tl wknd over 2f out* **8/1**[3]
13 *31* **Believe In Me** 2-8-1 0 [1] AdamBeschizza(3) 5
(Julia Feilden) *s.s: outpcd: t.o* **50/1**

1m 14.93s (2.73) **Going Correction** +0.275s/f (Good) **13** Ran SP% **119.3**
Speed ratings (Par 93): **92,91,91,90,89 88,86,85,81,77 77,76,35**
Tote Swingers:1&2:£5.00, 2&3:£8.60, 1&3:£8.10 CSF £37.98 TOTE £9.40: £3.10, £2.20, £2.60; EX 28.90 Trifecta £223.80 Pool £565.68 - 1.87 winning units..
Owner Hillier, Lawrence, Turney & Goddard **Bred** Tom Wallace **Trained** Kimpton, Hants

FOCUS
An interesting 6f maiden auction stakes for juveniles. They went a solid gallop and the winning time was nearly 5 secs outside standard, which is nothing special on ground officially described as good to firm (good in places).

NOTEBOOK

Fortinbrass(IRE) was the most experienced contender in the field, having progressed from his modest 5f Kempton debut in April to produce an encouraging just over 2l fourth of 10 at Windsor nine days later, and he maintained that improvement stepping up to 6f. This Baltic King colt showed speed from a modest draw once again and came through with a sustained challenge inside the final furlong. He is a half-brother to the Listed-placed Coolminx who won over 5f as a 2yo and later over 7f. This 6f trip looks ideal at this stage and there should be more to come from him. (op 15-2)

Rhamnus ◆ ran a remarkable race on debut, as he was left 6l at the start from a poor draw, but jockey Richard Hughes let him gradually get himself back into contention, and the Sakhee's Secret colt came home really well into a very encouraging about 1/2-length second. He is a half-brother to several winners, most notably Penny's Gift who won the German 1000 Guineas. He looks to have a decent future. (tchd 7-2 and 5-1)

You're The Boss stayed on well into third on debut and is probably looking for further already. (op 13-2)

Excel Yourself(IRE) ran really well from a poor draw and simply faded close home into fourth. She filled the same position on her debut at Pontefract last month, but has gone the right way for a possible success over this trip in the near future. (tchd 11-1)

Becky Lou(USA) ◆ made a pleasing debut after a tardy start and this daughter of Johannesburg is one to note.

Jontleman(IRE) had a slightly troubled passage into a never-nearer sixth. (op 10-1 tchd 12-1)

Bentleysoysterboy(IRE) travelled notably well 2f out on his second start, but found little inside the final furlong, and may appreciate a drop back to 5f. Official explanation: jockey said that the colt lost his action (op 11-2)

Simply Dreaming Official explanation: trainer said that the filly didn't handle the track

2194 REDBOURN ENGINEERING LTD FILLIES' H'CAP — 1m

5:55 (5:56) (Class 5) (0-75,75) 3-Y-O — £2,587 (£770; £384; £192) Stalls Low

Form — RPR

41 **1** **Burke's Rock**[96] [523] 3-9-5 **73** ... RyanMoore 2 — 81+
(Jeremy Noseda) *racd far side: chsd ldrs: rdn over 2f out: overall ldr over 1f out: edgd lft ins fnl f: drvn out: 1st of 5 in gp* **13/8**[1]

60-3 **2** ¾ **Princess Caetani (IRE)**[26] [1531] 3-8-13 **70** ... AdamBeschizza(3) 17 — 76+
(David Simcock) *racd centre: hld up: hdwy over 1f out: rdn to ld that gp wl ins fnl f: nt rch wnr: 1st of 11 in gp* **16/1**

32-2 **3** nk **My Sharona**[22] [1607] 3-9-4 **72** ... LiamKeniry 9 — 77
(Sylvester Kirk) *racd centre: hld up in tch: rdn to ld ins fnl f: hdd towards fin: 2nd of 11 in gp* **11/1**[3]

614- **4** 1¼ **Cresta Star**[188] [7358] 3-9-6 **74** ... RichardHughes 3 — 76
(Richard Hannon) *overall ldr far side: rdn over 2f out: sn edgd lft: hdd over 1f out: styd on same pce: 2nd of 5 in gp* **20/1**

01- **5** shd **Operettist**[220] [6745] 3-9-7 **75** ... DaneO'Neill 7 — 77
(Richard Hannon) *racd far side: hld up in tch: rdn over 2f out: edgd lft over 1f out: styd on same pce: 3rd of 5 in gp* **16/1**

541- **6** hd **Strathnaver**[167] [7598] 3-9-4 **72** ... JamieSpencer 10 — 74
(Ed Dunlop) *racd in centre: hld up: hdwy over 1f out: rdn and edgd lft ins fnl f: styd on: 3rd of 11 in gp* **14/1**

01- **7** 1½ **Afnoon (USA)**[220] [6744] 3-9-5 **73** ... TadhgO'Shea 13 — 71+
(John Dunlop) *racd centre: hld up: r.o ins fnl f: nvr nrr 4th of 11 in gp* **14/1**

01-0 **8** ½ **Napoleon's Muse (IRE)**[24] [1565] 3-9-7 **75** ... RichardKingscote 14 — 72
(Ralph Beckett) *led centre gp tl rdn and hdd over 2f out: no ex fnl f: 5th of 11 in gp* **18/1**

30-0 **9** hd **Inffiraaj (IRE)**[62] [918] 3-8-13 **67** ... MartinHarley 12 — 64
(Mick Channon) *racd centre: hld up: nt clr run over 1f out: r.o ins fnl f: nvr nrr: 6th of 11 in gp* **25/1**

156- **10** 2 **Sinai (IRE)**[224] [6645] 3-9-4 **72** ... SilvestreDeSousa 1 — 64
(Geoffrey Harker) *racd far side: s.i.s: hld up: effrt over 2f out: no ex fnl f: 4th of 5 in gp* **33/1**

00-0 **11** ¾ **Amis Reunis**[35] [1331] 3-9-0 **68** ... WilliamCarson 16 — 58
(Anthony Carson) *racd centrem hld up: hdwy over 2f out: sn outpcd: styd on towards fin: 7th of 11 in gp* **50/1**

1114 **12** ¾ **Roedean (IRE)**[94] [547] 3-9-5 **73** ...(p) TomQueally 5 — 62
(William Stone) *racd centre: chsd ldrs: outpcd over 2f out: styd on ins fnl f: 8th of 11 in gp* **33/1**

42-3 **13** ½ **Symphony Time (IRE)**[22] [1612] 3-9-5 **73** ... MartinDwyer 15 — 60
(Brian Meehan) *racd centre: chsd ldrs: led over 2f out: rdn over 1f out: hdd & wknd ins fnl f: 9th of 11 in gp* **12/1**

12 **14** ½ **Frosty Berry**[26] [1531] 3-8-13 **67** ... NickyMackay 4 — 53
(Marco Botti) *racd far side: chsd ldr tl rdn over 2f out: wknd fnl f: last of 5 in gp* **14/1**

021- **15** 2¼ **Tiger Cub**[220] [6753] 3-9-3 **71** ...[1] GeorgeBaker 11 — 52
(Mikael Magnusson) *racd centre: chsd ldrs: rdn over 2f out: wknd over 1f out: 10th of 11 in gp* **22/1**

26-4 **16** ¾ **Amy Dorrit**[8] [1985] 3-9-7 **75** ... WilliamBuick 8 — 54
(John Gosden) *racd centre: hld up: hdwy over 2f out: wknd fnl f: last of 11 in gp* **8/1**[2]

1m 41.24s (2.64) **Going Correction** +0.275s/f (Good) — **16** Ran SP% **123.1**

Speed ratings (Par 96): **97,96,95,94,94 94,92,92,92,90 89,88,88,87,85 84**

Tote Swingers:1&2:£12.80, 2&3:£40.00, 1&3:£6.30 CSF £26.97 CT £246.55 TOTE £2.10: £1.10, £3.80, £2.30, £3.70; EX 39.20 Trifecta £331.30 Part won. Pool £447.70 - 0.40 winning units..

Owner S E Construction (Kent) Ltd **Bred** Brook Stud Bloodstock Ltd **Trained** Newmarket, Suffolk

FOCUS

An informative 1m fillies' handicap confined to 3yos. The 16-runner field split into two groups, five up the far side, and 11 up the nearside rail. There was little in it at the finish, but it is notable that the smaller group produced the winner. The winning time of nearly 6 secs outside standard was again nothing special on officially good to firm ground. Despite the split the form makes some sense.

Strathnaver Official explanation: jockey said that the that the filly hung left

2195 SIMON GIBSON H'CAP — 5f

6:25 (6:30) (Class 4) (0-85,85) 4-Y-O+ — £4,528 (£1,347; £673; £336) Stalls Low

Form — RPR

0310 **1** **Dancing Freddy (IRE)**[23] [1581] 5-9-2 **80** ...(tp) MartinHarley 4 — 91
(Richard Guest) *chsd ldrs: led ins fnl f: rdn out* **28/1**

2-32 **2** ½ **Arctic Lynx (IRE)**[85] [652] 5-9-1 **79** ... GeorgeBaker 1 — 90+
(John Best) *hld up: nt clr run over 1f out: swtchd rt and r.o wl ins fnl f: wnt 2nd nr fin: nt rch wnr* **6/1**[2]

4-00 **3** 1 **Sutton Veny (IRE)**[16] [1727] 6-9-5 **83** ... JamieSpencer 6 — 89
(Jeremy Gask) *hld up: hdwy over 1f out: sn rdn: r.o: lost 2nd nr fin* **5/1**[1]

5-54 **4** 2½ **Bronze Beau**[12] [1868] 5-9-0 **78** ...(t) JamesSullivan 3 — 75
(Linda Stubbs) *chsd ldr: rdn and ev ch 1f out: styd on same pce* **8/1**

5243 **5** ½ **Estonia**[50] [1073] 5-8-7 **71** oh1 ... LukeMorris 13 — 66
(Michael Squance) *s.i.s: hdwy 1/2-way: rdn over 1f out: styd on* **25/1**

6022 **6** hd **Desert Strike**[6] [2040] 6-8-7 **71** ...(p) KierenFallon 15 — 65+
(Charles Hills) *hld up: pushed along 1/2-way: r.o wl ins fnl f: nrst fin* **15/2**[3]

-000 **7** nk **Button Moon (IRE)**[16] [1727] 4-9-4 **82** ...(b) JamesDoyle 10 — 75
(Ian Wood) *s.i.s: sn mid-div: rdn over 1f out: edgd rt ins fnl f: styd on* **20/1**

4423 **8** shd **Love You Louis**[37] [1290] 6-8-8 **72** ... ShaneKelly 14 — 65
(J R Jenkins) *chsd ldrs: rdn over 1f out: no ex ins fnl f* **14/1**

0-30 **9** shd **Solemn**[20] [1643] 7-9-6 **84** ...(b) LiamKeniry 8 — 76
(Milton Bradley) *chsd ldrs: rdn over 1f out: no ex ins fnl f* **14/1**

01- **10** ½ **Bertoliver**[250] [5923] 8-8-13 **80** ... RyanClark(3) 5 — 70
(Stuart Williams) *led: rdn over 1f out: hdd & wknd ins fnl f* **25/1**

2062 **11** shd **West Coast Dream**[20] [1642] 5-9-7 **85** ... TomEaves 7 — 75
(Roy Brotherton) *sn prom: rdn over 1f out: wknd ins fnl f* **12/1**

053- **12** ½ **Drift And Dream**[220] [6761] 5-8-11 **75** ... TedDurcan 2 — 63
(Chris Wall) *hld up: rdn over 1f out: n.d* **6/1**[2]

625/ **13** 2½ **Ziggy Lee**[564] [7254] 6-9-4 **82** ... WilliamCarson 11 — 77+
(Giles Bravery) *stdd s: hld up: nt clr run and hmpd ins fnl f: eased* **14/1**

-530 **14** hd **Haajes**[20] [1642] 8-9-3 **81** ... MickyFenton 12 — 60
(Paul Midgley) *hld up: rdn 1/2-way: a in rr* **12/1**

1m 0.18s (1.08) **Going Correction** +0.275s/f (Good) — **14** Ran SP% **119.4**

Speed ratings (Par 105): **102,101,99,95,94 94,94,93,93,92 92,91,87,87**

Tote Swingers:1&2:£22.50, 2&3:£6.30, 1&3:£26.30 CSF £180.43 CT £1002.85 TOTE £27.10: £6.60, £2.40, £1.70; EX 258.10 Trifecta £390.20 Part won. Pool £527.34 - 0.63 winning units..

Owner Rakebackmypoker.com **Bred** Vincent Duignan **Trained** Stainforth, S Yorks

FOCUS

A competitive Class 4 5f handicap. They went a proper gallop up the far-side rail and the winning time was respectable. Three of the first four home came from three of the lowest four available stalls.

Desert Strike Official explanation: jockey said that the gelding was denied a clear run

Ziggy Lee Official explanation: jockey said that the gelding was denied a clear run

2196 CHASSIS CAB DAF 30TH ANNIVERSARY MAIDEN STKS (DIV I) — 1m 2f

7:00 (7:03) (Class 5) 3-Y-O — £3,234 (£962; £481; £240) Stalls Low

Form — RPR

32- **1** **Anomaly**[197] [7233] 3-9-3 0 ... SilvestreDeSousa 1 — 95+
(Mahmood Al Zarooni) *mde all: clr fr over 1f out: styd on wl* **5/2**[1]

2 4½ **Suegioo (FR)** 3-9-3 0 ... MartinHarley 5 — 86+
(Marco Botti) *a.p: rdn to chse wnr over 1f out: sn hung lft and no imp* **50/1**

4- **3** 7 **Cardinal Walter (IRE)**[198] [7209] 3-9-3 0 ... JamieSpencer 3 — 72+
(David Simcock) *s.s: hld up: hdwy over 1f out: styd on to go 3rd ins fnl f: nvr nrr* **14/1**

3 **4** 1 **Morocco**[50] [1068] 3-9-3 0 ... WilliamBuick 4 — 70+
(John Gosden) *chsd wnr tl rdn over 1f out: wknd fnl f* **12/1**[3]

0 **5** 2 **Sky Khan**[28] [1467] 3-9-3 0 ... GeorgeBaker 13 — 66
(Ed Dunlop) *hld up: styd on fr over 1f out: nvr on terms* **25/1**

6 2¾ **Emerald Invader** 3-9-3 0 ... MarcHalford 10 — 61+
(David Elsworth) *s.i.s: hld up: hdwy over 2f out: wknd over 1f out* **100/1**

06- **7** ½ **Layali Dubai (USA)**[203] [7118] 3-8-12 0 ... MickaelBarzalona 16 — 55
(Saeed Bin Suroor) *mid-div: hdwy over 2f out: wknd over 1f out* **20/1**

8 3¼ **Reigns Of Glory (IRE)** 3-9-3 0 ... RichardHughes 7 — 53
(Richard Hannon) *chsd ldrs: rdn over 2f out: wknd over 1f out* **16/1**

0-6 **9** 2 **Just When**[31] [1414] 3-9-3 0 ... LiamKeniry 11 — 49
(Andrew Balding) *hld up: pushed along over 4f out: nt clr run wl over 3f out: n.d* **20/1**

4- **10** nk **Paramythi (IRE)**[202] [7134] 3-8-10 0 ... HayleyBurton(7) 2 — 48+
(Luca Cumani) *chsd ldrs: pushed along over 4f out: wknd over 2f out* **33/1**

11 1¾ **Zanotti** 3-9-3 0 ... NeilCallan 9 — 45+
(Roger Varian) *dwlt: sn prom: rdn and wknd wl over 1f out* **12/1**[3]

12 5 **Al Qatari (USA)** 3-9-3 0 ... LiamJones 6 — 35
(William Haggas) *sn pushed along in rr: bhd fnl 4f* **40/1**

5 **13** 3 **Cape Explorer**[12] [1867] 3-9-3 0 ... KierenFallon 8 — 29
(James Tate) *plld hrd and prom: rdn over 3f out: sn wknd and eased* **33/1**

43- **14** 4 **Rawaafed (IRE)**[252] [5851] 3-9-3 0 ... TadhgO'Shea 15 — 21
(Brian Meehan) *prom over 6f* **3/1**[2]

00- **15** 14 **Jambobo**[299] [4330] 3-9-3 0 ... ShaneKelly 14
(William Knight) *hld up: effrt over 4f out: wknd over 3f out* **100/1**

2m 6.67s (0.87) **Going Correction** +0.275s/f (Good) — **15** Ran SP% **107.1**

Speed ratings (Par 99): **107,103,97,97,95 93,92,90,88,88 86,82,80,77,66**

Tote Swingers:1&2:£54.60, 2&3:£89.10, 1&3:£10.40 CSF £125.00 TOTE £3.40: £1.30, £15.20, £3.00; EX 177.70 TRIFECTA Not won..

Owner Godolphin **Bred** Darley **Trained** Newmarket, Suffolk

■ Continuum (6/1) was withdrawn after losing a plate. Deduct 10p in the £ under R4.

FOCUS

The first division of a slightly above average 1m2f 3yo maiden for the grade. It looked the stronger of the two divisions and was the fastest of the three C&D times. The winner looks potentially better than the handicapper.

Cape Explorer Official explanation: jockey said that the colt ran too free

Rawaafed(IRE) Official explanation: jockey said that the colt stopped quickly

2197 CHASSIS CAB DAF 30TH ANNIVERSARY MAIDEN STKS (DIV II) — 1m 2f

7:35 (7:37) (Class 5) 3-Y-O — £3,234 (£962; £481; £240) Stalls Low

Form — RPR

33- **1** **Circus Mondao (USA)**[204] [7094] 3-9-3 0 ... SilvestreDeSousa 14 — 88+
(Mahmood Al Zarooni) *mde virtually all: drvn out* **8/1**

333- **2** nk **Spoke To Carlo**[244] [6126] 3-9-3 80 ... TomQueally 12 — 87+
(Eve Johnson Houghton) *edgd lft s: hld up in tch: chsd wnr over 1f out: rdn to ld briefly 1f out: styd on u.p* **11/2**[3]

6- **3** 3¼ **Bayan (IRE)**[237] [6300] 3-9-3 0 ... MickaelBarzalona 3 — 80+
(Brian Meehan) *prom: nt clr run and lost pl wl over 3f out: hdwy over 1f out: r.o: eased nr fin* **3/1**[2]

4 2¾ **Signed Up** 3-9-3 0 ... JimCrowley 10 — 75+
(Amanda Perrett) *hld up: hdwy over 4f out: rdn over 1f out: styd on same pce* **40/1**

0 **5** 2¼ **Chapelle du Roi (USA)**[24] [1567] 3-9-3 0 ... TedDurcan 11 — 70
(David Lanigan) *chsd ldrs tl rdn and wknd over 1f out* **20/1**

6 1 **Glittering Gold** 3-9-3 0 ... RyanMoore 1 — 68+
(Sir Michael Stoute) *hld up: r.o ins fnl f: nvr nrr* **8/1**

7 2½ **Obboorr** 3-9-3 0 ... NeilCallan 5 — 63+
(Roger Varian) *hld up in tch: hmpd over 3f out: wknd over 1f out* **16/1**

05- **8** 4 **Saaboog**[183] [7431] 3-8-12 0 ... KierenFallon 15 — 50
(James Tate) *led: racd keenly: rdn and hdd over 2f out: wknd over 1f out* **33/1**

9 hd **Salford Dream** 3-9-3 0 ... WilliamBuick 8 — 55
(David Elsworth) *hld up: rdn over 2f out: sn wknd* **14/1**

46- **10** 2½ **Gucci D'Oro (USA)**[206] [7060] 3-9-3 0 ... MartinDwyer 2 — 50
(David Simcock) *hld up: rdn and wknd over 2f out* **66/1**

04- **11** ½ **Attraction Ticket**[204] 7094 3-9-3 0 ShaneKelly 7 49
(David Simcock) *hld up: rdn over 3f out: wknd over 2f out* **40/1**

2- **12** ½ **Moshaagib (USA)**[205] 7083 3-9-3 0 TadhgO'Shea 13 48
(John Gosden) *hmpd s: hld up: effrt over 3f out: wknd wl over 1f out* **11/4**[1]

0 **13** 4 **Red Mystique (IRE)**[16] 1737 3-8-12 0 AshleyMorgan(5) 9 40
(Ed Dunlop) *hld up: rdn over 3f out: sn wknd* **100/1**

14 nk **Zain Glory** 3-9-3 0 LukeMorris 6 39
(Gerard Butler) *mid-div: rdn over 3f out: wknd over 2f out* **50/1**

0- **15** 37 **Verona Bay (FR)**[279] 5013 3-9-0 0 AdamBeschizza(3) 4
(Julia Feilden) *chsd ldrs: rdn over 4f out: wknd wl over 3f out: t.o* **200/1**

2m 7.42s (1.62) **Going Correction** +0.275s/f (Good) **15** Ran SP% **119.3**
Speed ratings (Par 99): **104,103,101,98,97 96,94,91,91,89 88,88,85,84,55**
Tote Swingers:1&2:£7.50, 2&3:£7.50, 1&3:£2.30 CSF £18.37 TOTE £12.10: £3.50, £2.30, £2.10; EX 76.80 Trifecta £184.80 Pool £479.56 - 1.92 winning units..
Owner Godolphin **Bred** Mercedes Stables Llc **Trained** Newmarket, Suffolk

FOCUS
The second division of a slightly above average 1m2f 3yo maiden for the grade. They raced up the far-side rail. The winning time was 0.75secs slower than the first division but this looked up to scratch, with improvement from the first two.
Glittering Gold Official explanation: jockey said that the colt suffered interference shortly after the start

2198 ORBITAL FOOD MACHINERY CONDITIONS STKS 1m
8:05 (8:07) (Class 3) 3-Y-O **£7,762** (£2,310; £1,154) **Stalls** Low

Form RPR

20-1 **1** **Fort Bastion (IRE)**[11] 1889 3-8-12 106 RichardHughes 2 109
(Richard Hannon) *trckd ldrs: qcknd to ld wl over 2f out: sn clr: easily* **13/8**[2]

61- **2** 4 **Starboard**[198] 7209 3-8-12 97 WilliamBuick 3 102+
(John Gosden) *led 3f: ev ch wl over 2f out: sn rdn and outpcd* **8/13**[1]

10 **3** 13 **Minstrels Gallery (IRE)**[28] 1470 3-8-12 87 FrederikTylicki 1 70
(J R Jenkins) *chsd ldr tl led 5f out: hdd wl over 2f out: wknd over 1f out* **14/1**[3]

1m 39.5s (0.90) **Going Correction** +0.275s/f (Good) **3** Ran SP% **106.7**
Speed ratings (Par 103): **106,102,89**
CSF £3.04 TOTE £2.30; EX 2.00.
Owner Sir Robert Ogden **Bred** L White & D McGregor **Trained** East Everleigh, Wilts

FOCUS
A good quality Class 3 conditions contest for 3-y-os, despite the small field. The winning time was very respectable despite the tactical nature of the race. Fort Bastion rates a personal best.

NOTEBOOK
Fort Bastion(IRE) set the standard on his juvenile form, the pick of which was when second in the Group 3 Acomb Stakes at York in August. He won his maiden emphatically over 2f shorter at Salisbury this month and looks to have benefited from that confidence booster. The step up to 1m proved no problem, and he has a nice turn of foot, which was a handy tactical tool in such a small-field. In fact, when asked to go on 2f out he caught the favourite completely on the hop, and the race was very quickly over as a contest. He has a bright future in Group company over 7f/1m. (tchd 7-4 and 6-4 in a place)
Starboard was sent to the front, but it wasn't the most positive of moves, as he didn't settle that well on this first start since winning a Redcar maiden impressively last November. William Buick looked unsure whether to stick or twist, and the winner went by on his blind side whilst he was making up his mind. The colt has some lofty entries and set about the task of chasing down the winner in game fashion, but the bird had flown. He is not one to give up on, though. He has definite ability and the 1m2f of the Coral Eclipse looks more suitable than the 1m of the St James's Palace Stakes on this evidence. Whether he proves good enough for either is yet to be proven, however. (op 4-6 tchd 8-11 in a place)
Minstrels Gallery(IRE) was outclassed in this company as seemed likely beforehand. (tchd 12-1)

2199 EAST ANGLIAN DAILY TIMES H'CAP (BETFAIR 10 FURLONG FLAT SERIES QUALIFIER) 1m 2f
8:35 (8:38) (Class 5) (0-75,75) 4-Y-O+ **£2,587** (£770; £384; £192) **Stalls** Low

Form RPR

2134 **1** **Knowe Head (NZ)**[19] 1657 5-9-4 72 LiamJones 1 80
(James Unett) *racd far side: hld up in tch: rdn to ld ins fnl f: styd on* **13/2**[2]

23-2 **2** nk **Chatterer (IRE)**[36] 1314 4-9-5 73 HayleyTurner 15 80
(Marcus Tregoning) *racd far side: chsd ldrs: led over 3f out: rdn over 1f out: hdd ins fnl f: styd on: 2nd of 15 that side* **9/1**

2235 **3** hd **Red Shuttle**[59] 959 5-9-2 70 (t) JamieSpencer 3 77+
(Noel Quinlan) *racd far side: hld up: hdwy over 1f out: r.o wl: 3rd of 15 that side* **28/1**

2231 **4** ¾ **Eagle Nebula**[16] 1732 8-9-0 68 IanMongan 4 73
(Brett Johnson) *racd far side: chsd ldrs: rdn over 1f out: r.o: 4th of 15 that side* **20/1**

0510 **5** 2 ½ **Vanilla Rum**[33] 1381 5-9-2 70 (b) FrannyNorton 20 70
(John Mackie) *racd stands' side: chsd ldr of that gp tl rdn to ld those over 1f out: no ch w far side: 1st of 3 in gp* **25/1**

00-3 **6** ½ **Chain Of Events**[10] 1939 5-9-4 72 TomQueally 8 71+
(Sarah Humphrey) *racd far side: hld up: nt clr run over 1f out: r.o: nt trble ldrs: 5th of 15 that side* **8/1**[3]

100- **7** ¾ **Height Of Summer (IRE)**[217] 6822 4-9-4 72 TedDurcan 2 70
(Chris Wall) *racd far side: hld up in tch: rdn over 1f out: styd on: 6th of 16 that side* **25/1**

1242 **8** hd **Daniel Thomas (IRE)**[17] 1718 10-9-2 70 (tp) WilliamCarson 6 67
(Richard Guest) *racd far side: hld up: swtchd lft over 2f out: styd on: nt trble ldrs: 7th of 15 that side* **20/1**

1410 **9** nk **Patriotic (IRE)**[5] 2082 4-9-2 70 MichaelHills 19 67
(Chris Dwyer) *racd stands' side: hld up: rdn over 1f out: styd on: nt trble ldrs: 2nd of 3 in gp* **9/1**

6-13 **10** ¾ **Aldedash (USA)**[21] 1633 4-9-6 74 KierenFallon 5 69
(James Fanshawe) *racd far side: hld up: hdwy over 2f out: rdn over 1f out: styd on same pce: eased nr fin: 8th of 15 that side* **5/1**[1]

6130 **11** 4 ½ **Casual Mover (IRE)**[26] 1513 4-9-6 74 LukeMorris 7 60
(John Best) *racd far side: chsd ldrs: rdn and ev ch 2f out: wknd fnl f: 9th of 15 that side* **14/1**

326- **12** 4 ½ **Wiggy Smith**[213] 6922 13-9-7 75 DaneO'Neill 18 52
(Henry Candy) *racd far side: hld up: effrt over 2f out: wknd wl over 1f out: 10th of 15 that side* **20/1**

-046 **13** 3 ½ **Yes Chef**[15] 1752 5-9-6 74 JamesMillman 17 44
(Rod Millman) *led stands' side gp tl rdn and hdd over 1f out: sn wknd: last of 3 that side* **8/1**[3]

10-0 **14** 9 **Amoya (GER)**[19] 1652 5-9-4 75 (t) AdamBeschizza(3) 9 27
(Philip McBride) *racd far side: hld up in tch: rdn over 3f out: wknd 2f out: 11th of 15 that side* **33/1**

0004 **15** 30 **Calypso Magic (IRE)**[43] 1181 4-9-4 72 KirstyMilczarek 14
(Olivia Maylam) *racd far side: led over 6f: wknd over 2f out: t.o: 12th of 15 that side: t.o* **33/1**

10-0 **16** 1 **Odin (IRE)**[31] 1416 4-9-7 75 NickyMackay 11
(David Elsworth) *racd far side: hld up: rdn and wknd over 2f out: 13th of 15 that side: t.o* **16/1**

230- **17** 5 **Sweet Lavender (IRE)**[202] 7136 4-9-5 73 (v) NeilCallan 13
(Gay Kelleway) *racd far side: prom over 6f: 14th of 15 that side: t.o* **40/1**

-234 **P** **Broughtons Paradis (IRE)**[75] 786 6-9-5 73 StevieDonohoe 16
(Willie Musson) *racd far side: hld up: hdwy 2f out: sn wknd: p.u 1f out* **16/1**

2m 7.57s (1.77) **Going Correction** +0.275s/f (Good) **18** Ran SP% **124.4**
Speed ratings (Par 103): **103,102,102,102,100 99,99,98,98,98 94,90,88,80,56 56,52,**
Tote Swingers:1&2:£8.20, 2&3:£8.20, 1&3:£0.00 CSF £54.89 TOTE £13.90: £2.30, £2.60, £4.30, £6.20; EX 81.70 TRIFECTA Not won..
Owner Lord Stuart J Stone **Bred** Glazeley Farms Trust **Trained** Tedsmore Hall, Shropshire

FOCUS
A competitive Class 5 1m2f handicap for older horses. They went a decent gallop with the majority sticking to the seemingly favoured far-side rail. For the second time on the evening, three of the first four home came from three of lowest four available stalls. Straightforward form, a little limited for the track.
Chain Of Events Official explanation: jockey said that the gelding suffered interference in running
Aldedash(USA) Official explanation: trainer said that the gelding was unsuited by the good to firm, good in places ground
T/Plt: £69.40 to a £1 stake. Pool £58,554.70. 615.52 winning tickets. T/Qpdt: £29.00 to a £1 stake. Pool £4,792.40. 122.20 winning tickets. CR

1889 SALISBURY (R-H)
Thursday, May 17

OFFICIAL GOING: Good (good to soft between 4f & 7f)
False rail up to 12ft off far side rail up the straight.
Wind: virtually nil Weather: overcast

2200 FONTHILL STUD MAIDEN FILLIES' STKS (DIV I) 1m 1f 198y
1:40 (1:42) (Class 5) 3-Y-O+ **£2,911** (£866; £432; £216) **Stalls** Low

Form RPR

02- **1** **Varnish**[208] 7030 3-8-12 0 RichardHughes 1 74+
(Richard Hannon) *mid-div: pushed along over 4f out: rdn to chse ldrs over 3f out: led ins fnl f: styd on wl to assert towards fin* **2/1**[1]

33- **2** ½ **Berwin (IRE)**[241] 6215 3-8-12 0 LiamKeniry 9 73+
(Sylvester Kirk) *hld up towards rr: hdwy 3f out: sn swtchd lft: rdn over 1f out: edgd sltly lft: ev ch ins fnl f: kpt on* **6/1**[3]

0 **3** ½ **Junior Diary (USA)**[28] 1472 3-8-12 0 ShaneKelly 10 72
(Brian Meehan) *led tl over 5f out: trckd ldrs: rdn over 2f out: styd on ins fnl f* **9/1**

4 nk **Regal Aura** 3-8-12 0 RobertHavlin 13 71
(John Gosden) *trckd ldr: led over 5f out: rdn wl over 1f out: hdd ins fnl f: kpt on but no ex* **12/1**

0- **5** ½ **Saint Hilary**[208] 7025 3-8-12 0 HayleyTurner 2 70
(William Muir) *trckd ldrs: rdn whn outpcd over 2f out: styd on fnl f* **20/1**

5- **6** 3 ½ **Easter Diva (IRE)**[220] 6745 3-8-12 0 PatCosgrave 5 63
(Amanda Perrett) *trckd ldrs: snatched up whn short of room over 6f out: rdn over 2f out: kpt on tl no ex fnl 100yds* **8/1**

4- **7** 4 **Red Halo (IRE)**[209] 6985 3-8-12 0 PatDobbs 12 55
(Sir Michael Stoute) *mid-div: struggling whn sltly hmpd over 2f out: nvr gng pce to get involved* **7/2**[2]

8 3 ¼ **Across The Galaxy** 3-8-12 0 DarryllHolland 11 49
(Hughie Morrison) *s.i.s: towards rr: struggling over 3f out: nvr a factor* **16/1**

0 **9** 17 **Trio Of Trix**[34] 1360 3-8-12 0 TomMcLaughlin 8 15
(Malcolm Saunders) *a towards rr* **200/1**

000- **10** 2 **Ellies Girl (IRE)**[350] 2639 4-9-9 0 CPGeoghegan(3) 4 12
(Ronald Harris) *a towards rr* **200/1**

02/ **11** 15 **Rosaria**[526] 7755 4-9-12 0 JimCrowley 6
(Harry Dunlop) *trckd ldrs: rdn 3f out: wknd jst over 2f out* **33/1**

2m 11.55s (1.65) **Going Correction** -0.025s/f (Good)
WFA 3 from 4yo 14lb **11** Ran SP% **113.2**
Speed ratings (Par 100): **92,91,91,90,90 87,84,81,68,66 54**
toteswingers:1&2:£2.70, 2&3:£10.20, 1&3:£7.00 CSF £13.28 TOTE £2.00: £1.10, £3.00, £3.30; EX 19.10.
Owner Highclere Thoroughbred Racing - Eleanor **Bred** Carmel Stud **Trained** East Everleigh, Wilts

FOCUS
This first division of the fillies' maiden was steadily run and there was a bunched finish. Ordinary form at best, the first two close to their 2yo marks.

2201 BATHWICK TYRES BRITISH STALLION STUDS EBF FILLIES' H'CAP 1m 1f 198y
2:10 (2:11) (Class 4) (0-85,83) 3-Y-O **£6,469** (£1,925; £962; £481) **Stalls** Low

Form RPR

6-22 **1** **Traveller's Tales**[57] 982 3-9-0 76 RichardHughes 11 83+
(Richard Hannon) *mid-div: nudged along 4f out: chsd ldrs 3f out: sn rdn: led ent fnl f: styd on wl* **16/1**

21-1 **2** 1 ½ **The Giving Tree (IRE)**[36] 1322 3-9-2 78 LiamKeniry 4 82+
(Sylvester Kirk) *mid-div: rdn and hdwy 2f out: styd on fnl f: wnt 2nd fnl strides* **6/1**[2]

3-31 **3** shd **Dutch Diamond**[43] 1192 3-8-11 73 NickyMackay 7 77+
(John Gosden) *trckd ldrs: rdn for str chal fr over 2f out: ev ch ent fnl f: kpt on but no ex* **16/1**

2-1 **4** ¾ **Shestheman**[26] 1532 3-9-6 82 TedDurcan 6 85+
(David Lanigan) *s.i.s: sn trcking ldrs: led wl over 2f out: sn rdn whn hrd pressed: hdd ent fnl f: no ex fnl 75yds* **11/4**[1]

525- **5** 1 ¾ **Shannon Spree**[183] 7436 3-8-7 72 SeanLevey(3) 3 71
(Richard Hannon) *hld up towards rr: pushed along over 3f out: swtchd lft and hdwy over 2f out: sn rdn: styd on same pce fnl f* **20/1**

1-2 **6** 1 ½ **Little Dutch Girl**[20] 1647 3-9-0 76 (b) JohnFahy 10 72
(Clive Cox) *s.i.s: towards rr of midfield: hdwy 4f out: rdn to chse ldrs over 2f out: kpt on same pce fnl f* **9/1**

302- **7** ¾ **Coplow**[201] 7164 3-9-6 82 PatDobbs 2 77+
(Richard Hannon) *rdn over 2f out: a mid-div* **8/1**

0-51 **8** 3 ¼ **Jane Lachatte (IRE)**[22] 1607 3-8-7 69 WilliamCarson 12 57
(Stuart Williams) *towards rr: sme late prog past btn horses: nvr a factor* **20/1**

04-3 **9** 1 **Virginia Gallica (IRE)**[20] 1649 3-9-0 76 SebSanders 13 62
(J W Hills) *mid-div: rdn to chse ldrs over 2f out: wknd ent fnl f* **25/1**

45-2 **10** *3/4* **Candycakes (IRE)**[34] 1363 3-9-1 **77**................ HayleyTurner 8 62+
(Michael Bell) *trckd ldrs tl nt clr run and lost pl over 2f out: sn rdn: wknd over 1f out* **16/1**

513 **11** *1/2* **Danube River**[15] 1757 3-8-11 **73**................ JimCrowley 9 57
(Mark Johnston) *trckd ldr: led over 5f out: rdn and hdd wl over 2f out: wknd over 1f out* **13/2**[3]

100- **12** *4 1/2* **Zingana**[238] 6275 3-9-2 **78**................ FergusSweeney 5 53
(Eve Johnson Houghton) *led tl looked to nt handle bnd over 5f out: trckd ldrs tl rdn over 2f out: wknd over 1f out* **16/1**

250- **13** *23* **Mahkama (USA)**[227] 6573 3-9-7 **83**................ RobertHavlin 1 12
(Saeed Bin Suroor) *awkward leaving stalls: a towards rr: eased whn btn over 1f out* **25/1**

2m 8.97s (-0.93) **Going Correction** -0.025s/f (Good) 13 Ran SP% **116.1**
Speed ratings (Par 98): **102,100,100,100,98 97,96,94,93,92 92,88,70**
CSF £100.33 CT £1562.14 TOTE £12.70: £2.50, £1.70, £4.40; EX 70.20.
Owner The Queen **Bred** The Queen **Trained** East Everleigh, Wilts

FOCUS
An interesting fillies' handicap. It was run at a brisk pace and there was plenty of scrimmaging in the home straight. Most of these are open to improvement.

2202 GEORGE SMITH HORSE BOXES MAIDEN STKS 5f
2:40 (2:40) (Class 5) 2-Y-0 **£2,911** (£866; £432; £216) **Stalls** Centre

Form RPR

1 **Ask The Guru** 2-9-3 0................ JimCrowley 5 80
(Ralph Beckett) *disp ld: rdn 2f out: kpt on strly to be outrt ldr fnl 100yds: rdn out* **9/4**[1]

2 *3/4* **Bairam** 2-9-3 0................ ShaneKelly 9 77
(Brian Meehan) *disp ld: rdn 2f out: kpt on but no ex whn hdd fnl 100yds* **4/1**[2]

3 *3/4* **Echion (IRE)** 2-9-3 0................ KieranO'Neill 6 75+
(Richard Hannon) *trckd ldrs: rdn 2f out: kpt on ins fnl f: clsng on ldrs at fin* **14/1**

4 *2* **David Jack** 2-9-3 0................ TedDurcan 3 67
(Brian Meehan) *trckd ldrs: rdn 2f out: kpt on but nt gng pce to chal* **9/1**

5 *1 1/2* **Magic Channel (USA)** 2-9-3 0................ RichardHughes 4 62
(Richard Hannon) *trckd ldrs: rdn 2f out: sn one pce* **9/4**[1]

6 *nk* **Majestic Red (IRE)** 2-8-12 0................ TomMcLaughlin 7 56
(Malcolm Saunders) *hld up in tch: effrt in centre 2f out: hld whn edgd rt ent fnl f* **22/1**

7 *3 1/4* **Danz Choice (IRE)** 2-9-3 0................ PatDobbs 2 49
(Richard Hannon) *hld up in tch: rdn over 2f out: nt pce to get on terms: wknd ins fnl f* **8/1**[3]

1m 1.71s (0.71) **Going Correction** -0.025s/f (Good) 7 Ran SP% **113.7**
Speed ratings (Par 93): **93,91,90,87,85 84,79**
toteswingers:1&2:£2.80, 2&3:£6.80, 1&3:£8.10 CSF £11.41 TOTE £3.30: £1.20, £3.60; EX 14.30.
Owner The Quick Fill Partnership **Bred** Redmyre Bloodstock & Tweenhills Stud **Trained** Kimpton, Hants

FOCUS
All newcomers here and probably not a bad maiden.

NOTEBOOK
Ask The Guru attracted decent support and made all for a winning debut. He has plenty of speed in his pedigree, but such a display suggests an extra furlong will hold no fears this year and stepping up to a novice event will reveal more as to his potential. (op 7-2)

Bairam ◆ is already gelded. His sire injects speed into the pedigree, which he displayed from the gates, and it was a promising debut effort seeing as his dam's side is more about stamina. He ought to collect next time. (tchd 7-2)

Echion(IRE), by the same sire as the winner, fared best of the three from his stable and did more than enough to think he'll be going close next time out. Another furlong ought to suit before that long. (tchd 16-1)

David Jack, the runner-up's stablemate, is out of a 5f winner and half-brother to three fair winners up to 1m. He fell out of the stalls and badly needed the initial experience, but did some nice work late on. (op 8-1 tchd 10-1)

Magic Channel(USA) was the first string from his yard, but proved easy enough to back and lacked any sort of a gear change. He'll probably appreciate better ground. (op 15-8 tchd 5-2 in a place and 7-4)

2203 SHARP'S DOOM BAR CLAIMING STKS 6f 212y
3:10 (3:10) (Class 5) 3-Y-0 **£2,264** (£673; £336; £168) **Stalls** Centre

Form RPR

23-0 **1** **Daunt (IRE)**[8] 1985 3-9-3 73................ RichardHughes 2 68+
(Richard Hannon) *trckd ldrs: jnd ldrs and w.w 2f out: led ent fnl f: pushed clr: readily* **6/5**[1]

00-0 **2** *2 3/4* **Marah Music**[16] 1730 3-8-9 62................ DarryllHolland 3 52
(Peter Makin) *prom: led over 4f out: rdn over 2f out: hdd ent fnl f: nt gng pce of wnr: hld on gamely for 2nd* **12/1**

0-60 **3** *shd* **Joy To The World (IRE)**[12] 1843 3-8-6 55................ ChrisCatlin 6 49
(Paul Cole) *hld up in last pair but in tch: rdn whn nt clr run over 2f out: swtchd rt: kpt on ins fnl f* **12/1**

660 **4** *hd* **Jacasa Too**[50] 1067 3-7-12 42................ SimonPearce(3) 4 43
(Rod Millman) *trckd ldrs: rdn over 2f out: ev ch whn edgd rt ent fnl f: kpt on same pce* **40/1**

-340 **5** *3 1/4* **Barbarella Blue (IRE)**[34] 1363 3-8-4 66................ AndreaAtzeni 1 38
(Marco Botti) *led tl over 4f out: chsd ldr: rdn over 2f out: ch over 1f out: fdd fnl 120yds* **9/4**[2]

050- **6** *3* **High Five Prince (IRE)**[218] 6807 3-8-5 44................ DavidProbert 5 31
(Mark Usher) *awkward leaving stalls: trckd ldrs: rdn over 2f out: hung rt and fdd fnl f* **7/1**[3]

60- **7** *13* **Peg Peg**[281] 4912 3-8-8 0................ FergusSweeney 7
(Nerys Dutfield) *s.i.s: last but in tch: rdn over 2f out: wknd over 1f out* **33/1**

1m 29.11s (0.51) **Going Correction** -0.025s/f (Good) 7 Ran SP% **109.5**
Speed ratings (Par 99): **96,92,92,92,88 85,70**
toteswingers:1&2:£2.50, 2&3:£3.50, 1&3:£3.00 CSF £15.63 TOTE £1.90: £1.30, £4.10; EX 8.10.The winner was claimed by J J Quinn for £10,000. Jacasa Too was subject to a friendly claim. Marah Music was subject to a friendly claim.
Owner Highclere Thoroughbred Racing - Namid **Bred** Michael And John Fahy **Trained** East Everleigh, Wilts

FOCUS
A sixth winner in the race since 2004 for trainer Richard Hannon and his colt won comfortably. The winner did not need to match his 2yo form in this modest race.

2204 FONTHILL STUD MAIDEN FILLIES' STKS (DIV II) 1m 1f 198y
3:45 (3:45) (Class 5) 3-Y-0+ **£2,911** (£866; £432; £216) **Stalls** Low

Form RPR

1 **Reyamour**[124] 4-9-12 79................ FergusSweeney 10 83
(Alan King) *trckd ldrs: led 3f out: sn rdn and hrd pressed: kpt finding for press: styd on: jst hld on* **20/1**

2 *hd* **Infinitum** 3-8-12 0................ RobertHavlin 5 81+
(John Gosden) *dwlt: bhd: pushed along over 3f out: rdn and stdy prog fr 2f out: styd on strly fnl f: only jst failed* **8/1**

3 *2 1/2* **Rosie Probert** 3-8-12 0................ HayleyTurner 2 76+
(Roger Charlton) *racd green: sn pushed along towards rr: rdn 3f out: stdy prog fr 2f out: styd on strly fnl f: snatched 3rd fnl stride: improve* **16/1**

5- **4** *nse* **Keene Dancer**[201] 7165 3-8-12 0................ PatDobbs 4 76
(Sir Michael Stoute) *trckd ldrs: rdn to chse wnr fr over 2f out: kpt on tl no ex fnl 120yds: lost 3rd fnl stride* **7/2**[3]

5 **5** *nk* **Khazeena**[22] 1610 3-8-12 0................ KellyHarrison 9 76
(William Haggas) *mid-div: rdn 3f out to chse ldrs: styd on same pce fnl 2f* **3/1**[1]

0-34 **6** *2 1/4* **Hunt A Mistress (IRE)**[27] 1502 3-8-12 75................(t) StevieDonohoe 1 71
(Paul Cole) *in tch: rdn over 2f out: styd on same pce* **8/1**

4 **7** *1 1/2* **Sound Hearts (USA)**[26] 1532 3-8-12 0................ AndreaAtzeni 13 68
(Roger Varian) *sn trcking ldrs on outer: effrt over 2f out: wknd ent fnl f* **10/3**[2]

0-20 **8** *2 1/2* **Finity Run (GER)**[8] 1976 3-8-12 70................ DarryllHolland 6 63
(Mark Johnston) *led tl rdn 3f out: wknd over 1f out* **20/1**

0-0 **9** *6* **Despatch**[27] 1503 3-8-12 0................ JimCrowley 8 51
(Ralph Beckett) *mid-div: rdn over 2f out: no imp: wknd fnl f* **25/1**

- **10** *4* **Rhossili Bay** 3-8-12 0................ ChrisCatlin 3 43
(Martyn Meade) *a towards rr* **100/1**

6 **11** *hd* **Goodie Goodie**[56] 990 3-8-12 0................ DavidProbert 12 43
(Sylvester Kirk) *mid-div: rdn 5f out: wknd over 2f out* **66/1**

12 *3/4* **Luna Rosa (IRE)** 3-8-12 0................ JohnFahy 7 41
(Clive Cox) *a towards rr* **50/1**

00/ **13** *13* **Jessica Ashton**[568] 7177 4-9-12 0................ PatCosgrave 11 16
(Stuart Kittow) *trckd ldr: rdn wl over 3f out: sn wandered u.p: wknd over 2f out* **100/1**

2m 9.55s (-0.35) **Going Correction** -0.025s/f (Good)
WFA 3 from 4yo 14lb 13 Ran SP% **117.2**
Speed ratings (Par 100): **100,99,97,97,97 95,94,92,87,84 84,83,73**
toteswingers:1&2:£15.90, 2&3:£19.10, 1&3:£14.30 CSF £162.25 TOTE £16.40: £3.80, £3.40, £4.90; EX 269.70.
Owner Denis J Barry **Bred** Haras De La Perelle **Trained** Barbury Castle, Wilts

FOCUS
The second and quicker division of the fillies' maiden. There was a sound pace on and they got sorted out nearing the two-furlong marker. The winner showed he retains his French Flat ability.

2205 MANOR FARM MEATS H'CAP (DIV I) 6f
4:20 (4:21) (Class 5) (0-75,74) 3-Y-0 **£2,587** (£770; £384; £192) **Stalls** Low

Form RPR

500- **1** **Ivor's Princess**[218] 6806 3-8-9 **65**................(b[1]) SeanLevey(3) 3 76
(Rod Millman) *slowly away and wnt lft: sn in tch: rdn to ld over 1f out: drifted lft: kpt on wl* **20/1**

61-2 **2** *1 3/4* **Royal Reyah**[27] 1493 3-9-7 **74**................ FergusSweeney 8 79
(Stuart Kittow) *cl up: rdn 2f out: chsd wnr and swtchd rt ent fnl f: kpt on same pce* **9/4**[1]

4-51 **3** *3 1/2* **Wiltshire Life (IRE)**[17] 1709 3-8-11 **69**................(p) MatthewCosham(5) 1 63
(Jeremy Gask) *trckd ldrs: rdn over 2f out: kpt on same pce* **9/1**

0002 **4** *1 3/4* **Marinus (IRE)**[16] 1725 3-8-6 **62**................ SophieDoyle(3) 4 50
(Sylvester Kirk) *led: rdn and hdd over 1f out: no ex ins fnl f* **9/1**

-302 **5** *2* **Samba Night (IRE)**[5] 2085 3-8-11 **64**................ AndreaAtzeni 2 46
(James Eustace) *t.k.h trcking ldr: rdn 2f out: fdd ins fnl f* **9/2**[3]

-354 **6** *nk* **Le King Beau (USA)**[14] 1789 3-9-1 **68**................ KieranO'Neill 10 49
(John Bridger) *trckd ldr: rdn 2f out: fdd fnl f* **16/1**

565- **7** *1/2* **Generalyse**[194] 7294 3-9-6 **73**................ PatDobbs 6 52
(Ben De Haan) *squeezed up s: in tch: rdn over 2f out: nt pce to get on terms: fdd fnl f* **7/2**[2]

43-0 **8** *3/4* **Zammy**[16] 1728 3-8-10 **63**................ DarryllHolland 7 40
(Michael Wigham) *squeezed up s: in last 3 but tch: rdn 3f out: nvr gng pce to threaten* **20/1**

053- **9** *2 3/4* **Invincible Dream (IRE)**[240] 6237 3-8-12 **65**................ StevieDonohoe 5 33
(Robert Mills) *in tch: rdn over 2f out: wknd ent fnl f* **20/1**

004 **10** *2* **Seventeen Seventy**[16] 1739 3-8-7 **60** oh2................ ChrisCatlin 9 22
(Alan Coogan) *cl up: rdn over 2f out: wknd over 1f out* **33/1**

1m 14.46s (-0.34) **Going Correction** -0.025s/f (Good) 10 Ran SP% **114.3**
Speed ratings (Par 99): **101,98,94,91,89 88,87,86,83,80**
toteswingers:1&2:£11.10, 2&3:£4.40, 1&3:£20.20 CSF £61.14 CT £461.05 TOTE £31.40: £6.80, £1.10, £3.20; EX 92.50.
Owner P G Gibbins & W I M Perry **Bred** The Three Point Partnership **Trained** Kentisbeare, Devon

FOCUS
A modest 3-y-o sprint handicap, run at a fair pace and the first four came clear. The time was similar to division one. The winner is rated back to her best.
Generalyse Official explanation: jockey said that the colt, hung right

2206 MANOR FARM MEATS H'CAP (DIV II) 6f
4:55 (4:55) (Class 5) (0-75,73) 3-Y-0 **£2,587** (£770; £384; £192) **Stalls** Low

Form RPR

16-1 **1** **Love Tale**[21] 1622 3-9-3 **69**................ FergusSweeney 5 82
(Mark Rimell) *trckd ldr: rdn to ld 2f out: kpt on wl to assert fnl 120yds: rdn out* **11/4**[1]

2-02 **2** *2* **Ashpan Sam**[10] 1912 3-9-4 **73**................ SeanLevey(3) 3 79
(John Spearing) *trckd ldr: rdn to press wnr fr 2f out tl no ex fnl 120yds* **7/2**[2]

30-2 **3** *2* **New Decade**[122] 193 3-8-11 **63**................ StevieDonohoe 1 64
(Milton Bradley) *set str pce: rdn and hdd 2f out: kpt on same pce fnl f* **8/1**

03-0 **4** *1* **Little Rainbow**[29] 1445 3-8-13 **65**................ JohnFahy 9 62
(Clive Cox) *t.k.h in last pair: effrt 2f out: fdd ent fnl f* **14/1**

10-1 **5** *nk* **Atlantis Crossing (IRE)**[16] 1725 3-8-12 **64**................ PatCosgrave 6 60
(Jim Boyle) *slowly away: nudged along in last 3 1/2-way: effrt whn short of room briefly 2f out: kpt on same pce fnl f* **4/1**[3]

610- **6** *3* **Wordismybond**[194] 7294 3-9-4 **70**................ DarryllHolland 8 56
(Peter Makin) *in tch: rdn over 2f out: nt gng pce to get on terms: wknd ins fnl f* **8/1**

5-35 **7** 4 ½ **One Kool Dude**[26] 1529 3-8-4 **63** .... IanBurns(7) 2 35
(Michael Bell) *chsd ldrs tl outpcd 3f out* **10/1**
8 *hd* **Fight (IRE)**[236] 6363 3-9-1 **67** .... (b[1]) ChrisCatlin 4 38
(Jeremy Gask) *outpcd 1/2-way: nvr a threat* **11/1**
1m 14.51s (-0.29) **Going Correction** -0.025s/f (Good) 8 Ran SP% **115.2**
Speed ratings (Par 99): **100,97,94,93,92 88,82,82**
toteswingers:1&2:£2.90, 2&3:£5.10, 1&3:£6.80 CSF £12.55 CT £67.75 TOTE £2.10: £1.10, £1.80, £3.30; EX 12.80.
Owner Mark Rimell **Bred** Witney And Warren Enterprises Ltd **Trained** Leafield, Oxon
FOCUS
The second division of the modest 3-y-o sprint handicap. It was run at a brisk pace, but still the closers failed to land a blow. The winner continues to progress.

2207 CGA RACING EXCELLENCE APPRENTICE H'CAP (WHIPS SHALL BE CARRIED BUT NOT USED) 6f 212y
5:25 (5:31) (Class 5) (0-70,70) 4-Y-0+ **£2,587** (£770; £384; £192) **Stalls** Centre

Form RPR
0250 **1** **Ibiza Sunset (IRE)**[6] 2043 4-9-0 **65** .... GeorgeDowning 7 76
(Brendan Powell) *chsd ldrs: led over 1f out: kpt on strly: pushed out* **14/1**
-003 **2** 4 ½ **Cocohatchee**[10] 1935 4-9-2 **67** .... JakePayne 6 66
(Pat Phelan) *chsd ldrs: pushed along over 2f out: chsd wnr over 1f out: a being hld* **16/1**
46-2 **3** ¾ **The Name Is Frank**[11] 1895 7-8-8 **64** .... RyanWhile(5) 13 61
(Mark Gillard) *chsd ldrs: kpt on same pce fnl 2f: jst hld on for 3rd* **10/1**
316- **4** *nk* **Lady Bayside**[267] 5376 4-8-13 **67** .... NicoleNordblad(3) 9 63+
(Malcolm Saunders) *bhd: plenty to do 3f out: fin strly fr over 1f out: nrly snatched 3rd: nt rch ldrs* **12/1**
300- **5** 1 ½ **Grand Piano (IRE)**[182] 7448 5-8-7 **65** .... (v) JoeyHaynes(7) 12 57
(Andrew Balding) *bhd: stdy prog fr 2f out: styd on wl ins fnl f: nt rch ldrs* **20/1**
4212 **6** ¾ **Dancing Welcome**[10] 1934 6-8-6 **62** .... (b) TimClark(5) 3 52
(Milton Bradley) *led at gd pce: edgd lft 2f out: sn hdd: no ex ins fnl f* **9/2[1]**
2-03 **7** ½ **Comrade Bond**[6] 2043 4-8-12 **70** .... RobJFitzpatrick(7) 10 59
(Mark H Tompkins) *chsd ldr: pushed along fr 3f out: one pce fnl 2f* **10/1**
3020 **8** 1 **Secret Queen**[33] 1378 5-8-6 **62** .... (v) RyanTate(5) 5 48
(Martin Hill) *awkwardly away: sn mid-div: styd on same pce fnl 2f: nvr threatened* **20/1**
6045 **9** 7 **All Right Now**[23] 1587 5-8-9 **60** .... JackDuern 1 27
(Derek Haydn Jones) *chsd ldrs tl wknd over 1f out* **11/2[2]**
603- **10** ½ **Frozen Over**[197] 7235 4-8-13 **67** .... IanBurns(3) 8 33
(Stuart Kittow) *a towards rr* **6/1[3]**
2511 **11** 10 **Katmai River (IRE)**[14] 1769 5-9-2 **70** .... (v) ThomasBrown(3) 2
(Mark Usher) *a bhd: nvr any ch* **7/1**
0-00 **12** 7 **High On The Hog (IRE)**[21] 1626 4-8-11 **69** .... KirstenSmith(7) 4
(Paul Howling) *in tch tl wknd over 2f out* **50/1**
160- **13** 3 ½ **Mr Udagawa**[193] 7057 6-8-9 **67** .... (p) DanielMuscutt(7) 11
(Bernard Llewellyn) *struggling 1/2-way: a towards rr* **40/1**
00-6 **14** 2 ½ **George Thisby**[10] 1936 6-8-13 **67** .... JoshBaudains(3) 14
(Rod Millman) *a bhd* **12/1**
1m 27.78s (-0.82) **Going Correction** -0.025s/f (Good) 14 Ran SP% **120.4**
Speed ratings (Par 103): **103,97,97,96,94 94,93,92,84,83 72,64,60,57**
toteswingers:1&2:£63.00, 2&3:£20.80, 1&3:£27.60 CSF £211.57 CT £2405.63 TOTE £20.00: £6.70, £6.10, £2.60; EX 256.50.
Owner R H Kerswell **Bred** Mrs J A Dene **Trained** Upper Lambourn, Berks
FOCUS
This was a typically wide-open race of its type, run at a decent clip. The winner is rated back to his early best.
T/Plt: £206.10 to a £1 stake. Pool of £51,110.70 - 181.00 winning tickets. T/Qpdt: £45.70 to a £1 stake. Pool of £2,695.08 - 43.60 winning tickets. TM

2176 YORK (L-H)
Thursday, May 17
OFFICIAL GOING: Good (7.6)
Wind: Virtually nil Weather: Overcast and light rain showers

2208 BETFRED MOBILE SPORTS STKS (H'CAP) 5f
1:30 (1:30) (Class 2) (0-105,101) 4-Y-0+ **£12,938** (£3,850; £1,924; £962) **Stalls** Centre

Form RPR
54-2 **1** **Judge 'n Jury**[12] 1849 8-8-0 **87** .... (t) DarrenEgan(7) 5 97
(Ronald Harris) *sn led: rdn clr over 1f out: drvn ins fnl f: hld on wl* **10/1[2]**
5-31 **2** *nk* **Secret Witness**[1] 2177 6-9-6 **100** 6ex .... (b) LukeMorris 15 109
(Ronald Harris) *towards rr: pushed along 1/2-way: hdwy 2f out: rdn wl over 1f out: styd on strly ins fnl f* **10/1[2]**
01-1 **3** 1 ¼ **Magical Macey (USA)**[29] 1438 5-9-3 **97** .... (b) GrahamGibbons 14 101
(David Barron) *racd towards stands' rail: cl up: rdn wl over 1f out: kpt on u.p ins fnl f* **12/1**
30-6 **4** ½ **Racy**[29] 1438 5-8-13 **93** .... PhillipMakin 2 95
(Kevin Ryan) *lw: led early: cl up: rdn wl over 1f out: kpt on same pce ins fnl f* **8/1[1]**
00-5 **5** ½ **Doctor Parkes**[8] 1975 6-8-12 **92** .... JimmyFortune 7 92
(Eric Alston) *on toes: chsd ldrs: rdn wl over 1f out: kpt on same pce fnl f* **8/1[1]**
50-3 **6** *nk* **Bedloe's Island (IRE)**[20] 1642 7-8-2 **82** oh6 .... JamesSullivan 12 81
(Neville Bycroft) *hld up in midfield: hdwy 2f out: sn rdn and styd on fnl f: nrst fin* **40/1**
24-0 **7** *nk* **Irish Heartbeat (IRE)**[11] 1885 7-8-7 **90** .... LeeTopliss(3) 6 88
(Richard Fahey) *hld up in tch: hdwy to chse ldrs over 2f out: sn rdn and n.m.r: no imp ins fnl f* **8/1[1]**
01-3 **8** ½ **Steps (IRE)**[12] 1849 4-8-12 **92** .... NeilCallan 1 88
(Roger Varian) *on toes: in tch: gd hdwy on outer and cl up 2f out: sn rdn and ev ch tl wknd ent fnl f* **8/1[1]**
46-4 **9** *shd* **Hazelrigg (IRE)**[29] 1438 7-8-5 **85** .... (be) JoeFanning 3 81
(Tim Easterby) *chsd ldrs: effrt and n.m.r over 1f out: sn rdn and no imp* **16/1**
00-0 **10** ¾ **Ancient Cross**[46] 1157 8-9-5 **99** .... (t) PaulMulrennan 9 92+
(Michael Easterby) *dwlt and sltly hmpd s: in rr tl styd on fr wl over 1f out: nrst fin* **16/1**
0-50 **11** 2 ¼ **Fitz Flyer (IRE)**[8] 1975 6-8-13 **93** .... KierenFallon 4 78
(David Nicholls) *lw: in tch: rdn along 2f out: grad wknd* **11/1[3]**
00-3 **12** ½ **Swiss Franc**[6] 2024 7-9-0 **94** .... RyanMoore 10 77
(David Elsworth) *lw: b.hind: n.m.r and sltly hmpd s: a in rr after* **16/1**
40-0 **13** *hd* **Cocktail Charlie**[29] 1438 4-8-5 **85** .... DuranFentiman 11 68
(Tim Easterby) *chsd ldrs: rdn along over 2f out: sn wknd* **14/1**
00-6 **14** 2 **El Viento (FR)**[46] 1157 4-8-11 **91** .... (b) TonyHamilton 16 67
(Richard Fahey) *racd towards stands' rail: towards rr: sme hdwy 1/2-way: sn rdn and wknd* **16/1**
301- **15** ½ **Verinco**[215] 6865 6-8-12 **97** .... (v) JustinNewman(5) 8 71
(Bryan Smart) *chsd ldrs: rdn along over 2f out: sn edgd lft and wknd* **14/1**
240- **16** 1 **Gramercy (IRE)**[229] 6520 5-9-7 **101** .... JamieSpencer 13 71
(Kevin Ryan) *stdd s: hld up: a bhd* **16/1**
59.1s (-0.20) **Going Correction** +0.20s/f (Good) 16 Ran SP% **123.8**
Speed ratings (Par 109): **109,108,106,105,104 104,103,103,103,101 98,97,97,93,93 91**
toteswingers:1&2:£16.30, 2&3:£21.10, 1&3:£16.50 CSF £107.93 CT £1283.10 TOTE £10.90: £2.70, £2.90, £2.40, £2.40; EX 102.70 Trifecta £1554.10 Part won. Pool: £2100.20 - 0.80 winning units..
Owner Robert & Nina Bailey **Bred** C A Cyzer **Trained** Earlswood, Monmouths
FOCUS
A good-class, competitive sprint handicap. The race was a triumph for trainer Ron Harris, who was responsible for the first two home. Not many got involved. The winner showed his best form since 2010 and the second is in the form of his life.
NOTEBOOK
Judge 'n Jury made virtually all the running up the centre of the track and it was clear entering the last furlong that he was not stopping. He has come back in good form this season with the tongue-tie refitted and could go in again.
Secret Witness, who scored over 6f here the previous day and was carrying a penalty, compromised his chance by missing the break slightly, but picked up really well in the closing stages and would have won in another 25yds or so. He is clearly tough and at the top of his game. (op 11-1)
Magical Macey(USA) has progressed really well since last August and, after making the running nearer the stands' side, kept a strongly under pressure and is still on the upgrade. (op 11-1 tchd 10-1)
Racy is a consistent sort and goes really well here. He ran another good race and deserves to win a similar contest, but the losing sequence is now 17 and he might be worth trying in cheekpieces or some form of headgear to give him a helping hand. (op 17-2 tchd 9-1 in a place)
Doctor Parkes ◆ has run pretty well on his two starts this year now and will be of interest when the ground dries up. (op 9-1)
Bedloe's Island(IRE) had a tough task from 6lb out of the weights but ran creditably, having chased the fourth most of the way. He will be interesting back off his proper mark. (op 33-1)
Irish Heartbeat(IRE) races mainly over longer trips but did perform creditably behind today's runner-up over C&D last August. He again ran pretty well without quite having the pace to make an impact, and probably needs softer ground at this trip. (op 12-1)
Steps(IRE) showed up for a long way but was rather exposed on the outside of the field and could not sustain his effort in the closing stages.
Hazelrigg(IRE) is pretty consistent despite not always finding much off the bridle. He is gradually slipping back down the weights and quicker ground might enable him to last home better.
Ancient Cross was attempting to win for the second successive year, this time off a 10lb higher mark. He could never land a blow, but will be of interest when dropped a few pounds. (op 14-1)
Swiss Franc's rider reported that the gelding hung right. Official explanation: jockey said that the gelding hung right (tchd 18-1)

2209 BETFRED MIDDLETON STKS (GROUP 2) (F&M) 1m 2f 88y
2:00 (2:00) (Class 1) 4-Y-0+
£56,710 (£21,500; £10,760; £5,360; £2,690; £1,350) **Stalls** Low

Form RPR
31-1 **1** **Izzi Top**[11] 1883 4-8-12 110 .... WilliamBuick 6 116
(John Gosden) *warm: edgy: trckd ldr: smooth hdwy 3f out and sn and cl up; led 2f out: sn rdn and edgd lft wl over 1f out: styd on wl ins fnl f* **7/2[1]**
410- **2** 1 ½ **Sajjhaa**[285] 4789 5-8-12 112 .... FrankieDettori 5 113
(Saeed Bin Suroor) *trckd ldng pair: smooth hdwy 3f out: cl up 2f out: rdn and ev ch wl over 1f out: kpt on same pce ins fnl f* **9/2[2]**
642- **3** 1 **I'm A Dreamer (IRE)**[214] 6909 5-8-12 111 .... JimmyFortune 3 112+
(David Simcock) *swtg: hld up towards rr: pushed along and hdwy 3f out: trckd ldrs whn n.m.r and swtchd rt 2f out: sn nt clr run and sltly hmpd: rdn wl over 1f out: kpt on ins fnl f* **6/1[3]**
54-4 **4** ¾ **Barefoot Lady (IRE)**[12] 1851 4-8-12 108 .... TonyHamilton 11 110
(Richard Fahey) *in rr: pushed along 4f out: rdn and hdwy wl over 2f out: kpt on u.p fnl f* **20/1**
42-3 **5** 2 **Beatrice Aurore (IRE)**[28] 1471 4-8-12 111 .... RyanMoore 10 106
(John Dunlop) *lw: hld up and bhd: hdwy 3f out: sn rdn along: drvn to chse ldrs wl over 1f out: wknd fnl f* **6/1[3]**
112- **6** 1 **Set To Music (IRE)**[252] 5850 4-8-12 110 .... JamieSpencer 2 104
(Michael Bell) *in tch: hdwy on inner to chse ldrs 3f out: rdn over 2f out: sn wknd* **15/2**
614- **7** 4 ½ **Mohedian Lady (IRE)**[208] 7027 4-8-12 103 .... KierenFallon 9 96
(Luca Cumani) *led and sn clr: qcknd over 4f out: rdn 3f out: hdd 2f out and sn wknd* **20/1**
20-4 **8** 6 **Timepiece**[11] 1883 5-8-12 114 .... TomQueally 4 84
(Sir Henry Cecil) *lw: hld up in tch: wd st to r nr stands' rail: hdwy to chse ldng pair 2f out: sn rdn and wknd qckly over 1f out* **7/1**
315- **9** 20 **Sea Of Heartbreak (IRE)**[214] 6909 5-9-1 108 .... JamesDoyle 8 49+
(Roger Charlton) *bit bkwd: trckd ldrs: wd st to r nr stands' rail: hdwy over 3f out: rdn and n.m.r 2f out: sn wknd and bhd whn eased over 1f out* **10/1**
2m 11.62s (-0.88) **Going Correction** +0.20s/f (Good) 9 Ran SP% **111.9**
Speed ratings (Par 115): **111,109,109,108,106 106,102,97,81**
toteswingers:1&2:£4.50, 2&3:£5.90, 1&3:£4.00 CSF £18.16 TOTE £3.60: £1.90, £2.00, £2.40; EX 17.60 Trifecta £56.60 Pool: £1704.57 - 22.28 winning units..
Owner Helena Springfield Ltd **Bred** Meon Valley Stud **Trained** Newmarket, Suffolk
FOCUS
A cracking contest that was run at a decent gallop. It would be surprising if this didn't turn out to be strong form for the grade. Izzi Top continued her progress but a bit more is needed to win most fillies' Group 1s.
NOTEBOOK
Izzi Top ◆, whose dam Zee Zee Top won this race in 2003, had made a sound start to her 4-y-o season with success in the Dahlia Stakes at Newmarket only 11 days earlier and took another step up the ladder with a driving success, this after cruising up to the lead going strongly. She has appeared to improve for another winter behind her and a Group 1 must now be what connections are after. The trainer mentioned the Nassau Stakes and/or the Prix de l'Opera as possible targets, and in the interim something like the Pretty Polly at the Curragh would make sense. (op 3-1 tchd 11-4)
Sajjhaa, off since a disappointing performance in a Group 3 in early August 2011, was second in this race on her reappearance last year and repeated the feat here, making the winner work for the victory throughout the final furlong. She clearly goes well at the course so other Group contests here would suit her. (op 5-1)
I'm A Dreamer(IRE) ◆, who'd won first time out at three and four, finished her 2011 campaign with a narrow defeat in the Grade 1 E P Taylor Stakes at Woodbine. Sat in the chasing bunch, she looked a bit unlucky not to finish considerably closer as she met the long-time leader coming back towards her about 1f out which stopped her momentum. A race at this level is within her scope. (op 11-2)

Barefoot Lady(IRE) was disappointing at Goodwood on her previous start, so this was a lot better especially as she was out the back when her rivals quickened on in the home straight. (tchd 22-1 in a place)
Beatrice Aurore(IRE) ◆ sat last and could never make up the ground against Group-class fillies. There will be other days for her. (op 8-1)
Set To Music(IRE) landed the Galtres Stakes over 1m4f at the Ebor meeting here last year, but wasn't able to complete a five-timer in the Park Hill at Doncaster on her final outing of the season over a trip that may have stretched her. This looked a good starting point for her but she ran as though she needs further now. (tchd 8-1)
Mohedian Lady(IRE), off since late October, had a bit to find against some higher-rated rivals but did a pretty good job of ensuring the race wasn't run at a false pace. She'll surely face easier tasks.
Timepiece, the only Group 1 winner in the field, and third to Midday in this contest last season, was a below-par fourth to Izzi Top at Newmarket on her reappearance and failed to fire again her. Lord Grimthorpe said afterwards there was no good explanation for this performance apart from her hanging a little bit. She wasn't showing her normal exuberance and connections will now consider her future. Tom Queally reported that the mare hung left handed. Official explanation: jockey said that the mare hung left handed (op 13-2)
Sea Of Heartbreak(IRE) ended last season with a good fifth in a Grade 1 at Woodbine (not far behind I'm A Dreamer), but looked vulnerable under a penalty and so it proved. (op 12-1)

2210 BETFRED DANTE STKS (GROUP 2) 1m 2f 88y
2:30 (2:32) (Class 1) 3-Y-O

£85,065 (£32,250; £16,140; £8,040; £4,035; £2,025) **Stalls** Low

Form				RPR
13-	**1**		**Bonfire**[200] 7192 3-9-0 108 ... JimmyFortune 4	117+
			(Andrew Balding) *lw: trckd ldr: smooth hdwy 3f out: led over 2f out: sn jnd and shkn up over 1f out: rdn and kpt on wl ins fnl f* **3/1**[2]
10-1	**2**	¾	**Ektihaam (IRE)**[27] 1504 3-9-0 108 ... TadhgO'Shea 3	116
			(Roger Varian) *lw t.k.h: hld up in rr: gd hdwy on outer over 3f out: cl up 2f out: sn rdn to chal and ev ch tl one pce wl ins fnl f* **6/1**
13-6	**3**	4	**Fencing (USA)**[12] 1856 3-9-0 111 ... WilliamBuick 1	109
			(John Gosden) *lw: hld up in tch: hdwy on bit to trck ldrs over 2f out: chsd ldng pair over 1f out: sn rdn and one pce* **7/2**[3]
6-2	**4**	10	**Dream Tune**[26] 1506 3-9-0 0 ... AdamKirby 7	89
			(Clive Cox) *in tch: rdn along and outpcd 3f out: kpt on u.p fr wl over 1f out to take modest 4th nr line* **40/1**
2-40	**5**	½	**Ptolemaic**[12] 1856 3-9-0 109 ... (v) TomEaves 2	88
			(Bryan Smart) *t.k.h: chsd ldrs on inner: hdwy and cl up 3f out: rdn over 2f out: grad wknd: lost modest 4th nr line* **25/1**
1-	**6**	9	**Mandaean**[187] 7405 3-9-0 0 ... MickaelBarzalona 6	87
			(Mahmood Al Zarooni) *athletic: lw: trckd ldrs: effrt 3f out: sn rdn and wknd over 2f out: eased* **11/2**
7	14	**Ernest Hemingway (IRE)**[34] 1368 3-9-0 0 ... JPO'Brien 5	91
			(A P O'Brien, Ire) *well made: led and sn clr: pushed along and jnd over 2f out: sn hdd and rdn: wknd qckly wl over 1f out and sn eased* **11/4**[1]

2m 10.52s (-1.98) **Going Correction** +0.20s/f (Good) **7** Ran SP% **109.8**
Speed ratings (Par 111): **115,114,111,103,102 95,84**
toteswingers:1&2:£3.80, 2&3:£4.40, 1&3:£2.30 CSF £19.37 TOTE £3.70: £2.20, £2.60; EX 24.30.
Owner Highclere Thoroughbred Racing-Pocahontas **Bred** Highclere Stud And Floors Farming **Trained** Kingsclere, Hants

FOCUS
This Group 2 is often regarded as the principal Derby trial, with North Light, Motivator and Authorized all taking this en-route to Epsom glory. In addition two of the last four winners were placed and Cape Blanco later took the Irish Derby. The time was 1.1secs faster than the preceding Group 2 for older fillies and the field finished well strung out. This was an up-to-scratch Dante and Bonfire is the clear rival to Camelot in the Derby. Ektihaam improved again with Fencing helping to set the standard.

NOTEBOOK
Bonfire ◆, a half-brother to Musidora winner Joviality, had beaten several subsequent winners on his debut before finishing an unlucky third in the Group 1 Criterium International at Saint-Cloud last autumn, behind the subsequent Djebel winner and Guineas second French Fifteen. That form made him a major contender here and he lived up to it with a determined success. Always travelling well in the wake of the leader, he came through to lead going as well as anything and really knuckled down under pressure to hold off the runner-up, the pair clear. He looks sure to take his place in the Derby line-up, despite having a hard race, and although there are a few doubts from his pedigree about him truly getting the trip, he deserves to do so and will have a sound chance if he stays. (tchd 5-2)
Ektihaam(IRE) bounced back from a disappointing effort in the Dewhurst, when he reportedly did not handle the track, to bolt up in a conditions race at Newbury. After proving difficult to load he settled well and came to have every chance, only to find the winner just too strong. He drew clear of the rest and is clearly a high-class colt on a Flat track. Not in the Derby, the Prix du Jockey-Club looks a reasonable alternative, although he will have to be supplemented. (op 11-2)
Fencing(USA), third behind the Derby favourite Camelot in the Racing Post Trophy and sixth behind the same colt in the 2000 Guineas last time, provided a strong line to that form. He moved into contention travelling well but might not have quite got home. (op 4-1)
Dream Tune, the only maiden in the line-up, had run a good second to subsequent Listed winner Noble Mission on his reappearance. He was out the back for most of the way and merely picked up the pieces as others weakened. He should have no trouble winning races though. (op 33-1)
Ptolemaic finished sixth in the 2000 Guineas as a long-priced outsider, which meant on that form he was quite closely matched with today's third. He tracked the pace but could not pick up when the race began in earnest. (tchd 22-1 and 33-1)
Mandaean, unbeaten in two starts for Andre Fabre, including the Group 1 Criterium de Saint-Cloud over 1m2f on heavy ground in November, tracked the leaders and was a little keen early on this debut for a new trainer. However, when the pace picked up he could not respond under pressure and was the first beaten. This was disappointing. (op 5-1 tchd 6-1)
Ernest Hemingway(IRE) ◆, whose trainer had been responsible for three of the last six winners of this, had been the winner of his sole previous start in a Polytrack maiden at Dundalk. He made the running and travelled with enthusiasm, but appeared to do too much too soon, as when taken on he had nothing left and was eased once beaten. Joseph O'Brien reported that the colt lost its action, so he can be given another chance. Official explanation: jockey said that the colt lost its action (op 10-3 tchd 7-2 in a place)

2211 BETFRED HAMBLETON STKS (H'CAP) (LISTED RACE) 1m
3:00 (3:01) (Class 1) (0-110,107) 4-Y-O+**£19,536** (£7,388; £3,692; £1,844) **Stalls** Low

Form				RPR
-323	**1**		**Fury**[12] 1854 4-9-4 **104** ... RyanMoore 3	113
			(William Haggas) *trckd ldng pair: hdwy 3f out: rdn to chal wl over 1f out: drvn and edgd lft ins fnl f: led last 50yds: jst hld on* **3/1**[2]
541-	**2**	nse	**Prince Of Johanne (IRE)**[236] 6339 6-8-12 **98** ... (p) RobertWinston 4	107
			(Tom Tate) *trckd ldr: hdwy over 3f out: led over 2f out: jnd and rdn wl over 1f out: hdd last 50yds: rallied nr line: jst failed* **20/1**
142-	**3**	2½	**Mijhaar**[315] 3774 4-9-2 **102** ... NeilCallan 2	105
			(Roger Varian) *lw: trckd ldrs: hdwy 3f out: rdn 2f out: drvn and kpt on same pce fnl f* **2/1**[1]
0-20	**4**	hd	**Bridgefield (USA)**[117] 261 4-9-0 **100** ... MickaelBarzalona 10	103+
			(Mahmood Al Zarooni) *hld up towards rr: hdwy wl over 2f out: rdn over 1f out: kpt on ins fnl f: nrst fin* **16/1**
4004	**5**	¾	**Navajo Chief**[46] 1158 5-9-0 **100** ... AdamKirby 12	101
			(Alan Jarvis) *led: rdn along 3f out: hdd over 2f out: kpt on same pce appr fnl f* **8/1**[3]
-011	**6**	nk	**Justonefortheroad**[26] 1523 6-8-13 **99** ... TonyHamilton 1	99
			(Richard Fahey) *midfield: hdwy 3f out: rdn along 2f out: no imp appr fnl f* **17/2**
644-	**7**	1¼	**Trade Storm**[152] 7802 4-8-12 **98** ... WilliamBuick 5	95
			(David Simcock) *chsd ldrs: hdwy and cl up over 3f out: rdn over 2f out and ev ch tl drvn and wknd over 1f out* **12/1**
102-	**8**	5	**Common Touch (IRE)**[295] 4428 4-8-9 **95** ... FrederikTylicki 9	81
			(Richard Fahey) *lw: in tch: effrt 3f out: rdn along 2f out: sn wknd* **12/1**
/0-	**9**	7	**Bezique**[382] 1738 4-8-12 **98** ... KierenFallon 11	68
			(Luca Cumani) *hld up towards rr: hdwy over 3f out: rdn over 2f out: sn wknd* **20/1**
1-15	**10**	5	**Neutrafa (IRE)**[12] 1851 4-8-7 **93** ... HarryBentley 8	51
			(John Mackie) *lw: a towards rr* **14/1**
0/50	**11**	10	**Titus Mills (IRE)**[15] 1749 4-9-0 **100** ... (b[1]) JamieSpencer 7	35
			(Brian Meehan) *a towards rr* **28/1**

1m 39.27s (0.27) **Going Correction** +0.20s/f (Good) **11** Ran SP% **120.9**
Speed ratings (Par 111): **106,105,103,103,102 102,100,95,88,83 73**
toteswingers:1&2:£16.50, 2&3:£14.30, 1&3:£1.70 CSF £66.82 CT £150.60 TOTE £4.50: £1.90, £4.90, £1.30; EX 70.40 Trifecta £175.70 Pool: £2407.90 - 10.14 winning units..
Owner Cheveley Park Stud **Bred** Cheveley Park Stud Ltd **Trained** Newmarket, Suffolk
■ Stewards' Enquiry : Robert Winston two-day ban: use of whip (May 31 and June 3)

FOCUS
No hanging about in what look a competitive heat, which provided an exciting climax. The form is not quite as strong as might be expected for the grade. The first three were always prominent.

NOTEBOOK
Fury had been running well in good handicaps at about 1m, so this win didn't come out of turn. Always well placed, his attitude was good under strong pressure and he rallied in willing style to get on top close to the line. He is due to go back into Group company now, probably somewhere in France. (op 9-2 tchd 5-1 early in a place)
Prince Of Johanne(IRE), below par on two previous runs here, rounded 2011 off with victory in the Cambridgeshire at Newmarket and has returned in tremendous heart, only losing out in the latter stages despite giving his all. He could be the right type for the Royal Hunt Cup.
Mijhaar ◆ had had only had four starts, but looked a smart prospect on each occasion, albeit over further than this trip on his final three starts. Returning from a 315-day absence, he took quite a grip but stayed on under pressure to make a pleasing reappearance. This effort should have taken some of the fizz out of him, and hopefully we'll see even better when he's upped in distance again. He wants plenty of ease, however, so his best opportunities may come abroad during the summer. (op 5-2 tchd 11-4)
Bridgefield(USA) ran respectably in a couple of races at Meydan at the start of the year, and arguably could have been third here had Barzalona been a bit more vigorous in the final few yards.
Navajo Chief ◆, who'd gone well at this course in the past, had an uncontested lead but didn't get home. He is on a good mark now and it won't be long before he hits first place again. (op 7-1)
Justonefortheroad, a 7f winner here in the past, was chasing a hat-trick since being returned to turf but couldn't get on terms after being caught one-paced over 2f out. (op 8-1)
Trade Storm ◆, on his second start for David Simcock but having his first outing of the year, caught the eye and is the type to take a big handicap before the end of the season. Perhaps the Bunbury Cup will be a suitable target. (op 10-1)
Bezique won three from four in Italy, but had been unraced since disappointing on soft ground in the Italian 1000 Guineas in May of last year. Making her debut for Luca Cumani, she showed little but is presumably much better than this. The jockey reported his mount ran too freely. Official explanation: jockey said that the filly ran too free (op 16-1)
Titus Mills(IRE)'s rider reported that the colt moved poorly. Official explanation: jockey said that the colt moved poorly (op 25-1)

2212 BRITISH STALLION STUDS SUPPORTING BRITISH RACING EBF SPRINT CONDITIONS STKS 5f
3:35 (3:35) (Class 2) 3-Y-O **£12,938** (£3,850; £1,924; £962) **Stalls** Centre

Form				RPR
1-1	**1**		**Pearl Secret**[20] 1639 3-9-2 101 ... JamieSpencer 5	111+
			(David Barron) *str: lw: t.k.h early: hld up: swtchd lft and hdwy 2f out: qcknd wl to ld ent fnl f: impressive* **5/6**[1]
161-	**2**	1½	**Ponty Acclaim (IRE)**[229] 6518 3-9-4 105 ... DavidAllan 2	105
			(Tim Easterby) *on toes: prom: chsd ldr after 2f: rdn to ld 1 1/2f out: hdd ent fnl f: kpt on* **14/1**
3-26	**3**	1½	**Caledonia Lady**[12] 1857 3-9-2 104 ... TonyCulhane 6	98
			(Jo Hughes) *t.k.h: trckd ldrs: n.m.r and swtchd rt wl over 1f out: sn rdn and styd on wl fnl f* **5/1**[3]
0-11	**4**	2¾	**Es Que Love (IRE)**[29] 1457 3-9-2 98 ... SilvestreDeSousa 4	88
			(Mark Johnston) *chsd ldr: rdn along 2f out: sn edgd lft and one pce* **11/4**[2]
26-4	**5**	2	**Vocational (USA)**[11] 1877 3-9-0 104 ... JoeFanning 1	79
			(Mark Johnston) *led: rdn along 2f out: hdd 1 1/2f out and sn wknd* **25/1**
00-0	**6**	8	**North Star Boy (IRE)**[29] 1457 3-9-2 94 ... RyanMoore 3	52
			(Richard Hannon) *dwlt: a in rr: outpcd fr wl over 1f out* **20/1**

1m 0.49s (1.19) **Going Correction** +0.20s/f (Good) **6** Ran SP% **113.2**
Speed ratings (Par 105): **98,95,93,88,85 72**
CSF £14.84 TOTE £1.80: £1.10, £3.30; EX 8.00.
Owner Pearl Bloodstock Ltd **Bred** Whitsbury Manor Stud & Pigeon House Stud **Trained** Maunby, N Yorks

FOCUS
A tight conditions sprint despite the small field, although the time was 1.39secs slower than the opening handicap. All three previous winners of this had been fillies and, although they filled the places this time, the winner was a colt with the potential to win Group races. The form is perhaps not the most solid, with the fourth below par, but the winner impressed and is value for a bit extra.

NOTEBOOK
Pearl Secret, who won his debut here last year, beat the second in that race by further giving weight when taking a handicap on his reappearance. He travelled well in rear and, when asked to pick up, did so in the style of a good colt. Although he did not increase the margin in the latter stages, he had matters well in hand by then. (op 10-11 tchd Evens)
Ponty Acclaim(IRE) ◆, a four-time winner as a juvenile, including when taking the Group 3 Cornwallis Stakes on her final start, had a 7lb penalty to carry on this reappearance. She was quite keen early but came through well to lead, only to be immediately tackled by the winner. She did not go down without a fight, though, and the winner was not getting any further away from her in the latter stages. She looks to have trained on and could win more Group races. (op 12-1)
Caledonia Lady, who ran second to a subsequent Group 3 winner on her reappearance and then was sixth against older rivals in the Palace House, was another who was keen under restraint before staying on well in the closing stages. There are more Listed races to be won with her. (op 9-2 tchd 4-1)
Es Que Love(IRE) has done really well in handicaps at 6f, winning twice this season, but was outpaced at this trip in this grade. (op 7-2)

Vocational(USA), whose best effort in Group company was on Polytrack, set off in front and performed creditably, but could not hold off the challengers and may not prove easy to place in the short-term. (op 20-1)

2213 STRATFORD PLACE STUD FOR INTERNATIONAL GROUP 1 WINNERS EBF MAIDEN STKS 6f

4:10 (4:11) (Class 3) 2-Y-O **£7,762** (£2,310; £1,154; £577) **Stalls** Centre

Form RPR

1 **Funk Soul Brother** 2-9-3 0 MichaelHills 4 82+
(Charles Hills) *leggy: dwlt and sltly hmpd s: t.k.h in midfield: hdwy over 2f out: chal over 1f out: rdn to ld ent fnl f: kpt on* **8/1**[3]

2 ½ **Newstead Abbey** 2-9-3 0 RichardMullen 5 80+
(David Brown) *leggy: attr: trckd ldrs: hdwy wl over 2f out: rdn over 1f out: styd on wl fnl f* **9/2**[2]

3 ½ **Artigiano (USA)** 2-9-3 0 FrankieDettori 2 79+
(Mahmood Al Zarooni) *w'like: attr: towards rr: hdwy on outer wl over 2f out: rdn to chse ldrs over 1f out: kpt on fnl f: nrst fin* **8/1**[3]

4 *shd* **Star Of Rohm** 2-9-3 0 AdamKirby 12 79+
(Michael Bell) *w'like: cl cpld: trckd ldrs: hdwy to ld 2f out: rdn and hdd ent fnl f: no ex last 100yds* **25/1**

5 *10* **Red Paladin (IRE)** 2-9-3 0 PhillipMakin 9 49+
(Kevin Ryan) *str: lw: trckd ldrs: effrt 2f out: sn rdn and wknd* **20/1**

6 6 *1 ½* **Bispham Green**[12] 1842 2-9-3 0 TonyHamilton 14 44+
(Richard Fahey) *leggy: chsd ldrs: swtchd lft over 2f out: sn rdn: hung lft and wknd wl over 1f out* **9/1**

7 *3* **Skytrain** 2-9-3 0 SilvestreDeSousa 7 35+
(Mark Johnston) *athletic: lw: cl up: led after 2f: rdn along and hdd 2f out: sn wknd* **12/1**

8 *nk* **Wynyard Boy** 2-9-3 0 DavidAllan 8 34+
(Tim Easterby) *w'like: cl cpld: dwlt and in rr tl sme late hdwy* **25/1**

9 *3 ½* **Birdy Boy (USA)** 2-9-3 0 JoeFanning 6 24
(Mark Johnston) *tall: lengthy: on toes: chsd ldrs: rdn along wl over 2f out: sn wknd* **18/1**

10 *4 ½* **If You Can (IRE)** 2-9-3 0 DuranFentiman 10 10
(Tim Easterby) *leggy: dwlt: a in rr* **33/1**

11 *nse* **Glory Awaits (IRE)** 2-9-3 0 JamieSpencer 13 10
(Kevin Ryan) *tall: lengthy: on toes: dwlt: a in rr* **10/1**

5 12 *25* **Unidexter (IRE)**[10] 1903 2-9-3 0 SamHitchcott 3
(Mick Channon) *w'like: a in rr* **20/1**

32 13 *13* **Dust Whirl**[12] 1842 2-9-3 0 RyanMoore 11
(Richard Hannon) *lw: led 2f: cl up tl rdn along and wknd qckly over 2f out: sn bhd and heavily eased* **5/2**[1]

1m 14.68s (2.78) **Going Correction** +0.20s/f (Good) 13 Ran SP% **121.2**
Speed ratings (Par 97): **89,88,87,87,74 72,68,67,63,57 57,23,6**
toteswingers:1&2:£14.40, 2&3:£10.00, 1&3:£7.90 CSF £41.15 TOTE £6.80: £2.50, £2.40, £2.30; EX 55.90 Trifecta £237.90 Pool: £1691.28 - 5.26 winning units..
Owner Phil Cunningham **Bred** P M Cunningham **Trained** Lambourn, Berks

FOCUS
Some nice horses have taken this in the past, with Lord Shanakill sticking out as the best of them. Also, subsequent Dewhurst winner Beethoven finished third in 2009. The pace looked honest enough and four came upwards of 10l clear. The time was decent and this is surely strong form.

NOTEBOOK
Funk Soul Brother cost £65,000 as a yearling, and is by the owner's dual Guineas hero Cockney Rebel, out of a dam who won over 5f as a 2yo. Slowly into stride, he was soon in a prominent place and came home a good winner once Michael Hills asked his mount to lengthen. It remains to be seen what he has beaten, but one would imagine the Coventry Stakes will be next for him. (op 7-1)
Newstead Abbey, whose dam is closely related to the useful sprinter Leap For Joy, who is from the family of high-class sprinter College Chapel, kept on in pleasing style after racing a little greenly at times. His trainer also has the exciting New Pearl, so he ought to have a rough idea where he stands with Funk Soul Brother if both head to Ascot. (op 13-2)
Artigiano(USA), the first foal of a dual 4yo winner in the US, was the first juvenile runner of the season for the stable and he posted a solid debut after being given time to get into the contest. He will be of obvious interest next time. (op 7-1)
Star Of Rohm, a 32,000gns half-brother to a few winners, was in prime position 2f out and kept on gamely all the way to the line. He can win any ordinary maiden. (op 20-1)
Red Paladin(IRE) ran green and can do better. (op 16-1)
Bispham Green was another to run green and should benefit from the experience. (op 8-1)
Wynyard Boy is an interesting prospect considering he's a £21,000 half-brother to this year's Fred Darling winner Moonstone Magic. His effort wasn't without promise despite his finishing position, and he's another who'll derive plenty for his initial experience.
Dust Whirl had been placed in 5f maidens but dropped out alarmingly here when the pack surrounded him. His jockey wasn't hard on him once it was obvious he had no more to give and reported the colt ran flat. Official explanation: jockey said that the colt ran flat (op 10-3)

2214 INVESTEC SPECIALIST BANK STKS (H'CAP) 2m 2f

4:45 (4:45) (Class 4) (0-80,80) 4-Y-0+ **£7,762** (£2,310; £1,154; £577) **Stalls** Low

Form RPR

3-31 1 **Cloudy Spirit**[37] 1272 7-9-4 72 TonyCulhane 6 84
(Reg Hollinshead) *hld up towards rr: hdwy on inner over 3f out: chal wl over 1f out: sn rdn: drvn and kpt on to ld last 150yds: gamely* **13/2**[2]

2-22 2 *nk* **Dark Ranger**[91] 577 6-9-11 79 EddieAhern 15 91
(Tim Pitt) *lw: in tch: smooth hdwy 4f out: led over 2f out: sn jnd and rdn wl over 1f out: drvn ent fnl f: edgd lft and hdd last 150yds: no ex nr fin* **8/1**[3]

3 *8* **Bruslini (FR)**[51] 7-9-12 80 GrahamLee 11 83
(Brian Ellison) *led: rdn along over 3f out: hdd over 2f out: sn drvn and kpt on same pce* **16/1**

316- 4 *3 ¼* **Orsippus (USA)**[34] 7139 6-9-3 71 JoeFanning 9 70
(Michael Smith) *midfield: hdwy over 4f out: rdn to chse ldrs over 2f out: drvn and one pce fr wl over 1f out* **12/1**

64-1 5 *7* **Secret Tune**[20] 1640 8-9-11 79 (t) AdamKirby 16 71
(Charlie Longsdon) *hld up in rr: hdwy over 5f out: rdn and in tch wl over 2f out: sn drvn and n.d* **12/1**

500/ 6 *2 ½* **Cape Tribulation**[35] 7018 8-9-12 80 JimmyFortune 7 69
(Malcolm Jefferson) *lw: hld up towards rr: stdy hdwy 7f out: chsd ldrs 3f out: sn rdn and no imp* **5/2**[1]

0-02 7 *½* **Lady Amakhala**[20] 1640 4-9-7 78 AndrewMullen 14 66
(George Moore) *prom: cl up 5f out: rdn over 3f out: drvn over 2f out and sn wknd* **25/1**

4434 8 *1 ½* **Bedouin Bay**[20] 1640 5-9-2 70 (p) DanielTudhope 10 57
(Alan McCabe) *prom: rdn along 4f out: drvn wl over 2f out: grad wknd* **25/1**

40-1 9 *½* **Mr Crystal (FR)**[24] 1559 8-9-1 72 DaleSwift(3) 1 58
(Micky Hammond) *hld up: a in rr* **20/1**

600/ 10 *4* **Kayf Aramis**[28] 6926 10-9-5 80 (b) WilliamTwiston-Davies(7) 13 62
(Nigel Twiston-Davies) *midfield: sme hdwy 7f out: rdn and in tch over 4f out: wknd 3f out* **20/1**

0511 11 *hd* **Lifetime (IRE)**[12] 1850 4-9-0 78 DarrenEgan(7) 2 60
(Brian Ellison) *hld up towards rr: sme hdwy over 4f out: sn rdn and n.d* **12/1**

-433 12 *4 ½* **Sohcahtoa (IRE)**[12] 1846 6-8-13 72 LMcNiff(5) 12 49
(David Barron) *hld up: hdwy over 5f out: rdn along 4f out: nvr a factor* **12/1**

06/2 13 *8* **Dorset Square (IRE)**[8] 1991 8-9-3 71 (t) RichardMullen 5 39
(Sarah Humphrey) *a towards rr* **33/1**

00-3 14 *9* **Alsahil (USA)**[26] 1525 6-9-1 74 GarryWhillans(5) 4 32
(Micky Hammond) *chsd ldrs on inner: rdn along wl over 3f out: sn wknd* **33/1**

0-14 15 *13* **Zefooha (FR)**[28] 1485 8-9-4 72 (p) GrahamGibbons 18 16
(Tim Walford) *trckd ldrs: rdn along over 4f out: sn wknd* **33/1**

10-0 16 *19* **Hollins**[39] 1239 8-9-11 79 FrederikTylicki 17
(Micky Hammond) *midfield: rdn along 7f out: sn lost pl and bhd fnl 3f* **20/1**

14-1 17 *10* **Priceless Art (IRE)**[57] 902 7-9-10 78 RobertWinston 8
(Alan Swinbank) *midfield: rdn along 1/2-way: hdwy to chse ldrs 7f out: wknd 5f out: bhd fnl 3f* **20/1**

3m 56.85s (1.45) **Going Correction** +0.20s/f (Good)
WFA 4 from 5yo+ 3lb 17 Ran SP% **125.2**
Speed ratings (Par 105): **104,103,100,98,95 94,94,93,93,91 91,89,86,82,76 67,63**
toteswingers:1&2:£4.10, 2&3:£26.20, 1&3:£28.20 CSF £49.76 CT £807.62 TOTE £7.30: £1.70, £2.10, £3.70, £2.40; EX 46.10 Trifecta £1793.40 Pool: £2423.56 - 1.00 winning units..
Owner Mrs Norma Harris **Bred** Mrs Norma Harris **Trained** Upper Longdon, Staffs
■ Stewards' Enquiry : Eddie Ahern eleven-day ban: use of whip (1-9 June, 11-12 June)
Tony Culhane two-day ban: use of whip (31 May and June 3)

FOCUS
Only a fair long-distance handicap but pretty competitive, with just 10lb covering the entire field on ratings. The first two came clear and they finished well strung out, but the riders of the front pair both incurred bans for their use of the whip. The winner improved her Flat form in line with the jumps.
Priceless Art(IRE) Official explanation: jockey said that the gelding was never travelling
T/Jkpt: £11,875.80 to a £1 stake. Pool of £91,996.36 - 5.50 winning tickets. T/Plt: £50.10 to a £1 stake. Pool of £211,529.19 - 3,079.13 winning tickets. T/Qpdt: £14.60 to a £1 stake. Pool of £9,126.33 - 462.55 winning tickets. JR

2215 - 2221a (Foreign Racing) - See Raceform Interactive

BADEN-BADEN (L-H)

Thursday, May 17

OFFICIAL GOING: Turf: good to soft

2222a BADENER MEILE (GROUP 3) (3YO+) (TURF) 1m

6:00 (6:08) 3-Y-O+

£26,666 (£9,166; £4,583; £2,500; £1,666; £1,250)

RPR

1 **Worthadd (IRE)**[228] 6566 5-9-6 0 MircoDemuro 2 116+
(Sir Mark Prescott Bt) *sn trcking ldr in 2nd: impr to chal gng wl 2f out: rdn to ld over 1f out and qcknd clr: kpt on under hands and heels ins fnl f: easily* **2/5**[1]

2 *2 ½* **Neatico (GER)**[32] 1410 5-9-2 0 AStarke 6 106
(P Schiergen, Germany) *prom on outer: rdn to try and chal over 2f out: kpt on at one pce ins fnl 1 1/2f: wnt 2nd ins fnl 100yds: no ch w wnr* **66/10**[3]

3 *shd* **Sir Oscar (GER)**[14] 1809 5-9-2 0 JBojko 5 106
(T Potters, Germany) *slow to stride: hld up in last pair: rdn to improve over 2f out: r.o to go 3rd cl home* **144/10**

4 *1 ½* **Gereon (GER)**[18] 4-9-2 0 DPorcu 8 103
(C Zschache, Germany) *got across fr wd draw to ld: rdn 2f out: sn hdd: kpt on one pce: lost 2 pls ins fnl 100yds* **173/10**

5 *2* **Nafar (GER)**[18] 4-9-2 0 APietsch 7 98
(W Hickst, Germany) *midfield on outer: rdn to try and improve on turn into st: outpcd over 1 1/2f out: plugged on* **101/10**

6 *1 ¾* **Eigelstein**[32] 1410 4-9-2 0 FilipMinarik 1 94
(P Schiergen, Germany) *prom on inner: rdn over 2 1/2f out: no ex and btn over 1f out: fdd* **171/10**

7 *5* **Point Blank (GER)**[32] 1410 4-9-2 0 THellier 3 82
(Mario Hofer, Germany) *midfield on inner: rdn 2 1/2f out: no ex over 1f out: fdd* **107/10**

8 *1 ¾* **Ferro Sensation (GER)**[18] 6-9-0 0 ADeVries 4 76
(J Pubben, Holland) *v.s.a: hld up in last: rdn and outpcd over 2f out: plugged on: nvr a factor* **59/10**[2]

1m 37.74s (-1.37) 8 Ran SP% **134.1**
WIN (incl. 10 euro stake): 14. PLACES: 11, 13, 16. SF: 51.
Owner Diego Romeo **Bred** Compagnia Generale S R L **Trained** Newmarket, Suffolk

NOTEBOOK
Worthadd(IRE), debuting for Sir Mark Prescott, was ridden by Mirco Demuro, who rode him when trained in Italy. He had plenty in hand of his nearest rivals on official figures and won with the minimum of fuss. He should come on for the outing and has plenty of options between a mile and 1m2f.

2223 - (Foreign Racing) - See Raceform Interactive

2032 HAMILTON (R-H)

Friday, May 18

OFFICIAL GOING: Good to soft (soft in places; 6.6)
Fresh ground provided and races of one mile and beyond reduced by approximately 54yds.
Wind: Fresh, across Weather: Overcast, showers

2224 BRITISH STALLION STUDS SUPPORTING BRITISH RACING E B F MAIDEN STKS 5f 4y

5:45 (5:47) (Class 5) 2-Y-O **£3,234** (£962; £481; £240) **Stalls** High

Form RPR

5 1 **Lasilia (IRE)**[25] 1556 2-8-9 0 JulieBurke(3) 3 77+
(Kevin Ryan) *trckd ldrs: shkn up and hdwy to ld over 1f out: drew clr fnl f: readily* **11/4**[2]

03 2 *4* **Princess In Exile**[25] 1556 2-8-12 0 DuranFentiman 2 63
(George Foster) *trckd ldr: rdn and ev ch 2f out: chsd (clr) wnr ins fnl f: no imp* **10/1**

3 **3** *1* **Opt Out**[7] 2039 2-9-3 0 JoeFanning 4 64
(Mark Johnston) *led tl rdn and hdd over 1f out: one pce whn lost 2nd ins fnl f* **8/11**[1]

4 *4* **Oh Boy Oh Boy** 2-9-0 0 PaddyAspell 5 48+
(James Moffatt) *taken steadily to post: s.i.s: rn green and a outpcd* **18/1**

F **Finalize** 2-8-9 0 TomEaves 1
(Bryan Smart) *s.i.s: bhd and outpcd: struggling whn fell 1/2-way* **8/1**[3]

1m 4.83s (4.83) **Going Correction** +0.625s/f (Yiel) **5** Ran SP% **110.0**
Speed ratings (Par 93): **86,79,78,71,**
CSF £26.16 TOTE £4.50: £2.20, £2.70; EX 31.00.

Owner Ms Fionnuala Garvey **Bred** B Cloney **Trained** Hambleton, N Yorks

FOCUS
An overcast, dry, cool evening, and while the pace was solid for this juvenile sprint maiden, the time suggested the ground was riding a little slower than advertised. They came up the stands' side. The quality of the field was probably not up to the standard of subsequent Royal Ascot scorers Bapak Chinta and Frederick Engels, who contested last year's finish, or subsequent juvenile Listed scorer Corporal Maddox who won this in 2009, but the winner might be decent. The runner-up helps with the level.

NOTEBOOK
Lasilia(IRE) produced a thoroughly professional performance. From the stable who won this last year with the subsequent Norfolk Stakes winner, she had clearly benefited from her debut and, after tracking the leading pair, drew readily clear under the minimum of persuasion. This daughter of Acclamation had age on her side (January foal) but should handle a step up in class and will get further. (op 3-1)

Princess In Exile finished in front of the winner at Pontefract but it was a muddling affair and she looked flattered by her proximity to the winner. She improved from that and shaped well after racing a little keenly early on, but had no chance with the winner. She can win in novice company. (op 8-1)

Opt Out had been well backed on his Lingfield AW debut a week ago, when beaten 2l by a rival with experience. Well backed again, he appearing to have improved mentally for that experience and should not have been inconvenienced by switching to an easy turf surface, but he hung away from the rail in the early stages. He will get better with age (a May 15 foal), certainly improve over further and should make a useful handicapper. (op 10-11 tchd evens in places)

Oh Boy Oh Boy was taken to the start by a handler and missed the break. Very green in the early stages, he stayed on quite well. He needs more time. (op 14-1)

Finalize, the first foal of 5f juvenile winning dam Choisette, looked a neat, compact sort. She broke slowly and suffered a crashing fall when taking a misstep at half-way and broke her pelvis. (op 15-2)

2225 ELECTROLUX (S) H'CAP 6f 5y
6:15 (6:17) (Class 6) (0-60,58) 3-5-Y-O £2,045 (£603; £302) **Stalls** High

Form RPR

1 **1** **Hopes N Dreams (IRE)**[7] 2046 4-9-6 **55** JulieBurke(3) 9 77
(Tony Coyle) *prom: niggled 1/2-way: smooth hdwy to ld wl over 1f out: pushed along and sn clr: eased nr fin: readily* **11/10**[1]

3024 **2** *7* **Flow Chart (IRE)**[9] 1987 5-9-1 **47** RobbieFitzpatrick 11 47
(Peter Grayson) *dwlt: hld up: hdwy and swtchd rt over 1f out: chsd (clr) wnr ins fnl f: no imp* **10/1**

300- **3** *2* **Cheeky Wee Red**[225] 6646 4-9-3 **49** DavidNolan 5 42
(Richard Fahey) *in tch: drvn along and chsd wnr over 1f out to ins fnl f: no ex* **9/1**[3]

0-35 **4** *shd* **Coastal Passage**[10] 1961 4-9-4 **50** (tp) StevieDonohoe 3 43
(Richard Guest) *in tch on outside: effrt and rdn 2 out: btn ins fnl f* **12/1**

00-2 **5** *6* **Circuitous**[15] 1801 4-9-12 **58** (b) JoeFanning 6 32
(Keith Dalgleish) *disp ld to wl over 1f out: sn rdn and wknd* **5/1**[2]

0400 **6** *1 1/4* **Mark Anthony (IRE)**[14] 1823 5-9-5 **56** (p) DeanHeslop(5) 7 26
(Shaun Harris) *chsd ldrs: drvn and hung rt 1/2-way: sn wknd* **9/1**[3]

00-6 **7** *3 1/2* **Tinzo (IRE)**[7] 2036 4-8-6 **45** MatthewHopkins(7) 10
(Alan Berry) *in tch: rdn along 1/2-way: btn over 1f out* **40/1**

030- **8** *1 3/4* **Crabbies Ginger**[320] 3661 4-9-5 **51** PaddyAspell 4
(Lisa Williamson) *hld up: struggling over 2f out: sn btn* **50/1**

006- **9** *2 1/4* **Look'N'Listen (IRE)**[480] 281 4-8-13 **45** DuranFentiman 1
(Ian Semple) *wnt bdly rt s: sn led on outside: edgd lft and hdd wl over 1f out: sn wknd* **28/1**

-053 **10** *3 1/4* **Abernethy (IRE)**[7] 2034 4-8-13 **45** (bt) TomEaves 8
(Linda Perratt) *s.i.s: bhd: struggling over 2f out: sn btn* **14/1**

1m 16.38s (4.18) **Going Correction** +0.625s/f (Yiel) **10** Ran SP% **115.6**
Speed ratings (Par 101): **97,87,85,84,76 75,70,68,65,60**
toteswingers:1&2:£4.30, 1&3:£4.00, 2&3:£12.40 CSF £12.91 CT £70.86 TOTE £2.00: £1.10, £2.80, £3.10; EX 13.40.The winner was bought in for £8,000.

Owner Matt & Lauren Morgan **Bred** J & Mrs Brennan & Edward & Mrs O'Regan **Trained** Norton, N Yorks

■ Stewards' Enquiry : Dean Heslop one-day ban; careless riding (1st June)

FOCUS
A weak seller run at a fair pace, but they finished strung out and very tired. The winner confirmed her Nottingham improvement and the form could be underrated.

Mark Anthony(IRE) Official explanation: jockey said gelding hung right throughoutr.

2226 HAPPY BIRTHDAY DUNCAN FERGUSON OPEN MAIDEN STKS 1m 1f 36y
6:50 (6:50) (Class 5) 3-Y-O+ £3,234 (£962; £481; £240) **Stalls** Low

Form RPR

2-2 **1** **Fortieth And Fifth (IRE)**[20] 1676 3-9-0 0 StevieDonohoe 4 87
(Michael Bell) *sn trcking ldr: led over 3f out: rdn clr fr over 1f out* **10/11**[1]

2 *5* **Moratab (IRE)** 3-9-0 0 TomEaves 5 75
(Roger Varian) *in tch: hdwy to chse wnr over 2f out: sn rdn: outpcd fr over 1f out* **10/3**[2]

5 **3** *4 1/2* **Star Deal (IRE)**[13] 1864 3-9-0 0 AndrewElliott 1 65
(Alan Swinbank) *t.k.h: trckd ldrs: rdn over 2f out: outpcd wl over 1f out* **13/2**

4 *11* **Itstooearly**[119] 9-9-8 0 PaddyAspell 3 38
(James Moffatt) *missed break: sn in tch: struggling over 4f out: sn btn* **100/1**

0 **5** *19* **Bryer (IRE)**[18] 1704 3-9-0 0 JoeFanning 2
(Mark Johnston) *led at modest gallop: rdn and hdd over 3f out: wknd 2f out* **4/1**[3]

2m 8.45s (8.75) **Going Correction** +1.05s/f (Soft)
WFA 3 from 9yo 13lb **5** Ran SP% **109.8**
Speed ratings (Par 103): **103,98,94,84,67**
CSF £4.23 TOTE £1.80: £1.10, £3.00; EX 4.00.

Owner Colin Bryce **Bred** Airlie Stud **Trained** Newmarket, Suffolk

FOCUS
The very soft ground again made life very difficult for the participants and the time was slow. They finished strung out but the form of the first two should work out, although this was a weakish race.

2227 GOOD LUCK TO HEARTS TOMORROW H'CAP 1m 65y
7:25 (7:27) (Class 5) (0-75,72) 4-Y-0+ £3,408 (£1,006; £503) **Stalls** Low

Form RPR

0532 **1** **Copperwood**[6] 2083 7-8-13 **64** JoeFanning 5 72
(Mark Johnston) *trckd ldrs: hdwy and ev ch over 2f out: sn rdn: led ins fnl f: r.o* **11/4**[1]

36-3 **2** *1/2* **Free Art**[39] 1251 4-9-1 **66** SilvestreDeSousa 6 73
(Geoffrey Harker) *prom: hdwy on outside to ld over 2f out: rdn and edgd rt over 1f out: hdd ins fnl f: kpt on: hld nr fin* **4/1**[2]

0-33 **3** *3* **Coral Sands (IRE)**[101] 457 4-8-7 **58** AndrewElliott 1 58
(Alan Swinbank) *t.k.h: led: rdn over 3f out: hung lft and hdd over 2f out: rallied over 1f out: kpt on fnl f* **9/2**[3]

11-0 **4** *1 1/4* **Botham (USA)**[14] 1820 8-9-7 **72** GrahamLee 7 69
(Jim Goldie) *hld up in tch: rdn and outpcd over 2f out: rallied over 1f: nt pce to chal* **5/1**

000- **5** *hd* **High Resolution**[246] 6079 5-9-4 **69** TomEaves 8 66
(Linda Perratt) *s.i.s: hld up: stdy hdwy whn nt clr run over 2f out: effrt wl over 1f out: no ex fnl f* **8/1**

2010 **6** *5* **Just Five (IRE)**[22] 1636 6-9-2 **67** (v) DuranFentiman 4 52
(John Weymes) *pressed ldr: ev ch 3f out: wknd 2f out* **14/1**

6P-0 **7** *1 1/2* **Mangham (IRE)**[15] 1796 7-8-13 **64** (p) PaddyAspell 3 46
(George Foster) *missed break: sn rcvrd and hld up in tch: effrt over 2f out: wknd over 1f out* **10/1**

4410 **8** *7* **Goal (IRE)**[15] 1769 4-9-7 **72** (t) RobbieFitzpatrick 2 38
(Richard Guest) *plld hrd in tch: swtchd to r alone stands' rail bnd over 5f out: rdn and wknd over 3f out* **25/1**

1m 56.12s (7.72) **Going Correction** +1.05s/f (Soft) **8** Ran SP% **112.2**
Speed ratings (Par 103): **103,102,99,98,98 93,91,84**
toteswingers:1&2:£2.60, 1&3:£1.90, 2&3:£5.20 CSF £13.19 CT £46.33 TOTE £4.20: £2.00, £1.10, £1.50; EX 12.80.

Owner Always Trying Partnership VIII (E) **Bred** Hertford Offset Press **Trained** Middleham Moor, N Yorks

■ Stewards' Enquiry : Robbie Fitzpatrick one-day ban; careless riding (14th June)

FOCUS
A reasonable handicap run at a fair pace for the conditions and the market leaders were all to the fore. The front pair drew a little way clear and the form looks solid. The winner looks better than ever.

2228 WILLIAM HILL BRAVEHEART H'CAP (LISTED RACE) 1m 4f 17y
8:00 (8:07) (Class 1) (0-110,108) 4-Y-O+£23,680 (£8,956; £4,476; £2,236) **Stalls** Low

Form RPR

-251 **1** **Ithoughtitwasover (IRE)**[12] 1882 4-8-10 **94** 3ex SilvestreDeSousa 5 101+
(Mark Johnston) *trckd ldr: led gng wl over 2f out: pushed along and qcknd clr ins fnl f: kpt on strly: eased cl home* **15/8**[1]

/0-0 **2** *1 3/4* **Hillview Boy (IRE)**[48] 1139 8-8-10 **94** oh1 GrahamLee 6 96
(Jim Goldie) *t.k.h: hld up: hdwy on outside over 1f out: sn rdn: chsd (clr) wnr ins fnl f: kpt on: no imp* **9/1**

20-3 **3** *1/2* **Creme Anglaise**[13] 1848 4-8-10 **94** oh3 StevieDonohoe 7 95
(Michael Bell) *t.k.h: hld up in tch: effrt and swtchd lft over 1f out: kpt on fnl f: nvr able to chal* **12/1**

000- **4** *1 1/4* **Constant Contact**[25] 6339 5-8-10 **94** oh1 PaddyAspell 4 93
(Donald McCain) *led at stdy pce: rdn and hdd over 2f out: rallied: nt qckn fnl f* **9/1**

62-3 **5** *1 3/4* **Bridge Of Gold (USA)**[27] 1507 6-9-8 **106** GeorgeBaker 3 102
(Mikael Magnusson) *t.k.h: trckd ldrs: rdn and edgd rt 2f out: outpcd appr fnl f* **2/1**[2]

034- **6** *14* **Laaheb**[170] 7584 6-9-9 **107** TomEaves 2 81
(Roger Varian) *trckd ldrs: rdn over 3f out: wknd 2f out* **5/1**[3]

2m 49.05s (10.45) **Going Correction** +1.05s/f (Soft) **6** Ran SP% **112.5**
Speed ratings (Par 111): **107,105,105,104,103 94**
toteswingers:1&2:£2.80, 1&3:£5.00, 2&3:£12.00 CSF £18.80 TOTE £2.10: £1.40, £3.20; EX 11.20.

Owner Crone Stud Farms Ltd **Bred** Stonethorn Stud Farms Ltd **Trained** Middleham Moor, N Yorks

FOCUS
A decent and competitive handicap, despite the withdrawal of top weight Gulf Of Naples owing to the testing ground, but not strong form for the grade. There was very little pace and it was not a truly run affair, but while the form of the beaten horses may not be reliable, the winner was deeply impressive and should go on to much better things.

NOTEBOOK
Ithoughtitwasover(IRE) followed up his Newmarket victory 12 days ago in tremendous style. Always just off the pacesetter, his rider barely had to move a muscle and was oozing confidence with 2f to run when hitting the front. He had to be shaken up to fend off the staying-on runner-up but he was never in danger. He goes up 7lb today, and was 4lb well in here and won with much more than that in hand. He is clearly a horse going places and will get further. (op 7-4 tchd 2-1)

Hillview Boy(IRE) stayed on really well from way off the pace, looking back to the sort of form that saw him win this race two years ago his last success and was running off a mark 1lb lower than that mark (his last success). He is eight now and while relatively lightly raced - his only run last season was when well beaten in the Ebor at York - he won't be up to this level for much longer, but this was more like it. (op 17-2)

Creme Anglaise was running from well out of the weights but she really caught the eye, staying on very well. This was a marked improvement on her seasonal debut and she may still be improving.

Constant Contact set the pace, such as it was, but didn't have the turn of foot to live with the winner over this trip and may have been seen in a better light with more forcing tactics. (op 16-1)

Bridge Of Gold(USA) had been placed in the Group 3 John Porter at Newbury last time and was subsequently well backed. However, the ground was patently too soft for him and he tired quickly. he is better than this. (op 5-2)

Laaheb does not appear to be the force of old and has something to prove. The ground should not have been an issue, but this was his first run of the season, so an excuse can be made on that score. (op 4-1 tchd 11-2)

2229 GOOD LUCK TO HIBS TOMORROW H'CAP 6f 5y
8:35 (8:36) (Class 4) (0-85,83) 3-Y-O £5,175 (£1,540; £769; £384) **Stalls** High

Form RPR

-362 **1** **Galician**[9] 1983 3-9-0 **76** JoeFanning 6 85
(Mark Johnston) *chsd ldrs: drvn over 2f out: hdwy over 1f out: led ins fnl f: edgd lft and kpt on wl cl home* **4/1**[1]

106- **2** *nk* **Our Boy Jack (IRE)**[224] 6670 3-8-5 **67** SilvestreDeSousa 9 75+
(Richard Fahey) *hld up: pushed along over 3f out: hdwy whn nt clr run wl over 1f out: styd on fnl f: tk 2nd cl home* **6/1**[3]

1560 **3** *nse* **Dubai Sunshine (IRE)**[18] 1721 3-9-1 **77** StevieDonohoe 3 85
(Michael Bell) *hld up: effrt and hdwy over 1f out: chsd wnr ins fnl f tl no ex cl home* **16/1**

21-0 **4** 2 ¾ **Desert Philosopher**[30] 1457 3-9-1 **80**.......... JulieBurke(3) 7 79
(Kevin Ryan) *chsd ldr: led over 2f out to ins fnl f: nt qckn* **11/2**[2]
2-13 **5** nk **Joshua The First**[15] 1798 3-8-11 **73**.......... LeeNewman 8 71
(Keith Dalgleish) *trckd ldrs: rdn over 2f out: edgd lft and no ex over 1f out* **8/1**
5426 **6** ¾ **I'll Be Good**[13] 1858 3-9-7 **83**.......... GrahamLee 1 79
(Robert Johnson) *hld up: hdwy and swtchd rt wl over 1f out: sn rdn: no imp fnl f* **13/2**
05-0 **7** nk **Bop It**[38] 1271 3-9-4 **80**.......... TomEaves 4 75
(Bryan Smart) *t.k.h: led to over 2f out: rallied and ev ch to ins fnl f: no ex* **16/1**
2-03 **8** 15 **See Clearly**[21] 1639 3-8-13 **75**..........(p) DuranFentiman 10 22
(Tim Easterby) *in tch: rdn over 2f out: wknd wl over 1f out* **16/1**
-051 **9** ¾ **Rock Canyon (IRE)**[7] 2036 3-8-2 **64** 6ex.......... PaulQuinn 2
(Linda Perratt) *prom: drvn over 2f out: wknd wl over 1f out* **14/1**

1m 15.68s (3.48) **Going Correction** +0.625s/f (Yiel) **9** Ran SP% **98.4**
Speed ratings (Par 101): **101,100,100,96,96 95,95,75,74**
toteswingers:1&2:£4.00, 1&3:£11.30, 2&3:£15.50 CSF £20.02 CT £212.34 TOTE £3.10: £1.70, £2.00, £4.00; EX 21.20.
Owner Sheikh Hamdan Bin Mohammed Al Maktoum **Bred** Darley **Trained** Middleham Moor, N Yorks
■ Stewards' Enquiry : Lee Newman one-day ban; careless riding (14th June)

FOCUS
A good sprint handicap for the money and run at a solid time for the conditions. It produced a tight finish and form looks sound. The winner ran to his latest AW form.

2230 SAINTS & SINNERS RACENIGHT H'CAP 5f 4y
9:10 (9:16) (Class 5) (0-75,75) 4-Y-0+ **£3,234** (£962; £481; £240) **Stalls** High

Form RPR
00-2 **1** **Breezolini**[12] 1875 4-8-13 **65**.......... SilvestreDeSousa 10 75
(Geoffrey Harker) *cl up: drvn 1/2-way: hdwy to ld ins fnl f: kpt on strly* **5/2**[1]
1112 **2** ¾ **First In Command (IRE)**[10] 1954 7-8-12 **69**..........(t) MarkCoumbe(5) 1 76
(Daniel Mark Loughnane) *hld up in tch on outside: smooth hdwy over 1f out: ev ch and rdn ins fnl f: edgd lft: kpt on: hld cl home* **6/1**
-531 **3** 1 ½ **Crimson Knot (IRE)**[7] 2037 4-9-2 **75** 6ex.......... MatthewHopkins(7) 3 77+
(Alan Berry) *hld up: effrt whn nt clr run over 1f out: swtchd rt and styd on fnl f: nrst fin* **5/1**[3]
0-02 **4** shd **Weetentherty**[7] 2037 5-8-2 **54** oh2.......... DuranFentiman 6 56
(Linda Perratt) *prom: effrt and rdn over 1f out: ev ch whn hmpd ins fnl f: kpt on towards fin* **28/1**
25-0 **5** nk **Cayman Fox**[12] 1881 7-8-4 **59**.......... JulieBurke(3) 2 59
(Linda Perratt) *led and sn clr: rdn and hdd ins fnl f: kpt on same pce* **22/1**
2442 **6** ½ **Angelo Poliziano**[4] 2122 6-9-7 **73**..........(p) LeeNewman 5 72
(George Foster) *missed break: bhd: hdwy to chse ldrs over 1f out: kpt on same pce fnl f* **14/1**
0-00 **7** 4 ½ **The Nifty Fox**[13] 1868 8-9-3 **69**..........(p) TomEaves 11 58+
(Tim Easterby) *chsd clr ldr to over 1f out: one pce whn hmpd ins fnl f* **8/1**
-152 **8** 1 ¼ **Bouncy Bouncy (IRE)**[9] 1990 5-9-7 **73**..........(t) StevieDonohoe 7 58+
(Michael Bell) *hld up in tch: rdn over 2f out: nvr able to chal: eased whn btn ins fnl f* **11/4**[2]
3020 **9** 8 **Vhujon (IRE)**[29] 1481 7-8-8 **60**.......... RobbieFitzpatrick 9
(Peter Grayson) *bhd: rdn and hung rt fr over 2f out: nvr on terms* **28/1**

1m 3.63s (3.63) **Going Correction** +0.625s/f (Yiel) **9** Ran SP% **115.2**
Speed ratings (Par 103): **95,93,91,91,90 89,82,80,67**
toteswingers:1&2:£4.60, 1&3:£1.90, 2&3:£6.50 CSF £17.46 CT £67.97 TOTE £3.20: £1.40, £2.30, £2.20; EX 24.20.
Owner P Macklam **Bred** Hellwood Stud Farm **Trained** Thirkleby, N Yorks
■ Stewards' Enquiry : Duran Fentiman three-day ban; careless riding (3rd-5th June)

FOCUS
A modest sprint finale and the money spoke correctly. The winner is basically rated to his old best.
Bouncy Bouncy(IRE) Official explanation: jockey said mare lost her action.
T/Plt: £32.50 to a £1 stake. Pool:£44,648.51 - 1,000.76 winning tickets T/Qpdt: £3.70 to a £1 stake. Pool:£4,296.58 - 836.82 winning tickets RY

1506 NEWBURY (L-H)
Friday, May 18

OFFICIAL GOING: Round course - good to soft; straight course - good (good to soft in places)
Rails set out wide so Round course 8m longer than advertised.
Wind: Moderate behind Weather: Whire cloud

2231 HILDON MAIDEN STKS 6f 8y
1:40 (1:42) (Class 4) 2-Y-0 **£3,881** (£1,155; £577; £288) **Stalls** Centre

Form RPR
1 **Sir Patrick Moore (FR)** 2-9-3 0.......... HayleyTurner 15 77
(Harry Dunlop) *disp ld tl slt ld 1f out: hdd fnl 120yds: rallied to ld again clsng stages* **40/1**
2 ½ **Pay Freeze (IRE)** 2-9-3 0.......... MartinHarley 2 76
(Mick Channon) *chsd ldrs: drvn to chal 1f out: styd upsides tl slt advantage fnl 120yds: hdd and one pce clsng stages* **12/1**[2]
4 **3** 1 ¼ **Mysterial**[12] 1886 2-9-3 0.......... RichardHughes 4 72
(Richard Hannon) *in rr but in tch: drvn and hdwy 2f out: styd on to take 3rd jst ins fnl f: kpt on but no imp fnl 120yds* **8/11**[1]
4 3 ¾ **Lawful** 2-9-3 0.......... GeorgeBaker 9 61
(Paul Fitzsimons) *chsd ldrs: rdn over 2f out: styd on same pce fnl f* **66/1**
5 ¾ **Walter White (IRE)** 2-9-3 0.......... JimmyFortune 1 58
(Andrew Balding) *disp ld: rdn 2f out: bmpd appr fnl f and wknd sn after* **12/1**[2]
6 hd **Knight Charm** 2-9-3 0.......... JohnFahy 3 58
(Eve Johnson Houghton) *t.k.h: chsd ldrs: ev ch 2f out: green: edgd lft and wknd appr fnl f* **66/1**
7 shd **Freeport** 2-9-3 0.......... DarryllHolland 8 57
(Brian Meehan) *chsd ldrs: rdn and one pce 2f out: kpt on again clsng stages* **33/1**
8 shd **Cappadocia (IRE)** 2-9-3 0.......... PatCosgrave 13 57
(Mick Channon) *in rr: hdwy 3f out: kpt on fnl f but nvr a threat* **33/1**
9 ¾ **Silver Ridge (IRE)** 2-9-3 0.......... RichardThomas 7 55
(Ralph Beckett) *broke wl: sn dropped to rr: kpt on again fnl f* **14/1**[3]
10 nse **Star Breaker** 2-9-3 0.......... JamesDoyle 12 55
(Sylvester Kirk) *hld up in rr: pushed along over 2f out: sme prog fnl f* **16/1**
11 2 **Secret Symphony** 2-9-3 0.......... LiamKeniry 10 49+
(Sylvester Kirk) *in rr: sme prog over 2f out: nvr rchd ldrs* **40/1**
12 1 **Gold Roll (IRE)** 2-9-3 0.......... MarcHalford 6 46
(David Elsworth) *in rr: sme hdwy over 2f out: sn outpcd* **50/1**
13 6 **Secret Sign** 2-9-3 0.......... TadhgO'Shea 11 28
(Brian Meehan) *chsd ldrs over 3f* **40/1**
14 ½ **Nelsons Dockyard (USA)** 2-9-3 0.......... TomQueally 14 26
(Paul Cole) *s.i.s: outpcd* **14/1**[3]
15 9 **Bix (IRE)** 2-9-3 0.......... MickaelBarzalona 5
(Brian Meehan) *slowly away: rcvrd and in tch 1/2-way: sn green and wknd* **12/1**[2]

1m 16.2s (3.20) **Going Correction** +0.325s/f (Good) **15** Ran SP% **118.3**
Speed ratings (Par 95): **91,90,88,83,82 82,82,82,81,81 78,77,69,68,56**
Tote Swingers: 1&2 £41.70, 1&3 £18.70, 2&3 £5.00 CSF £440.27 TOTE £54.20: £8.30, £3.70, £1.10; EX 1443.10.
Owner The Astronomers **Bred** S F Bloodstock LLC **Trained** Lambourn, Berks

FOCUS
This is often a strong maiden and winners will doubtless emerge from this year's running, a lot of these looking sure to improve for the experience. However it was steadily run, in a time over five seconds outside standard, and it proved difficult to make ground from off the pace.

NOTEBOOK
Sir Patrick Moore(FR) was his trainer's first juvenile runner this year. He was always close up and knuckled down well to master the runner-up close home. The first foal of a 1m Listed winner in France, he qualifies for some lucrative premiums in that country so could be campaigned over there. (op 33-1)
Pay Freeze(IRE), a relatively cheap 7,500gns as a yearling, is a half-brother to winners out of an unraced sister to the smart My Branch. He did nothing wrong and looked likely to succeed 100 yards out before the winner fought back. His trainer's 2yos this year have been winning second time out and this one, who is not the biggest, could well follow suit. (op 10-1)
Mysterial, whose trainer Richard Hannon has won this maiden in recent years with Canford Cliffs and Strong Suit, was a highly promising fourth on his debut at Newmarket. He had the edge on experience on all his rivals and the extra furlong appeared in his favour. However, after coming under pressure he took a while to pick up and, although he was running on nicely, he was not going to reach the first two. The lack of a true gallop was against him here and a maiden should soon come his way. (op 5-6 tchd 10-11)
Lawful, a half-brother to Listed 5f scorer Sarson out of an Ayr Gold Cup winner, carried the owner's second colours. He was soon towards the fore and stuck on for fourth, although the principals pulled away from him late on.
Walter White(IRE)'s pedigree and he showed speed until fading in the final furlong, shortly after receiving a bump. (op 11-1 tchd 10-1)
Knight Charm, a half-brother to smart sprinter Morache Music, was one of four in line across the track over a furlong out befoer weakening. He had been rather keen.
Freeport, whose dam is a half-sister to Derby winner High-Rise, did best of his trainer's three runners. (op 28-1)
Secret Symphony will do better. (op 100-1)

2232 SWETTENHAM STUD FILLIES' TRIAL STKS (LISTED RACE) 1m 2f 6y
2:10 (2:16) (Class 1) 3-Y-0
£18,714 (£7,095; £3,550; £1,768; £887; £445) **Stalls** Low

Form RPR
4 **1** **Momentary**[28] 1503 3-8-12 0.......... HayleyTurner 4 99
(Michael Bell) *trckd ldr: drvn to chal 2f out: sn led: hrd pressed and rdn fnl 120yds: hld on wl cl home* **33/1**
21- **2** shd **Shirocco Star**[209] 7030 3-8-12 76.......... DarryllHolland 3 99
(Hughie Morrison) *stdd in tch: hdwy travelling wl 3f out: wnt 3rd sn after: trckd wnr ins fnl 2f: drvn and qcknd to chal fnl 120yds: kpt on but a jst hld* **5/1**[3]
1-42 **3** 3 ¾ **Starscope**[12] 1884 3-8-12 98.......... JimmyFortune 8 91
(John Gosden) *mounted in stalls: led and t.k.h: drvn and hdd ins fnl 2f: sn dropped to 3rd: fnd no ex and outpcd fnl f* **6/5**[1]
4 **4** 4 ½ **Gold Show**[27] 1506 3-8-12 0.......... MartinHarley 2 82
(Mick Channon) *t.k.h in rr: nt clr run and swtchd rt over 3f out: sn rdn and outpcd: styd on to snatch 4th clsng stages but nvr any threat* **25/1**
1-3 **5** nse **Lacily (USA)**[12] 1887 3-8-12 79.......... MickaelBarzalona 1 82
(Mahmood Al Zarooni) *chsd ldrs in 3rd: rdn 3f out: wknd ins fnl 2f* **7/1**
4-1 **6** 4 **Morant Bay (IRE)**[21] 1649 3-8-12 83.......... TomQueally 7 74
(Sir Henry Cecil) *stdd in rr: hdwy to chse ldrs 3f out: rdn 2f out: sn btn* **14/1**
213- **7** 11 **Firdaws (USA)**[238] 6299 3-8-12 101.......... TadhgO'Shea 5 52
(Roger Varian) *in rr: pushed along over 4f out: sn swtchd rt to outside: rdn over 3f out: sn btn* **3/1**[2]
0-5 **8** 5 **Young Lou**[28] 1502 3-8-12 0.......... RoystonFfrench 6 42
(Robin Dickin) *in tch: rdn and wkng whn bmpd over 3f out* **100/1**

2m 11.28s (2.48) **Going Correction** +0.325s/f (Good) **8** Ran SP% **114.1**
Speed ratings (Par 104): **103,102,99,96,96 93,84,80**
Tote Swingers: 1&2 £16.10, 1&3 £6.40, 2&3 £2.70 CSF £187.29 TOTE £25.50: £4.10, £1.30, £1.40; EX 146.60.
Owner The Queen **Bred** The Queen **Trained** Newmarket, Suffolk

FOCUS
This Listed race has produced some smart fillies. Last year's Oaks winner Dancing Rain was second in this to Izzi Top, who finished third at Epsom, while Eswarah took this on the way to winning the Oaks in 2005. This looked a good edition on paper, but both the market leaders disappointed and the form does not look that solid. Improvement from the first two.

NOTEBOOK
Momentary was always in the first two and, having moved ahead, she just held the runner-up's challenge. She had been fourth on her debut over C&D last month and the three who beat her have all been found wanting in Listed races since, but she improved for her initial experience and is clearly a smart filly. A granddaughter of the Queen's Oaks runner-up Flight Of Fancy, she is not entered at Epsom and the Ribblesdale at Royal Ascot appears the plan.
Shirocco Star ◆ looked set to reward her supporters when delivering her challenge in smooth fashion, but she was just held by a filly who had the advantage of racing against the rail. This Oaks entry looks sure to benefit for the step up to 1m4f and is fully entitled to come on for the outing, so the future looks bright. Her owners won this with Izzi Top. (tchd 11-2)
Starscope, runner-up in the 1000 Guineas, when two places ahead of stablemate The Fugue, was taking a sizeable drop in grade. Again fitted with a hood, she showed temperament on the way to post and needed some persuading to enter the stalls. Getting across to set just a modest tempo, she could not counter when headed but stuck on for third. She seemed to stay well enough but it could just be that the Guineas was her day in the sun. It will be interesting to see how she is campaigned now. (op 5-4 tchd Evens)
Gold Show had been fourth to Noble Mission on her debut over 1m here last month. Upped in grade, she was a little keen early but was running on well from the back at the end. It is reasonable to expect further improvement and she is an interesting prospect. (op 33-1)
Lacily(USA), a well held third to her stablemate Kailani in the Pretty Polly at Newmarket, was ridden differently here and failed to build on that run. She has yet to convince she stays this far in softish ground. (op 8-1)
Morant Bay(IRE) briefly appeared likely to get involved but a promising forward move came to nothing. Her Sandown win came in bad ground and the form has been let down by the runner-up. (tchd 10-1)

Firdaws(USA), a daughter of the aforementioned Eswarah, was third in last year's Fillies' Mile at Newmarket. Reported to have been working well prior to this reappearance, she was fitted with a blanket for stalls entry. She never really looked like picking up from the back and this was most disappointing. Hopefully she can leave this behind, perhaps on quicker ground, but she has questions to answer now. (tchd 7-2)

2233 EVENTS BAR MANAGEMENT H'CAP — 1m 2f 6y

2:40 (2:44) (Class 5) (0-70,70) 4-Y-0+ — **£2,587** (£770; £384; £192) **Stalls** Low

Form — RPR

146- **1** **Resplendent Light**[213] 6437 7-8-6 **62**...................(t) DanielMuscutt(7) 12 — 71
(Bernard Llewellyn) *chsd ldrs: pushed along to take 3rd 2f out: rdn to chal fnl 120yds: led last strides* **33/1**

0261 **2** *nk* **Cairanne**[8] 2013 4-8-0 **56** 6ex........................ DarrenEgan(7) 10 — 64
(Tom Keddy) *led: rdn over 2f out: hrd pressed fr ins fnl f but kpt slt ld tl hdd last strides* **12/1**

-112 **3** *hd* **Russian Storm**[22] 1635 4-8-6 **60**.......................... JemmaMarshall(5) 11 — 68
(Pat Phelan) *chsd ldrs: rdn: hung lft and chsd ldr fr 3f out: str chal fr ins fnl f: stl upsides fnl 75yds: no ex last strides* **12/1**

515- **4** *1* **Ambala**[238] 6303 4-9-2 **65**.. GeorgeBaker 1 — 71+
(Chris Wall) *n.m.r on rails after s and in rr: hdwy 3f out: rdn 2f out: styd on to take 4th 1f out: kpt on clsng stages but nt rch ldng trio* **10/1**

060- **5** *1 3/4* **Sunny Future (IRE)**[221] 6749 6-9-3 **66**....................... WilliamCarson 2 — 69+
(Malcolm Saunders) *hld up towards rr: hdwy on ins fr 3f out: kpt on u.p fr 2f out: kpt on fnl f bit nvr gng pce to rch ldrs* **14/1**

6 *4* **The High Man**[576] 7025 4-9-7 **70**................................ J-PGuillambert 5 — 65
(Ed Walker) *chsd ldrs: rdn 3f out: wknd over 1f out* **7/1**[2]

00-3 **7** *8* **Osgood**[17] 1743 5-9-0 **68**...................................... CharlesBishop(5) 14 — 47
(Mick Channon) *chsd ldr: rdn 3f out: styd disputing 2nd to 2f out: wknd over 1f out* **12/1**

2-60 **8** *1/2* **Choral Festival**[111] 349 6-9-3 **69**................................ SeanLevey(3) 16 — 47
(John Bridger) *chsd ldrs: rdn 3f out: wknd over 2f out* **20/1**

2143 **9** *6* **Broughton Sands**[25] 1566 4-9-6 **69**.................... MickaelBarzalona 13 — 35
(Willie Musson) *in rr: rdn and no prog fr 3f out* **8/1**[3]

-023 **10** *3/4* **Hurakan (IRE)**[14] 1829 6-9-2 **65**..(p) JamesDoyle 8 — 29
(Richard Price) *chsd ldrs: rdn 3f out: wknd sn after* **7/1**[2]

334- **11** *22* **Hawridge Song**[302] 4236 4-9-7 **70**.................................. JamesMillman 9
(Rod Millman) *s.i.s: in rr: rdn and sme prog whn hung lft over 3f out: sn wknd: eased whn no ch: t.o* **20/1**

/16- **12** *30* **Cheddar George**[39] 6916 6-9-4 **67**............................. JimmyFortune 6
(Peter Chapple-Hyam) *a towards rr: eased whn no ch fnl f: t.o* **8/1**[3]

063- **13** *3 3/4* **Greeley House**[221] 6754 4-8-12 **61**.................................. HayleyTurner 7
(Chris Wall) *plld hrd in rr: rapid hdwy to chse ldrs 1/2-way: wknd fr 3f out: t.o* **6/1**[1]

644- **P** **Misk Khitaam (USA)**[309] 4009 4-9-6 **69**............................ TomQueally 3
(John Dunlop) *p.u sn after s* **14/1**

2m 12.64s (3.84) **Going Correction** +0.325s/f (Good) — **14** Ran SP% **119.5**
Speed ratings (Par 103): **97,96,96,95,94 91,84,84,79,79 61,37,34,**
Tote Swingers: 1&2 £55.90, 1&3 £38.10, 2&3 £13.70 CSF £379.80 CT £4977.21 TOTE £61.30: £12.70, £3.50, £3.90; EX 752.30.
Owner B J Llewellyn **Bred** Usk Valley Stud **Trained** Fochriw, Caerphilly

FOCUS
An ordinary handicap for the track, in which it paid to race prominently. The time compared favourably with that of the Listed race. The form is rated around the first three.
Cheddar George Official explanation: jockey said gelding was never travelling.
Greeley House Official explanation: jockey said gelding ran too free and lost left hind shoe.

2234 LUCK GREAYER BLOODSTOCK SHIPPING FILLIES' CONDITIONS STKS — 5f 34y

3:10 (3:11) (Class 3) 2-Y-0 — **£5,602** (£1,677; £838; £419; £209; £105) **Stalls** Centre

Form — RPR

321 **1** **Lady Phill**[7] 2039 2-8-10 0.. KierenFox(3) 2 — 79
(Bill Turner) *mde all: drvn wl over 1f out: rdn ins fnl f: styd on strly* **6/1**[3]

2 *1/2* **Jillnextdoor (IRE)** 2-8-7 0... MartinHarley 1 — 71+
(Mick Channon) *trckd ldrs: drvn over 1f out: styd on to dispute 2nd fnl f: rdn fnl 120yds: chsd wnr fnl 30yds but no imp* **2/1**[1]

41 **3** *nk* **Ishi Honest**[7] 2047 2-8-10 0... JimmyFortune 3 — 73
(Mark Usher) *chsd wnr: rdn along fr 2f out: jnd for 2nd ins fnl f and no imp on wnr: outpcd into 3rd fnl 30yds* **6/1**[3]

4 *1* **Marishi Ten (IRE)** 2-8-7 0.. LiamKeniry 4 — 66+
(Andrew Balding) *hld up in tch: hdwy to cl on ldrs over 1f out: shkn up and edgd lft jst ins fnl f: kpt on same pce* **8/1**

5 *3* **Curl (IRE)** 2-8-8 0 ow1.. RichardHughes 5 — 57+
(Richard Hannon) *sn nudged along to styd trcking ldrs: drvn along 1/2-way: wknd over 1f out* **9/4**[2]

6 *hd* **Fadeintoinfinity** 2-8-2 0.. CharlesBishop(5) 6 — 55
(Mick Channon) *wnt rt s: green and sn pushed along in rr: drvn hung lft and wknd fr 2f out* **20/1**

1m 3.29s (1.89) **Going Correction** +0.325s/f (Good) — **6** Ran SP% **108.5**
Speed ratings (Par 94): **97,96,95,94,89 89**
Tote Swingers: 1&2 £2.70, 1&3 £2.40, 2&3 £2.00 CSF £17.22 TOTE £7.20: £2.90, £1.90; EX 20.20.
Owner Mrs M S Teversham **Bred** Mrs Monica Teversham **Trained** Sigwells, Somerset

FOCUS
This conditions event was won a year ago by Best Terms, who emulated Flashy Wings in 2005 in going on to take the Queen Mary and the Lowther. This year's race looks unlikely to produce any stars, however.

NOTEBOOK
Lady Phill broke her maiden third time out in an ordinary race on the Lingfield Polytrack, showing just fair form. Smartly away here, she responded well to pressure to make all. She's on the upgrade, but might not be the easiest to place successfully now. (tchd 11-2 and 13-2)
Jillnextdoor(IRE), a 40,000gns half-sister to the smart miler Commander Cave, ran a pleasing race and was closing on the winner close home. She is sure to win races and it's interesting to note that Nijoom Dubai, who finished second in this race for the stable in 2007, went on to take the Albany Stakes at Ascot. (op 11-8)
Ishi Honest, who took a Nottingham auction maiden a week ago, ran a game race but this looks as good as she is. She's a nursery type. (tchd 11-2)
Marishi Ten(IRE) made a pleasing introduction and was not knocked about when held. This Invincible Spirit filly, who cost 70,000 euros, will stay a bit further and should be paying her way later in the season.
Curl(IRE), represented the stable successful in the last three runnings. A 40,000 euro yearling, oyt of a winner at 1m2f, she was green and soon being niggled along at the back, but she did pick up late in the day and will surely leave this running behind. (op 7-2)
Fadeintoinfinity, a daughter of first-season sire Sixties Icon, shaped as if very much in need of the experience and is likely to need further. (op 18-1 tchd 16-1)

2235 BETTOR.COM H'CAP — 1m 3f 5y

3:45 (3:45) (Class 4) (0-85,84) 3-Y-0 — **£4,528** (£1,347; £673; £336) **Stalls** Low

Form — RPR

644- **1** **Pilgrims Rest (IRE)**[212] 6945 3-8-10 **73**...................... RichardHughes 8 — 87+
(Richard Hannon) *hld up in rr: hdwy 3f out: drvn to chal 1f out: slt ld fnl 120yds and edgd lft sn after: a jst doing enough* **22/1**

44-1 **2** *3/4* **Commitment**[16] 1754 3-9-3 **80**.. JimmyFortune 5 — 93+
(Luca Cumani) *trckd ldrs: wnt 2nd over 3f out: led over 2f out: rdn and jnd 1f out: narrowly hdd fnl 120yds: kpt on but a jst hld* **15/2**

3231 **3** *5* **Eshaab (USA)**[16] 1757 3-9-1 **78**...................................... TadhgO'Shea 6 — 82
(Ed Dunlop) *chsd ldrs: nt clr run: rdn and swtchd rt to outside over 1f out: kpt on to take wl hld 3rd ins fnl f* **9/1**

5511 **4** *shd* **Whipcrackaway (IRE)**[13] 1853 3-8-13 **76**............................ JohnFahy 2 — 80+
(Peter Hedger) *in tch: hdwy on ins 3f out: nt clr run and swtchd rt to outside 2f out: styd on fnl f to take 4th and cl on 3rd nr fin but nvr any ch w ldng duo* **9/1**

1- **5** *1/2* **Waterclock (IRE)**[210] 6994 3-9-7 **84**................................ JamesDoyle 1 — 87
(Roger Charlton) *chsd ldrs: pushed along and outpcd 4f out: drvn and styd on to chse ldrs over 2f out: wknd fnl f* **11/2**[3]

032- **6** *3* **Hint Of Mint**[236] 6373 3-8-12 **75**.. LiamKeniry 4 — 73
(Andrew Balding) *led 1f: trckd ldr: led over 3f out: hdd over 2f out: wknd over 1f out* **28/1**

61-2 **7** *4* **Deia Sunrise (IRE)**[12] 1888 3-9-2 **79**............................... RobertHavlin 7 — 69
(John Gosden) *s.i.s: t.k.h in rr: sme hdwy 3f out: nvr rchd ldrs and wknd 2f out* **13/8**[1]

0-60 **8** *2* **Wreaths Of Empire (IRE)**[13] 1853 3-8-7 **70** oh5............ KieranO'Neill 3 — 57
(Richard Hannon) *sn drvn to ld after 1f: rdn 5f out: hdd over 3f out: sn btn* **50/1**

01- **9** *33* **Expert Fighter (USA)**[218] 6812 3-9-1 **78**................. MickaelBarzalona 9
(Saeed Bin Suroor) *in rr: rdn 4f out: sn dropped away: eased whn no ch: t.o* **9/2**[2]

2m 27.51s (6.31) **Going Correction** +0.325s/f (Good) — **9** Ran SP% **113.2**
Speed ratings (Par 101): **90,89,85,85,85 83,80,78,54**
Tote Swingers: 1&2 £15.80, 1&3 £9.90, 2&3 £6.60 CSF £171.13 CT £1601.04 TOTE £21.90: £4.40, £2.30, £2.80; EX 146.90.
Owner Markus Jooste & Bernard Kantor **Bred** Annalee Bloodstock & Rockhart Trading Ltd **Trained** East Everleigh, Wilts

FOCUS
The ill-fated Census and multiple Group winner Allied Powers won this handicap during the first five years of its history, while Arctic Cosmos, third here, took the St Leger. This year's field contained some unexposed types and should produce winners, but the pace was only steady which inconvenienced some. The first two did well to pull clear and the form is rated on the positive side.

2236 BATHWICK TYRES CARNARVON STKS (LISTED RACE) — 6f 8y

4:20 (4:23) (Class 1) 3-Y-0 — **£18,714** (£7,095; £3,550; £1,768; £887; £445) **Stalls** Centre

Form — RPR

63-2 **1** **Swiss Spirit**[30] 1452 3-9-0 **98**..................................... MickaelBarzalona 3 — 106
(David Elsworth) *trckd ldrs: led over 1f out: hrd rdn fnl f: all out* **7/4**[1]

44-1 **2** *nk* **Lethal Force (IRE)**[28] 1492 3-9-0 **105**.................................... JohnFahy 5 — 105
(Clive Cox) *in rr: stdy hdwy over 2f out: sn drvn: styd on wl to chse wnr ins fnl f: kpt on but a jst hld* **9/2**[3]

20-0 **3** *nk* **Samminder (IRE)**[16] 1751 3-9-0 **98**................................ JimmyFortune 6 — 104
(Peter Chapple-Hyam) *in rr but in tch: hdwy over 1f out: rdn and styd on wl thrght fnl f: nt quite pce to rch wnr* **8/1**

20-3 **4** *1 3/4* **Burwaaz**[16] 1751 3-9-0 **109**.. TadhgO'Shea 8 — 98
(Ed Dunlop) *hld up in rr: drvn and hdwy over 1f out: styd on to take 3rd ins fnl f: nt pce to rch ldng trio* **4/1**[2]

00-1 **5** *nk* **Fanrouge (IRE)**[28] 1493 3-8-9 **89**.. JamesDoyle 9 — 92
(Malcolm Saunders) *in rr: drvn and hdwy over 1f out: styd on fnl f: nt rch ldrs* **33/1**

464- **6** *1 1/4* **Inetrobil (IRE)**[260] 5656 3-8-9 **102**...................................... FrannyNorton 2 — 88
(Kevin Ryan) *chsd ldr: led 2f out: sn rdn: hdd over 1f out: wknd ins fnl f* **12/1**

61 **7** *1 1/2* **Pretty Primo (IRE)**[21] 1637 3-8-9 **79**............................... RichardHughes 7 — 84
(Richard Hannon) *chsd ldrs: rdn 2f out: wknd fnl f* **20/1**

0-64 **8** *9* **West Leake Diman (IRE)**[16] 1751 3-9-0 **104**................ WilliamCarson 4 — 60
(Charles Hills) *chsd ldrs: rdn 2f out: wknd appr fnl f* **16/1**

14-0 **9** *2 3/4* **Bayleyf (IRE)**[16] 1751 3-9-0 **100**.. HayleyTurner 1 — 51
(John Best) *led tl hdd 2f out: sn btn: eased whn btn fnl f* **6/1**

1m 13.79s (0.79) **Going Correction** +0.325s/f (Good) — **9** Ran SP% **121.2**
Speed ratings (Par 107): **107,106,106,103,103 101,99,87,84**
Tote Swingers: 1&2 £2.50, 1&3 £4.50, 2&3 £7.00 CSF £10.35 TOTE £2.80: £1.70, £1.30, £2.50; EX 12.00.
Owner Lordship Stud **Bred** Lordship Stud **Trained** Newmarket, Suffolk

FOCUS
A Listed race that has produced some smart sprinters in recent years, including Sakhee's Secret who won it in 2007 before taking the July Cup. In 2010 Society Rock was second both here and in the Golden Jubilee Stakes, and when he won the latter race 12 months later he had Elzaam, who had landed this prize, back in fourth. The winner continued his improvement and the runner-up sets the standard.

NOTEBOOK
Swiss Spirit, runner-up in a valuable sales race last time, maintained his upwards curve, travelling well into the lead before holding off challengers on either side. A scopey, powerful colt, who just carried his head a shade high, he looks to have more improvement in him and his trainer is thinking of stepping him up to 7f for the Jersey Stakes at Ascot. (op 5-2)
Lethal Force(IRE) was a smart juvenile and he had little problem landing the odds at Bath on his return. Back up in grade, he raced a little keenly early but came through to have his chance. He holds Group 1 entries in the July Cup and Diamond Jubilee, but will need to improve considerably to play a part there. (tchd 4-1)
Samminder(IRE) failed to get a run at Kempton on his return and he had to wait for the gaps here. It probably wasn't enough to cost him victory but it did allow the winner to take first run. The best has yet to be seen of him and this looks his grade. (tchd 15-2)
Burwaaz had Samminder and two more of these behind when third at Newbury and was the form pick, with several placed efforts in Group company at two. He had excuses at Kempton and this straight track was expected to be in his favour, but he was a shade disappointing. He perhaps saw more daylight than was desirable on the near side of the bunch, but also gave the impression that he wasn't putting it all in. Some headgear may help. (op 9-2)
Fanrouge(IRE) had plenty on at the weights but ran on late from the rear and just missed out on fourth.
Inetrobil(IRE), tackling male opposition for the first time on this reappearance, showed speed before fading. She may not be easy to place.

Pretty Primo(IRE) faced a stiff task on form and was not discredited on only her third start. (op 14-1)
Bayleyf(IRE) showed his usual bright pace but fizzled out tamely. (op 10-1)

2237 CHRIS BEEK RACING APPRENTICE H'CAP 1m 4f 5y
4:55 (4:56) (Class 5) (0-75,74) 4-Y-0+ **£2,587** (£770; £384; £192) **Stalls** Low

Form RPR
41-3 **1** **Lady Rosamunde**[28] 1491 4-9-4 **74**..............................(p) NedCurtis(3) 10 88
(Marcus Tregoning) *broke wl: stdd towards rr: stdy hdwy on ins over 4f out: led ins fnl 3f: drvn and styd on wl fnl f: comf* **9/2**[2]
-660 **2** *1 1/2* **O Ma Lad (IRE)**[12] 1890 4-9-4 **74**.............................. ThomasBrown(3) 3 84
(Sylvester Kirk) *chsd ldrs: drvn and ev ch 3f out: sn drvn and one pce: kpt on fr over 1f out to take 2nd fnl 120yds but no ch w wnr* **11/1**
2010 **3** *2 1/2* **Resplendent Alpha**[7] 2051 8-8-7 **63** 6ex................. NicoleNordblad(3) 1 69
(Alastair Lidderdale) *in rr: stdy hdwy on ins fr 3f out: chsd wnr fr 2f out: no imp over 1f out: one pce and lost 2nd fnl 120yds* **16/1**
34-3 **4** *6* **Trend Line (IRE)**[134] 43 4-9-6 **73**.............................. DarrenEgan 11 69
(Peter Chapple-Hyam) *in tch drvn to chse ldrs and hung lft 3f out: wknd fr 2f out* **7/1**[3]
444- **5** *4* **Eastern Magic**[209] 7032 5-8-7 **60**.. JackDuern 9 50
(Reg Hollinshead) *chsd ldrs: wnt 2nd over 6f out: led over 4f out: hdd ins fnl 3f: wknd over 2f out* **4/1**[1]
36-0 **6** *1/2* **Lady of Burgundy**[7] 2051 6-9-0 **72**...................... JenniferFerguson(5) 6 61
(Mark Usher) *s.i.s: in rr: sme hdwy 3f out: nvr rchd ldrs: wknd fnl 2f* **8/1**
335- **7** *9* **Warne's Way (IRE)**[118] 6998 9-9-4 **71**........................ GeorgeDowning 7 46
(Brendan Powell) *led 2f: chsd ldrs tl wknd 5f out* **15/2**
665- **8** *1 3/4* **Tijori (IRE)**[321] 3642 4-8-9 **69**.............................. DanielMuscutt(7) 8 41
(Bernard Llewellyn) *chsd ldrs early: bhd fnl 6f* **16/1**
651 **9** *7* **Darsan (IRE)**[8] 2009 4-8-8 **61** 6ex.. JakePayne 5 22
(Phil McEntee) *t.k.h: led after 2f: hdd over 4f out: wknd 3f out* **9/1**
4230 **10** *hd* **Beggers Belief**[50] 1083 4-8-4 **64**..............................(b) JoeyHaynes(7) 4 24
(Eric Wheeler) *chsd ldrs over 7f* **16/1**
2560 **11** *12* **Prohibition (IRE)**[12] 1895 6-8-0 **60**.............................. SemiraPashai(7) 12
(Alastair Lidderdale) *v.s.a: racd wd: a towards rr* **28/1**
4145 **12** *26* **Thundering Home**[62] 944 5-8-12 **65**..............................(t) NatashaEaton 2
(Richard Mitchell) *in tch: chsd ldrs 6f out: wknd rapidly over 3f out: t.o* **18/1**

2m 41.3s (5.80) **Going Correction** +0.325s/f (Good) **12** Ran SP% **118.2**
Speed ratings (Par 103): **93,92,90,86,83 83,77,76,71,71 63,46**
Tote Swingers: 1&2 £8.20, 1&3 £15.80, 2&3 £38.20 CSF £53.38 CT £734.26 TOTE £5.70: £1.60, £4.30, £4.80; EX 73.00.
Owner Mr And Mrs A E Pakenham **Bred** Mr & Mrs A E Pakenham **Trained** Lambourn, Berks
■ Stewards' Enquiry : Thomas Brown four day ban; used whip above permitted level (3rd-6th June)

FOCUS
They went a strong initial pace in this apprentice handicap which suited those who came from the rear. They finished well strung out and the form is rated around the second and third.
T/Plt: £111.50 to a £1 stake. Pool: £62,018.00 - 405.68 winning tickets. T/Qpdt: £71.00 to a £1 stake. Pool: £3,474.00 - 36.20 winning tickets. ST

1380 NEWCASTLE (L-H)
Friday, May 18

OFFICIAL GOING: Soft (heavy in places; 4.6)
Wind: Moderate, half-behind Weather: steady rain

2238 PADON CONTRACTS NOVICE STKS 6f
5:35 (5:35) (Class 4) 2-Y-0 **£3,428** (£1,020; £509) **Stalls** Centre

Form RPR
12 **1** **All On Red (IRE)**[12] 1891 2-8-11 0.............................. RobertWinston 1 82+
(Tobias B P Coles) *trckd ldr: led over 1f out: sn pushed clr: comf* **4/7**[1]
61 **2** *9* **Rated**[36] 1330 2-9-2 0.. SamHitchcott 3 58
(Mick Channon) *led: rdn whn hdd over 1f out: sn btn* **13/8**[2]
3 *23* **Lord Roflow** 2-9-0 0.. PatrickMathers 2
(Robert Johnson) *v.s.a: a wl bhd* **25/1**[3]

1m 24.96s (10.36) **Going Correction** +0.975s/f (Soft) **3** Ran SP% **105.6**
Speed ratings (Par 95): **69,57,26**
CSF £1.73 TOTE £1.40; EX 1.50.
Owner Julian W H Broughton **Bred** Thomas Cahalan & Sophie Hayley **Trained** Newmarket, Suffolk

FOCUS
Winning jockey Robert Winston described the ground as 'heavy' after the first race and the time, nearly 13 seconds slower than standard, backs that up, although this was a steadily run affair. The form has been rated with the conditions in mind.

NOTEBOOK
All On Red(IRE) proved different class to her main rival. Her rider was happy to get a lead from Rated, and blew that rival away with a nice turn of foot inside the final furlong, skipping clear to win with consummate ease. She clearly loves this type of ground and deserves a crack at something better now, with connections reportedly considering the National Stakes at Sandown. (op 8-13 tchd 8-15)
Rated, whom we probably didn't see the best of , looked very tired in the final furlong and didn't take to the conditions as well as the winner. He is only modest but should be able to do better back on decent ground. (op 6-4 tchd 7-4)
Lord Roflow was awkward leaving the stalls and immediately a long way behind the front two. He is entitled to benefit for the experience and is bred to come into his own over middle distances down the line. (op 20-1)

2239 ESCOTT SIGNS H'CAP 1m 3y(S)
6:05 (6:05) (Class 6) (0-60,60) 4-Y-0+ **£1,681** (£500; £250; £125) **Stalls** Centre

Form RPR
/023 **1** **Woteva**[6] 2090 6-8-10 **56**..............................(p) EvaMoscrop(7) 6 70
(Nigel Tinkler) *trckd ldrs: led wl over 1f out: sn clr: rdn out* **9/2**[1]
446- **2** *14* **Edas**[217] 6833 10-9-2 **60**.. GarryWhillans(5) 10 45
(Thomas Cuthbert) *in tch: pushed along over 2f out: briefly short of room 2f out: plugged on to go remote 2nd fnl 75yds* **16/1**
2030 **3** *1* **Bygones For Coins (IRE)**[14] 1831 4-8-11 **50**............. PatrickMathers 7 33
(Robert Johnson) *led: hdd wl over 1f out: sn no ch w wnr: wknd ins fnl f: lost 2nd fnl 75yds* **16/1**
0-30 **4** *1 3/4* **Jupiter Fidius**[24] 1583 5-8-11 **57**.............................. GemmaTutty(7) 5 36
(Karen Tutty) *hld up: pushed along over 2f out: plugged on: wnt remote 4th post* **6/1**[2]
255- **5** *hd* **Celtic Step**[161] 7698 8-8-9 **48**.. SamHitchcott 4 26
(Peter Niven) *in tch: rdn over 3f out: plugged on: lost 4th post* **12/1**
/-00 **6** *3* **Dolly Royal (IRE)**[34] 1384 7-8-9 **53**.............................. LMcNiff(5) 1 25
(Robert Johnson) *hld up in rr: rdn over 3f out: bhd tl sme late hdwy* **11/1**
5-41 **7** *13* **Rub Of The Relic (IRE)**[24] 1583 7-9-4 **57**..................(v) MickyFenton 13
(Paul Midgley) *chsd ldrs: wknd over 3f out* **7/1**
040- **8** *4 1/2* **Tropical Duke (IRE)**[217] 6833 6-8-5 **47** oh1 ow1.... AdamBeschizza(3) 8
(Ron Barr) *s.i.s: sn midfield: pushed along over 4f out: sn btn* **20/1**
0430 **9** *2 1/4* **Red Scintilla**[6] 2091 5-8-13 **52**..............................(p) MichaelStainton 14
(Nigel Tinkler) *prom tl wknd over 2f out* **16/1**
0-01 **10** *9* **It's A Mans World**[6] 2091 6-9-0 **56** 6ex.............................. PaulPickard(3) 3
(Kevin M Prendergast) *midfield: wknd over 3f out* **13/2**[3]
/43- **11** *1 3/4* **Royal Holiday (IRE)**[449] 670 5-8-4 **46**.............................. AmyRyan(3) 12
(Marjorie Fife) *chsd ldrs: wknd over 2f out* **10/1**
440 **12** *13* **Linroyale Boy (USA)**[25] 1560 4-9-7 **60**.............................. RobertWinston 2
(Alan Swinbank) *hld up: a in rr: t.o* **16/1**
00-0 **13** *10* **Penton Hook**[37] 1294 6-8-8 **50**..............................(p) RossAtkinson(3) 11
(Barry Murtagh) *s.i.s: sn pushed along in rr: a wl bhd* **40/1**
040- **14** *24* **Dean Iarracht (IRE)**[199] 7215 6-8-13 **57**.............................. ShaneBKelly(5) 9
(Tracy Waggott) *slowly away: a bhd: t.o* **16/1**

1m 50.98s (7.58) **Going Correction** +0.975s/f (Soft) **14** Ran SP% **120.0**
Speed ratings (Par 101): **101,87,86,84,84 81,68,63,61,52 50,37,27,3**
toteswingers:1&2:£16.10, 1&3:£16.60, 2&3:£42.60 CSF £78.56 CT £1073.12 TOTE £4.40: £1.90, £5.60, £5.40; EX 89.10 TRIFECTA Not won..
Owner M Laverack **Bred** Oakhill Stud **Trained** Langton, N Yorks
■ Eva Moscrop's first winner.

FOCUS
Low-grade form and they were strung out like long-distance chasers. They came over to the stands' side and it proved impossible to come from off the pace as conditions found most of these out.
Rub Of The Relic(IRE) Official explanation: jockey said gelding was unsuited by ground (soft, heavy in places)
It's A Mans World Official explanation: jockey said gelding ran flat.
Linroyale Boy(USA) Official explanation: trainer said gelding was unsuited by ground (soft, heavy in places)

2240 T.S.G. MEDIAN AUCTION MAIDEN STKS 1m 2f 32y
6:40 (6:40) (Class 5) 3-Y-0 **£2,328** (£693; £346) **Stalls** Centre

Form RPR
-232 **1** **Rocktherunway (IRE)**[13] 1866 3-9-0 78.............................. LeeTopliss(3) 3 84
(Michael Dods) *mde all: pushed clr over 2f out: easily* **2/7**[1]
04 **2** *31* **Gangsterbanksters (FR)**[27] 1518 3-9-3 0.................. RobertWinston 4 60+
(Mrs K Burke) *trckd wnr: rdn over 3f out: sn outpcd: eased ins fnl f* **3/1**[2]
0 **3** *26* **Pioneer Boy (USA)**[12] 1878 3-8-12 0.............................. GarryWhillans(5) 1
(Alan Swinbank) *trckd wnr: pushed along and lost pl 5f out: sn wl bhd* **25/1**[3]

2m 27.54s (15.64) **Going Correction** +1.525s/f (Heav) **3** Ran SP% **106.6**
Speed ratings (Par 99): **98,73,52**
CSF £1.42 TOTE £1.30; EX 1.30.
Owner The Sedgewick & Dods Racing Partnership **Bred** J Hanly, A Stroud And T Stewart **Trained** Denton, Co Durham

FOCUS
The easy winner showed useful form.

2241 MITIE H'CAP 1m 2f 32y
7:15 (7:15) (Class 4) (0-80,79) 4-Y-0+ **£4,075** (£1,212; £606; £303) **Stalls** Centre

Form RPR
05-4 **1** **Oneofapear (IRE)**[34] 1381 6-9-2 **79**.............................. GarryWhillans(5) 4 86
(Alan Swinbank) *trckd ldng pair: led 3f out: rdn over 2f out: kpt on* **8/1**
0502 **2** *1 1/2* **European Dream (IRE)**[8] 2011 9-9-6 **78**..................(p) PhillipMakin 3 82
(Richard Guest) *hld up in rr: pushed along and hdwy over 2f out: rdn to chse wnr ins fnl f: kpt on: a hld* **8/1**
56-3 **3** *6* **Hakuna Matata**[10] 1958 5-8-11 **69**.. BarryMcHugh 2 61
(Brian Ellison) *hld up in tch: smooth hdwy to trck wnr over 2f out: rdn over 1f out: sn one pce: wknd and lost 2nd ins fnl f* **9/2**[3]
-020 **4** *13* **Ailsa Craig (IRE)**[11] 1913 6-8-12 **75**.............................. ShaneBKelly(5) 5 41
(Edwin Tuer) *hld up in tch: rdn 3f out: sn no imp: wknd over 1f out* **3/1**[2]
0251 **5** *2 1/2* **Amazing Blue Sky**[11] 1913 6-9-6 **78** 6ex.............................. JamesSullivan 1 39
(Ruth Carr) *led narrowly: rdn whn hdd 3f out: sn wknd* **9/4**[1]
1-U3 **6** *25* **Law To Himself (IRE)**[15] 1797 5-9-0 **72**.............................. RobertWinston 6
(Alan Swinbank) *w ldr: rdn over 3f out: sn wknd: eased* **5/1**

2m 26.82s (14.92) **Going Correction** +1.525s/f (Heav) **6** Ran SP% **112.8**
Speed ratings (Par 105): **101,99,95,84,82 62**
toteswingers:1&2:£8.90, 1&3:£8.80, 2&3:£5.80 CSF £66.05 TOTE £11.30: £4.60, £3.10; EX 48.80.
Owner Mrs I Gibson & Dr C Emmerson **Bred** Tyrone Molloy **Trained** Melsonby, N Yorks

FOCUS
They went a decent gallop in the conditions, which may help to explain why the front-running Amazing Blue Sky dropped away tamely up the straight.
Amazing Blue Sky Official explanation: trainer could offer no explanation as to poor run.
Law To Himself(IRE) Official explanation: trainer said gelding was unsuited by ground (soft, heavy in places)

2242 O'BRIEN RECYCLING H'CAP 2m 19y
7:50 (7:51) (Class 5) (0-70,66) 4-Y-0+ **£2,328** (£693; £346; £173) **Stalls** Low

Form RPR
3-34 **1** **Pokfulham (IRE)**[14] 1822 6-9-7 **63**..............................(v) DanielTudhope 4 78
(Jim Goldie) *led at stdy pce: 5 l clr on bit 4f out: rdn over 2f out: a in control* **11/4**[2]
26-3 **2** *2* **Rosairlie (IRE)**[25] 1272 4-8-13 **62**.............................. GarryWhillans(5) 9 75+
(Micky Hammond) *hld up: pushed along over 3f out: hdwy into 2nd 2f out: styd on wl: nt quite rch wnr* **2/1**[1]
52-0 **3** *14* **Tigerino (IRE)**[22] 1631 4-8-5 **49**.. JamesSullivan 8 45
(Chris Fairhurst) *t.k.h in midfield: briefly 2nd over 2f out: wknd over 1f out* **7/2**[3]
520- **4** *5* **Terenzium (IRE)**[262] 5595 10-8-12 **54**..............................(p) KellyHarrison 5 44
(Micky Hammond) *midfield: pushed along and outpcd 4 out: no threat after* **16/1**
0-43 **5** *8* **Dechiper (IRE)**[15] 1794 10-8-5 **47** oh1.............................. PatrickMathers 2 27
(Robert Johnson) *hld up: rdn over 3f out: sn btn* **8/1**
45-4 **6** *15* **Tower**[15] 1794 5-8-11 **53**..............................(be) PhillipMakin 7
(Chris Grant) *trckd wnr: rdn over 3f out: wknd over 2f out* **11/1**
00/0 **7** *61* **Ruff Diamond (USA)**[15] 1794 7-9-1 **57**.............................. RobertWinston 6
(David Thompson) *midfield: hdwy into 2nd 10f out: pushed along 6f out: sn lost pl and wknd: t.o* **14/1**

4m 2.24s (22.84) **Going Correction** +1.525s/f (Heav)
WFA 4 from 5yo+ 2lb **7** Ran SP% **114.2**
Speed ratings (Par 103): **103,102,95,92,88 81,50**
toteswingers:1&2:£1.80, 1&3:£2.50, 2&3:£2.30 CSF £8.67 CT £18.42 TOTE £3.50: £2.00, £1.50; EX 8.10 Trifecta £106.20 Pool: £269.91 - 1.88 winning units.
Owner Ambrose Turnbull **Bred** Killian Farm **Trained** Uplawmoor, E Renfrews

FOCUS
This had an open feel to it on paper.
Ruff Diamond(USA) Official explanation: jockey said gelding hung left.

2243 DELOITTE H'CAP 7f
8:25 (8:25) (Class 3) (0-90,89) 4-Y-0+ £7,439 (£2,213; £1,106; £553) Stalls Centre

Form RPR

-063 **1** **Capaill Liath (IRE)**[14] 1821 4-9-2 87..........(p) AmyRyan(3) 7 97
(Kevin Ryan) *hld up in tch: rdn and hdwy 2f out: led over 1f out: drvn and kpt on ins fnl f* **11/4**[1]

-106 **2** *2* **The Osteopath (IRE)**[13] 1863 9-8-10 78.......... PhillipMakin 2 83
(John Davies) *hld up in rr: pushed along over 2 out: hdwy over 1f out: chsd wnr ins fnl f: kpt on* **7/1**

-430 **3** *3 ½* **Prime Exhibit**[27] 1522 7-8-12 87.......... ShirleyTeasdale(7) 5 83
(David Nicholls) *trckd ldrs: stl gng wl 2f out: pushed along over 1f out: sn one pce* **10/1**

0- **4** *½* **Anderiego (IRE)**[247] 6073 4-8-8 76.......... GrahamGibbons 8 70
(David O'Meara) *prom: led over 2f out: rdn whn hdd over 1f out: wknd ins fnl f* **3/1**[2]

0543 **5** *3 ½* **Imperial Djay (IRE)**[7] 2025 7-9-5 87.......... JamesSullivan 9 72
(Ruth Carr) *hld up in tch: rdn over 2f out: sn no imp* **9/2**[3]

0522 **6** *4* **Levitate**[10] 1951 4-8-11 79..........(v) IPoullis 4 54
(Alan McCabe) *chsd ldrs: rdn over 3f out: wknd over 1f out: lost hind shoe* **9/1**

62-0 **7** *nk* **Chiswick Bey (IRE)**[37] 1321 4-9-2 89.......... ShaneBKelly(5) 6 63
(Richard Fahey) *prom: rdn over 2f out: wknd over 1f out* **12/1**

-032 **8** *11* **Rigolleto (IRE)**[17] 1741 4-8-12 80..........(v[1]) SamHitchcott 3 26
(Mick Channon) *hld up in tch: pushed along and outpcd over 4f out: wknd over 2f out* **14/1**

P-03 **9** *18* **Eastern Hills**[20] 1650 7-8-11 79..........(p) KirstyMilczarek 1
(Alan McCabe) *led: rdn whn hdd over 2f out: sn wknd: eased* **22/1**

1m 36.13s (8.33) **Going Correction** +1.175s/f (Soft) **9** Ran SP% **120.1**
Speed ratings (Par 107): **99,96,92,92,88 83,83,70,50**
toteswingers:1&2:£6.70, 1&3:£8.40, 2&3:£20.80 CSF £23.70 CT £173.80 TOTE £4.60: £1.80, £1.70, £4.10; EX 42.00 TRIFECTA Not won..
Owner T A Rahman **Bred** Stanley Estate & Stud Co & Mount Coote Stud **Trained** Hambleton, N Yorks

FOCUS
A good quality handicap run at a decent pace.

NOTEBOOK
Capaill Liath(IRE) ◆ handled conditions best of all to win for a fourth time. The son of Iffraaj has been working his way into form since joining Kevin Ryan earlier in the year and he signalled his turn was near with a really good run at Musselburgh last time. His high head carriage is a little disconcerting but it doesn't seem to stop him going forward and he saw this out really strongly to come clear in the final furlong. The form looks good for the grade and there could be more nice prizes in this grey before the season is out. (op 4-1)
The Osteopath(IRE) is a solid marker under these conditions and at this venue, where he has such a good record. He kept on well and looks to have run his race, but there isn't much leeway in his mark at the moment. (op 11-2)
Prime Exhibit, having his first run for David Nicholls, travelled well for a long way but didn't really pick up once shaken up. He has become dangerously well handicapped and it will be a surprise if his new connections can't get him back in the winners' enclosure. (tchd 9-1)
Anderiego(IRE), another making his debut for a new yard, shaped quite encouragingly before getting tired in the closing stages and is entitled to come on plenty for this first run since September. He, too, is appealingly handicapped. (op 4-1)
Imperial Djay(IRE) has been running well this season but couldn't get in a blow from off the pace this time. He ideally wants better ground. (tchd 4-1)
Levitate reportedly lost a hind shoe, according to the trainer's representative. Official explanation: trainers representive said gelding lost hind shoe. (op 8-1)

2244 NEWCASTLE AIRPORT FILLIES' H'CAP 5f
9:00 (9:00) (Class 5) (0-70,68) 3-Y-0+ £2,328 (£693; £346; £173) Stalls Centre

Form RPR

0063 **1** **Pivotal Prospect**[4] 2122 4-8-12 54 oh9.......... RobertWinston 7 67
(Tracy Waggott) *mde all: rdn over 1f out: kpt on wl* **10/1**

32-1 **2** *3 ¼* **Untold Melody**[45] 1173 3-9-4 68.......... PhillipMakin 9 66
(Kevin Ryan) *trckd wnr: rdn 2f out: drvn and kpt on one pce fnl f* **10/3**[1]

0534 **3** *2* **Sally's Swansong**[12] 1881 6-8-12 54 oh4..........(b) GrahamGibbons 6 48
(Eric Alston) *prom: rdn over 1f out: sn one pce* **4/1**[2]

016- **4** *¾* **Sparking**[242] 6213 5-9-8 64.......... RichardKingscote 5 55
(Tom Dascombe) *chsd ldrs: pushed along and lost pl over 1f out: plugged on again fnl f* **7/1**

00-2 **5** *½* **Foreign Rhythm (IRE)**[27] 1528 7-9-3 64.......... ShaneBKelly(5) 3 54
(Ron Barr) *in tch on outer: rdn over 2f out: wknd ins fnl f* **11/2**[3]

3245 **6** *¾* **Amazing Win (IRE)**[11] 1910 4-9-0 56.......... SamHitchcott 8 43
(Mick Channon) *in tch: rdn over 2f out: briefly chsd wnr over 1f out: wknd ins fnl f* **4/1**[2]

-044 **7** *1* **Ever Roses**[10] 1954 4-9-3 59..........(v) MickyFenton 2 53+
(Paul Midgley) *sn pushed along towards rr: minor hdwy whn short of room ins fnl f* **13/2**

1m 6.95s (5.85) **Going Correction** +1.175s/f (Soft)
WFA 3 from 4yo+ 8lb **7** Ran SP% **113.4**
Speed ratings (Par 100): **100,94,91,90,89 88,86**
toteswingers:1&2:£6.00, 1&3:£7.40, 2&3:£1.70 CSF £42.45 CT £156.95 TOTE £11.30: £3.70, £1.80; EX 55.60 TRIFECTA Not won..
Owner Christopher James Allan **Bred** Michael E Broughton **Trained** Spennymoor, Co Durham

FOCUS
Modest form.
Ever Roses Official explanation: jockey said filly was denied a clear run.
T/Plt: £155.00 to a £1 stake. Pool:£49,505.57 - 233.14 winning tickets T/Qpdt: £33.80 to a £1 stake. Pool:£4,571.45 - 100.00 winning tickets AS

[2193]NEWMARKET (R-H)
Friday, May 18

OFFICIAL GOING: Good to firm (good in places; 7.8)
Far side course used with stalls on Stands side except 1m 4f race: Centre
Wind: Fresh half-against Weather: Overcast

2245 CHEMTEST/BRITISH STALLION STUDS E B F MAIDEN FILLIES' STKS 6f
2:20 (2:21) (Class 4) 2-Y-0 £4,528 (£1,347; £673; £336) Stalls High

Form RPR

1 **Sandreamer (IRE)** 2-9-0 0.......... MatthewDavies 3 80+
(Mick Channon) *s.i.s: hdwy 1/2-way: led over 1f out: rdn and edgd lft ins fnl f: r.o* **5/1**[3]

2 *1* **Sharaarah (IRE)** 2-9-0 0.......... NeilCallan 8 77+
(Ed Dunlop) *hld up: swtchd rt and hdwy over 1f out: r.o* **5/1**[3]

3 *1* **Testamatta** 2-9-0 0.......... TedDurcan 5 76+
(Marco Botti) *s.s: swished tail and rn green in rr: rdn and r.o wl ins fnl f: nt rch ldrs* **9/1**

4 *½* **Tipping Over (IRE)** 2-9-0 0.......... MichaelHills 2 73+
(Hugo Palmer) *w ldr: rdn and ev ch over 1f out: styd on same pce ins fnl f* **25/1**

5 *nse* **New Falcon (IRE)** 2-9-0 0.......... KierenFallon 1 72+
(James Tate) *led: rdn and hdd over 1f out: styd on same pce ins fnl f* **4/1**[1]

6 *hd* **Summer Isles** 2-9-0 0.......... JamieSpencer 6 72+
(Ed Dunlop) *chsd ldrs: rdn over 1f olut: styd on* **10/1**

7 *nk* **Blue Nova** 2-9-0 0.......... RyanMoore 10 71+
(Jeremy Noseda) *chsd ldrs: rdn and swtchd rt over 1f out: styd on same pce ins fnl f* **9/2**[2]

8 *1 ½* **Sorcellerie** 2-9-0 0.......... DaneO'Neill 9 66
(David Elsworth) *s.i.s: sn pushed along in rr: styd on ins fnl f: nvr trbld ldrs* **12/1**

9 *5* **Wittgenstein (IRE)** 2-9-0 0.......... MartinDwyer 4 51+
(Brian Meehan) *prom: hmpd and lost pl wl over 4f out: n.d after* **9/1**

10 *5* **Tiger's Home** 2-9-0 0.......... LukeMorris 7 36
(Julia Feilden) *s.i.s: sn prom: pushed along 1/2-way: wknd over 1f out* **40/1**

1m 15.19s (2.99) **Going Correction** +0.175s/f (Good) **10** Ran SP% **114.6**
Speed ratings (Par 92): **87,85,84,83,83 83,82,80,74,67**
Tote Swingers: 1&2 £6.60, 1&3 £10.70, 2&3 £15.40 CSF £29.66 TOTE £5.30: £2.40, £1.70, £2.90; EX 40.10.
Owner Jon and Julia Aisbitt **Bred** Epona Bloodstock Ltd **Trained** West Ilsley, Berks

FOCUS
There was nothing to go on in terms of form heading into this race but a taking performance, despite the steady early pace.

NOTEBOOK
Sandreamer(IRE) provided her yard with yet another juvenile success. The daughter of Oasis Dream, who cost £85,000 as a yearling, enjoyed an untroubled passage throughout and showed a smart turn of foot to put the race to bed ahead of the arguably unfortunate Sharaarah. The winner, who holds entries in some of the leading sales races later in the year, stuck to her task admirably in the closing stages having struck the front fully 2f from home. Channon's juveniles have tended to need a run this season and the fact that she was able overcome her lack of experience, in a competitive race, suggests that she could be a more than useful recruit. Connections are likely to step her up in class for her next start. (op 11-2)
Sharaarah(IRE) ◆ didn't have things her own way but showed more than enough on this, her debut run, to suggest she's a filly to be reckoned with for the remainder of the campaign. Like the winner, she is by Oasis Dream and she will have learnt plenty from this outing. She was boxed in and travelling strongly when Sandreamer kicked for home and did well in the circumstances to finish as close as she did. She represents another yard not noted for their debutante winners and there should be plenty more to come. (op 9-2)
Testamatta shaped with considerable promise and it shouldn't be long before she gets off the mark. She was one of the first under pressure but she quickened up nicely as they hit the rising ground and is another to take out of the race. (op 11-1)
Tipping Over(IRE), a cheaply bought first foal, gave plenty of encouragement.
New Falcon(IRE) related to several speedy types, showed good speed and can build on this debut. (op 9-2)
Summer Isles, the first foal of a mile winner, ran as if a stiffer test of stamina would suit. (tchd 9-1)
Blue Nova, out of a half-sister to Fantasia and Pink Symphony; also ran as if a stiffer test of stamina would suit. (tchd 11-2)

2246 STREETS CHARTERED ACCOUNTANTS H'CAP 1m
2:50 (2:52) (Class 5) (0-75,75) 3-Y-0 £2,587 (£770; £384; £192) Stalls High

Form RPR

-613 **1** **Fennell Bay (IRE)**[7] 2021 3-9-4 72.......... MircoDemuro 15 83
(Mark Johnston) *hld up: hdwy over 2f out: led 1f out: r.o* **7/1**[3]

104- **2** *½* **Sardanapalus**[235] 6413 3-9-4 72.......... JamieSpencer 13 82+
(Kevin Ryan) *stdd s: hld up: hdwy on outer 2f out: rdn and hung lft ins fnl f: r.o* **14/1**

61- **3** *3 ½* **Feisty Champion (IRE)**[202] 7177 3-9-4 72.......... SebSanders 1 75+
(J W Hills) *chsd ldrs: rdn over 1f out: hmpd ins fnl f: styd on same pce* **25/1**

40-4 **4** *½* **Engrossing**[39] 1257 3-9-7 75.......... NickyMackay 10 76
(David Elsworth) *chsd ldrs: led 5f out: rdn and hdd 1f out: no ex ins fnl f* **25/1**

522- **5** *2* **Andalieb**[167] 7626 3-9-3 71.......... NeilCallan 16 68+
(David Simcock) *hld up: hdwy and hmpd 2f out: styd on: nt trble ldrs* **14/1**

50-0 **6** *1* **Fortrose Academy (IRE)**[13] 1862 3-9-4 72.......... DavidProbert 11 66
(Andrew Balding) *plld hrd and prom: rdn over 1f out: wknd ins fnl f* **33/1**

01-1 **7** *1* **Twelve Strings (IRE)**[20] 1661 3-9-5 73.......... KierenFallon 2 64+
(Luca Cumani) *hld up: pushed along and hdwy 1/2-way: hmpd and lost pl 2f out: n.d after* **7/2**[1]

24-5 **8** *nk* **Inniscastle Boy**[17] 1728 3-8-12 66.......... MartinDwyer 5 57
(William Muir) *prom: rdn over 3f out: wknd over 1f out* **16/1**

060- **9** *1* **Calculated Risk**[223] 6699 3-8-9 63.......... JamieMackay 9 51+
(Willie Musson) *hld up: nt clr run over 2f out: styd on ins fnl f:* **18/1**

-143 **10** *¾* **Incendiary (IRE)**[15] 1790 3-9-0 75.......... NoelGarbutt(7) 3 62+
(Hugo Palmer) *hld up: rdn over 2f out: n.d* **14/1**

44-0 **11** *¾* **Philipstown**[30] 1452 3-9-5 73.......... RyanMoore 6 58
(Richard Hannon) *chsd ldrs: rdn over 2f out: wknd fnl f* **14/1**

51- **12** *½* **Lawn Jamil (USA)**[240] 6259 3-9-5 73..........(t) MichaelHills 14 57
(Charles Hills) *chsd ldrs: rdn over 3f out: wknd over 1f out* **5/1**[2]

344- **13** *7* **Stormy Whatever (FR)**[193] 7326 3-9-4 72.......... FrederikTylicki 4 40
(James Given) *led 3f: chsd ldrs: rdn over 2f out: wknd fnl f* **40/1**

410- **14** *shd* **Feelthedifference**[216] 6864 3-9-4 **72** .... IanMongan 12 40+
(Sir Henry Cecil) *hld up: racd keenly: hdwy and hmpd 2f out: nt clr run over 1f out: n.d* **16/1**

32-0 **15** *1 ½* **Cappielow Park**[27] 1506 3-9-7 **75** .... LukeMorris 7 39
(William Jarvis) *prom: rdn over 2f out: wknd over 1f out* **12/1**

0-46 **16** *nk* **Rogue Reporter (IRE)**[17] 1728 3-9-0 **68** ....(t) SaleemGolam 8 31
(Stuart Williams) *mid-div: rdn over 3f out: wknd over 2f out* **28/1**

1m 40.66s (2.06) **Going Correction** +0.175s/f (Good) **16** Ran SP% **119.3**
Speed ratings (Par 99): **96,95,92,91,89 88,87,87,86,85 84,84,77,77,75 75**
Tote Swingers: 1&2 £18.60, 1&3 £30.30, 2&3 £84.50 CSF £92.90 CT £2403.63 TOTE £10.70: £2.80, £3.50, £4.40, £6.60; EX 139.10.
Owner Sheikh Hamdan Bin Mohammed Al Maktoum **Bred** J R Wills **Trained** Middleham Moor, N Yorks

FOCUS
A highly competitive 3yo handicap, but a rough renewal with plenty unable to show their form. Not a race to take at face value.

2247 SQUIRES RESTAURANT AT BEDFORD LODGE HOTEL NOVICE STKS 6f

3:20 (3:21) (Class 4) 2-Y-O **£3,881** (£1,155; £577; £288) **Stalls** High

Form RPR

01 **1** **Heavy Metal**[15] 1767 2-9-5 0 .... MircoDemuro 7 87+
(Mark Johnston) *mde all: rdn over 1f out: r.o* **13/8**[1]

2 *¾* **Rising Legend** 2-9-0 0 .... RyanMoore 6 80+
(Richard Hannon) *chsd wnr: rdn and ev ch wl over 1f out: r.o* **11/4**[2]

3 *1 ¼* **Birdman (IRE)** 2-9-0 0 .... JamieSpencer 4 76+
(David Simcock) *dwlt: hld up: r.o ins fnl f: nrst fin* **5/1**[3]

1 **4** *shd* **Threes Grand**[25] 1563 2-8-11 0 .... NickyMackay 2 73
(Scott Dixon) *a.p: pushed along and swtchd rt over 2f out: r.o* **8/1**

5 *3 ½* **Hajam** 2-9-0 0 .... KierenFallon 1 65
(James Tate) *chsd ldrs: rdn and ev ch wl over 1f out: edgd lft and wknd ins fnl f* **7/1**

6 *15* **Tuffan (USA)** 2-9-0 0 .... BrettDoyle 5 20
(Clive Brittain) *s.i.s: sn pushed along in rr: wknd and eased over 1f out* **33/1**

1m 13.8s (1.60) **Going Correction** +0.175s/f (Good) **6** Ran SP% **108.0**
Speed ratings (Par 95): **96,95,93,93,88 68**
Tote Swingers: 1&2 £1.50, 1&3 £1.90, 2&3 £2.40 CSF £5.71 TOTE £2.10: £2.10, £1.50; EX 5.80.
Owner Sheikh Hamdan Bin Mohammed Al Maktoum **Bred** Darley **Trained** Middleham Moor, N Yorks

FOCUS
Some interesting newcomers lined-up for this juvenile event but the winner had experience.

NOTEBOOK
Heavy Metal ran out a convincing winner. Mark Johnston's 2yo had improved massively from his first to his second start and he appears to still be on the upgrade, never really looking in any danger once breaking well from his rail draw. The son of Exceed And Excel, who had made all to win at Brighton earlier in the month, set a decent pace throughout but had more than enough in hand to repel the persistent challenge of Rising Legend. He holds an entry in the Group 1 Phoenix Stakes at The Curragh later in the year but will surely have to step up again if he's able to justify that engagement. That said, he has done nothing wrong on his last two starts and is clearly uncomplicated. (op 2-1 tchd 6-4, 9-4 in a place)
Rising Legend was not without support on this, his introduction, and he performed creditably. He was alert from the gates but never really looked like threatening the winner. He's sure to come on for this and shouldn't be underestimated next time, even if upped in class. (tchd 3-1)
Birdman(IRE) rattled home following a sluggish start. (op 7-2)
Threes Grand, a winner on her debut on mich softer ground, seemed to handle this faster surface and performed well against the colts. (tchd 10-1)
Hajam showed good pace but weakened relatively quickly. (op 6-1)

2248 EDMONDSON HALL SOLICITORS & SPORTS LAWYERS H'CAP 1m 2f

3:55 (3:57) (Class 3) (0-90,88) 4-Y-O+ **£7,762** (£2,310; £1,154; £577) **Stalls** High

Form RPR

25-0 **1** **Danadana (IRE)**[13] 1854 4-9-4 **85** .... KierenFallon 10 102+
(Luca Cumani) *hld up in tch: led 2f out: shkn up and r.o wl* **9/2**[1]

0-11 **2** *1 ¾* **Qaraaba**[48] 1133 5-9-7 **88** .... DaneO'Neill 9 102
(Seamus Durack) *hld up: hdwy over 1f out: rdn to chse wnr ins fnl f: r.o* **5/1**[2]

212- **3** *2* **Robin Hoods Bay**[218] 6822 4-9-4 **85** .... JamieSpencer 2 95+
(Ed Vaughan) *hld up: hdwy over 2f out: rdn and ev ch over 1f out: styd on same pce ins fnl f* **9/1**[3]

20-6 **4** *¾* **Fanny May**[27] 1513 4-9-3 **84** .... MircoDemuro 16 92
(Denis Coakley) *hld up in tch: rdn over 1f out: styd on* **28/1**

-011 **5** *¾* **John Louis**[86] 648 4-8-11 **78** .... RichardMullen 11 85
(Philip McBride) *prom: rdn over 2f out: styd on same pce ins fnl f* **33/1**

5-35 **6** *½* **Borug (USA)**[14] 1820 4-9-3 **84** .... SebSanders 15 90
(James Tate) *s.i.s: hld up: hdwy u.p over 1f out: nrst fin* **33/1**

1- **7** *shd* **Rawaki (IRE)**[333] 3236 4-9-2 **83** .... DavidProbert 6 88+
(Andrew Balding) *prom: outpcd over 2f out: styd on fr over 1f out* **28/1**

110- **8** *1 ½* **Proud Chieftain**[188] 7391 4-9-6 **87** .... IanMongan 14 89
(Clifford Lines) *hld up: rdn over 1f out: styd on ins fnl f* **20/1**

-354 **9** *1 ½* **Mataaleb**[34] 1374 5-9-0 **81** .... LukeMorris 17 80
(Lydia Pearce) *s.i.s: hld up: rdn over 2f out: nvr trbld ldrs* **16/1**

405- **10** *2 ½* **Nave (USA)**[240] 6249 5-9-1 **82** .... MartinLane 8 76
(David Simcock) *chsd ldr tl led 1/2-way: rdn and hdd 2f out: wknd fnl f* **22/1**

22-0 **11** *½* **Yojimbo (IRE)**[48] 1133 4-9-1 **82** .... MatthewDavies 1 75
(Mick Channon) *hld up: hdwy over 3f out: rdn and wknd fnl f* **40/1**

141- **12** *nse* **Jiwen (CAN)**[210] 6996 4-9-7 **88** .... NeilCallan 20 81
(Roger Varian) *hld up: hdwy over 3f out: rdn and wknd over 1f out* **16/1**

202- **13** *shd* **Fadhaa (IRE)**[247] 6063 4-9-4 **85** .... MichaelHills 4 78
(Charles Hills) *hld up: hdwy over 2f out: wknd fnl f* **9/1**[3]

001- **14** *2* **Novirak (IRE)**[241] 6242 4-8-10 **77** .... JackMitchell 13 66
(James Fanshawe) *chsd ldrs: rdn over 2f out: wknd over 1f out* **20/1**

30-0 **15** *nk* **Reflect (IRE)**[48] 1139 4-9-7 **88** ....(t) PatDobbs 7 76
(Richard Hannon) *led to 1/2-way: chsd ldr: ev ch 2f out: sn rdn and wknd* **20/1**

21-1 **16** *5* **Silken Thoughts**[20] 1680 4-9-4 **85** .... BrettDoyle 3 63
(John Berry) *hld up: rdn over 2f out: wknd over 1f out* **14/1**

200/ **17** *2 ¼* **Seeking The Buck (USA)**[581] 6889 8-8-13 **80** .... MartinDwyer 5 54
(Amy Weaver) *prom tl rdn and wknd 2f out* **66/1**

633- **18** *nk* **Arabian Heights**[221] 6755 4-9-3 **84** .... FergusSweeney 18 57
(Alan King) *s.i.s: hld up and a in rr* **33/1**

1-00 **19** *nk* **Dick Doughtywylie**[13] 1854 4-9-7 **88** .... RyanMoore 12 61
(John Gosden) *hld up: a in rr* **12/1**

321- **20** *17* **Yasir (USA)**[218] 6822 4-9-4 **85** ....(v) TedDurcan 19 24
(Saeed Bin Suroor) *prom tl rdn and wknd wl over 2f out: t.o* **12/1**

2m 5.07s (-0.73) **Going Correction** +0.175s/f (Good) **20** Ran SP% **126.9**
Speed ratings (Par 107): **109,107,106,105,104 104,104,103,101,99 99,99,99,97,97 93,91,91,91,77**
Tote Swingers: 1&2 £7.10, 1&3 £6.00, 2&3 £15.10 CSF £21.93 CT £204.95 TOTE £5.00: £1.70, £2.40, £1.90, £4.90; EX 29.10.
Owner Sheikh Mohammed Obaid Al Maktoum **Bred** Darley **Trained** Newmarket, Suffolk

FOCUS
A competitive 1m2f handicap, run at a fair pace, and won in decisive style. The first three are all on the up.

NOTEBOOK
Danadana(IRE) stepped up considerably on an average run behind Tullius here a fortnight previously. He had shown useful form in three starts as a 3-y-o and is clearly going the right way based on this evidence. He ran as if needing the outing when finishing in midfield over 1m1f at this track last time and appeared much more at home over this additional furlong. He picked up well once asked for his effort and looks set for a lofty rise in the weights. Last year's winner, Vita Nova, went on to finish second in the Group 1 Yorkshire Oaks and, while it would be foolish to believe he could make the same impact, it's very likely that he'll be plying his trade a higher level after this. (op 11-2)
Qaraaba continues to impress and ran a fine race in defeat. She was successful off a mark of only 76 at Kempton in March and beat the remainder handsomely. Another rise is likely but she's clearly capable and would not look out of place if lining up in Listed company on her next start, especially against her own sex. (op 6-1)
Robin Hoods Bay had a similar profile to the runner-up and he was another to excel. He lost valuable ground with a slow start but made headway easily and was only found out in the final furlong. He has a habit of sluggish starts and could yet prove much better than his current rating. (op 8-1)
Fanny May did best of the rest, staying on steadily up the hill.
Rawaki(IRE) ◆ really took the eye. A winner on his debut at Wolverhampton, he didn't enjoy the clearest of passages but stayed on nicely without being knocked around.

2249 ROBERT CATTON'S 70TH BIRTHDAY MAIDEN FILLIES' STKS 1m 4f

4:30 (4:36) (Class 5) 3-Y-O **£3,234** (£962; £481; £240) **Stalls** Centre

Form RPR

1 **Pink Damsel (IRE)** 3-9-0 0 .... JamieSpencer 6 82+
(Roger Varian) *s.s: hld up: hdwy over 4f out: led over 3f out: shkn up ins fnl f: jst hld on* **2/1**[1]

2 *hd* **Rippled** 3-9-0 0 .... NickyMackay 11 78+
(John Gosden) *hld up: hdwy over 3f out: chsd wnr over 1f out: r.o* **25/1**

54- **3** *2* **Toptempo**[214] 6914 3-9-0 0 .... TedDurcan 7 75+
(Mark H Tompkins) *hld up: pushed along and hung rt fr over 2f out: r.o to go 3rd post: nrst fin* **9/2**[2]

5- **4** *shd* **Openly**[210] 6984 3-9-0 0 .... JackMitchell 9 75+
(James Fanshawe) *hld up: rdn over 2f out: hdwy over 1f out: r.o: nt rch ldrs* **16/1**

6- **5** *nse* **Adeste**[210] 6984 3-9-0 0 .... DaraghO'Donohoe 5 75
(Noel Quinlan) *hld up: hdwy over 2f out: rdn and hung rt over 1f out: r.o* **66/1**

40 **6** *¾* **Black Mascara (IRE)**[23] 1610 3-9-0 0 .... PatDobbs 8 74
(Richard Hannon) *chsd ldr: rdn over 2f out: styd on* **33/1**

0 **7** *½* **Bite Of The Cherry**[27] 1532 3-9-0 0 .... LukeMorris 3 78+
(Michael Bell) *mid-div: hdwy over 4f out: nt clr run and lost pl over 3f out: hmpd over 2f out: r.o ins fnl f* **16/1**

4-0 **8** *½* **Popular**[28] 1503 3-9-0 0 .... IanMongan 10 72+
(Sir Henry Cecil) *hld up: racd keenly: hdwy over 3f out: rdn over 1f out: no ex fnl f* **12/1**

44 **9** *3 ¾* **Light Zabeel (USA)**[16] 1748 3-9-0 0 .... MatthewDavies 4 66
(Mick Channon) *chsd ldrs: rdn over 2f out: wknd over 1f out* **12/1**

6 **10** *13* **Require**[28] 1503 3-9-0 0 .... KierenFallon 2 45+
(Luca Cumani) *prom: pushed along over 3f out: wknd over 2f out* **11/2**[3]

0- **11** *¾* **Al Karlovyyh (IRE)**[190] 7343 3-9-0 0 .... BrettDoyle 1 44
(Clive Brittain) *chsd ldrs: rdn over 2f out: sn wknd* **150/1**

60 **12** *7* **Trulee Scrumptious**[9] 1981 3-8-9 0 .... RosieJessop(5) 13 33
(Peter Charalambous) *prom tl rdn and wknd wl over 2f out* **200/1**

3- **13** *25* **Zenaat**[270] 5320 3-9-0 0 .... RyanMoore 12
(Sir Michael Stoute) *led over 8f: wkng whn hmpd over 2f out: t.o* **9/2**[2]

2m 35.5s (3.50) **Going Correction** +0.175s/f (Good) **13** Ran SP% **121.7**
Speed ratings (Par 96): **95,94,93,93,93 92,92,92,89,81 80,75,59**
Tote Swingers: 1&2 £12.40, 1&3 £3.30, 2&3 £22.70 CSF £65.37 TOTE £3.00: £1.30, £6.70, £1.90; EX 56.40.
Owner Mrs Fitri Hay **Bred** Smythson **Trained** Newmarket, Suffolk

FOCUS
Favourites have dominated this race in recent seasons and this renewal proved no different. There are doubts over the bare form but the winner is potentially a lot better than these.
Zenaat Official explanation: jockey said filly lost left front shoe.

2250 RACING UK H'CAP 1m

5:05 (5:17) (Class 3) (0-95,95) 4-Y-O+ **£7,762** (£2,310; £1,154; £577) **Stalls** High

Form RPR

331- **1** **Arabian Star (IRE)**[238] 6302 4-9-0 **88** .... DavidProbert 12 97
(Andrew Balding) *racd stands' side: led that duo tl gps merged 1/2-way: chsd ldr: rdn over 1f out: led ins fnl f: r.o* **17/2**

361- **2** *1 ¼* **Boogie Shoes**[239] 6273 4-9-7 **95** .... NeilCallan 5 101
(Roger Varian) *racd centre tl gp merged w stands' side 1/2-way: chsd ldr tl led overall 2f out: rdn and hdd ins fnl f: styd on same pce* **13/2**[3]

2631 **3** *½* **Mawaakef (IRE)**[17] 1741 4-8-13 **87** .... FrederikTylicki 1 92
(J R Jenkins) *racd centre tl gp merged w stands' side 1/2-way: overall ldr tl hdd 2f out: sn rdn: styd on* **20/1**

U0-0 **4** *hd* **Unex El Greco**[11] 1924 4-9-0 **88** .... NickyMackay 9 92
(John Gosden) *s.i.s: racd centre tl gp merged w stands' side 1/2-way: hld up: hdwy over 1f out: r.o* **16/1**

20-1 **5** *hd* **Norse Blues**[48] 1128 4-9-2 **90** .... PatDobbs 11 94
(Sylvester Kirk) *racd stands' side: trckd ldr: rdn over 1f out: r.o* **7/1**

1244 **6** *¾* **Reachforthebucks**[16] 1752 4-8-10 **84** .... MartinDwyer 2 86
(Jane Chapple-Hyam) *racd centre tl gp merged w stands' side 1/2-way: chsd ldrs: rdn over 2f out: styd on* **11/2**[2]

00-6 **7** *½* **Duster**[32] 1416 5-8-11 **85** .... DaneO'Neill 3 86
(Hughie Morrison) *racd centre tl gp merged w stands' side 1/2-way: hld up: hdwy over 1f out: r.o* **8/1**

53-6 **8** *5* **Redvers (IRE)**[48] 1128 4-9-0 **88** .... KierenFallon 10 78
(Ed Vaughan) *racd centre tl gp merged w stands' side 1/2-way: hld up: hdwy over 2f out: rdn over 1f out: wknd ins fnl f* **11/1**

2-10 **9** *3 ¾* **Push Me (IRE)**[16] 1752 5-8-7 **81** oh4 .... MartinLane 8 62
(Jamie Poulton) *racd centre tl gp merged w stands' side 1/2-way: hld up in tch: rdn and wknd over 2f out* **50/1**

6/5- **10** ½ **Cockney Class (USA)**[419] 991 5-9-5 **93**.......... JamieSpencer 7 73
(Brian Meehan) *racd centre tl gp merged w stands' side 1/2-way: s.i.s: hld up: hdwy over 1f out: wknd and eased ins fnl f* **16/1**

0-06 **11** ½ **Imaginary World (IRE)**[20] 1652 4-8-0 **81** oh5.........(be) NoelGarbutt(7) 6 60
(Alan McCabe) *racd centre tl gp merged w stands' side 1/2-way: dwlt: hld up: effrt over 1f out: sn wknd* **33/1**

01/- **12** *16* **Garde Cotiere (USA)**[583] 6850 4-9-6 **94**.......... RyanMoore 4 36+
(Jeremy Noseda) *racd centre tl gp merged w stands' side 1/2-way: plld hrd and prom: wknd wl over 2f out* **3/1**[1]

1m 38.91s (0.31) **Going Correction** +0.175s/f (Good) **12** Ran SP% **117.6**
Speed ratings (Par 107): **105,103,103,103,102 102,101,96,92,92 91,75**
Tote Swingers: 1&2 £6.80, 1&3 £22.70, 2&3 £24.00 CSF £61.20 CT £1092.82 TOTE £8.80: £2.50, £2.10, £5.90; EX 66.90.
Owner Jackie & George Smith **Bred** G A E And J Smith Bloodstock Ltd **Trained** Kingsclere, Hants

FOCUS
Some useful handicappers on show. The winer and fifth were the only two to race on the rail, and the winner took another step forward.

NOTEBOOK
Arabian Star(IRE) continues to build on a prolific 3-y-o campaign. He won three times from eight runs last season, including in the Silver Cambridgeshire over 1m1f here in September, and enjoyed a dream run against the near-side rail and stayed on dourly to win. He was 13lb higher than when scoring the first of his successes at Lingfield last May but, always handily placed, knuckled down well when challenged and was value for a shade more the official winning margin. He clearly likes it here and ought to remain competitive off an adjusted mark, with this run expected to have brought him on. (op 10-1 tchd 11-1)
Boogie Shoes was another with a progressive profile and he ran a solid race back in second. He was relatively easy to back beforehand suggesting he'd need this first run for 239 days. However, he came to win his race approaching the furlong marker but was ultimately outstayed. (op 11-2)
Mawaakef(IRE) has been kept busy of late but he's holding his form well and posted a career-best effort. He has been running on much softer ground than he faced here but certainly wasn't inconvenienced. (tchd 25-1)
Unex El Greco was close up in behind, the former confirming the promise he'd shown at Kempton last time. (op 20-1)
Norse Blues also finished close up in behind, and arguably ran close to his Doncaster form off a higher mark. (op 9-1)
Garde Cotiere(USA), having his first start since October 2010, was sent off favourite but was encountering fast turf for the first time and did not help his chance by racing too keenly. Official explanation: jockey said colt ran too free. (op 2-1 tchd 7-2)

2251 RACING EXCELLENCE "HANDS AND HEELS" APPRENTICE SERIES H'CAP (THE RACING EXCELLENCE INITIATIVE) 6f
5:40 (5:41) (Class 5) (0-75,75) 4-Y-0+ **£2,587** (£770; £384; £192) **Stalls** High

Form RPR

-431 **1** **Trojan Rocket (IRE)**[102] 448 4-9-1 **69**.......... IanBurns 6 84
(Michael Wigham) *trckd ldrs: led ins fnl f: pushed out* **8/1**[3]

123- **2** 2½ **Golden Compass**[223] 6696 4-8-10 **64**.......... JoshBaudains 12 71
(Giles Bravery) *chsd ldrs: led over 1f out: hdd and unable qck ins fnl f* **9/1**

3041 **3** ½ **Showboating (IRE)**[14] 1827 4-9-7 **75**..........(tp) ThomasGarner 4 81
(Alan McCabe) *hld up: hdwy over 1f out: sn ev ch: styd on same pce ins fnl f* **9/1**

3025 **4** 1¾ **Hatta Stream (IRE)**[6] 2070 6-8-13 **67**.......... SophieSilvester 7 67
(Lydia Pearce) *hld up: styd on fr over 1f out: nt trble ldrs* **11/2**[2]

1601 **5** *2* **Imprimis Tagula (IRE)**[7] 2043 8-9-4 **75** 6ex..........(v) HannahNunn(3) 3 69
(Alan Bailey) *led: pushed along and hdd over 1f out: wknd ins fnl f* **10/1**

6-32 **6** *hd* **Midnight Rider (IRE)**[11] 1936 4-9-7 **75**.......... MichaelJMurphy 13 68
(Chris Wall) *s.i.s: hld up: shkn up over 1f out: styd on same pce* **3/1**[1]

/4-3 **7** 2¾ **Al Janadeirya**[14] 1824 4-9-3 **74**.......... TimClark(3) 1 58
(Peter Chapple-Hyam) *s.i.s: sn prom: ev ch over 1f out: wknd ins fnl f* **9/1**

-134 **8** 1½ **Silver Linnet (IRE)**[72] 823 5-8-8 **65**.......... AliceHaynes(3) 5 44
(John Butler) *plld hrd and prom: wknd over 1f out* **20/1**

2006 **9** *3* **The Strig**[65] 893 5-8-11 **70**.......... SiobhanMiller(5) 11 40
(Stuart Williams) *hld up: n.d* **25/1**

0005 **10** 1½ **Ocean Legend (IRE)**[25] 1564 7-9-1 **74**.......... BradleyBosley(5) 10 39
(Tony Carroll) *hld up: racd keenly: wknd over 1f out* **14/1**

55 **11** 1½ **Clear Ice (IRE)**[90] 624 5-8-6 **65**..........(b) RobJFitzpatrick(5) 8 25
(Gay Kelleway) *hld up: racd keenly: effrt over 2f out: sn wknd* **16/1**

356- **12** *4* **Darcey**[169] 7595 6-8-11 **68**.......... HayleyBurton(3) 9 15
(Amy Weaver) *awkward leaving stalls: hld up: swtchd lft 1/2-way: wknd over 2f out* **16/1**

00/4 **13** 4½ **Sundae**[71] 839 8-9-7 **75**.......... NoelGarbutt 2
(K F Clutterbuck) *chsd ldr over 3f: wknd wl over 1f out* **50/1**

1m 13.53s (1.33) **Going Correction** +0.175s/f (Good) **13** Ran SP% **119.6**
Speed ratings (Par 103): **98,94,94,91,89 88,85,83,79,77 75,69,63**
Tote Swingers: 1&2 £7.10, 1&3 £15.20, 2&3 £10.60 CSF £76.61 CT £692.48 TOTE £8.30: £2.10, £1.60, £3.90; EX 88.40.
Owner G D J Linder **Bred** J G F Fox **Trained** Newmarket, Suffolk

FOCUS
A competitive sprint handicap, won in convincing style, with the winner posting a clear personal best. The runners raced right across the track.
T/Plt: £204.10 to a £1 stake. Pool: £67,335.72 - 240.73 winning tickets. T/Qpdt: £12.40 to a £1 stake. Pool: £4,162.00 - 248.32 winning tickets. CR

2208 YORK (L-H)
Friday, May 18

OFFICIAL GOING: Good (7.7)
Rail moved out 3m from 9f to entrance to straight adding 7yds to distances of 1m and over.
Wind: Fresh half against Weather: Overcast

2252 LANGLEYS SOLICITORS LLP E B F MARYGATE FILLIES' STKS (LISTED) 5f
1:30 (1:31) (Class 1) 2-Y-0 **£17,760** (£6,717; £3,357; £1,677) **Stalls** Centre

Form RPR

241 **1** **Ceiling Kitty**[11] 1920 2-8-12 0.......... RichardKingscote 9 89
(Tom Dascombe) *trckd ldrs: swtchd lft and gd hdwy wl over 1f out: rdn ins fnl f: led last 100yds: kpt on strly* **20/1**

351 **2** *2* **Mayfield Girl (IRE)**[13] 1861 2-8-12 0.......... RobertWinston 1 82
(Mel Brittain) *racd alone centre: cl up: led after 1f: clr over 2f out: rdn wl over 1f out: hdd & wknd last 100yds* **22/1**

215 **3** *hd* **Effie B**[12] 1891 2-8-12 0.......... ChrisCatlin 6 81
(Mick Channon) *in tch: hdwy 2f out: sn rdn: styd on u.p fnl f* **20/1**

13 **4** *nk* **Woodland Mill (IRE)**[24] 1579 2-8-12 0.......... BarryMcHugh 7 80
(Richard Fahey) *in tch whn hmpd and lost pl after 1f: swtchd lft and rdn 2f out: styd on strly fnl f: nrst fin* **50/1**

1 **5** 3¼ **Ingleby Royale**[30] 1435 2-8-12 0.......... TonyHamilton 2 68
(Richard Fahey) *chsd ldrs: hdwy 2f out: sn rdn and one pce appr fnl f* **8/1**[2]

11 **6** 2½ **Baileys Jubilee**[30] 1451 2-8-12 0.......... SilvestreDeSousa 5 59
(Mark Johnston) *led and sn swtchd rt to stands' rail: hdd after 1f: cl up: rdn along 2f out: sn btn* **2/5**[1]

01 **7** 2¼ **Dream Vale (IRE)**[10] 1949 2-8-12 0.......... DuranFentiman 3 51
(Tim Easterby) *prom: rdn along over 2f out: grad wknd* **16/1**

1 **8** 2½ **Somethingboutmary**[38] 1277 2-8-12 0.......... AmyRyan 11 42
(Kevin Ryan) *towards rr and sn edging lft: hung bdly lft over 2f out: nvr a factor* **14/1**

5 **9** ½ **This Is Nice (IRE)**[13] 1842 2-8-12 0.......... JimCrowley 4 40
(Tom Dascombe) *a towards rr* **20/1**

10 ¾ **Ana Emaratiya** 2-8-12 0.......... PhillipMakin 8 38+
(Kevin Ryan) *dwlt and sltly hmpd s: a bhd* **10/1**[3]

1 **11** *9* **Lothian Countess**[46] 1164 2-8-12 0.......... JamesSullivan 10 5
(George Foster) *chsd ldrs: rdn along over 2f out: sn wknd* **20/1**

1m 1.46s (2.16) **Going Correction** +0.225s/f (Good) **11** Ran SP% **129.5**
Speed ratings (Par 98): **91,87,87,87,81 77,74,70,69,68 53**
Tote Swingers: 1&2 £45.70, 1&3 £26.20, 2&3 £30.50 CSF £393.98 TOTE £20.70: £3.50, £5.30, £4.10; EX 400.20 Trifecta £1344.00 Part won. Pool: £1,816.32 - 0.90 winning units..
Owner A Black & The Master Bettors **Bred** A Black **Trained** Malpas, Cheshire

FOCUS
This Listed 2yo fillies' sprint looked up to scratch. It was a messy race, though, and the form seems weak for the class with the favourite blowing out.

NOTEBOOK
Ceiling Kitty made it third time lucky on Polytrack at Kempton 11 days earlier and stepped up again with a gutsy success on this big step up in class. She tracked the hot favourite towards the stands' rail and found plenty when angled out as that rival began to wane nearing the final furlong. She then mowed down the runner-up towards the centre of the track and should be rated better than the bare margin. Tom Dascombe's juveniles this year have taken time to find their feet, but on recent evidence they are now starting to shine and look worth following. This one's dam became disappointing, but she does have a nice pedigree and ought to handle a sixth furlong before too long. Whether she'll be up to having a serious say in Group company, probably at Royal Ascot in the Queen Mary next month, remains to be seen, though.
Mayfield Girl(IRE) was placed in the Brocklesby on her debut and got off the mark at the third attempt at Thirsk 13 days earlier. She posted a bold bid under an aggressive ride down the middle of the track and was only collared late on. That was probably the place to be, but she's a hardy little filly and now has some valuable black type. (op 25-1)
Effie B was put in her place in a conditions event at Salisbury last time and, while this was a definite step back in the right direction and a personal-best, she does hold the form down somewhat. Her trainer's 2-y-os are going very well at present, however, and she too now has black type next to her name.
Woodland Mill(IRE) ◆ failed to really handle Fibresand behind a good colt last time out. She had beaten the winner readily on her Kempton debut the time before, though, and the way she motored home late after finding early trouble here would suggest she's now crying out for a stiffer test. She's in good hands and looks the one to take from the race with the immediate future in mind
Ingleby Royale was the first string from her yard according to the market and attracted each-way support. However, she lacked any sort of gear change and found it too sharp. (op 11-1)
Baileys Jubilee seemed to have an obvious chance of scoring again despite this being a tougher race. She shot out and made her way over to the near side, but it was clear around 2f out she was in trouble. Perhaps she did too much too soon and may not have been on the best ground, but does leave her with plenty to prove.
Dream Vale(IRE) showed plenty of early speed, but ultimately paid for running with the choke out and may have found the run coming too soon. She's not one to write off.

2253 SPORTINGBET JORVIK STKS (H'CAP) 1m 4f
2:00 (2:00) (Class 2) (0-105,103) 4-Y-0+**£28,463** (£8,470; £4,232; £2,116) **Stalls** Centre

Form RPR

16-1 **1** **Easy Terms**[16] 1756 5-8-10 **92**.......... JamesSullivan 7 100
(Edwin Tuer) *hld up in midfield: dropped to rr over 6f out: nt clr run over 3f out: gd hdwy on outer over 2f out: r.o to ld post* **14/1**

004- **2** *shd* **High Office**[126] 6151 6-8-6 **88**.......... BarryMcHugh 5 95
(Richard Fahey) *led 1f: chsd ldr: led over 3f out: edgd rt and hdd cl home* **33/1**

100- **3** *nk* **Crackentorp**[169] 7297 7-8-9 **91**.......... DavidAllan 1 98
(Tim Easterby) *trckd ldrs: drvn 3f out: upsides 1f out: styd on wl clsng stages* **16/1**

56-3 **4** *hd* **Very Good Day (FR)**[13] 1850 5-8-3 **85**.......... ChrisCatlin 2 92
(Mick Channon) *in rr: gd hdwy on inner over 3f out: upsides over 1f out: no ex clsng stages* **14/1**

040- **5** ¾ **Itlaaq**[195] 7297 6-8-9 **91**..........(t) PaulMulrennan 13 96
(Michael Easterby) *swtchd lft s: hld up in rr: hdwy over 2f out: chal appr fnl f: no ex last 50yds* **25/1**

0-00 **6** ¾ **Bridle Belle**[12] 1882 4-8-3 **85**.......... PatrickMathers 12 89
(Richard Fahey) *hld up in rr: swtchd lft after 1f: hdwy on outside over 2f out: chsng ldrs 1f out: one pce* **12/1**

222- **7** *nk* **Spifer (IRE)**[258] 5700 4-8-9 **91**.......... RobertWinston 4 95+
(Luca Cumani) *t.k.h in midfield: effrt and hung lft 4f out: chal over 1f out: kpt on same pce last 100yds* **6/1**[2]

060- **8** *hd* **Tepmokea (IRE)**[195] 7297 6-8-11 **93**.......... JimCrowley 8 96
(Mrs K Burke) *trckd ldrs: chal over 2f out: kpt on same pce fnl f* **6/1**[2]

560- **9** *2* **Lyric Street (IRE)**[237] 6333 4-9-0 **96**.......... AdamKirby 16 96
(Ed Dunlop) *sn trcking ldrs: fdd last 100yds* **12/1**

050- **10** *1* **Waldvogel (IRE)**[219] 6803 8-8-6 **88**.......... AndreaAtzeni 3 87
(Nicky Richards) *mid-div: effrt over 2f out: one pce fnl f* **16/1**

00-1 **11** 1¼ **Deauville Flyer**[38] 1273 6-8-10 **92**.......... GrahamGibbons 11 89
(Tim Easterby) *mid-div: hdwy over 3f out: sn chsng ldrs: fdd last 100yds* **8/1**[3]

/5-3 **12** 3¼ **Caucus**[12] 1882 5-9-4 **100**.......... WilliamBuick 14 91
(John Gosden) *sn trcking ldrs: wknd over 1f out* **9/2**[1]

502- **13** ½ **Warlu Way**[230] 6528 5-8-11 **93**.......... PhillipMakin 10 84
(John Dunlop) *stdd and swtchd lft s: in rr: hdwy over 3f out: n.m.r over 2f out: lost pl over 1f out* **20/1**

31-0 **14** *39* **Sadeek's Song (USA)**[13] 1855 4-9-7 **103**.......... FrankieDettori 9 31
(Mahmood Al Zarooni) *trckd ldrs: effrt over 3f out: lost pl 2f out: bhd whn heavily eased ins fnl f: t.o* **10/1**

03-0 **15** *15* **Kinyras (IRE)**[38] 1273 4-8-5 **87**.................................. SilvestreDeSousa 6
(Michael Easterby) *drvn to ld after 1f: hdd over 3f out: lost pl over 1f out: eased and sn bhd: t.o* **25/1**

2m 35.57s (2.37) **Going Correction** +0.225s/f (Good) **15** Ran SP% **122.8**
Speed ratings (Par 109): **101,100,100,100,100 99,99,99,97,97 96,94,93,67,57**
Tote Swingers: 1&2 £70.40, 1&3 £43.30, 2&3 £105.20 CSF £428.88 CT £7263.45 TOTE £13.90: £3.00, £12.40, £3.50; EX 666.30 Trifecta £1562.30 Part won. Pool: £2,111.29 - 0.60 winning units..
Owner E Tuer **Bred** T E Pocock **Trained** Birkby, N Yorks
■ Stewards' Enquiry : Barry McHugh two-day ban; used whip above permitted level (3rd-4th May).

FOCUS
A tight and competitive handicap, run at a decent pace. There was a bunch finish and the form is nothing out of the ordinary, but Easy Terms produced another personal best.

NOTEBOOK
Easy Terms, winner of five of her previous six starts including on last month's Pontefract reappearance, is now 33lb higher than for the first of those successes. Despite losing her place in the middle of the contest, she made relentless progress halfway up the home straight and maintained her effort to lead inside the last furlong, though she didn't have a lot to spare at the line. As a result of that she can't go up too much for this, but as a mare currently in irresistible form it's impossible to know how much there is still left. She is a credit to her connections. (op 11-1)
High Office hadn't been in great form on the Flat or over hurdles since last summer, but this was much better. Always handy, he seemed likely to drop away over a furlong out, but kept at it and made sure the mare had to pull out all the stops. It's worth noting that two of his four wins have come after a break so he may not come on much for it, but even a repeat should win him races.
Crackentorp, a dual winner over C&D last season and successful over hurdles when last seen in December, had every chance halfway up the straight and, after looking held, ran on again once his rider put his whip down. This should set him up for a repeat win in next month's Queen Mother's Cup over C&D, provided he isn't put up more than 4lb for this effort.
Very Good Day(FR) ◆, winless since landing his maiden in June 2010, showed a bit more on his Goodwood reappearance 13 days earlier and finished well from off the pace towards the far side of the track here. He seems to have rediscovered his form and a return to further won't hurt. (op 12-1)
Itlaaq, returning from 195 days off, did well considering he tried to come from last place. He won first time out in 2010 so can go well fresh, but this was still a decent reappearance. (op 40-1)
Bridle Belle ◆ came through to hold every chance over a furlong out and improved on her two previous starts this year. She is already due to drop another 2lb, so could be interesting if turned out again reasonably quickly. (tchd 14-1)
Spifer(IRE), last seen splitting a couple of subsequent winners at Ascot last September, took a keen hold early and, although just about in front over a furlong out, then started to duck and dive and didn't appear to fancy it. This isn't the first time he has looked less than straightforward and is one to avoid at present. (tchd 11-2)
Tepmokea(IRE), 3lb higher than when winning this race for Richard Fahey on his reappearance last season, came through to hold every chance and there seemed no excuses. (op 9-1)
Caucus is already due to go up 4lb following his encouraging return at Newmarket 12 days earlier, but he found nothing at all off the bridle and proved disappointing. Official explanation: trainer could offer no explanation as to poor run.
Sadeek's Song(USA) was completely out of his depth in the Jockey Club Stakes on his return, but ran terribly again despite this much less-exalted company. He wasn't the first stable representative to disappoint at the meeting. Official explanation: jockey said colt ran flat. (tchd 9-1)

2254 SPORTINGBET YORKSHIRE CUP (BRITISH CHAMPIONS SERIES) (GROUP 2) 1m 6f
2:30 (2:30) (Class 1) 4-Y-0+

£79,394 (£30,100; £15,064; £7,504; £3,766; £1,890) **Stalls** Low

Form RPR
23-2 **1** **Red Cadeaux**[16] 1750 6-9-0 115.................................. TomMcLaughlin 4 113+
(Ed Dunlop) *trckd ldrs: smooth hdwy over 3f out: cl up over 2f out: rdn to ld wl over 1f out: hung lft ins fnl f: kpt on strly* **4/1**[2]
5465 **2** *1* **Glen's Diamond**[8] 1994 4-9-0 106.................................. TonyHamilton 7 112
(Richard Fahey) *t.k.h: hld up in tch: effrt 3f out: rdn 2f out: styd on u.p fnl f: nrst fin* **25/1**
43-1 **3** *1 3/4* **Harris Tweed**[27] 1507 5-9-0 115.................................. LiamJones 2 109
(William Haggas) *set stdy pce: qcknd over 4f out: pushed along 3f out: rdn over 2f out: sn jnd and hdd wl over 1f out: hld whn hmpd ins fnl f: kpt on same pce* **9/4**[1]
315- **4** *2 1/2* **Times Up**[216] 6857 6-9-0 111.................................. EddieAhern 1 106+
(John Dunlop) *hld up in tch: hdwy 4f out: rdn to chse ldrs 2f out: kpt on same pce u.p appr fnl f* **9/2**[3]
6015 **5** *2* **Electrolyser (IRE)**[16] 1750 7-9-0 109.................................. AdamKirby 8 103
(Clive Cox) *trckd ldr: effrt and cl up over 3f out: sn rdn along and wknd over 2f out* **20/1**
6-45 **6** *5* **Blue Bajan (IRE)**[13] 1855 10-9-0 104.................................. DanielTudhope 5 96
(David O'Meara) *hld up in rr: sme hdwy 3f out: rdn over 2f out and no imp* **10/1**
11- **7** *41* **Be Fabulous (GER)**[208] 7049 5-9-1 113.................................. FrankieDettori 6 40
(Mahmood Al Zarooni) *hld up in rr: effrt over 3f out: sn rdn and btn* **7/1**
4-15 **8** *5* **Arctic Cosmos (USA)**[27] 1507 5-9-0 111..................(b) WilliamBuick 3 32
(John Gosden) *trckd ldng pair: hdwy over 3f out: rdn and edgd lft over 2f out: sn wknd and eased* **7/1**

3m 2.89s (2.69) **Going Correction** +0.225s/f (Good) **8** Ran SP% **111.7**
Speed ratings (Par 115): **101,100,99,98,96 94,70,67**
Tote Swingers: 1&2 £12.50, 1&3 £2.90, 2&3 £12.90 CSF £86.97 TOTE £4.80: £1.60, £3.90, £1.40; EX 96.00 Trifecta £409.10 Pool: £2,128.49 - 3.85 winning units..
Owner R J Arculli **Bred** Foursome Thoroughbreds **Trained** Newmarket, Suffolk
■ Stewards' Enquiry : Tom McLaughlin caution; careless riding.

FOCUS
This longstanding Group 2 for stayers looked wide-open this season. The early pace was sound and the form looks solid enough rated around the runner-up, without being a vintage renewal. Red Cadeaux scored a bit more cosily than the bare form.

NOTEBOOK
Red Cadeaux was nicely placed when the tempo became serious around 3f out and readily hit the front near the furlong pole. However, he drifted markedly left soon after and allowed the placed horses another chance. He was always doing enough, though, so most probably found himself in front plenty soon enough, as he did at Flemington last November, and it could be there's even better to come from him this year under more patient tactics. He somewhat surprisingly doesn't hold an entry in next month's Gold Cup at Royal Ascot, but he does have plenty of speed for a stayer and his season revolves around another crack at Group 1 races abroad such as the Melbourne Cup, as well as the Irish St Leger in which he was placed last year. Indeed he could try his luck next in the Coronation Cup at Epsom on Derby day, back over 1m4f. His victory here is also a definite boost to the chances of Godolphin's progressive grey Colour Vision, who readily beat him at Kempton and heads for the Gold Cup. (op 7-2)
Glen's Diamond took time to settle under restraint yet did some very pleasing late work. The winner hanging allowed him to finish so close, but he's long been well regarded and is clearly worth persevering with in staying races. (op 28-1)
Harris Tweed was a gutsy winner on his return at Newbury last month on bad ground and was well backed to follow up on this quicker surface. He got his own way out in front, but was readily headed when the winner hit top gear and really teed it up for that rival. This likeable 5yo rates the benchmark and fully deserves to win a race of this class, which could well happen when he's back on more testing ground. (op 11-4)
Times Up was going nicely as they swung into the home straight. John Dunlop's late-maturing 6yo has never been at his best first time up, however, and he flattened out as though markedly in need of the run from the furlong marker. He's also happiest on quicker ground and there should be another nice pot in him this year. The Irish St Leger really looks the race if the ground is suitable, but there would be a lot worse outsiders if he turns up next in the Gold Cup. His rider later confirmed he blew up and was changing his legs on the ground. (op 11-2)
Electrolyser(IRE) was always going to find it tough to dominate with Harris Tweed in attendance. He wasn't beaten quite as far than was the case behind the winner on Polytrack last time, but will probably have to venture abroad for easier pickings to win a Group race. (op 16-1)
Blue Bajan(IRE) was a bit free early and found very little for pressure, running close to his Nottingham form with Electrolyser.
Be Fabulous(GER) joined her leading connections after winning the Group 1 Prix Royal-Oak at Longchamp in October. She was penalised for that and conceded weight all round on this British debut, but still attracted support. It was a woeful display from her, however, and yet another high-profile flop from her stable. (op 8-1)
Arctic Cosmos(USA) was expected to finish closer to Harris Tweed on this better ground and had blinkers back on instead of cheekpieces. He did too much early on just off the pace, though, and now has something to prove. The trainer later suggested the horse twisted his back and he's now likely to be roughed off until the second half of term. (op 9-2)

2255 EQUINITY POWERED BY GARMIN FILLIES' STKS REGISTERED AS MICHAEL SEELY MEMORIAL STAKES (LISTED RACE) 1m
3:00 (3:00) (Class 1) 3-Y-O

£22,684 (£8,600; £4,304; £2,144; £1,076; £540) **Stalls** Low

Form RPR
2110 **1** **Laugh Out Loud**[12] 1884 3-8-12 96.................................. WilliamBuick 5 111+
(Mick Channon) *trckd ldr: hdwy to ld wl over 2f out and sn jnd: rdn over 1f out: styd on wl fnl f* **2/1**[1]
14-3 **2** *1* **Electrelane**[27] 1508 3-8-12 92.................................. JimCrowley 3 108
(Ralph Beckett) *trckd ldng pair: hdwy 3f out: chal 2f out: ev ch whn rdn and hung lft over 1f out: kpt on u.p fnl f* **8/1**
136- **3** *10* **Hello Glory**[237] 6337 3-8-12 99.................................. EddieAhern 2 85
(David Simcock) *hld up towards rr: hdwy 3f out: rdn along 2f out: sn no imp* **13/2**
16-2 **4** *nk* **Way Too Hot**[41] 1215 3-8-12 93.................................. AdamKirby 4 84
(Clive Cox) *hld up in rr: hdwy over 3f out: rdn to chse ldrs over 2f out: sn one pce* **6/1**
6-30 **5** *1 3/4* **Lily's Angel (IRE)**[12] 1884 3-9-1 98.................................. TonyHamilton 6 83
(Richard Fahey) *trckd ldrs on outer: effrt 3f out: rdn over 2f out and sn btn* **4/1**[2]
10-4 **6** *hd* **Tactfully (IRE)**[41] 1215 3-8-12 91.................................. FrankieDettori 1 80
(Mahmood Al Zarooni) *led: rdn along over 3f out: hdd wl over 2f out: sn wknd* **5/1**[3]
6-06 **7** *5* **What's Up (IRE)**[12] 1887 3-8-12 91.................................. PhillipMakin 7 68
(Kevin Ryan) *hld up: a in rr* **25/1**

1m 40.13s (1.13) **Going Correction** +0.225s/f (Good) **7** Ran SP% **112.6**
Speed ratings (Par 104): **103,102,92,91,89 89,84**
Tote Swingers: 1&2 £3.70, 1&3 £3.50, 2&3 £7.20 CSF £18.23 TOTE £2.90: £1.70, £3.90; EX 19.60.
Owner Ann Black,M Al Qatami & K M Al Mudhaf **Bred** Norman Court Stud **Trained** West Ilsley, Berks

FOCUS
An average contest for the class. The first pair, who came right away from the remainder in the final 2f, were always up there, and only they showed their form. Another step forward from the winner.

NOTEBOOK
Laugh Out Loud hit top gear nearing the final furlong and was always doing enough to hold off the runner-up from thereon. She took time to settle out wide in a handy early position, but that didn't stop her from producing a neat turn of foot and she was probably idling somewhat near the business end. This was just her second outing on turf, having pulled too hard when not disgraced in the 1000 Guineas last time, and she's evidently a cut about Listed class. The obvious next step would have to be the Group 1 Coronation Stakes at Royal Ascot next month for this dual AW winner. That would be shooting at the stars again, but she is entitled to have a crack and it's a race her trainer has a good record in. The track at Ascot also often suits those with Polytrack form. There is also the Listed Sandringham Handicap to consider there, although she would surely be close to top weight in that after being reassessed. (op 9-4 tchd 15-8)
Electrelane was a well-held third on her return behind stablemate Moonstone Magic in the Group 3 Fred Darling over 7f last month, but did stay this trip on her final outing at two on testing ground in France. She travelled sweetly on the inside and, while lacking the tactical pace of the winner, there was much to admire about the way she rallied late on. She finished a long way clear in second and is obviously up to going one better in this class. Perhaps she will now head for the Sandringham at Royal Ascot, but wouldn't want it quick there. (op 17-2 tchd 10-1)
Hello Glory, well entered up, caught the eye moving well towards the far side after turning for home. It was her first outing this year, though, and she petered out as the first pair quickened clear. It was also her first attempt at the longer trip and she ought to last longer next time. She too could be one for the Sandringham next month. (op 6-1 tchd 7-1)
Way Too Hot was closely matched with the winner on her previous Kempton form so this rates a backwards step, but is also an indication of that rival's improvement. (op 11-2)
Lily's Angel(IRE) was one place ahead of the winner in the 1000 Guineas 12 days earlier, but was 3lb worse off back down in class. She never looked that happy this time, wanting to hang in the home straight, and obviously wasn't near her best. (op 7-2)
Tactfully(IRE) was beaten two lengths by the winner at Kempton last time. She dictated the pace and was easily left behind when the race got serious, but still ran close enough to her last-time-out form with the fourth. Faster ground is probably what she wants. (op 7-1)
What's Up(IRE) Official explanation: jockey said filly was never travelling.

2256 RALPH RAPER MEMORIAL STKS (H'CAP) 5f
3:35 (3:39) (Class 4) (0-80,80) 3-Y-O **£7,762** (£2,310; £1,154; £577) **Stalls** Centre

Form RPR
-312 **1** **Morocco Moon**[49] 1110 3-8-11 70.................................. ShaneKelly 17 90
(Tim Pitt) *chsd ldrs: hdwy on outer 2f out: rdn to chal and edgd lft ins fnl f: drvn and kpt on to ld nr line* **28/1**
431- **2** *shd* **Annie Beach (IRE)**[227] 6598 3-9-2 75.................................. GrahamGibbons 4 95
(David Barron) *wnt rt s: a.p: hdwy to ld wl over 1f out: jnd and rdn ins fnl f: hdd and no ex nr line* **16/1**
2-1 **3** *4 1/2* **Dreaming Of Rubies**[56] 1016 3-8-12 71..................(t) WilliamBuick 5 75
(Ben Haslam) *mde most tl rdn and hdd wl over 1f out: kpt on same pce u.p fnl f* **12/1**[3]
1- **4** *1/2* **Lupin Pooter**[336] 3125 3-8-8 67.................................. LeeNewman 6 69
(David Barron) *wnt rt s: chsd ldrs: rdn wl over 1f out: kpt on fnl f* **25/1**

50-0 **5** *hd* **Tip Top Gorgeous (IRE)**27 1317 3 -9-477................. DanielTudhope 8 78
(David O'Meara) *in tch: hdwy to chse ldrs wl over 1f out: rdn and one pce ent fnl f* **20/1**

-423 **6** *1 ¼* **Phoenix Clubs (IRE)**14 1817 3 -8-766........................... BarryMcHugh 3 63
(Paul Midgley) *sltly hmpd s: chsd ldrs: hdwy over 2f out: rdn wl over 1f out: sn one pce* **12/1**3

7 *hd* **Bogini (IRE)**216 6880 3 -8-1372............................(b) SilvestreDeSousa 15 68
(M D O'Callaghan, Ire) *wnt rt s: hld up in tch: hdwy 2f out: rdn to chse ldrs over 1f out: one pce ins fnl f* **20/1**

00-0 **8** *2* **Nearly A Gift (IRE)**3 1862 3 -8-1170.............................(t) DavidAllan 19 59
(Tim Easterby) *hampered s and bhd: hdwy wl over 1f out: kpt on fnl f* **50/1**

-320 **9** *3 ¼* **Come On Dave (IRE)**27 1317 3 -8-268................ ShirleyTeasdale(7) 13 45
(David Nicholls) *cl up: disp ld 1/2-way: sn rdn and wkng whn n.m.r 1f out* **16/1**

414 **10** *2 ¼* **Wicked Wench**21 1644 3 -9-376..................................... TonyCulhane 12 45
(Jo Hughes) *prom: cl up 1/2-way: rdn wl over 1f out and grad wknd* **20/1**

35-3 **11** *¾* **Chooseday (IRE)**20 1658 3 -9-780................................. PhillipMakin 16 46
(Kevin Ryan) *hmpd s: a in rr* **16/1**

2101 **12** *½* **Towbee**11 1912 3 -9-073 6ex... JamesSullivan 10 38
(Michael Easterby) *towards rr: hdwy 1/2-way: rdn along 2f out: sn btn* **5/1**1

60-0 **13** *2 ¼* **Fayr Fall (IRE)**10 1241 3 -8-771.................................. AdamCarter(5) 14 27
(Tim Easterby) *midfield: rdn along over 2f out: nvr nr ldrs* **50/1**

6-33 **14** *¾* **Middleton Flyer (IRE)**1 1912 3 -8-867........................ MickyFenton 20 21
(Paul Midgley) *in tch on wd outside: rdn along 1/2-way: sn wknd* **50/1**

3223 **15** *nk* **Homeward Strut**18 1721 3 -8-367..............................(b) RaulDaSilva(5) 7 20
(Frank Sheridan) *hmpd s: a in rr* **25/1**

00-0 **16** *¾* **Kylesku (IRE)**11 1912 3 -8-672.......................................(t) KevinStott(7) 2 22
(Kevin Ryan) *s.i.s and bhd towards far side: hdwy over 2f out: rdn to chse ldrs wl over 1f out: sn wknd* **66/1**

1-36 **17** *½* **Sky Crossing**13 1862 3 -9-073.................................... PaulMulrennan 11 21
(James Given) *chsd ldrs: rdn along 2f out: wknd over 1f out* **25/1**

12-2 **18** *6* **Master Bond**20 1658 3 -9-280.................................... JustinNewman(5) 1
(Bryan Smart) *prom on far rail: rdn along 2f out: sn wknd* **7/1**2

1m 0.19s (0.89)**Going Correction** +0.225s/f (Good) **18**Ran SP% **98.8**
Speed ratings (Par 101): **101,100,93,92,92 90,90,87,81,78 77,76,72,71,70 69,68,59**
Tote Swingers: 1&2 £53.90, 1&3 £26.70, 2&3 £9.20 CSF £208.14 CT £2092.38 TOTE £33.70: £6.20, £3.00 , £2.10 , £5.00 ; EX 440.40 TRIFECTA Not won. .
Owner Saintly Racing **Bred** R J Cornelius **Trained** Newmarket, Suffolk

FOCUS
The complexion of the contest changed completely with the withdrawal of the hot-favourite Tioman Pearl after he got under his stall. It paid to race handily. The first two did well to pull clear and have been given credit for the form.

2257 SPORTINGBET.COM STKS (H'CAP) 1m 2f 88y
4:10 (4:10) (Class 3) (0-90,90) 4-Y-0+ **£8,409** (£2,502; £1,250 ; £625) **Stalls** Low

Form RPR

1-12 **1** **Media Hype**20 1657 5 -9-083.. PhillipMakin 12 99+
(Mrs K Burke) *in rr: hmpde and forced wd bnd after 1f: smooth hdwy over 3f out: trcking ldrs and swtchd rt over 1f out: qcknd to ld last 75yds* **6/1**1

54-2 **2** *1 ¾* **Troopingthecolour**20 1674 6 -9-689...................... SilvestreDeSousa 8 100
(Steve Gollings) *chsd ldrs: led over 2f out: hdd and no ex last 50yds* **7/1**3

12-6 **3** *1 ¼* **Muffin McLeay (IRE)**14 1820 4 -8-1382......................... LeeNewman 4 91
(David Barron) *in tch: hdwy to chse ldrs over 3f out: styd on same pce last 150yds* **16/1**

-013 **4** *3 ½* **Tres Coronas (IRE)**23 1605 5 -9-588....................... GrahamGibbons 11 90+
(David Barron) *t.k.h: in rr: hmpd bnd after 1f: hdwy to chse ldrs over 2f out: kpt on one pce fnl f* **14/1**

30-0 **5** *2* **Barren Brook**48 1130 5 -9-790.. JamesSullivan 1 88
(Michael Easterby) *hld up in mid-div: smooth hdwy on inner over 2f out: chsng ldrs over 1f out: sn fdd* **13/2**2

1-10 **6** *½* **Camborne**34 1381 4 -9-487... WilliamBuick 17 84
(John Gosden) *s.i.s: in rr: hdwy over 2f out: hung lft over 1f out: kpt on* **14/1**

51-0 **7** *3* **Shamdarley (IRE)**48 1128 4 -9-285.......................... PaulMulrennan 5 76
(Michael Dods) *t.k.h: trckd ldrs: chal over 2f out: wknd over 1f out* **13/2**2

500- **8** *1 ½* **Classic Colori (IRE)**88 7391 5 -9-689...................... DanielTudhope 10 78
(David O'Meara) *led: hdd over 2f out: wknd over 1f out* **22/1**

004- **9** *2 ¼* **Pendragon (USA)**181 7492 9 -9-487............................ BarryMcHugh 20 71
(Brian Ellison) *in rr: hdwy inner over 3f out: wknd over 1f out* **25/1**

1140 **10** *2 ½* **Maverik**27 1510 4 -9-083.. JimCrowley 7 62
(Ralph Beckett) *chsd ldrs: chal 3f out: wknd over 1f out* **12/1**

2153 **11** *hd* **Dunhoy (IRE)**27 1513 4 -8-1382........................... TomMcLaughlin 6 61
(Tony Newcombe) *hld up towards rr: t.k.h: edgd rt bnd after 1f: hdwy on outside 3f out: sn chsng ldrs: wknd over 1f out* **16/1**

043- **12** *¾* **Porgy**155 6445 7 -8-1281... ShaneKelly 18 59
(Tim Pitt) *slowly away and wnt rt s: hld up in last: stdy hdwy over 1f out: nvr a factor* **33/1**

60-6 **13** *1 ½* **Pleasant Day (IRE)**13 1854 5 -8-985................... GeorgeChaloner(7) 14 60
(Richard Fahey) *chsd ldrs: lost pl over 1f out* **20/1**

41-4 **14** *1* **Sandusky**12 1882 4 -9-588.. FrankieDettori 19 61
(Mahmood Al Zarooni) *sn mid-div: drvn over 3f out: lost pl wl over 1f out* **6/1**1

4/5- **15** *9* **Jaaryah (IRE)**380 1807 4 -9-588................................... AndreaAtzeni 15 44
(Roger Varian) *swtchd lft after s: in rr: hdwy on inner to chse ldrs over 2f out: sn wknd: eased whn bhd* **25/1**

64-0 **16** *13* **The Mellor Fella**20 1670 4 -8-1180................................ TonyHamilton 9 11
(Richard Fahey) *chsd ldrs: lost pl over 2f out: eased whn bhd ins fnl f* **28/1**

2m 12.9s (0.40)**Going Correction** +0.225s/f (Good) **16**Ran SP% **123.7**
Speed ratings (Par 107): **107,105,104,101,100 99,97,96,94,92 92,91,90,89,82 72**
Tote Swingers: 1&2 £10.30, 1&3 £22.50, 2&3 £29.60 CSF £42.74 CT £657.79 TOTE £7.10 : £1.90, £2.10 , £4.90 , £3.10 ; EX 46.40 Trifecta £1545.10 Pool: £2,296.84 - 1.10 winning units.
Owner Light Valley Stud & Mrs E Burke **Bred** Meon Valley Stud **Trained** Middleham Moor, N Yorks

FOCUS
Another hot handicap run at a good pace and the finish was fought out between two half-brothers. The form looks solid and the winner continues to progress. He looks better than the bare form.

NOTEBOOK
Media Hype was up another 3lb having probably been unlucky not to complete the hat-trick at Haydock last time, but he put matters right here. No that it was completely straightforward as he was knocked to the rear of the field when hampered after a furlong, but he nonetheless travelled into the race like a dream and was never going to fail once in front, despite hanging away to his left late on. (op 5-1)
Troopingthecolour appeared to run well above himself in a four-runner Ripon conditions event on last month's return, but at least that run would have put him straight for this. He battled right to the line having been up there from the off and coming off the bridle a fair way out. He is 9lb higher than for his last win in a handicap, but remains competitive off this mark. (op 9-1)
Muffin McLeay (IRE) didn't find the race panning out for him on his Musselburgh return, but he had every chance here and looked like winning coming to the last 2f before getting run out of it by the front pair. He is still lightly raced, but this looks about as far as he wants to go at present.
Tres Coronas (IRE) met trouble in running when third at Epsom last time, but had every chance here having been produced with his effort over a furlong from home, but he then drifted left and wasn't making any further impression. He could probably have done with the ground not drying out. (op 16-1)
Barren Brook was back up in trip after finishing seventh in the Lincoln on his return and nothing was travelling better halfway up the home straight, but he found less than expected off the bridle. Perhaps he needs a quicker surface in order to help him see out this trip. (tchd 7-1)
Camborne had questions to answer following his poor effort on his turf debut at Newcastle last time and again missed the break here, something he has done in all three previous starts. He eventually plugged on into a never-dangerous sixth, but his head carriage wasn't pretty and he also hung, so it's probably best just to watch him at present.
Shamdarley(IRE) ended last season with a C&D success and ran much better than his finishing position of seventh would suggest in the Spring Mile on his reappearance, but despite holding a decent position throughout he found disappointingly little off the bridle. He's worth another chance. (op 6-1)
Sandusky very much caught the eye on his Newmarket return 12 days earlier and was officially 3lb well in, but proved to be yet another from the yard to fold extremely tamely. Official explanation: jockey said colt had no more to give. (op 13-2 tchd 11-2)

2258 SPORTINGBET STKS (H'CAP) 1m 4f
4:45 (4:45) (Class 4) (0-80,79) 3-Y-0 **£7,762** (£2,310; £1,154 ; £577) **Stalls** Centre

Form RPR

0-31 **1** **Estedaama (IRE)**43 1206 3 -9-476.................................. FrankieDettori 9 83
(Marcus Tregoning) *hld up in tch: hdwy 3f out: chsd ldrs 2f out: rdn to chal ent fnl f: styd on wl to ld last 50yds* **6/1**3

13-3 **2** *nk* **Daneking**21 1647 3 -9-577.. WilliamBuick 6 84
(John Gosden) *t.k.h: trckd ldrs: hdwy over 3f out: slt ld wl over 1f out and sn rdn: wandered ins fnl f: drvn: edgd lft and hdd last 50yds* **10/3**1

41-0 **3** *1 ¼* **Rayvin Black**29 1470 3 -9-779.. EddieAhern 1 84
(Mark H Tompkins) *hld up in tch on inner: hdwy over 3f out: rdn to chse ldrs 2f out: ev ch over 1f out tl one pce ins fnl f* **10/1**

62-2 **4** *2 ¼* **Spanish Wedding**18 1707 3 -9-476...................................... AdamKirby 5 77
(Marco Botti) *cl up: rdn along over 2f out and ev ch tl one pce ent fnl f* **4/1**2

0521 **5** *shd* **Priestley's Reward (IRE)**7 2118 3 -8-1273 6ex.(v) MichaelMetcalfe(3) 8 74
(Mrs K Burke) *hld up towards rr: hdwy 4f out: rdn to chse ldrs 2f out: kpt on same pce* **15/2**

1-00 **6** *2* **Choisan (IRE)**20 1653 3 -9-375.. DavidAllan 2 73
(Tim Easterby) *hld up towards rr: hdwy 3f out: rdn 2f out: no imp* **20/1**

4-32 **7** *4* **Only Orsenfoolsies**16 1757 3 -8-265 oh2..................... NeilFarley(5) 10 57
(Micky Hammond) *plld hrd: chsd ldrs on outer: hdwy to ld 3f out: rdn 2f out: sn hdd & wknd appr fnl f* **16/1**

5523 **8** *10* **Green Mitas (ITY)**24 1589 3 -8-568............................... RaulDaSilva(5) 4 44
(Frank Sheridan) *s.i.s and in rr: hdwy on wd outside over 3f out: rdn to chse ldrs over 2f out: sn wknd* **33/1**

23-1 **9** *¾* **Blades Lad**20 1676 3 -9-577.. TonyHamilton 3 51
(Richard Fahey) *trckd ldng pair: cl up 4f out: rdn along over 3f out: edgd lft and wknd 2f out* **7/1**

5-21 **10** *3 ¼* **Key Gold**41 1223 3 -9-072.. SilvestreDeSousa 7 41
(Mark Johnston) *led: rdn along 4f out: hdd 3f out and sn wknd* **9/1**

50-0 **11** *9* **Sirious Oss**13 1866 3 -8-1169...................................... PaulMulrennan 11 24
(Michael Easterby) *hld up: a in rr: bhd fnl 2f* **40/1**

2m 38.81s (5.61)**Going Correction** +0.225s/f (Good) **11**Ran SP% **116.7**
Speed ratings (Par 101): **90,89,88,87,87 86,83,76,76,74 68**
Tote Swingers: 1&2 £5.20, 1&3 £12.30, 2&3 £7.30 CSF £25.55 CT £198.98 TOTE £6.20 : £2.60 , £1.50, £3.50 ; EX 20.80 Trifecta £605.10 Pool: £1,864.63 - 2.28 winning units. .
Owner Hamdan Al Maktoum **Bred** Shadwell Estate Company Limited **Trained** Lambourn, Berks

FOCUS
A fair 3-y-o handicap featuring largely unexposed sorts, and this is likely a good race for the grade. Improvement from the first two.
Blades Lad Official explanation: jockey said gelding hung left.
T/Jkpt: Not won. T/Plt: £12,695.00 to a £1 stake. Pool: £196,860.00 - 11.32 winning tickets.
T/Qpdt: £57.50 to £1. Pool: £14,210.00 - 182.74 w. tickets. JR 2259a Foreign Racing (See RI)

1841 DONCASTER (L-H)
Saturday, May 19

OFFICIAL GOING: Good (8.0)
Wind: Light half behind Weather: Overcast

2260 CROWNHOTEL-BAWTRY.COM APPRENTICE H'CAP 1m 4f
6:10 (6:10) (Class 5) (0-70,69) 4-Y-0+ **£3,067** (£905; £453) **Stalls** Low

Form RPR

5-00 **1** **Sedgwick**16 1792 10 -8-1063................................. ShirleyTeasdale(5) 16 71+
(Shaun Harris) *in tch: hdwy 4f out: chal 2f out: sn rdn and led over 1f out: spooked and jinked rt 50yds out: kpt on* **25/1**

010- **2** *nk* **Kayaan**27 6790 5 -9-365.. CPGeoghegan 19 70+
(Pam Sly) *stdd and swtchd lft to inner s: hld up towards rr: hdwy 3f out: nt clr run and hmpd over 2f out: sn swtchd rt and rdn: styd on strly fnl f* **12/1**

6-04 **3** *¾* **Bavarian Nordic (USA)**24 1598 7 -8-755 oh5..................(v) AmyRyan 7 60
(Richard Whitaker) *trckd ldrs: hdwy 4f out: cl up 3f out: led over 2f out and sn rdn: hdd appr fnl f and kpt on same pce* **20/1**

146- **4** *½* **Al Furat (USA)**218 6838 4 -8-1263........................... ShaneBKelly(3) 13 66
(Ron Barr) *in tch: smooth hdwy to trck ldrs over 3f out: effrt 2f out and ev ch: rdn ent fnl f: n.m.r and kpt on same pce* **16/1**

-322 **5** *¾* **Reset City**33 1418 6 -9-769... RyanClark 15 71
(Ian Williams) *hld up in rr: hdwy 3f out: rdn to chse ldrs wl over 1f out: one pce fnl f* **9/2**1

0134 **6** *1 ¼* **Kingaroo (IRE)**8 2048 6 -8-255 oh4.............................. DarrenEgan(5) 14 55
(Garry Woodward) *led: rdn along 4f out: drvn 3f out: hdd over 2f out and grad wknd* **16/1**

0-2 **7** *hd* **Landesherr (GER)**15 1829 5 -9-163.................................(t) LeeTopliss 8 63
(Steve Gollings) *cl up: rdn and ev ch over 2f out: drvn wl over 1f out and kpt on one pce* **15/2**3

443 **8** *nse* **Polurrian (IRE)**14 1867 5 -9-769................................. DeclanCannon 4 69
(David O'Meara) *hld up towards rr: hdwy 3f out: rdn over 2f out: kpt on same pce* **9/1**

-434 **9** ¾ **Embsay Crag**[28] 1525 6-9-4 **69** GarryWhillans(3) 17 67
(Kate Walton) *hld up and bhd: hdwy on outer wl over 2f out: sn rdn and kpt on: nrst fin* **11/2**[2]

240- **10** ¾ **Locum**[149] 7859 7-8-2 **57** RobJFitzpatrick(7) 12 54
(Mark H Tompkins) *in tch: pushed along 4f out: rdn wl over 2f out: sn one pce* **14/1**

0-50 **11** 3 **Maybeme**[12] 1913 6-8-9 **57** ow1 PaulPickard 3 49
(Neville Bycroft) *hld up and bhd: sme hdwy fnl 2f: nvr a factor* **16/1**

4010 **12** 2½ **Jeer (IRE)**[48] 1154 8-9-0 **67** (t) DavidSimmonson(5) 5 55
(Michael Easterby) *chsd ldrs: hdwy and cl up 5f out: rdn along 3f out: sn wknd* **12/1**

366- **13** 3¼ **Ferney Boy**[207] 7077 6-8-4 **55** oh5 JamesRogers(3) 10 38
(Chris Fairhurst) *in tch: rdn along 4f out: sn wknd* **25/1**

0-00 **14** 6 **Lady Norlela**[8] 2048 6-8-2 **55** oh3 JackDuern(5) 1 29
(Brian Rothwell) *hmpd on inner after 1f: sme hdwy into midfield 1/2-way: n.d* **33/1**

0-00 **15** nk **Sally Friday (IRE)**[16] 1797 4-9-3 **65** JulieBurke 18 38
(Edwin Tuer) *midfield: rdn along 5f out: wknd over 3f out* **22/1**

55-2 **16** 19 **Eijaaz (IRE)**[11] 1950 11-8-4 **59** (p) JordanNason(7) 11
(Geoffrey Harker) *hld up: a in rr* **16/1**

-550 **17** 1¼ **Baharat (IRE)**[51] 1083 4-8-6 **59** (t) NathanAlison(5) 2
(Richard Guest) *midfield: rdn along 4f out: sn wknd* **25/1**

00-0 **18** 29 **Last Destination (IRE)**[12] 1917 4-8-7 **62** DanielleMooney(7) 9
(Nigel Tinkler) *plld hrd: n.m.r in midfield after 1f and sddle slipped: sn cl up: pushed along over 4f out and sn wknd* **66/1**

2m 36.0s (1.10) **Going Correction** +0.15s/f (Good) **18** Ran SP% **126.0**
Speed ratings (Par 103): **102,101,101,100,100 99,99,99,98,98 96,94,92,88,88 75,74,55**
toteswingers:1&2:£61.40, 2&3:£127.20, 1&3:£127.20 CSF £288.20 CT £6043.92 TOTE £37.80: £6.10, £6.40, £4.40, £3.40; EX 466.50 TRIFECTA Not won..
Owner Wilf Hobson **Bred** G And Mrs Middlebrook **Trained** Carburton, Notts
■ Stewards' Enquiry : Shirley Teasdale two-day ban; careless riding (3rd-4th June)

FOCUS
The consensus among the jockeys was that the ground was riding on the slow side of good after 9mm of overnight rain fell on ground that inexplicably had been watered (5mm on the straight course) on Thursday despite the wettest April on record in Yorkshire and a very wet start to May. Ground conditions were good to firm at declaration time and those trainers and owners who were rightfully anticipating some rare fast ground after weeks of soft and heavy are entitled to feel angry and cheated. Mostly exposed performers in a run-of-the-mill handicap. The pace wasn't strong for all the field was soon strung out and it didn't pay to be too far back. Modest form with one or two doubts.
Reset City Official explanation: jockey said mare hung left handed.
Lady Norlela Official explanation: trainer said mare struck into herself.
Sally Friday(IRE) Official explanation: trainer said filly had a breathing problem.

2261 WELCOME HOME BARNEY MAIDEN AUCTION STKS 5f
6:40 (6:41) (Class 5) 2-Y-O **£2,911** (£866; £432; £216) **Stalls** High

Form RPR

1 **Reckless Abandon** 2-8-13 0 AdamKirby 4 91+
(Clive Cox) *t.k.h: mde virtually all centre: qcknd clr over 1f out: drifted lft and kpt on wl fnl f* **6/1**[3]

2 **2** 2 **Annunciation**[7] 2073 2-9-2 0 RyanMoore 16 87
(Richard Hannon) *in tch on nr side of centre gp: hdwy to chse (clr) wnr over 1f out: kpt on fnl f: no imp* **11/8**[1]

3 3½ **The Black Jacobin** 2-8-9 0 StevieDonohoe 10 67
(J S Moore) *hld up in tch centre: effrt over 2f out: kpt on fnl f: nt gng pce of first two* **100/1**

4 shd **Therapeutic** 2-8-4 0 NickyMackay 19 62
(Scott Dixon) *midfield towards stands' rail: rdn and effrt 1/2-way: kpt on fnl f: nvr able to chal* **50/1**

464 **5** 2 **Someone's Darling**[8] 2019 2-8-4 0 AndreaAtzeni 17 54
(Jim Goldie) *hld up towards nr side of centre gp: rdn 1/2-way: kpt on fnl f: nrst fin* **20/1**

6 nk **Monkey Bar Flies (IRE)** 2-8-10 0 LeeTopliss(3) 3 62
(Richard Fahey) *cl up centre: ev ch and rdn 1/2-way: no ex over 1f out* **16/1**

4 **7** 2¾ **Blue Lotus (IRE)**[15] 1818 2-8-11 0 DavidAllan 2 50
(Tim Easterby) *cl up on outside of centre gp: drvn along 1/2-way: wknd over 1f out* **5/1**[2]

0 **8** 1¼ **Starbotton**[21] 1671 2-8-6 0 AndrewElliott 5 41
(James Bethell) *t.k.h: in tch centre tl edgd lft and wknd wl over 1f out* **100/1**

9 3½ **Sulky Sheila (IRE)** 2-8-4 0 DuranFentiman 13 30+
(Tim Easterby) *prom nr side of centre gp: rdn over 2f out: wknd wl over 1f out* **80/1**

10 1 **Delores Rocket** 2-8-5 0 JulieBurke(3) 18 27
(Kevin Ryan) *s.i.s: sn outpcd towards stands' side: nvr on terms* **66/1**

2 **11** ½ **Dil Laney (IRE)**[16] 1795 2-8-8 0 DeclanCannon(3) 6 28
(David O'Meara) *in tch centre tl rdn and wknd over 2f out* **16/1**

12 nk **Blazing Knight (IRE)** 2-8-11 0 HayleyTurner 11 27
(Ralph Beckett) *midfield centre: drvn and outpcd 1/2-way: n.d after* **9/1**

13 1¼ **Loki's Strike** 2-8-9 0 ow3 MichaelMetcalfe(3) 8 23
(Mrs K Burke) *s.i.s: bhd and outpcd centre: sme late hdwy: nvr on terms* **66/1**

5 **14** hd **Baker's Pursuit**[15] 1818 2-8-6 0 LeeNewman 12 17
(Jim Goldie) *sn pushed along bhd ldng gp centre: struggling over 2f out: nvr on terms* **25/1**

0 **15** ¾ **Dha Chara (IRE)**[31] 1437 2-8-11 0 TonyCulhane 14 19
(Reg Hollinshead) *hld up in midfield in centre: struggling over 2f out: sn wknd* **50/1**

4 **16** 1¼ **Red Star Lady (IRE)**[49] 1136 2-8-4 0 WilliamCarson 7 7
(Mrs K Burke) *t.k.h: cl up centre tl wknd fr 2f out* **16/1**

17 3½ **Proventi** 2-8-11 0 SamHitchcott 15 2
(Alan McCabe) *s.i.s: bhd and a outpcd towards stands' side* **100/1**

18 4 **Tyson The Byson** 2-8-9 0 PaulMulrennan 9
(David C Griffiths) *hld up bhd ldng gp centre: struggling over 2f out: sn btn* **66/1**

1m 0.4s (-0.10) **Going Correction** +0.15s/f (Good) **18** Ran SP% **121.9**
Speed ratings (Par 93): **106,102,97,97,93 93,88,86,81,79 78,78,76,76,74 72,67,60**
toteswingers:1&2:£5.10, 2&3:£42.50, 1&3:£143.00 CSF £13.49 TOTE £8.20: £3.10, £1.20, £19.50; EX 20.30 TRIFECTA Not won..
Owner Miss J Deadman & S Barrow **Bred** Car Colston Hall Stud **Trained** Lambourn, Berks

FOCUS
A large field for a maiden auction. The field raced centre to stand side for all the first two were split by the width of the track at the line. Strong form for the grade, in a decent time.

NOTEBOOK
Reckless Abandon ◆, a colt by Exchange Rate out of a mare that won at 6f here and 1m in Canada, had reportedly been well backed during the day and it was easy to see why. Soon up with the leaders, he quickened clear impressively under hand riding and had he not run so green in front, ending up on the far rail, he'd have won by a fair bit further. He looks very speedy and will almost certainly be much better suited too by fast ground. He looks Royal Ascot material. (op 5-1 tchd 13-2)
Annunciation, set a decent standard on his Haydock second, but though he almost certainly at least reproduced that form he looked clear second best from some way out. He'll win a maiden but isn't anything special clearly and may prove better suited by 6f. (tchd 5-4)
The Black Jacobin, a gelding by Piccolo out of a 1m winner in France, showed a good attitude as he battled on to just edge third and will improve.
Therapeutic, a filly by Milk It Mick out of a Marju mare, took some time to get the hang of things before staying on steadily. She'll be better suited by 6f and is another entitled to improve.
Someone's Darling never really threatened and is starting to look exposed. She'll have more realistic claims dropped to claiming company. (op 25-1)
Monkey Bar Flies(IRE), a colt by Elusive City, showed a bit more than the result suggests, alongside the winner for a fair way before possibly needing the race, and he'll do better with this run behind him. (op 14-1)
Blue Lotus(IRE) found this a much warmer heat than the modest affair he made his debut in at Musselburgh and is probably more one for nurseries anyway. (op 13-2 tchd 9-2)
Starbotton clearly finds 5f inadequate as his pedigree suggests and is one for nurseries down the line.
Dil Laney(IRE) Official explanation: jockey said gelding was unsuited by good ground.
Tyson The Byson Official explanation: jockey said colt hung left handed.

2262 KAT COMMUNICATIONS KNOWLEDGE ABOUT TELECOMS MEDIAN AUCTION MAIDEN STKS 6f
7:15 (7:17) (Class 5) 3-4-Y-O **£2,911** (£866; £432; £216) **Stalls** High

Form RPR

1 **Sir Pedro** 3-9-3 0 MichaelHills 16 79+
(Charles Hills) *in tch: hdwy on outer over 2f out: rdn to ld appr fnl f: sn edgd lft and styd on strly* **7/4**[1]

20- **2** 3½ **Iffraam (IRE)**[196] 7293 3-9-3 0 PaulMulrennan 19 68+
(Michael Dods) *hmpd s and in rr: hdwy on outer wl over 2f out: sn rdn and styd on wl ins fnl f* **5/1**[3]

3 1 **Asian Trader** 3-9-3 0 RyanMoore 6 65+
(William Haggas) *dwlt and towards rr: gd hdwy 1/2-way: trckd ldrs over 2f out: effrt to chal over 1f out and ev ch: rdn jst ins fnl f and kpt on same pce* **10/3**[2]

0 **4** ¾ **Rich Again (IRE)**[28] 1521 3-9-3 0 AndrewElliott 2 62
(James Bethell) *trckd ldrs: effrt whn nt clr run and swtchd lft over 1f out: sn rdn and styd on fnl f: nrst fin* **16/1**

00-0 **5** 1½ **Niceonemyson**[11] 1953 3-9-0 47 JulieBurke(3) 5 58?
(Christopher Wilson) *trckd ldrs: effrt over 2f out: rdn whn n.m.r and swtchd lft over 1f out: kpt on same pce* **100/1**

45 **6** 1¾ **Fame Again**[7] 2095 4-9-12 0 PaddyAspell 9 54+
(Michael Easterby) *prom: rdn 2f out: grad wknd* **25/1**

00 **7** ¾ **Perfect Policy**[19] 1705 3-8-9 0 HarryBentley(3) 8 45
(Ralph Beckett) *prom: cl up 1/2-way: led wl over 2f out: rdn wl over 1f out: hdd & wknd appr fnl f* **28/1**

0-0 **8** 1 **Sapphire Seeker**[14] 1843 3-9-3 0 AndreaAtzeni 17 46
(Des Donovan) *chsd ldrs: rdn along over 2f out: grad wknd* **22/1**

04 **9** ½ **Warrick Brown**[14] 1864 3-9-3 0 DuranFentiman 3 45
(Tim Easterby) *led: rdn along 1/2-way: sn hdd and grad wknd fnl 2f* **20/1**

0 **10** hd **Hurricane Max (IRE)**[14] 1843 3-9-3 0 RoystonFfrench 12 44
(Chris Fairhurst) *in tch: rdn along over 2f out: no hdwy* **50/1**

00- **11** 1 **Poontoon (IRE)**[155] 7783 3-9-3 0 DavidNolan 14 41
(Richard Fahey) *a in midfield* **33/1**

63 **12** ½ **Dartrix**[39] 1274 3-8-12 0 TomEaves 4 34+
(Michael Dods) *in tch: hdwy to chse ldrs over 2f out: sn rdn and wknd* **14/1**

0- **13** ½ **Optimum Rose (IRE)**[353] 2617 3-8-12 0 DanielTudhope 15 33
(David O'Meara) *chsd ldrs: rdn along wl over 2f out: sn wknd* **25/1**

0 **14** ¾ **Kapunda**[14] 1843 4-9-12 0 GrahamLee 18 37
(Jedd O'Keeffe) *wnt rt s: a towards rr* **100/1**

15 hd **Rocquaine (IRE)** 3-8-12 0 PadraigBeggy 11 30
(David Evans) *s.i.s: a in rr* **50/1**

16 1¼ **Majestic Angel (IRE)** 3-8-12 0 BarryMcHugh 10 26
(Brian Rothwell) *chsd ldrs: rdn along wl over 2f out: sn wknd* **100/1**

46 **17** nk **Brother Superior**[11] 1953 3-9-3 0 DavidAllan 13 30
(Tim Easterby) *a towards rr* **50/1**

0- **18** 1¾ **Absolute Bearing (IRE)**[191] 7345 3-9-3 0 JamesSullivan 20 24
(Tim Etherington) *wnt lft s: a in rr* **100/1**

00- **19** 7 **Powerball (IRE)**[183] 7460 4-9-4 0 AmyRyan(3) 1
(Lisa Williamson) *cl up: rdn along wl over 2f out: sn wknd* **150/1**

20 29 **Dragon Spirit (IRE)** 3-9-3 0 LeeNewman 7
(Noel Wilson) *dwlt and in rr: hdwy after 2f and in tch 1/2-way: sn rdn and wknd* **66/1**

1m 14.41s (0.81) **Going Correction** +0.15s/f (Good)
WFA 3 from 4yo 9lb **20** Ran SP% **123.8**
Speed ratings (Par 103): **100,95,94,93,91 88,87,86,85,85 84,83,82,81,81 79,79,77,67,29**
toteswingers:1&2:£4.00, 2&3:£4.10, 1&3:£4.50 CSF £8.60 TOTE £2.40: £1.60, £1.60, £1.70; EX 14.10 Trifecta £70.40 Pool: £421.67 - 4.42 winning units..
Owner R Morecombe, J Netherthorpe, C Wright **Bred** C J Mills **Trained** Lambourn, Berks

FOCUS
A three-horse race according to the market and as anticipated those horses came to the fore, though there were varying bits of promise in behind. The runners raced in the centre of the track and the pace was on the steady side for a sprint. The first three may prove a bit better than the bare form.

2263 FRENCHGATE FIRST FOR FASHION H'CAP 1m (R)
7:45 (7:46) (Class 3) (0-95,92) 3-Y-O **£8,409** (£2,502; £1,250; £625) **Stalls** Low

Form RPR

1-16 **1** **Bronze Angel (IRE)**[42] 1221 3-9-2 **87** (p) HayleyTurner 14 93+
(Marcus Tregoning) *prom: hdwy to ld appr fnl f: pushed out* **10/1**

125- **2** ¾ **Ladys First**[254] 5849 3-9-1 **89** LeeTopliss(3) 4 93+
(Richard Fahey) *in tch: pushed along over 2f out: rallied and chsd wnr ins fnl f: kpt on: hld nr fin* **8/1**

2-16 **3** nk **Verse Of Love**[22] 1641 3-8-5 **76** LukeMorris 5 79
(David Evans) *towards rr: rdn over 2f out: hdwy on outside over 1f out: hung lft and kpt on fnl f: no ex towards fin* **25/1**

3-35 **4** ¾ **Hadaj**[14] 1860 3-9-5 **90** BrettDoyle 13 92
(Clive Brittain) *s.s: hld up: rdn and hdwy on outside over 1f out: hung lft and kpt on fnl f: nrst fin* **16/1**

1-44 **5** ¾ **Solar Deity (IRE)**[31] 1452 3-9-2 **87** TedDurcan 6 87
(Marco Botti) *in tch: rdn along and sltly outpcd 2f out: kpt on ins fnl f: nvr able to chal* **11/2**[3]

0-31 **6** ¾ **Shamaal Nibras (USA)**[42] 1217 3-9-0 **88** SeanLevey(3) 9 86
(Richard Hannon) *hld up towards rr: rdn over 2f out: kpt on fnl f: nvr rchd ldrs* **25/1**

23-1 **7** ¾ **Savanna Days (IRE)**[49] 1142 3-8-11 **82** MartinHarley 8 78
(Mick Channon) *restless in stalls: hld up on ins: stdy hdwy over 2f out: effrt over 1f out: one pce fnl f* **12/1**

1 **8** *nse* **Mississippi**[19] 1704 3-9-7 **92** MartinDwyer 3 88+
(Brian Meehan) *t.k.h: chsd ldr: led wl over 1f out to appr fnl f: wknd last 100yds* **5/1**[2]

2-1 **9** 2¾ **Dank**[24] 1610 3-9-3 **88** RyanMoore 12 78
(Sir Michael Stoute) *hld up towards ins: stdy hdwy over 2f out: effrt and swtchd lft over 1f out: sn n.d* **3/1**[1]

6-25 **10** 1¼ **Bank On Me**[21] 1653 3-8-11 **82** (t) ShaneKelly 1 69
(Philip McBride) *led: rdn over 2f out: hdd wl over 1f out: sn wknd* **20/1**

621- **11** 1¾ **Poetic Dancer**[211] 6995 3-9-4 **89** AdamKirby 10 72
(Clive Cox) *hld up in midfield on outside: hdwy and prom over 1f out: sn rdn: wknd ins fnl f* **12/1**

21-0 **12** 8 **Venetian View (IRE)**[26] 1565 3-8-11 **82** RichardMullen 11 47
(Gary Moore) *hld up: drvn over 2f out: btn whn edgd lft over 1f out* **25/1**

24-0 **13** ½ **Elkhart (IRE)**[14] 1860 3-9-0 **85** JoeFanning 2 49
(Mark Johnston) *trckd ldrs tl rdn and wknd fr 2f out* **25/1**

1m 40.69s (0.99) **Going Correction** +0.15s/f (Good) **13 Ran SP% 118.7**
Speed ratings (Par 103): **101,100,99,99,98 97,96,96,94,92 91,83,82**
toteswingers:1&2:£8.70, 2&3:£56.40, 1&3:£25.30 CSF £80.25 CT £1983.24 TOTE £11.00: £3.20, £3.00, £9.20; EX 60.00 TRIFECTA Not won..
Owner Lady Tennant **Bred** Rihana Partnership **Trained** Lambourn, Berks

FOCUS
An interesting handicap consisting mostly of unexposed types, several who looked potentially ahead of their marks. The pace was muddling initially but picked up far enough out for those held up not to be disadvantaged. The level is set around the third.

NOTEBOOK
Bronze Angel(IRE) had been a bit disappointing at Musselburgh last time but her rider had clearly learned from her experience there and had her mount much closer to the pace this time. He didn't do much once he hit the front which probably explains why he was wearing cheekpieces, and it wouldn't be a surprise if this progressive sort was to win again. He might be even better suited by 1m2f. (op 9-1 tchd 11-1)
Ladys First shaped very well on her reappearance. She took time to find her stride but was going on well close home and being out of a winner in France at 10.5f will do better still once she is upped again in trip. She'll go up in the weights for this but probably not enough to stop her winning a handicap. (tchd 13-2)
Verse Of Love probably ran his best race yet, like the runner-up taking time to get going. A strongly-run race at this trip on easy ground promise to be his ideal conditions. (op 28-1)
Hadaj found this company easier than that he had taken on at Newmarket last time and would have gone close to winning had things panned out more in his favour, having to make his run from last place after a very slow start and still going on at the end. He's probably got more to offer. (op 20-1)
Solar Deity(IRE) ran quite well trying 1m for the first time without ever threatening to finish much closer. He carried his head slightly high, possibly still through inexperience, but it wouldn't be a surprise if he is tried in headgear if his progress starts to stall. (op 6-1)
Shamaal Nibras(USA) looks on no more than a fair mark but at least proved his effectiveness on turf and had no problem with the trip. (op 22-1)
Mississippi was well backed and though slightly disappointing on the face of it, this was only his third race after a rather bloodless victory at Kempton last time. He only faded out of it late on and remains quite a useful prospect, not least dropped to 7f on faster ground than this. (tchd 9-2 and 11-2)
Dank wasn't ideally placed as the race developed and possibly didn't have much room trying for a daring run along the inside rail, but all the same didn't finish with the same flourish others did. Her Kempton win isn't particularly strong form and perhaps the official assessors were overly cautious rating her 88. Official explanation: jockey said filly was denied a clear run. (tchd 10-3)

2264 ROBINSONSOFBAWTRY.COM H'CAP 6f
8:20 (8:20) (Class 4) (0-80,80) 4-Y-0+ **£5,175** (£1,540; £769; £384) **Stalls** High

Form RPR

2361 **1** **Italian Tom (IRE)**[7] 2071 5-9-0 **78** DarrenEgan(5) 18 88
(Ronald Harris) *in tch: hdwy wl over 1f out: rdn to ld ins fnl f: kpt on wl* **14/1**

142- **2** *nk* **Cape Classic (IRE)**[232] 6495 4-9-7 **80** RyanMoore 11 89+
(William Haggas) *hld up: hdwy whn nt clr run 2f out: sn swtchd lft and rdn: styd on strly fnl f* **15/8**[1]

6-53 **3** *hd* **Jack Luey**[7] 2096 5-9-2 **75** FrederikTylicki 2 84+
(Lawrence Mullaney) *prom: effrt to chal 2f out: rdn and ev ch over 1f out tl drvn and no ex wl ins fnl f* **14/1**

-11 **4** *hd* **Alive And Kicking**[13] 1875 4-9-2 **75** TedDurcan 17 83
(James Bethell) *prom: led 1/2-way: rdn over 1f out: hdd ins fnl f: no ex towards fin* **7/1**[2]

60-5 **5** 1¼ **Rasaman (IRE)**[14] 1868 8-9-4 **77** GrahamLee 19 81
(Jim Goldie) *dwlt and in rr: hdwy 2f out: rdn over 1f out: styd on fnl f: nrst fin* **14/1**

364 **6** ¾ **Head Space (IRE)**[22] 1642 4-9-5 **78** JamesSullivan 13 80
(Ruth Carr) *in rr: hdwy wl over 1f out: sn rdn and kpt on wl fnl f: nrst fin* **12/1**

215- **7** *nk* **Mount Hollow**[170] 7595 7-8-11 **77** (p) JackDuern(7) 10 78
(Reg Hollinshead) *hld up: hdwy whn hmpd 2f out: styd on fnl f: nrst fin* **20/1**

1204 **8** *nse* **Master Of Disguise**[5] 2122 6-8-13 **75** (t) HarryBentley(3) 5 75
(Brian Baugh) *chsd ldrs: rdn along wl over 1f out: drvn and wknd ent fnl f* **16/1**

5443 **9** ½ **Close To The Edge (IRE)**[67] 883 4-9-7 **80** ShaneKelly 16 79
(Alan McCabe) *racd nr stands' rail: prom: rdn and ch over 1f out: wknd ins fnl f* **25/1**

1302 **10** 2½ **Even Stevens**[22] 1643 4-9-6 **79** RobertWinston 7 70
(Scott Dixon) *prom: effrt 2f out: sn rdn and ev ch tl wknd fnl f* **14/1**

0650 **11** 1 **Jack My Boy (IRE)**[7] 2070 5-9-0 **73** PadraigBeggy 9 61
(David Evans) *nvr bttr than midfield* **20/1**

04-0 **12** *hd* **Hotham**[134] 64 9-9-6 **79** BarryMcHugh 6 66
(Noel Wilson) *hld up: n.d* **50/1**

60-0 **13** 3¾ **Barkston Ash**[48] 1156 4-9-4 **77** DuranFentiman 12 52
(Eric Alston) *prom: rdn 2f out: wknd over 1f out* **40/1**

0-00 **14** 2¾ **Mr Optimistic**[30] 1478 4-9-2 **78** LeeTopliss(3) 14 44
(Richard Fahey) *in tch: rdn along over 2f out: sn wknd* **25/1**

04-0 **15** *hd* **Deliberation (IRE)**[22] 1643 4-9-1 **74** RoystonFfrench 15 40
(Mark Buckley) *led to 1/2-way: cl up tl rdn and wknd wl over 1f out* **66/1**

513- **16** 16 **L'Astre De Choisir (IRE)**[220] 6797 4-9-1 **74** PaulMulrennan 8
(Michael Easterby) *chsd ldrs: rdn along wl over 2f out: sn wknd* **33/1**

00-0 **17** 2¾ **Comptonspirit**[15] 1827 8-9-3 **76** J-PGuillambert 4
(Brian Baugh) *chsd ldrs: rdn along 2f out: sn wknd* **100/1**

0-60 **18** 3¾ **Able Master (IRE)**[30] 1476 6-9-6 **79** DanielTudhope 3
(David O'Meara) *rrd stalls and blind removed late: lost many l s: a bhd* **9/1**[3]

1m 14.66s (1.06) **Going Correction** +0.175s/f (Good) **18 Ran SP% 124.6**
Speed ratings (Par 105): **99,98,98,98,96 95,95,94,94,90 89,89,84,80,80 59,55,50**
toteswingers:1&2:£4.00, 2&3:£9.70, 1&3:£37.30 CSF £36.71 CT £420.02 TOTE £12.60: £2.70, £1.10, £3.40, £2.20; EX 34.30 TRIFECTA Not won..
Owner S & A Mares **Bred** Tom Radley **Trained** Earlswood, Monmouths
■ Stewards' Enquiry : Darren Egan four-day ban; used whip above permitted levels (3rd-6th June)

FOCUS
A competitive sprint and one in which the runners stayed centre to stand side. The pace didn't pick up in earnest until halfway and the runner-up looked a shade unfortunate. The winner rates better than ever.
Comptonspirit Official explanation: trainer said mare was unsuited by good going.

2265 ELEMENTS MEDISPA H'CAP 7f
8:50 (8:52) (Class 4) (0-85,85) 3-Y-0 **£5,175** (£1,540; £769; £384) **Stalls** High

Form RPR

-113 **1** **Laffan (IRE)**[41] 1241 3-8-8 **75** AmyRyan(3) 13 95+
(Kevin Ryan) *t.k.h early: mde all: rdn over 2f out: drew clr appr last 150yds* **9/1**

51-1 **2** 4½ **Famous Poet (IRE)**[24] 1612 3-9-7 **85** PaulHanagan 8 93+
(Saeed Bin Suroor) *hld up in tch: effrt over 2f out: drvn and chsd wnr over 1f out: no imp last 150yds* **13/8**[1]

34-1 **3** *nk* **Magic Destiny**[21] 1660 3-8-7 **71** oh1 MartinHarley 14 78
(Mrs K Burke) *hld up in midfield on nr side of gp: hdwy over 2f out: edgd lft and kpt on fnl f: nvr able to chal* **14/1**

231- **4** 1½ **Go Dutch (IRE)**[250] 5991 3-9-5 **83** AndreaAtzeni 4 86+
(Roger Varian) *hld up: shkn up and hdwy 2f out: kpt on fnl f: no imp* **8/1**[3]

66-4 **5** 1½ **Al's Memory (IRE)**[19] 1721 3-8-9 **73** PadraigBeggy 5 72
(David Evans) *prom: drvn over 2f out: nt qckn over 1f out* **40/1**

31-2 **6** *hd* **Lucky Henry**[24] 1612 3-9-6 **84** AdamKirby 3 82
(Clive Cox) *in tch on outside of gp: effrt and rdn over 2f out: no ex fnl f* **9/2**[2]

31- **7** *nk* **Shamahan**[278] 5111 3-9-1 **79** ShaneKelly 11 77+
(Gary Moore) *hld up in midfield: pushed along and outpcd over 2f out: kpt on fnl f: nvr able to chal* **12/1**

40-0 **8** 1 **Hot Sugar (USA)**[42] 1217 3-8-12 **76** PhillipMakin 10 71
(Kevin Ryan) *in tch: rdn over 2f out: wknd over 1f out* **40/1**

1-40 **9** 3½ **Right Result (IRE)**[14] 1858 3-9-0 **78** GrahamGibbons 1 63
(James Bethell) *hld up towards rr: rdn along over 2f out: nvr able to chal* **22/1**

6-05 **10** 2½ **Shamrocked (IRE)**[13] 1894 3-8-11 **75** SamHitchcott 9 54
(Mick Channon) *trckd ldrs tl rdn and wknd over 2f out* **50/1**

10-0 **11** ½ **Mr Maynard**[38] 1304 3-8-11 **75** RyanMoore 2 52
(Sir Michael Stoute) *bhd: rdn along over 3f out: edgd lft over 2f out: sn btn* **18/1**

513- **12** ½ **Dissent (IRE)**[184] 7445 3-9-3 **81** [1] LukeMorris 12 57
(Gerard Butler) *t.k.h: hld up: stdy hdwy over 2f out: sn rdn and wknd* **20/1**

60-0 **13** *nk* **Charitable Act (FR)**[42] 1217 3-9-6 **84** MartinDwyer 6 59
(William Muir) *hld up: rdn over 2f out: sn wknd* **40/1**

441- **14** 1¾ **Master Of Ages (IRE)**[207] 7081 3-9-3 **81** JoeFanning 7 51
(Mark Johnston) *cl up tl rdn and wknd qckly 2f out* **25/1**

1m 27.08s (0.78) **Going Correction** +0.175s/f (Good) **14 Ran SP% 119.2**
Speed ratings (Par 101): **102,96,96,94,93 92,92,91,87,84 83,83,83,81**
toteswingers:1&2:£4.10, 2&3:£6.20, 1&3:£19.10 CSF £21.95 CT £221.17 TOTE £13.70: £3.30, £1.10, £4.30; EX 38.20 Trifecta £468.30 Pool: £702.49 - 1.11 winning units..
Owner Mubarak Al Naemi **Bred** Vincent Dunne **Trained** Hambleton, N Yorks

FOCUS
Several unexposed sorts on show in what looks likely to prove an informative handicap. The runners again came centre to stand side and the pace looked a reasonable one. Little got involved from the rear. The winner impressed and produced a biggish step up.
T/Plt: £215.70 to a £1 stake. Pool of £93,518.63 - 316.36 winning units. T/Qpdt: £14.90 to a £1 stake. Pool of £7,632.24 - 376.80 winning units. JR

2231 NEWBURY (L-H)
Saturday, May 19

OFFICIAL GOING: Straight course - good (good to soft in places); round course - good to soft (6.1)
Rail moved overnight and Round course 27m longer than advertised.
Wind: Nil Weather: White cloud

2266 BET ON YOUR MOBILE AT BLUESQ.COM E B F MAIDEN STKS (DIV I) 1m 2f 6y
1:30 (1:30) (Class 4) 3-Y-0 **£5,369** (£1,597; £798; £399) **Stalls** Low

Form RPR

1 **Bishop Roko** 3-9-3 0 JamesDoyle 1 97+
(Roger Charlton) *w'like: tall: scope: in tch: hdwy 3f out: hmpd appr fnl 2f: sn rcvrd: led appr fnl f: pushed out: readily* **16/1**

44-2 **2** 6 **Mysterious Man (IRE)**[13] 1893 3-9-3 83 JimmyFortune 3 85
(Andrew Balding) *led tl hdd over 7f out: styd trcking ldr tl led again over 2f out: drvn and hdd appr fnl f: sn outpcd by wnr but kpt on wl for 2nd* **11/4**[1]

0- **3** 2 **Sun Central (IRE)**[207] 7083 3-9-3 0 JPO'Brien 6 81+
(William Haggas) *w'like: str: scope: warm: chsd ldrs: drvn edgd lft and green 2f out: styd on same pce for 3rd appr fnl f* **9/2**[3]

4 ½ **Nabucco** 3-9-3 0 RobertHavlin 5 80+
(John Gosden) *leggy: unf: hmpd s: in rr: gd hdwy whn hmpd over 2f out: rallying whn hmpd again over 1f out: styd on wl fnl f to cl on 4th nr fin but nvr any ch w wnr* **20/1**

2-0 **5** 3¼ **King Of Dudes**[28] 1511 3-9-3 0 TomQueally 2 74
(Sir Henry Cecil) *chsd ldrs: hmpd over 2f out: sn rdn: hung rt and wknd over 1f out* **9/1**

6 3¾ **After The Storm**[225] 6678 3-9-3 0 ChrisCatlin 7 66
(Rebecca Curtis) *str: hmpd s: in rr: hdwy to cl on ldrs whn hmpd over 2f out: wknd sn after* **66/1**

7 1¼ **Mashaari (IRE)** 3-9-3 0 TadhgO'Shea 10 64
(John Gosden) *w'like: scope: bit bkwd: s.i.s: in rr: rdn over 2f out: styng on whn green and hung rt over 1f out: sme late prog* **16/1**

0 **8** *6* **Viewpoint (IRE)**[30] 1467 3-9-3 0 RichardHughes 9 52
(Richard Hannon) *lw: chsd ldrs: reminders over 5f out: wknd over 2f out* **7/2**[2]

0- **9** *3* **Galleon**[248] 6059 3-9-3 0 PatDobbs 11 46
(Sir Michael Stoute) *rdn over 3f out: a towards rr* **13/2**

0 **10** *2* **Essell**[28] 1506 3-8-12 0 MatthewDavies 4 37
(Mick Channon) *in tch: rdn 3f out and sn wknd* **66/1**

0 **11** *3 ½* **Fuzzy Logic (IRE)**[28] 1512 3-9-3 0 NeilCallan 12 35
(William Muir) *a in rr* **100/1**

25-2 **12** *6* **Hyperlink (IRE)**[30] 1484 3-9-3 75 (b[1]) KierenFallon 8 23
(Mark Johnston) *t.k.h: pressed ldr tl led over 7f out: rdn: veered lft and hdd over 2f out: wknd qckly u.p* **10/1**

2m 11.88s (3.08) **Going Correction** +0.325s/f (Good) **12** Ran SP% **120.0**
Speed ratings (Par 101): **100,95,93,93,90 87,86,81,79,77 75,70**
toteswingers: 1&2 £10.10, 1&3 £15.70, 2&3 £4.60 CSF £59.82 TOTE £20.40: £5.20, £1.40, £2.40; EX 75.40 Trifecta £669.80 Part won. Pool: £905.24 - 0.40 winning units..
Owner Michael Pescod **Bred** P T Tellwright **Trained** Beckhampton, Wilts

FOCUS
The rail was moved out, so the round course was 27 metres longer than standard. They finished strung out and the bare form looks misleading with a few of these probably capable of better than they showed. The second sets a sound standard and the winner looks above average.
Nabucco ◆ Official explanation: jockey said colt suffered interference in running.

2267 JLT ASTON PARK STKS (LISTED RACE) 1m 5f 61y
2:00 (2:01) (Class 1) 4-Y-0+

£18,714 (£7,095; £3,550; £1,768; £887; £445) **Stalls** Low

Form RPR

261- **1** **Hawaafez**[204] 7136 4-8-7 97 KieranO'Neill 2 107
(Marcus Tregoning) *h.d.w: led after 1f: hdd over 5f out: racd alone far side and a up w pce: rdn to chal fr 2f out: def advanage wl over 1f out and hrd drvn: in n.d fnl 120yds: comf* **3/1**[2]

2 *4* **Meganisi (IRE)**[9] 5-8-12 0 NeilCallan 5 106
(Rebecca Curtis) *led 1f: styd cl 2nd and led again over 5f out: racd centre crse: rdn over 2f out: sn hanging bdly rt: hdd wl over 1f out: styd hanging to stands' rail and kpt on one pce* **16/1**

234- **3** *shd* **Nehaam**[217] 6857 6-8-12 110 TadhgO'Shea 4 106
(John Gosden) *chsd ldrs: rdn and dropped to 4th over 4f out: styd on again to take 3rd 2f out: styd on u.p fnl f to cl on 2nd last strides but no ch w wnr* **10/3**[3]

032- **4** *4* **Ibicenco (GER)**[237] 6396 4-8-12 112 KierenFallon 3 100
(Luca Cumani) *w'like: hld up in rr: pushed along and struggling 4f out and stl no prog over 2f out: drvn and grad impr fr over 1f out but nvr any ch* **9/5**[1]

236/ **5** *5* **Dreamspeed (IRE)**[539] 7594 5-8-12 100 JimmyFortune 1 92
(Andrew Balding) *in tch in 4th: hdwy to take 3rd 4f out: drvn and dropped to 4th again 2f out: sn btn* **6/1**

4103 **6** *2 ½* **Junoob**[48] 1159 4-9-1 101 (b) RichardKingscote 6 92
(Tom Dascombe) *rdn along 4f out: a bhd* **12/1**

2m 58.44s (6.44) **Going Correction** +0.325s/f (Good) **6** Ran SP% **111.7**
Speed ratings (Par 111): **93,90,90,88,84 83**
toteswingers: 1&2 £8.30, 1&3 £2.30, 2&3 £5.60 CSF £43.26 TOTE £4.30: £2.20, £5.00; EX 56.30.
Owner Hamdan Al Maktoum **Bred** Shadwell Estate Co Ltd **Trained** Lambourn, Berks
■ Stewards' Enquiry : Kieran O'Neill two-day ban; used whip above permitted level (3rd-4th June)

FOCUS
Gamut was the best recent winner of this Listed race, going on to score at Group 1 and Group 2 level, although a number of others subsequently took Group 3s. This was not the strongest renewal and proved something of a strange race, with the only filly in the race making virtually all and those held up never getting involved. Slight improvement from the winner, but not the most solid form.

NOTEBOOK
Hawaafez, a sizeable filly whose only disappointing effort was when tried over 2m, made the running and, sticking more towards the far side than the rest, beat off the third around 2f out and kept galloping strongly to score with a bit in hand. Having gained black type here, connections can now look towards Group races, particularly against her own sex, although her trainer is keen to run her in the Ascot Gold Cup. (op 7-2)
Meganisi(IRE), a lightly-raced gelding who had won over hurdles earlier in the month, raced prominently and wide of the winner. He tried to take the filly on early in the straight but drifted to the stands' side under pressure and, although he kept responding, was always being held. He now qualifies for a mark and it will be interesting to see what he is given. (tchd 20-1)
Nehaam, a smart handicapper but also previously placed at Group and Listed level, was the owner's first string on jockey bookings. He was easy in the market though and, after tracking the pace, took a long time to make any inroads on his stable companion. He is probably better on faster ground and can be given another chance. (op 15-8)
Ibicenco(GER), making his debut for the yard, was well backed having been runner-up in a Group 1 on soft ground in his native Germany. He was disappointing though as, after being held up, he was being ridden early in the straight and the colt did not respond until the race was over. (op 3-1)
Dreamspeed(IRE), having his first start since November 2010, made some headway early in the straight before his effort flattened out. He was allowed to come home in his own time once his chance had gone and the run should bring him on. (op 7-1 tchd 15-2)
Junoob improved considerably on the all-weather over the winter but had a tough task on the ratings, especially as he had a 3lb penalty to carry. Held up at the back on the softest ground he has encountered, he never got involved. (op 9-1)

2268 BLUESQ.COM H'CAP 6f 8y
2:30 (2:34) (Class 2) (0-100,100) 4-Y-0+

£9,337 (£2,796; £1,398; £699; £349; £175) **Stalls** Centre

Form RPR

1104 **1** **Palace Moon**[49] 1140 7-9-7 100 (t) TomQueally 9 111
(William Knight) *hld up in rr: hdwy: n.m.r and squeezed through ins fnl 2f: qcknd to chse ldr over 1f out: styd on strly clsng stages to ld last strides* **25/1**

30-0 **2** *hd* **Pabusar**[49] 1129 4-9-7 100 JimCrowley 6 110
(Ralph Beckett) *trckd ldrs: led ins fnl 2f: rdn ins fnl f: kpt on wl: hdd last strides* **14/1**

05-3 **3** *3 ¾* **Mac's Power (IRE)**[40] 1255 6-9-6 99 (t) KierenFallon 7 97
(James Fanshawe) *lw: in tch: hdwy fr 2f out: hmpd wl over 1f out: chsd ldng duo fnl f but no imp* **9/2**[2]

000- **4** *1 ¾* **Lutine Bell**[217] 6862 5-8-13 92 RichardHughes 4 84
(Mike Murphy) *lw: slowly away: in rr: hdwy fr 2f out: styng on whn edgd rt wl over 1f out: kpt on to take 4th fnl 120yds but nt trble ldng trio* **8/1**

/00- **5** *nk* **Edge Closer**[315] 3841 8-8-9 88 PatDobbs 11 79+
(Tony Carroll) *hld up in tch: shkn up over 1f out: kpt on to press for 4th clsng stages but nvr gng pce of ldrs* **33/1**

0-26 **6** *½* **Naabegha**[15] 1821 5-8-8 87 JamesDoyle 12 77
(Ed de Giles) *chsd ldrs: drvn and ev ch 2f out: wknd ins fnl f* **10/1**

10-0 **7** *2 ½* **Bertiewhittle**[13] 1885 4-8-12 91 JimmyFortune 2 73
(David Barron) *in rr but in tch: hdwy and rdn to chse ldrs whn edgd rt appr fnl f: sn outpcd* **7/2**[1]

-000 **8** *¾* **Bay Knight (IRE)**[79] 756 6-9-4 100 SophieDoyle(3) 15 79
(J S Moore) *in rr: pushed along 1/2-way: kpt on fnl f: nvr rchd ldrs* **40/1**

6-12 **9** *1 ¼* **Whaileyy (IRE)**[70] 871 4-9-4 97 (b) SilvestreDeSousa 8 72
(Marco Botti) *lw: chsd ldrs: ev ch 2f out: wknd 1f out* **7/1**

30-1 **10** *2 ¼* **Esprit De Midas**[19] 1708 6-8-11 90 NeilCallan 14 58+
(Dean Ivory) *in rr: sme hdwy whn rdn and hmpd 1f out: nt rcvr* **16/1**

630- **11** *1 ¼* **Sohraab**[243] 6224 8-8-11 90 RobertHavlin 13 54
(Hughie Morrison) *chsd ldrs over 3f* **20/1**

500- **12** *¾* **Kuanyao (IRE)**[223] 6723 6-8-7 86 oh1 ChrisCatlin 10 48
(Peter Makin) *pressed ldrs over 3f* **33/1**

2-00 **13** *nse* **Mac Gille Eoin**[49] 1141 8-8-7 86 oh1 JohnFahy 5 48
(John Gallagher) *w ldr tl led over 2f out: hdd & wknd ins fnl quarter m* **40/1**

3-30 **14** *2 ¾* **The Confessor**[13] 1885 5-8-11 90 FergusSweeney 1 43
(Henry Candy) *chsd ldrs: rdn over 2f out: sn wknd* **6/1**[3]

100- **15** *1* **Swiss Cross**[300] 4357 5-9-3 96 (t) RichardKingscote 3 46
(Phil McEntee) *led tl hdd over 2f out: sn wknd* **33/1**

1m 13.34s (0.34) **Going Correction** +0.325s/f (Good) **15** Ran SP% **122.3**
Speed ratings (Par 109): **110,109,104,102,102 101,98,97,95,92 90,89,89,85,84**
toteswingers: 1&2 £24.70, 1&3 £17.80, 2&3 £16.70 CSF £325.88 CT £1877.77 TOTE £22.60: £4.60, £4.60, £2.40; EX 248.80 Trifecta £1595.50 Pool: £2,156.18 - 1.00 winning units..
Owner Canisbay Bloodstock **Bred** Miss B Swire **Trained** Patching, W Sussex

FOCUS
A competitive sprint handicap, but it lacked unexposed types. The first two finished clear and the winner was not far off his best.

NOTEBOOK
Palace Moon, back on turf after 49 days off, handled the easy ground better than might have been expected and showed he's still a smart sprinter. It will be surprising if he follows up off a higher mark, however. (op 16-1)
Pabusar shaped significantly better than in a Doncaster Listed race on his reappearance. He's been lightly raced and has mainly struggled since a promising juvenile campaign, but maybe he'll go on from this. (op 12-1 tchd 11-1)
Mac's Power(IRE) didn't impress with his attitude when tried in a hood on his comeback. This was a lot better, especially as he didn't get any cover early on and ended up being switched towards the stands' side with his challenge, and he might come on again for the run. Following his second-place finish in this last year, he 'won' the race on the wrong side in the Wokingham, and Royal Ascot will surely be the aim once again. (op 6-1 tchd 13-2)
Lutine Bell was left with a lot to do after missing the break and this was a promising return from 217 days off. (op 12-1)
Edge Closer, debuting for a new stable after 315 days off, shaped nicely, especially as this ground may have been softer than ideal. He travelled as well as any, but just plugged on when belatedly asked for his effort, shaping as though the run was needed. There should be more to come, although he may bounce if out again within the next month or so. (op 40-1)
Naabegha had no obvious excuse on this drop in trip. (op 12-1)
Bertiewhittle was disappointing, not building on his comeback effort at Newmarket when he was denied a clear run. (op 9-2 tchd 5-1 and 11-2)
The Confessor again didn't shape like sprinter. (op 5-1)

2269 BLUE SQUARE LONDON GOLD CUP (H'CAP) 1m 2f 6y
3:05 (3:05) (Class 2) (0-105,89) 3-Y-O

£15,562 (£4,660; £2,330; £1,165; £582; £292) **Stalls** Low

Form RPR

3-11 **1** **Expense Claim (IRE)**[13] 1892 3-9-3 85 JimmyFortune 14 102
(Andrew Balding) *lw: trckd ldrs: led over 2f out: drvn and styd on strly fnl f* **7/1**

11 **2** *2* **Hajras (IRE)**[30] 1477 3-9-2 84 TadhgO'Shea 3 97
(Mark Johnston) *w'like: chsd ldrs: drvn over 3f out: bmpd and edgd lft fr over 2f out: stl hanging whn chsng wnr fnl f: no imp* **11/2**[3]

13 **3** *2 ¼* **Clayton**[15] 1819 3-9-5 87 NeilCallan 5 95
(Kevin Ryan) *w'like: str: lw: t.k.h: chsd ldrs: rdn and edgd rt over 2f out: kpt on to take 3rd over 1f out: sn one pce and no imp on ldng duo* **16/1**

1-11 **4** *1* **Rewarded**[14] 1860 3-9-7 89 RobertHavlin 6 99+
(James Toller) *in rr but in tch: hdwy 3f out: styng on whn hmpd over 2f out: swtchd rt over 1f out: styd on wl clsng stages* **5/1**[2]

01- **5** *shd* **Thomas Chippendale (IRE)**[221] 6771 3-9-4 86 TomQueally 9 92+
(Sir Henry Cecil) *lw: t.k.h: stdd md-div on outer: c wd into st and gd hdwy to trck ldrs travelling wl 3f out: rdn and hung lft fr over 2f out: one pce appr fnl f* **2/1**[1]

2-1 **6** *2 ¾* **Hurricane In Dubai (IRE)**[19] 1703 3-8-7 75 JohnFahy 4 75
(Denis Coakley) *unf: broke wl: stdd 6f out: hdwy 3f out: chsd ldrs and rdn 2 out: nt clr run and swtchd rt sn after: styd on same pce fnl f* **12/1**

33-0 **7** *nk* **Humungosaur**[31] 1456 3-9-2 84 PatDobbs 8 84?
(Richard Hannon) *stdd towards rr s: sme hdwy on ins fr 3f out: drvn fr 2f out: nvr rchd ldrs* **50/1**

6-00 **8** *½* **Mcvicar**[31] 1440 3-8-2 70 KieranO'Neill 13 69
(Mick Channon) *stdd s: in rr: rdn and hdwy over 2f out: styd on clsng stages* **40/1**

13-0 **9** *2 ¼* **Tidal Way (IRE)**[26] 1565 3-8-11 79 MatthewDavies 7 73
(Mick Channon) *pressed ldrs: slt ld 3f out: hdd over 2f out: wknd qckly over 1f out* **40/1**

62-1 **10** *1 ¾* **Almuftarris (USA)**[38] 1312 3-9-2 84 JimCrowley 11 75
(Ed Dunlop) *in rr: drvn and hdwy 3f out: wknd qckly 2f out* **11/1**

114- **11** *14* **Poetic Lord**[213] 6957 3-9-5 87 RichardHughes 2 50
(Richard Hannon) *led: rdn and narrowly hdd 3f out: wknd u.p over 2f out* **14/1**

16- **12** *11* **Al Saham**[215] 6914 3-9-6 88 SilvestreDeSousa 12 29
(Saeed Bin Suroor) *str: t.k.h: in tch: c wd into st and racd towards outside: rdn and btn 3f out: eased* **25/1**

31 **13** *27* **Icelander (USA)**[80] 737 3-8-11 79 KierenFallon 1
(Mark Johnston) *w'like: scope: chsd ldrs: rdn over 4f out: sn btn: eased* **14/1**

2m 13.32s (4.52) **Going Correction** +0.325s/f (Good) **13** Ran SP% **123.8**
Speed ratings (Par 105): **94,92,90,89,89 87,87,86,85,83 72,63,42**
toteswingers: 1&2 £5.40, 1&3 £13.20, 2&3 £18.30 CSF £45.88 CT £614.06 TOTE £7.70: £2.30, £2.40, £4.10; EX 42.80 Trifecta £631.40 Pool: £2,338.09 - 2.74 winning units..
Owner Another Bottle Racing 2 **Bred** Glending Bloodstock **Trained** Kingsclere, Hants

FOCUS
A typically competitive renewal of this good handicap despite the fact that the top weights were a long way short of the race ceiling, but in the end a very comfortable winner. Plenty to like about the form.

NOTEBOOK

Expense Claim(IRE) ◆ has improved on the promise of his juvenile season since upped in distance this year, and took another step forward in completing the hat-trick here. He was always travelling well close to the pace and, when he committed for home around the quarter-mile pole, soon put the race to bed. He scored with plenty in hand and the King George V Handicap at Ascot appeals as a logical target. (op 13-2 tchd 15-2)

Hajras(IRE) had won both his previous starts but was stepping up in trip and grade here and was no sure thing to get it on pedigree. However, he was ridden fairly positively and stayed on without seriously threatening the winner. He looks a decent prospect and should be winning again before long. (op 9-2)

Clayton, another inexperienced sort, had missed the break on his turf and handicap debut last time. He broke much better here and was never far away, keeping on steadily in the straight. He is another who can build on this effort. (op 20-1)

Rewarded was possibly the unlucky one in this race, as he had to be switched twice in the straight before staying on late. He would have finished closer but would not have beaten the winner. Robert Havlin later reported that the colt suffered interference in running. Official explanation: jockey said colt suffered interference in running. (op 15-2)

Thomas Chippendale(IRE) beat a horse that subsequently finished fourth in the Kentucky Derby last term, and strictly on that form looked thrown in here. However, he was posted wide for most of the way and, after having a chance over 2f out, had nothing in reserve. He can be given a chance to prove he can do better. (op 9-4 tchd 5-2)

Hurricane In Dubai(IRE), making his turf and handicap debut, was very keen early and was dropped towards the rear before he settled. He was noted staying on in the straight after not getting the clearest passage and should have learnt from this. (op 16-1)

Al Saham appeared to be pulling and hanging right for much of the way, although it could have been a tack problem and, after moving wide for a run, he dropped away tamely in the last quarter-mile. (op 33-1 tchd 20-1)

2270 JLT LOCKINGE STKS (BRITISH CHAMPIONS SERIES) (GROUP 1) 1m (S)

3:40 (3:40) (Class 1) 4-Y-0+

£99,242 (£37,625; £18,830; £9,380; £4,707; £2,362) **Stalls** Centre

Form				RPR
111-	**1**		**Frankel**[217] 6860 4-9-0 136 ... TomQueally 6	139+
			(Sir Henry Cecil) *lw: racd keenly trcking ldr tl led 2f out: sn qcknd: surged clr fnl f: easily* **2/7**[1]
12-1	**2**	*5*	**Excelebration (IRE)**[27] 1549 4-9-0 126 ... JPO'Brien 7	127
			(A P O'Brien, Ire) *disp 3rd tl drvn and qcknd to go 2nd appr fnl f: kpt on wl but nvr any ch w easy wnr* **10/3**[2]
4-04	**3**	*4*	**Dubawi Gold**[22] 1646 4-9-0 117 ... RichardHughes 2	119
			(Richard Hannon) *stdd s and hld up in rr: drvn and qcknd fr 2f out to take 3rd jst ins fnl f but no ch w ldng duo* **16/1**[3]
/00-	**4**	*3*	**Bullet Train**[217] 6860 5-9-0 106 ... IanMongan 5	111
			(Sir Henry Cecil) *led tl hdd 2f out: lost 2nd and fdd appr fnl f* **100/1**
00-0	**5**	*7*	**Ransom Note**[30] 1471 5-9-0 115 ... KierenFallon 3	95
			(Charles Hills) *disp 3rd: rdn over 3f out: btn over 2f out* **33/1**
-031	**6**	*2 ¼*	**Windsor Palace (IRE)**[12] 1946 7-9-0 104 ...(v[1]) SeamieHeffernan 4	90
			(A P O'Brien, Ire) *disp 3rd and pushed along 4f out: wknd wl over 2f out* **40/1**

1m 38.14s (-1.56) **Going Correction** +0.325s/f (Good) 6 Ran SP% **113.1**

Speed ratings (Par 117): **120,115,111,108,101 98**

toteswingers: 1&2 £1.10, 1&3 £1.60, 2&3 £1.50 CSF £1.59 TOTE £1.40: £1.02, £1.70; EX 1.80.

Owner K Abdulla **Bred** Juddmonte Farms Ltd **Trained** Newmarket, Suffolk

FOCUS

A straightforward reappearance for the brilliant Frankel. This effort rates on a par with his Queen Elizabeth II Stakes win last autumn.

NOTEBOOK

Frankel ◆ wasn't seriously tested as he improved his record to a perfect ten. The pace, set by the winner's stablemate and half-brother Bullet Train, looked just ordinary by top-level standards, but Frankel still settled better than was often the case last year, just in behind, before drawing away without being challenged. Sir Henry Cecil's colt had already proven himself the best miler around, and the uncompetitive nature of this race means it would be dangerous to suggest we learnt anything new, but it is possible he's even better this year. He defeated the race-fit runner-up and third by even further than in the Queen Elizabeth II Stakes, while Bullet Train, more sensibly ridden this time, was beaten by an identical margin. That's despite Frankel having missed work when suffering a career-threatening setback in April, suggesting he can rate higher. He's likely to be kept at 1m for the Queen Anne, but that should be another procession against the same old faces, and the hope is that we see something different this season. A dream match with Black Caviar seems unlikely, but he should have no trouble staying 1m2f, so a step up in trip would be a start, and the latest Classic crop will presumably have a crack at him in due course. In the longer term, a horse billed as the world's best deserves to prove himself outside of Britain.

Excelebration(IRE) was always behind the winner with no prospect of giving him anything to worry about. However how do you beat this great horse? Even if Windsor Palace had helped force a stronger gallop, the outcome would almost certainly have been the same.He didn't achieve much when winning a 7f Group 3 at the Curragh on his debut for Aidan O'Brien, and he proved no match for his old rival. He could do with the winner moving up in trip sooner rather than later.

Dubawi Gold had excuses for his first two starts of 2012 and this was better, but he was still outclassed. He will want to avoid the front two in future. (op 20-1 tchd 25-1)

Ransom Note again struggled - he wants better ground and lesser company. (op 50-1)

Windsor Palace(IRE), the Ballydoyle second-string, played no worthwhile part, instead racing more or less alongside his stable companion. (op 50-1)

2271 BET ON YOUR MOBILE AT BLUESQ.COM E B F MAIDEN STKS (DIV II) 1m 2f 6y

4:50 (4:50) (Class 4) 3-Y-0 **£5,369** (£1,597; £798; £399) **Stalls** Low

Form				RPR
1		**Valiant** 3-9-3 0 ... JPO'Brien 3	86+
			(William Haggas) *w'like: scope: chsd ldrs: drvn and hdwy over 2f out: styd on wl fnl f to ld fnl 30yds* **8/1**
50-	**2**	*1*	**Stature (IRE)**[238] 6334 3-9-3 0 ...[1] JimmyFortune 1	84
			(Andrew Balding) *led: drvn 2f out: kpt on u.p over 1f out: edgd lft u.p fnl 120yds: hdd and no ex fnl 30yds* **16/1**
3-	**3**	*1*	**Cathedral**[245] 6165 3-9-3 0 ... SeamieHeffernan 2	82
			(Brian Meehan) *lw: in rr: hdwy 4f out: chsd ldr over 2f out: styd on to chal ins fnl f: bmpd fnl 120yds: sn no ex* **13/2**[3]
2-2	**4**	*6*	**Widyaan (IRE)**[35] 1385 3-9-3 0 ...(b) TadhgO'Shea 11	70
			(John Gosden) *w'like: stdd and swtchd lft s: in rr: drvn: hdwy and nt clr run whn swtchd sharply rt over 2f out: styd on for wl-hld 4th fnl f* **16/1**
4	**5**	*3 ¼*	**Sash Of Honour (IRE)**[31] 1456 3-9-3 0 ... PatDobbs 6	64
			(Sir Michael Stoute) *lw: chsd ldr 7f out: rdn and lost 2nd over 2f out: wknd over 1f out* **15/8**[1]
3	**6**	*6*	**Border Legend**[28] 1512 3-9-3 0 ... JamesDoyle 12	52+
			(Roger Charlton) *in tch: drvn and hdwy to press ldrs 3f out: sn green and hung lft: wknd over 2f out* **7/2**[2]
6-	**7**	*2 ½*	**Bute Hall**[189] 7398 3-9-3 0 ... TomQueally 7	50+
			(Mark Johnston) *w'like: chsd ldr to 7f out: styd wl there tl wkng whn hmpd over 2f out* **25/1**
8	*12*	**Linn County** 3-8-12 0 ... RobertHavlin 10	18
			(John Gosden) *w'like: str: slowly away: a towards rr* **16/1**
05-	**9**	*5*	**Turned To Gold (IRE)**[211] 6993 3-9-3 0 ... JimCrowley 5	13
			(Alan Jarvis) *swtg: t.k.h in rr: rdn and bhd fnl 4f* **33/1**
3-	**10**	*6*	**Mossbrae**[207] 7083 3-9-3 0 ... NeilCallan 4
			(Roger Varian) *w'like: scope: chsd ldrs: rdn and wknd 3f out: eased nr fin* **8/1**

2m 13.67s (4.87) **Going Correction** +0.325s/f (Good) **10** Ran SP% **117.0**

Speed ratings (Par 101): **93,92,91,86,84 79,77,67,63,58**

toteswingers: 1&2 £16.20, 1&3 £7.10, 2&3 £21.30 CSF £127.42 TOTE £9.90: £2.90, £6.00, £2.80; EX 199.40 TRIFECTA Not won..

Owner Highclere Thoroughbred Racing-Herring **Bred** New England, Middle Park & Balmerino Bs **Trained** Newmarket, Suffolk

FOCUS

This contest has generally been the source of useful handicappers but the 2011 winner Fiorente went on to be placed at Group 2 level. The second division of this maiden was run 1.79secs slower than the first leg and 0.35secs slower than the earlier 3yo handicap. Several of those failed to build on promising debuts but the winner made an encouraging start. There are doubts over the bare form.

Border Legend Official explanation: jockey said gelding hung left

2272 GET YOUR BET ON AT BLUE SQUARE FILLIES' H'CAP 7f (S)

5:20 (5:22) (Class 4) (0-85,85) 3-Y-O **£5,175** (£1,540; £769; £384) **Stalls** Centre

Form				RPR
2123	**1**		**Emman Bee (IRE)**[12] 1906 3-8-7 **71** oh1 ... FergusSweeney 16	80
			(John Gallagher) *sn chsng ldrs: chal 2f out: slt ld 1f out: drvn and styd on strly fnl 120yds* **16/1**
140-	**2**	*nk*	**Dare To Dream**[203] 7169 3-9-0 **78** ... RichardHughes 13	86
			(Richard Hannon) *hld up in rr: drvn and hdwy fr 2f out: styd on strly fnl f to cl on wnr fnl 75yds but a jst hld* **8/1**[3]
0-55	**3**	*2 ¼*	**Red Larkspur (IRE)**[24] 1612 3-9-0 **78** ... JamesDoyle 12	80
			(Roger Teal) *chsd ldrs: drvn and hdwy to press ldrs over 1f out: chsd wnr u.p but no imp fnl 120yds: dropped to 3rd fnl 75yds* **20/1**
321-	**4**	*¾*	**Rhagori**[205] 7125 3-8-10 **74** ... JimCrowley 15	74+
			(Ralph Beckett) *lw: in rr: drvn and hdwy fr 2f out: styd on wl fnl f to take 4th clsng stages* **11/1**
21-5	**5**	*nk*	**Lollina Paulina**[14] 1862 3-8-11 **75** ow1 ... NeilCallan 8	74
			(Kevin Ryan) *chsd ldrs: led over 2f out: hdd u.p 1f out: wknd fnl 120yds* **16/1**
241-	**6**	*2 ¾*	**No Compromise**[191] 7350 3-8-13 **77** ... RobertHavlin 11	69
			(Hughie Morrison) *in rr: drvn and hdwy fr 2f out: kpt on fnl f: nt rch ldrs* **8/1**[3]
250-	**7**	*hd*	**Imelda Mayhem**[210] 7028 3-9-4 **82** ... SeamieHeffernan 10	73
			(J S Moore) *in rr: drvn and hdwy over 2f out: chsd ldrs over 1f out: wknd fnl f* **40/1**
2-1	**8**	*3 ¼*	**Vivid Blue**[10] 1989 3-8-12 **79** ... AdamBeschizza(3) 7	61
			(William Haggas) *chsd ldrs: rdn over 2f out: wknd 1f out* **15/2**[2]
5-05	**9**	*1 ¼*	**Stellar Express (IRE)**[35] 1392 3-8-13 **77** ... NeilChalmers 3	56
			(Michael Appleby) *pressed ldrs: led ins fnl 4f: hdd over 2f out: wknd appr fnl f* **25/1**
611-	**10**	*hd*	**Emmuska**[172] 7576 3-9-2 **80** ... PatDobbs 6	58
			(Richard Hannon) *chsd ldrs: chal u.p 2f out: wknd 1f out* **14/1**
31-6	**11**	*7*	**I'm So Glad**[29] 1500 3-8-13 **77** ... MatthewDavies 1	36
			(Mick Channon) *chsd ldrs over 4f* **11/1**
450-	**12**	*2 ¾*	**Gold Lace (IRE)**[264] 5571 3-9-2 **85** ... AshleyMorgan(5) 5	37
			(Ed Dunlop) *in tch over 4f* **33/1**
35-1	**13**	*4*	**Dance Company**[18] 1736 3-8-13 **77** ... TomQueally 18	18
			(William Knight) *in tch: shkn up 3f out: sn wknd* **3/1**[1]
-161	**14**	*2 ¼*	**Boudoir (IRE)**[18] 1733 3-8-10 **74** ... KieranO'Neill 9
			(Richard Hannon) *stmbld bdly leaving stalles: sn rcvrd and in tch 1/2-way: wknd qckly appr fnl 2f* **16/1**
124	**15**	*6*	**Majestic Zafeen**[49] 1142 3-8-12 **76** ... SilvestreDeSousa 17
			(Alastair Lidderdale) *bhd fr 1/2-way* **20/1**
15-5	**16**	*9*	**Viola D'Amour (IRE)**[35] 1375 3-9-0 **78** ... RichardKingscote 4
			(Tom Dascombe) *plld hrd: chsd ldrs 4f* **20/1**
20-2	**17**	*1 ½*	**Ziefhd**[16] 1790 3-9-2 **80** ... JimmyFortune 2
			(Paul Cole) *lw: led tl hdd ins fnl 4f: wknd: ins fnl 3f* **9/1**

1m 27.66s (1.96) **Going Correction** +0.325s/f (Good) **17** Ran SP% **133.5**

Speed ratings (Par 98): **101,100,98,97,96 93,93,89,88,88 80,77,72,69,63 52,51**

toteswingers: 1&2 £31.00, 1&3 £53.30, 2&3 £41.30 CSF £138.06 CT £1590.46 TOTE £23.40: £6.60, £1.70, £5.80, £3.20; EX 177.70 TRIFECTA Not won..

Owner Mark Benton **Bred** O Bourke **Trained** Chastleton, Oxon

■ Stewards' Enquiry : Seamie Heffernan caution; entered wrong stall.

FOCUS

A couple of recent winners of this went on to score at Listed level, but the best of those to take this in the last ten years was Red Evie, who subsequently became a Group 1 performer, taking the following season's Lockinge Stakes. This time a big field of fillies contested a tight handicap, and in the end those drawn high and racing more towards the stands' side dominated. The form looks fairly ordinary.

Boudoir(IRE) Official explanation: jockey said filly stumbled leaving stalls.

2273 BLUE SQUARE RICHARD HUGHES MY AUTOBIOGRAPHY MAIDEN STKS 7f (S)

5:50 (5:54) (Class 4) 3-Y-0 **£5,175** (£1,540; £769; £384) **Stalls** Centre

Form				RPR
1		**Well Painted (IRE)** 3-9-3 0 ... JPO'Brien 4	87+
			(William Haggas) *trckd ldrs: bmpd 4f out: drvn: qcknd to ld and hung rt ins fnl f: hld on wl* **15/2**[3]
22-2	**2**	*nk*	**Riot Of Colour**[30] 1472 3-8-12 87 ... JimCrowley 11	81+
			(Ralph Beckett) *in tch: drvn and hdwy to chal whn bmpd ins fnl f: kpt on again clsng stages: nt quite pce of wnr* **10/11**[1]
5	**3**	*1 ¾*	**Register (IRE)**[8] 2041 3-9-3 0 ... SilvestreDeSousa 16	81
			(William Muir) *pressed ldrs: led over 2f out: narrowly hdd and bmpd ins fnl f: styd on same pce fnl 120yds* **16/1**
00-	**4**	*2 ½*	**Tea Cup**[292] 4614 3-8-12 0 ... KieranO'Neill 1	72+
			(Richard Hannon) *in tch: bmpd 4f out: hdwy over 2f out: drvn to chal whn bdly hmpd ins fnl f: nt rcvr* **20/1**
2	**5**	*¾*	**Keyaadi**[14] 1864 3-9-3 0 ... NeilCallan 19	72
			(Roger Varian) *led tl hdd over 2f out: wknd fnl f* **9/2**[2]
6	*½*	**Niger (IRE)** 3-9-3 0 ... TomQueally 10	71+
			(Jeremy Noseda) *in tch: pushed along over 2f out: kpt on fnl f but nvr gng pce of ldrs* **8/1**
53	**7**	*nk*	**Princess Steph (IRE)**[45] 1182 3-8-12 0 ... JamesDoyle 5	65
			(Heather Main) *chsd ldrs: ev ch and drvn 2f out: wknd ins fnl f* **33/1**
4-	**8**	*nk*	**Red Hot Secret**[200] 7210 3-8-7 0 ... RaulDaSilva(5) 2	64
			(Jeremy Gask) *trckd ldrs: rdn 2f out: wknd fnl f* **33/1**

05- **9** *hd* **Bohemian Rhapsody (IRE)**[223] 6726 3-9-0 0 .... PatrickHills(3) 8 69+
(J W Hills) *in tch: pushed along 1/2-way: kpt on again in clsng stages* **20/1**

10 *nk* **Basingstoke (IRE)** 3-8-10 0 .... DanielMuscutt(7) 7 68+
(Andrew Balding) *s.i.s: in rr: pushed along and green over 2f out: styd on again clsng stages* **40/1**

4-0 **11** *1 3/4* **Sondeduro**[8] 2041 3-9-3 0 .... FergusSweeney 6 63+
(Jamie Osborne) *in tch: pushed along and no prog fr 2f out* **33/1**

30- **12** *hd* **Anton Chigurh**[225] 6673 3-9-3 0 .... RichardKingscote 12 63+
(Tom Dascombe) *s.i.s: t.k.h: sme late prog* **28/1**

13 *3 1/2* **Dame Shirley** 3-8-12 0 .... PatDobbs 9 48
(J W Hills) *outpcd* **100/1**

14 *9* **Ascription (IRE)** 3-9-3 0 .... JimmyFortune 17 29
(Ed Dunlop) *s.i.s: outpcd* **16/1**

15 *4 1/2* **Sword In Hand** 3-9-3 0 .... SeamieHeffernan 18 17
(Alan Jarvis) *racd alone stands' side: chsd ldrs 4f* **33/1**

16 *2 1/4* **Tickin Time** 3-9-3 0 .... IanMongan 3
(Michael Squance) *s.i.s: a in rr* **100/1**

0- **17** *2 1/4* **Imperial Elegance**[245] 6160 3-8-12 0 .... MatthewDavies 15
(Mick Channon) *chsd ldrs 4f* **100/1**

1m 28.97s (3.27) **Going Correction** +0.325s/f (Good) **17** Ran SP% **135.4**
Speed ratings (Par 101): **94,93,91,88,87 87,87,86,86,86 84,83,79,69,64 61,59**
toteswingers: 1&2 £4.30, 1&3 £38.80, 2&3 £12.60 CSF £14.79 TOTE £13.30: £3.10, £1.40, £6.60; EX 22.10 Trifecta £139.70 Pool: £539.92 - 2.86 winning units..
Owner Options O Syndicate **Bred** Round Hill Stud **Trained** Newmarket, Suffolk

FOCUS
The form looks just fair, but it was a competitive maiden and really ought to produce a few winners. The time was relatively slow though.
T/Plt: £489.60 to a £1 stake. Pool: £144,121.30. 214.88 winning tickets. T/Qpdt: £31.60 to a £1 stake. Pool: £8,393.37. 196.54 winning tickets. ST

2245 NEWMARKET (R-H)
Saturday, May 19

OFFICIAL GOING: Good to firm (good in places; 8.1)
Far side course used with stalls on Far side except for 1m 4fr & 1m 6f: Centre
Wind: Fresh ,half-behind Weather: Overcast

2274 POPTELECOM.CO.UK H'CAP 7f
1:40 (1:41) (Class 4) (0-80,81) 4-Y-0+ **£5,175** (£1,540; £769; £384) **Stalls** Low

Form RPR

5-21 **1** **Highland Colori (IRE)**[12] 1936 4-9-7 **80** .... DavidProbert 17 92
(Andrew Balding) *racd alone stands' side: chsd ldrs: rdn and hung rt fr over 2f out: led over 1f out: styd on* **7/1**[3]

1-65 **2** *1 1/4* **Great Expectations**[38] 1354 4-8-12 **71** .... FrederikTylicki 7 80+
(J R Jenkins) *hld up: hdwy u.p over 1f out: r.o to go 2nd wl ins fnl f: nt rch wnr* **7/2**[1]

00-0 **3** *nk* **Amazing Amoray (IRE)**[48] 1156 4-9-3 **76** .... RyanMoore 9 84
(David Barron) *led: rdn and hdd over 2f out: styd on u.p* **9/2**[2]

6-04 **4** *1/2* **Illustrious Prince (IRE)**[21] 1650 5-8-13 **77** .... NeilFarley(5) 2 83
(Declan Carroll) *chsd ldr tl led over 2f out: rdn and hdd over 1f out: styd on same pce ins fnl f* **14/1**

6-22 **5** *1/2* **Angelic Upstart (IRE)**[23] 1633 4-8-13 **72** .... WilliamBuick 4 77
(Andrew Balding) *hld up: hdwy over 2f out: rdn over 1f out: styd on* **17/2**

100- **6** *hd* **Mrs Greeley**[208] 7050 4-9-1 **74** .... WilliamCarson 3 79
(Eve Johnson Houghton) *a.p: rdn over 1f out: edgd rt ins fnl f: styd on* **28/1**

4-13 **7** *hd* **Snow Trooper**[21] 1680 4-8-13 **72** .... ShaneKelly 14 76
(Dean Ivory) *prom: rdn over 1f out: styd on* **8/1**

40-0 **8** *1 1/4* **Rough Rock (IRE)**[39] 1289 7-8-10 **72** .... HarryBentley(3) 15 73
(Chris Dwyer) *hld up in tch: rdn over 2f out: styd on same pce ins fnl f* **33/1**

100- **9** *2 3/4* **Easy Over (IRE)**[255] 5820 4-9-2 **75** .... SebSanders 5 68
(Ed McMahon) *hld up: hdwy u.p over 1f out: nvr trbld ldrs* **18/1**

-146 **10** *1/2* **Myboyalfie (USA)**[26] 1561 5-8-13 **72** ....(v) JoeFanning 12 64
(J R Jenkins) *hld up: rdn over 2f out: styd on nr fin: nvr nrr* **11/1**

105- **11** *3/4* **Chief Of Men**[315] 3871 4-8-11 **70** .... EddieAhern 8 60
(Denis Coakley) *chsd ldrs: rdn over 2f out: wknd fnl f* **25/1**

-120 **12** *2* **Hawk Moth (IRE)**[63] 942 4-8-9 **68** .... JamieSpencer 1 52
(John Spearing) *hld up: rdn over 2f out: nvr on terms* **25/1**

40-1 **13** *3/4* **Ongoodform (IRE)**[7] 2083 5-9-8 **81** .... PaulHanagan 10 63
(Paul D'Arcy) *chsd ldrs tl rdn and wknd over 1f out* **12/1**

1-00 **14** *21* **Sketchy Evidence (USA)**[4] 2146 4-8-2 **66** oh1 .... DarrenEgan(5) 13
(John Best) *in rr and sn pushed along: lost tch fr over 2f out: t.o* **50/1**

00-6 **15** *11* **Breakheart (IRE)**[23] 1633 5-9-1 **74** .... TomMcLaughlin 6
(Paul Howling) *s.s: outpcd: t.o* **33/1**

1m 24.96s (-0.44) **Going Correction** +0.075s/f (Good) **15** Ran SP% **122.5**
Speed ratings (Par 105): **105,103,103,102,102 101,101,100,97,96 95,93,92,68,55**
toteswingers: 1&2 £6.10, 1&3 £7.10, 2&3 £5.30 CSF £29.45 CT £126.93 TOTE £9.00: £3.00, £1.80, £2.10; EX 41.40.
Owner Evan M Sutherland **Bred** Rathbarry Stud **Trained** Kingsclere, Hants

FOCUS
This looked an open contest for fair sorts. The winner raced solo against the rail but this is still worth a personal best. It proved hard to make ground.
Breakheart(IRE) Official explanation: jockey said gelding was slowly away.
Zaheeb Official explanation: jockey said filly ran too free.

2275 POPTELECOM.CO.UK FAIRWAY STKS (LISTED RACE) 1m 2f
2:15 (2:15) (Class 1) 3-Y-O **£18,714** (£7,095; £3,550; £1,768; £887) **Stalls** Low

Form RPR

1-2 **1** **Thought Worthy (USA)**[21] 1678 3-9-0 106 .... WilliamBuick 4 108+
(John Gosden) *led: pushed along and hung rt fr over 3f out: rdn and hdd 2f out: rallied to ld wl ins fnl f: r.o* **15/8**[1]

2-11 **2** *nk* **Noble Mission**[14] 1859 3-9-5 102 .... EddieAhern 1 112+
(Sir Henry Cecil) *trckd ldrs: shkn up over 2f out: rdn over 1f out: r.o* **15/8**[1]

51- **3** *3/4* **Rugged Cross**[274] 5254 3-9-0 98 .... DaneO'Neill 3 106
(Henry Candy) *hld up: hdwy u.p over 1f out: unable qck nr fin* **9/2**[2]

115- **4** *hd* **Farhaan (USA)**[238] 6336 3-9-0 100 .... PaulHanagan 2 105
(John Dunlop) *chsd ldr tl led 2f out: sn rdn: hung rt and hdd wl ins fnl f: styd on same pce* **15/2**[3]

11-2 **5** *14* **Prince Alzain (USA)**[35] 1375 3-9-0 97 .... RyanMoore 5 77
(Gerard Butler) *hld up: plld hrd: outpcd fr over 3f out* **11/1**

2m 4.31s (-1.49) **Going Correction** +0.075s/f (Good) **5** Ran SP% **107.8**
Speed ratings (Par 107): **108,107,107,107,95**
CSF £5.23 TOTE £2.00: £1.10, £1.30; EX 3.00.
Owner George Strawbridge **Bred** George Strawbridge **Trained** Newmarket, Suffolk

FOCUS
The pace looked nothing more than ordinary early, and every horse except for the disappointing and hard-pulling Prince Alzain had a chance in the final furlong. This was a muddling renewal, rated around the race averages.

NOTEBOOK
Thought Worthy(USA) ◆ only got caught late on by the unbeaten Imperial Monarch in the Classic Trial at Sandown, the pair raced far apart on the track that day, and showed a really willing attitude here to fight on tenaciously and rally back to the front close to the line. He wants further like his brother Lucarno, and still appeared green once giving his all, the track may not have suited either, so remains an exciting prospect. (op 9-4 tchd 5-2 in a place)
Noble Mission was testing his Derby credentials after a decent run of form in the spring, but things didn't look promising even before he'd entered the stalls considering he was noticeably sweating on various places of his body. He got slightly outpaced as the tempo lifted once racing, but ran on really well under his 5lb penalty to post another solid effort. He won't run at Epsom now, and the King Edward VII Stakes is the aim. (op 13-8 tchd 6-4 and 2-1 in a place)
Rugged Cross, one of the first under pressure in this, did particularly well to get as close as he did at the end and has something to build on for the rest of the season. (op 5-1 tchd 11-2)
Farhaan(USA) ran below expectations when made favourite for the Royal Lodge last year, form that has been boosted since, and hadn't been seen out since. Making his 3yo debut, he appeared to be delivered at the right time, but one got the impression he was there a bit too long in the end and dossed as a result. The ability still looks intact and he should obviously come on for this. (op 13-2)

2276 CORALCHAMPIONSCLUB.CO.UK SPRINT TROPHY (H'CAP) 6f
2:45 (2:46) (Class 2) (0-105,98) 3-Y-O **£24,900** (£7,456; £3,728; £1,864; £932; £468) **Stalls** Low

Form RPR

12-2 **1** **Mince**[14] 1858 3-9-0 **91** .... FrankieDettori 6 98
(Roger Charlton) *hld up: swtchd lft and hdwy over 1f out: r.o to ld post* **3/1**[1]

-211 **2** *hd* **Bartolomeu**[19] 1721 3-8-12 **89** .... PatCosgrave 5 95
(Marco Botti) *hld up: hdwy 2f out: led over 1f out: sn rdn: hdd post* **12/1**

10-0 **3** *nse* **Top Cop**[31] 1457 3-8-13 **90** .... DavidProbert 10 96
(Andrew Balding) *a.p: rdn over 1f out: r.o* **12/1**

11-6 **4** *1/2* **Rafeej**[22] 1644 3-8-10 **87** .... PaulHanagan 2 91
(Mark Johnston) *chsd ldr tl led wl over 1f out: sn rdn and hdd: r.o* **20/1**

14-0 **5** *nse* **Tioman Legend**[14] 1858 3-9-1 **92** .... DaneO'Neill 8 96
(Roger Charlton) *s.s: hld up: hdwy over 1f out: r.o* **33/1**

4-10 **6** *1/2* **Accession (IRE)**[17] 1751 3-9-4 **95** .... AdamKirby 9 97
(Clive Cox) *hld up: rdn and r.o wl ins fnl f: nt rch ldrs* **18/1**

00-5 **7** *1 1/4* **Lady Gorgeous**[31] 1454 3-9-7 **98** .... MartinHarley 11 96
(Mick Channon) *mid-div: pushed along and nt clr run over 1f out: r.o ins fnl f: nt trble ldrs* **20/1**

13-3 **8** *nse* **Democretes**[14] 1858 3-8-11 **88** .... RyanMoore 7 86
(Richard Hannon) *hld up: swtchd lft and hdwy over 1f out: r.o* **11/2**[2]

351- **9** *3/4* **Pea Shooter**[258] 5756 3-8-10 **87** .... PhillipMakin 4 83
(Kevin Ryan) *hld up in tch: rdn over 1f out: styd on same pce ins fnl f* **6/1**[3]

-121 **10** *3/4* **Dark Castle**[31] 1449 3-8-7 **84** .... LiamKeniry 1 77
(Sylvester Kirk) *hld up in tch: rdn over 1f out: no ex ins fnl f* **8/1**

-033 **11** *3/4* **Church Music (IRE)**[8] 2028 3-8-7 **84** ....(p) MircoDemuro 12 75
(Michael Scudamore) *led: rdn and hdd wl over 1f out: wknd wl ins fnl f* **33/1**

5-50 **12** *1 1/4* **Alejandro (IRE)**[14] 1858 3-8-8 **92** .... LauraBarry(7) 13 79
(Richard Fahey) *chsd ldrs: rdn over 1f out: edgd lft and wknd ins fnl f* **25/1**

35-4 **13** *3/4* **Responsive**[31] 1457 3-8-8 **85** .... DarryllHolland 14 70
(Hughie Morrison) *mid-div: rdn and nt clr run over 1f out: nvr trbld ldrs* **12/1**

51-4 **14** *1* **Kimbali (IRE)**[9] 1998 3-8-8 **85** .... FrederikTylicki 17 66
(Richard Fahey) *mid-div: pushed along 1/2-way: rdn whn hmpd over 1f out: n.d* **16/1**

1-45 **15** *shd* **Hurry Up George**[14] 1858 3-9-4 **98** .... HarryBentley(3) 16 79
(Ralph Beckett) *chsd ldrs: pushed along over 2f out: edgd lft and wknd fnl f* **16/1**

6-11 **16** *1 1/2* **Dishy Guru**[37] 1331 3-8-3 **80** .... WilliamCarson 18 56
(Michael Blanshard) *s.i.s: hld up: hdwy over 2f out: ev ch wl over 1f out: wknd fnl f* **33/1**

1m 12.21s (0.01) **Going Correction** +0.075s/f (Good) **16** Ran SP% **128.1**
Speed ratings (Par 105): **102,101,101,101,100 100,98,98,97,96 95,93,92,91,91 89**
toteswingers: 1&2 £4.70, 1&3 £12.90, 2&3 £27.90 CSF £38.74 CT £393.21 TOTE £2.80: £1.40, £2.30, £3.10, £5.30; EX 45.40 Trifecta £964.10 Pool: £29,284.24 - 35.28 winning units..
Owner Lady Rothschild **Bred** The Rt Hon Lord Rothschild **Trained** Beckhampton, Wilts

FOCUS
There was never going to be anything other than a strong pace set from the outset with so many runners taking part, and the draw didn't seem to play an important part in the outcome. Strong handicap form.

NOTEBOOK
Mince had several of today's rivals behind her when going close in a strongly contested handicap here on reappearance, and went one place better this time, but only just. Keen in behind runners on the far side early, Dettori was at his absolute best, switching his mount towards the stands' side from the 4f marker before coming with a persistent effort throughout the latter stages to steal the prize on the line. There is a valuable 6f handicap at York in June that some previous winners have headed for next, but presumably some black type is also on the agenda for her if something suitable can be found. (op 7-2)
Bartolomeu ◆ was back on turf after showing good form on the Polytrack (three different courses), and is definitely progressing in the right direction. He may have hit the front a bit too early after moving up strongly, but there is no doubt he can win a race of this nature. (tchd 14-1 in a place)
Top Cop finished behind a few of these in a C&D handicap at the Craven meeting but did best of them this time, posting a pleasing performance with that initial effort under his belt. (op 14-1)
Rafeej, up in trip, ran a long way below market expectations on his seasonal reappearance (trainer feels his horse doesn't want easy ground to be at his best), but did much better on quicker going. One would expect to see him kept to a faster surface from now. (op 16-1)
Tioman Legend got much closer to Mince this time (said to have raced too freely on the last occasion), which was some achievement considering he was dropped out soon after exiting the stalls and gave his rivals a couple of lengths head start early on.
Accession(IRE) wasn't beaten far, despite filling last place, on Polytrack last time and kept on well here in the final stages. (op 16-1)
Lady Gorgeous finished a close fifth in the Nell Gwyn here on her reappearance, but ran here as though a bit too high in the weights, for all that she didn't have a clear passage in the latter stages.
Democretes was one place behind Mince last time but was hampered over 4f out in this and never got going quickly enough to get involved. Presumably he'll go up in trip again now. (op 6-1)
Pea Shooter, reported to have done well over the winter, had been gelded since his last run but one got the impression he did a bit too much early to get home in a race of this quality first-time-out. (op 13-2 tchd 11-2)

Dark Castle was having his first run away from Kempton, therefore his first on turf, and had every chance but either didn't get home in this class of contest or is on the right handicap mark to stop him winning. (op 15-2)
Responsive's jockey didn't seem to have the room when he wanted to make a bid, so his mount's effort can be marked up a bit. (tchd 16-1)

2277 POPTELECOM.CO.UK KING CHARLES II STKS (LISTED RACE) 7f
3:20 (3:20) (Class 1) 3-Y-O

£18,714 (£7,095; £3,550; £1,768; £887; £445) Stalls Low

Form					RPR
1-4	1		**Aljamaaheer (IRE)**[29] 1500 3-9-0 88 (Roger Varian) *hld up: racd keenly: hdwy over 1f out: shkn up to ld and edgd rt ins fnl f: comf* **10/3[2]**	PaulHanagan 6	108+
3-1	2	1 ½	**The Nile**[18] 1737 3-9-0 95 (John Gosden) *trckd ldrs: rdn and hung rt over 1f out: r.o* **2/1[1]**	WilliamBuick 7	103+
44-0	3	1 ¼	**Balty Boys (IRE)**[31] 1452 3-9-0 110 (Charles Hills) *led: pushed along over 2f out: hdd and unable qck ins fnl f* **8/1**	MichaelHills 4	100
62-0	4	hd	**Saigon**[14] 1856 3-9-4 108 (James Toller) *hld up: rdn over 1f out: r.o ins fnl f: nt rch ldrs* **7/2[3]**	RyanMoore 1	103
-124	5	½	**Mr Red Clubs (IRE)**[14] 1860 3-9-0 91 (Tim Pitt) *chsd ldrs: rdn over 1f out: styd on same pce ins fnl f* **25/1**	ShaneKelly 2	98
51	6	2	**Van Ellis**[15] 1834 3-9-0 0 (Mark Johnston) *chsd ldr: rdn and ev ch over 1f out: wknd wl ins fnl f* **8/1**	JoeFanning 5	92+
30-2	7	2 ½	**Silverheels (IRE)**[14] 1845 3-9-0 100 (Paul Cole) *chsd ldrs: rdn over 1f out: wknd fnl f* **9/1**	FrankieDettori 3	86

1m 24.66s (-0.74) **Going Correction** +0.075s/f (Good) 7 Ran SP% **114.7**
Speed ratings (Par 107): **107,105,103,103,103 100,97**
toteswingers: 1&2 £2.60, 1&3 £5.00, 2&3 £3.90 CSF £10.52 TOTE £3.20: £2.20, £1.80; EX 6.10.

Owner Hamdan Al Maktoum **Bred** Corrin Stud & Sean O'Keefe **Trained** Newmarket, Suffolk

FOCUS
This Listed contest has often proved a reasonable guide to the Jersey Stakes at Royal Ascot, with Jeremy and Tariq both following up their wins here at the Royal Meeting and Fokine and Codemaster finishing runner-up. Balty Boys and Saigon brought Group-race form into this contest but there were several lightly-raced colts with the potential for improvement. A smart effort from the winner, who should do better.

NOTEBOOK
Aljamaaheer(IRE) had been too keen on his handicap debut on soft ground last time. He settled much better in this higher-grade contest and picked up really well when produced to score with something in reserve. He looks capable of going on from this and is likely to follow a number of his predecessors by taking in the Jersey Stakes next. (op 11-4 tchd 7-2)
The Nile, who took his maiden on Polytrack at the beginning of the month, was quite keen and saw plenty of daylight on the outside of his field. He could not pick up as well as the winner in the closing stages and connections might look for a similar contest before stepping him up a level. (op 5-2, tchd 3-1 and 11-4 in places)
Balty Boys(IRE) had the highest official rating due to having finished fourth in the Middle Park Stakes. He made the running and, although sticking to his task, found two progressive types too good for him. (tchd 15-2)
Saigon, another with good juvenile form, having been placed in the Mill Reef and Horris Hill, was held up out the back and took a long while to pick up before staying on late. He did not appear to stay a mile in the 2,000 Guineas but looked to need further here. Possibly a more positive ride at this trip will be in his favour. (tchd 3-1)
Mr Red Clubs(IRE) had been progressive on Polytrack during the winter but looked to have a stiff task here. He ran pretty well in the circumstances but is likely to suffer at the hands of the handicapper for this.
Van Ellis showed up well but did not appear to get home up the hill. He might be better back at 6f or on a flatter track at this trip.
Silverheels(IRE), who came up against a potentially smart sort on his reappearance, was well enough placed early but dropped away tamely. He had quite a busy juvenile season and has to prove that he has truly trained on. (tchd 8-1 and 10-1)

2278 CHEAP BROADBAND @ POPTELECOM.CO.UK H'CAP 1m 6f
3:55 (3:57) (Class 2) (0-105,103) 4-Y-O+

£18,675 (£5,592; £2,796; £1,398; £699; £351) Stalls Centre

Form					RPR
404-	1		**Mount Athos (IRE)**[224] 6690 5-9-10 103 (Luca Cumani) *hld up: hdwy 3f out: led over 1f out: pushed out* **9/2[1]**	JamieSpencer 2	112
050-	2	2 ¼	**Harlestone Times (IRE)**[196] 7297 5-9-5 98 (John Dunlop) *prom: outpcd over 3f out: rallied over 1f out: r.o to go 2nd post* **11/1**	FrankieDettori 4	104
6-30	3	nse	**Hurricane Higgins (IRE)**[13] 1882 4-9-2 95 (Mark Johnston) *hld up: hdwy over 3f out: rdn over 1f out: styd on* **12/1**	JoeFanning 9	101
30-1	4	3 ¼	**Viking Storm**[56] 1037 4-8-7 86 (Harry Dunlop) *prom: rdn over 1f out: no ex fnl f* **28/1**	PaulHanagan 8	87
0-13	5	nk	**Midsummer Sun**[21] 1674 4-9-5 98 (Sir Henry Cecil) *chsd ldr after 1f tl led over 2f out: rdn and hdd over 1f out: no ex ins fnl f* **9/1**	EddieAhern 13	99
410-	6	½	**Western Prize**[273] 5283 4-8-0 82 (Ralph Beckett) *prom: rdn over 2f out: styd on same pce fr over 1f out* **5/1[2]**	HarryBentley(3) 5	82
106-	7	2 ¼	**Bowdler's Magic**[98] 7102 5-8-6 85 (Mark Johnston) *hld up: rdn over 2f out: n.d* **12/1**	MircoDemuro 6	82
0003	8	nk	**Montaff**[21] 1672 6-9-2 95 (Mick Channon) *hld up: hdwy over 2f out: sn rdn: wknd ins fnl f* **16/1**	MartinHarley 1	92
/0-0	9	1 ½	**Bernie The Bolt (IRE)**[13] 1882 6-9-0 93 (Andrew Balding) *hld up: drvn along over 3f out: nvr trbld ldrs* **6/1[3]**	DavidProbert 14	88
06-5	10	2	**Buthelezi (USA)**[35] 1374 4-9-6 99 (John Gosden) *chsd ldrs: rdn over 3f out: wknd over 2f out* **9/1**	WilliamBuick 3	91
00-0	11	2 ¾	**Activate**[42] 1214 5-8-10 89 (Kevin Ryan) *led: rdn and hdd over 2f out: hung rt and wknd over 1f out* **28/1**	PhillipMakin 11	77
31-2	12	8	**Spice Fair**[14] 1850 5-8-10 89 (Mark Usher) *hld up: rdn over 3f out: wknd over 2f out: sn hung lft: eased fnl f* **7/1**	RyanMoore 10	66

2m 57.07s (0.07) **Going Correction** +0.075s/f (Good) 12 Ran SP% **118.1**
Speed ratings (Par 109): **102,100,100,98,98 98,97,96,96,94 93,88**
toteswingers: 1&2 £12.90, 1&3 £10.30, 2&3 £26.90 CSF £54.00 CT £553.81 TOTE £4.50: £1.90, £4.60, £4.30; EX 62.70.
Owner Dr Marwan Koukash **Bred** David Magnier And Cobra Bloodstock **Trained** Newmarket, Suffolk

FOCUS
This looked a fascinating affair, as it contained a few horses with the ability to hold their own at a slightly higher level coming up against solid handicappers. It has been rated just an average race for the grade, though.

NOTEBOOK
Mount Athos(IRE), who finished fourth in the Cesarewitch on his final start when with David Wachman, won with plenty in hand after racing powerfully throughout. He landed his first race in 2011 but didn't win again thereafter (although he ran some cracking races), so it'll be interesting to see if he can improve again under the care of Luca Cumani. The owner confirmed afterwards that the long-term aim for the horse is the Melbourne Cup. (tchd 4-1)
Harlestone Times(IRE), off since finishing down the field in the November Handicap, hit a flat spot about 3f out and didn't really pick up until deep inside the final furlong. He does stay well but is probably in need of going down the weights a bit to hold an obvious chance of victory. (op 16-1)
Hurricane Higgins(IRE) was trying this distance for the first time and saw it out perfectly well. More options should now be available to Mark Johnston in an attempt to get another victory into his horse. (op 10-1)
Viking Storm ◆ almost certainly stayed without being quite up to this level. That said, he will surely find things a bit easier in lesser company. (op 22-1)
Midsummer Sun had excuses for his Ripon defeat last time and did better here, but the race distance appeared to stretch him. (op 8-1)
Western Prize has plenty of scope to improve again at four, and may well do so with this run under his belt. (op 8-1)
Bernie The Bolt(IRE) was a staying-on seventh over an inadequate trip here on his comeback but this return to further, which should have suited, didn't bring about a significantly better performance (op 15-2, tchd 8-1 in a place)
Buthelezi(USA) ran poorly. (op 8-1)
Spice Fair was ridden patiently out the back and never made the slightest impression. Ryan Moore reported that the gelding hung left throughout. Official explanation: jockey said gelding hung left throughout. (op 11-2 tchd 5-1)

2279 POPTELECOM.CO.UK MAIDEN STKS (DIV I) 1m
4:30 (4:30) (Class 5) 3-Y-O

£3,234 (£962; £481; £240) Stalls Low

Form					RPR
5-3	1		**Captain Cat (IRE)**[28] 1506 3-9-3 0 (Roger Charlton) *led stands' side: edgd rt and overall ldr over 2f out: pushed clr fnl f* **13/8[1]**	JamieSpencer 7	90+
	2	4 ½	**Lahaag** 3-9-3 0 (John Gosden) *racd stands' side: hld up: hdwy over 1f out: r.o to go 2nd wl ins fnl f: no ch w wnr* **11/2[2]**	PaulHanagan 14	79+
5	3	½	**Trend Is My Friend (USA)**[51] 1086 3-9-3 0 (Amanda Perrett) *racd centre: chsd ldrs: rdn over 1f out: styd on same pce ins fnl f* **9/1**	EddieAhern 2	78
00-	4	½	**Santarini (IRE)**[203] 7165 3-8-9 0 (Richard Hannon) *racd centre: chsd ldrs: rdn over 2f out: styd on same pce ins fnl f* **14/1**	SeanLevey(3) 8	72
53	5	nk	**Tharawal (IRE)**[8] 2042 3-9-3 0 (Terry Clement) *racd stands' side: chsd wnr: edgd rt over 2f out: rdn over 1f out: no ex ins fnl f* **8/1[3]**	MarcHalford 9	76
0	6	1 ½	**Wildomar**[30] 1467 3-9-3 0 (Jeremy Noseda) *racd stands' side: rdn and edgd rt over 2f out: no ex ins fnl f* **8/1[3]**	WilliamBuick 10	73+
0-5	7	2	**Plastiki**[17] 1754 3-9-3 0 (Sir Michael Stoute) *racd centre: chsd ldrs: shkn up over 2f out: sn outpcd* **16/1**	RyanMoore 4	68+
00-	8	½	**Kaylena**[223] 6726 3-8-12 0 (Jeremy Noseda) *racd centre: chsd ldrs: outpcd 3f out: styd on ins fnl f* **33/1**	ShaneKelly 5	62+
	9	2 ¾	**Guarda Pampa** 3-8-12 0 (William Haggas) *racd centre: hld up in tch: wknd over 2f out* **25/1**	KellyHarrison 1	55
00-	10	11	**Marhoona (USA)**[267] 5445 3-8-12 0 (John Dunlop) *overall ldr in centre over 5f: wknd over 1f out* **14/1**	DaneO'Neill 6	29
0-	11	4 ½	**Galletto (IRE)**[199] 7232 3-8-10 0 (Luca Cumani) *racd centre: hld up and a in rr: bhd fnl 3f* **40/1**	JordanTaylor(7) 11	23
	12	1 ¼	**Merchants Return** 3-9-0 0 (Lydia Pearce) *racd centre: s.s: hld up: wkng whn hung lft over 2f out* **100/1**	SimonPearce(3) 3	20
0	13	6	**Wasabi (IRE)**[28] 1512 3-8-12 0 (John Berry) *racd centre: hld up: plld hrd: rdn and wknd over 2f out* **28/1**	PatCosgrave 12	

1m 39.39s (0.79) **Going Correction** +0.075s/f (Good) 13 Ran SP% **118.6**
Speed ratings (Par 99): **99,94,94,93,93 91,89,89,86,75 70,69,63**
toteswingers: 1&2 £2.90, 1&3 £5.00, 2&3 £9.60 CSF £9.31 TOTE £1.80: £1.10, £2.30, £3.00; EX 12.50.
Owner Seasons Holidays **Bred** Azienda Agricola Mediterranea **Trained** Beckhampton, Wilts

FOCUS
Probably a fair contest, but it was slower than division II and rates as just ordinary maiden form. The stands' side was again best.

2280 POPTELECOM.CO.UK MAIDEN STKS (DIV II) 1m
5:05 (5:05) (Class 5) 3-Y-O

£3,234 (£962; £481; £240) Stalls Low

Form					RPR
2	1		**Mukhadram**[30] 1467 3-9-3 0 (William Haggas) *a.p: chsd ldr over 2f out: shkn up to ld over 1f out: r.o* **4/9[1]**	PaulHanagan 10	91+
3-0	2	1 ¼	**Ibtahaj**[28] 1506 3-9-3 0 (Saeed Bin Suroor) *led 7f out: rdn and hdd over 1f out: styd on* **12/1**	FrankieDettori 12	88
0-	3	5	**Skirmish**[211] 6983 3-9-3 0 (Mark Johnston) *chsd ldrs: rdn over 2f out: styd on same pce fr over 1f out* **16/1**	JoeFanning 1	76+
	4	¾	**Thraya Star (FR)** 3-8-12 0 (Mick Channon) *s.i.s: sn chsng ldrs: rdn over 2f out: styd on same pce appr fnl f* **33/1**	MartinHarley 14	69
	5	3 ¾	**Utterance** 3-9-3 0 (John Gosden) *hld up: shkn up over 2f out: r.o ins fnl f: nvr nr to chal* **10/1[3]**	WilliamBuick 11	65+
4-0	6	3	**Whispering Warrior (IRE)**[12] 1922 3-9-3 0 (Jeremy Noseda) *hld up: rdn over 2f out: styd on: nt trble ldrs* **33/1**	ShaneKelly 3	58
0-	7	1 ¾	**Langham Lily (USA)**[214] 6933 3-8-12 0 (Chris Wall) *prom: rdn over 2f out: wknd over 1f out* **50/1**	SebSanders 5	49+
	8	1 ¾	**Confluence** 3-8-12 0 (Clifford Lines) *hld up: n.d* **50/1**	DaneO'Neill 4	44
	9	hd	**My Manekineko** 3-9-3 0 (J R Jenkins) *chsd ldrs: rdn over 2f out: wknd wl over 1f out* **66/1**	FrederikTylicki 8	49
0	10	3 ¼	**Opus (IRE)**[12] 1922 3-9-3 0 (Amanda Perrett) *hld up in tch: lost pl over 3f out: wknd over 2f out* **100/1**	(t) EddieAhern 13	41
45	11	3 ¼	**Stormbound (IRE)**[12] 1922 3-8-12 0 (Paul Cole) *led 1f: chsd ldrs: rdn over 3f out: wknd over 2f out* **18/1**	DuilioDaSilva(5) 7	33
00-	12	¾	**Grand Liaison**[213] 6950 3-8-12 0 (John Berry) *hld up: hdwy over 4f out: rdn and wknd over 2f out* **100/1**	MartinLane 6	27
	13	¾	**Greatest (FR)** 3-9-3 0 (Sir Michael Stoute) *s.i.s: sn pushed along and a in rr* **9/1[2]**	RyanMoore 2	30

14 *hd* **Azerodegree (IRE)** 3-9-3 0 .... PatCosgrave 9 29
(Marco Botti) *prom tl rdn and wknd over 3f out* **25/1**

1m 39.05s (0.45) **Going Correction** +0.075s/f (Good) **14** Ran SP% **124.3**
Speed ratings (Par 99): **100,98,93,93,89 86,84,82,82,79 76,75,74,74**
toteswingers: 1&2 £4.00, 1&3 £2.90, 2&3 £9.10 CSF £6.90 TOTE £1.40: £1.10, £1.80, £4.30; EX 8.20.
Owner Hamdan Al Maktoum **Bred** Wardall Bloodstock **Trained** Newmarket, Suffolk

FOCUS
There wasn't much early pace in this, which casts a bit of doubt about the form, but it was still quicker than the first division. A similar level of form.

2281 POPTELECOM.CO.UK CHEAP INTERNATIONAL CALLS H'CAP 1m 4f
5:40 (5:42) (Class 3) (0-95,90) 3-Y-O **£8,409** (£2,502; £1,250; £625) **Stalls** Centre

Form RPR

1-04 **1** **Handsome Man (IRE)**[13] 1892 3-8-9 **78** .... FrankieDettori 1 88
(Saeed Bin Suroor) *hld up: wnt centre over 8f out: hdwy and jnd stands' side gp over 4f out: led over 1f out: rdn out* **8/1**

512- **2** *nk* **Maastricht (IRE)**[257] 5783 3-8-7 **76** .... JoeFanning 4 85+
(Mark Johnston) *prom: lft chsng far side ldr over 9f out: lft to r alone over 5f out but stl up w the pce: rdn over 1f out: hung lft wl ins fnl f: r.o* **25/1**

2-41 **3** *3 1/4* **Theturnofthesun (IRE)**[38] 1302 3-8-13 **82** .... (p) WilliamBuick 7 86
(John Gosden) *chsd ldrs wnt centre over 9f out: swtchd to stands' side and led that gp over 7f out: overall ldr wl over 1f out: sn rdn and hdd: styd on same pce ins fnl f* **10/1**

51 **4** *3/4* **Suraj**[21] 1655 3-9-6 **89** .... JamieSpencer 9 92
(Michael Bell) *hld up in tch: wnt centre over 9f out: swtchd to stands' side over 7f out: trckd ldr: rdn over 1f out: styd on same pce fr over 1f out* **2/1**[1]

51-4 **5** *1 1/2* **Aazif (IRE)**[30] 1473 3-8-13 **82** .... PaulHanagan 2 82
(John Dunlop) *hld up: wnt centre over 8f out: hdwy and jnd stands' side gp over 4f out: rdn over 2f out: no ex ins fnl f* **6/1**[3]

01-2 **6** *2 1/2* **Wrotham Heath**[29] 1504 3-9-7 **90** .... EddieAhern 6 86+
(Sir Henry Cecil) *chsd ldrs: wnt centre over 9f out: jopined stands' side gp over 4f out: led overall over 3f out: rdn and hdd wl over 1f out: wknd ins fnl f* **5/2**[2]

1122 **7** *13* **Cape Safari (IRE)**[17] 1756 3-8-11 **80** .... DarryllHolland 3 56
(Alan Bailey) *chsd ldrs: wnt centre and led that gp over 9f out: led overall over 6f out: jnd stands' side over 4f out: hdd over 3f out: wknd over 2f out* **16/1**

10 **8** *2 3/4* **Good Of Luck**[13] 1888 3-8-11 **80** .... PatCosgrave 8 51
(Mick Channon) *hld up: wnt centre over 9f out: swtchd stands' side over 7f out: hdwy over 3f out: rdn and wknd over 1f out* **33/1**

1 **9** *32* **Natasha Rostova**[37] 1340 3-8-2 **71** oh1 .... DavidProbert 11
(Andrew Balding) *s.i.s: sn pushed along in rr: wnt centre over 9f out: swtchd stands' side over 7f out: wknd over 3f out: t.o* **20/1**

44-0 **10** *25* **Autarch (USA)**[14] 1853 3-8-2 **71** oh3 .... MircoDemuro 5
(Amanda Perrett) *led: styd far side turning fior home: hdd over 6f out: swtchd centre over 5f out: jnd stands' side gp over 4f out: wknd over 2f out: t.o* **40/1**

2m 32.27s (0.27) **Going Correction** +0.075s/f (Good) **10** Ran SP% **116.3**
Speed ratings (Par 103): **102,101,99,99,98 96,87,85,64,47**
toteswingers: 1&2 £26.80, 1&3 £8.90, 2&3 £23.50 CSF £189.47 CT £2009.71 TOTE £9.70: £2.70, £6.60, £3.20; EX 153.50.
Owner Godolphin **Bred** Bloomsbury Stud **Trained** Newmarket, Suffolk

FOCUS
The last race on this track before action moves to the July course was a bit unsatisfactory, as heading down the home straight the field somehow split into three groups. Decent handicap form, but messy with a split field.

NOTEBOOK
Handsome Man(IRE) finished tailed off on his return in a sales race here last month but has improved since then and gained a determined victory after heading down the stands' rail. The step up in distance appeared to suit and a trip to Royal Ascot for one of the handicaps could be next. (op 10-1 tchd 11-1)
Maastricht(IRE) ◆, absent since early September, stuck to his route towards the far side alone and was only just beaten by a horse on the other side of the track. He ought to be winning soon considering he stayed on so well without any company. (op 28-1)
Theturnofthesun(IRE), with cheekpieces fitted for the first time, headed for the stands' rail and had his chance. There was nothing wrong with the way he stuck on, but he was readily held. (op 8-1 tchd 11-1)
Suraj easily won at Doncaster three weeks previously following a promising debut here, so this has to go down as slightly disappointing, albeit it was only his third racecourse outing. (op 5-2)
Aazif(IRE) kept on but may not come into his own until tried over 1m6f or further. (tchd 9-2)
Wrotham Heath, who was beaten 5l by the subsequent Dante second at Newbury on his seasonal reappearance, was going powerfully passing the 3f marker but shaped like a horse that doesn't stay 1m4f. (tchd 9-4 and 11-4)
T/Plt: £19.90 to a £1 stake. Pool: £122,992.48. 4,503.25 winning tickets. T/Qpdt: £10.10 to a £1 stake. Pool: £5,117.09. 372.22 winning tickets. CR

2091 THIRSK (L-H)
Saturday, May 19

OFFICIAL GOING: Good to soft (8.1)
Wind: Fresh, against Weather: Cloudy

2282 BRITISH STALLION STUDS SUPPORTING BRITISH RACING E B F MAIDEN FILLIES' STKS 5f
1:50 (1:52) (Class 4) 2-Y-O **£4,528** (£1,347; £673; £336) **Stalls** High

Form RPR

1 **Rhagori Aur** 2-9-0 0 .... TomEaves 6 80+
(Bryan Smart) *dwlt: sn trckd ldrs gng wl: pushed along over 1f out: drvn to ld fnl 100yds: r.o wl* **14/1**

5 **2** *2 3/4* **Lady Of The House (IRE)**[30] 1466 2-8-11 0 .... AmyRyan(3) 10 70
(Kevin Ryan) *led narrowly: rdn over 1f out: edgd lft ins fnl f: hdd fnl 100yds: sn no ch w wnr* **15/8**[1]

3 *nk* **Royal Rascal** 2-9-0 0 .... DavidAllan 3 69+
(Tim Easterby) *chsd ldrs: rdn 2f out: kpt on* **16/1**

4 *shd* **Ighraa (IRE)** 2-9-0 0 .... HayleyTurner 13 69
(Brian Meehan) *s.i.s: sn in tch: pushed along 2f out: kpt on fnl f* **5/1**[2]

5 *2 1/4* **Dusty Storm (IRE)** 2-9-0 0 .... GrahamGibbons 4 62
(Ed McMahon) *prom: rdn to chal over 1f out: sn edgd lft: wknd fnl 100yds* **14/1**

6 *hd* **Jollification (IRE)** 2-9-0 0 .... TedDurcan 2 60
(George Baker) *hld up in tch: pushed along and outpcd 3f out: hdwy over 1f out: one pce fnl f* **6/1**[3]

7 *hd* **Smallbrook Lane (IRE)** 2-9-0 0 .... TonyHamilton 7 59
(Richard Fahey) *sn pushed towards rr: bhd tl kpt on fnl f* **15/2**

8 *5* **Dark Eros (IRE)** 2-9-0 0 .... DuranFentiman 12 41+
(Tim Easterby) *midfield: pushed along over 2f out: wknd over 1f out* **16/1**

9 *1 1/4* **Sandy's Row (USA)** 2-9-0 0 .... FrannyNorton 11 37+
(Mark Johnston) *sn nudged along towards rr: nvr threatened* **8/1**

10 *1 1/4* **My Claire** 2-9-0 0 .... AndrewMullen 1 32
(Nigel Tinkler) *dwlt: sn pushed along towards rr: a bhd* **40/1**

04 **11** *18* **Only For You**[21] 1651 2-9-0 0 .... RobertWinston 9
(Alan Brown) *w ldr: lost pl over 2f out: wknd over 1f out: eased* **50/1**

1m 4.21s (4.61) **Going Correction** +0.85s/f (Soft) **11** Ran SP% **118.1**
Speed ratings (Par 92): **97,92,92,91,88 88,87,79,77,75 46**
toteswingers: 1&2 £8.30, 1&3 £36.60, 2&3 £2.90 CSF £40.62 TOTE £13.20: £2.80, £1.40, £3.70; EX 55.70.
Owner Ceffyl Racing **Bred** Usk Valley Stud **Trained** Hambleton, N Yorks

FOCUS
A Class 4 5f maiden fillies' stakes. They went a decent gallop and the winning time of six seconds above standard looks a fair indicator that the official going description of good to soft is accurate. The form is pitched at the top end of the race averages.

NOTEBOOK
Rhagori Aur raced in midfield, after being slightly slowly away, and wanted to go faster in the middle third of this race on debut. She followed the favourite until the 2f pole and then cut her down decisively to make a very encouraging start to her career. This daughter of Exceed And Excel, the origin of so many precocious/smart 2yos, is a half-sister to a modest 1m2f winner, but her dam Aberdovey (by 2,000 Guineas-winner Mister Baileys) was a fair sort who won over 6f as a juvenile and later at 1m. She looks a nice type of filly for trainer Bryan Smart. (op 12-1 tchd 16-1)
Lady Of The House(IRE) finished a very respectable fifth of eight in a race working out well on debut at Newmarket (5f, good to soft) last month (RPR 67), and she gives some substance to this form with a slightly improved effort in second. (op 9-4)
Royal Rascal reportedly looked well in the paddock. She tracked across to race prominently from a low draw and stayed on into a good third on debut. Trainer Tim Easterby won this race three times in the previous ten years. (tchd 20-1)
Ighraa(IRE) started slowly on debut and deserves credit for quickly regaining a prominent position. She is a half-sister to several winners, a couple of them useful, and looks one to note given the benefit of this experience. (op 7-1)

2283 PAVILION AT THIRSK RACECOURSE FOR WEDDING RECEPTIONS H'CAP 1m
2:20 (2:21) (Class 6) (0-65,70) 3-Y-O **£2,587** (£770; £384; £192) **Stalls** Low

Form RPR

033- **1** **Sabhan (IRE)**[214] 6937 3-9-5 **63** .... DanielTudhope 6 69
(Geoffrey Harker) *hld up in midfield: pushed along and gd hdwy on outer over 2f out: led jst ins fnl f: kpt on* **11/2**[3]

4-41 **2** *1/2* **Dubious Escapade (IRE)**[12] 1918 3-9-11 **69** .... GrahamLee 13 74
(Ann Duffield) *in tch: pushed along over 2f out: rdn to ld narrowly appr fnl f: sn hdd: kpt on but a jst hld* **4/1**[1]

2124 **3** *1 1/2* **Pelican Rock (IRE)**[24] 1597 3-9-2 **60** .... (t) DuranFentiman 12 61
(Andrew Crook) *trckd ldrs: led 3f out: sn rdn: hdd appr fnl f: kpt on* **20/1**

-603 **4** *nk* **Eightfold**[28] 1517 3-9-4 **62** .... (t) LukeMorris 11 63
(Seamus Durack) *s.i.s: hld up: pushed along and hdwy 3f out: drvn over 1f out: kpt on fnl f* **5/1**[2]

12-1 **5** *1 1/4* **Regal Acclaim (IRE)**[24] 1600 3-8-13 **57** .... TedDurcan 1 55
(Tim Easterby) *midfield: rdn over 3f out: chsd ldrs over 2f out: kpt on one pce* **4/1**[1]

03-1 **6** *1* **Lolita Lebron (IRE)**[12] 1916 3-9-12 **70** .... RobertWinston 7 66
(Lawrence Mullaney) *trckd ldrs: rdn over 2f out: drvn and ev ch over 1f out: wknd ins fnl f* **13/2**

1060 **7** *10* **Captain Cardington (IRE)**[14] 1853 3-9-5 **63** .... (v) SamHitchcott 5 36
(Mick Channon) *hld up: pushed along over 4f out: nvr threatened* **14/1**

00-0 **8** *1 3/4* **Kieron's Rock (IRE)**[21] 1661 3-9-0 **58** .... AndrewElliott 8 27
(Jedd O'Keeffe) *hld up: pushed along over 4f out: a towards rr* **20/1**

-200 **9** *5* **Always Ends Well (IRE)**[10] 1982 3-9-2 **60** .... FrannyNorton 2 17
(Mark Johnston) *trckd ldrs: rdn over 3f out: wknd over 2f out* **14/1**

050- **10** *9* **Golden Valley**[231] 6524 3-9-7 **65** .... DavidAllan 9
(Tim Easterby) *led: rdn whn hdd 3f out: sn wknd* **10/1**

-330 **11** *12* **Vena Amoris (USA)**[39] 1288 3-9-0 **58** .... AdrianNicholls 4
(Mark Johnston) *midfield early: sn pushed along and lost pl: bhd over 4f out* **40/1**

1m 47.22s (7.12) **Going Correction** +0.85s/f (Soft) **11** Ran SP% **119.8**
Speed ratings (Par 97): **98,97,96,95,94 93,83,81,76,67 55**
toteswingers: 1&2 £16.10, 1&3 £29.20, 2&3 £16.80 CSF £27.62 CT £425.55 TOTE £5.30: £1.80, £2.80, £4.70; EX 38.00.
Owner Sheikh Khaled Duaij Al Sabah **Bred** M Morrissey **Trained** Thirkleby, N Yorks

FOCUS
A Class 6 1m handicap confined to 3yos. They appeared to go a very respectable gallop on good to soft ground but the winning time was over 10 seconds outside standard.

2284 MARKET CROSS JEWELLERS H'CAP 6f
2:55 (2:57) (Class 3) (0-90,89) 4-Y-O+ **£8,506** (£2,531; £1,265; £632) **Stalls** High

Form RPR

1U05 **1** **Arganil (USA)**[5] 2133 7-9-5 **87** .... (p) BarryMcHugh 12 96
(Kevin Ryan) *hld up: hdwy over 1f out: drvn to ld ins fnl f: jst hld on* **12/1**

/0-0 **2** *hd* **Pearl Ice**[14] 1844 4-9-5 **87** .... GrahamGibbons 14 99+
(David Barron) *restless stalls: dwlt: hld up in rr towards rail: short of room 2f out tl 1f out: swtchd lft to outer ins fnl f: r.o strly fnl 100yds: jst failed: v unlucky* **5/2**[1]

0033 **3** *1* **Beckermet (IRE)**[5] 2119 10-9-1 **83** .... JamesSullivan 6 88
(Ruth Carr) *w ldr: led narrowly over 1f out: hdd ins fnl f: kpt on* **9/1**

50-3 **4** *nse* **Mon Brav**[14] 1863 5-8-12 **83** .... PaulPickard(3) 2 88
(Brian Ellison) *prom towards outer: rdn and ev ch over 1f out: kpt on* **5/1**[2]

6-00 **5** *1/2* **Mass Rally (IRE)**[28] 1522 5-9-7 **89** .... (v) PaulMulrennan 11 92+
(Michael Dods) *hld up: hdwy 2f out: gng wl whn short of room over 1f out tl jst ins fnl f: kpt on once clr* **14/1**

06-2 **6** *1/2* **Summerinthecity (IRE)**[14] 1844 5-9-4 **89** .... LeeTopliss(3) 4 92+
(Ed de Giles) *trckd ldrs: briefly short of room and lost pl appr fnl f: kpt on ins fnl f* **13/2**[3]

-000 **7** *1* **Marine Commando**[14] 1844 4-9-6 **88** .... TonyHamilton 10 86
(Richard Fahey) *midfield: pushed along over 1f out: kpt on fnl f* **20/1**

-001 **8** *1 3/4* **Masked Dance (IRE)**[8] 2024 5-9-3 **85** .... (p) RobertWinston 9 78
(Scott Dixon) *chsd ldrs: rdn 2f out: wknd ins fnl f* **9/1**

035- **9** *1 1/4* **Barney McGrew (IRE)**[210] 7018 9-9-3 **85** .... TomEaves 15 74+
(Michael Dods) *hld up towards rail: n.m.r over 1f out tl ins fnl f: no ch after:* **10/1**

01-0 **10** *nk* **Amenable (IRE)**[42] 1220 5-9-3 **85** .... AdrianNicholls 8 73
(David Nicholls) *led narrowly: hdd over 1f out: sn wknd* **33/1**

00-0 **11** *9* **Fred Willetts (IRE)**[26] 1558 4-8-12 **85** .... LMcNiff(5) 7 44
(David Barron) *hld up: pushed along over 3f out: wknd 2f out* **20/1**

6-00 **P** **Elusive Prince**[15] 1821 4-9-6 **88** .... LeeNewman 5
(David Barron) *slowly away: immediately eased and p.u after 1f* **22/1**

1m 17.37s (4.67) **Going Correction** +0.85s/f (Soft) **12 Ran SP% 118.8**
Speed ratings (Par 107): **102,101,100,100,99 99,97,95,93,93 81,**
toteswingers: 1&2 £14.30, 1&3 £18.50, 2&3 £8.00 CSF £40.05 CT £298.52 TOTE £17.10: £4.60, £1.40, £2.80; EX 57.70.
Owner M & Mrs C McGeever **Bred** Colt Neck Stables, Llc **Trained** Hambleton, N Yorks
■ Stewards' Enquiry : James Sullivan two-day ban; used whip above permitted level (3rd-4th June)
Robert Winston two-day ban; used whip down the shoulder (4th-5th June)

FOCUS
A Class 3 6f handicap for older horses. The winning time was over six seconds outside standard.

NOTEBOOK
Arganil(USA) was racing off a mark 7lb lower than his peak-winning rating of 94, which came over 5f on Fibresand at Southwell in January last year. He won a similar Redcar (6f, good to firm) contest off 82 on his turf reappearance in April, but was reportedly never travelling in a 5f Wolverhampton claimer five days ago. He is very versatile as regards ground at up to this 6f trip, and has simply returned to form, making the most of the cards dropping right for him, after coming through with a sustained winning run from midfield. (op 20-1 tchd 11-1)
Pearl Ice's backers will be tearing their hair out after this contest. The tale of woe began as he reared up in the stalls just before the start. The well-drawn, usually prominent runner, then missed the break and was soon noted stone last on the near rail behind a wall of horses. The next time he hit your line of vision he was travelling notably well over 1f out, and Graham Gibbons made the only available move open to him by coming round the entire field into a most unlucky diminishing second. (tchd 11-4)
Beckermet(IRE) ran well in third from a lower than ideal stall. (op 7-1)
Mon Brav ran well in fourth from a lower than ideal stalls. (op 6-1)
Mass Rally(IRE) travelled notably well and stayed on into a promising fifth after a less-than clear passage through. Official explanation: jockey said gelding was denied a clear run. (op 12-1 tchd 16-1)
Summerinthecity(IRE) Official explanation: jockey said gelding was denied a run.
Elusive Prince Official explanation: jockey said gelding injured head in the stalls.

2285 MARION GIBSON BROWN MEMORIAL H'CAP — 1m
3:30 (3:31) (Class 4) (0-85,85) 4-Y-0+ **£5,272** (£1,568; £784; £392) **Stalls** Low

Form / RPR
0015 **1** **Al Muheer (IRE)**[8] 2029 7-9-2 **80** ....(b) JamesSullivan 8 — 96
(Ruth Carr) *hld up and bhd: smooth hdwy on outside to ld over 1f out: shkn up: edgd lft and sn clr: readily* **5/1**[3]
326- **2** *6* **Swiftly Done (IRE)**[203] 7161 5-9-7 **85** .... DanielTudhope 6 — 87
(Declan Carroll) *hld up: stdy hdwy gng wl over 2f out: swtchd lft and effrt wl over 1f out: sn chsng wnr: no imp fnl f* **15/2**
00-5 **3** *5* **I'm Super Too (IRE)**[12] 1914 5-8-13 **82** .... GarryWhillans(5) 4 — 73
(Alan Swinbank) *prom: effrt over 2f out: rdn and ev ch wl over 1f out: sn outpcd* **12/1**
1062 **4** *4* **The Osteopath (IRE)**[1] 2243 9-9-0 **78** .... HayleyTurner 3 — 60
(John Davies) *hld up towards rr on ins: rdn and outpcd 1/2-way: rallied 2f out: kpt on fnl f: nvr able to chal* **3/1**[1]
000- **5** *9* **Vito Volterra (IRE)**[239] 6290 5-9-2 **80** .... AndrewMullen 5 — 41
(Michael Smith) *w ldr: led over 3f out to over 1f out: sn btn* **18/1**
0-60 **6** *hd* **Dolphin Rock**[21] 1670 5-9-2 **80** .... LeeNewman 10 — 40
(David Barron) *prom: pushed along over 3f out: rallied: wknd wl over 1f out* **9/2**[2]
-236 **7** *9* **Sound Amigo (IRE)**[32] 1431 4-9-4 **82** .... BarryMcHugh 7 — 22
(Ollie Pears) *hld up in tch: rdn and outpcd over 2f out: sn struggling* **7/1**
05/0 **8** *5* **Day Of The Eagle (IRE)**[14] 1863 6-8-12 **83** .... DavidSimmonson(7) 9 — 11
(Michael Easterby) *bhd: pushed along 5f out: nvr on terms* **33/1**
-210 **9** *½* **Nibani (IRE)**[118] 263 5-9-0 **78** ....(p) TedDurcan 14 — 5
(Alastair Lidderdale) *bhd and sn outpcd: rdn and swtchd rt over 2f out: nvr on terms* **16/1**
40-0 **10** *½* **Glenridding**[8] 2029 8-9-4 **82** .... PaulMulrennan 1 — 8
(James Given) *led to over 3f out: rdn and wknd over 2f out* **25/1**
14-0 **11** *7* **Orbit The Moon (IRE)**[38] 1321 4-9-7 **85** ....(t) TomEaves 2
(Michael Dods) *s.i.s: sn chsng ldrs: drvn over 3f out: wknd over 2f out* **33/1**
121- **12** *3* **Imperator Augustus (IRE)**[237] 6382 4-9-6 **84** .... DuranFentiman 13
(Patrick Holmes) *hld up on outside: rdn and outpcd over 3f out: btn fnl 2f* **11/1**

1m 45.15s (5.05) **Going Correction** +0.85s/f (Soft) **12 Ran SP% 121.0**
Speed ratings (Par 105): **108,102,97,93,84 83,74,69,69,68 61,58**
CSF £42.56 CT £431.54 TOTE £6.20: £2.20, £2.40, £4.90; EX 42.00.
Owner Sprint King Racing (Antigua Cavaliers) **Bred** Foursome Thoroughbreds **Trained** Huby, N Yorks

FOCUS
A Class 4 1m handicap for older horses. They went a solid gallop on testing ground. The winning time was significantly better than the previous 1m handicap.

2286 YORKSHIRE OUTDOORS ADVENTURE EXPERIENCES H'CAP — 5f
4:05 (4:05) (Class 2) (0-100,97) 4-Y-0+ **£13,067** (£3,888; £1,943; £971) **Stalls** High

Form / RPR
00-0 **1** **Partner (IRE)**[10] 1975 6-8-10 **86** ....(b) FrannyNorton 8 — 96
(Kevin Ryan) *trckd ldrs: rdn to ld jst ins fnl f: kpt on* **22/1**
1-13 **2** *½* **Magical Macey (USA)**[2] 2208 5-9-2 **97** ....(b) LMcNiff(5) 12 — 105
(David Barron) *w ldr: rdn to ld over 1f out: hdd jst ins fnl f: kpt on but a jst hld* **11/4**[1]
3-20 **3** *nk* **Doc Hay (USA)**[13] 1885 5-9-3 **93** .... DanielTudhope 7 — 100+
(David O'Meara) *s.i.s: hld up: pushed along and gd hdwy over 1f out: kpt on wl* **8/1**
-202 **4** *2¾* **Foxy Music**[10] 1975 8-9-3 **93** .... GrahamGibbons 3 — 90
(Eric Alston) *prom: rdn 2f out: stl ev ch appr fnl f: no ex fnl 100yds* **16/1**
0-31 **5** *1* **Lui Rei (ITY)**[14] 1849 6-9-7 **97** .... HayleyTurner 11 — 91
(Robert Cowell) *hld up: pushed along over 2f out: bhd tl kpt on fnl f: nrst fin* **6/1**[2]
0136 **6** *1¼* **Sugar Beet**[14] 1849 4-9-3 **93** .... LukeMorris 10 — 82
(Ronald Harris) *midfield: rdn over 2f out: kpt on fnl f: nvr threatened ldrs* **18/1**
0-40 **7** *nk* **Cheveton**[13] 1885 8-8-11 **90** .... LeeTopliss(3) 16 — 78+
(Richard Price) *half rrd s: hld up towards rail: sme late hdwy: nvr threatened* **10/1**
20-0 **8** *nse* **Marvellous Value (IRE)**[31] 1438 7-9-1 **91** .... PaulMulrennan 6 — 79
(Michael Dods) *midfield: rdn 2f out: no ex ins fnl f* **25/1**
40-3 **9** *¾* **Excel Bolt**[42] 1219 4-9-5 **95** .... TomEaves 17 — 80
(Bryan Smart) *led narrowly: hdd over 1f out: jst sing to weaken whn short of room ins fnl f* **7/1**[3]
-200 **10** *½* **Bathwick Bear (IRE)**[10] 1975 4-8-11 **87** .... PadraigBeggy 14 — 70
(David Evans) *sn pushed along in midfield: nvr on terms* **12/1**
-013 **11** *½* **Arctic Feeling (IRE)**[10] 1975 4-8-7 **88** .... ShaneBKelly(5) 9 — 69
(Richard Fahey) *midfield: rdn over 2f out: wknd over 1f out* **17/2**
00-0 **12** *¾* **Love Delta (USA)**[3] 2177 5-9-2 **92** .... GrahamLee 15 — 71
(Kevin Ryan) *hld up: nvr threatened* **33/1**
32-6 **13** *3* **What About You (IRE)**[139] 3 4-8-9 **85** .... TonyHamilton 13 — 53
(Richard Fahey) *trckd ldrs: lost pl over 1f out: sn wknd* **22/1**

1m 2.72s (3.12) **Going Correction** +0.85s/f (Soft) **13 Ran SP% 118.5**
Speed ratings (Par 109): **109,108,107,103,101 99,99,99,97,97 96,95,90**
toteswingers: 1&2 £18.00, 1&3 £48.80, 2&3 £9.80 CSF £78.31 CT £550.90 TOTE £33.40: £7.20, £1.20, £4.10; EX 214.10.
Owner Dr Marwan Koukash **Bred** Miss Joan Murphy **Trained** Hambleton, N Yorks

FOCUS
A Class 2 5f handicap for 4yo+ sprinters was the feature on the card. The pace was contested and suited closing types. The winning time was much faster than the juveniles managed in the first race over the same C&D.

NOTEBOOK
Partner(IRE) was having his second start for trainer Kevin Ryan, who was completing a 298-1 double on the card, after a troubled passage from a poor draw on debut for the yard at Chester's May meeting. This 6yo son of Indian Ridge appeared to appreciate the good to soft ground racing off a mark only 2lb higher than when winning a fair 5f handicap at Tipperary for previous handler David Marnane in Ireland in August 2010. They went plenty fast enough in this contest, and he benefited from his midfield position, before coming past tiring rivals. He made the most of a good opportunity and is a previous 6f winner on better ground. He holds an entry in the 'Dash' at Epsom on Derby Day. (op 25-1)
Magical Macey(USA) arrived at the top of his game and once again deserves credit for a thoroughly genuine effort in second. He raced prominently, as is his wont, and helped set some solid fractions. He may now be in the grip of the handicapper off 97, but the way he rallied close home was engaging. (op 7-2 tchd 5-2 and 4-1 in a place)
Doc Hay(USA) missed the break and kept on notably well into a close third. This is the second time this season that he has shaped like a future winner off around this mark under similar conditions (op 17-2)
Foxy Music paid a price close home for helping set fast early fractions. (op 14-1)
Lui Rei(ITY) won well at Goodwood (5f, soft) this month and produced another good display in a never-nearer fifth. (op 5-1)

2287 THIRSK RACECOURSE CONFERENCE ROOMS MAIDEN STKS (DIV I) — 1m 4f
4:40 (4:42) (Class 5) 3-Y-0+ **£2,943** (£875; £437; £218) **Stalls** Low

Form / RPR
3 **1** **Calico Cat**[8] 2027 4-9-7 0 .... KatiaScallan(7) 9 — 90
(Alastair Lidderdale) *hld up: hdwy over 4f out: led on outside over 1f out: rdn and edgd lft ins fnl f: hld on wl* **3/1**[2]
3-32 **2** *¾* **Hallmark Star**[26] 1557 3-8-11 82 .... PaulMulrennan 5 — 88
(Gerard Butler) *led: rdn over 2f out: hdd over 1f out: rallied: bmpd ins fnl f: kpt on: hld nr fin* **9/4**[1]
5 **3** *nk* **Noble Alan (GER)**[14] 1866 9-10-0 0 .... GrahamLee 8 — 88
(Nicky Richards) *reluctant to enter stalls: hld up: hdwy whn hmpd over 4f out: smooth hdwy and ev ch over 1f out: sn rdn: kpt on fnl f: hld towards fin* **6/1**[3]
30 **4** *19* **Kashgar**[17] 1754 3-8-11 0 .... HayleyTurner 4 — 57+
(Michael Bell) *trckd ldrs: effrt and pushed along over 3f out: wknd fr 2f out* **8/1**
3- **5** *7* **Between Us**[169] 7598 3-8-6 0 .... LukeMorris 12 — 41+
(Sir Mark Prescott Bt) *t.k.h: pressed ldr: rdn over 3f out: wknd 2f out* **3/1**[2]
0-3 **6** *1¾* **Madam Lilibet (IRE)**[21] 1676 3-8-6 0 .... JamesSullivan 3 — 38
(Sharon Watt) *bhd: rdn over 5f out: nvr able to chal* **66/1**
65 **7** *5* **Lucky For Some**[11] 1950 5-9-4 0 .... DeanHeslop(5) 11 — 31
(Marjorie Fife) *s.i.s: sn in tch: struggling over 5f out: sn btn* **100/1**
44 **8** *17* **Border Bandit (USA)**[13] 1878 4-10-0 0 .... PaddyAspell 1
(Tracy Waggott) *hld up: pushed along over 3f out: nvr on terms* **33/1**
065- **9** *7* **Decadence**[296] 4466 4-9-9 46 .... AndrewMullen 10
(Nigel Tinkler) *hld up on outside: stdy hdwy over 5f out: wknd over 4f out* **66/1**
4 **10** *dist* **Rufus Stone (USA)**[40] 1261 4-10-0 0 .... RobertWinston 7
(Jane Chapple-Hyam) *in tch to 1/2-way: sn rdn and struggling* **14/1**

2m 47.18s (10.98) **Going Correction** +0.85s/f (Soft)
WFA 3 from 4yo+ 17lb **10 Ran SP% 119.7**
Speed ratings (Par 103): **97,96,96,83,78 77,74,63,58,**
toteswingers: 1&2 £2.20, 1&3 £4.80, 2&3 £3.30 CSF £10.44 TOTE £4.30: £1.70, £1.10, £2.30; EX 11.40.
Owner Chris Beek Racing **Bred** Darley **Trained** Lambourn, Berks

FOCUS
The first division of a Class 5 1m4f maiden stakes for 3yos+. It looks much the stronger of the two divisions on exposed form. The winning time was over 15 seconds outside standard. The first three finished well clear.
Rufus Stone(USA) Official explanation: trainers representative said gelding was unsuited by good to soft ground.

2288 THIRSK RACECOURSE CONFERENCE ROOMS MAIDEN STKS (DIV II) — 1m 4f
5:15 (5:19) (Class 5) 3-Y-0+ **£2,943** (£875; £437; £218) **Stalls** Low

Form / RPR
3 **1** **New Youmzain (FR)**[13] 1893 3-8-11 0 .... SamHitchcott 4 — 82
(Mick Channon) *trckd ldrs: led over 3f out: rdn and strly pressed 2f out: hdd appr fnl f: sn regained ld: kpt on* **5/2**[2]
2 **2** *½* **Pistol (IRE)**[38] 1301 3-8-11 0 .... RichardMullen 10 — 81
(Sir Michael Stoute) *hld up in tch: hdwy whn sltly short of room over 3f out: swtchd to outer and sn challngd: rdn and hung persistently lft fr over 2f out: led appr fnl f: sn hdd: hld nr fin* **1/1**[1]
0/4 **3** *12* **Hawkeshead**[21] 1662 5-10-0 0 .... MichaelO'Connell 1 — 68
(Ian Williams) *trckd ldrs: pushed along 3f out: one pce and no match ldng pair fnl 2f* **11/1**
00 **4** *7* **Hulwa (USA)**[13] 1878 3-8-6 0 .... FrannyNorton 8 — 46
(Tracy Waggott) *midfield: pushed along and outpcd over 5f out: plugged on fr over 2f out* **100/1**
/0-0 **5** *nk* **Sposalizio (IRE)**[14] 1867 5-10-0 45 ....(v) PaddyAspell 6 — 51
(Colin Teague) *trckd ldrs: rdn over 3f out: grad wknd* **100/1**
6 *1½* **Anna's Arch (IRE)**[143] 5-10-0 0 .... RobertWinston 9 — 49
(Alan Swinbank) *midfield on outer: hdwy over 4f out: rdn to chal 3f out: wknd over 1f out* **16/1**
04 **7** *4* **Seventh Sign**[14] 1867 3-8-11 0 .... LiamJones 11 — 41+
(William Haggas) *hld up: pushed along over 5f out: nvr threatened* **6/1**[3]
5232 **8** *17* **King's Wharf (IRE)**[35] 1390 3-8-11 66 .... PadraigBeggy 7 — 15
(David Evans) *led: rdn whn hdd over 3f out: sn wknd* **16/1**
50 **9** *7* **Life Of Laughter (USA)**[50] 1113 4-10-0 0 .... JamieMackay 2
(Willie Musson) *trckd ldrs: lost pl over 5f out: wknd over 3f out* **25/1**

U **Josie Lennon** 3-8-6 0 .... AndrewMullen 3
(Michael Smith) *slowly away: bucked and uns rdr after 100yds* **50/1**

2m 48.63s (12.43) **Going Correction** +0.85s/f (Soft)
WFA 3 from 4yo+ 17lb **10** Ran SP% **120.7**
Speed ratings (Par 103): **92,91,83,79,78 77,75,63,59,**
toteswingers: 1&2 £1.80, 1&3 £4.20, 2&3 £4.20 CSF £5.48 TOTE £4.50: £1.70, £1.02, £1.80; EX 7.30.
Owner Jaber Abdullah **Bred** Sarl Haras De Saint-Faust **Trained** West Ilsley, Berks

FOCUS
The second division of a Class 5 1m4f maiden stakes for 3yos+ and the weaker of the two contests on exposed form. The winning time was significantly slower than the first division.
Anna's Arch(IRE) Official explanation: jockey said gelding hung left.

2289 THIRSK RACES "CHAMPAGNE TUESDAY" 19TH JUNE H'CAP 5f
5:45 (5:47) (Class 4) (0-85,85) 4-Y-0+ **£5,272** (£1,568; £784; £392) **Stalls** High

Form RPR
4-10 **1** **Mayoman (IRE)**[22] 1642 7-9-3 **82** .... (v) DanielTudhope 5 92
(David O'Meara) *in tch: hdwy to ld over 1f out: pushed out fnl f: comf* **8/1**
4/00 **2** *1* **Ertikaan**[22] 1643 5-9-3 **82** .... LukeMorris 11 88
(Ronald Harris) *midfield: rdn and hung lft fr 1/2-way: hdwy to chse wnr appr fnl f: kpt on: hld cl home* **11/2**[2]
-000 **3** *1 1/2* **No Hubris (USA)**[8] 2029 5-9-2 **81** .... (b) JamesSullivan 10 82
(Ruth Carr) *prom: effrt and rdn 2f out: checked over 1f out: kpt on same pce ins fnl f* **33/1**
6-40 **4** *hd* **Hazelrigg (IRE)**[2] 2208 7-9-1 **85** .... (be) AdamCarter(5) 13 85
(Tim Easterby) *in tch stands' rail: shkn up over 1f out: r.o fnl f: nt pce to chal* **4/1**[1]
3555 **5** *1* **Courageous (IRE)**[15] 1828 6-9-5 **84** .... (t) FrannyNorton 14 80
(Kevin Ryan) *led and swtchd to centre after 1f: rdn and hdd over 1f out: sn one pce* **8/1**
0-61 **6** *hd* **Noodles Blue Boy**[14] 1868 6-9-3 **82** .... PaddyAspell 12 78
(Ollie Pears) *prom: effrt and ev ch over 1f out: one pce fnl f* **6/1**[3]
3-20 **7** *1/2* **Whozthecat (IRE)**[28] 1522 5-9-3 **82** .... (v) GrahamGibbons 6 76
(Declan Carroll) *dwlt: bhd and sn pushed along: hdwy over 1f out: kpt on: nvr able to chal* **7/1**
45-3 **8** *2 1/4* **Flash City (ITY)**[22] 1643 4-9-3 **82** .... (v) TomEaves 9 68
(Bryan Smart) *dwlt: hld up: hdwy over 2f out: edgd lft: no imp over 1f out* **10/1**
0-03 **9** *4* **Taurus Twins**[24] 1602 6-9-3 **82** .... (b) RobertWinston 4 53
(Richard Price) *midfield: drvn over 2f out: wknd over 1f out* **10/1**
31-6 **10** *1 1/4* **Beauty Pageant (IRE)**[15] 1828 5-8-10 **82** .... GeorgeDowning(7) 2 49
(Ed McMahon) *cl up tl rdn and wknd fr 2f out* **14/1**
00-0 **11** *1* **Tyfos**[22] 1642 7-9-4 **83** .... TomMcLaughlin 8 46
(Brian Baugh) *in tch: checked after 1f: rdn and struggling fr 1/2-way* **22/1**
0210 **12** *hd* **Haadeeth**[24] 1602 5-8-11 **81** .... MatthewCosham(5) 3 43
(David Evans) *midfield on wd outside: struggling over 2f out: btn over 1f out* **33/1**

1m 3.8s (4.20) **Going Correction** +0.85s/f (Soft) **12** Ran SP% **119.5**
Speed ratings (Par 105): **100,98,96,95,94 93,92,89,82,80 79,79**
toteswingers: 1&2 £10.80, 1&3 £65.40, 2&3 £44.30 CSF £51.01 CT £1397.96 TOTE £12.20: £3.10, £1.80, £11.20; EX 78.00.
Owner Tom Tuohy **Bred** James Cosgrove **Trained** Nawton, N Yorks

FOCUS
A Class 4 5f handicap for olders horses concluded proceedings for the day. The winning time was respectable for the grade.
Haadeeth Official explanation: jockey said gelding was never travelling.
T/Jkpt: Not won. T/Plt: £128.90 to a £1 stake. Pool: £70,106.06. 396.91 winning tickets. T/Qpdt: £22.20 to a £1 stake. Pool: £3,669.86. 122.11 winning tickets. AS

2290 - 2298a (Foreign Racing) - See Raceform Interactive

PIMLICO (L-H)
Saturday, May 19

OFFICIAL GOING: Dirt: fast; turf: firm

2299a PREAKNESS STKS (GRADE 1) (3YO) (DIRT) 1m 1f 110y(D)
11:18 (12:00) 3-Y-0 **£387,096** (£129,032; £70,967; £38,709; £19,354)

RPR
1 **I'll Have Another (USA)**[14] 1872 3-9-0 0 .... MGutierrez 9 127+
(Doug O'Neill, U.S.A) **16/5**[2]
2 *nk* **Bodemeister (USA)**[14] 1872 3-9-0 0 .... MESmith 7 126+
(Bob Baffert, U.S.A) **17/10**[1]
3 *8 3/4* **Creative Cause (USA)**[14] 1872 3-9-0 0 .... JRosario 6 108
(Mike Harrington, U.S.A) **63/10**
4 *3* **Zetterholm (USA)**[43] 3-9-0 0 .... JAlvarado 4 102
(Richard Dutrow Jr, U.S.A) **205/10**
5 *3 1/4* **Teeth Of The Dog (USA)**[42] 1232 3-9-0 0 .... JBravo 2 96
(Michael Matz, U.S.A) **155/10**
6 *nk* **Optimizer (USA)**[14] 1872 3-9-0 0 .... CNakatani 10 95
(D Wayne Lukas, U.S.A) **233/10**
7 *2 1/4* **Cozzetti (USA)**[35] 1396 3-9-0 0 .... JLezcano 11 90
(Dale Romans, U.S.A) **27/1**
8 *7 1/2* **Tiger Walk (USA)**[42] 1232 3-9-0 0 .... (b[1]) RADominguez 1 75
(Ignacio Correas IV, U.S.A) **234/10**
9 *2 1/4* **Daddy Nose Best (USA)**[14] 1872 3-9-0 0 .... JRLeparoux 8 70
(Steven Asmussen, U.S.A) **111/10**
10 *3 1/4* **Went The Day Well (USA)**[14] 1872 3-9-0 0 .... (b) JRVelazquez 5 64
(H Graham Motion, U.S.A) **57/10**[3]
11 *3 3/4* **Pretension (USA)**[14] 3-9-0 0 .... (b) JavierSantiago 3 56
(Christopher W Grove, U.S.A) **34/1**

1m 55.94s (0.35) **11** Ran SP% **123.1**
PARI-MUTUEL (all including $2 stakes): WIN 8.40; PLACE (1-2) 3.80, 3.20; SHOW (1-2-3) 2.80, 2.80, 3.60; SF 18.60.
Owner Reddam Racing Llc **Bred** Harvey Clarke **Trained** USA

FOCUS
The same one-two as in the Kentucky Derby, but unlike at Churchill Downs when I'll Have Another had the race set up for him by Bodemeister going too fast, there is no question of this being a fluke result. The runner-up was allowed an uncontested lead and recorded modest fractions. Here are his sectionals along with his Derby splits in brackets: 23.79 (22.32), 47.68 (45.39) and 1:11.72 (1:09.80). The time for the opening half-mile was the slowest in the Preakness since Aloma's Ruler won from the front in 1982, and this much more sensible ride than last time allowed him to repeat the sort of time figure he produced when making all in the Arkansas Derby. Yet I'll Have Another was good enough to get past him.

NOTEBOOK
I'll Have Another(USA) hadn't previously recorded the sort of time expected of a worthy Triple Crown contender, but he put that right with a top-class display. He was awarded a preliminary Beyer Speed Figure of 109 which, if confirmed, would be the fastest Preakness performance since the brilliant Curlin in 2007. I'll Have Another reportedly came out of the race well and will now bid to become the first horse since Affirmed in 1978 to complete the Triple Crown - he's the 12th since then to have won the first two legs. The 1m4f trip should be within reach and he'll hold obvious claims with the division lacking depth, but it's with good reason that no horse has achieved the feat for over 30 years. It's an incredibly demanding challenge, and not every horse takes to Belmont's somewhat unique track.
Bodemeister(USA) enjoyed the run of the race and had no excuses this time. He won't be going to the Belmont Stakes and is surely due a rest.
Creative Cause(USA) won't be going to the Belmont either. This was a solid effort, and he looks a bit more straightforward than was the case earlier in his career, but he wasn't good enough. It wouldn't surprise to see him revert to shorter distances.

2300 - 2307a (Foreign Racing) - See Raceform Interactive

1670 RIPON (R-H)
Sunday, May 20

OFFICIAL GOING: Good to soft (soft in places; 7.3)
Rail on bend from back straight to home straight moved out 4m adding about 12m to distances on Round course.
Wind: Breezy, half against Weather: Overcast

2308 MARK LISTER & FRIENDS SUPPORTING WOODEN SPOON MAIDEN STKS 6f
2:10 (2:10) (Class 5) 2-Y-0 **£2,911** (£866; £432; £216) **Stalls** High

Form RPR
4242 **1** **Hillbilly Boy (IRE)**[13] 1903 2-8-10 0 .... RyanWhile(7) 9 81
(Bill Turner) *mde all: rdn over 1f out: edgd rt and kpt on strly fnl f* **9/4**[1]
2 *2* **Maputo** 2-9-3 0 .... JoeFanning 6 75+
(Mark Johnston) *noisy and green in paddock: chsd wnr thrght: effrt and rdn over 1f out: kpt on ins fnl f: bttr for r* **10/3**[2]
3 *1 1/2* **Two Pancakes** 2-9-3 0 .... GrahamGibbons 2 71+
(Declan Carroll) *dwlt and wnt rt s: bhd: hdwy over 2f out: shkn up and kpt on fnl f: nrst fin* **16/1**
4 *shd* **Tha'Ir (IRE)** 2-9-3 0 .... SilvestreDeSousa 4 70+
(Saeed Bin Suroor) *colty in paddock: t.k.h: in tch: effrt over 1f out: kpt on same pce fnl f* **4/1**[3]
5 *nk* **Off Art** 2-9-3 0 .... DavidAllan 8 69+
(Tim Easterby) *missed break: bhd: hdwy 1/2-way: shkn up and kpt on fnl f: improve* **11/1**
6 *6* **Mary's Daughter** 2-8-12 0 .... TonyHamilton 5 46
(Richard Fahey) *dwlt: sn chsng ldrs on ins: rdn over 2f out: wknd over 1f out* **17/2**
7 *1 3/4* **Poetic Star** 2-9-3 0 .... GrahamLee 7 46
(Ben Haslam) *t.k.h: prom: rdn and outpcd 1/2-way: struggling fnl 2f* **28/1**
8 *7* **Look Forward (IRE)** 2-8-12 0 .... DuranFentiman 1 20
(Tim Easterby) *s.i.s: bhd and outpcd: no ch fr 2f out* **40/1**
3 **9** *8* **Bapak Bangsawan**[29] 1515 2-9-3 0 .... PhillipMakin 3
(Kevin Ryan) *t.k.h: prom on outside: rdn over 2f out: wknd over 1f out* **8/1**

1m 18.14s (5.14) **Going Correction** +0.475s/f (Yiel) **9** Ran SP% **115.6**
Speed ratings (Par 93): **84,81,79,79,78 70,68,59,48**
toteswingers: 1&2 £4.10, 1&3 £7.80, 2&3 £6.70 CSF £9.70 TOTE £3.10: £1.20, £1.80, £4.00; EX 11.10 Trifecta £97.20 Pool: £519.30 - 3.95 winning units..
Owner E A Brook **Bred** Tipper House Stud **Trained** Sigwells, Somerset

FOCUS
Some interesting newcomers on show in this juvenile event but it was the most experienced horse in the race, Hillbilly Boy, who scored in decisive fashion.

NOTEBOOK
Hillbilly Boy(IRE) had already shown a useful level of ability in four outings and that experience proved vital as he made all against the nearside rail. The son of Haafhd had gone close on a couple occasions over 5f at Bath and Beverley earlier in the year and he had no problems seeing out this extra furlong. He wandered around in the final furlong but never stopped going forward. He's no world beater but represents a yard that excels with its youngsters. (op 11-4)
Maputo wasn't without support and he posted a creditable effort back in second. Mark Johnston has been in flying form of late and it shouldn't be long before this son Cape Cross gets his head in front. He wasn't given a hard time once beaten. (op 3-1 tchd 7-2)
Two Pancakes had raced keenly through the early stages but was finishing better than anything and ought to be up to winning a similar race next time. (op 14-1)
Tha'Ir(IRE) looked unfurnished in the preliminaries but ran with some promise. (op 9-2)

2309 SEABROOK CRISPS STIRRING CHILDREN'S SMILES CHARITY (S) STKS 6f
2:40 (2:41) (Class 6) 2-Y-0 **£2,587** (£770; £384; £192) **Stalls** High

Form RPR
63 **1** **Captain Blue**[13] 1904 2-8-7 0 .... RyanWhile(7) 7 61
(Bill Turner) *prom: effrt and rdn over 1f out: led ins fnl f: edgd rt: rdn out* **14/1**
32 **2** *2 1/2* **Out Of The Blocks**[40] 1284 2-9-0 0 .... RichardKingscote 2 54
(Tom Dascombe) *chsd ldrs: rdn thrght: hdwy to ld over 2f out to ins fnl f: kpt on same pce* **5/6**[1]
00 **3** *1* **Zero Rated (IRE)**[32] 1437 2-8-9 0 .... (b[1]) DavidAllan 8 46
(Tim Easterby) *bhd: drvn 1/2-way: hdwy over 1f out: no imp ins fnl f* **8/1**[3]
4 **4** *2 1/4* **Saltaire Lass**[25] 1594 2-8-9 0 .... MickyFenton 3 39
(Paul Midgley) *rrd over bef s: hld up on outside: rdn over 2f out: kpt on fnl f: nvr able to chal* **9/2**[2]
662 **5** *1 1/2* **Tiger Sunset (IRE)**[6] 2132 2-9-0 0 .... (p) LiamKeniry 1 40
(J S Moore) *chsd ldr: ev ch over 2f out: wknd appr fnl f* **8/1**[3]
046 **6** *1* **Cherryred Girl (IRE)**[14] 1891 2-8-6 0 .... (b[1]) RyanPowell(3) 6 32
(J S Moore) *in tch: effrt and drvn 2f out: edgd rt and wknd appr fnl f* **20/1**
35 **7** *nk* **Red Koko (IRE)**[25] 1594 2-8-9 0 .... TomEaves 4 31
(George Moore) *led to over 2f out: rdn and wknd over 1f out* **20/1**

1m 20.43s (7.43) **Going Correction** +0.475s/f (Yiel) **7** Ran SP% **111.1**
Speed ratings (Par 91): **69,65,64,61,59 58,57**
toteswingers: 1&2 £3.00, 1&3 £6.70, 2&3 £2.70 CSF £24.94 TOTE £17.00: £4.40, £1.30; EX 26.20 Trifecta £304.90 Pool: £642.96 - 1.56 winning units..The winner was bought in for £13,500. Out of The Blocks was claimed by Mrs Ruth A Carr for £6,000.
Owner Miss Karen Theobald **Bred** Miss Karen Theobald **Trained** Sigwells, Somerset

FOCUS
A modest seller, run at a fair pace.

NOTEBOOK
Captain Blue, up in trip, improved to get off the mark on his third start. (tchd 16-1)

Out Of The Blocks looked to have plenty going for him on paper but he was never travelling with any authority and was readily brushed aside by the son of Captain Marvellous. The winner had shaped with a modicum of promise in this grade at Bath last time and he, like the yard's earlier winner, appeared to benefit greatly from a step up to this distance. He's clearly got his limitations but appears to be steadily improving. (op 4-5 tchd 8-11 and 10-11)
Zero Rated(IRE) stayed on to grab third without ever threatening to win. She was trying first-time headgear and responded well to them. A step up in trip may suit. (op 9-1 tchd 10-1)
Saltaire Lass reared over backwards when loading in the stalls. She was allowed to take part but was slowly away and never got involved. (op 6-1 tchd 13-2)

2310 C. B. HUTCHINSON MEMORIAL CHALLENGE CUP (FILLIES' H'CAP) 6f
3:10 (3:10) (Class 3) (0-95,86) 3-Y-O+ £8,191 (£2,451; £1,225; £613; £305) Stalls High

Form RPR
4-40 1 **Misplaced Fortune**[15] 1844 7-9-12 **84** SilvestreDeSousa 6 93
(Nigel Tinkler) *hld up: gd hdwy to ld appr fnl f: drvn out* **8/1**
1/1- 2 1 **Hallelujah**[333] 3283 4-9-9 **81** RyanMoore 4 87
(James Fanshawe) *bhd: rdn over 3f out: hdwy and edgd rt over 1f out: chsd wnr ins fnl f: r.o* **7/2**[1]
20-2 3 2 1/2 **Spinatrix**[31] 1476 4-9-10 **82** TomEaves 5 80
(Michael Dods) *pressed ldr: led wl over 1f out to appr fnl f: edgd rt and one pce ins fnl f* **5/1**[2]
1-6 4 3/4 **Brick Tops**[29] 1508 3-8-13 **80** WilliamBuick 2 73
(David Simcock) *s.i.s: hld up on outside: rdn over 2f out: edgd rt and no imp fnl f* **10/1**
4-33 5 3/4 **Jedward (IRE)**[13] 1926 5-9-4 **81** ShaneBKelly(5) 1 74
(Richard Fahey) *trckd ldrs: rdn and ev ch over 1f out: outpcd ins fnl f* **6/1**[3]
-506 6 1 1/4 **Jeannie Galloway (IRE)**[26] 1581 5-9-13 **85** JoeFanning 8 74
(Keith Dalgleish) *led to wl over 1f out: sn rdn and no ex* **6/1**[3]
0-40 7 1 **Timeless Elegance (IRE)**[16] 1827 5-9-1 **73** GrahamGibbons 10 59
(David Barron) *in tch: effrt over 2f out: sn rdn: wknd over 1f out* **16/1**
330- 8 4 1/2 **Celtic Sixpence (IRE)**[198] 7262 4-9-7 **79** TomQueally 7 50
(Noel Quinlan) *trckd ldrs: nt clr run briefly over 2f out: sn rdn and wknd over 1f out* **25/1**
5-51 9 10 **Pearl Blue (IRE)**[23] 1642 4-10-0 **86** TedDurcan 3 25
(Chris Wall) *prom: rdn along over 2f out: wknd over 1f out: eased whn no ch ins fnl f* **5/1**[2]

1m 17.17s (4.17) **Going Correction** +0.475s/f (Yiel)
WFA 3 from 4yo+ 9lb **9** Ran SP% **114.1**
Speed ratings (Par 104): **91,89,86,85,84 82,81,75,62**
toteswingers: 1&2 £9.10, 1&3 £7.30, 2&3 £3.70 CSF £35.69 CT £155.15 TOTE £10.40: £3.50, £1.80, £1.30; EX 57.50 Trifecta £373.00 Part won. Pool: £504.09 - 0.40 winning units..
Owner W F Burton **Bred** Adrian Smith **Trained** Langton, N Yorks

FOCUS
A competitive fillies' handicap, run at a decent pace throughout and won for the second time in three years by Misplaced Fortune.

NOTEBOOK
Misplaced Fortune had landed this contest back in 2010 and she made light of this 7lb higher mark to win convincingly. The Nigel Tinkler-trained mare had performed creditably on her reappearance here last month but, having been well beaten at Doncaster last time, had something to prove. However, she clearly relishes the demands of this track and could be called the winner some way out as she moved up strongly. She knuckled down well once challenged late on and deserves plenty of credit with this ground arguably a bit slower than ideal. She had been apprentice-ridden on her first two starts of the season and benefited from this stronger handling. (op 9-1)
Hallelujah, chasing a hat-trick following wins at Yarmouth and Kempton, lost little in defeat. She was never travelling at any stage but stayed on determinedly for pressure and was, perhaps, a shade unfortunate to find one too good. She ran as if this trip was a bare minimum and she would make plenty of interest if upped in distance on her next outing. (op 4-1 tchd 9-2)
Spinatrix did best of the rest and clearly goes well in these conditions. She wasn't able to go with the principals late on but had plenty of use made of her early on. (op 9-2)
Brick Tops looks too high in the weights. (op 9-1)
Pearl Blue(IRE) Official explanation: trainer could offer no explination as to poor run.

2311 RIPON, YORKSHIRE'S GARDEN RACECOURSE H'CAP 1m
3:40 (3:40) (Class 2) (0-105,100) 4-Y-O+
£12,450 (£3,728; £1,864; £932; £466; £234) Stalls Low

Form RPR
3535 1 **Dubai Dynamo**[9] 2025 7-8-7 **86** JamesSullivan 7 99
(Ruth Carr) *hld up in tch: hdwy over 2f out: led over 1f out: edgd rt: drvn clr fnl f* **7/2**[1]
4-02 2 3 1/4 **Honeymead (IRE)**[16] 1821 4-8-9 **88** TonyHamilton 2 93+
(Richard Fahey) *dwlt: sn in tch on ins: stdy hdwy whn nt clr run over 2f out to over 1f out: rdn and chsd wnr last 100yds: r.o* **7/1**[2]
1-02 3 1/2 **Silvery Moon (IRE)**[22] 1670 5-8-4 **83** DuranFentiman 5 87
(Tim Easterby) *pressed ldr: ev ch over 2f out to over 1f out: kpt on same pce* **7/2**[1]
10-0 4 4 **Vainglory (USA)**[29] 1510 8-8-6 **92** AliceHaynes(7) 3 87
(David Simcock) *hld up on outside: shkn up over 2f out: edgd rt over 1f out: nt pce to chal* **10/1**
000- 5 1/2 **Dunn'o (IRE)**[267] 5474 7-9-2 **95** AdrianNicholls 4 89
(David Nicholls) *taken early to post: t.k.h: led to over 1f out: sn wknd* **18/1**
1-00 6 1 3/4 **Don't Call Me (IRE)**[15] 1865 5-8-7 **93** ShirleyTeasdale(7) 1 83
(David Nicholls) *hld up: shkn up over 2f out: nvr able to chal* **8/1**[3]
0-42 7 hd **Osteopathic Remedy (IRE)**[15] 1865 8-8-12 **91** TomEaves 6 80
(Michael Dods) *trckd ldrs tl rdn and wknd fr 2f out* **7/2**[1]
010- 8 20 **Polar Kite (IRE)**[260] 5730 4-8-5 **89** ShaneBKelly(5) 9 32
(Richard Fahey) *t.k.h: chsd ldrs tl rdn and wknd fr 2f out* **10/1**

1m 43.32s (1.92) **Going Correction** +0.475s/f (Yiel) **8** Ran SP% **113.7**
Speed ratings (Par 109): **109,105,105,101,100 99,98,78**
toteswingers: 1&2 £4.10, 1&3 £3.50, 2&3 £5.30 CSF £28.40 CT £91.18 TOTE £5.10: £2.10, £2.30, £2.00; EX 32.60 Trifecta £125.10 Pool: £541.15 - 3.25 winning units..
Owner The Bottom Liners **Bred** T K & Mrs P A Knox **Trained** Huby, N Yorks

FOCUS
A decent renewal of this mile handicap.

NOTEBOOK
Dubai Dynamo has been a model of consistency for connections over the last few seasons and goes especially well here, having finished second in the last two runnings of this race and won a similar event off a pound lower mark a year ago. His consistency means he gets little respite from the handicapper and he looks set for a hefty hike in the weights after arguably the most dominant display of his career. This was the softest ground he's ever won on and there could be even more to come later in the season once the ground comes more in his favour. He appreciates a strong pace to run at and wouldn't look out of place in one the big handicaps at Royal Ascot. (op 9-2)
Honeymead(IRE) ran on well to finish second but was no match for the winner. She was caught in traffic when the winner kicked for home but it's unlikely it made any difference. She has a progressive profile but is proving hard to win with. (op 15-2)
Silvery Moon(IRE) was always well positioned behind the front-running Dunn'o and had no excuses for this defeat. He has looked onepaced on his last two outings and might be worth another try over further. (tchd 4-1)
Osteopathic Remedy(IRE) found little for pressure. Official explanation: trainer could offer no explanation at to poor run. (op 3-1)

2312 MIDDLEHAM TRAINERS ASSOCIATION H'CAP 1m 1f 170y
4:10 (4:10) (Class 4) (0-85,90) 4-Y-O+ £5,175 (£1,540; £769; £384) Stalls Low

Form RPR
4413 1 **Veiled Applause**[15] 1841 9-8-12 **76** MichaelO'Connell 3 86
(John Quinn) *in tch on ins: effrt and swtchd lft over 2f out: led over 1f out: edgd rt: drvn out* **9/1**
31-0 2 2 1/4 **Cape Rising (IRE)**[39] 1295 5-8-11 **75** RyanMoore 2 80
(Alan Swinbank) *chsd ldrs: drvn along over 3f out: ev ch over 2f out: kpt on fnl f: nt pce of wnr* **11/1**
-004 3 2 **Jonny Lesters Hair (IRE)**[22] 1670 7-9-3 **81** DavidAllan 6 82
(Tim Easterby) *taken early to post: led to over 1f out: rdn and kpt on same pce* **11/2**[3]
42-4 4 2 **Ashiri (IRE)**[29] 1513 4-9-3 **81** WilliamBuick 11 78
(David Simcock) *in tch on outside: effrt 3f out: edgd rt and no imp over 1f out* **4/1**[2]
40-3 5 2 3/4 **Lady Chaparral**[22] 1656 5-9-4 **82** TomEaves 7 73
(Michael Dods) *t.k.h: trckd ldrs: wnt 2nd 1/2-way: ev ch over 2f out to over 1f out: sn outpcd* **17/2**
5001 6 7 **Licence To Till (USA)**[8] 2077 5-9-12 **90** SilvestreDeSousa 5 72
(Mark Johnston) *hld up: rdn and effrt over 2f out: no imp fnl 2f* **8/1**
2-0 7 1/2 **Tenhoo**[22] 1657 6-8-7 **76** NathanAlison(5) 8 51
(Eric Alston) *t.k.h: hld up on ins: rdn over 3f out: wknd fr 2f out* **28/1**
10-6 8 1 1/2 **Unknown Rebel (IRE)**[22] 1239 4-8-9 **80** (p) PaulMcGiff(7) 10 52
(Kevin Ryan) *chsd ldr to 1/2-way: rdn and wknd over 3f out* **20/1**
0135 9 16 **West End Lad**[15] 1841 9-9-7 **85** (b) RussKennemore 4 24
(Roy Bowring) *hld up on outside: hdwy and in tch over 3f out: wknd over 2f out: t.o* **16/1**
2/22 10 28 **Edmaaj (IRE)**[18] 1755 4-8-12 **76** DanielTudhope 9
(David O'Meara) *hld up: shkn up and struggling 4f out: sn lost tch* **7/2**[1]
/221 11 30 **Hunters Belt (IRE)**[73] 836 8-8-7 **71** BarryMcHugh 1
(Noel Wilson) *hld up: struggling over 4f out: sn lost tch: eased whn no ch fnl 2f* **20/1**

2m 9.75s (4.35) **Going Correction** +0.475s/f (Yiel) **11** Ran SP% **116.4**
Speed ratings (Par 105): **101,99,97,96,93 88,87,86,73,51 27**
toteswingers: 1&2 £15.90, 1&3 £12.90, 2&3 £13.80 CSF £99.48 CT £599.25 TOTE £12.80: £3.60, £4.20, £3.40; EX 119.60 TRIFECTA Not won..
Owner Far 2 Many Sues **Bred** P J McCalmont **Trained** Settrington, N Yorks

FOCUS
A competitive handicap, run at a strong pace and a second C&D success for the John Quinn-trained Veiled Applause.
Edmaaj(IRE) Official explanation: vet said gelding finished distressed.

2313 GOTTOHAVEDIAMONDS.COM MAIDEN STKS 1m 1f
4:40 (4:41) (Class 5) 3-Y-O £2,911 (£866; £432; £216) Stalls Low

Form RPR
0-24 1 **Star Date (IRE)**[11] 1976 3-9-3 80 LukeMorris 7 85+
(Gerard Butler) *hld up in tch: effrt over 2f out: sn chsng clr ldr: drvn to ld last 100yds: styd on wl* **11/2**[3]
4-2 2 4 1/2 **Commend**[39] 1312 3-9-3 0 RyanMoore 14 75+
(Sir Michael Stoute) *chsd clr ldr: led over 2f out: sn rdn clr: hdd and no ex last 100yds* **2/1**[1]
4-0 3 1 1/4 **Rosselli (IRE)**[40] 1270 3-8-10 0 ConorHarrison(7) 6 72
(Mrs K Burke) *hld up in tch: rdn 3f out: styd on fnl 2f: nrst fin* **66/1**
0-0 4 11 **King Of Paradise (IRE)**[11] 1976 3-9-3 0 GrahamGibbons 2 48
(Eric Alston) *t.k.h: prom: effrt and rdn over 2f out: wknd fnl f* **40/1**
0U 5 5 **Meljana (IRE)**[31] 1479 3-8-12 0 GarryWhillans(5) 4 37
(Alan Swinbank) *s.i.s: bhd tl styd on fnl 2f: nvr able to chal* **150/1**
0- 6 1/2 **Saloomy**[214] 6951 3-9-3 0 WilliamBuick 8 36
(David Simcock) *t.k.h: prom tl rdn and wknd fr 2f out* **10/1**
0-6 7 2 1/4 **Border Hill Jack**[22] 1676 3-9-3 0 DanielTudhope 13 31
(Robin Bastiman) *hld up: rdn and outpcd over 3f out: n.d after* **200/1**
8 2 **Artistic Dawn (IRE)** 3-8-12 0 JamesSullivan 9 22
(John Weymes) *s.i.s: bhd and sn outpcd: detached 1/2-way: plugged on fnl f: nvr on terms* **100/1**
2-5 9 3/4 **Isatis**[31] 1472 3-8-12 0 TomQueally 1 20
(Sir Henry Cecil) *midfield: rdn over 3f out: wandered and wknd 2f out* **7/1**
2 10 11 **Vital Calling**[31] 1479 3-9-3 0 LeeNewman 11 +
(David Barron) *t.k.h: led and sn clr: rn wd bnd ent st: hdd over 2f out: sn wknd* **10/1**
11 7 **Soapy Delight** 3-8-12 0 JoeFanning 5 +
(Mark Johnston) *bhd and sn pushed along: struggling 1/2-way: nvr on terms* **25/1**
12 2 1/4 **Portraitofmylove (IRE)** 3-8-12 0 IanMongan 3
(Sir Henry Cecil) *bhd and sn outpcd: detached 1/2-way: nvr on terms* **18/1**
6 13 1/2 **Voodoo (IRE)**[20] 1716 3-9-3 0 (t) ShaneKelly 16
(Daniel Mark Loughnane) *s.i.s: towards rr: struggling 4f out: sn btn* **100/1**
32- 14 28 **Almaas (USA)**[241] 6267 3-9-3 0 SilvestreDeSousa 10
(Saeed Bin Suroor) *in tch on outside: struggling 3f out: sn wknd and eased: t.o* **3/1**[2]

2m 0.1s (5.40) **Going Correction** +0.475s/f (Yiel) **14** Ran SP% **120.6**
Speed ratings (Par 99): **95,91,89,80,75 75,73,71,70,61 54,52,52,27**
toteswingers: 1&2 £30.70, 1&3 £3.60, 2&3 £32.50 CSF £16.64 TOTE £7.60: £1.90, £1.60, £14.60; EX 24.40 TRIFECTA Not won..
Owner Beetle N Wedge Partnership **Bred** Macquarie **Trained** Newmarket, Suffolk

FOCUS
A furiously run affair. The form looks a little shaky.
Isatis Official explanation: jockey said filly became unbalanced in the closing stages.
Voodoo(IRE) Official explanation: jockey said gelding had no more to give.
Almaas(USA) Official explanation: jockey said colt hung left.

2314 RIPON RUFC IN UNION WITH WOODEN SPOON H'CAP 5f
5:10 (5:11) (Class 5) (0-70,68) 4-Y-O+ £2,911 (£866; £432; £216) Stalls High

Form RPR
605- 1 **Bosun Breese**[244] 6212 7-9-2 **68** LMcNiff(5) 7 83
(David Barron) *mde virtually all on outside of stands' side gp: rdn clr over 1f out: kpt on strly: 1st of 9 in gp* **15/2**[2]
-032 2 2 1/2 **Fama Mac**[8] 2091 5-8-7 **54** oh3 SilvestreDeSousa 3 60+
(Neville Bycroft) *in tch far side: sn pushed along: hdwy over 1f out: styd on to ld that gp towards fin: nt rch stands' side wnr: 1st of 5 in gp* **5/2**[1]

5-00 **3** ½ **Choc'A'Moca (IRE)**[29] 1526 5-8-10 **57**..........................(v) MickyFenton 1 61
(Paul Midgley) *led far side: rdn over 2f out: kpt on fnl f: hdd that gp nr fin: 2nd of 5 in gp* **20/1**

30-0 **4** ½ **Novalist**[31] 1480 4-8-7 **54**..........................(b) LiamKeniry 6 50
(Robin Bastiman) *midfield stands' side gp: rdn and hung rt 2f out: kpt on fnl f: 2nd of 9 in gp* **16/1**

-063 **5** ¾ **Baybshambles (IRE)**[6] 2120 8-8-8 **55**.......................... TomEaves 12 55
(Ron Barr) *hld up in midfield stands' side: rdn over 2f out: kpt on ins fnl f: nvr able to chal: 3rd of 9 in gp* **9/1**

54-5 **6** 1 ¾ **Meandmyshadow**[29] 1526 4-9-6 **67**.......................... GrahamGibbons 15 60
(Alan Brown) *cl up stands' side gp tl rdn and one pce fr over 1f out: 4th of 9 in gp* **9/1**

0-44 **7** ½ **Just For Mary**[22] 1675 8-9-7 **68**.......................... ShaneKelly 8 59
(Daniel Mark Loughnane) *s.i.s: bhd and sn pushed along stands' side gp: styd on fnl f: nrst fin: 5th of 9 in gp* **17/2**[3]

5000 **8** 2 **Divertimenti (IRE)**[97] 544 8-9-1 **62**..........................(b) RussKennemore 13 46
(Roy Bowring) *w ldr stands' side to 2f out: hung rt and sn outpcd: 6th of 9 in gp* **28/1**

-010 **9** 1 **Prince James**[12] 1954 5-8-8 **62**.......................... DavidSimmonson(7) 9 43
(Michael Easterby) *sn drvn along bhd stands' side ldrs: struggling over 2f out: n.d after: 7th of 9 in gp* **25/1**

-030 **10** ½ **Calypso Cay**[8] 2096 4-8-10 **62**.......................... GarryWhillans(5) 14 41
(Peter Salmon) *dwlt: bhd stands' side: rdn over 2f out: sn no imp: 8th of 9 in gp* **10/1**

00-6 **11** ¾ **Ingenti**[12] 1954 4-8-4 **54** oh1.......................... JulieBurke(3) 4 30
(Christopher Wilson) *cl up far side gp tl edgd lft and wknd over 1f out: 3rd of 5 in gp* **18/1**

2-30 **12** 2 **Kyzer Chief**[31] 1480 7-8-7 **59**.......................... ShaneBKelly(5) 5 28
(Ron Barr) *prom far side gp: rdn over 2f out: wknd over 1f out: 4th of 5 in gp* **18/1**

00-5 **13** ¾ **On The High Tops (IRE)**[12] 1954 4-9-4 **65**.......................... JamesSullivan 2 31
(Ruth Carr) *t.k.h: cl up far side tl wknd over 1f out: last of 5 in gp* **17/2**[3]

500- **14** 9 **Mr Mo Jo**[260] 5719 4-9-0 **61**.......................... DuranFentiman 16
(Lawrence Mullaney) *prom stands' side gp tl rdn and wknd fr 2f out: last of 9 in gp* **20/1**

1m 2.59s (1.89) **Going Correction** +0.475s/f (Yiel) **14** Ran SP% **123.7**
Speed ratings (Par 103): **103,99,98,97,96 93,92,89,87,87 85,82,81,67**
toteswingers: 1&2 £5.30, 1&3 £43.20, 2&3 £12.40 CSF £25.73 CT £389.61 TOTE £9.10: £3.20, £1.30, £6.80; EX 36.40 Trifecta £614.40 Pool: £838.63 - 1.01 winning units..
Owner Harrowgate Bloodstock Ltd **Bred** Lady Lonsdale **Trained** Maunby, N Yorks

FOCUS
A low grade if competitive sprint handicap, run at a strong pace.
T/Plt: £40.80 to a £1 stake. Pool: £85,629.57. 1,531.14 winning tickets. T/Qpdt: £21.20 to a £1 stake. Pool: £5,260.21. 183.30 winning tickets. RY

2315 - 2317a (Foreign Racing) - See Raceform Interactive

1687 NAVAN (L-H)
Sunday, May 20

OFFICIAL GOING: Good

2318a VINTAGE CROP STKS (LISTED RACE) 1m 6f
4:05 (4:05) 4-Y-0+ **£21,666** (£6,333; £3,000; £1,000)

RPR

1 **Fame And Glory**[218] 6857 6-9-10 120.......................... JPO'Brien 6 115+
(A P O'Brien, Ire) *trckd ldr in 2nd: cl up and pressed ldr after 5f: led 5f out: clr 4f out: reduced advantage 3f out: rdn and chal over 1f out: kpt on wl u.p fnl f* **5/4**[1]

2 nk **Unaccompanied (IRE)**[21] 1694 5-9-0 103.......................... PatSmullen 4 105
(D K Weld, Ire) *chsd ldrs in 3rd: hdwy into 2nd 3f out: rdn to chal over 1f out: kpt on fnl f: no ex cl home* **11/8**[2]

3 3 **Steps To Freedom (IRE)**[41] 5573 6-9-3 101..........................(t) FranBerry 1 104
(Mrs John Harrington, Ire) *settled bhd ldrs in 4th: hdwy into 3rd 3f out: rdn 2f out: kpt on same pce fr over 1f out: no ex ins fnl f* **13/2**[3]

4 12 **Rising Wind (IRE)**[21] 1694 4-9-0 89.......................... ChrisHayes 2 84
(Kevin Prendergast, Ire) *settled bhd ldrs: 5th 1/2-way: rdn and no imp 4f out: kpt on one pce* **25/1**

5 12 **Lovers Peace (IRE)**[10] 2018 4-9-0 74.......................... WJLee 3 67
(Edmond Kent, Ire) *towards rr: rdn and no imp 5f out: kpt on one pce st* **66/1**

6 25 **Table Mountain (IRE)**[50] 4398 5-9-3 95..........................(tp) JohnnyMurtagh 5 35
(Robert Alan Hennessy, Ire) *led: strly pressed after 5f: rdn and hdd 5f out: 4th and no ex 3f out: wknd: eased ins fnl f* **28/1**

7 1 ¾ **Notable Graduate (IRE)**[329] 3442 4-9-3 103.......................... ShaneGorey 7 33
(D K Weld, Ire) *hld up towards rr: rdn in mod 6th and no imp 3f out: wknd 2f out* **14/1**

3m 6.9s (-8.10) **7** Ran SP% **115.3**
CSF £3.27 TOTE £2.00: £1.80, £1.02; DF 3.00.
Owner Mrs Fitri Hay **Bred** Ptarmigan Bloodstock And Miss K Rausing **Trained** Ballydoyle, Co Tipperary

FOCUS
It may have only been a Listed contest on paper but in reality it was so much more. The second and third have been rated to their best.

NOTEBOOK
Fame And Glory hasn't always been fully wound up for his seasonal debut and hasn't impressed on either of his reappearances in the last two years. But with Ballydoyle firing on all cylinders, there was always a chance he would strip much fitter this time around, and so it proved. Table Mountain was sent straight into a clear lead, which certainly helped as it made the race a true test of stamina. Joseph O'Brien decided the time was right to kick on passing the 5f pole and went clear, but when Unaccompanied appeared on the scene 2f out he needed to pull out all the stops to prevail, and the way he stuck his neck out and battled suggests that a successful defence of his Gold Cup crown may be on the cards. There doesn't appear to be anything on the other side of the water coming through in the staying division and this display suggests that he is every bit as good, if not better, than he was 12 months ago. (op 6/5 tchd 11/8)
Unaccompanied(IRE) is a mare of real quality and, while she didn't win, she lost very little in defeat. It was a little surprising to see Dermot Weld sidestep both Cheltenham and Punchestown in preference for a Flat campaign but, on this evidence, it was the right call. She settled well, moved to challenge 2f out but just couldn't get past the brave winner after a prolonged duel inside the final furlong. (op 11/8 tchd 5/4)
Steps To Freedom(IRE) promised much but delivered very little at the end of his novice hurdling campaign and was well beaten at both Cheltenham and Fairyhouse festivals when well fancied. Ground may have been the main contributor to those lacklustre efforts and he showed more sparkle on this livelier surface. He travelled well and found plenty off the bridle, something that hasn't always been the case in the past. (op 7/1)
Notable Graduate(IRE), thought good enough to line up in last year's Irish Derby, showed worryingly little here and was always out the back. Something may have been amiss as the run was simply too bad to be true.

2319 - 2321a (Foreign Racing) - See Raceform Interactive

2222 BADEN-BADEN (L-H)
Sunday, May 20

OFFICIAL GOING: Turf: good

2322a GROSSER PREIS DER BADISCHEN UNTERNEHMER (GROUP 2) (4YO+) (TURF) 1m 3f
3:45 (12:00) 4-Y-0+
£33,333 (£12,916; £5,416; £3,333; £2,083; £1,250)

RPR

1 **Danedream (GER)**[175] 7563 4-9-2 0.......................... AStarke 8 115
(P Schiergen, Germany) *t.k.h: trckd ldrs: rdn and qcknd to ld over 1f out: clr ins fnl f: drvn and reduced advantage fnl 100yds: a gng to hold rivals* **2/5**[1]

2 ¾ **Ovambo Queen (GER)**[197] 5-8-11 0.......................... ADeVries 3 109
(Dr A Bolte, Germany) *awkward leaving leaving stalls: hld up in last trio: effrt and swtchd sharply rt 2f out: str run fnl f: chsd wnr ins fnl f: clsng on qckly towards fin* **36/5**[2]

3 nk **Silvaner (GER)**[21] 1700 4-9-1 0.......................... THellier 2 112
(P Schiergen, Germany) *t.k.h: in tch in midfield: rdn and effrt 2f out: drvn and hdwy over 1f out: r.o strly ins fnl f: clsng on wnr towards fin* **15/2**[3]

4 2 ½ **Tesey**[210] 4-9-1 0.......................... APietsch 9 108
(M G Mintchev, Germany) *chsd ldr: rdn and effrt to chal 2f out: outpcd by wnr over 1f out: battled on same pce fnl f* **28/1**

5 hd **Russian Tango (GER)**[28] 5-9-1 0.......................... EPedroza 4 108
(A Wohler, Germany) *chsd ldrs: rdn and effrt to chal over 2f out: outpcd by wnr over 1f out: battling for placings tl one pce fnl f* **19/2**

6 nk **Mighty Mouse (GER)**[21] 1700 4-9-1 0.......................... FrederikTylicki 10 107
(P Vovcenko, Germany) *led: rdn and hrd pressed jst over 2f out: hdd and outpcd by wnr over 1f out: styd on same pce fnl f* **195/10**

7 5 **King's Hall**[28] 4-9-1 0.......................... JBojko 5 98
(A Wohler, Germany) *hld up in rr: rdn and sme hdwy 2f out: no imp fnl f* **33/1**

8 2 ½ **Sir Lando**[21] 1700 5-9-1 0.......................... FJohansson 1 94
(Wido Neuroth, Norway) *hld up in last pair: effrt but stl plenty to do whn bdly hmpd 2f out: nt rcvr and wl btn after* **135/10**

9 1 ¾ **Lindenthaler (GER)**[21] 1700 4-9-1 0.......................... FilipMinarik 6 90
(P Schiergen, Germany) *t.k.h: hld up in tch in midfield: rdn and effrt whn pushed rt and hmpd 2f out: nt rcvr and n.d after* **27/1**

10 7 **Roches Cross (IRE)**[329] 4-9-1 0.......................... DPorcu 7 78
(Josef Vana II, Czech Republic) *t.k.h: hld up wl in tch in midfield: rdn and struggling 3f out: wknd 2f out* **29/1**

2m 16.59s (-2.68) **10** Ran SP% **130.0**
WIN (incl. 10 euro stake): 14. PLACES: 10, 14, 14. SF: 72.
Owner Gestut Burg Eberstein & Teruya Yoshida **Bred** Gestut Brummerhof **Trained** Germany

NOTEBOOK
Danedream(GER), whose trainer claimed she was only 80% for this reapppearance, was being closed down at the finish but was never going to be beaten. This was a pleasing effort from last year's Arc winner, she should come on for it, and it'll be either the Grand Prix de Saint-Cloud or the King George next for her.

2106 CAPANNELLE (R-H)
Sunday, May 20

OFFICIAL GOING: Turf: good to soft

2323a PREMIO CARLO D'ALESSIO (GROUP 3) (4YO+) (TURF) 1m 4f
2:40 (12:00) 4-Y-0+ **£23,333** (£10,266; £5,600; £2,800)

RPR

1 **Lake Drop (USA)**[56] 4-8-9 0.......................... CristianDemuro 1 104
(S Botti, Italy) *stdd s and t.k.h: hld up in last pair: effrt on inner and n.m.r over 2f out: drvn to chse ldrs over 1f out: led ins fnl f: r.o wl* **19/4**

2 ¾ **Frankenstein**[21] 5-8-9 0.......................... FrankieDettori 9 103
(B Grizzetti, Italy) *in tch in midfield: rdn and hdwy to chse ldr over 2f out: edgd rt u.p over 1f out: drvn and led narrowly 1f out: hdd and one pce ins fnl f* **63/20**[2]

3 hd **Branderburgo (IRE)**[49] 5-8-9 0.......................... CFiocchi 7 102
(M Grassi, Italy) *led after 1f: clr fr 1/2-way: rdn and qcknd 3f out: hrd drvn and narrowly hdd 1f out: styd on same pce after* **119/10**

4 2 **Pattaya (ITY)**[49] 4-8-9 0.......................... FabioBranca 4 99
(S Botti, Italy) *stdd s: hld up in last pair: hdwy into midfield 1/2-way: rdn to chse ldrs 2f out: unable qck and n.m.r over 1f out: styd on same pce fnl f* **19/10**[1]

5 2 **Silver Arrow (ITY)**[49] 7-8-9 0.......................... FrancescoDettori 6 96
(R Menichetti, Italy) *led for 1f: chsd ldr after tl over 2f out: sn drvn and outpcd: kpt on again fnl f* **224/10**

6 ½ **Cima De Pluie**[49] 5-8-9 0.......................... DarioVargiu 8 95
(B Grizzetti, Italy) *chsd ldrs: rdn and outpcd over 2f out: kpt on again ins fnl f* **47/10**[3]

7 4 **Inorato (IRE)**[56] 4-8-9 0.......................... SDiana 2 89
(F Camici, Italy) *hld up towards rr: rdn and struggling 3f out: styd on same pce and n.d fnl 2f* **68/1**

8 nk **Viso Pallido (IRE)** 4-8-9 0.......................... MircoDemuro 5 88
(Cristiana Signorelli, Italy) *hld up towards rr: rdn and no imp over 2f out: kpt on fnl f but nvr trbld ldrs* **43/5**

9 1 **Lord Chaparral (IRE)**[49] 5-8-9 0.......................... UmbertoRispoli 3 87
(R Brogi, Italy) *chsd ldrs: rdn and effrt to chse ldr 3f out tl over 2f out: wknd over 1f out: eased ins fnl f* **103/20**

2m 30.0s (2.80) **9** Ran SP% **133.7**
WIN (incl. 1 euro stake): 5.73. PLACES: 2.22, 1.97, 3.46. DF: 12.88.
Owner Scuderia Siba **Bred** Azienda Agricola Antezzate Srl **Trained** Italy

2324a 129TH DERBY ITALIANO BETTER (GROUP 2) (3YO) (TURF) 1m 3f
4:35 (12:00) 3-Y-O £208,333 (£91,666; £50,000; £25,000)

RPR

1 **Feuerblitz (GER)**[21] 3-9-2 0 RobertHavlin 4 103
(M Figge, Germany) *midfield: smooth prog into 3rd over 2 1/2f out: rdn over 1 1/2f out: r.o to chal over 1f out: protracted duel w eventual 2nd thrght fnl f: got up to ld last strides* **99/10**[3]

2 *snk* **Wild Wolf (IRE)**[21] 3-9-2 0 (b) UmbertoRispoli 3 102
(S Botti, Italy) *broke wl to ld: sn hdd and trckd ldr in clr 2nd: rdn to chal over 2f out: led over 1f out: strly pressed thrght fnl f: hdd last strides* **25/1**

3 *1 1/4* **Smoking Joe (ITY)**[28] 1555 3-9-2 0 FabioBranca 7 100
(S Botti, Italy) *midfield early: qckly pushed up into clr ld: rdn over 2 1/2f out: hdd over 1f out: kpt on for 3rd ins fnl f* **125/10**

4 *hd* **Vola E Va**[21] 3-9-2 0 DarioVargiu 1 100
(B Grizzetti, Italy) *hld up towards rr on inner: rdn to improve over 2f out: r.o to go 4th ins fnl f: gng on at fin* **32/1**

5 *2 1/4* **Herrbuga**[26] 1592 3-9-2 0 ThomasHuet 2 96
(G Botti, Italy) *midfield on inner: rdn over 2 1/2f out: kpt on one pce for 5th ins fnl 1 1/2f* **17/1**

6 *1 3/4* **Real Solution (USA)**[21] 3-9-2 0 FrankieDettori 11 92
(Gianluca Bietolini, Italy) *midfield on outer: rdn over 2 1/2f out: kpt on one pce for 6th ins fnl 1 1/2f* **2/5**[1]

7 *6* **Warder (IRE)**[28] 1555 3-9-2 0 (b) CristianDemuro 10 82
(R Biondi, Italy) *hld up in last pair: rdn to try and improve over 3f out: outpcd over 2f out: plugged on* **107/10**

8 *8* **Sopran Montieri (IRE)** 3-9-2 0 MircoDemuro 8 67
(B Grizzetti, Italy) *s.i.s: hld up in last: rdn over 3 1/2f out: sn btn: nvr a factor* **59/10**[2]

9 *7* **Teixidor (ITY)**[21] 3-9-2 0 SSulas 9 55
(Ottavio Di Paolo, Italy) *hld up towards rr: rdn over 3f out: no ex and btn over 1 1/2f out: eased* **38/1**

10 *3/4* **Meraviglioso**[26] 3-9-2 0 (b) PierantonioConvertino 6 53
(B Grizzetti, Italy) *sn trcking ldrs in 3rd: rdn and outpcd over 2 1/2f out: no ex and btn over 1 1/2f out: eased* **63/1**

11 *1* **Il Romito (IRE)**[35] 3-9-2 0 DPerovic 5 51
(E Borromeo, Italy) *hld up towards rr on outer: rdn and struggling over 4f out: no ex over 2f out: eased whn btn* **19/1**

2m 19.0s (139.00) **11** Ran SP% **132.6**
WIN (incl. 1 euro stake): 10.88. PLACES: 3.67, 5.38, 3.19. DF: 271.74.
Owner Stall Eivissa **Bred** Gestut Park Wiedingen **Trained** Germany

2325a PREMIO TUDINI (GROUP 3) (3YO+) (TURF) 6f
5:10 (12:00) 3-Y-O+ £23,333 (£10,266; £5,600; £2,800)

RPR

1 **United Color (USA)**[22] 3-8-6 0 CFiocchi 5 102
(R Menichetti, Italy) *midfield: rdn and trying to improve between rivals whn short of room and forced to briefly check over 1 1/2f out: qckly rcvrd and r.o to ld ins fnl f: drvn out* **197/10**

2 *3/4* **Traditional Chic (IRE)**[189] 7408 4-9-0 0 CristianDemuro 6 101
(L Riccardi, Italy) *midfield: rdn to chal over 1 1/2f out: r.o to go 2nd ins fnl f: nt pce of wnr* **59/10**

3 *1 1/2* **Pandar**[22] 3-8-5 0 MircoDemuro 4 94
(B Grizzetti, Italy) *disp ld on inner: rdn and hdd over 2f out: rallied to ld again over 1f out: hdd and dropped to 3rd ins fnl f: kpt on wout matching front pair cl home* **43/5**

4 *1 1/2* **Amico Fritz (GER)**[201] 7221 6-9-0 0 FabriceVeron 8 91
(H-A Pantall, France) *midfield on outer: rdn and outpcd over 2 1/2f out: kpt on u.p ins fnl 1 1/2f* **53/20**[1]

5 *shd* **Il Supremo (IRE)**[7] 4-9-0 0 GBietolini 3 91
(L Riccardi, Italy) *hld up in last pair: rdn over 2 1/2f out: outpcd over 1 1/2f out: rallied and r.o strly ins fnl f: wnt 5th ins fnl 50yds* **59/10**

6 *3/4* **Choisir Shadow (IRE)**[201] 7220 3-8-4 0 DarioVargiu 9 86
(B Grizzetti, Italy) *prom: rdn to chal over 2f out: sn led: hdd over 1f out: stl ev ch tl no ex and fdd ins fnl f: ct for 5th ins fnl 50yds* **16/5**[3]

7 *1/2* **Moustache (IRE)**[21] 1698 3-8-5 0 FrankieDettori 2 85
(D Grilli, Italy) *hld up in last pair: rdn and outpcd in last over 2 1/2f out: plugged on ins fnl f* **59/20**[2]

8 *4* **Malikayah (IRE)**[7] 2112 4-8-10 0 SSulas 1 70
(D Camuffo, Italy) *midfield: t.k.h: prog to chse ldrs over 3 1/2f out: rdn to chal over 1 1/2f out: kpt on tl no ex and wknd ins fnl f: eased* **142/10**

9 *2* **Jiroft (ITY)**[22] 5-9-0 0 PierantonioConvertino 10 68
(A Marcialis, Italy) *disp ld on outer: hdd and rdn over 2f out: no ex and wknd over 1 1/2f out: eased ins fnl f* **103/20**

10 *2 1/2* **Caratteraccio (IRE)**[56] 4-9-0 0 FabioBranca 12 60
(E Botti, Italy) *prom on outer: rdn to chal over 2f out: no ex and btn over 1f out: eased ins fnl f* **43/5**

U **Airspace (IRE)**[22] 6-9-0 0 StefanoLandi 11
(Riccardo Barontini, Italy) *jinked as stalls opened and uns rdr* **66/1**

1m 9.0s (-1.30)
WFA 3 from 4yo+ 9lb **11** Ran SP% **155.5**
WIN (incl. 1 euro stake): 20.66. PLACES: 4.66, 3.37, 3.37. DF: 186.93.
Owner Razza Dell'Olmo **Bred** Adena Springs **Trained** Italy

KRANJI (L-H)
Sunday, May 20

OFFICIAL GOING: Turf: soft

2326a KRISFLYER INTERNATIONAL SPRINT (GROUP 1) (3YO+) (TURF) 6f
12:50 (12:00) 3-Y-O+
£283,582 (£100,746; £50,995; £24,875; £9,950; £4,975)

RPR

1 **Ato (SAF)**[21] 5-9-0 0 (t) BVorster 3 116
(Patrick Shaw, Singapore) *broke wl: settled in midfield towards inner: smooth prog to chal over 1 1/2f out: rdn over 1f out: r.o to ld ins fnl 150yds: gng away at fin* **16/1**

2 *1 1/2* **Mr Big (AUS)**[21] 4-8-10 0 (t) StephenBaster 2 107
(M Freedman, Singapore) *pushed up to trck ldr on rail: led over 3f out: rdn 1 1/2f out: hdd ins fnl 150yds: kpt on* **78/10**

3 *1 1/4* **Secret Asset (IRE)**[50] 1146 7-9-0 0 GeorgeBaker 1 107
(Jane Chapple-Hyam) *hld up in last trio on inner: prog into midfield over 2 1/2f out: rdn and ev ch over 1 1/2f out: kpt on wout matching ldng duo ins fnl f* **126/10**

4 *1 3/4* **Captain Obvious (AUS)**[94] 588 7-9-0 0 (t) OChavez 4 101+
(S Burridge, Singapore) *midfield: rdn to improve over 2f out: kpt on one pce ins fnl 1 1/2f* **68/10**[3]

5 *1 3/4* **Krypton Factor**[50] 1147 4-9-0 0 (b) KierenFallon 8 96+
(F Nass, Bahrain) *hld up in last pair on outer: rdn and outpcd 2f out: kpt on to go 5th ins fnl 1 1/2f: nvr able to chal* **3/5**[1]

6 *4 3/4* **Better Be The One (AUS)**[21] 6-9-0 0 (b) JoaoMoreira 9 81+
(M Freedman, Singapore) *trapped wd early: pushed up to trck ldr in 3rd after first f: rdn and no ex over 2f out: fdd* **54/10**[2]

7 *1 3/4* **Invincible Ash (IRE)**[50] 1146 7-8-10 0 (p) GaryCarroll 6 71+
(M Halford, Ire) *hld up in last towards inner: swtchd out and rdn to try and improve over 2f out: plugged on ins fnl f: nvr gng pce to chal* **17/1**

8 *6 1/4* **Perfect Pins (NZ)**[30] 7-9-0 0 (b) JVerenzuela 5 55+
(Leticia Dragon, Singapore) *midfield on outer: rdn and dropped to last over 2 1/2f out: n.d after* **28/1**

9 *20* **Yin Xin (NZ)**[30] 5-9-0 0 DannyBeasley 7 55+
(T Kieser, Singapore) *broke v wl to ld: hdd over 3f out: rdn over 2 1/2f out: no ex and wknd ins fnl 1 1/2f: heavily eased cl home* **136/10**

1m 10.57s (70.57) **9** Ran SP% **131.4**
PARI-MUTUEL (including 5 sgd stakes): WIN 85.00; PLACE 19.00, 11.00, 15.00; (including 2 sgd stakes): DF 106.00.
Owner Newbury Racing Stable **Bred** Maine Chance Farms (pty) Ltd **Trained** Singapore

NOTEBOOK
Ato(SAF) had a good draw and saved ground around the inner until switched out in the straight. He ran on well to score, but this doesn't look strong form for the grade.
Secret Asset(IRE) had the best draw and, although he struggled a little with the early pace, he saved ground towards the inside until swinging into the straight, which helped him pick up third late on.
Krypton Factor, winner of the Golden Shaheen, was well below his best. His draw didn't make things easy (caught wide), but it was the ground which did for him here.

2327 - (Foreign Racing) - See Raceform Interactive

1352 LEICESTER (R-H)
Monday, May 21

OFFICIAL GOING: Good to soft (good in places; 7.0)
Wind: Light, behind Weather: Fine

2328 G.D. GILES H'CAP 1m 1f 218y
6:20 (6:20) (Class 4) (0-80,79) 4-Y-0+ £4,528 (£1,347; £673; £336) Stalls Low

Form RPR

40-2 1 **King Zeal (IRE)**[10] 2051 8-8-12 70 (t) TomQueally 4 74
(Barry Leavy) *chsd ldr over 5f: sn rdn: wnt 2nd again over 3f out tl over 2f out: outpcd over 1f out: rallied ins fnl f: edgd rt and styd on to ld nr fin* **7/2**[2]

0-40 2 *1/2* **Mcbirney (USA)**[30] 1513 5-9-1 76 PatrickHills(3) 1 79
(Paul D'Arcy) *a.p: chsd ldr over 2f out: rdn to ld ins fnl f: edgd rt and hdd nr fin* **7/1**

/34- 3 *1 3/4* **Red Lover**[191] 7401 4-9-3 75 RyanMoore 3 76
(Ed Dunlop) *hld up: hdwy over 2f out: rdn over 1f out: nt clr run ins fnl f: styng on whn hmpd towards fin* **5/1**[3]

66-0 4 *hd* **Audacious**[51] 1134 4-9-5 77 PatCosgrave 7 76?
(Michael Quinn) *led: rdn over 1f out: hdd and unable qck ins fnl f* **40/1**

0-60 5 *9* **Spey Song (IRE)**[15] 1879 4-8-4 65 (p) AmyRyan(3) 5 46
(James Bethell) *hld up: rdn over 2f out: n.d* **12/1**

3311 6 *5* **Tilsworth Glenboy**[10] 2051 5-9-6 78 FrederikTylicki 2 49
(J R Jenkins) *hld up in tch: plld hrd: sddle slipped over 8f out: chsd ldr over 4f out tl rdr kicked feet out of irons wl over 3f out: wknd 2f out* **5/2**[1]

1101 7 *2 1/2* **Flying Applause**[13] 1950 7-9-4 79 (bt) LeeTopliss(3) 9 45
(Roy Bowring) *s.i.s: hld up: plld hrd: hdwy 7f out: lost pl over 4f out: sn bhd* **11/1**

1-26 8 *39* **Glass Mountain (IRE)**[16] 1841 4-9-3 75 JackMitchell 8
(James Fanshawe) *plld hrd and prom: wknd over 3f out: t.o* **15/2**

2m 12.25s (4.35) **Going Correction** +0.50s/f (Yiel) **8** Ran SP% **110.2**
Speed ratings (Par 105): **102,101,100,100,92 88,86,55**
toteswingers: 1&2 £6.90, 1&3 £5.30, 2&3 £12.00 CSF £25.89 CT £112.43 TOTE £5.60: £2.30, £3.90, £1.10; EX 35.10.
Owner Deborah Hart & Alan Jackson **Bred** Janus Bloodstock **Trained** Forsbrook, Staffs
■ Stewards' Enquiry : Frederik Tylicki jockey said that the saddle slipped

FOCUS
After a dry night and day the going was amended to Good to soft, good in places. The winning jockey reported it was riding as described after the opener. A tight little handicap in which the early pace was steady and it resulted in a close finish between the first four. The form, rated around the winner, is a bit shaky.

2329 JAMES WARD (S) STKS 1m 60y
6:50 (6:50) (Class 6) 3-Y-0+ £1,617 (£481; £240; £120) Stalls Low

Form RPR

-020 1 **Benandonner (USA)**[9] 2068 9-9-7 84 RyanMoore 3 83+
(Mike Murphy) *hld up: hdwy over 3f out: led over 2f out: edgd rt fr over 1f out: clr fnl f* **1/5**[1]

2300 2 *6* **Mighty Clarets (IRE)**[10] 2051 5-9-7 62 PatCosgrave 2 69
(Barry Leavy) *chsd ldrs: ev ch over 2f out: sn rdn: styd on same pce appr fnl f* **9/2**[2]

100- 3 *12* **Aussie Blue (IRE)**[66] 7146 8-9-7 63 MichaelStainton 6 42
(Charles Pogson) *chsd ldr tl led wl over 2f out: sn rdn and hdd: wknd over 1f out* **20/1**[3]

/000 4 *6* **Lady Brickhouse**[25] 1635 5-8-10 40 ow1 (p) HarryPoulton(7) 1 24
(Michael Squance) *led: rdn and hdd wl over 2f out: sn wknd* **50/1**

000- 5 *3 1/4* **Cat Island**[285] 4929 4-9-2 49 TomQueally 5 15
(Mark H Tompkins) *hld up: rdn over 3f out: sn wknd* **20/1**[3]

0-06 6 *5* **Centre Stage**[9] 2090 4-9-0 42 (b[1]) JackDuern(7) 4
(Michael Appleby) *s.s and rel to r: a wl bhd: t.o* **33/1**

1m 48.06s (2.96) **Going Correction** +0.50s/f (Yiel) **6** Ran SP% **115.9**
Speed ratings (Par 101): **105,99,87,81,77 72**
toteswingers: 1&2 £1.02, 1&3 £4.70, 2&3 £5.40 CSF £1.49 TOTE £1.10: £1.02, £1.80; EX 1.50.There was no bid for the winner.
Owner M Murphy **Bred** Gainsborough Farm Llc **Trained** Westoning, Beds

FOCUS
Only one counted based on the ratings in this uncompetitive seller, and the winner did not need to match his recent form.

2330 BRITISH STALLION STUDS SUPPORTING BRITISH RACING E B F MAIDEN STKS — 5f 2y

7:20 (7:20) (Class 4) 2-Y-O — £4,334 (£1,289; £644; £322) Stalls High

Form — RPR
2 **1** **Smoothtalkinrascal (IRE)**[31] 1499 2-9-3 0 ShaneKelly 10 90+
(Brian Meehan) *trckd ldrs: led 3f out: pushed out* **4/5**[1]
5 **2** 3 ¼ **Forray**[19] 1753 2-9-3 0 RichardMullen 2 78+
(Ed McMahon) *prom: rdn over 2f out: chsd wnr over 1f out: no imp* **4/1**[2]
3 *shd* **Ceelo** 2-9-3 0 RyanMoore 3 78+
(Richard Hannon) *mid-div: sn pushed along: hdwy over 1f out: styd on* **14/1**
4 3 ½ **Lincolnrose (IRE)** 2-8-12 0 JamesDoyle 8 60+
(Alan McCabe) *mid-div: hdwy over 1f out: nvr trbld ldrs* **40/1**
5 *nk* **Wrightington** 2-9-0 0 LeeTopliss[(3)] 9 64+
(Richard Fahey) *s.i.s: sn outpcd: nt clr run over 1f out: r.o ins fnl f: nrst fin* **22/1**
20 **6** 2 ¾ **Ouzinkie (IRE)**[16] 1842 2-9-3 0 MatthewDavies 7 54
(Mick Channon) *trckd ldrs: racd keenly: rdn 1/2-way: wknd fnl f* **16/1**
60 **7** ½ **Royal Jenray**[19] 1753 2-9-3 0 BarryMcHugh 5 53
(Jedd O'Keeffe) *led 2f: sn rdn: wknd 2f out* **150/1**
8 1 ½ **Dream Ally (IRE)** 2-9-3 0 TomQueally 11 47
(Jedd O'Keeffe) *sn outpcd* **22/1**
2 **9** *nk* **Sutton Sid**[10] 2039 2-9-3 0 PatCosgrave 1 46
(George Baker) *chsd ldrs: pushed along 1/2-way: wknd over 1f out* **7/1**[3]
10 5 **Setfiretotherain** 2-9-0 0 AmyRyan[(3)] 4 28
(Kevin Ryan) *chsd ldr: rdn 1/2-way: wknd over 1f out* **25/1**

1m 2.54s (2.54) **Going Correction** +0.40s/f (Good) **10** Ran SP% **116.2**
Speed ratings (Par 95): **95,89,89,84,83 79,78,75,75,67**
toteswingers: 1&2 £1.70, 1&3 £2.40, 2&3 £7.30 CSF £3.68 TOTE £1.40: £1.02, £1.10, £5.60; EX 4.70.
Owner Invictus **Bred** Tony Kilduff **Trained** Manton, Wilts

FOCUS
An interesting juvenile maiden over the minimum trip and a cosy winner with the field fairly strung out behind. He built on his debut promise and scored in good style.

NOTEBOOK
Smoothtalkinrascal(IRE), a half-brother to a 6f juvenile winner, had finished runner-up on his debut in a race that had already produced three subsequent winners and he added to that in emphatic fashion. He was always travelling strongly nearest the rail and settled matters before entering the final furlong. He looks capable of going on to better things. (tchd 8-11 and 5-6)
Forray had shown good pace on his debut but had not lasted home in the heavy ground. He was settled just off the pace this time but could not go with the winner and only just held on to second. Time may show he came up against a decent sort here. (op 6-1)
Ceelo, from the family of Breeders' Cup Turf winner Johar, missed a beat at the start and had to be ridden to get into the race. He stayed on steadily and should be sharper for the experience.
Lincolnrose(IRE), a half-sister to five winners including the sprinter Haajes, ran creditably, especially as she appeared to stumble at around the halfway mark.
Wrightington was another who dwelt slightly leaving the stalls, but this speedily bred gelding showed enough to suggest he can win races in time. (op 20-1)
Sutton Sid ran well against a subsequent winner on his all-weather debut but disappointed on this switch to turf. (op 8-1 tchd 9-1)

2331 JOHN FERNELEY H'CAP — 7f 9y

7:50 (7:51) (Class 4) (0-80,80) 3-Y-O — £4,528 (£1,347; £673; £336) Stalls High

Form — RPR
22-4 **1** **Dixie's Dream (IRE)**[26] 1612 3-9-4 77 RyanMoore 3 82
(Richard Hannon) *mid-div: pushed along 1/2-way: hdwy over 2f out: led over 1f out: rdn and hung lft ins fnl f: styd on* **11/4**[1]
-642 **2** ½ **Tight Lipped (IRE)**[10] 2021 3-9-1 74 JamesDoyle 9 78
(James Eustace) *chsd ldrs: rdn and ev ch over 1f out: styd on* **4/1**[2]
000- **3** 1 ½ **Ebony Clarets**[256] 5847 3-8-8 67 BarryMcHugh 5 67
(Richard Fahey) *plld hrd: led: rdn and hdd over 1f out: unable qck wl ins fnl f* **16/1**
033- **4** *nk* **Fabled City (USA)**[194] 7330 3-9-1 74 (t[1]) AdamKirby 1 73
(Clive Cox) *a.p: rdn and ev ch over 1f out: no ex wl ins fnl f* **12/1**
P1-0 **5** ½ **Brimstone Hill (IRE)**[26] 1612 3-9-2 75 WilliamCarson 4 72
(Anthony Carson) *s.i.s: hld up: hdwy over 1f out: r.o: nt rch ldrs* **33/1**
3-10 **6** 1 ½ **Fourth Of June (IRE)**[16] 1860 3-9-7 80 TomMcLaughlin 10 73
(Ed Dunlop) *hld up: hdwy over 1f out: r.o: eased towards fin* **6/1**[3]
6-35 **7** 6 **Chorister Sport (IRE)**[20] 1731 3-8-7 66 oh1 LeeNewman 6 43
(William Jarvis) *plld hrd and prom: pushed along 1/2-way: wknd over 1f out* **50/1**
1202 **8** *nk* **Alkadi (IRE)**[18] 1798 3-9-2 75 JoeFanning 2 51
(Mark Johnston) *w ldr tl rdn over 1f out: wknd fnl f* **4/1**[2]
203- **9** 4 **Amoure Medici**[184] 7491 3-9-3 76 TomQueally 8 42
(Noel Quinlan) *stdd s: hld up: plld hrd: wknd over 1f out* **8/1**
410- **10** 4 **Chandigarh (IRE)**[246] 6196 3-8-13 77 ShaneBKelly[(5)] 7 32
(Paul Fitzsimons) *chsd ldrs: rdn 1/2-way: wknd over 2f out* **25/1**

1m 30.28s (4.08) **Going Correction** +0.40s/f (Good) **10** Ran SP% **114.4**
Speed ratings (Par 101): **92,91,89,89,88 87,80,79,75,70**
toteswingers: 1&2 £1.70, 1&3 £10.20, 2&3 £58.90 CSF £13.04 CT £147.26 TOTE £3.80: £2.10, £1.70, £4.80; EX 16.10.
Owner William Stobart **Bred** Miss Joan Murphy **Trained** East Everleigh, Wilts

FOCUS
A competitive 3yo handicap and a good finish. Pretty straightforward form.

2332 SARTORIUS MAIDEN STKS — 5f 218y

8:20 (8:21) (Class 5) 3-Y-O — £2,385 (£704; £352) Stalls High

Form — RPR
32-3 **1** **Ladyship**[38] 1357 3-8-12 79 RyanMoore 3 90+
(Sir Michael Stoute) *chsd ldrs: rdn over 1f out: styd on to ld wl ins fnl f* **15/8**[1]
22- **2** ¾ **Tickled Pink (IRE)**[311] 4052 3-8-12 0 TomQueally 8 88+
(Sir Henry Cecil) *led 5f out: rdn over 1f out: hdd wl ins fnl f* **15/8**[1]
4 **3** 3 ¾ **Art Form**[16] 1843 3-8-12 0 (t) ShaneKelly 9 76
(Alan McCabe) *led 1f: chsd ldrs: rdn over 1f out: wkng whn hung rt ins fnl f* **25/1**
3 **4** 3 ½ **Catwalk (IRE)**[24] 1637 3-8-12 0 JamesDoyle 10 65
(James Fanshawe) *chsd ldrs: rdn over 2f out: wknd over 1f out* **7/2**[2]
24-0 **5** 1 ¾ **More Than Words (IRE)**[32] 1472 3-8-12 76 KieranO'Neill 7 59
(Richard Hannon) *sn pushed along in rr: hdwy 1/2-way: rdn and wknd over 1f out* **7/1**[3]
6 4 ½ **Duke Of Destiny (IRE)** 3-9-3 0 PatCosgrave 2 50
(Ed Walker) *s.i.s: hdwy over 4f out: rdn and wknd over 2f out* **50/1**
00 **7** 3 ½ **Roundelay**[42] 1257 3-8-12 0 WilliamCarson 6 34
(Anthony Carson) *chsd ldrs tl rdn and wknd over 2f out* **150/1**
0 **8** 3 ½ **College Doll**[16] 1843 3-8-9 0 AmyRyan[(3)] 1 22
(Christine Dunnett) *s.i.s: sn pushed along in rr: wknd 1/2-way* **150/1**
06 **9** 7 **Mystical Witch**[21] 1705 3-8-12 0 TomMcLaughlin 5
(Christine Dunnett) *plld hrd and prom: lost pl over 4f out: wknd 1/2-way* **200/1**

1m 15.19s (2.19) **Going Correction** +0.40s/f (Good) **9** Ran SP% **111.9**
Speed ratings (Par 99): **101,100,95,90,88 82,77,72,63**
toteswingers: 1&2 £1.30, 1&3 £6.50, 2&3 £7.60 CSF £5.18 TOTE £2.40: £1.10, £1.40, £6.60; EX 5.70.
Owner Cheveley Park Stud **Bred** Cheveley Park Stud Ltd **Trained** Newmarket, Suffolk

FOCUS
A fair maiden judged on the figures of those with ratings and several with decent pedigrees. All but one of the runners were fillies and the joint favourites had the race between them from well over a furlong out. The winner is the type to progress.

2333 HENRY ALKEN H'CAP — 1m 3f 183y

8:50 (8:50) (Class 5) (0-70,70) 3-Y-O — £2,264 (£673; £336; £168) Stalls Low

Form — RPR
-441 **1** **Bridgehampton**[6] 2141 3-8-8 57 5ex RyanMoore 7 63
(Michael Bell) *hld up: plld hrd: hdwy 9f out: stdd and lost pl over 6f out: pushed along and hdwy over 2f out: rdn to ld and hung rt fr over 1f out: styd on u.p* **8/13**[1]
4-06 **2** ½ **News Show**[14] 1906 3-9-1 64 MartinLane 3 69
(David Simcock) *hld up: hdwy over 3f out: rdn and ev ch fr over 1f out: styd on* **20/1**
-213 **3** ¾ **Naseem Alyasmeen (IRE)**[26] 1597 3-9-7 70 SamHitchcott 5 74
(Mick Channon) *hld up: hdwy over 4f out: rdn and ev ch over 1f out: styd on* **8/1**[3]
20-0 **4** ½ **Arley Hall**[38] 1363 3-9-2 68 LeeTopliss[(3)] 8 71
(Richard Fahey) *broke wl: stdd and lost pl after 1f: hld up: hdwy over 3f out: rdn and swtchd lft over 1f out: nt clr run ent fnl f: r.o* **22/1**
4234 **5** *shd* **Torero**[17] 1992 3-9-4 70 AmyRyan[(3)] 10 73
(Kevin Ryan) *chsd ldr tl led over 9f out: rdn and hdd over 1f out: styd on* **16/1**
0-31 **6** 6 **Like Clockwork**[20] 1726 3-8-12 61 TomQueally 6 54
(Mark H Tompkins) *prom: n.m.r and lost pl after 2f: hdwy u.p and hung rt over 1f out: no ex ins fnl f* **11/2**[2]
2213 **7** 8 **Za'Lan (USA)**[37] 1390 3-9-5 68 (b[1]) JoeFanning 1 49
(Mark Johnston) *sn pushed along to chse ldrs: rdn and ev ch over 2f out: wknd over 1f out* **14/1**
5-32 **8** 12 **Landown Littlerock**[12] 1992 3-8-6 62 JackDuern[(7)] 9 23
(Reg Hollinshead) *prom: racd keenly: rdn and wknd over 2f out* **14/1**
4-65 **9** ½ **Our Ivor**[10] 2049 3-8-7 56 oh2 WilliamCarson 2 17
(Michael Appleby) *led: racd keenly: hdd over 9f out: chsd ldr: rdn over 2f out: sn wknd* **80/1**

2m 40.76s (6.86) **Going Correction** +0.50s/f (Yiel) **9** Ran SP% **118.0**
Speed ratings (Par 99): **97,96,96,95,95 91,86,78,78**
toteswingers: 1&2 £6.10, 1&3 £2.00, 2&3 £18.60 CSF £19.48 CT £63.08 TOTE £1.40: £1.02, £2.70, £2.60; EX 18.90.
Owner M B Hawtin **Bred** The Kingwood Partnership **Trained** Newmarket, Suffolk

FOCUS
A modest but tightly knit contest and there were half a dozen spread across the track and still in contention 2f out. the winner did not match his Beverley form.
T/Plt: £7.80 to a £1 stake. Pool: £59,726.15. 5,542.68 winning tickets. T/Qpdt: £3.20 to a £1 stake. Pool: £4,965.90. 1,114.52 winning tickets. CR

2118 REDCAR (L-H)
Monday, May 21

OFFICIAL GOING: Good (7.8)
Wind: Virtually nil Weather: Overcast

2334 FOLLOW REDCARRACING ON FACEBOOK AND TWITTER MEDIAN AUCTION MAIDEN STKS — 6f

2:10 (2:11) (Class 5) 2-Y-O — £1,940 (£577; £288; £144) Stalls Centre

Form — RPR
4 **1** **Hiddon Coin (IRE)**[16] 1861 2-9-3 0 DanielTudhope 10 76+
(David O'Meara) *mde all: rdn over 1f out: kpt on wl* **15/8**[1]
2 ¾ **Lucy Minaj** 2-8-12 0 TomEaves 11 68+
(Bryan Smart) *trckd ldrs: smooth hdwy 2f out: rdn to chse wnr ins fnl f and sn ev ch: no imp towards fin* **8/1**
0 **3** 4 ½ **Lady Ibrox**[14] 1911 2-8-12 0 TonyHamilton 7 53
(Alan Brown) *hld up: t.k.h: hdwy over 2f out: rdn to chse ldrs over 1f out: one pce fnl f* **66/1**
F **4** 1 ¼ **Silver Fawn (IRE)**[23] 1651 2-9-3 0 DuranFentiman 5 54+
(John Weymes) *in tch: rdn along: lost pl and bhd 1/2-way: hdwy 2f out: styd on wl appr fnl f: nrst fin* **40/1**
5 1 **Eastern Dragon (IRE)** 2-9-0 0 JulieBurke[(3)] 3 51+
(Kevin Ryan) *s.i.s and in rr hdwy 2f out: kpt on appr fnl f: nrst fin* **15/2**[3]
6 *nk* **Indastar** 2-9-3 0 MartinLane 12 50+
(Kevin M Prendergast) *trckd ldrs: hdwy 2f out: rdn to chse wnr 1f out and ev ch: sn wknd* **14/1**
7 ¾ **Twinwood Star (IRE)** 2-8-12 0 LiamJones 1 43
(John Weymes) *cl up: rdn along 2f out: wknd appr fnl f* **40/1**
8 4 **Old Man Clegg** 2-9-3 0 PaddyAspell 4 35
(Michael Easterby) *s.i.s: a towards rr* **16/1**
9 4 ½ **Bollin Billy** 2-9-3 0 DavidAllan 2 20+
(Tim Easterby) *dwlt: a towards rr* **11/1**
0 **10** *nk* **Special Report (IRE)**[33] 1435 2-9-3 0 AndrewMullen 6 19
(Nigel Tinkler) *prom: rdn along bef 1/2-way: sn wknd* **66/1**
11 ½ **Red Highlites (IRE)** 2-8-12 0 GrahamLee 9 13
(Ann Duffield) *t.k.h: chsd ldrs: rdn along 1/2-way: sn wknd* **12/1**
66 **12** 14 **Brazilian Clown (IRE)**[12] 1972 2-9-3 0 RichardKingscote 13
(Tom Dascombe) *chsd ldrs on outer: rdn along bef 1/2-way: sn wknd* **4/1**[2]

1m 16.89s (5.09) **Going Correction** +0.50s/f (Yiel) **12** Ran SP% **114.1**
Speed ratings (Par 93): **86,85,79,77,76 75,74,69,63,62 62,43**
toteswingers: 1&2 £3.90, 1&3 £22.60, 2&3 £38.60 CSF £16.24 TOTE £1.90: £1.10, £3.40, £24.70; EX 14.80.
Owner Hambleton Racing Ltd - Three In One **Bred** Noel & Anthony O'Callaghan **Trained** Nawton, N Yorks

FOCUS
An ordinary 6f median auction maiden 2yo race and the first two finished clear. The form is rated around the mid point of the race averages and the first two can do better.

NOTEBOOK
Hiddon Coin(IRE), who finished strongly after a slow start and looking clueless on his debut at Thirsk, was a different proposition here. He knew his job and was always doing more than enough to hold the runner-up. Still unfurnished, he should improve again. (tchd 7-4 and 2-1 in a place)
Lucy Minaj, a daughter of Dylan Thomas out of a mare that won over 6f and 7f, was quite keen. She pulled clear with the winner and should have no difficulty going one better. (tchd 17-2)
Lady Ibrox, keen early, showed a lot more than on her debut.
Silver Fawn(IRE), who fell early on first time, stayed on from last and this will have taught him something. (tchd 33-1)
Eastern Dragon(IRE), a half-brother to a winner in Poland, stayed on in good style late on after a very sluggish start. He will be much sharper next time. (op 9-1)
Indastar, first foal of an unraced mare, showed plenty of toe before tiring. (op 16-1)
Brazilian Clown(IRE), having his third run, was under pressure at halfway and dropped right away before being eased. He seems to be going the wrong way. (op 7-2 tchd 5-1)

2335 WIN A VIP DAY OUT @ REDCARRACING.CO.UK MAIDEN FILLIES' STKS 7f
2:40 (2:43) (Class 5) 3-Y-0+ **£2,045** (£603; £302) **Stalls** Centre

Form RPR
2 **1** **Liliargh (IRE)**[26] 1595 3-9-0 0 DanielTudhope 2 74+
(Ben Haslam) *cl up: led wl over 2f out: rdn wl over 1f out: styd on* **6/4**[1]
4-0 **2** *1* **Sabore**[16] 1864 3-9-0 0 TonyHamilton 6 70
(Richard Fahey) *hld up in tch: hdwy 2f out: carried hd high and rdn wl over 1f out: styd on ent fnl f: edgd lft and hld nr fin* **20/1**
4 **3** *3 1/4* **Gladsome**[9] 2095 4-9-11 0 MichaelStainton 5 65
(Jason Ward) *led: pushed along and hdd wl over 2f out: rdn over 1f out: kpt on one pce fnl f* **12/1**
6 **4** *1 3/4* **Dolly Diva**[7] 2121 3-9-0 0 MickyFenton 15 57
(Paul Midgley) *wnt rt s and bhd: hdwy wl over 2f out: rdn wl over 1f out: styd on appr fnl f: nrst fin* **33/1**
2-0 **5** *3/4* **Srinagar Girl**[38] 1357 3-9-0 0 IanMongan 3 54
(Sir Henry Cecil) *in tch: hdwy to chse ldng pair over 2f out: rdn wl over 1f out: wknd appr fnl f* **9/4**[2]
6 *8* **Waveguide (IRE)** 3-9-0 0 MartinLane 7 33+
(David Simcock) *towards rr whn stmbld after 1f: hdwy and in tch 3f out: sn chsng ldrs: rdn over 2f out and sn wknd* **15/2**[3]
0- **7** *nse* **Majestic Bounty**[268] 5486 3-9-0 0 KellyHarrison 13 33
(Chris Fairhurst) *towards rr: hdwy over 2f out: sn rdn and plugged on: nvr nr ldrs* **66/1**
00 **8** *5* **Under Par**[28] 1560 4-9-4 0 DavidSimmonson(7) 4 23
(Michael Easterby) *cl up: rdn along wl over 2f out: grad wknd* **100/1**
000- **9** *1 1/2* **Queen's Princess**[263] 5649 4-9-11 25 PaddyAspell 12 19
(John Wainwright) *a towards rr* **150/1**
0-0 **10** *1* **Serendipity Blue**[60] 1001 3-9-0 0 GrahamGibbons 8
(John Weymes) *chsd ldrs: rdn along 3f out: sn wknd* **100/1**
11 *nk* **Double Proposition** 3-9-0 0 TomEaves 14
(Bryan Smart) *in tch on wd outside: rdn along 1/2-way: sn wknd* **25/1**
05-0 **12** *1 1/4* **Phair Winter**[13] 1953 4-9-6 45 GarryWhillans(5) 10
(Alan Brown) *chsd ldrs to 1/2-way: sn wknd* **50/1**
5- **13** *4* **Selective Spirit**[359] 2485 3-9-0 0 DuranFentiman 9
(John Weymes) *t.k.h: a towards rr* **18/1**
14 *3/4* **Awaywithefairies** 3-9-0 0 GrahamLee 11
(Richard Ford) *a towards rr* **40/1**
05 **15** *2 1/4* **Toodeloo**[7] 2121 3-8-11 0 JulieBurke(3) 1
(Kevin Ryan) *prom: rdn along bef 1/2-way and sn wknd* **25/1**

1m 29.18s (4.68) **Going Correction** +0.50s/f (Yiel)
WFA 3 from 4yo 11lb **15** Ran SP% **119.4**
Speed ratings (Par 100): **93,91,88,86,85 76,76,70,68,67 67,65,61,60,57**
toteswingers: 1&2 £7.30, 1&3 £4.00, 2&3 £9.00 CSF £39.38 TOTE £2.50: £1.30, £2.80, £3.40; EX 28.80.
Owner Middleham Park Racing XXVII **Bred** Camogue Stud Ltd **Trained** Middleham Moor, N Yorks

FOCUS
No strength in depth in this modest maiden fillies' race, and it's doubtful it took much winning. The form is rated around the third.

2336 JOHN SMITH'S REDCAR STRAIGHT-MILE H'CAP (QUALIFIER) 1m
3:10 (3:11) (Class 5) (0-70,70) 3-Y-0 **£1,940** (£577; £288; £144) **Stalls** Centre

Form RPR
00-3 **1** **Forget Me Not Lane (IRE)**[43] 1238 3-9-1 **64** GrahamLee 8 70+
(Kevin Ryan) *chsd ldrs: rdn and outpcd over 2f out: styd on to ld nr fin* **7/1**[3]
03-3 **2** *nk* **My Guardian Angel**[41] 1288 3-9-4 **67** DavidAllan 12 72+
(Mark H Tompkins) *trckd ldrs: chal over 2f out: led ins fnl f: hdd nr fin* **7/1**[3]
50-4 **3** *1/2* **Double Cee**[9] 2089 3-8-9 **58** TonyHamilton 3 62
(Richard Fahey) *chsd ldrs: drvn over 3f out: styd on ins fnl f* **15/2**
00-6 **4** *nk* **Baltic Fizz (IRE)**[128] 180 3-8-13 **65** MichaelMetcalfe(3) 13 68
(Mrs K Burke) *in rr: hdwy over 2f out: n.m.r appr fnl f: styd on wl towards fin* **16/1**
46-5 **5** *nk* **Brockwell**[26] 1606 3-9-5 **68** RichardKingscote 2 71+
(Tom Dascombe) *chsd ldrs: drvn 3f out: edgd rt over 1f out: kpt on ins fnl f* **4/1**[1]
20-6 **6** *1 1/4* **Bollin Tommy**[19] 1757 3-9-0 **63** GrahamGibbons 11 63
(Tim Easterby) *led: edgd rt over 1f out: hdd ins fnl f: wknd whn hmpd towards fin* **33/1**
600- **7** *3* **Roll Of Thunder**[210] 7051 3-8-5 **54** FrannyNorton 9 47
(John Quinn) *mid-div: hdwy over 2f out: nt clr run appr fnl f: kpt on towards fin* **16/1**
1-16 **8** *1 1/2* **Daddy Warbucks (IRE)**[43] 1241 3-9-6 **69** AdrianNicholls 14 58
(David Nicholls) *trckd ldrs: chal over 2f out: wknd fnl f* **6/1**[2]
3-66 **9** *1* **Millymonkin**[14] 1918 3-9-0 **63** PaddyAspell 4 50
(Michael Easterby) *s.i.s: sn mid-div: effrt over 2f out: wknd over 1f out* **20/1**
-060 **10** *1 3/4* **The Blue Banana (IRE)**[18] 1798 3-9-4 **70** JulieBurke(3) 7 53
(Edwin Tuer) *mid-div: nvr a factor* **8/1**
06-0 **11** *1* **Brailsford (IRE)**[40] 1322 3-9-6 **69** RoystonFfrench 10 50
(Ismail Mohammed) *t.k.h: hdwy to chse ldrs over 2f out: wknd over 1f out* **16/1**
30-0 **12** *5* **Shotley Music**[16] 1864 3-9-4 **67** MichaelO'Connell 16 36
(Neville Bycroft) *s.s: bhd and hung lft: nvr on terms* **33/1**
000- **13** *1* **True Bond**[178] 7541 3-8-11 **60** TomEaves 15 27
(Geoffrey Oldroyd) *a in rr: bhd fnl 2f* **33/1**
000 **14** *2 3/4* **Gone By Sunrise**[7] 2130 3-8-2 **51** oh2 (t) MartinLane 1 12
(Derek Shaw) *in rr: bhd whn eased over 1f out* **66/1**
040- **15** *11* **Ellastina (IRE)**[220] 6842 3-8-8 **64** GeorgeChaloner(7) 5
(Richard Fahey) *chsd ldrs: lost pl over 2f out* **16/1**
06-3 **16** *8* **Becksies**[26] 1596 3-8-2 **51** oh6 DuranFentiman 6
(Paul Midgley) *t.k.h: trckd ldrs: wknd 3f out: sn bhd* **33/1**

1m 43.4s (5.40) **Going Correction** +0.50s/f (Yiel) **16** Ran SP% **123.7**
Speed ratings (Par 99): **93,92,92,91,91 90,87,85,84,83 82,77,76,73,62 54**
toteswingers: 1&2 £8.30, 1&3 £13.70, 2&3 £9.80 CSF £52.43 CT £405.00 TOTE £7.60: £1.90, £2.60, £2.40, £4.80; EX 38.20.
Owner J Hanson **Bred** Mrs Arkada Partnership **Trained** Hambleton, N Yorks
■ Stewards' Enquiry : David Allan caution: careless riding. two-day ban: use of whip (4-5 June)

FOCUS
A competitive 51-70 3yo handicap with little between the first five at the line. Modest form, but pretty sound.
Gone By Sunrise Official explanation: jockey said that the gelding had a breathing problem

2337 VOLTIGEUR RESTAURANT £10.95 TWO COURSE SPECIAL H'CAP 5f
3:40 (3:40) (Class 3) (0-90,90) 3-Y-0+
£3,735 (£1,118; £559; £279; £139; £70) **Stalls** Centre

Form RPR
0-36 **1** **Bedloe's Island (IRE)**[4] 2208 7-8-12 **76** MichaelO'Connell 4 87
(Neville Bycroft) *trckd ldrs: smooth hdwy 2f out: qcknd to ld ins fnl f: kpt on strly* **2/1**[1]
-616 **2** *2 1/2* **Noodles Blue Boy**[2] 2289 6-9-4 **82** PaddyAspell 6 84
(Ollie Pears) *cl up: rdn to ld over 2f out: drvn and hdd ins fnl f: kpt on* **8/1**
16-0 **3** *nk* **Another Wise Kid (IRE)**[24] 1643 4-9-5 **83** MickyFenton 3 84
(Paul Midgley) *trckd ldng pair: hdwy over 2f out: rdn wl over 1f out: one pce fnl f* **10/3**[2]
0066 **4** *3 1/4* **Captain Scooby**[24] 1643 6-8-13 **77** KellyHarrison 2 66
(Richard Guest) *towards rr: hdwy over 2f out: sn rdn and kpt on: nvr nr ldrs* **14/1**
4406 **5** *1/2* **Electric Qatar**[10] 2028 3-8-5 **77** RichardKingscote 8 65
(Tom Dascombe) *rrd s: sn in tch: hdwy 2f out: sn rdn and no imp over 1f out* **16/1**
40- **6** *1/2* **Azzurra Du Caprio (IRE)**[256] 5852 4-9-8 **86** GrahamLee 1 72
(Ben Haslam) *in tch: effrt 2f out: sn rdn and no hdwy* **9/2**[3]
5/-0 **7** *8* **Nosedive**[12] 1977 5-9-12 **90** AdrianNicholls 7 47
(David Nicholls) *hld up: a in rr* **20/1**
60-0 **8** *4* **Master Rooney (IRE)**[33] 1438 6-9-8 **86** TomEaves 5 29
(Bryan Smart) *led: rdn along 1/2-way: sn hdd & wknd* **8/1**

1m 0.18s (1.58) **Going Correction** +0.50s/f (Yiel)
WFA 3 from 4yo+ 8lb **8** Ran SP% **114.1**
Speed ratings (Par 107): **107,103,102,97,96 95,82,76**
toteswingers: 1&2 £4.20, 1&3 £2.40, 2&3 £4.40 CSF £18.86 CT £50.57 TOTE £3.30: £1.20, £1.10, £2.00; EX 16.10.
Owner J G Lumsden & M F Hogan **Bred** Dr Dean Harron **Trained** Brandsby, N Yorks

FOCUS
A 77-90 sprint handicap and a very ready still unexposed winner who set a personal best.

NOTEBOOK
Bedloe's Island(IRE) had finished a very good sixth in a much more competitive handicap at York four days earlier when 6lb wrong. He travelled supremely well and took this with the minimum of fuss - his three career wins have now come over this C&D. Clearly a late developer, he should continue to give a good account of himself. (op 5-2)
Noodles Blue Boy, who ended a lengthy losing run from a favourable draw two outings ago at Thirsk, had finished only sixth on a return there two days ago. He mastered the pacesetter, but was just a target for the winner. (op 6-1)
Another Wise Kid(IRE), a winner four times last year, showed he is back in form and he should add to his record this time when the ground firms up. (op 3-1 tchd 4-1)
Captain Scooby stayed on down the outside when it was all over and needs a return to six. (op 16-1)
Electric Qatar, who has proved a major let down, ruined his chance by rearing at the start.
Azzurra Du Caprio(IRE), who won first time out last year, has started her 4yo career on a stiff-looking mark. (op 7-1)

2338 RACING UK ON CHANNEL 432 MAIDEN CLAIMING STKS 5f
4:10 (4:11) (Class 6) 2-Y-0 **£1,704** (£503; £251) **Stalls** Centre

Form RPR
30 **1** **Lexi The Princess (IRE)**[11] 1997 2-8-10 0 FrannyNorton 3 66+
(Kevin Ryan) *led: rdn along 2f out: hdd over 1f out: rallied ins fnl f to ld nr fin* **7/2**[1]
2 *1/2* **Jamesbo's Girl** 2-8-6 0 AdrianNicholls 1 58
(David Nicholls) *cl up: led over 1f out: sn rdn and edgd rt ins fnl f: wknd and hdd nr fin* **13/2**
3 *3* **Reconsider Baby (IRE)** 2-8-10 0 MartinLane 2 51
(Mrs K Burke) *wnt lft s: in tch: hdwy 2f out: sn rdn and kpt on fnl f* **8/1**
4 **4** *nk* **Spray Tan**[14] 1903 2-8-6 0 LiamJones 6 46
(Tony Carroll) *wnt lft s: prom: rdn 2f out: grad wknd* **4/1**[2]
5 *2 3/4* **Riponian** 2-8-11 0 MichaelO'Connell 4 41
(Kate Walton) *dwlt and hmpd s: in rr tl hdwy 2f out: rdn and hung rt over 1f out: no imp* **14/1**
6 *1 1/4* **Blades Rose** 2-8-0 0 JulieBurke(3) 5 29
(Richard Fahey) *hmpd s: hld up towards rr: hdwy whn n.m.r and hmpd over 1f out: one pce after* **6/1**[3]
46 **7** *11* **Maggies Gem (IRE)**[26] 1594 2-8-1 0 ow1 DuranFentiman 8
(Paul Midgley) *chsd ldrs on outer: rdn along 1/2-way: sn wknd and towards rr whn hmpd over 1f out* **22/1**
260 **8** *4* **Stripped Bear (IRE)**[14] 1911 2-8-11 0 RichardKingscote 7
(Tom Dascombe) *chsd ldrs: rdn along 1/2-way: sn wknd and towards rr whn hmpd over 1f out* **4/1**[2]

1m 2.85s (4.25) **Going Correction** +0.50s/f (Yiel) **8** Ran SP% **112.0**
Speed ratings (Par 91): **86,85,80,79,75 73,55,49**
toteswingers: 1&2 £9.70, 1&3 £4.70, 2&3 £7.60 CSF £25.32 TOTE £2.90: £1.10, £3.70, £5.50; EX 33.10.
Owner Dr Marwan Koukash **Bred** Mountarmstrong Stud **Trained** Hambleton, N Yorks

FOCUS
A low-grade 2yo claimer with all but one of the eight runners fillies. The second was unlucky to bump into the winner at this level.

NOTEBOOK
Lexi The Princess(IRE), who swerved badly from the outside draw at Chester, had finished third in maiden company on her debut on the all-weather at Wolverhampton. Her rider never picked up his whip and put her head in front near the line. She will be suited by a step up to 6f or even 7f. (op 9-2)
Jamesbo's Girl, a bargain basement purchase, went on soon after halfway. She edged right and hung fire in front before being nabbed near the line. She will certainly win a seller. (op 5-1 tchd 7-1 and 15-2 in a place)

Reconsider Baby(IRE), out of an unraced mare, missed a beat at the start. She will come on for the outing and should win a seller. (tchd 7-1)
Spray Tan, fourth in a weak auction maiden at Bath, was much too keen for her own good. (op 7-2)
Riponian, the only colt in the line-up, made a satisfactory debut after a tardy start. (op 16-1)
Blades Rose, out of a mare that never saw a racetrack, showed a glimmer of ability first time. (tchd 11-2)

2339 LADIES' DAY ON SATURDAY 23RD JUNE MEDIAN AUCTION MAIDEN STKS 1m

4:40 (4:41) (Class 6) 3-5-Y-O **£1,704** (£503; £251) **Stalls** Centre

Form RPR
060- **1** **Kathlatino**209 7078 5-9-8 47 KellyHarrison 3 64
(Micky Hammond) *trckd ldrs: hdwy and cl up 1/2-way: led over 2f out: sn jnd and rdn over 1f out: drvn ins fnl f: sltly hmpd and hld on wl towards fin* **33/1**
200- **2** *shd* **Come Here Yew (IRE)**227 6674 4-9-13 76 DanielTudhope 10 69
(Declan Carroll) *trckd ldrs: hdwy and cl up over 2f out: rdn to chal over 1f out and ev ch: drvn and hung lft ins fnl f: no ex nr fin* **4/6**1
3 *1 1/2* **Anychanceofabirdie (USA)** 3-9-1 0 MartinLane 8 62
(David Simcock) *in tch: hdwy 3f out: rdn to chse ldng pair wl over 2f out: kpt on fnl f* **5/1**2
4 *9* **Special Mix**131 4-9-6 0 DavidSimmonson(7) 9 45
(Michael Easterby) *hld up: hdwy 3f out: rdn 2f out: kpt on appr fnl f: n.d* **12/1**
000 **5** *5* **Icewan**16 1864 3-9-1 0 MickyFenton 1 30
(Paul Midgley) *s.i.s and bhd tl sme late hdwy* **16/1**
0 **6** *1 1/4* **Certainly Elusive (IRE)**9 2095 3-8-10 0 GarryWhillans(5) 4 27
(Alan Swinbank) *prom on outer: rdn along 1/2-way: sn wknd* **10/1**3
7 *3/4* **Medecis Mountain** 3-9-1 0 PaddyAspell 5 26
(John Wainwright) *in tch: pushed along over 3f out: sn wknd* **66/1**
0 **8** *1 1/4* **Jerry Ellen (IRE)**16 1843 3-9-1 0 DavidAllan 11 23
(Tim Easterby) *cl up: led wl over 3f out: rdn and hdd wl over 2f out: sn wknd* **20/1**
9 *9* **Airmyles** 4-9-13 0 TomEaves 6
(Tracy Waggott) *s.i.s: a in rr* **25/1**
10 *1/2* **Tomasini** 3-9-1 0 DuranFentiman 2
(John Weymes) *chsd ldrs on outer: rdn along 1/2-way: sn wknd* **28/1**
11 *30* **Western Apache (IRE)**14 5-9-13 0 MichaelO'Connell 7
(Simon West) *led: rdn along 1/2-way: sn hdd & wknd* **100/1**

1m 43.73s (5.73) **Going Correction** +0.50s/f (Yiel)
WFA 3 from 4yo+ 12lb **11** Ran SP% **116.8**
Speed ratings (Par 101): **91,90,89,80,75 74,73,72,63,62 32**
toteswingers: 1&2 £11.60, 1&3 £26.20, 2&3 £2.50 CSF £53.82 TOTE £48.90: £7.80, £1.10, £1.60; EX 97.20.
Owner M D Hammond **Bred** Mrs Jayce Haley **Trained** Middleham Moor, N Yorks

FOCUS
A very weak median auction maiden totally lacking any strength in depth and an unlikely winner. The second is rated 10lb off his best.

2340 YORKSHIRE RACING SUMMER FESTIVAL 21ST - 29TH JULY H'CAP (DIV I) 1m 2f

5:10 (5:11) (Class 6) (0-55,55) 3-Y-O **£1,704** (£503; £251) **Stalls** Low

Form RPR
0-63 **1** **Lady Kashaan (IRE)**37 1386 3-8-10 49 AndrewElliott 15 57
(Alan Swinbank) *trckd ldrs on outer: outpcd over 3f out: hdwy over 2f out: r.o to ld last 50yds* **10/1**
0-23 **2** *3/4* **Rosie's Lady (IRE)**26 1600 3-8-13 52 GrahamLee 3 59
(David O'Meara) *s.i.s: sn mid-div: hdwy on ins to chse ldrs 3f out: nt clr run: swtchd rt over 1f out: kpt on towards fin* **8/1**
066- **3** *1* **Capriska**212 7038 3-8-12 51 JamieMackay 8 55
(Willie Musson) *mid-div: drvn 6f out: hdwy and c outside over 3f out: led over 1f out: hdd and no ex last 50yds* **6/1**3
553- **4** *hd* **Red Hermes (IRE)**158 7769 3-8-7 46 DavidAllan 10 51
(Mark H Tompkins) *mid-div: outpcd over 3f out: hdwy 2f out: nt clr run and swtchd rt 1f out: styd on wl towards fin* **16/1**
4-53 **5** *1 1/4* **Red Tyke (IRE)**14 1918 3-8-11 50 MichaelO'Connell 5 51
(John Quinn) *chsd ldrs: kpt on same pce fnl 100yds* **9/1**
6-03 **6** *nk* **Remember Rocky**7 2118 3-9-2 55 (v1) TomEaves 9 56
(Steve Gollings) *chsd ldrs: kpt on same pce appr fnl f* **6/1**3
5251 **7** *2 1/2* **Skyeron**5 2162 3-9-2 55 6ex LiamJones 1 51
(Mark Brisbourne) *led: hdd over 1f out: wknd fnl 50yds* **5/1**2
0-06 **8** *9* **Oops Caroline (IRE)**14 1916 3-9-0 53 DanielTudhope 7 31
(David O'Meara) *in rr: styd on fnl 3f: nvr nr ldrs* **20/1**
0-00 **9** *14* **Gabrial's Layla (IRE)**14 1915 3-8-8 47 FrannyNorton 11
(Mark Johnston) *in rr: bhd fnl 4f* **25/1**
30-0 **10** *1 1/2* **Brasingaman Espee**26 1600 3-8-7 46 oh1 AndrewMullen 14
(George Moore) *chsd ldrs: wknd over 3f out* **66/1**
0-45 **11** *1 1/4* **Divine Success (IRE)**14 1918 3-9-1 54 TonyHamilton 4
(Richard Fahey) *in tch: lost pl over 6f out: sn bhd* **18/1**
4532 **12** *1 1/4* **Martha's Way**26 1600 3-9-2 55 GrahamGibbons 2
(Michael Easterby) *s.i.s: sn trcking ldrs: wknd 2f out* **9/2**1
0-05 **13** *29* **Actor (IRE)**26 1597 3-8-7 46 oh1 (t) DuranFentiman 6
(John Weymes) *s.i.s: wl bhd fnl 4f: t.o* **66/1**
02-5 **14** *4* **Istan Star (USA)**12 1992 3-9-0 53 RoystonFfrench 13
(Julie Camacho) *in tch on outer: lost pl over 6f out: sme hdwy over 3f out: sn wknd and bhd* **33/1**

2m 13.75s (6.65) **Going Correction** +0.50s/f (Yiel) **14** Ran SP% **119.3**
Speed ratings (Par 97): **93,92,91,91,90 90,88,81,69,68 67,66,43,40**
toteswingers: 1&2 £16.80, 1&3 £23.30, 2&3 £16.50 CSF £82.90 CT £528.69 TOTE £11.70: £4.60, £1.30, £3.10; EX 89.00.
Owner G Brogan **Bred** Corduff Stud Ltd & J Corcoran **Trained** Melsonby, N Yorks
■ Stewards' Enquiry : Andrew Elliott two-day ban: use of whip (4-5 June)

FOCUS
Part one of a rock bottom 46-55 3yo handicap, and slightly the faster. There were seven in with a chance entering the final furlong. The first two came from the same Newcastel race.
Martha's Way Official explanation: trainer's representative could offer no explanation for the filly's performance

2341 YORKSHIRE RACING SUMMER FESTIVAL 21ST - 29TH JULY H'CAP (DIV II) 1m 2f

5:40 (5:43) (Class 6) (0-55,55) 3-Y-O **£1,704** (£503; £251) **Stalls** Low

Form RPR
00-4 **1** **Fine Altomis**40 1320 3-9-2 55 TomEaves 3 66
(Michael Dods) *mde all: rdn clr 3f out: drvn ins fnl f: kpt on* **2/1**1
0-00 **2** *1 1/4* **Penang Pegasus**37 1385 3-8-7 46 oh1 RoystonFfrench 1 55
(David O'Meara) *hld up and bhd: hung rt and wd home turn: hdwy 3f out: rdn to chse ldrs over 2f out: drvn to chse wnr and edgd lft ent fnl f: kpt on* **16/1**
6-00 **3** *8* **Hopes Rebellion**26 1596 3-8-11 50 GrahamGibbons 6 43
(Declan Carroll) *midfield: hdwy over 3f out: rdn to chse ldrs over 2f out: sn drvn and one pce* **33/1**
400 **4** *2 1/4* **Ossie's Dancer**40 1301 3-8-5 47 AdamBeschizza(3) 10 35
(Robert Cowell) *hld up towards rr: hdwy over 3f out: rdn to chse ldrs 2f out: sn drvn and kpt on one pce* **14/1**
600- **5** *4 1/2* **Pearl Catcher (IRE)**263 5645 3-8-11 50 DavidAllan 13 29
(Tim Easterby) *hld up in rr: hdwy 3f out: rdn to chse ldrs 2f out: sn no imp* **20/1**
05-3 **6** *7* **No Plan B (IRE)**35 1424 3-9-2 55 GrahamLee 5 20
(Noel Quinlan) *trckd ldrs: hdwy to chse wnr 4f out: rdn along 3f out: grad wknd fnl 2f* **6/1**2
0536 **7** *2 3/4* **Corn Maiden**12 1982 3-8-5 51 (t) LewisWalsh(7) 12
(Phil McEntee) *s.i.s: a in rr* **10/1**
-560 **8** *2* **My Pearl (IRE)**26 1596 3-8-7 49 JulieBurke(3) 4
(Kevin Ryan) *prom: rdn along over 3f out: wknd over 2f out* **17/2**
00-0 **9** *4 1/2* **Art Of Gold**38 1357 3-8-7 46 AdrianNicholls 11
(Amy Weaver) *a in rr* **33/1**
00-0 **10** *3 1/4* **Graylyn Olivaa**138 30 3-8-7 46 oh1 PaoloSirigu 2
(Robert Eddery) *midfield: hdwy and in tch 1/2-way: rdn along over 3f out: sn wknd* **33/1**
04-2 **11** *18* **Lithograph (USA)**74 833 3-9-2 55 FrannyNorton 14
(Mark Johnston) *chsd ldrs: rdn along over 3f out: sn wknd* **13/2**3
06-6 **12** *1/2* **Only A Round (IRE)**26 1596 3-8-8 47 KellyHarrison 7
(Micky Hammond) *midfield: rdn along 4f out: sn wknd* **20/1**
000- **13** *2 3/4* **Iberian Rock**217 6911 3-9-1 54 TonyHamilton 15
(Alan Brown) *chsd ldrs: rdn along over 4f out: sn wknd* **33/1**
0460 **14** *53* **Burning Passion**7 2118 3-9-0 53 (b1) PaddyAspell 9
(Michael Easterby) *s.i.s and reminders s: hdwy to join ldr after 3f: cl up tl rdn along and wknd 4f out: sn bhd and virtually p.u fnl f* **33/1**

2m 14.52s (7.42) **Going Correction** +0.50s/f (Yiel) **14** Ran SP% **117.3**
Speed ratings (Par 97): **90,89,82,80,77 71,69,67,64,61 47,46,44,2**
toteswingers: 1&2 £8.20, 1&3 £19.00, 2&3 £118.00 CSF £32.94 CT £789.30 TOTE £3.00: £1.30, £6.10, £8.10; EX 42.00.
Owner Steve Catchpole & Keith Hanson **Bred** Aston House Stud **Trained** Denton, Co Durham

FOCUS
Part two and the first pair finished well clear. The time was slower than the first division despite being run at what looked a fierce pace. Fairly weak form.
Lithograph(USA) Official explanation: trainer's representative could offer no explanation for the filly's poor performance
T/Plt: £14.80 to a £1 stake. Pool: £47,163.45. 2,322.60 winning tickets. T/Qpdt: £5.60 to a £1 stake. Pool: £3,067.44. 401.93 winning tickets. JR

2124WINDSOR (R-H)

Monday, May 21

OFFICIAL GOING: Good (good to firm in places; 8.1)
Wind: Light, behind Weather: Fine, pleasant

2342 SKYBET.COM CLAIMING STKS 6f

6:10 (6:11) (Class 5) 3-Y-O+ **£2,264** (£673; £336; £168) **Stalls** Low

Form RPR
2601 **1** **Efistorm**6 2146 11-9-2 77 HayleyTurner 9 73
(Conor Dore) *broke wl but restrained into 5th: prog 1/2-way: shkn up and led 1f out: cajoled along and a doing enough* **10/3**1
04-5 **2** *1/2* **Scarlet Rocks (IRE)**46 1204 4-8-9 66 (p) PadraigBeggy 1 64
(David Evans) *trckd ldrs: drvn 2f out: looking for room over 1f out and swtchd rt: r.o to press wnr ins fnl f: a hld* **9/2**2
120 **3** *hd* **Speedy Yaki (IRE)**37 1392 3-8-10 72 (bt) RichardHughes 5 71
(Daniel Mark Loughnane) *trckd ldrs: nt qckn 2f out and lost pl: drvn and r.o to press wnr ins fnl f: a hld* **9/1**
10-0 **4** *1* **Polar Annie**54 1066 7-8-7 79 SeanLevey(3) 7 61
(Malcolm Saunders) *led: drvn 2f out: edgd lft and hdd 1f out: nt qckn* **10/3**1
0-30 **5** *3* **Julius Geezer (IRE)**27 1587 4-9-7 78 J-PGuillambert 3 63
(Tom Dascombe) *rousted along to chse ldr: hrd rdn 2f out: lost 2nd over 1f out: cl up but hld whn squeezed out ent fnl f: fdd* **11/2**3
0000 **6** *1* **Highland Harvest**18 1769 8-8-12 59 KierenFox(3) 6 53
(Jamie Poulton) *a in last pair: rdn on outer 2f out: no prog and sn btn* **33/1**
550- **7** *3 1/4* **Durgan**241 6310 6-8-9 49 (p) GeorgeDowning(7) 4 44
(Linda Jewell) *s.i.s: mostly in last: struggling over 1f out* **100/1**

1m 12.81s (-0.19) **Going Correction** -0.10s/f (Good)
WFA 3 from 4yo+ 9lb **7** Ran SP% **93.7**
Speed ratings (Par 103): **97,96,96,94,90 89,85**
toteswingers: 1&2 £2.10, 1&3 £3.90, 2&3 £5.60 CSF £11.94 TOTE £3.40: £2.00, £2.20; EX 10.30 Trifecta £47.10.Polar Annie was claimed by Miss Helen Cross for £6,000. Scarlet Rocks was subject to a friendly claim.
Owner Sean J Murphy **Bred** E Duggan And D Churchman **Trained** Hubbert's Bridge, Lincs
■ Stewards' Enquiry : Padraig Beggy four-day ban: use of whip (4-7 June)

FOCUS
The inner rail of the straight was dolled out 12 yards at the 6f point and 4 yards at the winning post. The top bend was dolled out 11 yards from normal inner configuration, adding 43 yards to race distances at 1m-plus. This claimer was weakened when Falasteen had to be withdrawn (5/1, deduct 15p in the £ under R4) after bursting through the front of his stall, but it was still a fair race of its type. The winner is rated a length off last year's best.

2343 E B F SPICEMERCHANTGROUP.COM MAIDEN FILLIES' STKS 5f 10y

6:40 (6:43) (Class 5) 2-Y-O **£3,299** (£981; £490; £245) **Stalls** Low

Form RPR
2 **1** **Miss Diva**7 2124 2-9-0 0 RichardHughes 4 85+
(Richard Hannon) *disp ld after 1f: shkn up to ld over 1f out: wl in command and pushed out last 150yds* **5/6**1
2 *1 1/2* **Hoyam** 2-9-0 0 HayleyTurner 5 80+
(Michael Bell) *s.i.s: chsd ldrs: prog 1/2-way: wnt 2nd jst over 1f out: rn green and hung lft: styd on but readily hld* **5/1**2
3 *2* **Bridge Night** 2-9-0 0 WilliamBuick 9 72
(Eve Johnson Houghton) *gd spd fr wd draw: w wnr after 1f to over 1f out: one pce after* **25/1**

4 1/2 **Three Crowns** 2-8-11 0 .... SeanLevey(3) 7 71+
(Ian Wood) *towards rr: effrt on outer 1/2-way: wnt 4th 1f out: kpt on same pce* **33/1**

5 2 **Snow Angel (IRE)** 2-9-0 0 .... SebSanders 1 63
(J W Hills) *t.k.h: hld up in tch: outpcd and urged along 2f out: no ch after* **14/1**

6 1 1/4 **Meet Me Halfway** 2-9-0 0 .... EddieAhern 3 59
(Chris Wall) *towards rr: shkn up and effrt wl over 1f out: sn no prog and btn* **14/1**

7 nk **Kalahari Breeze (IRE)** 2-9-0 0 .... MartinDwyer 6 58+
(William Muir) *s.i.s: mostly last: pushed along 2f out: kpt on fnl f* **33/1**

8 nse **Puteri Nur Laila (IRE)** 2-9-0 0 .... NeilCallan 2 58
(Paul Cole) *fastest away and led 1f: sn lost pl and rdn: hung lft and rn green over 1f out: wknd* **12/1**

9 6 **Shrimpton** 2-9-0 0 .... MartinHarley 8 36
(Mick Channon) *pressed ldng pair after 1f tl wknd rapidly wl over 1f out* **13/2[3]**

1m 0.78s (0.48) **Going Correction** -0.10s/f (Good) **9** Ran SP% **115.3**
Speed ratings (Par 90): **92,89,86,85,82 80,79,79,70**
toteswingers: 1&2 £1.50, 1&3 £6.40, 2&3 £14.30 CSF £5.00 TOTE £1.80: £1.02, £1.20, £9.40; EX 4.90 Trifecta £47.70.
Owner Mrs E Roberts **Bred** C J Mills **Trained** East Everleigh, Wilts

FOCUS
A maiden that should produce a few winners. Only one of these fillies had the benefit of previous experience and that was the winner. The bare form is only ordinary.

NOTEBOOK
Miss Diva, the only one with a previous outing, won well enough to confirm the promise of her debut second over C&D on soft ground the previous week. She looks quite useful. (op Evens)
Hoyam, a 55,000gns half-sister to a moderate 6f Fibresand winner, out of a 5f 2yo scorer, went left under pressure, showing her inexperience, but clearly has plenty of ability. She should be well up to winning a similar race before long. (tchd 11-2)
Bridge Night, an April foal, quickly recovered from a sluggish start to show loads of natural pace. Her speed should see win a race like this.
Three Crowns ◆ is a half-sister to Royal Award, who won twice over 5f as a 2yo for this yard, and the dam was a multiple sprint winner, including for these connections. She was caught widest of all for a lot of the way and was noticeably green, but she showed plenty of ability without being given a hard ride. (tchd 28-1)
Snow Angel(IRE), closely rated to a 5f 2yo debut winner (Listed placed over 6f), made an adequate introduction and should come on for the run. (tchd 12-1)
Kalahari Breeze(IRE), an April foal, showed some ability after starting slowly.
Puteri Nur Laila(IRE) was not given a hard ride once held. (op 14-1)

2344 SKYBET MOBILE FOR IPHONE AND ANDROID MAIDEN FILLIES' STKS — 1m 67y
7:10 (7:13) (Class 5) 3-Y-0+ **£2,264** (£673; £336; £168) **Stalls** Low

Form RPR

1 **Irish History (IRE)** 3-8-7 0 .... AntiocoMurgia(5) 2 96+
(Mahmood Al Zarooni) *nt that wl away but sn trckd ldng quartet: smooth prog to ld wl over 1f out: readily drew clr: promising* **8/1**

2 6 **Belle De Crecy (IRE)** 3-8-12 0 .... RichardHughes 11 80
(Richard Hannon) *chsd ldrs in 7th but nt on terms: rdn and prog 3f out: styd on to take 2nd fnl f: no ch w wnr* **14/1**

0-3 3 1 **Al Baidaa**[21] 1704 3-8-12 0 .... NeilCallan 10 78
(Roger Varian) *trckd ldng pair: rdn to chal jst over 2f out: sn outpcd by wnr: kpt on* **5/1[2]**

2-3 4 nse **Disposition**[26] 1610 3-8-12 0 .... WilliamBuick 3 78+
(John Gosden) *led at str pce: drvn and hdd wl over 1f out: one pce after* **2/1[1]**

4 5 9 **Chigun**[14] 1923 3-8-12 0 .... EddieAhern 4 57
(Sir Henry Cecil) *cl up bhd ldng pair: shkn up 3f out: steadily wknd fnl 2f* **13/2**

6 1 3/4 **Emirates Queen** 3-8-12 0 .... KierenFallon 5 53+
(Luca Cumani) *dismntd and walked to post: dwlt: racd in 10th and wl off the pce: pushed along 3f out: kpt on but nvr nr ldrs* **6/1[3]**

64 7 1 1/4 **Aarti (IRE)**[20] 1736 3-8-12 0 .... MichaelHills 12 50+
(William Haggas) *w ldr at str pce to over 2f out: steadily wknd* **7/1**

8 2 1/4 **Riviera Romance** 3-8-12 0 .... SebSanders 14 45
(J W Hills) *dwlt: wl off the pce in 8th: pushed along 3f out: lost little grnd after* **100/1**

9 2 1/4 **Suedehead** 3-8-12 0 .... MartinDwyer 6 40
(William Muir) *dwlt: long way adift in 12th: virtually t.o 1/2-way: pushed along and sme hdwy 3f out: rn green and no prog 2f out* **80/1**

10 6 **Flashy Star** 3-8-12 0 .... MartinHarley 13 26
(Mick Channon) *dwlt: sn long way adrift in last pair: virtually t.o 1/2-way: sme late prog* **40/1**

11 2 **My Espoir** 3-8-12 0 .... JohnFahy 8 22
(Clive Cox) *chsd ldrs in 6th but nt on terms: urged along over 3f out: wknd* **40/1**

12 1 1/4 **Imperial Wave (IRE)** 3-8-12 0 .... DaneO'Neill 9 19
(David Lanigan) *s.i.s: sn long way adrift in last pair: virtually t.o 1/2-way: nvr a factor* **28/1**

13 3 1/4 **Kaypea** 3-8-12 0 .... HayleyTurner 1 11
(Simon Dow) *dwlt: wl off the pce in 11th: shkn up and no prog sn after 1/2-way* **50/1**

53- 14 15 **Mae Rose Cottage (IRE)**[301] 4386 3-8-12 0 .... DaraghO'Donohoe 7
(Barney Curley) *stdd after s and sn wl off the pce in 9th: wknd over 2f out: t.o* **50/1**

1m 41.85s (-2.85) **Going Correction** -0.10s/f (Good) **14** Ran SP% **122.4**
Speed ratings (Par 100): **110,104,103,102,93 92,90,88,86,80 78,77,73,58**
toteswingers: 1&2 £17.90, 1&3 £10.60, 2&3 £15.50 CSF £112.01 TOTE £10.00: £2.80, £4.50, £2.20; EX 120.00 Trifecta £697.00.
Owner Godolphin **Bred** Kilcarn Stud **Trained** Newmarket, Suffolk

FOCUS
This didn't look a strong fillies' maiden, but Irish History made a winning start with ease and recorded the only time on the card that dipped under standard. That's no mean feat for a debutante, even with the pace being quick. They finished unusually well strung out for a Windsor maiden.
Emirates Queen Official explanation: jockey said filly was never travelling and moved poorly in the closing stages

2345 LONDON IRISH CONDITIONS STKS — 5f 10y
7:40 (7:41) (Class 2) 2-Y-0 **£7,762** (£2,310; £1,154) **Stalls** Low

Form RPR

31 1 **Graphic Guest**[10] 2020 2-8-9 0 .... MartinHarley 4 95+
(Mick Channon) *settled in 3rd and sn 4 l bhd ldng pair: clsd fr 2f out: rdn to ld ins fnl f: won gng away* **3/1[2]**

1 2 1 3/4 **Hairy Rocket**[7] 2124 2-8-9 0 .... RichardHughes 2 89
(Richard Hannon) *broke wl: led at decent pce but hdd after 1f: rdn to ld again over 1f out: hdd and no ex ins fnl f* **4/9[1]**

2512 3 11 **Just Past Andover (IRE)**[12] 1972 2-8-11 0 .... KierenFallon 1 51
(Bill Turner) *nt as wl away as ldr but gd spd to ld after 1f: hdd & wknd qckly over 1f out* **13/2[3]**

59.66s (-0.64) **Going Correction** -0.10s/f (Good) **3** Ran SP% **107.6**
Speed ratings (Par 99): **101,98,80**
CSF £4.96 TOTE £5.10; EX 4.60.
Owner John Guest Racing **Bred** Barry Taylor **Trained** West Ilsley, Berks

FOCUS
The pace, set initially by Hairy Rocket and then by Just Past Andover, looked much too fast and this was set up for the more sensibly ridden Graphic Guest. The final time was 1.12 seconds faster than the earlier maiden, and almost identical to the later Class 4 handicap for older horses, supporting the view the beaten runners went off fast. The winner built on her debut promise and the second confirmed her debut ability.

NOTEBOOK
Graphic Guest recorded a very useful effort, even allowing for the race setting up for her. She could now head to Royal Ascot. (tchd 11-4 and 10-3)
Hairy Rocket ◆'s C&D maiden win (on soft ground) was franked by the runner-up earlier on the card, and this was a decent performance in defeat. She did extremely well to finish so close. (op 1-2)
Just Past Andover(IRE), runner-up in the Lily Agnes, can be excused. (op 6-1 tchd 8-1)

2346 DAVISBAKERYCARIBBEAN.COM H'CAP — 1m 3f 135y
8:10 (8:10) (Class 3) (0-95,94) 4-Y-0+ **£6,792** (£2,021; £1,010; £505) **Stalls** Low

Form RPR

4-35 1 **Ramona Chase**[26] 1605 7-8-12 85 .... (t) NickyMackay 4 92
(Michael Attwater) *trckd ldng pair: wnt 2nd over 3f out: rdn to cl on ldr over 1f out: disp ld ins fnl f: kpt on to gain narrow advantage last strides* **12/1**

0-04 2 hd **Fattsota**[16] 1854 4-9-3 90 .... SebSanders 9 96
(Marco Botti) *chsd ldng trio: rdn over 3f out: responded to press to cl 2f out: chal and disp ld ins fnl f: jst pipped* **9/2[1]**

10-0 3 3/4 **Purification (IRE)**[23] 1654 4-8-12 85 .... WilliamBuick 6 90
(John Gosden) *trckd ldng quartet: shkn up wl over 2f out: prog to chal and upsides ent fnl f: nt qckn last 75yds* **9/2[1]**

01-6 4 1 3/4 **All The Winds (GER)**[29] 187 7-8-8 81 .... HayleyTurner 10 83
(Shaun Lycett) *s.s: detached in last early: rdn and prog fr 3f out: tried to cl on ldrs 2f out: kpt on same pce after* **16/1**

3255 5 nse **Uphold**[14] 1939 5-8-10 83 ow1 .... (vt) NeilCallan 8 85
(Gay Kelleway) *led at str pce: at least 2 l clr over 2f out: hdd and no ex jst ins fnl f* **33/1**

00-0 6 1 3/4 **Jehanbux (USA)**[51] 1139 4-9-1 88 .... RichardHughes 1 87
(Richard Hannon) *w.w in midfield: tried to cl on ldrs over 2f out: rdn and nt qckn over 1f out* **9/1[3]**

14-6 7 1/2 **Mountain Range (IRE)**[15] 1882 4-8-13 86 .... EddieAhern 3 84
(John Dunlop) *hld up in midfield: drvn and effrt wl over 2f out: kpt on but nvr able to threaten* **9/2[1]**

6022 8 3 **First Avenue**[26] 1603 7-8-13 86 .... IanMongan 12 79
(Laura Mongan) *hld up in last trio: last 3f out: pushed along over 2f out: kpt on: nvr involved* **10/1**

636- 9 nk **Greylami (IRE)**[218] 6528 7-9-1 88 .... MartinDwyer 2 81
(Robert Mills) *rrd s: hld up in last trio: shkn up wl over 3f out: no prog over 2f out: wl btn after* **25/1**

/00- 10 13 **Australia Day (IRE)**[37] 4778 9-9-3 90 .... KierenFallon 11 60
(Paul Webber) *walked to post and mounted at s: chsd ldr: rdn 4f out: sn lost 2nd and wknd: eased fnl 2f: t.o* **16/1**

31- 11 1 1/2 **Sandbanks Sizzler (IRE)**[239] 6377 4-9-4 94 .... HarryBentley(3) 5 62
(Ralph Beckett) *taken down early: sweating: dwlt: nvr beyond midfield: wknd over 2f out: t.o* **5/1[2]**

2m 26.86s (-2.64) **Going Correction** -0.10s/f (Good) **11** Ran SP% **116.5**
Speed ratings (Par 107): **104,103,103,102,102 101,100,98,98,89 88**
toteswingers: 1&2 £14.50, 1&3 £11.60, 2&3 £13.30 CSF £64.72 CT £285.46 TOTE £13.60: £4.30, £2.70, £1.50; EX 93.40 Trifecta £464.00.
Owner Bagden Wood Building Services Limited **Bred** Ridgecourt Stud **Trained** Epsom, Surrey
■ Stewards' Enquiry : Nicky Mackay two-day ban: use of whip (4-5 June)
Seb Sanders two-day ban: use of whip (4-5 June)

FOCUS
An ordinary handicap for the class run at what seemed a fair gallop. Just about the winner's best turf form since he was a 3yo.

NOTEBOOK
Ramona Chase didn't get the clearest of runs in the City And Suburban at Epsom last time, and prior to that he'd made a promising reappearance in the Rosebery, so this win was no great surprise. However, it was just the fourth of his career and he's not an obvious one to follow up.
Fattsota didn't try to dominate this time, but he still had his chance and ran well. This looks about as good as he is for now. (tchd 5-1)
Purification(IRE) improved a good deal on the form he showed on soft ground on his reappearance, but was worried out of it in a close finish. It's possible he still has a bit more to offer, but he doesn't appeal as one to follow. (op 7-1)
All The Winds(GER) fared best of those from well off the pace, but he seemingly needs to be delivered late and wasn't unlucky. (op 14-1)
Mountain Range(IRE) just didn't pick up well enough and probably found the ground too quick. (tchd 5-1)
Australia Day(IRE) Official explanation: jockey said that the gelding hung right
Sandbanks Sizzler(IRE), absent since winning an Epsom maiden by 14l last September, got warm and was taken to post early. He lost ground with an awkward start and rather raced in snatches thereafter before coming wide into the straight. It basically seemed as though he found this all too much on his return and it will be surprising if he can't do better. (op 6-1)

2347 DAVIS WEST INDIAN BAKERY H'CAP — 5f 10y
8:40 (8:46) (Class 4) (0-85,85) 3-Y-0 **£4,851** (£1,443; £721; £360) **Stalls** Low

Form RPR

140 1 **Wicked Wench**[3] 2256 3-8-5 76 .... JoshBaudains(7) 14 83
(Jo Hughes) *racd on outer: pressed ldrs: led 2f out: sn clr: urged along fnl f: advantage dwindling but nvr threatened* **25/1**

51-0 2 1 **Kyleakin Lass**[21] 1721 3-9-0 78 .... RichardHughes 4 85+
(Ian Wood) *hld up in midfield: lost pl fr 1/2-way and wl in rr over 1f out but gng easily: gd prog fnl f: tk 2nd nr fin and clsd on wnr: too much to do* **11/1**

0-33 3 1/2 **Signifer (IRE)**[31] 1493 3-9-7 85 .... (v[1]) MartinHarley 1 86
(Mick Channon) *hld up in rr: gng strly 2f out but effrt delayed: prog to chse clr wnr ins fnl f: styd on but lost 2nd nr fin* **12/1**

0-50 4 1/2 **Mister Musicmaster**[12] 1983 3-9-2 80 .... JamesMillman 11 79
(Rod Millman) *racd on outer in midfield: rdn and effrt 2f out: styd on: nvr able to chal* **33/1**

3-15 **5** ½ **Red Senor (IRE)**[40] 1317 3-9-0 **78**.................................... MichaelHills 3 76+
(Charles Hills) *taken down early: t.k.h: hld up in rr: gng strly 2f out: tried to weave through fr over 1f out: styd on: nrst fin* **12/1**

1113 **6** shd **Bella Ophelia (IRE)**[62] 977 3-8-13 **77**.......................... DarryllHolland 10 74
(Hughie Morrison) *wnt awkwardly to post: wl in rr: rdn on outer 1/2-way: styd on fnl f: nvr able to chal* **12/1**

-623 **7** hd **Lupo D'Oro (IRE)**[20] 1739 3-8-11 **75**.............................. HayleyTurner 7 72
(John Best) *mde most to 2f out: lost 2nd and wknd ins fnl f* **9/1**

3110 **8** nk **Heartsong (IRE)**[16] 1858 3-9-5 **83**.. NeilCallan 5 78
(John Gallagher) *prom: rdn 2f out: sn outpcd: fdd* **10/1**

4-00 **9** 1 **Marygold**[14] 1921 3-8-11 **78**.. KierenFox(3) 9 70
(Lee Carter) *pressed ldr to 2f out: sn outpcd: fdd* **50/1**

132- **10** 1¼ **O'Gorman**[267] 5505 3-9-6 **84**.. PhillipMakin 8 71
(Kevin Ryan) *trckd ldrs: drvn and nt qckn wl over 1f out: steadily lost pl* **3/1**[1]

-460 **11** 1 **Bubbly Ballerina**[10] 2028 3-9-6 **84**.................................. SebSanders 13 68
(Alan Bailey) *pressed ldrs to 2f out: wkng whn n.m.r ins fnl f* **33/1**

5-05 **12** 1¼ **Indian Tinker**[23] 1658 3-9-1 **79**...................................... WilliamBuick 2 58
(Robert Cowell) *cl up bhd ldrs on inner: steadily wknd fr 2f out* **12/1**

1-06 **13** 1½ **Jinker Noble**[21] 1721 3-9-0 **78**.. JohnFahy 16 52
(Clive Cox) *s.i.s: in tch on outer: wknd over 1f out* **8/1**[3]

10-5 **14** ½ **Judas Jo (FR)**[52] 1125 3-9-1 **79**...................................... DavidProbert 6 51
(Gay Kelleway) *stdd s: hld up in rr: no real prog fnl 2f* **40/1**

610- **15** 8 **Sandfrankskipsgo**[186] 7445 3-9-0 **78**.............................. IanMongan 12 21+
(Peter Crate) *dwlt: rcvrd to chse ldrs: wkng whn hmpd 1f out: eased* **7/1**[2]

59.62s (-0.68) **Going Correction** -0.10s/f (Good) **15** Ran SP% **120.9**
Speed ratings (Par 101): **101,99,98,97,97 96,96,96,94,92 90,88,86,85,72**
toteswingers: 1&2 £94.90, 1&3 £65.90, 2&3 £21.50 CSF £270.01 CT £3545.71 TOTE £36.10: £10.10, £2.80, £3.80; EX 430.20 TRIFECTA Not won..
Owner James Hearne **Bred** Rainsbrook Bloodstock **Trained** Lambourn, Berks

FOCUS
A fair, competitive sprint handicap.
Red Senor(IRE) Official explanation: jockey said that the colt was slowly away and was denied a clear run
Indian Tinker Official explanation: jockey said that the gelding was denied a clear run and never travelling thereafter
T/Plt: £434.40 to a £1 stake. Pool: £84,927.17. 142.68 winning tickets. T/Qpdt: £228.70 to a £1 stake. Pool: £5,006.92. 16.20 winning tickets. JN

2130 WOLVERHAMPTON (A.W) (L-H)

Monday, May 21

OFFICIAL GOING: Standard
Wind: Light, against Weather: Sunny

2348 BOOK TICKETS ONLINE AT WOLVERHAMPTON-RACECOURSE.CO.UK AMATEUR RIDERS' CLASSIFIED CLAIMING STKS 1m 4f 50y(P)

2:30 (2:31) (Class 6) 4-Y-0+ **£1,646** (£506; £253) **Stalls** Low

Form RPR

-054 **1** **Sir Boss (IRE)**[10] 2031 7-10-7 72........................ MissMMullineaux(3) 12 78
(Michael Mullineaux) *stdd s: hld up in rr: hdwy over 4f out: rdn and effrt over 1f out: led fnl 100yds: r.o strly* **9/1**

-503 **2** 3 **Scamperdale**[21] 1718 10-10-10 74........................(p) MissSBrotherton 11 73
(Brian Baugh) *hld up in rr: hdwy 5f out: pressed ldr 3f out: rdn to ld 2f out: hdd and outpcd by wnr fnl 100yds* **9/2**[2]

1120 **3** 1 **Overrule (USA)**[16] 1846 8-10-1 75..................(p) MissFrancesHarper(7) 6 70
(Jason Ward) *broke wl: led for 1f: chsd ldng pair after tl led wl over 3f out: hdd 2f out: no ex ent fnl f: plugged on same pce after* **7/2**[1]

0/0- **4** ¾ **King Fingal (IRE)**[66] 1746 7-10-10 75................................ MrSWalker 2 70
(John Quinn) *hld up in midfield: rdn 4f out: hdwy and drvn over 1f out: kpt on same pce fnl f* **9/2**[2]

3334 **5** 1 **Ahlawy (IRE)**[21] 1718 9-9-11 67..................................(t) MrFMitchell(5) 10 61
(Frank Sheridan) *hld up in midfield: lost pl 6f out: rdn and hdwy on outer over 3f out: styd on same pce fr over 1f out* **8/1**

60-4 **6** 1½ **On The Feather**[6] 2149 6-9-11 66.................................. MrPMillman(5) 7 58
(Rod Millman) *in tch: rdn and unable qck ent fnl 2f: wknd over 1f out* **6/1**[3]

60-0 **7** 3¾ **Applaude**[10] 2048 7-9-9 40....................................(b) MatthewStanley(5) 9 50
(Chris Bealby) *t.k.h: hld up in midfield: hdwy to press ldrs 3f out: edgd rt and wknd over 1f out* **50/1**

420 **8** 4 **Polly Holder (IRE)**[18] 1794 4-9-13 57.........................(p) MrsRWilson(7) 3 50
(Paul D'Arcy) *pressed ldr and wnt clr after 1f: led 9f out tl hdd wl over 3f out: wknd over 2f out* **10/1**

463- **9** 1¼ **Appointment**[319] 3769 7-9-7 48.................................. MrsKGoldstein(7) 5 42
(Zoe Davison) *in tch in midfield on outer: wknd over 2f out* **40/1**

4212 **10** 4½ **Dunaskin (IRE)**[20] 1744 12-9-11 50..............................(b) MrsAGuest(7) 4 39
(Richard Guest) *taken down early and led to post: s.i.s: a bhd* **25/1**

4200 **11** 8 **Carlton Scroop (FR)**[61] 984 9-9-9 49..........................(b) MissMBryant(5) 8 22
(Paddy Butler) *chsd ldrs: wnt 2nd 6f out tl 4f out: sn wknd* **33/1**

0406 **12** 17 **Angelena Ballerina (IRE)**[31] 1496 5-9-9 45.............(p) MrLMichael(7) 1
(Dai Williams) *led after 1f and wnt clr w rival: hdd 9f out: lost 2nd 6f out and steadily lost pl: bhd 3f out: t.o* **100/1**

2m 42.74s (1.64) **Going Correction** +0.05s/f (Slow) **12** Ran SP% **115.3**
Speed ratings (Par 101): **96,94,93,92,92 91,88,86,85,82 76,65**
toteswingers: 1&2 £9.60, 1&3 £8.70, 2&3 £5.20 CSF £46.22 TOTE £15.20: £2.90, £2.80, £1.10; EX 42.30 Trifecta £179.20 Pool: £443.36 - 1.83 winning units..
Owner Miss M Mullineaux, P Lawton, I Ross **Bred** Mrs E R Cantillon **Trained** Alpraham, Cheshire

FOCUS
A classified claimer for amateur riders. It was run at a brisk pace and the form looks straightforward enough. The first two ran their best races since last year.

2349 BETFRED MOBILE MAIDEN AUCTION STKS 5f 20y(P)

3:00 (3:01) (Class 5) 2-Y-0 **£2,264** (£673; £336; £84; £84) **Stalls** Low

Form RPR

1 **Time For Lambrini (IRE)** 2-8-4 0.................................... AmyRyan(3) 6 74+
(Lisa Williamson) *mde all: shkn up and wnt clr over 1f out: r.o strly: comf* **25/1**

2 3¼ **Jet Acclaim (IRE)** 2-8-4 0.. NickyMackay 10 63
(Marco Botti) *chsd ldng trio: rdn and effrt wl over 1f out: edgd lft and chsd clr wnr ins fnl f: kpt on but no threat to wnr* **7/2**[1]

340 **3** 3½ **Jamnean**[28] 1556 2-8-4 0.. ChrisCatlin 8 50
(John Holt) *pressed ldr tl 2f out: sn drvn and outpcd: wl hld and plugged on same pce fnl f* **8/1**

0 **4** 1½ **Shirley's Pride**[10] 2047 2-8-4 0.................................... KieranO'Neill 3 45
(John Holt) *chsd ldrs: wnt 2nd and rdn 2f out: outpcd by wnr and btn over 1f out: wknd ins fnl f* **14/1**

6 **4** dht **Mission Bell**[7] 2135 2-8-4 0.. DavidProbert 4 45
(Mark Usher) *sn niggled along in midfield: drvn and no imp wl over 1f out: plugged on fnl f* **15/2**

2343 **6** ½ **Suivez L'Argent**[25] 1629 2-8-1 0.................................. HarryBentley(3) 1 43
(Joseph Tuite) *bustled along and struggling to go pce whn short of room after 1f and lost pl: bhd and rdn after: n.d* **7/2**[1]

7 13 **Supercruiser (IRE)** 2-8-12 0.................................. SilvestreDeSousa 2
(Nigel Tinkler) *t.k.h: hld up in midfield: rdn 1/2-way: wknd qckly wl over 1f out: eased ins fnl f* **6/1**[3]

8 10 **Tonkalili** 2-8-2 0 ow1.. DeclanCannon(3) 5
(James Unett) *dwlt: a bhd: lost tch 1/2-way* **16/1**

9 6 **Windforpower (IRE)** 2-9-1 0.. LukeMorris 7 +
(Ronald Harris) *s.i.s: a bhd: lost tch 1/2-way: eased fnl f: sddle slipped* **9/2**[2]

1m 2.59s (0.29) **Going Correction** +0.05s/f (Slow) **9** Ran SP% **116.2**
Speed ratings (Par 93): **99,93,88,85,85 85,64,48,38**
toteswingers: 1&2 £14.00, 1&3 £28.40, 2&3 £6.40 CSF £111.62 TOTE £44.10: £10.20, £1.70, £1.10; EX 182.70 TRIFECTA Not won..
Owner Halewood International Ltd **Bred** J Joyce **Trained** Saighton, Cheshire

FOCUS
This looked a weak juvenile maiden overall and few landed a serious blow. The third and averages help with the level.

NOTEBOOK
Time For Lambrini(IRE) became just the second juvenile winner for her yard in the last five years. She's also bred to want further, but certainly knew her job and showed decent early speed to lead. She was nicely on top inside the final furlong and clearly has a good future. This saw her jockey Amy Ryan ride out her claim.
Jet Acclaim(IRE), half-sister to a 7f winner, wasn't helped by having to race wide off the home turn and never threatened the winner. She was doing some decent late work, though, and finished a clear second-best. (op 10-3 tchd 3-1)
Jamnean duelled with the winner and, while firmly put in her place, this was better again from her back on Polytrack. She sets the standard. (op 7-1)
Shirley's Pride appreciated this sounder surface, but dropped out in the home straight and looks to want more time. (op 10-1)
Mission Bell, despite breaking better, still showed signs of greenness and ought to go forward again for the experience. (op 10-1)
Suivez L'Argent lacked zip from the gates and that saw her badly hampered on the inside as Supercruiser came across her. She was done with thereafter. (op 10-3 tchd 4-1)
Windforpower(IRE) Official explanation: jockey said that the gelding's saddle slipped

2350 BETFRED STILL TREBLE ODDS ON LUCKY 15'S H'CAP 5f 216y(P)

3:30 (3:30) (Class 6) (0-55,54) 4-Y-0+ **£1,704** (£503; £251) **Stalls** Low

Form RPR

000 **1** **Irie Ute**[21] 1702 4-9-4 **54**.. JamesDoyle 2 62
(Sylvester Kirk) *chsd ldrs: rdn and effrt to chse ldr 2f out: drvn and chal over 1f out: sltly hmpd ent fnl f: led fnl 50yds: drvn out* **15/2**

2600 **2** nk **Little Perisher**[12] 1987 5-8-12 **48**..........................(p) TomMcLaughlin 4 55
(Paul Howling) *towards rr: hdwy u.p ent fnl f: str run to press wnr cl home: nt quite rch wnr* **12/1**

0404 **3** hd **Steel City Boy (IRE)**[10] 2046 9-9-4 **54**............................ LukeMorris 10 60
(Garry Woodward) *led: drvn over 1f out: edgd rt ent fnl f: battled on gamely u.p tl hdd and no ex fnl 50yds* **12/1**

5236 **4** 1½ **Just Timmy Marcus**[32] 1487 6-9-4 **54**................................ TedDurcan 9 56
(Brian Baugh) *sn wl outpcd in last pair and rdn: hdwy 1f out: r.o wl ins fnl f: nt rch ldrs* **11/2**[2]

36-0 **5** nse **Pinball (IRE)**[15] 1881 6-9-0 **53**..(v) AmyRyan(3) 1 54
(Lisa Williamson) *fly-jmpd leaving stalls and slowly away: hdwy into midfield 1/2-way: rdn over 1f out: kpt on wl ins fnl f: nt rch ldrs* **14/1**

6536 **6** ½ **Slatey Hen (IRE)**[18] 1787 4-9-2 **52**..........................(p) WilliamCarson 5 52
(Richard Guest) *in tch in midfield: rdn 1/2-way: drvn and hdwy 2f out: chsd ldng pair after 1f: one pce fnl f* **11/1**

-200 **7** 1½ **Sleights Boy (IRE)**[9] 2091 4-8-13 **52**......................(v) DeclanCannon(3) 6 47
(Ian McInnes) *in tch: rdn 4f out: outpcd and lost pl 2f out: rallied and styd on again ins fnl f* **8/1**

6560 **8** nse **Bold Diva**[21] 1722 7-8-13 **49**.. AdamKirby 7 44
(Tony Carroll) *sn outpcd and rdn along in rr: hdwy ent fnl f: styd on fnl f: nvr trbld ldrs* **10/1**

6300 **9** ½ **Dingaan (IRE)**[54] 1061 9-9-0 **50**.................................. RobbieFitzpatrick 8 43
(Peter Grayson) *stdd s: sn outpcd in rr: rdn and effrt wd 2f out: kpt on fnl f: nvr trbld ldrs* **33/1**

0441 **10** nk **Avonlini**[37] 1387 6-8-13 **52**.. HarryBentley(3) 12 44
(Brian Baugh) *pressed ldr tl 2f out: sn struggling u.p: fdd ins fnl f* **7/1**[3]

0-25 **11** 1¾ **Circuitous**[3] 2225 4-9-0 **50**..(b) JoeFanning 3 37
(Keith Dalgleish) *in tch in midfield: rdr looking down and nt asked for effrt over 1f out: short of room ins fnl f: eased: sddle slipped* **4/1**[1]

20-0 **12** 1¼ **Miss Firefly**[31] 1497 7-9-4 **54**..................................(p) ChrisCatlin 13 37
(Ron Hodges) *chsd ldrs on outer: wknd u.p wl over 1f out: fdd fnl f* **25/1**

1m 15.24s (0.24) **Going Correction** +0.05s/f (Slow) **12** Ran SP% **117.0**
Speed ratings (Par 101): **100,99,99,97,97 96,94,94,93,93 91,89**
toteswingers: 1&2 £32.10, 1&3 £17.80, 2&3 £38.60 CSF £93.01 CT £1085.46 TOTE £14.00: £3.80, £4.80, £3.40; EX 96.30 TRIFECTA Not won..
Owner I A N Wight **Bred** Poulton Farm Stud **Trained** Upper Lambourn, Berks

FOCUS
A moderate handicap that looked wide-open. There was a strong pace on and the principals fought out a tight finish. Straightforward form.
Circuitous Official explanation: jockey said that the gelding's saddle slipped

2351 BETFRED MOBILE SPORTS H'CAP 5f 216y(P)

4:00 (4:01) (Class 6) (0-60,60) 3-Y-0 **£1,704** (£503; £251) **Stalls** Low

Form RPR

-040 **1** **Kai**[11] 2010 3-8-13 **52**..(v[1]) LukeMorris 2 58
(Michael Bell) *sn rdn along: in tch: hrd drvn and hdwy jst over 1f out: styd on to ld wl ins fnl f* **7/1**

605 **2** 1¾ **Dear Ben**[52] 1111 3-8-11 **50**.. WilliamCarson 6 50
(Brian Baugh) *led after 1f: drvn wl over 1f out: hdd and no ex wl ins fnl f* **16/1**

33-3 **3** nk **Dark Ages (IRE)**[20] 1731 3-9-1 **59**..............................(t) DavidKenny(5) 1 58
(George Baker) *chsd ldrs: nt clr run and shuffled bk over 1f out: swtchd rt and rdn 2f out: drvn and kpt on ins fnl f* **6/1**[2]

545 **4** shd **Julier Pass (IRE)**[10] 2036 3-9-4 **60**................................ GaryBartley(3) 4 59
(Hugh McWilliams) *towards rr: rdn and effrt on outer 2f out: hdwy ent fnl f: kpt on u.p* **8/1**

2446 **5** ¾ **Maria Montez**[20] 1731 3 -9-3**56**.. JoeFanning 7 53
(J W Hills) *stdd s: midfield: rdn and effrt to chse ldrs 2f out: kpt on same pce u.p ins fnl f* **9/1**

-000 **6** ½ **Applaudere**[7] 2130 3 -8-3**47** ow1............................(b) LeonnaMayor(5) 10 42
(Jamie Osborne) *sn outpcd in rr: stl plenty to do but hdwy 1f out: edgd rt but r.o fnl f: nt rch ldrs* **40/1**

06-0 **7** 1 **Shamakat**[38] 1357 3 -9-7**60**.. ChrisCatlin 12 52
(Rae Guest) *sn outpcd in last trio: hdwy 1f out: styd on ins fnl f: nvr trbld ldrs* **22/1**

1444 **8** nk **Umph (IRE)**[20] 1725 3 -9-5**58**..(b) JamesDoyle 5 49
(David Evans) *chsd ldrs: rdn to chse ldr 1/2-way tl ins fnl f: fdd fnl 100yds* **7/2**[1]

5321 **9** 3 ½ **Emma Jean (IRE)**[7] 2130 3 -9-7**60** 6ex................(bt) SilvestreDeSousa 9 40
(Frank Sheridan) *sn outpcd in last trio: n.d* **13/2**[3]

00-0 **10** 14 **Goal Hanger**[23] 1660 3 -8-13**57**..................................(e[1]) RaulDaSilva(5) 3
(William Kinsey) *led for 1f: chsd ldr tl 1/2-way: sn lost pl u.p: bhd fnl f* **25/1**

1m 15.76s (0.76)**Going Correction** +0.05s/f (Slow) **10**Ran SP% **100.0**
Speed ratings (Par 97): **96,93,93,93,92 91,90,89,85,66**
toteswingers: 1&2 £15.20, 1&3 £7.60, 2&3 £8.50 CSF £83.31 CT £491.46 TOTE £9.60 : £3.60, £6.60, £1.50 ; EX 93.60 TRIFECTA Not won.
Owner Raymond Tooth **Bred** Kirtlington Stud Ltd **Trained** Newmarket, Suffolk

FOCUS
A weak 3yo sprint handicap, run at a brisk early pace. A step up from the winner in the visor.
Goal Hanger Official explanation: jockey said that the filly hung right-handed

2352 BETFRED MOBILE CASINO H'CAP 5f 20y (P)
4:30 (4:30) (Class 6) (0-60,60) 4-Y-0+ **£1,704** (£503; £251) **Stalls** Low

Form RPR

0152 **1** **Almaty Express**[32] 1483 10 -9-5**58**................................(b) KieranO'Neill 3 65
(John Weymes) *broke fast: sn hdd and steadily lost pl: in rr and rdn 1/2-way: hdwy over 1f out: drvn and r.o fnl f to ld last stride* **6/1**[3]

0065 **2** shd **Loyal Royal (IRE)**[20] 1735 9 -9-3**56**................................(bt) LiamKeniry 2 63
(Milton Bradley) *t.k.h: hld up in midfield: hdwy to trck ldrs 2f out: rdn to ld 1f out: r.o u.p tl hdd last stride* **20/1**

000 **3** ½ **Legal Eagle (IRE)**[32] 1481 7 -9-4**60**........................(p) RobertLButler(3) 5 65
(Paul Green) *racd in last quartet: rdn 4f out: drvn over 2f out: hdwy u.p 1f out: r.o wl fnl 100yds* **12/1**

3013 **4** hd **Invigilator**[30] 1516 4 -9-2**55**... JoeFanning 7 59
(Derek Shaw) *stdd s: hld up in rr: hdwy on outer wl over 1f out: styd on wl u.p fnl f* **7/2**[2]

-004 **5** ½ **Sharp Shoes**[10] 2032 5 -9-3**56**................................(p) SilvestreDeSousa 4 58
(Ann Duffield) *in tch in midfield: rdn wl over 1f out: kpt on u.p ins fnl f* **3/1**[1]

4300 **6** 2 **Decider (USA)**[14] 1910 9 -9-5**58**...(b) LukeMorris 1 53
(Ronald Harris) *t.k.h: chsd ldrs: wnt 2nd 2f out: rdn and ev ch ent fnl f: nt qckn and wknd fnl 75yds* **15/2**

/004 **7** nse **Tagula Breeze (IRE)**[10] 2037 6 -9-7**60**........................ GeorgeBaker 9 55
(Ian McInnes) *stdd s: hld up in rr: hdwy over 1f out: swtchd lft and rdn 1f out: no imp fnl 100yds* **9/1**

3-40 **8** 10 **Missile Attack (IRE)**[18] 1800 4 -9-4**60**.................... DeclanCannon(3) 11 19
(Ian Semple) *dwlt: sn rcvrd to chse ldrs: rdn wl over 3f out: struggling 2f out: sn wknd* **10/1**

00-1 **9** 1 **Instructress**[18] 1787 4 -9-3**56**... PatCosgrave 8 11
(Robert Cowell) *chsd ldr tl 2f out: sn rdn and nt qckn: wknd over 1f out: fdd fnl f* **12/1**

000- **10** ¾ **Six Diamonds**[467] 477 5 -9-2**55**..................................(t) WilliamCarson 10
(Richard Guest) *led and crossed to inner: rdn wl over 1f out: hdd 1f out: sn fdd* **18/1**

1m 2.28s (-0.02)**Going Correction** +0.05s/f (Slow) **10**Ran SP% **117.8**
Speed ratings (Par 101): **102,101,101,100,99 96,96,80,79,77**
toteswingers: 1&2 £12.60, 1&3 £13.20, 2&3 £26.60 CSF £118.19 CT £1398.66 TOTE £6.80 : £2.40, £4.20 , £6.00 ; EX 88.90 TRIFECTA Not won.
Owner Highmoor Racing 4 & Tag Racing **Bred** P G Airey **Trained** Middleham Moor, N Yorks

FOCUS
An ordinary sprint handicap run at a searching pace. Sound enough form.

2353 PAT LOWE BIRTHDAY H'CAP 1m 1f 103y (P)
5:00 (5:01) (Class 6) (0-60,60) 3-Y-0 **£1,617** (£481; £240 ; £120) **Stalls** Low

Form RPR

00-5 **1** **Melodrama (IRE)**[35] 1424 3 -9-2**55**...................................(b) TedDurcan 5 63
(David Lanigan) *dwlt: racd in last quartet: hdwy over 3f out: rdn to go 3rd over 1f out: chsd clr ldr ins fnl f: led wl ins fnl f: sn in command and gng away at fin* **9/1**

0-53 **2** 2 **Lean On Pete (IRE)**[7] 2131 3 -9-7**60**................................ KieranO'Neill 9 64+
(Ollie Pears) *t.k.h: hld up in tch tl plld out and qcknd to ld over 3f out: sn clr: rdn over 1f out: drvn ins fnl f: hdd wl ins fnl f: sn btn* **2/1**[1]

502 **3** 1 ¼ **Song Of Joy (IRE)**[12] 1979 3 -9-7**60**.................................... AdamKirby 8 61
(Paul D'Arcy) *taken down early: dwlt: in tch in midfield: rdn 3f out: hdwy u.p over 1f out: styd on wl ins fnl f* **7/1**[3]

-204 **4** 1 **Parque Atlantico**[35] 1424 3 -8-7**46** oh1.......................(v) DavidProbert 13 45
(Andrew Balding) *chsd ldrs: wnt 2nd 5f out tl over 3f out: rdn to chse clr wnr 2f out tl ins fnl f: one pce* **9/1**

0-00 **5** 1 ¼ **Desert Red (IRE)**[20] 1736 3 -9-1**54**.. LukeMorris 2 51
(Michael Bell) *in tch: rdn and unable qck jst over 2f out: styd on same pce fr over 1f out* **4/1**[2]

0-64 **6** ¾ **La Confession**[11] 2014 3 -8-8**47**.. ChrisCatlin 4 42
(Rae Guest) *t.k.h: hld up in last quartet: rdn wl over 2f out: styd on ins fnl f: nvr trbld ldrs* **33/1**

4-45 **7** nk **Ferdy (IRE)**[62] 973 3 -8-3**47** oh1 ow1............................ RaulDaSilva(5) 1 41
(Paul Green) *t.k.h: chsd ldrs: rdn and struggling over 2f out: wknd wl over 1f out* **33/1**

005- **8** 1 ½ **Hollywood All Star (IRE)**[165] 7673 3 -8-7**46** oh1........... JoeFanning 12 37
(William Muir) *hld up in rr: stl bhd and rdn wl over 2f out: sme hdwy fnl f: n.d* **33/1**

050 **9** 3 ½ **Scripturist**[75] 827 3 -8-8**47**... WilliamCarson 10 31
(William Jarvis) *racd in last quartet: rdn over 6f out: u.p 5f out: struggling over 3f out: wl btn fnl 2f* **25/1**

05-3 **10** 1 ½ **Fu Fic Fas**[33] 1436 3 -9-7**60**..(t) GeorgeBaker 3 41
(Paul Fitzsimons) *led tl over 3f out: rdn and lost 2nd 2f out: sn wknd* **10/1**

00-0 **11** 18 **Choisirez (IRE)**[41] 1278 3 -8-9**53**........................... MatthewCosham(5) 6
(David Evans) *chsd ldr tl 5f out: sn rdn and lost pl: bhd fnl 2f* **80/1**

0-40 **12** 10 **Bevis Marks (USA)**[40] 1320 3 -9-5**58**........................ SilvestreDeSousa 7
(Mark Johnston) *a towards rr: drvn 4f out: sn toiling: lost tch 3f out: t.o* **10/1**

2m 2.04s (0.34)**Going Correction** +0.05s/f (Slow) **12**Ran SP% **117.9**
Speed ratings (Par 97): **100,98,97,96,95 94,94,92,89,88 72,63**
toteswingers: 1&2 £7.40, 1&3 £7.60, 2&3 £4.40 CSF £26.07 CT £138.87 TOTE £10.90 : £4.50 , £1.70, £2.70 ; EX 45.30 Trifecta £152.00 Pool: £908.31 - 4.42 winning units.
Owner Mrs John Magnier & Bob Lanigan **Bred** Tullamaine Castle Stud And Orpendale **Trained** Upper Lambourn, Berks

FOCUS
A moderate 3-y-o handicap. The early pace was average and those held up out the back were at a disadvantage. Pretty sound form overall.
Melodrama(IRE) Official explanation: trainer's representative said, regarding the apparent improvement of form, that the filly had made a noise on its last run and did not in this race.

2354 BOOK HOSPITALITY AT WOLVERHAMPTON RACECOURSE H'CAP (DIV I) 7f 32y (P)
5:30 (5:31) (Class 5) (0-75,75) 4-Y-0+ **£2,264** (£673; £336 ; £168) **Stalls** High

Form RPR

0-30 **1** **Smalljohn**[14] 1917 6 -8-11**70** ow1..............................(v) JustinNewman(5) 2 79
(Bryan Smart) *pressed ldr and sn clr: led over 3f out: drvn wl over 1f out: styd on wl fnl f* **4/1**[2]

1430 **2** 1 ¾ **Lastkingofscotland (IRE)**[9] 2083 6 -9-5**73**..................(b) LukeMorris 8 78
(Conor Dore) *chsd clr ldng pair: rdn and clsd over 2f out: chsd wnr ins fnl f: no imp fnl 100yds* **5/1**[3]

2130 **3** 1 **Piccolo Express**[17] 1830 6 -8-8**62**.................................... WilliamCarson 1 64
(Brian Baugh) *chsd ldng trio: rdn and clsd to chse wnr over 2f out tl ins fnl f: no ex* **11/1**

2222 **4** ½ **Unlimited**[27] 1586 10 -9-2**70**.. AdamKirby 6 71
(Tony Carroll) *hld up off the pce in midfield: rdn and effrt 3f out: hdwy u.p over 1f out: kpt on ins fnl f: nt rch ldrs* **15/2**

323- **5** nk **My Learned Friend (IRE)**[174] 7579 8 -8-8**69**.............. JoeyHaynes(7) 4 69
(Andrew Balding) *hld up off the pce in midfield: rdn and effrt over 2f out: chsd ldrs and swtchd rt 1f out: one pce ins fnl f* **10/1**

032 **6** 2 **Charlcot**[41] 1278 4 -8-9**63**... SilvestreDeSousa 5 57
(James Bethell) *racd off the pce in midfield: drvn over 3f out: sme hdwy over 1f out: swtchd and no imp ins fnl f* **7/2**[1]

3100 **7** 12 **Khandaq (USA)**[15] 1875 5 -9-6**74**.......................................(v[1]) JoeFanning 10 36
(Keith Dalgleish) *v.s.a: a bhd: rdn and modest hdwy over 1f out: wl btn and eased ins fnl f* **7/1**

0-01 **8** 1 ¼ **Addikt (IRE)**[40] 1299 7 -8-7**66**.. DavidKenny(5) 7 25
(Michael Scudamore) *a outpcd in last trio: n.d* **16/1**

2404 **9** ½ **One Way Or Another (AUS)**[62] 800 9 -8-13**72**(b) MatthewCosham(5) 11 29
(David Evans) *sn led: hdd over 3f out: lost 2nd and hung bdly rt over 2f out: sn dropped out and bhd* **14/1**

0200 **10** 2 ¾ **Ensnare**[37] 1378 7 -8-8**62**.. ChrisCatlin 9 12
(Willie Musson) *a outpcd in last trio: n.d* **22/1**

1m 29.38s (-0.22)**Going Correction** +0.05s/f (Slow) **10**Ran SP% **117.5**
Speed ratings (Par 103): **103,101,99,99,98 96,82,81,80,77**
toteswingers: 1&2 £5.00, 1&3 £6.90, 2&3 £10.00 CSF £24.61 CT £209.49 TOTE £3.50 : £1.10 , £2.20, £2.80 ; EX 26.80 Trifecta £119.60 Pool: £557.99 - 3.45 winning units.
Owner B Smart **Bred** W H R John And Partners **Trained** Hambleton, N Yorks

FOCUS
A moderate handicap, run at a searching early pace. The winner is rated back towards his best.
Khandaq(USA) Official explanation: jockey said that the gelding missed the break
Addikt(IRE) Official explanation: jockey said that the gelding missed the break

2355 BOOK HOSPITALITY AT WOLVERHAMPTON RACECOURSE H'CAP (DIV II) 7f 32y (P)
6:00 (6:01) (Class 5) (0-75,74) 4-Y-0+ **£2,264** (£673; £336 ; £168) **Stalls** High

Form RPR

2300 **1** **Jungle Bay**[28] 1564 5 -9-6**73**...(p) TedDurcan 4 81
(Jane Chapple-Hyam) *chsd ldr tl over 2f out: swtchd rt over 1f out and rdn to chal 1f out: drvn ahd fnl 100yds: drvn out* **3/1**[1]

4300 **2** ¾ **Satwa Laird**[10] 2044 6 -9-2**69**... LukeMorris 8 75
(Conor Dore) *in tch in midfield: rdn and hdwy to press ldrs over 2f out: drvn over 1f out: kpt on same pce ins fnl f* **9/1**

3102 **3** ½ **Waabel**[18] 1773 5 -9-2**69**...(t) WilliamCarson 9 74
(Richard Guest) *chsd ldng pair: wnt 2nd over 2f out: rdn to chal over 1f out: led ent fnl f: hdd and no ex fnl 100yds* **8/1**[3]

00-0 **4** ¾ **Sir Bruno (FR)**[33] 1094 5 -9-5**72**....................................... DavidProbert 3 75
(Bryn Palling) *hld up in tch towards rr: effrt over 2f out: drvn over 1f out: styd on ins fnl f: nt rch ldrs* **10/1**

5543 **5** hd **Restless Bay (IRE)**[17] 1827 4 -9-7**74**............................(e) GeorgeBaker 7 76+
(Reg Hollinshead) *taken down early: stdd s: hld up in last pair: hdwy over 1f out: swtchd lft and rdn to chse ldrs ins fnl f: no imp fnl 75yds* **3/1**[1]

610 **6** shd **Chookie Avon**[40] 1293 5 -9-4**71**......................................(p) AdamKirby 1 73
(Keith Dalgleish) *chsd ldng trio: rdn and unable qck wl over 1f out: styd on u.p ins fnl f* **7/1**[2]

3001 **7** ¾ **Powerful Pierre**[32] 1481 5 -8-12**68**........................(b) DeclanCannon(3) 6 68
(Ian McInnes) *in tch in midfield: drvn and unable qck over 1f out: kpt on ins fnl f* **14/1**

U050 **8** 2 ¾ **Lucky Dan (IRE)**[13] 1954 6 -8-10**63**........................ SilvestreDeSousa 2 55
(Paul Green) *t.k.h: hld up in midfield: effrt on inner over 1f out: no imp and btn whn nt clr run ins fnl f* **20/1**

00-0 **9** ½ **Dhhamaan (IRE)**[13] 1951 7 -8-8**61**.....................................(b) ChrisCatlin 5 52
(Ruth Carr) *led: rdn wl over 1f out: hdd ent fnl f: wknd* **16/1**

00-0 **10** 2 **Conry (IRE)**[13] 1958 6 -8-10**63**................................ RobbieFitzpatrick 10 49
(Daniel Mark Loughnane) *hld up in last trio: rdn wl over 2f out: no prog and wl hld whn edgd lft ins fnl f* **50/1**

450- **11** 1 ¼ **Ellies Image**[216] 6939 5 -8-9**62**.. KieranO'Neill 11 44
(Brian Baugh) *stdd s: hld up in rr: rdn and no hdwy over 2f out: n.d* **22/1**

1m 29.86s (0.26)**Going Correction** +0.05s/f (Slow) **11**Ran SP% **116.3**
Speed ratings (Par 103): **100,99,98,97,97 97,96,93,92,90 89**
toteswingers: 1&2 £6.70, 1&3 £9.20, 2&3 £10.80 CSF £30.34 CT £201.17 TOTE £4.30 : £1.40 , £3.80, £2.40 ; EX 37.50 Trifecta £59.40 Pool: £504.77 - 3.94 winning units.
Owner S Brewster & D Charlesworth **Bred** Stowell Hill Ltd & Major & Mrs R B Kennard **Trained** Dalham, Suffolk

FOCUS
This second division of the 7f handicap was another ordinary affair, and was the slower division. Those racing handy looked best off. The runner-up sets the standard.
T/Jkpt: Not won. T/Plt: £446.50 to a £1 stake. Pool: £71,662.95. 117.15 winning tickets. T/Qpdt: £93.30 to £1. Pool: £4,515.20. 35.78 w. tickets. SP

2356a-2359a Foreign Racing (See RI)

^{1767}BRIGHTON (L-H)

Tuesday, May 22

OFFICIAL GOING: Good to firm (firm in places; 8.2)

Wind: Fresh, behind Weather: Sunny and warm

2360 BETFAIR BRINGS YOU BETTER VALUE H'CAP — 5f 59y

2:00 (2:00) (Class 5) (0-70,69) 4-Y-0+ — **£2,264** (£673; £336; £168) **Stalls** Low

Form — RPR

0-44 **1** — **Ginzan**^{15} 1910 4-9-0 **62** .... TomMcLaughlin 7 — 72
(Malcolm Saunders) *disp ld: narrow ld after 2f: jnd fnl f: kpt on gamely u.p: jst hld on* **7/2**^{1}

1 **2** *nse* **Cut Across (IRE)**^{101} 524 4-9-5 **67** .... NeilCallan 10 — 77+
(Nick Littmoden) *dwlt: sn in midfield: hdwy and wnt lft over 1f out: jnd wnr fnl f: kpt on wl u.p: jst pipped* **4/1**^{2}

104 **3** *1 1/4* **Mother Jones**^{8} 2133 4-9-1 **68** .... MatthewCosham$^{(5)}$ 1 — 73
(David Evans) *chsd ldrs: hrd rdn over 1f out: nt qckn fnl f* **17/2**

40-5 **4** *1 1/2* **Imaginary Diva**^{35} 1428 6-9-0 **62** .... IanMongan 8 — 62
(George Margarson) *chsd ldrs: rdn over 2f out: styd on same pce* **12/1**

6214 **5** *3/4* **Court Applause (IRE)**^{55} 1073 4-9-4 **66** .... GeorgeBaker 2 — 64+
(William Muir) *hld up towards rr: promising hdwy and nt clr run over 1f out: fnd gap: no ex ins fnl f* **8/1**

0-60 **6** *1* **Bravo King (IRE)**^{112} 371 4-9-3 **65** ....(t) WilliamCarson 6 — 59
(Richard Guest) *stdd s: bhd tl sme late hdwy* **18/1**

304- **7** *1/2* **Stonecrabstomorrow (IRE)**^{209} 7097 9-9-3 **65** .... KierenFox 5 — 57
(Michael Attwater) *bhd: effrt and nt clr run over 1f out: nt rch ldrs* **14/1**

3-36 **8** *3/4* **Bobby's Doll**^{19} 1788 5-8-13 **68** .... GeorgeanBuckell$^{(7)}$ 4 — 58
(Terry Clement) *prom tl wknd wl over 1f out* **10/1**

3303 **9** *shd* **Sherjawy (IRE)**^{19} 1787 8-8-9 **57** ....(b) LukeMorris 9 — 46
(Zoe Davison) *in tch on outer: rdn over 2f out: sn wknd* **20/1**

0451 **10** *2 1/4* **Welsh Inlet (IRE)**^{19} 1773 4-9-4 **69** .... SeanLevey$^{(3)}$ 3 — 50
(John Bridger) *w ldrs tl hung bdly rt and proving unrideable over 1f out: virtually p.u* **9/2**^{3}

1m 1.3s (-1.00) **Going Correction** -0.20s/f (Firm) **10** Ran SP% **115.5**

Speed ratings (Par 103): **100,99,97,95,94 92,91,90,90,86**

Tote Swingers:1&2:£4.70, 2&3:£9.20, 1&3:£9.40 CSF £17.15 CT £111.58 TOTE £2.90: £1.10, £2.20, £3.70; EX 20.80.

Owner Paul Nicholas **Bred** Hedsor Stud **Trained** Green Ore, Somerset

■ Stewards' Enquiry : Neil Callan one-day ban; careless riding (5th June)

FOCUS

A modest sprint handicap.

Stonecrabstomorrow(IRE) Official explanation: jockey said gelding was denied a clear run.

Welsh Inlet(IRE) Official explanation: jockey said filly hung right

2361 WEATHERBYS BLOODSTOCK INSURANCE MAIDEN STKS — 5f 213y

2:30 (2:30) (Class 5) 3-Y-0+ — **£2,264** (£673; £336; £168) **Stalls** Low

Form — RPR

2 **1** — **Miliika**^{17} 1843 3-8-10 0 .... SebSanders 3 — 80+
(Rae Guest) *hld up in 5th: effrt 2f out: rdn to ld ent fnl f: comf* **1/2**^{1}

4445 **2** *2 1/2* **Millibar (IRE)**^{11} 2045 3-8-10 67 ....(p) NeilCallan 5 — 72
(Nick Littmoden) *disp ld: led over 2f out tl ent fnl f: sn outpcd by wnr* **7/1**^{3}

0- **3** *6* **Atmanna**^{263} 5689 3-8-10 0 .... BrettDoyle 4 — 53
(Clive Brittain) *chsd ldng pair: hrd rdn 2f out: one pce* **20/1**

5-0 **4** *3/4* **Tenderly Place**^{22} 1705 3-8-5 0 ....^{1} DavidKenny$^{(5)}$ 1 — 50
(William Knight) *hld up in rr: rdn and edgd rt over 1f out: styd on fnl f: nvr nrr* **20/1**

2304 **5** *1* **Diamond Marks (IRE)**^{26} 1622 3-9-1 59 .... JohnFahy 8 — 52
(John Gallagher) *plld hrd: disp ld tl over 2f out: hrd rdn and btn over 1f out* **10/1**

236 **6** *4* **Pashan Garh**^{11} 2041 3-9-1 72 .... LukeMorris 7 — 39
(Pat Eddery) *hld up in 6th: rdn 3f out: btn whn carried rt over 1f out* **9/2**^{2}

0 **7** *3 1/4* **Nawarah**^{33} 1472 3-8-10 0 .... DarryllHolland 6 — 24
(Michael Wigham) *stdd s: chsd ldrs: rdn over 2f out: sn wknd* **12/1**

00 **8** *2 1/4* **Starlight Secret**^{7} 2147 3-8-10 0 .... RaulDaSilva$^{(5)}$ 2 — 22
(Simon Earle) *sn outpcd and bhd* **66/1**

1m 8.32s (-1.88) **Going Correction** -0.20s/f (Firm) **8** Ran SP% **125.1**

Speed ratings (Par 103): **104,100,92,91,90 85,80,77**

Tote Swingers:1&2:£2.10, 2&3:£19.80, 1&3:£3.90 CSF £5.62 TOTE £1.80: £1.02, £1.90, £5.20; EX 5.00.

Owner Bradmill Ltd **Bred** C J Mills **Trained** Newmarket, Suffolk

FOCUS

A weak maiden.

Pashan Garh Official explanation: jockey said colt suffered interference in running.

Nawarah Official explanation: jockey said filly lost fore shoe.

2362 DANDY DICK THEATRE ROYAL BRIGHTON ATGTICKETS.COM FILLIES' H'CAP — 7f 214y

3:00 (3:00) (Class 5) (0-70,70) 4-Y-0+ — **£2,264** (£673; £336; £168) **Stalls** Low

Form — RPR

4-26 **1** — **Methayel (IRE)**^{21} 1729 4-9-7 **70** .... SebSanders 3 — 78
(Clive Brittain) *hld up in 4th: rdn over 3f out: led wl over 1f out: all out* **2/1**^{1}

00-5 **2** *1 1/2* **Sasheen**^{13} 1980 5-8-13 **62** .... DarryllHolland 6 — 67
(Jeremy Gask) *chsd ldr tl 2f out: kpt on u.p: regained 2nd fnl 75yds* **4/1**^{3}

5-40 **3** *3/4* **National Hope (IRE)**^{39} 1358 4-9-0 **63** ....(vt^{1}) PatCosgrave 7 — 66
(George Baker) *rdn to ld: drvn along over 3f out: hdd wl over 1f out: one pce ins fnl f* **17/2**

4002 **4** *shd* **Cut The Cackle (IRE)**^{6} 2171 6-8-7 **56** ....(bt) WilliamCarson 1 — 59
(Richard Guest) *stdd s: chsd ldrs: rdn over 3f out: nt clr run 2f out: styd on u.p fnl f* **11/2**

110- **5** *11* **Olney Lass**^{222} 6814 5-8-9 **61** .... SimonPearce$^{(3)}$ 2 — 39
(Lydia Pearce) *a last: rdn 4f out: n.d fnl 2f* **9/4**^{2}

1m 34.88s (-1.12) **Going Correction** -0.20s/f (Firm) **5** Ran SP% **110.0**

Speed ratings (Par 100): **97,95,94,94,83**

CSF £10.19 TOTE £2.80: £1.60, £1.70; EX 11.50.

Owner Saeed Manana **Bred** Lynchbages Edgeridge Ltd & Glenvale Stud **Trained** Newmarket, Suffolk

FOCUS

This isn't strong form.

Olney Lass Official explanation: jockey said mare was never tarvelling.

2363 WEATHERBYS BANK H'CAP — 1m 3f 196y

3:30 (3:30) (Class 5) (0-70,70) 4-Y-0+ — **£2,264** (£673; £336; £168) **Stalls** High

Form — RPR

2565 **1** — **St Ignatius**^{11} 2031 5-9-1 **64** ....(p) DarryllHolland 4 — 71
(Alan Bailey) *mde all: hld on gamely u.p fnl 2f* **14/1**

20-0 **2** *2* **Filun**^{36} 1418 7-9-7 **70** .... JohnFahy 3 — 74
(Anthony Middleton) *hld up in midfield: stdy hdwy on bridle fr 2f out to chal ent fnl f: nt sustain run* **11/1**

246- **3** *3* **The Calling Curlew**^{226} 6729 4-9-1 **69** .... AmyScott$^{(5)}$ 2 — 68
(Henry Candy) *prom: hrd rdn over 2f out: one pce* **13/2**

001- **4** *nk* **Navigation Track**^{287} 4888 4-9-1 **64** .... MartinLane 8 — 63
(David Simcock) *hld up in rr: rdn and hdwy over 1f out: styd on: nrst fin* **6/1**^{3}

6-24 **5** *2 1/2* **White Diamond**^{51} 1154 5-9-5 **68** .... WilliamCarson 9 — 63
(Michael Appleby) *prom: wnt 2nd 5f out tl 3f out: hrd rdn and btn 2f out* **14/1**

2036 **6** *3 1/2* **Silver Alliance**^{19} 1792 4-9-2 **68** .... AdamBeschizza$^{(3)}$ 10 — 57
(Julia Feilden) *chsd ldrs: wnt 2nd 3f out: wknd over 1f out* **12/1**

3221 **7** *5* **Byrd In Hand (IRE)**^{19} 1771 5-8-10 **62** .... SeanLevey$^{(3)}$ 5 — 43
(John Bridger) *mid-div: effrt on outer over 2f out: sn btn* **3/1**^{1}

3252 **8** *1 3/4* **Shabak Hom (IRE)**^{22} 1719 5-9-2 **70** .... MatthewCosham$^{(5)}$ 6 — 48
(David Evans) *a bhd* **12/1**

424- **9** *8* **Wily Fox**^{17} 6469 5-9-5 **68** .... LukeMorris 7 — 33
(James Eustace) *chsd ldrs: rdn over 4f out: sn lost pl* **9/2**^{2}

45-5 **10** *7* **Pelham Crescent (IRE)**^{138} 43 9-9-2 **65** .... DavidProbert 1 — 19
(Bryn Palling) *fly-jmpd and missed break: a bhd* **14/1**

2m 30.96s (-1.74) **Going Correction** -0.20s/f (Firm) **10** Ran SP% **114.5**

Speed ratings (Par 103): **97,95,93,93,91 89,86,84,79,74**

Tote Swingers:1&2:£29.10, 2&3:£13.10, 1&3:£14.50 CSF £155.27 CT £1099.64 TOTE £17.10: £4.30, £4.20, £3.00; EX 171.70.

Owner A J H **Bred** Simon And Helen Plumbly **Trained** Newmarket, Suffolk

FOCUS

A modest race.

2364 BETFAIR DON'T SETTLE FOR LESS H'CAP — 1m 1f 209y

4:00 (4:00) (Class 6) (0-60,60) 4-Y-0+ — **£1,617** (£481; £240; £120) **Stalls** High

Form — RPR

0103 **1** — **Resplendent Alpha**^{4} 2237 8-8-13 **57** .... AmyScott$^{(5)}$ 7 — 71
(Alastair Lidderdale) *hld up in rr: pushed along 3f out: rapid hdwy over 1f out: led ent fnl f: sn clr: easily* **5/1**^{2}

3300 **2** *4 1/2* **Potentiale (IRE)**^{15} 1919 8-9-0 **60** ....(v) Leah-AnneAvery$^{(7)}$ 11 — 65
(J W Hills) *sn pressing ldr: led 2f out tl ent fnl f: no ch w wnr* **11/1**

6600 **3** *shd* **Prince Of Thebes (IRE)**^{53} 1106 11-8-9 **48** .... KierenFox 8 — 52
(Michael Attwater) *led tl 2f out: nt qckn ent fnl f* **25/1**

0-12 **4** *1/2* **Lord Of The Storm**^{19} 1771 4-8-13 **59** .... JakePayne$^{(7)}$ 3 — 65+
(Bill Turner) *hld up in midfield: gd hdwy to press ldrs on rail whn gap clsd and squeezed out jst over 1f out: styd on fnl f* **4/1**^{1}

1334 **5** *2 1/2* **So Is She (IRE)**^{8} 2137 4-8-12 **51** ....(be) DarryllHolland 12 — 49
(Alan Bailey) *chsd ldrs: rdn and one pce fnl 2f* **7/1**^{3}

5022 **6** *1 1/4* **Cahala Dancer (IRE)**^{15} 1907 4-9-2 **55** .... KieranO'Neill 4 — 50
(Roger Teal) *bhd: pushed along 3f out: sme hdwy 2f out: nt rch ldrs* **4/1**^{1}

14-3 **7** *2 1/4* **Penang Cinta**^{15} 2115 9-9-1 **59** .... MatthewCosham$^{(5)}$ 2 — 50
(David Evans) *prom: drvn along over 3f out: wknd over 2f out* **8/1**

434 **8** *1* **Prince Namid**^{15} 1907 10-9-0 **53** ....(p) LukeMorris 5 — 42
(Jonathen de Giles) *chsd ldrs: rdn and btn over 2f out* **20/1**

36-5 **9** *1 1/2* **Corrib (IRE)**^{15} 1908 9-9-0 **53** ....(p) DavidProbert 6 — 39
(Bryn Palling) *a towards rr* **20/1**

1303 **10** *3 1/4* **Celtic Charlie (FR)**^{26} 1631 7-8-13 **52** .... IanMongan 1 — 31
(Pat Phelan) *rrd in stalls: s.s: hdwy into midfield after 3f: wnt prom 4f out: rdn and wknd over 1f out* **8/1**

6560 **11** *9* **Dichoh**^{41} 1309 9-8-7 **49** .... SeanLevey$^{(3)}$ 10 — 10
(Michael Madgwick) *mid-div: wknd over 3f out: sn bhd* **40/1**

2m 2.76s (-0.84) **Going Correction** -0.20s/f (Firm) **11** Ran SP% **115.5**

Speed ratings (Par 101): **95,91,91,90,88 87,86,85,84,81 74**

Tote Swingers:1&2:£14.90, 2&3:£63.80, 1&3:£24.30 CSF £54.13 CT £1248.50 TOTE £4.50: £2.20, £4.00, £5.10; EX 70.40.

Owner Chris Beek Racing **Bred** Sunley Stud **Trained** Lambourn, Berks

■ Stewards' Enquiry : Kieren Fox one-day ban; careless riding (5th June)

FOCUS

A moderate handicap.

2365 BETTER PRICES ON BETFAIR MOBILE H'CAP (DIV I) — 7f 214y

4:30 (4:31) (Class 6) (0-60,60) 4-Y-0+ — **£1,617** (£481; £240; £120) **Stalls** Low

Form — RPR

0/0- **1** — **Toga Tiger (IRE)**^{185} 7484 5-8-4 **48** .... RaulDaSilva$^{(5)}$ 9 — 58
(Jeremy Gask) *plld hrd: prom: led over 1f out: rdn out* **2/1**^{1}

2043 **2** *1 1/4* **Do More Business (IRE)**^{6} 2171 5-9-0 **53** .... IanMongan 10 — 60
(Alison Batchelor) *in tch: effrt 2f out: styd on to press wnr ins fnl f: a hld* **6/1**^{3}

0522 **3** *3/4* **Brown Pete (IRE)**^{19} 1772 4-9-2 **55** .... WilliamCarson 4 — 60
(Richard Guest) *plld hrd: prom: led over 3f out tl over 1f out: kpt on same pce* **9/4**^{2}

5-00 **4** *2 1/4* **Vertibes**^{21} 1743 4-8-12 **58** ....(b^{1}) KatiaScallan$^{(7)}$ 11 — 58
(Marcus Tregoning) *mid-div: rdn and styd on fnl 2f: nvr nrr* **8/1**

00-6 **5** *4 1/2* **Fonterutoli (IRE)**^{19} 1771 5-8-12 **56** .... NathanAlison$^{(5)}$ 6 — 46
(Roger Ingram) *s.s: outpcd and bhd: rdn and hdwy 2f out: no imp* **25/1**

4440 **6** *shd* **Toms River Tess (IRE)**^{26} 1628 4-8-4 **46** oh1 .... SimonPearce$^{(3)}$ 2 — 36
(Zoe Davison) *chsd ldr: led after 1f tl over 3f out: hrd rdn over 2f out: wknd over 1f out* **33/1**

5564 **7** *2 1/4* **Aggbag**^{26} 1634 8-8-2 **48** ow1 ....(p) RichardOliver$^{(7)}$ 8 — 32
(Michael Appleby) *led 1f: prom tl wknd 2f out* **14/1**

6000 **8** *12* **Justcallmehandsome**^{16} 1895 10-8-4 **48** ....(v) AmyScott$^{(5)}$ 12
(Dominic Ffrench Davis) *dwlt: a trailing* **28/1**

-000 **9** *6* **Cuthbert (IRE)**^{26} 1628 5-9-4 **57** .... KierenFox 7
(Michael Attwater) *dwlt: a bhd: no ch fnl 3f* **14/1**

3356 **10** *2 1/2* **Porthgwidden Beach (USA)**^{8} 2133 4-8-7 **46** oh1...(tp) LeeNewman 13
(Anthony Middleton) *sddle slipped early and racd v wd: mid-div: wknd 5f out: sn bhd: rdr fin wout irons* **25/1**

1m 34.34s (-1.66) **Going Correction** -0.20s/f (Firm) **10** Ran SP% **116.9**

Speed ratings (Par 101): **100,98,98,95,91 91,88,76,70,68**

Tote Swingers:1&2:£3.40, 2&3:£4.10, 1&3:£3.30 CSF £13.89 CT £29.73 TOTE £2.40: £1.10, £1.70, £1.80; EX 17.60.

Owner For Sale **Bred** Daniel Spaight **Trained** Sutton Veny, Wilts

FOCUS

A moderate, uncompetitive handicap.

Porthgwidden Beach(USA) Official explanation: jockey said saddle slipped in the early stages.

2366 SHARES IN DUKE OF MARMALADE @HEARTOFTHEOSUTH.NET H'CAP (DIV II OF 4.30PM) 7f 214y

5:00 (5:00) (Class 6) (0-60,60) 4-Y-0+ **£1,617** (£481; £240; £120) **Stalls** Low

Form RPR

060/ **1** **Ansells Pride (IRE)**[627] 5732 9-8-11 **57**.......................... JakePayne(7) 6 67
(Bill Turner) *mde all: sn 3 l clr: stl travelling wl in front over 2f out: drvn along and hld on fnl 150yds: jst lasted* **14/1**

51-0 **2** ½ **Lightning Spirit**[26] 1625 4-9-0 **53**....................................(p) NeilCallan 10 62
(Gary Moore) *mid-div: rdn over 2f out: hdwy over 1f out: wnt 2nd 100yds out: clsng on wnr at fin* **7/1[2]**

3224 **3** *nk* **Chandrayaan**[41] 1310 5-8-6 **48**..................................(v) SimonPearce(3) 2 56
(John E Long) *in tch: rdn and styd on wl fnl 2f: gng on at fin* **8/1[3]**

1000 **4** *1* **Having A Ball**[22] 1702 8-8-9 **48**.. JohnFahy 5 54
(Jonathan Portman) *bhd: rdn 3f out: gd late hdwy* **5/1[1]**

363 **5** 1¾ **Jumeirah Liberty**[19] 1772 4-9-7 **60**................................ SebSanders 11 62
(Zoe Davison) *chsd wnr: rdn over 3f out: lost 2nd and one pce fnl 100yds* **8/1[3]**

3100 **6** ½ **Holyfield Warrior (IRE)**[22] 1702 8-8-7 **46** oh1.................. KierenFox 12 47
(Michael Attwater) *mid-div on outer: hrd rdn 2f out: styd on fnl f* **20/1**

-041 **7** ½ **Titan Diamond (IRE)**[15] 1907 4-8-5 **49**................... RachealKneller(5) 9 49
(Mark Usher) *chsd ldrs: outpcd over 2f out: hld after* **7/1[2]**

0626 **8** ¾ **Inquisitress**[16] 1895 8-8-11 **50**.. KieranO'Neill 7 48
(John Bridger) *s.s: bhd: sme hdwy over 1f out: no ex fnl f* **8/1[3]**

020 **9** *1* **Fault**[6] 2170 6-8-11 **55**.. JemmaMarshall(5) 1 51
(Alastair Lidderdale) *prom tl outpcd 2f out* **5/1[1]**

0034 **10** *6* **Cristaliyev**[19] 1768 4-9-1 **54**..(b) PatCosgrave 3 36
(Jim Boyle) *t.k.h towards rr: hrd rdn over 2f out: sn bhd* **8/1[3]**

1m 34.06s (-1.94) **Going Correction** -0.20s/f (Firm) **10** Ran SP% **114.2**
Speed ratings (Par 101): **101,100,100,99,97 96,96,95,94,88**
Tote Swingers:1&2:£17.50, 2&3:£9.60, 1&3:£26.00 CSF £106.29 CT £861.38 TOTE £22.90: £7.30, £2.20, £1.30; EX 226.40.
Owner Ansells Of Watford **Bred** E Lonergan **Trained** Sigwells, Somerset

FOCUS
Division two of this moderate handicap and the time was 0.28 seconds faster than the first leg.

2367 CHECK BETFAIR BEFORE YOU BET H'CAP 6f 209y

5:30 (5:31) (Class 6) (0-60,60) 3-Y-O **£1,617** (£481; £240; £120) **Stalls** Low

Form RPR

0-46 **1** **Esprit Danseur**[21] 1733 3-9-6 **59**.. PatCosgrave 3 65
(Jim Boyle) *chsd ldrs: led over 1f out: drvn out* **9/1**

04 **2** ¾ **Collectable**[8] 2131 3-8-11 **50**... LeeNewman 7 54
(Jonathan Portman) *mid-div: hdwy 2f out: r.o wl to snatch 2nd on post* **14/1**

-466 **3** *nk* **Represent (IRE)**[8] 2136 3-9-4 **57**............................... MatthewDavies 13 60
(Mick Channon) *in tch: effrt on rail and n.m.r fr over 1f out: r.o* **9/1**

0054 **4** *hd* **Rainbow Riches (IRE)**[21] 1740 3-8-0 **46**..................... JoshBaudains(7) 2 49
(Roger Curtis) *disp ld tl over 1f out: kpt on u.p: lost 2nd on post* **40/1**

633 **5** 1½ **Sudden Wish (IRE)**[13] 1979 3-9-2 **55**........................... DarryllHolland 15 54
(Alan Bailey) *bhd: gd hdwy fr over 1f out: nrst fin* **7/1[3]**

4-65 **6** 1½ **Whatsofunny (IRE)**[25] 1637 3-9-5 **58**................................... NeilCallan 8 53
(Roger Varian) *chsd ldrs: one pce appr fnl f* **2/1[1]**

3 **7** *hd* **Temuco (IRE)**[22] 1716 3-9-2 **60**.............................. MatthewCosham(5) 9 54
(David Evans) *bhd: r.o fnl f: nvr nrr* **16/1**

0-36 **8** 4½ **Pius Parker (IRE)**[10] 2089 3-9-7 **60**....................................(v[1]) JohnFahy 1 42
(John Gallagher) *disp ld tl wknd over 1f out* **18/1**

52-0 **9** ¾ **Possibly**[21] 1733 3-9-7 **60**.. KierenFox 14 40
(Peter Chapple-Hyam) *outpcd and wl bhd tl styd on fnl f* **20/1**

0-00 **10** ¾ **Zuzu Angel (IRE)**[39] 1365 3-9-6 **59**................................. SebSanders 10 37
(William Knight) *in rr gp tl sme late hdwy* **14/1**

60-0 **11** *nk* **Chater Garden (IRE)**[43] 1260 3-8-7 **49**................ AdamBeschizza(3) 12 26
(Alan Jarvis) *s.s: a towards rr* **25/1**

0-35 **12** *1* **Love Grows Wild (USA)**[31] 1531 3-9-3 **56**.................. HayleyTurner 11 30
(Michael Bell) *mid-div: outpcd fnl 2f* **6/1[2]**

3006 **13** 1½ **Armiger**[18] 1826 3-8-10 **49**.. WilliamCarson 4 19
(William Muir) *prom tl wknd 2f out* **33/1**

506- **14** 2¼ **Gypsy Rider**[272] 5374 3-8-12 **56**................................ RaulDaSilva(5) 6 20
(Bryn Palling) *in tch tl wknd 2f out* **40/1**

000- **15** 3¼ **Refreshestheparts (USA)**[237] 6441 3-8-13 **57**........(t) DavidKenny(5) 16 12
(George Baker) *mid-div tl wknd 2f out* **33/1**

6-04 **16** *5* **Purley Queen (IRE)**[8] 2130 3-9-3 **59**.......................... SophieDoyle(3) 5
(Sylvester Kirk) *a towards rr: n.d fnl 2f* **20/1**

1m 22.09s (-1.01) **Going Correction** -0.20s/f (Firm) **16** Ran SP% **128.7**
Speed ratings (Par 97): **97,96,95,95,93 92,91,86,85,85 84,83,81,79,75 69**
Tote Swingers:1&2:£13.70, 2&3:£17.40, 1&3:£10.70 CSF £125.57 CT £1242.89 TOTE £15.70: £2.50, £5.00, £1.40, £8.90; EX 214.60.
Owner The 'In Recovery' Partnership **Bred** Sir Eric Parker **Trained** Epsom, Surrey

FOCUS
A moderate handicap - only one of the 16 runners had previously won a race.
Represent(IRE) Official explanation: jockey said filly was denied a clear run.
Rainbow Riches(IRE) Official explanation: jockey said saddle slipped.
Temuco(IRE) ◆ Official explanation: trainers representative reported gelding did not handle track.
Gypsy Rider Official explanation: jockey said gelding hung left.
T/Plt: £178.60 to a £1 stake. Pool £74,560.40. 304.64 winning tickets. T/Qpdt: £70.80 to a £1 stake. Pool £5,169.56. 53.98 winning tickets. LM

[2145]KEMPTON (A.W) (R-H)

Tuesday, May 22

OFFICIAL GOING: Standard
Wind: Moderate, against Weather: Fine, warm

2368 RACING PLUS PROUDLY SPONSORS MILLWALL MEDIAN AUCTION MAIDEN STKS 1m 2f (P)

6:00 (9:07) (Class 5) 3-4-Y-O **£2,264** (£673; £336; £168) **Stalls** Low

Form RPR

5-2 **1** **Handsome Ransom**[19] 1793 3-9-0 0............................... WilliamBuick 11 80+
(John Gosden) *mde virtually all: upped the tempo over 3f out: kicked on over 2f out and only one rival after: shkn up to draw clr fnl f* **2/5[1]**

5 **2** 4½ **Broadway Babe (IRE)**[19] 1793 3-8-9 0................. SilvestreDeSousa 10 66
(Harry Dunlop) *awkward s: sn chsd wnr: rdn 3f out: only danger over 2f out: btn off jst over 1f out: kpt on* **16/1[3]**

66 **3** 3¾ **Sign Manual**[16] 1893 3-9-0 0.. LukeMorris 1 63
(Michael Bell) *trckd ldrs: outpcd wl over 2f out: chsd ldng pair 2f out but nowhere nr them: no imp: clung on to 3rd nr fin* **10/1[2]**

4 ½ **Ghusoon** 3-8-9 0.. TadhgO'Shea 13 57+
(John Gosden) *slowest away: mostly in last trio: rdn 3f out and wl off the pce: wd bnd 2f out: styd on fr over 1f out: tk 4th and clsd on 3rd nr fin* **16/1[3]**

44 **5** *1* **Joe The Coat**[8] 2125 3-9-0 0.. TedDurcan 12 60
(Mark H Tompkins) *racd wd: cl up: outpcd wl over 2f out: rdn and disp modest 4th over 1f out: one pce* **10/1[2]**

6 *nk* **Elegant Ophelia** 3-8-9 0..(t) AndreaAtzeni 7 54
(Marco Botti) *dwlt: trckd ldrs: outpcd wl over 2f out: disp modest 4th over 1f out: one pce* **25/1**

03 **7** *2* **Geordie Boy**[36] 1415 3-9-0 0...................................... RichardMullen 9 55
(Sheena West) *a in midfield: outpcd and pushed along wl over 2f out: nvr on terms after: bttr for r* **16/1[3]**

0 **8** 1½ **Black Motive**[13] 1981 3-9-0 0..[1] StevieDonohoe 6 52
(Michael Bell) *dwlt: a in midfield: outpcd and rdn wl over 2f out: n.d after* **66/1**

00 **9** ½ **Red Mystique (IRE)**[5] 2197 3-8-9 0......................... AshleyMorgan(5) 2 51+
(Ed Dunlop) *a in midfield: pushed along 4f out: outpcd wl over 2f out: n.d after* **50/1**

10 *nse* **Wijaya** 3-8-9 0.. EddieAhern 14 46+
(James Fanshawe) *mostly in last trio: pushed along over 2f out: kpt on one pce after* **25/1**

11 *nse* **Any Given Dream (IRE)** 3-9-0 0....................................... MartinLane 3 51+
(David Simcock) *hld up in last trio: stl there but gng bttr than many 3f out: nudged along and kpt on steadily fnl 2f* **33/1**

12 *22* **Southerly** 3-8-11 0.. PatrickHills(3) 8
(Luca Cumani) *dwlt: a in tch in midfield: rn green and urged along fr 1/2-way: wknd qckly over 2f out: t.o* **33/1**

13 2¼ **Orla (IRE)**[18] 4-9-9 0... JamesDoyle 5
(Dominic Ffrench Davis) *mostly in 3rd tl wknd rapidly over 2f out: t.o* **100/1**

2m 8.88s (0.88) **Going Correction** -0.05s/f (Stan)
WFA 3 from 4yo 14lb **13** Ran SP% **125.3**
Speed ratings (Par 103): **94,90,87,87,86 85,84,83,82,82 82,65,63**
Tote Swingers:1&2:£3.70, 2&3:£5.20, 1&3:£1.90 CSF £8.95 TOTE £1.40: £1.02, £4.80, £2.30; EX 14.00 Trifecta £60.90 Pool £1,231.00 - 14.96 winning units..
Owner Normandie Stud Ltd **Bred** Normandie Stud Ltd **Trained** Newmarket, Suffolk

FOCUS
Few landed a blow in this uncompetitive maiden.
Geordie Boy Official explanation: jockey said gelding hung left.
Southerly Official explanation: jockey said colt did not handle kickback.

2369 MILLWALL RACEDAY AT KEMPTON PARK H'CAP 5f (P)

6:30 (9:07) (Class 4) (0-80,83) 4-Y-0+ **£4,528** (£1,347; £673; £336) **Stalls** Low

Form RPR

1030 **1** **Royal Bajan (USA)**[61] 991 4-9-2 **74**........................... FrederikTylicki 5 83
(James Given) *mde all: rdn over 1f out: fnd enough and a holding on fnl f* **7/1[3]**

00-5 **2** ½ **Befortyfour**[55] 1073 7-8-13 **71**...................................(t) RobbieFitzpatrick 7 78
(Richard Guest) *chsd ldrs: wnt 3rd over 1f out: drvn and r.o to take 2nd fnl strides* **20/1**

625- **3** ½ **Osiris Way**[175] 7575 10-9-3 **75**.. GeorgeBaker 8 80
(Patrick Chamings) *pressed wnr: rdn over 1f out: nt qckn and no imp after: lost 2nd last strides* **13/2[2]**

0-20 **4** 1¼ **Speightowns Kid (USA)**[18] 1828 4-9-2 **74**........(e[1]) SilvestreDeSousa 10 75
(Matthew Salaman) *chsd ldrs on outer: rdn 1/2-way: kpt on u.p: nvr able to chal* **10/1**

2435 **5** *nk* **Estonia**[5] 2195 5-9-3 **75**.. LukeMorris 2 75
(Michael Squance) *hld up in midfield on inner: n.m.r briefly 2f out: rdn over 1f out: kpt on: n.d* **8/1**

2403 **6** ½ **Fair Passion**[13] 1990 5-9-7 **79**... DaneO'Neill 6 77+
(Derek Shaw) *awkward s: mostly in last trio: drvn 2f out: kpt on fr over 1f out: nrst fin* **17/2**

2412 **7** *nk* **Black Cadillac (IRE)**[33] 1481 4-9-2 **74**........................... DavidProbert 12 71+
(Andrew Balding) *racd on outer in midfield: rdn 2f out: one pce and no imp on ldrs* **4/1[1]**

125- **8** *nk* **Rebecca Romero**[217] 6932 5-8-10 **68**................................ EddieAhern 4 64+
(Denis Coakley) *hld up in rr: jst pushed along fr over 1f out: kpt on: nvr actively involved* **7/1[3]**

05-0 **9** *2* **Macdillon**[15] 1936 6-9-4 **76**... FergusSweeney 11 65
(Stuart Kittow) *racd wd fr poor draw and sn in last trio: shkn up 2f out: one pce and no imp* **10/1**

26-3 **10** 2¼ **Wooden King (IRE)**[39] 1362 7-9-1 **73**........................ TomMcLaughlin 1 54
(Malcolm Saunders) *awkward s: a in last trio: shkn up and no prog over 1f out* **17/2**

25-0 **11** *1* **Baby Queen (IRE)**[18] 1828 6-8-13 **71**.......................... SamHitchcott 3 48
(Brian Baugh) *chsd ldng pair to over 1f out: wknd rapidly* **20/1**

59.64s (-0.86) **Going Correction** -0.05s/f (Stan) **11** Ran SP% **118.2**
Speed ratings (Par 105): **104,103,102,100,99 99,98,98,94,91 89**
Tote Swingers:1&2:£24.10, 2&3:£33.50, 1&3:£12.50 CSF £137.69 CT £946.83 TOTE £8.40: £2.50, £8.90, £3.30; EX 196.00 Trifecta £495.20 Part won. Pool £669.28 - 0.20 winning units..
Owner Danethorpe Racing Partnership **Bred** West Wind Farm **Trained** Willoughton, Lincs

FOCUS
A modest sprint where those drawn low held a significant advantage and once again on the inner course here it paid to race on the pace.
Black Cadillac(IRE) Official explanation: jockey said gelding hung right.

2370 BARRY KITCHENER MEMORIAL MAIDEN AUCTION STKS 6f (P)

7:00 (9:07) (Class 5) 2-Y-O **£2,264** (£673; £336; £168) **Stalls** Low

Form RPR

1 **London Citizen (USA)** 2-8-10 0.. LukeMorris 2 79+
(Mrs K Burke) *trckd ldrs: wnt 2nd over 1f out: drvn to ld jst ins fnl f: drew away last 100yds* **15/2**

025 **2** 2¼ **Marvelino**[10] 2069 2-8-13 0... DaneO'Neill 5 75
(Pat Eddery) *v difficult to load into stalls: broke wl: led 2f: stdd: led again 2f out and kicked on: hdd jst ins fnl f: no ex last 100yds* **5/2[2]**

3 *7* **Stupenda** 2-8-6 0... TadhgO'Shea 6 47
(Denis Coakley) *s.s: rapid prog to ld after 2f: hdd 2f out: wknd but hld on for 3rd* **14/1**

3 **4** 2¼ **Ace Pearl (USA)**[14] 1955 2-8-12 0.............................. MichaelStainton 8 46
(David Brown) *trckd ldr 2f: styd handy: pushed along 1/2-way: wknd wl over 1f out* **7/1[3]**

	5	nk	**Hasopop (IRE)** 2-8-12 0 ... SilvestreDeSousa 9 (Marco Botti) *dwlt: trckd ldrs: drvn over 2f out: wknd wl over 1f out* **2/1**[1]	45+
	6	hd	**Mumbai Star (IRE)** 2-8-11 0 ... FergusSweeney 4 (Paul Fitzsimons) *dwlt: off the pce in rr gp: n.d fr 1/2-way: kpt on fnl f* **25/1**	44
	7	2	**Bountybeamadam** 2-8-8 0 ... TedDurcan 3 (George Baker) *dwlt: hld up and a wl in rr: nvr a factor* **25/1**	35
66	8	2	**Lea Valley Black**[36] 1411 2-8-12 0 ... JamesDoyle 10 (Tom Dascombe) *a off the pce in rr gp: no ch fr 1/2-way* **14/1**	33
	9	½	**Orla's Rainbow (IRE)** 2-9-0 0 ... BrettDoyle 1 (John Berry) *a off the pce in rr: struggling bef 1/2-way* **20/1**	33
	10	13	**Bogsnog (IRE)** 2-8-12 0 ... EddieAhern 7 (Linda Stubbs) *s.s: rn green and a bhd: t.o* **40/1**	

1m 12.75s (-0.35) **Going Correction** -0.05s/f (Stan) **10** Ran SP% **114.4**
Speed ratings (Par 93): **100,97,87,84,84 84,81,78,78,60**
Tote Swingers:1&2:£2.70, 2&3:£7.90, 1&3:£16.60 CSF £24.90 TOTE £7.60: £1.70, £1.50, £3.90; EX 33.40 Trifecta £693.70 Part won. Pool £937.45 - 0.93 winning units..
Owner Hubert John Strecker **Bred** Stonestreet Thoroughbred Holdings LLC **Trained** Middleham Moor, N Yorks

FOCUS
There was no hanging about in this juvenile maiden and the first pair came well clear from the furlong marker.

NOTEBOOK
London Citizen(USA) ◆ was nicely drawn and he ran out a taking debut winner. He was going nicely turning for home, but took time to get the hang of things when asked for an effort. It was clear entering the final furlong he would master the more experienced runner-up, though, and he was well on top at the finish. The first foal of a South African Group 2 winner, he's entitled to improve a deal and it will be interesting to see where he pitches up next as he appears to have a bright future. It could well be the Listed Woodcote Stakes at Epsom on Derby day next month. (op 7-1 tchd 8-1)
Marvelino, on his first outing over 6f, was the one to aim at back on Polytrack. He delayed the start by having a hind shoe removed and then very nearly refused to enter the stalls. Once the gates opened he pinged out to lead, however, and made a bold bid. He is starting looking exposed, but was a clear second-best on and time may well tell he faced a stiff task. (tchd 9-4)
Stupenda didn't go unbacked for her debut. She did plenty early on after being rushed up and paid nearing the final furlong, leaving an impression the drop to 5f may suit in the short term. (op 11-1)
Ace Pearl(USA), who made his debut on Fibresand, proved very easy to back up in trip. He failed to see out the extra furlong racing at such pace and is now looking more of one for nurseries in due course. (op 13-2 tchd 15-2)
Hasopop(IRE), for whom there was plenty of money, was caught out wide early on and always looked to be going that stride too quick. Better was presumably expected and he ought to come on. (op 5-2)
Mumbai Star(IRE) did best of those that struggled to go the early pace and looks sure to improve
Lea Valley Black Official explanation: jockey said colt was slowly away.

2371 RACING PLUS OUT ON SATURDAY FOR JUST £1 H'CAP 2m (P)
7:30 (9:07) (Class 6) (0-60,59) 4-Y-0+ £1,617 (£481; £240; £120) Stalls Low

Form				RPR
0034	1		**Blackstone Vegas**[11] 1272 6-9-3 55 ... DaneO'Neill 5 (Derek Shaw) *trckd ldrs: wnt 3rd over 3f out: rdn to ld 2f out: kpt on to assert ins fnl f* **5/1**	63
-063	2	2	**Rodrigo De Freitas (IRE)**[119] 278 5-9-2 54 ...(v) PatCosgrave 1 (Jim Boyle) *trckd ldng pair: wnt 2nd over 3f out: rdn to chal over 2f out but hanging: chsd wnr sn after: nt qckn and hld fnl f* **14/1**	60
0034	3	1 ½	**Bengal Tiger**[63] 968 6-8-6 51 ... GeorgeDowning(7) 4 (Tony Carroll) *patiently rdn: prog to chse ldng trio wl over 2f out: sn rdn and nt qckn: kpt on one pce to take 3rd 1f out* **14/1**	55
6241	4	¾	**Delagoa Bay (IRE)**[8] 2134 4-8-12 52 6ex ... WilliamBuick 7 (Sylvester Kirk) *hld up in last: prog out wd 6f out: rdn over 4f out and sn dropped to rr again: styd on fr over 1f out to take 4th nr fin* **3/1**[1]	55
6333	5	1	**Waldsee (GER)**[6] 2175 7-9-6 58 ... JamesDoyle 3 (Paul Rich) *pressed ldr: led 5f out but hanging: hdd and nt qckn 2f out: fdd* **7/2**[3]	60
4/0-	6	1 ½	**Manjam (IRE)**[6] 8-8-7 45 ...(tp) SamHitchcott 2 (Chris Gordon) *led: rdn and hdd 5f out: lost pl over 3f out: one pce after* **25/1**	45
2124	7	2 ¼	**Broughtons Bandit**[6] 2175 5-9-3 55 ... StevieDonohoe 8 (Willie Musson) *trckd ldrs: rdn and lost pl 3f out: struggling after* **10/3**[2]	52
235-	8	13	**Formidable Guest**[160] 7761 8-9-0 59 ... CharlotteJenner(7) 6 (Jamie Poulton) *hld up in last pair: n.m.r after 5f: wknd over 3f out: t.o* **14/1**	41

3m 30.82s (0.72) **Going Correction** -0.05s/f (Stan)
WFA 4 from 5yo+ 2lb **8** Ran SP% **110.8**
Speed ratings (Par 101): **96,95,94,93,93 92,91,85**
Tote Swingers:1&2:£11.80, 2&3:£7.30, 1&3:£5.80 CSF £65.73 CT £873.84 TOTE £5.80: £1.50, £4.60, £3.10; EX 57.80 Trifecta £431.00 Pool £599.96 - 1.03 winning units..
Owner Shakespeare Racing **Bred** Elms Stud Co Ltd **Trained** Sproxton, Leics
■ Stewards' Enquiry : Charlotte Jenner five-day ban; used whip when out of contention (5th-9th June)
Dane O'Neill two-day ban; excessive use of whip (5th-6th June)

FOCUS
A weak staying handicap, run at a routine pace.

2372 SOUTHWARK NEWS PROUDLY SUPPORTS MILLWALL H'CAP 1m 4f (P)
8:00 (9:07) (Class 5) (0-75,75) 3-Y-0 £2,264 (£673; £336; £168) Stalls Centre

Form				RPR
045-	1		**Arch Villain (IRE)**[195] 7329 3-9-0 68 ... JimCrowley 6 (Amanda Perrett) *trckd ldng quartet: nt clr run over 2f out and again wl over 1f out: r.o wl whn in the clr fnl f: led post* **8/1**	76+
0-31	2	nse	**Hector's Chance**[13] 1982 3-8-11 65 ... JamesDoyle 11 (Heather Main) *t.k.h: hld up in 6th: prog jst over 2f out: drvn to ld ins fnl f: kpt on: hdd post* **17/2**	70+
01-5	3	½	**Awesome Pearl (USA)**[11] 2038 3-9-3 74 ... HarryBentley(3) 1 (Sir Mark Prescott Bt) *trckd ldng pair: wnt 2nd 2f out to 1f out and pressed ldr: styd on same pce fnl f: a hld* **13/2**	78
-665	4	hd	**Holly Martins**[16] 1892 3-8-11 72 ...(t) NicoleNordblad(7) 8 (Hans Adielsson) *led: kpt on wl whn pressed 2f out: hdd ins fnl f: no ex and lost 2 pls last strides* **20/1**	76
2-45	5	1 ¼	**Harry Buckle**[22] 1707 3-8-13 67 ... RichardMullen 10 (Philip McBride) *hld up in 10th: rdn on outer over 2f out: styd on fr over 1f out: nvr gng pce to chal* **12/1**	69+
00-1	6	nse	**Ukrainian (IRE)**[28] 1591 3-9-7 75 ... SilvestreDeSousa 9 (Mark Johnston) *hld up in 8th: shkn up on outer over 2f out: styd on fr over 1f out: nvr gng pce to threaten* **5/1**[2]	77+
3253	7	¾	**Dartford (USA)**[22] 1707 3-9-6 74 ... WilliamBuick 4 (John Gosden) *trckd ldng trio: drvn and effrt over 2f out: nt qckn wl over 1f out: fdd fnl f* **9/2**[1]	75
3215	8	2 ½	**Zain Princess (IRE)**[20] 1757 3-9-4 72 ... NickyMackay 3 (Gerard Butler) *hld up in last: rdn over 2f out: one pce and no ch w ldrs* **9/1**	69
1236	9	1 ½	**Beauchamp Castle**[22] 1707 3-9-2 70 ...(t) GeorgeBaker 2 (Hans Adielsson) *hld up in 9th: shkn up over 2f out: no prog over 1f out: wknd fnl f* **11/1**	64
0-12	10	1 ¼	**Topanga Canyon**[33] 1486 3-9-4 72 ...(v) LiamKeniry 5 (Andrew Balding) *trckd ldr to 2f out: sn wknd* **6/1**[3]	64
02-3	11	4 ½	**My Destination (IRE)**[40] 1340 3-9-7 75 ...(p) EddieAhern 7 (Ismail Mohammed) *hld up in 7th: rdn and no prog over 2f out: wknd wl over 1f out* **22/1**	60

2m 33.8s (-0.70) **Going Correction** -0.05s/f (Stan) **11** Ran SP% **119.2**
Speed ratings (Par 99): **100,99,99,99,98 98,98,96,95,94 91**
Tote Swingers:1&2:£4.60, 2&3:£6.60, 1&3:£13.10 CSF £75.39 CT £518.70 TOTE £9.20: £2.90, £3.20, £2.20; EX 69.10 Trifecta £518.70 Pool £883.20 - 1.26 winning units..
Owner Mr & Mrs F Cotton, Mr & Mrs P Conway **Bred** Summerhill Bloodstock **Trained** Pulborough, W Sussex

FOCUS
This wasn't a bad 3yo handicap. However, it was run at an ordinary pace, which resulted in a dash for home, and there was a bunched finish.

2373 UK HOMES FOR HEROES H'CAP 7f (P)
8:30 (9:07) (Class 6) (0-65,65) 4-Y-0+ £1,617 (£481; £240; £120) Stalls Low

Form				RPR
1122	1		**Diplomatic (IRE)**[54] 1088 7-9-3 61 ... LukeMorris 1 (Michael Squance) *trckd ldrs: strly rdn over 2f out: wnt 2nd over 1f out on inner: led last 150yds: styd on wl* **4/1**[1]	73
0502	2	1 ½	**Dvinsky (USA)**[6] 2170 11-9-2 60 ...(b) TomMcLaughlin 2 (Paul Howling) *led: styd on wl whn chal over 2f out: hdd and no ex last 150yds* **11/1**	68
0050	3	1 ¼	**West Leake (IRE)**[21] 1729 6-9-2 60 ... LiamKeniry 7 (Paul Burgoyne) *wl in tch bhd ldrs: outpcd 2f out: styd on fr over 1f out to take 3rd ins fnl f* **13/2**[3]	65
04-0	4	¾	**Spirit Of Gondree (IRE)**[38] 1391 4-9-3 61 ... FergusSweeney 12 (Milton Bradley) *stdd s: t.k.h and dropped into last pair fr wd draw: prog on inner over 2f out: styd on fnl f: nvr able to chal* **33/1**	64
6-35	5	1 ½	**Links Drive Lady**[7] 2146 4-9-7 65 ... ShaneKelly 5 (Dean Ivory) *reluctant to enter stalls: chsd ldr: chal and upsides over 2f out: lost 2nd over 1f out: wknd* **15/2**	64
0421	6	nk	**Loyal N Trusted**[22] 1722 4-9-4 62 ...(p) JimCrowley 6 (Richard Price) *towards rr: rdn wl over 2f out: styd on u.p fr over 1f out: nvr able to threaten* **11/2**[2]	60
2001	7	¾	**Gallantry**[22] 1702 10-9-3 61 ... AmirQuinn 3 (Paul Howling) *trckd ldrs: nt qckn over 2f out and outpcd by ldng trio: one pce after* **25/1**	57
0515	8	1 ¼	**Saucy Buck (IRE)**[19] 1772 4-9-3 61 ... MartinLane 10 (Jamie Poulton) *hld up and sn last: pushed along and mde sme prog fr over 2f out: rdn fnl f: kpt on but nvr involved* **14/1**	53
2525	9	2 ½	**Perfect Ch'l (IRE)**[19] 1788 5-9-7 65 ... JamesDoyle 4 (Ian Wood) *nvr beyond midfield: struggling to hold pl bef 1/2-way: wl btn fnl 2f* **13/2**[3]	51
434-	10	2 ¼	**Fenella Fudge**[174] 7587 4-9-6 64 ... DaneO'Neill 8 (Derek Shaw) *racd wd towards rr: struggling over 2f out: sn no ch* **14/1**	43
6060	11	3	**Doctor Hilary**[19] 1768 10-8-11 55 ...(v) RobertHavlin 11 (Mark Hoad) *racd wd: a in rr: struggling fr 3f out* **40/1**	26
1100	12	½	**Rise To Glory (IRE)**[14] 1961 4-9-0 58 ... DuranFentiman 9 (Shaun Harris) *racd wd: trckd ldng pair to over 2f out: wknd* **28/1**	28
05-0	13	1 ½	**Beautiful Lando (FR)**[115] 353 4-9-5 63 ...(b) SilvestreDeSousa 14 (Heather Main) *racd wd: wl there tl wknd over 2f out* **8/1**	29

1m 25.12s (-0.88) **Going Correction** -0.05s/f (Stan) **13** Ran SP% **119.3**
Speed ratings (Par 101): **103,101,99,99,97 96,96,94,91,89 85,85,83**
Tote Swingers:1&2:£7.00, 2&3:£26.40, 1&3:£2.00 CSF £47.09 CT £294.98 TOTE £4.10: £2.00, £2.60, £2.90; EX 45.20 Trifecta £304.20 Pool £978.66 - 2.38 winning units..
Owner K Squance & R Favarulo **Bred** Darley **Trained** Newmarket, Suffolk

FOCUS
An ordinary handicap and a wide-open looking race. There was an average pace on and the form looks straightforward enough.

2374 RACINGPLUS.CO.UK H'CAP 1m (P)
9:00 (9:07) (Class 6) (0-55,58) 3-Y-0 £1,617 (£481; £240; £120) Stalls Low

Form				RPR
00-0	1		**Watanee**[17] 1843 3-9-1 52 ... EddieAhern 2 (Clive Brittain) *trckd ldrs: rdn and prog to ld over 1f out: sn jnd: fnd more and asserted last 100yds* **5/1**[2]	62+
2502	2	1 ¾	**Songbird Blues**[27] 1608 3-9-4 55 ... DavidProbert 10 (Mark Usher) *t.k.h: hld up in midfield: gd prog fr 2f out to chal and w wnr 1f out: nt qckn and hld last 100yds: kpt on* **8/1**	61
0-05	3	1 ¼	**Adverse (IRE)**[29] 1560 3-8-8 52 ... IanBurns(7) 13 (Michael Bell) *t.k.h: racd on outer: trckd ldrs: effrt over 2f out: nt qckn over 1f out: styd on to take 3rd ins fnl f* **20/1**	55
060	4	shd	**Tom Red**[36] 1414 3-9-2 53 ... ShaneKelly 4 (Dean Ivory) *wl plcd bhd ldrs: gng strly 2f out: rdn and nt qckn over 1f out: kpt on to press for 3rd fnl f* **16/1**	56
00-6	5	¾	**Dana's Present**[21] 1725 3-9-4 55 ... LiamKeniry 6 (George Baker) *t.k.h: hld up in midfield on inner: effrt over 2f out: styd on same pce fr over 1f out* **15/2**	56
06-0	6	¾	**Tigertoo (IRE)**[21] 1740 3-9-4 55 ... WilliamCarson 9 (Stuart Williams) *t.k.h: stdd sn after s and hld up in last pair: pushed along over 2f out: styd on fnl 2f: no ch of rching ldrs* **25/1**	54
5-61	7	1 ½	**Lucifers Shadow (IRE)**[8] 2131 3-9-7 58 6ex ... JamesDoyle 1 (Sylvester Kirk) *led to over 4f out: styd cl up: rdn to chal and upsides over 1f out: wknd fnl f* **2/1**[1]	54
40-0	8	1 ¼	**Get The Trip**[27] 1608 3-8-8 50 ... RaulDaSilva(5) 5 (Anthony Carson) *racd in ldng trio: nrly upsides wl over 1f out: wknd fnl f* **33/1**	43
0-00	9	1 ¾	**Verge (IRE)**[36] 1420 3-9-0 51 ... TedDurcan 14 (Ed Vaughan) *t.k.h: hld up bhd ldrs: shkn up over 2f out: fdd over 1f out: eased* **40/1**	40
26-4	10	2	**Sweet Grace**[14] 1959 3-9-3 54 ...(t) MichaelStainton 7 (David Brown) *s.i.s: a in rr: rdn and struggling wl over 2f out* **20/1**	38
-064	11	hd	**Hurriya**[38] 1386 3-9-0 51 ... SilvestreDeSousa 12 (Mark Johnston) *t.k.h: prog out wd to ld over 4f out: hdd over 1f out: wknd qckly* **7/1**[3]	35
040-	12	2 ¾	**Music Girl**[273] 5343 3-9-0 51 ... DaneO'Neill 3 (Michael Blanshard) *s.i.s: a in rr: rdn and no prog over 2f out* **40/1**	29

050 **13** *2 ½* **Norse Song**[39] 1357 3-9-2 **53**.................................... MarcHalford 8 25
(David Elsworth) *a wl in rr: no prog on wd outside over 2f out* **20/1**

400- **14** *11* **Sally Pepper (USA)**[214] 6984 3-9-4 **55**........................ FrederikTylicki 11
(James Given) *a in rr: drvn over 4f out: t.o* **33/1**

1m 39.72s (-0.08) **Going Correction** -0.05s/f (Stan) **14** Ran SP% **120.2**
Speed ratings (Par 97): **98,96,95,94,94 93,91,90,88,86 86,83,81,70**
Tote Swingers:1&2:£7.90, 2&3:£16.10, 1&3:£20.30 CSF £39.14 CT £758.71 TOTE £6.60: £2.30, £2.60, £7.30; EX 44.60 Trifecta £331.00 Pool £1,100.64 - 2.46 winning units..
Owner Saeed Manana **Bred** Meon Valley Stud **Trained** Newmarket, Suffolk

FOCUS
A weak 3-y-o handicap on paper, but there were potential improvers lurking and three of the first four were handicap newcomers.
Watanee Official explanation: trainers representative said regarding apparent improvement in form that the filly is improving and was suited to the all-weather track.
Norse Song Official explanation: jockey said filly would not face kickback.
T/Plt: £259.00 to a £1 stake. Pool £64,584.05. 182.00 winning tickets T/Qpdt: £138.50 to a £1 stake. Pool £5,640.85. 30.12 winning tickets JN

2084 NOTTINGHAM (L-H)
Tuesday, May 22

OFFICIAL GOING: Good to firm (firm in places; 9.3)
Wind: Light, half-behind Weather: Warm and sunny

2375 BOOK FOR FAMILY DAY 3RD JUNE H'CAP (BETFAIR SPRINT FLAT SERIES QUALIFIER) 6f 15y
1:45 (1:46) (Class 5) (0-75,73) 3-Y-O **£3,234** (£962; £481; £240) **Stalls** High

Form RPR

2432 **1** **Available (IRE)**[33] 1482 3-9-1 **67**.................................... FrannyNorton 4 77
(John Mackie) *t.k.h: prom: effrt to chal wl over 1f out: rdn to ld ins fnl f: styd on* **14/1**

1-52 **2** *2* **Dancheur (IRE)**[22] 1709 3-9-0 **66**.................................... MartinHarley 1 70
(Mrs K Burke) *in tch: hdwy on outer to trck ldrs over 2f out: rdn over 1f out: styd on fnl f* **7/2**[2]

3311 **3** *1 ¼* **First Bid**[11] 2045 3-9-5 **71**.................................(b) J-PGuillambert 13 71
(James Given) *cl up: led after 2f: rdn over 1f out: hdd ins fnl f: kpt on same pce* **10/1**

14-6 **4** *1 ¾* **Relentless Harry (IRE)**[13] 1985 3-9-7 **73**....................(t) FrankieDettori 8 67+
(George Baker) *sltly hmpd and wnt lft s: in rr and swtchd rt after 2f: hdwy on outer over 2f out: rdn wl over 1f out: no imp fnl f* **11/4**[1]

03-2 **5** *nse* **Dora's Sister (IRE)**[20] 1758 3-8-12 **64**........................ TomQueally 10 58+
(John Quinn) *rrd and wnt lft s: towards rr: hdwy to chse ldrs 1/2-way: rdn 2f out: sn one pce* **9/2**[3]

26-0 **6** *1 ½* **Star City (IRE)**[29] 1560 3-9-3 **69**.................................... TomEaves 11 58
(Michael Dods) *hld up in rr: hdwy 2f out: styd on fnl f: nrst fin* **10/1**

3324 **7** *shd* **Man Of My Word**[49] 1176 3-9-0 **66**............................(p) PaulHanagan 12 55
(Scott Dixon) *led 2f: cl up tl rdn along over 2f out and grad wknd* **18/1**

14-4 **8** *¾* **Little China**[36] 1412 3-9-6 **72**.................................... MartinDwyer 2 59
(William Muir) *chsd ldrs: rdn along 1/2-way: sn wknd* **20/1**

00-6 **9** *2 ¼* **Sanad (IRE)**[34] 1445 3-8-12 **67**.................................... DominicFox(3) 14 47
(Anthony Carson) *a towards rr* **28/1**

1-20 **10** *1 ¼* **First Fast Now (IRE)**[15] 1912 3-8-4 **63**........................ EvaMoscrop(7) 6 39
(Nigel Tinkler) *a towards rr* **33/1**

33-6 **11** *2* **Knight Vision**[42] 1285 3-9-3 **69**.................................... AdrianNicholls 5 38
(David Nicholls) *prom: rdn along 1/2-way: sn wknd* **20/1**

1m 12.85s (-2.05) **Going Correction** -0.35s/f (Firm) **11** Ran SP% **113.1**
Speed ratings (Par 99): **99,96,94,92,92 90,90,89,86,84 81**
Tote Swingers:1&2:£8.10, 2&3:£7.70, 1&3:£13.00 CSF £57.26 CT £530.64 TOTE £17.70: £4.70, £1.40, £3.60; EX 50.60 Trifecta £231.40 Part won. Pool £213.83 - 0.50 winning units..
Owner Derbyshire Racing V **Bred** Carrigbeg Stud & David Powell **Trained** Church Broughton , Derbys

FOCUS
An average 6f handicap confined to 3yos. They raced up the middle to nearside at a decent gallop and the first three were always prominent. A small personal best from the winner.

2376 E B F THINK TAXI THINK DG 01159500500 MAIDEN STKS 6f 15y
2:15 (2:15) (Class 5) 2-Y-O **£3,234** (£962; £481; £240) **Stalls** High

Form RPR

1 **Windhoek** 2-9-3 0.................................... JoeFanning 10 86+
(Mark Johnston) *racd towards stands' rail: a.p: hdwy to ld over 1f out: sn rdn: green and hung persistently lft thrght fnl f: hld on wl towards fin* **11/1**

3 **2** *shd* **Janoub Nibras (IRE)**[10] 2069 2-9-3 0.................................... RichardHughes 2 86
(Richard Hannon) *trckd ldrs: hdwy on outer and cl up 2f out: rdn to ld briefly 1 1/2f out: hdd appr fnl f: ev ch whn carried lft ins fnl f: no ex nr fin* **11/8**[1]

3 **3** *4 ½* **Gold Hunter (IRE)**[16] 1886 2-9-3 0.................................... FrankieDettori 9 72
(Saeed Bin Suroor) *trckd ldrs: hdwy 1/2-way: led briefly 2f out: sn rdn and hdd wl over 1f out: n.m.r jst ins fnl f: one pce after* **3/1**[2]

23 **4** *½* **Well Acquainted (IRE)**[39] 1352 2-9-3 0.................................... AdamKirby 7 71
(Clive Cox) *in tch: pushed along over 2f out: sn swtchd lft and rdn: hdwy to chse ldrs over 1f out: swtchd rt ins fnl f: kpt on same pce* **13/2**[3]

44 **5** *6* **Indian Affair**[6] 2164 2-9-3 0.................................... RichardKingscote 3 53
(Milton Bradley) *led: rdn along wl over 2f out: sn hdd: wknd and hung rt ins fnl f* **25/1**

6 *¾* **Pearl Ransom (IRE)** 2-9-0 0.................................... HarryBentley(3) 1 50
(Kevin Ryan) *in tch: pushed along: green and outpcd 2f out: styd on appr fnl f* **25/1**

7 *1 ¾* **Pearl Reward (USA)** 2-9-3 0.................................... JimCrowley 8 45
(Stuart Williams) *cl up: rdn over 2f out: sn wknd* **40/1**

0 **8** *1 ½* **Cuisine (IRE)**[16] 1886 2-9-3 0.................................... JimmyFortune 5 41
(Andrew Balding) *cl up: rdn along 1/2-way: sn wknd* **33/1**

0 **9** *2 ¼* **Stand N Applaude**[18] 1818 2-9-3 0.................................... AdrianNicholls 4 34
(David Nicholls) *dwlt and a in rr* **100/1**

4 **10** *3 ¼* **Betty Boo (IRE)**[11] 2047 2-8-12 0.................................... RobbieFitzpatrick 12 19
(Shaun Harris) *racd towards stands' rail: in tch: pushed along 1/2-way: sn outpcd and bhd fnl 2f* **100/1**

11 *10* **Vandross (IRE)** 2-9-3 0.................................... TedDurcan 11
(Chris Wall) *sn outpcd and bhd fr 1/2-way* **100/1**

12 *dist* **Winged Icarus (USA)** 2-9-3 0.................................... ShaneKelly 6
(Alan McCabe) *sltly hmpd s: in rr whn virtually p.u after 1 1/2f: t.o* **14/1**

1m 12.87s (-2.03) **Going Correction** -0.35s/f (Firm) **12** Ran SP% **111.5**
Speed ratings (Par 93): **99,98,92,92,84 83,80,78,75,71 58,**
Tote Swingers:1&2:£4.60, 2&3:£2.10, 1&3:£4.50 CSF £23.99 TOTE £12.10: £3.80, £1.10, £1.80; EX 35.70 Trifecta £107.50 Pool £864.65 - 5.95 winning units..
Owner Sheikh Hamdan Bin Mohammed Al Maktoum **Bred** Horizon Bloodstock Limited **Trained** Middleham Moor, N Yorks

FOCUS
An above-average 6f juvenile maiden for the grade. The winning time was almost identical to the previous 6f handicap.

NOTEBOOK
Windhoek looked well in the preliminaries and raced prominently a few lanes off the nearside rail. The race developed inside the final 2f and inexperience brought him towards the centre of the course as he strode out towards the line, coming close to the second and carrying him slightly across the track close home in a tight finish, but there was no actual interference and after the stewards had a look the placings remained unaltered. The colt is the first foal out of the well-related Kahlua Kiss (Listed-placed over 7f juvenile/1m2f winner by Mister Baileys). He is entered in a valuable sales' contest over 7f in October and that appears a suitable target this term. (op 14-1 tchd 10-1)
Janoub Nibras(IRE) looked well and was sent off 11-8 market leader. The Acclamation colt ran a fine race when third over 5f at Ascot on soft ground on debut this month (RPR 80) and appeared to reproduce a similar level of form, as the front two came over 4l clear of the third. He looks likely to be suited by sticking to 6f for now and has an entry in Redcar's Two-Year-Old Trophy over the that trip later on this term. (tchd 6-4)
Gold Hunter(IRE), having finished about 5l third of 12 in a Newmarket maiden this month, may have just replicated that effort. (op 11-4 tchd 5-2)
Well Acquainted(IRE) shaped encouragingly for a step up beyond this trip, possibly 1m later this term. (tchd 7-1)
Winged Icarus(USA) Official explanation: jockey said colt lost his action

2377 WARREN BOARD NEW DIMENSION H'CAP 5f 13y
2:45 (2:46) (Class 6) (0-65,65) 4-Y-O+ **£1,617** (£481; £240; £120) **Stalls** High

Form RPR

456- **1** **Bilash**[255] 5914 5-9-5 **63**.................................... TonyCulhane 9 72
(Reg Hollinshead) *in tch: hdwy over 2f out: rdn to ld appr fnl f: sn edgd lft and drvn out* **6/1**[2]

0000 **2** *hd* **Divertimenti (IRE)**[2] 2314 8-9-1 **62**............................(b) LeeTopliss(3) 14 70
(Roy Bowring) *in tch: hdwy wl over 1f out: sn rdn and styd on strly fnl f: jst hld* **15/2**[3]

2303 **3** *1 ¼* **Avonvalley**[21] 1735 5-8-10 **54**.................................... RobbieFitzpatrick 12 58
(Peter Grayson) *in rr: hdwy wl over 1f out: sn rdn and styd on strly fnl f: nrst fin* **14/1**

0-36 **4** *½* **Two Turtle Doves (IRE)**[124] 212 6-8-11 **58**.............. HarryBentley(3) 3 60
(Michael Mullineaux) *trckd ldrs: hdwy on outer wl over 1f out: rdn to chse wnr ins fnl f: sn drvn and one pce* **11/1**

5-43 **5** *¾* **Danzoe (IRE)**[21] 1735 5-9-2 **60**.................................... ChrisCatlin 8 59
(Christine Dunnett) *towards rr: hdwy wl over 1f out: sn rdn and styd on fnl f: nrst fin* **12/1**

000- **6** *¾* **Atlantic Cycle (IRE)**[167] 7649 5-9-4 **62**................(t) RichardKingscote 11 59
(Milton Bradley) *led to 1/2-way: led again over 2f out: rdn and hdd appr fnl f: sn hung lft and wknd* **20/1**

6155 **7** *½* **Bertie Southstreet**[10] 2092 9-9-1 **59**............................(b) MickyFenton 13 54
(Paul Midgley) *in rr: hdwy over 1f out: sn rdn and no imp fnl f* **18/1**

6242 **8** *¾* **Boucher Garcon (IRE)**[10] 2084 4-9-2 **65**........................ NeilFarley(5) 1 57
(Declan Carroll) *cl up: led 1/2-way: rdn and hdd jst over 2f out: drvn and wknd over 1f out* **9/4**[1]

420 **9** *1 ¼* **Methaaly (IRE)**[53] 1116 9-9-3 **61**............................(be) RichardHughes 16 49
(Michael Mullineaux) *a in rr* **8/1**

-540 **10** *nse* **Griffin Point (IRE)**[15] 1934 5-9-1 **59**.................................... MartinDwyer 6 46
(William Muir) *a in midfield* **10/1**

0-00 **11** *nk* **Speedyfix**[21] 1734 5-8-13 **57**............................(v) MartinHarley 10 43
(Christine Dunnett) *chsd ldrs: rdn along 2f out: sn wknd* **40/1**

42-0 **12** *1 ½* **Duke Of Rainford**[38] 1383 5-8-7 **51** oh1.................................... TomEaves 5 32
(Michael Herrington) *dwlt: a towards rr* **25/1**

3-66 **13** *3 ¾* **Itum**[13] 1986 5-8-5 **52**.................................... DominicFox(3) 15 19
(Christine Dunnett) *a towards rr* **28/1**

59.55s (-1.45) **Going Correction** -0.35s/f (Firm) **13** Ran SP% **119.5**
Speed ratings (Par 101): **97,96,94,93,92 91,90,89,87,87 86,84,78**
Tote Swingers:1&2:£9.40, 2&3:£21.60, 1&3:£13.90 CSF £48.24 CT £612.81 TOTE £4.80: £1.40, £3.60, £4.30; EX 42.80 Trifecta £373.40 Pool £605.63 - 1.20 winning units..
Owner M Pyle & Mrs T Pyle **Bred** M Pyle & Mrs T Pyle **Trained** Upper Longdon, Staffs

FOCUS
A modest 5f handicap for older horses. They went a solid gallop and the form is straightforward.
Methaaly(IRE) Official explanation: jockey said gelding moved poorly.

2378 WINNING WAY WITH DG CARS H'CAP 2m 9y
3:15 (3:17) (Class 5) (0-75,74) 4-Y-O+ **£2,264** (£673; £336; £168) **Stalls** Low

Form RPR

340- **1** **Maoi Chinn Tire (IRE)**[266] 5609 5-9-0 **64**........................ PaulHanagan 1 74
(Jennie Candlish) *plld hrd: hld up in rr: swtchd to outer and hdwy to trck ldr after 3f: led wl over 2f out: rdn clr wl over 1f out: kpt on wl towards fin* **6/1**

0252 **2** *¾* **Hallstatt (IRE)**[28] 1588 6-9-2 **66**................................(t) GrahamLee 6 75
(John Mackie) *trckd ldrs on inner: hdwy 3f out: rdn to chse wnr wl over 1f out: drvn and kpt on fnl f: nt quite rch wnr* **11/2**[3]

0-12 **3** *5* **Veloce (IRE)**[15] 1925 4-9-4 **70**................................(v[1]) FrannyNorton 2 73
(Ian Williams) *hld up towards rr: hdwy 3f out: rdn over 2f out: drvn and kpt on to take 3rd ins fnl f* **9/4**[1]

3261 **4** *1 ¾* **Talbot Green**[19] 1791 4-8-10 **62**.................................... MartinDwyer 11 63
(William Muir) *led: pushed along and qcknd 4f out: rdn 3f out: sn hdd: drvn 2f out and grad wknd* **12/1**

0-04 **5** *½* **Action Front (USA)**[34] 1446 4-9-6 **72**.................................... JoeFanning 7 72
(Derek Shaw) *hld up and bhd: hdwy over 3f out: swtchd lft and rdn over 2f out: plugged on: nvr nr ldrs* **10/1**

00-6 **6** *7* **Mistoffelees**[29] 1559 6-9-6 **70**................................(t) J-PGuillambert 13 62
(James Given) *chsd ldng pair: effrt over 3f out: rdn wl over 2f out and sn wknd* **33/1**

0-03 **7** *3 ½* **Descaro (USA)**[29] 1559 6-9-7 **71**................................(v) DanielTudhope 9 59
(David O'Meara) *hld up in tch: rdn along 3f out: sn wknd* **5/1**[2]

21-0 **8** *3* **Rose Of Sarratt (IRE)**[15] 1925 4-8-13 **65**........................ ChrisCatlin 3 49
(Rae Guest) *t.k.h: hld up: effrt 4f out: sn rdn and btn 3f out* **12/1**

30-2 **9** *5* **Spruzzo**[19] 1794 6-8-8 **58**.................................... DuranFentiman 4 36
(Chris Fairhurst) *trckd ldrs: rdn along over 3f out: sn wknd* **11/1**

3m 30.71s (0.41) **Going Correction** -0.15s/f (Firm) course record
WFA 4 from 5yo+ 2lb **9** Ran SP% **112.9**
Speed ratings (Par 103): **92,91,89,88,88 84,82,81,78**
Tote Swingers:1&2:£6.60, 2&3:£3.10, 1&3:£3.20 CSF £37.92 CT £95.18 TOTE £8.60: £2.00, £1.90, £1.70; EX 40.80 Trifecta £124.10 Pool £800.24 - 4.77 winning units..
Owner Alan Baxter **Bred** Mrs E Thompson **Trained** Basford Green, Staffs

FOCUS
An average staying handicap. They didn't make this much of a stamina test with a steady gallop.

2379 MEET PEPPA PIG ON FAMILY DAY FILLIES' H'CAP 1m 2f 50y
3:45 (3:46) (Class 4) (0-80,77) 3-Y-O £4,075 (£1,212; £606; £303) Stalls Low

Form RPR

422- **1** **Dulkashe (IRE)**[208] 7118 3-9-7 **77** KierenFallon 7 84+
(Luca Cumani) *dwlt and hld up in rr: gd hdwy on outer 3f out to ld over 2f out: jnd and rdn over 1f out: styd on wl towards fin* **7/2**[1]

323- **2** *nk* **Eluding**[192] 7396 3-9-7 **77** MickaelBarzalona 2 83
(Mahmood Al Zarooni) *hld up in rr: effrt and nt clr run 3f out: sn swtchd rt to outer and hdwy 2f out: rdn to chal ent fnl f: ev ch tl drvn and no ex nr fin* **7/2**[1]

36-4 **3** *1 ½* **Corsetry (USA)**[16] 1893 3-9-4 **74** TomQueally 5 77
(Sir Henry Cecil) *chsd ldrs: led after 2f: pushed along and hdd 4f out: rallied to chal and ev ch over 1f out: drvn and no ex wl ins fnl f* **8/1**

25-5 **4** *2* **Shannon Spree**[5] 2201 3-9-2 **72** RichardHughes 3 71
(Richard Hannon) *prom: pushed along and lost pl over 4f out: swtchd rt and rdn 2f out: styd on fnl f* **9/2**[2]

1-41 **5** *½* **Al Jabreiah**[31] 1531 3-9-2 **72** LiamJones 4 70
(William Haggas) *trckd ldrs: hdwy over 3f out: rdn 2f out and sn no imp* **5/1**[3]

0-46 **6** *2 ¾* **Rythmic**[20] 1756 3-9-3 **73** JoeFanning 1 66
(Mark Johnston) *trckd ldrs on inner: effrt 3f out: sn rdn and wknd 2f out* **12/1**

00-5 **7** *1* **Symphony Star (IRE)**[39] 1364 3-8-7 **63** PaulHanagan 9 54
(Paul D'Arcy) *prom: rdn along 4f out: wknd wl over 2f out* **10/1**

450 **8** *9* **Findeln**[32] 1502 3-8-11 **67** JimCrowley 8 40
(Eve Johnson Houghton) *led 2f: cl up tl led again 4f out: rdn and hdd wl over 2f out: sn wknd* **33/1**

2m 10.54s (-1.16) **Going Correction** -0.15s/f (Firm) course record 8 Ran SP% **110.1**
Speed ratings (Par 98): **98,97,96,94,94 92,91,84**
Tote Swingers:1&2:£2.30, 2&3:£5.00, 1&3:£6.00 CSF £14.42 CT £82.47 TOTE £5.30: £1.70, £1.80, £3.40; EX 10.10 Trifecta £59.90 Pool £591.25 - 7.30 winning units..
Owner Sheikh Mohammed Obaid Al Maktoum **Bred** Max Morris Esq & Cheveley Park Stud Ltd **Trained** Newmarket, Suffolk

FOCUS
This was the feature on the card. They went a solid gallop.

2380 WARREN BOARD WORLD OF BOARD MAIDEN STKS (DIV I) 1m 75y
4:15 (4:17) (Class 5) 3-Y-O £2,264 (£673; £336; £168) Stalls Centre

Form RPR

1 **Marine Girl** 3-8-12 0 TomQueally 2 75+
(Sir Henry Cecil) *s.i.s and t.k.h early: hld up: hdwy 3f out: rdn to chse ldrs wl over 1f out: str run ins fnl f to ld on line* **11/1**[3]

26-6 **2** *nse* **Kaafel (IRE)**[52] 1132 3-9-3 75 PaulHanagan 10 80
(Charles Hills) *a.p: effrt 2f out: rdn to ld ins fnl f: hdd on line* **13/8**[1]

3 *nk* **Suffice (IRE)** 3-9-3 0 TonyHamilton 4 79
(Richard Fahey) *in tch: hdwy to chse ldrs 3f out: rdn over 2f out: kpt on wl fnl f* **20/1**

022- **4** *1* **Journalistic (USA)**[237] 6462 3-9-3 78 MartinDwyer 7 77
(Marcus Tregoning) *a.p: hdwy to ld 2f out: sn jnd and rdn: drvn and hdd ins fnl f: kpt on same pce* **7/4**[2]

0-0 **5** *1 ¾* **Rock Band**[31] 1512 3-9-3 0 RichardHughes 9 73
(Richard Hannon) *racd wd early and sn led: rdn along 3f out: hdd 2f out: drvn appr fnl f and grad wknd* **12/1**

60 **6** *7* **Pursue**[11] 2041 3-9-3 0 KierenFallon 8 57
(William Haggas) *trckd ldrs: hdwy on outer wl over 2f out: sn rdn and wknd over 1f out* **12/1**

7 *hd* **Card Sweep** 3-9-3 0 RoystonFfrench 3 56
(Ismail Mohammed) *a towards rr* **40/1**

0 **8** *½* **Tatting**[11] 2041 3-9-3 0 LiamKeniry 1 55
(Chris Dwyer) *a towards rr* **200/1**

66 **9** *18* **Bridal Medic**[42] 1270 3-9-3 0 GrahamLee 5 14
(John Mackie) *a in rr* **66/1**

10 *3 ¾* **Oasis Love (IRE)** 3-9-3 0 JoeFanning 6
(Mark Johnston) *in tch: chsd ldrs 3f out: sn rdn and wknd* **16/1**

1m 45.7s (0.10) **Going Correction** -0.15s/f (Firm) 10 Ran SP% **113.3**
Speed ratings (Par 99): **93,92,92,91,89 82,82,82,64,60**
Tote Swingers:1&2:£3.60, 2&3:£7.20, 1&3:£13.00 CSF £28.02 TOTE £10.80: £2.60, £1.30, £6.00; EX 33.40 Trifecta £460.80 Pool £1,083.55 - 1.74 winning units..
Owner Black Type Partnership II **Bred** D R Tucker **Trained** Newmarket, Suffolk

FOCUS
The first division of an interesting maiden. They appeared to go a decent gallop, though the winning time was around a second slower than the second division.
Bridal Medic Official explanation: trainer said gelding was unsuited by going (good to firm (firm in places)

2381 WARREN BOARD WORLD OF BOARD MAIDEN STKS (DIV II) 1m 75y
4:45 (4:48) (Class 5) 3-Y-O £2,264 (£673; £336; £168) Stalls Centre

Form RPR

52- **1** **Westwiththenight (IRE)**[213] 7025 3-8-12 0 RichardHughes 5 76+
(William Haggas) *hld up towards rr: smooth hdwy over 3f out: effrt 2f out: rdn to chal ent fnl f: styd on to ld last 50yds* **1/1**[1]

5 **2** *½* **Ukrainian Princess**[24] 1676 3-8-12 0 TomQueally 10 75
(Sir Henry Cecil) *chsd ldrs: hdwy to ld 2f out: sn hung lft and rdn: jnd ent fnl f: hdd and no ex last 50yds* **12/1**

2- **3** *2 ¾* **Yanabeeaa (USA)**[237] 6440 3-8-12 0 PaulHanagan 12 68+
(Sir Michael Stoute) *hld up towards rr: hdwy 3f out: rdn over 1f out: kpt on fnl f: nrst fin* **15/8**[2]

4 *1 ¼* **Thereabouts (USA)** 3-9-3 0 MartinHarley 8 71
(Marco Botti) *trckd ldrs: hdwy 3f out: sn cl up: rdn wl over 1f out and kpt on same pce* **28/1**

25 **5** *2 ¼* **Emily Carr (IRE)**[16] 1878 3-8-12 0 JoeFanning 1 60
(Mark Johnston) *chsd ldrs on inner: led after 2f: hdd 4f out: rdn wl over 2f out: grad wknd* **10/1**[3]

00- **6** *2 ¾* **Thane Of Cawdor (IRE)**[202] 7233 3-9-3 0 MickyFenton 11 59
(Tom Tate) *led 2f: cl up tl led again 4f out: rdn 3f out: hdd 2f out and grad wknd* **50/1**

0- **7** *hd* **Perfect Example (IRE)**[210] 7080 3-8-12 0 RoystonFfrench 4 54
(Ismail Mohammed) *prom: rdn 3f out: wknd 2f out* **66/1**

8 *18* **Mankini (IRE)** 3-9-3 0 KierenFallon 3 17
(Luca Cumani) *a towards rr: outpcd fnl 3f* **14/1**

9 *1* **First Voice (IRE)** 3-9-3 0 J-PGuillambert 7 15
(James Given) *plld hrd and hung bdly rt thrght: racd wd and chsd ldrs to 1/2-way: sn bhd* **66/1**

0 **10** *¾* **Pinot**[10] 2095 3-9-3 0 TonyHamilton 2 13
(Richard Fahey) *in tch: rdn along 4f out: sn wknd* **100/1**

1m 44.76s (-0.84) **Going Correction** -0.15s/f (Firm) course record 10 Ran SP% **117.6**
Speed ratings (Par 99): **98,97,94,93,91 88,88,70,69,68**
Tote Swingers:1&2:£4.10, 2&3:£4.30, 1&3:£1.30 CSF £15.14 TOTE £2.20: £1.30, £2.50, £1.40; EX 17.40 Trifecta £23.20 Pool £1,452.80 - 46.16 winning units..
Owner A E Oppenheimer **Bred** Hascombe And Valiant Studs **Trained** Newmarket, Suffolk

FOCUS
The second division of the maiden. The gallop looked an honest one and the winning time was around a second faster than the first leg.
First Voice(IRE) Official explanation: jockey said gelding ran too free

2382 REWARDS4RACING.COM CLASSIFIED STKS 1m 75y
5:15 (5:24) (Class 6) 3-Y-O £1,617 (£481; £240; £120) Stalls Centre

Form RPR

04-5 **1** **Bitaphon (IRE)**[133] 112 3-8-11 63 ow2 JustinNewman(5) 3 73
(John Balding) *mde most: rdn along 3f out: jnd wl over 1f out: drvn ent fnl f and hld on gamely* **28/1**

3204 **2** *¾* **Purple Affair (IRE)**[57] 1046 3-9-0 63 (b[1]) MartinHarley 9 70
(J S Moore) *trckd ldrs: hdwy 3f out: cl up 2f out: rdn and ev ch ent fnl f: kpt on same pce towards fin* **14/1**

65-4 **3** *nk* **Raffinn**[38] 1392 3-9-0 65 LiamKeniry 8 69
(Sylvester Kirk) *trckd ldrs: smooth hdwy 3f out: cl up 2f out: chal over 1f out: rdn and ev ch ins fnl f: sn drvn and one pce towards fin* **3/1**[1]

5434 **4** *5* **Bapak Pintar**[20] 1757 3-9-0 65 PhillipMakin 15 58
(Kevin Ryan) *prom: effrt whn n.m.r and sltly hmpd over 2f out: sn rdn and one pce* **7/1**

25-0 **5** *3 ½* **Rocky Reef**[21] 1728 3-9-0 64 (v) JimmyFortune 14 49
(Andrew Balding) *bhd: hdwy over 2f out: sn rdn and nvr nr ldrs* **10/1**

506- **6** *3* **Maccabees**[243] 6280 3-9-0 65 JamesMillman 5 43
(Rod Millman) *cl up: rdn along 3f out: drvn over 2f out and grad wknd* **14/1**

15-4 **7** *nk* **Winter Hill**[53] 1115 3-9-0 65 (b[1]) RichardKingscote 1 42
(Tom Dascombe) *s.i.s: nvr a factor* **14/1**

0-44 **8** *9* **City Dazzler (IRE)**[15] 1906 3-9-0 65 RichardHughes 10 21
(Richard Hannon) *a towards rr* **6/1**[3]

40-0 **9** *6* **Yes It's The Boy (USA)**[15] 1916 3-9-0 65 J-PGuillambert 12
(Ed Walker) *a towards rr* **33/1**

5-04 **10** *1 ¾* **Thecornishcockney**[19] 1793 3-9-0 65 (p) JackMitchell 6
(John Ryan) *chsd ldrs: rdn along 1/2-way: sn wknd* **11/1**

600 **11** *7* **Art News (IRE)**[41] 1312 3-9-0 62 (p) TomQueally 2
(Gary Moore) *chsd ldrs: lost pl 1/2-way and sn bhd* **20/1**

000- **12** *3 ¼* **Kung Hei Fat Choy (USA)**[214] 6983 3-9-0 62 PaulHanagan 11
(James Given) *plld hrd: chsd ldrs 3f: sn lost pl and bhd fnl 3f* **9/2**[2]

650- **13** *42* **Sugar Loaf**[194] 7343 3-9-0 65 MartinDwyer 13
(William Muir) *a in rr* **33/1**

1m 43.84s (-1.76) **Going Correction** -0.15s/f (Firm) course record 13 Ran SP% **121.5**
Speed ratings (Par 97): **102,101,100,95,92 89,89,80,74,72 65,62,20**
Tote Swingers:1&2:£58.00, 2&3:£11.70, 1&3:£28.40 CSF £371.46 TOTE £38.60: £8.50, £2.40, £2.30; EX 514.90 Trifecta £526.10 Part won. Pool £711.07 - 0.20 winning units..
Owner Mrs Debbie Sanderson **Bred** Pitrizzia Partnership **Trained** Scrooby, Notts

FOCUS
A modest classified stakes, but the gallop was a solid one and the winning time was respectable for the grade.
Bapak Pintar Official explanation: jockey said colt hung left.
Yes It's The Boy(USA) Official explanation: jockey said gelding was never travelling.
Sugar Loaf Official explanation: jockey said filly lost her action.
T/Jkpt: Not won. T/Plt: £59.30 to a £1 stake. Pool £71,047.37. 873.70 winning tickets. T/Qpdt: £13.10 to a £1 stake. Pool £5,103.13. 287.86 winning tickets. JR

CHEPSTOW (L-H)
Wednesday, May 23

OFFICIAL GOING: Good (good to soft in places) changing to good after race 1 (2.10)
Wind: Nil Weather: Sunny

2384 32REDPOKER.COM MAIDEN AUCTION STKS 6f 16y
2:10 (2:10) (Class 5) 2-Y-O £2,264 (£673; £336; £168) Stalls High

Form RPR

1 **Beedee** 2-8-10 0 WilliamTwiston-Davies(7) 3 77+
(Richard Hannon) *in rr: stdy hdwy appr fnl 2f: qcknd to ld fnl 150yds: comf* **13/2**[3]

05 **2** *1 ½* **Baltic Gin (IRE)**[7] 2163 2-8-3 0 RaulDaSilva(5) 8 64
(Malcolm Saunders) *trckd ldrs: pushed along 2f out: styd on fnl f to take 2nd last stride but no ch w wnr* **14/1**

3 *nse* **Cio Cio San (IRE)** 2-8-10 0 PatDobbs 2 66
(Richard Hannon) *in rr early: hdwy 3f out: qcknd to chal ins fnl 2f: qcknd to ld wl over 1f out: hdd fnl 150yds: styd on to dispute 2nd: dropped to 3rd last stride* **9/1**

6 **4** *3 ½* **Lucky Suit (IRE)**[30] 1563 2-8-9 0 RichardHughes 10 54
(Richard Hannon) *trckd ldrs: rdn over 2f out and led sn after: sn jnd: hdd wl over 1f out: wknd ins fnl f* **11/4**[1]

0 **5** *1* **Poetic Verse**[9] 2124 2-8-5 0 MartinLane 9 47
(Rod Millman) *in tch: pushed along 1/2-way: styd on ins fnl f: nvr a threat* **9/2**[2]

6 *nk* **Black Dave (IRE)** 2-9-2 0 PadraigBeggy 4 57
(David Evans) *plld hrd: chsd ldr over 3f: rdn 2f out: wknd fnl f* **13/2**[3]

0 **7** *1 ¾* **I'm Watching**[33] 1495 2-8-6 0 ow1 MickaelBarzalona 7 42
(George Baker) *led: rdn 3f out: jnd over 2f out and rdn: sn hdd: wknd fnl f* **12/1**

8 *2 ½* **Lagrima (IRE)** 2-8-5 0 DavidProbert 1 33
(J S Moore) *s.i.s and green: taken to r on stands' side fr over 3f out: a outpcd* **25/1**

0 **9** *2 ¼* **Tomway**[13] 1997 2-9-3 0 RichardKingscote 6 39
(Tom Dascombe) *chsd ldrs over 3f: sn rdn and btn* **12/1**

10 *8* **Luckster** 2-8-11 0 HayleyTurner 5 9
(David Evans) *rdn 1/2-way: a in rr* **20/1**

1m 12.0s **Going Correction** -0.15s/f (Firm) 10 Ran SP% **112.2**
Speed ratings (Par 93): **94,92,91,87,85 85,83,79,76,66**
Tote Swingers: 1&2 £16.00, 1&3 £13.20, 2&3 £17.10 CSF £89.30 TOTE £5.60: £2.00, £4.70, £2.30; EX 88.20.
Owner Derek And Jean Clee **Bred** D D & Mrs J P Clee **Trained** East Everleigh, Wilts

FOCUS
Nothing more than a modest contest.

NOTEBOOK
Beedee, a half-brother to a 6f to 1m US stakes winner, out of a useful mare, wasn't the quickest into stride, but his jockey took his time to get his mount racing before they came with a strong challenge towards the centre of the track before edging right. He'll get further and appears a nice prospect. (tchd 7-1)
Baltic Gin(IRE) hadn't shown enough in a couple of Bath maidens to think she would be taking this, but the extra furlong seemed to bring out some improvement. (tchd 12-1)
Cio Cio San(IRE), the second foal of a mare who was placed over middle distances, hit the front a furlong out but didn't quite see it out. A similar race ought to be won with her, although she will stay further. (op 15-2)
Lucky Suit(IRE) showed some pace on debut but weakened, and did much the same again. (op 3-1)
Poetic Verse kept on but was never dangerous. (op 15-2)
Black Dave(IRE), who cost £20,000 as a 2yo, has a bit of size about him and is entitled to come on for this. (op 6-1 tchd 5-1)

2385 32REDBET.COM CLASSIFIED STKS (DIV I) 7f 16y
2:40 (2:40) (Class 6) 3-Y-0+ **£1,617** (£481; £240; £120) **Stalls** High

Form RPR
0-30 **1** **Percythepinto (IRE)**[44] 1260 3-8-10 55..................(t) RichardHughes 10 53
(George Baker) *stdd s and hld up wl off pce: stl plenty to do 2f out: drvn and gd hdwy over 1f out: qcknd between horse to ld fnl 120yds: readily* **7/1**
05-0 **2** 3/4 **Valdaw**[32] 1533 4-9-7 55.. MartinLane 7 55
(Tony Carroll) *in rr: stl plenty to do whn pushed along 2f out: hdwy over 1f out: drvn and upsides in 7-horse chal fnl 150yds: chsd wnr but no imp fnl 30yds* **11/1**
6224 **3** 1/2 **Polar Auroras**[55] 1084 4-9-7 54..(t) DavidProbert 5 54
(Tony Carroll) *in tch: drvn and hdwy over 1f out: upsides in 7-horse chal fnl 150yds: chsd wnr fnl 120yds: no imp and dropped to 3rd fnl 30yds* **11/2**[3]
6-55 **4** 1/2 **Set To Go**[118] 307 5-9-7 45..(b) HayleyTurner 1 52
(Brendan Powell) *chsd ldr: chal fr 2f out: stl upsides u.p in 7-horse chal fnl 150yds: one pce fnl 50yds* **9/1**
241- **5** 1/2 **Croeso Mawr**[218] 6938 6-9-7 55.. NeilCallan 9 51
(John Spearing) *t.k.h: trckd ldrs: drvn over 1f out: upsides u.p in 7-horse chal fnl 150yds: wknd fnl 50yds* **11/4**[1]
4442 **6** hd **Son Of May**[28] 1596 3-8-10 53..(b) TonyCulhane 6 46
(Jo Hughes) *sn led: jnd 2f out and u.p: stl upsides in 7-horse chal fnl 150yds: wknd fnl 50yds* **7/2**[2]
0-06 **7** 1/2 **Perfect Honour (IRE)**[16] 1908 6-9-7 45..........................[1] JoeFanning 4 49
(Des Donovan) *in tch: drvn to chse ldrs and rdn 2f out: stl upsides in 7-horse chal fnl 150yds: wknd fnl 75yds* **12/1**
650- **8** 21 **Treasure Act**[210] 7096 4-9-7 52.. FergusSweeney 2
(Patrick Chamings) *t.k.h early: sn bhd* **14/1**
0-00 **9** 4 1/2 **Green Pearl (IRE)**[17] 1895 4-9-2 49..........................(t) JamesRogers[(5)] 3
(Ralph Beckett) *a bhd* **33/1**

1m 23.36s (0.16) **Going Correction** -0.15s/f (Firm)
WFA 3 from 4yo+ 11lb **9** Ran SP% **112.4**
Speed ratings (Par 101): **93,92,91,91,90 90,89,65,60**
Tote Swingers: 1&2 £9.90, 1&3 £7.30, 2&3 £13.50 CSF £77.78 TOTE £7.60: £2.10, £4.10, £1.30; EX 94.00.
Owner Seaton Partnership **Bred** Stone Ridge Farm **Trained** Whitsbury, Hants

FOCUS
None of these had solid credentials for various reasons, but three went off too quickly and the closers got on top in the final stages.
Percythepinto(IRE) Official explanation: trainer said regarding apparent improvement in form that the gelding was suited by a change in tactics and faster ground.

2386 32REDBET.COM CLASSIFIED STKS (DIV II) 7f 16y
3:10 (3:10) (Class 6) 3-Y-0+ **£1,617** (£481; £240; £120) **Stalls** High

Form RPR
0-40 **1** **Archina (IRE)**[40] 1357 3-8-10 49.. DavidProbert 5 60
(Andrew Balding) *chsd ldrs: drvn to go 2nd 2f out: drvn to ld appr fnl f: kpt on strly* **6/1**
300- **2** 2 1/4 **Picura**[231] 6628 3-8-10 48.. RichardKingscote 10 54
(Ralph Beckett) *led: drvn over 2f out: hdd appr fnl f: kpt on wl for 2nd but no ch w wnr* **8/1**
40-0 **3** 1 1/2 **Border Abby**[27] 1624 4-9-7 55.. NeilCallan 9 54
(Rae Guest) *in tch: drvn and hdwy fr 2f out to chse ldrs over 1f out: no imp and outpcd ins fnl f* **15/8**[1]
00 **4** nk **Volcanic Jack (IRE)**[103] 498 4-9-7 55.......................... PadraigBeggy 7 53
(Tony Carroll) *chsd ldrs: drvn to go 2nd 3f out: sn rdn: one pce fnl f* **11/2**[3]
/002 **5** 2 **Yanza**[16] 1910 6-9-2 50.. LauraPike[(5)] 6 48
(Pam Ford) *chsd ldr: rdn 4f out: edgd lft but styd prom: wknd fnl f* **9/1**
-603 **6** 2 3/4 **Joy To The World (IRE)**[6] 2203 3-8-5 55.................. DuilioDaSilva[(5)] 8 36
(Paul Cole) *t.k.h: sn in tch: drvn to dispute 2nd 3f out: wknd over 1f out* **9/2**[2]
0/00 **7** 3 1/2 **Our Georgie Girl**[16] 1908 5-9-7 37..........................(v[1]) JamesMillman 3 31
(Rod Millman) *a towards rr* **40/1**
00-0 **8** 2 1/4 **Aaranyow (IRE)**[16] 1907 4-9-7 45.. MartinLane 2 25
(Bryn Palling) *pressed ldrs over 3f: wknd 3f out* **20/1**

1m 23.16s (-0.04) **Going Correction** -0.15s/f (Firm)
WFA 3 from 4yo+ 11lb **8** Ran SP% **110.9**
Speed ratings (Par 101): **94,91,89,89,87 83,79,77**
Tote Swingers: 1&2 £6.80, 1&3 £4.00, 2&3 £5.70 CSF £49.34 TOTE £8.60: £2.60, £1.60, £1.50; EX 43.70.
Owner Dr Philip Brown **Bred** Good Breeding **Trained** Kingsclere, Hants
■ Stewards' Enquiry : David Probert two-day ban; used whip above permitted level (6th-7th June)

FOCUS
Ordinary stuff but the winner is probably a bit better than this level.

2387 £32 BONUS AT 32RED.COM MEDIAN AUCTION MAIDEN STKS 1m 14y
3:40 (3:40) (Class 5) 3-5-Y-0 **£2,264** (£673; £336; £168) **Stalls** High

Form RPR
6-5 **1** **Autumn Fire**[22] 1737 3-8-10 0.. DavidProbert 1 62+
(Andrew Balding) *trckd ldrs: drvn to go 2nd over 2f out: led 1f out: drvn out* **10/3**[3]
6-0 **2** 3/4 **Finlodex**[119] 292 5-9-13 0.. FergusSweeney 10 68
(Murty McGrath) *in tch: rdn and hdwy fr 2f out: styd on clsng stages to take 2nd but no imp on wnr* **20/1**
3 1/2 **Christingle** 3-8-10 0.. RichardHughes 8 59+
(William Haggas) *s.i.s: in rr: hdwy over 2f out: styd on wl appr fnl f: tk 3rd clsng stages and gng on at fin* **9/4**[2]
5 **4** 1/2 **Upper Grosvenor**[16] 1937 3-9-1 0.. NeilCallan 6 63+
(Roger Varian) *t.k.h: trckd ldr: led over 2f out: hdd 1f out: one pce into 4th clsng stages* **5/4**[1]
-60 **5** 2 **Call Me April**[22] 1724 4-9-8 0.. TomMcLaughlin 5 56
(Karen George) *chsd ldrs: rdn over 2f out: hung rt and outpcd appr fnl f* **14/1**
6 25 **Ifan (IRE)**[67] 4-9-13 0..(v[1]) MartinLane 3
(Bryn Palling) *sn led: hdd over 2f out: wkng whn hmpd appr fnl f: heavily eased sn after: t.o* **16/1**
7 5 **Vital Merlin** 3-9-1 0.. JamieGoldstein 2
(Nicky Vaughan) *slowly away: wl bhd tl mod prog past btn horses fnl f: t.o* **50/1**
0 **8** 1 1/2 **Captain Cavallo**[37] 1422 5-9-13 0.. TonyCulhane 9
(Nicky Vaughan) *s.i.s: sn bhd: t.o* **66/1**
00 **9** shd **Gravie**[23] 1716 4-9-8 0.. RussKennemore 4
(Brian Baugh) *a in rr: t.o* **66/1**
00- **10** 7 **Glitter (IRE)**[275] 5325 3-8-10 0.. JamesRogers[(5)] 7
(Laura Young) *chsd ldrs 4f: sn wknd: t.o* **80/1**

1m 35.07s (-1.13) **Going Correction** -0.15s/f (Firm)
WFA 3 from 4yo+ 12lb **10** Ran SP% **121.8**
Speed ratings (Par 103): **99,98,97,97,95 70,65,63,63,56**
Tote Swingers: 1&2 £8.00, 1&3 £3.40, 2&3 £9.70 CSF £69.77 TOTE £3.30: £1.10, £4.60, £2.10; EX 78.50.
Owner The Queen **Bred** The Queen **Trained** Kingsclere, Hants

FOCUS
Only three made any serious appeal.
Ifan(IRE) Official explanation: jockey said gelding hung left.

2388 32RED.COM H'CAP 5f 16y
4:10 (4:10) (Class 6) (0-60,59) 3-Y-0 **£1,617** (£481; £240; £120) **Stalls** High

Form RPR
5524 **1** **Trending (IRE)**[32] 1529 3-8-9 **52**..................................(b) RaulDaSilva[(5)] 2 60
(Jeremy Gask) *s.i.s as rdr ct lft boot in stalls: in rr: hdwy over 2f out: drvn and str run fnl f to ld fnl 50yds* **4/1**[1]
34-6 **2** 1/2 **Monty Fay (IRE)**[126] 201 3-9-2 **54**..........................(t) FergusSweeney 8 60
(Derek Haydn Jones) *sn led: rdn over 1f out: hdd and outpcd fnl 50yds* **6/1**
4005 **3** 1/2 **One Last Dream**[7] 2166 3-8-7 **45**.......................... RichardKingscote 12 49
(Ron Hodges) *chsd ldrs: rdn 2f out: wnt 2nd over 1f out but no imp: one pce into 3rd fnl 50yds* **16/1**
0040 **4** 1 3/4 **Seventeen Seventy**[6] 2205 3-9-6 **58**.......................... RussKennemore 6 56
(Alan Coogan) *s.i.s: in rr: rdn and hdwy over 1f out: kpt on fnl f: nvr gng pce to rch ldng trio* **33/1**
0456 **5** nk **First Rebellion**[29] 1585 3-8-7 **45**.. DavidProbert 10 42
(Tony Carroll) *chsd ldrs: rdn over 2f out: kpt on same pce fnl f* **5/1**[2]
0502 **6** 3/4 **Ghazeer (IRE)**[29] 1585 3-9-3 **55**.. JoeFanning 4 49+
(Derek Shaw) *in rr: drvn over 1f out: kpt on fnl f: nvr gng pce to get into contention* **11/2**[3]
0-50 **7** 3/4 **Periwinkle Way**[98] 564 3-8-2 **45**.......................... NathanAlison[(5)] 1 36
(Jim Boyle) *chsd ldrs: rdn 2f out: wknd fnl f* **20/1**
5044 **8** nk **Waspy**[27] 1625 3-8-7 **45**..........................(t) MickaelBarzalona 3 35+
(George Baker) *in tch: outpcd 1/2-way: shkn up and styd on fnl f: nvr a threat* **10/1**
344 **9** nk **Marie's Fantasy**[35] 1444 3-9-7 **59**.......................... JamieGoldstein 9 48
(Zoe Davison) *s.i.s: sn chsng ldrs: wknd over 1f out* **20/1**
004- **10** 2 **Verus Delicia (IRE)**[203] 7231 3-8-7 **45**.......................... PadraigBeggy 13 27
(Daniel Mark Loughnane) *in rr: pushed along 3f out: nvr gng pce to get into contention* **16/1**
600 **11** 1 3/4 **Tumbleowtashoes**[8] 2139 3-8-7 **45**..................................(t) MartinLane 5 21
(John Ryan) *chsd ldrs: rdn 3f out: wknd fr 2f out* **100/1**
400 **12** nk **Exkaliber**[22] 1723 3-9-3 **55**.. NeilCallan 7 30
(Jeremy Gask) *chsd ldrs 3f* **8/1**
55-0 **13** 3 3/4 **Jawim**[7] 2166 3-9-2 **54**.. TomMcLaughlin 11 15
(Malcolm Saunders) *chsd ldrs tl wknd wl over 1f out* **16/1**

59.42s (0.12) **Going Correction** -0.15s/f (Firm) **13** Ran SP% **117.6**
Speed ratings (Par 97): **93,92,91,88,88 86,85,85,84,81 78,78,72**
Tote Swingers: 1&2 £5.90, 1&3 £13.20, 2&3 £21.50 CSF £25.76 CT £360.81 TOTE £5.70: £2.00, £2.70, £5.70; EX 32.80.
Owner The Twitterati **Bred** Thomas Hassett **Trained** Sutton Veny, Wilts

FOCUS
Not a strong race using the third and fourth as a guide.

2389 32RED CASINO H'CAP 1m 2f 36y
4:40 (4:40) (Class 5) (0-70,70) 4-Y-0+ **£2,264** (£673; £336; £168) **Stalls** Low

Form RPR
00-6 **1** **Bold Cross (IRE)**[19] 1830 9-8-7 **61**.......................... MatthewCosham[(5)] 12 69
(Edward Bevan) *in rr: hdwy over 2f out: rdn and swtchd rt 1f out: str run fnl f: led fnl 25yds* **10/1**
1-03 **2** nk **Hamilton Hill**[16] 1908 5-8-2 **56** oh3.......................... RaulDaSilva[(5)] 6 63
(Dai Burchell) *s.i.s: in rr: hdwy on outside 2f out: str run to press ldrs fnl 120yds: tk 2nd fnl 25yds but nt quite pce of wnr* **11/2**[2]
400- **3** nk **Circle Of Angels**[173] 7603 4-8-10 **59**.. JoeFanning 4 65
(Ian Williams) *in rr: hdwy 3f out: rdn over 2f out: slt ld u.p 1f out: hrd pressed fnl 120yds: hdd and outpcd into 3rd fnl 25yds* **9/1**
43-2 **4** 3/4 **Cuckoo Rock (IRE)**[13] 2009 5-8-11 **60**..........................(p) LeeNewman 9 65
(Jonathan Portman) *chsd ldrs: rdn over 2f out: led appr fnl f: sn hdd: no ex fnl 120yds* **11/2**[2]
-640 **5** 4 **Lisselan Pleasure (USA)**[7] 2167 5-8-2 **58**.............(t) DanielMuscutt[(7)] 3 55
(Bernard Llewellyn) *in rr: hdwy fr 3f out: slt ld ins fnl 2f: hdd over 1f out: wknd fnl f* **20/1**
500- **6** 2 **Spring Secret**[201] 7264 6-9-0 **63**.. DavidProbert 7 56
(Bryn Palling) *in tch: rdn over 2f out: sme prog fnl f* **14/1**
6-3 **7** 1 1/4 **Ashkalara**[14] 1980 5-8-11 **60**.. RichardHughes 11 50
(Stuart Howe) *chsd ldrs: rdn over 2f out: wknd over 1f out* **7/2**[1]
210- **8** 1/2 **Sweet World**[10] 7263 8-9-1 **64**.. MartinLane 10 53
(Bernard Llewellyn) *chsd ldrs: rdn 3f out: wknd ins fnl 2f* **7/1**[3]
00-5 **9** 1 **Phluke**[20] 1771 11-9-1 **64**.. NeilCallan 13 51
(Eve Johnson Houghton) *led at str pce: rdn over 3f out: hdd ins fnl 2f: wknd over 1f out* **18/1**
-304 **10** 3/4 **Yourinthewill (USA)**[15] 1956 4-9-6 **69**.......................... PadraigBeggy 2 55
(Daniel Mark Loughnane) *chsd ldrs: rdn 3f out: wknd 2f out* **16/1**
11 2 3/4 **Taroum (IRE)**[296] 6687 5-8-10 **66**.......................... AidenBlakemore[(7)] 5 46
(Tony Carroll) *towards rr most of way* **33/1**
311- **12** 3 1/2 **Bernisdale**[169] 2565 4-9-4 **67**.. RussKennemore 8 40
(John Flint) *chsd ldr: rdn 4f out: wknd 3f out* **20/1**

160- **13** *1* **Urban Space**[262] 5761 6-9-7 **70** .... TonyCulhane 1 41
(John Flint) *a towards rr* **25/1**

2m 8.67s (-1.93) **Going Correction** -0.15s/f (Firm) **13** Ran SP% **118.7**
Speed ratings (Par 103): **101,100,100,99,96 95,94,93,92,92 90,87,86**
Tote Swingers: 1&2 £7.80, 1&3 £23.90, 2&3 £7.60 CSF £60.45 CT £522.96 TOTE £12.10: £3.30, £2.20, £3.00; EX 51.70.
Owner E G Bevan **Bred** M Hosokawa **Trained** Ullingswick, H'fords

FOCUS
A few of these appeared to come into this off a fair effort so, for the class, the form is solid.

2390 32RED H'CAP 1m 4f 23y
5:10 (5:10) (Class 4) (0-85,84) 3-Y-O **£4,528** (£1,347; £673; £336) **Stalls** Low

Form RPR
3221 **1** **Ruacana**[30] 1557 3-9-7 **84** .... HayleyTurner 3 89+
(Michael Bell) *trckd ldr after 2f: drvn and styd on fr 2f out: chal u.p fnl 75yds: led clsng strides* **5/4**[1]
3211 **2** *nk* **Scatter Dice (IRE)**[44] 1267 3-9-1 **78** .... JoeFanning 5 82+
(Mark Johnston) *led: rdn over 2f out: kpt on fnl f tl hdd and no ex clsng strides* **2/1**[2]
03-1 **3** *3* **Rei D'Oro (USA)**[110] 404 3-8-12 **75** .... MartinLane 4 74
(David Simcock) *s.i.s: trckd ldrs in 3rd after 4f: rdn and effrt to press for 2nd fr 3f out: nvr rchd ldr: btn appr fnl f* **7/2**[3]
002- **4** *28* **Pinseeker (IRE)**[245] 6245 3-8-9 **72** .... MickaelBarzalona 1 26
(Brendan Powell) *chsd ldrs: dropped to last pl after 4f: rdn and effrt to cl 3f out: nvr on term and wknd over 2f out* **12/1**

2m 35.94s (-3.06) **Going Correction** -0.15s/f (Firm) **4** Ran SP% **107.7**
Speed ratings (Par 101): **104,103,101,83**
CSF £3.99 TOTE £3.70; EX 4.50.
Owner Sheikh Marwan Al Maktoum **Bred** Darley **Trained** Newmarket, Suffolk

FOCUS
Only four runners but a good pace was set by Scatter Dice.

2391 DIGIBET.COM H'CAP 1m 4f 23y
5:45 (5:45) (Class 6) (0-52,52) 4-Y-O+ **£1,617** (£481; £240; £120) **Stalls** Low

Form RPR
000/ **1** **Passato (GER)**[46] 3569 8-8-13 **49** ....(t) HayleyTurner 5 59
(Jo Davis) *trckd ldr: led 3f out: sn drvn: styd on wl u.p fnl f: all out* **11/4**[1]
1326 **2** *½* **Mayan Flight (IRE)**[9] 2137 4-8-9 **52** .... GeorgeDowning[(7)] 1 61
(Tony Carroll) *s.i.s: in rr: hdwy on outside over 2f out: str run to chse wnr fnl f: no imp clsng stages* **10/1**
2120 **3** *½* **Asterales**[27] 1631 5-9-2 **52** .... JamieMackay 9 60
(Willie Musson) *in rr: hdwy over 2f out: styd on to take 3rd ins fnl f: kpt on clsng stages but nt rch ldng duo* **12/1**
5566 **4** *2½* **If What And Maybe**[22] 1744 4-9-0 **50** ....(v) TomMcLaughlin 15 54
(John Ryan) *sn drvn to chse ldrs: rdn 3f out: wknd ins fnl f* **25/1**
6403 **5** *1* **Josie's Dream (IRE)**[12] 2048 4-8-12 **48** .... TonyCulhane 16 50
(Jo Hughes) *chsd ldrs: rdn 3f out: wknd ins fnl f* **8/1**[2]
-403 **6** *nk* **Iguacu**[16] 1919 8-9-0 **50** ....(p) JoeFanning 7 52
(Richard Price) *chsd ldrs: rdn 3f out: wknd appr fnl f* **9/1**[3]
0/0- **7** *4* **Tallulah Mai**[19] 5947 5-9-1 **51** .... LeeNewman 3 47
(Matthew Salaman) *chsd ldrs: rdn 3f out: wknd 2f out* **14/1**
/00- **8** *1¾* **Waterford Star (IRE)**[385] 1819 4-9-2 **52** ....(b) RoystonFfrench 17 45
(Ian Williams) *in rr: pushed along over 3f out: sme late prog* **16/1**
/5-0 **9** *¾* **Crimson Monarch (USA)**[20] 1792 8-9-0 **50** .... RussKennemore 8 42
(Peter Hiatt) *chsd ldr: drvn to chal 3f out: wknd ins fnl 2f* **12/1**
332- **10** *2¼* **Captain Oats (IRE)**[286] 4951 9-8-11 **52** .... LauraPike[(5)] 13 40
(Pam Ford) *s.i.s: in rr: rdn 4f out and no prog* **14/1**
0404 **11** *hd* **Magnitude**[71] 889 7-8-12 **48** ....(v) KellyHarrison 2 36
(Brian Baugh) *rdn 4f out: nvr beyond mid-div* **14/1**
436- **12** *3¼* **Aureate**[13] 6873 8-8-12 **48** .... NeilChalmers 6 30
(Brian Forsey) *in tch over 1m* **33/1**
006- **13** *1¾* **Oak Leaves**[46] 5612 5-8-12 **48** .... DavidProbert 4 28
(Nikki Evans) *led tl hdd 3f out: sn wknd* **25/1**
U0-0 **14** *10* **Into The Wind**[32] 1534 5-9-1 **51** .... JamesMillman 10 15
(Rod Millman) *a in rr* **10/1**
406- **15** *8* **Gabrielle Da Vinci**[483] 309 6-8-11 **47** .... MarcHalford 14
(Andrew Price) *a in rr* **50/1**
0064 **16** *7* **Carr Hall (IRE)**[42] 1299 9-8-10 **46** .... NeilCallan 12
(Tony Carroll) *s.i.s: a in rr* **10/1**

2m 36.7s (-2.30) **Going Correction** -0.15s/f (Firm) **16** Ran SP% **128.9**
Speed ratings (Par 101): **101,100,100,98,98 97,95,93,93,91 91,89,88,81,76 71**
Tote Swingers: 1&2 £8.90, 1&3 £10.40, 2&3 £18.10 CSF £30.68 CT £306.94 TOTE £4.70: £1.50, £1.50, £4.70, £5.70; EX 36.80.
Owner P Ponting **Bred** Gestut Hof Ittlingen **Trained** East Garston, Berks

FOCUS
A big field but basically moderate types.
T/Plt: £330.60 to a £1 stake. Pool: £59,977.98 - 132.41 winning tickets. T/Qpdt: £38.90 to a £1 stake. Pool: £4,894.75 - 92.90 winning tickets. ST

2168 LINGFIELD (L-H)
Wednesday, May 23

OFFICIAL GOING: Turf course - good to firm (good in places); all-weather - standard
Wind: Almost nil Weather: Sultry

2392 CITIPOST DIRECT DISTRIBUTIONS CLASSIFIED (S) STKS (TURF) 1m 2f
2:00 (2:00) (Class 6) 3-Y-O+ **£1,704** (£503; £251) **Stalls** Low

Form RPR
140/ **1** **Reaction**[800] 6977 6-8-12 63 ....(p) HarryPoulton[(7)] 1 63
(Sheena West) *mde all: rdn whn pressed over 3f out and drew 2 l clr: pressed again 1f out: hld on wl* **9/2**[3]
2210 **2** *½* **Dazzling Valentine**[23] 1719 4-9-11 68 .... LiamJones 3 68
(Alan Bailey) *trckd wnr: chal 4f out: rdn and nt qckn 3f out: tried to have anther go 1f out: a hld* **5/6**[1]
1002 **3** *1¾* **Marvo**[7] 2168 8-9-11 66 ....(b) EddieAhern 4 64
(Mark H Tompkins) *hld up in last: coaxed along 3f out: asked for effrt over 1f out: sn rdn and fnd nil* **2/1**[2]

2m 13.11s (2.61) **Going Correction** -0.25s/f (Firm) **3** Ran SP% **106.1**
Speed ratings (Par 101): **79,78,77**
CSF £8.56 TOTE £5.90; EX 7.10.No bid for the winner.
Owner Gerald West **Bred** Mrs Brid Cosgrove **Trained** Falmer, E Sussex

FOCUS
There were question marks over each of these, and it was the outsider of three who came out on top under a well-judged front-running ride.

2393 NEWS INTERNATIONAL MAIDEN STKS (TURF) 1m 3f 106y
2:30 (2:33) (Class 5) 3-Y-O+ **£2,385** (£704; £352) **Stalls** High

Form RPR
1 **Clowance Estate (IRE)** 3-8-11 0 .... JamesDoyle 2 81+
(Roger Charlton) *trckd ldng trio: smooth prog fr 4f out to ld over 2f out: sn pressed: shkn up and assert fnl f* **2/1**[1]
3 **2** *1¼* **Scottish Vespers (IRE)**[37] 1414 3-8-11 0 .... RyanMoore 6 76
(Sir Michael Stoute) *in tch in 6th: reminders 1/2-way: rdn and prog over 3f out: wnt 2nd 2f out and sn chalng: styd on but hld fnl f* **3/1**[2]
00- **3** *11* **Tokyo Brown (USA)**[238] 6462 3-8-11 0 .... StevieDonohoe 1 58
(Heather Main) *in tch in 7th: outpcd fr 1/2-way: drvn over 3f out: styd on fnl 2f to take 3rd last stride* **100/1**
0- **4** *nk* **Onertother**[215] 6993 3-8-11 0 .... SamHitchcott 8 57
(Joseph Tuite) *settled in midfield: lft bhd whn ldr stretched the field 1/2-way: modest 8th over 3f out: stdy prog after: chsd clr ldng pair ins fnl f: lost 3rd post* **100/1**
0 **5** *2* **Encouraging (IRE)**[34] 1467 3-8-11 0 .... WilliamBuick 10 54
(David Elsworth) *settled in midfield: lft bhd whn ldr stretched the field 1/2-way: remote 9th over 3f out: wandered u.p but kpt on fnl 2f* **12/1**
30-6 **6** *½* **Poetic Power (IRE)**[42] 1312 3-8-11 79 .... NickyMackay 4 53
(David Elsworth) *led: stretched field fr 1/2-way and sn clr: hdd and btn over 2f out* **3/1**[2]
-000 **7** *2¾* **Unex Renoir**[7] 2174 4-9-12 76 ....(p) J-PGuillambert 13 48
(Michael Attwater) *chsd ldng pair to 3f out: steadily wknd* **16/1**
60 **8** *8* **Khamseen**[19] 1824 5-9-7 0 .... DavidKenny[(5)] 7 34
(Karen George) *hld up in last pair: t.o fr 5f out: shkn up and styd on fnl 2f: gng on at fin* **100/1**
0-05 **9** *1¼* **Gadreel (IRE)**[44] 1259 3-8-8 43 .... AdamBeschizza[(3)] 12 32
(Anthony Middleton) *chsd ldr to 3f out: steadily wknd* **100/1**
6 **10** *14* **Al Faylasoof (USA)**[34] 1484 3-8-11 0 .... JamieSpencer 11
(David Simcock) *a in last quartet: t.o fr 5f out* **25/1**
11 *11* **Pursuitoexcellence (IRE)** 4-9-12 0 .... KierenFallon 3
(Sir Michael Stoute) *rn v green and sn pushed along: a wl in rr: t.o fr 5f out* **6/1**[3]
12 *nk* **Dalayir (FR)**[717] 5-9-12 0 .... AmirQuinn 5
(Gary Moore) *chsd ldrs in 5th tl wknd rapidly 4f out: t.o* **25/1**
13 *2* **Across The Straits (FR)**[90] 8-9-12 0 .... RobertHavlin 9
(Jonathan Geake) *s.v.s: a in last quartet: t.o fr 5f out* **100/1**

2m 27.34s (-4.16) **Going Correction** -0.25s/f (Firm)
WFA 3 from 4yo+ 15lb **13** Ran SP% **123.8**
Speed ratings (Par 103): **105,104,96,95,94 94,92,86,85,75 67,66,65**
Tote Swingers: 1&2 £2.80, 1&3 £40.20, 2&3 £34.30 CSF £8.17 TOTE £3.50: £1.60, £1.50, £21.70; EX 12.20.
Owner Seasons Holidays **Bred** Woodcote Stud Ltd **Trained** Beckhampton, Wilts

FOCUS
There didn't appear to be much strength in depth to this maiden, but the first two finished nicely clear.

2394 MENZIES SELECT H'CAP (DIV I) (TURF) 1m 3f 106y
3:00 (3:01) (Class 6) (0-60,59) 4-Y-O+ **£1,704** (£503; £251) **Stalls** High

Form RPR
00-5 **1** **Steely**[28] 1613 4-9-3 **55** .... RyanMoore 2 67
(Gary Moore) *mde all: drvn clr wl over 2f out: hd high but maintained gallop: unchal* **3/1**[2]
3222 **2** *3¾* **Laser Blazer**[16] 1919 4-9-4 **56** ....(p) JamieSpencer 9 62
(Jeremy Gask) *hld up in 6th: rdn over 2f out: prog on inner after: styd on to take 2nd jst ins fnl f: no ch w wnr* **5/2**[1]
2106 **3** *1¼* **Cantor**[28] 1613 4-9-5 **57** ....(b) WilliamCarson 4 61
(Giles Bravery) *trckd ldng pair: rdn over 2f out: chsd clr wnr wl over 1f out to jst ins fnl f: one pce* **16/1**
0046 **4** *nk* **Pahente**[32] 1534 4-8-9 **47** .... LukeMorris 8 50
(Tony Carroll) *hld up in 5th: rdn and struggling 3f out: styd on fr over 1f out* **12/1**
200- **5** *2¼* **Saloon (USA)**[181] 7527 8-9-2 **54** ....(p) GeorgeBaker 6 54
(Jane Chapple-Hyam) *hld up in 7th and detached: rdn over 2f out: kpt on fr over 1f out: n.d* **8/1**
304 **6** *1½* **Total Obsession**[22] 1732 5-8-8 **46** .... RobertHavlin 3 43
(Mark Hoad) *trckd ldng pair: rdn to chse wnr over 2f out to wl over 1f out: wknd* **50/1**
300- **7** *2½* **Aine's Delight (IRE)**[56] 7805 6-9-0 **55** .... SimonPearce[(3)] 7 48
(Andy Turnell) *stdd s: hld up in last and detached: rdn and no prog 3f out: no ch after* **8/1**
311- **8** *7* **Shouda (IRE)**[244] 6287 6-9-7 **59** .... TomQueally 5 40
(Barney Curley) *chsd wnr to over 2f out: wkng qckly whn reminder over 1f out* **7/2**[3]

2m 31.6s (0.10) **Going Correction** -0.25s/f (Firm) **8** Ran SP% **113.6**
Speed ratings (Par 101): **89,86,85,85,83 82,80,75**
Tote Swingers: 1&2 £2.10, 1&3 £9.40, 2&3 £8.30 CSF £10.78 CT £98.01 TOTE £4.00: £1.80, £1.10, £3.30; EX 11.80.
Owner E A Condon **Bred** Mrs S E Barclay **Trained** Lower Beeding, W Sussex

FOCUS
The first division of this moderate handicap was run 4.26secs slower than the earlier maiden over the same trip.

2395 MENZIES SELECT H'CAP (DIV II) (TURF) 1m 3f 106y
3:30 (3:34) (Class 6) (0-60,57) 4-Y-O+ **£1,704** (£503; £251) **Stalls** High

Form RPR
425- **1** **Reggie Perrin**[143] 6926 4-9-4 **54** ....(v[1]) IanMongan 2 64
(Pat Phelan) *trckd ldng pair: urged along at various stages fr 1/2-way: rdn 3f out: clsd to ld wl over 1f out: styd on wl and on top fnl f* **9/4**[1]
0550 **2** *3* **Kucharova (IRE)**[42] 1310 4-9-0 **50** .... ChrisCatlin 9 54
(Seamus Mullins) *hld up in 7th: prog over 2f out: plld out and drvn to chse wnr jst over 1f out: styd on but no imp* **12/1**
-605 **3** *2* **Glens Wobbly**[16] 1907 4-8-2 **45** .... KatiaScallan[(7)] 5 46
(Jonathan Geake) *trckd ldrs: rdn over 3f out: lost pl and struggling over 2f out: kpt on to take 3rd ins fnl f* **16/1**
350- **4** *nse* **Cardi King**[181] 7527 4-9-5 **55** ....(t) JamesDoyle 7 56
(Ian Wood) *trckd ldrs: drvn and nt qckn wl over 2f out: kpt on fr over 1f out to press for 3rd fnl f* **15/2**[3]
0-05 **5** *½* **Barbirolli**[20] 1770 10-8-9 **45** .... WilliamCarson 3 45
(William Stone) *hld up disputing 5th: rdn and nt qckn wl over 2f out: kpt on to press for 3rd fnl f* **25/1**

003 **6** 2½ **Eurhythmic (IRE)**[20] 1771 5-9-7 **57**.................................. GeorgeBaker 8 53
(Jim Old) *pressed ldr: led over 2f out gng strly: hdd and rdn wl over 1f out: wknd* **11/1**

0352 **7** 3 **Heading To First**[20] 1770 5-8-10 **46**................................(p) RyanMoore 1 39
(Paddy Butler) *led to over 2f out: sn btn: eased whn no ch last 100yds* **10/3[2]**

3-00 **8** 3¾ **Notabadlad**[27] 1624 5-9-3 **56**.................................. AdamBeschizza(3) 4 40
(Simon Dow) *reluctant to enter stalls: dropped out in last: rdn and no prog over 3f out* **12/1**

2m 31.35s (-0.15) **Going Correction** -0.25s/f (Firm) **8** Ran SP% **99.1**
Speed ratings (Par 101): **90,87,86,86,85 84,81,79**
Tote Swingers: 1&2 £5.20, 1&3 £6.50, 2&3 £21.10 CSF £21.89 CT £209.04 TOTE £3.10: £1.60, £3.40, £2.50; EX 26.40.
Owner Ermyn Lodge Stud **Bred** Ermyn Lodge Stud Limited **Trained** Epsom, Surrey

FOCUS
There was a 10p rule 4 deduction from all bets after Trefoil refused to enter the stalls. This second leg of the handicap was run a quarter of a second faster than the first division.
Cardi King Official explanation: trainer said gedling was unsuited by ground (good to firm (good in places)

2396 MENZIES DISTRIBUTION H'CAP 1m 6f
4:00 (4:00) (Class 5) (0-70,70) 4-Y-0+ **£2,385** (£704; £352) **Stalls** High

Form RPR
40-1 **1** **Alfraamsey**[7] 2175 4-8-9 **58** 6ex.................................. JimmyFortune 5 70+
(Sheena West) *trckd ldr after 3f: led over 5f out: shkn up and decisive advantage over 3f out: drvn out* **5/2[1]**

000/ **2** ¾ **Our Folly**[55] 7179 4-8-2 **51** oh6..................................(t) LukeMorris 2 60
(Stuart Kittow) *detached in last pair early and nt gng that wl: rdn 5f out: prog fr 3f out to chse clr wnr 2f out: styd on and grad clsd fnl f* **40/1**

20-6 **3** 3¼ **Marcus Antonius**[72] 521 5-9-3 **66**.................................. PatCosgrave 1 70
(Jim Boyle) *trckd ldrs: rdn wl over 2f out: styd on u.p to take 3rd jst over 1f out: n.d to ldng pair* **6/1**

035 **4** 3¼ **Dream Catcher (SWE)**[75] 849 9-8-13 **62**....................(p) RyanMoore 3 61
(Jonjo O'Neill) *w.w in tch: rdn and no prog wl over 2f out: plugged on fr over 1f out* **8/1**

-002 **5** ¾ **Not Til Monday (IRE)**[28] 1598 6-9-7 **70**....................(v) FrederikTylicki 4 68
(J R Jenkins) *led to over 5f out: sn dropped to 3rd: drvn to chse wnr over 3f out to 2f out: fdd* **11/4[2]**

0513 **6** nk **Bute Street**[33] 1496 7-8-5 **54**.................................. ChrisCatlin 9 52
(Ron Hodges) *lost pl after 4f: rapid prog on outer to go 2nd 5f out to over 3f out: steadily wknd fnl 2f* **9/1**

1120 **7** shd **El Libertador (USA)**[65] 963 6-8-7 **56**....................(b) WilliamCarson 6 54
(Eric Wheeler) *hld up in detached last pair: tried to cl on ldng gp over 4f out: no prog over 2f out: plugged on* **20/1**

-461 **8** 74 **Frederick William**[65] 963 4-9-7 **70**....................(p) JamieSpencer 10
(Chris Gordon) *trckd ldr 3f: prom tl wknd rapidly 5f out: t.o whn virtually p.u fnl 2f* **11/2[3]**

3m 5.39s (-4.61) **Going Correction** -0.25s/f (Firm) **8** Ran SP% **113.2**
Speed ratings (Par 103): **103,102,100,98,98 98,98,55**
Tote Swingers: 1&2 £15.60, 1&3 £6.10, 2&3 £36.70 CSF £90.24 CT £544.31 TOTE £3.50: £1.40, £7.60, £1.20; EX 119.10.
Owner Tapestry Partnership **Bred** G Hedley & Mike Channon Bloodstock Limited **Trained** Falmer, E Sussex

FOCUS
A modest staying handicap and positive tactics once again paid dividends.
Frederick William Official explanation: jockey said gelding was never travelling.

2397 CITIBET - NEW WEEKLY FOOTBALL BETTING MAGAZINE FILLIES' H'CAP 6f (P)
4:30 (4:31) (Class 5) (0-70,70) 3-Y-O **£2,385** (£704; £352) **Stalls** Low

Form RPR
0-44 **1** **Subtle Knife**[23] 1709 3-9-0 **63**.................................. WilliamCarson 2 68
(Giles Bravery) *settled in 4th and off the pce: rdn over 2f out: clsd fr over 1f out: drvn ahd last 75yds* **8/1**

0-66 **2** ¾ **Kyanight (IRE)**[25] 1658 3-9-5 **68**.................................. JohnFahy 10 71
(Clive Cox) *trckd clr ldng pair: clsd to ld on inner jst over 1f out: drvn and hdd last 75yds* **16/1**

6435 **3** 1 **Chester'Slittlegem (IRE)**[42] 1313 3-9-2 **65**.................... TomQueally 3 64
(Ed de Giles) *settled in 5th and off the pce: rdn over 2f out: styd on to take 3rd ins fnl f: unable to chal* **8/1**

0-36 **4** nk **Fine Painting (IRE)**[12] 2045 3-9-7 **70**.................................. RyanMoore 6 68
(Gary Moore) *hld up in rr and off the pce: drvn on outer over 2f out: kpt on fr over 1f out: nvr able to chal* **5/2[1]**

0-04 **5** 1½ **Wrapped Up**[8] 2147 3-8-7 **56** oh3.................................. StevieDonohoe 7 50
(Heather Main) *wl off the pce in rr: drvn over 2f out: kpt on one pce fr over 1f out: n.d* **12/1**

-114 **6** ½ **Sweet Ovation**[91] 659 3-8-13 **67**.................................. LeeNewnes(5) 9 59
(Mark Usher) *hld up in last pair and wl off the pce: shkn up 2f out: styd on ins fnl f: nvr nr ldrs* **11/2[3]**

3623 **7** ½ **Trail Of Tears (IRE)**[14] 1986 3-9-4 **67**....................(b[1]) WilliamBuick 4 57
(John Gosden) *w ldr at str pce and clr of rest: drvn and hanging bnd 2f out: stl upsides jst over 1f out: sn wknd* **4/1[2]**

0-14 **8** 4 **Pucon**[16] 1941 3-9-2 **65**.................................. JimCrowley 1 43
(Roger Teal) *led at str pce but hrd pressed: hdd & wknd rapidly jst over 1f out* **10/1**

3200 **9** ½ **Arabian Flight**[22] 1725 3-8-11 **60**.................................. KieranO'Neill 5 36
(John Bridger) *a in rr: rdn bef 1/2-way: no prog* **16/1**

1m 13.29s (1.39) **Going Correction** +0.225s/f (Slow) **9** Ran SP% **114.7**
Speed ratings (Par 96): **99,98,96,96,94 93,92,87,86**
Tote Swingers: 1&2 £20.00, 1&3 £7.30, 2&3 £28.20 CSF £124.23 CT £1063.12 TOTE £12.80: £4.10, £6.40, £1.60; EX 123.00.
Owner D B Clark & Russel Grant **Bred** Mrs F Bravery **Trained** Newmarket, Suffolk

FOCUS
A competitive, if modest, AW fillies' handicap in which they appeared to go too fast early.

2398 MAIL PUBLISHER SOLUTIONS CLAIMING STKS 7f (P)
5:00 (5:00) (Class 6) 3-Y-O+ **£1,704** (£503; £251) **Stalls** Low

Form RPR
6051 **1** **Legal Legacy**[7] 2168 6-9-5 72.................................. StevieDonohoe 9 78
(John Ryan) *stdd s fr wd draw and hld up last: gd prog over 1f out: drvn and r.o wl to ld nr fin* **11/4[2]**

1211 **2** ½ **Red Somerset (USA)**[41] 1342 9-9-7 77.................................. KieranO'Neill 4 79
(Mike Murphy) *led at mod pce: kicked on over 2f out: r.o fnl f but hdd nr fin* **9/4[1]**

6443 **3** 2½ **Aquilifer (IRE)**[7] 2168 4-9-4 70..................................(tp) JimCrowley 1 69
(Mrs K Burke) *t.k.h: trckd ldr to over 2f out and again wl over 1f out: no imp and lost 2nd ins fnl f* **5/1**

6015 **4** hd **Imprimis Tagula (IRE)**[5] 2251 8-9-7 78..................................(v) LiamJones 5 71
(Alan Bailey) *t.k.h: trckd ldng pair: wnt 2nd over 2f out to wl over 1f out: nt qckn* **3/1[3]**

0006 **5** ½ **Highland Harvest**[2] 2342 8-9-3 67.................................. IanMongan 8 66
(Jamie Poulton) *hld up in tch: drvn and nt qckn wl over 1f out: one pce after* **20/1**

6601 **6** ¾ **Moment In The Sun**[14] 1979 3-8-7 61..................................(b) LukeMorris 6 61
(David Flood) *chsd ldrs: rdn sn after 1/2-way: nvr any imp* **8/1**

1m 27.66s (2.86) **Going Correction** +0.225s/f (Slow)
WFA 3 from 4yo+ 11lb **6** Ran SP% **115.0**
Speed ratings (Par 101): **92,91,88,88,87 86**
Tote Swingers: 1&2 £1.90, 1&3 £3.10, 2&3 £2.40 CSF £9.73 TOTE £3.70: £3.20, £1.10; EX 11.50.The winner was claimed by Mr. Richard Rowe for £8,000.
Owner M M Foulger **Bred** D Dowling **Trained** Newmarket, Suffolk

FOCUS
Withdrawals meant the field was reduced by a third in this fair claimer but the sextet that took part all had course wins to their name.

2399 SMITHS NEWS H'CAP 1m (P)
5:30 (5:31) (Class 5) (0-75,74) 4-Y-O+ **£2,385** (£704; £352) **Stalls** High

Form RPR
30-1 **1** **Scottish Glen**[140] 33 6-9-7 **74**.................................. JimCrowley 6 85
(Patrick Chamings) *settled in midfield disputing 6th: prog on outer over 2f out: swept into the ld jst over 1f out: styd on wl* **7/1**

5-40 **2** 1¼ **Whitby Jet (IRE)**[25] 1680 4-9-7 **74**.................................. RyanMoore 9 82
(Ed Vaughan) *hld up in last trio: drvn and prog fr 2f out: r.o to take 2nd last 75yds: no ch to chal* **9/2[1]**

50-0 **3** 1 **Catchanova (IRE)**[28] 1611 5-9-2 **69**.................................. TomQueally 7 75
(Eve Johnson Houghton) *hld up in 8th: prog on outer 2f out: rdn and r.o to take 2nd briefly 100yds out: one pce after* **15/2**

0-61 **4** 1¾ **Bloodsweatandtears**[20] 1772 4-9-7 **74**.................................. SebSanders 4 76+
(William Knight) *won battle for ld but hdd after 2f: hrd rdn to ld again wl over 1f out: hdd and fdd jst over 1f out* **11/2[2]**

2333 **5** 1¾ **Hereford Boy**[20] 1769 8-9-6 **73**..................................(v) JamieSpencer 1 71
(Dean Ivory) *hld up in last and wl off the pce: effrt 2f out: styd on but no threat* **6/1[3]**

1-33 **6** 1¼ **Perfect Mission**[132] 131 4-9-4 **71**..................................(v) JimmyFortune 10 66
(Andrew Balding) *t.k.h: trckd ldng pair: rdn over 2f out: nt qckn over 1f out: lost pl fnl f* **9/2[1]**

4200 **7** ½ **Mishrif (USA)**[62] 991 6-9-5 **72**..................................(b) FrederikTylicki 3 66
(J R Jenkins) *trckd ldrs disputing 4th: nt clr run briefly over 2f out: sltly hmpd wl over 1f out: drvn and sme prog after: no hdwy ins fnl f* **16/1**

1025 **8** 3¾ **Spinning Ridge (IRE)**[7] 2168 7-9-6 **73**..................................(v) LukeMorris 8 58
(Ronald Harris) *nvr bttr than midfield: rdn 3f out: no prog and btn over 1f out: eased* **16/1**

222- **9** 2 **Leelu**[239] 6434 6-8-13 **66**.................................. JamesDoyle 11 46
(David Arbuthnot) *taken down early: racd wd early: led after 2f: hdd & wknd wl over 1f out* **16/1**

0204 **10** 2½ **L'Hirondelle (IRE)**[12] 2044 8-9-2 **69**..................................[1] J-PGuillambert 5 44
(Michael Attwater) *a wl in rr and nvr gng wl: nvr a factor* **14/1**

04-0 **11** ½ **Greek Islands (IRE)**[12] 2043 4-9-3 **70**..................................(p) JohnFahy 2 44
(Ed de Giles) *trckd ldrs disputing 4th: drvn over 2f out: wknd over 1f out* **18/1**

1m 38.53s (0.33) **Going Correction** +0.225s/f (Slow) **11** Ran SP% **119.9**
Speed ratings (Par 103): **107,105,104,103,101 100,99,95,93,91 90**
Tote Swingers: 1&2 £9.30, 1&3 £13.50, 2&3 £6.40 CSF £39.33 CT £249.02 TOTE £9.50: £2.70, £2.30, £3.30; EX 53.50.
Owner The Foxford House Partnership **Bred** Mrs Ann Jenkins **Trained** Baughurst, Hants

FOCUS
A fair and competitive handicap but a clear-cut winner in the end.
T/Plt: £189.80 to a £1 stake. Pool: £46,568.02 - 179.02 winning tickets. T/Qpdt: £20.90 to a £1 stake. Pool: £4,639.18 - 163.92 winning tickets. JN

1986 SOUTHWELL (L-H)
Wednesday, May 23

OFFICIAL GOING: Standard
Wind: Light across Weather: Fine and dry

2400 FOLLOW US ON TWITTER @SOUTHWELL_RACES H'CAP 6f (F)
2:20 (2:21) (Class 4) (0-85,78) 3-Y-O **£4,075** (£1,212; £606; £303) **Stalls** Low

Form RPR
1251 **1** **Abi Scarlet (IRE)**[50] 1176 3-9-7 78.................................. DarryllHolland 4 90
(Hughie Morrison) *chsd ldng pair: pushed along over 2f out: rdn to chse ldr over 1f out: led ent fnl f: styd on* **1/1[1]**

2213 **2** 2½ **Reve Du Jour (IRE)**[50] 1176 3-8-10 70.................................. SeanLevey(3) 2 74
(Alan McCabe) *led: rdn along 2f out: drvn and hdd ent fnl f: kpt on same pce* **4/1[2]**

0202 **3** 1¼ **Feeling Good**[15] 1959 3-8-11 71.................................. DaleSwift(3) 6 71+
(Brian Ellison) *sn outpcd and pushed along in rr: rdn and wd st: kpt on u.p fnl 2f: tk 3rd nr fin* **5/1[3]**

3042 **4** nk **Beau Mistral (IRE)**[15] 1960 3-8-12 69.................................. SilvestreDeSousa 5 68
(Paul Green) *in tch: rdn to chse ldrs 2f out: sn one pce: lost 3rd nr line* **8/1**

4205 **5** 5 **Adranian (IRE)**[14] 1983 3-9-6 77..................................(v) MartinDwyer 1 60
(David C Griffiths) *cl up: rdn along 2f out: sn wknd* **20/1**

2220 **6** 1¼ **Flying Pickets (IRE)**[26] 1641 3-8-7 71..................................(be) NoraLooby(7) 3 50
(Alan McCabe) *dwlt: a in rr* **14/1**

1m 15.31s (-1.19) **Going Correction** -0.125s/f (Stan) **6** Ran SP% **109.2**
Speed ratings (Par 101): **102,98,97,96,89 88**
Tote Swingers: 1&2 £1.90, 1&3 £2.40, 2&3 £1.70 CSF £4.87 TOTE £2.30: £1.30, £1.10; EX 4.50.
Owner The Boot Inn Partnership **Bred** Henry O'Callaghan **Trained** East Ilsley, Berks

FOCUS
A straightforward 3yo sprint handicap.

2401 FINAL WHISTLE PUB SOUTHWELL H'CAP 7f (F)
2:50 (2:51) (Class 6) (0-55,54) 4-Y-O+ **£1,704** (£503; £251) **Stalls** Low

Form RPR
-003 **1** **Clear Spring (IRE)**[27] 1625 4-8-7 **45**.................................. AdrianNicholls 11 63+
(John Spearing) *cl up on outer: led over 2f out and sn rdn clr: drvn out* **13/2[3]**

000- **2** *1 ½* **Bishopbriggs (USA)**[295] 4651 7-9-2 **54**............................. AdamKirby 4 68
(K F Clutterbuck) *chsd ldr: hdwy over 2f out: rdn wl over 1f out: chsd wnr appr fnl f: kpt on towards fin* **4/1**[2]

1003 **3** *4* **Putin (IRE)**[14] 1988 4-8-11 **49**................................(bt) SilvestreDeSousa 6 52
(Phil McEntee) *prom: effrt and cl up over 2f out: sn rdn and one pce fr wl over 1f out* **10/3**[1]

0060 **4** *3 ¼* **Tenancy (IRE)**[20] 1787 8-8-11 **49**.................................(b) PaddyAspell 13 44
(Shaun Harris) *led: rdn along 3f out: hdd over 2f out and grad wknd* **28/1**

0001 **5** *½* **Hilbre Court (USA)**[14] 1988 7-9-1 **53**........................(v) DuranFentiman 9 47
(Brian Baugh) *towards rr and sn pushed along: rdn 1/2-way: sme hdwy and wd st: drvn over 2f out: n.d* **4/1**[2]

035- **6** *½* **Norcroft**[168] 7656 10-8-6 **47**..(p) DominicFox(3) 2 39
(Christine Dunnett) *midfield: hdwy 3f out: rdn over 2f out: sn one pce* **16/1**

-306 **7** *5* **Princess Willow**[85] 732 4-8-13 **51**............................. RichardThomas 7 30
(John E Long) *a towards rr* **11/1**

5-5 **8** *nk* **Adam De Beaulieu (USA)**[29] 1584 5-8-12 **50**..............(t) PhillipMakin 1 29
(Ben Haslam) *in tch: rdn along 3f out: sn wknd* **12/1**

00/4 **9** *1 ¼* **Amber Moon**[15] 1961 7-8-7 **45**.....................................(b) TomEaves 10 20
(Ann Stokell) *in tch: rdn along 1/2-way: sn wknd* **16/1**

000 **10** *11* **Miss Tooty Fruiti (IRE)**[23] 1718 4-8-0 **45**..................... JakePayne(7) 12
(Simon Hodgson) *a towards rr* **100/1**

00-6 **11** *¾* **Queen's Choice (IRE)**[15] 1961 4-8-7 **45**.....................(t) SaleemGolam 5
(Anabel K Murphy) *dwlt and a in rr* **33/1**

0-50 **12** *3 ½* **Fathey (IRE)**[134] 113 6-8-4 **47** ow2.............................. AdamCarter(5) 8
(Charles Smith) *a in rr* **28/1**

1m 29.29s (-1.01) **Going Correction** -0.125s/f (Stan) 12 Ran SP% **115.0**
Speed ratings (Par 101): **100,98,93,90,89 88,83,82,81,68 67,63**
Tote Swingers: 1&2 £32.90, 1&3 £6.00, 2&3 £4.80 CSF £30.69 CT £161.30 TOTE £5.50: £1.40, £2.10, £1.60; EX 102.30 Trifecta £161.30 Pool: £444.90 - 2.04 winning units..
Owner H James **Bred** Rocal Bloodstock **Trained** Kinnersley, Worcs

FOCUS
A moderate 46-55 handicap in which not many got involved.
Hilbre Court(USA) Official explanation: jockey said gelding was never travelling.

2402 BRITISH STALLION STUDS SUPPORTING BRITISH RACING E B F MAIDEN STKS 6f (F)
3:20 (3:21) (Class 5) 2-Y-O **£3,234** (£962; £481; £240) **Stalls** Low

Form RPR
32 **1** **Polski Max**[21] 1753 2-9-3 0.. TonyHamilton 3 86+
(Richard Fahey) *mde most: rdn 2f out: drvn and styd on wl fnl f* **10/11**[1]

02 **2** *2 ¼* **Secret Destination**[29] 1579 2-8-9 0.................................. DaleSwift(3) 8 74
(Brian Ellison) *in tch: hdwy 1/2-way: cl up 2f out: sn rdn and ev ch tl drvn and one pce ins fnl f* **7/1**[3]

323 **3** *8* **Marchwood**[7] 2163 2-9-3 0.. LiamKeniry 1 55
(J S Moore) *trckd ldrs on inner: hdwy and cl up over 2f out: sn rdn and ev ch tl drvn and outpcd wl over 1f out* **12/1**

4 *4* **Kalicamix** 2-9-3 0... PhillipMakin 6 43
(Paul Cole) *sn swtchd to outer: green and pushed along after 2f: wd st: sme hdwy fnl 2f: n.d* **16/1**

2 **5** *nk* **Ryedale Valley**[15] 1955 2-9-3 0.. DavidAllan 5 42
(Tim Easterby) *chsd ldrs: rdn along 1/2-way: sn wknd* **14/1**

6 *4* **Annie Besant** 2-8-12 0... MartinDwyer 7 25+
(David C Griffiths) *dwlt and swtchd lft after s: in rr tl hdwy to trck ldrs wl over 2f out: sn rdn and wknd* **33/1**

5464 **7** *1 ¾* **Until It Sleeps**[9] 2135 2-8-9 0.. SeanLevey(3) 4 20
(Alan McCabe) *cl up: rdn along 1/2-way: sn wknd* **50/1**

8 *9* **Wellingrove (IRE)** 2-9-3 0...................................... SilvestreDeSousa 2
(Mark Johnston) *dwlt: green and sn pushed along: a in rr* **3/1**[2]

1m 15.66s (-0.84) **Going Correction** -0.125s/f (Stan) 8 Ran SP% **115.0**
Speed ratings (Par 93): **100,97,86,81,80 75,72,60**
Tote Swingers: 1&2 £1.20, 1&3 £7.90, 2&3 £14.50 CSF £8.23 TOTE £2.10: £1.40, £1.10, £3.10; EX 5.70 Trifecta £47.90 Pool: £742.96 - 11.46 winning units..
Owner Market Avenue Racing & Tremousser **Bred** Mike J Beadle **Trained** Musley Bank, N Yorks

FOCUS
An ordinary maiden, but the form horses filled the frame and the first two pulled clear.

NOTEBOOK
Polski Max had been placed in two 5f turf maidens including when chasing home the previous week's York scorer Lastchancelucas at Pontefract earlier this month. Having been up on the pace from the off, he had to battle to see off the runner-up, but showed a willing attitude and can continue to improve. (op Evens tchd 5-6)
Secret Destination chased home a long odds-on shot in a four-runner maiden over 5f here last month and was brought through to hold every chance inside the last 2f, but again she found herself up against a fair sort for a routine Southwell maiden. (op 13-2)
Marchwood, placed in three 5f turf maidens, pressed the pace for a long way but didn't appear to see out the extra furlong on this slow surface. (op 9-1)
Kalicamix, a 30,000gns half-brother to two winners at up to 1m2f, ran in snatches on the wide outside and should benefit from the experience. He ought to appreciate further. (tchd 18-1)
Ryedale Valley, second of four on his debut over 5f here earlier this month, was shaken off 2f from home over this stiffer test. (op 16-1)
Wellingrove(IRE), a 115,000gns half-brother to three winners at up to 1m including one on Fibresand, proved horribly green on this debut. (op 7-2 tchd 4-1)

2403 CPMG NOTTINGHAM ARCHITECTS CLAIMING STKS 1m 4f (F)
3:50 (3:50) (Class 5) 3-Y-0+ **£2,385** (£704; £352) **Stalls** Low

Form RPR
1-11 **1** **La Estrella (USA)**[92] 643 9-10-0 89.................................. DaneO'Neill 1 84
(Don Cantillon) *trckd ldng pair: smooth hdwy over 3f out: cl up over 2f out: rdn to chal over 1f out: led ent fnl f: styd on* **1/2**[1]

-010 **2** *1 ¼* **Jack Dawkins (USA)**[28] 1598 7-9-12 70........................ AdrianNicholls 5 80
(David Nicholls) *led 1 1/2f: trckd ldr tl led again 4f out: jnd and rdn over 2f out: drvn over 1f out: hdd ent fnl f: kpt on same pce* **7/2**[2]

30-0 **3** *18* **Enroller (IRE)**[12] 1214 7-10-0 85..................................... MartinDwyer 4 62
(William Muir) *cl up: led after 1 1/2f: pushed along and hdd 4f out: rdn over 2f out: outpcd wl over 1f out: sn eased* **6/1**[3]

4 *31* **Aragorn Rouge**[82] 778 4-9-7 78.................................. AdamCarter(5) 3
(John Wainwright) *in tch: rdn along and outpcd over 4f out: sn bhd* **16/1**

2m 39.69s (-1.31) **Going Correction** -0.125s/f (Stan) 4 Ran SP% **109.1**
Speed ratings (Par 103): **99,98,86,65**
CSF £2.59 TOTE £1.40; EX 2.70.
Owner Don Cantillon **Bred** Five Horses Ltd And Theatrical Syndicate **Trained** Newmarket, Suffolk

FOCUS
This four-runner claimer was all about one horse.

2404 GREEN FEE OFFERS AT SOUTHWELLGOLFCLUB.COM CLASSIFIED (S) STKS 7f (F)
4:20 (4:20) (Class 6) 3-Y-O **£1,704** (£503; £251) **Stalls** Low

Form RPR
3-30 **1** **Sweetnessandlight**[32] 1517 3-9-4 63......................... MichaelStainton 2 61
(Jason Ward) *trckd ldng pair: hdwy 1/2-way: led over 1f out: kpt on* **4/11**[1]

-000 **2** *3 ½* **Medam**[32] 1531 3-8-12 45.. PaddyAspell 4 43
(Shaun Harris) *cl up: led after 2f: rdn along and hdd over 1f out: drvn and wknd appr fnl f* **16/1**

3656 **3** *4* **Jeremy Sue**[7] 2166 3-8-12 43......................................(tp) DaneO'Neill 3 33
(Derek Haydn Jones) *in tch: rdn along wl over 2f out: sn one pce* **15/2**[3]

-000 **4** *32* **Fine Kingdom**[8] 2141 3-8-12 52.. TomEaves 1
(Michael Dods) *led: hanging rt and hdd after 2f: sn pushed along and hung bdly rt 1/2-way: bhd and wd st: t.o* **5/1**[2]

1m 30.07s (-0.23) **Going Correction** -0.125s/f (Stan) 4 Ran SP% **107.6**
Speed ratings (Par 97): **96,92,87,50**
CSF £6.89 TOTE £1.30; EX 8.70.The winner was bought in for £5,750.
Owner Mrs Jill Ward **Bred** Dxb Bloodstock Ltd **Trained** Middleham, N Yorks

FOCUS
Little to get excited about in this classified seller.
Fine Kingdom Official explanation: jockey said gelding hung badly right

2405 MILLWARD INTEGRATED ENGINEERING CONSULTANTS H'CAP 1m (F)
4:50 (4:50) (Class 4) (0-80,80) 4-Y-0+ **£4,075** (£1,212; £606; £303) **Stalls** Low

Form RPR
6043 **1** **The Lock Master (IRE)**[12] 2051 5-9-5 **78**.............. SilvestreDeSousa 10 88
(Michael Appleby) *in tch: rdn along 3f out: hdwy to chse clr ldr 2f out: drvn over 1f out: styd on to ld nr fin* **5/2**[1]

261 **2** *½* **Alpha Tauri (USA)**[15] 1958 6-9-2 **75**................................(t) AdamKirby 8 84+
(Richard Guest) *trckd ldr: led over 3f out: qcknd clr wl over 2f out: rdn wl over 1f out: drvn ins fnl f: wknd last 75yds: hdd nr fin* **11/2**[3]

1460 **3** *6* **Myboyalfie (USA)**[4] 2274 5-8-13 **72**...............................(v) DaneO'Neill 2 67
(J R Jenkins) *in tch: hdwy over 3f out: rdn to chse ldng pair 2f out: sn rdn and no imp* **4/1**[2]

0060 **4** *6* **On The Cusp (IRE)**[7] 2168 5-8-4 **70**..........................(tp) NoraLooby(7) 5 51
(Richard Guest) *chsd ldrs and sn pushed along: rdn 3f out: sn one pce* **33/1**

3330 **5** *1 ¾* **Mcconnell (USA)**[20] 1771 7-8-4 **68**............................(b) DeanHeslop(5) 6 45
(Richard Guest) *towards rr: wd st: hdwy 2f out: sn rdn and n.d* **10/1**

0410 **6** *shd* **Bold Marc (IRE)**[25] 1659 10-8-8 **74**.......................... ConorHarrison(7) 4 51
(Mrs K Burke) *trckd ldrs 1f: sn swtchd to outer: lost pl and bhd 1/2-way: wd st: rdn 2f out: n.d* **14/1**

0310 **7** *½* **Standpoint**[11] 2083 6-9-7 **80**..(p) TomEaves 9 56
(Conor Dore) *midfield: rdn along wl over 2f out: n.d* **12/1**

0450 **8** *19* **All Right Now**[6] 2207 5-8-10 **69**..................................(b[1]) AndreaAtzeni 3
(Derek Haydn Jones) *led: rdn along and hdd over 3f out: sn wknd* **11/2**[3]

-030 **9** *4 ½* **Eastern Hills**[5] 2243 7-9-3 **79**....................................(p) SeanLevey(3) 1
(Alan McCabe) *chsd ldrs on inner: rdn along 3f out: sn wknd* **16/1**

10 *3 ¼* **Handheld**[532] 5-9-7 **80**.. LiamKeniry 7
(Ed de Giles) *dwlt: a in rr* **25/1**

1m 40.86s (-2.84) **Going Correction** -0.125s/f (Stan) 10 Ran SP% **115.5**
Speed ratings (Par 105): **109,108,102,96,94 94,94,75,70,67**
Tote Swingers: 1&2 £4.60, 1&3 £3.80, 2&3 £3.60 CSF £16.06 CT £46.70 TOTE £3.90: £1.70, £1.90, £1.10; EX 18.40 Trifecta £46.70 Pool: £749.10 - 11.87 winning units..
Owner K G Kitchen **Bred** Patrick F Kelly **Trained** Danethorpe, Notts

FOCUS
A decent handicap and there was no hiding place with several established trailblazers in opposition.
All Right Now Official explanation: jockey said gelding hung left.

2406 FIND US ON FACEBOOK SOUTHWELL RACECOURSE H'CAP 6f (F)
5:20 (5:20) (Class 6) (0-60,60) 4-Y-0+ **£1,704** (£503; £251) **Stalls** Low

Form RPR
3322 **1** **Gracie's Gift (IRE)**[14] 1987 10-8-6 **48**.....................(v) DeclanCannon(3) 6 57
(Richard Guest) *chsd ldng pair: hdwy 2f out: rdn to chse clr ldr over 1f out: styd on wl to ld last 75yds* **9/2**[2]

0363 **2** *1 ¼* **Bookiesindex Boy**[14] 1987 8-9-2 **55**............................ DaneO'Neill 2 60
(J R Jenkins) *stmbld s: trckd ldrs: hdwy over 2f out: rdn wl over 1f out: kpt on fnl f* **7/1**[3]

0000 **3** *½* **Hab Reeh**[15] 1961 4-8-7 **46** oh1.................................(bt) JamesSullivan 3 49
(Ruth Carr) *led at str pce and sn clr: rdn wl over 1f out: drvn ins fnl f: hdd and no ex last 75yds* **14/1**

2100 **4** *hd* **Blueberry Fizz (IRE)**[28] 1601 4-9-3 **56**.............................(p) AdamKirby 5 59
(John Ryan) *chsd ldr: rdn wl over 2f out: drvn over 1f out: kpt on fnl f* **12/1**

-630 **5** *2 ¾* **Efisio Princess**[56] 1070 9-9-2 **55**................................. RichardThomas 7 49
(John E Long) *chsd ldrs: wd st: rdn and hdwy over 2f out: drvn over 1f out: no imp fnl f* **12/1**

6011 **6** *nk* **Lindoro**[15] 1961 7-9-4 **60**... AmyRyan(3) 8 53
(Brian Ellison) *a in rr* **4/5**[1]

40-0 **7** *6* **Avec Moi**[14] 1987 5-8-4 **46** oh1...(p) DominicFox(3) 4 20
(Christine Dunnett) *a in rr* **50/1**

0-06 **8** *11* **Passing Moment**[14] 1989 4-8-7 **46** oh1......................... DuranFentiman 9
(Brian Baugh) *a in rr* **66/1**

500- **9** *1 ½* **Imogen Louise (IRE)**[162] 7748 4-9-0 **58**........................ DeanHeslop(5) 1
(Richard Guest) *in tch on inner: rdn 1/2-way: sn wknd* **40/1**

1m 16.24s (-0.26) **Going Correction** -0.125s/f (Stan) 9 Ran SP% **114.2**
Speed ratings (Par 101): **96,94,93,93,89 89,81,66,64**
Tote Swingers: 1&2 £4.10, 1&3 £2.10, 2&3 £12.50 CSF £35.03 CT £128.20 TOTE £5.20: £1.90, £1.50, £2.90; EX 22.80 Trifecta £128.20 Pool: £754.19 - 4.35 winning units..
Owner S Hussey **Bred** Richard O'Hara **Trained** Stainforth, S Yorks

FOCUS
A moderate sprint handicap, but they went a searing pace and it was crucial to be handy.
Lindoro Official explanation: jockey said gelding was outpaced.

T/Plt: £5.60 to a £1 stake. Pool: £43,196.26 - 5,545.10 winning tickets. T/Qpdt: £2.70 to a £1 stake. Pool: £2,570.00 - 682.81 winning tickets. JR

[1847]GOODWOOD (R-H)

Thursday, May 24

OFFICIAL GOING: Straight course - good; round course - good to firm

Wind: Almost nil Weather: Glorious

2407 BRITISH STALLION STUDS SUPPORTING BRITISH RACING E B F MAIDEN FILLIES' STKS — 6f

2:00 (2:00) (Class 5) 2-Y-O — **£3,234** (£962; £481; £240) **Stalls** High

Form — RPR

1 **Sky Lantern (IRE)** 2-9-0 0 ... RichardHughes 3 — 82+
(Richard Hannon) *w ldr: led 1/2-way: pushed clr fr 2f out: readily* **1/1**[1]

2 *3½* **Cruck Realta** 2-9-0 0 ... SamHitchcott 2 — 69
(Mick Channon) *chsd ldng pair: rdn to go 2nd over 1f out: no ch w wnr* **8/1**

3 *1¼* **Indignant** 2-9-0 0 ... RyanMoore 4 — 65
(Richard Hannon) *led to 1/2-way: shkn up and lost 2nd over 1f out: one pce* **3/1**[2]

4 *nk* **Glen Ginnie (IRE)** 2-9-0 0 ... MichaelHills 5 — 64
(Charles Hills) *s.s: t.k.h and hld up in 4th: plld out and effrt 2f out: rn green but kpt on to press for 3rd fnl f* **9/2**[3]

5 *47* **Sweet Alabama** 2-9-0 0 ... JamesMillman 1
(Rod Millman) *dwlt: rn green and sn bhd: t.o* **20/1**

1m 14.8s (2.60) **Going Correction** +0.025s/f (Good) — **5** Ran SP% **109.1**

Speed ratings (Par 90): **83,78,76,76,13**

CSF £9.42 TOTE £1.90: £1.10, £3.60; EX 8.30.

Owner B Keswick **Bred** Tally-Ho Stud **Trained** East Everleigh, Wilts

FOCUS

This maiden, dominated by Richard Hannon in recent times, was run at a steady pace. The winner can do better but this bare form may not be worth any more.

NOTEBOOK

Sky Lantern(IRE) won in the style of a decent type and gave her trainer his fifth successive winner in the race. Hannon has run two fillies in this contest for each of the last five seasons, and Richard Hughes has chosen correctly every time. Hughes was happy to take a lead from stablemate Indignant, but cruised to the front 2f out and drew clear. The yard's juveniles have tended to need their first run more than in recent times, so this was a fine effort. The Albany looks the obvious target for Royal Ascot, a race that Memory won, having landed this contest for the stable in 2010. (op 10-11 tchd 11-10)

Cruck Realta, who hails from a yard enjoying a fine season with their 2yos, made a most encouraging debut. A half-sister to the stable's 2yo winner Universal Circus, she travelled nicely into the race but could not quicken as well as the winner. She should come on plenty for this. (tchd 15-2 and 9-1)

Indignant showed plenty of speed to lead early, but was always doing a bit too much. She looks a precocious type, but may be better over 5f. (op 7-2 tchd 11-4)

Glen Ginnie(IRE), sister to the yard's 5f AW winner Red Senor, travelled nicely behind the principles and ran well to the line. She will come on a good deal for this. (op 5-1 tchd 11-2)

Sweet Alabama was green from the off and struggling from an early stage. Her future looks to be over further. (op 16-1)

2408 HAZEL WIGLEY MEMORIAL STKS (H'CAP) — 1m 1f

2:35 (2:35) (Class 4) (0-85,83) 3-Y-O

£4,668 (£1,398; £699; £349; £174; £87) **Stalls** Low

Form — RPR

1-0 1 **Beaufort Twelve**[35] [1470] 3-9-4 **83** ... HarryBentley(3) 6 — 96
(William Jarvis) *hld up disputing 7th: prog on wd outside over 2f out: led over 1f out: r.o wl fnl f: jst hld on* **15/2**

51- 2 *shd* **Silver Lime (USA)**[256] [5959] 3-9-3 **79** ... JamesDoyle 7 — 92
(Roger Charlton) *hld up in rr disputing 9th: prog on wd outside over 2f out: pressed wnr fnl f: r.o wl nr fin: jst failed* **6/1**[2]

01- 3 *2½* **Goodwood Atlantis (IRE)**[287] [4968] 3-9-2 **78** ... TedDurcan 10 — 85
(John Dunlop) *hld up in last trio: pushed along and no prog over 2f out: rdn and hdwy over 1f out: r.o wl fnl f to take 3rd last strides* **7/1**[3]

041- 4 *nk* **Eurystheus (IRE)**[234] [6588] 3-9-3 **79** ... RichardHughes 4 — 85
(Richard Hannon) *trckd ldrs disputing 5th: effrt over 2f out: wl on terms over 1f out: chsd ldng pair fnl f: outpcd and lost 3rd last strides* **5/1**[1]

01-6 5 *2½* **Jupiter Storm**[18] [1888] 3-9-4 **80** ... TomQueally 11 — 81+
(Gary Moore) *trckd ldng trio and clr of rest: effrt 2f out: drvn and upsides over 1f out: fdd fnl f* **8/1**

1-0 6 *3* **Attenborough (USA)**[53] [1160] 3-9-4 **80** ... RyanMoore 14 — 74
(Jeremy Noseda) *trckd ldrs disputing 5th: effrt and wl there 2f out: wknd jst over 1f out* **8/1**

001- 7 *½* **Hidden Justice (IRE)**[162] [7758] 3-8-11 **73** ... EddieAhern 13 — 66+
(Amanda Perrett) *hld up in last trio: pushed along and no prog wl over 2f out: styd on fr over 1f out: n.d* **33/1**

1416 8 *1* **Masters Blazing**[9] [2150] 3-9-1 **77** ... (p) BrettDoyle 3 — 68
(John Ryan) *trckd ldng pair: rdn wl over 2f out: led briefly over 1f out: sn wknd* **33/1**

21-3 9 *½* **California English (IRE)**[43] [1304] 3-9-3 **79** ... MartinDwyer 2 — 69
(Marco Botti) *pushed up to ld after 2f: hdd & wknd qckly on inner over 1f out* **10/1**

043- 10 *1¼* **Mr Churchill (IRE)**[228] [6726] 3-8-10 **72** ... MickaelBarzalona 5 — 59
(Mahmood Al Zarooni) *s.i.s: mostly last and nvr gng wl: hanging bdly u.p 2f out* **7/1**[3]

33-1 11 *¾* **Paloma's Prince (IRE)**[31] [1565] 3-9-2 **78** ... PatCosgrave 15 — 64
(Jim Boyle) *led 2f: trckd ldr: reminder over 3f out: wknd qckly over 1f out* **14/1**

0-35 12 *6* **Serene Oasis (IRE)**[15] [1985] 3-8-11 **73** ... TonyCulhane 8 — 45
(Mick Channon) *hld up in rr disputing 9th: pushed along and no prog over 2f out: hld together after* **50/1**

4-20 13 *5* **Titus Star (IRE)**[24] [1707] 3-8-9 **71** ... (p) LiamKeniry 1 — 32
(J S Moore) *t.k.h: hld up in midfield on inner disputing 7th: wknd rapidly over 2f out* **33/1**

1m 55.39s (-0.91) **Going Correction** +0.025s/f (Good) — **13** Ran SP% **116.5**

Speed ratings (Par 101): **105,104,102,102,100 97,97,96,95,94 93,88,84**

toteswingers:1&2:£10.00, 2&3:£6.70, 1&3:£14.30 CSF £49.23 CT £331.79 TOTE £7.90: £2.70, £2.60, £2.00; EX 72.00 Trifecta £420.20 Part won. Pool: £567.91 - 0.50 winning units..

Owner Tony Foster & John Kelsey-Fry **Bred** Limestone Stud **Trained** Newmarket, Suffolk

FOCUS

Plenty of unexposed types in this competitive handicap, and a decent pace suited those coming from behind. The form is rated on the positive side.

2409 WRIGHT JOINERY COMPANY STKS (H'CAP) — 7f

3:10 (3:11) (Class 2) (0-100,100) 4-Y-O+ **£12,938** (£3,850; £1,924; £962) **Stalls** Low

Form — RPR

21 1 **Primaeval**[54] [1140] 6-8-13 **92** ... (v) HayleyTurner 4 — 104+
(James Fanshawe) *trckd ldng pair: gng easily fr over 2f out: produced to ld jst over 1f out: pushed along firmly and sn clr* **5/2**[1]

00-6 2 *2* **Noble Citizen (USA)**[23] [1741] 7-8-6 **90** ... (be) LauraPike(5) 9 — 96
(David Simcock) *stdd s: hld up in last pair: effrt and nt clr run over 1f out: r.o wl fnl f to take 2nd last strides* **33/1**

14-0 3 *½* **Citrus Star (USA)**[31] [1558] 5-9-0 **93** ... WilliamBuick 11 — 98
(Chris Wall) *t.k.h: hld up in 9th: prog whn nt clr run briefly over 1f out: r.o fnl f: tk 3rd post* **9/1**[3]

151- 4 *nse* **Yair Hill (IRE)**[208] [7171] 4-8-8 **87** ... TedDurcan 1 — 92+
(John Dunlop) *dwlt: sn wl there on inner: trckd ldng pair and looking for a run 2f out: rdn to chse wnr ins fnl f: no imp and lost 2 pls nr fin* **9/1**[3]

-041 5 *1¾* **Bronze Prince**[12] [2082] 5-9-5 **98** ... JimCrowley 6 — 98
(Michael Attwater) *mde most tl hdd and fdd jst over 1f out* **12/1**

01-2 6 *hd* **Bonnie Brae**[12] [2068] 5-9-7 **100** ... RyanMoore 8 — 100
(David Elsworth) *hld up in last pair: plld out wd 2f out: drvn and prog over 1f out: nt rch ldrs and effrt flattened out last 100yds* **5/1**[2]

3-44 7 *3* **Global City (IRE)**[75] [874] 6-9-2 **95** ... (t) MickaelBarzalona 7 — 87
(Saeed Bin Suroor) *impeded s: snatched up in last trio over 5f out: effrt on inner over 2f out: no real prog* **20/1**

4101 8 *shd* **Thunderball**[13] [2023] 6-9-0 **93** ... (p) TomQueally 12 — 84
(Scott Dixon) *chsd ldrs disputing 5th: rdn over 2f out: wknd over 1f out* **9/1**[3]

600- 9 *1½* **Mr David (USA)**[222] [6862] 5-8-11 **90** ... JamesDoyle 10 — 77
(Jamie Osborne) *in tch in midfield disputing 7th: rdn over 2f out: wknd over 1f out* **14/1**

0-20 10 *1½* **Axiom**[47] [1212] 8-9-5 **98** ... J-PGuillambert 5 — 81
(Ed Walker) *impeded s: stmbld in midfield over 5f out: effrt on inner over 2f out: sme prog over 1f out: wknd quite qckly fnl f* **16/1**

100- 11 *nse* **Rulesn'regulations**[173] [7628] 6-8-8 **87** ... RichardMullen 3 — 70
(Matthew Salaman) *awkward and veered lft leaving stalls: trckd ldng pair to over 2f out: steadily wknd* **20/1**

5-60 12 *1* **Kakatosi**[12] [2068] 5-9-0 **93** ... (v[1]) DavidProbert 2 — 73
(Andrew Balding) *racd freely: w ldr to 2f out: wknd rapidly over 1f out* **9/1**[3]

1m 26.49s (-0.51) **Going Correction** +0.025s/f (Good) — **12** Ran SP% **117.9**

Speed ratings (Par 109): **103,100,100,100,98 97,94,94,92,90 90,89**

CSF £106.49 CT £667.66 TOTE £3.10: £1.60, £9.20, £3.70; EX 102.20 Trifecta £762.40 Pool: £1205.57 - 1.17 winning units..

Owner The Foncey Syndicate **Bred** Stowell Park Stud **Trained** Newmarket, Suffolk

FOCUS

This competitive handicap was run at a decent pace. A number of the field were hampered early on, but the winner was impressive and looks progressive. Straightforward form with the winner not quite needing to match his Polytrack best.

NOTEBOOK

Primaeval took full advantage of a mark lower than on the AW. While he was always nicely positioned, the next four home all came from off the pace, and this performance can be upgraded. He is entered in the Hunt Cup, for which he is 10-1 favourite, but could take his chance in the Buckingham Palace. (tchd 9-4)

Noble Citizen(USA) ran on nicely from an unpromising position, having been briefly hampered a furlong out. He is clearly not straightforward but possesses plenty of ability and could be competitive in a big handicap, especially if returning to his favoured Ascot. (op 40-1)

Citrus Star(USA) was nicely supported in the morning and was closing well without ever looking threatening, having been denied a clear passage a furlong out. He can step up on this. (op 13-2 tchd 10-1)

Yair Hill(IRE) travelled nicely behind the principals and looked dangerous before tiring inside the final furlong. He will come on for this first run in 208 days. (op 12-1)

Bronze Prince was involved in a tussle up front with Kakatosi and both those runners paid for that. (op 10-1)

Bonnie Brae can be rated better than this as she was hampered early and had to come wide up the straight. She looked dangerous a furlong out, but her exertions took their toll late on. (tchd 9-2)

Axiom was one of the worst sufferers of the early interference and should be given credit for closing on the principals 2f out, before tiring late on. Official explanation: jockey said that the gelding stumbled (op 14-1)

2410 HEIGHT OF FASHION STKS (LISTED RACE) (FILLIES) — 1m 1f 192y

3:45 (3:45) (Class 1) 3-Y-O — **£20,720** (£7,836; £3,916; £1,956) **Stalls** Low

Form — RPR

411- 1 **Coquet**[208] [7169] 3-9-3 94 ... RobertHavlin 7 — 105+
(Hughie Morrison) *hld up in 4th: prog 3f out: chal on inner over 1f out: led jst ins fnl f: drvn and r.o wl* **10/3**[1]

14-0 2 *nk* **Minidress**[36] [1454] 3-9-0 97 ... MickaelBarzalona 6 — 101
(Mahmood Al Zarooni) *t.k.h: hld up in last pair: prog on outer wl over 2f out: clsd on ldrs over 1f out: edgd rt sn after: pressed wnr ins fnl f: a jst hld* **9/2**[3]

41- 3 *1¼* **Gathering (USA)**[250] [6168] 3-9-0 91 ... (p) WilliamBuick 2 — 99
(John Gosden) *t.k.h: trckd ldr: clsd to ld over 1f out: sn hung rt u.p: hdd and no ex jst ins fnl f* **7/1**

1-20 4 *6* **Nayarra (IRE)**[18] [1884] 3-9-5 103 ... MartinDwyer 5 — 92
(Mick Channon) *broke on terms but sn restrained into last pair and tk quite t.k.h: trapped bhd rival 3f out: outpcd whn in the clr 2f out: pushed along to take modest 4th nr fin* **4/1**[2]

1-5 5 *¾* **Zimira (IRE)**[12] [2079] 3-9-0 0 ... RyanMoore 4 — 85
(Ed Dunlop) *trckd ldr: hld up in last pair: struggling 3f out: grad wknd* **20/1**

51-3 6 *nse* **Estrela**[12] [2079] 3-9-0 90 ... JamesDoyle 1 — 85
(Roger Charlton) *led at gd pce: drew clr over 4f out: hdd & wknd qckly over 1f out* **11/2**

2-21 7 *1¼* **Zaina (IRE)**[54] [1132] 3-9-0 85 ... DaneO'Neill 3 — 82
(Gerard Butler) *dwlt: t.k.h and hld up in tch: no prog over 2f out: sn btn* **5/1**

2m 7.34s (-0.76) **Going Correction** +0.025s/f (Good) — **7** Ran SP% **110.6**

Speed ratings (Par 104): **104,103,102,97,97 97,96**

toteswingers:1&2:£3.20, 2&3:£5.60, 1&3:£3.20 CSF £17.19 TOTE £3.90: £2.10, £3.00; EX 19.10.

Owner Hon Mary Morrison & Partners **Bred** Meon Valley Stud **Trained** East Ilsley, Berks

FOCUS

This Oaks Trial was run at a sound pace with the first three home pulling a long way clear, with all three looking useful. This race was the last chance for fillies to stake their claim for the Epsom Classic, and has been won by Love Divine and Snow Fairy in the past 12 years en-route to Classic glory. Only two of the seven runners held entries at Epsom. The form is rated around the race averages and makes some sense. Another step forward from the progressive Coquet.

NOTEBOOK

Coquet was a brave winner, booking her place in the Oaks line-up. Having her first start for 208 days, she looked big enough in the paddock, but travelled well through the race and battled on to the line when pressed inside the final furlong. Conceding 3lb to the next two home, she looks to be progressing nicely with her racing, although quotes of 25-1 for the Oaks in eight days' time show she will have to step up on this performance to give her handler his first Classic success. Hughie Morrison will also be represented by Shirocco Star, another 25-1 chance for the race. (op 4-1)

Minidress met trouble in the Nell Gwyn on her seasonal reappearance at Newmarket and ran a fine race here. She did not seem to be enjoying herself turning for home but stayed on in fine style to press the winner all the way to the line. This effort suggests that a step up in trip will see further improvement. (tchd 11-2)

Gathering(USA), representing the stable who won this in 2003 and 2008, does not hold any Pattern entries but ran well. She looked to be travelling best two furlongs from home, but was unable to quicken on her first start for 250 days. (tchd 13-2 and 15-2)

Nayarra(IRE), a small, compact filly, looked to face a tough task carrying a 5lb penalty for her Group 1 success in the Premio Gran Criterium last season and she was never able to get competitive. She did not enjoy the best of passages when entering the home straight but made some late progress when the race was over. On this performance a step up in trip will suit. (tchd 7-2 and 9-2)

Estrela had the benefit of a recent run and kicked 4l clear turning for home, but she was unable to sustain her run and may be better served by being ridden with more restraint. (op 6-1 tchd 5-1)

Zaina(IRE) was a decent winner of a Doncaster maiden in March, but found this tougher. The lightly raced filly was unable to pick up when the pace quickened and is another who may appreciate further. (op 4-1)

2411 HIPPO WASTE STKS (H'CAP) (DIV I) — 2m

4:20 (4:20) (Class 4) (0-85,85) 4-Y-0+ — £4,851 (£1,443; £721; £360) Stalls High

Form				RPR
01-1	1		**Al Khawaneej**[38] 1421 4-9-8 **85**........ MickaelBarzalona 9 (David Simcock) *hld up in 5th: prog on outer fr 3f out: rdn to ld over 1f out: styd on wl* **6/1**	94
	2	1 1/4	**Pascha Bere (FR)**[75] 9-8-11 **72**........ RichardMullen 2 (Nick Gifford) *stdd s: hld up in last pair: prog on outer fr 3f out: rdn to press wnr over 1f out: styd on but no imp after* **10/1**	79
3115	3	1 3/4	**Rasheed**[47] 1214 4-9-3 **80**........ WilliamBuick 5 (John Gosden) *trckd ldrs: wnt 2nd 5f out: led 3f out: drvn and hdd over 1f out: one pce* **3/1**[2]	85
/0-5	4	nse	**Natural High (IRE)**[34] 1505 7-9-5 **80**........ JamesDoyle 1 (Paul Rich) *hld up in 6th: clsd on ldrs 3f out: nt qckn wl over 1f out: kpt on to press for 3rd nr fin* **7/1**	85
2-06	5	1 3/4	**Saborido (USA)**[17] 1905 6-9-4 **79**........ EddieAhern 8 (Amanda Perrett) *trckd ldr to 5f out: styd on inner in st: effrt 3f out: steadily outpcd fnl 2f* **11/2**[3]	82
100-	6	1 1/4	**May Contain Nuts**[210] 7120 4-8-10 **73**........ FergusSweeney 4 (Brendan Powell) *led 2f: styd handy: rdn to chal over 2f out: wknd over 1f out* **14/1**	75
455/	7	2	**Golan Way**[35] 6878 8-8-6 **70**........ HarryBentley(3) 7 (Sheena West) *prog to ld after 2f: hdd 3f out: dropped rt out and sn last: styd on again fnl f* **11/4**[1]	69
12-0	8	2 1/2	**Shesha Bear**[29] 1603 7-9-2 **77**........(p) HayleyTurner 6 (Jonathan Portman) *hld up in last pair: cl up 3f out: stl in tch and jst pushed along 2f out: wknd* **20/1**	73

3m 33.53s (4.53) **Going Correction** +0.025s/f (Good)
WFA 4 from 6yo+ 2lb — **8** Ran SP% **114.4**
Speed ratings (Par 105): **89,88,87,87,86 85,84,83**
toteswingers:1&2:£9.00, 2&3:£6.30, 1&3:£3.00 CSF £63.09 CT £214.28 TOTE £6.90: £1.90, £3.50, £1.50; EX 79.20 Trifecta £202.80 Pool: £1244.32 - 4.54 winning units..
Owner Ahmad Al Shaikh **Bred** Cliveden Stud Ltd **Trained** Newmarket, Suffolk

FOCUS

The first division of this 2m handicap was run at a steady pace and the field were well grouped passing the furlong pole. It was the slower division and there were one or two doubts over the form, but the winner is useful.

2412 HIPPO WASTE STKS (H'CAP) (DIV II) — 2m

4:55 (4:55) (Class 4) (0-85,80) 4-Y-0+ — £4,851 (£1,443; £721; £360) Stalls High

Form				RPR
216-	1		**Astromagick**[229] 6707 4-8-13 **72**........ EddieAhern 1 (Mark H Tompkins) *hld up in 5th: prog on outer to ld narrowly 3f out: edgd rt over 1f out: styd on wl: holding rival fnl f* **7/2**[1]	81
3530	2	1/2	**Wild Desert (FR)**[19] 1846 7-9-9 **80**........ ChrisCatlin 3 (Charlie Longsdon) *trckd ldng pair gng strly: chal and upsides 3f out: chsd wnr after: styd on wl but a jst hld fnl f* **16/1**	88
225-	3	3 3/4	**Mohanad (IRE)**[37] 6171 6-9-4 **78**........ HarryBentley(3) 6 (Sheena West) *trckd ldng trio: tried to chal 3f out: nt qckn and sn outpcd: kpt on to win battle for 3rd* **4/1**[2]	82
060-	4	nse	**High Samana**[3] 6377 4-8-6 **65** ow1........(p) RichardMullen 8 (Seamus Mullins) *hld up in last pair: prog 3f out: outpcd over 2f out: kpt on to press for 3rd fnl f* **8/1**	68
01-3	5	1/2	**Blazing Field**[34] 1505 4-9-7 **80**........ JohnFahy 9 (Clive Cox) *hld up in last trio: drvn on outer over 2f out: one pce but pressed for 3rd fnl f* **7/2**[1]	83
3313	6	1/2	**Gilded Age**[17] 1905 6-9-1 **72**........(tp) HayleyTurner 4 (Chris Gordon) *led: hdd 3f out: steadily outpcd* **8/1**	74
1-00	7	1 1/2	**Hidden Valley**[8] 2174 4-8-13 **72**........(v) DavidProbert 5 (Andrew Balding) *hld up in last pair: effrt on outer 3f out: hanging and no prog 2f out: fdd* **7/1**[3]	72
-026	8	3 1/4	**Battleoftrafalgar**[73] 745 5-9-4 **75**........(b) J-PGuillambert 2 (Michael Attwater) *t.k.h: hld up in tch: prog on inner 3f out: one pce but chal for 3rd 2f out: wknd fnl f* **33/1**	72
/0-0	9	4	**Spirit Of Adjisa (IRE)**[34] 1505 8-9-8 **79**........ AndreaAtzeni 7 (Tim Vaughan) *pressed ldr: upsides over 3f out: losing pl whn squeezed out 2f out: wknd and eased* **20/1**	71

3m 31.9s (2.90) **Going Correction** +0.025s/f (Good)
WFA 4 from 5yo+ 2lb — **9** Ran SP% **112.8**
Speed ratings (Par 105): **93,92,90,90,90 90,89,87,85**
CSF £58.30 CT £230.39 TOTE £4.70: £1.70, £4.50, £1.70; EX 61.80 Trifecta £771.70 Part won. Pool: £1042.93 - 0.80 winning units..
Owner Mystic Meg Limited **Bred** Mystic Meg Limited **Trained** Newmarket, Suffolk

FOCUS

As in the first division of this 2m handicap, the pace was steady and there were plenty in contention passing the 2f pole, although the front two home pulled a long way clear inside the final furlong. It was the faster division and the form is rated around the runner-up.

2413 SAUNDERS CONSTRUCTION APPRENTICE STKS (H'CAP) — 6f

5:30 (5:31) (Class 5) (0-70,69) 4-Y-0+ — £2,911 (£866; £432; £216) Stalls High

Form				RPR
2456	1		**Amazing Win (IRE)**[6] 2244 4-8-7 **55** oh1........ CharlesBishop 3 (Mick Channon) *hld up bhd ldrs: hanging but clsd 2f out: urged into ld 1f out: kpt on wl* **9/2**[1]	64
4300	2	1 3/4	**Kyllachy Storm**[17] 1908 8-8-2 **55** oh1........ RyanTate(5) 9 (Ron Hodges) *hld up off the pce: no prog 2f out: rdn over 1f out: gd burst fnl f: r.o to take 2nd last strides* **6/1**[3]	59
4646	3	hd	**Speak The Truth (IRE)**[8] 2165 6-9-0 **65**........(p) NathanAlison(3) 5 (Jim Boyle) *hld up bhd ldrs: clsd 2f out: chsd wnr ins fnl f: no imp last 100yds: lost 2nd fnl strides* **10/1**	68
0435	4	1	**Silvee**[18] 1895 5-8-7 **55** oh2........ RosieJessop 8 (John Bridger) *sn in last on outer: effrt over 2f out: kpt on fr over 1f out: nvr able to chal* **14/1**	55
3-05	5	nk	**Drakes Drum**[13] 2043 4-9-5 **67**........(p) LucyKBarry 6 (Clive Cox) *racd freely: led after 2f and maintained str pce: wandered 2f out: hdd and fdd 1f out* **5/1**[2]	66+
040-	6	1/2	**Reginald Claude**[300] 4511 4-9-0 **65**........ RachealKneller(3) 2 (Mark Usher) *hld up in rr: prog on outer fr 2f out: tried to cl over 1f out: one pce after* **16/1**	62
5-04	7	1/2	**Volito**[23] 1734 6-9-3 **65**........ MatthewCosham 4 (Anabel K Murphy) *hld up in rr: tried to cl on outer fr 2f out: no prog fnl f* **5/1**[2]	61
6543	8	hd	**Even Bolder**[92] 658 9-8-10 **65**........ JoeyHaynes(7) 10 (Eric Wheeler) *racd freely: chsd ldng pair: lost pl 2f out: sn btn* **14/1**	60
-600	9	1 1/2	**Rio Royale (IRE)**[92] 658 6-8-7 **55** oh2........(b) RaulDaSilva 1 (Amanda Perrett) *blased off in front but hdd after 2f: fdd fnl 2f* **10/1**	45
0-00	10	6	**Da Ponte**[26] 1680 4-9-7 **69**........(p) DavidKenny 11 (Michael Scudamore) *racd alone against nr side rail: struggling fr 1/2-way: sn no ch* **14/1**	40

1m 11.86s (-0.34) **Going Correction** +0.025s/f (Good) — **10** Ran SP% **109.9**
Speed ratings (Par 103): **103,100,100,99,98 98,97,97,95,87**
toteswingers:1&2:£5.50, 2&3:£13.30, 1&3:£8.50 CSF £28.04 CT £223.59 TOTE £5.70: £2.00, £1.80, £3.40; EX 32.40 Trifecta £434.70 Part won. Pool of £587.48 - 0.20 winning units..
Owner Mrs Theresa Burns **Bred** J Repard **Trained** West Ilsley, Berks

FOCUS

This weak handicap, confined to apprentice riders, was run at sound pace and won in decisive fashion. The winner rates a turf personal best.

T/Plt: £91.80 to a £1 stake.Pool of £64,341.95 - 511.26 winning tickets. T/Qpdt: £31.90 to a £1 stake. Pool of £4,634.30 - 107.20 winning tickets. JN

2073 HAYDOCK (L-H)

Thursday, May 24

OFFICIAL GOING: Good to firm (9.6)

Wind: Nil Weather: Hot and Sunny

2414 CHILL OUT SPA H'CAP — 1m 2f 95y

2:20 (2:22) (Class 5) (0-75,75) 4-Y-0+ — £2,264 (£673; £336; £168) Stalls High

Form				RPR
10-3	1		**Elspeth's Boy (USA)**[12] 2094 5-8-11 **70**........ GarryWhillans(5) 15 (Philip Kirby) *hld up: hdwy over 3f out: led wl over 1f out: rdn whn pressed ins fnl f: kpt on gamley towards fin* **14/1**	81
0-22	2	3/4	**Jack's Revenge (IRE)**[28] 1636 4-9-6 **74**........(bt[1]) KierenFallon 7 (George Baker) *hld up in midfield: rdn over 2f out: hdwy to chse wnr over 1f out: hung lft whn chalng ins fnl f: nt qckn and hld towards fin* **9/1**[3]	83
04-1	3	1 3/4	**The Galloping Shoe**[26] 1657 7-9-5 **73**........ MichaelO'Connell 14 (Alistair Whillans) *racd keenly: hld up: hdwy whn nt clr run over 2f out: rdn over 1f out: styd on to chse ldng pair fnl 150yds: unable to mount serious chal* **3/1**[1]	79
-605	4	3 3/4	**Spey Song (IRE)**[3] 2328 4-8-11 **65**........(b[1]) JamieSpencer 2 (James Bethell) *missed break: bhd: rdn and hdwy over 1f out: kpt on fnl f: nt trble ldrs* **14/1**	64
0-15	5	2 1/4	**Saint Thomas (IRE)**[24] 1719 5-8-10 **64**........ JoeFanning 6 (John Mackie) *prom: chalng over 2f out: styd on same pce fnl f* **14/1**	59
00-0	6	1	**Amistress**[38] 1418 4-9-1 **69**........ NeilCallan 1 (Eve Johnson Houghton) *in midfield: rdn over 3f out: no imp* **12/1**	62
50-0	7	nse	**Goldenveil (IRE)**[44] 1275 4-8-12 **66**........(b[1]) TonyHamilton 11 (Richard Fahey) *hld up: rdn over 2f out: kpt on fnl f: nvr able to chal* **25/1**	59
0-00	8	hd	**Gala Casino Star (IRE)**[16] 1951 7-8-9 **70**........(p) JordanNason(7) 5 (Geoffrey Harker) *trckd ldrs: effrt over 3f out: led over 2f out: hdd wl over 1f out: no ex ins fnl f: eased whn btn fnl 100yds* **16/1**	62
0604	9	2	**Sartingo (IRE)**[15] 1988 5-8-8 **62**........ RobertWinston 12 (Alan Swinbank) *midfield: rdn and hdwy 4f out: sn chsd ldrs: hung lft 2f out: one pce ent fnl f: eased whn btn fnl 150yds* **7/1**[2]	56
10-6	10	7	**My Mate Jake (IRE)**[13] 2051 4-8-13 **67**........ PaulMulrennan 13 (James Given) *midfield: pushed along and outpcd over 3f out: nvr a threat* **20/1**	42
2-00	11	2 3/4	**Vittachi**[20] 1822 5-8-7 **61** oh1........ TomEaves 10 (Alistair Whillans) *hld up: u.p over 3f out: nvr a threat* **40/1**	31
10-0	12	1 1/4	**Kodicil (IRE)**[53] 1154 4-8-10 **64**........ DuranFentiman 4 (Tim Walford) *prom: pushed along over 4f out: rdn and wknd 3f out* **11/1**	32
31-0	13	6	**One Pursuit (IRE)**[26] 1657 4-9-7 **75**........ AdrianNicholls 3 (David Nicholls) *led: rdn and hdd over 2f out: sn wknd* **12/1**	31
3345	14	4 1/2	**Ahlawy (IRE)**[3] 2348 9-8-7 **61** oh2........(t) MircoDemuro 9 (Frank Sheridan) *missed break: a rdn along and bhd* **14/1**	9
560-	15	3	**Oriental Cavalier**[269] 5568 6-9-6 **74**........(v) GrahamLee 16 (Mark Buckley) *prom tl rdn and wknd over 3f out* **14/1**	16

2m 9.03s (-6.47) **Going Correction** -0.60s/f (Hard) — **15** Ran SP% **121.5**
Speed ratings (Par 103): **103,102,101,98,96 95,95,95,93,88 85,84,80,76,74**
CSF £132.13 CT £488.32 TOTE £19.70: £4.20, £2.40, £1.50; EX 126.00.
Owner Preesall Garage **Bred** S M D Ltd **Trained** Castleton, N Yorks

FOCUS

A moderate but competitive opener which was run at true gallop and the form looks solid. The winner is getting back towards last year's form.

2415 SOLARKING L.E.D. MAIDEN STKS 6f

2:55 (2:58) (Class 5) 2-Y-O £2,264 (£673; £336; £168) Stalls Centre

Form RPR

1 **Morawij** 2-9-3 0 NeilCallan 10 82+
(Roger Varian) *in tch: effrt 2f out: rdn to ld ent fnl f: sn edgd lft: kpt on gamley* **11/5**[1]

3 2 *nk* **Fraserburgh (IRE)**[9] 2138 2-9-3 0 JoeFanning 8 81
(Mark Johnston) *w ldr: rdn over 1f out: stl chalng ins fnl f: jst hld cl home* **11/4**[2]

3 *3/4* **Glass Office** 2-9-3 0 JamieSpencer 9 79+
(David Simcock) *trckd ldrs: led 2f out: hdd ent fnl f: kpt on tl no ex cl home* **5/1**[3]

4 *1/2* **Mandy Layla (IRE)** 2-8-12 0 TomEaves 5 72
(Bryan Smart) *led: hdd 2f out: rdn over 1f out: styd on same pce ins fnl f* **12/1**

5 *1 1/2* **Master Of War** 2-9-3 0 KieranO'Neill 3 73+
(Richard Hannon) *dwlt: in rr: rdn 2f out: hdwy to chse ldrs and sn hung lft over 1f out: kpt on ins fnl f: nt gng pce to chal front quartet* **14/1**

6 *4 1/2* **Index Waiter** 2-9-3 0 KierenFallon 6 59+
(Brian Meehan) *dwlt: hld up in tch: rdn over 2f out: green and one pce fnl f* **12/1**

5 7 *1 1/2* **Jordanstown**[47] 1218 2-9-3 0 PhillipMakin 12 55
(Kevin Ryan) *prom: rdn and nt qckn over 2f out: wknd over 1f out* **16/1**

8 *nk* **Rocket Ronnie (IRE)** 2-9-3 0 AdrianNicholls 7 54
(David Nicholls) *dwlt: racd keenly: hld up in rr: nvr able to get on terms w ldrs* **40/1**

9 *nk* **Millie N Aire** 2-8-12 0 AndrewElliott 13 48+
(Danielle McCormick) *dwlt and wnt rt s: sn in tch: rdn over 2f out: sn btn* **66/1**

05 10 *9* **Hats Off**[19] 1847 2-9-3 0 RobertWinston 2 26
(John Best) *plld hrd: prom: rdn over 2f out: wknd wl over 1f out: eased whn btn fnl f* **25/1**

11 *nk* **Mick Dundee (IRE)** 2-9-3 0 MircoDemuro 4 25
(J W Hills) *in tch tl rdn and wknd 2f out* **33/1**

12 *8* **Colours Of Nature** 2-9-3 0 DavidAllan 1 1
(Eric Alston) *prom: rdn over 2f out: sn wknd* **80/1**

1m 14.58s (0.78) **Going Correction** -0.025s/f (Good) 12 Ran SP% **114.5**
Speed ratings (Par 93): **93,92,91,90,88 82,80,80,80,68 67,57**
toteswingers:1&2:£2.40, 2&3:£3.00, 1&3:£3.00 CSF £7.42 TOTE £3.10: £1.60, £1.40, £1.80; EX 8.80.

Owner Sheikh Ahmed Al Maktoum **Bred** Dunchurch Lodge Stud Co **Trained** Newmarket, Suffolk

FOCUS

An interesting maiden which went to the well-regarded favourite, but several showed promise in behind. There was a fairly compressed finish.

NOTEBOOK

Morawij, a 120,000gns yearling, justified favouritism on his debut in workmanlike style to give his trainer a winner with his first 2-y-o runner of the season. A big, powerful colt, he was keen early but did enough to win. He has plenty of scope and shaped very much as though he would improve significantly for the experience. He holds a Listed entry in the Redcar Two-Year-Old Trophy. (op 9-4 tchd 5-2)

Fraserburgh(IRE) set the standard on his debut third at Beverley over 5f and saw out the longer trip well, just finding the winner too strong. (tchd 5-2)

Glass Office ◆, a 60,000euros purchase, was prominent in the betting. He held the lead over 2f out but just lacked the pace of the front two close home. The way he travelled suggests he has plenty of ability and he can win his maiden. (op 9-2)

Mandy Layla(IRE) ◆ made a highly encouraging debut, leading the field until after halfway and keeping on resolutely. She will find easier opportunities against her own sex. (op 14-1 tchd 11-1)

Master Of War was weak in the market but ran a race full of promise. He was green throughout but wasn't beaten far, and he'll be much wiser next time.

2416 SIMPLY COTTON H'CAP 7f

3:30 (3:31) (Class 4) (0-80,80) 3-Y-O £4,075 (£1,212; £606; £303) Stalls Low

Form RPR

6-61 1 **Xinbama (IRE)**[21] 1790 3-9-1 74 GrahamLee 5 79
(J W Hills) *hld up: rdn and hdwy over 2f out: styd on ins fnl f to ld fnl 100yds* **7/1**[3]

113- 2 *1 1/2* **Lady Layla**[223] 6826 3-9-5 78 JamieSpencer 1 79
(Bryan Smart) *bmpd s: chsd ldrs: rdn and chalng fr 1f out: disp ld briefly ins fnl f: hld towards fin* **11/4**[1]

6514 3 *1/2* **Boots And Spurs**[83] 764 3-9-2 75 (v) NeilCallan 11 75
(Mrs K Burke) *chsd ldrs: rdn over 2f out: chalng 1f out: disp ld briefly ins fnl f: hld towards fin* **10/1**

421- 4 *1 3/4* **Takealookatmenow (IRE)**[213] 7058 3-8-8 67 AdrianNicholls 6 62
(David Nicholls) *racd keenly: chse ldrs: led 3f out: rdn over 1f out: hdd ins fnl f: one pce fnl 50yds* **14/1**

-121 5 *3* **Half A Billion (IRE)**[21] 1798 3-9-2 78 LeeTopliss(3) 4 65
(Michael Dods) *led: hdd 3f out: rdn 2f out: fdd ins fnl f* **9/2**[2]

3230 6 *3* **Falcon's Reign (FR)**[78] 827 3-8-11 70 RussKennemore 7 49
(Michael Appleby) *stdd s: hld up: failed to pick-up over 2f out: kpt on past btn horses ins fnl f* **33/1**

2230 7 *1/2* **Homeward Strut**[6] 2256 3-8-8 67 (b) MircoDemuro 2 44
(Frank Sheridan) *bmpd s: in midfield: rdn over 3f out: wknd over 1f out* **15/2**

1-06 8 *2* **Sheikh The Reins (IRE)**[15] 1983 3-9-4 77 RobertWinston 9 49
(John Best) *hld up: lft bhd over 3f out* **9/1**

210- 9 *1 1/2* **Passionada**[230] 6670 3-9-0 73 LeeNewman 8 41
(David Barron) *midfield: rdn over 3f out: wknd over 2f out* **10/1**

2-10 10 *dist* **Marford Missile (IRE)**[14] 1998 3-9-7 80 KierenFallon 10
(Tom Dascombe) *hld up: hung bdly rt and almost off the crse after 2f: t.o after* **10/1**

1m 27.22s (-3.48) **Going Correction** -0.60s/f (Hard) 10 Ran SP% **116.0**
Speed ratings (Par 101): **95,93,92,90,87 83,83,81,79,**
CSF £26.40 CT £198.42 TOTE £9.10: £2.50, £1.60, £3.40; EX 30.20.

Owner Tony Waspe Partnership **Bred** P Heffernan **Trained** Upper Lambourn, Berks

FOCUS

A moderate 3yo handicap run at a strong gallop, and that suited the winner who was ridden with restraint. The second and third ran as well as ever.

Sheikh The Reins(IRE) Official explanation: jockey said that the colt slipped on the bend

2417 HATTONS SOLICITORS GOLD MEMBERSHIP H'CAP 1m

4:05 (4:06) (Class 3) (0-90,89) 4-Y-O+ £6,663 (£1,982; £990; £495) Stalls Low

Form RPR

-403 1 **Oriental Scot**[20] 1820 5-9-0 82 WilliamCarson 8 92
(William Jarvis) *hld up: hdwy 3f out: led over 1f out: r.o ins fnl f* **7/1**[3]

5435 2 *1 1/2* **Imperial Djay (IRE)**[6] 2243 7-9-7 89 JamesSullivan 13 96
(Ruth Carr) *hld up: hdwy 2f out: r.o for press ins fnl f: nt rch wnr* **16/1**

004- 3 *nse* **Desert Romance (IRE)**[211] 7110 6-9-0 82 DanielTudhope 10 88
(David O'Meara) *led early: prom: led 3f out: rdn and hdd wl over 1f out: stl ch ins fnl f: kpt on same pce cl home* **4/1**[2]

053- 4 *nk* **Lord Aeryn (IRE)**[250] 6150 5-9-1 88 ShaneBKelly(5) 3 94
(Richard Fahey) *midfield: hmpd after 2f: hdwy 3f out: edgd lft 2f out: sn led: hdd over 1f out: kpt on for press tl no ex cl home* **7/1**[3]

60-3 5 *nk* **Indian Jack (IRE)**[17] 1924 4-9-7 89 KierenFallon 2 95+
(Luca Cumani) *hmpd after 2f: hld up: pushed along over 3f out: hdwy over 1f out: styd on but nt gng pce to chal ldrs* **3/1**[1]

4505 6 *1* **Prince Of Burma (IRE)**[12] 2082 4-9-5 87 (b) PhillipMakin 6 90
(Jeremy Gask) *hld up: hdwy 2f out: rdn to chse ldrs over 1f out: one pce ins fnl f* **12/1**

-025 7 *4* **Kiwi Bay**[19] 1865 7-9-7 89 TomEaves 7 83
(Michael Dods) *pictched coming out of stalls: sn prom: chalng 3f out: no imp over 1f out: no ex ins fnl f* **16/1**

66-0 8 *1/2* **Euston Square**[20] 1820 6-8-8 76 PaulMulrennan 9 68
(Alistair Whillans) *hld up: bhd over 2f out: pushed along over 1f out: kpt on modly ins fnl f: no imp on ldrs* **22/1**

-060 9 *4 1/2* **Sam Nombulist**[19] 1863 4-8-9 80 AmyRyan(3) 1 62
(Richard Whitaker) *handy: hmpd after 2f: rdn and wknd 2f out* **16/1**

00-0 10 *1/2* **Soweto Star (IRE)**[9] 2151 4-8-9 77 RobertWinston 5 58
(John Best) *in tch: rdn over 2f out: sn wknd* **40/1**

00-0 11 *3/4* **Kalk Bay (IRE)**[19] 1863 5-8-8 83 DavidSimmonson(7) 12 62
(Michael Easterby) *trckd ldrs tl rdn and wknd 2f out* **33/1**

-000 12 *3 1/4* **Light From Mars**[13] 2025 7-9-7 89 JamieSpencer 11 61
(John Quinn) *sn led: trckd across to ins rail over 6f out: hdd 3f out: wknd over 1f out* **8/1**

20-0 13 *2* **Golden Tempest (IRE)**[47] 1212 4-9-5 87 NeilCallan 4 54
(Eve Johnson Houghton) *midfield: rdn and wknd over 2f out* **25/1**

1m 39.88s (-3.82) **Going Correction** -0.60s/f (Hard) 13 Ran SP% **120.0**
Speed ratings (Par 107): **95,93,93,93,92 91,87,87,82,82 81,78,76**
toteswingers:1&2:£10.40, 2&3:£19.40, 1&3:£6.60 CSF £109.05 CT £514.80 TOTE £9.30: £2.40, £4.00, £1.60; EX 81.60.

Owner Dr J Walker **Bred** Miss K Rausing **Trained** Newmarket, Suffolk

■ Stewards' Enquiry : Jamie Spencer four-day ban: careless riding (7-9 and 11 June)

FOCUS

An open handicap run at a solid tempo. The runners fanned out across the track in the straight in a race that favoured those ridden with restraint. Straightforward form.

NOTEBOOK

Oriental Scot, 3lb higher than his last winning mark, still looked well treated on the pick of his form and proved good enough to land his second C&D victory. Held up towards the rear in the early stages, he gradually wore down the leaders with a sustained run and stayed on strongly once hitting the front. (tchd 15-2)

Imperial Djay(IRE) is better known as a 7f specialist but ran a blinder upped in trip from his wide draw. Judging on this evidence he's capable of winning over 1m on an easier track.

Desert Romance(IRE) fared best of those ridden prominently and deserves credit. He clearly goes well fresh, having won off a 2lb higher mark on his seasonal debut in 2011, but wouldn't be certain to repeat this next time. (op 5-1)

Lord Aeryn(IRE), another who goes well fresh, enjoyed the quick ground and raced up the far rail. He tried hard inside the final furlong but lost two places close home. (op 10-1)

Indian Jack(IRE) made an encouraging return on his debut for this yard at Kempton and was fancied on his return to turf. He appeared to get outpaced in the straight, and wasn't helped when Lord Aeryn hampered him at the 2f pole, but responded to Kieren Fallon's urgings, suggesting he may be suited by a step up in trip. (op 11-4 tchd 4-1 in a place)

Prince Of Burma(IRE), a three-time winner on Polytrack, was last entering the straight and put in some good late work.

Kiwi Bay's rider reported that the gelding slipped leaving the stalls. Official explanation: jockey said that the gelding slipped leaving the stalls (op 14-1)

2418 GPW RECRUITMENT MAIDEN STKS 1m 3f 200y

4:40 (4:42) (Class 5) 3-Y-O+ £2,264 (£673; £336; £168) Stalls Centre

Form RPR

223 1 **Gabrial The Hero (USA)**[26] 1662 3-8-11 75 NeilCallan 4 77+
(David Simcock) *mde all: drew clr over 1f out: r.o wl: eased down towards fin* **11/10**[1]

0- 2 *7* **Al Mamzar (IRE)**[218] 6953 3-8-11 0 JamieSpencer 1 65+
(David Simcock) *hld up in tch: hdwy 3f out: wnt 2nd over 1f out: no ch w wnr* **5/4**[2]

4-0 3 *1 3/4* **Incitement**[19] 1866 4-10-0 0 DanielTudhope 9 63
(Andrew Crook) *trckd ldrs: rdn to take 2nd over 2f out: no imp and lost 2nd over 1f out: one pce* **8/1**[3]

0- 4 *2 1/4* **Astrogold**[208] 7164 3-8-6 0 JoeFanning 10 54
(Mark H Tompkins) *racd keenly: hld up: hung lft most of way in st: pushed along over 3f out: kpt on modly fnl f: nvr a threat* **20/1**

5 *1* **Big Time Billy (IRE)**[208] 6-9-9 0 WilliamCarson 7 53
(Mike Hammond) *missed break: in rr: rdn over 4f out: kpt on modly ins fnl f* **14/1**

00-6 6 *1 1/4* **Fleeting Fashion**[129] 195 3-8-9 52 ow3 RussKennemore 3 53
(Michael Appleby) *prom: rdn over 3f out: wknd over 1f out* **66/1**

5-4 7 *nk* **Bollistick**[35] 1484 6-10-0 0 GrahamLee 6 56?
(Michael Mullineaux) *prom: pushed along over 3f out: wknd 2f out* **28/1**

50 8 *12* **Omid**[19] 1866 4-10-0 0 (t) PhillipMakin 8 36
(Nicky Vaughan) *hld up: pushed and bhd over 3f out: nvr a threat* **16/1**

9 *11* **Byron Get One Free** 3-8-11 0 FrederikTylicki 5
(Richard Ford) *hld up: toiling and wl bhd over 4f out* **50/1**

2m 29.94s (-3.86) **Going Correction** -0.60s/f (Hard)
WFA 3 from 4yo+ 17lb 9 Ran SP% **127.4**
Speed ratings (Par 103): **89,84,83,81,81 80,79,71,64**
CSF £3.03 TOTE £2.00: £1.10, £1.50, £2.30; EX 3.70.

Owner Dr Marwan Koukash **Bred** Kirk Wycoff & Deby Wycoff **Trained** Newmarket, Suffolk

FOCUS

A weak maiden with little strength-in-depth and, as the betting suggested, it gave trainer David Simcock a 1-2. The winner did not need to improve much.

Big Time Billy(IRE) Official explanation: jockey said that the mare missed the break

2419 TAYLORMADE BETTING H'CAP 1m 3f 200y
5:15 (5:15) (Class 4) (0-85,85) 4-Y-0+ **£4,075** (£1,212; £606; £303) **Stalls** Centre

Form RPR
56-3 **1** **Number Theory**26 1657 4-8-12 **76** RussKennemore 12 92+
(John Holt) *hld up: hdwy 3f out: led wl over 1f out: edgd lft and drew clr ins fnl f: r.o wl* **9/2**1
202- **2** *5* **Loden**26 3286 5-9-0 **78** GrahamLee 3 86
(Donald McCain) *hld up: pushed along over 2f out: styd on and prog ins fnl f: tk 2nd fin: no ch w wnr* **28/1**
-612 **3** *hd* **Arizona John (IRE)**43 1295 7-8-11 **75** JoeFanning 6 82
(John Mackie) *trckd ldrs: led over 2f out: hdd wl over 1f out: styd on same pce ins fnl f* **5/1**2
5-63 **4** *½* **Rio's Rosanna (IRE)**22 1756 5-8-10 **77** AmyRyan(3) 11 83
(Richard Whitaker) *racd keenly in midfield: in tch w ldrs after 2f: rdn to chal over 2f out: nt qckn over 1f out: styd on same pce ins fnl f* **11/2**3
-501 **5** *nk* **Refractor (IRE)**24 1706 4-8-12 **76** MartinLane 8 82
(James Fanshawe) *hld up: hdwy over 2f out: wnt 2nd over 1f out: no imp on wnr ins fnl f: lost 2nd and no ex fnl 75yds* **17/2**
62-0 **6** *1 ¼* **Flying Power**12 2093 4-8-11 **75** PaddyAspell 13 79
(John Norton) *trckd ldrs: dropped to midfield after 2f: effrt over 2f out: edgd lft over 1f out: one pce* **25/1**
0-61 **7** *¾* **Fourth Generation (IRE)**13 2035 5-8-11 **75** AndrewElliott 1 78+
(Alan Swinbank) *hld up: nt clr run 3f out and over 2f out: sn rdn: kpt on same pce ins fnl f and no imp on ldrs* **11/1**
06-5 **8** *8* **Braveheart Move (IRE)**12 2077 6-9-3 **81** (v1) RobertWinston 7 71
(Geoffrey Harker) *sn led: hdd after 2f: remained prom: regained ld over 3f out: hdd over 2f out: wknd over 1f out* **14/1**
10-2 **9** *2* **Battery Power**26 1656 4-9-0 **78** NeilCallan 4 65
(Mark H Tompkins) *hld up: hdwy over 3f out: rdn over 2f out: no imp on ldrs: wknd over 1f out* **12/1**
2515 **10** *1 ¼* **Amazing Blue Sky**6 2241 6-9-0 **78** JamesSullivan 9 63
(Ruth Carr) *led early: racd keenly and prom: rdn and wknd over 2f out* **16/1**
21-0 **11** *2* **Yasir (USA)**6 2248 4-9-7 **85** (v) TadhgO'Shea 5 67
(Saeed Bin Suroor) *hld up: rdn over 2f out: no imp* **11/1**
20-0 **12** *4 ½* **Royal Trooper (IRE)**19 1846 6-9-1 **79** (b1) PaulMulrennan 2 53
(James Given) *racd keenly in midfield: rdn and wknd 2f out* **16/1**
4-03 **13** *11* **Pintrada**13 2031 4-8-10 **74** KierenFallon 10 31
(James Bethell) *racd keenly: trckd ldrs: led after 2f: hdd over 3f out: wknd over 2f out* **8/1**

2m 25.53s (-8.27) **Going Correction** -0.60s/f (Hard) course record **13 Ran SP% 122.0**
Speed ratings (Par 105): **104,100,100,100,100 99,98,93,92,91 89,86,79**
toteswingers:1&2:£31.20, 2&3:£16.90, 1&3:£5.20 CSF £135.41 CT £668.02 TOTE £6.20: £2.20, £6.00, £1.70; EX 118.90.
Owner Mohan Fonseka **Bred** R Haim **Trained** Peckleton, Leics

FOCUS
A wide-open handicap run at a good tempo in a fast time. The winner was impressive and the form looks solid through the third and fourth.
T/Jkpt: £39,629.10 to a £1 stake. Pool of £223,262.70 - 4.00 winning tickets. T/Plt: £26.60 to a £1 stake. Pool of £74,120.88 - 2,032.22 winning tickets. T/Qpdt: £12.60 to a £1 stake. Pool of £3,631.88 - 212.63 winning tickets DO

2200 SALISBURY (R-H)
Thursday, May 24

OFFICIAL GOING: Firm (good to firm in places in the last 5f)
Wind: virtually nil Weather: warm and sunny

2420 BETFAIR BOOSTS PRIZE MONEY AT SALISBURY E B F MAIDEN STKS 5f
6:10 (6:10) (Class 4) 2-Y-0 **£4,884** (£1,453; £726; £363) **Stalls** Low

Form RPR
0 **1** **Bungle Inthejungle**34 1499 2-9-3 0 MatthewDavies 10 84
(Mick Channon) *led after 1f: rdn over 1f out: sn hrd pressed: kpt on wl: rdn out* **8/1**
3 **2** *nk* **Jubilee Brig**17 1920 2-9-3 0 GeorgeBaker 6 83
(Gary Moore) *travelled wl bhd ldrs: swtchd lft wl over 2f out: rdn to press wnr ent fnl f: kpt on but nt gng pce to get by* **5/1**2
34 **3** *1 ¾* **Regal Dan (IRE)**19 1842 2-8-12 0 MatthewLawson(5) 9 77
(Charles Hills) *trckd ldrs: rdn and ev ch over 1f out: kpt on same pce fnl f* **6/1**3
2 **4** *2 ¾* **Black Monk (IRE)**43 1315 2-9-3 0 PatDobbs 3 67
(Richard Hannon) *led for 1f: chsd ldrs: rdn over 2f out: nt pce to chal: fdd fnl 100yds* **11/10**1
0 **5** *3 ½* **Deepest Blue**54 1131 2-9-3 0 AdamKirby 8 54
(Jamie Osborne) *prom: edgd lft 2f out: sn rdn: wknd ent fnl f* **20/1**
6 *5* **Pearl Bounty (IRE)** 2-9-3 0 JimmyFortune 4 36
(Andrew Balding) *little slowly away: in last pair: pushed along 3f out: nvr any imp on ldrs* **5/1**2
06 **7** *4 ½* **Icanboogie**17 1903 2-9-3 0 DarryllHolland 7 20
(Karen George) *s.i.s: a outpcd in rr* **100/1**
0 **8** *2 ½* **Tough Question**13 2039 2-9-3 0 JamieGoldstein 5 11
(Michael Madgwick) *chsd ldrs tl hung bdly lft and wknd over 2f out* **200/1**
0 **9** *13* **Shearian**18 1886 2-9-3 0 PatCosgrave 2
(Brian Meehan) *sn pushed along in midfield: wknd over 2f out* **40/1**

59.65s (-1.35) **Going Correction** -0.325s/f (Firm) **9 Ran SP% 115.0**
Speed ratings (Par 95): **97,96,93,89,83 75,68,64,43**
toteswingers:1&2:£8.90, 2&3:£4.60, 1&3:£6.40 CSF £46.30 TOTE £10.80: £2.70, £2.00, £1.80; EX 52.00.
Owner Christopher Wright & Miss Emily Asprey **Bred** Stratford Place Stud **Trained** West Ilsley, Berks

FOCUS
A warm run up to a meeting that took place on very fast ground and Pat Dobbs, who rode the fourth, reported: "It's as close as it gets to firm ground". A race that threw up smart sorts in Sir Parky (Group 3 Somerville Tattersall winner) in 2009 and Group 2 Norfolk/Gimcrack scorer Approve the following year and this year's winner may be able to hold his own in slightly stronger company. The pace was sound throughout and the form fits with the race averages.

NOTEBOOK
Bungle Inthejungle ◆ attracted a bit of support and stepped up considerably on the form shown in soft ground on his debut. He's a bit better than these bare facts give him credit for too, as he overcame a wide draw, jumped a path before halfway and both set and sustained a decent gallop after racing keenly. He'll be just as effective over 6f, has a bit of physical scope and can win more races. (op 10-1 tchd 12-1)
Jubilee Brig, who didn't get the rub of things when third to a subsequent winner at Kempton on his debut, was a bit edgy before the start but got a good tow into the race and bettered that form on this turf debut. He'll stay 6f (dam Listed placed over 7f) and is sure to win a race. (op 4-1)
Regal Dan(IRE) had shown fair form in two previous outings and seemed to give it his best shot on the quickest ground he's encountered to date. He should continue to give a good account and has the ability to win an uncompetitive race in this grade. (op 7-1)
Black Monk(IRE), whose trainer was bidding for a fourth win in the last five runnings of this race, failed to build on the form he showed on his debut at Nottingham in April. He's clearly nothing special but will be worth another chance. (tchd 10-11)
Deepest Blue didn't show much in the Brocklesby but left that debut form behind on this first run since and on this much quicker ground. He'll be one to take into nurseries at some point. (op 22-1 tchd 25-1)
Pearl Bounty(IRE), a 120,000gns half-brother to useful 6f Polytrack winner Hoot, attracted a bit of support in the day but was easy to back near the off and was never involved after a tardy start. It's fair to assume he'll do better over further at some point. (op 6-1 tchd 7-1)

2421 BETFAIR SPONSORS THE STABLE STAFF CANTEEN H'CAP 6f
6:40 (6:41) (Class 6) (0-65,65) 4-Y-0+ **£2,264** (£673; £336; £168) **Stalls** Low

Form RPR
60-0 **1** **My Own Way Home**27 1638 4-9-1 **59** PadraigBeggy 5 68
(David Evans) *s.i.s: sn mid-div: hdwy 3f out: sn rdn: r.o to ld towards fin: drvn out* **14/1**
6-40 **2** *nk* **Sarangoo**35 1481 4-9-1 **59** TomMcLaughlin 15 67
(Malcolm Saunders) *mid-div: hdwy 2f out: sn rdn: r.o to dispute narrow ld fnl 100yds: hdd towards fin* **18/1**
20-4 **3** *shd* **Annes Rocket (IRE)**36 1447 7-9-1 **59** (p) PatDobbs 6 67
(Jimmy Fox) *hld up towards rr: hdwy fr jst over 2f out: sn rdn: r.o to dispute narrow ld fnl 100yds: hdd towards fin* **10/1**3
-142 **4** *½* **Cheers**8 2165 4-9-5 **63** DaneO'Neill 12 69+
(Oliver Sherwood) *mid-div: hdwy 2f out but nt clrest of runs: sn rdn: r.o on wl ins fnl f* **7/2**1
005- **5** *½* **Dream Catcher (FR)**183 7519 4-9-6 **64** FergusSweeney 13 68
(Henry Candy) *mid-div: hdwy 3f out: rdn 2f out: kpt on fnl 100yds* **7/2**1
0056 **6** *nk* **Dreams Of Glory**50 1185 4-8-13 **60** SimonPearce(3) 4 63
(Ron Hodges) *pressed ldr: rdn 2f out: ev ch ent fnl f: no ex fnl 75yds* **22/1**
20-5 **7** *½* **Madame Kintyre**29 1609 4-9-4 **62** JamesMillman 3 64
(Rod Millman) *trckd ldrs: rdn over 1f out: ch jst ins fnl f: no ex fnl 75yds* **12/1**
2205 **8** *nse* **Catalinas Diamond (IRE)**23 1734 4-9-5 **63** (t) GeorgeBaker 11 65
(Pat Murphy) *hld up towards rr: hdwy 2f out: sn swtchd lft and rdn: kpt on same pce fnl f* **18/1**
55-0 **9** *nse* **Bermondsey Bob (IRE)**45 1254 6-9-5 **63** CathyGannon 8 65
(John Spearing) *led: rdn 2f out: kpt on gamely tl no ex whn hdd fnl 100yds* **14/1**
350- **10** *3 ¾* **Dualagi**145 7943 8-9-1 **59** StevieDonohoe 2 49
(Martin Bosley) *nvr bttr than mid-div* **40/1**
356 **11** *shd* **Choice Words (USA)**18 1889 4-9-7 **65** MickyFenton 17 54
(Emma Lavelle) *hld up towards rr: swtchd lft and sme hdwy 2f out: sn rdn: edgd rt and fdd fnl f* **16/1**
1033 **12** *1 ¾* **Spin Again (IRE)**9 2146 7-9-5 **63** MickaelBarzalona 9 47
(Daniel Kubler) *chsd ldrs: rdn 3f out: wknd ent fnl f* **9/1**2
10-3 **13** *1* **Glastonberry**138 87 4-8-11 **58** SophieDoyle(3) 18 38
(Geoffrey Deacon) *mid-div: rdn over 2f out: wknd ent fnl f* **33/1**
05-0 **14** *5* **Ever The Optimist (IRE)**29 1614 4-9-2 **60** AdamKirby 10 24
(Tony Newcombe) *s.i.s: t.k.h in rr early: rdn over 3f out: nvr any imp* **10/1**3
600- **15** *15* **Botanist**144 7237 5-9-5 **63** PatCosgrave 1
(Milton Bradley) *s.i.s: a towards rr: eased whn btn over 1f out* **18/1**
00-0 **16** *2 ¼* **Regency Art (IRE)**125 232 5-9-7 **65** JamesDoyle 7
(Milton Bradley) *hung lft over 1f out: sn eased: a in rr* **40/1**

1m 13.2s (-1.60) **Going Correction** -0.325s/f (Firm) **16 Ran SP% 127.5**
Speed ratings (Par 101): **97,96,96,95,95 94,94,94,93,88 88,86,85,78,58 55**
toteswingers:1&2:£77.70, 2&3:£38.80, 1&3:£31.60 CSF £247.97 CT £2745.20 TOTE £22.30: £4.40, £3.70, £1.50, £1.80; EX 250.00.
Owner L Audus **Bred** Theresa Fitsall **Trained** Pandy, Monmouths
■ Stewards' Enquiry : Padraig Beggy seven-day ban: use of whip (8,9,11- 145 June)

FOCUS
Mainly exposed performers in a modest handicap. The gallop was sound and, although the field raced centre-to-far side, the draw was of little significance. Straightforward form.
Regency Art(IRE) Official explanation: jockey said the gelding lost its action

2422 BETFAIR SUPPORTS OAKSEY HOUSE MAIDEN FILLIES' STKS 6f
7:15 (7:15) (Class 5) 3-Y-0+ **£2,911** (£866; £432; £216) **Stalls** Low

Form RPR
2- **1** **Swan Song**216 6991 3-8-12 0 JimmyFortune 5 82
(Andrew Balding) *narrow ld most of way: shkn up jst over 1f out: kpt on strly to assert fnl 120yds* **4/5**1
4-4 **2** *1 ¼* **Supreme Quest**17 1921 3-8-12 82 JamesDoyle 4 78
(Roger Charlton) *upsides wnr: ev ch whn rdn jst over 1f out: kpt on but no ex fnl 120yds* **7/5**2
0-4 **3** *4 ½* **Cynthia Calhoun**24 1705 3-8-12 0 AdamKirby 2 64
(Clive Cox) *trckd ldrs: rdn over 2f out: kpt on same pce: hung rt fnl f* **16/1**3
4- **4** *1* **Norlander**190 7435 3-8-12 0 RichardThomas 6 60
(Ralph Beckett) *trckd ldrs: rdn over 2f out: kpt on same pce* **16/1**3
00 **5** *4 ½* **Ishi**12 2065 3-8-12 0 JamesMillman 3 46
(Rod Millman) *in tch: rdn over 3f out: wknd over 1f out* **50/1**
600 **6** *8* **Smarty Time**18 1889 5-9-7 53 JohnFahy 7 22
(John Bridger) *dwlt: sn struggling: a in rr* **100/1**
0 **7** *12* **Doyle's Dream**34 1501 3-8-12 0 JamieGoldstein 1
(Michael Madgwick) *chsd ldrs: rdn over 2f out: sn wknd* **100/1**

1m 13.19s (-1.61) **Going Correction** -0.325s/f (Firm)
WFA 3 from 5yo 9lb **7 Ran SP% 112.9**
Speed ratings (Par 100): **97,95,89,88,82 71,55**
toteswingers:1&2:£1.10, 2&3:£1.90, 1&3:£1.60 CSF £2.06 TOTE £1.70: £1.10, £1.30; EX 2.50.
Owner J C Smith **Bred** Littleton Stud **Trained** Kingsclere, Hants

FOCUS
A race won by subsequent dual Listed winner Cartimandua in 2007 but the form of this uncompetitive event, in which the two market leaders pulled clear in the last furlong and a half, looks no more than fair. They finished in betting order and the form is rated around the second. The gallop was a reasonable one.
Smarty Time Official explanation: jockey said that the mare was slowly away

2423 BETFAIR FUNDS THE PJA DOCTOR H'CAP 1m 6f 21y
7:45 (7:45) (Class 4) (0-85,85) 4-Y-0+ **£4,722** (£1,405; £702; £351)

Form RPR
-10 **1** **Kangaroo Court (IRE)**8 2174 8-8-12 **76** MickyFenton 4 84
(Emma Lavelle) *mde all: styd on strly fnl f: rdn out* **12/1**

143- **2** 2 3/4 **Miss Topsy Turvy (IRE)**209 7136 4-8-12 76 DaneO'Neill 8 80
(John Dunlop) *mid-div: trckd ldrs over 6f out: rdn wl over 2f out: styd on to go 2nd ent fnl f: a being hld by wnr* **8/1**

410/ **3** nk **Monterey (IRE)**706 3145 5-9-7 85 RobertHavlin 3 88
(Robert Mills) *hld up towards rr: rdn in last pair over 2f out: sn hung lft: veered bdly lft wl over 1f out: hdwy on stands' side rails sn after: styd on wl fnl f* **17/2**

60-5 **4** 1 1/4 **Sunny Future (IRE)**6 2233 6-8-2 66 CathyGannon 1 67
(Malcolm Saunders) *hld up towards rr: hdwy over 3f out: rdn over 2f out: styd on but nvr threatened ldrs* **5/1**1

100- **5** 1 1/4 **Praxiteles (IRE)**54 4998 8-8-12 81 (tp) BrendanPowell(5) 10 81
(Rebecca Curtis) *trckd ldrs: disp 2nd 3f out: sn rdn: lost 2nd and no ex ent fnl f* **14/1**

0-50 **6** 3/4 **Sherman McCoy**19 1846 6-9-2 80 JamesMillman 2 79
(Rod Millman) *trckd wnr: rdn wl over 3f out: lost disp 2nd over 1f out: no ex* **13/2**3

010- **7** 3 1/4 **Blimey O'Riley (IRE)**209 7139 7-8-12 76 EddieAhern 9 70
(Mark H Tompkins) *mid-div: rdn wl over 2f out: wknd fnl f* **15/2**

015- **8** 3 1/2 **Hawridge King**209 7139 10-8-8 72 FergusSweeney 11 61
(Stuart Kittow) *mid-div: rdn 4f out: nvr gng pce to get on terms: wknd fnl f* **12/1**

24-0 **9** 1 1/4 **Four Nations (USA)**19 1850 4-9-1 79 PatDobbs 7 66
(Amanda Perrett) *racd keenly: mid-div: trckd ldrs over 6f out: rdn over 3f out: grad fdd fr 2f out* **11/2**2

000/ **10** 10 **Brett Vale (IRE)**627 5035 6-8-6 70 JohnFahy 5 43
(Peter Hedger) *rdn over 3f out: a last* **50/1**

150- **P** **Danvilla**258 5878 5-9-4 82 GeorgeBaker 6
(Paul Webber) *trckd wnr tl lost action and p.u over 6f out* **13/2**3

3m 0.84s (-6.56) **Going Correction** -0.325s/f (Firm) course record **11 Ran SP% 116.1**
Speed ratings (Par 105): **105,103,103,102,101 101,99,97,96,91**
toteswingers:1&2:£8.70, 2&3:£18.70, 1&3:£43.20 CSF £103.32 CT £866.56 TOTE £11.30: £2.50, £1.90, £3.00; EX 40.20.
Owner N Mustoe **Bred** Brian Wilson **Trained** Hatherden, Hants

FOCUS
The race was started by a flip start. A useful handicap in which the winner set no more than a reasonable gallop. He is entitled to be winning races on the Flat from this sort of mark.
Danvilla Official explanation: jockey said that the mare hung left

2424 BETFAIR SPONSORS THE OWNERS & TRAINERS BAR H'CAP 1m 4f
8:20 (8:21) (Class 6) (0-65,65) 3-Y-O **£2,264** (£673; £336; £168) **Stalls** Low

Form RPR

5-04 **1** **Dovils Date**15 1982 3-9-4 62 JamesMillman 11 76
(Rod Millman) *hld up bhd: swtchd to centre and hdwy fr over 3f out: rdn to press ldr whn drifted rt over 1f out: styd on wl to ld wl ins fnl f: all out* **16/1**

4-02 **2** hd **Bathwick Street**13 2049 3-8-11 55 StevieDonohoe 12 68
(David Evans) *sn rousted along to sit promly: led after 3f: (rn green whn in front): veered lft over 2f out: wandered u.p but kpt finding whn chal: hdd wl ins fnl f* **18/1**

6-52 **3** 6 **Cheviot Quest (IRE)**9 2141 3-8-13 57 LeeNewman 10 61
(William Jarvis) *mid-div: bmpd after 2f: sn nudged along: hdwy u.p over 3f out: styd on same pce fnl 2f* **5/1**2

5-52 **4** nk **Fleur De La Vie (IRE)**23 1726 3-8-13 60 HarryBentley(3) 7 63+
(Ralph Beckett) *mid-div: short of room over 4f out: hdwy over 3f out: sn rdn: styd on same pce fnl 2f* **15/2**3

0-04 **5** 3/4 **Jennifer J**110 429 3-9-5 63 EddieAhern 8 65
(Mark H Tompkins) *hld up towards rr: hdwy over 3f out: sn rdn: styd on same pce fnl 2f* **8/1**

00-5 **6** 3 **Curly Come Home**38 1414 3-9-5 63 GeorgeBaker 2 60
(Chris Wall) *trckd ldrs: rdn to chse ldr 3f out tl wl over 1f out: wknd fnl f* **10/1**

00-2 **7** 4 **Burnham**10 2126 3-9-4 62 DarryllHolland 13 53
(Hughie Morrison) *s.i.s: sn pushed into mid-div: lost pl whn squeezed out after 2f: towards rr: hdwy over 3f out: sn rdn to chse ldrs: wknd fnl f* **10/3**1

004 **8** 15 **Morilles**38 1414 3-9-7 65 AdamKirby 6 32
(Clive Cox) *mid-div: rdn 3f out: wknd 2f out* **10/1**

3325 **9** hd **Ctappers**30 1591 3-9-3 61 MatthewDavies 5 27
(Mick Channon) *mid-div: squeezed up after 2f: rdn over 3f out: sn wknd* **28/1**

-600 **10** 4 1/2 **Wreaths Of Empire (IRE)**6 2235 3-9-7 65 (b1) JimmyFortune 4 24
(Richard Hannon) *trckd ldrs: rdn over 3f out: wknd 2f out* **11/1**

01-0 **11** 2 1/2 **Welsh Nayber**24 1707 3-9-6 64 PatDobbs 9 19
(Amanda Perrett) *in tch: rdn over 3f out: wknd 2f out* **16/1**

00-0 **12** 1 **Chocolat Chaud (IRE)**38 1424 3-9-0 58 DaneO'Neill 1
(J W Hills) *trckd ldrs: rdn over 3f out: sn wknd* **25/1**

02-0 **13** 13 **Cato Minor**23 1726 3-8-11 55 (b) PatCosgrave 3
(Amanda Perrett) *a in rr* **50/1**

56-0 **14** 5 **Zamarelle**15 1982 3-9-3 61 JamesDoyle 14
(Roger Charlton) *racd freely: led for over 3f: trckd ldrs: rdn over 3f out: sn wknd* **14/1**

2m 34.65s (-3.35) **Going Correction** -0.325s/f (Firm) **14 Ran SP% 122.1**
Speed ratings (Par 97): **98,97,93,93,93 91,88,78,78,75 73,73,64,61**
toteswingers:1&2:£29.80, 2&3:£10.00, 1&3:£10.60 CSF £276.19 CT £1663.08 TOTE £24.60: £4.40, £6.10, £1.90; EX 336.20.
Owner Always Hopeful Partnership **Bred** Cranford Stud **Trained** Kentisbeare, Devon

FOCUS
A modest handicap in which a decent early gallop steadied after about 4f. The first two pulled clear in the closing stages. The first two in the market disappointed but there are grounds for thinking the form is sound.
Wreaths Of Empire(IRE) Official explanation: jockey said that the colt ran too free
Welsh Nayber Official explanation: jockey said the gelding hung badly left up the straight

2425 BETFAIR SUPPORTS THE GREATWOOD CHARITY CLASSIFIED STKS 1m 1f 198y
8:50 (8:51) (Class 5) 3-Y-O **£2,911** (£866; £432; £216) **Stalls** Low

Form RPR

2240 **1** **Devote Myself (IRE)**15 1976 3-9-0 69 CathyGannon 3 68
(David Evans) *racd freely: led: rn wd on bnd 6f out: sn 6 l clr: rdn 2f out: jnd sn after: kpt on v gamely: all out* **8/1**3

-424 **2** 3/4 **Santadelacruze**66 959 3-9-0 66 FergusSweeney 7 66
(Gary Moore) *hld up: rdn and hdwy fr 3f out: pressed wnr ent fnl f: kpt on: hld towards fin* **20/1**

04-4 **3** nk **Travelling**10 2136 3-9-0 70 AdamKirby 2 65
(Marco Botti) *chsd clr ldr: rdn and hdwy fr 3f out: ev ch fr over 1f out: no ex fnl 75yds* **11/4**1

0-23 **4** 1 1/2 **Aliante**9 2148 3-9-0 69 DaneO'Neill 4 62
(Mark Johnston) *chsd ldr: rdn over 3f out: sn outpcd: styd on fnl f* **7/1**2

3140 **5** 6 **Bramshill Lass**24 1707 3-9-0 70 PatDobbs 9 50
(Amanda Perrett) *cl up in chsng gp: rdn over 3f out: nvr threatened: wknd ent fnl f* **14/1**

45-0 **6** 13 **It's A Girl Thing (IRE)**43 1319 3-8-9 67 (v1) DavidKenny(5) 1 24
(George Baker) *cl up in chsng gp: rdn over 3f out: wknd over 1f out* **40/1**

2m 9.65s (-0.25) **Going Correction** -0.325s/f (Firm) **6 Ran SP% 64.1**
Speed ratings (Par 99): **88,87,87,85,81 70**
toteswingers:1&2:£7.40, 2&3:£6.50, 1&3:£1.60 CSF £38.97 TOTE £5.90: £2.70, £3.40; EX 24.40.
Owner Jason Tucker **Bred** D And Mrs D Veitch **Trained** Pandy, Monmouths

FOCUS
A modest classified event in which two of the three market leaders, McVicar and Porcini, were withdrawn after getting upset in the stalls. The winner was soon allowed to establish a large advantage off just an ordinary gallop. This rates a small personal best.
T/Plt: £1,344.80 to a £1 stake. Pool of £54,916.55 - 29.81 winning tickets. T/Qpdt: £109.70 to a £1 stake. Pool of £5,059.45 - 34.10 winning tickets. TM

1677 SANDOWN (R-H)
Thursday, May 24

OFFICIAL GOING: Straight course - good (good to firm in places); round course - good to firm (good in places)
Wind: Nil Weather: Fine

2426 BRITISH STALLION STUDS SUPPORTING BRITISH RACING E B F MAIDEN FILLIES' STKS 5f 6y
6:00 (6:01) (Class 5) 2-Y-O **£3,234** (£962; £481; £240) **Stalls** Low

Form RPR

1 **Upward Spiral** 2-9-0 0 RichardKingscote 9 84+
(Tom Dascombe) *mde all: rdn over 1f out: hung lft fnl f: styd on* **10/3**1

2 1 1/2 **Jubilee Diamond (IRE)** 2-9-0 0 RichardHughes 1 79+
(Richard Hannon) *chsd wnr: rdn and swished tail over 1f out: styd on same pce ins fnl f* **7/2**2

3 5 **Give Way Nelson (IRE)** 2-9-0 0 MartinDwyer 3 61+
(Brian Meehan) *s.i.s: sn pushed along in rr: rdn 1/2-way: nvr trbld ldrs* **4/1**3

4 1 **Sand And Deliver** 2-9-0 0 IanMongan 5 57+
(Peter Crate) *chsd ldrs: rdn over 1f out: wknd fnl f* **16/1**

5 nk **Exotic Isle** 2-9-0 0 JimCrowley 8 56
(Ralph Beckett) *chsd ldrs: rdn and edgd lft over 1f out: wknd ins fnl f* **7/2**2

6 4 1/2 **Little Miss Zuri (IRE)** 2-9-0 0 LiamKeniry 2 40
(Sylvester Kirk) *s.i.s: nvr on terms* **20/1**

7 13 **Barbs Princess** 2-9-0 0 MichaelHills 4
(Charles Hills) *s.s: outpcd* **15/2**

1m 1.2s (-0.40) **Going Correction** -0.325s/f (Firm) **7 Ran SP% 109.9**
Speed ratings (Par 90): **90,87,79,78,77 70,49**
toteswingers:1&2:£2.90, 2&3:£3.10, 1&3:£2.60 CSF £14.03 TOTE £5.70: £3.70, £1.50; EX 20.20 Trifecta £65.10 Pool: £7507.09 - 85.31 winning units..
Owner Trinity Hammers **Bred** Horizon Bloodstock Limited **Trained** Malpas, Cheshire

FOCUS
The front pair drew clear in what was no more than a fair juvenile maiden for the course. The race averages and the time help with the level.

NOTEBOOK
Upward Spiral, whose trainer won this in 2009, is bred for further (dam 7f winner), but she knew her job early, doing well to get across from stall nine, and despite wandering left late on, always looked to be doing enough. She should have more to offer and has the option of either the Queen Mary or Albany at Royal Ascot. (op 9-2 tchd 3-1 in places)
Jubilee Diamond(IRE), uneasy in the market, made no particular appeal on breeding and was easy in the market, but knew her job from stall one and made a satisfactory start. She isn't the biggest, but should go one better in a maiden. (op 3-1)
Give Way Nelson(IRE), a first runner for Eclipse-winning sire Mount Nelson, is a half-sister to a couple of useful sprint winners and was expected to need this debut run. Slowly away, she duly showed signs of greenness before keeping on and should improve plenty, with an extra furlong likely to suit. (op 3-1)
Sand And Deliver ◆, a sister to 7f Group 2 winner Finjaan, travelled strongly just in behind the speed before proving unable to quicken. She should show the benefit of this initial experience and can win a maiden.
Exotic Isle, an 80,000gns half-sister to 5f 2yo winner Princess Banu, raced widest throughout and looked clueless when asked for her effort. She reportedly looked fit but should still improve. (op 4-1 tchd 10-3)
Little Miss Zuri(IRE), closely related to three winners, including Listed-placed 5f winner Joyce, was slowly into stride and always struggling. (op 25-1 tchd 16-1)
Barbs Princess, a half-sister to numerous 5f-7f winners, became increasingly detached following a slow start and offered little short-term promise. (tchd 7-1 and 8-1)

2427 TELLISFORD H'CAP 1m 6f
6:30 (6:33) (Class 4) (0-85,82) 3-Y-O **£4,075** (£1,212; £606; £303) **Stalls** Low

Form RPR

10-4 **1** **Winner's Wish**31 1557 3-8-12 73 WilliamBuick 1 80
(Jeremy Noseda) *chsd ldr tl led over 3f out: rdn over 1f out: sn hung rt: styd on* **4/1**2

1-41 **2** 2 1/4 **Flying Trader (USA)**24 1707 3-9-2 77 LukeMorris 2 81
(Jane Chapple-Hyam) *a.p: rdn over 2f out: chsd wnr over 1f out: styd on same pce ins fnl f* **7/2**1

30-0 **3** 1 **Dollar Bill**24 1707 3-8-9 70 (p) RyanMoore 7 73
(Andrew Balding) *hld up: hdwy 8f out: rdn over 2f out: edgd rt fnl f: styd on same pce* **8/1**

4-15 **4** 5 **Juno The Muffinman (IRE)**15 1978 3-8-12 73 RichardKingscote 3 69
(Tom Dascombe) *prom: hmpd after 1f: rdn over 2f out: wknd over 1f out* **7/2**1

5-51 **5** 5 **Ballyheigue (IRE)**15 1981 3-9-4 79 (b) ShaneKelly 5 68
(Brian Meehan) *led: rdn and hdd over 3f out: wknd wl over 1f out* **9/1**

41 **6** 3 **Nice Rose**40 1380 3-9-7 82 SilvestreDeSousa 6 66
(Mark Johnston) *hld up: plld hrd: rdn over 3f out: wknd over 2f out* **11/2**3

-461 **7** 1 3/4 **Spanish Fork (IRE)**13 2049 3-8-5 66 SamHitchcott 4 48
(Mick Channon) *hld up: pushed along over 5f out: rdn over 3f out: sn wknd* **8/1**

3m 4.5s **Going Correction** -0.05s/f (Good) **7 Ran SP% 112.1**
Speed ratings (Par 101): **98,96,96,93,90 88,87**
toteswingers:1&2:£4.80, 2&3:£6.80, 1&3:£6.20 CSF £17.58 TOTE £5.10: £2.30, £2.30; EX 26.60.
Owner Abdulla Al Mansoori **Bred** Ashbrittle Stud **Trained** Newmarket, Suffolk

FOCUS
Having gone steady early the pace increased from a fair way out.A few of these failed to give their running in what was a fair staying handicap for 3yos and not form to get carried away with. Improvement from the winner with the second to form.

2428 FERNOX TFL H'CAP 1m 14y
7:05 (7:05) (Class 4) (0-85,82) 3-Y-O £4,075 (£1,212; £606; £303) Stalls Low

Form				RPR
10-0	1		**Jacob Cats**[36] 1452 3-9-5 **80** RichardHughes 3 (Richard Hannon) *hld up: nt clr run over 2f out: swtchd lft and hdwy over 1f out: r.o u.p to ld nr fin* **9/1**	94+
2-65	2	¾	**Ocean Tempest**[18] 1888 3-9-1 **76** BrettDoyle 1 (John Ryan) *chsd ldrs: led over 1f out: sn rdn: hdd towards fin* **33/1**	86
25-3	3	¾	**Lelaps (USA)**[54] 1132 3-9-5 **80** SilvestreDeSousa 5 (Marco Botti) *chsd ldr: rdn and ev ch over 1f out: styd on* **11/4**[1]	88
21-1	4	1	**Takeitfromalady (IRE)**[17] 1938 3-9-4 **79** (b) JimCrowley 9 (Ralph Beckett) *hld up: hdwy over 2f out: rdn over 1f out: edgd rt: styd on* **7/1**	85
1-25	5	shd	**Johnno**[9] 2150 3-9-3 **78** SebSanders 4 (J W Hills) *a.p: led over 2f out: rdn and hdd over 1f out: no ex towards fin* **13/2**[3]	84
6422	6	2 ¼	**Tight Lipped (IRE)**[3] 2331 3-8-13 **74** LukeMorris 12 (James Eustace) *chsd ldrs: rdn over 2f out: styd on same pce fnl f* **12/1**	75
10-4	7	2 ½	**Halling Dancer**[13] 2021 3-9-3 **78** FrankieDettori 6 (Lee Carter) *led over 5f: sn rdn: wknd ins fnl f* **16/1**	73
2-01	8	½	**Flaxen Flare (IRE)**[17] 1937 3-9-7 **82** (p) RyanMoore 7 (Andrew Balding) *hld up: hdwy 1/2-way: rdn over 1f out: wknd ins fnl f* **9/1**	76
5-52	9	1 ½	**Daliance (IRE)**[24] 1703 3-8-13 **74** RichardKingscote 8 (Tom Dascombe) *hld up: hdwy u.p over 2f out: wknd fnl f* **6/1**[2]	64
130-	10	1 ½	**Croquembouche (IRE)**[254] 6031 3-9-1 **76** LiamKeniry 11 (Ed de Giles) *hld up: plld hrd: rdn over 2f out: wknd over 1f out* **40/1**	63
346	11	1 ½	**Mutafaakir (IRE)**[24] 1703 3-9-5 **80** (tp) PaulHanagan 10 (John Gosden) *hld up: rdn over 2f out: n.d* **10/1**	64
50-0	12	¾	**Cape Rainbow**[29] 1607 3-8-11 **72** (v[1]) DavidProbert 2 (Mark Usher) *mid-div: rdn over 3f out: wknd over 2f out* **50/1**	54
01-	13	¾	**Keepax**[227] 6742 3-9-3 **78** ChrisCatlin 13 (Chris Wall) *hld up: rdn over 2f out: n.d* **33/1**	58

1m 44.15s (0.85) **Going Correction** -0.025s/f (Good) **13 Ran SP% 119.7**
Speed ratings (Par 101): **94,93,92,91,91 89,86,86,84,83 81,80,80**
toteswingers:1&2:£80.20, 2&3:£19.90, 1&3:£5.60 CSF £283.95 CT £834.70 TOTE £10.80: £4.30, £14.70, £1.50; EX 387.60 Trifecta £1784.50 Pool: £2917.97 - 1.21 winning units..
Owner Michael Pescod & Justin Dowley **Bred** Highclere Stud **Trained** East Everleigh, Wilts

FOCUS
Not that many got into what had looked a good, competitive handicap, with the pace being quite ordinary. The effort of the winner can therefore be upgraded. The second matched his best AW form and the third progressed from his sound maiden form.
Mutafaakir(IRE) Official explanation: jockey said that the colt hung right

2429 LOVEREADING.CO.UK H'CAP 1m 2f 7y
7:35 (7:40) (Class 4) (0-85,81) 3-Y-O £4,075 (£1,212; £606; £303) Stalls Low

Form				RPR
421-	1		**Freddy Q (IRE)**[256] 5967 3-9-4 **81** SeanLevey(3) 10 (Richard Hannon) *hld up: hdwy over 1f out: rdn to ld ins fnl f: r.o* **20/1**	89
51-	2	¾	**Willie Wag Tail (USA)**[223] 6837 3-9-5 **79** J-PGuillambert 7 (Ed Walker) *s.i.s: hld up: rdn over 2f out: hdwy over 1f out: ev ch ins fnl f: styd on same pce towards fin* **10/1**	86
-140	3	nk	**Ex Oriente (IRE)**[35] 1468 3-9-4 **78** (b) WilliamBuick 4 (John Gosden) *hld up: hdwy u.p over 2f out: ev ch ins fnl f: styd on same pce* **20/1**	84
55-0	4	1 ¾	**Counsel (IRE)**[27] 1641 3-8-13 **73** RyanMoore 9 (Sir Michael Stoute) *chsd ldr tl led over 2f out: rdn over 1f out: hdd and no ex ins fnl f* **7/1**[3]	76+
33-0	5	2	**Mizbah**[36] 1440 3-9-3 **77** (v[1]) FrankieDettori 1 (Saeed Bin Suroor) *led over 5f: wknd ins fnl f* **15/2**	76
04-3	6	1 ½	**Dynamic Duo (IRE)**[9] 2150 3-9-1 **75** RichardHughes 3 (Richard Hannon) *chsd ldrs: rdn over 1f out: wknd ins fnl f* **7/2**[2]	71+
52-4	7	1 ¾	**Mubaraza (IRE)**[18] 1888 3-9-7 **81** PaulHanagan 2 (John Dunlop) *prom: rdn over 3f out: wknd fnl f* **5/2**[1]	73
0-50	8	3 ¾	**Tingo In The Tale (IRE)**[27] 1647 3-9-1 **75** JimCrowley 6 (David Arbuthnot) *prom: lost pl 8f out: hdwy over 2f out: sn rdn and wknd* **25/1**	60
01-	9	¾	**Lancaster Gate**[156] 7835 3-9-3 **77** TomQueally 8 (Amanda Perrett) *hdwy over 7f out: rdn and wknd over 2f out* **12/1**	60

2m 9.83s (-0.67) **Going Correction** -0.025s/f (Good) **9 Ran SP% 105.2**
Speed ratings (Par 101): **101,100,100,98,97 95,94,91,90**
toteswingers:1&2:£15.10, 2&3:£29.60, 1&3:£49.40 CSF £172.37 CT £3225.02 TOTE £12.10: £2.90, £3.80, £4.40; EX 99.80 Trifecta £333.40 Pool: £ 3185.96- 7.07 winning units..
Owner H R Hunt **Bred** John Martin McLoughney **Trained** East Everleigh, Wilts

FOCUS
They appeared to go a decent gallop, courtesy of Frankie Dettori aboard Mizbah, and the race set up nicely for the closers. The third sets the standard and the winner is rated up 5lb on his previous best.

2430 "HEREDITARY SPASTIC PARAPLEGIA" AWARENESS MAIDEN STKS 1m 2f 7y
8:10 (8:13) (Class 5) 3-4-Y-O £2,587 (£770; £384; £192) Stalls Low

Form				RPR
3	1		**Trade Commissioner (IRE)**[54] 1138 4-9-12 0 WilliamBuick 9 (John Gosden) *chsd ldrs: shkn up to ld ins fnl f: r.o* **15/8**[2]	87+
043-	2	½	**Mawaqeet (USA)**[209] 7134 3-8-12 0 PaulHanagan 8 (Sir Michael Stoute) *hld up: hdwy u.p over 1f out: r.o to go 2nd nr fin: nt rch wnr* **10/1**	82
0	3	1	**Bedazzled**[17] 1923 3-8-7 0 SilvestreDeSousa 6 (James Fanshawe) *trckd ldrs: racd keenly: rdn over 1f out: styd on* **25/1**	75
2	4	¾	**Lucanin**[33] 1512 3-8-12 0 RyanMoore 12 (Sir Michael Stoute) *led over 2f: chsd ldr tl led again 3f out: rdn over 1f out: hdd and unable qck ins fnl f* **11/8**[1]	79
	5	2 ¼	**Minority Interest** 3-8-12 0 FrankieDettori 3 (Sir Michael Stoute) *chsd ldr tl led over 7f out: hdd 3f out: no ex ins fnl f* **9/1**[3]	74
06	6	nk	**Aegaeus**[19] 1866 3-8-12 0 HayleyTurner 2 (Ed Dunlop) *hld up in tch: racd keenly: rdn over 2f out: no ex ins fnl f* **20/1**	73
	7	6	**Semeen** 3-8-12 0 J-PGuillambert 1 (Luca Cumani) *s.s: hld up: hdwy over 2f out: wknd fnl f* **25/1**	61+
	8	¾	**Take The Stage (IRE)** 3-8-12 0 RichardHughes 13 (Jeremy Noseda) *hld up: hdwy over 2f out: sn rdn: edgd rt and wknd fnl f* **25/1**	60+
0-0	9	2	**Mount Mayday (IRE)**[49] 1206 3-8-12 0 SaleemGolam 11 (Stuart Williams) *hld up: plld hrd: nvr on terms* **100/1**	56
0-	10	nse	**Karistar (IRE)**[219] 6934 3-8-7 0 ow3 RyanClark(3) 5 (Tom Keddy) *mid-div: rdn over 3f out: wknd over 2f out* **100/1**	54
	11	8	**Carmen's Concerto** 3-8-7 0 DavidProbert 7 (Andrew Balding) *hld up: rdn and wknd over 3f out* **66/1**	35
5-0	12	1	**Princely Sum (IRE)**[10] 2125 3-8-12 0 (t) NickyMackay 4 (Stuart Williams) *hld up: a in rr: wknd over 3f out* **100/1**	38

2m 14.72s (4.22) **Going Correction** -0.025s/f (Good)
WFA 3 from 4yo 14lb **12 Ran SP% 116.7**
Speed ratings (Par 103): **82,81,80,80,78 78,73,72,71,71 64,63**
toteswingers:1&2:£4.70, 2&3:£15.90, 1&3:£7.90 CSF £18.63 TOTE £3.30: £1.30, £2.70, £4.30; EX 25.10 Trifecta £291.80 Pool: £922.78 - 2.34 winning units..
Owner Lady Rothschild **Bred** Kincorth Investments Inc **Trained** Newmarket, Suffolk

FOCUS
A strong maiden that should produce plenty of good winners. The steady pace resulted in something of a sprint finish and quite a few should show themselves better than the bare form in time. The form is rated around the race averages with the winner building on his debut promise.
Mount Mayday(IRE) Official explanation: trainer said that the gelding ran too free

2431 FERNOX FILLIES' H'CAP 1m 1f
8:40 (8:43) (Class 5) (0-75,75) 3-Y-O+ £2,587 (£770; £384; £192) Stalls Low

Form				RPR
1312	1		**Miss Cato**[33] 1519 3-8-9 **69** ChrisCatlin 6 (Rae Guest) *chsd ldrs: led over 1f out: r.o wl* **7/2**[1]	86
14-4	2	3 ¾	**Cresta Star**[7] 2194 3-9-0 **74** RichardHughes 12 (Richard Hannon) *a.p: chsd wnr over 1f out: edgd rt and styd on same pce fnl f* **7/2**[1]	83
0-54	3	5	**Bondi Mist (IRE)**[17] 1937 3-8-3 **63** LukeMorris 3 (Jonathan Portman) *hld up: hdwy over 2f out: rdn over 1f out: styd on same pce* **33/1**	61
2111	4	1	**Abigails Angel**[69] 919 5-9-9 **75** MarkCoumbe(5) 9 (Brett Johnson) *led: hdd over 5f out: rdn and ev ch over 1f out: no ex ins fnl f* **11/1**	73
350-	5	¾	**Buzkashi (IRE)**[236] 6526 3-9-0 **74** [1] TedDurcan 8 (David Lanigan) *hld up: rdn over 2f out: r.o ins fnl f: nvr nrr* **6/1**[3]	68
55-0	6	¾	**Winter Dress**[23] 1733 3-8-6 **66** PaulHanagan 1 (Roger Teal) *hld up in tch: plld hrd: rdn over 2f out: styd on same pce fr over 1f out* **15/2**	59
-305	7	shd	**Altona (IRE)**[17] 1906 3-8-9 **69** SamHitchcott 4 (Mick Channon) *hld up: hdwy u.p over 2f out: styd on same pce fr over 1f out* **33/1**	61
10-0	8	hd	**Secret Era**[17] 1919 5-8-8 **60** RaulDaSilva(5) 11 (William Muir) *chsd ldrs: rdn over 2f out: no ex ins fnl f* **25/1**	54
00-2	9	1 ¾	**Pearl Opera**[15] 1980 4-8-9 **56** oh1 SilvestreDeSousa 2 (Denis Coakley) *s.i.s: hld up: plld hrd: hdwy over 2f out: rdn and wknd over 1f out* **25/1**	46
10	10	1 ¼	**Ogaritmo**[27] 1641 3-9-0 **74** RyanMoore 5 (Marco Botti) *hld up: rdn over 2f out: nvr on terms* **5/1**[2]	68+
0-43	11	4 ½	**Midas Moment**[21] 1792 4-9-12 **73** MartinDwyer 10 (William Muir) *plld hrd and prom: led over 5f out: clr 4f out: rdn and hdd over 1f out: wknd fnl f* **20/1**	50
3220	12	11	**Imtithal (IRE)**[20] 1819 3-8-12 **72** WilliamBuick 7 (James Tate) *hld up: rdn over 2f out: sn lost tch* **25/1**	

1m 56.65s (0.95) **Going Correction** -0.025s/f (Good)
WFA 3 from 4yo+ 13lb **12 Ran SP% 117.7**
Speed ratings (Par 100): **94,90,86,85,84 84,83,83,82,81 77,67**
toteswingers:1&2:£2.60, 2&3:£32.10, 1&3:£22.00 CSF £13.50 CT £345.38 TOTE £4.20: £1.70, £1.80, £5.70; EX 17.40 Trifecta £574.40 Part won. Pool: £776.25 - 0.10 winning units..
Owner A H Bennett **Bred** A H Bennett **Trained** Newmarket, Suffolk

FOCUS
The pace increased once Midas Moment was allowed to stride on towards the end of the back and two progressive types drew clear. Decent form for the grade from the first two, but not much depth.
Ogaritmo Official explanation: jockey said that the filly was denied a clear run in the final furlong
T/Plt: £616.40 to a £1 stake. Pool of £58,223.66 - 68.95 winning tickets. T/Qpdt: £111.20 to a £1 stake. Pool of £5,977.22 - 39.76 winning tickets. CR

2432 - 2435a (Foreign Racing) - See Raceform Interactive

1949 CATTERICK (L-H)
Friday, May 25

OFFICIAL GOING: Good to firm (9.0)
Wind: Moderate, half behind Weather: Fine and sunny

2436 SUPPORT THE HOUSE THAT JACK BUILT APPRENTICE H'CAP 5f
6:35 (6:36) (Class 6) (0-60,60) 4-Y-O+ £1,704 (£503; £251) Stalls Low

Form				RPR
6006	1		**Chosen One (IRE)**[14] 2032 7-8-3 **47** ShirleyTeasdale(5) 1 (Ruth Carr) *mde all: clr 2f out: styd on wl: unchal* **5/1**[2]	61
-500	2	2 ¾	**Sophie's Beau (USA)**[13] 2092 5-8-2 **46** (bt) EvaMoscrop(5) 7 (Michael Chapman) *s.i.s: mid-div: hdwy over 1f out: styd on to take 2nd nr fin* **25/1**	50
022	3	1 ¼	**The Magic Of Rio**[45] 1280 6-8-7 **46** oh1 MatthewCosham 4 (John Balding) *chsd wnr: kpt on same pce fnl f* **5/1**[2]	46
0045	4	nk	**Sharp Shoes**[4] 2352 5-9-7 **60** (p) LucyAlexander 5 (Ann Duffield) *chsd ldrs: kpt on same pce appr fnl f* **4/1**[1]	59
3050	5	3 ¾	**Spirit Of Coniston**[47] 1242 9-8-11 **55** NedCurtis(5) 13 (Paul Midgley) *wnt lft s: mid-div: hung bdly lft 2f out: nvr a threat* **6/1**[3]	40
-300	6	nse	**Kyzer Chief**[5] 2314 7-9-6 **59** ShaneBKelly 10 (Ron Barr) *hmpd s: outpcd and bhd: styd on fnl f: nvr nr ldrs* **8/1**	44
0-01	7	1	**Dotty Darroch**[19] 1881 4-8-13 **55** AdamCarter(3) 14 (Robin Bastiman) *mid-div on outer: wknd over 1f out* **5/1**[2]	36
26-0	8	1	**Triskaidekaphobia**[47] 1242 9-8-5 **47** (t) LeonnaMayor(3) 11 (Wilf Storey) *hmpd s: bhd: kpt on fnl f* **18/1**	25
000-	9	4	**Hereselle (IRE)**[168] 7691 4-8-2 **46** oh1 NoraLooby(5) 6 (Michael Chapman) *wnt rt s: chsd ldrs: wknd over 1f out* **40/1**	
06-0	10	4 ½	**Stella Marris**[16] 1987 5-8-7 **46** oh1 AshleyMorgan 8 (Christopher Wilson) *in rr: bhd fnl 2f* **40/1**	

66-0 **11** *1 1/4* **Lady By Red (IRE)**[41] 1383 4-8-7 51.......................... ConorHarrison(5) 3
(David Thompson) *v free to post: chsd ldrs: wknd and hmpd over 1f out: eased* **28/1**

58.27s (-1.53) **Going Correction** -0.20s/f (Firm) **11** Ran SP% **112.8**
Speed ratings (Par 101): **104,99,97,97,91 91,89,87,81,74 72**
toteswingers: 1&2 £21.50, 1&3 £4.60, 2&3 £18.50 CSF £124.25 CT £657.63 TOTE £7.10: £1.90, £7.90, £1.20; EX 113.20 TRIFECTA Not won..
Owner Bridget Houlston, Chris Jeffery & Co **Bred** Carl Holt **Trained** Huby, N Yorks

■ Stewards' Enquiry : Matthew Cosham £650: changed boots after weighing out
Ashley Morgan £650: changed boots after weighing out

FOCUS
A weak apprentice riders' sprint where those drawn low held a big advantage. The winner had plummeted in the weights and showed his first real form this year.
Chosen One(IRE) Official explanation: trainer could offer no explanation for the apparent improvement of form.

2437 BRITISH STALLION STUDS SUPPORTING BRITISH RACING E B F MAIDEN FILLIES' STKS 5f
7:05 (7:06) (Class 5) 2-Y-O £3,203 (£946; £473) **Stalls** Low

Form RPR
1 **Satsuma** 2-9-0 0.. MichaelStainton 6 80+
(David Brown) *chsd ldrs: led over 1f out: styd on strly* **14/1**
05 **2** *2 3/4* **Lady Poppy**[36] 1474 2-9-0 0.. AndrewMullen 4 68
(George Moore) *led: edgd lft after 100yds: hdd over 1f out: sn outpcd* **14/1**
3 *3 1/2* **Denbigh Raur (IRE)** 2-9-0 0.. DavidNolan 5 56
(Ann Duffield) *mid-div: hdwy over 2f out: chsng ldng pair over 1f out: kpt on same pce* **40/1**
4 *1 1/4* **Mixed Message (IRE)** 2-9-0 0.................................... RichardMullen 8 51
(Ed McMahon) *dwlt: in rr: kpt on wl fnl 2f: will improve* **10/1**
4 **5** *2 1/4* **Annie Gogh**[36] 1474 2-9-0 0.. DuranFentiman 1 50+
(Tim Easterby) *chsd ldrs: bdly hmpd and lost pl after 100yds: hdwy over 1f out: swtchd rt jst ins fnl f: kpt on* **7/4[1]**
45 **6** *1 1/4* **La Sylphe**[14] 2047 2-9-0 0..(b[1]) GrahamGibbons 2 38
(David Barron) *chsd ldr: hmpd and edgd lft after 100yds: wknd over 1f out* **7/2[2]**
43 **7** *1 1/4* **Hellolini**[11] 2123 2-9-0 0.. LeeNewman 7 34
(Robin Bastiman) *chsd ldrs: wknd over 1f out* **12/1**
8 *nk* **Dinkie** 2-9-0 0.. TomEaves 13 33
(Ollie Pears) *in rr: sme hdwy over 2f out: nvr on terms* **33/1**
9 *5* **Kendal Princess (IRE)** 2-9-0 0.................................. DanielTudhope 12 15
(David O'Meara) *s.i.s: sn outpcd and bhd: nvr on terms* **20/1**
05 **10** *2* **Sound Affects**[17] 1949 2-9-0 0.. TonyHamilton 9 8
(Alan Brown) *chsd ldrs: wknd 2f out* **100/1**
4 **11** *2 1/4* **Must Be Me**[22] 1767 2-9-0 0.. AdrianNicholls 11
(Eve Johnson Houghton) *s.i.s: swtchd lft after s: reminders over 2f out: nvr on terms* **7/1[3]**
65 **12** *hd* **Mace The Ace**[18] 1911 2-8-11 0.. DaleSwift(3) 10
(David C Griffiths) *mid-div: hung rt and lost pl 2f out* **20/1**

58.38s (-1.42) **Going Correction** -0.20s/f (Firm) **12** Ran SP% **117.1**
Speed ratings (Par 90): **103,98,93,91,87 85,83,82,74,71 68,67**
toteswingers: 1&2 £23.50, 1&3 £12.70, 2&3 £117.00 CSF £179.82 TOTE £20.80: £5.10, £4.00, £10.60; EX 171.70 TRIFECTA Not won..
Owner John Kilbride, Adam Watson, James Hughes **Bred** Sarah Stoneham **Trained** Averham Park, Notts

■ Stewards' Enquiry : Andrew Mullen three-day ban: careless riding (8, 9, 11 June)

FOCUS
This ordinary juvenile fillies' maiden saw few land a blow and those racing on the pace near the far rail proved at a real advantage.

NOTEBOOK
Satsuma ran out a taking debut winner. She showed decent early dash and got over to the inside. She went clear without her rider needing to get overly serious with her and, while this was a messy affair, she clearly has a decent engine. Quick ground looks important to her cause and she has a deal of scope. (op 16-1 tchd 20-1)
Lady Poppy also got across early and went with the winner for a long way, but was ultimately well outclassed. She had plenty go her way, but it was her best display to date switched to quick ground. (op 12-1)
Denbigh Raur(IRE) shaped nicely and looks sure to come on for the initial experience. She ought to get another furlong this year.
Mixed Message(IRE) didn't have the best draw for his debut and proved easy to back. She did her best to get involved and left the impression he would be plenty sharper next time. (op 12-1)
Annie Gogh had the plum draw and proved popular with quicker ground expected to suit. She lost out when the door shut on her early on, however, and she's no doubt better than this. (op 9-4 tchd 11-4 in a place)

2438 FOLLOW US ON FACEBOOK AND TWITTER (S) STKS 7f
7:35 (7:36) (Class 6) 3-4-Y-0 £1,704 (£503; £251) **Stalls** Centre

Form RPR
03-0 **1** **Ballista (IRE)**[20] 1844 4-9-5 87.................................... GrahamGibbons 8 68+
(Tom Dascombe) *led 1f: w ldr: led over 4f out: clr over 2f out: eased towards fin* **5/6[1]**
652- **2** *4* **Cathcart Castle**[163] 7496 4-9-11 56.................................. DanielTudhope 6 59
(Simon West) *chsd ldrs: kpt on to take 2nd last 100yds* **10/1**
00- **3** *3 1/2* **Oakbrook**[266] 5681 3-8-8 0.. TonyHamilton 9 40
(Ann Duffield) *mid-div: hdwy over 2f out: styd on same pce fnl f* **50/1**
6-30 **4** *3/4* **Becksies**[4] 2336 3-8-3 42.. PatrickMathers 12 33
(Paul Midgley) *chsd ldrs: one pce fnl 2f* **14/1**
-500 **5** *hd* **Maggie Mey (IRE)**[18] 1917 4-9-6 63...........................(b[1]) MickyFenton 7 42
(Paul Midgley) *chsd ldrs: wnt 2nd over 2f out: wknd fnl f* **9/2[2]**
/P0- **6** *nse* **Jan Smuts (IRE)**[48] 7214 4-9-5 45..............................(tp) JamesSullivan 3 41
(Wilf Storey) *s.s: reminders after s: hdwy over 2f out: swtchd rt over 1f out: nrst fin* **66/1**
5000 **7** *2 1/4* **Stamp Duty (IRE)**[13] 2091 4-9-8 54.................................. DaleSwift(3) 4 41
(Suzzanne France) *sn in rr: kpt on fnl 2f: nvr a factor* **14/1**
5414 **8** *3 1/2* **Point At Issue (IRE)**[42] 1353 3-9-0 66..........................(b) AdrianNicholls 2 28
(David Nicholls) *chsd ldrs: sn drvn along: hmpd bnd over 4f out: wknd over 1f out* **7/1[3]**
0 **9** *1 1/4* **Dragon Spirit (IRE)**[6] 2262 3-8-8 0................................ LeeNewman 10 18
(Noel Wilson) *s.i.s: a in rr* **50/1**
500- **10** *8* **Indycisive**[215] 5489 4-9-5 42.. KellyHarrison 11
(Simon West) *s.s: sn wl bhd: t.o over 3f out* **50/1**
2-00 **11** *25* **Italian Ice**[10] 2139 3-8-3 41.. DuranFentiman 1
(Bryan Smart) *led after 1f: hdd over 4f out: lost pl over 2f out: sn heavily eased: t.o* **40/1**

1m 25.89s (-1.11) **Going Correction** -0.20s/f (Firm)
WFA 3 from 4yo 11lb **11** Ran SP% **117.5**
Speed ratings (Par 101): **98,93,89,88,88 88,85,81,80,71 42**
toteswingers: 1&2 £2.80, 1&3 £22.40, 2&3 £84.10 CSF £10.19 TOTE £1.80: £1.10, £2.60, £11.60; EX 13.00 Trifecta £227.00 Pool: £411.12 - 1.34 winning units..The winner was bought in for 11,000gns.
Owner Well Done Top Man Partnership **Bred** Sj Partnership **Trained** Malpas, Cheshire

FOCUS
An ordinary seller and the winner won as he was entitled to.
Maggie Mey(IRE) Official explanation: jockey said that the filly hung left

2439 PIN POINT RECRUITMENT H'CAP 5f
8:05 (8:06) (Class 4) (0-80,80) 3-Y-0+ £4,075 (£1,212; £606; £303) **Stalls** Low

Form RPR
0-01 **1** **Nomoreblondes**[17] 1954 8-8-12 73..............................(v) NedCurtis(7) 13 81
(Paul Midgley) *chsd ldrs: chal 1f out: styd on to ld wl ins fnl f* **16/1**
-544 **2** *nk* **Bronze Beau**[8] 2195 5-9-10 78......................................(t) JamesSullivan 6 85
(Linda Stubbs) *led: hdd and no ex towards fin* **7/2[1]**
4-02 **3** *1 1/2* **Select Committee**[10] 2140 7-9-3 71..........................(v) MichaelO'Connell 5 74
(John Quinn) *chsd ldrs: n.m.r 1f out and ins fnl f: kpt on* **5/1[3]**
0-40 **4** *nk* **Lost In Paris (IRE)**[30] 1602 6-9-12 80.........................(p) DuranFentiman 12 80+
(Tim Easterby) *dwlt: in rr: hdwy on outer over 1f out: styd on wl towards fin* **12/1**
00-0 **5** *1 1/2* **Lucky Numbers (IRE)**[36] 1478 6-9-12 80..............(v[1]) DanielTudhope 11 75+
(David O'Meara) *chsd ldrs: outpcd over 3f out: swtchd rt and kpt on fnl f* **4/1[2]**
02-0 **6** *nk* **Tabaret**[53] 1168 9-8-12 66 oh1.. TonyCulhane 14 60
(Richard Whitaker) *mid-div: hdwy over 1f out: kpt on wl ins fnl f* **25/1**
00-0 **7** *1* **Indian Trail**[20] 1868 12-9-8 76.......................................(b) PaulQuinn 8 66
(David Nicholls) *in rr-div: hdwy 2f out: kpt on same pce: nvr a threat* **12/1**
1-0 **8** *1 1/2* **Bertoliver**[8] 2195 8-9-9 80.. RyanClark(3) 3 65
(Stuart Williams) *chsd ldrs: edgd rt and fdd fnl f* **8/1**
25-0 **9** *1* **Black Annis Bower**[13] 2084 4-9-1 69.............................. DavidNolan 7 50
(Michael Easterby) *chsd ldrs: wknd over 1f out* **28/1**
562- **10** *3/4* **Irish Boy (IRE)**[240] 6456 4-8-12 66.................................. MickyFenton 1 45
(Paul Midgley) *mid-div: hdwy over 2f out: wknd over 1f out* **11/2**
/6-0 **11** *2 3/4* **Nickel Silver**[21] 1828 7-9-7 75......................................(v) TomEaves 4 44
(Bryan Smart) *in rr: sme hdwy 2f out: wknd over 1f out* **20/1**

58.31s (-1.49) **Going Correction** -0.20s/f (Firm)
WFA 3 from 4yo+ 8lb **11** Ran SP% **118.7**
Speed ratings (Par 105): **103,102,100,99,97 96,95,92,91,89 85**
toteswingers: 1&2 £9.90, 1&3 £23.10, 2&3 £4.70 CSF £70.50 CT £338.32 TOTE £18.50: £5.40, £1.90, £1.60; EX 117.50 Trifecta £205.80 Part won. Pool: £278.12 - 0.64 winning units..
Owner Anthony D Copley **Bred** P John And Redmyre Bloodstock **Trained** Westow, N Yorks

FOCUS
A modest but strong-run sprint and the first pair dominated late on against the far rail. The bare form could possibly be worth a bit more.
Lucky Numbers(IRE) Official explanation: trainer's representative said said that the gelding was unsuited by the good to firm ground

2440 LESLIE PETCH H'CAP 1m 3f 214y
8:35 (8:36) (Class 5) (0-75,74) 3-Y-0+ £2,264 (£673; £336; £168) **Stalls** Low

Form RPR
6602 **1** **O Ma Lad (IRE)**[7] 2237 4-9-3 70................................ ThomasBrown(7) 14 79
(Sylvester Kirk) *in rr: hdwy over 3f out: styd on to ld last 100yds: hld on towards fin* **11/4[1]**
040- **2** *nk* **Raleigh Quay (IRE)**[265] 5729 5-8-10 61......................... ShaneBKelly(5) 4 69
(Micky Hammond) *in rr: hdwy over 7f out: drvn over 5f out: outpcd over 3f out: hdwy and edgd lft 2f out: ev ch on ins fnl f: no ex towards fin* **22/1**
00-1 **3** *hd* **Yahrab (IRE)**[13] 2093 7-9-11 71.................................... GrahamGibbons 2 79
(Declan Carroll) *drvn along early: hdwy to chse ldrs 7f out: outpcd and lost pl over 3f out: hdwy on outside over 1f out: kpt on wl towards fin* **9/2[3]**
536- **4** *1* **King's Counsel (IRE)**[155] 4612 6-9-7 67..................(v) DanielTudhope 13 73
(David O'Meara) *sn chsng ldr: upsides over 5f out: led 4f out: hdd ins fnl f: no ex* **12/1**
0135 **5** *1 1/4* **Light The City (IRE)**[13] 2093 5-9-6 66............................. JamesSullivan 8 70
(Ruth Carr) *trckd ldrs: wnt 2nd over 3f out: kpt on one pce fnl f* **6/1**
66-3 **6** *nse* **Zaplamation (IRE)**[54] 1154 7-9-2 62......................... MichaelO'Connell 15 66
(John Quinn) *trckd ldrs: kpt on one pce fnl f* **10/1**
-000 **7** *5* **Pertuis (IRE)**[32] 1562 6-8-8 61.................................... KatieDowson(7) 9 57
(Micky Hammond) *dwlt: in rr: kpt on fnl 2f: nvr a factor* **66/1**
503- **8** *3 1/2* **The Oil Magnate**[209] 7162 7-9-10 70............................... TomEaves 11 61
(Michael Dods) *hld up in rr: nvr on terms* **25/1**
500- **9** *4* **Dynamic Drive (IRE)**[149] 7002 5-9-5 70........................ LucyAlexander(5) 10 54
(Barry Murtagh) *hld up in rr: hdwy 7f out: lost pl over 3f out* **28/1**
000- **10** *16* **Comical**[244] 6345 3-8-11 74... SilvestreDeSousa 3 33
(Mark Johnston) *led: drvn and hdd 4f out: lost pl over 2f out: eased whn bhd ins fnl f* **3/1[2]**
400- **11** *9* **Spiders Star**[221] 6915 9-9-1 61...................................... KellyHarrison 1
(Simon West) *chsd ldrs: drvn over 5f out: lost pl 3f out: sn bhd: eased ins fnl f* **33/1**

2m 35.31s (-3.59) **Going Correction** -0.20s/f (Firm)
WFA 3 from 4yo+ 17lb **11** Ran SP% **117.0**
Speed ratings (Par 103): **103,102,102,102,101 101,97,95,92,82 76**
toteswingers: 1&2 £19.80, 1&3 £1.80, 2&3 £22.30 CSF £69.72 CT £268.91 TOTE £3.20: £1.50, £6.60, £1.30; EX 92.00 TRIFECTA Not won..
Owner John Duddy **Bred** Mrs Brid Cosgrove **Trained** Upper Lambourn, Berks

FOCUS
A competitive handicap, run at a strong pace and it saw a tight finish. The winner was well in and did not quite need to match his Newbury run.
Light The City(IRE) Official explanation: jockey said that the gelding finished lame

2441 ELLERY HILL RATING RELATED MAIDEN STKS 7f
9:05 (9:07) (Class 6) 3-Y-0+ £2,045 (£603; £302) **Stalls** Centre

Form RPR
205- **1** **Dutch Rose (IRE)**[268] 5613 3-8-11 62............................ DanielTudhope 2 64+
(David O'Meara) *trckd ldrs: led after 2f: hung rt bnd and wd 3f out: sn hdd: led ins fnl f: hld on towards fin* **15/8[1]**
43-4 **2** *1/2* **Love Island**[18] 1912 3-8-11 65.. TonyCulhane 4 62
(Richard Whitaker) *sn chsng ldrs: upsides over 2f out: led narrowly appr fnl f: hdd last 100yds: no ex cl home* **9/1**

4-0 **3** shd **Rex Romanorum (IRE)**[13] 2095 4-9-11 62 PJMcDonald 8 69
(Patrick Holmes) *led 1f: chsd ldrs: slt ld over 2f out: hdd appr fnl f: no ex clsng stages* **14/1**
65-0 **4** ½ **Charles De Mille**[34] 1523 4-9-11 62 AndrewMullen 7 68+
(George Moore) *hld up in rr-div: drvn over 3f out: hdwy over 2f out: upsides over 1f out: kpt on same pce last 75yds* **25/1**
65-0 **5** 2¾ **Magic Bounty**[23] 1758 3-9-0 60 DuranFentiman 5 56
(Tim Easterby) *mid-div: hdwy over 3f out: chsng ldrs on outer over 1f out: fdd fnl f* **16/1**
0343 **6** ½ **Glennten**[25] 1709 3-9-0 65 LeeNewman 9 55
(Sylvester Kirk) *chsd ldrs: sn pushed along: rdn over 2f out: fdd fnl f* **4/1**[2]
603- **7** 4½ **Seattle Sounder (IRE)**[204] 7248 3-8-11 62 DaleSwift(3) 11 43
(Ann Duffield) *mid-div: outpcd and lost pl over 3f out: sme hdwy 2f out: nvr on terms* **6/1**[3]
06-0 **8** ¾ **Benidorm**[23] 1755 4-9-11 55 (b[1]) TonyHamilton 13 45
(John Wainwright) *s.i.s: sme hdwy 2f out: nvr on terms* **50/1**
030- **9** 2½ **Rock Of Monet**[266] 5690 3-9-0 64 (v[1]) MickyFenton 3 34
(Michael Bell) *w ldr: led after 1f: hdd after 2f: upsides over 2f out: wknd over 1f out* **16/1**
000- **10** 1½ **Rain Dance**[256] 6001 3-8-11 62 SilvestreDeSousa 10 27
(Eve Johnson Houghton) *in rr: drvn over 3f out: lost pl 2f out* **16/1**
0-50 **11** 12 **Praxios**[45] 1269 4-9-11 62 KellyHarrison 6
(Noel Wilson) *s.i.s: a bhd* **14/1**
0046 **R** **Pulsatilla**[21] 1823 4-9-8 59 (b) TomEaves 1
(Bryan Smart) *ref to r: lft in stalls: tk no part* **20/1**

1m 25.73s (-1.27) **Going Correction** -0.20s/f (Firm)
WFA 3 from 4yo 11lb 12 Ran SP% **120.6**
Speed ratings (Par 101): **99,98,98,97,94 94,88,88,85,83 69,**
toteswingers: 1&2 £7.00, 1&3 £6.80, 2&3 £11.80 CSF £19.79 TOTE £2.20: £1.40, £3.10, £2.80; EX 15.40 TRIFECTA Not won..
Owner Favourites Racing XXIV **Bred** Joseph Kennedy **Trained** Nawton, N Yorks

FOCUS
An ordinary maiden and pretty limited form with few solid. The winner's best form since her debut.
T/Jkpt: £25,000.00 to a £1 stake. Pool: £7,124.15. 1.00 winning tickets. T/Plt: £363.30 to a £1 stake. Pool £51,726.78. 103.92 winning tickets. T/Qpdt: £8.90 to a £1 stake. Pool £4,492.90. 371.98 winning tickets. WG

2407 GOODWOOD (R-H)

Friday, May 25

OFFICIAL GOING: Straight course - good (good to firm in places); round course - good to firm
Wind: Fresh, across (towards stands) Weather: Glorious

2442 GOODWOOD MAIDEN AUCTION STKS 5f
2:00 (2:00) (Class 5) 2-Y-O **£3,234** (£962; £481; £240) **Stalls** High

Form RPR
5 **1** **Tommy's Secret**[15] 1997 2-8-11 0 ow2 RichardHughes 3 77
(Jane Chapple-Hyam) *racd towards outer: chsd ldng pair: wnt 2nd wl over 1f out: rdn to ld jst ins fnl f: styd on wl* **5/2**[1]
2 2¾ **Whistling Buddy** 2-9-1 0 SebSanders 4 71+
(Peter Makin) *green preliminaries: chsd ldr: led 1/2-way: urged along over 1f out: hdd and one pce jst ins fnl f* **10/1**
33 **3** 1¼ **Fiducia**[22] 1767 2-8-8 0 HayleyTurner 6 60
(Simon Dow) *chsd ldrs but nt on terms: wnt 3rd over 1f out: one pce and no imp after* **4/1**[3]
4 3½ **Smiling Shark (USA)** 2-8-11 0 RyanMoore 1 50+
(Robert Cowell) *sn last: effrt on wd outside 2f out: sn no prog and btn* **11/4**[2]
03 **5** ½ **Emperor's Daughter**[11] 2135 2-7-13 0 DarrenEgan(5) 5 41
(Tim Pitt) *racd towards nr side rail: led to 1/2-way: wknd over 1f out* **8/1**
6 10 **Con Leche** 2-8-11 0 WilliamBuick 2 12
(Scott Dixon) *a in rr: effrt 2f out: sn wknd rapidly: eased ins fnl f: t.o* **6/1**

58.22s (-1.98) **Going Correction** -0.075s/f (Good) 6 Ran SP% **109.7**
Speed ratings (Par 93): **98,93,91,86,85 69**
Tote Swingers: 1&2 £4.50, 1&3 £2.10, 2&3 £6.40 CSF £25.26 TOTE £3.50: £2.60, £4.50; EX 23.50.
Owner Mrs Jane Chapple-Hyam **Bred** Henry And Mrs Rosemary Moszkowicz **Trained** Dalham, Suffolk

FOCUS
Quite an ordinary juvenile maiden for the course. The form looks quite straightforward.

NOTEBOOK
Tommy's Secret shaped with enough promise on his soft-ground debut at Chester to suggest there'd be a maiden in him, and he improved for the quicker surface, picking up quite nicely to get well on top late. The fact Richard Hughes weighed in 2lb heavier (girth strap was changed) means his effort needs to be marked up and he's clearly a fair prospect for one who cost so little. (op 11-4 tchd 3-1)
Whistling Buddy, half-brother to Silk Bounty, placed over 5f as a 2yo, out of a 5f-6f winner, was green beforehand but showed plenty of ability in the race, just losing out to one with more experience. He displayed a ton of speed and can probably win a small maiden. (op 8-1 tchd 11-1)
Fiducia helps to set the level of the form, having already finished third twice coming into the race. She should be helped by 6f, but may struggle to win a maiden. (tchd 9-2)
Smiling Shark(USA), whose dam is an unraced half-sister to a couple of US Grade 3 winners over 7f & 1m, was solid in the market but couldn't go the early gallop and made only modest late headway. (op 3-1 tchd 5-2)
Emperor's Daughter showed plenty of early pace, but the stands' rail probably wasn't the place to be and she stopped quite quickly once headed. (op 15-2 tchd 7-1)
Con Leche, whose dam was a 5f winner on her 2yo debut, was soon behind and the first one beaten. (op 13-2 tchd 7-1)

2443 TURFTV FOR BETTING SHOPS BONUS H'CAP 5f
2:35 (2:35) (Class 5) (0-75,75) 3-Y-O **£3,234** (£962; £481; £240) **Stalls** High

Form RPR
221- **1** **Blanc De Chine (IRE)**[175] 7607 3-9-2 **70** JimmyFortune 4 78
(Peter Makin) *hld up bhd ldrs: prog to ld jst ins fnl f: rdn and r.o wl* **7/2**[1]
3546 **2** 1¼ **Le King Beau (USA)**[8] 2205 3-8-11 **68** SeanLevey(3) 1 71
(John Bridger) *pressed ldng pair on outer: rdn 2f out: nt qckn over 1f out: styd on to take 2nd nr fin* **12/1**
2124 **3** shd **Ring For Baileys**[34] 1514 3-8-10 **64** HayleyTurner 8 66
(Chris Dwyer) *racd towards nr side: pressed ldr: narrow ld fr 2f out to jst ins fnl f: kpt on* **9/1**
1262 **4** nk **Welease Bwian (IRE)**[9] 2166 3-8-8 **62** (t) WilliamCarson 3 63
(Stuart Williams) *hld up bhd ldrs on outer and racd awkwardly: plld out and drvn over 1f out: styd on: nvr able to chal* **4/1**[2]
2-00 **5** 1½ **Hannibal Hayes (USA)**[20] 1843 3-8-9 **63** RyanMoore 6 59
(Jeremy Noseda) *wl in tch: rdn and nt qckn 2f out: kpt on same pce after* **11/2**[3]
-421 **6** hd **Bookiesindexdotnet**[58] 1063 3-9-7 **75** RichardHughes 5 70
(J R Jenkins) *led: narrowly hdd and pushed along 2f out: wl on terms and stl pushed along 1f out: fdd last 100yds* **11/2**[3]
4-25 **7** 2¼ **Christopher Chua (IRE)**[29] 1622 3-8-13 **67** SebSanders 2 54
(Simon Dow) *awkward s then stdd: hld up in last pair and detached: effrt 2f out: no hdwy after: fdd fnl f* **16/1**
1-23 **8** 6 **Hey Fiddle Fiddle (IRE)**[84] 769 3-8-10 **64** (b) MichaelHills 7 30
(Charles Hills) *awkward s: detached in last pair: no prog 2f out: sn wl bhd* **6/1**

57.81s (-2.39) **Going Correction** -0.075s/f (Good) 8 Ran SP% **110.9**
Speed ratings (Par 99): **101,99,98,98,95 95,92,82**
Tote Swingers: 1&2 £9.20, 1&3 £5.10, 2&3 £17.90 CSF £42.44 CT £334.04 TOTE £4.00: £1.40, £3.30, £2.50; EX 56.50 TRIFECTA Not won..
Owner R P Marchant & Mrs E Lee **Bred** Newlands House Stud **Trained** Ogbourne Maisey, Wilts

FOCUS
Just a modest 3yo sprint handicap, but it should produce winners at a similar level. The second and third set the standard.

2444 WILLIS LEASE FINANCE CORPORATION H'CAP 7f
3:10 (3:10) (Class 4) (0-85,85) 4-Y-O+ **£4,851** (£1,443; £721; £360) **Stalls** Low

Form RPR
1600 **1** **Shifting Star (IRE)**[18] 1924 7-9-4 **85** SeanLevey(3) 8 93
(John Bridger) *mde all: styd on far rail in st: rdn 2f out: kpt on wl to hold on fnl f* **18/1**
4410 **2** nk **Piscean (USA)**[19] 1885 7-9-4 **82** GeorgeBaker 3 89
(Tom Keddy) *hld up in last quartet: stdy prog gng wl fr 3f out: wnt 2nd 1f out: rdn and nt qckn last 150yds* **8/1**[3]
0-56 **3** hd **Corporal Maddox**[14] 2029 5-9-4 **82** StevieDonohoe 9 88
(Jamie Osborne) *hld up in last pair: sme prog 2f out: weaved through fnl f: swtchd rt 100yds out: fin wl* **10/1**
11-0 **4** ¾ **Konstantin (IRE)**[25] 1708 4-9-1 **79** HayleyTurner 7 83
(Marcus Tregoning) *trckd wnr: asked to chal over 2f out but hanging and sn lost 2nd: styd cl up after but nvr qcknd* **5/1**[1]
6040 **5** 1¼ **Kingscroft (IRE)**[20] 1865 4-9-6 **84** MircoDemuro 11 85
(Mark Johnston) *trckd ldrs: rdn 2f out: tried to cl over 1f out: one pce after* **11/1**
26-4 **6** ½ **Kingsdine (IRE)**[14] 2023 5-9-6 **84** TomMcLaughlin 12 84
(Malcolm Saunders) *t.k.h: racd on outer: prom: disp 2nd over 2f out to 1f out: fdd last 100yds* **8/1**[3]
0-00 **7** hd **George Baker (IRE)**[23] 1752 5-9-0 **78** FrankieDettori 5 80
(George Baker) *hld up in last quartet: looking for room 3f out: prog 2f out: one pce and hld fnl f: bmpd last 100yds* **8/1**[3]
-050 **8** 1 **Space Station**[13] 2068 6-9-2 **80** (b) SebSanders 6 76
(Simon Dow) *racd on outer: trckd ldrs: rdn over 2f out: no imp wl over 1f out: one pce* **11/1**
4311 **9** 1 **Indian Art (IRE)**[31] 1587 6-9-1 **79** RichardHughes 10 73
(Sylvester Kirk) *racd on outer: hld up in midfield: rdn and no prog 2f out: one pce after* **11/2**[2]
00-0 **10** hd **Rougette**[23] 1752 4-9-1 **79** MichaelHills 1 77
(Charles Hills) *prom on inner: effrt over 2f out: cl up but hld 1f out: fading whn hmpd last 100yds* **22/1**
3-10 **11** hd **Rafaaf (IRE)**[28] 1642 4-9-0 **78** AndreaAtzeni 2 71
(Robert Eddery) *hld up in last pair: rdn on inner over 2f out: no prog* **9/1**
5-20 **12** 16 **Bunce (IRE)**[13] 2071 4-8-13 **77** (p) WilliamBuick 4
(Paul Fitzsimons) *trckd ldrs: rdn and losing pl whn squeezed out 2f out: eased: t.o* **16/1**

1m 26.5s (-0.50) **Going Correction** -0.075s/f (Good) 12 Ran SP% **116.6**
Speed ratings (Par 105): **99,98,98,97,96 95,95,94,93,92 92,74**
Tote Swingers: 1&2 £32.30, 1&3 £24.60, 2&3 £22.00 CSF £152.94 CT £1554.98 TOTE £23.80: £5.60, £2.90, £3.70; EX 210.10 TRIFECTA Not won..
Owner Night Shadow Syndicate **Bred** Hardys Of Kilkeel Ltd **Trained** Liphook, Hants
■ Stewards' Enquiry : Sean Levey two-day ban: use of whip (June 8-9)
Michael Hills one-day ban: careless riding (June 8)

FOCUS
A good, competitive handicap run at a fair gallop. The first three have all run well here before.

2445 CASCO COCKED HAT STKS (LISTED RACE) (C&G) 1m 3f
3:45 (3:45) (Class 1) 3-Y-O **£19,848** (£7,525; £3,766; £1,876) **Stalls** High

Form RPR
3 **1** **Michelangelo**[20] 1859 3-9-0 0 WilliamBuick 1 106+
(John Gosden) *s.s and rousted along to rcvr: chsd ldr 1/2-way: outpcd and rdn over 3f out: grad clsd fr 2f out: drvn ahd last 100yds* **4/6**[1]
-111 **2** ½ **Expense Claim (IRE)**[6] 2269 3-9-0 85 JimmyFortune 5 105
(Andrew Balding) *led: stretched away 4f out and sn 4 l clr: drvn 2f out: edgd rt 1f out: collared last 100yds* **9/4**[2]
12-6 **3** 1¼ **Perennial**[37] 1455 3-9-0 105 MichaelHills 4 103
(Charles Hills) *hld up and sn last: outpcd whn wnt 3rd 3f out: clsd w wnr on ldr fr 2f out: rdn and nt qckn jst over 1f out: one pce* **5/1**[3]
0-00 **4** 32 **Polydamos**[11] 2129 3-9-0 70 (b[1]) MircoDemuro 3 45
(Harry Dunlop) *restless stalls: chsd ldr to 1/2-way: dropped to last and wknd 3f out: t.o* **100/1**

2m 24.61s (-1.89) **Going Correction** -0.075s/f (Good) 4 Ran SP% **108.4**
Speed ratings (Par 107): **103,102,101,78**
CSF £2.45 TOTE £1.60; EX 2.30.
Owner B E Nielsen **Bred** Denford Stud And Balmerino Bloodstock **Trained** Newmarket, Suffolk

FOCUS
Not much of a Derby trial, but a likeable effort from the lightly-raced Michelangelo, who can surely do better still. This is probably not form to take too literally though.

NOTEBOOK
Michelangelo was slowly away and had to be rousted to get into his stride, but still proved good enough to reel in a bang in-form horse who had enjoyed an easy lead and stolen a vital few lengths running down the hill. Having made a really pleasing debut against smart types in a Listed race at Newmarket, he still displayed obvious signs of greenness (looked a bit lost on the track) and certainly appears more of a long-term project, so there's a good chance the King Edward VII at Royal Ascot will come too soon in his development. Stamina looks his forte at present and the fact Masked Marvel, representing the same owner/trainer/jockey combination, took this last year en route to landing the St Leger, suggests Doncaster may be on this one's agenda later in the campaign also. He is a fine prospect. (op 5-6 tchd Evens in a place)
Expense Claim(IRE), 3-3 this year and reappearing just six days after readily landing the London Gold Cup from a mark of just 85, was gifted an easy lead and Jimmy Fortune was probably right to kick when he did, appearing to have them all beaten with 2f to run. However, near the far rail probably wasn't the place to be, and the horse's stamina slowly ebbed away. This still represented a further step forward and he could be a type for the Hampton Court Stakes at Royal Ascot. (op 15-8)

Perennial ran poorly in the Fielden Stakes on his reappearance and this was a truer reflection of his capabilities. A half-brother to Canadian International winner Redwood, he'll benefit from a truer test in future. (tchd 6-1)

Polydamos was making up the numbers and duly struggled in the first-time blinkers.

2446 IBA H'CAP — 6f

4:20 (4:20) (Class 2) (0-105,105) 3-Y-O+

£12,450 (£3,728; £1,864; £932; £466; £234) **Stalls** High

Form — RPR

1032 **1** **Chilli Green**[14] 2024 5-8-5 **87**.....(p) DarrenEgan(5) 3 — 92
(Lee Carter) *pressed ldr and racd towards outer: narrow ld over 2f out: jnd 1f out: edgd rt but jst prevailed* **8/1**

00-0 **2** *nse* **Oneladyowner**[20] 1844 4-8-9 **86** oh2..... WilliamBuick 1 — 91
(David Brown) *racd wdst of all: prog fr last pair 1/2-way: drvn to chal over 1f out: w wnr thrght fnl f: jst pipped* **7/1**

050- **3** *½* **Piazza San Pietro**[264] 5758 6-9-1 **92**..... RyanMoore 8 — 95
(Zoe Davison) *hld up in last pair and racd towards nr side: plld out and drvn over 1f out: r.o and edgd rt fnl f: tk 3rd last strides* **25/1**

0-00 **4** *½* **Fathsta (IRE)**[13] 2068 7-8-11 **88**..... StevieDonohoe 2 — 90
(David Simcock) *taken down early: trckd ldrs and racd on outer: drvn to chal over 1f out: tried to find way between first pair ins fnl f: hld whn no room last 50yds* **11/2**[3]

210- **5** *hd* **Ahtoug**[83] 791 4-9-5 **96**..... FrankieDettori 7 — 97
(Mahmood Al Zarooni) *racd towards nr side rail: hld up bhd ldrs: effrt 2f out: shkn up and styd on same pce: nvr able to chal* **7/2**[2]

0-15 **6** *1 ¼* **Fanrouge (IRE)**[7] 2236 3-8-3 **89**..... KieranO'Neill 6 — 84
(Malcolm Saunders) *pressed ldr: upsides over 2f out to over 1f out: fdd fnl f* **12/1**

-454 **7** *2 ¼* **Parisian Pyramid (IRE)**[19] 1885 6-9-0 **91**..... JimmyFortune 9 — 81
(Kevin Ryan) *racd towards nr side rail: led to over 2f out: steadily lost pl* **15/8**[1]

25-5 **8** *3 ¾* **Triple Aspect (IRE)**[44] 1316 6-10-0 **105**..... LiamJones 5 — 83
(Jeremy Gask) *hld up in rr: prog on outer fr 1/2-way: cl up 2f out: wknd rapidly jst over 1f out* **20/1**

1m 10.32s (-1.88) **Going Correction** -0.075s/f (Good)
WFA 3 from 4yo+ 9lb — 8 Ran SP% **112.3**
Speed ratings (Par 109): **109,108,108,107,107 105,102,97**
Tote Swingers: 1&2 £7.70, 1&3 £14.20, 2&3 £16.50 CSF £59.92 CT £1330.64 TOTE £9.10: £2.10, £2.20, £4.90; EX 90.70 Trifecta £879.60 Part won. Pool: £1,118.74 - 0.40 winning units..

Owner Peter M Crane **Bred** P M Crane **Trained** Epsom, Surrey

■ Stewards' Enquiry : Darren Egan three-day ban: careless riding (8, 9, 11 June)

FOCUS

Further evidence that the stands' rail wasn't the place to be with favourite Parisian Pyramid and the strong-travelling Ahtoug both finding little against it. The main action unfolded centre-track. Weakish form for the grade, if sound amongst the principals.

NOTEBOOK

Chilli Green, worn down late from the same mark on soft ground at Ascot the time before, appreciated the faster surface and was registering her first victory on turf. She shouldn't go up much and can continue to give a good account. (op 12-1)

Oneladyowner, 2lb out of the handicap and well beaten on his reappearance, showed a marked improvement in form and would have won had he been able to run from his correct mark. He's decent on his day. (op 8-1 tchd 9-1)

Piazza San Pietro, making his seasonal reappearance, was held up on the stands' rail early, but picked up really well once switched away from it. This was a promising debut for his new trainer. (op 22-1)

Fathsta(IRE) had his chance and was held, albeit set to finish close up, when squeezed out by the front pair late on. (op 6-1 tchd 13-2)

Ahtoug fared better than the bare result, traveling strongly on the slowest ground, and deserves another chance. (tchd 3-1)

Parisian Pyramid(IRE) was probably on the slowest ground and stopped too quickly for this to be his true form. (op 13-8)

2447 TURFTV BONUS H'CAP — 1m 4f

4:55 (4:55) (Class 4) (0-85,84) 4-Y-O+ **£4,851** (£1,443; £721; £360) **Stalls** High

Form — RPR

21-2 **1** **Figaro**[20] 1841 4-9-5 **82**..... RyanMoore 2 — 97+
(William Haggas) *mde all: rdn 2f out: styd on strly fr over 1f out* **2/1**[1]

1-31 **2** *2* **Lady Rosamunde**[7] 2237 4-8-11 **74**.....(p) TadhgO'Shea 8 — 86+
(Marcus Tregoning) *hld up disputing 6th: prog fr 4f out: rdn to chse wnr 2f out: 2 l down whn hung bdly rt fnl f: no imp after* **2/1**[1]

00-4 **3** *7* **Kathleen Frances**[18] 1940 5-8-12 **75**..... TedDurcan 4 — 76
(Mark H Tompkins) *chsd wnr: rdn and no imp whn lost 2nd 2f out: wknd fnl f: fin tired* **13/2**[2]

32-2 **4** *4 ½* **Woop Woop (IRE)**[67] 960 4-9-0 **77**..... WilliamBuick 10 — 71
(Ian Williams) *hld up in last pair: rapid prog on outer fr 4f out to chse ldrs 3f out: wknd 2f out* **9/1**[3]

264- **5** *hd* **Stentorian (IRE)**[146] 7139 4-8-6 **72**..... HarryBentley(3) 6 — 65
(Gary Moore) *chsd ldng pair to 3f out: steadily wknd* **25/1**

224- **6** *shd* **Crafty Roberto**[27] 4-8-12 **75**..... RichardHughes 9 — 68
(Noel Quinlan) *trckd ldrs disputing 4th: no imp 3f out: lost pl and btn over 2f out: wknd* **16/1**

-030 **7** *1 ¼* **Almail (USA)**[41] 1374 6-9-6 **83**..... FergusSweeney 7 — 74
(Jamie Osborne) *trckd ldrs disputing 4th: effrt 3f out: n.m.r and no prog over 2f out: sn wknd* **25/1**

410- **8** *¾* **Alshazah**[178] 7577 4-9-3 **80**..... JamesMillman 1 — 70
(Rod Millman) *hld up disputing 6th: gng wl enough over 4f out: effrt over 3f out: wknd over 2f out* **12/1**

510- **9** *4 ½* **Gunslinger (FR)**[188] 7017 7-9-2 **84**..... DavidKenny(5) 11 — 67
(Michael Scudamore) *stdd s: t.k.h: hld up in last pair: rdn and no prog over 3f out: no ch after* **28/1**

2m 37.1s (-1.30) **Going Correction** -0.075s/f (Good) — 9 Ran SP% **114.7**
Speed ratings (Par 105): **101,99,95,92,91 91,90,90,87**
Tote Swingers: 1&2 £2.30, 1&3 £3.50, 2&3 £3.40 CSF £5.38 CT £20.06 TOTE £3.00: £1.20, £1.20, £2.10; EX 6.80 Trifecta £24.50 Pool: £1,345.70 - 40.62 winning units..

Owner A Duke & R Smith **Bred** Cheveley Park Stud Ltd **Trained** Newmarket, Suffolk

FOCUS

Two progressive types pulled clear in a modest handicap run at an even tempo. There was little depth to the race.

2448 GOLF AT GOODWOOD FILLIES' H'CAP — 1m

5:30 (5:30) (Class 4) (0-80,77) 3-Y-O

£4,668 (£1,398; £699; £349; £174; £87) **Stalls** Low

Form — RPR

254- **1** **Amber Silk (IRE)**[240] 6440 3-9-5 **75**..... MichaelHills 11 — 84
(Charles Hills) *dropped in fr wd draw and hld up disputing 8th: prog over 2f out: quick move to ld wl over 1f out: in command fnl f: rdn out* **13/2**[3]

21 **2** *¾* **Roxelana (IRE)**[97] 620 3-9-1 **71**..... JimmyFortune 9 — 78+
(Jeremy Noseda) *settled in last pair: urged along 3f out: prog u.p on outer fr 2f out: r.o fnl f to take 2nd nr fin* **7/2**[1]

01- **3** *¾* **Cantal**[211] 7124 3-9-6 **76**..... RyanMoore 4 — 82
(Sir Michael Stoute) *trckd ldrs disputing 5th: quick move to chal 2f out: pressed wnr after: nt qckn and hld fnl f: lost 2nd nr fin* **4/1**[2]

-423 **4** *2 ½* **Play Street**[20] 1853 3-8-7 **63**..... HayleyTurner 5 — 63
(Jonathan Portman) *trckd clr ldng pair: rdn over 2f out: tried to cl over 1f out but outpcd: kpt on one pce after* **16/1**

1-50 **5** *3 ½* **Tinzapeas**[30] 1612 3-9-0 **70**..... MatthewDavies 12 — 62
(Mick Channon) *hld up in last pair: prog over 2f out: outpcd by ldrs over 1f out: wl hld in 5th fnl f: fdd last 100yds* **14/1**

001- **6** *2 ¾* **Forgive**[220] 6934 3-9-7 **77**..... RichardHughes 8 — 63+
(Richard Hannon) *hld up disputing 8th: pushed along over 3f out: clsd 2f out but sn outpcd: wknd fnl f* **4/1**[2]

-04U **7** *2* **Tweet Lady**[24] 1728 3-8-12 **68**..... JamesMillman 2 — 49+
(Rod Millman) *hld up disputing 5th: effrt on inner over 2f out: hld whn bdly hmpd over 1f out: kpt on nr fin* **25/1**

10 **8** *2* **Perfect Fantasy (IRE)**[16] 1985 3-9-2 **72**..... JohnFahy 1 — 48
(Clive Cox) *trckd clr ldng pair: clsd to chal 2f out: wknd over 1f out* **10/1**

403- **9** *½* **Glad Eye Gladys**[286] 5029 3-8-11 **67**..... TedDurcan 10 — 42
(Scott Dixon) *mostly in 7th: rdn over 3f out: sn struggling: wl btn fnl 2f* **20/1**

-214 **10** *½* **Hikma (USA)**[70] 920 3-9-1 **71**..... MircoDemuro 3 — 45
(Mark Johnston) *led after 1f at str pce: hdd & wknd rapidly wl over 1f out* **20/1**

332- **11** *18* **Cockney Rhyme**[189] 7454 3-9-7 **77**..... WilliamBuick 6
(Heather Main) *led 1f: w ldr at str pce to 2f out: wknd rapidly: t.o* **12/1**

1m 38.78s (-1.12) **Going Correction** -0.075s/f (Good) — 11 Ran SP% **118.3**
Speed ratings (Par 98): **102,101,100,98,94 91,89,87,87,86 68**
Tote Swingers: 1&2 £4.90, 1&3 £7.90, 2&3 £4.50 CSF £28.78 CT £106.50 TOTE £6.60: £1.80, £1.70, £2.00; EX 41.60 Trifecta £125.00 Pool: £812.41 - 4.80 winning units..

Owner Jeremy Gompertz **Bred** Mrs J Dempsey **Trained** Lambourn, Berks

FOCUS

A good-looking fillies' handicap, run at a fast pace, and likely decent form for the grade with an unexposed trio clear.

Tweet Lady Official explanation: jockey said that the filly suffered interference in running

T/Plt: £605.70 to a £1 stake. Pool: £60,531.00 - 72.95 winning tickets. T/Qpdt: £83.70 to a £1 stake. Pool: £5,145.00 - 45.45 winning tickets. JN

2414 HAYDOCK (L-H)

Friday, May 25

OFFICIAL GOING: Good to firm (9.6)

Wind: Moderate, behind Weather: Hot and Sunny

2449 PHS WASHROOM SERVICES H'CAP (BETFAIR 10 FURLONG FLAT SERIES QUALIFIER) — 1m 2f 95y

2:20 (2:21) (Class 5) (0-75,78) 3-Y-O **£3,234** (£962; £481; £240) **Stalls** Centre

Form — RPR

004- **1** **Watheeq (USA)**[188] 7493 3-8-12 **66**..... PaulHanagan 6 — 74+
(Roger Varian) *hld up: hdwy 3f out: led over 1f out: edgd lft ins fnl f: hld on wl nr fin* **6/1**[3]

6131 **2** *nk* **Fennell Bay (IRE)**[7] 2246 3-9-10 **78** 6ex..... SilvestreDeSousa 1 — 85+
(Mark Johnston) *midfield: outpcd 3f out: rallied 2f out: styd on ins fnl f: str chal ins fnl 75yds: jst hld* **11/4**[1]

6-30 **3** *1 ½* **Chelsea Mick**[44] 1320 3-8-6 **67**..... JoshBaudains(7) 15 — 71
(John Mackie) *hld up: pushed along and hdwy 3f out: chsd ldrs over 1f out: kpt on ins fnl f: nt quite pce of ldrs* **20/1**

26-0 **4** *½* **Scrupul (IRE)**[28] 1641 3-9-6 **74**..... KierenFallon 2 — 77+
(Luca Cumani) *ref to settle: a handy: nt qckn over 2f out: rallied to chal 1f out: hld whn sltly short of room fnl 100yds: kpt on same pce* **10/1**

0-40 **5** *nk* **Tallevu (IRE)**[18] 1906 3-8-10 **64**..... RichardKingscote 12 — 67+
(Tom Dascombe) *midfield: stmbld over 5f out: clsd to chse ldrs u.p over 1f out: kept on same pce ins fnl f* **66/1**

50-0 **6** *2 ½* **Romantic (IRE)**[25] 1707 3-9-1 **69**.....(b) TomQueally 10 — 67
(Sir Henry Cecil) *s.i.s: hld up: rdn over 2f out: hdwy and hung lft over 1f out: chsd ldrs and hung lft ins fnl f: one pce* **20/1**

-531 **7** *nk* **Fisher**[10] 2144 3-9-0 **68** 6ex..... AdrianNicholls 4 — 65
(David Nicholls) *led at stdy pce: rdn and hdd over 1f out: btn ins fnl f* **10/1**

41-4 **8** *6* **Instrumentalist (IRE)**[14] 2038 3-9-7 **75**..... MickaelBarzalona 7 — 61+
(John Best) *prom: pushed along over 3f out: rdn 2f out: chsng ldrs but nt qckning whn n.m.r and hmpd over 1f out: sn eased* **8/1**

416- **9** *¾* **Never Perfect (IRE)**[217] 6986 3-9-6 **74**..... JamieSpencer 13 — 58+
(Tom Tate) *s.i.s: racd keenly: hld up: effrt on outer 3f out: no imp whn hung rt over 1f out: nvr a threat* **5/1**[2]

10 *nse* **Watt Broderick (IRE)**[258] 5956 3-8-7 **61** oh1..... TomEaves 11 — 45+
(Ian Williams) *in tch: effrt to chal 2f out: carried hd high and losing pl whn n.m.r and hmpd over 1f out: sn dropped away* **10/1**

26-0 **11** *3* **Saffa Hill (IRE)**[36] 1479 3-9-4 **72**..... DanielTudhope 9 — 51
(Tim Easterby) *in rr: u.p 3f out: nvr a threat* **25/1**

040- **12** *1 ¾* **Northern Jewel (IRE)**[230] 6702 3-8-8 **62**..... TonyHamilton 14 — 37
(Richard Fahey) *hld up: u.p 3f out: nvr a threat* **33/1**

043- **13** *1* **Abdul Malik**[147] 7929 3-8-13 **67**..... MichaelO'Connell 3 — 40
(Kate Walton) *hld up: pushed along and outpcd 3f out: nvr a threat* **66/1**

50-4 **14** *30* **King Vahe (IRE)**[65] 981 3-9-1 **69**..... AdamKirby 5
(Alan Jarvis) *racd keenly: trckd ldrs: pushed along 4f out: wknd 3f out: t.o* **33/1**

2m 10.46s (-5.04) **Going Correction** -0.525s/f (Hard) — 14 Ran SP% **118.2**
Speed ratings (Par 99): **101,100,99,99,98 96,96,91,91,91 88,87,86,62**
Tote Swingers: 1&2 £6.60, 1&3 £20.20, 2&3 £20.40 CSF £20.60 CT £313.74 TOTE £7.40: £3.30, £1.10, £8.70; EX 20.70.

Owner Hamdan Al Maktoum **Bred** Shadwell Farm LLC **Trained** Newmarket, Suffolk

■ Stewards' Enquiry : Kieren Fallon caution: careless riding

FOCUS
The meeting took place on watered fast ground and all races were run on the inner home straight. A fair but interesting handicap featuring a number of unexposed types. They did not appear to go that fast early and it developed into something of a rough race in the closing stages, but the time still dipped under standard. It looked a good race for the grade and the form is rated on the positive side.

King Vahe(IRE) Official explanation: jockey said that the gelding stopped quickly

2450 E B F PHS COMPLIANCE MAIDEN FILLIES' STKS — 6f
2:55 (2:58) (Class 5) 2-Y-O — **£3,234** (£962; £481; £240) **Stalls** Centre

Form — RPR

1 **Kosika (USA)** 2-9-0 0 .... MickaelBarzalona 7 — 74+
(Mahmood Al Zarooni) *racd keenly: hld up in tch travelling wl: effrt 2f out: led and drifted lft over 1f out: r.o ins fnl f: a doing enough* **9/2**[1]

2 *hd* **Ayr Missile** 2-9-0 0 .... PhillipMakin 4 — 74+
(Kevin Ryan) *chsd ldrs: led wl over 2f out: hdd over 1f out: r.o and stl chalng ins fnl f: jst hld* **20/1**

5 **3** *1 1/2* **Curl (IRE)**[7] 2234 2-9-0 0 .... PatDobbs 3 — 69+
(Richard Hannon) *hld up: rdn and hdwy over 2f out: styd on ins fnl f: nt pce of front two* **9/2**[1]

6 **4** *hd* **Fadeintoinfinity**[7] 2234 2-9-0 0 .... TonyCulhane 11 — 68+
(Mick Channon) *hld up: pushed along over 2f out: rdn and hdwy over 1f out: styd on ins fnl f: nt pce to chal* **13/2**[2]

5 *1* **Annie's Fortune (IRE)** 2-9-0 0 .... KierenFallon 1 — 65+
(Alan Jarvis) *chsd ldrs: effrt 2f out: no ex fnl 75yds* **7/1**[3]

6 *3/4* **Open Letter (IRE)** 2-9-0 0 .... SilvestreDeSousa 6 — 63+
(Mark Johnston) *in tch: pushed along 1/2-way: sn outpcd: kpt on ins fnl f but no imp* **8/1**

35 **7** *4* **Blue Clumber**[16] 1972 2-9-0 0 .... GrahamGibbons 9 — 51
(Shaun Harris) *w ldrs tl rdn over 1f out: wknd ins fnl f* **12/1**

8 *3* **Showtime Girl (IRE)** 2-9-0 0 .... DanielTudhope 10 — 42+
(Tim Easterby) *edgy and uns rdr twice on way to post: w ldr: led bef 1/2-way: hdd wl over 2f out: wknd over 1f out* **16/1**

9 *hd* **Bayan Kasirga (IRE)** 2-9-0 0 .... TonyHamilton 2 — 42
(Richard Fahey) *in tch tl pushed along and outpcd over 2f out* **33/1**

10 *4* **Autumn Shadow (IRE)** 2-9-0 0 .... PaulHanagan 8 — 30+
(Richard Fahey) *missed break: rn green: a outpcd and bhd* **13/2**[2]

6 **11** *8* **Al Khisa (IRE)**[37] 1437 2-9-0 0 .... JamieSpencer 5 — 36
(Kevin Ryan) *led: hdd bef 1/2-way: wknd 2f out: eased whn wl btn ins fnl f* **16/1**

12 *61* **Amelia Jay** 2-9-0 0 .... AndrewElliott 12
(Danielle McCormick) *missed break: a outpcd and bhd: t.o* **100/1**

1m 12.34s (-1.46) **Going Correction** -0.425s/f (Firm) — **12** Ran SP% **114.8**
Speed ratings (Par 90): **92,91,89,89,88 87,81,77,77,72 61,**
Tote Swingers: 1&2 £16.90, 1&3 £5.40, 2&3 £16.50 CSF £96.99 TOTE £5.60: £2.20, £6.90, £1.20; EX 90.00.
Owner Godolphin **Bred** Betz Thoroughbred Et Al **Trained** Newmarket, Suffolk

FOCUS
Three of the four previous winners of this fillies' maiden went on to place at Group level and a number of major yards were represented this time. The bare form looks likely to prove pretty ordinary for the track.

NOTEBOOK
Kosika(USA)a $170,000 half-sister to three winners in the USA, was well backed on this debut and, having been held up, swept through to lead despite drifting left. Once in front she kept finding and should be capable of going on from this. (tchd 4-1)

Ayr Missile ◆, the first foal of a half-sister to Fontley and a couple of other winners, made a really promising debut. Always up with the pace, she kept battling and was not beaten far. She should be well up to winning a similar contest at least. (op 16-1)

Curl(IRE) was bustled along early before staying on. She confirmed her superiority over Fadeintoinfinity and helps set the level of the form, but looked in need of further again here. (tchd 11-2)

Fadeintoinfinity, who finished well having been held up at the back, looks in need of further. (op 7-1)

Annie's Fortune(IRE), whose immediate pedigree suggests she could be a middle-distance filly, does have some speed further back. She came through to deliver a challenge over a furlong out before fading and can be expected to improve on this. (op 8-1 tchd 13-2)

Open Letter(IRE), a 100,000gns daughter of a 7f winner out of a mare who finished third in the Marcel Boussac, chased the pace and did not run badly, but should benefit from the experience and an extra furlong in time. (tchd 9-1)

Autumn Shadow(IRE) was the better fancied of her trainer's two runners, but missed the break and could never go the pace on this debut. (op 7-1 tchd 6-1)

2451 PHS WATERLOGIC CLASSIFIED STKS — 6f
3:30 (3:31) (Class 4) 3-Y-O — **£4,075** (£1,212; £606; £303) **Stalls** Centre

Form — RPR

21-0 **1** **Decision By One**[15] 1998 3-9-0 80 ....(t) RichardKingscote 9 — 85
(Tom Dascombe) *racd alone on nr side rail: mde all: rdn over 1f out: r.o and a in control ins fnl f* **9/2**[3]

0-05 **2** *1/2* **Tip Top Gorgeous (IRE)**[7] 2256 3-9-0 77 .... DanielTudhope 7 — 83
(David O'Meara) *chsd ldrs: rdn 2f out: wnt 2nd wl ins fnl f: styd on but a hld* **4/1**[2]

3235 **3** *3/4* **Waseem Faris (IRE)**[18] 1921 3-9-0 80 .... TonyCulhane 2 — 81
(Mick Channon) *in tch: effrt over 1f out: kpt on ins fnl f: nt quite pce of first two* **7/1**

1-40 **4** *2 3/4* **Spykes Bay (USA)**[14] 2022 3-9-0 78 .... PaulHanagan 1 — 72
(Mrs K Burke) *gd spd and prom: rdn over 1f out: fdd ins fnl 100yds* **9/1**

1-50 **5** *1/2* **Gabbiano**[16] 1983 3-8-9 77 .... RaulDaSilva(5) 6 — 71
(Jeremy Gask) *hld up in rr: hung lft whn rdn and hdwy to chse ldrs over 1f out: one pce ins fnl f* **14/1**

1-04 **6** *4* **Desert Philosopher**[7] 2229 3-9-0 80 .... JamieSpencer 5 — 58
(Kevin Ryan) *hld up: rdn and failed to pick-up over 1f out: nvr a threat* **11/8**[1]

31-0 **7** *4* **Knocker Knowles (IRE)**[44] 1317 3-9-0 80 .... PadraigBeggy 3 — 45
(David Evans) *chsd ldrs: rdn over 2f out: wknd over 1f out* **33/1**

41P- **8** *33* **Especially Red (IRE)**[292] 4824 3-9-0 70 .... AdamKirby 4
(Lisa Williamson) *hld up: struggling over 2f out: wl bhd over 1f out* **66/1**

1m 11.01s (-2.79) **Going Correction** -0.425s/f (Firm) — **8** Ran SP% **113.9**
Speed ratings (Par 101): **101,100,99,95,95 89,84,40**
Tote Swingers: 1&2 £4.40, 1&3 £2.60, 2&3 £5.50 CSF £22.64 TOTE £3.70: £1.20, £1.50, £2.80; EX 28.50.
Owner The Half A Third Partnership **Bred** G E Amey **Trained** Malpas, Cheshire

FOCUS
A very tight classified stakes in which most were rated within 3lb of each other. The majority of the field raced up the centre, but the winner was the only one to come towards the stands' rail. He was entitled to win this and rates a small personal best. The time was just outside standard and 1.33secs faster that the preceding juvenile fillies' maiden.

2452 PHS DIRECT H'CAP — 1m
4:05 (4:07) (Class 4) (0-85,82) 3-Y-O — **£4,075** (£1,212; £606; £303) **Stalls** Low

Form — RPR

102 **1** **Basseterre (IRE)**[10] 2150 3-9-2 77 .... KierenFallon 8 — 86+
(Charles Hills) *hld up: hdwy over 2f out: led wl over 1f out: sn edgd lft: r.o wl: eased down cl home* **11/4**[2]

33-0 **2** *1 1/2* **Devdas (IRE)**[20] 1860 3-9-5 80 .... AdamKirby 7 — 85+
(Clive Cox) *hld up: stmbld over 2f out: sn rdn: hdwy over 1f out: hung lft and wnt 2nd ins fnl f: no imp on wnr* **6/1**[3]

51-0 **3** *1/2* **Nelson's Bay**[19] 1888 3-9-5 80 ....(t) MickaelBarzalona 6 — 83
(Brian Meehan) *hld up: rdn over 2f out: hdwy over 1f out: styd on ins fnl f: nt quite rch ldrs* **25/1**

21-0 **4** *1 1/2* **Third Half**[16] 1978 3-8-12 73 .... RichardKingscote 1 — 73
(Tom Dascombe) *led: rdn and hdd wl over 1f out: no ex ins fnl f* **8/1**

31-3 **5** *nk* **Farang Kondiew**[27] 1653 3-9-2 77 .... GrahamGibbons 4 — 76
(Declan Carroll) *racd keenly: trckd ldrs: rdn and nt qckn over 1f out: kpt on same pce ins fnl f* **5/2**[1]

0-22 **6** *1* **Dance The Rain**[13] 2076 3-9-7 82 .... TomEaves 2 — 81+
(Bryan Smart) *s.i.s: sn trckd ldrs: rdn 2f out: sltly short of room over 1f out: wknd ins fnl f* **13/2**

3310 **7** *1 1/4* **Three Bards (IRE)**[27] 1653 3-9-1 76 .... SilvestreDeSousa 5 — 70
(Mark Johnston) *prom: rdn 2f out: wknd ins fnl f* **20/1**

10-5 **8** *4 1/2* **Now My Sun**[14] 2021 3-8-11 72 .... PaulHanagan 9 — 56
(Mrs K Burke) *prom on outer: wknd wl over 1f out: eased whn wl btn ins fnl f* **9/1**

1m 39.11s (-4.59) **Going Correction** -0.525s/f (Hard) — **8** Ran SP% **112.6**
Speed ratings (Par 101): **101,99,99,97,97 96,94,90**
Tote Swingers: 1&2 £4.30, 1&3 £12.20, 2&3 £20.90 CSF £19.00 CT £330.99 TOTE £3.40: £1.20, £1.60, £5.00; EX 20.00.
Owner H R Mould **Bred** D G Hardisty Bloodstock **Trained** Lambourn, Berks

FOCUS
A decent handicap, but ultimately a comfortable winner. The first three were last at halfway and the winner is rated to his AW latest.

Farang Kondiew Official explanation: jockey said that the colt was denied a clear run
Dance The Rain Official explanation: jockey said that the filly was denied a clear run

2453 PHS DATASHRED MAIDEN STKS — 1m 2f 95y
4:40 (4:40) (Class 5) 3-Y-O+ — **£2,264** (£673; £336; £168) **Stalls** Centre

Form — RPR

3-04 **1** **Qaadira (USA)**[18] 1922 3-8-9 82 .... PaulHanagan 4 — 68+
(John Gosden) *racd in 2nd pl: led narrowly on bit 2f out: effrtlessly extended advantage ins fnl f: v easily* **4/7**[1]

0-0 **2** *3 3/4* **Master Chipper**[36] 1479 3-9-0 0 .... PJMcDonald 1 — 57
(Michael Dods) *led: rdn and hdd narrowly 2f out: a fighting losing battle: no ch w wnr fnl f* **66/1**

4 **3** *4 1/2* **M'Lady Eliza**[25] 1718 7-9-9 0 .... PadraigBeggy 3 — 45
(David Evans) *hld up in rr: kpt on take remote 3rd over 1f out: no threat to ldrs* **12/1**

00 **4** *4* **Morlotti**[18] 1923 3-9-0 0 .... KierenFallon 2 — 41
(Luca Cumani) *chsd ldrs: lost tch w front pair fr 3f out: lost 3rd over 1f out: nvr nr to chal* **6/1**[3]

00 **5** *9* **Almost Gemini (IRE)**[16] 1976 3-9-0 0 .... JamieSpencer 6 — 24
(Roger Varian) *hld up: pushed along 5f out: wl bhd fnl 3f* **7/2**[2]

2m 14.74s (-0.76) **Going Correction** -0.525s/f (Hard)
WFA 3 from 4yo+ 14lb — **5** Ran SP% **109.3**
Speed ratings (Par 103): **84,81,77,74,67**
CSF £31.64 TOTE £1.60: £1.02, £8.70; EX 32.10.
Owner Hamdan Al Maktoum **Bred** Shadwell Farm LLC **Trained** Newmarket, Suffolk

FOCUS
Three non-runners and a rather uncompetitive all-aged maiden. Weak form behind the winner. The steady early pace resulted in a time much slower than the opening handicap.

Morlotti Official explanation: jockey said that the gelding was unsuited by the good to firm ground.

2454 PHS TREADSMART H'CAP (FOR LADY AMATEUR RIDERS) — 1m 3f 200y
5:15 (5:16) (Class 5) (0-70,70) 4-Y-O+ — **£2,183** (£677; £338; £169) **Stalls** Centre

Form — RPR

25-6 **1** **Call Of Duty (IRE)**[11] 2134 7-9-9 58 .... MissECSayer 1 — 63
(Dianne Sayer) *led early: sn hld up in chsng gp: rdn and hdwy over 2f out: led over 1f out: styd on ins fnl f* **9/2**[3]

60-0 **2** *1* **Amana (USA)**[36] 1485 8-10-1 67 .... MissBeckyBrisbourne(3) 4 — 70
(Mark Brisbourne) *racd keenly: in tch in chsng gp: clsd 2f out: chalng ins fnl f: kpt on* **5/1**

250- **3** *3/4* **Houston Dynimo (IRE)**[181] 4360 7-10-2 68 .... MissJRRichards(3) 12 — 70
(Nicky Richards) *hld up: rdn and hdwy over 2f out: ev ch 1f out: nt qckn ins fnl f* **10/3**[1]

0-46 **4** *4* **Guga (IRE)**[25] 1718 6-9-0 56 oh4 ....(v) MissABlakemore(7) 8 — 51
(John Mackie) *plld hrd: sn led: hdd over 10f out: chsd clr ldr after: clsd on ldr but rdn and lost 2nd over 1f out: one pce ins fnl f* **11/1**

0300 **5** *2 1/2* **Swords**[51] 1189 10-9-2 58 oh11 ow2 .... MissSPeacock(7) 10 — 49?
(Ray Peacock) *hdwy to ld over 10f out: sn wl clr: reduced advantage 2f out: hdd over 1f out: wknd fnl f* **33/1**

4064 **6** *2* **Brouhaha**[13] 2077 8-10-0 70 .... MissALMurphy(7) 6 — 58
(Tom Dascombe) *handy in chsng gp: pushed along over 2f out: no imp fnl f* **4/1**[2]

1050 **7** *nk* **Lil Ella (IRE)**[22] 1794 5-9-3 57 .... MrsFreyaBrewer(5) 11 — 45
(Patrick Holmes) *hld up: rdn over 3f out: kpt on modly ins fnl f: nvr a threat* **9/1**

00-1 **8** *4 1/2* **Ptolomeos**[14] 2048 9-9-1 57 ....(p) MissEmmaBedford(7) 7 — 38
(Sean Regan) *prom in chsng gp: wknd 3f out* **8/1**

0-60 **9** *25* **Jobekani (IRE)**[57] 1096 6-9-4 56 oh11 ....(p) MissMMullineaux(3) 2
(Lisa Williamson) *a bhd* **20/1**

2m 35.46s (1.66) **Going Correction** -0.525s/f (Hard) — **9** Ran SP% **115.1**
Speed ratings (Par 103): **74,73,72,70,68 67,66,63,47**
Tote Swingers: 1&2 £4.20, 1&3 £3.50, 2&3 £4.60 CSF £27.17 CT £83.92 TOTE £5.70: £1.80, £1.40, £1.40; EX 27.50.
Owner T W Rebanks **Bred** Gainsborough Stud Management Ltd **Trained** Hackthorpe, Cumbria

FOCUS
A modest handicap for lady amateurs in which the early pace was slow. The winner probably only needed to run to his latter 2010 form.

T/Plt: £36.20 to a £1 stake. Pool: £56,111.00 - 1,129.00 winning tickets. T/Qpdt: £12.30 to a £1 stake. Pool: £3,589.00 - 215.09 winning tickets. DO

[1817]MUSSELBURGH (R-H)

Friday, May 25

OFFICIAL GOING: Good to firm (6.6)

Wind: Light, behind Weather: Fine and dry

2455 GORDON HALLIDAY FLOORING APPRENTICE H'CAP — 1m

6:45 (6:47) (Class 5) (0-65,65) 4-Y-0+ **£2,587** (£770; £384; £192) **Stalls** Low

Form — RPR

566- **1** **Mia Madonna**[258] 5915 4-8-11 **60** JustinNewman(5) 8 — 71
(Bryan Smart) *midfield: rdn along 3f out: hdwy wl over 1f out: styd on to chal ins fnl f: led nr fin* **9/1**

0-23 **2** *nk* **What's The Point**[38] 1432 4-9-7 **65** (p) JulieBurke 1 — 75+
(Ollie Pears) *cl up on inner: rdn along over 2f out: swtchd lft and hdwy to ld jst ins fnl f: sn drvn: hdd and no ex nr fin* **6/1**[3]

105- **3** *2* **Barton Bounty**[56] 7788 5-8-0 **51** oh5 FrancescaWoliter(7) 4 — 57
(Peter Niven) *towards rr: hdwy 3f out: rdn over 1f out: styd on ins fnl f: nrst fin* **33/1**

30-4 **4** *1 1/2* **Social Rhythm**[22] 1799 8-8-8 **55** LMcNiff(3) 2 — 57
(Alistair Whillans) *towards rr: hdwy 3f out: nt clr run over 2f out: rdn to chse ldrs and nt clr run over 1f out: kpt on ins fnl f* **7/1**

-260 **5** *2 1/2* **Beautiful Day**[14] 2033 4-9-4 **62** AmyRyan 5 — 59
(Kevin Ryan) *trckd ldng pair: hdwy 3f out: rdn to ld wl over 1f out: hdd jst ins fnl f and sn wknd* **13/5**[1]

0-03 **6** *3/4* **Whats For Pudding (IRE)**[13] 2091 4-8-5 **52** DeanHeslop(3) 10 — 47
(Declan Carroll) *chsd ldrs: hdwy on wd outside 3f out: rdn 2f out and sn no imp* **12/1**

0004 **7** *nk* **Joe Le Taxi (IRE)**[17] 1958 4-8-9 **58** DarylByrne(5) 7 — 52
(Mark Johnston) *in tch: rdn along over 2f out: sn one pce* **16/1**

3244 **8** *1 1/2* **Georgebernardshaw (IRE)**[19] 1879 7-9-3 **61** DeclanCannon 9 — 52
(Richard Guest) *chsd ldrs: rdn along wl over 2f out: sn wknd* **5/1**[2]

46-2 **9** *1 1/4* **Edas**[7] 2239 10-8-13 **60** GarryWhillans(3) 12 — 48
(Thomas Cuthbert) *a towards rr* **11/1**

36-0 **10** *1 3/4* **Byron Bear (IRE)**[21] 1831 4-8-8 **52** RossAtkinson 11 — 36
(Paul Midgley) *s.i.s: a towards rr* **20/1**

5454 **11** *2* **Pitkin**[21] 1830 4-8-9 **58** (b[1]) DavidSimmonson(5) 6 — 37
(Michael Easterby) *led and set str pce: clr 1/2-way: rdn wl over 2f out: hdd wl over 1f out and sn wknd* **18/1**

30-0 **12** *43* **Glenluji**[19] 1879 7-8-13 **57** LeeTopliss 13
(Jim Goldie) *a bhd* **14/1**

1m 42.14s (0.94) **Going Correction** -0.025s/f (Good) **12** Ran SP% **122.8**
Speed ratings (Par 103): **94,93,91,90,87 86,86,85,83,82 80,37**
toteswingers: 1&2 £57.30, 1&3 £9.40, 2&3 £41.10 CSF £64.50 CT £1761.03 TOTE £11.70: £3.40, £2.40, £11.90; EX 104.40.
Owner Jeffrey Hobby **Bred** Brightwalton Stud **Trained** Hambleton, N Yorks
■ Stewards' Enquiry : Daryl Byrne one-day ban: careless riding (8 June)

FOCUS
The pace was overly quick in this apprentice handicap. The winner is rated back to form.
Byron Bear(IRE) Official explanation: jockey said that the gelding reared as the stalls opened
Glenluji Official explanation: vet said that the gelding had a fibrillating heart

2456 BERNARD HUNTER CRANE HIRE OPEN MAIDEN STKS — 5f

7:15 (7:15) (Class 5) 2-Y-0 **£3,234** (£962; £481; £240) **Stalls** High

Form — RPR

3 **1** **Surely Speightful (USA)**[14] 2020 2-8-12 0 PhillipMakin 5 — 70+
(Kevin Ryan) *cl up: led over 1f out: clr whn hung rt ins fnl f* **4/9**[1]

2 *2 1/2* **Cracking Choice (IRE)** 2-9-3 0 PaulMulrennan 4 — 67+
(Michael Dods) *dwlt: sn chsng ldng pair: hdwy wl over 1f out: swtchd rt ent fnl f: styd on wl towards fin* **9/1**[3]

3 *3 1/4* **Sugar Blaze** 2-8-12 0 GrahamLee 6 — 48+
(Jim Goldie) *dwlt and in rr: hdwy wl over 1f out: swtchd rt and rdn ins fnl f: kpt on: nrst fin* **16/1**

35 **4** *nk* **Crystal Cove**[10] 2138 2-9-3 0 DavidAllan 3 — 52
(Tim Easterby) *slt ld: rdn along 2f out: hdd over 1f out: sn edgd lft and wknd* **4/1**[2]

0 **5** *1/2* **El Molino Blanco**[10] 2138 2-8-12 0 PaddyAspell 1 — 45
(Michael Easterby) *towards rr: hdwy 1/2-way: rdn over 1f out: kpt on same pce* **33/1**

0 **6** *2* **Hashegotanymoney**[10] 2138 2-8-10 0 DavidSimmonson(7) 2 — 43
(Michael Easterby) *wnt rt s: chsd ldrs on outer: rdn along 1/2-way: wknd wl over 1f out* **50/1**

1m 0.14s (-0.26) **Going Correction** -0.10s/f (Good) **6** Ran SP% **110.0**
Speed ratings (Par 93): **98,94,88,88,87 84**
toteswingers: 1&2 £1.40, 1&3 £2.50, 2&3 £2.90 CSF £5.14 TOTE £1.40: £1.10, £3.80; EX 6.30.
Owner Mrs R G Hillen **Bred** Kinsman Farm **Trained** Hambleton, N Yorks

FOCUS
An uncompetitive maiden, and the bare form is ordinary, but a potentially useful winner.

NOTEBOOK
Surely Speightful(USA) may well have gone off quick enough considering the other runner who helped force the speed, Crystal Cove, dropped right away, but she kept on strongly, and that's despite being inclined to go right under pressure. She had finished third of four on her debut at Ascot (5f, soft) and that form was boosted when the winner followed up with a very useful effort. There should be more to come. (op 1-2 tchd 4-7 in places)
Cracking Choice(IRE), the first living foal of a modest triple 5f winner (including here) for the same owner (and once for this trainer), shaped nicely. He was running on from off a hot pace, so it would be dangerous to get carried away, but he clearly has plenty of ability. (tchd 10-1)
Sugar Blaze's trainer has bred and trained four winners from her dam and three of them won over C&D. This was a respectable introduction and she can improve plenty. (tchd 14-1)
Crystal Cove tried to match strides with the winner from an early stage, and tanked along, but he didn't have the rail and failed to see his race out. He looks to have plenty of ability, but isn't getting home and might do better if he can relax in behind a quick pace. (op 7-2)
El Molino Blanco is probably one for nurseries in due course.

2457 PENTLAND LAND ROVER H'CAP — 1m 6f

7:45 (7:45) (Class 4) (0-85,82) 4-Y-0+ **£7,115** (£2,117; £1,058; £529) **Stalls** Centre

Form — RPR

324- **1** **Amazing King (IRE)**[70] 5273 8-8-13 **79** GarryWhillans(5) 11 — 86
(Philip Kirby) *hld up in rr: gd hdwy 3f out: trckd ldrs wl over 1f out: rdn to ld ins fnl f: kpt on* **16/1**

351- **2** *1/2* **Los Nadis (GER)**[29] 7102 8-9-1 **76** GrahamLee 9 — 82
(Jim Goldie) *cl up: led over 3f out: rdn and hdd wl over 1f out: rallied and ev ch ins fnl f: kpt on* **11/4**[1]

4-14 **3** *1 1/2* **Golden Future**[20] 1846 9-8-4 **68** DeclanCannon(3) 7 — 72
(Peter Niven) *trckd ldrs: hdwy 3f out: chal 2f out and ev ch tl rdn and one pce fnl f* **8/1**

56-1 **4** *1/2* **Bradbury (IRE)**[22] 1797 4-8-10 **71** (p) PhillipMakin 5 — 74
(James Bethell) *hld up towards rr: stdy hdwy towards outer 3f out: chal wl over 1f out: sn rdn and ev ch tl one pce ins fnl f* **9/1**

106- **5** *3/4* **Mojolika**[14] 5453 4-8-12 **73** PaulMulrennan 2 — 75
(Tim Easterby) *hld up in tch: hdwy on outer over 2f out: sn rdn to chse ldrs: drvn and one pce fnl f* **20/1**

040- **6** *3 1/4* **Forrest Flyer (IRE)**[230] 6707 8-8-7 **68** AmyRyan 3 — 66
(Jim Goldie) *chsd ldng pair: rdn along 3f out: wknd 2f out* **11/1**

0-55 **7** *6* **My Arch**[18] 1905 10-9-3 **81** JulieBurke(3) 1 — 70
(Ollie Pears) *in rr: pushed along 1/2-way: n.d* **10/1**

0-26 **8** *10* **Spirit Of A Nation (IRE)**[19] 1880 7-9-2 **77** PaddyAspell 6 — 52
(James Moffatt) *led: rdn along over 4f out: hdd over 3f out: wknd over 2f out* **22/1**

23-1 **9** *1 1/4* **Royal Swain (IRE)**[20] 1846 6-9-3 **78** RobertWinston 10 — 52
(Alan Swinbank) *trckd ldrs: effrt on outer 3f out: cl up and rdn 2f out: sn wknd* **7/2**[2]

3005 **10** *21* **The Bells O Peover**[15] 1993 4-9-7 **82** FrederikTylicki 8 — 26
(Mark Johnston) *hld up in rr: pushed along over 5f out: bhd fnl 3f* **11/2**[3]

3m 3.14s (-2.16) **Going Correction** -0.025s/f (Good) **10** Ran SP% **117.8**
Speed ratings (Par 105): **105,104,103,103,103 101,97,92,91,79**
toteswingers: 1&2 £10.30, 1&3 £19.00, 2&3 £3.20 CSF £60.58 CT £393.91 TOTE £16.20: £5.20, £1.40, £2.80; EX 79.30.
Owner Amazing Optimists **Bred** Kraemer Partnership **Trained** Castleton, N Yorks

FOCUS
A reasonable handicap run at a fair pace. The first two have good records here and this is straightforward form.
Royal Swain(IRE) Official explanation: jockey said that the gelding was unsuited by the track

2458 EDINBURGH EVENING NEWS H'CAP — 5f

8:15 (8:16) (Class 6) (0-65,65) 4-Y-0+ **£2,587** (£770; £384; £192) **Stalls** High

Form — RPR

4531 **1** **Sandwith**[14] 2032 9-8-11 **60** (p) LMcNiff(5) 9 — 68
(George Foster) *cl up: led wl over 1f out: drvn ins fnl f: hld on gamely* **9/2**[2]

06-5 **2** *1/2* **Lees Anthem**[19] 1881 5-8-9 **53** PaddyAspell 1 — 59
(Colin Teague) *chsd ldrs: hdwy 2f out: rdn over 1f out: chal ent fnl f and ev ch tl nt qckn nr fin* **17/2**[3]

0-62 **3** *1/2* **Here Now And Why (IRE)**[19] 1881 5-9-0 **58** (p) RobertWinston 3 — 62
(Ian Semple) *hld up in tch: hdwy whn nt clr run wl over 1f out: effrt and n.m.r ent fnl f: sn rdn and ev ch: no ex towards fin* **3/1**[1]

-660 **4** *nk* **Drumpellier (IRE)**[19] 1881 5-8-3 **47** oh1 ow1 (e) AmyRyan 8 — 50
(Simon West) *chsd ldrs: rdn and hdwy over 1f out: drvn ins fnl f: kpt on* **16/1**

4005 **5** *1/2* **Amno Dancer (IRE)**[14] 2037 5-8-1 **48** (b[1]) DeclanCannon(3) 6 — 52+
(Ian Semple) *towards rr: hdwy whn nt clr run wl over 1f out: swtchd rt and n.m.r ent fnl f: rdn and styng on whn squeezed out and snatched up nr fin* **25/1**

40 **6** *hd* **You'relikemefrank**[56] 1116 6-9-7 **65** (p) GrahamLee 2 — 66
(Richard Ford) *awkward and hmpd s: towards rr: swtchd wd and hdwy 2f out: rdn to chal appr fnl f: ev ch tl drvn and no ex last 75yds* **9/1**

00-0 **7** *1 3/4* **Distant Sun (USA)**[22] 1800 8-8-11 **55** PhillipMakin 7 — 49
(Linda Perratt) *a towards rr* **20/1**

360- **8** *shd* **Myjestic Melody (IRE)**[223] 6874 4-8-6 **50** JoeFanning 5 — 44+
(Noel Wilson) *dwlt and towards rr: hdwy 2f out: effrt whn nt clr run over 1f out: n.d after* **10/1**

5-05 **9** *2 3/4* **Cayman Fox**[7] 2230 7-8-11 **58** JulieBurke(3) 10 — 42
(Linda Perratt) *led 1f: cl up: rdn 2f out and sn wknd* **9/2**[2]

-400 **10** *2* **Missile Attack (IRE)**[4] 2352 4-8-13 **57** (v[1]) PaulMulrennan 4 — 34
(Ian Semple) *cl up: led after 1f: rdn 2f out: sn drvn and hdd wl over 1f out: wknd* **10/1**

59.76s (-0.64) **Going Correction** -0.025s/f (Good) **10** Ran SP% **114.6**
Speed ratings (Par 101): **101,100,99,98,98 97,95,94,90,87**
toteswingers: 1&2 £6.00, 1&3 £3.70, 2&3 £4.80 CSF £41.72 CT £134.31 TOTE £5.60: £1.80, £3.20, £1.30; EX 50.10.
Owner Stoneypath Racing Club **Bred** R R Whitton **Trained** Haddington, East Lothian
■ Stewards' Enquiry : Paddy Aspell caution: careless riding

FOCUS
A moderate but competitive sprint handicap, and it was sound run. The winner is rated to his best form of the past two seasons.
Amno Dancer(IRE) Official explanation: jockey said that the gelding was denied a clear run
Myjestic Melody(IRE) Official explanation: that the filly was denied a clear run.

2459 FASTER GREENER CENTRAL TAXIS H'CAP — 7f 30y

8:45 (8:46) (Class 5) (0-70,75) 3-Y-0 **£3,881** (£1,155; £577; £288) **Stalls** Low

Form — RPR

06-2 **1** **Our Boy Jack (IRE)**[7] 2229 3-9-1 **67** LeeTopliss(3) 2 — 83+
(Richard Fahey) *trckd ldrs: hdwy on wd outside 3f out: led over 2f out: sn rdn and hung rt: clr appr fnl f* **7/4**[1]

324 **2** *3 1/2* **Outlaw Torn (IRE)**[22] 1798 3-8-2 **54** (e) DeclanCannon(3) 6 — 59
(Richard Guest) *prom: chsd ldr after 2f: effrt and cl up over 2f out: rdn wl over 1f out: swtchd lft appr f and kpt on: no ch w wnr* **8/1**

-341 **3** *2 1/4* **On The Hoof**[10] 2143 3-9-12 **75** 6ex PaulMulrennan 3 — 74+
(Michael Easterby) *hld up: hdwy on inner over 2f out: rdn over 1f out: kpt on fnl f* **5/1**[3]

6155 **4** *1/2* **Ghost Train (IRE)**[25] 1721 3-9-5 **68** JoeFanning 4 — 66
(Mark Johnston) *t.k.h: hld up in rr: hdwy wl over 2f out: rdn wl over 1f out and sn no imp* **6/1**

-311 **5** *2 1/4* **Art Dzeko**[17] 1960 3-9-6 **69** DavidAllan 7 — 61
(Tim Easterby) *led: rdn along 3f out: hdd over 2f out and sn wknd* **4/1**[2]

0-60 **6** *3* **Al Shaqab (IRE)**[23] 1758 3-9-7 **70** AmyRyan 1 — 53
(Kevin Ryan) *chsd ldng pair: rdn along wl over 2f out: sn wknd* **12/1**

16-0 **7** *1 3/4* **For Shia And Lula (IRE)**[36] 1477 3-9-7 **70** FrederikTylicki 5 — 49
(Daniel Mark Loughnane) *a towards rr* **16/1**

1m 30.21s (1.21) **Going Correction** -0.025s/f (Good) **7** Ran SP% **112.0**
Speed ratings (Par 99): **92,88,85,84,82 78,76**
toteswingers: 1&2 £4.40, 1&3 £3.10, 2&3 £4.50 CSF £15.88 TOTE £2.80: £1.50, £3.50; EX 18.40.
Owner Middleham Park Racing XXXVI **Bred** Mrs Ian Fox **Trained** Musley Bank, N Yorks

FOCUS
A modest handicap and the pace looked a bit too strong. It might not have taken too much winning and the form is rated around the runner-up.

Art Dzeko Official explanation: jockey said that the gelding was unsuited by the ground (good to firm)

2460 SUZANNE & NIGEL WEDDING ANNIVESARY H'CAP 5f

9:15 (9:17) (Class 6) (0-65,61) 3-Y-O **£2,587** (£770; £384; £192) **Stalls** High

Form RPR

300- **1** **Koolgreycat (IRE)**[267] 5646 3-9-4 **58**............................ FrederikTylicki 7 64
(Noel Wilson) *mde all: rdn wl over 1f out: drvn and edgd rt ins fnl f: kpt on* **12/1**

000- **2** ¾ **Premier Choice**[224] 6836 3-9-7 **61**.. DavidAllan 5 64
(Tim Easterby) *hmpd s and bhd: hdwy 2f out: rdn over 1f out: drvn to chal ins fnl f: sn edgd rt and no ex* **9/4**[1]

0-61 **3** 1 **Made In The Shade**[10] 2139 3-8-12 **57** 6ex.......................... LMcNiff(5) 6 56
(Paul Midgley) *cl up: rdn wl over 1f out and ev ch tl drvn and one pce wl ins fnl f* **7/2**[2]

000- **4** ½ **Pavers Star**[213] 7072 3-8-2 **45**... JulieBurke(3) 4 42
(Noel Wilson) *cl up outer: effrt 2f out: sn rdn and ev ch tl one pce ins fnl f* **18/1**

330 **5** 1 **Miserere Mei (IRE)**[31] 1585 3-8-9 **52**.....................(e) DeclanCannon(3) 8 46
(Richard Guest) *chsd ldrs: hdwy on inner 2f out: rdn ent fnl f and sn one pce* **9/2**[3]

4-50 **6** 5 **Gran Canaria Queen**[21] 1817 3-8-13 **53**.......................... GrahamLee 1 29
(Ian Semple) *in tch: rdn along over 2f out: n.d* **12/1**

03-0 **7** 6 **Busy Bimbo (IRE)**[44] 1296 3-9-1 **55**................................ PhillipMakin 2
(Alan Berry) *a towards rr* **8/1**

54-6 **8** 6 **Lowtherwood**[134] 138 3-9-1 **55**.................................... PaulMulrennan 3
(Bryan Smart) *cl up: rdn along 1/2-way: sn wknd* **15/2**

1m 0.33s (-0.07) **Going Correction** -0.10s/f (Good) **8** Ran SP% **114.7**
Speed ratings (Par 97): **96,94,93,92,90 82,73,63**
CSF £39.52 CT £117.86 TOTE £13.00: £3.80, £1.10, £2.00; EX 51.30.
Owner J R Owen & M Wormald **Bred** Canice Farrell Jnr **Trained** Middleham, N Yorks

FOCUS
The time was the slowest of three races at the trip but did not compare badly with that clocked by older handicappers. The form is rated around the third.
T/Plt: £74.80 to a £1 stake. Pool: £40,922.81. 399.06 winning tickets. T/Qpdt: £7.20 to a £1 stake. Pool: £4,183.08. 424.46 winning tickets. JR

2008 YARMOUTH (L-H)

Friday, May 25

OFFICIAL GOING: Good to firm changing to firm (good to firm in places in back straight) after race 4 (3.55)
Wind: fresh, across Weather: sunny

2461 GREAT YARMOUTH TOURIST AUTHORITY MEDIAN AUCTION MAIDEN STKS 6f 3y

2:10 (2:12) (Class 6) 3-5-Y-O **£1,617** (£481; £240; £120) **Stalls** Centre

Form RPR

64- **1** **Pawprints (IRE)**[228] 6743 3-8-9 0............................ AdamBeschizza(3) 2 55
(William Haggas) *t.k.h: hld up in tch: rdn and effrt ent fnl 2f: led over 1f out: r.o wl* **4/7**[1]

445- **2** 2 **Tiberius Claudius (IRE)**[242] 6407 4-9-12 70.....................[1] NeilCallan 4 56
(George Margarson) *t.k.h: hld up in tch towards rr: rdn and effrt wl over 1f out: chsd wnr and drvn ins fnl f: no imp* **7/2**[2]

00-0 **3** ½ **Ooi Long**[15] 2010 3-9-3 44...(t) LukeMorris 7 52
(Mark Rimmer) *t.k.h: chsd ldrs: rdn to ld 2f out: hdd and edgd lft over 1f out: styd on same pce fnl f* **50/1**

3404 **4** nse **Miakora**[93] 657 4-9-7 46.. NickyMackay 6 49
(Michael Quinn) *stdd s: t.k.h: hld up in tch in rr: rdn and effrt 2f out: chsd ldrs and drvn 1f out: styd on same pce* **20/1**

5 1 ¼ **Avalanche** 3-9-3 0.. J-PGuillambert 3 48
(Luca Cumani) *dwlt: bhd: rdn 3f out: hdwy 1f out: styd on steadily ins fnl f: nvr trbld ldrs* **8/1**[3]

00- **6** 2 ¼ **Ottavino (IRE)**[240] 6448 3-8-10 0.................................... LewisWalsh(7) 9 41
(Jane Chapple-Hyam) *led for 1f: chsd ldr tl rdn ent fnl 2f: unable qck over 1f out: wknd 1f out* **12/1**

7 5 **Bonbon Bonnie** 4-9-0 0.. DannyBrock(7) 1 22
(Phil McEntee) *rn green thrght: s.i.s: t.k.h and sn rcvrd to ld after 1f: hdd and rdn ent fnl 2f: wknd over 1f out* **25/1**

1m 14.65s (0.25) **Going Correction** -0.275s/f (Firm)
WFA 3 from 4yo+ 9lb **7** Ran SP% **115.2**
Speed ratings (Par 101): **87,84,83,83,81 78,72**
Tote Swingers: 1&2 £1.20, 1&3 £6.90, 2&3 £7.90 CSF £2.82 TOTE £1.50: £1.10, £1.60; EX 2.70.
Owner Bill Eason, Michael Pallett & Partners **Bred** Henry Power & Balmerino Bloodstock **Trained** Newmarket, Suffolk

FOCUS
One of the weakest maiden races you'll ever see, run at a steady pace. The form is limited by the proximity of the third and fourth.

2462 SCROBY SANDS (S) STKS 5f 43y

2:45 (2:45) (Class 6) 2-Y-O **£1,617** (£481; £240; £120) **Stalls** Centre

Form RPR

3436 **1** **Suivez L'Argent**[4] 2349 2-8-3 0 ow1......................... CharlesBishop(5) 1 58
(Joseph Tuite) *led for 1f: pressed ldr tl shkn up to ld again 2f out: rdn clr ent fnl f: r.o wl: comf* **5/2**[2]

2 2 **Napinda** 2-8-7 0.. DavidProbert 2 50+
(Des Donovan) *bmpd sn after s: in tch: rdn and effrt wl over 1f out: chsd wnr ent fnl f: kpt on but a hld* **4/1**[3]

0466 **3** 3 **Cherryred Girl (IRE)**[5] 2309 2-8-7 0..............................(b) LukeMorris 5 39
(J S Moore) *chsd ldrs: rdn and unable qck 2f out: wknd 1f out* **9/1**

4 8 **Hippie Chick** 2-8-3 0 ow3.. RyanWhile(7) 4 13
(Bill Turner) *racd freely: led after 1f tl hdd 2f out: rn green and unbalanced wl over 1f out: sn wknd: eased ins fnl f* **15/8**[1]

5 1 ½ **My Lagan Love (IRE)** 2-8-4 0...................................... RyanPowell(3) 3
(J S Moore) *wnt lft and bmpd rival sn after s: rn green and a bhd* **13/2**

1m 3.49s (0.79) **Going Correction** -0.275s/f (Firm) **5** Ran SP% **106.7**
Speed ratings (Par 91): **82,78,74,61,58**
CSF £11.71 TOTE £3.30: £1.80, £1.90; EX 12.40.The winner was bought in 5,100gns.
Owner Shefford Valley Racing **Bred** Genesis Green Stud Ltd **Trained** Great Shefford, Berks

FOCUS
A lowly juvenile seller, run at a strong pace. The bare form is very moderate.

NOTEBOOK
Suivez L'Argent had shown only a modicum of ability in five previous starts, but she had more than enough to see off the newcomer Napinda. She had finished in the first three on three occasions previously but, having already been beaten in this grade at Redcar and Warwick, clearly has her limitations. She was the subject of good support prior to the off and she kept on well in the closing stages, despite wandering around. There might still be a degree of improvement to come, but she'd probably struggle if tried in nurseries later in the year. (op 9-4)

Napinda ran a sound race to fill second spot, but was firmly put in her place by the winner. She will improve for this experience and should remain competitive in this sort of company for the remainder of the campaign. (op 7-1 tchd 7-2)

Hippie Chick looked all over the place on this debut. (op 2-1 tchd 13-8)

2463 GRANGE FREEHOUSE UNDER NEW MANAGEMENT H'CAP (DIV I) 1m 3y

3:20 (3:20) (Class 6) (0-60,60) 4-Y-0+ **£1,617** (£481; £240; £120) **Stalls** Centre

Form RPR

000- **1** **Carpentras**[191] 7437 4-8-11 **50** ow1.............................. DarryllHolland 10 57
(Dr Jon Scargill) *t.k.h: hld up in tch: rdn 3f out: led over 1f out: hld on wl fnl 100yds: rdn out* **16/1**

063 **2** hd **Wind Star**[25] 1717 9-8-12 **56**..................................... MarkCoumbe(5) 12 62
(Brendan Powell) *stdd s: hld up in rr: rdn wl over 2f out: switching lft and hdwy over 1f out: str chal fnl 100yds: hld cl home* **7/1**[3]

0006 **3** 1 ½ **Kwik Time**[22] 1801 4-8-4 **46** oh1...................................(t) RyanPowell(3) 9 49
(Robin Bastiman) *led tl 1/2-way: rdn and ev ch ent fnl 2f: led wl over 1f out: sn hdd and styd on same pce after* **28/1**

-305 **4** 2 **Big Bay (USA)**[64] 991 6-9-2 **55**...................................... NeilCallan 1 53
(Jane Chapple-Hyam) *t.k.h: in tch: rdn wl over 2f out: unable qck over 1f out: styd on same pce fnl f* **2/1**[1]

3640 **5** hd **The Which Doctor**[29] 1634 7-9-2 **55**............................(e) CathyGannon 8 53
(Richard Guest) *s.i.s: hld up in rr: rdn and hdwy towards centre wl over 1f out: no imp fnl f* **9/1**

-430 **6** 1 **Henry's Hero**[37] 1447 6-8-7 **46** oh1................................ SaleemGolam 11 42
(Chris Dwyer) *taken down early: racd against stands' rail thrght: chsd ldrs: rdn wl over 2f out: wknd ent fnl f* **25/1**

3551 **7** 2 ¼ **Land Hawk (IRE)**[29] 1635 6-9-4 **60**............................ SimonPearce(3) 7 50
(Lydia Pearce) *t.k.h: chsd ldrs: lost pl and rdn wl over 2f out: plugged on fnl f but no threat to ldrs* **5/1**[2]

6400 **8** 1 ¼ **See The Storm**[22] 1801 4-8-9 **48** ow1............................ JackMitchell 4 36
(Lisa Williamson) *t.k.h: hld up in tch: hdwy to ld 1/2-way: rdn and hdd wl over 1f out: sn wknd* **17/2**

5006 **9** 5 **Gay Gallivanter**[57] 1096 4-8-7 **46**.................................. NickyMackay 5 22
(Michael Quinn) *hld up in tch in midfield: lost pl and rdn wl over 2f out: wknd wl over 1f out* **20/1**

1132 **10** 3 ½ **Warden Bond**[88] 725 4-9-4 **57**...................................(p) MartinLane 3 26
(William Stone) *t.k.h: hld up in tch towards rr: rdn and unable qck over 2f out: wknd wl over 1f out* **8/1**

1m 40.36s (-0.24) **Going Correction** -0.275s/f (Firm) **10** Ran SP% **112.1**
Speed ratings (Par 101): **90,89,88,86,86 85,82,81,76,73**
Tote Swingers: 1&2 £15.80, 1&3 £41.50, 2&3 £36.00 CSF £115.52 CT £2022.37 TOTE £21.50: £4.50, £1.90, £8.40; EX 150.30.
Owner D J Meilton **Bred** Lostford Manor Stud Ltd **Trained** Newmarket, Suffolk

FOCUS
A modest handicap, run only at a fair pace and something of upset. The runner-up looks the best guide to the level.

Carpentras Official explanation: trainer said, regarding the apparent improvement of form, that that the filly had strengthened up over the winter

The Which Doctor Official explanation: jockey said that the gelding was slowly away

Land Hawk(IRE) Official explanation: jockey said that the gelding was unsuited by the good to firm ground

2464 GRANGE FREEHOUSE UNDER NEW MANAGEMENT H'CAP (DIV II) 1m 3y

3:55 (3:58) (Class 6) (0-60,60) 4-Y-0+ **£1,617** (£481; £240; £120) **Stalls** Centre

Form RPR

5223 **1** **Brown Pete (IRE)**[3] 2365 4-9-2 **55**..............................(e) CathyGannon 8 67
(Richard Guest) *t.k.h: hld up in tch: rdn and effrt over 2f out: chsd ldr over 1f out: led 1f out: r.o strly* **9/4**[1]

0033 **2** 3 ¾ **Putin (IRE)**[2] 2401 4-8-10 **49**...(bt) JimCrowley 10 52
(Phil McEntee) *led: rdn ent fnl 2f: hdd 1f out: sn outpcd by wnr and btn but kpt on for clr 2nd* **10/1**

6-42 **3** 3 ¼ **Kyllachykov (IRE)**[18] 1908 4-8-10 **49** ow1............................ NeilCallan 7 45
(Robin Bastiman) *awkward leaving stalls: sn in tch: rdn and effrt 3f out: chsd ldng pair and edgd lft over 1f out: no imp and wl hld 1f out* **3/1**[2]

3600 **4** 1 ¾ **Tanforan**[27] 1659 10-8-13 **52**.. JackMitchell 4 44
(Brian Baugh) *hld up in rr: rdn and effrt over 2f out: no ch w ldrs but kpt on u.p fnl f* **18/1**

3511 **5** hd **Join Up**[13] 2090 6-9-3 **56**... ShaneKelly 1 47
(Mark Brisbourne) *t.k.h: chsd ldr: rdn and unable qck ent fnl 2f: btn over 1f out: fdd fnl f* **7/1**[3]

4426 **6** 1 ½ **Storm Runner (IRE)**[79] 821 4-9-2 **58**.......................... RyanPowell(3) 5 46
(George Margarson) *hld up in rr: rdn and effrt ent fnl 2f: no imp and wl btn 1f out* **14/1**

245- **7** 9 **Scarborough Lily**[185] 7507 4-9-7 **60**............................(v[1]) LukeMorris 2 27
(Ed Vaughan) *t.k.h: hld up in tch: rdn and nt qckn 3f out: wknd wl over 1f out: wl btn and eased ins fnl f* **15/2**

06-2 **8** 4 **Chez Vrony**[79] 822 6-8-4 **46**.................................(t) AdamBeschizza(3) 3
(Dave Morris) *hld up in last trio: rdn and effrt wl over 2f out: wknd wl over 1f out: wl btn and eased wl ins fnl f* **16/1**

6560 **9** hd **Godwit**[31] 1588 4-8-7 **46** oh1... ChrisCatlin 6
(Eugene Stanford) *in tch: rdn and lost pl 1/2-way: bhd fnl 2f: eased ins fnl f* **22/1**

4000 **10** 3 ¼ **Hot Tub**[79] 829 4-8-4 **46** oh1.. DominicFox(3) 11
(Christine Dunnett) *chsd ldrs: rdn and losing pl 1/2-way: bhd fnl 2f* **50/1**

6-06 **11** 10 **Salford Prince (IRE)**[62] 1036 4-9-2 **55**............................ MarcHalford 9
(David Elsworth) *chsd ldrs tl 1/2-way: sn lost pl: bhd fnl 2f: wl bhd and eased ins fnl f: t.o* **33/1**

1m 38.2s (-2.40) **Going Correction** -0.275s/f (Firm) **11** Ran SP% **116.2**
Speed ratings (Par 101): **101,97,94,92,92 90,81,77,77,74 64**
Tote Swingers: 1&2 £7.10, 1&3 £2.50, 2&3 £7.40 CSF £25.10 CT £69.05 TOTE £3.90: £1.70, £3.90, £1.80; EX 28.50.
Owner Rakebackmypoker.com **Bred** Jim Halligan **Trained** Stainforth, S Yorks

FOCUS
A modest if fairly competitive handicap, run at a strong pace which produced an exciting finish. The winner is rated to the best of his British form with the second to his AW mark.

2465 TRAFALGAR RESTAURANT AT GREAT YARMOUTH RACECOURSE FILLIES' H'CAP — 1m 3y
4:30 (4:32) (Class 4) (0-85,82) 4-Y-0+ **£4,075** (£1,212; £606; £303) **Stalls** Centre

Form RPR

0-00 **1** **Amoya (GER)**[8] 2199 5-8-11 **75**.............................(t) AdamBeschizza(3) 3 82
(Philip McBride) *mde all: rdn ent fnl 2f: styd on strly ins fnl f: rdn out* **11/1**

6-21 **2** 2 ¾ **Viking Rose (IRE)**[24] 1742 4-8-10 **71**................................ LukeMorris 1 72
(James Eustace) *chsd ldrs: rdn 3f out: drvn and chsd wnr over 1f out: no ex and btn ins fnl f: wknd fnl 100yds* **10/3**[2]

330- **3** nk **Our Gal**[185] 7510 4-9-7 **82**.. MartinLane 4 82
(Noel Quinlan) *hld up in tch in last pair: rdn and effrt over 2f out: swtchd lft and drvn to chse ldrs over 1f out: styd on same pce fnl f* **15/2**

21-0 **4** 2 ¾ **Hayaku (USA)**[48] 1213 4-9-2 **77**...................................(bt) JimCrowley 6 71
(Ralph Beckett) *chsd ldr: rdn wl over 2f out: ev ch and unable qck 2f out: wknd fnl f* **11/4**[1]

0-23 **5** 1 **Batgirl**[15] 2011 5-8-13 **74**.. EddieAhern 7 65
(John Berry) *in tch: rdn and unable qck 2f out: outpcd and btn over 1f out: wknd fnl f* **7/2**[3]

-060 **6** 1 ¼ **Imaginary World (IRE)**[7] 2250 4-9-1 **76**.........................(be) NeilCallan 2 64
(Alan McCabe) *in tch in rr: switching rt and effrt over 2f out: no prog and btn over 1f out: wknd fnl f* **6/1**

0-50 **7** 5 **Ela Gonda Mou**[34] 1533 5-8-7 **68** oh1................................ ChrisCatlin 5 45
(Peter Charalambous) *hld up in tch in last trio: rdn and struggling over 2f out: wknd wl over 1f out* **20/1**

1m 38.06s (-2.54) **Going Correction** -0.275s/f (Firm) **7** Ran SP% **111.1**
Speed ratings (Par 102): **101,98,97,95,94 92,87**
Tote Swingers: 1&2 £7.30, 1&3 £11.00, 2&3 £2.40 CSF £44.74 TOTE £14.10: £5.60, £2.00; EX 41.70.
Owner Black Star Racing **Bred** Gestut Ebbesloh **Trained** Newmarket, Suffolk

FOCUS
Not the strongest of handicaps for this grade and the runner-up looks the best guide to the level.
Amoya(GER) Official explanation: trainer said, regarding the apparent improvement of form, that the mare settled better in this race and appreciated being dropped back to a mile

2466 ODDSCHECKER.COM H'CAP — 7f 3y
5:05 (5:05) (Class 5) (0-70,69) 4-Y-0+ **£2,264** (£673; £336; £168) **Stalls** Centre

Form RPR

0024 **1** **Cut The Cackle (IRE)**[3] 2362 6-8-8 **56**.......................(bt) CathyGannon 9 66
(Richard Guest) *j. awkwardly leaving stalls: wnt lft and rdr lost iron: bhd: rcvrd iron after 1f: hdwy to ld 4f out: mde rest: drvn wl over 1f out: battled on wl fnl f* **10/1**

4311 **2** nk **Trojan Rocket (IRE)**[7] 2251 4-9-0 **69**................................ IanBurns(7) 6 78
(Michael Wigham) *stdd s: hld up in tch in rr: hdwy wl over 1f out: chsd ldrs 1f out: rdn and pressing wnr wl ins fnl f: kpt on wl* **6/4**[1]

-131 **3** 1 **First Class**[92] 664 4-8-7 **55**... DavidProbert 4 61
(Rae Guest) *hld up in tch towards rr: rdn and effrt 2f out: swtchd rt and drvn to chse ldrs over 1f out: kpt on: wnt 3rd cl home* **17/2**

1444 **4** ½ **Zaheeb**[24] 1729 4-9-1 **63**..(b[1]) NeilCallan 2 70
(Dave Morris) *chsd ldrs: chsd wnr 1/2-way: ev ch and rdn 2f out: continually hung into wnr after and nt qckn: hld whn hung into wnr: hmpd and plld out rt wl ins fnl f: lost 3rd cl home* **9/1**

2501 **5** 2 ¼ **Ibiza Sunset (IRE)**[8] 2207 4-8-10 **65**...................... GeorgeDowning(7) 1 64
(Brendan Powell) *chsd ldrs: rdn and keeping on whn sltly hmpd and swtchd rt 1f out: no ex ins fnl f* **7/2**[2]

3-0 **6** ¾ **Amba**[42] 1358 6-9-1 **63**...[1] EddieAhern 11 60
(Des Donovan) *led tl 4f out: rdn wl over 2f out: edgd lft over 1f out: wknd fnl f* **33/1**

3002 **7** shd **Satwa Laird**[4] 2355 6-9-7 **69**.. LukeMorris 8 66
(Conor Dore) *in tch but sn bustled along: rdn over 2f out: wknd u.p ent fnl f* **13/2**[3]

0541 **8** 7 **Custom House (IRE)**[22] 1768 4-8-9 **57**...................... RichardThomas 5 35
(John E Long) *chsd ldrs: rdn 1/2-way: struggling u.p 2f out: sn wknd* **28/1**

050- **9** 5 **Mudhish (IRE)**[312] 4160 7-8-13 **61**................................(b) BrettDoyle 7 25
(Clive Brittain) *in tch in midfield: rdn and fnd little over 2f out: sn edgd lft and wknd* **33/1**

1m 24.55s (-2.05) **Going Correction** -0.275s/f (Firm) **9** Ran SP% **114.5**
Speed ratings (Par 103): **100,99,98,97,95 94,94,86,80**
Tote Swingers: 1&2 £5.80, 1&3 £6.50, 2&3 £3.60 CSF £24.88 CT £135.73 TOTE £11.90: £3.00, £1.30, £2.60; EX 34.40.
Owner Rakebackmypoker.com **Bred** Mountarmstrong Stud **Trained** Stainforth, S Yorks

FOCUS
Some in-form sprinters on show in this handicap. The form is rated around the winner and fourth.

2467 ODDSCHECKER.MOBI H'CAP — 1m 2f 21y
5:40 (5:40) (Class 6) (0-55,55) 4-Y-0+ **£1,617** (£481; £240; £120) **Stalls** Low

Form RPR

0054 **1** **Sky Diamond (IRE)**[13] 2090 4-8-6 **52**.................(b) GeorgeDowning(7) 1 58
(John Mackie) *mde all: wnt wl clr 1/2-way: rdn ent fnl 2f: kpt on tl tired ins fnl f: a holding on: rdn out* **4/1**[1]

3345 **2** 1 ¼ **So Is She (IRE)**[3] 2364 4-8-12 **51**..............................(be) DarryllHolland 6 54
(Alan Bailey) *racd off the pce in midfield: rdn 3f out: edgd rt over 1f out: chsd clr wnr 1f out: kpt on u.p: nvr looked like getting to wnr* **4/1**[1]

6205 **3** 4 ½ **Market Puzzle (IRE)**[14] 2048 5-8-11 **55**.................(p) RachealKneller(5) 9 49
(Mark Brisbourne) *hld up wl off the pce in last pair: effrt 3f out: rdn over 1f out: styd on to go 3rd wl ins fnl f: no threat to wnr* **9/2**[2]

4-04 **4** ¾ **Coupland Lass (IRE)**[63] 1004 4-9-2 **55**........................ JamieMackay 11 48
(Willie Musson) *racd off the pce in midfield: rdn over 3f out: plugged on u.p fnl 2f but no imp on wnr* **22/1**

5502 **5** ½ **Director's Dream (IRE)**[15] 2013 4-8-11 **53**............ AdamBeschizza(3) 3 45
(Mark Rimmer) *t.k.h: chsd wnr: rdn over 3f out: drvn and no imp over 2f out: lost 2nd 1f out and plugged on same pce after* **9/2**[2]

0-33 **6** nk **Tinkerbell Will**[29] 1624 5-8-10 **49**................................ RichardThomas 7 40
(John E Long) *prom in main gp: rdn wl over 3f out: no imp: keeping on same pce and hld whn nt clr run and hmpd over 1f out: plugged on* **5/1**[3]

/45- **7** 3 **Young Jackie**[396] 1572 4-8-7 **49**... RyanPowell(3) 5 34
(George Margarson) *bustled along leaving stalls: a off the pce in last quartet: rdn over 3f out: no prog and unbalanced over 2f out: n.d* **12/1**

000- **8** 20 **Harry Lime**[198] 7333 4-9-0 **53**.. CathyGannon 8
(Chris Dwyer) *stdd s: hld up wl off the pce in rr: pushed along 4f out: edgd lft u.p and no hdwy wl over 2f out: wl bhd and eased fnl f* **10/1**

2m 9.21s (-1.29) **Going Correction** -0.275s/f (Firm) **8** Ran SP% **114.2**
Speed ratings (Par 101): **94,93,89,88,88 88,85,69**
Tote Swingers: 1&2 £3.30, 1&3 £6.80, 2&3 £5.00 CSF £20.01 CT £73.66 TOTE £5.60: £2.20, £1.10, £1.90; EX 20.50.
Owner W I Bloomfield **Bred** David Bourke **Trained** Church Broughton , Derbys

FOCUS
A wide open handicap, despite the small field. The runner-up is rated close to his recent AW best.
Harry Lime Official explanation: jockey said that the gelding was unsuited by the firm, good to firm in places in the back straight ground

2468 BEST ODDS @ ODDSCHECKER.COM H'CAP — 1m 6f 17y
6:15 (6:16) (Class 6) (0-60,60) 4-Y-0+ **£1,617** (£481; £240; £120) **Stalls** High

Form RPR

5421 **1** **Bilidn**[56] 1112 4-9-3 **56**... ChrisCatlin 9 67
(Noel Quinlan) *a gng wl: in tch: led 4f out: drvn wl over 1f out: styd on wl and drew clr ins fnl f* **9/4**[1]

3-40 **2** 4 ½ **Cotton Grass**[45] 1272 4-9-7 **60**.. EddieAhern 10 65
(Mark H Tompkins) *t.k.h early: in tch: hdwy to chse ldrs 4f out: rdn and ev ch 2f out: no ex and btn jst ins fnl f: plugged on to hold on for 2nd* **5/1**[2]

2415 **3** 1 **Six Of Clubs**[35] 1496 6-8-13 **59**.....................................(b) JakePayne(7) 6 62
(Bill Turner) *in tch in midfield: hdwy to chse ldrs 4f out: rdn over 2f out: drvn over 1f out: no ex and btn jst ins fnl f: plugged on* **11/2**[3]

5561 **4** 12 **Satwa Ballerina**[24] 1744 4-8-12 **54**.......................(b) AdamBeschizza(3) 7 41
(Mark Rimmer) *hld up in rr: rdn and effrt over 3f out: outpcd by ldrs and wl btn 2f out: plugged on to go modest 4th wl ins fnl f: n.d* **11/1**

-654 **5** ¾ **Minstrel Lad**[16] 1984 4-8-11 **53**...................................... SimonPearce(3) 3 38
(Lydia Pearce) *hld up in last trio: rdn and effrt over 3f out: drvn and no ch w ldng trio 2f out: wnt modest 4th over 1f out tl wl ins fnl f* **15/2**

/00- **6** ¾ **Old Boy Ted**[176] 7212 4-8-2 **48**................................ RobJFitzpatrick(7) 4 32
(Mark H Tompkins) *hld up in last trio: hit rail 6f out: rdn and effrt 3f out: sn outpcd and no ch w ldng trio over 2f out* **33/1**

640 **7** 10 **Icy Quiet**[71] 908 4-8-13 **52**..(t) NeilCallan 2 22
(Tobias B P Coles) *t.k.h: chsd ldrs: ev ch 4f out: rdn and struggling 2f out: sn wknd: fdd bdly ent fnl f* **7/1**

105- **8** 4 **Torran Sound**[63] 6104 5-9-2 **55**..(v) LukeMorris 8 20
(James Eustace) *chsd ldr tl led 11f out: hdd 4f out: wknd u.p 3f out: wl bhd over 1f out* **15/2**

05-0 **P** **Cragganmore Creek**[128] 200 9-8-7 **46** oh1...................... MartinLane 1
(Dave Morris) *led tl 11f out: chsd ldr tl lost pl rapidly over 4f out: wl t.o and p.u over 1f out* **80/1**

3m 5.9s (-1.70) **Going Correction** -0.275s/f (Firm) **9** Ran SP% **111.4**
Speed ratings (Par 101): **93,90,89,83,82 82,76,74,**
Tote Swingers: 1&2 £3.40, 1&3 £3.80, 2&3 £5.90 CSF £12.55 CT £51.75 TOTE £2.40: £1.30, £1.20, £1.80; EX 15.50.
Owner Patrick Wilmott **Bred** Meon Valley Stud **Trained** Newmarket, Suffolk

FOCUS
A moderate staying handicap, run only a steady pace. The third is rated to his latest turf mark.
Cragganmore Creek Official explanation: jockey said that the gelding lost action
T/Plt: £86.00 to a £1 stake. Pool: £46,625.00 - 395.54 winning tickets. T/Qpdt: £43.20 to a £1 stake. Pool: £4,130.00 - 70.64 winning tickets. SP

2025 CHESTER (L-H)
Saturday, May 26

OFFICIAL GOING: Good to firm
Wind: Moderate behind Weather: Fine and sunny

2469 COCA COLA E B F MAIDEN STKS — 6f 18y
2:25 (2:25) (Class 4) 2-Y-0 **£4,528** (£1,347; £673; £336) **Stalls** Low

Form RPR

1 **Odooj (IRE)** 2-9-3 0.. TadhgO'Shea 6 80+
(William Haggas) *a.p: swtchd lft over 1f out: led 1f out: rdn out* **11/4**[2]

2 **2** 2 ¾ **Mandy Lexi (IRE)**[16] 1997 2-8-12 0................................ StevieDonohoe 3 66
(Bryan Smart) *chsd ldrs: rdn over 2f out: styd on same pce ins fnl f* **4/5**[1]

3 1 ¼ **Dream Maker (IRE)** 2-8-12 0................................. RichardKingscote 5 62
(Tom Dascombe) *sn pushed along to chse ldr: led over 2f out: rdn and hdd 1f out: no ex* **8/1**[3]

4 1 **Sojoum** 2-8-12 0.. ChrisCatlin 2 59
(Mick Channon) *sn outpcd: tk clsr order over 2f out: sn outpcd: r.o ins fnl f* **9/1**

0 **5** 11 **Tyson The Byson**[7] 2261 2-9-3 0.. GrahamLee 1 31
(David C Griffiths) *led: rdn and hdd over 2f out: wkng whn n.m.r over 1f out* **16/1**

1m 17.63s (3.83) **Going Correction** +0.40s/f (Good) **5** Ran SP% **109.2**
Speed ratings (Par 95): **90,86,84,83,68**
toteswinger: 1&2 £3.60. CSF £5.27 TOTE £4.90: £2.90, £1.02; EX 5.40.
Owner Hamdan Al Maktoum **Bred** Shadwell Estate Company Limited **Trained** Newmarket, Suffolk

FOCUS
An ordinary small-field maiden to open proceedings, but in all likelihood the winner is above average.

NOTEBOOK
Odooj(IRE), whose dam was a 1m Listed winner, was the stable's first juvenile runner of the year. Happy to take a lead, he was presented with an inviting gap on the inside as the leader hung off the rail turning in and he made no mistake. There should be plenty more to come from him. (op 3-1, tchd 10-3 in a place)
Mandy Lexi(IRE) only just failed to get up on her debut over 5f here earlier this month and was all the rage to go one better, but she was being niggled along before reaching the home bend and couldn't match the winner once into the straight. Admittedly this ground was different to first time, but it's more likely she found herself up against a nice colt. (op 5-6 tchd 10-11)
Dream Maker(IRE), retained for 1,000GBP as a yearling, ran well having been on the pace for a long way but she did show signs of inexperience, getting upset in the stalls and running green on a couple of occasions. She is bred to need middle-distances judging by the dam's side of her pedigree. (op 13-2)
Sojoum, a half-sister to the very useful Fork Handles (6f winner but stays middle-distances) and a winning 1m3f plater/hurdler, ran green early but she showed definite ability in the later stages of the contest yet was by no means knocked about. (tchd 8-1)

2470 MATTHEW CLARK MAIDEN STKS — 6f 18y
2:55 (2:58) (Class 4) 3-Y-0 **£5,175** (£1,540; £769; £384) **Stalls** Low

Form RPR

5-3 **1** **All Or Nothin (IRE)**[21] 1864 3-9-3 0.......................... MichaelO'Connell 3 68+
(John Quinn) *mde all: rdn over 1f out: styd on wl* **5/2**[2]

06 **2** *1 ¾* **Taizong (IRE)**[21] 1843 3-9-3 0 .... StevieDonohoe 4 63
(Ian Williams) *chsd ldrs: rdn over 1f out: styd on u.p to take 2nd ins fnl f* **9/1**

3545 **3** *½* **Economic Crisis (IRE)**[17] 1986 3-8-12 51 .... GrahamLee 5 56
(Alan Berry) *chsd wnr: rdn over 1f out: styd on same pce ins fnl f* **40/1**

0 **4** *3 ¾* **Ptolemy**[21] 1843 3-9-3 0 .... JoeFanning 8 49+
(David Barron) *hld up: rdn over 1f out: r.o ins fnl f: nvr nrr* **20/1**

562 **5** *½* **Elegant Girl (IRE)**[12] 2121 3-8-12 65 .... DuranFentiman 6 42
(Tim Easterby) *mid-div: rdn over 1f out: kpt on ins fnl f* **17/2**[3]

5 **6** *shd* **John Coffey (IRE)**[45] 1296 3-9-3 0 .... TadhgO'Shea 10 47+
(David Nicholls) *s.i.s: hld up: nt clr run over 2f out: styng on whn hung lft ins fnl f: nvr nrr* **16/1**

3 **7** *hd* **Asian Trader**[7] 2262 3-9-3 0 .... LiamJones 1 46
(William Haggas) *trckd ldrs: plld hrd: rdn over 1f out: wknd ins fnl f* **11/10**[1]

3-0 **8** *¾* **Multi Bene**[14] 2085 3-9-3 0 .... RichardKingscote 7 44
(Tom Dascombe) *prom: rdn over 2f out: wknd over 1f out* **25/1**

40 **9** *6* **Ambitious Boy**[127] 231 3-9-3 0 .... ChrisCatlin 9 25
(Reg Hollinshead) *s.i.s: outpcd* **25/1**

0- **10** *2 ¾* **Red All Over (IRE)**[256] 6025 3-8-5 0 .... MatthewHopkins(7) 2
(Alan Berry) *s.s: outpcd* **66/1**

1m 17.0s (3.20) **Going Correction** +0.40s/f (Good) **10** Ran SP% **119.0**
Speed ratings (Par 101): **94,91,91,86,85 85,84,83,75,72**
toteswingers: 1&2 £7.10, 1&3 £9.20, 2&3 £9.20. CSF £23.84 TOTE £2.90: £1.10, £4.10, £12.90; EX 31.00.
Owner Ross Harmon **Bred** Ballyhane Stud **Trained** Settrington, N Yorks
■ Stewards' Enquiry : Matthew Hopkins four-day ban: use of whip (9, 11-14)

FOCUS
This didn't look a strong 3yo maiden and the first three home just about held those positions throughout. The proximity of the third limits the form.

2471 ONE COST H'CAP — 1m 3f 79y
3:25 (3:27) (Class 4) (0-85,81) 3-Y-O **£5,175** (£1,540; £769; £384) **Stalls** Low

Form RPR

52-3 **1** **Singalat**[33] 1557 3-9-7 **76** .... GrahamLee 2 84
(James Given) *led: rdn and hdd 1f out: rallied to ld wl ins fnl f* **5/1**

2116 **2** *nk* **Gabrial's King (IRE)**[33] 1557 3-8-11 **66** .... StevieDonohoe 1 73
(Ian Williams) *trckd ldrs: racd keenly: rdn to ld 1f out: hdd wl ins fnl f* **3/1**[2]

3-00 **3** *4* **Tidal Way (IRE)**[7] 2269 3-9-4 **73** .... NeilCallan 4 73
(Mick Channon) *hld up: hdwy and nt clr run over 2f out: rdn over 1f out: styd on same pce* **11/4**[1]

3-16 **4** *hd* **Rapid Heat Lad (IRE)**[17] 1978 3-9-0 **69** .... ChrisCatlin 5 68
(Reg Hollinshead) *chsd wnr tl rdn over 1f out: no ex fnl f* **7/2**[3]

2140 **5** *7* **Moataz (USA)**[45] 1319 3-8-13 **68** .... JoeFanning 3 55
(Mark Johnston) *hld up: nt clr run over 2f out: wknd over 1f out* **12/1**

2-16 **6** *2* **Enery (IRE)**[28] 1661 3-9-5 **74** .... LiamJones 6 57
(Mark Johnston) *prom: pushed along over 2f out: wknd over 1f out* **11/2**

2m 29.99s (5.19) **Going Correction** +0.40s/f (Good) **6** Ran SP% **113.6**
Speed ratings (Par 101): **97,96,93,93,88 87**
toteswingers: 1&2 £1.60, 1&3 £7.60, 2&3 £2.10. CSF £20.66 TOTE £5.00: £1.30, £1.70; EX 16.50.
Owner Danethorpe Racing Partnership **Bred** Mrs S Clifford **Trained** Willoughton, Lincs

FOCUS
Despite the withdrawal of recent Haydock winner Gabrial The Hero, Dr Marwan Koukash still owned 50% of the field. They didn't go much of a pace in this handicap and the first two from Pontefract dominated the finish, with a narrow personal best from the winner.

2472 MATTHEW CLARK H'CAP — 7f 2y
4:00 (4:04) (Class 2) (0-105,103) 4-Y-0+ **£12,938** (£3,850; £1,924; £962) **Stalls** Low

Form RPR

4352 **1** **Imperial Djay (IRE)**[2] 2417 7-8-7 **89** .... PJMcDonald 12 98
(Ruth Carr) *s.i.s: hld up: str run to ld wl ins fnl f* **9/1**

23-6 **2** *1* **Louis The Pious**[15] 2025 4-8-12 **94** .... GrahamLee 4 101
(Kevin Ryan) *chsd ldrs: rdn to ld over 1f out: hdd wl ins fnl f* **9/2**[2]

000 **3** *hd* **Mabait**[14] 2068 6-8-6 **95** .... AliceHaynes(7) 6 101
(David Simcock) *hld up: n.m.r and r.o wl ins fnl f: nrst fin* **28/1**

0001 **4** *½* **Pintura**[15] 2025 5-8-13 **95** .... StevieDonohoe 7 100
(David Simcock) *prom: rdn over 1f out: r.o* **10/1**

0-02 **5** *½* **Grissom (IRE)**[15] 2025 6-8-10 **92** .... DuranFentiman 9 95
(Tim Easterby) *chsd ldr: rdn and ev ch ins fnl f: no ex towards fin* **12/1**

1401 **6** *2 ¾* **Viva Ronaldo (IRE)**[15] 2029 6-8-8 **90** .... FrederikTylicki 2 86
(Richard Fahey) *hld up: rdn over 2f out: r.o ins fnl f: nvr nrr* **5/1**[3]

6-00 **7** *½* **Hot Rod Mamma (IRE)**[21] 1865 5-8-5 **87** .... AndrewElliott 1 82+
(Dianne Sayer) *hld up: nt clr run over 1f out tl ins fnl f: nvr able to chal* **25/1**

52-5 **8** *nk* **Eton Forever (IRE)**[56] 1130 5-9-7 **103** .... NeilCallan 3 97+
(Roger Varian) *chsd ldrs: nt clr run and stmbld over 1f out: running on whn hmpd ins fnl f: eased* **9/4**[1]

3-00 **9** *nk* **High Standing (USA)**[37] 1469 7-9-6 **102** .... LiamJones 11 95
(Jeremy Gask) *hld up: hdwy over 2f out: rdn over 1f out: no ex fnl f* **25/1**

01-5 **10** *1 ½* **Xilerator (IRE)**[35] 1523 5-9-1 **97** .... JoeFanning 5 86
(David Nicholls) *led: rdn and hdd over 1f out: wkng whn n.m.r ins fnl f* **10/1**

1m 27.56s (1.06) **Going Correction** +0.40s/f (Good) **10** Ran SP% **112.6**
Speed ratings (Par 109): **109,107,107,107,106 103,102,102,102,100**
toteswingers: 1&2 £5.40, 1&3 £8.60, 2&3 £8.60. CSF £46.41 CT £1107.57 TOTE £14.40: £2.50, £1.10, £12.00; EX 43.40.
Owner Hollinbridge Partnership **Bred** D Veitch And Musagd Abo Salim **Trained** Huby, N Yorks

FOCUS
A hot contest and the key to it proved to be the handicap run over half a furlong further at the big meeting earlier in the month, as that race produced the winner, second, fourth and fifth here. In a race as tight as this, room was always likely to be at a premium and they went a serious pace. The winner is rated back to his best.

NOTEBOOK
Imperial Djay(IRE) just lost out in a three-way photo behind Pintura and Grissom here a fortnight earlier, but had run twice in the meantime including when runner-up at Haydock two days previously. Dropped in from the outside stall, the strong pace proved ideal and the better ground helped him too, but his rider still did really well to find the gaps when he needed them and he made full use of them when they did appear. (op 8-1)
Louis The Pious ◆ finished around 8l behind Pintura, Grissom and Imperial Djay a fortnight earlier, but was conceding race-fitness to the trio that day and this quicker ground was in his favour. Ridden much closer to the pace than the winner, he never stopped trying and deserves to get his head back in front.
Mabait ◆, unplaced in his last ten starts, ran his best race for a long time, running on from well off the pace under his apprentice rider. Whilst it would be asking too much for him to recapture the glory days, he does seem to have reached the sort of mark he can win off. (tchd 33-1)
Pintura failed to confirm the form with the front pair from their meeting here last time, but he had every chance once switched out for his effort a furlong from home and ran his race.
Grissom(IRE) was the other member of the quartet who met here earlier in the month and, after racing prominently, again had every chance a furlong out, but he faded near the line and could probably have done without the ground firming up. (tchd 11-1)
Viva Ronaldo(IRE), a three-time winner at the track and in the frame on four other occasions from nine visits, was off the bridle a fair way out and came wide into the straight, but he was 6lb higher than when winning over C&D a fortnight earlier and that was probably a bigger problem. (op 9-2)
Hot Rod Mamma(IRE) ◆ has been mainly disappointing since racking up a five-timer between July and September last year and is still 7lb above her last winning mark, but she can be rated better than her finishing position here as she firstly got caught behind the weakening Xilerator over a furlong out and then by Eton Forever as he was eased off. Official explanation: jockey said that the mare was denied a clear run
Eton Forever(IRE)'s effort can be ignored as he ran into trouble at every turn when looking for a gap and eventually his rider gave up in disgust. He is still lightly raced for a 5-y-o and hopefully there will be another day. Official explanation: jockey said that that the gelding suffered interference in running (op 11-4 tchd 3-1)

2473 RED BULL H'CAP — 1m 2f 75y
4:35 (4:35) (Class 4) (0-85,85) 4-Y-0+ **£5,175** (£1,540; £769; £384) **Stalls** High

Form RPR

00-0 **1** **Watered Silk**[52] 1186 4-9-0 **78** .... RichardMullen 1 85
(Marcus Tregoning) *mde all: rdn over 1f out: styd on gamely* **10/1**

1341 **2** *¾* **Knowe Head (NZ)**[9] 2199 5-8-11 **75** .... LiamJones 3 81
(James Unett) *trckd ldrs: racd keenly: chsd wnr over 1f out: edgd rt: rdn: hung lft and ev ch ins fnl f: no ex nr fin* **3/1**[1]

1-4 **3** *1 ¼* **Elizabeth Coffee (IRE)**[16] 1999 4-8-10 **74** .... StevieDonohoe 8 77
(Ian Williams) *chsd ldrs: rdn over 1f out: r.o* **10/1**

2013 **4** *1 ½* **Calaf**[16] 1999 4-9-0 **85** .... GeorgeChaloner(7) 9 85+
(Richard Fahey) *hld up: hdwy on outer over 1f out: rdn and edgd lft ins fnl f: styd on same pce* **13/2**[3]

63-0 **5** *1 ¾* **Look Left**[42] 1381 4-9-1 **79** .... NeilCallan 2 76
(David Simcock) *hld up in tch: rdn over 1f out: styd on same pce fnl f:* **6/1**[2]

04-0 **6** *½* **Dhaular Dhar (IRE)**[14] 2068 10-9-4 **82** .... GrahamLee 10 78
(Jim Goldie) *s.i.s: hld up: hmpd after 2f: hdwy and nt clr run wl over 1f out: styd on same pce* **12/1**

04-6 **7** *hd* **Early Applause**[16] 1999 4-8-13 **77** .... RobertWinston 4 72
(Charles Hills) *plld hrd: sn w wnr: rdn over 2f out: no ex fnl f* **8/1**

0-53 **8** *hd* **I'm Super Too (IRE)**[7] 2285 5-9-2 **80** .... AndrewElliott 5 75
(Alan Swinbank) *plld hrd and prom: rdn over 2f out: sn outpcd* **9/1**

160- **9** *1 ½* **Iulus**[252] 6155 4-8-11 **75** .... MichaelO'Connell 6 67
(John Quinn) *hld up: rdn over 1f out: n.d* **25/1**

-031 **10** *¾* **Fazza**[14] 2094 5-8-12 **81** .... AdamCarter(5) 7 71
(Edwin Tuer) *hld up: rdn over 1f out: nvr on terms* **15/2**

306- **11** *31* **Mahadee (IRE)**[185] 7518 7-9-2 **80** .... (b) FrederikTylicki 11
(Ed de Giles) *chsd ldrs: rdn over 2f out: wknd wl over 1f out: eased: t.o* **25/1**

2m 13.93s (2.73) **Going Correction** +0.40s/f (Good) **11** Ran SP% **119.1**
Speed ratings (Par 105): **105,104,103,102,100 100,100,100,98,98 73**
toteswingers: 1&2 £17.90, 1&3 £17.90, 2&3 £4.10. CSF £40.58 CT £313.55 TOTE £12.40: £2.80, £1.10, £3.80; EX 42.40.
Owner Mr And Mrs A E Pakenham **Bred** Mr & Mrs A E Pakenham **Trained** Lambourn, Berks

FOCUS
They didn't go much of an early pace in this handicap, which caused a few to pull, and it may have played into the winner's hands. The form makes sense rated around the first three.
Iulus Official explanation: jockey said that the gelding suffered interference in running

2474 DUVAL-LEROY CHAMPAGNE H'CAP — 1m 5f 89y
5:10 (5:10) (Class 3) (0-90,87) 4-Y-0+ **£8,409** (£2,502; £1,250; £625) **Stalls** Low

Form RPR

0-31 **1** **Star Commander**[10] 2174 4-8-12 **78** .... RobertWinston 4 90
(Mark H Tompkins) *a.p: chsd ldr over 2f out: led wl over 1f out: sn rdn: styd on* **10/3**[2]

123- **2** *1 ¼* **Qahriman**[243] 6410 4-9-7 **87** .... J-PGuillambert 8 97+
(Luca Cumani) *dwlt: hld up: swtchd rt and hdwy over 1f out: rdn and hung lft ins fnl f: r.o* **5/1**[3]

364/ **3** *3 ½* **Cape Express (IRE)**[11] 5004 7-9-4 **84** .... NeilCallan 2 89
(Nicky Henderson) *prom: pushed along over 3f out: rdn to chse wnr over 1f out: no ex ins fnl f* **3/1**[1]

30-5 **4** *9* **Rosewin (IRE)**[29] 1640 6-9-0 **80** .... MichaelO'Connell 6 72
(Ollie Pears) *hld up: hdwy to chse wnr 8f out: rdn over 2f out: wknd over 1f out* **20/1**

-111 **5** *hd* **Chabada (JPN)**[77] 872 4-9-7 **87** .... StevieDonohoe 3 78
(Ian Williams) *chsd ldr: led after 2f: rdn and hdd wl over 1f out: wknd fnl f* **5/1**[3]

3306 **6** *2* **English Summer**[15] 2031 5-9-3 **83** .... JoeFanning 9 71
(Mark Johnston) *prom: pushed along 7f out: wknd wl over 1f out* **6/1**

51/4 **7** *9* **Silk Drum (IRE)**[23] 1797 7-8-5 **71** .... DuranFentiman 1 46
(Dianne Sayer) *led 2f: chsd ldrs: rdn over 3f out: wknd wl over 1f out* **13/2**

2m 54.37s (1.67) **Going Correction** +0.40s/f (Good) **7** Ran SP% **113.8**
Speed ratings (Par 107): **110,109,107,101,101 100,94**
toteswingers: 1&2 £3.40, 1&3 £1.80, 2&3 £2.00. CSF £20.03 CT £53.94 TOTE £4.90: £2.60, £4.00; EX 21.40.
Owner John Brenchley **Bred** Mary-Ann Penfold **Trained** Newmarket, Suffolk

FOCUS
A decent staying handicap in which the front three came clear. The runner-up is unexposed and can do better.

NOTEBOOK
Star Commander ◆ had gained both previous wins on Polytrack including narrowly off 2lb higher at Lingfield ten days earlier (now rated 7lb higher on sand), but he has some decent form on turf too. Never too far off the pace, his rider committed him off the final bend and that enabled him to get first run on the second. He stays well and handles fast ground, so there should be more to come from him. (op 9-2)
Qahriman ◆ is the one to take from the race. He didn't seem to handle the soft ground when last seen at Ffos Las 243 days earlier, but although this ground was more suitable the track certainly wasn't, and he was also inclined to pull hard at the back of the field. The fact that he put in a strong finishing effort down the centre of the track, despite so much being against him, suggests he will be winning again sooner rather than later. (op 11-2 tchd 6-1)
Cape Express(IRE) was having his first try on the Flat since August 2009 when rated 12lb higher, but he had run twice over hurdles for his new yard this year including winning at Southwell 11 days earlier. One of his two successes on the level came under today's rider and he was brought to hold every chance turning in, but lacked the pace to trouble the front pair. (op 5-2 tchd 10-3)
Rosewin(IRE) was allowed to go prominent starting the final circuit, but she had been keen enough through the early stages and that eventually took its toll. (op 16-1)

Chabada(JPN) was making her turf debut off 7lb higher after completing a hat-trick on the AW earlier in the year, but after making much of the running she was swamped turning for home. Her trainer reported that the filly was unsuited by the ground. Official explanation: jockey said the filly was unsuited by the good to firm ground (op 9-2 tchd 4-1)
English Summer had been beaten in all ten starts since winning this race off 6lb higher a year ago and never threatened this time. (op 11-2 tchd 5-1)
Silk Drum(IRE) didn't build on his promising return to the Flat at Musselburgh, but may not have found this tight track to his liking. (op 8-1)

2475 BEEFEATER H'CAP (DIV I) 6f 18y

5:45 (5:46) (Class 5) (0-75,75) 4-Y-0+ **£4,043** (£1,203; £601; £300) **Stalls** Low

Form RPR
-002 **1** **Green Park (IRE)**[14] [2092] 9-9-4 **72**....................(b) JoeFanning 8 82
(Declan Carroll) *hmpd sn after s: sn prom: led over 1f out: rdn out* **7/2**[1]
5023 **2** 1 ½ **Whipphound**[10] [2165] 4-8-1 **62**.................... JackDuern(7) 5 67
(Mark Brisbourne) *mid-div: hdwy over 2f out: chsd wnr fnl f: styd on* **4/1**[2]
20-0 **3** 2 ½ **Vizean (IRE)**[29] [1638] 4-8-11 **65**.................... MichaelO'Connell 3 61
(John Mackie) *chsd ldrs tl led over 3f out: rdn and hdd over 1f out: no ex fnl f* **5/1**[3]
0003 **4** nk **Legal Eagle (IRE)**[5] [2352] 7-9-4 **75**....................(p) RobertLButler(3) 4 70
(Paul Green) *led 1f: chsd ldrs: rdn over 1f out: styd on same pce* **8/1**
640- **5** 2 **Rutterkin (USA)**[225] [6841] 4-8-1 **62**.................... MatthewHopkins(7) 2 49
(Alan Berry) *hld up: styd on fr over 1f out: nvr nrr* **16/1**
3060 **6** ½ **Waking Warrior**[14] [2071] 4-9-5 **73**....................(tp) StevieDonohoe 1 59+
(Kevin Ryan) *chsd ldrs: hmpd and lost pl wl over 4f out: n.d after* **7/2**[1]
505 **7** ¾ **Absa Lutte (IRE)**[14] [2084] 9-9-1 **69**.................... LiamJones 11 52
(Michael Mullineaux) *s.i.s: hdwy over 2f out: wknd over 1f out* **20/1**
4-00 **8** 30 **Deliberation (IRE)**[7] [2264] 4-9-2 **70**....................(p) GrahamLee 10
(Mark Buckley) *mid-div: rdn and wknd over 2f out: t.o* **20/1**
50P- **9** nk **Jack Smudge**[227] [6801] 4-9-0 **68**.................... FrederikTylicki 12
(James Given) *hld up: rdn over 2f out: sn wknd: t.o* **10/1**
00-0 **10** 12 **Spanish Acclaim**[35] [1526] 5-8-7 **61** oh1....................(b) PJMcDonald 6
(Ruth Carr) *led 5f out: hdd over 3f out: rdn and wknd over 2f out: t.o* **20/1**

1m 16.71s (2.91) **Going Correction** +0.40s/f (Good) **10** Ran SP% **121.5**
Speed ratings (Par 103): **96,94,90,90,87 86,85,45,45,29**
toteswingers: 1&2 £4.00, 1&3 £5.80, 2&3 £5.80. CSF £17.79 CT £68.00 TOTE £3.20: £2.20, £1.10, £1.80; EX 12.60.
Owner G A Fixings Ltd **Bred** James Burns And A Moynan **Trained** Sledmere, E Yorks

FOCUS
An ordinary sprint handicap and a couple didn't enjoy the smoothest of trips. The winner is rated to last year's form with the second close to recent marks.

2476 BEEFEATER H'CAP (DIV II) 6f 18y

6:15 (6:16) (Class 5) (0-75,74) 4-Y-0+ **£4,043** (£1,203; £601; £300) **Stalls** Low

Form RPR
0500 **1** **Lucky Dan (IRE)**[5] [2355] 6-8-10 **63**.................... JoeFanning 2 78
(Paul Green) *chsd ldr tl led over 1f out: pushed clr fnl f* **13/2**[3]
1-60 **2** 3 ¼ **Song Of Parkes**[14] [2096] 5-9-3 **70**.................... MickyFenton 9 75
(Eric Alston) *hld up in tch: racd keenly: rdn over 1f out: edgd lft ins fnl f: wnt 2nd nr fin: no ch w wnr* **10/1**
0123 **3** ¾ **Red Cape (FR)**[12] [2133] 9-9-5 **72**....................(b) PJMcDonald 6 74
(Ruth Carr) *sn led: rdn and hdd over 1f out: no ex ins fnl f: lost 2nd nr fin* **9/2**[1]
4200 **4** 2 **Methaaly (IRE)**[4] [2377] 9-8-8 **61**....................(be) LiamJones 4 57
(Michael Mullineaux) *stmbld s: sn mid-div: pushed along 1/2-way: rdn over 1f out: kpt on: nt pce to chal* **16/1**
5342 **5** ½ **Steelcut**[12] [2133] 8-9-2 **69**....................(p) MichaelO'Connell 5 63
(Mark Buckley) *hld up: r.o ins fnl f: nvr nrr* **6/1**[2]
4230 **6** 1 ½ **Blown It (USA)**[48] [1237] 6-9-4 **71**.................... RobertWinston 1 60
(Keith Dalgleish) *prom: pushed along over 1f out: wknd ins fnl f* **6/1**[2]
30-0 **7** nse **Ballinargh Girl (IRE)**[14] [2094] 4-9-7 **74**.................... AndrewElliott 8 63
(Danielle McCormick) *hld up: rdn over 1f out: nvr nrr* **9/1**
4-56 **8** ¾ **Meandmyshadow**[6] [2314] 4-9-0 **67**.................... StevieDonohoe 10 54
(Alan Brown) *chsd ldrs: rdn over 1f out: wknd fnl f* **14/1**
600- **9** ½ **Stilettoesinthemud (IRE)**[225] [6847] 4-8-9 **62**.................... FrederikTylicki 3 47
(James Given) *s.i.s: hld up: rdn over 1f out: n.d* **16/1**
5-03 **10** 2 ¾ **Boundaries**[28] [1675] 4-9-6 **73**....................(e) DuranFentiman 7 49
(Tim Easterby) *hld up: a in rr* **6/1**[2]
1-41 **11** ½ **Stevie Gee (IRE)**[132] [186] 8-9-6 **73**....................(b) GrahamLee 11 48
(Mark Buckley) *mid-div: rdn over 2f out: wknd wl over 1f out* **8/1**

1m 15.6s (1.80) **Going Correction** +0.40s/f (Good) **11** Ran SP% **123.0**
Speed ratings (Par 103): **104,99,98,96,95 93,93,92,91,87 87**
toteswingers: 1&2 £25.60, 1&3 £7.60, 2&3 £12.50. CSF £73.32 CT £336.78 TOTE £5.50: £2.30, £5.20, £1.10; EX 57.80.
Owner Paul Green (Oaklea) **Bred** Mountarmstrong Stud **Trained** Lydiate, Merseyside

FOCUS
The winning time was 1.11 seconds faster than the first division. Few got involved and the first two are rated to last year's form.
Stilettoesinthemud(IRE) Official explanation: jockey said that the filly anticipated the start and hit the gate
T/Plt: £154.90 to a £1 stake. Pool £51,193.36. 241.14 winning tickets. T/Qpdt: £33.80 to a £1 stake. Pool £3,248.58. 71.06 winning tickets. CR

2442 GOODWOOD (R-H)

Saturday, May 26

OFFICIAL GOING: Round course - good to firm; straight course - good (good to firm in places)
Wind: medium behind Weather: sunny

2477 32RED CASINO H'CAP 1m 1f 192y

2:15 (2:15) (Class 2) (0-100,90) 3-Y-0 **£12,938** (£3,850; £1,924; £962) **Stalls** Low

Form RPR
21-4 **1** **Grandeur (IRE)**[29] [1645] 3-9-5 **88**.................... WilliamBuick 3 98
(Jeremy Noseda) *hld up in tch: rdn and effrt ent fnl 2f: chal over 1f out: led jst ins fnl f: r.o strly to go clr and edgd rt fnl 100yds* **4/1**[1]
31-6 **2** 2 ¼ **Trader Jack**[29] [1645] 3-9-5 **88**.................... EddieAhern 4 93
(Roger Charlton) *t.k.h: hld up in tch: jnd ldrs travelling strly over 3f out: led 3f out: hrd pressed and drvn over 1f out: hdd jst ins fnl f: outpcd fnl 100yds* **7/1**
10-0 **3** 1 ¼ **Ghost Protocol (IRE)**[21] [1860] 3-9-5 **88**.................... HayleyTurner 7 91
(David Simcock) *stdd s: hld up in last pair: effrt on inner and rdn wl over 2f out: nt clr run and switching lft fr 2f out: styd on to go 3rd fnl 100yds* **16/1**
11- **4** 1 **Misdemeanour (IRE)**[234] [6623] 3-9-2 **85**.................... PatDobbs 2 86
(Richard Hannon) *chsd ldrs: rdn and effrt over 2f out: unable qck over 1f out: kpt on same pce fnl f* **6/1**
06-1 **5** ¾ **Opinion (IRE)**[33] [1567] 3-9-2 **85**.................... RyanMoore 5 84
(Sir Michael Stoute) *chsd ldr: rdn and ev ch over 3f out: unable qck over 1f out: 3rd and btn 1f out: wknd fnl 100yds* **9/2**[2]
-354 **6** 1 ¼ **Hadaj**[7] [2263] 3-9-7 **90**.................... TomQueally 8 87
(Clive Brittain) *hld up in tch: rdn and effrt over 2f out: hung rt and no prog wl over 1f out: nvr threatened ldrs* **4/1**[1]
-340 **7** shd **Kinloch Castle**[10] [2182] 3-9-0 **83**.................... SilvestreDeSousa 1 79
(Mark Johnston) *led: hdd and rdn 3f out: styd pressing ldrs tl outpcd wl over 1f out: wknd 1f out* **14/1**
1-43 **8** 12 **Mr Spiggott (IRE)**[14] [2076] 3-9-0 **83**.................... MatthewDavies 6 55
(Mick Channon) *hld up in tch in rr: rdn and no prog over 2f out: btn over 1f out: eased ins fnl f* **11/2**[3]

2m 5.6s (-2.50) **Going Correction** -0.30s/f (Firm) **8** Ran SP% **112.9**
Speed ratings (Par 105): **98,96,95,94,93 92,92,83**
Tote Swingers: 1&2 £7.80, 1&3 £12.50, 2&3 £17.50 CSF £31.24 CT £397.88 TOTE £4.50: £1.60, £2.90, £4.70; EX 37.40 Trifecta £386.30 Part won. Pool: £522.12 - 0.40 winning units..
Owner Miss Yvonne Jacques **Bred** Mrs Cherry Faeste **Trained** Newmarket, Suffolk

FOCUS
This was a good-quality 3-y-o handicap. They went a fair pace and the form looks solid rated around the third and fourth.

NOTEBOOK
Grandeur(IRE) showed the benefit of his seasonal debut last month and completed the task readily, landing his second success from just four career starts. He took time to settle, but responded strongly when angled out nearing the final furlong and could soon be called the winner. The step up in trip was clearly up his street and, in good hands, looks likely to rate a fair deal higher this year. (op 9-2 tchd 5-1)
Trader Jack made his move 3f out and gave his all, finishing a clear second-best. He clearly stays this trip well and should enjoy getting back on some easier ground. (op 13-2 tchd 5-1)
Ghost Protocol(IRE), who made a tardy start, showed up a lot better again on this second run back since his winter break and would have been a little closer with a better passage around 2f out. (op 14-1)
Misdemeanour(IRE) was making her turf debut and shaped as though she would be plenty sharper for this seasonal return. She got the trip without much fuss. (op 15-2)
Opinion(IRE) was making his handicap debut after winning a Windsor maiden on his return last month, but proved easy to back. He lacked any sort of gear change on this quicker ground and may well appreciate stepping up in trip. (tchd 5-1)
Hadaj was well backed up in trip, but never looked entirely comfortable on this course and was beaten 3f out. (tchd 7-2)
Kinloch Castle didn't go down without a fight but was free in the early lead and sweated up beforehand, which cant have helped his cause. (op 12-1)
Mr Spiggott(IRE) was beaten well before stamina became a real issue and something looked to go amiss. However, his best form has all come on softer ground. (tchd 6-1)

2478 32RED FESTIVAL STKS (LISTED RACE) 1m 1f 192y

2:45 (2:46) (Class 1) 4-Y-0+

£19,848 (£7,525; £3,766; £1,876; £941; £472) **Stalls** Low

Form RPR
14-1 **1** **Jet Away**[37] [1475] 5-8-12 114.................... TomQueally 7 116
(Sir Henry Cecil) *dwlt and pushed along early: in tch: wnt 3rd 1/2-way: jnd ldr 4f out: rdn to ld 2f out: qcknd ahd over 1f out: clr and r.o wl fnl f* **11/4**[3]
22-6 **2** 2 ¾ **Fiorente (IRE)**[21] [1855] 4-8-12 108.................... RyanMoore 3 110
(Sir Michael Stoute) *hld up in tch in rr: rdn and effrt 3f out: hdwy u.p to press wnr 2f out: drvn and unable qck over 1f out: chsd wnr and one pce ins fnl f* **7/4**[1]
55-1 **3** nse **Retrieve (AUS)**[14] [2081] 5-8-12 113.................... SilvestreDeSousa 5 110
(Saeed Bin Suroor) *t.k.h early: hld up in tch: swtchd lft and effrt to press wnr 2f out: sn drvn and unable qck over 1f out: styd on same pce fnl f* **5/2**[2]
146- **4** 5 **Opera Gal (IRE)**[248] [6247] 5-8-7 101.................... DavidProbert 4 95
(Andrew Balding) *chsd ldng pair: rdn and unable qck 3f out: outpcd u.p over 2f out: styd on same pce and no threat to ldrs after* **10/1**
20-6 **5** 1 ¾ **Halfsin (IRE)**[31] [1605] 4-8-12 97.................... SebSanders 6 96
(Marco Botti) *led: rdn and qcknd whn jnd 4f out: hdd 2f out: sn outpcd and u.p: wknd jst over 1f out* **9/1**
5455 **6** 30 **Sos Brillante (CHI)**[14] [2066] 7-8-7 74.................... JamieMackay 1 31
(Terry Clement) *t.k.h: chsd ldr tl over 4f out: sn lost pl: wl bhd fnl 2f: t.o* **100/1**

2m 3.51s (-4.59) **Going Correction** -0.30s/f (Firm) **6** Ran SP% **111.7**
Speed ratings (Par 111): **106,103,103,99,98 74**
Tote Swingers: 1&2 £1.20, 1&3 £1.10, 2&3 £1.50 CSF £7.90 TOTE £3.00: £1.30, £1.50; EX 8.00 Trifecta £14.80 Pool: £491.63 - 24.42 winning units..
Owner K Abdulla **Bred** Juddmonte Farms Ltd **Trained** Newmarket, Suffolk

FOCUS
A Listed race run at a sound pace and the form makes sense rated around the first two, although nothing special for the grade.

NOTEBOOK
Jet Away made it 2-2 for the year and registered a career-best success under a fine tactical ride. Things didn't look to go to plan early as he was sluggish from the stalls, but Tom Queally made a positive move at the top of the home straight and got him into a lovely rhythm. He dug deep to fend off his two main-market rivals, but was nicely on top of the finish and evidently enjoys this venue as he finished runner-up at this meeting last year. He was top rated in the race so was entitled to score, but he could nick a Group race this year on similar ground. (op 10-3)
Fiorente(IRE) was back over the same C&D that saw him narrowly miss out in a Group 3 here last summer and was expected to enjoy the return to quick ground after flopping on his Newmarket return. He laboured once asked for maximum effort, though, and would probably have been better off racing more positively on this drop back in trip. There's little doubt he's been over-hyped, though. (op 15-8 tchd 13-8)
Retrieve(AUS) won nicely on his comeback at Lingfield a fortnight earlier. He didn't look as happy back on turf, but still ran right up to his previous level and should be able to pick up a race of this class. (op 9-4)
Opera Gal(IRE) couldn't get near the front on this seasonal debut and the run was needed. (op 14-1)
Halfsin(IRE) did plenty from the front and wasn't disgraced as he had a lot to find. (op 10-1)

2479 32RED.COM H'CAP 1m 4f

3:20 (3:25) (Class 2) (0-105,99) 4-Y-0+ **£19,407** (£5,775; £2,886; £1,443) **Stalls** High

Form RPR
30-0 **1** **Life And Soul (IRE)**[31] [1603] 5-8-8 **86**.................... HayleyTurner 5 95
(Amanda Perrett) *led tl 6f out: led again 5f out: hrd pressed and drvn over 2f out: hdd over 1f out: stl ev ch whn hung rt into rail ins fnl f: battled on gamely to ld again last stride* **7/1**[3]

23-1 **2** *shd* **Grumeti**^{14} [2072] 4-8-11 **89**.. RyanMoore 3 98+
(Alan King) *hld up in last trio: rdn and effrt over 2f out: drvn to ld narrowly over 1f out: edgd rt u.p ins fnl f: hdd last stride* **5/4**^{1}

2511 **3** *1 ¼* **Ithoughtitwasover (IRE)**^{8} [2228] 4-9-7 **99**............... SilvestreDeSousa 7 107+
(Mark Johnston) *hld up in tch: rdn over 2f out: ev ch over 1f out: no ex fnl 100yds: hld whn short of room and eased cl home* **7/2**^{2}

110- **4** *3 ¾* **Cosimo de Medici**^{231} [6690] 5-8-11 **89**......................(t) DarryllHolland 1 90
(Hughie Morrison) *t.k.h: hld up towards rr: hdwy to chse ldrs 8f out: rdn over 2f out: outpcd and btn over 1f out: one pce fnl f* **12/1**

5212 **5** *nse* **Sand Skier**^{10} [2174] 5-7-9 **80**...................................... NicoleNordblad$^{(7)}$ 6 81
(Hans Adielsson) *hld up in tch in last trio: rdn and effrt on outer over 2f out: hung rt and sme hdwy over 1f out: kpt on but no threat to ldrs fnl f* **20/1**

30-5 **6** *¾* **Woolfall Treasure**^{21} [1850] 7-9-1 **93**............................(v) WilliamBuick 9 93
(Gary Moore) *s.i.s: rdn along and hdwy to chse ldr after 1f: led 6f out tl 5f out: wknd over 1f out* **22/1**

143- **7** *2 ¼* **Late Telegraph (IRE)**^{198} [7347] 4-9-3 **95**.......................... TomQueally 4 91
(Sir Henry Cecil) *t.k.h: hld up in tch: trckd ldrs gng wl 4f out: rdn and fnd little over 2f out: wknd 2f out* **9/1**

-462 **8** *2 ¾* **Romeo Montague**^{10} [2176] 4-8-10 **88**......................... TomMcLaughlin 8 80
(Ed Dunlop) *reluctant to go to s: s.i.s: hld up in tch: effrt on inner 3f out: wknd 2f out* **10/1**

040- **9** *5* **Hanoverian Baron**^{185} [7523] 7-8-13 **91**............................ DavidProbert 2 75
(Tony Newcombe) *in tch: rdn and unable qck 3f out: wknd 2f out* **16/1**

2m 34.94s (-3.46) **Going Correction** -0.30s/f (Firm) **9** Ran SP% **120.9**
Speed ratings (Par 109): **99,98,98,95,95 95,93,91,88**
Tote Swingers: 1&2 £3.70, 1&3 £3.20, 2&3 £2.30 CSF £16.96 CT £38.43 TOTE £8.10: £2.50, £1.10, £1.70; EX 25.10 Trifecta £97.20 Pool: £2,040.21 - 15.52 winning units..
Owner A D Spence **Bred** Kildaragh Stud **Trained** Pulborough, W Sussex

FOCUS
This decent handicap looked to be run at something of an uneven pace, but the right horses still pulled clear in a battling finish. The winner is rated to his 2010 form with the placed horses still improving.

NOTEBOOK
Life And Soul(IRE) ran out a brave winner under a cracking ride from Hayley Turner. He set out to make all, but looked vulnerable as the pack closed up 3f out. He was headed and looked held 1f out, but rallied most gamely and got up on the inside despite being tight for room late in the day. This showed his flop on testing ground first time back a month earlier to be all wrong and he was well treated on old form. (tchd 8-1)
Grumeti, the top-rated 2m juvenile hurdler from the last jumps season, capitalised on a lenient mark back on the level at Ascot a fortnight previously and had finished third twice before on the track for his previous trainer. He was heavily backed again despite a 6lb rise, and was produced with every chance from well off the pace. The winner saw out the trip that bit better, however, and perhaps this ground was quicker than he ideally cares for. (op 15-8)
Ithoughtitwasover(IRE) was another 5lb higher and proved easy to back late on. He was given every chance and only wilted at the business end, rating a solid benchmark for the race. (op 10-3 tchd 3-1)
Cosimo de Medici is much more effective over staying trips these days and so it was a promising enough comeback display. (op 14-1)

2480 E B F ANTHONY SIMMONS MAIDEN STKS (SPONSORED BY TELECOM UK) 6f
3:55 (3:57) (Class 4) 2-Y-O **£5,175** (£1,540; £769; £384) **Stalls** High

Form RPR

1 **Mister Marc (IRE)** 2-9-3 0.. RyanMoore 2 80+
(Richard Hannon) *chsd ldrs: wnt 2nd 4f out: rdn and ev ch 2f out: led jst ins fnl f: r.o wl to assert fnl 100yds: rdn out* **7/2**^{2}

5 **2** *1* **Kimberella**^{20} [1886] 2-9-3 0.. HayleyTurner 11 77
(Michael Bell) *broke fast and led against stands' rail: rdn and jnd 2f out: hdd jst ins fnl f: styd on same pce after* **9/2**^{3}

3 *nk* **The Gold Cheongsam (IRE)** 2-8-12 0...................... WilliamBuick 12 71+
(Jeremy Noseda) *s.i.s: sn in tch in midfield: rdn and nt clr run over 2f out: swtchd rt and hdwy over 1f out: pressed wnr ins fnl f: no ex fnl 100yds* **2/1**^{1}

4 *shd* **Nile Knight** 2-9-3 0... TedDurcan 7 76+
(Marcus Tregoning) *in tch towards rr: rdn and effrt over 2f out: hdwy 1f out: styng on wl fin* **12/1**

5 *1 ½* **Club House (IRE)** 2-9-3 0... TomQueally 5 71
(Robert Mills) *wnt lft s: sn chsng ldrs: rdn and pressing ldrs 2f out: unable qck 1f out: one pce fnl f* **25/1**

32 **6** *shd* **Strong Conviction**^{10} [2164] 2-9-3 0........................... MatthewDavies 10 71+
(Mick Channon) *chsd ldr for 2f: styd chsng ldrs: rdn and unable qck whn edgd rt and hmpd over 1f out: one pce after* **7/1**

7 *½* **Zanetto** 2-9-3 0.. DavidProbert 4 70
(Andrew Balding) *s.i.s and rn green early: towards rr and pushed along: hdwy 1/2-way and rdn to chse ldrs 2f out: unable qck over 1f out: one pce after* **25/1**

8 *4 ½* **Dark Emerald (IRE)** 2-9-3 0...................................... KirstyMilczarek 1 56
(Brendan Powell) *s.i.s: bhd: clsd and in tch after 2f: rdn and effrt over 2f out: wknd over 1f out: fdd ins fnl f* **50/1**

5 **9** *3* **Rioja Day (IRE)**^{19} [1920] 2-9-3 0....................................... SebSanders 3 47
(J W Hills) *chsd ldrs: rdn and unable qck over 2f out: fdd qckly jst over 1f out* **40/1**

10 *shd* **Hot Diggity (FR)** 2-9-3 0.. EddieAhern 9 47
(Peter Chapple-Hyam) *in tch towards rr: rdn and effrt over 2f out: wknd over 1f out* **14/1**

11 *dist* **Ronaldinho (IRE)** 2-9-3 0... PatDobbs 6
(Richard Hannon) *bmpd s: moving bdly and sn lost tch: virtually p.u fnl 5f* **12/1**

1m 12.03s (-0.17) **Going Correction** -0.30s/f (Firm) **11** Ran SP% **120.4**
Speed ratings (Par 95): **89,87,87,87,85 85,84,78,74,74**
Tote Swingers: 1&2 £2.40, 1&3 £3.70, 2&3 £3.80 CSF £19.54 TOTE £4.50: £1.90, £1.80, £1.40; EX 16.40.
Owner Andrew Russell **Bred** Rathbarry Stud **Trained** East Everleigh, Wilts

FOCUS
This looked a decent juvenile maiden and the pace was solid.

NOTEBOOK
Mister Marc(IRE), who was carrying some condition, handed champion trainer Richard Hannon a fifth straight winner in the race and a sixth since 2002. He got across early and Ryan Moore always looked confident from the furlong marker. This son of Acclamation proved happy on the quick ground, he seems sure to improve and one would have to think the Coventry Stakes at Royal Ascot will come into consideration. (op 9-2)
Kimberella ◆ was always likely to relish this extra furlong and so it proved as he made a bold bid from the front against the stands' rail. He acted on the quicker ground, but may be happiest over this trip back on a slightly easier surface and can soon go one better. (op 5-1)
The Gold Cheongsam(IRE) ◆, the sole filly, was well fancied for this racecourse debut and turned in a promising display. She came with every chance 1f out, but her inexperience told and she ought to repay any backers next time out. (op 15-8 tchd 9-4 and 5-2 in a place)
Nile Knight ◆ is bred for further. However, his yard is currently going great guns and he finished strongly from off the pace. He looks potentially useful. (op 14-1)
Club House(IRE), out of a 1m-1m2f winner, shaped encouragingly and ought to prove a deal sharper next time. (op 28-1)
Strong Conviction was just about the form pick. This was a better race than he's faced so far, though, and he was beaten 1f out after showing early speed. (op 8-1)
Zanetto ran green on this debut and did some pleasing late work. He's yet another here that ought to get closer on his next assignment.
Ronaldinho(IRE) Official explanation: jockey said that the colt knocked itself leaving the stalls

2481 SOUTHERN DAILY ECHO TAPSTER STKS (LISTED RACE) 1m 4f
4:25 (4:27) (Class 1) 4-Y-O+ **£20,720** (£7,836; £3,916; £1,956) **Stalls** High

Form RPR

132- **1** **Sea Moon**^{203} [7305] 4-9-0 121.. RyanMoore 1 111
(Sir Michael Stoute) *led: hdd and rdn 3f out: drvn ahd again wl over 1f out: sn hrd pressed: hdd jst ins fnl f: kpt on gamely u.p to ld again towards fin* **2/7**^{1}

00-3 **2** *hd* **Dandino**^{45} [1318] 5-9-0 110.. HayleyTurner 4 110
(James Fanshawe) *hld up in tch: rdn and effrt wl over 2f out: str chal over 1f out: led jst ins fnl f: r.o wl tl hdd and no ex towards fin* **4/1**^{2}

114- **3** *5* **Berling (IRE)**^{259} [5921] 5-9-0 99.. EddieAhern 2 102
(John Dunlop) *hld up in tch: rdn and chsng ldrs whn nt clr run on inner 2f out: gap opened over 1f out: no ex 1f out: wknd fnl 100yds* **20/1**^{3}

363- **4** *2 ¼* **Cill Rialaig**^{212} [7129] 7-8-9 104...................................... DarryllHolland 3 93
(Hughie Morrison) *chsd wnr: rdn to ld 3f out: sn edgd rt: drvn and hdd wl over 1f out: sn wknd* **20/1**^{3}

2m 36.14s (-2.26) **Going Correction** -0.30s/f (Firm) **4** Ran SP% **107.3**
Speed ratings (Par 111): **95,94,91,90**
CSF £1.70 TOTE £1.30; EX 1.60.
Owner K Abdulla **Bred** Juddmonte Farms Ltd **Trained** Newmarket, Suffolk

FOCUS
A tactical Listed event and both of the principals were below their best.

NOTEBOOK
Sea Moon was last seen finishing second to St Nicholas Abbey at the Breeders' Cup 203 days earlier and had been found a golden opportunity for this 4-y-o debut. He had to make his own running, though, and looked bang in trouble for nearly all of the final 3f. However, to his credit he fought off Cill Rialaig and then rallied to fend off the runner-up, ultimately winning a touch cosily. This clearly isn't the way to ride him, but Ryan Moore was left with little choice and he looks certain to improve for the outing. It also wouldn't at all surprise if he proves a horse that peaks later in the year, and connections can still look forward to racing him at the top level again. (tchd 1-3)
Dandino, who got warm beforehand, looked to have been produced with a perfectly timed challenge inside the final furlong but the winner probably always just had his measure. This was just his second outing for the yard and he's clearly back on track. (op 9-2)
Berling(IRE) ◆ moved powerfully on the inside and was short of room when trying to challenge nearing the final furlong. It was his first run back, though, and fitness ultimately told as he weakened. There's every chance he'll peak this year and is one to side with next time out. (op 16-1)
Cill Rialaig put it up to the winner 3f out and got him at it. She paid the price in between the final 2f, but is entitled to come on plenty. (tchd 18-1)

2482 HAMPSHIRE CHRONICLE H'CAP 6f
5:00 (5:02) (Class 4) (0-80,80) 6-Y-O+ **£6,469** (£1,925; £962; £481) **Stalls** High

Form RPR

-455 **1** **Beat The Bell**^{19} [1935] 7-8-10 **74**................................. LeonnaMayor$^{(5)}$ 3 86
(Jamie Osborne) *in tch in midfield: hdwy over 2f out: rdn to chal over 1f out: led jst ins fnl f: r.o wl* **14/1**

4122 **2** *¾* **My Kingdom (IRE)**^{32} [1587] 6-9-6 **79**...........................(t) DarryllHolland 2 89
(Ian Williams) *hld up: hdwy jst over 2f out: swtchd rt and effrt u.p in centre over 1f out: chsd wnr ins fnl f: r.o* **7/2**^{1}

21-1 **3** *3 ¾* **Aye Aye Digby (IRE)**^{23} [1789] 7-9-6 **79**............................ SebSanders 5 77
(Patrick Chamings) *led: rdn ent fnl 2f: hrd pressed and drvn over 1f out: hdd jst ins fnl f: wknd* **7/2**^{1}

0146 **4** *1 ¼* **Mata Hari Blue**^{14} [2070] 6-8-12 **71**....................................(t) MichaelHills 7 65
(John Holt) *chsd ldr: rdn and edgd rt jst over 2f out: btn ent fnl f: wknd* **10/1**

5215 **5** *1* **Masai Moon**^{15} [2023] 8-9-7 **80**......................................(b) JamesMillman 8 70
(Rod Millman) *in tch: rdn and edgd rt ent fnl 2f: wknd over 1f out* **8/1**^{3}

3263 **6** *2 ½* **The Happy Hammer (IRE)**^{32} [1587] 6-8-4 **66** oh3....... HarryBentley$^{(3)}$ 1 48
(Eugene Stanford) *hld up in rr and grad switching towards stands' rail effrt u.p 2f out: no imp fr over 1f out* **10/1**

-624 **7** *½* **Emiratesdotcom**^{14} [2070] 6-9-3 **76**.. PatDobbs 6 57
(Milton Bradley) *in tch towards rr: effrt u.p jst over 2f out: no prog and wl hld fr over 1f out* **11/1**

460- **8** *4* **Ryan Style (IRE)**^{253} [6113] 6-9-6 **79**.............................. JackMitchell 11 47
(Lisa Williamson) *chsd ldrs: rdn and fnd little jst over 2f out: sn edgd rt and wknd: bhd fnl f* **25/1**

00-0 **9** *½* **Victorian Bounty**^{20} [1885] 7-9-0 **80**............. WilliamTwiston-Davies$^{(7)}$ 13 46
(Tony Newcombe) *chsd ldrs: rdn and struggling over 2f out: wknd and edgd rt 2f out: sn bhd* **20/1**

0-00 **10** *½* **Seamus Shindig**^{10} [2165] 10-8-5 **69**................................. AmyScott$^{(5)}$ 9 34
(Henry Candy) *a bhd: shkn up 2f out: rdr looking bhd and nt pushed ent fnl f: n.d* **16/1**

0-60 **11** *2* **Alfresco**^{73} [893] 8-8-9 **68**...(b) DavidProbert 10 26
(John Best) *t.k.h: hld up in tch: wknd u.p jst over 2f out: wl bhd fnl f* **15/2**^{2}

1m 9.63s (-2.57) **Going Correction** -0.30s/f (Firm) **11** Ran SP% **115.0**
Speed ratings: **105,104,99,97,96 92,92,86,86,85 82**
Tote Swingers: 1&2 £16.30, 1&3 £17.70, 2&3 £2.40 CSF £55.90 CT £158.55 TOTE £19.40: £5.70, £1.40, £1.70; EX 99.30.
Owner Leslie Marshall **Bred** D J P Turner **Trained** Upper Lambourn, Berks

FOCUS
A typically open-looking sprint handicap. The riders didn't want to know the stands' rail and the main action came down the centre. The runner-up, to his 6f best, sets the standard.
Seamus Shindig Official explanation: jockey said that the gelding lost action
Alfresco Official explanation: jockey said that the gelding was never travelling

2483 BRIGHTON ARGUS MAIDEN FILLIES' STKS 7f
5:35 (5:35) (Class 5) 3-Y-O
£3,112 (£932; £466; £233; £116; £58) **Stalls** Low

Form RPR

022 **1** **Sputnik Sweetheart**^{15} [2041] 3-9-0 73................................. PatDobbs 10 81
(Richard Hannon) *mde all: rdn and fnd ex over 1f out: r.o wl and in command fnl f: rdn out* **7/2**^{2}

2 **2** *2* **Ensejaam (CAN)**[36] [1501] 3-9-0 0 .... MichaelHills 1 75
(Charles Hills) *taken down early: sn chsng wnr: clsd and tried to chal over 2f out: unable qck over 1f out: one pce and wl hld fnl f* **5/4**[1]

0-0 **3** *4 ½* **Sangrail**[43] [1357] 3-9-0 0 .... JackMitchell 7 63
(William Muir) *racd off the pce in midfield after 1f: rdn to chse clr ldng pair 3f out: kpt on but no imp* **50/1**

4 *½* **Port Charlotte** 3-9-0 0 .... DarryllHolland 8 62+
(Hughie Morrison) *rn green: racd off the pce in last quartet and pushed along: hdwy 2f out: styd on wl fnl f: nvr trbld ldrs* **16/1**

0 **5** *4* **Majestic South**[15] [2050] 3-9-0 0 .... TomQueally 4 51+
(Mick Channon) *t.k.h early: racd off the pce in midfield: rdn 3f out: wnt modest 4th over 1f out: no imp and lost 4th ins fnl f* **20/1**

0 **6** *2 ½* **Wyebridge**[11] [2145] 3-9-0 0 .... AmirQuinn 9 44+
(Gary Moore) *rn green: racd wl off the pce in last quartet: sme modest hdwy fnl f: n.d* **50/1**

7 *4* **Poly Pomona** 3-8-7 0 .... WilliamTwiston-Davies(7) 12 33+
(Richard Hannon) *wnt lft leaving stalls and slowly away: rn green and bhd: sme hdwy fnl f: n.d* **15/2**

0 **8** *6* **Blissamore**[36] [1501] 3-9-0 0 .... TravisBlock 2 17
(Hughie Morrison) *racd keenly: chsd ldrs tl 3f out: sn wknd* **25/1**

9 *8* **Ebtisama (USA)** 3-8-11 0 .... HarryBentley(3) 11 +
(Marcus Tregoning) *awkward leaving stalls and slowly away: rn green and a bhd* **4/1**[3]

0 **10** *4* **Boragh Waters (IRE)**[11] [2145] 3-9-0 0 .... WilliamBuick 3
(Brian Meehan) *chsd ldrs for 1f: sn off the pce in midfield: wknd over 2f out: wl bhd fnl f: t.o* **40/1**

1m 25.07s (-1.93) **Going Correction** -0.30s/f (Firm) **10** Ran SP% **119.3**
Speed ratings (Par 96): **99,96,91,91,86 83,79,72,63,58**
Tote Swingers: 1&2 £2.40, 1&3 £33.50, 2&3 £17.00 CSF £19.79 TOTE £4.50: £1.60, £1.10, £11.80; EX 10.60.
Owner Michael Pescod **Bred** Ecurie I M Fares **Trained** East Everleigh, Wilts

FOCUS
There was no hanging about in this fillies' maiden, but it still paid to race on the pace. A step forward from the winner with the second a small improver.
T/Plt: £14.00 to a £1 stake. Pool: £87,172.00 - 4,528.20 winning tickets. T/Qpdt: £2.80 to a £1 stake. Pool: £4,503.00 - 1,172.30 winning tickets. SP

2449 HAYDOCK (L-H)
Saturday, May 26

OFFICIAL GOING: Good to firm (firm in places) changing to firm after race 1 (2.00).
Wind: Fresh 1/2 behind Weather: Fine and sunny, breezy but very warm

2484 BETFRED MOBILE SPORTS H'CAP 1m 3f 200y
2:00 (2:01) (Class 3) (0-90,88) 3-Y-O
£9,337 (£2,796; £1,398; £699; £349; £175) **Stalls** Centre

Form RPR

2-54 **1** **Montaser (IRE)**[17] [1978] 3-8-12 79 .... JimCrowley 3 93
(David Simcock) *hld up: hdwy on ins 4f out: chsd ldrs over 2f out: styd on to ld nr fin* **9/2**[3]

0-03 **2** *nk* **Rainbow Gold**[21] [1866] 3-8-10 77 .... MircoDemuro 1 91
(Mark Johnston) *t.k.h: trckd ldrs: led over 3f out: edgd lft fnl f: hdd and no ex towards fin* **16/1**

31-2 **3** *8* **Beyond Conceit (IRE)**[29] [1641] 3-9-7 88 .... JamieSpencer 5 89
(Tom Tate) *led: qcknd pce over 4f out: hdd over 3f out: kpt on same pce fnl 2f* **4/1**[2]

2-10 **4** *2 ¼* **Almuftarris (USA)**[7] [2269] 3-8-11 78 .... PaulHanagan 2 76
(Ed Dunlop) *trckd ldrs: drvn over 3f out: one pce* **5/1**

10 **5** *3 ¾* **Bob's World**[17] [1978] 3-8-8 75 .... TomEaves 7 67
(Jennie Candlish) *stdd s: hld up in rr: pushed along over 6f out: outpcd over 3f out: wknd over 1f out* **8/1**

511 **6** *nse* **Last Shadow**[14] [2088] 3-9-1 82 .... MartinDwyer 6 74
(William Muir) *trckd ldrs: drvn over 4f out: outpcd over 3f out: sn btn* **11/2**

031- **7** *¾* **Moidore**[213] [7109] 3-8-11 78 .... RichardMullen 4 68
(Roger Charlton) *hld up in rr: effrt 4f out: nvr a threat: hung lft and wknd over 1f out* **11/4**[1]

2m 28.69s (-5.11) **Going Correction** -0.35s/f (Firm) **7** Ran SP% **113.9**
Speed ratings (Par 103): **103,102,97,95,93 93,92**
toteswingers: 1&2 £28.50, 1&3 £2.30, 2&3 £28.50. CSF £67.40 TOTE £3.40: £2.70, £6.10; EX 109.30.
Owner Dr Marwan Koukash **Bred** Airlie Stud **Trained** Newmarket, Suffolk

FOCUS
The time for the opener was just a fraction outside the standard, confirming that the ground was riding quick. There was a strong wind pretty much behind the runners in the home straight too. Following the first race the official going description was amended to firm all over. This was only the fourth running of this good handicap, but a couple of the early winners, Opinion Poll and Brown Panther, have gone on to much better things. Some progressive types contested this renewal, which was run at a sound pace. A couple failed to do themselves justice but the first two drew well clear. The form is fluid but the third is rated close to his Doncaster mark.

NOTEBOOK
Montaser(IRE) went after the leader with two to run and, heldped by having the rail to run against, grabbed him with a couple of strides left. Unlucky not to have finished closer at Chester last time, he was suited by this much quicker ground. He's proving consistent this year. (op 5-1)
Rainbow Gold, still a maiden, went for home plenty soon enough and still looked in command approaching the final furlong, but his jockey seemed reluctant to go for his stick as his lead was being whittled away and the colt was worn down in the last strides. This was a most creditable handicap debut, but one that he perhaps should have won, and he'll be up in the weights for this.
Beyond Conceit(IRE) made the running at a generous pace but was quickly no threat once headed. The step up in trip oughtn't to have been a problem but he was racing off an 8lb higher mark than when narrowly beaten at Doncaster, and the ground could not have been more different. (op 9-2 tchd 11-2 early in a place)
Almuftarris(USA), dropped 6lb since his last run and a King Edward VII Stakes entry, raced somewhat keenly through the early stages and could not raise his game in the straight. (op 7-1)
Bob's World was never a factor and was much further behind Montaser than he had been at Chester.
Last Shadow, a dual Nottingham winner this spring, was 5lb higher on this rise in grade. He was in trouble before the home turn, certainly before this disappointing effort could be attributed to the longer trip. (op 5-1)
Moidore, described as mentally immature at two, has been gelded since his last appearance. Royal Ascot had been mentioned, but that was before this lacklustre performance. His maiden win came on fast ground so underfoot conditions should not have posed him too many problems. Richard Mullen reported that the gelding was never travelling. Official explanation: jockey said that the gelding was never travelling (op 5-2)

2485 BETFRED SILVER BOWL H'CAP 1m
2:30 (2:31) (Class 2) 3-Y-O
£37,350 (£11,184; £5,592; £2,796; £1,398; £702) **Stalls** Low

Form RPR

0-02 **1** **Gabrial (IRE)**[16] [1996] 3-9-1 91 .... JamieSpencer 2 104+
(Richard Fahey) *hld up in rr: plld outside and gd hdwy over 2f out: hung bdly lft over 1f out: styd on wl to ld last 75yds* **9/2**[2]

1-26 **2** *1 ¾* **Lucky Henry**[7] [2265] 3-8-7 83 .... PaulMulrennan 11 92
(Clive Cox) *trckd ldrs: led over 1f out: hdd and no ex ins fnl f* **20/1**

1503 **3** *2 ¾* **Switzerland (IRE)**[16] [1996] 3-9-5 95 .... MircoDemuro 10 98
(Mark Johnston) *w ldrs: led over 6f out: hdd over 1f out: kpt on same pce* **14/1**

13-3 **4** *¾* **Frog Hollow**[21] [1860] 3-9-0 90 .... JimCrowley 5 91+
(Ralph Beckett) *hld up in rr: hdwy over 2f out: sltly hmpd over 1f out: kpt on ins fnl f* **3/1**[1]

6-33 **5** *¾* **Tidentime (USA)**[15] [2022] 3-9-3 93 .... MartinHarley 1 92
(Mick Channon) *rr-div: hdwy on ins over 3f out: sn chsng ldrs: kpt on one pce fnl f* **10/1**

-230 **6** *hd* **Hazaz (IRE)**[14] [2080] 3-9-6 96 .... RobertWinston 3 95
(Clive Brittain) *chsd ldrs: one pce over 1f out* **20/1**

12-0 **7** *1* **Nemushka**[28] [1653] 3-8-5 81 .... (p) JamesSullivan 13 78+
(Richard Fahey) *in rr: hdwy on outer over 3f out: bdly hmpd and lost pl over 1f out: kpt on ins fnl f* **25/1**

00-1 **8** *1 ¼* **Apostle (IRE)**[20] [1894] 3-9-0 90 .... LukeMorris 16 84
(Michael Bell) *prom on outer: one pce fnl 2f* **14/1**

050- **9** *¾* **Wise Venture (IRE)**[217] [7026] 3-8-9 85 .... FergusSweeney 6 77
(Alan Jarvis) *led tl over 6f out: chsd ldrs: wknd fnl f* **33/1**

0-10 **10** *½* **Chapter Seven**[37] [1468] 3-9-0 90 .... FrederikTylicki 12 84+
(Richard Fahey) *towards rr: drvn 4f out: one pce whn hmpd and lost pl over 1f out* **16/1**

1-54 **11** *nk* **Lord Ofthe Shadows (IRE)**[15] [2022] 3-9-4 97 .... SeanLevey(3) 9 87
(Richard Hannon) *in tch: one pce whn nt clr run over 1f out* **20/1**

313- **12** *9* **Mabaany**[228] [6766] 3-8-13 89 .... PaulHanagan 15 58
(William Haggas) *t.k.h on outer: stdd into mid-div over 5f out: wknd over 1f out: eased whn bhd* **6/1**[3]

12-5 **13** *4* **Abishena (IRE)**[15] [2022] 3-9-3 93 .... PhillipMakin 14 53
(Mark Johnston) *in tch: lost pl over 1f out: eased whn bhd ins fnl f* **20/1**

1m 41.27s (-2.43) **Going Correction** -0.35s/f (Firm) **13** Ran SP% **111.6**
Speed ratings (Par 105): **98,96,93,92,92 91,90,89,88,88 88,79,75**
toteswingers: 1&2 £18.80, 1&3 £3.30, 2&3 £63.90. CSF £890.20 CT £890.20 TOTE £3.70: £1.50, £5.30, £3.20; EX 28.00 Trifecta £670.40 Part won. Pool: £906.01 - 0.20 winning units..
Owner Dr Marwan Koukash **Bred** B Kennedy **Trained** Musley Bank, N Yorks

FOCUS
Another competitive edition of this valuable 3yo handicap, although it was weakened a little by the non-runners. It was run at a searching pace and was around a second outside the standard. The winner impressed and the runner-up sets the level, despite recording a narrow personal-best.

NOTEBOOK
Gabrial(IRE), wanting nothing to do with the initial pace, was still last with three to run. When his initial choice of path was blocked Jamie Spencer switched his mount to the wide outside and the colt quickened up smartly, but he hung badly to his left as he did so and took out a couple of his stablemates on his inner. His erratic course did not stem his rapid progress and he won readily. He had hung at Chester and is obviously quirky, but he is smart too, as befits a horse named after the owner's son. The obvious race for him would be the Brittania Handicap at Royal Ascot - Sagramor completed the double last year - and a stands' side draw would be to his benefit. (op 4-1)
Lucky Henry ◆ travelled strongly before being let down to lead, but had not reckoned on the winner. With ground and trip in his favour he beat the rest well enough, and with more improvement to come he should be borne in mind for similar races.
Switzerland(IRE), half a length behind Gabrial at Chester and a pound better off now, was in front before the straight and kept going for third once headed. He handles most ground but has yet to convince that he truly wants a mile.
Frog Hollow was expected to improve on his reappearance at Newmarket, in a race Balducci had run in before winning this in 2010. Held up, he made late progress without troubling the principals, after being slightly inconvenienced when the winner went across him. The stiff mile at Ascot would suit him. (tchd 7-2 in places)
Tidentime(USA) kept on up the inside and this was a better effort, with this first try at a mile and the sound surface both obvious factors. (op 12-1)
Hazaz(IRE) ran respectably back at a more suitable trip, but isn't going to be easy to place successfully. His trainer has vast experience with this type, however, and there could yet be a nice race waiting for him somewhere along the line. (op 22-1)
Nemushka was badly hampered when the winner, her stablemate, hung across her, but still gathered herself and ran on in pleasing fashion. (op 20-1)
Apostle(IRE) was found wanting from a 5lb higher mark, with a wide draw not aiding his cause. (op 12-1)
Mabaany one of just two in the field without a previous run this season, and making his handicap debut, was a bit keen and can improve on this. (op 15-2)

2486 BETFRED.COM TEMPLE STKS (BRITISH CHAMPIONS SERIES) (GROUP 2) 5f
3:00 (3:04) (Class 1) 3-Y-O+
£45,368 (£17,200; £8,608; £4,288; £2,152; £1,080) **Stalls** High

Form RPR

220- **1** **Bated Breath**[167] [7730] 5-9-4 118 .... GeorgeBaker 2 121
(Roger Charlton) *trckd ldrs: t.k.h: led over 1f out: edgd lft ins fnl f: hld on wl* **2/1**[1]

0-22 **2** *nk* **Sole Power**[56] [1146] 5-9-4 115 .... PaulHanagan 4 120
(Edward Lynam, Ire) *n.m.r and lost pl after 100yds: hld up in rr: hdwy 2f out: nt clr run and swtchd outside appr fnl f: chsd wnr jst ins fnl f: no ex towards fin* **3/1**[2]

-224 **3** *3 ½* **Spirit Quartz (IRE)**[21] [1857] 4-9-4 106 .... JimCrowley 5 108
(Robert Cowell) *chsd ldrs: upsides over 1f out: styd on same pce* **14/1**

-052 **4** *hd* **Borderlescott**[17] [1977] 10-9-4 105 .... RobertWinston 12 107
(Robin Bastiman) *mid-div: hdwy over 2f out: chsng ldrs over 1f out: kpt on same pce* **20/1**

-061 **5** *½* **Confessional**[17] [1975] 5-9-4 101 .... (be) PaulMulrennan 6 105
(Tim Easterby) *mid-div: hdwy 2f out: swtchd lft: kpt on ins fnl f* **28/1**

2-63 **6** *2 ¼* **Elusivity (IRE)**[21] [1857] 4-9-4 107 .... ShaneKelly 8 97
(Brian Meehan) *towards rr: kpt on fnl 2f: edgd lft appr fnl f: nvr nr to chal* **14/1**

011- **7** ½ **Tangerine Trees**[237] 6563 7-9-8 115..............................(v) TomEaves 7 99
(Bryan Smart) *led: hdd over 1f out: sn wknd* **12/1**
020- **8** 1¼ **Masamah (IRE)**[237] 6563 6-9-4 113.............................. JamieSpencer 13 91
(Kevin Ryan) *chsd ldrs: hung lft: n.m.r and wknd appr fnl f* **7/1**[3]
110- **9** 2 **Bapak Chinta (USA)**[231] 6688 3-8-10 109........................ PhillipMakin 3 80
(Kevin Ryan) *chsd ldrs: lost pl 2f out* **20/1**
5-50 **10** 2 **Best Terms**[14] 2078 3-8-7 113.................................... KieranO'Neill 10 70
(Richard Hannon) *sn outpcd and bhd: kpt on fnl 2f: nvr on terms* **14/1**
2442 **11** 7 **Monsieur Joe (IRE)**[13] 2112 5-9-4 110............................ PatCosgrave 1 51
(Robert Cowell) *chsd ldrs on outer: sn drvn along: lost pl over 1f out* **20/1**
02-1 **12** 2½ **Swiss Dream**[14] 2087 4-9-1 103....................................... NickyMackay 9 39
(David Elsworth) *chsd ldrs: rdn and wknd 2f out* **20/1**

56.39s (-4.41) **Going Correction** -0.35s/f (Firm) course record
WFA 3 from 4yo+ 8lb **12 Ran SP% 121.0**
Speed ratings (Par 115): **121,120,114,114,113 110,109,107,104,101 89,85**
toteswingers: 1&2 £3.40, 1&3 £11.00, 2&3 £12.10. CSF £6.98 TOTE £2.90: £1.50, £1.60, £5.30; EX 11.20 Trifecta £221.70 Pool: £3,293.50 - 10.99 winning units..
Owner K Abdulla **Bred** Juddmonte Farms Ltd **Trained** Beckhampton, Wilts

FOCUS
A quality renewal of this Grade 2 sprint, which has been run at Haydock since 2008. The inaugural winner at this venue was Fleeting Spirit, and the track record she set that day was shattered by 0.76sec. The form looks solid with the first two, the form horses coming into this, pulling clear of the remainder, while the next three home are rated close to their marks.

NOTEBOOK
Bated Breath was beaten half a length or less in three top-level sprints last term, including the Betfred Sprint Cup here, and he deserved this victory which came on only his second run over 5f. He travelled very smoothly behind the pace and quickened up to lead before sticking his neck out to repel the runner-up's late burst. This confirms he is fully effective at this trip and the King's Stand is likely to be his race at Royal Ascot rather than taking on Black Caviar in the Diamond Jubilee. He is admirably suited by fast ground and there should be a Group One for him at some stage. (tchd 11-4 in a place)
Sole Power last year's winner, nearly emulated Mind Games who remains the only dual winner of this. Runner-up in both his outings in Dubai this spring, he had his ideal conditions of a strong-run 5f on quick ground here and, after tracking the winner through and just letting him take first run, he was finishing well. He had been squeezed out early on, and that maybe proved costly. The Nunthorpe, which he won in 2010, would be the obvious target, but Bated Breath might well take him on again at York. (op 7-2)
Spirit Quartz(IRE) represented connections rather than Prohibit and he did them proud, travelling nicely and sticking on for third behind two cracking sprinters. This was his first run on ground quicker than good. (op 12-1)
Borderlescott remains capable of high-class form and has now reached the frame in all five renewals of this race at Haydock, without managing to get his head in front. (tchd 22-1)
Confessional won a Chester handicap in bad ground off 95 last time and had a lot on at the weights, but he is improving and he was running on at the end here. (op 25-1 tchd 33-1)
Elusivity(IRE) is another sprinter on the upgrade and he backed up his Palace House third with another creditable effort. He won't mind returning to 6f.
Tangerine Trees was up against it on his seasonal debut conceding a 4lb penalty for his win in last autumn's Prix de l'Abbaye. He faded after showing pace and this should have put him spot-on for Royal Ascot. (op 11-1 tchd 9-1)
Masamah(IRE) was without the cheekpieces he wore when last seen in the Abbaye. He was drawn nearest the stands' rail but, after showing his customary pace, hung across the track. Official explanation: jockey said that the gelding hung left-handed (op 8-1)
Bapak Chinta(USA) faced a tall order against older sprinters on only the fourth outing of his career, and was found wanting. The quick ground was by no means ideal and, although he has plenty to prove now, it's to be hoped he can fulfil the abundant potential he showed when winning last year's Norfolk Stakes. (op 12-1)
Best Terms had the second-best chance on BHA ratings, but she was soon trailing on this drop back to sprint distances. She did pass a couple of rivals late on, but she continues to operate below her best and it remains to be seen how long connections persevere with this likeable filly. (tchd 16-1)
Monsieur Joe(IRE), the third's stablemate, was not helped by racing on the outside. (op 16-1)
Swiss Dream weakened after showing pace in this better grade. (op 18-1)

2487 BETFRED "THE BONUS KING" H'CAP (DIV I) 6f
3:30 (3:34) (Class 4) (0-85,85) 4-Y-0+ **£5,175** (£1,540; £769; £384) **Stalls** High

Form RPR
30-0 **1** **L'Ami Louis (IRE)**[21] 1844 4-9-4 82.............................. FergusSweeney 3 92
(Henry Candy) *mde all: edgd lft fnl f: hld on towards fin* **7/2**[1]
0-00 **2** nk **Fred Willetts (IRE)**[7] 2284 4-9-4 82..............................(v) LeeNewman 5 91
(David Barron) *s.s: sn chsng ldrs: edgd lft fnl f: no ex towards fin* **20/1**
3646 **3** 1¼ **Head Space (IRE)**[7] 2264 4-8-13 77........................... JamesSullivan 17 82+
(Ruth Carr) *chsd ldrs stands' side: edgd rt and kpt on wl fnl f* **5/1**[2]
10-6 **4** 2½ **Yurituni**[19] 1926 5-9-2 80..............................(v) PaulHanagan 10 77
(Eve Johnson Houghton) *chsd ldrs: outpcd over 1f out: kpt on last 150yds* **25/1**
-600 **5** nk **Able Master (IRE)**[7] 2264 6-9-1 79.............................. PhillipMakin 7 75+
(David O'Meara) *sn outpcd: n.m.r 2f out: edgd rt: styd on wl fnl f* **16/1**
35-0 **6** ½ **Barney McGrew (IRE)**[7] 2284 9-9-6 84........................... TomEaves 14 78
(Michael Dods) *dwlt: hdwy over 2f out: kpt on same pce fnl f* **10/1**
044- **7** nk **Who's Shirl**[245] 6355 6-8-10 74...................................... PaulMulrennan 2 68
(Chris Fairhurst) *in rr on outer: styd on appr fnl f: nvr a factor* **20/1**
-000 **8** 1¾ **Mac Gille Eoin**[7] 2268 8-9-5 83.. ShaneKelly 11 71
(John Gallagher) *reluctant to load: chsd ldrs: hung lft and wknd over 1f out* **16/1**
2644 **9** ½ **Kylladdie**[14] 2071 5-8-8 77.. RaulDaSilva(5) 16 63
(Steve Gollings) *towards rr: kpt on fnl f: nvr on terms* **10/1**
30-0 **10** 2 **King Of Eden (IRE)**[20] 1885 6-9-3 81............................. PatCosgrave 15 61
(Eric Alston) *towards rr: drvn over 2f out: nvr a factor* **13/2**[3]
/002 **11** 1 **Ertikaan**[7] 2289 5-9-7 85.. LukeMorris 1 62
(Ronald Harris) *chsd ldrs on outside: lost pl over 1f out* **15/2**
-444 **12** 6 **Azrael**[21] 1844 4-9-6 84.. MartinHarley 9 42
(Alan McCabe) *chsd ldrs: drvn 3f out: hung lft and lost pl wl over 1f out* **13/2**[3]
00-0 **13** 2¾ **Ginger Ted (IRE)**[21] 1844 5-9-5 83..............................(p) J-PGuillambert 6 32
(Stuart Williams) *mid-div: lost pl 3f out* **16/1**

1m 10.83s (-2.97) **Going Correction** -0.35s/f (Firm) **13 Ran SP% 126.5**
Speed ratings (Par 105): **105,104,102,99,99 98,98,95,95,92 91,83,79**
toteswingers: 1&2 £24.40, 1&3 £6.90, 2&3 £43.90. CSF £85.33 CT £377.58 TOTE £4.80: £2.00, £6.60, £2.60; EX 117.30.
Owner First Of Many Partnership **Bred** J M Carroll **Trained** Kingston Warren, Oxon

FOCUS
Ordinary sprint handicap form, although the winner can do better if going on from this while the second is holding his form well.
Mac Gille Eoin Official explanation: jockey said that the horse hung left-handed
Azrael Official explanation: jockey said that the gelding was unsuited by the firm ground

2488 BETFRED "THE BONUS KING" H'CAP (DIV II) 6f
4:05 (4:07) (Class 4) (0-85,85) 4-Y-0+ **£5,175** (£1,540; £769; £384) **Stalls** High

Form RPR
-420 **1** **Mappin Time (IRE)**[15] 2029 4-9-3 81.......................(p) PaulMulrennan 16 92
(Tim Easterby) *w ldrs: led over 1f out: kpt on wl towards fin* **20/1**
21-2 **2** 1 **Seeking Magic**[51] 1203 4-9-6 84..................................(t[1]) AdamKirby 9 92
(Clive Cox) *trckd ldrs: chal appr fnl f: no ex last 50yds* **5/1**[1]
100- **3** 1½ **Noverre To Go (IRE)**[230] 6723 6-9-4 82....................(bt[1]) LukeMorris 13 85
(Ronald Harris) *v awkward s: in rr: hdwy over 2f out: kpt on wl fnl f* **10/1**
41-4 **4** ¾ **Paradise Spectre**[47] 1254 5-8-9 73.............................. MartinHarley 8 74
(Mrs K Burke) *hmpd s: in rr: hdwy 2f out: kpt on wl ins fnl f* **9/1**
6416 **5** hd **Sulis Minerva (IRE)**[15] 2023 5-8-11 80........................... RaulDaSilva(5) 5 80
(Jeremy Gask) *in rr: hdwy over 2f out: kpt on wl fnl f* **16/1**
-140 **6** nse **Another Try (IRE)**[42] 1373 7-9-5 83.............................. JimCrowley 14 83
(Alan Jarvis) *prom: effrt over 2f out: one pce appr fnl f* **22/1**
0-4 **7** shd **Anderiego (IRE)**[8] 2243 4-8-12 76.............................. JamieSpencer 2 75+
(David O'Meara) *hmpd s: sn bhd: gd hdwy far side over 1f out: nt rch ldrs* **15/2**[2]
0-30 **8** 1¼ **Blues Jazz**[21] 1863 6-8-13 80.. DaleSwift(3) 17 75
(Ian Semple) *sn wl outpcd and in rr: hdwy 2f out: kpt on: eased towards fin* **20/1**
-200 **9** 2¼ **Whozthecat (IRE)**[7] 2289 5-9-3 81..............................(v) ShaneKelly 12 69
(Declan Carroll) *dwlt: in rr: sme hdwy over 1f out: nvr a factor* **8/1**[3]
10-0 **10** ½ **Sacrosanctus**[56] 1141 4-9-7 85.................................... NickyMackay 15 72
(Scott Dixon) *hld up: hdwy to chse ldrs stands' side over 3f out: wknd appr fnl f* **20/1**
0-00 **11** ¾ **Barkston Ash**[7] 2264 4-8-11 75.................................... MartinDwyer 7 59
(Eric Alston) *led: hdd over 1f out: sn wknd* **33/1**
5025 **12** 6 **Klynch**[18] 1951 6-9-4 82...(b) JamesSullivan 3 47
(Ruth Carr) *chsd ldrs: wknd over 1f out* **10/1**
0-23 **13** 3¼ **Midnight Feast**[19] 1936 4-8-13 77.............................. PaulHanagan 4 32
(Eve Johnson Houghton) *stmbld s: sn chsd ldrs: lost pl over 1f out* **9/1**
0-00 **14** ¾ **Damika (IRE)**[20] 1885 9-9-7 85.................................... MichaelStainton 11 37
(David Brown) *sn drvn along in rr: bhd fnl 3f* **16/1**
0-00 **15** ½ **Star Rover (IRE)**[17] 1975 5-9-5 83..............................(v) PadraigBeggy 6 34
(David Evans) *mid-div: drvn over 2f out: lost pl over 1f out* **20/1**
5555 **16** 4½ **Courageous (IRE)**[7] 2289 6-9-5 83..............................(t) WilliamCarson 1 19
(Kevin Ryan) *edgd rt s: chsd ldrs: lost pl and eased over 1f out* **16/1**
500- **17** 9 **Invincible Force (IRE)**[208] 7199 8-8-13 77..............(b) MircoDemuro 10
(Paul Green) *chsd ldrs: wknd over 2f out: eased ins fnl f* **40/1**

1m 11.1s (-2.70) **Going Correction** -0.35s/f (Firm) **17 Ran SP% 124.1**
Speed ratings (Par 105): **104,102,100,99,99 99,99,97,94,93 92,84,80,79,78 72,60**
toteswingers: 1&2 £16.00, 1&3 £27.50, 2&3 £13.10. CSF £109.42 CT £1132.56 TOTE £20.90: £5.40, £1.70, £3.70, £2.70; EX 117.50.
Owner P Baillie **Bred** J Jamgotchian **Trained** Great Habton, N Yorks
■ Stewards' Enquiry : Adam Kirby four-day ban: use of whip (9, 11-13 June)

FOCUS
The second division of this sprint was run in a slightly slower time than the first. The winner is rated to his former best backed up by the second.
Anderiego(IRE) Official explanation: trainers's representative said that the gelding was unsuited by the firm ground
Whozthecat(IRE) Official explanation: jockey said that the gelding suffered interference in running
Midnight Feast Official explanation: jockey said that the gelding stumbled leaving the stalls

2489 BETFRED GOALS GALORE H'CAP 7f
4:40 (4:41) (Class 3) (0-90,90) 4-Y-0+ **£8,409** (£2,502; £1,250; £625) **Stalls** Low

Form RPR
2620 **1** **Tamareen (IRE)**[15] 2029 4-8-10 79.............................. PaulHanagan 2 88
(Richard Fahey) *wnt rt s: chsd ldrs: chal over 2f out: led over 1f out: edgd lft: kpt on wl clsng stages* **11/1**
0-61 **2** 1½ **Farlow (IRE)**[21] 1844 4-9-6 89.. JimCrowley 1 94
(Ralph Beckett) *chsd ldrs: upsides on inner over 1f out: styd on same pce last 75yds* **4/1**[2]
-600 **3** 1 **Greensward**[42] 1373 6-9-4 87.. MartinDwyer 6 89+
(Mike Murphy) *mid-div: drvn 3f out: styng on whn nt clr run 1f out: kpt on wl towards fin* **20/1**
04-0 **4** ¾ **Treadwell (IRE)**[143] 29 5-9-7 90.............................. FergusSweeney 8 90
(Jamie Osborne) *s.i.s: mid-div: effrt over 2f out: kpt on same pce fnl f* **25/1**
3-60 **5** 1¼ **Redvers (IRE)**[8] 2250 4-9-3 86.. LukeMorris 7 83
(Ed Vaughan) *chsd ldrs: effrt over 2f out: kpt on one pce appr fnl f* **14/1**
0-00 **6** ½ **Glenridding**[7] 2285 8-8-10 79.. MartinHarley 12 75
(James Given) *led: hdd over 1f out: grad wknd* **50/1**
0401 **7** 1½ **Bawaardi (IRE)**[32] 1586 6-8-11 80.............................. PadraigBeggy 5 71
(David Evans) *chsd ldrs: drvn 3f out: wknd last 100yds* **25/1**
0-1 **8** ½ **Shahzan (IRE)**[21] 1843 4-9-4 87.................................... AndreaAtzeni 4 77
(Roger Varian) *trckd ldrs: t.k.h: drvn over 2f out: hung lft: wknd fnl f: n.m.r nr fin* **5/2**[1]
-140 **9** nk **Karaka Jack**[22] 1821 5-9-2 85.. GeorgeBaker 13 74
(David Nicholls) *hld up in rr: kpt on fnl 2f: nvr a factor* **12/1**
10-0 **10** 1 **Shesastar**[14] 2067 4-9-3 86.. PaulMulrennan 11 73
(David Barron) *hld up in rr: kpt on fnl 2f: nvr a factor* **9/1**
0151 **11** 3 **Al Muheer (IRE)**[7] 2285 7-9-7 90..............................(b) JamesSullivan 10 68
(Ruth Carr) *hld up in rr: t.k.h: nvr on terms* **13/2**[3]
2530 **12** 38 **Layla's Hero (IRE)**[21] 1844 5-9-4 87.............................. JamieSpencer 14
(John Quinn) *in rr: swtchd lft after s: last and drvn over 4f out: sn bhd: virtually p.u over 1f out: tailed rt off* **17/2**

1m 29.06s (-1.64) **Going Correction** -0.35s/f (Firm) **12 Ran SP% 119.5**
Speed ratings (Par 107): **95,93,92,91,89 89,87,87,86,85 82,38**
toteswingers: 1&2 £9.40, 1&3 £50.20, 2&3 £19.90. CSF £52.90 CT £890.89 TOTE £16.00: £4.00, £1.50, £7.90; EX 67.60.
Owner Dr Marwan Koukash **Bred** Mcdonnell Cbs Bloodstock **Trained** Musley Bank, N Yorks

FOCUS
Another ordinary handicap rated around the first two.

NOTEBOOK
Tamareen(IRE) tracked the leader into the straight before asserting approaching the final furlong. Generally pretty consistent, he had floundered in the soft ground at Chester but was much more home on this lightning-quick surface. (op 12-1)
Farlow(IRE) ran well off this 3lb higher mark for this Doncaster win and this good effort on his first try at 7f increases the options open to this progressive type. (op 11-2)
Greensward was stopped in his run before finishing nicely. He had fallen to his last winning mark and the return to turf suited him. (op 16-1)
Treadwell(IRE), off the track since January, made pleasing late headway. He is nicely handicapped on his old form now.
Redvers(IRE) had been dropped 2lb but remains 12lb above his previous winnng turf mark. (op 12-1)

Shahzan(IRE), a lightly raced handicap debutant, failed to settle satisfactorily and faded steadily once the chips were down. A return to 6f may suit him. (op 2-1)
Al Muheer(IRE)'s 10lb rise for his Thirsk win did not look insurmountable, but he was always towards the back of the field. It may pay to afford him another chance. James Sullivan reported that the gelding ran too freely. Official explanation: jockey said the gelding ran too freely (tchd 7-1)

2490 BETFRED "BONUS KING BINGO" H'CAP 7f
5:15 (5:16) (Class 3) (0-95,88) 3-Y-O **£8,409** (£2,502; £1,250; £625) **Stalls** Low

Form RPR
60-0 **1** **Hamza (IRE)**[16] 1998 3-9-3 **84**....................(b[1]) PaulMulrennan 3 92
(Kevin Ryan) *mde all: jnd 2f out: kpt on towards fin* **33/1**
2-14 **2** *1* **Glen Moss (IRE)**[16] 1996 3-9-6 **87**.................... WilliamCarson 6 92+
(Charles Hills) *dwlt: swtchd lft after s: in rr: hdwy over 3f out: chal 2f out: kpt on same pce last 50yds* **9/2**[2]
4-23 **3** *½* **Three Am Tour (IRE)**[10] 2182 3-9-3 **87**.................... SeanLevey(3) 4 91+
(Richard Hannon) *chsd ldrs: nt clr run and edgd rt 1f out: kpt on towards fin* **5/1**[3]
10-0 **4** *1* **Wahylah (IRE)**[38] 1452 3-8-13 **80**.................... MartinDwyer 2 81+
(Clive Brittain) *chsd ldrs on ins: nt clr run 2f out: keeping on wl whn n.m.r thrght fnl f* **16/1**
01 **5** *1 ¾* **Hometown Glory**[22] 1824 3-9-1 **82**.................... ShaneKelly 11 78
(Brian Meehan) *chsd ldrs: kpt on same pce appr fnl f* **7/1**
-050 **6** *2* **Cravat**[20] 1888 3-9-5 **86**.................... MircoDemuro 1 77
(Mark Johnston) *towards rr: drvn over 3f out: kpt on fnl 2f: nvr a threat* **10/1**
10-0 **7** *2 ½* **Elusive Flame**[36] 1500 3-9-3 **84**.................... NickyMackay 5 68
(David Elsworth) *chsd ldrs: wknd appr fnl f* **25/1**
4-30 **8** *5* **Gabrial's Gift (IRE)**[20] 1894 3-8-10 **77**.................... MartinHarley 10 48
(David Simcock) *hld up towards rr: hdwy 3f out: sn chsng ldrs: edgd lft and wknd over 1f out* **16/1**
1104 **9** *¾* **Kickingthelilly**[49] 1221 3-9-2 **83**.................... ChrisCatlin 13 52
(Rae Guest) *in rr: nvr a factor* **16/1**
4-00 **10** *3 ¼* **Ralphy Boy (IRE)**[10] 2182 3-9-7 **88**.................... LeeNewman 9 48
(David Nicholls) *chsd ldrs: wknd over 1f out* **20/1**
103- **11** *1 ¼* **Brocklebank (IRE)**[296] 4717 3-9-4 **88**.................... JulieBurke(3) 12 44
(Kevin Ryan) *in rr: drvn and outpcd over 3f out: nvr on terms* **25/1**
0-06 **12** *5* **Worthington (IRE)**[15] 2022 3-9-1 **82**.................... JamesSullivan 7 25
(Richard Fahey) *in rr: bhd fnl 4f* **33/1**
01- **13** *2 ½* **Afaal (USA)**[228] 6768 3-9-0 **81**.................... PaulHanagan 8 17
(William Haggas) *t.k.h: trckd ldrs: dropped to rr 4f out: sn drvn and lost pl* **5/2**[1]

1m 28.04s (-2.66) **Going Correction** -0.35s/f (Firm) 13 Ran SP% **121.0**
Speed ratings (Par 103): **101,99,99,98,96 93,91,85,84,80 79,73,70**
toteswingers: 1&2 £38.00, 1&3 £34.80, 2&3 £4.90. CSF £170.24 CT £895.06 TOTE £49.30: £12.20, £1.90, £1.70; EX 307.50.
Owner Mubarak Al Naemi **Bred** Castlemartin Stud And Skymarc Farm **Trained** Hambleton, N Yorks

FOCUS
A fair handicap run at a brisk pace and in a time a second quicker than the older handicappers took in the preceding race. A year ago the finish was contested by subsequent Grade 1 winner Western Aristocrat and Rhythm Of Light, who won the Sandringham at Royal Ascot on her next start, but the progressive types were eclipsed here. A slight personal -best from the winner backed up by the third and fourth.

NOTEBOOK
Hamza(IRE) cut little ice on his 3-y-o reappearance, but the step up to 7f and fitting of first-time blinkers elicited an improved run. He made all the running and fought on well, but it remains to be seen if the headgear works as well again.
Glen Moss(IRE) missed the break and travelled up well but hung in a little when challenging and was just held. He missed the break and was ridden off the pace, and seemed to settle better as a result. (op 6-1)
Three Am Tour(IRE) had to switch before running on. This was another sound effort, but she didn't get close enough for her aptitude for a battle to be tested. (op 6-1)
Wahylah(IRE), whose last three runs had been in valuable sales races, ran creditably on this handicap debut back up in trip. She was short of room on the rail late on, but for which she would have finished closer.
Hometown Glory, a Wolverhampton maiden winner, loomed up looking a threat, but could not quicken when required. This was only his third run and he still has something to offer. (op 11-2)
Cravat had ground and trip to suit and stepped up in recent efforts, albeit only marginally. (op 12-1)
Afaal(USA), a maiden winner when last seen in October, was in trouble by halfway and this was surely not his running. The representative of William Haggas reported that the gelding was unsuited by the firm ground. Official explanation: jockey said the gelding was unsuited by the firm ground (op 9-4 tchd 2-1)

2491 BETFRED MOBILE CASINO H'CAP 1m
5:50 (5:52) (Class 4) (0-80,80) 4-Y-0+ **£5,175** (£1,540; £769; £384) **Stalls** Low

Form RPR
0-01 **1** **Cono Zur (FR)**[22] 1830 5-8-10 **69**.................... JamesSullivan 8 81
(Ruth Carr) *mde all: qcknd 4f out: styd on to forge clr over 1f out: unchal* **9/1**
-500 **2** *3* **Musnad (USA)**[11] 2151 4-8-9 **71**.................... DaleSwift(3) 12 76+
(Brian Ellison) *in rr: outpcd 4f out: hdwy on ins over 2f out: styd on fnl f: tk 2nd post* **10/1**
6400 **3** *shd* **Gritstone**[19] 1914 5-8-7 **73**.................... LauraBarry(7) 17 78
(Richard Fahey) *chsd ldrs: wnt 2nd over 1f out: kpt on same pce* **12/1**
4-20 **4** *2* **Madam Macie (IRE)**[18] 1951 5-9-2 **80**.................... LucyAlexander(5) 10 80
(David O'Meara) *trckd ldrs: drvn and outpcd 4f out: kpt on same pce fnl 2f* **8/1**[3]
25-0 **5** *2 ¾* **My Single Malt (IRE)**[22] 1820 4-9-3 **76**.................... PaulHanagan 4 70
(Julie Camacho) *hld up in rr: hdwy over 2f out: kpt on fnl f* **10/1**
500- **6** *4 ½* **Venutius**[213] 7110 5-9-4 **80**.................... SeanLevey(3) 2 64
(Ed McMahon) *s.i.s: sn mid-div: outpcd over 2f out: no threat after* **12/1**
00-4 **7** *4* **Fastnet Storm (IRE)**[107] 480 6-9-0 **73**.................... MartinHarley 9 47
(David Barron) *chsd ldrs: wknd appr fnl f* **14/1**
-311 **8** *3 ¼* **Toymaker**[46] 1269 5-9-2 **75**.................... PaulMulrennan 11 42
(James Given) *in rr: drvn and outpcd over 3f out: no threat after* **3/1**[1]
4311 **9** *8* **Thackeray**[28] 1659 5-8-8 **67**.................... MichaelStainton 14 16
(Chris Fairhurst) *prom on outside: drvn and lost pl over 3f out* **4/1**[2]
0-16 **10** *1 ½* **President Lincoln (USA)**[18] 1951 4-9-6 **79**.................... ShaneKelly 1 24
(Declan Carroll) *wnt rt s: chsd ldrs: wknd 2f out* **8/1**[3]
300- **11** *6* **Izzy The Ozzy (IRE)**[244] 6383 4-9-4 **77**.................... LeeNewman 6
(David Barron) *chsd ldrs: drvn over 3f out: lost pl 2f out* **14/1**

1m 41.77s (-1.93) **Going Correction** -0.35s/f (Firm) 11 Ran SP% **124.1**
Speed ratings (Par 105): **95,92,91,89,87 82,78,75,67,65 59**
toteswingers: 1&2 £10.80, 1&3 £27.70, 2&3 £17.40. CSF £101.09 CT £1122.91 TOTE £10.20: £2.50, £3.50, £4.80; EX 145.50.
Owner Ruth Carr Racing **Bred** Jean-Pierre-Joseph Dubois **Trained** Huby, N Yorks

FOCUS
Just fair handicap form but fairly sound, rated around the first three.
Toymaker Official explanation: jockey said the gelding failed to pick up in the home straight
T/Jkpt: Not won. T/Plt: £581.40 to a £1 stake. Pool £128,198.23. 160.95 winning tickets. T/Qpdt: £24.80 to a £1 stake. Pool £7,779.91. 231.55 winning tickets. WG

2392 LINGFIELD (L-H)
Saturday, May 26

OFFICIAL GOING: Turf course - firm; all-weather - standard
Wind: Light breeze, half ahead Weather: Very warm

2492 BETFRED MOBILE BRITISH STALLION STUDS E B F MAIDEN FILLIES' STKS (TURF) 6f
5:55 (5:55) (Class 5) 2-Y-O **£3,881** (£1,155; £577; £288) **Stalls** High

Form RPR
1 **Lovely Pass (IRE)** 2-9-0 0.................... SilvestreDeSousa 4 80+
(Mahmood Al Zarooni) *racd green: slowly away and veered lft s: bhd: swtchd lft and gd hdwy over 2f out: sn led but hung bdly lft: r.o strly whn stened up: drew clr: comf* **8/11**[1]
2 *2 ¼* **Desert Sunrise** 2-9-0 0.................... RyanMoore 6 65
(Sir Michael Stoute) *s.i.s and hmpd s: sn pushed along in last pair: hdwy 3f out: ev ch wl over 1f out: sn rdn: nt pce of wnr* **11/4**[2]
3 *shd* **Spiritual Girl** 2-9-0 0.................... HayleyTurner 3 65
(Michael Bell) *prom: ev ch wl over 1f out: kpt on same pce fnl f* **11/1**
4 *9* **Ana Shababiya (IRE)** 2-9-0 0.................... EddieAhern 8 36
(Ismail Mohammed) *prom for 2f: rdn to chse ldrs 3f out: outpcd fr 2f out* **17/2**[3]
0 **5** *nk* **Harleys Rocket**[12] 2124 2-8-9 0.................... DavidKenny(5) 2 35
(Brendan Powell) *t.k.h: led: rdn and hdd jst over 2f out: sn outpcd* **22/1**
6 *4* **Strawberry Duck (IRE)** 2-9-0 0.................... KirstyMilczarek 1 22
(Amy Weaver) *chsd ldrs: rdn 3f out: wknd over 1f out* **40/1**
5 **7** *9* **Symphony Of Dreams**[19] 1904 2-9-0 0.................... MarcHalford 7
(Dai Burchell) *wnt lft leaving stalls: trckd ldrs: pushed along 3f out: rdn whn carried lft jst over 2f out: sn wknd* **66/1**

1m 11.48s (0.28) **Going Correction** -0.20s/f (Firm) 7 Ran SP% **111.7**
Speed ratings (Par 90): **90,87,86,74,74 69,57**
toteswingers: 1&2 £1.10, 1&3 £1.60, 2&3 £3.30. CSF £2.68 TOTE £1.70: £1.10, £2.10; EX 2.60.
Owner Godolphin **Bred** Stowell Park Stud **Trained** Newmarket, Suffolk

FOCUS
With three good stables filling the places, and the first two in particular having a decent pedigree, this was probably an above-average maiden despite the smallish field. The winner can do better if going the right way but the form is just ordinary.

NOTEBOOK
Lovely Pass(IRE), out of a winning miler, and a half-sister to winners at 7f/1m, was backed to make a winning debut but proved to be very green. She should benefit greatly from this and even better can be expected in future. (op 10-11)
Desert Sunrise ◆, a 75,000gns half-sister to high-class juveniles Primo Valentino and Dora Carrington, has plenty to live up to but this was a promising start. She will be hard to beat next time. (tchd 9-4)
Spiritual Girl has two middle-distance winners in the family but she showed plenty of speed on this debut. She should stay 7f later in the summer but this trip didn't look too sharp at present. (op 9-1 tchd 12-1)
Ana Shababiya(IRE), a 33,000gns half-sister to a modest 5f winner, was well beaten by the first three. She will have to improve to win a maiden but she showed enough to give some hope in nurseries later in the season. (op 7-1)
Harleys Rocket has a bit of early toe but 5f may be her trip at present and in any case she is some way short of winning a maiden. (op 25-1 tchd 28-1 and 20-1)

2493 BERNARD COUGHLAN 60TH BIRTHDAY FILLIES' H'CAP (TURF) 6f
6:30 (6:30) (Class 5) (0-75,75) 4-Y-0+ **£3,067** (£905; £453) **Stalls** High

Form RPR
2-06 **1** **Piddie's Power**[22] 1827 5-9-6 **74**.................... RyanMoore 2 83
(Ed McMahon) *hld up: pushed along and hdwy over 2f out: rdn to ld ent fnl f: r.o wl: readily* **7/2**[2]
02-0 **2** *2 ¾* **Amosite**[140] 88 6-8-7 **61**....................(p) KirstyMilczarek 6 61
(J R Jenkins) *led: rdn wl over 1f out: hdd ent fnl f: kpt on but nt pce of wnr* **12/1**
-066 **3** *1 ¾* **Nine Before Ten (IRE)**[39] 1428 4-8-5 **64**....................(t) NathanAlison(5) 4 58
(Richard Guest) *racd keenly: prom: rdn and ev ch 2f out: bmpd ent fnl f: kpt on same pce* **25/1**
31-2 **4** *½* **Oh So Spicy**[46] 1289 5-9-5 **73**.................... TedDurcan 5 66
(Chris Wall) *chsd ldrs: rdn over 2f out: nt pce to get on terms* **13/8**[1]
2126 **5** *½* **Dancing Welcome**[9] 2207 6-8-11 **65**....................(b) HayleyTurner 3 56
(Milton Bradley) *sn pushed along in last trio: rdn over 2f out: r.o fnl f: nvr threatened ldrs* **7/2**[2]
4016 **6** *1 ½* **Flashbang**[16] 2012 4-8-13 **67**....................(b) SilvestreDeSousa 7 53
(Paul Cole) *chsd ldrs: effrt to chal over 2f out: sn edgd lft: fdd ins fnl f* **13/2**[3]
000- **7** *3 ½* **Primo Lady**[248] 6256 4-9-7 **75**....................(v) EddieAhern 8 50
(Gay Kelleway) *sn pushed along in last trio: rdn 3f out: wknd and eased ins fnl f* **16/1**

1m 9.87s (-1.33) **Going Correction** -0.20s/f (Firm) 7 Ran SP% **113.3**
Speed ratings (Par 100): **100,96,94,93,92 90,86**
toteswingers: 1&2 £7.60, 1&3 £13.80, 2&3 £17.20. CSF £41.97 CT £896.62 TOTE £3.80: £1.70, £5.60; EX 47.20.
Owner The Brookfield Stud & Partners **Bred** The Dunnet Lads **Trained** Lichfield, Staffs

FOCUS
This wasn't greatly competitive, and many of the runners are inconsistent. The winner recorded a narrow personal-best.
Oh So Spicy Official explanation: jockey said that the mare was unsuited by the firm ground
Flashbang Official explanation: jockey said that the filly hung left

2494 VINOLS CROSS INN H'CAP (TURF) 5f
7:00 (7:02) (Class 5) (0-75,74) 3-Y-0+ **£3,067** (£905; £453) **Stalls** High

Form RPR
1430 **1** **Triple Dream**[14] 2084 7-9-8 **70**....................(tp) HayleyTurner 9 78
(Milton Bradley) *racd stands' side: chsd ldrs: rdn 2f out: sn edgd lft: str run ins fnl f: led fnl stride* **18/1**
-115 **2** *nse* **Howyadoingnotsobad (IRE)**[22] 1827 4-9-4 **71**.......... DavidKenny(5) 13 79
(Karen George) *racd stands' side: led: rdn and hung lft over 1f out: kpt on: ct fnl stride* **5/1**[2]
10-5 **3** *½* **Best Be Careful (IRE)**[15] 2040 4-9-3 **70**.................... RachealKneller(5) 8 76
(Mark Usher) *racd stands' side: mid-div: rdn whn swtchd rt ent fnl f: r.o: wnt 3rd nr fin* **12/1**

0060 **4** *1* **The Strig**[8] 2251 5-9-5 **67**......(v) BrettDoyle 12 69
(Stuart Williams) *racd stands' side: s.i.s: towards rr: rdn over 2f out: r.o ins fnl f: wnt 4th nr fin* **20/1**

00-5 **5** *½* **Picabo (IRE)**[19] 1936 4-9-6 **73**...... AmyScott(5) 3 74
(Henry Candy) *racd centre: s.i.s and wnt lft s: towards rr: rdn and hdwy fr 2f out: kpt on same pce fnl f* **6/1**[3]

53-0 **6** *hd* **Drift And Dream**[9] 2195 5-9-12 **74**...... TedDurcan 10 74
(Chris Wall) *racd stands' side: mid-div: rdn 2f out: no imp tl r.o ins fnl f* **5/1**[2]

6-30 **7** *¾* **Wooden King (IRE)**[4] 2369 7-9-10 **72**...... TomMcLaughlin 7 69
(Malcolm Saunders) *racd stands' side: chsd ldrs: rdn 2f out: fdd fnl 75yds* **10/1**

0501 **8** *nk* **Billy Red**[59] 1073 8-9-9 **71**......(b) JamieGoldstein 6 67
(J R Jenkins) *racd stands' side: chsd ldr: rdn 2f out: no ex ins fnl f* **20/1**

0226 **9** *1 ¾* **Desert Strike**[9] 2195 6-9-8 **70**......(p) RyanMoore 2 65
(Charles Hills) *racd centre: chsd ldrs: rdn over 2f out: keeping on at same pce whn short of room and snatched up ins fnl f* **5/1**[2]

3030 **10** *¾* **Sherjawy (IRE)**[4] 2360 8-8-12 **60** oh3......(b) KirstyMilczarek 5 47
(Zoe Davison) *racd stands' side: sn struggling: a in rr* **33/1**

40-3 **11** *1 ¾* **Whitecrest**[14] 2084 4-9-8 **70**...... EddieAhern 11 51
(John Spearing) *racd stands' side: mid-div: rdn over 2f out: wknd fnl f* **9/2**[1]

00-0 **12** *7* **Cape Royal**[14] 2084 12-8-13 **68**......(tp) TimClark(7) 4 24
(Milton Bradley) *racd centre: chsd ldrs tl wknd 2f out* **40/1**

57.23s (-0.97) **Going Correction** -0.20s/f (Firm) 12 Ran SP% **119.4**
Speed ratings (Par 103): **99,98,98,96,95 95,94,93,90,89 86,75**
toteswingers: 1&2 £11.80, 1&3 £34.00, 2&3 £12.40. CSF £102.11 CT £1163.57 TOTE £18.10: £4.80, £2.10, £2.50; EX 178.40.
Owner J M Bradley **Bred** Hesmonds Stud Ltd **Trained** Sedbury, Gloucs

FOCUS
This was a routine sprint handicap, with the runner-up only just failing to cash in on the usually-favoured highest stall. The form is ordinary but straightforward.
Triple Dream Official explanation: trainer said, regarding the apparent improvemnent of form, that the gelding was suited by today's ground
Desert Strike Official explanation: jockey said that the gelding was denied a clear run
Sherjawy(IRE) Official explanation: jockey said that the gelding lost its action

2495 THAKEHAM HOMES WITH CUBITT & WEST (S) STKS 1m 4f (P)
7:35 (7:35) (Class 6) 3-Y-O **£2,181** (£644; £322) **Stalls Low**

Form RPR
6-35 **1** **Cades Reef (IRE)**[12] 2129 3-8-12 70...... DavidProbert 4 52+
(Andrew Balding) *broke wl: led for 1f: settled in 4th: hdwy to ld over 2f out: kpt on: pushed out* **2/13**[1]

000- **2** *2* **Silver Six**[213] 7108 3-8-12 47...... EddieAhern 2 49
(Sheena West) *trckd ldrs: rdn over 2f out: sn chsng wnr: kpt on but a being hld* **16/1**[3]

5305 **3** *shd* **Angel Cake (IRE)**[25] 1740 3-8-7 48......(p) HayleyTurner 5 44
(Phil McEntee) *settled in last pair after 1f: hdwy on outer fr over 2f out: rdn to press for 2nd over 1f out: kpt on same pce fnl f* **6/1**[2]

00-0 **4** *3 ½* **Shek O Lad**[45] 1303 3-8-12 46...... DarryllHolland 1 43
(Alan Jarvis) *w wnr for 1f: trckd ldrs: rdn over 2f out: kpt on same pce fr over 1f out* **20/1**

0-50 **5** *32* **Trove (IRE)**[25] 1731 3-8-12 55...... SilvestreDeSousa 6
(Mark Hoad) *led after 1f: rdn over 3f out: hdd over 2f out: wknd wl over 1f out: t.o* **25/1**

00-0 **6** *7* **Ben Croy**[45] 1303 3-8-12 55......(be[1]) TomMcLaughlin 3
(Murty McGrath) *sn trcking ldr: rdn to press ldr briefly 3f out: wknd wl over 1f out: t.o* **33/1**

2m 36.88s (3.88) **Going Correction** +0.25s/f (Slow) 6 Ran SP% **118.4**
Speed ratings (Par 97): **97,95,95,93,71 67**
toteswingers: 1&2 £2.20, 1&3 £1.10, 2&3 £3.60. CSF £5.02 TOTE £1.20: £1.02, £6.80; EX 4.70.The winner was bought in for 8,600gns.
Owner Mick and Janice Mariscotti **Bred** Gerrardstown House Stud **Trained** Kingsclere, Hants
■ Stewards' Enquiry : Tom McLaughlin two-day ban: careless riding (9, 11 June)

FOCUS
The winner stood out beforehand in this weak seller but was unimpressive.

2496 JILL AND CLIVE'S SILVER ANNIVERSARY MAIDEN STKS 1m (P)
8:10 (8:12) (Class 5) 3-Y-O+ **£3,067** (£905; £453) **Stalls High**

Form RPR
42 **1** **Hill Street (IRE)**[19] 1923 3-9-1 0...... WilliamBuick 7 81+
(John Gosden) *trckd ldrs: shkn up to ld ent fnl f: kpt on wl: pushed out* **4/6**[1]

00 **2** *3* **Viewpoint (IRE)**[7] 2266 3-9-1 0...... TedDurcan 1 74
(Richard Hannon) *trckd ldr tl rdn over 2f out: kpt on to regain 2nd towards fin* **11/1**

0 **3** *½* **Muhdiq (USA)**[15] 2041 3-9-1 0...... SilvestreDeSousa 11 73
(Brian Meehan) *led: rdn over 2f out: hdd ent fnl f: sn hld by wnr: no ex whn lost 2nd nring fin* **9/1**[3]

4- **4** *nk* **Abbraccio**[395] 1605 4-9-13 0...... HayleyTurner 8 75
(James Fanshawe) *in tch: rdn 3f out: styd on wl ins fnl f: nt rch ldrs* **10/3**[2]

5 *shd* **Caskelena (IRE)** 3-8-10 0......[1] RyanMoore 5 67+
(Sir Michael Stoute) *s.i.s: towards rr: quite keen after 1f: hdwy over 3f out: sn rdn: styd on wl fnl f: nt rch ldrs* **11/1**

3-0 **6** *4 ½* **Paddyfrommenlo (IRE)**[38] 1450 3-9-1 0...... EddieAhern 12 62
(J W Hills) *towards rr: sme late prog: nvr trbld ldrs* **25/1**

7 *10* **Turama** 3-8-10 0...... TomMcLaughlin 4 34+
(Ed Dunlop) *s.i.s: racd green: bhd and sn pushed along: hdwy into midfield 2f out: wknd ent fnl f* **25/1**

0 **8** *1 ¾* **Beach Rhythm (USA)**[15] 2042 5-9-13 0...... JamesMillman 3 38
(Jim Allen) *in tch: rdn over 3f out: wknd over 2f out* **100/1**

0 **9** *2 ¼* **Perfect Outlook**[26] 1704 4-9-8 0...... DarryllHolland 6 27
(Jeremy Gask) *mid-div: rdn over 3f out: sn wknd* **66/1**

0 **10** *4 ½* **American Bling (USA)**[26] 1704 3-9-1 0...... AmirQuinn 9 22
(Gary Moore) *mid-div: pushed along over 3f out: wknd over 2f out* **66/1**

1m 38.94s (0.74) **Going Correction** +0.25s/f (Slow)
WFA 3 from 4yo+ 12lb 10 Ran SP% **121.4**
Speed ratings (Par 103): **106,103,102,102,102 97,87,85,83,79**
toteswingers: 1&2 £3.20, 1&3 £3.00, 2&3 £5.90. CSF £10.13 TOTE £1.70: £1.02, £4.10, £2.80; EX 10.40.
Owner H R H Princess Haya Of Jordan **Bred** Darley **Trained** Newmarket, Suffolk

FOCUS
These were lightly raced late-developers, which always raises some questions, but the first five have some potential if they thrive on their racing. The placed horses are improvers while the fourth is rated to last year's debut.

2497 THAKEHAM HOMES PRESENTS FRANKLINS GARDENS H'CAP 1m 2f (P)
8:40 (8:43) (Class 6) (0-60,60) 3-Y-O **£2,181** (£644; £322) **Stalls Low**

Form RPR
000- **1** **Tis Rock 'N' Roll (USA)**[185] 7521 3-9-7 **60**...... TedDurcan 1 73+
(David Lanigan) *trckd ldr: led 2f out: pushed clr: heavily eased towards fin* **6/5**[1]

2000 **2** *4* **Always Ends Well (IRE)**[7] 2283 3-9-5 **58**...... SilvestreDeSousa 2 60
(Mark Johnston) *led: rdn and hdd 2f out: kpt on but sn no ch w wnr* **8/1**

60-0 **3** *1 ¼* **Shomberg**[17] 1979 3-9-4 **57**...... EddieAhern 9 57
(Mark H Tompkins) *trckd ldrs: rdn over 2f out: kpt on same pce* **11/2**[2]

06-0 **4** *2* **You Got The Love**[10] 2162 3-8-5 **47**......(bt) HarryBentley(3) 6 43
(Jeremy Gask) *chsd ldrs: rdn 3f out: one pce fnl 2f* **20/1**

4634 **5** *1* **Never Satisfied**[60] 1055 3-9-4 **57**......(b) DarryllHolland 4 51
(Charles Hills) *mid-div: rdn over 2f out: nvr any imp* **7/1**[3]

00-6 **6** *2* **Arbeejay**[30] 1625 3-8-1 **47** oh1 ow1......(t) JakePayne(7) 3 37
(Simon Hodgson) *hld up towards rr: sme hdwy into midfield over 2f out: rdn wl over 1f out: no further imp* **40/1**

000- **7** *3* **Lana Mae**[158] 7830 3-8-10 **49**...... KirstyMilczarek 8 33
(Brendan Powell) *unruly gng to s and dismntd: tk str hold: rdn 3f out: a towards rr* **20/1**

40-4 **8** *2 ¾* **Vicgernic**[59] 1067 3-8-7 **46**......(p) BrettDoyle 7 24
(Gary Moore) *a towards rr* **8/1**

530- **9** *85* **Hesperides**[185] 7514 3-9-7 **60**...... WilliamBuick 5
(Harry Dunlop) *mid-div: rdn over 3f out: wknd qckly and eased over 2f out* **10/1**

2m 10.9s (4.30) **Going Correction** +0.25s/f (Slow) 9 Ran SP% **116.6**
Speed ratings (Par 97): **92,88,87,86,85 83,81,79,11**
toteswingers: 1&2 £3.60, 1&3 £3.70, 2&3 £7.80. CSF £11.33 CT £40.44 TOTE £2.40: £1.10, £2.50, £1.60; EX 14.10.
Owner Catesby W Clay **Bred** Runnymede Farm Inc **Trained** Upper Lambourn, Berks
■ Stewards' Enquiry : Ted Durcan trainer said, regarding the apparent improvement of form, thatthe colt had strenghthened up over the winter

FOCUS
This was a modest race in which prominent runners dominated and there were few changes in the placings from start to finish. The winner looked a cut above the rest.
T/Plt: £94.50 to a £1 stake. Pool £57,761.84. 445.77 winning tickets. T/Qpdt: £11.50 to a £1 stake. Pool £4,557.31. 291.90 winning tickets. TM

2266 NEWBURY (L-H)
Saturday, May 26

OFFICIAL GOING: Good to firm (firm in places back straight)
Wind: Brisk behind Weather: Sunny

2498 BROADBASE AMATEUR RIDERS' H'CAP 1m 2f 6y
6:10 (6:11) (Class 5) (0-70,70) 4-Y-O+ **£2,807** (£870; £435; £217) **Stalls Centre**

Form RPR
4254 **1** **Maven**[14] 2093 4-10-9 **70**...... MrWEasterby(5) 16 81
(Tim Easterby) *hld up in rr: swtchd rt to outer and hdwy 3f out: pushed along and styd on wl to ld ins fnl f: pushed out* **5/1**[1]

435- **2** *2 ½* **Laverre (IRE)**[298] 4626 5-10-5 **68**...... MrSamDavis(7) 1 74
(Lucy Wadham) *trckd ldrs: drvn to ld over 2f out: hdd ins fnl f: kpt on wl for 2nd but no ch w wnr* **12/1**

1216 **3** *¾* **Sail Home**[28] 1656 5-10-13 **69**...... MrRBirkett 13 74
(Julia Feilden) *chsd ldrs: drvn and styd on fnl 2f: kpt on to take 3rd fnl 120yds but no imp on ldng duo* **20/1**

00-P **4** *2* **South Cape**[23] 1792 9-10-7 **68**...... MissHayleyMoore(5) 7 69
(Gary Moore) *plld hrd and stdd in rr s: hdwy wd into st 5f out: styd in centre of crse and kpt on fnl 2f but nvr gng pce to rch ldrs* **22/1**

00-2 **5** *½* **Moody Tunes**[15] 2043 9-10-7 **70**...... MissALMurphy(7) 15 70
(Tom Dascombe) *led tl hdd over 2f out: sn one pce: lost 4th clsng stages* **16/1**

46-1 **6** *1 ¾* **Resplendent Light**[8] 2233 7-10-5 **66**......(t) MrJackSalmon(5) 9 62
(Bernard Llewellyn) *mid-div: hdwy towards outside fr 2f out: styd on fnl f: nvr a threat* **9/1**

156- **7** *½* **James Pollard (IRE)**[7] 7816 7-10-11 **67**......(t) RobertWilliams 3 62
(Bernard Llewellyn) *in tch: hdwy 3f out: no imp 2f out and styd on same pce* **8/1**[3]

24-0 **8** *3 ¼* **Larkrise Star**[15] 2044 5-10-5 **68**...... MissECrossman(7) 14 57
(Dean Ivory) *chsd ldr tl ins fnl 3f: sn rdn: wknd wl over 1f out* **20/1**

-644 **9** *7* **Highlife Dancer**[15] 2051 4-10-7 **68**...... MissSMDoolan(5) 4 43
(Mick Channon) *in tch: rdn 3f out: sn btn* **8/1**[3]

0322 **10** *nk* **Royal Etiquette (IRE)**[31] 1613 5-10-4 **63**...... MissRachelKing(3) 5 37
(Lawney Hill) *a towards rr* **12/1**

06-0 **11** *27* **Guilded Warrior**[15] 2043 9-10-8 **69**...... MissMBryant(5) 11
(Paddy Butler) *in tch: hdwy on outside 6f out: wknd over 4f out: t.o* **66/1**

5-56 **12** *2 ¼* **Muftarres (IRE)**[23] 1796 7-10-4 **63**......(b) MissWGibson(3) 10
(Paul Midgley) *t.k.h in rr: sme hdwy 3f out: sn wknd: t.o* **10/1**

2041 **13** *12* **Aviso (GER)**[19] 2117 8-10-8 **64**...... MrsEEvans 6
(David Evans) *chsd ldrs tl wknd qckly 3f out t.o* **33/1**

2315 **14** *7* **Penbryn (USA)**[19] 1919 5-10-6 **62**......(p) MissSBrotherton 8
(Nick Littmoden) *a in rr: t.o* **10/1**

2424 **U** **Edgeworth (IRE)**[26] 1719 6-10-11 **70**...... MrMJJSmith(3) 12
(David Bridgwater) *stmbld and uns rdr s* **13/2**[2]

2m 6.19s (-2.61) **Going Correction** -0.15s/f (Firm) 15 Ran SP% **120.0**
Speed ratings (Par 103): **104,102,101,99,99 98,97,95,89,89 67,65,56,50,**
toteswingers: 1&2 £11.10, 1&3 £42.30, 2&3 £43.10. CSF £59.72 CT £1118.38 TOTE £4.90: £1.40, £5.10, £7.40; EX 82.90 TRIFECTA Not won..
Owner Habton Farms **Bred** Habton Farms **Trained** Great Habton, N Yorks

FOCUS
A dry and warm run up to a meeting that saw the ground change to good to firm, firm in places in the back straight before the opener. The rail on the inside of the bend from the 1m to the 5f has been moved in so the round course distances are 10m longer than advertised. Exposed performers in a modest handicap in which second favourite Edgeworth stumbled and unseated his rider leaving the stalls. The gallop was soon reasonable.

2499 RELYON CLEANING NEWBURY MAIDEN AUCTION FILLIES' STKS 6f 8y
6:45 (6:47) (Class 5) 2-Y-O **£2,911** (£866; £432; £216) **Stalls** Centre

Form RPR

1 **Light Up My Life (IRE)** 2-8-11 0 PatCosgrave 4 80+
(Richard Hannon) *sn pressing for ld: str chal fnl 2f tl slt ld fnl 100yds: hld on all out* **16/1**

53 2 *nk* **Vestibule**[33] [1563] 2-8-4 0 NeilChalmers 11 72
(Eve Johnson Houghton) *pressed ldrs: led over 3f out: styd hrd pressed and rdn over 1f out: narrowly hdd fnl 100yds: styd on wl but nt quite pce of wnr* **14/1**

3 3 *½* **Faithfilly (IRE)**[19] [1911] 2-8-11 0 RichardKingscote 13 78
(Ed Walker) *slt ld tl hdd over 3f out: styd pressing ldrs and str chal fnl 2f tl one pce fnl 100yds* **13/2**[3]

4 *nk* **Annecdote** 2-8-4 0 LukeMorris 6 70+
(Jonathan Portman) *s.i.s: in rr: hdwy 3f out: n.m.r 2f out: gd hdwy fnl f: fin wl: gng on clsng stages* **18/1**

5 *1 ¼* **Momalorka** 2-8-4 0 KellyHarrison 8 66+
(William Haggas) *in tch: hdwy 2f out: styd on clsng stages: nt rch ldrs* **14/1**

6 *1 ½* **Front Page News** 2-8-6 0 AndreaAtzeni 3 63
(Robert Eddery) *in rr: hdwy over 1f out: kpt on fnl f: nvr gng pce to rch ldrs* **33/1**

3 7 *1* **Cio Cio San (IRE)**[3] [2384] 2-8-6 0 KieranO'Neill 5 60
(Richard Hannon) *chsd ldrs: rdn 2f out: wknd fnl f* **11/4**[1]

0 8 *3* **Sorcellerie**[8] [2245] 2-8-8 0 LiamKeniry 2 53+
(David Elsworth) *in tch: rdn and outpcd 2f out: styd on again clsng stages* **12/1**

0 9 *shd* **Lagrima (IRE)**[3] [2384] 2-8-1 0 RyanPowell(3) 1 49
(J S Moore) *chsd ldrs: rdn 2f out: sn btn* **100/1**

10 *½* **We Are City** 2-8-11 0 JamieSpencer 7 55
(Michael Bell) *in rr: sme hdwy on outside over 2f out: nvr rchd ldrs: wknd fnl f* **7/2**[2]

11 *nse* **Lady Bonanova (IRE)** 2-8-1 0 JemmaMarshall(5) 12 50
(Pat Phelan) *in rr: pushed along 2f out: styd on wl clsng stages* **100/1**

0 12 *3 ¾* **Devout (IRE)**[10] [2163] 2-8-5 0 SophieDoyle(3) 16 40
(Jamie Osborne) *chsd ldrs over 3f* **50/1**

4 13 *2* **Lobelia**[10] [2163] 2-8-4 0 JamieMackay 14 30
(Brian Meehan) *s.i.s: bhd most of way* **33/1**

3 14 *2 ½* **Peep N Creep (IRE)**[21] [1861] 2-8-4 0 PaulQuinn 15 23
(Tim Easterby) *chsd ldrs 3f* **15/2**

15 *16* **Michael's Song (IRE)** 2-8-3 0 CharlesBishop(5) 9
(Mick Channon) *slowly away: a green in rr* **22/1**

1m 11.76s (-1.24) **Going Correction** -0.15s/f (Firm) **15** Ran SP% **120.3**
Speed ratings (Par 90): **102,101,100,100,98 96,95,91,91,90 90,85,83,79,58**
toteswingers: 1&2 £41.00, 1&3 £17.50, 2&3 £11.30. CSF £211.94 TOTE £13.50: £3.10, £4.10, £2.40; EX 351.30 TRIFECTA Not won..
Owner D Boocock **Bred** D Boocock **Trained** East Everleigh, Wilts

FOCUS
A maiden that has often thrown up a decent performer, the pick being Group 3 winner Dhanyata in 2006 and Group 1 winner Margot Did in 2010 but the bare form of this race, where several finished in a heap, is only fair at best. The gallop was a reasonable one and the field soon merged into one group in the centre. Jamie Spencer reported the ground was riding "fast". Not the best recent renewal of this with the second having just modest form previously but the fourth and fifth showed promise.

NOTEBOOK
Light Up My Life(IRE), a 23,000gns half-sister to last year's useful winning (6f) juvenile Money Never Sleeps, showed fair form and a good attitude to beat a couple of more experienced rivals on this racecourse debut. She should have no problems with 7f and should be able to step up on this.
Vestibule, up in trip and back on fast ground, had the run of the race and turned in her best effort yet. She's likely to remain vulnerable to the better types in this grade but should be able to pick up a minor event at some point.
Faithfilly(IRE) fully confirmed debut promise over this longer trip on this much quicker ground and she should continue to give a good account. (op 7-1)
Annecdote ◆, a half-sister to several winners, including debut scorer Meglio Ancora and from a yard that won this race in 2008 and 09, shaped pleasingly on this racecourse debut after meeting trouble and she's entitled to improve for this experience.
Momalorka, an 800GBP yearling out of a half-sister to several winners, showed ability without being knocked about on this racecourse debut. She should stay 7f and is open to improvement. (op 16-1)
Front Page News, who cost 8,000GBP and is a half-sister to dual sprint winner Briery Lane and to multiple winner (from 5f-1m4f) St Ignatius, was far from disgraced on this racecourse debut. She should stay at least 7f and should do better. (op 40-1)
Cio Cio San(IRE) had shown form bordering on fair on her debut but was unable to build on that turned out quickly. This may well have come too soon and she'll be worth another chance in ordinary company. (op 7-2)
We Are City, a 22,000gns purchase out of a dam who won over 7f, looks a bit better than the bare facts suggest after a tardy start and after making up ground on the wide outside. Newcomers from this yard often improve a fair bit for their debut outings and she's worth another chance. (op 3-1 tchd 4-1)

2500 BATHWICK TYRES H'CAP 1m 7y(R)
7:15 (7:17) (Class 4) (0-85,85) 4-Y-O+ **£5,175** (£1,540; £769; £384) **Stalls** Centre

Form RPR

6-23 1 **Ree's Rascal (IRE)**[24] [1752] 4-9-1 79 PatCosgrave 10 86
(Jim Boyle) *in tch: rdn and hdwy 2f out: str run u.p fnl f: led fnl 120yds: r.o wl* **11/1**

05-2 2 *¾* **Sam Sharp (USA)**[28] [1679] 6-9-5 83 JamieSpencer 11 89+
(Ian Williams) *in rr: nt clr run ins fnl 2f: swtchd rt appr fnl f: r.o u.p fnl 120yds to take 2nd last stride: nt rch wnr* **7/2**[1]

2-00 3 *nse* **Yojimbo (IRE)**[8] [2248] 4-9-1 79 MatthewDavies 2 84
(Mick Channon) *w ldr: chal 4f out: stl upsides fr 2f out: slt ld ins fnl f: hdd fnl 120yds: lost 2nd last stride* **5/1**[2]

55-2 4 *1 ½* **Good Authority (IRE)**[25] [1729] 5-8-10 74 SebSanders 5 76
(Karen George) *in rr: hdwy over 1f out: hung lft ins fnl f: kpt on but nt rch ldrs* **12/1**

3-00 5 *1 ¼* **Perfect Cracker**[19] [1924] 4-9-5 83 AdamKirby 7 82
(Clive Cox) *in tch: rdn to chse ldrs 2f out: no imp and one pce fnl f* **9/1**

0300 6 *nk* **First Post (IRE)**[24] [1752] 5-9-5 83 AndreaAtzeni 3 81
(Derek Haydn Jones) *t.k.h: sn slt ld: jnd over 4f out: rdn and stl hrd pressed 2f out: hdd and faltered u.p ins fnl f: sn wknd* **7/1**[3]

064- 7 *nk* **Mubtadi**[258] [5970] 4-8-12 81 (t) AntiocoMurgia(5) 1 80+
(Ismail Mohammed) *chsd ldrs: nt clr run 2f out: styng on whn carried lft and hmpd ins fnl f: nt rcvr* **16/1**

2005 8 *3 ½* **Dozy Joe**[14] [2083] 4-9-2 80 LukeMorris 12 69
(Ian Wood) *chsd ldrs: rdn 2f out: hld whn hmpd ins fnl f* **20/1**

21/6 9 *shd* **Scottish Boogie (IRE)**[32] [1228] 5-8-12 76 PatDobbs 9 65
(Sylvester Kirk) *in rr: styd on fr over 1f out: nvr a threat* **16/1**

033- 10 *1* **John Biscuit (IRE)**[282] [5199] 4-9-1 79 LiamKeniry 6 66
(Andrew Balding) *t.k.h: chsd ldrs: rdn 2f out: wkng whn hmpd ins fnl f* **11/1**

0-40 11 *1 ½* **Orpen'Arry (IRE)**[11] [2151] 4-8-9 73 KieranO'Neill 8 56
(Jimmy Fox) *in rr: effrt on ins over 2f out: sn wknd* **25/1**

0-01 12 *¾* **Cruiser**[19] [1924] 4-9-7 85 MartinDwyer 4 67
(William Muir) *in tch: rdn over 2f out: btn whn hmpd ins fnl f* **8/1**

1m 36.46s (-2.24) **Going Correction** -0.15s/f (Firm) **12** Ran SP% **117.2**
Speed ratings (Par 105): **105,104,104,102,101 101,100,97,97,96 94,94**
toteswingers: 1&2 £11.80, 1&3 £10.30, 2&3 £4.10. CSF £48.71 CT £225.06 TOTE £14.50: £3.50, £1.80, £2.00; EX 62.20 Trifecta £332.90 Part won. Pool: £449.91 - 0.64 winning units..
Owner Walter Hayford **Bred** Pier House Stud **Trained** Epsom, Surrey
■ Stewards' Enquiry : Seb Sanders two-day ban: careless riding (9, 11 June)

FOCUS
Mainly exposed performers in a useful handicap. The gallop was an ordinary one.

2501 BATHWICK TYRES MAIDEN STKS 6f 8y
7:50 (7:51) (Class 5) 3-Y-O **£2,911** (£866; £432; £216) **Stalls** Centre

Form RPR

2-03 1 **Cheworee**[11] [2147] 3-8-12 73 LiamKeniry 11 80
(David Elsworth) *racd towards stands' side: trckd ldrs: qcknd to ld 1f out: pushed clr: easily* **14/1**

333- 2 *4 ½* **Juvenal (IRE)**[241] [6463] 3-9-3 77 KieranO'Neill 12 70
(Richard Hannon) *chsd ldrs: rdn over 1f out: styd on fnl f to take 2nd cl home but no ch w wnr* **9/2**[2]

2 3 *¾* **Zhiggy's Stardust**[20] [1889] 3-9-3 0 FergusSweeney 9 68
(Henry Candy) *pressed ldrs: led ins fnl 2f: sn rdn: hdd 1f out: sn outpcd by wnr: no ex and lost 2nd cl home* **11/1**

0 4 *1* **Nocturn**[38] [1452] 3-9-3 0 JamieSpencer 6 65+
(Jeremy Noseda) *s.i.s: in rr: stdy hdwy fr 2f out: green and edgd lft ins fnl f: styd on wl to take 4th clsng stages* **11/2**[3]

5 *nk* **River Pageant** 3-8-12 0 SebSanders 13 59
(Eve Johnson Houghton) *s.i.s: racd towards stands' side: hdwy to cl fr 2f out: kpt on same pce ins fnl f* **50/1**

0-33 6 *1* **Sandbetweenourtoes (IRE)**[17] [1985] 3-9-3 75 MartinDwyer 4 61
(Brian Meehan) *led: hdd ins fnl 2f: wknd ins fnl f* **4/1**[1]

0- 7 *1* **Scarabocio**[203] [7292] 3-9-0 0 AshleyHamblett(3) 7 57
(Peter Chapple-Hyam) *chsd ldrs: drvn over 2f out: wknd u.p appr fnl f* **12/1**

0 8 *2* **Rocquaine (IRE)**[7] [2262] 3-8-12 0 AndreaAtzeni 1 46
(David Evans) *pushed along towards rr over 2f out: sme hdwy ins fnl f* **100/1**

6-0 9 *½* **Invincible Beauty (IRE)**[67] [969] 3-8-12 0 LukeMorris 3 44
(Seamus Durack) *s.i.s: in rr: rdn: hung rt and green over 1f out: sme late prog* **33/1**

04 10 *1 ½* **Selfara**[15] [2041] 3-8-12 0 PatDobbs 5 40
(Roger Charlton) *in tch: rdn along over 2f out: sn btn* **8/1**

0 11 *1 ½* **Oceana Dreamer (IRE)**[20] [1889] 3-9-3 0 PatCosgrave 2 40
(Andrew Balding) *chsd ldrs: rdn over 2f out and sn btn* **18/1**

6- 12 *16* **Daffyd**[218] [6991] 3-9-3 0 GeorgeBaker 8
(Roger Charlton) *awkward leaving stalls: hld up in rr: shkn up over 2f out: no rspnse and dropped away qckly* **9/2**[2]

0-0 13 *½* **Imperial Elegance**[7] [2273] 3-8-12 0 MatthewDavies 10
(Mick Channon) *s.i.s: in rr: rdn over 3f out: lost tch over 2f out* **100/1**

1m 11.71s (-1.29) **Going Correction** -0.15s/f (Firm) **13** Ran SP% **117.7**
Speed ratings (Par 99): **102,96,95,93,93 91,90,87,87,85 83,61,61**
toteswingers: 1&2 £12.20, 1&3 £26.90, 2&3 £4.80. CSF £74.30 TOTE £20.30: £4.90, £2.20, £2.00; EX 117.10 Trifecta £328.90 Part won. Pool: £444.47 - 0.74 winning units..
Owner S Stoneham,E Van Cutsem,A Hoctor-Duncan **Bred** Sarah Stoneham **Trained** Newmarket, Suffolk

FOCUS
Not much strength in depth to this fair maiden but an improved effort from the winner. The gallop was soon reasonable and the winner raced towards the near side of the group.
Nocturn ◆ Official explanation: jockey said that the colt was slowly away and hung left handed
Invincible Beauty(IRE) Official explanation: jockey said that the filly moved poorly

2502 KKA-HIGHPOINT H'CAP 1m 5f 61y
8:25 (8:25) (Class 5) (0-75,75) 4-Y-O+ **£2,911** (£866; £432; £216) **Stalls** Centre

Form RPR

13-1 1 **Maydream**[10] [2167] 5-8-11 65 KieranO'Neill 5 75+
(Jimmy Fox) *hld up in rr: stdy hdwy on ins to trck ldrs fr 3f out: nt clr run and swtchd rt over 1f out: qcknd to ld ins fnl f: shkn up and a doing enough: edgd lft cl home* **9/2**[1]

544- 2 *nk* **Phonic (IRE)**[163] [7766] 5-8-8 62 MartinDwyer 11 68
(John Dunlop) *in tch: hdwy 4f out: ev ch fr 2f out and stl chalng fnl 120yds: nt pce of wnr clsng stages but hld on wl for 2nd* **14/1**

101- 3 *hd* **Ninfea (IRE)**[36] [7603] 4-8-12 66 LiamKeniry 6 72
(David Bridgwater) *in rr early: stdy hdwy to trck ldrs 3f out: ev ch fr 2f out and stl chalng fnl 120yds: no ex and one pce into 3rd nr fin* **20/1**

0-54 4 *¾* **Shades Of Grey**[10] [2167] 5-8-12 66 AdamKirby 12 71
(Clive Cox) *trckd ldrs: led 3f out: rdn 2f out: hdd ins fnl f: no ex clsng stages and hld whn hmpd nr fin* **5/1**[2]

2314 5 *1 ¾* **Eagle Nebula**[9] [2199] 8-9-0 68 LukeMorris 4 70
(Brett Johnson) *in rr: hdwy and hmpd 2f out: swtchd rt and hdwy u.p over 1f out: sn chsng ldrs: wknd fnl 75yds* **8/1**[3]

-032 6 *1 ¾* **Hamilton Hill**[3] [2389] 5-7-12 57 oh3 ow1 RaulDaSilva(5) 1 57+
(Dai Burchell) *in rr: hdwy and hmpd over 2f out: sn swtchd rt: styd on u.p fnl f: nt rch ldrs* **9/2**[1]

324 7 *6* **Mister Fizz**[17] [1981] 4-8-11 70 MatthewCosham(5) 8 61
(Edward Bevan) *chsd ldrs: rdn 3f out: wknd 2f out* **20/1**

0-33 8 *3 ¾* **Laughing Jack**[26] [1706] 4-9-0 75 GeorgeDowning(7) 10 60
(Tony Carroll) *t.k.h: in rr: rapid hdwy to chse ldrs 7f out: hung lft and wknd over 2f out* **9/1**

524- 9 *nk* **Castlemorris King**[157] [7839] 4-8-8 67 MarkCoumbe(5) 7 52
(Michael Attwater) *chsd ldrs: rdn 3f out: sn btn* **20/1**

0-00 **10** *2* **Magicalmysterytour (IRE)**41 577 9-9-1 **69**................ TonyCulhane 3 51
(Willie Musson) *s.i.s: in rr: sme hdwy whn hmpd over 2f out: no ch after* **14/1**

-041 **11** *3 1/4* **Timocracy**40 1418 7-8-12 **71**...................... LeonnaMayor(5) 14 48
(Alastair Lidderdale) *led tl hdd 3f out: sn btn* **8/1**3

300- **12** *79* **Cookieshake**196 7388 4-8-10 **64** ow1.............. PatCosgrave 2
(Peter Hiatt) *chsd ldrs: wknd qckly over 3f out: t.o* **33/1**

00-0 **13** *38* **First Battalion (IRE)**10 2174 4-8-13 **67**..............(b) SebSanders 9
(Paul Rich) *t.k.h: chsd ldrs tl wknd rapidly 4f out: t.o* **16/1**

2m 50.72s (-1.28) **Going Correction** -0.15s/f (Firm) **13** Ran SP% **121.7**
Speed ratings (Par 103): **97,96,96,96,95 94,90,88,87,86 84,36,12**
toteswingers: 1&2 £17.80, 1&3 £13.20, 2&3 £18.70. CSF £65.52 CT £1166.46 TOTE £6.10: £2.60, £3.70, £7.00; EX 90.00 TRIFECTA Not won..
Owner The Dancing Partners **Bred** The Dancing Partners **Trained** Collingbourne Ducis, Wilts

FOCUS
An ordinary handicap run at a fair gallop.
Hamilton Hill ◆ Official explanation: jockey said that the gelding was denied a clear run
Magicalmysterytour(IRE) Official explanation: jockey saidthat the gelding was denied a clear run

2503 ALEXANDER CONSULTING FILLIES' H'CAP 7f (S)
8:55 (8:58) (Class 5) (0-75,77) 3-Y-0+ **£2,911** (£866; £432; £216) **Stalls** Centre

Form RPR

0546 **1** **Avonrose**31 1609 5-9-4 **65**..............................(v) GeorgeBaker 10 78
(Derek Shaw) *mde virtually all: hrd pressed fr 2f out: rdn fnl f: styd on wl fnl 120yds* **16/1**

111- **2** *1/2* **Rivas Rhapsody (IRE)**163 7767 4-9-10 **71**.................. MartinDwyer 11 83
(Ian Wood) *chsd ldrs: drvn to chal fr 2f out: stl ev ch ins fnl f: no ex fnl 120yds* **7/2**2

00-2 **3** *1 1/2* **Saratoga Slew (IRE)**25 1733 3-9-1 **73**....................... JamieSpencer 3 77
(Marco Botti) *in rr: hdwy 2f out: chsd ldng duo fnl f but no imp* **7/1**3

2235 **4** *3 1/4* **Tenbridge**32 1589 3-8-10 **68**...................................(p) AndreaAtzeni 1 63
(Derek Haydn Jones) *pressed wnr: rdn 2f out: outpcd appr fnl f: kpt on again clsng stages* **50/1**

4-45 **5** *2 1/2* **Amphora**25 1730 3-8-10 **68**... LiamKeniry 2 56
(Andrew Balding) *in tch: pushed along over 2f out: rdn over 1f out: styd on same pce* **20/1**

0-00 **6** *1* **Sonning Rose (IRE)**31 1609 4-9-9 **70**........................ MatthewDavies 6 60
(Mick Channon) *in rr: hdwy 2f out: one pce fnl f* **10/1**

1362 **7** *hd* **Bint Alzain (IRE)**12 2136 3-8-7 **70**...............................1 RaulDaSilva(5) 14 55
(Gerard Butler) *in rr: hdwy appr fnl f: styd on clsng stages* **14/1**

026- **8** *shd* **Blue Maisey**206 7235 4-9-8 **69**.. SebSanders 16 58
(Peter Makin) *in tch: styd on to chse ldrs fr 2f out: hung lft and wknd ins fnl f* **20/1**

1231 **9** *1/2* **Emman Bee (IRE)**7 2272 3-9-5 **77**.............................. FergusSweeney 4 61
(John Gallagher) *chsd ldrs: rdn 2f out: sn wknd* **11/4**1

05-0 **10** *3 1/4* **Top Frock (IRE)**15 2050 3-8-13 **71**.................................... AdamKirby 12 46
(Clive Cox) *in tch: rdn and wkng whn hmpd ins fnl f* **40/1**

4-52 **11** *1 1/2* **Scarlet Rocks (IRE)**5 2342 4-9-0 **66**...............(p) MatthewCosham(5) 15 41
(David Evans) *s.i.s: in rr: nt clr run and swtchd rt over 1f out: nvr in contention* **20/1**

42-1 **12** *3/4* **By Invitation (USA)**143 26 3-8-13 **71**.............................. JimCrowley 13 46
(Ralph Beckett) *in tch: rdn and wkng whn hmpd ins fnl f* **16/1**

50-6 **13** *2 1/4* **Alice's Dancer (IRE)**20 1894 3-9-3 **75**............................ JackMitchell 7 38
(William Muir) *chsd ldrs over 4f* **25/1**

0-14 **14** *4* **Jumeirah Palm Star**23 1790 3-9-2 **74**................................ PatDobbs 8 26
(Richard Hannon) *pressed wnr: rdn 3f out: wknd over 2f out* **11/1**

100- **15** *12* **Aquasulis (IRE)**224 6864 3-9-0 **72**..................................... LukeMorris 9
(David Evans) *early spd: bhd fr 1/2-way* **50/1**

1m 25.27s (-0.43) **Going Correction** -0.15s/f (Firm)
WFA 3 from 4yo+ 11lb **15** Ran SP% **121.7**
Speed ratings (Par 100): **96,95,93,90,87 86,85,85,85,81 79,78,76,71,57**
toteswingers: 1&2 £18.70, 1&3 £32.30, 2&3 £6.10. CSF £66.07 CT £453.93 TOTE £21.20: £5.60, £2.00, £2.40; EX 110.20 TRIFECTA Not won..
Owner Moorland Racing **Bred** Mrs Mary Taylor **Trained** Sproxton, Leics

FOCUS
A fair handicap featuring a couple of unexposed sorts. The gallop was an ordinary one and those held up never figured.
Jumeirah Palm Star Official explanation: jockey said that the filly hung right in the final furlong
T/Plt: £805.40 to a £1 stake. Pool £61,061.71. 55.34 winning tickets. T/Qpdt: £20.60 to a £1 stake. Pool £5,238.38. 188.10 winning tickets. ST

2252 YORK (L-H)
Saturday, May 26

OFFICIAL GOING: Good to firm (8.1)
Wind: Light half against Weather: Sunny and dry

2504 BEAUMONTS INSURANCE BROKERS H'CAP 1m 4f
2:05 (2:05) (Class 3) (0-90,88) 4-Y-0+ **£8,409** (£2,502; £1,250; £625) **Stalls** Centre

Form RPR

21-5 **1** **Franciscan**20 1882 4-9-6 **87**.. KierenFallon 12 96+
(Luca Cumani) *hld up towards rr: hdwy over 3f out: chsd ldrs over 1f out: sn rdn and styd on ins fnl f to ld nr line* **7/2**1

40-3 **2** *hd* **Eltheeb**14 2093 5-8-13 **80**.. MickaelBarzalona 14 89
(David O'Meara) *hld up in rr: gd hdwy on wd outside 3f out: led 1 1/2f out: rdn ins fnl f: hdd and no ex nr line* **8/1**3

1-30 **3** *nk* **Royal Peculiar**20 1890 4-9-7 **88**...................................... FrankieDettori 17 96
(Sir Henry Cecil) *hld up: smooth hdwy over 4f out: trckd ldrs over 2f out: effrt to chal wl over 1f out: sn rdn and ev ch tl drvn and no ex towards fin* **6/1**2

0-26 **4** *3/4* **Certral**14 2067 4-8-12 **79**... AmyRyan 15 86
(Brian Ellison) *hld up in rr: hdwy on inner over 4f out: swtchd rt 3f out: effrt to chse ldrs wl over 1f out: rdn and ch whn edgd lft ent fnl f: kpt on* **20/1**

00-0 **5** *1 3/4* **Antigua Sunrise (IRE)**24 1756 6-8-9 **76**....................... PatrickMathers 7 82+
(Richard Fahey) *hld up in rr: hdwy whn nt clr run wl over 2f out: swtchd rt and rdn wl over 1f out: styd on fnl f: nrst fin* **20/1**

24-5 **6** *2 1/4* **Hong Kong Island (IRE)**20 1880 5-8-11 **83**............ GarryWhillans(5) 18 84
(Micky Hammond) *in tch: hdwy on outer to trck ldrs 1/2-way: pushed along 3f out: rdn over 2f out and kpt on same pce* **12/1**

6-26 **7** *1* **Iron Condor**10 2174 5-8-4 **76**.. DarrenEgan(5) 16 75
(James Eustace) *hld up towards rr: hdwy on outer over 4f out: in tch and rdn wl over 2f out: drvn and no imp fr over 1f out* **25/1**

50-0 **8** *2 3/4* **Granston (IRE)**10 2180 11-9-1 **82**................................ GrahamGibbons 5 77
(James Bethell) *prom: hdwy to ld wl over 2f out: rdn and hdd 1 1/2f out: sn wknd* **16/1**

2-00 **9** *2 1/4* **Meetings Man (IRE)**15 2031 5-8-9 **75**............................ KellyHarrison 6 66
(Micky Hammond) *cl up: pushed along 3f out: rdn 2f out: wknd and hld whn n.m.r and hmpd ent fnl f* **33/1**

6-00 **10** *3/4* **Red Jade**10 2180 7-8-10 **80**..................................(v1) MichaelMetcalfe(3) 8 70
(Mrs K Burke) *midfield: hdwy and in tch over 4f out: rdn along 3f out: wknd over 2f out* **14/1**

0-00 **11** *2 1/4* **Majestic Dream (IRE)**10 2176 4-9-2 **83**........................... PaddyAspell 4 69
(Michael Easterby) *trckd ldrs on inner: hdwy over 4f out: rdn along 3f out: sn wknd* **25/1**

420- **12** *8* **Mr Perceptive (IRE)**281 5242 4-8-5 **77**.................... JamesRogers(5) 10 50
(Micky Hammond) *dwlt: a in rr* **40/1**

42-2 **13** *2 1/2* **Getabuzz**20 1880 4-8-11 **78**... DavidAllan 3 47
(Tim Easterby) *hld up towards rr: hdwy over 3f out: in tch and rdn wl over 2f out: sn wknd* **6/1**2

/01- **14** *3 3/4* **Ultimate**71 6155 6-9-0 **84**.. LeeTopliss(3) 11 47
(Brian Ellison) *led: rdn along over 4f out: hdd wl over 3f out and sn wknd* **14/1**

-121 **15** *1* **Illustrious Forest**57 1114 4-8-12 **79**............................. TonyCulhane 13 41
(John Mackie) *prom: led wl over 3f out: rdn and hdd wl over 2f out: sn wknd* **14/1**

101- **16** *1 1/2* **Suhaili**217 7022 4-9-6 **87**.. TonyHamilton 2 46
(David Lanigan) *in tch: trckd ldrs 5f out: pushed along 4f out: rdn 3f out and sn wknd* **10/1**

2m 33.79s (0.59) **Going Correction** +0.225s/f (Good) **16** Ran SP% **127.2**
Speed ratings (Par 107): **107,106,106,106,105 103,102,101,99,99 97,92,90,88,87 86**
Tote Swingers: 1&2 £7.70, 1&3 £3.90, 2&3 £8.00 CSF £28.96 CT £172.51 TOTE £3.90: £1.60, £2.10, £1.90, £5.10; EX 22.10 Trifecta £227.70 Pool: £1,499.08 - 4.87 winning units..
Owner Dr Marwan Koukash **Bred** Fittocks Stud **Trained** Newmarket, Suffolk
■ Stewards' Enquiry : Kelly Harrison one-day ban: careless riding (9 June)

FOCUS
Rail from 1m1f to entrance to home straight moved out 3m adding 7yds to distances of 1m 4f and over. Drying ground all the time with Kieren Fallon feeling it to be "fast" while Graham Gibbons described it as "rattling". A good, competitive handicap, and although the pace was just an ordinary one, those held up emerged late on. The form looks solid, with the right horses coming to the fore.

NOTEBOOK
Franciscan, in need of the run when a good fifth at Newmarket on his reappearance, was short of room and slightly squeezed 3f out, conceding first run to Eltheeb, but he has long looked in need of trips in excess of this, and his extra stamina, as well as a strong ride from Kieren Fallon, enabled him to get up late. He'll be competing from marks in the 90s now, but should have plenty more to give in top 1m4f/1m6f handicaps. (tchd 3-1)
Eltheeb looked a bit unlucky on his reappearance at Thirsk and was again somewhat unfortunate, appearing to have made a winning run widest of all only to be claimed in the final strides. He's clearly progressing but will be nudged up the handicap for this. (op 7-1)
Royal Peculiar ◆ managed to show his last-time-out Salisbury running to be wrong, appreciating the return to faster ground. He's lightly raced and remains capable of better judging by the way he travelled. (op 7-1)
Certral showed improved form for the return to this distance and certainly seemed happier back on quick ground.
Antigua Sunrise(IRE) ◆, in-foal to Pastoral Pursuits, was unlucky not to finish closer, failing to get a run when needed, and she may be able to take advantage of her current mark if turned out fairly quickly.
Hong Kong Island(IRE) had his chance and kept on as though a return to further would suit. (tchd 14-1)
Iron Condor, who is effective up to 2m, was another who needs further than this.
Granston(IRE) didn't last long in front. (op 14-1 tchd 18-1)
Getabuzz, who is ideally suited by softer ground, probably found the ground too fast. Official explanation: jockey said the gelding was unsuited by the good to firm ground.
Suhaili, a the lightly raced 4-y-o, may also have found the ground a bit lively on this debut for David Lanigan.

2505 CLOISTERS SPA PARSONAGE ESCRICK NOW OPEN STKS (CONDITIONS RACE) 7f
2:35 (2:51) (Class 3) 3-Y-0+ **£9,703** (£2,887; £1,443; £721) **Stalls** Low

Form RPR

-034 **1** **Smarty Socks (IRE)**14 2075 8-9-2 100............................ KierenFallon 6 100
(David O'Meara) *in tch: hdwy 3f out: cl up wl over 1f out: sn rdn and led ins fnl f: kpt on strly towards fin* **6/1**

2-20 **2** *1 1/4* **Boomerang Bob (IRE)**21 1856 3-8-5 112............... MickaelBarzalona 5 93
(J W Hills) *stdd s and hld up in rr: hdwy on outer over 2f out: rdn to chal over 1f out: drvn and ev ch ins fnl f tl no ex last 50yds* **5/2**2

000- **3** *shd* **Dubai Hills**232 6672 6-8-11 87.................................. JustinNewman(5) 4 96?
(Bryan Smart) *trckd ldr: hdwy to ld wl over 2f out: drvn and hdd ins fnl f: no ex last 75yds* **25/1**

0-14 **4** *1 1/4* **Brae Hill (IRE)**14 2068 6-9-2 99...................................... TonyHamilton 7 93
(Richard Fahey) *led: pushed along 1/2-way: rdn and hdd wl over 2f out: sn drvn and kpt on u.p fnl f* **5/1**3

/0-2 **5** *4 1/2* **Saamidd**24 1749 4-9-2 114..(t) FrankieDettori 3 81
(Saeed Bin Suroor) *hld up in rr: hdwy 3f out: rdn to chal on outer wl over 1f out: sn drvn and wknd appr fnl f* **11/8**1

4002 **6** *17* **Regal Parade**14 2074 8-9-2 107...................................... AdrianNicholls 1 35
(David Nicholls) *trckd ldrs: hdwy 3f out: sn rdn and wknd 2f out* **6/1**

-600 **7** *1 1/2* **Reignier**22 1821 5-8-11 85...............................(p) ConorHarrison(7) 8 33
(Mrs K Burke) *chsd ldng pair: rdn along 3f out: sn wknd* **66/1**

1m 25.27s (-0.03) **Going Correction** +0.225s/f (Good)
WFA 3 from 4yo+ 11lb **7** Ran SP% **121.3**
Speed ratings (Par 107): **109,107,107,106,100 81,79**
Tote Swingers: 1&2 £5.00, 1&3 £18.00, 2&3 £14.70 CSF £23.11 TOTE £6.10: £1.80, £2.00; EX 33.70 Trifecta £526.00 Pool: £1,933.68 - 2.72 winning units..
Owner Direct Racing Club **Bred** Mick McGinn **Trained** Nawton, N Yorks

FOCUS
There was over a 15 minute delay to this conditions event, following an unfortunate incident that saw Captain Dimitrios collapse in the stalls. With the horses standing around for the extra time on a very hot day, it's probably unwise to read too much into the form. Those challenging nearer the stands' side came out on top. A muddling race with the first two below their best and the proximity of the third limiting things.

NOTEBOOK
Smarty Socks(IRE), down in grade having contested a Listed event at Haydock the time before, sustaining his effort best despite appearing to have a stiff task against the runner-up at the weights. (op 8-1)
Boomerang Bob(IRE), well beaten in the 2000 Guineas, was the only 3-y-o in the field and had his chance, it being somewhat disappointing he gave way a horse rated 12lb his inferior. (op 7-2 tchd 4-1)

Dubai Hills, rated just 87 and off for 232 days, was well positioned throughout and appeared to run above himself. He hasn't won since completing a four-timer on the Fibresand in January 2011 and it's hoped the handicapper doesn't read too much into this. (op 50-1)

Brae Hill(IRE) may have run just below his Victoria Cup-fourth level. (op 6-1 tchd 13-2)

Saamidd was unable to build on his Kempton second, finding little, but he had been in the stall next to Captain Dimitrios and probably deserves another chance. Official explanation: jockey said that the colt ran flat (op 11-10 tchd 6-4)

Regal Parade failed to build on his Haydock second returned to faster ground. Official explanation: jockey said that the gelding was unsuited by the good/firm going (tchd 7-1)

2506 STOWE FAMILY LAW LLP GRAND CUP (LISTED RACE) 1m 6f

3:10 (3:19) (Class 1) 4-Y-0+ **£19,848** (£7,525; £3,766; £1,876; £941) **Stalls** Low

Form				RPR
5-20	**1**		**Cavalryman**[56] 1149 6-9-0 113 .... FrankieDettori 2	109
			(Saeed Bin Suroor) *hld up in rr: smooth hdwy 3f out: chal on bit 2f out: led over 1f out: sn rdn and styd on* **9/4**[2]	
31	**2**	*2*	**Calico Cat**[7] 2287 4-9-0 95 .... MickaelBarzalona 6	106
			(Alastair Lidderdale) *hld up in rr: hdwy on outer 3f out: led 2f out: rdn and hdd appr fnl f: sn drvn and one pce* **11/1**	
-213	**3**	*4 ½*	**Gulf Of Naples (IRE)**[17] 1974 4-9-0 107 .... KierenFallon 1	100
			(Mark Johnston) *chsd ldr: rdn along 3f out: outpcd over 2f out: kpt on u.p fnl f* **6/4**[1]	
-040	**4**	*1*	**Barbican**[17] 1974 4-9-3 107 .... SamHitchcott 3	102
			(Alan Bailey) *led: clr 1/2-way: rdn along 3f out: hdd 2f out and sn wknd* **3/1**[3]	
00-0	**5**	*15*	**Mystery Star (IRE)**[17] 1974 7-9-0 91 .... DavidAllan 5	78
			(Mark H Tompkins) *prom: hdwy to chse ldr over 3f out: rdn wl over 2f out: sn wknd* **12/1**	

3m 1.24s (1.04) **Going Correction** +0.225s/f (Good) **5** Ran SP% **111.8**

Speed ratings (Par 111): **106,104,102,101,93**

CSF £23.80 TOTE £2.90: £1.70, £2.20; EX 21.50.

Owner Godolphin **Bred** Darley **Trained** Newmarket, Suffolk

FOCUS

Unreliable form potentially, with neither Barbican or Gulf Of Naples running to their mark.

NOTEBOOK

Cavalryman, who was third to Sea The Stars in the Arc at the height of his powers and has failed to match that level since joining Godolphin, but he's used to contesting stronger heats than this, and enjoyed a confidence-boosting victory. He'll go back up in grade now. (op 6-4)

Calico Cat, and for all that it looks as though he's been underrated, he shouldn't really have been able to run a horse of the winner's caliber so close. He had only made his debut a couple of weeks previously, appearing to finish a highly flattered third to Memphis Tennessee in the Ormonde Stakes, but he ran to a decent level when winning his maiden at Thirsk not long after, and this effort seemed to confirm he's at least very useful. Being so lightly raced, it's likely he has further improvement in him. (op 12-1)

Gulf Of Naples(IRE) may still have been feeling the effects of what was a huge effort in the Chester Cup. Down in trip and back on much faster ground, he couldn't dominate, but to his credit did keep on having been outpaced, and he may yet make a Pattern-class performer. (op 13-8)

Barbican, carrying a 3lb penalty, has been struggling to find his form this year and did little more than set it up for the others. (op 7-2)

Mystery Star(IRE) remains woefully out of sorts. (op 22-1 tchd 11-1)

2507 SKY BET MOBILE SPRINT H'CAP 5f

3:45 (3:51) (Class 2) (0-105,105) 3-Y-0+**£25,876** (£7,700; £3,848; £1,924) **Stalls** Centre

Form				RPR
3101	**1**		**Dancing Freddy (IRE)**[9] 2195 5-8-10 87 ....(tp) SaleemGolam 13	95
			(Richard Guest) *chsd ldrs: hdwy 2f out: rdn to ld ins fnl f: drvn and kpt on gamely towards fin* **28/1**	
461-	**2**	*½*	**Catfish (IRE)**[302] 4498 4-8-11 88 .... MickaelBarzalona 4	94
			(Brian Meehan) *racd wd: in tch: hdwy wl over 1f out: rdn and n.m.r ent fnl f: sn ev ch: drvn and kpt on* **10/1**	
2000	**3**	*nse*	**Bathwick Bear (IRE)**[7] 2286 4-8-9 86 oh2 .... CathyGannon 1	92
			(David Evans) *prom on wd outside: rdn along wl over 1f out: ev ch ent fnl f: sn drvn and kpt on same pce towards fin* **20/1**	
266-	**4**	*½*	**Celerina (IRE)**[49] 1226 5-9-3 94 .... FrankieDettori 6	98+
			(T Stack, Ire) *hmpd s and towards rr: hdwy 2f out: rdn over 1f out: styd on wl fnl f* **4/1**[1]	
420-	**5**	*nk*	**Albany Rose (IRE)**[238] 6522 4-8-7 87 .... RyanClark[(3)] 18	90+
			(Rae Guest) *racd nr stands' rail: towards rr: hdwy wl over 1f out: sn rdn and styd on fnl f: nrst fin* **20/1**	
0-36	**6**	*nse*	**Tax Free (IRE)**[17] 1975 10-9-2 93 .... AdrianNicholls 8	96
			(David Nicholls) *cl up: led 2f out: sn rdn: hdd and no ex ins fnl f* **16/1**	
25/0	**6**	*dht*	**Ziggy Lee**[9] 2195 6-8-4 86 oh6 .... JamesRogers[(5)] 5	89
			(Giles Bravery) *wnt rt s: towards rr: rdn and hdwy wl over 1f out: styd on wl fnl f: nrst fin* **25/1**	
0-00	**8**	*1 ¼*	**Ancient Cross**[9] 2208 8-9-0 98 ....(t) DavidSimmonson[(7)] 15	96+
			(Michael Easterby) *dwlt and towards rr: hdwy wl over 1f out: sn rdn and styd on fnl f: nrst fin* **12/1**	
6-45	**9**	*nk*	**Vocational (USA)**[9] 2212 3-8-11 96 .... SamHitchcott 3	90
			(Mark Johnston) *prom: rdn along 2f out: drvn appr fnl f: sn wknd* **33/1**	
-404	**10**	*½*	**Hazelrigg (IRE)**[7] 2289 7-8-9 86 oh2 ....(be) DavidAllan 2	82
			(Tim Easterby) *dwlt: towards rr and pushed along 1/2-way: rdn wl over 1f out: kpt on fnl f: n.d* **16/1**	
6-00	**11**	*nk*	**Johannes (IRE)**[21] 1844 9-8-9 86 oh1 .... TonyHamilton 16	80
			(Richard Fahey) *hld up: hdwy wl over 1f out: sn rdn and kpt on fnl f: n.d* **10/1**	
00-4	**12**	*shd*	**Lexi's Hero (IRE)**[17] 1975 4-9-9 100 ....(p) KierenFallon 14	94
			(Kevin Ryan) *chsd ldrs: rdn along wl over 1f out: grad wknd* **11/2**[2]	
-312	**13**	*nk*	**Secret Witness**[9] 2208 6-9-11 105 ....(b) CPGeoghegan[(3)] 19	98
			(Ronald Harris) *racd towards stands' rail: in rr: hdwy over 2f out: sn rdn and n.d* **8/1**[3]	
0-34	**14**	*1*	**Mon Brav**[7] 2284 5-8-4 86 oh3 ....(p) DarrenEgan[(5)] 9	75
			(Brian Ellison) *in tch: rdn along wl over 2f out: sn wknd* **14/1**	
-132	**15**	*hd*	**Magical Macey (USA)**[7] 2286 5-9-10 101 ....(b) GrahamGibbons 11	90
			(David Barron) *led: rdn along and hdd 2f out: sn wknd* **10/1**	
0104	**16**	*2*	**Fratellino**[11] 2159 5-9-1 92 ....(t) AndrewMullen 7	74
			(Alan McCabe) *hmpd s and a in rr* **33/1**	
00-	**17**	*2 ¾*	**Perfect Blossom**[307] 4357 5-8-9 86 .... PatrickMathers 17	58
			(Ian McInnes) *racd towards stands' rail: gd spd: rdn along over 2f out: sn wknd* **50/1**	
010-	**18**	*½*	**La Fortunata**[230] 6723 5-8-10 87 .... TonyCulhane 12	57
			(Mike Murphy) *prom: rdn along over 2f out: sn wknd* **20/1**	

58.63s (-0.67) **Going Correction** +0.10s/f (Good)

WFA 3 from 4yo+ 8lb **18** Ran SP% **129.3**

Speed ratings (Par 109): **109,108,108,107,106 106,106,104,104,103 103,102,102,100,100 97,92,92**

Tote Swingers: 1&2 £44.80, 1&3 £168.00, 2&3 £63.40 CSF £277.14 CT £5840.87 TOTE £22.50: £3.70, £3.00, £6.20, £1.70; EX 372.90 Trifecta £19687.80 Pool: £53,210.21 - 2.00 winning units..

Owner Rakebackmypoker.com **Bred** Vincent Duignan **Trained** Stainforth, S Yorks

■ Stewards' Enquiry : Saleem Golam four-day ban: use of whip (9, 11, 12, 13 June)

FOCUS

A typically open sprint handicap for the course. The winner is better than ever and the third is on a fair mark.

NOTEBOOK

Dancing Freddy(IRE) returned to turf with victory from 7lb lower at Newmarket recently and he found himself well positioned to strike in this more competitive heat. He's clearly improving, but whether he can complete a hat-trick remains to be seen.

Catfish(IRE), off since winning a 5f Goodwood handicap from 6lb lower 302 days earlier, was clearly ready for this reappearance and travelled nicely. She briefly had to wait for a run when starting to challenge, but had her chance. (tchd 9-1)

Bathwick Bear(IRE), racing from 2lb wrong, was soon up there from his low draw and enjoyed a good battle alongside Catfish. The return to better ground clearly helped. (op 18-1)

Celerina(IRE) didn't get the breaks, being hampered early and then made to wait when beginning to challenge, keeping on well once switched. She'd probably have won with a bit more fortune. (op 11-2 tchd 6-1)

Albany Rose(IRE), returning from 238 days off, was progressive last year and looks to have more to offer judging by this promising reappearance, making good late headway nearer the stands' rail.

Ziggy Lee, behind the winner at Newmarket on his return from a lengthy absence, made good late gains from 6lb wrong and will be of interest in a lesser event. (tchd 14-1)

Tax Free(IRE) showed plenty of pace and may be ready to win again once dropped a further few pounds. (tchd 14-1)

Vocational(USA) showed a ton of pace and will surely find easier opportunities. (op 66-1)

Lexi's Hero(IRE) didn't race with his usual zest and was below par. (op 15-2 tchd 5-1)

Secret Witness, who has been in good form but couldn't pick up.

Magical Macey(USA) went fast and failed to reproduce his best. (op 9-1)

2508 YORKSHIRE REGIMENT E B F MEDIAN AUCTION MAIDEN STKS 6f

4:15 (4:22) (Class 3) 2-Y-0 **£7,439** (£2,213; £1,106; £553) **Stalls** Centre

Form				RPR
2	**1**		**Pay Freeze (IRE)**[8] 2231 2-9-3 0 .... SamHitchcott 8	90+
			(Mick Channon) *mde most: rdn clr appr fnl f: kpt on strly* **13/8**[1]	
	2	*5*	**Mollyvator (IRE)** 2-8-9 0 .... MichaelMetcalfe[(3)] 2	70+
			(Mrs K Burke) *trckd ldrs: hdwy and cl up 2f out: rdn and ev ch wl over 1f out: edgd rt and one pce fnl f* **5/1**[2]	
6	**3**	*2 ¾*	**Finaz**[22] 1818 2-9-3 0 .... RussKennemore 9	67
			(Paul Midgley) *chsd ldrs: rdn along 2f out: kpt on same pce appr fnl f* **12/1**	
	4	*1*	**Tussie Mussie** 2-8-12 0 .... KierenFallon 7	59+
			(Mark Johnston) *dwlt: towards rr: hdwy 1/2-way: green and rdn to chse ldrs wl over 1f out: sn no imp* **5/1**[2]	
	5	*2 ¾*	**Sandsend (IRE)** 2-9-3 0 .... TonyHamilton 4	56
			(Richard Fahey) *prom: rdn along over 2f out: wknd wl over 1f out* **8/1**[3]	
	6	*1 ¾*	**Art Mistress (IRE)** 2-8-12 0 .... DavidAllan 1	45
			(Tim Easterby) *cl up on wd outside: effrt 2f out and ev ch tl rdn and wknd over 1f out* **11/1**	
0	**7**	*8*	**Harrogate Fair**[20] 1886 2-9-3 0 .... SaleemGolam 11	26
			(Michael Squance) *s.i.s: a in rr* **20/1**	
6	**8**	*7*	**Strasbourg Place**[11] 2138 2-8-12 0 .... AndrewMullen 5	
			(Nigel Tinkler) *in tch: green: stmbld and pushed along after 2f: sn lost pl: bhd and outpcd fr 1/2-way* **25/1**	
0	**9**	*5*	**Another Ponty**[28] 1671 2-8-12 0 .... GrahamGibbons 6	
			(Tim Easterby) *chsd ldrs: rdn along wl over 2f out: sn wknd* **33/1**	
	10	*1 ¾*	**Valetto (IRE)** 2-9-3 0 .... DavidNolan 10	
			(Tim Easterby) *in tch: green and pushed along 1/2-way: sn wknd* **28/1**	
	11	*½*	**No Reply** 2-9-3 0 .... AdrianNicholls 3	
			(David Nicholls) *t.k.h: chsd ldrs to 1/2-way: sn wknd* **16/1**	

1m 12.42s (0.52) **Going Correction** +0.10s/f (Good) **11** Ran SP% **119.4**

Speed ratings (Par 97): **100,93,89,88,84 82,71,62,55,53 52**

Tote Swingers: 1&2 £3.30, 1&3 £5.30, 2&3 £10.90 CSF £9.13 TOTE £2.60: £1.20, £1.80, £1.40; EX 11.00 Trifecta £154.60 Pool: £1,734.65 - 8.30 winning units..

Owner Lord Ilsley Racing (Hern Syndicate) **Bred** Tally-Ho Stud **Trained** West Ilsley, Berks

FOCUS

Not a particularly strong juvenile maiden for the track, but still a race that should produce winners.

NOTEBOOK

Pay Freeze(IRE) proved much the best, building on the promise of his recent debut at Newbury and stretching well clear. He'll presumably go up in grade now, but is probably no more than a decent handicapper in the making. (op 15-8)

Mollyvator(IRE), by Motivator but with plenty of speed on the distaff side of her pedigree, impressed with the way she travelled but couldn't match the more experienced winner. She should learn plenty and can probably win a maiden, with a drop to 5f unlikely to inconvenience. (op 11-2 tchd 13-2)

Finaz was very green on his debut and showed the benefit of that experience over the extra furlong. He's probably one for nurseries.

Tussie Mussie, related to numerous winners for the yard, most notably Lovelace, made a pleasing enough debut following a sluggish start. She looks likely to benefit from 7f. (op 9-2)

Sandsend(IRE), whose half-brother won over 5f on his 2-y-o debut, showed plenty of pace and normal progress should see him capable of winning a minor maiden. (op 9-1)

Art Mistress(IRE), half-sister to a 6f 2-y-o winner, offered plenty of promise considering her trainer's juveniles often come on plenty for an outing. (op 10-1)

2509 FEDERATION OF BLOODSTOCK AGENTS STKS (H'CAP) 5f

4:50 (4:52) (Class 3) (0-95,93) 3-Y-O **£8,409** (£2,502; £1,250; £625) **Stalls** Centre

Form				RPR
0-60	**1**		**Powerful Wind (IRE)**[15] 2028 3-8-7 84 .... DarrenEgan[(5)] 1	88
			(Ronald Harris) *cl up: led wl over 1f out: rdn clr appr fnl f: kpt on* **22/1**	
5-50	**2**	*1 ¼*	**Last Bid**[15] 2028 3-9-6 92 .... DavidAllan 5	91
			(Tim Easterby) *in rr and reminders after 1f: swtchd lft and hdwy 2f out: sn rdn and styd on wl fnl f: nt rch wnr* **20/1**	
12-0	**3**	*½*	**Profile Star (IRE)**[16] 1998 3-8-7 79 ow1 .... GrahamGibbons 2	76
			(David Barron) *hld up: hdwy 2f out: rdn over 1f out: styd on fnl f: nrst fin* **33/1**	
15-	**4**	*1 ¼*	**Alaskan Bullet (IRE)**[262] 5826 3-9-6 92 ....[1] KierenFallon 3	86
			(Michael Bell) *dwlt and towards rr: hdwy 2f out: rdn to chse ldrs over 1f out: styng on whn nt clr run ins fnl f: kpt on towards fin* **8/1**	

4464 **5** 1 1/2 **Pale Orchid (IRE)**[15] 2028 3-9-4 **90**.............................. CathyGannon 10 77
(David Evans) *towards rr: hdwy 2f out: sn rdn and kpt on fnl f: nrst fin* **10/1**

51-0 **6** 1/2 **Pea Shooter**[7] 2276 3-9-1 **87**.. PhillipMakin 6 73
(Kevin Ryan) *chsd ldng pair: rdn along 2f out: sn drvn: edgd rt and wknd appr fnl f* **9/4**[1]

41-1 **7** 1/2 **Exceedance**[19] 1921 3-9-7 **93**.. TomEaves 4 77
(Bryan Smart) *led and set str pce: rdn along and hdd wl over 1f out: drvn: hung lft and wknd ent fnl f* **7/2**[2]

10-6 **8** 2 1/2 **Amadeus Denton (IRE)**[35] 1524 3-8-9 **84**...................... LeeTopliss(3) 7 59
(Michael Dods) *chsd ldrs: rdn along 2f out: grad wknd* **33/1**

4266 **9** nk **I'll Be Good**[8] 2229 3-8-9 **81**... PatrickMathers 11 55
(Robert Johnson) *hld up on outer: rdn along 2f out: n.d* **16/1**

1-00 **10** 1 1/2 **Muaamara**[21] 1858 3-9-1 **87**.. SamHitchcott 9 55+
(Mick Channon) *a towards rr* **10/1**

112- **11** hd **Billyrayvalentine (CAN)**[211] 7138 3-8-13 **85**..............(t) FrankieDettori 8 53
(George Baker) *hld up: a towards rr* **4/1**[3]

59.31s (0.01) **Going Correction** +0.10s/f (Good) **11** Ran SP% **123.2**
Speed ratings (Par 103): **103,101,100,98,95 95,94,90,89,87 87**
Tote Swingers: 1&2 £33.90, 1&3 £30.10, 2&3 £53.30 CSF £396.34 TOTE £22.70: £3.90, £4.30, £9.80; EX 592.20 TRIFECTA Not won..
Owner Anthony Cooke **Bred** Miss Ciara Doyle **Trained** Earlswood, Monmouths
■ Stewards' Enquiry : Phillip Makin three-day ban: careless riding (June 9, 11-12)

FOCUS
The early pace was electric in this 5f sprint handicap and the form may not be that strong, but is taken at face value for now.

NOTEBOOK
Powerful Wind(IRE) blasted off, along with Exceedance, and it was a remarkable effort to keep going. Twice well held on testing ground earlier this season, he was down in the weights, leaving him just 2lb above his last winning mark, and kept going despite visibly tiring late on. All about speed, he's now unbeaten in 5f handicaps when the ground is fast. (op 25-1)
Last Bid was another to leave this season's earlier effort behind returning to faster ground, keeping on well without ever looking likely to reach the winner. He likes this C&D. (op 18-1)
Profile Star(IRE), well beaten over 6f on soft ground at Chester, found this ground more to his liking but does look in need of the extra furlong. He's capable of winning from this sort of mark.
Alaskan Bullet(IRE), wearing a first-time hood on this handicap debut, got behind following a sluggish start, but finished his race with purpose and is still lightly raced enough to improve. (op 12-1)
Pale Orchid(IRE) was another making late gains having been outpaced.
Pea Shooter was disappointing considering he'd run well on last week's reappearance at Newmarket. (op 3-1 tchd 10-3)
Exceedance is all about speed, but his two wins had come on turning tracks on the AW, and he looked vulnerable here up 14lb for this return to turf. Having duelled with the winner, he found little. (op 11-4)
Muaamara had little room for the second half of the race and can be given another chance. (op 8-1)
Billyrayvalentine(CAN) should have had the race run to suit on this reappearance, but he was outpaced and then couldn't pick up. (op 5-1)

2510 JOHN WRIGHT ELECTRICAL APPRENTICE H'CAP 1m
5:25 (5:28) (Class 4) (0-80,80) 4-Y-0+ £6,469 (£1,925; £962; £481) Stalls Low

Form RPR

3-13 **1** **Alfred Hutchinson**[56] 1134 4-8-11 **75**....................... JustinNewman(5) 6 85+
(Geoffrey Oldroyd) *in tch: hdwy over 2f out: rdn to chse ldrs over 1f out: styd on ins fnl f to ld nr line* **9/2**[1]

036- **2** shd **Next Edition (IRE)**[150] 4608 4-8-12 **78**....................... EvaMoscrop(7) 18 88
(Philip Kirby) *trckd ldrs: hdwy on outer over 3f out: cl up over 2f out: rdn to ld jst over 1f out: edgd lft ins fnl f: hdd and no ex nr line* **33/1**

523 **3** 1 3/4 **Regal Swain (IRE)**[14] 2095 4-8-10 **72**........................ GarryWhillans(3) 1 79+
(Alan Swinbank) *hld up towards rr: hdwy 3f out: rdn 2f out: styd on wl appr fnl f* **16/1**

0-31 **4** 1 1/2 **Great Shot**[24] 1752 4-8-11 **75**...................................... ThomasBrown(5) 4 78
(Sylvester Kirk) *in tch: hdwy 3f out: led 2f out: rdn and hdd jst over 1f out: kpt on same pce fnl f* **10/1**

0-00 **5** hd **Oratory (IRE)**[28] 1657 6-8-9 **73**... NedCurtis(5) 2 75
(Paul Midgley) *hld up towards rr: hdwy on wd outside 2f out: rdn and styd on fnl f: nrst fin* **9/1**[3]

003- **6** 1/2 **Merchant Of Medici**[233] 6658 5-9-2 **78**....................... JamesRogers(3) 19 79+
(Micky Hammond) *hld up: hdwy on inner over 2f out: rdn over 1f out: kpt on ins fnl f: nrst fin* **16/1**

00-0 **7** 3/4 **Desert Vision**[14] 2094 8-8-8 **72**..........................(t) DavidSimmonson(5) 3 71
(Michael Easterby) *trckd ldrs on inner: hdwy 3f out and sn cl up: rdn 2f out: and kpt on same pce* **50/1**

5004 **8** nk **Aquarian Spirit**[12] 2119 5-9-3 **76**...................................... LeeTopliss 10 78+
(Richard Fahey) *towards rr: hdwy 3f out: rdn 2f out: kpt on fnl f: nt rch ldrs* **12/1**

-606 **9** 1 **Dolphin Rock**[7] 2285 5-9-2 **78**... LMcNiff(3) 14 74
(David Barron) *led: rdn along and jnd 4f out: hdd 3f out and grad wknd* **10/1**

13-2 **10** nse **Invincible Hero (IRE)**[47] 1249 5-9-2 **80**........................ JasonHart(5) 20 76
(Declan Carroll) *t.k.h: prom on outer: rdn to dispute ld over 3f out: wknd over 2f out* **6/1**[2]

2140 **11** 1 **Alhaban (IRE)**[40] 1416 6-8-12 **76**................................... DarrenEgan(5) 9 70
(Ronald Harris) *towards rr: hdwy 3f out: rdn along 2f out: n.d* **16/1**

10 **12** 1/2 **Thatcherite (IRE)**[55] 1158 4-8-12 **74**....................(t) BrendanPowell(3) 16 67
(Tony Coyle) *dwlt: hdwy into midfield 1/2-way: rdn along over 3f out: n.d* **20/1**

0-10 **13** 1/2 **Mujaadel (USA)**[21] 1863 7-9-0 **78**........................(p) ShirleyTeasdale(5) 11 69
(David Nicholls) *nvr bttr than midfield* **20/1**

2100 **14** 1 3/4 **Nibani (IRE)**[7] 2285 5-8-9 **75**.....................................(p) SemiraPashai(7) 8 62
(Alastair Lidderdale) *s.i.s: a in rr* **25/1**

6-10 **15** 2 **Just The Tonic**[19] 1917 5-8-12 **74**................................ AshleyMorgan(3) 7 57
(Marjorie Fife) *nvr nr ldrs* **20/1**

20-0 **16** 1 1/2 **Triple Eight (IRE)**[14] 2094 4-8-10 **72**........................(p) DeanHeslop(3) 12 51
(Philip Kirby) *cl up on inner: rdn along over 3f out: sn wknd* **28/1**

50-0 **17** nk **Shadowtime**[19] 1917 7-8-13 **72**...................................... DeclanCannon 17 51+
(Tracy Waggott) *trckd ldrs: hdwy 4f out: led 3f out: rdn and hdd 2f out: sn wknd* **20/1**

253- **18** 1/2 **Ingleby Exceed (IRE)**[262] 5820 4-9-3 **76**...................... RossAtkinson 13 54
(David O'Meara) *a towards rr* **14/1**

1-06 **19** 4 **Count Bertoni (IRE)**[19] 1913 5-9-2 **75**....................... CPGeoghegan 15 43
(David O'Meara) *a towards rr* **14/1**

1120 **20** 3 **Upper Lambourn (IRE)**[48] 1236 4-8-13 **72**.......................... AmyRyan 5 33
(Brian Ellison) *dwlt: a in rr* **25/1**

1m 39.58s (0.58) **Going Correction** +0.225s/f (Good) **20** Ran SP% **134.4**
Speed ratings (Par 105): **106,105,104,102,102 101,101,100,99,99 98,98,97,96,94 92,92,91,87,84**
Tote Swingers: 1&2 £58.10, 1&3 £14.60, 2&3 £126.80 CSF £175.77 CT £2328.95 TOTE £4.80: £1.50, £10.10, £5.30, £3.00; EX 351.00 TRIFECTA Not won..
Owner R C Bond **Bred** R C Bond **Trained** Brawby, N Yorks
■ Stewards' Enquiry : Eva Moscrop two-day ban: careless riding (9-11 June)

FOCUS
A wide-open apprentice handicap, run at a fair clip, and probably fair form for the grade. The form looks solid despite the presence of the surprise runner-up.
T/Plt: £3,187.60 to a £1 stake. Pool: £111,568.00 - 25.55 winning tickets. T/Qpdt: £232.40 to a £1 stake. Pool: £5,498.00 - 17.50 winning tickets. JR

2511 - (Foreign Racing) - See Raceform Interactive

1942 CURRAGH (R-H)
Saturday, May 26

OFFICIAL GOING: Good (good to firm in places)

2512a EMIRATES EQUESTRIAN EUROPEAN BREEDERS FUND MARBLE HILL STKS (LISTED RACE) 5f
2:10 (2:10) 2-Y-0 £28,437 (£8,312; £3,937; £1,312)

RPR

1 **Cay Verde**[14] 2069 2-9-3 .... RichardHughes 2 100+
(Mick Channon) *a.p: disp ld 1/2-way: led under 2f out: pushed out and kpt on wl fnl f: comf* **5/2**[2]

2 3/4 **Dylanbaru (IRE)**[23] 1802 2-9-3 ....(t) WayneLordan 1 97
(T Stack, Ire) *towards rr: wnt 5th on outer 2f out: sn rdn and 2nd 1f out: kpt on same pce u.p wout threatening wnr* **22/1**

3 1/2 **Infanta Branca (USA)**[34] 1545 2-9-0 .... JPO'Brien 5 93
(A P O'Brien, Ire) *trckd ldrs: 4th 1/2-way: rdn over 1f out and kpt on same pce into 3rd fnl f* **7/4**[1]

4 1/2 **Liberating**[49] 1227 2-9-0 .... FranBerry 3 91
(Mrs John Harrington, Ire) *led or disp ld: strly pressed and hdd under 2f out: u.p in 3rd 1f out: dropped to 4th fnl f: kpt on one pce* **11/4**[3]

5 1/2 **Lottie Dod (IRE)**[10] 2183 2-9-0 .... JohnnyMurtagh 4 89
(Charles O'Brien, Ire) *hld up in rr: hdwy into 5th over 1f out: rdn and kpt on same pce* **20/1**

6 1 3/4 **Katchy Lady**[37] 1488 2-9-0 .... NGMcCullagh 6 83
(P J Prendergast, Ire) *chsd ldrs: 6th and rdn 2f out: no imp and kpt on one pce fr over 1f out* **25/1**

7 3 3/4 **Verbal Honesty (IRE)**[23] 1802 2-9-0 .... KevinManning 8 69
(J S Bolger, Ire) *prom and disp ld: 3rd 2f out: no ex fr wl over 1f out* **14/1**

8 hd **Tennessee Wildcat (IRE)**[10] 2184 2-9-3 ....(b[1]) GaryCarroll 7 71
(G M Lyons, Ire) *prom early racing keenly: 6th 1/2-way: rdn and no imp fr over 1f out* **14/1**

59.66s (-3.24) **Going Correction** -0.125s/f (Firm) **8** Ran SP% **117.9**
Speed ratings: **103,101,101,100,99 96,90,90**
CSF £58.12 TOTE £3.20: £1.50, £4.60, £1.30; DF 80.30.
Owner Box 41 **Bred** Lady Whent **Trained** West Ilsley, Berks

FOCUS
They didn't hang around in this contest and the snugness of victory suggests it was a good race.

NOTEBOOK
Cay Verde ◆ had won convincingly in a bog at Ascot on his previous run, this was a good performance. He showed plenty of speed and always travelled well, quickening to the front a furlong out and winning snugly. He looks a pure sprinter at this stage, although one imagines that an extra furlong shouldn't take much out of him, but it took a smart colt to win this in the manner he did and how good he is will presumably be more evident at Ascot next month where he goes for the Norfolk Stakes. (op 9/4)
Dylanbaru(IRE) ran no race in the mud at Tipperary previously but this was a much more accurate depiction of how much he progressed as he quickened from just off the pace on the outer to get into contention a furlong out but was always being held quite comfortably by the winner. There is a good race in him on this evidence. (op 25/1 tchd 20/1)
Infanta Branca(USA) had every chance but she may well improve over an extra furlong. She travelled well just behind the lead for most of the way and did keep on well but never quite looked like winning. One would imagine though that she's still likely to go for the Queen Mary. (op 9/4)
Liberating showed the most speed but was unable to see off her rivals, but to her credit she rallied well enough when headed and perhaps this trip on a flatter track might just suit her better. The third filly improved past her. (op 5/2)
Lottie Dod(IRE) was covered up a bit more today and saw her race out that bit better. She wasn't good enough but wasn't beaten that far and there should be a maiden somewhere to be won with her. (op 20/1 tchd 25/1)
Katchy Lady does look like a filly that needs further, at least on ground like this.
Verbal Honesty(IRE) wasn't good enough. (op 14/1 tchd 12/1)
Tennessee Wildcat(IRE) had little left in the closing stages after being lit up by first time blinkers. (op 16/1)

2513a WEATHERBYS IRELAND GREENLANDS STKS (GROUP 3) 6f
2:40 (2:41) 3-Y-0+ £33,854 (£9,895; £4,687; £1,562)

RPR

1 **Tiddliwinks**[10] 2179 6-10-0 .... PatSmullen 2 116
(Kevin Ryan) *rrd whn leaving stalls and towards rr: hdwy on outer into 6th 2f out: rdn to ld ins fnl f: kpt on best u.p* **8/1**

2 1/2 **Jimmy Styles**[37] 1469 8-9-9 ....(p) RichardHughes 12 109
(Clive Cox) *led: strly pressed and hdd 2f out: dropped to 5th 1f out: rallied u.p ins fnl f to go 2nd cl home* **10/1**

3 hd **The Reaper (IRE)**[35] 1538 4-9-9 **101**........................(b) JohnnyMurtagh 8 108
(G M Lyons, Ire) *prom: 2nd 1/2-way: rdn and briefly chal over 1f out: 4th early fnl f: kpt on u.p* **16/1**

4 nk **Hitchens (IRE)**[56] 1147 7-9-12 .... FranBerry 6 110
(David Barron) *trckd ldrs: 3rd 1/2-way: hdwy to ld 2f out: sn rdn and jnd: hdd ins fnl f and no ex clsng stages* **7/2**[2]

5 1 **Six Of Hearts**[15] 2059 8-9-9 **99**.......................................(p) SamJames 7 104
(Cecil Ross, Ire) *chsd ldrs: 7th 1/2-way: rdn and no imp 1 1/2f out: kpt on u.p ins fnl f* **25/1**

6 1 **Fire Lily (IRE)**[13] 2109 3-9-0 **109**..................................... WayneLordan 3 99
(David Wachman, Ire) *trckd ldrs: 5th 1/2-way: 3rd 2f out: chal and ev ch over 1f out: no ex ins fnl f* **9/4**[1]

7 nk **Bulbul (IRE)**[19] 1944 3-8-11 **98**............................... DeclanMcDonogh 10 95
(Kevin Prendergast, Ire) *trckd ldrs on rail: 4th 1/2-way: no ex fr over 1f out* **20/1**

8 1 1/4 **Experience (IRE)**[49] 1226 3-9-0 **103**...................................... WJLee 4 94
(David Wachman, Ire) *towards rr: nvr a factor: kpt on one pce fnl f* **8/1**

9 *1* **Santo Padre (IRE)**[95] 1538 8 -9-9106 FergalLynch 9 93
(David Marnane, Ire) *chsd ldrs towards rr: nvr a factor* **14/1**
10 *nk* **Katla (IRE)**[35] 1538 4 -9-698 CO'Donoghue 5 89+
(J F Grogan, Ire) *mid-div: 8th 1/2-way: nt clr run over 1f out: no imp in 7th whn sltly checked ins fnl f* **20/1**
11 *5 1/2* **Crusade (USA)**[203] 7306 3 -9-5112 JPO'Brien 1 77
(A P O'Brien, Ire) *trckd ldrs on outer: 6th 1/2-way: rdn and no ex under 2f out: eased whn btn fnl f* **7/1**[3]

1m 11.87s (-3.63)**Going Correction** -0.125s/f (Firm)
WFA 3 from 4yo+ 9lb **11**Ran SP%**122.7**
Speed ratings: **111,110,110,109,108 107,106,104,103,103 95**
CSF £86.44 TOTE £9.80 : £2.80 , £3.20 , £4.60 ; DF 72.30 .
Owner Guy Reed **Bred** Guy Reed **Trained** Hambleton, N Yorks

FOCUS
Consistency wouldn't be the greatest attribute belonging to Tiddliwinks but having won both of his starts this year perhaps it's finally coming.

NOTEBOOK
Tiddliwinks fly-leapt at the gate a little bit but it may well have helped Smullen to settle him behind horses and he did make up his ground quite stylishly in the manner of a good horse. He had the ability to battle as well, which he showed when his main opponents fought back when he hit the front but he just had a gun too many. He may well have even got to the front a fraction too soon but he showed again that he's a sprinter with a lot of ability on his day. (op 7/1)
Jimmy Styles was quickly out of the gate and helped set a decent clip next to the rail. He really kept going strongly when challenged and when various challenges developed. He's started off the season as a model of consistency and it would have to be considered that any horse starting off the season with three consecutive seconds in three stakes races deserves a change of luck. He did nothing wrong. (op 9/1)
The Reaper (IRE)has fallen short against this sort of opposition before but this might just have been a career best effort. It was an uncomplicated enough effort as he was up there and travelling well throughout and just sustained his effort to the line. It just wasn't quite good enough on this occasion.
Hitchens(IRE) travelled well and close to the pace and he had every chance when asked for his effort over a furlong out. He kept going at the same pace in what was a high class effort but one not quite good enough on ground which might have been on the lively side. (op 10/3)
Six Of Hearts ran on from mid-division to be a very honourable fifth. The hope must be that the handicapper won't take too dim a view.
Fire Lily (IRE)was ridden positively but faded rather disappointingly late on. (op 10/3)
Bulbul(IRE) has a good deal of speed but didn't really get the run of the race towards the stands' rail. It was an encouraging effort and one would imagine she'll stick to this sort of trip. (op 16/1)
Experience(IRE) didn't have a huge amount of luck in running. (op 7/1)
Santo Padre (IRE) Official explanation: jockey said gelding did not act on today's ground

2514a ABU DHABI IRISH 2000 GUINEAS (GROUP 1) (ENTIRE COLTS & FILLIES) 1m
3:15 (3:17) 3-Y-0
£145,000 (£47,500; £22,500 ; £7,500 ; £5,000 ; £2,500)

RPR
1 **Power**[21] 1856 3 -9-0114 JPO'Brien 3 116
(A P O'Brien, Ire) *settled in mid-div off pce: mod 6th 1/2-way: clsr in 4th over 1f out: qcknd to ld ins fnl f: kpt on wl* **5/1**[3]
2 *1* **Foxtrot Romeo (IRE)**[252] 6162 3 -9-0 NGMcCullagh 2 113
(Bryan Smart) *chsd ldrs in 3rd: clsr over 1f out: kpt on same pce u.p ins fnl f* **33/1**
3 *3/4* **Reply (IRE)**[231] 6688 3 -9-0109 FranBerry 5 112+
(A P O'Brien, Ire) *in rr of mid-div: mod 8th 1/2-way: hdwy and clsr in 5th 1f out: kpt on u.p ins fnl f* **25/1**
4 *nk* **Daddy Long Legs (USA)**[31] 1872 3 -9-0117 CO'Donoghue 7 111
(A P O'Brien, Ire) *led and set str pce: drvn along over 2f out: strly pressed and hdd ins fnl f: no ex* **7/1**
5 *1/2* **Born To Sea (IRE)**[31] 1856 3 -9-0105 [1] PatSmullen 1 110+
(John M Oxx, Ire) *hld up in rr: 9th 2f out: kpt on wl ins fnl f* **9/1**
6 *1 1/2* **Hermival (IRE)**[21] 1856 3 -9-0 GregoryBenoist 9 106
(M Delzangles, France) *settled towards rr: mod 7th 1/2-way: nvr a factor: rdn and kpt on same pce fr over 1f out* **4/1**[2]
7 *nk* **Wrote (IRE)**[13] 2102 3 -9-0112 SeamieHeffernan 11 106
(A P O'Brien, Ire) *chsd ldr in 2nd and clr of remainder: rdn 2f out: no ex fnl f and wknd* **12/1**
8 *nk* **Alkazim (IRE)**[37] 1468 3 -9-095 WayneLordan 6 105
(David Wachman, Ire) *a towards rr: nvr a factor* **40/1**
9 *nse* **Takar (IRE)**[19] 1943 3 -9-0105 (t) JohnnyMurtagh 10 105
(John M Oxx, Ire) *chsd ldrs: mod 5th 1/2-way: rdn and no imp wl over 1f out: no ex* **6/1**
10 *3/4* **Trumpet Major (IRE)**[21] 1856 3 -9-0 RichardHughes 8 103
(Richard Hannon) *settled in 4th wl off pce: rdn over 2f out and sn no ex* **9/4**[1]

1m 39.04s (-6.96)**Going Correction** -0.725s/f (Hard) **10**Ran SP%**121.1**
Speed ratings: **105,104,103,102,102 100,100,100,100,99**
CSF £162.61 TOTE £6.30 : £1.70 , £11.00 , £10.20 ; DF 146.70 .
Owner Michael Tabor & Derrick Smith & Mrs John Magnier **Bred** Norelands & Hugo Lascelles **Trained** Ballydoyle, Co Tipperary

FOCUS
Not exactly the most straightforward of Classics and it may well take some time to find some context for it.

NOTEBOOK
Power is not a horse that instantly quickens but he builds up momentum and finishes to some effect. A sound surface is essential and that's something he didn't get at Newmarket earlier this month. One would imagine that a truly run mile on top of the ground will suit him best and he's probably much more of a pure miler than Camelot. In truth, the 3-y-o division at this distance probably lacks a bit of strength in depth and there's little reason why he shouldn't be a force in races such as the St James Palace Stakes. Official explanation: trainer said, regarding the apparent improvement in form shown, that colt was having its firsr run of the season last time on ground softer than it handled last year; it tired in the latter stages possibly as a result of the ground. he added it raced at the same body weight as it was last time and that alll routine post-race examinations failed to show any abnormalities. (op 10/3)
Foxtrot Romeo (IRE)has obviously improved hugely. He was at the head of the chasing group for most of the way and really sustained his effort strongly from two furlongs out. One would say he can get a little bit further but one would imagine he can still improve considering his one win before this was in a Hamilton maiden. He could well be an interesting horse for the remainder of the season.
Reply(IRE) was ridden from a long way off the pace, more or less ridden to get the mile it seemed. He kept on really well to be on top of them close home but it seems likely that he's going to be dropped in trip from here on.
Daddy Long Legs (USA)wasn't the most advisable horse to give a lead to as he's the type of horse that could maintain an end-to-end gallop in a race like this. He couldn't quite see it out inside the last furlong and him coming off the far rail made things a fair bit easier for the winner in the last furlong. He'll step back up in trip. There's nothing to dislike about this horse with his uncomplicated style of running. (op 8/1 tchd 6/1)
Born To Sea (IRE)settled infinitely better in the hood, and maybe too well. Pat Smullen was able to switch him at the back of the field and it took some time to wake him up; he eventually came home better than most. (op 9/1 tchd 10/1)
Hermival(IRE) didn't get a lot of cover towards the outer but he couldn't pick up from off the pace. (op 5/1 tchd 7/2)
Wrote(IRE) chased the leader and just faded late on. (op 10/1)
Alkazim(IRE) probably wasn't good enough to get any closer. (op 33/1)
Takar(IRE) didn't pick up for pressure and it's a fair summation that he found the ground too lively. (op 11/2 tchd 13/2)
Trumpet Major (IRE)was off the pace but in a good position most of the way. He found nil when asked for his effort and was found to be coughing post race. Official explanation: vet said colt was found to be coughing post race (op 4/1)

2515a TRI EQUESTRIAN STKS (GROUP 3) (F&M) 1m
3:50 (3:51) 4-Y-0+ **£32,500** (£9,500; £4,500 ; £1,500)

RPR
1 **Emulous**[266] 5745 5 -9-5115 PatSmullen 3 108+
(D K Weld, Ire) *trckd ldrs in 5th: hdwy to chal and led ins fnl f: kpt on wl* **4/5**[1]
2 *1 3/4* **One Spirit (IRE)**[223] 6899 4 -9-097 NGMcCullagh 5 98
(G M Lyons, Ire) *trckd ldr in 2nd: rdn to ld 1 1/2f out: sn strly pressed and hdd ins fnl f: kpt on same pce u.p but no ch w wnr* **33/1**
3 *1/2* **Alanza (IRE)**[245] 6338 4 -9-3109 JohnnyMurtagh 8 101+
(John M Oxx, Ire) *settled in mid-div: 6th 1/2-way: pushed along and wnt 4th 1f out: kpt on into 3rd fnl f wout troubling wnr* **5/2**[2]
4 *2 1/4* **Law Of The Range**[20] 1883 5 -9-1 ow1 JPO'Brien 1 93
(Marco Botti) *led: rdn 2f out and sn hdd: no ex fnl f and dropped to 4th* **7/1**[3]
5 *hd* **Marvada (IRE)**[14] 2078 4 -9-0102 ShaneFoley 7 91+
(K J Condon, Ire) *trckd ldrs in 4th: rdn in 5th 1f out: no ex* **16/1**
6 *nk* **Winter's Night (IRE)**[21] 1851 4 -9-0 RichardHughes 9 91+
(Clive Cox) *t.k.h and trckd ldrs in 3rd: rdn and dropped to 6th over 1f out: no ex* **12/1**
7 *hd* **Spirit Of Cuba (IRE)**[20] 1896 4 -9-094 DeclanMcDonogh 4 90+
(Kevin Prendergast, Ire) *in rr: pushed along 2f out: nvr a factor: kpt on one pce* **50/1**
8 *nk* **Soul Custody (CAN)**[188] 5 -9-0 FranBerry 2 89+
(M J Grassick, Ire) *in rr of mid-div: 7th 1/2-way: no imp fr 1 1/2f out: kpt on one pce* **33/1**
9 *2* **Malayan Mist (IRE)**[20] 1896 4 -9-089 (b) KevinManning 6 85+
(D K Weld, Ire) *towards rr: rdn and no imp fr over 2f out* **40/1**

1m 41.23s (-4.77)**Going Correction** -0.725s/f (Hard) **9**Ran SP%**120.5**
Speed ratings: **95,93,92,90,90 90,89,89,87**
CSF £43.77 TOTE £1.70 : £1.02 , £7.70 , £1.50 ; DF 52.90 .
Owner K Abdulla **Bred** Juddmonte Farms Ltd **Trained** The Curragh, Co Kildare

FOCUS
Not much strength in depth in this Group 3.

NOTEBOOK
Emulous looked the pick of this field even with her Group 1 penalty and she did the job well on her first start of the season. It was a fourth win for her at this level on her first start since landing the Group 1 Matron Stakes at Leopardstown in September. Held up, her rider angled her to the left to deliver his challenge approaching the final furlong and with plenty of room to manoeuvre, she quickly asserted and was well in top at the finish. (op 9/10 tchd 1/1)
One Spirit (IRE) rated 18lb inferior to the winner, who was conceding 5lb, on official figures, had only a maiden win to her credit and she produced easily her best effort to date on her first start of the year. She raced in second place until responding for pressure to lead one and a half furlongs out. Although no match for the winner when headed inside the final furlong, she kept on to the line.
Alanza(IRE), winner of the Group 3 Sceptre Stakes and two Listed events last year, made an encouraging reappearance. Held up, she made headway from 2f out and ran on quite well without posing any real threat to the winner. She will improve and will be worth trying again at this level or higher. (op 2/1)
Law Of The Range was down in trip after a run in a 1m1f Group 3 at Newmarket on her previous start. She again made the running but after coming under pressure 2f out, she was soon headed and could make little impression over the final furlong.
Marvada(IRE), a four-time winner from 6f to this trip, ran a solid race, tracking the leaders before failing to make much impression for pressure from over 1f out. (op 16/1 tchd 20/1)
Winter's Night (IRE) Off. exp: jockey said filly lost its action.

2516a-2520a Foreign Racing (See RI)

1554 SAN SIRO (R-H)
Saturday, May 26
OFFICIAL GOING: Turf: good to soft

2521a PREMIO CARLO VITTADINI (EX EMILIO TURATI) (GROUP 2) (3YO+) (TURF) 1m
2:30 (12:00) 3-Y-0+ **£39,583** (£17,416; £9,500 ; £4,750)

RPR
1 **Vedelago (IRE)**[27] 1698 3 -8-70 MEsposito 5 111
(L Polito, Italy) *hld up in tch: rdn to improve 2 1/2f out: r.o to ld jst ins fnl f: wnt clr fnl 100yds* **6/4**[2]
2 *1 1/4* **Alianthus (GER)**[27] 7 -9-50 ADeVries 3 111
(J Hirschberger, Germany) *trckd ldr in clr 2nd: rdn and briefly outpcd over 2f out: led 1 1/2f out: hdd jst ins fnl f: kpt on wout matching wnr cl home* **3/5**[1]
3 *3/4* **Principe Adepto (USA)**[27] 4 -9-50 CristianDemuro 2 109
(E Botti, Italy) *trckd front pair in clr 3rd: rdn to chal 1 1/2f out: stl ev ch 1f out: no ex and fdd ins fnl f* **11/2**[3]
4 *nk* **Ransom Hope**[27] 7 -9-50 DarioVargiu 6 109
(L Riccardi, Italy) *hld up in last: rdn to improve on outer 3f out: outpcd over 1 1/2f out: kpt on ins fnl f: gng on at fin* **11/2**[3]
5 *4* **Regarde Moi**[13] 4 -9-50 NicolaPinna 4 99
(S Botti, Italy) *hld up in last pair: relegated to last and rdn 3f out: plugged on to go 5th cl home: nvr a factor* **35/1**
6 *1/2* **Billy Budd (IRE)**[27] 4 -9-50 FabioBranca 1 98
(S Botti, Italy) *led: rdn over 2f out: hdd 1 1/2f out: wkng whn short of room and forced to check jst over 1f out: qckly eased and dropped to last cl home* **96/10**

1m 35.0s (-7.10)
WFA 3 from 4yo+ 12lb **6**Ran SP%**145.5**
WIN (incl. 1 euro stake): 2.50. PLACES: 1.28, 1.14. DF: 4.17
Owner G T A **Bred** G T A Srl **Trained** Italy

2522a PREMIO OAKS D'ITALIA TROFEO SNAI (GROUP 2) (3YO FILLIES) (TURF) 1m 3f

3:45 (12:00) 3-Y-O £125,000 (£55,000; £30,000; £15,000)

RPR

1 **Cherry Collect (IRE)**[27] 1699 3-8-11 0 FabioBranca 9 105
(S Botti, Italy) *midfield on outer: rdn to improve over 2f out: r.o to ld ins fnl f: stretched clr cl home* **5/2**[2]

2 1 ½ **Angegreen (ITY)** 3-8-11 0 AStarke 10 102
(S Botti, Italy) *midfield on outer: rdn to chal 3f out: kpt on one pce fr over 2f out: wnt 2nd ins fnl 50yds* **77/10**

3 hd **Rosa Eglanteria**[230] 6740 3-8-11 0 DarioVargiu 13 102
(B Grizzetti, Italy) *prom: led 3f out: strly pressed and rdn 2f out: kpt on gamely: hdd ins fnl f: lost 2nd fnl 50yds* **67/10**

4 1 **Bay Vatoria (GER)** 3-8-11 0 J-PLopez 11 100+
(H Zappe, Austria) *midfield on inner: rdn to improve over 3 1/2f out: keeping on wl whn short of room and stmbld bdly jst ins fnl f: nt rcvr: gng on again at fin: unlucky* **188/10**

5 ½ **Aquila D'Oriente (ITY)**[175] 3-8-11 0 LManiezzi 8 99
(S Botti, Italy) *hld up in last on inner: rdn 2f out: rn to go 5th ins fnl f: nvr able to chal* **64/1**

6 ¾ **Wilddrossel (GER)**[27] 3-8-11 0 EFrank 2 98
(Markus Klug, Germany) *midfield on inner: rdn to maintain position over 4f out: outpcd over 2 1/2f out: plugged on under heavy press to go 6th post* **2/1**[1]

7 nse **Icebreaking (IRE)**[27] 1699 3-8-11 0 CristianDemuro 5 98
(L Riccardi, Italy) *hld up in last trio on outer: rdn to improve 2 1/2f out: kpt on one pce ins fnl 1 1/2f: pipped for 6th post* **26/1**

8 ½ **Rock My Heart (GER)**[48] 1243 3-8-11 0 APietsch 12 97
(W Hickst, Germany) *hld up towards rr on outer: prog into midfield 2 1/2f out: rdn to try and chal 2f out: kpt on tl sltly hmpd ins fnl f: no ex and fdd cl home* **67/10**

9 2 ¾ **Cubanita**[17] 1973 3-8-11 0 MartinLane 1 92
(Ralph Beckett) *trckd ldr in 3rd on inner: rdn over 2 1/2f out: outpcd over 1 1/2f out: no ex and wknd ins fnl f* **51/10**[3]

10 2 ½ **Freezy (IRE)**[20] 3-8-11 0 NicolaPinna 3 88
(S Botti, Italy) *midfield on inner: rdn over 3 1/2f out: no ex and wknd over 1 1/2f out: eased ins fnl f* **5/2**[2]

11 7 **Dan Loose Daughter**[20] 3-8-11 0 GArena 7 75
(B Grizzetti, Italy) *trckd ldr in 2nd: rdn 3f out: no ex and btn 2f out: wknd: eased ins fnl f* **67/10**

12 7 **Fularmada**[20] 3-8-11 0 PierantonioConvertino 4 62
(B Grizzetti, Italy) *hld up in last pair: last and rdn over 3f out: btn over 1 1/2f out: eased* **37/1**

13 1 ¼ **Miss Manduro (IRE)** 3-8-11 0 (b) SSulas 6 60
(A Di Dio, Italy) *led: rdn and hdd 3f out: qckly btn and wknd: eased* **206/10**

2m 14.2s (-4.40) **13 Ran SP% 174.9**
WIN (incl. 1 euro stake): 3.50 (Cherry Collect coupled with Freezy). PLACES: 1.60, 2.94, 2.30. DF: 30.00.
Owner Effevi **Bred** Razza Del Velino **Trained** Italy

2523 - (Foreign Racing) - See Raceform Interactive

2511 CURRAGH (R-H)

Sunday, May 27

OFFICIAL GOING: Good (good to firm in places; watered)

2524a AIRLIE STUD GALLINULE STKS (GROUP 3) 1m 2f

2:05 (2:05) 3-Y-O £28,437 (£8,312; £3,937; £1,312)

RPR

1 **Speaking Of Which (IRE)**[50] 1231 3-9-3 (bt[1]) PatSmullen 9 116+
(D K Weld, Ire) *t.k.h early and settled off pce in 5th: clsr 1/2-way and travelled wl to go 4th ent st: hdwy to ld 1 1/2f out and sn asserted: styd on wl to draw clr fnl f: easily* **7/1**[3]

2 9 **Soon (IRE)**[14] 2101 3-9-0 101 RyanMoore 6 95+
(A P O'Brien, Ire) *hld up in rr: 7th ent st: rdn in 5th over 1f out: hdwy between horses to go 2nd ins fnl f: kpt on same pce but no ch w easy wnr* **8/1**

3 1 ¾ **Athens (IRE)**[14] 2108 3-9-3 106 JPO'Brien 7 95
(A P O'Brien, Ire) *racd 2nd to clr ldr: clsr 1/2-way and disp appr st: led briefly 2f out: sn hdd u.p and no ch w easy wnr fr over 1f out: dropped to mod 3rd fnl f* **7/2**[2]

4 nk **Macbeth (IRE)**[45] 1350 3-9-3 92 ShaneFoley 5 94
(K J Condon, Ire) *chsd clr ldr: clsr in 3rd 1/2-way: rdn early st and no imp on easy wnr fr over 1f out: mod 4th ins fnl f* **8/1**

5 1 ¾ **Absolute Crackers (IRE)**[18] 1973 3-9-0 92 (p) FranBerry 3 87+
(Mrs John Harrington, Ire) *chsd clr ldr: clsr in 4th 1/2-way: 5th and drvn along ent st: no ex in 6th over 1f out: kpt on one pce u.p fnl f* **18/1**

6 2 ½ **Crius (IRE)**[38] 1470 3-9-6 RichardHughes 1 88
(Richard Hannon) *led racing keenly and sn clr: reduced advantage 1/2-way: jnd appr st: hdd 2f out and sn no ex* **13/8**[1]

7 2 ¾ **Cleofila (IRE)**[11] 2187 3-9-0 95 KevinManning 4 77
(J S Bolger, Ire) *chsd clr ldr: clsr in 6th 1/2-way: rdn ent st and no ex in 7th under 2f out* **9/1**

8 1 **Bible Black (IRE)**[114] 417 3-9-3 99 GaryCarroll 8 78
(G M Lyons, Ire) *hld up in rr: rdn ent st and sn no ex* **22/1**

2m 9.81s (-4.49) **Going Correction** -0.125s/f (Firm) **8 Ran SP% 114.7**
Speed ratings: **113,105,104,104,102 100,98,97**
CSF £61.09 TOTE £5.80: £1.90, £2.10, £1.50; DF 67.80.
Owner Moyglare Stud Farm **Bred** Moyglare Stud Farm Ltd **Trained** The Curragh, Co Kildare

FOCUS
This was a curious race in how it was run and the winner is probably a bit flattered although he was still mightily impressive.

NOTEBOOK
Speaking Of Which(IRE) ◆ was mightily impressive in the first-time visor. One could hardly have got carried away with his previous two efforts but he was transformed here, clearly enjoying the hold-up ride and the quick terrain. He barely broke a sweat to hit the front and quickly put this race to bed. A son of Invincible Spirit, the Irish Derby trip would surely be as far as he wants to go - indeed his trainer had toyed with the notion of running him in the Irish Guineas - but he is probably open to further improvement as he fills out and learns how to race. Dermot Weld, trainer: "He is a big, idle horse and that's why I tried a visor on him during work last week. The further he went in the visor the better he got. We'll come back here for the Irish Derby. He loves that ground." (op 13/2 tchd 6/1)
Soon(IRE) excelled herself again, rather like at Gowran two runs back when she finished a never-threatening second. She deserves to find another success and it could well be over this trip, which she was trying for the first time. (op 7/1)
Athens(IRE) was taken to dispute a long way from home and is possibly better than the form. His improvement seems to have peaked but he might have preferred it a bit easier underfoot.
Macbeth(IRE) was a shade out of his comfort zone but ran a decent race and it will probably encourage connections to have another go at Pattern company.
Absolute Crackers(IRE)was also a bit outclassed but ran respectably. This trip may stretch her a little. (op 16/1 tchd 20/1)
Crius(IRE) was given an unusually positive ride for a horse unraced beyond a mile. He was surely doing too much in the first half of the race and weakened badly in the straight. Official explanation: jockey said colt ran much too freely early on (op 7/4 tchd 15/8)

2525a TATTERSALLS GOLD CUP (GROUP 1) 1m 2f 110y

2:35 (2:35) 4-Y-O+ £108,500 (£33,250; £15,750; £5,250; £1,750)

RPR

1 **So You Think (NZ)**[57] 1150 6-9-1 125 JPO'Brien 3 127+
(A P O'Brien, Ire) *settled in 3rd off clr ldr: clsr 4f out and led ent st: in command fr over 1f out and styd on wl to stretch clr: v easily* **2/11**[1]

2 6 **Famous Name**[14] 2100 7-9-1 115 PatSmullen 4 115+
(D K Weld, Ire) *settled in 4th off clr ldr: clsr after 1/2-way and wnt 2nd early st: tried to chal 2f out but sn no ch w easy wnr: kpt on same pce* **7/1**[2]

3 7 ½ **Robin Hood (IRE)**[20] 1946 4-9-1 97 (b) SeamieHeffernan 5 101
(A P O'Brien, Ire) *sn led and clr after 3f: reduced advantage after 1/2-way and hdd ent st: rdn and no ex in 3rd under 2f out: kpt on one pce* **33/1**

4 1 ¾ **Bible Belt (IRE)**[225] 6859 4-8-12 113 FranBerry 2 95
(Mrs John Harrington, Ire) *hld up in rr: clsr after 1/2-way: 4th and rdn early st: sn no ex* **9/1**[3]

5 7 **Elusive Ridge (IRE)**[20] 1946 6-9-1 96 (p) ChrisHayes 1 84
(H Rogers, Ire) *chsd ldr in 2nd: clsr after 1/2-way: drvn along and dropped to 5th ent st: wknd* **66/1**

2m 15.65s (-4.35) **Going Correction** -0.125s/f (Firm) **5 Ran SP% 111.5**
Speed ratings: **111,106,101,99,94**
CSF £2.21 TOTE £1.40: £1.02, £2.20; DF 2.30.
Owner Smith/Magnier/Tabor/DatoTan/TunkuYahaya **Bred** M J Moran & Piper Farm Ltd **Trained** Ballydoyle, Co Tipperary

FOCUS
Nothing other than a formality on paper and so it proved.

NOTEBOOK
So You Think(NZ) sauntered to back-to-back wins in what again was a disappointingly uncompetitive renewal. Given a break since his Dubai exertions, this fine, big horse tracked a decent pace and everything seemed to go according to plan. He strode out well and was never remotely in danger of losing. This did not tell us much other than that he seems to retain his enthusiasm and he will go back to the Prince of Wales's Stakes with obvious claims. He is no superstar but seems to relish his racing and will no doubt be in good demand later on as a stallion in Australia. (op 1/5)
Famous Name, almost pulled out due to the quick ground, will likely never win a Group 1 but he got a soft top-level second-placed finish here. Pat Smullen was never going to give this fine servant a hard time as he was basically outclassed by the winner but travelled pretty well and seems as enthusiastic as ever.
Robin Hood(IRE) set a searching pace for his stablemate and, to his credit, kept on when headed. This seems his trip and he is an honest type.
Bible Belt(IRE), rated 16lb higher than Robin Hood, gave a rather laboured performance and was disappointing. (op 8/1)
Elusive Ridge(IRE) was a shade disappointing and is probably best on the all-weather.

2527a ETIHAD AIRWAYS IRISH 1,000 GUINEAS (GROUP 1) (FILLIES) 1m

3:40 (3:40) 3-Y-O

£145,000 (£47,500; £22,500; £7,500; £5,000; £2,500)

RPR

1 **Samitar**[14] 2109 3-9-0 MartinHarley 6 113
(Mick Channon) *trckd ldrs in 3rd: poised on rail travelling best 2f out: hdwy between horses and rdn to ld jst over 1f out: kpt on wl fnl f* **12/1**

2 1 ½ **Ishvana (IRE)**[20] 1944 3-9-0 95 SeamieHeffernan 1 110
(A P O'Brien, Ire) *chsd ldrs in 4th: rdn 2f out and wnt 2nd 1f out: kpt on same pce u.p but no imp on wnr* **33/1**

3 2 ¼ **Princess Sinead (IRE)**[14] 2101 3-9-0 102 FranBerry 7 105
(Mrs John Harrington, Ire) *settled in rr: 7th 1/2-way: hdwy into 4th 1f out: sn 3rd but no imp on first 2 ins fnl f* **25/1**

4 3 ¼ **Homecoming Queen (IRE)**[21] 1884 3-9-0 120 JPO'Brien 5 97+
(A P O'Brien, Ire) *led: pushed along 2f out: strly pressed and hdd jst over 1f out: sn no ex and dropped to 4th* **11/8**[1]

5 shd **After (IRE)**[14] 2109 3-9-0 109 RyanMoore 2 97
(A P O'Brien, Ire) *chsd ldrs in 6th: rdn in 7th under 2f out: kpt on u.p fnl f wout troubling ldrs* **11/2**

6 1 **La Collina (IRE)**[21] 1884 3-9-0 112 DeclanMcDonogh 8 95
(Kevin Prendergast, Ire) *trckd ldr in 2nd: drvn along over 2f out: sn no ex and dropped to 5th 1f out* **7/2**[2]

7 4 ¾ **Yellow Rosebud (IRE)**[14] 2101 3-9-0 109 PatSmullen 3 84
(D K Weld, Ire) *racd in 5th: rdn and no ex fr 2f out* **9/2**[3]

8 ½ **Janey Muddles (IRE)**[20] 1943 3-9-0 96 (t) KevinManning 4 83
(J S Bolger, Ire) *a towards rr and nvr a factor: rdn over 2f out and no threat* **33/1**

1m 38.55s (-7.45) **Going Correction** -0.725s/f (Hard) **8 Ran SP% 115.3**
Speed ratings: **108,106,104,101,100 99,95,94**
CSF £318.39 CT £9352.28 TOTE £13.80: £3.50, £6.10, £6.10; DF 457.00.
Owner Martin S Schwartz **Bred** Norman Court Stud **Trained** West Ilsley, Berks
■ Stewards' Enquiry : Ryan Moore severe caution: careless riding

FOCUS
Irish Guineas editions are rarely run on ground this fast and it certainly suited the winner. The form is held down by the runner-up, who is rated just 95.

NOTEBOOK
Samitar delivered in great style. While one can certainly pick holes in the form, she travelled like a smart type and there was no doubting her superiority. For a youngster having his first Classic ride, Martin Harley was admirably patient and happy to sit in third off the generous gallop. She moved closer around a quarter-mile out and moved to the immediate rear of the favourite travelling much the best. Once she got in the clear, Samitar was in no danger and, as has been the case before, she found plenty for driving. While one should not get carried away with what she achieved here, she had smart juvenile form and is clearly a force to fear on quickish ground over a mile off a strong pace. Mick Channon, trainer: "She needed some decent ground and will go for the Coronation Stakes at Royal Ascot. She was bought by the owner to go to America. The owner believed in me by putting Martin on and he got it spot-on - she was ridden with confidence."
Ishvana(IRE)'s proximity - she is, after all, rated 95 - drags down the form. She got a canny ride and travelled well, leaving previous form a long way behind on her ninth start. The chances are she is a bit flattered and her next race will tell us more. (op 40/1)

Princess Sinead(IRE) justified connections' long-held faith with a pleasing effort. Group 1-placed now, she left her Guineas Trial effort a long way behind and did a fine service for the National Stud, which owns her sire Jeremy. Ground-versatile, it is nevertheless hard to see her bettering this performance but she has generally been very consistent. (op 28/1)
Homecoming Queen(IRE) after this it seems fair to say she is at her best with dig underfoot. She could never really establish a foothold in the race here and, all things considered, ran respectably. Official explanation: jockey said filly did not handle today's ground (op 11/8 tchd 6/4)
After(IRE) was well backed but never threatened and looked a shade up against it on paper. She seemed to run her race. (op 13/2)
La Collina(IRE) was very disappointing, tracking the favourite and beaten a long way out. On the back of such a creditable effort at Newmarket, this performance suggests she may have found conditions too fast. (op 10/3 tchd 3/1)
Yellow Rosebud(IRE) never seemed happy at any stage and looked a different filly from the one who won the Guineas trial. Official explanation: jockey said filly did not handle today's ground (op 5/1 tchd 4/1)

2528 - 2530a (Foreign Racing) - See Raceform Interactive

1901 HOPPEGARTEN (R-H)
Sunday, May 27

OFFICIAL GOING: Turf: good

2531a DIANA-TRIAL (GROUP 2) (3YO FILLIES) (TURF) 1m 2f
3:45 (3:51) 3-Y-O
£33,333 (£12,916; £5,416; £3,333; £2,083; £1,250)

RPR

1 ½ **Wasimah (GER)** 3-9-2 0 WPanov 6 101
(H J Groschel, Germany) *hld up towards rr: rdn to improve 2 1/2f out: led over 1f out: hdd wl ins fnl f: kpt on* **33/10²**

2 ¾ **Nymphea (IRE)** 3-9-2 0 AStarke 7 100
(P Schiergen, Germany) *sn trcking ldr on outer: rdn to chal 2 1/2f out: led 2f out: hdd over 1f out: kpt on ins fnl f* **22/5³**

3 ¾ **Omana (FR)**³⁰ 3-9-2 0 FabriceVeron 2 98
(H-A Pantall, France) *prom on inner: rdn over 1 1/2f out: had to wait for clr run over 1f out: r.o to go 4th ins fnl f: gng on at fin* **105/10**

4 2 **High Heat (IRE)** 3-9-2 0 KKerekes 9 94
(W Figge, Germany) *hld up in last trio on wd outside: rdn to improve 2 1/2f out: kpt on one pce ins fnl 1 1/2f* **202/10**

5 ¾ **All For You (GER)**²¹⁰ 3-9-2 0 RobertHavlin 10 93
(P Harley, Germany) *unruly stalls: dropped in fr wd draw and hld up in last pair: last and rdn 2 1/2f out: outpcd over 1 1/2f out: styd on to go 6th ins fnl f* **195/10**

6 2 **Wanda's Girl**¹⁷¹ 3-9-2 0 MircoDemuro 8 89
(Manfred Hofer, Germany) *midfield on outer: rdn to chal over 2f out: kpt on tl no ex jst ins fnl f: fdd and dropped to 7th cl home* **19/2**

7 3 **Caitania (IRE)**²¹ 3-9-2 0 DavyBonilla 4 83
(C Sprengel, Germany) *slow to stride: hld up in last on inner: prog into midfield over 4f out: rdn over 2 1/2f out: short of room against rail and lost all ch over 1 1/2f out: coasted home ins fnl f* **104/10**

8 ½ **Faizeh (GER)** 3-9-2 0 FilipMinarik 5 82
(Andreas Lowe, Germany) *v slow to stride: drvn along to rcvr: t.k.h in midfield: rdn over 2 1/2f out: no ex and btn over 1 1/2f out: plugged on* **129/10**

9 2 ½ **Rila (FR)** 3-9-2 0 APietsch 1 77
(R Dzubasz, Germany) *drvn along early to ld: strly pressed 2 1/2f out: rdn whn hdd 2f out: qckly btn and wknd: eased ins fnl f* **31/5**

D **Monami (GER)**²³¹ 6737 3-9-2 0 JBojko 3 102
(A Wohler, Germany) *broke wl to dispute early ld: sn settled in midfield: rdn to improve 1 1/2f out: styd on strly to ld wl ins fnl f: drvn out* **12/5¹**

2m 4.8s (-1.90) **10** Ran SP% **128.9**
WIN (incl. 10 euro stake): 34. PLACES: 15, 15, 15. SF: 117.
Owner Frau Dr C Otto **Bred** Frau Dr C Otto **Trained** Germany

NOTEBOOK
Wasimah(GER) did not have the race run to suit and hit the front too soon.
Nymphea(IRE) is a late developer and can be expected to improve further.
Monami(GER) maintained her unbeaten record and is now clear favourite for the Preis der Diana. Connections wanted to run her in the German 1000 Guineas, but she missed her prep race for that following a setback, so they supplemented her for this. The pace was only steady but the filly quickened nicely and finally won with quite a bit in hand. She will have another race, probably at Hamburg, before the Diana.

2383 LONGCHAMP (R-H)
Sunday, May 27

OFFICIAL GOING: Turf: good

2532a MONTJEU COOLMORE PRIX SAINT-ALARY (GROUP 1) (3YO FILLIES) (TURF) 1m 2f
1:30 (12:00) 3-Y-O **£119,041** (£47,625; £23,812; £11,895; £5,958)

RPR

1 **Sagawara**²⁸ 1695 3-9-0 0 (p) Christophe-PatriceLemaire 8 107
(A De Royer-Dupre, France) *trckd ldr in 2nd on outer: rdn to chal 2f out: led 1f out: kpt on gamely u.p ins fnl f* **9/4²**

2 snk **Rjwa (IRE)**⁴⁰ 1434 3-9-0 0 ThierryJarnet 4 107
(F Rohaut, France) *settled in midfield on outer: rdn to improve over 2f out: r.o to go 2nd cl home: nt pce of wnr* **10/1³**

3 snk **Forces Of Darkness (IRE)**¹⁷ 3-9-0 0 GregoryBenoist 5 107
(F Vermeulen, France) *trckd ldr in 3rd on inner: rdn turn into st: r.o to chal wl ins fnl f: no ex and ct for 2nd cl home* **20/1**

4 ½ **La Peinture (FR)**³⁰ 3-9-0 0 OlivierPeslier 6 106
(F Rossi, France) *hld up in last on outer: rdn over 2f out: r.o to go 4th ins fnl f: nt pce to chal* **1/1¹**

5 1 ¼ **Crecy**⁴⁰ 1434 3-9-0 0 IoritzMendizabal 7 103
(Y Fouin, France) *hld up in last pair on inner: rdn to improve 2f out: kpt on one pce ins fnl 1 1/2f* **12/1**

6 1 ½ **Hasna (FR)**²⁷ 3-9-0 0 StephanePasquier 1 100
(P Bary, France) *led: set stdy pce: rdn over 2f out: hdd 1f out: no ex and fdd ins fnl f* **14/1**

7 1 ½ **Aigue Marine**³⁰ 3-9-0 0 ThierryThulliez 3 97
(N Clement, France) *midfield on outer: rdn turn into st: no ex and btn over 1f out: fdd* **12/1**

8 1 **Prima Noa (FR)**²⁸ 1695 3-9-0 0 GeraldMosse 9 95
(J Van Handenhove, France) *awkward s: midfield on inner: rdn over 2 1/2f out: sltly short of room 1 1/2f out: outpcd and fdd ins fnl f* **25/1**

2m 4.37s (0.37) **Going Correction** +0.05s/f (Good) **8** Ran SP% **120.5**
Speed ratings: **100,99,99,99,98 97,95,95**
WIN (incl. 1 euro stake): 3.10. PLACES: 1.60, 2.20, 4.00. DF: 11.70. SF: 15.50.
Owner H H Aga Khan **Bred** Haras De Son Altesse Aga Khan S C E A **Trained** Chantilly, France

NOTEBOOK
Sagawara, whose trainer employed cheekpieces for the first time in a Group race, was made plenty of use of an showed plenty of grit and determination to go repel a wall of challengers. She could now try and emulate Sarafina, who won the Saint-Alary two seasons ago before going on to lift the Prix de Diane.
Rjwa(IRE) was bouncing back to form after a below-par performance at Saint-Cloud last time and her trainer will also aim her at the Diane. Connections were disappointed with her run in the Prix Penelope where she didn't like going left-handed and didn't handle the very soft ground. His trainer is also responsible for Trois Lunes, who defeated Sagawara in the Prix Vanteaux last month.

2533a PRIX D'ISPAHAN (GROUP 1) (4YO+) (TURF) 1m 1f 55y
2:45 (12:00) 4-Y-O+ **£119,041** (£47,625; £23,812; £11,895; £5,958)

RPR

1 **Golden Lilac (IRE)**²⁸⁶ 5128 4-8-13 0 MaximeGuyon 1 119+
(A Fabre, France) *led early: pulling hrd: hdd after 1 1/2f: racd 3rd on rail under restraint: rdn 1 1/2f out: qcknd wl ent finaf f: chal for ld 150yds out: tk ld 100yds out: r.o strly* **6/1³**

2 ½ **Planteur (IRE)**⁵⁷ 1150 5-9-2 0 ChristopheSoumillon 3 119+
(Marco Botti) *settled in midfield on rail: swtchd away fr rail to make chal towards outside 1 1/2f out: r.o wl fnl f: nt rch ldrs* **5/1²**

3 ½ **No Risk At All (FR)**²⁶ 1746 5-9-2 0 IoritzMendizabal 5 118
(J-P Gallorini, France) *hld up towards rr: rdn and swtchd to rail over 1 1/2f out: r.o wl fnl f: nrest at fin* **50/1**

4 ¾ **Zinabaa (FR)**²⁶ 1746 7-9-2 0 YannickLetondeur 6 116
(M Mace, France) *settled in 2nd after 2f: rdn over 1 1/2f out: r.o fnl f: no threat to ldrs* **40/1**

5 1 ½ **Tin Horse (IRE)**²⁵⁹ 5988 4-9-2 0 ThierryJarnet 2 113
(D Guillemin, France) *settled in midfield: rdn but no ex fr 1 1/2f out: styd on at one pce fnl f* **20/1**

6 nk **Reliable Man**²⁸ 1696 4-9-2 0 GeraldMosse 8 113+
(A De Royer-Dupre, France) *hld up at rr of field: rdn over 1 1/2f out: no ex: styd on fnl f* **10/1**

7 6 **Penitent**³⁰ 1646 6-9-2 0 DanielTudhope 4 100
(David O'Meara) *settled in midfield: swtchd to outside ent st: rdn but no ex: fdd fnl f* **25/1**

D ¾ **Cirrus Des Aigles (FR)**²⁸ 1696 6-9-2 0 OlivierPeslier 7 120+
(Mme C Barande-Barbe, France) *2nd early: sent to ld after 1 1/2f: led into st: rdn over 1 1/2f out: qcknd wl: chal 150yds out: hdd 100yds out: r.o wl* **4/7¹**

1m 51.85s (-3.45) **Going Correction** +0.05s/f (Good) **8** Ran SP% **116.7**
Speed ratings: **117,115,115,114,113 113,107,116**
WIN (incl. 1 euro stake): 5.30. PLACES: 1.30, 1.10, 1.30. DF: 4.00. SF: 10.90.
Owner Gestut Ammerland **Bred** Ammerland Verwaltung Gmbh **Trained** Chantilly, France

NOTEBOOK
Golden Lilac(IRE) made a sparkling return to action when she surged past Cirrus Des Aigles inside the final furlong to win convincingly. She had not been seen on the track since last August and was keen in the early stages, but she settled much better when Guyon dropped her back in behind the leader and she picked up smartly when asked to close on the favourite. She might be supplemented for the Prince of Wales's Stakes or could perhaps wait for the Prix Jacques le Marois in August, although the Falmouth and Prix Rothschild come in between and might fit into her programme.
Planteur(IRE) finished well and is another who will benefit from a return to further. He has similar entries to the runner-up and could well meet him again at Ascot.
Cirrus Des Aigles(FR) made much of the running and attempted to kick from the front but could not match the finishing burst of the winner as she powered to the front inside the last furlong. He would be better over a bit further or on slightly softer ground. The Prince of Wales's Stakes and Eclipse are amongst his options.

2534a PRIX VICOMTESSE VIGIER (GROUP 2) (4YO+) (TURF) 1m 7f 110y
3:15 (12:00) 4-Y-O+ **£61,750** (£23,833; £11,375; £7,583; £3,791)

RPR

1 **Ivory Land (FR)**²⁸ 1697 5-8-11 0 StephanePasquier 7 114+
(A De Royer-Dupre, France) *settled in 2nd on outside of ldr: hrd rdn ent fnl f: chal for ld 100yds out: tk ld 50yds out: r.o wl* **8/1³**

2 ½ **Usuelo (FR)**²⁸ 1697 4-8-11 0 AntoineHamelin 6 115
(J-L Guillochon, France) *led fr s: qcknd wl in front 1 1/2f out: r.o wl ins fnl f: chal 100yds out: hdd 50yds out: r.o wl* **4/1¹**

3 1 ¾ **Prairie Star (FR)**²⁸ 1697 4-9-0 0 ChristopheSoumillon 5 116
(E Lellouche, France) *settled in 3rd on rail: rdn over 1f out: nt qckn: styd on fnl f* **4/1¹**

4 1 ¾ **Joshua Tree (IRE)**⁵⁷ 1144 5-8-11 0 OlivierPeslier 3 109
(Marco Botti) *settled in 6th: rdn over 1 1/2f out: r.o fnl f to take 4th: no threat to ldrs* **4/1¹**

5 snk **Tac De Boistron (FR)**²⁸ 1697 5-8-11 0 (p) ThierryJarnet 8 109
(A Lyon, France) *settled in midfield: rdn over 1 1/2f out: no ex: styd on fnl f* **12/1**

6 2 **Kasbah Bliss (FR)**⁵⁷ 1144 10-9-2 0 GeraldMosse 4 111
(F Doumen, France) *hld up at rr of field: rdn but no ex fr 1 1/2f out: styd on fnl f* **8/1³**

7 1 ¾ **Miss Lago (IRE)**²⁷ 1766 4-8-8 0 GregoryBenoist 2 103
(E Lellouche, France) *hld up towards rr: rdn but no ex fr 2f out: nvr a factor* **8/1³**

8 4 ½ **Altano (GER)**²¹ 1901 6-8-11 0 MaximeGuyon 1 99
(A Wohler, Germany) *settled in midfield: rdden over 2f out: no ex: nvr a factor* **13/2²**

3m 26.69s (5.19) **Going Correction** +0.05s/f (Good)
WFA 4 from 5yo+ 1lb **8** Ran SP% **114.4**
Speed ratings: **89,88,87,87,86 85,85,82**
WIN (incl. 1 euro stake): 6.30. PLACES: 1.70, 1.60, 1.60. DF: 23.60. SF: 50.00.
Owner Eduardo Fierro **Bred** Suc Z Hakam **Trained** Chantilly, France

NOTEBOOK
Ivory Land(FR) had finished behind a few of these last time in heavy ground, so presumably the going made all the difference. Afterwards connections were adamant they had no regrets about not having given the winner an entry in the Ascot race and he is likely to wait for another year.
Usuelo(FR) ran really well at the revised weights with the winner from their previous clash, and might be the best of these in the long term. He appears to act in most ground.

Prairie Star(FR) finished behind the runner-up for the second race in a row after appearing to hold every chance.
Joshua Tree(IRE) chased the leaders but took a while to hit top gear when Peslier asked for an effort. It's possible that he would have wanted a stronger gallop to chase.
Miss Lago(IRE) was disappointing but it's unlikely this was her true form.
Altano(GER) had an obvious form chance on going that had come right for him, but he ran a long way below what he should have done.

CARLISLE (R-H)

Monday, May 28

OFFICIAL GOING: Good to firm (firm in places last 4f; 7.9)
Wind: Breezy, across Weather: Hot, sunny

2535 ULTIMATE LADIES NIGHT ON AUGUST 6TH APPRENTICE H'CAP 7f 200y
6:20 (6:22) (Class 5) (0-70,70) 4-Y-0+ **£2,264** (£673; £336; £168) **Stalls** Low

Form RPR
6-33 **1** **Hakuna Matata**[10] 2241 5-9-4 **67** (p) AmyRyan 5 75
(Brian Ellison) *s.i.s: bhd: last and plenty to do over 3f out: gd hdwy on wd outside 2f out: led ins fnl f: edgd rt: pushed out* **8/1**
150- **2** ½ **Silly Gilly (IRE)**[243] 6453 8-8-13 **62** ShaneBKelly 12 68
(Ron Barr) *trckd ldrs: rdn over 2f out: led over 1f out to ins fnl f: kpt on: hld nr fin* **28/1**
00-2 **3** 1 ¼ **Broctune Papa Gio**[49] 1251 5-9-1 **64** DeclanCannon 14 67
(Keith Reveley) *hld up: rdn and hdwy 2f out: chsd ldrs ins fnl f: kpt on: hld towards fin* **6/1**[2]
2040 **4** 1 ¼ **Nezami (IRE)**[20] 1958 7-8-12 **66** NedCurtis(5) 10 66
(Paul Midgley) *in tch: effrt and rdn over 2f out: kpt on same pce fnl f* **9/1**
-402 **5** nse **Hayek**[30] 1659 5-8-13 **62** (b) AdamCarter 13 62
(Tim Easterby) *s.i.s: hld up: rdn and kpt on fr 2f out: nrst fin* **7/1**[3]
1-50 **6** ½ **Watts Up Son**[21] 1917 4-9-1 **69** (bt) JasonHart(5) 4 68
(Declan Carroll) *taken v early to post: s.i.s: effrt on outside over 3f out: edgd rt and n.m.r briefly over 1f out: kpt on fnl f* **16/1**
1230 **7** 2 ¾ **Qeethaara (USA)**[12] 2161 8-9-4 **67** (p) JamesRogers 7 59
(Mark Brisbourne) *prom: rdn along 2f out: outpcd fnl f* **22/1**
3-64 **8** ½ **Petsas Pleasure**[17] 2035 6-9-0 **63** JulieBurke 16 54
(Ollie Pears) *s.i.s: hld up: stdy hdwy on outside over 2f out: rdn over 1f out: sn one pce* **14/1**
6106 **9** ¾ **Chookie Avon**[7] 2355 5-8-13 **69** (p) PaulHainey(7) 3 58
(Keith Dalgleish) *hld up on ins: hmpd after 3f: rdn and hdwy on outside 2f out: no imp fnl f* **25/1**
2-13 **10** 2 ¾ **Le Chat D'Or**[25] 1796 4-9-4 **67** (t) LMcNiff 6 49
(Michael Dods) *hld up: checked after 3f: rdn and effrt over 2f out: wknd ins fnl f* **4/1**[1]
12-0 **11** 2 ¼ **Whispered Times (USA)**[49] 1251 5-9-2 **68** (p) JustinNewman(3) 8 44
(Tracy Waggott) *t.k.h: led 1f: led again over 2f out: rdn: edgd lft and hdd over 1f out: sn wknd* **16/1**
402 **12** 4 **Pursuit of Passion**[20] 1953 4-8-13 **62** LeeTopliss 15 28
(Richard Fahey) *prom: drvn and edgd lft over 2f out: wknd over 1f out* **20/1**
56-6 **13** 2 **Honest Deal**[22] 1879 4-9-6 **69** (b[1]) GarryWhillans 11 30
(Alan Swinbank) *t.k.h: led at decent gallop after 1f: rdn and hdd over 2f out: wknd over 1f out* **14/1**
-504 **14** ¾ **Desert Hunter (IRE)**[107] 531 9-8-0 **56** oh7 KatieDowson(7) 2 15
(Micky Hammond) *hld up on ins: checked after 3f: rdn 3f out: nvr on terms* **25/1**
045/ **P** **Billy Dane (IRE)**[631] 5789 8-9-7 **70** (v) LucyAlexander 9
(Barry Murtagh) *in tch tl broke down and p.u after 3f: fatally injured* **12/1**

1m 39.08s (-0.92) **Going Correction** -0.025s/f (Good) **15** Ran SP% **120.9**
Speed ratings (Par 103): **103,102,101,100,99 99,96,96,95,92 90,86,84,83,**
toteswingers:1&2:£20.30, 2&3:£31.30, 1&3:£8.50 CSF £224.96 CT £1478.32 TOTE £11.60: £3.20, £6.00, £3.20; EX 162.60.
Owner Sekura Group **Bred** Mrs J A Chapman **Trained** Norton, N Yorks

FOCUS
After another hot summer's day the ground continued to dry out. The opening 56-70 apprentice handicap was run under Racing Post standard, suggesting the ground was firm. A wide-open modest handicap.
Watts Up Son Official explanation: jockey said saddle slipped.
Chookie Avon Official explanation: jockey said gelding suffered interference in running.
Le Chat D'Or Official explanation: trainer said gelding was unsuited by good to firm (firm) ground.

2536 ALLAN ESTATE AGENTS A SMOOTH MOVE CLAIMING STKS 7f 200y
6:50 (6:50) (Class 6) 3-Y-0+ **£1,704** (£503; £251) **Stalls** Low

Form RPR
0201 **1** **Benandonner (USA)**[7] 2329 9-9-8 84 RobertWinston 2 71
(Mike Murphy) *plld hrd: hld up in tch on ins: swtchd to outside and hdwy 2f out: styd on wl fnl f to ld towards fin* **10/11**[1]
5540 **2** nk **River Ardeche**[21] 1917 7-8-12 64 ShaneBKelly(5) 4 65
(Tracy Waggott) *led at ordinary gallop: rdn and qcknd 2f out: kpt on wl fnl f: hdd towards fin* **20/1**
00-0 **3** 3 ¼ **Rasselas (IRE)**[16] 2094 5-9-6 64 AdrianNicholls 1 60
(David Nicholls) *trckd ldrs: rdn 2f out: kpt on ins fnl f: nt pce of first two* **14/1**[3]
00-2 **4** 2 **Carnival Dream**[49] 1248 7-9-0 46 GaryBartley(3) 6 52
(Hugh McWilliams) *t.k.h: cl up: rdn and edgd lft over 1f out: sn no ex* **50/1**
240- **5** ¾ **King Pin**[153] 7885 7-9-4 59 TomEaves 5 51
(Tracy Waggott) *prom: rdn over 2f out: no ex over 1f out* **25/1**
03-0 **6** 2 ¼ **Rowan Lodge (IRE)**[40] 1436 10-9-0 57 (b) JulieBurke(3) 3 45
(Ollie Pears) *plld hrd: hld up: stmbld over 6f out: effrt on outside over 2f out: nvr able to chal* **40/1**
6004 **7** 1 **Amazing Star (IRE)**[23] 1863 7-9-10 79 GrahamGibbons 8 49
(Declan Carroll) *s.i.s: t.k.h in rr: rdn over 2f out: no imp over 1f out* **4/1**[2]
000 **8** 2 ¼ **Silenceofthewind (USA)**[23] 1863 5-9-10 74 MichaelO'Connell 7 43
(Mrs K Burke) *t.k.h: prom on outside: stdy hdwy over 2f out: rdn and wknd qckly over 1f out* **4/1**[2]

1m 39.68s (-0.32) **Going Correction** -0.025s/f (Good) **8** Ran SP% **112.1**
Speed ratings (Par 101): **100,99,96,94,93 91,90,88**
toteswingers:1&2:£5.10, 2&3:£13.20, 1&3:£3.60 CSF £24.84 TOTE £2.10: £1.10, £8.70, £4.90; EX 18.00.River Ardeche was the subject of a friendly claim
Owner M Murphy **Bred** Gainsborough Farm Llc **Trained** Westoning, Beds

FOCUS
A claimer in which only three of the runners could be seriously fancied beforehand.

2537 OFFICE BAR CHAMPAGNES AND COCKTAILS MEDIAN AUCTION MAIDEN STKS 5f
7:20 (7:22) (Class 5) 2-Y-0 **£2,264** (£673; £336; £168) **Stalls** Low

Form RPR
2 **1** **Liber**[14] 2123 2-9-3 0 LukeMorris 8 85+
(Sir Mark Prescott Bt) *mde all: rdn and veered rt over 1f out: stened and kpt on strly to go clr fnl f* **10/11**[1]
6 **2** 4 ½ **Pastoral Prey**[25] 1795 2-9-3 0 LeeNewman 6 67
(George Foster) *noisy and green in preliminaries: cl up: effrt and ev ch 2f out: outpcd by wnr fnl f* **50/1**
0 **3** 2 **Yorkshire Icon**[13] 2138 2-9-3 0 PaddyAspell 3 61+
(Ann Duffield) *bhd and outpcd: plenty to do 1/2-way: gd hdwy fnl f: nrst fin* **22/1**
0 **4** 3 **Rat Catcher (IRE)**[13] 2138 2-9-3 0 DavidAllan 5 49
(Tim Easterby) *trckd ldrs: rdn over 2f out: edgd lft over 1f out: btn ins fnl f* **9/2**[3]
5 1 ¾ **Sleepy Haven (IRE)** 2-9-3 0 GrahamGibbons 1 43
(David Barron) *noisy and green in preliminaries: in tch: pushed along 1/2-way: btn fnl f* **14/1**
6 1 ¼ **Angel Grigio** 2-8-12 0 TomEaves 7 33
(Bryan Smart) *t.k.h: sn trcking ldrs: rdn and hung rt over 1f out: wknd ins fnl f* **4/1**[2]
7 1 ½ **Beadle** 2-9-3 0 GrahamLee 2 33
(Keith Dalgleish) *in tch: rdn along 1/2-way: wknd over 1f out* **20/1**
F4 **8** 1 ¼ **Silver Fawn (IRE)**[7] 2334 2-9-3 0 DuranFentiman 4 28
(John Weymes) *chsd ldng gp on outside: outpcd 1/2-way: btn over 1f out* **12/1**

1m 1.13s (0.33) **Going Correction** -0.175s/f (Firm) **8** Ran SP% **116.0**
Speed ratings (Par 93): **90,82,79,74,72 70,67,65**
toteswingers:1&2:£12.00, 2&3:£31.00, 1&3:£9.30 CSF £71.29 TOTE £1.80: £1.10, £11.70, £6.60; EX 53.70.
Owner William Charnley & Richard Pegum **Bred** Redmyre Bloodstock Ltd **Trained** Newmarket, Suffolk

FOCUS
Almost certainly a weak maiden but in the end a very ready, progressive winner. The runner-up sets the level.

NOTEBOOK
Liber, who has plenty of size about him, had finished runner-up first time in soft ground at Redcar. He bounced off the quick ground and, despite wandering slightly, in the end he came right away. His master trainer no doubt already has a plan mapped out for him. (tchd 6-5 and 5-4 in a place)
Pastoral Prey, unconsidered after finishing last of six first time at Musselburgh three weeks earlier, travelled almost as well as the winner though was no match in the end. A May foal, he will hopefully improve again.
Yorkshire Icon, on his second start, was soon detached in last. He made up a deal of ground in the final furlong and is already crying out for 6f. He will improve again. (op 20-1)
Rat Catcher(IRE), eighth of 13 first time, didn't really improve on that effort on much quicker ground. (op 13-2)
Sleepy Haven(IRE) showed his inexperience beforehand and the outing will not be lost on him. (tchd 11-1)
Angel Grigio tended to run with the choke out and was already on the retreat when brushed aside by the third. She looks very weak at present. (op 9-2 tchd 7-2)

2538 WATCH RACING UK ON SKY 432 H'CAP 5f 193y
7:50 (7:50) (Class 6) (0-65,65) 4-Y-0+ **£1,704** (£503; £251) **Stalls** Low

Form RPR
0405 **1** **Best Trip (IRE)**[24] 1823 5-8-9 **53** BarryMcHugh 16 71
(Brian Ellison) *t.k.h: trckd ldrs: smooth hdwy to ld over 1f out: rdn: edgd rt and kpt on strly fnl f* **4/1**[2]
4561 **2** 2 ¾ **Amazing Win (IRE)**[4] 2413 4-8-5 **54** CharlesBishop(5) 8 67+
(Mick Channon) *t.k.h: hld up towards rr: hdwy over 1f out: styd on fnl f to take 2nd nr fin: no ch w wnr* **9/4**[1]
1105 **3** ½ **Consistant**[39] 1481 4-9-4 **62** DuranFentiman 3 70
(Brian Baugh) *trckd ldrs: effrt and wnt 2nd over 1f out: kpt on fnl f: no ex and lost 2nd nr fin* **25/1**
-250 **4** 2 ¾ **Circuitous**[7] 2350 4-9-0 **58** (b) TomEaves 11 57
(Keith Dalgleish) *led: rdn and hdd over 1f out: sn outpcd* **20/1**
-023 **5** ¾ **Hellbender (IRE)**[24] 1823 6-9-3 **61** LeeNewman 7 58
(George Foster) *prom: rdn over 2f out: no ex over 1f out* **20/1**
0-04 **6** ½ **Ryedane (IRE)**[16] 2092 10-8-12 **63** (b) RachelRichardson(7) 10 58
(Tim Easterby) *hld up: stdy hdwy on outside over 2f out: sn rdn: kpt on ins fnl f: nvr able to chal* **16/1**
0-25 **7** ½ **Foreign Rhythm (IRE)**[10] 2244 7-8-13 **62** ShaneBKelly(5) 5 56
(Ron Barr) *bhd and pushed along: hdwy over 1f out: kpt on fnl f: nrest at fin* **22/1**
2500 **8** 2 ¼ **Dunmore Boy (IRE)**[49] 1251 4-8-11 **62** (p) GeorgeChaloner(7) 2 48
(Richard Fahey) *midfield on ins: rdn over 2f out: sn no imp: btn fnl f* **22/1**
0533 **9** 2 **Cerejeira (IRE)**[17] 2032 4-8-11 **55** (t) DavidAllan 4 35
(Eric Alston) *prom: lost pl over 2f out: n.d after* **12/1**
01-0 **10** nk **Henry Morgan**[22] 1875 5-9-2 **65** JustinNewman(5) 14 44
(Bryan Smart) *bhd on wd outside: rdn along 1/2-way: nvr able to chal* **17/2**
0232 **11** 1 ½ **Whipphound**[2] 2475 4-9-4 **62** LukeMorris 9 36
(Mark Brisbourne) *hld up: rdn over 2f out: sn no imp* **9/2**[3]
000- **12** 2 ¾ **Bay Of Fires (IRE)**[216] 7073 4-9-7 **65** PhillipMakin 12 30
(David O'Meara) *midfield: effrt over 2f out: wknd appr fnl f* **33/1**
630- **13** 18 **Nufoudh (IRE)**[246] 6382 8-9-7 **65** RobertWinston 13
(Tracy Waggott) *t.k.h: hld up on outside: shortlived effrt over 2f out: sn btn* **33/1**
3-00 **14** 1 ¼ **Cross Of Lorraine (IRE)**[20] 1954 9-9-3 **61** (b) TonyHamilton 15
(Chris Grant) *trckd ldrs tl rdn and wknd fr 2f out* **33/1**

1m 12.5s (-1.20) **Going Correction** -0.175s/f (Firm) **14** Ran SP% **123.9**
Speed ratings (Par 101): **101,97,96,93,92 91,90,87,85,84 82,78,54,53**
toteswingers:1&2:£5.60, 2&3:£15.30, 1&3:£16.30 CSF £12.02 CT £205.93 TOTE £3.40: £1.30, £2.10, £4.00; EX 21.00.
Owner Koo's Racing Club **Bred** Limetree Stud **Trained** Norton, N Yorks

FOCUS
A big field for this modest handicap. The winner had an outside draw to overcome, the favourite had a nightmare passage.

Best Trip(IRE) Official explanation: trainer said regarding apparent improvement in form that gelding settled better.

2539 NIGEL DEAN FILLIES' H'CAP (BETFAIR 10 FURLONG FLAT SERIES QUALIFIER) 1m 1f 61y

8:20 (8:20) (Class 4) (0-80,80) 3-Y-O+ **£5,175** (£1,540; £769; £384) **Stalls** Low

Form				RPR
-444	**1**		**Act Your Shoe Size**[16] 2076 3-8-9 **74** TomEaves 1 (Keith Dalgleish) *led to over 2f out: rallied and regained ld appr fnl f: hld on gamely towards fin* **7/1**	79
2-11	**2**	*hd*	**Love Your Looks**[19] 1980 4-10-0 **80** GrahamLee 8 (Mike Murphy) *hld up: stdy hdwy on outside over 2f out: effrt and rdn over 1f out: kpt on fnl f: jst hld* **9/2**[2]	86+
0-05	**3**	*shd*	**Snow Dancer (IRE)**[94] 694 8-9-6 **75** GaryBartley(3) 5 (Hugh McWilliams) *t.k.h: prom: effrt and rdn over 1f out: kpt on ins fnl f* **8/1**	81
0-30	**4**	*1 1/4*	**Sangar**[25] 1797 4-9-1 **67** MichaelO'Connell 7 (Ollie Pears) *trckd ldrs: wnt 2nd over 5f out: led over 2f out to appr fnl f: kpt on: no ex towards fin* **6/1**[3]	70
0-10	**5**	*hd*	**Cala Santanyi**[26] 1756 4-9-10 **76** (p) LukeMorris 6 (Gerard Butler) *t.k.h: cl up: rdn over 2f out: kpt on same pce fnl f* **12/1**	79
-466	**6**	*1 1/4*	**Rythmic**[6] 2379 3-8-8 **73** AdrianNicholls 9 (Mark Johnston) *hld up: rdn along and outpcd over 2f out: styd on fnl f: nvr able to chal* **16/1**	71
0-41	**7**	*1*	**Spavento (IRE)**[22] 1879 6-9-0 **66** oh4 DavidAllan 4 (Eric Alston) *in tch on ins: drvn over 2f out: rallied: no ex over 1f out* **11/1**	64
105-	**8**	*1/2*	**Adorable Choice (IRE)**[220] 6997 4-9-2 **71** RossAtkinson(3) 2 (Tom Dascombe) *s.i.s: towards rr on ins: drvn over 2f out: no imp over 1f out* **25/1**	68
2-55	**9**	*nse*	**Bountiful Girl**[16] 2076 3-8-11 **76** TonyHamilton 11 (Richard Fahey) *t.k.h: hld up: drvn and outpcd over 2f out: nvr on terms* **11/1**	71
5340	**10**	*1 1/2*	**Painted Tail (IRE)**[19] 1988 5-9-0 **66** oh1 RobertWinston 12 (Alan Swinbank) *hld up on outside: struggling over 2f out: sn n.d* **12/1**	60
4221	**11**	*13*	**Tidal Run**[12] 2161 4-9-6 **72** MatthewDavies 10 (Mick Channon) *prom: rdn over 3f out: wknd fr 2f out* **4/1**[1]	39

1m 56.36s (-1.24) **Going Correction** -0.025s/f (Good)
WFA 3 from 4yo+ 13lb **11** Ran SP% **117.9**
Speed ratings (Par 102): **104,103,103,102,102 101,100,100,99,98 87**
toteswingers:1&2:£8.30, 2&3:£10.00, 1&3:£12.10 CSF £38.62 CT £261.58 TOTE £9.90: £2.40, £3.00, £3.70; EX 59.80.

Owner Gordon McDowall **Bred** Gordon McDowall **Trained** Carluke, S Lanarks

■ Stewards' Enquiry : Tom Eaves two day ban; used whip above permitted level (11th-12 June)

FOCUS
A highly competitive fillies' handicap and a tight three-way finish.

Painted Tail(IRE) Official explanation: trainer said mare was unsuited by good to firm (firm) ground.

Tidal Run Official explanation: trainers representative could offer no explanation as to poor run.

2540 ALLAN LETTINGS RENT FOR SUCCESS H'CAP 6f 192y

8:50 (8:51) (Class 6) (0-60,60) 3-Y-O **£1,704** (£503; £251) **Stalls** Low

Form				RPR
0-10	**1**		**Johnny Cavagin**[45] 1359 3-9-5 **58** (t) RobertWinston 2 (Richard Guest) *t.k.h early: chsd ldr: led 2f out: sn drvn: hld on wl fnl f* **7/1**[2]	64
25-3	**2**	*shd*	**Mad For Fun (IRE)**[24] 1826 3-8-4 **50** NedCurtis(7) 7 (Paul Midgley) *chsd ldrs on outside: effrt over 1f out: rdn ins fnl f: kpt on under hands and heels nr fin: jst hld* **11/1**	56
0-06	**3**	*nk*	**Pendle Lady (IRE)**[14] 2130 3-9-2 **55** LukeMorris 6 (Mark Brisbourne) *trckd ldrs: effrt and pushed along over 2f out: edgd lft: rallied and ch ins fnl f: kpt on: hld nr fin* **16/1**	60
-240	**4**	*1/2*	**Orwellian**[45] 1359 3-9-3 **56** TomEaves 8 (Bryan Smart) *plld hrd: in tch on wd outside: effrt and rdn over 2f out: kpt on ins fnl f* **14/1**	59
03-3	**5**	*1/2*	**Zaffy (IRE)**[47] 1296 3-9-4 **57** DavidAllan 11 (Tim Easterby) *t.k.h: towards rr: drvn over 3f out: hdwy over 1f out: kpt on fnl f: no imp towards fin* **15/2**[3]	59+
4663	**6**	*3/4*	**Represent (IRE)**[6] 2367 3-9-4 **57** MatthewDavies 10 (Mick Channon) *hld up on outside: rdn and hdwy 2f out: edgd rt: no imp fnl f* **2/1**[1]	57
-244	**7**	*nk*	**Dansili Dutch (IRE)**[24] 1826 3-9-5 **58** GrahamGibbons 12 (David Barron) *bhd: rdn over 2f out: kpt on fnl f: nrest at fin* **11/1**	57
20-5	**8**	*2*	**Citybell (IRE)**[26] 1758 3-9-2 **60** ShaneBKelly(5) 13 (Richard Fahey) *t.k.h: hld up: rdn over 2f out: kpt on fnl f: nrest at fin* **10/1**	54
30-0	**9**	*1 1/4*	**Jay Kay**[16] 2095 3-8-11 **57** MatthewHopkins(7) 4 (Danielle McCormick) *t.k.h: in tch tl edgd rt and wknd wl over 1f out* **22/1**	47
03-0	**10**	*1/2*	**Spoken Words**[66] 1012 3-8-12 **54** ow1 GaryBartley(3) 1 (Hugh McWilliams) *led to 2f out: sn drvn: btn fnl f* **25/1**	43
045-	**11**	*6*	**Peters Pursuit (IRE)**[272] 5597 3-9-4 **57** TonyHamilton 3 (Richard Fahey) *midfield on ins: struggling wl over 2f out: sn wknd* **14/1**	30
52-0	**12**	*1/2*	**Great Nicanor (IRE)**[17] 2036 3-9-2 **55** GrahamLee 5 (Ian Semple) *in tch: rdn over 2f out: wknd wl over 1f out* **25/1**	26
4-00	**13**	*2 1/4*	**Elusive Bonus (IRE)**[33] 1599 3-9-1 **54** PhillipMakin 9 (David O'Meara) *t.k.h: hld up towards rr: struggling over 2f out: sn btn* **33/1**	19

1m 27.62s (0.52) **Going Correction** -0.025s/f (Good) **13** Ran SP% **117.6**
Speed ratings (Par 97): **96,95,95,94,94 93,93,90,89,88 82,81,78**
toteswingers:1&2:£13.50, 2&3:£34.30, 1&3:£15.70 CSF £76.35 CT £1193.48 TOTE £9.50: £2.90, £3.20, £1.80; EX 145.50.

Owner A Bell **Bred** A Bell **Trained** Stainforth, S Yorks

FOCUS
A blanket finish to this low-grade 3yo handicap.

Citybell(IRE) Official explanation: jockey said filly ran too freely.

T/Plt: £200.90 to a £1 stake. Pool £70,313.82 - 255.40 winning tickets. T/Qpdt: £44.60 to a £1 stake. Pool £4,829.31 - 80.02 winning tickets. RY

2368 KEMPTON (A.W) (R-H)

Monday, May 28

OFFICIAL GOING: Standard
Wind: Virtually nil Weather: warm and sunny

2541 BETFAIR MAIDEN FILLIES' STKS 6f (P)

2:15 (2:16) (Class 5) 2-Y-O **£2,264** (£673; £336; £168) **Stalls** Low

Form				RPR
2	**1**		**Sharaarah (IRE)**[10] 2245 2-9-0 0 PaulHanagan 5 (Ed Dunlop) *t.k.h: chsd ldr: rdn to ld wl over 1f out: r.o wl and drew clr ins fnl f: readily* **13/8**[1]	79
5	**2**	*2 1/2*	**New Falcon (IRE)**[10] 2245 2-9-0 0 NeilCallan 2 (James Tate) *led: rdn over 2f out: hdd wl over 1f out: kpt on u.p tl no ex ins fnl f: wknd towards fin* **4/1**[2]	72
	3	*1 1/2*	**Something Magic** 2-9-0 0 LiamKeniry 6 (Sylvester Kirk) *hld up in rr of main gp: rdn and hdwy jst over 2f out: kpt on wl fnl f: nt rch ldrs* **33/1**	67+
	4	*3/4*	**Pira Palace (IRE)** 2-9-0 0 RyanMoore 1 (Sir Michael Stoute) *in tch: rdn 1/2-way: chsd clr ldng pair 2f out: no imp: kpt on fnl f* **8/1**	65+
3223	**5**	*2*	**Poetic Princess**[17] 2047 2-9-0 0 TonyCulhane 7 (Jo Hughes) *chsd ldrs: rdn and outpcd ent fnl 2f: no threat to ldrs fr over 1f out* **11/1**	59
0	**6**	*1/2*	**World Freight Girl**[42] 1411 2-9-0 0 JimCrowley 3 (Dean Ivory) *in tch: rdn 1/2-way: outpcd and btn 2f out: n.d but kpt on again ins fnl f* **50/1**	57
	7	*1/2*	**Travel (USA)** 2-9-0 0 SilvestreDeSousa 8 (Mahmood Al Zarooni) *wnt bdly lft leaving stalls and lost many l s: clsd and in tch 1/2-way: outpcd over 2f out: no ch but kpt on again fnl f* **9/2**[3]	60+
0	**8**	*1*	**Melodee Princess (IRE)**[16] 2069 2-8-9 0 DarrenEgan(5) 4 (Ronald Harris) *hld up in tch: rdn and effrt 2f out: unable qck and sn outpcd: wl hld fnl f* **12/1**	53

1m 14.91s (1.81) **Going Correction** +0.10s/f (Slow) **8** Ran SP% **108.3**
Speed ratings (Par 90): **91,87,85,84,82 81,80,79**
toteswingers:1&2:£2.10, 2&3:£12.30, 1&3:£10.10 CSF £7.08 TOTE £2.50: £1.10, £2.60, £5.10; EX 8.10 Trifecta £59.10 Pool £900.13 - 11.26 winning units.

Owner Hamdan Al Maktoum **Bred** Shadwell Estate Company Limited **Trained** Newmarket, Suffolk

FOCUS
Probably a fair juvenile fillies' maiden for the track, and with the first two running similar racs to when meeting at Newmarket, the form fits in with the race average.

NOTEBOOK
Sharaarah(IRE) had shown plenty of promise when runner-up on her Newmarket debut ten days earlier and stepped up from that. Always on the shoulder of the leader, she was made to work in order to stamp her authority on the race once sent to the front over a furlong out, but she was well on top at the line. Her pedigree suggests that she wouldn't get much further than this, but she is likely to improve again. (op 11-8)
New Falcon(IRE) finished behind Sharaarah when fifth at Newmarket, having started favourite for that race, and again she tried to make all, but the result was just the same as she found her old rival too strong. The margin between the pair was slightly bigger than at Newmarket, but this was still probably a step forward. (op 5-1)
Something Magic, out of a winning miler, herself a half-sister to three high-class performers including the Breeders' Cup Juvenile Turf winner Donativum, was doing some solid late work and fared best of the three newcomers. (op 25-1)
Pira Palace(IRE), a 110,000euros half-sister to two winners at up to 7f, was always just being niggled along to hold her position on this debut, but should have learnt something from it. (tchd 7-1)
Poetic Princess had been placed in all four of her previous starts, including twice on Polytrack but, although she was forced to race wider than ideal, she was probably up against more progressive rivals. (op 9-1 tchd 14-1)
Travel(USA), a half-sister to two winners at up to 1m2f including the US Grade 2 winner Eight Belles, swerved violently away to her left exiting the stalls on her debut over 6f at Kempton and that was her chance gone. Official explanation: jockey said filly hung left leaving the stalls. (tchd 4-1)

2542 BETFAIR SUPPORTING GRASSROOTS RACING MAIDEN STKS (DIV I) 7f (P)

2:45 (2:48) (Class 5) 3-Y-O **£2,264** (£673; £336; £168) **Stalls** Low

Form				RPR
6-	**1**		**Fast Or Free**[222] 6951 3-9-3 0 PaulHanagan 6 (William Haggas) *mde all: rdn and kpt finding ex whn pressed 2f out: r.o wl fnl f* **15/8**[1]	85+
00	**2**	*1/2*	**Shy Rosa (USA)**[17] 2030 3-8-7 0 LeonnaMayor(5) 4 (Marcus Tregoning) *chsd ldrs: effrt on inner to chal wl over 1f out: kpt on wl but a jst hld fnl f* **16/1**	78
0-5	**3**	*4 1/2*	**Picture Dealer**[13] 2147 3-9-3 0 RyanMoore 14 (Gary Moore) *in tch: swtchd lft and effrt to chal 2f out: no ex ins fnl f: fdd fnl 100yds* **6/1**[3]	71+
0-3	**4**	*shd*	**Grey Seal (IRE)**[27] 1736 3-8-12 0 HayleyTurner 10 (James Fanshawe) *in tch: rdn and effrt 2f out: outpcd over 1f out: plugged on pressing for 3rd cl home* **9/2**[2]	66
042-	**5**	*1 3/4*	**Dark Don (IRE)**[247] 6344 3-9-3 73 WilliamCarson 2 (Charles Hills) *chsd ldrs: rdn and unable qck ent fnl 2f: wknd u.p jst over 1f out* **9/2**[2]	66
	6	*3 1/4*	**Tunnager Grove** 3-9-3 0 DarryllHolland 3 (Hughie Morrison) *in tch in midfield: rdn and outpcd over 2f out: 7th and no hdwy fr over 1f out* **40/1**	57
30-	**7**	*3/4*	**Take A Note**[186] 7526 3-9-3 0 GeorgeBaker 5 (Patrick Chamings) *hld up in last quartet: rdn and sme hdwy over 2f out: kpt on but no real imp fr over 1f out* **18/1**	55
	8	*1/2*	**Regalo Rosado** 3-8-12 0 PatDobbs 11 (Mike Murphy) *v.s.a: bhd: rdn and hdwy on inner 2f out: kpt on fnl f: n.d* **66/1**	49
0-	**9**	*1/2*	**Alnoomaas (IRE)**[289] 5051 3-9-0 0 CPGeoghegan(3) 13 (Ronald Harris) *t.k.h: hld up in midfield: swtchd lft and effrt over 2f out: sn outpcd and no threat to ldrs fnl 2f* **50/1**	53
05-	**10**	*shd*	**Superciliary**[187] 7520 3-9-3 0 JimCrowley 8 (Ralph Beckett) *chsd ldr tl wl over 1f out: wknd over 1f out: fdd ins fnl f* **9/1**	52
	11	*5*	**Bowstar** 3-8-12 0 J-PGuillambert 9 (Michael Attwater) *s.i.s: sn pushed along in rr: bhd fnl 2f* **50/1**	34
0	**12**	*1*	**Compton Crofter**[13] 2147 3-8-10 0 (t) NicoleNordblad(7) 12 (Hans Adielsson) *racd off the pce in midfield: pushed along 4f out: outpcd over 2f out: no threat to ldrs fnl 2f* **66/1**	36

0- **13** *24* **Tantrum (IRE)**[219] 7025 3-8-12 0 KirstyMilczarek 7
(Olivia Maylam) *chsd ldrs: hung lft and losing pl bnd 3f out: wl bhd and eased ins fnl f: t.o* **66/1**

0 **14** *4 1/2* **Baileys Bigishu**[35] 1560 3-9-3 0 PaulMulrennan 1
(James Given) *sn bhd: lost tch 1/2-way: t.o* **66/1**

1m 26.73s (0.73) **Going Correction** +0.10s/f (Slow) **14 Ran SP% 118.9**
Speed ratings (Par 99): **99,98,93,93,91 87,86,86,85,85 79,78,51,45**
toteswingers:1&2:£8.70, 2&3:£13.80, 1&3:£3.90 CSF £36.59 TOTE £2.60: £1.20, £6.00, £3.60; EX 41.70 Trifecta £517.10 Part won. Pool £698.88 - 0.10 winning units..
Owner Ian and Christine Beard **Bred** Usk Valley Stud **Trained** Newmarket, Suffolk

FOCUS
This ordinary maiden was dominated by those that raced handily. The form looks fluid with the form horse not running to his best.
Baileys Bigishu Official explanation: jockey said gelding missed break

2543 BETFAIR SUPPORTING GRASSROOTS RACING MAIDEN STKS (DIV II) 7f (P)
3:15 (3:17) (Class 5) 3-Y-O **£2,264** (£673; £336; £168) **Stalls** Low

Form RPR

5-56 **1** **Poole Harbour (IRE)**[23] 1852 3-9-3 80 RyanMoore 6 90+
(Richard Hannon) *mde all: rdn and qckned clr wl over 1f out: in command and r.o wl fnl f: rdn out* **3/1**[1]

4- **2** *4* **Henry Allingham**[205] 7293 3-9-3 0 NeilCallan 1 79
(Roger Varian) *t.k.h: sn chsng ldrs: chsd wnr over 2f out: sn rdn and edgd lft: outpcd by wnr and btn wl over 1f out: one pce after* **9/2**[2]

3 *1/2* **Admiralty** 3-9-3 0 RoystonFfrench 3 78
(Ismail Mohammed) *in tch in midfield: rdn and hdwy on inner over 2f out: wnt 3rd wl over 1f out: no ch w wnr but kpt on fnl f* **17/2**

4 *2 1/2* **Stirring Ballad** 3-8-12 0 DavidProbert 8 66+
(Andrew Balding) *stdd and dropped in bhd after s: hdwy 2f out: wnt 4th over 1f out: styd on but no ch w wnr* **16/1**

5 *5* **Charming (IRE)** 3-8-12 0 KirstyMilczarek 9 53
(Olivia Maylam) *t.k.h: chsd wnr tl 5f out: rdn 2f out: wknd wl over 1f out* **66/1**

04-2 **6** *3/4* **Levi Draper**[24] 1824 3-9-3 79 JackMitchell 7 56
(James Fanshawe) *t.k.h: hld up in tch: rdn and edgd lft ent fnl 2f: wknd wl over 1f out* **9/2**[2]

535 **7** *1 1/2* **Tharawal (IRE)**[9] 2279 3-9-3 81 DaneO'Neill 5 52
(Terry Clement) *dwlt: t.k.h: hld up in tch in midfield: swtchd lft and effrt over 2f out: wknd 2f out* **11/2**[3]

44-0 **8** *3 1/2* **Sequoia**[57] 1155 3-9-3 77 WilliamCarson 13 42
(Charles Hills) *slowly away: bhd: rdn and sme hdwy 2f out: n.d* **9/1**

0- **9** *4 1/2* **Caledonian Lad**[291] 4968 3-9-3 0 TravisBlock 2 30
(Hughie Morrison) *rn green: t.k.h in midfield: rdn over 2f out: sn wknd: bhd fnl f* **20/1**

0 **10** *3 1/2* **Geeaitch**[21] 1922 3-9-0 0 DominicFox(3) 10 21
(Anthony Carson) *in tch in midfield on outer: rdn and struggling 3f out: wknd over 2f out: bhd fnl f* **66/1**

0 **11** *1/2* **Pass The Time**[24] 1825 3-8-12 0 LiamKeniry 11 14
(Neil Mulholland) *dwlt: a bhd* **100/1**

0 **12** *3 1/4* **Tickin Time**[9] 2273 3-9-3 0 AndreaAtzeni 4 11
(Michael Squance) *a towards rr: rdn and wknd wl over 2f out: bhd fnl 2f* **66/1**

0 **13** *nk* **One Bid Too Many (USA)**[24] 1826 3-8-12 0 StevieDonohoe 14
(Derek Shaw) *s.i.s: a bhd* **66/1**

6 **14** *76* **Sun Seal**[33] 1610 3-8-12 0 DarryllHolland 12
(Hughie Morrison) *chsd wnr 5f out tl over 2f out: lost pl qckly: bhd and eased fnl 2f: t.o* **16/1**

1m 26.34s (0.34) **Going Correction** +0.10s/f (Slow) **14 Ran SP% 120.8**
Speed ratings (Par 99): **102,97,96,94,88 87,85,81,76,72 72,68,67,**
toteswingers:1&2:£4.10, 2&3:£9.80, 1&3:£6.90 CSF £15.58 TOTE £4.40: £1.50, £2.30, £2.50; EX 19.50 Trifecta £84.20 Pool £732.81 - 6.44 winning units..
Owner The Heffer Syndicate **Bred** Lisieux Stud **Trained** East Everleigh, Wilts

FOCUS
As in the first division, the winner made all and the winning time was 0.39 seconds faster. The form is again fluid with the 6th-8th below their marks.
Sun Seal Official explanation: trainer said filly finished lame.

2544 BETFAIR.COM H'CAP 1m 3f (P)
3:45 (3:46) (Class 5) (0-75,74) 3-Y-O **£2,264** (£673; £336; £168) **Stalls** Low

Form RPR

-312 **1** **Hector's Chance**[6] 2372 3-8-12 65 NeilCallan 10 76
(Heather Main) *chsd ldrs: rdn to ld 2f out: gng clr whn ducked rt u.p 1f out: r.o strly: readily* **11/4**[1]

5433 **2** *5* **Somemothersdohavem**[14] 2129 3-9-2 69 (p) BrettDoyle 5 71
(John Ryan) *hld up in tch: rdn and effrt 2f out: swtchd lft over 1f out: styd on to chse wnr wl ins fnl f: kpt on but no threat to wnr* **20/1**

15-6 **3** *3/4* **Night Flash (GER)**[16] 2088 3-9-4 71 PaulMulrennan 4 71
(James Given) *chsd ldr tl led over 2f out: rdn and hdd 2f out: outpcd by wnr and btn 1f out: lost 2nd wl ins fnl f* **12/1**

6-20 **4** *shd* **Haymarket**[65] 1031 3-9-3 70 SilvestreDeSousa 8 70
(Mark Johnston) *t.k.h: hld up in last quartet: rdn and hdwy u.p 2f out: styd on fnl f but no threat to wnr* **10/1**

60-4 **5** *2 1/4* **Tantamount**[42] 1422 3-9-0 67 RyanMoore 11 63
(Roger Charlton) *dwlt: t.k.h: hld up in midfield: rdn and unable qck over 2f out: wl hld over 1f out* **6/1**[2]

035- **6** *3/4* **No Time To Lose**[227] 6825 3-9-5 72 FergusSweeney 6 67
(Jamie Osborne) *racd in last trio: bustled along 8f out: rdn over 4f out: no ch but styd on fnl f* **8/1**

10 **7** *1* **Natasha Rostova**[9] 2281 3-9-3 70 DavidProbert 7 63
(Andrew Balding) *s.i.s and tail swishing leaving stalls: hld up in rr: swtchd lft 4f out: rdn and limited rspnse over 2f out: one pce and wl hld fnl 2f* **20/1**

6034 **8** *hd* **Eightfold**[9] 2283 3-8-8 61 (t) PaulHanagan 1 53
(Seamus Durack) *t.k.h: hld up in rr: sltly hmpd 4f out: rdn and no hdwy over 2f out: n.d* **13/2**[3]

0-25 **9** *hd* **Cape Samba**[35] 1567 3-9-7 74 (v[1]) RoystonFfrench 3 66
(Ismail Mohammed) *chsd ldrs: rdn and unable qck over 2f out: wknd wl over 1f out* **14/1**

6-20 **10** *3 1/2* **Sareeah (IRE)**[27] 1736 3-9-1 68 EddieAhern 2 54
(Clive Brittain) *in tch in midfield: rdn and struggling over 2f out: wknd wl over 1f out* **9/1**

-012 **11** *2 1/2* **Daring Damsel (IRE)**[19] 1982 3-8-13 66 (b) StevieDonohoe 9 47
(Paul Cole) *led tl over 2f out: wknd over 1f out: fdd and eased ins fnl f* **12/1**

2m 22.37s (0.47) **Going Correction** +0.10s/f (Slow) **11 Ran SP% 116.1**
Speed ratings (Par 99): **102,98,97,97,96 95,94,94,94,92 90**
toteswingers:1&2:£12.00, 2&3:£32.60, 1&3:£8.10 CSF £64.03 CT £559.98 TOTE £3.40: £1.60, £5.90, £3.80; EX 61.00 Trifecta £429.80 Pool £801.54 - 1.38 winning units.
Owner M Scott Russell **Bred** Wickham Stud **Trained** Kingston Lisle, Oxon

FOCUS
This ordinary middle-distance handicap developed into a one-horse race. The placed horses set the level.

2545 BETFAIR "DON'T SETTLE FOR LESS" H'CAP 7f (P)
4:15 (4:15) (Class 4) (0-85,85) 4-Y-O+ **£4,528** (£1,347; £673; £336) **Stalls** Low

Form RPR

04-0 **1** **My Son Max**[13] 2151 4-8-13 77 PatCosgrave 9 85
(P J O'Gorman) *stdd s: hld up in rr: stl plenty do wl over 1f out: gd hdwy jst over 1f out: chal fnl 100yds: r.o wl to ld cl home* **25/1**

-114 **2** *shd* **Ducal**[28] 1708 4-9-5 83 PatDobbs 13 90+
(Mike Murphy) *dwlt: sn rcvrd to chse ldrs: swtchd ins and qcknd to ld over 1f out: idled and drvn ins fnl f: fnd ex whn chal fnl f: hdd cl home* **7/1**

0-10 **3** *1 1/4* **Esprit De Midas**[9] 2268 6-9-7 85 JimCrowley 6 89
(Dean Ivory) *hld up in midfield: rdn and racd awkwardly u.p over 1f out: hdwy 1f out: styd on wl ins fnl f* **7/1**

6-30 **4** *3/4* **Dasho**[93] 711 4-9-4 82 NeilCallan 7 84
(Gay Kelleway) *chsd ldrs: chsd ldr over 2f out tl ins fnl f: styd on same pce fnl 150yds* **20/1**

3004 **5** *1 1/2* **Tevez**[45] 1354 7-8-11 82 (p) DanielMuscutt(7) 5 84+
(Des Donovan) *hld up of fthe pce in midfield: rdn and hdwy over 1f out: styng on whn hmpd ins fnl f: swtchd lft and styd on wl fnl 100yds* **14/1**

14-4 **6** *nse* **Flameoftheforest (IRE)**[32] 1627 5-9-2 80 (p) LiamKeniry 2 78
(Ed de Giles) *hld up in midfield: rdn and hdwy on inner wl over 1f out: styd on same pce ins fnl f* **20/1**

0050 **7** *shd* **Ocean Legend (IRE)**[10] 2251 7-8-9 80 GeorgeDowning(7) 3 78
(Tony Carroll) *in tch in midfield: effrt u.p 2f out: drvn and kpt on fnl f: nt pce to chal ldrs* **20/1**

4302 **8** *hd* **Lastkingofscotland (IRE)**[7] 2354 6-8-9 73 (b) HayleyTurner 1 70
(Conor Dore) *chsd ldr tl wl over 2f out: styd chsng ldrs: drvn over 1f out: wknd ins fnl f* **5/1**[2]

11-0 **9** *1 1/2* **Peace Seeker**[16] 2071 4-8-12 76 WilliamCarson 14 69
(Anthony Carson) *dropped in bhd after s: rdn over 2f out: hdwy ent fnl f: edgd rt and styd on ins fnl f: nvr threatened ldrs* **16/1**

1214 **10** *nse* **April Fool**[17] 2029 8-9-0 83 (b) DarrenEgan(5) 8 76
(Ronald Harris) *led: rdn over 2f out: hdd and drvn over 1f out: wknd ins fnl f* **11/2**[3]

000- **11** *1* **Rossetti**[159] 7841 4-8-13 77 JackMitchell 4 67
(James Fanshawe) *in tch in midfield: rdn and effrt ent fnl 2f: drvn and no rspnse over 1f out: wknd fnl f* **7/2**[1]

0103 **12** *3/4* **Aldermoor (USA)**[16] 2083 6-8-10 77 RyanClark(3) 11 65
(Stuart Williams) *rrd s: s.i.s: hld up in rr: effrt on inner 2f out: no imp and nvr trbld ldrs* **20/1**

04/3 **13** *1/2* **Cape Rock**[28] 1708 7-9-4 82 DarryllHolland 10 69
(William Knight) *in tch in midfield on outer: rdn and unable qck over 2f out: wknd over 1f out* **8/1**

20-6 **14** *6* **Silenzio**[27] 1727 4-8-13 77 RyanMoore 12 48
(Richard Hannon) *s.i.s: sn bustled along: a bhd* **16/1**

1m 26.33s (0.33) **Going Correction** +0.10s/f (Slow) **14 Ran SP% 131.7**
Speed ratings (Par 105): **102,101,100,99,97 97,97,97,95,95 94,93,93,86**
toteswingers:1&2:£48.30, 2&3:£7.00, 1&3:£52.30 CSF £194.70 CT £1437.48 TOTE £52.90: £10.40, £2.10, £3.10; EX 332.40 Trifecta £988.10 Part won. Pool £1,335.34 - 0.20 winning units..
Owner Racing To The Max **Bred** Mrs Fiona Denniff **Trained** Newmarket, Suffolk

FOCUS
A decent handicap and a fast pace was assured. The placed horses set the level.
Aldermoor(USA) Official explanation: jockey said gelding reared leaving stalls

2546 KEMPTON PARK FOR WEDDINGS H'CAP 7f (P)
4:45 (4:50) (Class 6) (0-65,65) 4-Y-O+ **£1,617** (£481; £240; £120) **Stalls** Low

Form RPR

5022 **1** **Dvinsky (USA)**[6] 2373 11-9-4 62 (b) TomMcLaughlin 12 69
(Paul Howling) *chsd ldr after 1f: rdn to ld wl over 1f out: battled on gamely u.p fnl f: all out* **17/2**

5250 **2** *nk* **Perfect Ch'I (IRE)**[6] 2373 5-9-7 65 (p) NeilCallan 4 71
(Ian Wood) *in tch: effrt u.p 2f out: chsd wnr ins fnl f: clsng grad fnl 100yds: nt quite get up* **7/1**[3]

4-00 **3** *1/2* **Dunseverick (IRE)**[62] 1052 4-9-2 60 TonyCulhane 2 64
(Jo Hughes) *v reluctant to go to s: t.k.h: hld up in tch: swtchd lft and effrt wl over 1f out: styd on wl u.p ins fnl f* **9/1**

1431 **4** *nk* **Lady Mango (IRE)**[12] 2171 4-9-0 63 DarrenEgan(5) 11 66+
(Ronald Harris) *in tch towards rr: rdn over 2f out: hdwy u.p 1f out: kpt on wl fnl 100yds: nt rch ldrs* **5/1**[1]

0-05 **5** *1 3/4* **Isingy Red (FR)**[12] 2173 4-9-4 62 PatCosgrave 1 61
(Jim Boyle) *broke fast and led for 1f: chsd ldrs: rdn and effrt to chal wl over 1f out: unable qck 1f out: wknd wl ins fnl f* **5/1**[1]

1500 **6** *1* **Archelao (IRE)**[12] 2173 4-9-7 65 AmirQuinn 6 61
(Richard Rowe) *hld up in rr of main gp: rdn and effrt 2f out: swtchd rt and styd on ins fnl f: nt rch ldrs* **10/1**

0345 **7** *hd* **Climaxfortackle (IRE)**[30] 1652 4-9-5 63 NickyMackay 8 58
(Derek Shaw) *in tch: effrt u.p on inner wl over 1f out: no imp ins fnl f* **10/1**

-004 **8** *1/2* **Kings 'n Dreams**[21] 1936 5-9-7 65 (b) GeorgeBaker 10 59
(Dean Ivory) *chsd ldrs on outer: hdwy to press ldrs and gng wl over 2f out: rdn and fnd nil over 1f out: wknd ins fnl f* **13/2**[2]

0-00 **9** *4 1/2* **Blue Deer (IRE)**[12] 2173 4-9-3 61 FrannyNorton 13 43
(Lee Carter) *s.i.s: a towards rr on outer: rdn over 2f out: wknd wl over 1f out* **14/1**

45-5 **10** *3/4* **Clumber Place**[18] 2012 6-9-7 65 PaulMulrennan 14 45
(James Given) *sn rdn along to ld after 1f: rdn and hdd wl over 1f out: wknd over 1f out* **20/1**

2000 **11** *nse* **Ensnare**[7] 2354 7-9-4 62 StevieDonohoe 9 42
(Willie Musson) *s.i.s: sn rdn and detached in last: n.d* **25/1**

-206 **12** *3 3/4* **Not My Choice (IRE)**[34] 1586 7-9-6 64 J-PGuillambert 7 34
(Paul Howling) *in tch in midfield: rdn wl over 2f out: no rspnse and btn whn eased over 1f out* **16/1**

1m 27.39s (1.39) **Going Correction** +0.10s/f (Slow) **12 Ran SP% 119.0**
Speed ratings (Par 101): **96,95,95,94,92 91,91,90,85,84 84,80**
toteswingers:1&2:£7.50, 2&3:£15.80, 1&3:£16.50 CSF £67.19 CT £564.28 TOTE £9.50: £2.50, £1.40, £5.30; EX 54.60 Trifecta £523.50 Part won. Pool £707.53 - 0.50 winning units..

Owner David Hardaker **Bred** Eclipse Bloodstock & Tipperary Bloodstock **Trained** Lee-On-The-Solent, Hants

FOCUS

A moderate handicap, but nonetheless a memorable result. The form is straightforward rated around the first two.

Not My Choice(IRE) Official explanation: trainer said gelding had a breathing problem.

2547 BETFAIR SUPPORTING GRASSROOTS RACING H'CAP 6f (P)

5:15 (5:15) (Class 6) (0-65,65) 3-Y-O £1,617 (£481; £240; £120) **Stalls** Low

Form RPR

030- **1** **Athenian (IRE)**^{222} [6946] 3-9-3 **61** ChrisCatlin 5 76
(Sir Mark Prescott Bt) *sn bustled up to ld: rdn 2f out: edgd lft but forged clr 1f out: styd on strly: readily* **7/2**^{3}

35-6 **2** *4* **Copper Falls**^{37} [1514] 3-8-10 **54** KirstyMilczarek 9 56
(Brendan Powell) *slowly away and dropped in bhd after s: swtchd ins and effrt 2f out: hdwy u.p over 1f out: wnt 2nd ins fnl f: no ch w wnr* **14/1**

2325 **3** *½* **Illustrious Lad (IRE)**^{27} [1725] 3-9-1 **59** PatCosgrave 3 59
(Jim Boyle) *chsd ldrs: rdn to chal 2f out: no ex and btn 1f out: outpcd and lost 2nd ins fnl f* **2/1**^{1}

1016 **4** *¾* **Russian Bullet**^{21} [1941] 3-9-7 **65** FergusSweeney 1 63
(Jamie Osborne) *hld up in last pair: hdwy 2f out: rdn over 1f out: kpt on ins fnl f: no threat to wnr* **11/4**^{2}

4-00 **5** *2 ½* **Gone To Ground**^{137} [132] 3-8-7 **51** oh6 (p) SaleemGolam 2 41
(Michael Squance) *in tch: rdn and unable qck over 2f out: wknd over 1f out* **40/1**

4333 **6** *13* **Faraway**^{84} [801] 3-9-2 **63** (b) CPGeoghegan$^{(3)}$ 7 11
(Ronald Harris) *stdd after s: hld up in last trio on outer: rdn and pushed lft over 2f out: drvn and wknd 2f out* **7/1**

0500 **7** *shd* **Dawn Lightning**^{21} [1912] 3-9-2 **60** (p) StevieDonohoe 4
(Alan McCabe) *t.k.h: hld up in midfield: rdn and unable qck over 2f out: drvn and wknd over 1f out* **16/1**

000 **8** *1 ¾* **Tumbleowtashoes**^{5} [2388] 3-8-7 **51** oh6 (tp) BrettDoyle 8
(John Ryan) *sn chsng ldr: rdn and unable qck over 2f out: wknd 2f out* **50/1**

105- **9** *15* **Mr Hendrix**^{151} [7905] 3-9-0 **58** WilliamCarson 6
(Mark Hoad) *t.k.h: chsd ldrs: rdn and edgd lft over 2f out: wknd 2f out and sn eased: t.o* **20/1**

1m 13.7s (0.60) **Going Correction** +0.10s/f (Slow) **9** Ran SP% **116.4**

Speed ratings (Par 97): **100,94,94,93,89 72,72,69,49**

toteswingers:1&2:£11.10, 2&3:£4.90, 1&3:£3.20 CSF £49.72 CT £123.80 TOTE £5.20: £1.40, £1.90, £1.20; EX 41.00 Trifecta £118.00 Pool £767.27 - 4.81 winning units..

Owner Axom (XXXI) **Bred** Keatly Overseas Ltd **Trained** Newmarket, Suffolk

■ Stewards' Enquiry : C P Geoghegan two-day ban; careless riding (11th-12th June)

FOCUS

Another modest handicap in which the placed horses set the level.

Copper Falls Official explanation: jockey said filly lost a front shoe.

Dawn Lightning Official explanation: jockey said filly lost her action in the home straight.

2548 KEMPTON LIVE H'CAP 1m (P)

5:45 (5:45) (Class 6) (0-60,60) 3-Y-O £1,617 (£481; £240; £120) **Stalls** Low

Form RPR

0-01 **1** **Watanee**^{6} [2374] 3-9-5 **58** 6ex EddieAhern 5 65+
(Clive Brittain) *chsd ldrs: rdn to ld over 1f out: drvn and kpt on wl ins fnl f* **5/4**^{1}

5022 **2** *nk* **Songbird Blues**^{6} [2374] 3-9-2 **55** HayleyTurner 14 61
(Mark Usher) *stdd s: t.k.h: hld up wl bhd: hdwy 2f out: drvn to press wnr wl ins fnl f: no ex and hld nr fin* **11/2**^{2}

025- **3** *½* **Trusting (IRE)**^{209} [7205] 3-9-4 **57** PatDobbs 8 62
(Eve Johnson Houghton) *in tch: hdwy to trck ldrs over 2f out: rdn and ev ch over 1f out: unable qck fnl 100yds* **7/1**^{3}

050- **4** *¾* **Roman Senate (IRE)**^{221} [6972] 3-8-10 **49** (b^{1}) StevieDonohoe 1 52
(Martin Bosley) *in tch: effrt to chse ldrs 2f out: drvn and kpt on same pce ins fnl f* **14/1**

00-3 **5** *1* **Men Don't Cry (IRE)**^{14} [2130] 3-9-7 **60** LiamKeniry 11 61
(Ed de Giles) *dwlt: sn pushed up into midfield: hdwy to chse ldrs and drvn over 1f out: no ex ins fnl f* **16/1**

005- **6** *2 ½* **April Ciel**^{278} [5375] 3-9-2 **60** DarrenEgan$^{(5)}$ 13 55
(Ronald Harris) *bhd: rdn and hdwy 2f out: edgd rt and r.o wl fnl f: nvr trbld ldrs* **14/1**

60-4 **7** *3* **Doc Hill**^{49} [1260] 3-8-7 **46** oh1 FrannyNorton 6 34
(Michael Blanshard) *chsd ldrs: wnt 2nd over 4f out: led over 2f out tl drvn and hdd over 1f out: wknd fnl f* **16/1**

6-02 **8** *½* **Artful Lady (IRE)**^{14} [2130] 3-8-10 **49** MartinLane 4 36
(George Margarson) *hld up in rr: swtchd ins and effrt 2f out: kpt on but nvr trbld ldrs* **16/1**

60-4 **9** *nk* **Emperors Waltz (IRE)**^{19} [1989] 3-9-3 **56** ChrisCatlin 3 42
(Rae Guest) *racd off the pce in midfield: effrt u.p over 2f out: styd on same pce and no imp fnl f* **14/1**

000- **10** *2 ½* **Dine Out**^{217} [7051] 3-9-7 **60** SaleemGolam 10 40
(Mark H Tompkins) *a off the pce towards rr: rdn and effrt over 2f out: plugged on but no imp* **40/1**

0-40 **11** *hd* **Vicgernic**^{2} [2497] 3-8-7 **46** (p) NickyMackay 9 26
(Gary Moore) *s.i.s: wl bhd: swtchd ins and nt clr run 2f out: plugged but n.d* **16/1**

4002 **12** *7* **King's Future**^{27} [1731] 3-9-0 **60** AaronChave$^{(7)}$ 12 24
(Lee Carter) *styd wd: led tl over 6f out: chsd ldrs after tl wknd 2f out* **20/1**

40-0 **13** *8* **Denton Dancer**^{48} [1288] 3-9-7 **60** (b^{1}) JackMitchell 2 6
(James Eustace) *sn rdn along: led over 6f out tl rdn and hdd over 2f out: sn wknd: wl bhd and eased ins fnl f* **40/1**

00-0 **14** *25* **Trioomph**^{21} [1918] 3-9-1 **54** PaulMulrennan 7
(James Given) *towards rr: reminders and hung lft bnd 5f out: lost tch over 2f out: eased fr over 1f out: t.o* **50/1**

1m 41.46s (1.66) **Going Correction** +0.10s/f (Slow) **14** Ran SP% **127.5**

Speed ratings (Par 97): **95,94,94,93,92 89,86,86,86,83 83,76,68,43**

toteswingers:1&2:£2.90, 2&3:£6.50, 1&3:£2.90 CSF £7.99 CT £41.32 TOTE £2.70: £1.30, £1.80, £2.40; EX 6.10 Trifecta £42.20 Pool £414.22 - 7.25 winning units..

Owner Saeed Manana **Bred** Meon Valley Stud **Trained** Newmarket, Suffolk

FOCUS

A moderate handicap in which only one of the 14 runners had previously been successful and that remained the case after the race. The pace was searing and the form is best rated around the fourth and fifth.

Songbird Blues Official explanation: jockey said filly hung right.

Vicgernic Official explanation: jockey said gelding was denied a clear run.

T/Jkpt: Not won. T/Plt: £113.80 to a £1 stake. Pool: £82,457.41 - 528.88 winning tickets. T/Qpdt: £52.00 to a £1 stake. Pool: £4,367.38 - 62.10 winning tickets. SP

2328 LEICESTER (R-H)

Monday, May 28

OFFICIAL GOING: Good to firm (firm in places; 9.2)

Wind: Nil Weather: Fine, turning showery race 5 onwards

2549 SHARNFORD H'CAP 7f 9y

2:00 (2:00) (Class 5) (0-70,70) 4-Y-0+ £2,264 (£673; £336; £168) **Stalls** High

Form RPR

53-0 **1** **Sairaam (IRE)**^{73} [927] 6-9-0 **63** CathyGannon 3 71
(Charles Smith) *mde all: shkn up over 2f out: rdn over 1f out: jst hld on* **15/2**^{3}

006- **2** *nse* **Daruband**^{169} [7727] 4-9-7 **70** (v) FrankieDettori 5 78
(Alan McCabe) *hld up: hdwy over 1f out: r.o wl: jst failed* **10/1**

5321 **3** *1 ¼* **Copperwood**^{10} [2227] 7-9-5 **68** JoeFanning 9 73
(Mark Johnston) *hld up: hdwy 1/2-way: rdn and hung rt over 1f out: r.o* **4/1**^{1}

1-06 **4** *2 ¼* **Hoppy's Flyer (FR)**^{31} [1638] 4-9-0 **63** MickyFenton 8 62
(Paul Midgley) *s.i.s: sn prom: outpcd over 2f out: rallied over 1f out: styd on* **10/1**

1050 **5** *1* **Mazovian (USA)**^{20} [1958] 4-8-11 **67** DannyBrock$^{(7)}$ 7 63
(Michael Chapman) *chsd ldrs: sn pushed along: outpcd 3f out: rallied over 1f out: r.o* **11/1**

50-0 **6** *3 ¼* **Ellies Image**^{7} [2355] 5-8-13 **62** FrederikTylicki 2 49
(Brian Baugh) *prom: rdn 1/2-way: wknd over 1f out* **16/1**

0002 **7** *hd* **Divertimenti (IRE)**^{6} [2377] 8-8-13 **62** (b) RussKennemore 4 49
(Roy Bowring) *prom: chsd wnr over 4f out: rdn over 1f out: wknd fnl f* **8/1**

5165 **8** *2 ¼* **Muhandis (IRE)**^{17} [2044] 4-9-3 **66** (v) RichardHughes 10 46
(Nick Littmoden) *s.i.s: hld up: rdn over 2f out: n.d* **8/1**

0-56 **9** *4* **Prince Of Passion (CAN)**^{28} [1702] 4-8-12 **61** TomQueally 11 31
(Derek Shaw) *s.i.s: hld up: a in rr* **9/1**

3446 **10** *10* **Dancing Maite**^{16} [2084] 7-9-3 **66** MartinDwyer 6
(Roy Bowring) *chsd wnr over 2f: remained handy tl rdn and wknd over 2f out* **11/2**^{2}

000- **11** *17* **Errigal Lad**^{223} [6940] 7-8-7 **56** oh7 KellyHarrison 1
(Garry Woodward) *hld up: a in rr: lost tch fr over 2f out: t.o* **66/1**

1m 24.48s (-1.72) **Going Correction** -0.15s/f (Firm) **11** Ran SP% **113.3**

Speed ratings (Par 103): **103,102,101,98,97 94,93,91,86,75 55**

toteswingers:1&2:£14.00, 2&3:£5.10, 1&3:£4.30 CSF £77.16 CT £347.67 TOTE £10.30: £2.60, £3.00, £1.20; EX 118.70.

Owner Phil Martin & Trev Sleath **Bred** Shadwell Estate Company Limited **Trained** Temple Bruer, Lincs

FOCUS

False rail on bend increased distances on Round course by 10yds. A moderate handicap and straightforward form rated around the first two. They raced at a respectable gallop up the middle-to-far side of the course. The jockeys afterwards reported the surface as good, fast ground.

Dancing Maite Official explanation: trainer said gelding lost a front shoe and was unsuited by good to firm (firm) ground.

2550 PYTCHLEY MAIDEN STKS 5f 218y

2:30 (2:31) (Class 4) 2-Y-O £3,428 (£1,020; £509; £254) **Stalls** High

Form RPR

3 **1** **Artigiano (USA)**^{11} [2213] 2-9-3 0 FrankieDettori 5 93+
(Mahmood Al Zarooni) *chsd ldrs: led over 1f out: pushed clr* **11/10**^{1}

2 **2** *6* **Pearl Noir**^{13} [2138] 2-9-3 0 FrederikTylicki 6 73
(Scott Dixon) *a.p: led over 2f out: rdn and hdd over 1f out: styd on same pce* **12/1**

3 *1* **Intimidate** 2-9-3 0 ChrisCatlin 8 70+
(Jeremy Noseda) *hld up: swtchd rt and hdwy over 1f out: hung lft ins fnl f: nvr trbld ldrs* **25/1**

4 **4** *¾* **Composed**^{21} [1920] 2-8-12 0 DuilioDaSilva$^{(5)}$ 11 68+
(Paul Cole) *edgd rt s: hld up: pushed along 1/2-way: unbalanced over 2f out: sn rdn: r.o ins fnl f: nvr nrr* **80/1**

5 *¾* **Gworn** 2-9-3 0 TomQueally 7 66+
(Ed Dunlop) *s.s: hld up: r.o ins fnl f: nrst fin* **20/1**

6 *3* **Haverstock** 2-9-3 0 JoeFanning 4 57
(Mark Johnston) *hld up: hdwy over 2f out: sn rdn: wknd over 1f out* **25/1**

7 *½* **Shooting Jacket (USA)** 2-9-3 0 MickaelBarzalona 3 55
(Mahmood Al Zarooni) *s.s: sn mid-div: rdn over 2f out: wkng whn bmpd over 1f out* **15/2**^{3}

3 **8** *2 ¼* **Symboline**^{17} [2019] 2-8-12 0 MartinHarley 10 43
(Mick Channon) *s.i.s and hmpd s: sn hld up in tch: rdn and wknd over 1f out* **11/1**

5 **9** *½* **Walter White (IRE)**^{10} [2231] 2-9-3 0 RichardHughes 2 47
(Andrew Balding) *chsd ldrs tl rdn and wknd over 1f out* **13/2**^{2}

0 **10** *9* **Forbidden Fruit (IRE)**^{16} [2069] 2-9-3 0 MartinDwyer 9 20
(Brian Meehan) *hmpd s: sn chsng ldrs: rdn and wknd over 2f out* **15/2**^{3}

0 **11** *2* **Proventi**^{9} [2261] 2-9-3 0 SamHitchcott 1 14
(Alan McCabe) *sn led: rdn and hdd over 2f out: wknd wl over 1f out* **200/1**

1m 11.26s (-1.74) **Going Correction** -0.15s/f (Firm) **11** Ran SP% **114.7**

Speed ratings (Par 95): **105,97,95,94,93 89,89,86,85,73 70**

toteswingers:1&2:£5.40, 2&3:£36.30, 1&3:£10.90 CSF £14.33 TOTE £2.00: £1.02, £4.70, £6.80; EX 13.60.

Owner Godolphin **Bred** Darley **Trained** Newmarket, Suffolk

FOCUS

An interesting maiden with some well-bred 2yos on show. They raced at a respectable pace up the middle of the track. The winning time was only a shade slower than standard and the winner was impressive, while the second is rated close to his debut mark.

NOTEBOOK

Artigiano(USA) ◆ reportedly looked well in the paddock and he was the clear form pick on the back of a promising third in a better race over this trip on good ground this month. He appreciated this faster surface, stretching out well in the final stages as if 7f will be no problem for him, and looks very useful. Frankie Dettori spoke in terms of Royal Ascot after the race, and he looks more than worthy of his place at that meeting after this stylish success. (op 10-11 tchd 6-5)

Pearl Noir raced prominently on this second career start over an extra furlong. This trip looks fine for him and it was a slightly better effort than on his debut. (op 16-1)

Intimidate was slightly fractious when the jockey tried to get on board in the parade ring. The colt is bred to be effective over 7f and shaped well for a try over that trip in a respectable debut third. (op 20-1)

Composed finished fourth over 5f at Kempton on his debut this month and it was an improved effort in this better company. He may appreciate 7f sooner rather than later. (op 66-1)

Gworn, easy to back on his debut, started notably slowly but finished his race off promisingly in fifth. He's well bred and should appreciate a step up to 7f/1m this year. (op 28-1 tchd 18-1)

2551 HICKLING (S) STKS — 5f 218y
3:00 (3:01) (Class 6) 3-5-Y-O — £1,704 (£503; £251) Stalls High

Form — RPR

-305 **1** **Julius Geezer (IRE)**[7] 2342 4-9-6 78 .... RichardKingscote 5 — 76
(Tom Dascombe) *a.p: chsd ldr over 2f out: led over 1f out: rdn out* **11/4**[2]

5435 **2** ½ **Restless Bay (IRE)**[7] 2355 4-9-6 74 .... (p) SamHitchcott 2 — 74
(Reg Hollinshead) *pushed along in rr early: hdwy over 4f out: n.m.r over 1f out: sn rdn and ev ch: r.o* **9/4**[1]

443 **3** 6 **Basle**[18] 2012 5-9-1 59 .... (t) RichardHughes 3 — 50
(Gay Kelleway) *hld up: hdwy u.p over 1f out: wnt 3rd wl ins fnl f: eased: nvr trbld ldrs* **10/3**[3]

5642 **4** 1 ¾ **Finefrenzyrolling (IRE)**[12] 2169 4-8-12 58 .... (p) MichaelMetcalfe(3) 7 — 44
(Mrs K Burke) *led: rdn: edgd rt and hdd over 1f out: wknd ins fnl f* **7/1**

0054 **5** 3 **Forty Proof (IRE)**[21] 2114 4-9-1 52 .... (v) MatthewCosham(5) 1 — 40
(David Evans) *stdd s: hld up: rdn over 2f out: n.d* **20/1**

5002 **6** ½ **Sophie's Beau (USA)**[3] 2436 5-9-6 46 .... (bt) RussKennemore 9 — 38
(Michael Chapman) *chsd ldr tl rdn over 2f out: hung rt and wknd over 1f out* **18/1**

3560 **7** 1 ¾ **Porthgwidden Beach (USA)**[6] 2365 4-9-1 45 .... (tp) KieranO'Neill 6 — 27
(Anthony Middleton) *mid-div: sn pushed along: wknd over 2f out* **66/1**

4440 **8** 11 **Umph (IRE)**[7] 2351 3-9-2 58 .... (b) CathyGannon 4
(David Evans) *sn pushed along and prom: wknd over 2f out* **16/1**

000/ **9** 8 **Gypsy Jazz (IRE)**[572] 7304 5-8-10 55 .... (p) AnnStokell(5) 8
(Ann Stokell) *sn pushed along in rr: bhd fr 1/2-way: t.o* **100/1**

1m 11.26s (-1.74) **Going Correction** -0.15s/f (Firm)
WFA 3 from 4yo+ 9lb — **9** Ran SP% **111.4**
Speed ratings (Par 101): **105,104,96,94,90 89,87,72,61**
toteswingers:1&2:£2.20, 2&3:£2.50, 1&3:£3.20 CSF £8.77 TOTE £4.00: £1.70, £1.10, £1.70; EX 9.20.The winner was bought in for 8,000gns
Owner Basing Bellman Stroud **Bred** Ballyhane Stud **Trained** Malpas, Cheshire

FOCUS
A slightly above-average seller open to three to 5-y-os. The winning time was very respectable for the grade and the second is rated to his AW level.

2552 BELVOIR CASTLE H'CAP — 1m 1f 218y
3:30 (3:31) (Class 4) (0-85,82) 3-Y-O — £4,528 (£1,347; £673; £336) Stalls Low

Form — RPR

44-1 **1** **Pilgrims Rest (IRE)**[10] 2235 3-9-7 **82** .... RichardHughes 3 — 92+
(Richard Hannon) *trckd ldr: shkn up to ld over 1f out: rdn and edgd rt ins fnl f: styd on* **6/4**[1]

6-55 **2** nk **Brockwell**[7] 2336 3-8-7 **68** .... RichardKingscote 4 — 77
(Tom Dascombe) *trckd ldrs: racd keenly: rdn and ev ch fr over 1f out: r.o* **7/2**[3]

53-4 **3** 8 **Touch Gold (IRE)**[37] 1511 3-9-2 **77** .... TomQueally 1 — 70
(Sir Henry Cecil) *s.s: hdwy over 3f out: rdn and hung rt over 1f out: wknd ins fnl f* **15/8**[2]

20-0 **4** 4 ½ **Long Lost Love**[27] 1728 3-8-12 **73** .... JoeFanning 5 — 57
(Mark Johnston) *led: shkn up over 2f out: rdn and hdd over 1f out: wknd fnl f* **9/1**

2m 7.34s (-0.56) **Going Correction** -0.15s/f (Firm) — **4** Ran SP% **107.0**
Speed ratings (Par 101): **96,95,89,85**
CSF £6.75 TOTE £1.90; EX 7.60.
Owner Markus Jooste & Bernard Kantor **Bred** Annalee Bloodstock & Rockhart Trading Ltd **Trained** East Everleigh, Wilts

FOCUS
An average small-field 1m2f handicap confined to 3-y-os. The winning time was nearly three seconds slower than standard, which is respectable and no more, on good to firm ground. The runner-up is rated an improver.
Touch Gold(IRE) Official explanation: vet said colt lost a near front shoe.

2553 BRITISH STALLION STUDS COPLOW EBF MAIDEN STKS — 1m 60y
4:00 (4:00) (Class 5) 3-Y-O — £3,557 (£1,058; £529; £264) Stalls Low

Form — RPR

22 **1** **Nine Realms**[21] 1922 3-9-3 0 .... LiamJones 11 — 97+
(William Haggas) *mde all: clr 1/2-way: pushed out: unchal* **11/10**[1]

6- **2** 5 **Razorbill (USA)**[220] 6983 3-9-3 0 .... MichaelHills 1 — 86+
(Charles Hills) *a.p: chsd wnr over 3f out: rdn over 1f out: no imp* **7/2**[2]

0-0 **3** 3 ½ **Highland Duke (IRE)**[57] 1155 3-9-3 0 .... FrankieDettori 4 — 76
(Clive Cox) *chsd ldrs: rdn over 2f out: styd on same pce* **10/1**

6-0 **4** 5 **Tafawuk (USA)**[21] 1923 3-9-3 0 .... TadhgO'Shea 9 — 64
(Roger Varian) *mid-div: hdwy over 2f out: wnt 4th over 1f out: no further prog* **20/1**

50 **5** 1 ½ **Cape Explorer**[11] 2196 3-9-3 0 .... JoeFanning 14 — 61
(James Tate) *chsd ldrs: rdn over 2f out: wknd over 1f out* **40/1**

6 6 **Elysian** 3-8-12 0 .... KierenFallon 8 — 42+
(Sir Michael Stoute) *hld up: hdwy over 2f out: wknd over 1f out* **9/2**[3]

0- **7** nk **Cape Joy (IRE)**[201] 7330 3-8-12 0 .... KieranO'Neill 13 — 42
(Richard Hannon) *hld up: nvr on terms* **40/1**

-00 **8** 1 ¾ **Capitol Gain (IRE)**[21] 1923 3-9-3 0 .... MartinDwyer 10 — 42
(Brian Meehan) *mid-div: pushed along 1/2-way: wknd over 2f out* **50/1**

5-0 **9** nk **Vickers Vimy**[38] 1502 3-8-12 0 .... RichardKingscote 7 — 37
(Ralph Beckett) *stdd s: hld up: nvr on terms* **40/1**

0 **10** 3 ½ **Scarborough Rock**[14] 2125 3-9-3 0 .... MickyFenton 6 — 34
(Tom Symonds) *a in rr* **100/1**

0 **11** 40 **Highly Skilled**[17] 2041 3-9-3 0 .... TomQueally 12
(Sir Henry Cecil) *trckd wnr tl rdn over 3f out: wknd over 2f out: t.o* **16/1**

12 1 **Bosonic** 3-9-3 0 .... MartinHarley 3
(Alan McCabe) *hld up: a in rr: t.o* **125/1**

00 **13** ¾ **Little Bucks**[19] 1989 3-9-3 0 .... CathyGannon 5
(Alan McCabe) *hld up: a in rr: t.o* **100/1**

1m 42.69s (-2.41) **Going Correction** -0.15s/f (Firm) — **13** Ran SP% **119.8**
Speed ratings (Par 99): **106,101,97,92,91 85,84,82,82,79 39,38,37**
toteswingers:1&2:£1.70, 2&3:£4.90, 1&3:£4.10 CSF £4.58 TOTE £2.10: £1.10, £1.50, £2.00; EX 5.30.
Owner Mr & Mrs D Hearson **Bred** Granham Farm Partnership **Trained** Newmarket, Suffolk

FOCUS
An informative 3yo maiden, which was run in driving rain. They went a decent gallop and the winning time was a shade faster than standard. The winner looked to improve again and the third might well set the standard long term.

2554 CHARNWOOD FOREST FILLIES' CONDITIONS STKS — 7f 9y
4:30 (4:30) (Class 3) 3-Y-O+ — £7,781 (£2,330; £1,165; £582; £291) Stalls High

Form — RPR

003 **1** **Dysphonia (AUS)**[16] 2078 6-8-13 110 .... (p) FrankieDettori 2 — 106+
(Saeed Bin Suroor) *hld up in tch: trckd ldr over 4f out: led on bit over 2f out: shkn up over 1f out: sn clr: easily* **30/100**[1]

/0-0 **2** 2 ¾ **Bezique**[11] 2211 4-8-13 95 .... KierenFallon 1 — 91
(Luca Cumani) *led over 4f: rdn over 1f out: sn outpcd* **10/3**[2]

50-0 **3** ¾ **Mortitia**[16] 2078 4-8-13 88 .... MartinDwyer 3 — 89?
(Brian Meehan) *plld hrd and prom: rdn over 1f out: styd on same pce* **20/1**[3]

2254 **4** 13 **Nevaeh**[16] 2065 3-8-2 67 .... (p) CathyGannon 4 — 50
(Pat Eddery) *chsd ldr over 2f: rdn and wknd over 2f out* **33/1**

5/36 **5** 7 **Hold The Star**[24] 1825 6-8-8 50 .... AnnStokell(5) 5 — 35
(Ann Stokell) *chsd ldrs to 1/2-way: bhd whn hung rt fnl 2f* **300/1**

1m 25.48s (-0.72) **Going Correction** -0.15s/f (Firm)
WFA 3 from 4yo+ 11lb — **5** Ran SP% **108.0**
Speed ratings (Par 104): **98,94,94,79,71**
CSF £1.45 TOTE £1.40: £1.02, £1.50; EX 1.60.
Owner Godolphin **Bred** Woodlands Stud NSW **Trained** Newmarket, Suffolk

FOCUS
A disappointing turnout for this 7f fillies' conditions stakes, which was the feature event on the card. They went a respectable enough gallop but the time was slow and the form looks muddling

NOTEBOOK
Dysphonia(AUS) came out 15lb clear according to adjusted official ratings on these terms. She was a multiple winner in Australia previously and placed in a Group 1 contest at Flemington on her final start there. She ran on well to finish third in a Group 3 contest over this 7f trip at Lingfield this month and built on that promise despite dropping in class. This mare by Lonhro settled behind the leader and was travelling all her rivals 2f out, before coming through for an easy success. A step up to 1m in Group 3 company may now be on the cards. (op 4-11)
Bezique progressed from her reappearance in a York handicap this month and may be up to winning a similar conditions or Listed contest over 1m this season. (tchd 3-1)
Mortitia progressed markedly from her reappearance and may be up to winning a similar race over 7f on fast ground this term. (op 12-1)

2555 SWANNINGTON H'CAP — 7f 9y
5:00 (5:01) (Class 6) (0-60,60) 4-Y-O+ — £1,617 (£481; £240; £120) Stalls High

Form — RPR

0-00 **1** **Master Of Song**[98] 636 5-9-4 **57** .... (p) RussKennemore 12 — 67
(Roy Bowring) *s.i.s: outpcd: hdwy over 1f out: r.o to ld wl ins fnl f* **33/1**

0010 **2** 1 ¾ **Yankee Storm**[34] 1587 7-9-2 **55** .... (b) FrankieDettori 6 — 60
(Michael Wigham) *hld up: hdwy 2f out: rdn and ev ch ins fnl f: nt qckn* **7/2**[1]

00-2 **3** ½ **Cadmium Loch**[39] 1487 4-9-0 **60** .... (p) JackDuern(7) 7 — 64
(Reg Hollinshead) *chsd ldrs: led 1/2-way: rdn: hung lft and hdd wl ins fnl f* **9/2**[2]

-030 **4** 4 ½ **Olynard (IRE)**[73] 929 6-9-2 **55** .... RichardKingscote 11 — 47
(Michael Mullineaux) *chsd ldrs: rdn over 2f out: styd on same pce fr over 1f out* **20/1**

241- **5** shd **Daffydowndilly**[167] 7748 4-9-7 **60** .... (bt) MickaelBarzalona 10 — 52
(Hughie Morrison) *s.i.s: swtchd rt and hdwy over 5f out: rdn over 2f out: wknd ins fnl f* **9/2**[2]

0603 **6** 1 ¾ **Rapid Water**[22] 1895 6-8-13 **59** .... WilliamTwiston-Davies(7) 15 — 46
(Pat Eddery) *hld up: hdwy over 4f out: rdn and wknd over 1f out* **12/1**[3]

624- **7** 2 ¼ **Tony Hollis**[306] 4431 4-9-4 **57** .... JamesMillman 5 — 38
(Rod Millman) *prom: rdn over 2f out: wknd over 1f out* **20/1**

-500 **8** 1 ¼ **Fathey (IRE)**[5] 2401 6-8-7 **46** oh1 .... JoeFanning 9 — 23
(Charles Smith) *led to 1/2-way: rdn and wknd over 1f out* **33/1**

6106 **9** 1 ¾ **Mr Chocolate Drop (IRE)**[19] 1988 8-8-10 **54** .... (t) NathanAlison(5) 14 — 27
(Mandy Rowland) *hdwy over 4f out: rdn over 2f out: wkng whn nt clr run ent fnl f* **12/1**[3]

6-50 **10** 3 ¼ **Alexs Rainbow (USA)**[12] 2170 4-8-13 **57** .... DavidKenny(5) 4 — 21
(Peter Hiatt) *chsd ldrs: pushed along 1/2-way: wknd over 1f out: eased ins fnl f* **25/1**

3/00 **11** 2 ¾ **Red Avalanche (IRE)**[12] 2165 5-9-4 **60** .... MichaelMetcalfe(3) 2 — 16
(Tony Newcombe) *chsd ldrs: rdn over 2f out: wknd over 1f out* **14/1**

4003 **12** hd **Gambatte**[32] 1634 5-8-4 **46** oh1 .... HarryBentley(3) 3
(Tony Carroll) *mid-div: rdn 1/2-way: wknd 2f out* **20/1**

6066 **13** 2 ½ **Jolie Etoile**[68] 985 4-8-2 **46** oh1 .... AmyScott(5) 1
(Tony Carroll) *sn outpcd* **33/1**

5640 **14** 1 **Aggbag**[6] 2365 8-8-2 **48** ow1 .... (p) RichardOliver(7) 8
(Michael Appleby) *prom: lost pl over 4f out: sn bhd* **33/1**

400 **15** 1 ½ **Kata Rock (USA)**[49] 1250 5-9-4 **57** .... FrederikTylicki 16
(Brian Rothwell) *mid-div: rdn over 4f out: wknd 3f out* **33/1**

5060 **16** 3 ¾ **Royal Box**[37] 1528 5-9-1 **54** .... (p) CathyGannon 13
(David Evans) *prom: lost pl over 4f out: bhd fr 1/2-way* **14/1**

1m 24.98s (-1.22) **Going Correction** -0.15s/f (Firm) — **16** Ran SP% **120.1**
Speed ratings (Par 101): **100,98,97,92,92 90,87,86,84,80 77,77,74,73,71 67**
toteswingers:1&2:£34.60, 2&3:£5.20, 1&3:£40.20 CSF £128.65 CT £633.92 TOTE £55.90: £9.10, £1.80, £1.10, £6.30; EX 273.00.
Owner S R Bowring **Bred** S R Bowring **Trained** Edwinstowe, Notts

FOCUS
A modest handicap with the winner rated close to his AW best. They appeared to go a solid gallop from the outset.
Red Avalanche(IRE) Official explanation: jockey said gelding hung left throughout.
T/Plt: £4.60 to a £1 stake. Pool: £57,142.76 - 8,927.48 winning tickets T/Qpdt: £2.40 to a £1 stake. Pool: £4,833.71 - 1,468.21 winning tickets C

2342 WINDSOR (R-H)
Monday, May 28

OFFICIAL GOING: Good to firm (8.5)
Wind: Light, behind Weather: Sunny, warm

2556 EBF DAVISBAKERYCARIBBEAN.COM NOVICE STKS — 5f 10y
6:10 (6:10) (Class 5) 2-Y-O — £3,299 (£981; £490) Stalls Low

Form — RPR

22 **1** **Annunciation**[9] 2261 2-9-0 0 .... RichardHughes 3 — 97+
(Richard Hannon) *fast away: mde all: briefly pushed along to draw clr over 1f out: eased ins fnl f* **4/6**[1]

2 **2** *6* **Emirates Echo**[22] 1886 2-9-0 0 NeilCallan 1 73
(David Simcock) *dwlt and also s.i.s: pushed along in last after 2f: effrt to chse wnr over 1f out: no ch* **2/1**[2]

3 *nse* **Quality Mark (USA)** 2-9-0 0 RyanMoore 2 73+
(Jeremy Noseda) *chsd wnr: pushed along 2f out: sn wl outpcd: jst lost out in battle for modest 2nd* **13/2**[3]

59.74s (-0.56) **Going Correction** -0.20s/f (Firm) **3** Ran SP% **106.7**
Speed ratings (Par 93): **96,86,86**
CSF £2.24 TOTE £1.70; EX 1.90.
Owner Middleham Park Racing XXXIX & James Pak **Bred** Abingdon & Witney College **Trained** East Everleigh, Wilts

FOCUS
Inner rail of straight dolled out 12yds at 6f and 4yds at winning post. Top bend dolled out 11yds from normal inner configuration adding 43yds to races of a mile and over. A fair novice event, despite there being just a trio of runners, and an impressive winner who looks capable of making up into a Pattern performer.

NOTEBOOK
Annunciation was quickly away and always going best. Clearly very speedy, he'd be entitled to take his chance in something at Royal Ascot, with the Windsor Castle perhaps likeliest, although a trip to Epsom next week for the Woodcote may come first. (op 8-11)
Emirates Echo showed plenty of ability behind an easy winner on his debut at Newmarket, but he was never matching Annunciation on faster ground here and will almost certainly benefit from an extra furlong. (tchd 9-4)
Quality Mark(USA), half-brother to a 7f AW winner, out of a mare who won from 5f-1m2f, showed enough to suggest he should win a standard maiden, with the experience unlikely to be lost on him. (op 6-1 tchd 11-2)

2557 DAVISBAKERYCARIBBEAN.COM H'CAP 1m 67y
6:40 (6:41) (Class 5) (0-75,75) 3-Y-O **£2,264** (£673; £336; £168) **Stalls** Low

Form RPR

4-00 **1** **Philipstown**[10] 2246 3-9-0 **71** SeanLevey(3) 3 82
(Richard Hannon) *wl in tch: prog over 3f out: led over 2f out: drvn and styd on wl fr over 1f out* **10/1**

6-25 **2** *2 ¾* **Good Luck Charm**[14] 2126 3-9-0 **68** TomQueally 8 73
(Gary Moore) *wl in tch: prog to trck ldrs 3f out: rdn 2f out: chsd wnr fnl f: styd on but no imp* **14/1**

346- **3** *1 ¼* **Gold Sceptre (FR)**[260] 5967 3-9-4 **72** RichardHughes 12 74
(Richard Hannon) *prom: rdn to chal 3f out: chsd wnr jst over 2f out: no imp over 1f out: pushed along in 3rd last 150yds* **6/1**

21-0 **4** *1 ½* **Tiger Cub**[11] 2194 3-9-2 **70** (t[1]) GeorgeBaker 7 69
(Mikael Magnusson) *mostly chsd ldr to 3f out: one pce fnl 2f* **18/1**

54-5 **5** *1 ¼* **Linkable**[19] 1976 3-9-5 **73** WilliamCarson 4 69
(Charles Hills) *hld up in rr early: prog bef 1/2-way: rdn to chal 3f out: nt qckn: one pce and hld fnl 2f* **11/2**[3]

-000 **6** *1 ¼* **Tidy Affair (IRE)**[13] 2150 3-9-7 **75** SamHitchcott 6 68
(Murty McGrath) *hld up wl in rr: shkn up over 2f out: styd on steadily after: nvr rchd ldrs* **28/1**

004- **7** *hd* **Poetry Writer**[201] 7329 3-9-0 **68** NeilCallan 2 60
(Michael Blanshard) *prom: lost pl and rdn over 3f out: nvr on terms w ldrs after* **40/1**

-230 **8** *nk* **Beau Duke (IRE)**[17] 2021 3-9-2 **70** DavidProbert 1 62
(Andrew Balding) *hld up off the pce in midfield: shkn up over 2f out: sme prog over 1f out: kpt on but nvr nr ldrs* **18/1**

6-31 **9** *3 ½* **Supaheart**[14] 2136 3-9-2 **70** DarryllHolland 13 54
(Hughie Morrison) *taken down early: led: hanging bdly lft bnd 6f out to over 4f out: continued to hang in home st: hdd over 2f out: wknd over 1f out* **9/2**[1]

25-0 **10** *7* **Tidal's Baby**[13] 2150 3-9-3 **71** JimCrowley 5 39
(Tony Carroll) *stdd s: t.k.h and hld up in last trio: nvr really figured* **28/1**

05-5 **11** *4* **Monymusk**[13] 2145 3-9-4 **72** SilvestreDeSousa 10 30
(David Elsworth) *hld up and sn detached in last and nt gng wl: briefest of effrts 3f out: nvr in it* **11/2**[3]

621- **12** *8* **Fairyinthewind (IRE)**[200] 7342 3-9-2 **70** RyanMoore 11 10
(Paul D'Arcy) *stmbld s: rdn towards rr 1/2-way: struggling after* **5/1**[2]

0-02 **13** *6* **Forest Edge (IRE)**[42] 1412 3-9-4 **72** PadraigBeggy 14
(David Evans) *prom 2f: sn lost pl and struggling bdly* **33/1**

1m 45.16s (0.46) **Going Correction** +0.05s/f (Good) **13** Ran SP% **118.5**
Speed ratings (Par 99): **99,96,95,93,92 91,90,90,87,80 76,68,62**
toteswingers:1&2:£14.20, 2&3:£7.40, 1&3:£24.50 CSF £135.74 CT £946.98 TOTE £18.90: £4.90, £2.90, £1.90; EX 197.20 TRIFECTA Not won..
Owner Dragon Gate **Bred** Whitsbury Manor Stud **Trained** East Everleigh, Wilts

FOCUS
Fair form for the grade and a race that should produce winners. The pace was honest and the form is rated around the placed horses.
Supaheart Official explanation: jockey said filly was unable to handle bend.
Tidal's Baby Official explanation: jockey said gelding was unable to handle bend.
Monymusk Official explanation: jockey said gelding was hampered leaving stalls and carries wide on bend.
Fairyinthewind(IRE) Official explanation: jockey said fill stumbled leaving stalls and was never travelling.
Forest Edge(IRE) Official explanation: jockey said gelding hung left.

2558 SKYBET.COM H'CAP 6f
7:10 (7:11) (Class 3) (0-95,92) 4-Y-O+ **£6,792** (£2,021; £1,010; £505) **Stalls** Low

Form RPR

42-2 **1** **Cape Classic (IRE)**[9] 2264 4-8-12 **83** RyanMoore 16 94+
(William Haggas) *sn chsd ldrs in 5th fr wd draw: hrd rdn over 2f out: clsd over 1f out: led last 150yds: drvn out* **5/2**[1]

0003 **2** *1 ¼* **Bathwick Bear (IRE)**[2] 2507 4-8-13 **84** KirstyMilczarek 3 92+
(David Evans) *trckd ldrs in 6th: looking for room fr 2f out: squeezed through ins fnl f: r.o to take 2nd nr fin* **6/1**[3]

1-02 **3** *nk* **Novellen Lad (IRE)**[107] 527 7-9-3 **88** NeilCallan 9 93
(Willie Musson) *sn off the pce in 9th: rdn over 2f out: taken out wd and prog fnl 2f: styd on: nrest at fin* **10/1**

34-0 **4** *1* **Ganas (IRE)**[27] 1727 4-9-0 **85** PatCosgrave 12 87
(Clive Cox) *chsd ldng pair: rdn to go 2nd over 2f out: tried to chal over 1f out: kpt on same pce fnl f* **16/1**

3-20 **5** *shd* **New Leyf (IRE)**[16] 2068 6-9-3 **88** J-PGuillambert 14 89
(Ed Walker) *pushed along in midfield by 1/2-way: prog on outer fr 2f out: styd on same pce fnl f: nvr able to chal* **15/2**

10-2 **6** *nk* **Camache Queen (IRE)**[21] 1926 4-8-10 **81** EddieAhern 1 82
(Denis Coakley) *trckd ldng trio on inner: clsd over 1f out and ch ent fnl f: nt qckn* **16/1**

14-5 **7** *½* **Fair Value (IRE)**[21] 1926 4-8-12 **83** SebSanders 8 82
(Simon Dow) *led at str pce: hdd last 150yds: fading whn nudged by rival sn after* **20/1**

00-0 **8** *1 ¼* **Kuanyao (IRE)**[9] 2268 6-8-12 **83** TomQueally 13 78
(Peter Makin) *mostly chsd ldr to over 2f out: styd pressing ldrs tl fdd fnl f* **33/1**

-025 **9** *½* **Elna Bright**[115] 405 7-9-0 **85** LiamKeniry 10 78
(Peter Crate) *stdd s: hld up in last pair: nudged along over 2f out: styd on takingly fnl f: nvr in it* **33/1**

06-0 **10** *¾* **Quasi Congaree (GER)**[145] 29 6-8-8 **82** (t) SeanLevey(3) 2 73
(Ian Wood) *sn off the pce in 10th: effrt on wd outside 1/2-way: nvr on terms* **40/1**

50-0 **11** *hd* **Main Beach**[13] 2151 5-8-8 **79** oh1 ow1 (t) StevieDonohoe 4 69
(Tobias B P Coles) *s.i.s: mostly in last pair and wl bhd: shkn up over 2f out: n.d but keeping on at fin* **20/1**

0-02 **12** *1* **Oneladyowner**[3] 2446 4-8-13 **84** SilvestreDeSousa 6 71
(David Brown) *a wl in rr: rdn and no prog over 2f out* **5/1**[2]

-304 **13** *1 ½* **Tagula Night (IRE)**[23] 1849 6-9-2 **87** (b) JimCrowley 11 69
(Dean Ivory) *racd on outer in midfield: no prog 2f out: fdd* **20/1**

024- **14** *7* **Golden Desert (IRE)**[175] 7636 8-9-7 **92** RichardHughes 7 52
(Simon Dow) *a in rr: wknd 2f out: eased* **33/1**

1m 10.68s (-2.32) **Going Correction** -0.20s/f (Firm) **14** Ran SP% **117.7**
Speed ratings (Par 107): **107,105,104,103,103 103,102,100,100,99 98,97,95,86**
toteswingers:1&2:£12.00, 2&3:£31.00, 1&3:£9.30 CSF £14.42 CT £132.65 TOTE £3.40: £1.80, £2.20, £2.90; EX 23.30 Trifecta £129.20 Pool £703.69 - 4.03 winning units..
Owner Bernard Kantor **Bred** Wentworth Racing **Trained** Newmarket, Suffolk

FOCUS
A fairly ordinary sprint handicap, run at a fast gallop. The form looks solid with the winner stepping up on his reappearance, backed up by the placed horses, with the second rated as finishing closer than the official margin.

NOTEBOOK
Cape Classic(IRE) ◆ should leave this form behind and progress to better things. A bit unlucky on his reappearance at Doncaster, Ryan Moore did well to get him to the position he did from stall 16, and he really put his stamp on the race late. He'll probably struggle to get into the Wokingham, but could be a leading player in the Stewards' Cup at Glorious Goodwood. It's worth noting his half-brother King's Apostle progressed really well with racing. (op 3-1)
Bathwick Bear(IRE), third at York two days earlier, was back up to 6f for this quick reappearance and looked unlucky not to finish closer, although his finishing position wasn't affected. (op 8-1 tchd 11-2)
Novellen Lad(IRE), in good form on AW over the winter, has run well here from this sort of mark in the past and he's entitled to come on for the outing, having been off for 107 days. (op 8-1)
Ganas(IRE), whose saddle slipped at Kempton the time before, ran a solid race on this return to turf and has more to offer as a sprinter. (op 12-1)
New Leyf(IRE) ought to be capable of winning from this mark on turf, but he was never quite going the pace. (op 9-1 tchd 10-1)
Camache Queen(IRE)'s previous turf win came on softer ground but she seemed okay on the quicker surface and could pick up a small race this summer. (op 20-1)
Elna Bright Official explanation: jockey said gelding was denied a clear run.

2559 DAVISBAKERYCARIBBEAN.COM LEISURE STKS (LISTED RACE) 6f
7:40 (7:40) (Class 1) 3-Y-O+ **£18,714** (£7,095; £3,550; £1,768; £887) **Stalls** Low

Form RPR

04-4 **1** **Markab**[16] 2074 9-9-0 107 DaneO'Neill 1 112
(Henry Candy) *mde all against nr side rail: hrd pressed 2f out: drvn over 1f out: styd on wl* **11/4**[2]

11-0 **2** *¾* **Elnawin**[12] 2179 6-9-0 110 RichardHughes 2 110
(Richard Hannon) *pressed wnr: rdn to chal 2f out: styd on but a hld ins fnl f* **7/2**[3]

003- **3** *¾* **Angels Will Fall (IRE)**[247] 6337 3-8-0 106 SilvestreDeSousa 3 102
(Charles Hills) *tk fierce hold bhd ldng pair: rdn to try to chal between rivals over 1f out: nt qckn fnl f* **7/2**[3]

50-0 **4** *shd* **Genki (IRE)**[39] 1469 8-9-0 114 (v) GeorgeBaker 6 107
(Roger Charlton) *hld up in 4th: cajoled along on outer 2f out: rdn and nt qckn over 1f out: kpt on but nvr landed a serious blow* **2/1**[1]

-505 **5** *1 ¾* **Medicean Man**[16] 2074 6-9-0 103 (b) HayleyTurner 4 101
(Jeremy Gask) *a last: rdn and nt on terms over 1f out: styd on same pce after* **12/1**

1m 10.14s (-2.86) **Going Correction** -0.20s/f (Firm)
WFA 3 from 6yo+ 9lb **5** Ran SP% **112.1**
Speed ratings (Par 111): **111,110,109,108,106**
CSF £12.77 TOTE £4.90: £2.40, £1.10; EX 14.70.
Owner Mosaic Racing **Bred** Shadwell Estate Company Limited **Trained** Kingston Warren, Oxon

FOCUS
A tight Listed sprint but the form looks rather shaky.

NOTEBOOK
Markab came out on top, bagging the rail in front and finding plenty for pressure. He'd clearly come on plenty for his Haydock reappearance and will reportedly seek a similar opportunity before possibly going back up in grade. (op 7-2)
Elnawin, well held in a Group 2 on his reappearance, stripped fitter this time and stuck on well to hold second. This is his level and he should find an opening this year. (op 100-30)
Angels Will Fall(IRE), winner of the Princess Margaret and third in the Cheveley Park, was receiving a stone from the older males and ran well considering she refused to settle early, just flattening out late on. This should have taken the fizz out of her but she won't be the easiest to place (op 100-30)
Genki(IRE) was the highest-rated of these on 114 but his best efforts have come in bigger fields and he couldn't quicken sufficiently when challenging wide. He'll probably take his chance in the Golden Jubilee again. (tchd 9-4)
Medicean Man, with blinkers back on, was never out of last. He's yet to recapture last year's best, but loves Ascot and is the type to run above himself in the King's Stand. (op 14-1)

2560 ANDREW GRANT COUNTRY HOMES SUPPORTING FITZROY MEDIAN AUCTION MAIDEN STKS 1m 2f 7y
8:10 (8:24) (Class 5) 3-Y-O **£2,264** (£673; £336; £168) **Stalls** Centre

Form RPR

4- **1** **Initiator**[290] 5011 3-9-3 0 RyanMoore 5 81+
(Jeremy Noseda) *ponied to s: trckd ldr: led 3f out and kicked clr: in n.d after: rdn out* **6/4**[1]

44 **2** *5* **Gold Show**[10] 2232 3-8-12 0 MartinHarley 3 66
(Mick Channon) *hld up in 6th: effrt 3f out: rdn and styd on to take 2nd nr fin: no ch w wnr* **9/4**[2]

0-0 **3** *nse* **Alvitude (USA)**[21] 1922 3-9-3 0 GeorgeBaker 6 71
(Roger Charlton) *trckd ldng trio: effrt to chse clr wnr 2f out: no imp: jst lost 2nd nr fin* **15/2**[3]

45 **4** *nk* **Sarmatian Knight (IRE)**[14] 2125 3-9-3 0 NeilCallan 1 70
(Ian Williams) *in tch in 7th: effrt 3f out: styd on to press for 2nd ins fnl f* **20/1**

0 **5** *4* **Iron Butterfly**[21] 1923 3-8-12 0 EddieAhern 12 57
(James Eustace) *trckd ldng quartet: shkn up to dispute 2nd over 2f out: sn fdd* **66/1**

The Form Book Flat, Raceform Ltd, Compton, RG20 6NL

00 **6** 1 **Imperial Ruby**[19] 1981 3-9-3 0 ..... SamHitchcott 14 60?
(Mick Channon) *led at stdy pce to 3f out: sn wl outpcd* **100/1**

0 **7** 2 1/2 **Salford Dream**[11] 2197 3-9-3 0 ..... SilvestreDeSousa 2 55
(David Elsworth) *s.s: rcvrd into midfield: stl looked green whn pushed along over 3f out: nvr on terms* **9/1**

-00 **8** 3 1/4 **Play Tiger (FR)**[25] 1793 3-9-3 0 ..... MartinLane 4 49
(David Simcock) *settled wl in rr: pushed along 3f out: nvr on terms* **100/1**

6 **9** 1 1/4 **Scarlett Fever**[12] 2172 3-8-12 0 ..... HayleyTurner 9 41
(Marcus Tregoning) *dwlt: a towards rr: pushed along and struggling over 3f out* **14/1**

00 **10** hd **Black Motive**[6] 2368 3-9-3 0 ..... StevieDonohoe 13 46
(Michael Bell) *sn in last pair: hanging at s of bnd over 6f out: nvr a factor* **66/1**

0-0 **11** 1 **Lady Ocarina**[12] 2172 3-8-12 0 ..... TedDurcan 11 39
(John Dunlop) *hld up: a wl in rr: pushed along and no prog over 2f out* **66/1**

12 4 **The Way To Be (IRE)** 3-9-3 0 ..... (p) DaneO'Neill 15 36
(Gerard Butler) *s.s: a in last pair: pushed along and struggling over 4f out* **20/1**

0 **13** 1 1/4 **Ecechera**[33] 1610 3-8-12 0 ..... JimCrowley 7 28
(Dean Ivory) *t.k.h: chsd ldng pair to over 3f out: wknd qckly over 2f out* **100/1**

2m 10.38s (1.68) **Going Correction** +0.05s/f (Good) **13** Ran SP% **116.2**
Speed ratings (Par 99): **95,91,90,90,87 86,84,82,81,80 80,76,75**
toteswingers:1&2:£1.10, 2&3:£4.20, 1&3:£3.20 CSF £4.32 TOTE £2.60: £1.30, £1.20, £2.20; EX 3.70 Trifecta £16.50 Pool £555.83 - 24.80 winning units..
Owner Cheveley Park Stud **Bred** D D & Mrs J P Clee **Trained** Newmarket, Suffolk

FOCUS
A moderate maiden, but taking winner. The time is modest and the level fluid, with trio immediately behind the placed horses likely to set the level long-term.
Iron Butterfly Official explanation: vet said filly sustained a cut to her right fore leg.

2561 SKYBET MOBILE FOR IPHONE & ANDROID H'CAP 1m 3f 135y
8:40 (8:48) (Class 4) (0-85,85) 4-Y-O+ **£4,851** (£1,443; £721; £360) **Stalls** Centre

Form RPR

41-0 **1** **Vasily**[12] 2180 4-9-3 **81** ..... AndreaAtzeni 1 91
(Robert Eddery) *t.k.h: trckd ldr: led over 2f out: sn rdn clr: styd on wl* **5/2**[2]

00-4 **2** 3 1/2 **New River (IRE)**[25] 1792 4-8-8 **72** ow1 ..... RichardHughes 3 76
(Richard Hannon) *trckd ldrs: sltly short of room over 2f out: swtchd lft and rdn to chse wnr over 1f out: no imp* **15/2**

65-5 **3** nk **Anton Dolin (IRE)**[49] 1258 4-9-2 **80** ..... EddieAhern 7 84
(John Dunlop) *hld up in midfield: rdn and effrt 3f out: styd on same pce fnl 2f to press for 2nd nr fin: no threat to wnr* **9/2**[3]

20-0 **4** 1/2 **Tasfeya**[12] 2174 4-8-13 **77** ..... StevieDonohoe 6 80
(Lee Carter) *led: drvn and hdd over 2f out: lost 2nd over 1f out: one pce* **16/1**

114- **5** 1 1/4 **Planetoid (IRE)**[270] 5641 4-9-7 **85** ..... TedDurcan 9 86
(David Lanigan) *hld up in rr: rdn and nt qckn 3f out: one pce and n.d fnl 2f* **9/4**[1]

300- **6** 2 **Kings Troop**[166] 6988 6-9-1 **79** ..... FergusSweeney 10 76
(Alan King) *trckd ldrs: drvn and effrt 3f out: nt qckn over 2f out: wknd over 1f out* **20/1**

643- **7** 1/2 **The Cayterers**[280] 5328 10-8-8 **79** ..... GeorgeDowning(7) 5 76
(Tony Carroll) *s.s: mostly detached in last to 3f out: kpt on one pce fnl 2f under tender handling* **11/1**

3110 **8** nk **Admirable Duque (IRE)**[62] 1056 6-8-6 **77** ..... (b) JoshBaudains(7) 2 73
(Dominic Ffrench Davis) *hld up in rr: rdn and effrt towards inner 3f out but nt clr run sn after: no prog 2f out: wknd* **25/1**

464- **9** 30 **Sohar**[290] 5001 4-8-11 **75** ..... KirstyMilczarek 8 20
(James Toller) *s.i.s: sn wl in tch: rdn and effrt on inner whn bdly hmpd over 2f out: nt rcvr and eased* **20/1**

2m 29.83s (0.33) **Going Correction** +0.05s/f (Good) **9** Ran SP% **116.9**
Speed ratings (Par 105): **100,97,97,97,96 94,94,94,74**
toteswingers:1&2:£5.40, 2&3:£6.80, 1&3:£4.30 CSF £21.21 CT £80.94 TOTE £4.50: £1.80, £1.90, £1.80; EX 26.40 Trifecta £43.80 Pool £521.54 - 8.79 winning units..
Owner Owen O'Brien & David Bannon **Bred** Cheveley Park Stud Ltd **Trained** Newmarket, Suffolk
■ Stewards' Enquiry : Kirsty Milczarek five-day ban; careless riding (11th-15th June)

FOCUS
A fair handicap, albeit one run at a steady early gallop, that should produce winners. The form is rated at something like face value, with the placed horses close to their marks.
Planetoid(IRE) Official explanation: jockey said gelding slipped leaving stalls.
T/Plt: £66.20 to a £1 stake. Pool £89,541.16 - 986.79 winning tickets. T/Qpdt: £9.40 to a £1 stake. Pool £7,680.04 - 598.62 winning tickets. JN

2562 - 2567a (Foreign Racing) - See Raceform Interactive

2107 COLOGNE (R-H)
Monday, May 28

OFFICIAL GOING: Turf: good

2568a MEHL-MULHENS-RENNEN (GERMAN 2,000 GUINEAS) (GROUP 2) (3YO COLTS & FILLIES) (TURF) 1m
4:15 (4:19) 3-Y-O **£83,333** (£25,000; £10,833; £5,833; £2,500)

RPR

1 **Caspar Netscher**[23] 1856 3-9-2 0 ..... ShaneKelly 1 114
(Alan McCabe) *slowly away: hld up in last pair on inner: smooth prog into midfield over 2f out: rdn to chse clr ldr over 1 1/2f out: r.o to ld ins fnl 100yds: wl on top at fin* **19/5**[2]

2 1 1/4 **Amarillo (IRE)**[43] 3-9-2 0 ..... AStarke 4 111
(P Schiergen, Germany) *prom on inner: led gng wl 2f out: rdn 1 1/2f out: kpt on u.p ins fnl f: hdd ins fnl 100yds: no ex and hld cl home* **5/1**

3 1 1/4 **Red Duke (USA)**[23] 1856 3-9-2 0 ..... JamieSpencer 6 108
(John Quinn) *midfield on outer: shuffled bk towards rr on turn into st: gng wl but forced to wait for gap over 2f out: in the clr and rdn over 1 1/2f out: r.o to go 3rd ins fnl 25yds: nvr able to chal* **54/10**

4 nk **Energizer (GER)**[36] 1553 3-9-2 0 ..... ADeVries 8 108
(J Hirschberger, Germany) *hld up in last trio on outer: rdn to improve over 2f out: kpt on ins fnl 1 1/2f: ct for 3rd ins fnl 25yds* **9/2**[3]

5 1 1/2 **Axiom (GER)** 3-9-2 0 ..... RPiechulek 3 104
(J Hirschberger, Germany) *pressed ldr on outer: rdn to ld 2 1/2f out: hdd 2f out: kpt on one pce ins fnl 1 1/2f* **236/10**

6 2 **Tai Chi (GER)**[198] 7405 3-9-2 0 ..... JohanVictoire 7 100
(Exors Of W Baltromei, Germany) *hld up in last on outer: rdn to improve over 2f out: outpcd over 1 1/2f out: plugged on to go 6th cl home* **27/10**[1]

7 1 1/2 **Pastorius (GER)**[36] 1553 3-9-2 0 ..... THellier 5 96
(Mario Hofer, Germany) *midfield on inner: rdn over 2f out: kpt on at one pce ins fnl 1 1/2f: ct for 6th cl home* **5/1**

8 1 1/2 **Kolonel (GER)**[36] 1553 3-9-2 0 ..... MircoDemuro 9 93
(A Wohler, Germany) *trckd ldng pair on outer: rdn over 2f out: jockey stopped riding for no apparent reason 1 1/2f out: coasted home ins fnl f* **167/10**

9 2 1/2 **Al Malek (FR)**[23] 3-9-2 0 ..... AndreBest 2 87
(Mario Hofer, Germany) *led: rdn and hdd 2 1/2f out: wknd* **167/10**

1m 34.4s (-3.99) **9** Ran SP% **130.4**
WIN (incl. 10 euro stake): 48. PLACES: 24, 18, 25. SF: 379.
Owner Charles Wentworth **Bred** Meon Valley Stud **Trained** Averham Park, Notts

NOTEBOOK
Caspar Netscher, whose only big race entry after this was in the July Cup, had yet to prove he stayed a truly run mile but, after being held up, he cruised up to challenge and won with plenty in hand once going on. This distance shouldn't be an issue now, although Cologne is fairly sharp, and he is clearly a tough individual.
Amarillo(IRE) has improved at three and did best of the German-trained runners after racing prominently.
Red Duke(USA) moved well chasing the leader before racing really freely off the final bend. He then got stuck in a pocket for a while, hit a flat spot and edged a bit right before coming home strongly. It's not difficult to argue he was a little unlucky.
Energizer(GER) is a reliable sort in Germany and probably ran up to his best.
Tai Chi(GER), comfortably the best of the German horses as a 2yo, came into this without a run this year and shaped disappointingly. He had a hard time as a juvenile, so needs to prove that he has trained on after this performance.
Pastorius(GER) looked really dangerous turning in but didn't pick up.
Al Malek(FR) led at what looked a reasonable pace before dropping right out. His form had looked decent previously, and a collateral line gave him the beating of Caspar Netscher, so this was moderate to say the least.

1745 MUNICH (L-H)
Monday, May 28

OFFICIAL GOING: Turf: good

2569a ONEXTWO.COM - BAVARIAN CLASSIC 2012 (GROUP 3) (3YO) (TURF) 1m 2f
3:30 (3:58) 3-Y-O
£26,666 (£9,166; £4,583; £2,500; £1,666; £1,250)

RPR

1 **Pakal (GER)**[22] 1900 3-9-2 0 ..... KKerekes 4 106
(W Figge, Germany) *pressed ldr early: sn racing in tch on heels of ldng gp: 3rd whn shkn up and sltly outpcd ent fnl 2f: r.o wl u.p fr over 1f out to ld fnl 50yds: all out* **108/10**

2 1/2 **Black Arrow (IRE)**[29] 3-9-2 0 ..... WilliamBuick 1 105
(A Wohler, Germany) *broke wl and led on ins: pressed fr over 2f out: sn rdn and hdd appr fnl f: rallied u.p to regain 2nd ins fnl 50yds: no ex cl home* **1/5**[1]

3 nk **Salon Soldier (GER)** 3-9-2 0 ..... FilipMinarik 3 104
(P Schiergen, Germany) *trckd ldr on ins of eventual wnr: rdn and pressed ldr on ins ent fnl 2f: sn hrd rdn and r.o: led appr fnl f: hdd fnl 50yds and lost 2nd sn after: no ex* **8/1**[2]

4 1 **Sharivar (GER)** 3-9-2 0 ..... RJuracek 7 102
(A Wohler, Germany) *reluctant to load: settled in 5th on outside: rdn to chse ldrs over 1f out: styd on ins fnl f: nt pce to chal* **112/10**

5 6 **Kolosseum (GER)** 3-8-13 0 ..... AntoineHamelin 5 87
(W Figge, Germany) *hld up in rr: no imp u.p fnl 2f: nvr threatened ldrs* **186/10**

6 3 **Lysino (GER)** 3-9-2 0 ..... GaetanMasure 6 84
(P Schiergen, Germany) *chsd ldrs towards outside: pressed ldr on outside over 3f out: rdn and nt qckn over 2f out: sn wknd* **43/5**[3]

7 43 **Showdancer (GER)** 3-9-2 0 ..... GHind 2
(N Sauer, Germany) *a bhd: lost tch fr 3f out: tailed-off* **39/1**

2m 5.27s (-3.70) **7** Ran SP% **129.1**
WIN (incl. 10 euro stake): 118. PLACES: 10, 10, 10. SF: 150.
Owner Stall Salzburg **Bred** Gestut Etzean **Trained** Germany

2156 SAINT-CLOUD (L-H)
Monday, May 28

OFFICIAL GOING: Turf: good to soft

2570a PRIX CORRIDA (GROUP 2) (4YO+ FILLIES & MARES) (TURF) 1m 2f 110y
2:55 (12:00) 4-Y-O+ **£61,750** (£23,833; £11,375; £7,583; £3,791)

RPR

1 **Solemia (IRE)**[20] 1971 4-8-9 0 ..... OlivierPeslier 3 111
(C Laffon-Parias, France) *hld up towards rr: stl wl off pce 2f out: rdn and qcknd wl over 1f out: str fin ins fnl f: led 50yds out: r.o wl: jst hld on to win by minimum margin* **3/1**[2]

2 nse **Shareta (IRE)**[28] 1766 4-8-11 0 ..... Christophe-PatriceLemaire 5 113+
(A De Royer-Dupre, France) *settled 4th on rail: rdn to s chal over 1 1/2f out: short of room: had to be stdd and swtchd arnd wkng Tempura: picked up wl 150yds out: fin strly: jst failed* **1/1**[1]

3 3/4 **Siyouma (IRE)**[31] 4-8-9 0 ..... ThierryJarnet 11 109
(F Doumen, France) *settled towards rr: swtchd to outside 2f out: picked up wl: r.o wl ent fnl f: got up for 3rd on line* **28/1**

4 shd **Andromeda Galaxy (FR)**[28] 1766 4-8-9 0 ..... AnthonyCrastus 9 109
(E Lellouche, France) *settled in midfield: rdn 2f out: qcknd wl to take ld over 1f out: hdd 50yds out: r.o* **22/1**

5 1 1/2 **Haya Landa (FR)**[28] 1766 4-8-9 0 ..... ThierryThulliez 6 106
(Mme L Audon, France) *settled in midfield: picked up wl 1 1/2f out: r.o ins fnl f: no threat to ldrs* **8/1**

6 nk **Kya One (FR)**[53] 1210 4-8-9 0 ..... StephanePasquier 4 105
(Y De Nicolay, France) *racd in midfield: picked up wl over 1 1/2f out: r.o strly ent fnl f: short of room: had to be stdd 100yds out: unlucky nt to be clsr* **16/1**

7 1/2 **Pagera (FR)**[29] 1696 4-8-9 0 ..... MaximeGuyon 1 105
(H-A Pantall, France) *v s.i.s: sn several l bhd rest of field: mde up grnd bef st: r.o u.p fnl 1 1/2f: nrest at fin* **20/1**

8 2 ½ **Aquamarine (JPN)**[28] 1766 4-8-11 0 ChristopheSoumillon 8 102
(M Delzangles, France) *settled in 2nd: several l off ldr: rdn to ld 1 1/2f out: sn hdd: eased ent fnl f* 11/2[3]

9 10 **Tempura (GER)**[41] 4-8-9 0 (b) FlavienPrat 7 80
(C Laffon-Parias, France) *sn led: wnt several l clr: stl wl clr ent st: rdn but no rspnse: hdd 1 1/2f out: eased fnl f* 50/1

10 2 **Divine Music (IRE)**[31] 5-8-9 0 (b) IoritzMendizabal 10 76
(P Van De Poele, France) *settled in 4th: rdn and no ex fr 2f out: sn fdd: eased fnl f* 16/1

2m 11.74s (-7.86) 10 Ran SP% **127.8**
WIN (incl. 1 euro stake): 3.60 (Solemia coupled with Tempura). PLACES: 1.40, 1.20, 3.80. DF: 3.40. SF: 6.90.
Owner Wertheimer & Frere **Bred** Wertheimer Et Frere **Trained** Chantilly, France

NOTEBOOK
Solemia(IRE) quickened up well, getting a jump on the favourite, and just held her off by the narrowest margin at the line. She's likely to come back for the Grand Prix de Saint-Cloud in late June.
Shareta(IRE) was unlucky in running, finished fast but the line came a fraction too soon. She will probably reoppose the winner in the Grand Prix de Saint-Cloud.

2384 CHEPSTOW (L-H)
Tuesday, May 29

OFFICIAL GOING: Good to firm (firm in places; watered; 9.2) changing to firm after race 4 (3.30)
Wind: Virtually nil Weather: Sunny periods

2571 DIGIBET.COM MAIDEN AUCTION STKS 5f 16y
2:00 (2:01) (Class 5) 2-Y-O **£2,264** (£673; £336; £168) **Stalls** High

Form RPR

6 1 **Majestic Red (IRE)**[12] 2202 2-8-5 0 CathyGannon 6 64+
(Malcolm Saunders) *sn trcking ldr: drvn and styd on appr fnl f: kpt on wl to ld last strides* 5/2[2]

2 hd **Bamurru (IRE)** 2-8-12 0 ow1 SebSanders 5 70
(Peter Makin) *sn led: tendency to hang lft: drvn over 1f out: kpt on: hdd last strides* 7/1

0 3 6 **Windforpower (IRE)**[8] 2349 2-8-5 0 DarrenEgan(5) 4 47
(Ronald Harris) *chsd ldrs: hung lft 2f out: sn drvn and no ch w ldng duo appr fnl f* 15/2

4 1 ¾ **Al Emirati (IRE)** 2-8-12 0 JamieSpencer 3 46+
(David Simcock) *broke wl sn pushed along: hung lft and outpcd over 2f out: swtchd rt over 1f out: mod prog clsng stages* 2/1[1]

5 6 **It's Only Business** 2-8-3 0 JakePayne(7) 1 19
(Bill Turner) *sn chsng ldrs and drvn: green: hung lft, hit rail and wknd over 2f out* 5/1[3]

6 1 **Northern Harbour (IRE)** 2-8-11 0 LukeMorris 2 16+
(J S Moore) *chsd ldrs: green: hung lft and wknd over 2f out* 16/1

1m 0.25s (0.95) **Going Correction** -0.225s/f (Firm) 6 Ran SP% **108.7**
Speed ratings (Par 93): **83,82,73,70,60 59**
Tote Swingers: 1&2 £3.40, 1&3 £3.40, 2&3 £11.10 CSF £18.35 TOTE £3.00: £2.00, £3.70; EX 19.60.
Owner The New Foursome Partnership 1 **Bred** Helen Smith & Sally Mullen **Trained** Green Ore, Somerset

FOCUS
Another warm day, and the winning jockey in the opener described the ground as "very quick". This maiden auction went to subsequent German 1,000 Guineas winner Penny's Gift in 2009, but there appeared little quality in this field and the form is weak. Only two of these had run before and they finished first and third. The runners raced centre to far side and the first two came clear. The form is rated about average for the race.

NOTEBOOK
Majestic Red(IRE), the only filly in the field, was sharper for her Salisbury experience. Chasing the runner-up near the centre of the track, she looked held entering the final fulong but ran on for a couple of cracks to get up close home. She may not be the easiest to place now until the nurseries start. (op 10-3)
Bamurru(IRE), considering how vocal and green he was in the preliminaries, made a creditable debut. He showed pace to lead, but hung to his left almost throughout and that cost him in the end. A grandson of Irish Oaks winner Vintage Tipple, he should get a bit further in time. (op 13-2 tchd 15-2)
Windforpower(IRE)'s saddle slipped on his recent debut at Wolverhampton. He was in third place for most of the way, but never looked comfortable on the track's undulations. (op 8-1 tchd 9-1)
Al Emirati(IRE), a 19,000GBP half-brother to the useful Liszt, could never make his presence felt but should come on a fair bit for the run. (op 15-8 tchd 7-4)
It's Only Business showed little, but was green both beforehand and in the race. He's not a bad type and will benefit from the outing. (op 9-2)
Northern Harbour(IRE), vocal beforehand and green in the race, will benefit from the outing. (tchd 18-1)

2572 WESTERN DAILY PRESS H'CAP 6f 16y
2:30 (2:31) (Class 5) (0-70,70) 4-Y-0+ **£2,264** (£673; £336; £168) **Stalls** High

Form RPR

16-4 1 **Lady Bayside**[12] 2207 4-9-4 67 TomMcLaughlin 9 75+
(Malcolm Saunders) *trckd ldrs: drvn 2f out: led appr fnl f: shkn up clsng stages and a doing enough* 11/2[2]

0430 2 ½ **Nubar Boy**[36] 1564 5-9-7 70 (v) PadraigBeggy 5 76
(David Evans) *in rr: hdwy fr 2f out: styd on wl u.p fnl f to chse wnr fnl 75yds but a hld* 20/1

1200 3 ¾ **Sole Danser (IRE)**[13] 2165 4-9-4 67 RichardKingscote 7 71+
(Milton Bradley) *s.i.s: in rr: drvn and gd hdwy wl over 1f out: str run ins fnl f to take 3rd clsng stages: nt rch ldng duo* 28/1

5-00 4 nk **Bermondsey Bob (IRE)**[5] 2421 6-9-0 63 CathyGannon 16 66
(John Spearing) *sn led: hdd over 3f out: one pce over 1f out: rallied ins fnl f: kpt on again clsng stages* 10/3[1]

200- 5 nse **Bateleur**[163] 7811 8-8-9 63 CharlesBishop(5) 10 65
(Mick Channon) *in tch: drvn and hdwy to dispute 2nd over 1f out: styd chsng wnr ins fnl f: one pce fnl 120yds* 25/1

560- 6 ¾ **Belle Bayardo (IRE)**[188] 7519 4-9-0 68 DarrenEgan(5) 13 68
(Ronald Harris) *chsd ldrs: rdn and hdwy over 1f out: styd on same pce fnl f* 14/1

2620 7 ¾ **Huzzah (IRE)**[13] 2171 7-8-9 58 MichaelStainton 2 59+
(Paul Howling) *in rr: swtchd rt towards stands' side over 3f out: styng on whn n.m.r ins fnl f: gng on clsng stages* 14/1

0235 8 1 **Going French (IRE)**[13] 2165 5-8-13 62 (t) SamHitchcott 15 56
(Dai Burchell) *prom: rdn 3f out: styd on fnl f but nvr gng pce to trble ldrs* 14/1

0203 9 ½ **Ghostwing**[26] 1789 5-9-3 69 (v) SophieDoyle(3) 17 62
(Ronald Harris) *chsd ldrs on stands' rail: rdn over 2f out: kpt on fnl f: nvr a threat* 8/1[3]

50-0 10 1 **Festival Dance**[22] 1910 4-8-6 58 HarryBentley(3) 12 48
(Ron Hodges) *w ldr: led over 3f out: hdd appr fnl f and wknd qckly* 28/1

56-0 11 1 ½ **Brandywell Boy (IRE)**[39] 1497 9-8-7 56 ChrisCatlin 11 41
(Dominic Ffrench Davis) *in tch: rdn over 2f out: sn wknd* 40/1

12 nk **Noble Four (IRE)**[12] 2219 4-9-7 70 WilliamCarson 8 54
(W McCreery, Ire) *in tch: rdn and sme hdwy over 2f out: sn wknd* 17/2

4-04 13 ½ **Spirit Of Gondree (IRE)**[7] 2373 4-8-12 61 FergusSweeney 6 43
(Milton Bradley) *a outpcd* 14/1

0024 14 1 **Diamond Vine (IRE)**[13] 2165 4-9-7 70 (p) LukeMorris 4 49
(Ronald Harris) *outpcd most of way* 12/1

3-50 15 3 ¼ **Colourbearer (IRE)**[13] 2165 5-8-13 62 (t) DaneO'Neill 3 31
(Milton Bradley) *s.i.s: outpcd* 18/1

1m 11.15s (-0.85) **Going Correction** -0.225s/f (Firm) 15 Ran SP% **117.7**
Speed ratings (Par 103): **96,95,94,93,93 92,91,90,89,88 86,86,85,84,79**
Tote Swingers: 1&2 £32.50, 1&3 £41.70, 2&3 £50.70 CSF £117.21 CT £2814.03 TOTE £4.80: £1.90, £5.70, £10.30; EX 85.40.
Owner Tim Bostwick **Bred** M Saunders & T Bostwick **Trained** Green Ore, Somerset

FOCUS
A very ordinary sprint handicap and not many came into this with solid recent form. The early pace was towards the stands' side of the group, but the winner was more towards the far side.

2573 WESTERN DAILY PRESS CLASSIFIED STKS 6f 16y
3:00 (3:00) (Class 6) 3-Y-0 **£1,617** (£481; £240; £120) **Stalls** High

Form RPR

3-33 1 **Dark Ages (IRE)**[8] 2351 3-9-0 65 (t) RichardHughes 8 69
(George Baker) *trckd ldrs: disp 2nd over 2f out: sn trcking ldr and pushed along to chal ins fnl f: drvn to ld fnl 120yds: kpt on wl* 13/8[1]

-050 2 ½ **Ocean Myth**[15] 2136 3-9-0 62 RichardKingscote 6 67
(Jonathan Portman) *led: drvn 2f out: jnd ins fnl f: hdd and no ex fnl 120yds* 6/1

20-0 3 2 ½ **Welsh Royale**[48] 1313 3-9-0 61 WilliamCarson 3 59
(William Muir) *in rr: rdn over 2f out: styd on appr fnl f: tk 3rd nr fin but no imp on ldng duo* 11/1

04-0 4 ¾ **Courtland King (IRE)**[38] 1529 3-9-0 62 (t) CathyGannon 5 57
(David Evans) *in tch: hdwy to dispute 2nd 2f out: styd on same pce: lost 3rd nr fin* 20/1

-163 5 5 **Ficelle (IRE)**[13] 2166 3-9-0 64 LukeMorris 1 41
(Ronald Harris) *chsd ldrs: rdn over 3f out: sn btn* 11/2[3]

0-23 6 1 **New Decade**[12] 2206 3-9-0 62 DaneO'Neill 2 37
(Milton Bradley) *chsd ldrs: rdn 2f out: wknd qckly appr fnl f* 3/1[2]

6-00 7 2 ¼ **Shamakat**[8] 2351 3-9-0 60 ChrisCatlin 7 30
(Rae Guest) *in rr: rdn 3f out: no ch after* 14/1

1m 11.73s (-0.27) **Going Correction** -0.225s/f (Firm) 7 Ran SP% **112.5**
Speed ratings (Par 97): **92,91,88,87,80 79,76**
Tote Swingers: 1&2 £3.30, 1&3 £3.70, 2&3 £6.50 CSF £11.54 TOTE £2.50: £1.60, £2.70; EX 15.10.
Owner Mrs C E S Baker **Bred** G W Robinson **Trained** Whitsbury, Hants

FOCUS
A typically tight classified stakes, and modest form.
Ficelle(IRE) Official explanation: jockey said filly suffered interference in running.

2574 MORGAN COLE H'CAP 1m 14y
3:30 (3:30) (Class 5) (0-70,68) 4-Y-0+ **£2,264** (£673; £336; £168) **Stalls** High

Form RPR

-000 1 **Hail Promenader (IRE)**[14] 2151 6-9-2 63 (p) WilliamCarson 6 73
(Anthony Carson) *trckd ldr: led over 5f out: rdn and kpt on strly fnl f* 10/1

000- 2 1 ¾ **Daneside (IRE)**[216] 7110 5-9-2 68 MatthewLawson(5) 7 74
(Gary Harrison) *chsd ldrs: wnt 2nd 4f out: rdn and no imp on wnr fr 2f out: hld on wl for 2nd clsng stages* 6/1[2]

/005 3 nk **Jalors (IRE)**[25] 1830 4-9-2 63 LukeMorris 11 68
(Ronald Harris) *in tch: rdn 2f out: styd on wl fnl f to cl on 2nd nr fin but no imp on wnr* 6/1[2]

3005 4 1 ½ **Shared Moment (IRE)**[22] 1909 6-9-0 61 (v) ChrisCatlin 3 63
(John Gallagher) *s.i.s: in rr: rdn over 3f out: hdwy over 1f out: styd on fnl f: nt rch ldrs* 20/1

6-23 5 2 **The Name Is Frank**[12] 2207 7-9-4 65 DaneO'Neill 4 62
(Mark Gillard) *led towards centre of crse tl hdd over 5f out: styd chsng ldrs: wknd fnl f* 13/2[3]

031- 6 1 ¼ **May Be Some Time**[214] 7137 4-9-6 67 FergusSweeney 10 62
(Stuart Kittow) *chsd ldrs: rdn over 2f out: btn fnl f* 11/4[1]

00-0 7 3 **Belle Park**[22] 1908 5-8-8 55 oh1 ow1 DarryllHolland 2 43
(Karen George) *in tch: rdn 3f out: sme hdwy fr 2f out: nvr rchd ldrs: wknd fnl f: eased whn no ch clsng stages* 22/1

54-4 8 5 **Budley**[26] 1772 4-9-5 66 AmirQuinn 5 42
(Bill Turner) *s.i.s: hdwy to chse ldrs 1/2-way: wknd over 2f out* 12/1

6010 9 3 ½ **May's Boy**[18] 2044 4-9-0 66 (p) RachealKneller(5) 8 34
(Mark Usher) *sn bhd* 6/1[2]

260- 10 shd **Bidable**[172] 7698 8-9-7 68 CathyGannon 9 36
(Bryn Palling) *sn bhd* 14/1

1m 33.61s (-2.59) **Going Correction** -0.225s/f (Firm) 10 Ran SP% **115.4**
Speed ratings (Par 103): **103,101,100,99,97 96,93,88,84,84**
Tote Swingers: 1&2 £12.40, 1&3 £8.90, 2&3 £6.20 CSF £68.14 CT £404.43 TOTE £11.20: £4.40, £2.20, £3.50; EX 98.30.
Owner Athos Racing **Bred** Rathbarry Stud **Trained** Newmarket, Suffolk

FOCUS
They raced in two groups in this modest handicap before converging at halfway.
Hail Promenader(IRE) Official explanation: trainer said regarding apparent improvement in form that gelding was better suited to a mile.

2575 YOLK RECRUITMENT H'CAP 2m 49y
4:00 (4:00) (Class 6) (0-60,59) 4-Y-0+ **£1,617** (£481; £240; £120) **Stalls** Low

Form RPR

5-00 1 **Sansili**[12] 1272 5-9-3 55 (tp) RichardHughes 7 65
(Peter Bowen) *in tch: hdwy 5f out: chsd ldr 3f out: rdn to chal 2f out: slt ld appr fnl f: sn hung lft u.p: in command of hmpd 2nd clsng stages* 8/1

/2-3 2 2 **Sainglend**[11] 772 7-9-6 58 JamieSpencer 11 67
(Paul Rich) *sn led: hdd 10f out: pushed along 7f out and again to ld over 4f out: rdn and jnd 2f out: narrowly hdd appr fnl f: looked hld whn hmpd ins fnl f: eased whn no ch w wnr clsng stages* 1/1[1]

60/2 3 3 ¼ **Tae Kwon Do (USA)**[13] 2175 6-8-10 48 (t) FergusSweeney 10 53
(Tim Vaughan) *s.i.s: in rr: hdwy 5f out: hdwy and nt clr run over 3f out: styd on to take one pce 3rd fr 2f out* 11/2[2]

-050 **4** ½ **Lucas Pitt**[25] 1831 5-8-4 **47** ow2 ....(v[1]) DavidKenny[(5)] 8 50
(Michael Scudamore) *in rr: hdwy on outside over 3f out: styd on to disp one pce 3rd fnl 2f: no ex and dropped to 4th ins fnl f* **28/1**
4035 **5** 9 **Josie's Dream (IRE)**[6] 2391 4-8-8 **48** .... TadhgO'Shea 3 40
(Jo Hughes) *chsd ldrs: rdn over 4f out: wknd fr 2f out* **15/2**[3]
-300 **6** 9 **Santera (IRE)**[42] 530 8-8-7 **45** .... CathyGannon 4 27
(Tony Carroll) *in rr: rdn 4f out and nvr gng pce to get into contention: no ch fnl 3f* **18/1**
/0-0 **7** 5 **Party Palace**[15] 2134 8-8-7 **45** .... LukeMorris 9 21
(Stuart Howe) *chsd ldrs: rdn over 4f out: sn btn* **22/1**
062- **8** ¾ **Princesse Fleur**[160] 4274 4-9-1 **55** .... JamieGoldstein 2 30
(Michael Scudamore) *chsd ldr: led 10f out: hdd over 4f out: sn btn* **33/1**
110- **9** 16 **Spinning Waters**[45] 6476 6-8-13 **51** ....(p) KellyHarrison 6
(Dai Burchell) *chsd ldrs 11f: sn bhd: t.o* **8/1**
00-0 **10** 52 **Nobbys Girl**[39] 1496 7-8-2 **45** .... DarrenEgan[(5)] 1
(Ronald Harris) *bhd fnl 9f: t.o* **100/1**

3m 31.95s (-6.95) **Going Correction** -0.40s/f (Firm)
WFA 4 from 5yo+ 2lb **10** Ran SP% **116.4**
Speed ratings (Par 101): **101,100,98,98,93 89,86,86,78,52**
Tote Swingers: 1&2 £2.80, 1&3 £7.00, 2&3 £2.10 CSF £15.93 CT £50.24 TOTE £6.30: £1.50, £1.20, £2.50; EX 18.00.
Owner Saith O Ni **Bred** Baron Von Oppenheim **Trained** Little Newcastle, Pembrokes

FOCUS
They went an ordinary pace in this low-grade staying handicap.
Sansili Official explanation: trainer said regarding apparent improvement in form that gelding benefited from being fitted with a tongue tieand the yard had come back to form.
Princesse Fleur Official explanation: jockey said filly was unsuited by firm ground.
Spinning Waters Official explanation: jockey said gelding ran flat.

2576 BREWIN DOLPHIN H'CAP 1m 2f 36y
4:30 (4:31) (Class 5) (0-75,75) 4-Y-0+ **£2,264** (£673; £336; £168) **Stalls** Low

Form RPR
346- **1** **Sammy Alexander**[293] 4908 4-9-1 **69** .... JamieSpencer 3 78+
(David Simcock) *hld up in rr: stdy hdwy and edgd rt 2f out whn clsng on ldrs: drvn to ld over 1f out: hrd drvn and styd on wl fnl f* **3/1**[2]
0-50 **2** 1¼ **Only You Maggie (IRE)**[25] 1830 5-8-3 **62** oh2 ow1(v) MatthewLawson[(5)] 2 68
(Gary Harrison) *s.i.s: in rr: wd into st 5f out: hdwy on outside over 2f out: styd on to chse wnr fnl 150yds: no imp clsng stages* **16/1**
0-00 **3** 2¾ **Aciano (IRE)**[14] 2151 4-9-6 **74** .... KirstyMilczarek 8 75
(Brendan Powell) *trckd ldr: rdn 2f out: chal fr wl over 1f out: wknd and dropped to 3rd fnl 150yds* **9/1**
0460 **4** 1¼ **Yes Chef**[12] 2199 5-9-4 **72** .... JamesMillman 1 70
(Rod Millman) *in tch: hdwy over 3f out: sn pushed along and one pce: swtchd rt over 1f out: kpt on fnl f: nver a threat* **9/4**[1]
04-6 **5** 2¾ **Ken's Girl**[22] 1939 8-9-5 **73** .... FergusSweeney 5 66
(Stuart Kittow) *led tl hdd & wknd over 1f out* **4/1**[3]
266- **6** 7 **Barachiel**[151] 7931 4-8-4 **63** .... DarrenEgan[(5)] 7 42
(Ronald Harris) *plld hrd: chsd ldrs: rdn 3f out: btn whn bmpd 2f out* **11/1**
-104 **7** 5 **Smart Step**[22] 1913 4-9-1 **69** .... MircoDemuro 6 38
(Mark Johnston) *in tch: rn wd into st 5f out: hdwy to chse ldrs 3f out: wknd 2f out* **6/1**

2m 6.66s (-3.94) **Going Correction** -0.40s/f (Firm) **7** Ran SP% **114.3**
Speed ratings (Par 103): **99,98,95,94,92 87,83**
Tote Swingers: 1&2 £6.30, 1&3 £5.70, 2&3 £12.80 CSF £46.68 CT £387.11 TOTE £2.30: £1.10, £11.00; EX 51.30.
Owner Mrs T A Foreman **Bred** Mrs T A Foreman **Trained** Newmarket, Suffolk

FOCUS
A fair handicap. The pace did not look strong, but the first two came from the back of the field.

2577 CHEPSTOW ANNUAL MEMBERS H'CAP (DIV I) 1m 4f 23y
5:00 (5:01) (Class 6) (0-60,60) 3-Y-0 **£1,617** (£481; £240; £120) **Stalls** Low

Form RPR
2503 **1** **Courtesy Call (IRE)**[14] 2141 3-9-5 **58** .... MircoDemuro 9 68
(Mark Johnston) *trckd ldr: led wl over 2f out: drvn 3 l clr appr fnl f: comf* **9/2**[1]
0-60 **2** 2½ **Looks Like Rain**[28] 1736 3-9-1 **54** .... JamieSpencer 1 60+
(Michael Bell) *s.i.s: hld up in rr: hdwy over 2f out: styd on to chse wnr ins fnl f: kpt on but nvr any ch* **9/2**[1]
3 2¼ **Linkup (IRE)**[10] 2293 3-8-2 **46** oh1 ....(b[1]) DarrenEgan[(5)] 7 48
(Paul W Flynn, Ire) *chsd ldrs: rdn and styd on to disp 2nd over 1f out: nvr any ch w wnr and outpcd into 3rd ins fnl f* **7/1**[3]
-130 **4** 1½ **Palmyra (IRE)**[22] 1915 3-9-6 **59** .... RichardHughes 8 59
(David Simcock) *towards rr but in tch: drvn and hdwy 3f out: chsd wnr 2f out: no imp and wknd into 4th ins fnl f* **10/1**
30-0 **5** 1 **Single Girl (IRE)**[43] 1424 3-8-13 **52** .... LeeNewman 11 50
(Jonathan Portman) *chsd ldrs: rdn over 3f out: wknd over 1f out* **14/1**
000- **6** 6 **Velvet Star (IRE)**[220] 7030 3-9-2 **55** .... ChrisCatlin 4 44
(Paul Cole) *sn led: hdd wl over 2f out: sn wknd* **8/1**
3612 **7** 3 **Alaam Al Wafa (IRE)**[35] 1591 3-9-7 **60** ....(p) LukeMorris 5 44
(Phil McEntee) *in rr but in tch: pushed along to hold position over 6f out: rdn and hdwy on ins 3f out: nvr rchd ldrs: wknd fr 2f out* **10/1**
-420 **8** 2½ **Rocco Breeze (IRE)**[20] 1982 3-8-11 **50** .... DaneO'Neill 10 30
(Philip McBride) *chsd ldrs: rdn 4f out: wknd over 2f out* **5/1**[2]
00-0 **9** 11 **Sea Fret**[36] 1567 3-8-7 **46** ....(p) DarryllHolland 3
(Hughie Morrison) *bhd most of way* **12/1**
06-0 **10** 60 **Miss Granger**[13] 2162 3-8-7 **49** .... SophieDoyle[(3)] 12
(Ronald Harris) *in rr: rdn and wd 5f out: t.o* **33/1**

2m 37.01s (-1.99) **Going Correction** -0.40s/f (Firm) **10** Ran SP% **112.1**
Speed ratings (Par 97): **90,88,86,85,85 81,79,77,70,30**
Tote Swingers: 1&2 £5.90, 1&3 £7.90, 2&3 £6.80 CSF £23.37 CT £136.94 TOTE £6.60: £1.80, £2.40, £3.40; EX 26.90.
Owner A D Spence **Bred** Mrs James Wigan **Trained** Middleham Moor, N Yorks

FOCUS
Division one of a low-grade handicap, which contained a few potential improvers. The pace was only steady and the time was slightly slower than that for division two.
Sea Fret Official explanation: jockey said filly was unsuited by firm ground.
Miss Granger Official explanation: jockey said filly was never travelling.

2578 CHEPSTOW ANNUAL MEMBERS H'CAP (DIV II) 1m 4f 23y
5:30 (5:33) (Class 6) (0-60,60) 3-Y-0 **£1,617** (£481; £240; £120) **Stalls** Low

Form RPR
605- **1** **Abundantly**[222] 6977 3-9-2 **55** .... DarryllHolland 8 66+
(Hughie Morrison) *hld up in rr: hdwy 3f out: styd on wl fr over 1f out to ld fnl 160yds: won gng away* **17/2**
0-64 **2** 2 **Micquus (IRE)**[28] 1726 3-8-11 **50** ....(v) RichardHughes 3 56
(Andrew Balding) *s.i.s: sn rcvrd to trck ldr after 2f: slt ld 3f out: rdn and hrd pressed 2f out: hdd over 1f out: dropped to cl 3rd ins fnl f: rallied to take 2nd fnl 120yds* **7/2**[2]
00-4 **3** 1¾ **Manbaa (USA)**[41] 1443 3-8-12 **51** .... TadhgO'Shea 9 54
(John Dunlop) *chsd ldrs: drvn to chal 2f out: led over 1f out and edgd rt u.p: hdd fnl 160yds: dropped to 3rd fnl 120yds* **6/1**[3]
0-31 **4** 3¾ **Kozmina Bay**[19] 2014 3-9-6 **59** .... LeeNewman 11 56
(Jonathan Portman) *chsd ldrs: rdn 3f out: nvr gng pce to chal: wknd over 1f out* **15/2**
0-22 **5** 3¼ **Mexican Wave**[35] 1590 3-8-7 **46** .... JamieSpencer 7 38
(Michael Bell) *in rr: hdwy 4f out: drvn to try and cl on ldrs over 2f out: no imp: wknd fnl f: eased whn hld clsng stages* **10/3**[1]
2146 **6** 1¼ **Excellent News (IRE)**[15] 2129 3-9-7 **60** .... SebSanders 2 50
(J W Hills) *chsd ldrs: rdn over 3f out: wknd ins fnl 2f* **13/2**
000- **7** 2¼ **Cash Injection**[192] 7494 3-9-1 **54** ....(t) TomMcLaughlin 6 43
(Karen George) *reluctant to enter stalls: in rr and rdn 6f out: mod prog 3f out: nvr nr ldrs: eased whn no ch fnl f* **16/1**
0-00 **8** 2¼ **Choisirez (IRE)**[8] 2353 3-9-0 **53** ....(v[1]) CathyGannon 5 36
(David Evans) *led tl hdd 3f out: wknd qckly 2f out* **40/1**
0-00 **9** ½ **Absolutely Me (IRE)**[28] 1737 3-8-10 **49** ....(t) ChrisCatlin 4 31
(Dominic Ffrench Davis) *in rr and wl bhd 4f out: mod prog fr 2f out* **20/1**
000 **10** 5 **Brave Kiss**[23] 1893 3-8-7 **46** oh1 .... FergusSweeney 1 20
(Mark Gillard) *chsd ldrs tl wknd qckly 3f out* **33/1**

2m 36.8s (-2.20) **Going Correction** -0.40s/f (Firm) **10** Ran SP% **111.2**
Speed ratings (Par 97): **91,89,88,86,83 83,81,80,79,76**
Tote Swingers: 1&2 £7.60, 1&3 £10.30, 2&3 £4.00 CSF £35.77 CT £187.16 TOTE £5.60: £1.90, £1.30, £2.80; EX 43.60.
Owner J Repard and S Dibb **Bred** J Repard & S Dibb **Trained** East Ilsley, Berks

FOCUS
Division two was run in a time 0.21sec quicker than the first, and it looked the better race.
T/Plt: £620.00 to a £1 stake. Pool: £53,539.00 - 63.03 winning tickets. T/Qpdt: £42.50 to a £1 stake. Pool: £4,441.00 - 77.20 winning tickets. ST

2492 LINGFIELD (L-H)
Tuesday, May 29

OFFICIAL GOING: Standard
Wind: virtually nil Weather: warm and sunny

2579 BETFRED STILL TREBLE ODDS ON LUCKY 15'S MEDIAN AUCTION MAIDEN STKS 5f (P)
2:20 (2:21) (Class 6) 2-Y-0 **£1,704** (£503; £251) **Stalls** High

Form RPR
3 **1** **Bridge Night**[8] 2343 2-8-12 0 .... WilliamBuick 8 78+
(Eve Johnson Houghton) *chsd ldr: chal 2f out: rdn over 1f out: led jst ins fnl f: r.o wl and gng away at fin* **11/8**[1]
0 **2** 2¾ **Puteri Nur Laila (IRE)**[8] 2343 2-8-12 0 .... NeilCallan 1 67
(Paul Cole) *led: jnd 2f out: sn rdn: hdd jst ins fnl f: sn outpcd and btn* **5/1**[3]
3 2 **Reliant Robin (IRE)** 2-9-3 0 .... StevieDonohoe 2 65
(Robert Mills) *chsd ldng trio: pushed along and wnt 3rd 2f out: no imp and styd on same pce fr over 1f out* **8/1**
4 4 **Petite Georgia (IRE)** 2-8-12 0 .... PatCosgrave 7 46
(George Baker) *awkward leaving stalls and dwlt: sn rcvrd to chse ldng pair: lost 3rd 2f out: sn rdn and wknd over 1f out* **15/2**
5 2 **Lord Avonbrook** 2-8-10 0 .... RyanWhile[(7)] 6 43+
(Bill Turner) *awkward leaving stalls: in tch towards rr on outer: wd bnd 2f out and lost pl: no imp u.p fr over 1f out* **4/1**[2]
0 **6** 2¼ **Cernanova (IRE)**[40] 1466 2-8-5 0 .... NoelGarbutt[(7)] 4 30
(Hugo Palmer) *rrd leaving stalls and dwlt: t.k.h early: rdn and struggling ent fnl 2f: sn wknd* **16/1**
0 **7** ½ **Gowertonian (IRE)**[22] 1903 2-9-0 0 .... CPGeoghegan[(3)] 3 33
(Ronald Harris) *s.i.s: a outpcd in rr* **40/1**
8 6 **Grandfathers Gift** 2-8-7 0 .... LauraPike[(5)] 5 7
(Michael Quinn) *in tch: rdn and struggling 1/2-way: wknd 2f out: wl bhd fnl f* **33/1**

1m 0.81s (2.01) **Going Correction** +0.275s/f (Slow) **8** Ran SP% **112.9**
Speed ratings (Par 91): **94,89,86,80,76 73,72,62**
Tote Swingers: 1&2 £2.30, 1&3 £1.10, 2&3 £14.20 CSF £8.25 TOTE £2.10: £1.02, £1.90, £3.30; EX 7.30 Trifecta £38.40 Pool: £441.08 - 8.48 winning units.
Owner S Emmet **Bred** S Emmet And Miss R Emmet **Trained** Blewbury, Oxon

FOCUS
Not much form to go on for this opening maiden and the pace was sound enough, with the field well strung out passing the line. While the winner won impressively, the form does not look that strong.

NOTEBOOK
Bridge Night had shown the best of the limited form on offer and she used her experience to get away quickly from her wide draw and sit handy. She had to be driven to pass the pace-setting runner-up, but won going away. She can continue to perform well over the minimum trip, but looks as though further will suit in time. (op 7-4 tchd 2-1)
Puteri Nur Laila(IRE) stepped up on her debut when eighth at Windsor, but was no match for the winner. She possesses raw natural speed and looks capable of landing a weak maiden. (op 13-2)
Reliant Robin(IRE), who was green entering the stalls, ran an encouraging race on his debut. His handler described him as "a nice little horse" and he should come on plenty for this run. (tchd 9-1)
Petite Georgia(IRE), who cost 37,000gns as a yearling, had to use up plenty of energy from her wide draw and raced wide throughout. The yard's runners tend to benefit from a run or two and this was a decent introduction. (tchd 13-2)
Lord Avonbrook was supported in the morning, but that surprised Bill Turner who said: "He's fit, but he's been a bit slow getting going and I think he might need it" and the handler's views were spot-on. He travelled well out wide but could not quicken entering the home straight and will have learnt a lot from this. (op 5-2)
Grandfathers Gift showed good early pace, albeit racing a bit keenly, and folded tamely up the straight. She looks a long term prospect.

2580 BETFRED MOBILE SPORTS (S) STKS 1m (P)
2:50 (2:50) (Class 6) 3-5-Y-0 **£1,704** (£503; £251) **Stalls** High

Form RPR
6016 **1** **Moment In The Sun**[6] 2398 3-8-7 **61** ....(b) MickaelBarzalona 1 67
(David Flood) *t.k.h early: chsd ldr for 1f: chsd ldrs after: rdn to ld over 1f out: clr fnl f: rdn out* **8/1**
131- **2** 2 **A Little Bit Dusty**[30] 717 4-8-12 **71** ....(b) RyanWhile[(7)] 3 65+
(Bill Turner) *detached in last pair: lost tch w ldng trio over 3f out: clsd and rdn along over 1f out: chsd wnr ins fnl f: kpt on* **3/1**[3]

05-0 **3** 3 ½ **Chief Of Men**[10] 2274 4-9-5 75 ....(vt¹) EddieAhern 4 57
(Denis Coakley) *chsd ldr after 1f: pressed ldr and hung rt whn rdn wl over 1f out: fnd little u.p: chsd clr wnr 1f out: lost 2nd and wknd fnl 150yds* **2/1**[2]

100- **4** 6 **Resuscitator (USA)**[384] 2000 5-9-5 77 ....(v) MichaelO'Connell 2 44
(Linda Stubbs) *broke fast: led: rdn and hdd over 1f out: sn btn: fdd fnl f* **7/4**[1]

56 **5** ½ **Multifac'Eted**[70] 974 3-7-13 0 .... RyanPowell(3) 5 34
(J S Moore) *detached in last pair: rdn 5f out: sn struggling: wl bhd 3f out: no ch but plugged on fnl f* **50/1**

1m 40.09s (1.89) **Going Correction** +0.275s/f (Slow)
WFA 3 from 4yo+ 12lb 5 Ran SP% **107.8**
Speed ratings (Par 101): **101,99,95,89,89**
CSF £30.07 TOTE £7.90: £5.00, £1.70; EX 17.80.No bid for the winner.
Owner Flood Family Racing Limited **Bred** Foursome Thoroughbreds **Trained** Exning, Suffolk

FOCUS
A competitive enough event for the grade despite the small field size and the pace was generous with the field well strung out passing the post.
Resuscitator(USA) Official explanation: jockey said gelding stopped quickly.

2581 CTP CLASSIFIED CLAIMING STKS 7f (P)
3:20 (3:20) (Class 6) 3-Y-0+ **£1,704** (£503; £251) **Stalls** Low

Form RPR
0330 **1** **Spin Again (IRE)**[5] 2421 7-9-2 70 .... MickaelBarzalona 9 75
(Daniel Kubler) *hld up in midfield: rdn and effrt to chse ldr wl over 1f out: led over 1f out: sn rdn and wnt clr: comf* **5/4**[1]

6011 **2** 3 ½ **Efistorm**[8] 2342 11-9-5 67 .... LiamKeniry 2 69
(Conor Dore) *hld up in last trio: rdn and hdwy wl over 1f out: chsd clr wnr ins fnl f: kpt on but no threat to wnr* **5/1**[3]

4433 **3** 2 ¼ **Aquilifer (IRE)**[6] 2398 4-9-5 68 ....(tp) ShaneKelly 1 63
(Mrs K Burke) *dwlt: pushed along: racd off the pce in last trio: rdn over 2f out: swtchd rt wl over 1f out: kpt on u.p fnl f: no threat to wnr* **4/1**[2]

1604 **4** nk **Zip Lock (IRE)**[13] 2169 6-8-10 70 .... LauraPike(5) 4 58
(Olivia Maylam) *plld hrd early: hld up towards rr: hdwy to chse ldng pair 5f out: rdn and unable qck 2f out: one pce fr over 1f out* **11/1**

2413 **5** 1 ¼ **Chjimes (IRE)**[13] 2169 8-9-3 66 ....(b) BrettDoyle 7 57
(Conor Dore) *t.k.h: hld up off the pce in last trio: rdn and effrt wl over 1f out: no imp* **12/1**

5240 **6** 1 ¾ **Elhamri**[21] 1958 8-8-12 67 .... SimonPearce(3) 5 50
(Conor Dore) *racd in midfield: rdn and unable qck 2f out: wknd over 1f out* **16/1**

53-0 **7** ½ **Invincible Dream (IRE)**[12] 2205 3-7-13 62 ....(b¹) DanielCremin(7) 8 47
(Robert Mills) *dashed up to ld after 1f: clr whn rn wd bnd 2f out: rdn and hdd wl over 1f out: wknd over 1f out* **25/1**

1360 **8** ¾ **Ace Of Spies (IRE)**[21] 1958 7-8-12 66 .... RyanPowell(3) 3 47
(Conor Dore) *chsd ldr tl wl over 1f out: sn wknd* **20/1**

1m 26.38s (1.58) **Going Correction** +0.275s/f (Slow)
WFA 3 from 4yo+ 11lb 8 Ran SP% **111.6**
Speed ratings (Par 101): **101,97,94,94,92 90,90,89**
Tote Swingers: 1&2 £2.30, 1&3 £1.10, 2&3 £4.00 CSF £7.23 TOTE £3.50: £1.50, £1.10, £1.10; EX 8.90 Trifecta £19.10 Pool: £641.89 - 24.83 winning units.Spin Again (IRE) claimed by Mr J. Ryan for £5,000. Zip Lock (IRE) claimed by Mr A. J. D. Lidderdale for £4,000.
Owner David Dacosta **Bred** Barry Lyons **Trained** Whitsbury, Hants

FOCUS
Many of the runners looked in with a chance judges on official ratings, but off the strong early pace few were able to get competitive.
Zip Lock(IRE) Official explanation: vet said gelding lost a right front shoe.

2582 BREATHE SPA AT MARRIOTT LINGFIELD H'CAP 7f (P)
3:50 (3:50) (Class 6) (0-55,58) 3-Y-0 **£1,704** (£503; £251) **Stalls** Low

Form RPR
0440 **1** **Waspy**[6] 2388 3-8-7 45 ....(t) MickaelBarzalona 1 51
(George Baker) *chsd ldrs: rdn to chal jst over 1f out: sustained chal to ld fnl 75yds: r.o wl* **17/2**

640- **2** 1 **Green Mountain (IRE)**[150] 7937 3-8-4 45 ....(t) AdamBeschizza(3) 2 48
(Philip McBride) *chsd ldr: rdn to press ldr 2f out: led jst over 1f out: sn hrd drvn: kpt on wl tl hdd and no ex fnl 75yds* **12/1**

01-6 **3** ½ **My Scat Daddy (USA)**[125] 294 3-8-13 51 .... WilliamBuick 10 53+
(Brett Johnson) *in tch in midfield but stuck on outer: lost pl bnd 2f out: rallied and hdwy u.p 1f out: edging lft but styd on wl fnl f* **5/2**[1]

000- **4** ¾ **Norfolk Sky**[239] 6588 3-8-7 45 .... PaulHanagan 13 45+
(Chris Wall) *racd on outer in last trio: stl plenty to do and rdn over 1f out: styd on wl ins fnl f: nt rch ldrs* **11/2**[2]

000- **5** 3 **Knoydart (USA)**[233] 6725 3-8-7 45 .... MartinDwyer 6 37
(Amanda Perrett) *t.k.h: chsd ldrs: rdn and unable qck 2f out: wknd ins fnl f* **7/1**

0-00 **6** shd **Get The Trip**[7] 2374 3-8-9 50 .... DominicFox(3) 9 41
(Anthony Carson) *led: rdn and hrd pressed wl over 1f out: hdd jst over 1f out: fdd fnl 100yds* **25/1**

5000 **7** 1 ½ **Thecornishcowboy**[19] 2010 3-9-0 52 ....(tp) BrettDoyle 3 39
(John Ryan) *in tch in last trio: pushed along and hdwy on inner over 2f out: drvn and clsd over 1f out: no imp 1f out: wknd fnl 100yds* **33/1**

00-5 **8** 1 **Enthrall (IRE)**[19] 2010 3-8-7 45 .... JoeFanning 7 30
(Denis Coakley) *t.k.h: chsd ldrs: rdn and struggling ent fnl 2f: wknd over 1f out* **17/2**

0401 **9** 1 ¾ **Kai**[8] 2351 3-8-13 58 6ex ....(v) IanBurns(7) 5 38
(Michael Bell) *in tch in midfield: rdn 3f out: wknd u.p over 1f out* **6/1**[3]

2105 **10** ¾ **Flying Kitty**[34] 1608 3-9-1 53 .... KieranO'Neill 8 31
(John Bridger) *stdd s: hld up in tch in last quartet: rdn wl over 2f out: no rspnse: wknd over 1f out* **12/1**

550- **11** 4 **Princess Palmer**[228] 6842 3-8-9 52 .... JamesRogers(5) 12 19
(Giles Bravery) *v awkward leaving stalls and s.i.s: plld hrd: hld up in tch in last quartet: wknd wl over 1f out* **25/1**

1m 27.84s (3.04) **Going Correction** +0.275s/f (Slow) 11 Ran SP% **117.8**
Speed ratings (Par 97): **93,91,91,90,87 86,85,84,82,81 76**
Tote Swingers: 1&2 £12.90, 1&3 £6.10, 2&3 £9.80 CSF £103.39 CT £337.99 TOTE £6.20: £1.70, £6.10, £1.60; EX 152.20 TRIFECTA Not won..
Owner Patrick Milmo **Bred** Jeremy Gompertz **Trained** Whitsbury, Hants

FOCUS
This uncompetitive low-grade handicap was run at a sensible pace and it paid to race handy.
Thecornishcowboy Official explanation: trainer said gelding was struck into.
Princess Palmer Official explanation: jockey said filly ran too free.

2583 BETFRED BONUS KING BINGO H'CAP 7f (P)
4:20 (4:21) (Class 5) (0-75,75) 3-Y-0 **£2,385** (£704; £352) **Stalls** Low

Form RPR
412- **1** **Delft**[164] 7799 3-9-7 75 .... RyanMoore 5 83+
(Jeremy Noseda) *chsd ldr: rdn to chal wl over 1f out: led over 1f out: r.o wl fnl f: rdn out* **11/8**[1]

40-4 **2** ¾ **Light Burst (USA)**[47] 1331 3-8-8 62 .... RoystonFfrench 4 68
(Ismail Mohammed) *in tch: swtchd rt and effrt to chse ldrs 2f out: sltly hmpd over 1f out: r.o wl u.p ins fnl f: wnt 2nd fnl 50yds* **50/1**

1430 **3** hd **Incendiary (IRE)**[11] 2246 3-9-7 75 .... GeorgeBaker 13 80+
(Hugo Palmer) *in tch in midfield: swtchd rt and effrt over 1f out: drvn and r.o wl ins fnl f: wnt 3rd cl home* **13/2**[3]

21-4 **4** ½ **Dark Falcon (IRE)**[24] 1862 3-9-4 72 .... KierenFallon 2 76
(James Tate) *in tch: rdn and effrt over 1f out: drvn to chse wnr ins fnl f: kpt on same pce and lost 2 pls fnl 50yds* **8/1**

-164 **5** 1 ½ **Manomine**[28] 1728 3-8-13 67 ....(b¹) BrettDoyle 3 67
(Clive Brittain) *broke fast and led: hdd wl over 2f out: stl pressing ldrs and drvn wl over 1f out: wknd ins fnl f* **25/1**

41-6 **6** nse **Strathnaver**[12] 2194 3-9-4 72 .... WilliamBuick 7 72+
(Ed Dunlop) *jostled leaving stalls: grad swtchd to inner and hld up in midfield: stuck bhd a wall of horses over 2f out: hdwy over 1f out: swtchd rt and r.o ins fnl f* **6/1**[2]

255- **7** ¾ **Flavius Victor (IRE)**[279] 5385 3-8-11 72 ..... WilliamTwiston-Davies(7) 10 70
(Richard Hannon) *stdd and wnt lft s: t.k.h: hld up in tch towards rr: rdn and effrt wl over 1f out: edgd lft and styd on ins fnl f* **20/1**

-440 **8** 1 **City Dazzler (IRE)**[7] 2382 3-8-11 65 .... PatDobbs 6 60
(Richard Hannon) *chsd ldrs tl led wl over 2f out: drvn and hdd over 1f out: wknd ins fnl f* **20/1**

3611 **9** 2 ¾ **One More Roman (IRE)**[28] 1731 3-8-10 64 ....(bt) MartinDwyer 8 52
(Gay Kelleway) *jostled leaving stalls: sn swtchd lft and dropped in bhd: rdn and effrt 2f out: kpt on but nvr trbld ldrs* **12/1**

0-06 **10** 1 **Fortrose Academy (IRE)**[11] 2246 3-9-2 70 .... DavidProbert 1 55
(Andrew Balding) *in tch in midfield: drvn and unable qck wl over 1f out: wknd ins fnl f* **16/1**

1305 **11** 4 ½ **Fugitive Motel (IRE)**[43] 1419 3-8-6 67 .... NicoleNordblad(7) 12 40
(Hans Adielsson) *t.k.h: hld up in tch in rr: n.d* **80/1**

32-0 **12** 1 **Flamborough Breeze**[18] 2045 3-9-2 70 .... NeilCallan 11 40
(Ed Vaughan) *in tch in midfield: rdn over 2f out: wknd wl over 1f out* **25/1**

1200 **13** 1 **Lionrock (FR)**[26] 1790 3-9-1 69 .... JoeFanning 9 37
(Mark Johnston) *short of room: hmpd and dropped to last sn after s: racd on outer and a bhd* **14/1**

1m 26.65s (1.85) **Going Correction** +0.275s/f (Slow) 13 Ran SP% **121.5**
Speed ratings (Par 99): **100,99,98,98,96 96,95,94,91,90 85,84,82**
Tote Swingers: 1&2 £22.10, 1&3 £2.60, 2&3 £58.80 CSF £118.07 CT £389.51 TOTE £2.40: £1.20, £12.50, £3.50; EX 76.30 Trifecta £438.60 Part won. Pool: £592.80 - 0.40 winning units..
Owner Cheveley Park Stud **Bred** Cheveley Park Stud Ltd **Trained** Newmarket, Suffolk

FOCUS
A competitve handicap run at a sound pace where once again it paid to race handily. The form looks strong.

2584 FOLLOW US ON TWITTER @LINGFIELDPARK MAIDEN STKS (DIV I) 1m 2f (P)
4:50 (4:52) (Class 5) 3-Y-0 **£2,385** (£704; £352) **Stalls** Low

Form RPR
0- **1** **Inthar (USA)**[217] 7082 3-9-3 0 .... FrankieDettori 11 88+
(Saeed Bin Suroor) *midfield early: hdwy to chse ldrs over 7f out: wnt 3rd 2f out: drvn ent fnl f: styd on wl to ld fnl 75yds: rdn out* **2/1**[1]

2 ¾ **Presume** 3-8-12 0 .... RyanMoore 5 81+
(Sir Michael Stoute) *chsd ldr: rdn and ev ch 2f out: drvn ahd over 1f out: hrd pressed ins fnl f: hdd and no ex fnl 75yds* **12/1**[3]

22- **3** 2 **Pulverize (USA)**[270] 5688 3-9-3 0 .... PaulHanagan 1 82
(Sir Michael Stoute) *t.k.h: broke fast: sn stdd bk and hld up in tch: rdn over 2f out: kpt on u.p ins fnl f: nt pce to rch ldrs* **2/1**[1]

0-3 **4** hd **Fearless Dream**[36] 1567 3-8-12 0 .... WilliamBuick 8 77
(John Gosden) *sn led: rdn and hrd pressed 2f out: hdd and drvn over 1f out: styd pressing ldrs tl btn fnl 100yds: hung rt and wknd towards fin* **4/1**[2]

5 5 **Castilo Del Diablo (IRE)** 3-9-3 0 .... EddieAhern 9 72+
(David Simcock) *dwlt: hld up in rr: pushed along and hdwy jst over 2f out: swtchd rt over 1f out: kpt on but nvr trbld ldrs* **66/1**

05 **6** 1 ¾ **Sky Khan**[12] 2196 3-9-3 0 .... GeorgeBaker 2 69+
(Ed Dunlop) *hld up in rr: rdn over 2f out: no threat to ldrs but styd on steadily fnl f* **14/1**

00- **7** 1 ½ **Ze King**[209] 7232 3-9-3 0 .... NeilCallan 3 66+
(Chris Wall) *chsd ldng pair tl 2f out: sn rdn and unable qck: btn 1f out: fdd fnl f* **80/1**

6 **8** 3 ¼ **Cool Sky**[22] 1923 3-9-3 0 .... JimCrowley 10 59
(William Knight) *t.k.h: hld up in midfield: rdn and struggling over 2f out: wknd over 1f out* **33/1**

4-0 **9** 2 ¼ **Paramythi (IRE)**[12] 2196 3-9-3 0 .... KierenFallon 4 55
(Luca Cumani) *chsd ldrs on outer: rdn along over 4f out: wknd ent fnl 2f: bhd fnl f* **20/1**

10 8 **Virginia Galilei (IRE)** 3-8-12 0 .... TedDurcan 7 34
(David Lanigan) *in tch in midfield: rdn and lost pl over 4f out: wknd ent fnl 2f: bhd and eased wl ins fnl f* **40/1**

11 6 **Imagery** 3-9-0 0 .... CPGeoghegan(3) 6 27
(Ronald Harris) *dwlt: a bhd* **100/1**

2m 7.47s (0.87) **Going Correction** +0.275s/f (Slow) 11 Ran SP% **114.9**
Speed ratings (Par 99): **107,106,104,104,100 99,98,95,93,87 82**
Tote Swingers: 1&2 £6.70, 1&3 £2.10, 2&3 £4.60 CSF £27.22 TOTE £2.80: £2.00, £4.10, £1.10; EX 38.10 Trifecta £307.10 Pool: £1,668.50 - 4.02 winning units..
Owner Godolphin **Bred** Darley **Trained** Newmarket, Suffolk

FOCUS
This maiden was run at a decent pace and the form looks strong, with the four principals pulling well clear up the home straight.

Fearless Dream Official explanation: jockey reported filly hung badly right from four furlong marker.

2585 FOLLOW US ON TWITTER @LINGFIELDPARK MAIDEN STKS (DIV II) 1m 2f (P)
5:20 (5:21) (Class 5) 3-Y-O **£2,385** (£704; £352) **Stalls** Low

Form RPR
0 **1** **Lashyn (USA)**[39] 1501 3-8-12 0 RyanMoore 11 70+
(Sir Michael Stoute) *awkward leaving stalls: sn rcvrd and chsd ldr: led wl over 2f out: rdn 2 l clr 2f out: kpt on wl tl rn green and hung rt wl ins fnl f: hld on cl home* **11/4**[2]
44-3 **2** *nk* **Muntasir (IRE)**[22] 1923 3-9-3 78 FrankieDettori 4 72
(Saeed Bin Suroor) *chsd ldrs: rdn and effrt to chse ldng pair 2f out: drvn and chsd wnr ins fnl f: keeping on and pressing wnr whn carried rt wl ins fnl f: kpt on cl home* **4/5**[1]
5-0 **3** *3/4* **Energlze (FR)**[38] 1512 3-9-3 0 (t) PatDobbs 3 71
(Richard Hannon) *chsd ldrs: rdn to chse wnr 2f out tl ins fnl f: kpt on u.p* **9/1**[3]
4 *3 3/4* **Caphira** 3-8-12 0 JimCrowley 7 58
(William Knight) *in tch in midfield: hdwy to chse ldrs 2f out: rdn and outpcd by ldng trio over 1f out: kpt on steadily ins fnl f* **11/1**
5 *2 1/4* **Cannizaro House (IRE)** 3-9-3 0 LiamKeniry 10 59
(Terry Clement) *dwlt: hld up in tch in last trio: hdwy on outer over 2f out: outpcd wl over 2f out: no threat to ldrs but swtchd rt and kpt on fnl f* **100/1**
00 **6** *1* **Opus (IRE)**[10] 2280 3-9-3 0 (t) EddieAhern 5 57
(Amanda Perrett) *in tch in midfield: rdn to chse ldrs 2f out: sn outpcd: wknd fnl f* **33/1**
0-0 **7** *4* **Al Karlovyyh (IRE)**[11] 2249 3-8-12 0 MartinDwyer 1 44
(Clive Brittain) *in tch: rdn and outpcd ent fnl 2f: wl btn 1f out* **66/1**
66 **8** *nk* **Sporting Gold (IRE)**[15] 2125 3-9-3 0 NeilCallan 9 48
(Roger Varian) *hld up in tch in last trio: rdn and struggling over 2f out: wknd 2f out* **16/1**
0 **9** *3 3/4* **Soho Spirit**[41] 1456 3-8-12 0[1] RobertHavlin 2 35
(James Toller) *led tl wl over 2f out: rdn and wknd 2f out: fdd over 1f out* **50/1**
00 **10** *47* **Extremely Alert**[18] 2042 3-9-3 0 JoeFanning 8
(Michael Bell) *hld up in tch in last trio: rdr looking down 3f out: sn lost tch: t.o fnl 2f* **50/1**

2m 9.36s (2.76) **Going Correction** +0.275s/f (Slow) **10** Ran SP% **115.8**
Speed ratings (Par 99): **99,98,98,95,93 92,89,89,86,48**
Tote Swingers: 1&2 £1.70, 1&3 £2.80, 2&3 £2.70 CSF £5.13 TOTE £3.30: £1.80, £1.02, £2.20; EX 6.10 Trifecta £29.10 Pool: £1,556.66 - 39.57 winning units..
Owner Nurlan Bizakov **Bred** Charles H Wacker **Trained** Newmarket, Suffolk

FOCUS
This maiden was run at a steady pace and, as in the first division, the principals pulled clear up the home straight. The winner survived a lengthy stewards' enquiry having edged markedly to her right late on, hampering the runner up in the process. It is hard to be certain whether the second would have won, but the stewards erred on the side of caution.

2586 LINGFIELDPARK.CO.UK H'CAP 1m (P)
5:50 (5:50) (Class 6) (0-60,60) 4-Y-O+ **£1,704** (£503; £251) **Stalls** High

Form RPR
6025 **1** **Karate (IRE)**[20] 1984 4-9-6 59 (t) JimCrowley 4 67
(Hans Adielsson) *in tch: swtchd lft and drvn to chal ent fnl f: led ins fnl f: r.o wl: rdn out* **10/3**[1]
0503 **2** *1 1/4* **West Leake (IRE)**[7] 2373 6-9-7 60 LiamKeniry 10 65
(Paul Burgoyne) *stdd and dropped in bhd after s: hld up in last pair: swtchd rt and effrt over 1f out: kpt on u.p to go 2nd cl home* **10/3**[1]
0-01 **3** *hd* **Footstepsofspring (FR)**[29] 1717 5-9-3 56 TonyCulhane 6 60
(Willie Musson) *t.k.h: chsd ldrs: wnt 2nd over 4f out: rdn and ev ch wl over 1f out: chsd wnr ins fnl f: one pce and lost 2nd cl home* **6/1**[3]
0/0- **4** *3/4* **Cottonfields (USA)**[163] 7810 6-9-2 55 (b[1]) NeilCallan 2 58
(Heather Main) *in tch: effrt u.p to chse ldrs 1f out: styd on same pce ins fnl f* **9/1**
3-33 **5** *2* **Ymir**[13] 2170 6-9-3 56 (tp) J-PGuillambert 5 54
(Michael Attwater) *chsd ldr tl led after 2f: rdn wl over 1f out: hdd ins fnl f: wknd fnl 75yds* **7/2**[2]
4601 **6** *1 1/2* **Querido (GER)**[23] 1895 8-9-3 59 (tp) RobertLButler[(3)] 1 54
(Paddy Butler) *in tch: rdn and effrt ent fnl f: no imp ins fnl f* **16/1**
06-0 **7** *3/4* **Fitz**[29] 1702 6-9-5 58 WilliamBuick 8 51
(Matthew Salaman) *s.i.s and sn rdn along: sme hdwy on outer 4f out: rdn and struggling 2f out: wknd over 1f out* **10/1**
0000 **8** *1/2* **Rasteau (IRE)**[19] 2009 4-8-7 49 oh1 ow3 RyanClark[(3)] 7 41
(Tom Keddy) *rdn along leaving stalls: sn chsng ldrs: rdn over 3f out: outpcd u.p over 1f out: wknd fnl f* **25/1**
000- **9** *13* **A B Celebration**[243] 6472 4-8-7 46 oh1 KieranO'Neill 3
(John Bridger) *led for 2f: chsd ldrs after tl lost pl over 2f out: wl bhd fnl f* **66/1**

1m 40.85s (2.65) **Going Correction** +0.275s/f (Slow) **9** Ran SP% **113.0**
Speed ratings (Par 101): **97,95,95,94,92 91,90,90,77**
Tote Swingers: 1&2 £4.70, 1&3 £4.20, 2&3 £3.90 CSF £14.27 CT £62.41 TOTE £2.60: £1.10, £1.30, £3.00; EX 16.10 Trifecta £77.60 Pool: £948.83 - 9.04 winning units..
Owner Erik Penser **Bred** C J Foy **Trained** Kingston Lisle, Oxon

FOCUS
This handicap was run at a sound pace and there were plenty in contention at the furlong pole. This form looks modest.
T/Plt: £12.20 to a £1 stake. Pool: £48,584.00 - 2,884.62 winning tickets. T/Qpdt: £4.20 to a £1 stake. Pool: £3,942.00 - 694.16 winning tickets. SP

[2308] RIPON (R-H)
Tuesday, May 29

OFFICIAL GOING: Good to firm (good in places; watered; 8.6)
Wind: light 1/2 behind Weather: fine

2587 BRITISH STALLION STUDS SUPPORTING BRITISH RACING E B F MAIDEN STKS 5f
2:10 (2:13) (Class 5) 2-Y-O **£3,557** (£1,058; £529; £264) **Stalls** High

Form RPR
6 **1** **Body And Soul (IRE)**[18] 2047 2-8-12 0 DavidAllan 4 71+
(Tim Easterby) *chsd ldrs: wnt 2nd 1f out: styd on wl to ld last 100yds* **13/2**[2]
00 **2** *1* **Limit Up**[17] 2069 2-9-3 0 SilvestreDeSousa 10 72
(Mark Johnston) *led: hung rt over 1f out: hdd and no ex ins fnl f* **15/2**[3]
3 *3/4* **Dream Scenario** 2-8-12 0 RobertWinston 12 65+
(Mel Brittain) *mid-div: hung rt and hdwy over 2f out: kpt on fnl f: tk 3rd nr fin* **20/1**
26 **4** *shd* **Botanic Garden**[13] 2181 2-9-3 0 RichardMullen 8 69+
(David Brown) *chsd ldrs: hung rt and kpt on same pce fnl f* **9/1**
4 **5** *1/2* **Star Of Rohm**[12] 2213 2-9-3 0 HayleyTurner 1 68+
(Michael Bell) *wnt rt s: mid-div: sn drvn along: outpcd over 2f out: kpt on wl fnl f* **8/13**[1]
5 **6** *1* **Clock Opera (IRE)**[18] 2019 2-8-12 0 MartinHarley 11 60+
(Mrs K Burke) *chsd ldrs: outpcd over 2f out: kpt on ins fnl f: will improve* **16/1**
7 *3 3/4* **Penny Garcia** 2-8-12 0 DuranFentiman 5 45+
(Tim Easterby) *in rr: sme hdwy on wd outside 2f out: nvr a factor* **80/1**
0 **8** *2 1/4* **Red Highlites (IRE)**[8] 2334 2-8-12 0 GrahamLee 6 37
(Ann Duffield) *mid-div: outpcd over 2f out: no threat after* **40/1**
9 *hd* **Bonnie Lesley (IRE)** 2-8-12 0 TomEaves 7 37
(Keith Dalgleish) *dwlt: a in rr* **40/1**
10 *3/4* **Ena Sharples** 2-8-12 0 AndrewMullen 2 34
(David Nicholls) *s.i.s: a bhd* **100/1**
0 **11** *1 3/4* **I'Ve No Money (IRE)**[25] 1818 2-9-3 0 PhillipMakin 3 33
(David C Griffiths) *wnt rt s: in rr: sme hdwy 2f out: sn wknd* **100/1**

59.55s (-1.15) **Going Correction** -0.225s/f (Firm) **11** Ran SP% **115.8**
Speed ratings (Par 93): **100,98,97,97,96 94,88,85,84,83 80**
Tote Swingers: 1&2 £4.80, 1&3 £8.70, 2&3 £9.40 CSF £50.54 TOTE £10.00: £2.60, £3.20, £6.70; EX 60.00.
Owner Ryedale Partners No 5 **Bred** Michael Downey & Roalso Ltd **Trained** Great Habton, N Yorks

FOCUS
Rail at innermost position and distances as advertised. A modest maiden, run at a decent pace and those racing handily proved to be at an advantage. The main action was stands' side early, but the leaders drifted towards the centre late on. The first pair set the standard and also limit the form.

NOTEBOOK
Body And Soul(IRE) ran below expectations on her debut at Nottingham 18 days earlier, but that was on soft ground and she showed it to be all wrong with a gutsy effort on this quicker surface. She did well to get out early from her draw and deserves credit for getting on top after the runner-up carried her into the middle of the track. There should be more to come. (op 8-1)
Limit Up led against the stands' rail for most of the way and held every chance. However, he spoilt his cause by handing right inside the final furlong and it's hoped that was still down to greenness, as this was his best effort to date. (op 13-2)
Dream Scenario ◆ fared best of the newcomers and was doing some decent work late on. She ended up widest of all, despite being drawn against the stands' rail, and this speedily bred filly looks one to side with next time. (op 16-1)
Botanic Garden returned to the sort of form that saw him finish runner-up over C&D on easy ground last month and helps to set the level of this form. (tchd 8-1)
Star Of Rohm posted a decent debut display at York over 6f 12 days earlier and was all the rage here. His outside stall wasn't ideal, but ultimately it was the dropping back to the minimum which found him out. (op 4-6 tchd 8-11)
Clock Opera(IRE) lasted longer for the switch to quicker ground and left the clear impression she would got forward again for this experience. (tchd 14-1)

2588 FOLLOW @RIPONRACES ON TWITTER H'CAP 1m 1f 170y
2:40 (2:40) (Class 5) (0-70,69) 4-Y-O+ **£2,911** (£866; £432; £216) **Stalls** Low

Form RPR
0-60 **1** **Searing Heat (USA)**[18] 2051 4-9-1 63 TomQueally 13 73
(Sir Henry Cecil) *chsd ldrs: effrt and hung rt over 2f out: wnt 2nd over 1f out: kpt on to ld nr fin* **10/1**
5020 **2** *nk* **Brockfield**[17] 2093 6-9-6 68 RobertWinston 3 77
(Mel Brittain) *led 1f: chsd ldrs: led over 2f out: edgd rt fnl f: hdd and no ex towards fin* **5/1**[1]
-410 **3** *2* **Rub Of The Relic (IRE)**[11] 2239 7-8-7 55 (v) AmyRyan 18 60
(Paul Midgley) *chsd ldrs: effrt over 2f out: kpt on same pce appr fnl f* **20/1**
6-32 **4** *3/4* **Free Art**[11] 2227 4-9-7 69 SilvestreDeSousa 12 72
(Geoffrey Harker) *mid-div: hdwy over 3f out: kpt on same pce appr fnl f* **8/1**[3]
022- **5** *hd* **Sinatramania**[241] 6536 5-8-9 57 FrederikTylicki 10 60
(Tracy Waggott) *in tch: effrt over 2f out: kpt on fnl f* **14/1**
0-00 **6** *3/4* **Cosmic Moon**[25] 1823 4-8-8 56 TonyHamilton 20 57+
(Richard Fahey) *swtchd rt s: in rr: hdwy over 2f out: kpt on fnl f* **40/1**
3600 **7** *1 1/2* **Transmit (IRE)**[49] 1269 5-8-8 56 DavidAllan 16 54
(Tim Easterby) *w ldrs: led after 1f: hdd after 2f: led over 3f out: hdd over 2f out: wknd fnl f* **50/1**
233- **8** *shd* **Pinotage**[151] 7931 4-9-2 64 GrahamLee 4 62
(Peter Niven) *in rr: hdwy over 2f out: kpt on fnl f* **8/1**[3]
1300 **9** *1* **Moral Issue**[13] 2173 4-9-5 67 (p) PatrickMathers 9 63
(Ian McInnes) *in rr: hdwy on outer over 2f out: nvr nr ldrs* **28/1**
4 **10** *1 1/2* **The Lodge Road (IRE)**[17] 2094 4-9-5 67 PhillipMakin 2 60+
(Martin Todhunter) *in rr: effrt 3f out: kpt on fnl f: nvr a threat* **7/1**[2]
0-63 **11** *2* **Norton Girl**[84] 809 4-8-4 55 oh10 DeclanCannon[(3)] 7 44
(Tracy Waggott) *chsd ldrs: wknd over 1f out* **100/1**
4-00 **12** *1/2* **Hail Bold Chief (USA)**[26] 1796 5-9-4 66 PJMcDonald 14 54
(Alan Swinbank) *in tch: effrt 3f out: wknd over 1f out* **10/1**
41-0 **13** *2 1/2* **Xpres Maite**[46] 1358 9-8-11 59 (b) RussKennemore 19 41
(Roy Bowring) *racd wd: led after 2f: hdd over 2f out: sn wknd* **16/1**
14 *1 1/2* **Tazaamun (IRE)**[335] 3529 4-8-10 58 DanielTudhope 11 37
(David O'Meara) *trckd ldrs: effrt over 2f out: sn ev ch: hung lft: wknd and eased ins fnl f* **7/1**[2]
1000 **15** *3 3/4* **Khandaq (USA)**[8] 2354 5-9-3 65 TomEaves 5 36
(Keith Dalgleish) *s.i.s: a in rr* **25/1**
301- **16** *3 1/4* **Valantino Oyster (IRE)**[218] 7061 5-9-0 67 (p) ShaneBKelly[(5)] 6 31
(Tracy Waggott) *a towards rr* **16/1**
0-00 **17** *2 1/4* **Last Destination (IRE)**[10] 2260 4-8-2 57 DanielleMooney[(7)] 15 17
(Nigel Tinkler) *t.k.h towards rr: bhd fnl 4f* **50/1**
4500 **18** *dist* **Yorksters Prince (IRE)**[22] 1913 5-9-2 64 (b) BarryMcHugh 1
(Tony Coyle) *in rr: lost pl and t.o after 3f: virtually p.u* **20/1**

2m 3.09s (-2.31) **Going Correction** -0.225s/f (Firm) **18** Ran SP% **124.7**
Speed ratings (Par 103): **100,99,98,97,97 96,95,95,94,93 91,91,89,88,85 82,80,**
Tote Swingers: 1&2 £15.70, 1&3 £40.80, 2&3 £36.00 CSF £54.85 CT £1014.59 TOTE £11.30: £3.00, £2.30, £5.00, £2.20; EX 101.40.
Owner K Abdulla **Bred** Juddmonte Farms Inc **Trained** Newmarket, Suffolk

FOCUS
A moderate handicap. Despite the large field few landed a serious blow and it paid to race up with the pace.
Searing Heat(USA) Official explanation: trainer said regarding apparent improvement in form that colt was better suited by going good to firm (good) in places.

Yorksters Prince(IRE) Official explanation: jockey said gelding moved poorly throughout.

2589 WEATHERBYS BANK H'CAP — 1m 1f 170y
3:10 (3:11) (Class 4) (0-80,77) 3-Y-O — **£4,528** (£1,347; £673; £336) **Stalls** Low

Form				RPR
01-2	**1**		**Eastern Destiny**[15] 2118 3-9-2 **72** .... TonyHamilton 5 (Richard Fahey) *trckd ldrs: wnt 2nd over 1f out: styd on fnl f: led cl home* **11/2**	82
0-03	**2**	½	**Indepub**[41] 1440 3-9-5 **75** .... (p) AmyRyan 7 (Kevin Ryan) *led: edgd rt after 1f: drvn clr over 2f out: edgd lft: hdd and no ex nr fin* **5/1**[3]	84
2-21	**3**	3	**Fortieth And Fifth (IRE)**[11] 2226 3-9-7 **77** .... HayleyTurner 8 (Michael Bell) *dwlt: swtchd rt sn after s: hld up in rr: effrt on ins whn nt clr run over 2f out: swtchd lft: styd on appr fnl f: tk 3rd last 100yds* **5/4**[1]	83+
0600	**4**	1 ½	**The Blue Banana (IRE)**[8] 2336 3-9-0 **70** .... JamesSullivan 2 (Edwin Tuer) *in rr: drvn 4f out: kpt on fnl 2f: nvr a threat* **16/1**	70
5130	**5**	4 ½	**Danube River**[12] 2201 3-9-3 **73** .... SilvestreDeSousa 6 (Mark Johnston) *racd wd: sn chsng ldr: wknd over 1f out* **9/2**[2]	63
54-0	**6**	7	**Dr Irv**[14] 2144 3-8-4 **60** .... AndrewMullen 1 (Kate Walton) *chsd ldrs: lost pl over 1f out* **18/1**	35
01-	**7**	14	**Swift Encounter (IRE)**[293] 4898 3-9-3 **73** .... GrahamLee 3 (Ann Duffield) *chsd ldrs: sn drvn along: lost pl after 3f: wknd wl over 1f out: eased* **20/1**	19
43-0	**8**	3	**Abdul Malik**[4] 2449 3-8-11 **67** .... PJMcDonald 4 (Kate Walton) *hld up in rr: effrt over 3f out: lost pl wl over 1f out: eased* **33/1**	

2m 3.06s (-2.34) **Going Correction** -0.225s/f (Firm) — **8** Ran SP% **113.5**
Speed ratings (Par 101): **100,99,97,96,92 86,75,73**
Tote Swingers: 1&2 £4.20, 1&3 £2.20, 2&3 £2.30 CSF £32.51 CT £54.44 TOTE £7.00: £2.00, £1.40, £1.10; EX 26.20.

Owner B H Farr **Bred** Worksop Manor Stud **Trained** Musley Bank, N Yorks

FOCUS
Not a bad 3-y-o handicap. It was run at an average pace, again suiting those racing prominently and the first pair came clear.

Fortieth And Fifth(IRE) Official explanation: jockey said gelding was denied a clear run.

Swift Encounter(IRE) Official explanation: trainer said gedling had a breathing problem.

2590 WILMOT-SMITH MEMORIAL H'CAP — 1m
3:40 (3:40) (Class 3) (0-95,92) 4-Y-O- **£6,931** (£2,074; £1,037; £519; £258) **Stalls** Low

Form				RPR
1-50	**1**		**Emilio Largo**[17] 2082 4-9-5 **90** .... TomQueally 2 (Sir Henry Cecil) *trckd ldrs: t.k.h: wnt 2nd 1f out: styd on to ld towards fin* **3/1**[1]	95+
0-00	**2**	nk	**Snow Bay**[25] 1821 6-8-6 **84** .... ShirleyTeasdale(7) 1 (David Nicholls) *led: qcknd 3f out: edgd lft over 1f out: hdd and no ex clsng stages* **9/2**[2]	88
6-66	**3**	½	**Extraterrestrial**[24] 1865 8-9-5 **90** .... FrederikTylicki 5 (Richard Fahey) *mid-div: effrt 3f out: styd on wl ins fnl f* **9/1**	93
6612	**4**	½	**Toto Skyllachy**[14] 2142 7-9-1 **86** .... DanielTudhope 7 (David O'Meara) *chsd ldrs: wnt 2nd 2f out: kpt on same pce ins fnl f* **15/2**	88
5351	**5**	1 ¾	**Dubai Dynamo**[9] 2311 7-9-7 **92** 6ex .... JamesSullivan 9 (Ruth Carr) *hld up: hdwy over 2f out: edgd rt and kpt on same pce ins fnl f* **3/1**[1]	90
03-6	**6**	2 ½	**Merchant Of Medici**[3] 2510 5-8-7 **78** .... SilvestreDeSousa 8 (Micky Hammond) *s.i.s: swtchd rt after s: in rr: drvn 4f out: outpcd over 2f out: styd on clsng stages* **11/2**[3]	70
-600	**7**	shd	**Askaud (IRE)**[24] 1854 4-9-7 **92** .... (p) PJMcDonald 6 (Scott Dixon) *chsd ldr: wknd fnl f* **20/1**	84
00-0	**8**	shd	**City Of The Kings (IRE)**[31] 1670 7-9-1 **86** .... GrahamLee 3 (Ollie Pears) *s.i.s: in rr: hdwy on ins over 4f out: one pce over 1f out* **22/1**	78

1m 38.08s (-3.32) **Going Correction** -0.225s/f (Firm) — **8** Ran SP% **114.4**
Speed ratings (Par 107): **107,106,106,105,103 101,101,101**
Tote Swingers: 1&2 £3.80, 1&3 £6.40, 2&3 £9.20 CSF £16.66 CT £107.03 TOTE £3.90: £1.50, £1.30, £2.60; EX 18.50.

Owner Malcolm C Denmark **Bred** Mrs M Chaworth-Musters **Trained** Newmarket, Suffolk

FOCUS
A fair handicap, run at a sound pace.

NOTEBOOK
Emilio Largo picked up strongly half a furlong out on the far rail and got on top near the finish, handing his leading trainer a double at a track he does very well at. He was much better than his previous outing on Polytrack 17 days earlier when a beaten favourite and had advertised his versatility regards ground with back-to-back wins last year. This came off a 4lb higher mark than the last of those and his finishing effort suggests there may be more to come from him in a handicap with greater value again now. (op 10-3 tchd 7-2 and 11-4)

Snow Bay arrived looking out of sorts, but likes this venue and was third off 10lb higher in this race last year. He made a bold bid from the front, but ultimately paid late on for taking a keen hold through the race. (op 13-2)

Extraterrestrial gave his all and posted a solid effort at a track that's probably not ideal for him. He could do with some respite from the handicapper, though. (op 8-1 tchd 10-1)

Toto Skyllachy came here in top form and he held every chance under a positive ride, rating a sound benchmark for the form. (op 7-1 tchd 8-1)

Dubai Dynamo, last year's winner, has been given a similar campaign to that of last term, but this time around he won on his previous outing and a penalty took him to a 7lb higher mark. He was compromised by racing keenly under restraint and having to come widest of all in the final 3f. (op 5-2 tchd 9-4)

2591 WEATHERBYS BLOODSTOCK INSURANCE H'CAP — 6f
4:10 (4:11) (Class 5) (0-75,75) 3-Y-O — **£2,911** (£866; £432; £216) **Stalls** High

Form				RPR
05-1	**1**		**Dutch Rose (IRE)**[4] 2441 3-9-0 **68** 6ex .... DanielTudhope 4 (David O'Meara) *wnt lft s: chsd ldrs: n.m.r appr fnl f: swtchd lft: r.o to ld post* **2/1**[1]	81+
341-	**2**	nse	**Springheel Jake**[202] 7337 3-9-6 **74** .... DavidNolan 2 (Ann Duffield) *chsd ldrs: chal over 1f out: led ins fnl f: edgd lft and hdd post* **13/2**[3]	84
3-56	**3**	2 ½	**Blue Shoes (IRE)**[22] 1912 3-8-9 **63** .... DavidAllan 3 (Tim Easterby) *chsd ldrs: led over 1f out: hdd ins fnl f: one pce* **14/1**	65
20-0	**4**	4	**Just Like Heaven (IRE)**[34] 1599 3-8-9 **63** .... DuranFentiman 8 (Tim Easterby) *led: hdd over 1f out: wknd last 100yds* **14/1**	52
633-	**5**	nk	**Endless Applause**[237] 6627 3-8-7 **61** oh4 .... AmyRyan 10 (Richard Whitaker) *chsd ldrs: one pce fnl 2f* **10/1**	49
00-0	**6**	1 ½	**Vite (IRE)**[58] 1155 3-8-10 **64** .... PhillipMakin 1 (David C Griffiths) *chsd ldrs on outside: drvn over 2f out: wknd over 1f out* **9/1**	47
33-0	**7**	2 ½	**Sir Windsorlot (IRE)**[41] 1441 3-8-7 **61** .... TomEaves 5 (John Quinn) *hmpd s: sn chsng ldrs: outpcd over 3f out: wknd over 2f out* **10/1**	36
0-05	**8**	6	**Niceonemyson**[10] 2262 3-8-11 **65** .... PaddyAspell 9 (Christopher Wilson) *w ldr: wknd over 1f out* **40/1**	21
2032	**9**	7	**Henry Bee**[24] 1862 3-9-2 **75** .... ShaneBKelly(5) 7 (Richard Fahey) *wnt rt s: sn drvn along and bhd* **5/1**[2]	
0-50	**10**	50	**Monnoyer**[29] 1721 3-9-5 **73** .... (v) TomQueally 6 (Scott Dixon) *t.k.h in rr: lost pl over 3f out: sn eased: virtually p.u: t.o* **17/2**	

1m 11.58s (-1.42) **Going Correction** -0.225s/f (Firm) — **10** Ran SP% **117.8**
Speed ratings (Par 99): **100,99,96,91,90 88,85,77,68,1**
Tote Swingers: 1&2 £3.70, 1&3 £9.40, 2&3 £13.10 CSF £15.22 CT £137.32 TOTE £3.70: £1.60, £1.40, £4.00; EX 15.10.

Owner Favourites Racing XXIV **Bred** Joseph Kennedy **Trained** Nawton, N Yorks

■ Stewards' Enquiry : David Nolan two-day ban; used whip above permitted level (12th-13th June)

FOCUS
The leaders set up this modest sprint handicap for those racing just off the early pace and there was a bobbing finish between the first pair, who came away from the rest.

Niceonemyson Official explanation: trainer said gelding was unsuited by the track.

Henry Bee Official explanation: jockey said gelding was never travelling.

Monnoyer Official explanation: jockey said gelding lost his action.

2592 SIS LIVE MAIDEN STKS — 1m
4:40 (4:42) (Class 5) 3-Y-O — **£2,587** (£770; £384; £192) **Stalls** Low

Form				RPR
2-6	**1**		**Cosmic Halo**[50] 1250 3-8-12 0 .... TonyHamilton 1 (Richard Fahey) *chsd ldrs: effrt over 2f out: styd on to ld towards fin* **7/2**[1]	63
53	**2**	nk	**Star Deal (IRE)**[11] 2226 3-9-3 0 .... PJMcDonald 11 (Alan Swinbank) *led: rdn over 2f out: no ex and hdd towards fin* **7/2**[1]	67
0-6	**3**	nk	**Running Reef (IRE)**[23] 1878 3-9-3 0 .... TomEaves 6 (Tracy Waggott) *t.k.h: trckd ldrs: nt clr run on inner over 1f out: swtchd lft: styd on wl towards fin* **9/1**	66
66	**4**	6	**Go On Gilbert**[14] 2143 3-9-3 0 .... PaddyAspell 2 (John Wainwright) *hld up in midfield: hdwy over 3f out: wknd fnl f* **15/2**	53
0	**5**	6	**Alpha Arion (IRE)**[14] 2143 3-9-3 0 .... DavidAllan 3 (Tim Easterby) *mid-div: hdwy to chse ldrs over 2f out: wknd over 1f out* **9/1**	39
0U5	**6**	¾	**Meljana (IRE)**[9] 2313 3-8-12 0 .... GarryWhillans(5) 9 (Alan Swinbank) *rr-div: sme hdwy over 3f out: wknd 2f out* **18/1**	37
0	**7**	¾	**Oasis Love (IRE)**[7] 2380 3-9-3 0 .... SilvestreDeSousa 7 (Mark Johnston) *chsd ldrs: drvn over 4f out: hmpd over 1f out: sn wknd* **6/1**[3]	35
	8	10	**Joyful Motive** 3-9-3 0 .... MickyFenton 5 (Tom Tate) *s.i.s: in rr: drvn and outpcd over 3f out: sn bhd* **5/1**[2]	12
	9	2 ¼	**Stars Legacy** 3-8-12 0 .... AndrewMullen 10 (George Moore) *dwlt: in rr and plunged 1st f: bhd fnl 3f* **25/1**	
0	**10**	11	**High Meadow Prince**[34] 1595 3-9-3 0 .... PatrickMathers 8 (Ron Barr) *mid-div: drvn over 3f out: lost pl over 2f out: sn bhd* **100/1**	

1m 40.9s (-0.50) **Going Correction** -0.225s/f (Firm) — **10** Ran SP% **117.3**
Speed ratings (Par 99): **93,92,92,86,80 79,78,68,66,55**
Tote Swingers: 1&2 £2.10, 1&3 £7.40, 2&3 £6.20 CSF £15.36 TOTE £3.30: £1.10, £1.90, £2.40; EX 11.40.

Owner The Cosmic Cases **Bred** The Cosmic Cases **Trained** Musley Bank, N Yorks

FOCUS
A weak 3yo maiden and yet another race on the card where it was a must to race handily.

2593 LADIES DAY 21ST JUNE BOOK NOW H'CAP — 1m 4f 10y
5:10 (5:11) (Class 5) (0-70,70) 4-Y-O+ — **£2,911** (£866; £432; £216) **Stalls** Low

Form				RPR
606-	**1**		**Bright Applause**[216] 7099 4-8-9 **58** .... FrederikTylicki 2 (Tracy Waggott) *led 1f: chsd ldrs: led 3f out: hld on wl* **11/1**	71
40-2	**2**	1 ¼	**Raleigh Quay (IRE)**[4] 2440 5-8-7 **61** .... ShaneBKelly(5) 8 (Micky Hammond) *chsd ldrs: effrt over 3f out: wnt 2nd over 1f out: kpt on: no real imp* **7/2**[1]	72
0-00	**3**	3 ½	**Coax**[26] 1796 4-8-11 **60** .... DanielTudhope 1 (Patrick Holmes) *in rr: effrt on ins over 3f out: styd on fnl f: tk 3rd nr fin* **14/1**	65
2-01	**4**	nk	**La Bacouetteuse (FR)**[25] 1822 7-9-3 **66** .... (p) DavidAllan 9 (Iain Jardine) *in rr: reminders after 3f: drvn 4f out: hdwy over 1f out: kpt on* **7/2**[1]	71+
60-6	**5**	1 ¾	**Operateur (IRE)**[36] 1562 4-8-9 **58** .... PhillipMakin 7 (Ben Haslam) *led after 1f: hdd over 7f out: led over 4f out: hdd 3f out: wknd fnl 75yds* **10/1**[3]	60
06-0	**6**	23	**Stanley Rigby**[34] 1598 6-8-12 **64** .... (b) LeeTopliss(3) 5 (Richard Fahey) *chsd ldrs: chal over 3f out: lost pl 2f out* **25/1**	29
-333	**7**	1 ¼	**Coral Sands (IRE)**[11] 2227 4-8-9 **58** .... PJMcDonald 4 (Alan Swinbank) *chsd ldrs: wknd 2f out* **7/2**[1]	21
1-50	**8**	17	**Betteras Bertie**[17] 2094 9-9-0 **63** .... (p) BarryMcHugh 10 (Tony Coyle) *dwlt: t.k.h: racd wd: hdwy to ld over 7f out: hung lft bnd and hdd over 4f out: lost pl over 2f out: sn bhd* **10/1**[3]	
-335	**9**	63	**Doctor Zhivago**[22] 1913 5-9-7 **70** .... (p) TomEaves 3 (Ian McInnes) *s.i.s: in rr: reminders after s: bhd 8f out: t.o whn virtually p.u3f out* **15/2**[2]	

2m 34.25s (-2.45) **Going Correction** -0.225s/f (Firm) — **9** Ran SP% **115.5**
Speed ratings (Par 103): **99,98,95,95,94 79,78,66,24**
Tote Swingers: 1&2 £9.10, 1&3 £16.70, 2&3 £13.20 CSF £49.42 CT £551.46 TOTE £14.30: £4.10, £1.10, £5.50; EX 67.20.

Owner Littlethorpe Park Racing **Bred** Old Mill Stud **Trained** Spennymoor, Co Durham

FOCUS
This was an ordinary handicap, run at a routine pace.

T/Jkpt: £14,065.30 to a £1 stake. Pool: £59,431.00 - 3.00 winning tickets. T/Plt: £92.00 to a £1 stake. Pool: £84,878.00 - 673.07 winning tickets. T/Qpdt: £7.50 to a £1 stake. Pool: £62,77.00 - 614.67 winning tickets. WG

AYR (L-H)

Wednesday, May 30

OFFICIAL GOING: Good to firm (firm in places; 9.7)

Wind: Breezy, across Weather: Overcast, cool

2594 BRITISH STALLION STUDS SUPPORTING BRITISH RACING E B F MAIDEN STKS 6f

2:10 (2:12) (Class 4) 2-Y-O £4,463 (£1,328; £663; £331) Stalls Low

Form RPR

4 1 **Party Royal**[20] 1997 2-9-3 0 MircoDemuro 8 78+
(Mark Johnston) *mde all: shkn up over 1f out: edgd lft and kpt on strly fnl f: readily* 5/4[1]

0 2 2 **Cappadocia (IRE)**[12] 2231 2-9-3 0 MatthewDavies 7 70
(Mick Channon) *prom: pushed along over 2f out: chsd wnr over 1f out: kpt on: no imp* 9/2[2]

3 1 ½ **Mazeppa** 2-9-3 0 TomEaves 2 65
(Keith Dalgleish) *hld up in tch: effrt and pushed along 2f out: kpt on fnl f: nvr able to chal* 80/1

322 4 ¾ **Out Of The Blocks**[10] 2309 2-9-3 0 PJMcDonald 6 63+
(Ruth Carr) *bhd: outpcd over 3f out: hdwy over 1f out: kpt on fnl f: nrst fin* 14/1

4645 5 ½ **Someone's Darling**[11] 2261 2-8-12 0 GrahamLee 1 57
(Jim Goldie) *w wnr: rdn over 2f out: no ex fnl f* 16/1

0 6 2 ½ **Nelsons Dockyard (USA)**[12] 2231 2-9-3 0 StevieDonohoe 4 54
(Paul Cole) *dwlt and blkd s: chsd ldng gp: rdn over 2f out: no imp fr over 1f out* 14/1

0 7 ¾ **Hitherto**[25] 1842 2-9-3 0 GrahamGibbons 3 52
(David Barron) *chsd ldrs: rdn over 2f out: wknd over 1f out* 25/1

8 4 **Bapak Besar (CAN)** 2-9-3 0 PhillipMakin 9 40+
(Kevin Ryan) *dwlt: sn in tch on outside: rdn over 2f out: sn no imp: btn fnl f* 13/2

9 3 ¼ **Makinson Lane (IRE)** 2-9-3 0 TonyHamilton 5 30+
(Richard Fahey) *blkd s: chsd ldng gp: rdn over 2f out: sn wknd* 5/1[3]

1m 11.74s (-0.66) **Going Correction** -0.175s/f (Firm) 9 Ran SP% 116.9
Speed ratings (Par 95): **97,94,92,91,90 87,86,81,76**
toteswingers: 1&2 £2.40, 1&3 £21.60, 2&3 £36.60. CSF £7.08 TOTE £2.40: £1.50, £2.30, £11.60; EX 8.90 Trifecta £189.20 Pool: £480.73 - 1.88 winning units..
Owner D & G Mercer 1 **Bred** Old Mill Stud & S Williams & J Parry **Trained** Middleham Moor, N Yorks

FOCUS
Course at full width. Probably a fair juvenile maiden and form worth taking a positive view of.

NOTEBOOK
Party Royal confirmed the promise of his previous effort to win this maiden with the minimum of fuss. The son of Royal Applause certainly wasn't best drawn but he showed plenty of early pace and travelled nicely before clearing away from his rivals. He was finishing to good effect at Chester and he put all of that experience to use with an accomplished display. He was value for a shade more the official winning margin and should be capable of better, be it over this distance or when upped another furlong. (op 2-1)
Cappadocia(IRE)'s yard's juvenile team has been in excellent form this season and he was another to build on only an average introduction. He had finished in midfield on his debut at Newbury and stepped up on that here. He was no match for the winner but could still be learning and shouldn't be long getting off the mark. (op 6-1)
Mazeppa shaped with promise back in third. (op 66-1)
Out Of The Blocks ◆ was the real eyecatcher. He has run well on all four starts so far and shouldn't be too harshly treated once switched to nurseries. (op 8-1)

2595 MONEY BACK IF SPAIN WIN AT BETVICTOR.COM H'CAP 6f

2:40 (2:41) (Class 6) (0-60,60) 3-Y-O £1,704 (£503; £251) Stalls Low

Form RPR

3000 1 **Sunny Side Up (IRE)**[42] 1441 3-8-11 57 LauraBarry(7) 4 68
(Richard Fahey) *t.k.h early: mde all: rdn 2f out: clr whn rdr dropped whip ins fnl f: styd on strly* 11/4[1]

-506 2 2 ¼ **Ambitious Icarus**[28] 1758 3-9-4 60 DeclanCannon(3) 6 64
(Richard Guest) *prom: effrt over 2f out: chsd wnr over 1f out: kpt on fnl f: no imp* 13/2[3]

040- 3 2 ¾ **Schmooze (IRE)**[255] 6186 3-9-3 56 FrederikTylicki 5 51
(Linda Perratt) *dwlt: bhd and outpcd: hdwy over 1f out: r.o fnl f: nrst fin* 9/1

044- 4 1 ½ **Selinda**[301] 4658 3-9-0 53 MatthewDavies 2 43
(Mick Channon) *cl up: rdn 2f out: outpcd fnl f* 10/1

00-4 5 1 ¼ **Madam Bonny (IRE)**[26] 1817 3-8-7 46 oh1 KellyHarrison 1 32
(Jim Goldie) *cl up: rdn over 2f out: no ex appr fnl f* 14/1

00-0 6 nk **Angel Kiss (IRE)**[26] 1817 3-8-8 47 oh1 ow1 TomEaves 3 32
(Colin Teague) *in tch: drvn over 2f out: outpcd appr fnl f* 66/1

0510 7 2 ¼ **Rock Canyon (IRE)**[12] 2229 3-9-7 60 PhillipMakin 7 38
(Linda Perratt) *cl up: rdn over 2f out: edgd lft and wknd over 1f out* 4/1[2]

000- 8 ½ **Captain Baldwin**[231] 6786 3-8-12 51 GrahamLee 8 27
(Jim Goldie) *dwlt: bhd and pushed along: no imp fr over 2f out* 10/1

-566 9 shd **After Timer (IRE)**[68] 1010 3-8-7 46 oh1 (v[1]) JamesSullivan 9 22
(Julie Camacho) *in tch tl rdn and wknd wl over 1f out* 25/1

6-43 10 2 ¾ **Brunswick Vale (IRE)**[15] 2139 3-8-12 51 (b) MickyFenton 10 18
(Paul Midgley) *dwlt: bhd on outside: struggling over 2f out: sn btn* 7/1

1m 12.2s (-0.20) **Going Correction** -0.175s/f (Firm) 10 Ran SP% 112.7
Speed ratings (Par 97): **94,91,87,85,83 83,80,79,79,75**
toteswingers: 1&2 £2.40, 1&3 £6.00, 2&3 £13.30. CSF £19.95 CT £138.43 TOTE £2.10: £1.10, £2.40, £3.70; EX 25.20 Trifecta £338.20 Part won. Pool: £457.14 - 0.94 winning units..
Owner Jim McGrath, Roger & Dianne Trevitt **Bred** Jim McGrath & Reg Griffin **Trained** Musley Bank, N Yorks

FOCUS
A desperately poor handicap, but it was a run at a strong early pace.
Brunswick Vale(IRE) Official explanation: jockey said filly hung right throughout

2596 BET MOBILE AT BETVICTOR.COM H'CAP 5f

3:10 (3:11) (Class 3) (0-90,88) 4-Y-O+ £6,663 (£1,982; £990; £495) Stalls Low

Form RPR

0-05 1 **Diman Waters (IRE)**[16] 2119 5-8-3 70 KellyHarrison 3 81
(Eric Alston) *hld up far side: hdwy 2f out: led wl ins fnl f: pushed out* 5/1[1]

05-1 2 ¾ **Bosun Breese**[10] 2314 7-8-7 74 6ex GrahamGibbons 7 82
(David Barron) *led and overall ldr far side: rdn over 1f out: hdd wl ins fnl f: r.o* 15/2

-000 3 ½ **The Nifty Fox**[12] 2230 8-8-2 69 oh3 (p) JamesSullivan 4 75
(Tim Easterby) *trckd far side ldrs: effrt and rdn over 1f out: kpt on ins fnl f* 16/1

1/0- 4 1 **Liberty Island (IRE)**[229] 6849 7-8-0 70 (p) DeclanCannon(3) 12 73
(Ian Semple) *led centre gp: rdn and edgd lft over 1f out: kpt on same pce ins fnl f* 20/1

1-20 5 hd **Style And Panache (IRE)**[44] 1417 4-8-7 74 MircoDemuro 14 76
(David Evans) *cl up on nr side of centre gp: rdn 2f out: r.o fnl f: nrst fin* 14/1

2100 6 hd **Haadeeth**[11] 2289 5-8-8 80 MatthewCosham(5) 2 81
(David Evans) *trckd far side ldrs: rdn over 2f out: kpt on same pce fnl f* 20/1

241- 7 1 ¼ **Le Toreador**[155] 7883 7-9-7 88 (p) PhillipMakin 13 85
(Kevin Ryan) *cl up centre: drvn over 2f out: nt qckn fnl f* 7/1[3]

00-0 8 hd **Medici Time**[14] 2177 7-9-3 84 (v) TomEaves 10 80
(Tim Easterby) *missed break: hld up centre gp: rdn over 2f out: kpt on fnl f: nrst fin* 15/2

5313 9 ½ **Crimson Knot (IRE)**[12] 2230 4-8-1 75 MatthewHopkins(7) 11 69
(Alan Berry) *hld up in tch centre gp: rdn 2f out: kpt on same pce fnl f* 20/1

2-60 10 shd **What About You (IRE)**[11] 2286 4-9-2 83 (v[1]) TonyHamilton 6 77
(Richard Fahey) *chsd far side ldr: rdn 2f out: no ex fnl f* 18/1

0003 11 1 ¼ **No Hubris (USA)**[11] 2289 5-9-0 81 (b) PJMcDonald 5 70
(Ruth Carr) *dwlt: bhd far side gp: rdn over 2f out: nvr able to chal* 10/1

0-23 12 ½ **Rothesay Chancer**[18] 2070 4-8-12 79 GrahamLee 8 66
(Jim Goldie) *in tch far side gp: rdn over 2f out: wknd fnl f* 6/1[2]

-101 13 ¾ **Go Go Green (IRE)**[18] 2092 6-8-10 77 FrederikTylicki 9 62
(Jim Goldie) *chsd centre ldrs: rdn over 2f out: wknd fnl f* 8/1

57.61s (-1.79) **Going Correction** -0.175s/f (Firm) 13 Ran SP% 119.3
Speed ratings (Par 107): **107,105,105,103,103 102,100,100,99,99 97,96,95**
toteswingers: 1&2 £9.70, 1&3 £10.40, 2&3 £16.60. CSF £40.11 CT £549.47 TOTE £5.70: £2.20, £3.40, £6.30; EX 51.50 Trifecta £346.00 Part won. Pool: £467.62 - 0.72 winning units..
Owner Buist, Long, Thompson **Bred** Mrs Chris Harrington **Trained** Longton, Lancs

FOCUS
A competitive sprint handicap.

NOTEBOOK
Diman Waters(IRE) travelled sweetly throughout before unleashing a smart turn of foot. He had plenty of supporters and those that got involved had very few anxious moments as he loomed alongside the front-running Bosun Breeze with a furlong to run. He only had to be shaken up to go clear and clearly appreciated the drop in trip, having been tried over 7f on his first two starts this season. This was only his second success from 23 attempts but he could well be a sprinter to follow for the rest of the year. His trainer has a good record with horses of this type and he'd make plenty of appeal if turned out under a penalty. (op 13-2 tchd 7-1)
Bosun Breese showed some blistering pace and was perhaps a shade unfortunate to find one too good. He was 6lb higher than when collecting at Ripon previously and is in great heart. He holds numerous entries and could prove hard to catch if lining up at Musselburgh, a track that suits pace horses well. (op 7-1 tchd 8-1)
The Nifty Fox continues to perform with credit in races such as this and he turned in yet another solid display. He has gone well in this contest previously but should be suited by a return to his favoured Catterick. (op 18-1 tchd 20-1 in a place)

2597 PLAY CASINO AT BETVICTOR.COM H'CAP 7f 50y

3:40 (3:44) (Class 4) (0-85,81) 4-Y-O+ £4,075 (£1,212; £606; £303) Stalls High

Form RPR

040- 1 **Ginger Jack**[222] 6989 5-9-0 78 PJMcDonald 10 85
(Geoffrey Harker) *trckd ldrs: rdn 2f out: styd on wl fnl f to ld cl home* 5/1[2]

-250 2 shd **Santefisio**[26] 1821 6-9-7 85 (p) PhillipMakin 8 92
(Keith Dalgleish) *t.k.h in midfield: gd hdwy on outside over 1f out: styd on to ld briefly towards fin: jst ct* 10/1

-025 3 hd **Celtic Sultan (IRE)**[26] 1821 8-9-6 84 MickyFenton 6 90
(Paul Midgley) *led: rdn and edgd rt over 1f out: hdd and no ex towards fin* 7/1[3]

4-00 4 shd **Orbit The Moon (IRE)**[11] 2285 4-9-2 80 (t) TomEaves 4 86
(Michael Dods) *trckd ldrs: effrt and chal over 1f out: kpt on fnl f: hld cl home* 40/1

0333 5 shd **Beckermet (IRE)**[11] 2284 10-9-5 83 JamesSullivan 1 89
(Ruth Carr) *hld up in midfield: hdwy on ins over 1f out: r.o wl fnl f: hld cl home* 11/1

-300 6 2 ¾ **Blues Jazz**[4] 2488 6-8-11 80 GarryWhillans(5) 5 79
(Ian Semple) *hld up towards rr: rdn over 2f out: kpt on fnl f: nvr able to chal* 5/1[2]

0-03 7 shd **Amazing Amoray (IRE)**[11] 2274 4-8-13 77 GrahamGibbons 11 76
(David Barron) *cl up: effrt and rdn 2f out: kpt on same pce fnl f* 4/1[1]

4010 8 2 ¼ **Bawaardi (IRE)**[4] 2489 6-8-11 80 MatthewCosham(5) 3 73
(David Evans) *s.i.s: bhd: rdn over 2f out: nvr able to chal* 16/1

0-04 9 nk **Polar Annie**[9] 2342 7-9-1 79 KellyHarrison 9 71
(Jim Goldie) *in tch: rdn and outpcd 2f out: n.d after* 33/1

-211 10 hd **No Poppy (IRE)**[16] 2119 4-8-9 78 AdamCarter(5) 12 69
(Tim Easterby) *s.i.s: hld up in midfield on outside: rdn 3f out: wknd over 1f out* 14/1

0-01 11 2 ½ **Northern Fling**[27] 1796 8-8-9 73 GrahamLee 2 58
(Jim Goldie) *hld up on ins: rdn over 2f out: sn wknd* 7/1[3]

00-6 12 16 **Silver Rime (FR)**[19] 2035 7-9-0 78 FrederikTylicki 7 21
(Linda Perratt) *s.i.s: bhd: struggling wl over 2f out: sn btn* 18/1

1m 28.07s (-5.33) **Going Correction** -0.625s/f (Hard) course record 12 Ran SP% 118.9
Speed ratings (Par 105): **105,104,104,104,104 101,101,98,98,98 95,76**
toteswingers: 1&2 £14.90, 1&3 £8.80, 2&3 £15.40. CSF £54.66 CT £355.20 TOTE £3.90: £1.20, £5.30, £3.10; EX 92.30 Trifecta £276.40 Pool: £694.76 - 1.86 winning units..
Owner C H McGhie **Bred** Darley **Trained** Thirkleby, N Yorks

FOCUS
A strong race and it served up a thrilling finish.
Bawaardi(IRE) Official explanation: trainer's rep said gelding was unsuited by the good to firm (firm in places) ground
Northern Fling Official explanation: trainer's rep had no explanation for the poor form shown

2598 BEST ODDS AT BETVICTOR.COM FILLIES' H'CAP 1m

4:10 (4:11) (Class 5) (0-70,70) 4-Y-O+ £2,264 (£673; £336; £168) Stalls Low

Form RPR

0-44 1 **Social Rhythm**[5] 2455 8-8-7 56 oh1 PJMcDonald 8 63
(Alistair Whillans) *hld up: hdwy on outside over 2f out: rdn to ld appr fnl f: kpt on wl* 7/2[1]

60-1 2 ½ **Kathlatino**[9] 2339 5-8-7 56 6ex KellyHarrison 1 62
(Micky Hammond) *chsd ldrs: drvn over 2f out: rallied fnl f: styd on wl to take 2nd cl home* 7/2[1]

461- 3 ½ **All For You (IRE)**[298] 4784 6-9-3 66 GrahamLee 2 70
(Jim Goldie) *hld up in tch: hdwy on ins 2f out: sn rdn: kpt on same pce ins fnl f* 7/2[1]

000- 4 hd **Emeralds Spirit (IRE)**[163] 7820 5-8-12 61 PhillipMakin 3 65
(John Weymes) *t.k.h: led: rdn over 2f out: hdd appr fnl f: kpt on same pce* 12/1[3]

0/1- **5** *nk* **Ykikamoocow**[371] 2399 6-9-7 **70** .... TonyHamilton 4 73
(Geoffrey Harker) *t.k.h: trckd ldrs: ev ch over 2f out to appr fnl f: sn no ex* **7/2**[1]

00-0 **6** *2 ½* **Sabratha (IRE)**[27] 1796 4-9-5 **68** .... FrederikTylicki 6 66
(Linda Perratt) *hld up in tch: stdy hdwy over 2f out: rdn and no ex over 1f out* **7/1**[2]

1m 40.05s (-3.75) **Going Correction** -0.625s/f (Hard) **6** Ran SP% **109.1**
Speed ratings (Par 100): **93,92,92,91,91 89**
toteswingers: 1&2 £2.80, 1&3 £2.40, 2&3 £2.10. CSF £14.77 CT £39.72 TOTE £4.00: £1.90, £1.10; EX 15.40 Trifecta £68.80 Pool: £631.31 - 6.79 winning units..

Owner Mrs L M Whillans **Bred** A And B Fairfields **Trained** Newmill-On-Slitrig, Borders

FOCUS
This looked a tightly knit handicap beforehand and so it proved with a couple of lengths covering the first five home.

2599 WATCH LIVE RACING AT BETVICTOR.COM H'CAP 1m 7f
4:40 (4:40) (Class 6) (0-60,60) 4-Y-0+ **£1,704** (£503; £251) **Stalls** Low

Form RPR

-000 **1** **Vittachi**[6] 2414 5-9-2 **60** .... GarryWhillans(5) 2 66
(Alistair Whillans) *trckd ldrs: smooth hdwy to ld over 2f out: sn rdn: kpt on wl fnl f* **11/4**[2]

600- **2** *nk* **Nay Secret**[28] 3487 4-8-6 **46** oh1 .... JamesSullivan 5 52
(Jim Goldie) *t.k.h: chsd clr ldr: hdwy and ev ch over 2f out: sn rdn: kpt on wl fnl f* **22/1**

23-0 **3** *2 ¼* **Bandanaman (IRE)**[53] 366 6-9-7 **60** ....(p) PJMcDonald 3 63
(Alan Swinbank) *missed break: hld up: rdn and hdwy over 2f out: styd on fnl f: nt rch first two* **9/2**[3]

/2-5 **4** *1 ¼* **Toshi (USA)**[27] 1794 10-8-9 **48** ow2 .... GrahamLee 8 49
(Jim Goldie) *stdd s: hld up: stdy hdwy 3f out: rdn and outpcd wl over 1f out: kpt on fnl f: no imp* **9/4**[1]

/05- **5** *½* **Wind Shuffle (GER)**[109] 3658 9-9-4 **57** .... TonyHamilton 4 57
(Richard Fahey) *t.k.h: hld up: hdwy on outside over 2f out: edgd lft and no ex over 1f out* **8/1**

000/ **6** *1 ¾* **Sydney Cove (IRE)**[7] 5331 6-8-8 **47** oh1 ow1 ....(p) GrahamGibbons 7 45
(Iain Jardine) *prom: drvn over 2f out: edgd lft and outpcd wl over 1f out* **9/1**

00-0 **7** *2 ½* **Rare Coincidence**[52] 1240 11-8-0 **46** oh1 .... MatthewHopkins(7) 1 41
(Alan Berry) *led and clr to 5f out: hdd over 2f out: wknd over 1f out* **16/1**

400- **8** *8* **Ballade De La Mer**[62] 6876 6-8-7 **46** oh1 ....(p) KellyHarrison 6 30
(George Foster) *hld up in tch: struggling 3f out: sn btn* **14/1**

3m 18.17s (-2.23) **Going Correction** -0.625s/f (Hard)
WFA 4 from 5yo+ 1lb **8** Ran SP% **113.6**
Speed ratings (Par 101): **80,79,78,77,77 76,75,71**
toteswingers: 1&2 £10.70, 1&3 £3.00, 2&3 £12.50. CSF £57.62 CT £263.73 TOTE £6.30: £2.70, £6.00, £1.10; EX 78.90 TRIFECTA Pool: £684.11 - 1.26 winning units..

Owner Sutherland Five **Bred** London Thoroughbred Services Ltd **Trained** Newmill-On-Slitrig, Borders

FOCUS
A modest staying handicap.

2600 HAPPY 70TH BIRTHDAY EILEEN WEDLOCK APPRENTICE H'CAP 1m 1f 20y
5:10 (5:11) (Class 6) (0-60,58) 4-Y-0+ **£1,704** (£503; £251) **Stalls** Low

Form RPR

3551 **1** **Harare**[26] 1831 11-8-12 **54** ....(v) GemmaTutty(5) 2 62
(Karen Tutty) *midfield: outpcd 3f out: rallied over 1f out: led ins fnl f: pushed out* **8/1**

05-3 **2** *nk* **Barton Bounty**[5] 2455 5-8-4 **46** .... FrancescaWolter(5) 7 53
(Peter Niven) *bhd: last and plenty to do ent st: gd hdwy over 1f out: styd on wl fnl f: jst hld* **3/1**[1]

45/5 **3** *hd* **Shaker Style (USA)**[18] 2091 6-9-1 **55** .... NedCurtis(3) 8 62
(Martin Todhunter) *hld up: rdn over 2f out: hdwy over 1f out: styd on wl fnl f: nrst fin* **4/1**[2]

-051 **4** *1 ¾* **Indian Giver**[19] 2033 4-9-7 **58** .... GeorgeDowning 6 61
(Hugh McWilliams) *prom: hdwy to ld appr fnl f: hdd ins fnl f: one pce* **9/2**[3]

0-00 **5** *1 ¼* **Glenluji**[5] 2455 7-9-6 **57** .... NoraLooby 3 57
(Jim Goldie) *trckd ldrs: hdwy to ld over 2f out: hdd appr fnl f: kpt on same pce* **14/1**

-004 **6** *1* **Deep Applause**[19] 2033 4-9-5 **56** ....(v[1]) DarylByrne 12 54
(Michael Dods) *hld up in tch: effrt on outside over 2f out: edgd lft over 1f out: sn no imp* **14/1**

0530 **7** *1* **Abernethy (IRE)**[12] 2225 4-8-4 **46** ow1 ....(t) RossSmith(5) 11 42
(Linda Perratt) *s.i.s: hld up: stdy hdwy over 2f out: sn pushed along: one pce over 1f out* **33/1**

00-0 **8** *17* **Viking Dancer**[57] 1178 5-8-5 **47** .... KevinLundie(5) 4
(Ruth Carr) *cl up on outside tl rdn and wknd over 2f out* **16/1**

400- **9** *1 ¾* **Sheedal (IRE)**[298] 4783 4-8-5 **45** .... DavidSimmonson(3) 10
(Ian Semple) *t.k.h: led to over 2f out: sn wknd* **66/1**

00-5 **10** *3 ¼* **Naafetha (IRE)**[53] 1222 4-9-4 **55** .... GeorgeChaloner 1
(George Foster) *in tch: drvn and outpcd over 3f out: struggling fnl 2f* **17/2**

10- **11** *23* **Diamond Sunrise (IRE)**[242] 6545 4-8-12 **52** .... ConorHarrison(3) 5
(Noel Wilson) *t.k.h: trckd ldr tl rdn and wknd qckly over 2f out* **14/1**

1m 55.47s (-2.03) **Going Correction** -0.625s/f (Hard) **11** Ran SP% **115.1**
Speed ratings (Par 101): **84,83,83,82,80 80,79,64,62,59 39**
toteswingers: 1&2 £4.20, 1&3 £6.10, 2&3 £3.50. CSF £31.45 CT £111.59 TOTE £7.70: £2.50, £2.30, £1.60; EX 29.50 TRIFECTA Pool: £66.72 - 5.39 winning units..

Owner Thoroughbred Homes Ltd **Bred** Limestone Stud **Trained** Osmotherley, N Yorks

FOCUS
A poor apprentice handicap.

Sheedal(IRE) Official explanation: jockey said filly hung right-handed

Diamond Sunrise(IRE) Official explanation: jockey said saddle slipped

T/Jkpt: Part won. £9,723.60 to a £1 stake. Pool: £25,000.00 - 0.50 winning tickets. T/Plt: £170.80 to a £1 stake. Pool: £72,104.71 - 308.10 winning tickets. T/Qpdt: £64.70 to a £1 stake. Pool: £4,719.75 - 53.90 winning tickets. RY

2138 BEVERLEY (R-H)
Wednesday, May 30

OFFICIAL GOING: Firm (good to firm in places; 8.7)
Wind: Light half behind Weather: Cloudy

2601 IT'S LUCKY IN LOVE NIGHT TONIGHT MAIDEN FILLIES' STKS 7f 100y
6:35 (6:37) (Class 5) 3-Y-0+ **£2,264** (£673; £336; £168) **Stalls** Low

Form RPR

6- **1** **Rugosa**[207] 7292 3-8-12 0 .... MichaelHills 5 71+
(Charles Hills) *wnt rt s: trckd ldr: hdwy to ld over 2f out: edgd rt over 1f out: sn rdn and styd on fnl f* **3/1**[2]

04- **2** *2 ¼* **Sigurwana (USA)**[168] 7757 3-8-12 0 .... JoeFanning 1 65+
(William Haggas) *led: pushed along and hdd over 2f out: swtchd lft and rdn wl over 1f out: kpt on same pce* **4/1**[3]

62-3 **3** *2 ¾* **Salacia (IRE)**[41] 1472 3-8-12 85 .... SilvestreDeSousa 9 58
(Mahmood Al Zarooni) *t.k.h and awkward early: chsd ldrs on outer: hdwy to chse ldng pair 3f out: rdn 2f out: sn no imp* **8/13**[1]

0600 **4** *3 ¾* **Merrjanah**[16] 2137 4-9-4 50 .... ShaneBKelly(5) 7 53
(John Wainwright) *in tch: rdn along wl over 2f out: nvr nr ldrs* **33/1**

6-44 **5** *2 ¾* **April Leyf (IRE)**[32] 1673 3-8-12 34 .... ShaneKelly 8 42
(Mark Brisbourne) *a towards rr* **80/1**

0305 **6** *nse* **Ellielusive (IRE)**[14] 2161 5-9-9 47 .... PaulMulrennan 3 46?
(Mark Brisbourne) *sltly hmpd s: sn in tch: rdn along 1/2-way: sn wknd* **66/1**

0 **7** *3* **Little Miss Mayhem (IRE)**[35] 1610 3-8-9 0 .... AdamBeschizza(3) 4 35
(Philip McBride) *hmpd s: a in rr* **20/1**

00-0 **8** *15* **Queen's Princess**[9] 2335 4-9-9 25 .... PaddyAspell 6
(John Wainwright) *a in rr* **150/1**

1m 32.12s (-1.68) **Going Correction** -0.275s/f (Firm)
WFA 3 from 4yo+ 11lb **8** Ran SP% **118.0**
Speed ratings (Par 100): **98,95,92,88,84 84,81,64**
toteswingers: 1&2 £1.60, 173 £1.40, 2&3 £1.40. CSF £15.14 TOTE £3.70: £1.10, £1.10, £1.02; EX 16.40 Trifecta £24.20 Pool: £1,652.82 - 50.38 winning units..

Owner K Abdulla **Bred** Millsec Limited **Trained** Lambourn, Berks

FOCUS
The inner rail around the bottom bend was moved in to provide fresh ground, adding 21 yards to all distances beyond 5f. This only concerned the front three, but a steady pace meant they couldn't show their true superiority over the others.

Ellielusive(IRE) Official explanation: jockey said mare spread a plate

2602 WEATHERBYS BLOODSTOCK INSURANCE CONDITIONS STKS 5f
7:05 (7:06) (Class 3) 3-Y-0+
£8,092 (£2,423; £1,211; £605; £302; £152) **Stalls** Low

Form RPR

3-46 **1** **Cheviot (USA)**[18] 2074 6-8-12 97 ....(p) RobertWinston 5 106
(Ian Semple) *trckd ldrs: hdwy 2f out: n.m.r and swtchd lft over 1f out: rdn and qcknd wl to ld last 100yds* **14/1**

1505 **2** *¾* **Addictive Dream (IRE)**[21] 1977 5-8-5 110 .... ShirleyTeasdale(7) 4 103
(David Nicholls) *t.k.h: led 1f: cl up: led over 1f out: shkn up ins fnl f: hdd and nt qckn last 100yds* **11/4**[3]

-203 **3** *½* **Doc Hay (USA)**[11] 2286 5-8-12 97 .... DanielTudhope 2 102
(David O'Meara) *in tch: hdwy 1/2-way: swtchd lft and rdn wl over 1f out: ev ch whn sltly hmpd ent fnl f: kpt on same pce* **5/2**[2]

0-U0 **4** *½* **Astrophysical Jet**[25] 1857 5-8-7 94 .... JoeFanning 1 95
(Ed McMahon) *cl up on inner: led after 1f: rdn along and hdd over 1f out: one pce fnl f* **2/1**[1]

0131 **5** *7* **Gorgeous Goblin (IRE)**[21] 1990 5-8-7 77 ....(t) KirstyMilczarek 6 70
(David C Griffiths) *wnt lft s: sn pushed along and a in rr* **33/1**

0-43 **6** *1 ¾* **Shoshoni Wind**[21] 1977 4-8-4 95 .... JulieBurke(3) 3 63
(Kevin Ryan) *chsd ldrs: rdn along over 2f out: wknd wl over 1f out* **6/1**

1m 0.62s (-2.88) **Going Correction** -0.35s/f (Firm) **6** Ran SP% **112.5**
Speed ratings (Par 107): **109,107,107,106,95 92**
toteswingers: 1&2 £6.60, 1&3 £7.80, 2&3 £3.30. CSF £52.32 TOTE £14.50: £4.90, £2.50; EX 59.80.

Owner Mrs J Penman, R Reid, W Robinson **Bred** Darley **Trained** Carluke, S Lanarks

■ Stewards' Enquiry : Robert Winston one-day ban: careless riding (Jun 13)

FOCUS
The time was only half a second outside the track record, but this looks muddling form. Few of these seemed likely to appreciate the rattling quick ground, and the lead was contested by the runner-up (well below his official mark of 110) and fourth.

NOTEBOOK
Cheviot(USA), who was well off the pace early, won despite having to wait for a run. He was below form last time, but had previously shaped well when fourth in the Abernant on his reappearance. (op 12-1 tchd 10-1)

Addictive Dream(IRE) was taken on for the lead, raced a bit keenly and did not look comfortable on the ground. It's no surprise he was below his best and he can be given another chance. (op 5-2 tchd 2-1)

Doc Hay(USA) ran okay, but should be capable of even better back on less quick ground. (tchd 3-1)

Astrophysical Jet was well backed despite having mainly struggled since last winning in 2010, and perhaps punters felt she was most likely to be suited by the conditions. She didn't run badly considering she was taken on for the lead, but it's looking doubtful she'll ever return to her best. (op 7-2)

Gorgeous Goblin(IRE), a winner on Fibresand off 71 last time, had a lot to find and the ground was also a worry. (op 25-1 tchd 40-1)

Shoshoni Wind presumably didn't act on the ground. (op 9-2)

2603 HILARY NEEDLER TROPHY (CONDITIONS STKS) (FILLIES) 5f
7:35 (7:37) (Class 2) 2-Y-0
£13,383 (£4,007; £2,003; £1,001; £500; £251) **Stalls** Low

Form RPR

1 **1** **Jadanna (IRE)**[37] 1556 2-8-12 0 .... PaulMulrennan 9 85+
(James Given) *prom: led over 2f out: rdn clr ent fnl f: drvn and kpt on towards fin* **7/1**[3]

350 **2** *1* **Blue Clumber**[5] 2450 2-8-12 0 .... JoeFanning 4 82
(Shaun Harris) *prom: rdn 2f out: chsd wnr over 1f out: kpt on u.p fnl f* **100/1**

14 **3** *nse* **Threes Grand**[12] 2247 2-8-12 0 .... KierenFallon 8 81
(Scott Dixon) *hmpd s and towards rr: gd hdwy on wd outside over 1f out: rdn and edgd rt ins fnl f: styd on wl* **12/1**

010 **4** 2 1/4 **Dream Vale (IRE)**[12] 2252 2-8-12 0 DuranFentiman 2 73
(Tim Easterby) *midfield: hdwy 2f out: rdn to chse ldrs over 1f out: swtchd rt and drvn ent fnl f: kpt on* **33/1**

3512 **5** 1 1/2 **Mayfield Girl (IRE)**[12] 2252 2-8-12 0 RobertWinston 13 67
(Mel Brittain) *wnt lft s and towards rr: hdwy on outer 2f out: rdn wl over 1f out: styd on: nearest fin* **15/2**

11 **6** hd **Judy In Disguise**[24] 1891 2-8-12 0 RyanWhile 1 67
(Bill Turner) *led 1f: pushed along whn hdd and sn unbalanced: rdn 1/2-way: n.d after* **15/8**[1]

134 **7** 1 **Woodland Mill (IRE)**[12] 2252 2-8-12 0 BarryMcHugh 10 63
(Richard Fahey) *towards rr: sme hdwy 2f out: sn rdn and no imp* **9/2**[2]

8 1 **Our Diane (IRE)** 2-8-9 0 DanielTudhope 12 56
(David O'Meara) *prom on wd outside: led after 1f: hdd and pushed along 1/2-way: sn rdn and wknd over 1f out* **7/1**[3]

51 **9** 2 **Lasilia (IRE)**[12] 2224 2-8-12 0 AmyRyan 11 52
(Kevin Ryan) *prom: led briefly 1/2-way: sn hdd and rdn: wknd appr fnl f* **12/1**

331 **10** shd **Sylvia Pankhurst (IRE)**[16] 2135 2-8-12 0 HayleyTurner 6 52
(David C Griffiths) *wnt bdly lft s: a towards rr* **25/1**

14 **11** 21 **Tharawal Lady (IRE)**[21] 1972 2-8-12 0 MichaelO'Connell 7
(John Quinn) *hmpd s: a in rr* **14/1**

1m 2.69s (-0.81) **Going Correction** -0.35s/f (Firm) **11** Ran SP% **119.6**
Speed ratings (Par 96): **92,90,90,86,84 84,82,80,77,77 43**
toteswingers: 1&2 £26.70, 1&3 £14.50, 2&3 £33.80. CSF £578.53 TOTE £8.50: £2.80, £12.20, £2.20; EX 902.30 TRIFECTA Not won..
Owner Danethorpe Racing Partnership **Bred** Rathasker Stud **Trained** Willoughton, Lincs

FOCUS
The bare form doesn't look anything special, but Jadanna is much better than the result indicates. She got caught up in a three-way battle for the lead (the other two finished eighth and ninth respectively), yet was able to skip clear of her rivals over a furlong out, looking much the best filly in the race, before understandably getting tired and running green. The form is rated around the third and fourth.

NOTEBOOK
Jadanna(IRE) ◆'s performance is all the more creditable considering she reportedly suffered a setback after her likeable debut win in soft ground at Pontefract, and there should be plenty more to come. She can have a big say in the Queen Mary. (op 6-1)
Blue Clumber left her previous form well behind, and that's despite still looking a bit green, although she's flattered to get so close to the winner. She was thought good enough to contest the Lily Agnes (presumably unsuited by testing ground), and this was the first time she's raced over 5f on a quick surface, so it would be dangerous to assume this was a fluke.
Threes Grand looks a bit flattered as she raced well off the hot pace, although she did cover a lot of ground, eventually challenging wide. (tchd 11-1 and 14-1 in a place)
Dream Vale(IRE) ran with credit but basically wasn't good enough.
Mayfield Girl(IRE), who was possibly flattered when second in a York Listed race on her previous start, never got involved from an unhelpful draw. Official explanation: jockey said filly was restless in stalls (op 8-1 tchd 13-2)
Judy In Disguise won her maiden on quick ground, but that was a weak race and the form of her second win, gained on easy ground, was much stronger. She didn't seem to appreciate these conditions, and it didn't help that her rider (aboard for first two wins) couldn't claim his usual 7lb allowance. Official explanation: trainer said filly was unsuited by the firm (good to firm in places) ground (op 5-2)
Woodland Mill(IRE) never looked comfortable and was presumably unsuited by the ground. She's ready for 6f. (op 5-1 tchd 4-1)
Our Diane(IRE) ◆, a 20,000GBP half-sister to a winner in the US, out of a champion juvenile in Brazil, showed blistering pace but it was a big ask to sustain such speed on her debut and she duly faded. There was a lot of money for her and she can be expected to do better. (op 8-1 tchd 10-1)
Lasilia(IRE), a recent Haydock maiden winner, was the sole representative for a trainer who had won this three times in the last six years, but she paid for going too fast and the ground was probably livelier than ideal. (op 9-1)
Tharawal Lady(IRE) Official explanation: jockey said filly hung left-handed

2604 KC LIGHTSTREAM H'CAP 1m 100y
8:05 (8:06) (Class 5) (0-70,70) 3-Y-O **£2,264** (£673; £336; £168) **Stalls** Low

Form RPR
33-1 **1** **Sabhan (IRE)**[11] 2283 3-9-4 **67** DanielTudhope 3 79+
(Geoffrey Harker) *t.k.h early: in tch: hdwy 3f out: swtchd lft to outer and rdn wl over 1f out: drvn to chse ldr ins fnl f: styd on gamely to ld on line* **15/8**[1]

-210 **2** shd **Captivity**[42] 1440 3-9-6 **69** JoeFanning 8 77
(Mark Johnston) *led: rdn clr 2f out: drvn ins fnl f: hdd and nt qckn on line* **17/2**

0-40 **3** 4 **Madame St Clair (IRE)**[25] 1853 3-9-0 **63** (b) ShaneKelly 4 62
(Brian Meehan) *trckd ldng pair: chsd ldr 1/2-way: rdn wl over 1f out: kpt on same pce* **14/1**

50-0 **4** 2 3/4 **Mokbil (IRE)**[30] 1703 3-9-7 **70** TadhgO'Shea 6 63
(Roger Varian) *trckd ldrs: hdwy to chse ldng pair 1/2-way: rdn over 2f out: sn one pce* **14/1**

0-43 **5** 6 **Double Cee**[9] 2336 3-8-4 **58** ShaneBKelly(5) 9 37+
(Richard Fahey) *towards rr: pushed along and bhd over 3f out: hdwy over 2f out: sn rdn and nvr nr ldrs* **4/1**[3]

000- **6** 1 1/4 **Firefly**[242] 6532 3-9-0 **63** DuranFentiman 1 40
(John Weymes) *a towards rr* **33/1**

004 **7** 1/2 **Haywain**[15] 2143 3-9-6 **69** AmyRyan 2 44
(Kevin Ryan) *prom: unbalanced and lost pl bnd at 1/2-way: rdn over 3f out and sn wknd* **7/2**[2]

4-63 **8** nk **Sygnature**[22] 1959 3-9-3 **66** RobertWinston 7 41
(Alan Swinbank) *a in rr* **11/1**

024- **9** 9 **Hunting Gonk**[219] 7066 3-9-7 **70** PaulMulrennan 5 24
(James Given) *a towards rr* **16/1**

1m 45.59s (-2.01) **Going Correction** -0.275s/f (Firm) **9** Ran SP% **118.0**
Speed ratings (Par 99): **99,98,94,92,86 84,84,84,75**
toteswingers: 1&2 £2.70, 1&3 £6.60, 2&3 £12.10. CSF £19.62 CT £178.42 TOTE £2.30: £1.10, £1.50, £4.40; EX 19.60 Trifecta £365.30 Pool: £612.22 - 1.24 winning units..
Owner Sheikh Khaled Duaij Al Sabah **Bred** M Morrissey **Trained** Thirkleby, N Yorks

FOCUS
A modest handicap run at what seemed a solid, even enough gallop thanks to Captivity.
Hunting Gonk Official explanation: trainer said colt was unsuited by the firm (good to firm in places) ground

2605 BEVERLEY MIDDLE DISTANCE SERIES H'CAP 1m 4f 16y
8:35 (8:35) (Class 5) (0-70,70) 3-Y-O **£2,587** (£770; £384; £192) **Stalls** Low

Form RPR
1513 **1** **Quiet Appeal (IRE)**[21] 1992 3-8-10 **59** SilvestreDeSousa 2 66
(Mark Johnston) *chsd clr ldr: tk clsr order 4f out: led over 2f out and sn rdn clr: drvn ins fnl f: jst hld on* **12/1**

-631 **2** shd **Lady Kashaan (IRE)**[9] 2340 3-8-7 **56** 6ex AndrewElliott 10 62
(Alan Swinbank) *in tch: hdwy wl over 3f out: rdn to chse ldrs 2f out: sn sltly outpcd: drvn and styd on strly ent fnl f: jst failed* **11/2**[3]

-455 **3** 1 1/4 **Harry Buckle**[8] 2372 3-9-4 **67** RichardMullen 5 71
(Philip McBride) *trckd ldrs: hdwy and cl up 3f out: rdn wl over 1f out: edgd rt and drvn appr fnl f: kpt on* **10/3**[1]

0-30 **4** 1/2 **Lost Highway (IRE)**[23] 1915 3-8-9 **58** JoeFanning 1 62
(Mark Johnston) *trckd ldrs: hdwy over 2f out: rdn and n.m.r over 1f out and ins fnl f: kpt on* **16/1**

2-00 **5** 3 **Cappielow Park**[12] 2246 3-9-7 **70** KierenFallon 6 69
(William Jarvis) *dwlt and in rr: hdwy over 3f out: in tch whn nt clr run on inner wl over 1f out: sn rdn and no imp* **6/1**

50-5 **6** 1/2 **Byron Blue (IRE)**[25] 1853 3-9-4 **67** HayleyTurner 9 65
(Jamie Osborne) *s.i.s and bhd: hdwy 3f out: rdn over 2f out: kpt on: nrst fin* **5/1**[2]

0-64 **7** 5 **Spirit Na Heireann (IRE)**[15] 2144 3-8-8 **62** ShaneBKelly(5) 3 52
(Richard Fahey) *in tch: effrt on inner 3f out: sn rdn and wknd 2f out* **8/1**

-452 **8** 3 3/4 **Minnie Diva (IRE)**[23] 1915 3-9-0 **63** PaulMulrennan 7 47
(Kevin Ryan) *led and sn clr at str pce: rdn along over 3f out: hdd over 2f out and sn wknd* **11/2**[3]

0-05 **9** 16 **Twin Ivan (IRE)**[16] 2118 3-8-3 **57** (p) DeanHeslop(5) 4
(Marjorie Fife) *a towards rr* **28/1**

2m 37.06s (-2.74) **Going Correction** -0.275s/f (Firm) **9** Ran SP% **112.9**
Speed ratings (Par 99): **98,97,97,96,94 94,91,88,77**
toteswingers: 1&2 £3.90, 1&3 £6.00, 2&3 £7.70. CSF £74.74 CT £271.25 TOTE £8.60: £2.50, £1.90, £1.60; EX 54.50 Trifecta £91.70 Pool: £393.22 - 3.17 winning units..
Owner T T Bloodstocks Bred Corduff Stud Ltd & T J Rooney **Trained** Middleham Moor, N Yorks
■ Stewards' Enquiry : Richard Mullen two-day ban: used whip above permitted level (Jun 13-14)

FOCUS
The early pace looked strong, thanks to Minnie Diva, and then seemed to slow before the straight, but there was no particular run-style that appeared favoured.
Cappielow Park ◆ Official explanation: jockey said colt hung right-handed
Minnie Diva(IRE) Official explanation: trainer's rep said filly was unsuited by the firm (good to firm places) ground

2606 COLLECT YOUR KEY AND PADLOCK H'CAP 1m 1f 207y
9:05 (9:07) (Class 4) (0-85,84) 4-Y-O+ **£4,075** (£1,212; £606; £303) **Stalls** Low

Form RPR
-000 **1** **Landaman (IRE)**[19] 2035 4-8-12 **75** SilvestreDeSousa 3 95+
(Mark Johnston) *mde all: rdn and qcknd clr 2f out: easily* **6/1**[3]

0115 **2** 8 **John Louis**[12] 2248 4-9-0 **77** RichardMullen 2 79
(Philip McBride) *a.p: effrt to chse wnr over 3f out: rdn over 2f out: drvn over 1f out: kpt on same pce* **3/1**[1]

0-21 **3** hd **Carragold**[15] 2142 6-9-0 **77** RobertWinston 6 79+
(Mel Brittain) *dwlt and in rr: gd hdwy on inner over 2f out: rdn to chse ldrs over 1f out: kpt on* **4/1**[2]

-010 **4** 3/4 **Tapis Libre**[27] 1797 4-8-8 **71** PaulMulrennan 10 71
(Michael Easterby) *trckd ldrs: effrt over 3f out: rdn over 2f out: kpt on same pce* **33/1**

160- **5** 2 3/4 **Red Inca**[32] 6409 4-8-9 **72** BarryMcHugh 11 67
(Brian Ellison) *dwlt and bhd: hdwy on outer over 2f out: rdn wl over 1f out: kpt on fnl f: nrst fin* **14/1**

10-0 **6** 1 **Tartan Gigha (IRE)**[14] 2180 7-9-1 **78** JoeFanning 9 71
(Geoffrey Harker) *hld up: hdwy over 4f out: rdn over 2f out: kpt on fnl f: n.d* **20/1**

2-63 **7** nk **Muffin McLeay (IRE)**[12] 2257 4-9-6 **83** LeeNewman 7 75
(David Barron) *midfield: effrt over 3f out: rdn over 2f out: sn no imp* **4/1**[2]

0-60 **8** 1/2 **Unknown Rebel (IRE)**[10] 2312 4-9-0 **80** (p) JulieBurke(3) 1 71
(Kevin Ryan) *prom: chsd wnr over 3f out: rdn wl over 2f out: wknd over 1f out* **10/1**

1350 **9** 10 **West End Lad**[10] 2312 9-9-7 **84** (b) RussKennemore 5 55
(Roy Bowring) *chsd ldrs on inner: rdn along over 3f out: sn wknd* **25/1**

1010 **10** 14 **Flying Applause**[9] 2328 7-9-2 **79** (b) AndreaAtzeni 8 22
(Roy Bowring) *sn in tch on outer: chsd ldrs 1/2-way: rdn along over 3f out: sn wknd* **33/1**

2m 2.91s (-4.09) **Going Correction** -0.275s/f (Firm) **10** Ran SP% **109.5**
Speed ratings (Par 105): **105,98,98,97,95 94,94,94,86,75**
toteswingers: 1&2 £5.50, 1&3 £3.90, 2&3 £2.80. CSF £20.76 CT £68.12 TOTE £8.40: £2.70, £1.10, £2.10; EX 27.30 Trifecta £76.80 Pool: £656.73 - 6.32 winning units..
Owner Sheikh Hamdan Bin Mohammed Al Maktoum **Bred** Darley **Trained** Middleham Moor, N Yorks

FOCUS
The winner was able to set a modest pace in an uncontested and raced with his ears pricked for much of the way, saving plenty, before drawing clear.
T/Plt: £154.10 to a £1 stake. Pool: £66,055.70 - 312.79 winning tickets. T/Qpdt: £44.40 to a £1 stake. Pool: £5,851.00 - 97.50 winning tickets. JR

1330 FOLKESTONE (R-H)
Wednesday, May 30

OFFICIAL GOING: Straight course - good to firm; round course - firm (good to firm in places)
Wind: Almost nil Weather: Sunny spells

2607 LEAS CLIFF HALL, PREMIER ENTERTAINMENT VENUE H'CAP 7f (S)
5:45 (5:45) (Class 6) (0-60,60) 4-Y-O+ **£1,704** (£503; £251) **Stalls** High

Form RPR
/00- **1** **Takitwo**[504] 129 9-8-13 **52** DaneO'Neill 10 65
(Jonathan Portman) *t.k.h: chsd ldrs: led 2f out: drvn clr: comf* **6/1**[2]

1031 **2** 7 **Ereka (IRE)**[14] 2170 4-8-9 **48** LukeMorris 9 42
(John Best) *in tch: effrt and hrd rdn 2f out: wnt 2nd over 1f out: no ch w wnr* **11/8**[1]

4406 **3** 1 1/2 **Toms River Tess (IRE)**[8] 2365 4-8-4 **46** oh1 SimonPearce(3) 2 36
(Zoe Davison) *led tl 2f out: one pce* **6/1**[2]

000- **4** 3/4 **Trust Me Boy**[200] 7387 4-8-7 **46** oh1 JohnFahy 1 34
(John E Long) *chsd ldr 3f: rdn and btn over 2f out* **25/1**

5310 **5** 1 **Lisselton Cross**[97] 665 4-9-0 **53** (v) LiamKeniry 6 38
(Martin Bosley) *stdd s: t.k.h in rr: rdn over 2f out: nvr able to chal* **8/1**[3]

-000 **6** nk **Crazy Chris**[69] 1002 7-8-9 **53** (b[1]) DarrenEgan(5) 4 38
(Milton Bradley) *a in last pair: rdn over 2f out: n.d* **6/1**[2]

055 **7** 3 3/4 **Simple Rhythm**[14] 2169 6-8-8 **47** (p) BrettDoyle 3 21
(John Ryan) *plld hrd: cl up: jnd ldr over 2f out: wknd wl over 1f out* **11/1**

1m 27.0s (-0.30) **Going Correction** -0.25s/f (Firm) **7** Ran SP% **108.3**
Speed ratings (Par 101): **91,83,81,80,79 78,74**
toteswingers: 1&2 £2.30, 1&3 £6.00, 2&3 £3.10. CSF £13.12 CT £43.70 TOTE £9.00: £3.80, £1.30; EX 10.30.

Owner P D Cundell **Bred** Roden House Stud **Trained** Compton, Berks
FOCUS
A moderate handicap was weakened when the four top weights were all withdrawn.

2608 FREEBETS.CO.UK H'CAP 7f (S)
6:15 (6:15) (Class 4) (0-85,85) 4-Y-0+ £4,528 (£1,347; £673; £336) Stalls High

Form RPR
3200 1 **Escape To Glory (USA)**[14] 2177 4-9-5 83 WilliamBuick 9 94
(Mikael Magnusson) *hld up towards rr: hdwy 3f out: swtchd rt and led wl over 1f out: drvn out* 7/4[1]
10-4 2 1 1/2 **Mingun Bell (USA)**[22] 1951 5-9-0 78 LiamKeniry 8 84
(Ed de Giles) *in tch: rdn 3f out: chsd wnr over 1f out: kpt on* 4/1[2]
0511 3 1/2 **Legal Legacy**[7] 2398 6-9-0 78 6ex AmirQuinn 4 83
(Richard Rowe) *stdd s and swtchd lft: hld up in rr: rdn and hdwy over 1f out: styd on* 16/1
150- 4 1 3/4 **Golden Delicious**[221] 7031 4-9-7 85 DarryllHolland 3 85
(Hughie Morrison) *prom: led over 3f out tl wl over 1f out: one pce* 5/1[3]
-526 5 1 1/4 **Kakapuka**[18] 2083 5-9-3 81 LukeMorris 6 78
(Anabel K Murphy) *towards rr: rdn over 2f out: nvr able to chal* 18/1
5-10 6 1 **Kingswinford (IRE)**[19] 2029 6-9-2 80 CathyGannon 7 74
(David Evans) *led tl over 3f out: rdn and btn 2f out* 10/1
23-5 7 3 1/2 **My Learned Friend (IRE)**[9] 2354 8-8-4 75 JoeyHaynes(7) 2 59
(Andrew Balding) *chsd ldr 3f: wknd 2f out* 25/1
-000 8 8 **Pat's Legacy (USA)**[51] 1249 6-9-4 82 TonyCulhane 5 45
(Jo Hughes) *mid-div: rdn over 2f out: n.d after* 12/1
1-00 9 15 **The Guru Of Gloom (IRE)**[18] 2083 4-9-2 80 RichardHughes 1
(William Muir) *in tch in centre tl wknd over 2f out: eased whn no ch 1f out* 10/1

1m 24.55s (-2.75) **Going Correction** -0.25s/f (Firm) 9 Ran SP% **113.9**
Speed ratings (Par 105): **105,103,102,100,99 98,94,85,67**
toteswingers: 1&2 £2.90, 1&3 £3.70, 2&3 £4.00. CSF £8.35 CT £80.69 TOTE £3.00: £1.30, £1.70, £4.10; EX 10.10.
Owner Eastwind Racing Ltd And Martha Trussell **Bred** Castleton Lyons **Trained** Upper Lambourn, Berks
FOCUS
A decent, competitive handicap run 2.45secs faster than the opening contest.
The Guru Of Gloom(IRE) Official explanation: jockey said gelding slipped galf-way and lost its action

2609 GREENMAN SOLAR LLAMA MAIDEN AUCTION STKS 6f
6:45 (6:45) (Class 6) 2-Y-0 £2,045 (£603; £302) Stalls High

Form RPR
1 **Maxentius (IRE)** 2-8-12 0 WilliamBuick 3 77+
(Peter Chapple-Hyam) *chsd ldr: led wl over 1f out: qcknd clr fnl f: easily* 10/11[1]
6 2 4 **Alexandrakollontai (IRE)**[14] 2164 2-8-8 0 LiamKeniry 6 58
(J S Moore) *in tch: rdn and hung rt 2f out: styd on fnl f: tk 2nd nr fin: nt trble wnr* 25/1
3 1 1/2 **Red Adair (IRE)** 2-9-2 0 RichardHughes 4 61+
(Richard Hannon) *in rr: rdn and hdwy towards centre over 2f out: chal wl over 1f out: no ex ins fnl f* 3/1[2]
0 4 nk **Bix (IRE)**[12] 2231 2-9-2 0 PaulHanagan 1 60+
(Brian Meehan) *chsd ldrs: outpcd fnl 2f* 15/2[3]
4 dht **Warrant Officer** 2-8-13 0 MartinHarley 5 57+
(Mick Channon) *hld up in 5th: rdn over 2f out: nvr able to chal* 11/1
52 6 1 **Otto The First**[29] 1738 2-9-0 0 LukeMorris 2 55
(John Best) *led tl wl over 1f out: sn wknd* 17/2

1m 12.73s (0.03) **Going Correction** -0.25s/f (Firm) 6 Ran SP% **111.9**
Speed ratings (Par 91): **89,83,81,81,81 79**
toteswingers: 1&2 £6.90, 1&3 £1.20, 2&3 £11.30. CSF £25.71 TOTE £2.30: £2.00, £7.40; EX 30.60.
Owner Tony Elliott **Bred** Barronstown Stud **Trained** Newmarket, Suffolk
FOCUS
A small field of juveniles for this maiden auction and those that had run had shown distinctly moderate form, so it was no surprise to see a newcomer take this. The time was faster than the following 3-y-o handicap over the trip and the winner was impressive.
NOTEBOOK
Maxentius(IRE) ◆, who was retained relatively cheaply as a yearling, is very much bred to be a middle-distance performer on his dam's side but clearly has inherited the precocity of his sire. Connections clearly knew what they had, as he was heavily backed into odds-on and, always travelling smoothly, found plenty when asked, despite showing signs of greenness. He deserves extra credit as he spread a plate beforehand and ran on three shoes. Presumably connections will be looking at better things for him after this, although he has no fancy entries as yet. (op 13-8 tchd 7-4)
Alexandrakollontai(IRE), named after the first female in Europe to become a government minister and later an ambassador, built on her debut effort and was staying on nicely at the finish. She can win a similar race, maybe against fillies. (tchd 22-1)
Red Adair(IRE), who was easy to back on this debut, was being niggled at before halfway but, once he saw daylight, ran on to challenge the winner before tiring. He should benefit from the experience and will face easier tasks in maidens. (op 9-4)
Warrant Officer, from the family of Gimcrack winner Bannister, ran like another who will benefit from the experience. (op 6-1 tchd 11-2)
Bix(IRE) looked in good shape beforehand but rather missed the break and then ran a bit free before fading. He looks to need a bit more time. (op 6-1 tchd 11-2)

2610 C-ELECT ASSOCIATES BUILDING MAINTENANCE SERVICES H'CAP 6f
7:15 (7:16) (Class 6) (0-65,65) 3-Y-0 £2,045 (£603; £302) Stalls High

Form RPR
4465 1 **Maria Montez**[9] 2351 3-9-1 56 MartinLane 7 61
(J W Hills) *trckd ldrs: nt clr run 2f out tl 1f out: fnd gap and qcknd through to ld ins fnl f: rdn out* 16/1
0404 2 1 1/2 **Seventeen Seventy**[7] 2388 3-9-0 55 LiamKeniry 4 55
(Alan Coogan) *t.k.h in rr: rdn and hdwy over 1f out: r.o ins fnl f* 8/1
-461 3 hd **Esprit Danseur**[8] 2367 3-9-10 65 6ex PatCosgrave 8 64
(Jim Boyle) *led: rdn and hdd ins fnl f: no ex* 11/8[1]
413- 4 3/4 **Uncle Timmy**[201] 7364 3-9-7 62 (t) CathyGannon 5 59
(David Evans) *chsd ldrs: rdn over 2f out: one pce fnl f* 9/2[3]
6-05 5 1/2 **Cambridge Duchess**[131] 219 3-9-1 56 WilliamCarson 3 51
(Stuart Williams) *restrained in rr: stmbld after 100yds: sn swtchd to stands' rail: rdn over 2f out: gng on at fin* 12/1
60-0 6 hd **Willow Beauty**[119] 376 3-8-9 51 PaulHanagan 6 45
(J R Jenkins) *pressed ldr tl no ex ent fnl f* 16/1
0-13 7 4 1/2 **Oneniteinheaven (IRE)**[20] 2010 3-8-10 58 LewisWalsh(7) 2 38
(Jane Chapple-Hyam) *last tl swtchd to centre and hdwy 3f out: wknd over 1f out* 4/1[2]

1m 12.98s (0.28) **Going Correction** -0.25s/f (Firm) 7 Ran SP% **110.9**
Speed ratings (Par 97): **88,86,85,84,84 83,77**
toteswingers: 1&2 £9.10, 1&3 £5.60, 2&3 £2.80. CSF £124.82 CT £282.29 TOTE £24.70: £9.20, £5.90; EX 119.10.
Owner John M Cole **Bred** D R Tucker **Trained** Upper Lambourn, Berks
FOCUS
A moderate sprint handicap where again it paid to race close to the stands' rail. The time was a quarter of a second slower than the preceding 2-y-o contest.

2611 MIRROR PUNTERS CLUB MAIDEN STKS 6f
7:45 (7:45) (Class 5) 3-Y-0+ £2,385 (£704; £352) Stalls High

Form RPR
00 1 **Rum Punch**[18] 2065 3-8-12 JohnFahy 9 62
(Eve Johnson Houghton) *in tch: rdn over 2f out: styd on to ld jst ins fnl f: drvn clr* 11/2[2]
0-20 2 2 3/4 **Miss Noble**[18] 2065 3-8-12 69 WilliamCarson 8 54
(Stuart Williams) *chsd ldr: rdn over 2f out: nt qckn fnl f* 10/1[3]
006- 3 1/2 **Abadejo**[175] 7652 4-9-12 55 PaulHanagan 7 59
(J R Jenkins) *racd freely: led tl jst ins fnl f: no ex* 20/1
32-4 4 1/2 **Backtrade (IRE)**[29] 1723 3-9-3 75 DavidProbert 5 57
(Andrew Balding) *chsd ldrs: rdn and sltly outpcd 2f out: tried to rally and nt clr run fr over 1f out* 4/9[1]
60 5 1 **Temple Road (IRE)**[24] 1889 4-9-12 DaneO'Neill 4 54
(Milton Bradley) *bhd: rdn and hdwy in centre 2f out: wknd fnl f* 12/1
04 6 4 1/2 **Petrarchan**[24] 1889 4-9-12 (t) LukeMorris 1 40
(Milton Bradley) *a in last pair: struggling fnl 2f* 16/1

1m 12.41s (-0.29) **Going Correction** -0.25s/f (Firm)
WFA 3 from 4yo 9lb 6 Ran SP% **112.1**
Speed ratings (Par 103): **91,87,86,86,84 78**
toteswingers: 1&2 £2.60, 1&3 £5.30, 2&3 £4.20. CSF £53.86 TOTE £6.70: £2.20, £2.10; EX 34.80.
Owner Mr & Mrs C J Hue Williams **Bred** Mrs C J Hue Williams **Trained** Blewbury, Oxon
FOCUS
An ordinary sprint maiden for older horses.

2612 FOLKESTONE SPORTS CENTRE, RUBY ANNIVERSARY MAIDEN STKS 1m 4f
8:15 (8:15) (Class 5) 3-Y-0 £2,264 (£673; £336; £168) Stalls High

Form RPR
6 1 **Glittering Gold**[13] 2197 3-9-3 RyanMoore 6 88+
(Sir Michael Stoute) *trckd ldr: led wl over 1f out: rdn out* 6/5[1]
5 2 2 **Rule Book (IRE)**[39] 1511 3-9-3 RichardHughes 5 85
(Richard Hannon) *hld up in 5th: swtchd outside and hdwy into 3rd 4f out: effrt and awkward hd carriage in st: kpt on to take 2nd 75yds out* 4/1[3]
-235 3 1 **Safarjal (IRE)**[21] 1973 3-8-12 83 PaulHanagan 3 78
(Charles Hills) *racd freely and restained in front: led tl wl over 1f out: nt qckn ins fnl f* 7/4[2]
6- 4 15 **Queen's Star**[208] 7257 3-8-9 SimonPearce(3) 7 54
(Andrew Balding) *dwlt: sn in tch in 4th: wknd over 2f out* 25/1
-0 5 11 **Rhossili Bay**[13] 2204 3-8-12 DaneO'Neill 1 36
(Martyn Meade) *dwlt: a bhd* 50/1
0 6 8 **Linton Hill (IRE)**[19] 2042 3-9-3 LiamKeniry 4 29
(Murty McGrath) *chsd ldrs: lost pl 4f out: sn bhd* 100/1

2m 37.58s (-3.32) **Going Correction** -0.325s/f (Firm) 6 Ran SP% **108.6**
Speed ratings (Par 99): **98,96,96,86,78 73**
toteswingers: 1&2 £1.60, 1&3 £1.10, 2&3 £1.20. CSF £5.95 TOTE £1.60: £1.02, £2.60; EX 6.80.
Owner The Queen **Bred** The Queen **Trained** Newmarket, Suffolk
FOCUS
A fair 3-y-o maiden based on the form of those with official ratings and a decisive winner in the Royal colours the week before the Diamond Jubilee celebrations.

2613 SPIRE ST SAVIOUR'S HOSPITAL HYTHE H'CAP 1m 4f
8:45 (8:45) (Class 5) (0-75,74) 3-Y-0 £2,264 (£673; £336; £168) Stalls High

Form RPR
2133 1 **Naseem Alyasmeen (IRE)**[9] 2333 3-9-3 70 MartinHarley 4 80+
(Mick Channon) *t.k.h: chsd ldr: led after 2f and sn 4 l clr: shkn up over 1f out: styd on* 9/4[2]
0-30 2 3 **Bounty Seeker (USA)**[30] 1707 3-9-7 74 FrannyNorton 2 78
(Mark Johnston) *led 2f: chsd wnr tl 4f out: regained 2nd 2f out: kpt on u.p: a hld* 4/1[3]
4332 3 3/4 **Somemothersdohavem**[2] 2544 3-9-0 67 (p) BrettDoyle 3 69
(John Ryan) *hld up in last: hdwy over 3f out: hrd rdn and hung rt in st: kpt on: a hld* 6/1
-333 4 4 **Viola Da Gamba (IRE)**[21] 1981 3-8-12 70 DavidKenny(5) 1 66
(William Knight) *hld up in 4th: rdn and outpcd fnl 3f* 14/1
320 5 11 **Kudoz**[24] 1893 3-9-6 73 AdamKirby 5 51
(Clive Cox) *chsd ldng pair: wnt 2nd 4f out: wknd 2f out* 13/8[1]

2m 37.24s (-3.66) **Going Correction** -0.325s/f (Firm) 5 Ran SP% **109.8**
Speed ratings (Par 99): **99,97,96,93,86**
CSF £11.31 TOTE £3.20: £2.40, £5.70; EX 9.40.
Owner Jaber Abdullah **Bred** Patrick Byrnes **Trained** West Ilsley, Berks
FOCUS
A tight little handicap on paper run 0.34 secs faster than the earlier maiden over the trip, but they finished well strung out.
T/Plt: £260.50 to a £1 stake. Pool: £53,736.23 - 150.56 winning tickets. T/Qpdt: £72.40 to a £1 stake. Pool: £5,345.26 - 54.60 winning tickets. LM

2594 AYR (L-H)
Thursday, May 31

OFFICIAL GOING: Good to firm (9.6)
Wind: Light, half against Weather: Cloudy

2614 BRITISH STALLION STUDS SUPPORTING BRITISH RACING E B F MAIDEN STKS 5f
1:40 (1:41) (Class 4) 2-Y-0 £4,463 (£1,328; £663; £331) Stalls High

Form RPR
32 1 **Hototo**[19] 2069 2-9-3 0 PhillipMakin 2 89+
(Kevin Ryan) *t.k.h: trckd ldrs: plld out and effrt over 1f out: rdn to ld ins fnl f: hld on wl* 11/8[2]

2 **2** *hd* **Jillnextdoor (IRE)**[13] 2234 2-8-12 0 MatthewDavies 4 82+
(Mick Channon) *prom: hdwy to ld over 2f out: sn pushed along: hdd ins fnl f: rallied: jst hld* **5/4**[1]

02 **3** *6* **Red Style (IRE)**[43] 1437 2-9-3 0 MickyFenton 1 66
(Paul Midgley) *t.k.h: led after 1f to over 2f out: wknd fnl f* **25/1**

6 **4** *1* **Monkey Bar Flies (IRE)**[12] 2261 2-9-3 0 FrederikTylicki 6 62
(Richard Fahey) *noisy in preliminaries: led 1f: cl up tl rdn and wknd appr fnl f* **7/1**[3]

5 *7* **Classy Anne** 2-8-12 0 LeeNewman 3 32
(Jim Goldie) *noisy in preliminaries: dwlt: in tch: hung lft thrght: wknd fr 2f out* **66/1**

50 **6** *3¼* **Baker's Pursuit**[12] 2261 2-8-12 0 GrahamLee 5 20
(Jim Goldie) *bhd and sn outpcd: no ch fr 1/2-way* **40/1**

58.72s (-0.68) **Going Correction** -0.20s/f (Firm) **6** Ran SP% **106.8**
Speed ratings (Par 95): **97,96,87,85,74 69**
toteswingers:1&2:£1.10, 1&3:£2.80, 2&3:£2.50 CSF £3.01 TOTE £2.50: £1.20, £1.10; EX 3.00.
Owner Kenneth Macpherson **Bred** B P Hammond **Trained** Hambleton, N Yorks

FOCUS
Course at full width. A small-field maiden, but the front pair look above average and pulled nicely clear.

NOTEBOOK
Hototo ◆'s second to Cay Verde at Ascot last time was made to look even better by the winner's subsequent success in a Curragh Listed event. This ground would have been very different to his previous two starts, but he coped with it well enough and showed a determined attitude after being switched left over a furlong out, batting on gamely. There is plenty of middle-distance winning form on the dam's side of his pedigree so he could well improve even more for further. (op 6-4)
Jillnextdoor(IRE) ◆, who was taking on previous winners when narrowly beaten in a Newbury conditions event on her debut, was produced to win her race over a furlong out and never gave in once headed by the winner. She should get a bit further and her winning turn is merely delayed. (op 11-10 tchd Evens)
Red Style(IRE) ran above his 25-1 odds when runner-up in a soft-ground Beverley maiden last month and ran another solid race under a prominent ride. He was up against a couple of nice sorts here and should find easier opportunities. (op 20-1)
Monkey Bar Flies(IRE) showed plenty of promise when sixth of 18 on his recent Doncaster debut and, though this may not seem to have been much of an improvement, time may show that this was a hot race of its type for the track. (op 8-1 tchd 9-1)

2615 DOWNLOAD THE BLUE SQUARE APP H'CAP 5f
2:10 (2:11) (Class 5) (0-70,70) 3-Y-O **£2,264** (£673; £336; £168) **Stalls** High

Form RPR

1-4 **1** **Lupin Pooter**[13] 2256 3-9-4 **67** GrahamGibbons 3 81+
(David Barron) *prom on outside: pushed along over 2f out: hdwy to ld ins fnl f: hld on wl* **6/5**[1]

5312 **2** *shd* **Wild Sauce**[27] 1817 3-9-3 **66** (b) TomEaves 9 80
(Bryan Smart) *led: rdn and hdd ins fnl f: rallied: jst hld* **9/2**[2]

0 **3** *2½* **Bogini (IRE)**[13] 2256 3-9-0 **70** (b) DavidSimmonson(7) 2 75
(M D O'Callaghan, Ire) *cl up on outside: effrt and ev ch over 1f out: nt qckn ins fnl f* **6/1**[3]

-330 **4** *1½* **Middleton Flyer (IRE)**[13] 2256 3-8-9 **65** NedCurtis(7) 10 64
(Paul Midgley) *cl up: drvn along over 2f out: one pce fnl f* **11/1**

-506 **5** *1* **Gran Canaria Queen**[6] 2460 3-8-1 **53** (b[1]) JulieBurke(3) 7 49
(Ian Semple) *plld hrd early: prom: rdn and hung lft over 1f out: outpcd fnl f* **33/1**

4-34 **6** *nk* **Majestic Breeze (IRE)**[36] 1599 3-8-2 **51** oh1 CathyGannon 6 46
(Brian Ellison) *blkd s: bhd and sn pushed along: hdwy over 1f out: kpt on ins fnl f: nrst fin* **10/1**

0-45 **7** *2¼* **Madam Bonny (IRE)**[1] 2595 3-8-2 **51** oh6 JamesSullivan 5 37
(Jim Goldie) *chsd ldng gp: drvn along over 2f out: btn over 1f out* **33/1**

0-00 **8** *½* **Nearly A Gift (IRE)**[13] 2256 3-9-5 **68** (t) PJMcDonald 11 53
(Tim Easterby) *cl up tl rdn and wknd appr fnl f* **8/1**

3-00 **9** *3* **Busy Bimbo (IRE)**[6] 2460 3-7-13 **55** (b[1]) MatthewHopkins(7) 1 29
(Alan Berry) *bhd on outside: struggling after 2f: nvr on terms* **66/1**

58.44s (-0.96) **Going Correction** -0.20s/f (Firm) **9** Ran SP% **113.8**
Speed ratings (Par 99): **99,98,94,92,90 90,86,85,81**
toteswingers:1&2:£2.20, 1&3:£2.80, 2&3:£4.30 CSF £6.40 CT £22.50 TOTE £2.40: £1.20, £1.90, £1.40; EX 6.20 Trifecta £14.10 Pool: £729.39 - 38.11 winning units..
Owner Liam & Dermot Kelly **Bred** John Starbuck **Trained** Maunby, N Yorks

FOCUS
An ordinary sprint handicap, but the winner can rate higher. Four of these met at York earlier this month and that race provided the winner, third and fourth here.

2616 BET AT BLUESQUARE.COM H'CAP 6f
2:40 (2:40) (Class 4) (0-85,83) 3-Y-O **£4,075** (£1,212; £606; £303) **Stalls** High

Form RPR

3621 **1** **Galician**[13] 2229 3-9-4 **80** MircoDemuro 4 93+
(Mark Johnston) *cl up on outside: hdwy to ld 2f out: pushed clr fnl f: comf* **7/2**[2]

2-03 **2** *3* **Profile Star (IRE)**[5] 2509 3-9-2 **78** GrahamGibbons 8 82+
(David Barron) *in tch on ins: effrt whn nt clr run appr 2f out: squeezed through and hdwy to chse (clr) wnr ins fnl f: r.o* **9/2**

3-30 **3** *¾* **Whisky Bravo**[21] 1998 3-9-1 **77** PJMcDonald 3 78
(David Brown) *prom on outside: effrt and disp 2nd pl over 1f out to ins fnl f: one pce* **20/1**

2-41 **4** *1¼* **Colbyor**[19] 2085 3-8-7 **69** FrederikTylicki 5 66
(Richard Fahey) *in tch: hdwy over 2f out: rdn and chsd wnr over 1f out to ins fnl f: sn outpcd* **10/1**

211 **5** *1½* **Jack Dexter**[21] 1998 3-9-7 **83** GrahamLee 6 75
(Jim Goldie) *hld up: effrt whn nt clr run over 2f out to over 1f out: effrt appr fnl f: kpt on same pce* **4/1**[3]

2-54 **6** *2* **Discression**[27] 1824 3-9-1 **77** PhillipMakin 7 62
(Kevin Ryan) *trckd ldrs: nt clr run over 2f out to over 1f out: sn no imp* **17/2**

00-5 **7** *3¼* **Cockney Fire**[34] 1639 3-9-1 **77** CathyGannon 1 52
(David Evans) *swtchd rt after 1f: disp ld to 2f out: wknd over 1f out* **33/1**

50-3 **8** *½* **Springinmystep (IRE)**[51] 1271 3-9-5 **81** TomEaves 2 54
(Michael Dods) *crossed over to stands' rail after 1f: led to 2f out: wkng whn hmpd over 1f out* **11/4**[1]

1m 10.83s (-1.57) **Going Correction** -0.20s/f (Firm) **8** Ran SP% **114.4**
Speed ratings (Par 101): **102,98,97,95,93 90,86,85**
toteswingers:1&2:£3.80, 1&3:£7.10, 2&3:£9.60 CSF £19.67 CT £272.76 TOTE £4.10: £1.20, £1.70, £3.80; EX 24.00 Trifecta £623.80 Pool: £859.85 - 1.02 winning units..
Owner Sheikh Hamdan Bin Mohammed Al Maktoum **Bred** Darley **Trained** Middleham Moor, N Yorks
■ Stewards' Enquiry : Graham Gibbons one-day ban: careless riding (Jun 14)

FOCUS
A fair handicap, but quite a rough race. The winning time was significantly faster than both divisions of the older-horse handicap and the third and fourth are rated close to form and set the level.
Jack Dexter Official explanation: trainer said gelding was unsuited by the good to firm ground
Springinmystep(IRE) Official explanation: trainer said colt ran too free

2617 GET YOUR BET ON AT BLUE SQUARE H'CAP (DIV I) 6f
3:15 (3:15) (Class 6) (0-60,60) 4-Y-O+ **£1,704** (£503; £251) **Stalls** High

Form RPR

2266 **1** **Argentine (IRE)**[25] 1875 8-9-7 **60** (v) TomEaves 4 66
(Ian Semple) *hld up stands' rail: nt clr run fr over 2f out: qcknd between horses to ld ent fnl f: r.o wl* **12/1**

5-50 **2** *¾* **Saxonette**[20] 2032 4-9-3 **56** PJMcDonald 8 60
(Linda Perratt) *hld up in tch: rdn and hdwy over 1f out: ev ch ent fnl f: kpt on fin* **25/1**

0-05 **3** *½* **Insolenceofoffice (IRE)**[25] 1875 4-9-1 **59** (p) LMcNiff(5) 9 61
(Richard Ford) *chsd clr ldng pair: drvn over 2f out: edgd lft wl over 1f out: ev ch ent fnl f: kpt on* **5/1**[3]

5300 **4** *1½* **Memphis Man**[40] 1528 9-9-2 **55** CathyGannon 2 52
(David Evans) *hld up: rdn and effrt whn nt clr run over 1f out: kpt on ins fnl f* **14/1**

00-0 **5** *1¾* **Colamandis**[97] 690 5-8-7 **46** oh1 AndrewElliott 5 38
(Hugh McWilliams) *hld up on outside: effrt and hdwy over 1f out: rdn and no imp fnl f* **80/1**

-024 **6** *2* **Weetentherty**[13] 2230 5-8-12 **54** JulieBurke(3) 3 44+
(Linda Perratt) *s.i.s: bhd and outpcd: hdwy whn swtchd rt appr fnl f: r.o: nvr able to chal* **8/1**

30-0 **7** *3½* **Crabbies Ginger**[13] 2225 4-8-9 **48** FrederikTylicki 6 22
(Lisa Williamson) *prom: effrt and rdn over 2f out: wknd ent fnl f* **40/1**

0061 **8** *shd* **Chosen One (IRE)**[6] 2436 7-8-8 **47** JamesSullivan 7 21+
(Ruth Carr) *disp ld: led over 1f out to ent fnl f: sn wknd* **5/2**[2]

612 **9** *1¼* **Alpha Tauri (USA)**[8] 2405 6-8-11 **50** (t) GrahamGibbons 1 20+
(Richard Guest) *led at str gallop: hdd over 1f out: eased whn btn ins fnl f* **2/1**[1]

1m 11.83s (-0.57) **Going Correction** -0.20s/f (Firm) **9** Ran SP% **111.6**
Speed ratings (Par 101): **95,94,93,91,89 86,81,81,79**
toteswingers:1&2:£13.50, 1&3:£11.30, 2&3:£22.50 CSF £247.27 CT £1665.89 TOTE £16.60: £3.80, £4.20, £1.10; EX 142.30 TRIFECTA Not won..
Owner Jim Hampson, Robert Reid **Bred** Tony Hirschfeld & L K Piggott **Trained** Carluke, S Lanarks
■ Stewards' Enquiry : L McNiff two-day ban: careless riding (Jun 14-15)
P J McDonald one-day ban: careless riding (Jun 14)

FOCUS
The most notable aspect of this moderate handicap was the pace they went with Alpha Tauri and Chosen One cutting each other's throats. The winner is rated close to recent AW form but the form is not entirely solid.
Chosen One(IRE) Official explanation: trainer said gelding was unsuited by the fast early pace

2618 GET YOUR BET ON AT BLUE SQUARE H'CAP (DIV II) 6f
3:45 (3:45) (Class 6) (0-60,60) 4-Y-O+ **£1,704** (£503; £251) **Stalls** High

Form RPR

2504 **1** **Circuitous**[3] 2538 4-9-5 **58** (v[1]) GrahamGibbons 3 66
(Keith Dalgleish) *mde all: sn crossed to stands' rail: rdn over 1f out: hrd pressed ins fnl f: kpt on wl* **9/2**[2]

5612 **2** *½* **Amazing Win (IRE)**[3] 2538 4-9-1 **54** MatthewDavies 6 60
(Mick Channon) *pressed wnr: rdn over 1f out: ev ch ins fnl f: kpt on: hld nr fin* **4/7**[1]

0055 **3** *1½* **Amno Dancer (IRE)**[6] 2458 5-8-9 **48** (b) TomEaves 1 50
(Ian Semple) *stdd s: hld up: swtchd rt after 2f: effrt over 1f out: kpt on fnl f: nt rch first two* **7/1**[3]

/000 **4** *3¾* **Whiteoak Lady (IRE)**[20] 2046 7-8-13 **52** (b) CathyGannon 7 42
(David Evans) *prom: rdn over 2f out: one pce appr fnl f* **12/1**

05-0 **5** *3¾* **Face East (USA)**[25] 1881 4-8-0 **46** oh1 MatthewHopkins(7) 2 24
(Alan Berry) *hld up on outside: rdn over 2f out: no imp fr over 1f out* **66/1**

0-00 **6** *nk* **Spanish Acclaim**[5] 2475 5-9-7 **60** (e[1]) JamesSullivan 4 37
(Ruth Carr) *t.k.h: cl up: rdn over 2f out: edgd rt and wknd over 1f out* **16/1**

05-0 **7** *5* **Miss Pronounce**[20] 2032 4-8-4 **46** oh1 JulieBurke(3) 5
(Linda Perratt) *dwlt: sn in tch: drvn over 2f out: wknd wl over 1f out* **40/1**

0-00 **8** *2¾* **Chambers (IRE)**[28] 1799 6-8-8 **47** FrederikTylicki 9
(Richard Ford) *trckd ldrs tl rdn and wknd wl over 1f out* **18/1**

1m 12.34s (-0.06) **Going Correction** -0.20s/f (Firm) **8** Ran SP% **117.1**
Speed ratings (Par 101): **92,91,89,84,79 78,72,68**
toteswingers:1&2:£1.20, 1&3:£2.10, 2&3:£2.40 CSF £7.59 CT £17.70 TOTE £5.20: £1.20, £1.10, £1.70; EX 7.50 Trifecta £26.40 Pool: £1086.91 - 30.39 winning units..
Owner A R M Galbraith **Bred** Deepwood Farm Stud **Trained** Carluke, S Lanarks

FOCUS
This looked weaker than the first division and the winning time was over half a second slower. The winner looks the best guide.

2619 BET AT BLUE SQUARE ON YOUR MOBILE H'CAP 1m
4:20 (4:20) (Class 5) (0-75,75) 4-Y-O+ **£2,264** (£673; £336; £168) **Stalls** Low

Form RPR

0-00 **1** **Silverware (USA)**[19] 2083 4-9-7 **75** TomEaves 9 81
(Linda Stubbs) *mde all at ordinary gallop: hrd pressed fr 2f out: styd on wl fnl f* **5/1**

00-4 **2** *1½* **Heezararity**[20] 2043 4-8-11 **65** (t) CathyGannon 8 68
(David Evans) *trckd ldrs: rdn and ev ch over 1f out: kpt on ins fnl f* **9/2**[3]

03-4 **3** *1¼* **Fieldgunner Kirkup (GER)**[24] 1917 4-9-4 **72** GrahamGibbons 2 72
(David Barron) *t.k.h: trckd ldr: chal gng wl 2f out: rdn appr fnl f: one pce last 100yds* **10/3**[1]

350- **4** *hd* **Another For Joe**[199] 5014 4-9-1 **69** GrahamLee 7 68
(Jim Goldie) *hld up: effrt and shkn up over 1f out: rdn and kpt on ins fnl f: nvr able to chal* **12/1**

0-03 **5** *nk* **Retreat Content (IRE)**[20] 2033 4-8-7 **61** FrederikTylicki 4 60
(Linda Perratt) *hld up in tch: rdn over 2f out: rallied over 1f out: nvr able to chal* **12/1**

1-26 **6** *3½* **Royal Straight**[20] 2033 7-8-9 **66** (t) JulieBurke(3) 5 56
(Linda Perratt) *dwlt: hld up: rdn over 2f out: nvr able to chal* **9/1**

1-04 **7** *½* **Botham (USA)**[13] 2227 8-8-10 **71** NoraLooby(7) 3 60
(Jim Goldie) *prom on ins: struggling over 2f out: n.d after* **14/1**

1-03 **8** *7* **Ventura Sands (IRE)**[24] 1917 4-8-12 **71** ShaneBKelly(5) 6 44
(Richard Fahey) *t.k.h: cl up tl rdn and wknd wl over 1f out* **7/2**[2]

1m 40.25s (-3.55) **Going Correction** -0.45s/f (Firm) **8** Ran SP% **112.2**
Speed ratings (Par 103): **99,97,96,96,95 92,91,84**
toteswingers:1&2:£5.30, 1&3:£4.30, 2&3:£3.00 CSF £26.61 CT £84.64 TOTE £7.10: £2.30, £1.80, £1.20; EX 42.00 Trifecta £124.10 Pool: £1,033.81 - 6.16 winning units..
Owner Paul & Linda Dixon **Bred** Alliand Equine **Trained** Norton, N Yorks

FOCUS
An ordinary handicap, but few got into it and things rather played into the hands of the winner. He sets the level but the form is muddling.
Ventura Sands(IRE) Official explanation: trainer's rep said gelding was lame right-hind

2620 FOLLOW US ON TWITTER @BLUESQ H'CAP 1m 2f
4:55 (4:55) (Class 4) (0-80,82) 4-Y-0+ **£4,075** (£1,212; £606; £303) **Stalls** Low

Form RPR
44-0 **1** **Full Toss**[133] 216 6-8-10 **69** GrahamLee 7 79
(Jim Goldie) *chsd ldr: led over 2f out: drvn and hld on wl fnl f* **25/1**
0-64 **2** *nk* **Judicious**[27] 1820 5-9-5 **78** FrederikTylicki 4 87+
(Paul Midgley) *hld up: hdwy over 2f out: effrt and chsd wnr ins fnl f: clsng at fin but a hld* **9/4**[1]
20-3 **3** *3 ½* **Jo'Burg (USA)**[19] 2077 8-9-7 **80** GrahamGibbons 6 82
(David O'Meara) *hld up in tch on outside: hdwy: edgd lft and chsd wnr over 2f out to ins fnl f: one pce* **6/1**
11-6 **4** *3 ¾* **Miss Blink**[47] 1381 5-9-1 **74** LeeNewman 1 69
(Robin Bastiman) *prom: effrt and rdn over 2f out: one pce over 1f out: edgd lft and btn ins fnl f* **8/1**
05-5 **5** *4* **Hawdyerwheesht**[28] 1797 4-8-7 **66** oh1 JamesSullivan 2 53
(Jim Goldie) *prom: drvn and outpcd over 2f out: n.d after* **16/1**
4131 **6** *shd* **Veiled Applause**[11] 2312 9-9-2 **82** 6ex KevinLundie(7) 5 68
(John Quinn) *hld up: hdwy on outside wl over 2f out: hung lft: wknd wl over 1f out* **10/1**
-002 **7** *1 ½* **Good Boy Jackson**[20] 2035 4-9-6 **79** PhillipMakin 8 62
(Kevin Ryan) *led to over 2f out: rdn and wknd over 1f out* **11/2**[3]
35-2 **8** *4 ½* **Lucky Windmill**[27] 1820 5-9-5 **78** PJMcDonald 3 52
(Alan Swinbank) *s.i.s: hld up: struggling over 2f out: sn btn* **7/2**[2]
2m 6.05s (-5.95) **Going Correction** -0.45s/f (Firm) 8 Ran SP% **112.6**
Speed ratings (Par 105): **105,104,101,98,95 95,94,90**
toteswingers:1&2:£6.70, 1&3:£7.80, 2&3:£4.00 CSF £78.93 CT £395.16 TOTE £26.10: £5.30, £1.30, £1.40; EX 107.00 Trifecta £798.20 Part won. Pool: £1,078.69 - 0.40 winning units..
Owner J S Goldie **Bred** The Queen **Trained** Uplawmoor, E Renfrews
FOCUS
A fair handicap and the pace looked solid. The winner is rated in line with his AW form.
Lucky Windmill Official explanation: trainer's rep said gelding was unsuited by the good to firm ground

2621 SEE PIXIE LOTT HERE - 22ND JUNE H'CAP 7f 50y
5:25 (5:26) (Class 6) (0-60,60) 4-Y-0+ **£1,617** (£481; £240; £120) **Stalls** High

Form RPR
636- **1** **Burnwynd Boy**[230] 6847 7-8-12 **51** TomEaves 8 57+
(Ian Semple) *t.k.h: hld up: weaved through to chse ldr over 1f out: led ins fnl f: rdn and kpt on* **8/1**[3]
554- **2** *¾* **Goninodaethat**[188] 7099 4-8-13 **52** GrahamLee 2 56
(Jim Goldie) *led: clr over 4f out: rdn whn faltered wl over 1f out: hdd ins fnl f: r.o* **7/1**[2]
00-3 **3** *hd* **Cheeky Wee Red**[13] 2225 4-8-4 **48** ShaneBKelly(5) 10 51
(Richard Fahey) *hld up in tch: rdn along over 2f out: rallied over 1f out: kpt on ins fnl f* **16/1**
0/0- **4** *hd* **Shamo Hill Theatre**[349] 3128 5-8-7 **46** oh1 PJMcDonald 12 49
(Paul Midgley) *midfield: effrt and rdn over 2f out: kpt on ins fnl f* **25/1**
-036 **5** *2 ¼* **Whats For Pudding (IRE)**[6] 2455 4-8-13 **52** GrahamGibbons 3 49
(Declan Carroll) *in tch on ins: drvn and outpcd over 2f out: rallied fnl f: r.o* **7/1**[2]
00-0 **6** *nk* **Illawalla**[52] 1248 4-8-7 **46** oh1 AndrewElliott 6 42
(Hugh McWilliams) *chsd ldrs: effrt over 2f out: nt qckn appr fnl f* **100/1**
326/ **7** *1* **King Of The Moors (USA)**[578] 7251 9-9-7 **60** (p) KellyHarrison 5 53
(John Spearing) *chsd ldr to over 1f out: sn wknd* **7/1**[2]
0-65 **8** *½* **Florio Vincitore (IRE)**[47] 1384 5-9-3 **56** JamesSullivan 1 48+
(Brian Ellison) *t.k.h: hld up on ins: swtchd lft and effrt over 2f out: edgd lft and no imp over 1f out* **5/4**[1]
40-4 **9** *8* **Shunkawakhan (IRE)**[28] 1801 9-8-7 **46** oh1 (tp) FrederikTylicki 11 16
(Linda Perratt) *midfield on outside: struggling over 2f out: sn btn* **16/1**
00-0 **10** *1* **Powerball (IRE)**[12] 2262 4-8-7 **46** oh1 CathyGannon 9 14
(Lisa Williamson) *stdd s: plld hrd in rr: struggling whn hung lft over 2f out: sn btn* **66/1**
5300 **11** *2 ¼* **Abernethy (IRE)**[1] 2600 4-8-4 **46** oh1 (t) JulieBurke(3) 4
(Linda Perratt) *hld up: rdn over 2f out: sn wknd* **20/1**
0-60 **12** *1 ¾* **Tinzo (IRE)**[13] 2225 4-8-0 **46** oh1 MatthewHopkins(7) 7
(Alan Berry) *s.s: bhd: struggling over 3f out: sn btn* **100/1**
1m 31.3s (-2.10) **Going Correction** -0.45s/f (Firm) 12 Ran SP% **116.9**
Speed ratings (Par 101): **94,93,92,92,90 89,88,88,78,77 75,73**
toteswingers:1&2:£14.00, 1&3:£12.20, 2&3:£10.80 CSF £59.81 CT £888.65 TOTE £10.20: £2.60, £2.30, £5.10; EX 66.90 TRIFECTA Not won..
Owner Robert Reid **Bred** Mrs A F Tullie **Trained** Carluke, S Lanarks
FOCUS
A moderate handicap, but run at a reasonable pace. The winner is down to a career-low mark and the form looks shaky.
T/Plt: £76.30 to a £1 stake. Pool:£53,141.05 - 508.04 winning tickets T/Qpdt: £43.40 to a £1 stake. Pool:£3,147.36 - 53.58 winning tickets RY

2360 BRIGHTON (L-H)
Thursday, May 31

OFFICIAL GOING: Good to firm (watered; 7.8)
Wind: Fresh, against Weather: Overcast

2622 PLATINUM LACE GENTLEMAN'S CLUB BRIGHTON MAIDEN AUCTION STKS 5f 59y
2:00 (2:00) (Class 5) 2-Y-0 **£2,264** (£673; £336; £168) **Stalls** Centre

Form RPR
55 **1** **Bheleyf (IRE)**[38] 1563 2-8-7 0 HarryBentley(3) 4 72
(Joseph Tuite) *disp 2nd pl: led wl over 1f out: drvn clr: hrd rdn fnl f: jst hld on* **7/4**[2]
2 *hd* **Boleyn** 2-8-6 0 KieranO'Neill 1 67+
(Richard Hannon) *in last pair: rdn over 2f out: hdwy to go 2nd over 1f out: clsng on wnr thrght fnl f: nt quite get up* **1/1**[1]
3 *6* **Wordsaplenty (IRE)** 2-8-8 0 LiamKeniry 2 48
(J S Moore) *t.k.h: disp 2nd tl over 2f out: sn outpcd: kpt on again fnl 100yds* **17/2**[3]
64 **4** *3 ¼* **Mission Bell**[10] 2349 2-8-6 0 DavidProbert 3 34
(Mark Usher) *led tl wl over 1f out: sn wknd* **10/1**
5 *3 ¼* **Belle Voir** 2-8-12 0 MartinDwyer 5 28
(Gay Kelleway) *rn green in last pair: n.d fnl 2f* **22/1**
1m 5.1s (2.80) **Going Correction** +0.175s/f (Good) 5 Ran SP% **110.3**
Speed ratings (Par 93): **84,83,74,68,63**
CSF £3.87 TOTE £3.40: £1.40, £1.20; EX 5.30.
Owner Heart Of The South Racing **Bred** Eimear Mulhern & Abbeville Stud **Trained** Great Shefford, Berks
FOCUS
Rail dolled out by 4m from 6f to 2.5f increasing distances by 8yds. This didn't look a strong contest by any means and the form looks fluid.
NOTEBOOK
Bheleyf(IRE) made it third time lucky, but only just held on after gaining a few lengths advantage. She'd shown ability previously at a modest level, so was entitled to take this. (op 15-8 tchd 2-1)
Boleyn ◆, the first foal of an unraced dam, stayed on well once hitting top gear and almost got up, despite her jockey not resorting to his whip at all in the final furlong. She doesn't look a star but ought to find an opportunity. (op 6-5 tchd 10-11)
Wordsaplenty(IRE), a half-sister to a hurdles winner in France, raced as though the outing would bring her on and may need a bit further. (op 8-1 tchd 9-1)
Mission Bell faded after leading and will no doubt be more interesting in handicaps later on in the year. (tchd 14-1)
Belle Voir, whose dam is a half-sister to several winners, including Nova Hawk (fourth in both the English and French 1000 Guineas last year), ran green and didn't appear to act on the track. (op 20-1 tchd 25-1)

2623 CREATIVE FOOD COURTS LTD H'CAP 1m 3f 196y
2:30 (2:30) (Class 5) (0-75,75) 4-Y-0+ **£2,264** (£673; £336; £168) **Stalls** High

Form RPR
50-5 **1** **Boston Blue**[75] 521 5-9-2 **70** JimCrowley 4 78
(Tony Carroll) *hld up: hdwy 3f out: led 1f out: hung lft: drvn out* **11/4**[1]
00-0 **2** *1 ¼* **Dubai Glory**[15] 2174 4-9-7 **75** IanMongan 1 81
(Sheena West) *prom: led 5f out tl 1f out: kpt on u.p* **7/2**[2]
0024 **3** *5* **Bennelong**[15] 2174 6-9-0 **68** AmirQuinn 3 66
(Richard Rowe) *hld up: hdwy into 3rd 4f out: one pce appr fnl f* **15/2**
0-02 **4** *3 ½* **Filun**[9] 2363 7-9-2 **70** LiamKeniry 5 62
(Anthony Middleton) *patiently rdn in rr: sme hdwy 2f out: shkn up and fnd little* **4/1**[3]
-003 **5** *3* **Aciano (IRE)**[2] 2576 4-9-6 **74** KirstyMilczarek 2 62
(Brendan Powell) *prom: rdn 3f out: wknd 2f out* **4/1**[3]
6510 **6** *20* **Darsan (IRE)**[13] 2237 4-8-10 **64** SilvestreDeSousa 6 20
(Phil McEntee) *led tl 5f out: sn lost pl: bhd whn eased over 1f out* **9/1**
2m 36.28s (3.58) **Going Correction** +0.175s/f (Good) 6 Ran SP% **110.7**
Speed ratings (Par 103): **95,94,90,88,86 73**
toteswingers:1&2:£3.00, 1&3:£2.80, 2&3:£2.60 CSF £12.17 TOTE £4.30: £2.50, £2.80; EX 13.20.
Owner B J Millen **Bred** Ballykilbride Stud **Trained** Cropthorne, Worcs
FOCUS
A fair handicap in which the runner-up looks the best guide.
Aciano(IRE) Official explanation: vet said gelding lost a right-hind shoe

2624 WELLPOOL BUILDING AND MAINTENANCE SERVICES H'CAP (DIV I OF 3.35) 1m 1f 209y
3:05 (3:05) (Class 6) (0-65,65) 3-Y-0 **£1,617** (£481; £240; £60; £60) **Stalls** High

Form RPR
4-00 **1** **Autarch (USA)**[12] 2281 3-9-4 **62** JimCrowley 8 65
(Amanda Perrett) *chsd ldrs: rdn over 2f out: no imp tl styd on strly ins fnl f: led fnl 30yds* **7/1**
6420 **2** *¾* **Kelpie Blitz (IRE)**[22] 1982 3-9-6 **64** GeorgeBaker 1 65
(Seamus Durack) *prom: effrt on ins rail 2f out: led over 1f out: hrd rdn: hdd fnl 30yds* **9/4**[1]
0060 **3** *1* **Johanna Fosie (IRE)**[30] 1726 3-8-7 **51** oh1 MartinHarley 5 50
(Mick Channon) *led: hrd rdn 2f out: hdd over 1f out: one pce* **22/1**
31-0 **4** *½* **Chrissycross (IRE)**[24] 1906 3-9-7 **65** AdamKirby 7 63
(Roger Teal) *towards rr: pushed along 5f out: gd late hdwy* **9/1**
-646 **4** *dht* **La Confession**[10] 2353 3-8-7 **51** oh4 DavidProbert 6 49
(Rae Guest) *t.k.h: chsd ldr tl over 1f out: one pce* **33/1**
2-54 **6** *1* **Joyful Spirit (IRE)**[26] 1853 3-9-2 **60** (b[1]) TedDurcan 3 56
(John Dunlop) *t.k.h: hld up in 6th: rdn and no hdwy fnl 2f: btn whn hung lft ins fnl f* **4/1**[3]
6120 **7** *4 ½* **Aiaam Al Wafa (IRE)**[2] 2577 3-9-2 **60** (p) SilvestreDeSousa 9 47
(Phil McEntee) *in tch: rdn over 2f out: sn btn* **14/1**
65-0 **8** *3* **Arabic**[30] 1728 3-9-5 **63** KierenFallon 4 44
(James Fanshawe) *in tch: rdn 4f out: wknd over 2f out* **7/2**[2]
5-05 **9** *17* **Beckfield Point**[64] 1068 3-8-13 **57** (t) JamesDoyle 2
(Stuart Williams) *dwlt: hld up in rr: shkn up and sme hdwy on rail 2f out: n.m.r: sn lost pl: eased whn no ch* **25/1**
2m 6.99s (3.39) **Going Correction** +0.175s/f (Good) 9 Ran SP% **113.3**
Speed ratings (Par 97): **93,92,91,91,91 90,86,84,70**
toteswingers:1&2:£5.50, 1&3:£23.00, 2&3:£12.50 CSF £22.18 CT £328.48 TOTE £10.00: £2.50, £1.10, £5.20; EX 32.40.
Owner John Connolly & Odile Griffith **Bred** Woodbridge Bloodstock **Trained** Pulborough, W Sussex
FOCUS
The first division of a modest handicap and the form looks shaky.
Autarch(USA) Official explanation: trainer's rep said, regarding apparent improvement in form, that the gelding was better suited by the lower class.

2625 COAST TO COAST BRIGHTON MARINA H'CAP (DIV II OF 3.05) 1m 1f 209y
3:35 (3:35) (Class 6) (0-65,65) 3-Y-0 **£1,617** (£481; £240; £120) **Stalls** High

Form RPR
50-5 **1** **Chignon (IRE)**[20] 2050 3-9-1 **59** TomQueally 3 69+
(Sir Henry Cecil) *hld up towards rr: hdwy 2f out: qcknd wl to ld over 1f out: rdn out: a in control* **7/2**[1]
-040 **2** *¾* **Thecornishcockney**[9] 2382 3-9-7 **65** (p) StevieDonohoe 9 70
(John Ryan) *hld up in last: gd hdwy on outer over 1f out: chsd wnr ins fnl f: hung lft: clsng at fin but a hld* **6/1**[3]
4-00 **3** *3* **Renegotiate**[26] 1853 3-9-3 **61** DavidProbert 6 60
(Andrew Balding) *hld up abt 6th: hdwy over 2f out: hrd rdn over 1f out: one pce* **7/2**[1]
560- **4** *1* **Isobella**[168] 7763 3-8-12 **56** DarryllHolland 5 53
(Hughie Morrison) *s.i.s: hld up in rr: hdwy 3f out: chal and wandered 2f out: no ex over 1f out* **10/1**
0524 **5** *1 ¾* **Dalmo**[52] 1267 3-9-5 **63** GeorgeBaker 4 57
(Gary Moore) *in tch: outpcd over 2f out: kpt on again fnl f* **5/1**[2]
5-13 **6** *3 ¾* **Lady Sylvia**[48] 1364 3-9-6 **64** LiamKeniry 7 50
(Joseph Tuite) *pressed ldr: led 3f out tl ins fnl 2f: wknd over 1f out* **7/1**
-060 **7** *2 ¾* **Musically**[30] 1728 3-9-2 **60** MartinHarley 8 41
(Mick Channon) *chsd ldrs: led ins fnl 2f tl wknd over 1f out* **13/2**

0506 **8** 3 1/4 **Canning Vale**64 1062 3-8-4 51 oh4 AdamBeschizza(3) 2 25
(Julia Feilden) *prom tl wknd 2f out* **33/1**
-300 **9** 23 **Leading Star**22 1981 3-8-7 51 oh6 (v1) JohnFahy 1
(Michael Madgwick) *led tl 3f out: sn lost pl* **66/1**
2m 5.98s (2.38) **Going Correction** +0.175s/f (Good) **9** Ran SP% **114.8**
Speed ratings (Par 97): **97,96,94,93,91 88,86,84,65**
toteswingers:1&2:£5.10, 1&3:£2.70, 2&3:£6.30 CSF £24.65 CT £77.92 TOTE £4.00: £1.10, £2.10, £1.90; EX 36.60.
Owner Miss Yvonne Jacques **Bred** Naiff Sa & Newtown Stud **Trained** Newmarket, Suffolk
FOCUS
The second division was run in a quicker time than the first and the form is fluid with nothing very solid.
Chignon(IRE) ◆ Official explanation: trainer's rep said, regarding apparent improvement in form, that the filly was better suited by the drop in class.

2626 LILY FOUNDATION MAIDEN STKS 7f 214y
4:10 (4:10) (Class 5) 3-Y-0+ £2,264 (£673; £336; £168) Stalls Centre

Form RPR
3-02 **1** **Ibtahaj**12 2280 3-9-2 85 FrankieDettori 5 89+
(Saeed Bin Suroor) *trckd ldr gng wl: led on bit 2f out: sn clr: v easily* **1/3**1
0-00 **2** 3 1/2 **Mishhar (IRE)**20 2042 3-8-11 64 MartinDwyer 2 70
(Clive Brittain) *hld up in rr: hdwy over 2f out: wnt 2nd over 1f out: no ch w wnr: flattered by margin* **40/1**
2303 **3** 4 1/2 **Attain**36 1607 3-9-2 71 JimCrowley 1 64
(Julia Feilden) *in tch: outpcd over 2f out: sn btn* **12/1**3
40-2 **4** 2 1/4 **Gunner Will (IRE)**44 1427 3-9-2 78 JamesDoyle 3 59
(Jamie Osborne) *led tl 2f out: wknd over 1f out* **4/1**2
30 **5** 8 **Charles Tyrwhitt**26 1852 3-9-2 0 KierenFallon 4 41
(George Baker) *hld up in 5th: rdn over 2f out: sn wknd* **25/1**
000- **6** 43 **Trisha's Boy (IRE)**280 5411 3-9-2 50 SebSanders 6
(Simon Dow) *chsd ldng pair: rdn over 2f out: sn wknd: eased whn btn* **100/1**
1m 36.91s (0.91) **Going Correction** +0.175s/f (Good) **6** Ran SP% **110.0**
Speed ratings (Par 103): **102,98,94,91,83 40**
CSF £20.89 TOTE £1.50: £1.10, £11.60; EX 16.70.
Owner Godolphin **Bred** Newsells Park Stud **Trained** Newmarket, Suffolk
FOCUS
The market suggested this would be a straightforward task for the favourite, and so it proved. The winner scored without needing to improve and is value for more.

2627 READ RYAN MOORE EXCLUSIVELY ON BETFAIR H'CAP 7f 214y
4:45 (4:45) (Class 6) (0-60,57) 4-Y-0+ £1,617 (£481; £240; £120) Stalls Centre

Form RPR
1-02 **1** **Lightning Spirit**9 2366 4-9-3 53 (p) GeorgeBaker 4 63+
(Gary Moore) *hld up in rr: rdn over 2f out: rapid hdwy ent fnl f: str run to ld fnl 30yds* **9/4**1
0-65 **2** 1 **Fonterutoli (IRE)**9 2365 5-9-1 56 NathanAlison(5) 6 61
(Roger Ingram) *s.s: bhd: hdwy on outer 3f out: led ins fnl 2f: hdd and nt qckn fnl 30yds* **16/1**
2535 **3** nk **Warbond**15 2171 4-9-3 53 JamieGoldstein 12 57
(Michael Madgwick) *dwlt: towards rr: gd hdwy over 1f out: chsd ldr ins fnl f: kpt on* **6/1**3
-050 **4** 2 1/4 **Rainsborough**24 1919 5-8-9 45 JohnFahy 5 44
(Peter Hedger) *in tch: rdn to press ldrs over 1f out: one pce fnl f* **9/1**
-635 **5** 2 3/4 **Monashee Rock (IRE)**15 2170 7-9-7 57 LiamKeniry 10 50
(Patrick Chamings) *t.k.h: hld up in tch: effrt 2f out: no imp* **3/1**2
5204 **6** 1 3/4 **Sottovoce**31 1722 4-9-5 55 JimCrowley 8 44
(Simon Dow) *prom tl wknd 1f out* **14/1**
6000 **7** 3 1/4 **Danceyourselfdizzy (IRE)**21 2013 4-8-9 45 (vt) SilvestreDeSousa 1 26
(Phil McEntee) *chsd ldrs tl wknd over 1f out* **14/1**
000- **8** shd **Prana (USA)**248 6411 4-8-4 45 RaulDaSilva(5) 11 26
(Jeremy Gask) *chsd ldrs: rdn 3f out: wknd 2f out* **25/1**
6606 **9** 1 1/2 **Littleportnbrandy (IRE)**64 1074 4-8-9 45 (bt) WilliamCarson 3 23
(Richard Guest) *towards rr: sme hdwy on inner 2f out: sn rdn and btn* **25/1**
00-0 **10** 8 **Prophet In A Dream**28 1787 4-8-10 51 DavidKenny(5) 7 10
(Paddy Butler) *sn led: hdd & wknd ins fnl 2f* **66/1**
0-00 **11** 1/2 **Gee Major**50 1299 5-8-12 48 JamesDoyle 2
(Nicky Vaughan) *prom tl wknd over 2f out* **9/1**
1m 38.35s (2.35) **Going Correction** +0.175s/f (Good) **11** Ran SP% **118.5**
Speed ratings (Par 101): **95,94,93,91,88 86,83,83,82,74 73**
toteswingers:1&2:£9.40, 1&3:£3.90, 2&3:£15.10 CSF £40.76 CT £200.28 TOTE £3.40: £2.20, £7.00, £2.50; EX 41.90.
Owner Heart Of The South Racing **Bred** John And Caroline Penny **Trained** Lower Beeding, W Sussex
FOCUS
Nothing more than a moderate contest, but a few of these did arrive here in fair form. The winner is better than the bare form and is on the upgrade.

2628 LOUISE KESTON BIRTHDAY CELEBRATION H'CAP 6f 209y
5:15 (5:15) (Class 6) (0-65,65) 3-Y-0 £1,617 (£481; £240; £120) Stalls Centre

Form RPR
10-0 **1** **The New Black (IRE)**17 2128 3-9-5 63 (v1) JackMitchell 2 67
(Gay Kelleway) *s.s: bhd: cajoled along fr 4f out: hdwy in centre over 1f out: str run to ld fnl 75yds* **16/1**
4432 **2** 1 3/4 **Auntie Kathryn (IRE)**21 2010 3-8-2 51 oh6 RaulDaSilva(5) 3 50
(Stuart Williams) *led over 2f: chsd ldr: led again jst over 1f out: hdd and nt qckn fnl 75yds* **7/1**3
00-0 **3** 1 **Authoritarian**20 2042 3-9-1 59 KieranO'Neill 1 59+
(Richard Hannon) *a.p: disputing 3rd and hld whn n.m.r on rail ins fnl f* **12/1**
05-0 **4** 1/2 **Saaboog**14 2197 3-9-7 65 KierenFallon 8 60
(James Tate) *w ldrs: led over 4f out tl jst over 1f out: one pce* **13/8**1
12-6 **5** 3 1/4 **Intomist (IRE)**31 1709 3-9-6 64 PatCosgrave 6 50
(Jim Boyle) *chsd ldrs: rdn and one pce fnl 2f* **15/2**
61-0 **6** 1 **Choccywoccydoodah**17 2136 3-9-6 64 JimCrowley 9 47
(James Given) *hld up in rr: effrt 2f out: no imp* **8/1**
-000 **7** hd **Here Comes Jeanie**35 1625 3-8-4 51 oh6 SimonPearce(3) 4 34
(Michael Madgwick) *towards rr: rdn 3f out: n.d* **50/1**
60-3 **8** 1 1/4 **Lazeez (USA)**66 1048 3-9-4 62 MartinLane 5 42
(Clive Brittain) *in tch tl wknd over 2f out* **16/1**
00-0 **9** 2 **Whinging Willie (IRE)**17 2128 3-9-7 65 (p) GeorgeBaker 7 39
(Gary Moore) *t.k.h: prom tl wknd over 2f out* **4/1**2
1m 25.57s (2.47) **Going Correction** +0.175s/f (Good) **9** Ran SP% **114.9**
Speed ratings (Par 97): **92,90,88,88,84 83,83,81,79**
toteswingers:1&2:£10.30, 1&3:£11.40, 2&3:£10.90 CSF £122.30 CT £982.26 TOTE £21.60: £4.70, £1.20, £4.40; EX 50.00.
Owner P Kerridge,G Hodson,P Tyler,R Edwards **Bred** Tullamaine Castle Stud **Trained** Exning, Suffolk
■ Stewards' Enquiry : Kieren Fallon two-day ban: careless riding (Jun 14-15)
FOCUS
The early gallop didn't seem strong, so the winner gets extra credit for coming from off the pace. The runner-up is rated in line with his best AW form.

2629 RACING POST JUBILEE SPECIAL OUT TUESDAY H'CAP 5f 213y
5:45 (5:45) (Class 5) (0-75,80) 4-Y-0+ £2,264 (£673; £336; £168) Stalls Centre

Form RPR
04-0 **1** **Avonmore Star**45 1417 4-9-4 75 SeanLevey(3) 2 82
(Richard Hannon) *dwlt: sn chsng ldrs: led jst ins fnl f: rdn out* **5/2**2
1023 **2** 3/4 **Waabel**10 2355 5-9-1 69 (t) WilliamCarson 6 74
(Richard Guest) *in tch: rdn over 2f out: str run fnl f: nt quite rch wnr* **15/2**
-040 **3** nk **Cheylesmore (IRE)**38 1561 4-9-2 70 (v) JimCrowley 1 74
(Michael Wigham) *chsd ldr: drvn to chal over 1f out: kpt on* **5/1**3
0604 **4** 1 **The Strig**5 2494 5-8-13 67 (v) SebSanders 4 68
(Stuart Williams) *led: hung lft and hdd jst ins fnl f: one pce* **9/1**
4551 **5** 2 1/2 **Beat The Bell**5 2482 7-9-7 80 6ex LeonnaMayor(5) 3 73
(Jamie Osborne) *s.s: plld hrd in rr: rdn 2f out: nvr able to chal* **6/4**1
-040 **6** 3 1/4 **Volito**7 2413 6-8-11 65 (p) LiamKeniry 5 47
(Anabel K Murphy) *s.s: hld up in 5th: rdn and nt trble ldrs fnl 2f* **14/1**
1m 12.0s (1.80) **Going Correction** +0.175s/f (Good) **6** Ran SP% **113.7**
Speed ratings (Par 103): **95,94,93,92,88 84**
CSF £21.22 TOTE £2.70: £1.10, £4.20; EX 18.90.
Owner Ken Geering **Bred** Miss J R Tooth **Trained** East Everleigh, Wilts
FOCUS
A fair sprint run at a respectable pace with the runner-up setting the standard.
T/Plt: £11.30 to a £1 stake. Pool:£50,678.03 - 3,262.58 winning tickets T/Qpdt: £7.30 to a £1 stake. Pool:£3,951.74 - 396.18 winning tickets LM

2238 NEWCASTLE (L-H)
Thursday, May 31

OFFICIAL GOING: Good to firm changing to good to firm (good in places) after race 2 (6:35)
Wind: light across Weather: cloudy, with the odd shower

2630 DELOITTE NOVICE STKS 5f
6:05 (6:05) (Class 5) 2-Y-0 £2,393 (£712; £355; £177) Stalls Centre

Form RPR
1 **1** **Madam Mojito (USA)**35 1629 2-8-11 0 MichaelO'Connell 3 84
(John Quinn) *trckd ldr: pushed along 2f out: led appr fnl f: kpt on wl* **9/1**
2 1 1/4 **Exactement (IRE)** 2-8-9 0 NGMcCullagh 4 78+
(Mrs K Burke) *hld up in tch: pushed along and hdwy to chse wnr appr fnl f: kpt on but a jst hld* **11/10**1
41 **3** 4 **Hiddon Coin (IRE)**10 2334 2-9-2 0 DanielTudhope 5 70
(David O'Meara) *trckd ldr: pushed along 2f out: drvn appr fnl f: sn no ex* **2/1**2
15 **4** nk **Ingleby Royale**13 2252 2-8-11 0 TonyHamilton 2 64
(Richard Fahey) *hld up: rdn and outpcd 2f out: kpt on towards fin: nvr threatened* **5/1**3
10 **5** nk **Lothian Countess**13 2252 2-8-11 0 DuranFentiman 1 63
(George Foster) *led: rdn whn hdd appr fnl f: wknd* **33/1**
1m 0.42s (-0.68) **Going Correction** -0.175s/f (Firm) **5** Ran SP% **110.6**
Speed ratings (Par 93): **98,96,89,89,88**
CSF £19.80 TOTE £8.10: £2.60, £1.80; EX 22.90.
Owner Ross Harmon **Bred** John Tl Jones III & W S Farish **Trained** Settrington, N Yorks
FOCUS
Rail from 1m round start to bend in home straight moved a fraction to provide fresh ground. Around 8mm of rain resulted in the ground being eased to good to firm, with "quick" and "nice, good ground" being put forward as descriptions by riders after the first. The front pair pulled clear in what seemed a fairly ordinary novice event and the form is rated at face value through the fourth.
NOTEBOOK
Madam Mojito(USA)'s previous experience made the difference. A narrow winner at Wolverhampton on debut (value for more), she always looked to be holding the well-backed runner-up, and deserves to take her chance up in grade, with the Queen Mary and Super Sprint the primary objectives. (tchd 8-1)
Exactement(IRE), not sold at 110,000gns and out of a 5.5f Listed-placed mare, travelled keenly, but then took a while to pick up, showing obvious signs of greenness, and always looked held. Clear of the remainder, she should have no trouble going one better in a maiden, assuming connections opt to bypass Royal Ascot. (op 11-8 tchd 6-4)
Hiddon Coin(IRE), the only male in the line-up, had won a 6f maiden at Redcar and the drop to 5f worked against him. He'll be one for nurseries over further. (op 15-8 tchd 7-4)
Ingleby Royale was probably below her last-time-out York form and now looks ready for 6f. (op 9-2 tchd 11-2)
Lothian Countess again showed speed but has yet to build on a winning debut.

2631 NCR GROUP MAIDEN FILLIES' STKS 6f
6:35 (6:38) (Class 4) 2-Y-0 £3,428 (£1,020; £509; £254) Stalls Centre

Form RPR
1 **Elle Woods (IRE)** 2-9-0 0 PaulMulrennan 2 82+
(Michael Dods) *dwlt: hld up in tch: pushed along and hdwy over 1f out: r.o wl ins fnl f: led nr fin* **16/1**
2 1/2 **Boom And Bloom (IRE)** 2-9-0 0 TonyHamilton 9 78+
(Richard Fahey) *trckd ldrs: pushed along 2f out: rdn to ld fnl 100yds: kpt on: ct nr fin* **16/1**
33 **3** 1 **Faithfilly (IRE)**5 2499 2-9-0 0 J-PGuillambert 10 75
(Ed Walker) *prom: led over 2f out: sn rdn: drvn whn hdd fnl 100yds: no ex* **13/8**1
0 **4** 3 3/4 **Ana Emaratiya**13 2252 2-9-0 0 AmyRyan 13 63+
(Kevin Ryan) *in tch: rdn over 2f out: kpt on fnl f* **4/1**2
0 **5** 2 1/4 **Sandy's Row (USA)**12 2282 2-9-0 0 FrannyNorton 7 57+
(Mark Johnston) *hld up in tch: pushed along over 2f out: kpt on one pce: nvr threatened ldrs* **8/1**
0 **6** 2 1/2 **Taxiformissbyron**26 1861 2-9-0 0 BarryMcHugh 3 49
(Ollie Pears) *trckd ldrs: pushed along over 2f out: grad wknd* **16/1**
4 **7** 1/2 **Sojoum**5 2469 2-9-0 0 SamHitchcott 8 51+
(Mick Channon) *hld up in tch: pushed along over 3f out: dropped to rr over 1f out: kpt on ins fnl f* **13/2**3
8 hd **Synphonic Air (IRE)** 2-9-0 0 DuranFentiman 6 47
(John Weymes) *sn pushed along towards rr: bhd tl sme late hdwy* **100/1**
9 3/4 **Charlemagne Diva** 2-9-0 0 PaddyAspell 11 45
(Ann Duffield) *t.k.h early: trckd ldrs: pushed along over 2f out: wknd appr fnl f* **16/1**

032 **10** *hd* **Princess In Exile**[13] 2224 2-9-0 0................................ DanielTudhope 12 44
(George Foster) *led: rdn whn hdd over 2f out: wknd appr fnl f* **12/1**

0 **11** *3* **Chiming Hart**[16] 2138 2-9-0 0................................ DavidAllan 1 35
(Tim Easterby) *trckd ldrs: rdn over 2f out: wknd over 1f out* **33/1**

12 *5* **Creditas** 2-9-0 0................................ MichaelO'Connell 4 20
(Jedd O'Keeffe) *prom early: pushed along and lost pl over 3f out: sn struggling* **66/1**

13 *25* **Cos Im Cool** 2-9-0 0................................ PatrickMathers 5
(Robert Johnson) *s.i.s: sn pushed along in rr: bhd fr 1/2-way* **100/1**

1m 14.37s (-0.23) **Going Correction** -0.175s/f (Firm) **13** Ran SP% **120.2**
Speed ratings (Par 92): **94,93,92,87,84 80,80,79,78,78 74,67,34**
toteswingers:1&2:£17.70, 1&3:£8.30, 2&3:£10.30 CSF £247.82 TOTE £14.90: £4.30, £5.40, £1.30; EX 145.70.
Owner Andrew Tinkler **Bred** Ballylinch Stud **Trained** Denton, Co Durham

FOCUS
An average fillies' maiden but one than should produce winners. The third sets the level.

NOTEBOOK
Elle Woods(IRE) ◆, whose dam was a useful 5f-6f winner, looked held racing into the final furlong, but really came strong in the final 100 yards and got up to win with a bit in hand under a considerate ride. She'll want 7f before long and should have plenty of improvement in her. (tchd 18-1)
Boom And Bloom(IRE), whose dam was a very useful 7f-1m winner, threw down a strong challenge, appearing to know her job, and showed more than enough to suggest she can win a maiden granted normal progress. (tchd 14-1)
Faithfilly(IRE) set the standard and had her chance on this quick reappearance, being worn down by a classier rival. She has enough pace to cope with a drop to 5f, but is beginning to look exposed. (op 11-8 tchd 15-8)
Ana Emaratiya, slowly away and hampered in a 5f Listed race on debut, took a while to pick up, still looking green, but she saw it out nicely and looks capable of winning a small maiden. (op 13-2 tchd 7-2)
Sandy's Row(USA) improved on her debut effort, despite again not being the best away, and she should continue to learn. Whether it be a maiden or nursery, there are races to be won with her. (op 14-1)
Taxiformissbyron will be of more interest switched to nurseries following another run.
Sojoum may have found this coming too soon following a fairly promising debut effort and is another for nurseries in due course. (op 8-1 tchd 6-1)

2632 LOCKTON INSURANCE FOR NEPIC MEMBERS H'CAP 7f
7:10 (7:10) (Class 4) (0-85,81) 4-Y-0+ **£4,075** (£1,212; £606; £303) **Stalls** Centre

Form RPR

-066 **1** **Polish World (USA)**[16] 2142 8-9-6 **80**................................ MickyFenton 5 91
(Paul Midgley) *w ldr: rdn to ld 2f out: drvn and kpt on fnl f* **20/1**

0-40 **2** *2* **Anderiego (IRE)**[5] 2488 4-9-2 **76**................................ DanielTudhope 7 82
(David O'Meara) *in tch: tk clsr order over 2f out: rdn to chse wnr over 1f out: drvn and no further imp ins fnl f* **7/4**[1]

0-00 **3** *3* **King Of Eden (IRE)**[5] 2487 6-9-7 **81**................................ PaulMulrennan 3 79
(Eric Alston) *in tch: rdn over 2f out: kpt on one pce: nvr threatened ldng pair* **7/1**[3]

0320 **4** *½* **Rigolleto (IRE)**[13] 2243 4-9-5 **79**................................ SamHitchcott 1 76
(Mick Channon) *midfield: pushed along over 3f out: sme hdwy 2f out: kpt on one pce* **25/1**

21-0 **5** *3* **Chookie Royale**[23] 1951 4-9-4 **78**................................(p) RoystonFfrench 4 66
(Keith Dalgleish) *t.k.h early: in tch: rdn over 2f out: sn outpcd by ldrs: one pce fnl f* **20/1**

1-02 **6** *1½* **Little Jimmy Odsox (IRE)**[17] 2119 4-9-4 **78**................................ DavidAllan 9 62
(Tim Easterby) *hld up in tch: rdn over 2f out: no imp* **11/2**[2]

52-0 **7** *1½* **IndiesIad**[51] 1269 4-8-8 **68**................................(p) FrannyNorton 8 48
(Ann Duffield) *hld up in tch: rdn over 2f out: sn no imp* **14/1**

62-5 **8** *1* **Dream Win**[78] 899 6-8-11 **71**................................ BarryMcHugh 6 49
(Brian Ellison) *hld up: nvr threatened* **10/1**

00-5 **9** *½* **Vito Volterra (IRE)**[12] 2285 5-9-4 **78**................................ AndrewMullen 2 54
(Michael Smith) *led narrowly: rdn whn hdd 2 out: sn wknd* **14/1**

1-05 **10** *4½* **Ted's Brother (IRE)**[33] 1650 4-9-0 **74**................................ J-PGuillambert 10 38
(Richard Guest) *racd keenly: hld up: a towards rr* **11/2**[2]

1m 25.69s (-2.11) **Going Correction** -0.175s/f (Firm) **10** Ran SP% **115.4**
Speed ratings (Par 105): **105,102,99,98,95 93,91,90,90,85**
toteswingers:1&2:£7.80, 1&3:£21.60, 2&3:£6.90 CSF £53.47 CT £284.87 TOTE £25.80: £7.70, £1.10, £2.40; EX 105.10.
Owner C R Green **Bred** Racehorse Management, Llc **Trained** Westow, N Yorks

FOCUS
A truly run handicap and the form looks solid for the grade, with the winner rated to his best and the second to his Irish form.

2633 NEPIC MAIDEN FILLIES' STKS 1m 2f 32y
7:45 (7:48) (Class 5) 3-Y-0+ **£2,264** (£673; £336; £168) **Stalls** Centre

Form RPR

4-6 **1** **Dinvar Diva**[19] 2079 3-8-10 0................................ NickyMackay 7 77+
(John Gosden) *trckd ldrs: qcknd to ld appr fnl f: kpt on* **10/3**[2]

0-6 **2** *2* **Sequence (IRE)**[41] 1502 3-8-10 0................................ RichardMullen 6 73+
(Sir Michael Stoute) *trckd ldrs: pushed along over 2f out: kpt on fnl f: wnt 2nd towards fin* **11/2**[3]

6-24 **3** *¾* **Everlong**[22] 1973 3-8-10 88................................ RobertHavlin 1 71
(Peter Chapple-Hyam) *t.k.h early: trckd ldr: rdn to ld 2f out: hdd appr fnl f: one pce: lost 2nd towards fin* **8/11**[1]

0 **4** *2¾* **Artistic Dawn (IRE)**[11] 2313 3-8-10 0................................ PaulMulrennan 11 66?
(John Weymes) *led at stdy pce: pushed along whn hdd over 2f out: one pce* **66/1**

5 *4½* **Echo Of Footsteps** 3-8-10 0................................ TonyHamilton 9 57
(Michael Herrington) *midfield: pushed along over 2f out: kpt on one pce: nvr threatened ldrs* **20/1**

6 *¾* **Seagoing** 3-8-10 0................................ DavidAllan 8 55+
(Tim Easterby) *dwlt: rn green in rr tl sme late hdwy* **11/1**

7 *4* **Nakuru Breeze (IRE)**[286] 5256 3-8-10 0................................ DanielTudhope 2 47
(David Thompson) *hld up in midfield: sltly short of room over 2f out: nvr threatened* **25/1**

8 *1½* **Miss Mohawk (IRE)** 3-8-10 0................................ MickyFenton 4 44
(Alan Brown) *dwlt: hld up: nvr threatened* **66/1**

0- **9** *47* **Royal Gig**[197] 7431 3-8-10 0................................ MichaelO'Connell 3
(Tim Etherington) *midfield: wknd qckly over 3f out: t.o* **66/1**

2m 15.05s (3.15) **Going Correction** +0.10s/f (Good)
WFA 3 from 6yo 14lb **9** Ran SP% **117.8**
Speed ratings (Par 100): **91,89,88,86,83 82,79,78,40**
toteswingers:1&2:£1.60, 1&3:£2.00, 2&3:£1.80 CSF £21.15 TOTE £5.40: £1.50, £1.20, £1.10; EX 17.90.
Owner Jeffrey Hobby **Bred** Brightwalton Stud **Trained** Newmarket, Suffolk

FOCUS
A fair fillies' maiden, albeit one lacking depth, and the key players drew clear. The pace was steady, resulting in all of the principals racing keenly early and the first three would be expected to stretch their advantage over the remainder in a truly run race.

2634 THREE MILE INN H'CAP 1m 4f 93y
8:15 (8:16) (Class 4) (0-85,81) 3-Y-0 **£4,176** (£1,313; £707) **Stalls** Low

Form RPR

2-1 **1** **Grandiloquent**[30] 1724 3-9-7 **81**................................ RichardMullen 4 88+
(Sir Michael Stoute) *led: pushed along 3f out: hdd narrowly 2f out: led again 1f out: drvn and kpt on to assert fnl 100yds* **9/4**[2]

03-0 **2** *1¼* **Venegazzu (IRE)**[40] 1511 3-8-11 **71**................................ RobertHavlin 2 76
(Peter Chapple-Hyam) *trckd ldr: rdn to ld narrowly 2f out: hdd 1f out: kpt on but hld fnl 100yds* **11/1**[3]

510- **3** *1* **Ventura Spirit**[227] 6911 3-8-11 **71**................................ TonyHamilton 1 74
(Richard Fahey) *hld up in tch: rdn and ev ch over 1f out: one pce ins fnl f* **12/1**

-032 **P** **Rainbow Gold**[5] 2484 3-9-3 **77**................................ FrannyNorton 3
(Mark Johnston) *trckd ldr: wnt wrong and p.u 10f out: fatally injured* **4/7**[1]

2m 49.92s (4.32) **Going Correction** +0.10s/f (Good) **4** Ran SP% **110.4**
Speed ratings (Par 101): **89,88,87,**
CSF £19.83 TOTE £2.60; EX 22.70.
Owner K Abdulla **Bred** Juddmonte Farms Ltd **Trained** Newmarket, Suffolk

FOCUS
A fair handicap weakened by the sad demise of the favourite. The placed horses to their juvenile form set the level.

2635 BOOKER CASH & CARRY H'CAP 2m 19y
8:45 (8:45) (Class 6) (0-65,62) 4-Y-0+ **£1,681** (£500; £250; £125) **Stalls** Low

Form RPR

4211 **1** **Bilidn**[6] 2468 4-9-8 **62** 6ex................................ ChrisCatlin 6 75+
(Noel Quinlan) *hld up in rr: smooth hdwy on outer 3f out: led 2f out: pushed clr: easily* **13/8**[1]

232- **2** *9* **Falcun**[75] 5651 5-9-6 **58**................................(v) TomEaves 5 60
(Micky Hammond) *midfield: wnt in snatches: lost pl and dropped towards rr over 5f out: styd on fnl 2f: wnt 2nd 1f out: no ch w wnr* **15/2**

35-6 **3** *shd* **Shirls Son Sam**[23] 1952 4-8-10 **50**................................ KellyHarrison 3 52
(Chris Fairhurst) *tk str hold in rr tl plld way to front after 3f: hdd 9f out: remained prom: led again over 2f out: sn hdd and no ch w wnr: lost 2nd 1f out: kpt on* **6/1**[3]

-435 **4** *¾* **Dechiper (IRE)**[13] 2242 10-8-7 **45**................................ PatrickMathers 10 46
(Robert Johnson) *hld up in midfield: hdwy over 3f out: rdn over 2f out: kpt on one pce* **14/1**

00-5 **5** *1½* **Manager Mick (IRE)**[52] 1247 4-8-5 **45**................................ AmyRyan 2 44
(John Norton) *hld up: drvn in rr over 5f out: styd on fnl 2f: nvr threatened* **14/1**

3-10 **6** *2½* **Ad Value (IRE)**[27] 1822 4-9-8 **62**................................ PJMcDonald 1 58
(Alan Swinbank) *trckd ldrs: rdn over 3f out: wknd ins fnl f* **7/2**[2]

0-05 **7** *2* **Sposalizio (IRE)**[12] 2288 5-8-12 **50**................................(b[1]) PaddyAspell 7 44
(Colin Teague) *led for 3f: trckd ldrs: rdn over 3f out: wknd over 1f out* **33/1**

000/ **8** *3* **Bollin Julie**[13] 6356 5-8-6 **49**................................ GarryWhillans[(5)] 9 39
(Donald Whillans) *hld up in midfield: hdwy to trck ldrs 6f out: rdn over 3f out: sn wknd* **14/1**

2440 **9** *16* **Escape Artist**[50] 1309 5-9-0 **52**................................ DanielTudhope 4 23
(David Thompson) *midfield: hdwy to ld 9f out: hdd over 2f out: sn wknd* **16/1**

3m 40.57s (1.17) **Going Correction** +0.10s/f (Good)
WFA 4 from 5yo+ 2lb **9** Ran SP% **115.2**
Speed ratings (Par 101): **101,96,96,96,95 94,93,91,83**
toteswingers:1&2:£4.00, 1&3:£3.40, 2&3:£3.70 CSF £14.55 CT £59.28 TOTE £2.50: £1.10, £2.30, £2.20; EX 14.40.
Owner Patrick Wilmott **Bred** Meon Valley Stud **Trained** Newmarket, Suffolk

FOCUS
A moderate staying handicap run at a steady gallop early before hard-pullers Shirls Son Sam, and then Escape Artist strode on to inject some pace. The form does not look solid, with the runner-up a few pounds off his best.

2636 SENDRIG FILLIES' H'CAP 6f
9:20 (9:20) (Class 4) (0-85,90) 4-Y-0+ **£4,075** (£1,212; £606; £303) **Stalls** Centre

Form RPR

4430 **1** **Close To The Edge (IRE)**[12] 2264 4-9-0 **78**................................ ShaneKelly 7 83
(Alan McCabe) *mde all: arnd 4 l 1/2-way: rdn 2f out: drvn ins fnl f: hld on all out* **4/1**[3]

352- **2** *hd* **Hezmah**[278] 5476 4-9-7 **85**................................ TadhgO'Shea 2 89
(John Gosden) *hld up: rdn and hdwy over 2f out: chsd wnr over 1f out: drvn and kpt on fnl f: jst failed* **1/1**[1]

-401 **3** *1* **Misplaced Fortune**[11] 2310 7-9-5 **90** 6ex................................ DanielleMooney[(7)] 3 91
(Nigel Tinkler) *hld up: pushed along over 2f out: angled lft and hdwy over 1f out: kpt on: nrst fin* **7/1**

42-4 **4** *4½* **Mango Music**[17] 2120 9-8-11 **75**................................ DanielTudhope 4 62
(David Thompson) *in tch: rdn 2f out: wknd ins fnl f* **16/1**

2-10 **5** *3* **Abidhabidubai**[16] 2142 4-9-0 **78**................................ MichaelO'Connell 6 55
(John Quinn) *trckd ldr: rdn over 2f out: wknd over 1f out* **7/2**[2]

1m 13.39s (-1.21) **Going Correction** -0.175s/f (Firm) **5** Ran SP% **110.6**
Speed ratings (Par 102): **101,100,99,93,89**
CSF £8.57 TOTE £5.60: £1.80, £1.10; EX 11.30.
Owner Charles Wentworth **Bred** Martin Francis **Trained** Averham Park, Notts

FOCUS
Just an ordinary sprint handicap and the form looks muddling, being best rated around the winner and third.

T/Plt: £38.10 to a £1 stake. Pool:£51,061.54 - 976.42 winning tickets T/Qpdt: £20.70 to a £1 stake. Pool:£4,277.18 - 152.50 winning tickets AS

2426 SANDOWN (R-H)

Thursday, May 31

OFFICIAL GOING: Good to firm (good in places on round course; round 8.7; sprint 8.9)

Wind: medium, against Weather: cloudy

2637 BETFAIR SPONSORS THE STABLE STAFF CANTEEN H'CAP (BETFAIR 10 FURLONG FLAT SERIES QUALIFIER) 1m 2f 7y

6:15 (6:15) (Class 5) (0-75,75) 4-Y-0+ **£2,587** (£770; £384; £192) **Stalls** Low

Form				RPR
0-36	1		**Chain Of Events**[14] 2199 5-9-2 **70** HayleyTurner 14 (Sarah Humphrey) *swtg: taken down early: chsd ldrs: rdn to ld over 1f out: kpt on wl and a holding rival fnl f: rdn out* **9/2**[1]	80
1066	2	1 ¼	**Super Duplex**[18] 1735 5-8-9 **63** FergusSweeney 15 (Pat Phelan) *hld up in tch in midfield: hdwy 3f out: rdn to chse wnr over 1f out: kpt on same pce u.p fnl f* **20/1**	71
1-01	3	1 ½	**Scottish Star**[30] 1729 4-9-6 **74** LukeMorris 8 (James Eustace) *edgy: hld up in midfield: rdn 3f out: stuck bhd a wall of horses and switching lft over 2f out: hdwy 1f out: r.o strly ins fnl f: wnt 3rd cl home* **10/1**	80+
514-	4	nk	**Armoise**[240] 6607 4-9-6 **74** (t) AdamKirby 4 (Marco Botti) *in tch: rdn over 2f out: outpcd u.p over 1f out: rallied 1f out and swtchd lft ins fnl f: kpt on to chse ldng pair ins fnl f: lost 3rd nr fin* **8/1**[3]	78
6504	5	¾	**Edgewater (IRE)**[15] 2168 5-8-12 **66** KirstyMilczarek 7 (Lee Carter) *lw: t.k.h: hld up in tch: rdn over 2f out: outpcd u.p over 1f out: kpt on again ins fnl f: nt pce to chal* **12/1**	68
55-0	6	1	**Golden Waters**[31] 1706 5-9-2 **70** TomQueally 6 (Eve Johnson Houghton) *lw: in tch in midfield: swtchd rt and hdwy over 1f out: flashed tail u.p but kpt on fnl f* **15/2**[2]	70
5-61	7	½	**Understory (USA)**[28] 1792 5-9-7 **75** NeilCallan 1 (Tim McCarthy) *led: rdn and hdd over 1f out: 3rd and btn 1f out: wknd ins fnl f* **16/1**	74
154-	8	1	**Twice Bitten**[259] 6104 4-9-2 **70** RichardHughes 3 (James Toller) *hld up towards rr: sltly hmpd 7f out: rdn and effrt over 2f out: no imp wl over 1f out: kpt on ins fnl f but nvr gng pce to rch ldrs: eased nr fin* **9/2**[1]	67
1602	9	5	**Mafi (IRE)**[28] 1792 4-9-3 **71** IanMongan 13 (Mark Hoad) *on toes: chsd ldrs: rdn over 3f out: struggling and losing pl whn short of room over 1f out: wknd ent fnl f* **25/1**	58
26-2	10	hd	**Barathea Dancer (IRE)**[15] 2161 4-9-7 **75** DaneO'Neill 5 (Roger Teal) *chsd ldr tl jst over 2f out: struggling u.p 2f out: wknd jst over 1f out* **14/1**	62
00-0	11	¾	**Height Of Summer (IRE)**[14] 2199 4-9-2 **70** TedDurcan 10 (Chris Wall) *lw: hld up in midfield: rdn 4f out: sme hdwy u.p 2f out: no prog over 1f out: wl hld whn eased ins fnl f* **12/1**	56
6-60	12	½	**If You Whisper (IRE)**[31] 1706 4-8-7 **61** MartinDwyer 12 (Mike Murphy) *dwlt: a in rr: rdn and struggling over 2f out: n.d* **22/1**	46
-000	13	13	**High On The Hog (IRE)**[14] 2207 4-8-13 **67** TomMcLaughlin 2 (Paul Howling) *on toes: s.i.s: a bhd: lost tch over 2f out* **80/1**	26
-133	14	5	**Irons On Fire (USA)**[30] 1732 4-8-13 **67** StevieDonohoe 17 (Lee Carter) *lw: stdd after s: hld up in rr: lost tch over 2f out* **25/1**	16
0-60	15	4 ½	**Breakheart (IRE)**[12] 2274 5-9-4 **72** MichaelStainton 11 (Paul Howling) *hld up towards rr: sltly hmpd 7f out: struggling u.p 3f out: lost tch over 2f out* **33/1**	12
104-	16	35	**Songburst**[165] 7806 4-9-6 **74** PatDobbs 16 (Richard Hannon) *on toes: bit bkwd: t.k.h early: hld up in last quartet: lost tch over 2f out: sn eased: t.o* **12/1**	

2m 9.3s (-1.20) **Going Correction** +0.075s/f (Good) **16** Ran SP% **124.9**

Speed ratings (Par 103): **107,106,104,104,103 103,102,101,97,97 97,96,86,82,78 50**

toteswingers:1&2:£31.20, 1&3:£9.70, 2&3:£40.60 CSF £104.36 CT £882.60 TOTE £4.90: £2.00, £4.30, £1.90, £2.60; EX 133.20 TRIFECTA Not won..

Owner P J Edwards **Bred** Bishop Wilton Stud **Trained** West Wratting, Cambs

FOCUS

Rail at innermost configuration and distances as advertised. The going was good to firm, good in places on the round course, and good to firm on the sprint course ahead of an excellent evening meeting. They went a stop-start pace in this competitive handicap. Two runners who were second and third in this race last year filled the first two positions this time around and are rated to their respective turf bests in a straightforward race.

Height Of Summer(IRE) Official explanation: jockey said filly ran flat

Songburst Official explanation: jockey said colt moved poorly

2638 BETFAIR FUNDS THE PJA DOCTOR NATIONAL STKS (LISTED RACE) 5f 6y

6:45 (6:48) (Class 1) 2-Y-0

£13,043 (£4,945; £2,474; £1,232; £618; £310) **Stalls** Low

Form				RPR
1	1		**Sir Prancealot (IRE)**[15] 2164 2-9-0 0 RichardHughes 2 (Richard Hannon) *str: lw: midfield: rdn and gd hdwy 2f out: chsng ldrs whn nt clr run over 1f out: swtchd rt 1f out: sn qcknd to ld and stormed clr fnl f: impressive* **15/8**[1]	105+
534	2	4 ½	**Top Boy**[19] 2069 2-9-0 0 DaneO'Neill 6 (Derek Shaw) *w'like: swtg: bmpd s: bhd: rdn 1/2-way: hdwy u.p wl over 1f out: led 1f out: sn hdd and outpcd by wnr: kpt on for clr 2nd* **12/1**	87
2153	3	2 ½	**Effie B**[13] 2252 2-8-9 0 MartinHarley 5 (Mick Channon) *bmpd s and sn bhd: rdn 1/2-way: hdwy ent fnl f: wnt 3rd fnl 100yds: styd on wl but no ch w wnr* **11/1**[3]	73
0	4	hd	**Ocean Applause**[25] 1886 2-9-0 0 BrettDoyle 4 (John Ryan) *sn bustled along in rr: hdwy on inner over 1f out: battling for modest 3rd fnl 100yds: styd on but no ch w wnr* **100/1**	77
11	5	5	**Storm Moon (USA)**[37] 1579 2-9-0 0 JoeFanning 1 (Mark Johnston) *led: rdn over 1f out: hdd 1f out: sn btn and fdd fnl f* **15/8**[1]	59
3	6	nk	**Pixilated**[23] 1949 2-9-0 0 NeilCallan 7 (Gay Kelleway) *leggy: midfield: rdn 1/2-way: lost pl and towards rr whn n.m.r and swtchd lft over 1f out: no prog and wl btn after* **50/1**	58
116	7	½	**Baileys Jubilee**[13] 2252 2-8-9 0 SilvestreDeSousa 9 (Mark Johnston) *sn w ldr: ev ch and rdn over 1f out tl btn 1f out: sn fdd* **9/2**[2]	51
14	8	2 ¼	**Mossgo (IRE)**[29] 1747 2-9-0 0 LukeMorris 8 (John Best) *broke fast: chsd ldng pair: rdn 2f out: sn struggling: wknd jst over 1f out: fdd fnl f* **50/1**	48
361	9	2 ¼	**Mosstang (IRE)**[23] 1955 2-9-0 0 StevieDonohoe 3 (Robert Mills) *lengthy: chsd ldng trio: rdn 2f out: struggling wl over 1f out: fdd ent fnl f* **25/1**	40

1m 1.85s (0.25) **Going Correction** +0.075s/f (Good) **9** Ran SP% **112.5**

Speed ratings (Par 101): **101,93,89,89,81 81,80,76,73**

toteswingers:1&2:£4.80, 1&3:£2.60, 2&3:£5.90 CSF £26.42 TOTE £2.40: £1.10, £2.60, £1.90; EX 23.10 Trifecta £114.00 Pool: £5,087.53 - 33.02 winning units..

Owner Andrew Tinkler **Bred** Dermot Cantillon And Forenaghts Stud **Trained** East Everleigh, Wilts

FOCUS

The last winner of the National Stakes to follow up at Royal Ascot was Russian Valour in the Norfolk Stakes for in 2003, and this renewal did not have a great deal of strength in depth, but the winner was very impressive in a race where not much went right for him, and he could be a serious player at the Royal meeting. The form could be worth more.

NOTEBOOK

Sir Prancealot(IRE) ◆ readily justified favouritism in a 5.7f Bath maiden on debut. This was much tougher and this 140,000 euros colt ran into some traffic problems at a couple of stages, but he showed a sharp turn of foot to get into contention before quickening again to go clear and provide Richard Hannon with a fifth win in this race in the last 11 years. The downside to the form is that his two main rivals probably went off too fast and stopped quickly, but the style of the win was still very striking. Related to five winners at up to 1m2f, he looks a very smart prospect with a good cruising speed and lethal turn of foot. He could go for the Norfolk or the Coventry at Royal Ascot. (op 2-1 tchd 9-4 in a place)

Top Boy showed a fair level of ability in 5f slow-ground maidens on his last two starts and he ran a career-best to finish second on this big step up in class, despite being coltish beforehand. (op 8-1)

Effie B got caught a bit flat footed in mid-race before staying on well to record a second consecutive placed effort in Listed company. Her form has been generally progressive in five runs and this Sixties Icon filly should appreciate a step up in trip. (tchd 10-1)

Ocean Applause showed little after missing the break in a Newmarket maiden on debut and was thrown into the deep end here, but this was a promising run from a half-brother to a couple of decent 5f/7f winners. (op 80-1)

Storm Moon(USA), a clear-cut winner of a Musselburgh maiden and Southwell novice event in his two previous starts, was quickly away but he got involved in a front-running duel with his stablemate and faded in a disappointing bid to maintain his unbeaten record. (op 9-4)

Baileys Jubilee looked potentially smart when winning a maiden and Newmarket novice event on her first two starts, but she was disappointing at odds-on in a Listed fillies' event at York last time and it was a similar story here. (op 7-2)

2639 BETFAIR HENRY II STKS (GROUP 3) 2m 78y

7:20 (7:20) (Class 1) 4-Y-0+

£31,190 (£11,825; £5,918; £2,213; £2,213; £742) **Stalls** Centre

Form				RPR
2-21	1		**Opinion Poll (IRE)**[61] 1144 6-9-4 116 FrankieDettori 6 (Mahmood Al Zarooni) *lw: hld up in midfield: smooth hdwy to press ldrs gng wl 2f out: rdn and qcknd to ld jst ins fnl f: wnt rt but sn clr: eased nr fin* **5/4**[1]	119+
32-4	2	2 ¾	**Ibicenco (GER)**[12] 2207 4-9-0 112 KierenFallon 1 (Luca Cumani) *chsd ldr: rdn 3f out: pressing ldr and drvn 2f out: outpcd by wnr and btn jst ins fnl f: kpt on same pce u.p and wnt 2nd nr fin* **8/1**[3]	111
020-	3	hd	**Chiberta King**[229] 6857 6-9-2 108 JimmyFortune 5 (Andrew Balding) *led: rdn over 2f out: kpt on wl tl hdd and unable qck w wnr jst ins fnl f: kpt on same pce and lost 2nd nr finsh* **25/1**	111
15-4	4	nse	**Times Up**[13] 2254 6-9-2 111 RyanMoore 8 (John Dunlop) *hld up off the pce in last quartet: rdn and effrt over 2f out: styng on but hanging rt over 1f out: swtchd lft 1f out: styd on u.p and pressing for placings cl home: no ch w wnr* **4/1**[2]	111
13-2	4	dht	**Zuider Zee (GER)**[50] 1318 5-9-2 105 WilliamBuick 3 (John Gosden) *lw: chsd ldng pair: rdn and effrt over 2f out: drvn and pressing ldrs 2f out: outpcd by wnr jst ins fnl f: kpt on same pce after* **10/1**	111
165-	6	8	**Askar Tau (FR)**[350] 3066 7-9-2 110 (v) GeorgeBaker 4 (Marcus Tregoning) *stdd s: hld up off the pce in last quartet: rdn and effrt over 2f out: edgd rt and no prog over 1f out: nvr trbld ldrs* **8/1**[3]	101
026-	7	3 ¼	**Aaim To Prosper (IRE)**[308] 4469 8-9-2 107 MartinDwyer 10 (Brian Meehan) *t.k.h: hld up wl off the pce in last pair: rdn 7f out: no prog u.p over 2f out: wl hld fnl 2f* **66/1**	97
013-	8	19	**Ley Hunter (USA)**[242] 6562 5-9-4 115 MickaelBarzalona 7 (Saeed Bin Suroor) *on toes: stdd s: hld up off the pce in last quartet: rdn and effrt over 2f out: no prog and btn 2f out: bhd and eased wl ins fnl f* **16/1**	77
-456	9	nk	**Blue Bajan (IRE)**[13] 2254 10-9-2 103 SilvestreDeSousa 2 (David O'Meara) *chsd ldng trio: rdn and unable qck over 2f out: sn wknd: wl btn over 1f out: eased wl ins fnl f: t.o* **16/1**	74
01-1	10	22	**Old Hundred (IRE)**[43] 1446 5-9-2 95 (v) HayleyTurner 9 (James Fanshawe) *lw: stdd and dropped in bhd after s: hld up wl bhd in last pair: rdn and no hdwy wl over 2f out: sn lost tch: t.o and eased fnl f* **33/1**	48

3m 34.8s (-3.90) **Going Correction** +0.075s/f (Good)

WFA 4 from 5yo+ 2lb **10** Ran SP% **115.8**

Speed ratings (Par 113): **112,110,110,110,110 106,104,95,95,84**

toteswingers:1&2:£2.70, 1&3:£12.00, 2&3:£95.40 CSF £11.71 TOTE £1.80: £1.10, £2.40, £7.90; EX 13.00 Trifecta £233.20 Pool: £7,013.03 - 22.25 winning units..

Owner Godolphin **Bred** Darley **Trained** Newmarket, Suffolk

FOCUS

A high-quality edition of this Group 3 event. Five of the runners were rated above 110, but the favourite did the job in smooth style and won with plenty in hand from a tightly bunched group of four. The form looks solid with the third setting the standard.

NOTEBOOK

Opinion Poll(IRE) recorded a fourth Group 2/3 success when a comfortable winner of the Dubai Gold Cup last time. He had strong form claims back on turf after a short break and justified favouritism in good style under a confident ride. He is a classy and very consistent stayer who has won on ground ranging from heavy to good to firm. A runner-up in the Ascot Gold Cup last year, he would have solid each-way claims in that race again but he has a bit of work to do to reverse 2011 form with five-time Group 1 winner Fame And Glory. (op 11-8 tchd 6-5, 13-8 and 6-4 in a place)

Ibicenco(GER), a Group 1 runner-up over 1m4f on his final run in Germany, put in a game effort to come out on top in the chasing group on his second run for Luca Cumani. He is still lightly raced and unexposed at staying trips. (op 9-1 tchd 12-1)

Chiberta King dictated the pace and battled bravely in a good return from 229 days off. A patchy profile casts some doubt about whether he will build on this and he has not made a big impact in three skirmishes in Group company, but he beat Aaim To Prosper in a C&D Listed event last July and he could be a big factor if attempting a repeat success in that contest. (op 33-1)

Zuider Zee(GER) hit a new form high when a runaway winner of the November handicap last autumn. He came up a bit short in Listed company on his next two runs and the step up to 2m was an unknown factor here, but he ran a big race and could have more to offer at this trip. (op 9-1 tchd 11-1)

Times Up got tapped for speed before staying on strongly and would have snatched second in another couple of strides. He has not had many chances at 2m+ and is a half-brother to relentlessly progressive top-class stayer Give Notice, who won the 2m4f Prix Du Cadran at Longchamp as a 5-y-o for the same connections. (op 9-1 tchd 11-1)

Askar Tau(FR) couldn't get involved on return from almost a year off.

Blue Bajan(IRE) won this race last year but he was well beaten in this much stronger renewal. (op 18-1 tchd 20-1)

2640 BETFAIR BRIGADIER GERARD STKS (GROUP 3) 1m 2f 7y
7:55 (7:55) (Class 1) 4-Y-0+

£31,190 (£11,825; £5,918; £2,948; £1,479; £742) **Stalls** Low

Form RPR

134- **1** **Carlton House (USA)**340 3442 4-9-0 119 RyanMoore 2 115+
(Sir Michael Stoute) *lw: t.k.h: trckd ldng pair: gng best and wating for gap 2f out: rdn and qcknd between horses to ld 1f out: in command and r.o wl ins fnl f* **10/11**1

100- **2** 1 3/4 **Sagramor**250 6339 4-9-0 98 DarryllHolland 6 111
(Hughie Morrison) *stdd after s: hld up in last pair: rdn and outpcd 2f out: rallied jst ins fnl f: r.o wl to go 2nd wl ins fnl f* **25/1**

11-6 **3** 1 **Hunter's Light (IRE)**21 1994 4-9-0 110 FrankieDettori 4 109
(Saeed Bin Suroor) *t.k.h: stdd and hld up in 4th after 1f: hdwy to chal and rdn 2f out: outpcd by wnr jst ins fnl f: one pce fnl 150yds* **13/2**

42-3 **4** hd **I'm A Dreamer (IRE)**14 2209 5-8-11 111 JimmyFortune 5 106
(David Simcock) *chsd ldr tl led over 2f out: sn rdn: hdd 1f out: styd on same pce ins fnl f* **7/2**2

21-1 **5** 1 3/4 **Colombian (IRE)**33 1677 4-9-3 115 WilliamBuick 3 108
(John Gosden) *sn led and set stdy gallop: hdd and rdn over 2f out: unable qck and lost pl whn n.m.r over 1f out: no ex and btn fnl 150yds* **9/2**3

4556 **6** 14 **Sos Brillante (CHI)**5 2478 7-8-11 74 WilliamCarson 1 74
(Terry Clement) *taken down early: stdd s: hld up in last: rdn and effrt on outer 3f out: wknd 2f out* **250/1**

2m 8.38s (-2.12) **Going Correction** +0.075s/f (Good) **6** Ran SP% **110.4**
Speed ratings (Par 113): **111,109,108,108,107 96**
toteswingers:1&2:£4.40, 1&3:£2.20, 2&3:£13.20 CSF £25.25 TOTE £2.00: £1.10, £7.20; EX 21.60.

Owner The Queen **Bred** Darley **Trained** Newmarket, Suffolk

FOCUS
There were not many runners but this was a strong renewal of this Group 3 event. Former Derby hero Workforce won this in 2011 and last year's Derby third and Irish Derby fourth, Carlton House, scored in decent style on this comeback run to give Sir Michael Stoute back-to-back wins in this race. The form is not strong for the grade and is somewhat muddling.

NOTEBOOK
Carlton House(USA) raced a bit freely just behind the steady pace, but he did well to quicken through a late gap and score with some authority in a race that didn't really go to plan. This former Dante winner is a strong traveller who has record of 3-6 and still has a fair amount of potential. A strongly run 1m2f could prove ideal but if can settle a bit better this season he should also prove more potent at 1m4f. He looks the flagship horse for the Queen in her Diamond Jubilee year and should be able to add a Group 1 success at some point. He is entered in the Prince Of Wales's Stakes at Royal Ascot, but it is also interesting that he has the option of dropping back to 1m in the Queen Anne Stakes. (op 5-6 tchd 4-5)

Sagramor won the Britannia off 93 at Royal Ascot last year but he ended last season with a modest run in the Cambridgeshire. He had a tough task stepped up to 1m2f on this first skirmish in Group company, but he finished fast out wide from off the steady pace. He is out of a dual 1m4f-1m6f winner and this lightly raced 4-y-o could continue to progress at middle-distances this year. (op 33-1 tchd 40-1 in places)

Hunter's Light(IRE) ended 2011 on a high with back-to-back 1m2f Listed wins at Goodwood and Lingfield. He was well below form at Chester on his return but bounced back with a decent effort in a race that didn't set up for his closing style. His form figures of 83663 in Group 2/3 races are not very inspiring, but he is a tough and likeable sort who is unbeaten in three runs in Listed company. (op 15-2 tchd 8-1)

I'm A Dreamer(IRE) has been largely campaigned against her own sex but she ran a solid race behind the top-class colt in this contest. She is a likeable mare who is a four-time winner and was a close second in a Grade 1 at Woodbine last autumn. (op 4-1)

Colombian(IRE) showed a gritty attitude when grinding his way to victory on heavy-ground in the 1m2f Gordon Richards Stakes here on his reappearance last month. He dictated the steady pace in this contest but was comfortably overhauled and may have been inconvenienced by the switch back to fast ground. (tchd 4-1)

2641 BETFAIR HERON STKS (LISTED RACE) 1m 14y
8:25 (8:29) (Class 1) 3-Y-O

£18,714 (£7,095; £3,550; £1,768; £887; £445) **Stalls** Low

Form RPR

1 **1** **Cogito (USA)**43 1450 3-8-12 90 FrankieDettori 10 96+
(Brian Meehan) *t.k.h: hld up in midfield: rdn and effrt 2f out: drvn to chse ldrs over 1f out: sustained effrt u.p to ld towards fin* **8/1**

3-14 **2** nk **Stipulate**33 1678 3-9-3 103 TomQueally 4 100
(Sir Henry Cecil) *lw: t.k.h: chsd ldrs: drvn to chse ldr over 1f out: led jst ins fnl f: kpt on wl u.p tl hdd and no ex fnl 50yds* **14/1**

1- **3** 2 **Tales Of Grimm (USA)**293 4995 3-8-12 0 RyanMoore 6 91+
(Sir Michael Stoute) *lw: t.k.h: hld up in tch in last trio: rdn and effrt over 2f out: hdwy u.p ent fnl f: styd on u.p to go 3rd towards fin* **7/1**

4-1 **4** nk **Kahruman (USA)**24 1923 3-8-12 94 PaulHanagan 9 90
(William Haggas) *lengthy: t.k.h: chsd ldr: rdn to ld 2f out: drvn and hdd jst ins fnl f: wknd fnl 50yds* **12/1**

-652 **5** 3/4 **Ocean Tempest**7 2428 3-8-12 76 (p) BrettDoyle 7 88?
(John Ryan) *t.k.h: led: sn hdd: chsd ldr: rdn and edgd rt over 1f out: kpt on same pce u.p fnl f* **100/1**

2-04 **6** 3/4 **Saigon**12 2277 3-9-3 107 KirstyMilczarek 2 91+
(James Toller) *t.k.h: hld up in midfield: rdn and outpcd 2f out: rallied and edging rt ent fnl f: kpt on fnl 150yds* **20/1**

1 **7** 1 3/4 **Irish History (IRE)**10 2344 3-8-7 0 MickaelBarzalona 1 77+
(Mahmood Al Zarooni) *leggy: athletic: t.k.h: hld up in tch in midfield: rdn on inner to chse ldrs 2f out: nt clr run and hmpd over 1f out: nt rcvr and styd on same pce fnl f* **7/2**2

1-0 **8** 2 3/4 **Top Offer**26 1856 3-8-12 0 JamesDoyle 3 75
(Roger Charlton) *t.k.h: stdd after s: hld up in tch in rr: rdn and effrt on outer over 2f out: no imp* **3/1**1

3-13 **9** 3 1/2 **Eastern Sun (IRE)**42 1470 3-8-12 103 WilliamBuick 8 67
(John Gosden) *lw: t.k.h: sn led and set stdy gallop: qcknd 3f out: rdn and hdd 2f out: wknd jst over 1f out: fdd fnl f* **5/1**3

2-40 **10** 7 **Redact (IRE)**26 1856 3-8-12 109 RichardHughes 5 50
(Richard Hannon) *t.k.h: stdd s and hld up in tch in rr: hmpd after 2f: rdn and no rspnse over 2f out: lost tch over 1f out* **10/1**

1m 42.71s (-0.59) **Going Correction** +0.075s/f (Good) **10** Ran SP% **116.7**
Speed ratings (Par 107): **105,104,102,102,101 100,99,96,92,85**
toteswingers:1&2:£16.80, 1&3:£9.00, 2&3:£23.10 CSF £113.43 TOTE £8.90: £2.40, £3.50, £3.10; EX 58.70 Trifecta £788.00 Part won. Pool: £1,064.89 - 0.10 winning units..

Owner Reddam Racing Llc **Bred** Lazy Lane Farms Inc **Trained** Manton, Wilts

FOCUS
A fascinating Listed race, involving four runners who had already shown win or placed form at Listed/Pattern level and there were also a number of unexposed types in the line-up. The pace was not very strong and it got a bit messy in the closing stages but the very lightly raced winner maintained his unbeaten record in good style. The fourth sets the level rated at face value.

NOTEBOOK
Cogito(USA), a $165,000 colt who made an impressive winning debut in a 7f Newmarket maiden last month, travelled well before finding a surging run out wide to strike against a majority of more experienced rivals on this step up to Listed company. He still has plenty of potential at this trip and beyond and is a Giant's Causeway half-brother to Admiral's Cruise, who won the 1m5f Geoffrey Freer for the same trainer. (op 10-1)

Stipulate was disappointing on heavy ground in the Classic Trial here last time, but this year's wide-margin Feilden Stakes winner bounced back with a huge run and was just caught close home. A scopey and lightly raced colt, he seems to need fast ground and could prove equally effective at 1m-1m2f. (op 12-1)

Tales Of Grimm(USA) stayed on strongly from some way back to snatch third in a promising comeback run. This 320,000gns brother to UAE 1m Group 3 winner Do It All still has a lot of potential after just two runs and should stay further than this. (op 13-2 tchd 15-2)

Kahruman(USA) forged clear in a 1m Kempton maiden on his seasonal debut. His BHA rating of 94 gave him quite a bit to find up in class, but he was never far away and battled well. (tchd 10-1)

Ocean Tempest had a mountain to climb on adjusted figures but he ran a big race with cheekpieces reapplied. However, the downside is that he is probably flattered by his proximity in a steadily run race and this could have destructive impact on his mark.

Saigon Official explanation: jockey said colt was struck into and lost a hind shoe

Irish History(IRE) who was heavily backed, was still moving well when running into severe traffic problems. This very lightly raced filly is worth another chance. (op 5-1)

Top Offer didn't shine on slow ground in the 2000 Guineas, and he was laboured under a patient ride on this drop in grade and switch back to fast ground. (op 11-4 tchd 10-3 and 7-2 in places)

Eastern Sun(IRE), placed behind Trumpet Major in the Craven last month, got an easy lead but he dropped away quickly 2f out. (op 6-1 tchd 13-2)

2642 BETFAIR SUPPORTS OAKSEY HOUSE H'CAP 1m 14y
8:55 (8:57) (Class 3) (0-95,93) 4-Y-0+

£6,847 (£2,050; £1,025; £512; £256; £128) **Stalls** Low

Form RPR

-211 **1** **Highland Colori (IRE)**12 2274 4-8-13 **85** DavidProbert 1 92
(Andrew Balding) *mde all: hrd pressed and rdn 2f out: battled on gamely u.p fnl f: all out* **8/1**3

00-5 **2** nk **Directorship**24 1924 6-9-4 **90** GeorgeBaker 14 99+
(Patrick Chamings) *lw: stdd after s: hld up in rr: swtchd lft and effrt wl over 1f out: str run fnl f: wnt 2nd last strides: nt quite rch wnr* **7/1**2

2-01 **3** nk **Weapon Of Choice (IRE)**33 1679 4-9-4 **90** TomQueally 4 96
(Stuart Kittow) *dwlt: swtchd lft and hdwy on outer to chse wnr 6f out: rdn and ev ch 2f out: kpt on wl u.p: no ex cl home* **11/1**

3006 **4** 1 1/4 **First Post (IRE)**5 2500 5-8-11 **83** DaneO'Neill 9 86
(Derek Haydn Jones) *t.k.h: hld up in midfield: rdn and unable qck 2f out: hdwy 1f out: styd on wl to chse ldrs ins fnl f: no imp towards fin* **9/1**

14-0 **5** hd **Diverting**19 2067 4-8-11 **86** HarryBentley(3) 6 91+
(William Jarvis) *in tch: swtchd lft 2f out and nt clr run over 1f out tl hdwy 1f out: styd on wl ins fnl f: nt rch ldrs* **8/1**3

1210 **6** 3/4 **George Guru**40 1510 5-9-2 **93** MarkCoumbe(5) 3 94
(Michael Attwater) *hld up towards rr: effrt u.p on inner 2f out: styd on same pce ins fnl f* **12/1**

10-0 **7** shd **Cool Macavity (IRE)**21 1999 4-8-5 **82** MatthewLawson(5) 15 83+
(Charles Hills) *steadield after s: hld up in last pair: rdn and effrt 2f out: kpt on u.p fnl f: nt rch ldrs* **20/1**

0000 **8** 1 1/4 **Lowther**19 2082 7-9-4 **90** (b) IanMongan 7 88
(Brett Johnson) *t.k.h: chsd ldr tl 6f out: styd chsng ldrs: drvn and unable qck wl over 1f out: no ex and one pce fnl f* **33/1**

4-0 **9** 3/4 **Cool Marble (IRE)**19 2068 5-8-7 **84** RaulDaSilva(5) 12 80
(Jeremy Gask) *hld up in midfield: swtchd lft and effrt u.p 2f out: styd on same pce and no imp fr over 1f out* **14/1**

5-50 **10** 1 1/2 **Hung Parliament (FR)**36 1603 4-9-0 **86** RichardKingscote 8 79
(Tom Dascombe) *chsd ldrs: rdn and unable qck 2f out: wknd jst ins fnl f* **66/1**

6-50 **11** 1 3/4 **Chapter And Verse (IRE)**24 1924 6-8-10 **82** KieranO'Neill 13 71
(Mike Murphy) *stdd s: hld up in rr: swtchd lft and effrt in centre over 2f out: no imp: n.d* **12/1**

4001 **12** 3/4 **Sinfonico (IRE)**16 2151 4-8-12 **84** RichardHughes 2 71
(Richard Hannon) *in tch in midfield: switching lft and rdn whn n.m.r wl over 1f out: sn wknd* **10/1**

/1-2 **13** 5 **Terdaad (IRE)**24 1924 4-9-5 **91** (p) FrankieDettori 11 66
(Saeed Bin Suroor) *t.k.h: hld up in midfield: rdn and lost pl 3f out: wknd and bhd 2f out* **11/4**1

1m 42.5s (-0.80) **Going Correction** +0.075s/f (Good) **13** Ran SP% **120.1**
Speed ratings (Par 107): **107,106,106,105,104 104,104,102,102,100 98,98,93**
toteswingers:1&2:£11.10, 1&3:£9.50, 2&3:£12.70 CSF £62.35 CT £645.53 TOTE £8.90: £3.70, £2.50, £3.40; EX 65.70 Trifecta £794.80 Part won. Pool: £1,074.09 - 0.10 winning units..

Owner Evan M Sutherland **Bred** Rathbarry Stud **Trained** Kingsclere, Hants

FOCUS
A hot handicap. The pace was not very strong but the progressive winner put in a gritty display to complete a hat-trick. The form is rated around the first two.

NOTEBOOK
Highland Colori(IRE) was unfazed by a step up to 1m and a switch to forcing tactics and put in a determined effort to defy a 5lb rise for his 7f Newmarket win last month. He has been a big improver for Andrew Balding this season and seems versatile regarding ground, trip and tactics. (op 13-2)

Directorship stayed on well from some way back but was just denied back on fast turf. This strong finisher can be marked up for going close from off a steady gallop and he should be closing in on a fourth win. (op 8-1 tchd 13-2)

Weapon Of Choice(IRE) rallied gamely when winning a 1m heavy-ground handicap over C&D last time. It was a slight concern that all four of his wins have been in single-figure fields, but he was racing off just 1lb higher than last time and went close despite pulling hard early on. (op 10-1)

First Post(IRE) had not hit top form in five previous runs this year, but this was more like it from a 5-y-o who has form figures of 13314 at this track. (tchd 10-1)

Diverting ran into a some trouble but shaped with plenty of promise on her second run back from a break. She completed a four-timer in 1m-1m1f handicaps in the second half of last season, and she should be capable of further success this season. (op 7-1 tchd 15-2 in a place)

Terdaad(IRE), a close second off 1lb lower in a Kempton handicap on his recent comeback, was sent off favourite but he put in a lifeless display in his bid to improve his record to 3-6. This was too bad to be true. (op 3-1)
T/Jkpt: £25,000.00 to a £1 stake. Pool:£17,482.59 - 1.00 winning ticket T/Plt: £96.00 to a £1 stake. Pool:£119,604.97 - 908.55 winning tickets T/Qpdt: £10.10 to a £1 stake. Pool:£7,948.41 - 579.23 winning tickets SP

2643 - 2646a (Foreign Racing) - See Raceform Interactive

[2622] BRIGHTON (L-H)

Friday, June 1

OFFICIAL GOING: Good to firm (watered; 7.8)
Wind: Moderate, against Weather: Overcast, warm

2647 AT THE RACES SKY 415 H'CAP — 5f 59y
1:50 (1:52) (Class 5) (0-70,70) 3-Y-O+ — **£2,264** (£673; £336; £168) **Stalls** Centre

Form — RPR
6122 **1** **Amazing Win (IRE)**[1] 2618 4-8-7 **54** .... CharlesBishop(5) 2 — 66
(Mick Channon) *chsd ldrs: rdn over 1f out: led fnl 130yds: r.o strly* **6/5**[1]
6044 **2** 2 3/4 **The Strig**[1] 2629 5-9-8 **67** ....(v) RyanClark(3) 8 — 69
(Stuart Williams) *sn chsng ldrs: rdn and edgd lft jst over 1f out: led ins fnl f: hdd fnl 130yds: nt pce of wnr* **5/1**[2]
2260 **3** hd **Desert Strike**[6] 2494 6-9-9 **70** ....(p) MatthewLawson(5) 1 — 71
(Charles Hills) *hld up in last: rdn 2f out: r.o ent fnl f: fin strly* **11/2**[3]
344- **4** 2 3/4 **The Jailer**[175] 7690 9-8-12 **57** .... RyanPowell(3) 5 — 48
(John O'Shea) *chsd ldr: rdn 2f out: kpt on same pce fnl f* **9/1**
5366 **5** 1/2 **Slatey Hen (IRE)**[11] 2350 4-8-10 **52** ....(p) WilliamCarson 4 — 42
(Richard Guest) *chsd ldrs: rdn wl over 1f out: kpt on same pce* **12/1**
-045 **6** 2 1/4 **Wrapped Up**[9] 2397 3-8-6 **55** ....(bt[1]) CathyGannon 3 — 33
(Heather Main) *wnt rt s: in last pair but in tch: rdn wl over 1f out: nt pce to threaten* **9/1**
00-6 **7** 3 1/4 **Atlantic Cycle (IRE)**[10] 2377 5-9-6 **62** ....(tp) FergusSweeney 6 — 32
(Milton Bradley) *led: rdn over 1f out: hdd jst ins fnl f: wknd* **9/1**

1m 3.4s (1.10) **Going Correction** +0.25s/f (Good)
WFA 3 from 4yo+ 7lb — 7 Ran SP% **115.2**
Speed ratings (Par 103): **101,96,96,91,91 87,82**
CSF £7.65 CT £23.93 TOTE £1.80: £1.10, £3.00; EX 8.30.
Owner Mrs Theresa Burns **Bred** J Repard **Trained** West Ilsley, Berks

FOCUS
Rail dolled out by 4m from 6f to 2.5f increasing distances by 8yds. A low-grade sprint handicap in which the placed horses are close to their recent marks.

2648 1.4 MILLION ATTHERACES.COM USERS/BRITISH STALLION STUDS SUPPORTING BRITISH RACING EBF MAIDEN STKS — 5f 213y
2:25 (2:25) (Class 5) 2-Y-O — **£3,169** (£943; £471; £235) **Stalls** Centre

Form — RPR
3 **1** **Birdman (IRE)**[14] 2247 2-9-3 0 .... MartinLane 5 — 86+
(David Simcock) *stdd bhd ldrs s: tk clsr order 2f out: edgd lft and led ent fnl f: r.o wl: comf* **4/9**[1]
2 2 1/2 **Bornean (IRE)** 2-8-12 0 .... AntiocoMurgia(5) 3 — 74+
(Mahmood Al Zarooni) *trckd ldr: pushed along to chal 2f out: rdn and ev ch ent fnl f: kpt on but nt pce of wnr* **11/4**[2]
3 2 1/4 **Boomshackerlacker (IRE)** 2-9-3 0 .... PatCosgrave 1 — 68+
(George Baker) *dwlt: sn chsng ldrs: pushed along 2f out: ch ent fnl f: squeezed up fnl 120yds: kpt on but no ex* **16/1**
0 **4** 1 **Danz Choice (IRE)**[15] 2202 2-9-3 0 .... KieranO'Neill 2 — 64
(Richard Hannon) *led: rdn over 1f out: hdd ent fnl f: edgd lft: no ex fnl 100yds* **12/1**[3]
5 7 **Standing Bear (IRE)** 2-9-3 0 .... StevieDonohoe 4 — 42
(Paul Cole) *sn outpcd: a last* **20/1**

1m 12.82s (2.62) **Going Correction** +0.25s/f (Good) — 5 Ran SP% **114.3**
Speed ratings (Par 93): **92,88,85,84,75**
CSF £2.11 TOTE £1.50: £1.10, £1.60; EX 2.40.
Owner Anthony Hogarth **Bred** Lynchbages Edgeridge Ltd & Glenvale Stud **Trained** Newmarket, Suffolk

FOCUS
A half-decent juvenile maiden for the track. The form is fluid but the second can rate higher.

NOTEBOOK
Birdman(IRE), third in a Newmarket novice event on debut, won well enough and could be capable of leaving the bare form behind in time on a more conventional track. He was well on top at the finish and will likely stay 7f. (tchd 2-5)
Bornean(IRE), a half-brother to Chesham winner Champlain, moved nicely enough but couldn't match the winner for pace when it mattered. He should improve enough to win a maiden. (tchd 3-1)
Boomshackerlacker(IRE), a 65,000gns half-brother to a 6f juvenile winner, is reportedly quite a strong, compact sort with plenty of speed and he made a satisfactory start. Like the runner-up, he looks capable of winning a maiden.
Danz Choice(IRE) showed considerably more than on debut and may be capable of winning a maiden back at 5f.
Standing Bear(IRE), a 24,000gns son of Excellent Art, was said to want further beforehand by his trainer (without a 2-y-o debut winner in 14 months) and he was always toiling. (op 16-1)

2649 WATCH ROYAL ASCOT LIVE ON ATR H'CAP — 5f 213y
3:00 (3:00) (Class 5) (0-75,75) 3-Y-O — **£2,264** (£673; £336; £168) **Stalls** Centre

Form — RPR
3-31 **1** **Show Flower**[20] 2065 3-9-4 **74** .... PatCosgrave 5 — 79
(Mick Channon) *hld up in 4th: effrt 2f out: r.o to ld fnl 100yds: drvn out* **2/1**[2]
6-11 **2** 1/2 **Love Tale**[15] 2206 3-9-5 **75** .... FergusSweeney 2 — 78
(Mark Rimell) *trckd ldng pair: shkn up 2f out: hrd rdn fnl f: fin wl: jst snatched 2nd* **13/8**[1]
-022 **3** nk **Ashpan Sam**[15] 2206 3-9-4 **74** .... CathyGannon 4 — 76
(John Spearing) *plld hrd early: settled after 2f: trckd ldr: drvn to ld ins fnl 2f: hdd and nt qckn fnl 100yds* **4/1**[3]
00-0 **4** 2 **Right Regal (IRE)**[37] 1612 3-9-2 **72** ....(b[1]) NickyMackay 3 — 68
(Marco Botti) *led: rdn and hdd ins fnl 2f: no ex fnl f* **11/2**
203- **5** 5 **Poseidon Grey (IRE)**[233] 6787 3-9-3 **73** .... JohnFahy 1 — 53
(Clive Cox) *hld up in last: rdn over 2f out: sn wknd* **10/1**

1m 12.42s (2.22) **Going Correction** +0.25s/f (Good) — 5 Ran SP% **115.9**
Speed ratings (Par 99): **95,94,93,91,84**
CSF £6.06 TOTE £2.10: £2.50, £1.70; EX 5.70.
Owner Jaber Abdullah **Bred** Maywood Stud **Trained** West Ilsley, Berks

FOCUS
An ordinary 3-y-o sprint handicap and there was little between the front three at the line. The pace was steady and the form is muddling.

2650 AT THE RACES VIRGIN 534 CLASSIFIED (S) STKS — 1m 1f 209y
3:35 (3:35) (Class 6) 3-5-Y-O — **£1,617** (£481; £240; £120) **Stalls** High

Form — RPR
-542 **1** **Moresweets 'n Lace**[17] 2149 5-9-7 70 .... GeorgeBaker 3 — 57+
(Gary Moore) *t.k.h: trckd ldr: chal on bit 2f out: led jst over 1f out: sn in command: comf* **1/3**[1]
6405 **2** 1 3/4 **Lisselan Pleasure (USA)**[9] 2389 5-9-0 57 ....(t) DanielMuscutt(7) 1 — 53
(Bernard Llewellyn) *t.k.h: trckd ldrs in 3rd: pushed into ld ins fnl 2f: hdd jst over 1f out: sn outpcd by wnr* **8/1**[3]
0535 **3** hd **Pandorica**[16] 2167 4-9-7 61 .... MartinLane 2 — 53
(Bernard Llewellyn) *led: rdn and hdd ins fnl 2f: one pce* **7/2**[2]
3520 **4** 1 **Heading To First**[9] 2395 5-9-4 46 .... RobertLButler(3) 4 — 51
(Paddy Butler) *hld up in cl 4th: effrt 2f out: hrd rdn and no imp over 1f out* **20/1**

2m 18.05s (14.45) **Going Correction** +0.25s/f (Good) — 4 Ran SP% **113.1**
Speed ratings (Par 101): **52,50,50,49**
CSF £4.15 TOTE £1.20; EX 4.50.The winner was bought in for 5,500gns.
Owner Darrell Hinds **Bred** Jeremy Hinds **Trained** Lower Beeding, W Sussex

FOCUS
An uncompetitive seller that was very slowly ran and the form is meaningless.

2651 FOLLOW AT THE RACES ON TWITTER H'CAP — 1m 3f 196y
4:15 (4:15) (Class 6) (0-55,61) 4-Y-O+ — **£1,617** (£481; £240; £120) **Stalls** High

Form — RPR
0-51 **1** **Steely**[9] 2394 4-9-8 **61** 6ex .... GeorgeBaker 2 — 75
(Gary Moore) *fast away: mde all: qcknd clr ins fnl 2f: easily* **4/5**[1]
0464 **2** 5 **Pahente**[9] 2394 4-8-8 **47** .... MartinLane 5 — 52
(Tony Carroll) *hld up in 5th: hdwy over 3f out: chsd wnr wl over 1f out: no imp* **9/2**[3]
-055 **3** 5 **Barbirolli**[9] 2395 10-8-7 **46** oh1 .... WilliamCarson 4 — 43
(William Stone) *hld up in last: outpcd and rdn 4f out: wnt modest 3rd ins fnl f* **12/1**
5502 **4** 3/4 **Kucharova (IRE)**[9] 2395 4-8-11 **50** .... LiamKeniry 3 — 46
(Seamus Mullins) *pressed wnr tl easily outpcd wl over 1f out* **9/4**[2]
5/0- **5** 12 **Nicky Nutjob (GER)**[17] 6309 6-8-8 **47** .... FergusSweeney 1 — 23
(John O'Shea) *prom tl hrd rdn and wknd 3f out* **20/1**
000 **6** 9 **Littlemissperfect**[44] 1443 4-8-7 **46** oh1 .... JohnFahy 6
(Richard Rowe) *racd wd: chsd ldrs tl wknd 3f out* **40/1**

2m 36.67s (3.97) **Going Correction** +0.25s/f (Good) — 6 Ran SP% **119.4**
Speed ratings (Par 101): **96,92,89,88,80 74**
toteswingers:1&2:£1.90, 1&3:£2.00, 2&3:£3.90 CSF £5.62 TOTE £2.40: £3.50, £1.40; EX 5.50.
Owner E A Condon **Bred** Mrs S E Barclay **Trained** Lower Beeding, W Sussex

FOCUS
A low-grade handicap and a repeat of last week's Lingfield form. The form could be worth a bit more at face value.

2652 JOIN AT THE RACES ON FACEBOOK H'CAP — 6f 209y
4:45 (4:45) (Class 6) (0-65,63) 4-Y-O+ — **£2,264** (£673; £336; £168) **Stalls** Centre

Form — RPR
2343 **1** **Hierarch (IRE)**[36] 1636 5-9-0 **63** .... AliceHaynes(7) 7 — 72
(David Simcock) *towards rr: hdwy in centre over 2f out: led 1f out: pushed out* **9/2**[3]
4500 **2** nk **Jonnie Skull (IRE)**[16] 2171 6-8-3 **52** ....(vt) DannyBrock(7) 4 — 60+
(Phil McEntee) *plld hrd in 3rd: hrd rdn and lost pl 2f out: rallied and r.o strly ins fnl f* **14/1**
03-6 **3** 1/2 **Paperetto**[146] 88 4-8-7 **56** .... DanielCremin(7) 3 — 62
(Robert Mills) *t.k.h: led 1f: pressed ldr: led again 2f out tl 1f out: hrd rdn: kpt on* **10/1**
2224 **4** 1 3/4 **Unlimited**[11] 2354 10-9-5 **61** .... AdamKirby 6 — 63
(Tony Carroll) *in tch: rdn to press ldrs 2f out: one pce fnl f* **4/1**[2]
2231 **5** hd **Brown Pete (IRE)**[7] 2464 4-9-5 **61** 6ex ....(e) WilliamCarson 1 — 65+
(Richard Guest) *s.s: sn chsng ldrs: drvn to chal over 1f out: 4th and hld whn hit on nose by anther rdr's whip nr fin* **1/1**[1]
0400 **6** 4 1/2 **Kyncraighe (IRE)**[112] 503 4-8-2 **49** ....(tp) AmyScott(5) 2 — 38
(Joseph Tuite) *bhd: rdn to chse ldrs 2f out: wknd over 1f out* **33/1**
60/1 **7** 8 **Ansells Pride (IRE)**[10] 2366 9-9-0 **63** 6ex .... JakePayne(7) 5 — 30
(Bill Turner) *led after 1f tl 2f out: sn wknd* **9/2**[3]

1m 24.39s (1.29) **Going Correction** +0.25s/f (Good) — 7 Ran SP% **125.1**
Speed ratings (Par 101): **102,101,101,99,98 93,84**
toteswingers:1&2:£4.40, 1&3:£7.50, 2&3:£12.70 CSF £67.68 TOTE £4.80: £1.50, £5.70; EX 50.00.
Owner Tick Tock Partnership **Bred** Castlemartin Stud And Skymarc Farm **Trained** Newmarket, Suffolk
■ Stewards' Enquiry : Alice Haynes two-day ban: careless riding (Jun 15-16)

FOCUS
Moderate but competitive stuff, although the pace was sound and the third helps set the standard.

2653 ATTHERACES.COM EXCLUSIVE WILLIAM BUICK DERBY BLOG "HANDS AND HEELS" APPRENTICE SERIES H'CAP — 1m 1f 209y
5:15 (5:15) (Class 6) (0-60,60) 4-Y-O+ — **£1,617** (£481; £240; £120) **Stalls** High

Form — RPR
3242 **1** **Ostentation**[38] 1580 5-9-7 **60** ....(b) NicoleNordblad 3 — 68
(Alastair Lidderdale) *patiently rdn: given plenty to do in detached last: gd hdwy on ins rail to chse ldr 2f out: led over 1f out: pushed out* **9/4**[1]
0-30 **2** 2 3/4 **Entrance**[37] 1613 4-9-2 **55** .... ShirleyTeasdale 1 — 58
(Julia Feilden) *sn off the pce disputing 4th: rdn and hdwy 2f out: styd on to take 2nd ins fnl f* **9/2**[3]
3002 **3** 3/4 **Potentiale (IRE)**[10] 2364 8-8-13 **60** ....(v) Leah-AnneAvery(8) 4 — 61
(J W Hills) *modest 3rd most of way: effrt and clsd on clr ldr 2f out: kpt on fnl f* **9/4**[1]
-410 **4** 4 **Rigid**[62] 744 5-9-2 **55** .... WilliamTwiston-Davies 2 — 48
(Tony Carroll) *chsd clr ldr tl 2f out: no ex over 1f out* **15/2**
0332 **5** 4 **Putin (IRE)**[7] 2464 4-8-10 **49** ....(bt) AliceHaynes 5 — 34
(Phil McEntee) *led and sn wnt 8 l clr: 12 l ahd 4f out: wknd and hdd over 1f out* **7/2**[2]
2000 **6** 8 **Carlton Scroop (FR)**[11] 2348 9-8-10 **49** ....(b) RyanWhile 6 — 18
(Paddy Butler) *sn off the pce disputing 4th: rdn and wknd 3f out* **20/1**

2m 5.78s (2.18) **Going Correction** +0.25s/f (Good) — 6 Ran SP% **118.5**
Speed ratings (Par 101): **101,98,98,95,91 85**
toteswingers:1&2:£2.80, 1&3:£1.50, 2&3:£2.70 CSF £13.81 TOTE £2.50: £1.10, £2.20; EX 16.40.
Owner Chris Beek Racing **Bred** Wellsummers Stud **Trained** Lambourn, Berks

FOCUS
A low-grade handicap with the winner close to his old turf best.
T/Plt: £32.10 to a £1 stake. Pool:£39,215.78 - 889.16 winning tickets T/Qpdt: £19.70 to a £1 stake. Pool:£2,852.59 - 107.12 winning tickets LM

1602 EPSOM (L-H)
Friday, June 1

OFFICIAL GOING: Good (good to firm in places; 8.2)
Wind: virtually nil Weather: dry, overcast

2654 PRINCESS ELIZABETH STKS (SPONSORED BY INVESTEC) (GROUP 3) (F&M) 1m 114y
1:40 (1:41) (Class 1) 3-Y-0+

£31,190 (£11,825; £5,918; £2,948; £1,479; £742) **Stalls** Low

Form RPR
113- **1** **Clinical**[191] 7516 4-9-6 103 ...... LukeMorris 6 110
(Sir Mark Prescott Bt) *chsd ldr: rdn to ld 2f out: kpt on wl u.p fnl f: drvn out* **7/1**
640- **2** ¾ **Joviality**[283] 5366 4-9-6 109 ...... WilliamBuick 3 108+
(John Gosden) *in tch: rdn and effrt to chse ldrs 2f out: hanging lft over 1f out: plld out 1f out and stvd on u.p to chse wnr ins fnl f: kpt on* **9/2**[3]
4-44 **3** 1 **Barefoot Lady (IRE)**[15] 2209 4-9-6 108 ...... TonyHamilton 1 106
(Richard Fahey) *led: rdn and hdd 2f out: kpt on same pce u.p: lost 2nd ins fnl f* **4/1**[2]
30-5 **4** 2 ¼ **Navarra Queen**[32] 1766 4-9-6 106 ...... AStarke 8 101
(P Schiergen, Germany) *stdd s: hld up in last pair: rdn and hdwy over 2f out: chsd ldng trio 2f out: styd on same pce fr over 1f out* **16/1**
241- **5** 2 ½ **Lay Time**[261] 6061 4-9-6 109 ...... JimmyFortune 5 96
(Andrew Balding) *in tch: rdn and unable qck ent fnl 2f: sn outpcd: 5th and wl hld over 1f out: eased wl ins fnl f* **13/8**[1]
1452 **6** 3 ½ **Night Lily (IRE)**[20] 2078 6-9-6 81 ...... JimCrowley 2 88
(Paul D'Arcy) *stdd s: hld up in last trio: rdn and effrt on inner over 2f out: sn struggling: wknd wl over 1f out* **25/1**
010- **7** 2 ¾ **Valencha**[209] 7295 5-9-6 91 ...... DarrylHolland 7 82
(Hughie Morrison) *s.i.s: nvr gng wl in rr: rdn and effrt 3f out: no imp and wl btn fnl 2f* **16/1**
20-1 **8** 20 **Boastful (IRE)**[27] 1851 4-9-6 100 ...... NeilCallan 4 39
(Mrs K Burke) *t.k.h: in tch: rdn over 2f out: sn wknd: wl bhd and eased ins fnl f: t.o* **14/1**

1m 43.84s (-2.26) **Going Correction** -0.10s/f (Good) **8** Ran SP% **111.1**
Speed ratings (Par 113): **106,105,104,102,100 97,94,76**
toteswingers:1&2:£6.10, 1&3:£4.90, 2&3:£2.70 CSF £36.15 TOTE £8.40: £2.10, £1.70, £1.60; EX 44.50 Trifecta £170.30 Pool: £2,034.50 - 8.83 winning units..
Owner Cheveley Park Stud **Bred** Cheveley Park Stud Ltd **Trained** Newmarket, Suffolk

FOCUS
Rail dolled out in places up to 6yds from 8f to winning post adding about 8yds to distances. The course had been watered, with 6mm applied to the hill and home straight on Wednesday afternoon and 3mm put on the home straight on Thursday afternoon. The jockeys were largely very complimentary about the ground, describing it as "beautiful" and "perfect". Dual scorer Echelon and Eva's Request are recent winners of this distaff Group 3 who have gone on to Group 1 success. This looked a reasonable renewal, but it lacked any 3-y-o runners. The pace was only ordinary and the first three were always towards the fore, the form is nothing special for the grade with the placed horses close to their marks.

NOTEBOOK
Clinical, third in this last year before winning a trio of Listed events, was kept in training to try and pick up a Group victory. She achieved her aim first time out, always in the front two and running on willingly once moving past the leader. Royal Ascot's Windsor Forest Stakes, a Group 2 over the straight mile, is the natural target for this tough grey. (op 11-2)
Joviality, Bonfire's half-sister, made a pleasing return, running on to go second inside the last but always just being held by the winner. Although she had worked on the track last month she didn't look entirely at home here, hanging on the camber. She handled the quicker ground well enough though and may renew rivalry with Clinical in the Windsor Forest, where she would be suited by the stiff mile. Her rider thought she will come on for this run. (op 5-1 tchd 11-2)
Barefoot Lady(IRE), an old rival of the runner-up, was ridden differently than she had been at York, where her stamina for 1m2f had been in question. Making the running, she stuck on against the rail once headed without handling the track particularly well. She remains winless since last April's Nell Gwyn Stakes, but has proved pretty consistent in defeat. (op 9-2)
Navarra Queen, representing the German-based team behind Arc winner Danedream, did best of those to race in the rear. She was close enough with two to run but could not sustain her effort inside the last. The trip was on the sharp side for her. (op 11-1)
Lay Time, a winner in Listed company when last seen in September, was asked for her effort down the outside but failed to pick up. Jimmy Fortune reportedly felt the ground was riding a little loose, which did not suit his mount, while Andrew Balding felt his filly "hated the course". She is worth another chance. (op 7-4 tchd 15-8)
Night Lily(IRE) had a lot to find at the weights and is a better mare on sand. (op 28-1)
Valencha is another who was at a big disadvantage on these terms. (op 28-1)
Boastful(IRE) had a below-par Barefoot Lady behind when winning in Listed company at Goodwood, but she could not build on that on this different ground. She raced keenly, if not taking as keen a tug as she had last time, and was the first beaten. Official explanation: jockey said filly ran too free (op 11-1)

2655 INVESTEC WEALTH & INVESTMENT H'CAP 1m 2f 18y
2:15 (2:15) (Class 2) 4-Y-0+

£28,012 (£8,388; £4,194; £2,097; £1,048; £526) **Stalls** Low

Form RPR
14-1 **1** **Gatewood**[16] 2176 4-9-1 91 ...... WilliamBuick 8 101+
(John Gosden) *hld up in rr: stl plenty to do and nt clr run over 2f out: swtchd rt and hdwy over 1f out: str run fnl f to ld cl home: in command at fin* **9/4**[1]
/430 **2** nk **Ottoman Empire (FR)**[92] 755 6-9-10 100 ...... JamieSpencer 2 107
(David Simcock) *t.k.h: trckd ldrs: rdn and effrt on inner to ld over 2f out: hung rt u.p over 1f out: kpt on wl u.p tl hdd and no ex cl home* **20/1**
-356 **3** nk **Borug (USA)**[14] 2248 4-8-6 82 ......(p) KierenFallon 3 88
(James Tate) *s.i.s: hld up in rr: rdn and effrt over 2f out: edging lft and hdwy over 1f out: r.o wl ins fnl f: pressing ldrs and gng on cl home* **10/1**
4-44 **4** ¾ **Black Spirit (USA)**[43] 1475 5-9-10 100 ......(t) AdamKirby 14 105
(Clive Cox) *in tch in midfield on outer: rdn and effrt over 2f out: keeping on whn pushed sltly rt over 1f out: rallied and styd on wl ins fnl f: nvr quite gng pce to rch ldrs* **20/1**
103- **5** nk **Haylaman (IRE)**[251] 6342 4-8-11 87 ...... MickaelBarzalona 12 91
(David Simcock) *towards rr on outer: rdn and struggling whn pushed rt 3f out: rallied and hdwy in centre over 1f out: styd on wl ins fnl f: nt rch ldrs* **25/1**
0016 **6** nse **Licence To Till (USA)**[12] 2312 5-9-0 90 ...... MircoDemuro 11 94
(Mark Johnston) *chsd ldrs: effrt u.p over 2f out: pressed ldrs and unable qck over 1f out: styd on same pce fnl f* **33/1**
0-01 **7** 1 ¾ **Resurge (IRE)**[22] 1999 7-9-5 95 ...... IanMongan 9 96
(Stuart Kittow) *taken down early: in tch in midfield: effrt u.p on inner over 2f out: kpt on same pce and no imp fnl f* **6/1**[3]
100- **8** ¾ **Cry Fury**[251] 6339 4-9-7 97 ...... JamesDoyle 4 96+
(Roger Charlton) *hld up in tch towards rr: rdn 3f out: styng on but stl plenty to do whn nt clr run and hmpd over 1f out: edging lft and styd on ins fnl f: nvr gng pce to rch ldrs* **8/1**
612- **9** 1 ¾ **Pivotman**[223] 7029 4-9-5 95 ......(t) JimCrowley 1 91
(Amanda Perrett) *led tl rdn and hdd over 2f out: stl pressing ldr whn pushed rt and hmpd over 1f out: wknd ins fnl f* **16/1**
-351 **10** hd **Ramona Chase**[11] 2346 7-8-10 91 6ex ......(t) MarkCoumbe(5) 6 86
(Michael Attwater) *t.k.h: hld up in tch: rdn and unable qck over 2f out: hrd drvn and kpt on fr over 1f out: nvr gng pce to chal* **20/1**
0-33 **11** 1 **Creme Anglaise**[14] 2228 4-9-2 92 ...... HayleyTurner 13 85
(Michael Bell) *w ldr tl rdn and unable qck over 2f out: btn ent fnl f: wknd fnl 150yds* **20/1**
000- **12** 2 **Rumh (GER)**[265] 5928 4-9-10 100 ...... FrankieDettori 10 89
(Saeed Bin Suroor) *hld up in last quartet: rdn and dropped to last over 3f out: styd on same pce and n.d after* **14/1**
060- **13** 17 **Pekan Star**[209] 7297 5-9-2 92 ...... NeilCallan 5 47
(Roger Varian) *plld hrd: chsd ldrs: rdn and struggling over 2f out: wknd and hung bdly lft over 1f out: eased ins fnl f* **11/2**[2]

2m 7.19s (-2.51) **Going Correction** -0.10s/f (Good) **13** Ran SP% **119.0**
Speed ratings (Par 109): **106,105,105,104,104 104,103,102,101,101 100,98,85**
toteswingers:1&2:£13.40, 1&3:£5.70, 2&3:£35.50 CSF £58.20 CT £389.93 TOTE £3.00: £1.30, £6.70, £3.20; EX 56.20 Trifecta £1738.60 Pool: £2,701.96 - 1.15 winning units..
Owner George Strawbridge **Bred** George Strawbridge **Trained** Newmarket, Suffolk
■ Stewards' Enquiry : Jamie Spencer two-day ban: careless riding (Jun 15-16)
William Buick two-day ban: careless riding (Jun 15-16)

FOCUS
A red-hot handicap, even following the late withdrawal of Stand To Reason. The pace looked ordinary and, in a race as tight as this, room was always going to be at a premium in the home straight. Despite that the form looks pretty solid rated around the placed horses.

NOTEBOOK
Gatewood ◆ was the least-exposed runner in the field and was 5lb higher than when making a successful return from 297 days off at York last month. Ridden with a lot of confidence out the back of the field early, he would have been an unlucky loser as he was stuck in a pocket with nowhere to go when looking for room over 2f out. He gave quite a bump to Haylaman as he was pulled out soon afterwards, but managed to put in a withering run down the wide outside and hit the front around 20 yards from the line. He can be rated better than the winning margin and, with further improvement possible, he could well develop into a Pattern-race performer. (tchd 2-1, 3-1 and 11-4 in places)
Ottoman Empire(FR) missed the whole of 2011 and hadn't been seen since bleeding on his third and final start at Meydan in March, though his trainer reported that he had been working well. Always handy, he enjoyed a nice gap up the inside rail over 2f from and was soon through it and in front, but he then managed to hang up the camber under pressure and was run out of it on the run to the line. This performance confirmed his trainer's optimism and he should be able to win a nice handicap this term. (op 25-1 tchd 28-1 in a place)
Borug(USA) was on a losing run of ten coming into this despite a slipping mark, but had the cheekpieces back on and ran a blinder. Held up well off the pace, albeit with the winner behind him, he was briefly short of room over 2f out, but managed to find a clear run through when switched towards the inside and ran on to the line. He can win a nice handicap if building on this. (op 9-1)
Black Spirit(USA) has found life tough in Pattern/conditions events since his last win off 3lb lower in July 2010, but ran well here and stayed on gamely after coming off the bridle over 2f out. This was a good effort from the widest stall. (op 14-1)
Haylaman(IRE) ◆, making his debut for the yard after 251 days off, was back under probably his optimum conditions, but things didn't really go his way. Quite apart from racing wide throughout, he didn't handle Tattenham Corner at all well and then took a bump from the winner passing the 2f pole, but despite all of that he finished strongly down the wide outside and wasn't beaten far. His trainer had warned that he might need the run, so this was very encouraging and he is one to keep a close eye on. (op 28-1 tchd 33-1)
Licence To Till(USA) remains 7lb higher than when dominating in a small-field handicap at Haydock two starts ago, but this was a fair effort considering he was always close to the pace and kept on well for pressure.
Resurge(IRE) loves it here with three wins over C&D including this race off 2lb higher last year, but despite getting within striking distance of the leaders against the rail entering the final furlong he couldn't make the most of it. (op 7-1 tchd 5-1)
Cry Fury, gelded since disappointing when third-favourite for the Cambridgeshire, looked to be hating the track in the home straight and became short of room over a furlong out, but was staying on towards the end. He was having only his seventh career start here and should do much better back on a more conventional track. (op 7-1)
Pivotman ended last season in good form once the tongue-tie went on and has been gelded in the meantime, but having made much of the running he dropped out as though just needing it. (op 14-1)
Pekan Star proved disappointing in three subsequent starts after winning a hot York handicap on his return last season, but both of his wins had come after significant layoffs so his 209-day absence appeared a positive. However, he pulled hard early and eventually dropped out, suggesting there is a more fundamental problem. (op 8-1)

2656 INVESTEC DIOMED STKS (GROUP 3) 1m 114y
2:50 (2:50) (Class 1) 3-Y-0+

£31,190 (£11,825; £5,918; £2,948; £1,479; £742) **Stalls** Low

Form RPR
0-53 **1** **Side Glance**[30] 1749 5-9-4 113 ...... JimmyFortune 6 111
(Andrew Balding) *t.k.h: chsd ldrs: rdn and effrt over 2f out: drvn to ld ins fnl f: styd on wl* **4/1**[2]
5-60 **2** ¾ **Dance And Dance (IRE)**[106] 591 6-9-4 110 ...... RyanMoore 4 109
(Ed Vaughan) *stdd s: hld up in last pair: rdn and effrt over 2f out: drvn and chsd ldng pair over 1f out: wnt 2nd ins fnl f: hld fnl 75yds* **5/1**[3]
004- **3** ¾ **Mac Love**[191] 7516 11-9-4 100 ...... JamesDoyle 1 107
(Roger Charlton) *hld up in last pair: rdn over 2f out: swtchd rt over 1f out: styd on wl u.p ins fnl f: wnt 3rd cl home* **25/1**
05-1 **4** ½ **Worthadd (IRE)**[15] 2222 5-9-7 120 ...... MircoDemuro 3 109
(Sir Mark Prescott Bt) *t.k.h: chsd ldr tl led 2f out: sn rdn: hdd ins fnl f: no ex and wknd towards fin* **5/6**[1]
3651 **5** 4 ½ **Marcret (ITY)**[22] 1994 5-9-7 111 ...... JamieSpencer 2 99
(Marco Botti) *t.k.h: hld up in tch: rdn and effrt over 2f out: no imp and btn 1f out: eased wl ins fnl f* **12/1**

-602 **6** *3 1/4* **St Moritz (IRE)**[61] 1158 6-9-4 106.................................. AdrianNicholls 5 88
(David Nicholls) *led and set stdy gallop: rdn and qcknd 3f out: hdd 2f out: wknd jst over 1f out* **11/1**

1m 43.37s (-2.73) **Going Correction** -0.10s/f (Good) **6** Ran SP% **111.1**
Speed ratings (Par 113): **108,107,106,106,102 99**
toteswingers:1&2:£2.40, 1&3:£9.90, 2&3:£10.50 CSF £23.16 TOTE £5.60: £2.50, £2.30; EX 25.10.

Owner Pearl Bloodstock Ltd **Bred** Kingsclere Stud **Trained** Kingsclere, Hants

FOCUS
Not a strong field for this Group 3, as is quite often the case. They went a modest initial gallop and most of these took a bit of a tug. The time was around half a second quicker than the fillies took in the Princess Elizabeth II Stakes. The form is limited by the proximity of the third.

NOTEBOOK
Side Glance raced keenly in third place, set alight by Marcret on his inner, but knuckled down well when asked to master the favourite. Well suited by a sound surface, he was emulating his sire Passing Glance, who won the Diomed for this yard in 2004. This looks his level, but he is worth a crack at some of the place money on offer in the Queen Anne. (op 9-2)
Dance And Dance(IRE) bounced back from a couple of lesser efforts at Meydan, running on from the rear of the field. Unfortunate not to have won since taking the C&D handicap on this card a year ago, he had his chance but could definitely have done with a truer gallop and perhaps a bigger field. (op 11-2 tchd 6-1)
Mac Love, making his fourth appearance in the race, and the winner in 2009, is without a victory since September that year but retains his enthusiasm and a measure of his ability. He put up a pleasing effort on his reappearance, finishing well from the back, and a faster gallop would have suited him. (tchd 22-1)
Worthadd(IRE) was the disappointment of the race, as he had 4lb in hand on BHA ratings. Penalised for his win this month in the Badener Meile in Germany, he looked set to add to that when moving ahead, but he was collared at the furlong pole and his stride was shortening in the last 150 yards. He gave the impression that he would have liked to go faster early, taking a tug and racing with his usual low head carriage, while the course is another plausible excuse. Certainly Mirco Demuro felt that the track didn't suit his horse, while Sir Mark Prescott thought the ground was too firm. The grey is another Queen Anne entry. (op 10-11 tchd 4-5, evens in places)
Marcret(ITY), also penalised, was another who took a tug. That win came in heavy ground and he proved nothing like as effective back on a sound surface in what proved less of a stamina test. (op 10-1)
St Moritz(IRE) was runner-up in this in 2011. Reverting to front-running tactics after being held up at Doncaster, he set his own pace but was quickly beaten once headed. (op 9-1)

2657 INVESTEC MILE H'CAP — 1m 114y
3:25 (3:25) (Class 2) (0-105,100) 4-Y-0+

£15,562 (£4,660; £2,330; £1,165; £582; £292) **Stalls** Low

Form RPR

0-30 **1** **Highland Knight (IRE)**[41] 1510 5-9-4 **95**......................(t) DavidProbert 7 106
(Andrew Balding) *mde all: rdn and qcknd clr w rival over 2f out: battled on gamely u.p and a jst holding rival fnl f: all out* **13/2**[2]

6313 **2** *nk* **Mawaakef (IRE)**[14] 2250 4-8-10 **87**.................................. FrederikTylicki 4 97
(J R Jenkins) *in tch: chsd wnr over 3f out: wnt clr w wnr over 2f out: sustained chal and ev ch fr over 1f out: a jst hld* **20/1**

0-04 **3** *4* **Unex El Greco**[14] 2250 4-8-11 **88**.................................. WilliamBuick 12 90+
(John Gosden) *s.i.s: hld up wl bhd: hmpd and moved wd 4f out: rdn 3f out: hdwy over 1f out: r.o wl fnl f to snatch 3rd last stride: no threat to ldng pair* **10/1**

3-0 **4** *shd* **Deire Na Sli (IRE)**[34] 1670 4-8-6 **88**...........................(b) DarrenEgan(5) 1 90
(Martyn Meade) *hld up off the pce in midfield: rdn and effrt on inner over 2f out: wnt 3rd 1f out: kpt on but no threat to ldng pair: lost 3rd last stride* **33/1**

0-15 **5** *1/2* **Norse Blues**[14] 2250 4-8-13 **90**.. JamesDoyle 8 90
(Sylvester Kirk) *in tch: rdn and outpcd over 2f out: rallied ent fnl f: kpt on u.p but no threat to ldng pair* **17/2**

31-0 **6** *3/4* **Starwatch**[46] 1416 5-8-5 **85**.. SeanLevey(3) 15 84
(John Bridger) *chsd ldrs: rdn and effrt 3f out: sn outpcd by ldng pair: kpt on u.p but no threat to ldng pair fr over 1f out* **25/1**

1114 **7** *1* **Forceful Appeal (USA)**[25] 1924 4-8-11 **88**.................... HayleyTurner 6 85
(Simon Dow) *in tch: chsd ldng pair over 3f out: drvn and outpcd by ldng pair over 2f out: no imp after: lost 3rd 1f out: wknd ins fnl f* **18/1**

00/ **8** *3* **Prince Jock (USA)**[13] 2291 5-8-6 **83** ow1........................ KierenFallon 5 73
(John Patrick Shanahan, Ire) *chsd ldrs: rdn and unable qck over 3f out: outpcd by ldrs over 2f out: n.d after* **10/1**

-024 **9** *nk* **Kay Gee Be (IRE)**[27] 1865 8-8-10 **87**........................... TonyHamilton 16 77
(Richard Fahey) *hld up off the pce towards rr: rdn and effrt on inner 3f out: styd on but no real imp: nvr trbld ldrs* **20/1**

2-14 **10** *8* **Moone's My Name**[20] 2067 4-8-11 **88**............................. JimCrowley 17 60
(Ralph Beckett) *s.i.s: sme hdwy whn hmpd bnd 4f out: rdn and no prog over 3f out: n.d* **8/1**[3]

02-6 **11** *1 1/2* **Roayh (USA)**[20] 2082 4-9-4 **95**...................................... FrankieDettori 14 64
(Saeed Bin Suroor) *hld up off the pce towards rr: hdwy whn hmpd bnd 4f out: rdn and no prog over 3f out: n.d* **14/1**

-006 **12** *6* **Don't Call Me (IRE)**[12] 2311 5-9-2 **93**..........................(t) AdrianNicholls 3 49
(David Nicholls) *s.i.s: nvr gng wl in rr: hmpd 6f out: wl bhd fnl 3f: eased ins fnl f* **25/1**

3-60 **13** *5* **Field Of Dream**[62] 1130 5-9-6 **97**.................................. JamieSpencer 13 43
(Jamie Osborne) *v.s.a: a bhd: hmpd 6f out: no hdwy over 3f out: wl btn whn hung lft over 1f out: eased ins fnl f* **25/1**

0631 **14** *1/2* **Capaill Liath (IRE)**[14] 2243 4-9-1 **92**.................................(p) AmyRyan 9 36
(Kevin Ryan) *racd off the pce in midfield: pushed along whn slipped bdly on downhill run 4f out: nt rcvr and wl bhd fnl 3f* **16/1**

61-2 **15** *4 1/2* **Boogie Shoes**[14] 2250 4-9-5 **96**.. NeilCallan 2 31
(Roger Varian) *t.k.h: chsd ldrs: rdn over 2f out: wl btn and eased ent fnl f: t.o* **7/2**[1]

-200 **16** *8* **Axiom**[8] 2409 8-9-2 **100** ow2.................................... MichaelJMurphy(7) 10 18
(Ed Walker) *hld up wl bhd: hit rail 6f out: wl bhd after: t.o and eased fnl f* **33/1**

00-5 **17** *30* **Dunn'o (IRE)**[12] 2311 7-9-4 **95**... RyanMoore 11
(David Nicholls) *chsd wnr tl over 3f out: sn dropped to rr and lost tch: t.o and eased fr over 1f out* **20/1**

1m 42.99s (-3.11) **Going Correction** -0.10s/f (Good) **17** Ran SP% **124.9**
Speed ratings (Par 109): **109,108,105,105,104 103,103,100,100,93 91,86,81,81,77 70,43**
toteswingers:1&2:£41.80, 1&3:£17.60, 2&3:£45.20 CSF £136.76 CT £1347.85 TOTE £8.40: £2.20, £4.40, £3.00, £8.90; EX 163.30 Trifecta £2193.50 Part won. Pool: £2,964.26 - 0.30 winning units..

Owner J C Smith **Bred** Littleton Stud **Trained** Kingsclere, Hants
■ Stewards' Enquiry : David Probert two-day ban: used whip above permitted level (Jun15-16)

FOCUS
Considering how competitive this handicap looked beforehand, it was remarkable how few ever got into it. The pace was strong and the field was soon well spread out. The form is rated a little cautiously.

NOTEBOOK
Highland Knight(IRE), 8lb higher than when runner-up in this race last year, was partly responsible for the strong gallop alongside Dunn'o, but he had seen that rival off passing halfway. It was soon clear that he had only the runner-up to worry about all the way up the home straight and proved very game in holding him off all the way to the line. He had been very disappointing on soft ground at Newbury last time, but this surface suited him much better. (op 7-1)
Mawaakef(IRE) ◆, closely matched with three of these when third at Newmarket last month having tried to make all, had to be content with a stalking role this time, but considering he was off the bridle straightening up for home he did well to stick at it and was the only conceivable danger to the winner over the last 2f. Despite his best efforts, the winner wouldn't be denied but he deserves compensation. (tchd 16-1)
Unex El Greco, just behind Mawaakef at Newmarket, soon found himself with an awful lot to do and did very well to stay on down the wide outside and finish as close as he did, in a race where those held up were at a severe disadvantage. He was having only his eighth start here and, if he can be kept sound, there should be a decent handicap in him.
Deire Na Sli(IRE) showed nothing on her reappearance when debuting for the yard, but she stayed on from the middle of the field over the last couple of furlongs and this was much better. Her record of 1-19 isn't ideal, but her new stable may be able to eke a bit more improvement out of her.
Norse Blues finished just behind Mawaakef and Unex El Greco at Newmarket and kept staying on without looking a threat. He remains 5lb higher than when winning the Spring Mile on his Doncaster reappearance. (op 8-1 tchd 9-1)
Starwatch was in blinding form in the second-half of last season, winning five from six, and was entitled to need his Windsor reappearance. He was drawn wide here, which meant he saw plenty of daylight in a handy position and he took a bit of a hold as well. Under the circumstances he did well to hang in there for as long as he did and this was a step forward.
Forceful Appeal(USA), a triple winner on the Lingfield Polytrack earlier in the year, was having his first try on turf in this country and moved up to chase the front pair over 2f from home, but could make no further impression on them. He may not want the ground this quick. (op 14-1)
Prince Jock(USA) was 8lb higher than for his recent Wexford success, including the overweight, and couldn't get back into the race after losing his pitch at halfway. (op 12-1 tchd 8-1)
Field Of Dream Official explanation: jockey said gelding slipped at start
Capaill Liath(IRE) stumbled badly at halfway, so can be forgiven this effort. Official explanation: jockey said gelding slipped (op 20-1)
Boogie Shoes had the second, third and fifth behind him when runner-up at Newmarket last month on his return from 239 days off, but after pulling hard in a handy position early he eventually stopped as though something was amiss. Official explanation: jockey said gelding ran too free (op 4-1)
Axiom got hampered against the rail after a couple of furlongs. Official explanation: vet said gelding was struck into
Dunn'o(IRE) Official explanation: jockey said gelding lost its action

2658 INVESTEC OAKS (GROUP 1) (FILLIES) — 1m 4f 10y
4:05 (4:08) (Class 1) 3-Y-O

£207,842 (£78,797; £39,435; £19,644; £9,858; £4,947) **Stalls** Centre

Form RPR

3 **1** **Was (IRE)**[16] 2187 3-9-0 0.. SeamieHeffernan 10 114
(A P O'Brien, Ire) *led after 1f tl 10f out: chsd ldrs after: 3rd st: rdn and qcknd to ld over 2f out: drvn over 1f out: kpt on wl fnl f: all out* **20/1**

21-2 **2** *nk* **Shirocco Star**[14] 2232 3-9-0 104.................................. DarryllHolland 8 113
(Hughie Morrison) *t.k.h: hld up wl in tch: 6th st: rdn and effrt to chse ldrs 2f out: drvn and chsd wnr ins fnl f: kpt on wl* **16/1**

1-41 **3** *1/2* **The Fugue**[16] 2178 3-9-0 111.. WilliamBuick 2 112+
(John Gosden) *t.k.h: hld up in tch: hmpd 9f out: 9th st: rdn and hdwy over 2f out: chsd ldrs over 1f out: styd on wl ins fnl f: wnt 3rd fnl 50yds* **11/4**[1]

11 **4** *1* **Vow**[20] 2079 3-9-0 105.. JohnnyMurtagh 3 111
(William Haggas) *t.k.h: chsd ldrs: 4th st: rdn to chal jst over 2f out: drvn and unable qck over 1f out: btn and edgd lft ins fnl f* **9/2**[3]

11-3 **5** *2* **Maybe (IRE)**[26] 1884 3-9-0 114... JPO'Brien 11 108+
(A P O'Brien, Ire) *stdd s: t.k.h: hld up in tch in rr: hmpd over 8f out: 11th st: swtchd rt and effrt 3f out: hdwy and drvn to chse ldng quartet over 1f out: kpt on fnl f: nt pce to chal* **10/3**[2]

11-1 **6** *2* **Coquet**[8] 2410 3-9-0 94.. RobertHavlin 5 110+
(Hughie Morrison) *t.k.h: in tch: hmpd 9f out: 7th st: effrt on inner to chse ldrs and stl gng wl whn squeezed for room and bdly hmpd 2f out: dropped to last: swtchd rt and rallied 1f out: r.o wl but unable to rcvr* **18/1**

1-1 **7** *nk* **Kailani**[26] 1887 3-9-0 106... MickaelBarzalona 13 104+
(Mahmood Al Zarooni) *stdd s: hld up in tch in rr: hmpd over 8f out: 12th st: pushed rt and rdn 3f out: hdwy u.p 1f out: styd on fnl f but no threat to ldrs* **6/1**

2 **8** *nk* **Betterbetterbetter (IRE)**[23] 1973 3-9-0 0...................... CO'Donoghue 7 104
(A P O'Brien, Ire) *t.k.h: hld up in tch: hmpd 9f out: 8th st: effrt u.p 3f out: edgd lft and no prog over 1f out: one pce after* **22/1**

1-2 **9** *2 1/2* **Colima (IRE)**[20] 2079 3-9-0 98.. JimCrowley 4 100
(Ralph Beckett) *in tch: 5th st: rdn and unable qck 3f out: struggling and lost pl over 2f out: wknd wl over 1f out* **20/1**

46-2 **10** *1 1/2* **Devotion (IRE)**[19] 2101 3-9-0 107.................................. RichardHughes 12 97
(A P O'Brien, Ire) *stdd s: hld up in tch in rr: hmpd over 8f out: 10th st: rdn and effrt wl over 2f out: no imp 2f out: wknd over 1f out* **33/1**

22 **11** *3 1/4* **Twirl (IRE)**[16] 2178 3-9-0 103... PatSmullen 1 92
(A P O'Brien, Ire) *led for 1f: chsd ldr 10f out: 2nd st: rdn to press ldrs but unable qck 3f out: wkng whn edgd lft wl over 1f out* **25/1**

-204 **12** *1/2* **Nayarra (IRE)**[8] 2410 3-9-0 103.. MartinDwyer 9 91
(Mick Channon) *t.k.h: chsd ldr tl led 10f out: rdn and hdd over 2f out: wknd 2f out: in rr whn short of room and hmpd wl over 1f out: eased ins fnl f* **50/1**

2m 38.68s (-0.22) **Going Correction** -0.10s/f (Good) **12** Ran SP% **116.0**
Speed ratings (Par 110): **96,95,95,94,93 92,91,91,90,89 86,86**
toteswingers:1&2:£20.50, 1&3:£12.40, 2&3:£8.10 CSF £274.21 CT £1160.63 TOTE £27.90: £6.60, £3.50, £1.50; EX 453.40 Trifecta £2161.40 Pool: £13,436.11 - 4.60 winning units..

Owner Derrick Smith & Mrs John Magnier & Michael Tabor **Bred** Lodge Park Stud **Trained** Ballydoyle, Co Tipperary
■ Stewards' Enquiry : J P O'Brien four-day ban: careless riding (Jun 15-18)
Darryll Holland four-day ban: careless riding (Jun 15-18)

FOCUS
The winners of most of the recognised Oaks trials were present this year, the exceptions being those at Chester and Newbury, though the runners-up in both of those contests did take part. Three of these ran in the Newmarket 1000 Guineas, while Ballydoyle provided just the five contenders after the late withdrawal of Kissed. Only two of these had been successful at Group 1 level before, one of which was in Italy. However, what had looked an intriguing contest beforehand ended up a most unsatisfactory event with a dawdling early pace and plenty of trouble, whilst the feeling is that the best filly didn't win. The form is not the most solid and the level is fluid.

NOTEBOOK

Was(IRE) was given a well-judged ride in a steadily run race. She raced close to the moderate pace throughout and made full use of the gap that appeared next to the inside rail, as the leader Nayarra hung away from it passing the 2f pole. Although pressed late on, she was always doing just enough. She had suffered a setback before finishing third in a Naas Group 3 on last month's return and that form left her with plenty to find to win a race like this, but she had made a big impression when winning at the Curragh on her sole juvenile start and this helps justify her 1,200,000gns purchase price. The Irish Oaks would be the obvious next port of call. (op 18-1 tchd 16-1)

Shirocco Star only just failed in the Listed trial at Newbury on last month's reappearance and is bred to stay this far. Racing in midfield, though never too far off the pace, she moved up smoothly to challenge over 2f out and kept on strongly, but could never quite force her head past the winner. This effort paid a compliment to her Newbury conqueror Momentary, but she is capable of winning a big event in her own right. (op 14-1)

The Fugue ◆ could hardly have been more impressive when bolting up in the Musidora and is bred to get this trip, but her chance was severely dented when she was hampered as the free-running Shirocco Star carried Betterbetterbetter right across her around 1m from home and she was knocked to the back of the field. Considering how much ground she made up down the outside in the home straight and how close she came to winning, she was surely the best filly on the day and hopefully she will get the chance to prove it. (tchd 3-1)

Vow, unbeaten in both starts this spring having been unraced at two, is bred to relish this trip and duly saw it out well when beating Colima in the Lingfield Oaks Trial on Polytrack, despite hanging all over the place in the home straight. Although ridden close to the pace in a steadily run race, she might have been better off making use of her proven stamina and when it came to a test of speed over the last 2f, she was just found wanting. (op 4-1 tchd 5-1)

Maybe(IRE), the pick of Joseph O'Brien over her four stable companions and the highest-rated runner in the field on account of her unblemished record at two including her success in the Moyglare, was beaten a fair way into third by her stablemate Homecoming Queen when favourite for the 1000 Guineas, and though there is stamina in her pedigree her dam was a sprinter and her trainer wasn't sure she would stay. She seemed to be ridden with those stamina doubts in mind, but getting into a barging match with Kailani after around half a mile presumably wasn't in the script and it cannot have done either of their chances much good. She did stay on down the wide outside late, but it was laboured progress and it did seem that she didn't improve for the trip. Her trainer hinted that he was considering dropping her back to 1m for the Coronation Stakes. (op 11-4)

Coquet booked her placed in the line-up with a game success in the Listed trial at Goodwood eight days earlier, but was a prime candidate to 'bounce'. However, she didn't really get the chance to show her form, as firstly she got caught in the backwash behind Shirocco Star, Betterbetterbetter and The Fugue after half a mile, and then got pinched against the inside rail by the weakening Nayarra when trying to get closer passing the 2f pole. She remains one to be interested in for a Group contest. (op 20-1)

Kailani, out of the 1000 Guineas/Oaks winner Kazzia, came into this unbeaten in two starts and was very impressive when winning the Pretty Polly at Newmarket last month, but this quicker ground was a question mark. She was unlikely to have a problem with the trip, though, so it was puzzling to see her held up out the back at an early stage and the argy-bargy with Maybe around 1m out was the last thing she needed. In her defence, she was all over the place down the wide outside in the home straight and looked to be hating both the track and the quick ground. (op 8-1)

Betterbetterbetter(IRE), narrowly beaten by a 74-rated rival in the Cheshire Oaks, was always in about the same position and never looked like landing a blow. (op 20-1)

Colima(IRE)'s profile coming into this was almost identical to the stable's 2008 Oaks-winner Look Here, in that she had won her only start at two and finished runner-up in the Lingfield Oaks Trial (behind Vow) on her return, albeit on Polytrack. She appeared to hold a good position throughout, so it was disappointing that she found so little off the bridle. Perhaps the quick ground found her out. (op 25-1)

Devotion(IRE) finished runner-up in the Leopardstown 1000 Guineas Trial last month, but that form has since taken a hit and, although she got caught up in the melee between Maybe and Kailani around 1m from home, it's hard to say that she would have troubled the principals otherwise.

Twirl(IRE), beaten over 4l by The Fugue in the Musidora, held a decent position from the off, soon settling behind the leader just ahead of the winner, but she was seen off well over a furlong from home.

2659 INVESTEC SURREY STKS (LISTED RACE) 7f

4:50 (4:50) (Class 1) 3-Y-O

£18,714 (£7,095; £3,550; £1,768; £887; £445) **Stalls** Low

Form				RPR
14-3	**1**		**Producer**[44] 1455 3-8-13 99 ... RichardHughes 7	99
			(Richard Hannon) *chsd ldrs: wnt 2nd 4f out: jnd ldr 3f out: rdn to ld over 1f out: drvn clr 1f out: r.o wl: eased cl home* **2/1**[1]
420-	**2**	3 ¾	**Justineo**[237] 6688 3-8-13 102 ... RyanMoore 2	89+
			(William Haggas) *bhd: rdn 3f out: hdwy u.p over 1f out: styd on fnl f to go 2nd nr fin: no ch w wnr* **11/4**[2]
0-50	**3**	½	**Lady Gorgeous**[13] 2276 3-8-8 98 ... MartinHarley 6	87+
			(Mick Channon) *hld up in tch: rdn and effrt to chse ldrs over 2f out: edgd lft u.p and unable qck over 1f out: n.m.r ins fnl f: squeezed between horses fnl 5yds to snatch 3rd last stride* **5/1**
10-3	**4**	shd	**Lunar Deity**[26] 1894 3-8-13 80 ... NeilCallan 4	87?
			(Eve Johnson Houghton) *in tch: rdn to chse ldrs 3f out: drvn and unable qck over 1f out: battling for placings and styd on same pce fnl f* **25/1**
4-03	**5**	shd	**Balty Boys (IRE)**[13] 2277 3-8-13 107 ... MichaelHills 5	87
			(Charles Hills) *led: jnd and rdn 3f out: hdd and outpcd by wnr over 1f out: battling for placings and one pce fnl f* **3/1**[3]
-020	**6**	9	**Big Note (IRE)**[30] 1751 3-8-13 94 ... JimmyFortune 1	63
			(Andrew Balding) *t.k.h: chsd ldrs: rdn and struggling over 2f out: hung lft and wknd wl over 1f out: bhd and eased ins fnl f* **14/1**

1m 21.48s (-1.82) **Going Correction** -0.10s/f (Good) **6** Ran SP% **112.2**

Speed ratings (Par 107): **106,101,101,101,100 90**

toteswingers:1&2:£2.10, 1&3:£2.30, 2&3:£2.90 CSF £7.77 TOTE £2.60: £1.30, £1.90; EX 8.70.

Owner J Palmer-Brown **Bred** Cheveley Park Stud Ltd **Trained** East Everleigh, Wilts

FOCUS

Some decent types such as Shakespearean, Hooray and Galeota have won this Listed race in recent years, but this looked an ordinary edition overall. That said, the winner's performance was smart, and the time was relatively quick, although the proximity of the fourth suggests the fourth underperformed.

NOTEBOOK

Producer's three juvenile wins all came over C&D and this looked the ideal race for him. It proved pretty straightforward as he got over to track the pace, railed slickly, then found plenty to draw clear once let down. He was not disgraced over 1m1f on his return at Newmarket, but this seems his optimum trip and the Jersey Stakes could be the most suitable race for him at Ascot. (op 9-4)

Justineo, settled in last, still had only one behind him at the furlong pole, but finished well down the outside. The track was not ideal for him and he can step up on this reappearance, with his stamina for this trip proven now. He will be entered in the Jersey Stakes. (op 7-2)

Lady Gorgeous found a gap on the rail closing and then she was hampered when switched, the interrupted passage probably costing her second. Fillies' races over this trip could be the way forward with her. (op 9-2 tchd 11-2)

Lunar Deity, upped in grade, had easily the least chance at these weights, but he ran creditably and just missed out on some black type. The quicker ground suited.

Balty Boys(IRE), seven places ahead of Justineo when fourth in last autumn's Middle Park Stakes, had the best chance on official figures. Making the running, he could never shake off the winner but stuck on, confirming that he stays this trip. His running style suggests a drop back to 6f would suit, however. (op 11-4)

Big Note(IRE) is not going to fulfil his potential, or stay this trip, unless he can be got to settle. (op 12-1 tchd 16-1)

2660 INVESTEC ASSET MANAGEMENT H'CAP 7f

5:25 (5:26) (Class 2) (0-100,95) 3-Y-O

£12,450 (£3,728; £1,864; £932; £466; £234) **Stalls** Low

Form				RPR
1131	**1**		**Laffan (IRE)**[13] 2265 3-8-11 **85** ... AmyRyan 9	94
			(Kevin Ryan) *mde all: wnt clr over 2f out: drvn and hrd pressed over 1f out: kpt on gamely and forged ahd ins fnl f: r.o wl: drvn out* **7/1**[3]
516	**2**	1 ¼	**Van Ellis**[13] 2277 3-9-7 **95** ... KierenFallon 14	100+
			(Mark Johnston) *in tch: pushed along and struggling on downhill run over 4f out: rdn and hdwy to chse wnr 2f out: str chal u.p over 1f out: no ex and btn ins fnl f: hld on for 2nd cl home* **8/1**
1-25	**3**	½	**Prince Alzain (USA)**[13] 2275 3-9-2 **90** ...[1] LukeMorris 11	96+
			(Gerard Butler) *hld up towards rr: swtchd rt and effrt over 2f out: hdwy u.p over 1f out: r.o strly ins fnl f: wnt 3rd nr fin* **20/1**
1-12	**4**	nk	**Famous Poet (IRE)**[13] 2265 3-8-11 **85** ... FrankieDettori 12	88
			(Saeed Bin Suroor) *hld up in midfield: effrt and nt clr run briefly over 2f out: hdwy u.p over 1f out: kpt on wl ins fnl f* **11/4**[2]
-500	**5**	nse	**Alejandro (IRE)**[13] 2276 3-9-2 **90** ... TonyHamilton 2	93
			(Richard Fahey) *chsd ldrs: drvn and outpcd by wnr over 2f out: kpt on u.p fnl f* **28/1**
-060	**6**	½	**Sheikh The Reins (IRE)**[8] 2416 3-8-3 **77** ... HayleyTurner 5	79
			(John Best) *chsd ldrs: rdn and unable qck over 2f out: kpt on fnl f but nt pce to chal* **40/1**
1	**7**	½	**Dutch Old Master**[21] 2042 3-8-8 **82** ... JamesDoyle 8	82+
			(Gary Moore) *chsd ldrs: n.m.r 2f out: swtchd ins and rdn over 1f out: no imp tl styd on ins fnl f: nt pce to chal* **20/1**
42-1	**8**	½	**Sholaan (IRE)**[28] 1825 3-9-1 **89** ... RyanMoore 13	88+
			(William Haggas) *t.k.h: in tch in midfield: rdn and effrt over 2f out: hdwy u.p over 1f out: no imp ins fnl f* **5/2**[1]
2-23	**9**	hd	**My Sharona**[15] 2194 3-8-2 **76** oh1 ... KieranO'Neill 10	74
			(Sylvester Kirk) *hld up towards rr: effrt on inner 3f out: switching rt fr 2f out: styd on u.p ins fnl f: nvr threatened ldrs* **12/1**
21-2	**10**	4 ½	**Fire Ship**[25] 1938 3-8-3 **80** ... HarryBentley(3) 15	66
			(William Knight) *dwlt: niggled along in rr: rdn and sme hdwy over 2f out: wknd over 1f out* **17/2**
0-60	**11**	1 ¾	**Crown Dependency (IRE)**[21] 2022 3-9-7 **95** ... RichardHughes 1	76
			(Richard Hannon) *chsd wnr tl 2f out: sn wknd: bhd and eased ins fnl f* **16/1**
13-0	**12**	7	**Dissent (IRE)**[13] 2265 3-8-1 **80** ...(e[1]) DarrenEgan(5) 4	43
			(Gerard Butler) *stdd s: t.k.h: hld up in rr: rdn and hdwy over 2f out: wknd wl over 1f out: bhd and eased fnl f* **25/1**

1m 23.0s (-0.30) **Going Correction** -0.10s/f (Good) **12** Ran SP% **122.2**

Speed ratings (Par 105): **97,95,95,94,94 94,93,92,92,87 85,77**

toteswingers:1&2:£7.60, 1&3:£21.50, 2&3:£14.30 CSF £59.16 CT £1102.59 TOTE £8.00: £2.60, £2.80, £5.80; EX 80.90 Trifecta £644.80 Pool: £3,904.04 - 4.48 winning units..

Owner Mubarak Al Naemi **Bred** Vincent Dunne **Trained** Hambleton, N Yorks

■ Stewards' Enquiry : Frankie Dettori two-day ban: careless riding (Jun 15-16)

FOCUS

A decent handicap but perhaps not the strongest for the grade, with the top weight 5lb lower than the permitted maximum. They seemed to go a fair gallop but the time was a second and a half slower than the Listed race. The form is rated on the positive side, although the fifth and sixth will ultimately set the level.

NOTEBOOK

Laffan(IRE) got over from stall nine to grab the lead and never relinquished it, momentarily looking in danger of being swamped but keeping on strongly. He went up 10lb for his win at Doncaster and Amy Ryan, who excelled here, has lost her 3lb claim since, so effectively he was racing off a 13lb higher mark. While he will be up in the weights again, he is progressing very well and he may be ready for a crack at a Listed race before long. (op 13-2)

Van Ellis, who ran in Listed company last time, performed well under top weight. He did not come down the hill too smoothly, but ran on well in the straight without being able to peg back the winner. This was a decent run from a wide draw. (op 7-1)

Prince Alzain(USA), dropped 3f in trip after finishing behind Derby runners Thought Worthy and Rugged Cross at Newmarket, was fitted with a hood for the first time which seemed to settle him. Switched out after failing to get a run up the inner, he still had a pack of horses in front of him entering the final furlong but rolled home down the outside to snatch third. A mile could be his optimum. (tchd 16-1)

Famous Poet(IRE)'s mark remained unchanged after his Doncaster run and he was a lot better off with Laffan, but he could not cash in for all that he ran respectably. He is another who will be suited by further. (op 7-2)

Alejandro(IRE) showed pace from stall two but did not convince that this trip is what he wants, losing third place in the dying strides. He has been eased 5lb since the start of the season.

Sheikh The Reins(IRE) could not get to the lead, but this was a respectable effort and he is due to be dropped 2lb now. (tchd 33-1)

Dutch Old Master ran creditably on this handicap and turf debut, and has more to offer. It will be interesting to see which way they go with him trip-wise, as he has speed in his pedigree but was staying on here.

Sholaan(IRE)'s Wolverhampton maiden win has been given a sizeable boost by wins for the next three home, and he was of obvious interest on this handicap debut. He could never pick up the leaders, a wide draw not helping, and his trainer said beforehand that he could be given a try over 6f. (op 3-1 tchd 10-3 in places)

My Sharona, runner-up here in April and a pretty consistent type, was closing quite nicely once switched away from the rail. (tchd 10-1)

T/Jkpt: Not won. T/Plt: £135.30 to a £1 stake. Pool:£241,723.19 - 1,303.55 winning tickets
T/Qpdt: £32.00 to a £1 stake. Pool:£13,292.44 - 306.51 winning tickets SP

[2484]HAYDOCK (L-H)

Friday, June 1

OFFICIAL GOING: Good (good to firm in places) changing to good to firm after race 2 (6:50)

Wind: light 1/2 against Weather: fine and sunny

2661 BETDAQ HAYDOCK PARK APPRENTICE TRAINING SERIES H'CAP (PART OF THE RACING EXCELLENCE INITIATIVE) 1m 2f 95y

6:20 (6:20) (Class 5) (0-75,76) 4-Y-O+ **£2,264** (£673; £336; £168) **Stalls** Centre

Form RPR

5651 **1** **St Ignatius**[10] 2363 5-9-5 **70** 6ex....(p) NatashaEaton 2 77
(Alan Bailey) *mde all: drvn over 3f out: hld on gamely* **13/2**

042 **2** *3/4* **Entihaa**[20] 2095 4-9-8 **73**.... GarryWhillans 1 79
(Alan Swinbank) *dwlt: sn chsng ldrs: effrt on ins over 3f out: n.m.r over 1f out: kpt on same pce last 100yds* **12/1**

5-61 **3** *1 1/2* **Call Of Duty (IRE)**[7] 2454 7-8-11 **62** 6ex.... ShaneBKelly 5 65
(Dianne Sayer) *hld up: hdwy over 4f out: kpt on same pce fnl f* **9/1**

0-31 **4** *1 3/4* **Elspeth's Boy (USA)**[8] 2414 5-9-11 **76** 6ex.... KyleJames 8 76
(Philip Kirby) *trckd wnr: t.k.h: chal over 2f out: wknd fnl 100yds* **7/4**[1]

0-21 **5** *1* **King Zeal (IRE)**[11] 2328 8-9-11 **76** 6ex....(t) JamesRogers 3 74
(Barry Leavy) *racd in last: rn in snatches: drvn over 6f out: wknd appr fnl f* **7/2**[2]

31-0 **6** *1/2* **Spanish Plume**[52] 1275 4-9-10 **75**.... JackDuern 4 72
(Reg Hollinshead) *trckd ldrs: effrt over 2f out: wknd fnl f* **4/1**[3]

2m 13.32s (-2.18) **Going Correction** -0.25s/f (Firm) **6** Ran SP% **109.6**

Speed ratings (Par 103): **98,97,96,94,94 93**

toteswingers:1&2:£7.30, 1&3:£6.70, 2&3:£9.70 CSF £69.21 CT £647.10 TOTE £6.70: £2.80, £4.20; EX 65.70 Trifecta £153.40 Pool: £404.48 - 1.95 winning units..

Owner A J H **Bred** Simon And Helen Plumbly **Trained** Newmarket, Suffolk

FOCUS

All races oninner home straight and distances on round course increased by 7yds. A competitive little apprentice handicap in which four of the six runners were carrying penalties having won on their previous start. The three market leaders filled the last three places. The runner-up looked an improver with the runner-up rated in line with his maiden form backed up by the third to his latest.

2662 E B F MHA LIGHTING MAIDEN STKS 6f

6:50 (6:50) (Class 5) 2-Y-O **£3,234** (£962; £481; £240) **Stalls** Centre

Form RPR

5 **1** **Master Of War**[8] 2415 2-9-3 0.... DaneO'Neill 10 87+
(Richard Hannon) *trckd ldrs: led wl over 1f out: r.o wl: readily* **6/1**[3]

0 **2** *2 1/4* **Deauville Prince (FR)**[23] 1972 2-9-3 0.... RichardKingscote 4 80
(Tom Dascombe) *hmpd s: hdwy over 2f out: chsd wnr 1f out: no imp* **25/1**

3 *1* **Requested** 2-9-3 0.... SilvestreDeSousa 5 77+
(Mahmood Al Zarooni) *wnt lft s: t.k.h: effrt over 2f out: kpt on same pce fnl f* **9/1**

4 *nk* **Ayaar (IRE)** 2-9-3 0.... MatthewDavies 3 76+
(Mick Channon) *hmpd s: sn chsng ldrs: kpt on same pce appr fnl f* **25/1**

2 **5** *3 3/4* **Newstead Abbey**[15] 2213 2-9-3 0.... RichardMullen 6 65
(David Brown) *w ldrs: drvn over 3f out: led briefly 2f out: wknd last 100yds* **1/1**[1]

6 *2* **Dreamily (IRE)** 2-8-12 0.... FrannyNorton 1 54
(Mark Johnston) *dwlt: sn chsng ldrs: wknd over 1f out* **9/1**

3 **7** *1* **Fantacise**[18] 2124 2-8-12 0.... PaulHanagan 2 51
(Brian Meehan) *wnt rt s: w ldrs: wknd over 1f out* **9/2**[2]

5 **8** *1* **Wrightington**[11] 2330 2-9-0 0.... LeeTopliss[(3)] 7 53
(Richard Fahey) *mid-div: outpcd and lost pl over 2f out* **25/1**

4 **9** *2 3/4* **Tahaf (IRE)**[44] 1451 2-9-3 0.... BrettDoyle 9 45
(Clive Brittain) *led: hdd 2f out: sn wknd* **50/1**

10 *2* **Baltic Prince (IRE)** 2-9-3 0.... RussKennemore 8 39
(Paul Green) *in rr and drvn along: nvr on terms* **100/1**

1m 15.16s (1.36) **Going Correction** +0.20s/f (Good) **10** Ran SP% **117.0**

Speed ratings (Par 93): **98,95,93,93,88 85,84,82,79,76**

toteswingers:1&2:£17.80, 1&3:£4.70, 2&3:£28.90 CSF £143.61 TOTE £6.00: £2.40, £6.90, £3.70; EX 128.40 Trifecta £639.40 Part won. Pool: £864.12 - 0.50 winning units..

Owner M S Al Shahi **Bred** R J Cornelius **Trained** East Everleigh, Wilts

FOCUS

This looked quite a decent maiden based on the form of those that had run previously, plus there were several newcomers from major yards. The form is rated around the averages with the winner stepping up on his debut.

NOTEBOOK

Master Of War was relatively unfancied on his debut here the previous week and showed the benefit of that experience by scoring in good style this time. He was always travelling and found plenty when asked, giving the impression there is more to come. (op 13-2 tchd 5-1)

Deauville Prince(FR) ◆, possibly suffered worst of those squeezed out at the start, but picked up well in the closing stages to chase home the winner. This was a big step up on his debut effort and he can be expected to win races before long. (op 20-1)

Requested, a 110,000gns colt from a family of middle-distance performers, is a very late foal and did well, especially as he was another one to get involved in some early scrimmaging. (op 8-1)

Ayaar(IRE), a half-brother to a sprint winner from the family of Hatta Fort, was edgy beforehand and was hampered early, but ran promisingly on this debut. He showed a fair bit of knee action so might appreciate slightly easier ground in future. (op 33-1)

Newstead Abbey ran really well when a close second on his debut at York and the third that day had bolted up since. Sent off a well-backed favourite, he showed good pace but could not sustain it. On the face of it this was disappointing but the trainer's representative reported that the colt was unsuited by the good to firm ground. Official explanation: trainer's rep said colt was unsuited by the good to firm ground (op 11-10 tchd 6-5 and 5-4 in a place)

Dreamily(IRE), a 100,000gns half-sister to four winners including Calming Influence, was quite keen and saw plenty of daylight on the outside of her field. She can be expected to do better with this experience behind her.

Fantacise, a half-sister to nine winners including Queen Mary winners Romantic Myth and Romantic Liason, had run promisingly on a softer surface on her debut and showed up early here, but dropped away disappointingly, so possibly needs some cut in the ground. (op 5-1)

2663 E B F PIPER HEIDSIECK CHAMPAGNE MAIDEN STKS 5f

7:25 (7:27) (Class 5) 2-Y-O **£3,234** (£962; £481; £240) **Stalls** Centre

Form RPR

1 **Cosmic Chatter** 2-9-3 0.... GrahamGibbons 1 86+
(David Barron) *wnt lft s: mde all: pushed along over 1f out: hld on wl towards fin* **9/1**[3]

2 *1/2* **Ian's Dream (USA)** 2-9-3 0.... ShaneKelly 5 84+
(Jeremy Noseda) *t.k.h in rr: swtchd lft 2f out: chsd wnr 1f out: kpt on last 50yds: a hld* **2/1**[1]

3 *3 1/4* **Dansili Dual (IRE)** 2-9-3 0.... DaneO'Neill 8 73+
(Richard Hannon) *sn chsng wnr: kpt on same pce fnl f* **2/1**[1]

4 *2* **Mayaasem** 2-9-3 0.... PaulHanagan 7 65+
(Charles Hills) *dwlt: mid-div: drvn to chse ldrs over 2f out: hung rt and one pce* **11/4**[2]

050 **5** *9* **Sound Affects**[7] 2437 2-8-12 0.... FrannyNorton 2 28
(Alan Brown) *t.k.h in rr: effrt over 2f out: lost pl over 1f out* **50/1**

00 **6** *8* **Dha Chara (IRE)**[13] 2261 2-9-3 0.... TonyCulhane 6
(Reg Hollinshead) *stmbld s: lost pl 2f out* **33/1**

7 *2 3/4* **Hollydanfaye** 2-8-12 0.... SilvestreDeSousa 4
(Paul Green) *sn chsng ldrs: rdn and edgd lft over 2f out: sn wknd* **40/1**

1m 2.28s (1.48) **Going Correction** +0.20s/f (Good) **7** Ran SP% **110.7**

Speed ratings (Par 93): **96,95,90,86,72 59,55**

toteswingers:1&2:£3.30, 1&3:£3.80, 2&3:£1.10 CSF £25.70 TOTE £10.60: £3.10, £2.30; EX 31.40 Trifecta £98.10 Pool: £729.32 - 5.50 winning units..

Owner T D Barron **Bred** Harrowgate Bloodstock Ltd **Trained** Maunby, N Yorks

FOCUS

The going description was changed to Good to firm all over before this race. A couple of recent winners of this have gone on to score at Listed level, while last year's winner Shumoos subsequently scored at Group 3 level and the runner-up Frederick Engels scored at Royal Ascot and then at Group 2 level. With the two that had run showing very moderate form, this looked set to fall to a newcomer, with several big yards represented. The first four were all seeing a racecourse for the first time and finished clear. The form is pretty good and rated towards the top end of the averages.

NOTEBOOK

Cosmic Chatter is bred for this trip and knew his job on this debut. He broke well and made all the running, eventually scoring more cosily than the official margin suggests, as his rider never picked up his stick. Already gelded, he looks capable of making his mark in better 5f races. (op 10-1 tchd 12-1)

Ian's Dream(USA), a speedily bred $120,000 foal, was taken down very quietly last of all and had a stable handler to meet him at the start. He showed he has ability though, picking up well from off the pace and delivering a sustained late challenge. He should win races if going the right way from this debut. (tchd 9-4)

Dansili Dual(IRE) ◆ is bred to be speedy, being out of an Albany and Cherry Hinton winner, showed good pace but could not keep tabs on the winner and faded late on. He should come on for the outing and can be expected to win races. (op 15-8)

Mayaasem, a 90,000gns yearling, tracked the pace but could not pick up in the latter stages. He gives the impression that he will be suited by further in time. (op 3-1 tchd 5-2)

2664 MULTIPLEX ACHILLES STKS (LISTED RACE) 5f

8:00 (8:00) (Class 1) 3-Y-O+

£18,714 (£7,095; £3,550; £1,768; £887; £445) **Stalls** Centre

Form RPR

22-0 **1** **Excelette (IRE)**[44] 1454 3-8-5 **98**.... RoystonFfrench 7 105
(Bryan Smart) *chsd ldr: drvn 2f out: led jst ins fnl f: edgd rt: hld on nr fin* **12/1**

2243 **2** *nk* **Spirit Quartz (IRE)**[6] 2486 4-9-3 **106**.... RichardKingscote 5 112
(Robert Cowell) *stdd s: hld up: effrt 2f out: chsng ldrs whn n.m.r 1f out: wnt 2nd 75yds out: r.o: jst hld* **2/1**[2]

0-64 **3** *3 1/4* **Noble Storm (USA)**[23] 1977 6-9-3 **107**.... GrahamGibbons 6 100
(Ed McMahon) *led: hdd jst ins fnl f: no ex* **13/2**[3]

221- **4** *3/4* **Amour Propre**[278] 5524 6-9-3 **112**.... DaneO'Neill 3 98
(Henry Candy) *w ldrs: kpt on same pce fnl f* **15/8**[1]

20-1 **5** *2* **Duchess Dora (IRE)**[23] 1977 5-8-12 **102**.... TomQueally 1 85
(John Quinn) *chsd ldrs: rdn over 2f out: wknd last 100yds* **8/1**

1040 **6** *1/2* **Fratellino**[6] 2507 5-9-7 **92**....(v[1]) ShaneKelly 4 93
(Alan McCabe) *sn outpcd and in rr: sme hdwy and edgd lft over 2f out: nvr a factor* **40/1**

162- **7** *1 1/2* **Chunky Diamond (IRE)**[223] 7019 3-8-10 **104**.... PaulHanagan 2 80
(Peter Chapple-Hyam) *s.i.s: hdwy over 1f out: wknd jst ins fnl f* **10/1**

1m 0.36s (-0.44) **Going Correction** +0.20s/f (Good)

WFA 3 from 4yo+ 7lb **7** Ran SP% **111.8**

Speed ratings (Par 111): **111,110,105,104,100 100,97**

toteswingers:1&2:£4.20, 1&3:£11.60, 2&3:£2.40 CSF £34.82 TOTE £17.80: £7.90, £1.40; EX 36.40.

Owner Crossfields Racing **Bred** David John Brown **Trained** Hambleton, N Yorks

FOCUS

A reasonable Listed race with the majority rated in excess of 100. The winner is rated in line with last season's Redcar form.

NOTEBOOK

Excelette(IRE), placed in four Listed races as a juvenile, having won twice previously. Dropping back to the minimum trip having not got home in the Nell Gwyn on her reappearance, she showed plenty of pace alongside the leader and picked up well when asked to win her race, opening up sufficient advantage to hold the late surge of the runner-up. She looks capable of winning Group races if able to go on from this, and her next target is a Group 3 at the Curragh later in the month. (tchd 14-1)

Spirit Quartz(IRE) ran a fine race over C&D in the Group 2 Temple Stakes the previous weekend and has run consistently well in all his starts since coming from Italy. He picked up well in the closing stages but just too late. He deserves to win one of these. (op 11-4)

Noble Storm(USA) was bidding to follow up his 2011 success and set off in front as usual. However, he never got much peace and couldn't find anything extra in the last furlong. He is gradually running into form though. (tchd 6-1)

Amour Propre, having his first run since winning a Group 3 at the Curragh in August, seemed to be going well enough at halfway but his effort flattened out under pressure. The run should bring him on. (op 13-8 tchd 2-1 in a place)

Duchess Dora(IRE) finished well to score on her reappearance at Chester, but that was on soft ground and she was taken off her feet early on this faster surface. She does handle fast ground but probably needs a stiffer track over this trip when it rides like this. (tchd 9-1)

2665 ELECTROLUX MAIDEN STKS 1m

8:30 (8:34) (Class 5) 3-Y-O+ **£2,264** (£673; £336; £168) **Stalls** Low

Form RPR

2-4 **1** **Tawaasul**[16] 2172 3-8-12 0.... PaulHanagan 12 76+
(William Haggas) *mde all: qcknd over 3f out: kpt on wl fnl f* **5/4**[1]

03 **2** *1 1/2* **Standing Strong (IRE)**[21] 2041 4-10-0 0.... TomQueally 5 80
(Robert Mills) *trckd ldrs: wnt 2nd over 3f out: chal 2f out: hung lft and carried hd high: one pce ins fnl f* **2/1**[2]

0 **3** *6* **Cape Alex**[42] 1503 3-8-12 0.... BrettDoyle 8 58
(Clive Brittain) *s.i.s: hld up: outpcd and lost pl over 5f out: hdwy 3f out: kpt on to take 3rd last 100yds* **25/1**

0 **4** *1 3/4* **Sir Lexington (IRE)**[25] 1922 3-9-3 0.... DaneO'Neill 4 59
(Richard Hannon) *chsd ldrs: one pce fnl 3f* **8/1**[3]

5 *13* **Naburn**[72] 4-9-9 0.... GarryWhillans[(5)] 6 33
(Alan Swinbank) *s.i.s: t.k.h: sn trcking ldrs: wknd over 1f out* **8/1**[3]

6 3½ **One For The Girls** 3-9-3 0 .... RussKennemore 10 21
(Nicky Vaughan) *s.i.s: hld up in rr: edgd lft and kpt on fnl 2f: nvr a factor* **33/1**

0-00 7 3¼ **Red Alex**[34] 1655 3-9-3 40 .... GrahamLee 3 14
(James Given) *chsd ldrs: drvn over 3f out: wknd 2f out* **33/1**

60 8 3¼ **Voodoo (IRE)**[12] 2313 3-9-3 0 .... PadraigBeggy 9
(Daniel Mark Loughnane) *s.i.s: in tch: drvn over 5f out: wknd 3f out* **66/1**

0 9 5 **Crimson Cheer (USA)**[17] 2145 3-8-12 0 ....(t) TravisBlock 11
(Brian Meehan) *chsd ldrs: drvn over 5f out: wknd over 3f out* **66/1**

00 10 36 **Captain Cavallo**[9] 2387 5-10-0 0 .... TonyCulhane 1
(Nicky Vaughan) *in rr-div: lost pl over 5f out: sn bhd: t.o 3f out* **100/1**

1m 42.8s (-0.90) **Going Correction** -0.25s/f (Firm)
WFA 3 from 4yo+ 11lb **10 Ran SP% 113.7**
Speed ratings (Par 103): **94,92,86,84,71 68,65,61,56,20**
toteswingers:1&2:£1.40, 1&3:£5.70, 2&3:£10.10 CSF £15.32 TOTE £2.10: £1.02, £1.80, £6.10; EX 3.90 Trifecta £24.90 Pool: £376.43 - 11.17 winning units..
Owner Hamdan Al Maktoum **Bred** Shadwell Estate Company Limited **Trained** Newmarket, Suffolk

FOCUS
Not many with form in this all-aged maiden and they went long odds bar four. The market leaders had a good battle over the last 2f and came well clear of the remainder. The runner-up sets the level to his latest AW form.
Captain Cavallo Official explanation: jockey said gelding lost its action

2666 MADNESS IN CONCERT HERE 6TH JULY H'CAP 1m 6f
9:00 (9:00) (Class 5) (0-75,74) 4-Y-0+ **£2,264** (£673; £336; £168) **Stalls** Low

Form RPR

-123 1 **Veloce (IRE)**[10] 2378 4-9-3 **70** ....(v) FrannyNorton 1 80
(Ian Williams) *led: jnd 3f out: edgd rt ins fnl f: all out* **9/4**[1]

064- 2 hd **Emrani (USA)**[331] 3725 5-9-3 **70** ....(p) TomQueally 5 79
(Donald McCain) *mid-div: drvn to chse ldrs 6f out: chal over 1f out: kpt on towards fin: jst hld* **6/1**

2522 3 2¾ **Hallstatt (IRE)**[10] 2378 6-8-13 **66** ....(t) GrahamLee 2 71
(John Mackie) *trckd wnr: upsides 3f out: one pce fnl f* **3/1**[3]

3120 4 1 **Chookie Hamilton**[29] 1797 8-9-7 **74** .... PaulHanagan 6 78
(Ian Semple) *hld up in rr: hdwy 4f out: upsides over 1f out: one pce* **8/1**

50-0 5 3¼ **Harvey's Hope**[17] 1381 6-9-0 **72** .... ShaneBKelly(5) 4 71
(Keith Reveley) *dwlt: hld up in rr: hdwy 4f out: sn chsng ldrs: wknd fnl f* **11/4**[2]

00 6 24 **Rock Of Deauville (IRE)**[129] 285 5-9-0 **70** .... LeeTopliss(3) 3 36
(Julie Camacho) *trckd ldrs: wknd over 2f out: bhd whn eased ins fnl f: t.o* **28/1**

2m 59.91s (-2.09) **Going Correction** -0.25s/f (Firm) **6 Ran SP% 111.3**
Speed ratings (Par 103): **105,104,103,102,100 87**
toteswingers:1&2:£3.40, 1&3:£1.40, 2&3:£3.00 CSF £15.76 TOTE £3.60: £2.20, £2.80; EX 16.30.
Owner Dr Marwan Koukash **Bred** J Jamgotchian **Trained** Portway, Worcs
■ Stewards' Enquiry : Franny Norton two-day ban: used whip above permitted level (Jun 15-16)

FOCUS
A fair and tightly knit staying handicap in which they appeared to go a reasonable pace and it produced a good finish. The runner-up is rated through the fourth to his late 2011 form.
T/Plt: £693.10 to a £1 stake. Pool:£55,833.53 - 58.80 winning tickets T/Qpdt: £17.60 to a £1 stake. Pool:£5,626.94 - 235.80 winning tickets WG

2630 NEWCASTLE (L-H)
Friday, June 1

OFFICIAL GOING: Good (good to firm in places; 7.7)
Wind: Almost nil Weather: Overcast, cool

2667 DELOITTE MEDIAN AUCTION MAIDEN STKS 6f
1:30 (1:31) (Class 6) 2-Y-0 **£1,617** (£481; £240; £120) **Stalls** Centre

Form RPR

1 **Chelwood Gate (IRE)** 2-9-3 0 .... AndreaAtzeni 8 81+
(Roger Varian) *dwlt: rn green early bhd main gp: smooth hdwy over 2f out: led ins fnl f: pushed out* **13/2**[2]

2 1 **Lewisham** 2-9-3 0 .... ChrisCatlin 2 78+
(Noel Quinlan) *t.k.h: cl up on outside: led over 2f out: rdn over 1f out: hdd ins fnl f: kpt on same pce* **11/1**

3 4½ **Whitfield (USA)** 2-9-3 0 .... ShaneKelly 5 65+
(Jeremy Noseda) *t.k.h: trckd ldrs: ev ch gng wl over 2f out: sn rdn: edgd lft and outpcd over 1f out: hld ins fnl f* **1/2**[1]

6 4 6 **Space Artist (IRE)**[25] 1911 2-9-3 0 .... TomEaves 9 47
(Bryan Smart) *led to over 2f out: rdn and wknd over 1f out* **8/1**[3]

5 5 2½ **Eastern Dragon (IRE)**[11] 2334 2-9-3 0 .... PaulMulrennan 7 45+
(Kevin Ryan) *trckd ldrs: effrt over 2f out: wknd over 1f out* **13/2**[2]

0 6 13 **Cosmic Dream**[25] 1911 2-8-13 0 ow1 .... JustinNewman(5) 6
(David C Griffiths) *cl up tl rdn and wknd over 2f out* **33/1**

7 14 **Jomari (IRE)** 2-9-3 0 .... GrahamGibbons 3
(Declan Carroll) *dwlt: sn wl bhd: no ch fr 1/2-way* **22/1**

3 8 12 **Lord Roflow**[14] 2238 2-9-3 0 .... PatrickMathers 1
(Robert Johnson) *dwlt and wnt lft s: sn drvn and lost tch: nvr on terms* **66/1**

1m 14.78s (0.18) **Going Correction** -0.125s/f (Firm) **8 Ran SP% 121.6**
Speed ratings (Par 91): **93,91,85,77,74 57,38,22**
toteswingers:1&2:£10.40, 1&3:£1.90, 2&3:£2.80 CSF £75.24 TOTE £9.40: £2.90, £3.50, £1.10; EX 62.50.
Owner Mrs Fitri Hay **Bred** Jusoor Syndicate **Trained** Newmarket, Suffolk

FOCUS
Rail from 1m round start to bend in home straight moved a fraction to provide fresh ground. Little depth to this maiden, and hard to know exactly what the form's worth, but the leading pair certainly looked promising in pulling a long way clear of the rest.

NOTEBOOK
Chelwood Gate(IRE) ◆, a son of Aussie Rules, overcame greenness to make a winning start to his career, picking up nicely once he got the hang of things to overhaul the runner-up late on. He's in good hands and can surely only go one way from this. (op 7-1)
Lewisham ◆, a Sleeping Indian colt, made a most promising start to his career and should be tough to beat at a similar level next time, impressing with the way he travelled for most of the contest. He doesn't lack for speed and 5f probably wouldn't even inconvenience him at this stage of his career. (tchd 10-1)
Whitfield(USA), a half-brother to several winners in North America, was the all the rage beforehand but couldn't justify it, not having any obvious excuses on the day. He's clearly thought capable of a fair bit better, though, and is worth another chance. (op 4-6)
Space Artist(IRE) is a handicap prospects.
Eastern Dragon(IRE) might do better once going into handicaps. (op 7-1)

2668 S V RUTTER MEDIAN AUCTION MAIDEN STKS 1m 4f 93y
2:00 (2:00) (Class 6) 3-4-Y-O **£1,617** (£481; £240; £120) **Stalls** Low

Form RPR

6-0 1 **Bute Hall**[13] 2271 3-8-12 0 .... JoeFanning 3 82+
(Mark Johnston) *trckd ldrs: hdwy to join ldr after 4f: led over 3f out: sn qcknd clr: edgd lft and kpt on strly fr 2f out: eased last 100yds* **11/2**[3]

42 2 6 **Savida (IRE)**[23] 1981 3-8-7 0 .... RichardMullen 6 60
(Sir Michael Stoute) *t.k.h: led 4f: chsd ldrs: effrt and wnt 2nd over 2f out: sn no imp on wnr* **4/5**[1]

5- 3 4½ **Serjeant Buzfuz**[238] 6675 3-8-12 0 .... DavidNolan 5 58
(Richard Fahey) *dwlt: hld up in tch: hdwy over 2f out: sn pushed along and no imp* **13/2**

60-3 4 14 **Muhamee (IRE)**[31] 1724 3-8-12 70 ....(v[1]) ChrisCatlin 4 36
(Saeed Bin Suroor) *prom: drvn and outpcd over 3f out: sn wknd* **5/1**[2]

0-66 5 7 **Angel Warrior (IRE)**[101] 641 3-8-12 52 .... PJMcDonald 2 24
(Ben Haslam) *hld up in tch: rdn and struggling 3f out: sn btn* **100/1**

0-4 6 nk **Astrogold**[8] 2418 3-8-7 0 .... SaleemGolam 7 19
(Mark H Tompkins) *plld hrd: cl up: led after 4f to over 3f out: wknd over 2f out* **16/1**

2m 46.1s (0.50) **Going Correction** -0.025s/f (Good) **6 Ran SP% 107.8**
Speed ratings (Par 101): **97,93,90,80,76 75**
toteswingers:1&2:£10.40, 1&3:£1.90, 2&3:£2.80 CSF £9.56 TOTE £4.10: £1.40, £1.10; EX 13.20.
Owner Always Trying Partnership X **Bred** Southcourt Stud **Trained** Middleham Moor, N Yorks

FOCUS
A weak maiden in all probability, and a slightly disappointing effort from short-priced favourite. The winner was impressive but not easy to gauge what he achieved.

2669 NEWCASTLE FLOORING H'CAP (DIV I) 1m 4f 93y
2:35 (2:35) (Class 6) (0-60,64) 4-Y-0+ **£1,617** (£481; £240; £120) **Stalls** Low

Form RPR

60-6 1 **Politbureau**[28] 1831 5-8-11 **50** .... PaddyAspell 2 55
(Michael Easterby) *prom: hdwy over 3f out: effrt 2f out: led last 100yds: drvn out* **5/1**[2]

-003 2 hd **Coax**[3] 2593 4-9-7 **60** .... DanielTudhope 3 65
(Patrick Holmes) *hld up in midfield: stdy hdwy to chse ldrs 3f out: effrt and rdn over 1f out: kpt on fnl f: jst hld* **9/4**[1]

0303 3 ½ **Bygones For Coins (IRE)**[14] 2239 4-8-10 **49** .... PatrickMathers 11 53
(Robert Johnson) *led: rdn over 2f out: hdd last 100yds: kpt on: hld nr fin* **12/1**

-464 4 2½ **Guga (IRE)**[7] 2454 6-8-13 **52** ....(b) FrannyNorton 12 52
(John Mackie) *plld hrd: trckd ldrs: effrt and rdn over 2f out: kpt on same pce over 1f out* **11/2**[3]

04-6 5 ½ **Marina's Ocean**[145] 98 8-8-7 **46** oh1 ....(b) RoystonFfrench 9 45?
(Roy Bowring) *hld up towards rr: drvn over 3f out: styd on fnl 2f: nvr able to chal* **33/1**

400 6 1½ **Linroyale Boy (USA)**[14] 2239 4-9-4 **57** .... PJMcDonald 5 54
(Alan Swinbank) *bhd: pushed along over 4f out: styd on fnl 2f: nvr nr ldrs* **14/1**

5-55 7 2¾ **Dzesmin (POL)**[22] 2009 10-9-2 **58** ....(p) DeclanCannon(3) 13 50
(Richard Guest) *hld up in midfield: stdy hdwy over 4f out: rdn and outpcd over 2f out: n.d after* **15/2**

0-00 8 4 **Jewelled Dagger (IRE)**[18] 2134 8-9-2 **55** .... GrahamLee 1 41
(Sharon Watt) *cl up: rdn over 2f out: wknd wl over 1f out* **16/1**

65-0 9 3 **Decadence**[13] 2287 4-8-7 **46** oh1 .... AndrewMullen 4 27
(Nigel Tinkler) *midfield: rdn and outpcd over 3f out: btn fnl 2f* **33/1**

4040 10 7 **Magnitude**[9] 2391 7-8-9 **48** ....(b) DuranFentiman 6 18
(Brian Baugh) *dwlt: bhd and pushed along: struggling over 3f out: sn btn* **16/1**

65-5 11 6 **Henrys Gift (IRE)**[21] 2033 4-9-1 **54** ....(v[1]) TomEaves 7 14
(Michael Dods) *plld hrd: hld up: hmpd after 4f: rdn over 3f out: sn struggling* **10/1**

2m 44.92s (-0.68) **Going Correction** -0.025s/f (Good) **11 Ran SP% 115.7**
Speed ratings (Par 101): **101,100,100,98,98 97,95,93,91,86 82**
toteswingers:1&2:£8.00, 1&3:£12.40, 2&3:£11.20 CSF £16.26 CT £125.09 TOTE £6.90: £2.20, £1.10, £5.20; EX 18.70.
Owner W H & Mrs J A Tinning **Bred** Darley **Trained** Sheriff Hutton, N Yorks
■ Stewards' Enquiry : Patrick Mathers two-day ban: used whip above permitted level (Jun 15-16)

FOCUS
Run-of-the-mill fare. The pace looked sound enough but not many actually ever got into contention. The front-running third limits the form with the fourth close to recent levels.
Henrys Gift(IRE) Official explanation: jockey said gelding ran too free

2670 NEWCASTLE FLOORING H'CAP (DIV II) 1m 4f 93y
3:10 (3:10) (Class 6) (0-60,60) 4-Y-0+ **£1,617** (£481; £240; £120) **Stalls** Low

Form RPR

00-0 1 **Idealism**[52] 1276 5-8-7 **46** oh1 .... PJMcDonald 12 55+
(Micky Hammond) *t.k.h prom: lost couple of pls 1/2-way: hdwy and hung lft over 2f out: nt clr run and swtchd rt appr fnl f: styd on to ld last 50yds: r.o wl* **16/1**

-050 2 1¾ **Media Stars**[28] 1829 7-8-10 **52** ....(p) LeeTopliss(3) 9 56
(Robert Johnson) *hld up: hdwy over 2f out: hung lft and led appr fnl f: hung rt ins fnl f: hdd and no ex last 50yds* **22/1**

52-0 3 hd **Avison (IRE)**[26] 1879 4-9-6 **59** .... DavidNolan 10 63
(Richard Fahey) *t.k.h: prom: rdn and sltly outpcd over 2f out: rallied over 1f out: carried rt ins fnl f: kpt on towards fin* **5/1**[2]

-532 4 1¼ **Needwood Park**[36] 1631 4-9-1 **54** ....(p) PaddyAspell 13 56
(Ray Craggs) *cl up: led over 2f out to appr fnl f: kpt on same pce fnl f* **9/2**[1]

40-0 5 nk **Dean Iarracht (IRE)**[14] 2239 6-9-0 **56** ....(p) DaleSwift(3) 11 58
(Tracy Waggott) *s.i.s: bhd and sn pushed along: no imp tl styd on wl fnl 2f: nrst fin* **18/1**

0/00 6 1¼ **Yas Marina (USA)**[23] 1988 4-8-10 **49** .... DanielTudhope 8 49
(David O'Meara) *hld up towards rr: rdn over 3f out: styd on wl fnl 2f: nvr able to chal* **5/1**[2]

030- 7 3¾ **Donna Elvira**[76] 7357 5-8-10 **49** .... JamesSullivan 5 43
(Edwin Tuer) *trckd ldrs: rdn over 3f out: outpcd fnl 2f* **8/1**

00-4 8 1¼ **Dimashq**[2] 1950 10-8-7 **46** .... DuranFentiman 2 38
(Paul Midgley) *led to over 2f out: rdn and wknd over 1f out* **17/2**

6-60 9 1¼ **Seawood**[24] 1952 6-8-7 **46** oh1 .... RoystonFfrench 3 36
(Roy Bowring) *dwlt: sn pushed along in rr: struggling over 2f out: nvr on terms* **10/1**

040- 10 8 **Hal Of A Lover**[168] 7789 4-9-2 **55** .... TomEaves 7 32
(Lisa Williamson) *prom: effrt and rdn over 2f out: sn wknd* **33/1**

-006 **11** *26* **Dolly Royal (IRE)**[14] 2239 7-8-12 **51** PaulMulrennan 4
(Robert Johnson) *hld up: struggling over 3f out: sn btn: eased whn no ch last 2f* **13/2**[3]
2m 47.75s (2.15) **Going Correction** -0.025s/f (Good) **11** Ran SP% **114.0**
Speed ratings (Par 101): **91,89,89,88,88 87,85,84,83,78 61**
toteswingers:1&2:£56.00, 1&3:£13.40, 2&3:£20.60 CSF £313.10 TOTE £17.00: £6.40, £5.50, £1.80; EX 394.40.
Owner Hope Springs Eternal **Bred** Sheikh Abdulla Bin Isa Al Khalifa **Trained** Middleham Moor, N Yorks

FOCUS
A much steadier pace for the second division of this handicap but the three in the frame behind the winner give the race a fairly sound appearance.
Idealism Official explanation: trainer said, regarding apparent improvement in form, that the gelding benefited from the step up in trip and lower grade race.
Dolly Royal(IRE) Official explanation: jockey said mare hung right-handed throughout

2671 DELOITTE CLASSIFIED STKS 1m 2f 32y
3:45 (3:45) (Class 6) 3-Y-O **£1,617** (£481; £240; £120) **Stalls** Centre

Form RPR
0-31 **1** **Forget Me Not Lane (IRE)**[11] 2336 3-9-6 64 GrahamLee 6 78+
(Kevin Ryan) *cl up: effrt and pushed along over 2f out: led ins fnl f: comf* **85/40**[1]
-320 **2** *1 ½* **Only Orsenfoolsies**[14] 2258 3-9-0 63 PJMcDonald 1 69
(Micky Hammond) *t.k.h: led: rdn over 1f out: hdd ins fnl f: kpt on same pce* **7/2**[3]
2-50 **3** *4* **Ghalaa (IRE)**[21] 2045 3-9-0 63 TadhgO'Shea 2 61
(Mark Johnston) *in tch: rdn and outpcd over 3f out: edgd lft and rallied over 1f out: no imp fnl f* **13/2**
30-3 **4** *8* **Greyhope**[55] 1223 3-8-11 64 JulieBurke(3) 5 45
(Lucinda Russell) *bhd and sn pushed along: drvn and outpcd over 3f out: kpt on fnl f: nvr able to chal* **20/1**
1000 **5** *4 ½* **Wolf Spirit (IRE)**[18] 2118 3-9-0 65 JamesSullivan 4 36
(Ruth Carr) *t.k.h: in tch: drvn over 2f out: wknd wl over 1f out* **9/1**
060 **6** *10* **Bitter Harvest**[17] 2143 3-9-0 65 ShaneKelly 3 16
(Michael Bell) *cl up tl rdn and wknd qckly fr over 2f out* **5/2**[2]
2m 13.2s (1.30) **Going Correction** -0.025s/f (Good) **6** Ran SP% **110.9**
Speed ratings (Par 97): **93,91,88,82,78 70**
CSF £9.63 TOTE £2.90: £1.10, £2.70; EX 8.50.
Owner J Hanson **Bred** Mrs Arkada Partnership **Trained** Hambleton, N Yorks

FOCUS
An uncompetitive classified event overall, but the winner is going the right way and beat a reasonable yardstick for the grade in the runner-up. The runner-up is rated to his Pontefract form.

2672 NORTH SEA LOGISTICS FILLIES' H'CAP 1m 3y(S)
4:25 (4:25) (Class 5) (0-75,75) 3-Y-O **£2,264** (£673; £336; £168) **Stalls** Centre

Form RPR
54-2 **1** **Al Wajba (USA)**[25] 1937 3-9-4 **75** AdamBeschizza(3) 5 85
(William Haggas) *plld hrd: hld up in tch: hdwy over 2f out: led 1f out: drifted lft: drvn out* **3/1**[2]
0-03 **2** *nk* **Silvas Romana (IRE)**[18] 2136 3-9-2 **70** PaulMulrennan 3 79
(Mark Brisbourne) *led at modest gallop: rdn 2f out: hdd 1f out: rallied: carried lft ins fnl f: kpt on: jst hld* **10/1**
0-00 **3** *6* **Inffiraaj (IRE)**[15] 2194 3-8-11 **65** SamHitchcott 7 60
(Mick Channon) *in tch: stdy hdwy over 3f out: rdn and no imp fr 2f out* **5/2**[1]
240 **4** *3 ¾* **Majestic Zafeen**[13] 2272 3-9-6 **74** GrahamLee 2 61
(Alastair Lidderdale) *t.k.h: prom: rdn over 2f out: outpcd wl over 1f out* **15/2**
0-64 **5** *6* **Baltic Fizz (IRE)**[11] 2336 3-8-11 **68** ow3 MichaelMetcalfe(3) 6 41
(Mrs K Burke) *prom: rdn and outpcd over 2f out: sn struggling* **3/1**[2]
-210 **6** *¾* **Chatterati (USA)**[20] 2067 3-9-6 **74** JoeFanning 1 45
(Mark Johnston) *chsd ldrs tl rdn and wknd appr 2f out* **7/1**[3]
1m 41.81s (-1.59) **Going Correction** -0.125s/f (Firm) **6** Ran SP% **111.9**
Speed ratings (Par 96): **102,101,95,91,85 85**
toteswingers:1&2:£4.80, 1&3:£2.70, 2&3:£5.10 CSF £30.51 TOTE £2.90: £1.10, £5.30; EX 19.00.
Owner H E Sheikh Mishal Hamad Bin KH Al-Thani **Bred** Kinsman Farm **Trained** Newmarket, Suffolk

FOCUS
Another race on the card where there wasn't a great deal of depth, but the front two deserve some credit for quickening clear off what was no more than a modest pace for much of the way. The form is a bit fuid although the winner is a potential improver.

2673 H MALONE H'CAP 1m 3y(S)
5:00 (5:01) (Class 6) (0-60,59) 3-Y-O **£1,617** (£481; £240; £120) **Stalls** Centre

Form RPR
3242 **1** **Outlaw Torn (IRE)**[7] 2459 3-8-13 **54** (e) DeclanCannon(3) 6 62
(Richard Guest) *hld up: hdwy over 2f out: led over 1f out: sn rdn and edgd rt: kpt on wl fnl f* **5/1**[2]
56-0 **2** *1 ¼* **Dance For Georgie**[123] 358 3-8-9 **47** ChrisCatlin 3 52
(Ben Haslam) *hld up: gd hdwy and ev ch over 1f out: sn drvn along: kpt on same pce wl ins fnl f* **8/1**
0123 **3** *2 ½* **Luctor Emergo (IRE)**[109] 549 3-9-4 **56** (b) JoeFanning 5 54
(Keith Dalgleish) *hld up: hdwy and ev ch over 2f out: sn rdn: edgd rt and carried hd high over 1f out: kpt on ins fnl f* **15/2**
526 **4** *shd* **Ma Kellys (IRE)**[17] 2144 3-9-7 **59** PJMcDonald 13 57
(Micky Hammond) *hld up: hdwy over 2f out: edgd lft and prom over 1f out: kpt on same pce fnl f* **8/1**
00-0 **5** *¾* **Time To Excel**[37] 1596 3-8-10 **48** PaulMulrennan 12 44
(Michael Dods) *hld up in tch: effrt 2f out: kpt on same pce fnl f* **25/1**
-002 **6** *1 ¾* **Penang Pegasus**[11] 2341 3-8-7 **45** JamesSullivan 4 36
(David O'Meara) *in tch: hdwy to ld over 2f out: hdd over 1f out: edgd rt: kpt on same pce* **4/1**[1]
3420 **7** *¾* **Vexillum (IRE)**[16] 2162 3-9-7 **59** SamHitchcott 7 48
(Mick Channon) *in tch: rdn and outpcd over 2f out: kpt on fnl f: nvr able to chal* **13/2**[3]
55-6 **8** *4 ½* **Miss Ella Jade**[25] 1915 3-9-0 **52** PaulQuinn 9 29
(Richard Whitaker) *prom: rdn over 3f out: wknd over 2f out* **50/1**
00-0 **9** *2* **Blue Top**[17] 2144 3-9-5 **57** DuranFentiman 8 28
(Tim Walford) *t.k.h: cl up tl rdn and wknd over 2f out* **12/1**
-005 **10** *1 ¼* **Rano Pano (USA)**[18] 2131 3-8-7 **48** ow2 (p) PaulPickard(3) 2 16
(Brian Ellison) *led to over 2f out: sn rdn and wknd* **16/1**
00-0 **11** *nk* **Teacher (IRE)**[31] 1740 3-8-4 **45** (b[1]) AdamBeschizza(3) 1 12
(William Haggas) *hld up: drvn over 3f out: shortlived effrt over 2f out: sn btn* **8/1**
4060 **12** *11* **Essexvale (IRE)**[53] 1252 3-8-10 **48** PatrickMathers 11
(Robert Johnson) *t.k.h: cl up tl rdn and wknd over 2f out* **25/1**
1m 42.23s (-1.17) **Going Correction** -0.125s/f (Firm) **12** Ran SP% **118.3**
Speed ratings (Par 97): **100,98,96,96,95 93,92,88,86,85 84,73**
toteswingers:1&2:£9.50, 1&3:£4.70, 2&3:£14.50 CSF £43.85 CT £301.41 TOTE £4.80: £1.80, £3.50, £2.60; EX 56.70.
Owner Future Racing (Notts) Limited **Bred** Derek Veitch & Rory O'Brien **Trained** Stainforth, S Yorks

FOCUS
Low-grade fare, though relatively competitive for the level and sound enough for the grade.

2674 SLM PLC H'CAP 5f
5:35 (5:35) (Class 4) (0-85,83) 4-Y-O+ **£4,075** (£1,212; £606; £303) **Stalls** Centre

Form RPR
6463 **1** **Head Space (IRE)**[6] 2487 4-9-1 **77** JamesSullivan 7 88
(Ruth Carr) *hld up in last pl: gd hdwy over 1f out: kpt on wl fnl f: led towards fin* **2/1**[1]
50-0 **2** *½* **Commanche Raider (IRE)**[41] 1526 5-8-4 **66** (b) PatrickMathers 2 75
(Michael Dods) *in tch: rdn and hdwy over 1f out: ev ch wl ins fnl f: hld towards fin* **33/1**
0-00 **3** *nk* **Tyfos**[13] 2289 7-9-5 **81** DuranFentiman 3 89
(Brian Baugh) *gd spd centre: rdn and led over 1f out: kpt on fnl f: hdd and no ex towards fin* **25/1**
6162 **4** *1* **Noodles Blue Boy**[11] 2337 6-9-6 **82** PaddyAspell 4 86
(Ollie Pears) *chsd ldrs: effrt and ev ch over 1f out to ins fnl f: no ex* **7/1**
3-33 **5** *1 ¾* **Diamond Blue**[17] 2140 4-8-8 **70** PaulMulrennan 6 68
(Richard Whitaker) *prom: effrt and drvn 2f out: kpt on same pce fnl f* **11/2**[3]
4-30 **6** *½* **Hamoody (USA)**[43] 1478 8-9-7 **83** AndrewMullen 8 79
(David Nicholls) *dwlt and blkd s: bhd and pushed along 1/2-way: hdwy fnl f: nrst fin* **14/1**
5442 **7** *¾* **Bronze Beau**[7] 2439 5-9-1 **77** (t) MichaelO'Connell 10 71
(Linda Stubbs) *led tl rdn and hdd over 1f out: sn no ex* **10/3**[2]
65-0 **8** *¾* **Crimea (IRE)**[54] 1237 6-9-6 **82** PaulQuinn 9 73
(David Nicholls) *towards rr: drvn along 1/2-way: no imp fr wl over 1f out* **11/1**
-500 **9** *1 ¼* **Sleepy Blue Ocean**[27] 1868 6-8-6 **68** (p) TadhgO'Shea 5 54
(John Balding) *prom tl rdn and wknd over 1f out* **12/1**
59.84s (-1.26) **Going Correction** -0.125s/f (Firm) **9** Ran SP% **113.8**
Speed ratings (Par 105): **105,104,103,102,99 98,97,96,94**
toteswingers:1&2:£17.30, 1&3:£11.30, 2&3:£41.30 CSF £72.95 CT £1282.01 TOTE £2.50: £1.10, £8.70, £5.10; EX 79.00.
Owner The Bottom Liners & Mrs R Carr **Bred** Castlemartin Stud And Skymarc Farm **Trained** Huby, N Yorks

FOCUS
A fair sprint and there was never going to be any hanging around. The runner-up is rated to last year's form.
T/Plt: £41.10 to a £1 stake. Pool:£46,562.57 - 825.06 winning tickets T/Qpdt: £27.80 to a £1 stake. Pool:£3,712.78 0 98.70 winning tickets RY

1753 PONTEFRACT (L-H)
Friday, June 1

OFFICIAL GOING: Good to firm (8.7)
Wind: Virtually nil Weather: Overcast

2675 ST. JOHN AMBULANCE H'CAP 1m 4y
6:30 (6:30) (Class 5) (0-75,72) 4-Y-O+ **£2,264** (£673; £336; £168) **Stalls** Low

Form RPR
-341 **1** **Woolston Ferry (IRE)**[16] 2173 6-8-11 **62** LiamJones 5 71
(Henry Candy) *trckd ldrs: pushed along 3f out: rdn 2f out: styd on u.p to ld ins fnl f: hld on gamely* **5/2**[1]
2-36 **2** *hd* **Seldom (IRE)**[52] 1276 6-8-12 **63** RobertWinston 2 71
(Mel Brittain) *midfield: hdwy on inner wl over 2f out: swtchd rt wl over 1f out: swtchd bk ins and rdn ent fnl f: sn ev ch tl drvn and no ex towards fin* **13/2**[3]
0-00 **3** *1 ¾* **Shadowtime**[6] 2510 7-9-2 **72** LucyAlexander(5) 9 76
(Tracy Waggott) *in tch: hdwy wl over 1f out: rdn and styd on fnl f: nrst fin* **12/1**
0-00 **4** *hd* **Talent Scout (IRE)**[34] 1659 6-8-12 **63** PhillipMakin 10 67
(Tim Walford) *stdd s and hld up in rr: hdwy on outer over 2f out: rdn to chse ldrs over 1f out: drvn ins fnl f and kpt on same pce* **18/1**
-264 **5** *½* **Sir George (IRE)**[38] 1578 7-9-6 **71** BarryMcHugh 6 74
(Ollie Pears) *trckd ldrs on outer: hdwy to chse ldr 2f out: rdn to chal over 1f out: ev ch whn n.m.r ent fnl f: sn one pce* **7/1**
3310 **6** *2* **Wiseman's Diamond (USA)**[20] 2094 7-9-3 **68** (b) MickyFenton 4 66
(Paul Midgley) *hld up in midfield: hdwy 2f out: n.m.r and swtchd rt ent fnl f: no imp* **8/1**
3504 **7** *¾* **Elijah Pepper (USA)**[36] 1636 7-9-1 **71** LMcNiff(5) 3 68
(David Barron) *chsd ldrs on inner: rdn along 3f out: wknd 2f out* **4/1**[2]
00-3 **8** *4* **Aussie Blue (IRE)**[11] 2329 8-8-12 **63** MichaelStainton 8 50
(Charles Pogson) *led: rdn along 3f out: drvn over 1f out: n.m.r and hdd ins fnl f: wknd qckly* **33/1**
00/0 **9** *1 ½* **Loukoumi**[20] 2094 4-9-2 **67** (p) TomEaves 7 51
(Tim Easterby) *prom: trckd ldr after 2f: rdn along 3f out: wknd 2f out* **28/1**
4100 **10** *2 ¼* **Goal (IRE)**[14] 2227 4-9-4 **69** (t) KirstyMilczarek 1 48
(Richard Guest) *dwlt: a in rr* **14/1**
20-6 **11** *½* **Devonelli (IRE)**[98] 692 4-8-7 **63** LeonnaMayor(5) 11 41
(John Wainwright) *wnt rt s: a in rr* **22/1**
1m 46.78s (0.88) **Going Correction** +0.15s/f (Good) **11** Ran SP% **115.9**
Speed ratings (Par 103): **101,100,99,98,98 96,95,91,90,87 87**
toteswingers:1&2:£3.60, 1&3:£4.50, 2&3:£8.50 CSF £18.01 CT £167.41 TOTE £4.20: £1.70, £1.30, £3.00; EX 21.20.
Owner Ms L Burns **Bred** Tim Taylor **Trained** Kingston Warren, Oxon

FOCUS
The false rail was in place over the last 6f, out about 15ft, and added approximately 12 yards to all races distances. Times suggested the ground was not quite as fast as the official description. The visual impression was that Aussie Blue, who seemed to burst his stall open a fraction of a second before the others, set a steady pace but then quickened the tempo prematurely. Those stalking the early leader were favoured and the runner-up to his best form sets the standard.

2676 CONSTANT SECURITY SERVING YORKSHIRE RACECOURSES H'CAP 1m 4f 8y
7:00 (7:00) (Class 4) (0-85,84) 4-Y-O+ **£4,528** (£1,347; £673; £336) **Stalls** Low

Form RPR
15-0 **1** **Dark Dune (IRE)**51 1295 4-8-9 **72** DavidAllan 3 79
(Tim Easterby) *hld up in rr: hdwy on outer wl over 2f out: chal over 1f out: rdn to ld jst ins fnl f: styd on wl* **10/3**3
3-00 **2** *1 1/4* **King Kurt (IRE)**16 2180 4-9-3 **80** PhillipMakin 1 84
(Kevin Ryan) *trckd ldr: pushed along and sltly outpcd 3f out: hdwy wl over 1f out: cl up ent fnl f: sn rdn and kpt on same pce* **9/4**2
6123 **3** *hd* **Arizona John (IRE)**8 2419 7-8-12 **75** RobertWinston 4 79
(John Mackie) *trckd ldng pair: hdwy to trck ldr after 5f: cl up 4f out: led over 2f out: sn jnd and rdn wl over 1f out: drvn and hdd jst ins fnl f: kpt on same pce* **13/8**1
0-30 **4** *13* **Alsahil (USA)**15 2214 6-8-9 **72** TomEaves 2 55
(Micky Hammond) *led: pushed along and jnd 4f out: rdn 3f out: hdd over 2f out: sn wknd* **11/2**

2m 41.07s (0.27) **Going Correction** +0.15s/f (Good) 4 Ran SP% **107.3**
Speed ratings (Par 105): **105,104,104,95**
CSF £10.77 TOTE £3.00; EX 8.60.
Owner Miss Betty Duxbury **Bred** P Turley **Trained** Great Habton, N Yorks

FOCUS
This looks unreliable form. The pace, set by the below-par Alsahil, was steady (time over 5 secs above standard) and Dark Dune enjoyed just about the best trip of the others, despite being a touch keen early. The form is muddling but the placed horses help set the level.

2677 DIAMOND JUBILEE YOUNGSTERS CONDITIONS STKS 6f
7:35 (7:35) (Class 2) 2-Y-O **£7,470** (£2,236; £1,118) **Stalls** Low

Form RPR
1 **1** **Indian Jade**25 1911 2-8-12 0 PhillipMakin 4 88+
(Kevin Ryan) *trckd ldr: cl up 1/2-way: rdn to chal 2f out: led ent fnl f: kpt on wl* **13/2**2
1 **2** *1 1/2* **New Pearl (IRE)**26 1886 2-8-12 0 JohnnyMurtagh 1 83
(David Brown) *led: jnd over 2f out: rdn over 1f out: hdd ent fnl f: sn drvn and one pce* **1/6**1
3 **3** *1* **Luhaif**20 2073 2-8-12 0 SamHitchcott 3 80+
(Mick Channon) *chsd ldng pair: rdn along and sltly outpcd over 2f out: styd on fnl f* **14/1**3

1m 17.86s (0.96) **Going Correction** +0.15s/f (Good) 3 Ran SP% **105.7**
Speed ratings (Par 99): **99,97,95**
CSF £8.63 TOTE £4.40; EX 4.80.
Owner Michael Beaumont **Bred** Hillwood Thoroughbred Breeding Ltd **Trained** Hambleton, N Yorks

FOCUS
In 2006 this was won by Hellvelyn, who followed up in the Coventry, and last season subsequent Group-race winners Caspar Netscher and Red Duke finished second and third respectively. There was a shock result in this latest running with New Pearl failing to justify his short odds, but he looked to be beaten fair and square, simply not finding enough after leading at what seemed a fair pace. The form is tricky to assess with confidence though.

NOTEBOOK
Indian Jade had made a successful introduction in an ordinary 5f maiden at Beverley and proved well suited by this extra furlong. While the true worth of this form is unclear, he's seemingly very useful. (op 6-1 tchd 7-1)
New Pearl(IRE) looked a smart prospect when winning by over 4l on his debut at Newmarket (5f, good to soft), but that race had so far failed to produce a winner from a good few runners. It seems his current limitations were exposed, but only time will show just what he achieved behind the unbeaten Indian Jade. (op 1-4)
Luhaif wasn't as street-wise as the front two and lacked their pace, but he kept on nicely. He was confirming the promise he showed when third on his debut at Haydock and he can do better still. (op 17-2 tchd 8-1)

2678 CONSTANT SECURITY SERVICES H'CAP 1m 4y
8:10 (8:11) (Class 4) (0-85,80) 3-Y-O **£4,528** (£1,347; £673; £336) **Stalls** Low

Form RPR
0-35 **1** **Satanic Beat (IRE)**28 1819 3-9-2 **76** TomEaves 5 86
(Jedd O'Keeffe) *mde all: rdn 2f out and sn clr: styd on strly* **15/2**
4-66 **2** *4* **Deepsand (IRE)**16 2182 3-9-3 **77** (e1) DavidAllan 4 78
(Tim Easterby) *trckd ldng pair: effrt to chse wnr 3f out: rdn 2f out: drvn and one pce fr over 1f out* **7/2**2
4-00 **3** *3/4* **Elkhart (IRE)**13 2263 3-9-6 **80** JoeFanning 2 79
(Mark Johnston) *trckd wnr: rdn along 3f out: drvn and one pce fr wl over 1f out* **4/1**3
-250 **4** *nk* **Bank On Me**13 2263 3-9-2 **79** (t) AdamBeschizza(3) 1 77
(Philip McBride) *hld up towards rr: hdwy over 2f out: rdn wl over 1f out: sn no imp* **4/1**3
04-2 **5** *1/2* **Sardanapalus**14 2246 3-9-5 **79** PhillipMakin 3 76
(Kevin Ryan) *dwlt: hld up in rr: hdwy on outer 3f out: rdn wl over 1f out: sn edgd rt and btn* **15/8**1

1m 46.67s (0.77) **Going Correction** +0.15s/f (Good) 5 Ran SP% **108.8**
Speed ratings (Par 101): **102,98,97,96,96**
CSF £31.85 TOTE £6.80: £2.90, £2.40; EX 24.60 TRIFECTA .
Owner Caron & Paul Chapman **Bred** Patrick Gleeson **Trained** Middleham Moor, N Yorks

FOCUS
An ordinary race for the grade but the winner is likeable and there may be more to come.

2679 LOGIC LETTINGS PONTEFRACT FILLIES' H'CAP 1m 2f 6y
8:40 (8:41) (Class 5) (0-70,69) 3-Y-O+ **£2,264** (£673; £336; £168) **Stalls** Low

Form RPR
35-2 **1** **Laverre (IRE)**6 2498 5-9-11 **68** AdamBeschizza(3) 5 76
(Lucy Wadham) *trckd ldng pair: hdwy 3f out: rdn wl over 1f out: chsd ldr ent fnl f: sn drvn and styd on to ld last 75yds* **2/1**1
-200 **2** *1/2* **Finity Run (GER)**15 2204 3-9-1 **68** JoeFanning 4 74
(Mark Johnston) *chsd ldr: hdwy and cl up over 2f out: rdn to ld over 1f out: drvn ent fnl f: hdd and no ex last 75yds* **4/1**3
2102 **3** *4 1/2* **Dazzling Valentine**9 2392 4-10-0 **68** LiamJones 7 66
(Alan Bailey) *hld up: hdwy 1/2-way: pushed along to chse ldrs over 3f out: rdn 2f out: sn one pce* **9/1**
301 **4** *1* **Sweetnessandlight**9 2404 3-9-2 **69** 6ex MichaelStainton 1 64
(Jason Ward) *hld up in rr: hdwy 6f out: effrt to chse ldrs wl over 2f out: sn rdn and n.d* **6/1**
505- **5** *1 1/4* **Tamara Bay**254 6253 4-9-4 **58** KirstyMilczarek 8 52
(John Davies) *led: rdn along and jnd 3f out: drvn and hdd over 1f out: grad wknd* **20/1**
63-0 **6** *2* **Margo Channing**17 2141 3-8-1 **54** oh1 KellyHarrison 6 43
(Micky Hammond) *a towards rr* **9/1**
63-1 **7** *3 3/4* **Lady Arabella (IRE)**38 1590 3-8-10 **68** LeonnaMayor(5) 2 49
(Alastair Lidderdale) *stdd s and dropped out in rr: sme hdwy 1/2-way: rdn along in rr wl over 2f out: nvr a factor* **7/2**2

2m 14.53s (0.83) **Going Correction** +0.15s/f (Good)
WFA 3 from 4yo+ 13lb 7 Ran SP% **114.6**
Speed ratings (Par 100): **102,101,98,97,96 94,91**
toteswingers:1&2:£3.60, 1&3:£2.00, 2&3:£4.10 CSF £10.28 CT £56.86 TOTE £2.10: £2.00, £1.60; EX 8.60.
Owner Mr And Mrs A E Pakenham **Bred** Kilnamoragh Stud **Trained** Newmarket, Suffolk

FOCUS
A decent gallop (thanks to Tamara Bay) set this up quite nicely for Laverre, who raced in third for much of the way, although she made hard enough work of it, being pushed all the way by a typically tough Mark Johnston runner, who sat second for most of the contest. She sets the level.
Lady Arabella(IRE) Official explanation: trainer had no explanation for the poor form shown

2680 SINGLES NIGHT - MONDAY EVENING 11TH JUNE MAIDEN STKS 6f
9:10 (9:10) (Class 5) 3-Y-O **£2,264** (£673; £336; £168) **Stalls** Low

Form RPR
1 **Shena's Dream (IRE)** 3-8-12 0 LiamJones 6 69+
(William Haggas) *hld up in tch: hdwy on outer over 2f out: rdn to chal ent fnl f: sn edgd lft: styd on to ld last 50yds* **11/8**1
040 **2** *1/2* **Warrick Brown**13 2262 3-9-3 69 DavidAllan 5 69
(Tim Easterby) *led 1f: cl up on inner: rdn to ld again over 1f out: drvn ins fnl f: hdd and no ex last 50yds* **8/1**
64 **3** *2 1/2* **Dolly Diva**11 2335 3-8-12 0 MickyFenton 4 56
(Paul Midgley) *t.k.h: led after 1f: pushed along 2f out: rdn and hdd over 1f out: one pce fnl f* **7/1**
0-06 **4** *1 1/2* **Vite (IRE)**3 2591 3-8-12 64 JustinNewman(5) 2 56
(David C Griffiths) *dwlt and reminders s: hdwy to chse ldrs 2f out: rdn wl over 1f out: no imp* **9/2**3
00 **5** *nk* **Hurricane Max (IRE)**13 2262 3-9-3 0 JoeFanning 7 55
(Chris Fairhurst) *hld up: hdwy on inner 2f out: sn rdn and no imp fnl f* **14/1**
5-0 **6** *21* **Selective Spirit**11 2335 3-8-12 0 DuranFentiman 3
(John Weymes) *t.k.h: chsd ldrs: rdn along over 2f out: hung sharply rt wl over 1f out and sn wknd* **33/1**
0-0 **7** *7* **Scarabocio**6 2501 3-9-3 0 PhillipMakin 1
(Peter Chapple-Hyam) *plld hrd: chsd ldrs: lost pl 1/2-way and sn bhd* **4/1**2

1m 18.47s (1.57) **Going Correction** +0.15s/f (Good) 7 Ran SP% **113.5**
Speed ratings (Par 99): **95,94,91,89,88 60,51**
CSF £13.24 TOTE £2.40: £1.80, £3.70; EX 8.20.
Owner Miss Pat O'Kelly **Bred** Kilcarn Stud **Trained** Newmarket, Suffolk
■ Stewards' Enquiry : Justin Newman two-day ban: careless riding (Jun 15-16)

FOCUS
The bare form looks modest, but there was plenty to like about Shena's Dream on her debut. The placed horses set a modest standard.
T/Plt: £678.20 to a £1 stake. Pool:£38,844.65 - 41.81 winning tickets T/Qpdt: £46.70 to a £1 stake. Pool:£2,992.19 - 47.37 winning tickets JR

2681 - 2684a (Foreign Racing) - See Raceform Interactive

1592 MAISONS-LAFFITTE (R-H)
Friday, June 1

OFFICIAL GOING: Turf: good

2685a PRIX DE MERICOURT (CLAIMER) (4YO+) (TURF) 1m 5f
2:20 (12:00) 4-Y-O+ **£9,583** (£3,833; £2,875; £1,916; £958)

RPR
1 **Benjamin (FR)**78 7-8-6 0 (p) MarcLerner(5) 4 80
(L A Urbano-Grajales, France) **103/10**
2 *3/4* **Fabulous Siam (FR)**80 6-9-5 0 ThierryJarnet 1 87
(P Boisgontier, France) **5/2**1
3 *2* **Zimri (FR)**36 8-9-4 0 AlexisBadel 7 83
(Mme M Bollack-Badel, France) **43/10**2
4 *1/2* **Cartesien**10 5-9-1 0 OlivierPeslier 5 79
(Robert Collet, France) **78/10**
5 *3/4* **Uphold**11 2346 5-9-8 0 (b) IoritzMendizabal 3 85
(Gay Kelleway) *sn led: under restraint: led into st: rdn 2f out: hdd 1 1/2f out: r.o wl u.p fnl f* **13/2**3
6 *2* **Bluefields (FR)**18 11-8-11 0 (p) GregoryBenoist 2 71
(D Chenu, France) **9/1**
7 *snk* **Lord Emery (GER)**54 4-9-7 0 ElliotCanal(6) 9 87
(M Figge, Germany) **10/1**
8 *1* **Touching Kings (FR)**44 7-9-2 0 AntoineHamelin 8 74
(C Boutin, France) **12/1**
9 *3/4* **Poeme Du Berlais (FR)**18 4-9-3 0 (p) PaulineProd'homme(3) 6 77
(D Prod'Homme, France) **9/1**

2m 51.12s (171.12) 9 Ran SP% **117.8**
WIN (incl. 1 euro stake): 11.30. PLACES: 2.40, 1.50, 1.70. DF: 20.50. SF: 53.20.
Owner Luis A Urbano Grajales **Bred** Haras De Manneville **Trained** Pau, France

2601 BEVERLEY (R-H)
Saturday, June 2

OFFICIAL GOING: Good to firm (7.9)
Wind: Moderate behid Weather: Cloudy

2686 EQUI-TREK BRAMHAM INTERNATIONAL HORSE TRIALS MEDIAN AUCTION MAIDEN STKS 5f
2:00 (2:06) (Class 5) 2-Y-O **£3,234** (£962; £481; £240) **Stalls** Low

Form RPR
3 **1** **Dream Scenario**4 2587 2-8-12 0 PatCosgrave 8 76
(Mel Brittain) *trckd ldrs: hdwy 2f out: swtchd lft and rdn to chal ent fnl f: sn led: edgd rt and styd on strly* **9/2**2
4 **2** *2 3/4* **Therapeutic**14 2261 2-8-12 0 ShaneKelly 7 66
(Scott Dixon) *a cl up: rdn to ld over 1f out: drvn and hdd ins fnl f: kpt on same pce* **6/1**3

2 **3** 3/4 **Boxing Shadows**[29] 1818 2-9-3 0 TomEaves 9 68
(Bryan Smart) *led after 1f: rdn and hdd over 1f out: kpt on same pce u.p fnl f* **5/2**[1]

4 1 1/4 **Confidential Creek** 2-9-3 0 BarryMcHugh 5 64+
(Ollie Pears) *qckly away and led 1f: trckd ldng pair: hdwy 2f out: rdn to chal over 1f out: ev ch tl wknd ins fnl f* **6/1**[3]

206 **5** 1/2 **Ouzinkie (IRE)**[12] 2330 2-9-3 0 MatthewDavies 4 62
(Mick Channon) *chsd ldrs: rdn along wl over 1f out: kpt on same pce fnl f* **9/1**

4 **6** 2 3/4 **Tussie Mussie**[7] 2508 2-8-12 0 FranBerry 6 47
(Mark Johnston) *rrd and dwlt s: rdr lost irons: hdwy into midfield after 1f: swtchd to inner and chsd ldrs 2f out: sn rdn and no imp whn stmbld ins fnl f* **9/2**[2]

7 3 1/4 **Monsieur Royale** 2-9-0 0 DaleSwift(3) 14 41+
(Geoffrey Oldroyd) *dwlt and sn pushed along in rr: swtchd to inner wl over 1f out: styd on fnl f* **20/1**

8 shd **Tumblewind** 2-8-12 0 RussKennemore 15 37+
(Richard Whitaker) *wnt lft s: sn in tch: rdn along 1/2-way: sn wknd* **66/1**

30 **9** 1 1/4 **Peep N Creep (IRE)**[7] 2499 2-8-7 0 AdamCarter(5) 11 31
(Tim Easterby) *nvr bttr than midfield* **16/1**

0 **10** hd **Sulky Sheila (IRE)**[14] 2261 2-8-12 0 PaddyAspell 13 30
(Tim Easterby) *chsd ldrs: rdn along 2f out: sn wknd* **50/1**

11 hd **Vino Collapso (IRE)** 2-9-3 0 PaulMulrennan 2 34
(James Given) *a in rr* **18/1**

12 1 1/4 **Baltic Rose (IRE)** 2-8-12 0 PatrickMathers 10 25
(Ian McInnes) *dwlt: a in rr* **66/1**

0 **13** 2 1/2 **Bronte Belle**[28] 1842 2-8-12 0 JackMitchell 1 16
(Jedd O'Keeffe) *a in rr* **28/1**

1m 3.14s (-0.36) **Going Correction** -0.15s/f (Firm) **13** Ran SP% **127.8**
Speed ratings (Par 93): **96,91,90,88,87 83,78,77,75,75 75,73,69**
toteswingers:1&2:£8.40, 1&3:£7.00, 2&3:£5.50 CSF £32.95 TOTE £7.30: £2.60, £1.70, £1.60; EX 43.90.
Owner Northgate Black **Bred** R J Cornelius **Trained** Warthill, N Yorks

FOCUS
Inner rail round bottom bend moved in to provide fresh ground adding 21yds to all races beyond 5f. Inner rail round bottom bend moved in to provide fresh ground adding 21yds to all races beyond 5f. A useful-looking maiden for the track and they went quite hard up front. The form looks a little fluid, although the runner-up might prove the best guide.

NOTEBOOK
Dream Scenario ◆ sat just behind the pacesetters before finding plenty when pulled out to make her challenge and she was strong at the finish, suggesting another furlong wouldn't be a problem if connections wanted to go that route. She had shaped with promise at Ripon on her debut, has a speedy pedigree and she looks a nice prospect for the big juvenile sprint races. (op 5-1 tchd 11-2)
Therapeutic showed plenty of pace and can find a similar race. (op 5-1 tchd 13-2)
Boxing Shadows also showed enough speed to suggest he can win. (op 10-3)
Confidential Creek showed up well for a long way before tiring late on. Just normal improvement from this first run will see him a major force in similar company next time. (tchd 11-2 and 13-2)
Ouzinkie(IRE) was noted making good late headway from off the pace and he will be seen to better effect when faced with a stiffer test of stamina. (tchd 8-1)
Tumblewind Official explanation: jockey said filly hung right
Vino Collapso(IRE) Official explanation: jockey said colt ran green

2687 GRAHAM HALLETT'S BIRTHDAY CELEBRATION H'CAP 1m 1f 207y
2:30 (2:32) (Class 5) (0-75,81) 4-Y-O+ **£3,067** (£905; £453) **Stalls** Low

Form RPR

0001 **1** **Landaman (IRE)**[3] 2606 4-9-13 **81** 6ex FranBerry 3 94
(Mark Johnston) *mde all: rdn clr over 2f out: kpt on strly* **8/13**[1]

0202 **2** 2 1/2 **Brockfield**[4] 2588 6-9-0 **68** PatCosgrave 8 76
(Mel Brittain) *trckd ldng pair: hdwy to chse wnr over 2f out: rdn wl over 1f out: kpt on fnl f* **9/2**[2]

00-0 **3** 1 1/4 **King Of The Celts (IRE)**[42] 1525 4-9-2 **70** TomEaves 7 76
(Tim Easterby) *chsd ldrs: hdwy 4f out: rdn to chse ldng pair over 2f out: drvn and one pce fr wl over 1f out* **33/1**

0-63 **4** 1 1/4 **Tribal Myth (IRE)**[26] 1913 5-8-5 **66** PaulMcGiff(7) 9 69
(Kevin Ryan) *in tch: lost pl 1/2-way: hdwy to chse ldrs over 2f out: sn rdn and no imp* **15/2**[3]

20-5 **5** 2 1/4 **Skyfire**[21] 2094 5-8-12 **66** SebSanders 1 65
(Nick Kent) *in tch: rdn along wl over 2f out: n.d* **14/1**

5032 **6** 1 1/2 **Scamperdale**[12] 2348 10-9-3 **71** (p) JackMitchell 2 67
(Brian Baugh) *s.i.s: a towards rr* **20/1**

1-00 **7** nse **Xpres Maite**[4] 2588 9-8-5 **59** (b) CathyGannon 4 54
(Roy Bowring) *cl up: rdn along over 3f out: sn wknd* **20/1**

0204 **8** 3/4 **Ailsa Craig (IRE)**[15] 2241 6-9-3 **74** DaleSwift(3) 5 68
(Edwin Tuer) *a towards rr* **14/1**

2m 6.18s (-0.82) **Going Correction** -0.15s/f (Firm) **8** Ran SP% **117.7**
Speed ratings (Par 103): **97,95,94,93,91 90,89,89**
toteswingers:1&2:£1.80, 1&3:£15.30, 2&3:£14.60 CSF £3.69 CT £45.69 TOTE £1.80: £1.10, £1.10, £2.80; EX 3.40 TRIFECTA .
Owner Sheikh Hamdan Bin Mohammed Al Maktoum **Bred** Darley **Trained** Middleham Moor, N Yorks

FOCUS
This was all about the winner, who ran to a similar mark as when scoring earlier in the week, backed up by the second and fourth.

2688 BRIAN YEARDLEY CONTINENTAL TWO YEAR OLD TROPHY (CONDITIONS STKS) 5f
3:00 (3:03) (Class 2) 2-Y-O **£9,337** (£2,796; £1,398; £699; £349) **Stalls** Low

Form RPR

01 **1** **Bungle Inthejungle**[9] 2420 2-9-2 0 MatthewDavies 1 95
(Mick Channon) *cl up: led after 1 1/2f: rdn over 1f out: styd on strly* **7/2**[2]

3 **2** 3 3/4 **The Black Jacobin**[14] 2261 2-8-12 0 LiamKeniry 3 78
(J S Moore) *chsd ldrs: hdwy on inner wl over 1f out: rdn to chse wnr ins fnl f: no imp* **11/1**[3]

41 **3** 2 1/4 **Top Notch Tonto (IRE)**[18] 2138 2-9-2 0 PatrickMathers 6 76+
(Ian McInnes) *s.i.s: sn outpcd and rdn along in rr: hdwy over 1f out: kpt on fnl f: nrst fin* **16/1**

1 **4** 1 **Ask The Guru**[16] 2202 2-9-2 0 SebSanders 2 70
(Ralph Beckett) *led 1 1/2f: cl up: rdn wl over 1f out: grad wknd* **3/1**[1]

10 **5** 2 1/2 **Cumbrian Craic**[17] 2181 2-9-2 0 PaulMulrennan 5 61
(Tim Easterby) *cl up: rdn 2f out: sn wknd* **25/1**

1m 3.18s (-0.32) **Going Correction** -0.15s/f (Firm) **5** Ran SP% **65.3**
Speed ratings (Par 99): **96,90,86,84,80**
CSF £11.45 TOTE £2.50: £1.20, £2.90; EX 30.90.
Owner Christopher Wright & Miss Emily Asprey **Bred** Stratford Place Stud **Trained** West Ilsley, Berks
■ Smoothtalkinrascal (Evens) withdrawn; Rule 4 applies, deduction 45p in the £ from all bets.

FOCUS
This was weakened by the withdrawal of hot favourite Smoothtalkinrascal at the start. The winner scored fluently and the form is given a chance.

NOTEBOOK
Bungle Inthejungle produced his best performance so far to make it two wins from three starts. After travelling smoothly on the front end, he displayed a smart turn of foot to quicken away from these over a furlong out and connections clearly think plenty of this colt, given his Group 1 Phoenix Stakes entry. Next stop is Royal Ascot and this progressive sort would be bang in the mix. (op 4-1 tchd 9-2)
The Black Jacobin ◆ stepped up on his encouraging Doncaster debut with a really likeable effort in second, and a maiden success looks a formalty for this one. (op 16-1)
Top Notch Tonto(IRE) lost a lot of ground at the start but finished best of all into third and deserves a deal of credit. (op 12-1)
Ask The Guru showed up well early but dropped away quite tamely at the business end. (op 7-2)

2689 BERYL AND JOE TURNER MEMORIAL STKS (H'CAP) 7f 100y
3:35 (3:38) (Class 5) (0-70,70) 3-Y-O **£2,911** (£866; £432; £216) **Stalls** Low

Form RPR

25-3 **1** **Annie Walker (IRE)**[47] 1419 3-9-2 **65** TomEaves 2 75
(David Nicholls) *trckd ldrs on inner: hdwy 2f out: swtchd lft and rdn ent fnl f: sn hung lft: drvn and styd on strly last 100yds to ld nr line* **17/2**

3-35 **2** nk **Tortoni (IRE)**[29] 1825 3-9-4 **70** JulieBurke(3) 13 79
(Kevin Ryan) *trckd ldrs: chsd ldr after 2f out: effrt 2f out: rdn to ld jst ins fnl f: sn drvn: hdd and no ex nr line* **8/1**[3]

1554 **3** 2 3/4 **Ghost Train (IRE)**[8] 2459 3-9-3 **66** FranBerry 14 68
(Mark Johnston) *sn led: rdn clr 3f out: drvn over 1f out: hdd jst ins fnl f: one pce* **17/2**

3-16 **4** 1 1/2 **Lolita Lebron (IRE)**[14] 2283 3-9-7 **70** CathyGannon 11 68
(Lawrence Mullaney) *trckd ldrs: hdwy 3f out: rdn to chse ldng pair 2f out: drvn and one pce appr fnl f* **10/1**

-434 **5** 1 1/4 **Chester Aristocrat**[19] 2118 3-9-7 **70** PatCosgrave 9 65+
(Eric Alston) *dwlt and in rr: swtchd to outer and hdwy over 2f out: rdn wl over 1f out: kpt on fnl f: nrst fin* **9/1**

-160 **6** 1/2 **Daddy Warbucks (IRE)**[12] 2336 3-9-3 **66** PaulQuinn 8 60
(David Nicholls) *chsd ldrs: rdn wl over 2f out: drvn wl over 1f out: no imp* **11/1**

2042 **7** nse **Purple Affair (IRE)**[11] 2382 3-9-5 **68** (b) LiamKeniry 12 62
(J S Moore) *in tch on outer: hdwy over 2f out: rdn along wl over 1f out: no imp* **11/2**[2]

56-0 **8** 1 1/4 **Sinai (IRE)**[16] 2194 3-9-7 **70** SebSanders 3 61+
(Geoffrey Harker) *s.i.s and bhd: hdwy over 2f out: styd on fnl f: nt rch ldrs* **12/1**

2023 **9** 2 1/4 **Feeling Good**[10] 2400 3-9-4 **67** BarryMcHugh 4 52
(Brian Ellison) *in rr: rdn along 3f out: nvr a factor* **5/1**[1]

53-0 **10** hd **Crossley**[21] 2095 3-9-0 **66** DaleSwift(3) 7 51
(Geoffrey Oldroyd) *in tch: rdn along wl over 2f out: sn wknd* **22/1**

030 **11** 1 **Dream Prospector**[28] 1864 3-9-4 **67** ShaneKelly 5 49+
(James Tate) *dwlt: midfield whn bdly hmpd on inner after 2f: n.d after* **20/1**

0-66 **12** 6 **Bollin Tommy**[12] 2336 3-9-0 **63** (p) KellyHarrison 6 30+
(Tim Easterby) *midfield: rdn along 3f out: sn wknd* **14/1**

44-0 **13** 2 1/4 **Stormy Whatever (FR)**[15] 2246 3-9-7 **70** PaulMulrennan 10 32
(James Given) *a in rr* **25/1**

36-0 **14** 16 **Abhaath (USA)**[18] 2150 3-9-6 **69** JackMitchell 1
(Ed Dunlop) *in tch: rdn along 3f out: wknd 2f out: bhd and eased fnl f* **12/1**

1m 33.57s (-0.23) **Going Correction** -0.15s/f (Firm) **14** Ran SP% **126.6**
Speed ratings (Par 99): **95,94,91,89,88 87,87,86,83,83 82,75,72,54**
toteswingers:1&2:£25.20, 1&3:£11.10, 2&3:£14.10 CSF £76.97 CT £629.79 TOTE £8.10: £2.30, £2.80, £3.90; EX 130.60.
Owner D Nicholls & Mrs M C Jacobs **Bred** Round Hill Stud **Trained** Sessay, N Yorks

FOCUS
A modest and wide open handicap run at a strong pace thanks to Ghost Train who had this field strung out from an early stage. Nothing got seriously involved from the rear and the placed horses are the best guides to the level.

2690 KEVIN DONKIN MEMORIAL H'CAP (DIV I) 5f
4:30 (4:34) (Class 5) (0-75,76) 4-Y-O+ **£2,911** (£866; £432; £216) **Stalls** Low

Form RPR

4624 **1** **Bond Fastrac**[21] 2096 5-9-4 **75** DaleSwift(3) 9 83
(Geoffrey Oldroyd) *towards rr: hdwy on outer wl over 1f out: str run ent fnl f: led last 100yds* **5/1**[3]

-051 **2** 1 1/2 **Diman Waters (IRE)**[3] 2596 5-9-8 **76** 6ex KellyHarrison 10 79
(Eric Alston) *chsd ldrs: hdwy 2f out: rdn to chal over 1f out: and ev ch: drvn and kpt on same pce ins fnl f* **2/1**[1]

11 **3** hd **Hopes N Dreams (IRE)**[15] 2225 4-8-9 **70** KevinStott(7) 8 72
(Kevin Ryan) *awkward s and bhd: hdwy wl over 1f out: swtchd lft and rdn ent fnl f: styd on strly towards fin* **9/2**[2]

0343 **4** hd **Belinsky (IRE)**[52] 1305 5-8-4 **65** ow2 JacobButterfield(7) 6 66
(Julie Camacho) *towards rr: hdwy over 2f out: rdn to chse ldrs appr fnl f: kpt on wl towards fin* **12/1**

2040 **5** nk **Master Of Disguise**[14] 2264 6-9-6 **74** (t) JackMitchell 4 74
(Brian Baugh) *trckd ldrs on inner: hdwy 2f out: rdn to ld briefly ent fnl f: sn drvn: hdd and one pce* **6/1**

000 **6** 1 **Under Par**[12] 2335 4-8-2 **56** oh11 PatrickMathers 5 52
(Michael Easterby) *in tch: hdwy on inner to chse ldrs wl over 1f out: sn rdn and n.m.r ent fnl f: kpt on same pce* **50/1**

6400 **7** 2 1/2 **Ingleby Star (IRE)**[18] 2140 7-9-2 **73** (p) PaulPickard(3) 3 60
(Ian McInnes) *chsd ldrs: rdn and edgd lft 2f out: sn drvn and wknd* **12/1**

0-50 **8** 1/2 **On The High Tops (IRE)**[13] 2314 4-8-5 **62** (b) JulieBurke(3) 2 48
(Ruth Carr) *led and sn clr: rdn wl over 1f out: hdd ent fnl f and wknd* **9/1**

4043 **9** 2 **Steel City Boy (IRE)**[12] 2350 9-8-3 **57** CathyGannon 1 35
(Garry Woodward) *chsd ldrs: hdwy 2f out: sn cl up and ch tl drvn and wknd over 1f out* **14/1**

30-0 **10** 11 **Lady Kildare (IRE)**[18] 2140 4-8-11 **65** TomEaves 7
(Jedd O'Keeffe) *prom: rdn along 1/2-way: sn wknd* **20/1**

1m 2.48s (-1.02) **Going Correction** -0.15s/f (Firm) **10** Ran SP% **121.2**
Speed ratings (Par 103): **102,99,99,98,98 96,92,92,88,71**
CSF £16.05 CT £50.17 TOTE £8.10: £2.70, £1.10, £3.70; EX 23.00.
Owner R C Bond **Bred** Bond Thoroughbred Corporation **Trained** Brawby, N Yorks

FOCUS
The trailblazing On The High Tops probably went off too quick here and the picture changed dramatically in the final furlong as the hold-up horses stormed through. The winner up looks the best guide to the level.

2691 BRANTINGHAM CONDITIONS STKS 5f
5:05 (5:05) (Class 4) 3-Y-O £5,291 (£1,584; £792; £396) Stalls Low

Form RPR
1-13 1 **Free Zone**^{27} 1877 3-8-12 94 .... TomEaves 3 103
(Bryan Smart) *mde most: rdn and qcknd wl over 1f out: styd on strly fnl f* **4/1**^{2}
-015 2 2 1/4 **Dam Beautiful**^{22} 2028 3-8-12 97 .... JulieBurke$^{(3)}$ 2 98
(Kevin Ryan) *cl up: rdn wl over 1f out: drvn and one pce fnl f* **4/1**^{2}
-011 3 1 **Ballesteros**^{22} 2028 3-9-1 107 .... ShaneKelly 1 94
(Brian Meehan) *ponied to s: trckd ldng pair: effrt wl over 1f out: rdn ent fnl f and kpt on same pce* **1/2**^{1}
2134 4 11 **El McGlynn (IRE)**^{18} 2139 3-8-0 58 .... HannahNunn$^{(7)}$ 4 47
(Peter Salmon) *cl up: rdn along bef 1/2-way: sn outpcd* **66/1**^{3}
1m 1.97s (-1.53) **Going Correction** -0.15s/f (Firm) **4** Ran SP% **108.2**
Speed ratings (Par 101): **106,102,100,83**
CSF £18.05 TOTE £5.50; EX 18.40.
Owner Fromthestables.com Racing **Bred** R G Levin **Trained** Hambleton, N Yorks

FOCUS
Everything looked set for Ballesteros to complete the hat-trick, but the odds-on favourite just didn't pick up on this faster ground. The form is rated around the first two but looks a little shaky.
Ballesteros Official explanation: jockey said gelding ran flat

2692 QUEEN'S JUBILEE H'CAP 1m 100y
5:40 (5:41) (Class 5) (0-70,68) 4-Y-O+ £2,911 (£866; £432; £216) Stalls Low

Form RPR
330- 1 **Eeny Mac (IRE)**^{252} 6343 5-8-0 **50** .... JulieBurke$^{(3)}$ 14 63
(Neville Bycroft) *trckd ldr: tk clsr order over 2f out: rdn over 1f out: led ent fnl f: drvn out* **16/1**
6-32 2 2 **Cottam Donny**^{26} 1917 4-9-2 **63** .... PaulMulrennan 12 71
(Mel Brittain) *led: qcknd clr 3f out: rdn 2f out: drvn and hdd ent fnl f: kpt on same pce* **7/2**^{1}
6-00 3 1/2 **Byron Bear (IRE)**^{8} 2455 4-8-2 **49** .... PaulQuinn 15 56+
(Paul Midgley) *hld up in rr: hdwy on wd outside over 2f out: rdn over 1f out: styd on fnl f: nrst fin* **16/1**
5-32 4 1 3/4 **Barton Bounty**^{3} 2600 5-8-0 **50** .... SimonPearce$^{(3)}$ 13 53
(Peter Niven) *hld up towards rr: hdwy on outer wl over 2f out: rdn wl over 1f out: styd on appr fnl f: nrst fin* **7/1**^{3}
0003 5 1 1/2 **Nicholas Pocock (IRE)**^{23} 2013 6-8-2 **52** ....(p) DeclanCannon$^{(3)}$ 7 52
(Ian McInnes) *in tch: hdwy on inner over 3f out: rdn to chse ldrs over 2f out: drvn and no imp over 1f out* **33/1**
646- 6 3/4 **Izzet**^{232} 6840 4-8-7 **54** .... BarryMcHugh 9 52
(Ron Barr) *hld up: hdwy wl over 2f out: rdn to chse ldrs wl over 1f out: no imp fnl f* **25/1**
3000 7 2 1/2 **Moral Issue**^{4} 2588 4-9-6 **67** ....(p) PatrickMathers 10 59
(Ian McInnes) *towards rr: hdwy over 2f out: sn rdn and nvr nr ldrs* **10/1**
6620 8 5 **Myraid**^{21} 2090 5-7-11 **49** ....(b) NathanAlison$^{(5)}$ 3 30
(Ruth Carr) *t.k.h: chsd ldng pair: rdn along wl over 2f out: sn wknd* **25/1**
5053 9 2 3/4 **Ra Junior (USA)**^{30} 1799 6-8-1 **55** .... DanielleMooney$^{(7)}$ 1 29
(Paul Midgley) *a towards rr* **14/1**
6-10 10 1 1/2 **One Of Twins**^{63} 1135 4-8-12 **59** .... PaddyAspell 4 30
(Michael Easterby) *chsd ldrs: rdn along wl over 2f out: sn wknd* **5/1**^{2}
0231 11 1/2 **Woteva**^{15} 2239 6-9-0 **68** ....(p) EvaMoscrop$^{(7)}$ 2 38
(Nigel Tinkler) *chsd ldrs: rdn along 3f out: sn wknd* **8/1**
0653 12 4 1/2 **Kyle Of Bute**^{49} 1391 6-9-0 **61** .... CathyGannon 11 21
(Brian Baugh) *in tch: rdn along 3f out: sn wknd* **9/1**
-640 13 1/2 **Petsas Pleasure**^{5} 2535 6-9-2 **63** .... TomEaves 5 21
(Ollie Pears) *hld up: a in rr* **12/1**
52-2 14 7 **Cathcart Castle**^{8} 2438 4-8-9 **56** .... KellyHarrison 8
(Simon West) *chsd ldrs: rdn along wl over 2f out: sn wknd* **12/1**
1m 45.75s (-1.85) **Going Correction** -0.15s/f (Firm) **14** Ran SP% **126.0**
Speed ratings (Par 103): **103,101,100,98,97 96,94,89,86,84 84,79,79,72**
toteswingers:1&2:£4.80, 1&3:£24.50, 2&3:£24.50 CSF £73.25 CT £714.60 TOTE £18.70: £7.60, £2.30, £9.80; EX 142.60.
Owner Mrs J Dickinson **Bred** Kenneth Heelan **Trained** Brandsby, N Yorks

FOCUS
Not a strong handicap by any means and most of these struggle to win. Despite the fact that they appeared to go off quite hard, the front two dominated and set the level of the form.

2693 KEVIN DONKIN MEMORIAL H'CAP (DIV II) 5f
6:10 (6:11) (Class 5) (0-75,75) 4-Y-O+ £2,911 (£866; £432; £216) Stalls Low

Form RPR
3-05 1 **Caranbola**^{44} 1476 6-9-7 **75** .... PaulMulrennan 7 85
(Mel Brittain) *mde all: rdn over 1f out: drvn ins fnl f and kpt on gamely* **2/1**^{1}
0-52 2 1 1/4 **Befortyfour**^{11} 2369 7-9-5 **73** ....(t) SebSanders 6 78
(Richard Guest) *prom: cl up 1/2-way: rdn and ev ch over 1f out: drvn ins fnl f: no ex last 100yds* **7/2**^{2}
0-00 3 hd **Comptonspirit**^{14} 2264 8-9-1 **74** .... JamesRogers$^{(5)}$ 1 78
(Brian Baugh) *a.p: rdn wl over 1f out: kpt on u.p fnl f* **20/1**
2-06 4 3/4 **Tabaret**^{8} 2439 9-8-11 **65** .... RussKennemore 4 67
(Richard Whitaker) *chsd ldrs: hdwy 2f out: sn rdn and one pce fnl f* **8/1**
-306 5 2 3/4 **Mawjoodah**^{18} 2146 4-8-6 **60** .... BarryMcHugh 2 52
(Brian Ellison) *hld up: hdwy on inner 2f out: swtchd lft and rdn to chse ldrs over 1f out: sn drvn and one pce* **6/1**
0100 6 1 3/4 **Prince James**^{13} 2314 5-8-7 **61** .... PaddyAspell 9 46
(Michael Easterby) *a in rr* **20/1**
2062 7 1/2 **Northern Bolt**^{21} 2096 7-9-1 **69** ....(b) PatrickMathers 8 53
(Ian McInnes) *dwlt: a in rr* **11/1**
-023 8 shd **Select Committee**^{8} 2439 7-9-7 **75** ....(v) PatCosgrave 5 58
(John Quinn) *trckd ldrs: rdn wl over 1f out: sn wknd* **5/1**^{3}
1000 9 3/4 **Prigsnov Dancer (IRE)**^{22} 2046 7-7-11 **58** oh10 ow2 GarethEdwards$^{(7)}$ 3 39
(Garry Woodward) *t.k.h: towards rr: effrt and n.m.r wl over 1f out: nvr a factor* **50/1**
1m 2.81s (-0.69) **Going Correction** -0.15s/f (Firm) **9** Ran SP% **117.4**
Speed ratings (Par 103): **99,97,96,95,91 88,87,87,86**
toteswingers:1&2:£1.50, 1&3:Not won, 2&3:£21.70 CSF £8.89 CT £107.71 TOTE £2.20: £1.02, £2.90, £5.10; EX 9.70.
Owner Mel Brittain **Bred** T E Pocock **Trained** Warthill, N Yorks

FOCUS
A run-of-the-mill sprint handicap rated around the first two.

T/Plt: £267.30 to a £1 stake. Pool:£40,102.90 - 109.50 winning tickets T/Qpdt: £118.40 to a £1 stake. Pool:£1,952.12 - 12.20 winning tickets JR

2436 CATTERICK (L-H)
Saturday, June 2

OFFICIAL GOING: Good to firm (watered; 8.7) (last two races abandoned due to unsafe ground)
Wind: fresh half against Weather: Cloudy

2694 BET TOTESCOOP6 TEXT TOTE TO 89660 CLASSIFIED CLAIMING STKS 1m 3f 214y
1:45 (1:45) (Class 6) 4-Y-O+ £2,181 (£644; £322) Stalls Low

Form RPR
060- 1 **Herostatus**^{158} 4423 5-9-7 73 .... DanielTudhope 1 81
(David O'Meara) *mde all: rdn over 2f out: strly pressed thrght fnl f: hld on all out* **10/1**
5-20 2 hd **Eijaaz (IRE)**^{14} 2260 11-8-1 58 ....(p) DuranFentiman 6 61
(Geoffrey Harker) *midfield: chsd ldrs over 2f out: chal appr fnl f: upsides fnl 100yds: jst failed* **7/2**^{2}
-126 3 2 3/4 **Tricksofthetrade (IRE)**^{93} 751 6-9-2 75 .... GarryWhillans$^{(5)}$ 3 77
(Alan Swinbank) *in tch: hdwy to chse ldr over 2f out: sn rdn: chal strly jst ins fnl f: no ex fnl 100yds* **3/1**^{1}
1203 4 2 1/2 **Overrule (USA)**^{12} 2348 8-8-11 74 ....(p) MickyFenton 8 63
(Jason Ward) *hld up: pushed along over 3f out: hdwy over 2f out: kpt on one pce: nvr threatened ldrs* **5/1**
3200 5 14 **Visions Of Johanna (USA)**^{23} 2009 7-8-1 54 ....(tp) AndrewMullen 4 30
(Richard Guest) *trckd ldr: pushed along over 3f out: wknd over 1f out* **14/1**
0-66 6 1 3/4 **Mistoffelees**^{11} 2378 6-8-7 65 ....(t) JamesSullivan 5 33
(James Given) *trckd ldrs: pushed along 4f out: sn wknd* **12/1**
150/ 7 1 1/4 **Park Lane**^{15} 5986 6-8-7 75 .... FrederikTylicki 7 31
(Noel Quinlan) *hld up in tch: pushed along over 4f out: sn btn* **4/1**^{3}
0/0- 8 9 **Umverti**^{357} 2932 7-8-8 68 .... LeeNewman 2 18
(Joanne Foster) *rdr removed blindfold late: v.s.a: hld up: a towards rr* **25/1**
2m 37.54s (-1.36) **Going Correction** +0.10s/f (Good) **8** Ran SP% **111.2**
Speed ratings (Par 101): **108,107,106,104,95 93,93,87**
toteswingers:1&2:£12.10, 1&3:£7.20, 2&3:£4.40 CSF £42.47 TOTE £11.80: £4.10, £1.30, £1.10; EX 75.90.
Owner R Naylor **Bred** Darley **Trained** Nawton, N Yorks

FOCUS
An overcast, dry afternoon. The ground had been watered but rode as advertised. A modest claimer to start with, comprising several out-of-form horses. The pace was sound enough, the front trio were fanned out halfway across the track at the finish and the form is rated cautiously, with the winner running his best race on turf.
Umverti Official explanation: jockey said blindfold became stuck and mare was slowly away

2695 BET TOTEPOOL TEXT TOTE TO 89660 MEDIAN AUCTION MAIDEN STKS 5f
2:15 (2:17) (Class 6) 3-Y-O £2,181 (£644; £322) Stalls Low

Form RPR
0-04 1 **Just Like Heaven (IRE)**^{4} 2591 3-9-3 63 .... DuranFentiman 8 65
(Tim Easterby) *w ldr: led over 3f out: rdn over 2f out: kpt on* **3/1**^{2}
5 2 1 3/4 **Imperial Legend (IRE)**^{42} 1521 3-9-3 0 .... AndrewMullen 4 58
(David Nicholls) *led: hdd over 3f out: chsd wnr: kpt on but a jst hld* **5/1**
0-03 3 1 3/4 **Ooi Long**^{8} 2461 3-9-3 47 ....(t) FrederikTylicki 2 52
(Mark Rimmer) *chsd ldng pair: rdn over 2f out: kpt on one pce* **18/1**
00-4 4 4 **Pavers Star**^{8} 2460 3-9-3 43 .... LeeNewman 9 38
(Noel Wilson) *chsd ldng pair: rdn over 2f out: no ex fnl f* **25/1**
0-0 5 2 **Absolute Bearing (IRE)**^{14} 2262 3-9-3 0 .... JamesSullivan 5 30
(Tim Etherington) *midfield: rdn over 2f out: sn no imp* **66/1**
0 6 hd **New Lease Of Life**^{21} 2065 3-9-3 0 .... DanielTudhope 7 30
(Jim Goldie) *hld up: outpcd in rr 3f out: bhd tl sme late hdwy* **7/2**^{3}
00-6 7 1 1/4 **Tallula (IRE)**^{38} 1600 3-8-7 44 .... ShaneBKelly$^{(5)}$ 1 20
(Micky Hammond) *hld up: pushed along 3f out: nvr threatened* **20/1**
05-0 8 1/2 **Never In (IRE)**^{19} 2121 3-8-5 45 .... MatthewHopkins$^{(7)}$ 6 18
(Alan Berry) *hld up: nvr threatened* **100/1**
9 hd **Planetex (IRE)** 3-9-3 0 .... MichaelO'Connell 3 23
(John Quinn) *s.i.s: hld up: pushed along and minor hdwy over 2f out: wknd over 1f out* **15/8**^{1}
59.71s (-0.09) **Going Correction** -0.075s/f (Good) **9** Ran SP% **115.0**
Speed ratings (Par 97): **97,94,91,85,81 81,79,78,78**
toteswingers:1&2:£5.00, 1&3:£7.10, 2&3:£4.00 CSF £17.67 TOTE £4.60: £1.50, £1.40, £2.70; EX 18.30.
Owner D B Lamplough **Bred** Derek Veitch And Mark Tong **Trained** Great Habton, N Yorks

FOCUS
A modest sprint maiden, and they finished quite strung out. The form seems adequate for the grade with the winner and third the best guides.

2696 BET TOTEQUADPOT TEXT TOTE TO 89660 H'CAP 7f
2:45 (2:47) (Class 5) (0-75,72) 4-Y-O+ £3,067 (£905; £453) Stalls Centre

Form RPR
4540 1 **Pitkin**^{8} 2455 4-8-4 **58** ....(b) RossAtkinson$^{(3)}$ 8 68
(Michael Easterby) *in tch: smooth hdwy over 2f out: led appr fnl f: edgd lft: drvn and kpt on* **28/1**
2-33 2 nk **Viking Warrior (IRE)**^{42} 1520 5-8-11 **67** .... ShaneBKelly$^{(5)}$ 3 76
(Michael Dods) *prom: rdn over 2f out: kpt on* **4/1**^{2}
2522 3 nk **Save The Bees**^{21} 2094 4-9-6 **71** .... MichaelO'Connell 1 79
(Declan Carroll) *midfield: rdn over 2f out: hdwy over 1f out: kpt on fnl f* **11/4**^{1}
0066 4 3/4 **Dr Red Eye**^{18} 2151 4-9-1 **66** .... MickyFenton 12 73
(Scott Dixon) *led: rdn whn hdd appr fnl f: short of room and lost 3rd towards fin* **13/2**^{3}
-060 5 2 1/4 **Rio Cobolo (IRE)**^{25} 1951 6-9-5 **70** .... AndrewMullen 6 70
(David Nicholls) *prom: rdn over 2f out: no ex fnl f* **18/1**
-530 6 1 1/4 **Chosen Character (IRE)**^{21} 2096 4-9-6 **71** ....(vt) StephenCraine 10 68
(Tom Dascombe) *midfield: rdn over 2f out: kpt on one pce* **13/2**^{3}
6-12 7 3/4 **Drive Home (USA)**^{114} 478 5-8-13 **64** ....(p) DanielTudhope 11 59
(Noel Wilson) *hld up in tch: rdn over 2f out: nvr threatened* **12/1**
60-6 8 1/2 **Keys Of Cyprus**^{42} 1527 10-8-13 **71** .... ShirleyTeasdale$^{(7)}$ 4 65
(David Nicholls) *midfield: rdn over 2f out: no imp* **25/1**

0-00 **9** 3/4 **No Quarter (IRE)**[42] 1527 5-8-6 **60**............................ DeclanCannon(3) 9 52
(Tracy Waggott) *dwlt: hld up in tch: pushed along over 2f out: sn no imp* **20/1**

02-0 **10** 11 **Song Of The Siren**[35] 1652 4-9-0 **72**.......(b1) WilliamTwiston-Davies(7) 5 34
(David O'Meara) *sn pushed along towards rr: a bhd* **16/1**

0-00 **11** 9 **Dhhamaan (IRE)**[12] 2355 7-8-13 **64**.........................(b) JamesSullivan 14
(Ruth Carr) *sn midfield on outer: wknd over 2f out* **18/1**

0-10 **R** **Nadeen (IRE)**[30] 1796 5-8-13 **67**.............................. AdamBeschizza(3) 2
(Michael Smith) *ref to r: failed to come out of stalls* **9/1**

1m 26.85s (-0.15) **Going Correction** +0.10s/f (Good) **12** Ran SP% **119.5**
Speed ratings (Par 103): **104,103,103,102,99 98,97,97,96,83 73,**
toteswingers:1&2:£18.20, 1&3:£18.20, 2&3:£3.40 CSF £135.57 CT £428.07 TOTE £38.60: £11.10, £2.20, £1.10; EX 242.10.
Owner Steve Hull **Bred** New Mill Farm Stud **Trained** Sheriff Hutton, N Yorks
■ Stewards' Enquiry : Ross Atkinson caution: careless riding.

FOCUS
A competitive, if weak handicap, although the form looks straightforward. The pace was true and there was not much between the main protagonists, but there was a shock result.
Pitkin Official explanation: trainer's rep said, regarding apparent improvement in form, that the gelding appears to be coming back to form.

2697 TOTEPOOL MOBILE TEXT TOTE TO 89660 H'CAP 7f
3:20 (3:21) (Class 3) (0-90,88) 4-Y-0+ **£9,703** (£2,887; £1,443; £721) **Stalls** Centre

Form RPR

4-11 **1** **Powerful Presence (IRE)**[29] 1821 6-9-6 **87**............... DanielTudhope 1 95
(David O'Meara) *w ldr: led 3f out: rdn over 2f out: drvn appr fnl f: jst hld on* **15/8**[1]

0405 **2** nk **Kingscroft (IRE)**[8] 2444 4-9-2 **83**.................................. AndrewElliott 10 90
(Mark Johnston) *hld up: rdn and gd hdwy on outer over 1f out: kpt on fnl f: jst failed* **11/1**

3000 **3** shd **Clockmaker (IRE)**[28] 1865 6-9-7 **88**.............................. DuranFentiman 7 95
(Tim Easterby) *in tch: rdn 2f out: hdwy to chse wnr ins fnl f: kpt on* **10/1**

5-13 **4** 1 1/2 **Orpsie Boy (IRE)**[22] 2029 9-9-6 **87**............................. JamesSullivan 13 90
(Ruth Carr) *hld up: rdn and hdwy over 1f out: kpt on* **17/2**[3]

-044 **5** hd **Illustrious Prince (IRE)**[14] 2274 5-8-10 **77**............. MichaelO'Connell 5 79
(Declan Carroll) *trckd ldrs: rdn over 2f out: no ex fnl 100yds* **6/1**[2]

3-01 **6** 1 3/4 **Ballista (IRE)**[8] 2438 4-9-4 **85**................................ StephenCraine 8 83
(Tom Dascombe) *chsd ldrs: rdn over 2f out: wknd ins fnl f* **16/1**

00-0 **7** 1/2 **Mr David (USA)**[9] 2409 5-9-7 **88**...................................... LeeNewman 9 84
(Jamie Osborne) *midfield: rdn over 2f out: sn one pce* **11/1**

-100 **8** 1 **Mujaadel (USA)**[7] 2510 7-8-10 **77**............................(p) AndrewMullen 11 71
(David Nicholls) *midfield: rdn over 2f out: nvr threatened ldrs* **20/1**

0060 **9** 2 **Crown Choice**[40] 1558 7-9-7 **88**.................................... MickyFenton 14 76
(Paul Midgley) *hld up: nvr threatened* **33/1**

-006 **10** 10 **Glenridding**[7] 2489 8-8-10 **77**.. FrederikTylicki 2 38
(James Given) *led narrowly: hdd 3f out: wknd over 1f out* **33/1**

-000 **11** 13 **Oil Strike**[29] 1821 5-8-12 **82**.. RossAtkinson(3) 3
(Michael Easterby) *racd keenly: hld up in midfield: wknd over 2f out* **22/1**

2360 **12** 1 **Sound Amigo (IRE)**[14] 2285 4-8-8 **80**......................... ShaneBKelly(5) 4
(Ollie Pears) *w ldr: rdn over 2f out: sn wknd* **9/1**

1m 26.4s (-0.60) **Going Correction** +0.10s/f (Good) **12** Ran SP% **116.2**
Speed ratings (Par 107): **107,106,106,104,104 102,102,100,98,87 72,71**
toteswingers:1&2:£7.50, 1&3:£6.40, 2&3:£11.70 CSF £21.69 CT £165.03 TOTE £2.70: £1.20, £2.50, £3.30; EX 17.50.
Owner The Lawton Bamforth Partnership **Bred** Corduff Stud **Trained** Nawton, N Yorks

FOCUS
A competitive handicap run at a true pace and the form looks solid rated through the third to last year's course form.

NOTEBOOK
Powerful Presence(IRE), having won his previous two, the latter with authority at Musselburgh (7f, good to soft), was well supported. Taking advantage of his excellent draw, he was allowed to dominate on the rail and his rider injected pace to burn off his immediate pursuers turning into the home straight. Upped 6lb since his last victory, he looked a sitting duck when idling but found more when challenged to produce a career-best performance. Though in great heart, he had a hard race here. He might head to the Buckingham Palace Stakes at Royal Ascot. (op 5-2)
Kingscroft(IRE) ◆ had shown plenty of dash at Goodwood when beaten just over 2l (7f, good to firm) eight days previously and conditions were ideal for him off a 1lb lower mark. He was a little outpaced early but made good headway and challenged wide; nothing was going better at the death. He just failed and looks certain to find compensation shortly. (op 9-1)
Clockmaker(IRE) ran his best race for a while on ground that would be plenty quick enough, and has been dropped to a winning mark. He should not be long in scoring. (tchd 11-1)
Orpsie Boy(IRE), from a less-than-ideal draw in 13, managed to get a pitch on the rail and made good late headway when switched off it. Ideally, he would prefer more cut in the ground and does not look well handicapped. He continues to be penalised for his consistency and this was another gallant effort. (op 8-1 tchd 9-1)
Illustrious Prince(IRE) has improved with every run this term and appeared to do so again here, his run just flattening out inside the final half-furlong. One win from 21 starts on turf (that coming off a 5lb lower mark) means he is frustrating to follow. A drop in class might help his confidence. (tchd 11-2)
Ballista(IRE), a seller winner over this C&D, made a bold bid up the middle of the track but his run flattened out. He was not beaten far. (op 14-1)

2698 RACING POST FORM WITH TOTEPOOL MOBILE H'CAP 1m 7f 177y
4:20 (4:20) (Class 5) (0-70,68) 4-Y-0+ **£2,911** (£866; £432; £216) **Stalls** Centre

Form RPR

46-0 **1** **Callisto Moon**[26] 1925 8-9-6 **64**..............................(p) MichaelO'Connell 6 71
(Jo Hughes) *mde all: rdn over 2f out: strly pressed fnl 2f: hld on wl* **11/2**[2]

226- **2** hd **Finellas Fortune**[176] 5079 7-8-10 **54**............................ AndrewMullen 3 60
(George Moore) *midfield: hdwy 4f out: rdn to chal over 2f out: kpt on: a jst hld: fell sn after line* **8/1**[3]

116- **3** 1 **Strikemaster (IRE)**[201] 7415 6-9-1 **59**......................(t) DuranFentiman 10 64
(Lee James) *hld up in tch: rdn and hdwy 2f out: sn chsd ldng pair: kpt on fnl f* **10/1**

04 **4** 3 **Bocamix (FR)**[17] 1282 6-9-9 **67**...................................(t) DanielTudhope 2 69
(Andrew Crook) *midfield: rdn over 2f out: kpt on fnl f: nvr threatened ldrs* **10/1**

0/42 **5** 1 1/4 **One For Joules (IRE)**[44] 1485 5-9-2 **67**....... WilliamTwiston-Davies(7) 7 67
(Michael Scudamore) *hld up: hdwy on outer over 4f out: sn trckd ldr: rdn over 2f out: wknd ins fnl f* **15/8**[1]

440- **6** 2 1/4 **Heart Of Dubai (USA)**[40] 6095 7-8-5 **54** ow2...........(p) ShaneBKelly(5) 5 51
(Micky Hammond) *hld up in tch: rdn over 2f out: sn no imp* **10/1**

5614 **7** 2 **Satwa Ballerina**[8] 2468 4-8-9 **54**...............................(b) FrederikTylicki 8 49
(Mark Rimmer) *trckd ldrs tl wknd 3f out* **14/1**

00-0 **8** 32 **Spiders Star**[8] 2440 9-8-11 **55**.....................................(p) LeeNewman 9 12
(Simon West) *hld up: a bhd* **12/1**

6/20 **9** 9 **Dorset Square (IRE)**[16] 2214 8-9-6 **67**................(bt) AdamBeschizza(3) 4 13
(Sarah Humphrey) *trckd ldr: lost pl over 4f out: sn wknd* **8/1**[3]

3m 32.82s (0.82) **Going Correction** +0.10s/f (Good)
WFA 4 from 5yo+ 1lb **9** Ran SP% **114.0**
Speed ratings (Par 103): **101,100,100,98,98 97,96,80,75**
toteswingers:1&2:£14.70, 1&3:£13.00, 2&3:£14.70 CSF £48.08 CT £426.60 TOTE £6.50: £1.70, £4.00, £3.10; EX 49.30.
Owner B Bedford & Mrs Gill White **Bred** Barton Stud **Trained** Lambourn, Berks

FOCUS
A weak staying handicap run at a decent pace. The form does not look anything out of the ordinary with the runner-up and fourth setting a limited standard. The runner-up's fall prompted an inspection of the ground directly after the winning post and it was found that light drizzle had made the surface slippery. It was subsequently deemed too dangerous to continue and the final two races were abandoned.

2699 READ LATEST TOTESCOOP6 NEWS AT TOTEPOOL.COM H'CAP 5f 212y
() (Class 4) (0-85,) 4-Y-0+ £

2700 FOLLOW TOTEPOOL ON FACEBOOK AND TWITTER MEDIAN AUCTION MAIDEN FILLIES' STKS 5f 212y
() (Class 6) 3-4-Y-0 £

T/Plt: £57.40 to a £1 stake.Pool of £34,616.66 - 439.91 winning tickets. T/Qpdt: £11.80 to a £1 stake.Pool of £2445.76 - 153.32 winning tickets. AS

2654 EPSOM (L-H)
Saturday, June 2

OFFICIAL GOING: Good to firm (derby course 8.5, 5f course 8.8, home straight: far side 8.2, stands' side 8.8)
Wind: medium, behind Weather: overcast, dry

2701 DIAMOND JUBILEE H'CAP (SPONSORED BY INVESTEC) 1m 2f 18y
1:35 (1:37) (Class 2) (0-105,100) 3-Y-0
£24,900 (£7,456; £3,728; £1,864; £932; £468) **Stalls** Low

Form RPR

1-26 **1** **Wrotham Heath**[14] 2281 3-8-11 **90**.................................... TomQueally 7 101+
(Sir Henry Cecil) *lw: hld up in tch in midfield: hdwy to join ldr on bit 2f out: rdn to ld over 1f out: drvn ins fnl f: edgd lft and hld on wl fnl 100yds* **5/1**[3]

1-41 **2** nk **Grandeur (IRE)**[7] 2477 3-9-3 **96**...................................... WilliamBuick 13 106+
(Jeremy Noseda) *swtg: hld up in tch in last quartet: hdwy to chse ldrs over 2f out: drvn over 1f out: chsd wnr ins fnl f: str chal fnl 100yds: r.o but a jst hld* **7/2**[1]

33-2 **3** 3/4 **Spoke To Carlo**[16] 2197 3-8-3 **82**... JohnFahy 6 91
(Eve Johnson Houghton) *swtg: on toes: restless in stalls: in tch in midfield: rdn and hdwy to chse ldrs 2f out: swtchd ins and pressing ldrs 1f out: keeping on same pce whn nt clr run towards fin* **17/2**

12-3 **4** 1 1/4 **Open Water (FR)**[27] 1888 3-8-7 **86**.................................. HayleyTurner 5 93
(Andrew Balding) *lw: sn led: rdn and jnd 2f out: drvn and hdd over 1f out: keeping on same pce and hld whn short of room fnl 100yds* **4/1**[2]

1312 **5** 4 1/2 **Fennell Bay (IRE)**[8] 2449 3-8-3 **82**........................ SilvestreDeSousa 1 79
(Mark Johnston) *chsd ldr tl 7f out: rdn and effrt to chal 2f out: no ex and btn ent fnl f: wknd* **17/2**

3-10 **6** 8 **Blades Lad**[15] 2258 3-7-10 **78** ow1................................ RyanPowell(3) 12 59
(Richard Fahey) *t.k.h: hld up in rr: rdn and struggling 3f out: wknd 2f out* **40/1**

1-12 **7** nse **The Giving Tree (IRE)**[16] 2201 3-8-1 **80**......................... KieranO'Neill 4 61
(Sylvester Kirk) *t.k.h: chsd ldrs tl wnt 2nd 7f out tl over 2f out: sn wknd u.p: wl btn whn hung lft wl over 1f out* **12/1**

162- **8** 1 3/4 **Position**[241] 6623 3-8-6 **85**.. LukeMorris 8 62
(Sir Mark Prescott Bt) *lw: chsd ldng trio: rdn on downhill run 2f out: wknd over 2f out: wl btn over 1f out* **20/1**

-200 **9** 4 **Entifaadha**[44] 1468 3-9-7 **100**... PaulHanagan 3 69
(William Haggas) *b: b.hind: swtg: t.k.h: hld up in tch: rdn and struggling over 2f out: sn wknd: wl btn whn bdly hmpd wl over 1f out* **14/1**

-225 **10** 32 **Mister Music**[28] 1859 3-9-2 **95**... RyanMoore 10
(Richard Hannon) *dwlt: a in rr: rdn and effrt whn hmpd over 3f out: sn lost tch and nt pushed: t.o* **11/1**

241 **F** **Star Date (IRE)**[13] 2313 3-7-13 **83**.................................. DarrenEgan(5) 9
(Gerard Butler) *stdd s: hld up in tch towards rr: hdwy whn clipped heels and fell heavily over 3f out* **9/1**

2m 7.01s (-2.69) **Going Correction** -0.05s/f (Good) **11** Ran SP% **119.8**
Speed ratings (Par 105): **108,107,107,106,102 96,96,94,91,65**
toteswingers:1&2:£4.70, 2&3:£7.90, 1&3:£9.40 CSF £23.32 CT £149.08 TOTE £6.30: £1.80, £1.70, £3.00; EX 23.70 Trifecta £141.50 Pool: £3911.86 - 20.44 winning units..
Owner K Abdulla **Bred** Juddmonte Farms Ltd **Trained** Newmarket, Suffolk
■ Stewards' Enquiry : Kieran O'Neill five-day ban: careless riding (Jun 16-20)
Tom Queally two-day ban: careless riding (Jun 16-17)

FOCUS
Track at normal configuration and distances as advertised. A race that has on more than one occasion in recent years thrown up a future Pattern-class performer, and there's a chance it may have done so again, as the only one in the race with a Group race entry (Irish Derby), Wrotham Heath, won a shade cosily. The early pace wasn't that strong but the first three came from the second half of the field and this looks form to be positive about.

NOTEBOOK
Wrotham Heath looked a potential Derby contender after winning his maiden at two, but he was beaten by a good horse on his reappearance and seemed to find 1m4f too far at Newmarket last time. Back in distance, he showed himself to be well handicapped, travelling strongly into contention and finding for pressure. Clearly fast ground is no bother to him, despite earlier indications to the contrary, and now that his best distance has been discovered, there should be more to come. The Group 3 Tercentenary Stakes at Royal Ascot was mentioned, and that looks a suitable race for him. (tchd 11-2)
Grandeur(IRE) also looks to have plenty of potential to develop into a stakes horse. He couldn't quite get by the winner but, having been raised 8lb to 96 for his Goodwood win, this was a good effort off his new mark. It wouldn't be a surprise to see him reoppose the winner at Royal Ascot as he'd get a 6lb pull in the weights. On his second start last summer he won a Brighton maiden, and back in third that day, beaten just over three lengths, was Spoke To Carlo, who was making his racecourse debut. (op 9-2)
Spoke To Carlo, who got a bit upset in the stalls beforehand, had a 14lb pull in the weights with Grandeur and came here on the back of a good effort at Newmarket on his reappearance, but he couldn't quite reverse the form. There's a handicap in him, though, and his performance helps give the form a solid look. (op 10-1 tchd 8-1)

Open Water(FR) was allowed the run of things out in front but tended to hang right against the camber inside the final 2f. He finished well clear of the rest, though, and beat off his nearest pursuers (Fennell Bay, The Giving Tree, Entifaadha and Position) by a long way, so it was probably a good effort, and having had only four starts, there should be better to come. Official explanation: jockey said colt hung right (tchd 5-1)

Fennell Bay(IRE), another 4lb higher, didn't run badly and simply looked to come up against better handicapped rivals. He's another who can be used to set the level of the form. (op 8-1)

Blades Lad was never a factor, simply staying on past a few beaten horses late. (tchd 50-1)

The Giving Tree(IRE), the only filly in the line-up, was beaten off with over 2f to run and perhaps the ground was quicker than ideal. (op 10-1)

Entifaadha, again keen, was keeping on and would have probably been sixth when badly hampered against the rail inside the final 2f. (op 16-1)

Mister Music was hampered at the back of the field when Star Date clipped heels and fell just as they straightened up for home, and Ryan Moore soon eased his mount down. Official explanation: jockey said colt was hampered by faller 3f out (op 12-1 tchd 14-1)

2702 INVESTEC WOODCOTE STKS (LISTED RACE) 6f

2:05 (2:10) (Class 1) 2-Y-O

£14,177 (£5,375; £2,690; £1,340; £672; £337) **Stalls** High

Form				RPR
012	1		**Chilworth Icon**[31] 1747 2-9-0 0 .... MartinHarley 4 (Mick Channon) *chsd ldrs: rdn to chal 2f out: drvn ahd jst ins fnl f: hrd pressd and bmpd ins fnl f: hld on wl and edgd rt nr fin* **12/1**	98
011	2	*shd*	**Heavy Metal**[15] 2247 2-9-0 0 .... SilvestreDeSousa 8 (Mark Johnston) *tall: str: lw:c dwlt: sn rdn along and rcvrd to chse ldrs: drvn and hdwy to chal 1f out: ev ch whn edgd lft and bmpd wnr ins fnl f: stl ev ch whn whip knocked out of rdrs hand cl home* **11/4**[2]	98
21	3	1 ¼	**Liber**[5] 2537 2-9-0 0 .... LukeMorris 7 (Sir Mark Prescott Bt) *w'like: chsd ldr tl led 4f out: drvn jst over 1f out: hdd jst ins fnl f: no ex and btn fnl 100yds: one pce after* **5/1**[3]	94
1	4	2 ½	**Euxton Hall (IRE)**[21] 2073 2-9-0 0 .... PaulHanagan 1 (Richard Fahey) *athletic: dwlt: sn bustled along: swtchd rt and effrt u.p 2f out: chsd ldng trio and drvn wl over 1f out: no imp tl styd on ins fnl f: nt gng pce to chal* **7/4**[1]	86+
11	5	4 ½	**Lastchancelucas**[17] 2181 2-9-0 0 .... JasonHart 5 (Declan Carroll) *on toes: led for 2f: drvn and outpcd wl over 2f out: wknd 2f out* **13/2**	73
	6	1 ¾	**Scotland Forever (IRE)**[16] 2215 2-9-0 0 .... CO'Donoghue 6 (John Patrick Shanahan, Ire) *str: t.k.h: early: hld up in last pair: awkward on downhill run 4f out and lost tch over 3f out: n.d after* **33/1**	68+
31	7	8	**Surely Speightful (USA)**[8] 2456 2-8-9 0 .... JamieSpencer 2 (Kevin Ryan) *leggy: awkward leaving stalls and slowly away: a bhd: lost tch over 2f out: wl bhd fnl 2f: eased wl ins fnl f* **10/1**	39

1m 8.43s (-0.97) **Going Correction** -0.05s/f (Good) 7 Ran SP% **112.8**

Speed ratings (Par 101): **104,103,102,98,92 90,79**

toteswingers:1&2:£6.30, 2&3:£2.70, 1&3:£8.50 CSF £43.81 TOTE £16.30: £4.30, £2.00; EX 33.80 Trifecta £265.30 Pool: £3567.08 - 9.94 winning units..

Owner 7Rus **Bred** Norman Court Stud **Trained** West Ilsley, Berks

■ Stewards' Enquiry : Silvestre De Sousa two-day ban: used whip above permitted level (Jun 16-17)

FOCUS

The last ten winners of the Woodcote have all failed to win again at Listed level or better. This looked another ordinary edition, even if the form appears fairly solid.

NOTEBOOK

Chilworth Icon won despite not handling the track all that well - he was ill at ease running downhill and for much of the straight. He came into this with a progressive profile at 5f and just managed to see out this extra furlong. His St Leger-winning sire is proving a remarkable source of precocious types (notably for this trainer) with his first crop, although there's plenty of speed on the dam's side of this one's pedigree. There might be more to come back on a conventional track, but he'll do well to better this achievement. (op 11-1)

Heavy Metal, whose trainer had won this three times in the last ten years, was on a hat-trick after a couple of minor victories, but he just failed to get up. He was surely not helped by his rider having his whip knocked out of his hand late on, even though Silvestre de Sousa had already done enough to pick up a two-day whip ban. Whatever, he looks the type to go on improving, at least in the short term. (op 3-1)

Liber, who made all in a 5f Carlisle maiden five days earlier, was again given a forward ride and travelled well, but he didn't see his race out. Maybe a return to the minimum trip would suit. (tchd 11-2)

Euxton Hall(IRE) looked decent when winning on his debut over this trip on easy ground at Haydock (useful runner-up has since won), but he was never going the required pace this time. He can be given another chance to confirm that initial promise back on a flatter track and softer ground might also help. (op 2-1 tchd 9-4 in a place)

Lastchancelucas proved his big-price debut win wasn't a fluke when following up at York, but he struggled over this extra furlong on this further rise in class. (op 7-1)

Scotland Forever(IRE), the sole Irish challenger, was reported on his debut (7f, good to soft) to have pulled hard and ducked in the straight. He was well held that day, so this was a big ask, and he was again keen after getting behind. (op 16-1)

Surely Speightful(USA), the only filly in the line-up, had looked a nice enough sort when winning a weak Musselburgh maiden under positive tactics on her second start, but this time she was never going after starting awkwardly. (op 8-1)

2703 DIAMOND JUBILEE CORONATION CUP (SPONSORED BY INVESTEC) (GROUP 1) 1m 4f 10y

2:40 (2:40) (Class 1) 4-Y-O+

£170,130 (£64,500; £32,280; £16,080; £8,070; £4,050) **Stalls** Centre

Form				RPR
1-22	1		**St Nicholas Abbey (IRE)**[26] 1946 5-9-0 123 .... JPO'Brien 4 (A P O'Brien, Ire) *hld up in last pair: hdwy on outer bnd over 3f out: led 2f out and sn qcknd clr: in command whn rdr dropped whip over 1f out: rdn out hands and heels fnl f: comf* **8/11**[1]	126+
3-21	2	4 ½	**Red Cadeaux**[15] 2254 6-9-0 116 .... RyanMoore 6 (Ed Dunlop) *stdd s: hld up in last pair: 6th st: sn rdn and hdwy into 4th: outpcd 2f out: kpt on fr over 1f out: wnt 2nd ins fnl f: no threat to wnr* **8/1**[3]	118
10-0	3	3 ¼	**Masked Marvel**[28] 1855 4-9-0 121 .... WilliamBuick 1 (John Gosden) *lw: bustled along leaving stalls: sn chsng ldr: 2nd st: rdn and clsd over 3f out: led wl over 2f out: hdd and immediately outpcd by wnr 2f out: plugged on but no ch after: lost 2nd ins fnl f* **8/1**[3]	113
15-2	4	1 ½	**Quest For Peace (IRE)**[28] 1855 4-9-0 114 .... KierenFallon 5 (Luca Cumani) *chsd ldng pair: 3rd and rdn st: clsd to press ldrs wl over 2f out: outpcd by wnr 2f out and wl hld after: plugged on* **12/1**	110
11-6	5	27	**Beaten Up**[63] 1149 4-9-0 119 .... JohnnyMurtagh 2 (William Haggas) *lw: t.k.h: hld up in 4th: 5th and rdn st: sn btn: wl bhd and eased fnl f: t.o* **3/1**[2]	67
3/43	6	29	**Robin Hood (IRE)**[6] 2525 4-9-0 99 .... (v[1]) SeamieHeffernan 3 (A P O'Brien, Ire) *led and sn clr: rdn over 3f out: hdd wl over 2f out: sn dropped out and wl bhd: t.o and eased fnl f* **66/1**	21

2m 34.52s (-4.38) **Going Correction** -0.05s/f (Good) 6 Ran SP% **114.3**

Speed ratings (Par 117): **112,109,106,105,87 68**

toteswingers:1&2:£1.90, 2&3:£3.00, 1&3:£2.40 CSF £7.92 TOTE £1.70: £1.10, £3.80; EX 5.30.

Owner Derrick Smith & Mrs John Magnier & Michael Tabor **Bred** Barton Bloodstock & Villiers Synd **Trained** Ballydoyle, Co Tipperary

FOCUS

There wasn't much strength in depth with the second favourite too keen and both the runner-up and third essentially stayers, but this was still a top-class performance from St Nicholas Abey, probably his best yet. The final time was 0.62 seconds off the Derby, but hand-timed sectionals showed Robin Hood set a slower pace than the leader in the Classic, and this lot came home quicker. Indeed, from the top of the straight to the line the split was around 0.90 seconds faster than the Derby. This rates a personal best from the winner with the runner-up setting the standard.

NOTEBOOK

St Nicholas Abbey(IRE) ♦, who was following up his victory in this last year (when he faced one less rival), was forced wider than ideal into the straight, and Joseph O'Brien lost his whip over a furlong out, but it didn't matter. He won with ease, despite looking a bit awkward under pressure, and his performance is all the more creditable considering the modest early tempo. Clearly his recent defeat over an inadequate 1m2f at the Curragh (set a lot to do), in his first start since finishing second in the Sheema Classic, set him up nicely for this and the King George is the obvious target now. (tchd 8-13 and 4-5 in places)

Red Cadeaux was no match at all for the winner but stayed on past beaten rivals for second. He recently gained a deserved success in the Yorkshire Cup and shouldn't be long in breaking the £1m barrier for prize-money earned - he's now on £969,547. (op 9-1)

Masked Marvel, last year's St Leger winner, led the main pack behind the pacemaker, but he lacked anything like the winner's speed in the straight and gradually lost second to a more conservatively ridden rival. This was a marked improvement on the form he showed on unsuitably soft ground in the Jockey Club Stakes on his return, but it strongly suggested he won't be winning a Group 1 at this trip in Britain. It wouldn't surprise to see him go abroad and/or back up in distance. (op 15-2 tchd 7-1)

Quest For Peace(IRE), formerly a stablemate of the winner, sweated up (not for the first time) and failed to build on his well-held second in the Jockey Club Stakes on his reappearance. He's not up to this level in Britain, although he was having only his eighth start. (tchd 14-1)

Beaten Up had looked so promising when winning his three starts last year and was particularly impressive in the St Simon Stakes considering he drew clear of Al Kazeem (Group 2 winner already this season) despite having refused to settle. However, he still hasn't learnt to relax and consequently he's been unable to make the jump up to the top level. He was too keen in the Sheema Classic on his return and likewise here. (op 4-1 tchd 9-2)

2704 INVESTEC SPECIALIST BANK "DASH" (H'CAP) 5f

3:15 (3:15) (Class 2) 3-Y-O+

£46,687 (£13,980; £6,990; £3,495; £1,747; £877) **Stalls** High

Form				RPR
005-	1		**Stone Of Folca**[270] 5805 4-8-12 **93** .... LukeMorris 2 (John Best) *taken down early: chsd ldrs: rdn to ld over 1f out: drvn and kpt on wl fnl f* **50/1**	102
60-0	2	½	**Desert Law (IRE)**[62] 1157 4-9-2 **97** .... JimmyFortune 16 (Andrew Balding) *lw: chsd ldrs: n.m.r over 1f out: rdn and effrt to chse wnr ins fnl f: kpt on wl u.p* **11/1**	104
61-2	3	¾	**Catfish (IRE)**[7] 2507 4-8-7 **88** .... MickaelBarzalona 15 (Brian Meehan) *taken down early: racd in midfield: rdn and effrt 1/2-way: hdwy 1f out: swtchd lft ins fnl f: r.o wl: nt rch ldrs* **7/1**[1]	93
1102	4	1 ¼	**Taajub (IRE)**[38] 1602 5-8-11 **92** .... IanMongan 3 (Peter Crate) *in tch: rdn and effrt to chse ldrs over 1f out: keeping on whn pushed lft ins fnl f: kpt on same pce fnl 100yds* **25/1**	92
0615	5	½	**Confessional**[7] 2486 5-9-4 **99** 4ex .... (be) TedDurcan 7 (Tim Easterby) *hld up in midfield: clsd to chse ldrs and gng wl whn nt clr run 1f out: trying to rally whn nt clr run again and hmpd fnl 100yds: kpt on: unable to chal* **8/1**[2]	97+
53-4	6	½	**Jamesway (IRE)**[38] 1602 4-8-4 **85** .... LiamJones 18 (Richard Fahey) *taken down early: sn outpcd towards rr: rdn and hdwy ent fnl f: swtchd lft ins fnl f: r.o wl: nt rch ldrs* **8/1**[2]	81
15-0	7	nk	**York Glory (USA)**[17] 2177 4-9-1 **96** .... (b) JamieSpencer 4 (Kevin Ryan) *bmpd s: sn rcvrd and in midfield: rdn and effrt in centre to chse ldrs 1f out: one pce fnl 100yds* **12/1**	91+
450	8	1 ¼	**Vocational (USA)**[7] 2507 3-9-2 **104** .... SilvestreDeSousa 9 (Mark Johnston) *sn outpcd and rdn along towards rr: hdwy ent fnl f: styd on wl fnl f: nt gng pce to chal ldrs* **33/1**	92+
0-65	9	½	**Captain Dunne (IRE)**[43] 1498 7-9-10 **105** .... (p) DaneO'Neill 11 (Tim Easterby) *led at fast pce: rdn and hdd over 1f out: lost 2nd ins fnl f: wknd fnl 100yds* **11/1**	94
-500	10	*shd*	**Fitz Flyer (IRE)**[16] 2208 6-8-12 **93** .... KierenFallon 8 (David Nicholls) *sn pushed along in midfield: hmpd 3f out: swtchd lft and hdwy towards centre jst over 1f out: kpt on but nvr threatened ldrs* **20/1**	82
03-6	11	½	**Oor Jock (IRE)**[42] 1538 4-8-11 **92** .... CO'Donoghue 1 (John Patrick Shanahan, Ire) *chsd ldrs: drvn and unable qck over 1f out: wknd ins fnl f* **50/1**	79
30-0	12	*hd*	**Sohraab**[14] 2268 8-8-9 **90** .... KieranO'Neill 19 (Hughie Morrison) *bhd on stands' rail: nt clr run ent fnl 2f: kpt on fnl f: nvr trbld ldrs* **14/1**	76+
63-1	13	½	**Long Awaited (IRE)**[36] 1643 4-8-6 **87** .... MartinDwyer 13 (David Barron) *in tch: cl to chse ldrs over 1f out: sn rdn and unable qck whn short of room 1f out: wknd ins fnl f* **16/1**	71
-603	14	*hd*	**Diamond Charlie (IRE)**[22] 2040 4-8-4 **85** .... HayleyTurner 5 (Simon Dow) *bmpd and squeezed out after s: sn wl bhd: sme hdwy fnl f: n.d* **40/1**	69+
5550	15	nk	**Courageous (IRE)**[7] 2488 6-7-13 **85** ow1 .... (t) RaulDaSilva(5) 12 (Kevin Ryan) *racd in midfield: rdn and effrt whn n.m.r over 1f out: no imp after* **40/1**	68
1-50	16	1	**Living It Large (FR)**[24] 1975 5-8-8 **89** .... JohnFahy 10 (Ed de Giles) *sn rdn along to chse ldrs: struggling u.p over 1f out: wknd fnl f* **20/1**	68
4-21	17	¾	**Judge 'n Jury**[16] 2208 8-8-10 **91** 4ex .... (t) MartinHarley 14 (Ronald Harris) *chsd ldr tl drvn over 1f out: wknd fnl f* **10/1**[3]	67
2-05	18	1 ½	**Dickie's Lad (IRE)**[17] 2177 4-8-13 **94** .... (t) TomQueally 6 (Kevin Ryan) *taken down early: short of room sn after s: a outpcd towards rr* **16/1**	65+
0-12	19	2 ¾	**Bear Behind (IRE)**[36] 1644 3-9-2 **104** .... RichardKingscote 20 (Tom Dascombe) *broke fast: chsd ldrs but sn struggling to go pce: lost pl 1/2-way: bhd fnl f* **7/1**[1]	62

0130 **20** 3 3/4 **Arctic Feeling (IRE)**[14] 2286 4-8-7 **88**........................ PaulHanagan 17 35+
(Richard Fahey) *hmpd sn after s: nt rcvr and detached in last after* **25/1**
53.69s (-2.01) **Going Correction** -0.175s/f (Firm)
WFA 3 from 4yo+ 7lb **20** Ran SP% **128.1**
Speed ratings (Par 109): **109,108,107,105,104 103,102,100,100,99 99,98,98,97,97 95,94,92,87,81**
toteswingers:1&2:£133.00, 2&3:£19.90, 1&3:£55.40 CSF £506.97 CT £4408.75 TOTE £84.10: £13.10, £3.60, £1.90, £6.60; EX 747.70 Trifecta £14350.70 Pool: £65935.96 - 3.40 winning units..
Owner Folkestone Racecourse Owners Group **Bred** D R Botterill **Trained** Hucking, Kent

FOCUS
This valuable sprint handicap attracted the usual big field, and with the ground riding fast and a following wind it was no surprise to see a quick time, although the clock stopped at a particularly swift 53.69sec, making it just 0.09sec outside the hand-timed track record, recorded by Indigenous back in 1960. A high draw, and more importantly a stands' rail pitch is usually an advantage in this race, but two of the first four came from the lowest four boxes this time. The form looks pretty sound using the third and fourth as guides, despite the usual hard-luck stories in a race of this nature.

NOTEBOOK
Stone Of Folca was a speedy, Group-class juvenile (fourth in the Norfolk and runner-up in the Molecomb) but he went on the missing list at three, largely disappointing after breaking his maiden on his reappearance. However, he'd dropped a fair few pounds as a result and was having his first start since being gelded here. Showing bright pace from the off, he gradually crossed over from his disadvantageous stall position to race in the front rank, before taking over with a furlong and a half to run and keeping on strongly to hold off the runner-up, who'd travelled far less distance from his high draw. He should be rated better than the bare form and, with little to split the top handicappers and the pattern-class performers, he'll deserve to take his chance back up in grade. A sharp track will always suit him best, so another go at the King George Stakes at Goodwood appeals. (op 40-1)
Desert Law(IRE) was far too keen over 6f on his reappearance and dropping back to 5f off a strong pace proved a good move. The gap came soon enough for him if he was good enough, but the winner was always just holding on. He can win over this trip off this sort of mark, but his owner is keen to go for the King's Stand with him. (op 12-1)
Catfish(IRE), 2lb well-in at the weights, had a nice draw and finished well having not enjoyed the clearest of passages. She should remain competitive off her new mark, but might go chasing black type next as the Listed Land O'Burns Stakes at Ayr in three weeks' time is apparently in connections' minds. (op 15-2 tchd 13-2)
Taajub(IRE) drawn low like the winner, showed good all-round pace. He'd displayed a liking for the track here on his previous start when the ground was soft, and this performance on contrasting ground (also a winner on Polytrack) showcased his versatility. (op 28-1 tchd 33-1)
Confessional, who was second last year from stall 13, had stall seven to deal with this time. His rider had to sit and suffer as the gaps failed to materialise and he was never really able to ask his mount for maximum effort. He shaped better than his finishing position suggests, but was well-in under his penalty here and will have to race off 5lb higher in future. Official explanation: jockey said gelding was denied a clear run (op 9-1)
Jamesway(IRE) struggled with the early gallop but weaved his way between horses near the stands' rail to be nearest at the finish. To some extent his style of running means he's a serial eyecatcher, and two wins, and none in the last two years, is a disappointing return really. (op 15-2)
York Glory(USA) ◆, another drawn low, returned to form after a poor performance on his reappearance at York. Racing widest towards the middle of the track throughout, this was a really good effort, and he's not handicapped out of things off his current mark. (tchd 14-1)
Vocational(USA) is normally up with the pace, but she couldn't go the gallop this time and instead came from behind late, putting in some good work at the finish. Perhaps being ridden with more restraint, like this, is the way to go with her.
Captain Dunne(IRE), who won this last year off the same mark, showed his usual bright early pace to lead, but didn't see his race out as strongly this time. (op 12-1)
Fitz Flyer(IRE) endured a bit of a rough race, but he kept on out wide once in the clear.
Sohraab, who was fourth from stall one last year, had a better draw this time, but he was always going to be a hostage to fortune given his style of running. Sure enoug,h he found his path blocked on the stands' rail as he tried to make up ground from the rear, and he shaped better than his finishing position suggests. Official explanation: jockey said gelding was denied a clear run
Courageous(IRE) was another who didn't get much luck in running. (op 33-1 tchd 50-1)
Bear Behind(IRE) looked to have the ideal draw considering his style of running, but he was free to post and perhaps his race had been run prior to the off, for while he got the rail he was never in front and he weakened with over 2f to run. Official explanation: jockey said colt ran too free to post (op 15-2 tchd 9-1 in a place)

2705 INVESTEC DERBY (GROUP 1) 1m 4f 10y
4:00 (4:04) (Class 1) 3-Y-0

£751,407 (£284,875; £142,570; £71,020; £35,642; £17,887) **Stalls** Centre

Form RPR
1-1 **1** **Camelot**[28] 1856 3-9-0 121........................ JPO'Brien 5 128+
(A P O'Brien, Ire) *lw: stdd s: hld up in last trio: 7th st: effrt 3f out: rdn to chse clr ldr 2f out: drvn and clsd readily to ld 1f out: r.o strly and sn clr: eased towards fin* **8/13**[1]
1-11 **2** 5 **Main Sequence (USA)**[21] 2080 3-9-0 106........................ TedDurcan 3 118
(David Lanigan) *edgy: stdd s: hld up in last trio: hdwy 6f out: 5th st: rdn and effrt over 3f out: wnt 3rd 2f out but sn no imp: no ch w wnr but kpt on ins fnl f to go 2nd on post* **9/1**
33-1 **3** shd **Astrology (IRE)**[22] 2026 3-9-0 113........................ RyanMoore 7 118
(A P O'Brien, Ire) *lw: led and set gd gallop: drvn and fnd ex to go clr over 2f out: hdd 1f out: nt gng pce of wnr and sn btn: lost 2nd on post* **13/2**[3]
1-21 **4** 6 **Thought Worthy (USA)**[14] 2275 3-9-0 106........................ WilliamBuick 6 108
(John Gosden) *on toes: chsd ldr: 2nd and pressing ldr st: drvn and unable qck over 2f out: 4th and wknd wl over 1f out* **16/1**
1421 **5** 2 **Mickdaam (IRE)**[23] 1995 3-9-0 108........................ PaulHanagan 4 105
(Richard Fahey) *hld up in tch: lost pl 6f out: last and rdn st: outpcd and btn over 2f out: no ch whn hung lft over 1f out* **25/1**
13-1 **6** 1/2 **Bonfire**[16] 2210 3-9-0 119........................ JimmyFortune 8 104
(Andrew Balding) *ponied to s: chsd ldrs: 4th and rdn st: 5th and struggling 2f out: sn wknd* **9/2**[2]
215 **7** 1/2 **Minimise Risk**[23] 1995 3-9-0 96........................ JamieSpencer 9 103
(Andrew Balding) *lw: stdd s: hld up in rr: 8th st: sn rdn and no imp: wknd and bhd 2f out* **66/1**
51-3 **8** 2 **Rugged Cross**[14] 2275 3-9-0 104........................ DaneO'Neill 2 100
(Henry Candy) *t.k.h: chsd ldrs: 3rd straight: sn rdn and unable to quicken: 6th and struggling 2f out: sn wknd* **33/1**
11-3 **9** 3 1/2 **Cavaleiro (IRE)**[21] 2080 3-9-0 95........................ HayleyTurner 1 95
(Marcus Tregoning) *in tch: 6th and rdn st: sn dropped to rr: lost tch 2f out* **25/1**
2m 33.9s (-5.00) **Going Correction** -0.05s/f (Good) **9** Ran SP% **121.4**
Speed ratings (Par 113): **114,110,110,106,105 104,104,103,100**
toteswingers:1&2:£2.70, 2&3:£5.70, 1&3:£2.00 CSF £7.65 CT £24.22 TOTE £1.80: £1.10, £1.90, £2.00; EX 7.30 Trifecta £30.80 Pool: £53333.63 - 1277.38 winning units..
Owner Derrick Smith & Mrs John Magnier & Michael Tabor **Bred** Sheikh Abdulla Bin Isa Al-Khalifa **Trained** Ballydoyle, Co Tipperary

FOCUS
The smallest field for the Derby since 1907, and while the winners of the Dante, Lingfield Derby Trial, Chester Vase and Dee Stakes all made the line-up, the race revolved around 2000 Guineas winner Camelot, who was bidding to emulate post-war greats such as Sir Ivor, Nijinsky, Nashwan and Sea The Stars in completing the Guineas/Derby double, and duly did so. The time was 0.62sec faster than that recorded by St Nicholas Abbey in the Coronation Cup earlier on the card, and hand-timed sectionals suggest they reached the path after around 5f about a second faster, while they took around 0.9sec longer to reach the line from the top of the straight. The form is rated close to the best of recent Derby winning performances and the fourth rated to previous form setting the level.

NOTEBOOK
Camelot produced a performance of true class. He travelled well in rear and quickened up smartly to join the leader heading to the 2f pole and then left him for dead inside the last to win with authority, going away. He will have little trouble dropping back to 1m2f, and a clash with Frankel would be something to look forward to, but there's been plenty of talk already about the prospect of him becoming the first colt to win the Triple Crown since Nijinsky in 1970. With the bloodstock industry largely geared around breeding for speed, in recent years going for the St Leger with a Derby winner has been considered a no-no, as connections run scared of their future stallion being branded as slow. Camelot already has a Guineas win under his belt, though, so there's less to be afraid of on that front, and in any case, most significantly of all, his connections appear keen on the idea, place in history and all that. It's quite reasonable to assume that the Leger might well be the easiest of the three Classics for him to win and he could still run in the Arc three weeks later. (op 4-6)
Main Sequence(USA) lacked the winner's impressive turn of foot, but he kept on well to take second right on the line. He's not a flashy colt, but he's steadily progressed with every outing and this was another personal best. The King Edward VII or the Irish Derby look the obvious races for him.
Astrology(IRE) won the Dee Stakes in desperate ground, but his connections were sure he'd appreciate a sounder surface - something backed up by his pedigree – and, having made all at Chester, he was the natural pacesetter in the race. For a moment it looked like he'd got a jump on the field heading to the 2f pole, but Camelot soon closed him down. Having been headed by the winner he got tired late on and was caught for second close home, but considering the pace he set he shaped like the second best horse in the race, and like the runner-up one would expect him now to head for either the Irish Derby or the King Edward VII. (tchd 6-1)
Thought Worthy(USA) moved up alongside the leader running down the hill and attempted to get first run and exploit any stamina deficiencies in his rivals. He couldn't stay with Astrology, though, and wandered about as he weakened. This track probably didn't play to his strengths, but he's a brother to St Leger winner Lucarno and the final Classic could well be his long-term target too, perhaps providing Camelot is absent.
Mickdaam(IRE), the Chester Vase winner, dropped back to last running down the hill. Chopped for room around 2f out, he might have finished a little closer with a clear run, but was clearly not in the class of the first three. (op 28-1)
Bonfire, who was unlucky not to beat French Fifteen in a Group 1 at two, had little to find with Camelot on a line through that horse. Indeed, the official handicapper had them just 2lb apart, and RPRs 3lb, but he wasn't sure to appreciate the longer trip and off this strong pace he was found wanting for stamina. He didn't handle the track either and will appreciate dropping back to 1m2f on a more conventional course. The Eclipse would seem a natural target. (tchd 5-1)
Minimise Risk, who didn't handle the ground at Chester when well beaten in the Vase, is bred to stay well. Given a patient ride out the back, he hung left down the camber in the straight which hampered his finishing effort. He's another who'll do better back on a more galloping track, and in his case when upped in distance. (tchd 50-1)
Rugged Cross was keen. He didn't run badly for a long way, though, and can make his mark at a lower level over shorter. (tchd 50-1 in a place)
Cavaleiro(IRE) faced a stiff task on what he'd achieved to date and was never seriously involved. (op 33-1)

2706 INVESTEC ZEBRA H'CAP 1m 4f 10y
4:50 (4:52) (Class 2) (0-100,98) 4-Y-0+

£12,450 (£3,728; £1,864; £932; £466; £234) **Stalls** Centre

Form RPR
0050 **1** **Fiery Lad (IRE)**[38] 1605 7-9-7 **98**........................ KierenFallon 11 105
(Luca Cumani) *hld up towards rr: rdn and effrt 3f out: hdwy and drvn to chse ldrs over 1f out: eged lft u.p 1f out: str chal ins fnl f: r.o wl to ld cl home* **10/1**
232- **2** hd **A Boy Named Suzi**[224] 7017 4-8-12 **89**........................ LukeMorris 14 96
(James Eustace) *hld up in midfield: rdn and effrt to chal wl over 1f out: led 1f out: r.o wl u.p but edgd lft fnl 50yds: hdd and no ex cl home* **13/2**[2]
06-0 **3** 1 3/4 **Spanish Duke (IRE)**[28] 1854 5-9-6 **97**........................ RyanMoore 4 103+
(John Dunlop) *lw: t.k.h: hld up towards rr: hdwy whn nt clr run over 2f out tl over 1f out: running on whn swtchd rt again ins fnl f: r.o wl fnl 100yds: unable to chal* **8/1**
00-3 **4** 1 **Communicator**[38] 1603 4-8-9 **86**........................ JamieSpencer 10 89
(Andrew Balding) *lw: led for over 1f: chsd ldr tl led again over 3f out: drvn and hrd pressed 2f out: hdd 1f out: no ex and btn fnl 100yds: wknd towards fin* **7/2**[1]
4/22 **5** 1 3/4 **King's Warrior (FR)**[23] 1993 5-9-1 **92**........................ WilliamBuick 15 92
(Peter Chapple-Hyam) *in tch in midfield: effrt to chse ldrs over 2f out: pressing ldrs and drvn over 1f out: unable qck and squeezed for room ent fnl f: wknd ins fnl f* **7/1**[3]
13/5 **6** 2 1/2 **Mezzanisi (IRE)**[27] 1890 7-8-5 **82**........................ PaulHanagan 8 78
(Peter Bowen) *t.k.h: hld up in last trio: rdn and hdwy over 2f out: edgd lft u.p over 1f out: no imp fnl f* **20/1**
06-1 **7** 1/2 **Quiz Mistress**[26] 1940 4-8-6 **83**........................ KieranO'Neill 13 78
(Hughie Morrison) *stdd s: t.k.h: hld up in rr on outer: rdn and effrt over 2f out: drvn and styd on same pce fr over 1f out* **10/1**
06/0 **8** 3/4 **Toughness Danon**[13] 631 6-8-6 **88**........................ BrendanPowell(5) 3 82
(Brendan Powell) *in tch in midfield: rdn and effrt on inner over 2f out: no prog over 1f out: wknd 1f out* **66/1**
530- **9** 4 **Incendo**[206] 7328 6-8-7 **84**........................(t) HayleyTurner 12 71
(James Fanshawe) *t.k.h: chsd ldrs: wnt 2nd 3f out: sn rdn and unable qck: struggling 2f out: edgd lft and wknd over 1f out* **14/1**
201- **10** 2 3/4 **Seaside Sizzler**[247] 6485 5-8-11 **88**........................(bt) JimCrowley 7 71
(Ralph Beckett) *chsd ldrs: rdn and struggling 3f out: wknd 2f out* **9/1**
1324 **11** 3/4 **Layline (IRE)**[70] 1037 5-8-7 **84**........................ MartinDwyer 5 66
(Gay Kelleway) *stdd s: t.k.h: hld up in rr: rdn and effrt over 2f out: no imp and wl hld over 1f out* **25/1**
3003 **12** 12 **Oceanway (USA)**[23] 1993 4-9-0 **91**........................ SilvestreDeSousa 6 54
(Mark Johnston) *chsd ldrs: rdn 4f out: wknd ent fnl 2f: bhd and eased ins fnl f* **10/1**
520- **13** 10 **Crassula**[259] 6172 4-8-6 **83**........................ LiamJones 2 30
(Terry Clement) *led over 10f out tl over 3f out: lost pl qckly 3f out: wl bhd fnl f: t.o* **25/1**
2m 36.91s (-1.99) **Going Correction** -0.05s/f (Good) **13** Ran SP% **117.1**
Speed ratings (Par 109): **104,103,102,102,100 99,98,98,95,93 93,85,78**
toteswingers:1&2:£13.50, 2&3:£13.50, 1&3:£10.80 CSF £69.11 CT £552.36 TOTE £12.70: £3.50, £2.10, £2.80; EX 68.50 Trifecta £614.40 Pool: £6514.94 - 7.84 winning units..
Owner Samanda Racing **Bred** Ken Carroll **Trained** Newmarket, Suffolk

FOCUS
A good, competitive handicap run at an ordinary pace. The still progressive runner-up sets the level.

NOTEBOOK
Fiery Lad(IRE) had been lightly raced since winning over 1m2f here on Oaks day in 2010, starting just six times (including three times in Dubai), and testing ground was no use here in April, but he was 7lb lower than for that victory. The trip was a slight question mark, but he saw it out well. He may now go for the Duke of Edinburgh at Royal Ascot, but that will be tougher. Official explanation: trainer said, regarding apparent improvement in form, that the gelding was unsuited by the heavy ground on its previous run. (op 8-1)

A Boy Named Suzi ran a fine race after 224 days off, continuing his progression with another career best. This was only his 11th start and there should be more to come. (tchd 6-1)

Spanish Duke(IRE), trying this distance for only the second time in his career, didn't have the best of trips, not helping himself by racing keenly and then having to wait for a clear run in the straight. Perhaps a strongly run 1m2f suits him even better, but this was at least a big improvement on his Newmarket reappearance. (op 10-1 tchd 11-1)

Communicator ◆ didn't run badly considering he sweated up. Whilst he didn't exactly build on the form of his debut for this stable/reappearance, the feeling remains that he may yet do better. (op 4-1 tchd 9-2 in a place)

King's Warrior(FR), up in trip, was held when short of room late on and didn't prove his stamina. (op 13-2 tchd 11-2)

Mezzanisi(IRE) was a bit keen and never seriously threatened, but this wasn't a bad run.

Seaside Sizzler was having his first start for 247 days and needs more of a stamina test. He was seen winning over 1m6f off 3lb lower. (op 10-1)

2707 INVESTEC OUT OF THE ORDINARY H'CAP — 6f
5:25 (5:28) (Class 2) (0-100,97) 4-Y-O+
£12,450 (£3,728; £1,864; £932; £466; £234) **Stalls** High

Form — RPR

-315 **1** **Lui Rei (ITY)**[14] 2286 6-9-7 **97** JimCrowley 7 — 107
(Robert Cowell) *hld up in midfield: swtchd rt 3f out: hdwy 2f out: rdn to chse ldr 1f out: led ins fnl f: r.o strly* **9/1**[3]

0-00 **2** 1 ¼ **Sacrosanctus**[7] 2488 4-8-7 **83** SilvestreDeSousa 3 — 89
(Scott Dixon) *chsd ldr tl led 4f out: rdn and fnd ex to go clr 2f out: hdd ins fnl f: no ex: jst hld 2nd* **14/1**

00-6 **3** shd **Baldemar**[55] 1236 7-8-6 **82** PaulHanagan 9 — 88
(Richard Fahey) *in tch: rdn 3f out: chsd ldrs and edgd lft u.p ins fnl f: kpt on* **8/1**[2]

00-0 **4** nk **Swiss Cross**[14] 2268 5-9-4 **94** (t) RichardKingscote 14 — 99
(Phil McEntee) *hld up in tch in midfield: hdwy u.p over 1f out: edgd lft and kpt on ins fnl f* **22/1**

5362 **5** 1 ¼ **Baby Strange**[17] 2177 8-8-9 **88** SeanLevey(3) 8 — 89+
(Derek Shaw) *dwlt: towards rr: hdwy into midfield 1/2-way: rdn and effrt to chse ldrs jst over 1f out: kpt on ins fnl f: nvr able to chal* **7/1**[1]

4102 **6** 3 ¼ **Piscean (USA)**[8] 2444 7-8-8 **84** KierenFallon 5 — 74
(Tom Keddy) *in tch in midfield: rdn and effrt on inner 2f out: no imp ent fnl f: wknd ins fnl f* **7/1**[1]

-003 **7** hd **Sutton Veny (IRE)**[16] 2195 6-8-9 **85** LiamJones 1 — 75
(Jeremy Gask) *chsd ldrs: drvn and chsd clr ldr wl over 1f out tl 1f out: wknd ins fnl f* **8/1**[2]

6-26 **8** 1 **Summerinthecity (IRE)**[14] 2284 5-8-13 **89** JohnFahy 4 — 75
(Ed de Giles) *dwlt: sn bustled along and racd in midfield on inner: rdn and unable qck 2f out: no imp fr over 1f out* **10/1**

0250 **9** nse **Elna Bright**[5] 2558 7-8-4 **85** JemmaMarshall(5) 2 — 71
(Peter Crate) *led for 2f: chsd ldr tl 2f out: sn rdn and unable qck: wknd 1f out* **20/1**

00-3 **10** 2 ½ **Noverre To Go (IRE)**[7] 2488 6-8-6 **82** (tp) LukeMorris 12 — 60
(Ronald Harris) *hld up in tch towards rr of main gp: rdn and effrt over 3f out: no prog and outpcd over 2f out: n.d after* **7/1**[1]

-401 **11** 1 ¾ **Titus Gent**[29] 1828 7-8-2 **83** RaulDaSilva(5) 13 — 56
(Jeremy Gask) *towards rr of main gp: rdn and effrt in centre over 2f out: no imp: nvr trbld ldrs* **25/1**

-610 **12** nk **Mandalay King (IRE)**[28] 1868 7-8-2 **78** (p) KieranO'Neill 15 — 50
(Marjorie Fife) *stdd s: sn wl outpcd and bhd: styd on u.p fr over 1f out: nvr trbld ldrs* **33/1**

1-00 **13** 3 ¾ **Amenable (IRE)**[14] 2284 5-8-8 **84** MartinHarley 6 — 44
(David Nicholls) *chsd ldrs: rdn and struggling 3f out: wknd 2f out* **25/1**

0-04 **14** ½ **We Have A Dream**[32] 1727 7-8-9 **85** MartinDwyer 11 — 43
(William Muir) *in tch: bmpd 4f out: lost pl 3f out: sn rdn and wknd: wl btn 1f out* **16/1**

0-00 **15** 2 ¾ **Swilly Ferry (USA)**[44] 1476 5-8-6 **82** HayleyTurner 16 — 31
(David Nicholls) *stdd s: sn wl outpcd and bhd: wl bhd fr 1/2-way* **16/1**

540- **16** 9 **Fireback**[267] 5887 5-8-10 **86** MickaelBarzalona 10
(Daniel Kubler) *taken down early: j. v awkwardly leaving stalls and v.s.a: nt rcvr and a wl bhd: eased ins fnl f* **10/1**

1m 7.65s (-1.75) **Going Correction** -0.05s/f (Good) **16** Ran SP% **126.1**
Speed ratings (Par 109): **109,107,107,106,105 100,100,99,99,95 93,93,88,87,83 71**
toteswingers:1&2:£34.20, 2&3:£29.90, 1&3:£15.90 CSF £123.83 CT £1072.93 TOTE £12.10: £2.80, £4.20, £2.70, £6.00; EX 176.80 Trifecta £1622.80 Pool: £4722.44 - 2.15 winning units..
Owner Rei Of Sunshine Partnership **Bred** Az Ag Antezzate Srl **Trained** Six Mile Bottom, Cambs

FOCUS
A decent sprint handicap and there were surprisingly few hard-luck stories. The form looks straightforward rated around the third and fourth.

NOTEBOOK
Lui Rei(ITY) ◆ was a winner at Goodwood two starts back, but he was still 2lb lower than when fourth in this last year and won nicely after travelling well. He's just the type of horse his trainer has been doing particularly well with in recent seasons and he's in the Wokingham. (op 8-1)

Sacrosanctus stepped up significantly on the form he showed on his first two starts this year. He was only 1lb above his last winning mark. (op 16-1)

Baldemar came into this boasting a 3-4 record at the track, including this race off the same mark in 2009. He again ran well, but was never quite doing enough. (op 9-1)

Swiss Cross, 2lb higher than when winning this last year, improved a good deal on the form he showed when debuting for this yard after an absence. He could build on this. (op 18-1 tchd 25-1)

Baby Strange travelled strongly as usual, but he didn't pick up well enough. (op 8-1, tchd 13-2 in a place)

Piscean(USA) didn't see his race out after going enthusiastically. (op 4-1)

Noverre To Go(IRE) might have found this coming too soon after a promising reappearance just a week earlier, and this was his first start at Epsom. (op 8-1)

T/Plt: £123.10 to a £1 stake. Pool of £278,104.38 - 1,649.08 winning tickets. T/Qpdt: £18.60 to a £1 stake. Pool of £13,174.65 - 523.95 winning tickets. SP

2661 HAYDOCK (L-H)
Saturday, June 2

OFFICIAL GOING: Good to firm (8.6)
The outer home straight was used for this meeting.
Wind: light 1/2 behind Weather: overcast, light rain

2708 BLUE SQUARE MAIDEN STKS — 1m 3f 200y
1:40 (1:40) (Class 5) 3-Y-O+
£2,911 (£866; £432; £216) **Stalls** Centre

Form — RPR

4323 **1** **Fleeting Image**[24] 1976 3-8-1 78 (p) NatashaEaton(7) 8 — 79
(Alan Bailey) *led after 1f: mde rest: edgd lft ins fnl f: hld on wl* **14/1**

6-3 **2** ¾ **Bayan (IRE)**[16] 2197 3-8-13 0 FrankieDettori 12 — 83
(Brian Meehan) *s.i.s: sn trcking ldrs: drvn over 4f out: styd on same pce ins fnl f* **11/8**[1]

22 **3** ¾ **Pistol (IRE)**[14] 2288 3-8-13 0 RobertWinston 1 — 82
(Sir Michael Stoute) *led 1f: trckd ldrs: effrt over 3f out: rdn and hung lft over 2f out: keeping on same pce on ins whn nt clr run towards fin* **7/2**[2]

430- **4** ¾ **Dawn Gale (IRE)**[285] 5317 4-9-9 79 AdamKirby 4 — 76
(Hughie Morrison) *hld up towards rr: hdwy over 3f out: chsng ldrs over 1f out: kpt on same pce* **20/1**

53 **5** 5 **Noble Alan (GER)**[14] 2287 9-10-0 0 PhillipMakin 10 — 73
(Nicky Richards) *hld up in mid-div: hdwy 4f out: drvn and swtchd lft over 2f out: wknd over 1f out* **6/1**[3]

00-0 **6** 4 **Hard Road**[40] 1567 3-8-13 35 ChrisCatlin 2 — 66
(Chris Wall) *in rr: hdwy 4f out: wknd 2f out* **100/1**

0 **7** ¾ **Reigns Of Glory (IRE)**[16] 2196 3-8-13 0 RichardHughes 5 — 65
(Richard Hannon) *t.k.h in rr: hdwy over 3f out: wknd 2f out* **11/1**

3 **8** 2 ¼ **Stock Hill Fair**[19] 2125 4-10-0 0 FergusSweeney 6 — 62
(Brendan Powell) *s.i.s: hld up in rr: effrt over 3f out: wknd 2f out* **25/1**

5 **9** 1 ¾ **Big Time Billy (IRE)**[9] 2418 6-9-9 0 DavidNolan 3 — 54
(Mike Hammond) *chsd ldrs: drvn over 4f out: wknd over 2f out* **40/1**

-42 **10** shd **Star For Life (USA)**[24] 1976 3-8-13 0 (p) JamesDoyle 7 — 59
(Mikael Magnusson) *trckd ldrs: t.k.h: wknd over 2f out* **6/1**[3]

11 ¾ **Taigan (FR)**[150] 5-10-0 0 TonyCulhane 11 — 57
(Ian Williams) *hld up in rr: effrt over 3f out: bhd fnl 2f* **50/1**

2m 36.1s (2.30) **Going Correction** +0.05s/f (Good)
WFA 3 from 4yo+ 15lb **11** Ran SP% **119.5**
Speed ratings (Par 103): **94,93,93,92,89 86,86,84,83,83 82**
toteswingers:1&2:£6.00, 2&3:£1.90, 1&3:£8.00 CSF £33.61 TOTE £19.70: £3.90, £1.20, £1.60; EX 49.00.
Owner P T Tellwright **Bred** P T Tellwright **Trained** Newmarket, Suffolk

FOCUS
All races on stands' side home straight. Races on round course increased in distance by 58yds, except 2.10 race which increased by 63yds. A really interesting contest, which seems sure to throw up plenty of winners during the season and the form looks sound enough, with the first four close to their marks.
Pistol(IRE) Official explanation: jockey said gelding hung left-handed

2709 BET AT BLUESQUARE.COM STKS (H'CAP) — 2m 45y
2:10 (2:10) (Class 2) (0-100,99) 4-Y-O+ **£12,938** (£3,850; £1,924; £962) **Stalls** Low

Form — RPR

11-2 **1** **Lordofthehouse (IRE)**[21] 2093 4-8-7 **83** ChrisCatlin 11 — 94+
(William Haggas) *s.s: hdwy down wd outside to ld over 12f out: jnd over 3f out: styd on wl to pull away fnl f* **5/1**[3]

10-0 **2** 2 ½ **Dazinski**[24] 1974 6-8-13 **88** RobertWinston 2 — 94
(Mark H Tompkins) *mid-div: hdwy 7f out: styd on to take 2nd jst ins fnl f: no imp* **10/1**

42-3 **3** 1 ¼ **Palazzo Bianco**[45] 1446 4-8-10 **86** NickyMackay 1 — 90+
(John Gosden) *led over 3f: chsd ldrs: outpcd and lost pl over 2f out: only 8th 1f out: styd on strly to take 3rd in clsng stages* **9/2**[2]

00/4 **4** 1 **Swinging Hawk (GER)**[17] 2180 6-8-8 **83** JamesDoyle 6 — 86
(Ian Williams) *trckd ldrs: hung lft 1f out: kpt on same pce* **6/1**

2324 **5** 3 **Halla San**[21] 2086 10-8-9 **84** PhillipMakin 13 — 83
(Richard Fahey) *in rr: kpt on fnl f: nvr a threat* **20/1**

20-P **6** ¾ **Kazbow (IRE)**[24] 1974 6-9-4 **93** RichardHughes 10 — 92
(Chris Grant) *trckd ldrs: effrt 4f out: chal over 2f out: fdd fnl f* **25/1**

54-0 **7** 1 **Tominator**[24] 1974 5-9-10 **99** TonyCulhane 3 — 100+
(Reg Hollinshead) *hld up in rr: hdwy over 5f out: kpt on same pce fnl 2f: nt clr run 1f out: will do bttr* **11/1**

3-10 **8** 2 **Shubaat**[24] 1974 5-9-0 **89** NeilCallan 7 — 84
(Roger Varian) *trckd ldrs: chal over 3f out: wknd over 1f out* **7/2**[1]

0030 **9** hd **Montaff**[14] 2278 6-9-5 **94** SamHitchcott 5 — 89
(Mick Channon) *sn drvn along in rr: hdwy and in tch 7f out: one pce fnl 2f: nvr a factor* **10/1**

3066 **10** 21 **English Summer**[7] 2474 5-8-5 **80** (b[1]) WayneLordan 12
(Mark Johnston) *chsd ldrs: drvn 4f out: lost pl over 2f out: bhd whn eased: t.o* **12/1**

3m 31.39s (-2.91) **Going Correction** +0.05s/f (Good)
WFA 4 from 5yo+ 1lb **10** Ran SP% **114.2**
Speed ratings (Par 109): **109,107,107,106,105 104,104,103,103,92**
toteswingers:1&2:£13.80, 2&3:£7.40, 1&3:£2.60 CSF £52.88 CT £239.87 TOTE £4.40: £1.90, £3.30, £1.70; EX 60.50 Trifecta £115.90 Pool: £499.93 - 3.19 winning units..
Owner Lael Stable **Bred** Lael Stables **Trained** Newmarket, Suffolk

FOCUS
Most of these had some sort of chance on turning into the home straight. The form looks sound rated around the runner-up and fourth.

NOTEBOOK
Lordofthehouse(IRE) really dug in after being joined in front and rallied in gritty style to maintain his impressive progression. Considering the way he battled, he could even get a bit further. (op 4-1)

Dazinski, down the field in the Chester Cup, followed the winner up the inside rail but wasn't good enough to get to him. This trip on reasonably quick going appears to suit him best. (op 12-1)

Palazzo Bianco ◆ had the scope for improvement, but found himself locked in a pocket for a while about 2f out before needing to lose a bit of ground to go around horses. He can be given another chance. (op 5-1)

Swinging Hawk(GER), back up in trip after a fair effort at York last time over 1m4f, had every chance but could never reel in the leader. James Doyle reported that the gelding hung left-handed. Official explanation: jockey said gelding hung left-handed (tchd 11-2)

Halla San had been running consistently but was never close enough to worry those ahead of him. (tchd 16-1)

Kazbow(IRE) pulled up in the Chester Cup on his comeback when making his debut for Chris Grant (reportedly had breathing problem), but this was a lot better as he did come through to look dangerous before faltering. (op 20-1)

Shubaat weakened steadily from over 1f out, suggesting he may want easing in trip again off this sort of mark. (op 9-2)

2710 TIMEFORM JURY STKS (REGISTERED AS THE JOHN OF GAUNT STAKES) (GROUP 3) 7f

2:35 (2:37) (Class 1) 4-Y-0+

£31,190 (£11,825; £5,918; £2,948; £1,479; £742) **Stalls** Low

Form RPR

51-6 **1** **Pastoral Player**[21] 2068 5-9-0 107 .... DarryllHolland 2 115
(Hughie Morrison) *awkward s: hld up: hdwy on ins over 2f out: swtchd rt over 1f out: str run to ld last 100yds: r.o wl* **3/1**[2]

02-3 **2** 1 ½ **Majestic Myles (IRE)**[21] 2075 4-9-0 110 .... DavidNolan 8 111
(Richard Fahey) *swtchd lft after s: trckd ldrs: led over 2f out: hdd and no ex ins fnl f* **8/1**

04-0 **3** 1 ¼ **Doncaster Rover (USA)**[17] 2179 6-9-0 105 .... RobertWinston 7 108
(David Brown) *chsd ldrs: pushed along over 4f out: kpt on to take 3rd nr fin* **14/1**

2-31 **4** 1 **Red Jazz (USA)**[21] 2075 5-9-0 112 .... MichaelHills 1 105
(Charles Hills) *led: hdd over 2f out: wknd towards fin* **10/11**[1]

14-4 **5** 1 ½ **Royal Rock**[63] 1129 8-9-3 112 .... GeorgeBaker 4 104
(Chris Wall) *stdd s: hld up: hdwy over 2f out: rdn over 1f out: kpt on nvr a threat* **7/1**[3]

0-06 **6** 1 ½ **Perfect Tribute**[21] 2078 4-8-11 97 .... JamesDoyle 6 94
(Clive Cox) *trckd ldrs: nt clr run over 1f out: sn wknd* **33/1**

0-45 **7** 1 ¾ **Six Of Hearts**[7] 2513 8-9-0 101 ....(p) WayneLordan 3 92
(Cecil Ross, Ire) *hld up: effrt over 3f out: wknd fnl f* **25/1**

1m 29.18s (-1.52) **Going Correction** +0.05s/f (Good) 7 Ran SP% **114.4**
Speed ratings (Par 113): **110,108,106,105,104 102,100**
toteswingers:1&2:£2.50, 2&3:£2.70, 1&3:£6.90 CSF £26.73 TOTE £4.20: £2.60, £2.20; EX 29.40 Trifecta £352.40 Pool: £1276.54 - 2.68 winning units..
Owner The Pursuits Partnership **Bred** Whitsbury Manor Stud & Pigeon House Stud **Trained** East Ilsley, Berks

FOCUS
A hot little contest with almost everything holding a chance of going close. The placed horses set the standard.

NOTEBOOK
Pastoral Player was a respectable sixth in the Victoria Cup on his return and duly made the step up to Group level after showing a tidy change of gear to take this, although Darryll Holland was lucky the gap appeared up the inside rail when it did. The Criterion Stakes at the end of June seems a logical target, although a strongly run 6f would also suit, so connections might eye a crack at Black Caviar in the Diamond Jubilee Stakes, considering the horse goes well at Ascot. (op 4-1)
Majestic Myles(IRE) was well placed and stuck on really nicely to get the better of Red Jazz this time. (op 13-2)
Doncaster Rover(USA) never looked likely to win but kept on well after being hard ridden some way out. (tchd 12-1)
Red Jazz(USA) got an easy enough lead, so one can only conclude he went a bit too quickly considering he had little left at the end, eventually losing out on third. (op 11-10)
Royal Rock moved with menace turning into the home straight but lacked the gears to tag on to the leading few. (op 13-2)

2711 GROSVENOR CASINOS PINNACLE STKS (GROUP 3) (F&M) 1m 3f 200y

3:10 (3:12) (Class 1) 4-Y-0+

£31,190 (£11,825; £5,918; £2,948; £1,479; £742) **Stalls** Centre

Form RPR

55-2 **1** **Shimmering Surf (IRE)**[28] 1848 5-8-12 100 .... NeilCallan 8 108
(Roger Varian) *w ldr: led after 1f: hdd after 3f: led over 3f out: edgd lft appr fnl f: hld on nr fin* **9/1**

12-6 **2** ¾ **Set To Music (IRE)**[16] 2209 4-8-12 109 .... RichardHughes 6 107+
(Michael Bell) *hld up towards rr: hdwy over 3f out: nt clr run over 2f out: swtchd rt over 1f out: styd on wl to take 2nd nr fin* **2/1**[1]

2-2 **3** ½ **Molly Malone (FR)**[25] 1971 4-8-12 104 .... GregoryBenoist 5 106
(M Delzangles, France) *chsd ldrs: styd on wl fnl f to take 3rd nr fin* **12/1**

14-0 **4** ½ **Mohedian Lady (IRE)**[16] 2209 4-8-12 102 .... KirstyMilczarek 3 105
(Luca Cumani) *trckd ldrs: chsd wnr jst ins fnl f: kpt on same pce* **6/1**[3]

10-3 **5** ¾ **Primevere (IRE)**[27] 1883 4-8-12 105 .... JamesDoyle 11 104+
(Roger Charlton) *hld up in rr: hdwy 3f out: chsng ldrs over 1f out: kpt on same pce* **11/2**[2]

330- **6** 4 **Dorcas Lane**[284] 5366 4-8-12 108 .... RichardMullen 2 98
(David Lanigan) *s.i.s: hld up towards rr: hdwy 7f out: effrt on ins over 3f out: wknd fnl 100yds* **13/2**

5-00 **7** 2 ½ **Goldplated (IRE)**[34] 1694 4-8-12 94 .... WayneLordan 10 94
(John Joseph Murphy, Ire) *s.i.s: hld up in rr: effrt 4f out: nt clr run over 2f out: wknd fnl f* **33/1**

11-0 **8** 51 **Khawlah (IRE)**[27] 1883 4-8-12 110 .... FrankieDettori 4
(Saeed Bin Suroor) *led 1f: led after 3f: hdd over 3f out: lost pl over 2f out: eased whn wl bhd: t.o* **13/2**

30-0 **9** 12 **Polygon (USA)**[28] 1848 4-8-12 100 .... NickyMackay 7
(John Gosden) *chsd ldrs: lost pl 3f out: eased whn wl bhd: t.o* **25/1**

2m 31.91s (-1.89) **Going Correction** +0.05s/f (Good) 9 Ran SP% **114.1**
Speed ratings (Par 113): **108,107,107,106,106 103,102,68,60**
toteswingers:1&2:£5.80, 2&3:£2.50, 1&3:£37.20 CSF £27.04 TOTE £11.30: £2.70, £1.10, £2.70; EX 34.70 Trifecta £190.90 Pool: £1963.81 - 7.61 winning units..
Owner P Winkworth **Bred** Cathal Ryan **Trained** Newmarket, Suffolk
■ Stewards' Enquiry : Kirsty Milczarek two-day ban: used whip above permitted level (Jun 16-17)

FOCUS
A solid contest run at a fair gallop, nothing more and the runner-up, to her form at this trip, sets the level.

NOTEBOOK
Shimmering Surf(IRE) looked up against it here after racing a bit freely towards the front, but she responded well to pressure and won nicely. She has returned to her best form since joining Roger Varian and might come back for the Lancashire Oaks. (tchd 10-1)
Set To Music(IRE) ◆ was up in trip after a modest start to her 4-y-o campaign, albeit in a Group 2, and appeared a little unlucky here not to make the winner work a bit harder, as Richard Hughes didn't have a lot of room over 2f out and had to wait a few moments before pulling his mount out into clear space. (op 11-4)
Molly Malone(FR), who hadn't finished out of the first three in six outings in France on vastly different ground, won on her reappearance and followed that with a good second, before being demoted to third, in a Group 3 at Longchamp won by the talented Allied Powers. She made her bid wide of trouble once steered towards the middle of the track and stayed on in good style all the way to the line, helping set a decent level. (op 10-1)
Mohedian Lady(IRE) ◆ finished closer to Set To Music than she did at York on her previous outing and ran pretty well considering she took a keen hold just behind the leaders. She looks poised to strike soon. (op 5-1)
Primevere(IRE), trying this trip for the first time, was produced to have every chance but didn't see the 1m4f out as well as those in front of her. That said, she wasn't beaten far so is worth another try over the distance. (tchd 6-1)
Dorcas Lane ◆, making her seasonal debut for a new trainer after being sold out of the Lucy Wadham stable, was hampered at least twice by Mohedian Lady while Richard Mullen was trying to make progress up the inside rail, and is much better than the beaten distance suggests. (op 8-1)
Khawlah(IRE), who had raced only at less than 1m2f previously, reportedly lost her action on her first run for more than a year last time. She led here but tamely fell away and Frankie Dettori reported that she lost her action again. Official explanation: jockey said filly lost its action (op 11-2 tchd 9-2)

2712 BLUE SQUARE SANDY LANE STKS (LISTED RACE) 6f

3:40 (3:41) (Class 1) 3-Y-O

£18,714 (£7,095; £3,550; £1,768; £887; £445) **Stalls** High

Form RPR

2- **1** **Slade Power (IRE)**[31] 1760 3-9-0 99 .... WayneLordan 1 109
(Edward Lynam, Ire) *trckd ldrs: wnt 2nd over 1f out: styd on wl to ld nr fin* **5/1**[3]

-114 **2** nk **Es Que Love (IRE)**[16] 2212 3-9-0 98 .... MircoDemuro 7 108
(Mark Johnston) *led: edgd lft after 100yds: clr over 1f out: hdd towards fin* **8/1**

4-12 **3** 1 **Lethal Force (IRE)**[15] 2236 3-9-0 105 .... AdamKirby 4 105
(Clive Cox) *trckd ldrs: effrt and nt clr run over 1f out: swtchd lft 1f out: kpt on wl* **5/1**[3]

10-4 **4** 6 **Bogart**[17] 2179 3-9-3 110 .... PhillipMakin 5 89
(Kevin Ryan) *stmbld s: sn chsng wnr: effrt over 2f out: rdn over 1f out: sn wknd* **13/8**[1]

0-03 **5** 4 **Samminder (IRE)**[15] 2236 3-9-0 104 .... FrankieDettori 3 73
(Peter Chapple-Hyam) *dwlt: effrt over 2f out: lost pl over 1f out* **3/1**[2]

-156 **6** nk **Fanrouge (IRE)**[8] 2446 3-8-9 89 .... TomMcLaughlin 2 67
(Malcolm Saunders) *hld up: effrt over 2f out: lost pl over 1f out* **40/1**

5-04 **7** 1 ¼ **Roger Sez (IRE)**[21] 2087 3-9-0 102 ....(b) NeilCallan 6 68
(Tim Easterby) *dwlt: in rr and sn drvn along: nvr a factor* **25/1**

1m 11.17s (-2.63) **Going Correction** -0.225s/f (Firm) 7 Ran SP% **113.8**
Speed ratings (Par 107): **108,107,106,98,92 92,90**
toteswingers:1&2:£10.30, 2&3:£6.20, 1&3:£7.50 CSF £42.84 TOTE £7.10: £2.00, £4.20; EX 40.60.
Owner Mrs S Power **Bred** Mrs S Power **Trained** Dunshaughlin, Co Meath
■ Stewards' Enquiry : Wayne Lordan two-day ban: used whip above permitted level (Jun 16-17)

FOCUS
Probably a smart contest, but the favourite ran poorly. The third looks the best guide to the form.

NOTEBOOK
Slade Power(IRE), returning to 6f, had been beaten half a length by subsequent Irish 1000 Guineas second Ishvana when upped to 7f at Dundalk last time and probably enjoyed tracking a decent gallop here, but only just got to the front late on. A progressive individual, he is clearly effective at this trip and the Sprint Cup here later in the year could be on the agenda. (op 11-2 tchd 6-1)
Es Que Love(IRE) possibly found the drop back to 5f against him on his previous outing when faced with a potential sprinting star, and did a lot better here after setting solid fractions towards the centre of the track. (op 12-1)
Lethal Force(IRE) went close in a Listed contest at Newbury last time and has some entries for big sprint contests later on, but one got the impression he was comfortably held on this occasion by the first two despite being a little squeezed for room about 1f out. (tchd 9-2)
Bogart, down in class and up against just his own age group, soon went prominent after stumbling and appeared to be going a sensible pace behind the leader. However, once Phillip Makin asked for an effort, nothing was there and the colt produced a weak finish. (tchd 6-4 tchd 7-4 in a place)
Samminder(IRE) could never go the gallop and failed to get involved. (tchd 11-4 and 10-3)

2713 E B F PLAY POKER WITH GROSVENOR CASINOS STKS (REGISTERED AS THE CECIL FRAIL STAKES) (LISTED) 6f

4:40 (4:41) (Class 1) 3-Y-O+

£18,714 (£7,095; £3,550; £1,768; £887; £445) **Stalls** High

Form RPR

64-6 **1** **Inetrobil (IRE)**[15] 2236 3-8-9 100 ow1 ....(b[1]) PhillipMakin 4 100
(Kevin Ryan) *w ldrs: led over 1f out: hld on towards fin* **20/1**

11-5 **2** nk **Artistic Jewel (IRE)**[21] 2087 3-8-12 101 .... RichardMullen 1 102
(Ed McMahon) *chsd ldrs: drvn and edgd lft over 1f out: chal ins fnl f: no ex nr fin* **16/1**

10-3 **3** 1 ¾ **Ladies Are Forever**[21] 2087 4-9-2 108 .... RobertWinston 8 94+
(Geoffrey Oldroyd) *mid-div: nt clr run over 1f out: swtchd lft and r.o: tk 3rd last 75yds* **11/4**[2]

-131 **4** shd **Haamaat (IRE)**[26] 1926 4-9-2 87 .... TadhgO'Shea 7 94+
(William Haggas) *stdd s: hld up in rr: hdwy over 1f out: kpt on ins fnl f* **8/1**

00-0 **5** 1 ¼ **My Propeller (IRE)**[21] 2078 3-8-8 97 ....[1] AndreaAtzeni 6 88
(Peter Chapple-Hyam) *led over 4f out: hdd over 1f out: one pce* **25/1**

6-05 **6** ¾ **Villeneuve**[21] 2078 3-8-8 90 .... NickyMackay 5 86
(William Muir) *chsd ldrs: effrt over 2f out: kpt on one pce* **50/1**

2-21 **7** nse **Mince**[14] 2276 3-8-8 95 .... JamesDoyle 9 85
(Roger Charlton) *chsd ldrs: drvn over 2f out: wknd jst ins fnl f* **15/8**[1]

03-1 **8** 1 ¾ **Intense Pink**[40] 1560 3-8-8 90 .... ChrisCatlin 10 80
(Chris Wall) *mid-div: drvn over 2f out: nvr a factor* **7/1**[3]

2-62 **9** 1 **Sioux Rising (IRE)**[21] 2087 6-9-2 100 .... DavidNolan 2 79
(Richard Fahey) *led over 1f: chsd ldrs: lost pl over 1f out* **14/1**

00-6 **10** 6 **Pepper Lane**[21] 2087 5-9-2 100 .... FrankieDettori 3 72
(David O'Meara) *rrd s: hdwy over 2f out: sn chsng ldrs: wknd over 1f out: heavily eased in clsng stages* **12/1**

1m 11.87s (-1.93) **Going Correction** -0.225s/f (Firm)
WFA 3 from 4yo+ 8lb 10 Ran SP% **115.9**
Speed ratings (Par 111): **103,102,100,100,98 97,97,95,93,85**
toteswingers:1&2:£44.00, 2&3:£15.00, 1&3:£11.40 CSF £295.47 TOTE £24.60: £6.20, £2.70, £1.80; EX 136.40.
Owner Highclere Thoroughbred Racing & P Beirne **Bred** P Beirne **Trained** Hambleton, N Yorks
■ Stewards' Enquiry : Richard Mullen two-day ban: used whip above permitted level (Jun 16-17)

FOCUS
They appeared to go a decent pace from the start and the winner was always well placed. but the overall time was nothing special and there are doubts over the form.

NOTEBOOK
Inetrobil(IRE), tried in blinkers here and much more robust-looking than some of her rivals, produced a determined finish after coming under strong pressure over 1f out. Beaten a narrow distance by Irish 1000 Guineas winner Samitar in last year's Albany Stakes, she was more than entitled to take a race at this level despite, what her starting price suggested, and with Phillip Makin putting up 1lb overweight. (op 16-1)
Artistic Jewel(IRE), who started favourite at Nottingham in a race a few of these contested, reversed form with two she met there and ran somewhere close to her best. Perhaps she doesn't want really soft ground considering her last outing. It's also interesting that she is yet to run round a bend.
Ladies Are Forever was in front of the Ed McMahon runner last time but couldn't maintain her advantage over that rival. Her jockey was forced to wait to make his run but was out in the clear with about 1f to go. (op 3-1)

Haamaat(IRE) ◆, returning to turf, had a bit to find on official figures with some of these but put up a pleasing effort, staying on in good style a bit too late. A return to 7f at Listed level might help. (op 10-1)
My Propeller(IRE), in a first-time hood, was dropped in trip again and didn't get home after setting the pace.
Mince raced just behind the leaders and couldn't pick up. Perhaps those big performances at Newmarket in the spring had taken the edge off her for now. (op 2-1 tchd 9-4 in places)
Intense Pink was taking a big step up in grade after winning a maiden by 14l at Pontefract on her seasonal return and wasn't up to it. (op 13-2 tchd 15-2)
Sioux Rising(IRE) raced in the front rank but offered little under pressure. She is now 0-14 on a straight track and has never won at higher than class 3 level. (op 12-1)

2714 GROSVENOR G CASINO H'CAP — 6f
5:15 (5:16) (Class 3) (0-95,90) 3-Y-O — **£8,409** (£2,502; £1,250; £625) **Stalls** High

Form	Pos	Dist	Horse / details	RPR
41-2	1		**Safari Sunseeker (IRE)**[24] 1983 3-8-7 **79** HarryBentley(3) 11 — (William Knight) *w ldrs stands' side: led 2f out: edgd lft: clr jst ins fnl f: kpt on wl* **9/1**	96
2-51	2	2	**Red Quartet (IRE)**[28] 1858 3-9-5 **88** AndreaAtzeni 12 — (Robert Eddery) *in rr: hdwy over 2f out: edgd lft and wnt 2nd 150yds out: kpt on* **10/3**[1]	99
32-0	3	6	**O'Gorman**[12] 2347 3-9-1 **84** PhillipMakin 7 — (Kevin Ryan) *t.k.h in mid-div: effrt over 2f out: kpt on to take modest 3rd nr fin* **14/1**	76
4645	4	hd	**Pale Orchid (IRE)**[7] 2509 3-9-1 **89** MatthewCosham(5) 5 — (David Evans) *chsd ldrs: edgd lft 1f out: wknd towards fin* **20/1**	80
2241	5	¾	**Willies Wonder (IRE)**[32] 1730 3-8-10 **79** MichaelHills 6 — (Charles Hills) *w ldr: wknd over 1f out* **9/1**	68
16-3	6	½	**Heeraat (IRE)**[45] 1457 3-9-5 **88** TadhgO'Shea 1 — (William Haggas) *led: hdd 2f out: wknd fnl 100yds* **7/2**[2]	75
-110	7	5	**Dishy Guru**[14] 2276 3-8-11 **80** FergusSweeney 4 — (Michael Blanshard) *hmpd s: in rr: sme hdwy over 2f out: wknd over 1f out* **25/1**	51
610	8	¾	**Pretty Primo (IRE)**[15] 2236 3-9-0 **83** RichardHughes 13 — (Richard Hannon) *mid-div: effrt over 2f out: wknd over 1f out* **7/1**[3]	52
0606	9	1 ¾	**Boris Grigoriev (IRE)**[23] 1996 3-9-0 **90** DavidSimmonson(7) 2 — (Michael Easterby) *wnt rt s: in rr and drvn along: nvr on terms* **33/1**	53
0115	10	nse	**Rusty Rocket (IRE)**[23] 1998 3-8-11 **80** DarryllHolland 8 — (Paul Green) *chsd ldrs: wknd over 1f out* **14/1**	43
41-0	11	3 ½	**Master Of Ages (IRE)**[14] 2265 3-8-10 **79** MircoDemuro 14 — (Mark Johnston) *mid-div: lost pl over 2f out* **12/1**	31
0-20	12	nk	**Sans Loi (IRE)**[28] 1858 3-9-2 **85** (b[1]) RobertWinston 9 — (Alan McCabe) *dwlt: in rr: sme hdwy on ins over 2f out: lost pl over 1f out* **8/1**	36

1m 11.86s (-1.94) **Going Correction** -0.225s/f (Firm) **12** Ran SP% **121.5**
Speed ratings (Par 103): **103,100,92,92,91 90,83,82,80,80 75,75**
toteswingers:1&2:£11.50, 2&3:£8.60, 1&3:£20.50 CSF £39.15 CT £433.32 TOTE £11.50: £3.40, £1.70, £4.80; EX 46.10.
Owner P Winkworth **Bred** D J Sweeney **Trained** Patching, W Sussex

FOCUS
The majority of these had shown a decent level of ability already in 2012, so it's best to view this result positively, despite both the principals recording personal bests.

NOTEBOOK
Safari Sunseeker(IRE) was second on his seasonal return at Kempton and progressed nicely from that to produce a fine display here. Close up, the moment Harry Bentley asked for an effort the horse stormed clear and was never going to be caught. The handicapper is sure to take a dim view of the result, but William Knight's horse is unexposed on turf and may have more to come. Connections hope he could be a Stewards' Cup horse. (op 8-1 tchd 10-1)
Red Quartet(IRE) ◆ took his form to a new level when getting the better of 18 rivals in a hot Newmarket handicap last time. Up 7lb for that, Andrea Atzeni had his mount going well out the back but can't have expected the winner to streak clear, thus giving him no chance of catching up. He remains a horse to keep on the right side of. (op 7-2 tchd 11-4)
O'Gorman, trying 6f for the first time since his racecourse debut, was hard ridden over 1f out but kept on respectably. He's on about the right handicap mark judged on this effort.
Pale Orchid(IRE), up in trip again after a couple of decent performances over 5f, was never that far away but tended to edge left under pressure and finished towards the far rail. (op 16-1)
Willies Wonder(IRE), up 7l for victory on his handicap debut last time on Lingfield's Polytrack, didn't look to have too many excuses. (op 8-1)
Heeraat(IRE) shaped nicely on his return at the Craven meeting in April, raced a bit freely while leading and didn't see it out. He'll need to settle better or be tried over 5f. (op 6-1)
Pretty Primo(IRE) made no impression on her handicap debut. (tchd 8-1)
Boris Grigoriev(IRE) had been well beaten in a couple of handicaps recently, and was already down 11lb in four starts since the end of March for his new stable. Beaten a head when with Aidan O'Brien in a Listed race as a 2-y-o, and given an RPR of 97 for that run, he'll surely prove to be better than this. (op 25-1)
Rusty Rocket(IRE) Official explanation: trainer said colt was unsuited by the good to firm ground
T/Plt: £599.70 to a £1 stake. Pool:£93,707.09 - 114.06 winning tickets T/Qpdt: £162.20 to a £1 stake. Pool:£4,561.41 - 20.81 winning tickets WG

2455 MUSSELBURGH (R-H)

Saturday, June 2

OFFICIAL GOING: Good to soft (good in places; 6.9)
Wind: Breezy, half against Weather: Overcast, cool

2715 TOTEPLACEPOT EDINBURGH CASTLE CONDITIONS STKS — 5f
1:55 (1:56) (Class 2) 2-Y-O — **£12,450** (£3,728; £1,864; £932; £466) **Stalls** High

Form	Pos	Dist	Horse / details	RPR
	1		**Ahern** 2-8-8 0 GrahamGibbons 1 — (David Barron) *dwlt: sn chsng ldrs: effrt and swtchd lft appr fnl f: rdn and qcknd to ld wl ins fnl f: sn clr: readily* **8/1**	91+
1	2	2 ½	**Satsuma**[8] 2437 2-8-9 0 MichaelStainton 3 — (David Brown) *t.k.h: led: rdn over 1f out: hdd wl ins fnl f: nt gng pce of wnr* **4/1**[3]	80
121	3	4	**All On Red (IRE)**[15] 2238 2-8-9 0 StevieDonohoe 6 — (Tobias B P Coles) *unruly bef s: in tch: sn drvn along: swtchd to outside and effrt 1/2-way: rdn and edgd rt over 1f out: sn outpcd* **4/1**[3]	66
15	4	shd	**Tatlisu (IRE)**[17] 2181 2-9-0 0 TonyHamilton 5 — (Richard Fahey) *dwlt: sn drvn along in rr: sme late hdwy: nvr on terms* **10/3**[2]	70
1	5	shd	**Rhagori Aur**[14] 2282 2-8-9 0 RoystonFfrench 7 — (Bryan Smart) *pressed ldr: drvn over 2f out: one pce whn hmpd appr fnl f: sn btn* **7/4**[1]	65

59.28s (-1.12) **Going Correction** -0.15s/f (Firm) **5** Ran SP% **110.6**
Speed ratings (Par 99): **102,98,91,91,91**
CSF £38.12 TOTE £9.60: £1.80, £2.40; EX 46.00.
Owner Qatar Racing Limited **Bred** Hellwood Stud Farm **Trained** Maunby, N Yorks

FOCUS
Distances as advertised. There was 16mm of rain on Thursday and the going was good to soft, good in places. An interesting conditions race. Last year's winner Frederick Engels went on to win the Windsor Castle at Royal Ascot, and the previous three winners all finished in the frame in the Norfolk Stakes or the Queen Mary. This looked a fair renewal but the two market leaders ran well below form and a well-related newcomer put in a strong performance to take the prize. The runner-up looks the best guide to the level.

NOTEBOOK
Ahern ◆, an £80,000 Dutch Art half-brother to useful multiple sprint winners Ingleby Lady and Mey Blosson, showed signs of inexperience but he stayed on strongly when switched to the stands' rail and powered clear for a decisive debut win. The form is a questionable with the two market leaders disappointing but the style of the victory was striking from the scopey and powerfully built winner, who could prove to be smart. (op 13-2)
Satsuma, a debut winner of a Catterick fillies' maiden last week, showed plenty of speed and a decent attitude in a good run stepped up significantly in class. (op 9-2)
All On Red(IRE) made it two wins from three starts when romping clear at odds-on in three-runner novice on soft ground at Newcastle last time. She set the standard but she was a bit reluctant to go into the stalls and never really found her rhythm in a laboured effort. (op 10-3)
Tatlisu(IRE) stayed on well to beat a field of newcomers over C&D on his debut and did well to finish fifth after bucking and getting detached in a York novice event last time. He was solid in the market, but he was pushed along almost immediately and was never anywhere near the firing line. (op 3-1 tchd 7-2)
Rhagori Aur who made a winning debut when scoring at 14-1 in a Thirsk fillies' maiden last month, raced up with the pace but she came under pressure some way out before dropping away. This was disappointing from the heavily-backed favourite, who looked well suited by good to soft ground on her first run. (op 5-2 tchd 13-8)

2716 TOTEPOOL TRADESMAN'S DERBY (H'CAP) — 1m 4f 100y
2:25 (2:25) (Class 4) (0-80,80) 3-Y-O — **£12,938** (£3,850; £1,924; £962) **Stalls** Low

Form	Pos	Dist	Horse / details	RPR
2321	1		**Rocktherunway (IRE)**[15] 2240 3-9-4 **80** LeeTopliss(3) 10 — (Michael Dods) *trckd ldrs: effrt and rdn over 2f out: styd on wl fnl f: led nr fin* **9/2**[3]	88
00-5	2	shd	**Moon Trip**[40] 1557 3-8-13 **72** MichaelStainton 9 — (Mark Johnston) *led at ordinary gallop: rdn over 2f out: edgd lft ins fnl f: kpt on: hdd nr fin* **20/1**	80
0-21	3	1 ½	**Party Line**[26] 1915 3-8-12 **71** JoeFanning 6 — (Mark Johnston) *hmpd and dropped to last sn after s: hdwy over 4f out: effrt and ev ch ent fnl f: one pce last 75yds* **4/1**[2]	77+
-006	4	½	**Choisan (IRE)**[15] 2258 3-9-0 **73** PJMcDonald 2 — (Tim Easterby) *in tch: drvn over 3f out: rallied over 1f out: kpt on fnl f: nt gng pce to chal* **16/1**	78
1162	5	1 ¼	**Gabrial's King (IRE)**[7] 2471 3-8-10 **69** FrannyNorton 4 — (Ian Williams) *s.i.s: t.k.h in midfield: rdn over 3f out: swtchd lft and hdwy over 1f out: edgd lft: r.o fnl f* **17/2**	72
52-5	6	¾	**Aleksandar**[44] 1486 3-8-9 **68** J-PGuillambert 13 — (Luca Cumani) *hld up on outside: drvn over 3f out: styd on fnl 2f: nvr able to chal* **15/2**	70+
2345	7	¾	**Torero**[12] 2333 3-8-10 **69** GrahamLee 8 — (Kevin Ryan) *hld up: hdwy and cl up 1/2-way: rdn and hung rt 2f out: sn outpcd* **16/1**	70
-412	8	9	**Spirit Of The Law (IRE)**[21] 2088 3-9-7 **80** RoystonFfrench 3 — (Ed Dunlop) *plld hrd: hld up towards rr: struggling over 3f out: sn btn* **3/1**[1]	67
5215	9	1 ½	**Priestley's Reward (IRE)**[15] 2258 3-8-11 **73**....(v) MichaelMetcalfe(3) 12 — (Mrs K Burke) *sn pushed along towards rr: drvn along over 3f out: nvr on terms* **14/1**	57
5310	10	6	**Fisher**[8] 2449 3-8-9 **68** AdrianNicholls 14 — (David Nicholls) *cl up: rdn and ev ch 3f out: wknd wl over 1f out* **25/1**	43
04-2	11	1 ½	**Queen's Estate (GER)**[35] 1655 3-8-13 **72** RobertHavlin 11 — (Mark Johnston) *midfield: rdn and wandered over 2f out: sn wknd* **16/1**	45
-351	P		**Cades Reef (IRE)**[7] 2495 3-8-11 **70** DavidProbert 1 — (Linda Perratt) *trckd ldrs tl rdn and lost pl qckly over 5f out: sn p.u* **20/1**	

2m 47.35s (5.35) **Going Correction** +0.25s/f (Good) **12** Ran SP% **123.2**
Speed ratings (Par 101): **92,91,90,90,89 89,88,82,81,77 76,**
toteswingers:1&2:£38.00, 2&3:£7.20, 1&3:£5.70 CSF £97.56 CT £399.90 TOTE £6.10: £1.20, £6.10, £1.50; EX 143.60 Trifecta £665.90 Pool: £1156.32 - 1.28 winning units..
Owner The Sedgewick & Dods Racing Partnership **Bred** J Hanly, A Stroud And T Stewart **Trained** Denton, Co Durham
■ Stewards' Enquiry : Michael Stainton two-day ban: used whip above permitted level (Jun 16-17)
Lee Topliss seven-day ban: used whip above permitted level (Jun 16-22)
Franny Norton one-day ban: careless riding (Jun 17)

FOCUS
A competitive handicap. It was run at a stop-start gallop and the first two raced up with the pace. The runner-up sets the level, backed up by the fourth.
Spirit Of The Law(IRE) Official explanation: trainer's rep had no explanation for the poor form shown

2717 TOTESCOOP6 SCOTTISH SPRINT CUP (H'CAP) — 5f
2:55 (2:56) (Class 2) (0-105,96) 3-Y-O+
£24,900 (£7,456; £3,728; £1,864; £932; £468) **Stalls** High

Form	Pos	Dist	Horse / details	RPR
03-3	1		**Bajan Tryst (USA)**[70] 1033 6-9-10 **96** GrahamLee 15 — (Kevin Ryan) *rrd s: sn pushed into midfield: effrt and edgd rt over 1f out: swtchd lft ins fnl f: qcknd to ld towards fin: readily* **16/1**	106
5-30	2	1	**Flash City (ITY)**[14] 2289 4-8-9 **81**.....(v) RoystonFfrench 5 — (Bryan Smart) *led: rdn 2f out: edgd rt ins fnl f: kpt on u.p: hdd towards fin* **33/1**	87
000-	3	nk	**Burning Thread (IRE)**[266] 5927 5-9-5 **91** StevieDonohoe 12 — (Tim Etherington) *cl up: rdn over 2f out: effrt and ev ch ins fnl f: kpt on: hld nr fin* **22/1**	96
0-64	4	½	**Racy**[16] 2208 5-9-7 **93** AmyRyan 8 — (Kevin Ryan) *midfield on outside: effrt and rdn over 1f out: kpt on ins fnl f: hld cl home* **4/1**[1]	96
2024	5	nk	**Foxy Music**[14] 2286 8-9-7 **93** GrahamGibbons 14 — (Eric Alston) *chsd ldrs: rdn over 2f out: edgd rt over 1f out: kpt on same pce ins fnl f* **14/1**	95
-366	6	shd	**Tax Free (IRE)**[7] 2507 10-9-7 **93** AdrianNicholls 10 — (David Nicholls) *midfield: rdn over 2f out: n.m.r and swtchd rt over 1f out: styd on ins fnl f* **10/1**	95
52-0	7	shd	**Barnet Fair**[17] 2177 4-9-3 **89** J-PGuillambert 3 — (Richard Guest) *fly-jmpd s: sn pushed along in rr: effrt on wd outside over 1f out: r.o ins fnl f* **7/1**[3]	90+
-230	8	nk	**Rothesay Chancer**[3] 2596 4-8-7 **79** SaleemGolam 7 — (Jim Goldie) *hld up: hdwy whn nt clr run over 1f out: rdn and styd on fnl f: nrst fin* **16/1**	79+

-101 **9** *hd* **Mayoman (IRE)**14 2289 7-8-13 **88**............(v) LeeTopliss(3) 11 88
(David O'Meara) *in tch: drvn along and effrt over 1f out: no ex ins fnl f* **12/1**

1010 **10** *nse* **Go Go Green (IRE)**3 2596 6-8-5 **77**............ MartinLane 4 76
(Jim Goldie) *bhd and pushed along: no imp tl styd on fnl f: nrst fin* **25/1**

1011 **11** ½ **Dancing Freddy (IRE)**7 2507 5-9-5 **91**............(tp) WilliamCarson 16 89
(Richard Guest) *in tch: rdn along over 2f out: nt qckn over 1f out* **6/1**2

-400 **12** 1¼ **Cheveton**14 2286 8-9-2 **88**............ RobertHavlin 9 81+
(Richard Price) *s.i.s: bhd and pushed along: shortlived effrt 2f out: sn n.d* **14/1**

0-01 **13** *hd* **Partner (IRE)**14 2286 6-9-6 **92**............(b) FrannyNorton 13 84
(Kevin Ryan) *towards rr and sn pushed along: hdwy whn nt clr run over 1f out: n.d* **15/2**

-000 **14** 1½ **Nasri**21 2068 6-9-6 **92**............ PJMcDonald 17 79
(David Nicholls) *sn pushed along towards rr stands' rail: struggling 1/2-way: nvr on terms* **11/1**

-404 **15** 3¾ **Lost In Paris (IRE)**8 2439 6-8-8 **80**............(p) TonyHamilton 1 53
(Tim Easterby) *cl up on outside tl rdn and wknd over 1f out* **16/1**

0-30 **16** 5 **Excel Bolt**14 2286 4-9-2 **93**............ JustinNewman(5) 2 48
(Bryan Smart) *cl up tl rdn and wknd over 1f out* **14/1**

59.84s (-0.56) **Going Correction** -0.15s/f (Firm) **16** Ran SP% **132.4**
Speed ratings (Par 109): **98,96,95,95,94 94,94,93,93,93 92,90,90,87,81 73**
toteswingers:1&2:£67.60, 2&3:£87.20, 1&3:£81.60 CSF £501.34 CT £11511.52 TOTE £24.80: £4.70, £7.30, £8.20, £1.60; EX 639.20 TRIFECTA Not won..
Owner Mrs Margaret Forsyth & Mrs R G Hillen **Bred** William Patterson & James Glenn **Trained** Hambleton, N Yorks

FOCUS
A hot handicap rated around the first two. It was fast and furious and they all raced from the centre to the stands' side.

NOTEBOOK
Bajan Tryst(USA) had looked more potent on Polytrack in recent years but he scythed his way through the pack and finished fast to collect this valuable prize and record a first turf win since July 2009. He usually races more prominently than this but he showed a sharp turn of foot coming from behind in this race. As good as ever at the age of six, he is versatile regarding ground and could go well if taking his chance in the Wokingham.
Flash City(ITY) had plenty of competition for the lead but he put in a commendable bid and was just picked off. His sole win from 15 starts was off 8lb lower at Southwell in December 2010 but he has been a consistent performer in good sprint handicaps.
Burning Thread(IRE) had a string of noughts in his form figures and was returning from 266 days off, but he bounced back with a big run off 3lb lower than his 50-1 win in this race last year. (tchd 20-1)
Racy was always prominent and kept on well in a third decent effort of 2012. (op 5-1)
Foxy Music showed loads of speed and kept battling in the closing stages. This was another good run from this 8-y-o, but he has some work to do to defy this career-high mark and has an ordinary strike-rate of 4-48 for a horse of his ability.
Tax Free(IRE) still retains plenty of ability and ran a solid race here. He should continue to go well but this prolific winner has managed just one victory since May 2009. (op 11-1)
Dancing Freddy(IRE) raced near the stands' rail, but he lacked spark in his hat-trick bid and the slow ground may have blunted his powers.
Partner(IRE) blasted back to form with a 22-1 win at Thirsk last time, but he didn't get much luck off 6lb higher here and rates better than his finishing position. Official explanation: jockey said gelding was denied a clear run (op 8-1)

2718 TOTEPOOL.COM EDINBURGH CUP (H'CAP) 1m 4f 100y
3:30 (3:31) (Class 2) (0-105,93) 3-Y-O
£31,125 (£9,320; £4,660; £2,330; £1,165; £585) **Stalls** Low

Form RPR

2112 **1** **Scatter Dice (IRE)**10 2390 3-8-7 **79**............ MartinLane 9 94
(Mark Johnston) *trckd ldrs: effrt and rdn over 2f out: slt ld over 1f out: styd on gamely fnl f* **16/1**

133 **2** *nk* **Clayton**14 2269 3-9-2 **88**............ GrahamLee 5 102
(Kevin Ryan) *trckd ldr: rdn to ld over 2f out: hdd over 1f out: styd upsides: styd on wl fnl f: hld cl home* **7/1**

2211 **3** 6 **Ruacana**10 2390 3-9-1 **87**............ StevieDonohoe 2 92
(Michael Bell) *in tch on ins: rdn and hdwy over 2f out: styd on fnl f: nt rch first two* **8/1**

50-2 **4** ½ **Stature (IRE)**14 2271 3-8-10 **82**............ DavidProbert 8 86+
(Andrew Balding) *plld hrd towards rr: hdwy whn hung lft over 2f out: styd on fnl f: nvr rchd ldrs* **12/1**

2-12 **5** ½ **Silver Blaze**29 1819 3-9-1 **87**............ PJMcDonald 12 90+
(Alan Swinbank) *hld up: rdn 3f out: hdwy over 1f out: kpt on fnl f: nvr able to chal* **14/1**

1-11 **6** 1¾ **Sparkling Portrait**27 1888 3-9-7 **93**............ TonyHamilton 13 94+
(Richard Fahey) *sn pushed along towards rr on outside: hdwy whn hmpd over 2f out: kpt on fnl f: nrst fin* **3/1**1

1220 **7** ½ **Bordoni (USA)**24 1978 3-8-13 **85**............ RobertHavlin 1 85+
(Mark Johnston) *hld up: drvn along 3f out: styd on fnl f: nvr able to chal* **25/1**

4-12 **8** 2¾ **Commitment**15 2235 3-9-1 **87**............ J-PGuillambert 3 82
(Luca Cumani) *trckd ldrs: effrt and rdn over 2f out: wknd over 1f out* **4/1**2

2316 **9** 1¼ **Good Morning Star (IRE)**17 2178 3-9-2 **88**............ FrannyNorton 7 82
(Mark Johnston) *bhd: drvn along over 3f out: nvr rchd ldrs* **16/1**

12-2 **10** 1½ **Maastricht (IRE)**14 2281 3-8-9 **81**............ JoeFanning 6 72
(Mark Johnston) *led at ordinary gallop: rdn and hdd over 2f out: wknd over 1f out* **11/2**3

0-16 **11** 16 **Ukrainian (IRE)**11 2372 3-8-3 **75**............ AdrianNicholls 4 41
(Mark Johnston) *plld hrd in tch: struggling over 3f out: sn wknd: t.o* **18/1**

-322 **12** 23 **Hallmark Star**14 2287 3-8-10 **85**............(p) LeeTopliss(3) 10 16
(Gerard Butler) *plld hrd: midfield on outside: struggling over 3f out: sn btn: t.o* **12/1**

2m 45.38s (3.38) **Going Correction** +0.25s/f (Good) **12** Ran SP% **126.9**
Speed ratings (Par 105): **98,97,93,93,93 91,91,89,88,87 77,61**
toteswingers:1&2:£55.70, 2&3:£11.10, 1&3:£18.20 CSF £132.58 CT £993.38 TOTE £19.10: £4.60, £3.00, £3.20; EX 144.00 Trifecta £1246.60 Pool: £2089.03 - 1.24 winning units..
Owner Sheikh Hamdan Bin Mohammed Al Maktoum **Bred** Darley **Trained** Middleham Moor, N Yorks

FOCUS
A valuable handicap. Nine of the runners had won or finished placed on their latest start, but not many got involved and the first two pulled a long way clear. Nevertheless, the form looks sound enough, with the winner, third and fourth helping to set the level.

NOTEBOOK
Scatter Dice(IRE) was just held by Ruacana in her bid to make it 3-3 in handicaps at Chepstow last time. Racing off just 1lb higher here, she stalked the leaders before finding a sustained run to come out on top in a good battle with the runner-up. She looks an uncomplicated and tough filly who handles most ground and could continue to progress. (op 14-1)
Clayton raced near the pace and battled well but was just held. He did have the runs of things to a certain extent, but this was his third good placed effort off a climbing mark since his debut win in a 1m Southwell maiden. Another decent rise in mark will follow but he should continue to be a factor in 1m4f handicaps, although it is worth noting that he has raced exclusively on slow ground on turf. (op 15-2)
Ruacana got caught out when the pace increased before staying on again. This was a minor setback in his bid to remain unbeaten in handicaps, but the pace bias and track were not ideal for his hold-up style.
Stature(IRE) plugged on out very wide in a second-time hood on his handicap debut. He is an unexposed brother to Listed-placed 1m2f winner Stately Home, but he doesn't look entirely straightforward. (op 10-1)
Silver Blaze was never involved but he stayed on late and didn't seem to have any stamina issues on his first try at 1m4f.
Sparkling Portrait was well-backed in his bid for a hat-trick but he couldn't make any impression. However, there were mitigating circumstances because he was trapped wide for the most way and was also hampered by the veering Stature. (op 11-2)
Commitment was lacklustre off 7lb higher than his close second in a slow-ground 1m3f handicap at Newbury last time. Official explanation: jockey said gelding lost its action (op 3-1)
Maastricht(IRE) went close in 1m2f/1m4f handicaps on his last two runs but he dropped away this time, which was disappointing because another prominent racer Clayton was just held. (op 6-1)
Ukrainian(IRE) Official explanation: jockey said gelding ran too free

2719 TOTEEXACTA TARTAN TROPHY H'CAP (CONSOLATION RACE FOR THE TOTESCOOP6 SCOTTISH SPRINT CUP) 5f
4:25 (4:25) (Class 4) (0-105,77) 3-Y-O+ **£7,762** (£2,310; £1,154; £577) **Stalls** High

Form RPR

5-12 **1** **Bosun Breese**3 2596 7-9-3 **75**............ LMcNiff(5) 4 95
(David Barron) *mde all: pushed along and qcknd clr over 1f out: readily* **15/8**1

0-55 **2** 6 **Rasaman (IRE)**14 2264 8-9-10 **77**............1 GrahamLee 9 75
(Jim Goldie) *hld up: rdn 1/2-way: styd on wl fnl f to take 2nd nr fin: no ch w wnr* **7/2**2

3-65 **3** 1¼ **Wicked Wilma (IRE)**18 2140 8-9-4 **71**............ PJMcDonald 7 65
(Alan Berry) *pressed wnr: rdn 1/2-way: one pce fnl f: lost 2nd cl home* **5/1**3

06 **4** 1 **You'relikemefrank**8 2458 6-8-11 **64**............(p) TonyHamilton 3 54
(Richard Ford) *dwlt: bhd: rdn and hdwy on outside over 1f out: no imp fnl f* **14/1**

000- **5** ¾ **Midnight Dynamo**261 6076 5-9-0 **67**............ FrannyNorton 6 55
(Jim Goldie) *trckd ldrs: drvn along over 2f out: one pce over 1f out* **12/1**

-030 **6** ¾ **Boundaries**7 2476 4-9-5 **72**............(v) GrahamGibbons 8 57
(Tim Easterby) *prom: drvn and outpcd 1/2-way: styd on fnl f: no imp* **11/2**

0-00 **7** 3 **Distant Sun (USA)**8 2458 8-8-2 **55** ow2............(p) JoeFanning 1 29
(Linda Perratt) *hld up on outside: rdn over 2f out: shortlived effrt over 1f out: sn wknd* **33/1**

2306 **8** *nk* **Blown It (USA)**7 2476 6-9-2 **69**............ WilliamCarson 5 42
(Keith Dalgleish) *sn pushed along towards rr: no imp fr 1/2-way* **12/1**

0-00 **9** 6 **Indian Trail**8 2439 12-9-7 **74**............(v) AdrianNicholls 2 25
(David Nicholls) *trckd ldrs tl rdn and wknd over 1f out* **16/1**

59.01s (-1.39) **Going Correction** -0.15s/f (Firm) **9** Ran SP% **119.9**
Speed ratings (Par 105): **105,95,93,91,90 89,84,84,74**
toteswingers:1&2:£2.50, 2&3:£5.80, 1&3:£4.40 CSF £8.78 CT £29.11 TOTE £3.00: £1.80, £1.90, £1.70; EX 7.80.
Owner Harrowgate Bloodstock Ltd **Bred** Lady Lonsdale **Trained** Maunby, N Yorks

FOCUS
There was a relatively small-field for this Sprint Cup consolation race. Several of the runners had not been in great form this season but the strong favourite hammered his rivals under a forcing ride. The winner is rated back to his old best and had very much the run of things.

2720 QUEEN'S JUBILEE TOTEQUICKPICK H'CAP 1m 1f
5:00 (5:00) (Class 4) (0-85,85) 4-Y-O+ **£6,469** (£1,925; £962; £481) **Stalls** Low

Form RPR

5002 **1** **Musnad (USA)**7 2491 4-8-7 **71**............ AmyRyan 8 81+
(Brian Ellison) *hld up: hdwy whn no room wl over 1f out tl swtchd lft appr fnl f: styd on wl to ld cl home* **8/1**

4031 **2** *nk* **Oriental Scot**9 2417 5-9-7 **85**............ WilliamCarson 6 92
(William Jarvis) *in tch: rdn and hdwy over 2f out: led appr fnl f: edgd rt ins fnl f: hdd cl home* **7/2**2

3 2¼ **Charpoy (USA)**45 1465 4-9-4 **82**............ PJMcDonald 1 84
(Ian Semple) *prom: effrt and hdwy over 2f out: rdn and ev ch over 1f out: nt qckn ins fnl f* **10/1**

1-00 **4** 1 **Shamdarley (IRE)**15 2257 4-9-6 **84**............ TonyHamilton 5 84
(Michael Dods) *hld up in tch: effrt over 2f out: sn rdn and hung rt: kpt on same pce fnl f* **9/2**3

04-3 **5** 1¼ **Desert Romance (IRE)**9 2417 6-9-4 **82**............(v1) GrahamGibbons 7 79
(David O'Meara) *led at decent gallop and sn clr: rdn and wandered over 2f out: hdd appr fnl f: sn outpcd* **11/2**

25-1 **6** *nk* **Staff Sergeant**29 1820 5-9-5 **83**............ GrahamLee 4 79
(Jim Goldie) *chsd clr ldr: rdn and effrt over 2f out: nt qckn over 1f out* **5/2**1

1510 **7** 10 **Munsarim (IRE)**26 1924 5-9-4 **85**............(b) LeeTopliss(3) 3 59
(Richard Fahey) *towards rr: struggling over 3f out: sn btn* **14/1**

00-5 **8** 6 **High Resolution**15 2227 5-8-4 **68**............ JoeFanning 2 29
(Linda Perratt) *missed break: bhd: rdn along over 3f out: sn struggling* **16/1**

5022 **9** 18 **European Dream (IRE)**15 2241 9-9-1 **79**............(p) J-PGuillambert 9
(Richard Guest) *bhd and sn outpcd: lost tch after 4f: t.o* **14/1**

1m 54.85s (0.95) **Going Correction** +0.25s/f (Good) **9** Ran SP% **123.8**
Speed ratings (Par 105): **105,104,102,101,100 100,91,86,70**
toteswingers:1&2:£6.90, 2&3:£6.90, 1&3:£9.20 CSF £38.92 CT £298.56 TOTE £11.40: £2.80, £2.20, £2.20; EX 73.50.
Owner Dan Gilbert **Bred** Shadwell Farm LLC **Trained** Norton, N Yorks

FOCUS
A decent handicap in which the runner-up sets the standard. It was run at a strong pace which played into the hands of the hold-up performers.

T/Jkpt: Not won. T/Plt: £823.10 to a £1 stake.Pool of £86,206.17 - 76.45 winning tickets. T/Qpdt: £37.20 to a £1 stake. Pool of £5,212.32 - 103.60 winning tickets. RY

2721 - 2727a (Foreign Racing) - See Raceform Interactive

2532 LONGCHAMP (R-H)

Saturday, June 2

OFFICIAL GOING: Turf: good

2728a PRIX DU PALAIS-ROYAL (GROUP 3) (3YO+) (TURF) 7f

1:30 (12:00) 3-Y-O+ **£33,333** (£13,333; £10,000; £6,666; £3,333)

RPR

1 **Moonlight Cloud**[231] 6858 4-9-6 0 ThierryJarnet 9 120
(F Head, France) *midfield: rdn to improve over 1 1/2f out: qcknd stylishly under hands and heels to ld ins fnl 100yds: wnt clr cl home: v impressive* **11/5**[1]

2 2 **So Long Malpic (FR)**[36] 5-9-0 0 OlivierPeslier 7 109
(T Lemer, France) *midfield: gd prog into front rnk over 1 1/2f out: rdn to chal 1f out: r.o to go 2nd post: nt pce of wnr* **22/1**

3 nse **Aesop's Fables (USA)**[23] 3-8-7 0 MaximeGuyon 6 108
(A Fabre, France) *prom on outer: rdn and outpcd over 2 1/2f out: gd prog u.p to ld over 1f out: hdd ins fnl 100yds: ct for 2nd post* **8/1**

4 1 **Rosendhal (IRE)**[39] 1593 5-9-3 0 (b) StephanePasquier 3 109
(G Botti, Italy) *front rnk thrght: rdn to chal over 2f out: briefly disputing ld over 1f out: kpt on wout matching pce of front trio ins fnl f* **13/1**

5 ½ **Nova Hawk**[30] 1809 4-9-0 0 Christophe-PatriceLemaire 14 105
(Rod Collet, France) *dropped in fr wd draw and hld up towards rr: stl gng wl but plenty to do over 2f out: rdn to improve 1 1/2f out: r.o strly to go 5th post: nvr able to chal* **7/1**[3]

6 hd **Fred Lalloupet**[20] 2112 5-9-3 0 AnthonyCrastus 1 107
(D Smaga, France) *prom on inner: rdn over 1 1/2f out: kpt on one pce ins fnl f: ct for 5th post* **21/1**

7 ½ **Kendam (FR)**[20] 2109 3-8-6 0 FabriceVeron 10 101
(H-A Pantall, France) *slow to stride and rdn along early stages: hld up towards rr: rdn 3f out: kpt on one pce ins fnl 2 1/2f: wnt 7th post* **40/1**

8 hd **Firebeam**[21] 2075 4-9-3 0 ChristopheSoumillon 5 105
(William Haggas) *qckly into stride and sn led: set even pce: rdn over 2 1/2f out: hdd over 1f out: fdd ins fnl f: ct for 7th post* **9/2**[2]

9 1¼ **Nordic Truce (USA)**[32] 1745 5-9-3 0 AStarke 13 102
(P Schiergen, Germany) *midfield on outer: rdn over 2 1/2f out: wl positioned and stl ev ch whn jockey seemed to stop riding over 1 1/2f out: r.o under tender handling ins fnl f: keeping on at fin: strnge ride* **32/1**

10 ½ **Smooth Operator (GER)**[13] 6-9-5 0 (b) GeraldMosse 2 102
(Mario Hofer, Germany) *midfield on inner: rdn over 3f out: outpcd over 1 1/2f out: plugged on* **11/1**

11 **Barbayam**[23] 3-8-4 0 FlavienPrat 4
(F Head, France) *broke wl: sn trcking ldr in 2nd on inner: tk fierce hold: rdn and brief effrt over 2f out: btn over 1f out: fdd ins fnl f* **24/1**

12 **Gammarth (FR)**[26] 4-9-3 0 RonanThomas 15
(H-A Pantall, France) *hld up in last: stl in rr but gng wl 2 1/2f out: rdn over 2f out: kpt on ins fnl 1 1/2f: nvr able to chal* **44/1**

13 **Broox (IRE)**[11] 4-9-3 0 StephaneBreux 11
(E J O'Neill, France) *hld up in last gp on inner: rdn over 2 1/2f out: plugged on: nvr a factor* **61/1**

14 **Paraggi**[25] 1970 3-8-7 0 ThierryThulliez 8
(M Delzangles, France) *midfield on inner: rdn 3 1/2f out: no ex and btn 1 1/2f out: fdd: eased ins fnl f* **22/1**

15 **Cerveza**[254] 6288 4-9-0 0 TheoBachelot 12
(F Poulsen, France) *hld up in last gp on outer: prog into midfield over 3 1/2f out: rdn over 3f out: no ex and btn 1 1/2f out: dropped to last ins fnl f* **105/1**

1m 19.31s (-1.39)
WFA 3 from 4yo+ 10lb **15 Ran SP% 116.0**
WIN (incl. 1 euro stake): 3.20. PLACES: 1.70, 5.10, 3.00. DF: 44.80. SF: 55.90.
Owner George Strawbridge **Bred** George Strawbridge **Trained** France

NOTEBOOK
Moonlight Cloud won impressively on her reappearance, defying a Group 1 penalty in the process. Her main summer target is the Prix Maurice de Gheest at Deauville in August, but she could take in the Diamond Jubilee Stakes first. She wouldn't want the ground too quick at Ascot, while Black Caviar would also stand in her way.
Nova Hawk, who had a tough draw to overcome, finished well having been given a lot to do, and a return to 1m will be in her favour. She could go for the Windsor Forest Stakes next, although connections are also considering Hamburg's Group 3 Stutenmeile.

2375 NOTTINGHAM (L-H)

Sunday, June 3

OFFICIAL GOING: Good changing to good to soft after race 2 (2.50)
Wind: Fresh, behind Weather: Rain

2729 BRITISH STALLION STUDS SUPPORTING BRITISH RACING E B F MAIDEN STKS 5f 13y

2:20 (2:20) (Class 5) 2-Y-O **£3,234** (£962; £481; £240) **Stalls** High

Form RPR

1 **Alhebayeb (IRE)** 2-9-3 0 TadhgO'Shea 2 79+
(Richard Hannon) *wnt lft s: sn rcvrd to trck ldr: pushed along over 2f out: rdn and edgd lft over 1f out: led ins fnl f: kpt on* **4/9**[1]

0 2 nk **Hardy Red (IRE)**[18] 2164 2-9-3 0 FergusSweeney 6 75
(Jamie Osborne) *w ldr: rdn over 1f out: kpt on: jst hld* **12/1**

5 3 2 **Snow Angel (IRE)**[13] 2343 2-8-12 0 SebSanders 3 63
(J W Hills) *led narrowly: rdn over 1f out: hdd ins fnl f: no ex* **4/1**[2]

4 7 **Rosie Future (IRE)** 2-8-12 0 ChrisCatlin 4 38+
(Rae Guest) *sn pushed along towards rr: a bhd* **17/2**[3]

0 5 12 **Luckster**[11] 2384 2-9-3 0 PadraigBeggy 5
(David Evans) *prom: pushed along and lost pl over 3f out: bhd fnl 2f* **40/1**

1m 1.53s (0.53) **Going Correction** -0.05s/f (Good) **5 Ran SP% 109.9**
Speed ratings (Par 93): **93,92,89,78,58**
toteswingers: 1&2 £6.30 CSF £6.94 TOTE £1.30: £1.10, £4.90; EX 6.00.
Owner Hamdan Al Maktoum **Bred** Yeomanstown Stud **Trained** East Everleigh, Wilts

FOCUS
Outside (summer) course used. There was a tailwind up the straight. The bottom bend had been moved out, increasing race distances by about 10yds on the round course. The winner scored with a bit in hand and the third looks the best guide to the form.

NOTEBOOK
Alhebayeb(IRE) was champion trainer Richard Hannon's first runner for Sheikh Hamdan. Despite walking out of the stalls, going left and taking a good while to get the hang of what was required, he came through to win a shade cosily in the end and this half-brother to five winners, including six-time sprint winner Humidor, can only improve for the experience and for another furlong. (op 4-7)
Hardy Red(IRE), beaten out of sight by another Hannon-trained runner (Sir Prancealot) at Bath on his debut, showed the benefit of that outing and, with the rail to help, he proved to be the favourite's biggest threat. He was probably flattered to finish so close, though, and if they meet again the distance between them is likely to be greater. (tchd 11-1)
Snow Angel(IRE) shouldn't have minded the rain given her pedigree. She took them along for most of the way, but allowed the runner-up to take the rail position and was attacked on her outer by the winner. (op 3-1)
Rosie Future(IRE) finished a long way adrift of the first three, but she's not bred for 5f and can improve for time and distance. (tchd 9-1)

2730 JOCKEY CLUB CATERING AT NOTTINGHAM RACECOURSE H'CAP 5f 13y

2:50 (2:51) (Class 6) (0-65,64) 3-Y-O **£2,070** (£616; £307; £153) **Stalls** High

Form RPR

5662 1 **Demora**[25] 1986 3-9-2 **59** TomQueally 4 72
(Michael Appleby) *prom towards centre: rdn and edgd rt over 1f out: led ins fnl f: kpt on* **17/2**

2624 2 1¼ **Welease Bwian (IRE)**[9] 2443 3-9-4 **64** RyanClark(3) 14 72
(Stuart Williams) *narrow ldr towards stands' rail: rdn over 2f out: hdd ins fnl f: one pce* **7/2**[1]

60-0 3 5 **Cataract**[40] 1585 3-8-3 **46** (b) ChrisCatlin 6 36
(John Weymes) *bmpd s: racd towards centre: sn w ldr: rdn over 2f out: outpcd by ldng pair over 1f out: no ex fnl f* **50/1**

-130 4 1¾ **Persidha**[43] 1529 3-9-7 **64** (v) JoeFanning 8 48
(Derek Shaw) *wnt lft s: chsd ldrs: rdn over 2f out: plugged on* **13/2**[3]

3025 5 3 **Samba Night (IRE)**[17] 2205 3-9-6 **63** LukeMorris 2 36
(James Eustace) *in tch towards centre: rdn and outpcd over 2f out: no threat after* **11/2**[2]

-350 6 nse **One Kool Dude**[17] 2206 3-8-11 **61** IanBurns(7) 11 34
(Michael Bell) *chsd ldrs: wknd ins fnl f* **10/1**

13-4 7 ½ **Uncle Timmy**[4] 2610 3-9-5 **62** (t) CathyGannon 10 33
(David Evans) *chsd ldrs: wknd over 1f out* **7/2**[1]

305 8 7 **Miserere Mei (IRE)**[9] 2460 3-8-4 **50** (p) DeclanCannon(3) 13
(Richard Guest) *prom: wknd over 1f out* **11/1**

5550 9 4½ **Thorpe Bay**[34] 1709 3-9-5 **62** (bt) HayleyTurner 5
(Conor Dore) *bmpd s: hld up: brought towards stands' side over 2f out: nvr on terms* **25/1**

4000 10 hd **Exkaliber**[11] 2388 3-8-6 **54** (p) RaulDaSilva(5) 9
(Jeremy Gask) *prom: pushed along over 3f out: sn lost pl: wknd over 1f out* **16/1**

0150 11 18 **Chateau Lola**[43] 1514 3-8-9 **52** (v) RichardMullen 12
(Derek Shaw) *stmbld s: hld up: a wl bhd* **33/1**

1m 0.07s (-0.93) **Going Correction** -0.05s/f (Good) **11 Ran SP% 115.7**
Speed ratings (Par 97): **105,103,95,92,87 87,86,75,68,67 39**
toteswingers: 1&2 £7.40, 1&3 £43.90, 2&3 £31.60 CSF £37.13 CT £1441.14 TOTE £9.10: £3.20, £2.00, £11.50; EX 38.70 TRIFECTA Not won..
Owner Dallas Racing **Bred** A M Wragg **Trained** Danethorpe, Notts

FOCUS
Only a modest sprint with the runner-up pretty much to form.
Uncle Timmy Official explanation: jockey said gelding never travelled
Chateau Lola Official explanation: jockey said filly stumbled leaving stalls

2731 BOOK A BISTRO PACKAGE IN FRANKIE'S H'CAP 5f 13y

3:20 (3:23) (Class 3) (0-95,94) 4-Y-O+ **£8,409** (£2,502; £1,250; £625) **Stalls** High

Form RPR

-030 1 **Taurus Twins**[15] 2289 6-8-11 **84** ow2 (b) TomQueally 8 91
(Richard Price) *mde all against stands' rail: strly pressed ins fnl f: kpt on wl* **5/2**[2]

60-1 2 1 **Kingsgate Choice (IRE)**[23] 2040 5-9-1 **88** LiamKeniry 6 91
(Ed de Giles) *chsd ldr: rdn over 2f out: upsides jst ins fnl f: kpt on: hld nr fin* **7/4**[1]

0301 3 10 **Royal Bajan (USA)**[12] 2369 4-8-5 **78** FrannyNorton 3 45
(James Given) *in tch: bdly outpcd by ldng pair 3f out: sn struggling* **7/2**[3]

1006 4 ¾ **Haadeeth**[7] 2596 5-8-7 **80** PadraigBeggy 2 45
(David Evans) *sn outpcd towards rr: nvr threatened* **7/1**

0060 5 1 **Volcanic Dust (IRE)**[48] 1417 4-8-7 **80** RichardKingscote 1 41
(Milton Bradley) *in tch: bdly outpcd by ldng pair 3f out: sn btn* **8/1**

59.82s (-1.18) **Going Correction** -0.05s/f (Good) **5 Ran SP% 110.8**
Speed ratings (Par 107): **107,105,89,88,86**
toteswingers: 1&2 £4.60 CSF £7.36 TOTE £2.80: £1.90, £1.40; EX 7.00 Trifecta £25.30 Pool: £492.83 - 14.40 winning units..
Owner G E Amey & G D Bailey **Bred** G E Amey **Trained** Ullingswick, H'fords

FOCUS
Only two mattered from some way out here and the winner is rated to the best view of his previous form.

NOTEBOOK
Taurus Twins, aboard whom Tom Queally put up 2lb overweight, came out on top, sticking to the stands' rail and bravely holding off the challenge of Kingsgate Choice out wide. This was his third win from four starts at this track and, being versatile when it comes to ground conditions, the rain caused him no bother. (op 11-4)
Kingsgate Choice(IRE) likes fast ground on turf so the easing conditions probably hurt his chances. He ran well in the circumstances and remains in good form for his new stable. (op 2-1 tchd 9-4)
Royal Bajan(USA) was well beaten by the first two but came out best in the battle for third. A better horse on Polytrack, his only win on turf came on good to firm and the ground had gone against him here. (op 10-3)
Haadeeth was never seriously competitive and is another who prefers fast ground. (op 5-1)
Volcanic Dust(IRE) continues to struggle for form. (op 9-1)

2732 NOTTINGHAM RACECOURSE NOW AVAILABLE FOR WEDDINGS H'CAP 1m 6f 15y

3:50 (3:50) (Class 5) (0-70,76) 4-Y-O+ **£2,911** (£866; £432; £216) **Stalls** Low

Form RPR

1231 1 **Veloce (IRE)**[2] 2666 4-9-6 **76** 6ex (v) GeorgeDowning(7) 1 84
(Ian Williams) *trckd ldng pair: rdn 3f out: led over 1f out: kpt on wl* **6/5**[1]

1346 2 2¾ **Kingaroo (IRE)**[15] 2260 6-8-2 **51** LukeMorris 4 55
(Garry Woodward) *led for 2f: remained prom: rdn to ld again over 3f out: hdd over 1f out: no ex fnl 100yds* **8/1**

1220 3 1¾ **Holden Eagle**[25] 1984 7-8-9 **65** IanBurns(7) 2 67
(Tony Newcombe) *hld up: pushed along and hdwy 3f out: rdn and ev ch over 1f out: no ex ins fnl f* **7/1**

35-0 **4** *5* **Warne's Way (IRE)**[16] 2237 9-9-5 **68**..............(v) TomQueally 5 63
(Brendan Powell) *hld up in tch: rdn along over 4f out: sn btn* **4/1**[2]
20-1 **5** *3/4* **Dove Cottage (IRE)**[59] 1205 10-9-2 **65**.............. FergusSweeney 6 59
(Stuart Kittow) *trckd ldr: led after 2f: rdn whn hdd over 3f out: sn wknd* **9/2**[3]

3m 12.46s (6.16) **Going Correction** +0.525s/f (Yiel) **5** Ran SP% **107.2**
Speed ratings (Par 103): **103,101,100,97,97**
toteswingers: 1&2 £9.20 CSF £10.49 TOTE £1.90: £1.50, £3.20; EX 7.20.
Owner Dr Marwan Koukash **Bred** J Jamgotchian **Trained** Portway, Worcs

FOCUS
The ground was changed to good to soft before this race, an ordinary staying handicap. The form is not entirely solid with the race rated through the runner-up.

2733 BLACK & WHITE CHRISTMAS PARTY H'CAP 1m 75y
4:20 (4:21) (Class 5) (0-75,75) 3-Y-O £2,911 (£866; £432; £216) **Stalls** Centre

Form RPR
-050 **1** **Stellar Express (IRE)**[15] 2272 3-9-7 **75**.............. LukeMorris 6 87
(Michael Appleby) *dwlt: hld up in midfield: pushed along and hdwy over 3f out: chsd ldr over 1f out: led fnl 100yds: r.o wl* **6/1**[3]
-600 **2** *2 1/2* **Rockme Cockney**[18] 2162 3-7-12 **57**..............(p) RaulDaSilva(5) 5 64
(Jeremy Gask) *led: rdn over 3f out: hdd fnl 100yds: sn no ch w wnr* **28/1**
61-3 **3** *3/4* **Feisty Champion (IRE)**[16] 2246 3-9-4 **72**.............. SebSanders 10 77+
(J W Hills) *hld up in rr: stl lot to do 3f out: hdwy on outer 2f out: r.o wl fnl f: nrst fin* **9/2**[2]
45-3 **4** *3/4* **Lovage**[23] 2045 3-8-11 **65**.............. JamesDoyle 2 68
(Roger Charlton) *trckd ldr: rdn and ev ch over 2f out: sn one pce: lost 3rd towards fin* **9/2**[2]
6-45 **5** *4* **Al's Memory (IRE)**[15] 2265 3-9-4 **72**.............. CathyGannon 1 66
(David Evans) *midfield: rdn and hdwy to chse ldrs 3f out: no ex over 1f out* **9/1**
01-5 **6** *4* **Operettist**[17] 2194 3-9-7 **75**.............. RichardHughes 3 60
(Richard Hannon) *in tch: rdn over 3f out: wknd over 1f out* **4/1**[1]
42-0 **7** *1/2* **Scarlet Whispers**[54] 1270 3-9-6 **74**.............. MickyFenton 9 58
(Pam Sly) *trckd ldrs: pushed along and lost pl over 3f out: sn btn* **25/1**
1140 **8** *nk* **Roedean (IRE)**[17] 2194 3-9-2 **70**..............(p) MartinLane 8 53
(William Stone) *prom: rdn over 3f out: sn wknd* **22/1**
-530 **9** *2 3/4* **Darrow (IRE)**[23] 2045 3-9-1 **69**.............. DarryllHolland 11 46
(William Knight) *racd keenly: hld up: hdwy on inner 3f out: wknd over 1f out* **12/1**
3-55 **10** *11* **Mighty Motive**[34] 1716 3-8-4 **58**.............. FrannyNorton 13
(John Mackie) *midfield: rdn over 3f out: sn wknd* **16/1**
0 **11** *8* **Fight (IRE)**[17] 2206 3-8-11 **65**.............. DaneO'Neill 15
(Jeremy Gask) *midfield on outer: wknd over 3f out* **33/1**
055- **12** *12* **Operation Tracer**[263] 6048 3-8-13 **67**.............. HayleyTurner 14
(Michael Bell) *hld up: a towards rr* **17/2**
-205 **13** *32* **Tooley Woods (IRE)**[30] 1826 3-7-9 **60** oh1.............. NoraLooby(7) 16
(Alan McCabe) *tk str hold on outer: sddle sn slipped: trckd ldrs: wknd and eased over 3f out* **50/1**

1m 49.95s (4.35) **Going Correction** +0.525s/f (Yiel) **13** Ran SP% **121.3**
Speed ratings (Par 99): **99,96,95,95,91 87,86,86,83,72 64,52,20**
toteswingers: 1&2 £38.60, 1&3 £7.00, 2&3 £35.80 CSF £174.07 CT £837.98 TOTE £7.70: £3.00, £9.10, £1.10; EX 261.90 Trifecta £535.60 Part won. Pool: £723.87 - 0.65 winning units..
Owner Mr & Mrs James Sumsion **Bred** Adrian Purvis **Trained** Danethorpe, Notts

FOCUS
This looked a competitive handicap but they finished well spread out and the second offers the best guide to the level.
Tooley Woods(IRE) Official explanation: jockey said saddle slipped

2734 ROOFTOP RESTAURANT AT NOTTINGHAM RACECOURSE MAIDEN FILLIES' STKS 1m 75y
4:50 (4:53) (Class 5) 3-Y-O £2,911 (£866; £432; £216) **Stalls** Centre

Form RPR
0- **1** **Khione**[271] 5806 3-9-0 0.............. KirstyMilczarek 2 91+
(Luca Cumani) *dwlt: hld up in midfield: pushed along and rapid hdwy to chal 3f out: sn rdn: kpt on: led nr fin* **11/1**
45 **2** *hd* **Chigun**[13] 2344 3-9-0 0.............. TomQueally 4 90
(Sir Henry Cecil) *led: rdn 3f out: hung persistently lft fr over 1f out: kpt on: hdd nr fin* **7/2**[2]
23- **3** *10* **Fulney**[228] 6950 3-9-0 0.............. LukeMorris 8 67
(James Eustace) *trckd ldrs: rdn and outpcd over 3f out: plugged on fnl 2f: wnt modest 3rd fnl 100yds* **2/1**[1]
6- **4** *2 1/4* **Dalkova**[275] 5691 3-9-0 0.............. RichardHughes 3 62+
(Richard Hannon) *trckd ldrs: rdn 3f out: stl ev ch whn short of room on rail over 1f out: wknd: lost 3rd fnl 100yds* **10/1**
6- **5** *4 1/2* **Valley Queen**[218] 7164 3-9-0 0.............. LiamKeniry 11 52
(Mark Usher) *in tch: rdn over 3f out: sn one pce: edgd lft over 2f out: wknd over 1f out* **25/1**
00 **6** *8* **Rocquaine (IRE)**[8] 2501 3-9-0 0.............. PadraigBeggy 10 33
(David Evans) *hld up: pushed along into midfield over 3f out: nvr threatened* **100/1**
30- **7** *3/4* **Frosty Secret**[218] 7164 3-8-7 0.............. LewisWalsh(7) 12 32
(Jane Chapple-Hyam) *midfield: rdn over 3f out: sn no imp* **28/1**
00- **8** *3/4* **Dangerous To Know**[244] 6581 3-9-0 0.............. DarryllHolland 9 30
(Hughie Morrison) *hld up: nvr threatened* **33/1**
2 **9** *1 1/4* **Queen Cassiopeia**[25] 1989 3-9-0 0.............. FrederikTylicki 13
(J R Jenkins) *prom: rdn over 3f out: wknd fnl 2f* **18/1**
10 *3 1/4* **Symfony (IRE)** 3-9-0 0.............. AdamKirby 14
(Clive Cox) *hld up: a towards rr* **20/1**
0 **11** *5* **Imperial Wave (IRE)**[13] 2344 3-9-0 0.............. DaneO'Neill 5
(David Lanigan) *hld up: a towards rr* **33/1**
12 *3 1/2* **Miss Dashwood** 3-9-0 0.............. HayleyTurner 6
(James Fanshawe) *in tch: rdn over 3f out: sn wknd* **4/1**[3]
0 **13** *46* **Toppled (IRE)**[39] 1610 3-9-0 0.............. JoeFanning 1
(Brian Meehan) *midfield: rdn over 3f out: wknd and eased over 2f out* **20/1**

1m 49.53s (3.93) **Going Correction** +0.525s/f (Yiel) **13** Ran SP% **121.9**
Speed ratings (Par 96): **101,100,90,88,84 76,75,74,73,70 65,61,15**
toteswingers: 1&2 £9.90, 1&3 £7.70, 2&3 £3.40 CSF £46.74 TOTE £15.80: £4.20, £1.70, £1.40; EX 69.60 TRIFECTA Not won..
Owner Aston House Stud **Bred** Aston House Stud **Trained** Newmarket, Suffolk

FOCUS
With ground conditions very different to those expected when declarations were made, it was no surprise to see a few of these fillies struggle in the conditions. The form is rated around the second and the averages.

Symfony(IRE) Official explanation: jockey said filly's bandage came undone and he eased

2735 A NIGHT WITH BOBBY GEORGE H'CAP 1m 2f 50y
5:20 (5:20) (Class 6) (0-65,65) 4-Y-O+ £2,070 (£616; £307; £153) **Stalls** Low

Form RPR
633- **1** **Hydrant**[156] 7930 6-9-3 **61**.............. SebSanders 8 76+
(Peter Salmon) *trckd ldr: led wl over 2f out: sn rdn clr: easily* **7/1**[3]
563 **2** *7* **Laconicos (IRE)**[20] 2137 10-8-5 **54**..............(t) LauraPike(5) 4 53
(William Stone) *midfield: rdn and hdwy on outer over 2f out: wnt 2nd 1f out: kpt on: no ch w wnr* **11/1**
0-46 **3** *4* **On The Feather**[13] 2348 6-9-6 **64**.............. JamesMillman 13 55
(Rod Millman) *hld up: rdn and hdwy over 2f out: plugged on: wnt 3rd fnl 100yds* **7/1**[3]
564 **4** *2* **Cheers Buddy (IRE)**[54] 1269 4-8-12 **59**.............. DaleSwift(3) 1 46
(Tony Coyle) *trckd ldr: rdn in 2nd over 2f out: wknd and lost 2 pls fnl f* **4/1**[2]
35/4 **5** *3* **Mutanaker**[18] 149 5-9-2 **60**.............. LiamKeniry 2 42
(Ed de Giles) *midfield: rdn over 2f out: sn no imp* **20/1**
-300 **6** *2* **John Potts**[73] 1000 7-9-2 **60**.............. KellyHarrison 5 38
(Brian Baugh) *hld up: hdwy into midfield 4f out: sn rdn: no imp* **20/1**
6520 **7** *nk* **Hits Only Jude (IRE)**[23] 2048 9-8-0 **51**..............(v) MichaelKenny(7) 10 28
(Declan Carroll) *trckd ldrs: rdn over 3f out: wknd over 2f out* **16/1**
00-4 **8** *10* **Fairy Mist (IRE)**[22] 2091 5-8-6 **50**..............(p) CathyGannon 3 8
(Brian Rothwell) *led: rdn whn hdd wl over 2f out: sn wknd* **8/1**
00-0 **9** *1 1/2* **Femme Royale**[22] 2090 4-8-2 **46** oh1.............. LukeMorris 9
(Richard Price) *hld up: rdn over 6f out: nvr threatened* **50/1**
00-0 **10** *1/2* **Hurricane Thomas (IRE)**[30] 1829 8-8-2 **46** oh1.............. FrannyNorton 11
(Karen Tutty) *midfield: rdn over 3f out: sn wknd* **14/1**
235/ **11** *8* **My Manikato**[641] 5665 5-9-7 **65**.............. TomQueally 14
(Richard Phillips) *dwlt: hld up: a bhd* **14/1**
050 **12** *25* **Scribe (IRE)**[38] 1636 4-8-10 **59**.............. MatthewCosham(5) 7
(David Evans) *midfield: wknd qckly over 3f out* **7/2**[1]
00-0 **13** *9* **Emperor Of Rome (IRE)**[27] 1919 4-9-0 **58**.............. FrederikTylicki 6
(Tim Fitzgerald) *midfield: wknd qckly over 3f out* **28/1**

2m 18.05s (6.35) **Going Correction** +0.525s/f (Yiel) **13** Ran SP% **120.8**
Speed ratings (Par 101): **95,89,86,84,82 80,80,72,71,70 64,44,37**
toteswingers: 1&2 £12.90, 1&3 £7.40, 2&3 £20.20 CSF £78.75 CT £568.39 TOTE £6.30: £2.60, £3.90, £3.20; EX 73.10 Trifecta £450.40 Part won. Pool: £608.76 - 0.30 winning units..
Owner C Hatch **Bred** Lord Halifax **Trained** Kirk Deighton, W Yorks

FOCUS
A weak handicap but a lot of these might not have run their races on the unexpectedly soft ground, but it was still an impressive performance from the winner.
Scribe(IRE) Official explanation: trainer said gelding was unsuited by the good to soft ground
T/Plt: £24.30 to a £1 stake. Pool: £60,222.61. 1,802.83 winning tickets. T/Qpdt: £8.40 to a £1 stake. Pool: £3,942.14. 347.00 winning tickets. AS

2736 - 2740a (Foreign Racing) - See Raceform Interactive

2259 CHANTILLY (R-H)
Sunday, June 3

OFFICIAL GOING: Turf: good to soft

2741a PRIX DE ROYAUMONT (GROUP 3) (3YO FILLIES) (TURF) 1m 4f
1:20 (12:00) 3-Y-O £33,333 (£13,333; £10,000; £6,666; £3,333)

RPR
1 **Sediciosa (IRE)**[21] 2111 3-9-0 0.............. GregoryBenoist 2 106
(Y Barberot, France) *settled cl 3rd bhd ldrs: rdn 2f out: swtchd to rail 1 1/2f out: qcknd wl whn gap opened 1f out: led 100yds out: r.o wl: comf* **11/2**[3]
2 *1 1/4* **Yellow And Green**[21] 2111 3-9-0 0.............. ThierryThulliez 7 104
(N Clement, France) *hld up at rr of field: rdn over 2f out: swtchd to outside: r.o wl undser press fnl f: wnt 2nd 100yds out: r.o wl but no threat to wnr* **11/4**[2]
3 *1 1/2* **Mandistana (FR)**[21] 2111 3-9-0 0.............. Christophe-PatriceLemaire 1 102
(A De Royer-Dupre, France) *sent to ld after 1f: led into st: u.p 2f out: hdd 1 1/2f out: rallied ins fnl f to claim 3rd 50yds out: styd on* **6/4**[1]
4 *snk* **Indriya (FR)**[37] 3-9-0 0.............. StephanePasquier 4 101
(F Rohaut, France) *led 1f then settled in 2nd: r.o u.p to ld 1 1/2f out: hdd 100yds out: no ex clsng stages: lost 3rd 50yds out: styd on* **11/2**[3]
5 *1 1/2* **Gulsary (IRE)**[43] 3-9-0 0.............. OlivierPeslier 5 99
(S Wattel, France) *settled towards rr of field: qcknd wl 2f out to look a threat: wnt 3rd 1f out: no ex u.p fnl 100yds: styd on* **25/1**
6 *1 1/2* **Lilting (IRE)**[15] 3-9-0 0..............(p) RonanThomas 3 97
(J E Pease, France) *settled 4th: rdn over 2f out: r.o u.p ent fnl f: sn no ex: styd on* **16/1**
7 *18* **Best Of All (GER)**[35] 3-9-0 0.............. ChristopheSoumillon 6 68
(E Lellouche, France) *settled 5th: rdn over 2 1/2f out: no rspnse: sn wknd: eased fnl 1 1/2f* **9/1**

2m 30.0s (-1.00) **Going Correction** +0.075s/f (Good) **7** Ran SP% **117.2**
Speed ratings: **106,105,104,104,103 102,90**
WIN (incl. 1 euro stake): 6.20. PLACES: 2.40, 1.90. SF: 17.50.
Owner Maurice Lagasse **Bred** Ponchartrain Stud **Trained** France

FOCUS
The front-running third has been rated to her mark.

NOTEBOOK
Sediciosa(IRE) made it three wins from four starts, proving suited by the extra furlong.
Yellow And Green, only a short-head behind the winner last time (when that one was runner-up in a Listed race), finished further back on this occasion but still ran well.
Mandistana(FR) was behind the front two last time and couldn't reverse form, despite going off favourite.

2742a PRIX DE SANDRINGHAM (GROUP 2) (3YO FILLIES) (TURF) 1m
2:30 (12:00) 3-Y-O £61,750 (£23,833; £11,375; £7,583; £3,791)

RPR
1 **Laugh Out Loud**[16] 2255 3-8-11 0.............. WilliamBuick 4 113
(Mick Channon) *sn led: shkn up in front 1 1/2f out: wnt clr: r.o wl ins fnl f: comf* **7/1**
2 *2* **Mashoora (IRE)**[28] 1884 3-8-11 0.............. ChristopheSoumillon 2 108
(J-C Rouget, France) *settled 3rd: wnt 2nd early in st: rdn to chse ldr: r.o u.p fnl f: nvr threatened ldr* **7/2**[2]
3 *2* **Rock Me Baby**[35] 1695 3-8-11 0.............. FrankieDettori 5 103+
(X Thomas-Demeaulte, France) *settled midfield: 5th ent fnl 1 1/2f: shkn up and r.o wl fnl f to go 3rd 50yds out* **22/1**

4 *nk* **Bugie D'Amore**[231] 6904 3-8-11 0.................................. GeraldMosse 7 103
(A De Royer-Dupre, France) *settled 4th: wnt 3rd 1 1/2f out: styd on fnl f: lost 3rd 50yds out* **10/1**

5 *½* **Lily America (FR)**[68] 1059 3-8-11 0.................................. ThierryJarnet 8 102+
(F Rohaut, France) *settled midfield: wnt 5th u.p 1 1/2f out: styd on fnl f* **8/1**

6 *1 ½* **Poupee Flash (USA)**[19] 2156 3-8-11 0.................... StephanePasquier 6 98+
(P Bary, France) *settled towards rr: rdn 2f out: u.p 1 1/2f out: styd on one pce fnl f* **8/1**

7 *hd* **Topeka (IRE)**[21] 2109 3-8-11 0.................................. IoritzMendizabal 3 98+
(Robert Collet, France) *hld up towards rr under restraint: rdn but no ex fr 1 1/2f out: styd on fnl f* **3/1**[1]

8 *1 ½* **Dark Orchid (USA)**[19] 2157 3-8-11 0............................ MaximeGuyon 1 94
(A Fabre, France) *settled 3rd on rail: rdn over 1 1/2f out: no ex: fdd fnl f* **4/1**[3]

9 *1 ¼* **Zantenda**[21] 2112 3-8-11 0..(b) OlivierPeslier 9 91+
(F Head, France) *hld up at rr of field: pulling hrd: rdn but no ex fr 2f out: a bhd* **14/1**

1m 39.2s (1.20) **Going Correction** +0.075s/f (Good) **9** Ran SP% **122.0**
Speed ratings: **97,95,93,92,92 90,90,89,87**
WIN (incl. 1 euro stake): 11.80. PLACES: 4.30, 2.10, 5.10. DF: 33.70. SF: 62.10.
Owner Ann Black,M Al Qatami & K M Al Mudhaf **Bred** Norman Court Stud **Trained** West Ilsley, Berks

FOCUS
The time was poor, with the winner dictating. The second and third are a reasonable guide to the level of the form.

NOTEBOOK
Laugh Out Loud looked good in following up her recent York Listed win, taking her career record to 4-6, but she was allowed the run of the race and the time was slow, so it would be dangerous to get carried away. The Coronation Stakes will be on her agenda.
Mashoora(IRE) showed her 1000 Guineas running to be all wrong, but couldn't get to the front-running winner.

2743a PRIX DU JOCKEY CLUB (GROUP 1) (3YO COLTS & FILLIES) (TURF) 1m 2f 110y
3:15 (12:00) 3-Y-O **£714,250** (£285,750; £142,875; £71,375; £35,750)

RPR

1 **Saonois (FR)**[29] 1869 3-9-2 0...................................... AntoineHamelin 16 118
(J-P Gauvin, France) *hld up in rr gp: impr into midfield over 4f out: swtchd ins and gd prog on to heels of ldrs over 1 1/2f out: rdn to chal ins fnl f: r.o strly to ld ins fnl 100yds: gng away at fin* **25/1**

2 *¾* **Saint Baudolino (IRE)**[23] 2064 3-9-2 0........................ MaximeGuyon 3 117
(A Fabre, France) *midfield: short of room and bmpd over 2 1/2f out: rdn over 2f out: r.o to chal ins fnl f: kpt on but no match for wnr cl home: wnt 2nd post* **6/1**[2]

3 *hd* **Nutello (USA)**[21] 2110 3-9-2 0...(p) FlavienPrat 1 117
(C Laffon-Parias, France) *sn disputing ld on inner: dropped bk to trck ldrs over 5 1/2f out: stl gng wl in bhd horses 2f out: swtchd out and rdn to chal 1 1/2f out: kpt on wl u.p ins fnl f: wnt 3rd post* **50/1**

4 *nse* **Kesampour (FR)**[29] 1869 3-9-2 0............... Christophe-PatriceLemaire 5 117
(M Delzangles, France) *midfield: taken to outer over 3 1/2f out: smooth prog to trck ldrs 3f out: rdn to chal 2f out: r.o to ld over 1f out: kpt on one pce and hdd ins fnl 100yds: dropped to 4th post* **7/1**[3]

5 *1 ¼* **Top Trip**[21] 2108 3-9-2 0.. ThomasHuet 14 114
(F Doumen, France) *hld up towards rr on outer: last over 5f out: gd prog into midfield over 2 1/2f out: rdn over 2f out: r.o wl ins fnl 1 1/2f: wnt 5th ins fnl 100yds* **16/1**

6 *1 ½* **Hidden Flame (IRE)**[41] 3-9-2 0................................ IoritzMendizabal 20 111+
(Robert Collet, France) *wnt violently lft s: qckly rcvrd and hld up towards rr on inner: short of room over 2 1/2f out: rdn and reminders over 2f out: nt clrest of runs ins fnl 1 1/2f but kpt on to go 5th ins fnl 50yds* **150/1**

7 *nk* **Hard Dream (IRE)**[41] 1570 3-9-2 0.......................... StephanePasquier 4 111+
(F Rohaut, France) *prom early: shuffled bk to midfield over 4f out: rdn over 2 1/2f out: keeping on whn short of room and forced to check 1 1/2f out: rcvrd and r.o again to go 7th ins fnl 50yds* **16/1**

8 *nk* **Imperial Monarch (IRE)**[36] 1678 3-9-2 0............................ JPO'Brien 9 110+
(A P O'Brien, Ire) *settled towards rr: denied clr run on inner 2 1/2f out: shuffled bk through field and lost all momentum: rdn to try and rcvr over 2f out: r.o down wd outside ins fnl f: wnt 8th last strides: gng on at fin: tch unlucky* **9/2**[1]

9 *snk* **Lunayir (FR)**[16] 3-9-2 0....................................... JohnnyMurtagh 15 110+
(A De Royer-Dupre, France) *qckly across fr wd draw to be prom on outer: chal gng wl 2 1/2f out: rdn 2f out: led briefly 1 1/2f out: hdd over 1f out: kpt on tl squeezed out and fdd ins fnl 100yds: eased and lost 3 pls cl home* **20/1**

10 *nk* **French Fifteen (FR)**[29] 1856 3-9-2 0................. ChristopheSoumillon 13 109+
(N Clement, France) *settled in midfield on inner: sltly short of room 2 1/2f out: rdn to try and improve 2f out: sme prog u.p tl nt clr run ins fnl f and forced to check: nt rcvr and eased ins fnl 100yds* **9/2**[1]

11 *¾* **Sir Jade (FR)**[21] 2108 3-9-2 0.................................... ThierryThulliez 6 108
(J-M Capitte, France) *midfield: rdn to try and improve 2f out: awkward u.p and edgd lft ins fnl f: plugged on* **66/1**

12 *1* **Albion**[29] 1869 3-9-2 0.. FrankieDettori 17 106+
(A Fabre, France) *midfield on outer: prog to trck ldrs over 3f out: rdn to chal 2 1/2f out: kpt on tl no ex and btn 1f out: fdd: eased cl home* **16/1**

13 *3* **Sofast (FR)**[23] 2064 3-9-2 0.. OlivierPeslier 7 100+
(F Head, France) *restrained towards rr: t.k.h: prog into midfield over 3f out: nt clr run and shuffled bk over 1 1/2f out: fnlly in the clr and rdn 1f out: kpt on under hands and heels: eased ins fnl 100yds: nvr able to chal* **16/1**

14 *1 ¼* **Most Improved (IRE)**[239] 6689 3-9-2 0........................... KierenFallon 11 97+
(Brian Meehan) *midfield on outer: pushed along to maintain position over 3f out: bk on bridle and looking for room 2 1/2f out: swtchd ins and rdn over 2f out: keeping on whn again short of room over 1f out: nt rcvr* **11/1**

15 *snk* **Ektihaam (IRE)**[17] 2210 3-9-2 0...................................... PaulHanagan 2 97+
(Roger Varian) *prom on inner: shuffled bk into midfield over 5f out: rdn 3f out: sltly short of room and checked 2 1/2f out: nt clr run on rail and lost all ch over 1f out: eased ins fnl f* **9/1**

16 *hd* **Valdo Bere (FR)**[41] 1570 3-9-2 0................................... ThierryJarnet 12 97
(E Leenders, France) *hld up in last gp on outer: rdn to improve over 1 1/2f out: outpcd and btn over 1f out: eased ins fnl f* **66/1**

17 *1 ¼* **Amaron**[21] 2110 3-9-2 0... DavyBonilla 18 94
(Andreas Lowe, Germany) *prom on outer: impr to ld over 4f out: rdn and hdd 1 1/2f out: qckly btn and wknd: eased* **33/1**

18 *¾* **Gregorian (IRE)**[21] 2110 3-9-2 0................................... WilliamBuick 10 93
(John Gosden) *midfield on outer: rn v wd and lost grnd on home bnd: rdn over 2f out: no ex and btn over 1 1/2f out: fdd: eased cl home* **25/1**

19 *20* **Silver Northern (FR)**[23] 2064 3-9-2 0.............................. AlexisBadel 19 54
(D Chenu, France) *dropped in fr wd draw: detached in last and rdn along early: tacked on to main body of field over 5f out: rdn over 2 1/2f out: nt clr run and qckly eased over 1f: t.o* **150/1**

20 *dist* **Tifongo (FR)**[41] 1570 3-9-2 0.................................... MickaelBarzalona 8
(H-A Pantall, France) *sn led: hdd over 4f out: rdn over 3f out: wknd qckly over 2f out: heavily eased: t.o* **40/1**

2m 8.1s (-0.70) **Going Correction** +0.075s/f (Good) **20** Ran SP% **129.1**
Speed ratings: **105,104,104,104,103 102,102,101,101,101 100,100,98,97,97 96,95,95,80,**
WIN (incl. 1 euro stake): 33.70. PLACES: 7.80, 2.80, 12.30. DF: 123.50. SF: 333.30.
Owner Pascal Treyve **Bred** Earl Haras De Nonant Le Pin **Trained** France

FOCUS
This didn't look a strong running beforehand and the result most certainly failed to alter that view. The pace was modest, resulting in the first 12 finishers being covered by less than 7l at the line, and it was a rough race. A safety limit of 20 (was even increased to 23 a couple of years earlier) probably isn't a good idea. The seventh and 11th have been rated to their best, while the second, fourth and fifth are among the more promising French 3yos.

NOTEBOOK
Saonois(FR) was given a tremendous ride by Antoine Hamelin, being waited with to avoid most of the trouble and then finding just enough room to deliver a winning challenge. He had managed only fourth behind Kesampour and Albion in the Prix Greffulhe last time and it's hard to take this form seriously.
Saint Baudolino(IRE) did well to finish so close considering he was bumped early in the straight. He has a progressive profile, but we should learn more about him next time.
Nutello(USA) finished close up in a muddling Poule d'Essai des Poulains and did so again here. We still don't know whether he is really up to this class.
Kesampour(FR) looked the winner for much of the closing stages, but ultimately found others finishing quicker. He's bred for stamina and should do better when faced with more of a test.
Top Trip, the Prix Hocquart winner, ran on well without matching the speed of others. He can yet do better.
Hidden Flame(IRE) is one to take from the race. He'd only ever run twice, being beaten over 1m on both occasions, but he's a half-brother to Group winners Memphis Tennessee and Royal Bench (same connections), and finished strongly despite a troubled trip.
Hard Dream(IRE), successful in the Prix Noailles last time, was another who found his path blocked and otherwise could have had a say.
Imperial Monarch(IRE), from a stable with tremendous strength in depth in the Classic division, travelled nicely enough prior to losing his chance when denied a clear run against the inside rail early in the straight. He didn't have the speed to recover, losing his momentum and becoming detached from the main group, but the way he then ran on when switched wide suggests he would have otherwise gone close. His Sandown Classic Trial success came on really bad ground and his knee action suggests he won't want quick conditions.
French Fifteen(FR), runner-up to Camelot in the French 2000 Guineas, never had much room in the straight but kept on, even when his rider gave up some way from the finish.
Sofast(FR), closely matched with the runner-up, was another who didn't get a chance to show his true form, finding significant trouble.
Most Improved(IRE) was the subject of much hype before the 2000 Guineas, but missed the race through injury. Starting for the first time since finishing third in the Dewhurst, he was weak on Betfair but would have finished considerably closer granted a better trip. He raced wide and looked in trouble from some way out, perhaps not handling this first experience of a turning track, but still had something to offer when continually being blocked in the straight.
Ektihaam(IRE)'s second-place finish in the Dante was let down by the winner, Bonfire, in the Epsom Derby, but this colt can be excused being well beaten here as he was short of room on the final bend and early in the straight.
Gregorian(IRE), who went wide when not beaten far in the French 2000 Guineas, again raced wide and did not handle the penultimate bend. That cost him his chance.

2744a GRAND PRIX DE CHANTILLY (GROUP 2) (4YO+) (TURF) 1m 4f
4:00 (12:00) 4-Y-O+ **£61,750** (£23,833; £11,375; £7,583; £3,791)

RPR

1 **Aiken**[22] 2066 4-8-11 0.. WilliamBuick 4 115
(John Gosden) *led fr s: in front ent st: rdn 2f out: chal and hdd 1f out: rallied wl u.str ride to regain ld 100yds out: r.o wl* **9/4**[2]

2 *¾* **Maxios**[26] 4-8-11 0.. StephanePasquier 2 114
(J E Pease, France) *racd 2nd under restraint: rdn to chal 1 1/2f out: led 1f out: hdd 100yds out: r.o wl* **9/2**[3]

3 *2 ½* **Dunaden (FR)**[29] 1855 6-9-4 0..................... Christophe-PatriceLemaire 1 117+
(M Delzangles, France) *hld up at rr: rdn 1 1/2f out: r.o wl ins fnl f to go 3rd 75yds out: no threat to ldrs* **5/6**[1]

4 *¾* **Dance Moves**[26] 1971 4-8-11 0.. MaximeGuyon 5 109
(A Fabre, France) *settled 3rd: u.p over 1 1/2f out: r.o ins fnl f: nvr rchd ldrs: lost 3rd 75yds out* **16/1**

5 *1 ¾* **Allied Powers (IRE)**[26] 1971 7-8-11 0....................... IoritzMendizabal 3 106
(Michael Bell) *settled 4th under restraint: u.p over 1 1/2f out: nt qckn: styd on fnl f* **7/1**

2m 35.8s (4.80) **Going Correction** +0.075s/f (Good) **5** Ran SP% **121.9**
Speed ratings: **87,86,84,84,83**
WIN (incl. 1 euro stake): 3.60. PLACES: 2.20, 2.00. SF: 17.10.
Owner George Strawbridge **Bred** George Strawbridge **Trained** Newmarket, Suffolk

FOCUS
The winner dominated from the front and the time was slow. The second and fourth help set the level.

NOTEBOOK
Aiken benefited from a well-judged front-running ride, gaining his sixth win on the trot. He will be put into the Grand Prix de Saint-Cloud and the Hardwicke Stakes at Royal Ascot, but wouldn't want it too firm.
Maxios had won his first three starts of 2012 and didn't do much wrong behind the smart front-running winner.
Dunaden(FR) had a tough task under his penalty and was set too much to do off a slow pace.

2745a PRIX DU GROS-CHENE (GROUP 2) (3YO+) (TURF) 5f
4:35 (12:00) 3-Y-O+ **£61,750** (£23,833; £11,375; £7,583; £3,791)

RPR

1 **Wizz Kid (IRE)**[21] 2112 4-8-13 0...................................... GeraldMosse 5 113
(Robert Collet, France) *hld up: pushed up into midfield over 3f out: rdn whn short of room and bmpd over 2 1/2f out: in the clr and really str run on outer fr over 1 1/2f out: led ins fnl 150yds: won gng away* **3/1**[1]

2 *1 ¾* **Stepper Point**[29] 1857 3-8-10 0 ow1.................... ChristopheSoumillon 3 108
(William Muir) *midfield: on inner: rdn over 2f out: r.o to go 2nd wl ins fnl f: no ch w wnr* **14/1**

3 *½* **Hamish McGonagall**[29] 1857 7-9-2 0................................ DavidAllan 9 108
(Tim Easterby) *prom: on outer: rdn 2 1/2f out: kpt on to go 3rd ins fnl f* **12/1**

4 *1 ¼* **Eton Rifles (IRE)**[29] 1857 7-9-2 0.............................. WilliamCarson 1 103
(Stuart Williams) *sn chsng ldr: rdn to chal over 2f out: disputing ld over 1 1/2f out: hdd ins fnl 150yds: no ex and dropped to 4th cl home* **10/1**

5 snk **Noble Hachy**[49] 1409 3-8-6 0........ CristianDemuro 2 97
(L Riccardi, Italy) *prom in centre: rdn to chal over 2 1/2f out: disputing ld over 1 1/2f out: hdd ins fnl 150yds: no ex and dropped to 5th cl home* **8/1**
6 nse **Calahorra (FR)**[21] 2112 3-8-6 0........ ThierryJarnet 11 97
(C Baillet, France) *sropped in fr wd draw and hld up in last: rdn over 2f out: r.o u.p to go 6th ins fnl f* **12/1**
7 3/4 **Prohibit**[64] 1146 7-9-2 0........(p) WilliamBuick 4 100
(Robert Cowell) *midfield: rdn and outpcd over 2 1/2f out: r.o ins fnl f: wnt 7th cl home* **5/1**[3]
8 1 1/4 **Huma Bird**[21] 2112 3-8-6 0........(p) MickaelBarzalona 7 89
(H-A Pantall, France) *prom early: relegated to midfield over 3 1/2f out: rdn over 3f out: kpt on tl no ex and fdd ins fnl f: eased and dropped to 8th cl home* **16/1**
9 3 **Move In Time**[29] 1857 4-9-2 0........ RobertWinston 10 85
(Bryan Smart) *hld up in tch: rdn and outpcd over 2 1/2f out: no ex and btn over 1f out: eased ins fnl f* **16/1**
10 1 1/2 **Beyond Desire**[21] 2112 5-8-13 0........ NeilCallan 6 76
(Roger Varian) *mde most on rail to over 1 1/2f out: rdn whn hdd: wknd: eased cl home* **9/2**[2]
11 6 **Mar Adentro (FR)**[21] 2112 6-9-2 0........(b) OlivierPeslier 8 58
(R Chotard, France) *prom in centre: rdn and outpcd over 2f out: fdd: eased whn btn* **20/1**

59.5s (1.20) **Going Correction** +0.625s/f (Yiel)
WFA 3 from 4yo+ 7lb 11 Ran SP% **118.6**
Speed ratings: **115,112,111,109,109 109,107,105,101,98 89**
WIN (incl. 1 euro stake): 3.30. PLACES: 1.50, 2.10, 5.20. DF: 6.10. SF: 26.80.
Owner Mme Maeve Mahony **Bred** Ballylinch Stud **Trained** Chantilly, France

FOCUS
The winner has been rated in line with a better view of her Nunthorpe run, while the second has been rated as running a personal best. The third, fourth and sixth help set the level.

NOTEBOOK
Wizz Kid(IRE), who caught the eye on her reappearance at Longchamp when carrying a 6lb penalty, built on that effort and easily repeated last year's success in this race, despite becoming short of room and getting bumped at halfway. The King's Stand would be her obvious next port of call.
Stepper Point improved hugely for his reappearance in the Palace House Stakes, finishing his race off well without being able to get to the winner. He will now head for the King's Stand Stakes, where he could meet the winner again.
Hamish McGonagall bounced back from an ordinary effort in the Palace House Stakes on this more favourable track. Never too far away, he kept on well for third, probably ran close to his best and is a good marker for the form.
Eton Rifles(IRE), who had the ground in his favour, was up there for a long way before weakening late on. He'll appreciate a return to 6f.
Prohibit, runner-up in this race last year, was having his first outing since disappointing out in Dubai. Keeping on at the finish, he should come on for the run.
Beyond Desire, who made all in the Prix de Saint-Georges last time out on ground that looked better than the official good to soft, couldn't repeat the trick here, failing to get home on a surface that was probably softer than ideal.

1410 DUSSELDORF (R-H)
Sunday, June 3

OFFICIAL GOING: Turf: soft

2746a GERMAN 1000 GUINEAS (GROUP 2) (3YO FILLIES) (TURF) 1m
4:25 (4:28) 3-Y-O
£58,333 (£23,333; £11,666; £5,833; £2,916; £2,083)

RPR
1 **Electrelane**[16] 2255 3-9-2 0........ JimCrowley 2 104
(Ralph Beckett) *a.p on ins rail: shkn up ins fnl 2f and chal ldr fr 1 1/2f out: led appr fnl f: r.o wl u.p: hld on gamely cl home* **9/10**[1]
2 shd **Cherry Danon (IRE)**[33] 3-9-2 0........ AStarke 9 104
(P Schiergen, Germany) *sn led: chal on ins by eventual wnr fr 1 1/2f out: hdd appr fnl f: rallied gamely u.p last 100yds: jst failed to get bk up* **10/1**
3 5 **Waldtraut (GER)**[33] 3-9-2 0........ JBojko 4 92
(A Wohler, Germany) *settled in 6th towards outside: rdn and effrt on outside 1 1/2f out: kpt on u.p fnl f: nt pce to go w first two* **17/2**
4 1 1/4 **Lady Of Budysin (GER)**[21] 2107 3-9-2 0........ EFrank 6 89
(Andreas Lowe, Germany) *hld up towards rr on ins: rdn and no imp 2f out: styd on u.p fr over 1f out: tk 4th cl home: nt pce to chal ldrs* **148/10**
5 1 1/2 **Survey (GER)**[21] 2107 3-9-2 0........ THellier 8 86
(Mario Hofer, Germany) *a.p on outside: shkn up and nt qckn w front two ent fnl 2f: pressed for 3rd over 1 1/2f out: rdn and one pce fr 1f out: wknd fnl 75yds* **11/2**[2]
6 1/2 **Ilena (GER)**[21] 2107 3-9-2 0........ ADeVries 7 85
(Dr A Bolte, Germany) *w.w in rr: rdn and effrt on outside over 1 1/2f out: kpt on at one pce u.p fnl f: nvr on terms w ldrs* **83/10**
7 1/2 **Dessau (GER)**[33] 3-9-2 0........ ShaneKelly 1 84
(W Hickst, Germany) *settled in 5th on ins trcking eventual wnr: shkn up to dispute 3rd over 1 1/2f out: sn rdn and nt qckn: wknd ins fnl f* **59/10**[3]
8 3 1/2 **Paraisa**[21] 2107 3-9-2 0........ TedDurcan 5 76
(A Wohler, Germany) *trckd ldrs: 4th whn outpcd and hrd rdn over 1 1/2f out: wknd fnl f* **157/10**
9 2 1/2 **Molly Filia (GER)**[21] 2107 3-9-2 0........ FilipMinarik 3 70
(Uwe Ostmann, Germany) *chsd ldng gp early: sn settled towards rr: shkn up to keep in tch 2 1/2f out: hrd rdn and no imp fr 1 1/2f out: btn whn eased ins fnl f* **105/10**

1m 40.4s (-0.76) 9 Ran SP% **133.9**
WIN (incl. 10 euro stake): 19. PLACES: 13, 22, 23. SF: 209.
Owner Clipper Logistics **Bred** Bigwigs Bloodstock **Trained** Kimpton, Hants

NOTEBOOK
Electrelane, whose York form had been given a boost when Laugh Out Loud won a Group 2 in France two hours earlier, raced prominently from the outset and narrowly got the better of a battle with the runner-up which went on for a good furlong and a half. She had to survive a stewards enquiry, and her rider was done for overuse of the whip, but she was always holding the runner-up.

2535 CARLISLE (R-H)
Monday, June 4

OFFICIAL GOING: Good to firm (7.9) changing to good to firm (firm in places) after race 3 (2.55)
Wind: Breezy, half behind Weather: Cloudy, bright

2747 BRITISH STALLION STUDS SUPPORTING BRITISH RACING E B F MAIDEN STKS 5f
1:55 (1:58) (Class 5) 2-Y-O **£3,234** (£962; £481; £240) Stalls Low

Form RPR
03 1 **Lady Ibrox**[14] 2334 2-8-9 0........ DaleSwift(3) 1 76
(Alan Brown) *mde all: rdn over 1f out: drvn and hld on wl towards fin* **18/1**
52 2 hd **Lady Of The House (IRE)**[16] 2282 2-8-12 0........ AmyRyan 3 75
(Kevin Ryan) *chsd wnr: rdn over 2f out: styd on wl last 100yds: jst hld* **6/4**[1]
3 4 **Dark Opal (IRE)** 2-8-12 0........ GrahamLee 4 61+
(John Weymes) *dwlt: sn prom: rdn over 2f out: outpcd by first two fr over 1f out* **14/1**
0 4 1 3/4 **Smallbrook Lane (IRE)**[16] 2282 2-8-12 0........ TonyHamilton 7 58+
(Richard Fahey) *reluctant to enter stalls: prom: hmpd and swtchd rt after 1f: rdn and nt qckn fnl 2f* **4/1**[3]
3 5 6 **Denbigh Raur (IRE)**[10] 2437 2-8-12 0........ DavidNolan 5 33+
(Ann Duffield) *s.i.s: rdn in rr over 3f out: nvr able to chal* **15/2**
05 6 1 1/4 **Roland**[21] 2123 2-9-3 0........ FrederikTylicki 2 35+
(Kevin Ryan) *s.i.s: sn rdn along in rr: nvr on terms* **22/1**
0 7 10 **Pippy**[26] 1972 2-9-3 0........ TomEaves 6
(Tom Dascombe) *prom: hung bdly lft thrght and drifted to r alone stands' rail fr over 3f out: sn struggling: lost tch fr 1/2-way* **10/3**[2]

1m 1.78s (0.98) **Going Correction** +0.125s/f (Good) 7 Ran SP% **111.1**
Speed ratings (Par 93): **97,96,90,87,77 75,59**
toteswingers:1&2:£10.30, 1&3:£23.20, 2&3:£2.30 CSF £43.17 TOTE £16.50: £4.90, £1.80; EX 29.50.
Owner Rangers Racing **Bred** D Simpson **Trained** Yedingham, N Yorks
■ Stewards' Enquiry : Amy Ryan two-day ban: use of whip (18, 24 June)

FOCUS
Not a strong maiden by any means.

NOTEBOOK
Lady Ibrox improved again with the drop back to 5f being very much in her favour and she showed bright speed to make all. A sharper test will suit her even better if anything. (tchd 20-1)
Lady Of The House(IRE) is going to pick up a race at some point, but there's no obvious sign she's progressing, though 6f should will suit her as she was doing her best work at the finish here. (tchd 13-8)
Dark Opal(IRE), a daughter of Camacho, showed ability and is entitled to improve, though she'll have to step up a fair bit to go close in similar company next time. (tchd 16-1)
Smallbrook Lane(IRE) is perhaps worth another chance to show herself capable of better, as she was done no favours by the wayward Pippy early on. (op 9-2 tchd 7-2)
Denbigh Raur(IRE) failed to build on last month's Catterick debut, being always on the back foot after a slow start. Official explanation: jockey said that the filly was never travelling
Roland hasn't shown much so far, but wasn't knocked about and it wouldn't be the biggest surprise to see him come back after a break and improve in nurseries later on in the campaign. (op 20-1)
Pippy had been green on his Chester debut, but simply looked wayward here, hanging left throughout. A return to a left-handed track will help, but he'll still have something to prove next time. (op 4-1 tchd 3-1)

2748 HAPPY BIRTHDAY STACEY REYNOLDS H'CAP (DIV I) 5f
2:25 (2:26) (Class 6) (0-60,66) 3-Y-O+ **£1,704** (£503; £251) Stalls Low

Form RPR
-003 1 **Choc'A'Moca (IRE)**[15] 2314 5-9-8 **56**........(v) MickyFenton 7 68
(Paul Midgley) *mde all: drvn over 1f out: hld on wl fnl f* **9/2**[2]
60-4 2 1 **Cruise Tothelimit (IRE)**[23] 2084 4-9-12 **60**........ TonyHamilton 8 68
(Ian Williams) *pressed wnr thrght: effrt and ev ch over 1f out: kpt on ins fnl f: hld towards fin* **11/4**[1]
0-60 3 3/4 **Ingenti**[15] 2314 4-9-3 **51**........ PaddyAspell 6 56
(Christopher Wilson) *trckd ldrs on ins: nt clr run over 2f out to wl over 1f out: sn rdn: kpt on same pce fnl f* **20/1**
0-04 4 2 1/4 **Novalist**[15] 2314 4-9-5 **53**........(b) DanielTudhope 3 50
(Robin Bastiman) *prom: drvn and outpcd wl over 1f out: kpt on ins fnl f* **7/1**
2661 5 hd **Argentine (IRE)**[4] 2617 8-10-4 **66** 6ex........(v) TomEaves 10 62
(Ian Semple) *t.k.h: hld up on outside: shortlived effrt over 1f out: no ex ins fnl f* **5/1**[3]
-053 6 1/2 **Insolenceofoffice (IRE)**[4] 2617 4-9-11 **59**........(p) GrahamLee 2 54
(Richard Ford) *sn rdn towards rr: drvn and hdwy wl over 1f out: sn outpcd* **9/2**[2]
6-00 7 1 3/4 **Triskaidekaphobia**[10] 2436 9-8-7 **46** oh1........ ShaneBKelly(5) 1 34
(Wilf Storey) *rn wout declared tongue-tie: in tch: drvn 1/2-way: wknd over 1f out* **33/1**
4-60 8 2 **Running Water**[63] 1169 4-8-9 **46** oh1........ PaulPickard(3) 9 27
(Hugh McWilliams) *hld up: effrt on outside over 2f out: wknd over 1f out* **50/1**
426 9 12 **Son Of May**[12] 2385 3-8-12 **53**........(b) TonyCulhane 5
(Jo Hughes) *s.i.s: bhd and detached: no ch fr 1/2-way* **7/1**

1m 1.4s (0.60) **Going Correction** +0.125s/f (Good)
WFA 3 from 4yo+ 7lb 9 Ran SP% **114.4**
Speed ratings (Par 101): **100,98,97,93,93 92,89,86,67**
toteswingers:1&2:£4.00, 1&3:£15.30, 2&3:£5.20 CSF £16.78 CT £221.25 TOTE £5.40: £2.00, £1.10, £2.60; EX 20.00.
Owner John Milburn - Andrew Stephenson **Bred** Yeomanstown Stud **Trained** Westow, N Yorks

FOCUS
A modest sprint run in a time 0.6 seconds faster than division two. A handy pitch proved vital, the front three occupying those positions almost throughout.
Triskaidekaphobia Official explanation: jockey said the gelding had a breathing problem

2749 HAPPY BIRTHDAY STACEY REYNOLDS H'CAP (DIV II) 5f
2:55 (2:58) (Class 6) (0-60,60) 3-Y-O+ **£1,704** (£503; £251) Stalls Low

Form RPR
046 1 **Rio's Girl**[54] 1298 5-9-2 **53**........ DaleSwift(3) 8 62
(Tony Coyle) *towards rr: effrt and rdn 2f out: led wl ins fnl f: kpt on wl* **13/2**
0206 2 1 1/4 **Tom Sawyer**[32] 1800 4-9-12 **60**........(p) FrederikTylicki 4 65
(Julie Camacho) *in tch: rdn and outpcd 2f out: rallied appr fnl f: tk 2nd nr fin: nt rch wnr* **13/2**

30-0 **3** *shd* **Ballarina**[54] 1298 6-9-9 **57** KellyHarrison 1 61
(Eric Alston) *taken early to post: t.k.h: led: rdn and edgd lft over 1f out: edgd rt and hdd wl ins fnl f: no ex* **8/1**

6604 **4** *2* **Drumpellier (IRE)**[10] 2458 5-8-12 **46** (e) AmyRyan 10 43
(Simon West) *towards rr: rdn along and hdwy over 1f out: kpt on fnl f: nvr able to chal* **10/1**

6-52 **5** *½* **Lees Anthem**[10] 2458 5-9-6 **54** PaddyAspell 2 49
(Colin Teague) *trckd ldrs: effrt and rdn wl over 1f out: kpt on same pce fnl f* **6/1**[3]

0000 **6** *1 ½* **Green Warrior**[29] 1881 4-9-1 **52** (e) DeclanCannon(3) 6 42
(Richard Guest) *taken early to post: sn pushed along towards rr: hdwy over 1f out: no imp fnl f* **22/1**

0454 **7** *hd* **Sharp Shoes**[10] 2436 5-9-11 **59** (p) GrahamLee 3 48
(Ann Duffield) *prom: rdn and edgd rt wl over 1f out: sn outpcd* **9/2**[1]

041- **8** *½* **Emily Hall**[224] 7059 3-8-7 **48** TomEaves 9 35+
(Bryan Smart) *taken early to post: dwlt: bhd: hdwy on wd outside over 2f out: no imp fr over 1f out* **6/1**[3]

6-00 **9** *1 ¼* **Stella Marris**[10] 2436 5-8-7 **46** oh1 GarryWhillans(5) 7 29
(Christopher Wilson) *cl up tl rdn and wknd over 1f out* **50/1**

5454 **10** *nk* **Julier Pass (IRE)**[14] 2351 3-8-11 **55** PaulPickard(3) 5 37+
(Hugh McWilliams) *bmpd s and sn outpcd: nvr on terms* **11/2**[2]

1m 2.0s (1.20) **Going Correction** +0.125s/f (Good)
WFA 3 from 4yo+ 7lb **10** Ran SP% **115.3**
Speed ratings (Par 101): **95,93,92,89,88 86,86,85,83,82**
toteswingers:1&2:£9.30, 1&3:£8.30, 2&3:£11.70 CSF £47.80 CT £351.19 TOTE £9.40: £3.40, £3.80, £2.90; EX 65.40.
Owner W P S Johnson & Brian Kerr **Bred** Hellwood Stud Farm **Trained** Norton, N Yorks
■ Stewards' Enquiry : Frederik Tylicki two-day ban: use of whip (18, 24 June)
Paul Pickard one-day ban: arrived late at start (18 June)

FOCUS
The second division of this ordinary sprint handicap. It was run at a good pace.

2750 MADNESS LIVE ON 7TH JULY H'CAP (BETFAIR SPRINT FLAT SERIES QUALIFIER) 5f 193y
3:30 (3:35) (Class 5) (0-70,70) 4-Y-0+ **£3,234** (£962; £481; £240) **Stalls** Low

Form RPR

5001 **1** **Lucky Dan (IRE)**[9] 2476 6-9-7 **70** JoeFanning 3 80
(Paul Green) *trckd ldrs: rdn to ld appr fnl f: kpt on wl* **13/2**[3]

-043 **2** *½* **Needy McCredie**[23] 2092 6-8-9 **58** PaddyAspell 9 66
(James Turner) *hld up on outside: smooth hdwy over 2f out: chsd wnr fnl f: edgd rt: hld towards fin* **5/1**[2]

3-61 **3** *3 ¼* **Secret City (IRE)**[23] 2096 6-9-7 **70** (b) DanielTudhope 2 68
(Robin Bastiman) *trckd ldrs: drvn along 1/2-way: kpt on same pce fnl f* **5/1**[2]

3122 **4** *nk* **Da'Quonde (IRE)**[24] 2032 4-9-0 **68** JustinNewman(5) 5 65
(Bryan Smart) *slt ld to appr fnl f: sn one pce* **4/1**[1]

0241 **5** *1 ½* **Cut The Cackle (IRE)**[10] 2466 6-8-10 **59** (bt) FrederikTylicki 1 51+
(Richard Guest) *dwlt: sn in tch: drvn along 1/2-way: no imp whn nt clr run ent fnl f: styd on towards fin* **4/1**[1]

-000 **6** *½* **Another Citizen (IRE)**[23] 2096 4-9-5 **68** (p) DavidNolan 6 59
(Tim Easterby) *w ldrs: rdn over 2f out: wknd appr fnl f* **10/1**

000- **7** *dht* **Dubai Celebration**[243] 6634 4-8-13 **62** [1] GrahamLee 7 53
(Julie Camacho) *hld up in tch: effrt and rdn over 2f out: no imp fr over 1f out* **14/1**

3060 **8** *1 ¾* **Blown It (USA)**[2] 2719 6-9-6 **69** TomEaves 4 54
(Keith Dalgleish) *t.k.h: hld up in tch: effrt and rdn over 1f out: edgd rt ent fnl f: sn wknd* **14/1**

1m 13.96s (0.26) **Going Correction** +0.125s/f (Good) **8** Ran SP% **109.1**
Speed ratings (Par 103): **103,102,98,97,95 94,94,92**
toteswingers:1&2:£6.10, 1&3:£3.10, 2&3:£17.90 CSF £35.20 CT £159.98 TOTE £6.30: £1.80, £1.90, £1.50; EX 17.30.
Owner Paul Green (Oaklea) **Bred** Mountarmstrong Stud **Trained** Lydiate, Merseyside
■ Stewards' Enquiry : Justin Newman two-day ban: careless riding (18, 24 June)

FOCUS
Hardly a handicap with much depth to it, but the leading pair still deserve some credit for pulling a long way clear.

2751 EDINBURGH WOOLLEN MILL CUMBERLAND PLATE TRIAL H'CAP 1m 3f 107y
4:05 (4:06) (Class 4) (0-80,80) 4-Y-0+ **£6,469** (£1,925; £962; £481) **Stalls** High

Form RPR

0-06 **1** **Tartan Gigha (IRE)**[5] 2606 7-9-5 **78** JoeFanning 3 90
(Geoffrey Harker) *hld up: gd hdwy 3f out: led on outside wl over 1f out: sn drifted rt to far rail: styd on wl fnl f* **16/1**

0-13 **2** *2 ¾* **Yahrab (IRE)**[10] 2440 7-9-1 **74** DanielTudhope 5 81
(Declan Carroll) *hld up: rdn over 3f out: gd hdwy to chse wnr fnl f: kpt on: no imp* **13/2**[2]

1-02 **3** *3 ¼* **Cape Rising (IRE)**[15] 2312 5-8-12 **76** GarryWhillans(5) 15 77+
(Alan Swinbank) *prom: rdn and outpcd over 2f out: styd on fnl f: nt pce to chal* **6/1**[1]

-053 **4** *1 ½* **Snow Dancer (IRE)**[7] 2539 8-9-1 **75** ow2 GaryBartley(3) 4 82+
(Hugh McWilliams) *s.i.s: hld up: hdwy whn nt clr run over 1f out and appr fnl f: r.o: nrst fin* **10/1**

0-53 **5** *1* **Royal Opera**[24] 2035 4-8-9 **71** PaulPickard(3) 2 68+
(Brian Ellison) *chsd ldr: rdn and ev ch over 2f out: one pce over 1f out* **8/1**

4340 **6** *nk* **Embsay Crag**[16] 2260 6-8-9 **68** GrahamLee 8 65
(Kate Walton) *t.k.h: hld up on outside: rdn and outpcd over 2f out: edgd rt: styd on fnl f: no imp* **8/1**

3225 **7** *¾* **Reset City**[16] 2260 6-8-9 **68** (t) RoystonFfrench 9 63
(Ian Williams) *hld up in tch: hdwy on outside to ld over 2f out to wl over 1f out: outpcd appr fnl f* **12/1**

44-0 **8** *¾* **Fossgate**[23] 2093 11-8-11 **70** AmyRyan 1 64
(James Bethell) *hld up on ins: drvn and outpcd over 3f out: n.d after* **25/1**

02-0 **9** *nk* **Gold Rules**[20] 2142 5-8-11 **70** TonyHamilton 11 64
(Michael Easterby) *led at decent gallop to over 2f out: wknd appr fnl f* **28/1**

-000 **10** *1 ¼* **Meetings Man (IRE)**[9] 2504 5-8-12 **71** FrederikTylicki 13 63
(Micky Hammond) *trckd ldrs: effrt and ev ch over 2f out: wknd appr fnl f* **15/2**[3]

-00 **11** *½* **Tenhoo**[15] 2312 6-8-11 **75** NathanAlison(5) 6 66
(Eric Alston) *hld up on ins: rdn over 3f out: outpcd fnl 2f* **14/1**

0-35 **12** *1 ¾* **Lady Chaparral**[15] 2312 5-9-7 **80** TomEaves 10 68
(Michael Dods) *trckd ldrs: effrt and rdn over 2f out: wknd appr fnl f* **6/1**[1]

4430 **13** *8* **Polurrian (IRE)**[16] 2260 5-8-9 **68** PaddyAspell 14 42
(David O'Meara) *midfield: outpcd and lost pl over 3f out: sn struggling* **20/1**

20-0 **14** *29* **Mr Perceptive (IRE)**[9] 2504 4-9-0 **73** KellyHarrison 7
(Micky Hammond) *s.i.s: bhd: lost tch fr 1/2-way: t.o* **33/1**

2m 22.0s (-1.10) **Going Correction** 0.0s/f (Good) **14** Ran SP% **120.2**
Speed ratings (Par 105): **104,102,99,98,97 97,97,96,96,95 95,93,87,66**
toteswingers:1&2:£23.00, 1&3:£20.60, 2&3:£4.10 CSF £111.48 CT £710.96 TOTE £18.70: £6.50, £2.40, £2.40; EX 194.10 TRIFECTA .
Owner A S Ward **Bred** Gainsborough Stud Management Ltd **Trained** Thirkleby, N Yorks

FOCUS
A fair handicap and competitive enough for the level. They went a strong pace, the field being well strung out from an early stage, and it was set up for those coming from behind.
Royal Opera Official explanation: jockey said that the gelding hung right handed
Mr Perceptive(IRE) Official explanation: trainer said that the gelding was unsuited by the track

2752 CARLISLE-RACES.CO.UK FILLIES' H'CAP 7f 200y
4:40 (4:40) (Class 3) (0-90,87) 3-Y-0+ **£6,663** (£1,982; £990; £495) **Stalls** Low

Form RPR

-204 **1** **Madam Macie (IRE)**[9] 2491 5-9-5 **78** DanielTudhope 3 89+
(David O'Meara) *mde all: qcknd over 2f out: clr over 1f out: kpt on wl: unchal* **7/2**[1]

-000 **2** *5* **Hot Rod Mamma (IRE)**[9] 2472 5-9-9 **87** ShaneBKelly(5) 7 87
(Dianne Sayer) *hld up: stdy hdwy over 2f out: effrt and chsd (clr) wnr over 1f out: sn no imp* **6/1**

43-1 **3** *5* **Parley (USA)**[114] 533 3-8-11 **81** JoeFanning 1 66
(Mark Johnston) *trckd ldrs: effrt and wnt 2nd over 2f out to over 1f out: sn outpcd* **9/2**[3]

2-00 **4** *hd* **Nemushka**[9] 2485 3-8-11 **81** (p) TonyHamilton 6 65
(Richard Fahey) *t.k.h: prom: effrt and disp 2nd pl over 2f out to over 1f out: sn outpcd* **4/1**[2]

5066 **5** *2 ½* **Jeannie Galloway (IRE)**[15] 2310 5-9-5 **83** GarryWhillans(5) 2 65
(Keith Dalgleish) *hld up in tch: drvn over 2f out: btn over 1f out* **9/1**

0-10 **6** *¾* **She's A Character**[24] 2025 5-9-1 **81** LauraBarry(7) 5 61
(Richard Fahey) *hld up: rdn and outpcd over 3f out: sn n.d* **10/1**

13-2 **7** *6* **Lady Layla**[11] 2416 3-8-9 **79** TomEaves 4 42
(Bryan Smart) *chsd wnr to over 2f out: sn rdn: edgd rt and wknd* **4/1**[2]

1m 38.7s (-1.30) **Going Correction** 0.0s/f (Good)
WFA 3 from 5yo 11lb **7** Ran SP% **113.8**
Speed ratings (Par 104): **106,101,96,95,93 92,86**
toteswingers:1&2:£5.20, 1&3:£3.30, 2&3:£4.00 CSF £24.35 TOTE £5.40: £3.70, £4.50; EX 39.80.
Owner Direct Racing Club **Bred** Michael McGlynn **Trained** Nawton, N Yorks

FOCUS
This looked quite competitive beforehand, but turned out to be anything but.

NOTEBOOK
Madam Macie(IRE) made all to win unchallenged. A hefty rise beckons and whether she'll get her own way in front to such an extent next time remains to be seen, but she's clearly pretty useful on her day. (op 5-1)
Hot Rod Mamma(IRE) enjoyed a real purple patch last summer and looks to be peaking again now. She had no chance with the winner, but saw off the rest comfortably in the end. (tchd 5-1 and 7-1 in a place)
Parley(USA) had beaten the useful Zaina when making a winning start for this yard at Wolverhampton in February, but failed to build on that switched to handicaps on her return. It's still early days, though. (op 4-1)
Nemushka didn't have things go her way at Haydock, but there were no obvious excuses this time.
Jeannie Galloway(IRE) hasn't been at her best in a couple of her starts for her new yard. (op 11-1 tchd 8-1)
She's A Character was one of the first beaten and has been well below-par on both starts since her Doncaster win. (op 9-1)
Lady Layla was the disappointment of the race. There's got to be a chance she found this coming a little quick after her good reappearance, though, and she's not one to be giving up on just yet. Official explanation: trainer said that the filly was unsuited by the ground (good to firm, firm in places) (op 7-2)

2753 DIAMOND JUBILEE CARLISLE BELL TRIAL H'CAP (DIV I) 7f 200y
5:15 (5:15) (Class 4) (0-80,80) 4-Y-0+ **£4,851** (£1,443; £721; £360) **Stalls** Low

Form RPR

-005 **1** **Oratory (IRE)**[9] 2510 6-8-13 **72** MickyFenton 10 82
(Paul Midgley) *prom on outside: smooth hdwy to ld wl over 1f out: sn rdn: hld on wl u.p fnl f* **5/1**[2]

0116 **2** *½* **Lindoro**[12] 2406 7-8-6 **68** PaulPickard(3) 2 77
(Brian Ellison) *trckd ldrs: effrt on ins whn edgd lft over 1f out: ev ch ins fnl f: hld nr fin* **9/1**

-530 **3** *1 ½* **I'm Super Too (IRE)**[9] 2473 5-8-13 **77** GarryWhillans(5) 3 82
(Alan Swinbank) *in tch on ins: drvn over 2f out: kpt on fnl f: nt rch first two* **8/1**[3]

3-20 **4** *¾* **Invincible Hero (IRE)**[9] 2510 5-9-7 **80** DanielTudhope 5 84+
(Declan Carroll) *t.k.h: trckd ldr: effrt whn n.m.r over 1f out: kpt on same pce ins fnl f* **11/4**[1]

0333 **5** *1 ¼* **Moheebb (IRE)**[20] 2142 8-9-1 **74** (v) TonyHamilton 9 75
(Ruth Carr) *hld up: drvn and outpcd over 3f out: rallied fnl f: nrst fin* **8/1**[3]

1060 **6** *¾* **Chookie Avon**[7] 2535 5-8-9 **68** (p) JoeFanning 7 67
(Keith Dalgleish) *hld up: hdwy on outside 2f out: outpcd fnl f* **22/1**

00 **7** *1 ½* **Thatcherite (IRE)**[9] 2510 4-8-10 **72** (t) DaleSwift(3) 6 68
(Tony Coyle) *s.i.s: bhd: drvn over 3f out: sme late hdwy: nvr rchd ldrs* **16/1**

0-30 **8** *nk* **Miami Gator (IRE)**[48] 5-9-4 **80** (v) MichaelMetcalfe(3) 1 75
(Mrs K Burke) *led: rdn and jst hdd whn carried lft briefly over 1f out: outpcd fnl f* **9/1**

0-00 **9** *2 ½* **Kalk Bay (IRE)**[11] 2417 5-8-12 **78** DavidSimmonson(7) 4 67
(Michael Easterby) *hld up: drvn along over 2f out: btn over 1f out* **20/1**

-003 **10** *½* **Shadowtime**[3] 2675 7-8-10 **69** FrederikTylicki 8 57
(Tracy Waggott) *in tch on outside: hdwy and cl up 2f out: sn rdn: wknd fnl f* **5/1**[2]

1m 38.85s (-1.15) **Going Correction** 0.0s/f (Good) **10** Ran SP% **117.2**
Speed ratings (Par 105): **105,104,103,102,101 100,98,98,95,95**
toteswingers:1&2:£11.20, 1&3:£11.20, 2&3:£12.90 CSF £49.73 CT £366.41 TOTE £7.00: £2.20, £2.70, £1.40; EX 66.70.
Owner The Unique Partnership **Bred** Lynch Bages Ltd & Samac Ltd **Trained** Westow, N Yorks

FOCUS
A fair handicap which was run at a sound pace. The time was 0.58 seconds faster than the second division.

2754 DIAMOND JUBILEE CARLISLE BELL TRIAL H'CAP (DIV II) 7f 200y
5:50 (5:50) (Class 4) (0-80,80) 4-Y-0+ **£4,851** (£1,443; £721; £360) **Stalls** Low

Form RPR
0-40 **1** **Fastnet Storm (IRE)**[9] 2491 6-8-11 **70**........................ RoystonFfrench 3 81
(David Barron) *mde all: hrd pressed and rdn over 1f out: kpt on strly fnl f* **8/1**
-000 **2** *2 ¾* **Majestic Dream (IRE)**[9] 2504 4-8-13 **79**............. DavidSimmonson(7) 7 84
(Michael Easterby) *sn trcking wnr: rdn and ev ch over 1f out: kpt on same pce ins fnl f* **11/2**[3]
0103 **3** *1* **Solar Spirit (IRE)**[27] 1951 7-9-2 **80**............................... ShaneBKelly(5) 4 83
(Tracy Waggott) *plld hrd: sn prom: stdy hdwy over 2f out: effrt and rdn over 1f out: edgd rt: one pce fnl f* **5/1**[2]
3213 **4** *2 ¼* **Copperwood**[7] 2549 7-8-9 **68**..................................... JoeFanning 5 66
(Mark Johnston) *cl up: rdn over 2f out: nt qckn over 1f out* **10/3**[1]
1000 **5** *hd* **Nibani (IRE)**[9] 2510 5-8-13 **72**..(p) GrahamLee 8 69
(Alastair Lidderdale) *s.i.s: hld up: rdn over 2f out: styd on fnl f: nrst fin* **7/1**
0020 **6** *5* **Arabian Spirit**[28] 1914 7-8-9 **75**........................ GeorgeChaloner(7) 2 61
(Richard Fahey) *dwlt: hld up towards rr: drvn and outpcd over 2f out: sn btn* **11/2**[3]
0044 **7** *1 ¼* **Collateral Damage (IRE)**[20] 2142 9-8-12 **71**...............(t) KellyHarrison 9 54
(Tim Easterby) *in tch on outside: hdwy over 3f out: wknd fr 2f out* **5/1**[2]
0-60 **8** *9* **Flipping**[23] 2094 5-8-13 **72**... TomEaves 1 34
(Eric Alston) *hld up in tch on ins: rdn and struggling over 2f out: sn btn* **16/1**

1m 39.43s (-0.57) **Going Correction** 0.0s/f (Good) **8** Ran SP% **116.7**
Speed ratings (Par 105): **102,99,98,96,95 90,89,80**
toteswingers:1&2:£8.20, 1&3:£5.90, 2&3:£5.80 CSF £52.31 CT £245.23 TOTE £9.60: £3.10, £1.90, £1.70; EX 71.90.
Owner The Kittywake Partnership **Bred** Norelands Bloodstock **Trained** Maunby, N Yorks

FOCUS
This didn't have the look of a strong handicap for the level and the winning time was 0.58 seconds slower than the first division.
Fastnet Storm(IRE) Official explanation: trainer's representative could offer no explanation for the apparent improvement of form
T/Jkpt: Not won. T/Plt: £451.30 to a £1 stake. Pool £53,582.88 - 86.67 winning units. T/Qpdt: £172.20 to a £1 stake. Pool £3,166.25 - 13.60 winning units. RY

2571 CHEPSTOW (L-H)
Monday, June 4

OFFICIAL GOING: Soft changing to good to soft after race 2 (2.15)
Wind: Virtually nil Weather: Sunny spells

2755 BATH MARQUEES FILLIES' H'CAP 1m 4f 23y
2:40 (2:40) (Class 5) (0-75,75) 4-Y-0+ **£2,264** (£673; £336; £168) **Stalls** Low

Form RPR
31-0 **1** **Lily In Pink**[28] 1940 4-9-7 **75**... JamesDoyle 6 87
(Jonathan Portman) *in tch: hdwy 5f out: trckd ldr over 3f out: drvn to chal ins fnl 2f: sn led: clr whn reminder and hung lft ins fnl f: clr whn wandered rt fnl 100yds* **8/1**
4233 **2** *6* **Shy**[19] 2167 7-8-8 **62**...(b) CathyGannon 4 64
(Rod Millman) *led: rdn 3f out: jnd 2f out: hdd sn after and no ch w wnr but kpt on wl enough for 2nd* **3/1**[2]
50-0 **3** *1 ½* **Devoted (IRE)**[28] 1940 4-9-4 **72**..(p) JimCrowley 2 72
(Ralph Beckett) *chsd ldrs: drvn and awkward bnd 5f out: rdn and styd on to take 3rd over 1f out: no imp on ldng duo* **4/1**[3]
0-42 **4** *2 ¾* **New River (IRE)**[7] 2561 4-9-3 **71**.. PatDobbs 10 66
(Richard Hannon) *chsd ldr: rdn 4f out: little reponse and lost 2nd over 3f out: wknd 2f out* **11/4**[1]
5 *3 ¾* **Belleau (IRE)**[186] 7014 4-8-6 **65**.............................. CharlesBishop(5) 7 54
(Matt Sheppard) *slowly away: sn in tch: drvn and effrt 3f out: nvr rchd ldrs and sn no ch* **25/1**
000- **6** *2* **Astragal**[179] 7671 4-8-6 **60**.. DavidProbert 9 46
(Andrew Balding) *rdn 5f out: a in rr* **14/1**
32-2 **7** *4 ½* **Agadir Summer**[51] 1380 4-9-6 **74**...................................... MartinLane 3 53
(David Simcock) *in tch: rdn 6f out: btn fnl 4f* **5/1**

2m 39.57s (0.57) **Going Correction** +0.175s/f (Good) **7** Ran SP% **110.0**
Speed ratings (Par 100): **105,101,100,98,95 94,91**
toteswingers:1&2:£3.80, 2&3:£3.10, 1&3:£5.20 CSF £29.70 CT £102.80 TOTE £9.10: £2.50, £2.30; EX 34.40.
Owner Miss Sarah Lloyd **Bred** J Ford & Peter J Skinner **Trained** Compton, Berks

FOCUS
A weak fillies' handicap won by one of the least exposed.
Lily In Pink Official explanation: trainer said, regarding the apparent improvment of form, that the filly was sharper following her previous run, which was her first of the season.

2756 PREMIER FOOD COURTS LTD H'CAP 1m 14y
3:15 (3:16) (Class 5) (0-70,70) 3-Y-0 **£2,264** (£673; £336; £168) **Stalls** Centre

Form RPR
00-3 **1** **Derfenna Art (IRE)**[21] 2128 3-9-3 **66**..............................(t) JimCrowley 2 74
(Seamus Durack) *stdd in rr: hdwy to trck ldrs over 3f out: led over 2f out: rdn and styd on strly appr fnl f: kpt on wl* **8/1**
6-54 **2** *1 ½* **Emperor Vespasian**[29] 1894 3-9-7 **70**........................ DavidProbert 10 74
(Andrew Balding) *hld up in rr: pushed along over 2f out: styd on fnl f to chse wnr fnl 120yds: no imp in clsng stages* **15/2**
1-04 **3** *2 ½* **Tiger Cub**[7] 2557 3-9-7 **70**.......................................(t) GeorgeBaker 4 69
(Mikael Magnusson) *led tl hdd over 2f out: sn rdn: no ch w wnr over 1f out: lost 2nd fnl 120yds* **8/1**
6-00 **4** *1* **Netley Marsh**[21] 2126 3-9-1 **67**.. SeanLevey(3) 11 63
(Richard Hannon) *s.i.s: sn rcvrd: rdn to chse ldrs 3f out: one pce fnl 2f* **9/1**
30-6 **5** *shd* **Lady Percy (IRE)**[21] 2128 3-8-6 **58**............................ HarryBentley(3) 12 54
(Mark Usher) *pressed ldrs to 1/2-way: styd chsng ldrs: rdn and btn ins fnl 2f* **14/1**
0-20 **6** *2 ¾* **Uncle Roger (IRE)**[34] 1728 3-9-5 **68**.................................... LiamKeniry 7 58
(Eve Johnson Houghton) *chsd ldrs: rdn 3f out: wknd fr 2f out* **13/2**[2]
00-1 **7** *2 ½* **Golden Jubilee (USA)**[21] 2128 3-9-3 **66**............................. PatDobbs 8 50
(Richard Hannon) *broke wl: stdd in rr: rdn over 3f out: little rspnse and no ch after: mod prog fnl f* **5/2**[1]
00-0 **8** *3* **Marhoona (USA)**[16] 2279 3-9-5 **68**................................... TadhgO'Shea 5 45
(John Dunlop) *rdn over 3f out: a in rr* **25/1**
0-05 **9** *2 ½* **Wyndham Wave**[21] 2128 3-9-2 **65**..................................... JamesDoyle 3 36
(Rod Millman) *chsd ldrs: rdn 3f out: sn btn* **7/1**[3]
04-0 **10** *2 ½* **Poetry Writer**[7] 2557 3-9-5 **68**... DaneO'Neill 1 34
(Michael Blanshard) *chsd ldrs over 5f* **22/1**
04-0 **11** *3 ½* **Sir Dylan**[31] 1824 3-9-3 **66**... LukeMorris 9 23
(Ronald Harris) *rdn and bhd fr 1/2-way* **16/1**

1m 37.3s (1.10) **Going Correction** +0.175s/f (Good) **11** Ran SP% **119.1**
Speed ratings (Par 99): **101,99,97,96,95 93,90,87,85,82 79**
toteswingers:1&2:£9.00, 2&3:£8.60, 1&3:£5.80 CSF £67.74 CT £513.44 TOTE £8.90: £2.10, £3.00, £1.90; EX 57.10.
Owner Mrs Anne Cowley **Bred** M Gaffney **Trained** Baydon, Wilts

FOCUS
The pace was only steady in this moderate handicap which favoured those ridden prominently. The runners came up the centre of the track.

2757 BRITISH STALLION STUDS SUPPORTING BRITISH RACING E B F MAIDEN FILLIES' STKS 7f 16y
3:50 (3:51) (Class 5) 3-Y-0+ **£3,557** (£1,058; £529; £264) **Stalls** Centre

Form RPR
00-4 **1** **Tea Cup**[16] 2273 3-8-12 84.. PatDobbs 8 72+
(Richard Hannon) *t.k.h in tch: hdwy 3f out: chsd ldr 2f out: drvn to ld ins fnl f: readily* **5/4**[1]
40 **2** *¾* **Swift Act**[52] 1363 3-8-12 0.. JamesDoyle 4 67
(Ronald Harris) *chsd ldr to 2f out: sn rdn: kpt on fnl f to retake 2nd in clsng stages but no ch w ready wnr* **16/1**
2544 **3** *1 ¼* **Nevaeh**[7] 2554 3-8-12 67..(p) LukeMorris 6 64
(Pat Eddery) *in tch: rdn and outpcd over 2f out: styd on again fnl f: gng on cl home to take 3rd but nvr a threat to wnr* **10/1**
0 **4** *nk* **Missus Mills (IRE)**[26] 1981 3-8-12 0.............................. PatCosgrave 1 63
(George Baker) *led: rdn over 1f out: hdd ins fnl f: wknd and lost two pls in clsng stages* **33/1**
0- **5** *shd* **Heyaaraat (IRE)**[219] 7165 3-8-12 0.................................. TadhgO'Shea 5 63
(Charles Hills) *s.i.s: in rr: rdn over 2f out: styd on ins fnl f but nvr gng pce to get into contention* **10/3**[2]
20- **6** *2 ¼* **Scarlet Belle**[221] 7124 3-8-9 0.................................. HarryBentley(3) 7 57
(Marcus Tregoning) *chsd ldrs: outpcd over 2f out: styd on again ins fnl f* **8/1**
4-0 **7** *9* **Red Hot Secret**[16] 2273 3-8-7 0.................................... RaulDaSilva(5) 9 33
(Jeremy Gask) *chsd ldrs 4f* **5/1**[3]
00 **8** *7* **Pass The Time**[7] 2543 3-8-13 0 ow1...................................... AdamKirby 2 15
(Neil Mulholland) *a in rr* **66/1**
9 *1 ¾* **Charity Rainbow**[68] 5-9-5 0... RyanPowell(3) 3
(Brendan Powell) *wnt lft s and slowly away: rcvrd and in tch 4f out: wknd 3f out* **50/1**

1m 25.71s (2.51) **Going Correction** +0.175s/f (Good)
WFA 3 from 5yo 10lb **9** Ran SP% **116.7**
Speed ratings (Par 100): **92,91,89,89,89 86,76,68,66**
toteswingers:1&2:£5.10, 2&3:£9.60, 1&3:£3.30 CSF £25.35 TOTE £2.10: £1.10, £3.60, £2.10; EX 12.10.
Owner P A Byrne **Bred** H Q Spooner **Trained** East Everleigh, Wilts

FOCUS
The ground had dried out prior to the this race and the official going was changed to Good to soft. A weak fillies' maiden and a slow time.

2758 MEDINET H'CAP 7f 16y
4:25 (4:25) (Class 5) (0-75,75) 4-Y-0+ **£2,264** (£673; £336; £168) **Stalls** Centre

Form RPR
4-01 **1** **George Benjamin**[54] 1294 5-8-12 **73**................................ RyanWhile(7) 4 81+
(Bill Turner) *trckd ldr: led over 3f out: shkn up fnl f: comf* **5/2**[1]
0250 **2** *1 ¼* **Spinning Ridge (IRE)**[12] 2399 7-9-2 **70**.......................(b) LukeMorris 2 75
(Ronald Harris) *chsd ldrs: rdn to chse wnr appr fnl f: kpt on but no ch w wnr* **17/2**
600- **3** *2* **Great Charm (IRE)**[362] 2806 7-9-6 **74**........................... GeorgeBaker 10 74
(Daniel Kubler) *racd on stands' rail: chsd wnr over 3f out: rdn 2f out: no imp on wnr: one pce into 3rd appr fnl f* **11/2**
0-04 **4** *¾* **Sir Bruno (FR)**[14] 2355 5-9-4 **72**.................................... DavidProbert 5 70
(Bryn Palling) *chsd ldrs: rdn 3f out: one pce fnl 2f* **11/2**
-150 **5** *1 ¼* **Aqua Ardens (GER)**[28] 1935 4-9-5 **73**............................. PatCosgrave 8 67
(George Baker) *in rr: rdn and sme hdwy fr 2f out: nvr gng pce to rch ldrs* **16/1**
0540 **6** *1 ¾* **Arctic Mirage**[19] 2171 4-8-5 **59**.. CathyGannon 7 48
(Michael Blanshard) *sn pushed along: in tch and stl drvn fr 3f out: kpt on same pce* **4/1**[2]
5350 **7** *9* **Fleetwoodsands (IRE)**[66] 1117 5-8-3 **60**.................(t) HarryBentley(3) 9 25
(Milton Bradley) *rrd s and slowly away: sn rcvrd and in tch 4f out: rdn 3f out: wknd 2f out* **5/1**[3]
0-00 **8** *16* **Regency Art (IRE)**[11] 2421 5-8-8 **62**...................................(p) LiamKeniry 3
(Milton Bradley) *chsd ldr tl wknd over 3f out* **40/1**

1m 24.61s (1.41) **Going Correction** +0.175s/f (Good) **8** Ran SP% **114.9**
Speed ratings (Par 103): **98,96,94,93,92 90,79,61**
toteswingers:1&2:£4.50, 2&3:£7.50, 1&3:£6.90 CSF £24.94 CT £107.99 TOTE £2.40: £1.70, £1.70, £2.30; EX 9.10.
Owner Anthony Knott **Bred** Mascalls Stud **Trained** Sigwells, Somerset

FOCUS
A moderate handicap run at a decent pace so the form should hold up. The runners tracked across to the stands' rail.

2759 ELITE RACING CLUB FILLIES' H'CAP 6f 16y
5:00 (5:00) (Class 5) (0-70,70) 3-Y-0 **£2,264** (£673; £336; £168) **Stalls** Centre

Form RPR
30-1 **1** **Athenian (IRE)**[7] 2547 3-9-4 **67** 6ex...................................... LukeMorris 3 77+
(Sir Mark Prescott Bt) *chsd ldrs: drvn along 3f out: led 2f out: rdn to assert fnl f: styd on strly* **8/13**[1]
1635 **2** *1 ¾* **Ficelle (IRE)**[6] 2573 3-9-1 **64**.. DavidProbert 4 68
(Ronald Harris) *in rr but in tch: rdn 2f out: styd on to chse wnr fnl f but no imp* **12/1**
3-04 **3** *1* **Little Rainbow**[18] 2206 3-9-0 **63**.. AdamKirby 10 64
(Clive Cox) *racd towards stands' side: hdwy to chse ldrs 3f out: rdn 2f out: kpt on same pce ins fnl f* **11/2**[2]
-513 **4** *2 ½* **Wiltshire Life (IRE)**[18] 2205 3-9-1 **69**......................(p) RaulDaSilva(5) 1 62
(Jeremy Gask) *led tl hdd 2f out: lost 2nd 1f out: wknd ins fnl f* **6/1**[3]
00-0 **5** *shd* **Aquasulis (IRE)**[9] 2503 3-9-7 **70**...................................... CathyGannon 5 62
(David Evans) *chsd ldr: rdn 3f out: lost 2nd 2f out: styd on same pce u.p* **33/1**
35-0 **6** *11* **Ida Inkley (IRE)**[34] 1733 3-8-13 **62**.................................... JamesDoyle 9 19
(Jonathan Portman) *racd stands' side: spd to 1/2-way* **25/1**

0-05 **7** *2* **Subtle Embrace (IRE)**[28] 1941 3-8-12 **61** JimCrowley 8 12
(Harry Dunlop) *in tch chsd ldrs over 3f out: sn wknd* **20/1**

6-50 **8** *3* **Molly Jones**[47] 1445 3-9-1 **64** DaneO'Neill 2
(Derek Haydn Jones) *rrd in stalls and slowly away: effrt to cl 1/2-way but a struggling and wknd sn after* **11/1**

1m 12.68s (0.68) **Going Correction** +0.175s/f (Good) **8** Ran SP% **119.2**
Speed ratings (Par 96): **102,99,98,95,94 80,77,73**
toteswingers:1&2:£2.60, 2&3:£4.10, 1&3:£1.90 CSF £10.07 CT £27.48 TOTE £1.70: £1.10, £2.80, £2.30; EX 12.20.
Owner Axom (XXXI) **Bred** Keatly Overseas Ltd **Trained** Newmarket, Suffolk

FOCUS
Little strength in depth to this 3yo fillies' handicap which went to the well-backed favourite.

2760 CHEPSTOW ANNUAL MEMBERS H'CAP (DIV I) 6f 16y
5:35 (5:35) (Class 6) (0-60,66) 4-Y-O+ **£1,617** (£481; £240; £120) **Stalls** Centre

Form RPR

4314 **1** **Lady Mango (IRE)**[7] 2546 4-9-3 **56** LukeMorris 6 65
(Ronald Harris) *in tch: rdn and outpcd over 3f out: rdn and rallied fr over 1f out: styd on wl u.p fnl f: edgd rt in clsng stages and led last strides* **9/2**[2]

0-01 **2** *shd* **Mary's Pet**[26] 1987 5-9-5 **58** (p) KierenFox 7 67
(Lee Carter) *led: rdn fnl f: kpt on tl hdd last strides* **9/2**[2]

50-0 **3** *2 1/4* **Greyemkay**[28] 1910 4-8-0 **53** DanielMuscutt(7) 9 47
(Richard Price) *in rr: hdwy 2f out: styd on to take 3rd ins fnl f but nt gng pce to rch ldng duo* **33/1**

00-3 **4** *1 3/4* **Trade Centre**[45] 1497 7-8-11 **50** DaneO'Neill 10 46
(Milton Bradley) *broke wl to chse ldr early: rdn and outpcd over 3f out: rallied u.p over 1f out: kpt on fnl f but nvr gng pce to chal* **7/2**[1]

0600 **5** *1 1/2* **Royal Box**[7] 2555 5-9-1 **54** (p) CathyGannon 5 45
(David Evans) *in rr: bdly outpcd and rdn over 3f out: hdwy over 1f out: keeping on whn nt clr run ins fnl f: swtchd rt: styd on again cl home* **7/1**

00-5 **6** *nk* **Quadra Hop (IRE)**[45] 1497 4-8-4 **48** RaulDaSilva(5) 12 38
(Bryn Palling) *chsd ldr 4f out: rdn 3f out: wknd ins fnl f* **8/1**

1302 **7** *nk* **Beachwood Bay**[27] 1958 4-9-7 **60** TadhgO'Shea 14 49
(Jo Hughes) *in tch: styd on to chse ldrs 1/2-way: wknd fnl f* **5/1**[3]

50-0 **8** *2* **Dualagi**[11] 2421 8-9-4 **57** GeorgeBaker 11 40+
(Martin Bosley) *in rr: hdwy on ins whn hmpd over 1f out: n.d after* **9/1**

0060 **9** *13* **Striking Willow**[124] 379 4-8-7 **46** oh1 DavidProbert 3
(Nikki Evans) *chsd ldrs over 3f* **40/1**

0244 **10** *8* **Deveze (IRE)**[81] 910 4-8-10 **49** (b) LiamKeniry 13
(Milton Bradley) *chsd ldrs: wknd 3f out: hung rt over 2f out* **25/1**

1m 12.98s (0.98) **Going Correction** +0.175s/f (Good) **10** Ran SP% **118.1**
Speed ratings (Par 101): **100,99,96,94,92 92,91,89,71,61**
toteswingers:1&2:£4.20, 2&3:£19.30, 1&3:£21.30 CSF £25.02 CT £600.78 TOTE £6.60: £1.90, £1.70, £6.00; EX 23.00.
Owner L Scadding & Mrs S Peachey-Scadding **Bred** Mount Coote Stud **Trained** Earlswood, Monmouths

FOCUS
Not many got into this with the runner-up setting a strong tempo only to be denied close home. The winning time was 0.18 seconds slower than the second division.

2761 CHEPSTOW ANNUAL MEMBERS H'CAP (DIV II) 6f 16y
6:05 (6:05) (Class 6) (0-60,60) 4-Y-O+ **£1,617** (£481; £240; £120) **Stalls** Centre

Form RPR

15-0 **1** **Full Shilling (IRE)**[46] 1481 4-9-6 **59** JamesDoyle 13 73
(John Spearing) *stdd s: hld up in rr: stdy hdwy fr 2f out: led 1f out: drvn clr ins fnl f* **3/1**[2]

0520 **2** *2 3/4* **Flaxen Lake**[45] 1497 5-8-13 **52** (p) LukeMorris 6 57
(Milton Bradley) *in rr: hrd rdn and hdwy fr 2f out: styd on u.p fnl f to take 2nd fnl 120yds but no ch w wnr* **8/1**

0-00 **3** *1 1/4* **Scommettitrice (IRE)**[35] 1722 4-8-7 **46** (b) CathyGannon 8 47
(David Evans) *chsd ldrs: chal fr 3f out and stl upsides over 1f out: outpcd by wnr ins fnl f and styd on one pce for 3rd fnl 120yds* **15/2**

0025 **4** *1 1/4* **Yanza**[12] 2386 6-8-8 **50** SeanLevey(3) 10 47
(Pam Ford) *chsd ldrs: chal fr 3f out tl narrow ld over 1f out: sn hdd: one pce ins fnl f* **7/1**[3]

0060 **5** *3/4* **Portrush Storm**[31] 1830 7-7-7 **46** oh1 DavidProbert 5 41
(Ray Peacock) *pressed ldr tl led narrowly fr 3f out: narrowly hdd over 1f out: stl ev ch tl wknd ins fnl f* **25/1**

6413 **6** *hd* **Gracie's Games**[24] 2046 6-8-12 **58** (v) DanielMuscutt(7) 3 52
(Richard Price) *in tch hdwy to trck ldrs and nt clr run over 1f out: sn shkn up and no imp fnl f* **11/4**[1]

0055 **7** *1/2* **Mucky Molly**[28] 1934 4-8-9 **48** LiamKeniry 1 40
(Olivia Maylam) *chsd ldrs: rdn 2f out: sn outpcd* **7/1**[3]

-000 **8** *6* **Decimate**[54] 1306 4-8-11 **57** DavidWarren(7) 12 30
(Andrew Reid) *a outpcd* **14/1**

00-0 **9** *11* **Botanist**[11] 2421 5-9-7 **60** DaneO'Neill 2
(Milton Bradley) *t.k.h: sn led: hdd & wknd 3f out* **14/1**

1m 12.8s (0.80) **Going Correction** +0.175s/f (Good) **9** Ran SP% **116.7**
Speed ratings (Par 101): **101,97,95,94,93 92,92,84,69**
toteswingers:1&2:£4.80, 2&3:£5.50, 1&3:£6.30 CSF £27.68 CT £166.65 TOTE £4.70: £1.80, £1.90, £2.60; EX 36.40.
Owner Not The Full Shilling Syndicate **Bred** Michael Dalton **Trained** Kinnersley, Worcs

FOCUS
A modest handicap but there was a contested lead which resulted in a strong pace, this favoured those ridden with restraint. The runners came up the centre of the track and the winning time was 0.18 seconds faster than the first division.

2762 BECOME AN ANNUAL MEMBER AT CHEPSTOW H'CAP 5f 16y
6:35 (6:35) (Class 6) (0-60,60) 3-Y-O **£1,617** (£481; £240; £120) **Stalls** Centre

Form RPR

4042 **1** **Seventeen Seventy**[5] 2610 3-9-2 **55** LiamKeniry 1 62
(Alan Coogan) *pressed ldrs: slt ld 2f out: hrd pressed fr over 1f out: asserted u.p ins fnl f: styd on wl* **9/2**[3]

4565 **2** *1* **First Rebellion**[12] 2388 3-8-7 **46** oh1 DavidProbert 3 49
(Tony Carroll) *prssed ldrs: str chal fr 2f out and stl upsides 1f out: nt gng pce of wnr ins fnl f: hld on wl for 2nd in clsng stages* **4/1**[2]

5241 **3** *hd* **Trending (IRE)**[12] 2388 3-8-12 **56** (b) RaulDaSilva(5) 6 58
(Jeremy Gask) *in rr: hdwy over 1f out: styd on u.p fnl f to press for 2nd in clsng stages but no imp on wnr* **1/1**[1]

-630 **4** *shd* **Bitter Lemon**[53] 1337 3-9-0 **53** DaneO'Neill 2 55
(Tony Newcombe) *in rr but in tch: hdwy to chse ldrs 2f out: chal 1f out: kpt on same pce ins fnl f and lost 3rd cl home* **12/1**

0-60 **5** *4 1/2* **Maltease Ah**[41] 1585 3-8-5 **51** DavidWarren(7) 7 37
(Andrew Reid) *s.i.s: sn chsng ldrs: wknd appr fnl f* **33/1**

3451 **6** *4* **My Name Is Sam**[46] 1482 3-9-7 **60** (b) LukeMorris 8 31
(Ronald Harris) *sn led: hdd 2f out: wknd wl over 1f out* **15/2**

00-6 **7** *2 1/4* **Ewenny Star**[66] 1111 3-8-0 **46** oh1 (b[1]) DanielMuscutt(7) 9
(Bryn Palling) *in tch to 1/2-way* **50/1**

1m 1.14s (1.84) **Going Correction** +0.175s/f (Good) **7** Ran SP% **112.5**
Speed ratings (Par 97): **92,90,90,89,82 76,72**
toteswingers:1&2:£2.60, 2&3:£1.60, 1&3:£2.00 CSF £21.97 CT £30.47 TOTE £5.20: £1.60, £1.70; EX 24.10.
Owner A B Coogan **Bred** Leydens Farm Stud **Trained** Soham, Cambs

FOCUS
Modest fare but the pace was solid thanks to My Name Is Sam, who predictably weakened after doing too much in the early stages.
T/Plt: £112.50 to a £1 stake. Pool £60,650.37 - 393.53 winning units. T/Qpdt: £4.70 to a £1 stake. Pool £4,552.64 - 715.90 winning units. ST

2549 LEICESTER (R-H)
Monday, June 4

OFFICIAL GOING: Soft (good to soft in places; 7.3)
Wind: Light half-behind Weather: Cloudy with sunny spells

2763 BEECHWOODMG.CO.UK MEDIAN AUCTION MAIDEN STKS 5f 2y
2:00 (2:00) (Class 6) 2-Y-O **£1,940** (£577; £288; £144) **Stalls** High

Form RPR

52 **1** **Forray**[14] 2330 2-9-3 0 RichardMullen 6 84
(Ed McMahon) *trckd ldr tl led 1/2-way: rdn and hung rt fr over 1f out: r.o* **9/4**[2]

3 **2** *2 3/4* **Echion (IRE)**[18] 2202 2-9-3 0 RyanMoore 4 74
(Richard Hannon) *led to 1/2-way: sn rdn: styd on same pce fnl f* **2/1**[1]

25 **3** *hd* **Barracuda Boy (IRE)**[23] 2073 2-9-3 0 RichardKingscote 3 73
(Tom Dascombe) *chsd ldrs: rdn and ev ch over 1f out: no ex ins fnl f* **17/2**[3]

2 **4** *1* **Bairam**[18] 2202 2-9-3 0 PaulHanagan 1 70
(Brian Meehan) *s.i.s: sn chsng ldrs: pushed along 1/2-way: rdn and ev ch over 1f out: no ex ins fnl f* **2/1**[1]

5 *12* **Miss Starry Eyed** 2-8-12 0 NeilCallan 5 22
(Derek Shaw) *s.s: sn prom: pushed along 1/2-way: wknd over 1f out* **100/1**

6 *21* **Star Maid** 2-8-12 0 MichaelO'Connell 2
(Tony Carroll) *hld up in tch: racd keenly: wknd 1/2-way: t.o* **150/1**

1m 3.24s (3.24) **Going Correction** +0.425s/f (Yiel) **6** Ran SP% **109.6**
Speed ratings (Par 91): **91,86,86,84,65 31**
toteswingers:1&2:£1.40, 2&3:£3.10, 1&3:£2.60 CSF £6.79 TOTE £3.30: £2.00, £1.90; EX 7.90.
Owner J C Fretwell **Bred** Anthony Morris **Trained** Lichfield, Staffs

FOCUS
Only four really mattered in this ordinary maiden.

NOTEBOOK
Forray improved from his debut to finish runner-up over C&D last month and took another step forward here. He still looked a bit green when hanging away to his right from over a furlong out, but was still much too good for these. There should be more to come, but he remains unproven on fast ground. (op 11-4)
Echion(IRE) finished just behind Bairam on his Salisbury debut and managed to turn that form around, but he was completely done for foot by the winner in the latter stages. (op 9-4 tchd 15-8)
Barracuda Boy(IRE) didn't see out the sixth furlong at Haydock on his second start and seemed happier back over the minimum, but he too couldn't match the winner's turn of foot. He is another yet to encounter quick ground. (op 9-1 tchd 8-1)
Bairam didn't confirm the promise of his Salisbury debut as might have been hoped, but he was being niggled at halfway and this trip looks too sharp for him now, which is backed up by his pedigree. (op 7-4)

2764 SMOOTH RADIO H'CAP 5f 218y
2:30 (2:31) (Class 4) (0-80,80) 3-Y-O **£5,175** (£1,540; £769; £384) **Stalls** High

Form RPR

5-14 **1** **Khubala (IRE)**[34] 1730 3-8-13 **72** (b[1]) RyanMoore 6 85
(Ed Dunlop) *hld up: hdwy over 2f out: led over 1f out: drvn out* **9/1**

6-21 **2** *1* **Our Boy Jack (IRE)**[10] 2459 3-9-4 **77** PaulHanagan 10 87
(Richard Fahey) *chsd ldrs: rdn over 2f out: styd on* **3/1**[1]

60-0 **3** *nk* **Goldream**[40] 1612 3-9-3 **76** KirstyMilczarek 4 85
(Luca Cumani) *hld up in tch: led 2f out: rdn and hdd over 1f out: styd on* **7/2**[2]

-504 **4** *2 3/4* **Mister Musicmaster**[14] 2347 3-9-6 **79** DarryllHolland 11 79
(Rod Millman) *prom: rdn over 2f out: styd on same pce fnl f* **10/1**

0-34 **5** *nk* **Lunar Deity**[3] 2659 3-9-7 **80** JohnFahy 7 79
(Eve Johnson Houghton) *hld up: swtchd rt over 2f out: sn rdn: hdwy over 1f out: nt trble ldrs* **7/2**[2]

2132 **6** *1 1/2* **Reve Du Jour (IRE)**[12] 2400 3-8-11 **70** ShaneKelly 12 64
(Alan McCabe) *chsd ldr tl led over 4f out: rdn and hdd 2f out: no ex fnl f* **12/1**

0-00 **7** *6* **Hot Sugar (USA)**[16] 2265 3-9-1 **74** NeilCallan 14 49
(Kevin Ryan) *led: hdd over 4f out: rdn and wknd over 1f out* **7/1**[3]

43-4 **8** *17* **Not Bad For A Boy (IRE)**[136] 230 3-9-1 **74** TomQueally 1
(Barry Leavy) *hld up: wknd 1/2-way* **20/1**

1m 15.4s (2.40) **Going Correction** +0.425s/f (Yiel) **8** Ran SP% **113.5**
Speed ratings (Par 101): **101,99,99,95,95 93,85,62**
toteswingers:1&2:£3.50, 2&3:£4.60, 1&3:£7.20 CSF £35.67 CT £113.48 TOTE £10.10: £2.60, £1.70, £1.80; EX 30.40.
Owner Miss P Araci **Bred** James F Hanly **Trained** Newmarket, Suffolk

FOCUS
This race was the hardest hit for non-runners with seven coming out on account of the ground, but an interesting handicap nonetheless.
Hot Sugar(USA) Official explanation: vet said gelding had lost a near fore shoe

2765 GILMORTON (S) STKS 1m 1f 218y
3:05 (3:06) (Class 6) 3-5-Y-O **£2,045** (£603; £302) **Stalls** Low

Form RPR

3002 **1** **Mighty Clarets (IRE)**[14] 2329 5-9-6 64 TomQueally 4 61
(Barry Leavy) *led 3f: chsd ldr tl led again over 2f out: rdn and hung rt fr over 1f out: all out* **2/1**[1]

60-0 **2** *3/4* **Iulus**[9] 2473 4-9-6 71 MichaelO'Connell 2 60
(John Quinn) *w ldr: led 7f out: hdd over 2f out: sn rdn: styd on same pce ins fnl f* **2/1**[1]

0-40 **3** *3/4* **No Time To Cry**[20] 2141 3-8-2 53 (p) PaulQuinn 8 52
(Ann Duffield) *chsd ldrs: rdn over 3f out: styd on* **17/2**[3]

6000 **4** *2 3/4* **Wreaths Of Empire (IRE)**[11] 2424 3-8-7 58 PaulHanagan 10 52
(Richard Hannon) *prom: rdn over 3f out: no ex fnl f* **7/2**[2]

00-0 **5** *6* **Ladram Bay (IRE)**[47] 1443 3-8-2 31 .... FrannyNorton 3 35
(Jonathan Portman) *hld up: bhd 1/2-way: hmpd over 2f out: n.d* **50/1**

00/0 **6** *1 3/4* **Jessica Ashton**[18] 2204 4-9-1 37 .... (b[1]) FergusSweeney 5 32
(Stuart Kittow) *s.i.s: hld up: hdwy over 3f out: sn rdn: wknd over 1f out* **40/1**

00- **7** *3* **Oakdown**[354] 3080 4-8-13 0 .... JacobButterfield(7) 6 31
(Richard Price) *prom: rdn 4f out: wknd 3f out: sn hung rt* **33/1**

8 *56* **Bez** 4-9-6 0 .... (b[1]) WilliamCarson 7
(Nicky Vaughan) *hld up: rdn over 4f out: sn wknd: t.o* **22/1**

2m 14.1s (6.20) **Going Correction** +0.425s/f (Yiel)
WFA 3 from 4yo+ 13lb **8** Ran SP% **111.1**
Speed ratings (Par 101): **92,91,90,88,83 82,80,35**
toteswingers:1&2:£2.10, 2&3:£4.10, 1&3:£3.50 CSF £5.60 TOTE £3.00: £1.70, £2.00, £1.20; EX 7.30.There was no bid for the winner
Owner Cops & Robbers **Bred** Ellesmere Bloodstock Ltd **Trained** Forsbrook, Staffs

FOCUS
A poor seller, dominated by the two best in at the weights, and there was never much between the pair throughout the contest.

2766 LEICESTER MERCURY FILLIES' H'CAP 7f 9y
3:40 (3:40) (Class 4) (0-80,79) 4-Y-O+
£4,980 (£1,491; £745; £372; £186; £93) **Stalls** High

Form RPR

5-03 **1** **Russian Rave**[23] 2067 6-9-6 **78** .... StephenCraine 3 89
(Jonathan Portman) *hld up: hdwy 1/2-way: rdn over 1f out: hung rt ins fnl f: r.o to ld post* **7/2[1]**

-210 **2** *shd* **Choral**[23] 2083 4-9-6 **78** .... RyanMoore 9 88
(Richard Hannon) *s.i.s: sn pushed along in rr: swtchd rt and hdwy over 2f out: led and edgd lft over 1f out: sn rdn: hdd post* **6/1[3]**

34-0 **3** *2 1/4* **Fenella Fudge**[13] 2373 4-8-6 **64** ow1 .... MartinDwyer 6 68
(Derek Shaw) *stdd s: hld up: hdwy over 1f out: r.o: nt rch ldrs* **20/1**

5240 **4** *nk* **Shes Rosie**[19] 2165 4-8-10 **68** .... FergusSweeney 7 71
(John O'Shea) *chsd ldr tl led over 2f out: rdn and hdd over 1f out: styd on same pce ins fnl f* **12/1**

-212 **5** *3 1/2* **Viking Rose (IRE)**[10] 2465 4-8-13 **71** .... WilliamBuick 10 65
(James Eustace) *trckd ldrs: rdn over 1f out: no ex ins fnl f* **7/2[1]**

0-13 **6** *2 3/4* **Miss Bootylishes**[19] 2161 7-9-2 **79** .... DavidKenny(5) 4 66
(Paul Burgoyne) *chsd ldrs tl rdn and wknd over 1f out* **16/1**

00-6 **7** *nk* **Mrs Greeley**[16] 2274 4-9-2 **74** .... WilliamCarson 2 60
(Eve Johnson Houghton) *prom: rdn over 1f out: wknd fnl f* **9/2[2]**

3-01 **8** *22* **Sairaam (IRE)**[7] 2549 6-8-11 **69** 6ex .... KirstyMilczarek 8
(Charles Smith) *led over 4f: wknd over 1f out: t.o* **12/1**

220- **9** *11* **Little Curtsey**[224] 7054 4-9-7 **79** .... DarryllHolland 1
(Hughie Morrison) *prom: pushed along over 2f out: rdn and wknd wl over 1f out: t.o* **7/1**

1m 28.74s (2.54) **Going Correction** +0.425s/f (Yiel) **9** Ran SP% **115.4**
Speed ratings (Par 102): **102,101,99,98,94 91,91,66,53**
toteswingers:1&2:£5.20, 2&3:£18.00, 1&3:£13.00 CSF £24.71 CT £365.87 TOTE £4.20: £1.20, £2.40, £7.10; EX 28.80.
Owner The Traditionalists **Bred** P A & M J Reditt & Morton Bloodstock **Trained** Compton, Berks

FOCUS
A fair fillies' handicap rated around the winner.
Sairaam(IRE) Official explanation: jockey said that the mare was unsuited by the ground, which was soft, good to soft in places
Little Curtsey Official explanation: vet said the filly bled from the nose

2767 LEICESTER MERCURY H'CAP 1m 1f 218y
4:15 (4:15) (Class 5) (0-70,69) 4-Y-O+ **£2,587** (£770; £384; £192) **Stalls** Low

Form RPR

2256 **1** **Cane Cat (IRE)**[15] 1533 5-8-5 **60** .... (t) GeorgeDowning(7) 11 69
(Tony Carroll) *hld up: nt clr run over 2f out: swtchd lft and hdwy over 1f out: edgd rt wl ins fnl f: styd on to ld nr fin* **14/1**

0431 **2** *3/4* **The Lock Master (IRE)**[12] 2405 5-9-3 **65** .... TomQueally 6 72
(Michael Appleby) *led 2f: chsd ldr tl led again over 2f out: sn rdn: hdd nr fin* **15/8[1]**

420- **3** *1/2* **Ice Nelly (IRE)**[203] 7413 4-9-4 **66** .... DarryllHolland 3 72
(Hughie Morrison) *trckd ldrs: racd keenly: rdn and ev ch ins fnl f: unable qck nr fin* **9/4[2]**

0-61 **4** *1 3/4* **Bold Cross (IRE)**[12] 2389 9-8-11 **64** .... MatthewCosham(5) 5 68
(Edward Bevan) *dwlt: hld up: hdwy 1/2-way: rdn over 1f out: styng on same pce whn hmpd wl ins fnl f* **7/1[3]**

2-00 **5** *2 1/2* **Arashi**[21] 2134 6-8-11 **59** .... MartinDwyer 9 57
(Derek Shaw) *chsd ldr tl led 8f out: rdn and hdd over 2f out: no ex fnl f* **14/1**

200- **6** *10* **Burza**[292] 5178 6-8-12 **60** .... FrannyNorton 7 38
(Pat Murphy) *chsd ldrs: rdn over 2f out: hmpd and wknd wl over 1f out* **9/1**

0 **7** *nk* **Taroum (IRE)**[12] 2389 5-8-8 **63** .... AidenBlakemore(7) 1 40
(Tony Carroll) *hld up: racd keenly: nvr on terms* **33/1**

3040 **8** *31* **Yourinthewill (USA)**[12] 2389 4-9-3 **65** .... ShaneKelly 8
(Daniel Mark Loughnane) *hld up in tch: rdn over 3f out: wknd over 2f out: eased: t.o* **11/1**

2m 12.34s (4.44) **Going Correction** +0.425s/f (Yiel) **8** Ran SP% **112.7**
Speed ratings (Par 103): **99,98,98,96,94 86,86,61**
toteswingers:1&2:£3.40, 2&3:£1.80, 1&3:£5.70 CSF £39.53 CT £83.33 TOTE £15.20: £2.70, £1.30, £1.20; EX 55.30.
Owner John W Egan **Bred** Mrs G P Booth And J Porteous **Trained** Cropthorne, Worcs
■ Stewards' Enquiry : Matthew Cosham four-day ban: careless riding (18, 24, 25 and 26th June)

FOCUS
An ordinary handicap run at a sound pace.
Yourinthewill(USA) Official explanation: vets said the gelding scoped dirty post-race

2768 SMOOTH RADIO E B F MAIDEN FILLIES' STKS 1m 3f 183y
4:50 (4:53) (Class 5) 3-Y-O+ **£3,557** (£1,058; £529; £264) **Stalls** Low

Form RPR

0-5 **1** **Saint Hilary**[18] 2200 3-8-12 0 .... MartinDwyer 12 85+
(William Muir) *chsd ldrs: led over 3f out: rdn and edgd lft over 1f out: styd on wl: comf* **14/1**

2 **2** *4* **Rippled**[17] 2249 3-8-12 0 .... WilliamBuick 11 78+
(John Gosden) *hld up in tch: chsd wnr over 2f out: sn rdn and ev ch: swtchd lft over 1f out: no ex ins fnl f* **4/7[1]**

60 **3** *1 3/4* **Require**[17] 2249 3-8-12 0 .... KirstyMilczarek 9 76+
(Luca Cumani) *racd keenly: led 1f: chsd ldrs: outpcd over 5f out: rallied and hung rt fr over 3f out: styd on* **14/1**

4 **4** *2* **Jorum**[25] 2008 3-8-12 0 .... TomQueally 3 72
(Sir Henry Cecil) *hld up: hdwy 1/2-way: outpcd over 3f out: rallied over 1f out: hung rt ins fnl f: styd on* **17/2[3]**

03 **5** *1/2* **Junior Diary (USA)**[18] 2200 3-8-12 0 .... ShaneKelly 8 72
(Brian Meehan) *led after 1f: rdn and hdd over 3f out: wknd fnl f* **12/1**

40-5 **6** *6* **Lily Potts**[20] 2148 3-8-12 67 .... FergusSweeney 5 62
(Chris Down) *prom: lost pl over 7f out: n.d after* **25/1**

320- **7** *11* **Parisian Princess (IRE)**[227] 6995 3-8-12 77 .... DarryllHolland 13 44
(Hughie Morrison) *hld up: hdwy over 5f out: rdn over 3f out: sn wknd* **8/1[2]**

0 **8** *1 3/4* **Moonshine Ruby**[37] 1655 6-9-13 0 .... WilliamCarson 10 42
(Peter Hiatt) *a in rr* **100/1**

9 *3/4* **Regal Diva** 4-9-13 0 .... RussKennemore 14 40
(Reg Hollinshead) *s.s: a in rr* **50/1**

0 **10** *1 1/4* **Linn County**[16] 2271 3-8-12 0 .... SaleemGolam 2 38
(John Gosden) *s.i.s: sn pushed along and prom: rdn and wknd over 2f out* **40/1**

60 **11** *21* **Goodie Goodie**[18] 2204 3-8-12 0 .... FrannyNorton 6
(Sylvester Kirk) *a in rr: bhd fnl 3f: t.o* **100/1**

12 *11* **Daghashah** 3-8-12 0 .... NeilCallan 15
(Clive Brittain) *mid-div: lost pl over 6f out: bhd fnl 3f: t.o* **20/1**

2m 37.5s (3.60) **Going Correction** +0.425s/f (Yiel)
WFA 3 from 4yo+ 15lb **12** Ran SP% **121.3**
Speed ratings (Par 100): **105,102,101,99,99 95,88,87,86,85 71,64**
toteswingers:1&2:£4.40, 2&3:£4.10, 1&3:£20.30 CSF £22.25 TOTE £16.70: £2.90, £1.20, £2.20; EX 37.00.
Owner Usk Valley Stud **Bred** Usk Valley Stud **Trained** Lambourn, Berks

FOCUS
Not the strongest of fillies' maidens outside of the winner though it was truly run.

2769 TIGERS APPRENTICE H'CAP 1m 3f 183y
5:20 (5:20) (Class 6) (0-60,54) 4-Y-O+ **£1,704** (£503; £251) **Stalls** Low

Form RPR

/0-0 **1** **Tallulah Mai**[12] 2391 5-8-13 **49** .... IanBurns(3) 3 56
(Matthew Salaman) *chsd ldrs: led over 3f out: hdd over 2f out: sn rdn: styd on to ld nr fin* **15/2**

5-00 **2** *1 1/4* **Crimson Monarch (USA)**[12] 2391 8-8-10 **46** .... (b) NoelGarbutt(3) 1 51
(Peter Hiatt) *chsd ldrs: led over 2f out: clr over 1f out: hdd nr fin* **11/2[3]**

3262 **3** *1* **Mayan Flight (IRE)**[12] 2391 4-9-7 **54** .... GeorgeDowning 5 57
(Tony Carroll) *s.i.s: hld up: hdwy over 2f out: rdn and hung rt over 1f out: styd on* **6/5[1]**

6000 **4** *1* **Port Hill**[44] 1534 5-8-9 **47** .... JacobButterfield(5) 4 49
(Mark Brisbourne) *led: hdd over 3f out: styd on same pce fnl f* **9/2[2]**

500- **5** *9* **Peaceful Means (IRE)**[233] 6876 9-9-2 **49** .... (t) JackDuern 6 36
(Mandy Rowland) *prom: rdn over 3f out: wknd 2f out* **14/1**

6605 **6** *10* **Four Steps Back**[44] 1534 5-8-12 **45** .... RachealKneller 7 16
(Mark Usher) *chsd ldrs tl wknd over 2f out* **17/2**

2m 41.06s (7.75) **Going Correction** +0.425s/f (Yiel) **6** Ran SP% **108.0**
Speed ratings (Par 101): **91,90,89,88,82 76**
toteswingers:1&2:£3.70, 2&3:£2.20, 1&3:£2.70 CSF £43.05 TOTE £8.30: £3.30, £1.90; EX 75.20.
Owner Oaktree Racing **Bred** Marshalla Salaman **Trained** Upper Lambourn, Berks

FOCUS
They went no pace in this moderate apprentice handicap and the winning time was over four seconds slower than the fillies' maiden.
Tallulah Mai Official explanation: trainer said, regarding the apparent improvement of form, that that this was a poor race, that the mare has been dropped in the weights, and the easier surface for this contest would appear to suit her
Four Steps Back Official explanation: trainer said the gelding finished distressed
T/Plt: £17.10 to a £1 stake. Pool £55,099.76 - 2,349.70 winning units. T/Qpdt: £3.40 to a £1 stake. Pool £3,706.71 - 803.16 winning units. CR

2334 REDCAR (L-H)
Monday, June 4

OFFICIAL GOING: Good to firm (good in places; 8.6)
Wind: moderate 1/2 against Weather: fine but breezy

2770 SUMMER WEDDING FAYRE HERE ON 29TH JULY MAIDEN AUCTION STKS 5f
2:15 (2:15) (Class 5) 2-Y-O **£2,385** (£704; £352) **Stalls** Centre

Form RPR

504 **1** **Lucky Lodge**[19] 2181 2-8-9 0 .... PaulMulrennan 3 69
(Mel Brittain) *mde all: rdn over 1f out: all out* **9/4[1]**

45 **2** *hd* **Annie Gogh**[10] 2437 2-8-7 0 .... DuranFentiman 8 67
(Tim Easterby) *w ldrs: styd on wl ins fnl f: jst hld* **9/2[3]**

3 **3** *1 1/4* **Dream Maker (IRE)**[9] 2469 2-8-7 0 .... GrahamGibbons 4 62
(Tom Dascombe) *wnt rt s: w ldrs: styd on same pce last 100yds* **9/2[3]**

0 **4** *1/2* **My Claire**[16] 2282 2-8-6 0 ow2 .... MickaelBarzalona 9 60
(Nigel Tinkler) *dwlt: in rr: hdwy and n.m.r over 1f out: styd on towards fin* **50/1**

20 **5** *3/4* **Dil Laney (IRE)**[16] 2261 2-8-12 0 .... KierenFallon 6 63
(David O'Meara) *w ldrs: drvn over 2f out: kpt on one pce fnl f* **4/1[2]**

6 **6** *nk* **Moss Quito (IRE)**[21] 2123 2-8-11 0 .... SilvestreDeSousa 10 60+
(David O'Meara) *chsd ldrs: outpcd over 3f out: kpt on fnl f* **14/1**

0 **7** *1* **Delores Rocket**[16] 2261 2-8-10 0 .... PhillipMakin 1 56
(Kevin Ryan) *sn outpcd and in rr: hdwy over 2f out: one pce fnl f* **14/1**

0 **8** *7* **Valetto (IRE)**[9] 2508 2-8-7 0 .... AdamCarter(5) 5 33
(Tim Easterby) *hmpd s: in rr: wknd over 1f out* **40/1**

0 **9** *3/4* **Twinwood Star (IRE)**[14] 2334 2-8-5 0 .... ChrisCatlin 11 23
(John Weymes) *mid-div stands' side: lost pl over 1f out* **33/1**

040 **10** *1* **Only For You**[16] 2282 2-8-4 0 .... PatrickMathers 7 18
(Alan Brown) *dwlt: hdwy over 3f out: lost pl over 1f out* **100/1**

11 *2* **Poppy's Purse** 2-8-1 0 .... JulieBurke(3) 2 11
(Ollie Pears) *w ldrs on outside: wknd appr fnl f: eased towards fin* **16/1**

1m 1.37s (2.77) **Going Correction** +0.175s/f (Good) **11** Ran SP% **114.7**
Speed ratings (Par 93): **84,83,81,80,79 79,77,66,65,63 60**
toteswingers:1&2:£2.70, 1&3:£3.00, 2&3:£5.80 CSF £11.69 TOTE £4.20: £1.90, £2.30, £2.40; EX 10.90 Trifecta £43.00 Pool £329.02 - 5.65 winning units..
Owner Mel Brittain **Bred** Mel Brittain **Trained** Warthill, N Yorks

FOCUS
This was not a very strong maiden and there was not much separating the first seven, but the leading form contender held off one of his main market rivals and the form looks solid enough.

NOTEBOOK

Lucky Lodge had leading claims on his fourth in a decent novice event at York last time and put in a determined effort under a positive ride to get off the mark on the fourth attempt. Out of a 2yo 5f winning half-sister to numerous sprint winners, he is generally progressive and his one blip was on soft ground. (op 5-2 tchd 11-4)

Annie Gogh didn't get any luck when heavily backed at Catterick last time, but she was always in the clear after a good break this time and stayed on resolutely to give the favourite a big scare close home. A Dutch Art filly out of a 1m-1m2f winner, she should continue to progress and her style suggests she should stay another furlong or two this season. (op 4-1)

Dream Maker(IRE), a fading third of five over 6f at Chester on her debut, gave it a decent try with an improved effort back at 5f. She is out of a modest middle-distance winner, but seems to have inherited plenty of speed from her sire Bahamian Bounty. (op 4-1)

My Claire was short of room approaching the final furlong, but she stayed on well when finding a gap. This was a much-improved second run by a half-sister to five winners, notably 1m Listed/7f Group 3 juvenile winner Klammer.

Dil Laney(IRE), a gelded son of Mujadil, bounced back with a solid run to confirm the promise of his debut second at Musselburgh. (op 5-1)

Moss Quito(IRE) still looked inexperienced, but he stayed on nicely against the nearside in an encouraging second run. (op 12-1)

2771 MARKET CROSS JEWELLERS MAIDEN H'CAP — 1m 6f 19y
2:45 (2:45) (Class 6) (0-65,63) 3-Y-O — **£1,704** (£503; £251) **Stalls** Low

Form — RPR

0-55 **1** **Flashman**[20] 2141 3-8-13 **58** .... LeeTopliss(3) 11 — 70
(Richard Fahey) *dwlt: sn trcking ldrs: t.k.h: chal over 2f out: led over 1f out: edgd lft: drvn out* **10/1**

-046 **2** *3* **Mr Snoozy**[20] 2141 3-8-10 **52** .... GrahamGibbons 8 — 60
(Tim Walford) *trckd ldrs: led over 2f out: hdd over 1f out: kpt on same pce* **9/1**[3]

-232 **3** *4* **Rosie's Lady (IRE)**[14] 2340 3-8-13 **55** .... KierenFallon 1 — 58
(David O'Meara) *in rr: drvn over 4f out: hdwy over 2f out: styd on to take 3rd last 100yds* **7/4**[1]

004 **4** *1 ½* **Hulwa (USA)**[16] 2288 3-8-1 **46** .... JulieBurke(3) 7 — 46
(Tracy Waggott) *led after 1f: hdd over 2f out: one pce* **20/1**

0-00 **5** *½* **Art Of Gold**[14] 2341 3-8-0 **45** .... (v[1]) DominicFox(3) 5 — 45
(Amy Weaver) *in rr: drvn over 5f out: kpt on fnl 2f: nvr nr ldrs* **66/1**

00-5 **6** *2 ½* **Pearl Catcher (IRE)**[14] 2341 3-8-5 **47** .... MickaelBarzalona 3 — 43
(Tim Easterby) *in rr: hdwy and swtchd rt over 3f out: one pce fnl 2f* **12/1**

-060 **7** *11* **Oops Caroline (IRE)**[14] 2340 3-8-8 **50** .... SilvestreDeSousa 6 — 31
(David O'Meara) *led 1f: sn mid-div: drvn 8f out: hdwy on ins over 3f out: hung rt and wknd over 1f out: eased towards fin* **10/1**

0-02 **8** *2 ½* **Shivsingh**[74] 998 3-9-7 **63** .... MartinHarley 2 — 40
(Mick Channon) *in rr: hdwy over 3f out: wknd over 1f out: eased towards fin* **11/2**[2]

0633 **9** *3 ½* **Lyrical Gangster (IRE)**[25] 2014 3-9-3 **59** .... JimmyFortune 4 — 31
(Peter Chapple-Hyam) *in rr: hdwy 4f out: sn drvn: wknd 2f out: eased towards fin* **18/1**

000 **10** *23* **Bollin Nancy**[30] 1864 3-8-3 **45** .... DuranFentiman 10
(Tim Easterby) *sn drvn along in rr: sme hdwy after 4f: lost pl over 6f out: sn bhd: eased fnl 2f: t.o* **11/1**

0-04 **11** *2* **Shek O Lad**[9] 2495 3-8-4 **46** .... ChrisCatlin 12
(Alan Jarvis) *chsd ldrs: hung lft and wknd 3f out: sn bhd: eased 2f out: t.o* **18/1**

0-00 **12** *39* **Shotley Music**[14] 2336 3-9-6 **62** .... PaulMulrennan 9
(Neville Bycroft) *hld up: sn trcking ldrs: reminders over 7f out: sn lost pl: t.o 4f out: sn eased: hopelessly t.o* **16/1**

3m 9.0s (4.30) **Going Correction** +0.175s/f (Good) — **12** Ran SP% **118.6**
Speed ratings (Par 97): **94,92,90,89,88 87,81,79,77,64 63,41**
toteswingers:1&2:£5.80, 1&3:£4.20, 2&3:£6.50 CSF £97.08 CT £234.19 TOTE £13.60: £4.10, £1.40, £1.50; EX 72.90 Trifecta £235.20 Part won. Pool £317.93 - 0.20 winning units..

Owner The G-Guck Group **Bred** Avenue Farm Stud **Trained** Musley Bank, N Yorks

FOCUS

A modest staying handicap. The pace looked strong and winner scored with authority from the clear second.

Flashman Official explanation: trainer's representative said, regarding the apparent improvement of form, that the gelding had hung badly left on its previous run at Beverley, which was reported, and he appreciated racing left-handed

Oops Caroline(IRE) Official explanation: jockey said that the filly hung right-handed

Shek O Lad Official explanation: jockey said that the gelding hung left-handed

2772 BUY YOUR TICKETS ON-LINE @ REDCARRACING.CO.UK H'CAP — 1m 2f
3:20 (3:20) (Class 4) (0-85,85) 3-Y-O — **£4,075** (£1,212; £606; £303) **Stalls** Low

Form — RPR

2115 **1** **Prussian**[23] 2088 3-9-7 **85** .... KierenFallon 7 — 90+
(Mark Johnston) *chsd ldr: led over 3f out: edgd rt fnl f: hld on wl* **9/2**[2]

2-41 **2** *½* **Ruscello (IRE)**[24] 2038 3-8-13 **77** .... J-PGuillambert 2 — 81+
(Ed Walker) *trckd ldrs: shkn up over 5f out: hdwy and nt clr run 4f out: chal 2f out: kpt on same pce ins fnl f* **5/1**[3]

6-00 **3** *nk* **Saffa Hill (IRE)**[10] 2449 3-8-5 **69** .... DuranFentiman 1 — 73
(Tim Easterby) *sn trcking ldrs: drvn over 3f out: swtchd rt over 1f out: styd on ins fnl f* **25/1**

3-05 **4** *3 ¾* **Mizbah**[11] 2429 3-8-12 **76** .... (v) SilvestreDeSousa 5 — 72
(Saeed Bin Suroor) *led: t.k.h: qcknd over 4f out: hdd over 3f out: rallied over 1f out: one pce* **11/2**

1 **5** *3 ¾* **Exclusive Dancer**[23] 2095 3-8-7 **71** .... PJMcDonald 6 — 60
(George Moore) *detached in last: drvn 6f out: hdwy to chse ldrs 3f out: wknd over 1f out* **14/1**

411 **6** *9* **Burke's Rock**[18] 2194 3-9-1 **79** .... JimmyFortune 4 — 50
(Jeremy Noseda) *trckd ldrs: effrt over 3f out: chal over 2f out: wknd over 1f out: heavily eased clsng stages* **10/11**[1]

2m 10.12s (3.02) **Going Correction** +0.175s/f (Good) — **6** Ran SP% **113.1**
Speed ratings (Par 101): **94,93,93,90,87 80**
toteswingers:1&2:£2.40, 1&3:£15.00, 2&3:Not won CSF £26.90 TOTE £6.40: £3.90, £1.90; EX 34.50.

Owner Sheikh Hamdan Bin Mohammed Al Maktoum **Bred** Darley **Trained** Middleham Moor, N Yorks

FOCUS

A decent handicap. The pace was not strong and they were tightly bunched 3f out. The hot favourite was disappointing, but the generally progressive winner bounced back with a gutsy display.

Burke's Rock Official explanation: jockey said that the filly was unsuited by the good to firm, good in places going

2773 TYREGIANT.COM ZETLAND GOLD CUP (H'CAP) — 1m 2f
3:55 (3:55) (Class 2) (0-105,100) 3-Y-O+**£16,172** (£4,812; £2,405; £1,202) **Stalls** Low

Form — RPR

5-01 **1** **Danadana (IRE)**[17] 2248 4-9-4 **94** .... KierenFallon 4 — 104+
(Luca Cumani) *hld up in mid-div: hdwy over 2f out: led over 1f out: hld on towards fin* **5/4**[1]

040- **2** *hd* **Mid Mon Lady (IRE)**[185] 7618 7-9-6 **96** .... ChrisCatlin 3 — 106+
(Sir Mark Prescott Bt) *dwlt: in rr: nt clr run over 3f out and over 2f out: only 6th and str run on outer over 1f out: edgd lft and r.o wl towards fin* **20/1**

/01- **3** *¾* **Con Artist (IRE)**[253] 6375 5-9-10 **100** .... SilvestreDeSousa 2 — 108
(Saeed Bin Suroor) *trckd ldrs: hdwy on ins to chal 2f out: styd on same pce last 100yds* **8/1**[3]

0045 **4** *¾* **Navajo Chief**[18] 2211 5-9-8 **98** .... PhillipMakin 8 — 105
(Alan Jarvis) *led: qcknd over 3f out: hdd over 1f out: styd on same pce* **16/1**

0-33 **5** *2 ¼* **Jo'Burg (USA)**[4] 2620 8-8-4 **80** .... PatrickMathers 5 — 82
(David O'Meara) *dwlt: hld up in rr: effrt on outer over 3f out: chsng ldrs over 1f out: wknd fnl 50yds* **20/1**

-306 **6** *1 ¾* **Northside Prince (IRE)**[19] 2176 6-8-12 **88** .... PJMcDonald 9 — 87
(Alan Swinbank) *trckd ldrs: one pce over 1f out* **20/1**

-105 **7** *7* **Mirrored**[19] 2176 6-8-12 **88** .... DuranFentiman 12 — 73
(Tim Easterby) *trckd ldrs: chal over 3f out: wknd 2f out* **14/1**

510- **8** *1* **Demolition**[182] 7297 8-9-3 **93** .... PaulMulrennan 1 — 76
(Noel Wilson) *trckd ldr: chal over 2f out: lost pl over 1f out* **33/1**

4023 **9** *1 ½* **Sirvino**[19] 2176 7-9-10 **100** .... GrahamGibbons 6 — 80+
(David Barron) *in tch: nt clr run over 2f out: wknd wl over 1f out* **8/1**[3]

0-32 **10** *hd* **Eltheeb**[9] 2504 5-8-7 **83** .... MickaelBarzalona 7 — 62
(David O'Meara) *in rr-div: effrt on outer over 2f out: lost pl over 1f out: lame* **7/1**[2]

6-20 **11** *7* **Fork Handles**[23] 2067 4-9-0 **90** .... MartinHarley 10 — 55
(Mick Channon) *dwlt: swtchd lft after s: in rr: hdwy on inner over 3f out: wknd 2f out: bhd whn eased nr fin* **14/1**

2m 7.29s (0.19) **Going Correction** +0.175s/f (Good) — **11** Ran SP% **115.6**
Speed ratings (Par 109): **106,105,105,104,102 101,95,95,93,93 88**
toteswingers:1&2:£6.20, 1&3:£3.20, 2&3:£33.40 CSF £34.31 CT £150.29 TOTE £2.30: £1.30, £5.80, £3.20; EX 37.20 Trifecta £429.50 Part won. Pool £580.47 - 0.70 winning units..

Owner Sheikh Mohammed Obaid Al Maktoum **Bred** Darley **Trained** Newmarket, Suffolk

FOCUS

A hot handicap, but it was run at just a fair pace with the heavily backed favourite just prevailing in an exciting finish.

NOTEBOOK

Danadana(IRE) travelled smoothly through the pack before quickening well and holding off a fast finisher to defy a 9lb rise for his stylish win in a 20-runner 1m Newmarket handicap last month. It looked like he was going to win by further when he made his move, but he showed fighting spirit to get the job done. This progressive colt is now 3-8 and has a similar profile to Forte Dei Marmi, who won this off a mark of 92 for Luca Cumani in 2010 before winning valuable handicaps at Sandown and Newbury later that year. His mark will move closer to the 100s after this, but this progressive son of Dubawi seems ideally suited by 1m2f on fast ground and could pick up another big prize this season. (op 6-4)

Mid Mon Lady(IRE) ran into some traffic problems, but she finished fast out wide and was just denied in a huge run without her regular blinkers on ground faster than ideal on her comeback/debut for Sir Mark Prescott. Her 26-run losing streak dates back to July 2010, but she was placed in Listed company in Ireland in the autumn and she could be a major force in a big handicap this summer. (op 22-1)

Con Artist(IRE) raced a bit freely early on, but he did well to go close under more patient tactics than usual on his return from 253 days off. A lightly raced son of Invincible Spirit, he is a triple winner at 1m-1m2f and this run proves that he is still feasibly treated off a mark 7lb higher than for his win at Epsom in September. (op 7-1)

Navajo Chief had the run of things up front, but he gave it a good shot and can be marked up a bit because he had previous form figures of 878 at 1m2f and all of his five wins have been at 5f-1m.. (op 14-1)

Jo'Burg(USA), beaten over 3l in a handicap at Ayr four days earlier, deserves credit for a good run out wide in this much stronger grade. He is on a long losing run, but is on a workable mark and went very close in a couple of 1m/1m2f handicaps last autumn. (op 18-1)

Northside Prince(IRE) had every chance before his run flattened out. (op 18-1)

Eltheeb was disappointing in his bid to repeat the form of his close call in a 1m4f York handicap last time, but he had an excuse because he was reported to be lame. Official explanation: jockey said that the gelding finished lame

2774 WIN A VIP DAY OUT @ REDCARRACING.CO.UK MEDIAN AUCTION MAIDEN STKS — 6f
4:30 (4:33) (Class 5) 3-Y-O — **£2,264** (£673; £336; £168) **Stalls** Centre

Form — RPR

04 **1** **Ptolemy**[9] 2470 3-9-3 0 .... GrahamGibbons 4 — 68
(David Barron) *chsd ldrs: effrt over 2f out: rdn and hung lft over 1f out: styd on to ld last 50yds: hld on* **7/4**[1]

0 **2** *nk* **Compton Time**[42] 1560 3-9-3 0 .... PaulMulrennan 6 — 67
(Michael Dods) *led 1f: chsd ldrs: styd on fnl f: no ex nr fin* **5/1**[3]

0320 **3** *hd* **Henry Bee**[6] 2591 3-9-0 75 .... (b[1]) LeeTopliss(3) 3 — 66
(Richard Fahey) *trckd ldrs: led over 3f out: rdn and edgd rt over 1f out: hdd and no ex last 50yds* **9/4**[2]

0466 **4** *4* **Tuibama (IRE)**[31] 1817 3-9-3 49 .... PhillipMakin 2 — 54
(Tracy Waggott) *stdd s: t.k.h early: effrt over 2f out: one pce* **12/1**

00 **5** *9* **Jerry Ellen (IRE)**[14] 2339 3-9-3 0 .... DuranFentiman 1 — 25
(Tim Easterby) *trckd ldrs: drvn over 2f out: wknd over 1f out* **22/1**

0 **6** *5* **Tomasini**[14] 2339 3-9-3 0 .... ChrisCatlin 7
(John Weymes) *sn outpcd and in rr: bhd fnl 3f* **33/1**

00- **7** *3 ¾* **Gentle Sands**[238] 6745 3-8-12 0 .... KierenFallon 5
(Ed McMahon) *w ldr: t.k.h: led after 1f: hdd over 3f out: wknd over 2f out: sn heavily eased* **9/1**

1m 13.63s (1.83) **Going Correction** +0.175s/f (Good) — **7** Ran SP% **108.8**
Speed ratings (Par 99): **94,93,93,88,76 69,64**
toteswingers:1&2:£2.20, 1&3:£2.10, 2&3:£3.80 CSF £9.80 TOTE £2.60: £2.00, £3.10; EX 9.40.

Owner Reg Gifford **Bred** R S E Gifford (wordsworth Hotel Ltd) **Trained** Maunby, N Yorks

FOCUS
The exposed 75-rated leading form contender was reeled in by a couple of well backed rivals in this ordinary maiden.

2775 COME RACING AGAIN TOMORROW H'CAP 1m 6f 19y
5:05 (5:05) (Class 6) (0-65,64) 4-Y-0+ £1,617 (£481; £240 ; £120) Stalls Low

Form RPR
02-4 1 **Madrasa (IRE)**[51] 1382 4 -9-259 ....(bt) PhillipMakin 4 72
(Keith Reveley) *hld up in mid-div: hdwy over 3f out: led 2f out: drew clr ins fnl f: readily* **5/1**[3]
0-00 2 5 **Tarantella Lady**[27] 1952 4 -9-259 ....(v) PJMcDonald 5 64
(George Moore) *chsd ldrs: drvn over 5f out: kpt on to take 2nd last 100yds* **20/1**
0503 3 2 **Dubara Reef (IRE)**[7] 1952 5 -8-851 ....(v) SilvestreDeSousa 9 53
(Paul Green) *chsd ldrs: drvn over 4f out: led briefly over 2f out: one pce* **9/2**[2]
0-00 4 8 **Kodicil (IRE)**[11] 2414 4 -9-562 .... GrahamGibbons 6 53
(Tim Walford) *trckd ldrs: chal over 2f out: wknd appr fnl f* **7/1**
66-0 5 3 **Ferney Boy**[16] 2260 6 -8-750 .... DuranFentiman 8 37
(Chris Fairhurst) *hld up in rr: hdwy 6f out: rdn over 3f out: wknd over 1f out* **20/1**
020- 6 ½ **Haka Dancer (USA)**[13] 6600 9 -7-945 ....(p) EvaMoscrop(7) 7 31
(Philip Kirby) *hld up in mid-div: sn t.k.h: hdwy and racd wd to ld 10f out: sn clr: hdd over 2f out: wknd over 1f out* **25/1**
01-4 7 11 **Navigation Track**[13] 2363 4 -9-464 .... AdamBeschizza(3) 3 35
(David Simcock) *stdd s: hld up in rr: effrt 4f out: sn rdn: nvr a factor: wknd over 1f out* **2/1**[1]
/006 8 5 **Yas Marina (USA)**[9] 2670 4 -8-649 ....(p) MickaelBarzalona 10 13
(David O'Meara) *mid-div: drvn over 5f out: wknd and eased 2f out* **11/2**
410- 9 21 **Brook Star (IRE)**[261] 6153 4 -8-1053 .... PaulMulrennan 1
(Michael Dods) *led 4f: chsd ldrs: hung lft and lost pl 2f out: sn bhd and eased: t.o* **20/1**
046- 10 12 **Andorn (GER)**[241] 5947 8 -9-264 ow1 .... KyleJames(5) 2
(Philip Kirby) *hld up in rr: drvn 4f out: sn bhd: eased* **14/1**

3m 6.53s (1.83) **Going Correction** +0.175s/f (Good) **10**Ran SP% **120.9**
Speed ratings (Par 101): **101,98,97,92,90 90,84,81,69,62**
toteswingers:1&2:£28.30, 1&3:£2.90, 2&3:£28.30 CSF £105.01 CT £490.54 TOTE £6.80 : £2.90, £7.60, £2.30 ; EX 138.50 Trifecta £279.10 Part won. Pool £377.19 - 0.10 winning units.
Owner M W Joyce **Bred** Paget Bloodstock **Trained** Lingdale, Redcar & Cleveland

FOCUS
A minor staying handicap with the favourite disappointing. The early pace was strong.
Yas Marina (USA) Official explanation: jockey said that the gelding had no more to give
Brook Star (IRE) Official explanation: jockey said that the filly hung left-handed
T/Plt: £43.40 to a £1 stake. Pool £48,449.57 - 814.74 winning units. T/Qpdt: £19.00 to a £1 stake. Pool £2,326.46 - 90.29 winning units. WG

2776a & 2778a - (Foreign Racing) - See Raceform Interactive

2183 NAAS (L-H)
Monday, June 4
OFFICIAL GOING: Good to yielding (yielding in places)

2777a OWENSTOWN STUD STKS (LISTED RACE) 7f
3:00 (3:00) 3-Y-0+ £23,020 (£6,729; £3,187 ; £1,062)

RPR
1 **One Spirit (IRE)**[9] 2515 4 -9-6100 .... NGMcCullagh 8 102+
(G M Lyons, Ire) *trckd ldr in 2nd: rdn to ld 1 1/2f out: drvn out and kpt on wl fnl f* **6/1**[2]
2 1 **Gordon Lord Byron (IRE)**[4] 2059 4 -9-9104 .... FranBerry 7 102+
(T Hogan, Ire) *in rr of mid-div on outer: 7th 2f out: gd hdwy to go 2nd 1f out: no imp on wnr ins fnl f: kpt on same pce* **4/1**[1]
3 1 ¼ **Glor Na Mara (IRE)**[9] 2516 4 -9-998 .... KevinManning 2 99+
(J S Bolger, Ire) *settled towards rr on inner: 9th 1/2-way: swtchd rt in st and 7th over 1f out: kpt on wl ins fnl f wout rching ldrs: wnt 3rd cl home* **7/1**[3]
4 nse **Billyford (IRE)**[9] 2516 7 -9-992 .... JohnnyMurtagh 10 98
(Liam Roche, Ire) *chsd ldrs: 6th 1/2-way: 4th 2f out: no imp on wnr fr over 1f out: kpt on one pce* **12/1**
5 1 ¾ **Simla Sunset (IRE)**[9] 2516 6 -9-684 ....(p) ChrisHayes 6 91
(P J Prendergast, Ire) *trckd ldrs on outer: 5th 1/2-way: 3rd early st: rdn and dropped to 5th 1f out: no imp ins fnl f* **20/1**
6 shd **Royal Blue Star (IRE)**[18] 2217 4 -9-695 .... JPO'Brien 5 90
(Mrs John Harrington, Ire) *led: rdn early st and hdd 1 1/2f out: 3rd and no imp 1f out: no ex ins fnl f* **10/1**
7 1 **Banna Boirche (IRE)**[9] 2516 6 -9-9106 .... ShaneFoley 3 91
(M Halford, Ire) *hld up in mid-div: 7th 1/2-way: swtchd rt and nt clr run over 1f out: nt persevered w whn btn ins fnl f* **4/1**[1]
8 ¾ **Barack (IRE)**[22] 2100 6 -9-1299 ....(bt) BenCurtis 1 92
(Francis Ennis, Ire) *trckd ldrs on inner: 3rd 1/2-way: rdn and dropped to 5th 2f out: no ex fr over 1f out* **12/1**
9 6 **Ahaaly**[54] 1324 3 -8-1092 .... DeclanMcDonogh 4 66
(Kevin Prendergast, Ire) *trckd ldrs racing keenly: 4th 1/2-way: 6th 2f out: sn rdn and no ex over 1f out: eased whn btn ins fnl f* **6/1**[2]
10 hd **Croisultan (IRE)**[24] 2059 6 -9-9105 ....(b) PatSmullen 9 72
(D K Weld, Ire) *settled in rr: nvr a factor: rdn early st and no ex fr wl over 1f out: eased whn btn ins fnl f* **8/1**

1m 23.38s (-4.12)
WFA 3 from 4yo+ 10lb **10**Ran SP% **121.4**
CSF £31.62 TOTE £6.80 : £2.20 , £1.70 , £2.20 ; DF 25.80 .
Owner Miss A H Marshall **Bred** F Dunne **Trained** Dunsany, Co. Meath

FOCUS
The winner and fourth have been rated to the better view of their recent form.

NOTEBOOK
One Spirit (IRE)'s rider adopted a positive approach by sending her to the front well over a furlong out and inviting the others to catch her. In the end she lengthened further and her winning margin of a length probably doesn't do her justice. She seems to have improved a good deal from three to four and is probably Group class. (op 13/2)
Gordon Lord Byron (IRE)was ridden for a finishing kick and, while not ideal to give the winner a few lengths early in the straight, that's the way it worked out. He couldn't be called unlucky as the winner continued to lengthen away inside the last and he just wasn't quite good enough to cope with her. It was another step up from him though and he shows no signs of declining. (op 3/1)
Glor Na Mara (IRE)was never seen with a chance but managed to come home better than most. One would be loath to make any predictions about this horse.
Billyford(IRE)'s trainer continues to get the best out of him. He didn't seem to get the best of luck in running at one point in the straight but he kept finding a bit and ran a fair race. There might be a stakes race over this type of trip for him this summer.
Simla Sunset (IRE)didn't have much cover on the outside but kept on reasonably well under pressure. This is about as good as she is.
Banna Boirche (IRE)couldn't make any real headway in the straight. Official explanation: jockey said gelding was denied a clear run in the straight
Ahaaly was a little bit keen early but dropped away tamely in the straight. Official explanation: vet said filly was found to be clinically abnormal post-race

2779a ALFRED NOBEL ROCHESTOWN (C&G) STKS (LISTED RACE) 6f
4:10 (4:14) 2-Y-0 £32,500 (£9,500; £4,500 ; £1,500)

RPR
1 **Dawn Approach (IRE)**[19] 2184 2 -9-3 .... KevinManning 1 105
(J S Bolger, Ire) *trckd ldr in 2nd: rdn to ld over 1f out: drvn out to assert ins fnl f: styd on wl* **4/9**[1]
2 2 ¾ **Mister Marc (IRE)**[9] 2480 2 -9-3 .... RichardHughes 2 97
(Richard Hannon) *led: strly pressed and hdd over 1f out: no imp on wnr ins fnl f* **5/1**[2]
3 4 ½ **Tennessee Wildcat (IRE)**[9] 2512 2 -9-3 ....(p) GaryCarroll 6 83
(G M Lyons, Ire) *chsd ldrs in 4th: 3rd 1/2-way: no ch w first 2 fr 2f out: kpt on one pce* **25/1**
4 3 **Yes Two**[30] 1842 2 -9-3 .... JamesMillman 5 74
(Rod Millman) *chsd ldrs in 3rd: pushed along in 4th 1/2-way: no imp fr 2f out: kpt on one pce* **16/1**
5 shd **Pedro The Great (USA)**2 -9-3 .... JPO'Brien 4 74+
(A P O'Brien, Ire) *chsd ldrs in 5th: drvn along bef 1/2-way: nvr a factor: kpt on one pce fr over 1f out* **8/1**[3]
6 9 **Spirit Of The Air (IRE)**[19] 2184 2 -9-3 ....(t) ShaneFoley 7 47
(John Joseph Murphy, Ire) *a in rr: sn outpcd and rdn along: nvr a factor* **66/1**

1m 11.48s (-1.72) **6**Ran SP% **108.3**
CSF £2.76 TOTE £1.20 : £1.10 , £1.30 ; DF 2.30 .
Owner Mrs J S Bolger **Bred** J S Bolger **Trained** Coolcullen, Co Carlow

FOCUS
This race lost some of its interest when Cougar Ridge refused to load. The winner already looks good enough to win a Chesham, if pointed that way.

NOTEBOOK
Dawn Approach (IRE)◆ was given a proper test as the runner-up took him on the whole way at a cut-throat gallop, but the winner began to get on top inside the last and the further they went the greater his superiority. This was a high-class performance on slowish ground and it will be fascinating to see how deep into the season he can keep this up. It would be hard to nominate a better one than him so far this campaign. (op 1/2)
Mister Marc (IRE)tried to do the winner for early speed and then hold on. But he was unable to get him off the bridle and was well stuffed by him in the end. He's probably more a 5f horse at this stage, but this is the sort of race that could have taken a lot out of him and caution might be exercised about whether he goes to Ascot. (op 13/2)
Tennessee Wildcat (IRE)was better than his bare form figures suggested and this was proved correct as he stuck at it well but was unable to lay a glove on the two principals. (op 33/1)
Yes Two struggled to go the pace a bit but stuck to his task reasonably well. (op 16/1 tchd 20/1)
Pedro The Great (USA)could never go the pace but didn't run badly. (op 5/1)

2780a COOLMORE STUD EUROPEAN BREEDERS FUND SPRINT STKS (LISTED RACE) (FILLIES) 6f
4:45 (4:45) 2-Y-0 £36,562 (£10,687; £5,062 ; £1,687)

RPR
1 **Sky Lantern (IRE)**[11] 2407 2 -9-0 .... RichardHughes 7 101+
(Richard Hannon) *trckd ldrs in 3rd: hdwy to ld over 1f out: sn strly pressed: kpt on wl and on top clsng stages* **11/8**[1]
2 ½ **True Verdict (IRE)**[9] 2183 2 -9-0 .... WJLee 3 99+
(David Wachman, Ire) *settled in rr: poised to chal on outer 2f out: wnt 2nd 1f out and sn rdn: kpt on u.p: no imp on wnr clsng stages* **4/1**[3]
3 3 **Liberating**[9] 2512 2 -9-0 .... FranBerry 5 90
(Mrs John Harrington, Ire) *chsd ldrs: 4th 1/2-way: rdn over 1f out: wnt 3rd ins fnl f but no imp on first 2* **7/2**[2]
4 2 **Nandiga (USA)**[9] 2511 2 -9-0 .... ChrisHayes 6 84
(P J Prendergast, Ire) *trckd ldr in 2nd: led 2f out: sn rdn and dropped to 3rd 1f out: no ex in 4th fnl f* **6/1**
5 1 ¼ **Scream Blue Murder (IRE)**[15] 2315 2 -9-0 .... WayneLordan 2 80
(T Stack, Ire) *chsd ldrs: 5th 1/2-way: rdn over 1f out and no ex ins fnl f* **5/1**
6 15 **Verbal Honesty (IRE)**[9] 2512 2 -9-0 .... KevinManning 4 35
(J S Bolger, Ire) *led racing keenly: drvn along and hdd 2f out: no imp whn short of room and snatched up over 1f out: eased whn btn fnl f* **16/1**

1m 11.56s (-1.64) **6**Ran SP% **121.2**
CSF £8.16 TOTE £2.00 : £1.20 , £1.90 ; DF 7.00 .
Owner B Keswick **Bred** Tally-Ho Stud **Trained** East Everleigh, Wilts

FOCUS
The winner should benefit from a further step up in trip. The form looks straightforward and the runner-up should have no problem winning a maiden, and possibly a Listed fillies' race.

NOTEBOOK
Sky Lantern (IRE)◆ looked vulnerable when the runner-up came to challenge but her stamina kicked in and any greenness she may have displayed was quickly dispelled as she picked up after getting a couple of backhanders. She won a shade cosily and clearly will improve for a step up in trip. She could yet be exciting and is clearly going the right way. (op 7/4 tchd 2/1)
True Verdict (IRE)would seem to be the best maiden in training. She appears to be much more of a speedy type than the winner. She laid up fairly effortlessly and travelled well to make her challenge but couldn't shake off the winner and her challenge flattened out up the hill. An easier 6f would suit her well and maybe better ground, but she'll win a good race. (op 9/2)
Liberating is looking more like an early season 2yo and maybe it was asking a bit for her to improve so much from her impressive Cork debut win in April. This was probably a better effort than her Marble Hill run, though, as she ran in a slightly more restrained manner and settled well. She kept on well inside the last without being good enough to trouble the first two.
Nandiga(USA) still looked quite green in the closing stages and raced with her head to one side. It would be a surprise if there wasn't some improvement in her. (op 6/1 tchd 11/2)
Scream Blue Murder (IRE)will have little trouble winning a maiden but she could never quite get involved here. (op 11/2)
Verbal Honesty (IRE)was squeezed up badly on the inside rail late on when she was dropping back. (op 14/1)

2781 - 2782a (Foreign Racing) - See Raceform Interactive

[2763]LEICESTER (R-H)

Tuesday, June 5

OFFICIAL GOING: Good to soft (7.1)

Wind: Light behind Weather: Overcast

2783 BRITISH STALLION STUDS SUPPORTING BRITISH RACING E B F MAIDEN FILLIES' STKS 5f 2y

2:10 (2:11) (Class 4) 2-Y-O **£4,334** (£1,289; £644; £322) **Stalls** High

Form RPR

6 **1** **Mary's Daughter**[16] 2308 2-9-0 0 DavidNolan 14 82+
(Richard Fahey) *a.p: led over 1f out: pushed clr ins fnl f: comf* **50/1**

2 *2 ¾* **Flirtinaskirt** 2-8-11 0 SeanLevey(3) 4 71
(Ed McMahon) *prom: pushed along over 3f out: rdn to chse wnr over 1f out: edgd lft ins fnl f: styd on* **20/1**

4 **3** *½* **Ighraa (IRE)**[17] 2282 2-9-0 0 PaulHanagan 6 69
(Brian Meehan) *prom: rdn 1/2-way: styd on* **11/2**[2]

0 **4** *nse* **Shrimpton**[15] 2343 2-9-0 0 MatthewDavies 10 69
(Mick Channon) *sn outpcd: swtchd rt and hdwy over 1f out: nt rch ldrs* **40/1**

532 **5** *¾* **Vestibule**[10] 2499 2-9-0 0 CathyGannon 13 66
(Eve Johnson Houghton) *prom: rdn over 1f out: no ex ins fnl f* **8/1**

6 *4* **Hot Secret** 2-9-0 0 JimmyFortune 1 52
(Andrew Balding) *s.s: bhd: hdwy over 1f out: wknd fnl f* **7/1**[3]

7 *¾* **Cut No Ice (IRE)** 2-9-0 0 StevieDonohoe 9 49
(Paul Cole) *sn outpcd: r.o ins fnl f: nrst fin* **33/1**

32 **8** *hd* **Steer By The Stars (IRE)**[25] 2020 2-9-0 0 JoeFanning 2 49
(Mark Johnston) *led 1f: led again 1/2-way: rdn and hdd over 1f out: wknd ins fnl f* **11/8**[1]

4 **9** *2* **Lincolnrose (IRE)**[15] 2330 2-9-0 0 JamesDoyle 5 41
(Alan McCabe) *chsd ldrs: rdn 1/2-way: wknd over 1f out* **16/1**

10 *2 ¼* **Henrietta Rose (USA)** 2-9-0 0 FrankieDettori 11 33
(Jeremy Noseda) *s.i.s: sn pushed along in rr: nvr on terms* **8/1**

11 *13* **Constant Dream** 2-9-0 0 PaulMulrennan 3
(James Given) *w ldr: led 4f out to 1/2-way: wknd over 1f out* **40/1**

1m 1.13s (1.13) **Going Correction** +0.10s/f (Good) **11** Ran SP% **112.6**
Speed ratings (Par 92): **94,89,88,88,87 81,79,79,76,72 52**
toteswingers:1&2:£36.10, 2&3:£40.90, 1&3:£17.40 CSF £761.64 TOTE £43.70: £7.40, £4.00, £1.40; EX 777.10.
Owner Mr And Mrs J D Cotton **Bred** Floors Farming And Dominic Burke **Trained** Musley Bank, N Yorks

FOCUS
This looked just a modest fillies' maiden, but it ought to produce a few winners. The action unfolded middle-to-stands' side, with the winner racing close to the rail.

NOTEBOOK
Mary's Daughter made huge improvement on her debut form to win easily, clearly being suited by this drop in trip. There's probably more to come. (tchd 66-1)
Flirtinaskirt, an 11,000GBP January foal, was always handy and kept on reasonably well, showing enough to suggest she can win a similar race. (tchd 18-1 and 22-1)
Ighraa(IRE) wasn't given anything like a hard time once held and maybe just hung onto third. She failed to really improve as expected from her Thirsk debut and maybe she wants better ground. (op 6-1)
Shrimpton failed to beat a rival on her debut at Windsor (5f, good) and this was obviously a lot better. (op 50-1 tchd 33-1)
Vestibule was well held on this drop back in trip and return to easy ground and she's already starting to look exposed, this being her fourth start. (tchd 17-2)
Hot Secret ◆, a late April foal, is related to some decent sprinters, notably Temple Meads (won the Mill Reef), and she showed plenty of ability. She had to use up a lot of energy after losing many lengths at the start and did well to finish as close as sixth. (op 13-2 tchd 8-1)
Cut No Ice(IRE) ◆, another late April foal, is related to loads of winners, the pick of them Haydock Sprint Cup heroine Pipalong. She soon got behind but there was much to like about the way she stayed on, and there should be significant improvement forthcoming. (tchd 28-1)
Steer By The Stars(IRE) split two subsequent winners when runner-up at Ascot (5f, soft) on her second start, so this was bitterly disappointing. (tchd 5-4 and 6-4)

2784 SMOOTH RADIO OADBY MAIDEN STKS 5f 218y

2:40 (2:40) (Class 4) 2-Y-O **£3,557** (£1,058; £529; £264) **Stalls** High

Form RPR

1 **Jalaa (IRE)** 2-9-3 0 PaulHanagan 10 84+
(Richard Hannon) *a.p: chsd ldr over 3f out: rdn to ld ins fnl f: r.o: readily* **2/1**[1]

0 **2** *2 ½* **Carlton Blue (IRE)**[46] 1499 2-9-3 0 StevieDonohoe 13 73
(Paul Cole) *chsd ldr: led over 4f out: hung rt fr 1/2-way: rdn over 1f out: hdd and unable qck ins fnl f* **11/1**

3 *½* **Stamford** 2-9-3 0 FrankieDettori 9 72+
(Mahmood Al Zarooni) *led: hdd over 4f out: chsd ldrs: rdn over 2f out: styng on same pce whn nt clr run ins fnl f* **85/40**[2]

4 *2* **Aseela (IRE)** 2-8-12 0 MartinDwyer 8 61
(Clive Brittain) *mid-div: sn pushed along: outpcd 1/2-way: styd on ins fnl f* **40/1**

5 *nk* **Hipster** 2-9-3 0 JimCrowley 5 65
(Ralph Beckett) *sn pushed along and prom: outpcd over 2f out: styd on ins fnl f* **9/1**

6 *1 ¼* **Red Avenger (USA)** 2-9-3 0 RyanMoore 7 61+
(Ed Dunlop) *sn outpcd: r.o ins fnl f: nrst fin* **13/2**[3]

7 *½* **Santo Prince (USA)** 2-9-3 0 JamieSpencer 1 59
(Michael Bell) *hld up: pushed along 1/2-way: nvr trbld ldrs* **14/1**

0 **8** *nk* **Getaway Car**[19] 2193 2-9-3 0 PaulMulrennan 2 58
(Gerard Butler) *hld up: pushed along 1/2-way: nvr on terms* **28/1**

9 *¾* **Iffley Fields** 2-9-3 0 ShaneKelly 12 56
(David Evans) *s.s: hung rt almost thrght: no ch fr 1/2-way* **66/1**

05 **10** *3 ¼* **Maypole Joe (IRE)**[61] 1202 2-9-3 0 CathyGannon 11 46
(David Evans) *prom to 1/2-way* **50/1**

1m 14.38s (1.38) **Going Correction** +0.10s/f (Good) **10** Ran SP% **113.0**
Speed ratings (Par 95): **94,90,90,87,86 85,84,84,83,78**
toteswingers:1&2:£2.80, 2&3:£3.60, 1&3:£1.80 CSF £23.24 TOTE £3.40: £1.60, £3.00, £1.40; EX 18.20.
Owner Hamdan Al Maktoum **Bred** Airlie Stud And R N Clay **Trained** East Everleigh, Wilts

FOCUS
Few got involved, but the winner and third, who were both representing powerful connections, were strongly fancied in the betting and this looks decent enough maiden form. The last two winners of this race (Roayh and most recently Roman Soldier) both subsequently finished placed in the Coventry Stakes. The field raced stands' side early, but the big players ended up more towards the middle.

NOTEBOOK
Jalaa(IRE), a 200,000gns half-brother to Dewhurst winner Intense Focus, had to be niggled to keep up with the strong travelling runner-up, but always looked likely to wear that one down despite being forced slightly right in the closing stages. He's a strong colt who very much looks the part and he rates a smart prospect. The Coventry is apparently on his agenda. (op 9-4)
Carlton Blue(IRE) built on the promise he showed at Newbury (5f, soft) on his debut, showing loads of pace yet travelling well within himself for a fair way. He edged right when getting tired and could yet do better. (op 9-1)
Stamford, a 200,000gns half-brother to a few winners, including the smart Champions Gallery (Group 1-placed at 1m2f), raced more towards the middle of the track than the front two and was always just held. There should be more to come and he looks a useful sort in the making. (op 15-8 tchd 9-4)
Aseela(IRE), a 30,000gns purchase who will probably want further, was the only filly in the line-up and shaped nicely enough. (tchd 50-1)
Hipster, a 20,000gns gelded son of a 6f juvenile winner, showed ability and is obviously open to improvement. (op 8-1)
Red Avenger(USA), a 175,000gns purchase, is a May foal. He soon got behind before finishing quite takingly and can do a lot better. (op 17-2)

2785 DIAMOND JUBILEE H'CAP 7f 9y

3:15 (3:16) (Class 4) (0-80,80) 3-Y-O **£6,301** (£1,886; £943; £472; £235) **Stalls** High

Form RPR

-225 **1** **Lady Loch**[25] 2030 3-8-11 **70** (b[1]) PaulHanagan 8 84
(Richard Fahey) *led: hdd over 5f out: chsd ldrs: rdn over 1f out: led ins fnl f: r.o* **12/1**

315- **2** *1* **Ruby Night (IRE)**[283] 5478 3-9-6 **79** JamieSpencer 1 90+
(Michael Bell) *a.p: led over 2f out: rdn over 1f out: hdd ins fnl f: styd on same pce* **11/1**

33-4 **3** *5* **Fabled City (USA)**[15] 2331 3-9-1 **74** (t) AdamKirby 9 72
(Clive Cox) *prom: rdn over 2f out: styd on same pce fnl f* **20/1**

114- **4** *nk* **Amadeus Wolfe Tone (IRE)**[235] 6829 3-9-6 **79** FergusSweeney 3 76
(Jamie Osborne) *hld up: hdwy over 2f out: rdn over 1f out: no ex fnl f* **11/1**

5-1 **5** *5* **Flexible Flyer**[57] 1256 3-9-2 **75** DarryllHolland 12 59+
(Hughie Morrison) *hmpd s: plld hrd: led over 5f out: rdn and hdd over 2f out: wknd fnl f* **5/2**[1]

-412 **6** *½* **Dubious Escapade (IRE)**[17] 2283 3-8-12 **71** JoeFanning 4 54
(Ann Duffield) *prom: rdn over 2f out: wknd over 1f out* **8/1**

4-24 **7** *4 ½* **Uprise**[27] 1983 3-9-1 **74** (v[1]) RyanMoore 11 45
(Sir Michael Stoute) *wnt lft s: hld up: rdn and hung rt over 1f out: nvr on terms* **4/1**[2]

35-3 **8** *2 ½* **Loyal Master (IRE)**[24] 2089 3-8-11 **75** JustinNewman(5) 2 40
(David C Griffiths) *chsd ldrs: rdn 1/2-way: wknd over 2f out* **18/1**

4633 **9** *2* **Lord Paget**[27] 1989 3-8-5 **64** RoystonFfrench 5 24
(Reg Hollinshead) *s.i.s: sn pushed along in rr: nvr nrr* **50/1**

430- **10** *7* **Theresnoneedfordat (IRE)**[239] 6743 3-8-12 **71** WilliamCarson 7 12
(Stuart Williams) *s.i.s: hld up: a in rr* **33/1**

1-60 **11** *shd* **Byronic Hero**[20] 2182 3-9-2 **75** PaulMulrennan 16 16
(Jedd O'Keeffe) *chsd ldrs: rdn 1/2-way: wknd over 2f out* **22/1**

1-44 **12** *11* **Dark Falcon (IRE)**[7] 2583 3-8-13 **72** KierenFallon 15
(James Tate) *chsd ldrs tl rdn and wknd over 2f out* **15/2**[3]

R-50 **13** *6* **Daraa (IRE)**[54] 1331 3-8-13 **72** MartinDwyer 6
(Clive Brittain) *hld up: plld hrd: wknd over 2f out* **80/1**

1m 25.11s (-1.09) **Going Correction** +0.10s/f (Good) **13** Ran SP% **116.3**
Speed ratings (Par 101): **110,108,103,102,97 96,91,88,86,78 78,65,58**
toteswingers:1&2:£16.00, 2&3:£31.30, 1&3:£16.30 CSF £126.39 CT £2678.21 TOTE £10.50: £2.60, £3.30, £5.40; EX 113.10.
Owner David W Armstrong **Bred** Jeremy Green And Sons **Trained** Musley Bank, N Yorks

FOCUS
They all raced up the middle. This was a fair 3yo handicap and the front two pulled clear.
Flexible Flyer Official explanation: jockey said colt ran too free
Dark Falcon(IRE) Official explanation: jockey said colt stopped quickly

2786 LEICESTER MERCURY CLAIMING STKS 7f 9y

3:50 (3:50) (Class 6) 3-Y-O **£1,617** (£481; £240; £120) **Stalls** High

Form RPR

-535 **1** **Compton Target (IRE)**[27] 1979 3-7-11 58 (t) NicoleNordblad(7) 6 55
(Hans Adielsson) *hld up: swtchd rt and hdwy over 2f out: rdn to ld over 1f out: edgd lft: pushed out* **5/1**[3]

0024 **2** *3 ¼* **Marinus (IRE)**[19] 2205 3-8-1 62 SophieDoyle(3) 7 46
(Sylvester Kirk) *chsd ldrs: rdn and ev ch over 1f out: styd on same pce ins fnl f* **9/2**[2]

0-50 **3** *1 ¼* **Enthrall (IRE)**[7] 2582 3-7-10 45 DominicFox(3) 9 38
(Denis Coakley) *led: rdn and hung rt fr over 2f out: hdd over 1f out: no ex fnl f* **20/1**

50-6 **4** *¾* **High Five Prince (IRE)**[19] 2203 3-8-0 42 ow1 RachealKneller(5) 1 42
(Mark Usher) *chsd ldrs: ev ch over 1f out: no ex fnl f* **40/1**

2421 **5** *nk* **Outlaw Torn (IRE)**[4] 2673 3-8-3 54 (e) DeclanCannon(3) 5 42
(Richard Guest) *hld up in tch: plld hrd: rdn over 2f out: styd on same pce fr over 1f out* **5/2**[1]

23-0 **6** *½* **Khazium (IRE)**[55] 1313 3-9-10 68 (p) ShaneKelly 3 59
(Pat Eddery) *hld up: hdwy over 4f out: outpcd 1/2-way: n.d after* **5/1**[3]

-360 **7** *5* **Pius Parker (IRE)**[14] 2367 3-8-4 59 (v) JoeFanning 4 25
(John Gallagher) *trckd ldrs: racd keenly: rdn and ev ch over 1f out: wknd fnl f* **8/1**

8 *19* **Hot Potato** 3-8-6 0 LukeMorris 10
(Tony Carroll) *prom: pushed along 1/2-way: wknd 2f out: t.o* **16/1**

2343 **9** *26* **Miss Purity Pinker (IRE)**[48] 1444 3-7-13 58 (v) CathyGannon 2
(David Evans) *sn pushed along in rr: bhd fr 1/2-way: eased: t.o* **10/1**

1m 27.31s (1.11) **Going Correction** +0.10s/f (Good) **9** Ran SP% **113.4**
Speed ratings (Par 97): **97,93,91,91,90 90,84,62,32**
toteswingers:1&2:£9.10, 2&3:£18.30, 1&3:£38.00 CSF £27.21 TOTE £4.70: £1.50, £2.10, £7.00; EX 27.00.Compton Target was claimed by J. M. Bradley for £5000.
Owner Erik Penser **Bred** R N Auld **Trained** Kingston Lisle, Oxon

FOCUS
A moderate claimer run in a time 2.20 seconds slower than the earlier Class 4 handicap for the 3yos. They raced middle-to-stands' side.
Khazium(IRE) Official explanation: jockey said colt lost a near-fore shoe
Miss Purity Pinker(IRE) Official explanation: jockey said filly moved poorly

2787 SMOOTH RADIO H'CAP (DIV I) 1m 1f 218y

4:20 (4:21) (Class 6) (0-65,65) 3-Y-O **£1,940** (£577; £288; £144) **Stalls** Low

Form RPR

600 **1** **Ultimate Destiny**[27] 1976 3-9-6 **64** JimCrowley 2 75
(Ralph Beckett) *mde all: rdn over 1f out: styd on wl* **9/1**

0-12 **2** *1 3/4* **Our Phylli Vera (IRE)**[20] 2162 3-9-4 **62**........................ FrankieDettori 4 69
(Harry Dunlop) *chsd wnr: rdn and ev ch over 1f out: styd on same pce ins fnl f* **4/1**[2]

4200 **3** *3 1/2* **Vexillum (IRE)**[4] 2673 3-9-1 **59**........................ SamHitchcott 15 59
(Mick Channon) *hld up: hdwy u.p over 2f out: r.o: nt rch ldrs* **7/1**[3]

0-06 **4** *shd* **Camrock Star (IRE)**[45] 1517 3-9-0 **58**........................ PaulMulrennan 17 58+
(David Evans) *s.i.s: hld up: hdwy over 1f out: r.o wl: nrst fin* **33/1**

05-0 **5** *1/2* **Leitrim King (IRE)**[41] 1606 3-9-4 **62**........................ ShaneKelly 13 61
(William Haggas) *prom: rdn over 3f out: sn outpcd: styd on u.p fnl f* **8/1**

6-06 **6** *shd* **Tigertoo (IRE)**[14] 2374 3-8-9 **53**........................ WilliamCarson 3 52
(Stuart Williams) *chsd ldrs: rdn over 2f out: no ex fnl f* **20/1**

2044 **7** *2 3/4* **Parque Atlantico**[15] 2353 3-7-13 **46** oh1........................(v) SimonPearce(3) 14 39
(Andrew Balding) *mid-div: hdwy over 4f out: rdn over 3f out: wknd fnl f* **18/1**

0402 **8** *1/2* **Thecornishcockney**[5] 2625 3-9-5 **63**........................(b) StevieDonohoe 12 55+
(John Ryan) *s.i.s: hld up: nt clr run over 2f out: swtchd lft over 1f out: nt clr run ins fnl f: nvr nr to chal* **7/1**[3]

2-55 **9** *1/2* **Foursquare Funtime**[113] 549 3-9-7 **65**........................ AdamKirby 10 56
(Reg Hollinshead) *hld up in tch: rdn over 2f out: wknd fnl f* **28/1**

000- **10** *1 1/2* **Solar View (IRE)**[235] 6828 3-8-6 **50**........................ LukeMorris 11 38
(Sir Mark Prescott Bt) *mid-div: lost pl 1/2-way: n.d after* **7/2**[1]

3446 **11** *3/4* **Arte Del Calcio**[53] 1353 3-9-4 **65**........................ SophieDoyle(3) 6 52
(Tony Carroll) *s.i.s: hld up: hdwy over 2f out: rdn and wknd over 1f out* **40/1**

040 **12** *5* **Purley Queen (IRE)**[14] 2367 3-8-11 **55**........................ JamesDoyle 1 32
(Sylvester Kirk) *hld up: rdn over 3f out: wknd over 1f out* **40/1**

00-0 **13** *6* **Delishuss**[50] 1415 3-8-2 **46**........................(b[1]) RichardThomas 9 11
(Dominic Ffrench Davis) *chsd ldrs: rdn over 3f out: wknd over 2f out* **66/1**

-003 **14** *1 1/2* **Hopes Rebellion**[15] 2341 3-8-4 **48**........................ PaulHanagan 16 10
(Declan Carroll) *hld up: rdn over 2f out: sn wknd* **25/1**

0-00 **15** *4* **Highly Likely (IRE)**[20] 2162 3-8-2 **46** oh1........................ CathyGannon 5
(John Dunlop) *chsd ldrs: rdn over 3f out: wknd over 2f out* **18/1**

2m 11.43s (3.53) **Going Correction** +0.10s/f (Good) **15** Ran SP% **120.2**
Speed ratings (Par 97): **89,87,84,84,84 84,82,81,81,80 79,75,70,69,66**
toteswingers:1&2:£8.00, 2&3:£7.70, 1&3:£10.90 CSF £41.43 CT £274.93 TOTE £7.90: £2.10, £1.80, £2.90; EX 54.70.
Owner D & J Newell **Bred** Derek & Judith Newell **Trained** Kimpton, Hants

FOCUS
The first two raced in the front pair throughout and the time was 1.49 seconds slower than the second division. The winner improved on his handicap debut and the second for the longer trip.
Ultimate Destiny Official explanation: trainer's rep said, regarding apparent improvement in form, that the gelding was better suited by the draw and good to soft ground.

2788 SMOOTH RADIO H'CAP (DIV II) — 1m 1f 218y
4:55 (4:57) (Class 6) (0-65,65) 3-Y-O **£1,940** (£577; £288; £144) **Stalls** Low

Form RPR

0-60 **1** **Sea Fever (IRE)**[20] 2172 3-9-6 **64**........................ KierenFallon 3 76+
(Luca Cumani) *hld up: hdwy over 3f out: led over 2f out: edgd rt over 1f out: shkn up ins fnl f: r.o* **5/2**[1]

00-0 **2** *1/2* **Grand Liaison**[17] 2280 3-7-13 **46** oh1........................ DominicFox(3) 13 57
(John Berry) *hld up: hdwy over 2f out: rdn to chse wnr over 1f out: r.o* **33/1**

600- **3** *3* **Neige D'Antan**[167] 7838 3-8-9 **53**........................ LukeMorris 2 58+
(Sir Mark Prescott Bt) *s.i.s: sn pushed along in rr: hdwy u.p over 2f out: wnt 3rd over 1f out: no imp ins fnl f* **6/1**[3]

00-0 **4** *10* **Kaiser Wilhelm (IRE)**[36] 1703 3-9-4 **62**........................ StevieDonohoe 14 47
(Paul Cole) *hld up: hdwy u.p over 1f out: nvr trbld ldrs* **33/1**

4344 **5** *7* **Bapak Pintar**[14] 2382 3-9-6 **64**........................ JamieSpencer 6 35
(Kevin Ryan) *hld up in tch: nt clr run over 3f out: swtchd rt over 2f out: wknd over 1f out* **4/1**[2]

0-00 **6** *6* **Kieron's Rock (IRE)**[17] 2283 3-8-9 **53**........................ PaulMulrennan 1 12
(Jedd O'Keeffe) *chsd ldr tl led 8f out: rdn and hdd over 2f out: wknd over 1f out* **40/1**

3053 **7** *10* **Angel Cake (IRE)**[10] 2495 3-7-12 **49** oh1 ow3.........(p) DannyBrock(7) 17
(Phil McEntee) *s.i.s: sn prom: chsd ldr over 3f out: rdn and ev ch over 2f out: wknd wl over 1f out: t.o* **28/1**

3140 **8** *2* **Cool Hand Luke (IRE)**[55] 1319 3-9-7 **65**...........(b[1]) RichardKingscote 11
(Tom Dascombe) *chsd ldrs: rdn over 2f out: sn wknd: eased: t.o* **16/1**

66-1 **9** *1 1/4* **Kingscombe (USA)**[56] 1278 3-9-6 **64**........................ AdamKirby 16
(Pat Eddery) *led 2f: chsd ldr tl rdn over 3f out: wkng whn nt clr run over 2f out: eased: t.o* **9/1**

-036 **10** *1 1/4* **Remember Rocky**[15] 2340 3-8-11 **55**........................(p) PaulHanagan 15
(Steve Gollings) *mid-div: lost pl over 6f out: n.d after: t.o* **7/1**

00-0 **11** *8* **Rain Dance**[11] 2441 3-8-10 **59**........................ AmyScott(5) 4
(Eve Johnson Houghton) *prom: racd keenly: hung lft and lost pl 6f out: bhd fnl 3f: t.o* **50/1**

0-24 **12** *3 1/2* **White Flight**[22] 2128 3-9-6 **64**........................ JimCrowley 12
(Jonathan Portman) *prom: rdn over 2f out: sn wknd and eased: t.o* **12/1**

5-00 **13** *2 1/4* **Princely Sum (IRE)**[12] 2430 3-9-4 **62**........................ WilliamCarson 8
(Stuart Williams) *s.i.s: hld up: rdn over 4f out: sn wknd: t.o* **33/1**

0-40 **14** *41* **Mariannes**[20] 2162 3-8-2 **46** oh1........................ CathyGannon 10
(John Dunlop) *a in rr: bhd and drvn along 1/2-way: sn lost tch: t.o* **28/1**

2m 9.94s (2.04) **Going Correction** +0.10s/f (Good) **14** Ran SP% **119.1**
Speed ratings (Par 97): **95,94,92,84,78 73,65,64,63,62 55,53,51,18**
toteswingers:1&2:£21.90, 2&3:£39.50, 1&3:£4.40 CSF £102.97 CT £464.72 TOTE £3.00: £1.70, £11.50, £3.20; EX 110.50.
Owner De La Warr Racing **Bred** K And Mrs Cullen **Trained** Newmarket, Suffolk

FOCUS
They finished strung out in a time 1.49 seconds faster than the first division and there should be plenty more to come from the winner, who was making his handicap debut. The first pair came clear.
Sea Fever(IRE) ◆ Official explanation: trainer's rep said, regarding apparent improvement in form, that the colt appeared to benefit from racing on turf and over a longer trip.
Kieron's Rock(IRE) Official explanation: jockey said gelding hung left
Rain Dance Official explanation: jockey said filly hung left

2789 LEICESTER MERCURY H'CAP — 5f 2y
5:25 (5:25) (Class 5) (0-75,73) 4-Y-O+ **£2,587** (£770; £384; £192) **Stalls** High

Form RPR

2042 **1** **Silvanus (IRE)**[33] 1800 7-9-3 **69**........................ PaulHanagan 1 84
(Paul Midgley) *trckd ldrs: plld hrd: led ins fnl f: rdn out* **11/2**[3]

0-30 **2** *1 1/4* **Whitecrest**[10] 2494 4-9-2 **68**........................ CathyGannon 9 78
(John Spearing) *racd alone on stands' side: chsd ldrs: rdn over 1f out: edgd rt: r.o* **9/1**

1464 **3** *2 3/4* **Mata Hari Blue**[10] 2482 6-9-4 **70**........................(t) LukeMorris 11 70
(John Holt) *s.i.s: hdwy 1/2-way: rdn over 1f out: styd on same pce ins fnl f* **5/2**[1]

6144 **4** *2 1/4* **Rylee Mooch**[32] 1828 4-9-2 **71**........................(e) DeclanCannon(3) 8 63
(Richard Guest) *chsd ldrs: led over 1f out: rdn and hdd ins fnl f: wknd towards fin* **12/1**

0-42 **5** *3/4* **Cruise Tothelimit (IRE)**[1] 2748 4-8-8 **60**........................ PaulMulrennan 7 49
(Ian Williams) *chsd ldrs: rdn 1/2-way: wknd ins fnl f* **11/4**[2]

1043 **6** *3/4* **Mother Jones**[14] 2360 4-9-1 **67**........................(p) JamesDoyle 10 54
(David Evans) *s.i.s: hld up: swtchd rt and hdwy over 1f out: sn rdn: wknd ins fnl f* **15/2**

4230 **7** *2 1/4* **Love You Louis**[19] 2195 6-9-5 **71**........................ ShaneKelly 4 50
(J R Jenkins) *chsd ldrs: rdn over 1f out: wknd fnl f* **10/1**

5-00 **8** *9* **Baby Queen (IRE)**[14] 2369 6-9-7 **73**........................ WilliamCarson 5 19
(Brian Baugh) *led over 3f: sn wknd* **28/1**

2145 **9** *1 3/4* **Court Applause (IRE)**[14] 2360 4-8-12 **64**........................ MartinDwyer 3
(William Muir) *s.i.s: outpcd* **16/1**

1m 0.7s (0.70) **Going Correction** +0.10s/f (Good) **9** Ran SP% **118.5**
Speed ratings (Par 103): **98,96,91,88,86 85,82,67,64**
toteswingers:1&2:£11.30, 2&3:£9.00, 1&3:£3.10 CSF £55.33 CT £156.31 TOTE £4.20: £1.90, £2.80, £1.10; EX 63.30.
Owner Colin Alton **Bred** Barronstown Stud And Mrs T Stack **Trained** Westow, N Yorks

FOCUS
They raced middle-to-stands' side in this modest sprint handicap. The winner rates back to his old best.
Rylee Mooch Official explanation: jockey said gelding lost both front shoes
T/Jkpt: Not won. T/Plt: £663.00 to a £1 stake. Pool of £87,357.41 - 96.18 winning tickets. T/Qpdt: £127.90 to a £1 stake. Pool of £6,184.26 - 35.78 winning tickets. CR

2770 REDCAR (L-H)
Tuesday, June 5

OFFICIAL GOING: Good to firm (good in places; watered; 8.5)
Wind: Light, half-behind Weather: Cloudy

2790 BRITISH STALLION STUDS SUPPORTING BRITISH RACING E B F MEDIAN AUCTION MAIDEN FILLIES' STKS — 6f
2:05 (2:05) (Class 5) 2-Y-O **£2,975** (£885; £442; £221) **Stalls** Centre

Form RPR

1 **Projectisle (IRE)** 2-9-0 0........................ PhillipMakin 3 74+
(Kevin Ryan) *mde all: rdn over 1f out: sn strly pressed: kpt on* **9/2**[2]

64 **2** *shd* **Fadeintoinfinity**[11] 2450 2-9-0 0........................ MartinHarley 4 74
(Mick Channon) *trckd ldr: rdn to chal over 1f out: kpt on but a jst hld* **13/8**[1]

3 *5* **Lady Margaeux (IRE)** 2-9-0 0........................ DanielTudhope 10 58+
(David O'Meara) *s.i.s: hld up: pushed along over 2f out: hdwy over 1f out: kpt on fnl f: wnt 3rd fnl 75yds* **11/1**

3403 **4** *1 3/4* **Jamnean**[15] 2349 2-9-0 0........................ RussKennemore 1 52
(John Holt) *prom: rdn 2f out: sn outpcd by ldng pair: no ex fnl f: lost 3rd fnl 75yds* **20/1**

00 **5** *nk* **Another Ponty**[10] 2508 2-9-0 0........................ DuranFentiman 2 51
(Tim Easterby) *dwlt: hld up in tch: pushed along and hdwy over 1f out: kpt on fnl f* **50/1**

2235 **6** *3/4* **Poetic Princess**[8] 2541 2-9-0 0........................ TonyCulhane 9 49+
(Jo Hughes) *prom: rdn and outpcd over 2f out: grad wknd fr over 1f out* **9/2**[2]

6 **7** *nk* **Blades Rose**[15] 2338 2-9-0 0........................ TonyHamilton 6 48
(Richard Fahey) *in tch: pushed along over 2f out: sn no imp* **20/1**

8 *7* **Ayasha** 2-9-0 0........................ TomEaves 7 25
(Bryan Smart) *dwlt: sn chsd ldrs: wknd over 1f out* **9/1**[3]

9 *1* **Double Happiness** 2-9-0 0........................ BarryMcHugh 5 22
(Brian Rothwell) *sn pushed along towards rr: a bhd:* **80/1**

0 **10** *1* **Kendal Princess (IRE)**[11] 2437 2-9-0 0........................ SilvestreDeSousa 8 19
(David O'Meara) *sn pushed along towards rr: a bhd* **14/1**

1m 11.95s (0.15) **Going Correction** -0.10s/f (Good) **10** Ran SP% **112.2**
Speed ratings (Par 90): **95,94,88,85,85 84,84,74,73,72**
toteswingers: 1&2 £3.50, 1&3 £10.40, 2&3 £6.20 CSF £11.21 TOTE £7.20: £1.90, £1.20, £2.80; EX 11.80.
Owner Mrs Angie Bailey **Bred** K B Lynch **Trained** Hambleton, N Yorks

FOCUS
The track had escaped any overnight rain and the going remained on the quick side. A median auction 2yo fillies' maiden with previous worthwhile form thin on the ground.

NOTEBOOK
Projectisle(IRE), a sister to three winners, was comfortably the pick of the paddock. She knew her job and the post came just in time, with the first two clear. She looked to be carrying some condition and she should go on from here. (op 4-1)
Fadeintoinfinity ◆, who recorded an RPR of 72 when fourth on her second start at Haydock, stuck to her task and would have got there in one more stride. She will surely go one better. (op 15-8 tchd 6-4)
Lady Margaeux(IRE), who has stamina on her dam's side, came from last to snatch third spot near the line. This will have taught her plenty and she will well suited by a seventh furlong. (op 10-1 tchd 12-1)
Jamnean, who had run poorly on her only previous turf start on soft ground (modest form in three AW runs also), will likely find easier opportunities down in grade. (tchd 22-1)
Another Ponty, well beaten on her two previous starts, shaped much better and appeals as a likely nursery type.
Poetic Princess, having her sixth start, looked rather light and is not progressing. (op 11-2)
Blades Rose, well beaten in a claimer first time, shaped much better despite racing keenly early on. On this showing she will win a claimer or a seller. (op 16-1)

2791 RACING UK SKY 432 (S) STKS — 7f
2:35 (2:35) (Class 6) 3-5-Y-O **£1,704** (£503; £251) **Stalls** Centre

Form RPR

0-00 **1** **Main Beach**[8] 2558 5-9-6 77........................(t) TomQueally 8 64
(Tobias B P Coles) *dwlt: hld up in tch: smooth hdwy 3f out: led 2f out: sn rdn clr: comf* **1/1**[1]

0650 **2** *4* **Thrust Control (IRE)**[24] 2091 5-8-13 49........................ JacobButterfield(7) 10 53
(Tracy Waggott) *led narrowly: rdn whn hdd 2f out: sn no ch w wnr: kpt on one pce* **25/1**

040- **3** *shd* **Bridge Valley**[159] 7911 5-9-1 49........................(b[1]) ShaneBKelly(5) 5 53
(Jason Ward) *pushed along leaving stall: hld up: rdn over 3f out: edgd rt to stands' rail over 2f out: kpt on: nrst fin* **66/1**

5005 **4** *3/4* **Maggie Mey (IRE)**[11] 2438 4-8-8 60........................ NedCurtis(7) 7 46
(Paul Midgley) *w ldr: rdn over 2f out: sn one pce: no ex and lost 3rd nr fin* **4/1**[2]

400- **5** 2 1/4 **Logans Legend (IRE)**[182] 7646 4-9-3 63........................(p) DaleSwift(3) 6 45
(Lawrence Mullaney) *racd keenly: trckd ldrs: rdn over 2f out: sn one pce: no ex ins fnl f* **18/1**

0-06 **6** 7 **Boga (IRE)**[55] 1294 5-8-8 44.......................... GemmaTutty(7) 9 21
(Karen Tutty) *trckd ldrs: rdn 3f out: wknd over 1f out* **33/1**

0-03 **7** 4 1/2 **Rasselas (IRE)**[8] 2536 5-9-6 64...................... AdrianNicholls 2 14
(David Nicholls) *prom: rdn over 3f out: wknd 2f out* **5/1**[3]

003 **8** 5 **Dunseverick (IRE)**[8] 2546 4-9-6 60.............................(e1) TonyCulhane 1
(Jo Hughes) *prom: rdn over 3f out: wknd over 2f out* **15/2**

000- **9** 2 1/4 **Saxby (IRE)**[283] 5490 5-8-13 45.......................... GeorgeChaloner(7) 3
(Alan Lockwood) *hld up a towards rr* **100/1**

000- **10** 6 **Valentine's Gift**[225] 7061 4-8-13 48...................... TerenceFury(7) 4
(Neville Bycroft) *hld up: a towards rr* **50/1**

1m 24.84s (0.34) **Going Correction** -0.10s/f (Good) **10** Ran SP% **114.9**
Speed ratings (Par 101): **94,89,89,88,85 77,72,67,64,57**
toteswingers: 1&2 £6.20, 1&3 £12.80, 2&3 £45.70 CSF £36.18 TOTE £2.00: £1.02, £7.30, £12.90; EX 24.00.The winner was sold to Paul Midgley for 8,200gns.

Owner Mrs R Coles **Bred** Miss J Chaplin **Trained** Newmarket, Suffolk

FOCUS
A one-horse seller on official ratings and so it proved. The winner did not need to match his best turf form.

2792 SUMMER WEDDING FAYRE HERE ON 29TH JULY H'CAP 1m 1f
3:10 (3:10) (Class 5) (0-75,75) 4-Y-O+ **£1,940** (£577; £288; £144) **Stalls** Low

Form RPR

46-4 **1** **Al Furat (USA)**[17] 2260 4-8-4 **63**...................... ShaneBKelly(5) 8 71
(Ron Barr) *dwlt: hld up: angled wd and gd hdwy 2f out: led 1f out: r.o wl* **8/1**

-402 **2** 1 3/4 **Whitby Jet (IRE)**[13] 2399 4-9-7 **75**...................... TomQueally 6 79
(Ed Vaughan) *hld up: stl gng wl towards rr 2f out: pushed along and hdwy over 1f out: chsd wnr ins fnl f: kpt on* **9/2**[1]

22-5 **3** 3 1/2 **Sinatramania**[7] 2588 5-8-3 **57**...................... FrannyNorton 11 53
(Tracy Waggott) *midfield: rdn 2f out: kpt on* **8/1**

-060 **4** 3/4 **Count Bertoni (IRE)**[10] 2510 5-9-5 **73**...................... DanielTudhope 7 68
(David O'Meara) *prom: rdn to ld over 2f out: hdd 1f out: no ex* **12/1**

-200 **5** 3/4 **Goodness**[32] 1822 4-8-13 **67**...................(v1) GrahamLee 2 60
(David O'Meara) *trckd ldrs: rdn over 2f out: one pce* **25/1**

00-2 **6** 2 1/2 **Come Here Yew (IRE)**[15] 2339 4-8-12 **73**...................... JasonHart(7) 4 61
(Declan Carroll) *trckd ldrs: rdn and lost pl over 2f out: no imp after* **13/2**[2]

24-0 **7** 1/2 **Tartan Gunna**[133] 285 6-9-7 **75**...................... JamesSullivan 10 61
(James Given) *hld up in midfield: rdn over 2f out: sn no imp* **14/1**

606- **8** 1 3/4 **Buzz Law (IRE)**[206] 7397 4-9-6 **74**...................... PhillipMakin 1 57
(Mrs K Burke) *dwlt: hld up in midfield towards inner: rdn over 2f out: no imp* **9/2**[1]

1466 **9** hd **I Confess**[42] 1587 7-9-5 **73**...................(b) SilvestreDeSousa 3 57
(Geoffrey Harker) *led: rdn whn hdd over 2f out: wknd and eased ins fnl f* **7/1**[3]

6000 **10** 3/4 **Transmit (IRE)**[7] 2588 5-7-9 **56**...................(b) GaryMahon(7) 5 36
(Tim Easterby) *in tch: rdn over 3f out: wknd over 1f out* **25/1**

6440 **11** 1/2 **Highlife Dancer**[10] 2498 4-8-12 **66**...................... MartinHarley 9 45
(Mick Channon) *midfield: rdn 3f out: wknd over 1f out* **8/1**

1m 53.68s (0.68) **Going Correction** +0.175s/f (Good) **11** Ran SP% **117.6**
Speed ratings (Par 103): **103,101,98,97,97 94,94,92,92,91 91**
toteswingers: 1&2 £6.10, 1&3 £8.30, 2&3 £5.10 CSF £43.89 CT £303.11 TOTE £11.00: £3.10, £1.50, £2.80; EX 31.00.

Owner P Cartmell **Bred** Philip Brown **Trained** Seamer, N Yorks

FOCUS
A wide-open handicap and the pace was strong. The first two were in the last pair turning for home. A personal best from the winner.

2793 FOLLOW REDCARRACING ON FACEBOOK & TWITTER H'CAP 5f
3:45 (3:46) (Class 4) (0-85,84) 4-Y-O+ **£4,075** (£1,212; £606; £303) **Stalls** Centre

Form RPR

-121 **1** **Bosun Breese**[3] 2719 7-8-13 **81** 6ex...................... LMcNiff(5) 10 91
(David Barron) *mde all: rdn 2f out: kpt on wl* **5/2**[1]

-064 **2** 3/4 **Tabaret**[3] 2693 9-8-3 **66** ow1...................(p) AmyRyan 7 74
(Richard Whitaker) *chsd ldrs: rdn and ev ch appr fnl f: kpt on* **16/1**

/40- **3** 1 1/4 **Secret Venue**[395] 1899 6-8-3 **66**...................... JamesSullivan 6 69
(Jedd O'Keeffe) *chsd ldrs: rdn over 2f out: kpt on* **66/1**

0230 **4** hd **Select Committee**[3] 2693 7-8-12 **75**...................(v) MichaelO'Connell 8 77
(John Quinn) *chsd ldrs: rdn over 2f out: kpt on* **16/1**

0003 **5** nk **The Nifty Fox**[6] 2596 8-8-3 **66**...................(p) SilvestreDeSousa 12 67
(Tim Easterby) *in tch: rdn 2f out: kpt on* **13/2**[3]

6-00 **6** 1 3/4 **Nickel Silver**[11] 2439 7-8-9 **72**...................(v) TomEaves 5 67
(Bryan Smart) *prom towards centre: rdn over 2f out: no ex ins fnl f* **50/1**

1-60 **7** 3/4 **Beauty Pageant (IRE)**[17] 2289 5-8-11 **81**.............. GeorgeChaloner(7) 9 73
(Ed McMahon) *midfield: hdwy to chse wnr 2f out: sn rdn and one pce* **12/1**

0-00 **8** nk **Lady Royale**[32] 1828 4-9-0 **80**...................(b) DaleSwift(3) 4 71
(Geoffrey Oldroyd) *hld up: rdn over 2f out: nvr threatened* **12/1**

115- **9** nse **Swendab (IRE)**[249] 6500 4-9-2 **79**...................(v) GrahamLee 3 70
(John O'Shea) *hld up: rdn over 2f out: nvr threatened* **12/1**

6211 **10** hd **Mercers Row**[21] 2140 5-8-13 **76**...................... DanielTudhope 2 66
(Noel Wilson) *chsd ldrs: rdn over 2f out: wknd ins fnl f* **9/1**

-361 **11** shd **Bedloe's Island (IRE)**[15] 2337 7-9-7 **84**...................... BarryMcHugh 11 74
(Neville Bycroft) *dwlt: hld up: nvr threatened* **9/2**[2]

311- **12** nk **Cool In The Shade**[237] 6801 4-8-9 **72**...................(b) TonyHamilton 13 61
(Paul Midgley) *prom: rdn over 2f out: wknd appr fnl f* **16/1**

620- **13** 3 3/4 **Eland Ally**[241] 6703 4-9-4 **81**...................... TomQueally 1 56
(Tom Tate) *hld up towards outer: rdn over 2f out: sn no imp: eased fnl f* **14/1**

57.39s (-1.21) **Going Correction** -0.10s/f (Good) **13** Ran SP% **120.9**
Speed ratings (Par 105): **105,103,101,101,101 98,97,96,96,96 95,95,89**
toteswingers: 1&2 £11.40, 1&3 £34.50, 2&3 £72.60 CSF £47.50 CT £2157.25 TOTE £4.50: £1.80, £5.30, £12.90; EX 56.00.

Owner Harrowgate Bloodstock Ltd **Bred** Lady Lonsdale **Trained** Maunby, N Yorks

FOCUS
A highly competitive sprint handicap with middle-to-stands' side seemingly at an advantage. The winner backed up his impressive Musselburgh win.

2794 BUY YOUR TICKETS ON-LINE @ REDCARRACING.CO.UK MEDIAN AUCTION MAIDEN STKS 1m 2f
4:15 (4:16) (Class 5) 3-5-Y-O **£1,940** (£577; £288; £144) **Stalls** Low

Form RPR

60- **1** **Mixora (USA)**[231] 6933 3-8-9 0...................... TomQueally 5 57
(Sir Henry Cecil) *trckd ldr: led narrowly over 2f out: pushed along whn strly pressed over 1f out: drvn and kpt on fnl f* **13/8**[2]

06-0 **2** 1/2 **Graceful Act**[64] 1170 4-9-5 54...................... DaleSwift(3) 3 56
(Ron Barr) *hld up in tch: pushed along and hdwy 3f out: rdn and upsides over 1f out: kpt on but a jst hld fnl f* **22/1**

0 **3** 5 **Airmyles**[15] 2339 4-9-8 0...................... ShaneBKelly(5) 2 51
(Tracy Waggott) *hld up in tch: rdn over 2f out: kpt on to go 3rd ins fnl f: no threat ldng pair* **66/1**

4 **4** 1 1/2 **Outback (IRE)**[70] 1053 3-9-0 79...................... GrahamLee 4 48
(Ann Duffield) *led at stdy pce: pushed along whn hdd over 2f out: sn struggling: wknd and lost 3rd ins fnl f* **11/10**[1]

5 7 **Variety Show (IRE)** 3-8-9 0...................... J-PGuillambert 1 32
(Sir Henry Cecil) *trckd ldr: pushed along over 3f out: wknd over 1f out: eased* **5/1**[3]

2m 13.0s (5.90) **Going Correction** +0.175s/f (Good)
WFA 3 from 4yo 13lb **5** Ran SP% **108.2**
Speed ratings (Par 103): **83,82,78,77,71**
CSF £27.33 TOTE £1.70: £1.10, £6.20; EX 21.50.

Owner K Abdulla **Bred** Millsec Ltd **Trained** Newmarket, Suffolk

FOCUS
A very weak median auction maiden run at a very steady pace to halfway. The winner probably didn't have to improve.

2795 WIN A VIP DAY OUT @ REDCARRACING.CO.UK H'CAP 6f
4:50 (4:53) (Class 5) (0-70,70) 3-Y-O **£1,940** (£577; £288; £144) **Stalls** Centre

Form RPR

-522 **1** **Dancheur (IRE)**[14] 2375 3-9-4 **67**...................... MartinHarley 1 82+
(Mrs K Burke) *mde all: rdn clr over 1f out: kpt on* **6/1**[3]

2-15 **2** 2 1/2 **Regal Acclaim (IRE)**[17] 2283 3-8-8 **57**...................... SilvestreDeSousa 5 64
(Tim Easterby) *trckd ldrs: rdn to chse wnr over 1f out: kpt on* **5/1**[2]

5-11 **3** 2 1/4 **Dutch Rose (IRE)**[7] 2591 3-9-5 **68** 6ex...................... DanielTudhope 13 68+
(David O'Meara) *hld up in tch: rdn over 2f out: hdwy over 1f out: kpt on* **7/4**[1]

-443 **4** 1 3/4 **Tahnee Mara (IRE)**[24] 2065 3-9-2 **65**...................... PhillipMakin 15 59
(Kevin Ryan) *chsd ldrs: rdn over 2f out: kpt on one pce* **18/1**

0-20 **5** 1 **Kyllachy Dancer**[29] 1912 3-8-10 **59**...................(v1) MichaelO'Connell 4 50
(John Quinn) *midfield: rdn over 2f out: kpt on* **33/1**

05-0 **6** 1 **Dazzlin Bluebell (IRE)**[22] 2130 3-8-2 **51** oh1...................... DuranFentiman 6 39
(Tim Easterby) *w ldr: rdn over 2f out: grad wknd over 1f out* **66/1**

-200 **7** nk **First Fast Now (IRE)**[14] 2375 3-8-8 **60**...................... DaleSwift(3) 10 47
(Nigel Tinkler) *hld up: rdn and sme hdwy over 1f out: one pce fnl f* **50/1**

346- **8** 1 **Oddysey (IRE)**[272] 5817 3-8-10 **62**...................... LeeTopliss(3) 12 46
(Michael Dods) *hld up: rdn over 2f out: nvr threatened* **14/1**

1-0 **9** 2 1/4 **La Salida**[33] 1798 3-9-5 **68**...................... GrahamGibbons 2 44
(David Barron) *chsd ldrs: rdn 3f out: wknd over 1f out* **16/1**

40-0 **10** 4 **New Romantic**[22] 2131 3-8-2 **51**...................... JamesSullivan 14 15
(Julie Camacho) *hld up: rdn over 3f out: a towards rr* **40/1**

041- **11** 3/4 **Fifteentwo**[244] 6628 3-9-7 **70**...................... AdrianNicholls 11 31
(David Nicholls) *dwlt: hld up: rdn over 3f out: nvr threatened* **10/1**

0-5 **12** 1/2 **Two Cities (IRE)**[21] 2143 3-9-2 **65**...................... GrahamLee 8 24
(Ann Duffield) *midfield: rdn over 3f out: sn wknd* **12/1**

0-46 **13** shd **Young Freddie (IRE)**[31] 1864 3-8-10 **59**...................... TomEaves 7 18
(Bryan Smart) *chsd ldrs: wknd over 2f out* **16/1**

-606 **14** 11 **Al Shaqab (IRE)**[11] 2459 3-9-2 **65**...................(b1) AmyRyan 9
(Kevin Ryan) *sn pushed along towards rr: bhd fnl 2f* **25/1**

1m 10.5s (-1.30) **Going Correction** -0.10s/f (Good) **14** Ran SP% **120.5**
Speed ratings (Par 99): **104,100,97,95,94 92,92,90,87,82 81,80,80,66**
toteswingers: 1&2 £4.00, 1&3 £3.50, 2&3 £3.10 CSF £34.73 CT £77.30 TOTE £7.80: £2.70, £1.90, £1.10; EX 35.80.

Owner Mark James & Mrs Elaine Burke **Bred** A F O'Callaghan **Trained** Middleham Moor, N Yorks

FOCUS
Quite a competitive 3yo handicap, but in the end a decisive all-the-way winner. He's rated up 8lb.

2796 VOLTIGEUR RESTAURANT 2 COURSES FOR £10.95 AMATEUR RIDERS' MAIDEN H'CAP 6f
5:20 (5:22) (Class 6) (0-65,63) 4-Y-O+ **£1,646** (£506; £253) **Stalls** Centre

Form RPR

0003 **1** **Hab Reeh**[13] 2406 4-10-0 **49** oh4...................(bt) MissSBrotherton 7 58
(Ruth Carr) *led after 1f: mde rest: clr over 2f out: drvn fnl f: hld on all out* **9/2**[2]

50- **2** hd **Sovereign Street**[347] 3347 4-10-9 **63**...................... MrGRSmith(5) 1 71
(Ann Duffield) *midfield: hdwy over 2f out: chsd wnr ins fnl f: kpt on: jst hld* **5/1**[3]

002- **3** 3 **Karate Queen**[371] 2593 7-9-9 **49** oh4...................... MissVBarr(5) 9 47
(Ron Barr) *midfield: hdwy to chse wnr over 1f out: kpt on one pce* **12/1**

0-60 **4** 5 **Spread Boy (IRE)**[25] 2033 5-9-7 **49** oh2...................... MrMAllan(7) 6 31
(Alan Berry) *led for 1f: remained prom: rdn and outpcd over 2f out: plugged on fnl f* **20/1**

6-00 **5** shd **Lady By Red (IRE)**[11] 2436 4-10-0 **49** oh2...................... MrFWindsorClive 14 31
(David Thompson) *prom: rdn over 2f out: plugged on* **28/1**

6004 **6** 1 1/4 **Merrjanah**[6] 2601 4-9-8 **50**...................... MrAFrench(7) 8 28
(John Wainwright) *hld up: rdn over 2f out: kpt on fnl f: nvr threatened* **11/2**

6-00 **7** 1 **Benidorm**[11] 2441 4-9-13 **53**...................(b) MrNSlatter(5) 12 28
(John Wainwright) *chsd ldrs: rdn over 2f out: wknd fnl f* **14/1**

0006 **8** 1/2 **Under Par**[3] 2690 4-10-0 **49** oh4...................... MissJCoward 3 22
(Michael Easterby) *w ldr: rdn and lost pl 3f out: no threat after* **7/2**[1]

500- **9** 1 3/4 **Isle Of Ellis (IRE)**[245] 6602 5-9-11 **49** oh4.........(v) MissMMullineaux(3) 5 17
(Ron Barr) *hld up: nvr threatened* **25/1**

/00- **10** 2 1/4 **Zoom In**[225] 7063 4-9-9 **49** oh4...................... MrAaronJames(5) 11
(Lee James) *hld up: nvr threatened* **50/1**

0-00 **11** 3 3/4 **Deslaya (IRE)**[36] 1717 4-9-7 **49**...................... MissMKeegan(7) 15
(Linda Stubbs) *sn pushed along towards rr: a bhd* **8/1**

0/6- **12** nk **Kheya (IRE)**[511] 119 4-10-2 **56**...................... MissRSmith(5) 2
(Micky Hammond) *chsd ldrs: wknd over 2f out* **33/1**

-600 **13** 5 **Tinzo (IRE)**[5] 2621 4-9-7 **49** oh4...................... MissFrancesHarper(7) 13
(Alan Berry) *slowly away: a towards rr* **33/1**

0-60 14 *10* **Field Finner**[117] 478 4-9-7 **49** oh1 MissKMargarson(7) 4
(Scott Dixon) *v.s.a: a wl bhd* **20/1**

1m 11.6s (-0.20) **Going Correction** -0.10s/f (Good) **14** Ran SP% **122.6**
Speed ratings (Par 101): **97,96,92,86,85 84,82,82,79,76 71,71,64,51**
toteswingers: 1&2 £5.10, 1&3 £4.30, 2&3 £6.50 CSF £25.34 CT £268.41 TOTE £7.00: £1.70, £3.50, £3.50; EX 45.70.
Owner Mrs Ruth A Carr **Bred** The Anglo Irish Choral Society **Trained** Huby, N Yorks

FOCUS
A rock-bottom amateurs' maiden handicap for 4yos and up. Only five of the 14 runners carried their correct mark and the first three finished clear. In common with the other sprints on the card the winner made virtually all.
T/Plt: £22.20 to a £1 stake. Pool: £53,830.19. 1,769.33 winning tickets. T/Qpdt: £13.50 to a £1 stake. Pool £3,176.23. 173.66 winning tickets. AS

2461 YARMOUTH (L-H)
Tuesday, June 5

OFFICIAL GOING: Good to firm (good in places; 7.3)
Wind: fresh, against Weather: dry, breezy

2797 BRITISH STALLION STUDS SUPPORTING BRITISH RACING E B F NOVICE STKS 6f 3y
2:20 (2:21) (Class 5) 2-Y-O **£3,234** (£962; £481; £240) **Stalls** Centre

Form RPR

1 **Amazonas (IRE)** 2-8-9 0 HayleyTurner 2 76+
(Ed Dunlop) *dropped in after s: t.k.h: hld up wl in tch: swtchd lft and effrt over 1f out: led fnl 100yds: r.o wl: pushed out* **7/1**

2 *¾* **Living Desert** 2-9-0 0 KirstyMilczarek 5 79+
(James Toller) *t.k.h: hld up wl in tch in rr: effrt and rn green over 1f out: hdwy to chal ins fnl f: kpt on* **17/2**

1 3 *¾* **Beedee**[13] 2384 2-8-9 0 WilliamTwiston-Davies(7) 6 78
(Richard Hannon) *sn pressing ldr: rdn and led narrowly wl over 1f out: hdd fnl 100yds: no ex* **6/4**[1]

4 *½* **Shafaani** 2-8-9 0 BrettDoyle 7 70
(Clive Brittain) *t.k.h: led tl hdd and rdn wl over 1f out: stl ev ch but unable qck 1f out: one pce ins fnl f* **16/1**

5 *2½* **Mowhoob** 2-9-0 0 WilliamBuick 4 67+
(John Gosden) *chsd ldrs: pushed along and lost pl 1/2-way: rdn and flashed tail ent fnl f: styd on same pce fnl f* **9/2**[3]

6 *nk* **Admiralofthesea (USA)** 2-9-0 0 AndreaAtzeni 8 67
(Robert Eddery) *in tch: rdn and effrt to press ldrs over 1f out: unable qck 1f out: wknd ins fnl f* **7/2**[2]

44 7 *4½* **Windsor Rose (IRE)**[52] 1388 2-8-9 0 TomMcLaughlin 1 48
(Mark Brisbourne) *t.k.h: hld up in tch in rr: rdn and no prog 2f out: wknd over 1f out* **50/1**

631 8 *5* **Captain Blue**[16] 2309 2-8-7 0 RyanWhile(7) 3 38
(Bill Turner) *sn bustled along to chse ldrs: rdn 2f out: wknd over 1f out: bhd fnl f* **25/1**

1m 16.62s (2.22) **Going Correction** +0.125s/f (Good) **8** Ran SP% **115.1**
Speed ratings (Par 93): **90,89,88,87,84 83,77,70**
toteswingers:1&2:£9.50, 1&3:£3.20, 2&3:£3.80 CSF £64.47 TOTE £8.40: £2.30, £2.90, £1.20; EX 82.80 Trifecta £151.20 Pool £541.63 - 2.65 winning units..
Owner Sir Robert Ogden **Bred** Sir Robert Ogden **Trained** Newmarket, Suffolk

FOCUS
Bottom bend dolled out 1.5m. Four of the previous five winners of this race had won their only previous starts, but this time the first two home were newcomers.

NOTEBOOK
Amazonas(IRE) is out of a winning juvenile over this trip and she certainly knew her job, travelling well off the pace and quickening when asked. She did this nicely and looks capable of even better. (op 6-1 tchd 8-1)
Living Desert, a 100,000gns colt out of a 1m4f Listed winner, attracted market support but showed signs of greenness and did well to stay on for a promising second. His pedigree suggests he will improve for further. (op 12-1 tchd 8-1)
Beedee made a winning debut over this trip at Chepstow last month under William Twiston-Davies and as that was a Class 5 contest, he incurred just a 2lb penalty. Soon in front, he battled on gamely when challenged but the two newcomers proved too strong for him late on. (op 7-4 tchd 11-8)
Shafaani, a half-sister to the stable's smart filly Elshabakiya, came with a promising challenge and may have hit the front for a few strides around a furlong out, but couldn't maintain it. This was encouraging enough. (tchd 20-1)
Mowhoob, a 65,000gns colt out of a 7f Fibresand winner, was the stable's first 2yo runner of the season and attracted support, but he didn't find much off the bridle and one crack with the whip resulted in a swish of the tail. He will need to have learnt something from this. (op 11-2 tchd 4-1)
Admiralofthesea(USA), retained for 32,000GBP as a 2yo, is out of a winner at up to 1m2f but looked too green to do himself justice on this debut. (op 3-1 tchd 4-1)

2798 WEDDINGS AT GREAT YARMOUTH RACECOURSE (S) STKS 6f 3y
2:50 (2:50) (Class 6) 2-Y-O **£1,617** (£481; £240; £120) **Stalls** Centre

Form RPR

6625 1 **Tiger Sunset (IRE)**[16] 2309 2-8-4 0 (p) AliceHaynes(7) 4 60
(J S Moore) *t.k.h: in tch: chsd ldr 1/2-way: led jst over 2f out: pressed and rdn ins fnl f: fnd ex and kpt on* **7/1**

6 2 *1* **Strawberry Duck (IRE)**[10] 2492 2-8-6 0 KirstyMilczarek 5 52
(Amy Weaver) *chsd ldrs: rdn and chsd wnr over 1f out: pressed wnr fnl 100yds: no ex and one pce after* **12/1**

4361 3 *3½* **Suivez L'Argent**[11] 2462 2-8-9 0 HarryBentley(3) 7 47
(Joseph Tuite) *awkward leaving stalls and dwlt: in tch in last pair: hdwy to chse ldrs 1/2-way: chsd wnr 2f out: wandered and fnd little u.p over 1f out: wknd ins fnl f* **6/4**[1]

5 4 *2* **Lord Avonbrook**[7] 2579 2-8-4 0 RyanWhile(7) 3 40+
(Bill Turner) *broke wl: chsd ldr tl lost pl and short of room 1/2-way: trying to rally and edging lft over 1f out: no prog fnl f* **3/1**[2]

4663 5 *6* **Cherryred Girl (IRE)**[11] 2462 2-8-3 0 (b) RyanPowell(3) 1 17
(J S Moore) *led tl jst over 2f out: wkng whn edgd rt jst over 1f out: fdd fnl f* **12/1**

344 6 *1½* **Reberty Lee**[35] 1738 2-8-11 0 (p) ChrisCatlin 2 18
(Noel Quinlan) *hld up in tch in last pair: drvn and fnd little over 1f out: wknd ent fnl f* **9/2**[3]

1m 17.48s (3.08) **Going Correction** +0.125s/f (Good) **6** Ran SP% **111.1**
Speed ratings (Par 91): **84,82,78,75,67 65**
toteswingers:1&2:£6.20, 1&3:£2.60, 2&3:£3.90 CSF £76.10 TOTE £9.20: £2.80, £4.80; EX 54.20.The winner was bought in for 4,600gns.
Owner G V March & J S Moore **Bred** D G Iceton **Trained** Upper Lambourn, Berks

FOCUS
This was a poor seller with the winning time 0.86 seconds slower than the opener.

NOTEBOOK
Tiger Sunset(IRE) had shown precious little ability in four previous starts in varied company (his second place at Wolverhampton came in a three-runner event) but, having got a nice lead from his stable-companion, he was sent for home over 2f out and kept on finding just enough. He was bought in for 4,600gns, but will be very fortunate to find another race as bad as this. (op 6-1 tchd 15-2)
Strawberry Duck(IRE), dropped in grade after finishing well beaten in a Lingfield turf maiden on debut, kept hounding the winner throughout the last furlong but couldn't quite force her head in front. (tchd 16-1)
Suivez L'Argent, penalised for winning a seller here 11 days earlier, was trying 6f for the first time and had every chance but didn't see it out. Her penalty is likely to remain a problem in races like this. (op 7-4)
Lord Avonbrook was expected to need the run when a well-beaten fifth of eight on his recent Lingfield Polytrack debut, but his trainer wasted no time in dropping him in class. He was well backed, but didn't appear to be helping his rider at all and failed to make much impression once asked for an effort. (op 4-1 tchd 11-4)

2799 INJURED JOCKEYS FUND MAIDEN STKS (DIV I) 1m 3y
3:25 (3:26) (Class 5) 3-Y-O+ **£2,264** (£673; £336; £168) **Stalls** Centre

Form RPR

5 1 **Utterance**[17] 2280 3-9-1 0 WilliamBuick 7 81+
(John Gosden) *t.k.h: chsd ldrs: led over 1f out: rdn ent fnl f: styd on strly and drew clr ins fnl f* **4/9**[1]

6-0 2 *3¼* **Tin Pan Alley**[36] 1703 4-9-12 0 AmirQuinn 9 77
(Giles Bravery) *chsd ldr tl led over 2f out: rdn and hdd over 1f out: kpt on u.p tl no ex fnl 150yds: battled on to hold 2nd* **14/1**

0 3 *nk* **Ascription (IRE)**[17] 2273 3-9-1 0 HayleyTurner 6 73
(Ed Dunlop) *stdd s: hld up in rr: hdwy jst over 2f out: rdn to chse ldng pair over 1f out: styd on same pce ins fnl f* **5/1**[2]

0-0 4 *10* **Langham Lily (USA)**[17] 2280 3-8-10 0 RichardMullen 3 45
(Chris Wall) *hld up in rr: rdn: edgd lft and effrt over 2f out: outpcd by ldng trio and wl btn 1f out: plugged on* **12/1**[3]

0 5 *¾* **Mankini (IRE)**[14] 2381 3-8-8 0 HayleyBurton(7) 5 49+
(Luca Cumani) *in tch towards rr: outpcd 2f out and sn wl btn: plugged on ins fnl f* **20/1**

\- 6 *1* **Bubbly Bounty** 3-8-10 0 LiamJones 2 41
(Alan Bailey) *in tch in midfield: rdn and struggling 2f out: sn outpcd and wl btn ent fnl f* **33/1**

0 7 *6* **My Manekineko**[17] 2280 3-9-1 0 FrederikTylicki 1 32
(J R Jenkins) *hld up in tch in midfield: rdn and struggling over 2f out: wl bhd over 1f out* **20/1**

8 *16* **Spark Of Genius** 3-8-10 0 (t) KirstyMilczarek 10
(James Toller) *towards rr: hdwy into midfield 5f out: rdn and wknd over 2f out: t.o and eased ins fnl f* **14/1**

00 9 *14* **Tatting**[14] 2380 3-9-1 0 LiamKeniry 8
(Chris Dwyer) *led tl over 2f out: sn wknd: t.o and eased ins fnl f* **100/1**

6 10 *7* **Al Sirat**[57] 1261 6-9-12 0 NeilChalmers 4
(Michael Appleby) *chsd ldrs: rdn and lost pl 3f out: wl bhd 2f out: t.o and eased ins fnl f* **50/1**

1m 40.45s (-0.15) **Going Correction** +0.125s/f (Good)
WFA 3 from 4yo+ 11lb **10** Ran SP% **122.4**
Speed ratings (Par 103): **105,101,101,91,90 89,83,67,53,46**
toteswingers:1&2:£5.30, 1&3:£3.50, 2&3:£9.70 CSF £8.69 TOTE £1.50: £1.10, £2.60, £1.60; EX 9.10 Trifecta £62.80 Pool £776.58 - 9.14 winning units..
Owner George Strawbridge **Bred** George Strawbridge **Trained** Newmarket, Suffolk

FOCUS
A modest maiden and none of the eight to have run before had managed to make the frame. The winning time was still 1.8 seconds faster than the second division.

2800 INJURED JOCKEYS FUND MAIDEN STKS (DIV II) 1m 3y
4:00 (4:02) (Class 5) 3-Y-O+ **£2,264** (£673; £336; £168) **Stalls** Centre

Form RPR

2 1 **Lahaag**[17] 2279 3-9-1 0 TadhgO'Shea 3 83
(John Gosden) *in tch: rdn to chse ldng pair wl over 1f out: led ins fnl f: styd on wl: rdn out* **15/8**[2]

2 *2* **Barkis**[272] 3-9-1 0 MircoDemuro 2 78
(Luca Cumani) *chsd ldr: rdn and ev ch over 1f out: unable qck and styd on same pce ins fnl f* **15/2**

0 3 *3¾* **Azerodegree (IRE)**[17] 2280 3-9-1 0 AndreaAtzeni 9 69
(Marco Botti) *hld up in tch: rdn and outpcd wl over 1f out: kpt on but no imp fnl f* **20/1**

53 4 *1¾* **Register (IRE)**[17] 2273 3-9-1 0 NeilCallan 8 65
(William Muir) *t.k.h: chsd ldrs tl led over 2f out: rdn over 1f out: hdd jst ins fnl f: fdd fnl 100yds* **7/4**[1]

06 5 *9* **Wildomar**[17] 2279 3-9-1 0 WilliamBuick 4 43
(Jeremy Noseda) *s.i.s: hld up in rr: rdn and effrt over 2f out: 5th and wl btn over 1f out* **11/2**[3]

0 6 *6* **Pont Menai**[20] 2172 3-9-1 0 FrederikTylicki 5 29
(J R Jenkins) *t.k.h: hld up in tch: j. path over 5f out: rdn and lost tch over 2f out* **66/1**

7 *7* **Angel Of Mercy** 4-9-4 0 AdamBeschizza(3) 6
(Julia Feilden) *s.i.s: sn rdn along and rn green in rr: lost tch over 2f out: t.o and eased fnl f* **50/1**

8 *7* **Tysoe Lad**[70] 4-9-12 0 NeilChalmers 10
(Michael Appleby) *chsd ldrs tl 3f out: sn lost pl and bhd 2f out: t.o and eased ins fnl f* **125/1**

-0 9 *18* **Fauran (IRE)**[62] 1182 3-8-10 0 BrettDoyle 1
(Clive Brittain) *led tl over 2f out: sn dropped out and bhd: t.o and eased fnl f* **20/1**

1m 42.25s (1.65) **Going Correction** +0.125s/f (Good)
WFA 3 from 4yo 11lb **9** Ran SP% **112.1**
Speed ratings (Par 103): **96,94,90,88,79 73,66,59,41**
toteswingers:1&2:£16.40, 1&3:£10.60, 2&3:£38.00 CSF £14.55 TOTE £3.50: £1.40, £1.30, £6.40; EX 14.40 Trifecta £93.10 Pool £1,037.16 - 8.24 winning units..
Owner Hamdan Al Maktoum **Bred** Shadwell Estate Company Limited **Trained** Newmarket, Suffolk

FOCUS
A couple in this division had already been placed, but the winning time was 1.8 seconds slower than the first leg.

Wildomar Official explanation: trainer's rep said colt was unsuited by the good to firm ground

2801 ANNUAL MEMBERSHIP AT GREAT YARMOUTH RACECOURSE H'CAP 1m 3y

4:30 (4:30) (Class 4) (0-80,80) 4-Y-0+ **£4,075** (£1,212; £606; £303) **Stalls** Centre

Form RPR

6-12 **1** **Barwick**[38] 1680 4-9-3 **76**........ TedDurcan 6 87+
(Mark H Tompkins) *hld up in last pair: smooth hdwy to join ldrs on bit 2f out: rdn to ld over 1f out: edging lft but styd on wl fnl f* **7/4**[1]

4100 **2** 1 ½ **Patriotic (IRE)**[19] 2199 4-8-9 **68**........ MichaelHills 4 74
(Chris Dwyer) *in tch in last trio: hdwy over 2f out: rdn and ev ch over 1f out: unable qck w wnr 1f out: styd on same pce fnl f* **8/1**

0-03 **3** 2 ½ **Catchanova (IRE)**[13] 2399 5-8-9 **68**........ JohnFahy 5 68
(Eve Johnson Houghton) *hld up in tch in last trio: rdn and hdwy over 2f out: chsd ldng trio and edgd lft u.p over 1f out: 3rd and one pce fnl f* **8/1**

33-0 **4** 2 ¼ **John Biscuit (IRE)**[10] 2500 4-9-5 **78**........ DavidProbert 3 73
(Andrew Balding) *taken down early: hld up in tch: rdn and effrt whn n.m.r 2f out: drvn and outpcd jst over 1f out: wl hld fnl f* **5/1**[2]

-402 **5** 6 **Mcbirney (USA)**[15] 2328 5-9-1 **77**........ PatrickHills(3) 9 58
(Paul D'Arcy) *in tch: hdwy and rdn to ld 2f out: hdd and drvn over 1f out: wknd fnl f* **6/1**[3]

-001 **6** 2 ¾ **Amoya (GER)**[11] 2465 5-9-4 **80**........(t) AdamBeschizza(3) 1 55
(Philip McBride) *chsd ldr tl over 2f out: sn drvn: wknd qckly over 1f out: wl btn fnl f* **9/1**

56-0 **7** 15 **Darcey**[18] 2251 6-8-7 **66**........ KirstyMilczarek 8
(Amy Weaver) *led tl rdn and hdd 2f out: sn wknd u.p: wl btn fnl f* **28/1**

6-04 **8** 11 **Audacious**[15] 2328 4-9-3 **76**........ PatCosgrave 7
(Michael Quinn) *chsd ldrs tl rdn and lost pl 3f out: wl bhd 2f out: t.o* **20/1**

00-1 **9** 9 **Maz**[89] 842 4-8-0 **66**........ NatashaEaton(7) 10
(Alan Bailey) *in tch: rdn 5f out: lost pl and bhd over 3f out: virtually p.u ins fnl f: t.o* **16/1**

1m 40.43s (-0.17) **Going Correction** +0.125s/f (Good) **9** Ran SP% **113.6**
Speed ratings (Par 105): **105,103,101,98,92 90,75,64,55**
toteswingers:1&2:£8.80, 1&3:£12.60, 2&3:£24.10 CSF £16.12 CT £88.16 TOTE £2.50: £1.50, £3.10, £1.60; EX 18.70 Trifecta £97.80 Pool £946.51 - 7.16 winning units..
Owner Steve Ashley **Bred** Dullingham Park **Trained** Newmarket, Suffolk

FOCUS
A fair handicap in which the winning time was fractionally faster than the first division of the maiden and much faster than the second.
Mcbirney(USA) Official explanation: trainer said gelding was unsuited by the good to firm ground

2802 ODDSCHECKER.MOBI H'CAP 1m 3y

5:05 (5:06) (Class 6) (0-60,60) 3-Y-0 **£1,617** (£481; £240; £120) **Stalls** Centre

Form RPR

0 **1** **Watt Broderick (IRE)**[11] 2449 3-9-5 **58**........ FrederikTylicki 7 70+
(Ian Williams) *hld up in rr: hdwy 3f out: chal and hung rt over 1f out: rdn to ld jst ins fnl f: kpt edging rt: fnd ex u.p wl ins fnl f: rdn out* **4/1**[1]

-440 **2** nk **Speedi Mouse**[27] 1979 3-9-5 **58**........ RichardMullen 8 69
(Philip McBride) *hld up towards rr: hdwy over 2f out: rdn and chsd ldrs over 1f out: ev ch ins fnl f: r.o but hld towards fin* **16/1**

-053 **3** 3 ½ **Adverse (IRE)**[14] 2374 3-8-6 **52**........ IanBurns(7) 12 55
(Michael Bell) *hld up in tch: hdwy to chse ldrs 3f out: rdn to ld 2f out: hdd over 1f out: wknd ins fnl f* **11/1**

335 **4** 2 ¾ **Sudden Wish (IRE)**[14] 2367 3-8-9 **55**........ NatashaEaton(7) 9 52
(Alan Bailey) *chsd ldrs: wnt 2nd over 3f out: rdn and ev ch wl over 1f out: edgd lft and unable qck over 1f out: wknd fnl f* **9/1**

-401 **5** 1 ¼ **Archina (IRE)**[13] 2386 3-9-2 **55**........ DavidProbert 4 49
(Andrew Balding) *led tl rdn and hdd 2f out: drvn and no ex over 1f out: wknd fnl f* **15/2**

0-30 **6** 5 **Coach Montana (IRE)**[35] 1740 3-8-12 **54**........ AdamBeschizza(3) 10 36
(Jane Chapple-Hyam) *in tch: rdn and effrt over 2f out: 6th and no prog wl over 1f out: wknd over 1f out* **16/1**

042 **7** 5 **Collectable**[14] 2367 3-8-12 **51**........ LeeNewman 2 22
(Jonathan Portman) *chsd ldrs: rdn and unable qck over 2f out: outpcd and btn wl over 1f out: sn wknd* **6/1**[3]

0000 **8** 1 ¼ **Thecornishcowboy**[7] 2582 3-8-13 **52**........(bt[1]) BrettDoyle 11 20
(John Ryan) *in tch in midfield: rdn and effrt over 2f out: no prog and wknd wl over 1f out* **40/1**

00-5 **9** 1 ¼ **Coup De Grace (IRE)**[31] 1852 3-9-7 **60**........(p) NeilCallan 3 25
(Amanda Perrett) *chsd ldr tl over 3f out: sn struggling u.p: wknd over 2f out: no ch fnl 2f* **10/1**

000- **10** nk **Critical Point**[202] 7431 3-8-7 **46** oh1........ ChrisCatlin 6 10
(Sir Mark Prescott Bt) *sn bhd and rdn along 5f out: struggling 1/2-way: modest hdwy fnl f: n.d* **16/1**

005- **11** 1 **Tresabella**[225] 7066 3-8-8 **47** oh1 ow1........ NeilChalmers 1 9
(Michael Appleby) *chsd ldrs: rdn and struggling over 3f out: wknd wl over 2f out: no ch fnl 2f* **50/1**

0-03 **12** ¾ **Authoritarian**[5] 2628 3-8-13 **59**........ WilliamTwiston-Davies(7) 15 19
(Richard Hannon) *in tch in midfield: rdn and fnd little over 2f out: sn wknd: wl btn over 1f out* **11/2**[2]

0-00 **13** 10 **Graylyn Olivaa**[15] 2341 3-8-7 **46** oh1........(b[1]) AndreaAtzeni 5
(Robert Eddery) *in tch: rdn and wknd over 2f out: wl bhd fnl 2f* **80/1**

0-35 **14** 10 **Men Don't Cry (IRE)**[8] 2548 3-9-7 **60**........(b[1]) LiamKeniry 14
(Ed de Giles) *in tch: rdn and struggling 3f out: sn lost pl: wl bhd and eased ins fnl f: t.o* **16/1**

46-6 **15** 11 **Fen Flyer**[35] 1740 3-8-7 **46** oh1........ MartinLane 13
(Chris Dwyer) *in tch: rdn and struggling 1/2-way: wl bhd over 2f out: t.o and eased ins fnl f* **66/1**

2-00 **16** 8 **Possibly**[14] 2367 3-9-2 **58**........ HarryBentley(3) 16
(Peter Chapple-Hyam) *in tch: rdn and lost pl over 3f out: t.o and eased fnl f* **33/1**

1m 42.62s (2.02) **Going Correction** +0.125s/f (Good) **16** Ran SP% **122.5**
Speed ratings (Par 97): **94,93,90,87,86 81,76,74,73,73 72,71,61,51,40 32**
toteswingers:1&2:£19.00, 1&3:£7.50, 2&3:£19.70 CSF £69.63 CT £671.04 TOTE £5.20: £1.40, £3.20, £2.70, £1.60; EX 91.00 Trifecta £777.50 Part won. Pool £1,050.76 - 0.20 winning units..
Owner Patrick Kelly **Bred** Joe Fogarty **Trained** Portway, Worcs

FOCUS
A moderate handicap, but this big field finished well spread out and a gamble was landed.
Watt Broderick(IRE) Official explanation: trainer said, regarding apparent improvement in form, that the gelding benefited from a drop back in trip.

Archina(IRE) Official explanation: jockey said filly ran too free

2803 ODDSCHECKER.COM H'CAP 7f 3y

5:35 (5:37) (Class 6) (0-60,60) 3-Y-0 **£1,617** (£481; £240; £120) **Stalls** Centre

Form RPR

0-66 **1** **Mr Fickle (IRE)**[24] 2065 3-9-6 **59**........ GeorgeBaker 8 68+
(Gary Moore) *stdd s: hld up in rr: hdwy over 2f out: rdn to chse ldrs over 1f out: drvn and ev ch ins fnl f: r.o wl to ld towards fin* **7/2**[1]

-063 **2** nk **Pendle Lady (IRE)**[8] 2540 3-9-2 **55**........ TomMcLaughlin 12 63
(Mark Brisbourne) *hld up towards rr: hdwy 3f out: rdn and chsd ldrs wl over 1f out: ev ch 1f out: led ins fnl f: kpt on wl tl hdd and no ex towards fin* **10/1**

354 **3** 3 ½ **Kashmiri Star**[24] 2086 3-9-0 **53**........ PatCosgrave 7 52
(Michael Quinn) *in tch in midfield: rdn to chse ldr 2f out: drvn and unable qck over 1f out: plugged on same pce fnl f: wnt 3rd last strides* **14/1**

6-05 **4** nk **Moody Dancer**[22] 2136 3-9-7 **60**........ DavidProbert 1 58
(William Muir) *chsd ldr tl led 3f out: rdn 2f out: drvn and hdd ins fnl f: wknd fnl 75yds and lost 3rd last strides* **7/1**[2]

0-24 **5** 1 ¾ **Silver Lace (IRE)**[39] 1637 3-9-6 **59**........ TedDurcan 15 52
(Chris Wall) *hld up in rr: rdn and hdwy over 2f out: 5th and no imp fr over 1f out* **8/1**[3]

0-00 **6** 5 **Sapphire Seeker**[17] 2262 3-9-5 **58**........ AndreaAtzeni 13 38
(Des Donovan) *in tch in midfield: rdn and effrt over 2f out: no imp wl over 1f out: sn wknd* **16/1**

0544 **7** 8 **Rainbow Riches (IRE)**[14] 2367 3-8-1 **47** ow1........ JoshBaudains(7) 9 5
(Roger Curtis) *chsd ldrs: rdn to go 2nd 3f out tl 2f out: wknd over 1f out: eased fnl f* **9/1**

5-46 **8** 1 ¾ **Indiana Guest (IRE)**[22] 2131 3-8-12 **54**........ RyanPowell(3) 11 7
(George Margarson) *v.s.a: bhd: swtchd lft and hdwy over 2f out: drvn and btn wl over 1f out: sn wknd* **22/1**

-350 **9** 1 **Love Grows Wild (USA)**[14] 2367 3-9-1 **54**........ HayleyTurner 14 4
(Michael Bell) *hld up in rr: swtchd lft and rdn wl over 2f out: no prog whn nt clr run and hmpd ent fnl 2f: no ch after* **10/1**

0-05 **10** 13 **Strictly Mine**[20] 2162 3-8-9 **48**........(p) LeeNewman 3
(Jonathan Portman) *led tl rdn and hdd 3f out: wknd and wl bhd 2f out: t.o and eased fnl f* **7/1**[2]

060 **11** 1 ½ **Mystical Witch**[15] 2332 3-9-2 **55**........ ChrisCatlin 2
(Christine Dunnett) *chsd ldrs tl 1/2-way: sn toiling and lost pl: t.o fnl f* **66/1**

600- **12** nk **La Sonadora**[208] 7342 3-8-11 **50**........ LiamJones 4
(John Spearing) *in tch: rdn and lost pl qckly over 2f out: t.o and eased ins fnl f* **40/1**

0-00 **13** 1 **Denton Dancer**[8] 2548 3-9-7 **60**........(b) JackMitchell 5
(James Eustace) *restless in stalls: chsd ldr tl 3f out: sn lost pl u.p: t.o and eased fnl f* **50/1**

40-0 **14** 8 **Ellastina (IRE)**[15] 2336 3-9-7 **60**........ FrederikTylicki 10
(Richard Fahey) *in tch in midfield: rdn 3f out: sn btn and bhd fnl 2f: t.o and eased fnl f* **20/1**

406 **15** 7 **Tatty**[25] 2050 3-9-5 **58**........ NeilCallan 16
(Ian Wood) *chsd ldrs tl 1/2-way: sn lost pl: wl bhd fnl 2f: t.o and eased fnl f* **14/1**

1m 27.86s (1.26) **Going Correction** +0.125s/f (Good) **15** Ran SP% **120.7**
Speed ratings (Par 97): **97,96,92,92,90 84,75,73,72,57 55,55,54,45,37**
toteswingers:1&2:£8.80, 1&3:£12.60, 2&3:£24.10 CSF £36.30 CT £447.87 TOTE £4.60: £2.10, £3.30, £2.30; EX 43.70 Trifecta £293.20 Pool £1,287.81 - 3.25 winning units..
Owner Tony Perkins **Bred** M Duffy **Trained** Lower Beeding, W Sussex

FOCUS
Only one of these had won a race before, but quite a few were entitled to improve for the switch to handicapping.
Mr Fickle(IRE) Official explanation: trainer's rep said, regarding apparent improvement in form, that the gelding benefited from the step up to 7f and the good to firm ground.
Rainbow Riches(IRE) Official explanation: trainer said filly finished distressed
Indiana Guest(IRE) Official explanation: trainer said gelding was slowly away
La Sonadora Official explanation: stewards noted that the blindfold which had become trapped between rider's leg and saddle dislodged approaching 4f out.
Denton Dancer Official explanation: trainer said gelding bled from the nose

2804 BEST ODDS @ ODDSCHECKER.COM H'CAP 1m 2f 21y

6:05 (6:05) (Class 6) (0-55,55) 4-Y-0+ **£1,617** (£481; £240; £120) **Stalls** Low

Form RPR

0-34 **1** **The Ducking Stool**[52] 1379 5-8-4 **46**........ AdamBeschizza(3) 8 56
(Julia Feilden) *led for 2f: chsd ldr after tl rdn to ld ent fnl 2f: drvn and kpt on wl fnl f* **8/1**

06-0 **2** 2 **Camera Shy (IRE)**[27] 1984 8-8-12 **54**........ AshleyHamblett(3) 11 60
(Kevin Morgan) *racd in last trio: hdwy over 2f out: rdn to chse clr ldng pair wl over 1f out: chsd wnr ins fnl f: kpt on but no imp* **10/1**

2044 **3** 2 **Avon Supreme**[26] 2013 4-8-10 **49**........ JackMitchell 1 51
(Gay Kelleway) *t.k.h: chsd ldrs: rdn to chse wnr ent fnl 2f: unable qck over 1f out: lost 2nd and wknd ins fnl f* **11/1**

0060 **4** 9 **Gay Gallivanter**[11] 2463 4-8-7 **46** oh1........(p) AndreaAtzeni 9 30
(Michael Quinn) *chsd ldrs: rdn and unable qck over 2f out: 5th and wl btn over 1f out: plugged on to go 4th ins fnl f* **33/1**

3452 **5** 1 ¼ **So Is She (IRE)**[11] 2467 4-8-13 **52**........(be) LiamKeniry 2 34
(Alan Bailey) *in tch in midfield: drvn and outpcd 3f out: plugged on but no ch w ldrs fnl 2f* **3/1**[1]

0541 **6** hd **Sky Diamond (IRE)**[11] 2467 4-8-9 **55**........(b) GeorgeDowning(7) 12 36
(John Mackie) *chsd ldr tl led after 2f: drvn and hdd ent fnl 2f: sn struggling: 4th and wl btn over 1f out* **7/2**[2]

3430 **7** ¾ **General Tufto**[27] 1988 7-8-12 **51**........(b) MartinLane 4 31
(Charles Smith) *bhd: rdn 5f out: no ch but plugged on fr over 1f out: n.d* **14/1**

2053 **8** 3 ¼ **Market Puzzle (IRE)**[11] 2467 5-9-1 **54**........(p) TedDurcan 3 27
(Mark Brisbourne) *hld up off the pce in midfield: rdn and effrt 4f out: no prog and wl btn 2f out* **6/1**[3]

0000 **9** 14 **Rasteau (IRE)**[7] 2586 4-8-7 **46** oh1........(b[1]) LiamJones 5
(Tom Keddy) *a towards rr: rdn and toiling 4f out: wl bhd fnl 2f* **40/1**

-044 **10** 7 **Coupland Lass (IRE)**[11] 2467 4-8-13 **52**........ NeilCallan 6
(Willie Musson) *t.k.h: hld up in midfield: rdn and no prog 4f out: wknd and wl bhd fnl 2f* **7/1**

-465 **11** 29 **Phoenix Flame**[103] 675 4-8-11 **50**........(t) KirstyMilczarek 10
(Brendan Powell) *a bhd: lost tch over 3f out: t.o fnl 2f* **20/1**

2m 9.38s (-1.12) **Going Correction** -0.075s/f (Good) **11** Ran SP% **119.4**
Speed ratings (Par 101): **101,99,97,90,89 89,88,86,75,69 46**
toteswingers:1&2:£19.00, 1&3:£7.50, 2&3:£19.70 CSF £84.75 CT £891.41 TOTE £8.90: £2.80, £4.20, £3.00; EX 109.90 Trifecta £1002.90 Part won. Pool £1,355.38 - 0.40 winning units..
Owner Mrs S McGuiness **Bred** Cheveley Park Stud Ltd **Trained** Exning, Suffolk

FOCUS
A moderate handicap.

Phoenix Flame Official explanation: trainer's rep said filly had a breathing problem
T/Plt: £264.30 to a £1 stake. Pool:£62,833.55 - 173.51 winning tickets T/Qpdt: £11.50 to a £1 stake. Pool:£5,448.62 - 350.50 winning tickets SP

LE LION-D'ANGERS (R-H)

Tuesday, June 5

OFFICIAL GOING: Turf: soft

2805a PRIX URBAN SEA (LISTED RACE) (4YO+ FILLIES & MARES) (TURF) 1m 2f

1:35 (12:00) 4-Y-0+ **£21,666** (£8,666; £6,500; £4,333; £2,166)

RPR

1 **Brasileira**[29] 4-8-11 0 .... AlexisBadel 10 103
(J-M Beguigne, France) **18/5**[2]

2 *1 ½* **Amare**[19] 5-8-11 0 .... (b) StephanePasquier 5 100
(P Harley, Germany) **7/2**[1]

3 *1 ½* **Street Secret (USA)**[36] 1766 4-8-11 0 .... Jean-BernardEyquem 2 97
(Mme Pia Brandt, France) **15/1**

4 *shd* **Yukatana (FR)**[28] 4-8-11 0 .... AlexandreRoussel 8 97
(C Lotoux, France) **16/1**

5 *¾* **Calipatria**[37] 5-8-11 0 .... FabriceVeron 3 95
(H-A Pantall, France) **6/1**[3]

6 *2* **Oekaki (FR)**[28] 5-9-2 0 .... AdrienFouassier 4 96
(Y Barberot, France) **9/1**

7 *1 ½* **Footsteppy (IRE)**[222] 4-8-11 0 .... FredericSpanu 7 91
(J E Hammond, France) **27/1**

8 *10* **Fleur Enchantee (FR)**[29] 8-8-11 0 .... (b) RonanThomas 6 71
(P Van De Poele, France) **6/1**[3]

9 *15* **Katmandoune (FR)**[70] 4-9-2 0 .... JohanVictoire 9 46
(Mme M Bollack-Badel, France) **18/1**

10 *3* **Tameen**[24] 2066 4-8-11 0 .... JulienAuge 1 35
(Ed Dunlop) *sn led: hld a narrow ld tl hdd over 2f out: no rspnse u.p: eased fnl 1 1/2f* **63/10**

2m 11.03s (131.03) **10 Ran SP% 117.2**
WIN (incl. 1 euro stake): 4.60. PLACES: 1.80, 1.80, 3.30. DF: 8.40. SF: 19.60.
Owner Ecurie Serval **Bred** Petra Bloodstock Agency Ltd **Trained** France

2806 - (Foreign Racing) - See Raceform Interactive

TABY (R-H)

Tuesday, June 5

OFFICIAL GOING: Turf: heavy

2807a JR FORVALTNING STOCKHOLMS STORA PRIS (GROUP 3) (4YO+) (TURF) 1m 1f 165y

8:12 (12:00) 4-Y-0+ **£56,179** (£28,089; £13,483; £8,988; £5,617)

RPR

1 **Sir Lando**[16] 2322 5-9-2 0 .... FJohansson 8 112
(Wido Neuroth, Norway) *hld up in last trio: rdn to improve over 2 1/2f out: r.o to ld jst ins fnl f: bounded clr: impressive* **78/10**[3]

2 *5 ½* **Without Fear (FR)**[243] 4-9-2 0 .... JacobJohansen 9 101
(Arnfinn Lund, Norway) *midfield on outer: rdn over 2 1/2f out: kpt on to go 2nd ins fnl f: no ch w wnr* **7/10**[1]

3 *2* **Bank Of Burden (USA)**[117] 486 5-9-2 0 .... Per-AndersGraberg 3 97
(Niels Petersen, Norway) *hld up towards rr on inner: prog into midfield over 4f out: rdn to chal 2f out: kpt on one pce ins fnl f* **81/10**

4 *1* **Tertullus (FR)**[38] 9-9-2 0 .... RafaelSchistl 2 95
(Rune Haugen, Norway) *broke wl: stdd and settled in midfield on inner: prog to trck ldng pair over 3f out: rdn to chal 2f out: briefly led over 1f out: hdd jst ins fnl f: no ex and dropped to 4th cl home* **11/2**[2]

5 *1 ¾* **Touch Of Hawk (FR)**[240] 6-9-2 0 .... LennartHammer-Hansen 4 91
(Wido Neuroth, Norway) *midfield on outer: smooth prog to chal over 2 1/2f out: rdn over 2f out: outpcd over 1f out: plugged on* **32/1**

6 *nk* **Peas And Carrots (DEN)**[21] 2160 9-9-2 0 .... EspenSki 6 91
(Lennart Reuterskiold Jr, Sweden) *hld up in last on outer: rdn to improve over 3f out: outpcd over 1 1/2f out: r.o to go 7th wl ins fnl f: gng on at fin* **115/10**

7 *3* **Palermo (GER)**[240] 6-9-2 0 .... CarlosLopez 7 85
(Cathrine Erichsen, Norway) *led: rdn over 3f out: hdd over 1f out: fdd: eased cl home* **47/1**

8 *1 ¾* **Boxing Day**[38] 5-9-2 0 .... ManuelMartinez 5 81
(Bent Olsen, Denmark) *prom in main body of field: lost pl qckly over 3f out: rdn over 2f out: sn btn* **55/1**

9 *7* **Energia Central (BRZ)**[445] 5-9-2 0 .... AStarke 1 67
(Fabricio Borges, Sweden) *hld up in last pair on inner: rdn and outpcd in last over 4f out: nvr a factor* **81/10**

10 *dist* **Falmouth Bay (USA)**[329] 3959 4-9-2 0 .... RafaeldeOliveira 10
(Catharina Vang, Sweden) *trckd ldr in clr 2nd: rdn and lost pl over 3f out: wknd and dropped to last in st: t.o* **178/10**

2m 3.9s (4.60) **10 Ran SP% 127.8**
PARI-MUTUEL (all including 1sek stake): WIN 8.82; PLACE 2.15, 1.40, 2.36; SF 21.63.
Owner Stall Perlen **Bred** Stowell Hill Ltd **Trained** Norway

2541 KEMPTON (A.W) (R-H)

Wednesday, June 6

OFFICIAL GOING: Standard
Wind: Fresh, half behind Weather: Fine but cloudy

2808 WIN BIG WITH BETDAQ MULTIPLES MEDIAN AUCTION MAIDEN STKS 5f (P)

6:00 (6:00) (Class 6) 2-Y-0 **£1,617** (£481; £240; £120) **Stalls** Low

Form RPR

32 1 **Jubilee Brig**[13] 2420 2-9-3 0 .... RyanMoore 5 84
(Gary Moore) *mde virtually all: rdn to assert jst over 1f out: drvn clr* **4/7**[1]

4 2 *2 ½* **Three Crowns**[16] 2343 2-8-12 0 .... JamesDoyle 6 70
(Ian Wood) *pressed wnr: stl chalng over 1f out: one pce and wl hld fnl f* **17/2**[3]

2 3 *3 ½* **Napinda**[12] 2462 2-8-12 0 .... NeilCallan 1 57
(Des Donovan) *trckd ldng pair: rdn 2f out: one pce and no imp fr over 1f out* **33/1**

4 *¾* **Kicken Off (IRE)** 2-9-3 0 .... AdamKirby 3 60
(Phil McEntee) *slowest away and wl bhd early: rchd 4th 2f out: pushed along and kpt on same pce after* **66/1**

5 *2 ½* **Lilly May (IRE)** 2-8-5 0 .... DannyBrock(7) 2 46
(Phil McEntee) *s.i.s: outpcd and bhd early: nvr a factor: tk modest 5th fnl f* **66/1**

4 6 *2 ¾* **Augustinian**[26] 2039 2-9-3 0 .... RichardHughes 4 41
(Richard Hannon) *s.i.s: sn pushed along in 4th and nvr gng wl: dropped to last fnl f* **11/4**[2]

1m 0.05s (-0.45) **Going Correction** -0.075s/f (Stan) **6 Ran SP% 106.8**
Speed ratings (Par 91): **100,96,90,89,85 80**
toteswingers: 1&2 £4.80, 1&3 £1.60, 2&3 £2.00 CSF £5.49 TOTE £1.70: £1.10, £2.90; EX 5.10.
Owner Lookout Partnership **Bred** Sir Eric Parker **Trained** Lower Beeding, W Sussex

FOCUS
The front two disputed the lead from the off, but still finished clear of the others in a time 0.08 seconds quicker than the following Class 5 handicap for older horses.

NOTEBOOK
Jubilee Brig ran third behind a subsequent Listed winner over C&D on his debut, and was then beaten only a neck at Salisbury (5f, firm) behind a horse who followed up in a conditions race, so he set a decent standard. He was pressed for much of the way by the runner-up, but had the advantage of the rail and was always doing enough, winning in the manner of a pretty useful sprinter. There was a suggestion afterwards he'll be considered for a race at Royal Ascot. (op 4-9)
Three Crowns showed plenty of pace to match strides with the winner, but that rival had the rail and proved too strong. She was confirming the promise of her debut fourth at Windsor and can be expected to do better again. Her connections suggested she could take her chance in the Windsor Castle. (op 9-1 tchd 10-1)
Napinda, runner-up in a Yarmouth seller on her debut, was well placed behind the duelling leaders but just wasn't good enough. (op 20-1)
Kicken Off(IRE), a half-brother to a winner of a 6f juvenile seller, showed ability after missing the break. He should build on this.
Lilly May(IRE), a 5,500gns purchase, has a pedigree that's a mix of speed and stamina. This was a respectable introduction.
Augustinian shaped okay on his debut at Lingfield, but was never going at any stage this time. (op 7-2)

2809 BACK OR LAY BETDAQ.COM H'CAP 5f (P)

6:30 (6:33) (Class 5) (0-70,70) 3-Y-0+ **£2,264** (£673; £336; £168) **Stalls** Low

Form RPR

0060 1 **Pick A Little**[22] 2146 4-9-9 **65** .... RichardHughes 1 74
(Brian Ellison) *led: pushed along and hdd over 1f out: rdn and styd on wl to ld again ins fnl f: gng away fin* **3/1**[2]

3 2 *1 ¼* **Black Baccara**[37] 1720 5-9-11 **70** .... (be) RyanClark(3) 4 71
(Phil McEntee) *mostly trckd wnr: moved up to ld over 1f out gng easily: rdn and fnd nil: hdd ins fnl f: wknd nr fin* **14/1**

3560 3 *¾* **Choice Words (USA)**[13] 2421 4-9-11 **67** .... KieranO'Neill 8 68
(Emma Lavelle) *t.k.h: hld up in tch: effrt 2f out: disp 3rd jst over 1f out but nt qckn: kpt on nr fin* **13/2**[3]

4510 4 *shd* **Welsh Inlet (IRE)**[15] 2360 4-9-5 **64** .... SeanLevey(3) 2 65
(John Bridger) *cl up: trckd ldng pair 2f out: nt qckn over 1f out: kpt on ins fnl f* **14/1**

1-50 5 *3 ¼* **Jolly Ranch**[21] 2165 6-9-3 **59** .... FergusSweeney 10 48
(Tony Newcombe) *hld up fr wd draw and in last pair early: prog after 2f: wnt 5th 2f out: no imp on ldrs after: lost grnd fnl f* **14/1**

-600 6 *1 ¾* **Lucky Art (USA)**[84] 890 6-9-8 **67** .... HarryBentley(3) 12 50
(Conor Dore) *settled in rr fr wd draw: outpcd 2f out: pushed along and no imp after* **33/1**

000- 7 *nse* **Gottcher**[224] 7104 4-9-10 **66** .... RyanMoore 6 49
(David Barron) *racd wd: prom: lost grnd bnd over 2f out: sn btn* **15/8**[1]

226 8 *1 ¾* **Cliffords Reprieve**[83] 912 4-9-5 **61** .... (b) SebSanders 9 37
(Eric Wheeler) *racd wd: in tch tl wknd quite qckly over 1f out* **10/1**

0004 9 *¾* **With Hindsight (IRE)**[22] 2146 4-9-5 **66** .... DavidKenny(5) 3 40
(Michael Scudamore) *w.w and wl in rr: pushed along over 1f out: nvr in it* **25/1**

402- 10 *1 ¼* **Ishetoo**[224] 7106 8-10-0 **70** .... AdamKirby 5 39
(Peter Grayson) *v reluctant to enter stalls: slowest away: a in last pair: nvr a factor* **20/1**

2110 11 *6* **Punching**[30] 1934 8-9-13 **69** .... GeorgeBaker 7 17
(Conor Dore) *racd wd: prom to 1/2-way: sn lost pl qckly: t.o* **20/1**

1m 0.13s (-0.37) **Going Correction** -0.075s/f (Stan) **11 Ran SP% 118.5**
Speed ratings (Par 103): **99,97,95,95,90 87,87,84,83,81 71**
toteswingers: 1&2 £7.20, 1&3 £6.20, 2&3 £21.10 CSF £42.01 CT £265.13 TOTE £4.30: £1.90, £2.80, £2.70; EX 41.70 Trifecta £299.70 Pool: £494.20 - 1.22 winning units..
Owner The K A C Partnership **Bred** D R Tucker **Trained** Norton, N Yorks

FOCUS
A few of these lost their chance by going wide.

2810 BETDAQ MOBILE APPS H'CAP 1m 2f (P)

7:00 (7:00) (Class 3) (0-95,94) 4-Y-0+
£6,411 (£1,919; £959; £479; £239; £120) **Stalls** Low

Form RPR

40-0 1 **Tropical Beat**[30] 1924 4-8-12 **85** .... WilliamBuick 9 95
(John Gosden) *hld up in 9th: prog on wd outside fr over 2f out: hd at awkward angle but sustained run to ld last 100yds* **13/2**[3]

10-0 2 *¾* **Proud Chieftain**[19] 2248 4-8-12 **85** .... (p) JamesDoyle 5 93
(Clifford Lines) *hld up in 5th: prog over 2f out: rdn to ld over 1f out: styd on but hdd and outpcd last 100yds* **8/1**

6150 3 *2* **Tappanappa (IRE)**[31] 1882 5-9-4 **91** .... (v) JimmyFortune 2 95
(Andrew Balding) *pushed up to chse ldng trio: rdn and effrt 2f out: styd on fr over 1f out: tk 3rd ins fnl f: one pce last 100yds* **11/1**

4222 4 *2 ¼* **Tinshu (IRE)**[67] 1137 6-9-7 **94** .... (p) FergusSweeney 11 94+
(Derek Haydn Jones) *hld up in last and wl off the pce: looking for room 2f out: stl last jst over 1f out: r.o fnl f: tk 4th nr fin: no ch* **16/1**

054/ 5 *¾* **Nafaath (IRE)**[385] 6710 6-9-3 **90** .... SebSanders 8 88
(Neil King) *s.i.s: hld up in 8th: looking for room 2f out: prog over 1f out: styd on same pce fnl f* **66/1**

444 6 *1 ½* **Suits Me**[21] 2176 9-9-6 **93** .... RichardHughes 4 88
(David Barron) *led at gd pce: tried to kick on 2f out: hdd & wknd over 1f out* **6/1**[2]

1530 7 *1* **Dunhoy (IRE)**[19] 2257 4-8-8 **81** .... MartinLane 3 74
(Tony Newcombe) *rousted along early: sn in 6th: rdn 1/2-way: struggling over 2f out: n.d over 1f out* **9/1**

1252 8 *1* **Megalala (IRE)**[63] 1186 11-8-5 **78** .... KieranO'Neill 10 69
(John Bridger) *mostly chsd ldr to wl over 1f out: wknd* **25/1**

3100 **9** 2 ¼ **Standpoint**[14] 2405 6-8-2 **78**........(p) HarryBentley(3) 6 65
(Conor Dore) *chsd ldng pair to wl over 1f out: wknd* **50/1**

2/1- **10** 3 ¼ **Laatafreet (IRE)**[328] 4023 4-9-7 **94**........ FrankieDettori 7 74
(Saeed Bin Suroor) *s.i.s: settled in 7th: rdn over 2f out: sn no prog: wknd over 1f out* **5/4**[1]

2m 4.46s (-3.54) **Going Correction** -0.075s/f (Stan) **10** Ran SP% **114.7**
Speed ratings (Par 107): **111,110,108,107,106 105,104,103,101,99**
toteswingers: 1&2 £17.10, 1&3 £12.10, 2&3 £13.10 CSF £55.69 CT £561.97 TOTE £7.00: £1.60, £3.10, £3.50; EX 68.70 TRIFECTA Not won..
Owner Normandie Stud Ltd **Bred** Normandie Stud Ltd **Trained** Newmarket, Suffolk

FOCUS
The pace was overly strong (only time on the card to dip under standard) with Suits Me hassled by Megalala.

NOTEBOOK
Tropical Beat was only 1-9 coming into this, but he was in the right place for much of the way considering how the race unfolded and won despite going wide into the straight and carrying his head high. He doesn't appeal as one to follow. (op 6-1 tchd 11-2)
Proud Chieftain, in cheekpieces for the first time, raced closer to the pace than the winner, but he was probably second best anyway. Whatever, he might have a bit more to offer.
Tappanappa(IRE) has gained both his wins to date over 1m4f and was one-paced over this shorter trip, despite the strong gallop. (op 14-1)
Tinshu(IRE), returning from 67 days off, finished well after having to wait for a clear run and would surely have finished closer had she enjoyed a smoother trip, although she was closing off a quick pace. (op 12-1)
Nafaath(IRE) made a respectable debut for new connections after a lengthy absence. (op 50-1)
Laatafreet(IRE) looked potentially smart when winning a Leicester maiden last July, but he hadn't been seen since and ran no sort of race on this return. He had run well here on his debut, so the surface shouldn't have been an issue. Official explanation: jockey said colt never travelled (op 6-4)

2811 BETDAQ CASINO GAMES H'CAP 7f (P)

7:30 (7:37) (Class 6) (0-65,65) 4-Y-0+ **£1,617** (£481; £240; £120) **Stalls** Low

Form RPR

-506 **1** **Zing Wing**[34] 1769 4-9-2 **65**........ DuilioDaSilva(5) 3 74
(Paul Cole) *chsd ldr: rdn over 2f out: wanting to hang over 1f out: kpt on to ld ins fnl f* **6/1**[3]

5-00 **2** ½ **Beautiful Lando (FR)**[15] 2373 4-9-3 **61**........(b) StevieDonohoe 6 69
(Heather Main) *chsd ldrs in 5th: clsd fr 2f out: chal and upsides ins fnl f: edgd rt and nt qckn* **4/1**[2]

0010 **3** 1 ½ **Gallantry**[15] 2373 10-9-3 **61**........ TomMcLaughlin 10 65
(Paul Howling) *settled wl in rr: rdn over 2f out: styd on fr over 1f out to take 3rd nr fin* **16/1**

00P- **4** ¾ **Imjin River (IRE)**[232] 6939 5-8-11 **60**........ AshleyMorgan(5) 2 62
(William Stone) *chsd ldng trio: clsd on inner fr 2f out: chal 1f out: no ex last 150yds* **33/1**

2502 **5** nk **Perfect Ch'l (IRE)**[9] 2546 5-9-6 **64**........(v[1]) NeilCallan 11 65
(Ian Wood) *racd freely: led at gd pce: rdn and hung bdly lft fr 2f out: hdd and fdd ins fnl f* **7/1**

540- **6** 1 **Paphos**[249] 6543 5-9-3 **64**........(v) RyanClark(3) 8 62
(Stuart Williams) *wl in rr: rdn over 2f out: tried to cl over 1f out: no hdwy fnl f* **9/1**

051- **7** ½ **Micky P**[259] 6257 5-9-5 **63**........(v) SaleemGolam 9 60
(Stuart Williams) *wl in rr: effrt over 2f out: tried to cl u.p over 1f out: no hdwy after* **16/1**

23-2 **8** 4 **Golden Compass**[19] 2251 4-9-6 **64**........ WilliamCarson 5 50
(Giles Bravery) *trckd ldng pair: urged along and nt qckn over 2f out: wknd over 1f out* **5/2**[1]

200 **9** ½ **Vhujon (IRE)**[19] 2230 7-9-1 **59**........ AdamKirby 4 44
(Peter Grayson) *towards rr: rdn and tried to cl on ldrs 2f out: wknd fnl f* **11/1**

-403 **10** 13 **National Hope (IRE)**[15] 2362 4-9-5 **63**........(vt) PatCosgrave 13 12
(George Baker) *got stuck in stalls and lft at least 20 l: nvr able to rcvr: t.o* **10/1**

1303 **11** 2 ¼ **Piccolo Express**[16] 2354 6-9-4 **62**........ J-PGuillambert 14
(Brian Baugh) *chsd ldrs on outer: lost grnd rapidly fr 1/2-way and wd bnd 3f out: t.o* **16/1**

1m 26.08s (0.08) **Going Correction** -0.075s/f (Stan) **11** Ran SP% **123.4**
Speed ratings (Par 101): **96,95,93,92,92 91,90,86,85,70 68**
toteswingers: 1&2 £5.40, 1&3 £43.50, 2&3 £69.90 CSF £31.84 CT £385.67 TOTE £7.70: £1.90, £2.40, £6.50; EX 43.40 Trifecta £115.90 Part won. Pool: £156.68 - 0.50 winning units..
Owner P F I Cole Ltd **Bred** Deepwood Farm Stud **Trained** Whatcombe, Oxon

FOCUS
There was a false start after West Leake burst his stall open, and Imjin River had to be withdrawn as he couldn't be pulled up before passing the winning post. The pace was strong, but this is form to wary of.

2812 BRITISH STALLION STUDS SUPPORTING BRITISH RACING E B F MAIDEN FILLIES' STKS 6f (P)

8:00 (8:03) (Class 5) 2-Y-0 **£3,299** (£981; £490; £245) **Stalls** Low

Form RPR

1 **Exceptionelle** 2-9-0 0........ NeilCallan 4 84+
(Roger Varian) *fractious preliminaries: hld up in midfield: prog gng strly 2f out: led jst ins fnl f: pushed out firmly to assert* **9/4**[1]

2 1 ¼ **Sugar House (USA)** 2-9-0 0........ MickaelBarzalona 12 81+
(Mahmood Al Zarooni) *wnt lft s: rn green in rr: drvn and gd prog on wd outside fr 2f out: styd on to take 2nd last 50yds: no real threat to wnr* **8/1**

3 **3** ½ **Indignant**[13] 2407 2-9-0 0........ RyanMoore 10 79
(Richard Hannon) *w ldr: led 2f out: rdn and hdd jst ins fnl f: kpt on but lost 2nd last 50yds* **10/1**

4 2 ¾ **Mystical Moment** 2-9-0 0........ RichardHughes 5 71+
(Richard Hannon) *mde most to 2f out: fdd fnl f* **7/1**

5 hd **Masarah (IRE)** 2-9-0 0........ MartinDwyer 1 71+
(Clive Brittain) *hld up in midfield: effrt over 2f out: swtchd rt and cl up over 1f out: fdd* **33/1**

22 **6** 2 ¾ **Back In The Frame**[44] 1556 2-9-0 0........ JimCrowley 2 64+
(Tom Dascombe) *restrained bhd ldng pair: effrt over 2f out: hld whn hmpd on inner over 1f out: fdd* **9/2**[2]

4 **7** 1 **Glen Ginnie (IRE)**[13] 2407 2-9-0 0........ WilliamBuick 3 59
(Charles Hills) *in tch towards rr: shkn up over 2f out: sn outpcd and btn* **7/1**

2 **8** nk **Jet Acclaim (IRE)**[16] 2349 2-9-0 0........ AdamKirby 9 58
(Marco Botti) *tk fierce hold: cl up tl wknd 2f out* **6/1**[3]

9 ½ **Our Golden Girl** 2-9-0 0........ LiamKeniry 6 56
(Mark Usher) *mostly in last: nvr a factor* **100/1**

10 7 **Assertive Agent** 2-9-0 0........ TedDurcan 7 35
(David Lanigan) *restless stalls: s.s: in tch to over 2f out: wknd qckly* **40/1**

1m 13.09s (-0.01) **Going Correction** -0.075s/f (Stan) **10** Ran SP% **114.8**
Speed ratings (Par 90): **97,95,94,91,90 87,85,85,84,75**
toteswingers: 1&2 £6.90, 1&3 £6.80, 2&3 £18.10 CSF £20.57 TOTE £4.00: £2.50, £2.20, £2.10; EX 33.30 Trifecta £150.90 Pool: £448.80 - 2.20 winning units..
Owner Thurloe Thoroughbreds XXX **Bred** The Kingwood Partnership **Trained** Newmarket, Suffolk
■ Stewards' Enquiry : Martin Dwyer two-day ban: careless riding (Jun 24-25)

FOCUS
At least a fair fillies' maiden and an impressive winner.

NOTEBOOK
Exceptionelle ◆ could hardly have impressed any more with the way she travelled through the race. She was still tanking along at the furlong pole and although she didn't draw away once off the bridle, she did enough to please her rider who punched the air on crossing the line (a rare sight in a maiden). This 85,000gns purchase is a half-sister to a 1m Group 3 winner, out of a 7f juvenile scorer who was later placed in the German 1,000 Guineas. She looks Royal Ascot material. (op 15-8)
Sugar House(USA), who is out of a multiple 6f-1m stakes winner (including Grade 1) on dirt in the US, shaped nicely despite running green and covering a lot of ground from the widest stall, but still finishing well. (op 10-1)
Indignant built on the promise she showed behind subsequent Irish Listed winner Sky Lantern on her debut at Goodwood. (op 14-1)
Mystical Moment looked the stable's first string on jockey bookings, but faded after being given a forward ride on this debut. A 30,000gns first foal of a 1m winner, she should improve a fair bit. (op 11-1)
Masarah(IRE), out of a useful 1m-1m2f winner, made a pleasing introduction. (op 40-1)
Back In The Frame had finished runner-up on her first two starts, but this was tougher. She was held when short of room late on, but would otherwise have finished slightly closer. (op 4-1 tchd 5-1)
Jet Acclaim(IRE) was too keen and didn't build on her debut second at Wolverhampton. (tchd 13-2)

2813 READ HAYLEY AT RACINGUK.COM EVERY FRIDAY H'CAP (LONDON MILE QUALIFIER) 1m (P)

8:30 (8:30) (Class 4) (0-85,85) 3-Y-0 **£4,075** (£1,212; £606; £303) **Stalls** Low

Form RPR

5-21 **1** **Curzon Line**[22] 2150 3-9-5 **83**........ MickaelBarzalona 2 90+
(Mahmood Al Zarooni) *trckd ldrs: rdn and prog to ld 1f out: styd on wl: readily* **7/2**[1]

01 **2** 1 **Roserrow**[21] 2172 3-9-7 **85**........ JimmyFortune 3 89
(Andrew Balding) *pressed ldr: rdn over 2f out: nt qckn as wnr wnt by 1f out: kpt on to take 2nd again last 75yds* **12/1**

1-30 **3** ¾ **California English (IRE)**[13] 2408 3-9-1 **79**........ AdamKirby 9 81+
(Marco Botti) *hld up in midfield: effrt on inner 2f out: drvn and styd on fnl f to take 3rd nr fin* **17/2**

3-31 **4** nk **Mizwaaj (IRE)**[26] 2041 3-9-6 **84**........ FrankieDettori 1 86
(Saeed Bin Suroor) *mde most: rdn 2f out: hdd 1f out: one pce and lost 2 pls last 75yds* **9/2**[2]

-000 **5** ½ **Ghostwriting (USA)**[32] 1860 3-9-6 **84**........ WilliamBuick 4 84
(John Gosden) *sweating: cl up: rdn over 2f out: nt qckn over 1f out: styd on same pce fnl f* **20/1**

14 **6** ½ **Main Line**[22] 2150 3-9-1 **79**........ TedDurcan 13 78+
(David Lanigan) *dropped in fr wd draw and hld up in last pair: angled out over 2f out w hd quite high: making sme prog whn impeded 1f out: kpt on: nrst fin* **6/1**[3]

1-00 **7** hd **Venetian View (IRE)**[18] 2263 3-9-7 **85**........(b[1]) RyanMoore 10 84
(Gary Moore) *hld up in last: urged along 3f out: prog on outer whn bmpd 1f out: kpt on but nvr any ch: nrst fin* **10/1**

1-50 **8** 1 **Finbar**[25] 2088 3-9-3 **81**........ PaulMulrennan 8 77
(James Given) *hld up in midfield: effrt 2f out: swtchd lft jst over 1f out: one pce fnl f* **33/1**

34-1 **9** 3 ½ **Obliterieght (IRE)**[28] 1985 3-9-4 **82**........ JimCrowley 5 70
(William Knight) *pressed ldrs: drvn over 2f out: btn over 1f out: wknd qckly fnl f* **6/1**[3]

32-0 **10** 1 ¼ **Cockney Rhyme**[12] 2448 3-8-11 **75**........ NeilCallan 7 60
(Heather Main) *hld up in midfield: effrt on inner over 2f out: wknd over 1f out* **40/1**

642- **11** 1 ½ **Opera Buff**[215] 7258 3-8-13 **77**........ LiamKeniry 6 58
(Sylvester Kirk) *a in rr: shkn up and no prog over 2f out: wknd over 1f out* **25/1**

512- **12** 5 **Gloriam (USA)**[207] 7390 3-9-7 **85**........ MartinLane 11 54
(David Simcock) *settled in rr and racd on outer: shkn up and no prog over 2f out: wknd rapidly over 1f out* **25/1**

1m 38.66s (-1.14) **Going Correction** -0.075s/f (Stan) **12** Ran SP% **114.1**
Speed ratings (Par 101): **102,101,100,99,99 98,98,97,94,93 91,86**
toteswingers: 1&2 £4.80, 1&3 £7.30, 2&3 £37.90 CSF £41.23 CT £333.66 TOTE £5.10: £1.90, £3.20, £4.80; EX 48.50 Trifecta £304.40 Part won. Pool: £411.35 - 0.10 winning units..
Owner Godolphin **Bred** Darley **Trained** Newmarket, Suffolk

FOCUS
A fair 3yo handicap, but the pace seemed just modest and those held up were at a disadvantage.

2814 KEMPTONLIVE.CO.UK APPRENTICE H'CAP 1m 4f (P)

9:00 (9:00) (Class 6) (0-65,65) 4-Y-0+ **£1,617** (£481; £240; £120) **Stalls** Centre

Form RPR

4133 **1** **Khun John (IRE)**[27] 2009 9-9-3 **58**........ RaulDaSilva 6 66
(Willie Musson) *t.k.h: hld up in tch: rdn to go 3rd wl over 1f out: looked hld tl styd on wl to ld last strides* **3/1**[1]

0662 **2** nk **Super Duplex**[6] 2637 5-9-5 **63**........ JakePayne(3) 9 70
(Pat Phelan) *t.k.h: hld up in rr: prog 4f out: led over 2f out: hdd ins fnl f: upsides nr fin: jst outpcd* **4/1**[2]

521- **3** nse **Decana**[183] 7645 4-9-2 **64**........ ChristianSewell(7) 7 71
(Hughie Morrison) *led at slow pce to over 7f out: styd cl up: pushed along to chal 2f out: led ins fnl f: kpt on but hdd last strides* **11/2**

0-25 **4** 3 ¼ **Mafeteng**[22] 2149 4-9-4 **64**........ NedCurtis(5) 3 66
(John Dunlop) *t.k.h: cl up: lost pl bef 1/2-way: last over 3f out: rdn and kpt on fnl 2f: no ch* **9/2**[3]

1063 **5** 1 **Cantor**[14] 2394 4-9-1 **56**........(b) JamesRogers 2 58
(Giles Bravery) *hld up in rr: outpcd fr 3f out: urged along and styd on fr over 1f out: n.d* **12/1**

50-6 **6** ¾ **Rasam Aldaar**[7] 984 4-8-4 **50**........(tp) AliceHaynes(5) 12 49
(Neil King) *cl up: chal over 3f out: upsides over 2f out: fdd over 1f out* **25/1**

00-6 **7** 1 ½ **Rather Cool**[22] 2149 4-8-9 **50**........ DavidKenny 11 47
(John Bridger) *cl up tl outpcd fr 2f out* **25/1**

0235 **8** 1 ¼ **Lytham (IRE)**[33] 1831 11-8-8 **52**........ GeorgeDowning(3) 10 47
(Tony Carroll) *plld hrd: hld up in rr: stl pulling 4f out: wknd 2f out* **9/1**

2-62 **9** *6* **Lakeman (IRE)**[29] 1956 6-9-7 **62**......................................(b) KyleJames 5 47
(Brian Ellison) *t.k.h: wl in tch tl wknd fr over 2f out* **12/1**

02/0 **10** *1 ½* **Rosaria**[20] 2200 4-9-5 **65**................................ WilliamTwiston-Davies(5) 8 48
(Harry Dunlop) *plld hrd: cl up: led over 7f out but at no str pce: hdd & wknd qckly over 2f out* **25/1**

2m 39.38s (4.88) **Going Correction** -0.075s/f (Stan) **10** Ran SP% **115.5**
Speed ratings (Par 101): **80,79,79,77,76 76,75,74,70,69**
toteswingers: 1&2 £2.40, 1&3 £4.00, 2&3 £9.40 CSF £14.25 CT £60.40 TOTE £5.60: £2.10, £2.30, £2.00; EX 15.50 Trifecta £74.90 Pool: £653.31 - 6.45 winning units..
Owner The Strawberries To A Donkey Partnership **Bred** Sti Engineering Srl **Trained** Newmarket, Suffolk

FOCUS
A slowly run race and the form needs treating with caution.
Lytham(IRE) Official explanation: jockey said gelding ran too free
T/Plt: £518.10 to a £1 stake. Pool £56,367.83. 79.42 winning tickets. T/Qpdt: £195.00 to a £1 stake. Pool: £4,613.81. 17.50 winning tickets. JN

2729 NOTTINGHAM (L-H)

Wednesday, June 6

OFFICIAL GOING: Good to soft (soft in places; 7.0)
Wind: Moderate against Weather: Cloudy periods

2815 PLAY BIG MONEY TOTEJACKPOT AT TOTEPOOL.COM H'CAP 6f 15y

2:00 (2:06) (Class 5) (0-70,70) 4-Y-O+ **£2,264** (£673; £336; £168) **Stalls** High

Form RPR

00-0 **1** **Errigal Lad**[9] 2549 7-8-2 **51** oh2...................................... KellyHarrison 12 64
(Garry Woodward) *s.i.s and bhd: stdy hdwy 2f out: swtchd lft and rdn over 1f out: styd on to chal ins fnl f whn carried bdly lft: led towards fin: gamely* **40/1**

14- **2** *nk* **Prodigality**[168] 7842 4-9-7 **70**... LukeMorris 6 82+
(Ronald Harris) *in tch: hdwy 1/2-way: pushed along to ld over 1f out: edgd rt ent fnl f: sn rdn and hung bdly lft last 100yds: hdd towards fin: 2nd of 12 in gp* **11/2**[2]

-030 **3** *4* **Comrade Bond**[20] 2207 4-9-7 **70**... TedDurcan 4 69
(Mark H Tompkins) *trckd ldrs: hdwy 2f out: rdn and ev ch over 1f out: kpt on same pce: 3rd of 12* **6/1**[3]

4136 **4** *shd* **Gracie's Games**[2] 2761 6-8-5 **61** ow3.................(v) MichaelJMurphy(7) 5 60
(Richard Price) *dwlt and swtchd rt s: towards rr: hdwy on outer 1/2-way: rdn and ev ch over 1f out: wknd ins fnl f: 4th of 12 in gp* **6/1**[3]

-004 **5** *4* **Bermondsey Bob (IRE)**[5] 2572 6-8-13 **62**.................. CathyGannon 11 48
(John Spearing) *cl up: led 2f out: rdn and hdd over 1f out: grad wknd: 5th of 12 in gp* **9/2**[1]

20-0 **6** *¾* **Arch Walker (IRE)**[48] 1481 5-8-13 **62**..........................(b) DarryllHolland 3 46
(John Weymes) *trckd ldr far side: led that gp wl over 2f out and prom tl rdn and wknd appr fnl f: 1st of 2 in gp* **20/1**

-006 **7** *1 ¼* **Spanish Acclaim**[6] 2618 5-8-6 **55**................................ JamesSullivan 14 35
(Ruth Carr) *towards rr: sme hdwy over 1f out: nvr a factor: 6th of 12 in gp* **28/1**

1004 **8** *nk* **Blueberry Fizz (IRE)**[14] 2406 4-8-3 **52**...................(v) KirstyMilczarek 16 31
(John Ryan) *a towards rr: 7th of 12 in gp* **20/1**

0430 **9** *shd* **Steel City Boy (IRE)**[4] 2690 9-8-8 **57**........................ WilliamCarson 17 35
(Garry Woodward) *led: rdn along and hdd 2f out: sn wknd: 8th of 12 in gp* **20/1**

-000 **10** *nk* **Seamus Shindig**[11] 2482 10-8-13 **67**................................ AmyScott(5) 9 44
(Henry Candy) *in tch: rdn along over 2f out: sn wknd: 9th of 12 in gp* **8/1**

4460 **11** *1* **Dancing Maite**[9] 2549 7-9-3 **66**...............................(b) RussKennemore 15 40
(Roy Bowring) *chsd ldrs: rdn along wl over 2f out: sn wknd: 10th of 12 in gp* **10/1**

356- **12** *4 ½* **Royal Liaison**[285] 5442 4-8-13 **62**.................................... KierenFallon 10 22
(James Fanshawe) *a towards rr: 11th of 12 in gp* **11/1**

6114 **13** *¾* **Kipchak (IRE)**[84] 900 7-9-0 **63**...............................(b) HayleyTurner 13 20
(Conor Dore) *chsd ldrs: rdn along and lost pl bef 1/2-way: sn bhd: 12th of 12 in gp* **22/1**

-660 **14** *9* **Itum**[15] 2377 5-7-13 **51** oh2.. DominicFox(3) 2
(Christine Dunnett) *led far side gp: hdd wl over 2f out and sn wknd: 2nd of 2 in gp* **80/1**

1m 15.83s (0.93) **Going Correction** +0.075s/f (Good) **14** Ran SP% **116.4**
Speed ratings (Par 103): **96,95,90,90,84 83,82,81,81,81 79,73,72,60**
toteswingers:1&2:£48.60, 1&3:£51.00, 2&3:£7.40 CSF £225.62 CT £1579.12 TOTE £60.70: £14.00, £2.80, £1.60; EX 395.90 TRIFECTA Not won..
Owner Mrs Elisabeth Cash **Bred** Robin Lawson **Trained** Bolham, Notts
■ Stewards' Enquiry : Luke Morris caution: careless riding.
Cathy Gannon two-day ban: careless riding (Jun 24-25)

FOCUS
Outside (summer) course used and bottom bend moved out adding about 10yds to distances on Round course. An ordinary sprint handicap, but a good-sized field.
Errigal Lad Official explanation: trainer said, regarding apparent improvement in form, that the gelding was better suited by the shorter trip
Dancing Maite Official explanation: trainer said gelding had been struck into

2816 FREE RACING POST FORM AT TOTEPOOL.COM H'CAP 5f 13y

2:30 (2:31) (Class 5) (0-75,74) 3-Y-O **£2,264** (£673; £336; £168) **Stalls** High

Form RPR

1051 **1** **Cats Eyes**[21] 2166 3-9-1 **68**.. ShaneKelly 5 78+
(Robert Cowell) *trckd ldrs: n.m.r 2f out: chal on bit over 1f out: shkn up and qcknd to ld ins fnl f: cleverly* **3/1**[2]

6621 **2** *½* **Demora**[3] 2730 3-8-13 **66** 6ex.. LukeMorris 1 72+
(Michael Appleby) *slt ld: rdn along wl over 1f out: hdd ins fnl f: sn drvn and kpt on* **11/8**[1]

4065 **3** *2* **Electric Qatar**[16] 2337 3-9-7 **74**.............................. RichardKingscote 6 72
(Tom Dascombe) *rrd and dwlt s: in rr: hdwy 1/2-way: rdn to chse ldng pair ent fnl f: kpt on: nrst fin* **4/1**[3]

-503 **4** *2* **Lady Gibraltar**[36] 1730 3-9-6 **73**...................................... KierenFallon 4 64
(Alan Jarvis) *trckd ldrs: swtchd lft to outer 1/2-way: effrt and ev ch wl over 1f out: sn rdn and wknd appr fnl f* **6/1**

4216 **5** *2 ¼* **Bookiesindexdotnet**[12] 2443 3-9-6 **73**.................................. PatDobbs 3 56
(J R Jenkins) *cl up: rdn along 2f out: wknd over 1f out* **8/1**

1m 1.41s (0.41) **Going Correction** +0.075s/f (Good) **5** Ran SP% **112.5**
Speed ratings (Par 99): **99,98,95,91,88**
CSF £7.79 TOTE £3.30: £2.40, £1.70; EX 7.70 Trifecta £17.20 Pool £529.18 - 22.76 winning units..
Owner Manor Farm Stud (rutland) **Bred** Manor Farm Stud & Mrs A J Ralli **Trained** Six Mile Bottom, Cambs

FOCUS
A competitive sprint handicap for 3yos was weakened by three withdrawals.

2817 E B F PLAY TOTEQUADPOT AT TOTEPOOL.COM MAIDEN STKS 5f 13y

3:05 (3:07) (Class 5) 2-Y-O **£3,234** (£962; £481; £240) **Stalls** High

Form RPR

1 **Dashing David (IRE)** 2-9-3 0... PatDobbs 5 85+
(Richard Hannon) *s.i.s: green and rdn along in rr: hdwy wl over 1f out: swtchd lft ins fnl f and styd on strly to ld last 50yds* **2/1**[2]

3 **2** *1 ¼* **Trinityelitedotcom (IRE)**[27] 1997 2-9-3 0.............. RichardKingscote 2 77
(Tom Dascombe) *led: rdn clr ent fnl f: hdd and no ex last 50yds* **11/10**[1]

60 **3** *5* **Bentleysoysterboy (IRE)**[20] 2193 2-9-3 0.........(b[1]) SilvestreDeSousa 4 59
(David Elsworth) *dwlt: t.k.h and sn trcking ldrs: effrt 2f out: sn rdn and edgd lft wl over 1f out: one pce* **7/2**[3]

4 **4** *3 ¼* **Jimmy Elder**[32] 1847 2-9-3 0... KieranO'Neill 3 47
(Richard Hannon) *cl up: rdn and ev ch wl over 1f out: wknd appr fnl f* **8/1**

00 **5** *1* **Proventi**[9] 2550 2-8-10 0.. NoelGarbutt(7) 1 44
(Alan McCabe) *cl up on outer: rdn along 2f out: sn wknd* **66/1**

1m 2.88s (1.88) **Going Correction** +0.075s/f (Good) **5** Ran SP% **115.8**
Speed ratings (Par 93): **87,85,77,71,70**
CSF £4.91 TOTE £3.00: £1.80, £1.10; EX 5.30.
Owner Sir David Seale **Bred** Hascombe And Valiant Studs **Trained** East Everleigh, Wilts

FOCUS
This race has attracted small fields in each of its three runnings, but the two previous winners both went on to be rated in excess of 100, with last year's scorer, Bear Behind, being placed at Listed level. It proved to be a race of changing fortunes.

NOTEBOOK
Dashing David(IRE), a 64,000gns breeze-up purchase from a good family, was the only runner in the field without previous experience and was outpaced in the early stages as his inexperience showed. However, he gradually got the idea of what was required and picked up well as his rivals started to tread water, eventually scoring comfortably. He should get further than this and can go on to better things. (op 10-3)
Trinityelitedotcom(IRE), who made the running when third at Chester on his debut in a contest that has thrown up three subsequent winners, was sent off favourite and was soon in front here. He looked to have beaten off his rivals entering the last furlong, only to be run down late. He was racing into a headwind here and can be given a chance to make it third time lucky. (op 5-4 tchd 11-8)
Bentleysoysterboy(IRE) failed to build on the promise of his debut effort when upped in trip and on faster ground last time and had blinkers on dropped back to the minimum trip. He was keen to post, though, proved difficult to load and then ran too free before finding little for pressure. He is looking one to be wary of until proving more amenable. (op 3-1 tchd 5-2)
Jimmy Elder, a stable companion of the winner, was expected to improve for his debut and was sharper this time, but could not sustain his effort. (tchd 6-1 and 17-2)

2818 FIND LIVE TOTEJACKPOT INFORMATION AT TOTEPOOL.COM H'CAP 1m 6f 15y

3:40 (3:41) (Class 5) (0-70,70) 3-Y-O **£2,264** (£673; £336; £168) **Stalls** Low

Form RPR

-022 **1** **Bathwick Street**[13] 2424 3-8-11 **60**.................................. CathyGannon 1 70
(David Evans) *led 2f: cl up tl led again over 2f out: sn rdn clr: styd on wl* **4/1**[1]

4520 **2** *5* **Minnie Diva (IRE)**[7] 2605 3-9-0 **63**...................................... GrahamLee 4 66
(Kevin Ryan) *sn pushed along to chse ldng pair: cl up 1/2-way: rdn over 3f out: drvn to chse wnr 2f out: no imp* **5/1**[2]

6320 **3** *¾* **Chankillo**[28] 1982 3-8-13 **62**.. TedDurcan 6 64
(Mark H Tompkins) *hld up in midfield: hdwy 5f out: rdn to chse ldng pair over 2f out: sn one pce* **12/1**

4610 **4** *7* **Spanish Fork (IRE)**[13] 2427 3-9-3 **66**............................. SamHitchcott 7 58
(Mick Channon) *in rr and sn rdn along: hdwy into midfield over 4f out: sn drvn along: plugged on: nvr a factor* **8/1**

0-24 **5** *3 ¼* **Wayne Manor (IRE)**[23] 2129 3-9-1 **64**.............................[1] JimCrowley 8 52
(Ralph Beckett) *trckd ldrs: effrt over 5f out: rdn along 4f out: sn drvn and no hdwy* **5/1**[2]

06-6 **6** *½* **Maccabees**[15] 2382 3-8-13 **62**.. JamesMillman 5 49
(Rod Millman) *prom: led after 2f: rdn along 4f out: hdd over 2f out and sn wknd* **11/1**

00-3 **7** *13* **Stickleback**[26] 2049 3-8-2 **51** oh1................................ KirstyMilczarek 10 20
(Harry Dunlop) *hld up: a in rr* **9/1**

02-4 **8** *1* **Pinseeker (IRE)**[14] 2390 3-9-6 **69**.. LukeMorris 11 36
(Brendan Powell) *a in rr* **33/1**

30-0 **9** *41* **Hurricane Emerald (IRE)**[22] 2144 3-9-3 **66**............ SilvestreDeSousa 9
(Mark Johnston) *a towards rr* **9/1**

00-3 **10** *51* **Tokyo Brown (USA)**[14] 2393 3-9-2 **65**.............................. KierenFallon 2
(Heather Main) *in tch: rdn along 1/2-way: sn lost pl and bhd whn eased 4f out* **15/2**[3]

3m 9.89s (3.59) **Going Correction** +0.25s/f (Good) **10** Ran SP% **115.2**
Speed ratings (Par 99): **99,96,95,91,89 89,82,81,58,29**
toteswingers:1&2:£5.00, 1&3:£8.90, 2&3:£15.00 CSF £23.29 CT £219.51 TOTE £4.60: £1.60, £1.40, £4.10; EX 26.50 Trifecta £382.90 Pool £838.26 - 1.62 winning units..
Owner Wayne Clifford **Bred** Mrs D Du Feu **Trained** Pandy, Monmouths

FOCUS
A modest staying handicap for 3yos in which few got involved and they finished pretty tired in the conditions.

2819 TOTEPOOL.COM SPORTS, GAMES, BINGO & MORE CONDITIONS STKS 1m 75y

4:15 (4:15) (Class 2) 3-Y-O+
£9,835 (£2,945; £1,472; £736; £368; £184) **Stalls** Centre

Form RPR

4220 **1** **Rodrigo De Torres**[25] 2068 5-9-1 **98**................................ MartinHarley 6 104
(Mrs K Burke) *trckd ldr: cl up 3f out: led 2f out: sn rdn clr and styd on strly* **7/1**

202- **2** *3 ¾* **Invisible Man**[276] 5777 6-9-1 **107**...........................(b) MickaelBarzalona 2 95
(Saeed Bin Suroor) *hld up in rr: hdwy over 3f out: sn pushed along: styd on to chse wnr over 1f out: sn drvn and no imp* **2/1**[1]

3515 **3** *nk* **Dubai Dynamo**[8] 2590 7-9-1 **93**..................................... JamesSullivan 3 95
(Ruth Carr) *trckd ldng pair: hdwy over 3f out: rdn 2f out: drvn and kpt on same pce fnl f* **4/1**[3]

0000 **4** *2 ½* **Bay Knight (IRE)**[18] 2268 6-9-7 **97**..................................... SophieDoyle 4 95
(J S Moore) *t.k.h: led: rdn along 3f out: hdd 2f out: sn drvn and grad wknd* **28/1**

6026 **5** *4* **St Moritz (IRE)**[5] 2656 6-9-1 **106**.................................. AdrianNicholls 5 80
(David Nicholls) *hld up: hdwy on outer to chse ldrs over 3f out: sn rdn and btn 2f out* **7/2**[2]

0-35 **6** *7* **Graphic (IRE)**[32] 1854 3-8-13 95 .... PatDobbs 1 70
(Richard Hannon) *trckd ldrs: effrt over 3f out: sn rdn along and wknd over 2f out* **9/2**

1m 48.91s (3.31) **Going Correction** +0.25s/f (Good)
WFA 3 from 5yo+ 11lb **6** Ran SP% **109.7**
Speed ratings (Par 109): **93,89,88,86,82 75**
toteswingers:1&2:£2.90, 1&3:£3.60, 2&3:£2.20 CSF £20.47 TOTE £9.20: £4.30, £2.00; EX 24.60.
Owner M Gittins & Mrs E Burke **Bred** Worksop Manor Stud **Trained** Middleham Moor, N Yorks

FOCUS
A slowly run conditions event with the time just 0.45 seconds faster than the following 69-83 handicap for 3yo fillies.

NOTEBOOK
Rodrigo De Torres had not won for over two years but has been in good form this season and, with his ability to handle soft ground not in doubt, he coped with the step up in trip to score readily. He was always close to the pace but his rider was not keen to go on too early. However, when he did commit the response was decisive and he was in control from that point. He seems best in small fields and is entered in a forethcoming Group 3 in Ireland. (op 11-2)
Invisible Man's trainer has a good record in conditions races at this track, and his three winners in the last ten years (Dubai Destination, Librettist and Rio De La Plata), all went on to score at Group 1 level later that season, but along with St Moritz (the other rated in the 100s) the ground was a question mark. He was held up and keen early, but was being ridden along soon after turning into the straight and, although staying on, he never looked like catching the winner. (op 9-4)
Dubai Dynamo, better known as a handicapper and with the lowest official rating of these, was proven on soft ground and ran his usual honest race without being good enough. He looks the best guide to the form. (tchd 7-2)
Bay Knight(IRE) handles any ground, but is yet to find his form for new connections since coming from Ireland and had a difficult task giving weight all round plus his rider was unable to claim. He made the running and did not totally drop away once headed, so might be gradually finding his feet. (op 33-1)
St Moritz(IRE), often a front runner, has been varying the tactics since his return to action this season and was held up here. He made a forward move around 3f out, but his effort petered out fairly tamely. The ground is the obvious excuse. (op 5-2)
Graphic(IRE), the only 3yo, travelled well enough early but found nothing when asked. He has handled testing ground previously so may have had other excuses. (op 13-2)

2820 E B F PLAY BLACKJACK AND ROULETTE AT TOTEPOOL.COM FILLIES' H'CAP 1m 75y

4:45 (4:45) (Class 4) (0-85,83) 3-Y-O £**4,528** (£1,347; £673; £336) **Stalls** Centre

Form RPR
0501 **1** **Stellar Express (IRE)**[3] 2733 3-9-5 **81** 6ex .... LukeMorris 9 89
(Michael Appleby) *sn led: mde most: rdn 2f out: drvn ent fnl f: kpt on gamely* **5/2**[1]
5-40 **2** *1 ¼* **Negin**[36] 1736 3-8-7 **69** .... ChrisCatlin 8 74
(Ed Dunlop) *dwlt: hld up and bhd: tk clsr order 4f out: gd hdwy on inner over 2f out: swtchd rt and rdn to chal wl over 1f out: ev ch tl drvn and one pce wl ins fnl f* **20/1**
1 **3** *½* **Secret Quest**[26] 2050 3-9-4 **80** .... MickaelBarzalona 4 84
(James Fanshawe) *hld up in rr: pushed along 5f out: hdwy on wd outside 3f out: rdn to chse ldng pair wl over 1f out: kpt on fnl f: nrst fin* **9/2**[2]
221- **4** *6* **Al Mahmeyah**[278] 5689 3-9-1 **77** .... PatDobbs 7 67
(Richard Hannon) *in tch on outer: hdwy 3f out: rdn over 2f out: drvn and no imp fr over 1f out* **12/1**
5-20 **5** *nk* **Candycakes (IRE)**[20] 2201 3-9-0 **76** .... HayleyTurner 1 65
(Michael Bell) *dwlt: a towards rr* **8/1**
24-1 **6** *3 ¾* **Balady (IRE)**[32] 1852 3-9-3 **79** .... TadhgO'Shea 5 60
(John Dunlop) *t.k.h early: chsd wnr: rdn along 3f out: wknd over 2f out* **11/2**[3]
010- **7** *4 ½* **Whimsical (IRE)**[228] 7028 3-9-7 **83** .... JimCrowley 6 53
(Richard Hannon) *trckd ldrs: hdwy to chse wnr 1/2-way: rdn wl over 2f out: sn wknd* **12/1**
1 **8** *7* **Hawaiian Storm**[48] 1479 3-8-8 **73** .... MichaelMetcalfe(3) 3 27
(Mrs K Burke) *chsd ldrs: rdn along over 3f out: sn wknd* **9/2**[2]

1m 49.36s (3.76) **Going Correction** +0.25s/f (Good) **8** Ran SP% **111.6**
Speed ratings (Par 98): **91,89,89,83,82 79,74,67**
toteswingers:1&2:£10.40, 1&3:£3.00, 2&3:£13.80 CSF £52.60 CT £209.79 TOTE £2.60: £1.10, £6.70, £1.90; EX 62.00 Trifecta £581.10 Part won. Pool £785.28 - 0.40 winning units..
Owner Mr & Mrs James Sumsion **Bred** Adrian Purvis **Trained** Danethorpe, Notts

FOCUS
Just a fair fillies' handicap, although a couple of recent winners did make their mark at Listed level, and there were a couple of unexposed fillies making their handicap debuts.

2821 DEAL OR NO DEAL AT TOTEPOOL.COM "HANDS AND HEELS" APPRENTICE SERIES H'CAP 1m 2f 50y

5:15 (5:15) (Class 5) (0-65,65) 4-Y-O+ £**1,940** (£577; £288; £144) **Stalls** Low

Form RPR
0-03 **1** **Matavia Bay (IRE)**[37] 1702 4-8-6 **58** .... MichaelJMMurphy(8) 6 71
(Alan Jarvis) *mde all: rdn over 2f out: styd on strly fnl f* **8/1**
4312 **2** *6* **The Lock Master (IRE)**[2] 2767 5-8-13 **65** .... RichardOliver(8) 7 67
(Michael Appleby) *trckd ldrs: hdwy 1/2-way: chsd wnr fr wl over 3f out: rdn fnl 2f: no imp fnl f* **10/11**[1]
66-6 **3** *nk* **Barachiel**[8] 2576 4-9-5 **63** .... DanielMuscutt 1 64
(Ronald Harris) *prom: chsd wnr after 3f: rdn along over 3f out: kpt on same pce fnl 2f* **10/1**
0-60 **4** *4* **My Mate Jake (IRE)**[13] 2414 4-9-7 **65** .... DavidSimmonson 2 58
(James Given) *trckd ldrs: effrt over 3f out: sn rdn along and one pce fnl 2f* **11/2**[2]
0030 **5** *¾* **Gambatte**[9] 2555 5-8-2 **46** oh1 .... NicoleNordblad 4 38
(Tony Carroll) *t.k.h: hld up towards rr: hdwy to chse ldrs after 3f: rdn along 3f out: grad wknd* **20/1**
0 **6** *6* **Squirrel Wood (IRE)**[21] 2167 4-9-6 **64** .... WilliamTwiston-Davies 8 45
(Mary Hambro) *midfield: rdn along over 4f out: sn outpcd* **7/1**[3]
0-60 **7** *24* **Queen's Choice (IRE)**[14] 2401 4-8-2 **46** oh1 .... (t) AliceHaynes 10
(Anabel K Murphy) *v.s.a: a bhd* **40/1**
5645 **8** *16* **Sofias Number One (USA)**[28] 1988 4-8-2 **46** oh1 .... (b) NoelGarbutt 5
(Roy Bowring) *chsd ldrs: lost pl 1/2-way: bhd fnl 3f* **14/1**

2m 16.68s (4.98) **Going Correction** +0.25s/f (Good) **8** Ran SP% **114.3**
Speed ratings (Par 103): **90,85,84,81,81 76,57,44**
toteswingers:1&2:£2.80, 1&3:£8.70, 2&3:£3.50 CSF £15.72 CT £75.87 TOTE £9.00: £2.30, £1.30, £2.00; EX 17.30 Trifecta £108.30 Pool £524.30 - 3.58 winning units..
Owner Geoffrey Bishop & Jarvis Associates **Bred** Limestone & Tara Studs **Trained** Twyford, Bucks

FOCUS
A moderate 'hands and heels' apprentice handicap in which they appeared to go a sound gallop, but the winner made virtually all.
T/Plt: £33.40 to a £1 stake. Pool:£54,721.69 - 1,192.85 winning tickets T/Qpdt: £5.70 to a £1 stake. Pool:£3,573.37 - 457.23 winning tickets JR

2587 RIPON (R-H)

Wednesday, June 6

OFFICIAL GOING: Good changing to good to soft after race 2 (7.10)
Wind: Almost nil Weather: Overcast, heavy showers 1st 3

2822 BRITISH STALLION STUDS SUPPORTING BRITISH RACING E B F MAIDEN STKS 6f

6:40 (6:42) (Class 5) 2-Y-O £**3,557** (£1,058; £529; £264) **Stalls** High

Form RPR
4 **1** **Tha'Ir (IRE)**[17] 2308 2-9-3 0 .... FrederikTylicki 1 95+
(Saeed Bin Suroor) *mde all: swtchd lft after 1f: drvn clr fnl f* **6/1**
2 *4 ½* **Bircham (IRE)** 2-9-3 0 .... SilvestreDeSousa 4 83+
(Mahmood Al Zarooni) *chsd wnr: kpt on same pce appr fnl f: no imp* **7/2**[1]
0 **3** *3 ¼* **Freeport**[19] 2231 2-9-3 0 .... DarryllHolland 7 72
(Brian Meehan) *chsd ldrs: sn drvn along: one pce fnl 2f* **9/2**[2]
4 *¾* **Specialty (IRE)** 2-8-12 0 .... MickyFenton 6 66+
(Pam Sly) *wnt rt s: in rr: hdwy 2f out: styd on towards fin: will improve* **14/1**
5 *4* **Mushaakis (IRE)** 2-9-3 0 .... PaulHanagan 3 58+
(Mark Johnston) *chsd ldrs on outer: wknd over 1f out* **5/1**[3]
6 *1 ¾* **Flighty Clarets (IRE)** 2-8-12 0 .... TonyHamilton 5 48
(Richard Fahey) *dwlt: t.k.h: sn trcking ldrs: wandered and wknd over 1f out* **25/1**
0 **7** *¾* **Rocket Ronnie (IRE)**[13] 2415 2-9-3 0 .... AdrianNicholls 8 50
(David Nicholls) *chsd ldrs: wknd wl over 1f out* **18/1**
8 *9* **Archie Stevens** 2-9-3 0 .... RichardKingscote 10 23
(Tom Dascombe) *wnt rt s: in rr: sme hdwy on outside over 2f out: sn wknd* **7/1**
0 **9** *1* **Bollin Billy**[16] 2334 2-9-3 0 .... DavidAllan 11 20
(Tim Easterby) *sn outpcd in rr: bhd fnl 2f* **40/1**
F40 **10** *nk* **Silver Fawn (IRE)**[9] 2537 2-9-3 0 .... DuranFentiman 2 19
(John Weymes) *chsd ldrs: outpcd over 3f out: lost pl 2f out* **66/1**
0 **11** *1* **Glory Awaits (IRE)**[20] 2213 2-9-3 0 .... JamieSpencer 9 22
(Kevin Ryan) *s.i.s: sn drvn along in rr: bhd fnl 2f* **8/1**

1m 14.43s (1.43) **Going Correction** 0.0s/f (Good) **11** Ran SP% **114.7**
Speed ratings (Par 93): **90,84,79,78,73 71,70,58,56,56 54**
toteswingers: 1&2 £1.90, 1&3 £2.20, 2&3 £5.50 CSF £26.18 TOTE £5.60: £2.20, £1.50, £2.10; EX 18.90.
Owner Godolphin **Bred** Lodge Park Stud **Trained** Newmarket, Suffolk

FOCUS
Rail at innermost position and distances as advertised. Although the ground was unchanged, despite 4mm of overnight rain and a wet run up to the opening race, the time suggested conditions were on the easy side and Paul Hanagan reported: "The rain is already getting in and it's on the soft side."A race that often throws up a decent sort and this winner, who improved a fair bit from his debut run, looks useful at least. It's worth being positive about the form.

NOTEBOOK
Tha'Ir(IRE), who showed ability over C&D on his debut, stepped up a fair way on that level to win a stronger looking contest with plenty in hand, despite drifting right in the closing stages. This Derby entry isn't the biggest of individuals and has yet to encounter quick ground but he'll be at least as good over 7f and may be able to hold his own in slightly stronger company. (op 5-1)
Bircham(IRE) ◆, who cost 120,000gns and is the first foal of a winner in France up to 1m, attracted support and showed a fair level of ability on this racecourse debut. He's a scopey type who should come on a fair bit for this debut experience and he's sure to pick up a similar event. (op 5-1)
Freeport showed ability in a race that has already thrown up a winner at Newbury on his debut and, while he stepped up on that level, he again left the impression that the step up to 7f would be more to his liking. He should be able to pick up an ordinary event. Official explanation: trainer's rep said colt was unsuited by the track (op 4-1 tchd 7-2 and 11-2)
Specialty(IRE), the second foal of the yard's 1000 Guineas winner Speciosa, showed ability, despite her apparent greenness on this racecourse debut. The step up to 7f should be more to her liking and she should be able to better this bare form. (op 16-1)
Mushaakis(IRE), the first foal of a useful Polytrack winner, showed ability before tiring in the conditions. He travelled strongly until lack of peak fitness told on this racecourse debut in this rain-soaked ground and he's the type to win races in due course. (op 6-1 tchd 7-1)
Archie Stevens Official explanation: jockey said gelding missed the break

2823 EURA AUDIT UK (S) H'CAP 1m 4f 10y

7:10 (7:11) (Class 6) (0-60,59) 4-5-Y-O £**1,940** (£577; £288; £144) **Stalls** Low

Form RPR
0-02 **1** **Stansonnit**[26] 2034 4-9-7 **59** .... PJMcDonald 7 63
(Alan Swinbank) *trckd ldrs: led 2f out: jnd ins fnl f: all out* **9/2**[2]
53- **2** *hd* **Commander Veejay**[227] 6229 4-8-11 **49** .... (p) BarryMcHugh 8 53
(Brian Rothwell) *in tch: chal over 1f out: kpt on towards fin: jst hld* **12/1**
1203 **3** *2 ¾* **Asterales**[14] 2391 5-9-1 **53** .... JamieMackay 1 53
(Willie Musson) *hld up in rr: drvn and outpcd over 3f out: hdwy and edgd lft over 1f out: kpt on ins fnl f: nt rch 1st 2* **5/4**[1]
54-5 **4** *1 ¾* **Lady Gargoyle**[60] 1223 4-8-9 **47** ow2 .... GrahamLee 5 44
(Jim Goldie) *chsd ldrs: pushed along over 3f out: kpt on one pce over 1f out* **10/1**
5-00 **5** *3 ¼* **Decadence**[5] 2669 4-8-7 **45** .... SilvestreDeSousa 9 37
(Nigel Tinkler) *trckd ldr: chal 4f out: led briefly over 2f out: wknd fnl f* **15/2**[3]
-500 **6** *¾* **Rapturous Applause**[110] 602 4-8-11 **49** .... FrederikTylicki 10 39
(Micky Hammond) *in rr: hdwy over 3f out: one pce fnl 2f* **17/2**
0-20 **7** *¾* **Arizona High**[14] 97 4-9-0 **52** .... DanielTudhope 3 41
(Andrew Crook) *led: t.k.h: hdd over 2f out: wknd appr fnl f* **18/1**
P0-6 **8** *1* **Jan Smuts (IRE)**[12] 2438 4-8-7 **45** .... (tp) JamesSullivan 6 33
(Wilf Storey) *in tch: drvn 6f out: fdd over 1f out* **33/1**
5-50 **9** *16* **Adam De Beaulieu (USA)**[14] 2401 5-8-7 **45** .... (t) TomEaves 4
(Ben Haslam) *dwlt: t.k.h in last: drvn over 3f out: sn bhd: eased ins fnl f* **16/1**

2m 43.86s (7.16) **Going Correction** +0.625s/f (Yiel) **9** Ran SP% **115.8**
Speed ratings: **101,100,99,97,95 95,94,94,83**
CSF £56.89 CT £105.28 TOTE £3.90: £1.20, £3.80, £1.10; EX 81.50.There was no bid for the winner. Asterales was claimed by Mrs Joanna Hughes for £6,000.
Owner The Twopin Partnership **Bred** R G Percival And Mrs A Lockhart **Trained** Melsonby, N Yorks

FOCUS
Mainly exposed performers in a moderate seller and a race run in driving rain. The form is rated negatively. The gallop was fair but the final time was just over 10 seconds above Racing Post Standard and the ground was then changed to "good to soft".

Adam De Beaulieu(USA) Official explanation: jockey said gelding ran too free

2824 RIPON FARM SERVICES H'CAP 6f
7:40 (7:41) (Class 4) (0-85,86) 3-Y-O **£4,528** (£1,347; £673; £336) **Stalls** High

Form RPR
21-4 **1** **Takealookatmenow (IRE)**[13] 2416 3-8-8 **67**............ AdrianNicholls 11 77
(David Nicholls) *mde all stands' side: styd on strly: readily* **10/1**
5-30 **2** *1 3/4* **Chooseday (IRE)**[19] 2256 3-9-6 **79**.................. PhillipMakin 6 83
(Kevin Ryan) *chsd wnr: kpt on same pce fnl f* **14/1**
3-42 **3** *1* **Love Island**[12] 2441 3-8-3 **62**.................. AmyRyan 4 63
(Richard Whitaker) *dwlt: hdwy on outer to chse 1st 2 over 2f out: kpt on same pce fnl f* **12/1**
41-2 **4** *1 1/2* **Springheel Jake**[8] 2591 3-9-1 **74**.................. DavidNolan 8 70
(Ann Duffield) *chsd ldrs: effrt over 2f out: kpt on same pce over 1f out* **5/1**[2]
6211 **5** *3 3/4* **Galician**[6] 2616 3-9-13 **86** 6ex.................. JoeFanning 3 70
(Mark Johnston) *chsd ldrs on outer: drvn and outpcd 3f out: wknd jst ins fnl f* **2/1**[1]
-030 **6** *1* **See Clearly**[19] 2229 3-8-13 **72**..................(p) DavidAllan 9 53
(Tim Easterby) *in rr-div: sn pushed along: hdwy over 2f out: nvr a factor* **25/1**
0000 **7** *2 1/4* **Parc De Launay**[21] 2182 3-9-7 **80**..................(p) JamieSpencer 7 54
(Tom Tate) *chsd ldrs: drvn over 2f out: wknd and eased appr fnl f* **6/1**[3]
03-6 **8** *1/2* **Alabanda (IRE)**[49] 1441 3-8-7 **66**.................. DuranFentiman 2 38
(Tim Easterby) *prom on outer: effrt and outpcd 3f out: wknd appr fnl f* **28/1**
31-0 **9** *2 3/4* **Indego Blues**[57] 1271 3-9-3 **76**.................. PaulQuinn 12 39
(David Nicholls) *t.k.h in rr stands' side: sme hdwy over 2f out: fdd appr fnl f* **8/1**
05P- **10** *11* **Almond Branches**[281] 5591 3-9-1 **74**.................. PJMcDonald 10
(George Moore) *dwlt: towards rr: lost pl over 1f out: sn eased* **28/1**
4321 **11** *3 1/2* **Available (IRE)**[15] 2375 3-9-1 **74**.................. FrannyNorton 5
(John Mackie) *mid-div: lost pl 2f out: eased whn bhd* **11/1**
0-60 **12** *9* **Amadeus Denton (IRE)**[11] 2509 3-9-7 **80**.................. TomEaves 1
(Michael Dods) *t.k.h in rr: wknd 2f out: eased whn bhd* **50/1**

1m 15.15s (2.15) **Going Correction** +0.40s/f (Good) **12** Ran SP% **119.9**
Speed ratings (Par 101): **101,98,97,95,90 89,86,85,81,67 62,50**
toteswingers: 1&2 £26.30, 1&3 £11.40, 2&3 £23.30 CSF £137.28 CT £1732.28 TOTE £9.00: £2.40, £5.40, £2.80; EX 68.30.
Owner D Nicholls & Mrs S J Barker **Bred** Ian W Glenton **Trained** Sessay, N Yorks

FOCUS
A useful handicap run at decent gallop - though the hold-up horses never figured - and a race in which the first four pulled clear of the disappointing market leader. The form is rated around the first two.
Available(IRE) Official explanation: jockey said filly never travelled

2825 DIRECTORS CUP H'CAP STKS 6f
8:10 (8:11) (Class 3) (0-95,95) 4-Y-O-**£6,931** (£2,074; £1,037; £519; £258) **Stalls** High

Form RPR
0-02 **1** **Pearl Ice**[18] 2284 4-9-2 **90**.................. GrahamGibbons 10 105+
(David Barron) *trckd ldrs: qcknd to ld over 1f out: r.o strly* **5/2**[1]
3335 **2** *2 3/4* **Beckermet (IRE)**[7] 2597 10-8-9 **83**.................. PJMcDonald 3 89
(Ruth Carr) *hmpd and swtchd rt after s: led 2 others on far side: kpt on wl fnl f: no ch w wnr* **18/1**
-200 **3** *nk* **Advanced**[25] 2068 9-9-4 **95**.................. JulieBurke(3) 7 100
(Kevin Ryan) *chsd ldrs: kpt on same pce fnl f* **14/1**
3350 **4** *3/4* **Tajneed (IRE)**[21] 2177 9-9-1 **89**.................. AdrianNicholls 11 92
(David Nicholls) *mid-div: hdwy over 2f out: nt clr run over 1f out: kpt on* **8/1**[3]
1010 **5** *shd* **Thunderball**[13] 2409 6-8-12 **93**..................(p) JordanUys(7) 8 95
(Scott Dixon) *in rr: hdwy on outer over 2f out: sn chsng ldrs: kpt on same pce fr over 1f out* **25/1**
00-0 **6** *nk* **Roker Park (IRE)**[21] 2177 7-9-0 **88**.................. DanielTudhope 4 89
(David O'Meara) *swtchd rt after s: racd w 2 others on far side: outpcd over 2f out: kpt on fnl f: 2nd of 3 that gp* **12/1**
0-66 **7** *1/2* **Coolminx (IRE)**[21] 2177 5-9-0 **88**.................. PaulHanagan 1 88
(Richard Fahey) *half-rrd s: switch rt and racd far side w 2 others: chsd ldrs: kpt on same pce over 1f out: 3rd of 3 that gp* **8/1**[3]
U051 **8** *2* **Arganil (USA)**[18] 2284 7-9-3 **91**..................(p) PhillipMakin 12 84
(Kevin Ryan) *in rr: hdwy over 1f out: nvr a factor* **25/1**
0-00 **9** *3 3/4* **Cocktail Charlie**[20] 2208 4-8-8 **82**..................(p) FrederikTylicki 2 63+
(Tim Easterby) *swtchd lft after 100yds and racd stands' side: sn chsng ldrs: wknd over 1f out* **16/1**
0103 **9** *dht* **Fast Shot**[21] 2177 4-8-13 **87**.................. DavidAllan 6 68+
(Tim Easterby) *in rr: effrt over 2f out: hmpd over 1f out: sn wknd* **9/1**
0620 **11** *nk* **West Coast Dream**[20] 2195 5-8-11 **85**.................. TomEaves 9 65
(Roy Brotherton) *chsd overall ldr stands' side: wknd over 1f out* **50/1**
-114 **12** *4 1/2* **Alive And Kicking**[18] 2264 4-8-3 **77**.................. AmyRyan 13 43
(James Bethell) *overall ldr stands' rail: hdd and lost pl over 1f out* **9/2**[2]
440 **13** *4* **Global City (IRE)**[13] 2409 6-9-5 **93**..................(t) SilvestreDeSousa 14 46
(Saeed Bin Suroor) *in rr-div: effrt on inner over 2f out: swtchd rt over 1f out: no imp whn heavily eased 1f out* **16/1**

1m 14.3s (1.30) **Going Correction** +0.40s/f (Good) **13** Ran SP% **120.0**
Speed ratings (Par 107): **107,103,102,101,101 101,100,98,93,93 92,86,81**
toteswingers: 1&2 £12.90, 1&3 £9.10, 2&3 £44.60 CSF £52.02 CT £559.38 TOTE £4.60: £1.20, £4.90, £4.10; EX 58.90.
Owner Laurence O'Kane & Paul Murphy **Bred** Canary Thoroughbreds **Trained** Maunby, N Yorks
■ Stewards' Enquiry : Frederik Tylicki one-day ban: careless riding (Jun 25)

FOCUS
A very useful handicap in which the gallop was sound and, although the winner scored in clear-cut fashion against the stands rail, there was nothing between the trio who raced on the far side and the principals in the larger stands side group. The winner could be competitive in top handicaps.

NOTEBOOK
Pearl Ice ◆, a most unlucky loser at Thirsk, made amends for his in-form trainer from this 3lb higher mark in decisive fashion, impressing with both the way he went through the race and with the way he quickened clear. He's a lightly raced sort and, although he has to prove he's as good on fast ground, he appeals strongly as the sort to win a decent handicap this season. (tchd 9-4 and 11-4)
Beckermet(IRE) was no match for the ready winner but he's a reliable yardstick who fared best of the remainder after going to the front on the far side. He won't always bump into one so progressive and, despite his advancing years, this confirmed he's capable of winning races in this grade. (op 16-1 tchd 20-1)
Advanced, back in trip, returned to the form that saw him finish second to Colonel Mak on his reappearance in April. He's a very useful sort but one that is vulnerable to an improver and he may struggle to win a competitive handicap from this mark. (tchd 16-1)
Tajneed(IRE) hasn't won since 2010 but he goes well here and had underfoot conditions to suit so it was no surprise to see him give a good account to extend his current run of form returned to this track for the first time this year. He's not at his very best but he's slipped to on a decent mark. (op 7-1)
Thunderball hadn't been at his best over 7f on quick ground on his previous start but fared much better back in trip with give underfoot. He doesn't have much in hand of his current mark, though. (tchd 20-1)
Roker Park(IRE) had been well held on his reappearance but showed a fair bit more this time after racing in the smaller far side group. He'll be spot on next time and he's worth another try over 7f on this evidence. (op 14-1)
Fast Shot, who is usually a consistent sort, wasn't able to show his best after meeting trouble at a crucial stage. He acts on most ground and, although 6lb higher than his last win, is worth another chance away from progressive sorts. Official explanation: jockey said gelding was denied a clear run (op 10-1 tchd 11-1)

2826 SIS LIVE MAIDEN STKS 1m 1f 170y
8:40 (8:44) (Class 5) 3-Y-O+ **£2,587** (£770; £384; £192) **Stalls** Low

Form RPR
40- **1** **Amaze**[259] 2735 4-9-10 0.................. BarryMcHugh 6 83
(Brian Ellison) *hld up in mid-div: hdwy to trck ldrs over 3f out: chal over 1f out: styd on to ld last 50yds* **50/1**
3-4 **2** *3/4* **Stencive**[32] 1859 3-8-11 0.................. LiamJones 11 80
(William Haggas) *dwlt: sn chsng ldrs: led over 7f out: rdn over 2f out: hdd and no ex wl ins fnl f* **8/11**[1]
2 **3** *shd* **Moratab (IRE)**[19] 2226 3-8-11 0.................. AndreaAtzeni 9 80
(Roger Varian) *in rr: hdwy 5f out: chsd ldrs over 2f out: kpt on towards fin* **15/2**
4 **4** *nk* **Kunegunda**[26] 2050 3-8-6 0.................. SilvestreDeSousa 3 74
(James Fanshawe) *trckd ldrs: drvn 4f out: sn outpcd: hdwy over 2f out: sn chsng ldrs: swtchd rt and styd on last 50yds* **6/1**[3]
5 *6* **Bobs Her Uncle** 3-8-7 0 ow1.................. GrahamGibbons 5 63
(James Bethell) *s.i.s: swtchd rt after s: lost pl 4f out: sme hdwy over 2f out: one pce* **33/1**
3- **6** *13* **Saslong**[179] 7709 3-8-11 0.................. JoeFanning 2 39+
(Mark Johnston) *trckd ldrs: wknd over 1f out: eased ins fnl f* **16/1**
06 **7** *2 1/4* **Certainly Elusive (IRE)**[16] 2339 3-8-11 0..................(b) PJMcDonald 7 35
(Alan Swinbank) *drvn along in rr: nvr on terms* **66/1**
0- **8** *1 1/4* **There's No Rules**[209] 7350 3-8-8 0.................. DeclanCannon(3) 4 32
(Richard Guest) *in rr: lost pl 4f out: sn bhd* **100/1**
40 **9** *8* **Rufus Stone (USA)**[18] 2287 4-9-10 0.................. MichaelO'Connell 8 16
(Jane Chapple-Hyam) *sn chsng ldrs: drvn over 4f out: lost pl 3f out: sn bhd* **50/1**
2-3 **10** *23* **Yanabeeaa (USA)**[15] 2381 3-8-6 0.................. PaulHanagan 1
(Sir Michael Stoute) *led tl over 7f out: drvn over 3f out: wknd over 2f out: sn heavily eased: t.o* **5/2**[2]

2m 10.83s (5.43) **Going Correction** +0.625s/f (Yiel)
WFA 3 from 4yo 13lb **10** Ran SP% **127.8**
Speed ratings (Par 103): **103,102,102,102,97 86,85,84,77,59**
toteswingers: 1&2 £16.00, 1&3 £28.80, 2&3 £1.60 CSF £96.41 TOTE £99.50: £17.60, £1.10, £1.60; EX 388.40.
Owner A Farrell, A Williamson, H Lynn **Bred** Cheveley Park Stud Ltd **Trained** Norton, N Yorks

FOCUS
Several decent performers have taken this maiden, the pick being Godolphin's Group 2 dirt winner Jalil in 2007 but it'll be a surprise if this winner turns out to be smart. The gallop was an ordinary one and the first four, who pulled clear, finished in a heap. The second was a long way below his previous form and the race is rated around the third and fourth.
Yanabeeaa(USA) Official explanation: trainer's rep said filly was unsuited by the good to soft ground

2827 LADIES DAY 21ST JUNE BOOK NOW H'CAP 2m
9:10 (9:10) (Class 5) (0-75,71) 4-Y-O+ **£2,911** (£866; £432; £216) **Stalls** High

Form RPR
6-32 **1** **Rosairlie (IRE)**[19] 2242 4-8-12 **65**.................. GarryWhillans(5) 7 81
(Micky Hammond) *hld up in tch: effrt 4f out: wnt 2nd over 2f out: sn led: kpt on fnl f: jst hld on* **7/2**[2]
16-4 **2** *nse* **Orsippus (USA)**[20] 2214 6-9-10 **71**.................. SilvestreDeSousa 6 87
(Michael Smith) *trckd ldrs: drvn over 4f out: chsd wnr 1f out: styd on wl towards fin: jst denied* **3/1**[1]
0-20 **3** *8* **Spruzzo**[15] 2378 6-8-9 **56**.................. DuranFentiman 3 62
(Chris Fairhurst) *led: hdd 2f out: one pce appr fnl f* **12/1**
4330 **4** *2 1/2* **Sohcahtoa (IRE)**[20] 2214 6-9-10 **71**.................. GrahamGibbons 4 74
(David Barron) *mid-div: drvn over 4f out: hdwy over 3f out: edgd lft over 1f out: one pce* **4/1**[3]
2-30 **5** *1 3/4* **Mohawk Ridge**[33] 1822 6-9-4 **68**.................. LeeTopliss(3) 8 69
(Michael Dods) *trckd ldrs: wnt 2nd over 4f out: fdd appr fnl f* **13/2**
6-14 **6** *17* **Bradbury (IRE)**[12] 2457 4-9-8 **70**..................(p) PaulHanagan 5 51
(James Bethell) *mid-div: drvn 7f out: lost pl over 3f out: sn bhd* **6/1**
20-4 **7** *10* **Terenzium (IRE)**[19] 2242 10-8-5 **52** oh1..................(p) KellyHarrison 10 21
(Micky Hammond) *racd in last: wl bhd fnl 3f* **33/1**
-006 **8** *5* **Munaawib**[34] 1794 4-8-1 **52** oh7.................. JulieBurke(3) 1 15
(David C Griffiths) *trckd ldrs: t.k.h: effrt over 4f out: lost pl over 3f out: sn bhd* **40/1**
423- **9** *78* **Stormy Morning**[92] 7032 6-9-1 **62**..................(p) MichaelO'Connell 9
(Philip Kirby) *in rr: hdwy on outside 9f out: sn drvn: lost pl over 4f out: sn bhd: t.o 3f out: eventually completed* **16/1**

3m 40.55s (8.75) **Going Correction** +0.625s/f (Yiel)
WFA 4 from 6yo+ 1lb **9** Ran SP% **113.8**
Speed ratings (Par 103): **103,102,98,97,96 88,83,80,41**
toteswingers: 1&2 £2.00, 1&3 £6.50, 2&3 £3.70 CSF £14.19 CT £110.13 TOTE £5.00: £1.80, £1.30, £4.70; EX 11.70.
Owner The Bay Horse Masham **Bred** Airlie Stud **Trained** Middleham Moor, N Yorks

FOCUS
A fair handicap in which the gallop was just an ordinary one in the softening conditions. The first two deserve credit for pulling clear in the closing stages and there are grounds for thinking they can both do better.

T/Jkpt: Not won. T/Plt: £69.50 to a £1 stake. Pool: £88,320.75. 926.58 winning tickets. T/Qpdt: £45.00 to a £1 stake. Pool: £6,173.94. 101.35 winning tickets. WG

2828a - 2836a (Foreign Racing) - See Raceform Interactive

2224 HAMILTON (R-H)

Thursday, June 7

OFFICIAL GOING: Good to firm (good in places; 9.4)

Wind: Fresh, half against Weather: Overcast

2837 WEATHERBYS BANK MAIDEN AUCTION STKS 6f 5y

2:00 (2:00) (Class 6) 2-Y-O £2,587 (£770; £384 ; £192) Stalls High

Form RPR

4 1 **Mandy Layla (IRE)**[14] 2415 2 -8-10[0] TomEaves 3 75+
(Bryan Smart) *mde all: rdn over 1f out: edgd lft ins fnl f: kpt on wl* **5/6**[1]

62 2 1 1/4 **Pastoral Prey**[10] 2537 2 -8-9[0] LeeNewman 8 68
(George Foster) *coltish and unruly in paddock: chsd ldrs: effrt over 1f out: hung lft ins fnl f: styd on to take 2nd towards fin* **17/2**

0 3 hd **Bayan Kasirga (IRE)**[13] 2450 2 -8-6[0] PatrickMathers 2 65+
(Richard Fahey) *sn pushed along bhd ldng gp: hdwy over 1f out: styd on wl fnl f: nrst fin* **28/1**

4 nk **Tough Lady (IRE)** 2-8-8[0] JoeFanning 4 66+
(Mark Johnston) *pressed wnr: rdn wl over 1f out: kpt on same pce ins fnl f: lost two pls towards fin* **4/1**[2]

6455 5 4 **Someone's Darling**[8] 2594 2 -8-4[0] PaulQuinn 5 50
(Jim Goldie) *chsd ldrs: rdn over 2f out: outpcd fnl f* **8/1**

6 2 **Bernardino** 2 -8-9[0] GrahamGibbons 6 49
(David Barron) *sn rn green bhd ldng gp: rdn 1/2-way: outpcd fr 2f out* **7/1**[3]

0 7 6 **Amelia Jay**[13] 2450 2 -8-4[0] JamesSullivan 1 26
(Danielle McCormick) *s.i.s: sn wl bhd: sme late hdwy: nvr on terms* **200/1**

0 8 1 **Beadle**[10] 2537 2 -8-13[0] GrahamLee 7 32
(Keith Dalgleish) *upset in stalls: trckd ldrs: rdn over 2f out: wknd over 1f out* **28/1**

1m 12.42s (0.22) **Going Correction** -0.25s/f (Firm) 8Ran SP% 116.1
Speed ratings (Par 91): **88,86,86,85,80 77,69,68**
toteswingers:1&2:£2.60, 1&3:£6.60, 2&3:£12.60 CSF £9.16 TOTE £2.00 : £1.40 , £2.30 , £5.80 ; EX 7.30 .
Owner Dr Marwan Koukash **Bred** Mrs E J O'Grady **Trained** Hambleton, N Yorks

FOCUS

All races beyond 6f were run over 25 yards shorter than advertised. This looked a modest heat using the runner-up and fourth as a guide. The winner was the form choice.

NOTEBOOK

Mandy Layla (IRE) who made an encouraging debut when fourth in a 6f Haydock maiden a fortnight previously, was quickly into stride and saw it out well. Lightly framed and not overly big, she'll surely be given a sterner test next time. (op 4-5 tchd 10-11 and evens)

Pastoral Prey, up to 6f, came under pressure over 2f out but kept on. He probably ran close to the level of his previous outing, despite being coltish in the paddock. (op 15-2)

Bayan Kasirga (IRE) improved for her initial outing with a strong-finishing third here. She shapes as though another furlong in due course will suit. (op 25-1)

Tough Lady (IRE)◆, who cost 22,000euros as a foal and then 12,000gns as a yearling, is a first foal of a dam who won over 7f on the AW. She dueled with the winner early before fading inside the final furlong. There should be more to come with this experience under her belt. (op 11-2)

Someone's Darling, by far the most experienced of these, wasn't beaten far but never looked dangerous. (op 9-1)

Bernardino's rider reported that the gelding hung right throughout. Official explanation: jockey said gelding hung right throughout. (op 11-1)

Amelia Jay Official explanation: jockey said filly missed the break.

2838 LANARKSHIRE CHAMBER OF COMMERCE CLAIMING STKS 6f 5y

2:30 (2:31) (Class 6) 3-5-Y-0 £2,045 (£603; £302)Stalls Centre

Form RPR

0002 1 **Frequency**[32] 1876 5 -9-10[72] (b) RobertWinston 5 79+
(Keith Dalgleish) *covered up in tch: stdy hdwy over 1f out: plld out and qckned to ld last 75yds: comf* **5/2**[2]

2200 2 1 3/4 **Falasteen (IRE)**[29] 1975 5 -9-7[87] (t) PhillipMakin 2 71
(Kevin Ryan) *w ldr: led over 3f out to appr fnl f: rallied: styd on to take 2nd nr fin: nt pce of wnr* **11/4**[3]

0232 3 hd **Waabel**[7] 2629 5 -9-6[70] (t) LeeNewman 1 69
(Richard Guest) *trckd ldrs: rdn to ld appr fnl f to last 75yds: kpt on same pce* **9/4**[1]

0015 4 3 **Qubuh (IRE)**[24] 2120 4 -9-3[64] MichaelO'Connell 4 63
(Linda Stubbs) *prom: effrt whn nt clr run and swtchd lft over 1f out: rdn and outpcd ins fnl f* **4/1**

0-05 5 12 **Colamandis**[7] 2617 5 -8-12[38] (p) AndrewElliott 3 13
(Hugh McWilliams) *led to over 3f out: outpcd whn hmpd over 1f out: sn lost tch: b.b.v* **125/1**

1m 11.88s (-0.32) **Going Correction** -0.25s/f (Firm) 5Ran SP% 106.8
Speed ratings (Par 101): **92,89,89,85,69**
CSF £9.07 TOTE £4.20 : £1.70 , £1.90 ; EX 8.40 .
Owner Mrs Francesca Mitchell **Bred** Manor Farm Stud (rutland) **Trained** Carluke, S Lanarks

FOCUS

A trappy little event. This could rate a turf best from the winner, but there are doubts.

Colamandis Official explanation: trainers representative said mare bled from nose.

2839 WEATHERBYS BLOODSTOCK INSURANCE H'CAP 5f 4y

3:00 (3:02) (Class 6) (0-65,63) 3-Y-0+ £2,045 (£603; £302)Stalls Centre

Form RPR

5311 1 **Sandwith**[13] 2458 9 -9-9[63] (p) LMcNiff[(5)] 6 72
(George Foster) *chsd ldrs: effrt and led wl over 1f out: rdn along and hld on wl fnl f* **4/1**[2]

-000 2 1/2 **Distant Sun (USA)**[7] 2719 8 -8-13[53] (p) ShaneBKelly[(5)] 9 60
(Linda Perratt) *prom: effrt over 2f out: chsd wnr fnl f: kpt on: hld towards fin* **18/1**

5450 3 3/4 **M J Woodward**[57] 1292 3 -9-0[56] JoeFanning 1 57
(Paul Green) *racd alone centre: cl up: rdn along 2f out: kpt on ins fnl f* **16/1**

-623 4 shd **Here Now And Why (IRE)**[8] 2458 5 -9-9[58] (v[1]) RobertWinston 8 62
(Ian Semple) *prom: effrt and rdn wl over 1f out: keeping on whn nt clr run ins fnl f: kpt on* **2/1**[1]

4006 5 2 1/2 **Mark Anthony (IRE)**[20] 2225 5 -9-6[55] GrahamGibbons 11 50
(Shaun Harris) *cl up: led 1/2-way to wl over 1f out: sn drvn along: one pce fnl f* **9/1**

0553 6 1/2 **Amno Dancer (IRE)**[7] 2618 5 -8-13[48] (b) TomEaves 2 41
(Ian Semple) *hld up: pushed along and effrt over 2f out: no imp fr over 1f out* **8/1**[3]

-056 7 1/2 **Andrasta**[24] 2120 7 -8-4[46] MatthewHopkins[(7)] 4 37
(Alan Berry) *hld up on outside of main gp: pushed along over 2f out: no imp over 1f out* **33/1**

0246 8 2 1/2 **Weetentherty**[7] 2617 5 -9-5[54] PhillipMakin 3 36
(Linda Perratt) *hld up: rdn along over 2f out: nvr rchd ldrs* **8/1**[3]

-050 9 5 **Cayman Fox**[13] 2458 7 -9-8[57] PJMcDonald 7 21
(Linda Perratt) *prom: rdn and edgd rt over 2f out: sn wknd* **10/1**

00-0 10 29 **Six Diamonds**[17] 2352 5 -9-3[52] LeeNewman 10
(Richard Guest) *wnt keenly to post: led to 1/2-way: sn lost pl and struggling: t.o* **28/1**

59.7s (-0.30) **Going Correction** -0.25s/f (Firm)
WFA 3 from 4yo+ 7lb 10Ran SP% 112.2
Speed ratings (Par 101): **92,91,90,89,85 85,84,80,72,25**
toteswingers:1&2:£11.90, 1&3:£8.90, 2&3:£23.40 CSF £69.90 CT £1050.53 TOTE £5.50 : £1.80 , £4.20, £3.90 ; EX 69.80 .
Owner Stoneypath Racing Club **Bred** R R Whitton **Trained** Haddington, East Lothian
■ Stewards' Enquiry : L McNiff one-day ban; careless riding (24th June)

FOCUS

Only three or four of these came into this ordinary sprint off the back of a decent effort, so it remains to be seen whether the form is strong. The winner caontinues his revival.

Six Diamonds Official explanation: trainers representative said mare had a breathing problem.

2840 WEATHERBYS BANK FILLIES' H'CAP 1m 65y

3:30 (3:32) (Class 5) (0-70,67) 3-Y-0+ £3,881 (£1,155; £577 ; £288) Stalls Low

Form RPR

-410 1 **Spavento (IRE)**[10] 2539 6 -9-9[62] DavidAllan 9 70
(Eric Alston) *sn pushed along in rr: hdwy 2f out: styd on wl to ld cl home* **4/1**[1]

50-2 2 nk **Silly Gilly (IRE)**[10] 2535 8 -9-4[62] ShaneBKelly[(5)] 2 69
(Ron Barr) *t.k.h: trckd ldrs: led over 2f out: rdn over 1f out: styd on fnl f: hdd cl home* **9/2**[2]

2415 3 3/4 **Cut The Cackle (IRE)**[6] 2750 6 -9-6[59] (bt) LeeNewman 6 65
(Richard Guest) *dwlt: sn prom: hdwy on outside to chse ldr wl over 1f out: edgd rt: kpt on same pce ins fnl f* **6/1**

0514 4 1 1/4 **Indian Giver**[8] 2600 4 -9-2[58] PaulPickard[(3)] 7 61
(Hugh McWilliams) *hld up in tch: rdn over 2f out: hdwy on outside over 1f out: no imp fnl f* **11/2**[3]

2140 5 6 **Hikma (USA)**[13] 2448 3 -9-3[67] JoeFanning 5 53
(Mark Johnston) *cl up: rdn and outpcd over 2f out: n.d after* **6/1**

61-3 6 2 3/4 **All For You (IRE)**[8] 2598 6 -9-13[66] GrahamLee 8 49
(Jim Goldie) *hld up: stdy hdwy over 3f out: sn rdn: no imp 2f out: btn fnl f* **4/1**[1]

3405 7 9 **Barbarella Blue (IRE)**[21] 2203 3 -8-10[63] JulieBurke[(3)] 3 22
(Alan Berry) *hld up on ins: drvn over 3f out: wknd over 2f out* **50/1**

0-03 8 nk **More Bottle (IRE)**[31] 1916 3 -8-1[51] PaulQuinn 4
(Tom Tate) *t.k.h: led tl hung lft and hdd over 2f out: sn wknd* **14/1**

00-0 9 8 **Sheedal (IRE)**[8] 2600 4 -8-9[48] oh3 TomEaves 10
(Ian Semple) *hld up in tch: struggling wl over 2f out: sn btn* **100/1**

1m 46.17s (-2.23) **Going Correction** -0.25s/f (Firm)
WFA 3 from 4yo+ 11lb 9Ran SP% 111.8
Speed ratings (Par 100): **101,100,99,98,92 89,80,80,72**
toteswingers:1&2:£4.80, 1&3:£3.40, 2&3:£6.00 CSF £21.04 CT £104.07 TOTE £4.30 : £1.70 , £2.10, £2.20 ; EX 20.20 .
Owner Whitehills Racing Syndicate **Bred** E Prosser, J Singh, & N & E Kent **Trained** Longton, Lancs
■ Stewards' Enquiry : Paul Quinn caution; careless riding.

FOCUS

A modest fillies' handicap but it was sound run. Limited if sound form.

All For You (IRE) Official explanation: trainer could offer no explination as to poor run.

Sheedal(IRE) Official explanation: jockey said filly hung right.

2841 WEATHERBYS PRINTING H'CAP 6f 5y

4:00 (4:02) (Class 5) (0-75,73) 4-Y-0+ £3,881 (£1,155; £577 ; £288 Stalls Centre

Form RPR

113 1 **Hopes N Dreams (IRE)**[9] 2690 4 -9-1[70] JulieBurke[(3)] 10 85+
(Kevin Ryan) *dwlt: sn in tch: hdwy to ld 1/2-way: rdn and clr over 1f out: kpt on wl: eased nr fin* **5/2**[2]

-000 2 3 3/4 **Barkston Ash**[12] 2488 4 -8-13[72] JasonHart[(7)] 2 75
(Eric Alston) *cl up: rdn over 2f out: sn chsng wnr: kpt on fnl f: nt pce to chal* **17/2**

0-00 3 2 **Ballinargh Girl (IRE)**[12] 2476 4 -9-6[72] JamesSullivan 7 69
(Danielle McCormick) *in tch: rdn over 2f out: edgd lft and hdwy wl over 1f out: kpt on fnl f: no imp* **25/1**

4352 4 nk **Restless Bay (IRE)**[10] 2551 4 -9-7[73] (p) GrahamLee 1 69
(Reg Hollinshead) *hld up: shkn up and hdwy over 1f out: kpt on fnl f: nvr able to chal* **9/1**

-101 5 6 **Bandstand**[121] 458 6 -9-7[73] TomEaves 8 49
(Bryan Smart) *cl up: drvn over 2f out: edgd rt and wknd over 1f out* **12/1**

511- 6 1 1/4 **Hills Of Dakota**[263] 6190 4 -9-7[73] GrahamGibbons 4 45
(David Barron) *cl up: drvn and outpcd 1/2-way: n.d after* **2/1**[1]

0-66 7 hd **Sea Salt**[26] 2096 9 -8-8[65] ShaneBKelly[(5)] 9 37
(Ron Barr) *sn bhd and struggling stands' rail: nvr a factor* **28/1**

0034 8 4 1/2 **Legal Eagle (IRE)**[12] 2475 7 -9-7[73] (p) JoeFanning 6 30
(Paul Green) *anticipated s: dwlt: sn pushed along in rr: no ch fr 1/2-way* **8/1**[3]

-502 9 4 1/2 **Saxonette**[7] 2617 4 -8-5[57] ow1 PJMcDonald 5
(Linda Perratt) *led to 1/2-way: sn rdn and lost pl* **28/1**

4426 10 1 1/2 **Angelo Poliziano**[20] 2230 6 -9-5[71] (p) LeeNewman 3
(George Foster) *cl up: rdn over 3f out: wknd over 2f out* **33/1**

1m 10.23s (-1.97) **Going Correction** -0.25s/f (Firm) 10Ran SP% 114.9
Speed ratings (Par 103): **103,98,95,94,86 85,85,79,73,71**
toteswingers:1&2:£4.60, 1&3:£11.70, 2&3:£26.00 CSF £22.45 CT £436.52 TOTE £3.50 : £1.60 , £2.60, £5.70 ; EX 23.20 .
Owner JCG Chua & CK Ong **Bred** J & Mrs Brennan & Edward & Mrs O'Regan **Trained** Hambleton, N Yorks

FOCUS

An open-looking contest was taken with some ease. A tricky race to pin down but the winner posted a personal best.

Legal Eagle (IRE) Official explanation: jockey said gelding hit his head on stalls.

2842 PRESTIGE SCOTLAND H'CAP 1m 5f 9y

4:30 (4:30) (Class 5) (0-70,70) 4-Y-0+ £3,234 (£962; £481 ; £240) Stalls Low

Form RPR

-014 1 **La Bacouetteuse (FR)**[9] 2593 7 -9-3[66] (p) DavidAllan 3 75
(Iain Jardine) *hld up in tch: effrt and rdn over 2f out: wnt 2nd and edgd lft appr fnl f: styd on wl fnl f: led cl home* **2/1**[2]

-341 **2** *nse* **Pokfulham (IRE)**[20] 2242 6-9-7 **70**..............................(v) DanielTudhope 5 79
(Jim Goldie) *led at stdy pce: rdn along and qcknd 3f out: styd on fnl f: hdd cl home* **9/5**[1]
-035 **3** *8* **Cadgers Brig**[118] 500 4-9-5 **68**..(p) JoeFanning 1 65
(Keith Dalgleish) *chsd ldr: rdn over 2f out: outpcd and lost 2nd appr fnl f* **7/1**
00-0 **4** *7* **Dynamic Drive (IRE)**[13] 2440 5-8-10 **64**..................... GarryWhillans[(5)] 4 51
(Barry Murtagh) *chsd ldrs: rdn 3f out: wknd wl over 1f out* **10/1**
4-00 **5** *12* **Damascus Symphony**[30] 1952 4-9-0 **63**.................... GrahamGibbons 2 32
(James Bethell) *in tch: rdn along over 2f out: sn wknd* **4/1**[3]

2m 50.03s (-3.87) **Going Correction** -0.25s/f (Firm) **5** Ran SP% **110.6**
Speed ratings (Par 103): **101,100,96,91,84**
CSF £6.05 TOTE £1.80: £1.10, £1.90; EX 6.00.
Owner Miss S A Booth **Bred** Sarl Classic Breeding & Maria R Mendes **Trained** Bonchester Bridge, Borders
■ Stewards' Enquiry : David Allan four-day ban; used whip above permitted level (24th-27th June)

FOCUS
An even gallop, nothing more, was set by the leader, and two pulled well clear in the final stages. No depth, but the first two are entitled to rate this high.

2843 READ HAYLEY AT RACINGUK.COM EVERY FRIDAY H'CAP 1m 3f 16y
5:00 (5:00) (Class 6) (0-65,64) 3-Y-O **£2,045** (£603; £302) **Stalls** Low

Form RPR
5031 **1** **Courtesy Call (IRE)**[9] 2577 3-9-7 **64** 6ex........................... JoeFanning 2 73+
(Mark Johnston) *chsd clr ldr: hdwy to ld 3f out: sn clr: pushed out: unchal* **7/4**[1]
3445 **2** *4½* **Bapak Pintar**[2] 2788 3-9-4 **64**... JulieBurke[(3)] 1 65
(Kevin Ryan) *led and clr to 1/2-way: hdd 3f out: kpt on same pce fnl 2f* **11/4**[2]
-450 **3** *4½* **Ferdy (IRE)**[17] 2353 3-8-2 **45**... PatrickMathers 4 38
(Paul Green) *in tch chsng gp: hdwy on outside over 3f out: rdn and wknd wl over 1f out* **20/1**[3]
0-41 **4** *2¼* **Fine Altomis**[17] 2341 3-9-4 **61**... TomEaves 6 50
(Michael Dods) *cl up chsng gp: rdn and outpcd 3f out: n.d after* **7/4**[1]
06-5 **5** *17* **Landaho**[40] 1660 3-8-2 **45**.. JamesSullivan 5
(Hugh McWilliams) *hld up in tch chsng gp: hdwy over 4f out: wknd over 3f out: sn lost tch* **50/1**

2m 22.55s (-3.05) **Going Correction** -0.25s/f (Firm) **5** Ran SP% **106.1**
Speed ratings (Par 97): **101,97,94,92,80**
CSF £6.36 TOTE £2.40: £1.10, £1.60; EX 6.10.
Owner A D Spence **Bred** Mrs James Wigan **Trained** Middleham Moor, N Yorks

FOCUS
The betting suggested only three could be realistically expected to win.
T/Plt: £68.10 to a £1 stake. Pool:£43,946.37 - 471.00 winning tickets T/Qpdt: £24.70 to a £1 stake. Pool:£2,775.12 - 82.96 winning tickets RY

2579 LINGFIELD (L-H)
Thursday, June 7

OFFICIAL GOING: Turf course - good to soft (7.1) changing to soft after race 1 (2:20); all-weather - standard
The softening conditions on the straight turf course appeared to bring the low-drawn runners into play more than can be the case here.
Wind: virtually nil changing to fresh behind after 4th Weather: rain

2844 LINGFIELDPARK.CO.UK MEDIAN AUCTION MAIDEN STKS 6f
2:20 (2:22) (Class 6) 2-Y-O **£1,704** (£503; £251) **Stalls** High

Form RPR
3 **1** **Reliant Robin (IRE)**[9] 2579 2-9-3 0............................ StevieDonohoe 12 72+
(Robert Mills) *broke wl: chsd ldrs tl shuffled bk into midfield after 2f: effrt and swtchd sharply lft over 1f out: gd hdwy to ld wl ins fnl f: hld on wl cl home* **7/1**
2 *nse* **Super Simon (IRE)** 2-9-3 0.. NeilCallan 4 72+
(Paul D'Arcy) *wnt lft s: in tch: rdn and effrt over 1f out: styd on u.p and ev ch ins fnl f: r.o wl but jst hld cl home* **33/1**
3 *¾* **Prince Regal** 2-9-3 0... KierenFallon 2 70
(Alan Jarvis) *chsd ldrs: wnt 2nd 4f out: rdn and ev ch over 1f out: led ins fnl f: hdd and styd on same pce wl ins fnl f* **7/2**[2]
4 *hd* **Frege (USA)** 2-8-12 0.. FrankieDettori 1 64
(Brian Meehan) *chsd ldrs: rdn and effrt to chal over 1f out: ev ch fnl f tl no ex fnl 50yds* **7/1**
0 **5** *1* **Tiger's Home**[20] 2245 2-8-9 0..................................... AdamBeschizza[(3)] 6 61
(Julia Feilden) *sn bustled along to ld: drvn and hrd pressed over 1f out: hdd ins fnl f: one pce fnl 100yds* **80/1**
0 **6** *1* **Gold Roll (IRE)**[20] 2231 2-9-3 0.. MarcHalford 13 68+
(David Elsworth) *dwlt: hld up in tch towards rr: hdwy 2f out: styng on whn bdly hmpd jst over 1f out: kpt on ins fnl f: unable to chal* **25/1**
5 **7** *½* **Magic Channel (USA)**[21] 2202 2-9-3 0..................... RichardHughes 10 62
(Richard Hannon) *in tch: rdn and effrt over 1f out: no imp 1f out: styd on same pce fnl f* **3/1**[1]
8 *3½* **Attenshun (IRE)** 2-9-3 0..(b[1]) RichardKingscote 5 51+
(Tom Dascombe) *s.i.s: bhd and sn u.p: hdwy ent fnl f: styd on past btn horses fnl f: nvr trbld ldrs* **33/1**
9 *¾* **Claude Greenwood** 2-9-3 0... JamesDoyle 3 49+
(Sylvester Kirk) *awkward leaving stalls and bmpd s: midfield: rdn and lost pl over 2f out: hdwy ent fnl f: styd on past btn horses fnl f* **50/1**
10 *1* **Rafale** 2-9-3 0.. RyanMoore 8 46
(Richard Hannon) *in tch: rdn and effrt wl over 1f out: no imp and btn over 1f out: wknd fnl f* **10/1**
00 **11** *hd* **I'm Watching**[15] 2384 2-8-12 0................................. MickaelBarzalona 7 43
(George Baker) *chsd ldrs: rdn and unable qck wl over 1f out: btn and eased ins fnl f* **33/1**
4 **12** *¾* **Lawful**[20] 2231 2-9-3 0... WilliamBuick 9 43
(Paul Fitzsimons) *in tch in midfield: rdn and effrt over 2f out: no imp and btn over 1f out: wknd fnl f* **9/2**[3]
4 **13** *1* **Frosted Off**[57] 1315 2-9-0 0... RyanClark[(3)] 11 40
(John Spearing) *in tch towards rr: rdn over 2f out: wknd u.p over 1f out:* **33/1**

1m 14.13s (2.93) **Going Correction** +0.325s/f (Good) **13** Ran SP% **118.3**
Speed ratings (Par 91): **93,92,91,91,90 89,88,83,82,81 81,80,78**
toteswingers:1&2:£30.00, 1&3:£7.40, 2&3:£25.40 CSF £221.11 TOTE £9.90: £2.80, £7.30, £2.00; EX 173.90.
Owner Pinehurst Racing & Mrs B B Mills **Bred** Rathbarry Stud **Trained** Headley, Surrey
■ Stewards' Enquiry : Stevie Donohoe three-day ban; carless riding (24th-26th June)

FOCUS
Persistent rain had already eased the ground, and it was further changed from "good to soft" to "soft" after this opening race. Though this was a routine turf maiden, there were some likeable performances, but the finishing order would undoubtedly have been different on faster ground. The form is just modest to fair.

NOTEBOOK
Reliant Robin(IRE), whose debut was over 5f on Polytrack, appreciated the extra furlong and really took off when switched. He looks a progressive sort and should stay even further in due course. (op 13-2 tchd 6-1 and 8-1)
Super Simon(IRE), a 34,000GBP yearling from a winning family, only just failed to make it a winning debut. Because of the softening conditions, his low draw probably wasn't the disadvantage it usually is here, but it was still a cracking effort and it will be interesting to see if he can repeat this on faster ground.
Prince Regal, whose dam won over 6f as a 2yo, has several other winners in the family. He didn't quite get home on this debut, but he showed plenty of speed and should last the full trip when conditions are less testing. (op 10-3)
Frege(USA), a 60,000gns half-sister to four winners, had been given the normally near-impossible number one stall, but the rain brought the low-drawn runners right into play. She probably did a bit too much too soon in these conditions, but she looks a likely winner before long. (op 8-1 tchd 13-2)
Tiger's Home improved greatly on her debut, when she finished last. More is needed to win a maiden, but she is going in the right direction and clearly acts well on soft. (op 100-1)
Gold Roll(IRE) didn't get the run of the race, and is worth a look next time. (op 33-1)
Magic Channel(USA) was backed to improve significantly from his debut, but the softer ground and extra furlong combined to beat him. (tchd 7-2)
Lawful showed more than this on his debut, so he deserves another chance on better ground. (op 11-2)

2845 LINGFIELD PARK MARRIOTT HOTEL & COUNTRY CLUB (S) STKS 7f
2:50 (2:52) (Class 6) 3-Y-O+ **£1,704** (£503; £251) **Stalls** High

Form RPR
0-0U **1** **Llewellyn**[22] 2165 4-9-2 67.. NathanAlison[(5)] 8 76
(Jim Boyle) *restless in stalls: sn chsng ldr: led over 1f out: sn rdn and wnt clr: in command fnl f: rdn out* **10/1**[3]
4433 **2** *3½* **Basle**[10] 2551 5-9-2 59...(t) NeilCallan 4 62
(Gay Kelleway) *hld up in tch: trckd ldng pair 2f out: rdn to chse wnr jst over 1f out: one pce and no imp after* **5/1**[2]
2011 **3** *nk* **Benandonner (USA)**[10] 2536 9-9-13 84............................ RyanMoore 9 72
(Mike Murphy) *led tl hdd and rdn over 1f out: sn outpcd and btn: 3rd and plugged on same pce fnl f* **2/7**[1]
0060 **4** *10* **Armiger**[16] 2367 3-8-11 46... SilvestreDeSousa 7 36
(William Muir) *chsd ldrs: rdn and struggling over 2f out: wknd wl over 1f out: wl btn fnl f* **20/1**
3-50 **5** *1½* **Navaho Spirit**[70] 1086 3-8-6 67... LauraPike[(5)] 2 32
(Terry Clement) *in tch in midfield: rdn and struggling over 2f out: wknd u.p wl over 1f out: no ch 1f out* **10/1**[3]
0430 **6** *2¼* **Divine Rule (IRE)**[96] 781 4-9-13 53...............................(b) IanMongan 5 36
(Laura Mongan) *dwlt and short of room sn after s: hld up in tch: hdwy into midfield after 1f: rdn and fnd little 2f out: drvn and wknd wl over 1f out* **20/1**
0-00 **7** *3½* **Chater Garden (IRE)**[16] 2367 3-8-11 47......................... DarryllHolland 6 17
(Alan Jarvis) *s.i.s: bhd and pushed along: stmbld after 2f: rdn and lost tch ent fnl 2f* **25/1**
0000 **8** *½* **Danceyourselfdizzy (IRE)**[7] 2627 4-9-2 41..........(vt) LeonnaMayor[(5)] 3 20
(Phil McEntee) *stdd s: hld up in tch in rr: rdn and short-lived effrt over 2f out: sn wknd and bhd* **25/1**

1m 24.87s (1.57) **Going Correction** +0.325s/f (Good)
WFA 3 from 4yo+ 10lb **8** Ran SP% **129.8**
Speed ratings (Par 101): **104,100,99,88,86 83,79,79**
toteswingers:1&2:£3.60, 1&3:£2.60, 2&3:£1.30 CSF £62.25 TOTE £11.50: £2.10, £1.50, £1.02; EX 77.00.There was no bid for the winner. Benandonner was claimed by Mr P. Butler for £6,000.
Owner Elite Racing Club **Bred** Elite Racing Club **Trained** Epsom, Surrey

FOCUS
The favourably weighted and in-form favourite seemed to dominate this otherwise poor seller, but he was well beaten. The winner perhaps ran a small personal best.

2846 MIRROR PUNTERS CLUB FILLIES' H'CAP 7f
3:20 (3:20) (Class 5) (0-75,75) 3-Y-O **£2,385** (£704; £352) **Stalls** High

Form RPR
2354 **1** **Tenbridge**[12] 2503 3-8-13 **67**...(p) AndreaAtzeni 11 75
(Derek Haydn Jones) *chsd ldrs: wnt 2nd over 2f out: rdn and ev ch over 1f out: sustained chal fnl f and r.o to ld last stride* **16/1**
-230 **2** *nse* **My Sharona**[6] 2660 3-9-7 **75**... JamesDoyle 14 83
(Sylvester Kirk) *led: rdn 1f out: hrd pressed and drvn ins fnl f: r.o u.p: hdd last stride* **2/1**[1]
2-23 **3** *3½* **Shaleek**[24] 2121 3-9-7 **75**...(b[1]) NeilCallan 8 74
(Roger Varian) *hld up in tch: hdwy to press ldrs over 1f out: drvn and unable qck 1f out: outpcd by ldng pair fnl 150yds* **8/1**[3]
-616 **4** *2¾* **Ermyn Flyer**[33] 1853 3-8-1 **60**...................................... JemmaMarshall[(5)] 2 52
(Pat Phelan) *chsd ldrs: rdn and unable qck 2f out: unable qck and btn 1f out: wknd* **7/1**[2]
55-5 **5** *1* **Arrow Lake (FR)**[28] 2014 3-8-9 **63**.......................... DaraghO'Donohoe 12 52
(Noel Quinlan) *dwlt and swtchd rt after s: bhd: hdwy into midfield 1/2-way: drvn and hdwy 2f out: plugged on but no real imp fr over 1f out* **50/1**
4-00 **6** *2* **Basantee**[40] 1653 3-9-5 **73**....................................... RichardKingscote 10 57
(Tom Dascombe) *chsd ldr tl over 2f out: sn struggling u.p: wknd over 1f out* **22/1**
-364 **7** *1½* **Fine Painting (IRE)**[15] 2397 3-9-1 **69**................................ RyanMoore 13 49
(Gary Moore) *t.k.h: hld up in midfield: rdn and no prog wl over 1f out: wl hld 1f out* **8/1**[3]
0-00 **8** *3½* **Amis Reunis**[21] 2194 3-8-8 **65**... DominicFox[(3)] 7 36
(Anthony Carson) *swtchd rt after s: bhd: sme hdwy u.p over 2f out: no prog and wl hld fnl 2f* **40/1**
6-40 **9** *½* **Amy Dorrit**[21] 2194 3-9-4 **72**...(b[1]) WilliamBuick 4 42
(John Gosden) *towards rr: j. path over 4f out: rdn and no prog over 2f out: no threat to ldrs fnl 2f* **12/1**
4400 **10** *8* **City Dazzler (IRE)**[9] 2583 3-8-6 **63**................................ SeanLevey[(3)] 16 12
(Richard Hannon) *in tch in midfield: rdn and struggling over 2f out: sn wknd* **10/1**
00-0 **11** *4* **Zingana**[21] 2201 3-9-7 **75**... TomQueally 18 13
(Eve Johnson Houghton) *s.i.s: bhd and sn pushed along: rdn and wknd over 2f out: t.o fnl f* **11/1**
065- **12** *3¾* **Caterina**[321] 4263 3-9-4 **72**.. RichardHughes 15
(Richard Hannon) *in tch: rdn and btn over 2f out: wl bhd and eased fnl f: t.o* **12/1**

122- **13** 2¾ **Cristal Gem**[183] 7657 3-9-0 **75** .... DavidWarren(7) 6
(Andrew Reid) *dwlt and bmpd s: bhd: hdwy to chse ldrs in centre 1/2-way: wknd qckly over 2f out: t.o fnl f* **33/1**

1m 26.21s (2.91) **Going Correction** +0.325s/f (Good) 13 Ran SP% **118.4**
Speed ratings (Par 96): **96,95,91,88,87 85,83,79,79,69 65,61,57**
toteswingers:1&2:£9.80, 1&3:£13.00, 2&3:£5.00 CSF £46.32 CT £291.48 TOTE £24.20: £4.80, £1.50, £2.10; EX 76.50.
Owner Mrs E M Haydn Jones **Bred** Mrs M L Parry **Trained** Efail Isaf, Rhondda C Taff

FOCUS
None of these was a regular winner beforehand and there was little depth. The form is rated around the first two.

2847 WATCH ROYAL ASCOT ON AT THE RACES H'CAP 7f 140y
3:50 (3:52) (Class 5) (0-70,70) 4-Y-0+ **£2,385** (£704; £352) **Stalls** Centre

Form RPR

4603 **1** **Myboyalfie (USA)**[15] 2405 5-9-6 **69** ....(v) FrederikTylicki 4 83
(J R Jenkins) *chsd ldrs tl led 3f out: mde rest: r.o wl and drew clr fnl f: rdn out* **4/1**[1]

5410 **2** 3 **Custom House (IRE)**[13] 2466 4-8-8 **57** .... JohnFahy 11 62
(John E Long) *chsd ldr: chsd wnr over 2f out: drvn and tried to chal over 1f out: outpcd and btn fnl f* **25/1**

0-00 **3** 4 **Rough Rock (IRE)**[19] 2274 7-9-2 **70** .... RaulDaSilva(5) 10 65
(Chris Dwyer) *in tch: rdn and effrt 2f out: 3rd and styd on same pce fr over 1f out* **8/1**[3]

3635 **4** ¾ **Jumeirah Liberty**[16] 2366 4-8-9 **58** .... JamieGoldstein 9 51
(Zoe Davison) *in tch: rdn and hdwy 2f out: kpt on ins fnl f: no ch w wnr* **14/1**

03-0 **5** 4½ **Frozen Over**[21] 2207 4-9-3 **66** .... FergusSweeney 2 47
(Stuart Kittow) *in tch in centre: rdn and struggling 2f out: wknd over 1f out* **10/1**

4354 **6** ½ **Silvee**[14] 2413 5-8-4 **53** .... KieranO'Neill 6 33
(John Bridger) *bhd: rdn and hdwy over 2f out: no imp and btn over 1f out: wknd fnl f* **14/1**

4444 **7** 3 **Zaheeb**[13] 2466 4-9-0 **63** ....(b) TomQueally 7 36
(Dave Morris) *hld up in tch: rdn and short-lived effrt 2f out: sn no prog and wl btn over 1f out* **5/1**[2]

2040 **8** 2½ **L'Hirondelle (IRE)**[15] 2399 8-8-11 **60** ....(p) J-PGuillambert 3 26
(Michael Attwater) *chsd ldrs: rdn along 4f out: sn struggling: wknd wl over 2f out* **16/1**

600 **9** ¾ **Opus Maximus (IRE)**[27] 2044 7-8-12 **66** .... LauraPike(5) 15 31
(Conor Dore) *hld up bhd: swtchd to centre and effrt over 2f out: no prog and no ch fnl 2f* **8/1**[3]

0024 **9** *dht* **Kielty's Folly**[22] 2170 8-8-11 **60** ....(p) JackMitchell 14 25
(Brian Baugh) *sn bustled along in midfield: lost pl over 2f out: bhd and no ch fnl 2f* **11/1**

0040 **11** 1½ **Calypso Magic (IRE)**[21] 2199 4-9-5 **68** ....(t) KirstyMilczarek 16 29
(Olivia Maylam) *taken down early: dropped in bhd after s: rdn and no hdwy over 2f out: wl bhd fnl 2f* **9/1**

26-0 **12** 7 **Blue Maisey**[12] 2503 4-9-5 **68** .... SebSanders 1 11
(Peter Makin) *taken down early: in tch in midfield: rdn and wknd over 2f out: wl bhd fnl f* **16/1**

4500 **13** 4 **Comadoir (IRE)**[77] 995 6-8-11 **60** ....(p) ChrisCatlin 13
(Jo Crowley) *led tl 3f out: sn lost pl: t.o fnl f* **14/1**

1m 35.14s (2.84) **Going Correction** +0.325s/f (Good) 13 Ran SP% **121.9**
Speed ratings (Par 103): **98,95,91,90,85 85,82,79,79,79 77,70,66**
toteswingers:1&2:£19.50, 1&3:£6.20, 2&3:£37.40 CSF £111.78 CT £784.10 TOTE £3.00: £1.10, £8.80, £3.50; EX 116.40.
Owner D Badham **Bred** Robert Pierz & Robert Brooks **Trained** Royston, Herts

FOCUS
This was a modest race, won by a runner who thrives in the soft. He is rated close to his reappearance effort.

2848 LINGFIELD PARK OWNERS CLUB MAIDEN FILLIES' STKS (DIV I) 1m 2f (P)
4:20 (4:22) (Class 5) 3-Y-0+ **£2,385** (£704; £352) **Stalls** Low

Form RPR

4-00 **1** **Popular**[20] 2249 3-8-9 78 .... TomQueally 8 81
(Sir Henry Cecil) *chsd ldrs: wnt 2nd 8f out: rdn and ev ch over 1f out: drvn to ld ins fnl f: styd on wl and asserted wl ins fnl f: rdn out* **3/1**[2]

2 ½ **Hippy Hippy Shake** 3-8-9 0 .... KierenFallon 11 80+
(Luca Cumani) *t.k.h early: hld up in tch in midfield: rdn and effrt on outer wl over 2f out: wnt 5th 2f out: styd on wl ins fnl f: chsd wnr wl ins fnl f: gng on fin but nvr quite getting to wnr* **9/2**[3]

55 **3** ½ **Khazeena**[21] 2204 3-8-9 0 .... FrankieDettori 5 79
(William Haggas) *led: hrd pressed and rdn over 1f out: kpt on wl tl drvn and hdd ins fnl f: no ex and lost 2nd wl ins fnl f* **10/1**

23-2 **4** 1½ **Eluding**[16] 2379 3-8-9 80 .... MickaelBarzalona 1 76
(Mahmood Al Zarooni) *t.k.h: chsd ldrs: rdn and effrt 2f out: drvn and unable qck over 1f out: styd on same pce fnl f* **9/4**[1]

3-0 **5** *shd* **Zenaat**[20] 2249 3-8-9 0 .... RyanMoore 2 76+
(Sir Michael Stoute) *hld up in tch: rdn and outpcd ent fnl 2f: tried to rally u.p 1f out: styd on same pce and no imp fnl f* **14/1**

3-2 **6** 1 **Croftamie**[108] 635 3-8-9 0 .... SilvestreDeSousa 3 74+
(Mark Johnston) *chsd ldrs: rdn and effrt 2f out: unable qck u.p over 1f out: styd on same pce fnl f* **14/1**

5-0 **7** 5 **Gallipot**[48] 1502 3-8-9 0 .... WilliamBuick 9 64+
(John Gosden) *hld up in tch in midfield: rdn and outpcd 2f out: pushed along: one pce and no threat to ldrs fr over 1f out* **5/1**

8 ¾ **Raving Monsun** 3-8-10 0 ow1 .... SebSanders 6 63+
(Marco Botti) *hld up in tch towards rr: rdn and hdwy over 2f out: styng whn swtchd rt 1f out: kpt on but no threat to ldrs* **40/1**

0 **9** 1 **Confluence**[19] 2280 3-8-9 0 .... JamesDoyle 4 60+
(Clifford Lines) *stdd after s: hld up in last trio: outpcd 2f out: pushed along and swtchd rt over 1f out: kpt on* **66/1**

10 3¼ **Omega Omega** 3-8-6 0 .... AdamBeschizza(3) 10 54
(Julia Feilden) *v.s.a and rdn along early: in tch in rr: rdn and outpcd over 2f out: wknd 2f out* **100/1**

00- **11** 2 **Swift Winged**[222] 7177 3-8-9 0 .... DarryllHolland 12 50
(Hughie Morrison) *hld up in tch towards rr: rdn and hdwy 3f out: no imp 2f out: one pce and no threat to ldrs* **100/1**

00- **12** *dist* **Balaton**[229] 7030 3-8-9 0 .... NeilCallan 7
(Brian Meehan) *chsd ldr tl lost pl and reminder over 4f out: lost tch and virtually p.u fnl 3f: wl t.o: b.b.v* **100/1**

2m 6.62s (0.02) **Going Correction** +0.125s/f (Slow) 12 Ran SP% **119.9**
Speed ratings (Par 100): **104,103,103,102,101 101,97,96,95,93 91,**
toteswingers:1&2:£4.40, 1&3:£7.60, 2&3:£8.90 CSF £17.17 TOTE £3.30: £1.20, £1.60, £2.50; EX 22.20.
Owner K Abdulla **Bred** Juddmonte Farms Ltd **Trained** Newmarket, Suffolk

FOCUS
This was steadily run and is probably not form to take too literally, but it contained some well-bred fillies and is worth checking out for future winners, albeit at a lower level than would have been the original intention.
Balaton Official explanation: trainer said filly bled from nose.

2849 LINGFIELD PARK OWNERS CLUB MAIDEN FILLIES' STKS (DIV II) 1m 2f (P)
4:50 (4:54) (Class 5) 3-Y-0+ **£2,385** (£704; £352) **Stalls** Low

Form RPR

1 **Minoan Dancer (IRE)** 3-8-9 0 .... RyanMoore 3 76+
(Sir Michael Stoute) *t.k.h: hld up in tch in last quartet: gd hdwy 2f out: chsd ldrs 1f out: wnt between horses and str run fnl 100yds to ld last strides* **10/1**

5- **2** *hd* **Silent Moment (USA)**[232] 6953 3-8-9 0 .... FrankieDettori 5 76
(Saeed Bin Suroor) *led and set stdy gallop: rdn and qckng 2f out: drvn ins fnl f: hdd last strides* **7/4**[1]

40 **3** ½ **Sound Hearts (USA)**[21] 2204 3-8-9 0 .... NeilCallan 1 75
(Roger Varian) *in tch: rdn and effrt to chse wnr over 1f out: swtchd rt 1f out: kpt on fnl 100yds* **6/1**[3]

0- **4** 3 **Dusty Red**[229] 7030 3-8-9 0 .... JimCrowley 4 69+
(William Knight) *in tch: rdn and effrt to chse ldr whn hung rt bnd wl over 1f out: outpcd and hung rt ins fnl f* **20/1**

4 **5** 1½ **Ghusoon**[16] 2368 3-8-9 0 .... WilliamBuick 9 66+
(John Gosden) *s.i.s and rdn along early: grad rcvrd and hdwy into midfield on outer 7f out: rdn and effrt whn carried wd bnd wl over 1f out: keeping on same pce and hld whn pushed rt again ins fnl f* **3/1**[2]

00- **6** *hd* **Angelic Note (IRE)**[229] 7025 3-8-9 0 .... DarryllHolland 10 66
(Brian Meehan) *chsd ldr: rdn 4f out: drvn and lost 2nd 2f out: no ex and btn whn sltly hmpd 1f out: wknd ins fnl f* **33/1**

7 1½ **Chella Thriller (SPA)** 3-8-9 0 .... JamesDoyle 8 63+
(Alastair Lidderdale) *hld up in tch in last quartet: hdwy and wdst of all 3f out: carried wdr bnd wl over 1f out: sn rdn: rn green and edgd lft: styd on same pce after* **12/1**

0 **8** ¾ **Carmen's Concerto**[14] 2430 3-8-9 0 .... JimmyFortune 11 61+
(Andrew Balding) *in tch: rdn and effrt over 2f out: unable qck u.p 2f out: outpcd and btn over 1f out* **50/1**

0 **9** *shd* **Guarda Pampa**[19] 2279 3-8-9 0 .... KellyHarrison 7 61+
(William Haggas) *t.k.h: hld up in tch: rdn 4f out: outpcd over 2f out: one pce and no threat to ldrs fnl 2f* **40/1**

10 1¾ **Natural Bloom (IRE)** 3-8-9 0 .... TomQueally 2 57
(Sir Henry Cecil) *t.k.h: chsd ldrs: rdn and struggling ent fnl 2f: sn wknd* **10/1**

11 16 **Dubai Emerald (USA)** 3-8-2 0 .... IanBurns(7) 6 25
(Michael Bell) *s.i.s and rdn along early: clsd and in tch 7f out: rdn and lost tch 3f out* **50/1**

0 **12** 7 **Wijaya**[16] 2368 3-8-9 0 .... HayleyTurner 12
(James Fanshawe) *chsd ldrs on outer: rdn and losing pl whn hmpd bnd 2f out: sn wknd* **22/1**

2m 8.52s (1.92) **Going Correction** +0.125s/f (Slow) 12 Ran SP% **119.9**
Speed ratings (Par 100): **97,96,96,94,92 92,91,90,90,89 76,71**
toteswingers:1&2:£4.80, 1&3:£9.30, 2&3:£3.20 CSF £26.52 TOTE £7.10: £1.60, £1.20, £2.20; EX 32.40.
Owner Cheveley Park Stud **Bred** Lodge Park Stud **Trained** Newmarket, Suffolk

FOCUS
As in division one, some good stables were represented and the race was above-average for an AW maiden. However, the pace was slack, with the runner-up dictating it. It was slower than division I and it's hard to rate the form too positively.
Guarda Pampa Official explanation: jockey said filly suffered interference ton the first bend.

2850 ROYAL ASCOT LIVE ON ATR SKY 415 H'CAP 1m 4f (P)
5:20 (5:21) (Class 6) (0-60,60) 3-Y-0 **£1,704** (£503; £251) **Stalls** Low

Form RPR

3-24 **1** **Astroscarlet**[120] 472 3-8-10 **49** .... DarryllHolland 12 62
(Mark H Tompkins) *chsd ldrs early: losing pl and dropping towards rr whn hmpd bnd 9f out: racd in last quartet tl gd hdwy to chse ldr 4f out: rdn to ld and wnt clr 2f out: styd on wl* **14/1**

1-23 **2** 2¾ **Better Be Mine (IRE)**[37] 1726 3-9-1 **54** .... RyanMoore 5 63
(John Dunlop) *hld up in midfield: rdn and effrt over 2f out: chsd clr wnr 2f out: no imp fnl f but kpt on for clr 2nd* **4/1**[3]

-602 **3** 6 **Looks Like Rain**[9] 2577 3-9-1 **54** .... HayleyTurner 4 53+
(Michael Bell) *chsd ldrs: drvn 4f out: outpcd 2f out: no ch w wnr but plugged on to go modest 3rd ins fnl f* **7/2**[2]

60-0 **4** 1 **Tazweed (IRE)**[29] 1979 3-9-1 **54** .... NeilCallan 3 51+
(Roger Varian) *in tch in midfield: rdn and outpcd over 2f out: rallied ent fnl f: styd on but no ch w wnr* **12/1**

023 **5** ¾ **Song Of Joy (IRE)**[17] 2353 3-9-7 **60** .... AdamKirby 13 56
(Paul D'Arcy) *stdd s: hld up in rr: hdwy 3f out: drvn and outpcd 2f out: wl btn but pressing for placings fr over 1f out* **8/1**

-642 **6** *nse* **Micquus (IRE)**[9] 2578 3-8-11 **50** ....(v) JimmyFortune 8 46
(Andrew Balding) *chsd ldr tl led over 3f out: rdn clr w wnr 3f out: hdd 2f out: sn drvn and outpcd: 3rd and wl btn over 1f out: wknd* **10/3**[1]

5001 **7** 1½ **Run Of The Day**[29] 1992 3-9-1 **59** .... AmyScott(5) 7 53
(Eve Johnson Houghton) *hld up in rr: rdn and effrt jst over 2f out: plugged on but nvr a threat to ldrs* **16/1**

440- **8** 11 **Beacon Lady**[252] 6471 3-8-6 **50** .... DavidKenny(5) 1 26
(William Knight) *hld up in midfield: nt clr run: shuffled bk and lost any ch 3f out: wl bhd fnl 2f* **33/1**

-203 **9** *hd* **Green Legacy (USA)**[71] 1062 3-9-5 **58** .... SebSanders 10 34
(Amanda Perrett) *hld up in rr: rdn and short-lived effrt over 2f out: no prog 2f and wl btn after* **12/1**

0002 **10** 13 **Always Ends Well (IRE)**[12] 2497 3-9-5 **58** .... SilvestreDeSousa 2 13
(Mark Johnston) *led tl over 3f out: wknd qckly over 2f out: wl bhd and eased fnl f: t.o* **12/1**

3-30 **11** 84 **Pearl Frost**[77] 993 3-9-3 **56** .... IanMongan 9
(Laura Mongan) *s.i.s: t.k.h: hld up: hdwy to chse ldrs after 2f: rdn and lost pl over 4f out: t.o and eased fnl 2f* **28/1**

40-0 **12** 9 **Music Girl**[16] 2374 3-8-9 **48** .... FergusSweeney 6
(Michael Blanshard) *in tch: pushed along 10f out: rdn and wknd wl over 2f out: bhd and eased fr 2f out: t.o and virtually p.u fnl f* **66/1**

2m 32.62s (-0.38) **Going Correction** +0.125s/f (Slow) 12 Ran SP% **119.9**
Speed ratings (Par 97): **106,104,100,99,99 98,97,90,90,81 25,19**
toteswingers:1&2:£9.30, 1&3:£12.20, 2&3:£3.40 CSF £69.34 CT £247.64 TOTE £11.50: £3.60, £1.80, £2.00; EX 77.40.
Owner Mystic Meg Limited **Bred** Mystic Meg Limited **Trained** Newmarket, Suffolk

FOCUS
This low-grade contest was run at a modest early pace but, when the tempo quickened, all the runners were off the bridle at the 3f pole. The way the race was run meant that few were in contention late on. A clear personal best from the winner.
Pearl Frost Official explanation: jockey said gelding suffered interference in running.
Music Girl Official explanation: jockey said filly lost her action.

2851 ROYAL ASCOT LIVE ON VIRGIN 534 H'CAP 1m 4f (P)
5:50 (5:51) (Class 6) (0-55,55) 4-Y-0+ £1,704 (£503; £251) Stalls Low

Form RPR
0023 1 **Oneiric**[35] 1791 4-8-9 55 IanBurns(7) 12 63
(Brett Johnson) *dwlt and rdn along early: hdwy to chse ldr after 2f: rdn to ld over 1f out: sn clr: styd on wl: rdn out* 10/1
-002 2 2 1/4 **Crimson Monarch (USA)**[3] 2769 8-8-7 46 (b) ChrisCatlin 2 50
(Peter Hiatt) *t.k.h: chsd ldrs: effrt u.p 2f out: unable qck over 1f out: no threat to wnr but kpt on ins fnl f to go 2nd wl ins fnl f* 9/2[1]
3060 3 nk **Gower Rules (IRE)**[29] 1984 4-9-2 55 KieranO'Neill 9 59
(John Bridger) *led: rdn and jnd over 2f out: drvn and hdd over 1f out: sn outpcd and btn 1f out: styd on same pce and lost 2nd towards fin* 8/1
50-4 4 3/4 **Cardi King**[15] 2395 4-9-1 54 (t) SilvestreDeSousa 3 56+
(Ian Wood) *hld up in midfield: effrt and rdn in 5th 2f out: styng on whn swtchd rt ins fnl f: kpt on but no threat to wnr* 17/2
-124 5 1 **Lord Of The Storm**[16] 2364 4-8-7 53 RyanWhile(7) 11 54+
(Bill Turner) *hld up in tch on outer: outpcd over 1f out: rdn and effrt 1f out: sn nt clr run and swtchd lft: kpt on but no threat to wnr* 5/1[2]
3/00 6 hd **Rulbin Realta**[27] 2041 5-8-13 52 IanMongan 5 52
(Pat Phelan) *in tch: rdn and chsd ldrs over 2f out unable qck 2f out: plugged on same pce but no threat to wnr fr over 1f out* 6/1[3]
2034 7 3 **Regal Rave (USA)**[31] 1919 5-8-11 50 (v) JimmyFortune 13 46+
(Peter Hedger) *stdd and dropped in bhd after s: t.k.h and hld up in rr: rdn and hdwy over 1f out: kpt on fnl f: nvr trbld ldrs* 9/2[1]
3046 8 nse **Total Obsession**[15] 2394 5-8-0 46 oh1 (p) NoelGarbutt(7) 7 42
(Mark Hoad) *hld up in tch in last quartet: rdn and effrt over 2f out: plugged on but no imp fnl 2f* 50/1
5025 9 1 1/2 **Director's Dream (IRE)**[13] 2467 4-8-13 52 FrederikTylicki 8 45
(Mark Rimmer) *stdd s: hld up in midfield: rdn and effrt over 2f out: no prog and styd on same pce fnl 2f* 16/1
450/ 10 4 1/2 **Adorabella (IRE)**[411] 5180 9-9-0 53 (t) FergusSweeney 4 39
(Paul Rich) *bhd: rdn and effrt over 2f out: no prog fnl 2f: nvr trbld ldrs* 14/1
00-0 11 1 1/2 **Harry Lime**[13] 2467 4-8-8 52 RaulDaSilva(5) 1 36
(Chris Dwyer) *in tch in midfield: rdn and struggling over 2f out: wknd 2f out* 28/1
00/0 12 3/4 **Sahara Sunshine**[25] 1184 7-8-2 46 oh1 (vt[1]) AmyScott(5) 10 28
(Laura Mongan) *dwlt: t.k.h: hld up in rr: rdn and no prog over 2f out: wl btn 2f out* 40/1
550 13 1/2 **Redinessence (IRE)**[55] 1363 4-9-2 55 JamieMackay 6 37
(Willie Musson) *in tch in midfield: rdn and lost pl over 4f out: bhd over 2f out* 25/1

2m 34.42s (1.42) **Going Correction** +0.125s/f (Slow) 13 Ran SP% **122.3**
Speed ratings (Par 101): **100,98,98,97,97 97,95,94,93,90 89,89,89**
toteswingers:1&2:£6.80, 1&3:£20.80, 2&3:£18.00 CSF £54.32 CT £390.97 TOTE £11.60: £2.60, £2.30, £3.40; EX 62.50.
Owner Suresh Sivagnanam **Bred** A D G Oldrey **Trained** Epsom, Surrey

FOCUS
This was effectively a seller without the auction, but the winner has some potential at a low level. It was steadily run and is rated around the first three.
T/Plt: £78.60 to a £1 stake. Pool:£64,159.98 - 595.26 winning tickets T/Qpdt: £28.10 to a £1 stake. Pool:£4,371.12 - 114.88 winning tickets SP

2637 SANDOWN (R-H)
Thursday, June 7

OFFICIAL GOING: Soft (heavy in places on home bend)
Wind: Across, moderate becoming fresh Weather: Heavy rain before racing; mostly overcast

2852 WEST END MAIDEN AUCTION STKS 5f 6y
6:15 (6:16) (Class 5) 2-Y-0 £2,264 (£673; £336; £168) Stalls Low

Form RPR
2 1 **Rhamnus**[21] 2193 2-9-2 0 RichardHughes 2 86+
(Richard Hannon) *racd against rail: trckd ldr 2f: styd cl up: urged along 2f out: sn in 2nd again: swtchd arnd ldr and led jst ins fnl f: forged clr* 1/1[1]
02 2 3 3/4 **Fletcher Christian**[33] 1847 2-9-2 0 JohnFahy 7 72
(John Gallagher) *wl away fr wd draw: led and crossed to far rail after 2f: kicked on 2f out: hdd and outpcd jst ins fnl f: kpt on* 16/1
22 3 2 1/2 **Uncomplicated**[27] 2047 2-8-6 0 MickaelBarzalona 6 53
(Jim Boyle) *sltly hmpd s: racd wdst of all: in tch: rdn to go 3rd jst over 1f out: one pce and no imp after* 5/1[2]
0252 4 2 **Marvelino**[16] 2370 2-8-11 0 KierenFox 4 50
(Pat Eddery) *dwlt: sn prom: disp 2nd after 2f to 2f out: grad fdd* 6/1[3]
5 shd **Beau Select (IRE)** 2-8-9 0 AndreaAtzeni 1 48
(Robert Eddery) *in rr: shkn up and outpcd fr 2f out: no ch after: plugged on nr fin* 33/1
02 6 1 **Cappadocia (IRE)**[8] 2594 2-8-12 0 ow1 MatthewDavies 5 47
(Mick Channon) *wnt lft s: prom: disp 2nd after 2f to 2f out: grad fdd* 5/1[2]
0 7 7 **The Manx Missile**[26] 2069 2-8-13 0 MartinHarley 9 23
(Michael Bell) *sltly hmpd s: in tch over 3f: wknd* 16/1
0 8 25 **Prince Of Prophets (IRE)**[32] 1886 2-8-9 0 SaleemGolam 10
(Stuart Williams) *a last: wknd 1/2-way: t.o* 100/1

1m 6.99s (5.39) **Going Correction** +1.05s/f (Soft) 8 Ran SP% **113.3**
Speed ratings (Par 93): **98,92,88,84,84 83,71,31**
toteswingers: 1&2 £6.10, 1&3 £1.10, 2&3 £3.50. CSF £19.87 TOTE £2.20: £1.10, £2.90, £1.10; EX 14.80 Trifecta £43.00 Pool: £6,143.70 - 105.51 winning units..
Owner Rockcliffe Stud **Bred** Capt A L Smith-Maxwell **Trained** East Everleigh, Wilts

FOCUS
Rail on Round course home bend moved out 3yds and 5yd up home straight adding 5yds to distances on that course. This was not an overly strong juvenile maiden for the course. The form fits with the race averages.

NOTEBOOK
Rhamnus ◆ was most unfortunate when beaten on his Newmarket debut, having lost many lengths on exiting the stalls, and he had little trouble going one better, despite looking far from happy on the ground. Clearly promising, he's got a bit of size about him and apparently won't be rushed up in grade. (op 10-11 tchd 11-10)
Fletcher Christian handles some cut and kept on having shown good speed, running his best race.
Uncomplicated, slightly impeded early, ran well considering she raced widest of all, but isn't necessarily progressing. (tchd 9-2)
Marvelino probably found the testing ground against him but is fairly well exposed now. (op 11-2 tchd 5-1)
Beau Select(IRE), whose dam was a 7f winner, tried to make some late headway and should improve.
Cappadocia(IRE) was unable to build on his Ayr second, the softer ground clearly not helping. (op 13-2)

2853 PERFORMANCE PR 10TH ANNIVERSARY H'CAP 5f 6y
6:50 (6:52) (Class 4) (0-85,85) 3-Y-0+ £4,075 (£1,212; £606; £303) Stalls Low

Form RPR
-300 1 **Solemn**[21] 2195 7-9-12 83 (b) LiamKeniry 10 95
(Milton Bradley) *mde all and crossed fr wd draw to rail after 2f: rdn clr 2f out: in n.d after: eased last 100yds* 25/1
0330 2 6 **Church Music (IRE)**[19] 2276 3-9-5 83 (p) SebSanders 4 70
(Michael Scudamore) *chsd wnr thrght: lft bhd fr 2f out: clung on for 2nd* 7/1[3]
1520 3 1/2 **Bouncy Bouncy (IRE)**[20] 2230 5-9-7 78 (t) SaleemGolam 1 67
(Michael Bell) *racd against rail: hld up in tch: rdn 2f out: pressed for 2nd fnl f: kpt on* 15/2
3611 4 1 1/2 **Italian Tom (IRE)**[19] 2264 5-9-8 82 CPGeoghegan(3) 11 65+
(Ronald Harris) *hld up and racd wd: trbld passage most of way: styd on fnl f: nrst fin* 9/1
-333 5 nk **Signifer (IRE)**[17] 2347 3-9-7 85 (v) MartinHarley 5 64
(Mick Channon) *hld up in tch: effrt 2f out: fnd nil and no imp on plcd horses fnl f* 11/2[2]
0-03 6 nse **Alpha Delta Whisky**[35] 1773 4-8-12 69 JohnFahy 7 51
(John Gallagher) *prom: pressed runner-up tl jst over 1f out: wknd* 9/1
5-00 7 1 1/4 **Macdillon**[16] 2369 6-9-3 74 MickaelBarzalona 13 51
(Stuart Kittow) *racd wd: in tch: rdn and struggling 2f out: no ch after* 7/1[3]
0223 8 4 1/2 **Ashpan Sam**[6] 2649 3-8-10 74 KierenFox 12 32
(John Spearing) *racd wd: prom: drvn 1/2-way: wknd over 1f out: 8th and no ch whn hmpd ins fnl f* 9/1
/21- 9 2 3/4 **Expose**[356] 3136 4-9-11 82 RichardHughes 9 33
(William Haggas) *hld up in rr: rdn 1/2-way: sn btn* 7/2[1]
2111 10 1 1/4 **Lesley's Choice**[24] 2133 6-9-1 77 (b) MatthewLawson(5) 6 24
(Paul Rich) *struggling after 2f: sn bhd* 14/1

1m 6.17s (4.57) **Going Correction** +1.05s/f (Soft)
WFA 3 from 4yo+ 7lb 10 Ran SP% **114.9**
Speed ratings (Par 105): **105,95,94,92,91 91,89,82,78,76**
toteswingers: 1&2 £31.40, 1&3 £55.20, 2&3 £9.10. CSF £187.88 CT £1494.43 TOTE £39.00: £10.20, £3.40, £4.10; EX 292.90 Trifecta £1550.10 Pool: £3,896.24 - 1.86 winning units..
Owner E A Hayward **Bred** Cheveley Park Stud Ltd **Trained** Sedbury, Gloucs

FOCUS
Few got into this ordinary sprint handicap and it's not form to put much faith in going forward. The winner is rated to the best view of his previous form.

2854 CHELSEA FC FOUNDATION H'CAP 7f 16y
7:25 (7:28) (Class 4) (0-85,86) 3-Y-0 £4,075 (£1,212; £606; £303) Stalls Low

Form RPR
1-20 1 **Fire Ship**[6] 2660 3-9-3 80 JimCrowley 9 87
(William Knight) *led: jnd over 3f out and sn shkn up: fought off first chal but hdd u.p jst ins fnl f: tail swishing but rallied to ld nr fin* 9/4[2]
1-25 2 3/4 **Tartiflette**[22] 2182 3-9-6 83 SebSanders 2 88+
(Ed McMahon) *hld up and last to 1/2-way: effrt to chse wnr over 1f out: led jst ins fnl f and looked sure to win: drvn and hdd nr fin* 11/8[1]
5-40 3 8 **Responsive**[19] 2276 3-9-7 84 DarryllHolland 5 68
(Hughie Morrison) *trckd wnr after 1f: chal and upsides over 3f out to 2f out: wknd over 1f out* 8/1
31-0 4 1 1/2 **Shamahan**[19] 2265 3-9-2 79 RyanMoore 8 59
(Gary Moore) *chsd wnr 1f: dropped to last 1/2-way: sn btn* 3/1[3]

1m 35.92s (6.42) **Going Correction** +0.925s/f (Soft) 4 Ran SP% **109.0**
Speed ratings (Par 101): **100,99,90,88**
toteswinger: 1&2 £2.40. CSF £5.79 TOTE £3.00; EX 3.80.
Owner IGP Partnership & P Winkworth **Bred** Yorton Farm **Trained** Patching, W Sussex

FOCUS
A depleted line-up and again form that shouldn't be taken at face value. The field took the long route around the outside of the course, under the trees, and they certainly covered more than the advertised distance, which favoured the winner more than the runner-up. Only the first two showed their form.
Responsive Official explanation: jockey said filly lost her action.

2855 PERFORMANCEPR.COM H'CAP 1m 14y
7:55 (7:55) (Class 4) (0-85,81) 4-Y-0+ £4,075 (£1,212; £606; £303) Stalls Low

Form RPR
0-42 1 **Spa's Dancer (IRE)**[27] 2029 5-9-7 81 LiamKeniry 3 94
(Ed de Giles) *led after 1f and racd quite freely: clr over 2f out: reminders over 1f out: kpt up to work tl eased last 50yds* 7/4[1]
/1-4 2 4 **Jawhar (IRE)**[28] 2011 4-9-3 77 PaulHanagan 5 81
(William Haggas) *disp 3rd bhd clr ldng pair: rdn to chse wnr over 2f out: no imp after* 4/1[2]
20-0 3 2 **Hurricane Lady (IRE)**[40] 1652 4-9-4 78 KierenFallon 2 77
(Mike Murphy) *fast away: led 1f: chsd wnr: styd in centre for first part of home st: lost 2nd over 2f out: one pce after* 8/1
2346 4 4 **Salient**[22] 2173 8-8-7 67 KierenFox 9 57
(Michael Attwater) *disp 3rd bhd clr ldng pair: rdn 3f out: no real imp after* 17/2
0-00 5 3 1/2 **Rougette**[13] 2444 4-9-2 76 FrankieDettori 7 58
(Charles Hills) *disp 3rd bhd clr ldng pair: rdn wl over 2f out: sn struggling* 9/1
00-2 6 1 **Daneside (IRE)**[9] 2574 5-8-3 68 MatthewLawson(5) 6 48
(Gary Harrison) *a in 6th: wl off the pce and styd centre in st: no prog* 9/2[3]
0000 7 4 **Epsom Salts**[31] 1939 7-8-12 72 (p) IanMongan 8 42
(Pat Phelan) *dwlt: a in last and t.o by 1/2-way: plugged on fnl f* 20/1

1m 49.71s (6.41) **Going Correction** +0.925s/f (Soft) 7 Ran SP% **110.9**
Speed ratings (Par 105): **104,100,98,94,90 89,85**
toteswingers: 1&2 £1.30, 1&3 £6.00, 2&3 £7.40. CSF £8.22 CT £39.78 TOTE £2.90: £2.40, £1.90; EX 7.40 Trifecta £25.20 Pool: £3,413.59 - 99.85 winning units..
Owner T Gould **Bred** Giacinto Gugliemi **Trained** Ledbury, H'fords

FOCUS
The runners again came stands' side in the straight, although this time having cut the home bend. This was not overly competitive and the form shouldn't be taken too literally.

Rougette Official explanation: trainer said filly finished distressed.

2856 BRITISH STALLION STUDS SUPPORTING BRITISH RACING EBF MAIDEN STKS 1m 2f 7y
8:30 (8:31) (Class 5) 3-Y-O **£3,557** (£1,058; £529; £264) **Stalls** Low

Form				RPR
4	1		**Signed Up**[21] 2197 3-9-3 0 JimCrowley 13 (Amanda Perrett) *led or disp thrght: grabbed nr side rail in st: def advantage wl over 1f out: hrd pressed fnl f: hld on wl* **8/1**[3]	91
4	2	½	**Nabucco**[19] 2266 3-9-3 0 WilliamBuick 9 (John Gosden) *chsd ldrs in 6th: prog over 2f out: drvn to chse wnr over 1f out: persistent chal fnl f: hld last 50yds* **7/2**[1]	90
	3	2 ½	**Livery (IRE)** 3-9-3 0 JimmyFortune 2 (Jeremy Noseda) *stdd s: hld up in last: striking prog fr 3f out gng wl: reminders fnl f: r.o to take 3rd post* **25/1**	85+
	4	nk	**Dr Yes (FR)** 3-9-3 0 TomQueally 10 (Sir Henry Cecil) *settled in midfield: prog fr 3f out: shkn up and chsd ldng pair 1f out: no imp: lost 3rd post* **14/1**	84+
4	5	1 ¾	**Cactus Valley (IRE)**[38] 1703 3-9-3 0 JamesDoyle 4 (Roger Charlton) *dwlt: wl in rr but gng wl enough: stdy prog over 3f out: shkn up 2f out: rchd 5th 1f out: no imp after* **9/1**	81+
3-3	6	1	**Cathedral**[19] 2271 3-9-3 0 FrankieDettori 17 (Brian Meehan) *prom: disp ld after 2f: rdn and w wnr over 2f out: lost 2nd and fdd over 1f out* **4/1**[2]	79
6-24	7	10	**Dream Tune**[21] 2210 3-9-3 93 AdamKirby 11 (Clive Cox) *trckd ldrs in 5th: cl up and shkn up over 2f out: wknd over 1f out* **7/2**[1]	59
0-0	8	5	**Astra Hall**[24] 2125 3-8-12 0 RichardThomas 15 (Ralph Beckett) *trckd ldrs: steadily wknd fr 3f out* **66/1**	44
	9	3 ¼	**Stunning View (USA)** 3-8-12 0 PaulHanagan 3 (John Gosden) *a in rr: no prog 3f out: wl btn after* **14/1**	37
	10	1 ½	**Maria's Choice (IRE)** 3-9-3 0 RyanMoore 6 (Sir Michael Stoute) *s.i.s: a towards rr: struggling over 2f out* **16/1**	39
0-4	11	4 ½	**Onertother**[15] 2393 3-8-10 0 JacobMoore(7) 16 (Joseph Tuite) *prom: styd in centre in st: wknd qckly fnl 2f* **66/1**	30
	12	2	**Cellist** 3-9-3 0 KierenFallon 8 (William Haggas) *dwlt: rcvrd into midfield: tk inner line into st: wknd over 2f out* **22/1**	26
	13	7	**Soldier Spy** 3-9-3 0 IanMongan 1 (Mark Usher) *sn in midfield: tk inner line into st: wknd over 2f out* **100/1**	12
0	14	32	**Take The Stage (IRE)**[14] 2430 3-9-3 0 SilvestreDeSousa 12 (Jeremy Noseda) *disp ld 2f: w ldrs tl wknd v rapidly 3f out: t.o* **33/1**	

2m 16.32s (5.82) **Going Correction** +0.925s/f (Soft) 14 Ran SP% 119.9
Speed ratings (Par 99): **113,112,110,110,108 108,100,96,93,92 88,87,81,55**
toteswingers: 1&2 £13.40, 1&3 £73.30, 2&3 £28.30. CSF £34.23 TOTE £11.00: £3.50, £1.10, £9.70; EX 42.60 TRIFECTA Not won..

Owner K Abdulla **Bred** Juddmonte Farms Ltd **Trained** Pulborough, W Sussex

FOCUS
The long route was again taken around the outside under the trees. They finished well strung out off what looked a good pace on bad ground. This was likely an above-average maiden that should produce winners.

2857 CLAYGATE H'CAP (BETFAIR 10 FURLONG FLAT SERIES QUALIFIER) 1m 2f 7y
9:00 (9:00) (Class 4) (0-80,80) 4-Y-0+ **£4,075** (£1,212; £606; £303) **Stalls** Low

Form				RPR
-600	1		**Choral Festival**[20] 2233 6-8-9 68 KieranO'Neill 9 (John Bridger) *trckd ldrs: clsd on inner over 2f out: edgd rt but led over 1f out: hrd pressed ins fnl f: hld on wl* **25/1**	79
021	2	shd	**O Ma Lad (IRE)**[13] 2440 4-9-2 75 NeilCallan 8 (Sylvester Kirk) *hld up in rr: rdn over 2f out: prog wl over 1f out: tk 2nd fnl f: clsd on wnr fin: jst failed* **11/2**[3]	85
503-	3	4 ½	**Cashpoint**[297] 5103 7-9-1 74 StevieDonohoe 1 (Ian Williams) *pressed ldr: led 6f out: edgd rt and hdd over 1f out: fdd fnl f* **6/1**	75
3116	4	½	**Tilsworth Glenboy**[17] 2328 5-9-5 78 FrederikTylicki 11 (J R Jenkins) *hld up in last pair: effrt whn nt clr run 3f out: rdn and prog fr 2f out: kpt on but nvr on terms* **3/1**[1]	78
-614	5	2 ¼	**Bloodsweatandtears**[15] 2399 4-9-1 74 SebSanders 4 (William Knight) *led 4f: pressed ldr after: stl chalng over 2f out: wknd over 1f out* **8/1**	69
234-	6	3	**Bouggatti**[248] 6577 4-8-8 67 PaulHanagan 6 (Lady Herries) *trckd ldrs: rdn wl over 2f out: sn struggling* **10/1**	56
15-	7	½	**Antarctic (IRE)**[365] 2819 4-9-6 79 WilliamBuick 3 (John Gosden) *prom: rdn wl over 2f out: steadily wknd fnl 2f* **7/2**[2]	67
150-	8	7	**Significant Move**[260] 6249 5-9-7 80 IanMongan 2 (Stuart Kittow) *t.k.h early: hld up in midfield: rdn and struggling over 2f out* **9/1**	54
-000	9	10	**The Tichborne (IRE)**[47] 1510 4-9-7 80 JackMitchell 7 (Roger Teal) *hld up: last and struggling fr 1/2-way: wl bhd fr 3f out* **20/1**	34

2m 18.45s (7.95) **Going Correction** +0.925s/f (Soft) 9 Ran SP% 115.7
Speed ratings (Par 105): **105,104,101,100,99 96,96,90,82**
toteswingers: 1&2 £15.00, 1&3 £25.50, 2&3 £8.10. CSF £156.85 CT £949.86 TOTE £38.50: £8.90, £2.40, £3.20; EX 140.40 TRIFECTA Not won..

Owner Mrs Liz Gardner **Bred** Cheveley Park Stud Ltd **Trained** Liphook, Hants

■ Stewards' Enquiry : Frederik Tylicki two-day ban; careless riding (24th-25th June)

FOCUS
Despite it being a clear advantage to get as near to the stands' side as possible throughout the evening, runners in this average handicap ended up more centre-track. The first two came clear but the form is rated cautiously.

Choral Festival Official explanation: trainer said regarding apparent improvement in form that filly needed the run on her last start.

T/Jkpt: Not won. T/Plt: £564.60 to a £1 stake. Pool:£88,939.50 - 114.98 winning tickets T/Qpdt: £68.20 to a £1 stake. Pool:£6,577.81 - 71.30 winning tickets JN

2348 WOLVERHAMPTON (A.W) (L-H)
Thursday, June 7

OFFICIAL GOING: Standard
Wind: Fresh against Weather: Light rain

2858 WOLVERHAMPTON-RACECOURSE.CO.UK H'CAP 1m 141y(P)
2:10 (2:11) (Class 6) (0-60,60) 4-Y-0+ **£1,704** (£503; £251) **Stalls** Low

Form				RPR
1060	1		**Mr Chocolate Drop (IRE)**[10] 2555 8-9-7 60 (t) RussKennemore 7 (Mandy Rowland) *s.i.s: hld up: hdwy over 1f out: sn rdn: r.o to ld post* **16/1**	68
-212	2	nk	**Goldstorm**[38] 1717 4-9-4 57 WilliamCarson 13 (Brian Baugh) *chsd ldr 1f: remained handy: rdn over 1f out: edgd rt and led ins fnl f: hdd post* **5/2**[1]	64+
50-0	3	¾	**Mudhish (IRE)**[13] 2466 7-9-6 59 (b) MartinDwyer 12 (Clive Brittain) *plld hrd and a.p: led wl over 2f out: rdn and hdd ins fnl f: styd on* **25/1**	65
2364	4	2	**Just Timmy Marcus**[17] 2350 6-9-1 54 TonyCulhane 9 (Brian Baugh) *s.i.s: hld up: hdwy over 1f out: r.o: nt rch ldrs* **11/1**	55
6554	5	shd	**Gazboolou**[22] 2171 8-9-0 53 DaneO'Neill 2 (Henry Candy) *chsd ldrs: rdn over 2f out: styd on* **13/2**[2]	54
2500	6	hd	**Beetuna (IRE)**[29] 1988 7-9-6 59 (tp) ShaneKelly 10 (Daniel Mark Loughnane) *chsd ldrs: rdn over 1f out: hmpd ins fnl f: no ex* **11/1**	59
0-00	7	½	**Secret Era**[14] 2431 5-9-4 57 GeorgeBaker 1 (William Muir) *hld up: r.o ins fnl f: nvr nrr* **13/2**[2]	56
6303	8	nk	**Monsieur Pontaven**[31] 1907 5-9-0 53 (b) LiamKeniry 8 (Robin Bastiman) *hld up in tch: lost pl 6f out: rdn over 1f out: r.o* **8/1**[3]	51
0000	9	1	**Justcallmehandsome**[16] 2365 10-8-9 55 (be) NicoleNordblad(7) 11 (Dominic Ffrench Davis) *dwlt: hld up: hdwy 4f out: shkn up over 1f out: no ex ins fnl f* **33/1**	51
5115	10	1 ¾	**Join Up**[13] 2464 6-9-3 56 TomMcLaughlin 5 (Mark Brisbourne) *led: racd keenly: hdd over 4f out: rdn over 1f out: wknd and eased ins fnl f* **17/2**	48
500-	11	shd	**Totally Trusted**[177] 7748 4-9-0 53 (p) LukeMorris 6 (Scott Dixon) *mid-div: rdn over 2f out: wknd over 1f out* **16/1**	45
/64-	12	11	**Dance To Destiny**[502] 262 4-8-12 56 AntiocoMurgia(5) 3 (K F Clutterbuck) *chsd ldr over 7f out tl led over 4f out: hdd wl over 2f out: wknd over 1f out* **25/1**	23

1m 51.16s (0.66) **Going Correction** -0.05s/f (Stan) 12 Ran SP% 115.9
Speed ratings (Par 101): **95,94,94,92,92 92,91,91,90,88 88,79**
toteswingers:1&2:£16.70, 1&3:£42.50, 2&3:£18.40 CSF £53.59 CT £1040.99 TOTE £28.70: £6.60, £1.70, £8.70; EX 79.80 TRIFECTA Not won..

Owner Miss M E Rowland **Bred** P J Munnelly **Trained** Lower Blidworth, Notts

FOCUS
A low-grade opener run at an average gallop. The runner-up traded at 1.01 close home. Pretty limited form, rated around the winner.

2859 DOWNLOAD OUR IPHONE APP FILLIES' H'CAP 1m 141y(P)
2:40 (2:40) (Class 5) (0-75,73) 4-Y-0+ **£2,264** (£673; £336; £168) **Stalls** Low

Form				RPR
-261	1		**Methayel (IRE)**[16] 2362 4-9-7 73 MartinDwyer 7 (Clive Brittain) *a.p: led over 1f out: edgd lft ins fnl f: r.o* **3/1**[3]	79
-430	2	1 ½	**Midas Moment**[14] 2431 4-9-7 73 GeorgeBaker 5 (William Muir) *hld up: hdwy over 2f out: rdn over 1f out: edgd lft ins fnl f: styd on* **2/1**[1]	76
0-10	3	nk	**Ssafa**[40] 1652 4-9-6 72 MichaelHills 1 (J W Hills) *chsd ldrs: rdn and ev ch over 1f out: styd on* **11/4**[2]	74
3450	4	1 ¼	**Climaxfortackle (IRE)**[10] 2546 4-8-11 63 (v) NickyMackay 3 (Derek Shaw) *hld up: nt clr run ins fnl f: r.o: nvr able to chal* **5/1**	62
560-	5	1	**Out Of Nothing**[33] 3358 9-8-13 65 SamHitchcott 6 (Dai Burchell) *led: rdn and hdd over 1f out: no ex ins fnl f* **18/1**	62
0/40	6	½	**Amber Moon**[15] 2401 7-8-2 54 oh9 (b) CathyGannon 2 (Ann Stokell) *trckd ldr: racd keenly: rdn and ev ch over 1f out: no ex ins fnl f* **50/1**	50?

1m 50.64s (0.14) **Going Correction** -0.05s/f (Stan) 6 Ran SP% 108.9
Speed ratings (Par 100): **97,95,95,94,93 92**
toteswingers:1&2:£1.40, 1&3:£3.60, 2&3:£1.90 CSF £8.82 TOTE £3.90: £2.70, £2.40; EX 7.50.

Owner Saeed Manana **Bred** Lynchbages Edgeridge Ltd & Glenvale Stud **Trained** Newmarket, Suffolk

FOCUS
This didn't look a strong fillies' handicap and they finished in a bunch so the form needs to be treated with caution. The winner at least confirmed her Brighton improvement.

2860 BOOK HOSPITALITY AT WOLVERHAMPTON RACECOURSE H'CAP 1f 103y(P)
3:10 (3:10) (Class 5) (0-75,73) 3-Y-O **£2,264** (£673; £336; £168) **Stalls** Low

Form				RPR
23-4	1		**Talk Of The North**[43] 1607 3-9-0 66 MichaelHills 7 (Hugo Palmer) *hld up in tch: shkn up over 2f out: edgd lft ins fnl f: styd on to ld nr fin* **12/1**	74
6654	2	¾	**Holly Martins**[16] 2372 3-8-13 72 (t) NicoleNordblad(7) 12 (Hans Adielsson) *led: clr 2f out: rdn over 1f out: hdd nr fin* **11/1**	78
00-1	3	2	**Tis Rock 'N' Roll (USA)**[12] 2497 3-9-3 69 TedDurcan 3 (David Lanigan) *chsd ldrs: rdn over 2f out: edgd lft ins fnl f: styd on* **5/2**[1]	71
30-6	4	nk	**Supreme Luxury (IRE)**[55] 1363 3-9-4 70 AmyRyan 8 (Kevin Ryan) *hld up: rdn over 2f out: hdwy and swtchd lft over 1f out: r.o* **18/1**	71
-126	5	1	**Sheila's Buddy**[32] 1892 3-9-6 72 LiamKeniry 11 (J S Moore) *hld up: rdn and r.o ins fnl f: nrst fin* **16/1**	71+
05-6	6	2 ¼	**April Ciel**[10] 2548 3-8-8 60 LukeMorris 2 (Ronald Harris) *hld up: rdn over 3f out: hdwy over 1f out: nvr trbld ldrs* **18/1**	54
2102	7	2 ½	**Captivity**[8] 2604 3-9-5 71 MircoDemuro 9 (Mark Johnston) *hld up: hdwy over 3f out: rdn over 2f out: wknd fnl f* **9/2**[2]	60
5230	8	¾	**Green Mitas (ITY)**[20] 2258 3-9-0 66 CathyGannon 13 (Frank Sheridan) *chsd ldr: rdn over 2f out: wknd fnl f* **66/1**	54
155	9	2 ¼	**Rockgoat (IRE)**[43] 1607 3-9-5 71 (b[1]) PatCosgrave 6 (Marco Botti) *hmpd s: hdwy over 7f out: rdn over 3f out: wknd 2f out* **20/1**	54
51-0	10	1 ¼	**Lawn Jamil (USA)**[20] 2246 3-9-7 73 (t) TadhgO'Shea 5 (Charles Hills) *hmpd s: hld up: hdwy over 2f out: sn wknd* **14/1**	53
2150	11	1 ½	**Zain Princess (IRE)**[16] 2372 3-9-5 71 NickyMackay 1 (Gerard Butler) *mid-div: lost pl whn hmpd wl over 3f out: eased* **13/2**[3]	48+

-320 **12** ¾ **Landown Littlerock**[17] 2333 3-8-10 **62** ow1 TonyCulhane 4 37
(Reg Hollinshead) *wnt rt s: hld up: a in rr* **28/1**
5-63 **13** *45* **Night Flash (GER)**[10] 2544 3-9-5 **71** PaulMulrennan 10
(James Given) *chsd ldrs: rdn 4f out: sn hung lft: wknd and eased: t.o* **8/1**
2m 0.15s (-1.55) **Going Correction** -0.05s/f (Stan) **13** Ran SP% **120.0**
Speed ratings (Par 99): **104,103,101,101,100 98,96,95,93,92 91,90,50**
toteswingers:1&2:£6.70, 1&3:£11.10, 2&3:£10.20 CSF £135.75 CT £442.02 TOTE £14.70: £4.10, £5.30, £1.10; EX 226.50 TRIFECTA Not won..
Owner Northern Folly **Bred** Hascombe And Valiant Studs **Trained** Newmarket, Suffolk

FOCUS
The runner-up was given a fine ride from the front in a contest where it proved beneficial to race close to the pace. The form among the principals makes sense.
Zain Princess(IRE) Official explanation: jockey said filly suffered interference in running.\n\x\x vet said filly moved poorly after race.
Night Flash(GER) Official explanation: jockey said colt hung left throughout.

2861 LIKE US ON FACEBOOK WOLVERHAMPTON RACECOURSE CLAIMING STKS 5f 20y(P)
3:40 (3:40) (Class 6) 3-Y-O+ **£1,704** (£503; £251) **Stalls** Low

Form RPR
1114 **1** **Redair (IRE)**[48] 1493 3-8-10 78 CathyGannon 4 78
(David Evans) *chsd ldrs: pushed along 1/2-way: rdn to ld and hung lft ins fnl f: r.o* **3/1**[1]
-600 **2** ¾ **What About You (IRE)**[8] 2596 4-9-3 83 TonyHamilton 8 78
(Richard Fahey) *chsd ldr: rdn over 1f out: r.o* **10/3**[2]
5-00 **3** *shd* **Crimea (IRE)**[6] 2674 6-9-8 82 AdrianNicholls 5 83
(David Nicholls) *led: rdn over 1f out: hdd ins fnl f: r.o* **6/1**
0-00 **4** 1¼ **Love Delta (USA)**[19] 2286 5-9-4 88 AmyRyan 2 74
(Kevin Ryan) *chsd ldrs: rdn over 1f out: n.m.r and hung lft ins fnl f: styd on same pce* **9/2**[3]
4036 **5** 2½ **Fair Passion**[16] 2369 5-9-6 78 DaneO'Neill 6 67
(Derek Shaw) *s.i.s: hld up: hung rt tl over 1f out: sn rdn and hung lft: nt trble ldrs* **13/2**
/2-5 **6** ¾ **Matsunosuke**[27] 2024 10-9-4 90 TonyCulhane 3 63
(Dr Richard Newland) *hld up: shkn up over 1f out: nvr trbld ldrs* **20/1**
0 **7** *6* **Green Wave (ITY)**[24] 2133 3-8-11 0 (bt) MircoDemuro 7 38
(Frank Sheridan) *prom: hung rt 1/2-way: sn wknd* **250/1**
1200 **8** 2½ **Upper Lambourn (IRE)**[12] 2510 4-9-4 75 BarryMcHugh 1 32
(Brian Ellison) *sn outpcd* **7/1**
1m 1.77s (-0.53) **Going Correction** -0.05s/f (Stan)
WFA 3 from 4yo+ 7lb **8** Ran SP% **111.5**
Speed ratings (Par 101): **102,100,100,98,94 93,83,79**
toteswingers:1&2:£2.80, 2&3:£10.60, 1&3:£4.80 CSF £12.50 TOTE £4.20: £1.20, £1.20, £1.90; EX 12.90 Trifecta £48.20 Pool £552.17 - 8.47 winning units..
Owner J & J Potter & The late Mrs S Edwards **Bred** Noel O'Callaghan **Trained** Pandy, Monmouths

FOCUS
The usual doubts over the grade and current form of these, but the winner is rated close to form.
Fair Passion Official explanation: jockey said mare hung right on bend.

2862 SPONSOR A RACE BY CALLING 01902 390000 H'CAP 5f 216y(P)
4:10 (4:11) (Class 6) (0-60,59) 3-Y-O **£1,704** (£503; £251) **Stalls** Low

Form RPR
0002 **1** **Medam**[15] 2404 3-8-0 **45** ShirleyTeasdale(7) 1 54
(Shaun Harris) *a.p: shkn up over 1f out: rdn to ld wl ins fnl f: r.o* **25/1**
400 **2** 1¼ **Ambitious Boy**[12] 2470 3-9-7 **59** RussKennemore 9 64+
(Reg Hollinshead) *s.i.s: hdwy over 2f out: r.o ins fnl f: wnt 2nd nr fin: nt rch wnr* **20/1**
4322 **3** ¾ **Auntie Kathryn (IRE)**[7] 2628 3-8-7 **45** NickyMackay 10 48
(Stuart Williams) *chsd ldrs: led over 1f out: sn rdn: hdd and unable qck wl ins fnl f* **7/2**[1]
5-52 **4** ½ **Red Shadow**[23] 2139 3-8-13 **54** DaleSwift(3) 12 55
(Alan Brown) *chsd ldrs: rdn over 2f out: styd on* **12/1**
5050 **5** 1½ **Hugenot (IRE)**[37] 1725 3-9-3 **55** (b[1]) MickyFenton 7 52
(Tobias B P Coles) *sn led: rdn and hdd over 1f out: no ex ins fnl f* **10/1**
0-02 **6** ¾ **Marah Music**[21] 2203 3-9-7 **59** MircoDemuro 3 53
(Peter Makin) *mid-div: rdn over 1f out: r.o: nt trble ldrs* **15/2**[3]
0-00 **7** 1¼ **Aubrietia**[24] 2131 3-8-7 **45** LukeMorris 2 35
(Ed Vaughan) *s.i.s: sn pushed along in rr: hdwy u.p over 2f out: nt clr run wl over 1f out: n.d after* **5/1**[2]
0-40 **8** *nk* **Doc Hill**[10] 2548 3-8-7 **45** FrannyNorton 11 34
(Michael Blanshard) *broke wl enough: sn lost pl: n.d after* **14/1**
6052 **9** *5* **Dear Ben**[17] 2351 3-8-12 **50** WilliamCarson 6 23
(Brian Baugh) *led early: chsd ldrs: rdn over 2f out: wknd over 1f out* **5/1**[2]
00-3 **10** *nse* **Oakbrook**[13] 2438 3-8-8 **46** TonyHamilton 5 19
(Ann Duffield) *mid-div: rdn and wknd over 2f out* **22/1**
0006 **11** 2¼ **Applaudere**[17] 2351 3-8-7 **45** (b) RichardMullen 4 11
(Jamie Osborne) *hld up: nvr on terms* **25/1**
05-0 **12** 1¾ **Best In Show**[24] 2131 3-9-3 **55** MichaelHills 8 15
(J W Hills) *hld up: effrt on outer over 2f out: sn wknd* **12/1**
00-0 **13** *11* **Minty Jones**[23] 2143 3-9-6 **58** SamHitchcott 13
(Michael Mullineaux) *mid-div: rdn and wknd over 2f out* **25/1**
1m 14.35s (-0.65) **Going Correction** -0.05s/f (Stan) **13** Ran SP% **119.1**
Speed ratings (Par 97): **102,100,99,98,96 95,94,93,86,86 83,81,66**
toteswingers:1&2:£38.70, 1&3:£11.40, 2&3:£17.60 CSF £429.26 CT £2243.92 TOTE £44.40: £12.80, £6.40, £1.90; EX 286.80 TRIFECTA Not won..
Owner Burton Agnes Bloodstock **Bred** Burton Agnes Stud Co Ltd **Trained** Carburton, Notts

FOCUS
This low-grade handicap was run at a decent gallop. Limited form but it makes some sense.

2863 FOLLOW US ON TWITTER @WOLVESRACES H'CAP 1m 5f 194y(P)
4:40 (4:41) (Class 4) (0-80,80) 4-Y-O+ **£4,204** (£1,251; £625; £312) **Stalls** Low

Form RPR
3540 **1** **Mataaleb**[20] 2248 5-9-2 **78** SimonPearce(3) 3 89
(Lydia Pearce) *s.i.s: hld up: hdwy over 5f out: swtchd rt over 1f out: rdn to ld wl ins fnl f: r.o* **11/4**[2]
11 **2** ½ **Teak (IRE)**[34] 1829 5-8-7 **66** FrannyNorton 5 76
(Ian Williams) *chsd ldrs: led 1f out: sn rdn: hdd wl ins fnl f* **9/4**[1]
232- **3** *3* **Reem Star**[191] 7577 4-9-6 **79** AmyRyan 10 85
(Kevin Ryan) *a.p: chsd ldr 7f out: led over 3f out: rdn and hdd 1f out: styd on same pce* **8/1**[3]
0541 **4** 2¾ **Sir Boss (IRE)**[17] 2348 7-9-5 **78** CathyGannon 8 80
(Michael Mullineaux) *s.i.s: hld up: hdwy over 2f out: rdn ins fnl f: nt trble ldrs* **12/1**
455 **5** 3¾ **Saint Helena (IRE)**[22] 2174 4-9-0 **73** LukeMorris 2 70
(Harry Dunlop) *prom: chsd ldr over 2f out: sn rdn: wknd over 1f out* **17/2**
122- **6** 2¾ **Money Money Money**[308] 4719 6-9-5 **78** JamesMillman 1 71
(Rod Millman) *hld up: hdwy over 5f out: rdn and wknd over 1f out* **12/1**
-116 **7** 4½ **Steady Gaze**[105] 673 7-8-9 **68** AmirQuinn 11 55
(Richard Rowe) *hld up: rdn over 2f out: sn wknd* **28/1**
20-0 **8** *4* **Cozy Tiger (USA)**[103] 714 7-8-11 **70** TonyCulhane 9 51
(Willie Musson) *hld up: drvn along 3f out: sn wknd* **25/1**
30-0 **9** *3* **Sweet Lavender (IRE)**[21] 2199 4-8-13 **72** PatCosgrave 7 49
(Gay Kelleway) *hld up: rdn over 4f out: wknd over 3f out* **50/1**
00-0 **10** *16* **Jacobs Son**[31] 1939 4-9-2 **75** RobertHavlin 4 29
(Robert Mills) *led: hdd over 8f out: lft in ld 7f out: hdd over 3f out: sn rdn and wknd: t.o* **16/1**
0050 **11** 1¾ **The Bells O Peover**[13] 2457 4-9-7 **80** (v[1]) MircoDemuro 6 32
(Mark Johnston) *chsd ldr: shkn up to ld over 8f out: sn pushed clr: eased and hdd 7f out: sn bhd: t.o: rdr rode fin a circ too sn* **10/1**
3m 1.25s (-4.75) **Going Correction** -0.05s/f (Stan) **11** Ran SP% **118.7**
Speed ratings (Par 105): **111,110,109,107,105 103,101,98,97,88 87**
toteswingers:1&2:£2.80, 1&3:£5.40, 2&3:£4.30 CSF £9.26 CT £43.88 TOTE £3.20: £1.10, £1.50, £2.10; EX 11.20 Trifecta £84.20 Pool £861.45 - 7.57 winning units..
Owner Killarney Glen **Bred** Shadwell Estate Company Limited **Trained** Newmarket, Suffolk
■ Stewards' Enquiry : Mirco Demuro 12-day ban; rode finish a circuit too soon (21st June-2nd July).

FOCUS
Not a competitive handicap but it was run at a decent tempo, the two last-time-out winners pulled clear and the form looks solid, rated around the third.
Sweet Lavender(IRE) Official explanation: vet said filly lost both front shoes.

2864 BOOK HORIZONS RESTAURANT AT WOLVERHAMPTON RACECOURSE MAIDEN STKS (DIV I) 7f 32y(P)
5:10 (5:13) (Class 5) 3-Y-O+ **£2,264** (£673; £336; £168) **Stalls** High

Form RPR
20-2 **1** **Iffraam (IRE)**[19] 2262 3-9-1 74 PaulMulrennan 4 75
(Michael Dods) *sn chsng ldr: rdn over 1f out: styd on to ld towards fin* **8/11**[1]
-336 **2** ½ **Sandbetweenourtoes (IRE)**[12] 2501 3-9-1 74 (p) ShaneKelly 8 73
(Brian Meehan) *chsd ldrs: rdn to ld ins fnl f: hdd towards fin* **7/2**[2]
3 2½ **Citizen Smith (IRE)** 3-8-8 0 NatashaEaton(7) 5 67+
(Alan Bailey) *s.i.s: hld up: edgd lft over 2f out: hdwy over 1f out: hung lft ins fnl f: r.o: nt rch ldrs* **20/1**
43 **4** 1½ **Art Form**[17] 2332 3-8-10 0 (t) PatCosgrave 11 58
(Alan McCabe) *sn led: rdn over 1f out: hdd and no ex ins fnl f* **9/2**[3]
5 *hd* **Pearl Nation (USA)** 3-9-1 0 WilliamCarson 9 65+
(Brian Baugh) *hld up: hdwy over 1f out: hmpd ins fnl f: nvr trbld ldrs* **14/1**
6 1½ **Monzino (USA)**[87] 4-9-11 0 AmirQuinn 2 62
(Michael Chapman) *s.i.s: sn pushed along in rr: styd on ins fnl f* **200/1**
7 ¾ **Little Red Nell (IRE)** 3-8-10 0 LukeMorris 6 51
(Martin Bosley) *prom: drvn along 1/2-way: wknd ins fnl f* **66/1**
00- **8** *nk* **Glaze**[230] 6992 3-8-10 0 TravisBlock 7 50
(Hughie Morrison) *mid-div: rdn over 2f out: wknd over 1f out* **20/1**
00 **9** 1¼ **Compton Crofter**[10] 2542 3-8-8 0 (t) NicoleNordblad(7) 10 52
(Hans Adielsson) *chsd ldrs: rdn over 2f out: wknd fnl f* **100/1**
45 **10** *9* **Fushicho**[58] 1278 3-9-1 0 MichaelHills 1 27
(Michael Wigham) *hld up: bhd whn nt clr run wl over 1f out: nvr nr to chal* **50/1**
0-0 **11** 2¼ **Perfect Example (IRE)**[16] 2381 3-8-10 0 RoystonFfrench 3 16
(Ismail Mohammed) *prom: rdn and lost pl whn hmpd over 2f out: sn bhd* **28/1**
12 *2* **Silver Threepence** 4-9-6 0 RussKennemore 12 15
(Roy Brotherton) *s.i.s: sn pushed along and a in rr: eased fnl 2f* **50/1**
1m 29.7s (0.10) **Going Correction** -0.05s/f (Stan)
WFA 3 from 4yo 10lb **12** Ran SP% **124.8**
Speed ratings (Par 103): **97,96,93,91,91 89,89,88,87,77 74,72**
toteswingers:1&2:£1.20, 1&3:£7.40, 2&3:£8.60 CSF £3.44 TOTE £2.40: £1.10, £1.10, £4.70; EX 6.00 Trifecta £53.80 Pool £1,251.27 - 17.21 winning units..
Owner Andrew Tinkler **Bred** Roalso Ltd **Trained** Denton, Co Durham
■ Stewards' Enquiry : Natasha Eaton four-day ban; careless riding (24th-27th June)

FOCUS
There was little strength in depth to this maiden and the market leaders dominated. The time was slower than division II.
Perfect Example(IRE) Official explanation: jockey said filly suffered interference in running.

2865 BOOK HORIZONS RESTAURANT AT WOLVERHAMPTON RACECOURSE MAIDEN STKS (DIV II) 7f 32y(P)
5:40 (5:42) (Class 5) 3-Y-O+ **£2,264** (£673; £336; £168) **Stalls** High

Form RPR
/365 **1** **Hold The Star**[10] 2554 6-9-1 50 AnnStokell(5) 7 64
(Ann Stokell) *chsd ldr tl led over 2f out: rdn out* **100/1**
6 **2** 1¼ **Niger (IRE)**[19] 2273 3-9-1 0 MircoDemuro 8 61+
(Jeremy Noseda) *hld up: hdwy over 2f out: rdn over 1f out: r.o to go 2nd wl ins fnl f: nt rch wnr* **6/5**[1]
6-06 **3** ½ **Star City (IRE)**[16] 2375 3-9-1 67 PaulMulrennan 5 60
(Michael Dods) *chsd ldrs: rdn over 1f out: edgd lft: styd on* **8/1**
3 **4** ½ **Admiralty**[10] 2543 3-9-1 0 RoystonFfrench 12 59
(Ismail Mohammed) *hld up: hdwy over 2f out: sn rdn: styd on* **9/4**[2]
00 **5** *5* **Blissamore**[12] 2483 3-8-10 0 DaneO'Neill 10 40
(Hughie Morrison) *hld up: hdwy over 2f out: hung lft over 1f out: nt trble ldrs* **22/1**
6 4½ **Precision Five** 3-8-10 0 (p) PatCosgrave 1 28
(Jeremy Gask) *hld up: no ch whn nt clr run ins fnl f: nvr nrr* **50/1**
25 **7** 1½ **Piece Of Cake**[37] 1736 3-8-10 0 MichaelHills 4 24
(Charles Hills) *led: hdd over 2f out: wknd fnl f* **7/1**[3]
0 **8** *nk* **Bonbon Bonnie**[13] 2461 4-8-13 0 DannyBrock(7) 6 28
(Phil McEntee) *chsd ldrs: rdn 1/2-way: wknd over 1f out: hung lft fnl f* **66/1**
9 *6* **Kodiac Island** 3-8-10 0 AdrianNicholls 9
(Ed McMahon) *chsd ldrs tl rdn and wknd 2f out* **25/1**
0 **10** *5* **Anniesuella (IRE)**[37] 1736 3-8-10 0 LukeMorris 3
(Martin Bosley) *s.i.s: nvr on terms* **100/1**
11 *4* **Blackthorn Stick (IRE)** 3-9-1 0 MickyFenton 11
(John Butler) *s.i.s: a in rr* **25/1**
00- **12** 1¾ **Secret Lodge**[266] 6097 4-9-6 0 TomMcLaughlin 2
(Garry Woodward) *mid-div: rdn 1/2-way: wknd over 2f out* **200/1**
1m 28.73s (-0.87) **Going Correction** -0.05s/f (Stan)
WFA 3 from 4yo+ 10lb **12** Ran SP% **117.8**
Speed ratings (Par 103): **102,100,100,99,93 88,86,86,79,73 69,67**
toteswingers:1&2:£26.80, 1&3:£15.30, 2&3:£2.80 CSF £216.07 TOTE £96.20: £9.80, £1.30, £1.90; EX 437.20 TRIFECTA Not won..
Owner Ms Caron Stokell **Bred** Gainsborough Stud Management Ltd **Trained** Brompton-on-Swale, N Yorks

FOCUS
The second division of the maiden again lacked depth and the winner returned at 100-1. It was surely more down to the failures of others rather than the winner dramatically improving.
Hold The Star Official explanation: trainer said regarding apparent improvement in form that mare was suited by a return to the all-weather.
Star City(IRE) Official explanation: jockey said gelding was hanging both directions.
T/Plt: £13.80 to a £1 stake. Pool:£55,406.93 - 2,914.56 winning tickets T/Qpdt: £6.80 to a £1 stake. Pool:£3,533.76 - 380.00 winning tickets CR

[2161] BATH (L-H)
Friday, June 8

OFFICIAL GOING: Good to soft (soft in places; 7.1)
Wind: Very strong ahead Weather: Overcast

2866 BATH ALES BREWERY CLASSIFIED STKS — 1m 2f 46y
6:00 (6:00) (Class 6) 3-Y-O — **£1,704** (£503; £251) **Stalls** Low

Form — RPR

4-00 **1** **Sondeduro**[20] 2273 3-9-0 74 ... FergusSweeney 9 — 82
(Jamie Osborne) *mde virtually all: jnd fr 2f out and sn drvn: rdn to keep narrow advantage fnl f: styd on wl clsng stages and a doing enough* **7/1**[3]

2-16 **2** *nk* **Hurricane In Dubai (IRE)**[20] 2269 3-9-0 74 ... JohnFahy 8 — 81
(Denis Coakley) *in tch: hdwy over 5f out: chsd ldrs 2f out: chal u.p fnl f: nt pce of wnr clsng stages but styd on wl for 2nd* **15/8**[1]

6210 **3** *¾* **Take Two**[24] 2144 3-9-0 74 ... LukeMorris 1 — 79
(John O'Shea) *s.i.s: in rr: hdwy 4f out: chsd ldrs 3f out: chal fr 2f out and stl ev ch ins fnl f: edgd rt and styd on same pce clsng stages* **11/2**[2]

332 **4** *1 ¾* **Angel Gabrial (IRE)**[130] 362 3-9-0 75 ... FrannyNorton 4 — 78
(Ian Williams) *t.k.h in rr: hdwy over 1f out: styng on one pce whn hmpd clsng stages* **8/1**

54-2 **5** *3 ½* **Isthmus**[28] 2038 3-9-0 74 ... MartinDwyer 5 — 69
(Amanda Perrett) *chsd ldrs: wnt 2nd 6f out: chal 2f out: wknd ins fnl f* **11/2**[2]

32-6 **6** *4 ½* **Hint Of Mint**[21] 2235 3-9-0 74 ... LiamKeniry 2 — 60
(Andrew Balding) *chsd ldr 4f: wknd 2f out* **8/1**

33-2 **7** *6* **Berwin (IRE)**[22] 2200 3-9-0 75 ... JamesDoyle 3 — 48
(Sylvester Kirk) *broke wl: dropped to rr after 4f: rdn 3f out and sn dropped away* **8/1**

2m 17.2s (6.20) **Going Correction** +0.60s/f (Yiel) — 7 Ran SP% **111.4**
Speed ratings (Par 97): **99,98,98,96,93 90,85**
Tote Swingers: 1&2 £3.80, 1&3 £8.10, 2&3 £2.90 CSF £19.51 TOTE £8.10: £4.10, £1.80; EX 28.10.
Owner Lady Blyth **Bred** Ballygallon Stud Ltd **Trained** Upper Lambourn, Berks

FOCUS
After heavy rain throughout the week the going was good to soft, soft in places. There was a strong gusting wind head on into the horses up the straight. They went just a fair pace in this classified event. The runners were tightly grouped around the final bend and there was not much separating the first three. Probably ordinary form on balance.

2867 BATH ALES SALAMANDER H'CAP — 1m 2f 46y
6:30 (6:30) (Class 5) (0-70,70) 4-Y-O+ — **£2,264** (£673; £336; £168) **Stalls** Low

Form — RPR

424U **1** **Edgeworth (IRE)**[13] 2498 6-9-0 **70** ... GeorgeDowning(7) 1 — 77
(David Bridgwater) *sn led: hdd ins fnl 6f: led again 3f out: rdn 2f out: hrd pressed ins fnl f: kpt on wl clsng stages* **7/1**[3]

56-0 **2** *¾* **James Pollard (IRE)**[13] 2498 7-8-10 **66** ...(t) AliceHaynes(7) 7 — 72
(Bernard Llewellyn) *towards rr but in tch 5f out: hdwy fr 3f out: styd on u.p to take 2nd clsng stages but a hld by wnr* **12/1**

0053 **3** *½* **Jalors (IRE)**[10] 2574 4-9-0 **63** ... LukeMorris 13 — 68
(Ronald Harris) *chsd ldr to 6f out: styd cl up in 3rd: chsd wnr ins fnl 2f: chal 1f out: kpt on same pce for 3rd ins fnl f* **6/1**[2]

6-16 **4** *shd* **Resplendent Light**[13] 2498 7-8-10 **66** ...(t) DanielMuscutt(7) 11 — 70
(Bernard Llewellyn) *in tch: hdwy 3f out: styd on fr 2f out to press wnr jst ins fnl f: no ex and one pce into 4th: clsng stages* **9/1**

0-P4 **5** *¾* **South Cape**[13] 2498 9-9-3 **66** ... JamesDoyle 3 — 69
(Gary Moore) *in tch rdn over 3f out: hdwy u.p fr 2f out: kpt on same pce ins fnl f* **8/1**

-502 **6** *hd* **Only You Maggie (IRE)**[10] 2576 5-8-5 **59** ...(v) MatthewLawson(5) 6 — 61
(Gary Harrison) *s.i.s: t.k.h in rr: rdn over 3f out: hdwy on stands' rail whn nt clr run and swtchd lft appr fnl f: kpt on but nt pce to rch ldrs* **9/1**

0-24 **7** *1 ½* **Signora Frasi (IRE)**[30] 1980 7-8-12 **61** ... FergusSweeney 4 — 60
(Tony Newcombe) *in rr rdn over 2f out: hdwy over 1f out: styd on fnl f but nvr gng pce to chal* **14/1**

642/ **8** *¾* **Gordon Flash**[650] 5536 5-9-0 **63** ... WilliamCarson 12 — 61
(Charles Hills) *in rr: rdn and hdwy over 2f out: styng on whn nt clr run on stands' rail appr fnl f: no ch after* **8/1**

2300 **9** *5* **Beggers Belief**[21] 2237 4-8-4 **60** ...(b) JoeyHaynes(7) 10 — 48
(Eric Wheeler) *s.i.s: in rr: hdwy 3f out: sme hdwy over 2f out: nvr rchd ldrs: wknd fnl f* **28/1**

2421 **10** *¾* **Ostentation**[7] 2653 5-8-4 **60** ...(b) NicoleNordblad(7) 8 — 46
(Alastair Lidderdale) *in rr: hdwy 4f out: styd along far side fr 3f out: sn rdn along and no ch after* **11/4**[1]

005- **11** *5* **Gallego**[226] 7113 10-8-8 **62** ... RachealKneller(5) 2 — 38
(Richard Price) *slowly away: plld hrd and chsd ldrs 7f out: led ins fnl 6f: hdd 3f out: wknd ins fnl 2f: no ch whn hung rt over 1f out* **40/1**

2m 19.33s (8.33) **Going Correction** +0.60s/f (Yiel) — 11 Ran SP% **115.9**
Speed ratings (Par 103): **90,89,89,88,88 88,86,86,82,81 77**
Tote Swingers: 1&2 £24.90, 1&3 £9.50, 2&3 £16.10 CSF £86.61 CT £535.19 TOTE £8.80: £2.40, £3.90, £2.10; EX 96.50.
Owner J Star **Bred** Yvonne & Gerard Kennedy **Trained** Icomb, Gloucs

FOCUS
The early pace was steady. Gallego opened up a clear cut lead 4f out before fading and there was a bunch finish in this handicap. Straightforward form.
Ostentation Official explanation: jockey said gelding ran too free in slowly run race and oost its action on bottom bend
Gallego Official explanation: jockey said gelding hung right

2868 BATH ALES HOP POLE/BRITISH STALLION STUDS E B F MAIDEN STKS — 5f 11y
7:00 (7:03) (Class 5) 2-Y-O — **£3,234** (£962; £481; £240) **Stalls** Centre

Form — RPR

00 **1** **Cuisine (IRE)**[17] 2376 2-9-3 0 ... DavidProbert 9 — 74
(Andrew Balding) *pressed ldrs: led 2f out: narrowly hdd wl over 1f out: styd on u.p fnl f to ld again cl home* **13/2**

3 **2** *nk* **Dansili Dual (IRE)**[7] 2663 2-9-3 0 ... PatDobbs 8 — 73
(Richard Hannon) *trckd ldrs: chal 2f out: led wl over 1f out: stl hrd pressed ins fnl f: hdd cl home* **6/4**[1]

326 **3** *½* **Strong Conviction**[13] 2480 2-9-3 0 ... SamHitchcott 3 — 71
(Mick Channon) *rdn along fr s and struggling to go pce in rr over 3f out: swtchd lft over 1f out: str run to chse ldrs ins fnl f: gng on clsng stages* **5/2**[2]

03 **4** *3 ½* **Windforpower (IRE)**[10] 2571 2-9-3 0 ...(v1) LukeMorris 1 — 59
(Ronald Harris) *wnt lft s: chsd ldrs but styd alone far side tl hdwy u.p and c rt to join main gp fr 2f out: chal fr over 1f out tl wknd ins fnl f* **20/1**

0 **5** *1 ¾* **Khefyn (IRE)**[23] 2164 2-9-0 0 ... CPGeoghegan(3) 7 — 52
(Ronald Harris) *s.i.s: sn pressing ldrs: led over 2f out: sn hdd: wknd fnl f* **25/1**

6 *5* **Buy Art** 2-9-3 0 ... JamesDoyle 4 — 34
(Gary Moore) *sn led: hdd over 2f out: styd pressing ldrs tl wknd fnl f* **4/1**[3]

05 **7** *7* **Kwanto**[23] 2164 2-8-12 0 ... TomMcLaughlin 5
(Malcolm Saunders) *uns rdr bef s: spd to 1/2-way* **33/1**

1m 6.27s (3.77) **Going Correction** +0.60s/f (Yiel) — 7 Ran SP% **113.5**
Speed ratings (Par 93): **93,92,91,86,83 75,64**
Tote Swingers: 1&2 £4.70, 1&3 £4.20, 2&3 £1.02 CSF £16.50 TOTE £6.40: £4.30, £1.60; EX 18.80.
Owner Brook Farm Bloodstock **Bred** M Ryan **Trained** Kingsclere, Hants

FOCUS
The well-backed Richard Hannon-trained favourite was just run down in a tight three-way finish in this maiden which was run at a good pace in the conditions. The form is rated a shade negatively.

NOTEBOOK
Cuisine(IRE) had been beaten 15l or more in a pair of slow-ground maidens at Newmarket and Nottingham and was weak in the market here, but he found a sustained run against the near side to get off the mark with a much improved effort. A Holy Roman Emperor colt who is a first foal of a 6f 2yo winning half-sister to Nassau/Musidora winner Zahrat Dubai, he is open to more progress and should stay quite a bit further than this in time. (op 11-2 tchd 7-1)
Dansili Dual(IRE) had fair claims on his debut 2-1 third in a 5f Haydock maiden last week. He was heavily backed and looked likely to collect when making his move inside the final 2f but he was reeled in close home. (op 7-4)
Strong Conviction got a bit tapped for speed back at 5f before staying on strongly in a creditable fourth run. He is developing a consistent profile and has quite a bit of stamina on his dam's side, so should appreciate a step back up in trip. (op 9-4 tchd 11-4)
Windforpower(IRE) seemed to find a bit of improvement with a visor applied on his third run. (op 14-1)
Khefyn(IRE) showed some speed and ability before fading on his second start. (tchd 28-1)
Buy Art, a second foal of 6f winning half-sister to several winners at up to 1m including US 1m stakes winner Solar Bound, attracted support and showed some pace and promise before getting tired on his debut run. (op 7-1)

2869 BATH ALES GEM FILLIES' H'CAP — 5f 11y
7:35 (7:35) (Class 5) (0-70,70) 3-Y-O — **£2,264** (£673; £336; £168) **Stalls** Centre

Form — RPR

03 **1** **Bogini (IRE)**[8] 2615 3-9-2 **70** ...(b) MatthewCosham(5) 1 — 86
(M D O'Callaghan, Ire) *trckd ldr: chal over 2f out: led travelling smoothly wl over 1f out: drvn clr and edgd lft ins fnl f: comf* **7/2**[2]

41-0 **2** *5* **I See You**[39] 1709 3-9-1 **64** ... SebSanders 3 — 62
(Peter Makin) *s.i.s: in rr but in tch: drvn and hdwy over 1f out: tk 2nd ins fnl f but nvr any ch w wnr* **11/2**[3]

-230 **3** *2* **Hey Fiddle Fiddle (IRE)**[14] 2443 3-9-0 **63** ...(b) WilliamCarson 8 — 54
(Charles Hills) *led: rdn and jnd 2f out: hdd wl over 1f out and no ch w wnr: one pce and lost 2nd ins fnl f* **10/1**

6352 **4** *shd* **Ficelle (IRE)**[4] 2759 3-9-1 **64** ... LukeMorris 4 — 54
(Ronald Harris) *chsd ldrs: rdn and effrt 2f out: no ch w wnr over 1f out: one pce appr fnl f* **11/4**[1]

0502 **5** *shd* **Ocean Myth**[10] 2573 3-8-13 **62** ... JamesDoyle 6 — 52
(Jonathan Portman) *pressed ldrs: rdn and ev ch over 2f out: no ch w wnr over 1f out and styd on same pce* **7/2**[2]

-662 **6** *9* **Kyanight (IRE)**[16] 2397 3-9-7 **70** ... JohnFahy 5 — 28
(Clive Cox) *unsuitable grnd* **11/2**[3]

1m 5.43s (2.93) **Going Correction** +0.60s/f (Yiel) — 6 Ran SP% **111.0**
Speed ratings (Par 96): **100,92,88,88,88 74**
Tote Swingers: 1&2 £4.90, 1&3 £4.60, 2&3 £8.30 CSF £21.87 CT £165.38 TOTE £4.20: £2.10, £4.10; EX 25.60.
Owner Michael O'Callaghan **Bred** Mountarmstrong Stud **Trained** Rathangan, Co. Kildare

FOCUS
This looked a tight 3yo fillies' handicap but there was a runaway winner, who is rated in line with her Irish 2yo best.

2870 BATH ALES SUMMER'S HARE H'CAP — 5f 161y
8:10 (8:11) (Class 4) (0-85,85) 3-Y-O+ — **£4,075** (£1,212; £606; £303) **Stalls** Centre

Form — RPR

02-4 **1** **Crew Cut (IRE)**[35] 1827 4-8-11 **73** ... RaulDaSilva(5) 11 — 84+
(Jeremy Gask) *trckd ldrs: rdn and outpcd wl over 1f out: rallied tl press and str run fnl 120yds to ld last strides* **9/2**[1]

6-03 **2** *nk* **Apollo D'Negro (IRE)**[27] 2071 4-9-6 **77** ...(v) JohnFahy 4 — 85
(Clive Cox) *in rr: hdwy 2f out: str run ins fnl f to chal last strides but nt quite pce of wnr* **5/1**[2]

60-0 **3** *hd* **Barons Spy (IRE)**[28] 2029 11-9-10 **81** ... JamesDoyle 1 — 88
(Richard Price) *chsd ldrs: drvn along fr 3f out: styd on towards centre of crse to take narrow ld 1f out: kpt on u.p fnl f: hdd last strides* **9/1**

6-00 **4** *¾* **Quasi Congaree (GER)**[11] 2558 6-9-6 **82** ...(t) BrendanPowell(5) 13 — 87
(Ian Wood) *in tch: hdwy to chse ldrs fr 2f out: chal 1f out: no ex fnl 75yds* **16/1**

1100 **5** *1 ½* **Heartsong (IRE)**[18] 2347 3-9-2 **81** ... MartinDwyer 9 — 79
(John Gallagher) *chsd ldrs: chal over 1f out: no ex fnl 75yds* **9/1**

1500 **6** *½* **Night Trade (IRE)**[27] 2070 5-9-5 **76** ... LukeMorris 3 — 74
(Ronald Harris) *in rr: drvn over 2f out: hdwy to chse ldrs 1f out: one pce ins fnl f* **14/1**

0400 **7** *¾* **Roodee Queen**[24] 2146 4-9-1 **72** ...(b1) CathyGannon 14 — 67
(Milton Bradley) *sn led: rdn 2f out: hdd 1f out: wknd ins fnl f* **18/1**

-206 **8** *nse* **Mambo Spirit (IRE)**[71] 1091 8-8-10 **72** ... DavidKenny(5) 6 — 67
(Tony Newcombe) *stmbld s: in rr: rdn over 2f out: styd on fnl f: nvr a threat* **33/1**

15-0 **9** *½* **Mount Hollow**[20] 2264 7-8-12 **76** ...(p) JackDuern(7) 10 — 70
(Reg Hollinshead) *s.i.s: rdn and styd on appr fnl f: nvr rchd ldrs* **6/1**[3]

0020 **10** *3 ¼* **Ertikaan**[13] 2487 5-9-11 **85** ... CPGeoghegan(3) 12 — 68
(Ronald Harris) *chsd ldrs: rdn 2f out: stl ev ch over 1f out* **8/1**

00-0 **11** *1 ¾* **Rulesn'regulations**[15] 2409 6-9-7 **85** ...(b) ThomasGarner(7) 15 — 62
(Matthew Salaman) *pressed ldr: rdn 1/2-way: wknd 2f out: eased whn no ch ins fnl f* **12/1**

-106 **12** *3 ½* **Divine Call**[27] 2071 5-9-6 77....(p) LiamKeniry 2 43
(Milton Bradley) *s.i.s: outpcd* **9/1**

1m 13.99s (2.79) **Going Correction** +0.60s/f (Yiel)
WFA 3 from 4yo+ 8lb **12** Ran SP% **118.7**
Speed ratings (Par 105): **105,104,104,103,101 100,99,99,98,94 92,87**
Tote Swingers: 1&2 £2.90, 1&3 £7.30, 2&3 £6.30 CSF £26.41 CT £200.13 TOTE £4.40: £1.40, £2.80, £3.10; EX 21.90.
Owner Carstairs, Page & HFR **Bred** Rathbarry Stud **Trained** Sutton Veny, Wilts

FOCUS
A decent sprint handicap. The fast pace set by Roodee Queen and Rulesn'regulations played into the hands of the hold-up performers and there was an exciting finish. The form looks sound.
Quasi Congaree(GER) Official explanation: starter said gelding ran without tongue strap which had come adrift and couldn't be re-ftted
Mambo Spirit(IRE) Official explanation: jockey said gelding was slowly away

2871 BRITISH STALLION STUDS SUPPORTING BRITISH RACING E B F MAIDEN FILLIES' STKS 5f 161y
8:40 (8:46) (Class 5) 3-Y-O+ **£3,557** (£1,058; £529; £264) **Stalls** Centre

Form RPR
4452 **1** **Millibar (IRE)**[17] 2361 3-9-0 67....(p) TomMcLaughlin 6 70
(Nick Littmoden) *s.i.s: in rr: rdn and no prog 3f out: hdwy over 1f out: swtchd lft and str run fnl f: led last strides* **9/4**[1]
2 *nk* **Miss Complex** 3-9-0 0.... MartinDwyer 1 69
(Brian Meehan) *trckd ldrs: wnt 2nd ins fnl 3f: led jst ins fnl 2f: hrd drvn fnl f: hdd last strides* **7/2**[2]
0 **3** *hd* **Gladiatrix**[24] 2147 3-9-0 0.... JamesMillman 7 68
(Rod Millman) *chsd ldr: rdn 2f out: rallied to chal ins fnl f: kpt on: no ex clsng stages* **7/1**
4 *3* **Funcheon Vale (IRE)** 3-9-0 0.... RobertHavlin 2 61+
(Hughie Morrison) *trckd ldrs: drvn to chal over 1f out: green: hung lft and wknd ins fnl f* **9/1**
36- **5** *7* **Rode Two Destiny (IRE)**[236] 6890 3-9-0 0.... SebSanders 9 35
(Peter Makin) *led tl hdd jst ins fnl 2f: wknd appr fnl f* **9/2**[3]

1m 15.79s (4.59) **Going Correction** +0.60s/f (Yiel)
WFA 3 from 4yo 8lb **5** Ran SP% **93.7**
Speed ratings (Par 100): **93,92,92,88,79**
CSF £7.17 TOTE £2.80: £1.70, £2.20; EX 8.90.
Owner Mrs Linda Francis **Bred** Martin Francis **Trained** Newmarket, Suffolk

FOCUS
A number of non-runners and some late withdrawals reduced this ordinary maiden to just five runners. The favourite looked in trouble some way out but got on top in the closing stages. The time was relatively slow, and this is modest form.

2872 BATH ALES SWAN H'CAP 1m 5f 22y
9:10 (9:10) (Class 6) (0-60,58) 4-Y-O+ **£1,617** (£481; £240; £120) **Stalls** High

Form RPR
5136 **1** **Bute Street**[16] 2396 7-9-2 53.... WilliamCarson 9 64
(Ron Hodges) *trckd ldr: led over 2f out: pushed out* **5/1**[3]
32-0 **2** *2 ¾* **Captain Oats (IRE)**[16] 2391 9-8-10 52.... RachealKneller(5) 1 59
(Pam Ford) *s.i.s: in rr: hdwy and drvn over 3f out: tk 3rd over 2f out: styd on fnl f to take 2nd fnl 100yds: no ch w wnr* **6/1**
00/1 **3** *1 ¼* **Passato (GER)**[16] 2391 8-9-3 54....(t) JamesDoyle 8 59
(Jo Davis) *led tl rdn and hdd over 2f out: sn no ch w wnr: lost 2nd fnl 100yds* **1/1**[1]
4 *5* **Perfect Buttons (IRE)**[20] 6316 6-8-8 45.... FergusSweeney 2 43
(Tim Vaughan) *chsd ldrs in 3rd: rdn rdn over 3f out: wknd and dropped to 4th over 2f out* **9/1**
2414 **5** *hd* **Delagoa Bay (IRE)**[17] 2371 4-9-4 55.... MartinDwyer 6 52
(Sylvester Kirk) *chsd ldrs: rdn 3f out: btn over 2f out* **9/2**[2]
6040 **6** *7* **Bashama**[30] 1984 4-9-2 53.... DavidProbert 5 40
(Nikki Evans) *rdn 4f out: a in rr* **14/1**

3m 4.68s (12.68) **Going Correction** +0.60s/f (Yiel) **6** Ran SP% **115.8**
Speed ratings (Par 101): **84,82,81,78,78 74**
Tote Swingers: 1&2 £3.50, 1&3 £2.80, 2&3 £3.90 CSF £34.93 CT £52.68 TOTE £6.30: £3.80, £1.90; EX 34.00.
Owner J W Mursell **Bred** J W Mursell **Trained** Charlton Mackrell, Somerset

FOCUS
A minor staying handicap which was weakened by a stack of withdrawals. The winner raced near the pace and the hold-up runners couldn't get involved. The winner is rated to his old turf best.
T/Plt: £93.30 to a £1 stake. Pool: £50,794.00 - 397.22 winning tickets. T/Qpdt: £12.00 to a £1 stake. Pool: £4,279.00 - 262.78 winning tickets. ST

2694 CATTERICK (L-H)
Friday, June 8

OFFICIAL GOING: Good to soft (soft in places; 7.4)
Wind: Breezy, half against Weather: Overcast, raining

2873 BRITISH STALLION STUDS SUPPORTING BRITISH RACING E B F MAIDEN STKS 5f
2:00 (2:00) (Class 5) 2-Y-O **£3,169** (£943; £471; £235) **Stalls** Low

Form RPR
052 **1** **Lady Poppy**[14] 2437 2-8-12 0.... PJMcDonald 1 74
(George Moore) *mde all: rdn over 1f out: styd on strly fnl f* **3/1**[2]
3 **2** *1 ½* **Mazeppa**[9] 2594 2-9-3 0.... TomEaves 2 74
(Keith Dalgleish) *dwlt: sn chsng wnr: effrt and rdn over 1f out: kpt on ins fnl f* **5/2**[1]
U **3** *4 ½* **Panama Cat (USA)**[24] 2138 2-8-12 0.... PhillipMakin 3 52+
(Kevin Ryan) *chsd ldng gp: pushed along 1/2-way: hdwy over 1f out: kpt on fnl f: nt rch first two* **9/2**[3]
354 **4** *6* **Crystal Cove**[14] 2456 2-9-3 0.... PaulMulrennan 10 36
(Tim Easterby) *stdd in tch: effrt and rdn 1/2-way: no imp fr wl over 1f out* **8/1**
5 *2* **Pacquiao (IRE)** 2-9-3 0.... MichaelO'Connell 9 29+
(John Quinn) *dwlt: rn green in rr: sme late hdwy: nvr on terms* **10/1**
2 **6** *nse* **Cymeriad**[25] 2135 2-8-12 0.... JamesSullivan 5 23
(Michael Easterby) *prom tl rdn and wknd wl over 1f out* **8/1**
6 **7** *3* **Indastar**[18] 2334 2-9-0 0.... PaulPickard(3) 4 18
(Kevin M Prendergast) *hld up on outside: rdn and edgd lft over 2f out: sn struggling* **22/1**
8 *12* **Holding Fast (IRE)** 2-9-3 0.... RobertWinston 7
(Tobias B P Coles) *cl up tl rdn and wknd qckly 2f out: eased fnl f* **16/1**

1m 1.97s (2.17) **Going Correction** +0.325s/f (Good) **8** Ran SP% **113.3**
Speed ratings (Par 93): **95,92,85,75,72 72,67,48**
Tote Swingers: 1&2 £3.30, 1&3 £2.30, 2&3 £4.50 CSF £10.72 TOTE £4.00: £1.20, £1.70, £2.00; EX 12.20.
Owner Ingham Racing Syndicate **Bred** Whatton Manor Stud **Trained** Middleham Moor, N Yorks

FOCUS
Only a modest maiden, run in testing conditions and won in good style. the first two finished clear but the race lacked strength in depth.

NOTEBOOK
Lady Poppy never sighted another rival. George Moore isn't renowed for his record in this sphere but this daughter of Kyllachy had clearly learnt plenty from her three previous outings and never really looked in any danger once grabbing the favoured far-side rail. She has a likeable attitude and she's entitled to remain competitive, especially if sticking to sharp tracks such as this. (op 11-4 tchd 10-3)
Mazeppa was the only one to pose any sort of threat and he kept on pluckily on ground that would have been slower than ideal. He has now posted solid efforts on fast ground and soft ground and ought to be capable of winning a small race before too long. (op 3-1)
Panama Cat(USA), who had unshipped her rider early on at Beverley on her debut, showed a bit of promise on what was effectively her first outing. (tchd 5-1)
Pacquiao(IRE) was seen putting in some good late work having run green throughout. (op 12-1)
Holding Fast(IRE)'s trainer reported that the colt was unsuited by the ground. Official explanation: trainer said colt was unsuited by the good to soft (soft in places) ground

2874 YORKSHIRE-OUTDOORS.CO.UK (S) STKS 1m 5f 175y
2:35 (2:35) (Class 6) 4-Y-O+ **£1,704** (£503; £251) **Stalls** Low

Form RPR
0/0- **1** **Private Story (USA)**[65] 3013 5-8-12 88.... DanielTudhope 6 66
(David O'Meara) *sn trcking ldr: rdn to ld 3f out: sn brought field to stands' side: rdn and hld on wl fnl 2f* **11/4**[2]
-202 **2** *1 ¼* **Eijaaz (IRE)**[6] 2694 11-8-12 58....(p) DuranFentiman 1 64
(Geoffrey Harker) *hld up in tch: hdwy and shkn up over 2f out: chsng wnr whn effrt and swtchd lft ent fnl f: kpt on: hld nr fin* **2/1**[1]
456- **3** *4* **Bijou Dan**[227] 7075 11-8-12 59.... PJMcDonald 7 58
(George Moore) *trckd ldrs: effrt and chsd wnr over 2f out to 1f out: sn outpcd* **9/1**
-050 **4** *10* **Sposalizio (IRE)**[8] 2635 5-8-12 50....(b) PaddyAspell 5 44
(Colin Teague) *led: rdn and hdd 3f out: wknd appr 2f out* **33/1**
5-14 **5** *6* **Dew Reward (IRE)**[76] 465 4-8-11 60.... RyanWhile(7) 3 42
(Bill Turner) *prom whn stmbld: hmpd and lost pl bnd after 5f: sn detached: sme late hdwy: nvr on terms* **10/1**
553/ **6** *16* **Veloso (FR)**[617] 6516 10-8-12 72.... PaulMulrennan 8 14
(Noel Wilson) *trckd ldrs tl rdn and wknd fr 3f out* **3/1**[3]

3m 11.82s (8.22) **Going Correction** +0.325s/f (Good) **6** Ran SP% **107.0**
Speed ratings (Par 101): **89,88,86,80,76 67**
Tote Swingers: 1&2 £2.10, 1&3 £5.60, 2&3 £2.60 CSF £7.80 TOTE £4.40: £1.50, £1.70; EX 7.90.The winner was bought in for 5,000gns.
Owner Middleham Park Racing XXXII **Bred** Gail Peters Beitz **Trained** Nawton, N Yorks

FOCUS
A weakish seller, run only at a steady pace, but they came stands' side in the straight and produced a slow-motion finish. The runner-up sets the standard.

2875 LIONWELD KENNEDY H'CAP 5f
3:10 (3:12) (Class 5) (0-70,70) 3-Y-O+ **£2,264** (£673; £336; £168) **Stalls** Low

Form RPR
463- **1** **Oldjoesaid**[171] 7834 8-10-0 70.... PhillipMakin 7 83
(Paul Midgley) *wnt rt s: prom: effrt and swtchd rt over 1f out: led ins fnl f: drvn out* **13/8**[1]
0610 **2** *2* **Chosen One (IRE)**[8] 2617 7-8-13 55.... JamesSullivan 4 61
(Ruth Carr) *led: rdn over 1f out: hdd ins fnl f: kpt on same pce* **4/1**[3]
5-00 **3** *hd* **Black Annis Bower**[14] 2439 4-9-4 67.... DavidSimmonson(7) 5 72
(Michael Easterby) *cl up: drvn along fr 1/2-way: kpt on same pce ins fnl f* **13/2**
3200 **4** *4 ½* **Come On Dave (IRE)**[21] 2256 3-9-3 66.... AdrianNicholls 6 51
(David Nicholls) *dwlt: sn trcking ldrs: effrt and rdn over 1f out: outpcd appr fnl f* **11/4**[2]
0-00 **5** *11* **Kylesku (IRE)**[21] 2256 3-9-1 67.... JulieBurke(3) 8 13
(Kevin Ryan) *carried rt s: bhd: drvn and outpcd after 2f: sn lost tch* **8/1**

1m 2.18s (2.38) **Going Correction** +0.40s/f (Good)
WFA 3 from 4yo+ 7lb **5** Ran SP% **109.2**
Speed ratings (Par 103): **96,92,92,85,67**
CSF £8.23 TOTE £2.80: £1.70, £1.60; EX 7.10.
Owner The Unique Partnership **Bred** Mrs R D Peacock **Trained** Westow, N Yorks

FOCUS
A modest sprint handicap, decimated by non-runners. The winner only had to run to somehting like last year's reappearance form.

2876 PIN POINT RECRUITMENT H'CAP 5f 212y
3:45 (3:45) (Class 4) (0-85,85) 4-Y-O+ **£4,204** (£1,251; £625; £312) **Stalls** Low

Form RPR
1033 **1** **Solar Spirit (IRE)**[4] 2754 7-8-11 80.... ShaneBKelly(5) 2 89
(Tracy Waggott) *trckd ldrs: rdn to ld over 1f out: hld on wl fnl f* **9/2**[3]
-266 **2** *hd* **Naabegha**[20] 2268 5-9-7 85.... ChrisCatlin 10 93
(Ed de Giles) *t.k.h: cl up: led after 2f to over 1f out: sn rdn and rallied: kpt on fnl f: jst hld* **3/1**[1]
0021 **3** *shd* **Green Park (IRE)**[13] 2475 9-8-12 76....(b) JoeFanning 5 84
(Declan Carroll) *trckd ldrs: effrt and rdn over 1f out: ev ch ins fnl f: r.o fin* **8/1**
0-05 **4** *1 ¼* **Lucky Numbers (IRE)**[14] 2439 6-9-2 80....(v) DanielTudhope 4 84
(David O'Meara) *hld up in tch: effrt and rdn over 2f out: kpt on fnl f: no imp* **7/2**[2]
0250 **5** *½* **Klynch**[13] 2488 6-9-2 80....(b) JamesSullivan 7 82
(Ruth Carr) *hld up: hdwy on outside of gp over 1f out: kpt on same pce ins fnl f* **5/1**
4-04 **6** *9* **Saucy Brown (IRE)**[33] 1876 6-8-13 77.... AdrianNicholls 6 50
(David Nicholls) *led 2f: cl up tl rdn and wknd over 1f out* **16/1**
1233 **7** *1 ¼* **Red Cape (FR)**[13] 2476 9-8-7 71....(b) PJMcDonald 1 40
(Ruth Carr) *trckd ldrs: styd alone far side and rdn ent st: sn struggling* **9/1**
-000 **8** *2* **Mr Optimistic**[20] 2264 4-8-8 75.... LeeTopliss(3) 9 38
(Richard Fahey) *hld up on outside: struggling over 2f out: sn btn* **16/1**

1m 15.24s (1.64) **Going Correction** +0.40s/f (Good) **8** Ran SP% **114.9**
Speed ratings (Par 105): **105,104,104,102,102 90,88,85**
Tote Swingers: 1&2 £6.20, 1&3 £7.60, 2&3 £5.40 CSF £18.54 CT £104.52 TOTE £5.50: £1.70, £1.60, £2.40; EX 25.40.
Owner Christopher James Allan **Bred** Paul Hensey **Trained** Spennymoor, Co Durham

FOCUS
A fairly competitive handicap given the number of runners and it served up a thrilling finish. The winner's best figure for three years.

2877 40 YEARS OF EXCELLENCE - NAGS HEAD PICKHILL MAIDEN STKS 1m 3f 214y
4:20 (4:20) (Class 5) 3-Y-O+ £2,264 (£673; £336; £168) Stalls Low

Form RPR
0/43 1 **Hawkeshead**[20] 2288 5-9-12 73 MichaelO'Connell 2 73
(Ian Williams) *cl up: led after 5f: drvn and styd on strly fr 2f out* 5/1[3]
6 2 1 1/4 **Anna's Arch (IRE)**[20] 2288 5-9-7 0 GarryWhillans(5) 8 69
(Alan Swinbank) *hld up in tch: effrt on outside over 2f out: edgd lft: chsd wnr fnl f: kpt on: no imp* 14/1
4 3 2 3/4 **Special Mix**[18] 2339 4-9-5 0 DavidSimmonson(7) 5 64
(Michael Easterby) *trckd ldrs: hmpd wl over 3f out: effrt 2f out: kpt on same pce fnl f* 28/1
4-03 4 shd **Incitement**[15] 2418 4-9-12 68 DanielTudhope 1 64
(Andrew Crook) *trckd ldrs: wnt 2nd over 2f out: rdn over 2f out: one pce fnl f* 8/1
2002 5 3 1/4 **Finity Run (GER)**[7] 2679 3-8-6 68 JoeFanning 4 54
(Mark Johnston) *led 5f: cl up: rdn over 3f out: edgd lft and outpcd wl over 1f out* 5/4[1]
0 6 2 **In The Crowd (IRE)**[33] 1878 3-8-11 0 PJMcDonald 3 56
(Alan Swinbank) *chsd ldng gp: drvn and outpcd over 3f out: n.d after* 16/1
3-5 7 2 3/4 **Between Us**[20] 2287 3-8-6 0 ChrisCatlin 7 46
(Sir Mark Prescott Bt) *hld up in tch: nt handle paddock bnd after 4f: hdwy on outside to chse ldrs 1/2-way: rdn and wknd over 2f out* 3/1[2]
00-6 8 16 **Isolde's Return**[37] 1754 3-8-6 30 JamesSullivan 9 21
(George Moore) *bhd: struggling 4f out: sn btn: lost tch over 2f out* 100/1

2m 47.67s (8.77) **Going Correction** +0.475s/f (Yiel)
WFA 3 from 4yo+ 15lb 8 Ran SP% **114.2**
Speed ratings (Par 103): **89,88,86,86,84 82,80,70**
Tote Swingers: 1&2 £6.10, 1&3 £11.60, 2&3 £16.10 CSF £69.88 TOTE £7.00: £1.20, £2.90, £4.70; EX 52.40.
Owner Mr & Mrs G Middlebrook **Bred** Mr & Mrs G Middlebrook **Trained** Portway, Worcs

FOCUS
A poor maiden, won in dominant fashion. The winner probably didn't need to improve on his debut form.

2878 GO RACING IN YORKSHIRE H'CAP 5f 212y
4:55 (4:56) (Class 6) (0-65,65) 3-Y-O+ £2,045 (£603; £302) Stalls Low

Form RPR
0031 1 **Choc'A'Moca (IRE)**[4] 2748 5-9-11 62 6ex (v) MickyFenton 2 71
(Paul Midgley) *wnt rt s: pressed ldr: drvn and effrt 2f out: led ins fnl f: kpt on wl u.p* 2/1[1]
00-0 2 hd **Bay Of Fires (IRE)**[11] 2538 4-10-0 65 DanielTudhope 6 73
(David O'Meara) *led: rdn 2f out: hdd ins fnl f: rallied: jst hld* 8/1
0/0- 3 4 1/2 **Ursus**[361] 2670 7-8-13 50 (p) PaddyAspell 9 44
(Christopher Wilson) *trckd ldrs: effrt and drvn wl over 1f out: outpcd fnl f* 16/1
40-5 4 1 1/2 **Rutterkin (USA)**[13] 2475 4-9-6 60 JulieBurke(3) 4 49
(Alan Berry) *dwlt: bhd: struggling over 3f out: styd on fr over 1f out: n.d* 5/1[3]
2-00 5 nse **Mecca's Team**[36] 1800 4-9-9 63 LeeTopliss(3) 5 52+
(Michael Dods) *blkd s: bhd and sn pushed along: styd on fr over 1f out: nvr able to chal* 9/2[2]
0603 6 1 **Greenhead High**[44] 1601 4-9-11 62 AdrianNicholls 12 48
(David Nicholls) *chsd ldng gp: pushed along 1/2-way: effrt and hung lft wl over 1f out: sn btn* 6/1
5-05 7 2 1/4 **Magic Bounty**[14] 2441 3-8-13 58 DuranFentiman 10 35
(Tim Easterby) *in tch: rdn over 2f out: wknd wl over 1f out* 6/1

1m 17.16s (3.56) **Going Correction** +0.55s/f (Yiel)
WFA 3 from 4yo+ 8lb 7 Ran SP% **113.7**
Speed ratings (Par 101): **98,97,91,89,89 88,85**
Tote Swingers: 1&2 £4.10, 1&3 £7.10, 2&3 £10.20 CSF £18.68 CT £197.58 TOTE £3.20: £2.60, £2.70; EX 16.00.
Owner John Milburn - Andrew Stephenson **Bred** Yeomanstown Stud **Trained** Westow, N Yorks

FOCUS
A low-grade sprint handicap, run at a fast pace given the conditions. Straightforward form.

2879 WE RACE AGAIN ON JULY 4TH H'CAP 7f
5:30 (5:31) (Class 5) (0-70,68) 3-Y-O+ £2,385 (£704; £352) Stalls Centre

Form RPR
-332 1 **Viking Warrior (IRE)**[6] 2696 5-9-10 67 LeeTopliss(3) 9 76
(Michael Dods) *cl up on outside: led over 2f out: rdn over 1f out: styd on wl fnl f* 9/4[1]
0-04 2 1 **Balti's Sister (IRE)**[32] 1916 3-8-4 54 JamesSullivan 11 56
(Michael Easterby) *trckd ldrs: effrt over 2f out: edgd lft and kpt on fnl f* 13/2[3]
5-04 3 1 1/4 **Charles De Mille**[14] 2441 4-9-8 62 PJMcDonald 1 65
(George Moore) *prom: effrt and rdn over 2f out: hung lft: kpt on same pce fnl f* 12/1
-000 4 1 **No Quarter (IRE)**[6] 2696 5-9-1 60 ShaneBKelly(5) 10 60
(Tracy Waggott) *hld up: hdwy 3f out: n.m.r and swtchd lft wl over 1f out: kpt on ins fnl f* 20/1
2134 5 1 3/4 **Copperwood**[4] 2754 7-10-0 68 JoeFanning 7 64
(Mark Johnston) *cl up: rdn over 2f out: no ex over 1f out* 9/2[2]
-064 6 1/2 **Hoppy's Flyer (FR)**[11] 2549 4-9-9 63 MickyFenton 6 57
(Paul Midgley) *hld up: effrt over 2f out: no imp fr over 1f out* 8/1
0365 7 1/2 **Whats For Pudding (IRE)**[8] 2621 4-8-5 52 JasonHart(7) 8 45
(Declan Carroll) *bhd and sn pushed along: sme late hdwy: nvr on terms* 8/1
-010 8 3 1/4 **It's A Mans World**[21] 2239 6-8-12 55 PaulPickard(3) 4 39
(Kevin M Prendergast) *hld up: rdn and outpcd over 2f out: sn wknd* 18/1
0-00 9 17 **Cara's Request (AUS)**[41] 1659 7-9-10 64 AdrianNicholls 2
(David Nicholls) *led to over 2f out: sn rdn and wknd* 9/1

1m 30.55s (3.55) **Going Correction** +0.625s/f (Yiel)
WFA 3 from 4yo+ 10lb 9 Ran SP% **112.2**
Speed ratings (Par 103): **104,102,101,100,98 97,97,93,74**
Tote Swingers: 1&2 £4.40, 1&3 £5.50, 2&3 £18.10 CSF £16.31 CT £140.46 TOTE £2.30: £1.30, £2.00, £3.60; EX 16.60.
Owner Transpennine Partnership **Bred** Darley **Trained** Denton, Co Durham
■ Stewards' Enquiry : James Sullivan two-day ban: careless riding (Jun 24-25)

FOCUS
Only modest 7f handicap but it was run at good pace. A small personal best from the winner, who was the first to grab the stands' rail.

T/Plt: £58.00 to a £1 stake. Pool: £47,555.00 - 597.55 winning tickets. T/Qpdt: £35.00 to a £1 stake. Pool: £2,836.00 - 59.94 winning tickets. RY

2260 DONCASTER (L-H)
Friday, June 8

OFFICIAL GOING: Good to soft (soft in places) changing to soft (good to soft in places) after race 1 (6.40)
Wind: Moderate half against Weather: Overcast and showers

2880 YORKSHIRE RADIO SUPPORTING YORKSHIRE RACING MAIDEN STKS 6f
6:40 (6:40) (Class 5) 2-Y-O £2,264 (£673; £336; £168) Stalls High

Form RPR
1 **The Taj (USA)** 2-9-3 0 PaulHanagan 3 83+
(Richard Hannon) *cl up: led wl over 1f out: sn jnd and rn green: rdn ent fnl f: styd on wl* 5/6[1]
5 2 2 1/4 **Hasopop (IRE)**[17] 2370 2-9-3 0 WilliamBuick 2 74+
(Marco Botti) *hld up towards rr: hdwy to trck ldrs 1/2-way: rdn to chal wl over 1f out: ev ch tl one pce ins fnl f* 13/2[3]
3 1 **Mickstathetricksta** 2-9-3 0 RobertWinston 5 71+
(Scott Dixon) *s.i.s and green in rr: smooth hdwy 1/2-way: rdn to chse ldrs over 1f out: kpt on ins fnl f* 20/1
4 1/2 **Quintilian (IRE)** 2-9-3 0 MickaelBarzalona 6 70+
(Mahmood Al Zarooni) *towards rr: hdwy to chse ldrs 1/2-way: rdn wl over 1f out: one pce ins fnl f* 4/1[2]
66 5 1 3/4 **Bispham Green**[22] 2213 2-9-3 0 TonyHamilton 7 65
(Richard Fahey) *mde most tl rdn and hdd wl over 1f out: grad wknd fnl f* 8/1
6 1 **Spivey Cove** 2-9-3 0 PaulMulrennan 9 62+
(Ed McMahon) *trckd ldrs: rdn along 2f out: sn wknd* 12/1
06 7 7 **Hashegotanymoney**[14] 2456 2-9-3 0 DavidNolan 4 41
(Michael Easterby) *pushed along after 2f: a in rr* 66/1
0 8 3 1/2 **Mill End Dancer**[25] 2135 2-8-12 0 GrahamGibbons 11 25
(Michael Easterby) *cl up: rdn along wl over 2f out: sn wknd* 50/1
00 9 7 **Clock On Tom**[24] 2138 2-8-10 0 DavidSimmonson(7) 10
(Michael Easterby) *chsd ldrs: lost pl bef 1/2-way: sn in rr* 80/1

1m 17.98s (4.38) **Going Correction** +0.65s/f (Yiel) 9 Ran SP% **116.1**
Speed ratings (Par 93): **96,93,91,91,88 87,78,73,64**
Tote Swingers: 1&2 £3.40, 1&3 £3.30, 2&3 £12.40 CSF £6.77 TOTE £2.00: £1.10, £2.20, £3.10; EX 8.30.
Owner Hamdan Al Maktoum **Bred** Summer Wind Farm **Trained** East Everleigh, Wilts

FOCUS
Probably just a fair maiden with those that had run not setting an exacting standard but the winner impressed and is surely bound for much better things. The pace wasn't strong with the field well bunched to 2f out and the runners came down the centre. The fifth ran pretty much to his debut mark but the level is fluid.

NOTEBOOK
The Taj(USA) ◆, a $200,000 colt by Street Cry out of a useful winner in the States, is from a yard that can do little wrong with its youngsters right now and looks another useful addition to their arsenal. Always travelling comfortably and only asked to do enough to win his race, he left the impression he'd have won by a fair bit further had the pace been stronger or had his rider so desired. He'll stay 7f but clearly isn't short of speed, given his rider almost had to take a pull under 2f out, and though Ascot will probably come too quick for him, he didn't look as if he would be out of place there. (op 8-11 tchd Evens)
Hasopop(IRE) showed more like the form the market had expected of him first time up but he still looked green and some way from the finished article, not quite seeing his race out after briefly threatening the winner, and is sure to improve again. (tchd 7-1)
Mickstathetricksta ◆, a cheaply-bought son of Milk It Mick out of a dual 7f winner on Polytrack, wasn't so inconvenienced by his slow start as he might have been given the early gallop, but all the same he showed a good attitude to be nearest at the finish. He looks a sure improver. (op 16-1)
Quintilian(IRE), a 200,000 gns son of Cape Cross out of a mare that stayed 1m4f in Ireland and a three-parts sister to the Doncaster Cup winner Saddler's Rock, looked inexperienced early on but picked up steadily once the penny dropped. All the same, he looked a tad short of pace and if he's to win a maiden it's more likely to be at 7f. (op 5-1)
Bispham Green showed the benefit of his experience by taking the field along, but was flattered to finish so close on account of the steady gallop and it might be his nursery mark suffers as a result. Given he's by Green Desert, though, he might still do better on faster ground. (op 11-1)
Spivey Cove ◆ who cost 50,000 gns as a yearling and is a half-brother to a juvenile sprint winner, shaped encouragingly under a considerate ride on ground that he never really looked comfortable on, creeping closer late. He might well be a different proposition next time. (tchd 11-1)

2881 ROYAL ASCOT LIVE ON ATR SKY 415 MAIDEN STKS 7f
7:10 (7:13) (Class 5) 3-Y-O £2,264 (£673; £336; £168) Stalls High

Form RPR
3 1 **Unex Annigoni (IRE)**[34] 1852 3-9-3 0 WilliamBuick 10 79+
(John Gosden) *t.k.h early: cl up: chal 2f out: rdn and qcknd to ld ent fnl f: kpt on* 6/5[1]
20 2 1/2 **Vital Calling**[19] 2313 3-9-3 0 GrahamGibbons 9 75+
(David Barron) *t.k.h early: trckd ldrs: hdwy 2f out: shkn up and sltly outpcd over 1f out: styd on u.p fnl f* 4/1[2]
0-6 3 1 1/2 **Saloomy**[19] 2313 3-9-3 0 RichardMullen 3 71
(David Simcock) *led: pushed along over 2f out: rdn wl over 1f out: hdd ent fnl f and kpt on same pce* 6/1[3]
05 4 7 **Alpha Arion (IRE)**[10] 2592 3-9-3 0 DavidAllan 5 53
(Tim Easterby) *towards rr: hdwy over 3f out: rdn 2f out: kpt on fnl f: nt rch ldrs* 25/1
5 1 1/4 **Well Bank (IRE)** 3-9-0 0 DeclanCannon(3) 15 50
(Colin Teague) *t.k.h early: towards rr: hdwy wl over 2f out: rdn: green and swtchd rt over 1f out: styd on ins fnl f: nrst fin* 100/1
0-42 6 nk **Last Supper**[28] 2030 3-8-12 69 TomEaves 2 44
(James Bethell) *cl up: rdn along 2f out: grad wknd* 6/1[3]
7 1/2 **Dream On Paddy** 3-9-0 0 DaleSwift(3) 11 48
(Ian McInnes) *s.i.s and bhd: rdn along 1/2-way: sme late hdwy* 20/1
8 3/4 **Malindi** 3-8-12 0 PaulMulrennan 1 41
(James Given) *dwlt: sn in tch: rdn along 2f out: sn wknd* 16/1
0 9 7 **Medecis Mountain**[18] 2339 3-9-3 0 PaddyAspell 12 28
(John Wainwright) *a towards rr* 100/1
10 1 1/2 **Austerity Boy** 3-9-3 0 MartinHarley 13 24
(Des Donovan) *a towards rr* 50/1
0-0 11 1 1/2 **Majestic Bounty**[18] 2335 3-8-12 0 RobertWinston 8 15
(Chris Fairhurst) *towards rr: hdwy and in tch over 2f out: sn rdn and wknd* 50/1
12 1 3/4 **Military Green (FR)** 3-9-3 0 DuranFentiman 7 15
(Tim Easterby) *s.i.s and bhd: sme hdwy 3f out: sn rdn and wknd* 33/1

13 *11* **Libby's Lad** 3-9-3 0 DavidNolan 4
(David C Griffiths) *chsd ldrs: rdn along over 3f out: sn wknd* **50/1**

1m 30.46s (4.16) **Going Correction** +0.65s/f (Yiel) **13** Ran SP% **119.3**
Speed ratings (Par 99): **102,101,99,91,90 89,89,88,80,78 77,75,62**
Tote Swingers: 1&2 £3.60, 1&3 £4.10, 2&3 £1.10 CSF £5.36 TOTE £2.70: £1.30, £1.60, £1.10; EX 9.00.

Owner W J Gredley **Bred** Keatly Overseas Ltd **Trained** Newmarket, Suffolk

FOCUS
A maiden more about potential than proven form and the market only wanted to know four, three of whom finished clear. Once again the pace wasn't strong and the runners came down the centre. The form is ordinary but the first two look potential improvers.

2882 BILL FOURACRES H'CAP — 1m (S)
7:45 (7:45) (Class 3) (0-95,90) 4-Y-0+ **£6,792** (£2,021; £1,010; £505) **Stalls** High

Form				RPR
26-2	**1**		**Swiftly Done (IRE)**[20] 2285 5-9-2 **85** GrahamGibbons 13 (Declan Carroll) *hld up in rr: gd hdwy wl over 2f out: trckd ldrs wl over 1f out: swtchd rt and rdn to ld ins fnl f: kpt on* **9/1**	96+
00-0	**2**	½	**Classic Colori (IRE)**[21] 2257 5-9-4 **87** DanielTudhope 4 (David O'Meara) *dwlt: hld up in rr: hdwy over 2f out: rdn wl over 1f out: styd on fnl f: nrst fin* **8/1**	96
00-1	**3**	¾	**Making Eyes (IRE)**[27] 2067 4-9-6 **89** IanMongan 3 (Hugo Palmer) *hld up in tch: hdwy 3f out: chal wl over 1f out: rdn to ld briefly jst ins fnl f: sn hdd: drvn and one pce* **6/1**[2]	96
-022	**4**	1 ¼	**Honeymead (IRE)**[19] 2311 4-9-5 **88** PaulHanagan 7 (Richard Fahey) *prom: effrt to ld 2f out: sn rdn and hdd jst ins fnl f: kpt on same pce* **13/2**[3]	92
0-04	**5**	2 ¾	**Vainglory (USA)**[19] 2311 8-9-2 **90** LauraPike(5) 11 (David Simcock) *trckd ldrs: rdn along over 2f out: drvn over 1f out and sn wknd* **18/1**	88
2-00	**6**	1 ¾	**Chiswick Bey (IRE)**[21] 2243 4-9-4 **87** TonyHamilton 9 (Richard Fahey) *in tch: effrt 3f out: rdn along 2f out: sn no imp* **33/1**	81
0-10	**7**	1	**Ashva (USA)**[32] 1924 4-9-3 **86** (t) PaulMulrennan 8 (Michael Dods) *trckd ldrs: pushed along wl over 2f out: rdn and wknd wl over 1f out* **16/1**	78
-023	**8**	2	**Silvery Moon (IRE)**[19] 2311 5-9-0 **83** DavidAllan 6 (Tim Easterby) *led: rdn along and hdd 2f out: sn wknd* **13/2**[3]	70
/30-	**9**	½	**Obligada (IRE)**[217] 7277 4-9-3 **86** RobertWinston 5 (Tobias B P Coles) *dwlt: a towards rr* **16/1**	72
5/00	**10**	2	**Day Of The Eagle (IRE)**[20] 2285 6-8-9 **78** JamesSullivan 12 (Michael Easterby) *a in rr* **50/1**	59
0250	**11**	½	**Kiwi Bay**[15] 2417 7-9-4 **87** TomEaves 2 (Michael Dods) *hld up: a towards rr* **20/1**	67
0-35	**12**	1	**Indian Jack (IRE)**[15] 2417 4-9-6 **89** KierenFallon 14 (Luca Cumani) *trckd ldrs: cl up after 2f: rdn along wl over 2f out: wknd qckly* **11/4**[1]	67

1m 43.0s (3.70) **Going Correction** +0.65s/f (Yiel) **12** Ran SP% **115.4**
Speed ratings (Par 107): **107,106,105,104,101 100,99,97,96,94 94,93**
Tote Swingers: 1&2 £11.40, 1&3 £15.80, 2&3 £11.60 CSF £75.54 CT £475.60 TOTE £12.70: £3.60, £2.20, £1.80; EX 89.80.

Owner D Watts, Miss C King, J Syme & M Syme **Bred** Joe Fogarty **Trained** Sledmere, E Yorks

FOCUS
A useful handicap run at a decent gallop in the conditions and the advantage was with those horses that were patiently ridden. The runners again came down the centre and the form is rated on the positive side with the runner-up to last year's best.

NOTEBOOK
Swiftly Done(IRE) had shaped well on his reappearance and though that form hasn't worked out too well he took a step forward with a slightly ready win under a confident ride, and that despite finding a bit of trouble. Progressive last year and still lightly raced for his age, he could end up useful by the end of the season and will be worth a look whatever grade of handicap he contests whenever conditions are testing. (tchd 10-1)

Classic Colori(IRE) shaped with much more encouragement than on his comeback and still looked to have a bit of running in him passing the line after being switched, but he's a slightly tricky customer and probably needs things to fall just right. (op 10-1)

Making Eyes(IRE) travelled well throughout and ran a solid race without having any excuses. (op 11-2)

Honeymead(IRE) fared best of those up with the pace throughout and continues to run well without quite getting her head in front. (tchd 6-1)

Vainglory(USA) ◆ got closer to Honeymead under an aggressive ride than he had at Ripon last time and looks to be running himself into form, so is one to keep a close eye on. (tchd 20-1)

Chiswick Bey(IRE) never really threatened to finish any closer and continues to under-perform. (op 40-1)

Ashva(USA) looked sure to be involved in the finish for a long way but didn't find what looked likely and continues to be hit and miss. (op 14-1)

Silvery Moon(IRE) dropped out after racing at the head of affairs early on so can have his effort excused to some degree (op 6-1)

Indian Jack(IRE) was another who dropped out after racing close to the head of affairs early on, so can have his effort excused to some degree on ground that might well be too soft nowadays. Official explanation: jockey said gelding had no more to give (op 10-3)

2883 ATTHERACES.COM EXCLUSIVE WILLIAM BUICK BLOG H'CAP — 1m (R)
8:20 (8:21) (Class 5) (0-75,75) 3-Y-O **£2,264** (£673; £336; £168) **Stalls** Low

Form				RPR
22-5	**1**		**Andalieb**[21] 2246 3-9-3 **71** WilliamBuick 7 (David Simcock) *hld up in rr: smooth hdwy on outer 3f out: chal and hung sharply rt over 1f out: rdn and qcknd wl to ld last 100yds: sn clr* **4/1**[2]	83+
-441	**2**	2 ¼	**Peter Anders**[31] 1959 3-9-4 **72** JoeFanning 9 (Mark Johnston) *hld up in tch: hdwy over 3f out: rdn to ld wl over 1f out: drvn ent fnl f: hdd and one pce last 100yds* **13/2**[3]	79
4303	**3**	nk	**Incendiary (IRE)**[10] 2583 3-9-7 **75** IanMongan 2 (Hugo Palmer) *hld up in tch: hdwy 3f out: rdn to chse ldrs wl over 1f out: kpt on u.p fnl f* **8/1**	81+
06-3	**4**	4 ½	**Exning Halt**[38] 1737 3-9-5 **73** KierenFallon 3 (James Fanshawe) *dwlt: hld up towards rr: hdwy on inner over 3f out: rdn to chse ldrs 2f out: wknd appr fnl f* **15/2**	69
4-51	**5**	3 ¼	**Bitaphon (IRE)**[17] 2382 3-8-13 **72** JustinNewman(5) 8 (John Balding) *led: rdn along 3f out: sn hdd & wknd fnl 2f* **8/1**	60
4-13	**6**	hd	**Magic Destiny**[20] 2265 3-9-2 **70** MartinHarley 1 (Mrs K Burke) *trckd ldrs: hdwy over 3f out: led wl over 2f out: rdn and hdd wl over 1f out: sn wknd* **7/4**[1]	58
5-30	**7**	6	**Loyal Master (IRE)**[3] 2785 3-9-7 **75** (t) AdrianNicholls 6 (David C Griffiths) *chsd ldr: rdn along 3f out: wkng whn n.m.r and hmpd over 2f out: sn bhd* **16/1**	49
00-6	**8**	1	**Thane Of Cawdor (IRE)**[17] 2381 3-8-11 **65** MickyFenton 4 (Tom Tate) *chsd ldrs: rdn along over 3f out: sn wknd* **25/1**	37

1m 43.51s (3.81) **Going Correction** +0.40s/f (Good) **8** Ran SP% **113.4**
Speed ratings (Par 99): **96,93,93,88,85 85,79,78**
Tote Swingers: 1&2 £6.30, 1&3 £6.00, 2&3 £7.80 CSF £29.47 CT £196.84 TOTE £4.80: £1.20, £2.00, £2.00; EX 22.30.

Owner Ziad A Galadari **Bred** Galadari Sons Stud Company Limited **Trained** Newmarket, Suffolk

FOCUS
Several progressive performers came to the fore in a handicap run at a reasonable pace and this is almost certainly strong form for the grade. The runner-up matched his previous turf best.

Magic Destiny Official explanation: jockey said filly ran too free

2884 FREEBETS.CO.UK FILLIES' H'CAP — 1m 2f 60y
8:50 (8:51) (Class 3) (0-95,92) 4-Y-O+ **£6,792** (£2,021; £1,010; £505) **Stalls** Low

Form				RPR
-112	**1**		**Qaraaba**[21] 2248 5-9-7 **92** GeorgeBaker 9 (Seamus Durack) *hld up in rr: stdy hdwy 3f out: trckd ldrs on bit 2f out: led appr fnl f: sn clr: easily* **1/1**[1]	108+
6-13	**2**	3	**Dragonera**[27] 2072 4-9-4 **89** WilliamBuick 6 (Ed Dunlop) *trckd ldng pair: hdwy over 3f out: led wl over 2f out: rdn wl over 1f out: hdd and drvn appr fnl f: kpt on same pce* **5/1**[3]	97+
2541	**3**	1 ¾	**Maven**[13] 2498 4-8-6 **77** DavidAllan 8 (Tim Easterby) *hld up towards rr: hdwy 4f out: rdn to chse ldr wl over 2f out: sn drvn and kpt on same pce* **12/1**	81
6000	**4**	5	**Askaud (IRE)**[10] 2590 4-9-7 **92** (p) IanMongan 2 (Scott Dixon) *hld up in tch: hdwy 3f out: rdn along over 2f out: sn btn* **16/1**	86
3-65	**5**	¾	**Bolivia (GER)**[34] 1848 6-9-0 **85** (t) GrahamLee 3 (Lucy Wadham) *trckd ldr: led over 3f out: rdn and hdd wl over 2f out: sn wknd* **8/1**	78
0-56	**6**	4 ½	**El Torbellino (IRE)**[23] 2180 4-8-9 **80** DanielTudhope 5 (David O'Meara) *led: rdn along over 4f out: hdd over 3f out: wknd wl over 2f out* **9/2**[2]	64
30-3	**7**	4 ½	**Our Gal**[14] 2465 4-8-10 **81** RobertWinston 10 (Noel Quinlan) *trckd ldrs: effrt 4f out: rdn along 3f out: sn wknd* **16/1**	56

2m 12.22s (2.82) **Going Correction** +0.40s/f (Good) **7** Ran SP% **115.4**
Speed ratings (Par 104): **104,101,100,96,95 92,88**
Tote Swingers: 1&2 £2.00, 1&3 £2.70, 2&3 £5.20 CSF £6.55 CT £37.34 TOTE £2.10: £1.40, £1.70; EX 6.20.

Owner P A Deal **Bred** Shadwell Estate Company Limited **Trained** Baydon, Wilts

FOCUS
A fairly useful handicap but one turned into a procession by one who relishes the conditions and was very well handicapped. Again the runners stayed clear of the far rail. The winner impressed and the third is rated close to his latest Newbury form.

NOTEBOOK
Qaraaba has been in great form this season and faced a much easier task here than when conceding 3lb to the subsequent Zetland Gold Cup winner Danadana at Newmarket last time, shrugging off the 4lb rise in her mark with terrific ease. The runner-up is a reliable type so she might just be eligible for the Wolferton at Ascot, but connections are probably thinking more of finding some black type after this. (op 5-4 tchd 11-8)

Dragonera was given a good ride over a trip just on the sharp side in the conditions and ran her usual game race without proving any match for the winner. There was no disgrace in this defeat. (op 11-2)

Maven found this an altogether stiffer task than when winning a 0-70 handicap for amateurs at Newbury last time and was readily put in her place once asked for her effort. She was progressive before this but needs to have her sights lowered. (tchd 10-1)

Askaud(IRE) was asked for her effort more towards the stands' side than the rest, but that doesn't excuse another lacklustre effort. (op 14-1)

Bolivia(GER) can at least have her effort upgraded a tad on account of faring better of the duo that took each other on in front. (tchd 7-1)

El Torbellino(IRE) has form on this surface but ran poorly. (tchd 11-2)

Our Gal seemed to go wrong and was eased. Official explanation: jockey said filly hung right throughout

2885 ROYAL ASCOT LIVE ON VIRGIN 534 H'CAP — 1m 4f
9:20 (9:21) (Class 5) (0-70,76) 3-Y-O **£2,264** (£673; £336; £168) **Stalls** Low

Form				RPR
6-22	**1**		**Nicholascopernicus (IRE)**[34] 1853 3-9-6 **69** WilliamBuick 4 (Ed Walker) *hld up in rr: smooth hdwy wl over 2f out: rdn to ld 1 1/2f out: sn clr easily* **15/8**[1]	82+
0-10	**2**	3 ¾	**Dorry K (IRE)**[24] 2144 3-9-5 **68** GrahamGibbons 3 (David Barron) *hld up in tch: hdwy to chse ldrs wl over 2f out: sn rdn and sltly outpcd wl over 1f out: styd on u.p fnl f: no ch w wnr* **7/1**[3]	71
1331	**3**	½	**Naseem Alyasmeen (IRE)**[9] 2613 3-9-13 **76** 6ex MartinHarley 6 (Mick Channon) *hld up in tch: hdwy 4f out: chal wl over 2f out: sn rdn and one pce* **7/2**[2]	78
2323	**4**	nk	**Rosie's Lady (IRE)**[4] 2771 3-8-7 **56** ow1 TomEaves 1 (David O'Meara) *t.k.h: trckd ldng pair: hdwy on inner and cl up 3f out: rdn to chal 2f out: sn drvn and one pce* **9/1**	58
0-04	**5**	hd	**Arley Hall**[18] 2333 3-9-5 **68** PaulHanagan 5 (Richard Fahey) *t.k.h: trckd ldr: cl up over 4f out: rdn along wl over 2f out: sn drvn and one pce* **7/2**[2]	69
-234	**6**	¾	**Aliante**[15] 2425 3-9-6 **69** JoeFanning 2 (Mark Johnston) *led: jnd and pushed along 4f out: rdn wl over 2f out: drvn and hdd 1 1/2f out: sn wknd* **11/1**	69

2m 44.7s (9.80) **Going Correction** +0.40s/f (Good) **6** Ran SP% **110.1**
Speed ratings (Par 99): **83,80,80,79,79 79**
Tote Swingers: 1&2 £4.50, 1&3 £1.90, 2&3 £2.60 CSF £14.82 TOTE £2.50: £1.50, £3.90; EX 17.50.

Owner Greenwood, Halsall and Pegum **Bred** Mrs E J O'Grady **Trained** Newmarket, Suffolk

FOCUS
A modest finale and something of an muddling affair but the winner is clearly well ahead of his current mark and looks sure to rate a fair bit higher in time. The far rail was ignored again but the form looks sound with those in the frame behind the winner close to their marks.

T/Plt: £58.20 to a £1 stake. Pool: £57,223.00 - 717.62 winning tickets. T/Qpdt: £35.30 to a £1 stake. Pool: £4,129.00 - 86.34 winning tickets. JR

[2477]GOODWOOD (R-H)

Friday, June 8

OFFICIAL GOING: Good to soft (7.1)

Wind: very strong against in relation to straight Weather: overcast

2886 BIBENDUM AMATEUR RIDERS' STKS (H'CAP) 1m 1f

6:20 (6:24) (Class 5) (0-70,70) 4-Y-0+ **£2,495** (£774; £386; £193) **Stalls** Low

Form RPR

0-25 **1** **Moody Tunes**[13] 2498 9-10-5 **68**.................................. MissALMurphy(7) 3 78
(Tom Dascombe) *led: rdn over 2f out: hdd ent fnl f: rallied to regain ld towards fin: game* **7/1**

0023 **2** ½ **Potentiale (IRE)**[7] 2653 8-9-10 **59**.......................(v) MrEdwardSibbick(7) 2 68
(J W Hills) *mid-div: hdwy 3f out: rdn to chse wnr over 2f out: led ent fnl f: no ex whn hdd towards fin* **15/2**

0366 **3** 4 **Silver Alliance**[17] 2363 4-10-11 **67**...................................... MrRBirkett 12 67
(Julia Feilden) *hld up towards rr: gd hdwy on inner over 4f out: rdn over 2f out: wnt 3rd over 1f out: styd on same pce fnl f* **8/1**

2210 **4** 3 **Byrd In Hand (IRE)**[17] 2363 5-10-3 **62**.................................. MrCMartin(3) 6 56
(John Bridger) *racd keenly: trckd wnr: rdn 3f out: styd on same pce fnl 2f* **9/2[2]**

/60- **5** ½ **Sentosa**[24] 2872 5-10-5 **64**.. MrNdeBoinville(3) 8 56
(Michael Blanshard) *mid-div: squeezed up 4f out: rdn 3f out: styd on but nvr gng pce to threaten ldrs* **40/1**

0530 **6** 1¾ **Market Puzzle (IRE)**[3] 2804 5-9-9 **54**.......(p) MissBeckyBrisbourne(3) 14 43
(Mark Brisbourne) *mid-div: rdn over 3f out: styd on same pce fnl 2f: nvr trbld ldrs* **13/2[3]**

2000 **7** 1½ **Northern Spy (USA)**[43] 1626 8-9-13 **60**.............. MrJCoffill-Brown(5) 15 45
(Simon Dow) *mid-div: hdwy on outer over 6f out: effrt over 3f out: one pce fnl 2f* **14/1**

00-0 **8** 1½ **Cobbs Quay**[28] 2051 4-10-11 **67**................................ MissSBrotherton 11 49
(Daniel Kubler) *nudged along towards rr: swtchd lft over 4f out: sn rdn into midfield: no further imp fnl 2f* **7/2[1]**

0-60 **9** 1¾ **George Thisby**[22] 2207 6-10-4 **65**.................................... MrPMillman(5) 7 43
(Rod Millman) *chsd ldrs: rdn over 3f out: wknd 2f out* **16/1**

3435 **10** 4½ **Lisahane Bog**[36] 1792 5-9-7 **56** ow1.....................(b) MrLiamJennings(7) 4 24
(Peter Hedger) *dwlt bdly: a in rr* **16/1**

-142 **11** 11 **Bert The Alert**[32] 2115 4-10-7 **70**.................................. MrGGorman(7) 10 14
(Gary Moore) *hld up towards rr: hmpd on bnd 4f out: sn rdn: wknd 3f out* **16/1**

00-0 **12** 26 **A B Celebration**[10] 2586 4-9-2 **51** oh6..........................(v[1]) MrAJones(7) 5
(John Bridger) *chsd ldrs tl rdn over 4f out: sn btn* **100/1**

2m 1.35s (5.05) **Going Correction** +0.45s/f (Yiel) **12** Ran SP% **116.9**

Speed ratings (Par 103): **95,94,91,88,87 86,85,83,82,78 68,45**

Tote Swingers: 1&2 £5.40, 1&3 £11.30, 2&3 £13.80 CSF £57.85 CT £437.77 TOTE £6.60: £2.20, £2.70, £2.80; EX 33.40 Trifecta £482.80 Part won. Pool: £652.53 - 0.30 winning units..

Owner Paul Murphy **Bred** Llety Stud **Trained** Malpas, Cheshire

■ Amy Murphy's first winner.

■ Stewards' Enquiry : Mr Liam Jennings five-day ban: used whip when out of contention (tbn)
Mr A Jones three-day ban: careless riding (tbn)

FOCUS

First 2f of Mile course moved out 5yds. A modest handicap run at a steady pace. The first four raced near the far rail but the form is pretty straightforward.

Lisahane Bog Official explanation: jockey said gelding was slowly away

Bert The Alert Official explanation: jockey said gelding suffered interference in running

2887 GORDON'S STKS (H'CAP) 1m 4f

6:50 (6:53) (Class 4) (0-85,82) 4-Y-0+ **£5,175** (£1,540; £769; £384) **Stalls** High

Form RPR

4-02 **1** **Roberto Pegasus (USA)**[32] 1940 6-9-3 **78**................ RichardHughes 3 89
(Pat Phelan) *racd in 4th: hdwy to ld 3f out: rdn 2f out: styd on wl fnl f* **5/2[1]**

2 **2** 1½ **Luggers Hall (IRE)**[28] 2031 4-9-0 **75**.................................... JimCrowley 6 83
(Tony Carroll) *stdd s: in last: rdn and hdwy 3f out: chsd wnr 2f out: kpt on but a being hld fnl f* **4/1[2]**

05-0 **3** 4½ **Nave (USA)**[21] 2248 5-9-3 **78**.. HayleyTurner 4 79
(David Simcock) *led: rdn whn hdd 3f out: chsd wnr tl 2f out: no ex fnl f* **5/2[1]**

0-01 **4** 1½ **Watered Silk**[13] 2473 4-9-7 **82**.. KieranO'Neill 1 81
(Marcus Tregoning) *w ldr tl over 6f out: pushed bk upsides 4f out: sn rdn: edgd lft whn keeping on at same pce fr over 1f out* **7/1[3]**

4-46 **5** 2 **Achalas (IRE)**[32] 1940 4-8-12 **73**.. NeilCallan 5 68
(Heather Main) *s.i.s: sn trcking ldrs: wnt 2nd over 6f out: upsides 4f out: sn rdn: keeping on at same pce whn wandering u.p fr over 1f out* **12/1**

031- **6** ¾ **Mons Calpe (IRE)**[240] 6790 6-8-10 **71**........................ StevieDonohoe 8 65
(Paul Cole) *s.i.s: in tch: rdn 3f out: nvr gng pce to get involved* **20/1**

43-0 **7** 4½ **Porgy**[21] 2257 7-9-4 **79**.. AdamKirby 2 66
(Tim Pitt) *in last pair: rdn 3f out: nvr any imp on ldrs* **10/1**

2m 42.28s (3.88) **Going Correction** +0.45s/f (Yiel) **7** Ran SP% **111.2**

Speed ratings (Par 105): **105,104,101,100,98 98,95**

Tote Swingers: 1&2 £3.30, 1&3 £1.20, 2&3 £2.50 CSF £11.95 CT £25.08 TOTE £3.90: £2.30, £2.70; EX 14.50 Trifecta £80.70 Pool: £581.55 - 5.33 winning units..

Owner J Daniels **Bred** Gigginstown House Stud **Trained** Epsom, Surrey

FOCUS

A stronger pace to this 1m4f contest and it was won by a horse who looks to be improving now. The winner took a small step forward.

2888 FAIR TRADE PRACTICE E B F MAIDEN STKS 6f

7:25 (7:25) (Class 5) 2-Y-0 **£3,234** (£962; £481; £240) **Stalls** High

Form RPR

1 **Olympic Glory (IRE)** 2-9-3 0...................................... RichardHughes 2 90+
(Richard Hannon) *s.i.s: sn swtchd to stands' side rails: in last pair: cruised upsides 2f out: sn shkn up to ld: r.o strly: quite impressive* **6/4[1]**

0 **2** 3¼ **Dark Emerald (IRE)**[13] 2480 2-9-3 0........................ KirstyMilczarek 6 78
(Brendan Powell) *trckd ldrs: rdn over 2f out: swtchd rt to chal sn after: kpt on but nt pce of wnr fnl f* **20/1**

3 nk **Shrewd** 2-9-3 0.. HayleyTurner 5 77
(Michael Bell) *led: rdn whn hdd over 2f out: kpt on but nt pce of wnr fnl f* **8/1**

4 ¾ **Millers Wharf (IRE)** 2-9-3 0.. DaneO'Neill 7 75+
(Richard Hannon) *s.i.s: last but in tch: swtchd lft to chal 2f out: sn rdn: kpt on same pce fnl f* **11/2[3]**

4 **5** 3¾ **Nile Knight**[13] 2480 2-9-3 0.. KieranO'Neill 8 64
(Marcus Tregoning) *prom: rdn and ev ch 2f out: wknd ent fnl f* **2/1[2]**

6 5 **Aussie Reigns (IRE)** 2-9-3 0.. JimCrowley 3 49
(William Knight) *trckd ldrs: rdn over 2f out: wknd jst over 1f out* **10/1**

1m 15.48s (3.28) **Going Correction** +0.45s/f (Yiel) **6** Ran SP% **113.7**

Speed ratings (Par 93): **96,91,91,90,85 78**

Tote Swingers: 1&2 £4.40, 1&3 £2.70, 2&3 £15.10 CSF £30.86 TOTE £2.60: £1.80, £5.40; EX 35.40 Trifecta £149.80 Pool: £328.11 - 1.62 winning units..

Owner Mrs J Wood **Bred** Denis McDonnell **Trained** East Everleigh, Wilts

FOCUS

A potentially useful maiden in which Richard Hannon often introduces a decent newcomer. Olympic Glory impressed and could be very useful.

NOTEBOOK

Olympic Glory(IRE) ◆ absolutely bolted up and has the potential to be very smart. Easily the pick of the paddock, where he looked a size bigger than his rivals, this Choisir colt travelled smoothly up the stands' rail before showing a bright turn of foot to shoot clear in the final furlong and win most impressively. Royal Ascot is less then two weeks away, but it would be no surprise should this good-looking colt make a quick return to the track and line up for a big prize. (op 2-1 tchd 9-4)

Dark Emerald(IRE) took a major step forward from his modest debut run over C&D and maybe these slower conditions suited him.

Shrewd was quite coltish in the preliminaries and was on edge when going out onto the track, which must have taken something out of him. He travelled well for a long way before tiring in the final furlong. This was a very promising debut given what went on beforehand. (op 15-2 tchd 13-2)

Millers Wharf(IRE), a stablemate to the winner, was a little green early but he he made ground from off the pace, widest of all, and shaped with some promise. He cost 95,000gns, so it will be disappointing if he can't build on this. (op 5-1)

Nile Knight set quite a good standard on his debut third here but he couldn't reproduce that level of form on this slower ground and was disappointing. It's way too early to be writing him off and he'll probably be seen to better effect back on decent ground and over further. (tchd 15-8 and 9-4)

2889 CRIMBOURNE STUD STKS (H'CAP) 1m 4f

8:00 (8:00) (Class 4) (0-85,84) 3-Y-0 **£5,175** (£1,540; £769; £384) **Stalls** High

Form RPR

2-24 **1** **Spanish Wedding**[21] 2258 3-8-13 **76**...........................(b[1]) AndreaAtzeni 8 86
(Marco Botti) *trckd ldr: rdn to chal over 2f out: led over 1f out: styd on wl: rdn out* **9/1**

01-0 **2** 2 **Hidden Justice (IRE)**[15] 2408 3-8-7 **70**............................ JimCrowley 1 77+
(Amanda Perrett) *cl up: nt clr run bhd fr pair 2f out: swtchd lft and rdn over 1f out: styd on to go 2nd ins fnl f: a being hld by wnr* **8/1**

-213 **3** 1½ **Party Line**[6] 2716 3-8-8 **71**.. SilvestreDeSousa 2 76
(Mark Johnston) *led: rdn whn pressed over 2f out: hdd over 1f out: no ex fnl f* **9/4[1]**

6-12 **4** 2 **Man Of Plenty**[25] 2129 3-9-3 **80**.. DaneO'Neill 4 81
(John Dunlop) *trckd ldrs: rdn 2f out: nt quite pce to chal: no ex ins fnl f* **13/2[3]**

3-00 **5** 2 **Humungosaur**[20] 2269 3-9-2 **79**.................................... RichardHughes 9 77
(Richard Hannon) *stdd s: last: effrt to cl on ldrs over 2f out: nvr gng pce to get on terms* **7/1**

1-26 **6** nk **Little Dutch Girl**[22] 2201 3-8-13 **76**...................................(b) AdamKirby 5 74
(Clive Cox) *s.i.s: towards rr: hdwy whn nt clr run fr 3f out tl rdn 2f out: no further imp* **8/1**

5114 **7** 13 **Whipcrackaway (IRE)**[21] 2235 3-8-13 **76**............................ NeilCallan 6 53
(Peter Hedger) *hld up: hmpd after 1f: nudged along after being awkward rnding bnd over 5f out: nvr travelling after: eased whn btn fnl f* **5/1[2]**

3-13 **8** ½ **Rei D'Oro (USA)**[16] 2390 3-8-11 **74**................................ MartinLane 3 50
(David Simcock) *s.i.s: abt to trck ldrs whn squeezed out after 1f: in tch: rdn 3f out: btn whn eased ins fnl f* **10/1**

2m 45.1s (6.70) **Going Correction** +0.45s/f (Yiel) **8** Ran SP% **114.6**

Speed ratings (Par 101): **95,93,92,91,90 89,81,80**

Tote Swingers: 1&2 £17.60, 1&3 £4.80, 2&3 £6.00 CSF £77.83 CT £217.64 TOTE £10.60: £2.60, £2.50, £1.30; EX 106.60 Trifecta £425.50 Part won. Pool: £575.03 - 0.50 winning units..

Owner Khalifa Dasmal **Bred** Miss K Rausing **Trained** Newmarket, Suffolk

FOCUS

A competitive 3yo handicap run at a reasonable gallop, but it proved difficult to make ground from off the pace with the first four home having filled those positions throughout. The form has been given a chance.

2890 BRITISH STALLION STUDS SUPPORTING BRITISH RACING E B F FILLIES' STKS (H'CAP) 6f

8:30 (8:30) (Class 3) (0-95,94) 3-Y-0+ **£7,762** (£2,310; £1,154; £577) **Stalls** High

Form RPR

/1-2 **1** **Hallelujah**[19] 2310 4-9-3 **83**.. HayleyTurner 1 96+
(James Fanshawe) *cl up: pushed along to ld ent fnl f: kpt on: a enough in hand to hold on: rdn out* **7/2[2]**

44-1 **2** nk **Moretta Blanche**[27] 2070 5-9-1 **81**..................................(t) JimCrowley 7 93
(Ralph Beckett) *slowly away: last: hdwy 2f out: rdn jst over 1f out: r.o wl fnl f: clsng on wnr nring fin* **7/1**

31-5 **3** 1¾ **Free Verse**[27] 2067 3-8-11 **85**...................................... RichardHughes 10 89+
(Richard Hannon) *trckd ldrs: rdn over 2f out: sn outpcd: r.o ins fnl f* **3/1[1]**

-410 **4** 2¼ **Interakt**[27] 2071 5-8-7 **76**.. HarryBentley(3) 4 75
(Joseph Tuite) *trckd ldrs: rdn to ld over 1f out: hdd ent fnl f: no ex* **12/1**

06-0 **5** shd **Dreamwriter (USA)**[62] 1215 3-9-2 **90**................................ KieranO'Neill 8 87
(Richard Hannon) *in last pair but in tch: rdn over 2f out: swtchd rt over 1f out: styd on but nvr gng pce to threaten* **25/1**

6660 **6** 3¾ **Cochabamba (IRE)**[27] 2067 4-9-5 **85**................................ JackMitchell 9 72
(Roger Teal) *trckd ldrs: rdn over 2f out: wknd ins fnl f* **8/1**

500 **7** 1¼ **Vocational (USA)**[6] 2704 3-9-6 **94**............................ SilvestreDeSousa 2 75
(Mark Johnston) *prom: led over 3f out: sn swtchd to stands' side rails and rdn: hung rt: hdd over 1f out: wknd ins fnl f* **4/1[3]**

20-6 **8** 2 **Bless You**[44] 1602 4-9-3 **83**.. DaneO'Neill 12 60
(Henry Candy) *led tl rdn over 3f out: chsd ldrs: hld whn short of room and snatched up ent fnl f* **7/1**

1m 14.38s (2.18) **Going Correction** +0.45s/f (Yiel)

WFA 3 from 4yo+ 8lb **8** Ran SP% **114.9**

Speed ratings (Par 104): **103,102,100,97,97 92,90,87**

Tote Swingers: 1&2 £2.70, 1&3 £2.00, 2&3 £6.50 CSF £28.23 CT £81.39 TOTE £3.60: £1.40, £2.00, £1.60; EX 27.60 Trifecta £86.30 Pool: £432.70 - 1.20 winning units..

Owner Chippenham Lodge Stud **Bred** Chippenham Lodge Stud Ltd **Trained** Newmarket, Suffolk

FOCUS

They went a decent gallop here and the finish was dominated by horses who came from off the pace. Another step forward from the winner.

NOTEBOOK

Hallelujah, the least exposed runner in the field and racing on the outside of the field throughout, found a smart change of gear to quicken clear entering the final furlong. Although her lead was eroded in the closing stages, the race was already in the bag and she has now won three of her four starts. She has the potential to develop into a pattern-class sprinter if maintaining this kind of progression. (op 10-3 tchd 4-1)

Moretta Blanche finished strongly from off the pace and ran a blinder off 4lb higher than at Ascot. She shaped like she'll do better again on a slightly stiffer track. (tchd 13-2)

Free Verse took too long to get going but was full of running at the finish. She looks nailed on to win more races granted a stiffer test. (tchd 7-2)
Interakt isn't as progressive as the front three and couldn't live with those rivals in the closing stages having held every chance. (op 14-1)
Vocational(USA) dropped away having made the running and either set too strong a gallop or just didn't act as well up in trip on slower ground than she's used to. Official explanation: jockey said filly lost its action (op 11-2)

2891 CAPITAL FM MAIDEN FILLIES' STKS 1m
9:00 (9:02) (Class 5) 3-Y-0+ **£2,587** (£770; £384; £192) **Stalls** Low

Form				RPR
	1		**Selfsame (USA)** 3-8-12 0 ... JimCrowley 1 (Amanda Perrett) *s.i.s: towards rr: hdwy on far rails fr 2f out: rdn and r.o strly ins fnl f: swtchd lft and squeezed through gap to ld fnl 30yds* **9/1**	74+
00-4	2	½	**Santarini (IRE)**[20] 2279 3-8-12 70 ... RichardHughes 2 (Richard Hannon) *mid-div: rdn and gd run up far rails 3f out: led over 2f out: hrd drvn whn hdd fnl 30yds: no ex* **6/1**[3]	73
02-	3	nk	**Baheeja**[234] 6934 3-8-12 0 ... NeilCallan 13 (Roger Varian) *in tch: wandered whn rdn over 2f out: sn mde prog: styd on to hold ev ch wl ins fnl f: kpt on* **2/1**[1]	72+
0-	4	1 ¾	**All Time**[420] 1364 4-9-9 0 ... StevieDonohoe 3 (Sir Henry Cecil) *trckd ldrs: lost pl sltly whn nt clr run over 2f out: sn rdn and edgd lft: styd on fnl f* **9/4**[2]	71
00	5	1	**Guiletta (IRE)**[32] 1923 3-8-9 0 ... RyanClark(3) 9 (Rae Guest) *hld up towards rr: rdn and stdy prog fr over 2f out: styd on wl fnl f* **20/1**	66+
6	6	2 ½	**Divine Pamina (IRE)**[49] 1501 3-8-12 0 ... HayleyTurner 5 (Jim Boyle) *trckd ldrs: rdn 3f out: one pce fnl 2f* **10/1**	60
00	7	4	**Perfect Outlook**[13] 2496 4-9-9 0 ... KieranO'Neill 12 (Jeremy Gask) *hld up towards rr: sme late prog: nvr trbld ldrs* **66/1**	53
4-	8	¾	**Present Day**[242] 6745 3-8-12 0 ... AdamKirby 7 (Clive Cox) *led: rdn and hdd over 2f out: fdd fnl f* **14/1**	48
0	9	1 ¾	**Ebtisama (USA)**[13] 2483 3-8-12 0 ... JackMitchell 8 (Marcus Tregoning) *mid-div: effrt wl over 2f out: wknd fnl f* **20/1**	44
0	10	1 ½	**Luna Rosa (IRE)**[22] 2204 3-8-12 0 ...[1] DaneO'Neill 10 (Clive Cox) *trckd ldrs: rdn over 2f out: wknd over 1f out* **20/1**	40
00	11	3 ¾	**Miss Socialite**[28] 2050 3-8-12 0 ... MartinLane 11 (Jeremy Gask) *racd keenly: prom: rdn over 2f out: grad fdd* **33/1**	31
06	12	2 ¼	**Wyebridge**[13] 2483 3-8-9 0 ... HarryBentley(3) 4 (Gary Moore) *s.i.s: a towards rr* **25/1**	26

1m 42.77s (2.87) **Going Correction** +0.45s/f (Yiel)
WFA 3 from 4yo 11lb **12** Ran SP% **126.7**
Speed ratings (Par 100): **103,102,102,100,99 96,92,92,90,88 85,82**
Tote Swingers: 1&2 £9.60, 1&3 £5.80, 2&3 £4.20 CSF £60.61 TOTE £13.50: £3.00, £2.20, £1.40; EX 66.10 Trifecta £285.30 Pool: £462.74 - 1.20 winning units..
Owner K Abdulla **Bred** Millsec Ltd **Trained** Pulborough, W Sussex

FOCUS
Probably just an ordinary maiden, won by the only debutante in the race. The form is rated around the runner-up.
Perfect Outlook Official explanation: jockey said filly was denied a clear run
T/Jkpt: £139,921.60 to a £1 stake. Pool: £197,073.00 - 1.00 winning ticket. T/Plt: £35.30 to a £1 stake. Pool: £66,074.00 - 1,364.81 winning tickets. T/Qpdt: £5.80 to a £1 stake. Pool: £4,244.00 - 541.18 winning tickets. TM

2274 NEWMARKET (R-H)
Friday, June 8

OFFICIAL GOING: Soft (7.3)
Wind: behind, strong Weather: rain, clearing

2892 LLOYDS TSB COMMERCIAL E B F MAIDEN FILLIES' STKS 6f
1:40 (1:42) (Class 4) 2-Y-0 **£4,528** (£1,347; £673; £336) **Stalls** High

Form				RPR
	1		**Newfangled (USA)** 2-9-0 0 ... WilliamBuick 3 (John Gosden) *chsd ldrs: rdn to ld over 1f out: styd on strly under hands and heels riding and drew clr fnl f* **10/1**	95+
	2	4 ½	**Fleeting Smile (USA)** 2-9-0 0 ... PaulHanagan 8 (Richard Hannon) *led tl over 3f out: chsd ldr after: rdn over 1f out: drvn and chsd wnr 1f out: no imp and wknd fnl 100yds but stl clr 2nd* **1/1**[1]	81+
	3	2 ½	**Summer Dream (IRE)** 2-9-0 0 ... TedDurcan 7 (Marco Botti) *hld up in last trio: rdn and effrt 2f out: hdwy and swtchd rt ins fnl f: styd on steadily to go 3rd nr fin* **16/1**	74+
6	4	½	**Summer Isles**[21] 2245 2-9-0 0 ... RyanMoore 10 (Ed Dunlop) *in tch: rdn and effrt 2f out: no ch w wnr but kpt on steadily fnl f* **15/2**[2]	72
5	5	2 ¼	**Annie's Fortune (IRE)**[14] 2450 2-9-0 0 ... KierenFallon 6 (Alan Jarvis) *chsd ldr tl led over 3f out: drvn and hdd over 1f out: fdd ins fnl f* **9/1**	65
	6	1 ½	**Trucanini** 2-9-0 0 ... SebSanders 4 (Chris Wall) *in tch in last trio: pushed along and hdwy into midfield over 2f out: outpcd and btn over 1f out: plugged on* **50/1**	61
	7	3 ½	**Red Eclipse (IRE)** 2-9-0 0 ... DarryllHolland 5 (Alan Bailey) *awkward leaving stalls and slowly away: in tch: rdn over 2f out: sn struggling: wknd over 1f out: fdd fnl f* **40/1**	50
	8	2 ½	**Glossy Posse** 2-9-0 0 ... PatCosgrave 2 (Richard Hannon) *wnt rt s: in tch: rdn and struggling over 2f out: wknd over 1f out: fdd fnl f* **9/1**	43
	9	¾	**Singapura (USA)** 2-9-0 0 ... SilvestreDeSousa 1 (Mahmood Al Zarooni) *wnt rt s: in tch in midfield: rdn and struggling 2f out: sn wknd and bhd fnl f* **8/1**[3]	41
	10	1	**Lilly White (USA)** 2-9-0 0 ... ShaneKelly 9 (Brian Meehan) *in tch in midfield: rdn and lost pl 1/2-way: wknd and bhd over 1f out* **33/1**	38

1m 15.67s (3.17) **Going Correction** +0.55s/f (Yiel) **10** Ran SP% **115.2**
Speed ratings (Par 92): **100,94,90,90,87 85,80,77,76,74**
Tote Swingers:1&2:£4.10, 2&3:£6.20, 1&3:£16.40 CSF £19.95 TOTE £10.40: £3.30, £1.10, £3.70; EX 29.00 Trifecta £466.70 Pool: £1,122.78 - 1.78 winning units..
Owner H R H Princess Haya Of Jordan **Bred** Darley **Trained** Newmarket, Suffolk

FOCUS
Stands' side track of July course used. Stalls on far side except 1m2f &1m4f which were in centre. With plenty of rain about and a strong wind half behind, conditions proved testing - after riding in the first race Ryan Moore and Paul Hanagan reported the ground to be soft. There was a well-backed favourite in this fillies' maiden, but she was turned over. The form is taken at face value for now, with the fourth and fifth the best guides.

NOTEBOOK
Newfangled(USA) ◆ won in impressive style on her debut. Looking very professional, she travelled well, handled the ground and only had to be pushed out with hands and heels to score by a clear margin. A daughter of New Approach, she looks Royal Ascot class, and the Albany looks the ideal target. (op 9-1 tchd 12-1)
Fleeting Smile(USA), in whom there was plenty of confidence (backed from 9-2 in the morning), cost $500,000 and is out of a champion US older mare, but while she kept on well near the far rail she had no chance with the easy winner. Perhaps the ground was softer than she would ideally like. Either way, she shouldn't have too much trouble going one better. (op 11-8)
Summer Dream(IRE), held up further back than the first two, was also staying on well at the finish. Out of a sister to 2000 Guineas third Olympian Odyssey, she can only improve for this debut effort. (op 14-1)
Summer Isles had the benefit of a previous outing, and help give the form some substance. However, as a daughter of Exceed And Excel she might not want the ground this soft. (op 7-1 tchd 13-2)
Annie's Fortune(IRE) also had the benefit of a previous outing, and helps give the form some substance. However, as a daughter of Montjeu, further should suit her in time. (op 8-1)
Trucanini didn't shape badly on her debut. Her stable isn't known for first-time-out 2-y-o winners so there should be improvement in her. (op 40-1)
Singapura(USA) ran green and appeared to find conditions pretty tiring. She's bred for fast ground.

2893 COUNTRYSIDE ALLIANCE BRITISH STALLION STUDS E B F FILLIES' H'CAP (DIV I) 6f
2:10 (2:12) (Class 4) (0-85,85) 3-Y-0 **£4,528** (£1,347; £673; £336) **Stalls** High

Form				RPR
5-13	1		**Charlotte Rosina**[32] 1921 3-9-2 80 ... SebSanders 5 (Roger Teal) *mde all: rdn wl over 1f out: drvn and styd on wl fnl f: eased cl home* **20/1**	92
0-11	2	1 ¼	**Athenian (IRE)**[4] 2759 3-8-9 73 12ex ... LukeMorris 1 (Sir Mark Prescott Bt) *wnt rt s and slowly away: sn rcvrd and chsd ldrs: rdn and pressing wnr over 1f out: no ex ins fnl f and kpt on same pce fnl 100yds* **2/1**[1]	81
1-60	3	½	**I'm So Glad**[20] 2272 3-8-11 75 ... MartinHarley 2 (Mick Channon) *hld up in tch: rdn and effrt to chse ldng pair 1f out: flashed tail u.p and styd on same pce fnl f* **8/1**	82
10-2	4	4	**Place In My Heart**[32] 1921 3-9-7 85 ... FrankieDettori 6 (George Baker) *stdd after s: hld up in tch: rdn and effrt 2f out: no imp and btn 1f out: plugged on to go modest 4th ins fnl f* **13/2**[3]	79
1-64	5	nk	**Brick Tops**[19] 2310 3-9-0 78 ... WilliamBuick 4 (David Simcock) *hld up in rr: swtchd rt and effrt wl over 1f out: no prog and no ch w ldrs 1f out: plugged on ins fnl f* **7/1**	71
060-	6	1 ¼	**Besito (IRE)**[224] 7135 3-9-0 81 ...[1] HarryBentley(3) 9 (William Jarvis) *broke wl and chsd ldrs early: steadily lost pl and towards rr 1/2-way: rdn and hdwy 2f out: sn struggling and wknd 1f out* **16/1**	70
	7	2	**Bahama Spirit (IRE)**[215] 7319 3-9-1 79 ... IanMongan 7 (Jeremy Gask) *chsd ldr tl over 1f out: sn drvn and struggling: fdd ins fnl f* **25/1**	62
1	8	2 ½	**Isola Verde**[25] 2121 3-8-8 72 ... KierenFallon 8 (James Fanshawe) *t.k.h early: hld up in tch: rdn and effrt on far rail over 2f out: btn over 1f out: fdd fnl f* **5/1**[2]	47
-052	9	shd	**Tip Top Gorgeous (IRE)**[14] 2451 3-9-2 80 ... SilvestreDeSousa 3 (David O'Meara) *s.i.s: in tch in rr: rdn and struggling over 2f out: wknd over 1f out* **8/1**	54

1m 15.17s (2.67) **Going Correction** +0.55s/f (Yiel) **9** Ran SP% **112.5**
Speed ratings (Par 98): **104,102,101,96,95 94,91,88,88**
Tote Swingers:1&2:£6.60, 2&3:£5.60, 1&3:£17.80 CSF £58.58 CT £360.65 TOTE £23.50: £5.40, £1.50, £3.20; EX 76.80 Trifecta £791.80 Part won. Pool: £1,070.06 - 0.40 winning units..
Owner Edward Hyde **Bred** Edward Hyde **Trained** Ashtead, Surrey

FOCUS
The early pace wasn't that strong and it paid to race prominently. The third, to her juvenile form is the best guide.

2894 COUNTRYSIDE ALLIANCE BRITISH STALLION STUDS E B F FILLIES' H'CAP (DIV II) 6f
2:45 (2:48) (Class 4) (0-85,82) 3-Y-0 **£4,528** (£1,347; £673; £336) **Stalls** High

Form				RPR
1-55	1		**Lollina Paulina**[20] 2272 3-8-13 74 ... NeilCallan 3 (Kevin Ryan) *broke fast: mde all: rdn over 1f out: hung rt fnl f: bmpd rival fnl 100yds: battled on gamely and hld on towards fin* **4/1**[2]	80
1136	2	½	**Bella Ophelia (IRE)**[18] 2347 3-9-1 76 ... DarryllHolland 6 (Hughie Morrison) *taken down early: chsd ldrs: rdn to chal ent fnl f: carried rt fnl f: ev ch whn bmpd and n.m.r fnl 100yds: kpt on but hld towards fin* **5/1**	80+
-553	3	2	**Red Larkspur (IRE)**[20] 2272 3-9-3 78 ... FrankieDettori 9 (Roger Teal) *in tch: effrt to chal over 1f out: unable qck ins fnl f: styd on same pce fnl 100yds* **9/4**[1]	76
-031	4	½	**Cheworee**[13] 2501 3-9-5 80 ... RyanMoore 1 (David Elsworth) *s.i.s: in tch in rr: rdn and effrt to chse ldrs over 1f out: carried rt 1f out: swtchd lft ins fnl f: styd on same pce fnl 100yds* **9/2**[3]	76
10-0	5	shd	**Princess Of Orange**[34] 1858 3-9-7 82 ...[1] TedDurcan 8 (Rae Guest) *t.k.h: chsd wnr tl 2f out: styd on same pce and hung rt fnl f* **20/1**	78
50-0	6	½	**Imelda Mayhem**[20] 2272 3-9-6 81 ... ShaneKelly 2 (J S Moore) *in tch: effrt u.p 2f out: drvn and one pce ent fnl f* **9/1**	75
2-30	7	9	**Symphony Time (IRE)**[22] 2194 3-8-11 72 ... MickaelBarzalona 4 (Brian Meehan) *t.k.h: hld up in tch: rdn and effrt wl over 1f out: wknd 1f out: fdd ins fnl f* **8/1**	37

1m 15.94s (3.44) **Going Correction** +0.55s/f (Yiel) **7** Ran SP% **111.5**
Speed ratings (Par 98): **99,98,95,95,94 94,82**
Tote Swingers:1&2:£4.40, 2&3:£3.20, 1&3:£2.90 CSF £22.82 CT £52.96 TOTE £5.60: £2.70, £3.50; EX 23.10 Trifecta £68.30 Pool: £1,063.30 - 11.51 winning units..
Owner The Paulina Partnership **Bred** Newsells Park Stud **Trained** Hambleton, N Yorks
■ Stewards' Enquiry : Neil Callan four-day ban: careless riding (Jun 24-27)

FOCUS
Once again the race was dominated from the front, and the winning time was 0.77sec slower than the first division. The form is rated around the winner and third, backed up by the fourth.

2895 COUNTRYSIDE ALLIANCE FOUNDATION MAIDEN STKS 1m 4f
3:20 (3:20) (Class 5) 3-Y-0 **£3,234** (£962; £481; £240) **Stalls** Centre

Form				RPR
2-22	1		**Shantaram**[27] 2080 3-9-3 104 ... WilliamBuick 5 (John Gosden) *in tch: hdwy to chse ldng pair 2f out: sn rdn: drvn to chal 1f out: led ins fnl f: asserted and forged ahd fnl 100yds* **1/8**[1]	86+

0 **2** *3/4* **Mashaari (IRE)**[20] 2266 3-9-3 0 RobertHavlin 3 85
(John Gosden) *chsd ldrs: wnt 2nd 3f out: rdn and ev ch 2f out: edgd lft and bmpd rival over 1f out: led 1f out: hdd and stl edging lft ins fnl f: no ex fnl 100yds* **12/1**[3]

406 **3** *2* **Black Mascara (IRE)**[21] 2249 3-8-12 80 JimmyFortune 2 77
(Richard Hannon) *led: rdn and hrd pressed 2f out: bmpd over 1f out: hdd 1f out: no ex and btn ins fnl f* **10/1**[2]

4 *3 1/4* **White Nile (IRE)** 3-9-3 0 MartinLane 9 77+
(David Simcock) *hld up in rr: rdn and hdwy over 2f out: chsd ldng trio wl over 1f out: styd on steadily fnl f but no threat to ldrs* **10/1**[2]

00 **5** *11* **Salford Dream**[11] 2560 3-9-3 0 MickaelBarzalona 11 59
(David Elsworth) *in tch: swtchd lft and effrt over 2f out: no imp whn rdr dropped whip over 1f out: wknd and rn green fnl f* **20/1**

0 **6** *1 3/4* **Card Sweep**[17] 2380 3-9-3 0 RoystonFfrench 8 56
(Ismail Mohammed) *hld up in tch: rdn and effrt wl over 2f out: wknd 2f out: 6th and wl btn 1f out* **50/1**

05 **7** *14* **Encouraging (IRE)**[16] 2393 3-9-3 0 MarcHalford 10 34
(David Elsworth) *t.k.h: hld up in tch: rdn and wknd wl over 2f out: wl bhd fnl f* **20/1**

0-3 **8** *12* **Edraaq**[36] 1793 3-9-3 0 TadhgO'Shea 6 15
(Brian Meehan) *chsd ldr tl 3f out: sn u.p and struggling: wknd 2f out: t.o and eased fnl f* **14/1**

0 **9** *5* **The Way To Be (IRE)**[11] 2560 3-9-3 0 (p) DarryllHolland 4
(Gerard Butler) *hld up in tch: rdn and wknd over 3f out: t.o and eased fnl f* **50/1**

0-0 **10** *26* **Verona Bay (FR)**[22] 2197 3-9-0 0 AdamBeschizza(3) 7
(Julia Feilden) *chsd ldrs tl rdn and lost pl over 3f out: t.o over 1f out: eased ins fnl f* **66/1**

2m 37.9s (5.00) **Going Correction** +0.55s/f (Yiel) **10** Ran SP% **136.4**
Speed ratings (Par 99): **105,104,103,101,93 92,83,75,71,54**
Tote Swingers:1&2:£2.40, 2&3:£5.10, 1&3:£2.10 CSF £4.83 TOTE £1.10: £1.02, £2.70, £2.20; EX 5.00 Trifecta £19.30 Pool: £1,323.94 - 50.58 winning units..
Owner Lady Bamford **Bred** Lady Bamford **Trained** Newmarket, Suffolk

FOCUS
The winner was the standout on form but made hard work of this and the level is a bit fluid.

2896 LLOYDS TSB CARDNET H'CAP 7f
3:55 (3:56) (Class 3) (0-95,95) 4-Y-O+ **£7,762** (£2,310; £1,154; £577) **Stalls** High

Form RPR

50-0 **1** **Paramour**[41] 1670 5-8-8 82 DarryllHolland 4 91
(Alan Bailey) *mde all and grad led field across to stands' rail: rdn over 1f out: edgd lft but styd on wl fnl f* **9/1**

0445 **2** *1* **Illustrious Prince (IRE)**[6] 2697 5-7-12 77 NeilFarley(5) 10 83
(Declan Carroll) *chsd ldrs: rdn over 1f out: drvn and chsd wnr ins fnl f: styd on same pce fnl 100yds* **5/1**[2]

-605 **3** *shd* **Redvers (IRE)**[13] 2489 4-8-11 85 (b) RyanMoore 12 91+
(Ed Vaughan) *hld up in rr: rdn and effrt over 1f out: drvn and pressing for 2nd ins fnl f: kpt on* **8/1**

6005 **4** *nk* **Able Master (IRE)**[13] 2487 6-8-3 77 SilvestreDeSousa 9 82
(David O'Meara) *taken down early: chsd wnr: rdn over 2f out: drvn and unable qck over 1f out: styd on same pce ins fnl f* **10/1**

4-01 **5** *2 1/2* **My Son Max**[11] 2545 4-8-9 83 6ex PatCosgrave 5 82
(P J O'Gorman) *hld up in tch towards rr: rdn and effrt over 1f out: styd on same pce and no imp ins fnl f* **11/1**

2001 **6** *2* **Escape To Glory (USA)**[9] 2608 4-9-1 89 6ex WilliamBuick 1 83
(Mikael Magnusson) *hld up in tch: rdn over 2f out: drvn and no imp over 1f out: wknd ins fnl f* **3/1**[1]

64-0 **7** *5* **Mubtadi**[13] 2500 4-8-6 80 (t) RoystonFfrench 11 61
(Ismail Mohammed) *t.k.h: hld up in tch: rdn 2f out: drvn and no prog over 1f out: wknd fnl f* **8/1**

520- **8** *1 1/4* **Atlantic Sport (USA)**[251] 6521 7-9-7 95 TonyCulhane 2 72
(Mick Channon) *trckd ldrs: rdn and fnd little over 1f out: btn 1f out and wknd fnl f* **8/1**

00-0 **9** *13* **Theladyinquestion**[27] 2078 5-9-1 89 JimmyFortune 8 33
(Andrew Balding) *hld up in tch: btn 2f out: sn lost tch and nt pushed: eased ins fnl f* **7/1**[3]

1m 28.17s (2.47) **Going Correction** +0.55s/f (Yiel) **9** Ran SP% **114.9**
Speed ratings (Par 107): **107,105,105,105,102 100,94,93,78**
Tote Swingers: 1&2 £12.20, 1&3 £18.70, 2&3 £8.00 CSF £53.23 CT £379.85 TOTE £11.40: £4.20, £1.70, £3.20; EX 82.50 TRIFECTA Not won..
Owner Richard Jeffrey **Bred** Cheveley Park Stud Ltd **Trained** Newmarket, Suffolk

FOCUS
A decent handicap with the winner back to his early best with the second to this year's form.

NOTEBOOK
Paramour, despite having finished tailed off at Ripon on his only previous start this year when briefly with David Nicholls, did not go unbacked on his debut for Alan Bailey. Based on the best of his form from last year when trained by David O'Meara he was on a fair mark and, although racing prominently, was clearly an advantage on this card, he is unexposed over this sort of distance, is lightly raced for his age and could have more improvement in him. His trainer has the Ayr Gold Cup in mind for him later in the season, and an ability to stay 7f has proven an asset in that race in the past. (op 12-1 tchd 14-1 and 16-1 in a place)
Illustrious Prince(IRE), prominent more towards the centre of the track, seems to go on most ground and ran another solid race. Being up with the pace was a plus on this card, so any further rise in the weights won't help his cause. (op 7-1)
Redvers(IRE) deserves credit as he got into third having been held up in last position early on. He's another who receives no gifts from the handicapper, but at least he's in top form. (op 7-1 tchd 13-2)
Able Master(IRE) ran well upped to 7f, but he was another who benefited from racing prominently. (op 8-1)
My Son Max, in contrast, was out the back for much of the race and struggled to land a meaningful blow. He might be happier back on better ground. (op 8-1)
Escape To Glory(USA), who won at Folkestone last time out on good to firm, didn't look comfortable on this more testing surface. He was also reported to have lost a front shoe. Official explanation: trainer's rep said colt was unsuited by the soft ground and had lost a front shoe (op 4-1)
Theladyinquestion Official explanation: trainer's rep said mare was unsuited by the soft ground

2897 LLOYDS TSB FOR JOURNEY H'CAP 1m 2f
4:30 (4:32) (Class 3) (0-95,93) 3-Y-O **£7,762** (£2,310; £1,154; £577) **Stalls** Centre

Form RPR

01-5 **1** **Thomas Chippendale (IRE)**[20] 2269 3-9-0 86 TomQueally 5 101+
(Sir Henry Cecil) *stdd s: hld up in tch in last trio: smooth hdwy to join ldrs over 1f out: sn led: rdn and qcknd clr 1f out: r.o strly: readily* **13/8**[1]

3213 **2** *3 1/2* **Valley Of Destiny**[32] 1938 3-8-7 79 TedDurcan 6 83
(Richard Hannon) *chsd ldrs: rdn and effrt 2f out: no ch w wnr but kpt on u.p ins fnl f to go 2nd last strides* **12/1**

-110 **3** *hd* **Samba King**[33] 1888 3-9-7 93 MickaelBarzalona 7 96
(Mahmood Al Zarooni) *in tch: rdn and effrt to press ldrs over 1f out: drvn and outpcd by wnr 1f out: styd on same pce after: edgd lft cl home* **15/2**[3]

01 **4** *1 1/4* **Sheikhzayedroad**[33] 1878 3-8-4 76 MartinLane 3 78+
(David Simcock) *stdd s: hld up in tch in rr: grad swtchd to outer and hdwy to press ldrs over 1f out: drvn and outpcd by wnr 1f out: battling for 2nd and one pce after: sltly hmpd and wknd cl home* **9/1**

3125 **5** *3/4* **Fennell Bay (IRE)**[6] 2701 3-8-10 82 SilvestreDeSousa 1 81+
(Mark Johnston) *led for 2f: chsd ldrs after: rdn and n.m.r 2f out: edgd lft and unable qck u.p over 1f out: no ch w wnr and styd on same pce fnl f* **8/1**

1-04 **6** *hd* **Just Fabulous**[27] 2088 3-8-13 85 AndrewElliott 9 84
(George Moore) *t.k.h: chsd ldr after 2f tl led 5f out: rdn and hdd whn edgd lft and sltly hmpd over 1f out: no ch w wnr and one pce fnl f* **16/1**

1-5 **7** *2 3/4* **Jungle Beat (IRE)**[51] 1455 3-9-4 90 WilliamBuick 4 84
(John Gosden) *hld up in tch in rr: rdn and effrt 2f out: drvn and no imp over 1f out: nvr trbld ldrs* **6/1**[2]

61- **8** *1 3/4* **Trois Vallees (USA)**[263] 6216 3-8-11 83 FrankieDettori 8 73
(Mahmood Al Zarooni) *hld up in tch in rr: rdn and effrt over 2f out: drvn and unable qck over 1f out: wknd fnl f* **17/2**

14-0 **9** *33* **Poetic Lord**[20] 2269 3-8-12 84 RyanMoore 2
(Richard Hannon) *chsd ldr tl led after 2f: hdd 5f out but styd upsides ldrs tl rdn and btn over 1f out: virtually p.u ins fnl f* **20/1**

2m 10.16s (4.66) **Going Correction** +0.55s/f (Yiel) **9** Ran SP% **114.1**
Speed ratings (Par 103): **103,100,100,99,98 98,96,94,68**
Tote Swingers: 1&2 £6.40, 1&3 £4.00, 2&3 £11.70 CSF £22.67 CT £115.67 TOTE £2.80: £1.60, £2.00, £2.70; EX 26.30 Trifecta £183.10 Pool: £1,739.63 - 7.03 winning units..
Owner Sir Robert Ogden **Bred** Premier Bloodstock **Trained** Newmarket, Suffolk

FOCUS
A good quality handicap and a smart performance from the winner. The third and sixth help set the standard.

NOTEBOOK
Thomas Chippendale(IRE) ◆ shaped better than his finishing position in a strong handicap at Newbury on his return and proved himself a well-handicapped horse here by bolting up off the same mark. A step up to 1m4f is expected to suit the son of Dansili and Henry Cecil seemed keen on going for the King Edward VII next, even though the King George V handicap might seem a more obvious option, so the regard in which he is held is clear. (op 2-1)
Valley Of Destiny appreciates plenty of give in the ground and ran well to come out best of the rest behind a rival who is clearly far better than this class. The longer trip suited him well. (op 11-1)
Samba King, who had no chance last time when racing alone on the wrong side, travelled up well and, while put in his place by the winner, posted a solid enough effort in defeat. All six of his races so far have come with give in the ground, so presumably it's thought to be important to him. (op 8-1)
Sheikhzayedroad came through from off the pace but didn't quite see his race out on the climb to the line. This was a decent effort straight out of winning his maiden on his second start, though, and he's entitled to step up on it next time. (op 8-1)
Fennell Bay(IRE), more exposed than most in this field, got no run close to the stands' rail and looked to finish with something left in the tank. A little more improvement can't be discounted. (op 10-1)
Just Fabulous, who has been kept exclusively to softish ground so far in her career, disputed the lead for a long way, but racing keenly early didn't help her chances of seeing her race out. (tchd 20-1)
Jungle Beat(IRE) didn't settle through the early stages and that probably compromised his finishing effort to some extent. (op 9-2 tchd 4-1)
Trois Vallees(USA) lacks a bit of size and might not want the ground this soft. (op 9-1)

2898 LLOYDS TSB CARDNET CLASSIFIED STKS 1m
5:05 (5:07) (Class 5) 3-Y-O **£2,587** (£770; £192; £192; £192) **Stalls** High

Form RPR

1 **1** **Dellbuoy**[79] 981 3-9-0 75 IanMongan 2 83+
(Pat Phelan) *stdd s: hld up in tch towards rr: hdwy over 2f out: led over 1f out: rn green ent fnl f: rdn and styd on wl to draw clr fnl 150yds: readily* **10/1**

5-04 **2** *3* **Counsel (IRE)**[15] 2429 3-9-0 73 RyanMoore 5 76
(Sir Michael Stoute) *in tch: rdn and effrt over 2f out: racd awkwardly u.p and unable qck 2f out: styd on ins fnl f: wnt 2nd last strides* **3/1**[1]

2122 **3** *hd* **Mayo Lad (IRE)**[30] 1985 3-9-0 75 TomQueally 9 76
(Richard Hannon) *chsd ldr: rdn and chsd wnr over 1f out: one pce fnl f* **4/1**[2]

21-0 **3** *dht* **Amoralist**[46] 1557 3-9-0 75 TedDurcan 12 76
(Ed Dunlop) *hld up in tch towards rr: hdwy 3f out: drvn and chsd ldrs over 1f out: styd on same pce ins fnl f* **9/1**

3-06 **3** *dht* **Paddyfrommenlo (IRE)**[13] 2496 3-9-0 74 FrankieDettori 7 76+
(J W Hills) *hld up in tch in rr: rdn over 2f out: no imp tl styd on wl ins fnl f* **10/1**

2020 **6** *1 1/4* **Alkadi (IRE)**[18] 2331 3-9-0 75 SilvestreDeSousa 6 73
(Mark Johnston) *chsd ldrs: drvn to press ldrs over 2f out: no ex and btn ins fnl f* **11/1**

50-3 **7** *5* **Acer Diamonds (IRE)**[32] 1937 3-9-0 72 DarryllHolland 11 62
(Julia Feilden) *led tl rdn and hdd over 1f out: wknd ins fnl f* **14/1**

2-24 **8** *3* **Widyaan (IRE)**[20] 2271 3-9-0 74 (p) TadhgO'Shea 1 55
(John Gosden) *hld up in tch: hdwy to chse ldrs and pushed rt over 1f out: wknd 1f out: fdd fnl f* **9/2**[3]

00-5 **9** *6* **Underwritten**[48] 1512 3-9-0 72 JimmyFortune 3 41
(Andrew Balding) *chsd ldrs: rdn over 2f out: wknd over 1f out: bhd fnl f* **11/1**

1m 43.4s (3.40) **Going Correction** +0.55s/f (Yiel) **9** Ran SP% **114.7**
CSF £39.89 TOTE £13.60: £2.90, £1.70; EX 27 Trifecta £Owner Timesquare Ltd Bred.

FOCUS
A modest race but a pleasing performance. The level is bit fluid with the dead-heaters helping to set the standard.

2899 RACING UK H'CAP 1m 2f
5:40 (5:43) (Class 5) (0-75,76) 4-Y-O+ **£2,726** (£805; £402) **Stalls** Centre

Form RPR

0-30 **1** **Osgood**[21] 2233 5-8-12 66 TonyCulhane 11 75
(Mick Channon) *in tch: hdwy to trck ldrs 2f out: rdn to chal 1f out: led ins fnl f: all out and hld on cl home* **14/1**

0-62 **2** *hd* **Lieutenant Kojak**[38] 1743 4-8-8 67 RosieJessop(5) 8 75
(Peter Charalambous) *hld up in tch: hdwy to chse ldrs and nt clr run over 1f out: swtchd lft and sustained chal fnl f: jst hld cl home* **6/1**

46P/ **3** *1 3/4* **Sacrilege**[35] 4201 7 -8-10**67**.......................................(b) RyanPowell(3) 12 72
(Daniel O'Brien) *chsd ldrs: wnt 2nd 6f out: rdn to ld over 1f out: hdd ins fnl f: styd on same pce fnl 100yds* **33/1**

0-00 **4** *1* **Odin (IRE)**[22] 2199 4 -9-4**72**... MarcHalford 3 75
(David Elsworth) *in tch: rdn and chse ldrs over 1f out: styd on same pce ins fnl f* **22/1**

5105 **5** *shd* **Vanilla Rum**[22] 2199 5 -9-1**69**.......................................(b) MircoDemuro 6 72
(John Mackie) *hmpd s: hld up in tch in rr: hdwy 3f out: chsd ldrs and drvn over 1f out: one pce and no imp fnl f* **9/1**

2612 **6** *11* **Cairanne**[21] 2233 4 -8-2**58** ow1................................. AdamBeschizza(3) 1 40
(Tom Keddy) *led: rdn and hdd over 1f out: fdd fnl f* **7/2**[2]

1320 **7** *7* **Warden Bond**[14] 2463 4 -7-13**56**.................................(p) DominicFox(3) 7 23
(William Stone) *chsd ldrs: struggling u.p 3f out: wl btn fnl 2f* **25/1**

60-0 **8** *2* **Marhaba Malyoon (IRE)**[33] 1880 4 -9-7**75**..................... TadhgO'Shea 4 38
(David Simcock) *hld up towards rr: rdn and short-lived effrt over 2f out: no prog and wl btn fnl 2f* **16/1**

34-3 **9** *nse* **Red Lover**[18] 2328 4 -9-7**75**... RyanMoore 10 38
(Ed Dunlop) *stdd s: hld up in last trio: rdn and short-lived effrt over 2f out: no prog and wl btn 2f out* **5/2**[1]

0000 **10** *5* **Final Drive (IRE)**[37] 1755 6 -9-0**68**................................(t) ShaneKelly 14 21
(John Butler) *stdd and dropped in bhd after s: rdn over 2f out: no hdwy and sn wl btn* **25/1**

/46- **11** *4* **Victorian Number (FR)**[27] 4 -9-6**74**..............................(p) PatCosgrave 2 19
(Geoffrey Deacon) *chsd ldr tl 6f out: lost pl and bhd over 3f out: wl bhd fnl 2f: t.o* **66/1**

-601 **12** *12* **Searing Heat (USA)**[10] 2588 4 -9-1**69** 6ex........................ TomQueally 5
(Sir Henry Cecil) *in tch tl wknd qckly over 2f out: wl bhd and eased fnl f: t.o* **5/1**[3]

2m 9.93s (4.43)**Going Correction** +0.55s/f (Yiel) **12**Ran SP% **120.8**
Speed ratings (Par 103): **104,103,102,101,101 92,87,85,85,81 78,68**
Tote Swingers: 1&2 £14.90, 1&3 £44.80, 2&3 £44.40 CSF £92.26 CT £2750.61 TOTE £16.80: £4.40, £2.80 , £10.20 ; EX 138.50 Trifecta £445.00 Part won. Pool: £601.47 - 0.62 winning tickets..
Owner Billy Parish **Bred** Eurostrait Ltd **Trained** West Ilsley, Berks
■ Stewards' Enquiry : Adam Beschizza five-day ban: used whip when filly showed no response (Jun 22-26)

FOCUS
A modest handicap run at a good gallop but the form does not look that solid or reliable.
Red Lover Official explanation: jockey said gelding never travelled
T/Plt: £106.90 to a £1 stake. Pool: £57,649.00 - 393.40 winning tickets. T/Qpdt: £28.50 to a £1 stake. Pool: £4,411.00 - 114.46 w. tickets. SP 2900a-2902a Foreign Racing (See RI)

[2099]LEOPARDSTOWN (L-H)
Friday, June 8

OFFICIAL GOING: Heavy

2903a SEAMUS & ROSEMARY MCGRATH MEMORIAL SAVAL BEG STKS (LISTED RACE) 1m 6f
7:35 (7:35) 4-Y-0+ **£25,729** (£7,520; £3,562 ; £1,187)

RPR

1 **Midnight Soprano (IRE)**[12] 2526 5 -9-0**100**..................... ChrisHayes 7 108
(P D Deegan, Ire) *racd in 3rd: clsr appr st: rdn and hdwy on outer to ld under 2f out: edgd lft u.p ins fnl f: kpt on best* **5/1**[3]

2 *1/2* **Saddler's Rock (IRE)**[273] 5884 4 -9-10**114**...............(t) JohnnyMurtagh 2 117+
(John M Oxx, Ire) *hld up in 4th: clsr appr st: pushed along in 3rd over 1f out: wnt 2nd ins fnl f: kpt on same pce wout really threatening wnr* **4/1**[2]

3 *1* **Unaccompanied (IRE)**[19] 2318 5 -9-0**105**......................... PatSmullen 3 106
(D K Weld, Ire) *trckd ldr in 2nd: 4 l down 1/2-way: much clsr appr st: pushed along to chal early st: dropped to 3rd and no imp whn short of room ins fnl f* **5/6**[1]

4 *3 1/4* **Eternal Heart (IRE)**[30] 1974 4 -9-3... JPO'Brien 6 104
(Mark Johnston) *led and sn 4 l clr: reduced advantage appr st: rdn and hdd under 2f out: sn dropped to 4th and no ex ins fnl f* **5/1**[3]

3m 20.35s (19.35)**Going Correction** +1.40s/f (Soft) **4**Ran SP% **107.9**
Speed ratings: **100,99,99,97**
CSF £22.17 TOTE £5.00 ; DF 23.50 .
Owner J Monaghan **Bred** J Monaghan **Trained** The Curragh, Co Kildare

FOCUS
A depleted field with four of the eight declared non-runners because of the very testing conditions. The winning time was almost 22 seconds slower than when Fame And Glory won the race on good ground a year ago. The runner-up has been rated just off his best on his seasonal reappearance.

NOTEBOOK
Midnight Soprano (IRE)came out on top and stretched her winning sequence to five. Four of her five previous wins were achieved on yielding or soft ground, but this was her first time on heavy and her first attempt over this distance and at this level. Sent to the front under 2f out, after twice edging left she kept on well inside the final furlong. Trainer Paul Deegan intends aiming her at another Listed event, the Martin Molony Stakes, over 1m3f at Limerick on June 22. (op 11/2 tchd 6/1)
Saddler's Rock (IRE)◆ had missed his intended seasonal reappearance in the Vintage Crop Stakes last month due to a minor setback. His trainer expected him to need this run and had also expresssed serious doubts about the testing ground. Held up behind his three rivals, he began his effort off the last bend and after looking held he warmed to his task inside the final furlong and was closing near the finish. John Oxx said "Considering the ground, which he hates, and the lack of a previous run this season, I'm very pleasesd. He blew up and then got his second wind and finished with a good rattle. He'll take his chance in the Ascot Gold Cup." (op 3/1)
Unaccompanied(IRE) had run Fame And Glory to a neck in the Vintage Crop Stakes at Navan last month and this versatile mare, a dual Grade 1 winner over hurdles and a Listed winner over 1m2f at the Curragh last season, was sent off favourite. She had every chance and, although done no favours by the winner on a couple of occasions early in the final furlong, she was already beginning to struggle. A stewards inquiry was called but, predictably, there was no change to the result. While she appreciates cut, these conditions were possibly too testing for her to produce her best. (op 4/5)
Eternal Heart (IRE)set off in front and was soon clear. His advantage was reduced before the straight and he had no more to offer when tackled and headed under 2f out. (op 6/1 tchd 7/1)

2904 - 2908a (Foreign Racing) - See Raceform Interactive

[2469]CHESTER (L-H)
Saturday, June 9

OFFICIAL GOING: Soft (6.4)
Wind: Fresh, half against Weather: Overcast

2909 CRABBIES "SPIFFING" ALCOHOLIC GINGER BEER FILLIES' H'CAP 1m 4f 66y
2:00 (2:00) (Class 4) (0-85,84) 4-Y-0+ **£5,822** (£1,732; £865 ; £432) **Stalls** Low

Form RPR

1 **1** **Reyamour**[23] 2204 4 -9-3**80**.. FergusSweeney 1 85
(Alan King) *trckd ldrs: led over 1f out: r.o ins fnl f: in command towards fin* **4/1**[2]

0-43 **2** *1 1/2* **Kathleen Frances**[15] 2447 5 -8-11**74**.................................. TedDurcan 9 77
(Mark H Tompkins) *hld up in rr: hdwy on outer 2f out: wnt 2nd and chalng over 1f out: no ex fnl 50yds* **5/2**[1]

12-2 **3** *1* **Sugar Hiccup (IRE)**[28] 2077 4 -8-10**73**......................... FrannyNorton 5 74
(David Simcock) *chsd ldr: pushed along 2f out: tried to chal but lost 2nd over 1f out: nt qckn ent fnl f: styd on same pce after* **5/2**[1]

/5-0 **4** *nk* **Jaaryah (IRE)**[22] 2257 4 -9-7**84**.. JackMitchell 7 85
(Roger Varian) *racd keenly: hld up: pushed along over 1f out: kpt on ins fnl f: nt gng pce to chal* **12/1**

1-43 **5** *hd* **Elizabeth Coffee (IRE)**[14] 2473 4 -8-11**74**..................... TonyHamilton 3 75
(Ian Williams) *racd keenly: hld up in tch: pushed along and outpcd over 1f out: kpt on u.p ins fnl f but no real imp* **11/2**[3]

1040 **6** *5* **Smart Step**[11] 2576 4 -8-5**68**.. JoeFanning 4 61
(Mark Johnston) *led: pushed along and hdd over 1f out: wknd fnl 150yds* **8/1**

2m 47.54s (9.04)**Going Correction** +0.50s/f (Yiel) **6**Ran SP% **111.3**
Speed ratings (Par 102): **89,88,87,87,87 83**
toteswingers:1&2:£4.60, 2&3:£2.60, 1&3:£2.30 CSF £14.15 CT £27.82 TOTE £5.60 : £3.00 , £1.90; EX 18.90 .
Owner Denis J Barry **Bred** Haras De La Perelle **Trained** Barbury Castle, Wilts

FOCUS
Rail at innermost and distances as advertised. After 11mm of overnight rain the ground was officially soft. There was fresh ground to race on though, with the rails back to the inside. The winning jockey reported ground was really testing and the grass was quite long. A fair fillies' handicap that was taken by the subsequent Cesarewitch winner Never Can Tell in 2011, but the field was reduced by a third due to withdrawals. The pace was very steady early on and did not pick up until the last half-mile, as evidenced by the time being 12.74secs above standard, so there must be doubts over the bare form. The winner took a step forward.

2910 WILLOW WATER H'CAP 7f 122y
2:35 (2:35) (Class 2) (0-105,98) 3-Y-0+ **£16,172** (£4,812; £2,405 ; £1,202) **Stalls** Low

Form RPR

3521 **1** **Imperial Djay (IRE)**[14] 2472 7 -9-9**93**............................. PJMcDonald 5 102
(Ruth Carr) *midfield: hdwy whn nt clr run and swtchd rt over 1f out: str run ins fnl f: got up to ld post* **8/1**

0014 **2** *nse* **Pintura**[14] 2472 5 -9-11**95**... FrannyNorton 1 103
(David Simcock) *led: rdn 2f out: jst over 2 l clr 1f out: all out towards fin: ct post* **4/1**[1]

0003 **3** *1 1/2* **Clockmaker (IRE)**[7] 2697 6 -9-6**90**................................ DanielTudhope 2 94
(Tim Easterby) *trckd ldrs: wnt 2nd wl over 2f out: rdn and nt qckn whn j. path over 1f out: lost 2nd fnl 100yds: styd on same pce towards fin* **8/1**

5153 **4** *1* **Dubai Dynamo**[3] 2819 7 -9-9**93**.. JamesSullivan 8 95
(Ruth Carr) *hld up: rdn 2f out: hdwy over 1f out: styd on ins fnl f: nrst fin* **9/1**

5-24 **5** *nk* **Kyllachy Star**[29] 2025 6 -9-7**91**.. TonyHamilton 4 92
(Richard Fahey) *midfield: hdwy over 2f out: rdn to chse ldrs over 1f out: styd on same pce ins fnl f* **7/1**[3]

5162 **6** *2* **Van Ellis**[8] 2660 3 -9-2**97**.. JoeFanning 7 90
(Mark Johnston) *chsd ldrs: effrt over 1f out: no ex fnl 100yds* **11/2**[2]

-134 **7** *1/2* **Orpsie Boy (IRE)**[7] 2697 9 -9-0**87**...................................... DaleSwift(3) 3 82
(Ruth Carr) *in tch: rdn over 1f out: one pce ins fnl f* **14/1**

0506 **8** *2 1/4* **Cravat**[14] 2490 3 -8-3**84**.. LiamJones 14 70
(Mark Johnston) *in rr: rdn and edgd rt over 1f out: kpt on u.p ins fnl f: nvr able to trble ldrs* **25/1**

4016 **9** *3* **Viva Ronaldo (IRE)**[14] 2472 6 -8-12**89**................. GeorgeChaloner(7) 12 71
(Richard Fahey) *hld up: pushed along 2f out: nvr a threat* **16/1**

2-00 **10** *nk* **Pravda Street**[28] 2068 7 -9-1**85**.. BarryMcHugh 10 66
(Brian Ellison) *sn pushed along: racd in rr div: nvr gng pce to trble ldrs* **9/1**

100- **11** *1 1/4* **Rakaan (IRE)**[358] 3109 5 -10-0**98**.. TedDurcan 9 76
(Jamie Osborne) *n.m.r s: hld up: pushed along 2f out: no imp on ldrs: eased whn wl btn fnl 100yds* **40/1**

-420 **12** *5* **Osteopathic Remedy (IRE)**[20] 2311 8 -9-7**91**................. TomEaves 13 56
(Michael Dods) *prom: pushed along on outer and wknd over 2f out* **16/1**

00-0 **13** *34* **One Scoop Or Two**[29] 2029 6 -9-0**84**.....................(p) RussKennemore 6
(Reg Hollinshead) *prom tl wknd over 2f out: t.o* **33/1**

1m 35.82s (2.02)**Going Correction** +0.50s/f (Yiel)
WFA 3 from 4yo+ 11lb **13**Ran SP% **117.8**
Speed ratings (Par 109): **109,108,107,106,106 104,103,101,98,98 96,91,57**
toteswingers:1&2:£4.60, 2&3:£10.00, 1&3:£22.40 CSF £38.65 CT £223.60 TOTE £8.20 : £2.90 , £1.90, £3.40 ; EX 22.80 Trifecta £316.30 Pool: £1,021.62 - 2.39 winning units. .
Owner Hollinbridge Partnership **Bred** D Veitch And Musagd Abo Salim **Trained** Huby, N Yorks

FOCUS
A good, competitive handicap with a big field for the track, and the form looks sound amongst the principals. The draw again proved significant as the first three were all drawn in the five lowest stalls.

NOTEBOOK
Imperial Djay (IRE)was meeting the runner-up for the third time here this season and made the score 2-1 with a last-gasp victory. Held up near the rail, he had to be switched when the third went across him over a furlong out but, once in the clear, he picked up strongly to snatch the race on the line. The first two both deserve plenty of credit for running so consistently, whatever the ground. (op 13-2)
Pintura goes on the track and took advantage of the rail draw to make the running. His rider kicked rounding the home turn and he opened up an advantage that looked to be a winning one entering the final furlong, only for the winner to catch him on the line. This consistent performer did everything right and deserves to gain compensation before long. (op 9-2, tchd 5-1 in places)
Clockmaker(IRE) goes well on sharp tracks and had his chance but could not produce another gear. He is probably handicapped to his limit on turf at present. (op 10-1)
Dubai Dynamo, another consistent sort who has been in good form, ran his race again and was not far off previous course form with the principals. He ideally needs a slightly stiffer test. (tchd 10-1)

Kyllachy Star, another who was involved in the race at the May meeting that included three of the first four here, ran well again and should win a race, possibly around this track, at some point soon, if he can avoid his old rivals. (op 6-1)

Van Ellis ◆, having his first try on soft ground and taking on older rivals, tracked the pace but had nothing more to offer in the latter stages. He still did well for one so relatively inexperienced and will be of interest in a similar contest back on better ground. (op 13-2 tchd 7-1)

Orpsie Boy (IRE) has been running well this season and was close to previous form with the third, but he could do with being dropped a couple of pounds to aid his chance of scoring again. 16-1)

Cravat had to be held up from his outside draw and, although he ran on quite well for pressure, could never get close enough to land a blow. (op 28-1)

Rakaan(IRE) Official explanation: jockey said gelding had no more to give

2911 JOHN HALEWOOD MEMORIAL H'CAP — 1m 2f 75y

3:10 (3:11) (Class 2) (0-105,97) 4-Y-O+ **£31,505** (£9,430; £4,715; £2,360; £1,175) **Stalls** High

Form | | | | RPR

0166 **1** **Licence To Till (USA)**[8] 2655 5 -9-390 .... JoeFanning 8 100
(Mark Johnston) *mde all: rdn ins fnl f: r.o and a in command after* **16/1**

54 **2** 1 1/2 **Robemaker**[30] 1993 4 -9-188 .... LukeMorris 3 95
(John Gosden) *midfield: hdwy 3f out: rdn over 1f out: styd on to take 2nd fnl 100yds: nt rch wnr* **17/2**

0030 **3** 3/4 **Oceanway (USA)**[7] 2706 4 -9-289 .... SamHitchcott 1 95
(Mark Johnston) *prom: pushed along 3f out: wnt 2nd over 1f out: unable to chal wnr: lost 2nd wl ins fnl f: styd on same pce* **16/1**

1-12 **4** nk **Stand To Reason (IRE)**[20] 1999 4 -9-794 .... TedDurcan 2 99
(Mikael Magnusson) *coltish in padddock: racd keenly: trckd ldrs: rdn and nt qckn over 1f out: styd on same pce ins fnl f* **7/4**[1]

0134 **5** 1 **Tres Coronas (IRE)**[22] 2257 5 -9-087 .... LeeNewman 4 90
(David Barron) *in tch: effrt over 1f out: kpt on u.p ins fnl f: one pce fnl 50yds* **8/1**[3]

-010 **6** 3/4 **Resurge (IRE)**[8] 2655 7 -9-794 .... FergusSweeney 9 96
(Stuart Kittow) *hld up: rdn over 1f out: prog ins fnl f: styd on towards fin: nvr able to threaten ldrs* **12/1**

2-00 **7** 1/2 **Las Verglas Star (IRE)**[25] 1854 4 -8-1386 .... TonyHamilton 7 88
(Richard Fahey) *hld up: pushed along over 2f out: rdn and sme hdwy ins fnl f: eased whn no imp fnl 50yds* **33/1**

0134 **8** nse **Calaf**[14] 2473 4 -8-1184 .... FrannyNorton 11 84
(Richard Fahey) *plld hrd: hld up: bumnped wl over 5f out: effrt into midfield over 1f out: no imp fnl f* **25/1**

01-1 **9** 1 **War Poet**[42] 1654 5 -9-794 .... DanielTudhope 6 93
(David O'Meara) *in rr: pushed along over 2f out: nvr trbld ldrs* **6/1**[2]

3123 **10** 2 1/4 **Memory Cloth**[26] 2127 5 -9-996 .... BarryMcHugh 5 90
(Brian Ellison) *prom: chsd wnr after 2f: rdn and lost 2nd over 1f out: wknd ins fnl f* **6/1**[2]

3412 **11** 3 3/4 **Knowe Head (NZ)**[14] 2473 5 -8-477 .... LiamJones 13 64
(James Unett) *midfield: pushed along over 2f out: wknd over 1f out* **25/1**

2m 15.08s (3.88) **Going Correction** +0.50s/f (Yiel) **11**Ran SP% **116.7**
Speed ratings (Par 109): **104,102,102,101,101 100,100,100,99,97 94**
toteswingers:1&2:£7.30, 2&3:£16.00, 1&3:£11.00 CSF £141.16 CT £2216.95 TOTE £16.80 : £5.60, £3.20 , £5.30 ; EX 121.60 Trifecta £947.20 Pool: £1,408.07 - 1.10 winning units. .
Owner The Vine Accord **Bred** John Hettinger **Trained** Middleham Moor, N Yorks

FOCUS

Very healthy prize-money resulted in a decent field for this good-class handicap. Mark Johnston took this with Jutland last year and he was doubly represented this time, and his pair finished first and third. The three lowest stalls filled the frame behind the winner, who finally matched his AW form.

NOTEBOOK

Licence To Till (USA) ran well at Epsom the previous week, but a return to front-running tactics under a jockey who is formidable from the front enabled him to get back to winning ways off 7lb higher than for his previous success. Connections might be thinking in terms of Royal Ascot and then possibly the John Smith's Cup at York next month for him now. (op 12-1)

Robemaker finished behind today's third over C&D last time but reversed the form despite being worse off at the weights. He came out of the pack to chase the winner but could make little impression. (op 9-1)

Oceanway(USA) ◆ had to be ridden to hold her place from the inside stall, but got a good pitch and kept plugging away having been ridden a fair way from home. She can build on this on better ground and could be the type to figure at Goodwood later on. (op 18-1 tchd 20-1)

Stand To Reason (IRE) touched off by Resurge at the May meeting here, was prominent and keen early, and he could not pick up once in line for home. He can be forgiven this and is likely to do better on a stiffer track with a stronger pace. (op 9-4)

Tres Coronas (IRE) ran another solid race and connections will be hoping to find a race for him at Newcastle's Northumberland Plate meeting at the end of the month, as he likes that track and won at the meeting last year. (op 11-1)

Resurge(IRE) won here earlier in the season but, despite adopting similar tactics this time, could only stay on past beaten rivals in the straight. (op 10-1)

Las Verglas Star (IRE) had not shown much previously this spring but this was a better effort and he might be running back into form.

War Poet, raised 8lb for his recent win, was easy to back and never got involved, having been held up in the rear. This sharper track and the way the race was run probably did not suit his running style. (op 9-2)

Memory Cloth played up before going in the stalls and was a little keen just behind the leaders in the early stages. He weakened quite quickly in the last furlong as if he did not stay this longer trip. (tchd 13-2)

2912 LAMB'S NAVY RUM MAIDEN STKS — 5f 16y

3:40 (3:43) (Class 4) 2-Y-O **£5,175** (£1,540; £769 ; £384) **Stalls** Low

Form | | | | RPR

264 **1** **Botanic Garden**[11] 2587 2 -9-30 .... RichardMullen 6 79+
(David Brown) *hld up: hdwy wl over 1f out: sn led: r.o wl and edgd rt ins fnl f: wl in command towards fin* **10/3**[2]

2 2 3/4 **Starlight Angel (IRE)** 2 -8-120 .... LukeMorris 2 64
(Ronald Harris) *trckd ldrs: rdn and wnt 2nd over 1f out: nt gng pce of wnr fnl f* **5/1**

0 **3** 1 **Capo Rosso (IRE)**[36] 1818 2 -9-30 .... FrannyNorton 4 66
(Tom Dascombe) *w ldr tl rdn over 1f out: styd on same pce ins fnl f* **6/1**

0 **4** 2 1/4 **Colours Of Nature**[16] 2415 2 -9-30 .... TedDurcan 5 57
(Eric Alston) *in rr: rdn and hdwy to chse ldrs over 1f out: one pce ins fnl f* **25/1**

0 **5** 1 1/4 **Our Diane (IRE)**[10] 2603 2 -8-120 .... DanielTudhope 7 48+
(David O'Meara) *racd keenly: chsd ldrs: effrt on outer wl over 1f out: sn wknd* **9/2**[3]

0 **6** 1/2 **Showtime Girl (IRE)**[15] 2450 2 -8-120 .... TonyHamilton 8 46
(Tim Easterby) *in rr: pushed along over 2f out: nvr a threat* **12/1**

002 **7** 2 1/4 **Limit Up**[11] 2587 2 -9-30 .... JoeFanning 3 43
(Mark Johnston) *led: hung rt and hdd over 1f out: wknd ins fnl f: eased whn btn fnl 75yds* **9/4**[1]

1m 4.39s (3.39) **Going Correction** +0.50s/f (Yiel) **7**Ran SP% **114.5**
Speed ratings (Par 95): **92,87,86,82,80 79,76**
toteswingers:1&2:£4.10, 2&3:£4.40, 1&3:£3.00 CSF £20.31 TOTE £6.00 : £3.50 , £2.50 ; EX 21.60.
Owner J C Fretwell **Bred** The Kathryn Stud Ltd **Trained** Averham Park, Notts

FOCUS

The majority of the field in this juvenile maiden had experience, although their previous form was nothing more than fair. Not much depth but the winner produced a personal best.

NOTEBOOK

Botanic Garden had not appeared to go on from his debut effort, but that run was on soft ground and the return to a similar surface for the first time since worked the oracle. He missed the break and had to be ridden along, and was then too keen behind the leaders at halfway. However, he responded when asked for his effort and, when the gap opened near the rail as the leader wandered, he took full advantage. A novice event, possibly over 6f, may be on the agenda for him now. (op 4-1 tchd 9-2)

Starlight Angel (IRE) ◆, a 22,000GBP half-sister to a couple of useful juveniles, showed plenty of ability on this debut, chasing the leader and knowing her job. She was slightly hampered when that rival weakened, but stuck to her task and should be up to winning a maiden at least. (op 15-2)

Capo Rosso (IRE) showed ability on his debut and did so again here, especially as he had to race wide for much of the way. He may be of more interest on a faster surface. Franny Norton reported that the colt hung right on the bend. Official explanation: jockey said colt hung right on bend (op 13-2 tchd 11-2)

Colours Of Nature finished tailed off last on his debut and ran better this time, although he only stayed on from the back late. (op 18-1)

Our Diane (IRE) who made her debut in the Hilary Needler and ran well to a point, was encountering much slower ground this time and was easy in the market. She failed to pick up and might be more of a nursery type on faster going after another run. (op 7-2)

Limit Up jumped quickly and made the running but then faltered and hung right off the home turn and dropped away quickly, as if he had a problem. Joe Fanning reported that the colt stopped quickly in the home straight. Official explanation: jockey said colt stopped quickly in home straight (op 5-2)

2913 TSINGTAO CHINESE BEER CLASSIFIED CLAIMING STKS — 7f 2y

4:15 (4:15) (Class 4) 3-Y-O+ **£5,175** (£1,540; £769 ; £384) **Stalls** Low

Form | | | | RPR

4-46 **1** **Flameoftheforest (IRE)**[12] 2545 5 -9-779 ....(p) JoeFanning 4 86
(Ed de Giles) *hld up in tch: impr to ld over 1f out: r.o wl: in command towards fin* **4/1**[2]

0040 **2** 2 3/4 **Amazing Star (IRE)**[12] 2536 7 -9-477 .... FergusSweeney 2 76
(Declan Carroll) *dwlt: hld up: swtchd rt and hdwy over 1f out: styd on ins fnl f: tk 2nd towards fin: nt trble wnr* **17/2**

40-0 **3** 3/4 **Koo And The Gang (IRE)**[26] 2119 5 -9-575 .... BarryMcHugh 11 75
(Brian Ellison) *in tch: wnt prom over 4f out: ev ch 2f out: rdn over 1f out: styd on same pce ins fnl f* **14/1**

3204 **4** 1/2 **Rigolleto (IRE)**[9] 2632 4 -9-578 .... SamHitchcott 14 74
(Mick Channon) *pushed along early to go prom: led over 5f out: hdd over 1f out: no ex fnl 75yds* **8/1**

4260 **5** hd **Lockantanks**[91] 866 5 -9-1078 .... LukeMorris 3 78
(Michael Appleby) *trckd ldrs: rdn over 1f out: kpt on same pce ins fnl f* **5/1**[3]

3001 **6** 1 1/4 **Jungle Bay**[19] 2355 5 -9-677 ....(p) TedDurcan 1 71
(Jane Chapple-Hyam) *led: hdd over 5f out: remained prom: rdn whn n.m.r over 1f out: nt qckn: one pce ins fnl f: eased whn btn fnl 50yds* **11/4**[1]

6106 **7** 8 **Marksbury**[24] 2161 5 -8-1057 .... MatthewLawson(5) 7 45
(Mark Brisbourne) *in rr: u.p over 2f out: nvr on terms* **50/1**

-335 **8** 8 **Jedward (IRE)**[20] 2310 5 -9-580 .... FrannyNorton 6 28
(Richard Fahey) *racd keenly: handy: hmpd after 1f: u.p over 3f out: wknd over 2f out* **4/1**[2]

1m 30.12s (3.62) **Going Correction** +0.50s/f (Yiel)
WFA 3 from 4yo+ 10lb **8**Ran SP% **113.6**
Speed ratings (Par 105): **99,95,95,94,94 92,83,74**
toteswingers:1&2:£8.20, 2&3:£13.10, 1&3:£8.70 CSF £36.91 TOTE £4.40 : £1.10 , £2.30 , £4.00 ; EX 39.10 .
Owner Mrs Hugh McAlister **Bred** Western Bloodstock **Trained** Ledbury, H'fords
■ Stewards' Enquiry : Sam Hitchcott two-day ban: careless riding (Jun 24-25)

FOCUS

What had looked a competitive classified claimer was weakened by the withdrawal of five of the runners, including the 2011 winner. The form is rated slightly negatively.

Jedward(IRE) Official explanation: jockey said mare lost its action in home straight

2914 LAMBRINI ORIGINAL H'CAP — 5f 16y

4:50 (4:51) (Class 3) (0-95,90) 3-Y-O **£8,409** (£2,502; £1,250 ; £625) **Stalls** Low

Form | | | | RPR

0424 **1** **Beau Mistral (IRE)**[17] 2400 3 -8-271 oh2 .... CathyGannon 1 84
(Paul Green) *mde all: rdn over 1f out: r.o wl: in command fnl 110yds* **11/1**

2-12 **2** 2 3/4 **Sonko (IRE)**[29] 2028 3 -9-285 ....(p) FrannyNorton 6 88
(Tim Pitt) *chsd ldrs: wnt 2nd over 1f out: sn rdn and lugged in bhd wnr: one pce fnl 110yds* **11/4**[2]

1150 **3** 1 1/4 **Rusty Rocket (IRE)**[7] 2714 3 -8-1079 .... JoeFanning 7 78+
(Paul Green) *hld up: rdn and hdwy 1f out: kpt on to take 3rd wl ins fnl f: nt rch ldrs* **5/1**[3]

4600 **4** 1/2 **Bubbly Ballerina**[19] 2347 3 -8-1382 .... LiamJones 5 79
(Alan Bailey) *chsd ldrs: rdn and outpcd 2f out: edgd rt ins fnl f: kpt on but no imp on ldrs* **16/1**

3335 **5** 3 3/4 **Signifer (IRE)**[2] 2853 3 -9-285 ....(v) SamHitchcott 4 68
(Mick Channon) *hld up: rdn and hdwy 2f out: chsd ldrs over 1f out: nvr able to chal: wknd wl ins fnl f: eased whn btn towards fin* **6/1**

1-22 **6** 8 **Royal Reyah**[23] 2205 3 -8-776 .... FergusSweeney 2 31+
(Stuart Kittow) *in rr: pushed along over 3f out: eased whn wl btn ins fnl f* **5/2**[1]

-601 **7** 17 **Powerful Wind (IRE)**[14] 2509 3 -9-790 .... LukeMorris 3
(Ronald Harris) *w wnr: rdn 2f out: lost 2nd over 1f out: sn wknd: eased whn wl btn ins fnl f* **8/1**

1m 3.24s (2.24) **Going Correction** +0.55s/f (Yiel) **7**Ran SP% **111.5**
Speed ratings (Par 103): **104,99,97,96,90 78,50**
toteswingers:1&2:£5.50, 2&3:£2.00, 1&3:£8.90 CSF £39.33 TOTE £20.10 : £7.00 , £1.80 ; EX 58.30.
Owner The Winsor Not Group **Bred** John McEnery **Trained** Lydiate, Merseyside

FOCUS

A good 3yo sprint handicap, despite the smallish field, but a rather surprise winner. There seemed no fluke about this.

NOTEBOOK

Beau Mistral(IRE) had shown she could handle cut in the ground in the past but had appeared most effective on fast going. However, she jumped well from the inside stall and made all the running, finding extra when asked to see off the runner-up. This was a decent effort from 2lb out of the handicap but she has struggled off higher marks in the past and will need things to fall as well as they did here to follow up, although she does go well for Cathy Gannon, who is now 2-3 on her. (op 12-1 tchd 14-1)

Sonko(IRE) is most effective when leading but wasn't able to this time. However, she looked the likely winner when produced to challenge the leader over a furlong out, only to have nothing in reserve when the winner found more. (op 5-2 tchd 9-4)

Rusty Rocket(IRE) ran pretty well considering he had to race wide for most of the way, having been drawn on the outside. He has scored over 7f and is worth another try over further. (op 6-1)

Bubbly Ballerina goes well on a sharp track but is arguably better on a sounder surface and had nothing more to offer in the straight. (op 12-1)

Signifer(IRE) was easy in the market and never got involved. It is possible his run two days previously had taken the edge off him. (tchd 11-2 and 15-2)

Royal Reyah missed the break and was always at the back. This was disappointing on ground he handles. Fergus Sweeney reported that the colt was never travelling. Official explanation: jockey said colt never trravelled (op 3-1)

Powerful Wind(IRE) tried to stay with the winner but dropped away quickly in the straight and was eased. He is much better on fast ground. Luke Morris reported that the colt stopped quickly. Official explanation: jockey said colt stopped quickly (op 7-1)

2915 HALEWOOD INTERNATIONAL FILLIES' H'CAP — 1m 2f 75y

5:25 (5:26) (Class 5) (0-70,69) 4-Y-O+ — **£4,528** (£1,347; £673; £336) — **Stalls** High

Form — RPR

1551 **1** **Isdaal**[25] [2149] 5-9-1 **66** ... AshleyHamblett(3) 9 — 74
(Kevin Morgan) *hld up: hdwy on outer over 1f out: r.o ins fnl f to ld last strides* **14/1**

3123 **2** *hd* **Favorite Girl (GER)**[81] [978] 4-9-4 **66** ... LukeMorris 3 — 74
(Michael Appleby) *midfield: hdwy 3f out: effrt to chse ldrs over 2f out: sn n.m.r: rdn over 1f out: led ent fnl f: sn edgd lft: hdd fnl strides* **9/2**[2]

-250 **3** *2* **Sacco D'Oro**[2] [767] 6-8-2 **50** oh5 ... (b) CathyGannon 5 — 54
(Michael Mullineaux) *missed break: in rr: rdn and hdwy over 1f out: styd on ins fnl f: tk 3rd towards fin: nt rch front pair* **33/1**

15-4 **4** *1* **Ambala**[22] [2233] 4-9-4 **66** ... TedDurcan 7 — 68+
(Chris Wall) *chsd ldrs: led over 2f out: rdn over 1f out: hdd ent fnl f: one pce fnl 75yds* **4/1**[1]

2205 **5** *1* **Zenarinda**[39] [1743] 5-8-11 **64** ... HarryPoulton(5) 4 — 64
(Mark H Tompkins) *broke wl: in tch: outpcd over 2f out: edgd lft and clsd to chse ldrs over 1f out: kpt on same pce ins fnl f* **12/1**

1023 **6** *2* **Dazzling Valentine**[8] [2679] 4-9-5 **67** ... LiamJones 8 — 63
(Alan Bailey) *midfield: pushed along 3f out: one pce u.p ins fnl f* **11/1**

-304 **7** *1 ½* **Sangar**[12] [2539] 4-9-5 **67** ... BarryMcHugh 10 — 60
(Ollie Pears) *midfield: hdwy 4f out: chalng 2f out: rdn over 1f out: wknd ins fnl f* **7/1**

0-00 **8** *4* **Goldenveil (IRE)**[16] [2414] 4-9-0 **62** ... (b) TonyHamilton 1 — 47
(Richard Fahey) *racd keenly: chsd ldrs: n.m.r and hmpd 2f out: wknd over 1f out* **7/1**

6133 **9** *6* **Mount Abora (IRE)**[126] [433] 5-9-7 **69** ... FrannyNorton 2 — 43
(Ian Williams) *chsd ldr: led over 3f out: hdd over 2f out: wknd over 1f out* **11/2**[3]

6-30 **10** *10* **Ashkalara**[17] [2389] 5-8-11 **59** ... JoeFanning 6 — 13
(Stuart Howe) *hld up: u.p 4f out: nvr a threat* **12/1**

3056 **11** *46* **Ellielusive (IRE)**[10] [2601] 5-8-2 **50** ... (p) PaulQuinn 11
(Mark Brisbourne) *sn led: pushed along 5f out: hdd over 3f out: sn wknd: wl bhd 2f out: t.o* **33/1**

2m 17.91s (6.71) **Going Correction** +0.55s/f (Yiel) — **11** Ran SP% **114.8**

Speed ratings (Par 100): **95,94,93,92,91 90,88,85,80,72 36**

toteswingers:1&2:£12.70, 2&3:£12.30, 1&3:£48.20 CSF £74.20 CT £2035.17 TOTE £19.40: £4.00, £1.90, £10.00; EX 88.30.

Owner Roemex Ltd **Bred** Shadwell Estate Company Limited **Trained** Gazeley, Suffolk

FOCUS

A modest but competitive fillies' handicap run 2.83secs slower than the earlier feature race. The winner carried over her AW progress.

T/Plt: £1,569.10 to a £1 stake. Pool of £83,744.67 - 38.96 winning tickets. T/Qpdt: £295.50 to a £1 stake. Pool of £4,696.91 - 11.76 winning tickets. DO

2880 DONCASTER (L-H)

Saturday, June 9

OFFICIAL GOING: Soft (good to soft in places) changing to good to soft (soft in places) after race 1 (2.05)

Wind: Fresh against Weather: Cloudy with sunny periods

2916 FREEBETS.CO.UK H'CAP — 1m (S)

2:05 (2:05) (Class 2) (0-105,98) 3-Y-O — **£12,938** (£3,850; £1,924; £962) — **Stalls** High

Form — RPR

-100 **1** **Chapter Seven**[14] [2485] 3-8-11 **88** ... RobertWinston 8 — 96+
(Richard Fahey) *hld up in rr: nt clr run over 2f out and sn swtchd lft: effrt and hdwy to chse ldrs whn hmpd jst ins fnl f: swtchd rt and rdn: qcknd wl to ld last 50yds* **10/1**

1 **2** *¾* **Well Painted (IRE)**[21] [2273] 3-8-13 **93** ... AdamBeschizza(3) 7 — 98
(William Haggas) *hld up: hdwy over 2f out: rdn to chal over 1f out: drvn to ld ins fnl f: hdd and nt qckn last 50yds* **9/1**

2250 **3** *¾* **Mister Music**[7] [2701] 3-9-4 **95** ... PatDobbs 5 — 99
(Richard Hannon) *trckd ldrs: hdwy 2f out: rdn and ev ch whn edgd lft jst ins fnl f: kpt on same pce* **22/1**

1040 **4** *nk* **Kickingthelilly**[14] [2490] 3-8-4 **81** ... ChrisCatlin 6 — 84
(Rae Guest) *towards rr: hdwy on wd outside wl over 1f out: rdn to chal and ev ch ins fnl f: drvn and no ex last 100yds* **33/1**

-316 **5** *½* **Shamaal Nibras (USA)**[21] [2263] 3-8-11 **88** ... JimmyFortune 1 — 90+
(Richard Hannon) *stdd s and hld up towards rr: stdy hdwy on outer 3f out: led 2f out: sn rdn and hung bdly rt to rails wl over 1f out: drvn and hdd ins fnl f: kpt on same pce* **16/1**

1410 **6** *4 ½* **Warfare**[24] [2182] 3-8-4 **81** ... AmyRyan 3 — 73
(Kevin Ryan) *t.k.h: prom: cl up 3f out: rdn along over 2f out and sn wknd* **8/1**[3]

1-6 **7** *4* **Assizes**[28] [2076] 3-8-11 **88** ... GrahamLee 9 — 70
(Mark Johnston) *led: rdn along 3f out: hdd 2f out: wkng whn bdly hmpd wl over 1f out: bhd after* **22/1**

226- **8** *1 ¼* **Gold City (IRE)**[252] [6535] 3-9-7 **98** ... SilvestreDeSousa 4 — 77
(Saeed Bin Suroor) *trckd ldrs: hdwy and cl up 3f out: rdn along and hld whn bdly hmpd wl over 1f out: bhd after* **8/1**[3]

01 **9** *1 ½* **Mawasem**[33] [1922] 3-9-4 **95** ... PaulHanagan 2 — 71
(Sir Michael Stoute) *prom on outer: effrt and cl up 3f out: rdn along 2f out: drvn whn hmpd wl over 1f out: wknd after* **11/4**[2]

6-11 **10** *1 ¼* **Grey Mirage**[43] [1645] 3-8-12 **89** ... WilliamBuick 10 — 62
(Marco Botti) *trckd ldrs on inner: hdwy 3f out: rdn along 2f out: n.m.r and sltly hmpd wl over 1f out: sn btn* **9/4**[1]

1m 42.67s (3.37) **Going Correction** +0.45s/f (Yiel) — **10** Ran SP% **116.3**

Speed ratings (Par 105): **101,100,99,99,98 94,90,88,87,86**

Tote Swingers: 1&2 £17.40, 1&3 £39.60, 2&3 £26.90 CSF £93.43 CT £1931.77 TOTE £12.00: £3.30, £3.00, £4.40; EX 107.90 TRIFECTA Not won..

Owner T G & Mrs M E Holdcroft **Bred** Bearstone Stud **Trained** Musley Bank, N Yorks

■ Stewards' Enquiry : Jimmy Fortune four-day ban: careless riding (Jun 24-27)

Pat Dobbs two-day ban: careless riding (Jun 24-25)

FOCUS

This looked a decent 3-y-o handicap and it produced a thrilling finish, but it was also quite a rough race. The fourth helps to set the level.

NOTEBOOK

Chapter Seven had the ground come right for him and would have been an unlucky loser. Ridden with plenty of patience, he had to be manoeuvred to try to find racing room well over 1f from home and was hampered when the gap between the second and third closed inside the last, but he managed to get through and put in a sustained run. It does seem he needs cut to show his best. (tchd 11-1)

Well Painted(IRE), winner of a 7f Newbury maiden on his debut last month (race has produced a couple of subsequent winners), had every chance once switched left over 1f out and this was another decent effort, given his inexperience. (op 8-1)

Mister Music's effort at Epsom seven days earlier could be ignored and this staying-on effort was much more like it back on a soft surface, but he lacks the scope of a few of these. (op 25-1 tchd 20-1)

Kickingthelilly stayed on well from off the pace towards the outside and wasn't beaten far. This confirms she isn't just a Polytrack filly, but she is another lacking the scope for further improvement of some of her rivals.

Shamaal Nibras(USA) looked the one to beat when hitting the front on the outside over 1f out, but once there he hung away to his right, ended up against the stands' rail, and was run right out of it. He has so far shown his best form on Polytrack. Official explanation: jockey said colt hung right-handed (tchd 18-1)

Warfare may have had excuses for his modest effort at York last time and was proven in the ground, but didn't get home after racing keenly early. (tchd 15-2)

Mawasem was hampered when Shamaal Nibras hung across him over a furlong from home, but looked to have run his race by then. The ground may have found him out. Official explanation: jockey said colt hung right-handed (op 3-1 tchd 5-2)

Grey Mirage, bidding for a hat-trick off a 7lb higher mark, showed when winning at Sandown last time that he could cope with testing ground, so this poor effort is hard to explain. His rider reported that the colt stopped quickly. Official explanation: jockey said colt stopped quickly (op 5-2 tchd 11-4)

2917 E B F CROWNHOTEL-BAWTRY.COM MAIDEN FILLIES' STKS — 6f 110y

2:40 (2:41) (Class 5) 2-Y-O — **£3,946** (£1,174; £586; £293) — **Stalls** High

Form — RPR

1 **Go Angellica (IRE)** 2-9-0 0 ... MartinLane 12 — 81+
(David Simcock) *towards rr: hdwy 1/2-way: chsd ldng pair over 1f out and sn rdn: styd on u.p fnl f to ld nr fin* **22/1**

34 **2** *½* **Rio's Pearl**[26] [2124] 2-8-11 0 ... HarryBentley(3) 13 — 80+
(Ralph Beckett) *led: rdn over 1f out: clr whn edgd lft wl ins fnl f: hdd and no ex nr fin* **6/1**[2]

2 **3** *½* **Cruck Realta**[16] [2407] 2-9-0 0 ... MatthewDavies 11 — 78
(Mick Channon) *trckd ldr: effrt 2f out: rdn over 1f out: kpt on same pce ins fnl f* **15/2**[3]

6 **4** *3 ¾* **Art Mistress (IRE)**[14] [2508] 2-9-0 0 ... DavidAllan 9 — 68+
(Tim Easterby) *towards rr: hdwy 2f out: nt clr run and swtchd rt jst over 1f out: styd on fnl f: nrst fin* **12/1**

2 **5** *2 ¼* **Ayr Missile**[15] [2450] 2-9-0 0 ... GrahamLee 15 — 62
(Kevin Ryan) *trckd ldrs: hdwy 2f out: sn rdn and one pce fr over 1f out* **4/1**[1]

53 **6** *hd* **Curl (IRE)**[15] [2450] 2-9-0 0 ... PatDobbs 14 — 61
(Richard Hannon) *trckd ldrs: effrt 2f out: rdn along wl over 1f out: sn one pce* **6/1**[2]

0 **7** *¾* **Penny Garcia**[11] [2587] 2-9-0 0 ... DuranFentiman 6 — 59
(Tim Easterby) *in tch: rdn along on outer 1/2-way: sn outpcd* **50/1**

8 *1 ½* **Hundredsnthousands (IRE)** 2-9-0 0 ... MichaelO'Connell 10 — 55
(John Quinn) *dwlt: a towards rr* **16/1**

9 *nk* **Eghnaa** 2-9-0 0 ... PaulHanagan 7 — 54
(Ed Dunlop) *t.k.h early: hld up: sme hdwy 1/2-way: sn rdn and btn* **8/1**

6 **10** *5* **Open Letter (IRE)**[15] [2450] 2-9-0 0 ... SilvestreDeSousa 8 — 40
(Mark Johnston) *prom: rdn along wl over 2f out: sn wknd* **4/1**[1]

11 *3* **Grey Street** 2-9-0 0 ... DavidNolan 2 — 32
(Richard Fahey) *dwlt: sn cl up on outer: rdn along 1/2-way: sn wknd* **14/1**

1m 23.0s (3.10) **Going Correction** +0.45s/f (Yiel) — **11** Ran SP% **118.0**

Speed ratings (Par 90): **100,99,98,94,92 91,90,89,88,83 79**

Tote Swingers: 1&2 £26.70, 1&3 £28.80, 2&3 £9.60 CSF £149.46 TOTE £28.10: £7.00, £2.60, £2.50; EX 242.90.

Owner Ahmed Jaber **Bred** Rabbah Bloodstock Limited **Trained** Newmarket, Suffolk

FOCUS

This extended 6f trip into a headwind on easy ground would have been quite a stamina test for these 2-y-o fillies. The level is fluid with the runner-up the best guide.

NOTEBOOK

Go Angellica(IRE) ◆, a half-sister to a 2-y-o 6f winner, was off the bridle over 2f from home, so it was some effort from her to stick at it and outstay two rivals with previous experience in these conditions. She can only improve. (op 25-1 tchd 20-1)

Rio's Pearl was disappointing at Windsor on her second start considering how well she ran in a Salisbury conditions event on her debut, but this was more like it and having hit the gates running and set the pace, she looked likely to score coming to the last furlong. However, she then started to wobble and hang away to her left, giving the winner the chance she needed. She was racing beyond the minimum trip for the first time, but it would be harsh to blame a lack of stamina and she can surely find a race at some stage. (op 5-1)

Cruck Realta found only the subsequent Listed winner Sky Lantern too good in a five-runner maiden on her Goodwood debut and kept battling away, having been handy from the start. She should find a race before long. (op 8-1)

Art Mistress(IRE) ◆ ran well for a long way on her York debut, but was held up this time. She was noted making some decent late progress and a race should be found for her before long. (op 14-1)

Ayr Missile didn't really progress from her debut, but the ground was very different here.

Open Letter(IRE) finished behind both Ayr Missile and Curl at Haydock and was in trouble some way out. Her rider reported that the filly hung right-handed. Official explanation: jockey said filly hung right-handed (op 5-1 tchd 11-2)

2918 BRENDA ARMSTRONG 75TH BIRTHDAY MAIDEN STKS 5f
3:15 (3:16) (Class 5) 3-Y-O+ **£2,911** (£866; £432; £216) **Stalls** High

Form				RPR
522	1		**Sir Maximilian (IRE)**[28] 2065 3-9-3 77 WilliamBuick 8	84+
			(Ed Dunlop) *in tch: hdwy 1/2-way: trckd ldrs and nt clr run over 1f out: swtchd lft and qcknd to ld ent fnl f: sn clr: easily* **11/10**[1]	
	2	6	**Vanity's Girl (IRE)** 3-8-12 0 GrahamLee 3	54+
			(John Quinn) *dwlt and in rr: hdwy wl over 1f out: rdn and styd on wl fnl f: no ch w wnr* **16/1**	
03-	3	1/2	**Million Faces**[257] 6406 3-8-12 0 ChrisCatlin 7	53
			(Rae Guest) *slt ld: rdn wl over 1f out: drvn and hdd ent fnl f: kpt on same pce* **11/4**[2]	
52	4	1	**Imperial Legend (IRE)**[7] 2695 3-9-3 0 AdrianNicholls 10	54
			(David Nicholls) *cl up: rdn 2f out and ev ch tl wknd ent fnl f* **7/1**[3]	
0	5	1 3/4	**Majestic Angel (IRE)**[21] 2262 3-8-5 0 JasonHart(7) 4	43
			(Brian Rothwell) *chsd ldrs: rdn along 2f out: sn outpcd* **50/1**	
0	6	hd	**Planetex (IRE)**[7] 2695 3-9-3 0 MichaelO'Connell 1	47
			(John Quinn) *cl up: rdn wl over 1f out and ev ch tl wknd appr fnl f* **12/1**	
4	7	2	**Mon Duchess**[26] 2121 4-9-5 0 DavidNolan 2	35
			(Lawrence Mullaney) *chsd ldrs: rdn along 2f out: sn wknd* **14/1**	
0-	8	29	**Too Ambitious**[196] 7555 3-8-5 0 JackDuern(7) 6	
			(Reg Hollinshead) *awkward and fly leapt s: s.i.s and a bhd* **25/1**	

1m 1.98s (1.48) **Going Correction** +0.45s/f (Yiel)
WFA 3 from 4yo+ 7lb **8** Ran SP% **112.8**
Speed ratings (Par 103): **106,96,95,94,91 90,87,41**
Tote Swingers: 1&2 £4.20, 1&3 £1.60, 2&3 £8.30 CSF £21.27 TOTE £2.00: £1.10, £3.30, £1.40; EX 17.40.

Owner Sir Robert Ogden **Bred** Holborn Trust Co **Trained** Newmarket, Suffolk

FOCUS
An uncompetitive maiden, and the favourite duly bolted up. The form is rated around the winner to the best of his previous form.

Too Ambitious Official explanation: jockey said filly was slowly away

2919 FREEBETS.CO.UK FREE BETS H'CAP 7f
3:45 (3:45) (Class 2) (0-105,102) 4-Y-O+ **£12,938** (£3,850; £1,924; £962) **Stalls** High

Form				RPR
1-10	1		**Tariq Too**[28] 2068 5-8-7 91 HarryBentley(3) 7	103
			(Amy Weaver) *dwlt: hld up: smooth hdwy wl over 2f out: chsd ldr jst over 1f out: rdn to chal ent fnl f: kpt on u.p to ld last 100yds* **7/2**[1]	
2565	2	hd	**Scarf (AUS)**[28] 2075 5-9-7 102 SilvestreDeSousa 9	113
			(Saeed Bin Suroor) *t.k.h early: trckd ldrs: hdwy over 2f out: rdn to ld wl over 1f out: jnd and drvn ins fnl f: hdd and no ex last 100yds* **18/1**	
53-4	3	3 1/4	**Lord Aeryn (IRE)**[16] 2417 5-8-7 88 PaulHanagan 3	91
			(Richard Fahey) *hld up towards rr: hdwy 2f out: rdn over 1f out: styd on fnl f: nrst fin* **5/1**[2]	
1400	4	3/4	**Karaka Jack**[14] 2489 5-8-3 84 AdrianNicholls 5	85
			(David Nicholls) *hld up in rr: hdwy 2f out: rdn wl over 1f out: styd on fnl f: nrst fin* **14/1**	
-025	5	3/4	**Grissom (IRE)**[14] 2472 6-8-11 92 DavidAllan 8	91
			(Tim Easterby) *hld up in tch: hdwy to chse ldrs over 2f out: sn rdn and no imp fr over 1f out* **7/1**	
-004	6	1 1/2	**Fathsta (IRE)**[15] 2446 7-8-7 88 WilliamBuick 11	83
			(David Simcock) *hld up in rr: sme hdwy wl over 1f out: sn rdn and n.d* **11/2**[3]	
4303	7	1/2	**Prime Exhibit**[22] 2243 7-7-13 87 ShirleyTeasdale(7) 10	80
			(David Nicholls) *led: rdn along over 2f out: hdd wl over 1f out: grad wknd* **9/1**	
3-62	8	1 1/2	**Louis The Pious**[14] 2472 4-9-0 95 GrahamLee 6	85
			(Kevin Ryan) *trckd ldrs: rdn along over 2f out: sn btn* **13/2**	
4052	9	3 3/4	**Kingscroft (IRE)**[7] 2697 4-8-4 85 AndrewElliott 2	65
			(Mark Johnston) *chsd ldrs: rdn along wl over 2f out: sn wknd* **9/1**	
0004	10	7	**Bay Knight (IRE)**[3] 2819 6-8-13 97 SophieDoyle(3) 4	59
			(J S Moore) *cl up: rdn along wl over 2f out: sn wknd* **20/1**	

1m 27.77s (1.47) **Going Correction** +0.45s/f (Yiel) **10** Ran SP% **116.8**
Speed ratings (Par 109): **109,108,105,104,103 101,101,99,95,87**
Tote Swingers: 1&2 £12.10, 1&3 £4.30, 2&3 £11.60 CSF £70.06 CT £325.71 TOTE £4.80: £1.70, £4.80, £1.60; EX 79.40 Trifecta £746.20 Part won. Pool: £1,008.50 - 0.62 winning units..

Owner Bringloe Clarke Spain Hensby Partridge **Bred** D R Botterill **Trained** Newmarket, Suffolk

FOCUS
A decent handicap, run at a good pace, and the form looks solid.

NOTEBOOK
Tariq Too didn't run at all badly in the Victoria Cup last time when bidding for a hat-trick and the ground appeared to have come right for him, as he wasn't going to run if there was insufficient rain. Ridden with a lot of confidence, he had to work hard to get to the runner-up and found that rival a tough nut to crack, but he was always doing just enough. He may not have conditions in his favour for much longer if summer ever arrives, but this was a nice prize to win. (op 4-1 tchd 9-2)

Scarf(AUS) ◆, back in a handicap after a couple of unsuccessful tries at Listed level, ran a blinder. Keen early, he carted himself to the front over 1f out, but despite his earlier exertions he fought back gamely when headed. He's in the Wokingham, and although he hasn't run over 6f since winning over it in Australia a year ago, he could be interesting in that contest if the ground came up soft. (op 16-1)

Lord Aeryn(IRE) stayed on over the last 2f and ran a nice race on ground that may have been softer than ideal. (op 9-2 tchd 6-1)

Karaka Jack had been disappointing in his last two starts after starting off the season so well, but this staying-on effort was much better, especially as he was trying to come from last place. (op 16-1 tchd 12-1)

Grissom(IRE) finished behind Louis The Pious on fast ground at Chester last time, having been ahead of that rival on soft ground the time before. He had his chance over 1f from home, but couldn't go through with it and this mark is proving just beyond him, while he may prefer an easier 7f when the going is testing. (tchd 13-2)

Fathsta(IRE) never got into it and is on a losing run of 15. (tchd 5-1 and 6-1)

Prime Exhibit is well handicapped these days and ran well on his debut for the yard last time, but he was easily picked off here after making the running and isn't easy to win with (3-29). (op 11-1 tchd 12-1)

Louis The Pious dropped away after holding every chance and probably found the ground against him. (op 6-1)

Kingscroft(IRE) was in trouble at halfway. (op 11-1 tchd 8-1)

2920 FREE BETTING WITH FREEBETS.CO.UK CONDITIONS STKS 1m 2f 60y
4:20 (4:20) (Class 2) 3-Y-O **£12,938** (£3,850; £1,924; £962) **Stalls** Low

Form				RPR
61-2	1		**Starboard**[23] 2198 3-8-12 97 WilliamBuick 3	105+
			(John Gosden) *trckd ldr: cl up over 3f out: chal 2f out: rdn to ld ent fnl f: drvn and edgd rt last 100yds: kpt on* **6/4**[2]	
1-13	2	3/4	**Kingsdesire (IRE)**[29] 2026 3-8-12 94 (t) PaulHanagan 4	103
			(Marco Botti) *hld up in rr: hdwy on outer over 2f out: rdn to chal over 1f out: drvn and ev ch ins fnl f: no ex last 50yds* **11/2**[3]	
1112	3	1 1/4	**Expense Claim (IRE)**[15] 2445 3-8-12 97 JimmyFortune 1	101
			(Andrew Balding) *led: rdn and qcknd over 2f out: drvn over 1f out: hdd ent fnl f: no ex last 100yds* **5/4**[1]	
3-13	4	10	**Counterglow (IRE)**[91] 873 3-9-1 104 SilvestreDeSousa 2	85
			(Mahmood Al Zarooni) *trckd ldng pair: effrt over 2f out: rdn wl over 1f out: wknd appr fnl f* **15/2**	

2m 11.86s (2.46) **Going Correction** +0.15s/f (Good) **4** Ran SP% **111.6**
Speed ratings (Par 105): **96,95,94,86**
CSF £9.49 TOTE £2.00; EX 11.80.

Owner K Abdulla **Bred** Juddmonte Farms Ltd **Trained** Newmarket, Suffolk

FOCUS
Luca Cumani had won the two previous runnings with horses who respectively went on to win and finish second in the Hampton Court at Royal Ascot. The Newmarket trainer did not have a runner this year, but this looked a classy little contest, even though the quartet strolled around for 7f before things picked up. The third is rated close to his latest Goodwood form.

NOTEBOOK
Starboard was up more than 2f in trip after getting turned over at odds-on in a three-runner Newmarket conditions event on his reappearance, but showed that running to be all wrong here. Always on the shoulder of the leader, his attitude when asked to go to win his race was impressive, as he had to dig deep to get on top of the third horse and then withstand the runner-up. He holds entries in the King Edward VII and the Eclipse, and while he will need to come on plenty to figure in races like those, it does show the regard in which he is held. (op 7-4 tchd 2-1)
Kingsdesire(IRE) appeared to be dropped out last on purpose and although he was the first of the quartet off the bridle, he responded once switched out wide and stayed on to press the winner all the way to the line. He had looked all at sea in the deep ground when beaten a long way into third of four behind Astrology in the Dee Stakes, but while this ground wasn't anything like as testing it still may be that he needs a sounder surface to show his best. (tchd 5-1)
Expense Claim(IRE) has been highly progressive so far this season and lost little in defeat when narrowly beaten in a four-runner Listed contest at Goodwood last time. Having been left alone to do his own thing out in front again, he tried to quicken from the front passing the 3f pole and kept on battling until the last half-furlong. He is very game, but may not be the easiest to place now. (tchd 11-8)
Counterglow(IRE) hadn't been seen since running two good races at Meydan in March and ended up well beaten. His two wins have come when fresh, so fitness should not have been an issue, but he may not have liked the ground. (op 7-1)

2921 KAT COMMUNICATIONS KNOWLEDGE ABOUT TELECOMS H'CAP 1m 4f
4:55 (4:55) (Class 4) (0-85,84) 4-Y-O+ **£5,175** (£1,540; £769; £384) **Stalls** Low

Form				RPR
-106	1		**Camborne**[22] 2257 4-9-7 84 (p) WilliamBuick 5	104+
			(John Gosden) *trckd ldrs: hdwy 3f out: rdn to ld over 1f out: clr ins fnl f: easily* **5/1**[2]	
0-20	2	7	**Battery Power**[16] 2419 4-9-0 77 JimmyFortune 1	84
			(Mark H Tompkins) *hld up towards rr: hdwy 3f out: chsd ldrs 2f out: rdn and styd on fnl f: no ch w wnr* **15/2**	
2-20	3	1 1/2	**Getabuzz**[14] 2504 4-9-1 78 DavidAllan 6	82
			(Tim Easterby) *hld up in tch: hdwy 3f out: rdn to chse ldrs 2f out: sn drvn and kpt on same pce* **4/1**[1]	
0-00	4	1/2	**Royal Trooper (IRE)**[16] 2419 6-9-0 77 PaulMulrennan 7	80
			(James Given) *trckd ldrs: hdwy to ld 3f out: rdn 2f out: hdd over 1f out: grad wknd* **14/1**	
/0-0	5	hd	**Bollin Felix**[24] 2180 8-8-10 80 RachelRichardson(7) 4	83
			(Tim Easterby) *towards rr: hdwy and in tch 1/2-way: rdn to chse ldrs 3f out: drvn 2f out and no imp* **20/1**	
1-64	6	2 3/4	**All The Winds (GER)**[19] 2346 7-9-3 80 RussKennemore 8	78
			(Shaun Lycett) *dwlt and in rr: hdwy on inner over 3f out: rdn over 2f out: n.d* **10/1**	
5150	7	1 3/4	**Amazing Blue Sky**[16] 2419 6-8-11 77 DaleSwift(3) 12	73
			(Ruth Carr) *led: rdn along over 3f out: sn hdd & wknd* **12/1**	
21-0	8	2 1/4	**Snow Hill**[47] 1566 4-9-1 78 PaulHanagan 10	70
			(Chris Wall) *hld up in rr: hdwy over 4f out: rdn along wl over 2f out: sn btn* **6/1**[3]	
-001	9	3 1/2	**Sedgwick**[21] 2260 10-7-11 67 ShirleyTeasdale(7) 3	53
			(Shaun Harris) *hld up: a towards rr* **10/1**	
04-0	10	nse	**Pendragon (USA)**[22] 2257 9-9-3 83 PaulPickard(3) 2	69
			(Brian Ellison) *trckd ldng pair: rdn along over 3f out: wknd over 2f out* **9/1**	
54-0	11	10	**Twice Bitten**[9] 2637 4-8-6 69 KirstyMilczarek 9	39
			(James Toller) *prom: chsd ldr after 2f: rdn along 4f out: sn wknd* **8/1**	

2m 33.86s (-1.04) **Going Correction** +0.15s/f (Good) **11** Ran SP% **121.1**
Speed ratings (Par 105): **109,104,103,103,102 101,99,98,96,96 89**
Tote Swingers: 1&2 £7.80, 1&3 £4.70, 2&3 £8.20 CSF £43.83 CT £168.19 TOTE £5.30: £1.50, £2.80, £2.40; EX 47.00.

Owner H R H Princess Haya Of Jordan **Bred** Southill Stud **Trained** Newmarket, Suffolk

FOCUS
This had looked a competitive handicap and the pace was solid, but it was turned into a rout. The runners came down the centre on reaching the home straight. The form looks sound rated around the placed horses.

Snow Hill Official explanation: jockey said gelding hung left-handed
Twice Bitten Official explanation: jockey said gelding stopped very quickly
T/Plt: £451.90 to a £1 stake. Pool: £85,529.00 - 138.15 winning tickets. T/Qpdt: £14.40 to a £1 stake. Pool: £5,463.00 - 279.56 winning tickets. JR

2667 NEWCASTLE (L-H)
Saturday, June 9

OFFICIAL GOING: Soft (6.1)
Wind: Light, half behind Weather: Cloudy

2922 NESTLE CONFECTIONERY FAWDON H'CAP 1m 3y(S)
6:15 (6:15) (Class 5) (0-70,70) 4-Y-O+ **£2,911** (£866; £432; £216) **Stalls** Centre

Form				RPR
-130	1		**Le Chat D'Or**[12] 2535 4-9-4 67 (t) TomEaves 14	78
			(Michael Dods) *in tch: hdwy to chal over 2f out: led over 1f out: rdn and veered rt ent fnl f: drvn and styd on wl towards fin* **5/1**[2]	

-331 **2** ¾ **Hakuna Matata**[12] 2535 5-9-7 **70**........(p) AmyRyan 3 79
(Brian Ellison) *dwlt: hld up midfield: hdwy on outside to chse ldrs 2f out: effrt and ev ch whn hung rt ins fnl f: kpt on: hld nr fin* **2/1**[1]

0-00 **3** 2½ **Triple Eight (IRE)**[14] 2510 4-9-5 **68**........(p) MichaelO'Connell 12 71
(Philip Kirby) *hld up: rdn over 2f out: styd on fnl f: no imp last 100yds* **14/1**

020- **4** 1¼ **Monthly Medal**[221] 7216 9-8-7 **59**........(t) DeclanCannon(3) 16 59
(Wilf Storey) *t.k.h: hld up on nr side of gp: hdwy to ld over 2f out: hdd over 1f out: carried rt ins fnl f: one pce* **28/1**

0000 **5** 1 **Khandaq (USA)**[11] 2588 5-8-6 **62**........ PaulHainey(7) 9 60
(Keith Dalgleish) *dwlt: bhd: rdn over 2f out: hdwy over 1f out: kpt on fnl f: no imp* **40/1**

2230 **6** 1½ **Master Of Dance (IRE)**[103] 722 5-9-6 **69**........(p) ShaneKelly 5 64
(Keith Dalgleish) *trckd ldrs: rdn and outpcd over 2f out: rallied appr fnl f: no imp* **10/1**[3]

-362 **7** 2 **Seldom (IRE)**[8] 2675 6-9-2 **65**........ DuranFentiman 7 55
(Mel Brittain) *in tch: drvn and outpcd over 2f out: sme late hdwy: nvr rchd ldrs* **10/1**[3]

2310 **8** nk **Woteva**[7] 2692 6-8-12 **68**........(p) DanielleMooney(7) 6 57
(Nigel Tinkler) *led to over 2f out: sn rdn and outpcd* **11/1**

40-5 **9** 1½ **King Pin**[12] 2536 7-8-4 **58**........ ShaneBKelly(5) 2 44
(Tracy Waggott) *bhd: struggling over 2f out: sn n.d* **16/1**

0060 **10** 1¾ **Dolly Royal (IRE)**[8] 2670 7-8-2 **51** oh6........(p) KellyHarrison 13 33
(Robert Johnson) *disp ld to over 2f out: sn rdn and wknd* **33/1**

2605 **11** ½ **Beautiful Day**[15] 2455 4-8-10 **59**........ GrahamLee 8 40
(Kevin Ryan) *t.k.h: trckd ldrs tl rdn and wknd 2f out* **5/1**[2]

6200 **12** 7 **Myraid**[7] 2692 5-8-2 **51** oh3........ JamesSullivan 10 16
(Ruth Carr) *bhd: struggling over 3f out: sn btn* **33/1**

P-00 **13** 37 **Mangham (IRE)**[22] 2227 7-8-13 **62**........(p) LeeNewman 1
(George Foster) *cl up on outside tl rdn and wknd over 2f out: t.o* **28/1**

1m 44.1s (0.70) **Going Correction** +0.175s/f (Good) **13** Ran SP% **120.9**
Speed ratings (Par 103): **103,102,99,98,97 96,94,93,92,90 89,82,45**
toteswingers:1&2:£2.80, 2&3:£6.70, 1&3:£9.60 CSF £14.72 CT £140.80 TOTE £7.20: £2.90, £1.60, £4.20; EX 19.70.
Owner Calum Stewart Anne Gillespie **Bred** Dr A Gillespie **Trained** Denton, Co Durham
■ Stewards' Enquiry : Amy Ryan two-day ban: used whip above permitted level (Jun 25-26)

FOCUS
Slight rail movement in back straight. After a very wet spell the going was changed to soft resulting in wholesale non-runners. After the opener the ground was described as soft. They raced in one group towards the centre in this modest 51-70 handicap. The form is little fluid with the third and fourth having done better already this year.

2923 TOFFEE CRISP MAIDEN AUCTION STKS 6f
6:45 (6:45) (Class 5) 2-Y-O **£2,911** (£866; £432; £216) **Stalls** Centre

Form RPR

1 **Silent Footsteps (IRE)** 2-9-3 0........ TomEaves 6 73+
(Michael Dods) *hld up last: smooth hdwy over 2f out: rdn to ld appr fnl f: styd on strly to go clr last 100yds* **5/1**[3]

2 3½ **Red Joker (IRE)** 2-9-3 0........ PJMcDonald 8 63
(Alan Swinbank) *prom: pushed along over 2f out: hdwy to chal over 1f out: kpt on same pce last 100yds* **6/1**

03 **3** ½ **Yorkshire Icon**[12] 2537 2-8-11 0........ PaddyAspell 13 55+
(Ann Duffield) *plld hrd: hld up in tch: rdn and outpcd over 2f out: rallied appr fnl f: styd on: nrst fin* **3/1**[1]

4 1¼ **Marabout (IRE)** 2-8-13 0........ GrahamLee 14 53
(Mel Brittain) *in tch: effrt over 2f out: rdn and rn green over 1f out: no imp ins fnl f* **7/2**[2]

0 **5** ¾ **Look Forward (IRE)**[20] 2308 2-8-4 0........ DuranFentiman 9 42
(Tim Easterby) *led at ordinary gallop: rdn and hdd appr fnl f: sn outpcd* **33/1**

00 **6** 2¼ **Hitherto**[10] 2594 2-8-13 0........ LeeNewman 3 44
(David Barron) *in tch: drvn along over 2f out: shortlived effrt appr fnl f: sn no imp* **11/2**

0 **7** 1¾ **Poetic Star**[20] 2308 2-8-11 0........ AmyRyan 5 37
(Ben Haslam) *cl up: rdn over 2f out: wknd appr fnl f* **12/1**

0 **8** 2½ **Jomari (IRE)**[8] 2667 2-8-6 0........ NeilFarley(5) 11 30
(Declan Carroll) *trckd ldrs: rdn along over 2f out: wknd over 1f out* **12/1**

1m 18.59s (3.99) **Going Correction** +0.375s/f (Good) **8** Ran SP% **111.9**
Speed ratings (Par 93): **88,83,82,81,80 77,74,71**
toteswingers:1&2:£7.10, 2&3:£5.00, 1&3:£6.60 CSF £33.27 TOTE £7.50: £2.40, £1.30, £2.00; EX 31.50.
Owner Kevin Kirkup **Bred** Mrs M McWey **Trained** Denton, Co Durham

FOCUS
Due to the soft ground half of the intended 16-runners were absent. Again they raced in one group up the centre in this modest 2-y-o maiden auction event. The form looks modest and might be anchored by the proximity of the third and fifth.

NOTEBOOK
Silent Footsteps(IRE) came from last to first on his debut. Dropped in and making his way to the stands' side in the end he came right away. On this showing he will be even better over 7f. (op 11-2)
Red Joker(IRE), his trainer's first juvenile runner this year, cost 16,000euros. He knew his job but, after striking the front, he was soon overwhelmed by the winner. He can surely go one better. (op 5-1)
Yorkshire Icon, having his third start, was quite keen. As at Carlisle he was putting in all his best work at the finish and he is crying out for 7f. (op 7-2)
Marabout(IRE), on his first start, looked fit. He hit a flat spot before keeping on in good style late on. This will have taught him plenty. (tchd 4-1)
Look Forward(IRE), well beaten first time, knew her job this time and took them along until tiring noticeably in the closing stages. There ought to be better to come from this bargain basement purchase. (op 40-1)

2924 LIGHTHOUSE PROJECT H'CAP 7f
7:15 (7:15) (Class 5) (0-75,73) 4-Y-O+ **£2,911** (£866; £432; £216) **Stalls** Centre

Form RPR

3-43 **1** **Fieldgunner Kirkup (GER)**[9] 2619 4-8-13 **70**........ LMcNiff(5) 11 84
(David Barron) *hld up: hdwy to ld 1f out: drifted to stands rail ins fnl f: kpt on strly* **9/2**[2]

0235 **2** 3¾ **Hellbender (IRE)**[12] 2538 6-8-3 **60**........ NeilFarley(5) 12 64
(George Foster) *hld up: drvn and outpcd 1/2-way: rallied over 1f out: rdn and chsd wnr last 100yds: kpt on: no imp* **12/1**

100- **3** ¾ **Brave Battle**[259] 6343 4-8-5 **62**........ ShaneBKelly(5) 14 64
(Ron Barr) *hld up: rdn along over 2f out: sn outpcd: rallied fnl f: kpt on fin* **40/1**

5-05 **4** nse **Daring Dream (GER)**[29] 2035 7-9-6 **72**........ GrahamLee 15 74
(Jim Goldie) *dwlt: t.k.h in rr: hung lft thrght: drifted to r alone far rail 3f out: effrt and ev ch over 1f out to ins fnl f: no ex* **8/1**

1-06 **5** shd **Reason To Believe (IRE)**[109] 646 4-8-11 **63**........(b) PJMcDonald 5 65
(Ben Haslam) *t.k.h: led: rdn and hdd 1f out: sn one pce* **9/1**

0606 **6** nk **Chookie Avon**[5] 2753 5-9-2 **68**........(p) AmyRyan 8 69
(Keith Dalgleish) *hld up: rdn over 2f out: hdwy over 1f out: kpt on fnl f: no imp* **13/2**

0404 **7** hd **Nezami (IRE)**[12] 2535 7-8-6 **65**........ NedCurtis(7) 2 66
(Paul Midgley) *awkward s: sn prom: drvn along over 2f out: one pce fr over 1f out* **11/2**[3]

-000 **8** 6 **Dhhamaan (IRE)**[7] 2696 7-8-10 **62**........(b) JamesSullivan 3 47
(Ruth Carr) *hld up in tch: hdwy over 3f out: rdn and wknd over 1f out* **33/1**

0-62 **9** ¾ **Steel Stockholder**[49] 1520 6-8-12 **64**........ DuranFentiman 13 47
(Mel Brittain) *trckd ldrs: rdn over 3f out: wknd over 2f out* **4/1**[1]

2-00 **10** 2½ **Whispered Times (USA)**[12] 2535 5-9-0 **66**........(p) PatrickMathers 9 43
(Tracy Waggott) *trckd ldrs: rdn 1/2-way: hung lft and wknd 2f out* **25/1**

130 **11** 8 **Andiamo Via**[93] 834 5-8-12 **64**........ LeeNewman 7 20
(Michael Smith) *trckd ldrs tl rdn and wknd qckly over 2f out* **17/2**

1m 30.33s (2.53) **Going Correction** +0.375s/f (Good) **11** Ran SP% **115.5**
Speed ratings (Par 103): **100,95,94,94,94 94,94,87,86,83 74**
toteswingers:1&2:£6.60, 2&3:£73.10, 1&3:£29.50 CSF £55.11 CT £1900.48 TOTE £6.50: £1.90, £3.30, £10.50; EX 64.40.
Owner Kevin Kirkup **Bred** I And D Meinke **Trained** Maunby, N Yorks

FOCUS
They set off in one group up the centre in this modest 60-72 handicap but the winner hung right and ended under the stands' side rail. Graham Lee was left with little option but to take Daring Dream to race alone on the far side rail at the halfway mark. The runner-up is rated close to his April C&D form.
Daring Dream(GER) Official explanation: jockey said gelding hung left-handed throughout
Reason To Believe(IRE) Official explanation: trainer said gelding finished distressed
Dhhamaan(IRE) Official explanation: jockey said gelding missed the break having anticipated the start
Steel Stockholder Official explanation: trainer's rep said gelding coughed

2925 ROWNTREE'S FRUIT PASTILLES H'CAP 2m 19y
7:45 (7:46) (Class 6) (0-65,72) 4-Y-O+ **£2,070** (£616; £307; £153) **Stalls** Low

Form RPR

2111 **1** **Bilidn**[9] 2635 4-10-2 **72**........ ChrisCatlin 9 86+
(Noel Quinlan) *t.k.h: hld up: smooth hdwy to ld over 1f out: pushed along and kpt on strly fnl f* **9/4**[1]

3224 **2** 5 **Three White Socks (IRE)**[32] 1952 5-9-6 **61**........ AmyRyan 5 66
(Brian Ellison) *midfield: sn pushed along: hdwy over 4f out: led over 2f out to over 1f out: kpt on fnl f: nt pce of wnr* **3/1**[2]

02/- **3** 3¼ **Royal Curtsy**[22] 2466 9-8-11 **52**........ PaulMulrennan 7 53
(Stuart Coltherd) *midfield: hdwy on ins over 3f out: rdn and kpt on fnl 2f: no imp* **16/1**

00-2 **4** ¾ **Nay Secret**[10] 2599 4-8-6 **48**........ JamesSullivan 4 48
(Jim Goldie) *chsd ldrs: effrt and ev ch over 2f out: rdn and no ex over 1f out* **11/1**

2-03 **5** 11 **Tigerino (IRE)**[22] 2242 4-8-5 **47**........ DuranFentiman 11 34
(Chris Fairhurst) *hld up: hdwy and prom over 3f out: rdn and wknd over 1f out* **15/2**[3]

3033 **6** 19 **Bygones For Coins (IRE)**[8] 2669 4-8-8 **50**........ SilvestreDeSousa 10 14
(Robert Johnson) *t.k.h: led at decent gallop: rdn and hdd over 2f out: sn wknd* **12/1**

3-25 **7** nk **Dan's Heir**[32] 1952 10-8-4 **50**........(t) ShaneBKelly(5) 6 14
(Wilf Storey) *bhd: pushed along 1/2-way: nvr rchd ldrs* **11/1**

005- **8** 1½ **Short Supply (USA)**[27] 7340 6-8-5 **53**........(p) GemmaTutty(7) 2 15
(Tim Walford) *midfield: drvn and outpcd over 6f out: sn struggling* **16/1**

1-00 **9** 41 **Rose Of Sarratt (IRE)**[18] 2378 4-9-4 **63**........ AdamBeschizza(3) 12
(Rae Guest) *hdwy to chse ldr after 2f and sn clr of rest: rdn and lost 2nd over 3f out: sn wknd* **12/1**

400- **10** 10 **Minkie Moon (IRE)**[70] 3268 4-8-13 **55**........ GrahamLee 8
(Mark Campion) *midfield: rdn along over 6f out: lost tch last 4f* **28/1**

3m 43.84s (4.44) **Going Correction** +0.375s/f (Good)
WFA 4 from 5yo+ 1lb **10** Ran SP% **114.8**
Speed ratings (Par 101): **103,100,98,98,93 83,83,82,62,57**
toteswingers:1&2:£3.10, 2&3:£7.60, 1&3:£9.40 CSF £8.61 CT £83.16 TOTE £3.30: £1.10, £1.70, £5.40; EX 11.20.
Owner Patrick Wilmott **Bred** Meon Valley Stud **Trained** Newmarket, Suffolk

FOCUS
A modest 47-72 stayers' handicap with the two leaders clear until the final half-mile but a very confidently clear-cut winner, who is several steps ahead of the handicapper. The runner-up to this year's form is the best guide.
Dan's Heir Official explanation: trainer said gelding resented the first-time tongue strap

2926 BLUE RIBAND H'CAP 1m 2f 32y
8:15 (8:15) (Class 5) (0-75,72) 4-Y-O+ **£2,911** (£866; £432; £216) **Stalls** High

Form RPR

-006 **1** **Cosmic Moon**[11] 2588 4-8-4 **55**........ PatrickMathers 8 66
(Richard Fahey) *s.i.s: hld up: hdwy on outside to ld over 2f out: rdn and styd on wl fnl f* **6/1**[2]

40 **2** 1¼ **The Lodge Road (IRE)**[11] 2588 4-9-0 **65**........ PaulMulrennan 7 73
(Martin Todhunter) *hld up in tch: hdwy to chal over 2f out: sn rdn: kpt on: hld fnl 100yds* **6/1**[2]

-035 **3** 6 **Retreat Content (IRE)**[9] 2619 4-8-8 **59**........ TomEaves 5 55
(Linda Perratt) *in tch: drvn over 4f out: rallied 2f out: kpt on fnl f: nt pce of first two* **10/1**

2022 **4** 1 **Brockfield**[7] 2687 6-9-7 **72**........ DuranFentiman 2 66+
(Mel Brittain) *t.k.h early: chsd ldr: effrt and ev ch over 2f out: wknd ins fnl f* **15/8**[1]

6-60 **5** 2 **Honest Deal**[12] 2535 4-9-0 **65**........ PJMcDonald 1 55
(Alan Swinbank) *trckd ldrs: rdn 3f out: wknd over 1f out* **7/1**[3]

01-0 **6** 2¼ **Valantino Oyster (IRE)**[11] 2588 5-9-0 **65**........(p) JamesSullivan 11 51
(Tracy Waggott) *hld up: rdn and outpcd over 3f out: hung lft: sme late hdwy: nvr rchd ldrs* **12/1**

0300 **7** 11 **Calypso Cay**[20] 2314 4-8-5 **59**........ AdamBeschizza(3) 10 23
(Peter Salmon) *led tl rdn and hdd over 2f out: wknd wl over 1f out* **18/1**

4-43 **8** 1¼ **Bring Sweets (IRE)**[21] 1580 5-8-2 **53** oh3........(p) AmyRyan 3 14
(Brian Ellison) *hld up: rdn along over 3f out: sn struggling* **7/1**[3]

2m 20.58s (8.68) **Going Correction** +0.575s/f (Yiel) **8** Ran SP% **110.4**
Speed ratings (Par 103): **88,87,82,81,79 78,69,68**
toteswingers:1&2:£6.50, 2&3:£13.30, 1&3:£12.60 CSF £38.61 CT £332.72 TOTE £7.00: £1.80, £2.20, £2.80; EX 72.30.
Owner The Cosmic Cases **Bred** The Cosmic Cases **Trained** Musley Bank, N Yorks

FOCUS
This modest 53-72 handicap was run in a heavy rain shower. A step up from the winner.

2927 ACTION FOR CHILDREN MAIDEN STKS — 1m 2f 32y
8:45 (8:45) (Class 5) 3-Y-0+ — **£2,911** (£866; £432; £216) **Stalls** High

Form — RPR

25 **1** **Right To Rule (IRE)**[34] 1893 3-8-12 0 ShaneKelly 9 77+
(William Haggas) *trckd ldrs: rdn to ld appr fnl f: styd on wl* **10/11**[1]

5- **2** ¾ **Headline News (IRE)**[242] 6772 3-8-7 0 ChrisCatlin 10 70
(Rae Guest) *t.k.h: hld up in tch: stdy hdwy over 2f out: chsd wnr ins fnl f: r.o* **3/1**[2]

3 3½ **New Drama (IRE)** 3-8-7 0 SilvestreDeSousa 2 63
(Mark Johnston) *cl up: led over 3f out: rdn: edgd lft and hdd appr fnl f: sn outpcd* **6/1**[3]

4 3¾ **Generous Dream**[39] 4-9-6 0 DavidAllan 7 57
(Mel Brittain) *hld up: pushed along over 3f out: styd on fnl 2f: nvr able to chal* **33/1**

5 24 **Mr Flintstone** 3-8-12 0 DuranFentiman 1 13
(Tim Walford) *in tch: rdn and outpcd 3f out: sn btn* **40/1**

6 4 **Quan (IRE)** 3-8-12 0 PJMcDonald 4
(Alan Swinbank) *t.k.h: hld up: hdwy to ld after 2f: hung bdly rt and hdd bnd over 3f out: sn struggling* **10/1**

0-00 **7** 17 **Mount Mayday (IRE)**[16] 2430 3-8-12 0 PaulMulrennan 3
(Stuart Williams) *t.k.h: hld up: struggling wl over 2f out: sn btn* **33/1**

00 **F** **Dragon Spirit (IRE)**[15] 2438 3-8-12 0 TomEaves 8
(Linda Perratt) *led 2f: cl up: rdn and wkng whn fell 2f out* **40/1**

2m 21.1s (9.20) **Going Correction** +0.575s/f (Yiel)
WFA 3 from 4yo 13lb — **8** Ran SP% **111.5**
Speed ratings (Par 103): **86,85,82,79,60 57,43,**
toteswingers:1&2:£2.20, 2&3:£3.10, 1&3:£1.40 CSF £3.42 TOTE £1.90: £1.10, £1.40, £1.70; EX 4.40.
Owner Right Tack Partnership **Bred** Max Morris **Trained** Newmarket, Suffolk

FOCUS
No strength in depth in this maiden race, which was run as the rain continued to fall. The form is rated through the winner.
Quan(IRE) Official explanation: jockey said gelding hung right-handed
Mount Mayday(IRE) Official explanation: jockey said gelding ran too free

2928 BREAKAWAY H'CAP — 5f
9:15 (9:15) (Class 5) (0-75,73) 3-Y-0 — **£2,911** (£866; £432; £216) **Stalls** Centre

Form — RPR

5-23 **1** **Gowanharry (IRE)**[29] 2036 3-8-13 **65** (t) PaulMulrennan 5 73+
(Michael Dods) *cl up centre: led over 2f out: rdn and kpt on wl fnl f* **9/4**[2]

3334 **2** ¾ **Celestial Dawn**[32] 1960 3-8-2 **54** oh1 JamesSullivan 6 59
(John Weymes) *racd centre: in tch: rdn and outpcd over 3f out: rallied over 1f out: chsd wnr ins fnl f: r.o* **7/1**

5625 **3** nk **Elegant Girl (IRE)**[14] 2470 3-8-13 **65** DavidAllan 8 69
(Tim Easterby) *swtchd to r w one other stands rail after 1f: cl up: rdn and ev ch over 1f out: nt qckn ins fnl f* **6/1**[3]

5100 **4** nse **Rock Canyon (IRE)**[10] 2595 3-8-6 **58** (p) PJMcDonald 4 62
(Linda Perratt) *bhd and sn outpcd: plenty to do 1/2-way: gd hdwy over 1f out: r.o ins fnl f* **8/1**

450- **5** 3 **Holy Angel (IRE)**[229] 7059 3-8-6 **58** DuranFentiman 9 51
(Tim Easterby) *swtchd to r w stands side ldr after 1f: effrt and rdn over 1f out: no ex last 100yds* **8/1**

2-13 **6** 15 **Dreaming Of Rubies**[22] 2256 3-9-5 **71** (t) TomEaves 7
(Ben Haslam) *led centre to 1/2-way: rdn and wknd over 1f out: eased whn no ch* **2/1**[1]

1m 4.34s (3.24) **Going Correction** +0.575s/f (Yiel) — **6** Ran SP% **113.1**
Speed ratings (Par 99): **97,95,95,95,90 66**
CSF £18.15 CT £81.79 TOTE £3.80: £1.50, £3.00; EX 21.50.
Owner Les Waugh **Bred** L Waugh **Trained** Denton, Co Durham

FOCUS
The evening ended with the rain still falling. A modest 54-71 3yo sprint handicap. Two of the runners were switched to race under the stands' side rail. The winner is rated close to her Thirsk form but form that is not rated too positively.
T/Plt: £34.90 to a £1 stake. Pool of £57,990.44 - 1,210.45 winning tickets. T/Qpdt: £17.60 to a £1 stake. Pool of £4,523.43 - 189.40 winning tickets. RY

2892 NEWMARKET (R-H)
Saturday, June 9

OFFICIAL GOING: Good to soft (7.3)
Wind: medium to fresh, behind Weather: overcast

2929 FLY LONDON SOUTHEND TO BELFAST E B F MAIDEN STKS (DIV I) — 6f
1:45 (1:45) (Class 4) 2-Y-0 — **£4,528** (£1,347; £673; £336) **Stalls** High

Form — RPR

4 **1** **Tipping Over (IRE)**[22] 2245 2-8-12 0 MichaelHills 3 83+
(Hugo Palmer) *racd in centre: mde all: rdn over 1f out: edgd lft but styd on strly fnl f: rdn out* **9/1**

2 2 **Ask Dad** 2-9-3 0 RichardHughes 8 82+
(Richard Hannon) *hld up in tch: rdn and hdwy 2f out: chsd wnr jst over 1f out: trying to chal whn edgd lft u.p ins fnl f: no ex and btn fnl 100yds: jst hld 2nd* **3/1**[1]

3 nse **King Dragon (IRE)** 2-9-3 0 MartinDwyer 14 82+
(Brian Meehan) *hld up in tch towards rr: rdn and switching rt 2f out: swtchd bk lft and hdwy ent fnl f: styd on strly fnl 100yds* **25/1**

4 2¼ **Bourbon (IRE)** 2-9-3 0 MickaelBarzalona 9 75+
(Mahmood Al Zarooni) *sn bhd: pushed along 1/2-way: rdn and gd hdwy over 1f out: chsd ldrs and drvn 1f out: no ex and wknd fnl 100yds* **9/2**[2]

2065 **5** ¾ **Ouzinkie (IRE)**[7] 2686 2-9-3 0 MartinHarley 4 73
(Mick Channon) *chsd ldrs: chsd wnr 1/2-way tl unable qck u.p over 1f out: styd on same pce fnl f* **20/1**

4 **6** ¾ **Kalicamix**[17] 2402 2-9-3 0 StevieDonohoe 2 71
(Paul Cole) *racd alone nrest stands' rail: chsd wnr tl 1/2-way: sn u.p and outpcd 2f out: kpt on but no threat to wnr fnl f* **25/1**

32 **7** 3¼ **Fraserburgh (IRE)**[16] 2415 2-9-3 0 MircoDemuro 6 61
(Mark Johnston) *chsd ldrs: drvn and unable qck wl over 1f out: btn ent fnl f: wknd* **3/1**[1]

8 2¾ **Shebebi (USA)** 2-9-3 0 TadhgO'Shea 5 53+
(John Dunlop) *v.s.a: rn green and sn detached in last: sme hdwy fnl f: n.d* **20/1**

4 **9** nk **Ana Shababiya (IRE)**[14] 2492 2-8-12 0 RoystonFfrench 13 47
(Ismail Mohammed) *in tch: rdn 1/2-way: struggling u.p 2f out: wknd over 1f out* **66/1**

10 3¾ **Meridius (IRE)** 2-9-3 0 RyanMoore 12 41
(Jeremy Noseda) *s.i.s: rn green and rdn along early: clsd and in tch in rr after 1f: rdn and struggling 2f out: sn wknd* **8/1**[3]

11 16 **Rock Up (IRE)** 2-9-3 0 FrankieDettori 11
(David Elsworth) *wnt lft s: in tch in midfield: rdn and wknd 2f out: bhd and eased ins fnl f* **10/1**

1m 13.99s (1.49) **Going Correction** +0.05s/f (Good) — **11** Ran SP% **117.1**
Speed ratings (Par 95): **92,89,89,86,85 84,79,76,75,70 49**
toteswingers:1&2:£5.90, 2&3:£11.10, 1&3:£3.50 CSF £33.64 TOTE £10.00: £3.10, £1.80, £5.80; EX 48.50 TRIFECTA Not won..
Owner Anglia Bloodstock Syndicate **Bred** Jude Doherty **Trained** Newmarket, Suffolk

FOCUS
Stands' side track of July course used. Stalls Far side except 1m2f, 1m4f and 1m7f Centre. This was the first division of what was probably quite an ordinary juvenile maiden by course standards with the fifth used as a marker. The pace was decent, though, and the race should still produce its share of winners.

NOTEBOOK
Tipping Over(IRE) pressed on a fair way out and always looked to be doing enough, confirming the promise of last month's debut on the Rowley Mile. She's not overly big but is very professional and her action suggests there may be even more to come back on a drier surface. (op 17-2)
Ask Dad ◆, a brother to useful 6f-7f winner Tell Dad and Group placed 5f-6f 2yo Khawatim, is by a speedy mare and these conditions wouldn't have been ideal. He picked up well to challenge before edging left and should come on plenty for the outing, marking him down as hard to beat in something similar. (op 7-2)
King Dragon(IRE), an already gelded half-brother to a 7f 2yo winner, showed plenty and, like many from the yard, should come on a good deal for this initial experience. He'll want better ground too. (op 33-1)
Bourbon(IRE), a half-brother to winners Roscoff (7.5f Listed placed) and Carnac (1m4f-2m), was green through the first half of the race and dropped off the back of the main group. The fact he saw the race out nicely bodes well and he can win an ordinary maiden on better ground with 7f likely to suit. (op 4-1)
Ouzinkie(IRE) travelled well on this first try at 6f and helps set the level of the form. He doesn't look to be progressing and modest nurseries may be more his thing. (op 16-1)
Kalicamix raced more centre to stands' side with the winner but couldn't maintain the gallop anywhere near as well. Still, this was a big step up on his debut effort.
Fraserburgh(IRE) took a step backwards, being niggled from an early stage and perhaps disliking the ground. (tchd 7-2)
Shebebi(USA), a half-brother to two winners from 7f-1m, shaped promisingly considering how slowly away he was. (op 18-1)
Meridius(IRE), a half-brother to useful middle-distance runner Stotsfold, was slowly away and ran green.

2930 FLY LONDON SOUTHEND TO IBIZA H'CAP — 1m
2:20 (2:22) (Class 3) (0-90,90) 3-Y-0 — **£9,703** (£2,887; £1,443; £721) **Stalls** High

Form — RPR

6-1 **1** **Fast Or Free**[12] 2542 3-8-11 **80** RyanMoore 6 92
(William Haggas) *chsd clr ldr: clsd 2f out: rdn to ld jst over 1f out: styd on wl fnl f: drvn out* **7/1**[2]

1-14 **2** 1½ **Takeitfromalady (IRE)**[16] 2428 3-8-10 **79** (b) JimCrowley 16 87
(Ralph Beckett) *in tch on far side of field: effrt u.p over 1f out: chsd ldng pair 1f out: chsd wnr ins fnl f: no imp* **15/2**[3]

0043 **3** 1 **Zakreet**[28] 2088 3-8-7 **79** (b[1]) JulieBurke(3) 7 85
(Kevin Ryan) *racd freely: led and sn clr: rdn and hdd jst over 1f out: no ex and one pce ins fnl f* **16/1**

1-20 **4** 1½ **Deia Sunrise (IRE)**[22] 2235 3-9-2 **85** RobertHavlin 11 88
(John Gosden) *hld up towards rr: hdwy to chse ldrs over 2f out: rdn and unable qck over 1f out: styd on same pce u.p fnl f* **7/1**[2]

21 **5** 1 **Legendary**[91] 869 3-8-13 **82** KierenFallon 15 82
(Ed Vaughan) *stdd s: t.k.h: hld up in tch in midfield: hdwy to chse ldrs 2f out: sn drvn and unable qck: wknd ins fnl f* **16/1**

612- **6** 1 **Chil The Kite**[261] 6268 3-9-3 **86** DarryllHolland 12 84+
(Hughie Morrison) *t.k.h early: hld up in midfield: rdn and unable qck over 1f out: no threat to ldrs and styd on same pce fnl f* **7/1**[2]

6525 **7** 1¼ **Ocean Tempest**[9] 2641 3-8-11 **80** (p) BrettDoyle 10 75
(John Ryan) *hld up towards rr: hdwy 3f out: chsd ldrs and unable qck u.p over 1f out: wknd ins fnl f* **12/1**

1-66 **8** nk **Campanology**[35] 1860 3-8-12 **88** WilliamTwiston-Davies(7) 1 82+
(Richard Hannon) *stdd and swtchd lft s: hld up in rr: hdwy over 2f out: in tch and rdn over 1f out: no prog: pushed along and one pce fnl f* **20/1**

0-10 **9** 1 **Apostle (IRE)**[14] 2485 3-9-7 **90** TomQueally 2 82+
(Michael Bell) *hld up in rr: swtchd rt and rdn 2f out: hdwy over 1f out: edging lft but styd on fnl f: nvr gng pce to chal* **12/1**

31-4 **10** ½ **Go Dutch (IRE)**[21] 2265 3-9-0 **83** NeilCallan 13 74
(Roger Varian) *in tch in midfield: rdn and unable qck 2f out: one pce and no threat to ldrs fnl f* **6/1**[1]

1-03 **11** 9 **Nelson's Bay**[15] 2452 3-8-11 **80** (t) MickaelBarzalona 9 50
(Brian Meehan) *in tch: rdn and losing pl over 2f out: bhd fnl f* **20/1**

2-41 **12** ¾ **Dixie's Dream (IRE)**[19] 2331 3-8-12 **81** RichardHughes 8 50+
(Richard Hannon) *hld up towards rr: rdn 3f out: no hdwy and btn over 1f out: wl btn fnl f* **9/1**

11-0 **13** 11 **Asifa (IRE)**[42] 1653 3-9-2 **85** (p) FrankieDettori 14 28
(Saeed Bin Suroor) *chsd ldrs tl 3f out: sn lost pl: wl bhd and eased ins fnl f* **18/1**

103 **14** ¾ **Minstrels Gallery (IRE)**[23] 2198 3-9-2 **85** FrederikTylicki 5 26
(J R Jenkins) *in tch in midfield: u.p and lost pl 3f out: wl bhd and eased fnl f* **25/1**

10-4 **15** 12 **Right Divine (IRE)**[122] 471 3-8-13 **82** MartinDwyer 4
(Brian Meehan) *restless in stalls: in tch in midfield: rdn and lost pl wl over 2f out: t.o and eased fnl f* **40/1**

1m 39.62s (-0.38) **Going Correction** +0.05s/f (Good) — **15** Ran SP% **121.8**
Speed ratings (Par 103): **103,101,100,99,98 97,95,95,94,93 84,84,73,72,60**
toteswingers:1&2:£13.70, 2&3:£27.10, 1&3:£15.20 CSF £56.01 CT £844.62 TOTE £8.30: £2.40, £2.10, £7.80; EX 71.30 Trifecta £160.70 Pool: £1,184.05 - 5.45 winning units..
Owner Ian and Christine Beard **Bred** Usk Valley Stud **Trained** Newmarket, Suffolk

FOCUS
A decent 3yo handicap run at a good pace and the form looks solid even if little managed to get into it from off the pace. They raced in two groups early but had merged before halfway, and as in the first race, the winner came more centre-to-stands' side. The third is probably the guide rated to the best of his juvenile form.

NOTEBOOK
Fast Or Free showed a really likeable attitude when winning his maiden over 7f at Kempton 12 days earlier and the longer trip on a slower surface was of no inconvenience on this handicap debut. He can expect to find himself on a mark in the high-80s following this and the Britannia will surely come under consideration. (tchd 13-2)

Takeitfromalady(IRE) challenged far side and seemed to appreciate returning to ground with some cut in it. He's run really well in defeat the last twice now and may benefit from 1m2f. (op 6-1)
Zakreet didn't hang around in first-time blinkers and it was most commendable that he kept on the way he did once headed. Slow ground and a good test at 1m or an easy 1m2f suits him best. (op 14-1)
Deia Sunrise(IRE) apparently found 1m3f too far at Newbury last time, having earlier run really well over 1f shorter. He was off his new 6lb higher mark this time, though, and lacked the pace returning to this trip. (op 9-1)
Legendary, like the runner-up, raced more far side and he ran nicely on this handicap/turf debut considering it was his first start in 91 days and his trainer had warned the ground wouldn't suit. There should be more to come.
Chil The Kite, off for 261 days, has a good deal of talent but isn't straightforward, much like his half-brother Pastoral Player. He was very keen early, caught between the two groups, and didn't run badly considering. Hopefully this will have taken the fizz out of him and he remains capable of better. (op 6-1)
Ocean Tempest's 4lb rise for his close-up effort in a 1m Listed race at Sandown looked fair, but he couldn't match that form on slower ground.
Go Dutch(IRE) was disappointing considering he's a soft-ground winner and had made a promising reappearance. (op 7-1 tchd 15-2)

2931 FLY LONDON SOUTHEND TO BARCELONA H'CAP — 6f

2:55 (2:56) (Class 2) (0-105,106) 3-Y-O+**£19,407** (£5,775; £2,886; £1,443) **Stalls** High

Form — RPR

-120 **1** — **Mirza**[34] 1885 5-9-6 **98** .... RichardHughes 13 — 105
(Rae Guest) *chsd ldr: rdn to chal over 1f out: led narrowly 1f out: battled on gamely ins fnl f and asserted fnl 75yds: styd on* **7/1**

1142 **2** 3/4 **Es Que Love (IRE)**[7] 2712 3-9-6 **106** .... MircoDemuro 4 — 109
(Mark Johnston) *led: jnd and rdn over 1f out: narrowly hdd and drvn 1f out: battled on gamely tl no ex and btn fnl 75yds* **5/1**[2]

5055 **3** hd **Medicean Man**[12] 2559 6-9-5 **102** .... RaulDaSilva(5) 3 — 106
(Jeremy Gask) *chsd ldng pair: rdn and effrt to chal jst over 1f out: ev ch after tl no ex and one pce fnl 75yds* **25/1**

-000 **4** shd **High Standing (USA)**[14] 2472 7-9-8 **100** ....(p) RyanMoore 15 — 104+
(Jeremy Gask) *stdd s: hld up in last pair: rdn and hdwy over 1f out: swtchd rt ins fnl f: r.o strly fnl 100yds: nt rch ldrs* **16/1**

0-60 **5** 1 3/4 **El Viento (FR)**[23] 2208 4-8-11 **89** .... TomQueally 14 — 87
(Richard Fahey) *in tch: rdn: edgd rt and outpcd over 1f out: kpt on same pce u.p fnl f* **20/1**

4-00 **6** 2 3/4 **Irish Heartbeat (IRE)**[23] 2208 7-8-11 **89** .... FrederikTylicki 11 — 79
(Richard Fahey) *stdd s: hld up wl in tch: rdn and unable qck whn edgd rt over 1f out: sn outpcd and btn 1f out* **13/2**[3]

1020 **7** 1/2 **Shropshire (IRE)**[24] 2177 4-9-3 **95** .... MichaelHills 10 — 83
(Charles Hills) *stdd s: t.k.h: hld up in tch towards rr: nt clr run ent fnl 2f: swtchd rt and effrt over 1f out: styd on same pce and no threat to ldrs fnl f* **15/2**

-021 **8** 1/2 **Pearl Ice**[3] 2825 4-9-4 **96** 6ex .... GrahamGibbons 7 — 82
(David Barron) *in tch in midfield: rdn 1/2-way: struggling and losing pl whn sltly hmpd over 1f out: one pce and no threat to ldrs after* **6/4**[1]

020- **9** 7 **Breathless Kiss (USA)**[210] 7392 5-9-2 **97** .... JulieBurke(3) 1 — 61
(Kevin Ryan) *in tch in midfield: rdn and lost pl 2f out: sn wknd and bhd fnl f* **33/1**

0-30 **10** 1/2 **Swiss Franc**[23] 2208 7-9-0 **92** .... MickaelBarzalona 2 — 54
(David Elsworth) *t.k.h: hld up in last pair: rdn and no rspnse wl over 1f out: sn btn: bhd fnl f* **16/1**

1m 12.68s (0.18) **Going Correction** +0.05s/f (Good)
WFA 3 from 4yo+ 8lb — **10** Ran SP% **117.6**
Speed ratings (Par 109): **100,99,98,98,96 92,91,91,81,81**
CSF £41.27 CT £862.26 TOTE £7.70: £2.30, £1.80, £5.80; EX 44.10 Trifecta £528.00 Pool: £1,919.68 - 2.68 winning units..
Owner C J Mills **Bred** C J Mills **Trained** Newmarket, Suffolk

FOCUS
The field raced far side and, in keeping with the earlier contests, little got into it from off the pace with the front three being up there throughout. The runner-up confirmed his latest Listed personal-best.

NOTEBOOK
Mirza recorded back-to-back career bests in April, but he was below par when last seen and the short break was clearly needed. He got a nice tow from the runner-up and looks to have earned himself another crack at Pattern company. (op 13-2 tchd 8-1)
Es Que Love(IRE) was up 8lb having finished second at Listed level a week earlier and he'd probably have won had he had his favoured sound surface. He too can mix it back at pattern level. (op 6-1)
Medicean Man ◆ is the horse to take from the race. Best suited by 5f on good, fast ground, he's been struggling to recapture last season's best in 2012, but this looked more like the progressive sprinter of last year, and it's not out of the question he could run a big race at huge odds in the King's Stand given his love of Ascot. (op 20-1)
High Standing(USA) ◆, rated 113 at a peak in 2009-10, is another who's been struggling to find some form, but he ran really well considering where he raced relative to the front three. He's only a few pounds higher than when winning the Wokingham in 2009 and could easily go well in the race once more. (op 14-1)
El Viento(FR) is only just above his last winning mark and there was promise in this run. (tchd 25-1)
Irish Heartbeat(IRE) is tricky to win with and the way the race played out didn't suit. (op 7-1)
Shropshire(IRE) didn't have much go right and can be given another chance. (op 7-1 tchd 13-2)
Pearl Ice made up for an unlucky second at Thirsk when bolting home at Ripon just three days earlier and he was out again quickly in an attempt to get into the Wokingham. The race clearly came too soon, but he retains potential and can be given another chance. Official explanation: trainer's rep said, regarding running, that the colt had raced only three days previously and this may have come too soon. (op 15-8)

2932 FLY LONDON SOUTHEND TO FARO H'CAP — 1m 2f

3:30 (3:30) (Class 3) (0-95,92) 4-Y-O+ **£9,703** (£2,887; £1,443; £721) **Stalls** Centre

Form — RPR

1152 **1** — **John Louis**[10] 2606 4-8-1 **77** .... RaulDaSilva(5) 3 — 91
(Philip McBride) *mde all: sn clr: c bk to field 3f out: rdn and fnd ex 2f out: styd on strly ins fnl f: rdn out* **12/1**

4-22 **2** 2 1/2 **Troopingthecolour**[22] 2257 6-9-7 **92** .... FrankieDettori 7 — 101
(Steve Gollings) *chsd wnr thrght: clsd on wnr 3f out: rdn and hung lft fr over 1f out: no ex and btn ins fnl f: wknd towards fin* **4/1**[2]

31 **3** 1 1/2 **Trade Commissioner (IRE)**[16] 2430 4-9-1 **86** .... RyanMoore 8 — 92
(John Gosden) *t.k.h: chsd ldrs: drvn and unable qck over 1f out: 3rd and wl hld ins fnl f: kpt on fnl 100yds* **9/4**[1]

40-3 **4** 1/2 **Little Rocky**[42] 1654 4-9-2 **87** .... TomQueally 9 — 92
(David Simcock) *in tch in midfield: rdn and effrt 2f out: battling for 3rd but no ch w wnr ins fnl f: kpt on* **5/1**[3]

-002 **5** 1 1/2 **Shavansky**[25] 2151 8-9-3 **88** .... JamesMillman 1 — 90
(Rod Millman) *in tch in midfield: hdwy and rdn over 2f out: outpcd by ldng pair and btn 1f out: plugged on same pce fnl f* **16/1**

1-40 **6** 6 **Sandusky**[22] 2257 4-9-6 **91** .... MickaelBarzalona 6 — 81
(Mahmood Al Zarooni) *taken down early: t.k.h: hld up in tch in midfield: rdn and unable qck wl over 2f out: no threat to ldrs and one pce fr over 1f out* **9/1**

4620 **7** 2 1/4 **Romeo Montague**[14] 2479 4-9-3 **88** ....(v) RichardHughes 11 — 74
(Ed Dunlop) *stdd s: hld up in rr: hdwy into midfield 3f out: rdn and no prog over 1f out: fdd and eased ins fnl f* **12/1**

16-0 **8** 1 3/4 **Camberley Two**[33] 1924 4-9-0 **85** .... JamesDoyle 4 — 67
(Roger Charlton) *t.k.h: hld up in last trio: rdn and no imp over 2f out: wl hld fr over 1f out* **12/1**

0-55 **9** 3/4 **Silver Grey (IRE)**[30] 1999 5-8-2 **76** .... RyanPowell(3) 12 — 57
(Martyn Meade) *chsd ldrs: rdn and clsd on wnr 3f out: struggling u.p 2f out: btn over 1f out: fdd fnl f* **25/1**

31-0 **10** 3 1/4 **Sandbanks Sizzler (IRE)**[19] 2346 4-9-3 **88** ....[1] JimCrowley 5 — 62
(Ralph Beckett) *s.i.s: a bhd: lost tch wl over 1f out* **25/1**

2m 6.02s (0.52) **Going Correction** +0.05s/f (Good) — **10** Ran SP% **114.1**
Speed ratings (Par 107): **99,97,95,95,94 89,87,86,85,83**
CSF £58.30 CT £148.04 TOTE £14.80: £3.70, £1.50, £1.40; EX 66.50 Trifecta £211.00 Pool: £1,771.24 - 6.21 winning units..
Owner Four Winds Racing **Bred** Wood Farm Stud (Waresley) **Trained** Newmarket, Suffolk

FOCUS
Another race where racing prominently paid off with the first three more of less holding their positions throughout. The action unfolded centre to far side. The runner-up to his latest York form sets the standard.

NOTEBOOK
John Louis soon asserted into a clear lead, setting a decent clip, and having been given a breather and allowed to come back to the field, kicked again over 2f out and always looked the winner thereafter. He brought solid form into the race (albeit beaten 8l by Landaman, who was a non-runner, at Beverley previously), and the slow ground was clearly no bother. (op 10-1 tchd 14-1)
Troopingthecolour gave chase throughout and ran yet another solid race, registering his third consecutive second placing having ended up on the far rail. He deserves to win one but will probably be nudged up the handicap again. (op 9-2 tchd 7-2 tchd 5-1 in a place)
Trade Commissioner(IRE) created a strong impression when winning his maiden at Sandown, and an opening mark of 86 looked fair. However, he'd been a non-runner because of good to soft ground in the past, and having raced a touch keener than ideal, he looked far from happy on the surface when asked to quicken up. He got warm beforehand and still looks a bit inexperienced, so should learn again and can leave this form behind on quicker ground. (op 2-1 tchd 15-8)
Little Rocky likes some cut in the ground and again ran well enough to suggest he can defy this mark in the right company. (tchd 6-1)
Shavansky was never able to challenge.
Sandusky, who went to post early, was far too free and has now run poorly on back-to-back outings. He was progressive last year and ran really well on his reappearance so may be worth giving one last chance to. (op 11-1)
Romeo Montague Official explanation: jockey said gelding stopped quickly
Camberley Two, who was keen, didn't exactly shape as though this was the sort of test he wanted.

2933 FLY LONDON SOUTHEND TO DUBLIN LEVY BOARD H'CAP — 1m 4f

4:00 (4:01) (Class 2) (0-105,102) 4-Y-O+**£32,345** (£9,625; £4,810; £2,405) **Stalls** Centre

Form — RPR

13-4 **1** — **High Jinx (IRE)**[42] 1654 4-9-0 **92** .... RyanMoore 13 — 104+
(James Fanshawe) *hld up towards rr: shkn up and hdwy 4f out: rdn and hdwy to chse ldrs 2f out: drvn and chal 1f out: drew clr w runner-up ins fnl f: led fnl 50yds: styd on wl: drvn out* **7/2**[1]

11-0 **2** nk **Anatolian**[34] 1882 4-9-4 **96** .... FrankieDettori 9 — 108
(Mahmood Al Zarooni) *hld up in tch: hdwy to join ldrs 2f out: rdn and led jst over 1f out: drvn and wnt clr w wnr ins fnl f: hdd and no ex fnl 50yds* **10/1**

04-2 **3** 5 **High Office**[22] 2253 6-8-12 **90** .... FrederikTylicki 5 — 94
(Richard Fahey) *hld up in tch in midfield: rdn and effrt over 2f out: nt clr run and swtchd rt over 1f out: styd on u.p ins fnl f: wnt 3rd wl ins fnl f* **20/1**

53-1 **4** 3/4 **Mulaqen**[24] 2180 4-9-5 **97** .... TadhgO'Shea 3 — 100
(Marcus Tregoning) *chsd ldrs: jnd ldrs over 3f out: rdn and led 2f out: drvn and hdd jst over 1f out: unable qck and outpcd by ldng pair 1f out: plugged on same pce fnl f* **5/1**[3]

5113 **5** 3/4 **Ithoughtitwasover (IRE)**[14] 2479 4-9-10 **102** .... MircoDemuro 1 — 104+
(Mark Johnston) *in tch in midfield tl short of room and dropped to rr after 2f: hdwy 5f out: pressing ldrs and rdn over 2f out: unable qck u.p ent fnl f: outpcd by ldng pair and plugged on fnl f* **10/1**

22-0 **6** 1/2 **Spifer (IRE)**[22] 2253 4-8-12 **90** .... KierenFallon 16 — 91
(Luca Cumani) *stdd s: hld up in tch in last quartet: pushed along and hdwy over 3f out: chsng ldrs over 1f out: drvn and hung rt ent jst over 1f out: nt qckn and edgd bk lft 1f out: sn btn and one pce after* **9/2**[2]

3-6 **7** hd **Western Pearl**[35] 1848 5-9-0 **92** .... NeilCallan 12 — 92
(William Knight) *hld up in tch: chsng ldrs and n.m.r ent fnl 2f: rdn and unable qck over 1f out: plugged on same pce but no threat to ldrs fnl f* **28/1**

10-0 **8** 2 1/2 **Qushchi**[35] 1848 4-9-3 **95** .... WilliamCarson 2 — 91
(William Jarvis) *led tl rdn and hdd 2f out: no ex u.p and btn 1f out: fdd ins fnl f* **25/1**

43-0 **9** 1 3/4 **Late Telegraph (IRE)**[14] 2479 4-8-13 **91** .... TomQueally 4 — 85
(Sir Henry Cecil) *t.k.h: hld up in midfield: rdn and effrt 2f out: unable qck whn slighjtly hmpd and swtchd rt over 1f out: sn outpcd and btn jst ins fnl f* **14/1**

015- **10** 2 1/2 **Classic Vintage (USA)**[217] 7297 6-9-3 **95** .... JimCrowley 8 — 85
(Amanda Perrett) *in tch in midfield: rdn and lost pl 3f out: no threat to ldrs fnl 2f* **25/1**

503- **11** 1 **Classic Punch (IRE)**[224] 7170 9-9-8 **100** .... MartinHarley 11 — 88
(David Elsworth) *chsd ldr: racd against stands' rail fr 8f out: styd prom tl wknd wl over 1f out* **28/1**

0005 **12** 1/2 **Lyssio (GER)**[42] 1677 5-8-7 **90** .... MarkCoumbe(5) 14 — 77
(Michael Attwater) *t.k.h: chsd ldrs: rdn and unable qck over 2f out: wknd wl over 1f out* **66/1**

1-01 **13** 14 **Vasily**[12] 2561 4-8-9 **87** .... AndreaAtzeni 6 — 52
(Robert Eddery) *t.k.h: chsd ldrs tl struggling over 2f out: sn wknd: bhd and eased ins fnl f* **9/1**

242- **14** 1/2 **Ermyn Lodge**[245] 6690 6-9-3 **95** ....(v) IanMongan 10 — 59
(Pat Phelan) *stdd s: hld up in rr: lost tch over 2f out* **12/1**

610- **15** *9* **Swingkeel (IRE)**[317] [4469] 7-9-9 **101** .... DaneO'Neill 7 51
(John Dunlop) *a towards rr: lost tch 3f out: t.o* **40/1**

2m 30.6s (-2.30) **Going Correction** +0.05s/f (Good) **15** Ran SP% **122.9**
Speed ratings (Par 109): **109,108,105,104,104 104,104,102,101,99 98,98,89,88,82**
toteswingers:1&2:£12.00, 2&3:£49.70, 1&3:£26.90 CSF £36.40 CT £632.82 TOTE £4.60: £2.00, £3.10, £4.80; EX 40.90 Trifecta £804.00 Pool: £56,031.78 - 51.57 winning units..
Owner Mr & Mrs W J Williams **Bred** Haras De La Perelle **Trained** Newmarket, Suffolk

FOCUS
A strong-looking middle-distance handicap run at a decent clip with the front two drawing clear from 1f out. All bar Classic Punch raced centre-field. The third and fourth set a solid standard.

NOTEBOOK
High Jinx(IRE) ◆ was the first winner on the day to come from off the pace. Off for 42 days having made a really encouraging return over an inadequate 1m2f, the bit of cut in the ground was in his favour and he very much won in the style of a horse with more to come, needing every yard of this trip. His rating will be nudging 100 once reassessed, so the Northumberland Plate and Ebor will presumably come under consideration. He could end up in pattern races. (op 4-1)
Anatolian had been a bit disappointing on his reappearance and this was more like it. He sat more prominently than the winner and committed sooner, always looking set to come off second best. Clear of the third, he's as effective at 1m2f but will need to find further progress as his rating seems sure to be around 100 now. (tchd 9-1)
High Office travelled well and ran right up to form behind a couple of younger, less-exposed rivals.
Mulaqen smashed lesser opposition on his reappearance at York and always seemed likely to come up short in a better race from his 13lb higher mark, not to say he didn't run well. (tchd 11-2)
Ithoughtitwasover(IRE) has proven most progressive this season and his effort needs upgrading considering he was short of room and lost his position early. He used his finishing effort to get to the leaders and may yet be capable of winning from this sort of mark. (op 9-1)
Spifer(IRE) has his quirks and didn't travel as well as he can. This wasn't the big step forward on last month's debut that was expected and, although he shouldn't be written off yet, he's left with a bit to prove.
Western Pearl has missed a few engagements because of fast ground and she showed more than on last month's reappearance in Listed company at Goodwood. (op 33-1)
Qushchi ran creditably here from the front. (op 28-1)
Late Telegraph(IRE) was keen and things didn't really go his way, so he is probably worth another chance.
Classic Punch(IRE) loves it here and took the solo route against the stands' rail. He was on terms for most of the straight, but ultimately the lack of a run told. A drop back to 1m2f may suit him best. (op 33-1 tchd 25-1)
Vasily raced keenly and may not have liked the soft ground. Official explanation: trainer said colt was unsuited by the good to soft ground (tchd 8-1)
Ermyn Lodge was warming up for the Ascot Stakes, but considering his fine record fresh, it would have been nice to see a little more. (op 16-1)

2934 FLY LONDON SOUTHEND TO BELFAST E B F MAIDEN STKS (DIV II) 6f
4:35 (4:36) (Class 4) 2-Y-O **£4,528** (£1,347; £673; £336) **Stalls** High

Form RPR
1 **Havana Gold (IRE)** 2-9-3 0 .... RyanMoore 6 84+
(Richard Hannon) *hld up towards rr: hdwy and trcking ldrs waiting for gap over 1f out: rdn and qcknd to ld jst over 1f out: r.o wl: rdn out* **16/1**
2 *1 ½* **Pearl Acclaim (IRE)** 2-9-3 0 .... RichardHughes 2 79+
(Richard Hannon) *in tch: effrt and rdn to chse wnr jst over 1f out: drvn ins fnl f: r.o but a hld: eased cl home* **4/5**[1]
3 *2 ½* **Sejalaat (IRE)** 2-9-3 0 .... DaneO'Neill 7 75+
(John Dunlop) *hld up towards rr: hdwy to press ldrs and stl gng wl whn pushed lft and hmpd jst over 1f out: rallied and r.o ins fnl f: wnt 3rd towards fin* **33/1**
5 **4** *nk* **Club House (IRE)**[14] [2480] 2-9-3 0 .... RobertHavlin 4 71
(Robert Mills) *led: rdn: hung lft and hdd jst over 1f out: outpcd by ldng pair and no ex fnl f: lost 3rd towards fin* **10/1**[3]
5 *shd* **Brazen** 2-9-3 0 .... FrankieDettori 3 71+
(David Simcock) *hld up towards rr: hdwy and rdn over 2f out: outpcd by ldng pair and btn 1f out: kpt on same pce fnl 150yds* **7/1**[2]
6 *2 ¼* **Ferjaan** 2-9-3 0 .... TadhgO'Shea 10 64+
(John Gosden) *stdd s: hld up in tch in rr: hdwy and chsng ldrs whn nt clr run and swtchd rt jst over 1f out: one pce and no threat to ldrs after* **10/1**[3]
7 *6* **Woody Bay** 2-9-3 0 .... JimCrowley 11 46+
(James Given) *chsd ldrs: rdn 2f out: struggling and losing pl whn sltly hmpd over 1f out: sn wknd* **20/1**
8 *1 ¾* **Sennockian Star** 2-9-3 0 .... MircoDemuro 5 41+
(Mark Johnston) *racd keenly: chsd ldr: rdn and ev ch wl over 1f out: stl pressing ldr but unable qck whn carried lft jst over 1f out: sn btn and fdd ins fnl f* **16/1**
6 **9** *5* **Index Waiter**[16] [2415] 2-9-3 0 .... KierenFallon 13 26
(Brian Meehan) *chsd ldrs: rdn and ev ch 2f out: wknd over 1f out: fdd fnl f* **14/1**
10 *1 ½* **Whitford (IRE)** 2-9-3 0 .... AndreaAtzeni 1 21
(Chris Dwyer) *wnt sharply rt s: in tch in rr: lost tch wl over 1f out* **66/1**
11 *11* **Sekumkum (IRE)** 2-9-3 0 .... MickaelBarzalona 12
(Marco Botti) *rn green and sn rdn along in rr: lost tch 2f out* **16/1**

1m 14.54s (2.04) **Going Correction** +0.05s/f (Good) **11** Ran SP% **119.7**
Speed ratings (Par 95): **88,86,82,82,82 79,71,68,62,60 45**
toteswingers:1&2:£5.00, 2&3:£12.10, 1&3:£36.30 CSF £29.36 TOTE £13.70: £3.10, £1.10, £10.00; EX 34.30 Trifecta £281.90 Pool: £1,295.34 - 3.40 winning units..
Owner Carmichael Humber **Bred** Sir Eric Parker **Trained** East Everleigh, Wilts
■ Stewards' Enquiry : Robert Havlin two-day ban: careless riding (Jun 24-25)

FOCUS
Not much between this and division one. A solid start from the runner-up with the third rated a little better having been hampered, with the fourth close to his debut figure.

NOTEBOOK
Havana Gold(IRE), a half-brother to prolific 5f winner Rocker, picked up nicely once asked and is clearly a useful prospect. He's the type to go hunting big pots in valuable sales races.
Pearl Acclaim(IRE), a 165,000gns yearling, was strong in the betting, but he was initially very keen on exiting the stalls and then looked to struggle to pick up on the slow surface. It may be a different story on quicker ground and he can go one better in a maiden. (op 5-6 tchd 8-11)
Sejalaat(IRE), a half-brother to 5f Group-placed 2-y-o winner Nassem Sea, was unlucky not to have gone quite a bit closer. He was closing strongly when badly hampered by the fourth and couldn't recover in time. He'll no doubt prove popular when bidding for compensation.
Club House(IRE) fared best of those with previous experience, although it was down to him veering left that cost the third the race.
Brazen, a half-brother to six winners, most notably Doctor Brown (very useful over 6f as a 2yo), came with a decent-looking charge from the rear only to flatten out on the run to the line. He should improve enough to land a standard maiden. (tchd 15-2)
Ferjaan, a half-brother to 6f AW winner Ghazwah, wasn't the best away but did keep on and should benefit from drier ground. (tchd 12-1)
Woody Bay, whose dam was a 1m winner, ran better than the bare result. (op 16-1)
Sennockian Star, who is a half-brother to a couple of middle-distance winners, ran well for a long way and should improve.

2935 FLY LONDON SOUTHEND TO MALAGA MAIDEN FILLIES' STKS 7f
5:10 (5:12) (Class 5) 3-Y-O **£3,234** (£962; £481; £240) **Stalls** High

Form RPR
3-4 **1** **Poisson D'Or**[29] [2042] 3-9-0 0 .... JamesDoyle 8 84
(Rae Guest) *in tch: hdwy to join ldrs over 1f out: rdn to ld 1f out: r.o strly and drew clr fnl f: readily* **4/1**[2]
2 *2 ¾* **Medhyaar** 3-9-0 0 .... TadhgO'Shea 12 76+
(William Haggas) *v.s.a: t.k.h: clsd and in rr of main gp after 1f: hdwy and chsng ldrs whn nt clr run over 1f out: rdn and m green jst over 1f out: styd on wl ins fnl f: wnt 2nd cl home* **16/1**
-23 **3** *½* **Ihtifal**[33] [1922] 3-9-0 0 .... (t) MickaelBarzalona 5 75
(Saeed Bin Suroor) *in tch: hdwy to press ldrs over 2f out: rdn to ld over 1f out: sn hung lft u.p and hdd 1f out: one pce and sn brushed aside by wnr: lost 2nd cl home* **2/1**[1]
4 *3* **Quality Pearl (USA)** 3-9-0 0 .... KierenFallon 1 67+
(Luca Cumani) *in tch: pushed along 3f out: rdn and outpcd over 1f out: no threat to ldrs but styd on steadily ins fnl f* **5/1**[3]
0 **5** *1 ¾* **Poly Pomona**[14] [2483] 3-9-0 0 .... KieranO'Neill 2 62
(Richard Hannon) *chsd ldrs tl led 2f out: sn hdd: rdn and pushed lft: continued to hang lft and btn 1f out: wknd* **10/1**
6 *nk* **Shore Performer (IRE)** 3-9-0 0 .... MircoDemuro 7 61+
(William Haggas) *v slowly: away: bhd: stdy prog fr 4f out: chsd ldrs and rdn over 1f out: sn btn and nt pushed ins fnl f* **11/1**
0 **7** *4* **Litmus (USA)**[40] [1705] 3-9-0 0 .... WilliamCarson 10 50
(Charles Hills) *t.k.h: chsd ldrs: rdn and struggling 2f out: wknd over 1f out* **20/1**
8 *¾* **Rose Madder** 3-9-0 0 .... MartinHarley 6 48
(Michael Bell) *t.k.h: hld up in tch: nt clr run over 2f out: rdn and unable qck wl over 1f out: sn wknd* **25/1**
9 *3 ¾* **Secret Jubilee** 3-9-0 0 .... StevieDonohoe 4 38
(Philip McBride) *v.s.a: rn green in rr: n.d* **25/1**
00- **10** *nk* **Connishka**[235] [6933] 3-9-0 0 .... DarryllHolland 15 37
(Alan Bailey) *in tch: rdn and struggling ent fnl 2f: sn wknd: fdd fnl f* **40/1**
0- **11** *3 ¾* **Dark Orchid**[220] [7233] 3-9-0 0 .... RobertHavlin 11 27
(Peter Chapple-Hyam) *led tl 2f out: sn lost pl and btn: bhd fnl f* **12/1**
00 **12** *1* **Boragh Waters (IRE)**[14] [2483] 3-9-0 0 .... MartinDwyer 3 25
(Brian Meehan) *chsd ldrs tl over 2f out: sn rdn and lost pl: bhd fnl f* **66/1**

1m 26.56s (0.86) **Going Correction** +0.05s/f (Good) **12** Ran SP% **117.4**
Speed ratings (Par 96): **97,93,93,89,87 87,82,82,77,77 73,72**
toteswingers:1&2:£5.80, 2&3:£8.20, 1&3:£2.50 CSF £60.33 TOTE £5.10: £1.50, £4.90, £1.20; EX 74.50 Trifecta £226.70 Pool: £1,375.74 - 4.49 winning units..
Owner The Family Fish **Bred** New England, Stanley House & Mount Coote Studs **Trained** Newmarket, Suffolk

FOCUS
This is likely to be quite a decent fillies' maiden with several promising performances in behind and the race should produce winners. The level is a bit fluid with the third below her AW mark.

2936 FLY LONDON SOUTHEND TO WATERFORD H'CAP 1m 6f 175y
5:40 (5:43) (Class 4) (0-85,85) 4-Y-O+ **£5,175** (£1,540; £769; £192; £192) **Stalls** Centre

Form RPR
10/3 **1** **Monterey (IRE)**[16] [2423] 5-9-7 **85** .... (b[1]) RobertHavlin 11 93
(Robert Mills) *t.k.h: hld up in midfield: wnt to r alone on far rail 7f out: rdn and chsng ldrs over 1f out: led ins fnl f: rdn out* **8/1**
50-P **2** *1 ¼* **Danvilla**[16] [2423] 5-9-4 **82** .... WilliamCarson 6 88
(Paul Webber) *chsd ldrs tl led 4f out: rdn and hdd over 2f out: hung lft u.p over 1f out: kpt on to go 2nd again cl home* **12/1**
61-3 **3** *½* **Knightly Escapade**[24] [2174] 4-9-0 **78** .... IanMongan 9 83+
(John Dunlop) *hld up in tch: hdwy to join ldr gng wl 3f out: led over 2f out: rdn 2f out: drvn and hdd ins fnl f: no ex and lost 2nd cl home* **13/2**[3]
350- **4** *¾* **Arab League (IRE)**[28] [4719] 7-9-0 **78** .... (p) NeilCallan 13 82
(David Pipe) *in tch: rdn and unable qck 3f out: kpt on u.p ins fnl f* **4/1**[1]
25-3 **4** *dht* **Mohanad (IRE)**[16] [2412] 6-9-0 **78** .... FrankieDettori 1 82
(Sheena West) *hld up in tch: rdn and unable qck 3f out: swtchd lft and rallied 1f out: kpt on u.p fnl f* **6/1**[2]
-045 **6** *2* **Action Front (USA)**[18] [2378] 4-8-5 **69** .... MartinLane 2 71
(Derek Shaw) *hld up in tch in rr: hdwy 6f out: drvn and outpcd over 2f out: plugged on ins fnl f* **20/1**
-216 **7** *4 ½* **Boss's Destination**[43] [1640] 5-9-4 **82** .... KierenFallon 8 78
(Alan Swinbank) *chsd ldrs: wnt 2nd 10f out tl 3f out: sn u.p and unable qck: wknd wl over 1f out* **6/1**[2]
1153 **8** *14* **Rasheed**[16] [2411] 4-9-2 **80** .... MarcHalford 5 58
(John Gosden) *in tch in midfield: rdn and unable qck 3f out: wknd 2f out: eased ins fnl f* **10/1**
06-0 **9** *½* **Bowdler's Magic**[21] [2278] 5-9-6 **84** .... MircoDemuro 12 61
(Mark Johnston) *s.i.s: a bhd: n.d* **11/1**
-024 **10** *1 ½* **Taikoo**[35] [1850] 7-9-6 **84** .... DarryllHolland 3 59
(Hughie Morrison) *led tl 10f out: chsd ldr tl lost pl 3f out: sn btn and eased fnl 2f* **15/2**
2310 **11** *47* **Crunched**[24] [2180] 5-9-1 **79** .... MartinDwyer 4
(Tim Pitt) *chsd ldrs tl led 10f out: hdd 4f out and sn dropped out: t.o and virtually p.u fnl 2f* **33/1**

3m 9.85s (1.45) **Going Correction** +0.05s/f (Good) **11** Ran SP% **117.6**
Speed ratings (Par 105): **98,97,97,96,96 95,93,85,85,84 59**
toteswingers:1&2:£18.80, 2&3:£18.10, 1&3:£10.80 CSF £99.95 CT £665.64 TOTE £10.90: £3.40, £4.30, £2.00; EX 126.20 Trifecta £820.70 Part won. Pool: £1,109.13 - 0.50 winning units..
Owner Mrs B B Mills, J Humphreys, B Ecclestone **Bred** Swettenham Stud **Trained** Headley, Surrey

FOCUS
An open staying handicap. Perhaps not form to get carried away with with the winner racing alone far side and arguably the best horse at the weights finishing third. A messy race with a moderate time and the form looks pretty ordinary overall.

T/Jkpt: Not won. T/Plt: £162.10 to a £1 stake. Pool of £134,710.38 - 606.65 winning tickets. T/Qpdt: £22.90 to a £1 stake. Pool of £7,732.46 - 249.46 winning tickets. SP

[2556]WINDSOR (R-H)

Saturday, June 9

OFFICIAL GOING: Soft changing to good to soft after race 2 (6.30)

The runners often head to the far side in soft ground, but conditions were drying well, and after the first race they mainly raced in the stands' side half.

Wind: Moderate, behind Weather: Fine

2937 FEGENTRI WORLD CUP OF NATIONS STKS (AMATEUR RIDERS' H'CAP) (IN MEMORY OF JOHN CIECHANOWSKI) 1m 2f 7y

6:00 (6:01) (Class 6) (0-65,62) 4-Y-0+ £2,305 (£709; £354) Stalls High

Form RPR

6304 1 **Shirataki (IRE)**[40] 1706 4-11-9 61 MrsCamillePeltier 7 69
(Peter Hiatt) *mde all: clr 1/2-way: styd towards centre in st: rdn and hrd pressed fnl f: hld on wl* 11/2[3]

0603 2 *nk* **Gower Rules (IRE)**[2] 2851 4-11-3 55 MrFabrizioPerego 2 62
(John Bridger) *hld up last: prog 4f out: styd in centre and chsd wnr 2f out: str chal fnl f: nt qckn nr fin* 9/2[2]

2315 3 *3* **Brown Pete (IRE)**[8] 2652 4-11-10 62 (e) MrAlessandroRuiu 1 63
(Richard Guest) *hld up in rr: prog 4f out: wnt towards far side initially in st but c bk to centre 2f out: tk 3rd 1f out: no imp on ldng pair* 4/1[1]

4104 4 *5* **Rigid**[8] 2653 5-11-2 54 MrPMadden 6 45
(Tony Carroll) *sn chsd wnr: wnt towards far side briefly in st: lost 2nd 2f out: wknd* 7/1

5106 5 *6* **Darsan (IRE)**[9] 2623 4-11-10 62 MrDennisSchiergen 4 41
(Phil McEntee) *trckd ldrs: wnt to far side in st and sn no ch: c bk to centre in wl btn 5th fnl f* 11/2[3]

3030 6 *5* **Celtic Charlie (FR)**[18] 2364 7-10-12 50 MrFMitchell 5 19
(Pat Phelan) *hld up in midfield: prog to chse ldng pair 1/2-way: wnt to far side in st and sn no ch* 6/1

00-0 7 *1* **Cookieshake**[14] 2502 4-11-3 55 MrsSilkeBruggemann 3 22
(Peter Hiatt) *trckd ldrs: wnt to far side in st and sn no ch* 16/1

5440 8 *½* **Rosy Dawn**[44] 1624 7-10-7 45 MrMikaelMescam 8 11
(John Bridger) *prom 4f: sn lost pl and pushed along: struggling whn wnt to far side in st: no ch after* 16/1

300/ 9 *3 ¼* **Underscore (USA)**[2099] 5205 10-10-8 46 MlleBrittanyTrimble 9
(Ann Stokell) *hld up in rr: effrt over 3f out: wnt to far side in st and sn no ch* 20/1

2m 11.08s (2.38) **Going Correction** +0.15s/f (Good) 9 Ran SP% 112.3

Speed ratings (Par 101): **96,95,93,89,84 80,79,79,76**

toteswingers:1&2:£3.70, 2&3:£1.50, 1&3:£5.40 CSF £29.34 CT £108.10 TOTE £5.10: £2.00, £1.90, £1.30; EX 37.70 Trifecta £193.60 Pool: £540.86 - 2.06 winning units..

Owner Carl Dcmczak **Bred** Deerfield Farm **Trained** Hook Norton, Oxon

FOCUS

Top bend dolled out 2yds from inner line adding 7yds to races of 1m and over. Rest of track at normal configuration and course at maximum width. In a weak race run at a solid if unspectacular pace, the runners fanned out across the track in the final 3f, but those who went wide in search of faster ground must have been left wondering why. Though some way off the stands' rail, the winner stayed nearest to it, with the runner-up the next-closest. The form is rated around the first two.

2938 MATT CLEGG MEMORIAL MAIDEN FILLIES' STKS 5f 10y

6:30 (6:32) (Class 5) 2-Y-0 £2,911 (£866; £432; £216) Stalls Low

Form RPR

1 **City Image (IRE)** 2-9-0 0 RichardHughes 4 80+
(Richard Hannon) *dwlt: pushed along to dispute 4th but sme way off the pce: clsd jst over 1f out: r.o to ld last 100yds* 3/1[1]

2 *1 ½* **Botanica (IRE)** 2-9-0 0 RyanMoore 2 78+
(Richard Hannon) *slowest away: bdly outpcd in 7th: pushed along and prog over 1f out: styd on wl to take 2nd last 50yds* 9/2[2]

4 3 *2* **Sand And Deliver**[16] 2426 2-9-0 0 LiamKeniry 6 67+
(Peter Crate) *mde most and clr w one rival: stl clr of rest 1f out: hdd & wknd last 100yds* 8/1

4 *1 ½* **Star Up In The Sky (USA)** 2-9-0 0 TomQueally 7 62+
(Kevin Ryan) *w ldr and clr of rest: stl upsides and clr 1f out: wknd qckly last 100yds* 11/2

3 5 *2 ½* **Spiritual Girl**[14] 2492 2-9-0 0 HayleyTurner 5 53+
(Michael Bell) *chsd ldng pair and clr of rest: shkn up and no imp 2f out: wknd fnl f* 9/2[2]

6 *shd* **Cross Pattee (IRE)** 2-9-0 0 NickyMackay 9 53
(John Gosden) *taken down early and steadily to post: disp 4th but outpcd: shkn up 2f out: no real prog* 5/1[3]

7 *12* **Madam Moreton** 2-9-0 0 TomMcLaughlin 3
(George Margarson) *disp 4th but outpcd: no prog 2f out: wknd rapidly fnl f* 33/1

8 *2 ½* **Marguerite St Just** 2-9-0 0 MickyFenton 1
(Olivia Maylam) *rn green and t.o in last over 3f out: fin w a flourish* 66/1

1m 1.05s (0.75) **Going Correction** +0.15s/f (Good) 8 Ran SP% 109.0

Speed ratings (Par 90): **100,97,94,92,88 87,68,64**

toteswingers:1&2:£2.80, 2&3:£6.80, 1&3:£5.00 CSF £14.90 TOTE £3.80: £1.50, £1.60, £2.30; EX 11.20 Trifecta £59.90 Pool: £932.68 - 11.51 winning units..

Owner P A Byrne **Bred** Patrick Byrnes **Trained** East Everleigh, Wilts

FOCUS

The two leaders duelled in front and went a blistering gallop, particularly for the conditions. It was no surprise that they were retreating fast at the finish. The front two impressed but the third and fourth rather set it up for them.

NOTEBOOK

City Image(IRE) is an Elusive City daughter of a winner in France around 1m1f, and there are other winners in the family from 6f to 1m2f, so she will stay at least an additional furlong. Richard Hughes wasn't tempted into chasing the furious early gallop, and what stamina she does have at this stage of her career came in handy as the both leaders folded late on. (tchd 11-4)

Botanica(IRE), a 28,000GBP half-sister to five winners, is bred to be speedy and this was a sterling first effort. She should stay 6f before long, and on this occasion the strong gallop eventually helped her overcome a slowish start

Sand And Deliver has what it takes to win over 5f, but she overdid the early tempo and didn't get home. Her speed will be a great asset in races to come. (op 7-1)

Star Up In The Sky(USA), purchased this year for 55,000GBP, is a half-sister to two winners in the US. She has speed to burn and should make good use of it when she saves a bit more than she did on this debut. (tchd 13-2)

Spiritual Girl has the speed of a sprinter, but she got home better at 6f on fast ground first time out. She may have lasted longer had she not chased the tearaway leading pair. (op 4-1 tchd 7-2)

Cross Pattee(IRE), a half-sister to the Pattern-class middle-distance performer Bronze Cannon and four other winners, made a satisfactory if never-dangerous debut. She will do better at 6f, and even further later in her career. (tchd 11-2)

2939 READING POST (S) STKS 6f

7:00 (7:00) (Class 6) 3-Y-0+ £2,070 (£616; £307; £153) Stalls Low

Form RPR

-200 1 **Bunce (IRE)**[15] 2444 4-9-8 76 RaulDaSilva(5) 4 66
(Paul Fitzsimons) *trckd ldr after 1f: chal 2f out: sn drvn: narrow ld ins fnl f: hld on* 8/11[1]

0112 2 *shd* **Efistorm**[11] 2581 11-9-13 77 HayleyTurner 3 65
(Conor Dore) *led: cajoled along and edgd lft whn chal over 1f out: narrowly hdd ins fnl f: styd on: jst hld* 7/4[2]

2244 3 *1* **Unlimited**[8] 2652 10-9-13 60 TomQueally 2 62
(Tony Carroll) *rrd s: last tl wnt 3rd 1/2-way: drvn to chal 2f out: nt qckn over 1f out: swtchd rt and styd on* 8/1[3]

00/0 4 *3* **Gypsy Jazz (IRE)**[12] 2551 5-9-3 52 (p) AnnStokell(5) 1 47
(Ann Stokell) *t.k.h: trckd ldr 1f: dropped to last 1/2-way: one pce after* 33/1

1m 14.44s (1.44) **Going Correction** +0.15s/f (Good) 4 Ran SP% 108.3

Speed ratings (Par 101): **96,95,94,90**

CSF £2.25 TOTE £1.80; EX 2.40.There was no bid for the winner. Efistorm was claimed by D. J. Ffrench Davis for £6000.

Owner Raymond Tooth **Bred** John Doyle **Trained** Upper Lambourn, Berks

FOCUS

The first two home are well above the standard normally seen in this grade. The form is rated cautiously through the third to his latest turf form.

2940 DAVISCARIBBEAN.COM H'CAP 6f

7:30 (7:30) (Class 4) (0-80,80) 4-Y-0+ £5,175 (£1,540; £769; £384) Stalls Low

Form RPR

00-4 1 **Cardinal**[33] 1935 7-8-8 67 JamesDoyle 9 78
(Robert Cowell) *hld up in midfield: prog over 2f out: drvn to press ldr over 1f out: narrow ld ins fnl f: hld on* 8/1[3]

1- 2 *shd* **Magic Secret**[239] 6839 4-9-3 76 MickyFenton 12 87
(Jeremy Gask) *sn led: drvn wl over 1f out: narrowly hdd ins fnl f: jst hld* 7/1[2]

6-41 3 *1 ½* **Lady Bayside**[11] 2572 4-8-12 71 TomMcLaughlin 3 77
(Malcolm Saunders) *w ldrs: chal 2f out: drifted lft and one pce fnl f* 9/1

-326 4 *hd* **Midnight Rider (IRE)**[22] 2251 4-9-5 78 GeorgeBaker 5 83+
(Chris Wall) *hld up bhd ldrs: looking for room fr 2f out: rdn to cl 1f out: one pce fnl f* 11/2[1]

6240 5 *½* **Emiratesdotcom**[14] 2482 6-9-3 76 RyanMoore 10 80+
(Milton Bradley) *chsd ldrs: drvn 2f out: swtchd outside and tried to chal 1f out: one pce* 10/1

5402 6 *hd* **Rambo Will**[59] 1305 4-8-13 72 DaneO'Neill 1 75
(J R Jenkins) *racd against nr side rail: mostly pressed ldr to 2f out: steadily fdd* 20/1

0-60 7 *1 ¼* **Silenzio**[12] 2545 4-9-2 75 RichardHughes 15 74
(Richard Hannon) *hld up and grad swtchd fr wd draw to inner: prog over 2f out: rdn over 1f out: hanging lft and nt qckn* 7/1[2]

-230 8 *3* **Midnight Feast**[14] 2488 4-9-4 77 TomQueally 11 66
(Eve Johnson Houghton) *hld up in midfield: effrt over 2f out: tried to cl over 1f out: edgd lft and fnd nil u.p* 8/1[3]

0-00 9 *3* **Ginger Ted (IRE)**[14] 2487 5-9-7 80 (p) J-PGuillambert 2 60
(Stuart Williams) *sn pushed along in last quartet: nvr on terms* 20/1

4054 10 *½* **Intercept (IRE)**[28] 2083 4-9-5 78 (t) NickyMackay 4 56
(John Gosden) *w ldrs tl wknd u.p 2f out* 17/2

0664 11 *1* **Captain Scooby**[19] 2337 6-9-3 76 MartinHarley 7 51
(Richard Guest) *hld up in last quartet: pushed along and no prog fnl 2f* 16/1

2206 12 *1 ¾* **Hinton Admiral**[24] 2168 8-8-13 72 HayleyTurner 6 41
(Conor Dore) *a in last quartet: rdn and no prog over 2f out* 25/1

2300 13 *7* **Earlsmedic**[28] 2070 7-8-8 70 (v) RyanClark(3) 13 17
(Stuart Williams) *a in last quartet: taken to wd outside and drvn over 2f out: sn wknd* 33/1

4165 14 *6* **Sulis Minerva (IRE)**[14] 2488 5-9-1 79 RaulDaSilva(5) 14 7
(Jeremy Gask) *towards rr: effrt on wd outside over 2f out: sn wknd rapidly and eased: t.o* 20/1

1m 13.01s (0.01) **Going Correction** +0.15s/f (Good) 14 Ran SP% 119.2

Speed ratings (Par 105): **105,104,102,102,101 101,100,96,92,91 90,87,78,70**

toteswingers:1&2:£18.90, 2&3:£17.80, 1&3:£18.40 CSF £57.12 CT £535.25 TOTE £9.90: £2.70, £3.60, £3.80; EX 85.20 Trifecta £363.30 Part won. Pool: £491.01 - 0.20 winning units..

Owner Mrs J May **Bred** The Queen **Trained** Six Mile Bottom, Cambs

FOCUS

This was a competitive sprint handicap of a reasonable standard. The form looks ordinary but straightforward.

Silenzio Official explanation: jockey said colt hung left

2941 SKYBET.COM MAIDEN STKS 1m 67y

8:00 (8:01) (Class 5) 3-Y-0 £2,911 (£866; £432; £216) Stalls Low

Form RPR

36 1 **Border Legend**[21] 2271 3-9-3 0 JamesDoyle 1 82
(Roger Charlton) *w ldr: gng best 3f out: led 2f out: clr whn hung lft fnl f: rdn out* 5/1

0-2 2 *1* **Eagle Power (IRE)**[40] 1704 3-9-3 0 HayleyTurner 13 78
(James Fanshawe) *trckd ldng pair: rdn over 2f out: styd on to chse wnr fnl f: clsng at fin* 9/2[3]

00-0 3 *2 ¼* **Dance With Me (IRE)**[70] 1138 3-9-3 73 LiamKeniry 6 73
(Andrew Balding) *t.k.h: hld up in midfield: effrt on outer over 2f out: drvn and styd on to take 3rd nr fin* 16/1

0- 4 *hd* **Proximity**[224] 7164 3-8-12 0 TomQueally 4 68+
(Sir Michael Stoute) *trckd ldrs in 6th: pushed along over 2f out and no prog: reminder and r.o fnl f: fin wl* 14/1

5 *½* **Hummingbird** 3-8-12 0 MichaelHills 7 66
(William Haggas) *trckd ldng trio: rdn over 2f out: no imp over 1f out: one pce* 11/1

4-36 6 *nse* **Dynamic Duo (IRE)**[16] 2429 3-9-3 74 RichardHughes 9 71
(Richard Hannon) *mde most: rdn and hdd 2f out: lost 2nd fnl f: pushed along and lost pls nr fin* 10/3[1]

0-2 7 *1* **Cufflink**[29] 2050 3-8-12 0 RichardKingscote 14 64+
(Rae Guest) *restrained fr wd draw into last trio: stl only 10th over 1f out: reminder and r.o fnl f: fin wl* 7/2[2]

00 8 *¾* **Essell**[21] 2266 3-8-12 0 MartinHarley 8 62
(Mick Channon) *trckd ldrs in 5th: shkn up over 2f out: no imp wl over 1f out: one pce* 66/1

0 **9** ¾ **Modern Tutor**[49] 1506 3-9-3 0 RyanMoore 11 65+
(Sir Michael Stoute) *hld up towards rr: shkn up on outer over 2f out: kpt on but nvr on terms* **17/2**

0 **10** 3¾ **Albonny (IRE)**[40] 1703 3-9-3 0 DaneO'Neill 12 56
(Alan Jarvis) *dwlt: mostly in last pair: shkn up over 2f out: modest late prog* **100/1**

0 **11** 3 **Semeen**[16] 2430 3-9-3 0 KierenFallon 3 49
(Luca Cumani) *dwlt: hld up towards rr: pushed along over 2f out: no prog over 1f out: wknd* **11/1**

0-0 **12** 1¾ **Caledonian Lad**[12] 2543 3-9-3 0 DarryllHolland 10 45
(Hughie Morrison) *wl in tch in midfield: lost pl over 3f out: struggling in rr fnl 2f* **22/1**

00 **13** 10 **Trio Of Trix**[23] 2200 3-8-12 0 TomMcLaughlin 2 16
(Malcolm Saunders) *dwlt: a in last pair: t.o* **200/1**

1m 45.53s (0.83) **Going Correction** +0.15s/f (Good) **13** Ran SP% **127.2**
Speed ratings (Par 99): **101,100,97,97,97 97,96,95,94,90 87,86,76**
toteswingers:1&2:£6.70, 2&3:£30.70, 1&3:£25.70 CSF £29.50 TOTE £7.00: £2.00, £2.00, £6.40; EX 29.70 Trifecta £361.60 Part won. Pool: £488.76 - 0.85 winning units..
Owner The Queen **Bred** The Queen **Trained** Beckhampton, Wilts

FOCUS
The runners in this 3yo maiden hadn't been overexposed, and improvement is likely from a number of them. The pace was good early on but slackened a bit around the bend, as is usually the case. The form looks ordinary rated around the third and sixth.

2942 SKYBET MOBILE FOR IPHONE & ANDROID H'CAP 1m 2f 7y
8:30 (8:33) (Class 4) (0-80,80) 3-Y-O **£5,175** (£1,540; £769; £384) **Stalls** High

Form RPR

4-42 **1** **Cresta Star**[16] 2431 3-9-4 **77** RichardHughes 1 83
(Richard Hannon) *t.k.h: led to 1/2-way: rdn to ld again 2f out: jnd over 1f out: styd on wl fnl f* **5/1**[2]

0-50 **2** 1 **Plastiki**[21] 2279 3-8-8 **67** (v[1]) RyanMoore 3 71
(Sir Michael Stoute) *cl up: effrt to go 2nd over 1f out and sn upsides wnr: drvn and nt qckn ins fnl f* **11/1**

01-0 **3** ¾ **Keepax**[16] 2428 3-9-2 **75** GeorgeBaker 6 77
(Chris Wall) *dropped out in last: prog 3f out: rdn and styd on fr over 1f out to take 3rd ins fnl f* **20/1**

1-10 **4** 1 **Twelve Strings (IRE)**[22] 2246 3-9-2 **75** KierenFallon 13 75
(Luca Cumani) *hld up in midfield: awkward bnd 1/2-way: rdn and tried to cl on ldrs 2f out: disp 3rd fnl f: one pce* **3/1**[1]

05-0 **5** ½ **Bohemian Rhapsody (IRE)**[21] 2273 3-9-3 **79** PatrickHills(3) 10 78+
(J W Hills) *hld up in rr: effrt on inner and n.m.r 3f out: sme prog whn nt clr run over 1f out: rdn and kpt on: n.d* **14/1**

05-6 **6** 3¼ **Quick Bite (IRE)**[42] 1653 3-9-7 **80** IanMongan 2 73
(Hugo Palmer) *t.k.h: hld up in midfield tl quick move to ld 1/2-way: hdd 2f out: wknd fnl f* **10/1**

4-20 **7** 2¾ **Shot In The Dark (IRE)**[26] 2128 3-8-12 **71** LiamKeniry 9 58
(Andrew Balding) *chsd ldr to 1/2-way: styd prom tl wknd over 1f out* **16/1**

3-36 **8** 7 **Yaa Salam**[52] 1456 3-9-4 **77** (vt[1]) MickaelBarzalona 5 50+
(Mahmood Al Zarooni) *bmpd s: hld up in midfield: prog on inner to go 4th over 3f out: tried to find way through against rail over 2f out but nowhere to go: wknd over 1f out* **8/1**

322- **9** 18 **Blank Czech (IRE)**[272] 5967 3-9-5 **78** JimCrowley 12 15
(Amanda Perrett) *hld up in rr: shkn up and no prog wl over 2f out: sn wknd: t.o* **6/1**

1 **10** 37 **Marine Girl**[18] 2380 3-9-4 **77** TomQueally 7
(Sir Henry Cecil) *v restless in stalls: dwlt: rcvrd and in tch on outer: wknd rapidly 3f out: eased and t.o* **11/2**[3]

2m 9.76s (1.06) **Going Correction** +0.15s/f (Good) **10** Ran SP% **117.2**
Speed ratings (Par 101): **101,100,99,98,98 95,93,88,73,44**
toteswingers:1&2:£14.40, 2&3:£35.30, 1&3:£26.90 CSF £59.08 CT £1015.73 TOTE £4.60: £1.70, £3.80, £8.10; EX 82.90 Trifecta £384.90 Part won. Pool: £520.17 - 0.65 winning units..
Owner P T Tellwright **Bred** P T Tellwright **Trained** East Everleigh, Wilts
■ Stewards' Enquiry : Mickael Barzalona two-day ban: careless riding (Jun 24-25)

FOCUS
Several of the more inexperienced runners in this race will be worth keeping an eye on after their initial appearance in handicap company here. The pace was medium and the form is a bit muddling, so has been rated cautiously.
Keepax Official explanation: jockey said gelding hung right
Twelve Strings(IRE) Official explanation: jockey said gelding hung right
Bohemian Rhapsody(IRE) Official explanation: jockey said colt hung right

2943 LONGLEAT LM FILLIES' H'CAP 5f 10y
9:00 (9:02) (Class 5) (0-70,69) 3-Y-O+ **£2,911** (£866; £432; £216) **Stalls** Low

Form RPR

-441 **1** **Ginzan**[18] 2360 4-9-11 **66** TomMcLaughlin 2 74
(Malcolm Saunders) *prom on inner: rdn 2f out: led jst over 1f out: hrd pressed fnl f: hld on* **4/1**[1]

0-50 **2** hd **Madame Kintyre**[16] 2421 4-9-6 **61** (b) JamesMillman 3 68
(Rod Millman) *t.k.h: hld up bhd ldrs: prog to chal fnl f: styd on: jst hld* **7/1**[3]

0-00 **3** 1¼ **Festival Dance**[11] 2572 4-9-1 **56** HayleyTurner 4 59
(Ron Hodges) *hld up in midfield: prog over 1f out: drvn to go 3rd fnl f: one pce last 150yds* **8/1**

5104 **4** nk **Welsh Inlet (IRE)**[3] 2809 4-10-0 **69** RichardHughes 11 70
(John Bridger) *racd towards outer in midfield: drvn and effrt over 1f out: styd on but nvr able to chal* **6/1**[2]

0-54 **5** shd **Imaginary Diva**[18] 2360 6-9-5 **60** TomQueally 13 61
(George Margarson) *hld up in tch: shkn up and nt qckn wl over 1f out: styd on fnl f: nrst fin* **15/2**

60-0 **6** nk **Superior Edge**[24] 2165 5-9-0 **60** (p) RaulDaSilva(5) 7 60
(Christopher Mason) *pressed ldr to 1/2-way: sn rdn and lost pl styd on again last 150yds* **16/1**

0-60 **7** ¾ **Atlantic Cycle (IRE)**[8] 2647 5-8-11 **59** (tp) GeorgeDowning(7) 6 56
(Milton Bradley) *led: edgd lft fr over 1f out and sn hdd: wknd last 100yds* **16/1**

16-4 **8** nse **Sparking**[22] 2244 5-9-8 **63** RichardKingscote 12 60
(Tom Dascombe) *racd wdst of all: pushed along in midfield bef 1/2-way: effrt u.p over 1f out: kpt on one pce* **9/1**

0-00 **9** nk **Miss Firefly**[19] 2350 7-8-8 **52** (p) RyanClark(3) 9 48
(Ron Hodges) *fractious to post: t.k.h: hld up in midfield: hrd rdn 2f out: one pce* **25/1**

1340 **10** ¾ **Silver Linnet (IRE)**[22] 2251 5-9-8 **63** (p) MickyFenton 8 56
(John Butler) *blindfold off shade late and dwlt: hld up at bk of main gp: reminders over 1f out: styd on fnl f: nvr nr ldrs* **22/1**

0-00 **11** nk **Six Diamonds**[2] 2839 5-8-11 **52** MartinHarley 15 44
(Richard Guest) *hld up in last: shkn up over 1f out: kpt on fnl f: nvr nr ldrs* **40/1**

0003 **12** 1½ **Baby Dottie**[39] 1734 5-9-2 **57** IanMongan 10 44
(Pat Phelan) *hld up: a in rr: shkn up and no prog over 1f out* **6/1**[2]

5400 **13** 3¼ **Griffin Point (IRE)**[18] 2377 5-9-1 **56** MartinDwyer 5 31
(William Muir) *a in rr: rdn and struggling sn after 1/2-way* **22/1**

1m 1.46s (1.16) **Going Correction** +0.15s/f (Good)
WFA 3 from 4yo+ 7lb **13** Ran SP% **120.7**
Speed ratings (Par 100): **96,95,93,93,93 92,91,91,90,89 89,86,81**
toteswingers:1&2:£5.40, 2&3:£20.80, 1&3:£5.70 CSF £30.15 CT £184.78 TOTE £6.20: £2.10, £3.20, £3.70; EX 46.20 Trifecta £304.70 Part won. Pool: £411.81 - 0.10 winning units..
Owner Paul Nicholas **Bred** Hedsor Stud **Trained** Green Ore, Somerset

FOCUS
This was the sort of sprint handicap where the runners generally just win in their turn, but the in-form winner made it two in a row. There wasn't much separating the first 11 at the finish but the form looks pretty straightforward.
Welsh Inlet(IRE) Official explanation: jockey said filly hung right
T/Plt: £266.80 to a £1 stake. Pool of £68,405.51 - 187.10 winning tickets. T/Qpdt: £51.80 to a £1 stake. Pool of £5,078.50 - 72.48 winning tickets. JN

2944 - 2950a (Foreign Racing) - See Raceform Interactive

2741 CHANTILLY (R-H)
Saturday, June 9
OFFICIAL GOING: Turf: soft; polytrack: standard

2951a PRIX PAUL DE MOUSSAC (GROUP 3) (3YO COLTS & GELDINGS) (TURF) 1m
4:50 (12:00) 3-Y-O **£33,333** (£13,333; £10,000; £6,666; £3,333)

RPR

1 **Xanadou (IRE)**[29] 2064 3-8-10 0 ChristopheSoumillon 2 113
(J-C Rouget, France) *racd midfield: mde smooth prog to chal ldr 1f out: tk ld 100yds out: r.o wl: comf* **41/10**[3]

2 1¼ **Archbishop (USA)**[35] 1860 3-8-10 0 DavyBonilla 7 110
(Brian Meehan) *led fr s: rdn 1 1/2f out: picked up wl: chal and hdd 100yds out: r.o wl* **24/1**

3 1¼ **Coupe De Ville (IRE)**[27] 2110 3-8-10 0 OlivierPeslier 8 107
(Richard Hannon) *racd promly bhd ldr: wnt 2nd 1f out: r.o wl wout troubling ldrs* **5/1**

4 ½ **So Beautiful (FR)**[35] 3-8-10 0 ThierryJarnet 6 106
(Mlle S-V Tarrou, France) *racd towards rr: mde gd progress ent fnl f: r.o wl fnl 100yds: nrest at fin* **16/1**

5 1¾ **Mustaheel (IRE)**[46] 1592 3-8-10 0 Francois-XavierBertras 1 102
(F Rohaut, France) *broke wl to follow ldr for 2f then settled midfield on rail: rdn and mde prog 2f out: no ex ins fnl f: fdd* **33/10**[2]

6 2 **Coup De Theatre (FR)**[55] 1408 3-8-10 0 RonanThomas 3 97
(P Van De Poele, France) *settled cl up bhd ldr: picked up wl 2f out: rdn over 1f out: no ex: nt hrd rdn fnl 100yds* **23/1**

7 2 **Hippolyte (FR)**[22] 2259 3-8-10 0 FlavienPrat 4 93
(T Clout, France) *hld up in rr for first 2f then sent up on outside to take prom position: rdn over 1 1/2f: no ex: r.o one pce* **23/10**[1]

8 8 **Malossol (USA)**[41] 1698 3-8-13 0 IoritzMendizabal 5 77
(G Botti, Italy) *hld up in rr: rdn over 2f out: no ex: eased ent fnl f* **7/1**

1m 38.3s (0.30) **8** Ran SP% **116.4**
WIN (incl. 1 euro stake): 5.10. PLACES: 2.10, 4.70, 2.20. DF: 52.60. SF: 128.00.
Owner Daniel-Yves Treves **Bred** Yeguada Milagro **Trained** Pau, France

NOTEBOOK
Xanadou(IRE) had underfoot conditions to suit and did it well.
Archbishop(USA), back up in grade, made the running and only gave best in the last half-furlong.
Coupe De Ville(IRE), not beaten far when seventh in the Poulains over C&D, could not build on that form.

2952 - 2953a (Foreign Racing) - See Raceform Interactive

2565 BELMONT PARK (L-H)
Saturday, June 9
OFFICIAL GOING: Turf: firm; dirt: fast

2954a BELMONT STKS (GRADE 1) (3YO) (DIRT) 1m 4f (D)
11:40 (12:00) 3-Y-O **£387,096** (£129,032; £70,967; £38,709; £19,354)

RPR

1 **Union Rags (USA)**[35] 1872 3-9-0 0 JRVelazquez 3 123+
(Michael Matz, U.S.A) **11/4**[2]

2 nk **Paynter (USA)**[21] 3-9-0 0 MESmith 9 122
(Bob Baffert, U.S.A) **43/10**[3]

3 1¾ **Atigun (USA)**[35] 3-9-0 0 JRLeparoux 4 119
(Kenneth McPeek, U.S.A) **205/10**

4 5½ **Street Life (USA)**[28] 3-9-0 0 (b) JLezcano 1 111
(Chad C Brown, U.S.A) **98/10**

5 2½ **Five Sixteen (USA)**[52] 3-9-0 0 (b) RosieNapravnik 7 107
(Dominick A Schettino, U.S.A) **193/10**

6 1 **Unstoppable U (USA)**[43] 3-9-0 0 JAlvarado 2 105
(Kenneth McPeek, U.S.A) **119/10**

7 hd **Dullahan (USA)**[35] 1872 3-9-0 0 JJCastellano 5 105
(Dale Romans, U.S.A) **5/2**[1]

8 7¼ **My Adonis (USA)**[35] 3-9-0 0 (b) RADominguez 11 93
(Kelly Breen, U.S.A) **197/10**

9 3¾ **Ravelo's Boy (USA)**[91] 3-9-0 0 (b) ASolis 6 87
(Manuel J Azpurua, U.S.A) **27/1**

10 8¾ **Optimizer (USA)**[21] 2299 3-9-0 0 CNakatani 10 73
(D Wayne Lukas, U.S.A) **144/10**

P **Guyana Star Dweej (USA)**[43] 3-9-0 0 (b) KDesormeaux 8
(Doodnauth Shivmangal, U.S.A) **232/10**

2m 30.42s (1.46) **11** Ran SP% **119.7**
PARI-MUTUEL (all including $2 stakes): WIN 7.50; PLACE (1-2) 4.20, 5.10; SHOW (1-2-3) 3.40, 3.90, 10.60; SF 31.40.
Owner Chadds Ford Stable **Bred** Phyllis M Wyeth **Trained** USA

FOCUS

All of the attention should have been directed towards one horse, I'll Have Another, who would have been bidding to become the 12th horse to complete the American Triple Crown and the first since 1978, but he was found the previous day to have developed tendonitis in his near-fore and was retired. Given the question marks against the stamina of several in this contest, the pace set by the runner-up was steady and the fractions were sensible: 23.72, 49.23, 1:14.72, 1:38.85 and 2:04.39, whilst the final time of 2:30.42 was slow given a fast track.

NOTEBOOK

Union Rags (USA)s problems were only just beginning when he stumbled and missed the break in the Kentucky Derby and under the circumstances he did well to finish as close as seventh. Having swerved the Preakness to wait for this, he had a new jockey in John Velasquez (replacing Julien Leparoux, who was aboard Atigun) and the switch paid off. The colt was always travelling nicely not too far off the pace and, having crept closer on the inside rounding the home bend, just needed a gap to appear. Fortunately the leader accommodatingly hung off the rail, giving him his chance, and he seized it. In view of the troubled runs he endured in both the Florida Derby and Kentucky Derby, he richly deserved this.

Paynter(USA) has always been highly regarded, reportedly ahead of the Kentucky and Preakness runner-up Bodemeister, but his stamina for this wasn't guaranteed. Despite that he was sent straight to the front and had a fairly easy time of it, apart from when pressed by Unstoppable U around half a mile from home, but he still looked likely to see it out starting up the stretch. However, he edged away from the rail under pressure and, under circumstances that must have stirred up painful images for connections of Bodemeister being mugged late on by I'll Have Another at Churchill Downs and Pimlico, he had the big prize snatched from him in the shadow of the post.

Atigun(USA) ran a blinder considering he took a fierce hold early and found himself nearly last after losing his place in the backstretch, but he managed to get into a challenging position after switching out wide turning for home and wasn't shaken off until well inside the last furlong.

Street Life (USA)s a confirmed stretch-runner and being held up well off the pace in a steadily run race was never going to be ideal for him, so it was little surprise to see him plug on late for a never-dangerous fourth.

Dullahan(USA), the Kentucky Derby third, was the big disappointment of the race. Like his old rival the winner, he had skipped the Preakness to wait for this and had a new jockey in the shape of Javier Castellano, but after dropping to the rear of the field in the backstretch he barely picked up at all once put under pressure. It's probably no coincidence that his two wins have been gained on the synthetic surface at Keeneland.

2955 - 2957a (Foreign Racing) - See Raceform Interactive

2523 CURRAGH (R-H)

Sunday, June 10

OFFICIAL GOING: Round course - soft; straight course - soft to heavy

2958a IRISH STALLION FARMS EUROPEAN BREEDERS FUND 2YO MAIDEN — 6f

2:20 (2:20) 2-Y-0 **£9,487** (£2,200; £962 ; £550)

RPR

1 **Gale Force Ten**[23] [2300] 2 -9-5 ... JPO'Brien 1 89
(A P O'Brien, Ire) *sn cl up and disp ld: u.p in 2nd over 1f out: chal ins fnl f: styd on best to edge on clsng stages* **7/2**[3]

2 3/4 **Leitir Mor (IRE)**[4] [2523] 2 -9-5 ... KevinManning 10 87
(J S Bolger, Ire) *sn disp ld: def ldr wl over 1f out: pressed ins fnl f: hdd and kpt on same pce clsng stages* **11/10**[1]

3 2 3/4 **Hard Yards (IRE)** 2 -9-5 ... ChrisHayes 6 79+
(A Oliver, Ire) *sn trckd ldrs: no imp u.p in 4th fr over 1f out: kpt on wout threatening fnl f* **16/1**

4 2 1/2 **Newberry Hill (IRE)**[14] [2523] 2 -9-5 ... FranBerry 3 71
(Mrs John Harrington, Ire) *prom: chal but struggling fr 2f out: no imp in 5th and kpt on same pce fr over 1f out* **11/4**[2]

5 1/2 **Nabat Sultan** 2 -9-0 ... DeclanMcDonogh 2 65
(Kevin Prendergast, Ire) *w.w: impr to chal 2f out: no imp u.p in 3rd and kpt on same pce fr over 1f out* **14/1**

6 1/2 **Bedecked (IRE)**[23] [2300] 2 -9-0 ... RoryCleary 8 63
(J S Bolger, Ire) *chsd ldrs: no imp u.p and kpt on same pce fr 2f out* **33/1**

7 1 1/4 **Cool Metallic (IRE)** 2 -9-5 ... PatSmullen 4 65
(D K Weld, Ire) *dwlt: towards rr: no imp and kpt on same pce u.p fr 2f out* **14/1**

8 2 1/2 **Sherzam** 2 -9-0 ... NGMcCullagh 5 52
(Thomas Carmody, Ire) *s.i.s: sn towards rr: no imp u.p and kpt on same pce fr 2f out* **25/1**

1m 17.44s (1.94) **Going Correction** +0.525s/f (Yiel) 8Ran SP% 122.5
Speed ratings: **100,99,95,92,91 90,89,85**
CSF £8.37 TOTE £4.00 : £1.60 , £1.10 , £4.00 ; DF 9.60 .
Owner Michael Tabor **Bred** S Tindall, D Ludlow & Stowell Hill Ltd **Trained** Ballydoyle, Co Tipperary

FOCUS

A good maiden won impressively.

NOTEBOOK

Gale Force Ten looked probably second best when the runner-up found a bit and went on by a length a furlong out but he saw it out far better than the runner-up. He's an improving colt who will be much better suited by goodish ground although plans to drop him back to 5f look ambitious as he would have little trouble staying 7f on this evidence. Winning trainer Aidan O'Brien: "We were very worried about the ground for him so that was a pleasant surprise. We thought he could be an Ascot horse and he'll either go for the Norfolk or the Windsor Castle." (op 9/2)

Leitir Mor (IRE)suffered his third straight narrow defeat. Most things went in his favour here and when he went on over a furlong out with the stands' side rail to help him he shouldn't really have been beaten. He has questions to answer. (op 1/1 tchd 5/4)

Hard Yards (IRE)was a bit coltish in the paddock but he ran well. Tracking the pace on the inside, he didn't really get going until inside the final furlong but he came home well. He'll improve. (op 20/1)

Newberry Hill (IRE)was well supported in the market but he looked a handful in the paddock and to an extent going down to the start. He raced handily but was off the bridle early and looked one-paced. He might improve a bit more on better ground. (op 11/4 tchd 3/1)

Nabat Sultan closed up nicely after halfway but he dropped away rather tamely inside the last furlong.

2959 - 2964a (Foreign Racing) - See Raceform Interactive

2568 COLOGNE (R-H)

Sunday, June 10

OFFICIAL GOING: Turf: good

2965a SILBERNES BAND DES RHEINLANDES (LISTED RACE) (4YO+) (TURF) — 1m 7f

2:00 (12:00) 4-Y-0+ **£10,833** (£3,333; £1,666 ; £833)

RPR

1 **Slight Advantage (IRE)**[258] [6410] 4 -8-6[0] ... JBojko 5 101
(A Wohler, Germany) **10/1**

2 2 **Tres Rock Danon (FR)**[35] [1901] 6 -9-2[0] ... THellier 4 108
(W Hickst, Germany) **3/5**[1]

3 hd **Hot Blood (IRE)**[25] [2191] 4 -8-10[0] ... AStarke 1 102
(P Schiergen, Germany) **43/10**[3]

4 3 1/2 **All My Heart**[211] [7406] 4 -8-8[0] ... LukeMorris 2 95
(Sir Mark Prescott Bt) *settled in 4th and wl in tch: wnt on after 2 1/2f: scrubbed along to hold advantage whn chal on both sides 3f out: sn hrd rdn and hdd over 2f out: no ex u.p fnl f* **13/5**[2]

5 2 **Aviator (GER)**[35] [1901] 4 -8-9[0] ... (b) EPedroza 3 94
(P Harley, Germany) **56/10**

3m 8.9s (188.90) 5Ran SP% 133.4
WIN (incl. 10 euro stakje): 110. PLACES: 23, 14,. SF: 219 .
Owner Stiftung Gestut Fahrhof **Bred** Airlie Stud **Trained** Germany

NOTEBOOK

All My Heart found the ground much too lively, according to her rider.

2966a OPPENHEIM-UNION-RENNEN (GROUP 2) (3YO) (TURF) — 1m 3f

3:40 (12:00) 3-Y-0 **£50,000** (£17,500; £8,333 ; £4,166 ; £2,083 ; £1,250)

RPR

1 **Novellist (IRE)**[35] [1900] 3 -9-2[0] ... EPedroza 8 109
(A Wohler, Germany) *hld up towards rr: stdy prog to chse ldrs over 2 1/2f out: rdn to ld over 1f out: streaked clr ins fnl f: v impressive* **1/5**[1]

2 5 **Munic Boy (USA)**[66] 3 -9-2[0] ... FrederikTylicki 7 100
(Manfred Hofer, Germany) *led: rdn over 2 1/2f out: hdd over 1f out: kpt on wl for 2nd ins fnl f: outclassed by wnr* **154/10**

3 hd **Nexius (IRE)**[42] 3 -9-2[0] ... THellier 4 100
(W Hickst, Germany) *prom on inner: stmbld and lost pl over 4f out: sn rcvrd: rdn 2 1/2f out: kpt on to go 3rd ins fnl f: no ch w wnr* **208/10**

4 shd **Girolamo (GER)**[22] [2296] 3 -9-2[0] ... AStarke 1 99
(P Schiergen, Germany) *midfield: rdn and outpcd over 2f out: flashed home to snatch 4th fnl strides* **129/10**

5 1/2 **Mano Diao**[35] [1900] 3 -9-2[0] ... OlivierPeslier 3 99
(Mario Hofer, Germany) *hld up in last: rdn over 3f out: r.o down wd outside to go 5th on post* **36/5**[2]

6 shd **Andolini (GER)**[22] [2296] 3 -9-2[0] ... JBojko 5 98
(A Wohler, Germany) *trckd ldr on outer: rdn to chal over 2 1/2f out: kpt on tl no ex and fdd wl ins fnl f: lost 2 pls last strides* **112/10**[3]

7 7 **Andreas (GER)** 3 -9-2[0] ... EFrank 2 86
(Markus Klug, Germany) *hld up towards rr on inner: rdn and outpcd over 3f out: plugged on ins fnl 2f: nvr a factor* **121/10**

8 3 1/2 **Le Pursang (GER)**[22] [2296] 3 -9-2[0] ... MrDennisSchiergen 6 79
(P Schiergen, Germany) *midfield on outer: rdn over 2 1/2f out: outpcd and btn over 1 1/2f out: wknd* **28/1**

2m 14.1s (-6.70) 8Ran SP% 132.7
WIN (incl. 10 euro stake): 12. PLACES: 11, 17, 24. SF: 155 .
Owner Dr Christoph Berglar **Bred** Christoph Berglar **Trained** Germany

NOTEBOOK

Novellist(IRE) ran out a convincing winner of Germany's premier Derby trial. Maintaining his unbeaten record, he now looks likely to start the hottest favourite in many years for the Hamburg Classic.

2967a Foreign Racing (See Raceform Interactive)

2521 SAN SIRO (R-H)

Sunday, June 10

OFFICIAL GOING: Turf: soft

2968a GRAN PREMIO DI MILANO SNAI (GROUP 1) (3YO+) (TURF) — 1m 4f

2:55 (12:00) 3-Y-0+ **£79,166** (£34,833; £19,000 ; £9,500)

RPR

1 **Earl Of Tinsdal (GER)**[42] [1700] 4 -9-7[0] ... WilliamBuick 1 116
(A Wohler, Germany) *mde all: set stdy pce: rdn to increase tempo 3f out: over 2 l clr 2f out: kpt on wl u.p ins fnl 1 1/2f: increased advantage cl home: nvr chal* **53/20**[2]

2 3 1/2 **Quiza Quiza Quiza**[28] [2106] 6 -9-4[0] ... CristianDemuro 9 107
(L Riccardi, Italy) *hld up in last trio: impr to trck ldr in 2nd after 4f: rdn over 2 1/2f out: kpt on wl u.p ins fnl 1 1/2f: no ch w wnr* **63/10**

3 nk **Vadamar (FR)**[63] [1245] 4 -9-7[0] ... Christophe-PatriceLemaire 8 110
(M Delzangles, France) *prom early: dropped to midfield over 5f out: rdn to improve 3f out: kpt on u.p ins fnl 2f: nt pce of wnr* **4/5**[1]

4 1 1/2 **Joshua Tree (IRE)**[14] [2534] 5 -9-7[0] ... AdamKirby 7 107
(Marco Botti) *hld up in last pair on outer: rdn to improve over 2 1/2f out: kpt on one pce ins fnl 2f: no ex cl home* **4/1**[3]

5 9 **Sopran Montieri (IRE)**[7] 3 -8-6[0] ... DarioVargiu 5 93
(B Grizzetti, Italy) *midfield on outer: towards rr over 6f out: rdn to try and improve over 3 1/2f out: outpcd 2f out: eased whn btn ins fnl f* **129/10**

6 3 1/2 **Frankenstein**[21] [2323] 5 -9-7[0] ... GArena 3 87
(B Grizzetti, Italy) *hld up in last pair on inner: rdn over 3f out: outpcd over 1 1/2f out: sn btn: eased ins fnl f* **40/1**

7 2 **Saratoga Black (IRE)**[28] [2106] 5 -9-7[0] ... FabioBranca 2 84
(B Grizzetti, Italy) *prom on inner: rdn over 3f out: no ex and btn over 1 1/2f out: wknd and eased over 1f out* **269/10**

2m 30.0s (-1.50)
WFA 3 from 4yo+ 15lb 7Ran SP% 129.9
WIN (incl. 1 euro stake): 3.65. PLACES: 1.22, 1.25, 1.09. DF: 13.75 .
Owner Sunrace Stables **Bred** Hannes K Gutschow **Trained** Germany

NOTEBOOK
Earl Of Tinsdal(GER), last year's German Derby runner-up, made all under William Buick. Having cranked up the tempo from 3f out, he never looked in danger of being caught.
Joshua Tree(IRE) made some headway from the rear inside the final three furlongs but could only keep on at the same pace once push came to shove.

2607 FOLKESTONE (R-H)

Monday, June 11

OFFICIAL GOING: Soft (round course 6.1; straight course: stands' side 6.4, far side 5.8)
Wind: almost nil Weather: overcast

2970 STERLING SERVICE CHAUFFEURS MAIDEN STKS — 5f
2:15 (2:15) (Class 5) 2-Y-0 — **£2,385** (£704; £352) **Stalls** High

Form — RPR

1 **Joey's Destiny (IRE)** 2-9-3 0 ... DaneO'Neill 4 — 89+
(George Baker) *chsd ldr: pushed along to ld 2f out: readily drew clr 1f out* **7/1**[3]

00 **2** *5* **Pippy**[7] 2747 2-9-3 0 ... RichardKingscote 2 — 68
(Tom Dascombe) *slow away: in tch: outpcd over 3f out: pushed along over 2f out: plugged on one pce and swtchd rt 1f out: tk 2nd ins fnl f: nvr any hope of catching wnr* **8/1**

02 **3** *nk* **Hardy Red (IRE)**[8] 2729 2-9-3 0 ... FergusSweeney 3 — 67
(Jamie Osborne) *cl up: pushed along over 2f out: rdn to chse wnr over 1f out: one pce and lost 2nd ins fnl f* **5/4**[1]

4 **4** *3 ½* **Smiling Shark (USA)**[17] 2442 2-9-3 0 ... NeilCallan 5 — 54
(Robert Cowell) *broke wl and led: grabbed stands' side rail: pushed along and hdd 2f out: wknd and lost 2nd over 1f out* **2/1**[2]

5 *14* **Royal Mizar (SPA)** 2-9-3 0 ... LukeMorris 1 — 22+
(Alastair Lidderdale) *slow away and wnt rt s: hung rt thrght and sn floundering: t.o fnl 2f* **16/1**

1m 2.5s (2.50) **Going Correction** +0.40s/f (Good) — **5** Ran SP% **107.3**
Speed ratings (Par 93): **96,88,87,81,59**
CSF £50.92 TOTE £12.40: £3.40, £4.10; EX 71.20.
Owner Delancey **Bred** Brian Wallace **Trained** Whitsbury, Hants

FOCUS
With the market leaders disappointing in this maiden the form is hard to gauge, but the winner could hardly have been more impressive and could prove pretty useful. Improvement from the second.

NOTEBOOK
Joey's Destiny(IRE) ◆, retained for £40,000 as a 2yo, has a pedigree that is all speed and he certainly showed that with the way he galloped away from his rivals over the last furlong or so. The vibes beforehand suggested this wasn't expected and his stable isn't noted for winning juvenile debutants (2-58 in past five seasons), so he is likely to progress and will now take his chance in the Windsor Castle. (op 8-1 tchd 17-2)
Pippy, last in both of his first two starts, got restless in the stalls and fly-jumped exiting them, but he eventually managed to stay on past beaten rivals for a distant second. It seems that he does possess a little ability and this was handy with the nurseries less than a month away. (op 17-2)
Hardy Red(IRE) was only just beaten by a long odds-on shot on his second start, but he dropped tamely away after coming off the bridle at halfway and this was disappointing. The ground may have been an issue, but he now has a bit to prove. (op 6-5 tchd 11-8)
Smiling Shark(USA), outpaced when fourth of six on his Goodwood debut, also dropped out after showing early speed and unless the ground was to blame this was a step backwards. (tchd 15-8)

2971 BHEST RACING TO SCHOOL H'CAP — 5f
2:45 (2:45) (Class 6) (0-55,54) 3-Y-0+ — **£1,704** (£503; £251) **Stalls** High

Form — RPR

3033 **1** **Avonvalley**[20] 2377 5-9-7 **54** ... GeorgeBaker 11 — 65
(Peter Grayson) *hld up against stands' side rail: hdwy over 2f out: pushed along and pressed ldr over 1f out: rdn to ld ins fnl f: kpt on wl* **5/2**[1]

3632 **2** *1* **Bookiesindex Boy**[19] 2406 8-8-12 **45** ... FrederikTylicki 12 — 52
(J R Jenkins) *chsd ldr against stands' side rail: swtchd rt over 1f out: pushed along and chsd wnr ins fnl f: no imp fnl 75yds* **7/2**[2]

6000 **3** *3* **Spic 'n Span**[35] 1910 7-8-13 **46** ... (b) LukeMorris 10 — 43
(Ronald Harris) *taken down early: led against stands' side rail: pushed along over 1f out: drvn and hdd ins fnl f: grad wknd* **16/1**

-060 **4** *5* **Perfect Honour (IRE)**[19] 2385 6-8-9 **45** ... AdamBeschizza(3) 2 — 24
(Des Donovan) *taken down early: slow away and in rr: pushed along after 2f: drvn and plodded on past toiling rivals fr over 1f out* **17/2**

536- **5** *nk* **See Vermont**[230] 7086 4-9-3 **50** ... NeilCallan 4 — 28
(Robin Bastiman) *in tch: swtchd lft after 2f: drvn 2f out: no imp fnl f* **8/1**

-000 **6** *1 ½* **Speedyfix**[20] 2377 5-9-7 **54** ... (tp) TomMcLaughlin 7 — 26
(Christine Dunnett) *in rr: rdn along early: struggling over 3f out: wl btn fnl 2f* **25/1**

4063 **7** *2 ¼* **Toms River Tess (IRE)**[12] 2607 4-8-9 **45** ... SimonPearce(3) 9
(Zoe Davison) *cl up: urged along 2f out: drvn and wknd over 1f out* **10/1**

000- **8** *2 ¾* **Grayfriars**[200] 7525 4-8-7 **45** ... DarylByrne(5) 8
(J R Jenkins) *in rr: rdn over 2f out: sn struggling and btn* **40/1**

0000 **9** *shd* **Litotes**[39] 1768 4-8-7 **45** ... (v) MarkCoumbe(5) 6
(Michael Attwater) *in tch: rdn 3f out: struggling and no ch fnl 2f* **50/1**

003 **10** *1 ¾* **Scommettitrice (IRE)**[7] 2761 4-8-13 **46** ... (b) CathyGannon 5
(David Evans) *in tch: rdn and lost pl 3f out: struggling and wl btn wl over 1f out* **7/1**[3]

550 **11** *nk* **Simple Rhythm**[12] 2607 6-8-9 **45** ... (p) RyanPowell(3) 1
(John Ryan) *in tch on outer: drvn and struggling 3f out: sn dropped away* **12/1**

1m 1.88s (1.88) **Going Correction** +0.40s/f (Good)
WFA 3 from 4yo+ 7lb — **11** Ran SP% **115.8**
Speed ratings (Par 101): **100,98,93,85,85 82,79,74,74,71 71**
toteswingers:1&2:£2.90, 2&3:£10.70, 1&3:£8.30 CSF £10.50 CT £109.77 TOTE £3.90: £1.40, £2.00, £4.60; EX 10.80 Trifecta £93.50 Pool: £693.74 - 5.49 winning units..
Owner Richard Teatum **Bred** Ercan Dogan **Trained** Formby, Lancs

FOCUS
A moderate sprint handicap and the draw was crucial with the leading trio starting from the three stalls closest to the stands' rail. The time was good for the grade but this was still a pretty weak race.

Toms River Tess(IRE) Official explanation: trainer's rep said filly was unsuited by the soft ground

2972 TKM PLUMBERS MERCHANTS LTD CLAIMING STKS — 6f
3:15 (3:15) (Class 6) 3-Y-0+ — **£1,704** (£503; £251) **Stalls** High

Form — RPR

-0U1 **1** **Llewellyn**[4] 2845 4-8-10 67 ... NathanAlison(5) 3 — 74+
(Jim Boyle) *hld up: nt clr run and short of room 2f out: swtchd lft and pushed along over 1f out: led fnl 100yds: pushed out hands and heels: comf* **1/1**[1]

0240 **2** *2 ¼* **Diamond Vine (IRE)**[13] 2572 4-9-2 69 ... (p) LukeMorris 4 — 68
(Ronald Harris) *cl up: pushed along 3f out: drvn and pressed ldr 2f out: led 1f out: hdd fnl 100yds and no ch w wnr* **11/4**[2]

10-0 **3** *3* **Chandigarh (IRE)**[21] 2331 3-8-2 75 ... (b[1]) KieranO'Neill 1 — 50
(Paul Fitzsimons) *slt bump s: led: drvn 2f out: hdd & wknd 1f out: no ch fnl 100yds* **7/2**[3]

0400 **4** *2 ½* **Microlight**[46] 1628 4-9-1 47 ... (v[1]) RichardThomas 5 — 49
(John E Long) *pressed ldr tl 2f out: sn drvn and wknd: wl btn fnl f* **40/1**

4010 **5** *¾* **Kai**[13] 2582 3-8-4 57 ... (v) HayleyTurner 2 — 42
(Michael Bell) *slt bump s: a in last: rdn over 4f out: nt looking keen and wl btn fnl 2f* **10/1**

1m 15.94s (3.24) **Going Correction** +0.525s/f (Yiel)
WFA 3 from 4yo 8lb — **5** Ran SP% **110.4**
Speed ratings (Par 101): **99,96,92,88,87**
CSF £4.04 TOTE £2.30: £1.60, £1.20; EX 4.50.Llewellyn was claimed by K. M. F. Burke for £6000.
Owner Elite Racing Club **Bred** Elite Racing Club **Trained** Epsom, Surrey

FOCUS
A moderate claimer and shaky form with plenty of doubts.

2973 JOHN L HAVERY 60TH BIRTHDAY H'CAP — 6f
3:45 (3:45) (Class 6) (0-65,65) 4-Y-0+ — **£1,704** (£503; £251) **Stalls** High

Form — RPR

3222 **1** **Caramelita**[32] 2012 5-9-3 **61** ... (v) FrederikTylicki 9 — 72
(J R Jenkins) *hld up: short of room 2f out: rdn over 1f out: swtchd rt and produced w str run to ld fnl 75yds: r.o wl* **7/2**[2]

-012 **2** *3* **Mary's Pet**[7] 2760 5-8-7 **58** ... (p) WilliamTwiston-Davies(7) 10 — 59
(Lee Carter) *led: pushed along over 1f out: drvn and hdd fnl 75yds: nt gng pce of wnr* **11/4**[1]

6240 **3** *1 ¼* **Anjomarba (IRE)**[26] 2170 5-9-0 **58** ... HayleyTurner 12 — 55
(Conor Dore) *cl up against rail: rdn over 2f out: drvn and unable qck over 1f out* **7/2**[2]

-044 **4** *½* **Novalist**[7] 2748 4-8-10 **54** ow1 ... (b) NeilCallan 2 — 50
(Robin Bastiman) *cl up on outer: rdn 2f out: one pce and no imp fnl f* **8/1**

1265 **5** *1* **Dancing Welcome**[16] 2493 6-8-13 **64** ... (b) GeorgeDowning(7) 11 — 57
(Milton Bradley) *in tch: rdn 3f out: plugged on one pce ins fnl 2f: nvr a threat* **5/1**[3]

0040 **6** *1 ¼* **Blueberry Fizz (IRE)**[5] 2815 4-8-1 **52** ... (v) BradleyBosley(7) 5 — 41
(John Ryan) *cl up: drvn over 1f out: wknd ins fnl f* **33/1**

-500 **7** *2 ¼* **Colourbearer (IRE)**[13] 2572 5-9-1 **59** ... (t) LukeMorris 4 — 40
(Milton Bradley) *in tch: rdn over 2f out: sn struggling: btn fnl f* **14/1**

3000 **8** *½* **Dingaan (IRE)**[21] 2350 9-8-5 **49** ... CathyGannon 3 — 29
(Peter Grayson) *hld up: rdn 2f out: no ch whn short of room over 1f out* **22/1**

0-00 **9** *5* **Avec Moi**[19] 2406 5-7-13 **46** oh1 ... DominicFox(3) 1 — 10
(Christine Dunnett) *outpcd in rr: drvn and no ch fnl 3f* **66/1**

1m 15.39s (2.69) **Going Correction** +0.525s/f (Yiel) — **9** Ran SP% **114.3**
Speed ratings (Par 101): **103,99,97,96,95 93,90,90,83**
toteswingers:1&2:£2.70, 2&3:£4.20, 1&3:£3.90 CSF £13.18 CT £35.02 TOTE £5.00: £1.80, £1.70, £1.80; EX 11.50 Trifecta £28.30 Pool: £840.47 - 21.93 winning units..
Owner La Senoritas **Bred** R B Hill **Trained** Royston, Herts

FOCUS
Another moderate sprint handicap dominated by those drawn high, even though the winner made her finishing effort down the centre of the track. The winner has a good record here and is rated back to her best.

2974 HP TECHNOLOGY MEDIAN AUCTION MAIDEN STKS — 7f (S)
4:15 (4:18) (Class 6) 3-4-Y-0 — **£1,704** (£503; £251) **Stalls** High

Form — RPR

4-2 **1** **Henry Allingham**[14] 2543 3-9-3 0 ... NeilCallan 10 — 82+
(Roger Varian) *led against rail: pushed along over 1f out: rdn clr ins fnl f: comf* **4/6**[1]

53-2 **2** *4* **Kalokagathia (IRE)**[137] 308 3-9-3 75 ... DaneO'Neill 1 — 71
(Jo Crowley) *cl up on outer: pushed along to chse wnr 3f out: drvn and ev ch over 1f out: no imp ins fnl f* **3/1**[2]

3 *3 ¼* **Exceedexpectations (IRE)** 3-9-3 0 ... HayleyTurner 6 — 63
(Michael Bell) *cl up: rdn 3f out: pushed along and readily outpcd by ldng pair: plugged on one pce fnl f* **7/1**[3]

6 **4** *3 ¾* **Duke Of Destiny (IRE)**[21] 2332 3-9-0 0 ... SimonPearce(3) 5 — 53
(Ed Walker) *in tch: pushed along 3f out: wknd 2f out an stl running green: sn btn* **14/1**

5 *hd* **Bazron (IRE)** 4-9-5 0 ... AdamBeschizza(3) 2 — 51
(Des Donovan) *cl up: drvn along 3f out: no imp and wknd over 1f out* **40/1**

6 *7* **Mrs Bridges** 3-8-12 0 ... RobertHavlin 7 — 29
(Roger Ingram) *dumped rdr twice bef s and taken v steadily to post: a in rr: wl btn fnl 3f* **20/1**

0- **7** *7* **Tijuca (IRE)**[262] 6291 3-8-12 0 ... LiamKeniry 8 — 11
(Ed de Giles) *slowly away and a in rr* **50/1**

1m 30.9s (3.60) **Going Correction** +0.65s/f (Yiel)
WFA 3 from 4yo 10lb — **7** Ran SP% **113.3**
Speed ratings (Par 101): **105,100,96,92,92 84,76**
toteswingers:1&2:£1.60, 2&3:£1.50, 1&3:£2.60 CSF £2.77 TOTE £1.70: £1.60, £2.00; EX 2.70 Trifecta £5.90 Pool: £1121.21 - 139.22 winning units..
Owner R Baines, J Collins & N Horsfall **Bred** Red House Stud **Trained** Newmarket, Suffolk

FOCUS
An uncompetitive maiden and the form horses dominated. Improvement from the winner, who can do a bit better still.

2975 O'CONNELL'S DRYWALL THERMAL RENDERING H'CAP — 7f (S)
4:45 (4:45) (Class 4) (0-85,87) 3-Y-0+ — **£4,851** (£1,443; £721; £360) **Stalls** High

Form — RPR

0-60 **1** **Duster**[24] 2250 5-9-12 **83** ... DarryllHolland 3 — 88
(Hughie Morrison) *slowly away: pushed along to go prom: drvn along 2f out: pressed ldr 1f out: battled on wl and led cl home* **4/1**[2]

-421 **2** *shd* **Spa's Dancer (IRE)**[4] 2855 5-10-2 **87** 6ex ... LiamKeniry 4 — 92
(Ed de Giles) *sn led: grabbed rail 3f out: rdn over 1f out: hanging lft u.p and strly pressed ins fnl f: hdd cl home* **7/4**[1]

0045 **3** 1 1/4 **Tevez**[14] 2545 7-9-7 **81**........(p) AdamBeschizza(3) 9 82
(Des Donovan) *in rr: pushed along 4f out: hdwy 3f out: drvn and ev ch over 1f out: no ex fnl 100yds: jst hld on for 3rd* **5/1**[3]
04-0 **4** *shd* **Sir Glanton (IRE)**[72] 1142 3-9-1 **82**........ HayleyTurner 7 79
(Amanda Perrett) *uns rdr on way to s: midfield: rdn along over 2f out: outpcd 2f out: kpt on 1f out: pressed for 3rd ins fnl f* **16/1**
0-00 **5** *nse* **Soweto Star (IRE)**[18] 2417 4-9-1 **72**........ LiamJones 10 73
(John Best) *in rr: rdn 3f out: struggling 2f out: drvn and kpt on ins fnl f to cl on plcd horses* **20/1**
-106 **6** *nk* **Fourth Of June (IRE)**[21] 2331 3-8-12 **79**........ TomMcLaughlin 1 75
(Ed Dunlop) *hld up: hdwy over 3f out: drvn and chsd ldrs over 1f out: kpt on one pce to press for pls ins fnl f* **10/1**
4604 **7** *7* **Yes Chef**[13] 2576 5-8-13 **70**........ DaneO'Neill 2 52
(Chris Gordon) *cl up: rdn 3f out: wknd 2f out* **10/1**
0-00 **8** *1* **Golden Tempest (IRE)**[18] 2417 4-9-13 **84**........ NeilCallan 6 64
(Eve Johnson Houghton) *cl up: rdn over 2f out: wl btn ins fnl f* **25/1**
041- **9** *21* **Chalk And Cheese (USA)**[247] 6699 3-8-8 **75**........(p) ChrisCatlin 5
(Stuart Williams) *in tch: pushed along and wknd over 3f out: sn toiling and detached: t.o* **20/1**
22-0 **10** *8* **Regal Approval**[41] 1727 4-9-7 **78**........ ShaneKelly 8
(Jim Boyle) *in rr: rdn 4f out: sn toiling and t.o* **25/1**

1m 30.48s (3.18) **Going Correction** +0.65s/f (Yiel)
WFA 3 from 4yo+ 10lb **10** Ran SP% **114.3**
Speed ratings (Par 105): **107,106,105,105,105 104,96,95,71,62**
toteswingers:1&2:£2.90, 2&3:£3.80, 1&3:£4.50 CSF £10.43 CT £34.32 TOTE £5.90: £1.80, £1.10, £2.10; EX 10.50 Trifecta £51.30 Pool: £956.30 - 13.78 winning units..
Owner M T Bevan **Bred** Paddock Space **Trained** East Ilsley, Berks

FOCUS
A competitive handicap and a stirring finish. The winner is rated close to his best.

2976 LADIES LOVE KMFM H'CAP — 2m 93y
5:15 (5:15) (Class 5) (0-75,70) 4-Y-0+ **£2,385** (£704; £352) **Stalls** High

Form RPR
2-05 **1** **Kadouchski (FR)**[28] 1925 8-8-3 **58**........ HannahNunn(7) 2 66
(John Berry) *t.k.h: hld up: urged along 7f out: pushed along 3f out: pressed ldrs on inner 2f out: rdn to ld ins fnl f: r.o wl* **17/2**
55/0 **2** 3/4 **Golan Way**[18] 2411 8-9-7 **69**........ ChrisCatlin 3 75
(Sheena West) *cl up: led after 2f: drvn along 6f out: strly pressed fnl 2f: hdd ins fnl f: no ex fnl 50yds* **9/4**[1]
0025 **3** 1 1/4 **Not Til Monday (IRE)**[19] 2396 6-9-7 **69**........(v) FrederikTylicki 6 75
(J R Jenkins) *led tl hdd after 2f: remained cl up tl shuffled bk 6f out: pushed along 3f out: drvn and no ex ins fnl 2f* **10/3**[3]
0-63 **4** 3/4 **Marcus Antonius**[19] 2396 5-9-4 **66**........ DaneO'Neill 4 70
(Jim Boyle) *in tch: dropped to rr after 5f: hdwy 4f out: produced to chal on outer over 2f out: ev ch over 1f out: no ex ins fnl f* **3/1**[2]
-544 **5** *5* **Shades Of Grey**[16] 2502 5-9-5 **67**........ JohnFahy 5 65
(Clive Cox) *mounted outside paddock: cl up: jnd ldr 6f out: drvn 3f out: wknd ins fnl 2f* **7/2**

3m 52.23s (15.03) **Going Correction** +0.775s/f (Yiel)
WFA 4 from 5yo+ 1lb **5** Ran SP% **111.6**
Speed ratings (Par 103): **93,92,92,91,89**
CSF £28.10 TOTE £5.30: £2.00, £1.70; EX 14.30.
Owner John Berry **Bred** Henrietta Charlet & Danny Charlesworth **Trained** Newmarket, Suffolk

FOCUS
An ordinary staying event run at a modest gallop. The form is rated at face value.
T/Plt: £34.80 to a £1 stake. Pool of £55,323.31 - 1,157.57 winning tickets. T/Qpdt: £1.60 to a £1 stake. Pool of £6,130.81 - 2,798.38 winning tickets. CS

2675 PONTEFRACT (L-H)
Monday, June 11

OFFICIAL GOING: Good (7.5)
False rail in place over last 6f, about 5yds from inside line and added about 12yds to advertised distances of all races.
Wind: Moderate half against Weather: Overcast

2977 RADIO AIRE BREAKFAST SHOW MAIDEN AUCTION FILLIES' STKS — 6f
6:50 (6:52) (Class 5) 2-Y-O **£2,385** (£704; £352) **Stalls** Low

Form RPR
1 **Agent Allison** 2-8-10 0........ WilliamBuick 3 91+
(Peter Chapple-Hyam) *trckd ldrs: hdwy 2f out: rdn to ld ent fnl f: sn clr: styd on strly* **13/8**[1]
22 **2** *7* **Throwing Roses**[34] 1949 2-8-4 0........ JamesSullivan 8 61
(Ollie Pears) *led: rdn wl over 1f out: hdd ent fnl f: kpt on* **8/1**[3]
0 **3** *1* **Senafe**[25] 2193 2-8-4 0........ NickyMackay 4 58
(Marco Botti) *chsd ldr: rdn along 2f out: drvn and one pce fnl f* **10/1**
4 *shd* **Disko Dasko (FR)** 2-8-6 0........ SilvestreDeSousa 1 60
(Mrs K Burke) *chsd ldrs: rdn along 2f out: kpt on same pce* **16/1**
5 2 3/4 **Awakened Spirit (IRE)** 2-8-6 0........ WayneLordan 7 51+
(David Wachman, Ire) *in tch: rdn along over 2f out: drvn wl over 1f out and no hdwy* **7/2**[2]
6 *15* **Lucky Prize** 2-8-4 0........ FrannyNorton 2
(Mel Brittain) *a towards rr* **22/1**
7 *nk* **Princess Hollow** 2-8-5 0 ow1........ BarryMcHugh 6
(Tony Coyle) *dwlt and wnt rt s: a in rr* **40/1**
8 3 1/2 **Hi Candy (IRE)** 2-8-6 0........ PJMcDonald 5
(Ben Haslam) *s.i.s: a in rr* **50/1**
0 **9** *6* **Dark Eros (IRE)**[23] 2282 2-8-4 0........ DuranFentiman 11
(Tim Easterby) *a in rr* **16/1**
U **Fenwick Gale (IRE)** 2-8-8 0........ PaulMulrennan 10
(Kevin Ryan) *swvd bdly rt s: fly-leapt and bucked and uns rdr ins first f* **8/1**[3]

1m 18.16s (1.26) **Going Correction** +0.325s/f (Good) **10** Ran SP% **112.1**
Speed ratings (Par 90): **104,94,93,93,89 69,69,64,56,**
toteswingers:1&2:£3.50, 2&3:£9.40, 1&3:£5.70 CSF £14.30 TOTE £2.10: £1.02, £2.40, £3.00; EX 13.00.
Owner Mrs Fitri Hay **Bred** D R Botterill **Trained** Newmarket, Suffolk

FOCUS
A false rail was in place from 6f out, adding around 12yds to all races. The track had missed all the rain and the ground was largely described as "good" by those who rode in the first, although Barry McHugh felt it was "on the slow side". No more than an ordinary juvenile maiden, with the runner-up helping with the level, but the winner impressed and is clearly useful.

NOTEBOOK
Agent Allison, half-sister to a 1m winner, was conceding weight all round yet stretched right away in the style of a useful filly. Royal Ascot's not far away but she'd fully entitled to take her chance in the Albany. (op 7-4 tchd 6-4)
Throwing Roses appeared to run to form, not necessarily improving for the step up to 6f. (op 7-1)
Senafe improved markedly on her debut effort, looking to know a lot more this time, and she's a likely type for nurseries. (tchd 9-1)
Disko Dasko(FR), a half-sister to French winners at 4.5f and 1m2f, seemed to know her job well enough and ought to benefit from 7f. (op 20-1)
Awakened Spirit(IRE), whose dam managed no more than a fourth over 5f from two starts, proved one-paced and was a little disappointing considering she'd come across from Ireland.

2978 TONY BETHELL MEMORIAL H'CAP — 2m 1f 22y
7:20 (7:20) (Class 4) (0-80,80) 4-Y-0+ **£4,204** (£1,251; £625; £312) **Stalls** Low

Form RPR
0341 **1** **Blackstone Vegas**[20] 2371 6-8-5 **61** oh2........ JoeFanning 13 71
(Derek Shaw) *hld up in rr: stdy hdwy 4f out: chsd ldrs 2f out: swtchd to outer and rdn to chal over 1f out: styd on to ld ins fnl f: kpt on wl* **14/1**
06-5 **2** 1 1/4 **Mojolika**[17] 2457 4-9-0 **71**........ GrahamGibbons 12 79
(Tim Easterby) *stdd s: hld up in rr: stdy hdwy 5f out: chsd ldrs 2f out: rdn over 1f out: kpt on fnl f* **14/1**
0500 **3** *5* **The Bells O Peover**[4] 2863 4-9-9 **80**........(v) SilvestreDeSousa 9 83
(Mark Johnston) *trckd ldr: led 4f out: rdn clr 2f out: drvn ent fnl f: sn hdd and one pce* **12/1**
006- **4** 3/4 **Petella**[238] 6915 6-8-10 **66**........ PJMcDonald 10 68
(George Moore) *hld up in rr: hdwy over 6f out: effrt on outer to chse ldrs 3f out: rdn along wl over 1f out: sn one pce* **25/1**
10-0 **5** 1 3/4 **Blimey O'Riley (IRE)**[18] 2423 7-9-4 **74**........ TedDurcan 5 74
(Mark H Tompkins) *in tch: hdwy to trck ldrs over 4f out: rdn to chse ldr wl over 1f out: drvn and wknd ent fnl f* **5/1**[2]
-030 **6** *2* **Descaro (USA)**[20] 2378 6-8-12 **68**........ MichaelO'Connell 3 66
(David O'Meara) *hld up towards rr: hdwy on inner whn n.m.r over 4f out: rdn 2f out: styd on to chse ldrs over 1f out: no imp fnl f* **14/1**
0-13 **7** *9* **Passion Play**[27] 2149 4-8-9 **66**........ WilliamBuick 2 54
(William Knight) *prom: effrt 3f out: rdn along over 2f out: sn wknd* **12/1**
-550 **8** 1 1/2 **My Arch**[17] 2457 10-9-9 **79**........ TomQueally 6 65
(Ollie Pears) *in tch on outer: rdn along over 7f out: lost pl and bhd 4f out* **10/1**[3]
64-2 **9** 3/4 **Emrani (USA)**[10] 2666 5-9-5 **75**........(b) GrahamLee 4 60
(Donald McCain) *hld up towards rr: hdwy into midfield 1/2-way: rdn along 4f out: sn btn* **5/1**[2]
044 **10** *31* **Bocamix (FR)**[9] 2698 6-8-10 **66**........(t) RobertWinston 1 17
(Andrew Crook) *chsd ldrs on inner: rdn along 5f out: sn wknd* **20/1**
30-0 **11** *8* **Wells Lyrical (IRE)**[37] 1846 7-9-7 **77**........ PaulHanagan 8 19
(Bryan Smart) *led: rdn along and hdd 4f out: sn wknd* **9/2**[1]
00-6 **12** *13* **May Contain Nuto**[18] 2411 4-9-0 **71**........ KirstyMilczarek 7
(Brendan Powell) *trckd ldrs: hdwy 4f out: chsd ldr 3f out: sn rdn and wknd qckly wl over 1f out* **11/1**
-065 **13** *50* **Saborido (USA)**[18] 2411 6-9-7 **77**........ PaulMulrennan 11
(Amanda Perrett) *chsd ldrs: rdn along 6f out: sn lost pl and bhd: t.o fnl 3f* **10/1**[3]

3m 53.87s (9.27) **Going Correction** +0.325s/f (Good)
WFA 4 from 5yo+ 1lb **13** Ran SP% **122.0**
Speed ratings (Par 105): **91,90,88,87,86 85,81,81,80,66 62,56,32**
toteswingers:1&2:£36.40, 2&3:£12.70, 1&3:£59.10 CSF £200.60 CT £2432.78 TOTE £19.80: £4.80, £4.10, £4.00; EX 369.10.
Owner Shakespeare Racing **Bred** Elms Stud Co Ltd **Trained** Sproxton, Leics

FOCUS
A typically open staying handicap for the course, and despite the early pace being far from frantic, the race set up for the closers. Pretty straightforward form.
Saborido(USA) Official explanation: jockey said gelding ran flat

2979 MR WOLF SPRINT H'CAP — 6f
7:50 (7:52) (Class 3) (0-90,88) 3-Y-O **£7,115** (£2,117; £1,058; £529) **Stalls** Low

Form RPR
5-31 **1** **All Or Nothin (IRE)**[16] 2470 3-8-9 **76**........ MichaelO'Connell 2 90
(John Quinn) *in tch: hdwy 2f out: swtchd lft and rdn to chal ent fnl f: sn led: drvn out* **8/1**
0-30 **2** 3/4 **Springinmystep (IRE)**[11] 2616 3-9-0 **81**........(t) PaulMulrennan 1 93
(Michael Dods) *trckd ldng pair on inner: hdwy 2f out: rdn and squeezed through to chal ent fnl f: ev ch tl drvn and no ex last 75yds* **11/2**[3]
1215 **3** 4 1/2 **Half A Billion (IRE)**[18] 2416 3-8-8 **78**........ LeeTopliss(3) 4 76
(Michael Dods) *led: rdn along wl over 1f out: drvn and hdd jst ins fnl f: sn one pce* **11/1**
-302 **4** 1 1/4 **Chooseday (IRE)**[5] 2824 3-8-12 **79**........ AmyRyan 5 73
(Kevin Ryan) *cl up: rdn 2f out: ev ch tl drvn and wknd ent fnl f* **4/1**[2]
2353 **5** 2 1/2 **Waseem Faris (IRE)**[17] 2451 3-8-12 **79**........ MartinHarley 3 65
(Mick Channon) *hld up: hdwy to chse ldrs 2f out: rdn over 1f out and sn btn* **9/1**
-400 **6** 1 3/4 **Right Result (IRE)**[23] 2265 3-8-8 **75**........ GrahamGibbons 6 55
(James Bethell) *dwlt and in rr: hdwy 2f out: sn rdn and kpt on appr fnl f* **10/1**
0-01 **7** *8* **Orders From Rome (IRE)**[33] 1986 3-8-12 **79**........ TomQueally 9 33
(Eve Johnson Houghton) *dwlt: a towards rr* **22/1**
-303 **8** *4* **Whisky Bravo**[11] 2616 3-8-10 **77**........ RobertWinston 7 19
(David Brown) *a towards rr* **16/1**
1-64 **9** 1 1/2 **Rafeej**[23] 2276 3-9-7 **88**........ PaulHanagan 8 25
(Mark Johnston) *chsd ldrs: rdn along over 2f out: sn wknd* **11/4**[1]

1m 18.27s (1.37) **Going Correction** +0.325s/f (Good) **9** Ran SP% **110.8**
Speed ratings (Par 103): **103,102,96,94,91 88,78,72,70**
toteswingers:1&2:£5.10, 2&3:£12.30, 1&3:£7.60 CSF £48.35 CT £464.71 TOTE £9.90: £3.40, £2.60, £3.20; EX 56.10.
Owner Ross Harmon **Bred** Ballyhane Stud **Trained** Settrington, N Yorks

FOCUS
A decent 3yo sprint handicap and the first two finished clear. The winner was unexposed.

NOTEBOOK
All Or Nothin(IRE), all-the-way winner of a Chester maiden over this trip, improved again to make a winning handicap debut from a mark of 76. He ought to prove as effective back at 7f and looks the type with more to give.
Springinmystep(IRE) bounced back from a poor effort at Ayr, returning to the level of his earlier C&D form. The return of the tongue-tie clearly helped and his trainer's on a fine run at present. (op 13-2 tchd 7-1)
Half A Billion(IRE) had plenty of use made of him on this drop in trip but lacked the pace late on. (op 12-1)
Chooseday(IRE) was unable to build on his Ripon second from five days earlier. (tchd 7-2)
Right Result(IRE) Official explanation: jockey said gelding missed the break

Rafeej was conceding 7lb or more to his rivals but that was no excuse for such a tame effort, being in trouble by halfway and dropping right out. This clearly wasn't his true form. Official explanation: jockey said colt never travelled (op 9-4)

2980 READ HAYLEY AT RACINGUK.COM EVERY FRIDAY H'CAP — 1m 2f 6y

8:20 (8:21) (Class 4) (0-80,78) 3-Y-O — **£4,528** (£1,347; £673; £336) **Stalls** Low

Form — RPR

-311 **1** **Forget Me Not Lane (IRE)**[10] 2671 3-9-2 **73** .... GrahamLee 2 — 81+
(Kevin Ryan) *cl up on inner: led after 1 1/2f: rdn over 1f out: drvn ins fnl f: hld on gamely* **5/1**[1]

4-32 **2** *1/2* **Muntasir (IRE)**[13] 2585 3-9-7 **78** .... SilvestreDeSousa 6 — 85+
(Saeed Bin Suroor) *hld up towards rr: hdwy 2f out: rdn over 1f out: styd on strly ins fnl f: nt quite rch wnr* **8/1**

6-43 **3** *1 1/2* **Corsetry (USA)**[20] 2379 3-9-3 **74** .... TomQueally 9 — 78
(Sir Henry Cecil) *trckd ldrs: hdwy 2f out: rdn to chse wnr ent fnl f: sn edgd lft and one pce* **13/2**[3]

-405 **4** *1 1/2* **Tallevu (IRE)**[17] 2449 3-8-8 **65** .... RichardKingscote 4 — 66
(Tom Dascombe) *trckd ldrs: hdwy 2f out: rdn wl over 1f out: drvn and one pce fnl f* **25/1**

-303 **5** *hd* **Chelsea Mick**[17] 2449 3-8-5 **69** .... IanBurns(7) 1 — 70
(John Mackie) *trckd ldrs on inner: hdwy 2f out: rdn over 1f out: kpt on same pce fnl f* **9/1**

5-40 **6** *1 1/2* **Petaluma**[36] 1887 3-9-2 **73** .... MartinHarley 3 — 71
(Mick Channon) *hld up: hdwy over 2f out: rdn wl over 1f out: sn no imp* **8/1**

16-0 **7** *nk* **Never Perfect (IRE)**[17] 2449 3-9-1 **72** .... MickyFenton 8 — 70+
(Tom Tate) *s.i.s and bhd: hdwy over 2f out: rdn wl over 1f out: kpt on: nrst fin* **16/1**

1-5 **8** *4* **Gabrial's Star**[54] 1440 3-9-7 **78** .... FrannyNorton 10 — 67
(Bryan Smart) *hld up: a in rr* **6/1**[2]

3100 **9** *4 1/2* **Three Bards (IRE)**[17] 2452 3-9-1 **72** .... JoeFanning 5 — 52
(Mark Johnston) *led 1 1/2f: cl up: rdn along 2f out: sn drvn and wknd* **14/1**

2313 **10** *21* **Eshaab (USA)**[24] 2235 3-9-7 **78** .... PaulHanagan 11 — 16
(Ed Dunlop) *chsd ldrs: rdn along wl over 2f out: sn wknd* **13/2**[3]

22-4 **11** *53* **Journalistic (USA)**[20] 2380 3-9-7 **78** .... WilliamBuick 7
(Marcus Tregoning) *hld up: a in rr: eased and bhd fnl 1 1/2f* **14/1**

2m 15.78s (2.08) **Going Correction** +0.325s/f (Good) — **11** Ran SP% **112.9**
Speed ratings (Par 101): **104,103,102,101,101 99,99,96,92,76 33**
toteswingers:1&2:£9.50, 2&3:£3.40, 1&3:£5.60 CSF £42.57 CT £260.04 TOTE £5.20: £2.00, £2.50, £2.40; EX 37.20.
Owner J Hanson **Bred** Mrs Arkada Partnership **Trained** Hambleton, N Yorks

FOCUS
Few got into what looked a decent,competitive 3yo handicap. The winner took another step forward.
Never Perfect(IRE) Official explanation: jockey said gelding was denied a clear run
Journalistic(USA) Official explanation: jockey said colt never travelled

2981 FAMILY DAY PACKAGES ON SUNDAY JUNE 24TH H'CAP — 6f

8:50 (8:51) (Class 5) (0-70,69) 3-Y-O+ — **£2,385** (£704; £352) **Stalls** Low

Form — RPR

5401 **1** **Pitkin**[9] 2696 4-9-5 **60** .... (b) PaulMulrennan 12 — 77+
(Michael Easterby) *cl up: slt ld after 1f: rdn wl over 1f out: drvn and styd on wl fnl f* **13/2**[2]

1053 **2** *2 1/4* **Consistant**[14] 2538 4-9-7 **62** .... DuranFentiman 1 — 71
(Brian Baugh) *led 1f: cl up on inner: rdn wl over 1f out and ev ch tl drvn and one pce ins fnl f* **8/1**[3]

0065 **3** *2 1/2* **Mark Anthony (IRE)**[4] 2839 5-9-0 **55** .... (p) JoeFanning 6 — 56+
(Shaun Harris) *dwlt and in rr: hdwy 2f out: rdn to chse ldrs over 1f out: kpt on u.p fnl f: nrst fin* **10/1**

0505 **4** *1 1/4* **Mazovian (USA)**[14] 2549 4-9-10 **65** .... SilvestreDeSousa 10 — 62
(Michael Chapman) *prom: rdn along 2f out: drvn wl over 1f out: kpt on same pce* **17/2**

0010 **5** *3/4* **Powerful Pierre**[21] 2355 5-9-9 **67** .... (b) DaleSwift(3) 3 — 62
(Ian McInnes) *chsd ldrs on inner: rdn along 2f out: sn one pce* **12/1**

0020 **6** *nk* **Divertimenti (IRE)**[14] 2549 8-9-7 **65** .... (b) LeeTopliss(3) 2 — 59
(Roy Bowring) *prom: chsd ldng pair 1/2-way: rdn 2f out and sn wknd* **9/1**

0-23 **7** *1/2* **Cadmium Loch**[14] 2555 4-8-12 **60** .... (p) JackDuern(7) 4 — 52
(Reg Hollinshead) *chsd ldrs: rdn along 2f out: sn drvn and wknd* **7/2**[1]

0620 **8** *1* **Northern Bolt**[9] 2693 7-10-0 **69** .... PatrickMathers 5 — 58
(Ian McInnes) *nvr bttr than midfield* **20/1**

61- **9** *1* **Taro Tywod (IRE)**[282] 5726 3-9-6 **69** .... DavidNolan 11 — 53
(Ann Duffield) *nvr nr ldrs* **8/1**[3]

2636 **10** *3/4* **The Happy Hammer (IRE)**[16] 2482 6-9-8 **63** .... GrahamLee 8 — 46
(Eugene Stanford) *a in rr* **9/1**

3240 **11** *shd* **Man Of My Word**[20] 2375 3-9-1 **64** .... (p) TomQueally 9 — 45
(Scott Dixon) *chsd ldrs: rdn along 2f out: sn wknd* **16/1**

0-06 **12** *1 3/4* **Cottam Stella**[31] 2046 4-8-10 **51** oh5 ow1 .... RobertWinston 13 — 28
(Mel Brittain) *a in rr* **50/1**

1m 19.19s (2.29) **Going Correction** +0.325s/f (Good)
WFA 3 from 4yo+ 8lb — **12** Ran SP% **117.7**
Speed ratings (Par 103): **97,94,90,89,88 87,86,85,84,83 83,80**
toteswingers:1&2:£5.10, 2&3:£14.80, 1&3:£10.40 CSF £57.33 CT £526.79 TOTE £6.60: £1.70, £2.40, £4.10; EX 56.80.
Owner Steve Hull **Bred** New Mill Farm Stud **Trained** Sheriff Hutton, N Yorks

FOCUS
The field was soon strung out in this sprint handicap, the pace being a good one, but the leaders kept going. The winner stepped up on his latest form.
Cadmium Loch Official explanation: jockey said gelding ran flat

2982 KIDS PICNIC PACKAGE FOR £5 H'CAP — 5f

9:20 (9:20) (Class 5) (0-75,73) 4-Y-O+ — **£2,385** (£704; £352) **Stalls** Low

Form — RPR

0-02 **1** **Commanche Raider (IRE)**[10] 2674 5-9-3 **69** .... (b) PaulMulrennan 4 — 75
(Michael Dods) *hld up in rr: hdwy over 1f out: rdn and str run ins fnl f to ld nr line* **9/2**[1]

0050 **2** *shd* **Sir Geoffrey (IRE)**[30] 2084 6-8-13 **65** .... (p) RobertWinston 6 — 71
(Scott Dixon) *hld up towards rr: hdwy 2f out: rdn over 1f out: chal ins fnl f and ev ch tl drvn and nt qckn nr line* **12/1**

0405 **3** *hd* **Master Of Disguise**[9] 2690 6-9-7 **73** .... (t) DuranFentiman 8 — 78
(Brian Baugh) *sn led: rdn wl over 1f out: drvn ins fnl f: hdd and nt qckn nr line* **5/1**[2]

0-00 **4** *1 1/2* **Lady Kildare (IRE)**[9] 2690 4-8-10 **62** .... AndrewElliott 9 — 62
(Jedd O'Keeffe) *trckd ldrs: effrt 2f out: rdn and ch over 1f out: drvn and one pce fnl f* **28/1**

2304 **5** *1/2* **Select Committee**[6] 2793 7-9-7 **73** .... (v) MichaelO'Connell 3 — 71
(John Quinn) *cl up: ev ch 2f out tl rdn and one pce ins fnl f* **11/2**[3]

461 **6** *3/4* **Rio's Girl**[7] 2749 5-8-7 **59** 6ex .... BarryMcHugh 5 — 54
(Tony Coyle) *n.m.r and hmpd sn after s: in rr: hdwy on outer to chse ldrs over 2f out: rdn wl over 1f out: kpt on same pce appr fnl f* **8/1**

1006 **7** *6* **Prince James**[9] 2693 5-8-8 **60** .... JamesSullivan 10 — 34
(Michael Easterby) *in tch: rdn along over 2f out: sn wknd* **20/1**

4000 **8** *3/4* **Ingleby Star (IRE)**[9] 2690 7-9-0 **71** .... (p) JustinNewman(5) 1 — 42
(Ian McInnes) *cl up on inner: ev ch 2f out: rdn and wknd over 1f out* **10/1**

56-1 **9** *1 1/2* **Bilash**[20] 2377 5-9-1 **67** .... GrahamLee 2 — 32
(Reg Hollinshead) *a towards rr* **5/1**[2]

550- **10** *4* **Mr Wolf**[263] 6276 11-8-13 **65** .... (p) TonyHamilton 7 — 16
(Paul Midgley) *chsd ldrs: rdn along 2f out: sn wknd* **9/1**

1m 5.86s (2.56) **Going Correction** +0.325s/f (Good) — **10** Ran SP% **113.0**
Speed ratings (Par 103): **92,91,91,89,88 87,77,76,73,67**
toteswingers:1&2:£9.90, 2&3:£12.20, 1&3:£6.40 CSF £56.69 CT £277.28 TOTE £4.70: £1.60, £4.30, £1.90; EX 68.00.
Owner Doug Graham **Bred** Epona Bloodstock Ltd **Trained** Denton, Co Durham
■ Stewards' Enquiry : Robert Winston two-day ban: used whip above permitted level (Jun 25-26)

FOCUS
A modest but competitive sprint handicap. The winner had dropped to a good mark but there are doubts over the form.
T/Jkpt: Part won. £27,164.40 to a £1 stake. Pool £38,259.72 - 0.50 winning units. T/Plt: £905.80 to a £1 stake. Pool £82,656.65 - 66.61 winning units. T/Qpdt: £64.90 to a £1 stake. Pool £5,870.60 - 66.90 winning units. JR

2937 WINDSOR (R-H)

Monday, June 11

OFFICIAL GOING: Soft (heavy in places; 5.5)
Top bend dolled out 2yds from normal inner configuration adding 7yds to race distances of 1m and over.
Wind: Light, behind Weather: Overcast, drizzly

2983 EBF COOLMORE ALFRED NOBLE MEDIAN AUCTION MAIDEN STKS — 6f

6:10 (6:12) (Class 5) 2-Y-O — **£3,234** (£962; £481; £240) **Stalls** Low

Form — RPR

0 **1** **Silver Ridge (IRE)**[24] 2231 2-9-3 0 .... JimCrowley 9 — 82+
(Ralph Beckett) *mde virtually all: shkn up and drew clr over 1f out: readily* **5/2**[1]

0 **2** *5* **Ronaldinho (IRE)**[16] 2480 2-9-0 0 .... SeanLevey(3) 4 — 66+
(Richard Hannon) *dwlt: sn prom: rdn to chse wnr wl over 1f out: one pce and sn no imp* **14/1**

3 *1/2* **Red Refraction (IRE)** 2-9-3 0 .... RichardHughes 11 — 65
(Richard Hannon) *hld up in rr: prog 1/2-way: shkn up 2f out: kpt on to take 3rd fnl f: n.d* **7/2**[2]

5 **4** *1* **Standing Bear (IRE)**[10] 2648 2-8-12 0 .... DuilioDaSilva(5) 6 — 62+
(Paul Cole) *outpcd and bhd in last: stl there 2f out: pushed along and gd prog over 1f out: styd on wl to take 4th nr fin* **40/1**

5 *1 1/4* **The Sixties** 2-9-3 0 .... TonyCulhane 14 — 60+
(Mick Channon) *dwlt: bhd early: prog fr 1/2-way: pushed along and styd on steadily fnl 2f* **16/1**

5 **6** *1 1/2* **It's Only Business**[13] 2571 2-8-10 0 .... JakePayne(7) 8 — 53+
(Bill Turner) *stirrup leather broke sn after s: pressed wnr to wl over 1f out: wknd fnl f* **66/1**

7 *3/4* **Secret Beau** 2-9-3 0 .... JamesDoyle 7 — 51
(George Baker) *prom: shkn up to dispute 2nd wl over 1f out: rn green and wknd sn after* **20/1**

44 **8** *2 1/2* **Composed**[14] 2550 2-9-3 0 .... StevieDonohoe 2 — 44
(Paul Cole) *in tch: pushed along bef 1/2-way: struggling over 2f out* **9/2**[3]

00 **9** *1 1/4* **Devout (IRE)**[16] 2499 2-8-7 0 .... LeonnaMayor(5) 15 — 35
(Jamie Osborne) *w ldrs to 2f out: wknd* **33/1**

10 *1/2* **Keene's Pointe** 2-9-3 0 .... MartinLane 10 — 38
(J W Hills) *chsd ldrs: pushed along 1/2-way: wknd 2f out* **20/1**

11 *3* **Overrider** 2-9-3 0 .... LukeMorris 12 — 29
(Charles Hills) *difficult to load into stalls: pushed along to chse ldrs: wknd 2f out* **14/1**

12 *1 3/4* **Noble Bull (IRE)** 2-9-3 0 .... MichaelHills 5 — 24
(Charles Hills) *dwlt: outpcd and a bhd* **9/1**

13 *3 1/2* **Cardmaster (IRE)** 2-9-3 0 .... CathyGannon 16 — 14
(Eve Johnson Houghton) *chsd ldrs over 2f: sn wknd qckly* **25/1**

1m 18.12s (5.12) **Going Correction** +0.70s/f (Yiel) — **13** Ran SP% **118.4**
Speed ratings (Par 93): **93,86,85,84,82 80,79,76,74,74 70,67,63**
toteswingers:1&2:£7.50, 2&3:£8.20, 1&3:£3.10 CSF £35.86 TOTE £2.70: £1.10, £5.20, £2.10; EX 34.70 Trifecta £130.90 Pool £491.91 - 2.78 winning units..
Owner The Pickford Hill Partnership **Bred** Ballykilbride Stud **Trained** Kimpton, Hants

FOCUS
There was 19mm of rain overnight and another 5mm in the morning, and the ground, previously described as good to soft, had eased to soft, heavy in places (mainly around top bends in 1m+ races), with the GoingStick reading moving from 6.9 to 5.5. The top bend was dolled out 2yds from its normal configuration, adding 7yds to race distances of 1m+; the remainder of the running rail was back at its normal configuration. Some good horses have won this maiden in the last ten years, including subsequent Listed winner Privy Seal, Group 3 winner Scarlet Runner, Group 2 winner Assertive and dual Group 1 winner Dick Turpin. Silver Ridge fits with the race averages and plenty ran with promise behind.

NOTEBOOK
Silver Ridge(IRE) won easily, stepping up greatly on his debut effort at Newbury. By Verglas out of an Indian Ridge mare, clearly the testing conditions suited him well, and his trainer suggested he'll be kept to this sort of ground if possible. (op 3-1 tchd 100-30)
Ronaldinho(IRE), whose trainer had won four of the previous ten renewals of this maiden, had an excuse for finishing well beaten on his debut as he apparently kicked himself leaving the stalls and this was a better reflection of his ability. He should come on for this and ought to get further in time (dam 1m4f winner). (op 10-1)
Red Refraction(IRE) looked the Hannon first string, but he had two handlers in the paddock, didn't impress going down to the start and was weak in the betting. He didn't run badly all things considered, and there should be better to come on faster ground. (tchd 3-1 and 4-1)
Standing Bear(IRE) struggled to go the pace early and was detached in last at one point, but he finished his race off in eyecatching style. Bred to want further in time, the way he ran underlined the impression that he'll be interesting once eligible for nurseries and stepped up to 7f.
The Sixties was awkward from the stalls and lost ground. Kidded along, he was too green to do himself complete justice, but he was keeping on nicely at the finish and looks sure to improve a bundle for this debut outing. (tchd 14-1)

It's Only Business's rider had his right leg out of the iron (stirrup leather broke) from when the stalls opened. Naturally this hampered his ability to ride a finish and in the circumstances the colt ran well. Official explanation: jockey said stirrup leathers snapped leaving stalls
Secret Beau, who was a bit keen, showed ability and might do better on quicker ground. (op 22-1)
Composed will be of more interest in nurseries in due course.

2984 TEXT WISH TO 70123 CLAIMING STKS 1m 2f 7y
6:40 (6:40) (Class 5) 3-Y-0+ **£2,264** (£673; £336; £168) **Stalls** High

Form RPR
3145 **1** **Eagle Nebula**[16] 2502 8-9-7 68 IanMongan 4 72
(Brett Johnson) *chsd clr ldr: led wl over 2f out: hrd rdn over 1f out: in command fnl f: eased last strides* **8/1**
2 *1 1/4* **Offbeat Safaris (IRE)**[38] 4-9-6 0 GeorgeDowning(7) 2 75
(Brendan Powell) *s.s: hld up in last pair: prog 4f out: chsd wnr over 2f out: tried to chal on inner over 1f out but no room: no imp fnl f* **15/2**
543- **3** *nk* **Foxhaven**[208] 7430 10-9-9 77 (v) GeorgeBaker 5 70
(Patrick Chamings) *prom: chsd wnr over 2f out: sn rdn and nt qckn: kpt on but jst lost out in battle for 2nd* **7/2[2]**
3106 **4** *4* **Call To Reason (IRE)**[32] 1993 5-9-7 81 JimCrowley 1 60
(Ian Williams) *hld up in rr: prog to go 4th wl over 1f out: rdn and no hdwy after* **5/2[1]**
0-60 **5** *4* **Cashelgar (IRE)**[128] 427 6-9-6 92 DeclanCannon(3) 9 54
(Richard Guest) *t.k.h early: hld up in tch: pushed along over 2f out: fdd* **4/1[3]**
413/ **6** *6* **King's Masque**[651] 5591 6-8-9 75 DanielMuscutt(7) 8 35
(Bernard Llewellyn) *t.k.h: hld up in tch: wknd over 2f out* **6/1**
-2P0 **7** *18* **Royal Alcor (IRE)**[50] 850 5-9-2 63 (b) LeonnaMayor(5) 7
(Alastair Lidderdale) *led and clr: styd towards nr side early in st: hdd & wknd rapidly wl over 2f out: t.o* **16/1**

2m 16.22s (7.52) **Going Correction** +0.55s/f (Yiel) **7 Ran SP% 113.8**
Speed ratings (Par 103): **91,90,89,86,83 78,64**
toteswingers:1&2:£4.30, 2&3:£6.00, 1&3:£2.10 CSF £63.92 TOTE £9.00: £3.20, £3.10; EX 80.10 Trifecta £207.20 Part won. Pool £280.12 - 0.64 winning units..
Owner Tann Racing **Bred** Juddmonte Farms Ltd **Trained** Epsom, Surrey

FOCUS
The higher-rated runners failed to come up to scratch here. It was a fair race on paper, but there are the usual doubts over the form, which is rated around the winner.

2985 PERTEMPS NETWORK H'CAP 1m 2f 7y
7:10 (7:10) (Class 4) (0-80,79) 4-Y-0+ **£4,204** (£1,251; £625; £312) **Stalls** High

Form RPR
2520 **1** **Megalala (IRE)**[5] 2810 11-9-6 78 KieranO'Neill 7 84
(John Bridger) *mde all: rdn whn pressed over 2f out: gained upper hand over 1f out: eased nr fin* **9/4[1]**
60-0 **2** *1 3/4* **Urban Space**[19] 2389 6-8-11 69 KierenFox 6 72
(John Flint) *n.m.r after 2f and dropped to last: prog 1/2-way: chsd wnr over 3f out: drvn to chal over 2f out: no ex over 1f out* **3/1[2]**
1000 **3** *14* **Standpoint**[5] 2810 6-9-4 76 (p) LukeMorris 3 51
(Conor Dore) *t.k.h early: trckd ldng pair: rdn 4f out: lft bhd fnl 3f* **11/2[3]**
4210 **4** *2 1/2* **Ostentation**[3] 2867 5-8-7 65 (b) MartinLane 8 35
(Alastair Lidderdale) *chsd wnr to over 3f out: sn btn: flat out in remote 4th fnl 2f* **3/1[2]**
-136 **5** *24* **Miss Bootylishes**[7] 2766 7-9-2 79 DavidKenny(5) 4
(Paul Burgoyne) *in tch: effrt over 3f out: sn wknd: wl bhd last 2f: eased and t.o* **7/1**

2m 14.03s (5.33) **Going Correction** +0.55s/f (Yiel) **5 Ran SP% 108.7**
Speed ratings (Par 105): **100,98,87,85,66**
CSF £8.94 TOTE £2.40: £1.80, £2.00; EX 7.80 Trifecta £37.70 Pool £352.49 - 6.90 winning units..
Owner Tommy Ware **Bred** Joseph Gallagher **Trained** Liphook, Hants

FOCUS
A modest contest dominated from the front. The winner didn't need to improve.

2986 JOHN SUNLEY MEMORIAL H'CAP 5f 10y
7:40 (7:40) (Class 4) (0-85,85) 3-Y-0 **£4,851** (£1,443; £721; £360) **Stalls** Low

Form RPR
1-02 **1** **Kyleakin Lass**[21] 2347 3-9-3 81 RichardHughes 9 90+
(Ian Wood) *hld up in last pair: swtchd arnd rivals and prog jst over 1f out: decisive move to ld last 100yds: eased fnl strides* **5/2[1]**
21 **2** *nk* **Miliika**[20] 2361 3-9-2 80 ChrisCatlin 7 88+
(Rae Guest) *hld up in last pair: looking for room wl over 1f out: prog and got through fnl f: tk 2nd last 75yds: r.o but too late to chal* **7/2[2]**
401 **3** *1* **Wicked Wench**[21] 2347 3-9-3 81 TonyCulhane 2 83
(Jo Hughes) *cl up: led main gp on far side over 1f out: hdd and outpcd last 100yds* **11/1**
0-50 **4** *3/4* **Cockney Fire**[11] 2616 3-8-9 73 CathyGannon 4 72
(David Evans) *led: styd in centre 1/2-way: edgd across and stl on terms jst over 1f out: one pce after* **20/1**
6242 **5** *2* **Welease Bwian (IRE)**[8] 2730 3-7-11 66 oh2 RaulDaSilva(5) 1 58+
(Stuart Williams) *pressed ldr: styd alone on nr side fr 1/2-way: on terms over 1f out: no ex* **6/1[3]**
-155 **6** *3/4* **Red Senor (IRE)**[21] 2347 3-8-13 77 MichaelHills 8 66
(Charles Hills) *prom: pressed ldr on far side over 2f out to over 1f out: fdd* **6/1[3]**
251- **7** *1 1/2* **Tango Sky (IRE)**[205] 7482 3-8-12 76 (p) JimCrowley 3 60
(Ralph Beckett) *prom: led far side gp 1/2-way: hdd & wknd over 1f out* **7/2[2]**

1m 3.65s (3.35) **Going Correction** +0.70s/f (Yiel) **7 Ran SP% 114.7**
Speed ratings (Par 101): **101,100,98,97,94 93,90**
toteswingers:1&2:£1.30, 2&3:£2.20, 1&3:£6.20 CSF £11.52 CT £79.04 TOTE £3.60: £1.90, £2.00; EX 8.40 Trifecta £56.70 Pool £643.18 - 8.38 winning units..
Owner C R Lambourne, M Forbes, D Losse **Bred** West Dereham Abbey Stud **Trained** Upper Lambourn, Berks

FOCUS
There was a decent pace on here. The winner reversed C&D form with the third, who sets the standard.

2987 STARLIGHT CLASSIFIED STKS 6f
8:10 (8:10) (Class 5) 3-Y-0 **£2,264** (£673; £336; £168) **Stalls** Low

Form RPR
-603 **1** **I'm So Glad**[3] 2893 3-9-0 75 MatthewDavies 2 79
(Mick Channon) *trckd clr ldr: clsd 2f out: rdn to ld 1f out: edgd lft and flashed tail u.p: asserted last 100yds* **10/11[1]**
1-00 **2** *1 1/4* **Knocker Knowles (IRE)**[17] 2451 3-9-0 75 CathyGannon 1 75
(David Evans) *taken down early: led and sn 3 l clr: rdn 2f out: hdd 1f out: no ex last 100yds* **12/1**
201- **3** *1* **Lucky Money**[277] 5863 3-9-0 75 LukeMorris 3 72
(Sir Mark Prescott Bt) *chsd ldng pair: rdn and no imp 2f out: edgd lft over 1f out: styd on last 100yds* **9/4[2]**
313- **4** *13* **Topflight Princess**[176] 7808 3-9-0 75 IanMongan 5 30
(Jeremy Gask) *dwlt: a 4th: rdn and no prog 2f out: sn wknd* **17/2[3]**
01- **5** *15* **Four Richer**[349] 3490 3-9-0 75 FergusSweeney 4
(Jamie Osborne) *veered bdly lft s: nt rcvr and a t.o* **9/1**

1m 17.84s (4.84) **Going Correction** +0.70s/f (Yiel) **5 Ran SP% 111.4**
Speed ratings (Par 99): **95,93,92,74,54**
CSF £12.72 TOTE £1.80: £1.10, £4.50; EX 13.10 Trifecta £32.80 Pool £391.09 - 8.82 winning units..
Owner Chris Wright & The Hon Mrs J M Corbett **Bred** Stratford Place Stud **Trained** West Ilsley, Berks

FOCUS
There was nothing between these five runners on official ratings as they all came into the race rated 75. The winner probably didn't need to improve on his latest run.
Four Richer Official explanation: jockey said colt hung badly left leaving stalls

2988 ST JOHN H'CAP 1m 67y
8:40 (8:40) (Class 5) (0-75,75) 4-Y-0+ **£2,264** (£673; £252; £252) **Stalls** Low

Form RPR
-130 **1** **Snow Trooper**[23] 2274 4-9-3 71 ShaneKelly 1 82
(Dean Ivory) *hld up: prog to chse ldr over 2f out and sn chalng: hd high but led over 1f out: rdn clr fnl f* **7/4[1]**
1114 **2** *8* **Abigails Angel**[18] 2431 5-9-0 73 MarkCoumbe(5) 2 66
(Brett Johnson) *led 1f: pushed along to ld again 3f out: hdd u.p over 1f out: wknd qckly last 100yds* **4/1[3]**
404- **3** *3 1/4* **Diddums**[295] 5298 6-7-9 56 (p) KatiaScallan(7) 7 41
(Alastair Lidderdale) *hld up in last: effrt 3f out: sn lft bhd* **12/1**
0005 **3** *dht* **Nibani (IRE)**[7] 2754 5-8-13 72 (b) LeonnaMayor(5) 8 57
(Alastair Lidderdale) *racd freely: led after 1f: hdd 3f out: sn btn* **13/2**
1/60 **5** *8* **Scottish Boogie (IRE)**[16] 2500 5-9-7 75 LiamKeniry 4 42
(Sylvester Kirk) *t.k.h: cl up: rdn and nt qckn wl over 2f out: sn wknd* **2/1[2]**

1m 48.4s (3.70) **Going Correction** +0.55s/f (Yiel) **5 Ran SP% 110.7**
Speed ratings (Par 103): **103,95,91,91,83**
CSF £9.11 TOTE £3.10: £1.70, £2.00; EX 7.50 Trifecta £62.50 Pool £461.82 - 5.46 winning units..
Owner K B Taylor **Bred** Ashridge Farm Stud **Trained** Radlett, Herts

FOCUS
A modest contest and unconvincing form, despite the wide margin of victory.
T/Plt: £70.70 to a £1 stake. Pool:£68,823.95 - 710.53 winning tickets T/Qpdt: £4.40 to a £1 stake. Pool:£5,444.16 - 905.51 winning tickets JN

2806 LONGCHAMP (R-H)
Monday, June 11

OFFICIAL GOING: Turf: very soft

2989a LA COUPE (GROUP 3) (4YO+) (TURF) 1m 2f
2:20 (12:00) 4-Y-0+ **£33,333** (£13,333; £10,000; £6,666; £3,333)

RPR
1 **No Risk At All (FR)**[15] 2533 5-8-11 0 IoritzMendizabal 3 121+
(J-P Gallorini, France) *hld up towards rr: qcknd wl over 2f out: cruised to ld 1 1/2f out: sn wnt clr: easily* **7/2[2]**
2 *3 1/2* **Meandre (FR)**[37] 1855 4-8-11 0 MaximeGuyon 5 114
(A Fabre, France) *settled 4th: qcknd wl on outside early in st: tk ld 2f out: chal and hdd 1 1/2f out: unable qck: styd on fnl f* **10/11[1]**
3 *8* **Sortilege (IRE)**[25] 2223 4-8-8 0 EPedroza 6 95
(A Wohler, Germany) *hld up at rr: r.o wl u.p fr 2f out: wnt 3rd 1f out: styd on fnl f* **20/1**
4 *2 1/2* **Poet**[44] 1677 7-8-11 0 PatCosgrave 1 93
(Clive Cox) *rdn to ld fr s: sn several l clr: stl wl clr ent st: sn u.p: fnd no ex: hdd 2f out: styd on one pce fnl f* **5/1[3]**
5 *2* **Abdel (FR)**[22] 4-8-11 0 OlivierPeslier 4 89
(J-M Osorio, Spain) *settled 3rd: rdn early in st: no ex: nvr a factor fnl 1 1/2f* **8/1**
6 *10* **Mighty Mouse (GER)**[22] 2322 4-8-11 0 FilipMinarik 2 69
(P Vovcenko, Germany) *settled in 2nd: u.p bef st over 2 1/2f out: hrd rdn but fnd no ex: wknd qckly* **18/1**

2m 8.95s (4.95) **6 Ran SP% 112.4**
WIN (incl. 1 euro stake): 4.60. PLACES: 1.60, 1.20. SF: 9.40.
Owner J-P Gallorini **Bred** Mme Sylvia Wildenstein **Trained** France

NOTEBOOK
No Risk At All(FR)strode clear of his five rivals to stake a claim for major middle distance honours in the second half of the season.\n\x\x The lightly-raced 5-y-o was stepping up in trip after excellent efforts in the Prix du Muguet and most recently when fourth to Golden Lilac in the Prix d'Ispahan. He has been entered in the Arc and that is the target at this stage.
Meandre(FR) proved at his most effective last season when coming off a fast pace on good ground and, while Poet set the race up, he never appeared to be travelling as well as the winner on ground officially described as very soft.
Poet was again ridden positively but went off quite hard and could not maintain the advantage.

2990 - 2993a (Foreign Racing) - See Raceform Interactive

2647 BRIGHTON (L-H)
Tuesday, June 12

OFFICIAL GOING: Soft (6.0)
Wind: medium, across Weather: overcast, dry

2994 32RED H'CAP 5f 59y
6:00 (6:01) (Class 5) (0-75,75) 3-Y-0+ **£2,458** (£731; £365; £182) **Stalls** Low

Form RPR
5010 **1** **Billy Red**[17] 2494 8-9-10 71 (b) FergusSweeney 2 80
(J R Jenkins) *t.k.h: chsd ldrs tl led 1/2-way: mde rest: rdn wl over 1f out: kpt on wl fnl f* **9/1**
-302 **2** *3/4* **Whitecrest**[7] 2789 4-9-7 68 CathyGannon 5 74
(John Spearing) *broke fast: led tl 1/2-way: rdn and edgd lft wl over 1f out: pressed wnr ins fnl f: styd on same pce and hld fnl 75yds* **2/1[1]**
221 **3** *3/4* **Amazing Win (IRE)**[11] 2647 4-8-8 60 CharlesBishop(5) 6 64
(Mick Channon) *prom: rdn and ev ch wl over 1f out: drvn ent fnl f: no ex and btn fnl 100yds: wknd towards fin* **9/4[2]**

44-6 **4** 1 **Magical Speedfit (IRE)**[63] 1290 7-9-2 **70**...................... RichardOld(7) 3 70
(George Margarson) *stdd after s: hld up in last pair: rdn and effrt jst over 1f out: kpt on wl ins fnl f: nt rch ldrs* **14/1**

0442 **5** shd **The Strig**[11] 2647 5-9-4 **65**...(v) SebSanders 7 65
(Stuart Williams) *dwlt: t.k.h: hld up in tch: rdn and effrt against stands' rail over 1f out: drvn and no imp fnl f* **7/1**

0312 **6** ¾ **Clear Praise (USA)**[68] 1204 5-10-0 **75**............................ TomQueally 4 72
(Simon Dow) *t.k.h: hld up in tch in last pair: shkn up and effrt 2f out: drvn and no prog over 1f out: styd on same pce after* **6/1**3

1m 4.54s (2.24) **Going Correction** +0.525s/f (Yiel) 6 Ran SP% **107.6**
Speed ratings (Par 103): **103,101,100,99,98 97**
toteswingers:1&2:£5.20, 2&3:£1.30, 1&3:£4.00 CSF £25.17 TOTE £15.80: £7.40, £1.10; EX 30.20.
Owner Mrs Irene Hampson **Bred** D R Tucker **Trained** Royston, Herts

FOCUS
A tight sprint handicap. They unsurprisingly came stands' side after straightening for home. The winner is rated back to his old turf best.

2995 32RED.COM MEDIAN AUCTION MAIDEN STKS 5f 59y
6:30 (6:30) (Class 5) 2-Y-O **£2,458** (£731; £365) **Stalls** Low

Form RPR

1 **Belle Intrigue** 2-8-12 0... RyanMoore 2 66+
(Amanda Perrett) *hld up bhd rivals: nt clr run 2f out tl swtchd lft to chal between horses and rn green fnl 100yds: r.o wl to ld last stride* **5/2**2

4 **2** shd **Kicken Off (IRE)**[6] 2808 2-9-3 0...................................... CathyGannon 1 71
(Phil McEntee) *chsd ldr: rdn 2f out: drvn 1f out and styd on to ld fnl 100yds: hdd last stride* **15/2**3

2 **3** 1¼ **Whistling Buddy**[18] 2442 2-9-3 0..................................... SebSanders 4 66
(Peter Makin) *led: looked to be gng best and rdn over 1f out: hdd fnl 100yds: wknd towards fin* **8/15**1

1m 5.28s (2.98) **Going Correction** +0.525s/f (Yiel) 3 Ran SP% **105.6**
Speed ratings (Par 93): **97,96,94**
CSF £12.05 TOTE £3.00; EX 8.90.
Owner Mr & Mrs F Cotton, Mr & Mrs P Conway **Bred** T E Cooper **Trained** Pulborough, W Sussex

FOCUS
An ordinary little juvenile maiden, run at a sound pace. Again they came stands' side in the home straight. The bare form has been given the benefit of the doubt.

NOTEBOOK
Belle Intrigue got up on the line and any backers have Ryan Moore to thank, who was at his very best aboard her. She broke well enough, but advertised her inexperience throughout much of the home straight. It was clear nearing the final furlong that Moore was desperate for an opening having elected to race on the rail after straightening up, however, and one came just in time as he lifted her home. Despite her sire's influence there is stamina in her pedigree and no doubt her yard will be over the moon as this was its first 2-y-o runner of the season. (op 3-1)
Kicken Off(IRE) showed the clear benefit of his debut experience at Kempton last time out and very nearly scored. The soft ground clearly held no fears and he's entitled to improve again, so could well nick a small maiden. (op 8-1 tchd 7-1)
Whistling Buddy was all the rage to go one better than his promising debut second at Goodwood 18 days previously. He set out to make all and appeared the one to be on halfway up the home straight. However, his stride shortened markedly inside the final half furlong and this deeper surface along with the stiffer finish was probably to blame. (op 2-5)

2996 32REDPOKER.COM MEDIAN AUCTION MAIDEN STKS 5f 213y
7:00 (7:00) (Class 5) 3-5-Y-O **£2,458** (£731; £365; £182) **Stalls** Low

Form RPR

0-53 **1** **Picture Dealer**[15] 2542 3-9-3 70....................................... RyanMoore 2 73+
(Gary Moore) *in tch: rdn and effrt to chse ldr 2f out: chal over 1f out: led 1f out: r.o wl and drew clr fnl 100yds: comf* **4/7**1

40 **2** 2¼ **Ta Ajabb**[28] 2145 3-9-0 0.......................................(b1) AdamBeschizza(3) 3 66
(William Haggas) *in tch: swtchd lft and rdn wl over 1f out: drvn and styd on ins fnl f to go 2nd fnl 50yds: no ch w wnr* **9/4**2

0-00 **3** 1 **Yes It's The Boy (USA)**[21] 2382 3-9-3 61..................... J-PGuillambert 5 63
(Ed Walker) *led: jnd and rdn over 1f out: hdd 1f out: sn outpcd and btn fnl 100yds: lost 2nd fnl 50yds* **33/1**

05 **4** 1 **Majestic South**[17] 2483 3-8-12 0...................................... MartinHarley 6 54
(Mick Channon) *chsd ldr tl 2f out: sn rdn and unbalanced: outpcd and btn over 1f out: kpt on but no ch w wnr fnl f* **12/1**3

5 5 **Rowan Rhapsody** 3-8-12 0... PatCosgrave 4 38
(Jim Boyle) *dwlt: a bhd: sn rdn along and rn green: wknd over 1f out: eased wl ins fnl f* **33/1**

1m 12.64s (2.44) **Going Correction** +0.525s/f (Yiel) 5 Ran SP% **108.0**
Speed ratings (Par 103): **104,101,99,98,91**
CSF £1.95 TOTE £1.30: £1.10, £1.50; EX 2.60.
Owner R A Green **Bred** L Ellinas & Old Mill Stud **Trained** Lower Beeding, W Sussex

FOCUS
A moderate 3yo maiden. Once again the stands' side was the favoured route in the home straight and the form looks straightforward enough, with improvement from the winner.

2997 £32 BONUS AT 32RED.COM H'CAP 1m 3f 196y
7:30 (7:30) (Class 6) (0-65,65) 4-Y-O+ **£1,940** (£577; £288; £144) **Stalls** High

Form RPR

0243 **1** **Bennelong**[12] 2623 6-9-7 **65**.. AmirQuinn 8 71+
(Richard Rowe) *stdd s: hld up in last pair: hdwy to trck ldrs on bit 2f out: led 1f out: rdn and qcknd clr ins fnl f: r.o wl: comf* **5/2**1

-606 **2** 3 **Royal Defence (IRE)**[33] 2009 6-8-13 **57**......................... PatCosgrave 3 58
(Michael Quinn) *led: hdd over 4f out: drvn and led again wl over 1f out: hdd 1f out: edgd lft and outpcd by wnr fnl f* **10/1**

11-0 **3** shd **Shouda (IRE)**[20] 2394 6-9-1 **59**... TomQueally 5 60
(Barney Curley) *stdd s: t.k.h: hld up in last pair: rdn 3f out: hdwy u.p to chse ldrs over 1f out: styd on same pce ins fnl f* **7/1**

0553 **4** 1½ **Barbirolli**[11] 2651 10-8-4 **48** oh1 ow2.................................. MartinLane 7 46
(William Stone) *in tch: rdn and unable qck over 2f out: rallied u.p to chse ldrs over 1f out: one pce and btn fnl f* **16/1**

6140 **5** 1¼ **Satwa Ballerina**[10] 2698 4-8-8 **52**................................(b) LukeMorris 4 48
(Mark Rimmer) *t.k.h: chsd ldrs: rdn and unable qck wl over 2f out: edgd lft and tried to rally over 1f out: wknd ins fnl f* **3/1**2

1062 **6** 8 **Spartan King (IRE)**[29] 2134 4-9-0 **58**......................... StevieDonohoe 2 42
(Ian Williams) *in tch: hdwy to chse ldr 5f out: led over 4f out: rdn over 2f out: hdd wl over 1f out: wknd ent fnl f: fdd* **4/1**3

0 **7** 21 **Dalayir (FR)**[20] 2393 5-9-7 **65**....................................(v1) GeorgeBaker 1 15
(Gary Moore) *t.k.h: chsd ldr tl 5f out: rdn and wknd over 2f out: wl bhd and eased fr over 1f out: t.o* **9/1**

2m 42.2s (9.50) **Going Correction** +0.525s/f (Yiel) 7 Ran SP% **111.0**
Speed ratings (Par 101): **89,87,86,85,85 79,65**
toteswingers:1&2:£8.30, 2&3:£14.40, 1&3:£3.00 CSF £26.05 CT £147.27 TOTE £5.40: £2.30, £3.30; EX 26.00 Trifecta £89.70 Pool: £502.31 - 4.14 winning units..
Owner Miss Victoria Baalham **Bred** The National Stud **Trained** Sullington, W Sussex

FOCUS
A weak handicap with an open look about it. The winner may not have had to improve on his recent form.
Spartan King(IRE) Official explanation: jockey said gelding ran too free

2998 DFSK LOAD HOPPER VANS RYANDFSK.CO.UK H'CAP 1m 1f 209y
8:00 (8:01) (Class 6) (0-55,54) 4-Y-O+ **£1,940** (£577; £288; £144) **Stalls** High

Form RPR

0-00 **1** **Ryedale Lass**[36] 1937 4-9-0 **52**... LiamKeniry 8 58
(Joseph Tuite) *hld up in last pair: rdn and effrt against stands' rail over 1f out: led ins fnl f: qcknd clr under hands and heels riding fnl 100yds: eased cl home* **6/1**

336/ **2** 2 **Devon Diva**[543] 7918 6-8-4 **49**................................. GeorgeDowning(7) 7 51
(David Bridgwater) *in tch: rdn and effrt to chal 2f out: led ent fnl f: hdd and outpcd by wnr ins fnl f: hld on for 2nd* **17/2**

632 **3** nk **Laconicos (IRE)**[9] 2735 10-8-11 **54**.................................(t) LauraPike(5) 5 55
(William Stone) *led tl hdd 2f out: sn outpcd u.p: swtchd lft and rallied ins fnl f: no ch w wnr but pressing for 2nd cl home* **5/2**2

5204 **4** ½ **Heading To First**[11] 2650 5-8-8 **46**................................... CathyGannon 6 46
(Paddy Butler) *chsd ldr: rdn and ev ch ent fnl 2f: styd on same pce u.p ins fnl f* **9/4**1

6260 **5** 7 **Inquisitress**[21] 2366 8-8-8 **49**... SeanLevey(3) 9 35
(John Bridger) *t.k.h: hld up in last pair: hdwy to chse ldrs 1/2-way: rdn to ld 2f out: sn drvn and hdd ent fnl f: fdd fnl f* **3/1**3

2m 10.61s (7.01) **Going Correction** +0.525s/f (Yiel) 5 Ran SP% **109.2**
Speed ratings (Par 101): **92,90,90,89,84**
toteswingers:1&2:£5.00, 2&3:£5.30, 1&3:£2.40 CSF £47.34 TOTE £7.20: £3.60, £3.20; EX 40.50 Trifecta £533.50 Part won. Pool: £721.02 - 0.74 winning units..
Owner Racing Green Horseracing Partnerships **Bred** Mayden Stud, J A And D S Dewhurst **Trained** Great Shefford, Berks

FOCUS
A very weak handicap. It was run at an average pace and the stands' rail proved the place to be. Dubious form.
Ryedale Lass Official explanation: trainer's rep said, regarding apparent improvement in form, that the filly had benefited from a step up in trip and being held up.

2999 SEABAY CORPORATION H'CAP 1m 1f 209y
8:30 (8:30) (Class 5) (0-70,70) 3-Y-O **£2,458** (£731; £365; £182) **Stalls** High

Form RPR

5-16 **1** **Moment In Time (IRE)**[36] 1938 3-9-7 **70**............................ MartinLane 6 76+
(David Simcock) *hld up in tch in last pair: rdn and effrt wl over 2f out: ev ch and carried lft over 1f out: led ins fnl f: hld on wl cl home* **6/1**

050- **2** hd **Seven Veils (IRE)**[260] 6400 3-8-8 **57**.................................. LukeMorris 3 63+
(Sir Mark Prescott Bt) *sn chsng ldr: rdn 4f out: ev ch and drvn wl over 1f out: pressing wnr and hung bdly lft ins fnl f: styd on wl cl home* **5/2**2

1-00 **3** 1¾ **Welsh Nayber**[19] 2424 3-8-13 **62**....................................(b1) JimCrowley 2 64
(Amanda Perrett) *chsd ldr: rdn to ld wl over 1f out: hung bdly lft over 1f out: hdd ins fnl f: no ex and btn fnl 100yds* **8/1**

0-51 **4** 1 **Chignon (IRE)**[12] 2625 3-9-1 **64**....................................... TomQueally 9 64
(Sir Henry Cecil) *t.k.h: hld up in tch: rdn and effrt wl over 2f out: drvn and styd on same pce fnl f* **2/1**1

3050 **5** 2¼ **Altona (IRE)**[19] 2431 3-9-3 **66**... MartinHarley 7 62
(Mick Channon) *hld up in tch in last pair: rdn and effrt over 3f out: styd on same pce and no imp fr over 1f out* **4/1**3

6-04 **6** 5 **You Got The Love**[17] 2497 3-8-2 **51** oh6....................(bt) CathyGannon 5 37
(Jeremy Gask) *t.k.h: sn led: hdd: rdn and wandered wl over 1f out: wknd over 1f out* **40/1**

2m 11.16s (7.56) **Going Correction** +0.525s/f (Yiel) 6 Ran SP% **109.7**
Speed ratings (Par 99): **90,89,88,87,85 81**
toteswingers:1&2:£1.40, 2&3:£4.40, 1&3:£6.40 CSF £20.36 CT £109.93 TOTE £8.20: £3.00, £1.30; EX 25.00 Trifecta £163.20 Pool: £930.76 - 4.22 winning units..
Owner Mrs Julia Annable **Bred** L K I Bloodstock Ltd **Trained** Newmarket, Suffolk

FOCUS
A modest 3-y-o handicap, but still an interesting affair for the grade. There was a routine pace on until half a mile out and, despite the field originally coming stands' side, this time the main action developed nearer the far rail. The form is rated around the third.

3000 MID SUSSEX GOLF CLUB H'CAP 6f 209y
9:00 (9:00) (Class 5) (0-70,70) 3-Y-O+ **£2,458** (£731; £365; £182) **Stalls** Low

Form RPR

0403 **1** **Cheylesmore (IRE)**[12] 2629 4-10-0 **70**...........................(v) TomQueally 8 80
(Michael Wigham) *mde all: rdn and fnd ex over 1f out: in command fnl f: r.o wl: comf* **7/4**1

0065 **2** 2 **Highland Harvest**[20] 2398 8-9-2 **58**.................................(b1) IanMongan 7 63
(Jamie Poulton) *chsd ldng pair: rdn and effrt over 2f out: chsd wnr 2f out: styd on wl but no imp on wnr fnl f* **9/1**

0-03 **3** 4½ **Welsh Royale**[14] 2573 3-8-9 **61**.. MartinDwyer 2 49
(William Muir) *s.i.s: sn bustled along in rr: hdwy to r against stands' rail and chsd ldrs over 2f out: wknd jst over 1f out* **7/2**3

5110 **4** 1¾ **Katmai River (IRE)**[26] 2207 5-9-9 **70**...........................(v) LeeNewnes(5) 3 58
(Mark Usher) *sn bustled along in last pair and nvr gng wl: rdn and outpcd 3f out: plugged on but no ch fnl f* **2/1**2

6-00 **5** 1 **Guilded Warrior**[17] 2498 9-9-2 **65**............................ GeorgeDowning(7) 5 50
(Paddy Butler) *chsd ldr tl 2f out: wknd u.p over 1f out* **14/1**

1m 26.83s (3.73) **Going Correction** +0.525s/f (Yiel)
WFA 3 from 4yo+ 10lb 5 Ran SP% **108.6**
Speed ratings (Par 103): **99,96,91,89,88**
CSF £16.18 TOTE £2.90: £1.10, £2.90; EX 16.30 Trifecta £49.00 Pool: £464.36 - 7.01 winning units..
Owner A Jalil Al Mallah **Bred** John Cullinan **Trained** Newmarket, Suffolk

FOCUS
This was decimated by non-runners and the first pair came clear. The winner rates a personal best.

T/Plt: £728.20 to a £1 stake. Pool of £57,111.91 - 57.25 winning tickets. T/Qpdt: £103.10 to a £1 stake. Pool of £5,758.95 - 41.30 winning tickets. SP

2844 LINGFIELD (L-H)
Tuesday, June 12

OFFICIAL GOING: Turf course - heavy; all-weather - standard
Wind: Almost Nil Weather: Overcast, drizzly

3001 STARR COMPANIES MEDIAN AUCTION MAIDEN STKS (TURF) 1m 1f
2:15 (2:16) (Class 6) 3-5-Y-O £1,704 (£503; £251) Stalls Low

Form RPR
44 1 Anya[38] 1852 3-8-10 0 LukeMorris 6 71
(Ed Walker) *hld up in 4th: moved up to chal 3f out: drvn ahd jst over 2f out: drew clr fnl f* 3/1[3]
-052 2 4 It's A Privilege[29] 2128 3-9-1 71 (b[1]) RyanMoore 2 67
(Ralph Beckett) *led: styd on inner in st: hdd and nt qckn jst over 2f out: no ch w wnr fnl f* 13/8[1]
30 3 1 3/4 Stock Hill Fair[10] 2708 4-9-13 0 FergusSweeney 3 65
(Brendan Powell) *trckd ldr: chal 4f out to 3f out: sn dropped to 3rd: one pce after* 8/1
600 4 1 1/4 Khamseen[20] 2393 5-9-8 0 DavidKenny(5) 1 62
(Karen George) *hld up in last pair: drvn 3f out and sn in 4th: no imp on ldng trio tl kpt on fnl f* 50/1
0-24 5 8 Gunner Will (IRE)[12] 2626 3-9-1 74 JamieSpencer 5 43
(Jamie Osborne) *chsd ldng pair to over 3f out: steadily wknd* 5/2[2]
60 6 13 Scarlett Fever[15] 2560 3-8-3 0 KatiaScallan(7) 4
(Marcus Tregoning) *a in last pair: pushed along by 1/2-way: wknd qckly 3f out: t.o* 20/1

2m 2.28s (5.68) **Going Correction** +0.80s/f (Soft)
WFA 3 from 4yo+ 12lb 6 Ran SP% 109.5
Speed ratings (Par 101): **106,102,100,99,92 81**
toteswingers:1&2:£1.40, 2&3:£1.80, 1&3:£2.90 CSF £7.86 TOTE £5.20: £1.70, £1.60; EX 9.00.
Owner Mrs L Alexander **Bred** Mrs L M Alexander **Trained** Newmarket, Suffolk

FOCUS
The turf races were allowed to go ahead following a 6.30am inspection. This was a weak maiden and it was noticeable that the runners took the home bend very carefully. The form is rated around the second.

3002 VISIT ATTHERACES.COM/ASCOT H'CAP (TURF) 1m 1f
2:45 (2:46) (Class 5) (0-70,70) 3-Y-O £2,385 (£704; £352) Stalls Low

Form RPR
2306 1 Falcon's Reign (FR)[19] 2416 3-9-5 68 JamesDoyle 10 72
(Michael Appleby) *hld up disputing 6th: plld out and prog gng strly over 2f out: led over 1f out but sn jnd: drvn and jst hld on* 14/1
0600 2 shd Musically[12] 2625 3-8-8 57 SamHitchcott 6 60
(Mick Channon) *hld up in rr: plld out wd 3f out: drvn and prog over 2f out: jnd wnr over 1f out: persistent chal after: jst failed* 22/1
04U0 3 nk Tweet Lady[18] 2448 3-9-2 65 JamesMillman 7 69
(Rod Millman) *mounted on crse and taken down early: hld up disputing 6th: looking for room and lost pl over 2f out: prog over 1f out: wnt 3rd ins fnl f: clsng on ldng pair fin* 12/1
-542 4 3 1/2 Emperor Vespasian[8] 2756 3-9-7 70 RyanMoore 5 65
(Andrew Balding) *t.k.h: hld up wl in rr: taken out wd and drvn over 2f out: plugged on to take modest 4th nr fin: nvr a threat* 7/4[1]
5-10 5 nk Northern Territory (IRE)[29] 2126 3-9-1 64 JamieSpencer 9 58
(Jim Boyle) *trckd ldng trio: cl enough over 2f out: nt qckn over 1f out: fdd* 4/1[2]
6046 6 1/2 Darnathean[42] 1730 3-9-6 69 (be) StevieDonohoe 12 62
(Paul D'Arcy) *taken down early: led: rdn over 2f out: hdd over 1f out: steadily wknd* 14/1
6-64 7 shd Titus Bolt (IRE)[34] 1979 3-8-9 58 FergusSweeney 11 51
(Jim Boyle) *mostly chsd ldng pair: styd on inner in st: lost pl 2f out: steadily fdd* 13/2[3]
6000 8 14 Art News (IRE)[21] 2382 3-8-11 60 (v[1]) ShaneKelly 13 22
(Gary Moore) *trckd ldng trio tl wknd over 2f out: t.o* 25/1
-600 9 nse Jay Bee Blue[32] 2045 3-8-13 65 SophieDoyle(3) 14 27
(Paul Rich) *dwlt: rousted along to rcvr and sn chsd ldr: wknd 3f out: t.o* 9/1
1-00 10 3 1/4 Equity Card (FR)[31] 2089 3-9-4 67 SilvestreDeSousa 2 22
(Mark Johnston) *sn wl in rr: rdn and wknd 3f out: t.o* 14/1
000- 11 28 Fine Finale[186] 7697 3-8-2 51 oh6 (p) JamieMackay 1
(Michael Squance) *sn detached in last: a wl bhd: wl t.o* 66/1

2m 3.86s (7.26) **Going Correction** +0.80s/f (Soft) 11 Ran SP% 117.1
Speed ratings (Par 99): **99,98,98,95,95 94,94,82,82,79 54**
toteswingers:1&2:£38.40, 2&3:£32.10, 1&3:£25.20 CSF £284.15 CT £3760.81 TOTE £9.50: £2.60, £6.40, £3.20; EX 259.50.
Owner T R Pearson **Bred** Rabbah Bloodstock Ltd **Trained** Danethorpe, Notts

FOCUS
A moderate handicap and the winning time was 1.58 seconds slower than the opening maiden. The winner is rated back to his debut form.

3003 ATR ROYAL ASCOT MICROSITE NOW LIVE H'CAP (TURF) 1m 3f 106y
3:15 (3:18) (Class 5) (0-75,74) 3-Y-O £2,385 (£704; £352) Stalls High

Form RPR
-500 1 Tingo In The Tale (IRE)[19] 2429 3-9-4 71 JamesDoyle 9 76
(David Arbuthnot) *hld up in last: quick prog on outer to go 2nd 1/2-way: led over 2f out: drvn and jnd ins fnl f: jst prevailed* 15/2[3]
-424 2 shd Cyrus Sod[29] 2126 3-9-6 73 RyanMoore 8 78+
(Ed Dunlop) *trckd ldng pair: dropped to last 5f out: urged along and wl bhd over 3f out: r.o over 2f out to join wnr ins fnl f: jst pipped* 1/1[1]
2130 3 2 1/4 Za'Lan (USA)[22] 2333 3-8-10 63 SilvestreDeSousa 1 64
(Mark Johnston) *led at gd pce: styd on inner in st: hdd over 2f out: one pce and lost 2nd fnl f* 9/1
-510 4 1 1/2 Jane Lachatte (IRE)[26] 2201 3-9-2 69 JamieSpencer 6 67
(Stuart Williams) *dwlt: hld up: trckd ldng pair sn after 1/2-way: cl enough over 2f out: nt qckn over 1f out* 9/4[2]
1405 5 10 Bramshill Lass[19] 2425 3-8-12 65 StevieDonohoe 3 46
(Amanda Perrett) *chsd ldr to 1/2-way: wknd over 2f out* 16/1

2m 44.31s (12.81) **Going Correction** +0.80s/f (Soft) 5 Ran SP% 108.4
Speed ratings (Par 99): **85,84,83,82,74**
CSF £15.26 TOTE £6.80: £2.70, £1.20; EX 17.30.
Owner George S Thompson **Bred** Brian Williamson **Trained** Beare Green, Surrey

FOCUS
A modest 3yo handicap, but still quite competitive despite the small field following multiple defections. They went a fair gallop, with the pace really picking up running down the hill. The winner was on a good mark on his 2yo best.

Bramshill Lass Official explanation: trainer said filly was unsuited by the heavy ground

3004 STARR COMPANIES H'CAP 7f (P)
3:50 (3:51) (Class 2) (0-100,100) 4-Y-O+ £10,221 (£3,041; £1,519; £759) Stalls Low

Form RPR
1142 1 Ducal[15] 2545 4-8-7 86 JohnFahy 9 94+
(Mike Murphy) *t.k.h: trckd ldrs on outer: wnt 2nd over 2f out: led wl over 1f out and sn 2 l clr: jst hld on* 4/1[1]
-563 2 nk Corporal Maddox[18] 2444 5-8-5 84 CathyGannon 8 91+
(Jamie Osborne) *dwlt: hld up in last pair: tried to make prog 2f out: bhd rivals 1f out: plld wd 150yds out: r.o strly after: jst failed* 6/1[3]
5300 3 nk Mia's Boy[38] 1854 8-9-7 100 GeorgeBaker 6 106
(Chris Dwyer) *hld up in tch on outer: prog 2f out: chsd wnr fnl f: clsd but lost 2nd nr fin* 9/1
-002 4 2 Sacrosanctus[10] 2707 4-8-6 85 SilvestreDeSousa 7 86
(Scott Dixon) *t.k.h: trckd ldr: led 4f out: drvn and hdd wl over 1f out: one pce* 5/1[2]
3316 5 1/2 Caldercruix (USA)[72] 1161 5-8-5 84 (v) LukeMorris 2 84
(James Evans) *trckd ldrs: rdn over 2f out: outpcd over 1f out: n.d after* 9/1
1026 6 1/2 Piscean (USA)[10] 2707 7-9-3 96 JamieSpencer 3 94+
(Tom Keddy) *sn restrained to last pair: stl there gng easily 1f out but stuck bhd rivals: plld out and r.o last 100yds: nvr in it* 8/1
6001 7 hd Shifting Star (IRE)[18] 2444 7-8-6 88 SeanLevey(3) 5 86
(John Bridger) *led to 4f out: lost 2nd over 2f out: one pce and lost pls fr over 1f out* 8/1
3625 8 3/4 Baby Strange[10] 2707 8-8-5 84 MartinDwyer 4 83
(Derek Shaw) *hld up towards rr: rdn on inner 2f out: trying to make prog but no ch whn hmpd and eased wl ins fnl f* 8/1
0250 9 1/2 Bravo Echo[60] 1354 6-9-4 97 (t) J-PGuillambert 1 91
(Michael Attwater) *t.k.h: trckd ldng pair to wl over 2f out: sn rdn and struggling: btn whn bmpd and eased ins fnl f* 12/1

1m 24.16s (-0.64) **Going Correction** +0.075s/f (Slow) 9 Ran SP% 112.0
Speed ratings (Par 109): **106,105,105,103,102 101,101,100,100**
toteswingers:1&2:£5.40, 2&3:£10.90, 1&3:£7.30 CSF £26.62 CT £199.21 TOTE £4.50: £2.00, £2.30, £2.60; EX 29.40.
Owner The Icebreakers **Bred** Cheveley Park Stud Ltd **Trained** Westoning, Beds

FOCUS
This looked a cracking 81-100 handicap beforehand, but the early pace wasn't strong and a few of these endured horrible passages. The form should therefore be treated with some caution. The level is set around the third and fourth.

NOTEBOOK
Ducal was up another 3lb to a new career-high mark, having been in great form at Kempton and Wolverhampton in recent months, but he ran poorly in his only previous try here. However, he was given a well-judged ride, sweeping around the outside to lead over 1f out and getting first run on the second and third. It wasn't his fault that several of his rivals got into trouble so he deserved this for being given the most sensible ride.

Corporal Maddox came into this on a losing run of 18, but he is off a feasible mark these days. Held up early, he didn't see any daylight at all when still going well 1f out and took a long time in being pulled wide. He flew home when in the clear, but the post was always going to beat him. He deserves compensation. (op 13-2 tchd 11-2)

Mia's Boy, back on Polytrack after a couple of moderate efforts on turf, was doing all his best work late and didn't have too many excuses other than he is better over further. (op 10-1 tchd 11-1)

Sacrosanctus carted his way into a handy position early, which can't have done him any favours, and he did well to keep on going for fourth. He has won over this trip on turf, but his four Polytrack wins have come over shorter. (op 11-2)

Caldercruix(USA) also did plenty early so wasn't disgraced, but his main problem is that his handicap mark suffered following his Southwell romp in March. (tchd 17-2)

Piscean(USA) doesn't race over 7f very often, but was unbeaten in two previous starts over the trip on Polytrack. Unfortunately his style of running requires luck and there was none of that around for him here. This can be ignored. Official explanation: jockey said gelding was denied a clear run (op 13-2)

Shifting Star(IRE) had the run of the race out in front.

3005 CHARLOTTE'S HAPPY BIRTHDAY (S) STKS 6f (P)
4:20 (4:20) (Class 6) 3-Y-O £1,704 (£503; £251) Stalls Low

Form RPR
331 1 Dark Ages (IRE)[14] 2573 3-8-12 60 (t) JamieSpencer 5 73
(George Baker) *trckd ldng pair: clsng whn lft in ld wl over 1f out: shkn up and wl in command fnl f* 11/10[1]
400 2 1 3/4 Purley Queen (IRE)[7] 2787 3-8-7 59 SilvestreDeSousa 4 62
(Sylvester Kirk) *hld up towards rr: prog on outer over 2f out: chsd wnr over 1f out: r.o and drew clr of rest but no imp* 8/1[3]
3045 3 7 Diamond Marks (IRE)[21] 2361 3-8-12 63 IanMongan 10 45
(John Gallagher) *stdd s: hld up in rr: prog jst over 2f out: wnt 3rd jst over 1f out: lft further bhd by ldng pair* 9/2[2]
5145 4 1 1/4 Tiablo (IRE)[55] 1444 3-8-12 63 LukeMorris 2 41
(David Evans) *chsd ldrs: shkn up over 2f out: easily outpcd fr wl over 1f out* 8/1[3]
600- 5 3/4 Dubai Rythm[277] 5896 3-8-12 0 (b[1]) JackMitchell 9 39
(Michael Appleby) *t.k.h: w ldr: led 1/2-way: rn wd bnd 2f out and sn hdd: fdd* 33/1
6 1 1/4 Alfie Joe 3-8-9 0 RyanClark(3) 1 35
(Ron Hodges) *s.s: reluctant to exert himself and sn detached in last: stl same 2f out: r.o fnl 150yds* 33/1
-005 7 hd Gone To Ground[15] 2547 3-8-12 42 KirstyMilczarek 7 34
(Michael Squance) *chsd ldrs: rdn over 2f out: sn lft bhd* 40/1
4-04 8 1 3/4 Courtland King (IRE)[14] 2573 3-8-12 60 (t) CathyGannon 6 28
(David Evans) *taken down early: reluctant to leave the stalls and lost at least 10 l: nvr able to rcvr* 10/1
3600 9 11 Pius Parker (IRE)[7] 2786 3-8-9 59 (b[1]) SeanLevey(3) 8
(John Gallagher) *t.k.h: led to 1/2-way: pressed ldr to jst over 2f out: wknd rapidly: t.o* 10/1

1m 11.79s (-0.11) **Going Correction** +0.075s/f (Slow) 9 Ran SP% 114.5
Speed ratings (Par 97): **103,100,91,89,88 87,86,84,69**
toteswingers:1&2:£3.30, 2&3:£5.30, 1&3:£2.60 CSF £10.38 TOTE £2.10: £1.10, £3.00, £1.70; EX 12.00.The winner was bought by S Adams for 9,000gns.
Owner Mrs C E S Baker **Bred** G W Robinson **Trained** Whitsbury, Hants

FOCUS
A weak seller. The winner only needed to run somewhwere near her turf latest.

Courtland King(IRE) Official explanation: jockey said gelding planted in stalls and was slowly away

3006 WATCH ROYAL ASCOT ON AT THE RACES H'CAP (DIV I) 7f (P)
4:50 (4:50) (Class 6) (0-65,65) 4-Y-0+ £1,704 (£503; £251) Stalls Low

Form RPR

2050 **1** **Catalinas Diamond (IRE)**[19] 2421 4-9-4 62 (t) GeorgeBaker 6 69
(Pat Murphy) *w.w in 4th: trckd clr ldng pair 2f out: clsd over 1f out: rdn to ld ins fnl f: fnd enough to hold on* **16/5**[1]

0221 **2** *nk* **Dvinsky (USA)**[15] 2546 11-9-7 65 (b) J-PGuillambert 10 71
(Paul Howling) *trckd ldr and sn clr of rest: drvn to chal 2f out: upsides ins fnl f: battled on wl: jst hld* **7/1**

5 **3** *3/4* **Demoiselle Bond**[110] 665 4-8-9 53 ow2 RobertHavlin 2 57
(Lydia Richards) *led at str pce and clr w one rival: drvn 2f out: hdd ins fnl f: kpt on* **9/1**

-200 **4** *3/4* **Bedibyes**[27] 2170 4-8-11 55 KirstyMilczarek 4 57
(Richard Mitchell) *settled in last pair: prog on inner over 2f out: drvn to go 4th fnl f w tail whirling: styd on but nvr quite able to chal* **8/1**

04-3 **5** *3 1/2* **Diddums**[1] 2988 6-7-10 47 (p) KatiaScallan(7) 7 40
(Alastair Lidderdale) *dwlt: hld up in last pair: effrt on wd outside over 2f out: kpt on fr over 1f out: no ch* **6/1**[3]

000- **6** *hd* **Rafella (IRE)**[237] 6944 4-9-5 63 (p) JamieSpencer 5 55
(Michael Scudamore) *nvr bttr than midfield: u.p 3f out: n.d fr over 1f out* **12/1**

4-35 **7** *hd* **Pastoral Jet**[117] 578 4-8-4 48 JohnFahy 8 39
(Richard Rowe) *trckd ldrs in 5th: rdn over 2f out: no imp over 1f out* **4/1**[2]

3105 **8** *1/2* **Lisselton Cross**[13] 2607 4-8-9 53 (v) LukeMorris 9 43
(Martin Bosley) *nvr bttr than midfield: shkn up and no prog wl over 2f out: n.d after* **14/1**

3600 **9** *4* **Ace Of Spies (IRE)**[14] 2581 7-9-1 64 DavidKenny(5) 3 43
(Conor Dore) *chsd clr ldng pair to 2f out: wknd over 1f out* **20/1**

0000 **10** *1 3/4* **Ensnare**[15] 2546 7-9-2 60 StevieDonohoe 1 35
(Willie Musson) *nvr bttr than midfield: dropped to last and struggling 3f out: no ch after* **20/1**

1m 24.48s (-0.32) **Going Correction** +0.075s/f (Slow) 10 Ran SP% **115.6**
Speed ratings (Par 101): **104,103,102,101,97 97,97,96,92,90**
toteswingers:1&2:£4.50, 2&3:£6.10, 1&3:£6.60 CSF £25.58 CT £183.27 TOTE £5.00: £1.80, £2.20, £2.50; EX 16.90.
Owner Briton International **Bred** Sean Gorman **Trained** East Garston, Berks
■ Stewards' Enquiry : J-P Guillambert two-day ban: used whip above permitted level (Jun 26-27)

FOCUS
Very few got into this moderate handicap with the second and third soon tearing off into a clear lead. Those two set the standard, and it was the pick of the C&D times.

3007 WATCH ROYAL ASCOT ON AT THE RACES H'CAP (DIV II) 7f (P)
5:20 (5:21) (Class 6) (0-65,64) 4-Y-0+ £1,704 (£503; £251) Stalls Low

Form RPR

3546 **1** **Silvee**[5] 2847 5-8-7 53 SeanLevey(3) 6 66
(John Bridger) *prom: trckd ldr 1/2-way: led 2f out: rdn and drew clr fr over 1f out* **9/2**[2]

-355 **2** *4 1/2* **Links Drive Lady**[21] 2373 4-9-6 63 ShaneKelly 8 64
(Dean Ivory) *trckd ldrs: effrt over 2f out: rdn to chse wnr over 1f out: sn lft bhd* **7/2**[1]

330- **3** *shd* **Patavium Prince (IRE)**[167] 7895 9-9-4 61 IanMongan 2 62
(Jo Crowley) *trckd ldrs: effrt 2f out: drvn to dispute 2nd jst over 1f out: no ch w wnr* **9/2**[2]

56-0 **4** *2* **Louphole**[27] 2170 10-9-0 57 JamieSpencer 4 52
(J R Jenkins) *stdd s: tk fierce hold early: hld up in last pair: prog on inner over 1f out: tk 4th ins fnl f: no ch* **15/2**

5356 **5** *nk* **Grand Honour (IRE)**[83] 986 6-8-2 45 KierenFox 3 39
(Paul Howling) *t.k.h: hld up in last pair: plld out wd 2f out: plugged on to take 5th nr fin* **25/1**

000- **6** *nk* **My Vindication (USA)**[253] 6586 4-9-6 63 JackMitchell 9 57
(Gay Kelleway) *led at mod pce to over 5f out: chsd ldr to 1/2-way: lost pl u.p over 1f out* **10/1**

/0-6 **7** *3/4* **Red Rhythm**[34] 1987 5-8-9 52 (t) LukeMorris 1 44
(David Evans) *hld up in last quartet: rdn and no prog wl over 2f out: struggling after* **5/1**[3]

1330 **8** *hd* **Irons On Fire (USA)**[12] 2637 4-9-7 64 AmirQuinn 7 55
(Lee Carter) *hld up in last quartet: jst pushed along fr 2f out: kpt on one pce: nvr nr ldrs* **12/1**

4006 **9** *3/4* **Kyncraighe (IRE)**[11] 2652 4-8-0 48 (tp) LeonnaMayor(5) 5 37
(Joseph Tuite) *hld up in midfield: prog on wd outside over 2f out: wknd over 1f out* **25/1**

5/6- **10** *7* **Stargazy**[427] 1283 8-8-0 48 AmyScott(5) 10 18
(Alastair Lidderdale) *stdd s: plld way through fr last to ld over 5f out and sn clr: hdd & wknd rapidly 2f out* **40/1**

1m 25.55s (0.75) **Going Correction** +0.075s/f (Slow) 10 Ran SP% **113.9**
Speed ratings (Par 101): **98,92,92,90,90 89,88,88,87,79**
toteswingers:1&2:£4.10, 2&3:£3.50, 1&3:£4.60 CSF £19.67 CT £75.51 TOTE £5.40: £1.60, £2.10, £2.10; EX 19.20.
Owner Mr & Mrs K Finch **Bred** Mr And Mrs K Finch **Trained** Liphook, Hants
■ Stewards' Enquiry : Kieren Fox two-day ban: careless riding (Jun 26-27)

FOCUS
The early pace in this second division was strong, but the final time was over a second slower than the first leg. The winner is rated in line with her old best, taking into account the jockey's claim.

3008 LINGFIELD MARRIOTT HOTEL & COUNTRY CLUB H'CAP 5f (P)
5:50 (5:50) (Class 6) (0-65,65) 4-Y-0+ £1,704 (£503; £251) Stalls High

Form RPR

05-5 **1** **Autocracy**[89] 910 5-8-4 48 (bt) MickaelBarzalona 2 58
(Daniel Kubler) *trckd ldrs gng wl: produced 1f out: drvn ahd ins fnl f: styd on* **10/1**

4135 **2** *1* **Chjimes (IRE)**[14] 2581 8-9-7 65 (b) JamieSpencer 4 71
(Conor Dore) *hld up in rr: gng wl 2f out: effrt on inner over 1f out: sltly checked jst ins fnl f: styd on to take 2nd nr fin* **5/1**[2]

5430 **3** *nk* **Even Bolder**[19] 2413 9-9-7 65 GeorgeBaker 1 70
(Eric Wheeler) *trckd ldrs on inner: cl up in 3rd 2f out: drvn to dispute 2nd 1f out: kpt on same pce* **9/2**[1]

3006 **4** *shd* **Decider (USA)**[22] 2352 9-8-12 56 (b) LukeMorris 5 61
(Ronald Harris) *led: hrd rdn over 1f out: hdd and one pce ins fnl f* **6/1**[3]

0300 **5** *nse* **Sherjawy (IRE)**[17] 2494 8-8-11 55 SamHitchcott 6 59
(Zoe Davison) *sn rdn in rr: no prog tl styd on u.p ins fnl f: nrst fin* **13/2**

00-5 **6** *1* **Bateleur**[14] 2572 8-8-13 57 MatthewDavies 3 58
(Mick Channon) *dwlt: last tl urged along and effrt over 1f out: kpt on same pce: n.d* **6/1**[3]

6-00 **7** *3/4* **Brandywell Boy (IRE)**[14] 2572 9-8-9 53 JamesDoyle 10 51
(Dominic Ffrench Davis) *dwlt: racd wd: rdn bef 1/2-way: effrt u.p over 1f out: nvr able to threaten* **10/1**

0-10 **8** *1/2* **Instructress**[22] 2352 4-8-11 55 ShaneKelly 7 51
(Robert Cowell) *chsd ldr to over 1f out: sn lost pl and btn* **7/1**

0500 **9** *3/4* **Replicator**[120] 544 7-8-4 48 (e) JamieMackay 8 42
(Patrick Gilligan) *chsd ldng pair to jst over 2f out: sn lost pl u.p* **20/1**

2406 **10** *3/4* **Elhamri**[14] 2581 8-9-2 65 DavidKenny(5) 9 56
(Conor Dore) *sn rdn: a struggling towards rr* **25/1**

58.97s (0.17) **Going Correction** +0.075s/f (Slow) 10 Ran SP% **116.0**
Speed ratings (Par 101): **101,99,98,98,98 97,95,95,93,92**
toteswingers:1&2:£5.40, 2&3:£3.30, 1&3:£8.40 CSF £59.12 CT £222.47 TOTE £8.90: £3.80, £1.70, £1.10; EX 31.00.
Owner Mr & Mrs G Middlebrook **Bred** Mr & Mrs G Middlebrook **Trained** Whitsbury, Hants

FOCUS
A moderate sprint handicap, but competitive enough and they finished in a heap. Straightforward form.
T/Plt: £208.20 to a £1 stake. Pool of £61,539.00 - 215.76 winning tickets. T/Qpdt: £5.40 to a £1 stake. Pool of £6,334.00 - 862.56 winning tickets. JN

[2420] SALISBURY (R-H)
Tuesday, June 12

OFFICIAL GOING: Soft (heavy in places; 7.1)
Wind: mild breeze Weather: overcast

3009 DOUGLAND MAIDEN AUCTION STKS (DIV I) 6f
2:00 (2:01) (Class 5) 2-Y-O £2,587 (£770; £384; £192) Stalls Low

Form RPR

1 **Pasaka Boy** 2-8-9 0 LeeNewman 8 74
(Jonathan Portman) *mid-div: hdwy over 2f out: swtchd rt over 1f out: chal ent fnl f: kpt on to ld nring fin: rdn out* **50/1**

5 **2** *nk* **Hipster**[7] 2784 2-9-2 0 JimCrowley 4 80
(Ralph Beckett) *a.p: rdn wl over 1f out: narrow advantage ent fnl f: kpt on but no ex whn hdd nring fin* **9/4**[1]

2 **3** *1/2* **Boleyn**[12] 2622 2-8-4 0 KieranO'Neill 9 67
(Richard Hannon) *taken rt leaving stalls bef switching bk lft to ld on stands' side rails: rdn and hrd pressed fr 2f out: narrowly hdd ent fnl f: kpt on but no ex towards fin* **5/1**[3]

6 **4** *1 1/2* **Jontleman (IRE)**[26] 2193 2-8-9 0 MartinHarley 6 67+
(Mick Channon) *trckd ldrs: nt clr run over 2f out and over 1f out: rdn and kpt on fnl f: nvr able to mount chal* **5/2**[2]

5 *3 1/2* **Haatefina** 2-8-7 0 DavidProbert 2 55+
(Mark Usher) *s.i.s: mid-div: rdn and hdwy 2f out: one pce fnl f* **33/1**

0 **6** *2* **Epsom Flyer**[32] 2039 2-8-4 0 JemmaMarshall(5) 10 51+
(Pat Phelan) *hld up towards rr: rdn whn nt clr run over 1f out: kpt on same pce fnl f: nvr threatened ldrs* **66/1**

64 **7** *1* **Lucky Suit (IRE)**[20] 2384 2-8-7 0 HayleyTurner 12 46
(Richard Hannon) *towards rr: pushed along over 3f out: nvr gng pce to get on terms* **9/1**

052 **8** *3 1/2* **Baltic Gin (IRE)**[20] 2384 2-8-4 0 TadhgO'Shea 3 32
(Malcolm Saunders) *trckd ldrs: chal 3f out tl 2f out: wknd ent fnl f* **10/1**

9 *1/2* **Sakhee's Ichigou** 2-8-5 0 ow1 ChrisCatlin 1 32
(Michael Blanshard) *in tch tl lost pl over 3f out: rdn over 2f out: wknd fnl f* **100/1**

10 *2* **Spithead** 2-8-9 0 LiamJones 11 30+
(William Haggas) *s.i.s: a towards rr* **16/1**

11 *4 1/2* **Roz** 2-8-11 0 DaneO'Neill 5 18
(Harry Dunlop) *awkward leaving stalls: sn mid-div: hdwy over 2f out: sn rdn: wknd over 1f out* **20/1**

1m 18.85s (4.05) **Going Correction** +0.625s/f (Yiel) 11 Ran SP% **113.1**
Speed ratings (Par 93): **98,97,96,94,90 87,86,81,80,78 72**
toteswingers:1&2:£23.60, 2&3:£3.40, 1&3:£23.60 CSF £153.09 TOTE £67.20: £12.10, £1.30, £1.80; EX 277.20 TRIFECTA Not won..
Owner RWH Partnership **Bred** G Wickens And J Homan **Trained** Compton, Berks

FOCUS
The going was soft, heavy in places, as backed up by those who rode in the first. The stalls for the 1m2f & 1m4f races were on the outside, while for the remaining races the stalls were on the inside. All the runners raced up the near-side rail with the front four pulling clear of the field in what looked a fair maiden. The form fits in with the race averages.

NOTEBOOK
Pasaka Boy, whose handler felt would want further in time (out of multiple 1m4f winner Shesha Bear - ran in the 5.05), ran out a willing winner having been driven in midfield at the 2f pole, showing a game attitude when coming between horses over 1f out. With the next three home having all run before, and being prominent in the market, the form looks solid.
Hipster stayed on well when fifth in a 6f Leicester maiden on debut and he ran another encouraging race. He showed early speed from stall four to bag the stands' rail and looked the winner 1f out, just losing out in a tight finish. He should be capable of landing a maiden. (op 11-4)
Boleyn, who found the 5f at Brighton too sharp on debut, did well to find a decent position from her draw, but couldn't quicken as well as the front two. She ultimately looked to pay for doing too much through the first half of the race. (op 9-2 tchd 11-2)
Jontleman(IRE) was hampered on debut at Newmarket and again did not endure the best of passages when looking to close. His handler is adept at improving his juveniles and this was another promising effort. (op 9-4)
Haatefina, a half-sister to 6f-1m winner Flipping, showed promise, travelling nicely behind the principals before staying on into a clear fifth. Her yard has a 5% strike-rate with 2yos and she can build on this. (op 40-1)
Epsom Flyer was noted making good late progress once the race was over, and should be seen to better effect once handicapped.
Lucky Suit(IRE) was under pressure a long way from home but kept responding to her rider's urgings, suggesting that a step up in trip is needed. (op 17-2 tchd 8-1)
Spithead, a half-brother to prolific 5f winner Judge 'n Jury, looked big in the paddock and should come on for this. (op 18-1)
Roz, whose dam was a 7f-1m winner, was forced to race wide and will learn plenty from this run. (op 25-1)

3010 DOUGLAND MAIDEN AUCTION STKS (DIV II) 6f
2:30 (2:30) (Class 5) 2-Y-O £2,587 (£770; £384; £192) Stalls Low

Form RPR

23 **1** **Cruck Realta**[3] 2917 2-8-4 0 RoystonFfrench 6 79+
(Mick Channon) *trckd ldrs: led 2f out: sn rdn: kpt on wl* **2/1**[1]

5 **2** *2 1/2* **Momalorka**[17] 2499 2-8-4 0 KellyHarrison 11 72+
(William Haggas) *wnt sltly rt s: trckd ldr: rdn 2f out: styd on to chse wnr jst ins fnl f: a being hld* **5/2**[2]

3 **3** *3½* **Red Adair (IRE)**[13] 2609 2-9-2 0 RichardHughes 8 72
(Richard Hannon) *trckd ldrs: rdn over 2f out: sn swtchd rt to chse wnr: no ex whn lost 2nd jst ins fnl f: jst hld on for 3rd* **7/2**[3]

0 **4** *hd* **Bountybeamadam**[21] 2370 2-8-7 0 HayleyTurner 1 62
(George Baker) *rrd leaving stalls: sn led: rdn and hdd 2f out: kpt on same pce: nrly snatched 3rd* **25/1**

3 **5** *2½* **Stupenda**[21] 2370 2-8-4 0 TadhgO'Shea 7 52
(Denis Coakley) *little slowly away: sn mid-div: rdn and hdwy wl over 1f out to chse ldrs: hung lft and fdd fnl 120yds:* **10/1**

6 **6** *4* **Mumbai Star (IRE)**[21] 2370 2-8-9 0 LeeNewman 9 45
(Paul Fitzsimons) *s.i.s: sn trcking ldrs: rdn over 2f out: wknd over 1f out* **22/1**

7 *6* **Branson (IRE)** 2-9-2 0 PatDobbs 4 34
(Richard Hannon) *sn pushed along: a towards rr* **14/1**

8 *5* **Karl Marx (IRE)** 2-8-12 0 DavidProbert 2 15
(Mark Usher) *chsd ldrs: rdn wl over 2f out: wknd wl over 1f out* **22/1**

9 *4* **Incognita** 2-8-5 0 ow1 ChrisCatlin 10
(Chris Down) *s.i.s: sn pushed along: a towards rr* **40/1**

1m 18.17s (3.37) **Going Correction** +0.625s/f (Yiel) **9** Ran SP% **114.9**
Speed ratings (Par 93): **102,98,94,93,90 85,77,70,65**
toteswingers:1&2:£2.10, 2&3:£3.30, 1&3:£1.90 CSF £6.69 TOTE £3.30: £1.10, £1.40, £1.60; EX 6.70 Trifecta £19.50 Pool: £499.94 - 18.88 winning units..
Owner Anne & Steve Fisher **Bred** Wansdyke Farms Limited **Trained** West Ilsley, Berks

FOCUS
Division two of this juvenile maiden was run at a decent pace with the time 0.68 seconds quicker than the opener. As in the first, all the runners headed to the stands' side, with the field well strung out at the line. The winner looked well in on her Doncaster form.

NOTEBOOK
Cruck Realta had shown promise in two previous starts, the most recent of which was only three days earlier, and she put that experience to good use with an impressive success. She was not helped by having to race wide throughout, but was always travelling nicely and quickened well, in truth hitting the front earlier than ideal. She could be a Chesham type. (op 5-2)
Momalorka kept on well when fifth on her debut over 6f at Newbury on quicker ground, and stepped up on that effort here. She travelled nicely through the race and, although unable to pick up quite as well as her more experienced rival, she is in the right hands to continue her development. (op 3-1)
Red Adair(IRE), who was green on debut before tiring at Folkestone, looked as though this experience would also bring him on. He seemed a bit unbalanced on this softer ground when the pace quickened and could be seen to better effect on drier ground. (op 3-1)
Bountybeamadam, stepped up on her debut effort, showing good early pace to lead before fading inside the final furlong. She stayed on well enough and looks to be progressing with racing. (op 22-1)
Stupenda was not helped by racing wide but stayed on well enough under pressure, showing some promise, and may be seen to better effect once the ground firms up. (op 9-1 tchd 8-1)
Mumbai Star(IRE), half-brother to 1m2f/triple bumper winner Donatis Comet, was described as a lazy type who would be suited by 7f in time. He was slightly disappointing and it looks as though time will certainly be needed with him. (op 18-1)

3011 EMPRISE SERVICES CLAIMING STKS 6f 212y
3:00 (3:00) (Class 5) 3-Y-0+ **£2,264** (£673; £336; £168) **Stalls** Low

Form RPR

106 **1** **Kingswinford (IRE)**[13] 2608 6-8-13 79 MatthewCosham(5) 1 84
(David Evans) *mde all: rdn whn hrd pressed fr 2f out: kpt on gamely to assert towards fin* **5/1**

-011 **2** *1* **George Benjamin**[8] 2758 5-8-9 73 RyanWhile(7) 2 79
(Bill Turner) *prom: rdn for str chal 2f out: drifted rt fr 1f out: kpt on but hld fnl 120yds* **15/8**[1]

6-46 **3** *2½* **Kingsdine (IRE)**[18] 2444 5-9-9 83 TomMcLaughlin 5 80
(Malcolm Saunders) *stdd s: trckd ldrs: rdn for str chal fr 2f out: ev ch ent fnl f: drifted rt: no ex fnl 120yds* **7/2**[2]

2001 **4** *3½* **Bunce (IRE)**[3] 2939 4-9-4 76 JimmyFortune 4 66
(Paul Fitzsimons) *trckd ldrs: rdn wl over 1f out: fdd fnl f* **4/1**[3]

3110 **5** *¾* **Indian Art (IRE)**[18] 2444 6-9-7 79 RichardHughes 3 67
(Sylvester Kirk) *prom for 2f: trckd ldrs: struggling over 2f out: sn btn* **9/2**

0/06 **6** *2½* **Jessica Ashton**[8] 2765 4-8-11 37 (b) PatCosgrave 6 50?
(Stuart Kittow) *trckd ldrs: snatched up on rails 5f out: rdn over 3f out: wknd jst over 1f out* **100/1**

1m 32.2s (3.60) **Going Correction** +0.625s/f (Yiel) **6** Ran SP% **112.8**
Speed ratings (Par 103): **104,102,100,96,95 92**
toteswingers:1&2:£2.50, 2&3:£1.90, 1&3:£3.30 CSF £15.02 TOTE £5.60: £2.50, £1.60; EX 16.60.George Benjamin was claimed by C. N. Kellett for £5000.
Owner J E Abbey **Bred** J Costello **Trained** Pandy, Monmouths

FOCUS
A competitive claimer run at a sound pace and won in game fashion by the 2010 victor. The form is rated around the first two and looks more solid than most claimers.

3012 CUSTOM SECURITY SERVICES OF VERWOOD MAIDEN STKS 6f 212y
3:30 (3:31) (Class 5) 3-Y-0+ **£2,911** (£866; £432; £216) **Stalls** Low

Form RPR

333- **1** **Cool Rhythm**[231] 7073 4-9-13 69 JimCrowley 3 81
(Ralph Beckett) *squeezed up s: towards rr: pushed along over 2f out: hdwy over 1f out: styd on wl to ld fnl 120yds* **4/1**[3]

33-2 **2** *¾* **Juvenal (IRE)**[17] 2501 3-9-3 77 RichardHughes 4 75
(Richard Hannon) *mid-div: struggling to hold pl whn pushed along over 3f out: rdn and hdwy over 2f out: led over 1f out: hrd drvn and no ex whn hdd fnl 120yds* **1/1**[1]

0-44 **3** *1* **Engrossing**[25] 2246 3-9-3 75 PatDobbs 2 72
(Richard Hannon) *trckd ldrs: rdn to chal over 1f out: kpt on but no ex fnl 120yds* **3/1**[2]

4 **4** *2½* **Bajan Story**[42] 1737 3-9-3 0 DaneO'Neill 12 66
(Michael Blanshard) *towards rr: hdwy on rails over 3f out: rdn whn nt clr run and swtchd rt over 1f out: styd on same pce fnl f* **18/1**

5 *6* **Village Green** 3-9-3 0 KierenFallon 7 50
(Charles Hills) *trckd ldrs: rdn 3f out: wknd ins fnl f* **14/1**

04 **6** *nk* **Missus Mills (IRE)**[8] 2757 3-8-12 0 PatCosgrave 1 45
(George Baker) *led: rdn 2f out: hdd over 1f out: wknd ins fnl f* **11/1**

00 **7** *8* **Beach Rhythm (USA)**[17] 2496 5-9-8 0 JamesRogers(5) 6 33
(Jim Allen) *prom: rdn over 3f out: wknd over 1f out* **150/1**

6 **8** *¾* **Tunnager Grove**[15] 2542 3-9-3 0 HayleyTurner 10 27
(Hughie Morrison) *prom: rdn over 2f out: edgd rt: wknd over 1f out* **20/1**

00 **9** *28* **Flag Is Up**[32] 2041 3-8-12 0 (v[1]) MarkCoumbe(5) 13
(Brett Johnson) *pushed along 5f out: a towards rr: t.o* **200/1**

1m 32.74s (4.14) **Going Correction** +0.625s/f (Yiel)
WFA 3 from 4yo+ 10lb **9** Ran SP% **121.2**
Speed ratings (Par 103): **101,100,99,96,89 88,79,78,46**
toteswingers:1&2:£2.20, 2&3:£2.00, 1&3:£2.50 CSF £8.79 TOTE £4.50: £1.40, £1.10, £1.60; EX 12.20 Trifecta £30.10 Pool: £1040.12 - 25.55 winning units..
Owner Cromhall Stud **Bred** Derek R Price **Trained** Kimpton, Hants

FOCUS
This uncompetitive-looking maiden was run at a steady pace, with plenty struggling a long way from home, and the front four pulled a long way clear. An 8lb personal best from the winner.

3013 BRITISH STALLION STUDS SUPPORTING BRITISH RACING E B F MARGADALE FILLIES' H'CAP 1m 1f 198y
4:05 (4:05) (Class 4) (0-85,84) 3-Y-0+ **£4,851** (£1,443; £721) **Stalls** Low

Form RPR

0-32 **1** **Princess Caetani (IRE)**[26] 2194 3-8-5 74 RoystonFfrench 1 83
(David Simcock) *trckd ldng pair: pushed along to chal 2f out: led over 1f out: styd on strly: pushed out* **9/4**[2]

-221 **2** *7* **Traveller's Tales**[26] 2201 3-8-13 82 RichardHughes 4 83
(Richard Hannon) *trckd ldr: led over 2f out: sn rdn: hdd over 1f out: sn hld: eased fnl 120yds* **10/11**[1]

0-10 **3** *11* **Miss Aix**[45] 1656 4-10-0 84 HayleyTurner 6 63
(Michael Bell) *led: rdn and hdd over 2f out: sn btn* **3/1**[3]

2m 13.63s (3.73) **Going Correction** +0.625s/f (Yiel)
WFA 3 from 4yo+ 13lb **3** Ran SP% **108.2**
Speed ratings (Par 102): **110,104,95**
CSF £4.73 TOTE £2.70; EX 3.60.
Owner Favourites Racing **Bred** Barronstown Stud **Trained** Newmarket, Suffolk

FOCUS
Despite the small field (five non-runners) this fillies' handicap was run at an honest pace with the runners racing up the far side of the track for the majority of the race, before coming across to the stands rail 3f from home. The winner is rated up 8lb but it's hard to know how literally to take this form.

3014 CASTLEPOINTSHOPPING.COM H'CAP 6f 212y
4:35 (4:36) (Class 6) (0-65,65) 3-Y-0 **£1,940** (£577; £288; £144) **Stalls** Low

Form RPR

30 **1** **Temuco (IRE)**[21] 2367 3-8-9 58 MatthewCosham(5) 12 71
(David Evans) *trckd ldrs: rdn over 2f out: drifted to centre and racd alone sn after: styd on wl to ld nring fin: drvn out* **9/1**[3]

5-05 **2** *½* **Rocky Reef**[21] 2382 3-9-4 62 (v) JimmyFortune 8 73
(Andrew Balding) *a.p: led over 3f out: rdn over 1f out: kpt on but no ex whn hdd towards fin* **5/1**[2]

0632 **3** *1¾* **Pendle Lady (IRE)**[7] 2803 3-8-12 56 TomMcLaughlin 15 63
(Mark Brisbourne) *mid-div: pushed along and hdwy over 2f out: sn rdn: styd on fnl f* **7/2**[1]

0-60 **4** *2* **Saint Irene**[34] 1979 3-8-13 57 DaneO'Neill 13 58
(Michael Blanshard) *mid-div: rdn over 2f out: hdwy over 1f out: styd on same pce fnl f* **11/1**

-301 **5** *1½* **Percythepinto (IRE)**[20] 2385 3-9-0 58 (t) RichardHughes 4 56
(George Baker) *hld up towards rr: pushed along for stdy prog fr over 2f out: rdn over 1f out: edgd lft: kpt on same pce ins fnl f* **5/1**[2]

0-64 **6** *¾* **High Five Prince (IRE)**[7] 2786 3-8-2 46 oh1 HayleyTurner 2 42
(Mark Usher) *trckd ldrs: led 5f out: rdn and hdd over 3f out: fdd ins fnl f* **9/1**[3]

00-0 **7** *1* **Bajan Hero**[7] 1319 3-8-13 57 LeeNewman 3 50
(David Evans) *chsd ldrs: rdn over 3f out: wknd ins fnl f* **40/1**

04 **8** *1* **Jacasa Too**[26] 2203 3-8-2 49 SimonPearce(3) 14 39
(Rod Millman) *chsd ldrs: rdn over 3f out: fdd ins fnl f* **25/1**

4000 **9** *1½* **City Dazzler (IRE)**[5] 2846 3-9-5 63 PatDobbs 10 50
(Richard Hannon) *hld up towards rr: pushed along and hdwy over 2f out: sn rdn: wknd over 1f out* **9/1**[3]

60-0 **10** *3¾* **Peg Peg**[26] 2203 3-7-9 46 oh1 NoelGarbutt(7) 5 23
(Nerys Dutfield) *chsd ldrs: effrt over 2f out: wknd over 1f out* **50/1**

062- **11** *3¼* **Vergrigio (IRE)**[236] 6977 3-9-7 65 RoystonFfrench 6 33
(David Pipe) *struggling over 4f out: a towards rr* **12/1**

00-5 **12** *40* **Knoydart (USA)**[14] 2582 3-8-2 46 oh1 KieranO'Neill 11
(Amanda Perrett) *led for 2f: trckd ldrs: rdn 3f out: sn btn: eased over 1f out* **14/1**

1m 32.85s (4.25) **Going Correction** +0.625s/f (Yiel) **12** Ran SP% **116.5**
Speed ratings (Par 97): **100,99,97,95,93 92,91,90,88,84 80,34**
toteswingers:1&2:£9.10, 2&3:£4.80, 1&3:£8.20 CSF £51.88 CT £192.90 TOTE £15.10: £3.80, £2.00, £1.10; EX 60.40 Trifecta £406.30 Pool: £1180.61 - 2.15 winning units..
Owner Mrs E Evans **Bred** Thomas McDonogh **Trained** Pandy, Monmouths

FOCUS
A moderate handicap run at a steady pace, with the field again coming stands' side, although the winner was taken noticeably wide to challenge. The winner is rated in line with his Irish 2yo form.
City Dazzler(IRE) Official explanation: jockey said filly clipped heels 2f out
Knoydart(USA) Official explanation: jockey said gelding hung right

3015 CASTLEPOINT SHOPPING PARK A3060 BOURNEMOUTH H'CAP 1m 4f
5:05 (5:05) (Class 5) (0-75,75) 4-Y-0+ **£2,587** (£770; £384; £192) **Stalls** Low

Form RPR

-465 **1** **Achalas (IRE)**[4] 2887 4-9-5 73 (b[1]) TadhgO'Shea 3 77
(Heather Main) *slowly away: bhd: hdwy over 2f out: rdn to ld ent fnl f: styd on wl* **9/2**[3]

2-00 **2** *1* **Shesha Bear**[19] 2411 7-9-7 75 (p) LeeNewman 2 77
(Jonathan Portman) *in last pair: hdwy over 3f out: sn rdn: drifted rt: styd on to chse wnr ins fnl f: hld towards fin* **8/1**

0260 **3** *2¼* **Battleoftrafalgar**[19] 2412 5-9-4 72 (b) KierenFallon 6 70
(Michael Attwater) *led: qcknd pce over 3f out: rdn over 2f out: hdd ent fnl f: no ex* **10/1**

2-05 **4** *nk* **Persian Herald**[16] 1940 4-9-1 69 JimCrowley 4 67
(William Muir) *in tch: sltly outpcd 3f out: styd on fnl f: clsng on ldrs at fin* **4/1**[2]

00-6 **5** *6* **Kings Troop**[15] 2561 6-9-7 75 JimmyFortune 7 63
(Alan King) *in tch: disp 2nd over 3f out: sn rdn: wknd fnl f* **6/1**

6-63 **6** *9* **Korngold**[31] 2086 4-9-1 69 TedDurcan 5 43
(John Dunlop) *trckd ldrs: outpcd wl over 2f out: wknd wl over 1f out* **15/8**[1]

2030 **7** *3¼* **Mazij**[31] 2093 4-9-2 70 ChrisCatlin 8 39
(Peter Hiatt) *trckd ldr: j. path after 1f: rdn 3f out: wknd over 1f out* **22/1**

2m 44.54s (6.54) **Going Correction** +0.625s/f (Yiel) **7** Ran SP% **111.8**
Speed ratings (Par 103): **103,102,100,100,96 90,88**
toteswingers:1&2:£5.00, 2&3:£6.90, 1&3:£5.40 CSF £37.33 CT £334.27 TOTE £4.60: £1.60, £4.70; EX 40.10 Trifecta £159.60 Pool: £1167.25 - 5.41 winning units..
Owner Mr & Mrs D R Guest **Bred** Stonethorn Stud Farms Ltd **Trained** Kingston Lisle, Oxon

FOCUS
An fair handicap that looked competitive beforehand and was run at a sound pace, with the front four coming a long way clear. The winner is rated back to form in the blinkers.

Korngold Official explanation: jockey said colt stopped quickly

3016 CGA RACING EXCELLENCE APPRENTICE H'CAP (WHIPS SHALL BE CARRIED BUT NOT USED) 6f

5:35 (5:35) (Class 5) (0-75,75) 4-Y-O+ £2,587 (£770; £384; £192) Stalls Low

Form RPR

0032 1 **Cocohatchee**[26] 2207 4-9-1 66 JakePayne 2 74
(Pat Phelan) *tk str hold: mde virtually all: kpt on gamely fnl f: pushed out* 3/1[2]

-402 2 2 **Sarangoo**[19] 2421 4-8-11 62 IanBurns 11 64
(Malcolm Saunders) *hld up but wl in tch: hdwy over 2f out: sn shkn up: styd on to go 2nd fnl 120yds: a being hld by wnr* 5/1[3]

-600 3 1 **Silenzio**[3] 2940 4-9-10 75 WilliamTwiston-Davies 1 73
(Richard Hannon) *trckd ldrs: effrt over 2f out: sn chsng wnr: lost 2nd whn no ex fnl 120yds* 5/2[1]

5015 4 1 1/2 **Ibiza Sunset (IRE)**[18] 2466 4-9-4 72 ThomasGarner(3) 5 66
(Brendan Powell) *hld up but wl in tch: hdwy over 2f out: sn pushed along: kpt on same pce fnl f* 17/2

2320 5 1 **Whipphound**[15] 2538 4-8-11 62 JackDuern 7 52
(Mark Brisbourne) *chsd ldrs: pushed along over 2f out: sn one pce* 9/1

040 6 1/2 **One Way Or Another (AUS)**[22] 2354 9-9-0 70 (bt) AliceHaynes(5) 6 59
(David Evans) *awkward leaving stalls: in tch: pushed along over 2f out: nvr gng pce to get involved* 14/1

0-00 7 5 **Dualagi**[8] 2760 8-7-13 57 KirstenSmith(7) 4 30
(Martin Bosley) *prom for 2f: chsd ldrs tl wknd jst over 1f out* 25/1

4-05 8 7 **Homeboy (IRE)**[48] 1614 4-8-8 59 (p) NedCurtis 8
(Marcus Tregoning) *plld hrd: w wnr for 2f: trckd ldrs: drifted to stands' side rails and wknd 2f out* 7/1

1m 17.96s (3.16) **Going Correction** +0.625s/f (Yiel) 8 Ran SP% 113.8
Speed ratings (Par 103): **103,100,99,97,95 95,88,79**
toteswingers:1&2:£4.20, 2&3:£3.30, 1&3:£2.50 CSF £18.23 CT £41.75 TOTE £5.40: £2.00, £1.80, £1.10; EX 16.40 Trifecta £34.80 Pool: £1035.32 - 21.98 winning units..
Owner John James (Cranborne) **Bred** Henry And Mrs Rosemary Moszkowicz **Trained** Epsom, Surrey

FOCUS
This apprentice handicap was run at a steady pace with plenty of the runners keen for their heads early. When the tempo increased few were able to get competitive. The winner's best effort since last summer.
Homeboy(IRE) Official explanation: jockey said gelding hung left
T/Plt: £22.50 to a £1 stake. Pool of £52,121.48 - 1,689.09 winning tickets. T/Qpdt: £11.30 to a £1 stake. Pool of £3,434.87 - 224.06 winning tickets. TM

965 COMPIEGNE (L-H)

Tuesday, June 12

OFFICIAL GOING: Turf: heavy

3017a PRIX AMBER RAMA (CONDITIONS) (2YO) (TURF) 7f

11:00 (12:00) 2-Y-O £15,416 (£6,166; £4,625; £3,083; £1,541)

RPR

1 **Sir Patrick Moore (FR)**[25] 2231 2-8-11 0 ChristopheSoumillon 2 89
(Harry Dunlop) *broke wl: sn led: set stdy pce: shkn up over 1 1/2f out: given a couple of reminders ent fnl f: qcknd wl: sn wnt clr: easily* 2/1[2]

2 2 **Kamran (FR)**[20] 2-9-2 0 OlivierPeslier 5 89
(F Head, France) 3/5[1]

3 1/2 **Halloween Chope (FR)**[29] 2-8-8 0 IoritzMendizabal 3 80
(D Prod'Homme, France) 10/1

4 1 1/2 **Just One Wish (IRE)**[20] 2-8-8 0 StephanePasquier 1 76
(H De Nicolay, France) 8/1[3]

5 3 1/2 **Haring (SPA)**[6] 2-8-11 0 JohanVictoire 4 71
(C Boutin, France) 26/1

1m 30.86s (90.86) 5 Ran SP% 119.7
WIN (incl. 1 euro stake): 3.00. PLACES: 1.20, 1.10. SF: 3.70.
Owner The Astronomers **Bred** S F Bloodstock LLC **Trained** Lambourn, Berks

NOTEBOOK
Sir Patrick Moore(FR) made all under Christophe Soumillon to land this juvenile contest over 7f from the favourite. Having already won his maiden at Newbury, Dunlop can now look at stepping the colt up in class again. The trainer is looking at returning for Deauville in August maybe a Listed race at the July meeting before then.

2686 BEVERLEY (R-H)

Wednesday, June 13

OFFICIAL GOING: Good to soft (6.7)
Inside rail around bottom bend moved out adding 19yds to race distances further than 5f.
Wind: Light half-against Weather: Overcast

3018 JINYU - TYREGIANT.COM H'CAP (DIV I) 5f

2:00 (2:01) (Class 6) (0-65,65) 3-Y-O+ £1,940 (£577; £288; £144) Stalls Low

Form RPR

0026 1 **Sophie's Beau (USA)**[16] 2551 5-8-2 46 (b) EvaMoscrop(7) 2 57
(Michael Chapman) *wnt lft s: trckd ldrs: swtchd lft and hdwy to chal jst over 1f out: rdn to ld jst ins fnl f: sn clr: kpt on wl* 9/1

-010 2 3 3/4 **Dotty Darroch**[19] 2436 4-9-4 55 DanielTudhope 5 53
(Robin Bastiman) *cl up: led 1/2-way: rdn and hdd jst ins fnl f: kpt on same pce* 3/1[2]

00/0 3 1 1/4 **Pawan (IRE)**[35] 1987 12-8-8 50 (be) AnnStokell(5) 6 43
(Ann Stokell) *chsd ldrs on outer: rdn along and sltly outpcd wl over 1f out: styd on on fnl f: nrst fin* 25/1

00-0 4 shd **Mr Mo Jo**[24] 2314 4-9-8 59 RobertWinston 1 52
(Lawrence Mullaney) *slt ld to 1/2-way: cl up: rdn and ev ch over 1f out: wknd ins fnl f* 11/1

0134 5 hd **Invigilator**[23] 2352 4-9-1 52 GrahamGibbons 8 44
(Derek Shaw) *hld up: effrt 2f out: swtchd rt to inner and rdn over 1f out: kpt on u.p ins fnl f: n.d* 5/2[1]

0-40 6 1 1/4 **Fair Bunny**[32] 2091 5-8-12 49 (b) AndrewElliott 9 36
(Alan Brown) *dwlt: sn chsng ldrs: rdn along over 2f out: wknd and hung rt over 1f out* 4/1[3]

0206 7 1 1/2 **Divertimenti (IRE)**[2] 2981 8-9-11 65 (b) DaleSwift(3) 3 47
(Roy Bowring) *sltly hmpd s: chsd ldrs: rdn along over 2f out: sn btn* 5/1

1m 5.18s (1.68) **Going Correction** +0.40s/f (Good)
WFA 3 from 4yo+ 7lb 7 Ran SP% 112.4
Speed ratings (Par 101): **102,96,94,93,93 91,89**
toteswingers:1&2:£9.50, 1&3:£37.50, 2&3:£5.40 CSF £34.89 CT £650.94 TOTE £7.70: £3.80, £3.40; EX 46.70.
Owner Mrs M Chapman **Bred** Steve C Snowden & Doug Wilson **Trained** Market Rasen, Lincs

FOCUS
Nothing more than a moderate start to the day.

3019 ADMIRAL - TYREGIANT.COM CLAIMING STKS 5f

2:30 (2:33) (Class 6) 2-Y-O £1,617 (£481; £240; £120) Stalls Low

Form RPR

54 1 **Lord Avonbrook**[8] 2798 2-8-4 0 RyanWhile(7) 5 63
(Bill Turner) *trckd ldng pair: cl up 1/2-way: chal over 1f out: rdn to ld ent fnl f: sn edgd lft: styd on wl* 12/1

00 2 3 **Sulky Sheila (IRE)**[11] 2686 2-8-6 0 JamesSullivan 2 47
(Tim Easterby) *led: rdn along and edgd rt 2f out: jnd over 1f out: drvn and hdd ent fnl f: kpt on same pce* 6/1[2]

205 3 nk **Dil Laney (IRE)**[9] 2770 2-8-11 0 DanielTudhope 1 53
(David O'Meara) *cl up on inner: pushed along 1/2-way: rdn whn n.m.r and hmpd on rail wl over 1f out: sn swtchd lft and sltly outpcd: drvn and kpt on fnl f* 4/6[1]

003 4 9 **Zero Rated (IRE)**[24] 2309 2-8-6 0 (b) DavidAllan 4 14
(Tim Easterby) *sn pushed along in rr: rdn along after 1 1/2f and sn outpcd: bhd fnl 2f* 15/2[3]

1m 6.24s (2.74) **Going Correction** +0.40s/f (Good) 4 Ran SP% 93.7
Speed ratings (Par 91): **94,89,88,74**
CSF £46.32 TOTE £13.50; EX 51.10.
Owner Mrs M S Teversham **Bred** Mrs Monica Teversham **Trained** Sigwells, Somerset

FOCUS
Not a race to dwell on for too long, especially as Saltaire Lass played up at the start and failed to load into the stalls. The filly cannot run now until the day after passing a stalls test. A weak race and limited form, but the winner delivered and it was no fluke.

NOTEBOOK
Lord Avonbrook was comfortably held in selling grade last time but took this with a bit in hand after showing even pace throughout. It was another good bit of placing by the astute Bill Turner, and some low-grade nurseries later in the season will probably suit the horse. (op 10-1)
Sulky Sheila(IRE) had been beaten over 13l on both starts, so this appeared to be better, although she was treading water in the latter stages. (op 8-1)
Dil Laney(IRE) looked the best of these on previous form, but got hampered up the inside rail at a crucial stage of the contest by the runner-up and wasn't able to get going quickly enough once switching positions to cause the winner any problems. (op 4-5 tchd 8-13 and 5-6 in places)
Zero Rated(IRE) was struggling from an early stage. (op 6-1)

3020 JINYU - TYREGIANT.COM H'CAP (DIV II) 5f

3:00 (3:01) (Class 6) (0-65,63) 3-Y-O+ £1,940 (£577; £288; £144) Stalls Low

Form RPR

4664 1 **Tuibama (IRE)**[9] 2774 3-8-7 49 (p) FrannyNorton 4 55
(Tracy Waggott) *mde all: rdn over 1f out: drvn and styd on wl towards fin* 8/1

6044 2 hd **Drumpellier (IRE)**[9] 2749 5-8-11 46 DanielTudhope 7 54
(Simon West) *dwlt and in rr: hdwy on outer wl over 1f out: sn rdn: str run ins fnl f: jst failed* 17/2

0031 3 1 **Hab Reeh**[8] 2796 4-9-2 51 6ex (bt) JamesSullivan 6 56
(Ruth Carr) *prom: chsd wnr fr 1/2-way: rdn over 1f out: drvn ins fnl f: kpt on* 5/2[1]

0604 4 3 **Perfect Honour (IRE)**[2] 2971 6-8-10 45 MichaelO'Connell 3 39
(Des Donovan) *prom: rdn along wl over 1f out: sn drvn and one pce* 9/2[2]

3364 5 2 3/4 **Highland Warrior**[29] 2140 13-10-0 63 MickyFenton 1 47
(Paul Midgley) *chsd ldrs: hdwy over 1f out: sn rdn and one pce fnl f* 11/2[3]

6-05 6 1 1/2 **Pinball (IRE)**[23] 2350 6-9-4 53 (p) TonyHamilton 5 32
(Lisa Williamson) *hld up in tch: hdwy on inner to chse ldrs wl over 1f out: sn rdn and no imp* 9/1

54-0 7 hd **Wotatomboy**[36] 1961 6-9-0 49 AmyRyan 2 27
(Richard Whitaker) *dwlt: a towards rr* 10/1

0040 8 2 1/2 **Tagula Breeze (IRE)**[23] 2352 6-9-6 58 DaleSwift(3) 8 27
(Ian McInnes) *t.k.h: chsd ldrs: rdn along wl over 1f out: grad wknd* 14/1

603- 9 4 **Lujiana**[187] 7691 7-8-3 45 JordanHibberd(7) 9
(Mel Brittain) *chsd ldrs on outer: rdn along bef 1/2-way: sn lost pl and bhd* 25/1

1m 5.83s (2.33) **Going Correction** +0.40s/f (Good)
WFA 3 from 4yo+ 7lb 9 Ran SP% 113.4
Speed ratings (Par 101): **97,96,95,90,85 83,83,79,72**
toteswingers:1&2:£16.30, 1&3:£5.60, 2&3:£7.10 CSF £72.24 CT £218.26 TOTE £10.00: £3.20, £3.80, £1.50; EX 113.50.
Owner H Conlon **Bred** J F Tuthill **Trained** Spennymoor, Co Durham

FOCUS
This appeared the stronger of the two divisions, with more horses coming into it in good heart, although the winning time was a bit slower.
Highland Warrior Official explanation: jockey said gelding lost its action

3021 MARSHAL - TYREGIANT.COM H'CAP 7f 100y

3:30 (3:30) (Class 5) (0-70,65) 4-Y-O+ £2,587 (£770; £384; £192) Stalls Low

Form RPR

4-03 1 **Fenella Fudge**[9] 2766 4-9-5 63 GrahamGibbons 7 74
(Derek Shaw) *awkward and sltly hmpd s: sn swtchd rt to rails in rr: hdwy on inner 2f out: rdn to chse ldrs over 1f out: swtchd lft to chal ent fnl f: sn drvn and styd on gamely to ld on line* 5/1[2]

11-5 2 shd **Eastward Ho**[64] 1269 4-9-4 62 TonyHamilton 1 73
(Jason Ward) *sn led: rdn wl over 1f out: drvn ins fnl f: hdd and no ex nr line* 6/1[3]

06-0 3 3 **Gadobout Dancer**[32] 2091 5-8-8 52 JamesSullivan 2 55
(Tony Coyle) *chsd ldrs: rdn wl over 2f out: styd on to chal over 1f out: ev ch tl drvn and one pce ins fnl f* 10/1

-560 4 5 **Meandmyshadow**[18] 2476 4-9-7 65 FrannyNorton 3 56
(Alan Brown) *hld up: hdwy over 2f out: rdn wl over 1f out: kpt on: n.d* 14/1

-322 5 1 3/4 **Cottam Donny**[11] 2692 4-9-5 63 RobertWinston 5 49
(Mel Brittain) *t.k.h: cl up: rdn to chal 2f out: ev ch tl drvn and wknd appr fnl f* 11/8[1]

50-0 6 hd **Lady Gar Gar**[60] 1384 4-8-12 59 (v) DaleSwift(3) 4 45
(Geoffrey Oldroyd) *chsd ldrs: effrt over 2f out: sn rdn and wknd wl over 1f out* 7/1

3122 **7** 1 1/2 **Bonnie Prince Blue**[36] 1961 9-9-2 **60**........................(b) DanielTudhope 8 42
(Ian McInnes) *in tch: rdn along over 2f out: sn btn* **16/1**

0000 **8** 8 **Transmit (IRE)**[8] 2792 5-8-4 **55**........................(b) GaryMahon(7) 6 17
(Tim Easterby) *wnt lft s: a in rr: rdn along 4f out: outpcd and bhd fnl 3f* **25/1**

1m 36.05s (2.25) **Going Correction** +0.40s/f (Good) **8** Ran SP% **111.0**
Speed ratings (Par 103): **103,102,99,93,91 91,89,80**
toteswingers:1&2:£6.40, 1&3:£11.70, 2&3:£17.40 CSF £32.74 CT £279.51 TOTE £9.00: £2.60, £1.10, £3.20; EX 34.10.

Owner Brian Johnson (Northamptonshire) **Bred** Onslow, Given, Stratton & Cashin **Trained** Sproxton, Leics

FOCUS
A modest contest.

3022 INFINITY - TYREGIANT.COM H'CAP 1m 1f 207y
4:00 (4:00) (Class 5) (0-70,65) 4-Y-0+ **£2,587** (£770; £384; £192) **Stalls** Low

Form RPR

-500 **1** **Maybeme**[25] 2260 6-8-10 **54**........................ AmyRyan 4 62
(Neville Bycroft) *dwlt and towards rr: stdy hdwy 1/2-way: chsd ldrs over 2f out: rdn over 1f out: styd on to ld jst ins fnl f: drvn out* **4/1**[2]

3122 **2** nk **The Lock Master (IRE)**[7] 2821 5-9-7 **65**........................ GrahamGibbons 2 72
(Michael Appleby) *hld up in rr: stdy hdwy 3f out: chsd ldrs over 1f out: rdn ent fnl f: sn ev ch tl drvn and no ex towards fin* **11/4**[1]

6-36 **3** 1 1/4 **Zaplamation (IRE)**[6] 2440 7-9-4 **62**........................ MichaelO'Connell 6 67
(John Quinn) *trckd ldng pair: hdwy over 3f out: rdn to ld wl over 1f out: drvn and hdd jst ins fnl f: kpt on same pce* **11/4**[1]

4300 **4** 4 **General Tufto**[8] 2804 7-8-7 **51**........................(b) AndrewElliott 5 48
(Charles Smith) *in rr: pushed along 3f out: rdn and hdwy 2f out: styd on fnl f: nrst fin* **22/1**

01-1 **5** nk **Rockweiller**[37] 1919 5-9-7 **65**........................(v) TonyHamilton 8 61
(Steve Gollings) *cl up: led wl over 2f out: sn rdn: hdd wl over 1f out: drvn and wknd ent fnl f* **6/1**[3]

-000 **6** 1/2 **Xpres Maite**[11] 2687 9-8-13 **57**........................(b) AmirQuinn 9 52
(Roy Bowring) *prom: led after 2f: rdn along 3f out: sn hdd and grad wknd fnl 2f* **16/1**

52-3 **7** 5 **Tobrata**[97] 836 6-9-2 **60**........................ RobertWinston 7 45
(Mel Brittain) *chsd ldrs: rdn along on outer 4f out: wknd wl over 2f out* **8/1**

/0-0 **8** 1 **Umverti**[11] 2694 7-9-1 **59**........................ DanielTudhope 3 42
(Joanne Foster) *led 2f: trckd ldng pair: rdn along 3f out: grad wknd* **16/1**

2m 11.34s (4.34) **Going Correction** +0.40s/f (Good) **8** Ran SP% **114.8**
Speed ratings (Par 103): **98,97,96,93,93 92,88,88**
toteswingers:1&2:£3.60, 1&3:£3.60, 2&3:£3.10 CSF £15.52 CT £34.47 TOTE £4.30: £1.90, £1.10, £1.10; EX 17.20.

Owner Mrs J Dickinson **Bred** Harts Farm And Stud **Trained** Brandsby, N Yorks

■ Stewards' Enquiry : Graham Gibbons two-day ban: used whip above permitted level (Jun 27-28)

FOCUS
Quite an interesting result, as what had looked to be Neville Bycroft's first string Eeny Mac was taken out earlier in the day because of the going, despite having form in soft ground, and his other runner won after being nicely backed in the lead up to the off.

3023 SAILUN - TYREGIANT.COM H'CAP (PART OF THE BEVERLEY MIDDLE DISTANCE SERIES) 1m 4f 16y
4:30 (4:30) (Class 6) (0-55,55) 3-Y-O **£2,587** (£770; £384; £192) **Stalls** Low

Form RPR

0-66 **1** **Fleeting Fashion**[20] 2418 3-8-8 **52**........................ ShirleyTeasdale(7) 11 58
(Michael Appleby) *trckd ldrs: hdwy over 2f out: rdn to chal ent fnl f: sn led and kpt on wl* **10/1**

-535 **2** 1 3/4 **Red Tyke (IRE)**[23] 2340 3-8-12 **49**........................ MichaelO'Connell 1 52
(John Quinn) *t.k.h: trckd ldrs: hdwy 3f out: rdn 2f out: styd on to ld over 1f out: drvn ent fnl f: sn hdd and kpt on same pce* **3/1**[2]

0462 **3** hd **Mr Snoozy**[9] 2771 3-9-1 **52**........................ GrahamGibbons 5 55+
(Tim Walford) *trckd ldrs on inner whn n.m.r and hmpd after 1f: in tch: pushed along over 3f out: rdn and outpcd 2f out: drvn and styd on wl fnl f: tk 3rd on line* **11/4**[1]

0600 **4** nse **Oops Caroline (IRE)**[9] 2771 3-8-13 **50**........................(b[1]) DanielTudhope 2 53
(David O'Meara) *in tch: rapid hdwy to ld over 6f out: rdn over 2f out: drvn and hdd over 1f out: rallied ins fnl f: no ex last 75yds: lost 3rd on line* **14/1**

0-40 **5** 1 **Emperors Waltz (IRE)**[16] 2548 3-9-4 **55**........................ DavidAllan 12 56
(Rae Guest) *prom: hdwy to trck ldr 1/2-way: chal over 2f out: rdn wl over 1f out and ev ch tl drvn and wknd ent fnl f* **7/1**[3]

500- **6** 1 1/4 **Astonished Harry (GER)**[266] 6260 3-9-1 **55**........................ PaulPickard(3) 4 54
(Reg Hollinshead) *t.k.h: towards rr: hdwy on wd outside over 2f out: sn rdn and no imp appr fnl f* **28/1**

0-00 **7** 5 **Brasingaman Espee**[23] 2340 3-8-9 **46** oh1........................ AndrewElliott 8 37
(George Moore) *midfield: rdn along over 3f out: n.d* **40/1**

0000 **8** 7 **Bollin Nancy**[9] 2771 3-8-6 **48** oh1 ow2........................ AdamCarter(5) 9 28
(Tim Easterby) *led: hdd over 6f out: cl up tl rdn along and wknd over 2f out* **40/1**

0 **9** 1 1/4 **Nickeys On Time (IRE)**[30] 2130 3-8-12 **49**........................ StephenCraine 6 27
(Daniel Mark Loughnane) *dwlt: a towards rr* **28/1**

0-36 **10** 3 **Madam Lilibet (IRE)**[25] 2287 3-8-9 **46**........................ TonyHamilton 3 19
(Sharon Watt) *a in rr* **22/1**

006- **11** 6 **Eastern Seel**[280] 5818 3-8-10 **47**........................ JamesSullivan 7 11
(Tim Easterby) *towards rr: sme hdwy into midfield over 5f out: rdn along and wknd over 4f out* **11/1**

4004 **12** 1 1/4 **Ossie's Dancer**[23] 2341 3-8-9 **46** oh1........................ RobertWinston 10 8
(Robert Cowell) *towards rr: hdwy into midfield over 5f out: in tch over 3f out: sn rdn and wknd* **7/1**[3]

2m 48.05s (8.25) **Going Correction** +0.40s/f (Good) **12** Ran SP% **116.9**
Speed ratings (Par 97): **88,86,86,86,86 85,81,77,76,74 70,69**
toteswingers:1&2:£2.60, 1&3:£2.70, 2&3:£2.30 CSF £37.43 CT £106.61 TOTE £10.90: £3.80, £1.10, £1.10; EX 50.90.

Owner P J & Mrs J P Haycock **Bred** P J Haycock **Trained** Danethorpe, Notts

■ Stewards' Enquiry : Andrew Elliott caution: entered wrong stall.

FOCUS
Low-grade but interesting stuff, as quite a few unexposed types capable of improvement took their chance. The early gallop was poor and it developed into a sprint.

Fleeting Fashion Official explanation: trainer said, regarding apparent improvement in form, that the filly had strengthened up over the winter and had come on for its first run of the season.

Madam Lilibet(IRE) Official explanation: jockey said filly hung left

Ossie's Dancer Official explanation: jockey said gelding lost its action

3024 ROTALLA - TYREGIANT.COM MAIDEN STKS 7f 100y
5:00 (5:03) (Class 5) 3-Y-O+ **£2,393** (£712; £355; £177) **Stalls** Low

Form RPR

- **1** **Miss Ellany (IRE)**[194] 7611 3-8-9 0........................ DanielTudhope 5 80
(David O'Meara) *trckd ldr: led over 2f out: rdn clr appr fnl f: kpt on strly* **2/1**[2]

43 **2** 6 **Gladsome**[23] 2335 4-9-5 0........................ RobertWinston 3 69
(Jason Ward) *hld up in tch: hdwy 3f out: rdn to chse wnr wl over 1f out: sn edgd rt and no imp* **5/2**[3]

4-02 **3** 2 1/4 **Sabore**[23] 2335 3-8-9 72........................ TonyHamilton 1 60
(Richard Fahey) *trckd ldrs on inner: hdwy 3f out: rdn 2f out: drvn over 1f out and one pce* **7/4**[1]

0-00 **4** 7 **Derek The Diamond**[50] 1590 3-9-0 45........................ GrahamGibbons 4 47
(Michael Appleby) *led: rdn along 3f out: hdd over 2f out and sn wknd* **20/1**

06- **5** 13 **Rosa Luxemburg**[174] 7856 4-9-5 0........................(e[1]) MichaelO'Connell 6
(Lawrence Mullaney) *a in rr* **50/1**

0 **6** 9 **Alaskan Prince (IRE)**[32] 2095 7-9-10 0........................ AndrewElliott 7
(Peter Salmon) *wnt bdly lft s: t.k.h and sn chsng ldng pair: cl up over 4f out: rdn along and wknd over 3f out* **100/1**

6 **7** 29 **Monzino (USA)**[6] 2864 4-9-5 0........................ AnnStokell(5) 2
(Michael Chapman) *in tch: rdn along 1/2-way: sn hung lft: wknd and bhd* **25/1**

1m 35.53s (1.73) **Going Correction** +0.40s/f (Good)
WFA 3 from 4yo+ 10lb **7** Ran SP% **109.8**
Speed ratings (Par 103): **106,99,96,88,73 63,30**
toteswingers:1&2:£1.50, 1&3:£1.70, 2&3:£1.40 CSF £6.67 TOTE £3.50: £2.50, £1.40; EX 6.80.

Owner W O'Brien **Bred** Miss Debbie Kitchin **Trained** Nawton, N Yorks

FOCUS
Probably just a modest affair.

Monzino(USA) Official explanation: jockey said gelding ran flat

3025 HULL FC LUCKY 13 LOTTERY H'CAP 1m 100y
5:30 (5:31) (Class 6) (0-65,63) 3-Y-O **£1,704** (£503; £251) **Stalls** Low

Form RPR

0-65 **1** **Lady Advocate (IRE)**[37] 1916 3-8-13 **55**........................(b) DavidAllan 5 63
(Tim Easterby) *led 3f: cl up tl led again 3f out: jnd 2f out and sn rdn: drvn ins fnl f and kpt on gamely* **12/1**

003- **2** nk **Bada Bing**[253] 6611 3-8-9 **51**........................ RobertWinston 2 58
(Scott Dixon) *trckd ldrs on inner: hdwy 3f out: chal 2f out: sn rdn and ev ch tl drvn and no ex wl ins fnl f* **12/1**

-403 **3** 6 **No Time To Cry**[9] 2765 3-8-11 **53**........................(p) FrannyNorton 4 47
(Ann Duffield) *chsd ldng pair: rdn along over 2f out: drvn over 1f out and sn one pce* **9/2**[2]

06-1 **4** 1 3/4 **Kian's Joy**[60] 1386 3-8-10 **52**........................ AndrewElliott 8 41
(Jedd O'Keeffe) *towards rr: pushed along on outer whn hung lft bnd at 1/2-way: bhd 3f out: rdn and hdwy 2f out: swtchd wd and drvn over 1f out: kpt on wl u.p fnl f: nrst fin* **3/1**[1]

0130 **5** 1/2 **My New Angel (IRE)**[37] 1918 3-8-6 **48**........................ AmyRyan 7 36
(Paul Green) *in tch on outer: hdwy 3f out: rdn to chse ldrs over 2f out: drvn and no imp fr over 1f out* **16/1**

0005 **6** 1/2 **Icewan**[23] 2339 3-9-0 **56**........................(p) MickyFenton 12 43+
(Paul Midgley) *towards rr: rdn along whn nt clr run 2f out: sn swtchd lft to wd outside: kpt on fnl f: nrst fin* **14/1**

045- **7** hd **Catramis**[254] 6572 3-8-13 **58**........................ DaleSwift(3) 11 45
(Geoffrey Oldroyd) *hld up in rr effrt and nt clr run on inner 2f out: sn swtchd lft and rdn: sme late hdwy* **9/1**[3]

0-03 **8** nk **So Cheeky**[33] 2030 3-8-8 **57**........................ HannahNunn(7) 1 43
(Peter Salmon) *hld up towards rr: hdwy on inner wl over 2f out: sn rdn and nvr nr ldrs* **9/1**[3]

-050 **9** 2 1/2 **Twin Ivan (IRE)**[14] 2605 3-8-6 **53**........................ DeanHeslop(5) 10 33
(Marjorie Fife) *chsd ldrs: rdn along 1/2-way: sn wknd* **20/1**

45-0 **10** 4 1/2 **Peters Pursuit (IRE)**[16] 2540 3-8-13 **55**........................ TonyHamilton 6 25
(Richard Fahey) *in tch: rdn along over 3f out: sn wknd* **10/1**

415 **11** 11 **Source Of Light (IRE)**[105] 739 3-9-6 **62**........................ StephenCraine 3
(Daniel Mark Loughnane) *towards rr: sme hdwy 3f out: rdn over 2f out: nvr a factor* **12/1**

00-0 **12** 6 **King Laertis (IRE)**[127] 459 3-7-12 **45**........................ NeilFarley(5) 14
(Tracy Waggott) *chsd ldrs: hdwy and cl up 1/2-way: rdn along wl over 2f out: sn wknd* **16/1**

-400 **13** 26 **Forever Janey**[50] 1585 3-8-3 **45**........................ JamesSullivan 13
(Paul Green) *chsd ldrs: cl up after 2f: led after 3f: rdn along and hdd 3f out: sn wknd* **33/1**

1m 51.73s (4.13) **Going Correction** +0.40s/f (Good) **13** Ran SP% **121.5**
Speed ratings (Par 97): **95,94,88,86,86 85,85,85,82,78 67,61,35**
toteswingers:1&2:£20.60, 1&3:£10.50, 2&3:£12.50 CSF £150.94 CT £565.54 TOTE £15.10: £4.40, £3.40, £2.20; EX 98.50.

Owner S A Heley **Bred** Michael O'Dwyer & Knockainey Stud **Trained** Great Habton, N Yorks

FOCUS
A modest event where it paid to be handy turning in.

Kian's Joy Official explanation: trainer said gelding did not act on the track

T/Plt: £1,439.20 to a £1 stake. Pool:£47,021.79 - 23.85 winning tickets T/Qpdt: £12.70 to a £1 stake. Pool:£4,905.67 - 284.26 winning tickets JR

2837 HAMILTON (R-H)
Wednesday, June 13

OFFICIAL GOING: Good (good to firm in places; 9.3)

All races of a mile and beyond reduced in distance by about 25yds.
Wind: Almost nil Weather: Overcast

3026 JOIN HAMILTON PARK ON FACEBOOK AMATEUR RIDERS' H'CAP 6f 5y
6:20 (6:22) (Class 6) (0-60,60) 4-Y-O+ **£1,975** (£607; £303) **Stalls** Centre

Form RPR

4153 **1** **Cut The Cackle (IRE)**[6] 2840 6-10-6 **59**........(bt) MissKMargarson(7) 11 68
(Richard Guest) *dwlt: sn pushed along in midfield: hdwy over 1f out: led wl ins fnl f: pushed out* **7/2**[1]

5/1- **2** 1/2 **Bid For Gold**[366] 2990 8-10-7 **60**........................ MissEmmaBedford(7) 4 67
(Jedd O'Keeffe) *cl up: rdn to ld over 1f out: hdd wl ins fnl f: r.o* **16/1**

00-0 **3** 1 1/4 **Isle Of Ellis (IRE)**[8] 2796 5-9-9 **46** oh1........................(v) MissRSmith(5) 8 49
(Ron Barr) *chsd ldrs: rdn and outpcd 2f out: styd on ins fnl f* **40/1**

2352 **4** *nk* **Hellbender (IRE)**[4] 2924 6-10-11 **60** MrMEnnis(3) 9 62
(George Foster) *sn pushed along towards rr: edgd rt and hdwy over 1f out: kpt on fnl f: nt gng pce to chal* **6/1**[3]
-364 **5** *hd* **Two Turtle Doves (IRE)**[22] 2377 6-10-9 **58** MissMMullineaux(3) 3 59
(Michael Mullineaux) *bhd: hdwy on wd outside 2f out: sn pushed along: no imp ins fnl f* **15/2**
-000 **6** *nk* **Lizzie (IRE)**[32] 2096 4-10-9 **60** (b) MrWEasterby(5) 13 60
(Tim Easterby) *in tch: rdn over 2f out: styd on ins fnl f: nvr able to chal* **4/1**[2]
02-3 **7** *1* **Karate Queen**[8] 2796 7-9-9 **46** oh1 MissVBarr(5) 15 43
(Ron Barr) *overall ldr stands' rail tl hdd over 1f out: sn outpcd* **9/1**
4000 **8** *1 3/4* **See The Storm**[19] 2463 4-9-9 **46** (p) MrJHamilton(5) 10 38
(Lisa Williamson) *cl up: effrt and ev ch 2f out: wknd ins fnl f* **20/1**
-604 **9** *nse* **Spread Boy (IRE)**[8] 2796 5-9-8 **47** MrMAllan(7) 2 38
(Alan Berry) *spd on outside: outpcd over 2f out: sme late hdwy: no imp* **28/1**
3550 **10** *1 3/4* **Blue Noodles**[111] 666 6-9-9 **48** MrAFrench(7) 6 34
(John Wainwright) *in tch tl rdn and wknd over 2f out* **20/1**
-105 **11** *nk* **Avoncreek**[33] 2046 8-10-3 **49** (v) MissSBrotherton 5 34
(Brian Baugh) *t.k.h: hld up: struggling over 2f out: sn btn* **14/1**
0560 **12** *3* **Andrasta**[6] 2839 7-9-11 **46** MissWGibson(3) 7 21
(Alan Berry) *bhd: swtchd lft over 3f out: sn rdn and struggling* **25/1**
00-0 **13** *3 3/4* **Striking Priorite**[35] 1988 4-9-8 **47** oh1 ow1 (e[1]) MrDLevey(7) 12 10
(Tim Fitzgerald) *s.i.s: bhd: struggling 1/2-way: nvr on terms* **50/1**

1m 12.63s (0.43) **Going Correction** -0.20s/f (Firm) **13** Ran SP% **112.0**
Speed ratings (Par 101): **89,88,86,86,86 85,84,81,81,79 79,75,70**
toteswingers:1&2:£15.70, 1&3:£60.20, 2&3:£101.20 CSF £47.90 CT £1683.17 TOTE £5.00: £1.30, £4.80, £12.80; EX 45.50.
Owner Rakebackmypoker.com **Bred** Mountarmstrong Stud **Trained** Stainforth, S Yorks
■ Cheyenne Red was withdrawn (14/1, upset in stalls). Deduct 5p in the £ under R4. Katie Margarson's first winner.
■ Stewards' Enquiry : Mr M Ennis caution: entered wrong stall.

FOCUS
Central Scotland had escaped much of the rain and after this low-grade amateur riders' sprint handicap the ground was reckoned to be just on the quick side of good. They set off in two groups but converged into one towards the stands' side by halfway.

3027 STEPS AND PETER ANDRE LIVE ON SAT 7 JULY H'CAP 6f 5y
6:50 (6:51) (Class 4) (0-80,80) 4-Y-0+ **£5,175** (£1,540; £769; £384) **Stalls** Centre

Form RPR
3051 **1** **Julius Geezer (IRE)**[16] 2551 4-9-2 **75** RichardKingscote 5 88
(Tom Dascombe) *mde all: rdn along 2f out: hung lft ins fnl f: kpt on wl* **16/1**
3130 **2** *1 3/4* **Crimson Knot (IRE)**[14] 2596 4-9-2 **75** GrahamLee 8 82
(Alan Berry) *chsd ldrs: effrt and hdwy over 1f out: chsd wnr ins fnl f: r.o* **28/1**
0002 **3** *nk* **Barkston Ash**[6] 2841 4-8-6 **72** JasonHart(7) 9 78
(Eric Alston) *trckd ldrs: effrt and edgd rt over 1f out: checked ins fnl f: kpt on same pce towards fin* **11/2**[1]
1-05 **4** *2 3/4* **Chookie Royale**[13] 2632 4-9-3 **76** [1] PaulMulrennan 11 73
(Keith Dalgleish) *sn pushed along in midfield: effrt and edgd rt 2f out: kpt on same pce fnl f* **14/1**
00-3 **5** *3/4* **North Central (USA)**[33] 2037 5-8-6 **65** (p) BarryMcHugh 4 60
(Jim Goldie) *hld up towards rr: rdn and outpcd over 2f out: styd on fnl f: nvr able to chal* **40/1**
3006 **6** *nk* **Blues Jazz**[14] 2597 6-9-1 **79** GarryWhillans(5) 6 73
(Ian Semple) *sn rdn in rr: no imp tl styd on last 150yds: nvr rchd ldrs* **8/1**[3]
0-21 **7** *nk* **Breezolini**[26] 2230 4-8-13 **72** DuranFentiman 2 65
(Geoffrey Harker) *in tch: drvn along over 2f out: no imp appr fnl f* **14/1**
0035 **8** *1/2* **The Nifty Fox**[8] 2793 8-8-11 **70** (p) TomEaves 3 61
(Tim Easterby) *hld up: nt clr run over 2f out: rdn over 1f out: n.d* **22/1**
0000 **9** *1 3/4* **Oil Strike**[11] 2697 5-9-0 **80** DavidSimmonson(7) 7 66
(Michael Easterby) *chsd wnr: rdn over 1f out: wknd ins fnl f* **33/1**
0-10 **10** *3/4* **Jarrow (IRE)**[38] 1885 5-9-7 **80** AdrianNicholls 12 63
(David Nicholls) *t.k.h: hld up: short-lived effrt over 2f out: btn fnl f* **6/1**[2]

1m 10.19s (-2.01) **Going Correction** -0.20s/f (Firm) **10** Ran SP% **73.2**
Speed ratings (Par 105): **105,102,102,98,97 97,96,96,93,92**
toteswingers:1&2:£50.60, 1&3:£3.10, 2&3:£50.60 CSF £156.81 CT £644.91 TOTE £10.80: £2.90, £4.50, £1.80; EX 143.70.
Owner Basing Bellman Stroud **Bred** Ballyhane Stud **Trained** Malpas, Cheshire
■ Hopes N Dreams was withdrawn (11/8F, upset in stalls). Deduct 40p in the £ under R4.

FOCUS
A competitive sprint handicap and again they raced in one group towards the stands' side.

3028 HAMILTON-PARK.CO.UK H'CAP 5f 4y
7:20 (7:22) (Class 6) (0-65,61) 3-Y-O **£2,045** (£603; £302) **Stalls** Centre

Form RPR
1004 **1** **Rock Canyon (IRE)**[4] 2928 3-8-13 **58** (p) ShaneBKelly(5) 2 66
(Linda Perratt) *hld up: swtchd rt and effrt 1/2-way: led ins fnl f: hung lft: r.o strly* **11/2**[3]
-041 **2** *2 1/4* **Just Like Heaven (IRE)**[11] 2695 3-9-7 **61** DuranFentiman 8 61
(Tim Easterby) *led tl drvn and hdd over 1f out: rallied ins fnl f to take 2nd nr fin: nt rch wnr* **7/4**[1]
5065 **3** *hd* **Gran Canaria Queen**[13] 2615 3-8-10 **50** (v[1]) BarryMcHugh 1 49
(Ian Semple) *plld hrd: cl up: swtchd lft sn after s: led over 1f out to ins fnl f: no ex* **14/1**
5453 **4** *3/4* **Economic Crisis (IRE)**[18] 2470 3-9-1 **55** GrahamLee 3 51
(Alan Berry) *upset in stalls: prom: pushed along and sltly outpcd whn checked briefly over 1f out: kpt on same pce ins fnl f* **13/2**
-050 **5** *2 1/4* **Niceonemyson**[15] 2591 3-9-6 **60** PaddyAspell 7 48
(Christopher Wilson) *trckd ldrs: rdn and outpcd 2f out: kpt on fnl f: no imp* **9/1**
00-0 **6** *2 1/4* **Elusive Island (USA)**[77] 1067 3-9-2 **56** (p) PaulMulrennan 5 36
(Ann Duffield) *in tch: rdn and outpcd over 2f out: n.d after* **5/1**[2]
41-0 **7** *1/2* **Emily Hall**[9] 2749 3-8-8 **48** TomEaves 6 26
(Bryan Smart) *bhd on ins: drvn over 2f out: nvr rchd ldrs* **8/1**
0600 **8** *3 1/4* **Essexvale (IRE)**[12] 2673 3-8-2 **45** JulieBurke(3) 4 12
(Robert Johnson) *missed break: bhd and outpcd: nvr on terms* **25/1**

59.27s (-0.73) **Going Correction** -0.20s/f (Firm) **8** Ran SP% **113.4**
Speed ratings (Par 97): **97,93,93,91,88 84,83,78**
toteswingers:1&2:£3.00, 1&3:£13.20, 2&3:£6.10 CSF £15.27 CT £126.65 TOTE £6.70: £2.00, £1.10, £3.60; EX 14.80.
Owner Mrs Helen Perratt **Bred** Patrick J Connolly **Trained** East Kilbride, S Lanarks

3029 TOM JONES LIVE ON FRIDAY 6TH JULY H'CAP 1m 3f 16y
7:50 (7:53) (Class 6) (0-65,65) 4-Y-0+ **£2,726** (£805; £402) **Stalls** High

Form RPR
0-22 **1** **Raleigh Quay (IRE)**[15] 2593 5-9-2 **65** ShaneBKelly(5) 3 74
(Micky Hammond) *hld up: rdn and hdwy on outside over 2f out: edgd rt and led over 1f out: styd on wl u.p fnl f* **3/1**[2]
-000 **2** *1/2* **Hail Bold Chief (USA)**[15] 2588 5-9-5 **63** PJMcDonald 1 71
(Alan Swinbank) *prom: rdn and hdwy over 2f out: chsd wnr fnl f: kpt on: hld towards fin* **11/4**[1]
05-5 **3** *3 1/2* **Wind Shuffle (GER)**[14] 2599 9-8-11 **55** PaulMulrennan 8 57
(Richard Fahey) *plld hrd: cl up: led after 2f to over 1f out: sn one pce* **9/1**
50-0 **4** *2 1/4* **Goodlukin Lucy**[30] 2134 5-8-9 **53** GrahamLee 2 51
(Dianne Sayer) *hld up: rdn and outpcd over 2f out: styd on fnl f: nvr able to chal* **8/1**
3-2 **5** *3/4* **Commander Veejay**[7] 2823 4-8-5 **49** (b) BarryMcHugh 5 45
(Brian Rothwell) *dwlt: t.k.h and sn in tch: rdn whn n.m.r 2f out: sn no imp* **10/1**
2-03 **6** *1/2* **Avison (IRE)**[12] 2670 4-8-13 **60** LeeTopliss(3) 10 55
(Richard Fahey) *t.k.h: chsd ldrs: effrt and ev ch over 2f out: sn rdn: wknd over 1f out* **9/2**[3]
-505 **7** *1* **Downtown Boy (IRE)**[48] 1635 4-8-4 **47** ow1 (p) JoeFanning 9 42
(Ray Craggs) *hld up: hdwy and ev ch over 3f out: rdn and wkng whn hmpd over 1f out* **9/1**
00/6 **8** *1/2* **Sydney Cove (IRE)**[14] 2599 6-8-2 **46** oh1 (p) DuranFentiman 7 39
(Iain Jardine) *led 2f: cl up tl rdn and wknd over 2f out* **14/1**

2m 23.14s (-2.46) **Going Correction** -0.275s/f (Firm) **8** Ran SP% **116.7**
Speed ratings (Par 101): **97,96,94,92,91 91,90,90**
toteswingers:1&2:£3.50, 1&3:£7.10, 2&3:£11.90 CSF £12.01 CT £65.68 TOTE £3.60: £1.10, £1.50, £2.90; EX 13.10.
Owner S T Brankin & J Zuppinger **Bred** S O'Sullivan **Trained** Middleham Moor, N Yorks
■ Stewards' Enquiry : Shane B Kelly 1st incident, one-day ban: careless riding (Jun 27); 2nd, two-day ban: careless riding (Jun 28-29); two-day ban: used whip above permitted level (Jun 30-Jul 1)

FOCUS
A low-grade middle distance handicap run at a steady pace early on.

3030 RACING UK (S) STKS 1m 1f 36y
8:20 (8:21) (Class 6) 4-Y-0+ **£1,940** (£577; £288; £144) **Stalls** Low

Form RPR
4-00 **1** **Pendragon (USA)**[4] 2921 9-9-3 83 BarryMcHugh 6 78
(Brian Ellison) *mde all at stdy pce: rdn and qcknd 2f out: kpt on strly fnl f* **1/1**[1]
6-02 **2** *2 3/4* **Bella Noir**[46] 1652 5-8-9 72 MichaelMetcalfe(3) 3 67
(Mrs K Burke) *pressed wnr: effrt and ev ch over 2f out: sn rdn: one pce fnl f* **85/40**[2]
-266 **3** *1 3/4* **Royal Straight**[13] 2619 7-9-3 64 (t) GrahamLee 5 68
(Linda Perratt) *t.k.h: prom: effrt and rdn 2f out: sn one pce* **14/1**
0206 **4** *5* **Arabian Spirit**[9] 2754 7-9-0 75 LeeTopliss(3) 4 57
(Richard Fahey) *t.k.h: trckd ldrs: rdn and outpcd over 2f out: btn over 1f out* **5/1**[3]
5 *8* **Little Thief** 5-8-7 0 DuranFentiman 2 29
(Iain Jardine) *reluctant to enter stalls: t.k.h: hld up in tch: outpcd and hung lft fr 3f out: sn struggling* **33/1**

1m 59.95s (0.25) **Going Correction** -0.275s/f (Firm) **5** Ran SP% **108.3**
Speed ratings (Par 101): **87,84,83,78,71**
CSF £3.21 TOTE £2.50: £2.10, £1.10; EX 3.50.The winner was bought in for 6,000gns.
Owner Dan Gilbert & Kristian Strangeway **Bred** Flaxman Holdings Ltd **Trained** Norton, N Yorks

3031 TURFTV CLASSIFIED STKS 1m 1f 36y
8:50 (8:50) (Class 5) 3-4-Y-O **£4,090** (£1,207; £604) **Stalls** Low

Form RPR
0-4 **1** **Another For Joe**[13] 2619 4-9-7 67 GrahamLee 1 75
(Jim Goldie) *mde all: pushed along over 2f out: drvn and hld on gamely fnl f* **10/1**
1-04 **2** *nk* **Third Half**[19] 2452 3-8-9 70 RichardKingscote 7 72+
(Tom Dascombe) *t.k.h: hld up: rdn along over 3f out: gd hdwy on outside over 1f out: styd on wl fnl f: tk 2nd nr fin jst hld* **6/4**[1]
-324 **3** *1/2* **Free Art**[15] 2588 4-9-7 69 PJMcDonald 4 73
(Geoffrey Harker) *t.k.h: trckd ldrs: hdwy to chse wnr over 1f out: sn rdn: one pce ins fnl f: lost 2nd nr fin* **5/1**[3]
00-5 **4** *1* **District Attorney (IRE)**[44] 1703 3-8-9 69 PaulMulrennan 2 69
(William Haggas) *chsd wnr: rdn over 2f out: lost 2nd over 1f out: kpt on steadily fnl f* **7/2**[2]
2-61 **5** *2 1/4* **Cosmic Halo**[15] 2592 3-8-4 69 ShaneBKelly(5) 6 64
(Richard Fahey) *t.k.h: hld up in tch: rdn and outpcd over 2f out: plugged on fnl f: no imp* **7/1**
2106 **6** *3 1/2* **Chatterati (USA)**[12] 2672 3-8-9 70 JoeFanning 5 58
(Mark Johnston) *chsd ldrs: rdn 3f out: wknd over 1f out* **16/1**
00-6 **7** *7* **Cadore (IRE)**[27] 1797 4-9-7 69 (b[1]) TomEaves 8 43
(Lucinda Russell) *hld up: rdn along and outpcd wl over 2f out: sn btn* **20/1**

1m 56.51s (-3.19) **Going Correction** -0.275s/f (Firm)
WFA 3 from 4yo 12lb **7** Ran SP% **111.1**
Speed ratings (Par 103): **103,102,102,101,99 96,90**
toteswingers:1&2:£2.60, 1&3:£6.50, 2&3:£1.60 CSF £24.11 TOTE £10.80: £3.60, £1.70; EX 35.80.
Owner J S Goldie **Bred** G Merkel **Trained** Uplawmoor, E Renfrews

FOCUS
A tight-knit classified stakes with just 3lb between the seven runners on official ratings.

3032 BOOK NOW FOR SAINTS & SINNERS NIGHT H'CAP 1m 65y
9:20 (9:20) (Class 6) (0-60,60) 3-Y-0+ **£1,940** (£577; £288; £144) **Stalls** Low

Form RPR
0-04 **1** **King Of Paradise (IRE)**[24] 2313 3-8-9 **59** JasonHart(7) 4 64+
(Eric Alston) *plld hrd and sddle sn slipped forward: prom: rn wd over 4f out: effrt over 2f out: led wl ins fnl f: pushed out* **3/1**[1]
-000 **2** *1/2* **Last Destination (IRE)**[15] 2588 4-9-8 **54** PaulMulrennan 5 61
(Nigel Tinkler) *hld up towards rr: gd hdwy to ld 2f out: hdd wl ins fnl f: hld nr fin* **15/2**
-441 **3** *1* **Social Rhythm**[14] 2598 8-9-8 **59** GarryWhillans(5) 8 64
(Alistair Whillans) *s.i.s: hld up: hdwy to chal over 1f out: sn rdn: kpt on same pce wl ins fnl f* **4/1**[2]

-450 **4** *nk* **Madam Bonny (IRE)**[13] 2615 3-8-3 **46** oh1 .... DuranFentiman 2 49+
(Jim Goldie) *hld up in midfield on ins: effrt whn nt clr run over 2f out: swtchd lft and rdn over 1f out: styd on fnl f* **20/1**

0-00 **5** *3* **Viking Dancer**[14] 2600 5-9-0 **46** oh1 .... PJMcDonald 6 43
(Ruth Carr) *trckd ldrs: effrt and rdn 2f out: outpcd ins fnl f* **25/1**

0046 **6** *2 ½* **Deep Applause**[14] 2600 4-9-4 **53** ....(b[1]) LeeTopliss(3) 11 45
(Michael Dods) *dwlt: hld up: rdn whn hmpd and stmbld wl over 2f out: sme late hdwy: nvr on terms* **9/1**

0-40 **7** *2 ¼* **Fairy Mist (IRE)**[10] 2735 5-9-4 **50** ....(p) JoeFanning 3 36
(Brian Rothwell) *chsd ldr: rdn to ld briefly appr 2f out: wknd over 1f out* **9/2**[3]

2-00 **8** *1 ½* **Great Nicanor (IRE)**[16] 2540 3-8-7 **50** .... BarryMcHugh 10 30
(Ian Semple) *hld up: rdn and hdwy over 2f out: no imp over 1f out* **18/1**

03-0 **9** *½* **Seattle Sounder (IRE)**[19] 2441 3-9-3 **60** ....(v[1]) GrahamLee 7 39
(Ann Duffield) *midfield: rdn over 3f out: wknd 2f out* **9/1**

5-50 **10** *3 ¼* **Henrys Gift (IRE)**[12] 2669 4-9-6 **52** ....(b[1]) TomEaves 9 26
(Michael Dods) *led tl rdn and hdd appr 2f out: sn wknd* **14/1**

1m 46.84s (-1.56) **Going Correction** -0.275s/f (Firm)
WFA 3 from 4yo+ 11lb **10** Ran SP% **115.5**
Speed ratings (Par 101): **96,95,94,94,91 88,86,84,84,81**
toteswingers:1&2:£6.10, 1&3:£1.70, 2&3:£13.20 CSF £25.68 CT £90.77 TOTE £3.50: £1.10, £3.40, £1.80; EX 33.80.
Owner P G Buist **Bred** Sandro Garavelli **Trained** Longton, Lancs
■ Stewards' Enquiry : Garry Whillans four-day ban: careless riding (Jun 27-30)
Duran Fentiman two-day ban: careless riding (Jun 27-28)

FOCUS
A rock-bottom handicap.
T/Plt: £19.80 to a £1 stake. Pool:£52,818.84 - 1,946.92 winning tickets T/Qpdt: £7.40 to a £1 stake. Pool:£4,326.03 - 429.20 winning tickets RY

2708 HAYDOCK (L-H)
Wednesday, June 13

OFFICIAL GOING: Good to soft (good in places; 8.0)
All races on inner home straight and races on round course reduced in distance by 5yds.
Wind: Nil Weather: Cloudy

3033 NORTHERN TRUST INVESTMENT, DEVELOPMENT, LAND REGENERATION H'CAP 1m 6f
2:20 (2:22) (Class 4) (0-85,80) 3-Y-O **£4,075** (£1,212; £606; £303) **Stalls** Low

Form RPR

216- **1** **Gassin Golf**[231] 7095 3-9-3 **76** .... LukeMorris 5 87+
(Sir Mark Prescott Bt) *hld up: hdwy over 3f out: led over 2f out: rdn over 1f out: styd on dourly and in command towards fin* **11/4**[1]

231 **2** *2* **Gabrial The Hero (USA)**[20] 2418 3-9-7 **80** .... JamieSpencer 2 88
(David Simcock) *hld up in rr: hdwy over 2f out: rdn and chalng over 1f out: no ex fnl 75yds* **11/2**[2]

0-41 **3** *hd* **Winner's Wish**[20] 2427 3-9-5 **78** .... WilliamBuick 4 86
(Jeremy Noseda) *trckd ldrs: effrt 3f out: tail flashed u.p: nt qckn over 2f out: styd on towards fin* **11/4**[1]

3313 **4** *4* **Naseem Alyasmeen (IRE)**[5] 2885 3-9-3 **76** .... MartinHarley 1 78
(Mick Channon) *hld up: hdwy 4f out: effrt over 3f out: one pce u.p fr over 1f out* **13/2**[3]

-154 **5** *4 ½* **Juno The Muffinman (IRE)**[20] 2427 3-8-12 **71** ...(p) RichardKingscote 6 67
(Tom Dascombe) *led: shkn up 4f out: rdn 3f out: hdd over 2f out: sn wknd* **7/1**

0-1 **6** *14* **Countess Ferrama**[39] 1866 3-9-7 **80** .... KellyHarrison 3 57
(William Haggas) *chsd ldr to 7f out: remained handy: rdn over 3f out: wknd over 2f out* **8/1**

416 **7** *5* **Nice Rose**[20] 2427 3-9-7 **80** .... SilvestreDeSousa 7 50
(Mark Johnston) *trckd ldrs: racd in 2nd pl fr 7f out to 4f out: rdn and wknd over 3f out* **16/1**

2m 57.48s (-4.52) **Going Correction** -0.175s/f (Firm) **7** Ran SP% **111.5**
Speed ratings (Par 101): **105,103,103,101,98 90,88**
toteswingers:1&2:£3.50, 1&3:£2.60, 2&3:£1.90 CSF £17.26 TOTE £4.40: £2.60, £1.60; EX 16.20.
Owner J L C Pearce **Bred** J L C Pearce **Trained** Newmarket, Suffolk

FOCUS
A decent handicap for the grade, run at a fair pace and in a time 1.48 seconds outside standard. The first two came from the rear and most of the field ended up towards the stands' side in the latter stages. The form is rated positively and there looks more to come from the winner.

3034 E B F CLASSIC LODGES MAIDEN FILLIES' STKS 6f
2:50 (2:52) (Class 5) 2-Y-O **£3,234** (£962; £481; £240) **Stalls** Centre

Form RPR

1 **Chat (USA)** 2-9-0 0 .... WilliamBuick 8 82+
(John Gosden) *in tch: impr to ld over 2f out: rdn over 1f out: r.o ins fnl f: a in control* **15/8**[1]

2 *2* **Strictly Silca** 2-9-0 0 .... MartinHarley 9 76+
(Mick Channon) *s.s: hld up: hdwy to trck ldrs over 3f out: rdn and nt qckn over 2f out: hung lft over 1f out: styd on ins fnl f: tk 2nd towards fin: nt pce of wnr* **9/1**

30 **3** *¾* **Fantacise**[12] 2662 2-9-0 0 .... MartinDwyer 6 74
(Brian Meehan) *racd keenly: hld up in rr: hdwy over 3f out: rdn and chalng fr over 2f out: styd on same pce fnl 100yds* **9/1**

22 **4** *1 ¾* **Mandy Lexi (IRE)**[18] 2469 2-9-0 0 .... TomEaves 10 69
(Bryan Smart) *led: hdd over 2f out: rdn and stl chalng over 1f out: no ex fnl 100yds* **9/2**[3]

0 **5** *2* **Millie N Aire**[20] 2415 2-9-0 0 .... PJMcDonald 7 65+
(Danielle McCormick) *prom: rdn over 2f out: stl chalng over 1f out: wknd fnl 100yds* **66/1**

6 **6** *nk* **Dreamily (IRE)**[12] 2662 2-9-0 0 .... SilvestreDeSousa 1 62+
(Mark Johnston) *a shade restless in stalls: in tch: rdn over 2f out: sn outpcd* **7/1**

00 **7** *½* **Delores Rocket**[9] 2770 2-9-0 0 .... PhillipMakin 3 60+
(Kevin Ryan) *prom: pushed along and lost pl over 3f out: wknd over 2f out* **33/1**

4 **8** *1 ½* **Mixed Message (IRE)**[19] 2437 2-9-0 0 .... JamieSpencer 5 56
(Ed McMahon) *chsd ldrs: ev ch whn n.m.r and checked over 2f out: sn lost pl: wl btn fnl f* **4/1**[2]

9 *½* **Madame Elizabeth** 2-9-0 0 .... RussKennemore 4 54+
(Reg Hollinshead) *s.i.s: hld up: pushed along and outpcd over 2f out: sn btn* **66/1**

66 **10** *13* **Schottische**[28] 2163 2-9-0 0 .... LukeMorris 2 15
(Derek Haydn Jones) *handy: lost pl after 2f: bhd fr 1/2-way* **100/1**

1m 15.41s (1.61) **Going Correction** +0.025s/f (Good) **10** Ran SP% **112.4**
Speed ratings (Par 90): **90,87,86,84,81 80,80,78,77,60**
toteswingers:1&2:£5.50, 1&3:£6.10, 2&3:£12.90 CSF £19.10 TOTE £2.80: £1.60, £3.50, £2.70; EX 19.40 Trifecta £94.80 Pool: £825.13 - 6.44 winning units..
Owner George Strawbridge **Bred** Stone Farm **Trained** Newmarket, Suffolk

FOCUS
A fair fillies' maiden, run in a time 4.91 seconds slower than standard. It was dominated by those drawn high, although the runner-up ended up widest out in the centre. The third and the race averages dictate the level but the winner looks a fair recruit.

NOTEBOOK
Chat(USA), a $200,000 yearling, comes from the family of Rainbow View, who raced so successfully for the same connections. Soon positioned closest to the stands' rail, she took a little time to impose herself on the race but won comfortably in the end. She will have learned something from this and will have no problem with another furlong at this stage. (op 2-1 tchd 7-4)
Strictly Silca ◆ is out of a Moyglare Stud Stakes runner-up who was herself a half-sister to several smart performers in these colours, notably Golden Silca and Silca's Sister. After a slow start she edged to the centre of the track and finished strongly. Her stable's juveniles have been improving for their initial run and she looks sure to pick up a maiden before long. (op 15-2)
Fantacise disappointed over C&D on her second run and this was better, but she edged away from the rail when under pressure late on. The return to easier conditions seemed to suit her. (op 13-2)
Mandy Lexi(IRE) was the one to beat on form after finishing runner-up in a pair of Chester maidens last month. After showing pace she could not race on with the principals in the final furlong, and she may be worth dropping back to the minimum trip. (op 4-1)
Millie N Aire showed little on her debut over C&D, but knew a lot more this time and was in there fighting a furlong out before fading. (tchd 50-1)
Dreamily(IRE) again lacked cover from stall one, as she had on her debut over C&D, and she can perhaps be afforded another chance. (tchd 8-1)
Mixed Message(IRE) was expected to benefit from this extra furlong, but she was just starting to feel the pinch when she was short of room between rivals. (op 11-2)

3035 LEGENDS BLACKPOOL AT CENTRAL PIER SHOWBAR MAIDEN STKS 1m 3f 200y
3:20 (3:22) (Class 5) 3-Y-O+ **£2,264** (£673; £336; £168) **Stalls** Centre

Form RPR

4-3 **1** **Cardinal Walter (IRE)**[27] 2196 3-8-13 0 .... JamieSpencer 8 90+
(David Simcock) *hld up in midfield: pushed along 3f out: hdwy over 2f out: lugged in bhd ldr over 1f out: swtchd rt arnd ldr wl ins fnl f: r.o to get up fnl stride* **6/4**[1]

3 **2** *hd* **Swnymor (IRE)**[42] 1754 3-8-13 0 .... LiamJones 11 85+
(William Haggas) *trckd ldrs: led over 2f out: rdn over 1f out: strly pressed wl ins fnl f: hdd fnl stride* **9/2**[3]

4 **3** *4 ½* **Regal Aura**[27] 2200 3-8-8 0 .... WilliamBuick 2 73
(John Gosden) *led: hdd over 2f out: rdn and stl ch over 1f out: no ex fnl 100yds* **3/1**[2]

22-0 **4** *2 ¼* **Badea**[35] 1976 3-8-10 **78** .... LeeTopliss(3) 10 74
(Richard Fahey) *prom: rdn over 3f out: edgd lft over 2f out: one pce u.p over 1f out: no imp fnl f* **11/1**

5 *3 ¼* **Pete The Pastor**[53] 4-10-0 0 .... JoeFanning 6 69
(Hughie Morrison) *hld up: outpcd 4f out: styd on fnl 2f: nvr able to trble ldrs* **33/1**

0 **6** *½* **Taigan (FR)**[11] 2708 5-10-0 0 .... StevieDonohoe 3 68
(Ian Williams) *trckd ldrs: pushed along 4f out: wknd over 2f out* **33/1**

6 **7** *3 ¼* **Seagoing**[13] 2633 3-8-8 0 .... LukeMorris 4 58
(Tim Easterby) *midfield: pushed along over 4f out: outpcd over 2f out: no imp after* **20/1**

5 **8** *4 ½* **Naburn**[12] 2665 4-10-0 0 .... PJMcDonald 9 56
(Alan Swinbank) *hld up: struggling 3f out: nvr on terms w ldrs* **33/1**

0 **9** *2 ¼* **Bold Duke**[121] 546 4-9-9 0 .... MatthewCosham(5) 12 52
(Edward Bevan) *hld up: rdn over 4f out: a bhd* **150/1**

0 **10** *1* **Joyful Motive**[15] 2592 3-8-13 0 .... TomQueally 1 51
(Tom Tate) *trckd ldrs: niggled along briefly 7f out: pushed along 4f out: wknd over 3f out* **50/1**

11 *3 ¼* **Monicker** 3-8-8 0 .... SilvestreDeSousa 13 41
(Mark Johnston) *prom: pushed along over 4f out: edgd lft 3f out: wknd over 1f out* **16/1**

12 *¾* **Ewans Princess**[25] 5-9-9 0 .... TomEaves 5 39
(George Charlton) *struggling 3f out: a bhd* **100/1**

13 *1 ¼* **Buckshee**[14] 4-10-0 0 .... PhillipMakin 7 42
(Tim Easterby) *midfield: rdn and wknd 3f out* **66/1**

2m 31.62s (-2.18) **Going Correction** -0.175s/f (Firm)
WFA 3 from 4yo+ 15lb **13** Ran SP% **116.1**
Speed ratings (Par 103): **100,99,96,95,93 92,90,87,86,85 83,82,82**
toteswingers:1&2:£2.30, 1&3:£1.10, 2&3:£3.10 CSF £7.45 TOTE £2.40: £1.10, £1.70, £1.70; EX 8.20 Trifecta £20.70 Pool: £1,091.41 - 38.96 winning units..
Owner Mrs Fitri Hay **Bred** Max Morris Esq & Kildangan Stud **Trained** Newmarket, Suffolk

FOCUS
This maiden was won by subsequent Listed winner Wild Coco a year ago. It lacked strength in depth and not many became involved from the rear off an ordinary pace. The winner is potentially a fair bit better than the bare form and looks useful.

3036 TRUST INNS PUBLICANS H'CAP 1m 3f 200y
3:50 (3:50) (Class 3) (0-95,93) 4-Y-O+ **£6,663** (£1,982; £990; £495) **Stalls** Centre

Form RPR

6-31 **1** **Number Theory**[20] 2419 4-9-0 **86** .... RussKennemore 3 97
(John Holt) *hld up: hdwy on inner 3f out: rdn to ld over 1f out: r.o and in command towards fin* **7/2**[1]

312- **2** *1 ½* **Tmaam (USA)**[263] 6342 4-9-4 **90** .... JoeFanning 10 99
(Mark Johnston) *midfield: pushed along and outpcd over 4f out: hdwy 3f out: chalng over 1f out: nt qckn wl ins fnl f: hld towards fin* **13/2**

30-4 **3** *½* **Ittirad (USA)**[49] 1605 4-9-0 **86** .... NeilCallan 7 94
(Roger Varian) *chsd ldr: led 3f out: rdn over 2f out: hdd over 1f out: kpt on u.p: styd on same pce fnl 75yds* **4/1**[2]

0-03 **4** *2 ¼* **Purification (IRE)**[23] 2346 4-9-1 **87** ....(b[1]) WilliamBuick 9 91
(John Gosden) *a.p: rdn over 2f out: carried hd to one side and nt qckn over 1f out: kpt on same pce ins fnl f* **8/1**

3-10 **5** *1 ½* **Royal Swain (IRE)**[19] 2457 6-8-5 **77** .... PJMcDonald 4 79
(Alan Swinbank) *broke wl: in tch: rdn and outpcd over 2f out: kpt on modly fnl f* **16/1**

0-12 **6** *½* **Mica Mika (IRE)**[28] 2180 4-8-7 **86** .... LauraBarry(7) 8 87
(Richard Fahey) *midfield: lost pl over 5f out: rdn over 2f out: kpt on u.p fnl f: no imp* **7/1**

6-34 **7** *hd* **Very Good Day (FR)**[26] 2253 5-9-0 **86** .... MartinHarley 6 87
(Mick Channon) *hld up: rdn over 2f out: plugged on at one pce fr over 1f out: nvr able to chal* **9/2**[3]

224- **8** 2 **Bollin Greta**[236] 6988 7-8-13 **85**..(t) PhillipMakin 1 83
(Tim Easterby) *racd keenly: prom: rdn and nt qckning whn n.m.r and hmpd wl over 1f out: sn btn* **33/1**

002- **9** 22 **Alakhan (IRE)**[203] 7523 6-9-0 **86**................................ StevieDonohoe 2 48
(Ian Williams) *hld up in rr: hdwy 6f out: chsd ldrs 5f out: wknd over 3f out* **16/1**

3/40 **10** 6 **Eye Of The Tiger (GER)**[38] 1882 7-9-7 **93**........................ TomQueally 5 46
(Barney Curley) *sn led: hdd 3f out: wknd 2f out* **50/1**

2m 29.58s (-4.22) **Going Correction** -0.175s/f (Firm) **10** Ran SP% **114.0**
Speed ratings (Par 107): **107,106,105,104,103 102,102,101,86,82**
toteswingers:1&2:£6.40, 1&3:£3.50, 2&3:£4.70 CSF £25.85 CT £93.47 TOTE £5.60: £2.30, £2.60, £2.10; EX 35.20 Trifecta £100.30 Pool: £954.32 - 7.04 winning units..
Owner Mohan Fonseka **Bred** R Haim **Trained** Peckleton, Leics

FOCUS
A decent handicap run at a reasonable pace, and in a time two seconds quicker than the preceding maiden. Pretty solid form, with another personal best from the winner.

NOTEBOOK
Number Theory is developing into a Haydock specialist and has recorded all three of his wins at this track, as well as being placed on his other three visits. Coming through from the rear, he defied a 10lb rise for his latest C&D win with a little in hand. Versatile as far as ground conditions are concerned, he has a good attitude and is likely to come back here for the Old Newton Cup next month. (op 4-1)
Tmaam(USA) delivered his challenge down the outside up the straight and had every chance. The least experienced member of the field, he had not run since September and this has to rate a pleasing return. (op 11-2)
Ittirad(USA) was back up in trip after a fair reappearance in testing ground at Epsom. Getting to the front with three to run and boxing on, he was unable to hold off the front pair but is capable of winning off this sort of mark. (tchd 9-2)
Purification(IRE) was raised 2lb for finishing third at Windsor. Fitted with first-time blinkers, he raced prominently again but his attitude under pressure looked questionable. (op 13-2)
Royal Swain(IRE) ran better than he had on the unsuitable track at Musselburgh last time, but in truth never posed a serious threat. This trip is on the short side for him. (op 20-1)
Mica Mika(IRE) was held off a 3lb higher mark than when second to an unexposed rival at York. (tchd 13-2)
Very Good Day(FR) could not build on a pair of fair efforts this spring and remains winless since taking the maiden on this card two years ago. (op 11-2)
Bollin Greta would have been a little closer on this seasonal return had she not been hampered, but is not really one to be making excuses for.

3037 DIGGING, LIFTING, ROLLING WITH AMBROSE HIRE H'CAP 1m
4:20 (4:20) (Class 4) (0-85,84) 4-Y-0+ **£4,075** (£1,212; £606; £303) **Stalls** Low

Form RPR
1621 **1** **Postscript (IRE)**[103] 771 4-8-10 **73**................................ JamieSpencer 1 83
(Ian Williams) *mde all: rdn ins fnl f: r.o: in command fnl 150yds* **11/2**[3]

1162 **2** 1 ¾ **Lindoro**[9] 2753 7-8-5 **68**.. PJMcDonald 7 74
(Brian Ellison) *chsd wnr: chalng 2f out: rdn and nt qckn ins fnl f: hld fnl 150yds* **7/2**[2]

0064 **3** ¾ **First Post (IRE)**[13] 2642 5-9-5 **82**................................ LukeMorris 3 86
(Derek Haydn Jones) *chsd ldrs: u.p over 2f out: hung lft over 1f out: kpt on u.p but no real imp ins fnl f* **9/4**[1]

-040 **4** 2 ¾ **Icy Blue**[37] 1914 4-8-9 **72** ow2................................ RussKennemore 8 70
(Richard Whitaker) *stdd s: hld up: effrt over 1f out: no imp on ldrs: one pce fnl f* **8/1**

624 **5** hd **The Osteopath (IRE)**[25] 2285 9-9-1 **78**........................ PhillipMakin 5 75
(John Davies) *in tch: pushed along 3f out: one pce fnl 2f* **6/1**

6-00 **6** 1 ¼ **Point North (IRE)**[39] 1863 5-9-3 **80**........................(t) WilliamBuick 4 75
(John Balding) *hld up: effrt over 1f out: no imp on ldrs: wknd ins fnl f* **10/1**

0220 **7** 3 ½ **European Dream (IRE)**[11] 2720 9-9-2 **79**....................(p) MartinHarley 2 66
(Richard Guest) *hld up: rdn 2f out: no imp* **20/1**

1m 42.25s (-1.45) **Going Correction** -0.175s/f (Firm) **7** Ran SP% **107.6**
Speed ratings (Par 105): **100,98,97,94,94 93,89**
toteswingers:1&2:£2.60, 1&3:£2.70, 2&3:£2.30 CSF £22.00 CT £47.03 TOTE £5.00: £2.10, £2.90; EX 18.40 Trifecta £31.80 Pool: £750.87 - 17.42 winning units..
Owner Dr Marwan Koukash **Bred** Darley **Trained** Portway, Worcs

FOCUS
An ordinary handicap in which the first three occupied the same positions throughout. The winner built on his AW improvement and may do better yet.

3038 COLOROLL DESIGN H'CAP 1m 2f 95y
4:50 (4:50) (Class 4) (0-85,85) 4-Y-0+ **£4,075** (£1,212; £606; £303) **Stalls** High

Form RPR
6511 **1** **St Ignatius**[12] 2661 5-8-3 **74**................................(p) NatashaEaton(7) 4 80
(Alan Bailey) *led at gd pce for 2f: chsd ldr tl regained ld over 2f out: rdn over 1f out: all out cl home* **8/1**

6-00 **2** nk **Euston Square**[20] 2417 6-8-9 **73**................................ WilliamBuick 2 78
(Alistair Whillans) *s.s: hld up: pushed along over 2f out: swtchd rt over 1f out: prog and styd on ins fnl f: gng on at fin* **4/1**[3]

0020 **3** ¾ **Good Boy Jackson**[13] 2620 4-8-13 **77**........................ PhillipMakin 7 81
(Kevin Ryan) *w ldr setting gd pce: led after 2f: rdn and hdd over 2f out: kpt on and continued to chal ins fnl f: one pce cl home* **10/3**[2]

5/44 **4** hd **Steuben (GER)**[32] 2072 6-9-7 **85**................................ TomQueally 6 88?
(Barney Curley) *racd keenly: hld up: hdwy to chse ldrs over 3f out: rdn over 1f out: styd on ins fnl f but a hld: one pce fnl strides* **25/1**

423- **5** ½ **Kenyan Cat**[236] 6996 5-9-4 **82**.. NeilCallan 1 84
(Ed McMahon) *chsd ldrs: rdn over 2f out: nt qckn over 1f out: styd on u.p cl home but hld* **9/4**[1]

6 7 **Pirate Chest (IRE)**[553] 7769 4-9-0 **78**........................ LukeMorris 5 67
(Patrick Holmes) *chsd ldrs: pushed along over 4f out: lost pl over 3f out: bhd after* **14/1**

3-05 **7** 2 ¼ **Look Left**[18] 2473 4-8-12 **76**.. JamieSpencer 8 61
(David Simcock) *hld up in rr: pushed along 4f out: sme hdwy over 3f out: rdn over 2f out: no imp on ldrs: wl btn ins fnl f* **5/1**

2m 12.38s (-3.12) **Going Correction** -0.175s/f (Firm) **7** Ran SP% **112.1**
Speed ratings (Par 105): **105,104,104,104,103 98,96**
CSF £38.15 CT £126.89 TOTE £10.00: £3.90, £1.40; EX 50.90 Trifecta £212.60 Pool: £962.56 - 3.35 winning units..
Owner A J H **Bred** Simon And Helen Plumbly **Trained** Newmarket, Suffolk

FOCUS
After a brisk initial pace the leaders were paddling in the latter stages, and the first five finished in a heap. The bare form is not totally convincing but the winner continued his progress.
T/Plt: £62.40 to a £1 stake. Pool:£62,089.49 - 725.54 winning tickets T/Qpdt: £11.30 to a £1 stake. Pool:£4,753.46 - 308.91 winning tickets DO

2808 KEMPTON (A.W) (R-H)
Wednesday, June 13

OFFICIAL GOING: Standard
Wind: Moderate, half behind Weather: Fine

3039 WIN BIG WITH BETDAQ MULTIPLES APPRENTICE H'CAP 1m (P)
6:10 (6:11) (Class 5) (0-75,75) 4-Y-0+ **£2,264** (£673; £336; £168) **Stalls** Low

Form RPR
-631 **1** **Hurricane Spirit (IRE)**[89] 915 8-9-4 **72**................ NicoleNordblad(3) 13 83
(Hans Adielsson) *trckd ldr: led wl over 2f out and shkn up: in full command over 1f out: pushed out* **11/1**

0004 **2** 2 ½ **Guest Book (IRE)**[75] 1116 5-9-2 **67**........................(p) JamieJones 5 72
(Michael Scudamore) *trckd ldng trio: rdn to chse wnr 2f out: styd on but no imp* **4/1**[1]

036- **3** 2 ¼ **Cool Hand Jake**[209] 7447 6-9-1 **69**........................ LeonnaMayor(3) 10 69
(Jamie Osborne) *hld up in 10th: wl bhd in main gp over 2f out: gd prog over 1f out: r.o to take 3rd nr fin: no ch to chal* **16/1**

-330 **4** 1 ¼ **Laughing Jack**[18] 2502 4-9-6 **74**........................ GeorgeDowning(3) 3 71
(Tony Carroll) *chsd ldrs in 6th but off the pce: outpcd sn after 1/2-way: wl bhd in main gp over 2f out: styd on fr over 1f out: tk 4th last stride* **15/2**

0106 **5** nk **Just Five (IRE)**[26] 2227 6-9-2 **67**........................(v) RaulDaSilva 6 64
(John Weymes) *t.k.h: trckd ldng pair: rdn in 3rd over 1f out: fdd and lost pl last strides* **20/1**

4-00 **6** nse **Larkrise Star**[18] 2498 5-8-8 **66**................................ PaulBooth(7) 2 62
(Dean Ivory) *hld up disputing 5th: prog on inner and last of those w a ch over 2f out: tried to press for a pl fnl f: kpt on same pce* **12/1**

3535 **7** hd **Den's Gift (IRE)**[29] 2151 8-9-10 **75**........................(b) LucyKBarry 7 71
(Clive Cox) *led at gd pce: hdd wl over 2f out: steadily wknd fr over 1f out* **9/2**[2]

0100 **8** 9 **May's Boy**[15] 2574 4-9-0 **68**........................(p) RachealKneller(3) 12 43
(Mark Usher) *hld up in 9th: outpcd and wl bhd in main gp over 2f out: no prog* **20/1**

010 **9** 1 ¼ **Addikt (IRE)**[23] 2354 7-9-1 **66**................................ JamesRogers 4 38
(Michael Scudamore) *dwlt: wl in rr: wl bhd in main gp over 2f out: no ch after* **40/1**

-033 **10** 1 ¾ **Catchanova (IRE)**[8] 2801 5-9-3 **68**................................ AmyScott 11 36
(Eve Johnson Houghton) *dwlt: a wl in rr: wl bhd in main gp over 2f out* **11/2**[3]

2300 **11** 3 ½ **Qeethaara (USA)**[16] 2535 8-9-4 **72**........................(p) JackDuern(3) 14 32
(Mark Brisbourne) *hld up off the pce disputing 7th: outpcd and wl bhd in main gp over 2f out: no prog* **25/1**

-600 **12** 3 **Breakheart (IRE)**[13] 2637 5-8-13 **69**........ WilliamTwiston-Davies(5) 8 22
(Paul Howling) *s.s: a in last trio: wl bhd over 2f out* **20/1**

/0-0 **13** 2 ½ **Bramshaw (USA)**[76] 1087 5-9-10 **75**........................ JustinNewman 1 23
(Amanda Perrett) *chsd ldng quartet tl wknd rapidly 3f out* **11/1**

1m 38.6s (-1.20) **Going Correction** -0.075s/f (Stan) **13** Ran SP% **116.1**
Speed ratings (Par 103): **103,100,98,97,96 96,96,87,86,84 80,77,75**
toteswingers:1&2:£13.20, 1&3:£21.80, 2&3:£21.10 CSF £48.82 CT £737.15 TOTE £8.80: £3.90, £2.30, £5.00; EX 65.90 Trifecta £131.00 Pool: £467.66 - 2.64 winning units..
Owner Hans Adielsson A B **Bred** Knocktoran Stud **Trained** Kingston Lisle, Oxon

FOCUS
A fair apprentice handicap, run at a solid pace.
Bramshaw(USA) Official explanation: jockey said gelding hung left throughout

3040 BACK OR LAY BETDAQ.COM MAIDEN STKS 6f (P)
6:40 (6:40) (Class 5) 2-Y-0 **£2,264** (£673; £336; £168) **Stalls** Low

Form RPR
32 **1** **Janoub Nibras (IRE)**[22] 2376 2-9-3 0........................ RichardHughes 5 78+
(Richard Hannon) *cl up: led gng easily over 1f out: pushed out: comf* **2/9**[1]

2 1 ½ **Sadiigah** 2-8-12 0.. KirstyMilczarek 2 68
(Clive Brittain) *trckd ldr: led jst over 2f out to over 1f out: kpt on but no ch w wnr* **25/1**

3 nse **Bay Laurel (IRE)** 2-8-12 0................................ MickaelBarzalona 7 68
(Harry Dunlop) *green preliminaries: sn in last pair: shkn up on outer over 2f out: prog over 1f out: styd on to take 3rd ins fnl f and press runner-up* **16/1**

4 1 ½ **Moonlit Dancer (IRE)** 2-8-12 0................................ MartinLane 3 63
(J W Hills) *in tch: shkn up over 2f out: outpcd over 1f out: kpt on same pce fnl f* **20/1**

5 1 ¼ **Typhon (USA)** 2-9-3 0.. TedDurcan 1 64+
(David Lanigan) *awkward s: cl up: outpcd and rn green wl over 1f out: kpt on ins fnl f* **12/1**[3]

06 **6** ¾ **World Freight Girl**[16] 2541 2-8-12 0........................ JimCrowley 6 57
(Dean Ivory) *led at mod pce: hdd jst over 2f out: fdd fr over 1f out* **33/1**

7 ½ **Quiet Prayer** 2-9-3 0.. HayleyTurner 4 60
(Ed Dunlop) *hld up and sn in last: detached and urged along 2f out: styd on fnl f* **13/2**[2]

8 2 ½ **Vinifera (USA)** 2-8-12 0.. JamesDoyle 9 47
(Clive Brittain) *racd wd: cl up: chsd ldrs: shkn up 2f out: wknd qckly fnl f* **20/1**

1m 15.4s (2.30) **Going Correction** -0.075s/f (Stan) **8** Ran SP% **125.1**
Speed ratings (Par 93): **81,79,78,76,75 74,73,70**
toteswingers:1&2:£5.50, 1&3:£3.40, 2&3:£19.00 CSF £15.92 TOTE £1.20: £1.02, £8.20, £2.50; EX 14.90 Trifecta £65.50 Pool: £437.31 - 4.94 winning units..
Owner Saeed H Altayer **Bred** Rathbarry Stud **Trained** East Everleigh, Wilts

FOCUS
There were a couple of interesting newcomers on show for this juvenile event, but the field finished compressed in a slow time. The winner did not need to match his pre-race mark.

NOTEBOOK
Janoub Nibras(IRE) got off the mark with the minimum of fuss. Richard Hannon's representative travelled powerfully and, having been sent to the front at the 2f marker, only had to be pushed out under hands and heels to win. He was ideally positioned off a sluggish pace but won as he liked, pricking his ears throughout the final furlong. It's unclear if this was any improvement on what he'd already shown but he's certainly got ability and wouldn't look out of place in Listed company on his next start. (tchd 1-4 and 2-7 in a place)
Sadiigah produced a big run and should have no problem winning races. She will appreciate further.
Bay Laurel(IRE), a half-sister to Bathwick Bear, ran well and should win races.
Moonlit Dancer(IRE) did best of the rest.

Typhon(USA) stuck on well without being knocked around.

3041 BETDAQ MOBILE APPS H'CAP 6f (P)
7:10 (7:10) (Class 5) (0-75,75) 3-Y-O £2,264 (£673; £336; £168) Stalls Low

Form RPR

3- 1 **Fast Finian (IRE)**[194] 7613 3-9-3 71 JimCrowley 8 76+
(Paul D'Arcy) *hld up in last pair: taken wd over 2f out: prog wl over 1f out: drvn to ld ins fnl f: hld on* 7/2[1]

2300 2 nk **Homeward Strut**[20] 2416 3-8-13 67 (b) JamesDoyle 6 71
(Frank Sheridan) *trckd ldrs: drvn and effrt 2f out: got through to chal ins fnl f: styd on but a hld* 10/1

-201 3 hd **Dressed In Lace**[85] 970 3-9-3 71 IanMongan 1 74
(Jo Crowley) *trckd ldrs: drvn and effrt on inner 2f out: upsides jst ins fnl f: nt qckn last 100yds* 7/1

-505 4 ½ **Gabbiano**[19] 2451 3-9-2 75 (p) RaulDaSilva(5) 5 82+
(Jeremy Gask) *t.k.h: hld up last: prog on inner whn chopped off over 1f out: trapped bhd rivals after tl r.o in the clr fnl 50yds: fin full of running* 7/2[1]

3113 5 ½ **First Bid**[22] 2375 3-9-3 71 (b) J-PGuillambert 3 71
(James Given) *t.k.h early: mostly pressed ldr to over 1f out: nt qckn: kpt on same pce* 10/1

1610 6 ¾ **Boudoir (IRE)**[25] 2272 3-9-3 74 SeanLevey(3) 2 71
(Richard Hannon) *mde most in narrow ld: hrd pressed on all sides fr 2f out: hdd and fdd last 150yds* 5/1[2]

1-20 7 ½ **Lesotho (IRE)**[63] 1317 3-9-7 75 DaraghO'Donohoe 9 71
(Noel Quinlan) *racd on outer of three ldrs: def 2nd over 1f out and chalng: fdd fnl f* 14/1

40-0 8 1 ¼ **West Leake Hare (IRE)**[44] 1721 3-9-6 74 KierenFallon 7 66
(Charles Hills) *in tch: rdn and nt qckn over 2f out: struggling to stay on terms and n.d after* 13/2[3]

1m 12.93s (-0.17) **Going Correction** -0.075s/f (Stan) 8 Ran SP% 111.8
Speed ratings (Par 99): **98,97,97,96,96 95,94,92**
toteswingers:1&2:£6.70, 1&3:£5.20, 2&3:£8.40 CSF £37.38 CT £228.90 TOTE £5.30: £1.80, £3.40, £1.60; EX 40.00 Trifecta £91.10 Pool: £381.69 - 3.10 winning units..
Owner John W Kennedy **Bred** N Hartery **Trained** Newmarket, Suffolk

FOCUS
A fair 3yo handicap but the steady early fractions meant there wasn't much separating the entire field at the line.
Gabbiano Official explanation: jockey said gelding was denied a clear run

3042 BETDAQ CASINO GAMES H'CAP 1m 4f (P)
7:40 (7:40) (Class 4) (0-85,85) 3-Y-O £4,075 (£1,212; £606; £303) Stalls Centre

Form RPR

51-2 1 **Willie Wag Tail (USA)**[20] 2429 3-9-4 82 GeorgeBaker 3 95+
(Ed Walker) *hld up in midfield on inner: smooth prog over 2f out: led wl over 1f out: sn pressed and rdn: styd on wl fnl f* 9/2[1]

16-0 2 2 **Al Saham**[25] 2269 3-9-7 85 SilvestreDeSousa 1 94
(Saeed Bin Suroor) *hld up in rr: prog on inner over 2f out: tk 2nd over 1f out and pressed wnr: styd on but readily hld last 150yds* 16/1

1403 3 ¾ **Ex Oriente (IRE)**[20] 2429 3-9-3 81 (b) RichardHughes 2 89
(John Gosden) *t.k.h: hld up in last pair: prog on wd outside wl over 2f out: tried to chal over 1f out: edgd rt and one pce after* 12/1

5-31 4 2 ¼ **Cape Savannah**[114] 635 3-9-1 79 MartinLane 13 84
(David Simcock) *sn prom fr wd draw: rdn over 4f out: struggling wl over 2f out: styd on fr over 1f out* 25/1

62-0 5 ¾ **Position**[11] 2701 3-9-5 83 ChrisCatlin 4 86
(Sir Mark Prescott Bt) *led 1f: settled to trck ldrs: looking for room over 2f out: drvn and kpt on same pce fr over 1f out* 16/1

31-0 6 2 ¾ **Moidore**[18] 2484 3-9-0 78 JamesDoyle 9 77+
(Roger Charlton) *hld up in rr: tried to make prog on outer over 2f out but nt pce to do so: styd on same pce fr over 1f out* 8/1

1220 7 3 ½ **Cape Safari (IRE)**[25] 2281 3-9-2 80 (p) HayleyTurner 12 73
(Alan Bailey) *trckd ldr after 1f fr wd draw: led 3f out: drvn and hdd wl over 1f out: wknd* 14/1

2-31 8 2 ¼ **Singalat**[18] 2471 3-9-2 80 JimCrowley 7 70
(James Given) *wl plcd bhd ldrs: rdn over 5f out and sn lost pl: struggling after* 14/1

3121 9 1 ¼ **Hector's Chance**[16] 2544 3-8-10 74 KierenFallon 6 62
(Heather Main) *hld up towards rr: prog fr 5f out to trck ldrs over 3f out: drvn to chal over 2f out: wknd over 1f out: eased* 5/1[2]

1- 10 1 ¼ **Tamarrud**[312] 4798 3-9-0 78 MickaelBarzalona 11 64+
(Saeed Bin Suroor) *racd wd thrght: prog fr midfield to go prom 1/2-way: drvn to chal over 2f out: wknd over 1f out: eased* 11/2[3]

100 11 2 ¼ **Natasha Rostova**[16] 2544 3-8-4 68 DavidProbert 10 50
(Andrew Balding) *s.s: hld up in last: rdn and nt qckn 3f out: bhd after* 40/1

-413 12 8 **Theturnofthesun (IRE)**[25] 2281 3-9-4 82 (p) RobertHavlin 8 51
(John Gosden) *led after 1f to 3f out: wknd rapidly 2f out* 13/2

2m 31.13s (-3.37) **Going Correction** -0.075s/f (Stan) 12 Ran SP% 113.8
Speed ratings (Par 101): **108,106,106,104,104 102,100,98,97,96 95,90**
toteswingers:1&2:£12.70, 1&3:£5.70, 2&3:£29.80 CSF £73.81 CT £802.53 TOTE £4.70: £2.90, £6.50, £2.90; EX 94.40 Trifecta £399.50 Part won. Pool: £539.97 - 0.64 winning units..
Owner One Carat Partnership **Bred** Derry Meeting Farm & London Thoroughbred Services **Trained** Newmarket, Suffolk

FOCUS
A competitive handicap, run at an even pace.
Natasha Rostova Official explanation: jockey said filly missed the break

3043 KEMPTON LIVE H'CAP 1m 3f (P)
8:10 (8:14) (Class 6) (0-55,55) 4-Y-O+ £1,617 (£481; £240; £120) Stalls Low

Form RPR

-336 1 **Tinkerbell Will**[19] 2467 5-8-11 48 RichardThomas 2 57
(John E Long) *trckd ldrs: rdn and prog to press ldr wl over 1f out: led ins fnl f: hld on nr fin* 10/1

5466 2 hd **Ermyntrude**[63] 1299 5-9-1 52 IanMongan 3 61
(Pat Phelan) *trckd ldrs: wnt 3rd over 3f out: drvn to ld 2f out: sn hrd pressed: hdd ins fnl f: kpt on wl: jst hld* 8/1

0-60 3 2 ½ **Rather Cool**[7] 2814 4-8-13 50 KieranO'Neill 10 54
(John Bridger) *hld up in last pair: drvn and prog on wd outside fr over 2f out: styd on to take 3rd fnl f: no imp* 25/1

6036 4 3 ¼ **Rapid Water**[16] 2555 6-8-13 55 RaulDaSilva(5) 7 53
(Pat Eddery) *hld up wl in rr: rdn and prog over 3f out: chsd ldng trio 2f out: sn no imp* 9/1

5-U0 5 shd **Who Loves Ya Baby**[75] 1112 4-8-13 50 KirstyMilczarek 13 48
(Peter Charalambous) *reluctant to enter stalls: hld up in last pair: drvn and effrt on inner over 2f out: no real imp tl styd on fnl f: nrly grabbed 4th* 14/1

2350 6 3 **Lytham (IRE)**[7] 2814 11-9-1 52 JimCrowley 8 45
(Tony Carroll) *hld up in rr: sme prog out wd over 3f out: shkn up and nt qckn over 2f out: wl btn after* 7/1[3]

6545 7 ¾ **Minstrel Lad**[19] 2468 4-8-12 52 SimonPearce(3) 11 43
(Lydia Pearce) *trckd ldr after 4f: led over 3f out: drvn and hdd 2f out: wknd* 6/1[2]

6006 8 2 **Smarty Time**[20] 2422 5-8-13 53 SeanLevey(3) 4 41
(John Bridger) *racd freely: led to over 3f out: wknd over 2f out* 20/1

6003 9 1 ½ **Prince Of Thebes (IRE)**[22] 2364 11-8-13 50 KierenFox 1 35
(Michael Attwater) *w.w in midfield on inner: drvn and dropped to last over 2f out: no ch after* 12/1

0004 10 ½ **Port Hill**[9] 2769 5-8-10 47 TomMcLaughlin 6 31
(Mark Brisbourne) *chsd ldr 4f: lost pl qckly 4f out: no ch fnl 2f* 10/1

0-44 11 nk **Cardi King**[6] 2851 4-9-3 54 (t) JamesDoyle 12 51+
(Ian Wood) *racd wd in midfield: prog to chse ldng trio over 3f out: 6th and wkng whn bdly hmpd 1f out: eased* 5/1[1]

005/ 12 15 **Ildiko (USA)**[603] 7003 5-8-6 48 MatthewCosham(5) 9
(Dr Jeremy Naylor) *chsd ldrs: rdn over 4f out: wknd rapidly over 2f out: t.o* 50/1

2m 20.46s (-1.44) **Going Correction** -0.075s/f (Stan) 12 Ran SP% 107.7
Speed ratings (Par 101): **102,101,100,97,97 95,94,93,92,91 91,80**
toteswingers:1&2:£16.70, 1&3:£37.90, 2&3:£34.00 CSF £70.44 CT £1423.42 TOTE £11.90: £3.70, £2.80, £5.80; EX 93.80 TRIFECTA Not won..
Owner Mr & Mrs T H Bambridge **Bred** The Willow Stud **Trained** Caterham, Surrey
■ Trecase was withdrawn (6/1, ref to ents stalls). Deduct 10p in the £ under R4.
■ Stewards' Enquiry : Simon Pearce two-day ban: careless riding (Jun 27-28)

FOCUS
A lowly handicap but it was run at a strong pace and served up a good finish.
Minstrel Lad Official explanation: jockey said gelding lost a shoe
Port Hill Official explanation: jockey said gelding hung right
Cardi King Official explanation: jockey said gelding was hampered 1f out, lost its action and saddle slipped

3044 REWARDS4RACING.COM FILLIES' H'CAP 7f (P)
8:40 (8:41) (Class 5) (0-70,70) 3-Y-O £2,264 (£673; £336; £168) Stalls Low

Form RPR

620 1 **Bint Alzain (IRE)**[18] 2503 3-9-2 70 RaulDaSilva(5) 8 78
(Gerard Butler) *trckd ldng pair: plld out and decisive move to ld over 1f out: 3 l clr ins fnl f: rdn out* 6/1[2]

-441 2 ¾ **Subtle Knife**[21] 2397 3-9-4 67 WilliamCarson 12 73+
(Giles Bravery) *hld up in 10th: gd prog on outer jst over 2f out: r.o wl to take 2nd ins fnl f: nvr gng to rch wnr* 17/2[3]

0-01 3 2 ¼ **The New Black (IRE)**[13] 2628 3-9-4 67 (v) JackMitchell 11 67
(Gay Kelleway) *s.i.s: off the pce in last trio: nt clr run briefly over 2f out and plld out wd: styd on wl fr over 1f out to take 3rd last strides* 16/1

040 4 nk **Selfara**[18] 2501 3-9-4 67 JamesDoyle 1 66
(Roger Charlton) *led 2f: pressed ldr to wl over 1f out: sn outpcd* 5/2[1]

0-43 5 ¾ **Cynthia Calhoun**[20] 2422 3-9-5 68 JohnFahy 5 65
(Clive Cox) *hld up in midfield in abt 8th: rdn and sme prog over 2f out: nvr gng pce to threaten* 14/1

4353 6 nk **Chester'Slittlegem (IRE)**[21] 2397 3-9-2 65 LiamKeniry 9 61
(Ed de Giles) *w ldr: led after 2f out to over 1f out: fdd fnl f* 12/1

2-50 7 hd **Remix (IRE)**[30] 2136 3-9-2 65 MartinLane 6 61
(J W Hills) *chsd ldrs: rdn 1/2-way: 5th 2f out: sn outpcd* 14/1

5-00 8 ¾ **Top Frock (IRE)**[18] 2503 3-9-4 67 (b[1]) PatCosgrave 13 61
(Clive Cox) *trckd ldng pair to over 2f out: steadily wknd over 1f out* 33/1

2-00 9 10 **Flamborough Breeze**[15] 2583 3-9-4 67 RichardHughes 3 34
(Ed Vaughan) *sn lost decent pl: rdn towards rr 1/2-way: bmpd by rivals whn effrt over 2f out: sn btn* 9/1

0-26 10 hd **Absent Amy (IRE)**[53] 1529 3-9-1 64 KierenFallon 2 30
(Willie Musson) *dwlt: hld up in last pair: pushed along and no prog over 2f out: wl bhd after* 6/1[2]

50-0 11 1 ½ **Sugar Loaf**[22] 2382 3-9-2 65 HayleyTurner 4 27
(William Muir) *chsd ldrs: rdn and wknd rapidly over 2f out* 40/1

50-0 12 1 ½ **Pindrop**[61] 1357 3-8-13 62 TedDurcan 10 20
(Clive Cox) *racd wd: chsd ldrs: wknd qckly over 2f out: sn bhd* 25/1

1-06 13 1 ¼ **Choccywoccydoodah**[13] 2628 3-9-0 63 JimCrowley 14 18
(James Given) *dropped in fr wd draw and hld up in last pair: no prog 3f out: wl bhd after* 20/1

1m 25.44s (-0.56) **Going Correction** -0.075s/f (Stan) 13 Ran SP% 118.6
Speed ratings (Par 96): **100,99,96,96,95 95,94,93,82,82 80,78,77**
toteswingers:1&2:£8.40, 1&3:£11.00, 2&3:£11.90 CSF £53.36 CT £783.51 TOTE £7.90: £2.40, £2.90, £3.40; EX 78.10 TRIFECTA Not won..
Owner Asaad Al Banwan **Bred** Philip Brady **Trained** Newmarket, Suffolk

FOCUS
Only a modest 7f handicap.
Cynthia Calhoun Official explanation: jockey said filly hung right
Absent Amy(IRE) Official explanation: jockey said filly did not face the kickback

3045 READ NICK LUCK IN RACING PLUS H'CAP 7f (P)
9:10 (9:10) (Class 4) (0-80,80) 4-Y-O+ £4,075 (£1,212; £606; £303) Stalls Low

Form RPR

5-24 1 **Good Authority (IRE)**[18] 2500 5-9-1 74 TomMcLaughlin 8 81+
(Karen George) *hld up in last trio: prog fr 2f out: drvn and sustained effrt fnl f to ld nr fin* 11/2[3]

2102 2 nk **Choral**[9] 2766 4-9-5 78 RichardHughes 9 84
(Richard Hannon) *trckd ldrs: rdn over 2f out: clsd to chal fnl f: upsides 50yds out: jst outpcd* 4/1[2]

34-0 3 ½ **Ezdeyaad (USA)**[58] 1416 8-9-4 77 GeorgeBaker 5 82
(Ed Walker) *pressed ldr gng wl: rdn to take narrow ld over 1f out: hrd pressed fnl f: hdd nr fin* 12/1

-336 4 1 ¼ **Perfect Mission**[21] 2399 4-8-11 70 (v) DavidProbert 3 72
(Andrew Balding) *led: drvn and hdd over 1f out: hld after but kpt on ins fnl f* 8/1

0500 5 shd **Ocean Legend (IRE)**[16] 2545 7-9-5 78 KirstyMilczarek 4 79
(Tony Carroll) *trckd ldng pair: chal on inner over 1f out: nrly upsides jst ins fnl f: no ex last 100yds* 14/1

15-0 6 nk **Emkanaat**[37] 1935 4-9-1 77 DominicFox(3) 7 78
(Roger Varian) *chsd ldrs and racd on outer: drvn over 2f out: kpt on fr over 1f out: nvr able to chal* 20/1

0-40 7 2 ½ **Islesman**[58] 1416 4-9-5 78 (b[1]) KierenFallon 1 72
(Heather Main) *trckd ldrs: shkn up over 2f out: nt qckn and no imp on ldrs after* 7/2[1]

5515 8 ½ **Beat The Bell**[13] 2629 7-9-2 80 LeonnaMayor(5) 2 72
(Jamie Osborne) *dwlt: hld up in rr: effrt and drifted rt fr 2f out: nvr on terms but kpt on nr fin* 20/1

0 **9** *1 ¾* **Handheld**[21] 2405 5-9-2 **75**.......................... LiamKeniry 10 68+
(Ed de Giles) *s.s: hld up in last pair: effrt but n.d whn carried rt then hmpd over 1f out: nvr styd on nr fin* **66/1**

5113 **10** *½* **Legal Legacy**[14] 2608 6-9-4 **77**.......................... AmirQuinn 13 63
(Richard Rowe) *hld up in last pair fr wd draw: swtchd rt and shkn up over 1f out: no significant prog* **16/1**

1221 **11** *2 ¼* **Diplomatic (IRE)**[22] 2373 7-8-8 **67**.......................... SilvestreDeSousa 11 47
(Michael Squance) *drvn in midfield by 1/2-way: struggling after* **13/2**

0020 **12** *¾* **Satwa Laird**[19] 2466 6-8-12 **71**.......................... HayleyTurner 12 49
(Conor Dore) *prom on outer tl wknd over 2f out* **25/1**

1m 25.17s (-0.83) **Going Correction** -0.075s/f (Stan) **12** Ran SP% **117.2**
Speed ratings (Par 105): **101,100,100,90,90 00,06,04,02,02 80,88**
toteswingers:1&2:£4.10, 1&3:£8.60, 2&3:£14.90 CSF £26.06 CT £255.92 TOTE £7.80: £2.30, £1.30, £3.90; EX 33.20 Trifecta £468.80 Part won. Pool: £633.53 - 0.64 winning units..
Owner Adrian Parr & Karen George **Bred** Mountarmstrong Stud **Trained** Higher Eastington, Devon
■ Stewards' Enquiry : Leonna Mayor two-day ban: careless riding (Jun 27-28)

FOCUS
A competitive 7f handicap, run at a decent pace.
Handheld Official explanation: jockey said gelding was denied a clear run
T/Plt: £606.30 to a £1 stake. Pool:£58,588.92 - 70.54 winning tickets T/Qpdt: £169.70 to a £1 stake. Pool:£4,312.16 - 18.80 winning tickets JN

2797 YARMOUTH (L-H)
Wednesday, June 13

OFFICIAL GOING: Good to firm (7.4)
Back straight and bottom bend moved out 3metres.
Wind: fresh, behind Weather: bright and breezy

3046 BET IN-PLAY AT BETVICTOR.COM MAIDEN AUCTION STKS 5f 43y
2:10 (2:12) (Class 5) 2-Y-O **£2,264** (£673; £336; £168) **Stalls** Centre

Form RPR

36 **1** **Pixilated**[13] 2638 2-8-12 0.......................... JackMitchell 2 74+
(Gay Kelleway) *mde all: rdn along and wnt clr over 1f out: in command fnl f: comf* **10/3**[2]

2 *3 ¼* **Not Now Blondie** 2-8-7 0.......................... CathyGannon 1 60+
(Chris Dwyer) *outpcd in midfield: rdn 1/2-way: wnt modest 3rd 1f out: styd on wl to go 2nd wl ins fnl f: no threat to wnr* **14/1**

5 **3** *2* **Miss Starry Eyed**[9] 2763 2-8-1 0.......................... DeclanCannon(3) 3 47
(Derek Shaw) *chsd ldng pair: chsd wnr 2f out: sn rdn and edging lft: outpcd and btn 1f out: lost 2nd and wknd wl ins fnl f* **20/1**

5 **4** *1 ¼* **Lilly May (IRE)**[7] 2808 2-8-5 0.......................... ChrisCatlin 6 44+
(Phil McEntee) *sn outpcd and rdn along in last trio: styd on ins fnl f: n.d* **15/2**

5 *½* **Ritaach (IRE)** 2-8-7 0.......................... BrettDoyle 4 44+
(Clive Brittain) *s.i.s: sn rdn along: rn green and outpcd in last trio: styd on ins fnl f: n.d* **5/1**[3]

6 *3* **Purple Day** 2-9-0 0.......................... LiamKeniry 7 35
(Pam Sly) *chsd wnr tl 2f out: sn rdn and struggling: 3rd and btn over 1f out: fdd fnl f* **11/2**

00 **D** *1 ½* **Getaway Car**[8] 2784 2-8-13 0.......................... EddieAhern 5 44+
(Gerard Butler) *sn outpcd in rr: nvr on terms* **9/4**[1]

1m 1.94s (-0.76) **Going Correction** -0.475s/f (Firm) **7** Ran SP% **109.1**
Speed ratings (Par 93): **87,81,78,76,75 68,73**
toteswingers:1&2:£7.30, 1&3:£11.30, 2&3:£20.30 CSF £41.98 TOTE £2.90: £1.70, £7.20; EX 25.00.
Owner Patricia Crook & Francis Aspin **Bred** A Christou **Trained** Exning, Suffolk

FOCUS
This was an ordinary juvenile maiden and few landed a serious blow. The winner had a bit in hand at the line and the runner-up looks sure to improve.

NOTEBOOK
Pixilated, who reportedly got a kick in the stomach beforehand, made it third time lucky with a ready effort from the front. He was outclassed in the Listed National Stakes behind the promising Sir Prancealot at Sandown last time, but this was obviously a lot easier and it was his previous experience that won him the day as he was by some way the most professional in the race. He ought to get a bit further down the line and will find his level when the nurseries begin next month. His trainer later said he'll now likely head to Royal Ascot next week for the Windsor Castle Stakes. (op 11-4 tchd 7-2)
Not Now Blondie ◆ was the eyecatcher. She was starting off over a trip too sharp on breeding and that showed as she lacked the pace to go with the leaders. However, the penny dropped from 2f out and she finished with purpose. She's well up to winning races and ought to relish another furlong on this sort of ground. (op 11-1)
Miss Starry Eyed broke a lot better on this second outing and appreciated the quicker surface, turning in an improved effort. She'll struggle to win a maiden, though. (op 16-1 tchd 22-1)
Lilly May(IRE) again took time to get organised from the stalls, but did some pleasing late work on this switch to turf and ought to go forward again for the outing. (op 8-1 tchd 17-2)
Ritaach(IRE), speedily bred, lost out with the sluggish start and advertised her inexperience throughout more towards the far side of the track. (op 11-2 tchd 9-2)
Purple Day didn't go unbacked and knew his job, but dropped right out inside the final furlong and clearly needed this debut run. (op 7-1 tchd 5-1)
Getaway Car was faced with his easiest task to date and reverting to quicker ground. His fate was apparent in the first furlong as he was steadied from the stalls and thus allowed the leaders to get right away from him. The drop back in trip went against him, but he's a good deal better than he was able to show. (op 5-2 tchd 11-4)

3047 HOLLAND V GERMANY SPECIALS AT BETVICTOR.COM H'CAP 1m 2f 21y
2:40 (2:40) (Class 6) (0-65,64) 4-Y-0+ **£1,617** (£481; £240; £120) **Stalls** Low

Form RPR

-040 **1** **Five Hearts**[28] 2171 4-8-5 **48**..........................(b[1]) ChrisCatlin 6 57
(Mark H Tompkins) *stdd s: hld up in rr: hdwy and switching rt wl over 2f out: drvn to chse ldr 1f out: led ins fnl f: styd on wl* **25/1**

45-0 **2** *1 ¾* **Young Jackie**[19] 2467 4-8-4 **47**.......................... CathyGannon 4 52
(George Margarson) *t.k.h: chsd ldrs: rdn over 2f out: kpt on u.p fnl f: wnt 2nd cl home* **16/1**

-005 **3** *½* **Taqaat (USA)**[69] 1207 4-9-2 **59**.......................... PaulHanagan 11 63
(Tim McCarthy) *led: rdn 3f out: kpt on wl u.p tl hdd ins fnl f: no ex and one pce after: lost 2nd cl home* **14/1**

0256 **4** *½* **Kiss A Prince**[33] 2043 6-9-7 **64**..........................(p) ShaneKelly 2 67
(Dean Ivory) *hld up in last trio: effrt 2f out: chsd ldrs and rdn over 1f out: kpt on ins fnl f* **15/2**

6126 **5** *¾* **Cairanne**[5] 2899 4-8-12 **58**.......................... RyanClark(3) 10 60
(Tom Keddy) *s.i.s: t.k.h: sn rcvrd and in midfield: chsd ldr 7f out: rdn and ev ch 3f out: no ex 1f out: one pce and btn fnl 150yds* **3/1**[1]

5040 **6** *½* **Thank You Joy**[33] 2048 4-9-0 **57**..........................(v) FrederikTylicki 3 58
(J R Jenkins) *in tch in midfield: rdn and unable qck over 2f out: kpt on u.p ins fnl f: nvr gng pce to rch ldrs* **10/1**

3030 **7** *1* **Monsieur Pontaven**[6] 2858 5-8-8 **51** ow1.......................... DarryllHolland 9 50
(Robin Bastiman) *stdd s: hld up in last trio: effrt over 2f out: rdn over 1f out: kpt on ins fnl f: nvr trbld ldrs* **11/2**[3]

-004 **8** *1 ¾* **Vertibes**[22] 2365 4-8-13 **56**..........................(b) SebSanders 1 51
(Marcus Tregoning) *chsd ldr tl 2f out: styd chsng ldrs: ev ch and rdn over 2f out: no ex over 1f out: wknd ins fnl f* **5/1**[2]

0035 **9** *3 ½* **Nicholas Pocock (IRE)**[11] 2692 6-8-6 **52**..........................(p) DeclanCannon(3) 8 40
(Ian McInnes) *t.k.h: in tch: rdn and effrt over 3f out: no prog 2f out: sn wknd* **14/1**

2345 **10** *21* **Arkaim** 818 4-9-6 [illegible].......................... LiamKeniry 7
(Pam Sly) *t.k.h: hld up in midfield: lost pl and rdn 4f out: bhd fnl 2f: eased ins fnl f* **7/1**

2m 9.61s (-0.89) **Going Correction** -0.05s/f (Good) **10** Ran SP% **113.5**
Speed ratings (Par 101): **101,99,99,98,98 97,97,95,92,76**
toteswingers:1&2:£52.00, 1&3:£53.20, 2&3:£24.40 CSF £362.68 CT £5694.25 TOTE £28.80: £7.50, £6.10, £5.10; EX 286.60.
Owner TCWS Ltd **Bred** Dullingham Park **Trained** Newmarket, Suffolk

FOCUS
A moderate handicap, run at a sound pace.
Monsieur Pontaven Official explanation: trainer said gelding was unsuited by the good to firm ground

3048 BETVICTOR ON YOUR MOBILE APPRENTICE (S) STKS 1m 1f
3:10 (3:11) (Class 6) 3-Y-O **£1,617** (£481; £240; £120) **Stalls** Low

Form RPR

122- **1** **Purple 'n Gold (IRE)**[204] 7501 3-9-1 74..........................(v[1]) DavidKenny(3) 6 71
(George Baker) *trckd ldrs: chsd ldr and clr of field over 3f out: led and hung rt over 1f out: stl hanging but drvn and in command fnl 100yds: pushed out towards fin* **9/4**[1]

6 **2** *2 ¼* **Elegant Ophelia**[22] 2368 3-8-4 0..........................(t) TobyAtkinson(3) 1 55
(Marco Botti) *s.i.s: bhd: rdn over 3f out: hdwy and stl plenty to do over 1f out: styd on wl fnl f to go 2nd towards fin: no threat to wnr* **11/2**[3]

4642 **3** *nk* **Casa Bex**[61] 1365 3-8-12 63..........................(t) AdamBeschizza 2 59
(Philip McBride) *hld up bhd: rdn and effrt 3f out: hdwy but stl plenty to do over 1f out: styd on wl u.p ins fnl f: no threat to wnr* **10/3**[2]

200 **4** *½* **Aiaam Al Wafa (IRE)**[13] 2624 3-8-8 57..........................(p) DannyBrock(5) 7 59
(Phil McEntee) *chsd ldrs tl led 4f out and sn rdn clr: hdd over 1f out: kpt on u.p tl no ex ins fnl f: lost 2 pls towards fin* **22/1**

5-30 **5** *6* **Fu Fic Fas**[23] 2353 3-8-4 55.......................... AshleyMorgan(3) 11 40
(Paul Fitzsimons) *t.k.h: hld up in tch: lost pl and rdn 4f out: wl hld fnl 2f: plugged on fnl f* **11/1**

2510 **6** *nk* **Skyeron**[23] 2340 3-8-13 53.......................... DeclanCannon 10 45
(Mark Brisbourne) *led tl 4f out: sn outpcd u.p: 3rd and btn 2f out: wknd over 1f out* **7/1**

-445 **7** *3 ¼* **April Leyf (IRE)**[14] 2601 3-8-2 50.......................... NoelGarbutt(5) 3 32
(Mark Brisbourne) *in tch in midfield: rdn and struggling 4f out: no ch fnl 2f* **50/1**

3130 **8** *5* **Smart Affair**[35] 1982 3-8-6 50.......................... RobertTart(7) 4 27
(Alan Bailey) *racd in last trio: rdn and struggling over 3f out: no ch fnl 2f* **16/1**

0 **9** *nk* **Eight Letters (USA)**[54] 1502 3-8-2 0.......................... IanBurns(5) 12 21
(Michael Bell) *chsd ldr tl 4f out: sn wknd: wl bhd over 1f out* **33/1**

00-0 **10** *½* **Dine Out**[16] 2548 3-8-7 57.......................... RyanClark 5 19
(Mark H Tompkins) *a towards rr: rdn 5f out: sn struggling: bhd fnl 2f* **11/1**

1m 55.74s (-0.06) **Going Correction** -0.05s/f (Good) **10** Ran SP% **113.5**
Speed ratings (Par 97): **98,96,95,95,89 89,86,82,82,81**
toteswingers:1&2:£3.70, 1&3:£2.60, 2&3:£4.30 CSF £14.04 TOTE £3.30: £1.40, £2.30, £1.50; EX 17.70.The winner was bought in for 5,800gns. Elegant Ophelia was claimed by Mr Dean Ivory for £5,000.
Owner M Khan X2 **Bred** Stonethorn Stud Farms Ltd **Trained** Whitsbury, Hants
■ Stewards' Enquiry : Adam Beschizza two-day ban: used whip above permitted level (Jun 27-28)

FOCUS
The first four came well clear in this weak seller.

3049 BETVICTOR FOR EURO 2012 H'CAP 6f 3y
3:40 (3:41) (Class 3) (0-90,89) 3-Y-0+ **£6,490** (£1,942; £971; £486; £242) **Stalls** Centre

Form RPR

52-2 **1** **Hezmah**[13] 2636 4-9-11 **86**.......................... PaulHanagan 4 98
(John Gosden) *chsd ldrs: chal and stl gng wl over 1f out: hld hd high ins fnl f: drvn fnl 75yds: kpt on to ld last strides* **11/4**[1]

4-51 **2** *hd* **Nassau Storm**[29] 2145 3-8-4 **76**.......................... HarryBentley(3) 9 85
(William Knight) *in tch in midfield: rdn 1/2-way: hdwy to chal 1f out: drvn to ld fnl 100yds: kpt on tl hdd last strides* **16/1**

0-00 **3** *1 ¼* **Kuanyao (IRE)**[16] 2558 6-9-6 **81**.......................... SebSanders 8 88
(Peter Makin) *led: rdn wl over 1f out: drvn ent fnl f: hdd fnl 100yds: no ex* **16/1**

-000 **4** *½* **Johannes (IRE)**[18] 2507 9-9-8 **83**.......................... FrederikTylicki 1 88
(Richard Fahey) *taken down early: in tch in midfield: rdn 1/2-way: no prog tl styd on wl u.p fnl 100yds* **17/2**

0-00 **5** *1 ¼* **Flynn's Boy**[32] 2083 4-9-0 **75**.......................... RobertHavlin 13 76
(Rae Guest) *hld up towards rr: rdn and hdwy over 2f out: drvn to chse ldrs over 1f out: edgd lft and no imp ins fnl f* **20/1**

5-06 **6** *¾* **Barney McGrew (IRE)**[18] 2487 9-9-7 **82**.......................... RoystonFfrench 10 81
(Michael Dods) *taken down early: in tch in midfield: rdn and unable qck 1/2-way: kpt on u.p ins fnl f* **16/1**

0046 **7** *nk* **Fathsta (IRE)**[4] 2919 7-9-10 **88**.......................... AdamBeschizza(3) 2 86
(David Simcock) *taken down early: sn pushed along in rr: hdwy u.p over 1f out: kpt on fnl f: nvr trbld ldrs* **6/1**[3]

0-01 **8** *2 ¼* **L'Ami Louis (IRE)**[18] 2487 4-10-0 **89**.......................... DaneO'Neill 12 80
(Henry Candy) *chsd ldrs: rdn and unable qck over 2f out: wknd 1f out* **5/1**[2]

3040 **9** *1 ¼* **Tagula Night (IRE)**[16] 2558 6-9-11 **86**.......................... ShaneKelly 7 73
(Dean Ivory) *towards rr: rdn 1/2-way: plugged on fnl f: nvr trbld ldrs* **18/1**

0000 **10** *1 ½* **Button Moon (IRE)**[27] 2195 4-8-12 **80**..........................(v[1]) IanBurns(7) 6 62
(Ian Wood) *w ldr: ev ch and rdn wl over 1f out: struggling 1f out: fdd ins fnl f* **25/1**

100- **11** *1 ¼* **Master Mylo (IRE)**[270] 6173 5-9-8 **83**.......................... PatCosgrave 11 61
(Robert Cowell) *taken down early: in tch: rdn and struggling 1/2-way: wknd over 1f out:* **33/1**

-205 **12** *nse* **New Leyf (IRE)**[16] 2558 6-9-5 **87**.......................... MichaelJMurphy(7) 5 65
(Ed Walker) *sn pushed along and struggling towards rr: bhd and drvn 2f out: no prog and wl hld after* **7/1**

3-00 **13** *58* **Dissent (IRE)**[12] 2660 3-8-8 **77** EddieAhern 14
(Gerard Butler) *bhd: eased and lost tch 1/2-way: wl t.o and virtually p.u fnl f* **33/1**

1m 10.45s (-3.95) **Going Correction** -0.475s/f (Firm)
WFA 3 from 4yo+ 8lb **13** Ran SP% **118.0**
Speed ratings (Par 107): **107,106,105,104,102 101,101,98,96,94 93,92,15**
toteswingers:1&2:£8.10, 1&3:£6.00, 2&3:£23.70 CSF £47.86 CT £595.85 TOTE £2.90: £1.50, £7.30, £6.60; EX 58.60.
Owner Hamdan Al Maktoum **Bred** Andrew Buxton **Trained** Newmarket, Suffolk

FOCUS
This was a fair sprint handicap. It was run at a decent tempo and the form should work out.

NOTEBOOK
Hezmah narrowly missed out on her return at Newcastle 13 days earlier and she deservedly got the better of a tight finish this time off a 1lb higher mark. She travelled best through the race, but took time to get the job done and it made some sense that jockey Paul Hanagan later reported that she took a false step inside the final furlong. In the right hands, she can win more races as a sprinter as she's relatively lightly raced. (op 5-2 tchd 3-1)
Nassau Storm ◆ was only just denied on this handicap debut. He made all over 7f on Polytrack last month, but getting a lead off strong pace suited on this initial outing as a sprinter and he left the impression he would have followed up had he raced with more company inside the final furlong. It was just his sixth start to date, his second on turf, and he's one to follow (op 14-1)
Kuanyao(IRE) had dropped to a mark 3lb lower than when registering the last of his six straights wins in 2010 and sprung back to life with a gutsy effort under a positive ride. (op 20-1 tchd 14-1)
Johannes(IRE) is better than the bare form as this was a race where coming from well off the pace proved tricky. He's on a long losing run, but is nicely treated at present and an end to the drought may well be in sight. (op 8-1 tchd 9-1)
Flynn's Boy, from an in-form stable, is back on his last winning mark and this was much his best effort of the year. He should go closer over a stiffer 6f. (op 25-1)
L'Ami Louis(IRE) was 7lb higher than when making all at Haydock last month. He was unable to dominate and failed to confirm that form with Barney McGrew as a result. (tchd 9-2)
Dissent(IRE) Official explanation: jockey said colt lost its action

3050 BETVICTOR.COM - 7 PLACES AT US OPEN H'CAP 6f 3y
4:10 (4:12) (Class 6) (0-65,63) 3-Y-O **£1,617** (£481; £240; £120) **Stalls** Centre

Form RPR
00-6 **1** **Sarah Berry**[34] 2010 3-8-11 **53** DarryllHolland 8 62
(Chris Dwyer) *chsd ldrs: rdn and ev ch ent fnl f: kpt on wl to ld cl home* **28/1**
-033 **2** *½* **Ooi Long**[11] 2695 3-8-8 **50** (t) FrederikTylicki 4 57
(Mark Rimmer) *stdd after s: bmpd and pushed lft sn after s: t.k.h: hld up towards rr: hdwy 1/2-way: rdn and ev ch 2f out: led 1f out: drvn fnl f: hdd cl home* **7/1**[3]
00-1 **3** *1 ¼* **Dream Walker (FR)**[34] 2010 3-9-6 **62** PatrickMathers 3 65+
(Ian McInnes) *s.i.s: bdly bmpd and pushed lft sn after s: bhd: hdwy 1/2-way: drvn 2f out: kpt on wl ins fnl f: nt rch ldrs* **4/1**[1]
0255 **4** *nk* **Samba Night (IRE)**[10] 2730 3-9-7 **63** (v[1]) EddieAhern 9 65
(James Eustace) *led: hdd 1f out: no ex and btn fnl 100yds: one pce* **9/1**
-236 **5** *1* **New Decade**[15] 2573 3-9-4 **60** DaneO'Neill 2 59
(Milton Bradley) *in tch: effrt and drvn to chse ldrs over 1f out: styd on same pce ins fnl f* **6/1**[2]
30-0 **6** *2 ¼* **Rock Of Monet**[19] 2441 3-9-6 **62** (v) PatCosgrave 7 54
(Michael Bell) *wnt lft and bmpd rivals after s: hld up in tch: effrt over 2f out: drvn and unable qck over 1f out: wknd ins fnl f* **16/1**
0421 **7** *2* **Seventeen Seventy**[9] 2762 3-9-5 **61** 6ex LiamKeniry 15 46
(Alan Coogan) *in tch: rdn and effrt ent fnl 2f: edgd lft and no imp ent fnl f: wknd* **8/1**
5062 **8** *½* **Ambitious Icarus**[14] 2595 3-9-1 **60** DeclanCannon[(3)] 14 44
(Richard Guest) *s.i.s: hld up in rr: rdn and effrt nrest stands' rail 2f out: no prog and edgd lft over 1f out: wl hld fnl f* **11/1**
5-04 **9** *1 ¼* **Tenderly Place**[22] 2361 3-8-10 **57** (t[1]) DavidKenny[(5)] 5 37
(William Knight) *taken down early: bhd: rdn 1/2-way: plugged on but nvr trbld ldrs* **16/1**
0-50 **10** *¾* **Citybell (IRE)**[16] 2540 3-9-2 **58** PaulHanagan 12 35
(Richard Fahey) *taken down early: in tch in midfield: rdn and unable qck over 2f out: wknd over 1f out* **8/1**
-460 **11** *½* **Indiana Guest (IRE)**[8] 2803 3-8-12 **54** SebSanders 10 30
(George Margarson) *in tch in midfield: shuffled bk towards rr and nt clr run over 2f out: rdn over 1f out: no imp* **9/1**
6-60 **12** *1 ¼* **Fen Flyer**[8] 2802 3-7-10 **45** (b) IanBurns[(7)] 1 17
(Chris Dwyer) *racd alone towards far rail: midfield: rdn over 2f out: sn struggling and wl hld over 1f out: wknd* **50/1**
5-06 **13** *1 ½* **Ida Inkley (IRE)**[9] 2759 3-9-6 **62** LeeNewman 11 29
(Jonathan Portman) *chsd ldrs tl 1/2-way: sn rdn and struggling: wknd and bhd over 1f out* **33/1**
0000 **14** *1* **Tumbleowtashoes**[16] 2547 3-8-0 **45** (tp) RyanPowell[(3)] 13
(John Ryan) *chsd ldr tl 1/2-way: sn struggling u.p: bhd over 1f out* **100/1**
0600 **15** *9* **Mystical Witch**[8] 2803 3-8-13 **55** (p) TomMcLaughlin 16
(Christine Dunnett) *towards rr: rdn and struggling 1/2-way: wl bhd over 1f out* **50/1**

1m 12.22s (-2.18) **Going Correction** -0.475s/f (Firm) **15** Ran SP% **120.4**
Speed ratings (Par 97): **95,94,92,92,90 87,85,84,82,81 81,79,77,76,64**
toteswingers:1&2:£38.70, 1&3:£21.90, 2&3:£7.10 CSF £209.02 CT £973.52 TOTE £42.30: £11.30, £2.40, £1.60; EX 360.40.
Owner Strawberry Fields Stud **Bred** F B B White **Trained** Six Mile Bottom, Cambs

FOCUS
A moderate 3-y-o sprint handicap, run at a fair pace and the main action developed down the centre.
Sarah Berry Official explanation: trainer said, regarding apparent improvement in form, that the filly appreciated the good to firm ground having run on heavy last time.
Tenderly Place Official explanation: jockey said filly hung left

3051 BEST PRICES AT BETVICTOR.COM MAIDEN H'CAP 1m 3y
4:40 (4:40) (Class 6) (0-65,60) 4-Y-O+ **£1,617** (£481; £240; £120) **Stalls** Centre

Form RPR
-354 **1** **Handsome King**[97] 833 5-9-7 **60** (p) FrederikTylicki 1 65
(J R Jenkins) *led tl 3f out: rdn over 2f out: ev ch and drvn 1f out: kpt on u.p to ld last strides* **9/2**[3]
0000 **2** *hd* **Danceyourselfdizzy (IRE)**[6] 2845 4-7-13 **45** [1] DannyBrock[(7)] 2 49
(Phil McEntee) *chsd ldrs: wnt 2nd over 5f out: led 3f out: rdn over 1f out: hrd pressed ins fnl f: hdd last strides* **20/1**
0443 **3** *1 ¼* **Avon Supreme**[8] 2804 4-8-10 **49** ShaneKelly 9 50
(Gay Kelleway) *t.k.h: hld up in tch: rdn and chsd ldrs over 1f out: hanging lft and nt qckning 1f out: one pce and hld whn nt clr run towards fin* **10/3**[2]
-423 **4** *nk* **Kyllachykov (IRE)**[19] 2464 4-8-9 **48** PaulHanagan 10 49
(Robin Bastiman) *hld up in last pair: pushed along 1/2-way: rdn over 2f out: sme hdwy and swtchd lft 1f out: styd on fnl 100yds: nvr gng pce to rch ldrs* **11/10**[1]
0000 **5** *2 ½* **Rasteau (IRE)**[8] 2804 4-8-6 **48** ow3 RyanClark[(3)] 8 43
(Tom Keddy) *chsd wnr tl over 2f out: styd chsng ldrs: rdn and unable qck over 1f out: wknd ins fnl f* **22/1**
046 **6** *8* **Petrarchan**[14] 2611 4-9-4 **57** (t) DaneO'Neill 7 34
(Milton Bradley) *s.i.s: hld up in last trio: hdwy 3f out: rdn 2f out: drvn and no ex over 1f out: fdd fnl f* **8/1**
0000 **7** *6* **Hot Tub**[19] 2464 4-8-3 **45** (bt[1]) DominicFox[(3)] 5
(Christine Dunnett) *stdd s: hld up in tch: rdn over 3f out: wknd 2f out: wl bhd fnl f* **50/1**

1m 39.16s (-1.44) **Going Correction** -0.475s/f (Firm) **7** Ran SP% **111.1**
Speed ratings (Par 101): **88,87,86,86,83 75,69**
toteswingers:1&2:£4.700, 1&3:£2.80, 2&3:£6.3 CSF £75.47 CT £323.45 TOTE £5.40: £2.60, £7.20; EX 42.70.
Owner Roger Bradbury **Bred** Southill Stud **Trained** Royston, Herts

FOCUS
A very weak handicap, run at an ordinary pace.

3052 SIS LIVE H'CAP (DIV I) 7f 3y
5:10 (5:13) (Class 6) (0-60,60) 3-Y-O+ **£1,617** (£481; £240; £120) **Stalls** Centre

Form RPR
3301 **1** **Spin Again (IRE)**[15] 2581 7-10-0 **60** PatCosgrave 10 71
(John Ryan) *in tch: effrt to chse ldr 2f out: chal and wnt clr w rival over 1f out: rdn to ld ins fnl f: r.o wl* **4/1**[2]
3325 **2** *2 ½* **Putin (IRE)**[12] 2653 4-8-10 **49** (bt) DannyBrock[(7)] 11 53
(Phil McEntee) *racd keenly: led: rdn and drew clr w wnr over 1f out: hdd and one pce ins fnl f* **13/2**
40-2 **3** *4* **Green Mountain (IRE)**[15] 2582 3-8-1 **46** (t) AdamBeschizza[(3)] 5 35
(Philip McBride) *in tch: rdn and effrt wl over 2f out: outpcd by ldng pair: wnt 3rd over 1f out: kpt on but no imp* **11/2**
4266 **4** *2* **Storm Runner (IRE)**[19] 2464 4-9-11 **57** PaulHanagan 3 45
(George Margarson) *in tch: lost pl and rdn over 2f out: no threat to ldrs and plugged on same pce fr over 1f out* **9/2**[3]
-000 **5** *1* **Whiskey Junction**[33] 2046 8-9-11 **57** SebSanders 6 42
(Michael Quinn) *t.k.h: chsd ldr tl 2f out: sn wknd* **14/1**
6-00 **6** *4 ½* **Fleetwoodmaxi (USA)**[98] 828 5-9-7 **53** EddieAhern 2 26
(Peter Makin) *in tch: rdn and struggling over 2f out: sn wknd: wl btn and eased ins fnl f* **16/1**
00-4 **7** *½* **Norfolk Sky**[15] 2582 3-8-4 **46** oh1 CathyGannon 1 14
(Chris Wall) *a bhd: sn pushed along and nvr gng wl: rdn and no rspnse 3f out: no ch fnl 2f* **3/1**[1]
-060 **8** *1 ¾* **Passing Moment**[21] 2406 4-9-0 **46** oh1 FrederikTylicki 4 13
(Brian Baugh) *chsd ldrs tl over 2f out: sn wknd: bhd fnl f* **33/1**
0P-4 **9** *1 ¼* **Imjin River (IRE)**[7] 2811 5-9-6 **57** AshleyMorgan[(5)] 9 21
(William Stone) *hld up in last pair: hdwy 3f out: rdn and fnd nil over 2f out: sn wknd* **9/1**

1m 24.41s (-2.19) **Going Correction** -0.475s/f (Firm)
WFA 3 from 4yo+ 10lb **9** Ran SP% **117.4**
Speed ratings (Par 101): **93,90,85,83,82 77,76,74,73**
toteswingers:1&2:£6.00, 1&3:£3.30, 2&3:£6.80 CSF £30.76 CT £145.27 TOTE £6.20: £2.40, £2.30, £2.50; EX 29.20.
Owner M M Foulger **Bred** Barry Lyons **Trained** Newmarket, Suffolk

FOCUS
An ordinary handicap and another race on the day where it paid to be handy.

3053 SIS LIVE H'CAP (DIV II) 7f 3y
5:40 (5:40) (Class 6) (0-60,60) 3-Y-O+ **£1,617** (£481; £240; £120) **Stalls** Centre

Form RPR
5002 **1** **Jonnie Skull (IRE)**[12] 2652 6-9-0 **53** (vt) DannyBrock[(7)] 6 61
(Phil McEntee) *stdd s: t.k.h: hld up in tch: rdn and effrt to chal ent fnl f: led ins fnl f: edgd lft but r.o wl* **8/1**
0102 **2** *¾* **Yankee Storm**[16] 2555 7-9-10 **56** (b) DarryllHolland 5 62
(Michael Wigham) *t.k.h: trckd ldrs: nt clr run jst over 2f out: rdn and effrt to chal 1f out: ev ch ins fnl f: edgd lft and no ex fnl 50yds* **5/2**[1]
-652 **3** *2* **Fonterutoli (IRE)**[13] 2627 5-9-6 **57** NathanAlison[(5)] 11 58
(Roger Ingram) *t.k.h: chsd ldr: rdn to ld over 1f out: hdd ins fnl f: wknd fnl 75yds* **8/1**
00-1 **4** *1 ¼* **Takitwo**[14] 2607 9-9-13 **59** DaneO'Neill 10 56
(Jonathan Portman) *hld up in tch in rr: hdwy 2f out: rdn over 1f out: styd on same pce fnl f* **11/2**[3]
0035 **5** *1 ½* **Crocodile Bay (IRE)**[32] 2090 9-8-11 **46** (p) DeclanCannon[(3)] 2 39
(Richard Guest) *led at stdy gallop: rdn 2f out: hdd and unable qck over 1f out: wknd ins fnl f* **14/1**
050 **6** *nk* **Abriachan**[43] 1729 5-10-0 **60** CathyGannon 3 52
(Noel Quinlan) *in tch: lost pl 1/2-way: rdn and hdwy 2f out: one pce and no imp fnl f* **10/3**[2]
0500 **7** *2 ½* **Nothing's Simple**[53] 1530 3-7-11 **46** oh1 NoelGarbutt[(7)] 9 36
(Hugo Palmer) *in tch towards rr but sn pushed along: u.p 4f out: struggling and outpcd 2f out: n.d after* **40/1**
35-6 **8** *3* **Norcroft**[21] 2401 10-9-0 **46** oh1 (p) SebSanders 7 24
(Christine Dunnett) *in tch towards rr: rdn and outpcd over 2f out: no threat to ldrs fr over 1f out* **20/1**
-000 **9** *5* **Morermaloke**[97] 831 4-9-2 **48** PatrickMathers 4 12
(Ian McInnes) *t.k.h: chsd ldrs: rdn over 2f out: sn struggling: wknd over 1f out* **40/1**
1060 **10** *2 ¾* **Marksbury**[4] 2913 5-9-8 **57** RyanClark[(3)] 8 14
(Mark Brisbourne) *chsd ldrs: rdn and lost pl over 2f out: bhd over 1f out* **10/1**

1m 25.16s (-1.44) **Going Correction** -0.475s/f (Firm)
WFA 3 from 4yo+ 10lb **10** Ran SP% **114.7**
Speed ratings (Par 101): **89,88,85,84,82 82,79,76,70,67**
toteswingers:1&2:£2.80, 1&3:£10.00, 2&3:£6.60 CSF £27.33 CT £168.43 TOTE £11.70: £2.40, £1.40, £2.00; EX 22.40.
Owner Eventmaker Racehorses **Bred** Canice Farrell Jnr **Trained** Newmarket, Suffolk

FOCUS
This second division of the ordinary 7f handicap and it was run at a stronger early pace, which helped those coming from behind. Sound form.
Yankee Storm Official explanation: two-day ban: used whip down shoulder in the forehand (Jun 27-28)

T/Jkpt: Not won. T/Plt: £2,804.40 to a £1 stake. Pool:£67,229.49 - 17.50 winning tickets T/Qpdt: £69.40 to a £1 stake. Pool:£6,486.29 - 69.12 winning tickets SP

3054 - 3060a (Foreign Racing) - See Raceform Interactive

3033

HAYDOCK (L-H)

Thursday, June 14

OFFICIAL GOING: Good (good to firm in places)

All races on inner Home straight and distances on round course reduced in distance by 5yds.

Wind: Light to moderate, behind Weather: Cloudy, rained later

3061 BETDAQ HAYDOCK PARK APPRENTICE TRAINING SERIES H'CAP (PART OF THE RACING EXCELLENCE INITIATIVE) 1m 3f 200y

6:50 (6:50) (Class 5) (0-70,70) 4-Y-0+ **£2,264** (£673; £336; £168) **Stalls** Centre

Form RPR

0-05 **1** **Silver Tigress**[41] 1822 4-8-7 **53** GarryWhillans 1 65
(George Moore) *hld up: hdwy on inner 5f out: rdn to ld over 1f out: styd on u.p: hld on gamely at fin* **13/2**[3]

112 **2** *nk* **Teak (IRE)**[7] 2863 5-9-6 **66** MatthewCosham 4 78
(Ian Williams) *led for 2f at stdy pce: remained handy: regained ld 3f out: rdn and hdd over 1f out: styd on u.p: rallied wl ins fnl f: jst hld* **1/1**[1]

066- **3** *5* **Graceful Descent (FR)**[16] 7162 7-9-5 **70** GemmaTutty(5) 9 74
(Karen Tutty) *hld up: rdn over 2f out: hdwy over 1f out: wnt 3rd ins fnl f: nt trble front pair* **16/1**

25-6 **4** *1 1/4* **Aegean Destiny**[29] 2167 5-8-13 **59** JustinNewman 10 61
(John Mackie) *hld up in tch: effrt 3f out: styd on u.p over 1f out: no imp on ldrs: kpt on same pce ins fnl f* **7/1**

5033 **5** *5* **Dubara Reef (IRE)**[10] 2775 5-8-5 **51** (v) MatthewLawson 6 45
(Paul Green) *w ldr: led at stdy pce after 2f: hdd 3f out: rdn over 2f out: wknd fnl f* **11/2**[2]

-000 **6** *12* **Amir Pasha (UAE)**[52] 1562 7-8-10 **56** (p) ShaneBKelly 3 30
(Micky Hammond) *in tch: cl up 7f out: rdn over 2f out: wknd over 1f out* **10/1**

5-40 **7** *3 1/4* **Bollistick**[21] 2418 6-8-3 **52** NatashaEaton(3) 7 21
(Michael Mullineaux) *prom tl wknd over 3f out* **18/1**

110/ **8** *39* **Isitcozimcool (IRE)**[615] 705 7-8-12 **63** DavidSimmonson(5) 11
(Barry Murtagh) *racd keenly: handy: lost pl over 4f out: sn pushed along: bhd fnl 3f: t.o* **40/1**

2m 29.58s (-4.22) **Going Correction** -0.575s/f (Hard) **8** Ran SP% **113.9**

Speed ratings (Par 103): **91,90,87,86,83 75,73,47**

Swingers:1&2:£2.50, 2&3:£3.60, 1&3:£7.10 CSF £13.30 CT £99.93 TOTE £7.50: £2.50, £1.10, £2.90; EX 17.60 Trifecta £241.10 Part won. Pool: £325.88 - 0.41 winning units..

Owner A Crute & Partners **Bred** Mrs J M F Dibben & Mrs Amanda Brudenell **Trained** Middleham Moor, N Yorks

FOCUS

Following a dry night and day the ground was changed to "good, good to firm in places". All races were run on the inner track in the home straight, reducing distances on the round course by 5yds. A modest handicap run at an ordinary gallop and the first two pulled clear in the last quarter mile. The winner is rated back to her 3yo form.

3062 TONY CUNLIFFE 50TH BIRTHDAY CELEBRATION MAIDEN STKS (C&G) 7f

7:20 (7:20) (Class 5) 2-Y-0 **£2,264** (£673; £336; £168) **Stalls** Low

Form RPR

00 **1** **Glory Awaits (IRE)**[8] 2822 2-9-0 0 GrahamLee 9 86
(Kevin Ryan) *a.p: led over 1f out: r.o for pressurre ins fnl f: jst prevailed on the nod* **50/1**

5 **2** *nse* **Letstalkaboutmoney (IRE)**[62] 1352 2-8-11 0 (v[1]) MichaelMetcalfe(3) 5 86
(Mrs K Burke) *trckd ldrs: str chal fr over 1f out: r.o u.p: jst denied on the nod* **11/2**[3]

33 **3** *1 3/4* **Luhaif**[13] 2677 2-9-0 0 MartinHarley 3 81
(Mick Channon) *trckd ldrs: plld off rail to chal over 1f out: no ex fnl 75yds* **5/2**[2]

43 **4** *3 1/2* **Mysterial**[27] 2231 2-8-11 0 SeanLevey(3) 11 72
(Richard Hannon) *hld up: hdwy 3f out: rdn and edgd rt whn chsng ldrs over 1f out: edgd lft whn one pce ins fnl f* **2/1**[1]

5 **5** *1 1/2* **Mowhoob**[9] 2797 2-9-0 0 PaulHanagan 10 68
(John Gosden) *hld up: rdn 2f out: checked whn nt clr run briefly over 1f out: nvr nr to chal* **6/1**

6 **6** *1 1/2* **Haverstock**[17] 2550 2-9-0 0 JoeFanning 6 64
(Mark Johnston) *led: pressed 2f out: rdn and hdd over 1f out: wknd ins fnl f* **10/1**

25 **7** *8* **Ryedale Valley**[22] 2402 2-9-0 0 DavidAllan 7 44
(Tim Easterby) *racd keenly in midfield: rdn over 2f out: wknd over 1f out* **50/1**

0 **8** *nse* **If You Can (IRE)**[28] 2213 2-9-0 0 GrahamGibbons 8 43
(Tim Easterby) *ref to settle in midfield: wknd over 2f out* **100/1**

9 *3/4* **Cielo Rojo (IRE)** 2-9-0 0 TonyHamilton 1 42
(Richard Fahey) *s.s: rdn over 3f out: a bhd* **25/1**

10 *3/4* **Pearl Spice (IRE)** 2-8-11 0 HarryBentley(3) 2 40+
(Sir Mark Prescott Bt) *s.s: pushed along and a bhd* **12/1**

1m 27.76s (-2.94) **Going Correction** -0.575s/f (Hard) **10** Ran SP% **117.1**

Speed ratings (Par 93): **93,92,90,86,85 83,74,74,73,72**

Swingers:1&2:£17.30, 2&3:£6.80, 1&3:£59.80 CSF £304.86 TOTE £53.40: £6.70, £2.60, £1.60; EX 349.00 TRIFECTA Not won..

Owner Emerald Racing **Bred** J Fisher **Trained** Hambleton, N Yorks

FOCUS

An interesting maiden on paper but only a fair gallop saw those held up failed to land a blow and the two market leaders didn't improve as much for the step up to this trip as had seemed likely. The winner left his previous two runs behind.

NOTEBOOK

Glory Awaits(IRE), soundly beaten both outings over 6f, had the run of the race and showed much-improved form over this longer trip. He has a bit of size and scope and may do better still. Official explanation: trainer's representative said, reagarding the apparent improvement of form, that the colt was better suited by a galloping track and a step up to a seven furlong race (tchd 66-1)

Letstalkaboutmoney(IRE) hadn't shown much in a race that has worked out particularly well over 6f in soft ground at Leicester in April, fared a good deal better in the first-time visor over this longer trip on this much quicker ground. He's capable of making amends in ordinary company. (op 5-1)

Luhaif looked sure to be suited by the step up to this trip but, although not beaten far, proved a bit of a disappointment against two rivals that had previously shown precious little. Nevertheless he seemed to stay this trip well enough and remains capable of picking up a minor event. (op 3-1)

Mysterial ran well to chase home two subsequent winners at Newbury last time, travelled strongly for a long way but failed to improve in the anticipated manner for the step up to this trip once asked for an effort. (op 7-4 tchd 9-4)

Mowhoob, who showed ability at Yarmouth on his debut, failed to build on that over a trip that could have been expected to suit. However he's in good hands, should stay 1m in due course and is open to a bit of improvement. (op 13-2)

Cielo Rojo(IRE), a 19,000gns yearling and a half-brother to winners including very useful French and Austrian 1m winner Armigerent, offered little after a tardy start but should do better.

Pearl Spice(IRE), a 165,000euro yearling and half-brother to several winners, was easy to back and was too green to do himself justice on this racecourse debut. This Derby entry is sure to come on for this experience. (op 14-1)

3063 SILK MILL BAR (RIPPONDEN) H'CAP 7f

7:50 (7:51) (Class 4) (0-85,85) 3-Y-O **£4,204** (£1,251; £625; £312) **Stalls** Low

Form RPR

6-10 **1** **Ardmay (IRE)**[29] 2182 3-8-13 **77** AmyRyan 11 89+
(Kevin Ryan) *midfield: pushed along briefly over 5f out: lost pl ent st over 4f out: hdwy over 3f out: rdn to ld over 1f out: idled towards fin* **8/1**

03-6 **2** *1* **Strada Facendo (USA)**[41] 1824 3-8-12 **76** KirstyMilczarek 7 85+
(Luca Cumani) *s.i.s: hld up: hdwy 3f out: rdn to chal ent fnl f: nt qckn: hld cl home* **17/2**

3-1 **3** *1* **Dos Amigos (IRE)**[40] 1864 3-9-1 **79** PaulMulrennan 3 86+
(Michael Dods) *trckd ldrs: nt qckn 2f out: rdn over 1f out: styd on ins fnl f: nt quite pce of ldrs* **3/1**[1]

14-4 **4** *nk* **Amadeus Wolfe Tone (IRE)**[9] 2785 3-9-1 **79** GrahamLee 10 85
(Jamie Osborne) *hld up: pushed along over 2f out: hdwy to chse ldrs over 1f out: styd on ins fnl f: one pce cl home* **9/2**[2]

3142 **5** *3 3/4* **Berlusca (IRE)**[98] 841 3-8-8 **72** JoeFanning 4 68+
(Mark Brisbourne) *racd keenly in tch: n.m.r and lost pl over 2f out: kpt on ins fnl f: no imp* **20/1**

1-20 **6** *3* **Grizzle**[29] 2182 3-9-6 **84** MickaelBarzalona 5 72
(Mahmood Al Zarooni) *towards rr and niggled along most of way: sme hdwy over 1f out: one pce and no imp fnl f* **9/2**[2]

2212 **7** *2 3/4* **Gabrial's Bounty (IRE)**[35] 1998 3-9-2 **85** CharlesBishop(5) 8 65
(Mick Channon) *racd keenly: trckd ldrs: led 2f out: rdn and hdd over 1f out: wknd ins fnl f* **6/1**[3]

310- **8** *1 3/4* **Commanche**[321] 4496 3-8-8 **72** TomEaves 6 47
(Bryan Smart) *racd keenly: prom: led over 2f out: sn hdd: wknd over 1f out* **20/1**

00-3 **9** *2 3/4* **Ebony Clarets**[24] 2331 3-8-3 **67** PaulHanagan 9 35
(Richard Fahey) *midfield: pushed along over 2f out: wknd over 1f out* **11/1**

3-40 **10** *15* **Not Bad For A Boy (IRE)**[10] 2764 3-8-7 **74** SeanLevey(3) 2
(Barry Leavy) *led: hdd over 2f out: wknd over 1f out: eased whn wl btn ins fnl f* **40/1**

1m 26.49s (-4.21) **Going Correction** -0.575s/f (Hard) **10** Ran SP% **117.6**

Speed ratings (Par 101): **101,99,98,98,94 90,87,85,82,65**

Swingers:1&2:£6.30, 2&3:£8.10, 1&3:£9.70 CSF £72.53 CT £257.39 TOTE £10.00: £2.90, £3.10, £1.70; EX 100.30 TRIFECTA Not won..

Owner A C Henson **Bred** Tom Kelly **Trained** Hambleton, N Yorks

FOCUS

A useful handicap featuring a few unexposed sorts and this race should throw up winners. The gallop was just an ordinary one. The winner is rated back to his reappearance form.

Ardmay(IRE) ◆ Official explanation: trainer's representative said, regarding the apparent improvement of form, that he was unable to explain the poor run last time but that the gelding was better suited by the drop in class

3064 Y.P.O. PENNINE BEST OF BRITAIN H'CAP 1m

8:20 (8:20) (Class 3) (0-95,82) 3-Y-O **£7,115** (£2,117; £1,058; £529) **Stalls** Low

Form RPR

1-35 **1** **Farang Kondiew**[20] 2452 3-9-2 **77** DanielTudhope 3 85
(Declan Carroll) *in tch: pushed along over 2f out: r.o for press to ld ins fnl f: in command fnl strides* **3/1**[1]

2-11 **2** *3/4* **Trail Blaze (IRE)**[33] 2076 3-9-5 **80** AmyRyan 9 86
(Kevin Ryan) *led: hdd narrowly over 2f out: rdn and continued to chal: hld cl home* **4/1**[3]

01-6 **3** *nk* **Border Revia (IRE)**[41] 1819 3-9-2 **77** PaulHanagan 4 82
(Richard Fahey) *midfield: pushed along over 4f out: outpcd over 3f out: r.o for press ins fnl f: gng on at fin* **12/1**

-662 **4** *1/2* **Deepsand (IRE)**[13] 2678 3-9-0 **75** (e) DavidAllan 1 79
(Tim Easterby) *hld up: pushed along over 3f out: hdwy over 1f out: chsd ldrs ins fnl f: kpt on but a hld* **9/1**

5-33 **5** *nse* **Lelaps (USA)**[21] 2428 3-9-7 **82** MartinHarley 2 86
(Marco Botti) *hld up in rr: effrt over 2f out: chsd ldrs over 1f out: styd on towards fin* **7/2**[2]

-163 **6** *3/4* **Verse Of Love**[26] 2263 3-9-1 **76** CathyGannon 8 78
(David Evans) *prom: rdn and nosed ahd over 2f out: hdd ins fnl f: fdd fnl 75yds* **13/2**

-226 **7** *8* **Dance The Rain**[20] 2452 3-9-6 **81** TomEaves 6 65
(Bryan Smart) *s.i.s: sn prom: rdn over 2f out: wknd ins fnl f* **7/1**

1m 40.05s (-3.65) **Going Correction** -0.575s/f (Hard) **7** Ran SP% **110.7**

Speed ratings (Par 103): **95,94,93,93,93 92,84**

Swingers:1&2:£2.30, 2&3:£8.80, 1&3:£1.80 CSF £14.16 CT £115.51 TOTE £2.80: £2.30, £2.10; EX 20.30 Trifecta £149.00 Pool: £304.06 - 1.51 winning units..

Owner Kenny Mackay & Lee Ibbotson **Bred** The Lavington Stud **Trained** Sledmere, E Yorks

■ Stewards' Enquiry : Amy Ryan caution: careless riding

FOCUS

Another useful handicap and one in which an ordinary pace to the 3f pole saw the first six finish in a heap. The form looks sound nevertheless.

NOTEBOOK

Farang Kondiew ◆ would have preferred a stronger gallop but he turned in his best effort of the year to win a shade snugly in the end. He isn't fully exposed, is the type physically to make further progress, he should have no problems with another furlong and is more than capable of winning again. (op 10-3 tchd 7-2)

Trail Blaze(IRE)'s recent improvement has come on rain-soaked ground but he showed he's just as good on a sounder surface after being harried for the lead some way from home. He too is a scopey type who isn't fully exposed and he should continue to give a good account. (op 3-1)

Border Revia(IRE) had disappointed on his reappearance but fared a good deal better this time, for all that he looked inconvenienced by the muddling gallop on this quick ground. A stronger overall pace will suit and he's worth another chance over a bit further. (op 16-1)

Deepsand(IRE), with the headgear again fitted, for the second time in succession wasn't disgraced in a race run at an ordinary gallop. More of an end-to-end gallop would have suited but he's still to match the pick of his juvenile form. (op 11-1 tchd 8-1)

Lelaps(USA) failed to match the form of his Sandown run but this unexposed sort again shaped as though he'd be better suited by the return to 1m2f and he isn't one to be writing off just yet. (tchd 4-1)

Verse Of Love had the run of the race and wasn't totally disgraced but he's going to have to raise his game if he is to win a competitive handicap from his current mark. (op 17-2)

Dance The Rain Official explanation: trainer could offer no explanation for the gelding's performance

3065 RACE TO SUCCESS WITH AVNET H'CAP 5f
8:50 (8:52) (Class 4) (0-80,80) 3-Y-O+ **£4,204** (£1,251; £625; £312) **Stalls** Centre

Form RPR
5-00 **1** **Bop It**[27] 2229 3-9-5 **78** TomEaves 8 84
(Bryan Smart) *a.p: rdn ins fnl f: r.o to ld cl home* **13/2**[3]
4420 **2** *nk* **Bronze Beau**[13] 2674 5-10-0 **80** (t) JamesSullivan 6 88
(Linda Stubbs) *led: rdn ins fnl f: hdd cl home* **12/1**
1122 **3** *1 1/4* **First In Command (IRE)**[27] 2230 7-9-7 **73** (t) PaulHanagan 7 76
(Daniel Mark Loughnane) *hld up: hdwy over 1f out: chsd ldrs ins fnl f: styd on* **7/1**
630- **4** *1 3/4* **Quaroma**[309] 4909 7-9-4 **77** NedCurtis(7) 12 74
(Paul Midgley) *hld up in tch: rdn to chal over 1f out: no ex fnl 75yds* **6/1**[2]
0512 **5** *1/2* **Diman Waters (IRE)**[12] 2690 5-9-10 **76** KellyHarrison 1 71
(Eric Alston) *hld up: rdn over 1f out: styd on ins fnl f: nt pce to chal* **4/1**[1]
64 **6** *1 1/4* **You'relikemefrank**[12] 2719 6-8-11 **63** (p) GrahamLee 4 54
(Richard Ford) *hld up: rdn ins fnl f: kpt on: nvr trbld ldrs* **8/1**
2004 **7** *nse* **Methaaly (IRE)**[19] 2476 9-8-9 **61** oh2 AmyRyan 14 52
(Michael Mullineaux) *hld up: rdn 2f out: no imp* **25/1**
-205 **8** *3/4* **Style And Panache (IRE)**[15] 2596 4-9-7 **73** (p) CathyGannon 10 61
(David Evans) *chsd ldrs: pushed along 1/2-way: sn wknd* **17/2**
3020 **9** *1* **Even Stevens**[26] 2264 4-9-6 **79** (p) JordanUys(7) 5 63
(Scott Dixon) *wnt sideways and nrly uns rdr leaving stalls: chsd ldrs: rdn over 1f out: sn wknd* **8/1**
-653 **10** *3 1/4* **Wicked Wilma (IRE)**[12] 2719 8-9-4 **70** PJMcDonald 3 43
(Alan Berry) *prom tl rdn and wknd over 1f out* **14/1**
0011 **11** *15* **Lucky Dan (IRE)**[10] 2750 6-9-3 **76** 6ex RyanWhile(7) 11
(Paul Green) *rrd s and completely missed break: a wl bhd* **10/1**

59.68s (-1.12) **Going Correction** -0.075s/f (Good)
WFA 3 from 4yo+ 7lb **11** Ran SP% **120.2**
Speed ratings (Par 105): **105,104,102,99,98 96,96,95,94,88 64**
Swingers:1&2:£17.10, 2&3:£11.00, 1&3:£16.50 CSF £83.77 CT £570.70 TOTE £7.80: £1.90, £3.70, £2.10; EX 104.10 Trifecta £239.80 Part won. Pool: £324.18 - 0.10 winning units..
Owner A Turton, J Blackburn & R Bond **Bred** Bond Thoroughbred Corporation **Trained** Hambleton, N Yorks

FOCUS
A fair handicap run at a decent gallop throughout. Straightforward form, which looks sound overall.
Lucky Dan(IRE) Official explanation: jockey said that the gelding missed the break

3066 STEPS HERE ON 21ST JULY H'CAP 1m 2f 95y
9:20 (9:21) (Class 5) (0-70,70) 3-Y-O **£2,264** (£673; £336; £168) **Stalls** High

Form RPR
440- **1** **Clon Brulee (IRE)**[216] 7367 3-9-6 **67** GrahamGibbons 15 78+
(David Barron) *in tch: led over 2f out: flashed tail u.p and edgd rt ins fnl f: kpt on wl* **14/1**
-552 **2** *1 1/4* **Brockwell**[17] 2552 3-9-7 **60** RichardKingscote 14 77
(Tom Dascombe) *hld up: hdwy 3f out: chsd wnr over 1f out: nt qckn ins fnl f* **11/2**[3]
4055 **3** *1 1/4* **Maybeagrey**[38] 1915 3-9-2 **63** DuranFentiman 8 70+
(Tim Easterby) *s.i.s: hld up: hdwy over 1f out: styd on ins fnl f: nt quite pce to get to ldrs* **25/1**
0-50 **4** *hd* **Now My Sun**[20] 2452 3-9-4 **68** MartinHarley(3) 4 74
(Mrs K Burke) *dwlt: hld up in rr: hdwy over 2f out: rdn over 1f out: sn chsd ldrs: styd on ins fnl f: one pce fnl strides* **12/1**
264 **5** *3 1/2* **Ma Kellys (IRE)**[13] 2673 3-8-12 **59** BarryMcHugh 6 59
(Micky Hammond) *plld hrd: trckd ldrs: rdn over 2f out: no ex fnl 100yds* **16/1**
00-3 **6** *1 3/4* **Neige D'Antan**[9] 2788 3-8-6 **53** LukeMorris 11 49
(Sir Mark Prescott Bt) *dwlt: hld up: pushed along over 3f out: hdwy sn after: rdn and hung lft over 1f out: one pce fnl f* **3/1**[2]
1405 **7** *1 3/4* **Moataz (USA)**[19] 2471 3-9-3 **64** JoeFanning 9 57
(Mark Johnston) *sn led: hdd over 2f out: rdn over 1f out: wknd ins fnl f* **20/1**
6-40 **8** *1/2* **Sweet Grace**[23] 2374 3-8-4 **51** (t) JamesSullivan 10 43
(David Brown) *hld up: rdn 3f out: no imp* **33/1**
-601 **9** *3/4* **Sea Fever (IRE)**[9] 2788 3-9-9 **70** 6ex KirstyMilczarek 7 61
(Luca Cumani) *trckd ldrs: pushed along over 3f out: wknd over 1f out* **6/5**[1]
660 **10** *22* **Bridal Medic**[23] 2380 3-8-5 **52** FrannyNorton 5
(John Mackie) *in tch tl wknd 3f out* **25/1**
3-00 **11** *3/4* **Abdul Malik**[16] 2589 3-8-10 **57** PJMcDonald 12
(Kate Walton) *midfield: hdwy to go prom over 6f out: wknd 2f out* **50/1**
0-02 **12** *4* **Master Chipper**[20] 2453 3-9-6 **67** TomEaves 2
(Michael Dods) *racd keenly: prom tl wknd over 3f out* **40/1**

2m 13.45s (-2.05) **Going Correction** -0.575s/f (Hard) **12** Ran SP% **125.9**
Speed ratings (Par 99): **85,84,83,82,80 78,77,76,76,58 58,54**
Swingers:1&2:£11.40, 2&3:£21.50, 1&3:£48.40 CSF £88.05 CT £1960.76 TOTE £15.10: £3.90, £2.00, £8.10; EX 71.50 TRIFECTA Not won..
Owner Ms Colette Twomey **Bred** Collette Twomey **Trained** Maunby, N Yorks

FOCUS
A modest handicap which didn't take as much winning as seemed likely with the two market leaders disappointing. The gallop was no more than fair. The winner produced a clear personal best.
T/Jkpt: Not won. T/Plt: £166.70 to a £1 stake. Pool: £66,219.14 - 289.98 winning tickets. T/Qpdt: £49.70 to a £1 stake. Pool: £4,660.23 - 69.29 winning tickets. DO

[2498]NEWBURY (L-H)
Thursday, June 14

OFFICIAL GOING: Good to soft (soft in places; 6.3)
Rail moved out from 1m to 5f on round course to give fresh ground and distances on round course increased by about 23metres.
Wind: Brisk behind Weather: Overcast

3067 OUTWARD BOUND TRUST MAIDEN STKS 6f 110y
2:20 (2:21) (Class 4) 2-Y-O **£3,428** (£1,020; £509; £254) **Stalls** Centre

Form RPR
1 **Toronado (IRE)** 2-9-0 0 RichardHughes 7 95+
(Richard Hannon) *led tl hdd 4f out: styd trcking ldr: led again over 1f out: sn pushed along to assert: r.o strly clsng stages* **11/4**[2]
2 *2 3/4* **One Word More (IRE)** 2-9-0 0 WilliamCarson 6 84+
(Charles Hills) *chsd ldrs: rdn 2f out: styd on wl fnl f to take 2nd fnl 75yds but no ch w wnr* **18/1**
4 **3** *1* **Ayaar (IRE)**[13] 2662 2-9-0 0 MartinHarley 10 82
(Mick Channon) *trckd ldr: led 4f out: rdn 2f out: hdd over 1f out: sn outpcd by wnr: no ex and lost 2nd fnl 75yds* **9/4**[1]
4 *5* **Monsieur Rieussec** 2-9-0 0 JimmyFortune 8 68+
(Jonathan Portman) *s.i.s: in rr: pushed along 3f out: styd on fnl f but nvr any threat to ldng trio* **9/1**
0 **5** *1 1/4* **Santo Prince (USA)**[9] 2784 2-9-0 0 HayleyTurner 5 64
(Michael Bell) *in rr: pushed along 1/2-way: styd on fnl f: nvr any threat* **10/1**
6 *1 1/2* **Hands Of Time** 2-9-0 0 WilliamBuick 4 60
(Richard Hannon) *chsd ldrs: pushed along over 2f out: wknd appr fnl f* **10/3**[3]
5 **7** *3/4* **Royal Mizar (SPA)**[3] 2970 2-9-0 0 LukeMorris 3 58
(Alastair Lidderdale) *in rr: rdn over 3f out and nvr gng pce to get into contention* **100/1**
8 *1/2* **Shaolin (IRE)** 2-9-0 0 JimCrowley 9 56
(Seamus Durack) *chsd ldrs tl over 2f out: wknd sn after* **33/1**
9 *1 1/2* **Nine Iron (IRE)** 2-9-0 0 MatthewDavies 1 52
(Mick Channon) *s.i.s: sn in tch: wknd over 2f out* **25/1**
10 *12* **Exzachary** 2-9-0 0 TonyCulhane 2 19
(Jo Hughes) *chsd ldrs: rdn 3f out: wknd over 2f out* **40/1**

1m 20.62s (1.32) **Going Correction** +0.225s/f (Good) **10** Ran SP% **115.1**
Speed ratings (Par 95): **101,97,96,91,89 87,87,86,84,71**
Swingers:1&2:£8.10, 2&3:£6.10, 1&3:£1.90 CSF £47.44 TOTE £3.40: £1.30, £3.80, £1.10; EX 45.70 Trifecta £148.80 Pool: £768.57 - 3.82 winning units..
Owner Carmichael Humber **Bred** Paul Nataf **Trained** East Everleigh, Wilts

FOCUS
This maiden will often produce an above-average performer, usually a newcomer, and the winner looks a horse to follow. The first three finished clear.

NOTEBOOK
Toronado(IRE) ◆'s siblings had achieved a limited amount on the racecourse, although the dam is nicely related, but he made an eyecatching debut, coming right away from his rivals in the final furlong. His only big race entry is in next year's Derby, but connections did suggest the Chesham Stakes next week could come under consideration. (op 3-1 tchd 7-2)
One Word More(IRE) ◆, from the first crop of Thousand Words, who made a winning debut in the 2006 renewal of this contest, is a half-brother to a decent juvenile performer and got the idea late on to post a pleasing performance. (op 16-1 tchd 20-1)
Ayaar(IRE) probably built on his encouraging debut in a Haydock maiden - Richard Hannon trained the winner of that race - and helps to give the race some sort of level. (op 2-1)
Monsieur Rieussec, the first foal of a half-sister to Caster Sugar and Sir Royal, seemed a little green early but made some late progress when getting the hang of things. He'll get further in time and has plenty of size about him. (op 8-1)
Santo Prince(USA) was well beaten on his debut and again here, but did appear to make a bit of progress. (op 11-1)
Hands Of Time is related to six winners, notably his brother and Lockinge winner Virtual. Purchased for 150,000gns, he seemed the stable's second string on jockey arrangements and tended to edge left once William Buick asked for everything. (op 7-2 tchd 4-1)

3068 PERTEMPS NETWORK SUPPORTING OUTWARD BOUND H'CAP 1m (S)
2:50 (2:52) (Class 5) (0-75,75) 3-Y-O **£2,587** (£770; £384; £192) **Stalls** Centre

Form RPR
3-11 **1** **Tigers Tale (IRE)**[44] 1728 3-9-3 **71** (v) JamesDoyle 3 89
(Roger Teal) *bmpd s: mde all: c steadily clr in own time fr over 1f out: unchal* **9/2**[2]
0-50 **2** *9* **Coup De Grace (IRE)**[9] 2802 3-8-6 **60** HayleyTurner 1 57
(Amanda Perrett) *in rr: rdn over 2f out: styd on u.p fr over 1f out to take 2nd fnl 150yds but nvr any ch w unchal wnr* **18/1**
2360 **3** *3* **Beauchamp Castle**[23] 2372 3-9-0 **68** (bt[1]) WilliamBuick 7 58
(Hans Adielsson) *in rr: rdn over 3f out: gng nowhere over 2f out: styd on appr fnl f: tk wl-hld 3rd last stride* **9/1**
0-31 **4** *nse* **Derfenna Art (IRE)**[10] 2756 3-9-4 **72** 6ex (t) JimCrowley 5 62
(Seamus Durack) *bmpd s: chsd ldrs: wnt 2nd over 3f out: no ch w unchal wnr fr over 2f out: lost 2nd fnl 150yds: lost 3rd last stride* **5/2**[1]
4-50 **5** *3* **Inniscastle Boy**[27] 2246 3-8-11 **65** DavidProbert 4 48
(William Muir) *bmpd s: chsd ldrs: rdn 3f out: wknd 2f out* **17/2**
4-00 **6** *3* **Sequoia**[17] 2543 3-9-5 **73** WilliamCarson 2 49
(Charles Hills) *chsd ldrs and disp 2nd u.p over 2f out: wknd qckly appr fnl f* **10/1**
0-05 **7** *3* **Rock Band**[23] 2380 3-9-6 **74** RichardHughes 6 44
(Richard Hannon) *chsd ldrs: rdn to dispute 2nd over 2f out but nvr any ch w unchal wnr: wknd over 1f out* **8/1**[3]
522 **8** *31* **Cooler Climes**[30] 2145 3-9-7 **75** LukeMorris 8
(Pat Eddery) *wnt rt s: sn rcvrd to chse ldrs 1/2-way: rdn and wknd fr 3f out: eased whn btn over 1f out* **9/2**[2]

1m 42.75s (3.05) **Going Correction** +0.225s/f (Good) **8** Ran SP% **110.9**
Speed ratings (Par 99): **93,84,81,80,77 74,71,40**
Swingers:1&2:£13.40, 2&3:£22.80, 1&3:£7.90 CSF £73.38 CT £674.59 TOTE £4.20: £1.80, £5.00, £1.70; EX 84.90 Trifecta £153.90 Pool: £763.56 - 3.67 winning units..
Owner B Kitcherside & Big Cat Partnership **Bred** Butlersgrove Stud **Trained** Ashtead, Surrey

FOCUS
A modest contest but the winner scored with considerable ease. However there is some doubt as to what else ran their race, and the form is a bit guessy.
Cooler Climes Official explanation: jockey said that the colt was unsuited by the ground (good to soft – soft in places)

3069 LORD WEINSTOCK MEMORIAL STKS (REGISTERED AS THE BALLYMACOLL STUD STAKES) (LISTED RACE) (FILLIES) 1m 2f 6y
3:25 (3:25) (Class 1) 3-Y-O
£18,714 (£7,095; £3,550; £1,768; £887; £445) **Stalls** Centre

Form RPR
5-1 **1** **Great Heavens**[35] 2008 3-8-12 0 WilliamBuick 5 99+
(John Gosden) *mde all: drvn and c clr appr fnl f: r.o strly: unchal* **11/8**[1]
3121 **2** *2 1/4* **Miss Cato**[21] 2431 3-8-12 79 ChrisCatlin 1 95
(Rae Guest) *plld hrd: chsd ldrs: rdn over 3f out: chsd wnr fr 2f out: kpt on u.p but wl hld thrght fnl f* **6/1**[3]
210- **3** *2 1/2* **Albamara**[265] 6299 3-8-12 85 LukeMorris 2 90+
(Sir Mark Prescott Bt) *in tch: pushed along 3f out: sn swtchd rt to outside and styd on fr over 1f out: no imp on ldng duo* **5/2**[2]
-214 **4** *3 3/4* **Apothecary**[33] 2079 3-8-12 89 SaleemGolam 4 82
(John Gosden) *in tch: drvn and hdwy to disp 2nd wl over 2f out: wknd appr fnl f* **8/1**
-3 **5** *shd* **Devine Guest (IRE)**[55] 1502 3-8-12 0 MartinHarley 7 82?
(Mick Channon) *in rr: rdn and sme hdwy over 2f out: sn one pce* **17/2**

033- **6** *10* **Villa Royale**[192] [7634] 3-8-12 71 ... RichardHughes 6 62
(Harry Dunlop) *chsd ldrs: rdn 3f out: wknd over 2f out* **33/1**

2m 13.51s (4.71) **Going Correction** +0.275s/f (Good) **6** Ran SP% **109.5**
Speed ratings (Par 104): **92,90,88,85,85 77**
Swingers:1&2:£2.40, 2&3:£2.80, 1&3:£1.40 CSF £9.63 TOTE £1.80: £1.20, £2.50; EX 9.10.
Owner Lady Rothschild **Bred** Kincorth Investments Inc **Trained** Newmarket, Suffolk

FOCUS
No huge stars have emerged from this in the past and only Eleanora Duse, who subsequently landed an Irish Group 2, has managed another success after winning here since 2002. The time was modest and this looked a pretty ordinary race for the grade. The winner made all, which was the best place to be.

NOTEBOOK
Great Heavens looked to have a serious amount of potential considering her pedigree, let alone her racecourse achievements, and was allowed to dictate at an ordinary gallop. William Buick gradually wound things up and the filly kept finding for pressure, ultimately running out a clear winner. It remains to be seen if she can get another success in her profile considering the aforementioned record of this race, but she really should do and appears to appreciate some ease in the ground. (op 5-4 tchd 6-4)

Miss Cato was one of the worst sufferers of the slow gallop, tending to pull hard under restraint, but still had something left to give Great Heavens a fright at the furlong pole. She earned some valuable black type, not bad for a filly who started off her career by winning a seller in January, but it would appear that her future now lies in America. (op 15-2)

Albamara, not seen since finishing last of eight in the Fillies' Mile the previous September, got a bit outpaced while in behind but did keep on nicely when it was all too late. (tchd 2-1)

Apothecary, comfortably held by Vow in the Lingfield Oaks Trial on her last start, was trying turf for the first time and tended to travel a shade keenly early. She had her chance but wasn't good enough. (op 10-1 tchd 12-1)

Devine Guest(IRE) showed promise on her only start back in April at this course and didn't do too badly here after getting stuck in a pocket for a few strides when the tempo was quickening. Any ordinary maiden ought to be within her grasp at this time of the year. (op 8-1 tchd 9-1)

Villa Royale, off since early December, dropped right away and has plenty to prove. (tchd 40-1)

3070 REISSER MAIDEN FILLIES' STKS 1m 2f 6y
4:00 (4:00) (Class 4) 3-Y-O **£4,075** (£1,212; £606; £303) **Stalls** Centre

Form RPR
-322 **1** **Perfect Delight**[30] [2148] 3-9-0 83 ... JohnFahy 2 83
(Clive Cox) *trckd ldrs: chal 2f out: slt ld 1f out: hrd pressed ins fnl f: asserted fnl 75yds* **5/2**[1]
02-0 **2** *½* **Coplow**[28] [2201] 3-9-0 80 ... KieranO'Neill 9 82
(Richard Hannon) *trckd ldr: slt ld ins fnl 3f: rdn and narrowly hdd 1f out: styd pressing wnr tl outpcd fnl 75yds* **11/2**[3]
442 **3** *2 ¾* **Gold Show**[17] [2560] 3-9-0 86 ... MatthewDavies 4 76
(Mick Channon) *chsd ldrs: chal fr 2f out tl outpcd by ldng duo appr fnl f* **6/1**
3-43 **4** *6* **La Pampita (IRE)**[29] [2172] 3-9-0 76 ... HayleyTurner 1 64
(William Knight) *led: narrowly hdd ins fnl 3f: sn rdn: wknd over 1f out* **11/1**
5 *6* **We Used To Wait (USA)** 3-9-0 0 ... RichardHughes 8 52
(Peter Chapple-Hyam) *in tch: rdn 3f out: sn btn* **16/1**
2-34 **6** *½* **Disposition**[24] [2344] 3-9-0 79 ... WilliamBuick 3 51
(John Gosden) *in tch: rdn and effrt appr fnl 3f: btn sn after* **7/2**[2]
7 *nk* **Positively** 3-9-0 0 ... JimmyFortune 10 50
(Sir Michael Stoute) *in rr: drvn along 3f out: mod late prog* **6/1**
5-6 **8** *11* **Easter Diva (IRE)**[28] [2200] 3-9-0 0 ... JimCrowley 5 28
(Amanda Perrett) *in rr: rdn and brief effrt over 3f out: nvr in contention and sn dropped away* **25/1**

2m 11.77s (2.97) **Going Correction** +0.275s/f (Good) **8** Ran SP% **112.8**
Speed ratings (Par 98): **99,98,96,91,86 86,86,77**
Swingers:1&2:£3.60, 2&3:£6.20, 1&3:£2.40 CSF £16.09 TOTE £3.50: £1.20, £2.10, £1.50; EX 16.90 Trifecta £65.40 Pool: £973.31 - 10.99 winning units..
Owner Mildmay Racing & D H Caslon **Bred** Mildmay Bloodstock Ltd **Trained** Lambourn, Berks

FOCUS
With three of these fillies rated 80 or higher, this ought to be a useful contest. It was the fastest of the three C&D times and the form looks sound. The winner is rated to her best.

3071 BE WISER INSURANCE H'CAP 7f (S)
4:30 (4:33) (Class 5) (0-75,75) 3-Y-O **£2,587** (£770; £384; £192) **Stalls** Centre

Form RPR
-050 **1** **Shamrocked (IRE)**[26] [2265] 3-9-2 70 ... MatthewDavies 8 79
(Mick Channon) *mde all: rdn fnl f: hrd pressed fnl 120yds: kpt on wl clsng stages* **10/1**
2366 **2** *nk* **Pashan Garh**[23] [2361] 3-9-1 69 ... LukeMorris 5 77
(Pat Eddery) *chsd ldrs: wnt 2nd 2f out: hrd rdn to press wnr fnl 120yds: styd on one pce* **14/1**
0-40 **3** *3 ¾* **Halling Dancer**[21] [2428] 3-9-0 75 ... WilliamTwiston-Davies(7) 2 73
(Lee Carter) *chsd ldrs: disp 2nd over 2f out tl over 1f out: outpcd fnl f* **4/1**[2]
2-65 **4** *4* **Intomist (IRE)**[14] [2628] 3-8-3 62 ... NathanAlison(5) 9 50
(Jim Boyle) *chsd ldrs: rdn over 2f out: sn outpcd* **16/1**
4-05 **5** *nse* **More Than Words (IRE)**[24] [2332] 3-9-5 73 ... RichardHughes 6 61+
(Richard Hannon) *hld up in rr: pushed along and hdwy fr 2f out: kpt on fnl f: nvr gng pce to get into contention* **6/1**[3]
05-0 **6** *3* **Superciliary**[17] [2542] 3-9-2 70 ... JimCrowley 1 50
(Ralph Beckett) *in tch: rdn over 2f out: sn btn* **7/2**[1]
10-6 **7** *hd* **Wordismybond**[28] [2206] 3-8-13 67 ... WilliamBuick 11 47
(Peter Makin) *t.k.h: disp 2nd: rdn 2f out: sn btn* **7/1**
006- **8** *1* **Greatest Dancer (IRE)**[287] [5637] 3-8-13 67 ... HayleyTurner 3 44
(Jamie Osborne) *in rr: drvn along over 2f out: mod prog fnl f* **25/1**
000- **9** *½* **Plum Bay**[327] [4330] 3-8-6 60 ... KieranO'Neill 4 36
(David Elsworth) *a towards rr* **16/1**
-060 **10** *½* **Fortrose Academy (IRE)**[16] [2583] 3-8-13 67 ... DavidProbert 10 41
(Andrew Balding) *chsd ldrs 4f* **15/2**
310- **11** *13* **Idols Eye**[230] [7135] 3-9-4 72 ... JamesDoyle 7 13
(Martyn Meade) *a in rr* **25/1**

1m 27.45s (1.75) **Going Correction** +0.225s/f (Good) **11** Ran SP% **116.0**
Speed ratings (Par 99): **99,98,94,89,89 86,86,84,84,83 68**
Swingers:1&2:£23.50, 2&3:£14.00, 1&3:£9.90 CSF £139.46 CT £660.35 TOTE £12.20: £3.50, £5.10, £1.10; EX 177.70 TRIFECTA Not won..
Owner Box 41 **Bred** Lodge Park Stud **Trained** West Ilsley, Berks

FOCUS
A fair contest in which it paid to race handily. It rather lacked improving types and the form is rated loosely around the third.

3072 INSURE WISER H'CAP 1m 4f 5y
5:05 (5:05) (Class 5) (0-75,75) 3-Y-O **£2,587** (£770; £384; £192) **Stalls** Centre

Form RPR
221 **1** **Nicholascopernicus (IRE)**[6] [2885] 3-9-7 75 6ex ... WilliamBuick 3 93+
(Ed Walker) *hld up in tch: stdy hdwy to trck ldr 3f out: chal on bit wl over 2f out: sn led: shkn up and clr ins fnl f: eased clsng stages* **4/7**[1]
-041 **2** *1 ¼* **Dovils Date**[21] [2424] 3-9-0 68 ... JamesMillman 8 77
(Rod Millman) *slowly away: in rr but sn in tch: rdn and hdwy to chse ldrs 3f out: wnt 2nd appr fnl f: nvr any ch but clsd on eased down wnr clsng stages* **15/2**[3]
663 **3** *2 ¼* **Sign Manual**[23] [2368] 3-9-4 72 ... HayleyTurner 5 76
(Michael Bell) *in rr: hdwy 3f out: rdn to dispute 2nd wl over 1f out: styd on same pce fnl f* **12/1**
0-66 **4** *4 ½* **Poetic Power (IRE)**[22] [2393] 3-9-7 75 ... DavidProbert 9 72
(David Elsworth) *led after 2f: rdn 3f out: jnd by wnr 2f out: sn hdd: wknd over 1f out* **10/1**
0010 **5** *8* **Run Of The Day**[7] [2850] 3-8-5 59 ... ChrisCatlin 7 43
(Eve Johnson Houghton) *in tch rdn over 3f out: nvr gng pce to rch ldrs: sn btn* **40/1**
2-30 **6** *2 ½* **My Destination (IRE)**[23] [2372] 3-9-7 75 ... (b[1]) RoystonFfrench 2 55
(Ismail Mohammed) *led 2f: chsd ldr to 6f out: wknd over 3f out* **28/1**
4346 **7** *52* **Dynastic**[34] [2038] 3-9-5 73 ... RichardHughes 1
(Richard Hannon) *chsd ldrs wnt 2nd 6f out: wknd 3f out* **7/1**[2]

2m 41.82s (6.32) **Going Correction** +0.275s/f (Good) **7** Ran SP% **110.6**
Speed ratings (Par 99): **89,88,86,83,78 76,42**
Swingers:1&2:£2.00, 2&3:£3.30, 1&3:£3.00 CSF £5.03 CT £22.56 TOTE £1.40: £1.20, £2.30; EX 4.30 Trifecta £13.60 Pool: £1,048.45 - 56.95 winning units..
Owner Greenwood, Halsall and Pegum **Bred** Mrs E J O'Grady **Trained** Newmarket, Suffolk

FOCUS
This can often produce a decent stayer, indeed three of the winners since 2005 have gone on to contest the Melbourne Cup as older horses, Bauer standing out as being the best. The heavily eased winner was value for 6l and the form seems sound enough.

3073 BE WISER INSURANCE GENTLEMAN AMATEUR RIDERS' H'CAP 1m 2f 6y
5:35 (5:35) (Class 5) (0-70,70) 4-Y-O+ **£2,495** (£774; £386; £193) **Stalls** Centre

Form RPR
430- **1** **Sula Two**[262] [6405] 5-10-10 64 ... PhilipPrince(5) 1 84
(Ron Hodges) *trckd ldr: led 3f out: c wl clr fr 2f out: pushed out fnl f* **6/1**[3]
3-24 **2** *15* **Cuckoo Rock (IRE)**[22] [2389] 5-10-3 59 ... (p) MrJHarding(7) 2 51
(Jonathan Portman) *in rr: lost tch and last 5f out: hdwy on ins fr 3f out: styd on to chse wnr wl over 1f out but nvr any ch* **7/2**[2]
0046 **3** *2* **Merrjanah**[9] [2796] 4-9-11 53 ... MrAFrench(7) 3 41
(John Wainwright) *chsd ldrs: wnt 2nd 3f out: sn drvn and no ch w wnr: lost 2nd wl over 1f out* **25/1**
1445 **4** *6* **Mustajed**[31] [2137] 11-10-1 55 ... (b) MrPMillman(5) 5 31
(Rod Millman) *in rr: pushed along over 3f out: styd on fr 2f out: nvr gng pce to get into contention* **10/1**
3-12 **5** *1 ¾* **Spartan Spirit (IRE)**[77] [1083] 4-10-12 66 ... MrRPooles(5) 10 39
(Hughie Morrison) *t.k.h in rr: sme hdwy and drvn 3f out: nvr gng pce to get into contention and sn no ch* **11/4**[1]
2163 **6** *7* **Sail Home**[19] [2498] 5-11-7 70 ... MrRBirkett 6 30
(Julia Feilden) *in tch: rdn 3f out and sn btn* **13/2**
2104 **7** *nk* **Byrd In Hand (IRE)**[6] [2886] 5-10-10 62 ... MrCMartin(3) 9 21
(John Bridger) *chsd ldrs: rdn 4f out: wknd ins fnl 3f* **6/1**[3]
000- **8** *14* **Transfer**[148] [7441] 7-10-10 62 ... MrMPrice(3) 4
(Richard Price) *rdn 4f out: a in rr* **16/1**
4400 **9** *10* **Rosy Dawn**[5] [2937] 7-9-7 51 oh6 ... MrAJones(7) 7
(John Bridger) *led at str pce: hdd 3f out: wknd rapidly* **33/1**

2m 13.66s (4.86) **Going Correction** +0.275s/f (Good) **9** Ran SP% **112.6**
Speed ratings (Par 103): **91,79,77,72,71 65,65,54,46**
Swingers:1&2:£5.60, 2&3:£16.90, 1&3:£24.50 CSF £26.44 CT £482.28 TOTE £6.90: £2.40, £2.40, £8.20; EX 37.90 Trifecta £582.10 Part won. Pool: £786.69 - 0.20 winning units..
Owner Richard Prince **Bred** D R Tucker **Trained** Charlton Mackrell, Somerset

FOCUS
Quite a range of ability on show here, but the early pace set by Rosy Dawn was suicidal and ensured the field finished strung out. The winner is rated back to his old best, and is clearly worth more at face value.

T/Plt: £40.20 to a £1 stake. Pool: £51,569.00 - 935.61 winning tickets. T/Qpdt: £5.40 to a £1 stake. Pool: £3,235.00 - 436.21 winning tickets. ST

2815 NOTTINGHAM (L-H)
Thursday, June 14

OFFICIAL GOING: Good (good to soft in places; 7.4)
Outside (summer) course used and bottom bend moved out adding about 15yds to distances on round course.
Wind: Moderate across Weather: Cloudy with sunny periods

3074 BRITISH STALLION STUDS SUPPORTING BRITISH RACING EBF MAIDEN STKS 6f 15y
2:00 (2:02) (Class 5) 2-Y-O **£3,234** (£962; £481; £240) **Stalls** High

Form RPR
1 **Rayaheen** 2-8-12 0 ... PaulHanagan 13 83+
(Richard Hannon) *led early: cl up: effrt wl over 1f out: qcknd to ld appr fnl f: sn clr* **7/2**[2]
45 **2** *2 ½* **Star Of Rohm**[16] [2587] 2-9-3 0 ... PaulMulrennan 2 78
(Michael Bell) *qckly away and swtchd rt towards stands' rail: sn led: rdn wl over 1f out: hdd appr fnl f and kpt on same pce* **11/2**[3]
2 **3** *nk* **Super Simon (IRE)**[7] [2844] 2-9-3 0 ... NeilCallan 7 77
(Paul D'Arcy) *midfield: hdwy over 2f out: rdn along wl over 1f out: styd on ins fnl f: nrst fin* **10/1**
4 *1* **Yourartisonfire** 2-9-0 0 ... MichaelMetcalfe(3) 1 74+
(Mrs K Burke) *dwlt: sn prom: cl up 1/2-way: effrt over 2f out: sn rdn and ev ch tl wknd ent fnl f* **18/1**
5 **5** *2 ½* **Gworn**[17] [2550] 2-9-3 0 ... MickaelBarzalona 3 67+
(Ed Dunlop) *chsd ldrs on outer: effrt over 2f out: sn rdn: edgd lft and wknd over 1f out* **11/4**[1]
6 *1* **It's Taboo** 2-8-12 0 ... DaneO'Neill 4 59
(Mark Usher) *dwlt and towards rr: hdwy over 2f out: styd on fnl f: nrst fin* **100/1**

7 1 1/2 **Al Muntazah (IRE)** 2-9-3 0 CathyGannon 8 59
(Ronald Harris) *towards rr: hdwy and in tch 2f out: sn rdn and no imp* **40/1**

8 1 **Corn Snow (USA)** 2-9-3 0 SilvestreDeSousa 11 56
(Mahmood Al Zarooni) *t.k.h: trckd ldrs: effrt over 2f out: sn rdn and wknd over 1f out* **9/1**

9 nse **Zhuba (IRE)** 2-9-3 0 GeorgeBaker 9 56
(John Best) *chsd ldrs: rdn along over 2f out: sn wknd* **9/1**

0 10 1 1/4 **Winged Icarus (USA)**[23] 2376 2-9-3 0 IPoullis 6 55+
(Alan McCabe) *midfield: hdwy on wd outside and in tch 2f out: sn rdn and wknd: eased fnl f* **33/1**

11 nse **My Sweet Lord** 2-9-3 0 RichardKingscote 12 52
(Mark Usher) *s.i.s: a in rr* **100/1**

12 4 1/2 **Teetotal (IRE)** 2-9-3 0 KellyHarrison 10 38
(Nigel Tinkler) *a towards rr* **100/1**

13 11 **Trapeze** 2-8-12 0 NickyMackay 14
(John Gosden) *sn outpcd and bhd fr 1/2-way* **10/1**

14 2 **Salute To Seville (IRE)** 2-8-12 0 LiamKeniry 5
(J S Moore) *in tch: pushed along bef 1/2-way: sn wknd* **100/1**

1m 13.6s (-1.30) **Going Correction** -0.30s/f (Firm) **14** Ran SP% **117.1**
Speed ratings (Par 93): **96,92,92,90,87 86,84,82,82,81 81,75,60,57**
Swingers:1&2:£4.10, 2&3:£6.20, 1&3:£4.40 CSF £22.04 TOTE £4.70: £1.50, £2.30, £3.50; EX 16.70.
Owner Hamdan Al Maktoum **Bred** Shadwell Estate Company Limited **Trained** East Everleigh, Wilts

FOCUS
An interesting juvenile contest began proceedings, featuring runners with an experience advantage taking on some well-bred newcomers. They went an even pace and the winning time of just over a second slower than standard suggests the ground is generally good with slight cut. The winner impressed and the baclance of the next two sets the level.

NOTEBOOK
Rayaheen ◆ had the benefit of the rail to race against and ran out a pleasing winner on debut. The daughter of Nayef was always in a prominent position and lengthened clear of her field inside the final furlong in easy fashion. She is the first foal of Natagora (5f juvenile and 1000 Guineas winner) and holds an entry in the Queen Mary Stakes at Royal Ascot. It will be surprising if connections decide to drop her in trip, though, unless it is riding really testing in Berkshire, and a step up to 7f in better company looks more likely later in the season. (op 4-1)
Star Of Rohm failed to build on a pleasing fourth on his debut at York (6f, good) in May, when fifth on faster ground over 5f at Ripon later that month. This display was more like it though, and he should be capable of winning his maiden under similar conditions. (tchd 6-1)
Super Simon(IRE) was touched off over this 6f trip on good to soft ground at Lingfield on his debut earlier this month and has gone the right way for that initial experience. He is already looking for 7f and should go well over that trip later this season. (tchd 12-1)
Yourartisonfire reportedly impressed in the paddock and made a pleasing debut despite a slightly slow start. (op 20-1 tchd 12-1)
Gworn appeared inconvenienced by racing on the outside from a low draw. He failed to build on a decent Leicester (6f, good to firm) debut in May. (op 7-2 tchd 5-2)
Corn Snow(USA)'s rider reported that the colt's saddle had slipped during the race. Official explanation: jockey said that the colt's saddle had slipped during the race (op 8-1)
My Sweet Lord's rider reported that the gelding had missed the break. Official explanation: jockey said that the gelding had missed the break

3075 MAGNERS H'CAP (DIV I) 6f 15y
2:30 (2:31) (Class 6) (0-65,65) 3-Y-O+ **£1,940** (£577; £288; £144) **Stalls** High

Form RPR

2655 1 **Dancing Welcome**[3] 2973 6-10-0 **64** (b) RichardKingscote 1 74
(Milton Bradley) *trckd ldr: cl up 2f out: rdn to ld 1 1/2f out: sn clr: kpt on* **10/3**[3]

5-01 2 2 **Full Shilling (IRE)**[10] 2761 4-10-1 **65** 6ex NeilCallan 5 69+
(John Spearing) *bmpd s: hld up: n.m.r and swtchd lft to outer 2f out: rdn to chse wnr and hung bdly rt 1f out: sn no imp* **5/2**[1]

4-50 3 3 **Bartley**[57] 1441 3-9-2 **60** (p) TomEaves 2 52
(Bryan Smart) *trckd ldng pair: effrt 2f out: rdn along whn hmpd 1f out: kpt on same pce* **18/1**

2-15 4 3/4 **Les Verguettes (IRE)**[127] 473 4-9-12 **62** GeorgeBaker 10 54
(Chris Wall) *hld up: hdwy 2f out: rdn over 1f out and sn one pce* **3/1**[2]

150- 5 1 1/2 **Ridgeway Sapphire**[286] 5677 5-8-9 **50** (v) LeeNewnes(5) 4 37
(Mark Usher) *trckd ldng pair: rdn along 2f out: wkng whn n.m.r 1f out* **22/1**

4600 6 1/2 **Dancing Maite**[8] 2815 7-10-0 **64** (b) AmirQuinn 3 50
(Roy Bowring) *led: rdn along 2f out: hdd 1 1/2f out and sn wknd* **10/1**

4300 7 2 1/2 **Red Scintilla**[27] 2239 5-8-13 **49** (v[1]) SilvestreDeSousa 7 27
(Nigel Tinkler) *bmpd s: towards rr: rdn along and outpcd fr 1/2-way* **8/1**

66- 8 11 **Zafonic Star**[229] 7174 3-9-6 **64** MichaelO'Connell 8
(Ian Williams) *s.i.s: in rr and pushed along after 2f: sn outpcd and bhd* **12/1**

1m 13.71s (-1.19) **Going Correction** -0.30s/f (Firm)
WFA 3 from 4yo+ 8lb **8** Ran SP% **114.2**
Speed ratings (Par 101): **95,92,88,87,85 84,81,66**
Swingers:1&2:£4.60, 2&3:£29.20, 1&3:£20.20 CSF £12.06 CT £126.89 TOTE £4.20: £1.30, £1.60, £3.80; EX 12.70.
Owner J M Bradley **Bred** The Hon Mrs E J Wills **Trained** Sedbury, Gloucs

FOCUS
The first division of a modest sprint handicap. The winning time was marginally slower than that of the filly who won the juvenile race on her debut over the same C&D half-an-hour earlier. All four sprints were won from the front and the winner is rated back to her best.
Dancing Maite Official explanation: jockey said that the gelding had lost its action
Zafonic Star Official explanation: jockey said that the gelding was slowly away and hung left-handed throughout

3076 MAGNERS H'CAP (DIV II) 6f 15y
3:05 (3:06) (Class 6) (0-65,65) 3-Y-O+ **£1,940** (£577; £288; £144) **Stalls** High

Form RPR

4312 1 **Big Wave (IRE)**[42] 1788 4-9-13 **64** NeilCallan 5 73+
(Alison Hutchinson) *t.k.h: sn led: rdn clr ent fnl f: kpt on* **2/1**[1]

0-01 2 1 **Errigal Lad**[8] 2815 7-9-4 **55** 6ex KellyHarrison 2 61+
(Garry Woodward) *s.i.s and bhd: hdwy 2f out: sn rdn and styd on strly fnl f: nt rch wnr* **4/1**[2]

0254 3 hd **Yanza**[10] 2761 6-8-8 **50** LauraPike(5) 9 55
(Pam Ford) *trckd ldrs: effrt 2f out: sn rdn: chsd wnr ent fnl f: sn drvn and kpt on* **8/1**

40-6 4 3 1/4 **Reginald Claude**[21] 2413 4-9-7 **63** LeeNewnes(5) 7 58
(Mark Usher) *in tch: hdwy on outer 2f out: sn rdn and kpt on fnl f* **8/1**

5-00 5 shd **Ever The Optimist (IRE)**[21] 2421 4-9-6 **57** DaneO'Neill 4 51
(Tony Newcombe) *in tch: hdwy 2f out: sn rdn and no imp fnl f* **7/1**[3]

004/ 6 2 1/2 **Louis Vee (IRE)**[653] 5644 4-8-10 **47** LiamKeniry 1 33
(Ed de Giles) *a towards rr* **25/1**

0P-0 7 2 3/4 **Jack Smudge**[19] 2475 4-9-9 **65** ShaneBKelly(5) 3 42
(James Given) *chsd ldrs: rdn along wl over 1f out: sn wknd* **16/1**

060- 8 2 1/2 **Our Monica (IRE)**[224] 7252 3-8-1 **46** oh1 SilvestreDeSousa 6 13
(Ian Williams) *cl up: rdn along 2f out: sn wknd* **11/1**

/05- 9 2 1/4 **Depden (IRE)**[511] 233 4-8-7 **47** oh1 ow1 DaleSwift(3) 10
(Richard Price) *chsd ldrs: rdn along 1/2-way: sn wknd* **33/1**

645/ 10 11 **Berrymead**[801] 1112 7-8-8 **50** AnnStokell(5) 8
(Ann Stokell) *midfield: rdn along wl over 2f out: sn wknd* **33/1**

1m 13.86s (-1.04) **Going Correction** -0.30s/f (Firm)
WFA 3 from 4yo+ 8lb **10** Ran SP% **112.0**
Speed ratings (Par 101): **94,92,92,88,87 84,80,77,74,59**
Swingers:1&2:£1.80, 2&3:£3.80, 1&3:£4.00 CSF £8.88 CT £51.16 TOTE £2.50: £1.40, £1.40, £2.90; EX 7.00.
Owner Philip Carney **Bred** P De Vere Hunt **Trained** Exning, Suffolk
■ A first winner for trainer Alison Hutchinson with her first runner.

FOCUS
The second division of a lowly sprint handicap for 3yo plus. The winning time was marginally slower than the first division. The winner was less exposed than the rest and rates a small personal best.

3077 CAFFREYS H'CAP 1m 6f 15y
3:40 (3:40) (Class 5) (0-75,78) 4-Y-O+ **£2,264** (£673; £336; £168) **Stalls** Low

Form RPR

1111 1 **Bilidn**[5] 2925 4-9-13 **78** 6ex PaulHanagan 6 87+
(Noel Quinlan) *t.k.h: hld up in rr: hdwy on outer 3f out: rdn to ld over 1f out: styd on strly* **11/10**[1]

333- 2 2 1/4 **Suzi's A Class Act**[199] 7570 4-9-1 **66** (p) CathyGannon 1 70
(James Eustace) *hld up in rr: hdwy on inner 3f out: rdn wl over 1f out: chsd wnr ins fnl f: no imp towards fin* **7/1**

4-00 3 1 1/4 **Inside Knowledge (USA)**[83] 1011 6-8-2 **53** oh1 KellyHarrison 7 55
(Garry Woodward) *hld up towards rr: keen and hdwy after 4f: led after 6f: rdn along 3f out: drvn over 2f out: hdd over 1f out: kpt on same pce* **40/1**

0-24 4 1 1/4 **Henry San (IRE)**[26] 1505 5-9-4 **69** FergusSweeney 3 69
(Alan King) *trckd ldng pair: hdwy 4f out: cl up 3f out: rdn and ev ch over 2f out: drvn and one pce appr fnl f* **10/1**

2433 5 1 1/4 **Jamarjo (IRE)**[38] 1925 5-9-1 **66** (p) MickaelBarzalona 5 65
(Steve Gollings) *t.k.h: hld up: hdwy 4f out: rdn to chse ldrs wl over 2f out: sn drvn and one pce* **4/1**[2]

442/ 6 8 **Cubism**[25] 4990 6-8-9 **60** (t) KirstyMilczarek 2 47
(Brendan Powell) *prom: rdn along over 3f out: wknd wl over 2f out* **20/1**

46-3 7 3/4 **The Calling Curlew**[23] 2363 4-9-4 **69** DaneO'Neill 8 55
(Henry Candy) *led 6f: cl up: rdn 3f out: wknd 2f out* **13/2**[3]

3m 7.97s (1.67) **Going Correction** +0.175s/f (Good) **7** Ran SP% **109.7**
Speed ratings (Par 103): **102,100,100,99,98 94,93**
Swingers:1&2:£3.60, 2&3:£20.00, 1&3:£8.30 CSF £8.59 CT £165.81 TOTE £2.00: £1.50, £2.30; EX 6.90.
Owner Patrick Wilmott **Bred** Meon Valley Stud **Trained** Newmarket, Suffolk

FOCUS
An average staying handicap. The gallop was not strong but the winning time of nearly 11 secs slower than standard does suggest the ground was riding more akin to good to soft on the round course. There's a bit of doubt over how solid the form is given how slowly run the race was.
The Calling Curlew Official explanation: trainer could offer no explanation for the gelding's performance

3078 ABG LAW CLASSIC H'CAP 6f 15y
4:10 (4:12) (Class 2) (0-105,97) 4-Y-O+
£10,582 (£3,168; £1,584; £792; £396; £198) **Stalls** High

Form RPR

-000 1 **Damika (IRE)**[19] 2488 9-8-6 **82** (v[1]) PJMcDonald 3 93
(David Brown) *sn cl up: led over 3f out: rdn clr over 1f out: kpt on strly* **33/1**

-340 2 2 **Mon Brav**[19] 2507 5-8-7 **83** BarryMcHugh 10 88
(Brian Ellison) *led: hdd over 3f out: chsd wnr: rdn wl over 1f out: kpt on fnl f* **15/2**[3]

4540 3 1 1/4 **Docofthebay (IRE)**[52] 1558 8-9-1 **91** (b) FrederikTylicki 6 92+
(Scott Dixon) *towards rr: hdwy on outer 2f out: rdn over 1f out: styd on fnl f: nrst fin* **8/1**

5-00 4 hd **York Glory (USA)**[12] 2704 4-9-5 **95** (b) GrahamLee 11 95
(Kevin Ryan) *trckd ldrs: hdwy wl over 1f out: sn rdn and no imp fnl f* **9/4**[1]

1-30 5 shd **Steps (IRE)**[28] 2208 4-9-2 **92** NeilCallan 4 92
(Roger Varian) *trckd ldrs: effrt and n.m.r 2f out: sn swtchd lft and rdn: kpt on same pce* **9/2**[2]

4000 6 1/2 **Cheveton**[12] 2717 8-8-7 **86** DaleSwift(3) 1 84
(Richard Price) *prom: effrt over 2f out: sn rdn and ch tl drvn and one pce ent fnl f* **11/1**

2033 7 nk **Doc Hay (USA)**[15] 2602 5-9-7 **97** DanielTudhope 8 94
(David O'Meara) *dwlt and in rr: gd hdwy on inner 2f out: effrt and n.m.r over 1f out: sn rdn and n.d* **17/2**

50-3 8 1 1/2 **Piazza San Pietro**[20] 2446 6-9-2 **92** GeorgeBaker 7 91+
(Zoe Davison) *towards rr: hdwy over 2f out: rdn whn n.m.r over 1f out: n.d* **10/1**

0-04 9 nk **Swiss Cross**[12] 2707 5-9-5 **95** (t) RichardKingscote 9 87
(Phil McEntee) *cl up: rdn 2f out: grad wknd* **10/1**

0000 10 3 3/4 **Marine Commando**[26] 2284 4-8-11 **87** PaulHanagan 5 67
(Richard Fahey) *chsd ldrs: rdn along 2f out: sn wknd* **20/1**

0010 11 14 **Masked Dance (IRE)**[26] 2284 5-8-9 **85** (p) SilvestreDeSousa 2 20
(Scott Dixon) *prom: rdn along over 2f out: sn wknd* **20/1**

1m 11.74s (-3.16) **Going Correction** -0.30s/f (Firm) **11** Ran SP% **121.3**
Speed ratings (Par 109): **109,106,104,104,104 103,103,101,100,95 77**
Swingers:1&2:£39.50, 2&3:£11.10, 1&3:£41.30 CSF £266.22 CT £2239.41 TOTE £45.60: £9.50, £2.50, £2.50; EX 439.00.
Owner Miss Emily R Bullock **Bred** Patrick J Monahan **Trained** Averham Park, Notts

FOCUS
A decent sprint handicap for older horses and the feature on the card. The winning time was notably faster than standard and significantly quicker than the earlier races over the trip. The surprise winner bounced back to form from the front, with the second always in the front pair too.

NOTEBOOK
Damika(IRE) ◆ was taken straight to the front on the stands' rail from a modest draw and made all the running quite comfortably, despite his huge odds. He has won in Class 2 company on three previous occasions, including his last success over this trip at Ripon on good to soft ground off a 12lb higher rating in August 2010, and he put behind him three moderate efforts for new connections so far this season by bouncing back to form under suitable conditions wearing a first-time visor. He is entered up over the same trip in handicaps at Doncaster at the weekend and Thirsk next week. Provided the headgear has the same effect, he should go very well under a penalty in either contest. Official explanation: trainer said, reagarding the apparent improvement of form, that trainer's explanation that the gelding had benefitted from first time application of visor

Mon Brav raced prominently and had no excuses, but he remains in good form racing off a fair mark and looks likely to prove very competitive under similar conditions this summer. (op 9-1)
Docofthebay(IRE) headed a bunch finish contesting the minor honours and is nearing his last winning handicap mark over 1f further in October 2010. (op 9-1 tchd 10-1)
York Glory(USA) took a while to get a clear passage but failed to pick up as well as seemed likely. (op 5-2 tchd 11-4)
Steps(IRE) ◆ performed perfectly respectably having not had a clear run and being forced to make his effort more towards the centre of the track, and remains of interest under these conditions. (op 5-1 tchd 4-1)
Piazza San Pietro's rider reported that the gelding had been denied a clear run. Official explanation: jockey said that the gelding had been denied a clear run (op 9-1 tchd 11-1)

3079 CARLING ZEST MAIDEN STKS — 1m 75y
4:45 (4:47) (Class 5) 3-Y-0+ — **£2,264** (£673; £336; £168) **Stalls** Centre

Form — RPR

6-2 **1** **Razorbill (USA)**[17] 2553 3-9-0 0 ... MichaelHills 5 — 88+
(Charles Hills) *trckd ldrs on inner: hdwy over 3f out: led wl over 1f out: sn edgd rt and clr: eased towards fin* **5/4**[1]

2 4½ **Ruwaiyan (USA)** 3-9-0 0 ... SilvestreDeSousa 13 — 75+
(Mahmood Al Zarooni) *prom: led over 3f out: rdn over 2f out: hdd wl over 1f out and sn one pce* **5/1**[2]

3 nk **Voice From Above (IRE)** 3-8-9 0 ... DuranFentiman 7 — 69
(Patrick Holmes) *dwlt and towards rr: hdwy 1/2-way: rdn over 2f out: styd on wl appr fnl f: nrst fin* **200/1**

03 **4** 1¼ **Ascription (IRE)**[9] 2799 3-9-0 0 ... PaulMulrennan 10 — 71
(Ed Dunlop) *trckd ldrs: hdwy 3f out: rdn to chse ldng pair over 2f out: wknd wl over 1f out* **11/2**[3]

5 2¼ **Missouri Belle** 3-8-9 0 ... NickyMackay 8 — 61
(John Gosden) *towards rr: hdwy wl over 2f out: sn rdn and kpt on: nvr nr ldrs* **20/1**

6 1 **Chemistry Master** 4-9-11 0 ... RobertWinston 6 — 67+
(Jeremy Gask) *s.i.s and bhd: hdwy wl over 2f out: sn rdn and styd on: n.d* **50/1**

00 **7** ¾ **Fuzzy Logic (IRE)**[26] 2266 3-9-0 0 ... NeilCallan 3 — 62
(William Muir) *in tch: rdn along 3f out: sn no hdwy* **66/1**

03 **8** 4 **Azerodegree (IRE)**[9] 2800 3-9-0 0 ... FrannyNorton 2 — 53+
(Marco Botti) *towards rr tl sme late hdwy* **11/1**

4 **9** 4 **Thereabouts (USA)**[23] 2381 3-9-0 0 ... DaneO'Neill 11 — 43
(Marco Botti) *t.k.h: chsd ldrs: rdn along 3f out: sn wknd* **7/1**

0-0 **10** 2¾ **Alnoomaas (IRE)**[17] 2542 3-9-0 0 ... MarcHalford 9 — 37
(Ronald Harris) *led: rdn along and hdd over 3f out: sn wknd* **66/1**

5- **11** 5 **Spellmaker**[183] 7749 3-9-0 0 ... FergusSweeney 14 — 26
(Tony Newcombe) *s.i.s: a in rr* **50/1**

00 **12** ½ **Craniac**[45] 1716 5-9-11 0 ... (t) CathyGannon 4 — 27
(Frank Sheridan) *s.i.s: a in rr* **250/1**

00 **13** 63 **Manaar (USA)**[44] 1736 3-8-9 0 ... PaulHanagan 12
(John Gosden) *prom on outer: pushed along bef 1/2-way: sn lost pl and bhd fnl 3f* **14/1**

1m 46.36s (0.76) **Going Correction** +0.175s/f (Good)
WFA 3 from 4yo+ 11lb — **13** Ran SP% **116.6**
Speed ratings (Par 103): **103,98,98,96,94 93,92,88,84,82 77,76,13**
Swingers:1&2:£3.20, 2&3:£85.50, 1&3:£23.90 CSF £6.91 TOTE £2.80: £1.40, £3.00, £17.90; EX 10.50.
Owner K Abdulla **Bred** Juddmonte Farms Inc **Trained** Lambourn, Berks

FOCUS
Some noteworthy formlines converged in this 1m maiden for 3yo plus. The winning time was nearly four seconds slower than standard, which confirms the round course is riding much slower than the stands' side of the straight course. The winner set an above average standard and was value for a bit extra.
Manaar(USA) Official explanation: jockey said that the filly had a breathing problem

3080 GALLIFORD TRY FILLIES' H'CAP — 1m 2f 50y
5:15 (5:15) (Class 5) (0-75,75) 3-Y-0 — **£2,264** (£673; £336; £168) **Stalls** Low

Form — RPR

10- **1** **Ambivalent (IRE)**[253] 6623 3-9-4 72 ... [1] NeilCallan 8 — 90+
(Roger Varian) *hld up in rr: smooth hdwy 1/2-way: trckd ldrs 3f out: led 2f out: pushed clr ent fnl f: easily* **5/2**[1]

-313 **2** 5 **Dutch Diamond**[28] 2201 3-9-7 75 ... NickyMackay 1 — 80+
(John Gosden) *trckd ldrs: hdwy on inner over 4f out: led 3f out: rdn and hdd 2f out: sn drvn and kpt on same pce* **3/1**[2]

-312 **3** 8 **Mistress Of Rome**[30] 2144 3-9-2 70 ... PaulMulrennan 3 — 60
(Michael Dods) *chsd ldrs: rdn along and outpcd 3f out: drvn 2f out: kpt on one pce: tk mod 3rd nr fin* **4/1**[3]

55-2 **4** nse **Idyllic Star (IRE)**[45] 1716 3-9-1 69 ... LiamKeniry 6 — 59
(J S Moore) *prom: rdn along 3f out: drvn and one pce fnl 2f* **14/1**

1-00 **5** 1¾ **Napoleon's Muse (IRE)**[28] 2194 3-9-4 72 ... RichardKingscote 4 — 58
(Ralph Beckett) *prom on inner: led over 4f out: rdn along and hdd 3f out: drvn and one pce fnl 2f* **5/1**

0-40 **6** ½ **Indian Blossom**[44] 1737 3-8-2 56 oh1 ... KellyHarrison 2 — 41
(Harry Dunlop) *dwlt and in rr: hdwy 3f out: rdn and styd on fnl 2f: n.d* **50/1**

-100 **7** 19 **Arch Of Colours**[34] 2038 3-9-5 73 ... FrannyNorton 10 — 21
(Mark Johnston) *led: rdn along and hdd over 4f out: drvn over 3f out and sn wknd* **22/1**

01-6 **8** 1¼ **Forgive**[20] 2448 3-9-7 75 ... PatDobbs 5 — 21
(Richard Hannon) *in tch: rdn along wl over 3f out: sn wknd* **8/1**

00-0 **9** 20 **Sally Pepper (USA)**[23] 2374 3-8-2 56 oh5 ... (b[1]) JamesSullivan 9
(James Given) *chsd ldrs 3f: sn lost pl and bhd fnl 3f* **100/1**

2m 12.48s (0.78) **Going Correction** +0.175s/f (Good) — **9** Ran SP% **115.3**
Speed ratings (Par 96): **103,99,92,92,91 90,75,74,58**
Swingers:1&2:£2.80, 2&3:£3.40, 1&3:£4.50 CSF £10.01 CT £28.19 TOTE £4.20: £1.80, £1.10, £2.30; EX 13.60.
Owner Abdullah Saeed Belhab **Bred** Darley **Trained** Newmarket, Suffolk

FOCUS
A decent 1m2f fillies' handicap for the grade, confined to 3-y-os. Big improvement from the winner, but they were strung out and this is not easy form to pin down.
Mistress Of Rome Official explanation: jockey said that the filly hung left-handed throughout

3081 DG TAXIS GETTING YOU HOME SAFELY H'CAP — 1m 2f 50y
5:45 (5:45) (Class 6) (0-60,66) 4-Y-0+ — **£1,940** (£577; £288; £144) **Stalls** Low

Form — RPR

-500 **1** **Ela Gonda Mou**[20] 2465 5-9-7 60 ... RobertWinston 1 — 71
(Peter Charalambous) *trckd ldrs on inner: hdwy to ld over 3f out: rdn 2f out: drvn out* **11/2**[3]

6-63 **2** 2¼ **Barachiel**[8] 2821 4-9-7 60 ... MarcHalford 5 — 67
(Ronald Harris) *hld up in tch: hdwy over 3f out: chsd wnr over 2f out: rdn over 1f out: drvn and no imp ins fnl f* **5/1**[2]

64-0 **3** 5 **My Sister**[16] 653 5-8-2 46 ... RachealKneller(5) 4 — 43
(Mark Usher) *hld up towards rr: hdwy 3f out: rdn to chse ldng pair 2f out: sn drvn and no imp* **9/1**

0-10 **4** 3½ **Ptolomeos**[20] 2454 9-8-13 57 ... (p) AmyScott(5) 10 — 47
(Sean Regan) *dwlt and in rr: hdwy over 3f out: rdn over 2f out: kpt on appr fnl f: nvr gng pce to rch ldrs* **17/2**

10-0 **5** 1 **Brook Star (IRE)**[10] 2775 4-8-11 53 ... (p) LeeTopliss(3) 2 — 41
(Michael Dods) *led: rdn along and hdd over 3f out: drvn over 2f out and grad wknd* **20/1**

3006 **6** hd **John Potts**[11] 2735 7-9-7 60 ... KellyHarrison 8 — 48
(Brian Baugh) *in tch: hdwy 3f out: rdn along over 2f out: n.d* **25/1**

0-02 **7** 3½ **Penderyn**[34] 2048 5-8-0 45 ... JackDuern(7) 6 — 27
(Charles Smith) *prom: chsd ldr 1/2-way: rdn along on outer wl over 3f out: wknd wl over 2f out* **8/1**

5006 **8** 2 **Beetuna (IRE)**[7] 2858 7-9-1 59 ... (p) MarkCoumbe(5) 12 — 36
(Daniel Mark Loughnane) *dwlt and in rr: hdwy 3f out: rdn along over 2f out: n.d* **10/1**

63-0 **9** 38 **Greeley House**[27] 2233 4-9-7 60 ... GeorgeBaker 11
(Chris Wall) *hld up in tch: hdwy to trck ldrs over 4f out: rdn over 3f out: sn btn* **8/1**

0-0 **10** 17 **Reveal The Light**[86] 976 5-8-7 45 ... NickyMackay 3
(Garry Woodward) *cl up: rdn along over 4f out: sn wknd: t.o fnl 2f* **40/1**

2561 **11** 5 **Cane Cat (IRE)**[10] 2767 5-9-6 66 6ex ... (t) GeorgeDowning(7) 7
(Tony Carroll) *v.s.a and virtually ref to r: a t.o* **7/2**[1]

2m 13.02s (1.32) **Going Correction** +0.175s/f (Good) — **11** Ran SP% **117.2**
Speed ratings (Par 101): **101,99,95,92,91 91,88,87,56,43 39**
Swingers:1&2:£9.30, 2&3:£10.30, 1&3:£13.40 CSF £32.25 CT £245.88 TOTE £8.40: £2.90, £1.40, £3.20; EX 37.10.
Owner P Charalambous **Bred** Peter Charles **Trained** Newmarket, Suffolk

FOCUS
A lowly 1m2f handicap for older horses. The winner had slipped to a good mark and the first two were clear.
T/Plt: £88.80 to a £1 stake. Pool: £41,685.00 - 342.33 winning tickets. T/Qpdt: £47.10 to a £1 stake. Pool: £3,063.00 - 48.12 winning tickets. JR

3046 YARMOUTH (L-H)
Thursday, June 14

OFFICIAL GOING: Good to firm (7.7)
Back straight and bottom bend dolled out 3metres increasing distances on round course by 5metres.
Wind: medium, across Weather: bright and sunny

3082 £25 WELCOME BONUS AT BETVICTOR.COM MAIDEN STKS — 6f 3y
2:10 (2:17) (Class 5) 3-Y-0+ — **£2,264** (£673; £336; £168) **Stalls** Centre

Form — RPR

22-2 **1** **Tickled Pink (IRE)**[24] 2332 3-8-9 84 ... TomQueally 5 — 74+
(Sir Henry Cecil) *w ldr tl led on bit 2f out: pushed along hands and heels and in command fnl f: comf* **2/7**[1]

2 ¾ **Palmette** 3-8-9 0 ... RobertHavlin 1 — 71+
(John Gosden) *in tch: rdn and chsd ldng pair wl over 1f out: wnt 2nd ins fnl f: kpt on wl but a hld* **5/1**[2]

04 **3** 1¾ **Charity Box**[30] 2145 3-8-9 0 ... TedDurcan 2 — 65
(Chris Wall) *led at stdy gallop tl rdn and hdd wl over 1f out: styd on same pce after: lost 2nd ins fnl f* **16/1**

- **4** 3½ **Fairest (IRE)** 3-8-9 0 ... RyanMoore 4 — 54
(Jeremy Noseda) *hld up in tch: rdn and effrt over 2f out: outpcd and btn wl over 1f out: plugged on fnl f* **8/1**[3]

00 **5** ¾ **College Doll**[24] 2332 3-8-6 0 ... DominicFox(3) 3 — 51?
(Christine Dunnett) *t.k.h: chsd ldng pair: rdn over 2f out: outpcd and lost pl wl over 1f out: one pce and wl hld after* **200/1**

-600 **6** 11 **Luisa Tetrazzini (IRE)**[42] 1768 6-9-0 49 ... (b) AdamBeschizza(3) 6 — 16
(Terry Clement) *v awkward leaving stalls and rel to r: lost many l: clsd and in tch in midfield after 2f: rdn and wknd 2f out: bhd fnl f* **125/1**

1m 14.58s (0.18) **Going Correction** -0.20s/f (Firm)
WFA 3 from 6yo 8lb — **6** Ran SP% **112.7**
Speed ratings (Par 103): **90,89,86,82,81 66**
CSF £2.28 TOTE £1.30: £1.10, £2.20; EX 2.90.
Owner Trevor C Stewart **Bred** T Stewart **Trained** Newmarket, Suffolk

FOCUS
A modest maiden event, run at a sedate pace. The winner did not need to match her previous best.

3083 BETVICTOR FOR BEST PRICES CLASSIFIED STKS — 1m 3y
2:40 (2:43) (Class 6) 3-Y-0 — **£1,617** (£481; £240; £120) **Stalls** Centre

Form — RPR

4402 **1** **Speedi Mouse**[9] 2802 3-8-9 58 ... RaulDaSilva(5) 11 — 73
(Philip McBride) *hld up towards rr: swtchd lft and effrt 2f out: hdwy u.p to press ldrs over 1f out: led ins fnl f: hld on wl cl home* **5/2**[1]

606 **2** hd **Pursue**[23] 2380 3-9-0 65 ... (b[1]) LiamJones 13 — 72
(William Haggas) *hld up in tch: hdwy to chal 2f out: rdn to ld and hung rt ent fnl f: hdd ins fnl f: hung bk lft u.p but stl ev ch ins fnl f: hld cl home* **10/1**

36-0 **3** 3½ **Darling Grace**[30] 2143 3-9-0 65 ... RyanMoore 8 — 64+
(William Haggas) *hld up in tch: rdn and effrt 2f out: swtchd rt and drvn over 1f out: styd on u.p to snatch 3rd on line: no threat to ldng pair* **4/1**[2]

5-50 **4** nse **No Dominion (IRE)**[31] 2118 3-9-0 62 ... JamieSpencer 2 — 64
(James Given) *stdd s: hld up in rr: pushed along 1/2-way: swtchd lft and hdwy 2f out: chsd ldrs and drvn over 1f out: no ex and wknd fnl 100yds: lost 3rd on post* **8/1**

-003 **5** 3 **Inffiraaj (IRE)**[13] 2672 3-9-0 63 ... SamHitchcott 1 — 57
(Mick Channon) *in tch: jnd ldrs gng wl over 2f out: rdn over 1f out: sn drvn and nt qckn: fdd fnl 100yds* **15/2**

403 **6** shd **Madame St Clair (IRE)**[15] 2604 3-9-0 61 ... (b) ShaneKelly 10 — 57
(Brian Meehan) *chsd ldrs tl led over 3f out: rdn wl over 1f out: hdd ent fnl f: fdd fnl 100yds* **12/1**

05-0 **7** 12 **Tresabella**[9] 2802 3-9-0 30 ... PatCosgrave 12 — 29
(Michael Appleby) *stdd s: hld up in rr: hdwy 1/2-way: in midfield and rdn over 2f out: sn struggling: wknd over 1f out* **150/1**

0-03 **8** 2½ **Sangrail**[19] 2483 3-9-0 65 ... JackMitchell 5 — 24
(William Muir) *in tch: rdn and unable qck over 2f out: wknd u.p wl over 1f out: wl btn fnl f* **13/2**[3]

-240 **9** *1 ½* **White Flight**^{9} 2788 3-9-0 64 .... LeeNewman 4 20
(Jonathan Portman) *chsd ldrs: rdn and unable qck over 2f out: wknd wl over 1f out: wl btn fnl f* **22/1**

0300 **10** *5* **Dream Prospector**^{12} 2689 3-9-0 65 .... MartinDwyer 9
(James Tate) *t.k.h: chsd ldr tl 1/2-way: lost pl qckly u.p 3f out: bhd fnl 2f* **20/1**

4500 **11** *3* **Findeln**^{23} 2379 3-9-0 61 .... TomQueally 3
(Eve Johnson Houghton) *led tl over 3f out: sn lost pl: bhd fnl 2f* **25/1**

53-0 **12** *1* **Mae Rose Cottage (IRE)**^{24} 2344 3-9-0 61 .... DaraghO'Donohoe 6
(Barney Curley) *in tch in midfield: rdn and lost pl 3f out: bhd fnl 2f* **40/1**

1m 39.6s (-1.00) **Going Correction** -0.20s/f (Firm) 12 Ran SP% **117.6**
Speed ratings (Par 97): **97,96,93,93,90 90,78,75,74,69 66,65**
CSF £26.69 TOTE £4.00: £1.60, £3.70, £1.10; EX 36.40.
Owner P J McBride **Bred** Langham Hall Stud **Trained** Newmarket, Suffolk
■ Stewards' Enquiry : Liam Jones two-day ban: use of whip (28 and 29 June)

FOCUS
A low-grade classified stakes, run at a fair pace. Sound form for the grade.

3084 IN-PLAY EURO BETTING AT BETVICTOR (S) STKS 7f 3y
3:15 (3:17) (Class 6) 2-Y-O **£1,617** (£481; £240; £120) **Stalls** Centre

Form RPR

60 **1** **Missing Agent**^{66} 1253 2-8-11 0 .... ShaneKelly 7 55
(David Evans) *t.k.h: hld up in tch: swtchd lft and hdwy u.p over 1f out: chsd ldr ins fnl f: hrd drvn and r.o wl to ld towards fin* **20/1**

6251 **2** *½* **Tiger Sunset (IRE)**^{9} 2798 2-8-10 0 .... (p) AliceHaynes$^{(7)}$ 4 60
(J S Moore) *t.k.h: chsd ldr: pushed into ld over 1f out: hung rt and racing against stands' rail fnl f: rdn ins fnl f: hdd and no ex towards fin* **11/4**^{1}

050 **3** *2 ½* **Maypole Joe (IRE)**^{9} 2784 2-8-11 0 .... StevieDonohoe 1 48
(David Evans) *hld up in tch: rdn and effrt 2f out: drvn and chsd ldr 1f out tl ins fnl f: outpcd fnl 100yds* **3/1**^{2}

0 **4** *nse* **Believe In Me**^{28} 2193 2-8-3 0 .... AdamBeschizza$^{(3)}$ 5 42
(Julia Feilden) *sn led: rdn over 2f out: hdd and drvn over 1f out: hung rt and no ex fnl f* **20/1**

5 *5* **Pearl Of Phoenix** 2-8-6 0 .... TadhgO'Shea 3 29
(Jo Hughes) *in tch: rdn and effrt 2f out: unable qck over 1f out: sn wknd* **12/1**

6 *4 ½* **Ground To Garden** 2-8-1 0 .... RaulDaSilva$^{(5)}$ 6 18
(Gay Kelleway) *t.k.h: chsd ldrs tl rdn and unable qck jst over 2f out: wknd over 1f out* **11/4**^{1}

7 *8* **Eliya** 2-8-6 0 .... MircoDemuro 2
(Jo Hughes) *in tch in rr but looked to gng wl: reminders 4f out: lost tch 2f out* **6/1**^{3}

1m 28.93s (2.33) **Going Correction** -0.20s/f (Firm) 7 Ran SP% **109.8**
Speed ratings (Par 91): **78,77,74,74,68 63,54**
CSF £68.82 TOTE £30.20: £10.50, £2.80; EX 78.90.The winner was bought in for 4,800gns.
Owner Mrs E Evans **Bred** Jason Puckey **Trained** Pandy, Monmouths

FOCUS
A lowly juvenile seller, run only at a steady pace but it served up a good finish. The second and third set the level.

NOTEBOOK
Missing Agent just edged out the favourite. David Evans has an extremely good record with his runners in this grade and he enhanced that here with the relatively unfastened son of Misu Bond coming home fast and late to grab what had looked an unlikely success. The winner had been beaten a long way in this company on softer ground at his track last time and clearly benefited for this quicker surface. He stayed on powerfully and should have no problem seeing out a mile later in the campaign. A faster pace would also have suited. (op 12-1)
Tiger Sunset(IRE) traded at very low odds on the exchanges but was worn down in the dying strides. He had appeared to hold a decisive advantage when they hit the furlong but drifted across to the nearside rail, which had been considered the slowest part of the track. Stronger handling may have made the difference. (op 9-4)
Maypole Joe(IRE) ran with credit. (op 7-2)
Ground To Garden finished tamely and is one to avoid on this evidence. (op 7-2)

3085 SPAIN V IRELAND SPECIALS AT BETVICTOR.COM FILLIES' H'CAP 7f 3y
3:50 (3:52) (Class 4) (0-85,83) 3-Y-O+ **£4,075** (£1,212; £606; £303) **Stalls** Centre

Form RPR

2-10 **1** **Appealing (IRE)**^{68} 1215 3-9-3 82 .... AdamKirby 8 94
(Marco Botti) *t.k.h: chsd ldrs: rdn to ld over 1f out: clr and r.o wl fnl f: comf* **8/1**^{3}

01-3 **2** *2 ½* **Cantal**^{20} 2448 3-9-0 79 .... RyanMoore 4 83
(Sir Michael Stoute) *in tch: rdn and effrt to press ldrs wl over 1f out: outpcd by wnr 1f out: wnt 2nd and styd on same pce ins fnl f* **6/4**^{1}

0-04 **3** *nk* **Wahylah (IRE)**^{19} 2490 3-9-1 80 .... MartinDwyer 6 83
(Clive Brittain) *hld up in tch: rdn and effrt 2f out: kpt on wl u.p ins fnl f: no threat to wnr* **11/2**^{2}

5-10 **4** *1* **Dance Company**^{26} 2272 3-8-12 77 .... TomQueally 7 77
(William Knight) *hld up in tch: rdn 2f out: styd on u.p ins fnl f: no threat to wnr* **10/1**

350- **5** *1 ¼* **Saskia's Dream**^{260} 6457 4-9-0 76 .... LewisWalsh$^{(7)}$ 9 77
(Jane Chapple-Hyam) *w ldr tl led 5f out: rdn and hdd over 1f out: sn edgd lft and unable qck: wknd ins fnl f* **20/1**

50-0 **6** *½* **Mahkama (USA)**^{28} 2201 3-9-2 81 .... TedDurcan 1 77
(Saeed Bin Suroor) *t.k.h: hld up in tch in last trio: rdn and effrt over 1f out: styd on same pce and no imp fnl f* **33/1**

2-10 **7** *1 ¾* **Vivid Blue**^{26} 2272 3-8-12 77 .... LiamJones 5 68
(William Haggas) *led for 2f: chsd ldr tl wl over 1f out: sn rdn and unable qck: wknd ins fnl f* **11/2**^{2}

120- **8** *1* **Al Mayasah (IRE)**^{287} 5657 4-10-0 83 .... JamieSpencer 2 75
(David Simcock) *stdd s: t.k.h: hld up in tch in rr: rdn and effrt over 1f out: no prog and wl hld fnl f* **11/2**^{2}

-360 **9** *6* **Bobby's Doll**^{23} 2360 5-8-9 67 .... AdamBeschizza$^{(3)}$ 3 43
(Terry Clement) *hld up in tch in rr: rdn over 2f out: no rspnse and sn struggling: wknd over 1f out* **66/1**

1m 25.99s (-0.61) **Going Correction** -0.20s/f (Firm)
WFA 3 from 4yo+ 10lb 9 Ran SP% **115.6**
Speed ratings (Par 102): **95,92,91,90,89 88,86,85,78**
Swingers:1&2:£3.60, 2&3:£3.10, 1&3:£6.20 CSF £20.16 CT £74.45 TOTE £6.70: £2.50, £1.10, £2.40; EX 22.70.
Owner Miss Yvonne Jacques **Bred** Ms Michelle Lyons **Trained** Newmarket, Suffolk

FOCUS
Not the strongest of fillies' handicaps given the grad but the winner impressed and posted a clear turf best.

Mahkama(USA) Official explanation: jockey said that the filly ran too free

3086 BEST PRICES AT BETVICTOR.COM H'CAP 2m
4:20 (4:21) (Class 6) (0-60,60) 4-Y-O+ **£1,617** (£481; £240; £120) **Stalls** Centre

Form RPR

00-0 **1** **Waterford Star (IRE)**^{22} 2391 4-8-8 48 .... (v^{1}) JamieSpencer 1 57
(Ian Williams) *prom in main gp: clsd on ldr 3f out: rdn and ev ch 2f out: led over 1f out: sn drvn clr: kpt on fnl f* **5/1**^{3}

04-0 **2** *3 ¼* **Ponte Di Rosa**^{25} 151 4-8-12 52 .... StevieDonohoe 9 57
(Michael Appleby) *hld up wl off the pce in last quartet: rdn and effrt over 3f out: styng on and swtchd rt over 1f out: styd on wl fnl f to go 2nd fnl 75yds: no threat to wnr* **20/1**

00-6 **3** *1* **Old Boy Ted**^{20} 2468 4-7-13 46 .... RobJFitzpatrick$^{(7)}$ 11 50
(Mark H Tompkins) *s.i.s: hld up wl off the pce in last quartet: rdn over 3f out: hdwy over 2f out: kpt on wl ins fnl f to go 3rd towards fin: no threat to wnr* **33/1**

2614 **4** *¾* **Talbot Green**^{23} 2378 4-9-6 60 .... MartinDwyer 12 63
(William Muir) *chsd clr ldr: rdn along and clsd 3f out: led 2f out: sn hdd and unable qck: wknd ins fnl f and lost 2nd and 3rd fnl 75yds* **5/1**^{3}

0-00 **5** *1 ¾* **Mollyow (IRE)**^{9} 742 4-8-3 46 oh1 .... DominicFox$^{(3)}$ 5 47
(Terry Clement) *hld up wl off the pce in last quartet: rdn 3f out: hdwy and swtchd lft over 1f out: kpt on wl ins fnl f: nvr trbld ldrs* **10/1**

-402 **6** *4 ½* **Cotton Grass**^{20} 2468 4-9-6 60 .... EddieAhern 4 56
(Mark H Tompkins) *hld up off the pce in midfield: rdn and effrt over 3f out: plugged on same pce and no imp fr over 1f out* **3/1**^{1}

0632 **7** *½* **Rodrigo De Freitas (IRE)**^{23} 2371 5-9-3 56 .... (v) PatCosgrave 8 51
(Jim Boyle) *racd wl off the pce in midfield: hdwy to go prom in main gp and clsd on ldr 3f out: rdn to chse ldng pair 2f out: edgd lft and struggling over 1f out: wknd fnl f* **8/1**

000 **8** *7* **Spiritonthemount (USA)**^{29} 2175 7-8-4 46 .... (b) AdamBeschizza$^{(3)}$ 10 33
(Peter Hiatt) *v.s.a: sn rcvrd and led after 2f: sn clr: pushed along 4f out: rdn and hdd 2f out: sn wknd* **33/1**

500 **9** *36* **Omid**^{21} 2418 4-9-1 55 .... (t) TedDurcan 6
(Nicky Vaughan) *prom in main gp: rdn and struggling 4f out: wknd and wl bhd fnl 2f: eased ins fnl f: t.o* **14/1**

6663 **10** *1 ½* **Kavaloti (IRE)**^{51} 1588 8-9-7 60 .... (b) RyanMoore 2
(Gary Moore) *hld up wl off the pce in last quartet: no prog 4f out: wl bhd and eased fnl 2f: t.o* **9/2**^{2}

3m 34.44s (2.04) **Going Correction** -0.025s/f (Good)
WFA 4 from 5yo+ 1lb 10 Ran SP% **114.0**
Speed ratings (Par 101): **93,91,90,90,89 87,87,83,65,64**
Swingers:1&2:£22.20, 2&3:£44.50, 1&3:£11.70 CSF £98.81 CT £2911.21 TOTE £4.50: £1.90, £6.00, £8.20; EX 125.80.
Owner R S Brookhouse **Bred** Denis McDonnell **Trained** Portway, Worcs

FOCUS
A poor staying handicap, run at a furious pace. Not much solid form to race the rate around, but it appears sound enough.
Waterford Star(IRE) Official explanation: trainer's representative said, regarding the apparent improvment of form, that the gelding may have benefitted from a step up in trip to two miles from a mile and a half on its' previous run
Kavaloti(IRE) Official explanation: trainer's representative said that the gelding was unsuited by the good to firm ground

3087 BETVICTOR ON YOUR MOBILE H'CAP 1m 6f 17y
4:55 (4:55) (Class 5) (0-70,70) 3-Y-O **£2,264** (£673; £336; £168) **Stalls** Centre

Form RPR

3323 **1** **Somemothersdohavem**^{15} 2613 3-9-3 66 .... (p) AdamKirby 7 74
(John Ryan) *racd off the pce in midfield: clsd on ldr and 4th 2f out: swtchd rt 1f out: and drvn to chal ins fnl f: led fnl 50yds: r.o wl* **12/1**

-523 **2** *¾* **Cheviot Quest (IRE)**^{21} 2424 3-8-10 59 .... LeeNewman 3 66
(William Jarvis) *t.k.h early: chsd clr ldr: rdn and clsd on ldr over 2f out: drvn to ld ent fnl f: hdd and no ex fnl 50yds* **4/1**^{2}

-524 **3** *1* **Fleur De La Vie (IRE)**^{21} 2424 3-8-10 59 .... RyanMoore 2 64
(Ralph Beckett) *prom in main gp: chsd clr ldr 8f out: rdn 4f out: clsd on ldr over 2f out: pressing ldrs and drvn over 1f out: kpt on same pce ins fnl f* **5/2**^{1}

-210 **4** *1* **Key Gold**^{27} 2258 3-9-7 70 .... MircoDemuro 5 74
(Mark Johnston) *led: wnt clr 12f out: rdn over 2f out: drvn and hdd ent fnl f: no ex and lost 2 pls ins fnl f* **9/1**

2125 **5** *¾* **Quixote**^{30} 2144 3-9-4 67 .... MartinDwyer 11 70
(Clive Brittain) *racd off the pce in midfield: rdn 3f out: hdwy over 1f out: kpt on ins fnl f* **8/1**

0-56 **6** *¾* **Byron Blue (IRE)**^{15} 2605 3-9-2 65 .... JamieSpencer 10 69+
(Jamie Osborne) *stdd s: hld up wl off the pce in rr: hdwy and drvn 2f out: kpt on u.p fnl f: nt clr run and eased wl ins fnl f* **11/2**^{3}

0-05 **7** *shd* **Single Girl (IRE)**^{16} 2577 3-7-11 51 oh1 .... (p) RaulDaSilva$^{(5)}$ 8 53
(Jonathan Portman) *t.k.h early: hld up wl off the pce in last quartet: rdn and effrt over 2f out: styd on fnl f: nt pce to rch ldrs* **22/1**

-316 **8** *8* **Like Clockwork**^{24} 2333 3-8-11 60 .... EddieAhern 9 51
(Mark H Tompkins) *t.k.h: hld up wl off the pce in midfield: rdn and effrt 2f out: wknd over 1f out* **10/1**

3250 **9** *6* **Ctappers**^{21} 2424 3-8-10 59 .... SamHitchcott 12 41
(Mick Channon) *hld up wl off the pce in last quartet: rdn and no hdwy over 2f out: lost tch 2f out* **33/1**

0-04 **10** *11* **Kaiser Wilhelm (IRE)**^{9} 2788 3-8-13 62 .... StevieDonohoe 4 29
(Paul Cole) *t.k.h early: rdn and btn 3f out: lost tch 2f out* **12/1**

3m 7.46s (-0.14) **Going Correction** -0.025s/f (Good) 10 Ran SP% **116.8**
Speed ratings (Par 99): **99,98,98,97,97 96,96,91,88,82**
Swingers:1&2:£7.90, 2&3:£2.90, 1&3:£8.20 CSF £59.73 CT £162.07 TOTE £12.70: £2.70, £1.50, £1.20; EX 55.30.
Owner J Ryan **Bred** John And Susan Davis **Trained** Newmarket, Suffolk

FOCUS
An interesting 3yo handicap, run at at a brisk pace. Ordinary form, with a small personal best from the winner.
Kaiser Wilhelm(IRE) Official explanation: jockey said that the colt was unsuited by the good to firm ground

3088 TRAFALGAR RESTAURANT AT GREAT YARMOUTH RACECOURSE H'CAP 1m 3f 101y
5:25 (5:26) (Class 6) (0-65,65) 3-Y-O **£1,617** (£481; £240; £120) **Stalls** Low

Form RPR

0-56 **1** **Curly Come Home**^{21} 2424 3-9-5 63 .... SebSanders 12 72
(Chris Wall) *stdd s: hld up in tch in rr: hdwy on inner over 2f out: rdn and qcknd to ld over 1f out: in command ins fnl f: pushed out* **6/1**^{2}

-045 **2** *1* **Jennifer J**[21] 2424 3-9-4 **62** EddieAhern 2 70+
(Mark H Tompkins) *chsd ldrs: nt clr run 2f out tl over 1f out: rdn and hdwy 1f out: chsd wnr ins fnl f: r.o but nvr gng to rch wnr* **5/2**[1]

6-04 **3** *1 ½* **Tafawuk (USA)**[17] 2553 3-9-7 **65** TadhgO'Shea 4 70
(Roger Varian) *in tch in midfield: hdwy to join ldr on bit wl over 2f out: rdn and outpcd by wnr over 1f out: styd on same pce fnl f* **5/2**[1]

5245 **4** *½* **Dalmo**[14] 2625 3-9-2 **60** RyanMoore 8 64
(Gary Moore) *led: rdn over 2f out: hdd and unable qck over 1f out: styd on same pce fnl f* **7/1**

0660 **5** *6* **Arctic Galaxy (CAN)**[36] 1982 3-9-6 **64** RobertHavlin 7 58
(John Gosden) *hld up in tch: rdn and effrt to chse ldrs over 2f out: btn over 1f out: wknd fnl f* **10/1**

0-51 **6** *14* **Melodrama (IRE)**[24] 2353 3-9-3 **61** (b) TedDurcan 11 31
(David Lanigan) *hld up in tch in last trio: rdn and effrt over 2f out: no ex and btn over 1f out: wl btn and eased ins fnl f* **13/2**[3]

565 **7** *8* **Multifac'Eted**[16] 2580 3-7-13 **46** oh1 RyanPowell(3) 5
(J S Moore) *t.k.h early: hld up in tch: rdn and struggling over 3f out: lost tch 2f out: eased ins fnl f* **50/1**

006 **8** *6* **Imperial Ruby**[17] 2560 3-9-3 **61** SamHitchcott 9
(Mick Channon) *chsd ldr tl wl over 2f out: sn lost pl: wl bhd and eased ins fnl f* **22/1**

2m 29.31s (0.61) **Going Correction** -0.025s/f (Good) **8** Ran SP% **112.7**
Speed ratings (Par 97): **96,95,94,93,89 79,73,69**
Swingers:1&2:£5.00, 2&3:£3.20, 1&3:£6.30 CSF £20.75 CT £46.39 TOTE £8.40: £2.40, £1.02, £1.60; EX 24.10.
Owner The Hut Partnership & Partner **Bred** Farmers Hill Stud **Trained** Newmarket, Suffolk

FOCUS
Some big yards and interesting handicap debutants represented in this 0-65 handicap.
Curly Come Home Official explanation: trainer's representative said, reagarding the apparent improvement of form, that the filly was ridden with more restraint than on its' previous run at Salisbury, where it was ridden prominently
T/Plt: £170.90 to a £1 stake. Pool: £49,013.00 - 209.25 winning tickets. T/Qpdt: £135.50 to a £1 stake. Pool: £3,012.00 - 16.44 winning tickets. SP

3089 - 3090a (Foreign Racing) - See Raceform Interactive

2900 LEOPARDSTOWN (L-H)
Thursday, June 14

OFFICIAL GOING: Good changing to good to soft after race 1 (4.50) changing to soft after race 3 (5.55)

3091a BALLYCORUS STKS (GROUP 3) 7f
5:55 (5:56) 3-Y-O+ **£31,145** (£9,104; £4,312; £1,437)

RPR

1 **Alanza (IRE)**[19] 2515 4-9-9 109 JohnnyMurtagh 7 107+
(John M Oxx, Ire) *chsd ldrs in 4th: impr into 2nd and pushed along 1 1/2f out: rdn to ld under 1f out: styd on wl fnl f: comf at the line* **8/11**[1]

2 *nk* **Marvada (IRE)**[19] 2515 4-9-6 101 ShaneFoley 8 103
(K J Condon, Ire) *attempted to make all: rdn 1 1/2f out: hdd under 1f out: kpt on wl fnl f* **10/1**

3 *2 ½* **Glor Na Mara (IRE)**[10] 2777 4-9-9 98 KevinManning 1 99
(J S Bolger, Ire) *chsd ldrs in 3rd: rdn ent st: kpt on same pce in 3rd fr 1 1/2f out* **4/1**[2]

4 *1 ¾* **Singing Bird (IRE)**[38] 1948 3-8-10 WayneLordan 5 88+
(David Wachman, Ire) *settled in last: rdn ent st: wnt mod 4th 1f out: kpt on fnl f* **10/1**

5 *4 ½* **Rodrigo De Torres**[8] 2819 5-9-9 CO'Donoghue 6 82
(Mrs K Burke) *prom: 2nd 1/2-way: rdn ent st: wknd fr 2f out* **10/1**

6 *8* **Empowering (IRE)**[242] 6899 4-9-6 102 JPO'Brien 2 58
(A P O'Brien, Ire) *chsd ldrs in 5th: rdn 3f out: sn no imp: eased fnl f* **11/2**[3]

1m 30.3s (1.60) **Going Correction** +0.525s/f (Yiel)
WFA 3 from 4yo+ 10lb **6** Ran SP% **120.6**
Speed ratings: **111,110,107,105,100 91**
CSF £10.63 TOTE £1.60: £1.02, £5.90; DF 13.20.
Owner H H Aga Khan **Bred** His Highness The Aga Khan's Studs S C **Trained** Currabeg, Co Kildare

FOCUS
A decent race for the level. The third sets the standard, with the front-running runner-up rated as running a small turf personal best.

NOTEBOOK
Alanza(IRE) did enough to win and show there's probably still a fair bit to work on. She closed up nicely enough and didn't have to work very hard to get to the front but once getting there she didn't do very much and probably had to work marginally harder than she had to in order to see that filly off. She'll be seen to much better effect on a quicker surface and looks likely to be thrown back into Group 1 company next month. (op 8/11 tchd 4/5)
Marvada(IRE) keeps her form admirably on most surfaces and is a credit to her trainer. She got a positive ride here and managed to beat off all of her rivals except the winner, who just had too much class for her. It was still a fine effort. (op 10/1 tchd 12/1)
Glor Na Mara(IRE) ran a fair race and it's hard to know whether this is as good as he's capable of at this stage. He was outpaced fairly readily by the first two in the straight although the ground wasn't really in his favour.
Singing Bird(IRE) faced a very stiff task on just her second start but she didn't acquit herself badly at all. Held up, she made some headway in the straight but wasn't good enough on the night to challenge. She should have a good bit of improvement left in her.
Rodrigo De Torres raced freely in the front rank and didn't have much left for the closing stages.
Empowering(IRE) should have done better in the conditions but she was beaten early in the straight.

3092a BALLYOGAN STKS (GROUP 3) (F&M) 6f
6:25 (6:27) 3-Y-O+ **£31,145** (£9,104; £4,312; £1,437)

RPR

1 **Fire Lily (IRE)**[19] 2513 3-9-2 107 WayneLordan 1 113
(David Wachman, Ire) *chsd ldrs: cl 2nd on inner 2f out: rdn to ld 1f out: styd on wl fnl f* **9/4**[1]

2 *¾* **After (IRE)**[18] 2527 3-8-13 107 SeamieHeffernan 10 108+
(A P O'Brien, Ire) *mid-div: 6th 1/2-way: impr into cl 4th and rdn 2f out: wnt 2nd fnl f: styd on wl cl home* **6/1**[3]

3 *1 ¾* **Gossamer Seed (IRE)**[38] 1944 4-9-10 104 (t) ShaneFoley 3 107
(John Joseph Murphy, Ire) *chsd ldrs: rdn 2f out: mod 6th 2f out: kpt on wout threatening to go 3rd ins fnl f: nvr nrr* **10/1**

4 *nk* **Inetrobil (IRE)**[12] 2713 3-8-13 (b) PhillipMakin 6 101
(Kevin Ryan) *led early: hdd bef 1/2-way: rdn in cl 2nd over 2f out: no ex fr 1 1/2f out* **10/1**

5 *nse* **Swiss Dream**[19] 2486 4-9-7 FranBerry 2 103
(David Elsworth) *racd in 2nd early: led bef 1/2-way: rdn and strly pressed 2f out: hdd 1f out: no imp ins fnl f* **6/1**[3]

6 *2 ¾* **Lightening Pearl (IRE)**[39] 1884 3-9-6 109 KevinManning 5 99
(G M Lyons, Ire) *dwlt and in rr: rdn and no imp st* **4/1**[2]

7 *nse* **Katla (IRE)**[19] 2513 4-9-7 98 JPO'Brien 9 94
(J F Grogan, Ire) *hld up in 7th: rdn 3f out: no imp st* **7/1**

8 *1* **Rubina (IRE)**[32] 2101 3-8-13 100 (bt[1]) JohnnyMurtagh 7 89
(John M Oxx, Ire) *dwlt and sn adrift of field in last: no imp fr 3f out* **12/1**

9 *½* **Royal Blue Star (IRE)**[10] 2777 4-9-7 95 (p) PatSmullen 4 89
(Mrs John Harrington, Ire) *chsd ldrs: rdn ent st: wknd fr 2f out* **16/1**

1m 15.3s (1.20) **Going Correction** +0.525s/f (Yiel)
WFA 3 from 4yo 8lb **9** Ran SP% **123.6**
Speed ratings: **113,112,109,109,109 105,105,104,103**
CSF £17.57 TOTE £2.90: £1.10, £1.50, £3.90; DF 17.20.
Owner Michael Tabor **Bred** Beauty Is Truth Syndicate **Trained** Goolds Cross, Co Tipperary

FOCUS
The fourth looks the best guide, and the winner has been rated as running a personal best.

NOTEBOOK
Fire Lily(IRE) put her disappointing effort in the Greenlands Stakes at the Curragh well behind her with victory of more authority than her winning margin would suggest. She went about her job in a far more professional manner on this occasion and the easier surface probably helped her, and despite getting there a shade too soon a furlong out she saw it out well enough and was probably value for a little bit more than the margin of victory would suggest. She should be well able to hold her own at a higher level over 6f, although one suspects she might just be a little bit better over 7f. (op 3/1)
After(IRE) finished fractionally in front of the winner in the Poule D'Essai Des Pouliches, but over this shorter trip she wasn't able to confirm the placings. She raced quite handily and came there with a chance just over a furlong out but the winner displayed the better turn of foot and any impression this filly was able to make was a bit deceptive. (op 13/2)
Gossamer Seed(IRE) appreciated the underfoot conditions but probably would have appreciated an extra furlong. She raced close to the pace and kept on again in the straight having just lost her place turning in. She's a good filly and there's another decent race in her. (op 9/1)
Inetrobil(IRE) was just a bit one-paced. (op 7/1)
Swiss Dream was still just about in front a furlong out but she weakened a little bit more markedly. (op 11/2)
Lightening Pearl(IRE) didn't run that discouragingly on ground which was probably gone for her. She closed up behind the pace early in the straight but couldn't quite sustain it. She was retired afterwards. (op 4/1 tchd 7/2)

3093 - 3095a (Foreign Racing) - See Raceform Interactive

2755 CHEPSTOW (L-H)
Friday, June 15

OFFICIAL GOING: Heavy (5.2) changing to soft (heavy in places after race 4 (7.15)
Wind: Strong and blustery, varying direction Weather: Cloudy

3096 FREEBETS.CO.UK FILLIES' H'CAP 1m 14y
5:30 (5:30) (Class 5) (0-75,71) 4-Y-O+ **£2,264** (£673; £336; £168) **Stalls** High

Form RPR

4-65 **1** **Ken's Girl**[17] 2576 8-9-7 **71** IanMongan 1 78
(Stuart Kittow) *racd in centre of crse: led over 4f out: hrd drvn whn chal thrght fnl f: all out* **11/8**[1]

41-5 **2** *nk* **Croeso Mawr**[23] 2385 6-8-5 **55** CathyGannon 4 61
(John Spearing) *t.k.h: racd towards stands' side and chsd wnr over 3f out: styd on to cl u.p fnl f but a jst hld* **11/4**[2]

60-5 **3** *¾* **Out Of Nothing**[8] 2859 9-9-6 **70** DaneO'Neill 5 74
(Dai Burchell) *racd on stands' side and led tl over 4f out: rdn and lost 2nd over 3f out: outpcd over 2f out: rallied fnl f: gng on clsng stages but a jst hld by ldng duo* **11/2**

0054 **4** *27* **Shared Moment (IRE)**[17] 2574 6-8-9 **59** (v) MartinLane 7
(John Gallagher) *v.s.a: rcvrd and in tch after 2f: rdn 4f out: sn btn: t.o* **9/2**[3]

60-5 **5** *31* **Sentosa**[7] 2886 5-9-0 **64** LiamKeniry 2
(Michael Blanshard) *racd towards centre of crse: rdn 4f out: sn btn: t.o* **14/1**

1m 42.06s (5.86) **Going Correction** +0.825s/f (Soft) **5** Ran SP% **109.0**
Speed ratings (Par 100): **103,102,101,74,43**
CSF £5.25 TOTE £2.00: £1.10, £2.10; EX 4.70.
Owner Midd Shire Racing **Bred** D R Tucker **Trained** Blackborough, Devon

FOCUS
There was a strong headwind in the straight and after 14mm of rain overnight the going was changed to heavy. The well-backed favourite raced in isolation up the centre of the track for most of the way and showed a gritty attitude to hold on in this fillies' handicap. The winner is rated more in line with her latter 2011 form.

3097 BRITISH STALLION STUDS SUPPORTING BRITISH RACING E B F NOVICE STKS 6f 16y
6:05 (6:05) (Class 4) 2-Y-O **£4,398** (£1,309; £654; £327) **Stalls** High

Form RPR

31 **1** **Birdman (IRE)**[14] 2648 2-9-5 0 MartinLane 5 89+
(David Simcock) *hld up in rr but in tch: drvn over 2f out: styd on to chal ins fnl 2f: led wl over 1f out: pushed along and asserted ins fnl f: won gng away* **11/8**[1]

041 **2** *3 ¼* **Fortinbrass (IRE)**[29] 2193 2-8-11 0 JamesRogers(5) 2 76
(Ralph Beckett) *led: rdn and jnd 2f out: hdd wl over 1f out: no ch w wnr fnl f but kpt on wl for 2nd* **13/2**

13 **3** *1 ¼* **Beedee**[10] 2797 2-8-13 0 SeanLevey(3) 4 73
(Richard Hannon) *chsd ldrs: chal over 2f out: one pce u.p over 1f out: styd on for 3rd fnl 120yds* **4/1**[3]

50 **4** *¾* **Walter White (IRE)**[18] 2550 2-9-0 0 LiamKeniry 6 68
(Andrew Balding) *chsd ldrs: upsides fr 3f out and stl ev ch 2f out: outpcd into last pl over 1f out: kpt on again to take 4th fnl 75yds* **9/1**

413 **5** *2 ¾* **Ishi Honest**[28] 2234 2-8-11 0 DaneO'Neill 1 57
(Mark Usher) *chsd ldrs: drvn along and ev ch 2f out: wknd ins fnl f* **3/1**[2]

1m 17.44s (5.44) **Going Correction** +0.825s/f (Soft) **5** Ran SP% **110.4**
Speed ratings (Par 95): **96,91,90,89,85**
CSF £10.71 TOTE £2.30: £1.20, £3.90; EX 11.30.
Owner Anthony Hogarth **Bred** Lynchbages Edgeridge Ltd & Glenvale Stud **Trained** Newmarket, Suffolk

FOCUS
A decent novice event run at a fair pace in the conditions. The form is rated around the placed horses and the winner did it well.

NOTEBOOK

Birdman(IRE) finished third behind a subsequent close Listed second in a Newmarket novice stakes on debut before comfortably landing the odds in a Brighton maiden. Well backed again, he was one of the first under pressure but he showed a good attitude to fight his way into the lead before quickening clear to make it two wins from three starts. A brother to Group-placed maiden A Mind Of Her Own, he looks useful and should stay an extra furlong or two in time. (tchd 5-4 and 6-4)

Fortinbrass(IRE) continued his steady progression when winning a fast-ground 6f Newmarket maiden auction last month. This was quite a bit tougher but this half-brother to a couple of slow-turf winners showed good speed and fighting spirit to finish runner-up. This trip looks ideal for him at this stage and he has scope for further improvement. (op 8-1)

Beedee made a winning debut in a C&D maiden but he was held as favourite behind two newcomers in a fast-ground Yarmouth novice event last time and couldn't make an impact on his first run on testing ground here. (op 9-2 tchd 7-2)

Walter White(IRE), well held in a pair of 6f maidens, had plenty to find on form but he showed some speed against the stands' rail before plugging on in this tough event. (op 16-1)

Ishi Honest had decent claims on her close third in a Newbury fillies' conditions race last month but she was a bit marooned out wide and was well held taking on the boys for the first time on this step up to 6f. (op 11-4 tchd 10-3)

3098 FREEBETS.CO.UK MAIDEN H'CAP — 6f 16y

6:40 (6:40) (Class 5) (0-70,68) 3-Y-0+ — £2,264 (£673; £336; £168) Stalls High

Form — RPR

2350 **1** **Going French (IRE)**[17] 2572 5-9-6 **60**............(t) KellyHarrison 8 — 68
(Dai Burchell) *trckd ldr: led ins fnl 3f: drvn along and styd on wl fnl f* **15/2**

3-06 **2** *1* **Khazium (IRE)**[10] 2786 3-9-1 **68**............(p) MatthewCosham(5) 7 — 71
(Pat Eddery) *s.i.s and sn drvn along in rr: hdwy 2f out: rdn and kpt on to chse wnr fnl 175yds: no imp clsng stages* **6/1**[3]

0-60 **3** *3* **Red Rhythm**[3] 3007 5-8-12 **52**............ CathyGannon 1 — 47
(David Evans) *sn led: hdd ins fnl 3f: rdn and one pce fr 2f out: dropped to 3rd fnl 175yds* **7/1**

24-0 **4** *2* **Tony Hollis**[18] 2555 4-9-1 **55**............ JamesMillman 4 — 44
(Rod Millman) *chsd ldrs: rdn and hung rt over 2f out: sn one pce* **8/1**

3223 **5** *nk* **Auntie Kathryn (IRE)**[8] 2862 3-7-12 **51**............ RaulDaSilva(5) 5 — 37
(Stuart Williams) *hmpd and lost pl sn after s: hdwy and nt clr run over 2f out: kpt on same pce fr over 1f out* **7/2**[1]

3436 **6** *4* **Glennten**[21] 2441 3-9-1 **63**............ LiamKeniry 6 — 36
(Sylvester Kirk) *chsd ldrs: rdn over 3f out: wknd wl over 2f out* **5/1**[2]

0-03 **7** *nk* **Greyemkay**[11] 2760 4-8-2 **49** oh3............ DanielMuscutt(7) 2 — 23
(Richard Price) *chsd ldrs: rdn and btn over 2f out* **14/1**

4-62 **8** *1 1/2* **Monty Fay (IRE)**[23] 2388 3-8-8 **56**............(t) WilliamCarson 3 — 23
(Derek Haydn Jones) *hmpd and lost pl after 1f: racd towards centre of crse: hrd rdn and no prog 3f out: no ch fnl 2f* **5/1**[2]

1m 17.79s (5.79) **Going Correction** +0.825s/f (Soft)
WFA 3 from 4yo+ 8lb — 8 Ran SP% **111.9**
Speed ratings (Par 103): **94,92,88,86,85 80,79,77**
Tote Swingers:1&2:£7.70, 2&3:£9.50, 1&3:£8.90 CSF £49.32 CT £328.27 TOTE £10.40: £2.20, £2.50, £2.80; EX 49.50.
Owner Alan Shinton **Bred** Kilnamoragh Stud **Trained** Briery Hill, Blaenau Gwent

FOCUS

The runners had a combined record of 0-84 in this maiden handicap. However, the pace was decent and they finished quite well strung out, so the form could work out. The race is rated around the winner to his winter form.

Tony Hollis Official explanation: jockey said gelding hung right throughout

Monty Fay(IRE) Official explanation: jockey said gelding suffered interference shortly after start

3099 NFU MUTUAL H'CAP — 7f 16y

7:15 (7:16) (Class 5) (0-70,75) 4-Y-0+ — £2,264 (£673; £336; £168) Stalls High

Form — RPR

6031 **1** **Myboyalfie (USA)**[8] 2847 5-9-12 **75** 6ex............(v) IanMongan 1 — 83
(J R Jenkins) *in tch: hdwy over 2f out: rdn to ld over 1f out and edgd rt: in command whn edgd rt again clsng stages* **11/8**[1]

-122 **2** *1* **Douze Points (IRE)**[42] 1830 6-9-7 **70**............ AdamKirby 3 — 76
(John Butler) *in rr: rdn and outpcd over 3f out: hdwy over 1f out: styd on u.p fnl f to take 2nd clsng stages but no imp on wnr* **6/1**[3]

6005 **3** *hd* **Royal Box**[11] 2760 5-8-3 **52**............(p) CathyGannon 7 — 57
(David Evans) *crossed sn after s and swtchd lft: sn chsng ldr: led jst ins fnl 2f: hdd u.p appr fnl f: hld whn carried rt and lost 2nd clsng stages* **4/1**[2]

6523 **4** *2 3/4* **Fonterutoli (IRE)**[2] 3053 5-8-8 **57**............ RobertHavlin 8 — 55
(Roger Ingram) *in rr: hdwy 3f out: chal ins fnl 2f: one pce appr fnl f and hld whn carried rt clsng stages* **13/2**

502 **5** *2 1/4* **Spinning Ridge (IRE)**[11] 2758 7-9-7 **70**............(b) MarcHalford 4 — 62
(Ronald Harris) *in rr early: hdwy 3f out: chal 2f out: one pce u.p whn hmpd and swtchd lft appr fnl f* **14/1**

0001 **6** *3/4* **Hail Promenader (IRE)**[17] 2574 6-9-4 **67**............(b[1]) WilliamCarson 5 — 63+
(Anthony Carson) *wnt rt to stands' rail sn after s and led: rdn and jnd 2f out: sn hdd u.p wknd fnl f: btn whn hmpd and snatched up clsng stages* **9/1**

0466 **7** *3* **Petrarchan**[2] 3051 4-8-8 **57**............(t) RichardKingscote 2 — 39+
(Milton Bradley) *s.i.s: in rr: sme hdwy whn hmpd and swtchd rt over 1f out: no ch after* **20/1**

0/00 **8** *10* **Komreyev Star**[39] 1907 10-8-2 **51** oh6............(b[1]) MartinLane 6
(Ray Peacock) *pressed ldrs: rdn 4f out: sn btn tailed: off* **100/1**

1m 30.09s (6.89) **Going Correction** +0.825s/f (Soft) — 8 Ran SP% **112.1**
Speed ratings (Par 103): **93,91,91,88,85 85,81,70**
Tote Swingers:1&2:£2.80, 2&3:£3.80, 1&3:£3.30 CSF £9.63 CT £25.95 TOTE £2.00: £1.10, £1.90, £1.40; EX 9.90.
Owner D Badham **Bred** Robert Pierz & Robert Brooks **Trained** Royston, Herts

■ Stewards' Enquiry : William Carson two-day ban: careless riding (Jun 29-30)

FOCUS

The three market leaders filled the first three positions in this handicap and the form looks solid enough. It;s doubtful if the winner had to match the form of his latest win.

3100 FREEBETS.CO.UK MAIDEN FILLIES' STKS — 1m 4f 23y

7:50 (7:53) (Class 5) 3-Y-0+ — £2,264 (£673; £336; £168) Stalls Low

Form — RPR

2 **1** **Monshak (IRE)**[36] 2008 3-8-12 0............ SebSanders 6 — 69+
(Sir Michael Stoute) *in tch: pushed along and rn in snatches fr 4f out: rdn 3f out: styd on to take 3rd 2f out: outpcd over 1f out: rallied fnl f and kpt on to ld nr fin* **13/8**[1]

0- **2** *1/2* **Rose Season**[226] 7233 3-8-12 0............ NeilCallan 9 — 68+
(Roger Varian) *trckd ldrs: wnt 2nd over 2f out: chal fr over 1f out tl led u.p fnl 120yds: hdd nr fin* **11/4**[3]

3 **3** *1 1/2* **Rosie Probert**[29] 2204 3-8-12 0............ JamesDoyle 7 — 65+
(Roger Charlton) *trckd ldr: chal 4f out: led over 3f out: jnd over 1f out: rdn and hung lft u.p ins fnl f: hdd and no ex fnl 120yds: dropped to 3rd clsng stages* **9/4**[2]

50 **4** *4 1/2* **Big Time Billy (IRE)**[13] 2708 6-9-13 0............ WilliamCarson 1 — 58
(Mike Hammond) *in rr: hdwy 3f out and sn rdn: hung lft over 2f out: styd on same pce fr over 1f out* **22/1**

00 **5** *1/2* **David's Folly (IRE)**[77] 1113 3-8-7 0............ RaulDaSilva(5) 2 — 57?
(Bryn Palling) *chsd ldrs: rdn and outpcd over 3f out: styd on same pce u.p fr over 1f out* **50/1**

6-4 **6** *3* **Queen's Star**[16] 2612 3-8-9 0............ SimonPearce(3) 8 — 52
(Andrew Balding) *hld up in rr: hdwy on ins 4f out: sn rdn: wknd ins fnl 3f* **20/1**

0 **7** *4 1/2* **Across The Galaxy**[29] 2200 3-8-12 0............ RobertHavlin 5 — 45
(Hughie Morrison) *led: jnd 4f out: hdd over 3f out: wknd over 2f out* **16/1**

0 **8** *38* **Charity Rainbow**[11] 2757 5-9-8 0............ DavidKenny(5) 3
(Brendan Powell) *a in rr: lost tch fnl 4f: t.o* **66/1**

2m 50.22s (11.22) **Going Correction** +0.825s/f (Soft)
WFA 3 from 5yo+ 15lb — 8 Ran SP% **114.0**
Speed ratings (Par 100): **95,94,93,90,90 88,85,60**
Tote Swingers:1&2:£1.90, 2&3:£2.00, 1&3:£1.30 CSF £6.05 TOTE £2.00: £1.02, £1.40, £1.20; EX 6.20.
Owner Nurlan Bizakov **Bred** Ecurie Des Monceaux **Trained** Newmarket, Suffolk

FOCUS

The going was changed from heavy to soft, heavy in places. There didn't seem to be much strength in depth in this maiden but the three market leaders pulled clear in a race of changing fortunes and the form could be decent. Reinette O'Bry refused to enter the stalls and was withdrawn. The first three were clear but the fourth and fifth are likely to set the long-term level.

Queen's Star Official explanation: jockey said filly was denied a clear run

3101 BATH MARQUEES H'CAP — 1m 2f 36y

8:25 (8:25) (Class 5) (0-75,73) 4-Y-0+ — £2,264 (£673; £336; £168) Stalls Low

Form — RPR

0326 **1** **Hamilton Hill**[20] 2502 5-8-0 **57**............ RaulDaSilva(5) 4 — 69+
(Dai Burchell) *trckd ldr: led ins fnl 2f: pushed clr fnl f: v easily* **13/8**[2]

65-0 **2** *7* **Tijori (IRE)**[28] 2237 4-9-0 **66**............ NeilCallan 2 — 64
(Bernard Llewellyn) *led tl hdd ins fnl 2f: sn no ch w wnr but hrd pressed for 2nd: styd on to hold that position ins fnl f* **5/1**[3]

120- **3** *nk* **Taste The Wine (IRE)**[179] 7817 6-8-4 **63**............ DanielMuscutt(7) 3 — 60
(Bernard Llewellyn) *s.i.s: racd in 3rd: hdwy to chse ldrs 3f out: rdn and outpcd over 1f out: styd on fnl f to cl on 2nd clsng stages but nvr any ch w v easy wnr* **7/1**

46-1 **4** *1* **Sammy Alexander**[17] 2576 4-9-7 **73**............ MartinLane 5 — 68
(David Simcock) *s.i.s: racd in 4th: hdwy 3f out: disp 2nd appr fnl f but nvr any ch w v easy wnr: wknd bk into 4th fnl 50yds* **6/4**[1]

2m 24.06s (13.46) **Going Correction** +0.825s/f (Soft) — 4 Ran SP% **107.3**
Speed ratings (Par 103): **79,73,73,72**
CSF £9.12 TOTE £2.60; EX 11.90.
Owner T G Price **Bred** Middleton Stud **Trained** Briery Hill, Blaenau Gwent

FOCUS

There was a runaway winner in this small-field handicap, but it's hard to know what he achieved with the opposition unconvincing.

3102 FREEBETS.CO.UK H'CAP — 2m 49y

8:55 (8:55) (Class 6) (0-65,65) 4-Y-0+ — £1,617 (£481; £240; £120) Stalls Low

Form — RPR

00/2 **1** **Our Folly**[23] 2396 4-8-13 **55**............(t) IanMongan 5 — 66
(Stuart Kittow) *slowly away: sn rcvrd: hdwy to cl on ldrs 6f out: led wl over 2f out: rdn over 1f out: kpt on strly fnl f* **4/1**[3]

0-54 **2** *5* **Sunny Future (IRE)**[22] 2423 6-9-10 **65**............ TomMcLaughlin 4 — 70
(Malcolm Saunders) *in rr tl hdwy 1/2-way: wnt 2nd 7f out: led ins fnl 4f: hdd wl over 2f out: sn rdn: no ch w wnr fnl f but kpt on wl for clr 2nd* **9/4**[1]

360- **3** *12* **Maggie Aron**[170] 7894 6-8-13 **54**............ AdamKirby 10 — 45
(Tim Vaughan) *in tch: hdwy to chse ldrs 4f out: rdn 3f out: lost tch w ldng duo wl over 1f out* **10/1**

21-3 **4** *1 3/4* **Decana**[9] 2814 4-9-1 **64**............ ChristianSewell(7) 1 — 53
(Hughie Morrison) *hld up in rr: hdwy 4f out: chsd ldrs 3f out: sn rdn: wknd qckly fr 2f out* **3/1**[2]

-000 **5** *17* **Haafhd Decent (IRE)**[39] 1910 4-8-1 **46** oh1............ SimonPearce(3) 9 — 15
(Dai Williams) *chsd ldrs: lost position and dropped towards rr 5f out: hdwy to chse ldrs 3f out: sn rdn: wknd over 2f out* **50/1**

2314 **6** *13* **Blue Cossack (IRE)**[88] 963 4-8-13 **55**............ DaneO'Neill 7
(Mark Usher) *chsd ldrs: rdn and wknd 3f out* **7/1**

10-0 **7** *1 3/4* **Spinning Waters**[17] 2575 6-8-9 **50**............(p) KellyHarrison 6
(Dai Burchell) *led tl hdd & wknd ins fnl 4f* **8/1**

4m 4.33s (25.43) **Going Correction** +0.825s/f (Soft)
WFA 4 from 5yo+ 1lb — 7 Ran SP% **110.4**
Speed ratings (Par 101): **69,66,60,59,51 44,43**
Tote Swingers:1&2:£2.90, 2&3:£6.40, 1&3:£8.10 CSF £12.47 CT £75.79 TOTE £5.60: £2.80, £1.70; EX 14.70.
Owner Midd Shire Racing **Bred** D R Tucker **Trained** Blackborough, Devon

FOCUS

An ordinary staying handicap. The pace was not very strong but they finished well strung out. The winner showed a little more improvement and the form is rated around the second.

T/Plt: £42.80 to a £1 stake. Pool £38,634.88. 657.56 winning tickets T/Qpdt: £19.70 to a £1 stake. Pool £3,380.12. 126.96 winning tickets ST

2886 GOODWOOD (R-H)

Friday, June 15

OFFICIAL GOING: Good to soft (soft in places; 6.5)

First 2f of mile course and lower bend dolled out 5yds increasing distances by 10yds. Top bend out 3yds increasing distances on that course by 7yds.

Wind: Fresh, half-against Weather: breezy and dry

3103 GORDON'S APPRENTICE STKS (H'CAP) — 6f

6:15 (6:15) (Class 5) (0-70,70) 4-Y-0+ — £3,234 (£962; £481; £240) Stalls High

Form — RPR

3451 **1** **Jake The Snake (IRE)**[30] 2169 11-9-7 **67**............ LucyKBarry 1 — 73
(Tony Carroll) *stdd and dropped in after s: hld up in rr: hdwy in centre 1/2-way: rdn to ld ins fnl f: r.o wl: rdn out* **17/2**

4643 **2** *1 1/4* **Mata Hari Blue**[10] 2789 6-9-10 **70**............(t) MatthewLawson 6 — 72
(John Holt) *s.i.s: racd in midfield: clsd on ldrs 1/2-way: drvn and pressing ldr over 1f out: chsd wnr and one pce fnl 150yds* **3/1**[2]

3002 **3** *hd* **Kyllachy Storm**[22] 2413 8-8-4 **55**.. RyanTate(5) 4 56
(Ron Hodges) *led tl 1/2-way: outpcd and lost pl over 2f out: drvn and effrt over 1f out: styd on u.p ins fnl f* **5/1**

213 **4** *3/4* **Amazing Win (IRE)**[3] 2994 4-9-0 **60**............................ CharlesBishop 2 59
(Mick Channon) *w ldr tl led 1/2-way: rdn over 1f out: hdd ins fnl f: no ex and one pce fnl 150yds* **11/4**[1]

44-0 **5** *3 1/4* **Spitfire**[165] 13 7-9-7 **70**... DannyBrock(3) 7 58
(J R Jenkins) *chsd ldrs: clsd 1/2-way: shkn up and effrt 2f out: rdn: hung rt and fnd little over 1f out: stl hanging and wknd 1f out: wl btn and eased wl ins fnl f* **6/1**

0254 **6** *3/4* **Hatta Stream (IRE)**[28] 2251 6-9-1 **66**...................... SophieSilvester(5) 5 52
(Lydia Pearce) *chsd ldrs: clsd 1/2-way: rdn and pressing ldrs over 1f out: wknd 1f out* **9/2**[3]

1m 16.11s (3.91) **Going Correction** +0.75s/f (Yiel) **6** Ran SP% **111.3**
Speed ratings (Par 103): **103,101,101,100,95 94**
Tote Swingers:1&2:£3.50, 2&3:£3.30, 1&3:£8.30 CSF £33.35 CT £137.99 TOTE £6.40: £2.30, £2.40; EX 18.00 Trifecta £52.30 Pool £397.14 - 5.61 winning units..
Owner T P Ramsden **Bred** J F Tuthill **Trained** Cropthorne, Worcs
■ Stewards' Enquiry : Matthew Lawson two-day ban: used whip above permitted level (Jun 29-30)

FOCUS
The course soaked up 6mm of overnight rain and the time confirmed the ground was on the soft side. A modest handicap in which the gallop was a reasonable one in the conditions. The winner was close to his recent AW form.

3104 THREE FRIDAY NIGHTS CLASSIFIED STKS 1m 3f
6:50 (6:50) (Class 5) 3-Y-O **£2,726** (£805; £402) **Stalls** High

Form RPR
5-20 **1** **Hyperlink (IRE)**[27] 2266 3-9-0 73.................................... MircoDemuro 1 76
(Mark Johnston) *mde all: rdn and qcknd ent fnl f: clr over 1f out: r.o wl* **6/1**

1-02 **2** *2 1/4* **Hidden Justice (IRE)**[7] 2889 3-9-0 70.......................... EddieAhern 2 72
(Amanda Perrett) *hld up in 3rd: clsd on ldrs 5f out: chsd wnr over 3f out: rdn 2f out: drvn and styd on same pce fr over 1f out* **5/2**[2]

45-1 **3** *nse* **Arch Villain (IRE)**[24] 2372 3-9-0 75.................................. JimCrowley 4 72
(Amanda Perrett) *hld up in last: clsd on ldrs 5f out: rdn ent fnl 2f: kpt on same pce and no imp fr over 1f out* **6/4**[1]

-406 **4** *nk* **Petaluma**[4] 2980 3-9-0 73.. MartinHarley 3 71
(Mick Channon) *chsd wnr: c to stands' rail over 3f out: rdn over 2f out: styd on same pce and no imp fr over 1f out: hung rt ins fnl f* **3/1**[3]

2m 36.99s (10.49) **Going Correction** +0.60s/f (Yiel) **4** Ran SP% **107.9**
Speed ratings (Par 99): **85,83,83,83**
CSF £20.08 TOTE £6.80; EX 21.40.
Owner Sheikh Hamdan Bin Mohammed Al Maktoum **Bred** Airlie Stud **Trained** Middleham Moor, N Yorks

FOCUS
A fair classified event but a steady pace that only picked up passing the 2f pole means this bare form isn't reliable. It's unlikely the winner improved.

3105 CAPITAL FM STKS (H'CAP) 7f
7:25 (7:25) (Class 4) (0-85,84) 4-Y-O+ **£5,175** (£1,540; £769; £384) **Stalls** Low

Form RPR
1-06 **1** **Starwatch**[14] 2657 5-9-7 **84**.. KieranO'Neill 4 93
(John Bridger) *chsd clr ldng pair: clsd 3f out: rdn to ld 2f out: drvn over 1f out: r.o gamely to assert ins fnl f: rdn out* **7/1**

4-12 **2** *1 1/4* **Moretta Blanche**[7] 2890 5-9-4 **81**.............................(t) JimCrowley 8 87
(Ralph Beckett) *stdd s: hld up in rr: clsd on ldrs 3f out: upsides wnr and gng wl 2f out: rdn over 1f out: drvn and no ex ins fnl f: btn fnl 100yds* **5/2**[2]

-652 **3** *1 1/4* **Great Expectations**[27] 2274 4-8-10 **73**.......................... FrederikTylicki 7 75
(J R Jenkins) *hld up in midfield: clsd on ldrs 3f out: rdn and chsd ldrs over 1f out: edgd rt and btn ins fnl f* **2/1**[1]

5632 **4** *3* **Corporal Maddox**[3] 3004 5-9-7 **84**................................ RichardHughes 2 78
(Jamie Osborne) *stdd s: hld up in last pair: clsd on ldrs 3f out: trckd ldrs 2f out: swtchd lft and effrt over 1f out: no ex and btn whn pushed rt ins fnl f: wknd and eased towards fin* **3/1**[3]

3464 **5** *5* **Salient**[8] 2855 8-8-4 **67**... KierenFox 3 48
(Michael Attwater) *led and clr w rival: hdd after 2f but styd upsides ldr: rdn 3f out: wknd 2f out* **20/1**

6-04 **6** *15* **Batchelors Star (IRE)**[35] 2024 4-9-6 **83**........................... TomQueally 1 23
(Jim Boyle) *racd freely: sn clr w ldr tl led after 2f: rdn over 2f out: sn hdd & wknd: wl bhd and eased fnl 100yds* **14/1**

1m 30.26s (3.26) **Going Correction** +0.60s/f (Yiel) **6** Ran SP% **110.8**
Speed ratings (Par 105): **105,103,102,98,93 75**
Tote Swingers:1&2:£3.70, 2&3:£1.90, 1&3:£2.30 CSF £24.16 CT £45.45 TOTE £6.70: £2.30, £1.90; EX 21.20 Trifecta £48.50 Pool £344.67 - 5.25 winning units..
Owner J J Bridger **Bred** Mrs J A Chapman **Trained** Liphook, Hants

FOCUS
A useful handicap in which the two leaders ensured the gallop was a decent one. The winner continue's last year's remarkable progress.

3106 LEVY RESTAURANTS STKS (H'CAP) 1m 1f 192y
8:00 (8:02) (Class 3) (0-90,89) 3-Y-O **£7,762** (£2,310; £1,154; £577) **Stalls** Low

Form RPR
-340 **1** **Clare Island Boy (IRE)**[34] 2076 3-9-7 **86**............................ PatDobbs 1 91
(Richard Hannon) *mde all: rdn and qcknd 2f out: r.o wl and a holding rivals ins fnl f* **15/2**

03-2 **2** *nk* **Bank Bonus**[32] 2125 3-9-0 **79**.. JimmyFortune 3 83
(Andrew Balding) *chsd wnr: rdn and effrt on inner to chal ent fnl 2f: drvn and kpt on fnl f: a jst hld* **7/2**[2]

0-22 **3** *hd* **Sir Mike**[30] 2172 3-9-1 **80**.. JimCrowley 2 84
(Amanda Perrett) *chsd ldng pair: effrt to chal 2f out: ev ch and drvn over 1f out: kpt on but a jst hld fnl f* **11/2**[3]

52-1 **4** *2 1/2* **Westwiththenight (IRE)**[24] 2381 3-9-1 **80**......................... EddieAhern 6 79
(William Haggas) *hld up in 4th: hdwy on outer to press ldrs over 3f out: rdn and fnd little over 1f out: edgd rt and btn ins fnl f* **7/2**[2]

21-1 **5** *3 3/4* **Freddy Q (IRE)**[22] 2429 3-9-7 **86**.................................. RichardHughes 4 78
(Richard Hannon) *hld up in last: hdwy to join ldrs gng wl over 2f out: rdn and unable qck wl over 1f out: wknd 1f out: btn and eased wl ins fnl f* **6/4**[1]

2m 16.67s (8.57) **Going Correction** +0.60s/f (Yiel) **5** Ran SP% **111.6**
Speed ratings (Par 103): **89,88,88,86,83**
CSF £33.04 TOTE £10.10: £4.10, £2.70; EX 36.40.
Owner Middleham Park Racing XIV & James Pak **Bred** Norelands Bloodstock **Trained** East Everleigh, Wilts

FOCUS
Another useful handicap but the gallop was a steady one and this form doesn't look reliable. The race has been rated cautiously.

NOTEBOOK
Clare Island Boy(IRE) had been soundly beaten on his previous two starts but he was allowed the easiest of leads back over this longer trip and showed a good attitude in the closing stages. Things were stacked in his favour here but he shouldn't be going up too much for this and will be of interest in races when it looks as though he'll be able to dominate. (op 9-1)
Bank Bonusleft the impression a stronger gallop would have suited but he ran well, despite taking a good grip early on. He's a useful sort who should be able to pick up a similar event when the emphasis leans more towards stamina. (op 4-1)
Sir Mike ran right up to his best after taking a good hold in this muddling event on this handicap debut. He has a fair bit of physical scope and should be able to pick up a race. (op 9-2)
Westwiththenight(IRE) came into this race as a progressive maiden winner but he was too keen and proved and proved a bit disappointing on his handicap debut and first run in ground this testing. However he's in good hands and will be worth another chance back on a sound surface.
Freddy Q(IRE) raced with the choke out and was a long below the form of his reappearance win. He has won in soft ground but will be of more interest back over 1m in a more truly run race.
Official explanation: jockey said colt ran too free (op 7-4)

3107 FRANKIE'S 25TH ANNIVERSARY MAIDEN STKS 1m
8:35 (8:36) (Class 5) 3-Y-O **£2,911** (£866; £432; £216) **Stalls** Low

Form RPR
3-23 **1** **Spoke To Carlo**[13] 2701 3-9-3 84.. JohnFahy 5 87+
(Eve Johnson Houghton) *t.k.h: hld up in last pair: effrt on inner and qckd to ld wl over 1f out: rdn clr over 1f out: r.o strly: comf* **8/11**[1]

3 **2** *3 1/2* **Raheeba**[46] 1703 3-8-12 0.. MircoDemuro 1 74
(Mark Johnston) *chsd ldr: rdn to chal 2f out: outpcd by wnr over 1f out and styd on same pce after* **13/2**[3]

4 **3** *1/2* **Stirring Ballad**[18] 2543 3-8-12 0.. JimmyFortune 2 72
(Andrew Balding) *wnt lft s: led tl rdn and hdd wl over 1f out: outpcd by wnr over 1f out: r.o same pce after* **8/1**

5-03 **4** *3/4* **Energize (FR)**[17] 2585 3-9-3 75....................................... RichardHughes 6 76
(Richard Hannon) *wnt lft s: in tch in midfield: rdn and effrt ent fnl 2f: drvn and outpcd over 1f out: no ch w wnr and one pce after* **8/1**

0 **5** *2 1/2* **Bowstar**[18] 2542 3-8-12 0... J-PGuillambert 4 65
(Michael Attwater) *t.k.h: chsd ldng pair tl nt clr run and shuffled bk over 2f out: rdn and no hdwy wl over 1f out* **33/1**

6 *4 1/2* **Riddle Master** 3-9-3 0... TomQueally 3 59
(Sir Henry Cecil) *dwlt and rn green early: in tch in rr: effrt on outer to chse ldrs 3f out: rdn 2f out: sn btn and wknd* **11/2**[2]

1m 44.61s (4.71) **Going Correction** +0.60s/f (Yiel) **6** Ran SP% **111.8**
Speed ratings (Par 99): **100,96,96,95,92 88**
Tote Swingers:1&2:£1.50, 2&3:£5.00, 1&3:£2.40 CSF £6.00 TOTE £1.80: £1.10, £2.90; EX 6.30.
Owner Anthony Pye-Jeary And Mel Smith **Bred** Shareef Racing & Redmyre Bloodstock **Trained** Blewbury, Oxon

FOCUS
A race won by smart trio Indian Creek (2001), Three Graces (2003) and Dansili Dancer (2005) and threw up a very useful sort in Galiando last year but this was an uncompetitive event won by one that had previously had a few chances. The gallop was on the steady side. Sound enough form, with the winner not needing to match this year's best.

3108 DERMOT O'LEARY STKS (H'CAP) 6f
9:05 (9:05) (Class 4) (0-85,85) 3-Y-O **£5,175** (£1,540; £769; £384) **Stalls** High

Form RPR
-000 **1** **Muaamara**[20] 2509 3-9-7 **85**... MartinHarley 6 94
(Mick Channon) *stdd s: hld up in rr: clsd to trck ldrs over 1f out: wnt between horses and shkn up to ld 1f out: r.o wl: comf* **7/2**[3]

-112 **2** *2* **Love Tale**[14] 2649 3-8-12 **76**.. FergusSweeney 5 79
(Mark Rimell) *chsd ldrs: swtchd rt and rdn to chal over 1f out: chsd wnr and r.o same pce u.p fnl f* **9/4**[1]

062 **3** *1 3/4* **Taizong (IRE)**[20] 2470 3-8-2 **66** oh1.................................. NickyMackay 1 63
(Ian Williams) *w ldr: rdn to ld over 1f out: sn hdd: outpcd 1f out and sn btn* **11/4**[2]

0-20 **4** *3/4* **Ziefhd**[27] 2272 3-9-2 **80**.. StevieDonohoe 4 75
(Paul Cole) *t.k.h: hld up in tch: rdn and effrt over 1f out: drvn and no ex 1f out: wknd fnl f* **11/2**

5462 **5** *3 1/4* **Le King Beau (USA)**[21] 2443 3-8-5 **69**............................ KieranO'Neill 2 54
(John Bridger) *led: rdn 2f out: sn hdd: wknd 1f out* **11/2**

1m 16.34s (4.14) **Going Correction** +0.75s/f (Yiel) **5** Ran SP% **110.4**
Speed ratings (Par 101): **102,99,97,96,91**
CSF £11.78 TOTE £4.80: £2.50, £1.20; EX 12.00.
Owner M Al-Qatami & K M Al-Mudhaf **Bred** R J Cornelius **Trained** West Ilsley, Berks

FOCUS
A useful handicap in which the gallop was on the steady side for a sprint, and the time was slow. The winner got her act together and the second rates a small personal best.
T/Plt: £563.30 to a £1 stake. Pool £35,836.82. 46.44 winning tickets T/Qpdt: £24.50 to a £1 stake. Pool £3,614.70. 109.04 winning tickets SP

2715 MUSSELBURGH (R-H)
Friday, June 15

OFFICIAL GOING: Good to soft
Wind: Fresh, behind Weather: Heavy rain

3109 JENNERS & FRASERS H'CAP (DIV I) 5f
1:20 (1:24) (Class 5) (0-75,75) 3-Y-O+ **£5,175** (£1,540; £769; £384) **Stalls** High

Form RPR
/0-4 **1** **Liberty Island (IRE)**[16] 2596 7-9-11 **69**...........(p) DuranFentiman 2 79
(Ian Semple) *cl up: overall ldr on stands' side after 2f: rdn clr over 1f out: drvn out* **4/1**[3]

0421 **2** *1* **Silvanus (IRE)**[10] 2789 7-9-10 **75** 6ex.................................. NedCurtis(7) 8 81
(Paul Midgley) *towards rr: hdwy 1/2-way: rdn to chse ldrs over 1f out: swtchd rt ins fnl f: kpt on* **5/2**[1]

-435 **3** *1 1/4* **Scrooby Doo**[77] 1115 3-9-2 **67**.. LukeMorris 5 66
(Scott Dixon) *chsd ldrs: hdwy to chse wnr over 2f out: drvn over 1f out: kpt on same pce fnl f* **9/1**

0-03 **4** *2* **Ballarina**[11] 2749 6-8-8 **57**... DarylByrne(5) 1 52
(Eric Alston) *racd alone towards far side: led 2f: cl up: rdn along and edgd lft 2f out: wknd over 1f out* **10/1**

4260 **5** *2* **Angelo Poliziano**[8] 2841 6-9-13 **71**...............................(p) LeeNewman 6 59
(George Foster) *chsd ldr on stands' rail: rdn along 2f out: sn drvn and wknd* **16/1**

6102 **6** *2 1/4* **Chosen One (IRE)**[7] 2875 7-8-11 **55**............................. JamesSullivan 4 34
(Ruth Carr) *chsd ldrs: rdn along over 2f out: no hdwy* **7/1**

00-5 **7** *2 1/2* **Midnight Dynamo**[13] 2719 5-9-7 **65**...................................... GrahamLee 9 35+
(Jim Goldie) *a towards rr* **7/2**[2]

5020 **8** 3 ¼ **Saxonette**[8] 2841 4-9-0 58 BarryMcHugh 3 17
(Linda Perratt) *dwlt: a in rr* **25/1**
0002 **9** 1 ½ **Distant Sun (USA)**[8] 2839 8-8-9 53 oh1 (p) PaulMulrennan 10 6+
(Linda Perratt) *a towards rr* **12/1**
59.48s (-0.92) **Going Correction** -0.10s/f (Good)
WFA 3 from 4yo+ 7lb 9 Ran SP% 119.8
Speed ratings (Par 103): **103,101,99,96,93 89,85,80,77**
toteswingers:1&2:£3.20, 1&3:£7.50, 2&3:£6.50 CSF £15.05 CT £86.99 TOTE £5.70: £2.30, £1.40, £2.20; EX 20.10.
Owner Highland Racing 6 & Robert Reid **Bred** Pat Grogan **Trained** Carluke, S Lanarks
■ Stewards' Enquiry : Ned Curtis five-day ban: careless riding (Jun 29-Jul 3)

FOCUS
Not many got into this ordinary sprint handicap. The winner is rated to the best of his Irish form, backed up by the placed horses.

3110 BALFOUR BEATTY ENGINEERING (BBES) MAIDEN AUCTION STKS 5f

1:50 (1:51) (Class 5) 2-Y-O **£3,234** (£962; £481; £240) **Stalls** High

Form RPR
00 **1** **Starbotton**[27] 2261 2-8-6 0 AndrewElliott 11 70
(James Bethell) *cl up on stands' rail: led 1/2-way: rdn clr over 1f out: kpt on strly* **28/1**
0 **2** 2 ¼ **Bonnie Lesley (IRE)**[17] 2587 2-8-5 0 JoeFanning 10 61
(Keith Dalgleish) *in tch: hdwy 2f out: chsd ldrs over 1f out: swtchd rt and rdn ent fnl f: kpt on wl* **18/1**
66 **3** ½ **Moss Quito (IRE)**[11] 2770 2-8-10 0 GrahamLee 8 64
(David O'Meara) *in tch: hdwy on inner 1/2-way: rdn to chse ldrs over 1f out: kpt on wl fnl f* **14/1**
42 **4** ½ **Therapeutic**[13] 2686 2-8-5 0 LukeMorris 2 57
(Scott Dixon) *prom: chsd wnr over 2f out: rdn over 1f out: drvn and one pce fnl f* **5/2**[1]
5 ½ **Grievous Angel (IRE)** 2-8-8 0 ow1 PaulMulrennan 7 59
(Ann Duffield) *dwlt and towards rr: hdwy wl over 1f out: rdn and styd on fnl f: nrst fin* **25/1**
023 **6** ¾ **Red Style (IRE)**[15] 2614 2-8-2 0 NedCurtis(7) 4 57
(Paul Midgley) *in tch: hdwy to chse ldrs 1/2-way: rdn along wl over 1f out: wknd ent fnl f* **4/1**[2]
452 **7** 1 ¾ **Annie Gogh**[11] 2770 2-8-6 0 DuranFentiman 6 48
(Tim Easterby) *led: hdd 1/2-way and sn rdn along: wknd over 1f out* **5/1**[3]
8 1 **Charlie Em** 2-8-5 0 BarryMcHugh 9 43
(Richard Fahey) *s.i.s: a in rr* **8/1**
0 **9** 5 **Charlemagne Diva**[15] 2631 2-8-5 0 JamesSullivan 3 25
(Ann Duffield) *sltly hmpd s: a in rr* **12/1**
4 **10** 3 ½ **Confidential Creek**[13] 2686 2-8-12 0 TomEaves 1 19
(Ollie Pears) *wnt rt s: cl up on outer: rdn along 1/2-way: sn wknd* **5/1**[3]
59.87s (-0.53) **Going Correction** -0.10s/f (Good) 10 Ran SP% 119.9
Speed ratings (Par 93): **100,96,95,94,94 92,90,88,80,74**
toteswingers:1&2:£24.20, 1&3:£24.20, 2&3:£24.20 CSF £462.62 TOTE £32.60: £7.60, £3.80, £4.10; EX 407.70.
Owner Clarendon Thoroughbred Racing **Bred** Miss H Budgett & Kirtlington Stud Ltd **Trained** Middleham Moor, N Yorks

FOCUS
An interesting maiden auction event in which the form horses were eclipsed by some with more longer-term potential. The draw played its part too, with the first three starting from the four highest stalls. The third and fourth are the best guides to the level.

NOTEBOOK
Starbotton had finished well held in her first two outings and is bred to get much further than this, but the easing of the ground made it a bit more of a test and she made just about all to score. She should continue to improve, especially as she goes up in trip. Official explanation: trainer's rep had no explanation for the apparent improvement in form
Bonnie Lesley(IRE) ◆ was well beaten on her Ripon debut, but like the winner she is bred to stay much further as her dam won over middle-distances. Having got outpaced early, she stayed on nicely once switched out wide a furlong from home and can surely go one better before too long.
Moss Quito(IRE) finished sixth in a couple of Redcar maidens on varying ground (around 3l behind Annie Gogh in the second), but showed ability both times and again showed that he possesses some talent with the way he stayed on against the stands' rail. He could be just the type for a nursery when they begin next month. (op 12-1)
Therapeutic had shown plenty of ability in her first two starts and did best of the 'form' horses having been up there from the start, especially as she was drawn out in the centre of the track. She lacks the scope of those ahead of her, but could also be just the type for a nursery. (op 3-1)
Grievous Angel(IRE), a £12,000 2-y-o and half-sister to four winners (one at Listed level) over a variety of trips, was taken off her feet early but was noted doing some decent late work. She is one to keep an eye on. (op 33-1)
Red Style(IRE) was put in his place.
Annie Gogh made little impression after leading early. (op 11-2)

3111 HBJ CLAIM SOLUTIONS H'CAP 1m

2:20 (2:20) (Class 5) (0-70,69) 3-Y-O **£5,175** (£1,540; £769; £384) **Stalls** Low

Form RPR
3-45 **1** **Hi There (IRE)**[43] 1798 3-9-0 62 BarryMcHugh 13 71+
(Richard Fahey) *towards rr: hdwy over 2f out: sn in tch: swtchd rt and rdn to chse ldrs over 1f out: nt clr run 1f out: swtchd lft ins fnl f: styd on wl to ld nr fin* **7/1**
0052 **2** nk **Mick Slates (IRE)**[39] 1916 3-8-0 53 NeilFarley(5) 12 59
(Declan Carroll) *chsd ldr: cl up 3f out: rdn to ld 1 1/2f out: jnd and drvn ins fnl f: hdd and no ex nr fin* **14/1**
4345 **3** 1 ½ **Chester Aristocrat**[13] 2689 3-9-2 69 DarylByrne(5) 1 72
(Eric Alston) *trckd ldng pair: hdwy 2f out: rdn to chal over 1f out: drvn and ch ins fnl f: no ex last 75yds* **5/1**[3]
3-25 **4** 2 ½ **Dora's Sister (IRE)**[24] 2375 3-9-2 64 MichaelO'Connell 6 61
(John Quinn) *in tch: hdwy 3f out: chsd ldrs 2f out: nt clr run and edgd rt 1f out: chsd ldng pair whn hmpd and wknd ins fnl f* **4/1**[1]
0-04 **5** 3 ¼ **Long Lost Love**[18] 2552 3-9-4 66 JoeFanning 9 56
(Mark Johnston) *led: rdn along wl over 2f out: drvn and hdd 1 1/2f out: grad wknd* **8/1**
-660 **6** ½ **Bollin Tommy**[13] 2689 3-8-13 61 (p) DuranFentiman 5 49
(Tim Easterby) *chsd ldrs: rdn along wl over 2f out: wknd wl over 1f out* **25/1**
2404 **7** 1 ¼ **Orwellian**[18] 2540 3-8-8 56 TomEaves 11 42
(Bryan Smart) *midfield: hdwy on wd outside over 2f out: rdn to chse ldrs over 1f out: sn drvn and wknd* **10/1**
1233 **8** 2 ¼ **Luctor Emergo (IRE)**[14] 2673 3-8-8 56 (v[1]) PaulMulrennan 8 36
(Keith Dalgleish) *a towards rr* **8/1**
-532 **9** shd **Lean On Pete (IRE)**[25] 2353 3-9-1 63 GrahamLee 7 43
(Ollie Pears) *midfield: pushed along over 3f out: rdn over 2f out: sn wknd* **9/2**[2]
00-0 **10** nk **Roll Of Thunder**[25] 2336 3-8-5 53 ow1 AndrewElliott 14 33
(John Quinn) *a towards rr* **18/1**
00-0 **11** 9 **Captain Baldwin**[16] 2595 3-8-2 50 oh1 LukeMorris 4 9
(Jim Goldie) *a towards rr* **66/1**
0005 **12** ½ **Wolf Spirit (IRE)**[14] 2671 3-9-1 63 JamesSullivan 10 21
(Ruth Carr) *a in rr* **20/1**
1m 42.88s (1.68) **Going Correction** +0.20s/f (Good) 12 Ran SP% 120.7
Speed ratings (Par 99): **99,98,97,94,91 90,89,87,87,87 78,77**
CSF £100.49 CT £549.36 TOTE £6.50: £2.30, £4.20, £2.00; EX 112.90.
Owner Market Avenue Racing Club Ltd **Bred** J & J Waldron **Trained** Musley Bank, N Yorks
■ Stewards' Enquiry : Barry McHugh one-day ban: careless riding (Jun 29)

FOCUS
A modest handicap with eight of the 13 runners maidens coming into it. The placed horses look the best guides to the level.
Lean On Pete(IRE) Official explanation: jockey said gelding was unsuited by the good to soft ground

3112 M&F FUNERAL SERVICES E B F MAIDEN STKS 7f 30y

2:50 (2:50) (Class 5) 2-Y-O **£3,234** (£962; £481; £240) **Stalls** Low

Form RPR
32 **1** **Mazeppa**[7] 2873 2-9-3 0 TomEaves 5 74
(Keith Dalgleish) *led to 1/2-way: cl up: rdn to ld again over 1f out: edgd lft and drvn ins fnl f: kpt on* **11/5**[1]
0 **2** nk **Oasis Cannes**[34] 2073 2-9-3 0 LukeMorris 6 73+
(Sir Mark Prescott Bt) *chsd ldng pair: pushed along 3f out: rdn and sltly outpcd over 2f out: drvn and styd on to chal ins fnl f: no ex nr fin* **7/2**[2]
0 **3** 2 ¼ **Wellingrove (IRE)**[23] 2402 2-9-3 0 JoeFanning 9 68
(Mark Johnston) *cl up: led 1/2-way: rdn and edgd lft wl over 1f out: sn hdd: drvn and one pce fnl f* **6/1**[3]
4 2 **Fife Jo** 2-9-3 0 GrahamLee 3 63+
(Jim Goldie) *hld up in rr: stdy hdwy 2f out: rdn over 1f out: styd on ins fnl f: nrst fin* **14/1**
0 **5** nse **Orla's Rainbow (IRE)**[24] 2370 2-9-3 0 LeeNewman 4 63
(John Berry) *chsd ldng pair on inner: rdn along wl over 2f out: drvn and one pce fr wl over 1f out* **10/1**
6 1 ½ **Tiger Prince (IRE)** 2-9-3 0 PaulMulrennan 2 59
(Ann Duffield) *in tch: rdn along wl over 2f out: sn one pce* **14/1**
7 ½ **Oriental Romance (IRE)** 2-8-12 0 BarryMcHugh 1 53
(Richard Fahey) *a towards rr* **8/1**
3224 **8** 3 ¾ **Out Of The Blocks**[16] 2594 2-9-3 0 JamesSullivan 7 48
(Ruth Carr) *a towards rr* **6/1**[3]
1m 31.48s (2.48) **Going Correction** +0.25s/f (Good) 8 Ran SP% 115.6
Speed ratings (Par 93): **95,94,92,89,89 88,87,83**
toteswingers:1&2:£2.60, 1&3:£4.70, 2&3:£8.10 CSF £10.01 TOTE £3.40: £1.50, £1.70, £2.50; EX 11.00.
Owner Gordon McDowall **Bred** Gordon McDowall **Trained** Carluke, S Lanarks

FOCUS
An interesting maiden and this would have been quite a test for these juveniles. The fourth helps set the level.

NOTEBOOK
Mazeppa was up in trip after showing plenty of ability in his first two starts and was always towards the fore here. Despite hanging away to his left to follow the third horse over a furlong out, he kept on going well enough to just hold off the runner-up. He looks one for staying nurseries between now and the end of the season. (op 2-1 tchd 5-2)
Oasis Cannes, last of seven on last month's Haydock debut, is bred to be suited by this extra furlong and duly improved plenty. He was off the bridle a fair way out, but stuck at it and very nearly seized his chance as the leading pair started to hang. There should be a similar race in him. (op 4-1)
Wellingrove(IRE) ◆, very green when last of eight on his Fibresand debut last month, carted himself to the front after a couple of furlongs and again showed his immaturity by hanging about all over the place from over a furlong out. However, at least he showed that he possesses ability and there should be a lot more to come from him. (op 7-1)
Fife Jo, a £10,000 half-brother to a winning sprinter from the family of Monsieur Bond, came from last place to record a pleasing debut performance.
Orla's Rainbow(IRE) ran better than when well beaten on last month's Kempton debut and is bred to be suited by a proper test of stamina.

3113 JENNERS & FRASERS H'CAP (DIV II) 5f

3:25 (3:25) (Class 5) (0-75,73) 3-Y-O+ **£5,175** (£1,540; £769; £384) **Stalls** High

Form RPR
1224 **1** **Da'Quonde (IRE)**[11] 2750 4-9-9 68 TomEaves 6 84
(Bryan Smart) *led 1 1/2f: cl up: led again over 1f out: rdn and qcknd clr ins fnl f: easily* **9/4**[1]
4000 **2** 4 ½ **Missile Attack (IRE)**[21] 2458 4-8-9 54 (p) BarryMcHugh 5 54
(Ian Semple) *chsd ldng pair: rdn along 2f out: drvn over 1f out and kpt on same pce* **12/1**
3111 **3** hd **Sandwith**[8] 2839 9-9-5 69 6ex (p) NeilFarley(5) 8 68
(George Foster) *cl up on inner: led after 1 1/2f: rdn 2f out: hdd over 1f out: sn drvn and one pce* **7/2**[2]
0500 **4** ¾ **Cayman Fox**[8] 2839 7-8-12 57 (p) PaulMulrennan 7 54
(Linda Perratt) *in tch: hdwy 2f out: sn rdn and styd on fnl f: nrst fin* **10/1**
5-0 **5** 1 **Glenlini**[43] 1800 6-8-10 55 GrahamLee 2 48
(Jim Goldie) *sn outpcd and rdn along in rr: nvr a factor* **7/1**[3]
300- **6** 2 ¼ **Arriva La Diva**[286] 5719 6-9-2 61 LeeNewman 4 46
(Linda Perratt) *chsd ldrs: rdn along 2f out: sn drvn and wknd* **12/1**
6530 **7** 7 **Wicked Wilma (IRE)**[1] 3065 8-9-4 70 MatthewHopkins(7) 3 30+
(Alan Berry) *stmbld bdly and lost many l s: a bhd* **7/2**[2]
1m 0.19s (-0.21) **Going Correction** +0.05s/f (Good) 7 Ran SP% 112.2
Speed ratings (Par 103): **103,95,95,94,92 89,77**
toteswingers:1&2:£12.00, 1&3:£2.50, 2&3:£6.10 CSF £28.95 CT £90.66 TOTE £3.00: £1.80, £6.00; EX 28.10.
Owner The Barber Girls **Bred** Gestut Sohrenhof **Trained** Hambleton, N Yorks

FOCUS
The winning time was 0.71 seconds slower than the first division, though the ground would have deteriorated a bit in the meantime. The winner produced another step forward, while the third helps set the level.
Wicked Wilma(IRE) Official explanation: jockey said mare was slow away

3114 HBJ EMPLOYMENT SOLUTIONS LADIES DAY CUP (H'CAP) 1m 6f

4:00 (4:00) (Class 4) (0-85,84) 4-Y-O+ **£7,762** (£2,310; £1,154; £577) **Stalls** Centre

Form RPR
52-0 **1** **Blue Destination**[13] 1381 4-9-2 79 MichaelO'Connell 4 84
(John Quinn) *trckd ldrs: hdwy over 5f out: cl up over 2f out: rdn to chal wl over 1f out: drvn ins fnl f: kpt on to ld last 50yds* **17/2**

-143 2 ½ **Golden Future**[21] 2457 9-8-2 **68**................................. DeclanCannon(3) 1 72
(Peter Niven) *trckd ldng pair: hdwy 3f out: cl up 2f out: rdn to chal over 1f out: drvn ins fnl f and ev ch tl no ex last 50yds* **5/1**[3]

206- 3 nk **Stags Leap (IRE)**[5] 6379 5-8-2 **65** oh4......................... DuranFentiman 2 68
(Dianne Sayer) *trckd ldr: cl up over 3f out: led over 2f out: sn jnd and rdn: drvn ent fnl f: hdd and no ex last 50yds* **28/1**

33-4 4 1½ **Jonny Delta**[40] 1880 5-8-11 **74**.. GrahamLee 10 75
(Jim Goldie) *led: rdn along over 3f out: hdd over 2f out: drvn and kpt on same pce fr over 1f out* **2/1**[1]

0-00 5 nk **Activate**[27] 2278 5-9-7 **84**... BarryMcHugh 8 85
(Kevin Ryan) *hld up in rr: stdy hdwy over 4f out: rdn to chse ldrs 2f out: drvn and one pce fnl f* **7/1**

-061 6 7 **Tartan Gigha (IRE)**[11] 2751 7-9-6 **83** 6ex.......................... JoeFanning 5 74
(Geoffrey Harker) *hld up in rr: sme hdwy on inner wl over 2f out: swtchd lft over 1f out: no imp* **8/1**

1204 7 3¾ **Chookie Hamilton**[14] 2666 8-8-11 **74**.................................. TomEaves 3 60
(Ian Semple) *hld up in tch: hdwy 3f out: rdn along over 2f out: sn wknd* **7/1**

-260 8 4½ **Spirit Of A Nation (IRE)**[21] 2457 7-8-12 **75**.................... PaddyAspell 6 54
(James Moffatt) *trckd ldng pair: rdn along 4f out: sn wknd* **20/1**

50-0 9 10 **Waldvogel (IRE)**[28] 2253 8-9-7 **84**................................ PaulMulrennan 7 49
(Nicky Richards) *hld up: sme hdwy 3f out: sn rdn along and wknd* **4/1**[2]

3m 6.73s (1.43) **Going Correction** +0.25s/f (Good) **9** Ran SP% **124.8**
Speed ratings (Par 105): **105,104,104,103,103 99,97,94,89**
toteswingers:1&2:£10.30, 1&3:£22.90, 2&3:£5.90 CSF £54.86 CT £1177.38 TOTE £10.20: £2.80, £2.00, £5.10; EX 64.80.
Owner Maxilead Limited **Bred** Kirtlington Stud Ltd **Trained** Settrington, N Yorks

FOCUS
A decent staying handicap, run at an even pace, and a thrilling finish. The front four were prominent throughout but the form is held down by the proximity of the third from out of the weights.
Waldvogel(IRE) Official explanation: jockey said gelding had a fibrillating heart

3115 PENTLAND LAND ROVER H'CAP 7f 30y
4:30 (4:30) (Class 6) (0-65,65) 4-Y-0+ **£3,234** (£962; £481; £240) **Stalls** Low

Form RPR

-304 1 **Jupiter Fidius**[28] 2239 5-8-5 **56**..................................(p) GemmaTutty(7) 9 66
(Karen Tutty) *hld up towards rr: gd hdwy on outer over 3f out: led wl over 1f out: sn rdn clr: styd on* **10/1**

54-2 2 1¼ **Goninodaethat**[15] 2621 4-8-9 **53** ow1................................. GrahamLee 5 60
(Jim Goldie) *trckd ldrs: hdwy to chse ldr 3f out: led briefly over 2f out: sn rdn and hdd wl over 1f out: drvn and kpt on fnl f* **9/2**[2]

5-00 3 1½ **Iceblast**[34] 2096 4-9-2 **60**.. PaulMulrennan 2 63+
(Michael Easterby) *chsd ldrs: rdn along and sltly outpcd 2f out: drvn and kpt on fnl f* **3/1**[1]

503- 4 shd **Military Call**[233] 7099 5-9-1 **59**................................. MichaelO'Connell 12 62
(Alistair Whillans) *hld up towards rr: hdwy 3f out: rdn to chse ldng pair over 1f out: drvn and one pce fnl f* **10/1**

3650 5 2¼ **Whats For Pudding (IRE)**[7] 2879 4-8-2 **51**..................... NeilFarley(5) 6 48
(Declan Carroll) *in tch: rdn along wl over 2f out: kpt on same pce* **8/1**

0-10 6 3¾ **Cannon Bolt (IRE)**[34] 2091 4-9-2 **60**............................(b) LeeNewman 4 46
(Robin Bastiman) *led: rdn along 3f out: hdd over 2f out: grad wknd* **9/1**

5041 7 14 **Circuitous**[15] 2618 4-9-5 **63**..(v) JoeFanning 7 12
(Keith Dalgleish) *prom: pushed along 3f out: sn wknd* **7/1**

0-02 8 ¾ **Bay Of Fires (IRE)**[7] 2878 4-9-5 **63**.................................... LukeMorris 3 10
(David O'Meara) *hld up in tch: hdwy 3f out: rdn to chse ldng pair over 2f out: sn drvn and wknd* **5/1**[3]

140- 9 7 **Berbice (IRE)**[188] 7715 7-9-6 **64**...................................... BarryMcHugh 11
(Linda Perratt) *a in rr* **14/1**

1m 31.36s (2.36) **Going Correction** +0.25s/f (Good) **9** Ran SP% **118.3**
Speed ratings (Par 101): **96,94,92,92,90 85,69,69,61**
toteswingers:1&2:£15.80, 1&3:£13.40, 2&3:£5.20 CSF £55.95 CT £172.82 TOTE £17.00: £3.40, £1.50, £1.90; EX 99.40.
Owner N D Tutty **Bred** A C Birkle **Trained** Osmotherley, N Yorks

FOCUS
A moderate handicap, but with a few in here that like to force it a strong pace was always likely. The first two are rated to last year's form.
Jupiter Fidius Official explanation: trainer's rep said, regarding apparent improvement in form, that the gelding was better suited by the good to soft ground.

3116 SPRINGFIELD PROPERTIES H'CAP (FOR LADY AMATEUR RIDERS) 1m 4f 100y
5:05 (5:05) (Class 5) (0-70,70) 4-Y-0+ **£3,743** (£1,161; £580; £290) **Stalls** Low

Form RPR

0-10 1 **Talk Of Saafend (IRE)**[7] 2137 7-9-4 **53**........................... MissECSayer 5 61
(Dianne Sayer) *s.i.s and bhd: stdy hdwy over 4f out: effrt on wd outside 2f out: sn rdn and styd on to chal ent fnl f: led last 75yds* **4/1**[1]

350- 2 nk **Oddsmaker (IRE)**[295] 5405 11-9-4 **58**.............(t) MissAngelaBarnes(5) 11 66
(Maurice Barnes) *led and sn clr: pushed along wl over 2f out: rdn wl over 1f out: stl slt ld whn rdr appeared to mstke winning line and eased momentarily ins fnl 100yds: sn hdd and nt rcvr* **10/1**

05-0 3 4½ **Cool Baranca (GER)**[5] 2137 6-8-11 **51** oh2.......... MissRobynGray(5) 12 52
(Dianne Sayer) *chsd clr ldr: pushed along 3f out: rdn and sltly outpcd 2f out: styd on u.p fnl f* **6/1**[3]

00-R 4 nk **That'll Do Nicely (IRE)**[46] 1719 9-10-4 **70**............. MissJRRichards(3) 8 71
(Nicky Richards) *hld up towards rr: stdy hdwy over 4f out: rdn to chse ldrs wl over 1f out: kpt on same pce* **10/1**

2663 5 1¼ **Royal Straight**[2] 3030 7-9-8 **64**..................................(t) MissLSutcliffe(7) 14 63
(Linda Perratt) *hld up towards rr: smooth hdwy 3f out: chsd ldrs wl over 1f out: rdn over 1f out: sn btn* **7/1**

6-20 6 2¾ **Edas**[21] 2455 10-9-6 **58**... MissHCuthbert(3) 6 52
(Thomas Cuthbert) *trckd ldrs: hdwy to chse clr ldr over 3f out: rdn 2f out: wknd appr fnl f* **11/2**[2]

0-40 7 5 **Dimashq**[14] 2670 10-8-13 **51** oh6............................. MissWGibson(3) 10 38
(Paul Midgley) *in tch: hdwy to chse ldrs over 3f out: rdn over 2f out: sn wknd* **20/1**

0-60 8 5 **Mystified (IRE)**[11] 1247 9-9-2 **51** oh5.......................... MissSBrotherton 1 30
(Alan Berry) *prom: rdn along 3f out: wknd over 2f out* **16/1**

2-54 9 1¼ **Toshi (USA)**[16] 2599 10-9-2 **51** oh4..................................... MrsCBartley 13 28
(Jim Goldie) *chsd ldrs on outer: rdn along 3f out: wknd over 2f out* **8/1**

10 9 **Great Wisdom (IRE)**[13] 6341 6-10-3 **69**..................(p) MissCWalton(3) 4 32
(Lucinda Russell) *a towards rr* **16/1**

0/- 11 shd **Uncle Brit**[35] 1883 6-9-8 **60**................................... MissRJefferson(3) 2 23
(Malcolm Jefferson) *chsd ldrs: rdn along 1/2-way: sn lost pl and bhd fnl 3f* **10/1**

0-00 12 2¾ **Hurricane Thomas (IRE)**[12] 2735 8-8-11 **51** oh6(t) MissPhillipaTutty(5) 3 10
(Karen Tutty) *chsd ldrs: rdn along 4f out: sn wknd* **22/1**

2m 48.31s (6.31) **Going Correction** +0.25s/f (Good) **12** Ran SP% **121.4**
Speed ratings (Par 103): **88,87,84,84,83 81,78,75,74,68 68,66**
CSF £45.78 CT £244.31 TOTE £5.20: £2.10, £4.30, £2.60; EX 61.80.
Owner Dennis J Coppola **Bred** Michael Dalton **Trained** Hackthorpe, Cumbria
■ Stewards' Enquiry : Miss Angela Barnes ten-day ban: failed to ride out for 1st (tbn)

FOCUS
A modest contest, but at least the runner-up made sure the pace was good. he sets the standard and is rated as finishing upsides the winner.
Hurricane Thomas(IRE) Official explanation: jockey said gelding hung right
T/Jkpt: Quadpot: T/Plt: £2,354.90 to a £1 stake. Pool:£53,067.00 - 16.45 winning tickets
T/Qpdt: £49.00 to a £1 stake. Pool:£5,509.64 - 83.16 winning tickets JR

2852 SANDOWN (R-H)
Friday, June 15

OFFICIAL GOING: Soft (heavy in places on sprint course: sprint 5.2; round 6.2)
Sprint track full width. Round course dolled out 5yds from 9f to post adding about 8yds to distances. Home straight narrowed to 12yds bend to 2f pole.
Wind: Fresh, half-against Weather: Changeable, heavy rain during race 1

3117 BRITISH STALLION STUDS SUPPORTING BRITISH RACING E B F SPRINT MAIDEN STKS 5f 6y
2:10 (2:12) (Class 5) 2-Y-0 **£3,881** (£1,155; £577; £288) **Stalls** Low

Form RPR

333 1 **Faithfilly (IRE)**[15] 2631 2-8-12 0.. NeilCallan 4 83
(Ed Walker) *fast away: mde all against rail: pushed clr over 1f out: in n.d after: eased nr fin* **5/2**[2]

2 3¼ **Hasanan** 2-8-12 0.. BrettDoyle 1 69+
(Clive Brittain) *in tch: chsd wnr against rail 2f out: shkn up and no imp over 1f out* **7/2**

6 3 2¾ **Classic Art**[34] 2069 2-9-3 0... EddieAhern 5 64
(Roger Teal) *chsd wnr to 2f out: sn rdn and btn* **3/1**[3]

343 4 2¾ **Regal Dan (IRE)**[22] 2420 2-9-3 0...................................... MichaelHills 3 55
(Charles Hills) *t.k.h early: hld up and sn racd wd: disp 2nd 2f out: wknd over 1f out* **9/4**[1]

5 30 **Persian Marvel (IRE)** 2-9-3 0.. PatCosgrave 2
(Jim Boyle) *n.m.r after 1f and snatched up: sn lost tch: wl t.o* **16/1**

1m 7.44s (5.84) **Going Correction** +1.125s/f (Soft) **5** Ran SP% **112.4**
Speed ratings (Par 93): **98,92,88,84,36**
CSF £11.72 TOTE £2.60: £1.50, £2.10; EX 12.40.
Owner Laurence A Bellman **Bred** Deer Forest Stud **Trained** Newmarket, Suffolk
■ Stewards' Enquiry : Eddie Ahern three-day ban: careless riding (Jun 29-Jul 1)

FOCUS
The going was changed to soft, heavy in places after 6.5mm of overnight and morning rain and the time of the first confirmed that description. A small-field maiden and just fair form amongst those with experience, but one of those made it count and she sets the standard.

NOTEBOOK
Faithfilly(IRE), third on all three previous starts, absolutely pinged the gates and made all to score in comfortable fashion. She was not asked for a real effort until over a furlong out and picked up well in the conditions to score readily. She could go on from this in nurseries. (tchd 11-4)
Hasanan, by an Arc winner but a half-sister to a couple of juvenile winners from the family of Excellent Art, made a promising debut, chasing the winner throughout. She can certainly come on for the run and should get further. (tchd 3-1 and 4-1)
Classic Art, who ran green on his debut in a race that is working out well, showed up well until losing his place soon after halfway, and then rallied to some extent. (op 4-1)
Regal Dan(IRE) had to race furthest from the rail after being hampered early, but did not appear to like the conditions and his low action suggests a return to faster will be in his favour. (tchd 5-2)

3118 MEDIFORCE INDEPENDENT AMBULANCE H'CAP 5f 6y
2:40 (2:43) (Class 5) (0-75,76) 3-Y-0 **£2,587** (£770; £384; £192) **Stalls** Low

Form RPR

031 1 **Bogini (IRE)**[7] 2869 3-9-5 **76** 6ex..............................(b) MatthewCosham(5) 1 87
(M D O'Callaghan, Ire) *racd against rail: prom: trckd ldr over 1f out and sn plld out to chal: shkn up to ld jst ins fnl f: drew away* **13/8**[1]

41 2 2¼ **Jocasta Dawn**[45] 1739 3-9-7 **73**...................................... FergusSweeney 7 76+
(Henry Candy) *racd wd: hld up in 5th: rdn and prog to go 3rd over 1f out: styd on to take 2nd post* **7/2**[2]

-511 3 shd **Laura's Bairn**[51] 1599 3-9-5 **71**...................................(v) FrederikTylicki 4 73
(J R Jenkins) *led against rail: rdn over 1f out: hdd and one pce jst ins fnl f: lost 2nd post* **6/1**

-005 4 2½ **Hannibal Hayes (USA)**[21] 2443 3-8-9 **61**.................... RichardHughes 3 54+
(Jeremy Noseda) *hld up in 6th: plld out v wd and effrt 2f out: kpt on to take 4th fnl f: nvr on terms* **5/1**[3]

630 5 9 **Langley Vale**[45] 1723 3-9-0 **66**... SebSanders 2 27
(Roger Teal) *chsd ldr to over 3f out: rdn and lost pl sn after 1/2-way: wknd over 1f out* **8/1**

1P-0 6 2¾ **Especially Red (IRE)**[21] 2451 3-9-2 **68**............................. EddieAhern 5 19
(Lisa Williamson) *racd wd: prom: chsd ldr over 3f out to over 1f out: wknd qckly* **22/1**

50-0 7 5 **Baltic Flyer (IRE)**[35] 2045 3-8-10 **62**.................................. PaoloSirigu 6
(Robert Eddery) *hld up in last and racd wd: struggling bef 1/2-way: bhd whn hung rt over 1f out* **25/1**

1m 7.23s (5.63) **Going Correction** +1.125s/f (Soft) **7** Ran SP% **110.6**
Speed ratings (Par 99): **99,95,95,91,76 72,64**
toteswingers:1&2:£1.10, 1&3:£1.60, 2&3:£2.70 CSF £6.84 TOTE £2.60: £1.80, £2.20; EX 7.90.
Owner Michael O'Callaghan **Bred** Mountarmstrong Stud **Trained** Rathangan, Co. Kildare

FOCUS
Just a fair sprint handicap and the time was only just over a quarter of a second faster than the opening maiden. the form is rated around the winner and third.

3119 BRITISH STALLION STUDS SUPPORTING BRITISH RACING E B F MAIDEN STKS 7f 16y
3:15 (3:15) (Class 5) 2-Y-0 **£3,881** (£1,155; £577; £288) **Stalls** Low

Form RPR

1 **Operation Chariot (IRE)** 2-9-3 0................................. JimmyFortune 2 82+
(Andrew Balding) *s.i.s: sn trckd ldr: led 2f out and firmly pushed along: clr whn rdn out last 100yds* **11/4**[3]

2 5 **Sublimation (IRE)** 2-9-3 0... RichardHughes 1 72+
(Richard Hannon) *hld up in 3rd: rdn to chse wnr over 1f out: no imp and lost grnd last 150yds* **13/8**[1]

6 **3** *4* **Tuffan (USA)**[28] 2247 2-9-3 0 .... SebSanders 4 60
(Clive Brittain) *led: rdn and hdd 2f out: steadily fdd* **8/1**

4 *2 1/4* **Royal Prize** 2-9-3 0 .... JimCrowley 3 54
(Ralph Beckett) *dwlt: a in last: shkn up over 2f out: rn green and no prog over 1f out* **9/4**[2]

1m 38.12s (8.62) **Going Correction** +0.775s/f (Yiel) 4 Ran SP% **106.6**
Speed ratings (Par 93): **81,75,70,68**
CSF £7.41 TOTE £3.70; EX 7.10.
Owner P Brend & J Dwyer **Bred** Loughbrown Stud **Trained** Kingsclere, Hants

FOCUS
The best recent winner of this maiden was the Dante winner and Group 1 placed Magistretti, while several others have also been placed in Group races. The only one with previous experience in this small field had been well beaten on his sole start but there were a couple of well-bred types amongst the newcomers. It proved a real test for these inexperienced youngsters in the conditions and the form looks fluid at this stage.

NOTEBOOK
Operation Chariot(IRE), a sibling of five winners from 1m to 1m2f, was never far away and battled on tenaciously after hitting the front. Entered in the Derby, he is clearly well thought-of, and it will be interesting to see where he goes next. (op 3-1 tchd 5-2)
Sublimation(IRE), who traces to the family of Milligram, was sent off favourite on this debut and had his chance but could not pick up as well as the winner. (op 6-4 tchd 7-4)
Tuffan(USA), who had been slowly away on his debut, was sharper this time, made the running and came stands' side turning for home. It did not help him though as he was soon done with when headed inside the last quarter-mile. (op 11-1)
Royal Prize, a half-brother to a number of winners including the Group 3 winning stayer Gold Medallist, looked greenest of the four, having to be pushed along to find his stride, and was unable to pick up. He is likely to take time to find his feet and is probably one for next year. (op 2-1)

3120 MOUSETRAP CHALLENGE CUP FILLIES' H'CAP 1m 14y
3:50 (3:50) (Class 4) (0-85,81) 3-Y-0 **£4,075** (£1,212; £606; £303) **Stalls** Low

Form RPR
-032 **1** **Silvas Romana (IRE)**[14] 2672 3-9-0 **74** .... TomMcLaughlin 4 79
(Mark Brisbourne) *trckd ldr: led 3f out: urged along w no recrse to the whip fr over 1f out: hld on* **8/1**

10-5 **2** *nk* **Oojooba**[49] 1647 3-9-7 **81** .... NeilCallan 5 85
(Roger Varian) *t.k.h: trckd ldng pair: chsd wnr 2f out: no imp tl clsd gap nr fin: jst hld* **11/8**[1]

41-6 **3** *3 1/2* **No Compromise**[27] 2272 3-9-3 **77** .... JimmyFortune 3 73
(Hughie Morrison) *hld up in cl tch: shkn up and nt qckn over 2f out: wnt 3rd over 1f out: no imp fnl f* **9/4**[2]

11-0 **4** *3 1/4* **Emmuska**[27] 2272 3-9-6 **80** .... RichardHughes 2 69
(Richard Hannon) *led to 3f out: sn shkn up: fdd fnl 2f* **7/2**[3]

2-00 **5** *11* **Cockney Rhyme**[9] 2813 3-9-3 **77** .... StevieDonohoe 1 40
(Heather Main) *hld up in cl tch: shkn up wl over 2f out: sn wknd* **22/1**

1m 49.83s (6.53) **Going Correction** +0.775s/f (Yiel) 5 Ran SP% **110.6**
Speed ratings (Par 98): **98,97,94,90,79**
CSF £19.76 TOTE £8.30: £2.40, £1.50; EX 17.00.
Owner The Bourne Connection **Bred** Limetree Stud **Trained** Great Ness, Shropshire

FOCUS
A tight little fillies' handicap despite the small field; they came up the centre in the straight. The second and third help set the level.

3121 MEDIFORCE.ORG H'CAP 1m 2f 7y
4:20 (4:20) (Class 3) (0-90,86) 4-Y-0+ **£6,411** (£1,919; £959; £479; £239) **Stalls** Low

Form RPR
-361 **1** **Chain Of Events**[15] 2637 5-8-11 **76** .... JimCrowley 2 86
(Sarah Humphrey) *hld up initially but quick move to ld after 1f: mde rest: at least 3 l clr fr 1/2-way: wl in command 2f out: rdn out* **7/2**[3]

0-02 **2** *4 1/2* **Proud Chieftain**[9] 2810 4-9-6 **85** .... (p) JamesDoyle 4 86
(Clifford Lines) *led at slow pce for 1f: chsd wnr after: shkn up and no imp over 2f out* **5/2**[2]

4-60 **3** *2* **Mountain Range (IRE)**[25] 2346 4-9-5 **84** .... EddieAhern 1 81
(John Dunlop) *trckd ldng pair: shkn up to dispute 2nd 3f out: nt qckn over 2f out: wl hld after* **7/2**[3]

0-15 **4** *7* **Aldwick Bay (IRE)**[30] 2180 4-9-7 **86** .... RichardHughes 3 74
(Richard Hannon) *hld up in 4th: effrt 3f out: sn rdn and no prog: eased ins fnl f* **9/4**[1]

36-0 **5** *1 1/2* **Greylami (IRE)**[25] 2346 7-9-6 **85** .... StevieDonohoe 5 65
(Robert Mills) *awkward s: sn hld up in last: shkn up and wl detached 3f out: no prog* **16/1**

2m 19.17s (8.67) **Going Correction** +0.775s/f (Yiel) 5 Ran SP% **109.7**
Speed ratings (Par 107): **96,92,90,85,84**
CSF £12.45 TOTE £4.90: £2.40, £2.60; EX 14.20.
Owner P J Edwards **Bred** Bishop Wilton Stud **Trained** West Wratting, Cambs

FOCUS
A decent handicap with very little between four of the five runners on official ratings. The form is a bit fluid with the runner-up rated close to his turf form.

NOTEBOOK
Chain Of Events ◆ was soon taken to the front and dictated, and the order barely changed from that point on. A winner over C&D on fast ground at the end of last month off 6lb lower, he had form on a softer surface though, and once his rider kicked on rounding the home turn, he was always in charge. He has been placed on both his other starts here so is always one to consider at this track, and will be aimed at the £100,000 bonus in a race over C&D on 1st September. (op 9-2)
Proud Chieftain led early before settling in behind the winner, but could make no impression in the straight. This was his first try on soft ground and he is probably happier on faster.
Mountain Range(IRE) goes well on soft ground and has won over C&D, but his effort here was short-lived and he is not firing at present. (op 3-1, tchd 4-1 in places)
Aldwick Bay(IRE) was sent off favourite having scored on soft ground earlier this season but his effort flattened out after he briefly looked a threat around 2f out. This was disappointing, but possibly he is better suited by flat or sharp tracks and the stiff finish here was against him. (op 5-2 tchd 2-1)
Greylami(IRE) has not won for getting on for two years now and has only shown glimpses of his old form recently, despite a falling handicap mark. It might be worth trying cheekpieces or some form of headgear to try to spark a revival. (op 12-1)

3122 BECK H'CAP 1m 2f 7y
4:55 (4:55) (Class 5) (0-75,72) 3-Y-0 **£2,587** (£770; £384; £192) **Stalls** Low

Form RPR
6001 **1** **Ultimate Destiny**[10] 2787 3-9-5 **70** 6ex .... JimCrowley 7 80
(Ralph Beckett) *mde virtually all: jnd over 2f out: drvn and gd battle w runner-up after: gained upper hand last 50yds* **2/1**[1]

-003 **2** *3/4* **Tidal Way (IRE)**[20] 2471 3-9-6 **71** .... JimmyFortune 5 79
(Mick Channon) *pressed wnr to 1/2-way and again over 3f out: sustained chal and upsides fr over 2f out tl no ex last 50yds* **11/4**[2]

1-04 **3** *4 1/2* **Chrissycross (IRE)**[15] 2624 3-8-8 **64** .... (p) MarkCoumbe(5) 3 63
(Roger Teal) *in tch: pushed along over 4f out: prog to chse ldng pair over 2f out and cl enough: nt qckn over 1f out: steadily lft bhd fnl f* **10/1**

0006 **4** *6* **Tidy Affair (IRE)**[18] 2557 3-9-7 **72** .... TomMcLaughlin 2 59
(Murty McGrath) *hld up: styd on inner in bk st whn rest racd wd: rdn over 3f out: sn no prog: tk modest 4th nr fin* **12/1**

0-00 **5** *shd* **Chocolat Chaud (IRE)**[22] 2424 3-8-4 **55** .... KieranO'Neill 1 42
(J W Hills) *stdd s: hld up in last pair: shkn up over 3f out: no real prog* **14/1**

04-0 **6** *nk* **Attraction Ticket**[29] 2197 3-8-9 **60** .... FergusSweeney 8 46
(David Simcock) *in tch: rdn and effrt 3f out: wknd 2f out* **7/2**[3]

006 **7** *16* **Opus (IRE)**[17] 2585 3-8-11 **62** .... (t) PatCosgrave 6 16
(Amanda Perrett) *prom: chsd wnr 1/2-way to over 3f out: wknd qckly: t.o* **11/1**

2m 18.48s (7.98) **Going Correction** +0.775s/f (Yiel) 7 Ran SP% **114.0**
Speed ratings (Par 99): **99,98,94,90,89 89,76**
toteswingers:1&2:£1.80, 1&3:£3.90, 2&3:£3.90 CSF £7.63 CT £41.48 TOTE £3.10: £1.50, £2.40; EX 6.00.
Owner D & J Newell **Bred** Derek & Judith Newell **Trained** Kimpton, Hants

FOCUS
Quite a competitive 3yo handicap that produced a fine finish. The time was 0.69sec faster than the preceding handicap. The runner-up is rated close to his best juvenile form.
T/Plt: £73.00 to a £1 stake. Pool:£44,980.64 - 449.63 winning tickets T/Qpdt: £24.90 to a £1 stake. Pool:£2,386.89 - 70.90 winning tickets JN

2504 YORK (L-H)
Friday, June 15

OFFICIAL GOING: Good to soft (soft in places) changing to soft after race 3 (3.05)
Rail on round course moved to innermost line reducing distances of races of 1m and over by 27yds.
Wind: Moderate, half-behind Weather: ovdercast, changeable, heavy showers

3123 ACTURIS E B F MAIDEN STKS 5f
2:00 (2:01) (Class 3) 2-Y-O **£6,469** (£1,925; £962; £481) **Stalls** Centre

Form RPR
1 **Flyman** 2-9-3 0 .... PaulHanagan 2 91+
(Richard Fahey) *w ldr: led 3f out: shkn up 1f out: edgd lft: styd on strly* **15/8**[1]

2 *1 1/4* **Tanghan (IRE)** 2-9-3 0 .... DavidNolan 5 84+
(Richard Fahey) *dwlt: mid-div: hdwy over 2f out: chsd wnr 1f out: kpt on same pce last 75yds* **20/1**

04 **3** *2 1/2* **Shrimpton**[10] 2783 2-8-12 0 .... SamHitchcott 4 70
(Mick Channon) *wnt lft s: chsd ldrs: kpt on same pce appr fnl f* **8/1**

4 *6* **Masai King (IRE)** 2-9-3 0 .... DanielTudhope 11 56+
(Robin Bastiman) *in rr: hdwy and nt clr run over 1f out: swtchd lft: kpt on* **33/1**

36 **5** *1* **Inchy Coo**[44] 1753 2-8-12 0 .... DavidAllan 9 45
(Tim Easterby) *s.i.s: sn pushed along: hdwy over 2f out: nvr a factor* **14/1**

3 **6** *hd* **Prince Regal**[8] 2844 2-8-10 0 .... MichaelJMMurphy(7) 1 49
(Alan Jarvis) *led: hdd 3f out: edgd rt: wknd appr fnl f* **3/1**[2]

600 **7** *8* **Royal Jenray**[25] 2330 2-9-3 0 .... PhillipMakin 6 20
(Jedd O'Keeffe) *chsd ldrs: reminders 3f out: wknd over 1f out* **100/1**

5 **8** *2 1/2* **Sandsend (IRE)**[20] 2508 2-9-3 0 .... TonyHamilton 13 11
(Richard Fahey) *towards rr: sme hdwy over 2f out: sn wknd* **9/1**

4 **9** *7* **Tough Lady (IRE)**[8] 2837 2-8-12 0 .... SilvestreDeSousa 10
(Mark Johnston) *mid-div: sn outpcd and hung lft: lost pl over 3f out: bhd fnl 2f* **15/2**[3]

05 **10** *3/4* **El Molino Blanco**[21] 2456 2-8-5 0 .... DavidSimmonson(7) 7
(Michael Easterby) *s.i.s: outpcd and in rr: bhd fnl 2f* **80/1**

11 *1* **Grey Destiny** 2-9-3 0 .... RobertWinston 8
(Mel Brittain) *chsd ldrs: lost pl 2f out* **33/1**

1m 3.01s (3.71) **Going Correction** +0.675s/f (Yiel) 11 Ran SP% **112.2**
Speed ratings (Par 97): **97,95,91,81,79 79,66,62,51,50 48**
toteswingers:1&2:£11.00, 1&3:£4.20, 2&3:£25.00 CSF £45.53 TOTE £2.80: £1.20, £5.70, £2.40; EX 41.40 Trifecta £285.90 Pool: £687.77 - 1.78 winning units..
Owner George Murray **Bred** Coln Valley Stud **Trained** Musley Bank, N Yorks

FOCUS
The principals came nicely clear in this juvenile maiden and its worth taking a positive view about the form. The ground certainly looked on the easy side.

NOTEBOOK
Flyman rewarded solid support and got his career off to a perfect start. He showed natural early pace and travelled best in the race. He drifted left once asked to win the race, though, and had to dig deep near the business end. He evidently has plenty of speed, but his trainer was slightly worried about this sharp 5f beforehand and his dam did score over 7f. That all bodes well for his future and it will be interesting to see where he turns up next. (tchd 2-1 and 9-4 in a place)
Tanghan(IRE), a 20-1 shot, pushed the winner inside the final furlong and made it a 1-2 for the stable. He's bred to enjoy longer trips and so it wasn't surprising that he did his best work late on. It must rate a promising introduction. (op 18-1 tchd 22-1)
Shrimpton did some decent late work and fared best of those with previous experience, so rates a fair benchmark. She's improved with each of her three races to date. (tchd 9-1)
Masai King(IRE) is a half-brother to Chandlery, who landed the Group 2 Vintage Stakes over 7f for Richard Hannon at Glorious Goodwood last year. He broke well enough towards the near side, but got behind from halfway and then had to switch for his effort when well beaten. He did stride out nicely inside the final furlong, however, and looks sure to come on a bundle. A stiffer test can see him off the mark.
Inchy Coo was outpaced from a very early stage and looks ready for another furlong. (tchd 16-1)
Prince Regal ran well below his encouraging debut effort at Lingfield. He surely found the run coming too soon. (tchd 11-4 and 10-3 and 7-2 in a place)

3124 NEPTUNE INVESTMENT MANAGEMENT STKS (H'CAP) 1m 2f 88y
2:30 (2:30) (Class 2) (0-100,88) 3-Y-O **£12,938** (£3,850; £1,924; £962) **Stalls** Low

Form RPR
1 **1** **Valiant**[27] 2271 3-9-5 **86** .... RyanMoore 5 102
(William Haggas) *s.i.s: detached in last and sn pushed along: hdwy over 1f out: styd on wl to ld last 30yds* **7/4**[1]

-125 **2** *1 1/4* **Silver Blaze**[13] 2718 3-9-6 **87** .... PJMcDonald 4 100
(Alan Swinbank) *trckd ldrs: chal over 2f out: hung lft and led over 1f out: hdd and no ex wl ins fnl f* **13/2**

3-24 **3** *2 1/2* **Ahzeemah (IRE)**[49] 1641 3-9-4 **85** .... (p) SilvestreDeSousa 1 93
(Saeed Bin Suroor) *trckd ldrs: rdn over 3f out: ev ch over 1f out: kpt on one pce* **9/2**[3]

1-21 **4** *10* **Eastern Destiny**[17] 2589 3-8-10 **77** .... PaulHanagan 2 65
(Richard Fahey) *led: qcknd pce 4f out: hdd over 1f out: sn wknd* **11/2**

1-01 **5** *20* **Beaufort Twelve**[22] 2408 3-9-4 **88** .... HarryBentley(3) 6 36
(William Jarvis) *t.k.h: sn trcking ldr: drvn and outpcd over 3f out: sn lost pl and bhd: t.o* **3/1**[2]

2m 13.67s (1.17) **Going Correction** +0.20s/f (Good) **5** Ran SP% **108.3**
Speed ratings (Par 105): **103,102,100,92,76**
CSF £12.66 TOTE £2.30: £1.40, £2.70; EX 13.50.

Owner Highclere Thoroughbred Racing-Herring **Bred** New England, Middle Park & Balmerino Bs **Trained** Newmarket, Suffolk

FOCUS
This 3yo handicap usually throws up a winner to follow through the season, although the top weight this year was rated 12lb lower than the race ceiling.

NOTEBOOK
Valiant made it 2-2 on his handicap debut. However, any backers of the winner have Ryan Moore to thank, as he was at his very best and one will do well to see a better ride this year. The son of Galileo proved lazy from the stalls and got behind, with Moore continually niggling at him to close. Indeed, he was the first to get a reminder after straightening for home and looked well held 2f out. As the pace began to collapse in front of him, though, he finally responded to maximum pressure and mowed down the runner-up late on to win cosily. He needed all of this trip when landing his maiden last month and will no doubt appreciate a stiffer test as he matures, but it was greenness that so nearly cost him here and his future looks very bright as he's in the right hands. (op 2-1)

Silver Blaze was much better suited by this drop back in trip and has to rate somewhat unfortunate to have bumped into such a promising winner, as he battled gamely to master the leaders before being mugged. He has plenty of scope. (op 5-1)

Ahzeemah(IRE) appreciated this slightly easier ground and had every chance, but is now looking held by the handicapper. (op 5-1 tchd 4-1)

Eastern Destiny won well at Ripon last time out and was up 5lb. She went from the front this time, though, and while it was still a sound effort, the more positive tactics found her out in this company on the easier ground. (op 5-1)

Beaufort Twelve made it 2-3 when scraping home on his handicap debut at Goodwood 22 days earlier and was raised 5lb. He moved nicely into contention, but fell in a hole once put under pressure and this confirms he wants a quicker surface. Official explanation: trainer said that the colt was unsuitably by the good to soft (soft in places) ground (op 10-3 tchd 7-2)

3125 BOND TYRES STKS (H'CAP) 1m 6f
3:05 (3:06) (Class 2) (0-105,97) 4-Y-0+ **£12,938** (£3,850; £1,924; £962) **Stalls** Low

Form RPR

23-2 **1** **Qahriman**[20] 2474 4-9-0 **90** .... RyanMoore 7 100+
(Luca Cumani) *hld up in mid-div: effrt 4f out: wnt 2nd over 1f out: led last 100yds: styd on wl* **7/2**[2]

-006 **2** *2* **Bridle Belle**[28] 2253 4-8-8 **84** .... PaulHanagan 2 91
(Richard Fahey) *trckd ldrs: led over 2f out: hdd and no ex ins fnl f* **11/1**

000- **3** *5* **The Betchworth Kid**[195] 7297 7-9-7 **97** .... HayleyTurner 5 97
(Alan King) *s.i.s: in rr: drvn over 4f out: hdwy on wd outside over 1f out: styd on to take 3rd towards fin* **16/1**

1/22 **4** *½* **Local Hero (GER)**[34] 2072 5-8-13 **89** .... (p) RobertWinston 6 88
(Steve Gollings) *mid-div: hdwy over 4f out: chsng ldrs 3f out: one pce fnl 2f* **9/2**[3]

1-21 **5** *4* **Lordofthehouse (IRE)**[13] 2709 4-8-13 **89** .... ChrisCatlin 11 83+
(William Haggas) *s.v.s: hdwy to join ldrs 8f out: hung lft and wknd over 1f out* **3/1**[1]

0-10 **6** *3* **Deauville Flyer**[28] 2253 6-9-1 **91** .... (p) DavidAllan 8 81
(Tim Easterby) *chsd ldrs: drvn 4f out: wknd over 1f out* **10/1**

/055 **7** *¾* **Smokey Oakey (IRE)**[83] 1037 8-8-7 **83** .... TedDurcan 1 71
(Mark H Tompkins) *hld up in mid-div: smooth hdwy over 3f out: wknd over 1f out* **33/1**

-040 **8** *¾* **Address Unknown**[37] 1974 5-8-11 **94** .... (v) GeorgeDowning(7) 9 81
(Ian Williams) *hld up in rr: hdwy 7f out: wknd over 1f out* **40/1**

03-0 **9** *8* **Merchant Of Dubai**[37] 1974 7-9-3 **93** .... DanielTudhope 12 69
(Jim Goldie) *w ldr: led over 3f out: hdd over 2f out: wknd over 1f out* **12/1**

-510 **10** *7* **Persian Peril**[30] 2180 8-8-12 **88** .... PJMcDonald 4 54
(Alan Swinbank) *hld up in rr: hdwy on outer over 3f out: lost pl over 1f out* **33/1**

00-4 **11** *8* **Constant Contact**[28] 2228 5-9-1 **91** .... PhillipMakin 10 46
(Donald McCain) *led: drvn over 4f out: hdd over 3f out: wknd 2f out: eased whn bhd* **16/1**

-303 **12** *15* **Hurricane Higgins (IRE)**[27] 2278 4-9-7 **97** .... SilvestreDeSousa 3 31
(Mark Johnston) *chsd ldrs: checked on bnd over 4f out: lost pl over 3f out: bhd whn swvd rt over 2f out: eased: t.o* **12/1**

3m 5.95s (5.75) **Going Correction** +0.475s/f (Yiel) **12** Ran SP% **118.3**
Speed ratings (Par 109): **102,100,98,97,95 93,93,92,88,84 79,71**
toteswingers:1&2:£10.50, 1&3:£11.00, 2&3:£25.50 CSF £41.25 CT £551.74 TOTE £4.40: £2.00, £3.40, £5.50; EX 43.60 Trifecta £1066.30 Part won. Pool: £1,440.96 - 0.84 winning units..

Owner Sheikh Mohammed Obaid Al Maktoum **Bred** Darley **Trained** Newmarket, Suffolk

FOCUS
A decent staying handicap, run at a solid pace, and the form should work out with the first pair coming clear.

NOTEBOOK
Qahriman got up inside the final half furlong and got off the mark at the second time of asking for the campaign under another cracking ride from Ryan Moore, who completed a quick-fire double. He looked a winning waiting to happen when second on his comeback at Chester last month and this more galloping track back up in trip was sure to suit better. However, he did have something to prove on an easy surface. Moore rode him confidently, though, and he easily made up ground at the top of the home straight. He met trouble when initially looking for a way through and showed guts when in the clear to mow down the runner-up, so this was a very likeable display. No doubt the Ebor over C&D in August will now be on this scopey 4yo's agenda and he can develop into a leading player for that. (op 4-1 tchd 10-3)

Bridle Belle travelled beautifully and made a bold bid, but was a sitting duck for the winner from the furlong marker. She was back on her last winning mark here and will now go back up in the handicap, but was a clear second-best. A more patient ride over this sort of trip can see her deservedly back to winning ways. (op 14-1)

The Betchworth Kid was last seen over hurdles in December, but met support back on the level and he stayed on late in the day to turn in a promising effort on ground that suits. He's high enough in the weights, but is entitled to improve for the run. (op 14-1)

Local Hero(GER), a runner-up the last twice, goes well on this ground and had every chance. He has to rate as a non-stayer, however.

Lordofthehouse(IRE), 6lb higher back down in trip on slower ground, again blew the start, losing around six lengths, and being rushed up to be handy into the first turn wide of runners cannot have helped his finishing effort. He remains a stayer of promise, but does have some issues. (op 11-4 tchd 7-2)

3126 SKF ROUS (S) STKS 6f
3:40 (3:43) (Class 4) 2-Y-O **£6,469** (£1,925; £962; £481) **Stalls** Centre

Form RPR

642 **1** **Fadeintoinfinity**[10] 2790 2-8-6 0 .... SamHitchcott 11 71+
(Mick Channon) *hld up towards rr: hdwy stands' side over 3f out: styd on to ld jst ins fnl f: drvn out* **5/2**[1]

0 **2** *2¼* **Old Man Clegg**[25] 2334 2-8-11 0 .... PhillipMakin 15 68
(Michael Easterby) *swer rt s: in rr: hdwy stands' side over 2f out: styd on to take 2nd nr line* **18/1**

3 *½* **Balinka** 2-8-6 0 .... PJMcDonald 1 61+
(Mel Brittain) *led after 1f: hdd jst ins fnl f: lost 2nd nr fin* **33/1**

621 **4** *4* **Mad Jazz**[51] 1594 2-8-3 0 .... DominicFox(3) 10 49+
(Tony Coyle) *in tch: outpcd over 2f out: kpt on fnl f* **16/1**

11 **5** *1¼* **Severn Bore**[67] 1253 2-8-4 0 .... RyanWhile(7) 16 51
(Bill Turner) *trckd ldrs: edgd lft and wknd over 1f out* **6/1**[3]

2 **6** *2½* **Jamesbo's Girl**[25] 2338 2-8-6 0 .... AdrianNicholls 2 38
(David Nicholls) *in rr: kpt on fnl 2f: nvr nr ldrs* **11/1**

00 **7** *3* **Mill End Dancer**[7] 2880 2-8-6 0 .... AmyRyan 4 29
(Michael Easterby) *led 1f: chsd ldrs: wknd over 1f out* **50/1**

8 *7* **Edith Anne** 2-8-9 0 ow3 .... MickyFenton 12 11
(Paul Midgley) *s.i.s: sn mid-div: wknd 2f out* **40/1**

3 **9** *nk* **Reconsider Baby (IRE)**[25] 2338 2-8-6 0 .... RoystonFfrench 14 7
(Mrs K Burke) *in rr and sn pushed along: nvr on terms* **16/1**

324 **10** *18* **Fly Fisher (IRE)**[31] 2138 2-8-11 0 .... PaulHanagan 6
(Richard Fahey) *mid-div: drvn over 2f out: lost pl wl over 1f out: eased whn bhd* **3/1**[2]

00 **11** *2¼* **Special Report (IRE)**[25] 2334 2-8-11 0 .... SilvestreDeSousa 7
(Nigel Tinkler) *in rr: eased whn bhd* **100/1**

12 *2* **Haaf'n Haaf** 2-8-5 0 ow1 .... DavidSimmonson(7) 3
(Michael Easterby) *s.i.s: a in rr: eased whn bhd* **25/1**

523 **13** *1* **Shop Til You Drop**[51] 1594 2-8-6 0 .... KirstyMilczarek 9
(David Evans) *chsd ldrs: lost pl over 1f out: eased whn bhd* **25/1**

031 **14** *39* **Vanessa**[68] 1235 2-8-6 0 .... GrahamGibbons 17
(Jim Goldie) *virtually ref to r: a hopelessly t.o* **10/1**

1m 18.11s (6.21) **Going Correction** +0.775s/f (Yiel) **14** Ran SP% **118.3**
Speed ratings (Par 95): **89,85,84,79,77 74,70,61,60,36 33,30,29,**
toteswingers:1&2:£13.70, 1&3:£18.80, 2&3:£63.20 CSF £46.04 TOTE £3.50: £1.40, £6.30, £10.10; EX 73.10 TRIFECTA Not won..The winner was bought in for £12,500. Severn Bore was claimed by Michael Wigham for £12,000.

Owner Imperial **Bred** Imperial & Mike Channon Bloodstock Ltd **Trained** West Ilsley, Berks

FOCUS
Rain bucketed down prior to this juvenile seller and unsurprisingly the ground was officially changed to soft. There was no hanging about and most struggled on the deteriorating surface.

NOTEBOOK
Fadeintoinfinity was the clear form pick on this drop into plating company and she proved too strong for her rivals, winning readily. Her near-miss at Redcar ten days earlier was by far the best form on offer here and her yard's 2yos continue in decent form. She was subsequently bought in for £12,500. (op 7-2)

Old Man Clegg, whose yard won this last year, got going late on the near side and showed up a lot better than had been the case on his debut last month. He has some scope and should come on again for the experience. (op 25-1 tchd 28-1)

Balinka, speedily bred, shot out from her inside draw and posted a bold debut effort. She looks a sure-fire future winner.

Mad Jazz made all in a seller at Catterick 51 days earlier. Easy to back over this extra furlong, he hit a flat spot in mid-field before staying on late when the race was effectively over, and he should appreciate reverting to better ground. (op 11-1)

Severn Bore arrived having won two races of this class in April. He's bred to stay this trip no bother, so it was probably a case of the soft ground and needing the run that saw him tire from the furlong marker. (op 11-2)

Fly Fisher(IRE), the clear second favourite, struggled to pick up out of this ground and failed to get home. Official explanation: jockey said colt was never travelled (op 7-2)

Shop Til You Drop Official explanation: jockey said filly lost its action

3127 COOPERS MARQUEES STKS (H'CAP) 5f
4:10 (4:11) (Class 3) (0-95,94) 3-Y-0+ **£7,439** (£2,213; £1,106; £553) **Stalls** Centre

Form RPR

-210 **1** **Judge 'n Jury**[13] 2704 8-9-8 **93** .... (t) DarrenEgan(5) 17 102
(Ronald Harris) *w ldrs stands' side: led ins fnl f: jst hld on* **10/1**

4040 **2** *shd* **Hazelrigg (IRE)**[20] 2507 7-9-3 **83** .... (be) DavidAllan 1 92
(Tim Easterby) *chsd ldrs: kpt on ins fnl f: jst denied* **14/1**

0-00 **3** *½* **Sohraab**[13] 2704 8-9-7 **87** .... RyanMoore 6 94+
(Hughie Morrison) *hld up: hdwy far side over 2f out: chsng ldrs over 1f out: styd on towards fin* **6/1**[1]

-302 **4** *nk* **Flash City (ITY)**[13] 2717 4-9-3 **83** .... (v) RoystonFfrench 2 89
(Bryan Smart) *led: hdd ins fnl f: fdd fnl strides* **14/1**

0301 **5** *3½* **Taurus Twins**[12] 2731 6-9-5 **88** 6ex .... (b) DaleSwift(3) 9 81
(Richard Price) *chsd ldrs: wknd last 150yds* **25/1**

5300 **6** *1½* **Haajes**[29] 2195 8-8-13 **79** .... MickyFenton 15 67
(Paul Midgley) *towards rr: hdwy 2f out: kpt on ins fnl f* **18/1**

-420 **7** *2¾* **Blue Jack**[37] 1975 7-9-7 **94** .... (v) WilliamTwiston-Davies(7) 5 72
(Tom Dascombe) *s.i.s: in rr: swtchd lft over 1f out: kpt on* **20/1**

3610 **8** *nk* **Bedloe's Island (IRE)**[10] 2793 7-9-4 **84** .... SilvestreDeSousa 13 61
(Neville Bycroft) *dwlt: in rr: swtchd rt to stands' side over 1f out: kpt on: nvr nr ldrs* **14/1**

1010 **9** *2¼* **Mayoman (IRE)**[13] 2717 7-9-7 **87** .... (v) DanielTudhope 18 56+
(David O'Meara) *s.i.s: sme hdwy whn nt clr run over 1f out: nvr a factor* **25/1**

0245 **10** *1¾* **Foxy Music**[13] 2717 8-9-12 **92** .... ShaneKelly 7 55
(Eric Alston) *chsd ldrs: wknd over 1f out* **25/1**

0032 **11** *3¾* **Bathwick Bear (IRE)**[18] 2558 4-9-8 **88** .... KirstyMilczarek 12 37
(David Evans) *in rr: hdwy and swtchd stands' rails 2f out: sn wknd* **14/1**

-644 **12** *½* **Racy**[13] 2717 5-9-13 **93** .... PhillipMakin 16 40
(Kevin Ryan) *dwlt: sn mid-div: wknd over 1f out* **13/2**[2]

3-46 **13** *3¼* **Jamesway (IRE)**[13] 2704 4-9-4 **84** .... TonyHamilton 3 20
(Richard Fahey) *mid-div: effrt and n.m.r over 2f out: sn wknd* **8/1**[3]

0-00 **14** *nk* **Medici Time**[16] 2596 7-9-3 **83** .... RichardMullen 14 18
(Tim Easterby) *s.i.s: sme hdwy stands' side 2f out: sn wknd* **25/1**

41-0 **15** *½* **Le Toreador**[16] 2596 7-9-6 **86** .... (p) PaulHanagan 8 19
(Kevin Ryan) *in tch: effrt over 2f out: sn wknd* **20/1**

-000 **16** *3¼* **Cocktail Charlie**[9] 2825 4-9-2 **82** .... (p) TedDurcan 10 3
(Tim Easterby) *mid-div: effrt over 2f out: sn wknd* **16/1**

3-10 **17** *5* **Long Awaited (IRE)**[13] 2704 4-9-7 **87**.................... GrahamGibbons 20
(David Barron) *mid-div: wknd 2f out: eased whn bhd ins fnl f* **9/1**

1m 2.18s (2.88) **Going Correction** +0.775s/f (Yiel) **17** Ran SP% **120.5**
Speed ratings (Par 107): **107,106,106,105,99 97,93,92,89,86 80,79,74,73,73 67,59**
toteswingers:1&2:£38.50, 1&3:£8.00, 2&3:£28.40 CSF £124.81 CT £936.66 TOTE £9.20: £2.10, £4.10, £1.70, £2.80; EX 192.90 TRIFECTA Not won..
Owner Robert & Nina Bailey **Bred** C A Cyzer **Trained** Earlswood, Monmouths

FOCUS
Helping force the pace on the sprint track at York is never a bad idea and it once again proved hard to make up ground from out the back in this good sprint handicap. The first four were clear at the finish.

NOTEBOOK
Judge 'n Jury knuckled down bravely inside the final furlong and just did enough to hang on. He was well beaten at York on his previous outing, but had made all over C&D the time before and obviously this venue is right up his street. The 8yo deserves extra credit as the three behind were all drawn much lower and this race most often goes to a runner near the bottom of the handicap. He has won off a 5lb higher mark in the past and is clearly in top form. (tchd 9-1)
Hazelrigg(IRE), who missed the kick here last time out, raced handily and only just failed. He hasn't won since 2010 but ideally wants quicker ground and, on this showing, his turn looks to be nearing again. (op 16-1)
Sohraab ◆, better than the bare form when in front of the winner last time, had dropped to a mark 1lb lower than when taking this race in 2008 and attracted support with Ryan Moore back aboard. He did really well against the pace bias and can surely be found another opening this summer. (op 13-2)
Flash City(ITY) is a consistent sprinter and, posting a rock-solid effort, helps to set the level of this form. His sole win came on Fibresand in 2010, though. (op 16-1)
Taurus Twins blasted out down the centre of the track, but couldn't dominate as he tends to prefer and was ultimately found out by the penalty.
Haajes lacked the pace to land a telling blow, but stayed on late and wasn't disgraced from the foot of the weights. He looks to be creeping back near the top of his game. (op 14-1)
Racy tracked the winner early, but was toiling from halfway and needs better ground. Official explanation: jockey said that the gelding was unsuited by the good to soft (soft in places) ground (op 6-1 tchd 15-2 in a place)
Long Awaited(IRE) was beaten a long way out and has something to prove after this. Official explanation: trainer had no explanation for the poor form shown (tchd 10-1)

3128 RACING PLUS £1.20 ON SATURDAY STKS (H'CAP) 7f
4:45 (4:46) (Class 3) (0-95,91) 4-Y-0+ £7,439 (£2,213; £1,106; £553) Stalls Centre

Form RPR
0600 **1** **Sam Nombulist**[22] 2417 4-8-8 **78**....................(v) RobertWinston 12 90
(Richard Whitaker) *led after 1f: edgd lft and hld on wl clsng stages* **25/1**
-103 **2** *1* **Esprit De Midas**[18] 2545 6-9-5 **89**.............................. ShaneKelly 6 98
(Dean Ivory) *chsd ldrs: wnt 2nd over 1f out: no ex towards fin* **20/1**
11-1 **3** *7* **Green Howard**[38] 1951 4-8-13 **83**.............................. DanielTudhope 5 74
(Robin Bastiman) *in tch: effrt over 2f out: kpt on fnl f tk 3rd post* **4/1**[1]
00-3 **4** *shd* **Dubai Hills**[20] 2505 6-9-3 **87**.............................. RoystonFfrench 2 78
(Bryan Smart) *chsd ldrs: kpt on one pce over 1f out* **10/1**
0002 **5** *8* **Majestic Dream (IRE)**[11] 2754 4-8-9 **79**....................(v) GrahamGibbons 1 49
(Michael Easterby) *led 1f: chsd ldrs: wknd fnl f* **14/1**
2-00 **6** *¾* **Space War**[30] 2176 5-8-8 **85**.............................. DavidSimmonson(7) 8 53
(Michael Easterby) *mid-div: hdwy over 2f out: nvr nr ldrs* **33/1**
3352 **7** *3 ¼* **Beckermet (IRE)**[9] 2825 10-8-13 **83**.............................. PJMcDonald 16 42
(Ruth Carr) *mid-div on outer: lost pl over 4f out: edgd lft and kpt on fnl 2f* **16/1**
0510 **8** *8* **Arganil (USA)**[9] 2825 7-9-7 **91**.............................. PhillipMakin 13 30
(Kevin Ryan) *dwlt: in rr: sme hdwy over 2f out: nvr on terms* **25/1**
3-43 **9** *½* **Lord Aeryn (IRE)**[6] 2919 5-9-4 **88**.............................. PaulHanagan 15 25
(Richard Fahey) *s.i.s: in rr: sme hdwy over 2f out: nvr a factor* **8/1**[3]
0661 **10** *½* **Polish World (USA)**[15] 2632 8-9-2 **86**.............................. MickyFenton 14 22
(Paul Midgley) *chsd ldrs on outer: wknd over 1f out* **33/1**
1030 **11** *2* **Fast Shot**[9] 2825 4-9-3 **87**.............................. DavidAllan 18 18
(Tim Easterby) *s.i.s: kpt on fnl 2f: nvr on terms* **20/1**
2041 **12** *nk* **Madam Macie (IRE)**[11] 2752 5-9-0 **84** 6ex.............. SilvestreDeSousa 7 14
(David O'Meara) *in tch: effrt over 2f out: lost pl over 1f out* **12/1**
1406 **13** *3* **Another Try (IRE)**[20] 2488 7-8-5 **82**.............. MichaelJMMurphy(7) 9
(Alan Jarvis) *mid-div: effrt over 2f out: sn wknd* **40/1**
0033 **14** *6* **Clockmaker (IRE)**[6] 2910 6-9-6 **90**.............................. TedDurcan 10
(Tim Easterby) *in rr: nvr on terms* **11/1**
304- **15** *4* **Waltz Darling (IRE)**[275] 6046 4-8-8 **78**.............................. TonyHamilton 3
(Richard Fahey) *dwlt: a in rr* **33/1**
30-0 **16** *¾* **White Frost (IRE)**[34] 2068 4-9-6 **90**.............................. RyanMoore 11
(Charles Hills) *in rr: sme hdwy on wd outside over 2f out: sn wknd* **5/1**[2]
10-0 **17** *nk* **Polar Kite (IRE)**[26] 2311 4-9-2 **89**.............................. LeeTopliss(3) 4
(Richard Fahey) *s.i.s: effrt over 2f out: sn chsng ldrs: wknd over 1f out* **33/1**
440 **18** *1* **Azrael**[20] 2487 4-8-13 **83**.............................. RichardMullen 19
(Alan McCabe) *in rr-div on outer: nvr on terms* **33/1**
-002 **19** *1 ½* **Snow Bay**[17] 2590 6-9-1 **85**.............................. AdrianNicholls 17
(David Nicholls) *chsd ldrs on wd outside: lost pl 4f out* **20/1**

1m 27.33s (2.03) **Going Correction** +0.475s/f (Yiel) **19** Ran SP% **124.6**
Speed ratings (Par 107): **107,105,97,97,88 87,84,74,74,73 71,71,67,60,56 55,55,53,52**
toteswingers:1&2:£120.10, 1&3:£30.80, 2&3:£13.10 CSF £438.51 CT £2489.28 TOTE £34.40: £7.00, £4.20, £1.60, £2.40; EX 787.30 TRIFECTA Not won..
Owner Robert Macgregor **Bred** R F And S D Knipe **Trained** Scarcroft, W Yorks

FOCUS
This was a competitive-looking handicap and there was a decent pace on. However, most were found out by underfoot conditions and the first pair came well clear late on, both racing closest to the far side.

NOTEBOOK
Sam Nombulist arrived looking out of sorts and things didn't look good for his cause when he sweated up beforehand. He also failed to settle out in front, but that wasn't enough to stop him and he dug deep to repel the runner-up near the finish. This was a greatly improved effort, but both his wins have now come on such ground and the re-application of a visor clearly did the trick. Official explanation: trainer's rep said, regarding apparent improvement in form, that the gelding was better suited by the soft ground and had the run of the race.
Esprit De Midas has resumed in much better form this year and this was another decent effort back on turf, despite him being rated 4lb higher than on the AW. He was clear of the remainder at the finish.
Green Howard had won four of his last five previous outings and still looked fairly handicapped despite being another 4lb higher. This was his toughest task yet, but he left the impression he would have been bang there at the finish had he raced closer to the far side and he remains on an upward curve. (tchd 9-2)
Dubai Hills ran above himself in a decent conditions event on his seasonal debut over C&D last month. The handicapper left him alone for that, but he confirmed himself in decent heart with a sound effort back in handicap company. His sole success on turf came over 6f and perhaps a drop back to that trip may be worth a try. (tchd 8-1)
Lord Aeryn(IRE) never threatened after making a tardy start and getting behind. (op 7-1)
White Frost(IRE) was in trouble shortly after turning for home on the near side. Official explanation: jockey said colt lost its action (op 8-1)

3129 FUTURE CLEANING SERVICES APPRENTICE STKS (H'CAP) 1m 4f
5:15 (5:15) (Class 4) (0-80,80) 4-Y-0+ £5,239 (£1,559; £779; £389) Stalls Low

Form RPR
-634 **1** **Rio's Rosanna (IRE)**[22] 2419 5-9-6 **76**.............................. AmyRyan 8 91
(Richard Whitaker) *trckd ldrs: led over 2f out: drvn clr fnl f* **9/2**[1]
-202 **2** *3 ¾* **Battery Power**[6] 2921 4-9-0 **77**.............................. RobJFitzpatrick(7) 3 86
(Mark H Tompkins) *mid-div: hdwy to chse ldrs over 2f out: kpt on to take 2nd post* **6/1**[2]
33-1 **3** *nse* **Hydrant**[12] 2735 6-8-11 **67** 6ex.............................. AdamBeschizza 6 76
(Peter Salmon) *led 1f: chsd ldrs: led over 3f out: hdd over 2f out: one pce* **13/2**[3]
-000 **4** *5* **Magicalmysterytour (IRE)**[20] 2502 9-8-5 **66**.............. JackDuern(5) 5 67
(Willie Musson) *in rr: hdwy over 2f out: kpt on one pce over 1f out* **9/1**
0000 **5** *2 ½* **Meetings Man (IRE)**[11] 2751 5-8-12 **71**.............. ShaneBKelly(3) 7 68
(Micky Hammond) *prom: effrt over 3f out: one pce fnl 2f* **16/1**
0-05 **6** *4 ½* **Bollin Felix**[6] 2921 8-9-3 **80**..........................(b) RachelRichardson(7) 17 70
(Tim Easterby) *chsd ldrs: wknd over 1f out* **14/1**
-050 **7** *nk* **Grey Command (USA)**[42] 1822 7-8-7 **63**.............. HarryBentley 2 52
(Mel Brittain) *mid-div: drvn and lost pl 4f out: sme hdwy 2f out: nvr a factor* **25/1**
-535 **8** *4* **Royal Opera**[11] 2751 4-9-1 **71**.............................. PaulPickard 18 54
(Brian Ellison) *swtchd lft after s: sn chsng ldrs: wknd over 1f out* **10/1**
3412 **9** *7* **Pokfulham (IRE)**[8] 2842 6-8-9 **70**..........................(v) JasonHart(5) 16 42
(Jim Goldie) *swtchd lft after s: led after 1f: hdd over 3f out: wknd over 2f out* **8/1**
-620 **10** *¾* **Lakeman (IRE)**[9] 2814 6-8-1 **62**..........................(b) JakePayne(5) 4 33
(Brian Ellison) *chsd ldrs: drvn over 3f out: lost pl over 2f out* **33/1**
0010 **11** *½* **Sedgwick**[6] 2921 10-8-6 **67**.............................. ShirleyTeasdale(5) 14 37
(Shaun Harris) *mid-div: wknd over 2f out* **14/1**
0104 **12** *7* **Tapis Libre**[16] 2606 4-8-10 **71**.............................. DavidSimmonson(5) 10 30
(Michael Easterby) *s.i.s: in rr: whn hung lft over 3f out* **33/1**
1263 **13** *11* **Tricksofthetrade (IRE)**[13] 2694 6-9-2 **75**.............. GarryWhillans(3) 11 16
(Alan Swinbank) *hld up in rr: bhd fnl 2f: eased* **12/1**
0000 **14** *1 ¼* **Pertuis (IRE)**[21] 2440 6-7-12 **61** oh1.............................. KatieDowson(7) 1
(Micky Hammond) *half rrd s: in rr: lost pl 3f out: eased whn bhd* **50/1**
0-1 **15** *1 ¼* **Artisan**[95] 642 4-9-2 **72**.............................. LeeTopliss 9 9
(Brian Ellison) *in rr: bhd fnl 3f: eased* **12/1**

2m 37.03s (3.83) **Going Correction** +0.475s/f (Yiel) **15** Ran SP% **122.3**
Speed ratings (Par 105): **106,103,103,100,98 95,95,92,87,87 87,82,75,74,73**
toteswingers:1&2:£4.70, 2&3:£7.30, 1&3:£4.70 CSF £29.19 CT £180.43 TOTE £5.30: £1.90, £2.50, £2.40; EX 36.40 Trifecta £201.90 Pool: £930.43 - 3.41 winning units..
Owner James Marshall & Mrs Susan Marshall **Bred** Hellwood Stud Farm **Trained** Scarcroft, W Yorks

FOCUS
This was a modest handicap for apprentice riders and again underfoot conditions played a big part as those racing handily prospered. The form still looks sound enough, though, with the first three clear.
Artisan Official explanation: jockey said gelding was unsuited by the soft ground
T/Jkpt: £122,407.40 to a £1 stake. Pool:£344,809.69 - 2.00 winning tickets T/Plt: £144.20 to a £1 stake. Pool:£115,709.99 - 585.52 winning tickets T/Qpdt: £45.50 to a £1 stake. Pool:£6,562.02 - 106.68 winning tickets WG

3130 - 3136a (Foreign Racing) - See Raceform Interactive

2866 BATH (L-H)
Saturday, June 16

OFFICIAL GOING: Good (good to soft in places; 7.7)
Bottom bend realigned adding 12.5yds to race distances that include it.
Wind: Strong across Weather: Overcast

3137 BRANDONTRUST.ORG H'CAP 1m 2f 46y
2:10 (2:10) (Class 6) (0-55,58) 4-Y-0+ £2,181 (£644; £322) Stalls Low

Form RPR
01/5 **1** **Pindar (GER)**[37] 2013 8-8-7 **46**.............................. WilliamCarson 6 57
(Barney Curley) *trckd ldrs: led 4f out: rdn 2f out: hung bdly lft u.p fnl 120yds: kpt on wl* **10/1**
-001 **2** *2 ½* **Ryedale Lass**[4] 2998 4-9-5 **58** 6ex.............................. CathyGannon 5 67+
(Joseph Tuite) *in tch: hdwy on rails fr 3f out: chsd wnr appr fnl f: styng on to chal whn hmpd and snatched up fnl 120yds: nt rcvr* **7/2**[2]
0-03 **3** *1 ¾* **Border Abby**[24] 2386 4-9-0 **53**.............................. ChrisCatlin 11 56
(Rae Guest) *chsd ldrs: rdn over 2f out: chsd ldng duo appr fnl f: no imp* **10/3**[1]
6-50 **4** *1 ¾* **Corrib (IRE)**[25] 2364 9-8-12 **51**..........................(p) NeilChalmers 12 50
(Bryn Palling) *chsd ldrs: rdn 3f out: one pce fnl 2f* **17/2**[3]
5500 **5** *¾* **Redinessence (IRE)**[9] 2851 4-8-11 **50**.............................. StevieDonohoe 3 48
(Willie Musson) *chsd ldrs: drvn along 3f out: outpcd fnl 2f* **20/1**
0-00 **6** *nk* **Into The Wind**[24] 2391 5-8-10 **49** ow1.............................. JamesMillman 8 46+
(Rod Millman) *in rr: hdwy over 2f out: n.m.r over 1f out: kpt on ins fnl f: nvr a threat* **10/1**
0-00 **7** *¾* **Belle Park**[18] 2574 5-8-13 **52**.............................. TomMcLaughlin 4 47+
(Karen George) *slowly away: in rr: hdwy 2f out: kpt on fnl f: nvr a threat* **20/1**
0-00 **8** *¾* **Femme Royale**[13] 2735 4-8-2 **46** oh1.............................. RaulDaSilva(5) 2 40
(Richard Price) *chsd ldrs: rdn over 3f out: wknd 2f out* **40/1**
40-0 **9** *nk* **Night Sky**[86] 995 5-9-2 **55**.............................. PatDobbs 13 48
(Tony Carroll) *in rr: hdwy 3f out: sn rdn and dropped away* **16/1**
4-00 **10** *1 ¼* **Disturbia (IRE)**[44] 1771 4-8-2 **46** oh1.............................. LauraPike(5) 7 37
(Olivia Maylam) *in rr: pushed along and r.o fr over 1f out: kpt clsng stages* **22/1**
0305 **11** *3 ¾* **Gambatte**[10] 2821 5-8-2 **46** oh1..........................(b[1]) DarrenEgan(5) 10 29
(Tony Carroll) *v.s.a: in rr: mod prog over 2f out: nvr any ch* **16/1**
0006 **12** *1 ½* **Crazy Chris**[17] 2607 7-8-10 **49**..........................(b) RichardKingscote 16 29
(Milton Bradley) *chsd ldrs: wnt 2nd 3f out: sn u.p: wknd wl over 1f out* **16/1**
00-0 **13** *29* **Prana (USA)**[16] 2627 4-8-7 **46** oh1..........................(p) JohnFahy 15
(Jeremy Gask) *led to 4f out: sn btn: t.o* **33/1**
54-5 **14** *11* **Toucan Tango (IRE)**[165] 23 4-8-11 **50**.............................. DaneO'Neill 1
(Bernard Llewellyn) *a in rr: t.o* **12/1**

2m 14.42s (3.42) **Going Correction** +0.375s/f (Good) **14** Ran SP% **118.6**
Speed ratings (Par 101): **101,99,97,96,95 95,94,94,93,92 89,88,65,56**
toteswingers:1&2:£7.70, 1&3:£7.80, 2&3:£2.60 CSF £40.98 CT £145.70 TOTE £11.70: £3.70, £1.80, £2.30; EX 48.70.
Owner Curley Leisure **Bred** Gestut Schlenderhan **Trained** Newmarket, Suffolk
■ Stewards' Enquiry : William Carson two-day ban: careless riding (Jul 1-2)

FOCUS
A moderate event in which the early pace wasn't particularly strong. The third and fourth are the best guides to the level.

3138 BRITISH STALLION STUDS / BRANDON TRUST E B F NOVICE STKS 5f 11y
2:40 (2:41) (Class 4) 2-Y-O £4,463 (£1,328; £497; £497) Stalls Centre

Form RPR

31 **1** **Bridge Night**[18] 2579 2-8-11 0.. CathyGannon 2 87+
(Eve Johnson Houghton) *mde all: drvn 2f out: 3 l clr 1f out: r.o strly ins fnl f* **9/2[2]**

1 **2** 3/4 **Rebel Magic**[31] 2163 2-8-11 0.. PatDobbs 3 84+
(Richard Hannon) *trckd wnr 3f out: rdn and one pce whn wnr qcknd over 1f out: styd on clsng stages but a readily hld* **2/1[1]**

445 **3** 6 **Indian Affair**[25] 2376 2-9-0 0.. DaneO'Neill 1 66
(Milton Bradley) *chsd ldrs: wnt 3rd over 2f out: nvr gng pce of ldng duo fr over 1f out* **11/1**

65 **3** dht **Edged Out**[33] 2124 2-8-4 0.. RaulDaSilva(5) 6 61
(Bryn Palling) *in tch: rdn and outpcd over 2f out: styd on again fnl f to dead-heat for wl hld 3rd last stride* **9/1**

61 **5** 2 1/4 **Majestic Red (IRE)**[18] 2571 2-8-11 0.. TomMcLaughlin 7 55
(Malcolm Saunders) *in rr: drvn and sme hdwy 2f out: nvr rchd ldrs and kpt on same pce fnl f* **8/1**

001 **6** shd **Cuisine (IRE)**[8] 2868 2-9-5 0.. ChrisCatlin 9 62
(Andrew Balding) *in tch: chsd ldrs and rdn 2f out: styd on same pce u.p fnl f* **5/1[3]**

04 **7** 1 1/4 **Danz Choice (IRE)**[15] 2648 2-8-7 0.. WilliamTwiston-Davies(7) 5 53
(Richard Hannon) *chsd wnr to 3f out: wknd over 1f out* **18/1**

05 **8** 2 **Khefyn (IRE)**[8] 2868 2-8-9 0.. DarrenEgan(5) 4 46
(Ronald Harris) *outpcd* **33/1**

9 nk **Mullit (IRE)** 2-9-0 0.. RichardKingscote 8 44
(Tom Dascombe) *s.i.s: outpcd* **12/1**

1m 3.15s (0.65) **Going Correction** +0.225s/f (Good) **9** Ran SP% **113.5**
Speed ratings (Par 95): **103,101,92,92,88 88,86,83,82**
Place: Edge Out £1.10, Indian Affair £1.40. toteswingers:1&2:£1.90, 2&EO:£1.50, 1&IA:£5.80, 2&IA:£4.60, 1&EO:£4.30 CSF £13.62 TOTE £5.30: £2.30, £1.70; EX 14.00.

Owner S Emmet **Bred** S Emmet And Miss R Emmet **Trained** Blewbury, Oxon

FOCUS
With four previous winners taking their chance, this looked a strong contest for the class. The winner showed good speed and this looks decent form.

NOTEBOOK
Bridge Night broke smartly, showed a lot of pace and won quite nicely after having the run of the race. One would imagine she'll be at her best on speed-favouring tracks. (op 7-2)

Rebel Magic, a C&D winner on debut, travelled quite well close to the leader but hit a flat spot about 2f out before keeping on strongly. She's effective at 5f but will get further. (op 5-2)

Indian Affair had shown ability in maidens over both sprint trips here and confirmed he has ability again. A small handicap over 6f later on could be ideal. (op 14-1)

Edged Out looked sure to get into a clear third at one stage but took a while to get going. No doubt she'll find her level when nurseries start. (op 14-1)

Majestic Red(IRE) won an ordinary-looking event at Chepstow on her previous start, but hardly got involved here.

Cuisine(IRE) showed improved form to win over C&D last week but didn't back that performance up this time, albeit giving weight away to all rivals.

3139 BRANDON TRUST FAST FURLONG H'CAP 5f 161y
3:15 (3:24) (Class 4) (0-80,78) 3-Y-O+ £3,357 (£3,357; £769; £384) Stalls Centre

Form RPR

6-00 **1** **Rocket Rob (IRE)**[35] 2071 6-9-6 70.. StevieDonohoe 4 77
(Willie Musson) *s.i.s: in rr: hdwy over 2f out: drvn to dispute ld fnl 120yds: kpt on wl to force dead-heat* **11/4[1]**

0011 **1** dht **Valmina**[31] 2165 5-9-2 73..(t) GeorgeDowning(7) 5 80
(Tony Carroll) *reluctant to enter stalls: s.i.s: in rr: hdwy 2f out: str run to dispute ld fnl 120yds: kpt on wl to force dead-heat* **6/1[2]**

4411 **3** 3/4 **Ginzan**[7] 2943 4-9-6 70.. TomMcLaughlin 11 75
(Malcolm Saunders) *in tch: rdn and hdwy on outside over 1f out: str run fnl f to take 3rd clsng stages but nt rch winning duo* **6/1[2]**

2060 **4** shd **Mambo Spirit (IRE)**[8] 2870 8-9-6 70.. DaneO'Neill 16 75+
(Tony Newcombe) *s.i.s: in rr: hdwy: nt clr run and swtchd rt 1f out: str run on outside fnl f: kpt on clsng stages* **20/1**

2405 **5** hd **Emiratesdotcom**[7] 2940 6-9-11 75.. RichardKingscote 1 79
(Milton Bradley) *pressed ldrs: led over 3f out: rdn 2f out: jnd ins fnl f: hdd and nt qckn fnl 120yds* **7/1[3]**

2402 **6** shd **Diamond Vine (IRE)**[5] 2972 4-9-2 69..(p) CPGeoghegan(3) 12 73
(Ronald Harris) *in rr: hdwy on outside fr 2f out: styd on u.p fnl f: kpt on clsng stages* **22/1**

1122 **7** hd **Efistorm**[7] 2939 11-9-6 75.. JemmaMarshall(5) 10 78
(Joseph Tuite) *in rr: hdwy fr 2f out: kpt on wl clsng stages* **20/1**

5006 **8** 1/2 **Night Trade (IRE)**[8] 2870 5-9-6 75.. DarrenEgan(5) 6 76
(Ronald Harris) *in rr: hdwy on ins over 1f: kpt on same pce ins fnl f* **12/1**

15-0 **9** 1 1/4 **Swendab (IRE)**[11] 2793 4-9-11 78.. RyanPowell(3) 14 75
(John O'Shea) *chsd ldrs: drvn along fr 3f out: styd on same pce ins fnl f* **25/1**

0566 **10** 3 **Dreams Of Glory**[23] 2421 4-8-7 60.. SimonPearce(3) 13 47
(Ron Hodges) *sn slt ld: hdd over 3f out: styd chalng tl wknd ins fnl f* **14/1**

2050 **11** 6 **Style And Panache (IRE)**[2] 3065 4-9-9 73..(p) ShaneKelly 3 41
(David Evans) *chsd ldrs to 2f out* **12/1**

500- **12** 1 1/2 **Time Medicean**[192] 7660 6-9-12 76.. TonyCulhane 17 39
(Tony Carroll) *chsd ldrs: wkng on outside whn hmpd 1f out* **20/1**

1-00 **13** 1 1/4 **Peace Seeker**[19] 2545 4-9-11 75.. WilliamCarson 2 70+
(Anthony Carson) *chsd ldrs: btn whn hmpd 1f out* **12/1**

1m 12.3s (1.10) **Going Correction** +0.225s/f (Good)
WFA 3 from 4yo+ 7lb **13** Ran SP% **120.0**
Speed ratings (Par 105): **101,101,100,99,99 99,99,98,96,92 84,82,81**WIN: Valmina £3.60 Rocket Rob £1.60 PL: V £2.90, RR £2.10, G £2.00 EX: V/RR £11.90, RR/V £11.00 CSF: V/RR £10.37 RR/V £8.16, Tricast: V&RR&G £53.29, RR&V&G £47.05 toteswingers: V&RR £11.50, V&G £4.60, RR&G £4.10.

Owner Mayden Stud **Bred** Mayden Stud, J A And D S Dewhurst **Trained** Cropthorne, Worcs

FOCUS
Not a particularly ideal set of circumstances for these sprinters, as there was a lengthy delay when Belle Bayardo needed removing from the stalls for being unruly, and then another hold-up when one of the geldings that shared the prize proved difficult to load. The form looks fair despite the bunch finish.

3140 HEALTHCARE RM MAIDEN AUCTION STKS 5f 11y
3:50 (3:56) (Class 6) 2-Y-O £2,070 (£616; £307; £153) Stalls Centre

Form RPR

1 **Risky Rizkova** 2-8-9 0.. RichardKingscote 9 66
(Jonathan Portman) *in tch: hdwy 2f out: styd on strly ins fnl f: led last stride* **18/1**

0655 **2** shd **Ouzinkie (IRE)**[7] 2929 2-9-2 0.. MatthewDavies 8 73
(Mick Channon) *chsd ldr: rdn 2f out: chal ins fnl f: slt ld fnl 120yds: ct last stride* **3/1[2]**

034 **3** 1/2 **Windforpower (IRE)**[8] 2868 2-8-6 0..(p) DarrenEgan(5) 2 66+
(Ronald Harris) *chsd ldrs: rdn and one pce appr fnl f: rallied and styd on fnl 120yds: sn hung lft: kpt on* **12/1**

4 1/2 **Kodatish (IRE)** 2-9-0 0 ow1.. CPGeoghegan(3) 5 70+
(Ronald Harris) *in tch: hdwy over 1f out: styd on wl clsng stages: nt rch ldrs* **25/1**

3 **5** nse **Wordsaplenty (IRE)**[16] 2622 2-8-1 0.. RyanPowell(3) 11 57
(J S Moore) *in rr: hdwy over 1f out: sn hung lft: swtchd rt and styd on fnl 120yds: nt rch ldrs* **16/1**

44 **6** 1 3/4 **Jimmy Elder**[10] 2817 2-8-13 0.. PatDobbs 4 60
(Richard Hannon) *w ldr tl led over 3f out: kpt slt ld and drvn fr 2f out: hdd fnl 120yds: btn whn hmpd on ins sn after* **8/1[3]**

7 hd **Secretori** 2-8-11 0.. ShaneKelly 3 60+
(Matthew Salaman) *in rr: hdwy and hmpd 1f out: styd on again clsng stages* **20/1**

8 nk **Plexolini** 2-8-11 0.. StevieDonohoe 10 56
(Jo Hughes) *chsd ldrs tl wknd fnl f* **20/1**

9 1/2 **Frans Hals** 2-8-13 0.. DaneO'Neill 1 63+
(Dominic Ffrench Davis) *in rr: sme hdwy whn nt clr run appr fnl f: n.d after* **8/1[3]**

2 **10** 3 **Bamurru (IRE)**[18] 2571 2-8-13 0.. PatCosgrave 6 46
(Peter Makin) *slt ld tl narrowly hdd over 3f out: rdn over 2f out: btn sn after* **2/1[1]**

11 5 **Silverrica (IRE)** 2-8-8 0.. CathyGannon 7 23
(Malcolm Saunders) *slowly away: green and rn v wd bnd over 3f out: no ch after* **20/1**

1m 4.49s (1.99) **Going Correction** +0.225s/f (Good) **11** Ran SP% **117.5**
Speed ratings (Par 91): **93,92,92,91,91 88,88,87,86,81 73**
toteswingers:1&2:£12.90, 1&3:£34.70, 2&3:£7.90 CSF £67.71 TOTE £24.10: £7.00, £1.20, £3.70; EX 110.20.

Owner J R Walton **Bred** Whatton Manor Stud **Trained** Compton, Berks

FOCUS
Probably not a result to trust, as a couple caught the eye in behind and the favourite disappointed. A messy race and a modest time, so the form has been rated conservatively.

NOTEBOOK
Risky Rizkova, an already gelded half-brother to a 7f winner, needed pushing along at about halfway but responded to pressure and made an excellent start to his career by beating some more experienced rivals. That said, he'll probably need to up his game a bit if moved into stronger company. (op 20-1 tchd 16-1)

Ouzinkie(IRE), back down to 5f, had the most experience and gives the race a level of sorts considering he'd run to an RPR of 72 and 75 previously. (tchd 11-4)

Windforpower(IRE), with a visor replaced by cheekpieces, was a long way behind Bamurru at Chepstow when they last met but reversed that form. (op 10-1)

Kodatish(IRE), a half-brother to fair juvenile Sonoran Sands, definitely has ability and should build on this. (op 20-1)

Wordsaplenty(IRE) tended to wander and shapes as though she needs further.

Secretori was green early but kept on nicely. (tchd 16-1)

Frans Hals, who attracted market interest, met a bit of trouble when making progress. (op 12-1)

Bamurru(IRE) weakened as though something was amiss late on. (tchd 9-4)

3141 PEARCE BROTHERS H'CAP 5f 161y
4:20 (4:22) (Class 6) (0-55,54) 3-Y-O £2,181 (£644; £322) Stalls Centre

Form RPR

3342 **1** **Celestial Dawn**[7] 2928 3-9-2 54.. ChrisCatlin 9 66
(John Weymes) *trckd ldrs: drvn and qckned to chal 1f out: led sn after: rdn out* **11/2[2]**

5652 **2** 3 **First Rebellion**[12] 2762 3-8-3 46.. DarrenEgan(5) 1 48
(Tony Carroll) *chsd ldrs: led over 2f out: sn rdn: jnd 1f out and hdd sn after: no imp on wnr but styd on wl for 2nd clsng stages* **13/2[3]**

0053 **3** 1 **One Last Dream**[24] 2388 3-8-8 46.. RichardKingscote 8 45
(Ron Hodges) *chsd ldrs: rdn: hung rt and outpcd appr fnl f: rallied fnl 120yds to take 3rd clsng stages* **7/2[1]**

5-62 **4** 1/2 **Copper Falls**[19] 2547 3-8-11 54.. BrendanPowell(5) 2 51
(Brendan Powell) *s.i.s: sn in tch: stdy hdwy to trck ldrs travelling comf wl over 1f out: styd on same pce ins fnl f and lost 3rd clsng stages* **13/2[3]**

4401 **5** 3 1/2 **Waspy**[18] 2582 3-8-10 48..(t) PatCosgrave 10 34
(George Baker) *in tch: rdn and one pce fr 1/2-way* **7/1**

000 **6** 3 1/2 **Roundelay**[26] 2332 3-8-4 45.. DominicFox(3) 4 19
(Anthony Carson) *chsd ldrs: rdn over 2f out: wknd over 1f out* **16/1**

5440 **7** shd **Rainbow Riches (IRE)**[11] 2803 3-8-5 46.. RyanPowell(3) 5 20
(Roger Curtis) *in rr and sn rdn: a outpcd* **14/1**

-006 **8** 2 1/2 **Get The Trip**[18] 2582 3-8-9 47.. WilliamCarson 3 12
(Anthony Carson) *sn led: hdd over 2f out: wknd wl over 1f out* **10/1**

40-0 **9** 26 **Zigazag (IRE)**[33] 2131 3-9-1 53..(t) CathyGannon 12
(David Evans) *s.i.s: sn rdn: lost tch 3f out: t.o* **12/1**

5504 **P** **Russian Rumba (IRE)**[37] 2010 3-9-0 52.. PatDobbs 11
(Jonathan Portman) *in rr: lost action over 2f out: p.u and dismntd sn after: lame* **7/1**

1m 13.0s (1.80) **Going Correction** +0.225s/f (Good) **10** Ran SP% **118.6**
Speed ratings (Par 97): **97,93,91,91,86 81,81,78,43,**
toteswingers:1&2:£7.40, 1&3:£4.10, 2&3:£4.70 CSF £41.93 CT £148.05 TOTE £6.40: £1.90, £2.00, £1.70; EX 32.20.

Owner Grange Park Racing **Bred** The Welcome Alliance **Trained** Middleham Moor, N Yorks

FOCUS
The leaders went off at a quick tempo, which meant a few of these finish tired. The form is limited and does not look solid.

Zigazag(IRE) Official explanation: jockey said gelding missed the break

Russian Rumba(IRE) Official explanation: jockey said filly pulled up lame

3142 ALEX MCCRINDLE MEMORIAL H'CAP 1m 3f 144y

4:50 (4:51) (Class 5) (0-70,71) 3-Y-O **£2,911** (£866; £432; £216) **Stalls** High

Form RPR

5-66 **1** **April Ciel**[9] 2860 3-8-3 **57**.............................. DarrenEgan[(5)] 13 69
(Ronald Harris) *mde virtually all: travelling wl 2f out: drvn out ins fnl f* **15/2**

436- **2** *1 3/4* **Dora's Gift**[183] 7777 3-9-0 **63**.............................. ShaneKelly 8 72
(Hughie Morrison) *in rr: hdwy 7f out: chsd wnr fr 2f out: styd on wl u.p but no imp clsng stages* **17/2**

-050 **3** *2 1/4* **The Quarterjack**[31] 2162 3-7-13 **53** oh2 ow2.............................. RaulDaSilva[(5)] 1 58
(Ron Hodges) *in rr: drvn and hdwy over 2f out: kpt on u.p to take 3rd over 1f out: styd on same pce fnl f* **50/1**

00-0 **4** *1 1/2* **Cash Injection**[18] 2578 3-7-9 **51**..............................(t) KatiaScallan[(7)] 12 53
(Karen George) *in rr: rdn and c wd into st over 3f out: kpt on to take 4th clsng stages* **33/1**

0-00 **5** *1/2* **Brundon**[46] 1726 3-8-9 **58**.............................. DaneO'Neill 16 59
(Henry Candy) *prom early: lost position and dropped to rr 6f out: drvn and hdwy fr 3f out: disp one pce 3rd 1f out: nvr rchd ldng duo and sn no ex* **20/1**

0-03 **6** *shd* **Silver Samba**[38] 1982 3-8-10 **62**.............................. SimonPearce[(3)] 3 63
(Andrew Balding) *s.i.s: in rr: rdn 5f out: hdwy over 2f out: styd on same pce* **13/2**[2]

6-66 **7** *4 1/2* **Maccabees**[10] 2818 3-8-12 **61**.............................. JamesMillman 9 55
(Rod Millman) *s.i.s: in rr: rdn: hdwy and wd into st bnd over 3f out: nvr rchd ldrs and wknd over 1f out* **8/1**

3-41 **8** *1 1/2* **Talk Of The North**[9] 2860 3-9-3 **71**.............................. LauraPike[(5)] 10 62
(Hugo Palmer) *chsd ldrs fr 1/2-way: rdn 3f out: disp 2nd over 2f out: wknd over 1f out* **3/1**[1]

25-0 **9** *1* **Dont Take Me Alive**[42] 1853 3-9-4 **67**.............................. JohnFahy 15 56
(Clive Cox) *chsd ldrs: rdn over 3f out: wknd 2f out* **22/1**

-314 **10** *12* **Kozmina Bay**[18] 2578 3-8-10 **59**.............................. RichardKingscote 5 28
(Jonathan Portman) *in rr whn faltered 9f out: no ch after* **14/1**

5-54 **11** *1* **Shannon Spree**[25] 2379 3-9-7 **70**.............................. PatDobbs 11 37
(Richard Hannon) *rdn over 5f out: a bhd* **7/1**[3]

2-00 **12** *22* **Cato Minor**[23] 2424 3-8-1 **53**.............................. RyanPowell[(3)] 4
(Amanda Perrett) *chsd ldrs: rdn and wknd 5f out* **40/1**

0-20 **13** *2* **Hardy Plume**[31] 2162 3-8-3 **55**.............................. DominicFox[(3)] 2
(Denis Coakley) *chsd ldrs: rdn 4f out: wknd 3f out: eased whn no ch* **20/1**

0-45 **14** *6* **Tantamount**[19] 2544 3-9-3 **66**.............................. ChrisCatlin 14
(Roger Charlton) *chsd ldrs: hanging bdly rt fr 5f out: hung v wd off bnd over 3f out and sn t.o* **8/1**

2m 34.72s (4.12) **Going Correction** +0.375s/f (Good) **14 Ran SP% 123.2**
Speed ratings (Par 99): **101,99,98,97,97 96,93,92,92,84 83,68,67,63**
toteswingers:1&2:£16.70, 1&3:£48.60, 2&3:£37.40 CSF £65.44 CT £3005.83 TOTE £9.10: £3.30, £3.60, £15.00; EX 103.30.

Owner Paul & Ann de Weck **Bred** Paul And Ann De Weck **Trained** Earlswood, Monmouths

FOCUS

Lots of runners but not many got into this modest event. The runner-up stepped up on his juvenile form and the fifth is possibly the best guide to his maiden form.

April Ciel Official explanation: trainer said, regarding apparent improvement in form, that the gelding was unlcuky in its two previous runs on the all-weather over a shorter trip.

Tantamount Official explanation: jockey said colt hung badly right

3143 BRANDON TRUST GREAT WESTERN BIKE RIDE H'CAP 1m 3f 144y

5:25 (5:25) (Class 6) (0-60,60) 4-Y-O+ **£2,070** (£616; £307; £153) **Stalls** High

Form RPR

1361 **1** **Bute Street**[8] 2872 7-9-5 **58**.............................. WilliamCarson 5 67
(Ron Hodges) *mde all: pushed along 2f out: styd on wl u.p fnl f: unchal* **9/4**[1]

600/ **2** *2 1/2* **Blue Zealot (IRE)**[604] 7039 5-8-7 **46** oh1.............................. JohnFahy 4 51
(Anthony Honeyball) *chsd ldrs: rdn 3f out: styd on fr over 2f out: tk 2nd last strides but no imp on wnr* **7/1**

2033 **3** *nse* **Asterales**[10] 2823 5-9-0 **53**..............................(t) TonyCulhane 10 58
(Jo Hughes) *in tch early: dropped in rr 6f out: rdn and hdwy fr 2f out: styd on to chse wnr ins fnl 2f: no imp fnl f and lost 2nd last strides* **5/1**[2]

5353 **4** *3 1/2* **Pandorica**[15] 2650 4-9-0 **60**..............................(p) DanielMuscutt[(7)] 6 59
(Bernard Llewellyn) *t.k.h: towards rr: hdwy 3f out: chsd ldrs 2f out and sn disputing 2nd: no imp on wnr and one pce fnl f* **10/1**

0022 **5** *1* **Crimson Monarch (USA)**[9] 2851 8-8-9 **48**..............................(b) ChrisCatlin 2 45
(Peter Hiatt) *chsd ldrs: rdn 3f out: wknd over 1f* **5/1**[2]

4642 **6** *nse* **Pahente**[15] 2651 4-8-2 **46**.............................. DarrenEgan[(5)] 1 43
(Tony Carroll) *in rr: rdn over 3f out: hdwy over 2f out: nvr rchd ldrs* **6/1**[3]

4052 **7** *3* **Lisselan Pleasure (USA)**[15] 2650 5-9-3 **56**..............................(t) DaneO'Neill 8 48
(Bernard Llewellyn) *in rr: hdwy 3f out: chsd ldrs over 2f out: wknd over 1f out* **12/1**

8 *2 3/4* **Terra Bleu (IRE)**[10] 6824 5-8-7 **51**.............................. BrendanPowell[(5)] 13 38
(Brendan Powell) *chsd wnr tl over 3f out: wknd appr fnl 2f* **20/1**

603- **9** *9* **Madam Tessa (IRE)**[197] 7608 4-9-1 **54**.............................. NeilChalmers 7 26
(Bryn Palling) *bhd most of way* **18/1**

/0-5 **10** *2* **Nicky Nutjob (GER)**[15] 2651 6-8-4 **46** oh1.............................. RyanPowell[(3)] 12 15
(John O'Shea) *plld hrd: chsd ldrs 7f* **25/1**

00-0 **11** *30* **Ellies Girl (IRE)**[30] 2200 4-8-0 **46** oh1.............................. NicoleNordblad[(7)] 3
(Ronald Harris) *t.k.h: a in rr: lost tch fnl 3f* **40/1**

2m 37.51s (6.91) **Going Correction** +0.375s/f (Good) **11 Ran SP% 124.0**
Speed ratings (Par 101): **91,89,89,86,86 86,84,82,76,75 55**
toteswingers:1&2:£8.10, 1&3:£6.90, 2&3:£8.90 CSF £19.24 CT £76.33 TOTE £3.20: £1.40, £2.10, £2.20; EX 28.00.

Owner J W Mursell **Bred** J W Mursell **Trained** Charlton Mackrell, Somerset

FOCUS

Not a result to rely on, as the winning rider got everything right up front. The runner-up is rated to the best of his old form.

T/Plt: £110.10 to a £1 stake. Pool:£73,974.08 - 490.37 winning tickets T/Qpdt: £56.20 to a £1 stake. Pool:£4,135.55 - 54.40 winning tickets ST

2783 LEICESTER (R-H)

Saturday, June 16

3144 Meeting Abandoned - Waterlogged

3001 LINGFIELD (L-H)

Saturday, June 16

OFFICIAL GOING: Turf course - good (good to soft in places; 7.2); all-weather - standard

Wind: Strong, behind Weather: Overcast with showers

3150 CYPRIUM BAR AT MARRIOTT LINGFIELD MEDIAN AUCTION MAIDEN FILLIES' STKS 5f

6:35 (6:36) (Class 6) 2-Y-O **£2,181** (£644; £322) **Stalls** High

Form RPR

05 **1** **Harleys Rocket**[21] 2492 2-8-9 0.............................. DavidKenny[(5)] 4 69
(Brendan Powell) *pressed ldrs on outer: drvn over 1f out: clsd to ld last 150yds: kpt on* **10/1**

02 **2** *3/4* **Puteri Nur Laila (IRE)**[18] 2579 2-9-0 0.............................. NeilCallan 3 66+
(Paul Cole) *restless stalls: fast away: led and crossed to rail: hdd after 1f: rdn in 4th over 2f out and struggling: styd on to take 2nd last 100yds: unable to chal* **6/5**[1]

05 **3** *1 3/4* **Tiger's Home**[9] 2844 2-8-11 0.............................. AdamBeschizza[(3)] 2 60
(Julia Feilden) *led after 1f and crossed to rail: hdd wl over 1f out: one pce u.p* **5/2**[2]

04 **4** *1 1/2* **Shirley's Pride**[26] 2349 2-9-0 0.............................. RussKennemore 1 54
(John Holt) *w ldrs: rdn to ld wl over 1f out: hdd & wknd last 150yds* **8/1**[3]

5 **5** *4* **Belle Voir**[16] 2622 2-9-0 0.............................. JackMitchell 5 40
(Gay Kelleway) *outpcd and rdn in last after 2f: nvr a factor: modest late prog* **10/1**

6 *2 1/4* **Marvelous Miss (IRE)** 2-9-0 0.............................. TomMcLaughlin 8 32
(Christine Dunnett) *a in rr: hanging and rn green 2f out: wknd* **40/1**

0 **7** *2 1/4* **Grandfathers Gift**[18] 2579 2-8-7 0.............................. DannyBrock[(7)] 7 24
(Michael Quinn) *chsd ldrs 3f: wknd rapidly* **25/1**

59.71s (1.51) **Going Correction** +0.175s/f (Good) **7 Ran SP% 109.6**
Speed ratings (Par 88): **94,92,90,87,81 77,74**
toteswingers:1&2:£2.70, 1&3:£4.80, 2&3:£1.20 CSF £20.71 TOTE £11.90: £4.00, £1.50; EX 23.10.

Owner A A Byrne **Bred** Anthony Byrne **Trained** Upper Lambourn, Berks

FOCUS

Unlikely anything out of the ordinary will emerge from a maiden in which the runners, helped by a strong tailwind, unsurprisingly stayed near the stand rail. The pace looked muddling and the placed horses help set the level.

NOTEBOOK

Harleys Rocket showed much improved form, settling better than she had done in her previous races but not obviously having anything in hand passing the line. She's not up to winning a novice so will be best kept back for 5f nurseries. (tchd 11-1)

Puteri Nur Laila(IRE) was given a poor ride, restrained after breaking easily the best and losing pole position in front on the rail as a result. Possibly the softish ground wasn't ideal as she took a long time to get going but she began to stay on once switched wide and left the impression she was the best horse in the race. She would have won ridden more positively but maidens won't come much weaker than this. (tchd 11-10 and 5-4)

Tiger's Home was able to get across and bag the rail despite not breaking that sharply, but was made to look one paced once the race began in earnest. By Tiger Hill out of Kris mare, she found this test inadequate. (tchd 11-4)

Shirley's Pride looked sure to be involved once going to the front over 1f out but folded tamely and looks a short runner for now. Her trainer had reported on her debut soft ground isn't ideal for her. (op 9-1)

Belle Voir didn't show anything but is bred to need a fair bit further. (tchd 7-1)

Marvelous Miss(IRE) pulled too hard early on her debut. (op 28-1 tchd 50-1)

3151 ANGELA NICHOLLS "DON'T DISCLOSE I'M 40" H'CAP 6f

7:05 (7:06) (Class 6) (0-60,65) 3-Y-O+ **£2,181** (£644; £322) **Stalls** High

Form RPR

-435 **1** **Danzoe (IRE)**[25] 2377 5-9-10 **58**.............................. TomMcLaughlin 15 67
(Christine Dunnett) *hld up in midfield: prog fr 2f out: shkn up to ld 1f out: drifted lft nr fin: jst hld on* **16/1**

0550 **2** *shd* **Mucky Molly**[12] 2761 4-8-12 **46**.............................. NeilCallan 2 55+
(Olivia Maylam) *dwlt: drvn and wl in rr bef 1/2-way: swtchd lft and prog 2f out: styd on wl fnl f: jst failed* **22/1**

6200 **3** *nse* **Huzzah (IRE)**[18] 2572 7-9-10 **58**.............................. AmirQuinn 12 67
(Paul Howling) *stdd s: hld up in last and wl bhd: stdy prog on wd outside fr 1/2-way: shkn up and clsd ins fnl f: jst failed* **7/1**[3]

-661 **4** *1/2* **Mr Fickle (IRE)**[11] 2803 3-9-10 **65**.............................. GeorgeBaker 16 70+
(Gary Moore) *dwlt: rousted along and wl in rr bef 1/2-way: styd on wl fr over 1f out: gaining at fin* **15/8**[1]

2403 **5** *1* **Anjomarba (IRE)**[5] 2973 5-9-10 **58**.............................. HayleyTurner 13 62+
(Conor Dore) *led after 1f and grabbed rail: drvn and hdd 1f out: one pce* **6/1**[2]

4004 **6** *1 1/2* **Microlight**[5] 2972 4-8-13 **47**..............................(v) SamHitchcott 14 46
(John E Long) *chsd ldrs against rail: rdn and no prog 2f out: kpt on fnl f: n.d* **16/1**

5202 **7** *4* **Flaxen Lake**[12] 2761 5-9-4 **52**..............................(p) NickyMackay 8 42+
(Milton Bradley) *chsd ldrs: rdn and no prog whn hmpd wl over 1f out: kpt on after* **16/1**

6305 **8** *1 1/2* **Efisio Princess**[24] 2406 9-9-2 **50**.............................. RichardThomas 10 31
(John E Long) *cl up: rdn to dispute 2nd briefly 2f out: wknd over 1f out* **16/1**

0-00 **9** *3/4* **Pose (IRE)**[31] 2171 5-9-2 **55**..............................(t) MarkCoumbe[(5)] 9 34
(Roger Ingram) *trckd ldrs: rdn to dispute 2nd briefly 2f out: wknd jst over 1f out* **33/1**

00-0 **10** *3/4* **Johnny Splash (IRE)**[46] 1725 3-8-13 **54**..............................(b[1]) JackMitchell 17 29
(Roger Teal) *led against rail 1f: rdn sn after 1/2-way: wknd wl over 1f out* **33/1**

0004 **11** *1 1/4* **Whiteoak Lady (IRE)**[16] 2618 7-9-2 **50**..............................(b) CathyGannon 11 23
(David Evans) *dwlt: sn drvn and a struggling in rr* **14/1**

3253 **12** *4* **Illustrious Lad (IRE)**[19] 2547 3-9-3 **58**.............................. JimCrowley 6 16
(Jim Boyle) *chsd ldrs 4f: wknd and eased over 1f out* **9/1**

0-30 **13** *6* **Glastonberry**[23] 2421 4-9-6 **57**.............................. SophieDoyle[(3)] 1
(Geoffrey Deacon) *prom on wd outside: shkn up whn bmpd and slipped wl over 1f out: wknd and eased* **33/1**

06-3 **14** *11* **Abadejo**[17] 2611 4-9-12 **60**............ FergusSweeney 7
(J R Jenkins) *pressed ldr after 1f to 2f out: wknd rapidly and eased: t.o* **28/1**

1m 12.59s (1.39) **Going Correction** +0.175s/f (Good)
WFA 3 from 4yo+ 7lb **14** Ran SP% **118.4**
Speed ratings (Par 101): **97,96,96,96,94 92,87,85,84,83 81,76,68,53**
toteswingers:1&2:£58.00, 1&3:£12.80, 2&3:£17.30 CSF £334.93 CT £2727.67 TOTE £11.40: £3.10, £4.20, £3.00; EX 376.40.
Owner One For All **Bred** Miss Anne Ormsby **Trained** Hingham, Norfolk
■ Stewards' Enquiry : Neil Callan two-day ban: careless riding (Jun 30-Jul 1)

FOCUS
Low-grade fare with interesting horses thin on the ground and not the one-horse race the market suggested once the favourite got behind on the stand rail. The pace was strong and the first four all came from the back. The winner is rated in line with the best of her winter AW form.
Huzzah(IRE) Official explanation: jockey said gelding was slowly away and hung left

3152 SYLVIA BROWN MEMORIAL H'CAP — 7f
7:35 (7:40) (Class 6) (0-55,54) 3-Y-O+ **£2,181** (£644; £322) **Stalls** High

Form RPR

0031 **1** **Clear Spring (IRE)**[24] 2401 4-9-6 **51**............ NickyMackay 6 65
(John Spearing) *chsd ldr: led after 2f: racd against rail sn after and clr fr 3f out: rdn out last 100yds* **7/1**[3]

004 **2** *3 ½* **Volcanic Jack (IRE)**[24] 2386 4-9-7 **52**............ NeilCallan 13 57
(Tony Carroll) *taken down early: trckd ldrs: wnt 3rd over 2f out and sn clr of rest: styd on to chse wnr last 100yds: no ch* **10/1**

0226 **3** *1* **Cahala Dancer (IRE)**[25] 2364 4-9-4 **54**............ MarkCoumbe(5) 15 56
(Roger Teal) *trckd ldrs: chsd clr wnr 3f out: no imp: lost 2nd last 100yds* **11/4**[1]

0-00 **4** *3* **Renoir's Lady**[143] 293 4-9-5 **50**............ HayleyTurner 9 44
(Simon Dow) *hld up in rr of main gp: rdn and sme prog to take 4th 2f out: nvr on terms w ldrs* **25/1**

3060 **5** *2 ¾* **Princess Willow**[24] 2401 4-9-4 **49**............ RichardThomas 11 36
(John E Long) *towards rr: rdn over 2f out: kpt on but nvr a factor* **12/1**

2605 **6** *¾* **Inquisitress**[4] 2998 8-9-4 **49**............ JamieGoldstein 7 34
(John Bridger) *dwlt: wl in rr: rdn 3f out: kpt on fnl 2f: n.d* **20/1**

0060 **7** *4* **Smarty Time**[3] 3043 5-9-8 **53**............ KierenFox 17 27
(John Bridger) *chsd ldrs nr side: rdn and no prog 3f out: wl btn fnl 2f* **25/1**

5500 **8** *1 ¼* **Captainrisk (IRE)**[31] 2171 6-9-7 **52**............(v) TomMcLaughlin 8 23
(Christine Dunnett) *str reminders and detached in rr after 2f: modest late prog* **20/1**

4340 **9** *½* **Prince Namid**[25] 2364 10-9-0 **52**............ NatashaEaton(7) 4 21
(Jonathen de Giles) *racd centre: nvr on terms w ldrs: no ch fnl 2f* **16/1**

00-0 **10** *5* **Strategic Action (IRE)**[164] 38 3-8-12 **52**............ MartinLane 14
(Linda Jewell) *rdn in midfield 1/2-way: sn struggling: wknd over 1f out* **40/1**

3 **11** *1 ¾* **Demoiselle Bond**[4] 3006 4-9-6 **51**............ RobertHavlin 5
(Lydia Richards) *taken down early and put in stalls wl bef rest: racd centre: led 2f: lost 2nd 3f out: sn wknd and eased* **9/1**

0226 **12** *3 ¼* **Jackie Love (IRE)**[85] 1009 4-8-12 **48**............(b) LauraPike(5) 1
(Olivia Maylam) *dwlt: racd centre: a wl off the pce and nvr a factor* **20/1**

6-00 **13** *8* **Invincible Beauty (IRE)**[21] 2501 3-8-13 **53**............ ShaneKelly 18
(Seamus Durack) *taken steadily to post: a in rr nr side: wknd over 2f out: eased* **4/1**[2]

0000 **14** *33* **Cuthbert (IRE)**[25] 2365 5-9-8 **53**............(p) JimCrowley 2
(Michael Attwater) *s.s: initially taken towards far side then racd in centre: sn wl bhd: t.o* **25/1**

1m 24.23s (0.93) **Going Correction** +0.175s/f (Good)
WFA 3 from 4yo+ 9lb **14** Ran SP% **120.1**
Speed ratings (Par 101): **101,97,95,92,89 88,83,82,81,76 74,70,61,23**
toteswingers:1&2:£11.20, 1&3:£3.90, 2&3:£7.90 CSF £66.74 CT £247.74 TOTE £7.70: £2.60, £4.10, £1.60; EX 83.30.
Owner H James **Bred** Rocal Bloodstock **Trained** Kinnersley, Worcs

FOCUS
Thoroughly uninspiring fare with only two of the runners in this 0-55 having made the first three last time out. The runners again bunched towards the stand rail and despite the pace appearing decent little got into it. The runner-up looks the best guide with the winner full value for the margin of victory.
Smarty Time Official explanation: trainer said mare lost a front shoe
Invincible Beauty(IRE) Official explanation: jockey said filly hung right

3153 MASTER'S H'CAP — 1m (P)
8:05 (8:10) (Class 6) (0-60,60) 4-Y-O+ **£2,181** (£644; £322) **Stalls** High

Form RPR

-040 **1** **Spirit Of Gondree (IRE)**[18] 2572 4-9-6 **59**............(b[1]) CathyGannon 4 68
(Milton Bradley) *taken down early: mde all and set str pce: jnd 2f out: fought on wl to assert fnl f: hld on* **12/1**

-235 **2** *1* **The Name Is Frank**[18] 2574 7-9-4 **57**............ GeorgeBaker 10 64
(Mark Gillard) *taken down early: chsd ldrs in 6th: prog over 2f out: drvn and styd on fr over 1f out: tk 2nd last strides* **13/2**[2]

-000 **3** *nk* **Blue Deer (IRE)**[19] 2546 4-9-6 **59**............(p) AmirQuinn 11 65
(Lee Carter) *prom on outer: chsd wnr 3f out: clsd to chal 2f out: wandering and nt go by over 1f out: lost 2nd last strides* **7/1**[3]

5150 **4** *hd* **Saucy Buck (IRE)**[25] 2373 4-9-7 **60**............ ShaneKelly 7 66
(Jamie Poulton) *hld up in 7th: prog over 2f out: drvn and styd on fr over 1f out: nrst fin* **10/1**

-335 **5** *6* **Ymir**[18] 2586 6-9-3 **56**............(t) JimCrowley 6 48
(Michael Attwater) *prom: chsd wnr briefly over 3f out: wknd on inner over 1f out* **6/1**[1]

3200 **6** *½* **Warden Bond**[8] 2899 4-9-3 **56**............(p) MartinLane 8 47
(William Stone) *nvr beyond midfield: rdn and no prog wl over 2f out: wl hld after* **10/1**

2243 **7** *¾* **Polar Auroras**[24] 2385 4-8-10 **56**............(t) GeorgeDowning(7) 12 45
(Tony Carroll) *hld up in last trio: plenty to do whn shkn up over 2f out: kpt on fnl f: no ch* **7/1**[3]

5406 **8** *nk* **Arctic Mirage**[12] 2758 4-9-4 **57**............ FergusSweeney 3 45
(Michael Blanshard) *hld up in 9th: plenty to do whn shkn up 2f out: no great prog after* **16/1**

6355 **9** *nk* **Monashee Rock (IRE)**[16] 2627 7-9-1 **54**............ KierenFox 2 41
(Patrick Chamings) *s.i.s: drvn in last by 1/2-way: nvr a factor but plugged on fnl f* **9/1**

6354 **10** *nk* **Jumeirah Liberty**[9] 2847 4-9-4 **57**............ JamieGoldstein 1 44
(Zoe Davison) *prom: rdn and lost pl over 2f out: steadily fdd* **15/2**

0-00 **11** *29* **Botanist**[12] 2761 5-9-4 **57**............(e[1]) NickyMackay 5
(Milton Bradley) *chsd wnr to over 3f out: wknd rapidly: t.o* **25/1**

/0-4 **12** *2 ¾* **Cottonfields (USA)**[18] 2586 6-9-1 **54**............(bt) NeilCallan 9
(Heather Main) *awkward s: a wl in rr: wknd over 2f out: t.o* **11/1**

1m 38.65s (0.45) **Going Correction** +0.10s/f (Slow) **12** Ran SP% **118.3**
Speed ratings (Par 101): **101,100,99,99,93 93,92,91,91,91 62,59**
toteswingers:1&2:£18.60, 1&3:£18.30, 2&3:£4.60 CSF £87.85 CT £606.00 TOTE £15.10: £4.30, £2.40, £3.60; EX 119.70.
Owner Paul & Ann de Weck & Partner **Bred** Windflower Overseas Holdings Inc **Trained** Sedbury, Gloucs

FOCUS
The first race on the Polytrack but no upturn in quality unfortunately in another weak affair in which they bet 6/1 the field. The pace was mostly decent and few got into it from behind until very late. The first two and the fourth help set the level.
Cottonfields(USA) Official explanation: jockey said gelding hung both ways

3154 PATTENMAKERS H'CAP — 1m 2f (P)
8:35 (8:41) (Class 5) (0-70,73) 4-Y-O+ **£3,067** (£905; £453) **Stalls** Low

Form RPR

6 **1** **The High Man**[29] 2233 4-9-6 **69**............ GeorgeBaker 2 79+
(Ed Walker) *trckd ldng pair: trapped on inner briefly over 2f out: plld out and clsd over 1f out: rdn to ld jst ins fnl f: sn in command* **15/8**[1]

-440 **2** *1 ½* **Strike Force**[134] 400 8-9-5 **68**............(t) NeilCallan 6 73
(Alison Hutchinson) *trckd ldng pair: wnt 2nd over 2f out: rdn to ld over 1f out: hdd and one pce jst ins fnl f* **16/1**

6020 **3** *hd* **Mafi (IRE)**[16] 2637 4-9-7 **70**............ RobertHavlin 11 75
(Mark Hoad) *hld up in midfield disputing 6th: prog over 2f out: chsd ldng pair fnl f: nrly snatched 2nd* **7/1**[3]

0056 **4** *¾* **Al Aqabah (IRE)**[36] 2044 7-9-2 **68**............(b) AdamBeschizza(3) 12 72
(Brian Gubby) *dwlt: hld up in last pair: stl wl in rr 2f out: drvn and r.o fr over 1f out: fin wl* **16/1**

5006 **5** *hd* **Archelao (IRE)**[19] 2546 4-9-1 **64**............ AmirQuinn 13 67
(Richard Rowe) *t.k.h: hld up in last trio: prog on wd outside over 2f out: styd on fnl f: nvr able to chal* **10/1**

5220 **6** *¾* **D'Urberville**[64] 1358 5-9-5 **68**............ FergusSweeney 8 70
(J R Jenkins) *hld up in midfield disputing 6th: prog over 2f out: drvn and styd on fr over 1f out: nvr gng pce to chal* **20/1**

206- **7** *nk* **Peachez**[227] 7236 4-9-2 **70**............(p) AmyScott(5) 10 71
(Alastair Lidderdale) *hld up in 8th: gng wl enough but plenty to do over 2f out: styd on fr over 1f out: one pce last 100yds* **14/1**

0000 **8** *3* **Unex Renoir**[24] 2393 4-9-2 **65**............(b) NickyMackay 14 60
(Michael Attwater) *prog rnd outside to chse ldr after 2f: led over 3f out: hdd over 1f out: wknd* **20/1**

24U1 **9** *1 ½* **Edgeworth (IRE)**[8] 2867 6-9-3 **73**............ GeorgeDowning(7) 3 65
(David Bridgwater) *led: rdn and hdd over 3f out: sn lost pl and btn* **4/1**[2]

0103 **10** *½* **Gallantry**[10] 2811 10-8-12 **61**............ TomMcLaughlin 9 52
(Paul Howling) *dwlt: hld up in detached last: rdn over 2f out: nvr a factor* **20/1**

000 **11** *14* **Opus Maximus (IRE)**[9] 2847 7-9-0 **63**............ HayleyTurner 4 26
(Conor Dore) *racd wd mostly: chsd ldng pair: wknd over 3f out: t.o* **10/1**

2m 5.59s (-1.01) **Going Correction** +0.10s/f (Slow) **11** Ran SP% **118.2**
Speed ratings (Par 103): **108,106,106,106,105 105,105,102,101,101 89**
toteswingers:1&2:£6.10, 1&3:£6.60, 2&3:£15.20 CSF £34.57 CT £171.61 TOTE £3.00: £1.50, £4.30, £2.90; EX 39.30.
Owner Dubai Thoroughbred Racing **Bred** Cheveley Park Stud Ltd **Trained** Newmarket, Suffolk

FOCUS
The handicap highlight of the evening won by a progressive winner. The pace was rather uneven and it didn't pay to be held up too far back. The form is ordinary and the placed horses set the level.

3155 RACING & MUSIC NIGHTS AT LINGFIELD PARK MEDIAN AUCTION MAIDEN STKS — 7f (P)
9:05 (9:09) (Class 6) 3-4-Y-O **£2,181** (£644; £322) **Stalls** Low

Form RPR

32- **1** **Don Libre**[214] 7422 3-9-3 0............ NeilCallan 4 79
(Paul Cole) *mde all: drvn clr over 1f out: unchal after* **9/2**[2]

0 **2** *6* **Indigo Iris (IRE)**[32] 2145 3-9-3 0............ JimCrowley 12 63+
(Richard Hannon) *trckd ldrs: sltly outpcd over 2f out: styd on to take 2nd ins fnl f: no ch w wnr* **12/1**

60- **3** *1 ½* **Pastures New**[169] 7921 4-9-9 0............ AdamBeschizza(3) 9 62
(Des Donovan) *pressed wnr: drvn over 2f out: lft bhd over 1f out: lost 2nd ins fnl f* **100/1**

4 *1 ¾* **Certavi (IRE)**[56] 1535 3-9-3 0............ ShaneKelly 3 54
(Seamus Durack) *dwlt: t.k.h: hld up in midfield: outpcd over 2f out: sme prog over 1f out: one pce fnl f* **16/1**

0- **5** *½* **Two Sugars**[519] 158 4-9-12 0............ CathyGannon 1 56
(Louise Best) *trckd ldrs: outpcd over 2f out: no imp after* **80/1**

6 *2 ½* **Yogic Flyer** 3-8-12 0............ JackMitchell 8 41
(Gay Kelleway) *hld up in last trio: sme prog 2f out into midfield over 1f out: no hdwy after* **50/1**

0- **7** *1 ¾* **Saffron Park**[383] 2559 3-9-3 0............ HayleyTurner 14 42
(John Best) *racd v wd early: trckd ldrs: outpcd over 2f out: n.d after* **11/1**

2-UR **8** *1 ¼* **Aurens (IRE)**[57] 1492 3-9-3 0............(v[1]) AmirQuinn 6 38
(Gary Moore) *rel to r and lft several l: tk fierce hold and sn in tch on outer: no prog fnl 2f* **8/1**[3]

0 **9** *3* **Regal Art**[56] 1512 3-9-3 0............ FergusSweeney 5 30
(Jo Crowley) *hld up towards rr: outpcd over 2f out: nvr on terms after* **14/1**

0 **10** *nk* **Soldier Spy**[9] 2856 3-9-3 0............ MartinLane 11 29
(Mark Usher) *hld up in last trio: nvr on terms no prog fnl 2f* **33/1**

0 **11** *6* **Blackthorn Stick (IRE)**[9] 2865 3-9-3 0............ TomMcLaughlin 13 13
(John Butler) *dwlt: bmpd over 5f out whn in last pair: nvr a factor* **66/1**

0- **P** **Barberton (USA)**[302] 5254 3-9-3 0............ GeorgeBaker 2
(Jeremy Noseda) *hld up in midfield: p.u 1/2-way: dismntd* **4/5**[1]

1m 26.03s (1.23) **Going Correction** +0.10s/f (Slow)
WFA 3 from 4yo 9lb **12** Ran SP% **122.0**
Speed ratings (Par 101): **96,89,87,85,84 82,80,78,75,74 67,**
toteswingers:1&2:£10.70, 1&3:£19.60, 2&3:£114.80 CSF £57.84 TOTE £7.00: £1.60, £2.80, £11.90; EX 29.20.
Owner Mrs E A Bass **Bred** Mrs E A Bass **Trained** Whatcombe, Oxon

FOCUS
A fair maiden that lost much of its interest when the favourite \bBarberton\p was pulled up on the run down to the bottom turn apparently on account of a slipped saddle. The winner wound up a steady pace from the front and few ever got competitive. The form does not look solid behind the main players and is rated slightly negatively.
Barberton(USA) Official explanation: jockey said saddle slipped
T/Plt: £564.80 to a £1 stake. Pool:£94,376.24 - 121.98 winning tickets T/Qpdt: £59.70 to a £1 stake. Pool:£7,978.90 - 98.88 winning tickets JN

[3117] SANDOWN (R-H)

Saturday, June 16

OFFICIAL GOING: Soft (good to soft in places in back straight on round course; home straight: far side 6.4, centre 6.2, stands' side 6.2; round course 6.4)
Sprint track full width. Round course dolled out 5yds from 9f to post adding about 8yds to distances. Home straight narrowed to 12yds bend to 2f pole.
Wind: fresh, against Weather: dry and breezy

3156 BETFRED MOBILE SPORTS H'CAP 1m 1f

2:20 (2:21) (Class 3) (0-90,86) 3-Y-O

£9,337 (£2,796; £1,398; £699; £349; £175) **Stalls** Low

Form				RPR
6-15	1		**Opinion (IRE)**[21] 2477 3-9-5 **84**................ RyanMoore 3 (Sir Michael Stoute) *t.k.h early: chsd ldr tl 5f out: chsd ldrs after: rdn 3f out: hdwy u.p to press ldrs over 1f out: led ins fnl f: r.o wl: drvn out* **3/1**[2]	97
4120	2	1 3/4	**Spirit Of The Law (IRE)**[14] 2716 3-9-0 **79**................ HayleyTurner 9 (Ed Dunlop) *led tl hdd and rdn 2f out: led agin 1f out: sn hdd and styd on same pce fnl 150yds* **4/1**[3]	88
-301	3	1/2	**Hefner (IRE)**[44] 1793 3-9-2 **81**................ RichardHughes 2 (Richard Hannon) *in tch: rdn and effrt ent fnl 2f: swtchd rt and drvn 1f out: styd on u.p fnl f* **10/1**	89
6-1	4	1/2	**Dark Stranger (USA)**[84] 1031 3-9-7 **86**................ RobertHavlin 6 (John Gosden) *chsd ldrs tl hdwy to join ldr 4f out: led 2f out: sn rdn and edgd rt: hdd 1f out: styd on same pce ins fnl f* **15/2**	93
-142	5	nk	**Takeitfromalady (IRE)**[7] 2930 3-9-3 **82**................(b) JimCrowley 7 (Ralph Beckett) *s.i.s: in tch in rr: hdwy against stands' rail over 2f out: rdn ent fnl 2f: kpt on fnl f but nvr quite gng pce to rch ldrs* **2/1**[1]	88
10-3	6	2 1/4	**Ventura Spirit**[16] 2634 3-8-4 **69**................ TadhgO'Shea 5 (Richard Fahey) *stdd s: hld up in last pair: nt clr run over 2f out tl swtchd lft and rdn over 1f out: no ex 1f out: wknd ins fnl f* **16/1**	70
5-66	7	1 1/2	**Quick Bite (IRE)**[7] 2942 3-8-6 **78**................ NoelGarbutt(7) 4 (Hugo Palmer) *t.k.h: chsd ldrs tl wnt 2nd 5f out tl 4f out: rdn 2f out: outpcd and btn 1f out: wknd fnl f* **14/1**	76

1m 57.94s (2.24) **Going Correction** +0.40s/f (Good) **7** Ran SP% **111.7**
Speed ratings (Par 103): **106,104,104,103,103 101,99**
Swingers:1&2:£3.00, 2&3:£8.90, 1&3:£3.50 CSF £14.65 CT £101.26 TOTE £4.60: £3.20, £1.90; EX 16.20 Trifecta £114.80 Pool: £963.67 - 6.20 winning units..
Owner Highclere Thoroughbred Racing-Herring **Bred** Ballylinch Stud **Trained** Newmarket, Suffolk

FOCUS
The ground had dried out a little following a bright and breezy morning. The wind was in the horses' faces up the straight, making it a bit of a test. The time for the opener was 4.94sec outside the standard. Richard Hughes felt the ground was "dead", while Hayley Turner said the drying conditions had left the ground rather sticky. This decent handicap has been won in recent years by a couple of useful sorts in Steele Tango, who went on to win in Group company, and subsequent Royal Ascot scorer Beachfire. The field came over to the stands' side turning in, before ending up racing down the centre of the track.

NOTEBOOK
Opinion(IRE) on the inside of the group once into the straight, was being stoked along with three to run but responded well to tough it out. He is thoroughly at home in soft ground and got away with the drop in trip in the conditions. (op 10-3 tchd 11-4, 4-1 in a place)
Spirit Of The Law(IRE) made the running on this drop back in trip and, showing a willing attitude, even edged ahead again briefly before the winner took his measure. This was a return to form after a blip at Musselburgh. (op 5-1 tchd 11-2)
Hefner(IRE)'s Lingfield maiden win had been boosted by the subsequent victory of the runner-up, Handsome Ransom. The colt dropped back to last place turning into the straight but stayed on after switching to the inside of the group. (op 9-1)
Dark Stranger(USA) had been absent since winning his maiden on Polytrack in March. He travelled well into the lead, but could not retain his advantage for long. It could have been that the outing was just needed, and he is worth giving another chance to, particularly on better ground. (op 11-2 tchd 8-1)
Takeitfromalady(IRE), steadily progressive this year and raised a further 3lb, was slow to break and, although sticking on, was never able to land a blow. Official explanation: jockey said gelding was slowly away (tchd 9-4)
Ventura Spirit, dropping back from 1m4f, was another who failed to become seriously involved from the rear, although he didn't have much room in which to operate at one stage. (tchd 18-1)
Quick Bite(IRE), who raced a little keenly, continues to perform below her mark. (op 12-1 tchd 16-1)

3157 BETFRED THE BONUS KING H'CAP 1m 14y

2:50 (2:52) (Class 2) (0-100,98) 3-Y-0+

£21,787 (£6,524; £3,262; £1,631; £815; £409) **Stalls** Low

Form				RPR
1255	1		**Fennell Bay (IRE)**[8] 2897 3-8-1 **81**................ JoeFanning 11 (Mark Johnston) *led for 1f: chsd ldr tl led again over 2f out: rdn 2f out and sn clr: styd on wl ins fnl f: rdn out* **8/1**	93
311	2	1 3/4	**Prince Of Sorrento**[37] 2011 5-9-0 **84**................ RichardHughes 13 (Lee Carter) *styd wd early: in tch in midfield: rdn and hdwy 2f out: chsd clr ldr over 1f out: drvn and styd on to press wnr ins fnl f: no ex and btn fnl 100yds* **9/2**[2]	94
4004	3	3	**Karaka Jack**[7] 2919 5-8-13 **83**................ AdrianNicholls 7 (David Nicholls) *hld up in last pair: rdn and effrt 3f out: hdwy u.p over 1f out: kpt on fnl f to go 3rd nr fin: no threat to ldng pair* **14/1**	86
0-33	4	hd	**Stage Attraction (IRE)**[35] 2082 4-9-3 **87**................ RyanMoore 9 (Andrew Balding) *in tch in midfield: swtchd lft and rdn 2f out: hdwy u.p over 1f out: chsd clr ldng pair 1f out: no imp: lost 3rd nr fin* **4/1**[1]	90
5-22	5	5	**Sam Sharp (USA)**[21] 2500 6-9-0 **84**................ RoystonFfrench 3 (Ian Williams) *hld up in last pair: rdn over 3f out: drvn and sme hdwy 2f out: no threat to ldrs but plugged on u.p fnl f* **15/2**	76
0-00	6	2 1/4	**Fantasy Gladiator**[35] 2068 6-8-12 **82**................(p) MartinHarley 12 (Robert Cowell) *chsd ldrs: rdn over 2f out: no ex and btn over 1f out: fdd fnl f* **25/1**	68
-013	7	1/2	**Weapon Of Choice (IRE)**[16] 2642 4-9-7 **91**................ IanMongan 4 (Stuart Kittow) *t.k.h: chsd ldr tl led after 1f: rdn and hdd over 2f out: btn and wknd over 1f out: fdd fnl f* **7/1**[3]	76
1-00	8	2 1/2	**Take It To The Max**[56] 1510 5-9-6 **95**................ ShaneBKelly(5) 10 (Richard Fahey) *bhd in last quartet: rdn over 3f out: drvn and no prog 2f out: n.d* **22/1**	74
032	9	3/4	**Standing Strong (IRE)**[15] 2665 4-8-9 **79** oh1................ RobertHavlin 2 (Robert Mills) *taken down early: t.k.h: chsd ldrs: rdn and struggling over 2f out: wknd 2f out* **16/1**	57
00-0	10	nk	**Leviathan**[77] 1128 5-9-3 **87**................ MartinLane 8 (Tony Newcombe) *in tch in midfield: rdn and no rspnse over 2f out: wknd 2f out* **11/1**	64
0010	11	3 3/4	**Sinfonico (IRE)**[16] 2642 4-8-11 **81**................ JimCrowley 5 (Richard Hannon) *in tch in midfield: rdn and effrt nrest far rail wl over 2f out: no hdwy and btn 2f out: sn wknd* **16/1**	49
554/	12	10	**Morana (IRE)**[772] 1833 5-10-0 **98**................ EddieAhern 1 (Warren Greatrex) *a last quartet: rdn and no rspnse over 2f out: sn lost tch: eased ins fnl f* **28/1**	43
0000	13	9	**Lowther**[16] 2642 7-8-10 **87**................ AccursioRomeo(7) 6 (Brett Johnson) *t.k.h: chsd ldrs tl lost pl qckly over 2f out: t.o and eased ins fnl f* **33/1**	12

1m 45.04s (1.74) **Going Correction** +0.40s/f (Good)
WFA 3 from 4yo+ 10lb **13** Ran SP% **114.9**
Speed ratings (Par 109): **107,105,102,102,97 94,94,91,91,90 87,77,68**
Swingers:1&2:£6.80, 2&3:£6.80, 1&3:£24.30 CSF £40.09 CT £513.84 TOTE £8.70: £3.30, £1.50, £3.30; EX 47.50 Trifecta £1027.00 Pool: £1,582.25 - 1.14 winning units..
Owner Sheikh Hamdan Bin Mohammed Al Maktoum **Bred** J R Wills **Trained** Middleham Moor, N Yorks

FOCUS
A good handicap, but perhaps not the strongest race for the grade. Although they kept away from the inside rail, the runners did not come as wide in the home straight as they had in the opener. The first two came clear.

NOTEBOOK
Fennell Bay(IRE) was the sole 3yo in the race and was in receipt of plenty of weight from his elders. After striking the front he soon had only the runner-up to deal with, and he would have beaten him more comfortably had he not edged to his left late on. He had been running well in defeat over 1m2f since a win on the Rowley Mile and this victory proved his effectiveness on soft ground. (op 10-1)
Prince Of Sorrento won a much weaker race at Yarmouth last time and he ran with credit off a 9lb higher mark. It looked fleetingly when he emerged from the pack as if he would cut down the winner, but although he was unable to do so he kept going for second and finished clear of the rest. (op 7-1 tchd 4-1)
Karaka Jack was reverting to a mile. Racing nearer to the inside rail than most, he ran on from the rear of the field without threatening the first two. (op 12-1)
Stage Attraction(IRE) ran another solid race and is capable of winning from this type of mark, perhaps if given a chance at 1m2f. (op 7-2)
Sam Sharp(USA) turned into the straight in last place but was steadily picking off rivals late on without troubling the principals. Runner-up on his previous two starts, he remains in decent form. (op 7-1 tchd 13-2)
Fantasy Gladiator came just about widest into the straight and the ground was perhaps not ideal for him, so this was a reasonable effort. (op 28-1)
Weapon Of Choice(IRE), who made a good deal of the running, had no ground issues and was just 2lb higher than when pipping Sam Sharp over C&D in April. Ian Mongan reported that the gelding ran flat. Official explanation: jockey said gelding ran flat (op 11-2)
Morana(IRE) a one-time smart performer for Peter Chapple-Hyam and gelded since he was last seen in May 2010, showed little on this handicap debut. (op 33-1 tchd 25-1)

3158 NOVAE BLOODSTOCK INSURANCE SCURRY STKS (LISTED RACE) 5f 6y

3:25 (3:27) (Class 1) 3-Y-0

£18,714 (£7,095; £3,550; £1,768; £887; £445) **Stalls** Low

Form				RPR
1-11	1		**Pearl Secret**[30] 2212 3-8-13 108................ RichardHughes 7 (David Barron) *stdd s: t.k.h: hld up in last pair: hdwy 3f out: chal ent fnl f: rdn to ld ins fnl f: r.o under hands and heels riding fnl f: asserted towards fin* **1/3**[1]	108+
-131	2	nk	**Free Zone**[14] 2691 3-8-13 98................ TomEaves 5 (Bryan Smart) *led and set stdy gallop: rdn and qcknd 2f out: hrd pressed and drvn 1f out: sn hdd: battled on gamely u.p: hld cl home* **7/1**[2]	107
14-0	3	2	**Ultrasonic (USA)**[42] 1858 3-8-8 92................ RyanMoore 3 (Sir Michael Stoute) *t.k.h: hld up in tch: rdn and effrt wl over 1f out: hdwy u.p to chse ldng pair ins fnl f: no imp fnl 100yds* **8/1**[3]	95
4-00	4	1	**Bayleyf (IRE)**[29] 2236 3-8-13 97................[1] IanMongan 1 (John Best) *t.k.h: chsd ldrs: rdn and unable qck over 1f out: styd on same pce and btn fnl f* **33/1**	96
205-	5	3/4	**Rex Imperator**[259] 6518 3-8-13 99................ JimCrowley 4 (Roger Charlton) *t.k.h: hld up in last pair: rdn 2f out: swtchd lft 1f out: kpt on but no imp fnl f* **14/1**	94
62-0	6	1 1/2	**Chunky Diamond (IRE)**[15] 2664 3-8-13 104................ RobertHavlin 6 (Peter Chapple-Hyam) *dwlt: t.k.h: sn rcvrd to chse ldr: rdn 2f out: 3rd and unable qck ent fnl f: wknd ins fnl f* **25/1**	88

1m 5.31s (3.71) **Going Correction** +1.00s/f (Soft) **6** Ran SP% **112.1**
Speed ratings (Par 107): **110,109,106,104,103 101**
Swingers:1&2:£1.10, 2&3:£3.10, 1&3:£1.50 CSF £3.31 TOTE £1.30: £1.20, £2.10; EX 2.90 Trifecta £7.30 Pool: £1,435.89 - 143.89 winning units..
Owner Pearl Bloodstock Ltd **Bred** Whitsbury Manor Stud & Pigeon House Stud **Trained** Maunby, N Yorks

FOCUS
This Listed sprint was won last year by Margot Did, who took the Nunthorpe Stakes two months later, while Hoh Mike and Triple Aspect are other recent winners to have progressed to Group-race success.

NOTEBOOK
Pearl Secret came here three from three and his vastly experienced trainer has called him the best horse he's handled. The powerfully built chestnut didn't get much cover towards the rear of the field, taking a bit of a hold early on, but picked up ground in taking style. After he'd struck the front there was a worrying moment for his supporters as the runner-up fought back, but the favourite was always in command and was value for a considerably wider margin of victory. On the bare form this was not especially convincing, but he remains unbeaten and is progressing nicely through the ranks, although the July Cup is likely to be asking too much of him at this stage and the Nunthorpe, in which his trainer's Coastal Bluff dead-heated in 1997, is a more likely target. He looks the type with one burst and will be suited by being able to deliver it off a stronger pace in a bigger field. Better ground should be fine, although he is a heavy-topped type who would not want it too firm. (op 4-11)
Free Zone tried to make all and, after being headed by the favourite inside the last, he rallied bravely. While he was very likely flattered to have gone down by only a neck, this confirms him a smart and progressive sprinter, particularly as he was 10lb worse off with Pearl Secret than he would have been in a handicap. (op 13-2)
Ultrasonic(USA), a lightly raced filly, kept on from the back without convincing that the minimum trip is what she wants. This secures some black type for her. (op 10-1 tchd 12-1)
Bayleyf(IRE) was fitted with a hood for the first time and needed a rug for stalls entry. Normally such a pacey colt, he was reined back behind the leaders on this drop back in trip and was comfortably held by the principals, although this was an improvement on what he showed at Newbury. (op 25-1)
Rex Imperator had been off since October and his trainer had voiced concerns about the suitability of this ground. Again a little slowly away, the gelding was running on when it was all over, not convincing at all that he is a 5f performer. He warrants another chance. (op 16-1)

Chunky Diamond(IRE) ran freely chasing the pace before fading. He hasn't beaten a rival in two starts this season, but the ground was a possible excuse here. (op 16-1)

3159 BETFRED HAT TRICK HEAVEN ON THE EUROS H'CAP 5f 6y
4:00 (4:00) (Class 4) (0-80,77) 4-Y-0+ **£6,145** (£1,828; £913; £456) **Stalls** Low

Form RPR

0-41 **1** **Cardinal**[7] 2940 7-9-1 **71** JimCrowley 6 80
(Robert Cowell) *w ldr tl led 2f out: sn rdn: drvn and styd on wl to assert ins fnl f: drvn out* **4/1**[2]

4104 **2** *1* **Interakt**[8] 2890 5-9-2 **75** HarryBentley(3) 7 80
(Joseph Tuite) *in tch: hdwy to chse ldrs 2f out: sn drvn: kpt on ins fnl f: wnt 2nd on post* **6/1**[3]

-533 **3** *nse* **Jack Luey**[28] 2264 5-9-7 **77** RyanMoore 2 82
(Lawrence Mullaney) *led: hdd 2f out: stl ev ch and rdn over 1f out: drvn 1f out: no ex and btn fnl 100yds: edgd lft and lost 2nd on post* **13/8**[1]

5203 **4** *shd* **Bouncy Bouncy (IRE)**[9] 2853 5-9-7 **77** (t) HayleyTurner 3 82+
(Michael Bell) *chsd ldrs: effrt u.p over 1f out: hld by wnr but keeping on and pressing for 2nd whn nt clr run and eased cl home* **15/2**

6640 **5** *1 1/4* **Captain Scooby**[7] 2940 6-9-1 **74** DeclanCannon(3) 8 74
(Richard Guest) *stdd s: hld up in last pair: rdn and effrt over 1f out: styd on same pce ins fnl f* **8/1**

20-6 **6** *1 3/4* **Rash Judgement**[40] 1935 7-9-5 **75** RichardHughes 5 69
(Stuart Kittow) *t.k.h: hld up in tch: rdn and unable qck over 1f out: one pce and btn fnl f* **7/1**

2-56 **7** *3/4* **Matsunosuke**[9] 2861 10-9-5 **75** MartinHarley 1 66
(Dr Richard Newland) *stdd s: hld up in last pair: rdn and effrt over 1f out: no imp and wl hld fnl f* **33/1**

1m 5.94s (4.34) **Going Correction** +1.00s/f (Soft) 7 Ran SP% **110.7**
Speed ratings (Par 105): **105,103,103,103,101 98,97**
Swingers:1&2:£5.20, 2&3:£3.00, 1&3:£1.40 CSF £25.95 CT £50.17 TOTE £5.10: £2.70, £3.00; EX 27.40.
Owner Mrs J May **Bred** The Queen **Trained** Six Mile Bottom, Cambs

FOCUS
An ordinary handicap for the grade, run at what only looked a steady pace. The time was 0.63sec slower than the preceding Listed race. It proved difficult to make up ground from the rear.
Jack Luey Official explanation: jockey said gelding hung left
Bouncy Bouncy(IRE) Official explanation: jockey said mare was denied a clear run

3160 BETFRED DOUBLE DELIGHT ON THE EUROS H'CAP 7f 16y
4:30 (4:32) (Class 3) (0-90,88) 3-Y-0 **£9,337** (£2,796; £1,398; £699; £349) **Stalls** Low

Form RPR

3165 **1** **Shamaal Nibras (USA)**[7] 2916 3-9-7 **88** RichardHughes 2 98
(Richard Hannon) *hld up in last pair: rdn and effrt jst over 1f out: qcknd to ld ins fnl f: r.o strly and sn clr: eased cl home* **5/2**[2]

-252 **2** *2* **Tartiflette**[9] 2854 3-9-2 **83** SebSanders 5 87
(Ed McMahon) *stdd s: hld up in last pair: clsd to trck ldrs over 1f out: swtchd lft and effrt 1f out: chsd wnr fnl 100yds: no imp* **7/4**[1]

-212 **3** *1* **Our Boy Jack (IRE)**[12] 2764 3-8-7 **79** ShaneBKelly(5) 7 80
(Richard Fahey) *w ldr: rdn and ev ch over 2f out: led over 1f out: outpcd by wnr and styd on one pce ins fnl f* **10/3**[3]

5060 **4** *1 3/4* **Cravat**[7] 2910 3-9-0 **81** JoeFanning 6 78
(Mark Johnston) *chsd ldng pair: effrt to chal 2f out: drvn over 1f out: outpcd and btn ins fnl f* **7/1**

0520 **5** *2 1/2* **Tip Top Gorgeous (IRE)**[8] 2893 3-8-13 **80** JimCrowley 3 70
(David O'Meara) *led: rdn 2f out: sn hdd: wknd fnl f* **12/1**

1m 33.08s (3.58) **Going Correction** +0.40s/f (Good) 5 Ran SP% **108.2**
Speed ratings (Par 103): **95,92,91,89,86**
CSF £7.02 TOTE £3.90: £1.60, £1.40; EX 7.50.
Owner Tariq S Al Tayer **Bred** Andrew Cowen & Gary Tolchin **Trained** East Everleigh, Wilts

FOCUS
They went a fairly steady pace in this reasonable handicap, but the first two were able to come from the rear. The runners made for the centre of the track in the straight but the winner ended up next to the inside rail.

NOTEBOOK
Shamaal Nibras(USA) is not entirely straightforward, but a hold-up ride suits him and he quickened up nicely once switched for his run close to the inside rail. He is running consistently well this spring. The Hannon yard also won this prize 12 months ago. (op 7-2 tchd 4-1)
Tartiflette travelled well in the rear but the gap closed on her in the straight. Once Seb Sanders had switched her he seemed to delay asking her for full effort and the winner took first run on her. In the jockey's defence the filly had twice been denied when seeming set to win this season, including over C&D last time, and is not the type to find much in front. (op 13-8)
Our Boy Jack(IRE), back up to 7f, did a lot of running up with the pace and was picked off in the latter stages. He should continue to perform with credit and we know that he handles fast ground too. (op 11-4)
Cravat has been descending the weights and he had his chance, but is still not operating at his best. (op 6-1)
Tip Top Gorgeous(IRE) raced keenly on the front end and could not hit back when headed. She does not convince that she stays this far. (op 9-1)

3161 BETFRED MOBILE E B F MAIDEN STKS 1m 2f 7y
5:00 (5:02) (Class 5) 3-Y-0 **£3,881** (£1,155; £577; £288) **Stalls** Low

Form RPR

52 **1** **Rule Book (IRE)**[17] 2612 3-9-3 0 RichardHughes 9 86
(Richard Hannon) *sn led and set stdy gallop: rdn wl over 1f out: hdd and drvn 1f out: battled on gamely u.p to ld again wl ins fnl f: drvn out* **9/2**[3]

2 *nk* **Sir Quintin (IRE)** 3-9-3 0 HayleyTurner 5 85+
(Andrew Balding) *hld up in tch in last trio: swtchd lft 3f out: rdn and hdwy 2f out: led 1f out: sn drvn: r.o wl tl hdd and no ex wl ins fnl f* **20/1**

3 *3 3/4* **Zamdy Man** 3-9-3 0 EddieAhern 6 78+
(Venetia Williams) *chsd ldrs: shuffled bk into last quartet but stl wl in tch 4f out: hdwy u.p over 1f out: kpt on wl and wnt 3rd ins fnl f* **25/1**

0- **4** *3/4* **Top Billing**[241] 6954 3-9-3 0 RobertHavlin 2 76
(John Gosden) *in tch: rdn and effrt 2f out: outpcd by ldng pair 1f out: styd on same pce after* **4/1**[2]

5 *1/2* **Sea Smoke (IRE)** 3-9-0 0 PatrickHills(3) 3 75+
(Luca Cumani) *s.i.s and rn green early: sn clsd and in tch: hdwy into midfield 8f out: switching lft and rt looking for run fr 2f out: bdly hmpd and swtchd rt 1f out: kpt on* **22/1**

4 **6** *1* **Moonglow**[32] 2148 3-8-12 0 RyanMoore 7 68
(John Gosden) *chsd ldrs: rdn and unable qck 2f out: drvn and outpcd jst over 1f out: wl hld fnl f* **7/2**[1]

7 *3* **Educate** 3-9-3 0 TadhgO'Shea 11 70+
(Ismail Mohammed) *rn green: in tch in rr: hdwy and nt clr run 2f out: swtchd rt and sme hdwy over 1f out: swtchd bk lft jst ins fnl f: nt pushed and no prog after* **66/1**

8 *1/2* **Peninsula** 3-8-12 0 JimCrowley 10 61+
(Ralph Beckett) *in tch in midfield on outer: rdn and unable qck 2f out: outpcd and btn over 1f out: wknd fnl f* **10/1**

9 *1 1/2* **Checkpoint** 3-9-3 0 IanMongan 4 63+
(Sir Henry Cecil) *in tch in midfield: rdn and unable qck ent fnl 2f: wknd over 1f out* **7/1**

4-30 **10** *1/2* **Virginia Gallica (IRE)**[30] 2201 3-8-12 75 SebSanders 1 57
(J W Hills) *t.k.h: chsd ldrs tl hdwy to join wnr 8f out: rdn ent fnl 2f: fnd little and wknd over 1f out* **13/2**

2-05 **11** *7* **Silkee Supreme**[31] 2172 3-9-3 72 GeorgeBaker 12 48
(Richard Hannon) *t.k.h: chsd ldr for 2f: styd chsng ldrs: rdn and lost pl ent fnl 2f: towards rr whn hmpd wl over 1f out: wl btn and eased wl ins fnl f* **16/1**

004 **12** *17* **Morlotti**[22] 2453 3-9-3 0 J-PGuillambert 8 14+
(Luca Cumani) *in tch in last trio: effrt on outer whn squeezed and hmpd 2f out: sn btn: wl bhd and eased ins fnl f* **33/1**

2m 14.98s (4.48) **Going Correction** +0.40s/f (Good) 12 Ran SP% **118.6**
Speed ratings (Par 99): **98,97,94,94,93 92,90,90,88,88 82,69**
Swingers:1&2:£15.50, 2&3:£71.30, 1&3:£28.90 CSF £97.20 TOTE £5.30: £2.10, £4.30, £9.30; EX 65.90.
Owner Andrew Tinkler **Bred** Joseph Heavey **Trained** East Everleigh, Wilts

FOCUS
A modest maiden for the track, run at a steady pace, but there were a number of eye-catching performances and the race should produce winners. The first two came clear.
Sea Smoke(IRE) ◆ Official explanation: jockey said gelding was denied a clear run
Educate ◆ Official explanation: jockey said colt was denied a clear run

3162 BETFRED BONUS KING BINGO H'CAP 1m 6f
5:30 (5:31) (Class 4) (0-85,82) 4-Y-0+ **£6,145** (£1,828; £913; £456) **Stalls** Low

Form RPR

-655 **1** **Bolivia (GER)**[8] 2884 6-9-6 **81** (t) EddieAhern 2 92
(Lucy Wadham) *chsd ldr: clsd and gng best over 2f out: led wl over 1f out and sn rdn clr: wl in command 1f out: comf* **9/2**

5-34 **2** *7* **Mohanad (IRE)**[7] 2936 6-9-0 **78** HarryBentley(3) 5 79
(Sheena West) *chsd ldrs: rdn and unable qck 3f out: edgd lft u.p 2f out: chsd clr wnr 1f out: no imp* **4/1**[3]

10-1 **3** *1 1/2* **Rockfella**[41] 1890 6-9-7 **82** TadhgO'Shea 7 81
(Denis Coakley) *hld up in last trio: hdwy 8f out: rdn and no imp 3f out: no ch w wnr but plugged on to go modest 3rd ins fnl f* **7/2**[2]

/3-3 **4** *1 1/2* **Hawridge Star (IRE)**[41] 1890 10-9-0 **75** IanMongan 1 72
(Stuart Kittow) *hld up in rr: rdn 4f out: swtchd lft 2f out: plugged on u.p to go modest 4th ins fnl f: no ch w wnr* **11/4**[1]

5555 **5** *2* **Uphold**[15] 2685 5-9-7 **82** (vt) JackMitchell 3 76
(Gay Kelleway) *led: pushed clr 4f out: rdn and hdd wl over 1f out: sn btn: lost 2nd and wl btn 1f out: wknd and lost 2 pls ins fnl f* **10/1**

6145 **6** *6* **Cotton King**[61] 1421 5-9-1 **76** (t) RichardHughes 8 62
(Lady Herries) *chsd ldng pair early: steadily lost pl: 5th and effrt 3f out: no prog and wl btn fnl 2f* **6/1**

0-00 **7** *2* **Cozy Tiger (USA)**[9] 2863 7-8-4 **65** JamieMackay 4 48
(Willie Musson) *hld up in rr: swtchd lft and struggling 3f out: sn lost tch* **20/1**

3m 7.96s (3.46) **Going Correction** +0.40s/f (Good) 7 Ran SP% **115.2**
Speed ratings (Par 105): **106,102,101,100,99 95,94**
Swingers:1&2:£3.90, 2&3:£4.10, 1&3:£3.80 CSF £23.09 CT £69.67 TOTE £7.00: £2.90, £2.60; EX 27.60.
Owner Mr And Mrs A E Pakenham **Bred** Frau I U D Meinke **Trained** Newmarket, Suffolk

FOCUS
A fair handicap in which the fifth set a brisk gallop.
T/Plt: £118.00 to a £1 stake. Pool: £110,973.00 - 686.18 winning tickets. T/Qpdt: £12.30 to a £1 stake. Pool: £6,8011.00 - 407.27 winning tickets. SP

3123 YORK (L-H)
Saturday, June 16

OFFICIAL GOING: Soft (6.2; home straight: stands' side 6.0, centre 6.1, far side 6.1)
Rail on round course moved out 3m from 9f to entrance to home straight reducing distances of races of 1m and over by 22yds.
Wind: fresh 1/2 behind Weather: overcast, chageable, frequent showers

3163 QUEEN MOTHER'S CUP (LADY AMATEUR RIDERS) (H'CAP) 1m 4f
2:05 (2:05) (Class 3) (0-95,94) 3-Y-0+ **£12,478** (£3,870; £1,934; £968) **Stalls** Centre

Form RPR

00-3 **1** **Crackentorp**[29] 2253 7-10-13 **93** MissJCoward 20 102
(Tim Easterby) *trckd ldrs: effrt over 3f out: led over 2f out: drvn out* **10/1**

4-56 **2** *3/4* **Hong Kong Island (IRE)**[21] 2504 5-9-12 **81** MissRSmith(3) 18 89+
(Micky Hammond) *mid-div: plld wd outside over 3f out: chsd wnr over 1f out: edgd rt: no ex clsng stages* **20/1**

1316 **3** *2 1/4* **Veiled Applause**[16] 2620 9-10-2 **82** SamanthaDrake 8 86
(John Quinn) *chsd ldrs: upsides over 2f out: kpt on same pce* **25/1**

15-3 **4** *1 3/4* **Eagle Rock (IRE)**[31] 2180 4-9-11 **80** MissHayleyMoore(3) 15 81
(Tom Tate) *swtchd lft s: in tch: effrt over 3f out: sn chsng ldrs: kpt on same pce fnl 2f* **15/2**[2]

0-05 **5** *3/4* **Antigua Sunrise (IRE)**[21] 2504 6-9-7 **76** MissPhillipaTutty(3) 17 76
(Richard Fahey) *mid-div: styd on fnl 3f: nt rch ldrs* **12/1**

-000 **6** *1 1/4* **Red Jade**[21] 2504 7-9-9 **75** oh1 MissCWalton 13 73
(Mrs K Burke) *mid-div: effrt over 3f out: one pce fnl 2f* **16/1**

26-5 **7** *1* **Scrapper Smith (IRE)**[49] 1654 6-10-9 **89** MissADeniel 2 85
(Alistair Whillans) *hld up in rr: styd on fnl 3f: nvr nr ldrs* **12/1**

-222 **8** *1/2* **Troopingthecolour**[7] 2932 6-11-0 **94** (t) MissSBrotherton 11 90
(Steve Gollings) *in tch: effrt over 3f out: sn prom: wknd ins fnl f* **13/2**[1]

0-32 **9** *3/4* **Lexington Bay (IRE)**[59] 1446 4-10-2 **88** MissJMcLernon(6) 3 82
(Richard Fahey) *hld up in rr: kpt on fnl 3f: nvr a factor* **8/1**[3]

-026 **10** *1* **Odin's Raven (IRE)**[35] 2093 7-9-6 **75** oh1 MissHBethell(3) 19 68
(Brian Ellison) *rr-div: kpt on fnl 3f: nvr nr ldrs* **20/1**

3245 **11** *1 1/4* **Halla San**[14] 2709 10-9-10 **82** MissKMabon(6) 5 73
(Richard Fahey) *in rr: sme hdwy 3f out: nvr a factor* **33/1**

10-0 **12** *2 1/2* **Demolition**[12] 2773 8-10-7 **90** MissKBannon(3) 10 77
(Noel Wilson) *t.k.h in rr: sme hdwy over 2f out: wknd fnl f* **33/1**

5414 **13** *2* **Sir Boss (IRE)**[9] 2863 7-9-11 **77** MissMMullineaux 4 61
(Michael Mullineaux) *in rr: hdwy over 3f out: wknd 2f out* **40/1**

2200 **14** *3 3/4* **Cape Safari (IRE)**[3] 3042 3-9-0 **80** (p) MissLMasterton 9 58
(Alan Bailey) *led after 1f: hdd over 2f out: sn wknd* **11/1**

511/ **15** *14* **Ascalon**[1358] 6272 8-10-4 **90**.. MissELOwen(6) 14 45
(Pat Eddery) *sn w ldrs: wknd over 2f out: sn bhd* **25/1**

40-5 **16** *7* **Itlaaq**[29] 2253 6-10-9 **92**.. MissJoannaMason(3) 1 36
(Michael Easterby) *a in rr* **16/1**

0002 **17** *2 1/4* **Hot Rod Mamma (IRE)**[12] 2752 5-10-7 **87**.................... MissECSayer 7 27
(Dianne Sayer) *hld up in rr: nvr on terms* **20/1**

1-00 **18** *14* **Tiger Webb**[63] 1381 4-9-10 **76**............................ MrsAdeleMulrennan 12
(Michael Easterby) *trckd ldrs: lost pl over 3f out* **66/1**

40-0 **19** *dist* **Hanoverian Baron**[21] 2479 7-10-5 **85**...................... MissCHannaford 6
(Tony Newcombe) *led 1f: chsd ldrs: lost pl over 3f out: eased fnl 2f: hopelessly t.o (btn 99+)* **9/1**

2m 40.24s (7.04) **Going Correction** +0.375s/f (Good)
WFA 3 from 4yo+ 14lb **19** Ran SP% **122.6**
Speed ratings (Par 107): **91,90,89,87,87 86,85,85,85,84 83,81,80,78,68 64,62,53,**
Swingers:1&2:£55.10, 2&3:£113.40, 1&3:£66.00 CSF £201.99 CT £4807.79 TOTE £9.30: £2.50, £4.60, £6.20, £1.80; EX 336.00 TRIFECTA Not won..
Owner C H Stevens **Bred** C A Cyzer **Trained** Great Habton, N Yorks

FOCUS
As usual a competitive handicap for female amateurs. The winner recorded a personal-best with the placed horses setting the standard.

NOTEBOOK
Crackentorp, winner of the race last year and third back in 2010, is clearly very much at home at York. His rider did well to get him over from the outside stall and take a prominent position, and from 3f out it was clear he was going best. Despite reservations about his ability to cope with the ground he handled it well, and defying a career-high mark was no mean feat (10lb higher than last year). (op 9-1 tchd 8-1)
Hong Kong Island(IRE) edged both ways for pressure in the straight but kept on well to close the winner down. This was the first time he'd run on ground this soft and he coped with conditions well.
Veiled Applause, well placed just behind the leaders turning into the straight, put up a solid effort off a stiff looking mark. (op 20-1)
Eagle Rock(IRE) did best of those held up off the pace early. A mid-race move to go and track the winner proved sensible, and he stayed on well. (op 6-1)
Antigua Sunrise(IRE), who's in-foal to Pastoral Pursuits, often runs well here. (op 14-1 tchd 16-1)
Scrapper Smith(IRE) was given plenty to do from well off the pace. (op 14-1)
Troopingthecolour didn't quite get home and might be happier back over 1m2f. (op 8-1)
Lexington Bay(IRE) was staying on all too late and looks to need further these days. (op 9-1)
Hanoverian Baron Official explanation: jockey said gelding had no more to give

3164 LADBROKES.COM H'CAP 1m 208y
2:35 (2:36) (Class 2) (0-105,99) 3-Y-O+ **£17,466** (£5,197; £2,597; £1,298) **Stalls** Low

Form RPR

0454 **1** **Navajo Chief**[12] 2773 5-10-0 **99**.. KierenFallon 3 112
(Alan Jarvis) *trckd ldng pair: hdwy to ld 3f out: rdn and jnd over 1f out: drvn and hdd ins fnl f: rallied gamely to ld again nr fin* **6/1**[2]

21-0 **2** *nk* **Area Fifty One**[31] 2176 4-9-2 **87**.. PaulHanagan 8 99
(Richard Fahey) *a.p: trckd ldng pair 3f out: hdwy 2f out: chal over 1f out: rdn to ld ins fnl f: sn drvn: hdd and no ex nr fin* **10/1**

0-02 **3** *8* **Hillview Boy (IRE)**[29] 2228 8-9-8 **93**................................ GrahamLee 2 88
(Jim Goldie) *in tch on inner: hdwy over 3f out: rdn to chse ldng pair over 1f out: drvn and no imp ins fnl f* **8/1**

1534 **4** *2* **Dubai Dynamo**[7] 2910 7-9-7 **92**.. JamesSullivan 4 82
(Ruth Carr) *in tch: hdwy 3f out: rdn wl over 1f out: no imp* **8/1**

1120 **5** *1* **Colour Guard**[79] 1087 4-9-5 **90**.. MircoDemuro 13 78
(Mark Johnston) *hld up towards rr: hdwy on outer wl over 2f out: sn rdn and n.d* **16/1**

-663 **6** *1/2* **Extraterrestrial**[18] 2590 8-9-5 **90**................................... FrederikTylicki 5 77
(Richard Fahey) *in tch: effrt 3f out: sn rdn along and n.d* **10/1**

0-02 **7** *shd* **Classic Colori (IRE)**[8] 2882 5-9-5 **90**........................ DanielTudhope 10 77
(David O'Meara) *hld up: a towards rr* **11/2**[1]

5-16 **8** *3/4* **Staff Sergeant**[14] 2720 5-8-12 **83**.................................... LeeNewman 7 68
(Jim Goldie) *led: rdn along and hdd 3f out: wknd 2f out* **12/1**

2/5- **9** *6* **Fighter Boy (IRE)**[488] 542 5-10-0 **99**...................... GrahamGibbons 11 71
(Michael Easterby) *hld up: a in rr* **33/1**

0-05 **10** *5* **Barren Brook**[29] 2257 5-9-3 **88**...................................... PaulMulrennan 12 49
(Michael Easterby) *t.k.h early: hld up: a towards rr* **8/1**

2224 **11** *7* **Tinshu (IRE)**[10] 2810 6-9-6 **91**................................(p) AndreaAtzeni 1 37
(Derek Haydn Jones) *chsd ldrs: rdn along over 3f out: grad wknd* **16/1**

0-65 **12** *18* **Halfsin (IRE)**[21] 2478 4-9-12 **97**................................ MickaelBarzalona 6
(Marco Botti) *hld up: a towards rr* **7/1**[3]

1m 53.15s (1.15) **Going Correction** +0.375s/f (Good) **12** Ran SP% **116.1**
Speed ratings (Par 109): **109,108,101,99,98 98,98,97,92,87 81,65**
Swingers:1&2:£7.00, 2&3:£15.30, 1&3:£4.20 CSF £63.42 CT £491.07 TOTE £5.40: £2.20, £2.90, £2.70; EX 59.00 Trifecta £354.20 Pool: £2,159.08 - 4.51 winning units..
Owner Geoffrey Bishop **Bred** Eurostrait Ltd **Trained** Twyford, Bucks

FOCUS
The early pace wasn't frantic and, as has become the pattern, it paid to race prominently. The winner is rated in line with last year's career best.

NOTEBOOK
Navajo Chief was on a fair mark, had the ground in his favour, was back at a track he has run well at in the past, and was given a good ride. He also showed plenty of determination to rally and get back up after being headed by Area Fifty One. That said, this was his first win beyond a mile, and the John Smith's Cup, which is likely to be his next target, will put even more of a test on his stamina. (op 5-1 tchd 9-2 tchd 13-2 in a place)
Area Fifty One has been declared a non-runner on three occasions in the past when the ground was soft, but he took his chance here on his second start for Richard Fahey and showed himself to be perfectly at ease with plenty of give. Like the winner he was never far from the lead and, although he succumbed to the rally of the winner, he finished well clear of the rest and looks ready to strike again. (op 11-1)
Hillview Boy(IRE) was well behind the first two at the line but he's better suited by a longer trip than this. (op 15-2 tchd 7-1)
Dubai Dynamo has never won beyond a mile, and he looked to be getting a little tired at the end.
Colour Guard, a three-time winner on Fibresand, was having his first start on turf and struggled to land a blow from off the pace. (op 14-1)
Extraterrestrial doesn't boast a great strike-rate and the handicapper seems to have his measure at the moment. (op 9-1)
Classic Colori(IRE) was another who was given plenty to do considering the bias towards pace horses over the course of this two-day meeting. (op 7-1)
Halfsin(IRE) Official explanation: trainer's rep said gelding was unable to dominate

3165 BOND TYRES TROPHY (H'CAP) 6f
3:10 (3:10) (Class 2) (0-105,99) 3-Y-O **£51,752** (£15,400; £7,696; £3,848) **Stalls** Centre

Form RPR

2-10 **1** **Sholaan (IRE)**[15] 2660 3-8-9 **87**..(b[1]) LiamJones 4 106
(William Haggas) *trckd overall ldr towards far side: led over 2f out: clr over 1f out: drvn out* **10/1**[3]

22-1 **2** *5* **Gabriel's Lad (IRE)**[46] 1723 3-8-6 **84**.............................. KierenFallon 12 88
(Denis Coakley) *dwlt: t.k.h: sn trcking ldrs: chsd wnr over 1f out: styd on* **10/1**[3]

-142 **3** *3* **Glen Moss (IRE)**[21] 2490 3-8-12 **90**.................................. MichaelHills 9 85
(Charles Hills) *mid-div: effrt over 2f out: wnt 3rd over 1f out: kpt on same pce* **8/1**[2]

6060 **4** *3* **Boris Grigoriev (IRE)**[14] 2714 3-8-7 **85**...................... PaulMulrennan 17 71+
(Michael Easterby) *mid-div towards stands' side: hdwy over 2f out: hung lft: kpt on fnl f* **40/1**

-040 **5** *shd* **Roger Sez (IRE)**[14] 2712 3-9-7 **99**....................................(p) TedDurcan 1 85
(Tim Easterby) *racd towards far side: in rr and sn pushed along: kpt on fnl 2f* **20/1**

-502 **6** *2* **Last Bid**[21] 2509 3-9-2 **94**.. GrahamGibbons 10 74
(Tim Easterby) *mid-div: hdwy over 2f out: kpt on same pce* **33/1**

01-6 **7** *7* **Intransigent**[37] 1998 3-8-10 **88**.. LiamKeniry 14 47
(Andrew Balding) *hld up in mid-div: effrt over 2f out: nvr a threat* **10/1**[3]

-214 **8** *1 3/4* **Nameitwhatyoulike**[31] 2182 3-8-6 **84**..........................(b) JamesSullivan 3 37
(Michael Easterby) *overall ldr towards far side: hdd over 2f out: wknd over 1f out* **8/1**[2]

1-06 **9** *1 1/4* **Pea Shooter**[21] 2509 3-8-7 **85**.. AmyRyan 6 35+
(Kevin Ryan) *wnt rt s: racd centre: chsd ldrs on far side: wknd over 1f out* **10/1**[3]

40-0 **10** *3 1/2* **Queens Revenge**[70] 1221 3-8-12 **90**................................ DavidAllan 8 29
(Tim Easterby) *hmpd s: sn mid-div: effrt over 2f out: wknd over 1f out* **20/1**

-305 **11** *3 3/4* **Lily's Angel (IRE)**[29] 2255 3-8-13 **98**.......................... LauraBarry(7) 18 26
(Richard Fahey) *hld up towards stands' side: nvr a factor* **16/1**

01-1 **12** *2 3/4* **Priceless Jewel**[38] 1983 3-8-12 **90**................................ JamesDoyle 15 10+
(Roger Charlton) *mid-div: effrt over 2f out: wknd over 1f out* **5/1**[1]

6454 **13** *2* **Pale Orchid (IRE)**[14] 2714 3-8-9 **87**................................ PaulHanagan 11
(David Evans) *mid-div: effrt over 2f out: wknd over 1f out* **25/1**

-233 **14** *3/4* **Three Am Tour (IRE)**[21] 2490 3-8-8 **89**........................ SeanLevey(3) 19
(Richard Hannon) *mid-div stands' side: effrt over 2f out: sn wknd* **12/1**

0152 **15** *6* **Dam Beautiful**[14] 2691 3-9-3 **95**.. PhillipMakin 16
(Kevin Ryan) *mid-div: rdn over 2f out: sn lost pl* **28/1**

4-05 **16** *1/2* **Tioman Legend**[28] 2276 3-9-1 **93**.................................. DanielTudhope 7
(Roger Charlton) *hmpd s: hld up in rr towards far side: effrt 3f out: sn wknd: eased* **12/1**

0-03 **17** *1/2* **Top Cop**[28] 2276 3-9-1 **93**.. JimmyFortune 2
(Andrew Balding) *chsd ldrs towards far side: lost pl over 2f out: eased over 1f out* **8/1**[2]

1m 15.78s (3.88) **Going Correction** +0.95s/f (Soft) **17** Ran SP% **129.8**
Speed ratings (Par 105): **112,105,101,97,97 94,85,82,81,76 71,67,65,64,56 55,54**
Swingers:1&2:£40.40, 2&3:£19.40, 1&3:£28.30 CSF £103.18 CT £892.98 TOTE £13.40: £3.50, £2.50, £2.90, £12.20; EX 200.60 Trifecta £2534.60 Pool: £48,877.16 - 14.27 winning units..
Owner Sheikh Ahmed Al Maktoum **Bred** Kilnamoragh Stud **Trained** Newmarket, Suffolk

FOCUS
This valuable handicap didn't look to quite have the strength in depth of some recent seasons, and the testing ground knocked out several contenders. The field initially split in two, with the winner among a group of five that raced towards the far side, while the rest of the field raced more centre to stands' side, but the groups merged again at halfway. There seemed no obvious bias. The winner was impressive and could rate higher.

NOTEBOOK
Sholaan(IRE) bolted up. He'd shown when beating some useful types in a Wolverhampton maiden in May that he had ability, but had disappointed at Epsom last time, racing too keenly and failing to handle the track. Dropped back to 6f for the first time and with blinkers added, he showed good pace throughout, handled the ground no problem, took over in front at halfway and soon bounded clear. Sprinting is clearly his thing and, while a hefty rise is now inevitable, he's unexposed in this division and open to further improvement. (tchd 12-1)
Gabriel's Lad(IRE) had no chance with the winner but beat the rest handily. His trainer was concerned about the ground beforehand, but he handled it well, and there ought to be better to come from him as this was his debut in handicap company. (tchd 11-1)
Glen Moss(IRE), like the winner, has been doing his racing over further, and proved suited by a return to sprinting. He should continue to pose a threat off this sort of mark. (op 10-1)
Boris Grigoriev(IRE) ◆, whose rider wasn't overly animated in the closing stages (reported to have hung left), just held off Roger Sez for fourth on the line. His mark has come down a lot since joining the yard at the end of last season, 16lb to be precise, and there is presumably a plan for him. He's one to keep an eye on. Official explanation: jockey said gelding hung left
Roger Sez(IRE) struggled a little to go the pace early on but was keeping on well at the finish. This wouldn't be her ideal track (York favours pace horses) so it was a solid effort in the circumstances. (op 33-1)
Last Bid didn't look to be beaten for stamina. Better ground might suit him in future, though.
Intransigent, who had a tough trip at Chester last time, had no such excuse here, and proved disappointing, looking far from happy on the ground. (tchd 12-1)
Nameitwhatyoulike didn't have any trouble going the pace over this shorter trip as he was up there for a long way towards the far side, but he dropped away inside the final 2f. (tchd 7-1)
Pea Shooter has the right style of running for this place but he wasn't able to dominate this field.
Priceless Jewel held strong claims on her defeat of Safari Sunseeker and Galician at Kempton last time, and being by Selkirk there had to be a hope that she would handle the soft ground. She didn't, though (confirmed by trainer's representative afterwards), and it's probably wise to put a line through this, as she remains a promising filly for sprints back on a decent surface. Official explanation: trainer's rep said filly was unsuited by the soft ground (op 6-1 tchd 13-2 in a place)
Tioman Legend couldn't pick up on the ground and presumably found conditions too testing.
Top Cop was eased down some way out having also struggled to cope with conditions. Official explanation: jockey said colt never travelled

3166 IAN AND KATE HALL MACMILLAN GANTON STKS (LISTED RACE) 1m
3:45 (3:47) (Class 1) 3-Y-O+ **£19,536** (£7,388; £3,692) **Stalls** Low

Form RPR

2-11 **1** **Tullius (IRE)**[33] 2127 4-9-10 108.. JimmyFortune 5 116
(Andrew Balding) *set stdy pce: qcknd over 3f out: jnd 2f out: rdn over 1f out: kpt on wl fnl f* **8/13**[1]

4-03 **2** *2* **Doncaster Rover (USA)**[14] 2710 6-9-7 105................ RobertWinston 2 108
(David Brown) *trckd wnr: cl up 3f out: chal wl over 1f out: sn rdn and ev ch tl drvn and one pce ins fnl f* **5/1**[3]

-602 **3** *7* **Dance And Dance (IRE)**[15] 2656 6-9-7 110.................... LukeMorris 4 97
(Ed Vaughan) *trckd ldng pair: effrt 3f out and cl up tl rdn and outpcd fr wl over 1f out* **9/4**[2]

1m 43.0s (4.00) **Going Correction** +0.375s/f (Good)
WFA 3 from 4yo+ 10lb **3** Ran SP% **109.4**
Speed ratings (Par 111): **95,93,86**
CSF £3.87 TOTE £1.60; EX 3.50.
Owner Kennet Valley Thoroughbreds VI **Bred** Sc Archi Romani **Trained** Kingsclere, Hants

FOCUS
Following the withdrawal of three of the intended six runners a very small field went to post for this Listed race. The form is a bit muddling but another step forward from the winner.

NOTEBOOK

Tullius(IRE) completed a hat-trick, making all this time, in contrast to his previous two wins when ridden with more patience. This was a shrewd tactical move on a track and on ground that was delivering a big advantage to pace horses, and the fact that he didn't have to go particularly fast in front made his job easier. He's slowly climbing the ladder, and is clearly well suited by a nice bit of give underfoot. (op 10-11)

Doncaster Rover(USA), who had his stamina to prove over this longer trip, was aided by the steady early gallop. He drew up alongside the winner early in the straight, but could never quite edge ahead and in the end was just outstayed. It was a good effort, nevertheless. (op 4-1)

Dance And Dance(IRE), held up in third place, had most to do when the pace quickened in front. He's at his best coming from behind off a strong gallop, and things just didn't pan out in his favour here. The trainer's representative reported that the gelding was unsuited by the soft going. Official explanation: trainer's rep said gelding was unsuited by the soft ground (op 15-8)

3167 RICHARD HOWARD-VYSE MEMORIAL H'CAP — 1m 208y

4:15 (4:18) (Class 4) (0-80,80) 4-Y-0+ **£7,762** (£2,310; £1,154; £577) **Stalls** Low

Form				RPR
/220	**1**		**Edmaaj (IRE)**[27] 2312 4-9-1 **74** DanielTudhope 8 (David O'Meara) *trckd ldrs: effrt over 2f out: 4th 1f out: styd on strly to ld and forge clr clsng stages* **10/1**	86
30-3	**2**	*2 ½*	**Rustic Deacon**[32] 2151 5-9-4 **77** KierenFallon 3 (Willie Musson) *led: pushed 3 l clr 1f out: wknd and hdd last 40yds* **10/1**	84
6060	**3**	*nk*	**Dolphin Rock**[21] 2510 5-9-3 **76** LeeNewman 4 (David Barron) *chsd ldrs: wnt 2nd over 3f out: kpt on same pce ins fnl f* **12/1**	82
-213	**4**	*½*	**Carragold**[17] 2606 6-9-4 **77** RobertWinston 1 (Mel Brittain) *dwlt: hdwy to chse ldrs after 3f: drvn over 3f out: swtchd rt ins fnl f: styd on* **5/1**[1]	82
40-6	**5**	*nk*	**Robert The Painter (IRE)**[33] 2119 4-9-4 **77** DavidNolan 2 (David O'Meara) *chsd ldrs: kpt on same pce over 1f out* **20/1**	81
3335	**6**	*3*	**Moheebb (IRE)**[12] 2753 8-9-0 **73** (v) PJMcDonald 5 (Ruth Carr) *in rr: hdwy on inner over 3f out: sn chsng ldrs: one pce fnl 2f* **7/1**[2]	71+
3-66	**7**	*5*	**Merchant Of Medici**[18] 2590 5-9-3 **76** FrederikTylicki 16 (Micky Hammond) *in rr: hdwy over 2f out: nvr nr ldrs* **20/1**	63
2200	**8**	*1*	**European Dream (IRE)**[3] 3037 9-9-6 **79** (p) RobbieFitzpatrick 7 (Richard Guest) *mid-div: drvn 3f out: nvr a factor* **20/1**	63
-335	**9**	*1*	**Jo'Burg (USA)**[12] 2773 8-9-6 **79** GrahamGibbons 13 (David O'Meara) *dwlt: hld up in midfield: effrt 3f out: nvr nr ldrs* **10/1**	61
0021	**10**	*3 ¾*	**Musnad (USA)**[14] 2720 4-9-3 **76** AmyRyan 20 (Brian Ellison) *in rr: drvn 4f out: hung lft over 2f out: sme late hdwy* **9/1**[3]	50
0-03	**11**	*3 ½*	**Koo And The Gang (IRE)**[7] 2913 5-9-1 **74** BarryMcHugh 19 (Brian Ellison) *swtchd lft after s: a in rr* **25/1**	40
4-00	**12**	*1 ¼*	**Cool Marble (IRE)**[16] 2642 5-9-7 **80** JamesDoyle 11 (Jeremy Gask) *trckd ldrs: effrt over 3f out: wknd over 2f out* **14/1**	44
0043	**13**	*1 ½*	**Jonny Lesters Hair (IRE)**[27] 2312 7-9-7 **80** DavidAllan 10 (Tim Easterby) *chsd ldrs: wknd over 2f out* **10/1**	40
-360	**14**	*shd*	**Aerodynamic (IRE)**[33] 2119 5-9-2 **75** PaddyAspell 14 (Michael Easterby) *a towards rr* **20/1**	35
/000	**15**	*5*	**Day Of The Eagle (IRE)**[8] 2882 6-8-7 **73** DavidSimmonson(7) 6 (Michael Easterby) *mid-div: effrt 4f out: wknd 2f out: eased clsng stages* **50/1**	22
1-00	**16**	*12*	**Switchback**[63] 1381 4-9-2 **75** PaulMulrennan 17 (Michael Easterby) *in rr: bhd fnl 3f: eased over 1f out* **66/1**	
0040	**17**	*15*	**Aquarian Spirit**[21] 2510 5-9-2 **75** PaulHanagan 18 (Richard Fahey) *in rr: bhd fnl 3f: heavily eased* **16/1**	

1m 55.37s (3.37) **Going Correction** +0.375s/f (Good) **17** Ran SP% **122.1**
Speed ratings (Par 105): **100,97,97,97,96 94,89,88,87,84 81,80,79,78,74 63,50**
Swingers:1&2:£29.80, 2&3:£37.00, 1&3:£28.80 CSF £95.87 CT £1231.79 TOTE £12.60: £2.50, £2.20, £2.90, £1.80; EX 157.80 TRIFECTA Not won..
Owner K Nicholson **Bred** Airlie Stud **Trained** Nawton, N Yorks
■ Stewards' Enquiry : Lee Newman two-day ban: used whip above permitted level (Jun 30-Jul 1)

FOCUS

Once again it paid to race quite prominently.The form looks sound rated around the third, fourth and fifth.

Musnad(USA) Official explanation: trainer said gelding was unsuited by the soft ground
Jonny Lesters Hair(IRE) Official explanation: trainer had no explanation for the poor form shown

3168 REG GRIFFIN APPRECIATION E B F MAIDEN STKS — 6f

4:45 (4:50) (Class 3) 2-Y-0 **£7,439** (£2,213; £1,106; £553) **Stalls** Centre

Form				RPR
3	**1**		**Royal Rascal**[28] 2282 2-8-12 0 DavidAllan 10 (Tim Easterby) *prom: cl up 1/2-way: led wl over 2f out: rdn clr appr fnl f: edgd lft and styd on strly* **4/1**[2]	82+
63	**2**	*5*	**Finaz**[21] 2508 2-9-3 0 MickyFenton 1 (Paul Midgley) *led: hdd 1/2-way: rdn along 2f out: drvn over 1f out and kpt on: no ch w wnr* **11/2**[3]	72
55	**3**	*3 ¾*	**Eastern Dragon (IRE)**[15] 2667 2-9-3 0 PaulMulrennan 9 (Kevin Ryan) *cl up: led briefly 1/2-way: sn hdd and rdn: drvn and one pce fr wl over 1f out* **16/1**	61
	4	*2 ½*	**Complicator** 2-9-3 0 IPoullis 2 (Alan McCabe) *t.k.h: hld up in rr: hdwy on outer to trck ldrs 1/2-way: effrt on wd outside and cl up over 2f out: sn rdn and wknd wl over 1f out* **12/1**	53+
	5	*1 ½*	**Reggie Bond** 2-9-0 0 DaleSwift(3) 8 (Geoffrey Oldroyd) *dwlt and green in rr: pushed along and hdwy 1/2-way: rdn to chse ldrs over 2f out: sn edgd lft and no imp* **8/1**	49
	6	*10*	**Notional Demand** 2-9-3 0 DuranFentiman 4 (Tim Easterby) *a towards rr* **25/1**	19
	7	*1*	**Cash Is King** 2-9-3 0 TonyHamilton 7 (Richard Fahey) *chsd ldrs: rdn along bef 1/2-way: sn wknd* **6/1**	16
	8	*11*	**Marhaba Malayeen (IRE)** 2-9-3 0 PhillipMakin 3 (Kevin Ryan) *a towards rr* **6/1**	
	9	*2 ½*	**Orions Hero (IRE)** 2-9-3 0 PaulHanagan 5 (Richard Fahey) *chsd ldrs: rdn along bef 1/2-way: sn wknd* **3/1**[1]	

1m 18.64s (6.74) **Going Correction** +0.95s/f (Soft) **9** Ran SP% **117.5**
Speed ratings (Par 97): **93,86,81,78,76 62,61,46,43**
Swingers:1&2:£4.70, 2&3:£12.10, 1&3:£13.50 CSF £26.84 TOTE £5.10: £1.50, £2.30, £4.60; EX 34.50 Trifecta £255.70 Pool: £2,284.81 - 6.61 winning units..
Owner C H Stevens **Bred** Habton Farms **Trained** Great Habton, N Yorks

FOCUS

Probably not a strong maiden, and the first three home were the three in the field with previous experience. They all built on previous efforts.

NOTEBOOK

Royal Rascal had the benefit of a previous outing and, while the ground was softer than at Thirsk on her debut, she handled it well and quickened clear in good style when asked to go and win her race. She might not have beaten a great deal but she could be an interesting one for decent nurseries in due course. (op 9-2)

Finaz, third on fast ground over the C&D last time out, showed his versatility by coming home clear of the rest, but he's likely to remain vulnerable in maidens. (op 8-1)

Eastern Dragon(IRE) was another who had the advantage of racing experience. This was arguably his best effort to date, but modest handicaps will be his thing.

Complicator, who holds Royal Ascot entries, did best of the newcomers despite not settling early. He was entitled to get tired in the ground and better can be expected next time. (tchd 14-1)

Cash Is King travelled well enough in behind the leaders for the first half of the race, but then quickly dropped away. All four can do better for this experience. (op 5-1)

3169 CHARLES HENRY MEMORIAL H'CAP — 6f

5:15 (5:18) (Class 4) (0-80,80) 3-Y-0+ **£7,115** (£2,117; £1,058; £529) **Stalls** Centre

Form				RPR
2505	**1**		**Klynch**[8] 2876 6-9-6 **79** (b) JamesSullivan 15 (Ruth Carr) *mid-div: hdwy over 2f out: swtchd stands' side over 1f out: 4th 1f out: styd on to ld post* **9/1**	87
0213	**2**	*shd*	**Green Park (IRE)**[8] 2876 9-9-0 **78** (b) NeilFarley(5) 5 (Declan Carroll) *sn trcking ldrs: chal gng wl 2f out: led over 1f out: kpt on ins fnl f: hdd last stride* **10/1**	86
3350	**3**	*½*	**Jedward (IRE)**[7] 2913 5-9-6 **79** PaulHanagan 12 (Richard Fahey) *trckd ldrs: chal over 1f out: no ex last 50yds* **12/1**	85
0-35	**4**	*2 ¼*	**Defence Council (IRE)**[42] 1863 4-9-6 **79** RobertWinston 19 (Mel Brittain) *mid-div: hdwy over 2f out: chsng ldrs over 1f out: one pce* **16/1**	78
-402	**5**	*2 ½*	**Anderiego (IRE)**[16] 2632 4-9-5 **78** DanielTudhope 11 (David O'Meara) *chsd ldrs: effrt over 2f out: fdd over 1f out* **4/1**[1]	69
-054	**6**	*1 ¼*	**Lucky Numbers (IRE)**[8] 2876 6-9-6 **79** (b) DavidNolan 14 (David O'Meara) *led: 3 l clr 3f out: hdd over 1f out: wknd* **14/1**	66
-026	**7**	*3 ½*	**Little Jimmy Odsox (IRE)**[16] 2632 4-9-5 **78** (b[1]) DavidAllan 10 (Tim Easterby) *s.i.s: sn mid-div and drvn along: wknd over 1f out* **9/1**	54
6100	**8**	*5*	**Mandalay King (IRE)**[14] 2707 7-9-4 **77** (p) PhillipMakin 6 (Marjorie Fife) *in rr: hdwy 2f out: sn wknd* **25/1**	37
-051	**9**	*1 ¼*	**Caranbola**[14] 2693 6-9-6 **79** PaulMulrennan 13 (Mel Brittain) *chsd ldrs: drvn over 2f out: lost pl over 1f out* **16/1**	35
6241	**10**	*½*	**Bond Fastrac**[14] 2690 5-9-4 **80** DaleSwift(3) 18 (Geoffrey Oldroyd) *awkward s: mid-div: drvn over 2f out: sn btn* **16/1**	34
-046	**11**	*2 ½*	**Saucy Brown (IRE)**[8] 2876 6-9-2 **75** PaulQuinn 16 (David Nicholls) *a towards rr* **25/1**	21
-000	**12**	*nse*	**Ginger Ted (IRE)**[7] 2940 5-9-4 **77** (p) JamesDoyle 9 (Stuart Williams) *a outpcd and in rr* **10/1**	23
1306	**13**	*1 ½*	**Last Sovereign**[35] 2092 8-9-4 **77** PJMcDonald 20 (Ollie Pears) *sn bhd* **33/1**	18
0100	**14**	*4*	**Go Go Green (IRE)**[14] 2717 6-9-3 **76** KierenFallon 2 (Jim Goldie) *chsd ldrs: wknd over 1f out: heavily eased* **8/1**[3]	5
-003	**P**		**Toby Tyler**[58] 1478 6-9-5 **78** (v) MickyFenton 3 (Paul Midgley) *dwlt: in rr: lost pl over 2f out: eased and p.u and dismntd over 1f out* **13/2**[2]	

1m 16.75s (4.85) **Going Correction** +0.95s/f (Soft) **15** Ran SP% **125.3**
Speed ratings (Par 105): **105,104,104,101,97 96,91,84,83,82 79,79,77,71,**
Swingers:1&2:£23.50, 2&3:£24.90, 1&3:£21.10 CSF £97.41 CT £1133.32 TOTE £10.40: £4.30, £3.10, £4.80; EX 139.30 Trifecta £1425.70 Part won. Pool: £1,926.71 - 0.50 winning units..
Owner Douglas Renton **Bred** J C S Wilson Bloodstock **Trained** Huby, N Yorks

FOCUS

For once the winner came from well off the pace. The winning time was just under a second slower than that recorded by the 3yos in the Bond Tyres Trophy earlier on the card. The placed horses set the level having been well placed.

Go Go Green(IRE) Official explanation: jockey said gelding ran flat
Toby Tyler Official explanation: jockey said gelding lost its action
T/Jkpt: Not won. T/Plt: £437.20 to a £1 stake. Pool: £210,021.00 - 350.64 winning tickets.
T/Qpdt: £58.80 to a £1 stake. Pool: £9,203.00 - 115.66 winning tickets. WG

3175 - 3177a (Foreign Racing) - See Raceform Interactive

LYON PARILLY (R-H)

Saturday, June 16

OFFICIAL GOING: Turf: good

3178a GRAND PRIX DE LYON (LISTED RACE) (TURF) — 1m 4f

4:40 (12:00) 4-Y-0+ **£25,000** (£10,000; £7,500; £5,000; £2,500)

			RPR
1		**Lancelot (FR)**[58] 5-9-2 0 OlivierPeslier 9 (A De Mieulle, France) **5/2**[2]	108
2	*shd*	**War Is War (IRE)**[50] 4-9-2 0 ThomasHuet 1 (E J O'Neill, France) **16/1**	108
3	*snk*	**Jo All The Way**[30] 2223 5-8-11 0 (p) Christophe-PatriceLemaire 5 (E Lellouche, France) **2/1**[1]	103
4	*¾*	**Pump Pump Boy (FR)**[30] 2223 4-8-11 0 IoritzMendizabal 6 (M Pimbonnet, France) **31/1**	102
5	*nse*	**Victorinna (FR)**[37] 4-8-8 0 AnthonyCrastus 3 (C Laffon-Parias, France) **9/1**	98
6	*1 ½*	**Oppenort (IRE)**[240] 7114 4-8-11 0 GregoryBenoist 7 (M Delzangles, France) **10/1**	99
7	*3*	**Pagera (FR)**[19] 2570 4-8-8 0 StephanePasquier 10 (H-A Pantall, France) **44/5**[3]	91
8	*½*	**Sant'Alberto (ITY)**[30] 2223 4-8-11 0 UmbertoRispoli 4 (F Chappet, France) **23/1**	93
9	*6*	**Dangerous Midge (USA)**[231] 7170 6-8-11 0 DavyBonilla 2 (Brian Meehan) *racd 3rd on ins on settling: rdn bef st: given reminders 2f out: no ex: sn wknd* **12/1**	84
10	*1 ½*	**Selim (RUS)**[279] 4-8-11 0 RonanThomas 8 (D Sepulchre, France) **13/1**	81

2m 33.78s (0.27) **10** Ran SP% **119.2**
WIN (incl. 1 euro stake): 3.50. PLACES: 1.50, 2.70, 1.40. DF: 25.40. SF: 31.10.
Owner H H Sheikh Abdullah Bin Khalifa Al Thani **Bred** Jean-Charles Coude **Trained** France

2916 DONCASTER (L-H)

Sunday, June 17

OFFICIAL GOING: Good to soft (7.5)

Wind: Light against Weather: Cloudy

3180 CROWNHOTEL-BAWTRY.COM APPRENTICE H'CAP 1m 6f 132y

2:00 (2:00) (Class 5) (0-70,70) 4-Y-O+ **£2,911** (£866; £432; £216) **Stalls** Low

Form RPR

43-5 **1** **Handles For Forks (IRE)**[80] 1085 4-9-5 **68**........... CharlesBishop(3) 11 77
(Mick Channon) *hld up towards rr: hdwy 3f out: trckd ldrs 2f out: rdn over 1f out: styd on to ld ins fnl f* **9/1**

1232 **2** ¾ **Favorite Girl (GER)**[8] 2915 4-9-3 **68**............................ JackDuern(5) 14 76+
(Michael Appleby) *hld up in tch: gd hdwy over 3f out: led wl over 2f out: rdn and edgd lft over 1f out: hdd and no ex ins fnl f* **9/2**[2]

03-0 **3** 2 ¾ **The Oil Magnate**[23] 2440 7-9-5 **68**............................ ShaneBKelly(3) 3 72
(Michael Dods) *trckd ldrs: hdwy 3f out: rdn and ev ch wl over 1f out: n.m.r appr fnl f and kpt on same pce* **6/1**[3]

32-4 **4** 1 ¾ **Lady Bluesky**[43] 1057 9-8-13 **62**............................ GarryWhillans(3) 12 64
(Alistair Whillans) *trckd ldrs: hdwy and cl up 5f out: led 4f out: jnd and rdn 3f out: sn hdd and kpt on same pce* **11/4**[1]

0-01 **5** nk **Tallulah Mai**[13] 2769 5-8-8 **54**.................................... AdamBeschizza 10 56
(Matthew Salaman) *trckd ldng pair: hdwy over 3f out: rdn and ch over 2f out: sn one pce* **7/1**

5103 **6** 3 ½ **Carnac (IRE)**[39] 1991 6-8-8 **59**....................................(p) NoraLooby(5) 8 56
(Alan McCabe) *trckd ldrs: effrt over 3f out: sn rdn along and one pce* **25/1**

7 nse **Sinnamara (IRE)**[13] 3887 4-9-2 **65**............................(p) AdamCarter(3) 4 62
(John Wainwright) *in tch: pushed along wl over 2f out: sn one pce* **25/1**

3462 **8** 4 ½ **Kingaroo (IRE)**[14] 2732 6-8-5 **51**.................................... RyanPowell 13 42
(Garry Woodward) *led: pushed along and jnd 5f out: hdd 4f out: sn wknd* **12/1**

1000 **9** 1 ¾ **Goal (IRE)**[16] 2675 4-9-4 **67**.. NathanAlison(3) 7 56
(Charles Smith) *dwlt: a bhd* **50/1**

-140 **10** 7 **Zefooha (FR)**[19] 2214 8-9-3 **70**..................................(p) GemmaTutty(7) 1 50
(Tim Walford) *cl up: rdn along over 4f out: sn wknd* **16/1**

5001 **11** 9 **Maybeme**[4] 3022 6-8-7 **60** 6ex..................................... TerenceFury(7) 6 28
(Neville Bycroft) *dwlt: a in rr* **8/1**

3m 12.81s (5.41) **Going Correction** +0.225s/f (Good) **11** Ran SP% **116.0**
Speed ratings (Par 103): **94,93,92,91,91 89,89,86,85,82 77**
Swingers:1&2:£4.20, 2&3:£7.20, 1&3:£6.40 CSF £47.69 CT £266.05 TOTE £11.20: £2.40, £1.80, £2.00; EX 37.30 Trifecta £263.40 Part won. Pool: £355.95 - 0.20 winning units..
Owner M Channon **Bred** Manister House Stud **Trained** West Ilsley, Berks

FOCUS
A modest contest, in which the pace looked respectable.
Maybeme Official explanation: jockey said mare never travelled

3181 WILLIE MCKAY SPORTS MANAGEMENT MAIDEN STKS 1m 4f

2:30 (2:30) (Class 5) 3-Y-O+ **£2,911** (£866; £432; £216) **Stalls** Low

Form RPR

2 **1** **Biographer**[55] 1567 3-8-13 0... TedDurcan 5 82+
(David Lanigan) *trckd ldng pair: hdwy 4f out: led 3f out: pushed along 2f out: rdn over 1f out: styd on* **1/5**[1]

2 2 **Roc De Prince** 3-8-13 0... TonyHamilton 7 76
(Richard Fahey) *t.k.h early: hld up: hdwy to trck ldrs over 3f out: effrt to chal 2f out: ev ch tl rdn and one pce ent fnl f* **14/1**

3 10 **Native Eight (USA)** 3-8-13 0... NeilCallan 6 60
(Ian Williams) *hld up: hdwy over 3f out: sn rdn along: styd on appr fnl f: tk mod 3rd nr line* **20/1**

0-0 **4** nse **Lord Nandi**[42] 1893 3-8-13 0.. PatCosgrave 8 60
(Sir Henry Cecil) *led over 3f: trckd ldr tl rdn to ld again briefly over 3f out: sn drvn and hdd: one pce after: lost mod 3rd nr line* **12/1**[3]

62 **5** shd **Anna's Arch (IRE)**[9] 2877 5-9-8 0............................ GarryWhillans(5) 2 60
(Alan Swinbank) *trckd ldrs: rdn along over 3f out: kpt on same pce fnl 2f* **7/1**[2]

6 20 **Jim Tango (FR)**[18] 8-9-13 0..(tp) PJMcDonald 4 28
(Brian Storey) *towards rr: rapid hdwy to ld over 8f out: rdn along and hdd over 3f out: sn wknd and bhd* **50/1**

2m 38.38s (3.48) **Going Correction** +0.225s/f (Good)
WFA 3 from 5yo+ 14lb **6** Ran SP% **116.9**
Speed ratings (Par 103): **97,95,89,88,88 75**
Swingers:1&2:£1.60, 2&3:£9.70, 1&3:£2.90 CSF £5.38 TOTE £1.20: £1.10, £6.40; EX 4.10 Trifecta £23.30 Pool: £722.94 - 22.87 winning units..
Owner B E Nielsen **Bred** Bjorn E Nielsen **Trained** Upper Lambourn, Berks

FOCUS
An average maiden.

3182 COFFEE SHOP DORE VILLAGE SHEFFIELD E.B.F. MEDIAN AUCTION MAIDEN STKS 6f

3:00 (3:02) (Class 5) 2-Y-O **£3,946** (£1,174; £586; £293) **Stalls** High

Form RPR

52 **1** **Kimberella**[22] 2480 2-9-3 0.. JamieSpencer 18 84
(Michael Bell) *racd nr stands' rail: cl up: led after 2f: rdn over 1f out: styd on wl towards fin* **11/4**[1]

2 ½ **Ginger Goose** 2-9-3 0.. TonyHamilton 2 83+
(Richard Fahey) *midfield: hdwy 1/2-way: chsd ldrs 2f out: chal wl over 1f out: sn rdn and ev ch: nt qckn wl ins fnl f* **25/1**

2 **3** 1 ¼ **Lewisham**[16] 2667 2-9-3 0.. DaraghO'Donohoe 9 82+
(Noel Quinlan) *hld up in rr: swtchd to outer and gd hdwy 1/2-way: rdn to chal on wd outside wl over 1f out and ev ch tl drvn and one pce wl ins fnl f* **11/2**[2]

4 nk **Califante** 2-8-12 0.. PatDobbs 12 73+
(Richard Hannon) *in rr: hdwy over 2f out: swtchd rt and rdn wl over 1f out: styd on wl fnl f: nrst fin* **12/1**

5 3 ¾ **Athman (IRE)** 2-9-3 0.. MickaelBarzalona 8 68+
(Mahmood Al Zarooni) *towards rr: hdwy over 2f out: rdn to chse ldrs whn nt clr run and green 1f out: kpt on ins fnl f: nrst fin* **8/1**

6 nk **Trymyluck** 2-8-12 0.. MickyFenton 20 61
(Pam Sly) *racd nr stands' rail: chsd ldrs: rdn 2f out: kpt on same pce* **66/1**

25 **7** hd **Newstead Abbey**[16] 2662 2-9-3 0.. NeilCallan 10 65
(David Brown) *prom: rdn along over 2f out: wandered over 1f out and sn wknd* **11/4**[1]

00 **8** hd **Stand N Applaude**[26] 2376 2-8-10 0........................ ShirleyTeasdale(7) 17 65
(David Nicholls) *led 2f: cl up: rdn along 2f out: grad wknd* **100/1**

9 1 ½ **Eyeline** 2-9-3 0.. RussKennemore 1 60
(Reg Hollinshead) *dwlt and towards rr: hdwy and in tch 1/2-way: rdn along over 2f out: n.d* **100/1**

10 shd **Bain's Pass (IRE)** 2-9-3 0... PhillipMakin 11 60
(Kevin Ryan) *chsd ldrs: rdn along wl over 2f out: grad wknd* **25/1**

4 **11** nk **Warrant Officer**[18] 2609 2-9-3 0.................................... MartinHarley 16 59
(Mick Channon) *towards rr: hdwy and in tch 1/2-way: sn rdn along and wknd* **25/1**

3 **12** ¾ **Two Pancakes**[28] 2308 2-9-3 0.................................... GrahamGibbons 3 57
(Declan Carroll) *chsd ldrs: rdn along over 2f out: grad wknd* **12/1**

13 1 **Max The Machine** 2-9-3 0.. JoeFanning 7 60+
(Derek Shaw) *in tch: rdn along over 2f out: grad wknd* **33/1**

14 nse **Hazza The Jazza** 2-9-3 0... J-PGuillambert 13 54
(Richard Guest) *s.i.s: a towards rr* **80/1**

3 **14** dht **Mickstathetricksta**[9] 2880 2-9-3 0..................................... KierenFallon 14 54
(Scott Dixon) *in tch: rdn along 1/2-way: sn wknd* **7/1**[3]

1m 15.75s (2.15) **Going Correction** +0.175s/f (Good) **15** Ran SP% **126.9**
Speed ratings (Par 93): **92,91,89,89,84 83,83,83,81,81 80,79,78,78,78**
Swingers:1&2:£15.30, 2&3:£32.80, 1&3:£5.30 CSF £88.03 TOTE £4.30: £1.50, £3.50, £2.80; EX 98.80 Trifecta £388.50 Pool: £651.16 - 1.24 winning units..
Owner K J P Gundlach **Bred** P And Mrs A G Venner **Trained** Newmarket, Suffolk

FOCUS
A fair juvenile maiden and a slight step forward from the winner and the third fits in.

NOTEBOOK
Kimberella has progressed on each outing and won nicely after coming up the rail. One got the impression he was value for slightly more than the winning distance. (op 7-2 tchd 4-1)
Ginger Goose ◆ appeared to know his job on debut and showed plenty of ability towards the centre of the track. He promises to stay further and looks a nice type. (op 20-1)
Lewisham ◆, who lost ground at the start when tightened up, made a fast move around runners heading to the furlong marker that looked almost certain to see him take this, but he failed to get home. What happened leaving the stalls and racing keenly while under restraint obviously didn't help his cause. (op 5-1)
Califante ◆ made up some good late ground after racing towards the rear early and gave the impression she has the ability to win something. (op 10-1 tchd 9-1)
Athman(IRE), a half-brother to Exceedingly Good and Betty Brook, was green and then got hampered when making progress. He's no star but is better than his position suggests. (op 10-1 tchd 11-1)
Newstead Abbey is regressing after a decent debut effort. Neil Callan reported that his mount ran too free. Official explanation: jockey said colt ran too free (op 7-2)

3183 GCI COM EMPOWERING YOUR COMMUNICATIONS H'CAP 6f

3:35 (3:35) (Class 3) (0-95,92) 3-Y-O+ **£8,409** (£2,502; £1,250; £625) **Stalls** High

Form RPR

552 **1** **Rasaman (IRE)**[15] 2719 8-8-13 **77**.. GrahamLee 5 86
(Jim Goldie) *hld up in rr: hdwy wl over 1f out: effrt whn sltly hmpd ent fnl f: rdn and styd on to ld last 50yds* **12/1**

-005 **2** shd **Mass Rally (IRE)**[29] 2284 5-9-11 **89**.......................(v) PaulMulrennan 8 98
(Michael Dods) *hld up in rr: smooth hdwy 2f out: nt clr run over 1f out: swtchd lft ent fnl f: sn rdn and ev ch tl drvn and nt qckn nr fin* **20/1**

4631 **3** nk **Head Space (IRE)**[16] 2674 4-9-4 **82**................................. JamesSullivan 9 90+
(Ruth Carr) *in tch: hdwy to chse ldrs wl over 1f out: rdn to ld ins fnl f: drvn: hdd and no ex last 50yds* **8/1**

0-00 **4** nk **Bertiewhittle**[29] 2268 4-9-11 **89**................................. GrahamGibbons 11 96
(David Barron) *hld up: hdwy wl over 1f out: rdn and styd on strly ins fnl f: ev ch whn edgd lft and no ex last 50yds* **7/1**[3]

2000 **5** 1 ½ **Whozthecat (IRE)**[22] 2488 5-9-1 **79**........................(v) DanielTudhope 13 81
(Declan Carroll) *led: hdd wl over 2f out: cl up and rdn wl over 1f out: wknd fnl f* **16/1**

0001 **6** nk **Damika (IRE)**[3] 3078 9-9-10 **88** 6ex.............................(v) PJMcDonald 6 89
(David Brown) *cl up: led wl over 2f out: rdn and edgd rt 1f out: hdd & wknd ins fnl f* **12/1**

0105 **7** 1 ¼ **Thunderball**[11] 2825 6-10-0 **92**......................................(p) KierenFallon 17 89
(Scott Dixon) *hld up: hdwy over 2f out: n.m.r and swtchd rt over 1f out: rdn and styd on fnl f: nrst fin* **12/1**

-306 **8** hd **Hamoody (USA)**[16] 2674 8-8-10 **81**........................ ShirleyTeasdale(7) 14 78
(David Nicholls) *in tch: hdwy to chse ldrs over 1f out: sn rdn and one pce ins fnl f* **50/1**

-260 **9** hd **Summerinthecity (IRE)**[15] 2707 5-9-10 **88**....................... PhillipMakin 3 84
(Ed de Giles) *hld up: gd hdwy to join ldrs 2f out: rdn wl over 1f out: wknd ent fnl f* **14/1**

-510 **10** 1 ½ **Pearl Blue (IRE)**[28] 2310 4-9-8 **86**.................................. GeorgeBaker 1 77
(Chris Wall) *prom: rdn along 2f out: grad wknd* **16/1**

0-00 **11** nse **Marvellous Value (IRE)**[29] 2286 7-9-11 **89**........................ TomEaves 12 80
(Michael Dods) *sn trcking ldrs: effrt 2f out: rdn over 1f out and sn wknd* **20/1**

0-01 **12** 1 **Paramour**[9] 2896 5-9-7 **85**... FrankieDettori 4 73
(Alan Bailey) *hld up in midfield: hdwy 1/2-way: rdn over 2f out: sn btn* **6/1**[2]

0331 **13** nk **Solar Spirit (IRE)**[9] 2876 7-9-0 **83**............................ ShaneBKelly(5) 7 70
(Tracy Waggott) *prom: rdn along 2f out: sn wknd* **16/1**

-010 **14** 2 **Partner (IRE)**[15] 2717 6-10-0 **92**...............................(b) JamieSpencer 16 72
(Kevin Ryan) *hld up: a in rr* **16/1**

-660 **15** 3 ¼ **Coolminx (IRE)**[11] 2825 5-9-9 **87**.................................... BarryMcHugh 15 57
(Richard Fahey) *chsd ldrs: rdn along 1/2-way: sn wknd* **14/1**

0-10 **16** 12 **Shahzan (IRE)**[22] 2489 4-9-9 **87**.. NeilCallan 19 19
(Roger Varian) *chsd ldrs: rdn along wl over 2f out: sn wknd* **5/1**[1]

1m 13.52s (-0.08) **Going Correction** +0.175s/f (Good) **16** Ran SP% **126.0**
Speed ratings (Par 107): **107,106,106,106,104 103,102,101,101,99 99,98,97,95,90 74**
Swingers:1&2:£113.70, 2&3:£33.50, 1&3:£11.70 CSF £242.62 CT £2057.03 TOTE £14.90: £2.90, £5.00, £2.80, £1.90; EX 336.30 Trifecta £663.70 Part won. Pool: £896.94 - 0.40 winning units..
Owner Paul Moulton **Bred** Rasana Partnership **Trained** Uplawmoor, E Renfrews
■ Stewards' Enquiry : Paul Mulrennan one-day ban: careless riding (Jul 1)

NOTEBOOK
Rasaman(IRE) was ridden to perfection by Graham Lee and got to the front yards from the line. Jim Goldie's runner should still be interesting after a weight rise considering his previous victories. (op 16-1)
Mass Rally(IRE), with no success since November 2009, looked set to take this as he cruised up to the leaders. Paul Mulrennan tried to get his mount to quicken at the last moment but the gelding didn't pick up. He's the type of horse in-running punters need to be cautious about.
Head Space(IRE), who was a bit free in midfield, burst through to have every chance before finding two rivals just a bit too strong late on. (op 7-1)
Bertiewhittle came with a fine effort from off the pace, one that seemed likely to send him to the front, but he couldn't manage to get ahead.
Whozthecat(IRE), without a success since November 2010, had the run of the race out in front and ran pretty well.

Hamoody(USA) ◆ didn't shape too badly. He's back on a fair mark now so watch out for him in the coming weeks, especially if he heads to Goodwood.
Shahzan(IRE) Official explanation: jockey said colt ran flat

3184 FREEBETS.CO.UK H'CAP — 7f
4:10 (4:10) (Class 5) (0-70,68) 3-Y-0 — **£2,911** (£866; £432; £216) **Stalls** High

Form / RPR

0522 **1** **Mick Slates (IRE)**[2] 3111 3-8-1 **53** ... NeilFarley(5) 9 — 63+
(Declan Carroll) *t.k.h: cl up: rdn to ld jst over 1f out: kpt on wl u.p fnl f* — **9/2[2]**

-152 **2** ¾ **Regal Acclaim (IRE)**[12] 2795 3-8-10 **57** ... TedDurcan 8 — 65
(Tim Easterby) *trckd ldrs: hdwy 2f out: rdn over 1f out: kpt on u.p fnl f* — **9/4[1]**

042- **3** ¾ **Duke Of Aricabeau (IRE)**[297] 5399 3-9-4 **65** ... MartinHarley 4 — 71
(Mrs K Burke) *trckd ldrs: smooth hdwy on outer 1/2-way: led wl over 2f out: rdn and hdd jst over 1f out: wknd ins fnl f* — **10/1**

-042 **4** ½ **Balti's Sister (IRE)**[9] 2879 3-8-8 **55** ... PaulMulrennan 7 — 60+
(Michael Easterby) *hld up towards rr: hdwy over 2f out: rdn to chse ldrs over 1f out: drvn and one pce fnl f* — **11/1**

55-0 **5** 3¾ **Flavius Victor (IRE)**[19] 2583 3-9-7 **68** ... PatDobbs 10 — 62
(Richard Hannon) *t.k.h early: in tch: effrt over 2f out: sn rdn and no imp* — **8/1[3]**

1-00 **6** 1¼ **La Salida**[12] 2795 3-9-4 **65** ... GrahamGibbons 13 — 56
(David Barron) *hld up towards rr: sme hdwy 2f out: sn rdn and n.d* — **12/1**

640- **7** ½ **Baileys Over Ice**[228] 7223 3-9-1 **62** ... JamesSullivan 14 — 52
(James Given) *a towards rr* — **25/1**

600- **8** ½ **Ingleby Angel (IRE)**[257] 6611 3-8-3 **50** ... DuranFentiman 12 — 38
(David O'Meara) *t.k.h: prom: rdn along over 2f out: sn drvn and wknd* **33/1**

505 **9** 2¼ **Tinzapeas**[23] 2448 3-9-7 **68** ... MatthewDavies 1 — 50
(Mick Channon) *towards rr: hdwy wl over 2f out: sn rdn and n.d* — **9/1**

33-5 **10** 1½ **Endless Applause**[19] 2591 3-8-10 **57** ... AmyRyan 11 — 35
(Richard Whitaker) *chsd ldrs: rdn along 3f out: sn wknd* — **11/1**

-223 **11** 10 **Bond Style**[127] 536 3-9-3 **64** ... (p) TomEaves 2 — 15
(Bryan Smart) *dwlt: a in rr* — **20/1**

0-60 **12** 1¼ **Tallula (IRE)**[15] 2695 3-8-2 **49** oh4 ... KellyHarrison 6
(Micky Hammond) *led: rdn along and hdd 3f out: sn wknd* — **50/1**

1m 28.6s (2.30) **Going Correction** +0.175s/f (Good) — **12** Ran SP% **117.0**
Speed ratings (Par 99): **93,92,91,90,86 85,84,83,81,79 68,66**
Swingers:1&2:£3.10, 2&3:£4.90, 1&3:£10.70 CSF £14.11 CT £96.58 TOTE £5.00: £1.70, £1.20, £3.70; EX 12.40 Trifecta £97.20 Pool: £881.58 - 6.71 winning units..
Owner Ormskirk **Bred** Peter McCutcheon **Trained** Sledmere, E Yorks

FOCUS
A moderate handicap. The form looks reliable.

3185 FREEBETS.CO.UK FREE BETS H'CAP — 1m (R)
4:40 (4:40) (Class 4) (0-85,85) 4-Y-0+ — **£5,175** (£1,540; £769; £384) **Stalls** Low

Form / RPR

5226 **1** **Levitate**[30] 2243 4-9-3 **81** ... (v) MartinHarley 8 — 94
(Alan McCabe) *hld up in tch: hdwy over 2f out: swtchd rt and rdn over 1f out: styd on to ld last 100yds* — **10/1**

53-0 **2** 1 **Ingleby Exceed (IRE)**[22] 2510 4-8-11 **75** ... DanielTudhope 3 — 86
(David O'Meara) *hld up: gd hdwy on inner over 3f out: led wl over 2f out: rdn and edgd rt over 1f out: drvn ins fnl f: hdd and no ex last 100yds* **8/1**

2605 **3** 2 **Lockantanks**[8] 2913 5-9-0 **78** ... GrahamLee 6 — 87+
(Michael Appleby) *chsd ldrs: hdwy and nt clr run 2f out: sn swtchd lft and rdn: styd on fnl f* — **8/1**

-204 **4** 1¼ **Invincible Hero (IRE)**[13] 2753 5-9-1 **79** ... GrahamGibbons 1 — 82
(Declan Carroll) *led: rdn along and hdd wl over 2f out: drvn wl over 1f out: one pce* — **3/1[1]**

0404 **5** 1½ **Icy Blue**[4] 3037 4-8-6 **70** ... AmyRyan 9 — 70
(Richard Whitaker) *hld up: hdwy and in tch over 2f out: rdn wl over 1f out and sn one pce* — **6/1[2]**

0-50 **6** nk **Vito Volterra (IRE)**[17] 2632 5-8-12 **76** ... PatCosgrave 10 — 75
(Michael Smith) *cl up: rdn along 3f out: drvn over 2f out and grad wknd* — **16/1**

245 **7** ½ **The Osteopath (IRE)**[4] 3037 9-9-0 **78** ... PhillipMakin 5 — 76
(John Davies) *in tch: rdn along wl over 2f out: sn no imp* — **12/1**

-106 **8** 2¾ **She's A Character**[13] 2752 5-8-11 **80** ... ShaneBKelly(5) 4 — 72
(Richard Fahey) *dwlt: a in rr* — **8/1**

0440 **9** 7 **Collateral Damage (IRE)**[13] 2754 9-8-5 **69** ... (t) DuranFentiman 11 — 45
(Tim Easterby) *chsd ldrs on outer: rdn along 3f out: sn wknd* — **11/1**

5312 **10** 3¾ **St Oswald**[95] 899 4-8-13 **77** ... KierenFallon 13 — 44
(Alan Bailey) *a towards rr* — **15/2[3]**

0-00 **11** 20 **One Scoop Or Two**[8] 2910 6-9-2 **80** ... (p) RussKennemore 2
(Reg Hollinshead) *chsd ldrs: rdn along 3f out: sn wknd* — **40/1**

1m 40.34s (0.64) **Going Correction** +0.225s/f (Good) — **11** Ran SP% **117.8**
Speed ratings (Par 105): **105,104,102,100,99 98,98,95,88,84 64**
Swingers:1&2:£14.30, 2&3:£13.90, 1&3:£14.30 CSF £87.81 CT £679.26 TOTE £12.30: £3.60, £3.20, £2.80; EX 127.30 TRIFECTA Not won..
Owner Charles Wentworth **Bred** Cheveley Park Stud Ltd **Trained** Averham Park, Notts
■ Stewards' Enquiry : Graham Gibbons two-day ban: used whip with excessive force (Jul 1-2)

FOCUS
Probably just a fair contest using the runner-up as a guide.
One Scoop Or Two Official explanation: jockey said gelding stopped quickly

3186 FREE BETTING WITH FREEBETS.CO.UK CLASSIFIED STKS — 1m 2f 60y
5:15 (5:15) (Class 5) 3-Y-0 — **£2,911** (£866; £432; £216) **Stalls** Low

Form / RPR

3-32 **1** **My Guardian Angel**[27] 2336 3-9-0 69 ... TedDurcan 4 — 77+
(Mark H Tompkins) *hld up in rr: effrt and nt clr run on inner wl over 2f out: sn swtchd lft to outer and rdn: drvn over 1f out: styd on u.p ins fnl f to ld last 50yds* — **2/1[1]**

4-20 **2** 1½ **Queen's Estate (GER)**[15] 2716 3-9-0 70 ... JoeFanning 1 — 72
(Mark Johnston) *trckd ldr: hdwy 3f out: chal 2f out and sn rdn: drvn to ld 1f out: wknd ins fnl f: hdd and no ex last 50yds* — **11/2**

30-6 **3** 1½ **Buster Brown (IRE)**[34] 2126 3-9-0 70 ... PaulMulrennan 3 — 69
(James Given) *led: rdn along over 2f out: jnd and drvn over 1f out: hdd 1f out: kpt on same pce* — **7/1**

043 **4** 2¾ **Dropzone (USA)**[69] 1250 3-9-0 67 ... AndreaAtzeni 7 — 64
(Marco Botti) *chsd ldng pair: rdn along wl over 2f out: drvn and one pce fr over 1f out* — **3/1[2]**

2401 **5** ½ **Devote Myself (IRE)**[24] 2425 3-9-0 70 ... KierenFallon 2 — 63
(David Evans) *hld up: a in rr* — **4/1[3]**

24-0 **6** 5 **Hunting Gonk**[18] 2604 3-9-0 67 ... GrahamLee 6 — 53
(James Given) *chsd ldrs: rdn along 3f out: sn wknd* — **22/1**

2m 13.27s (3.87) **Going Correction** +0.225s/f (Good) — **6** Ran SP% **110.6**
Speed ratings (Par 99): **93,91,90,88,88 84**
Swingers:1&2:£3.90, 2&3:£4.30, 1&3:£3.70 CSF £12.94 TOTE £2.30: £1.40, £3.30; EX 13.00.
Owner Sarabex **Bred** Dullingham Park **Trained** Newmarket, Suffolk

FOCUS
A modest affair.
T/Jkpt: Not won. T/Plt: £93.50 to a £1 stake. Pool: £115,160.41 - 898.50 winning tickets. T/Qpdt: £45.60 to a £1 stake. Pool: £7,917.98 - 128.30 winning tickets. JR

3009 SALISBURY (R-H)
Sunday, June 17

OFFICIAL GOING: Good to soft (good in places) changing to good (good to soft in places) after race 1 (2.20)
Rail erected up straight 16ft off stands' side rail.
Wind: mild breeze against Weather: sunny with cloudy periods

3187 BATHWICK TYRES H'CAP — 1m 4f
2:20 (2:20) (Class 4) (0-85,84) 4-Y-0+ — **£5,175** (£1,540; £769; £384) **Stalls** High

Form / RPR

6-10 **1** **Quiz Mistress**[15] 2706 4-9-6 **83** ... RichardHughes 2 — 95
(Hughie Morrison) *hld up towards rr: swtchd lft after hdwy over 2f out: led wl over 1f out: styd on strly: pushed out* — **7/2[1]**

0-02 **2** 3 **Dubai Glory**[17] 2623 4-8-12 **75** ... ChrisCatlin 8 — 82
(Sheena West) *trckd clr ldr: clsd on ldr fr over 3f out: led 2f out: sn rdn and hdd: styd on but hld by wnr fnl f* — **8/1**

0-04 **3** 1½ **Tasfeya**[20] 2561 4-8-13 **76** ... AmirQuinn 10 — 81
(Lee Carter) *led: sn clr: rdn and hdd 2f out: styd on but no ex* — **22/1**

44-4 **4** ½ **Gosbeck**[53] 1603 4-9-7 **84** ... DaneO'Neill 4 — 88
(Henry Candy) *trckd ldrs: rdn over 2f out: styd on same pce fnl f* — **5/1[3]**

-432 **5** hd **Kathleen Frances**[8] 2909 5-8-12 **75** ... JimmyFortune 7 — 79
(Mark H Tompkins) *mid-div: hdwy over 2f out: rdn and ch whn bmpd wl over 1f out: kpt on same pce fnl f* — **4/1[2]**

2520 **6** 9 **Shabak Hom (IRE)**[26] 2363 5-8-6 **69** ... CathyGannon 1 — 58
(David Evans) *racd keenly: hld up towards rr: rdn 5f out: nvr any imp on ldrs* — **40/1**

3-11 **7** 1¾ **Maydream**[22] 2502 5-8-3 **71** ... RaulDaSilva(5) 5 — 57
(Jimmy Fox) *hld up towards rr: struggling over 4f out: nvr threatened ldrs* — **6/1**

3261 **8** 13 **Hamilton Hill**[2] 3101 5-7-11 **65** 6ex ... DarrenEgan(5) 6 — 31
(Dai Burchell) *s.i.s: towards rr: stdy prog fr 5f out: rdn 3f out: wknd over 1f out* — **7/1**

10-0 **9** 3½ **Gunslinger (FR)**[23] 2447 7-9-0 **82** ... DavidKenny(5) 3 — 42
(Michael Scudamore) *s.i.s: sn mid-div: rdn and hdwy 3f out: wknd over 1f out* — **33/1**

10-0 **10** ¾ **Alshazah**[23] 2447 4-8-12 **75** ... JamesMillman 9 — 34
(Rod Millman) *trckd ldrs: effrt over 2f out: wknd over 1f out* — **14/1**

2m 37.09s (-0.91) **Going Correction** +0.05s/f (Good) — **10** Ran SP% **113.2**
Speed ratings (Par 105): **105,103,102,101,101 95,94,85,83,82**
Swingers:1&2:£6.90, 2&3:£27.00, 1&3:£13.80 CSF £30.18 CT £527.08 TOTE £4.00: £1.60, £2.80, £6.40; EX 35.20.
Owner The Fairy Story Partnership **Bred** Deepwood Farm Stud **Trained** East Ilsley, Berks

FOCUS
Rail erected up straight 16ft off stands-side rail. The ground had dried out and jockeys in the first reported it to be riding good, perhaps slightly tacky. This fair handicap was run in a time just over three seconds outside standard.

3188 WESTOVER GROUP H'CAP — 5f
2:50 (2:51) (Class 4) (0-85,90) 3-Y-0+ — **£5,175** (£1,540; £769; £384) **Stalls** Low

Form / RPR

2662 **1** **Naabegha**[9] 2876 5-10-2 **87** ... LiamKeniry 5 — 100+
(Ed de Giles) *travelled wl bhd ldrs: shkn up to ld ent fnl f: r.o strly: readily* — **2/1[1]**

5-14 **2** 3 **Ray Of Joy**[41] 1926 6-9-10 **81** ... RichardHughes 1 — 83+
(J R Jenkins) *awkward leaving stalls and sn short of room: towards rr: hdwy 2f out: sn rdn and swtchd lft: r.o ins fnl f: snatched 2nd fnl stride* — **13/2[3]**

3001 **3** nse **Solemn**[10] 2853 7-10-5 **90** ... (b) DaneO'Neill 7 — 92
(Milton Bradley) *prom: rdn to dispute ld 2f out tl hdd ent fnl f: kpt on but nt pce of wnr: lost 2nd fnl stride* — **5/1[2]**

6200 **4** nk **West Coast Dream**[11] 2825 5-9-12 **83** ... IanMongan 6 — 84
(Roy Brotherton) *led for over 1f: rdn to dispute ld 2f out: hdd ent fnl f: kpt on but no ex* — **15/2**

1044 **5** 2¼ **Welsh Inlet (IRE)**[8] 2943 4-8-8 **68** ... SeanLevey(3) 4 — 61
(John Bridger) *trckd ldrs: rdn over 2f out: nt pce to chal: fdd fnl 75yds* — **14/1**

4010 **6** ½ **Titus Gent**[15] 2707 7-9-5 **81** ... RaulDaSilva(5) 2 — 72
(Jeremy Gask) *hld up: rdn and stdy prog fr 2f out: kpt on but nvr gng pce to threaten ldrs* — **9/1**

0-30 **7** 2 **Noverre To Go (IRE)**[15] 2707 6-9-5 **81** ... (bt) DarrenEgan(5) 8 — 65
(Ronald Harris) *little awkward leaving stalls: hdwy to ld after 1f: rdn: hung lft and hdd 2f out: sn btn* — **5/1[2]**

0-05 **8** 3¼ **Aquasulis (IRE)**[13] 2759 3-8-4 **67** ... CathyGannon 3 — 37
(David Evans) *hld up: rdn over 2f out: nvr any imp: wknd fnl f* — **33/1**

1m 1.05s (0.05) **Going Correction** +0.15s/f (Good)
WFA 3 from 4yo+ 6lb — **8** Ran SP% **111.4**
Speed ratings (Par 105): **105,100,100,99,96 95,92,86**
Swingers:1&2:£3.60, 2&3:£4.90, 1&3:£2.40 CSF £14.50 CT £54.60 TOTE £2.90: £2.10, £1.20, £1.90; EX 15.10.
Owner Tight Lines Partnership **Bred** Shadwell Estate Company Limited **Trained** Ledbury, H'fords

FOCUS
A fair sprint handicap for the grade.

3189 WATERAID MILDREN CONSTRUCTION MAIDEN FILLIES' STKS — 1m
3:25 (3:27) (Class 5) 3-Y-0 — **£2,911** (£866; £432; £216) **Stalls** Low

Form / RPR

452 **1** **Chigun**[14] 2734 3-9-0 80 ... IanMongan 6 — 92+
(Sir Henry Cecil) *mde all: rdn clr 2f out: wl in command after: comf* — **9/4[2]**

4 **2** 10 **Port Charlotte**[22] 2483 3-9-0 0 ... RichardHughes 1 — 69
(Hughie Morrison) *mid-div: rdn and stdy prog fr over 2f out: wnt 2nd ent fnl f: nvr any ch w wnr* — **8/1[3]**

22 **3** 2 ¼ **Ensejaam (CAN)**[22] 2483 3-9-0 0 .... PaulHanagan 2 64
(Charles Hills) *chsd wnr tl rdn wl over 2f out: styd on same pce* **7/4**[1]

6-5 **4** 2 ¼ **Valley Queen**[14] 2734 3-9-0 0 .... DaneO'Neill 8 59
(Mark Usher) *sweating: mid-div: rdn wl over 2f out: little imp tl styd on wl ins fnl f* **50/1**

6 **5** *nk* **Waveguide (IRE)**[27] 2335 3-9-0 0 .... MartinLane 11 58+
(David Simcock) *hld up towards rr: rdn and stdy prog fr over 2f out: styd on but nvr threatened ldrs* **33/1**

6 ½ **Treasured Dream** 3-9-0 0 .... EddieAhern 12 57+
(Amanda Perrett) *cl up: effrt over 2f out: sn one pce* **20/1**

30 **7** 1 ¼ **Secrets Away (IRE)**[36] 2079 3-9-0 0 .... AdamKirby 5 54
(Marco Botti) *chsd wnr: rdn over 2f out: fdd ins fnl f* **11/1**

0- **8** 4 **Sweet Liberta (IRE)**[295] 5479 3-9-0 0 ....[1] DavidProbert 3 45
(Andrew Balding) *towards rr: rdn 3f out: nvr a factor* **14/1**

9 *nse* **Albanka (USA)** 3-9-0 0 .... JimmyFortune 4 45+
(Sir Michael Stoute) *mid-div: rdn over 2f out: wknd over 1f out* **17/2**

00 **10** 1 ¼ **Wasabi (IRE)**[29] 2279 3-9-0 0 .... CathyGannon 13 42
(John Berry) *a towards rr* **50/1**

00- **11** 5 **Zarosa (IRE)**[211] 7493 3-9-0 0 .... JimmyQuinn 10 31
(John Berry) *a towards rr* **200/1**

00 **12** 3 ¾ **Ececheira**[20] 2560 3-9-0 0 .... LiamKeniry 9 22
(Dean Ivory) *mid-div: rdn over 2f out: sn wknd* **200/1**

13 21 **Spanish Trail** 3-8-11 0 .... PatrickHills(3) 14
(Christopher Kellett) *trckd wnr tl rdn 3f out: sn hung lft and wknd* **200/1**

1m 43.24s (-0.26) **Going Correction** +0.15s/f (Good) **13** Ran SP% **116.9**
Speed ratings (Par 96): **107,97,94,92,92 91,90,86,86,85 80,76,55**
Swingers:1&2:£4.70, 2&3:£3.10, 1&3:£1.60 CSF £19.58 TOTE £2.90: £1.10, £2.50, £1.20; EX 21.60.
Owner V I Araci **Bred** Whatton Manor Stud **Trained** Newmarket, Suffolk

FOCUS
An interesting fillies' maiden, although it lacked depth.

3190 BATHWICK TYRES CATHEDRAL STKS (LISTED RACE) 6f
4:00 (4:00) (Class 1) 3-Y-0+
£18,714 (£7,095; £3,550; £1,768; £887; £445) **Stalls** Low

Form RPR

0-50 **1** **Libranno**[32] 2179 4-9-4 109 .... RichardHughes 5 106
(Richard Hannon) *trckd ldr: rdn to ld jst over 1f out: hld on wl: drvn out* **7/1**

10-1 **2** *nk* **Our Jonathan**[36] 2074 5-9-4 114 .... FrannyNorton 1 105+
(Kevin Ryan) *in tch: nt clr run over 2f out: hdwy u.p whn squeezed up in barging match jst over 1f out: r.o wl ins fnl f: clsng on wnr at fin* **13/8**[1]

30-2 **3** *hd* **Definightly**[43] 1857 6-9-4 107 ....(b) JamesDoyle 7 104
(Roger Charlton) *led: rdn and hdd jst over 1f out: kpt on* **9/2**[2]

1-04 **4** *nk* **Eton Rifles (IRE)**[14] 2745 7-9-8 109 .... WilliamCarson 4 107+
(Stuart Williams) *trckd ldrs: swtchd lft whn nt clr run jst over 1f out and c off worst in barging match: kpt on wl fnl 75yds* **11/2**[3]

50-3 **5** ¾ **Morache Music**[36] 2074 4-9-4 105 .... SebSanders 9 101
(Peter Makin) *hld up: hdwy whn nt clr run briefly over 2f out: sn rdn: kpt on ins fnl f* **14/1**

50-4 **6** *hd* **Golden Delicious**[18] 2608 4-8-13 85 .... JimmyFortune 10 93
(Hughie Morrison) *hld up: hdwy on far rails 2f out: sn rdn: kpt on fnl f* **25/1**

1-52 **7** 1 **Artistic Jewel (IRE)**[15] 2713 3-8-10 102 .... SeanLevey 6 96
(Ed McMahon) *sn cl up: rdn to chse ldrs 2f out: keeping on at same pce whn recieved hefty bump jst over 1f out: sn no ex* **7/1**

5566 **8** 3 ½ **Sos Brillante (CHI)**[17] 2640 7-8-13 74 .... JimmyQuinn 3 81?
(Terry Clement) *s.i.s: hld up: rdn over 3f out: nvr any imp: wknd fnl f* **200/1**

0321 **9** 3 ¾ **Chilli Green**[23] 2446 5-8-13 89 ....(p) DarrenEgan 8 69
(Lee Carter) *in tch: rdn over 2f out: wknd ent fnl f* **20/1**

1m 14.49s (-0.31) **Going Correction** +0.15s/f (Good)
WFA 3 from 4yo+ 7lb **9** Ran SP% **112.4**
Speed ratings (Par 111): **108,107,107,106,105 105,104,99,94**
Swingers:1&2:£3.60, 2&3:£3.10, 1&3:£5.10 CSF £17.98 TOTE £9.00: £2.10, £1.40, £1.30; EX 12.40.
Owner Mcdowell Racing **Bred** O McDowell **Trained** East Everleigh, Wilts

FOCUS
The best recent winner of this Listed event was 2007 scorer Sakhee's Secret, who took the July Cup next time out. This looked a decent renewal, but it was a messy race and the form may not prove entirely straightforward. The time was just over 2 secs slower than standard.

NOTEBOOK
Libranno missed the trouble racing close to the pace and ran on in gritty style. He enhanced the fine record in this event of the Richard Hannon yard, who won it four years ago with Edge Closer and in 2011 with Elnawin, who had been second 12 months earlier. Tough and classy, Libranno had valid excuses for his two lacklustre runs earlier this season. He is just as effective at 7f and could run over that trip in the Criterion Stakes at Newmarket next before another crack at the July Cup, in which he was fourth last year. Official explanation: trainer's rep had no explanation for the apparent improvement in form. (op 13-2)
Our Jonathan, a winner on his return at Haydock, had 5lb in hand of Libranno on BHA ratings. Drawn in stall one, he found himself a little further from the front than desirable before becoming involved in a barging match at a crucial stage. When in the clear he ran on well, and he remains in good heart. He is a high-class sprinter when on song and no doubt all roads lead to Haydock's Sprint Cup in September. (op 11-8)
Definightly came here in preference to a race at Cork the same afternoon. Back over 6f, he ran well from the front and just missed out, despite the ground having gone against him a little. (tchd 4-1)
Eton Rifles(IRE) ◆, saddled with a 4lb penalty, clashed with old rival Our Jonathan when switching off the rail for a run. He came off worse, but to his credit he ran on strongly to the line. He's well capable of winning a Group race. (op 13-2 tchd 5-1)
Morache Music, third in Our Jonathan's Haydock race, ran well and would have been closer had he not met a bit of trouble when attempting to pick up. (op 16-1 tchd 12-1)
Golden Delicious held little realistic chance in this company, but she likes this track and was not beaten far. A fillies' Listed race could be the way forward for her.
Artistic Jewel(IRE) was another caught up in the bumping match approaching the final furlong, and it ended what chance she had. (op 9-1)

3191 BRIDGET SWIRE MEMORIAL MAIDEN STKS 6f
4:30 (4:30) (Class 3) 2-Y-0 **£7,762** (£2,310; £865; £865) **Stalls** Low

Form RPR

0 **1** **Star Breaker**[30] 2231 2-9-3 0 .... JamesDoyle 1 78+
(Sylvester Kirk) *led: rdn and narrowly hdd over 1f out: rallied v gamely u.str.p to regain ld nring fin* **5/1**[2]

2 *shd* **Martial Art (IRE)** 2-9-3 0 .... DavidProbert 3 78+
(Andrew Balding) *trckd ldr: racd green early: rdn to take narrow advantage over 1f out: kpt on but no ex whn hdd nring fin* **9/1**

3 3 ¼ **Bold Prediction (IRE)** 2-9-3 0 .... RichardHughes 4 68
(Richard Hannon) *trckd ldrs: rdn and ev ch 2f out: sn hld: kpt on same pce* **11/10**[1]

3 *dht* **Clement (IRE)** 2-9-3 0 .... SebSanders 5 68
(Eve Johnson Houghton) *s.i.s: last but in tch: rdn in cl 4th 2f out: kpt on same pce fnl f* **14/1**

06 **5** ½ **Gold Roll (IRE)**[10] 2844 2-9-3 0 .... MarcHalford 6 66
(David Elsworth) *cl up: outpcd 2f out: kpt on fnl f but nvr any threat after* **8/1**[3]

6 68 **Great Run** 2-9-3 0 .... DaneO'Neill 2
(Richard Hannon) *smething amiss almost immediately: virtually p.u in 1st 100yds* **5/1**[2]

1m 17.63s (2.83) **Going Correction** +0.15s/f (Good) **6** Ran SP% **108.7**
Speed ratings (Par 97): **87,86,82,82,81**
Swingers:1&2:£5.50, 2&BP £1.50, 1&BP £0.90, 2&C £5.40, 1&C £3.60 CSF £42.86 TOTE £4.90: £2.50, £4.60; EX 39.90.
Owner J C Smith **Bred** Jnp Bloodstock Ltd **Trained** Upper Lambourn, Berks

FOCUS
Just a small line-up for what was quite a valuable maiden, but it still looked an interesting race. It's unlikely there was anything in the field as good as last year's winner Harbour Watch, who later won the Richmond Stakes, but the first two came clear and looks fairly useful. The fifth and the averages are the best guides to the level.

NOTEBOOK
Star Breaker was down the field on his debut at Newbury a month ago but that race, won by Sir Patrick Moore, is throwing up winners. Warm before the start, and equipped with a cross-noseband, he made most of the running and fought back after being headed inside the last. He liked the ground and there may be further improvement in him. (op 4-1 tchd 7-2)
Martial Art(IRE)'s trainer has close family connections with the late Bridget Swire, after whom this race was named. The colt was in the first pair throughout and just missed out to an opponent who'd had the benefit of a previous run. Likely to stay further in time, he should soon find compensation. (tchd 8-1)
Bold Prediction(IRE) joined Clement on the line for third after being held together through the final furlong when his measure had been taken. He is no Harbour Watch - who won this for his yard a year ago - but a maiden should come his way, perhaps over 7f. (tchd 12-1)
Clement(IRE) kept on willingly after finding himself a little outpaced by the leaders. He's from the family of Duncan and Samuel and will appreciate a greater test of stamina in time. (tchd 12-1)
Gold Roll(IRE) had finished 3l behind Star Breaker on his debut at Newbury. When trying to improve down the outer he hung to his right, but he did keep on once reaching the rail. He looks a nursery type. (op 7-1 tchd 13-2)
Great Run, who looked the Hannon second string, came in for a bit of support, but he started awkwardly and was soon eased down. He was reported to have lost his action, but happily seemed sound when pulling up. Official explanation: jockey said colt lost its action (op 11-2)

3192 BATHWICK TYRES FILLIES' H'CAP 6f 212y
5:05 (5:06) (Class 5) (0-75,74) 3-Y-0+ **£2,911** (£866; £432; £216) **Stalls** Low

Form RPR

00-1 **1** **Ivor's Princess**[31] 2205 3-9-0 **72** ....(b) SeanLevey(3) 3 85
(Rod Millman) *s.i.s: sn in tch: rdn and hdwy over 2f out: led over 1f out: styd on strly to draw clr fnl f: comf* **8/1**

11-2 **2** 5 **Rivas Rhapsody (IRE)**[22] 2503 4-10-0 **74** .... JamesDoyle 1 77
(Ian Wood) *trckd ldr: swtchd lft over 1f out: sn rdn: kpt on but a being comf hld by wnr* **5/4**[1]

-235 **3** 3 ¾ **Batgirl**[23] 2465 5-9-12 **72** .... RichardHughes 6 64
(John Berry) *hld up bhd ldrs: hdwy 2f out: sn rdn: styd on same pce fnl f* **7/1**[3]

0-23 **4** *hd* **Saratoga Slew (IRE)**[22] 2503 3-9-4 **73** .... AdamKirby 5 62
(Marco Botti) *trckd ldr: led wl over 2f out: sn rdn: hdd over 1f out: fdd ins fnl f* **10/3**[2]

-005 **5** 2 **Amethyst Dawn (IRE)**[108] 753 6-9-10 **70** .... EddieAhern 9 56
(Andrew Reid) *cl up: rdn 2f out: sn one pce* **28/1**

0-01 **6** ½ **My Own Way Home**[24] 2421 4-9-3 **63** .... PadraigBeggy 7 48
(David Evans) *in tch: nt best of runs whn swtchd lft and rdn 2f out: nvr any imp* **16/1**

402 **7** ½ **Swift Act**[13] 2757 3-8-10 **70** .... DarrenEgan(5) 10 51
(Ronald Harris) *in tch: effrt over 2f out: sn one pce* **16/1**

0-03 **8** ¾ **Vizean (IRE)**[22] 2475 4-8-10 **63** .... WilliamTwiston-Davies(7) 4 45
(John Mackie) *led tl rdn wl over 2f out: wknd fnl f* **14/1**

1m 29.49s (0.89) **Going Correction** +0.15s/f (Good)
WFA 3 from 4yo+ 9lb **8** Ran SP% **113.0**
Speed ratings (Par 100): **100,94,90,89,87 86,86,85**
Swingers:1&2:£3.30, 2&3:£2.60, 1&3:£7.40 CSF £18.02 CT £74.97 TOTE £10.30: £2.40, £1.40, £1.70; EX 21.60.
Owner P G Gibbins & W I M Perry **Bred** The Three Point Partnership **Trained** Kentisbeare, Devon

FOCUS
A modest fillies' handicap run at a solid pace.

3193 BATHWICK TYRES RACING EXCELLENCE "HANDS AND HEELS" APPRENTICE SERIES H'CAP 1m
5:35 (5:36) (Class 6) (0-65,65) 3-Y-0 **£2,070** (£616; £307; £153) **Stalls** Low

Form RPR

0-65 **1** **Lady Percy (IRE)**[13] 2756 3-8-11 **55** .... DanielMuscutt 12 62
(Mark Usher) *jnd far side gp after racing in centre for 1f: mid-div: led briefly over 2f out: sn rdn to chse ldr: renewed effrt fnl 100yds: led fnl stride* **9/1**

301 **2** *nse* **Temuco (IRE)**[5] 3014 3-9-6 **64** 6ex .... AliceHaynes 8 73+
(David Evans) *hld up: swtchd lft and hdwy over 2f out: led over 1f out: drifted rt: ct fnl stride* **9/2**[2]

-136 **3** *nk* **Lady Sylvia**[17] 2625 3-9-0 **61** .... JacobMoore(3) 6 67
(Joseph Tuite) *hld up: hdwy over 2f out: sn rdn: styd on ins fnl f* **16/1**

6-51 **4** 5 **Autumn Fire**[25] 2387 3-9-2 **63** .... ThomasBrown(3) 9 58
(Andrew Balding) *prom: losing pl whn short of room 4f out: sn rdn: styd on same pce fnl 2f* **9/2**[2]

-122 **5** 3 **Our Phylli Vera (IRE)**[12] 2787 3-9-7 **65** .... WilliamTwiston-Davies 1 53
(Harry Dunlop) *led for 1f: prom: led briefly and rdn over 2f out: fdd fnl f* **10/3**[1]

00-6 **6** *shd* **Isola Bella**[32] 2162 3-8-2 **46** .... NicoleNordblad 5 33
(Jonathan Portman) *hld up: hdwy over 2f out: kpt on same pce: nvr trbld ldrs* **6/1**[3]

6036 **7** ¾ **Joy To The World (IRE)**[25] 2386 3-8-8 **52** .... RyanWhile 3 38
(Paul Cole) *chsd ldrs: rdn and ev ch 2f out: fdd ins fnl f* **25/1**

5351 **8** 4 **Compton Target (IRE)**[12] 2786 3-9-0 **58** ....(t) TimClark 2 34
(Milton Bradley) *trckd ldrs: rdn over 2f out: wknd over 1f out* **8/1**

-050 **9** 10 **Gadreel (IRE)**[25] 2393 3-8-2 **46** oh1 .... NoelGarbutt 4
(Anthony Middleton) *mid-div tl wknd 2f out* **40/1**

-230 **10** 2 **Macy Anne (IRE)**[65] 1365 3-8-8 **60** .... DanielCremin(8) 10
(Robert Mills) *led after 1f: hdd over 2f out: sn wknd* **25/1**

400- **11** *3* **King's Ciel**[185] 7763 3-9-4 62 .... ThomasGarner 11
(George Baker) *prom in centre: pushed along 4f out: wknd over 2f out*
28/1

1m 46.5s (3.00) **Going Correction** +0.15s/f (Good) **11** Ran SP% **114.3**
Speed ratings (Par 97): **91,90,90,85,82 82,81,77,67,65 62**
Swingers:1&2:£7.90, 2&3:£14.30, 1&3:£23.50 CSF £45.88 CT £653.68 TOTE £9.60: £2.70, £1.80, £5.10; EX 52.60.
Owner Ushers Court **Bred** Garry Chong **Trained** Upper Lambourn, Berks

FOCUS
A very modest apprentice handicap in which they were spread across the track in the latter stages. The first three finished clear but the form does not look particularly sound.
King's Ciel Official explanation: jockey said gelding hung right
T/Plt: £38.00 to a £1 stake. Pool: £82,042.98 - 1,574.76 winning tickets. T/Qpdt: £9.00 to a £1 stake. Pool: £6,597.08 - 128.30 winning tickets. TM

3194 - 3195a (Foreign Racing) - See Raceform Interactive

2058 CORK (R-H)
Sunday, June 17

OFFICIAL GOING: Round course - soft; sprint course - heavy (soft to heavy in places)

3196a GALTEE MIDSUMMER SPRINT STKS (LISTED RACE) 5f
3:15 (3:16) 3-Y-0+ **£24,375** (£7,125; £3,375; £1,125)

RPR

1 **Mirza**[8] 2931 5-9-7 .... FranBerry 2 107
(Rae Guest) *pushed along to chse ldrs early and sn disputing 2nd: rdn 2f out: styd on wl fnl f to ld nr line* **2/1**[1]

2 *½* **My Girl Anna (IRE)**[21] 2528 5-9-4 89 .... RoryCleary 3 102
(Muredach Kelly, Ire) *sn disputing 2nd: leaning rt but travelling wl 2f out: rdn to ld over 1f out: styd on wl: hdd nr line* **14/1**

3 *½* **Gossamer Seed (IRE)**[3] 3092 4-9-9 104 ....(t) ShaneFoley 7 105
(John Joseph Murphy, Ire) *chsd ldrs: rdn in 4th under 2f out: kpt on fnl f* **6/1**

4 *½* **Santo Padre (IRE)**[22] 2513 8-9-10 106 .... FergalLynch 8 104
(David Marnane, Ire) *in tch in rr: rdn 2f out: sme prog wout threatening to go 4th fnl f* **12/1**

5 *1 ¼* **Inxile (IRE)**[43] 1857 7-9-10 ....(p) AdrianNicholls 4 100
(David Nicholls) *broke wl and led: rdn and strly pressed 2f out: hdd over 1f out: no imp fnl f* **7/2**[2]

6 *1* **Borderlescott**[22] 2486 10-9-7 .... RobertWinston 9 93
(Robin Bastiman) *chsd ldrs: rdn in 6th 2f out: no imp over 1f out: checked briefly ins fnl f* **5/1**[3]

7 *3 ¾* **Caprella**[21] 2528 3-8-12 83 ....(b) ChrisHayes 6 77
(P D Deegan, Ire) *chsd ldrs: rdn and wknd fr 2f out* **33/1**

8 *1 ¼* **Roicead (USA)**[294] 5524 5-9-7 105 ....(t) KevinManning 1 75
(W McCreery, Ire) *chsd ldrs: rdn and wknd fr over 2f out* **9/1**

59.84s (0.64)
WFA 3 from 4yo+ 6lb **8** Ran SP% **113.8**
CSF £31.93 TOTE £2.70: £1.40, £2.60, £1.60; DF 21.10.
Owner C J Mills **Bred** C J Mills **Trained** Newmarket, Suffolk

FOCUS
There have been some smart sprinters in Ireland in recent seasons, but it is still the case that the better Irish sprints are highly vulnerable to challengers from Britain. Here we had the situation of a progressive handicapper proving good enough to justify favouritism in this Listed contest. The winner has been rated to his 5f mark, and the runner-up to a personal best.

NOTEBOOK
Mirza, with handicap wins under his belt this term at Newbury and Newmarket, came into the race with a more progressive profile than a couple of old warriors. He did not show instant speed, instead gradually warming to his task from around 2f out and getting on top in the closing stages. Bearing in mind that he stays 6f effectively there should be plenty of opportunities for him and it would be no surprise to see him back in Ireland later in the season. (op 2/1 tchd 13/8)
My Girl Anna(IRE) is enjoying a good campaign. Until now the highlight was provided by a handicap win at Navan off a relatively modest 81. She surpassed that with a definite career-best here, running prominently all the way and only just losing out after leading from a furlong out. She's not going to be easy to place after this, but she's proving a real credit to her trainer. (op 16/1)
Gossamer Seed(IRE), who won the Group 3 Athasi Stakes over 7f in April, has come down a furlong on each start since and this was a creditable performance on her first run over the minimum distance since she won a maiden at the venue in September 2010. She clearly takes her racing well, since this came only three days after finishing third in the Group 3 Ballyogan Stakes over 6f at Leopardstown. (op 7/1)
Santo Padre(IRE) won a similar race at Naas in April to record his first success since landing the Portland Handicap in 2009. He cut little ice at Group 3 level in the Greenlands on his next start and again seemed a bit below his best here, although the market did not indicate any real fancy for him. (op 10/1)
Inxile(IRE) was quickly away and made a lot of the running without managing to get away from his pursuers. He weakened into fifth and does not seem to have recovered his form after a spell in Dubai during the winter. (op 4/1 tchd 9/2)
Borderlescott was disappointing and it was all over before he suffered some late interference. (op 4/1)

3197a KERRY GROUP NOBLESSE STKS (GROUP 3) (F&M) 1m 4f
3:50 (3:50) 3-Y-0+ **£44,687** (£13,062; £6,187; £2,062)

RPR

1 **Sapphire (IRE)**[252] 6736 4-9-9 109 .... PatSmullen 1 113+
(D K Weld, Ire) *trckd ldrs in 3rd in inner: impr to ld travelling wl over 2f out: sn qcknd clr: styd on strly fnl f: v easily* **11/8**[1]

2 *4 ¾* **Betterbetterbetter (IRE)**[16] 2658 3-8-9 97 .... CO'Donoghue 4 105
(A P O'Brien, Ire) *trckd ldrs: 5th ent st: rdn in mod 3rd 2f out: wnt mod 2nd fnl f: nt trble easy wnr* **9/2**[3]

3 *3 ½* **Soon (IRE)**[21] 2524 3-8-9 99 .... SeamieHeffernan 8 99+
(A P O'Brien, Ire) *in rr: rdn in mod 6th 2f out: wnt mod 3rd ins fnl f: kpt on same pce* **8/1**

4 *1 ¼* **Remember Alexander**[35] 2101 3-8-12 102 .... ShaneFoley 7 100
(Mrs John Harrington, Ire) *chsd ldrs: 4th ent st: sn rdn: 5th 2f out: kpt on one pce* **9/1**

5 *nk* **Demurely (IRE)**[37] 2063 3-8-9 .... DavidMcCabe 5 97?
(A P O'Brien, Ire) *trckd ldr in 2nd: rdn over 2f out: no imp fr 1 1/2f out: kpt on one pce* **33/1**

6 *nk* **Eternal Bounty (IRE)**[231] 7184 3-8-9 90 .... WJLee 6 96
(David Wachman, Ire) *mid-div: rdn and no imp over 2f out* **10/1**

7 *2 ½* **Goldplated (IRE)**[15] 2711 4-9-9 94 .... BenCurtis 2 92
(John Joseph Murphy, Ire) *led: rdn and hdd over 2f out: dropped to mod 3rd 1 1/2f out: wknd* **66/1**

8 *½* **Ebalviyra (IRE)**[45] 1806 3-8-9 .... NGMcCullagh 3 92
(John M Oxx, Ire) *towards rr: rdn in 7th 2f out: no imp* **4/1**[2]

2m 35.93s (-11.97)
WFA 3 from 4yo 14lb **8** Ran SP% **114.9**
CSF £7.83 TOTE £1.70: £1.50, £1.02, £2.00; DF 9.10.
Owner Moyglare Stud Farm **Bred** Moyglare Stud Farm Ltd **Trained** The Curragh, Co Kildare

FOCUS
An impressive performance by a filly capable of winning at a higher level judged on this. It has been rated around the winner and second, with the third and fourth just off their pre-race marks.

NOTEBOOK
Sapphire(IRE) was impressive in landing this Group 3 prize with considerable authority on her seasonal debut. Sapphire's form at three, culminating in a handsome Listed win at the Curragh, had indicated a liking for soft ground and she confirmed that trait here. She could be a Group 1 filly in the making and the Pretty Polly is the logical next step before a likely international campaign, in the manner adopted by Weld with many top-class fillies in the past. (op 6/4 tchd 5/4)
Betterbetterbetter(IRE) was only touched off in the Cheshire Oaks and was not beaten that far behind stable companion Was at Epsom, so she represents a useful enough 3yo yardstick at this level. She was no match for the winner. (op 5/1 tchd 11/2)
Soon(IRE) kept on from the rear. (op 8/1 tchd 7/1)
Remember Alexander now has a bit to prove at Pattern level. (op 8/1 tchd 11/1)
Demurely(IRE) ran well enough to suggest she can be placed to win a maiden.
Ebalviyra(IRE) failed to cope with the rise in class. (op 4/1 tchd 7/2)

3198 - 3202a (Foreign Racing) - See Raceform Interactive

2951 CHANTILLY (R-H)
Sunday, June 17

OFFICIAL GOING: Turf: good to soft

3203a PRIX DE DIANE LONGINES (GROUP 1) (3YO FILLIES) (TURF) 1m 2f 110y
2:45 (12:00) 3-Y-0 **£476,166** (£190,500; £95,250; £47,583; £23,833)

RPR

1 **Valyra**[30] 3-9-0 0 .... JohnnyMurtagh 2 120
(J-C Rouget, France) *settled towards rr on ins fr s: swtchd away fr rail early in st: qcknd wl 2f out: began chal 1f out: chal ldr 150yds out: tk ld 120yds out: r.o wl: comf* **25/1**

2 *¾* **Beauty Parlour**[35] 2109 3-9-0 0 .... ChristopheSoumillon 9 119
(E Lellouche, France) *prom bhd ldrs fr s: mde smooth prog to ld 2f out: wnt clr: u.p 1f out: chal 150yds out: hdd 120yds out: styd on wl* **5/6**[1]

3 *3* **Rjwa (IRE)**[21] 2532 3-9-0 0 .... ThierryJarnet 3 113
(F Rohaut, France) *racd towards rr: qckhd wl u.p 2f out to chse ldr: r.o wl ins fnl f to go clr 3rd* **33/1**

4 *4* **Forces Of Darkness (IRE)**[21] 2532 3-9-0 0 .... IoritzMendizabal 1 105
(F Vermeulen, France) *racd in midfield: responded to str press ent fnl f: styd on wl to go 4th cl home* **66/1**

5 *nk* **Dalkala (USA)**[33] 2156 3-9-0 0 .... Christophe-PatriceLemaire 7 105
(A De Royer-Dupre, France) *hld up towards bk of field: mde gd prog to be prom 2f out: u.p ent fnl f: no ex: styd on fnl f: lost 4th cl home* **15/2**[3]

6 *snk* **Leaupartie (IRE)**[23] 3-9-0 0 .... GregoryBenoist 4 104
(F Chappet, France) *hld up towards bk of field: r.o u.p ent fnl 1 1/2f: styd on wl fnl f* **50/1**

7 *½* **Up (IRE)**[35] 2109 3-9-0 0 .... RyanMoore 11 103
(A P O'Brien, Ire) *hld up at rr of field: began to make prog 2f out: short of room 1f out: had to be stdd: swtchd to outside and r.o fnl f* **12/1**

8 *nk* **Sagawara**[21] 2532 3-9-0 0 ....(p) GeraldMosse 6 103
(A De Royer-Dupre, France) *sn prom on ins bhd ldrs: u.p 2f out: no ex: styd on at one pce fnl f* **22/1**

9 *10* **Petite Noblesse (FR)**[35] 2109 3-9-0 0 .... MaximeGuyon 12 83
(A Fabre, France) *a towards rr: hrd rdn 2f out: nvr a factor* **20/1**

10 *20* **Trois Lunes (FR)**[49] 1695 3-9-0 0 .... Francois-XavierBertras 8 44
(F Rohaut, France) *racd in midfield towards outside: rdn but no ex over 2f out: fdd* **25/1**

11 *dist* **Kissed (IRE)**[49] 1690 3-9-0 0 .... JPO'Brien 10
(A P O'Brien, Ire) *led fr s: set str pce: stl in front 2 1/2f out: hdd 2f out: rdn: no ex: grad fdd: eased fnl f* **200/1**

12 *1* **Best Of All (GER)**[14] 2741 3-9-0 0 ....(p) AnthonyCrastus 5
(E Lellouche, France) *prom on outside fr s: unable to hd ldr: swung wd into st: sn eased* **5/2**[2]

2m 10.11s (1.31) **Going Correction** +0.425s/f (Yiel) **12** Ran SP% **126.3**
Speed ratings: **112,111,109,106,106 106,105,105,98,83 ,**
WIN (incl. 1 euro stake): 4.20 (Valyra coupled with Sagawara & Dalkala). PLACES: 3.30, 1.20, 2.70. DF: 13.50.SF: 34.60.
Owner H H Aga Khan **Bred** Haras De S.A. Aga Khan Scea **Trained** Pau, France

FOCUS
The ground was nowhere near as soft as had been predicted. A strong edition that was run at a good gallop, this despite the favourite's pacemaker Best Of All fluffing the start and being rendered ineffective. Two of the four unbeaten fillies drew clear and they can be expected to at least hold their own against the boys later in the campaign. The runner-up has been rated to a small personal best, with the fourth roughly to her Prix Saint-Alary form.

NOTEBOOK
Valyra, the apparent Aga Khan third-string who had been supplemented, was unconsidered in the market, but she'd won both previous starts, including a 1m2f conditions race at the course the time before, and this victory confirmed her as a fast-improving filly. In deep for this first attempt at Group level, she produced a sustained burst to run down the favourite, who'd been committed plenty soon enough, and promises to improve again for a step up to 1m4f. She's not in the Irish Oaks, but races such as the Prix Vermeille and Arc/Prix de L'Opera seem likely autumn targets.
Beauty Parlour made it 4-4 in the Pouliches and promised to benefit from the extra yardage. However, having sat on the brisk pace throughout, she kicked for home soon on entering the straight and was worn down late. For a horse with acceleration going up in trip it was surprising her usually confident jockey opted for such a forward ride, and she'd have very good claims of reversing form with the winner were they to meet again. She too is a likely type for races such as the Prix Vermeille and Arc/Prix de L'Opera.
Rjwa(IRE) confirmed Prix Saint-Alary placings with Forces Of Darkness and looks capable of winning at Group 2 level.
Forces Of Darkness(IRE) couldn't reverse Prix Saint-Alary placings with Rjwa.
Dalkala(USA), the Aga Khan first string, was previously unbeaten and a Group 3 winner last time. From a good family, the drying ground was in her favour, so it was disappointing she couldn't fare any better.
Up(IRE) didn't get the best of runs.
Sagawara, the Prix Saint-Alary winner, raced keenly and was readily swept aside, failing to give her running.
Petite Noblesse(FR), dropped right out to get her settled, was never able to get involved.

Kissed(IRE), who skipped Epsom in the hope of softer ground here, wouldn't have welcomed the drying conditions and, having led into the straight, was quickly swept aside. It later emerged she'd sustained a fracture to her left fore and has therefore been retired.

3204a PRIX DU LYS (GROUP 3) (3YO COLTS & GELDINGS) (TURF) 1m 4f
4:05 (12:00) 3-Y-0 **£33,333** (£13,333; £10,000; £6,666; £3,333)

RPR

1 **Remus De La Tour (FR)**[32] 2192 3-8-11 0 DavyBonilla 2 111
(K Borgel, France) *sn led under restraint: set gd pce: shkn up 1 1/2f out: wnt clr: r.o wl: strly chal fnl 50yds: hld on wl* **14/1**

2 snk **Masterstroke (USA)**[35] 2108 3-8-11 0 MaximeGuyon 1 111
(A Fabre, France) *settled in 3rd on ins: wnt 2nd 1 1/2f out: lost pl ent fnl f: rallied u.p and wnt 2nd 100yds out: r.o wl: str chal fnl 50yds: a being hld by wnr* **8/11**[1]

3 3/4 **Ashkiyr (FR)**[17] 3-8-11 0 Christophe-PatriceLemaire 3 110
(A De Royer-Dupre, France) *settled in midfield on ins: shkn up 1 1/2f out: r.o wl fnl f: clst at fin* **3/1**[2]

4 2 1/2 **Propulsion (IRE)**[48] 3-8-11 0 (b[1]) OlivierPeslier 7 106
(F Head, France) *settled towards rr: qcknd wl 2f out: wnt 2nd 1 1/2f out: no ex fnl f: styd on* **8/1**[3]

5 1 3/4 **Rollex Borget (FR)**[26] 2383 3-8-11 0 GeraldMosse 5 103
(J Bertran De Balanda, France) *settled towards rr: swtchd to outside early in st: qcknd wl: ev ch 1 1/2f out: no ex u.p: styd on fnl f* **9/1**

6 3/4 **Mothman (IRE)**[26] 2383 3-8-11 0 FabriceVeron 6 102
(T Lemer, France) *racd in cl 2nd fr s: rdn 2f out: unable qck: sn lost pl: rallied fnl f: styd on again* **20/1**

7 3 **Mortga (FR)**[23] 3-8-11 0 ThierryJarnet 4 97
(P Bary, France) *upset in stalls and uns rdr: hld up in rr: rdn 2f out: r.o: began to fade 1f out: nt hrd rdn fnl f* **16/1**

2m 37.27s (6.27) **Going Correction** +0.425s/f (Yiel) 7 Ran SP% **121.3**
Speed ratings: **96,95,95,93,92 92,90**
WIN (incl. 1 euro stake): 15.90. PLACES: 3.70, 1.40. SF: 40.90.
Owner Barthelemy Vives **Bred** Mme A De Clermont Tonnerre **Trained** France

NOTEBOOK
Remus De La Tour(FR) followed up his win in a Listed race last time with an all-the-way success in this better company.
Masterstroke(USA), runner-up in the Prix Hocquart last time out, hit a flat spot but was closing well at the finish.
Ashkiyr(FR)'s rider appeared to overdo the waiting tactics.

3205a PRIX DU CHEMIN DE FER DU NORD (GROUP 3) (4YO+) (TURF) 1m
4:35 (12:00) 4-Y-0+ **£33,333** (£13,333; £10,000; £6,666; £3,333)

RPR

1 **Vagabond Shoes (IRE)**[99] 876 5-8-11 0 StephanePasquier 8 113
(Y Durepaire, Spain) *racd in midfield towards outside: qcknd wl to take ld 1f out: r.o wl: nvr threatened* **20/1**

2 3/4 **Moonwalk In Paris (FR)**[77] 1163 4-9-0 0 ChristopheSoumillon 3 114
(J-C Rouget, France) *hld up in rr: mde gd prog 2f out: r.o wl fnl f to go clr 2nd but wout threatening ldr* **9/4**[1]

3 1 1/4 **Evaporation (FR)**[47] 1746 5-8-8 0 OlivierPeslier 6 105
(C Laffon-Parias, France) *racd in midfield: qcknd wl 2f out: wnt 2nd 1f out: no ex ins fnl f: lost 2nd 100yds out* **11/4**[2]

4 snk **Shamalgan (FR)**[47] 1746 5-9-2 0 GregoryBenoist 2 113
(X Nakkachdji, France) *led fr s: rdn 1 1/2f out: unable qck: hdd 1f out: styd on at one pce fnl 100yds* **14/1**

5 1 1/2 **Fury**[31] 2211 4-8-11 0 RyanMoore 4 104
(William Haggas) *prom bhd ldrs fr s: styng on wl 1 1/2f out whn short of room: had to be stdd and swtchd towards rail: r.o again fnl 150yds* **5/1**

6 3/4 **Zinabaa (FR)**[21] 2533 7-9-2 0 YannickLetondeur 1 108
(M Mace, France) *prom on rail bhd ldrs: rdn but unable qck 2f out: styd on fnl f* **4/1**[3]

7 6 **Blue Soave (FR)**[47] 1746 4-8-11 0 ThierryThulliez 7 89
(F Chappet, France) *hld up towards rr: rdn but fnd no ex fr 2f out: fdd* **33/1**

8 1 1/2 **Maiguri (IRE)**[26] 4-8-11 0 JohanVictoire 5 85
(C Baillet, France) *racd towards rr: rdn but nt qckn in st: nvr a factor* **20/1**

9 6 **Glad Sky**[45] 1809 6-8-11 0 BriceRaballand 9 72
(J-L Pelletan, France) *prom fr s: rdn but sn wknd in st* **50/1**

10 snk **Ch'Tio Bilote (FR)**[10] 4-8-11 0 IoritzMendizabal 10 71
(J-P Gallorini, France) *a towards rr: nvr a factor* **12/1**

1m 38.78s (0.78) **Going Correction** +0.425s/f (Yiel) 10 Ran SP% **122.9**
Speed ratings: **113,112,111,110,109 108,102,101,95,94**
WIN (incl. 1 euro stake): 23.80. PLACES: 3.20, 1.40, 1.40. DF: 30.30. SF: 82.40.
Owner Javier Martinez Salmean **Bred** Almagro De Actividades Comerciales S A **Trained** Spain

NOTEBOOK
Vagabond Shoes(IRE), having his first outing since running at Meydan in the spring, showed a nice turn of speed to run them down. The plan had apparently been to go for the Prix Messidor, which he won last year, next, but he may have his sights raised now that he's already got another Group 3 under his belt.
Moonwalk In Paris(FR), seeking a four-timer, finished well from off the pace but couldn't seriously threaten the winner. He's a good marker for the form.
Evaporation(FR) could have done without the ground drying out as much as it had.
Fury, up in grade, didn't get the clearest of runs inside the final 2f.

DORTMUND (R-H)
Sunday, June 17

OFFICIAL GOING: Turf: good

3206a GROSSER PREIS DER WIRTSCHAFT (GROUP 3) (3YO+) (TURF) 1m 2f
4:10 (4:20) 3-Y-0+
£26,666 (£9,166; £4,583; £2,500; £1,666; £1,250)

RPR

1 **All Shamar**[42] 1900 3-8-6 0 ow1 AStarke 3 114
(W Hickst, Germany) *trckd ldr in 2nd on outer: led gng wl over 3f out: rdn over 2 1/2f out: kpt on wl u.p to maintain advantage ins fnl 2f: comf* **17/10**[2]

2 3 1/2 **Theo Danon (GER)**[35] 2106 4-9-5 0 FilipMinarik 2 109
(P Schiergen, Germany) *hld up in last pair: rdn to improve over 3f out: effrt to chal over 2f out: outpcd by wnr ins fnl 1 1/2f: kpt on* **131/10**

3 1/2 **Russian Tango (GER)**[28] 2322 5-9-5 0 THellier 5 108
(A Wohler, Germany) *midfield on outer: rdn over 3f out: effrt to chal over 2f out: outpcd over 1 1/2f out: plugged on to go 3rd cl home* **73/10**

4 3/4 **Scalo**[329] 4374 5-9-3 0 EPedroza 6 105
(A Wohler, Germany) *hld up in last: rdn to improve over 3f out: kpt on one pce ins fnl 2f: no ex and ct for 3rd cl home* **7/10**[1]

5 2 1/2 **Perfect Son**[8] 5-9-3 0 EFrank 4 100
(C Zeitz, Germany) *led: rdn and hdd over 3f out: no ex and btn over 1 1/2f out: fdd* **182/10**

6 13 **Tesey**[28] 2322 4-9-3 0 DPorcu 1 74
(M G Mintchev, Germany) *midfield on outer: lost pl over 3 1/2f out: rdn and outpcd in rr on turn into st: sn btn: t.o* **66/10**[3]

2m 6.09s (126.09)
WFA 3 from 4yo+ 12lb 6 Ran SP% **133.4**
WIN (incl. 10 euro stake): 27. PLACES: 18, 45. SF: 477.
Owner Stall Pregel **Bred** D R Tucker **Trained** Germany

NIORT
Sunday, June 17

OFFICIAL GOING: Turf: good

3207a PRIX DES PMU (PX CHEVAL LIBERTE) (CONDITIONS) (4YO+ FILLIES & MARES) (TURF) 1m 3f
4:45 (12:00) 4-Y-0+ **£2,916** (£1,166; £875; £583; £291)

RPR

1 **Paradise Tree (IRE)** 4-8-10 0 EnzoCorallo[(6)] 2 79
(P Sogorb, France) **17/10**[1]

2 1 **Sanisa (FR)**[119] 4-9-6 0 (b) AnthonyBernard 4 81
(J Boisnard, France) **2/1**[2]

3 2 1/2 **Mapenzi (FR)** 4-8-4 0 AntoineWerle[(7)] 5 68
(H-A Pantall, France) **73/10**

4 nk **Come On Mate (FR)**[12] 4-8-11 0 StephaneBreux 3 67
(E J O'Neill, France) **13/2**[3]

5 1 **Dundrum Dancer (IRE)**[7] 6599 5-8-9 0 AdrienFouassier 7 63
(Alex Hales) *chsd ldrs: qcknd to have ev ch 1 1/2f out: sn rdn and no ex: fdd fnl 150yds* **186/10**

6 4 **Lady Sol (FR)**[216] 7-9-0 0 SebastienCastellier 6 61
(F Monnier, France) **104/10**

F **Thisbe Des Sorinieres (FR)**[1092] 7-8-2 0 (p) ChristopherGrosbois[(7)] 1
(T Poche, France) **178/10**

2m 21.22s (141.22) 7 Ran SP% **114.9**
PARI-MUTUEL (all including 1 euro stakes): WIN 2.70; PLACE 1.80, 2.40; SHOW (1-2-3) 2.20, 2.10, 2.40; SF 7.20.
Owner Marquesa De Moratalla **Bred** Mise De Moratalla **Trained** France

2747 CARLISLE (R-H)
Monday, June 18

OFFICIAL GOING: Good to soft (soft in places; 6.9)
Old Stable bend moved out 2yds adding about 3yds to races of 7f and further.
Wind: Fresh, half against Weather: Cloudy, bright

3208 BOOK YOUR CONFERENCE AT CARLISLE RACECOURSE MAIDEN AUCTION STKS 5f 193y
2:15 (2:15) (Class 5) 2-Y-0 **£2,264** (£673; £336; £168) **Stalls** Low

Form RPR

1 **Elle Rebelle** 2-8-4 0 PaulQuinn 5 66+
(Mark Brisbourne) *dwlt: hld up: effrt whn nt clr run and swtchd rt over 2f out: hdwy to ld ent fnl f: kpt on strly* **14/1**

3 2 nk **Lady Margaeux (IRE)**[13] 2790 2-8-8 0 JoeFanning 11 69+
(David O'Meara) *cl up: rdn to ld over 1f out: hdd ent fnl f: edgd rt: rallied: kpt on fin* **15/8**[1]

0 3 1 **Team Challenge**[44] 1842 2-8-9 0 DavidAllan 13 67
(Tim Easterby) *dwlt: hld up: rdn over 2f out: hdwy over 1f out: kpt on: nrst fin* **12/1**

4 1 **Elusive Heir (IRE)** 2-9-2 0 TomEaves 7 71
(Bryan Smart) *prom on outside: effrt over 2f out: edgd lft over 1f out: kpt on same pce ins fnl f* **13/2**[3]

0 5 1/2 **Loki's Strike**[30] 2261 2-8-8 0 MichaelMetcalfe[(3)] 9 64
(Mrs K Burke) *t.k.h: hld up in tch on outside: effrt and rdn over 1f out: no imp ins fnl f* **8/1**

6 2 1/4 **Naughtybychoice** 2-8-11 0 PaulMulrennan 3 58+
(Ollie Pears) *noisy and green in preliminaries: hld up: rdn along over 2f out: styd on fnl f: nvr able to chal* **9/1**

6 7 hd **Bernardino**[11] 2837 2-8-9 0 GrahamGibbons 8 55
(David Barron) *cl up: led over 2f out to over 1f out: wknd ins fnl f* **11/2**[2]

8 1 1/4 **Senora Lobo (IRE)** 2-8-4 0 PatrickMathers 2 46+
(Lisa Williamson) *trckd ldrs: nt clr run and swtchd lft over 2f out: sn rdn: wknd ins fnl f* **66/1**

9 1 3/4 **Vision Of Judgment** 2-8-9 0 GrahamLee 12 46+
(Ollie Pears) *towards rr: drvn along over 2f out: nvr on terms* **33/1**

0 10 1 1/4 **Hi Candy (IRE)**[7] 2977 2-8-8 0 TonyHamilton 10 41+
(Ben Haslam) *rrd as stalls opened: wl bhd: sme hdwy over 1f out: nvr on terms* **100/1**

11 hd **Cromwell Rose (IRE)** 2-8-5 0 ow1 AndrewElliott 4 37
(John Weymes) *t.k.h: mde most to over 2f out: wknd over 1f out* **33/1**

12 3 1/4 **Pink Cadillac (IRE)** 2-8-6 0 JamesSullivan 1 29
(Ben Haslam) *sn pushed along in midfield: struggling over 2f out: sn wknd* **20/1**

05 13 11 **Look Forward (IRE)**[9] 2923 2-8-4 0 DuranFentiman 6
(Tim Easterby) *trckd ldrs: rdn along over 3f out: wknd appr 2f out* **20/1**

1m 17.43s (3.73) **Going Correction** +0.375s/f (Good) 13 Ran SP% **116.9**
Speed ratings (Par 93): **90,89,88,86,86 83,83,81,79,77 77,72,58**
toteswingers:1&2:£10.00, 2&3:£6.10, 1&3:£40.30 CSF £37.24 TOTE £24.60: £5.10, £1.60, £3.70; EX 84.30.
Owner The Bourne Connection **Bred** Mette Campbell-Andenaes **Trained** Great Ness, Shropshire
■ Stewards' Enquiry : Patrick Mathers one-day ban: careless riding (Jul 2)

FOCUS
Only a modest juvenile maiden but it was run at a decent pace.

NOTEBOOK

Elle Rebelle fended off the strong late challenge of the favourite. The daughter of Cockney Rebel cost only 3,500gns as a yearling and it remains to be seen how much this form is worth. However, she showed more than enough on this debut effort to suggest she's got a future and certainly didn't shirk the issue. Her trainer isn't renowned for his juvenile winners and she is entitled to sharpen up considerably for this experience. She ought to have no problem getting 7f before the end of the season. (op 20-1 tchd 22-1)

Lady Margaeux(IRE) was relatively easy to back in the ring but she ran with credit, despite coming up just short. She had stayed on in eyecatching fashion at Redcar on her debut and ran a similar race here. She didn't have the best of trips, but is only limited on what she's shown thus far. She looks the type to do better in low-grade nurseries. (op 11-8)

Team Challenge ran a pleasing race and showed no ill-effects from a unruly debut effort at Doncaster last month. He made ground down the wide outside and is another that should come on for this experience. (op 14-1 tchd 16-1)

Elusive Heir(IRE) ◆ made decent late gains and could well be the one to take out of this. He raced four wide throughout, but should be well up to winning a weak maiden before too long. (tchd 7-1)

Bernardino Official explanation: trainer's rep said gelding was struck into

Hi Candy(IRE) completely blew the start and was never able to get competitive. (op 80-1)

3209 WATCH RACING UK ON SKY 432 H'CAP (DIV I) 5f 193y

2:45 (2:45) (Class 6) (0-60,66) 3-Y-0+ **£1,704** (£503; £251) **Stalls** Low

Form RPR

4011 **1** **Pitkin**[7] 2981 4-10-4 **66** 6ex....(b) PaulMulrennan 6 73+
(Michael Easterby) *t.k.h: mde all: rdn over 1f out: styd on wl fnl f* **5/2**[1]

0600 **2** *2* **Dolly Royal (IRE)**[9] 2922 7-8-12 **46** oh1....(p) RobertWinston 9 46+
(Robert Johnson) *hld up: pushed along 1/2-way: effrt whn nt clr run over 1f out and ins fnl f: swtchd lft and styd on to chse wnr nr fin: no imp* **10/1**

3000 **3** *1* **Red Scintilla**[4] 3075 5-9-1 **49**....(p) GrahamLee 10 46
(Nigel Tinkler) *trckd ldrs: effrt and rdn 2f out: kpt on same pce ins fnl f* **12/1**

-000 **4** *nk* **Cross Of Lorraine (IRE)**[21] 2538 9-9-10 **58**....(p) TonyHamilton 3 54
(Chris Grant) *prom: effrt over 1f out: chsd wnr ins fnl f: no ex and lost two pls towards fin* **28/1**

3045 **5** *2 1/4* **Soopacal (IRE)**[65] 1383 7-9-5 **56**.... PaulPickard(3) 1 45
(Brian Ellison) *sn rdn to chse wnr: drvn over 2f out: lost 2nd and no ex ins fnl f* **11/2**

3524 **6** *2 1/4* **Hellbender (IRE)**[5] 3026 6-9-7 **60**.... NeilFarley(5) 8 42
(George Foster) *hld up in tch: rdn over 2f out: edgd lft: no imp over 1f out* **7/2**[2]

3-00 **7** *nk* **Spoken Words**[21] 2540 3-8-10 **51**.... AndrewElliott 5 32
(Hugh McWilliams) *hld up: rdn along over 2f out: nvr able to chal* **20/1**

0442 **8** *hd* **Drumpellier (IRE)**[5] 3020 5-8-12 **46**....(p) DanielTudhope 2 26
(Simon West) *t.k.h: hld up towards rr: drvn over 2f out: nvr able to chal* **4/1**[3]

00-0 **9** *11* **True Bond**[28] 2336 3-8-12 **56**....(v) DaleSwift(3) 7
(Geoffrey Oldroyd) *dwlt: bhd and sn drvn along: struggling fr 1/2-way* **20/1**

1m 15.78s (2.08) **Going Correction** +0.375s/f (Good)
WFA 3 from 4yo+ 7lb **9** Ran SP% **115.9**
Speed ratings (Par 101): **101,98,97,96,93 90,90,89,75**
toteswingers:1&2:£6.00, 2&3:£8.40, 1&3:£7.60 CSF £27.91 CT £255.85 TOTE £3.40: £1.20, £3.60, £3.30; EX 29.70.
Owner Steve Hull **Bred** New Mill Farm Stud **Trained** Sheriff Hutton, N Yorks

FOCUS
A poor handicap, but the fastest of the three races over C&D.

3210 WATCH RACING UK ON SKY 432 H'CAP (DIV II) 5f 193y

3:15 (3:15) (Class 6) (0-60,60) 3-Y-0+ **£1,704** (£503; £251) **Stalls** Low

Form RPR

134 **1** **Amazing Win (IRE)**[3] 3103 4-9-12 **60**.... TonyCulhane 8 68
(Mick Channon) *trckd ldrs gng wl: rdn to ld over 1f out: hld on wl fnl f* **2/1**[1]

-503 **2** *1/2* **Bartley**[4] 3075 3-9-5 **60**....(p) TomEaves 2 64
(Bryan Smart) *dwlt: bhd and sn drvn along: hdwy on outside over 1f out: edgd rt and chsd wnr ins fnl f: kpt on: hld towards fin* **3/1**[2]

0536 **3** *1 1/2* **Insolenceofoffice (IRE)**[14] 2748 4-9-6 **59**....(p) LMcNiff(5) 4 61
(Richard Ford) *cl up: rdn over 2f out: kpt on same pce ins fnl f* **5/1**[3]

6-00 **4** *1 1/2* **Misshollygolightly**[35] 2121 4-8-12 **46** oh1.... DuranFentiman 6 43
(Brian Baugh) *chsd ldng gp: effrt and rdn over 2f out: kpt on same pce fnl f* **50/1**

/0-3 **5** *3/4* **Ursus**[10] 2878 7-9-1 **49**....(p) PaddyAspell 5 43
(Christopher Wilson) *trckd ldrs: drvn and outpcd wl over 1f out: kpt on fnl f: no imp* **10/1**

03-0 **6** *1 1/2* **Dylan's Dream (IRE)**[66] 1359 3-8-11 **52**.... DavidAllan 1 40
(Tim Easterby) *chsd ldng gp: drvn and outpcd 1/2-way: sme late hdwy: nvr on terms* **12/1**

0-54 **7** *3/4* **Rutterkin (USA)**[10] 2878 4-9-3 **58**.... MatthewHopkins(7) 9 45
(Alan Berry) *bhd: rdn over 2f out: nvr able to chal* **12/1**

-005 **8** *1* **Lady By Red (IRE)**[13] 2796 4-8-12 **46** oh1.... DanielTudhope 7 30
(David Thompson) *taken early to post: t.k.h: led to over 1f out: wknd ins fnl f* **18/1**

4-00 **9** *1 1/2* **Wotatomboy**[5] 3020 6-9-1 **49**....(v) RobertWinston 3 28
(Richard Whitaker) *trckd ldrs: rdn along over 2f out: wknd over 1f out* **11/1**

1m 16.61s (2.91) **Going Correction** +0.375s/f (Good)
WFA 3 from 4yo+ 7lb **9** Ran SP% **115.0**
Speed ratings (Par 101): **95,94,92,90,89 87,86,85,83**
toteswingers:1&2:£2.00, 2&3:£4.20, 1&3:£2.90 CSF £7.87 CT £25.32 TOTE £2.80: £1.60, £1.50, £1.10; EX 9.10.
Owner Mrs Theresa Burns **Bred** J Repard **Trained** West Ilsley, Berks

FOCUS
The second division of this handicap didn't look as strong as the first leg.

3211 SCOTT TRAWLERS LTD H'CAP (BETFAIR SPRINT FLAT SERIES QUALIFIER) 5f

3:45 (3:45) (Class 5) (0-70,70) 3-Y-0+ **£3,234** (£962; £481; £240) **Stalls** Low

Form RPR

0-33 **1** **Red Roar (IRE)**[52] 1638 5-9-7 **65**.... GrahamLee 7 74
(Alan Berry) *in tch: pushed along 1/2-way: hdwy to ld ins fnl f: rdn out* **10/3**[2]

0322 **2** *1* **Fama Mac**[29] 2314 5-8-10 **54**.... JamesSullivan 5 59
(Neville Bycroft) *chsd ldrs: drvn along fr 1/2-way: chsd wnr last 100yds: kpt on towards fin* **5/2**[1]

5050 **3** *2 1/4* **Absa Lutte (IRE)**[23] 2475 9-9-9 **67**.... RobertHavlin 8 64
(Michael Mullineaux) *s.i.s: bhd and outpcd: no imp tl styd on wl last 150yds: nvr rchd ldrs* **20/1**

2420 **4** *nk* **Boucher Garcon (IRE)**[27] 2377 4-9-2 **65**.... NeilFarley(5) 2 61
(Declan Carroll) *led at str gallop: rdn over 2f out: hdd ins fnl f: sn no ex* **7/2**[3]

0006 **5** *1/2* **Another Citizen (IRE)**[14] 2750 4-9-7 **65**....(b) DavidAllan 9 59
(Tim Easterby) *disp ld: rdn over 2f out: no ex ins fnl f* **9/1**

0631 **6** *2 1/2* **Pivotal Prospect**[31] 2244 4-9-0 **63**.... ShaneBKelly(5) 1 48
(Tracy Waggott) *chsd ldrs: rdn along 1/2-way: wknd over 1f out: eased whn btn ins fnl f* **4/1**

1m 3.26s (2.46) **Going Correction** +0.375s/f (Good)
WFA 3 from 4yo+ 6lb **6** Ran SP% **108.6**
Speed ratings (Par 103): **95,93,89,89,88 84**
toteswingers:1&2:£2.00, 2&3:£5.40, 1&3:£6.50 CSF £11.25 CT £120.03 TOTE £4.20: £1.40, £1.90; EX 10.00.
Owner Sporting Kings **Bred** Tally-Ho Stud **Trained** Cockerham, Lancs

FOCUS
A fair sprint handicap, run at the expected strong pace.

Pivotal Prospect Official explanation: jockey said filly became unbalanced approaching final furlong and collided with the rail.

3212 ULTIMATE LADIES NIGHT ON 6TH AUGUST H'CAP 1m 3f 107y

4:15 (4:15) (Class 5) (0-70,68) 3-Y-0 **£2,264** (£673; £336; £168) **Stalls** High

Form RPR

6312 **1** **Lady Kashaan (IRE)**[19] 2605 3-8-12 **59**.... AndrewElliott 5 74+
(Alan Swinbank) *t.k.h: hld up in tch: hdwy to ld wl over 2f out: pushed clr: readily* **11/4**[1]

3234 **2** *8* **Rosie's Lady (IRE)**[10] 2885 3-8-9 **56** ow1.... GrahamLee 4 58
(David O'Meara) *trckd ldr: rdn and led briefly 3f out: rdn: edgd rt and no ch w wnr fr 2f out* **13/2**

4-06 **3** *4* **Dr Irv**[20] 2589 3-8-7 **54**.... KellyHarrison 3 49
(Kate Walton) *t.k.h: hld up: hdwy on outside 4f out: rdn and edgd rt over 2f out: sn no imp* **20/1**

05-1 **4** *1 3/4* **Abundantly**[20] 2578 3-9-2 **63**.... RobertHavlin 2 55
(Hughie Morrison) *dwlt: t.k.h: hld up on ins: effrt and swtchd rt over 2f out: sn no imp* **7/2**[3]

-102 **5** *5* **Dorry K (IRE)**[10] 2885 3-9-7 **68**.... GrahamGibbons 1 52
(David Barron) *chsd ldrs tl wknd fr 3f out* **3/1**[2]

042 **6** *13* **Gangsterbanksters (FR)**[31] 2240 3-9-6 **67**.... RobertWinston 6 28
(Mrs K Burke) *bhd on outside: detached after 3f: rdn over 4f out: n.d* **12/1**

-304 **7** *4 1/2* **Lost Highway (IRE)**[19] 2605 3-8-11 **58**....(b[1]) JoeFanning 7 12
(Mark Johnston) *led to 3f out: sn rdn and wknd* **11/1**

0-34 **8** *8* **Greyhope**[17] 2671 3-8-12 **59**.... TomEaves 8
(Lucinda Russell) *trckd ldrs tl rdn and wknd qckly over 3f out* **33/1**

2m 26.83s (3.73) **Going Correction** +0.30s/f (Good) **8** Ran SP% **111.0**
Speed ratings (Par 99): **98,92,89,88,84 74,71,65**
toteswingers:1&2:£3.20, 2&3:£13.60, 1&3:£9.60 CSF £19.73 CT £278.67 TOTE £3.60: £1.60, £2.00, £5.40; EX 15.40.
Owner G Brogan **Bred** Corduff Stud Ltd & J Corcoran **Trained** Melsonby, N Yorks

FOCUS
Only a fair handicap but an emphatic winner.

Dorry K(IRE) Official explanation: trainer's rep had no explanation for the poor form shown.

3213 CUMWHINTON H'CAP (BETFAIR 10 FURLONG FLAT SERIES QUALIFIER) 1m 1f 61y

4:45 (4:46) (Class 5) (0-70,70) 4-Y-0+ **£3,234** (£962; £481; £240) **Stalls** Low

Form RPR

-506 **1** **Watts Up Son**[21] 2535 4-8-13 **69**....(bt) JasonHart(7) 8 79
(Declan Carroll) *taken early to post: enterprisingly rdn: led at decent gallop and sn clr: rdn over 2f out: styd on wl fnl f* **8/1**[3]

3400 **2** *1 1/4* **Painted Tail (IRE)**[21] 2539 5-9-1 **64**.... RobertWinston 7 71
(Alan Swinbank) *prom: effrt and rdn over 2f out: chsd wnr over 1f out: kpt on fnl f: nt gng pce to chal* **9/2**[1]

2005 **3** *3 3/4* **Goodness**[13] 2792 4-9-2 **65**....(v) DanielTudhope 1 64
(David O'Meara) *chsd ldrs: effrt and wnt 2nd wl over 2f out: one pce fr over 1f out* **9/1**

-206 **4** *1/2* **Edas**[3] 3116 10-8-9 **58**.... AdrianNicholls 6 56
(Thomas Cuthbert) *hld up: hdwy on outside over 2f out: rdn and hung rt over 1f out: no imp ins fnl f* **20/1**

-613 **5** *2* **Call Of Duty (IRE)**[17] 2661 7-8-8 **62**.... ShaneBKelly(5) 2 56
(Dianne Sayer) *dwlt: midfield on ins: drvn along over 3f out: kpt on fnl 2f: no imp* **10/1**

-040 **6** *3/4* **Botham (USA)**[18] 2619 8-9-6 **69**.... GrahamLee 9 61
(Jim Goldie) *hld up towards rr: rdn over 3f out: no imp fr 2f out* **10/1**

0-50 **7** *1 1/2* **High Resolution**[16] 2720 5-9-3 **66**.... JamesSullivan 10 55
(Linda Perratt) *s.i.s: hld up: pushed along over 2f out: nvr on terms* **22/1**

-301 **8** *1 3/4* **Osgood**[10] 2899 5-9-7 **70**.... TonyCulhane 5 55
(Mick Channon) *hld up: rdn whn n.m.r briefly 3f out: sn outpcd* **9/2**[1]

0406 **9** *2 1/4* **Smart Step**[9] 2909 4-9-4 **67**.... JoeFanning 4 47
(Mark Johnston) *chsd wnr: rdn over 3f out: wknd over 2f out* **6/1**[2]

3110 **10** *nse* **Thackeray**[23] 2491 5-9-4 **67**.... KellyHarrison 11 47
(Chris Fairhurst) *s.i.s: bhd and sn pushed along: drvn over 3f out: nvr on terms* **6/1**[2]

360/ **11** *18* **Aggravation**[181] 6547 10-8-10 **59**.... TonyHamilton 3
(Chris Grant) *prom tl rdn and wknd over 2f out* **50/1**

1m 59.48s (1.88) **Going Correction** +0.30s/f (Good) **11** Ran SP% **115.3**
Speed ratings (Par 103): **103,101,98,98,96 95,94,92,90,90 74**
toteswingers:1&2:£9.30, 2&3:£9.40, 1&3:£14.00 CSF £42.01 CT £333.23 TOTE £10.50: £2.80, £2.00, £4.40; EX 53.00.
Owner L Ibbotson, D Watts & J Syme **Bred** West Dereham Abbey Stud **Trained** Sledmere, E Yorks

FOCUS
An interesting, if only fair handicap, run at a strong pace.

Edas Official explanation: jockey said gelding hung right

Osgood Official explanation: jockey said gelding ran flat

3214 JOIN NOW AT REWARDS4RACING.COM FILLIES' H'CAP 6f 192y

5:15 (5:15) (Class 4) (0-80,74) 3-Y-0 **£4,075** (£1,212; £606; £303) **Stalls** Low

Form RPR

-113 **1** **Dutch Rose (IRE)**[13] 2795 3-9-5 **72**.... DanielTudhope 8 91
(David O'Meara) *mde all: rdn clr 3f out: kpt on wl fnl f* **5/2**[1]

-136 **2** *1 3/4* **Magic Destiny**[10] 2883 3-9-0 **70**.... MichaelMetcalfe(3) 7 84
(Mrs K Burke) *prom: hdwy to chse wnr 2f out: sn rdn and edgd rt: kpt on fnl f: hld towards fin* **3/1**[2]

5-31 **3** *7* **Annie Walker (IRE)**[16] 2689 3-9-4 **71**.... AdrianNicholls 3 66
(David Nicholls) *trckd ldrs: effrt and edgd lft over 2f out: outpcd wl over 1f out* **11/2**[3]

20-0 **4** ½ **Parisian Princess (IRE)**[14] 2768 3-9-3 **70** RobertHavlin 1 64
(Hughie Morrison) *hld up in tch: rdn and effrt on outside wl over 2f out: sn no imp* **13/2**

3-60 **5** 9 **Alabanda (IRE)**[12] 2824 3-8-10 **63** DuranFentiman 5 32
(Tim Easterby) *hld up: drvn along over 3f out: sn outpcd: nvr able to chal* **10/1**

21 **6** 6 **Liliargh (IRE)**[28] 2335 3-9-7 **74** TomEaves 4 27
(Ben Haslam) *chsd wnr tl rdn and wknd over 2f out* **6/1**

-350 **7** 5 **Serene Oasis (IRE)**[25] 2408 3-9-3 **70** TonyCulhane 6
(Mick Channon) *t.k.h to post: hld up: struggling over 3f out: sn btn* **14/1**

4050 **8** 12 **Barbarella Blue (IRE)**[11] 2840 3-7-11 **57** MatthewHopkins(7) 2
(Alan Berry) *s.i.s: hld up: struggling over 3f out: sn wknd* **66/1**

1m 28.32s (1.22) **Going Correction** +0.30s/f (Good) **8** Ran SP% **113.8**
Speed ratings (Par 98): **105,103,95,94,84 77,71,57**
toteswingers:1&2:£3.10, 2&3:£4.40, 1&3:£2.40 CSF £10.03 CT £36.31 TOTE £3.80: £1.20, £1.30, £1.80; EX 11.50.
Owner Favourites Racing XXIV **Bred** Joseph Kennedy **Trained** Nawton, N Yorks

FOCUS
A fairly competitive fillies' handicap on paper.
Liliargh(IRE) Official explanation: trainer had no explanation for the poor form shown

3215 BELL & PLATE DAY NEXT WEDNESDAY H'CAP 7f 200y
5:45 (5:45) (Class 5) (0-70,70) 4-Y-0+ **£2,264** (£673; £336; £168) **Stalls** Low

Form RPR

1345 **1** **Copperwood**[10] 2879 7-9-4 **67** JoeFanning 6 79
(Mark Johnston) *mde all: rdn and qcknd over 1f out: hld on wl fnl f* **4/1**[2]

5144 **2** 1 ¼ **Indian Giver**[11] 2840 4-8-7 **59** ow1 PaulPickard(3) 4 68
(Hugh McWilliams) *hld up in tch: hdwy on outside over 2f out: chsd wnr and edgd rt over 1f out: kpt on and no imp towards fin* **5/1**[3]

-000 **3** 4 ½ **Mangham (IRE)**[9] 2922 7-8-3 **57** (p) NeilFarley(5) 3 56
(George Foster) *s.i.s: t.k.h: hld up on ins: effrt 2f out: kpt on fnl f: no imp* **16/1**

2306 **4** 2 ½ **Master Of Dance (IRE)**[9] 2922 5-9-4 **67** (p) TomEaves 2 60
(Keith Dalgleish) *in tch: drvn and outpcd over 2f out: r.o fnl f: nvr able to chal* **11/2**

3-06 **5** 1 ¼ **Strong Man**[37] 2094 4-9-0 **63** (b) PaddyAspell 7 53
(Michael Easterby) *t.k.h: chsd wnr to over 1f out: edgd rt and sn btn* **8/1**

46-6 **6** 3 ¼ **Izzet**[16] 2692 4-8-4 **53** ow1 PatrickMathers 8 36
(Ron Barr) *hld up in tch on outside: effrt and rdn over 2f out: wknd over 1f out* **5/1**[3]

/1-5 **7** 3 ¾ **Ykikamoocow**[19] 2598 6-9-7 **70** DanielTudhope 1 44
(Geoffrey Harker) *t.k.h: trckd ldrs: rdn over 2f out: sn btn: eased whn no ch fnl f* **7/2**[1]

0-06 **8** 5 **Ellies Image**[21] 2549 5-8-11 **60** DuranFentiman 9 23
(Brian Baugh) *s.i.s: hld up: rdn along 3f out: sn n.d* **16/1**

544- **9** 1 **Purkab**[266] 6415 4-8-2 **51** oh2 JamesSullivan 5 11
(Jim Goldie) *hld up: struggling over 3f out: sn btn* **25/1**

10 1 ½ **De Lesseps (USA)**[243] 4-8-11 **60** GrahamLee 10 17
(Alan Berry) *t.k.h: cl up tl rdn and wknd fr 3f out* **66/1**

1m 43.26s (3.26) **Going Correction** +0.30s/f (Good) **10** Ran SP% **119.2**
Speed ratings (Par 103): **95,93,89,86,85 82,78,73,72,71**
toteswingers:1&2:£5.70, 2&3:£12.00, 1&3:£18.90 CSF £25.02 CT £293.47 TOTE £4.10: £1.70, £1.70, £6.50; EX 25.20.
Owner Always Trying Partnership VIII (E) **Bred** Hertford Offset Press **Trained** Middleham Moor, N Yorks

FOCUS
A competitive if modest handicap, run at a steady pace.
Ykikamoocow Official explanation: jockey said mare hung left
T/Plt: £85.70 to a £1 stake. Pool of £63,788.54 - 543.22 winning tickets. T/Qpdt: £16.00 to a £1 stake. Pool of £5,258.62 - 241.94 winning tickets. RY

1253 WARWICK (L-H)
Monday, June 18

OFFICIAL GOING: Soft (heavy in places in the back straight)
Wind: half behind Weather: sunny

3216 JOCKEY CLUB CATERING AMATEUR RIDERS' H'CAP 1m 4f 134y
6:25 (6:25) (Class 6) (0-60,59) 4-Y-0+ **£1,646** (£506; £253) **Stalls** Low

Form RPR

0/13 **1** **Passato (GER)**[10] 2872 8-10-2 **54** (t) MrJAPonting(7) 6 69
(Jo Davis) *pressed ldr tl led 7f out: pressed on and drew clr w rival 3f out: kpt on wl and in n.d ins fnl f* **10/3**[2]

-341 **2** 7 **The Ducking Stool**[13] 2804 5-10-8 **53** MrRBirkett 4 61
(Julia Feilden) *reluctant to leave paddock: cl up: chsd wnr 6f out: rdn and drew clr w wnr 3f out: no ex fnl f and readily brushed aside* **3/1**[1]

50/0 **3** 7 **Adorabella (IRE)**[11] 2851 9-10-2 **50** (t) MissSallyRandell(3) 8 43
(Paul Rich) *in tch: hdwy to chse ldng pair 4f out: rdn and no imp fnl 2f: hld on for modest 3rd* **16/1**

4200 **4** ½ **Polly Holder (IRE)**[28] 2348 4-10-4 **56** (p) MrsRWilson(7) 1 49
(Paul D'Arcy) *wl in rr early: urged along 4f out: no imp and wl btn 8th 2f out: plugged on past toiling rivals ins fnl f* **9/1**

550 **5** 1 ¾ **Dzesmin (POL)**[17] 2669 10-10-3 **55** (p) MrsAGuest(7) 10 45
(Richard Guest) *v slow away and in rr: hdwy over 5f out: effrt over 3f out: rdn along and no imp fnl 2f* **14/1**

5-01 **6** 2 ½ **William's Way**[35] 2137 10-10-3 **51** (t) MrCMartin(3) 3 37
(Ian Wood) *in rr: tk clsr order 6f out: rdn along 4f out: unable qck fnl 3f* **6/1**[3]

0/6- **7** nk **Plug In Baby**[229] 6438 4-10-5 **50** MrRGHenderson 2 35
(Nick Mitchell) *in tch: hdwy 6f out: pushed along 4f out: drvn and wknd over 2f out* **25/1**

2503 **8** 12 **Sacco D'Oro**[9] 2915 6-10-1 **49** (b) MissMMullineaux(3) 9 16
(Michael Mullineaux) *wl in rr: last and rdn 6f out: sn no hope: t.o* **8/1**

2413 **9** 10 **Bold Adventure**[87] 1011 8-10-7 **55** MrPShea(3) 5
(Willie Musson) *in tch: urged along 5f out: pushed along and struggling 3f out: brought wd into st and sn t.o* **11/1**

500- **10** 60 **Runaway Tiger (IRE)**[364] 3233 4-10-3 **55** MissLucySaunders(7) 11
(Paul D'Arcy) *unruly bef s: led: hdd 7f out: wknd and dropped away qckly 6f out: sn hopelessly t.o* **18/1**

2m 53.74s (9.14) **Going Correction** +0.35s/f (Good) **10** Ran SP% **113.5**
Speed ratings (Par 101): **85,80,76,76,75 73,73,65,59,22**
Tote Swingers: 1&2 £1.80, 1&3 £30.10, 2&3 £14.70 CSF £13.32 CT £135.22 TOTE £5.00: £1.90, £1.20, £5.20; EX 13.70.
Owner P Ponting **Bred** Gestut Hof Ittlingen **Trained** East Garston, Berks

FOCUS
They were soon strung out in this low-grade amateur riders' handicap, but few got into it from off the pace.

3217 HARPER FIELDS CARE HOME - BALSALL COMMON MEDIAN AUCTION MAIDEN STKS 5f
6:55 (6:56) (Class 5) 2-Y-0 **£2,264** (£673; £336; £168) **Stalls** Low

Form RPR

6 **1** **Knight Charm**[31] 2231 2-9-3 0 JohnFahy 5 75+
(Eve Johnson Houghton) *in tch: hdwy 2f out: arrived on bit over 1f out: bmpd rival and led 1f out: sn hanging lft: drew clr and continued to r awkwardly* **5/2**[2]

6 **2** 2 ¼ **Hot Secret**[13] 2783 2-8-12 0 [1] JimmyFortune 2 60+
(Andrew Balding) *hld up: urged along and hdwy 2f out: rdn and ev ch over 1f out: drvn and nt pce of wnr fnl 100yds* **9/2**[3]

3 2 ½ **Avec Rose** 2-8-12 0 PaulHanagan 1 52
(Richard Fahey) *niggled along early: in tch: pushed along over 2f out: rdn and short of room over 1f out: sn btn and nt hrd pushed: rn green: do bttr* **10/11**[1]

0 **4** 1 ¾ **Baltic Prince (IRE)**[17] 2662 2-9-3 0 CathyGannon 3 50
(Paul Green) *led: pushed along 2f out: hanging rt and hdd and short of room 1f out: sn wknd* **33/1**

0 **5** 2 ½ **Constant Dream**[13] 2783 2-8-12 0 FrannyNorton 4 36
(James Given) *in tch: dropped last 3f out: sn struggling and btn* **33/1**

6 **6** 4 **Star Maid**[14] 2763 2-8-12 0 LukeMorris 7 21
(Tony Carroll) *chsd ldr: urged along over 2f out: drifted rt and wknd over 1f out* **100/1**

1m 3.24s (3.64) **Going Correction** +0.675s/f (Yiel) **6** Ran SP% **106.0**
Speed ratings (Par 93): **97,93,89,86,82 76**
Tote Swingers: 1&2 £1.50, 1&3 £1.10, 2&3 £1.60 CSF £12.01 TOTE £4.30: £1.70, £1.40; EX 11.00.
Owner Fairweather Friends **Bred** Michael E Broughton **Trained** Blewbury, Oxon

FOCUS
An ordinary juvenile maiden.

NOTEBOOK
Knight Charm travelled like a horse capable of taking higher rank and won with more in hand than the bare margin. He was hanging under pressure, still looking green, and could improve enough to take his chance in next month's Super Sprint. (op 9-4)
Hot Secret stepped up on her debut effort, the addition of a first-time hood helping. (op 7-2)
Avec Rose is bred for speed, her dam being a 5f winner, and reportedly came into this with a bit of a reputation, but she struggled to pick up sufficiently and was held when slightly hampered. She can improve on this and is well worth another chance on better ground. Official explanation: jockey said filly jumped the path about 1f out (op Evens tchd 11-10)

3218 AON HEWITT JUBILEE H'CAP 6f
7:25 (7:25) (Class 6) (0-65,64) 3-Y-0 **£1,704** (£503; £251) **Stalls** Low

Form RPR

2365 **1** **New Decade**[5] 3050 3-9-3 **60** LukeMorris 3 69
(Milton Bradley) *chsd ldr: led 4f out: rdn over 1f out: kpt on wl* **10/3**[2]

4210 **2** 2 ½ **Seventeen Seventy**[5] 3050 3-9-2 **59** AmirQuinn 10 60
(Alan Coogan) *t.k.h: cl up: chsd wnr over 2f out: drvn and ev ch ins fnl 2f: no ex fnl 100yds* **11/1**

6005 **3** 1 ¼ **Big Sylv (IRE)**[35] 2130 3-8-7 **50** LiamJones 4 49
(James Unett) *in tch on outer: pushed along over 2f out: drvn 1f out and unable qck: plugged on past btn rivals to take 3rd cl home* **18/1**

050 **4** 1 **Miserere Mei (IRE)**[15] 2730 3-8-2 **48** (e) DeclanCannon(3) 13 42
(Richard Guest) *midfield: hdwy on outer 3f out: rdn over 1f out: no imp ins fnl f* **33/1**

2000 **5** hd **First Fast Now (IRE)**[13] 2795 3-9-1 **58** SilvestreDeSousa 6 51
(Nigel Tinkler) *midfield: drvn 2f out: drifted rt 1f out and sn no imp* **8/1**

6522 **6** 1 ¾ **First Rebellion**[2] 3141 3-8-3 **46** FrannyNorton 1 36
(Tony Carroll) *unruly stalls and stmbld after a few strides: sn rcvrd and in tch on inner: rdn over 2f out: swtchd rt and lost pl over 1f out: eased and btn ins fnl f* **11/4**[1]

4002 **7** shd **Ambitious Boy**[11] 2862 3-9-4 **61** RussKennemore 8 48
(Reg Hollinshead) *in rr: pushed along over 2f out: sn toiling* **10/1**

6330 **8** nk **Lord Paget**[13] 2785 3-8-12 **62** (p) JackDuern(7) 12 48
(Reg Hollinshead) *in rr: rdn along over 3f out: drvn and no ex fnl 2f* **25/1**

4503 **9** 2 ½ **M J Woodward**[11] 2839 3-8-13 **56** CathyGannon 2 34
(Paul Green) *led tl hdd 4f out: drvn and sn lost pl: no ch fnl 2f* **6/1**[3]

0-60 **10** 6 **Sanad (IRE)**[27] 2375 3-9-6 **63** WilliamCarson 5 22
(Anthony Carson) *in rr: rdn 3f out: struggling and wl btn fnl 2f* **18/1**

-000 **11** 17 **Shamakat**[20] 2573 3-8-13 **56** PaulHanagan 9
(Rae Guest) *a in rr: struggling 3f out: sn floundering* **16/1**

1m 16.41s (4.61) **Going Correction** +0.675s/f (Yiel) **11** Ran SP% **115.8**
Speed ratings (Par 97): **96,92,91,89,89 87,86,86,83,75 52**
Tote Swingers: 1&2 £14.70, 2&3 £36.00 CSF £39.41 CT £584.57 TOTE £5.10: £1.70, £4.90, £7.40; EX 48.90.
Owner Darren Hudson-Wood **Bred** Cheveley Park Stud Ltd **Trained** Sedbury, Gloucs
■ Stewards' Enquiry : Franny Norton caution: careless riding.

FOCUS
The early pace appeared quite ordinary and few got into the race.
First Rebellion Official explanation: jockey said gelding stumbled on leaving stalls
Ambitious Boy Official explanation: trainer's rep said gelding was unsuited by the soft (heavy in places) ground

3219 VOUTE SALES WARWICKSHIRE OAKS STKS (LISTED RACE) (F&M) 1m 2f 188y
7:55 (7:55) (Class 1) 4-Y-0+
£18,714 (£7,095; £3,550; £1,768; £887; £445) **Stalls** Low

Form RPR

2-62 **1** **Set To Music (IRE)**[16] 2711 4-8-12 105 JamieSpencer 1 105
(Michael Bell) *chsd ldr: pushed along to ld over 1f out: sn forged clr: rdn out and in n.d fnl 150yds* **6/4**[1]

-132 **2** 3 ¾ **Dragonera**[10] 2884 4-8-12 89 PaulMulrennan 2 98
(Ed Dunlop) *led: pushed along over 2f out: drvn and hdd over 1f out: sn no ch w easy wnr* **8/1**[3]

40-2 **3** 1 ¼ **Mid Mon Lady (IRE)**[14] 2773 7-8-12 100 LukeMorris 8 96
(Sir Mark Prescott Bt) *hld up: hdwy on outer over 2f out: swtchd lft over 1f out: plugged on one pce fnl f* **7/2**[2]

00-0 **4** 4 ½ **Rumh (GER)**[17] 2655 4-8-12 95 FrankieDettori 4 88
(Saeed Bin Suroor) *in tch: rdn 3f out: drvn and struggling 2f out: sn btn* **10/1**

362- **5** *2 3/4* **Moment Of Time**[234] 7136 4-8-12 89 JimmyFortune 5 83
(Andrew Balding) *hld up: pushed along over 2f out: drvn over 1f out: one pce and btn ins fnl f* **20/1**

002 **6** *6* **Myplacelater**[39] 1994 5-8-12 107 FrannyNorton 7 72
(Richard Fahey) *chsd ldr: pushed along 4f out: drvn and sn struggling: dropped last 2f out and btn* **7/2**[2]

2m 22.34s (1.24) **Going Correction** +0.35s/f (Good) **6** Ran SP% **109.4**
Speed ratings (Par 111): **109,106,105,102,100 95**
Tote Swingers: 1&2 £1.40, 1&3 £2.10, 2&3 £3.30 CSF £13.47 TOTE £2.00: £1.40, £2.70; EX 9.70.
Owner The Queen **Bred** His Highness The Aga Khan's Studs S C **Trained** Newmarket, Suffolk

FOCUS
The early pace was ordinary and the runners came stands' side in the straight.

NOTEBOOK
Set To Music(IRE)'s class shone through, handling the ground well and readily asserting late on having got the stands' rail. She looks capable of breaking her Group-race duck at some stage, with further suiting ideally. (op 5-4 tchd 7-4)
Dragonera, progressive in handicaps, had 16lb to find with the winner on ratings but she handles soft ground well and had the run of it from the front. (tchd 9-1)
Mid Mon Lady(IRE) just missed out from a mark of 96 on her recent debut for the yard, but she challenged widest rounding the final bend and simply wasn't good enough. (op 9-2 tchd 3-1)
Rumh(GER) no longer looks up to Pattern level. (op 12-1)
Moment Of Time, rated just 89 and still a maiden, was no danger on this return from 234 days off. (op 28-1 tchd 33-1)
Myplacelater had run really well in a Group 3 at Chester the time before and handles soft ground well, so an excuse will presumably come to light for this miserable effort. (op 10-3 tchd 11-4)

3220 REWARDS4RACING.COM H'CAP 1m 2f 188y
8:25 (8:25) (Class 6) (0-65,65) 4-Y-O+ **£1,704** (£503; £251) **Stalls** Low

Form RPR

-242 **1** **Cuckoo Rock (IRE)**[4] 3073 5-9-1 59 (p) LeeNewman 8 67
(Jonathan Portman) *in tch: niggled along and briefly outpcd 3f out: drvn to ld 1f out: kpt on wl* **9/4**[1]

00-3 **2** *1 1/4* **Circle Of Angels**[26] 2389 4-9-1 59 JamieSpencer 5 65
(Ian Williams) *hld up: rdn along over 2f out: hdwy over 1f out: kpt on wl ins fnl f: nt rch wnr* **10/3**[2]

4504 **3** *1/2* **Climaxfortackle (IRE)**[11] 2859 4-9-3 61 (v) DaneO'Neill 4 66
(Derek Shaw) *hld up: pushed along and hdwy against rail 2f out: r.o wl ins fnl f: tk 3rd cl home* **6/1**

5610 **4** *nse* **Cane Cat (IRE)**[4] 3081 5-8-13 64 (t) GeorgeDowning(7) 6 69
(Tony Carroll) *midfield: drvn and outpcd 3f out: hdwy and ev ch 2f out: no ex ins fnl f* **10/1**

/5-4 **5** *1* **Finch Flyer (IRE)**[20] 1624 5-8-9 53 SilvestreDeSousa 11 56
(Aytach Sadik) *midfield: rdn and outpcd 3f out: effrt and short of room 1f out: plugged on* **12/1**

00-6 **6** *1 1/2* **Broughtons Swinger**[157] 150 5-9-7 65 JamieMackay 10 65
(Willie Musson) *cl up: hdwy to ld 2f out: pushed along and hdd 1f out: wknd qckly ins fnl f* **11/2**[3]

-000 **7** *1/2* **Femme Royale**[2] 3137 4-7-9 46 oh1 NoelGarbutt(7) 9 45
(Richard Price) *in tch: pushed along over 2f out: wknd 1f out* **25/1**

-666 **8** *nse* **Mistoffelees**[16] 2694 6-9-0 58 (t) JimmyFortune 2 57
(James Given) *led: hdd and rdn 2f out: sn wknd and short of room 1f out: no ex fnl 75yds* **14/1**

2m 27.65s (6.55) **Going Correction** +0.35s/f (Good) **8** Ran SP% **110.8**
Speed ratings (Par 101): **90,89,88,88,87 86,86,86**
Tote Swingers: 1&2 £3.00, 1&3 £1.70, 2&3 £7.00 CSF £9.04 CT £35.45 TOTE £3.20: £1.80, £1.10, £2.50; EX 11.40.
Owner Prof C D Green **Bred** Prof C Green **Trained** Compton, Berks

FOCUS
The field, which came stands' side, started to bunch inside the final 2f.
Finch Flyer(IRE) Official explanation: jockey said gelding suffered interference closing stages

3221 FUEL RECRUITMENT H'CAP 7f 26y
8:55 (8:56) (Class 4) (0-85,85) 4-Y-O+ **£4,075** (£1,212; £606; £303) **Stalls** Low

Form RPR

0-03 **1** **Barons Spy (IRE)**[10] 2870 11-9-5 83 LukeMorris 2 91
(Richard Price) *in tch: rdn 2f out: hdwy to press ldrs over 1f out: led ins fnl f: hld on wl* **17/2**

1222 **2** *hd* **My Kingdom (IRE)**[23] 2482 6-9-4 82 (t) JamieSpencer 1 90
(Ian Williams) *in rr: hdwy and gng best 2f out: pushed along and pressed ldr ins fnl f: jst failed* **6/4**[1]

5461 **3** *nk* **Avonrose**[23] 2503 5-8-6 70 (v) FrannyNorton 5 77
(Derek Shaw) *led: rdn over 1f out: hdd ins fnl f: battled on wl: no ex and hld fnl 50yds* **6/1**

2044 **4** *3 1/4* **Rigolleto (IRE)**[9] 2913 4-8-12 76 MatthewDavies 3 75
(Mick Channon) *in tch: drvn and ev ch over 1f out: unable to go w ldng trio and btn ins fnl f* **10/3**[2]

0520 **5** *6* **Kingscroft (IRE)**[9] 2919 4-9-7 85 SilvestreDeSousa 4 68
(Mark Johnston) *cl up: pushed along 3f out: drvn and lost pl 2f out: sn struggling and btn* **4/1**[3]

1m 28.34s (3.74) **Going Correction** +0.675s/f (Yiel) **5** Ran SP% **107.9**
Speed ratings (Par 105): **105,104,97,94,93**
CSF £21.00 TOTE £7.20: £2.10, £1.10; EX 16.70.
Owner Barry Veasey **Bred** Tally-Ho Stud **Trained** Ullingswick, H'fords

FOCUS
Modest form for the grade.
T/Plt: £62.20 to a £1 stake. Pool: £54,928.00 - 644.29 winning tickets. T/Qpdt: £16.70 to a £1 stake. Pool: £4,072.00 - 180.34 winning tickets. CS

2983 WINDSOR (R-H)
Monday, June 18

OFFICIAL GOING: Good to soft (good in places)
Inner of straight out 17yds at 6f and 7yds at Winning Post. Top bend dolled out 10yds adding 42yds to distances of 1m and over.
Wind: Light, half behind Weather: Fine

3222 DAVISBAKERYCARIBBEAN.COM APPRENTICE H'CAP 1m 3f 135y
6:10 (6:11) (Class 5) (0-70,70) 4-Y-O+ **£2,264** (£673; £336; £168) **Stalls** Centre

Form RPR

3220 **1** **Royal Etiquette (IRE)**[23] 2498 5-9-1 61 LeonnaMayor 1 70
(Lawney Hill) *hld up in rr: stdy prog fr 3f out and styd in centre: chsd ldr and hung lft to far side over 1f out: chal fnl f: styd on to ld nr fin* **16/1**

0-02 **2** *hd* **Urban Space**[7] 2985 6-9-9 69 GeorgeDowning 13 78
(John Flint) *hld up in midfield: prog 4f out: wnt to far side 3f out: overall ldr 2f out: worn down nr fin* **7/2**[1]

03/- **3** *2 3/4* **Dispol Diva**[517] 6662 6-8-2 51 oh5 (v) NedCurtis(3) 12 55
(Paul Midgley) *prom: styd nr side 3f out and gng strly: led gp over 2f out: clr of rest fnl f but nt on terms w far side pair* **25/1**

1430 **4** *2 1/2* **Broughton Sands**[31] 2233 4-9-2 67 LewisWalsh(5) 3 67
(Willie Musson) *prom: styd nr side 3f out: rdn to chal and upsides over 2f out: one pce* **7/1**[2]

00 **5** *shd* **Taroum (IRE)**[14] 2767 5-8-4 57 AidenBlakemore(7) 6 57
(Tony Carroll) *hld up in last: styd nr side 3f out: nudged along and styd on steadily fnl 2f: nrst fin* **66/1**

6032 **6** *1* **Gower Rules (IRE)**[9] 2937 4-8-8 57 ThomasBrown(3) 15 55
(John Bridger) *chsd ldrs: rdn 3f out and styd nr side: nt pce to threaten after but kpt on* **10/1**

24-0 **7** *hd* **Wily Fox**[27] 2363 5-9-6 66 [1] DarrenEgan 10 64
(James Eustace) *hld up wl in rr: taken to far side 3f out: kpt on but n.d* **16/1**

31-6 **8** *shd* **Mons Calpe (IRE)**[10] 2887 6-9-7 67 DarylByrne 5 64
(Paul Cole) *hld up in midfield: hmpd and snatched up bnd 5f out: styd nr side after: styd on fr 2f out* **11/1**

-511 **9** *1 1/2* **Steely**[17] 2651 4-9-7 70 WilliamTwiston-Davies(3) 2 65
(Gary Moore) *prom: rdn to chal over 3f out: styd nr side in st: wknd 2f out* **9/1**

6-06 **10** *4 1/2* **Lady of Burgundy**[31] 2237 6-9-9 69 RachealKneller 7 56
(Mark Usher) *s.i.s: mostly in last trio: wnt far side 3f out: nvr on terms* **17/2**[3]

3041 **11** *6* **Shirataki (IRE)**[9] 2937 4-9-4 64 IanBurns 4 41
(Peter Hiatt) *trckd ldr: led after 5f: styd nr side 3f out: hdd & wknd over 2f out* **17/2**[3]

/006 **12** *3 1/2* **Rulbin Realta**[11] 2851 5-8-5 51 JakePayne 14 22
(Pat Phelan) *prom: rdn and wd bnd over 5f out: sn lost pl and bhd* **16/1**

46-0 **13** *nk* **Victorian Number (FR)**[10] 2899 4-9-3 66 (p) ThomasGarner(3) 8 37
(Geoffrey Deacon) *nvr beyond midfield: u.p over 3f out: sn btn* **100/1**

0251 **14** *12* **Karate (IRE)**[20] 2586 4-9-2 62 (t) NicoleNordblad 11 12
(Hans Adielsson) *t.k.h: hld up wl in rr: pushed along and no prog 3f out: wknd: t.o* **16/1**

00-2 **15** *11* **If I Were A Boy (IRE)**[146] 281 5-9-10 70 (p) JoshBaudains 9 2
(Dominic Ffrench Davis) *led 5f: drvn and wknd rapidly over 3f out: t.o* **20/1**

2m 32.69s (3.19) **Going Correction** +0.45s/f (Yiel) **15** Ran SP% **117.8**
Speed ratings (Par 103): **107,106,105,103,103 102,102,102,101,98 94,92,91,83,76**
Tote Swingers: 1&2 £25.00, 1&3 £81.60, 2&3 £28.60 CSF £67.30 CT £1430.09 TOTE £23.60: £6.20, £1.10, £9.90; EX 130.50 TRIFECTA Not won..
Owner John Bull & Alan Hill **Bred** Windflower Overseas Holdings Inc **Trained** Aston Rowant, Oxon

FOCUS
There was a solid pace on here and the field spread across the home straight, but it was the pair that went far side that fought it out.
Mons Calpe(IRE) Official explanation: jockey said gelding suffered interference on back bend

3223 DAVISBAKERYCARIBBEAN.COM E B F MAIDEN STKS 5f 10y
6:40 (6:41) (Class 5) 2-Y-O **£3,234** (£962; £481; £240) **Stalls** Low

Form RPR

32 **1** **Dansili Dual (IRE)**[10] 2868 2-9-3 0 RichardHughes 1 78+
(Richard Hannon) *mde virtually all: taken to r against far side rail 1/2-way: drvn and hld on fnl f* **6/4**[2]

2 *nk* **Royal Aspiration (IRE)** 2-9-3 0 JimCrowley 2 77+
(William Haggas) *sn last and pushed along: prog 1/2-way: chsd wnr over 1f out: shkn up and clsd fnl f: jst hld* **12/1**

3 *2 1/2* **Sky Garden** 2-8-12 0 MichaelHills 6 63+
(William Haggas) *w wnr 2f: lost pl and pushed along in 4th 2f out: kpt on to take 3rd 1f out: n.d* **6/5**[1]

30 **4** *2 1/2* **Symboline**[21] 2550 2-8-12 0 MartinHarley 3 54
(Mick Channon) *cl up: chsd wnr over 2f out to over 1f out: fdd* **15/2**[3]

5 *1 3/4* **Why So Fast (IRE)** 2-8-9 0 HarryBentley(3) 5 48
(Stuart Williams) *green to post: s.s: sn rcvrd and in tch: rn green and fdd fnl 2f* **28/1**

1m 2.36s (2.06) **Going Correction** +0.225s/f (Good) **5** Ran SP% **108.4**
Speed ratings (Par 93): **92,91,87,83,80**
CSF £16.97 TOTE £2.40: £1.30, £4.20; EX 10.00.
Owner Andrew Tinkler **Bred** Denis Brosnan **Trained** East Everleigh, Wilts

FOCUS
A fair little juvenile maiden.

NOTEBOOK
Dansili Dual(IRE) saw it out professionally and made it third time lucky. He was only just held on similar ground at Bath last time and had clearly learned again for that experience as he quickened willingly when sent clear, bagging the far rail in the process. He was tying up close home, but is bred to enjoy a quicker surface and more improvement should be forthcoming when he reverting to better ground. (tchd 15-8)
Royal Aspiration(IRE) ◆ comfortably came out on top of the pair from his yard. He showed his inexperience early on, but did some decent late work and was eating into the winner's advantage near the finish. It's fair to expect this speedily bred colt to go one better next time out. (op 16-1 tchd 11-1)
Sky Garden is from a successful family her yard knows all about and being so heavily backed she was evidently expected to make a winning debut. She knew her job from the gates, but rather tamely allowed the winner to go clear when that one asserted and it looked a case of her needing the initial outing. A quicker surface may also suit. (tchd 11-10 and 5-4)
Symboline never seriously threatened back on easier ground, but should find her feet when the nurseries begin next month. (op 9-1 tchd 7-1)
Why So Fast(IRE) proved distinctly green from the preliminaries to the start, and in the race itself. Her yard's 2yos nearly always improve for their debut outings and another furlong should suit before too long. (op 25-1 tchd 20-1 and 33-1)

3224 MIRROR PUNTERS CLUB (S) STKS 6f
7:10 (7:37) (Class 5) 2-Y-O **£2,264** (£673; £336; £168) **Stalls** Low

Form RPR

640 **1** **Lucky Suit (IRE)**[6] 3009 2-8-6 0 MartinDwyer 5 60
(Richard Hannon) *w ldr: led 1/2-way: rdn 2f out: all out to hold on ins fnl f* **7/2**[2]

40 **2** *1/2* **Sojoum**[18] 2631 2-8-6 0 SamHitchcott 10 59
(Mick Channon) *hld up towards rr: nt clr run 1/2-way: sn rdn: prog and edgd lft over 1f out: chsd wnr u.p ins fnl f: nt qckn last 75yds* **9/4**[1]

3 *1 1/2* **Fruity Bun** 2-7-13 0 IanBurns(7) 6 54
(Matthew Salaman) *chsd ldrs: rdn over 2f out: chsd wnr 2f out: one pce and lost 2nd ins fnl f* **12/1**

6 **4** *1 ¼* **Northern Harbour (IRE)**[20] 2571 2-8-11 0......................(p) LiamKeniry 1 55
(J S Moore) *chsd ldrs: rdn and nt qckn jst over 2f out: kpt on same pce fr over 1f out* **33/1**

00 **5** *nk* **Myzamour**[56] 1563 2-8-6 0.. TadhgO'Shea 2 49
(J S Moore) *sn pushed along in last pair: kpt on steadily on outer fnl 2f: nrst fin* **16/1**

0 **6** *1 ¼* **Iffley Fields**[13] 2784 2-8-11 0.. ShaneKelly 9 51
(David Evans) *prom: rdn and losing pl whn bdly hmpd over 1f out: no ch after* **9/2**[3]

00 **7** *3* **Prince Of Prophets (IRE)**[11] 2852 2-8-11 0...............(t) SaleemGolam 4 42
(Stuart Williams) *dwlt: mostly in rr: rdn and no imp on ldrs fnl 2f* **40/1**

62 **8** *shd* **Strawberry Duck (IRE)**[13] 2798 2-8-3 0......................... DominicFox(3) 3 36
(Amy Weaver) *mostly towards rr: no prog 2f out: fdd* **8/1**

6 **9** *7* **Ground To Garden**[4] 3084 2-8-1 0................................ DarrenEgan(5) 7 20
(Gay Kelleway) *led to 1/2-way: chsd wnr to 2f out: losing pl whn bdly hmpd over 1f out: wknd* **14/1**

4 **10** *5* **Eloquent Star (IRE)**[69] 1284 2-8-11 0........................... PadraigBeggy 8 10
(David Evans) *restless stalls: s.s: rcvrd to chse ldrs after 2f: wkng whn hmpd over 1f out: bhd after* **14/1**

1m 15.87s (2.87) **Going Correction** +0.225s/f (Good) **10** Ran SP% **114.6**
Speed ratings (Par 93): **89,88,86,84,84 82,78,78,69,62**
Tote Swingers: 1&2 £2.40, 1&3 £25.60, 2&3 £19.90 CSF £11.52 TOTE £4.40: £1.70, £1.10, £4.90; EX 11.10 Trifecta £151.00 Pool: £1,013.78 - 4.96 winning units..No bid for the winner.
Owner B Bull **Bred** Mountarmstrong Stud **Trained** East Everleigh, Wilts

FOCUS
A weak 2yo seller.

NOTEBOOK
Lucky Suit(IRE) enhanced Richard Hannon's cracking record in the race, handing the trainer a quick-fire double in the process. She had not shown much in three previous outings, but this was an easier task and she displayed a plucky attitude under pressure from 2f out. Her sire's progeny are showing a real liking for easy ground and she's now clearly found her sort of level. (op 3-1)
Sojoum, having a first outing on an easy surface, was another taking a marked drop in class and got well backed. She got anything but the run of the race and would probably have prevailed had she got a better passage. She too now looks to have found her level. (op 11-4)
Fruity Bun was starting off at the bottom level, but is bred to appreciate longer trips so this was a fair debut effort. (op 14-1 tchd 16-1)
Northern Harbour(IRE), equipped with first-time cheekpieces, was not helped by the inside stall and is a little better than the bare form. (tchd 28-1)
Myzamour needs a stiffer test. (tchd 14-1)
Iffley Fields, well-supported, was looking held prior to being badly hampered by the runner-up. Official explanation: jockey said gelding suffered interference in running (op 13-2 tchd 7-1)
Ground To Garden Official explanation: jockey said filly suffered interference in running

3225 FREEBETS H'CAP 6f
7:40 (7:40) (Class 4) (0-85,85) 4-Y-O+ **£4,851** (£1,443; £721; £360) **Stalls** Low

Form RPR

6114 **1** **Italian Tom (IRE)**[11] 2853 5-8-13 **82**.............................. DarrenEgan(5) 9 91
(Ronald Harris) *hld up in last: rdn over 2f out: gd prog on wd outside after: led 1f out: styd on wl* **15/2**

1-44 **2** *1 ¼* **Paradise Spectre**[23] 2488 5-8-9 **73**................................ MartinHarley 5 78
(Mrs K Burke) *prom: pressed ldr over 3f out: rdn over 2f out: chal over 1f out: chsd wnr fnl f: readily hld* **3/1**[2]

-040 **3** *1* **We Have A Dream**[16] 2707 7-9-5 **83**................................ MartinDwyer 1 85+
(William Muir) *fast away: led: styd nr side 1/2-way: edgd lft fr 2f out: hdd and no ex 1f out* **9/1**

0321 **4** *nse* **Cocohatchee**[6] 3016 4-8-2 **66**.. TadhgO'Shea 7 68
(Pat Phelan) *t.k.h: prom on outer: pressed ldr over 3f out: nt qckn over 1f out: one pce after* **11/4**[1]

6500 **5** *1* **Jack My Boy (IRE)**[30] 2264 5-8-6 **70**............................ PadraigBeggy 6 68
(David Evans) *rdn in rr bef 1/2-way: styd on outer and sme prog over 1f out: one pce fnl f* **16/1**

4-04 **6** *¾* **Ganas (IRE)**[21] 2558 4-9-6 **84**... AdamKirby 4 80
(Clive Cox) *chsd ldr over 2f: rdn over 2f out: nt qckn wl over 1f out: fdd fnl f* **7/2**[3]

-463 **7** *1 ¾* **Kingsdine (IRE)**[6] 3011 5-9-5 **83**................................ TomMcLaughlin 3 73
(Malcolm Saunders) *hld up in rr: styd against nr side rail and delivered effrt over 1f out: no prog* **10/1**

0040 **8** *1 ¾* **Kings 'n Dreams**[21] 2546 5-8-2 **69**...............................(b) DominicFox(3) 8 54
(Dean Ivory) *a in last pair: rdn and no prog over 2f out* **25/1**

1m 13.57s (0.57) **Going Correction** +0.225s/f (Good) **8** Ran SP% **114.5**
Speed ratings (Par 105): **105,103,102,101,100 99,97,94**
Tote Swingers: 1&2 £6.10, 1&3 £3.70, 2&3 £6.20 CSF £30.35 CT £208.56 TOTE £4.80: £1.20, £1.80, £2.50; EX 32.20 Trifecta £106.90 Pool: £799.02 - 5.52 winning units..
Owner S & A Mares **Bred** Tom Radley **Trained** Earlswood, Monmouths

FOCUS
A modest sprint handicap. Surprisingly the field took time to head far side in the home straight and, while it saw a host of chances 1f out, the winner came widest of all.

3226 SKYBET.COM H'CAP 1m 67y
8:10 (8:10) (Class 4) (0-80,80) 4-Y-O+ **£4,204** (£1,251; £625; £312) **Stalls** Low

Form RPR

222 **1** **Jack's Revenge (IRE)**[25] 2414 4-9-5 **78**..................(bt) RichardHughes 1 87
(George Baker) *hld up in midfield: tending to hang 2f out: plld out wd and gd prog fnl f: r.o wl to ld last strides* **7/1**

6001 **2** *nk* **Choral Festival**[11] 2857 6-8-12 **74**................................ SeanLevey(3) 6 82
(John Bridger) *trckd ldng trio: shkn up on outer to ld wl over 1f out: over a l clr fnl f: idlded and hdd last strides* **12/1**

1301 **3** *1 ½* **Snow Trooper**[7] 2988 4-9-4 **77** 6ex................................... ShaneKelly 12 82
(Dean Ivory) *trckd ldrs: grabbed far side rail over 2f out: tried to chal wl over 1f out: one pce fnl f* **5/2**[1]

314 **4** *½* **Great Shot**[23] 2510 4-9-2 **75**... JamesDoyle 5 78
(Sylvester Kirk) *led to wl over 1f out: one pce after* **11/2**[3]

31-4 **5** *1* **Top Diktat**[34] 2151 4-9-7 **80**... RyanMoore 2 82
(Sir Michael Stoute) *trckd ldrs: rdn over 3f out: styd in tch but no imp whn sltly short of room over 1f out: kpt on* **11/4**[2]

1104 **6** *nk* **Katmai River (IRE)**[6] 3000 5-8-11 **70**............................ DavidProbert 10 70
(Mark Usher) *mostly chsd ldr to 2f out: steadily fdd over 1f out* **33/1**

3-0 **7** *¾* **The Cayterers**[21] 2561 10-9-6 **79**..................................... MartinLane 3 78
(Tony Carroll) *stdd s: hld up in last pair: shuffled along and styd on steadily fnl 2f: nvr in it* **16/1**

0000 **8** *5* **Pat's Legacy (USA)**[19] 2608 6-9-6 **79**........................ J-PGuillambert 8 66
(Jo Hughes) *awkward and stdd s: hld up in last pair: shkn up 3f out: nvr a factor* **25/1**

2-40 **9** *3 ½* **Peponi**[138] 374 6-8-13 **72**.. SebSanders 4 51
(Peter Makin) *hld up in midfield: shkn up over 2f out and no prog: wknd over 1f out* **25/1**

06-0 **10** *4 ½* **Mahadee (IRE)**[23] 2473 7-9-2 **75**..................................... LiamKeniry 11 44
(Ed de Giles) *hld up in midfield: rdn wl over 2f out: sn wknd* **40/1**

00-3 **11** *8* **Great Charm (IRE)**[14] 2758 7-9-1 **74**........................ MickaelBarzalona 9 24
(Daniel Kubler) *t.k.h: hld up in last trio: no prog 3f out: sn bhd* **20/1**

1m 47.18s (2.48) **Going Correction** +0.45s/f (Yiel) **11** Ran SP% **114.5**
Speed ratings (Par 105): **105,104,103,102,101 101,100,95,92,87 79**
Tote Swingers: 1&2 £16.60, 1&3 £4.20, 2&3 £7.10 CSF £77.61 CT £271.35 TOTE £7.00: £2.00, £3.70, £1.70; EX 103.80 Trifecta £435.40 Pool: £1,184.63 - 2.01 winning units..
Owner PJL Racing **Bred** Con Marnane **Trained** Whitsbury, Hants

FOCUS
A competitive handicap for the class. It was run at a fair pace and normal service was resumed as the entire field went far side in the home straight.

3227 SKYBET.COM MAIDEN STKS 1m 2f 7y
8:40 (8:46) (Class 5) 3-Y-O+ **£2,264** (£673; £336; £168) **Stalls** Centre

Form RPR

42 **1** **Nabucco**[11] 2856 3-9-0 0.. WilliamBuick 2 93+
(John Gosden) *trckd ldng pair: led 3f out: shkn up 2f out: r.o wl and in command fnl f* **4/7**[1]

2 *2* **Guarantee** 3-9-0 0.. MichaelHills 7 89+
(William Haggas) *trckd ldrs in 5th: moved up 3f out: chsd wnr wl over 1f out: r.o but no imp* **20/1**

44 **3** *1* **Kunegunda**[12] 2826 3-8-9 0.. JackMitchell 15 82
(James Fanshawe) *trckd ldng trio: shkn up over 2f out: styd on fr over 1f out: nvr able to chal* **20/1**

45 **4** *1 ¼* **Cactus Valley (IRE)**[11] 2856 3-9-0 0................................ JamesDoyle 8 84+
(Roger Charlton) *trckd ldrs in 6th: shkn up over 2f out: styd on steadily fnl 2f: likely to improve* **6/1**[3]

54- **5** *4* **Rysbrack (USA)**[301] 5327 6-9-12 0.............................. RichardHughes 11 76
(Paul Webber) *trckd ldr to 3f out: styd pressing wnr to wl over 1f out: wknd rapidly fnl f* **16/1**

45 **6** *2* **Sash Of Honour (IRE)**[30] 2271 3-9-0 0.......................... RyanMoore 14 72
(Sir Michael Stoute) *settled in midfield: pushed along 4f out: prog to chse ldrs 3f out: wknd over 1f out* **9/2**[2]

0 **7** *8* **Flashy Star**[28] 2344 3-8-9 0.. MartinHarley 16 51
(Mick Channon) *uns rdr bef ent stalls: wl in tch in midfield: no prog over 2f out: wknd over 1f out* **66/1**

0- **8** *4* **Phantom Ranch**[243] 6953 3-9-0 0..................................... SebSanders 3 48
(Hughie Morrison) *mde most to 3f out: sn wknd* **50/1**

9 *½* **Oh So Charming** 3-8-9 0....................................... MatthewLawson(5) 5 47
(Andy Turnell) *s.s: wl in rr: no ch fnl 2f but styd on fr over 1f out* **100/1**

10 *6* **Queen Hermione (IRE)**[12] 4-9-7 0................................ LiamKeniry 13 30
(Linda Jewell) *dwlt: in tch in midfield to 3f out: eased whn no ch fnl 2f* **150/1**

11 *nse* **Dee Ee Williams (IRE)**[29] 9-9-12 0.................................. JimCrowley 4 35
(Nick Gifford) *dwlt: hld up and a wl in rr: pushed along and no ch over 2f out* **33/1**

12 *2 ½* **Rusland (IRE)** 3-9-0 0.. RoystonFfrench 12 30
(Ismail Mohammed) *scratchy to post: hld up and sn last: nvr a factor* **66/1**

0 **13** *nk* **Imagery**[20] 2584 3-8-9 0... DarrenEgan(5) 9 29
(Ronald Harris) *reluctant to enter stalls: nvr bttr than midfield: shkn up 4f out: sn wknd* **150/1**

0- **14** *nse* **Amaroni**[263] 6473 4-9-12 0.. MattieBatchelor 10 29
(John E Long) *rel to r and slowest away: in tch in rr to over 3f out: sn wknd and bhd* **150/1**

15 *7* **No No Cardinal (IRE)** 3-9-0 0.. AdamKirby 1 15
(Peter Hedger) *plld hrd in midfield: wknd over 3f out: t.o* **150/1**

0 **16** *3 ¾* **Southerly**[27] 2368 3-8-7 0.. HayleyBurton(7) 6
(Luca Cumani) *hld up and sn wl in rr: t.o* **100/1**

2m 13.24s (4.54) **Going Correction** +0.45s/f (Yiel)
WFA 3 from 4yo+ 12lb **16** Ran SP% **124.0**
Speed ratings (Par 103): **99,97,96,95,92 90,84,81,80,76 75,73,73,73,68 65**
Tote Swingers: 1&2 £7.10, 1&3 £6.40, 2&3 £22.40 CSF £21.36 TOTE £1.70: £1.10, £4.80, £3.90; EX 17.00 Trifecta £175.00 Pool: £2,530.57 - 10.70 winning units..
Owner H R H Princess Haya Of Jordan **Bred** Darley **Trained** Newmarket, Suffolk

FOCUS
Not a bad maiden and straightforward enough form.
Rysbrack(USA) Official explanation: jockey said gelding stumbled inside final furlong

3228 DAVISBAKERYCARIBBEAN.COM H'CAP 1m 2f 7y
9:10 (9:11) (Class 5) (0-70,68) 3-Y-O **£2,264** (£673; £336; £168) **Stalls** Centre

Form RPR

0-20 **1** **Burnham**[25] 2424 3-9-3 **64**.. RichardHughes 3 70+
(Hughie Morrison) *sn prom: urged along fr 1/2-way and looked awkward: wnt 2nd 3f out: drvn ahd over 1f out: styd on* **6/4**[1]

0000 **2** *1 ½* **Thecornishcowboy**[13] 2802 3-8-2 **49**.............................(t) JimmyQuinn 6 52
(John Ryan) *hld up in midfield: prog over 2f out: chsd ldng pair over 1f out: styd on to take 2nd ins fnl f: no imp on wnr* **40/1**

0-02 **3** *nse* **Grand Liaison**[13] 2788 3-8-2 **52**...................................... DominicFox(3) 8 55+
(John Berry) *hld up in rr: prog over 3f out: taken to far rail over 2f out: drvn and styd on fr over 1f out to press for 2nd nr fin* **11/2**[3]

-000 **4** *¾* **Capitol Gain (IRE)**[21] 2553 3-9-4 **65**.............................. MartinDwyer 9 67
(Brian Meehan) *sn led: drvn over 2f out: hdd and one pce over 1f out* **16/1**

-460 **5** *¾* **Rogue Reporter (IRE)**[31] 2246 3-9-4 **65**...................... SaleemGolam 10 66
(Stuart Williams) *hld up in last pair: prog over 2f out: trying to cl on ldrs whn nt clr run briefly over 1f out: styd on* **33/1**

60-0 **6** *nse* **Calculated Risk**[31] 2246 3-9-0 **61**.............................. StevieDonohoe 7 61
(Willie Musson) *hld up in tch: effrt over 2f out: rdn and styd on same pce fr over 1f out: nvr able to chal* **9/2**[2]

5-06 **7** *6* **Winter Dress**[25] 2431 3-9-2 **63**.. JamesDoyle 2 51
(Roger Teal) *mostly chsd ldr to 3f out: wknd 2f out* **12/1**

3-00 **8** *1 ½* **Invincible Dream (IRE)**[20] 2581 3-8-8 **60**.............. JemmaMarshall(5) 1 45
(Pat Phelan) *hld up in last: shkn up 3f out: no real prog* **40/1**

-543 **9** *11* **Bondi Mist (IRE)**[25] 2431 3-9-0 **61**......................... MickaelBarzalona 11 24
(Jonathan Portman) *lost pl on outer over 5f out and dropped to rr: effrt again 4f out: wknd rapidly 2f out* **8/1**

-043 **10** *10* **Tiger Cub**[14] 2756 3-9-7 **68**...(t) WilliamBuick 4 11
(Mikael Magnusson) *trckd ldrs tl wknd rapidly over 2f out: t.o* **8/1**

2m 13.4s (4.70) **Going Correction** +0.45s/f (Yiel) **10** Ran SP% **117.2**
Speed ratings (Par 99): **99,97,97,97,96 96,91,90,81,73**
Tote Swingers: 1&2 £13.40, 1&3 £2.60, 2&3 £47.20 CSF £83.17 CT £273.26 TOTE £2.60: £1.20, £11.00, £2.20; EX 104.70 Trifecta £1118.50 Pool: £1,995.22 - 1.32 winning units..
Owner The Hill Stud **Bred** The Hill Stud **Trained** East Ilsley, Berks

FOCUS
A modest 3yo handicap, run at an ordinary pace.

T/Plt: £52.40 to a £1 stake. Pool: £86,948.00 -1,210.93 winning tickets. T/Qpdt: £9.60 to a £1 stake. Pool: £7,307.34 - 559.36 winning tickets. JN

2858 WOLVERHAMPTON (A.W) (L-H)

Monday, June 18

OFFICIAL GOING: Standard

Wind: Fresh behind Weather: Cloudy with sunny spells

3229 FOLLOW US AT LADBROKES NEWS H'CAP (DIV I) 7f 32y(P)

2:00 (1:40) (Class 5) (0-75,75) 3-Y-O+ **£2,264** (£673; £336; £168) **Stalls** High

Form RPR

-301 **1** **Smalljohn**[28] 2354 6-9-13 **74**............(v) PhillipMakin 9 82
(Bryan Smart) *mde all: rdn and hung rt fr over 1f out: styd on* **8/1**

1200 **2** ¾ **Hawk Moth (IRE)**[30] 2274 4-9-6 **67**............ CathyGannon 3 73+
(John Spearing) *hld up: hdwy over 1f out: rdn to go 2nd wl ins fnl f: nt rch wnr* **13/2**[3]

4203 **3** ¾ **Striker Torres (IRE)**[33] 2173 6-9-7 **68**............(v) JamesDoyle 1 72
(Ian McInnes) *chsd ldrs: rdn over 1f out: styd on same pce ins fnl f* **7/1**

3362 **4** *nse* **Sandbetweenourtoes (IRE)**[11] 2864 3-9-4 **74**............(p) ShaneKelly 11 75
(Brian Meehan) *prom: outpcd 2f out: rallied ins fnl f: r.o* **15/2**

0200 **5** *nk* **Satwa Laird**[5] 3045 6-9-10 **71**............ HayleyTurner 5 74
(Conor Dore) *chsd wnr tl rdn over 1f out: styd on same pce ins fnl f* **14/1**

00-0 **6** ½ **Rossetti**[21] 2545 4-10-0 **75**............ KierenFallon 4 77
(James Fanshawe) *hld up: hdwy over 2f out: rdn over 1f out: styd on* **4/1**[2]

2206 **7** *nk* **Flying Pickets (IRE)**[26] 2400 3-9-0 **70**............(be) JohnFahy 2 68
(Alan McCabe) *prom: lost pl 1/2-way: r.o u.p fnl f* **28/1**

00-0 **8** 2¾ **Easy Over (IRE)**[30] 2274 4-9-12 **73**............ NeilCallan 7 67
(Ed McMahon) *s.i.s: hdwy over 5f out: rdn over 2f out: styd on same pce fr over 1f out: eased whn hld nr fin* **7/2**[1]

-002 **9** ½ **Beautiful Lando (FR)**[12] 2811 4-9-3 **64**............(b) StevieDonohoe 12 56
(Heather Main) *s.i.s: hld up: rdn over 1f out: nvr on terms* **22/1**

3500 **10** 1¾ **Fleetwoodsands (IRE)**[14] 2758 5-9-8 **69**............(t) LukeMorris 6 57
(Milton Bradley) *hld up: rdn over 1f out: n.d* **22/1**

000 **11** 1¼ **Vhujon (IRE)**[12] 2811 7-8-10 **57**............ RobbieFitzpatrick 8 41
(Peter Grayson) *hld up: shkn up and hung rt over 2f out: a in rr* **66/1**

6-00 **12** 8 **Brailsford (IRE)**[26] 2336 3-8-9 **65**............(p) RoystonFfrench 10 25
(Ismail Mohammed) *chsd ldrs: rdn over 2f out: wknd over 1f out* **25/1**

1m 28.81s (-0.79) **Going Correction** -0.025s/f (Stan)
WFA 3 from 4yo+ 9lb **12** Ran **SP% 115.1**
Speed ratings (Par 103): **103,102,101,101,100 100,99,96,96,94 92,83**
toteswingers:1&2:£11.00, 2&3:£8.60, 1&3:£5.70 CSF £53.49 CT £388.79 TOTE £10.80: £2.30, £2.20, £2.20; EX 56.70 Trifecta £136.40 Pool: £306.03 - 1.66 winning units..
Owner B Smart **Bred** W H R John And Partners **Trained** Hambleton, N Yorks

FOCUS
A routine handicap of its type and not many got into it.

3230 FOLLOW US AT LADBROKES NEWS H'CAP (DIV II) 7f 32y(P)

2:30 (2:33) (Class 5) (0-75,75) 3-Y-O+ **£2,264** (£673; £336; £168) **Stalls** High

Form RPR

3020 **1** **Chambles**[89] 982 3-8-8 **64**............ KierenFallon 1 74
(Alan McCabe) *s.i.s: sn prom: led over 1f out: r.o: readily* **4/1**[1]

3-00 **2** ¾ **Multi Bene**[23] 2470 3-8-6 **62**............ RichardKingscote 6 70
(Tom Dascombe) *prom: pushed along 1/2-way: rdn and nt clr run over 1f out: edgd lft and r.o to go 2nd wl ins fnl f: nt rch wnr* **16/1**

01-5 **3** 2¼ **Four Richer**[7] 2987 3-9-5 **75**............(b[1]) FergusSweeney 3 77
(Jamie Osborne) *hld up: hdwy over 1f out: r.o wl: nt rch ldrs* **12/1**

0206 **4** ¾ **Alkadi (IRE)**[10] 2898 3-9-3 **73**............ SilvestreDeSousa 5 73
(Mark Johnston) *chsd ldrs: pushed along 1/2-way: rdn over 1f out: styd on same pce ins fnl f* **9/2**[2]

-044 **5** 3¼ **Sir Bruno (FR)**[14] 2758 5-9-10 **71**............ DavidProbert 4 65
(Bryn Palling) *mid-div: hdwy over 2f out: rdn and nt clr run over 1f out: wknd wl ins fnl f* **7/1**

3065 **6** ½ **Mawjoodah**[16] 2693 4-9-2 **63**............ BarryMcHugh 2 56
(Brian Ellison) *led: rdn and hdd over 1f out: wknd wl ins fnl f* **11/1**

000 **7** ½ **Thatcherite (IRE)**[14] 2753 4-9-13 **74**............(t) StephenCraine 10 66
(Tony Coyle) *s.i.s: hld up: rdn over 1f out: r.o ins fnl f: nvr nrr* **14/1**

3651 **8** 1½ **Hold The Star**[11] 2865 6-8-7 **59**............ AnnStokell[(5)] 9 46
(Ann Stokell) *chsd ldrs: wnt 2nd over 2f out tl rdn and edgd rt over 1f out: wknd fnl f* **10/1**

50 **9** ½ **Local Singer (IRE)**[37] 2070 4-9-6 **67**............ TomMcLaughlin 8 53
(Paul Howling) *sn pushed along in rr: bhd fr 1/2-way* **18/1**

3020 **10** 5 **Lastkingofscotland (IRE)**[21] 2545 6-9-12 **73**............(b) HayleyTurner 7 46
(Conor Dore) *hld up: rdn over 2f out: wknd over 1f out: eased* **6/1**[3]

4 **11** 1¾ **Aragorn Rouge**[26] 2403 4-9-6 **72**............ AdamCarter[(5)] 11 40
(John Wainwright) *s.i.s: outpcd* **25/1**

6-55 **12** 1¼ **Sweet Secret**[136] 403 5-9-4 **68**............(b) RaulDaSilva[(3)] 12 33
(Jeremy Gask) *chsd ldr tl rdn over 2f out: wknd wl over 1f out* **16/1**

1m 28.8s (-0.80) **Going Correction** -0.025s/f (Stan)
WFA 3 from 4yo+ 9lb **12** Ran **SP% 117.6**
Speed ratings (Par 103): **103,102,99,98,95 94,93,92,91,85 83,82**
toteswingers:1&2:£19.70, 2&3:£54.30, 1&3:£9.70 CSF £68.59 CT £723.46 TOTE £3.20: £1.10, £5.70, £4.50; EX 87.30 TRIFECTA Not won..
Owner A S Reid **Bred** A S Reid **Trained** Averham Park, Notts

FOCUS
The winning time was 1/100th of a second quicker than the first division.
Lastkingofscotland(IRE) Official explanation: trainer said gelding returned lame right-fore.

3231 ATR ROYAL ASCOT MICROSITE NOW LIVE (S) STKS 7f 32y(P)

3:00 (3:00) (Class 6) 3-Y-O+ **£1,704** (£503; £251) **Stalls** High

Form RPR

-650 **1** **Florio Vincitore (IRE)**[18] 2621 5-9-8 62............(v) BarryMcHugh 4 74
(Brian Ellison) *mde all: shkn up over 1f out: pushed out: eased nr fin* **4/1**[2]

0-04 **2** 2¾ **Right Regal (IRE)**[17] 2649 3-8-13 68............(b) AndreaAtzeni 3 64
(Marco Botti) *a.p: rdn to chse wnr over 1f out: no imp fnl f* **4/1**[2]

3524 **3** *nk* **Restless Bay (IRE)**[11] 2841 4-9-8 73............(p) ChrisCatlin 1 66
(Reg Hollinshead) *hld up: hdwy over 1f out: sn rdn: styd on* **13/8**[1]

3644 **4** 4 **Just Timmy Marcus**[11] 2858 6-9-8 53............ WilliamCarson 5 55
(Brian Baugh) *s.i.s: hdwy 1/2-way: rdn over 2f out: wknd over 1f out* **16/1**

406 **5** *nk* **One Way Or Another (AUS)**[6] 3016 9-9-8 70............(bt) CathyGannon 7 54
(David Evans) *hld up: rdn over 1f out: nvr on terms* **8/1**

31-2 **6** 1 **A Little Bit Dusty**[20] 2580 4-9-1 71............(b) RyanWhile[(7)] 8 51
(Bill Turner) *s.i.s: sn prom: jnd wnr 5f out tl pushed along over 2f out: wknd over 1f out:* **11/2**[3]

1m 29.03s (-0.57) **Going Correction** -0.025s/f (Stan)
WFA 3 from 4yo+ 9lb **6** Ran **SP% 110.5**
Speed ratings (Par 101): **102,98,98,93,93 92**
toteswingers:1&2:£2.40, 2&3:£2.20, 1&3:£2.40 CSF £19.39 TOTE £4.80: £2.10, £2.60; EX 17.20 Trifecta £42.50 Pool: £629.92 - 10.96 winning units..There was no bid for the winner. A Little Bit Dusty was claimed by J P. Evitt for £6000.
Owner L S Keys & Kristian Strangeway **Bred** Newsells Park Stud **Trained** Norton, N Yorks

FOCUS
A moderate seller and few got involved. The winning time was around a quarter of a second faster than both divisions of the handicap.

3232 LADBROKES GAME ON! MEDIAN AUCTION MAIDEN STKS 1m 4f 50y(P)

3:30 (3:30) (Class 5) 3-5-Y-O **£2,264** (£673; £336; £168) **Stalls** Low

Form RPR

422 **1** **Savida (IRE)**[17] 2668 3-8-8 73............(b[1]) RyanMoore 7 69
(Sir Michael Stoute) *a.p: led over 1f out: sn rdn and hung rt: styd on wl* **9/4**[2]

3 **2** 3 **New Drama (IRE)**[9] 2927 3-8-8 0............ SilvestreDeSousa 10 65
(Mark Johnston) *sn led: rdn and hdd over 1f out: styd on same pce ins fnl f* **11/2**[3]

23 **3** 3¾ **Moratab (IRE)**[12] 2826 3-8-13 0............ NeilCallan 6 66
(Roger Varian) *chsd ldrs: wnt 2nd over 2f out tl rdn wl over 1f out: no ex fnl f: eased nr fin* **11/10**[1]

0050 **4** 2¼ **Rano Pano (USA)**[17] 2673 3-8-8 44............ BarryMcHugh 4 55
(Brian Ellison) *hld up: hdwy over 2f out: rdn: hung lft and wknd over 1f out* **33/1**

43 **5** *hd* **Special Mix**[10] 2877 4-9-13 0............ PhillipMakin 5 60
(Michael Easterby) *hld up in tch: rdn over 3f out: wknd over 1f out* **14/1**

5-3 **6** 10 **Serjeant Buzfuz**[17] 2668 3-8-13 0............ DavidNolan 9 44
(Richard Fahey) *chsd ldr tl rdn over 2f out: wknd over 1f out* **11/1**

0 **7** 2¼ **Roman Around**[33] 2172 3-8-3 0............ DavidKenny[(5)] 8 35
(William Knight) *mid-div: pushed along 7f out: wknd over 2f out* **50/1**

8 *nk* **Barnacre** 3-8-13 0............ PJMcDonald 2 40
(Richard Ford) *hld up: rdn over 5f out: wknd over 3f out* **50/1**

0 **9** 27 **Polly Pease**[49] 1716 3-8-8 0............ DavidProbert 1
(Nikki Evans) *hld up: pushed along 5f out: wknd over 3f out: t.o* **150/1**

2m 41.36s (0.26) **Going Correction** -0.025s/f (Stan)
WFA 3 from 4yo 14lb **9** Ran **SP% 116.3**
Speed ratings (Par 103): **98,96,93,92,91 85,83,83,65**
toteswingers:1&2:£2.70, 2&3:£3.00, 1&3:£1.40 CSF £15.02 TOTE £3.20: £1.30, £1.90, £1.10; EX 15.30 Trifecta £28.00 Pool: £842.68 - 22.24 winning units..
Owner Miss A H Marshall **Bred** Frank Dunne **Trained** Newmarket, Suffolk

FOCUS
A modest middle-distance maiden run at a steady pace and the principals were always handy, though they were also the market leaders.

3233 VISIT ATTHERACES.COM/ASCOT H'CAP 1m 4f 50y(P)

4:00 (4:00) (Class 6) (0-60,60) 3-Y-O **£1,704** (£503; £251) **Stalls** Low

Form RPR

0-50 **1** **Zowaina**[142] 350 3-9-3 **56**............ NeilCallan 6 71
(Roger Varian) *a.p: led over 1f out: styd on wl* **8/1**[3]

50-2 **2** 2½ **Seven Veils (IRE)**[6] 2999 3-9-4 **57**............ LukeMorris 4 68
(Sir Mark Prescott Bt) *s.i.s and hmpd s: hld up: hdwy 1/2-way: rdn to chse wnr and hung lft fr over 1f out: styd on same pce* **11/8**[1]

0530 **3** 8 **Angel Cake (IRE)**[13] 2788 3-8-7 **46** oh1............(p) SilvestreDeSousa 11 44
(Phil McEntee) *hld up: hdwy over 1f out: sn rdn and hung lft: wnt 3rd wl ins fnl f: nvr nrr* **50/1**

5-05 **4** 1¾ **Leitrim King (IRE)**[13] 2787 3-9-7 **60**............(b[1]) ShaneKelly 3 55
(William Haggas) *s.i.s: hdwy to ld over 8f out: rdn and hdd over 1f out: wknd fnl f* **9/2**[2]

000 **5** 2½ **Black Motive**[21] 2560 3-9-4 **57**............ HayleyTurner 12 48
(Michael Bell) *trckd ldrs: racd keenly: wnt 2nd over 6f out: rdn and ev ch over 1f out: wknd fnl f* **25/1**

0440 **6** 12 **Parque Atlantico**[13] 2787 3-8-7 **46** oh1............(v) DavidProbert 9 18
(Andrew Balding) *chsd ldr: lost pl over 8f out: rdn over 5f out: wknd over 2f out: eased* **12/1**

0-03 **7** 7 **Shomberg**[23] 2497 3-9-2 **55**............ EddieAhern 5 16
(Mark H Tompkins) *mid-div: hdwy over 4f out: rdn and hung lft over 3f out: wknd over 2f out: t.o* **9/1**

0U56 **8** ½ **Meljana (IRE)**[20] 2592 3-8-8 **47**............ PJMcDonald 10 7
(Alan Swinbank) *s.i.s: rdn over 6f out: a in rr: t.o* **16/1**

00-5 **9** 1 **Bells Of Berlin**[80] 1113 3-9-1 **54**............(v[1]) KierenFallon 2 12
(Alan McCabe) *hld up in tch: racd keenly: rdn and wknd over 2f out: t.o* **16/1**

0603 **10** *nk* **Johanna Fosie (IRE)**[18] 2624 3-8-12 **51**............ MatthewDavies 1 9
(Mick Channon) *led over 3f: chsd ldrs tl rdn over 5f out: wknd 4f out: t.o* **20/1**

00-6 **11** ½ **Firefly**[19] 2604 3-9-5 **58**............ ChrisCatlin 7 15
(John Weymes) *hld up: a in rr: lost tch fr over 3f out: t.o* **33/1**

2m 39.67s (-1.43) **Going Correction** -0.025s/f (Stan) **11** Ran **SP% 114.4**
Speed ratings (Par 97): **103,101,96,94,93 85,80,80,79,79 78**
toteswingers:1&2:£3.80, 2&3:£8.40, 1&3:£19.50 CSF £18.04 CT £525.42 TOTE £15.20: £3.60, £1.02, £6.70; EX 24.50 Trifecta £839.60 Pool: £1134.63 - 0.10 winning units..
Owner Sheikh Ahmed Al Maktoum **Bred** Darley **Trained** Newmarket, Suffolk

FOCUS
A moderate middle-distance handicap run at a stop-start gallop, though the time was still 1.69 seconds quicker than the maiden. None of these had won a race before.
Zowaina Official explanation: trainer's rep said, regarding apparent improvement in form, that the filly benefited from the step up in trip.

3234 LADBROKES H'CAP 5f 20y(P)

4:30 (4:31) (Class 4) (0-80,79) 3-Y-O **£4,528** (£1,347; £673; £336) **Stalls** Low

Form RPR

0653 **1** **Electric Qatar**[12] 2816 3-9-0 **72**............ RichardKingscote 8 82
(Tom Dascombe) *s.i.s: hld up: rdn over 1f out: str run to ld wl ins fnl f: sn clr* **7/1**[3]

-240 **2** 2 **Uprise**[13] 2785 3-9-1 **73**............ RyanMoore 1 76
(Sir Michael Stoute) *sn pushed along in rr: rdn over 1f out: hung lft ins fnl f: swtchd rt and r.o wl to go 2nd nr fin: no ch w wnr* **2/1**[1]

4241 **3** ½ **Beau Mistral (IRE)**[9] 2914 3-9-7 **79**............ CathyGannon 6 80
(Paul Green) *chsd ldr tl rdn over 1f out: r.o* **10/1**

-060 **4** *hd* **Jinker Noble**[28] 2347 3-9-3 **75**............ JohnFahy 2 75+
(Clive Cox) *chsd ldrs: n.m.r and lost pl wl over 3f out: r.o u.p ins fnl f* **4/1**[2]

1243 **5** *shd* **Ring For Baileys**[24] 2443 3-8-4 **65** .... RaulDaSilva(3) 5 65
(Chris Dwyer) *chsd ldrs: rdn to ld ins fnl f: sn hdd and unable qck* **4/1**[2]

0-50 **6** *1* **Judas Jo (FR)**[28] 2347 3-9-4 **76** .... NeilCallan 7 72
(Gay Kelleway) *prom: rdn over 1f out: styd on same pce fnl f* **33/1**

2165 **7** *nk* **Bookiesindexdotnet**[12] 2816 3-9-3 **75** .... (t) KierenFallon 9 70
(J R Jenkins) *led: rdn and hdd ins fnl f: no ex* **16/1**

10-0 **8** *1 1/4* **Lexington Spirit (IRE)**[58] 1514 3-9-1 **73** .... DavidNolan 4 64
(Richard Fahey) *prom: rdn over 1f out: wknd ins fnl f* **14/1**

0-45 **9** *1 3/4* **Mitie Mouse**[61] 1449 3-8-12 **70** .... ShaneKelly 3 55
(Mike Murphy) *mid-div: pushed along and hung rt 1/2-way: wknd over 1f out* **20/1**

1m 1.62s (-0.68) **Going Correction** -0.025s/f (Stan) **9** Ran SP% **115.2**
Speed ratings (Par 101): **104,100,100,99,99 97,97,95,92**
toteswingers:1&2:£4.50, 2&3:£5.30, 1&3:£6.10 CSF £21.32 CT £142.41 TOTE £8.70: £2.10, £1.10, £2.20; EX 38.70 Trifecta £796.20 Pool: £1215.94 - 1.13 winning units..
Owner A Black & M Owen **Bred** Miss Nicola Kent **Trained** Malpas, Cheshire

FOCUS
A decent 3yo sprint handicap, but the leaders went off too quick and the first two home were last and last-but-one at halfway.
Mitie Mouse Official explanation: jockey said gelding hung right throughout

3235 ROYAL ASCOT LIVE ON AT THE RACES MAIDEN STKS 5f 216y(P)
5:00 (5:00) (Class 5) 3-Y-O+ **£2,264** (£673; £336; £168) **Stalls** Low

Form RPR

0-03 **1** **Goldream**[14] 2764 3-9-3 **78** .... KierenFallon 8 87+
(Luca Cumani) *a.p: chsd ldr over 2f out: shkn up to ld over 1f out: edgd lft: sn pushed clr* **1/1**[1]

5 **2** *3* **Pearl Nation (USA)**[11] 2864 3-9-3 **0** .... WilliamCarson 3 80+
(Brian Baugh) *prom: nt clr run and lost pl over 2f out: swtchd rt over 1f out: r.o to go 2nd towards fin: no ch w wnr* **10/1**[3]

5 **3** *1* **Charming (IRE)**[21] 2543 3-8-12 **0** .... KirstyMilczarek 7 69
(Olivia Maylam) *chsd ldrs: rdn over 1f out: styd on same pce fnl f* **33/1**

42 **4** *5* **Supreme Quest**[25] 2422 3-8-12 **80** .... JamesDoyle 12 53
(Roger Charlton) *led: shkn up and hdd over 1f out: nt clr run sn after: wknd fnl f* **2/1**[2]

00 **5** *4* **Oceana Dreamer (IRE)**[23] 2501 3-9-3 **0** .... DavidProbert 9 45
(Andrew Balding) *mid-div: hdwy over 2f out: rdn and wknd over 1f out* **16/1**

-064 **6** *1/2* **Vite (IRE)**[17] 2680 3-9-3 **62** .... SilvestreDeSousa 10 43
(David C Griffiths) *mid-div: hdwy u.p over 2f out: wkng whn hung lft over 1f out* **33/1**

00 **7** *3/4* **Lothair (IRE)**[44] 1864 3-9-3 **0** .... PJMcDonald 4 41
(Alan Swinbank) *chsd ldr tl rdn over 2f out: wknd over 1f out* **33/1**

0/03 **8** *5* **Beaux Yeux**[41] 1957 6-9-0 **42** .... (be1) AnnStokell(5) 2 22
(Ann Stokell) *sn outpcd* **200/1**

00 **9** *2 1/4* **Green Wave (ITY)**[11] 2861 3-8-12 **0** .... (bt) MircoDemuro 1
(Frank Sheridan) *hld up: edgd rt over 2f out: nvr nr to chal* **200/1**

0456 **10** *1* **Wrapped Up**[17] 2647 3-8-12 **52** .... (v1) StevieDonohoe 11
(Heather Main) *s.i.s: a in rr: lost tch over 2f out* **40/1**

11 *3/4* **Stoneacre Hull (IRE)** 3-8-12 **0** .... RobbieFitzpatrick 6
(Peter Grayson) *s.s: outpcd* **200/1**

3 **12** *2 1/2* **Citizen Smith (IRE)**[11] 2864 3-8-10 **0** .... NatashaEaton(7) 13
(Alan Bailey) *s.i.s: hdwy over 4f out: hung rt and wknd over 2f out* **14/1**

1m 14.29s (-0.71) **Going Correction** -0.025s/f (Stan)
WFA 3 from 4yo+ 7lb **12** Ran SP% **117.7**
Speed ratings (Par 103): **103,99,97,91,85 85,84,77,74,73 72,68**
toteswingers:1&2:£3.00, 2&3:£21.50, 1&3:£8.10 CSF £12.51 TOTE £1.80: £1.10, £2.10, £6.60; EX 12.50 Trifecta £97.90 Pool: £783.83 - 5.92 winning units..
Owner Tsega Horses **Bred** Tsega Breeding Limited **Trained** Newmarket, Suffolk

FOCUS
A very uncompetitive maiden despite the numbers and they finished well spread out.
Beaux Yeux Official explanation: jockey said mare was slowly away
Green Wave(ITY) Official explanation: jockey said filly hung right
Stoneacre Hull(IRE) Official explanation: jockey said filly was slowly away

3236 LADBROKES CASINO H'CAP 1m 1f 103y(P)
5:30 (5:30) (Class 6) (0-60,60) 4-Y-O+ **£1,704** (£503; £251) **Stalls** Low

Form RPR

6530 **1** **Kyle Of Bute**[16] 2692 6-9-7 **60** .... WilliamCarson 13 67
(Brian Baugh) *chsd ldr: rdn to ld over 1f out: edgd lft ins fnl f: jst hld on* **16/1**

55-5 **2** *shd* **Celtic Step**[31] 2239 8-9-4 **57** .... PhillipMakin 12 63
(Peter Niven) *sn led: rdn and hdd over 1f out: ev ch and edgd lft ins fnl f: r.o* **11/1**

6040 **3** *1* **Sartingo (IRE)**[25] 2414 5-9-7 **60** .... PJMcDonald 3 64
(Alan Swinbank) *a.p: rdn over 1f out: hung lft ins fnl f: r.o: wnt 3rd post* **3/1**[1]

-000 **4** *nse* **Secret Era**[11] 2858 5-9-0 **56** .... RaulDaSilva(3) 2 60
(William Muir) *chsd ldrs: rdn and ev ch over 1f out: styng on same pce whn n.m.r and eased nr fin* **8/1**

0020 **5** *2 3/4* **Harrys Yer Man**[45] 1831 8-8-6 **52** .... JackDuern(7) 9 50+
(Mark Brisbourne) *hld up: swtchd rt and hdwy over 1f out: rdn and edgd lft ins fnl f: r.o* **8/1**

6405 **6** *hd* **The Which Doctor**[24] 2463 7-9-1 **54** .... (b) AndreaAtzeni 10 52
(Richard Guest) *hld up: r.o ins fnl f: nvr nrr* **10/1**

5511 **7** *1 1/2* **Harare**[19] 2600 11-8-12 **58** .... (v) GemmaTutty(7) 5 53
(Karen Tutty) *hld up: hdwy 5f out: rdn and wknd fnl f* **7/1**[3]

00-6 **8** *3 1/2* **Burza**[14] 2767 6-9-2 **55** .... (t) FrannyNorton 1 43
(Pat Murphy) *chsd ldrs: rdn over 3f out: wknd over 1f out* **10/1**

500 **9** *3/4* **Scribe (IRE)**[15] 2735 4-9-5 **58** .... CathyGannon 8 44
(David Evans) *sn pushed along in rr: rdn over 1f out: n.d* **4/1**[2]

5260 **10** *1/2* **Petomic (IRE)**[94] 922 7-9-3 **56** .... (p) StephenCraine 11 41
(Daniel Mark Loughnane) *hld up: rdn over 1f out: n.d* **16/1**

506- **11** *1/2* **Chlodan**[22] 3469 5-8-6 **52** .... DavidSimmonson(7) 7 36
(Michael Easterby) *s.i.s: sn prom: rdn over 2f out: wknd over 1f out* **66/1**

2m 2.74s (1.04) **Going Correction** -0.025s/f (Stan) **11** Ran SP% **119.5**
Speed ratings (Par 101): **94,93,93,92,90 90,89,85,85,84 84**
toteswingers:1&2:£18.80, 2&3:£9.00, 1&3:£10.00 CSF £183.43 CT £681.66 TOTE £25.50: £5.30, £4.00, £2.00; EX 158.20 Trifecta £615.30 Pool: £939.73 - 1.13 winning units..
Owner J H Chrimes And Mr & Mrs G W Hannam **Bred** Chippenham Lodge Stud Ltd **Trained** Audley, Staffs

FOCUS
A moderate handicap run at a modest pace and the first four were always at the front.
T/Jkpt: Not won. T/Plt: £122.10 to a £1 stake. Pool of £78,324.57 - 467.96 winning tickets. T/Qpdt: £11.20 to a £1 stake. Pool of £7,336.71 - 481.68 winning tickets. CR

2065 ASCOT (R-H)
Tuesday, June 19

OFFICIAL GOING: Good to soft changing to straight course - good; round course - good to soft (good in places) after race 2 (3.05)
Rail on Round course moved out 3yds from 9f to bend turning into home straight adding 9yd to 1m 2f race and 12yds to1m 4f &2m 4f races.
Wind: virtually nil Weather: fine

3237 QUEEN ANNE STKS (BRITISH CHAMPIONS SERIES) (GROUP 1) 1m (S)
2:30 (2:34) (Class 1) 4-Y-O+
£198,485 (£75,250; £37,660; £18,760; £9,415; £4,725) **Stalls** Centre

Form RPR

11-1 **1** **Frankel**[31] 2270 4-9-0 **138** .... TomQueally 8 142+
(Sir Henry Cecil) *lw: trckd ldrs a gng wl: led over 2f out: shkn up over 1f out: sn qcknd clr: edgd sltly rt ins fnl f: extremely impressive* **1/10**[1]

2-12 **2** *11* **Excelebration (IRE)**[31] 2270 4-9-0 **125** .... JPO'Brien 3 117
(A P O'Brien, Ire) *a.p: wnt 2nd over 2f out: rdn and unable to go w wnr over 1f out: no ch fnl f: all out to hold on for 2nd* **5/1**[2]

-531 **3** *nk* **Side Glance**[18] 2656 5-9-0 **113** .... JimmyFortune 5 116
(Andrew Balding) *racd keenly in tch: effrt over 2f out: wnt 3rd over 1f out: styd on towards fin: pressed 2nd cl home* **33/1**

05-2 **4** *1* **Indomito (GER)**[65] 1410 6-9-0 **108** .... WilliamBuick 10 113
(A Wohler, Germany) *hld up: swtchd rt over 2f out: rdn and hdwy over 1f out: styd on towards fin: nvr able to chal* **50/1**

0316 **5** *3* **Windsor Palace (IRE)**[31] 2270 7-9-0 **104** .... (v) SeamieHeffernan 7 106
(A P O'Brien, Ire) *s.i.s: racd in rr div and niggled along most of way: prog ins fnl f: styd on: nvr gng pce to get competitive* **100/1**

00-4 **6** *3/4* **Bullet Train**[31] 2270 5-9-0 **111** .... IanMongan 6 105
(Sir Henry Cecil) *led: pushed along and hdd over 2f out: sn outpcd: no ch fnl f* **66/1**

0-0 **7** *nk* **Helmet (AUS)**[80] 1145 4-8-13 **119** .... (tp) MickaelBarzalona 9 103
(Mahmood Al Zarooni) *racd keenly: prom: pushed along 3f out: outpcd ent fnl 2f: no ch fnl f* **20/1**

0-11 **8** *1 1/2* **Premio Loco (USA)**[35] 2160 8-9-0 **113** .... GeorgeBaker 11 101
(Chris Wall) *midfield: pushed along over 2f out: sn outpcd: no imp after* **50/1**

-314 **9** *3/4* **Red Jazz (USA)**[17] 2710 5-9-0 **112** .... MichaelHills 4 99
(Charles Hills) *hld up in midfield: pushed along 3f out: wl btn over 1f out* **50/1**

110- **10** *1/2* **Strong Suit (USA)**[227] 7307 4-9-0 **123** .... RichardHughes 1 98
(Richard Hannon) *lw: stdd early on: hld up: effrt in midfield over 1f out: no imp: sn wknd* **10/1**[3]

5-14 **11** *1 1/2* **Worthadd (IRE)**[18] 2656 5-9-0 **118** .... FrankieDettori 2 94
(Sir Mark Prescott Bt) *lw: handy: rdn 2f out: wknd over 1f out* **20/1**

1m 37.85s (-2.95) **Going Correction** +0.175s/f (Good) course record**11** Ran SP% **137.5**
Speed ratings (Par 117): **121,110,109,108,105 104,104,103,102,101 100**
toteswingers:1&2:£1.10, 2&3:£11.50, 1&3:£6.10 CSF £1.78 CT £16.79 TOTE £1.10: £1.10, £1.30, £5.50; EX 1.90 Trifecta £15.10 Pool: £37438.42 - 1824.51 winning units..
Owner K Abdulla **Bred** Juddmonte Farms Ltd **Trained** Newmarket, Suffolk

FOCUS
Drying ground all the time on a hot, sunny day, with times suggesting it was pretty much good. The rail was out 3yds from the 9f marker to the home bend, increasing distances by 6yds on the Old Mile, 9yds over 1m2f, and 12yds over 1m4f and 2m4f. They raced centre-field in this opening event and the pace was a level one. This was the definition of starting the meeting with a bang. Frankel rates the best horse in the history of RPRs (Sea The Stars and Daylami next on 138) and can rate higher, as this bare form was limited to an extent by the fourth and fifth. Excelebration was clearly below form.

NOTEBOOK
Frankel, the world's highest-rated racehorse, absolutely murdered his rivals, with the 125-rated Excelebration, who has become something of a punching bag for the favourite, a whopping 11 lengths back in second. Although his price contracted all the way down to 1-10 (one of the shortest-priced runners in the history of the Royal meeting), he produced a performance that surely exceeded expectations, even of those closest to the him, effortlessly tanking to the front before powering clear for what was his most impressive performance to date, in terms of form anyway, and in a very good time. Rated 138 prior to the race and now unbeaten in 11 with seven Group 1-wins to his name, it's scary that his master trainer feels he's getting better all the time, and anyone planning on going up against him in the Sussex, a race he won last year, will think again following this. The tendon injury suffered in April, which led to premature speculation that he'd be retired, seems a distant memory now and it looks as though the racing public will finally get a chance to see him over 1m2f in August's Juddmonte International, with the Champion Stakes presumably the ultimate goal, assuming everything goes to plan. (op 1-8 tchd 1-6 in places and 1-7 in places)

Excelebration(IRE)'s only defeats since his debut have come in races contested by Frankel, this being the fourth time he's finished runner-up to him. A Group 1-winning miler and very high-class in his own right, he can be rated better than the bare result, paying late on for having tried to match the invincible winner, and surely connections won't be taking him on again. He hasn't necessarily improved for the switch to Aidan O'Brien this year, but there are suitable opportunities in France for him in the coming months, and hopefully he'll get some well-deserved glory in Britain later in the campaign, with Frankel exiting the mile scene.

Side Glance likes it here and looked to run a career-best. Winner of a Group 3 at Epsom on Oaks day, he was slightly flattered to finish so close to Excelebration, but is clearly on the up again following a slightly subdued start to the season, and the Group 2 Summer Mile over C&D next month (beaten favourite last year), looks the obvious aim.

Indomito(GER), yet to win above Listed level, was ridden to pick up the pieces late and he did well to finish fourth. (op 66-1)

Windsor Palace(IRE) wasn't the best away, but he stays further and it was no surprise to see him making late gains.

Bullet Train performed his pace-making duties admirably. (op 100-1)

Helmet(AUS), an ex-Australian colt, got warm and raced far too keenly on this British debut. (tchd 25-1)

Strong Suit(USA) was very disappointing. Winner of last year's Jersey (also won Coventry at two), and a dual Group 2 scorer subsequently, he hadn't run since finishing well held in last year's Breeders' Cup Mile (raced wide; hampered), but fitness shouldn't have been a problem and he simply didn't pick up. He's high-class on his day, but is now 0-5 at Group 1 level.

Worthadd(IRE) was disappointing in the Epsom race won by Side Glance and this represented a further step backwards. (tchd 25-1)

3238 KING'S STAND STKS (BRITISH CHAMPIONS SERIES & GLOBAL SPRINT CHALLENGE) (GROUP 1) 5f

3:05 (3:12) (Class 1) 3-Y-0+

£198,485 (£75,250; £37,660; £18,760; £9,415; £4,725) **Stalls** Centre

Form RPR

0/4- **1** **Little Bridge (NZ)**51 6-9-4 116..........(t) ZacPurton 7 124
(C S Shum, Hong Kong) *swtg: chsd ldr: rdn to ld 1f out: r.o wl and a holding rival fnl f: rdn out* **12/1**

20-1 **2** *3/4* **Bated Breath**24 2486 5-9-4 118.......... JamesDoyle 8 121
(Roger Charlton) *in tch: rdn and effrt over 1f out: pressed wnr 1f out: r.o u.p but a hld fnl f* **11/2**2

-222 **3** *1* **Sole Power**24 2486 5-9-4 115.......... JohnnyMurtagh 22 117+
(Edward Lynam, Ire) *hld up in rr: swtchd lft and effrt 2f out: hdwy to chse ldng pair u.p jst ins fnl f: r.o but no imp fnl 100yds* **8/1**3

0553 **4** *1 1/4* **Medicean Man**10 2931 6-9-4 103..........(p) LukeNolen 3 113
(Jeremy Gask) *swtg: stdd s: hld up in rr: rdn and hdwy 2f out: swtchd lft 1f out: r.o wl ins fnl f: nvr looked like rching ldrs* **33/1**

2432 **5** *1 1/2* **Spirit Quartz (IRE)**18 2664 4-9-4 106.......... FrankieDettori 6 108
(Robert Cowell) *in tch in midfield: rdn and hdwy 2f out: drvn and chsd ldrs jst over 1f out: no ex and outpcd fnl 150yds* **16/1**

6-55 **6** *3/4* **Night Carnation**45 1857 4-9-1 105.......... JimmyFortune 10 102
(Andrew Balding) *racd keenly: in tch: rdn and unable qck over 1f out: styd on same pce and no threat to ldrs fnl f* **33/1**

-263 **7** *nse* **Caledonia Lady**33 2212 3-8-9 102.......... PaulHanagan 17 100
(Jo Hughes) *s.i.s: sn pushed along and outpcd in rr: hdwy and swtchd rt over 1f out: r.o wl ins fnl f: nvr trbld ldrs* **33/1**

11-0 **8** *1/2* **Tangerine Trees**24 2486 7-9-4 115..........(v) TomEaves 9 103
(Bryan Smart) *led: rdn over 1f out: hdd 1f out: no ex and sn btn: fdd fnl 100yds* **20/1**

5/1 **9** *1* **Ortensia (AUS)**80 1146 7-9-1 115..........(b) CraigAWilliams 5 96
(Paul Messara, Australia) *swtg: in tch: effrt on far side to chse ldrs over 1f out: drvn and no ex 1f out: wknd ins fnl f* **9/2**1

2-51 **10** *3/4* **Wizz Kid (IRE)**16 2745 4-9-1 113.......... GeraldMosse 15 94
(Robert Collet, France) *swtg: sn niggled along in midfield: lost pl and towards rr whn nt clr run jst over 2f out: swtchd rt and sme hdwy over 1f out: no imp fnl f* **9/2**1

4420 **11** *hd* **Monsieur Joe (IRE)**24 2486 5-9-4 110.......... WilliamBuick 12 96
(Robert Cowell) *in tch in midfield: rdn and unable qck 2f out: styd on same pce and no imp fr over 1f out* **66/1**

61-2 **12** *3/4* **Ponty Acclaim (IRE)**33 2212 3-8-9 105.......... TedDurcan 1 88
(Tim Easterby) *chsd ldrs: rdn over 2f out: struggling and btn over 1f out: wknd fnl f* **33/1**

1-02 **13** *nk* **Stepper Point**16 2745 3-8-12 109.......... MartinDwyer 4 90
(William Muir) *lw: in tch: effrt and rdn 2f out: no imp and btn jst over 1f out: wknd fnl f* **50/1**

-203 **14** *hd* **Hamish McGonagall**16 2745 7-9-4 110.......... DavidAllan 14 91
(Tim Easterby) *in tch: drvn and struggling 1/2-way: outpcd and no threat to ldrs fr over 1f out: plugged on* **33/1**

4000 **15** *2 1/4* **Prohibit**16 2745 7-9-4 114..........(p) JimCrowley 13 83
(Robert Cowell) *in tch in midfield: rdn and no rspnse 2f out: swtchd rt over 1f out: no imp and wl hld after* **25/1**

/2-3 **16** *1 1/2* **Joy And Fun (NZ)**80 1146 9-9-4 117..........(p) BrettDoyle 16 78
(D Cruz, Hong Kong) *bhd: swtchd lft and stl plenty to do over 1f out: no imp after: n.d* **16/1**

10-0 **17** *nk* **Bapak Chinta (USA)**24 2486 3-8-12 109.......... PhillipMakin 2 75
(Kevin Ryan) *sn rdn along in midfield: lost pl u.p 2f out: no ch 1f out* **40/1**

05-1 **18** *hd* **Stone Of Folca**17 2704 4-9-4 100.......... LukeMorris 21 76
(John Best) *chsd ldrs: rdn and struggling 1/2-way: wknd over 1f out: bhd fnl f* **33/1**

6-03 **19** *2 1/2* **Secret Asset (IRE)**30 2326 7-9-4 112.......... GeorgeBaker 19 67
(Jane Chapple-Hyam) *in tch: rdn and struggling over 2f out: wknd over 1f out: bhd and eased wl ins fnl f* **33/1**

30-6 **20** *nk* **Dinkum Diamond (IRE)**69 1316 4-9-4 106.......... FergusSweeney 23 66
(Henry Candy) *bhd: rdn and no rspnse 1/2-way: n.d* **100/1**

-000 **21** *1* **Margot Did (IRE)**45 1857 4-9-1 114..........(v1) HayleyTurner 11 59
(Michael Bell) *in tch: rdn and no rspnse 2f out: sn drvn and wknd: wl btn and eased fnl 100yds* **25/1**

21-4 **22** *1* **Amour Propre**18 2664 6-9-4 112.......... DaneO'Neill 20 59
(Henry Candy) *chsd ldrs: rdn 1/2-way: wknd wl over 1f out: wl bhd and eased wl ins fnl f* **33/1**

59.69s (-0.81) **Going Correction** +0.175s/f (Good)
WFA 3 from 4yo+ 6lb **22 Ran SP% 125.2**
Speed ratings (Par 117): **113,111,110,108,105 104,104,103,102,100 100,99,98,98,95 92,92,91,87,87 85,84**
toteswingers:1&2:£14.30, 2&3:£8.40, 1&3:£25.40 CSF £63.78 CT £589.39 TOTE £16.20: £2.70, £2.30, £3.20; EX 51.50 Trifecta £521.00 Pool: £15781.59 -22.41 winning units..
Owner Ko Kam Piu **Bred** Llanhennock Trust **Trained** Hong Kong
■ The first winner in Britain for both Danny Shum and Zac Purton.

FOCUS

This major sprint was dominated by overseas raiders in the four years following the re-opening of the course after refurbishment, with three Australians and a Spanish-trained winner, and this year there were challengers from Australia, France and Hong Kong and it fell to one of the raiders from the latter province. The field eschewed the rails and came in one group up the centre, with those drawn low (towards the far side) having the best of it. The straight course was changed to Good from Good to soft after this race. The winner recorded a personal best in an ordinary renewal, while the second sets the level with the third just off his Haydock mark from a disadvantageous draw.

NOTEBOOK

Little Bridge(NZ), a Group-class Hong Kong-trained sprinter who is best on a sound surface, was quickly away and always in the leading group. He went on well over a furlong out and was always holding the challenge of the runner-up. He will be aimed at a race in Hong Kong in September. (tchd 14-1 in places and 10-1 in places)

Bated Breath had suffered narrow defeats in a couple of Group 1s last season at 6f, and impressed with how he travelled dropped to 5f when winning the Temple Stakes on his previous start. He was never far away here and had every chance, but could not reel in the winner. The July Cup looks a natural target next and he will have a sound chance of breaking his duck at this level. (tchd 5-1, 6-1 in places)

Sole Power ◆, a former Nunthorpe and Temple Stakes winner who was narrowly beaten by today's runner-up in the latter race this season, was suited by the drying ground and did best of those that were drawn high. He ran pretty close to his Haydock form despite the draw not being in his favour and can win another race at the top level on this evidence. (tchd 9-1 in places)

Medicean Man, a three-time course winner from five previous attempts (two wins and a narrow defeat in three tries over C&D), had been gradually running into form. He had the usual cheekpieces back on instead of the blinkers he wore last time and ran a fine race, finishing well having been held up. He seems to save his best for this track and might well reappear in the Wokingham. (op 25-1)

Spirit Quartz(IRE), an ex-Italian Group 3 winner, has been steadily progressing for his new yard this season and did best of the Cowell trio. He had a bit to find on Temple Stakes running with a couple of these and ran pretty much to that mark, helping to give the race a solid look. (op 20-1)

Night Carnation, a Group 3 winner over 5f who stays 6f, had a bit to find on recent form but ran really well, being in the firing line throughout and only tiring in the last furlong or so. The drying ground was in her favour here and she can win more Group races this term.

Caledonia Lady ◆, whose only win was in Listed company, had placed on both previous starts here, including being a close third in the Queen Mary at this meeting last year, and did best of the 3yos. She was last of all at halfway, but made relentless late progress and would have finished closer had she got going earlier. (op 40-1)

Tangerine Trees, who made all when winning the Prix de L'Abbaye on Arc day last season, had been well beaten behind today's runner-up on his return. He travelled powerfully in front until well past halfway, but could not sustain the effort. He is better on a flatter track, though, and should be a player in the Nunthorpe and the Abbaye once again.

Ortensia(AUS) the only Australian challenger, had beaten a number of these in the Al Quoz Sprint at Meydan. She stays 6f, but is effective at 5f and got the good pace to run at that suits. However, she only briefly looked a threat when switched to make her effort. Her trainer could offer no explanation for the performance. Official explanation: trainer said he had no explination as to poor run. (op 11-2 tchd 6-1 ion a place)

Wizz Kid(IRE), a dual Group 2 winning French sprinter who is best with cut in the ground, had run a good second over 6f here last autumn and was well supported. She was out the back early before staying on to good effect more towards the stands' side and could be back here again in the autumn. (op 11-2)

Monsieur Joe(IRE), narrowly beaten in a French Group 3 last month, showed up for a fair way before fading.

Ponty Acclaim(IRE) won the Group 3 Cornwallis Stakes over C&D on her only previous start here and showed plenty of early pace before tiring. She should be up to winning good races at a slightly lower level.

Hamish McGonagall ran his usual game race, keeping going despite being pushed along before halfway. This consistent sort has yet to win a Listed or Group race and is probably best on a flat track. (op 40-1)

Prohibit, last year's winner, was held by several of these on recent form and faded after chasing the pace.

Joy And Fun(NZ), the other Hong Kong-trained sprinter whose form linked closely with the winner, was ponied to the start but was then re-saddled and got in a bit of a stew beforehand. He had been injured in this race in 2010 and perhaps he was remembering it. (op 20-1)

Margot Did(IRE), the surprise Nunthorpe winner last season and placed on all three starts at this track (all over 6f), had been below par in Dubai this spring and was visored for the first time. She raced prominently early, but was on the retreat from 2f out.

3239 ST JAMES'S PALACE STKS (BRITISH CHAMPIONS SERIES) (GROUP 1) (ENTIRE COLTS) 1m (R)

3:45 (3:48) (Class 1) 3-Y-0

£167,294 (£63,425; £31,742; £15,812; £7,935; £3,982) **Stalls** Low

Form RPR

13-0 **1** **Most Improved (IRE)**16 2743 3-9-0 115.......... KierenFallon 15 118
(Brian Meehan) *lw: trckd ldrs: wnt 2nd over 4f out: led over 2f out: rdn over 1f out: kpt on wl and a doing enough towards fin* **9/1**

336 **2** *3/4* **Hermival (IRE)**24 2514 3-9-0 116.......... GregoryBenoist 2 116
(M Delzangles, France) *handy: rdn and nt qckn over 2f out: edgd rt whn clsng on ldrs ins fnl f: r.o to take 2nd fnl strides* **9/1**

-150 **3** *hd* **Gregorian (IRE)**16 2743 3-9-0 111.......... RyanMoore 12 116
(John Gosden) *midfield: clsd over 5f out: rdn and tried to chal over 2f out: no imp on wnr ins fnl f: lost 2nd fnl strides* **14/1**

2-05 **4** *1* **Born To Sea (IRE)**24 2514 3-9-0 110.......... JohnnyMurtagh 11 113
(John M Oxx, Ire) *lw: midfield: nt qckn over 2f out: effrt over 1f out: styd on ins fnl f: gng on at fin* **7/1**2

-021 **5** *2* **Gabrial (IRE)**24 2485 3-9-0 101.......... JamieSpencer 1 109
(Richard Fahey) *midfield: rdn over 2f out: effrt and swtchd rt over 1f out: chsd ldrs ins fnl f: styd on: nt gng pce to get to ldrs* **16/1**

44-2 **6** *nse* **Foxtrot Romeo (IRE)**24 2514 3-9-0 114.......... RichardHughes 6 109
(Bryan Smart) *sn chsd ldr: lost 2nd over 4f out: remained prom: rdn and tried to chal over 2f out: unable to get to wnr over 1f out: wknd fnl 100yds* **14/1**

-046 **7** *1/2* **Saigon**19 2641 3-9-0 104.......... KirstyMilczarek 4 107+
(James Toller) *hld up in midfield on inner: rdn over 2f out: edgd lft over 1f out: styd on ins fnl f: nt gng pce to chal ldrs* **100/1**

11 **8** *1* **Cogito (USA)**19 2641 3-9-0 104.......... MartinDwyer 13 105+
(Brian Meehan) *squeezed out s: in rr: hmpd over 2f out: rdn and styd on over 1f out: nvr able to get to ldrs* **22/1**

1 **9** *1 1/4* **Lucayan (FR)**37 2110 3-9-0 113..........(p) StephanePasquier 14 102
(F Rohaut, France) *w'like: hld up: hdwy on outer 5f out: rdn to chse ldrs over 2f out: no imp over 1f out: wknd ins fnl f* **16/1**

0-20 **10** *1* **Miblish**61 1470 3-9-0 90..........(t) TomQueally 9 100+
(Clive Brittain) *lw: in rr: pushed along 4f out: forced wd over 2f out: kpt on u.p over 1f out: nvr trbld ldrs* **200/1**

2-10 **11** *2 1/4* **Dragon Pulse (IRE)**37 2110 3-9-0 113.......... FranBerry 10 95
(M Delzangles, France) *lw: midfield: rdn over 2f out: sn no imp: wknd over 1f out* **8/1**3

2-01 **12** *7* **Power**24 2514 3-9-0 117.......... JPO'Brien 5 79+
(A P O'Brien, Ire) *lw: hld up: hmpd over 2f out: nvr able to get competitive after* **11/4**1

3-63 **13** *9* **Fencing (USA)**33 2210 3-9-0 110..........(t) FrankieDettori 7 58+
(John Gosden) *lw: hld up: bdly hmpd over 2f out: nt rcvr: sn eased* **12/1**

-330 **14** *6* **Wrote (IRE)**24 2514 3-9-0 112.......... SeamieHeffernan 16 44+
(A P O'Brien, Ire) *led at gd pce: rdn and hdd over 2f out: sn wknd* **33/1**

20-1 **15** *dist* **Arnold Lane (IRE)**40 1996 3-9-0 97.......... MartinHarley 8 +
(Mick Channon) *midfield: bdly hmpd over 2f out: lost pl qckly: virtually p.u whn t.o over 1f out* **40/1**

3-12 **P** **The Nile**31 2277 3-9-0 103.......... WilliamBuick 3
(John Gosden) *trckd ldrs: lost pl over 3f out: wnt wrong and p.u over 2f out: fatally injured* **10/1**

1m 40.14s (-0.56) **Going Correction** +0.275s/f (Good) **16 Ran SP% 123.4**
Speed ratings (Par 113): **113,112,112,111,109 109,108,107,106,105 103,96,87,81,**
toteswingers:1&2:£17.70, 2&3:£28.00, 1&3:£28.00 CSF £86.21 CT £1190.12 TOTE £10.80: £3.00, £3.30, £4.30; EX 120.30 Trifecta £2189.80 Pool: £18707.78 - 6.32 winning units..
Owner Iraj Parvizi **Bred** Skymarc Farm Inc And Ecurie Des Monceaux **Trained** Manton, Wilts
■ Kieren Fallon's first British Group 1 win since Yeats in the 2006 Gold Cup.

FOCUS

There's no standout performer in the 1m 3yo division and it was about as open a running of this as there's been in recent times, with the largest field in at least 60 years. Although the race featured winners of both the Irish and French Guineas, it didn't look a strong edition. The pace was a good one, Wrote going hard to get across from stall 16, but there was trouble on the home bend when The Nile broke down, causing notable interference to at least a handful of the runners at the rear. The form needs treating with a hint of caution. The form is a bit below average for the grade with the runner-up the best guide, backed up by the third and seventh.

NOTEBOOK

Most Improved(IRE), forced to miss the Guineas and then subject to poor luck in the French Derby on his recent reappearance (met trouble; lost both front shoes), looked to have been dealt another blow by drawing stall 15. However, he managed to obtain a good position chasing the pace, and was then always likely to take some passing once kicking for home, given he's bred to stay further. He's entitled to progress again, although he'd be wasting his time if lining up against Frankel in the Sussex, and 1m2f may prove his best trip in time. (op 8-1 tchd 10-1in places)

Hermival(IRE), the 2000 Guineas third, got too far back on ground faster than ideal in the Irish equivalent. He took a while to pick up (his rider not using the whip until over 1f out) and a more forward ride would have seen him go even closer. Soft ground suits him best. (tchd 10-1)

Gregorian(IRE), fifth in a messy French 2000 Guineas before finishing well beaten in their Derby (wide trip), had a nice run through and seemed suited by the drop in trip. It remains to be seen whether he's a genuine Group 1 performer, though. (tchd 16-1)

Born To Sea(IRE) benefited from quicker ground and a first-time hood when settling better in the Irish Guineas, and he stepped forward again on that, despite racing more keenly than ideal. Perhaps 1m2f may be his trip if learning to settle, but he's another yet to convince he's a genuine Group 1 horse. (op 8-1)

Gabrial(IRE), impressive winner of the Silver Bowl at Haydock from a mark of 91, justified being supplemented into the race, doing well to stay on considering he raced keenly and was a bit cramped for room on the inner. (tchd 20-1)

Foxtrot Romeo(IRE) was unable to build on his Irish Guineas second, possibly sitting too close to the pace.

Saigon Official explanation: jockey said colt suffered interference in running.

Cogito(USA), for whom little went right, ended up in last and was then hampered turning in. (op 20-1)

Lucayan(FR), whose French Guineas was a very messy race, used up his juice here in closing wide rounding the final bend. (op 14-1)

Dragon Pulse(IRE) had no excuses, failing to pick up. (op 10-1)

Power, the Irish Guineas winner, lost his position early and was then badly hampered straightening for home. He was unable to pick up thereafter and can be given another chance. Official explanation: jockey said colt suffered interference in running. (op 10-3 tchd 7-2 in places)

Fencing(USA), with the tongue-tie back on, was off the pace and had just come under pressure when badly hampered. Official explanation: jockey said colt suffered interference in running. (op 10-1)

Arnold Lane(IRE) Official explanation: jockey said colt suffered interference in running.

3240 COVENTRY STKS (GROUP 2) — 6f

4:25 (4:26) (Class 1) 2-Y-O

£48,203 (£18,275; £9,146; £4,556; £2,286; £1,147) **Stalls** Centre

Form				RPR
11	**1**		**Dawn Approach (IRE)**[15] 2779 2-9-1 0 KevinManning 13 (J S Bolger, Ire) *str: t.k.h: hld up in tch: rdn and effrt over 1f out: led ent fnl f: asserting whn hung lft ins fnl f: sn stened and r.o wl* **7/2**[2]	114+
1	**2**	¾	**Olympic Glory (IRE)**[11] 2888 2-9-1 0 DaneO'Neill 16 (Richard Hannon) *lw: leggy: in tch towards rr: rdn and effrt over 2f out: hdwy and swtchd lft jst over 1f out: styd on wl u.p ins fnl f: wnt 2nd last strides* **20/1**	112+
	3	*nk*	**Cristoforo Colombo (USA)**[30] 2315 2-9-1 0 JPO'Brien 6 (A P O'Brien, Ire) *leggy: hld up in tch: hdwy over 2f out: rdn and ev ch 1f out: hrd drvn and no ex ins fnl f: one pce and lost 2nd last strides* **13/2**[3]	111
11	**4**	2 ½	**Sir Prancealot (IRE)**[19] 2638 2-9-1 0 RichardHughes 21 (Richard Hannon) *lw: stdd s: t.k.h: hld up in tch towards rr: nt clr run and swtchd lft 2f out: hdwy u.p over 1f out: chsd ldrs but kpt on same pce and no imp ins fnl f* **3/1**[1]	103
31	**5**	¾	**Artigiano (USA)**[22] 2550 2-9-1 0 FrankieDettori 11 (Mahmood Al Zarooni) *lw: stdd s: hld up in tch: rdn over 2f out: drvn: edgd lft and hdwy over 1f out: styd on but no imp fnl 100yds* **12/1**	101
	6	1 ¾	**Lines Of Battle (USA)**[23] 2523 2-9-1 0 RyanMoore 9 (A P O'Brien, Ire) *str: hld up in tch: pushed along jst over 2f out: swtchd rt and hdwy to chse ldrs jst over 1f out: drvn and btn jst ins fnl f: wknd fnl 150yds* **10/1**	95
2	**7**	1	**Leitir Mor (IRE)**[9] 2958 2-9-1 0 (p) RonanWhelan 14 (J S Bolger, Ire) *str: t.k.h: chsd ldr tl rdn to ld over 2f out: drvn and hdd ent fnl f: wknd fnl 150yds* **66/1**	92
11	**8**	1	**Indian Jade**[18] 2677 2-9-1 0 PhillipMakin 10 (Kevin Ryan) *unf: chsd ldrs: rdn and unable qck wl over 1f out: btn ent fnl f: wknd fnl 150yds* **40/1**	89
51	**9**	½	**Master Of War**[18] 2662 2-9-1 0 JimmyFortune 1 (Richard Hannon) *in tch in midfield: rdn and struggling over 2f out: hdwy jst over 1f out: styd on but no threat to ldrs fnl f* **50/1**	87
1	**10**	*nk*	**The Taj (USA)**[11] 2880 2-9-1 0 PaulHanagan 23 (Richard Hannon) *str: t.k.h: led tl over 2f out: stl ev ch and rdn 2f out: wknd jst over 1f out: fdd ins fnl f* **20/1**	87+
0112	**11**	1	**Heavy Metal**[17] 2702 2-9-1 0 SilvestreDeSousa 17 (Mark Johnston) *lw: in tch in midfield: rdn 1/2-way: n.m.r and struggling over 2f out: plugged on fnl f but no threat to ldrs* **20/1**	83
02	**12**	*shd*	**Dark Emerald (IRE)**[11] 2888 2-9-1 0 FranBerry 3 (Brendan Powell) *s.i.s: rdn along and outpcd in rr: drvn over 2f out: styd on past btn horses fnl f: n.d* **200/1**	83
133	**13**	*hd*	**Baddilini**[41] 1972 2-9-1 0 GeorgeBaker 2 (Alan Bailey) *racd alone towards far rail for 2f: chsd ldrs tl 2f out: sn rdn and wknd over 1f out* **100/1**	83
3	**14**	¾	**Whitfield (USA)**[18] 2667 2-9-1 0 WilliamBuick 5 (Jeremy Noseda) *stdd s: t.k.h: hld up in rr: swtchd rt and effrt towards far side 2f out: no prog over 1f out and btn 1f out: wknd fnl f* **100/1**	80
1	**15**	½	**Englishman**[60] 1499 2-9-1 0 MichaelHills 4 (Charles Hills) *stdd after s: hld up towards rr: swtchd rt and gd hdwy to chse ldrs after 2f: ev ch and rdn 2f out: btn over 1f out: wknd fnl f* **8/1**	79
2	**16**	1 ½	**Living Desert**[14] 2797 2-9-1 0 KirstyMilczarek 12 (James Toller) *in tch: rdn and losing pl whn sltly hmpd over 2f out: wknd wl over 1f out* **100/1**	74
3	**17**	*hd*	**King Dragon (IRE)**[10] 2929 2-9-1 0 MartinDwyer 7 (Brian Meehan) *towards rr: rdn and effrt 2f out: no imp: nvr trbld ldrs* **50/1**	73
12	**18**	¾	**New Pearl (IRE)**[18] 2677 2-9-1 0 JohnnyMurtagh 20 (David Brown) *chsd ldrs tl ent fnl 2f: sn rdn and wknd over 1f out: fdd fnl f* **25/1**	71
1	**19**	*nk*	**Funk Soul Brother**[33] 2213 2-9-1 0 DarryllHolland 18 (Charles Hills) *lw: stdd and hmpd s: a in rr: hmpd again after 2f: rdn and no prog over 2f out: n.d* **20/1**	70
5342	**20**	½	**Top Boy**[19] 2638 2-9-1 0 JoeFanning 8 (Derek Shaw) *t.k.h: hld up in midfield early: hdwy to chse ldrs after 2f out: rdn 2f out: sn wknd* **100/1**	69
41	**21**	7	**Party Royal**[20] 2594 2-9-1 0 MircoDemuro 22 (Mark Johnston) *t.k.h: chsd ldrs tl 1/2-way: sn rdn and lost pl: wknd 2f out and bhd fnl f* **66/1**	47
13	**22**	9	**Mrs Brown's Boy**[34] 2181 2-9-1 0 LukeMorris 19 (Ronald Harris) *a towards rr: rdn and struggling 1/2-way: lost tch 2f out* **100/1**	19

1m 13.64s (-0.86) **Going Correction** +0.175s/f (Good) **22** Ran SP% **126.1**

Speed ratings (Par 105): **112,111,110,107,106 103,102,101,100,100 98,98,98,97,96 94,94,93,93,92 83,71**

toteswingers:1&2:£23.60, 2&3:£35.40, 1&3:£2.30 CSF £78.40 CT £464.53 TOTE £4.40: £1.80, £7.20, £2.50; EX 117.70 Trifecta £1282.60 Pool: £14744.11 - 8.50 winning units..

Owner Mrs J S Bolger & J P Spain **Bred** J S Bolger **Trained** Coolcullen, Co Carlow

FOCUS

The principal colts' juvenile contest of the meeting and in recent seasons it has had a major bearing on future events, producing subsequent classic winners Henrythenavigator, Canford Cliffs and Power, plus Group 1-winning sprinters Red Clubs and Art Connoisseur. A big field for this year's contest with 16 previous winners (and nine of them unbeaten) taking part. This time the field came more centre-to-stands' side and the first three drew clear. It was a cracking time and Dawn Approach continues to impress. It looks a race to be dlightly positive about.

NOTEBOOK

Dawn Approach(IRE) ◆, unbeaten in three starts coming into this, including a Listed race from three previous winners, had gained all those successes with cut in the ground. However, he handled this surface well and kept finding despite being under pressure a fair way from home. He should stay further and the National Stakes at the Curragh looks a likely target. (tchd 10-3, 4-1 in places)

Olympic Glory(IRE) ◆, one of four runners for the yard, won an easy-ground Goodwood maiden earlier this month. He came from a fair way back and finished strongly, suggesting he will appreciate another furlong in due course. The Superlative at Newmarket and the Vintage at Goodwood are possibilities.

Cristoforo Colombo(USA), whose sire won this race, had scored on his debut at Navan and appreciated the ground drying out. He did best of those drawn low, but would not have been helped by racing away from where the pace was and can be given extra credit for this. A half-brother to a Middle Park winner, he should be up to winning a Group race if going on from this.\ (op 6-1 tchd 11-2)

Sir Prancealot(IRE), unbeaten in two starts, was particularly impressive when bolting up in Listed National Stakes despite being hampered in running. Stepping up in trip but the stable first string on jockey bookings, he was keen under restraint early and then could not make up the leeway on the leaders. It will be interesting to see if he reverts to the minimum trip next time. (op 7-2 tchd 4-1 in places)

Artigiano(USA) made an encouraging debut behind Funk Soul Brother at York and then bolted up in a Leicester maiden. Held up early, he was ridden over 2f out before staying on as if he would not mind a longer trip now. (op 16-1)

Lines Of Battle(USA) won a Curragh maiden on his debut last month from Leitir Mor and confirmed that effort, staying on steadily. (tchd 11-1)

Leitir Mor(IRE), narrowly beaten in all three starts in Curragh maidens, had the tongue tie he had worn on his last two starts replaced by first-time cheekpieces. He made the running to the benefit of his stable companion, but kept going quite well and should be up to picking up a small race. (op 50-1)

Indian Jade was a winner on his debut before beating well regarded 1-6 shot New Pearl at Pontefract on his second outing. He showed up until fading in the latter stages. (tchd 33-1)

Master Of War improved on his debut to run out ready winner of a Haydock maiden and looks to be progressing. (op 40-1)

The Taj(USA) impressed when scoring at Doncaster earlier in the month on his debut, but was very keen up with the pace and paid for it in the latter stages.

Englishman, the winner of a Newbury maiden on his debut from five subsequent winners, was the stable number one on jockey bookings. He got into contention soon after halfway before fading. (op 17-2)

3241 ASCOT STKS (H'CAP) — 2m 4f

5:00 (5:03) (Class 2) (0-95,95) 4-Y-0+

£34,237 (£10,252; £5,126; £2,563; £1,281; £643) **Stalls** Low

Form				RPR
350-	**1**		**Simenon (IRE)**[25] 3396 5-9-10 **95** RyanMoore 7 (W P Mullins, Ire) *in tch: nt clr run over 3f out: plld out over 2f out: led over 1f out: sn edgd rt: powered clr ins fnl f: sn wl in command: styd on wl* **8/1**[3]	106
1-11	**2**	6	**Al Khawaneej**[26] 2411 4-9-3 **90** JamieSpencer 10 (David Simcock) *lw: hld up: hdwy on outer over 2f out: styd on to take 2nd ins fnl f and edgd rt: no imp on wnr* **8/1**[3]	95+
54/5	**3**	1 ¼	**Nafaath (IRE)**[13] 2810 6-9-2 **87** SebSanders 15 (Neil King) *hld up: rdn and hdwy over 2f out: styd on ins fnl f: nt quite get to ldrs* **40/1**	91
0/	**4**	½	**Scots Gaelic (IRE)**[13] 2835 5-9-1 **86** DannyGrant 16 (Patrick J Flynn, Ire) *swtg: in tch: lost pl 8f out: u.p 3f out: styd on over 1f out: clsd towards fin* **40/1**	89
60	**5**	*shd*	**Western Pearl**[10] 2933 5-9-5 **90** FrankieDettori 1 (William Knight) *trckd ldrs: wnt 2nd over 3f out: upsides 2f out: unable to go w wnr over 1f out: styd on same pce ins fnl f* **10/1**	93
1-20	**6**	¾	**Spice Fair**[31] 2278 5-9-4 **89** JimmyFortune 8 (Mark Usher) *hld up: rdn and swtchd lft over 2f out: hdwy over 1f out: styd on and edgd rt ins fnl f: gng on at fin: nt quite get to ldrs* **25/1**	91
110-	**7**	1 ¼	**Becausewecan (USA)**[134] 6690 6-9-7 **92** JoeFanning 6 (Mark Johnston) *trckd ldrs: rdn over 2f out: tail flashed u.p over 1f out: one pce after* **33/1**	93
600-	**8**	½	**Ashbrittle**[94] 7406 5-9-3 **88** (b) PaulHanagan 4 (David Pipe) *lw: midfield: niggled along over 4f out: nt qckn wl 2f out: sn n.m.r: hdwy and lost pl: styd on ins fnl f but no ch* **14/1**	91+
-222	**9**	*nk*	**Dark Ranger**[33] 2214 6-9-2 **87** TomQueally 12 (Tim Pitt) *swtg: hld up: hdwy 9f out: chsd ldrs over 5f out: no ex u.p over 1f out* **8/1**[3]	87
110-	**10**	¾	**Veiled**[68] 6690 6-9-10 **95** EddieAhern 17 (Nicky Henderson) *midfield: effrt 3f out: sltly intimidated over 2f out: no imp whn n.m.r wl ins fnl f: sn eased* **9/1**	95
300/	**11**	*hd*	**Call It On (IRE)**[96] 2027 6-9-0 **85** PhillipMakin 19 (Philip Kirby) *racd keenly: led: rdn and jnd over 2f out: hdd over 1f out: wknd fnl 100yds* **100/1**	84
-644	**12**	½	**Twin Soul (IRE)**[38] 2066 4-9-0 **87** DavidProbert 9 (Andrew Balding) *trckd ldrs: rdn 3f out: wknd 2f out* **33/1**	86

U30- **13** *1* **Tuscan Gold**[33] 6690 5-9-0 **85** IanMongan 11 84
(Laura Mongan) *racd keenly in midfield: pushed along over 2f out: no imp* **66/1**

600- **14** *5* **Elyaadi**[16] 2740 8-9-5 **90** FranBerry 2 83
(John Queally, Ire) *midfield: rdn on inner over 2f out and sme hdwy: nt trble ldrs: wl btn ins fnl f* **6/1**[1]

0/31 **15** *1 1/2* **Monterey (IRE)**[10] 2936 5-9-4 **89** (b) RobertHavlin 13 80
(Robert Mills) *hld up: rdn and hung bdly lft over 2f out: c over to stands' side: nvr a threat* **11/1**

600/ **16** *10* **Fiulin**[62] 1821 7-9-5 **90** RichardHughes 5 71
(David Pipe) *lw: trckd ldrs: rdn 5f out: wknd over 2f out: eased whn btn over 1f out* **16/1**

/0-1 **17** *4 1/2* **Private Story (USA)**[11] 2874 5-9-0 **85** SilvestreDeSousa 3 62+
(David O'Meara) *lw: chsd ldr: rdn over 4f out: lost 2nd over 3f out: wknd over 2f out: eased whn btn over 1f out* **66/1**

606- **18** *1/2* **Sentry Duty (FR)**[32] 6690 10-9-10 **95** KierenFallon 14 71
(Nicky Henderson) *hld up: pushed along over 3f out: carried lft whn no imp over 2f out: nvr a threat* **20/1**

0-P2 **19** *2 1/4* **Danvilla**[10] 2936 5-8-13 **84** WilliamCarson 20 58
(Paul Webber) *stdd s: hld up: u.p over 2f out: a bhd:* **16/1**

10-4 **20** *1/2* **Cosimo de Medici**[24] 2479 5-9-4 **89** (t) DarryllHolland 18 62
(Hughie Morrison) *racd keenly: hld up in last pl: pushed along over 3f out: nvr on terms* **15/2**[2]

4m 30.5s (5.70) **Going Correction** +0.275s/f (Good)
WFA 4 from 5yo+ 2lb **20** Ran SP% **128.6**
Speed ratings (Par 109): **99,96,96,95,95 95,95,94,94,94 94,94,93,91,91 87,85,85,84,84**
toteswingers:1&2:£12.70, 2&3:£87.00, 1&3:£92.80 CSF £67.09 CT £2477.37 TOTE £7.50: £2.10, £2.10, £13.40, £10.10; EX 86.60 Trifecta £10171.60 Part won. Pool: £13745.50 - 0.03 winning units..

Owner Wicklow Bloodstock Limited **Bred** Max Morris **Trained** Muine Beag, Co Carlow

■ Stewards' Enquiry : Ryan Moore three-day ban; careless riding (3rd-5th July)

FOCUS

A typically competitive running of this marathon handicap. The pace was a steady one and two of the market leaders came to the fore late, with the race again going to a dual-purpose horse. Personal-bests from the first two.

NOTEBOOK

Simenon(IRE), who did his previous Flat racing for Andrew Balding, ran to a smart level for his new yard over hurdles last jumps season, winning twice, and he turned in a much-improved display on this return to the level, showing acceleration for a stayer and drawing right away. He may hang around for the Queen Alexandra over 2f further on Saturday, assuming he's none the worse, and it's not hard to see him running another big race. (op 7-1)

Al Khawaneej looked fairly treated off 5lb higher than when winning over 2m at Goodwood, and his performance can be upgraded after he found himself shuffled back before the final bend and forced to race wide. He picked up extremely well in the straight, before flattening, and could yet make a Pattern performer back at shorter. the Cesarewitch was also mentioned.

Nafaath(IRE) made a really promising return from 13 months off over an inadequate 1m2f at Kempton, and the step up to this marathon trip (has won a 2m4f maiden hurdle) clearly suited him well, making really good late progress. (tchd 33-1 in places)

Scots Gaelic(IRE), up 9lb for winning a 1m4f Fairyhouse handicap, is proven up to 2m and he saw the extra 4f out well considering he raced a bit wide.

Western Pearl, racing beyond 1m7f for the first time, travelled strongly up on the pace and had her chance, stamina looking to desert her late on. She's got a win in her back at shorter. (op 12-1)

Spice Fair showed his last-time-out Newmarket running to be all wrong, seeing out the marathon trip well having got a bit far back.

Becausewecan(USA), well beaten in this last year from 2lb lower and 0-3 over hurdles last season, held a good position and ran as well as could have been expected.

Ashbrittle may not have won, but he was staying on well and would probably have been in the mix but for getting badly hampered 2f out. Official explanation: jockey said gelding suffered interference in running. (op 11-1)

Dark Ranger was below his best but not helped by being posted on the outside of the field for most of the way. (op 9-1)

Veiled, 7lb higher than when winning last year, may have paid for closing up quickly out wide, being short of room late. (op 10-1)

Call It On(IRE) had the run of things before fading.

Elyaadi, runner-up from 4lb higher in 2010, was popular in the market but failed to get involved. (op 7-1)

Monterey(IRE) tends to hang left, his Newmarket win last time coming when racing alone against the far-side rail, but he gave away too much ground here. Official explanation: jockey said gelding hung left. (op 12-1)

Fiulin travelled nicely around the inner, but his stamina didn't seem up to it. (op 12-1)

Sentry Duty(FR) Official explanation: jockey said gelding suffered interference in running.

Cosimo de Medici, the gamble of the race, was dropped out in last, raced keenly, and ideally needed a faster gallop, although he still proved most laboured. (op 8-1)

3242 WINDSOR CASTLE STKS (LISTED RACE) 5f

5:35 (5:38) (Class 1) 2-Y-O

£31,190 (£11,825; £5,918; £2,948; £1,479; £742) **Stalls** Centre

Form RPR

321 **1** **Hototo**[19] 2614 2-9-3 0 PhillipMakin 18 101
(Kevin Ryan) *broke wl: sn stdd and in tch: swtchd lft and effrt over 2f out: rdn to ld jst ins fnl f: hld on gamely fnl 100yds: all out* **14/1**

1 **2** *1/2* **Alhebayeb (IRE)**[16] 2729 2-9-3 0 PaulHanagan 4 99
(Richard Hannon) *w'like: stdd s: hld up in rr: rdn: hdwy and edgd rt 2f out: drvn and chsd ldrs 1f out: kpt on wl to go 2nd wl ins fnl f* **12/1**

2 **3** *1/2* **Dylanbaru (IRE)**[24] 2512 2-9-3 0 (t) WayneLordan 20 97
(T Stack, Ire) *w'like: leggy: hld up towards rr: rdn and hdwy over 2f out: drvn and hdwy over 1f out: edgd rt and styd on strly ins fnl f: wnt 3rd last strides* **16/1**

011 **4** *nk* **Bungle Inthejungle**[17] 2688 2-9-3 0 MatthewDavies 5 96
(Mick Channon) *chsd ldr tl led after 1f: rdn over 2f out: drvn over 1f out: hdd jst ins fnl f: kpt on gamely: no ex and lost 2 pls wl ins fnl f* **16/1**

5 **5** *shd* **Parliament Square (IRE)**[34] 2184 2-9-3 0 JPO'Brien 21 96
(A P O'Brien, Ire) *leggy: in tch: effrt 2f out: drvn to chal and hung rt 1f out: styd on same pce fnl 100yds* **7/1**[3]

2 **6** *hd* **Ask Dad**[10] 2929 2-9-3 0 RyanMoore 11 95
(Richard Hannon) *lw: stdd s: hld up in rr: rdn and effrt jst over 2f out: hdwy u.p over 1f out: chsd ldrs ins fnl f: no ex and one pce towards fin* **10/1**

213 **7** *nse* **Liber**[17] 2702 2-9-3 0 LukeMorris 10 95
(Sir Mark Prescott Bt) *lw: in tch: effrt u.p to chal over 1f out: no ex u.p and one pce fnl 100yds* **18/1**

21 **8** *2* **Smoothtalkinrascal (IRE)**[29] 2330 2-9-3 0 ShaneKelly 1 88
(Brian Meehan) *towards rr: sltly hmpd: swtchd lft and rdn 2f out: hdwy u.p 1f out: styd on fnl f but nvr gng pce to rch ldrs* **9/1**

21 **9** *nk* **Pay Freeze (IRE)**[24] 2508 2-9-3 0 JohnnyMurtagh 14 87
(Mick Channon) *stdd s: hld up in tch: hdwy and edging rt 2f out: chsng ldrs and stl edging rt u.p ent fnl f: no ex and btn fnl 100yds* **4/1**[1]

321 **10** *2* **Polski Max**[27] 2402 2-9-3 0 TonyHamilton 3 80
(Richard Fahey) *in tch: rdn jst over 2f out: drvn and unable qck over 1f out: one pce and hld fnl f* **20/1**

1 **11** *1* **Cosmic Chatter**[18] 2663 2-9-3 0 GrahamGibbons 9 76
(David Barron) *leggy: w ldrs: rdn ent fnl 2f: drvn and unable qck over 1f out: wknd ins fnl f* **14/1**

413 **12** *1/2* **Top Notch Tonto (IRE)**[17] 2688 2-9-3 0 PatrickMathers 6 74
(Ian McInnes) *dwlt: sn pushed along and rcvrd to r in midfield: drvn over 2f out: kpt on but nvr gng pce to trble ldrs* **100/1**

51 **13** *nk* **Tommy's Secret**[25] 2442 2-9-3 0 WilliamBuick 17 73
(Jane Chapple-Hyam) *towards rr: rdn and struggling over 2f out: bhd and hung rt 2f out: rallied and styd on ins fnl f: no threat to ldrs* **50/1**

14 *3/4* **Ajmany (IRE)** 2-9-3 0 KierenFallon 22 70
(Luca Cumani) *w'like: scope: str: bit bkwd: sn pushed and outpcd: detached in last 1/2-way: stl wl bhd over 1f out: styd on wl ins fnl f: nvr trbld ldrs* **14/1**

411 **15** *nse* **Lyric Ace (IRE)**[48] 1747 2-9-3 0 RichardHughes 7 70
(Richard Hannon) *comp: in tch: rdn and effrt to chse ldrs wl over 1f out: drvn and btn 1f out: wknd ins fnl f* **5/1**[2]

022 **16** *3/4* **Fletcher Christian**[12] 2852 2-9-3 0 NeilCallan 19 68
(John Gallagher) *awkward leaving stalls: in tch in midfield: rdn and unable qck ent fnl 2f: wknd over 1f out* **100/1**

32 **17** *1/2* **Trinityelitedotcom (IRE)**[13] 2817 2-9-3 0 RichardKingscote 23 66
(Tom Dascombe) *racd alone against stands' rail: broke fast and led for 1f: rdn and struggling 1/2-way: wknd wl over 1f out* **50/1**

22 **18** *5* **Pearl Noir**[22] 2550 2-9-3 0 FrederikTylicki 12 48
(Scott Dixon) *w ldrs: rdn over 2f out: wknd over 1f out: fdd fnl f* **80/1**

2524 **19** *3/4* **Marvelino**[12] 2852 2-9-3 0 (v[1]) DaneO'Neill 16 45
(Pat Eddery) *w ldrs tl over 2f out: sn rdn and hung rt 2f out: wknd over 1f out: fdd fnl f* **100/1**

6 **20** *1 3/4* **Little Miss Zuri (IRE)**[26] 2426 2-8-12 0 LiamKeniry 13 34
(Sylvester Kirk) *w'like: sn pushed along and struggling towards rr: wknd wl over 1f out* **100/1**

361 **21** *1* **Pixilated**[6] 3046 2-9-3 0 JackMitchell 15 35
(Gay Kelleway) *w ldrs: rdn 1/2-way: wknd over 1f out: fdd fnl f* **80/1**

140 **22** *3 3/4* **Mossgo (IRE)**[19] 2638 2-9-3 0 JimCrowley 2 22
(John Best) *in tch in midfield: rdn and struggling 2f out: sn wknd: bhd fnl f* **100/1**

23 *11* **Jackpot** 2-8-12 0 KirstyMilczarek 8
(Brendan Powell) *leggy: in tch for 2f: sn rdn and lost pl: bhd fnl 2f* **100/1**

1m 1.21s (0.71) **Going Correction** +0.175s/f (Good) **23** Ran SP% **130.1**
Speed ratings (Par 101): **101,100,99,98,98 98,98,95,94,91 89,89,88,87,87 86,85,77,76,73 71,65,48**
toteswingers:1&2:£42.10, 2&3:£52.90, 1&3:£44.00 CSF £172.76 CT £2772.27 TOTE £19.00: £4.90, £5.40, £4.40; EX 334.90 Trifecta £3216.30 Pool: £13430.59 - 3.09 winning units..

Owner Kenneth Macpherson **Bred** B P Hammond **Trained** Hambleton, N Yorks

FOCUS

Not one of the strongest races of the meeting (subsequent Group 2 winner Frederick Engels was the best recent scorer) but highly competitive nonetheless and this year's big field made it more so. The main group raced up the centre and there was no apparent advantage. A tyoical renewal and straightforward form, with the third the best guide.

NOTEBOOK

Hototo had improved with experience, being runner-up to the useful Cay Verde in a good race over C&D before getting off the mark at Ayr on fast ground. He travelled well off the pace before picking up to take the lead and scored a little cosily in the end. He has several entries in sales races and could take in one of those later in the year, with the Molecomb, Gimcrack and Flying Childers as possible options. (op 12-1 tchd 11-1)

Alhebayeb(IRE) ◆, winner of a Nottingham maiden on his debut from more experienced rivals, is a half-brother to the speedy Humidor amongst others and ran a decent race, finishing amongst more experienced rivals, especially as he missed a beat at the start. He should be able to score at this level before long. (op 10-1 tchd 14-1)

Dylanbaru(IRE) had won only one of four previous starts, a Polytrack maiden, but was narrowly beaten by Cay Verde in a Listed race on his previous outing and finished well. He looks as if he will get another furlong on this evidence. (op 14-1)

Bungle Inthejungle, bidding for a hat-trick and well suited by fast ground, showed plenty of pace throughout but was run out of it near the line. He looks the sort to figure in Newbury's Super Sprint next month. (op 14-1)

Parliament Square(IRE), fifth behind three previous winners on his debut after getting upset in the stalls, was an interesting runner for a major yard. He came to have every chance nearest to the stands' side, but could not sustain the effort in the closing half-furlong. (op 10-1)

Ask Dad, runner-up on his debut in a 6f easy ground maiden, was dropping in trip but is bred to be speedy. He stayed on nicely and a return to 6f should see him getting off the mark. (op 14-1 tchd 9-1)

Liber, a decent third over 6f in the Woodcote when he didn't quite get home, showed plenty of pace back at the minimum and stuck on under pressure. He can win again at a lower level. (op 14-1 tchd 20-1)

Smoothtalkinrascal(IRE), runner-up in a good Newbury maiden before scoring in fine style at Leicester from a subsequent winner, was an interesting contender. He was drawn on the outside of his field, but was tucked in early then failed to pick up as well as could have been expected. (op 8-1)

Pay Freeze(IRE) was beaten by a subsequent winner on his debut and got off the mark next time in easy fashion at York (6f). Dropping in trip here, he surprisingly faded late on after having his chance. (op 5-1 tchd 11-2)

Cosmic Chatter knew his job when making all to win a 5f maiden on his debut at Haydock, but was restive before the start here and was too keen in the race. He can be given another chance. Official explanation: jockey said gelding was unsettled at start. (op 12-1)

Lyric Ace(IRE) needed the experience when fourth in a race that has worked out well on his debut, but had scored twice since, beating subsequent winners both times. The stable first string on jockey bookings, he showed up before weakening over a furlong out. (op 9-2 tchd 4-1)

T/Jkpt: Not won. T/Plt: £872.90 to a £1 stake. Pool of £518,016.98 - 433.20 winning tickets. T/Qpdt: £388.40 to a £1 stake. Pool of £19,559.44 - 37.26 winning tickets. SP

2994 BRIGHTON (L-H)

Tuesday, June 19

OFFICIAL GOING: Good to firm (good in places)

Rail moved out 2m from 4.5f to 3.5f adding 5yds to all distances.

Wind: Moderate, half against Weather: Fine

3243 EURO 2012 IN-PLAY AT BETVICTOR.COM H'CAP 5f 59y
6:00 (6:00) (Class 6) (0-60,60) 3-Y-O+ £1,617 (£481; £240; £120) Stalls Low

Form RPR

-003 1 **Festival Dance**10 2943 4-9-5 56 HarryBentley(3) 13 67
(Ron Hodges) *prom on outside: rdn and hdwy to ld over 1f out: edgd lft: hld on wl fnl f* 5/2[1]

5-51 2 hd **Autocracy**7 3008 5-9-6 54 6ex (bt) MickaelBarzalona 3 64
(Daniel Kubler) *t.k.h: hld up bhd ldng gp: effrt and plld out over 1f out: chsd wnr ins fnl f: r.o* 13/2

5000 3 2 **Colourbearer (IRE)**8 2973 5-9-11 59 (tp) CathyGannon 6 62
(Milton Bradley) *plld hrd: hld up on outside: drvn and outpcd 2f out: styd on wl fnl f: nt pce of first two* 5/1[3]

-545 4 hd **Imaginary Diva**10 2943 6-9-8 59 RyanPowell(3) 5 62
(George Margarson) *chsd ldrs: effrt and rdn wl over 1f out: kpt on same pce ins fnl f* 7/2[2]

5500 5 2 1/4 **Simple Rhythm**8 2971 6-8-5 46 oh1 (v1) BradleyBosley(7) 10 41
(John Ryan) *t.k.h: led to over 1f out: edgd lft and no ex ins fnl f* 20/1

5600 6 nk **Porthgwidden Beach (USA)**22 2551 4-8-12 46 oh1 (tp) ChrisCatlin 1 40
(Anthony Middleton) *chsd ldr to 1/2-way: rdn and no ex over 1f out* 28/1

-040 7 1 1/4 **Courtland King (IRE)**7 3005 3-9-3 60 (t) MatthewCosham(3) 2 47
(David Evans) *sn in tch on ins: rdn over 2f out: no ex over 1f out* 14/1

-600 8 3 **Wishbone (IRE)**105 813 5-9-5 53 TonyCulhane 7 32
(Jo Hughes) *plld hrd: hld up on outside: pushed along and edgd lft 2f out: sn struggling* 7/1

0-00 9 2 3/4 **Zigazag (IRE)**3 3141 3-8-13 53 (t) AndreaAtzeni 9 20
(David Evans) *rrd as stalls opened: bhd: rdn 1/2-way: btn whn edgd lft over 1f out* 18/1

45/0 10 nk **Berrymead**5 3076 7-8-11 50 AnnStokell(5) 11 18
(Ann Stokell) *in tch: struggling wl over 2f out: sn no ch* 33/1

1m 2.88s (0.58) **Going Correction** -0.10s/f (Good)
WFA 3 from 4yo+ 6lb 10 Ran SP% **116.4**
Speed ratings (Par 101): **91,90,87,87,83 83,81,76,71,71**
Tote Swingers:1&2:£2.40, 2&3:£5.70, 1&3:£1.90 CSF £18.67 CT £77.89 TOTE £3.30: £1.10, £2.30, £1.90; EX 19.90 Trifecta £54.30 Pool £770.07 - 10.49 winning units..
Owner Mrs M Watt A Midgley & R J Hodges **Bred** M Watt & Exors Of The Late Miss J John **Trained** Charlton Mackrell, Somerset

FOCUS
This moderate sprint handicap was run at a decent pace, with surprisingly few able to close from behind.
Wishbone(IRE) Official explanation: jockey said mare ran too free.

3244 BRITISH STALLION STUDS SUPPORTING BRITISH RACING E B F MAIDEN STKS 5f 213y
6:30 (6:30) (Class 5) 2-Y-O £3,169 (£943; £471; £235) Stalls Low

Form RPR

6 1 **Buy Art**11 2868 2-9-3 GeorgeBaker 4 75
(Gary Moore) *plld hrd: prom: led after 2f: hung lft and jnd by runner-up over 1f out: hld on wl u.p* 7/1[3]

42 2 1/2 **Kicken Off (IRE)**7 2995 2-9-3 AdamKirby 1 73
(Phil McEntee) *led 2f: rejnd wnr over 1f out: kpt on u.p: nt qckn fnl 50yds* 3/1[2]

56 3 3 **It's Only Business**8 2983 2-8-10 JakePayne(7) 3 64
(Bill Turner) *chsd ldrs: rdn over 2f out: kpt on fnl f* 25/1

22 4 1 **Emirates Echo**22 2556 2-9-3 MickaelBarzalona 5 62
(David Simcock) *dwlt: pushed along in detached last and nvr going wl: sme hdwy in centre 2f out: edgd lft: no imp* 8/15[1]

00 5 7 **Tough Question**26 2420 2-9-3 JamieGoldstein 6 40
(Michael Madgwick) *chsd ldrs tl wknd over 2f out* 100/1

0 6 13 **Madam Moreton**10 2938 2-8-12 TomMcLaughlin 2
(George Margarson) *sn outpcd in 5th: effrt in centre over 2f out: wknd wl over 1f out* 66/1

1m 11.32s (1.12) **Going Correction** -0.10s/f (Good) 6 Ran SP% **109.1**
Speed ratings (Par 93): **88,87,83,82,72 55**
Tote Swingers:1&2:£2.10, 2&3:£3.40, 1&3:£3.80 CSF £26.02 TOTE £7.00: £3.20, £1.30; EX 30.70.
Owner R A Green **Bred** Mount Coote Stud & M & W Bell Racing **Trained** Lower Beeding, W Sussex

FOCUS
An uncompetitive maiden run at a sound pace, with the first two home dominating from the off.

NOTEBOOK
Buy Art had attracted support and showed some promise before getting tired on his debut, but had clearly learnt plenty from that outing. He proved keen enough early, but was travelling so well his rider sent him to the front fully 3f from home. He was briefly headed inside the final furlong, but fought back well to win and while his task was made easier by the disappointing run of the favourite, there was plenty to like about this run. (op 9-1 tchd 11-2)
Kicken Off(IRE) had just been beaten over 5f here on his last start and ran another sound race. While he does not possess the scope of the winner, he was clear of the third and may be capable of landing a small maiden, perhaps back at the minimum trip. (op 11-4 tchd 7-2)
It's Only Business's chance was ruined last time when his rider's stirrup leathers snapped leaving the stalls, hampering his ability to ride a finish. No such drama unfolded here, but he could never get competitive on this drying ground. He stayed on under pressure and his pedigree suggests he will need further in time. (tchd 20-1)
Emirates Echo had shown ability on his two previous starts and was heavily backed to score here, but ran a most disappointing race. Slowly out of the stalls, he had to be driven to get competitive but never looked comfortable on this undulating track. He kept hanging in behind runners when taken wide for his effort and never looked like picking the leaders off. He had run well on good to firm last time, so the ground was no excuse, and it could be that he needs an easier track to be seen to his best. (tchd 8-13)

3245 BETVICTOR ON YOUR MOBILE H'CAP 5f 213y
7:00 (7:00) (Class 5) (0-70,76) 3-Y-O+ £2,264 (£673; £336; £168) Stalls Low

Form RPR

0040 1 **Whiteoak Lady (IRE)**3 3151 7-8-9 51 oh1 (p) AndreaAtzeni 3 60
(David Evans) *mid-div: rdn and hdwy 2f out: r.o to ld nr fin* 20/1

0045 2 nk **Bermondsey Bob (IRE)**13 2815 6-9-5 61 SamHitchcott 7 69
(John Spearing) *chsd ldrs on outer: drvn to lead ins fnl f: ct nr fin* 3/1[2]

-050 3 1 3/4 **Homeboy (IRE)**7 3016 4-8-10 59 KatiaScallan(7) 5 61
(Marcus Tregoning) *towards rr: rdn 3f out: r.o fr over 1f out: nrst fin* 10/1

4031 4 nk **Cheylesmore (IRE)**7 3000 4-10-6 76 6ex (v) GeorgeBaker 4 77
(Michael Wigham) *led: hrd rdn and hdd ins fnl f: no ex* 11/4[1]

2323 5 2 **Waabel**12 2838 5-10-0 70 (t) SaleemGolam 2 65
(Richard Guest) *prom: rdn to chal 2f out: wknd fnl f* 11/2[3]

3-40 6 1 1/2 **Uncle Timmy**16 2730 3-8-8 60 (t) MatthewCosham(3) 8 48
(David Evans) *in tch: drvn along 2f out: one pce* 16/1

-044 7 2 1/4 **Smoky Cloud (IRE)**47 1769 5-9-6 65 SeanLevey(3) 6 48
(Tony Newcombe) *prom: rdn over 2f out: wknd wl over 1f out* 13/2

0/03 8 2 1/4 **Pawan (IRE)**6 3018 12-8-4 51 oh1 (be) AnnStokell(5) 11 27
(Ann Stokell) *dwlt: a in rr: n.d fnl 2f* 22/1

0-56 9 1/2 **Bateleur**7 3008 8-9-1 62 CharlesBishop(5) 10 36
(Mick Channon) *hld up in rr: hmpd after 1f: mod effrt 2f out: n.d* 12/1

260- 10 5 **Monessa (IRE)**279 6053 3-9-0 63 FergusSweeney 1 19
(Linda Jewell) *mid-div: wknd over 2f out: sn bhd* 33/1

1m 10.03s (-0.17) **Going Correction** -0.10s/f (Good)
WFA 3 from 4yo+ 7lb 10 Ran SP% **115.1**
Speed ratings (Par 103): **97,96,94,93,91 89,86,83,82,75**
Tote Swingers:1&2:£13.10, 2&3:£11.30, 1&3:£37.60 CSF £76.95 CT £655.10 TOTE £47.50: £11.70, £1.10, £4.10; EX 200.10 TRIFECTA Not won..
Owner Jason Tucker **Bred** Thomas J Reid **Trained** Pandy, Monmouths

FOCUS
A competitive sprint handicap run at a decent pace, with plenty keen to lead, suiting those coming from off the pace. The form looks modest.
Pawan(IRE) Official explanation: jockey said gelding was unsuited by good to firm (good in places) going.

3246 BET ENGLAND, BETVICTOR H'CAP 1m 1f 209y
7:30 (7:31) (Class 6) (0-65,65) 3-Y-O £1,617 (£481; £240; £120) Stalls Low

Form RPR

-003 1 **Renegotiate**19 2625 3-9-1 59 DavidProbert 10 68
(Andrew Balding) *hld up in tch: hdwy to ld over 1f out: drvn and hld on wl fnl f* 9/2[2]

05-0 2 3/4 **Hollywood All Star (IRE)**29 2353 3-8-0 47 oh1 ow1 RaulDaSilva(3) 8 55
(William Muir) *hld up: rdn over 2f out: hdwy over 1f out: chsd wnr ins fnl f: kpt on wl* 25/1

25-3 3 2 1/4 **Trusting (IRE)**22 2548 3-9-1 59 CathyGannon 3 62
(Eve Johnson Houghton) *trckd ldrs: effrt and rdn over 2f out: kpt on same pce ins fnl f* 6/1[3]

6464 4 3/4 **La Confession**19 2624 3-8-6 50 ChrisCatlin 15 52
(Rae Guest) *cl up: ev ch over 2f out to over 1f out: kpt on same pce ins fnl f* 14/1

1454 5 3 3/4 **Anginola (IRE)**112 727 3-9-2 63 MatthewCosham(3) 5 57
(David Evans) *hld up in midfield on ins: carried bk by wkng rival over 3f out: effrt over 2f out: kpt on fnl f: no imp* 33/1

-000 6 hd **Choisirez (IRE)**14 2578 3-8-2 46 oh1 (v) JamieMackay 2 40
(David Evans) *led to over 1f out: sn rdn and outpcd* 40/1

4202 7 1 1/4 **Kelpie Blitz (IRE)**19 2624 3-9-7 65 GeorgeBaker 16 56
(Seamus Durack) *fractious bef s: in tch on wd outside: rdn and effrt over 2f out: wknd over 1f out* 11/4[1]

2003 8 hd **Vexillum (IRE)**14 2787 3-8-13 57 PatCosgrave 6 48
(Mick Channon) *hld up in midfield: drvn along over 2f out: no imp fr over 1f out* 7/1

0-06 9 3/4 **Ben Croy**24 2495 3-8-2 46 oh1 [1] MartinLane 4 35
(Brian Meehan) *chsd ldrs tl rdn and wknd over 1f out* 33/1

-000 10 11 **Verge (IRE)**28 2374 3-8-4 48 AndreaAtzeni 12 15
(Ed Vaughan) *hld up: rdn over 2f out: edgd lft and sn wknd* 25/1

00-0 11 5 **Lana Mae**24 2497 3-7-13 46 SophieDoyle(3) 7
(Brendan Powell) *hld up: rdn and struggling over 3f out: sn btn* 66/1

6002 12 3/4 **Musically**7 3002 3-8-13 57 SamHitchcott 14
(Mick Channon) *hld up on wd outside: drvn and struggling over 2f out: sn btn* 17/2

00-0 13 6 **True Prince (USA)**83 1067 3-8-4 51 HarryBentley(3) 1
(Amanda Perrett) *prom tl rdn and wknd over 3f out* 14/1

000 14 7 **Saharan Air (IRE)**39 2042 3-9-5 63 (v1) LiamKeniry 11
(George Baker) *t.k.h: hld up: struggling over 3f out: nvr on terms* 12/1

-505 15 4 1/2 **Search And Rescue (USA)**116 683 3-8-5 49 MickaelBarzalona 13
(J W Hills) *in tch on outside tl wknd wl over 2f out: sn eased whn no ch* 33/1

2m 3.21s (-0.39) **Going Correction** -0.10s/f (Good) 15 Ran SP% **123.6**
Speed ratings (Par 97): **97,96,94,94,91 90,89,89,89,80 76,75,70,65,61**
Tote Swingers:1&2:£94.10, 2&3:£43.60, 1&3:£7.30 CSF £121.72 CT £699.53 TOTE £5.40: £1.80, £11.40, £2.20; EX 160.90 TRIFECTA Not won..
Owner Birkdale Racing Syndicate **Bred** Hillen, Galvin, Hatta Bs & Tweenhills **Trained** Kingsclere, Hants

FOCUS
Another competitive-looking handicap that was run at a steady pace, suiting those racing up with the gallop.
Search And Rescue(USA) Official explanation: jockey said colt had no more to give.

3247 ENGLAND OUTRIGHT AT BETVICTOR.COM H'CAP 7f 214y
8:00 (8:00) (Class 6) (0-65,64) 4-Y-O+ £2,264 (£673; £336; £168) Stalls Low

Form RPR

/0-1 1 **Toga Tiger (IRE)**28 2365 5-8-6 52 RaulDaSilva(3) 1 68+
(Jeremy Gask) *in tch: hdwy to ld over 1f out: qcknd clr fnl f: readily* 7/4[1]

41-5 2 4 1/2 **Daffydowndilly**22 2555 4-9-3 60 (t) DarryllHolland 4 66
(Hughie Morrison) *t.k.h early: prom: effrt on outside over 2f out: chsd wnr appr fnl f: kpt on* 5/1[2]

2626 3 1/2 **Hip Hip Hooray**47 1772 6-9-5 62 IanMongan 6 67+
(Luke Dace) *hld up: drvn along and hdwy over 1f out: kpt on fnl f: nvr able to chal* 16/1

3153 4 nk **Brown Pete (IRE)**10 2937 4-9-5 62 (e) SaleemGolam 10 66
(Richard Guest) *dwlt: hld up: rdn and hdwy over 1f out: no imp fnl f* 7/1[3]

-021 5 nse **Lightning Spirit**19 2627 4-9-1 58 (p) GeorgeBaker 5 62
(Gary Moore) *hld up: rdn and hdwy over 1f out: no imp ins fnl f* 5/1[2]

0-20 6 2 **Pearl Opera**26 2431 4-8-10 53 TadhgO'Shea 11 52
(Denis Coakley) *t.k.h: hld up in tch: effrt and rdn 2f out: sn no imp* 16/1

3252 7 5 **Putin (IRE)**6 3052 4-7-13 49 (bt) DannyBrock(7) 12 37
(Phil McEntee) *t.k.h: led: rdn and hdd over 1f out: sn btn* 17/2

00-6 8 3 **My Vindication (USA)**7 3007 4-9-6 63 JackMitchell 8 44
(Gay Kelleway) *rrd s: hld: rdn 3f out: nvr able to chal* 33/1

0-55 9 1/2 **Sentosa**4 3096 5-9-5 62 FergusSweeney 13 42
(Michael Blanshard) *hld up in tch: struggling over 2f out: sn btn* 50/1

2654 10 7 **Lutine Charlie (IRE)**109 761 5-9-1 61 (v) MatthewCosham(3) 2 25
(David Evans) *t.k.h: cl up tl rdn and wknd fr 2f out: eased whn no ch fnl f* 28/1

0000 **11** 2 1/2 **High On The Hog (IRE)**[19] 2637 4-9-7 **64**.................. J-PGuillambert 3 22
(Paul Howling) *t.k.h: prom tl rdn and wknd over 2f out* **50/1**
1m 34.55s (-1.45) **Going Correction** -0.10s/f (Good) **11** Ran SP% **114.8**
Speed ratings (Par 101): **103,98,98,97,97 95,90,87,87,80 77**
Tote Swingers:1&2:£3.90, 2&3:£9.10, 1&3:£10.10 CSF £9.59 CT £102.39 TOTE £2.10: £1.10, £1.20, £8.00; EX 14.60 Trifecta £51.60 Pool £327.17 - 4.69 winning units..
Owner For Sale **Bred** Daniel Spaight **Trained** Sutton Veny, Wilts
FOCUS
A moderate handicap run at a sound pace and won in fine style by the well-backed favourite.
Lutine Charlie(IRE) Official explanation: jockey said gelding ran too free.

3248 ENGLAND SPECIALS AT BETVICTOR.COM H'CAP 7f 214y
8:30 (8:30) (Class 5) (0-75,75) 3-Y-O **£2,264** (£673; £336; £168) **Stalls** Low

Form RPR
2-22 **1** **Zaeem**[49] 1737 3-9-7 **75**.................. MickaelBarzalona 3 84
(Mahmood Al Zarooni) *hld up in midfield: smooth hdwy to ld ins fnl 2f: sn qcknd clr: eased fnl 50yds* **11/4**[2]
-252 **2** 1/2 **Good Luck Charm**[22] 2557 3-9-1 **69** ow1.................. GeorgeBaker 5 74
(Gary Moore) *sn chsng ldr: regained 2nd over 1f out: clsd on easy wnr fnl f but flattered by margin* **9/4**[1]
-000 **3** 2 **Zuzu Angel (IRE)**[28] 2367 3-8-0 **57**.................. HarryBentley(3) 8 57
(William Knight) *t.k.h: prom: outpcd over 2f out: styd on fnl f* **25/1**
1-51 **4** 3 **Final Delivery**[70] 1287 3-9-3 **71**..................(p) LiamKeniry 7 65
(George Baker) *trckd ldrs in 4th: effrt 2f out: one pce appr fnl f* **14/1**
100 **5** 1 1/4 **Good Of Luck**[31] 2281 3-9-7 **75**.................. PatCosgrave 2 66
(Mick Channon) *in tch: rdn to dispute 2nd 2f out: sn outpcd* **6/1**[3]
000 **6** 1 **Essell**[10] 2941 3-8-11 **65**.................. SamHitchcott 9 53
(Mick Channon) *bhd: rdn 3f out: nvr rchd ldrs* **10/1**
0453 **7** nk **Diamond Marks (IRE)**[7] 3005 3-8-5 **59**.................. ChrisCatlin 4 47
(John Gallagher) *bhd: mod effrt 2f out: n.d* **20/1**
3-01 **8** 2 3/4 **Daunt (IRE)**[33] 2203 3-9-2 **73**.................. SeanLevey(3) 1 54
(Alison Hutchinson) *led: sn 5 l clr: hdd & wknd ins fnl 2f* **8/1**
6110 **9** 7 **One More Roman (IRE)**[21] 2583 3-8-10 **64**..................(bt) JackMitchell 6 29
(Gay Kelleway) *towards rr: rdn over 2f out: sn struggling* **16/1**
1m 35.36s (-0.64) **Going Correction** -0.10s/f (Good) **9** Ran SP% **113.1**
Speed ratings (Par 99): **99,98,96,93,92 91,90,88,81**
Tote Swingers:1&2:£2.40, 2&3:£16.70, 1&3:£23.90 CSF £9.11 CT £119.90 TOTE £2.40: £1.10, £2.00, £7.40; EX 8.70 Trifecta £103.30 Pool £364.42 - 2.61 winning units..
Owner Godolphin **Bred** Umm Qarn Management Co Ltd **Trained** Newmarket, Suffolk
FOCUS
Another competitive handicap, run at a sound pace, with few able to get competitive.

3249 BETVICTOR NUMBER 1 FOR FOOTBALL BETTING H'CAP 6f 209y
9:00 (9:00) (Class 6) (0-65,65) 4-Y-O+ **£1,617** (£481; £240; £120) **Stalls** Low

Form RPR
5000 **1** **Comadoir (IRE)**[12] 2847 6-9-0 **57**..................(p) NathanSweeney(5) 1 68
(Jo Crowley) *mde all: rdn and hld on wl fnl 2f* **10/1**
1531 **2** 2 1/4 **Cut The Cackle (IRE)**[6] 3026 6-9-13 **65** 6ex..................(bt) SaleemGolam 4 70
(Richard Guest) *in tch: effrt over 2f out: chsd wnr fnl f: no imp* **7/1**
0021 **3** 2 **Jonnie Skull (IRE)**[6] 3053 6-9-0 **59** 6ex..................(vt) DannyBrock(7) 2 59
(Phil McEntee) *prom: rdn over 2f out: styd on fnl f* **11/2**[3]
0311 **4** 3/4 **Clear Spring (IRE)**[3] 3152 4-9-5 **57** 6ex.................. NickyMackay 8 55
(John Spearing) *rrd and s.s: sn rcvrd into 4th: chsd wnr over 2f out tl 1f out: no ex* **6/5**[1]
2046 **5** 7 **Sottovoce**[19] 2627 4-9-0 **52**.................. DarryllHolland 3 31
(Simon Dow) *prom tl wknd over 2f out* **16/1**
0652 **6** 1 **Highland Harvest**[7] 3000 8-9-6 **58**..................(b) IanMongan 7 34
(Jamie Poulton) *hld up in 6th: rdn over 2f out: n.d* **14/1**
0053 **7** 2 1/2 **Royal Box**[4] 3099 5-9-0 **52**..................(b) CathyGannon 5 21
(David Evans) *sn rdn along: a bhd* **5/1**[2]
1m 22.96s (-0.14) **Going Correction** -0.10s/f (Good) **7** Ran SP% **111.6**
Speed ratings (Par 101): **96,93,91,90,82 81,78**
Tote Swingers:1&2:£3.10, 2&3:£3.90, 1&3:£8.00 CSF £72.32 CT £419.15 TOTE £17.00: £7.00, £2.60; EX 65.00 Trifecta £317.30 Part won. Pool £428.90 - 0.80 winning units..
Owner Mrs Liz Nelson **Bred** J S Bolger **Trained** Whitcombe, Dorset
FOCUS
An uncompetitive handicap to end the card, run at a sound pace with the winner making all under a well-judged ride.
Sottovoce Official explanation: jockey said filly lost her action..
Royal Box Official explanation: trainers representative said the gelding was unsuited by going (good to firm (good in places).
T/Plt: £164.10 to a £1 stake. Pool £54,311.13. 241.55 winning tickets T/Qpdt: £21.60 to a £1 stake. Pool £5,625.93. 191.98 winning tickets LM

2282 THIRSK (L-H)
Tuesday, June 19

OFFICIAL GOING: Good to soft (good in places; 8.0)
Rail moved out 3-4yds on both bends adding about 12yds to 7f races and 17yds to races in excess of a mile.
Wind: Light half behind Weather: Sunny periods

3250 BRITISH STALLION STUDS SUPPORTING BRITISH RACING E B F NOVICE STKS 5f
2:15 (2:16) (Class 4) 2-Y-O **£4,528** (£1,347; £673; £336) **Stalls** High

Form RPR
61 **1** **Body And Soul (IRE)**[21] 2587 2-9-0 0.................. DuranFentiman 6 89+
(Tim Easterby) *trckd ldrs: swtchd lft and hdwy 2f out: rdn over 1f out: led ins fnl f: styd on wl* **5/2**[2]
521 **2** 2 **Forray**[15] 2763 2-9-2 0.................. RichardMullen 2 84
(Ed McMahon) *sltly hmpd s: t.k.h and chsd ldrs: cl up over 2f out: led 1 1/2f out: sn rdn and edgd rt: hdd and one pce ins fnl f* **2/1**[1]
031 **3** 1 1/4 **Lady Ibrox**[15] 2747 2-8-11 0.................. DaleSwift(3) 3 78
(Alan Brown) *cl up on inner: effrt 1/2-way and sn ev ch: rdn and n.m.r appr fnl f: sn one pce* **16/1**
5125 **4** 1 1/4 **Mayfield Girl (IRE)**[20] 2603 2-8-11 0.................. RobertWinston 7 70
(Mel Brittain) *chsd ldrs: rdn along wl over 1f out: sn no imp* **4/1**[3]
0521 **5** 1 **Lady Poppy**[11] 2873 2-9-0 0.................. PJMcDonald 1 69
(George Moore) *wnt rt s: sn led: rdn along over 2f out: hdd wl over 1f out and sn wknd* **4/1**[3]
0 **6** 12 **No Reply**[24] 2508 2-9-0 0.................. AdrianNicholls 4 26+
(David Nicholls) *dwlt: sn outpcd and a bhd* **50/1**
59.89s (0.29) **Going Correction** +0.125s/f (Good) **6** Ran SP% **109.7**
Speed ratings (Par 95): **102,98,96,94,93 74**
toteswingers:1&2:£2.20, 2&3:£3.30, 1&3:£5.40 CSF £7.53 TOTE £3.30: £1.40, £2.50; EX 8.80.
Owner C H Stevens **Bred** Michael Downey & Roalso Ltd **Trained** Great Habton, N Yorks
FOCUS
Not a bad novice event with the winner taking a big step forward.
NOTEBOOK
Body And Soul(IRE) got on top nearing the business end and won going away. She did well to win at Ripon on her previous outing and that form needs upgrading as she beat two subsequent winners. Duran Fentiman's decision to reign her back early on paid off as the pace rather collapsed in front of her late on, and she's better than the bare form as she was forced widest with her challenge. Her connections think highly of her and this ground was probably as easy as she wants it, so it's a good bet she can rate a fair bit higher this year. The Super Sprint at Newbury is likely to be up next. (op 11-4 tchd 9-4)
Forray got off the mark at the third attempt at Leicester 15 days earlier and unsurprisingly proved popular. He could have done without the ground drying out, though, and didn't help his cause by getting warm beforehand. He also took time to settle which blunted his finishing effort, but he was conceding the progressive winner 2lb so this was another decent effort. (op 15-8)
Lady Ibrox, a winner at Carlisle last time out, held every chance against the favoured stands' rail and posted a career-best in defeat. There will be other days for this likeable filly. (op 14-1)
Mayfield Girl(IRE) lacked a gear change and may have been better off under a more positive ride, but it's understandable that her jockey held onto her as there was plenty of pace on early. She won her maiden here three runs back and this Listed-placed filly rates the benchmark. (tchd 9-2)
Lady Poppy was found out in this much better company. (op 9-2 tchd 5-1)

3251 BOOK NOW FOR LADIES' DAY 8TH SEPTEMBER (S) STKS 6f
2:50 (2:52) (Class 5) 2-Y-O **£2,587** (£770; £384; £192) **Stalls** High

Form RPR
26 **1** **Jamesbo's Girl**[4] 3126 2-8-9 0.................. AdrianNicholls 4 75+
(David Nicholls) *trckd ldrs: hdwy to ld 1 1/2f out: sn rdn clr: styd on strly* **2/1**[1]
60 **2** 7 **Blades Rose**[14] 2790 2-8-4 0.................. ShaneBKelly(5) 8 54
(Richard Fahey) *cl up on inner: led over 2f out: rdn and hdd 1 1/2f out: sn drvn and kpt on: no ch w wnr* **6/1**[2]
2053 **3** 5 **Dil Laney (IRE)**[6] 3019 2-9-0 0.................. DanielTudhope 7 44
(David O'Meara) *wnt lft s: cl up: rdn 2f out: drvn wl over 1f out and sn outpcd* **2/1**[1]
440 **4** 1 1/2 **Windsor Rose (IRE)**[14] 2797 2-8-9 0.................. FrannyNorton 5 35
(Mark Brisbourne) *in tch: rdn along wl over 2f out: outpcd fr wl over 1f out* **17/2**
00 **5** 1/2 **Valetto (IRE)**[15] 2770 2-8-9 0..................(b[1]) AdamCarter(5) 6 38
(Tim Easterby) *hmpd and dwlt s: in rr tl pushed along and hdwy 1/2-way: rdn to chse ldrs 2f out: sn wknd* **33/1**
300 **6** 3 3/4 **Peep N Creep (IRE)**[17] 2686 2-8-9 0..................(b[1]) DuranFentiman 3 22
(Tim Easterby) *chsd ldrs on outer: rdn along whn sltly hmpd over 2f out: sn wknd* **15/2**[3]
043 **7** 13 **Miss Penny Arcade**[36] 2132 2-8-9 0.................. PaulMulrennan 2
(Keith Dalgleish) *sn led: rdn along 1/2-way: sn hung lft and hdd: wknd qckly* **16/1**
1m 13.45s (0.75) **Going Correction** +0.125s/f (Good) **7** Ran SP% **112.1**
Speed ratings (Par 93): **100,90,84,82,81 76,59**
toteswingers:1&2:£3.50, 2&3:£2.70, 1&3:£1.20 CSF £14.23 TOTE £3.40: £2.20, £3.20; EX 18.00.There was no bid for the winner.
Owner Pinnacle Jamesbo's Partnership **Bred** Lady Juliet Tadgell **Trained** Sessay, N Yorks
FOCUS
The winner proved far too classy in this 2-y-o seller.
NOTEBOOK
Jamesbo's Girl bolted up. She couldn't operate on the deteriorating surface in a better race at York last week and was better judged on her debut second in May. She shot clear after making her way to the front and is clearly a deal better than this level, even if it was a desperate affair. (op 11-4 tchd 15-8)
Blades Rose was firmly outclassed by the winner on this drop in grade, but beat the rest readily enough and should pick up something similar for his powerful yard. (op 7-1 tchd 8-1)
Dil Laney(IRE) was hampered at a crucial stage when beaten at odds on at Beverley last time. He was conceding the winner 5lb, but it made little difference as he was blown away by that rival. This is evidently his sort of level and he rates the best guide for the form. (op 11-4)
Windsor Rose(IRE) was dropping in class, but was easily found out by returning to the minimum trip and should appreciate stepping back up a furlong in similar company. (op 9-1 tchd 8-1)

3252 BRITISH STALLION STUDS SUPPORTING BRITISH RACING E B F FILLIES' H'CAP 1m
3:25 (3:26) (Class 3) (0-90,88) 3-Y-O+ **£6,792** (£2,021; £1,010; £505) **Stalls** Low

Form RPR
4441 **1** **Act Your Shoe Size**[22] 2539 3-8-7 **77**.................. PaulMulrennan 8 85
(Keith Dalgleish) *led to 1/2-way: chsd ldr: rdn wl over 1f out: styd on to chal ent fnl f: led last 150yds: hld on gamely* **9/2**[3]
2110 **2** shd **No Poppy (IRE)**[20] 2597 4-8-13 **78**.................. AdamCarter(5) 3 88
(Tim Easterby) *trckd ldrs: hdwy 2f out: effrt on inner and rdn over 1f out: styd on to chal jst ins fnl f and ev ch tl drvn and nt qckn nr line* **16/1**
0410 **3** 3 3/4 **Madam Macie (IRE)**[4] 3128 5-9-13 **87**.................. DanielTudhope 5 88+
(David O'Meara) *chsd ldr tl led 1/2-way: pushed clr 3f out: rdn over 1f out: jnd ent fnl f and sn drvn: hdd & wknd last 150yds* **7/2**[2]
0224 **4** 3 1/2 **Honeymead (IRE)**[11] 2882 4-9-9 **88**.................. ShaneBKelly(5) 6 81+
(Richard Fahey) *trckd ldrs: hdwy 3f out: rdn 2f out and sn one pce* **9/4**[1]
10 **5** 1 3/4 **Hawaiian Storm**[13] 2820 3-8-0 **70**.................. JimmyQuinn 7 57
(Mrs K Burke) *chsd ldng pair: rdn along 3f out: grad wknd fr over 2f out* **20/1**
-006 **6** shd **Basantee**[12] 2846 3-7-11 **70**.................. DominicFox(3) 1 57
(Tom Dascombe) *dwlt: a in rr* **40/1**
1-35 **7** hd **Lacily (USA)**[32] 2232 3-9-2 **86**.................. AhmedAjtebi 4 73
(Mahmood Al Zarooni) *dwlt: hld up in rr: effrt on outer and sme hdwy wl over 2f out: sn rdn: hung lft and nvr a factor* **9/2**[3]
1-5 **8** 3 3/4 **Ihtiraam (IRE)**[47] 1790 3-8-8 **78**.................. RichardMullen 2 56
(Saeed Bin Suroor) *chsd ldrs: rdn along over 3f out: sn wknd* **9/1**
1m 41.48s (1.38) **Going Correction** +0.25s/f (Good)
WFA 3 from 4yo+ 10lb **8** Ran SP% **112.4**
Speed ratings (Par 104): **103,102,99,95,93 93,93,89**
toteswingers:1&2:£7.80, 2&3:£9.40, 1&3:£4.60 CSF £68.44 CT £279.83 TOTE £5.70: £1.70, £5.00, £1.40; EX 86.10.
Owner Gordon McDowall **Bred** Gordon McDowall **Trained** Carluke, S Lanarks
FOCUS
A modest fillies' handicap.
NOTEBOOK
Act Your Shoe Size was raised just 1lb for her success at Carlisle last time and she followed up with a brave effort. She likes to dominate, but was headed into the home turn by the third and looked in trouble. She picked up most gamely when asked to rally from 2f out, though, and stuck her head out where it mattered at the finish. She's clearly improving, but the handicapper will now have his say. (op 11-2 tchd 6-1)
No Poppy(IRE) appreciated getting back on some easy ground and, making a bold bid, was just held on the far rail at the line. She remains in decent heart and sets the level. (op 12-1)

Madam Macie(IRE) flopped at York last week, but showed her true colours here and ran up to her official mark. (tchd 4-1)
Honeymead(IRE) was racing against her own sex for the first time since her previous win in 2010. She tried to close off the home turn, but proved laboured and probably needs some respite in the weights. (op 2-1 tchd 5-2)
Lacily(USA) never figured and looks one to swerve. (tchd 5-1)

3253 THEAKSTON BEST BITTER H'CAP 1m 4f
4:00 (4:00) (Class 4) (0-80,80) 4-Y-0+ **£4,140** (£1,232; £615; £307) **Stalls** Low

Form RPR
0422 **1** **Entihaa**[18] 2661 4-9-2 **75** PJMcDonald 6 84
(Alan Swinbank) *hld up in tch: hdwy 4f out: chsd ldng pair wl over 2f out: n.m.r and swtchd rt over 1f out and sn rdn: drvn ent fnl f: styd on wl to ld last 50yds* **9/4**[1]
2-06 **2** 3/4 **Flying Power**[26] 2419 4-9-0 **73** PaddyAspell 7 81
(John Norton) *trckd ldng pair: hdwy over 3f out: led over 2f out and sn rdn: edgd lft over 1f out: drvn ent fnl f: hdd and no ex last 50yds* **5/1**[3]
60-1 **3** 1 1/4 **Herostatus**[17] 2694 5-9-7 **80** DanielTudhope 1 86
(David O'Meara) *sn led: hdd 5f out: cl up on inner: led again over 3f out: rdn along and hdd over 2f out: drvn and ev ch tl one pce wl ins fnl f* **8/1**
1500 **4** 1 3/4 **Amazing Blue Sky**[10] 2921 6-9-2 **75** JamesSullivan 2 78
(Ruth Carr) *cl up: led after 4f: hdd over 4f out: pushed along over 3f out: rdn over 2f out and kpt on same pce* **4/1**[2]
40-0 **5** 9 **Beat The Shower**[38] 2093 6-9-1 **74** GrahamLee 3 63
(Peter Niven) *hld up in tch: pushed along wl over 3f out: sn rdn and wknd* **7/1**
0500 **6** 2 1/4 **Grey Command (USA)**[4] 3129 7-8-4 **63** DuranFentiman 8 48
(Mel Brittain) *chsd ldrs: rdn along wl over 3f out: sn wknd* **14/1**
2210 **7** 10 **Hunters Belt (IRE)**[30] 2312 8-8-0 **64** NeilFarley(5) 5 33
(Noel Wilson) *a towards rr* **25/1**
0660 **8** 22 **English Summer**[17] 2709 5-9-4 **77** (b) FrannyNorton 4 11
(Mark Johnston) *a towards rr: rdn along over 4f out: sn outpcd and bhd* **8/1**

2m 39.87s (3.67) **Going Correction** +0.25s/f (Good) 8 Ran SP% **112.7**
Speed ratings (Par 105): **97,96,95,94,88 87,80,65**
toteswingers:1&2:£2.70, 2&3:£6.00, 1&3:£3.00 CSF £13.19 CT £73.85 TOTE £3.00: £1.70, £1.60, £2.30; EX 15.80.
Owner Elsa Crankshaw & G Allan **Bred** Wardall Bloodstock **Trained** Melsonby, N Yorks

FOCUS
This was run at a solid gallop, but still it paid to race handily and there was a cracking finish.
Hunters Belt(IRE) Official explanation: jockey said gelding was never travelling.

3254 "LIKE" THIRSK RACECOURSE OFFICIAL FACEBOOK PAGE H'CAP (DIV I) 7f
4:40 (4:41) (Class 5) (0-70,69) 3-Y-0+ **£2,587** (£770; £384; £192) **Stalls** Low

Form RPR
00-4 **1** **Emeralds Spirit (IRE)**[20] 2598 5-9-6 **61** PaulMulrennan 7 71
(John Weymes) *trckd ldrs: hdwy 3f out: chal over 2f out: rdn to ld over 1f out: drvn ins fnl f: kpt on wl towards fin* **6/1**[3]
4-34 **2** 1 1/2 **Horatio Carter**[161] 115 7-9-12 **67** DanielTudhope 9 73
(David O'Meara) *towards rr: hdwy on outer over 3f out: pushed along to chse ldrs 2f out: rdn and edgd lft over 1f out: styd on to chal ent fnl f: sn drvn and ev ch tl no ex last 100yds* **5/1**[2]
5-20 **3** 1 3/4 **First Class Favour (IRE)**[57] 1561 4-9-11 **66** DuranFentiman 5 67
(Tim Easterby) *chsd ldr: hdwy to chal 2f out: sn rdn and ev ch tl drvn and one pce fnl f* **8/1**
0000 **4** 3 1/2 **Dhhamaan (IRE)**[10] 2924 7-9-4 **59** (b) JamesSullivan 4 51
(Ruth Carr) *set gd pce: rdn along and jnd 2f out: hdd over 1f out and grad wknd* **7/1**
00-3 **5** 3 1/2 **Brave Battle**[10] 2924 4-9-1 **61** ShaneBKelly(5) 3 43
(Ron Barr) *in tch: rdn along over 2f out: sn one pce* **11/1**
0100 **6** 1 **It's A Mans World**[11] 2879 6-8-10 **54** (b[1]) PaulPickard(3) 6 34
(Kevin M Prendergast) *dwlt and in rr tl sme late hdwy* **16/1**
-043 **7** 1 1/4 **Charles De Mille**[11] 2879 4-9-7 **62** PJMcDonald 1 38
(George Moore) *in tch: hdwy to chse ldrs 3f out: rdn 2f out: sn wknd* **11/4**[1]
5-00 **8** 2 1/2 **Vantaa (IRE)**[50] 1702 4-8-9 **50** RobertWinston 8 20
(Mrs K Burke) *a towards rr* **14/1**
1140 **9** 6 **Kipchak (IRE)**[13] 2815 7-9-3 **63** DavidKenny(5) 2 16
(Conor Dore) *chsd ldng pair: rdn along over 3f out: sn wknd* **33/1**
0-60 **10** 6 **Keys Of Cyprus**[17] 2696 10-10-0 **69** AdrianNicholls 10
(David Nicholls) *hld up: a in rr* **14/1**

1m 28.38s (1.18) **Going Correction** +0.25s/f (Good) 10 Ran SP% **111.7**
Speed ratings (Par 103): **103,101,99,95,91 90,88,85,79,72**
toteswingers:1&2:£5.70, 2&3:£4.20, 1&3:£7.50 CSF £34.44 CT £236.35 TOTE £5.80: £2.10, £1.50, £2.40; EX 31.00.
Owner T A Scothern **Bred** Epona Bloodstock Ltd **Trained** Middleham Moor, N Yorks

FOCUS
An ordinary handicap. There was a solid pace on, but once more it proved an advantage to be handy.
Charles De Mille Official explanation: trainer said gelding finished lame.

3255 FOLLOW THIRSK ON TWITTER @THIRSKRACES H'CAP 6f
5:15 (5:15) (Class 4) (0-85,83) 3-Y-0+ **£4,140** (£1,232; £615; £307) **Stalls** High

Form RPR
-220 **1** **Trade Secret**[38] 2096 5-9-8 **78** RobertWinston 8 88
(Mel Brittain) *hld up: pushed along 1/2-way: swtchd to outer over 2f out: rdn to chse ldng pair over 1f out: styd on ins fnl f to ld last 40yds* **15/2**
0005 **2** 1/2 **Whozthecat (IRE)**[2] 3183 5-9-9 **79** (v) DanielTudhope 7 87
(Declan Carroll) *mde most: rdn clr wl over 1f out: drvn ins fnl f: hdd and no ex last 40yds* **3/1**[2]
2132 **3** 2 1/4 **Green Park (IRE)**[3] 3169 9-9-3 **78** (b) NeilFarley(5) 4 79
(Declan Carroll) *a.p: effrt to chse ldr 2f out: sn rdn and one pce fnl f* **4/1**[3]
-100 **4** 5 **Just The Tonic**[24] 2510 5-9-3 **73** AmyRyan 5 58
(Marjorie Fife) *prom: rdn along 1/2-way: drvn wl over 1f out and sn one pce* **22/1**
00-1 **5** 1/2 **Fol Hollow (IRE)**[36] 2122 7-9-1 **78** ShirleyTeasdale(7) 9 62
(David Nicholls) *cl up on inner: rdn along over 2f out: grad wknd* **14/1**
0030 **6** hd **No Hubris (USA)**[20] 2596 5-9-9 **79** (b) JamesSullivan 1 62
(Ruth Carr) *chsd ldrs on outer: rdn along 1/2-way: sn wknd* **25/1**
0-23 **7** 2 1/4 **Spinatrix**[30] 2310 4-9-11 **81** PaulMulrennan 10 57
(Michael Dods) *a towards rr* **9/4**[1]
1015 **8** 3 3/4 **Bandstand**[12] 2841 6-9-2 **72** RoystonFfrench 3 36
(Bryan Smart) *s.i.s: a in rr* **25/1**
303- **9** 19 **Bonnie Charlie**[246] 6917 6-9-11 **81** AdrianNicholls 2
(David Nicholls) *s.i.s: a bhd* **20/1**

1m 12.66s (-0.04) **Going Correction** +0.125s/f (Good) 9 Ran SP% **111.0**
Speed ratings (Par 105): **105,104,101,94,94 93,90,85,60**
toteswingers:1&2:£5.00, 2&3:£3.10, 1&3:£5.10 CSF £27.40 CT £98.93 TOTE £5.70: £1.60, £1.80, £1.10; EX 34.40.
Owner Mel Brittain **Bred** Whitsbury Manor Stud **Trained** Warthill, N Yorks

FOCUS
This competitive sprint handicap was run at a strong pace and the principals dominated from the furlong marker.
Trade Secret Official explanation: trainer had no explanation as to apparent improvement in form.
Spinatrix Official explanation: jockey could offer no explanation as to poor running.

3256 "SUMMER JAZZ" EVENING MEETING MONDAY 25TH JUNE H'CAP 5f
5:45 (5:46) (Class 6) (0-65,64) 3-Y-0+ **£2,045** (£603; £302) **Stalls** High

Form RPR
6641 **1** **Tuibama (IRE)**[6] 3020 3-9-2 **58** 6ex (p) FrannyNorton 14 68
(Tracy Waggott) *racd towards stands' rail: mde all: rdn clr wl over 1f out: kpt on strly* **8/1**
60-0 **2** 1 1/2 **Myjestic Melody (IRE)**[25] 2458 4-8-13 **49** DanielTudhope 12 56
(Noel Wilson) *midfield: hdwy whn hmpd 2f out: sn rdn and styd on chse wnr ins fnl f: no imp towards fin* **16/1**
00-2 **3** 1 3/4 **Besty**[59] 1526 5-9-8 **58** MickyFenton 4 59
(Paul Midgley) *midfield: hdwy 2f out: rdn to chse ldrs wl over 1f out: kpt on u.p fnl f* **6/1**[2]
2-00 **4** 1 1/2 **Duke Of Rainford**[28] 2377 5-8-13 **49** GrahamLee 10 44
(Michael Herrington) *towards rr: hdwy 2f out: sn rdn: styd on fnl f: nrst fin* **25/1**
3645 **5** nk **Two Turtle Doves (IRE)**[6] 3026 6-9-8 **58** JimmyQuinn 3 52
(Michael Mullineaux) *hld up: hdwy 2f out: sn rdn and kpt on fnl f* **7/1**[3]
0313 **6** 1/2 **Hab Reeh**[6] 3020 4-9-2 **52** (bt) JamesSullivan 9 44
(Ruth Carr) *chsd ldrs: pushed along and hmpd 2f out: sn swtchd lft and kpt on u.p fnl f* **3/1**[1]
0-06 **7** 1/2 **Arch Walker (IRE)**[13] 2815 5-9-12 **62** (b) PaulMulrennan 5 58
(John Weymes) *in tch: effrt whn hmpd wl over 1f out: kpt on ins fnl f* **16/1**
4300 **8** 1 **Steel City Boy (IRE)**[13] 2815 9-8-13 **54** LMcNiff(5) 8 41
(Garry Woodward) *nvr bttr than midfield* **20/1**
5-06 **9** 1/2 **Dazzlin Bluebell (IRE)**[14] 2795 3-8-7 **49** DuranFentiman 2 32
(Tim Easterby) *cl up on wd outside: rdn along 2f out: sn wknd* **20/1**
5343 **10** 1 1/4 **Sally's Swansong**[32] 2244 6-9-0 **50** (b) KellyHarrison 6 31
(Eric Alston) *a in rr* **11/1**
03-0 **11** shd **Lujiana**[6] 3020 7-8-9 **45** PJMcDonald 13 25
(Mel Brittain) *sn rdn along and a towards rr* **50/1**
0663 **12** 3/4 **Nine Before Ten (IRE)**[24] 2493 4-9-12 **62** RobbieFitzpatrick 7 40
(Charles Smith) *dwlt: a in rr* **25/1**
6006 **13** 3/4 **Lucky Art (USA)**[13] 2809 6-9-9 **64** DavidKenny(5) 11 39
(Conor Dore) *prom: rdn along 2f out: sn drvn and wknd* **16/1**
-525 **14** 5 **Lees Anthem**[15] 2749 5-9-3 **53** PaddyAspell 1 10
(Colin Teague) *a towards rr* **20/1**
0-04 **15** nk **Mr Mo Jo**[6] 3018 4-9-9 **59** RobertWinston 15 15
(Lawrence Mullaney) *chsd wnr: swtchd lft and rdn 2f out: sn wknd* **16/1**

1m 0.2s (0.60) **Going Correction** +0.125s/f (Good)
WFA 3 from 4yo+ 6lb 15 Ran SP% **118.7**
Speed ratings (Par 101): **100,97,94,92,91 91,90,88,87,85 85,84,83,75,74**
toteswingers:1&2:£30.20, 2&3:£21.50, 1&3:£5.10 CSF £112.63 CT £847.07 TOTE £11.40: £3.60, £5.50, £2.60; EX 124.90.
Owner H Conlon **Bred** J F Tuthill **Trained** Spennymoor, Co Durham
■ Stewards' Enquiry : James Sullivan two-day ban; careless riding (3rd-4th July)
Robert Winston two-day ban; careless riding (3rd-4th July)

FOCUS
This ordinary sprint handicap was a typically open contest for the class and it was something of a messy affair.
Nine Before Ten(IRE) Official explanation: jockey said filly missed the break.
Mr Mo Jo Official explanation: jockey said gelding hung left throughout.

3257 "LIKE" THIRSK RACECOURSE OFFICIAL FACEBOOK PAGE H'CAP (DIV II) 7f
6:15 (6:15) (Class 5) (0-70,69) 3-Y-0+ **£2,587** (£770; £384; £192) **Stalls** Low

Form RPR
-620 **1** **Steel Stockholder**[10] 2924 6-9-9 **64** RobertWinston 1 72
(Mel Brittain) *trckd ldng pair: hdwy over 2f out: sn rdn to chal: led ent fnl f: drvn and hld on wl towards fin* **5/2**[1]
0004 **2** 1/2 **No Quarter (IRE)**[11] 2879 5-9-2 **57** FrannyNorton 5 64
(Tracy Waggott) *hld up in tch: hdwy over 2f out: rdn to chse ldrs over 1f out: drvn to chal ins fnl f: ev ch tl no ex towards fin* **6/1**[3]
2440 **3** 1/2 **Georgebernardshaw (IRE)**[25] 2455 7-9-2 **60** DeclanCannon(3) 10 65
(Richard Guest) *prom: cl up 1/2-way: chal 2f out and ev ch: rdn ent fnl f and no ex last 150yds* **6/1**[3]
5-50 **4** 1 1/4 **Clumber Place**[22] 2546 6-9-8 **63** PaulMulrennan 9 65
(James Given) *sn led: jnd and rdn 2f out: drvn and hdd ent fnl f: kpt on same pce* **17/2**
-600 **5** 3 1/2 **Flipping**[15] 2754 5-9-12 **67** KellyHarrison 6 59
(Eric Alston) *bhd: hdwy on inner 2f out: sn rdn and kpt on fnl f: nvr nr ldrs* **14/1**
-120 **6** nk **Drive Home (USA)**[17] 2696 5-9-7 **62** (p) BarryMcHugh 8 54
(Noel Wilson) *in rr: hdwy 3f out: rdn 2f out: sn drvn and no imp on ldrs fr wl over 1f out* **7/1**
-046 **7** hd **Ryedane (IRE)**[22] 2538 10-8-13 **61** (b) RachelRichardson(7) 2 52
(Tim Easterby) *t.k.h: chsd ldrs tl one pce fr over 2f out* **14/1**
4-62 **8** 4 **Gulf Storm (IRE)**[43] 1918 3-8-5 **55** (t) RoystonFfrench 4 32
(Bryan Smart) *chsd ldrs tl hung rt bnd after 3f: in rr after* **4/1**[2]

1m 29.09s (1.89) **Going Correction** +0.25s/f (Good)
WFA 3 from 4yo+ 9lb 8 Ran SP% **113.5**
Speed ratings (Par 103): **99,98,97,96,92 92,91,87**
toteswingers:1&2:£4.30, 2&3:£8.70, 1&3:£4.50 CSF £17.51 CT £80.33 TOTE £2.60: £1.10, £3.60, £1.30; EX 20.90.
Owner Mel Brittain **Bred** Mrs Joan M Langmead **Trained** Warthill, N Yorks

FOCUS
The second division of the moderate 7f handicap. It was run at a solid pace, but yet again it proved a race on the round course where it was an advantage racing handy.
Gulf Storm(IRE) Official explanation: jockey said colt hung right round bend.
T/Plt: £89.60 to a £1 stake. Pool of £48,151.28 - 391.87 winning tickets. T/Qpdt: £14.20 to a £1 stake. Pool of £3,876.46 - 201.42 winning tickets. JR

3258 - 3264a (Foreign Racing) - See Raceform Interactive

3237 ASCOT (R-H)

Wednesday, June 20

OFFICIAL GOING: Good (stands' side 8.7, centre 8.9, farside 8.8, round 7.7)

Rail on Round course moved out 3yds from 9f to bend turning into home straight adding 9yd to 1m 2f race and 12yds to1m 4f &2m 4f races.

3265 JERSEY STKS (GROUP 3) 7f

2:30 (2:35) (Class 1) 3-Y-O

£39,697 (£15,050; £7,532; £3,752; £1,883; £945) **Stalls** Centre

Form RPR

-032 **1** **Ishvana (IRE)**[24] 2527 3-8-12 108 SeamieHeffernan 6 111
(A P O'Brien, Ire) *dwlt: towards rr early: stdy prog 5f out: rdn to ld ent fnl 2f: drvn and r.o gamely fnl f* **20/1**

11 **2** *1* **Sentaril**[46] 1845 3-8-12 108 JohnnyMurtagh 11 108+
(William Haggas) *lw: stdd s: t.k.h: hld up towards rr: nt clr run briefly 2f out: rdn and effrt over 1f out: drvn and r.o wl ins fnl f: wnt 2nd last stride* **5/1**[2]

1-41 **3** *shd* **Aljamaaheer (IRE)**[32] 2277 3-9-1 107 PaulHanagan 18 111+
(Roger Varian) *t.k.h: hld up in midfield: effrt and edgd rt 2f out: drvn over 1f out: r.o wl u.p fnl f: wnt 2nd cl home tl last stride* **4/1**[1]

-123 **4** *hd* **Lethal Force (IRE)**[18] 2712 3-9-1 103 (p) AdamKirby 10 110
(Clive Cox) *hld up in tch: rdn and effrt over 1f out: drvn and kpt on wl to chse wnr wl ins fnl f: no ex and lost 2 pls last strides* **16/1**

4-31 **5** *nk* **Producer**[19] 2659 3-9-1 109 RichardHughes 3 110
(Richard Hannon) *chsd ldrs: rdn to chse wnr wl over 1f out: kpt on but unable qck 1f out: styd on same pce and lost 3 pls wl ins fnl f* **14/1**

-503 **6** *½* **Lady Gorgeous**[19] 2659 3-8-12 98 MartinHarley 1 105
(Mick Channon) *stdd after s: hld up in midfield: rdn and effrt on far side 2f out: drvn and chsd ldrs 1f out: styd on same pce fnl 100yds* **80/1**

-202 **7** *½* **Boomerang Bob (IRE)**[25] 2505 3-9-1 110 SebSanders 5 107
(J W Hills) *hld up in tch: nt clr run 2f out tl over 1f out: hdwy u.p ent fnl f: r.o wl: nt rch ldrs* **20/1**

-405 **8** *hd* **Ptolemaic**[34] 2210 3-9-1 109 (v) TomEaves 24 106
(Bryan Smart) *lw: chsd ldrs: rdn 2f out: kpt on u.p fnl f but nt pce to threaten ldrs* **66/1**

0-21 **9** *shd* **Sovereign Debt (IRE)**[40] 2022 3-9-1 100 JamieSpencer 22 111+
(Michael Bell) *stdd s: hld up in rr: in tch whn nt clr run and swtchd lft and bmpd rival 2f out: plenty to do and hanging rt over 1f out: rdn and hdwy 1f out: r.o strly: nt clr run and eased cl home* **12/1**

-503 **10** *hd* **Red Duke (USA)**[23] 2568 3-9-6 109 TomQueally 13 111
(John Quinn) *chsd ldrs: nt clr run briefly over 2f out: drvn over 1f out: kpt on u.p fnl f but nt pce to threaten ldrs* **25/1**

11 **11** *nk* **Valbchek (IRE)**[63] 1452 3-9-1 100 RyanMoore 25 105
(Jeremy Noseda) *lw: stdd s: t.k.h: hld up towards rr: rdn and hdwy 2f out: chsng ldrs and edgd rt u.p jst over 1f out: no ex and one pce fnl f* **11/2**[3]

13-3 **12** *hd* **Reply (IRE)**[25] 2514 3-9-1 113 JPO'Brien 9 104
(A P O'Brien, Ire) *chsd ldrs: nt clr run and shuffled bk into midfield over 2f out: swtchd rt and effrt u.p over 1f out: kpt on fnl f but nt threaten ldrs* **11/2**[3]

10-4 **13** *1 ¼* **Rebellious Guest**[60] 1509 3-9-1 99 IanMongan 7 101
(George Margarson) *stdd s: t.k.h: hld up in tch towards rr: rdn and effrt over 1f out: kpt on ins fnl f: nvr trbld ldrs* **100/1**

-130 **14** *3 ¼* **Eastern Sun (IRE)**[20] 2641 3-9-1 98 WilliamBuick 8 92
(John Gosden) *hld up towards rr: rdn and struggling over 2f out: no threat to ldrs but rallied and styd on fnl f* **66/1**

0220 **15** *1 ¾* **Bannock (IRE)**[35] 2179 3-9-1 109 SilvestreDeSousa 23 87
(Mark Johnston) *lw: led tl ent fnl 2f: sn u.p and unable qck: wknd jst ins fnl f* **66/1**

213- **16** *nk* **Ewell Place (IRE)**[307] 5216 3-9-1 98 StevieDonohoe 4 87
(Robert Mills) *t.k.h: chsd ldrs: rdn and struggling whn pushed rt over 1f out: wknd ent fnl f* **100/1**

1311 **17** *hd* **Laffan (IRE)**[19] 2660 3-9-1 90 AmyRyan 14 86
(Kevin Ryan) *chsd ldr tl over 2f out: sn drvn and struggling: wknd over 1f out* **40/1**

3-21 **18** *½* **Swiss Spirit**[33] 2236 3-9-1 104 MickaelBarzalona 2 93
(David Elsworth) *lw: plld hrd: chsd ldrs: rdn and unable qck over 1f out: btn jst ins fnl f: eased fnl 75yds* **20/1**

2-10 **19** *3 ¾* **Telwaar**[38] 2110 3-9-1 100 ChristopheSoumillon 20 75
(Peter Chapple-Hyam) *stdd s: hld up in tch towards rr: no imp wl over 1f out: wl hld and eased fnl f* **33/1**

5-10 **20** *2 ¾* **Talwar (IRE)**[46] 1856 3-9-4 104 JimmyFortune 26 70
(Jeremy Noseda) *stdd and swtchd rt s: hld up in tch in rr: effrt and rdn whn sltly hmpd 2f out: n.d after* **66/1**

-400 **21** *1 ¼* **Redact (IRE)**[20] 2641 3-9-1 104 JimCrowley 21 64
(Richard Hannon) *in tch: rdn and struggling jst over 2f out: wknd over 1f out* **80/1**

20-2 **22** *hd* **Justineo**[19] 2659 3-9-1 102 FrankieDettori 12 63
(William Haggas) *swtg: stdd s: hld up in rr: swtchd rt and effrt wl over 1f out: no imp and sn btn: eased ins fnl f* **33/1**

1m 25.45s (-2.15) **Going Correction** -0.025s/f (Good) **22** Ran SP% **124.5**

Speed ratings (Par 109): **111,109,109,109,109 108,108,107,107,107 107,106,105,101,99 99,99,98,94,91 89,89**

toteswingers: 1&2 £33.10, 1&3 £22.70, 2&3 £3.50. CSF £105.20 CT £507.43 TOTE £25.40: £7.60, £2.60, £2.30; EX 178.30 Trifecta £1104.00 Pool: £7,216.50 - 4.77 winning units..

Owner Mrs A M O'Brien **Bred** Mrs Ann Marie O'Brien **Trained** Ballydoyle, Co Tipperary

■ Stewards' Enquiry : Seamie Heffernan seven-day ban: used whip above permitted levle (Jul 4-10)

Johnny Murtagh two-day ban: used whip above permitted level (Jul 4-5)

FOCUS

The ground continued to dry out and was officially Good all round, though one rider in the opener described the going as "Good to firm". Even with the four non-runners this was the biggest Jersey field for years, but despite that they raced as one group up the centre of the track. The early pace looked just fair, but the winning time was only around half a second outside the course record. There was a pretty compressed finish and there are one or two doubts, but most of the first ten were close to their marks. The winner confirmed her surprise Irish Guineas improevment.

NOTEBOOK

Ishvana(IRE) had appeared flattered when finishing runner-up at 33-1 in the Irish 1,000 Guineas, but this performance proved otherwise. Sent to the front over 2f from home, she was never going to stop with her stamina guaranteed and she proved game in holding off her pursuers. This was her tenth start, but she seems to have really come to herself now. (tchd 25-1)

Sentaril, impressive winner of a Newbury maiden and Doncaster conditions event, was held up and didn't see a lot of daylight just as the pace was quickening. She ran on very strongly once out in the clear, but the winner had gone beyond recall. Even though this trip isn't a problem for her, she is bred to be a sprinter and it will be fascinating to see how she is campaigned now. (op 9-2)

Aljamaaheer(IRE) looked just the type for this race when winning a Newmarket Listed event last month and the drying ground was in his favour. He was another to finish well from the middle of the field and there are Pattern races to be won with him. (op 9-2 tchd 5-1)

Lethal Force(IRE), back up in trip following fair efforts in a couple of 6f Listed races, had cheekpieces on for the first time and ran on strongly under pressure late on. This was only his second try at 7f and he looks worth persevering with over it, especially if the headgear continues to have a positive effect. (op 20-1)

Producer, who is 4-4 at Epsom, is now 0-4 elsewhere but it would be harsh to be anything but complimentary about this effort as he fared best of those that raced up with the pace throughout. (op 16-1 tchd 20-1 in a place)

Lady Gorgeous finished much closer to Producer than she had at Epsom last time with this more conventional track probably helping. She was staying on well in the closing stages and may be able to find a Pattern race back against her own sex. (tchd 100-1)

Boomerang Bob(IRE) hadn't built on his second in the Greenham on his seasonal return, but this was better as he was another staying on well towards the finish. (op 25-1)

Ptolemaic, back down in trip after good efforts in the Craven and 2,000 Guineas but a heavy defeat in the Dante, had every chance passing the 2f pole but lacked finishing pace. His ideal trip is uncertain and he may not be the easiest to place. (op 50-1)

Sovereign Debt(IRE) ◆ was put up 10lb after his impressive success off 90 in a handicap over C&D last month, but ran a strange race this time. Having travelled apparently well near the back of the field, he was just about last with a huge amount of ground to make up 2f from home. Once switched left, he fairly flew but faced an impossible task. He can be rated much better than his final position and his next start should be very informative.

Red Duke(USA) showed up for a long way, but his Group 2 penalty was always going to make this a difficult task. (op 28-1 tchd 33-1)

Valbchek(IRE), unbeaten in two starts over 6f, always had this race as his target and the stable had won this twice in the previous ten years, but he hung away to his left once put under pressure and was making no impression on the leaders inside the last furlong. (tchd 5-1 in places)

Reply(IRE) looked the one to beat having finished third in the Middle Park and Irish 2,000 Guineas in his last two starts, but he gradually lost his early prominent position and there was no way back. This was disappointing. (tchd 4-1 and 6-1 and 13-2 in a place)

Laffan(IRE) Official explanation: jockey said gelding lost its action

Swiss Spirit was stepping up to 7f for the first time, so the last thing he needed was to pull like a train early. (tchd 22-1)

3266 WINDSOR FOREST STKS (GROUP 2) (F&M) 1m (S)

3:05 (3:09) (Class 1) 4-Y-0+

£56,710 (£21,500; £10,760; £5,360; £2,690; £1,350) **Stalls** Centre

Form RPR

40-2 **1** **Joviality**[19] 2654 4-8-12 109 WilliamBuick 3 115
(John Gosden) *lw: racd keenly: trckd ldrs: led 2f out: rdn and hung lft fr over 1f out: jnd by runner-up ins fnl f: plld out more cl home* **11/1**

22-1 **2** *nk* **Chachamaidee (IRE)**[39] 2078 5-8-12 113 TomQueally 11 114
(Sir Henry Cecil) *lw: sluggish s: hld up: hdwy 2f out: drew level w wnr and chalng ins fnl f: hld cl home* **4/1**[2]

41-5 **3** *1* **Lay Time**[19] 2654 4-8-12 109 JimmyFortune 7 112+
(Andrew Balding) *handy: rdn and nt qckn 2f out: rdn and swtchd rt jst over 1f out to chse ldrs: styd on same pce cl home* **9/1**

-443 **4** *1 ¼* **Barefoot Lady (IRE)**[19] 2654 4-8-12 108 PaulHanagan 6 109
(Richard Fahey) *racd keenly: led: rdn and hdd 2f out: stl ev ch 1f out: kpt on u.p: one pce towards fin* **14/1**

2-35 **5** *hd* **Beatrice Aurore (IRE)**[34] 2209 4-8-12 109 RyanMoore 13 108+
(John Dunlop) *swtg: in rr: rdn and hdwy over 1f out: styd on ins fnl f: clsd towards fin but unable to chal ldrs* **18/1**

-264 **6** *3* **Law Of The Range**[25] 2515 5-8-12 104 SilvestreDeSousa 12 101
(Marco Botti) *prom: rdn wl over 1f out: edgd rt whn outpcd and btn ins fnl f* **50/1**

11-1 **7** *hd* **Emulous**[25] 2515 5-9-3 115 PatSmullen 8 106
(D K Weld, Ire) *str: in tch: effrt to chse ldrs over 2f out: wknd ins fnl f* **11/4**[1]

0031 **8** *1 ¾* **Dysphonia (AUS)**[23] 2554 6-8-12 110 (p) FrankieDettori 5 97
(Saeed Bin Suroor) *hld up: sme hdwy over 2f out: no imp on ldrs: one pce fnl f* **25/1**

112- **9** *nse* **Nahrain**[229] 7284 4-9-3 117 NeilCallan 2 102+
(Roger Varian) *prom: rdn and chalng over 2f out: nt qckn over 1f out: wknd ent fnl f* **13/2**[3]

13-1 **10** *¾* **Clinical**[19] 2654 4-8-12 109 LukeMorris 10 95
(Sir Mark Prescott Bt) *hld up: rdn 3f out: nvr able to get on terms w ldrs* **11/1**

024- **11** *½* **I Love Me**[369] 3106 4-8-12 107 DavidProbert 1 94
(Andrew Balding) *racd keenly: hld up in midfield: rdn and lost pl over 2f out: nvr a threat* **22/1**

2-05 **12** *¾* **Rhythm Of Light**[124] 617 4-8-12 107 RichardKingscote 4 92
(Tom Dascombe) *lw: hld up: rdn and hdwy 2f out: no imp on ldrs: wknd ins fnl f* **66/1**

0-12 **13** *17* **Captivator**[45] 1883 5-8-12 105 KierenFallon 9 53
(James Fanshawe) *hld up: u.p 2f out: wl bhd fnl f: nvr a threat* **16/1**

1m 38.37s (-2.43) **Going Correction** -0.025s/f (Good) **13** Ran SP% **116.1**

Speed ratings (Par 115): **111,110,109,108,108 105,105,103,103,102 102,101,84**

toteswingers: 1&2 £10.80, 1&3 £18.60, 2&3 £8.10. CSF £51.43 CT £436.08 TOTE £13.20: £3.90, £1.80, £3.40; EX 62.10 Trifecta £940.60 Pool: £12,977.82 - 10.21 winning units..

Owner H R H Princess Haya Of Jordan **Bred** Highclere Stud And Floors Farming **Trained** Newmarket, Suffolk

FOCUS

The ninth running of this event attracted a suitably classy line-up, with a spread of only 9lb between the field on BHA ratings. They raced down the centre of the course. Pretty straightforward form, the winner rated up 7lb on her 3yo best.

NOTEBOOK

Joviality had made a promising return to action when second at Epsom, where she failed to act on the camber, but that outing put her just right for this. Settling better once taken back just off the pace, she edged to her left when in front but held off the runner-up a shade more easily than the margin implies. There's something about her head carriage that hints that she isn't wholly straightforward, but she battles hard enough. None of the last four winners of this went on to Group 1 glory but she will bid for success at that level in races like the Falmouth Stakes and the Nassau, with the 1m2f of the latter event sure to suit. (op 12-1)

Chachamaidee(IRE), not for the first time, missed the break by several lengths. She travelled strongly in rear and looked like succeeding when coming with a strong burst on the near side of the group, but once upsides the winner she could not quite sustain her run. Second in this event a year ago too, she is admirably consistent at this trip or 7f, and a worthwhile prize should come her way this season. She could run in the Falmouth Stakes at Newmarket, where her trainer believes the dip in the course could suit her. (op 7-2)

Lay Time had finished nearly six lengths behind Joviality at Epsom, where both track and ground were put forward as possible excuses. Running on well through the final furlong, after being slightly short of room, this was more representative of her capabilities. She might get a bit further. (tchd 11-1)

Barefoot Lady(IRE) again made the running and did not fold when headed, but honourable frame efforts have been the story of her career since she took the Nell Gwyn in the spring of last year. She has clashed with Jovialty on five occasions and has finished behind her rival three times now. (op 25-1)

Beatrice Aurore(IRE) was staying on stoutly from the back and on this evidence she will surely benefit from a return to 1m2f. She finished runner-up at that trip in the Group 1 Premio Lydia Tesio in Rome last autumn, and another crack at that prize would make a lot of sense. (op 33-1)

Law Of The Range had the least chance on official figures. After racing prominently her measure was readily taken by the principals, but she is a trier and she kept on to the line. (tchd 66-1)

Emulous was well placed and moved nicely, but her challenge never really materialised. She was saddled with a Group 1 penalty, having taken the Matron Stakes at Leopardstown last September, and her defeat means that all seven fillies to have carried such a penalty in this race have been beaten. (tchd 3-1 tchd 7-2 in a place)

Dysphonia(AUS), a tall mare, took only a minor event last time and never figured on this step back up in grade. (tchd 20-1)

Nahrain had reportedly pleased in her preparations for this seasonal return, but she drifted in the market. Another with a Group 1 penalty, her effort fizzled out but she can be afforded another chance, perhaps back up in trip. She will be fresher than most for the rest of the season. (op 11-2)

Clinical had today's winner, third and fourth behind when winning Epsom's Princess Elizabeth Stakes earlier this month, but she handled that track better than most and never featured this time. She is the seventh winner of the Epsom race to have failed here. (op 14-1 tchd 10-1)

I Love Me, not seen since finishing fourth in the Coronation Stakes a year ago, took time to settle and was never seen with a winning chance. (tchd 20-1 and 25-1)

Rhythm Of Light never figured on this first start for four months.

Captivator failed to give her running. (tchd 14-1)

3267 150TH ANNIVERSARY OF PRINCE OF WALES'S STKS (BRITISH CHAMPIONS SERIES) (GROUP 1) 1m 2f

3:45 (3:50) (Class 1) 4-Y-0+

£283,550 (£107,500; £53,800; £26,800; £13,450; £6,750) **Stalls** Low

Form	Pos	Dist	Horse / Details	RPR
6-41	**1**		**So You Think (NZ)**[24] 2525 6-9-0 125 .... JPO'Brien 7 (A P O'Brien, Ire) *lw: chsd ldng pair: led gng wl 2f out: sn chal and rdn: qcknd clr w rival over 1f out: led ins fnl f: styd on strly and drew clr fnl 100yds* **4/5**[1]	127
34-1	**2**	*2 ¼*	**Carlton House (USA)**[20] 2640 4-9-0 119 .... RyanMoore 2 (Sir Michael Stoute) *t.k.h: hld up in midfield: swtchd lft and effrt over 2f out: rdn and qcknd to chal wl over 1f out: clr w wnr over 1f out: btn ins fnl f: tired and all out to hold 2nd cl home* **7/2**[2]	122
/1-1	**3**	*½*	**Farhh**[46] 1865 4-9-0 114 .... FrankieDettori 8 (Saeed Bin Suroor) *lw: rrd as stalls opened and slowly away: dropped in bhd: hdwy on inner 2f out: nt clr run over 1f out tl ins fnl f: gd hdwy and swtchd lft ins fnl f: gng on strly at fin* **6/1**[3]	123+
0-30	**4**	*nk*	**Reliable Man**[24] 2533 4-9-0 116 .... (t) GeraldMosse 9 (A De Royer-Dupre, France) *stdd s: hld up in last pair: rdn 2f out: swtchd lft and gd hdwy over 1f out: wnt 3rd fnl 100yds: r.o but lost 3rd cl home* **12/1**	121+
0-16	**5**	*1 ¼*	**Sri Putra**[38] 2106 6-9-0 115 .... NeilCallan 3 (Roger Varian) *lw: hld up in tch in last quartet: rdn and effrt 2f out: outpcd by ldng pair whn n.m.r and squeezed between horses over 1f out: no threat to wnr but kpt on u.p fnl f* **66/1**	118
2123	**6**	*¾*	**City Style (USA)**[81] 1148 6-9-0 116 .... MickaelBarzalona 11 (Mahmood Al Zarooni) *swtg: stdd and swtchd rt after s: hld up in midfield: effrt ent fnl 2f: outpcd by ldng pair and hung rt and nt clr run 1f out: swtchd lft and styd on ins fnl f: no threat to wnr* **33/1**	119+
0-33	**7**	*½*	**Planteur (IRE)**[24] 2533 5-9-0 121 .... ChristopheSoumillon 1 (Marco Botti) *swtg: t.k.h: hld up in tch in last quartet: rdn and effrt ent fnl 2f: outpcd by ldng pair wl over 1f out: wnt 3rd 1f out tl fnl 100yds: wknd towards fin* **10/1**	116
1-15	**8**	*1 ¾*	**Colombian (IRE)**[20] 2640 4-9-0 115 .... WilliamBuick 4 (John Gosden) *swtg: chsd ldrs: rdn and effrt whn pushed lft over 2f out: swtchd lft and no imp over 1f out: wknd ins fnl f* **40/1**	112
6443	**9**	*shd*	**Wigmore Hall (IRE)**[41] 1994 5-9-0 115 .... JamieSpencer 6 (Michael Bell) *hld up in tch: swtchd lft and effrt jst over 2f out: sn outpcd by ldng pair and drvn: wknd ins fnl f* **33/1**	112
	10	*6*	**Big Blue Kitten (USA)**[59] 4-9-0 105 .... (t) JohnnyMurtagh 10 (Chad C Brown, U.S.A) *str: swtg: chsd ldr tl rdn to ld over 2f out: hdd and drvn 2f out: sn outpcd by ldng pair: lost 3rd 1f out: fdd fnl f* **50/1**	100
/436	**11**	*22*	**Robin Hood (IRE)**[18] 2703 4-9-0 99 .... (v) SeamieHeffernan 5 (A P O'Brien, Ire) *led: rdn 3f out: hdd over 1f out: wknd and bhd over 1f out: eased fnl f: t.o* **200/1**	56

2m 3.86s (-3.54) **Going Correction** +0.125s/f (Good) **11** Ran SP% **121.1**

Speed ratings (Par 117): **119,117,116,116,115 114,114,113,113,108 90**

toteswingers: 1&2 £1.70, 1&3 £2.10, 2&3 £4.00. CSF £3.72 CT £10.98 TOTE £1.90: £1.10, £1.50, £1.70; EX 4.80 Trifecta £13.90 Pool: £24,981.36 - 1,327.59 winning units..

Owner Smith/Magnier/Tabor/DatoTan/TunkuYahaya **Bred** M J Moran & Piper Farm Ltd **Trained** Ballydoyle, Co Tipperary

FOCUS

The absence of Cirrus Des Aigles took something away from the quality of this contest, but it was still a fascinating renewal featuring a much-heralded international star, challengers from the US and France (who had won this three times in the previous five years) plus a fancied royal runner. They went a good gallop here with the pacemaker setting the tempo and the market leaders came to the fore. Another top-class figure for So You Think, who didn't need to match his best. Farhh looked second best and the fifth is the key to the form.

NOTEBOOK

So You Think(NZ) was just caught by Rewilding in this last year having been committed for home a fair way out, but he was held on to longer this time having got a nice lead in a handy position from his stablemate Robin Hood. After arriving with his effort still travelling well over a furlong out, he suddenly found himself with a battle on his hands, but when asked to exert himself he found plenty and was going away at the line. He landed the Eclipse and Irish Champion Stakes after his defeat here last year and he came into this off the back of a bloodless success in the Tattersalls Gold Cup, but this was as good a performance as he has put up outside Australia. Now the winner of five Group 1s in Europe and ten in all, he may not be seen here many more times before he takes up stallion duties. (op Evens tchd 11-10 in places)

Carlton House(USA) was returning from 340 days off when landing the odds in the Brigadier Gerard last month and was bidding to become the Queen's first domestic Group 1 winner since Dunfermline took the St Leger in 1977. He travelled very nicely off the pace and a famous win looked possible when he was delivered with his effort on the inside over a furlong from home. He seemed to be in front for a few strides, but once So You Think was asked for maximum effort he was made to look very much second best. There are certainly more Group races to be won with him over this trip, but he may not be quite up to winning a genuine Group 1. (op 10-3 tchd 4-1)

Farhh ◆, 3-3 coming into this, was up 2f in trip and taking a whopping step up in class after bolting up in the Thirsk Hunt Cup off a mark of 100, but he covered himself in glory and was perhaps unlucky not to do even better. Dropped out last early, he made good progress up the inside rail in the straight but was then stopped in his run by the hanging Planteur. He ran on strongly again once seeing daylight and although he would have had to go some in order to trouble So You Think, it does seem that he is a very smart performer after all and looks well worth another crack at the top level after this. Official explanation: jockey said colt missed the break (op 7-1)

Reliable Man had become disappointing after winning the French Derby and Prix Niel last term and finished behind Planteur in the Prix d'Ispahan. Given plenty to do here, he made good late progress down the wide outside but never looked like getting to the front. Even so, this wasn't a bad effort as he could probably have done without the ground drying out. (op 14-1)

Sri Putra finished third in this last year and has also been placed in the last two runnings of the Eclipse, so it wasn't a total surprise that he ran another big race, but it's frustrating that he can't take more advantage of seemingly easier opportunities.

City Style(USA), last seen finishing third behind Cityscape in the Dubai Duty Free, was trying beyond 1m1f for the first time. Patiently ridden, he didn't looked completely at ease on the drying ground on a couple of occasions in the home straight, but neither did he get the clearest of runs so he can be rated a length or so closer.

Planteur(IRE) finished around 7l behind So You Think when fourth in this last year and had run perfectly creditably when third in both the Dubai World Cup (just ahead of So You Think) and Prix d'Ispahan in his first two starts for his current yard. However, he got himself into a sweat beforehand and was keen enough during the race, so it may be best to give him the benefit of the doubt. (op 9-1)

Colombian(IRE), well held behind Carlton House in the Brigadier Gerard, was beaten off with over a furlong left to run and was another who could have done without the ground drying out. (op 50-1)

Wigmore Hall(IRE) gained his biggest payday when winning a Grade 1 at Woodbine last September and the drying ground should have helped him, but he found this all too much before the furlong pole and he doesn't look up to this level domestically. (tchd 28-1)

Big Blue Kitten(USA), an American challenger, won five in a row last year, but had never been successful above Grade 2 level and had never raced beyond 1m1f. Always handy, he found himself in front when the pacemaker dropped away over 2f out, but his moment of glory didn't last long.

3268 ROYAL HUNT CUP (HERITAGE H'CAP) 1m (S)

4:25 (4:27) (Class 2) 3-Y-0+

£77,812 (£23,300; £11,650; £5,825; £2,912; £1,462) **Stalls** Centre

Form	Pos	Dist	Horse / Details	RPR
41-2	**1**		**Prince Of Johanne (IRE)**[34] 2211 6-9-3 **100** .... (p) JohnFahy 33 (Tom Tate) *hld up in midfield: hdwy over 3f out: led 1f out: r.o and edgd rt ins fnl f: in command towards fin* **16/1**	110
20-0	**2**	*½*	**Excellent Guest**[39] 2068 5-8-11 **94** .... TomQueally 18 (George Margarson) *midfield: hdwy over 2f out: wnt 2nd and chalng ins fnl f: nt pce of wnr cl home* **33/1**	103
0060	**3**	*¾*	**Don't Call Me (IRE)**[19] 2657 5-8-8 **91** .... (t) SamHitchcott 21 (David Nicholls) *trckd ldrs: pushed along over 3f out: led over 1f out: sn hdd: stl ev ch ins fnl f: no ex towards fin* **50/1**	98
600	**4**	*nk*	**Field Of Dream**[19] 2657 5-9-0 **97** .... (b) JamieSpencer 13 (Jamie Osborne) *missed break: bhd: swtchd lft and hdwy over 1f out: r.o strly ins fnl f: clsd qckly towards finsh* **66/1**	104+
02-2	**5**	*½*	**Invisible Man**[14] 2819 6-9-10 **107** .... (b) FrankieDettori 10 (Saeed Bin Suroor) *lw: hld up in rr: rdn 2f out: hdwy over 1f out: fin wl: nt quite get to ldrs* **20/1**	112
1-23	**6**	*nk*	**Cai Shen (IRE)**[39] 2081 4-9-8 **105** .... RichardHughes 1 (Richard Hannon) *hld up: swtchd lft and hdwy 2f out: sn rdn: r.o ins fnl f: gng on at fin* **12/1**[3]	110+
3-00	**7**	*½*	**Stevie Thunder**[46] 1865 7-8-7 **93** .... RyanClark(3) 29 (Ian Williams) *chsd ldrs: chalng 3f out: stl ev ch over 1f out: one pce fnl 100yds* **50/1**	97
31-2	**8**	*½*	**Dimension**[39] 2082 4-9-1 **98** .... JohnnyMurtagh 7 (James Fanshawe) *in tch: effrt to chal over 1f out: styd on same pce fnl 100yds* **9/2**[1]	100+
6310	**9**	*nk*	**Capaill Liath (IRE)**[19] 2657 4-8-9 **92** .... (p) AmyRyan 28 (Kevin Ryan) *midfield: hdwy bef 1/2-way: sn chsd ldrs: chalng 2f out: one pce ins fnl f* **33/1**	94
-600	**10**	*1 ¼*	**Man Of Action (USA)**[81] 1130 5-9-2 **99** .... (v) SilvestreDeSousa 26 (Saeed Bin Suroor) *lw: missed break: in rr: pushed along 1/2-way: hdwy 2f out: in midfield over 1f out: styd on ins fnl f wout troubling ldrs* **25/1**	98
0-41	**11**	*1 ¼*	**Captain Bertie (IRE)**[60] 1510 4-8-10 **93** .... WilliamCarson 17 (Charles Hills) *lw: midfield: effrt over 2f out: styd on same pce ins fnl f* **12/1**[3]	89
2002	**12**	*nk*	**Belgian Bill**[102] 866 4-9-2 **99** .... (t) KierenFallon 32 (George Baker) *lw: midfield: hdwy 1/2-way: led 3f out: rdn and hdd over 1f out: wknd ins fnl f* **10/1**[2]	94+
4-05	**13**	*nse*	**Albaqaa**[37] 2127 7-8-9 **95** .... HarryBentley(3) 19 (P J O'Gorman) *midfield: rdn over 2f out: hdwy whn nt clr run and swtchd rt over 1f out: styd on ins fnl f: nt rch ldrs* **66/1**	91+
003	**14**	*2 ¾*	**Mabait**[25] 2472 6-8-13 **96** .... MartinLane 30 (David Simcock) *hld up: rdn 1/2-way: nvr able to rch ldrs* **16/1**	85
-144	**15**	*hd*	**Brae Hill (IRE)**[25] 2505 6-9-2 **99** .... TonyHamilton 23 (Richard Fahey) *led: hdd 3f out: wknd over 1f out* **33/1**	87
151-	**16**	*nk*	**Boom And Bust (IRE)**[327] 4494 5-9-2 **99** .... HayleyTurner 3 (Marcus Tregoning) *prom: rdn over 1f out: sn wknd* **16/1**	87
11-4	**17**	*nk*	**Edinburgh Knight (IRE)**[81] 1130 5-9-8 **105** .... JimCrowley 20 (Paul D'Arcy) *lw: midfield: rdn over 2f out: effrt to chse ldrs over 1f out: wknd ins fnl f* **12/1**[3]	92
/1-	**18**	*½*	**Rock Critic (IRE)**[48] 1808 7-9-6 **103** .... PatSmullen 12 (D K Weld, Ire) *trckd ldrs: rdn 2f out: n.m.r and hmpd over 1f out: edgd rt ins fnl f: eased fnl 75yds* **25/1**	89+
1-44	**19**	*½*	**King Torus (IRE)**[37] 2127 4-9-10 **107** .... MartinDwyer 22 (Richard Hannon) *lw: midfield: pushed along 3f out: wknd 2f out* **50/1**	92
1-26	**20**	*½*	**Bonnie Brae**[27] 2409 5-9-3 **100** .... RyanMoore 6 (David Elsworth) *hld up: rdn and swtchd rt 2f out: hdwy over 1f out: sn chsd ldrs: wknd ins fnl f* **20/1**	84+
-120	**21**	*½*	**Mull Of Killough (IRE)**[60] 1510 6-9-2 **99** .... ShaneKelly 8 (Jane Chapple-Hyam) *midfield early: pushed along and outpcd over 3f out* **20/1**	81
0116	**22**	*1 ¾*	**Justonefortheroad**[34] 2211 6-8-11 **99** .... ShaneBKelly(5) 5 (Richard Fahey) *hld up: pushed along and outpcd 3f out: rdn and hdwy over 1f out: sn wknd* **12/1**[3]	77
33/5	**23**	*3*	**Fair Trade**[81] 1137 5-9-9 **106** .... DarryllHolland 24 (Hughie Morrison) *prom: pushed along 3f out: wknd over 2f out* **33/1**	78
1-20	**24**	*4 ½*	**Boogie Shoes**[19] 2657 4-8-13 **96** ....[1] NeilCallan 11 (Roger Varian) *prom: rdn 2f out: wknd over 1f out* **25/1**	57

02-0 **25** 3/4 **Common Touch (IRE)**[34] 2211 4-8-12 **95**.................... PaulHanagan 16 54
(Richard Fahey) *midfield: rdn over 2f out: n.m.r and struggling to hold pl over 1f out: sn btn* **33/1**

31-1 **26** 9 **Arabian Star (IRE)**[33] 2250 4-8-9 **92**.............................. DavidProbert 9 31
(Andrew Balding) *prom: rdn 2f out: wknd over 1f out* **16/1**

44-0 **27** 6 **Trade Storm**[34] 2211 4-8-13 **96**....................................... WilliamBuick 25 21
(David Simcock) *lw: trckd ldrs: rdn over 2f out: sn wknd* **16/1**

24-0 **28** 10 **Golden Desert (IRE)**[23] 2558 8-8-9 **92**.......................... LukeMorris 15
(Simon Dow) *midfield: pushed along over 3f out: sn wknd* **100/1**

-244 **29** 37 **King's Trail (JPN)**[81] 1137 10-8-10 **93**.............................. ShaneFoley 2
(Takashi Kodama, Ire) *in tch tl wknd over 3f out* **100/1**

-204 **30** 71 **Bridgefield (USA)**[34] 2211 4-9-2 **99**................ MickaelBarzalona 14
(Mahmood Al Zarooni) *lw: hld up: effrt in midfield over 3f out: no imp: lost pl qckly over 2f out: sn wl bhd: t.o* **16/1**

1m 38.24s (-2.56) **Going Correction** -0.025s/f (Good) course record **30** Ran SP% **139.5**
Speed ratings (Par 109): **111,110,109,109,108 108,108,107,107,106 104,104,104,101,101 101,100,100,99,99 98,97,94,89,88**
toteswingers: 1&2 £87.00, 1&3 £609.00, 2&3 £609.00. CSF £489.50 CT £22723.09 TOTE £18.40: £3.80, £9.90, £18.50, £22.60; EX 1172.80 TRIFECTA Not won..
Owner David Storey **Bred** T J Rooney And Corduff Stud **Trained** Tadcaster, N Yorks
■ Stewards' Enquiry : John Fahy seven-day ban: used whip above permitted level (Jul 4-10)

FOCUS
A typically competitive edition of this historic event, and strong handicap form. The field quickly split into two groups, but the bunches soon merged into one. The place to be in this event proved to be the stands' side of the pack, although not actually that close to the rail, and the winner came from the highest stall. Straightforward form, with another personal best from the winner.

NOTEBOOK
Prince Of Johanne(IRE) came from the highest stall. A big field and decent ground suit this grey, who landed last autumn's Cambridgeshire in similar circumstances off a 9lb lower mark. He had been beaten a nose in a Listed handicap at York last month on his one run since and he confirmed form here with three opponents from that race, running on for pressure closest to the stands' side. (op 14-1)
Excellent Guest was below par on his return in the Victoria Cup here, but had been second off this mark in last summer's Bunbury Cup. He travelled smoothly and kept on well once let down, despite edging left late on. He likes this track and could turn out again in the Buckingham Palace Handicap here on Friday, in which he was second last year. The drop back to 7f would be in his favour, for all that he handled this mile well.
Don't Call Me(IRE) was a pound wrong at the weights and had not been at his best this term, but he was well treated on last autumn's Ayr win and showed a return to form. The drying ground had not been expected to prove ideal for him.
Field Of Dream fell out of the stalls and initially raced on the far side before Jamie Spencer brought him all the way over to the stands' side. He was still plumb last with over a quarter of a mile left, but finished fast and late for fourth. The refitted blinkers seemed to work and he was due to be dropped 2lb before this. (tchd 100-1 in a place)
Invisible Man, a running-on fifth off 12lb higher than when winning it two years ago, was also third last season. This was a fine effort off 107 and this event brings out the best in him.
Cai Shen(IRE) was drawn on the worse side as it turned out but ran a thoroughly commendable race, running on nicely once switched. Runner-up to Sagramor in last season's Britannia Handicap over C&D, he is fully effective at both this trip and 1m2f. (op 14-1)
Stevie Thunder, runner-up to Prince Of Johannes in the Cambridgeshire off a pound lower, was drawn close to his old rival and only faded out of the frame inside the final furlong.
Dimension, 3lb higher than when second on his return on the Lingfield Polytrack, came in for sustained support. He had his chance, but edged to his left after delivering his challenge and was held in the final 100 yards. While this was a decent run, he has been a beaten favourite in five of his last six starts. (op 6-1)
Capaill Liath(IRE) had an excuse at Epsom last time and he ran a commendable race, albeit helped by racing on the side where the pace was. (tchd 40-1 in a place)
Man Of Action(USA) was very slowly away before running on when it was all over.
Captain Bertie(IRE) failed to figure from an 8lb higher mark. (tchd 14-1 in a place)
Belgian Bill raced up with the pace towards the stands' side and showed ahead for a while, but he faded out of the picture. His lack of a run since March may have told. (op 12-1 tchd 14-1 in a place)
Albaqaa did some good late work without figuring. (op 50-1)
Mabait, who showed a return to form last time, could not make his high draw count.
Brae Hill(IRE), who went to post early, led the field down the centre for 5f.
Boom And Bust(IRE), winner of his last four handicaps but 29lb higher than the first of them, and not seen since Glorious Goodwood, is entitled to be sharper for this reappearance. (op 20-1)
Edinburgh Knight(IRE) had attracted considerable support in recent days having been laid out for this since finishing fourth in the Lincoln, but he never gave his supporters serious hopes.
Common Touch(IRE) Official explanation: jockey said gelding suffered interference in running
Bridgefield(USA) Official explanation: jockey said colt got upset in stalls

3269 QUEEN MARY STKS (GROUP 2) (FILLIES) 5f
5:00 (5:03) (Class 1) 2-Y-O

£42,532 (£16,125; £8,070; £4,020; £2,017; £1,012) **Stalls** Centre

Form RPR

2411 **1** **Ceiling Kitty**[33] 2252 2-8-12 0.................................... RichardKingscote 5 103
(Tom Dascombe) *racd far side: chsd ldrs: rdn to ld over 1f out: hung lft but kpt on wl u.p fnl f: drvn out* **20/1**

2 **2** 1 **Hoyam**[30] 2343 2-8-12 0.. JamieSpencer 17 99+
(Michael Bell) *lengthy: lw: racd centre to nr side gp: hld up in rr: swtchd lft 1/2-way: rdn and hdwy over 1f out: edging rt but r.o strly fnl f: wnt 2nd fnl 50yds: 1st of 11 in gp* **10/1**

12 **3** 1 **Hairy Rocket**[30] 2345 2-8-12 0.. RyanMoore 18 95
(Richard Hannon) *racd centre to nr side gp: chsd ldrs: led gp and chsd overall ldrs 2f out: styd on u.p to chse wnr ins fnl f: no ex and lost 2nd fnl 50yds: 2nd of 11 in gp* **11/1**

1 **4** 1/2 **Upward Spiral**[27] 2426 2-8-12 0.................................. JohnnyMurtagh 23 94+
(Tom Dascombe) *racd centre to nr side gp: in tch: rdn and chsd ldrs 1f out: kpt on same pce ins fnl f: 3rd of 11 in gp* **6/1**[2]

11 **5** 1/2 **Jadanna (IRE)**[21] 2603 2-8-12 0.................................. FrankieDettori 10 92
(James Given) *w'like: lw: racd far side: in tch: rdn ent fnl 2f: kpt on wl u.p ins fnl f: nt pce to rch ldrs: 2nd of 16 in gp* **10/1**

510 **6** 1 **Lasilia (IRE)**[21] 2603 2-8-12 0.. TonyHamilton 27 88
(Kevin Ryan) *leggy: racd centre to nr side gp: midfield: rdn 1/2-way: hdwy and carried rt 1f out: kpt on same pce fnl f: 4th of 11 in gp* **100/1**

12 **7** hd **Satsuma**[18] 2715 2-8-12 0.. WilliamBuick 2 87
(David Brown) *racd far side: chsd ldrs: rdn 2f out: styd on u.p to chse wnr jst over 1f out tl ins fnl f: wknd cl home: 3rd of 16 in gp* **12/1**

22 **8** hd **Jillnextdoor (IRE)**[20] 2614 2-8-12 0.......................... CraigAWilliams 4 87+
(Mick Channon) *unf: racd far side: in tch: effrt and rdn to chse ldrs over 1f out: no ex and btn ins fnl f: wknd towards fin: 4th of 16 in gp* **12/1**

11 **9** 3/4 **Madam Mojito (USA)**[20] 2630 2-8-12 0.................... MichaelO'Connell 11 84
(John Quinn) *racd far side: chsd ldr tl 1/2-way: sn rdn but styd prom tl wknd ins fnl f: 5th of 16 in gp* **25/1**

143 **10** 1 1/4 **Threes Grand**[21] 2603 2-8-12 0.. KierenFallon 19 79
(Scott Dixon) *racd centre to nr side gp tl swtchd to far side gp 1/2-way: chsd ldrs: rdn and struggling 2f out: wknd 1f out: 6th of 16 in gp* **25/1**

44 **11** 1/2 **Excel Yourself (IRE)**[34] 2193 2-8-12 0............................ MartinDwyer 9 78
(James Tate) *lw: racd far side: in tch: rdn 2f out: unable qck over 1f out: one pce and no imp fnl f: 7th of 16 in gp* **80/1**

21 **12** nse **Miss Diva**[30] 2343 2-8-12 0.. JimmyFortune 25 78
(Richard Hannon) *racd centre to nr side gp: in tch: rdn 2f out: unable qck u.p over 1f out: wknd ins fnl f: 5th of 11 in gp* **33/1**

1160 **13** 1/2 **Baileys Jubilee**[20] 2638 2-8-12 0................................ SilvestreDeSousa 1 76
(Mark Johnston) *racd far side: in tch in midfield: rdn over 2f out: nt clr run and bdly hmpd wl over 1f out: bhd after: rallied and styd on wl ins fnl f: nt rcvr: 8th of 16 in gp* **33/1**

3211 **14** 3/4 **Lady Phill**[33] 2234 2-8-12 0.. KierenFox 24 73
(Bill Turner) *racd centre to nr side gp: led gp and chsd ldrs overall tl 2f out: sn u.p: wknd fnl f: 6th of 11 in gp* **40/1**

15 nk **Mironica (IRE)**[35] 2183 2-8-12 0.................................... WayneLordan 15 72
(David Wachman, Ire) *leggy: swtg: racd centre to nr side gp: s.i.s: towards rr: swtchd to far side gp 1/2-way: sn u.p: plugged on but n.d: 9th of 16 in gp* **5/1**[1]

21 **16** nk **Sharaarah (IRE)**[23] 2541 2-8-12 0.................................... PaulHanagan 8 71
(Ed Dunlop) *racd far side: in tch: rdn and effrt wl over 1f out: drvn and no ex over 1f out: wknd ins fnl f: 10th of 16 in gp* **20/1**

4 **17** hd **Star Up In The Sky (USA)**[11] 2938 2-8-12 0....................... AmyRyan 3 70
(Kevin Ryan) *str: racd far side: in tch: rdn over 2f out: hung rt 2f out: sn struggling and wknd fnl f: 11th of 16 in gp* **33/1**

1 **18** 1 1/2 **Projectisle (IRE)**[15] 2790 2-8-12 0.................................... NeilCallan 12 65
(Kevin Ryan) *leggy: racd far side: hld up towards rr: rdn wl over 1f out: no imp: nvr trbld ldrs: 12th of 16 in gp* **40/1**

221 **19** nk **All Fur Coat**[42] 1972 2-8-12 0.. HayleyTurner 6 64
(Jo Hughes) *racd far side: overall ldr tl rdn and hdd over 1f out: fdd fnl f: 13th of 16 in gp* **33/1**

2 **20** 1/2 **Jubilee Diamond (IRE)**[27] 2426 2-8-12 0................. RichardHughes 14 62
(Richard Hannon) *lw: racd centre to nr side gp: towards rr: rdn and struggling whn swtchd to far side gp 1/2-way: flashed tail and wknd wl over 1f out: 14th of 16 in gp* **14/1**

2 **21** nk **Starlight Angel (IRE)**[11] 2912 2-8-12 0........................... LukeMorris 20 61
(Ronald Harris) *racd centre to nr side gp: chsd ldrs tl 2f out: sn u.p and wknd jst over 1f out: 7th of 11 in gp* **100/1**

311 **22** nse **Graphic Guest**[30] 2345 2-8-12 0...................................... MartinHarley 21 61
(Mick Channon) *racd centre to nr side gp: a towards rr: rdn and effrt 2f out: nvr trbld ldrs: 8th of 11 in gp* **15/2**[3]

5 **23** 1 3/4 **Masarah (IRE)**[14] 2812 2-8-12 0.. TomQueally 22 54
(Clive Brittain) *racd centre to nr side gp: sn outpcd in rr: n.d: 9th of 11 in gp* **100/1**

00 **24** nk **Melodee Princess (IRE)**[23] 2541 2-8-12 0.................... DarrenEgan 16 53
(Ronald Harris) *unf: racd centre to nr side gp: s.i.s: a outpcd in rr: 10th of 11 in gp* **150/1**

1 **25** 1 **Belle Intrigue**[8] 2995 2-8-12 0.. JimCrowley 13 50
(Amanda Perrett) *leggy: racd far side gp: in tch in midfield: struggling 1/2-way: bhd over 1f out: 15th of 16 in gp* **66/1**

0 **26** 4 **Modern Lady**[58] 1556 2-8-12 0.................................... J-PGuillambert 26 35
(Richard Guest) *unf: racd centre to nr side gp: sn rdn and struggling towards rr: wknd u.p 2f out: 11th of 11 in gp* **150/1**

27 6 **Delphica (IRE)** 2-8-12 0.. ShaneKelly 7 14
(Gary Moore) *racd far side: slowly away: a bhd: 16th of 16 in gp* **50/1**

59.18s (-1.32) **Going Correction** -0.025s/f (Good) **27** Ran SP% **134.1**
Speed ratings (Par 102): **109,107,105,105,104 102,102,101,100,98 97,97,97,95,95 94,94,92,91,90 90,90,87,87,85 79,69**
toteswingers: 1&2 £108.00, 1&3 £72.20, 2&3 £61.10. CSF £194.22 CT £2382.39 TOTE £27.00: £7.30, £7.50, £3.20; EX 553.90 Trifecta £7767.20 Part won. Pool: £10,496.22 - 0.21 winning units..
Owner A Black & The Master Bettors **Bred** A Black **Trained** Malpas, Cheshire

FOCUS
A bigger field than usual for this year's Queen Mary and they split into two equal-sized groups early. It seemed for much of the race as though those on the far side held sway and the winner came from that flank, but the other three who made the frame were all drawn high. The winning time was just 1/100th of a second outside the juvenile course record set in this race two years ago. Ceiling Kitty took another leap forward, with the second another big improver.

NOTEBOOK
Ceiling Kitty appeared to be improving coming into this and had successfully stepped up to Listed company at York last time, making her the only previous Pattern-race winner in this field. Always handy in the far-side group, she was committed for home inside the last 2f and, despite hanging away to her left in the closing stages, never looked likely to be caught. There is no telling when her progression might end.
Hoyam ◆ showed plenty of promise when chasing home Miss Diva on her Windsor debut and her trainer felt that she had come on a lot for that. He was proved right, but she was ridden in stark contrast to the winner and only had one behind her at halfway. She took off once asked for her effort and finished in great style, but the winner had gained too much of an advantage. Her trainer felt that she lacked experience and that she has a big future, with the Cherry Hinton and Princess Margaret possible options for her now. She is likely to eventually prove the best of these. (op 20-1)
Hairy Rocket was long odds-on when beaten by Graphic Guest in a three-runner Windsor conditions event last time and showed that running to be all wrong. Always handy in the nearside group, she never stopped trying and connections were delighted by this effort. The St Hugh's Stakes, Empress Stakes and Cherry Hinton were all mentioned as possible targets and she should certainly be up to winning a nice race or two. (op 12-1 tchd 14-1 in a places)
Upward Spiral ◆ confirmed the form of her Sandown debut success over Jubilee Diamond and was produced to hold every chance. She is entitled to still have improvement left in her and has a future. (op 7-1 tchd 15-2)
Jadanna(IRE), 2-2 after winning a Pontefract maiden and a Beverley conditions event on varying ground, was never far away in the far-side group and kept staying on. She should find easier opportunities. (op 11-1 tchd 9-1)
Lasilia(IRE) had already twice finished a long way behind Jadanna, but got much closer to her here having started from the stall closest to the stands' rail. She too can be found easier tasks.
Satsuma appeared to have her limitations exposed when runner-up in a Musselburgh conditions event last time, but ran creditably in the far-side group at this much higher level.
Jillnextdoor(IRE) had been narrowly beaten in her first two starts, including by Lady Phill on her Newbury debut, but her subsequent head defeat by Hototo at Ayr received a boost when the winner took the Windsor Castle here the previous day. She may not have been in the ideal place in trying to make up ground tight against the far rail, so this was a fair effort, but it may be best to try and win a maiden with her before tackling this sort of level again. (op 14-1)
Mironica(IRE), winner of a 6f Naas maiden on her debut last month when her trainer felt the easy ground was against her, never got into this and there seemed to be no excuses. (op 11-2 tchd 6-1 in a place)

Graphic Guest was bidding for a hat-trick after winning a C&D maiden and a Windsor conditions event, but proved disappointing. However, she did become restless in the stalls, which may have been the reason for this moderate effort. (tchd 8-1)

3270 SANDRINGHAM H'CAP (LISTED RACE) (FILLIES) 1m (S)

5:35 (5:36) (Class 1) (0-110,109) 3-Y-O

£31,190 (£11,825; £5,918; £2,948; £1,479; £742) Stalls Centre

Form RPR

4 **1** **Duntle (IRE)**[38] 2101 3-9-2 **104**.......... WayneLordan 18 112+
(David Wachman, Ire) *leggy: a travelling wl in midfield: hdwy wl over 2f out: led ent fnl 2f: r.o gamely ins fnl f: in control fnl 100yds* **4/1**[1]

-530 **2** ½ **Arsaadi (IRE)**[45] 1887 3-8-7 **95** oh3..........(b[1]) LiamJones 17 102
(William Haggas) *chsd ldr: rdn to ld over 2f out: hdd ent fnl 2f: continued to chal wnr: r.o for press but hld fnl 100yds* **12/1**

25-2 **3** 2½ **Ladys First**[32] 2263 3-8-7 **95** oh5.......... PaulHanagan 4 96+
(Richard Fahey) *chsd ldr in small gp of 4 towards far-side: led gp over 1f out: kpt on u.p: hld by front pair fnl 150yds* **7/1**[3]

-056 **4** 1 **Villeneuve**[18] 2713 3-8-7 **95** oh5.......... MartinDwyer 12 94
(William Muir) *racd keenly in midfield: hdwy over 3f out: rdn to chse ldrs over 2f out: styd on same pce fnl 150yds* **25/1**

-250 **5** nk **Pimpernel (IRE)**[63] 1454 3-9-2 **104**.......... FrankieDettori 7 102
(Mahmood Al Zarooni) *racd keenly: hld up: hdwy 3f out: rdn and no imp over 1f out: styd on ins fnl f: nvr able to rch ldrs* **10/1**

6-24 **6** 2¼ **Way Too Hot**[33] 2255 3-8-7 **95** oh2.......... NeilCallan 5 88
(Clive Cox) *hld up: rdn 2f out: hdwy over 1f out: one pce and no imp on ldrs fnl 100yds* **20/1**

5-10 **7** hd **Falls Of Lora (IRE)**[81] 1145 3-9-2 **104**.......... MickaelBarzalona 14 96
(Mahmood Al Zarooni) *midfield: pushed along over 4f out: effrt over 2f out: one pce ins fnl f* **16/1**

2-03 **8** 2½ **Semayyel (IRE)**[46] 1845 3-8-7 **95** oh1.......... MartinLane 3 82
(Clive Brittain) *led small gp of 4 towards far-side: rdn over 2f out: hdd over 1f out: wknd fnl f* **66/1**

36-3 **9** 4½ **Hello Glory**[33] 2255 3-8-8 **96**.......... JamieSpencer 11 72
(David Simcock) *s.i.s: hld up in rr: rdn over 2f out: plugged on at one pce fr over 1f out: no imp* **8/1**

30-4 **10** hd **Switcher (IRE)**[60] 1508 3-8-10 **98**.......... RichardKingscote 16 77
(Tom Dascombe) *chsd ldrs: rdn over 2f out: wknd over 1f out: eased whn btn ins fnl f* **16/1**

3-00 **11** 1¼ **Fillionaire**[39] 2078 3-8-7 **95** oh2.......... MartinHarley 13 68
(Mick Channon) *chsd ldrs: rdn 1/2-way: wknd over 2f out* **33/1**

0404 **12** 1¼ **Kickingthelilly**[11] 2916 3-8-7 **95** oh14.......... ChrisCatlin 1 65
(Rae Guest) *racd in last pl in small gp of 4 towards far-side: struggling to go pce over 5f out: plugged on over 1f out: nvr a threat* **50/1**

3163 **13** 2¼ **Esentepe (IRE)**[35] 2178 3-8-12 **100**.......... RichardHughes 9 65
(Richard Hannon) *midfield: rdn and wknd 2f out* **10/1**

330- **14** ½ **Kinetica**[269] 6389 3-8-10 **98**.......... LukeMorris 15 62
(Sir Mark Prescott Bt) *overall ldr: hdd over 2f out: wknd over 1f out* **16/1**

-060 **15** 1¾ **What's Up (IRE)**[33] 2255 3-8-8 **96** oh8 ow1.......... ShaneKelly 10 56
(Kevin Ryan) *hld up: pushed along over 4f out: wknd 2f out: eased whn btn fnl f* **66/1**

-321 **16** 6 **Electrelane**[17] 2746 3-9-7 **109**.......... JimCrowley 2 55
(Ralph Beckett) *chsd ldrs in small gp of 4 towards far-side: pushed along 3f out: wknd over 2f out* **13/2**[2]

6-20 **17** 19 **Devotion (IRE)**[19] 2658 3-9-3 **105**.......... JPO'Brien 6
(A P O'Brien, Ire) *hld up: pushed along 3f out: bhd and eased over 1f out: t.o* **9/1**

1m 37.9s (-2.90) **Going Correction** -0.025s/f (Good) course record **17** Ran SP% **127.0**
Speed ratings (Par 104): **113,112,110,109,108 106,106,103,99,99 97,96,94,93,92 86,67**
toteswingers: 1&2 £19.80, 1&3 £5.90, 2&3 £17.80. CSF £51.70 CT £350.69 TOTE £5.80: £2.00, £3.00, £1.70, £5.80; EX 91.80 Trifecta £695.30 Pool: £8,964.96 - 9.54 winning units..

Owner Niarchos Family **Bred** Airlie Stud **Trained** Goolds Cross, Co Tipperary

FOCUS

A good Listed handicap for fillies which has been part of the Royal Ascot programme since 2002. Eight of these raced from out of the handicap, and only four of the field had run in a handicap before. A group of four raced down the centre with the remainder in a group more towards the stands' side, and the first two came out of the two highest stalls. The form does not look as solid as it might have, but the time was quicker than both the Windsor Forest and the Hunt Cup and Duntle looks a smart filly. She was less exposed than most here.

NOTEBOOK

Duntle(IRE) was a wide-margin winner of a Dundalk AW maiden before finishing fourth in Leopardstown's 1000 Guineas Trial. Racing on the stands' side of the group, she travelled well before showing the right attitude as she fought it out with the runner-up. A lightly raced filly with more to offer, she will doubtless step back up in grade now. Several recent winners of this went on to win in Group 1 or Group 2 company, but it remains to be seen if she proves up to that level. Her future may lie in the USA. (op 9-2 tchd 5-1)

Arsaadi(IRE) was always towards the fore in the larger group and this was a big run in first-time blinkers. Racing from 3lb out of the weights, she was back in trip after a couple of runs at 1m2f. (tchd 14-1)

Ladys First, another who was wrong at the weights, in her case by 5lb, went a little keenly to post. Doing best of the four to race in the centre-to-far side, she had no company in the latter stages and deserves plenty of credit for this. (op 8-1)

Villeneuve, who was 5lb wrong, stepped up on her previous efforts over this longer trip, as her pedigree suggested she would. (op 33-1)

Pimpernel(IRE) went to post early. She travelled noticeably well on the stands'-side flank of the field but did not pick up as well as she had promised. This was still much more encouraging than her last two starts, albeit that this represented a drop in grade.

Way Too Hot ran respectably in this first handicap, keeping on quite well at the end and reversing York form behind Electrelane with Hello Glory.

Falls Of Lora(IRE), the UAE Oaks winner, then struggled in the equivalent race for colts but ran respectably back in a handicap.

Switcher(IRE) Official explanation: jockey said filly never travelled

Electrelane won her German Guineas in soft ground and she disappointed in these quicker conditions. The topweight had quite a hard race at Dusseldorf and was not helped by racing away from the main action here. Jim Crowley reported that the filly lost her action. Official explanation: jockey said filly lost its action (op 8-1)

Devotion(IRE), an Oaks also-ran since finishing ahead of Duntle at Leopardstown, failed to give her running and Joseph O'Brien reported that she was never travelling. Official explanation: jockey said filly never travelled (tchd 8-1)

T/Jkpt: Not won. T/Plt: £1,326.50 to a £1 stake. Pool £530,981.36. 292.19 winning tickets. T/Qpdt: £246.10 to a £1 stake. Pool £24,216.64. 72.80 winning tickets. SP

[3026] HAMILTON (R-H)

Wednesday, June 20

OFFICIAL GOING: Good (good to firm in places; 9.3)

All races of a mile and beyond reduced in distance by about 25yds.

Wind: Fresh, half behind Weather: Cloudy, bright

3271 BRITISH STALLION STUDS SUPPORTING BRITISH RACING E B F MAIDEN STKS 6f 5y

2:20 (2:22) (Class 5) 2-Y-O £3,234 (£962; £481; £240) Stalls High

Form RPR

320 **1** **Steer By The Stars (IRE)**[15] 2783 2-8-12 0.......... JoeFanning 6 74+
(Mark Johnston) *mde virtually all: rdn over 1f out: styd on wl fnl f* **4/1**[2]

4 **2** 1¾ **Gold Beau (FR)**[39] 2073 2-9-3 0.......... GrahamLee 7 74
(Linda Stubbs) *prom: outpcd over 2f out: rallied and edgd rt over 1f out: chsd wnr ins fnl f: r.o* **25/1**

03 **3** ½ **Capo Rosso (IRE)**[11] 2912 2-9-3 0.......... FrannyNorton 8 72
(Tom Dascombe) *chsd ldrs: rdn along and sltly outpcd over 1f out: rallied ins fnl f* **10/1**

4 1¼ **Montcliffe** 2-9-0 0.......... BarryMcHugh 5 65
(Richard Fahey) *noisy in preliminaries: dwlt: sn trcking ldrs: effrt and edgd rt over 1f out: sn one pce* **8/1**[3]

5 3¾ **Mysterious Wonder** 2-9-0 0.......... PhillipMakin 2 54
(Kevin Ryan) *t.k.h: w wnr: rdn over 2f out: wknd ent fnl f* **4/6**[1]

00 **6** 4½ **Rocket Ronnie (IRE)**[14] 2822 2-9-3 0.......... AdrianNicholls 3 44
(David Nicholls) *upset in stalls: chsd ldng gp: struggling after 2f: n.d after* **40/1**

1m 11.25s (-0.95) **Going Correction** -0.175s/f (Firm) **6** Ran SP% **106.5**
Speed ratings (Par 93): **99,96,96,94,89 83**
toteswingers: 1&2 £12.60, 1&3 £1.60, 2&3 £11.50. CSF £68.40 TOTE £6.80: £4.00, £13.40; EX 45.60.

Owner Capt Alasdair & Mrs Eliza Ross **Bred** Ms E Flynn **Trained** Middleham Moor, N Yorks

FOCUS

All races over further than 6f were approximately 25 yards less than the official distance. An interesting juvenile maiden began proceedings. The gallop appeared genuine on drying ground - two of the jockeys reported the going was riding lovely, good ground.

NOTEBOOK

Steer By The Stars(IRE) had to bounce back from a modest Leicester effort this month over a 1f longer trip on decent ground. She is the second foal out of a well-related French 1m winning dam, and appreciated the step up in trip in producing a comfortable first career success. She looks to have a fair future at up to 1m in handicaps. (op 7-2)

Gold Beau(FR) progressed on his fair fourth on debut over this trip on good to soft ground at Haydock last month. He may be able to land a similar contest over further, but has a future at up to at least 1m in handicaps in any case.

Capo Rosso(IRE) progressed to finish third in a Chester maiden on his second start this month and ran to a similar level on this much quicker ground. (op 8-1)

Montcliffe showed obvious signs of inexperience on debut, but performed respectably and can build on this effort. (op 9-1 tchd 10-1)

Mysterious Wonder looked well beforehand, but proved a most disappointing favourite on debut. A drop back to 5f may beckon. (op Evens tchd 11-10 in a place)

3272 SAM COLLINGWOOD-CAMERON H'CAP 6f 5y

2:55 (2:56) (Class 5) (0-75,81) 3-Y-O+ £3,234 (£962; £481; £240) Stalls High

Form RPR

0023 **1** **Barkston Ash**[7] 3027 4-9-2 **70**.......... JasonHart(7) 4 81
(Eric Alston) *trckd ldrs: led over 2f out: sn rdn: kpt on strly fnl f* **6/4**[1]

0-2 **2** 1¾ **Sovereign Street**[15] 2796 4-9-4 **65**.......... PaulMulrennan 7 70
(Ann Duffield) *t.k.h: chsd ldng gp: effrt and chsd wnr over 1f out: hung rt: kpt on fnl f: nt pce to chal* **15/2**[3]

0605 **3** 2 **Rio Cobolo (IRE)**[18] 2696 6-9-8 **69**.......... (v) AdrianNicholls 1 68
(David Nicholls) *led to over 2f out: sn drvn along: kpt on same pce fnl f* **17/2**

0511 **4** ¾ **Julius Geezer (IRE)**[7] 3027 4-10-1 **81** 6ex.......... GarryWhillans(5) 6 78
(Tom Dascombe) *in tch: rdn over 2f out: effrt over 1f out: no imp fnl f* **85/40**[2]

2460 **5** 1¼ **Weetentherty**[13] 2839 5-8-10 **57** oh4 ow1.......... PhillipMakin 9 50
(Linda Perratt) *hld up: rdn and hdwy over 1f out: nvr able to chal* **33/1**

050- **6** 1 **Gap Princess (IRE)**[202] 7596 8-9-9 **70**.......... RobertWinston 5 59
(Geoffrey Harker) *hld up bhd ldng gp: effrt on outside over 1f out: sn no imp* **14/1**

0505 **7** 1½ **Niceonemyson**[7] 3028 3-8-6 **60**.......... BarryMcHugh 3 43
(Christopher Wilson) *trckd ldrs: rdn over 2f out: wknd over 1f out* **28/1**

2-44 **8** nse **Mango Music**[20] 2636 9-9-11 **72**.......... (p) JoeFanning 2 56
(David Thompson) *cl up tl rdn and wknd over 1f out* **22/1**

1m 10.6s (-1.60) **Going Correction** -0.175s/f (Firm)
WFA 3 from 4yo+ 7lb **8** Ran SP% **111.7**
Speed ratings (Par 103): **103,100,98,97,95 94,92,91**
toteswingers: 1&2 £1.70, 1&3 £5.50, 2&3 £20.00. CSF £12.72 CT £69.76 TOTE £2.20: £1.02, £2.60, £1.40; EX 16.70.

Owner The Selebians **Bred** Jonathan Shack **Trained** Longton, Lancs

FOCUS

An average handicap.

3273 FOLLOW @HAMILTONPARKRC ON TWITTER MEDIAN AUCTION MAIDEN STKS 1m 1f 36y

3:30 (3:31) (Class 6) 3-5-Y-O £2,045 (£603; £302) Stalls Low

Form RPR

4-03 **1** **Rosselli (IRE)**[31] 2313 3-9-0 73.......... PhillipMakin 6 73
(Mrs K Burke) *trckd ldrs: effrt and wnt 2nd over 2f out: sn rdn: led ins fnl f: drvn out* **2/1**[2]

3 **2** ¾ **Suffice (IRE)**[29] 2380 3-9-0 0.......... DavidNolan 4 71
(Richard Fahey) *dwlt: hld up: plenty to do 4f out: sn pushed along: hdwy over 2f out: styd on wl to take 2nd towards fin* **5/4**[1]

44 **3** 1 **Outback (IRE)**[15] 2794 3-9-0 70.......... (p) GrahamLee 7 69
(Ann Duffield) *chsd ldrs: rdn and outpcd 3f out: rallied over 1f out: styd on towards fin* **7/1**[3]

3-6 **4** ¾ **Saslong**[14] 2826 3-9-0 0.......... JoeFanning 2 67
(Mark Johnston) *early ldr: led after 3f: rdn over 2f out: hdd ins fnl f: no ex and lost two pls towards fin* **17/2**

06 **5** 1¼ **In The Crowd (IRE)**[12] 2877 3-9-0 0.......... PJMcDonald 3 65
(Alan Swinbank) *hld up in tch: pushed along over 2f out: styd on steadily fnl f* **16/1**

00 **6** *21* **Medecis Mountain**[12] 2881 3-9-0 0 .... PaddyAspell 5 18
(John Wainwright) *settled midfield: struggling over 3f out: sn wknd* **100/1**

7 *3½* **Bandy Bob** 3-8-9 0 .... GarryWhillans(5) 8 11
(Iain Jardine) *t.k.h: hld up: struggling wl over 2f out: sn btn* **33/1**

8 *8* **Stormont Bridge**[83] 4-9-11 0 ....(t) PaulMulrennan 9
(Maurice Barnes) *sn led: hdd after 3f: chsd ldr tl wknd over 2f out* **100/1**

9 *27* **Lochluichart (IRE)** 3-9-0 0 .... BarryMcHugh 1
(Ian Semple) *missed break: t.k.h: hld up: struggling wl over 3f out: sn btn* **50/1**

1m 56.99s (-2.71) **Going Correction** -0.275s/f (Firm)
WFA 3 from 4yo 11lb **9** Ran SP% **113.6**
Speed ratings (Par 101): **101,100,99,98,97 79,75,68,44**
toteswingers: 1&2 £1.90, 1&3 £2.80, 2&3 £1.20. CSF £4.69 TOTE £2.60: £1.10, £1.90, £1.10; EX 6.60.
Owner Philip Richards **Bred** Philip Richards **Trained** Middleham Moor, N Yorks

FOCUS
A modest maiden. The winning time was very respectable for the grade, just over a second slower than standard.

3274 MCGHEE'S TEAZ H'CAP 1m 65y
4:10 (4:13) (Class 4) (0-80,79) 3-Y-0+ **£5,175** (£1,540; £769; £384) **Stalls** Low

Form RPR

-300 **1** **Miami Gator (IRE)**[16] 2753 5-9-5 **77** ....(v) ConorHarrison(7) 10 85
(Mrs K Burke) *mde all: rdn over 2f out: kpt on gamely fnl f* **25/1**

40-1 **2** *½* **Ginger Jack**[21] 2597 5-10-0 **79** .... PJMcDonald 7 86
(Geoffrey Harker) *prom: effrt and rdn over 2f out: chsd wnr ins fnl f: kpt on: hld nr fin* **9/2**[3]

3-00 **3** *1½* **Sound Advice**[47] 1819 3-9-4 **79** .... PaulMulrennan 6 80
(Keith Dalgleish) *chsd ldrs: effrt and chsd wnr over 1f out: hung rt: lost 2nd and no ex ins fnl f* **16/1**

5303 **4** *nse* **I'm Super Too (IRE)**[16] 2753 5-9-7 **77** .... GarryWhillans(5) 11 80
(Alan Swinbank) *in tch on outside: rdn along over 2f out: kpt on ins fnl f: nrst fin* **7/2**[2]

0-60 **5** *1* **Silver Rime (FR)**[21] 2597 7-9-10 **75** .... PhillipMakin 4 76
(Linda Perratt) *s.i.s: hld up: rdn and hdwy over 1f out: r.o ins fnl f: nvr able to chal* **40/1**

0030 **6** *1¼* **Shadowtime**[16] 2753 7-9-6 **71** .... FrannyNorton 9 69
(Tracy Waggott) *hld up in tch on ins: effrt over 2f out: nt clr run briefly 1f out: kpt on fnl f: no imp* **16/1**

3356 **7** *nk* **Moheebb (IRE)**[4] 3167 8-9-8 **73** .... JamesSullivan 2 70
(Ruth Carr) *hld up in midfield: rdn along over 2f out: no imp fr over 1f out* **5/1**

1-63 **8** *3¼* **Border Revia (IRE)**[6] 3064 3-9-2 **77** .... BarryMcHugh 3 65
(Richard Fahey) *sn pushed along in midfield: rdn over 2f out: edgd rt and wknd over 1f out* **10/3**[1]

-210 **9** *1½* **Hamis Al Bin (IRE)**[36] 2150 3-9-3 **78** .... JoeFanning 5 62
(Mark Johnston) *chsd ldr: rdn and edgd lft over 2f out: edgd rt and wknd appr fnl f* **14/1**

0-63 **10** *1* **Running Reef (IRE)**[22] 2592 3-8-12 **73** .... PaddyAspell 8 55
(Tracy Waggott) *hld up: drvn along over 3f out: sn struggling* **25/1**

1-00 **11** *1½* **One Pursuit (IRE)**[27] 2414 4-9-8 **73** .... AdrianNicholls 1 54
(David Nicholls) *s.i.s: bhd: struggling over 3f out: nvr on terms* **14/1**

1m 45.09s (-3.31) **Going Correction** -0.275s/f (Firm)
WFA 3 from 4yo+ 10lb **11** Ran SP% **115.4**
Speed ratings (Par 105): **105,104,103,102,101 100,100,97,95,94 93**
toteswingers: 1&2 £21.30, 1&3 £39.60, 2&3 £17.80. CSF £129.98 CT £1885.62 TOTE £37.70: £9.20, £2.30, £6.50; EX 146.50.
Owner Ontoawinner & Mrs E Burke **Bred** Newlands House Stud **Trained** Middleham Moor, N Yorks

FOCUS
This fair handicap was the feature race on the card. The winning time was only a shade outside standard.

3275 SAINTS & SINNERS RACENIGHT NEXT WEEK H'CAP 1m 65y
4:45 (4:46) (Class 6) (0-60,60) 3-Y-0 **£1,940** (£577; £288; £144) **Stalls** Low

Form RPR

-435 **1** **Double Cee**[21] 2604 3-9-6 **59** .... DavidNolan 12 73+
(Richard Fahey) *in tch: gd hdwy on outside to ld over 1f out: rdn and styd on strly to go clr fnl f* **7/2**[1]

0-3 **2** *4* **Schmooze (IRE)**[21] 2595 3-8-13 **55** .... DaleSwift(3) 5 58
(Linda Perratt) *dwlt: hld up: hdwy against far rail over 2f out: chsd (clr) wnr ins fnl f: no imp* **16/1**

00-0 **3** *1* **Critical Point**[15] 2802 3-8-2 **46** oh1 .... RosieJessop(5) 2 47
(Sir Mark Prescott Bt) *hld up in tch: pushed along 1/2-way: styd on fr 2f out: nrst fin* **14/1**

2330 **4** *¾* **Luctor Emergo (IRE)**[5] 3111 3-9-3 **56** .... PaulMulrennan 7 55
(Keith Dalgleish) *hld up in midfield on outside: rdn 3f out: styd on over 1f out: nvr able to chal* **9/2**[2]

0-00 **5** *½* **Al Doha**[149] 270 3-8-10 **49** .... BarryMcHugh 3 47
(Kevin Ryan) *led: rdn over 2f out: hdd over 1f out: sn no ex* **28/1**

664 **6** *½* **Go On Gilbert**[22] 2592 3-9-7 **60** .... PaddyAspell 4 57
(John Wainwright) *hld up towards rr: outpcd 3f out: rallied whn n.m.r briefly over 1f out: kpt on: nvr able to chal* **14/1**

050- **7** *1½* **Lord Franklin**[256] 6702 3-8-3 **49** .... JasonHart(7) 8 42
(Eric Alston) *s.i.s: bhd: outpcd 4f out: sme late hdwy: nvr rchd ldrs* **5/1**[3]

0020 **8** *1½* **Always Ends Well (IRE)**[13] 2850 3-9-4 **57** .... JoeFanning 1 47
(Mark Johnston) *trckd ldrs: rdn over 2f out: wknd over 1f out* **9/1**

060 **9** *¾* **Certainly Elusive (IRE)**[14] 2826 3-8-10 **49** ....(b) PJMcDonald 10 37
(Alan Swinbank) *cl up: ev ch and edgd rt 2f out: sn rdn and wknd* **16/1**

006- **10** *5* **Last Zak**[261] 6572 3-8-11 **50** .... JamesSullivan 13 27
(Michael Easterby) *sn pushed along towards rr: struggling 4f out: nvr on terms* **33/1**

5-36 **11** *3½* **No Plan B (IRE)**[30] 2341 3-9-1 **54** ....(p) FrannyNorton 11 23
(Noel Quinlan) *sn pushed along towards rr: sme hdwy over 3f out: sn n.d* **12/1**

4504 **12** *1¾* **Madam Bonny (IRE)**[7] 3032 3-8-7 **46** oh1 .... DuranFentiman 6
(Jim Goldie) *trckd ldrs: effrt and rdn over 2f out: wknd over 1f out* **7/1**

0-06 **13** *2* **Angel Kiss (IRE)**[21] 2595 3-8-0 **46** oh1 .... ShirleyTeasdale(7) 9
(Colin Teague) *hld up: drvn along over 3f out: sn wknd* **66/1**

1m 45.65s (-2.75) **Going Correction** -0.275s/f (Firm) **13** Ran SP% **120.2**
Speed ratings (Par 97): **102,98,97,96,95 95,93,92,91,86 83,81,79**
toteswingers: 1&2 £13.20, 1&3 £15.70, 2&3 £38.80. CSF £62.19 CT £741.29 TOTE £3.20: £1.10, £3.90, £7.10; EX 45.50.
Owner R A Fahey **Bred** Bearstone Stud **Trained** Musley Bank, N Yorks

FOCUS
A lowly handicap.

3276 BOOK NOW FOR LADIES NIGHT CLASSIFIED CLAIMING STKS 5f 4y
5:20 (5:20) (Class 6) 3-Y-0+ **£1,940** (£577; £288; £144) **Stalls** High

Form RPR

2330 **1** **Red Cape (FR)**[12] 2876 9-9-0 **70** ....(b) JamesSullivan 5 71
(Ruth Carr) *trckd ldr: rdn to ld over 1f out: styd on strly fnl f* **5/4**[1]

4534 **2** *2¼* **Economic Crisis (IRE)**[7] 3028 3-8-9 **55** .... PaddyAspell 2 62?
(Alan Berry) *chsd ldrs: rdn along over 2f out: chsd wnr ins fnl f: kpt on: no imp* **20/1**

00-6 **3** *1* **Arriva La Diva**[5] 3113 6-8-10 **61** .... DaleSwift(3) 6 58
(Linda Perratt) *led to over 1f out: kpt on same pce ins fnl f* **17/2**[3]

2605 **4** *¾* **Angelo Poliziano**[5] 3109 6-8-12 **70** ....(p) LMcNiff(5) 3 60
(George Foster) *blindold slow to remove: dwlt: in tch: effrt and rdn over 1f out: kpt on same pce fnl f* **3/1**[2]

6615 **5** *¾* **Argentine (IRE)**[16] 2748 8-8-11 **64** ....(v) PaulMulrennan 4 51
(Ian Semple) *taken early to post: rrd as stalls opened: sn in tch: effrt and rdn over 1f out: kpt on same pce* **3/1**[2]

58.93s (-1.07) **Going Correction** -0.175s/f (Firm)
WFA 3 from 6yo+ 6lb **5** Ran SP% **109.7**
Speed ratings (Par 101): **101,97,95,94,93**
toteswinger: 1&2 £8.20. CSF £23.94 TOTE £2.80: £1.80, £8.30; EX 22.50.
Owner Middleham Park Racing LVI **Bred** Gilles And Mrs Forien **Trained** Huby, N Yorks

FOCUS
A small-field claimer, in which the gallop appeared genuine throughout.
Angelo Poliziano Official explanation: jockey said gelding was being awkward and he was unable to remove blindfold just before gates opened

3277 TURFTV IN YOUR BETTING SHOP APPRENTICE H'CAP (ROUND 2 OF HAMILTON PARK APPRENTICE RIDER SERIES) 1m 4f 17y
5:55 (5:55) (Class 6) (0-60,60) 4-Y-0+ **£2,045** (£603; £302) **Stalls** Low

Form RPR

5110 **1** **Harare**[2] 3236 11-9-0 **58** ....(v) GemmaTutty(5) 7 68
(Karen Tutty) *hld up: pushed along over 2f out: gd hdwy over 1f out: led ins fnl f: kpt on wl* **7/2**[2]

0005 **2** *3½* **Khandaq (USA)**[11] 2922 5-9-0 **60** .... PaulHainey(7) 4 64
(Keith Dalgleish) *hld up: smooth hdwy to ld over 2f out: rdn over 1f out: hdd ins fnl f: sn no ex* **9/4**[1]

0504 **3** *2½* **Sposalizio (IRE)**[12] 2874 5-8-4 **46** oh1 ....(b) LauraBarry(3) 5 46
(Colin Teague) *led tl hung lft and hdd over 2f out: rallied over 1f out: sn no imp* **9/1**

4400 **4** *3¼* **Escape Artist**[13] 2635 5-8-5 **49** ow3 .... RossSmith(5) 3 44
(David Thompson) *hld up on ins: effrt over 2f out: no imp wl over 1f out* **25/1**

4-54 **5** *2¾* **Lady Gargoyle**[14] 2823 4-8-7 **46** oh1 .... JasonHart 8 37
(Jim Goldie) *plld hrd: restrained in tch: rdn along over 3f out: outpcd fr 2f out* **4/1**[3]

40-0 **6** *13* **Hal Of A Lover**[19] 2670 4-8-11 **50** ....(p) GeorgeChaloner 2 20
(Lisa Williamson) *trckd ldrs tl rdn and wknd over 2f out* **14/1**

0-04 **7** *2* **Dynamic Drive (IRE)**[13] 2842 5-9-1 **57** .... DavidSimmonson(3) 1 24
(Barry Murtagh) *chsd ldrs: effrt over 3f out: wknd fr 2f out* **6/1**

40-6 **8** *25* **Crabbies Gold (IRE)**[18] 2013 4-8-6 **48** ....(v[1]) ShirleyTeasdale(3) 6
(Lisa Williamson) *trckd ldrs tl rdn and wknd wl over 2f out: t.o* **12/1**

2m 36.82s (-1.78) **Going Correction** -0.275s/f (Firm) **8** Ran SP% **115.5**
Speed ratings (Par 101): **94,91,90,87,86 77,76,59**
toteswingers: 1&2 £3.40, 1&3 £6.30, 2&3 £6.70. CSF £11.95 CT £63.90 TOTE £3.10: £1.10, £1.80, £2.90; EX 16.90.
Owner Thoroughbred Homes Ltd **Bred** Limestone Stud **Trained** Osmotherley, N Yorks

FOCUS
The early gallop for this contest was strong and the complexion of the race changed in the final stages.
T/Plt: £110.80 to a £1 stake. Pool £37,675.23. 248.20 winning tickets. T/Qpdt: £17.20 to a £1 stake. Pool £3,533.25. 151.97 winning tickets. RY

3039 KEMPTON (A.W) (R-H)
Wednesday, June 20

OFFICIAL GOING: Standard
Wind: Fresh, half behind Weather: Fine

3278 WIN BIG WITH BETDAQ MULTIPLES APPRENTICE H'CAP 1m 2f (P)
6:10 (6:11) (Class 4) (0-80,80) 4-Y-0+ **£4,075** (£1,212; £606; £303) **Stalls** Low

Form RPR

2125 **1** **Sand Skier**[25] 2479 5-9-7 **80** .... NicoleNordblad(3) 7 89
(Hans Adielsson) *t.k.h: trckd ldr after 3f: led 4f out: kicked clr 2f out: styd on wl* **8/1**

3-04 **2** *1¾* **John Biscuit (IRE)**[15] 2801 4-9-5 **80** .... ThomasBrown(5) 10 86
(Andrew Balding) *trckd ldrs: rdn to chse wnr over 2f out: styd on but nvr able to chal* **8/1**

0230 **3** *1* **Hurakan (IRE)**[33] 2233 6-8-6 **67** ....(p) DanielMuscutt(5) 4 71
(Richard Price) *dwlt: hld up but sn wl in tch: rdn to chse ldng pair 2f out: kpt on but unable to chal* **7/1**[2]

-013 **4** *1¾* **Scottish Star**[20] 2637 4-9-2 **75** .... IanBurns(3) 5 75+
(James Eustace) *racd wd: hld up in rr: prog whn v wd bnd 2f out: kpt on to take 4th nr fin: no ch* **3/1**[1]

3304 **5** *¾* **Laughing Jack**[7] 3039 4-9-1 **74** .... GeorgeDowning(3) 9 73+
(Tony Carroll) *stdd s: hld up in last: prog over 2f out but ldrs already gone for home: styd on but no hope of threatening* **15/2**[3]

230- **6** *½* **Brigadoon**[174] 7908 5-9-3 **78** .... WilliamTwiston-Davies(5) 2 76
(William Jarvis) *trckd ldrs: rdn over 2f out: steadily outpcd after* **10/1**

4025 **7** *2* **Mcbirney (USA)**[15] 2801 5-8-13 **76** .... LouisSteward(7) 6 70
(Paul D'Arcy) *in tch towards rr: urged along fr over 2f out: one pce and no imp* **12/1**

41-4 **8** *½* **Sakhee's Pearl**[112] 733 6-9-6 **76** .... MatthewLawson 12 69
(Jo Crowley) *racd wd: chsd ldrs: rdn over 2f out: wknd over 1f out* **9/1**

00/0 **9** *shd* **Seeking The Buck (USA)**[33] 2248 8-8-13 **74** .... HayleyBurton(5) 1 66
(Amy Weaver) *dwlt: hld up in last pair: no prog whn wd bnd 2f out: kpt on fnl f* **28/1**

0000 **10** *17* **Epsom Salts**[13] 2855 7-8-13 **72** .... JakePayne(3) 3 30
(Pat Phelan) *lft in ld after 3f: hdd 4f out: wknd qckly over 2f out: t.o* **66/1**

105 **11** *64* **Cala Santanyi**[23] 2539 4-9-6 **76** ....(p) AshleyMorgan 11
(Gerard Butler) *in tch tl wknd rapidly 4f out: wl t.o whn virtually p.u fnl f* **11/1**

52-0 **12** *62* **Oetzi**[56] 1611 4-8-6 **67** .... MichaelJMMurphy(5) 8
(Alan Jarvis) *sddle slipped sn after s: led tl wd bnd after 3f: steadily dropped away: virtually p.u fnl 2f* **20/1**

2m 6.49s (-1.51) **Going Correction** -0.10s/f (Stan) **12** Ran SP% **116.3**
Speed ratings (Par 105): **102,100,99,98,97 97,95,95,95,81 30,**
toteswingers: 1&2 £6.90, 1&3 £11.10, 2&3 £11.80. CSF £67.88 CT £473.20 TOTE £3.50: £2.60, £3.40, £2.30; EX 79.30 Trifecta £498.60 Part won. Pool: £673.82 - 0.10 winning units..
Owner Erik Penser **Bred** Rabbah Bloodstock Limited **Trained** Kingston Lisle, Oxon

FOCUS
Quite a competitive apprentice handicap. Prominent runners were favoured through the card and the form is rated cautiously.
Cala Santanyi Official explanation: jockey said filly had no more to give
Oetzi Official explanation: jockey said saddle slipped

3279 BACK OR LAY AT BETDAQ.COM MAIDEN FILLIES' STKS 1m 2f (P)
6:40 (6:41) (Class 5) 3-Y-0+ **£2,264** (£673; £336; £168) **Stalls** Low

Form RPR
5-2 **1** **Silent Moment (USA)**[13] 2849 3-9-0 0 .... SilvestreDeSousa 2 85
(Saeed Bin Suroor) *mde all: gng best and looked in command 2f out: drvn out to hold on fnl f* **4/1**[2]
2-3 **2** *½* **Medea (IRE)**[40] 2050 3-9-0 0 .... RyanMoore 7 84
(Sir Michael Stoute) *mostly chsd wnr: rdn and no imp over 2f out: styd on to chal ins fnl f: jst hld* **3/1**[1]
0 **3** *2 ¼* **Four Leaves (IRE)**[61] 1502 3-9-0 0 .... AdamKirby 3 79
(Marco Botti) *mostly in 3rd: rdn to dispute 2nd over 2f out to over 1f out: one pce fnl f* **20/1**
03 **4** *2* **Amaraja (GER)**[41] 2008 3-9-0 0 .... TomQueally 5 75+
(Sir Henry Cecil) *chsd ldng quartet: rdn and outpcd over 2f out: kpt on to take 4th over 1f out: n.d* **4/1**[2]
0- **5** *¾* **Fleur De Cactus (IRE)**[235] 7164 3-9-0 0 .... RichardMullen 10 74
(Sir Michael Stoute) *in tch in 7th: shoved along by 1/2-way: kpt on for driving but nvr able to threaten* **6/1**[3]
6 *1* **Light Shine** 3-9-0 0 .... RobertHavlin 13 72+
(John Gosden) *s.s: hld up in last trio: pushed along in 9th wl over 1f out: styd on wl after: likely improver* **33/1**
0 **7** *3* **Stunning View (USA)**[13] 2856 3-9-0 0 .... KierenFallon 4 68
(John Gosden) *mostly in midfield: rdn and effrt over 2f out: no imp on ldrs over 1f out: eased whn no ch nr fin* **7/1**
4 **8** *1 ½* **Caphira**[22] 2585 3-9-0 0 .... ShaneKelly 11 63
(William Knight) *dwlt: rushed up to chse ldrs after 2f and racd wd: wknd jst over 2f out* **16/1**
0 **9** *1 ¼* **Raving Monsun**[13] 2848 3-9-0 0 .... SebSanders 9 60
(Marco Botti) *racd wd: chsd ldng trio tl wknd qckly 2f out* **25/1**
10 *3 ¼* **Douro** 3-9-0 0 .... JamesDoyle 12 54+
(Roger Charlton) *hld up in last: shkn up and no prog 3f out: bhd after* **25/1**
0 **11** *4* **Runway Girl (IRE)**[61] 1502 3-9-0 0 .... TedDurcan 14 46
(Roger Charlton) *a wl in rr: shkn up and no prog 3f out* **50/1**
12 *2 ¼* **Head Office** 3-9-0 0 .... IanMongan 1 41
(Pat Phelan) *a in rr: pushed along and no prog 3f out: no ch after* **150/1**
13 *nk* **Superstician** 3-9-0 0 .... JackMitchell 8 40
(James Fanshawe) *restless in stalls: s.s: a in last trio: struggling 3f out* **50/1**
14 *67* **Fierecilla** 3-8-11 0 .... RyanClark(3) 6
(Tom Keddy) *dwlt: in tch 6f: wknd rapidly and wl t.o* **125/1**

2m 6.46s (-1.54) **Going Correction** -0.10s/f (Stan) **14** Ran SP% **118.4**
Speed ratings (Par 100): **102,101,99,98,97 96,94,93,92,89 86,84,84,30**
toteswingers: 1&2 £2.00, 1&3 £27.00, 2&3 £15.00. CSF £14.90 TOTE £4.50: £2.10, £2.50, £11.00; EX 11.10 Trifecta £267.20 Part won. Pool: £361.14 - 0.10 winning units..
Owner Godolphin **Bred** Darley **Trained** Newmarket, Suffolk

FOCUS
Older horse maidens on this track are quite often interesting and plenty of major yards were represented in this fillies' event. The time was fractionally faster than the opening contest and those ridden prominently were at an advantage. The form is rated around the first three.

3280 BETDAQ MOBILE APPS H'CAP 1m 2f (P)
7:10 (7:11) (Class 4) (0-85,85) 3-Y-0 **£4,075** (£1,212; £606; £303) **Stalls** Low

Form RPR
-042 **1** **Counsel (IRE)**[12] 2898 3-8-10 **74** .... RyanMoore 3 87
(Sir Michael Stoute) *hld up in last pair early: prog fr 3f out: rdn to go 3rd 2f out: clsd to chal fnl f: drvn ahd last 75yds* **13/2**[3]
01-0 **2** *¾* **Expert Fighter (USA)**[33] 2235 3-9-0 **78** .... TedDurcan 2 89
(Saeed Bin Suroor) *awkward s: rcvrd to go prom: chsd ldr over 2f out: drvn ahd jst ins fnl f: hdd and no ex last 75yds* **20/1**
6-04 **3** *2 ¾* **Scrupul (IRE)**[26] 2449 3-8-11 **75** .... KierenFallon 7 81
(Luca Cumani) *prog to ld after 2f and crossed to inner: kicked on over 2f out: hdd and no ex jst ins fnl f* **12/1**
241F **4** *3 ½* **Star Date (IRE)**[18] 2701 3-9-2 **83** .... RaulDaSilva(3) 6 82
(Gerard Butler) *hld up in last: pushed along over 3f out: prog to go 4th over 1f out but n.d: one pce after* **7/1**
-003 **5** *2 ¾* **Elkhart (IRE)**[19] 2678 3-8-13 **77** .... MircoDemuro 5 70
(Mark Johnston) *trckd ldrs: rdn over 2f out: sn outpcd: fdd fnl f* **20/1**
-000 **6** *11* **Venetian View (IRE)**[14] 2813 3-9-6 **84** ....(b) GeorgeBaker 8 55
(Gary Moore) *intimidated and rn wd bnd after 3f: dropped to last pair: rdn and no prog 3f out: sn bhd* **9/1**
61-0 **7** *2 ½* **Trois Vallees (USA)**[12] 2897 3-9-1 **79** .... SilvestreDeSousa 4 45
(Mahmood Al Zarooni) *chsd ldrs: shoved along fr 1/2-way: wknd 3f out: sn last and bhd* **4/1**[2]
5-21 **8** *¾* **Handsome Ransom**[29] 2368 3-9-7 **85** .... WilliamBuick 1 50
(John Gosden) *led 2f: chsd ldr: rdn over 3f out: lost 2nd over 2f out and wknd: eased whn no ch* **6/4**[1]

2m 6.13s (-1.87) **Going Correction** -0.10s/f (Stan) **8** Ran SP% **113.0**
Speed ratings (Par 101): **103,102,100,97,95 86,84,83**
toteswingers: 1&2 £23.30, 1&3 £8.70, 2&3 £36.80. CSF £117.23 CT £1502.53 TOTE £8.00: £1.50, £9.80, £4.40; EX 134.50 TRIFECTA Not won..
Owner Highclere Thoroughbred Racing-Booklaw **Bred** Star Bloodstock **Trained** Newmarket, Suffolk

FOCUS
A good handicap in which the pace looked strong early but the overall time was just 0.33secs faster than the preceding maiden. A personal best from the winner.
Trois Vallees(USA) Official explanation: jockey said colt never travelled
Handsome Ransom Official explanation: jockey said colt lost its action

3281 BETDAQ CASINO GAMES H'CAP 7f (P)
7:40 (7:41) (Class 4) (0-85,85) 3-Y-0+ **£4,075** (£1,212; £606; £303) **Stalls** Low

Form RPR
-314 **1** **Mizwaaj (IRE)**[14] 2813 3-9-4 **84** .... SilvestreDeSousa 14 96
(Saeed Bin Suroor) *t.k.h: sn trckd ldr fr wdst draw: led over 2f out and kicked 2 l clr: hld on nr fin* **15/2**
41 **2** *nk* **Dutch Supreme**[36] 2147 3-9-5 **85** .... TedDurcan 12 96
(David Lanigan) *cut across fr wd draw to trck ldng pair on inner: nt qckn whn wnr kicked on over 2f out: wnt 2nd wl over 1f out: clsd fnl f: jst hld* **9/2**[3]
-144 **3** *1 ½* **Triple Charm**[50] 1741 4-9-13 **84** ....(p) RyanMoore 3 94+
(Jeremy Noseda) *hld up in last trio: gd prog fr 2f out: wnt 3rd ins fnl f: r.o: too much to do* **10/3**[1]
6324 **4** *1 ¼* **Corporal Maddox**[5] 3105 5-9-13 **84** .... JamieSpencer 7 91
(Jamie Osborne) *hld up in last trio: prog jst over 2f out: disp 3rd jst ins fnl f: styd on same pce after* **4/1**[2]
2003 **5** *1 ½* **Sole Danser (IRE)**[22] 2572 4-9-2 **73** .... RichardKingscote 1 76
(Milton Bradley) *hld up towards rr: prog 2f out: tried to chal for a pl 1f out: one pce after* **22/1**
1662 **6** *1* **Street Power (USA)**[39] 2071 7-9-4 **78** .... RaulDaSilva(3) 9 78
(Jeremy Gask) *hld up in rr: prog jst over 2f out: tried to cl and chal for a pl fnl f: fdd* **10/1**
0000 **7** *1 ¾* **The Tichborne (IRE)**[13] 2857 4-9-2 **73** .... JackMitchell 11 68
(Roger Teal) *settled in last trio: drvn and gng nowhere 3f out: styd on fnl 2f: n.d* **25/1**
1060 **8** *1* **Divine Call**[12] 2870 5-9-10 **81** ....(p) LukeMorris 2 73
(Milton Bradley) *prom: hrd rdn and 3rd briefly over 1f out on inner: wknd fnl f* **33/1**
0540 **9** *nse* **Intercept (IRE)**[11] 2940 4-9-9 **80** ....(t[1]) WilliamBuick 4 72
(John Gosden) *sn in midfield: rdn and effrt out wd over 2f out: no imp over 1f out* **8/1**
234- **10** *6* **Rondeau (GR)**[235] 7171 7-9-12 **83** .... GeorgeBaker 13 59+
(Patrick Chamings) *sn prom and racd wd: wl there over 2f out: jst pushed along and lost pl rapidly over 1f out* **16/1**
2-33 **11** *½* **Salacia (IRE)**[21] 2601 3-9-2 **82** .... RoystonFfrench 6 54
(Ismail Mohammed) *led to over 2f out: wknd qckly* **40/1**
2546 **12** *3 ¼* **Hatta Stream (IRE)**[5] 3103 6-9-4 **78** .... SimonPearce(3) 10 44
(Lydia Pearce) *racd wd in midfield: wknd over 2f out* **33/1**
200- **13** *9* **My Gacho (IRE)**[239] 7074 10-9-6 **77** ....(v) J-PGuillambert 5 19
(David Nicholls) *plld hrd early: cl up tl rdn and wknd rapidly over 2f out: t.o* **66/1**

1m 24.43s (-1.57) **Going Correction** -0.10s/f (Stan)
WFA 3 from 4yo+ 9lb **13** Ran SP% **117.1**
Speed ratings (Par 105): **104,103,101,100,98 97,95,94,94,87 87,83,73**
toteswingers: 1&2 £7.90, 1&3 £3.80, 2&3 £2.90. CSF £37.58 CT £140.14 TOTE £7.90: £2.70, £1.10, £1.50; EX 47.00 Trifecta £211.20 Part won. Pool: £285.47 - 0.30 winning units..
Owner Godolphin **Bred** Darley **Trained** Newmarket, Suffolk
■ Stewards' Enquiry : Ted Durcan one-day ban: careless riding (Jul 4)

FOCUS
A maximum field and another good handicap, and once again it paid to race close to the pace. Good form for the grade, and the first two are both progressing.
Hatta Stream(IRE) Official explanation: jockey said gelding never travelled

3282 BRITISH STALLION STUDS SUPPORTING BRITISH RACING E B F MAIDEN FILLIES' STKS 7f (P)
8:10 (8:12) (Class 5) 2-Y-0 **£3,234** (£962; £481; £240) **Stalls** Low

Form RPR
1 **Discernable** 2-9-0 0 .... SilvestreDeSousa 8 79+
(Mark Johnston) *mde all: pressed and rdn 2f out: r.o wl and in command fnl f* **11/4**[1]
2 *¾* **Savanna La Mar (USA)** 2-9-0 0 .... LukeMorris 5 77+
(Sir Mark Prescott Bt) *green in preliminaries: chsd ldrs: pushed along in 4th 1/2-way: styd on fr over 1f out to take 2nd last 100yds: nt rch wnr* **6/1**[2]
6 **3** *1 ¼* **Cross Pattee (IRE)**[11] 2938 2-9-0 0 .... WilliamBuick 10 74
(John Gosden) *sn chsd wnr: rdn to chal 2f out: hld 1f out: one pce and lost 2nd last 100yds* **6/1**[2]
4 *1 ¼* **Nardin** 2-9-0 0 .... PaulHanagan 4 71
(Ed Dunlop) *trckd ldrs: shkn up over 2f out: styd on same pce fr over 1f out* **15/2**
5 *¾* **Jathabah (IRE)** 2-9-0 0 .... SebSanders 2 69+
(Clive Brittain) *t.k.h early: hld up in midfield: chsd ldrs over 2f out: styd on fr over 1f out: nrst fin* **20/1**
03 **6** *nk* **Bayan Kasirga (IRE)**[13] 2837 2-9-0 0 .... TonyHamilton 6 68
(Richard Fahey) *chsd ldrs: rdn over 2f out: one pce and no imp after: kpt on* **7/1**[3]
0 **7** *1 ¾* **Wittgenstein (IRE)**[33] 2245 2-9-0 0 .... MartinDwyer 1 63
(Brian Meehan) *mostly chsd ldng pair to 2f out: steadily fdd* **8/1**
8 *3 ¼* **Wedding Speech (IRE)** 2-9-0 0 .... RyanMoore 14 55+
(Sir Michael Stoute) *chsd ldrs: rdn 3f out: no imp 2f out: wknd fnl f* **9/1**
0 **9** *3 ¼* **Marguerite St Just**[11] 2938 2-9-0 0 .... JackMitchell 12 47
(Olivia Maylam) *racd wd in midfield: v wd bnd 3f out and lost grnd: pushed along and nvr on terms after* **80/1**
10 *4* **Una Bella Cosa** 2-9-0 0 .... ShaneKelly 11 36
(Alan McCabe) *green in preliminaries: s.s: a in rr: lost tch over 2f out* **33/1**
11 *shd* **Alpine Mysteries (IRE)** 2-9-0 0 .... TedDurcan 13 36
(John Dunlop) *green in preliminaries: s.v.s: rn v green and detached in last: sme late prog* **28/1**
12 *4 ½* **Serenata (IRE)** 2-9-0 0 .... StevieDonohoe 7 24+
(Paul Cole) *in tch in midfield: wd bnd 3f out: sn wknd* **40/1**
13 *¾* **Diva Cavallina** 2-9-0 0 .... JohnFahy 3 22
(Alan McCabe) *a towards rr: wknd over 2f out* **33/1**
14 *9* **Dolly Bantry** 2-9-0 0 .... IPoullis 9
(Alan McCabe) *sn rdn in rr: nvr a factor: t.o* **40/1**

1m 26.67s (0.67) **Going Correction** -0.10s/f (Stan) **14** Ran SP% **120.8**
Speed ratings (Par 90): **92,91,89,88,87 87,85,81,77,73 72,67,66,56**
toteswingers: 1&2 £6.30, 1&3 £6.00, 2&3 £10.70. CSF £17.33 TOTE £5.70: £2.10, £1.10, £2.50; EX 23.70 Trifecta £114.00 Pool: £225.02 - 1.46 winning units..
Owner Sheikh Hamdan Bin Mohammed Al Maktoum **Bred** Newsells Park Stud **Trained** Middleham Moor, N Yorks

FOCUS
A 7f maiden for juvenile fillies with a number of well-bred sorts representing major yards, and this could be a race that throws up its share of future winners. It has been rated around the mid-point of the race averages.

NOTEBOOK

Discernable, a 160,000gns half-sister to a couple of winners in the US, was well backed on this debut and clearly knew her job. Her rider, who was completing a treble, was keen to make plenty of use of her and she responded really well for pressure, stretching out well in the closing stages. She could make up into a Group filly if she goes the right way. (op 7-2)

Savanna La Mar(USA), the first European runner for her sire Curlin, is out of a Listed winner and she showed signs of greenness before keeping on in good style in pursuit of the winner. She should have no difficulty winning races with this debut behind her.

Cross Pattee(IRE), a half-sister to Bronze Cannon amongst others, was stepping up 2f in trip from her debut but put that experience to good use to grab a prominent position early from her high draw. She probably ran into a couple of decent newcomers here and can find easier opportunities. (op 11-2 tchd 7-1)

Nardin, a 90,000gns half-sister to several winners was another who looked to need the experience, but showed enough on this debut to suggest she can make her mark. (op 6-1)

Jathabah(IRE), related to five winners, stayed on late from the back without threatening. (op 25-1)

Wedding Speech(IRE) was beaten by inexperience and the highest draw, which meant she raced on the outside of the pack and saw plenty of daylight. She can do better in time, and possibly over further. (op 8-1 tchd 7-1)

Serenata(IRE) Official explanation: jockey said bit slipped through filly's mouth

3283 PHIL GEDGE FAREWELL H'CAP — 2m (P)

8:40 (8:41) (Class 6) (0-65,65) 4-Y-O+ — £1,617 (£481; £240; £120) Stalls Low

Form — RPR

3-35 **1** **Reillys Daughter**[35] 2175 4-8-13 **57**.................................. IanMongan 1 — 66
(Laura Mongan) *trckd ldng pair: drvn over 2f out: wnt 2nd over 1f out: styd on u.p to ld last 100yds* **14/1**

0-11 **2** *1* **Alfraamsey**[18] 2396 4-9-6 **64**.. JimmyFortune 9 — 72
(Sheena West) *led at ordianry pce: kicked on over 2f out: edgd lft fr over 1f out: hdd and nt qckn last 100yds* **7/2**[2]

354 **3** *2 ¼* **Dream Catcher (SWE)**[28] 2396 9-9-3 **61**......................(p) HayleyTurner 5 — 66
(Jonjo O'Neill) *t.k.h: trckd ldr: rdn over 2f out: nt qckn and lost 2nd over 1f out: hld on for 3rd* **16/1**

2222 **4** *hd* **Laser Blazer**[28] 2394 4-8-12 **56**......................................(p) PatCosgrave 6 — 61
(Jeremy Gask) *tk fierce hold in 7th: stl taking t.k.h 5f out: rdn and nt qckn over 2f out: styd on fr over 1f out: nrly tk 3rd* **9/1**

44-2 **5** *1 ¼* **Phonic (IRE)**[25] 2502 5-8-13 **64**.. NedCurtis(7) 7 — 68
(John Dunlop) *trckd ldrs in 5th: pushed along and outpcd over 2f out: one pce and no real imp after* **5/1**[3]

0-00 **6** *1* **Sweet Lavender (IRE)**[13] 2863 4-9-7 **65**.................... JackMitchell 12 — 67
(Gay Kelleway) *chsd ldng trio on outer: rdn and nt qckn over 2f out: steadily fdd* **50/1**

-003 **7** *2 ¼* **Inside Knowledge (USA)**[6] 3077 6-8-8 **52**...................... LukeMorris 4 — 52
(Garry Woodward) *hld up in last trio: outpcd over 2f out: nvr on terms* **12/1**

3144 **8** *1 ¼* **Cloudy Start**[37] 2134 6-9-0 **63**...................................... LeonnaMayor(5) 2 — 61
(Jamie Osborne) *hld up in last: effrt on outer 3f out but sn outpcd: nvr on terms* **12/1**

3146 **9** *6* **Blue Cossack (IRE)**[5] 3102 4-9-3 **61**............................ DavidProbert 10 — 52
(Mark Usher) *s.s: hld up in last pair: effrt over 3f out: no prog over 2f out: sn wknd* **18/1**

5/11 **10** *1* **Fade To Grey (IRE)**[19] 1925 8-9-4 **62**...........................(t) KierenFallon 3 — 52
(Shaun Lycett) *hld up in 7th: pushed along over 3f out: sn struggling: bhd fnl 2f* **9/4**[1]

3m 34.1s (4.00) **Going Correction** -0.10s/f (Stan) — **10** Ran SP% **114.8**

Speed ratings (Par 101): **86,85,84,84,83 83,82,81,78,77**

toteswingers: 1&2 £13.30, 1&3 £8.70, 2&3 £16.70. CSF £61.70 CT £806.30 TOTE £18.30: £5.10, £1.30, £3.50; EX 54.60 Trifecta £224.50 Part won. Pool: £303.50 - 0.10 winning units..

Owner Condover Racing **Bred** P Cunningham **Trained** Epsom, Surrey

FOCUS

A modest stayers' handicap in which the first three held those positions throughout. The winner reversed Lingfield form with the runner-up.

Blue Cossack(IRE) Official explanation: jockey said gelding was slowly away

3284 IRISH NIGHT WITH ROLLERCOASTER 11.07.12 H'CAP — 6f (P)

9:10 (9:10) (Class 4) (0-85,85) 3-Y-O — £4,075 (£1,212; £606; £303) Stalls Low

Form — RPR

-046 **1** **Desert Philosopher**[26] 2451 3-9-4 **82**.............................. JamieSpencer 9 — 95
(Kevin Ryan) *fast away fr wd draw: mde all: drvn at least 2 l clr over 1f out: hld on nr fin* **14/1**

-020 **2** *hd* **Mezzotint (IRE)**[46] 1858 3-9-7 **85**.................................... AndreaAtzeni 5 — 97+
(Marco Botti) *chsd ldrs: crowded over 4f out: rdn to chse wnr 2f out: clsd u.p fnl f: jst failed* **9/2**[3]

2415 **3** *3 ¾* **Willies Wonder (IRE)**[18] 2714 3-9-0 **78**......................... WilliamBuick 2 — 78
(Charles Hills) *hld up in rr: prog over 2f out: chsd ldng pair over 1f out: one pce and no imp* **11/2**

001- **4** *1 ¾* **Solfilia**[341] 4069 3-9-2 **80**.. DarryllHolland 8 — 74+
(Hughie Morrison) *trying to get in fr wd draw whn slipped over 4f out: sn chsd ldng pair: wnt 2nd after 1/2-way to 2f out: easily outpcd* **20/1**

03-0 **5** *2* **Amoure Medici**[30] 2331 3-8-11 **75**.................................. JackMitchell 6 — 63
(Noel Quinlan) *t.k.h: chsd wnr to sn after 1/2-way: steadily wknd on inner* **33/1**

5054 **6** *½* **Gabbiano**[7] 3041 3-8-8 **75**.......................................(p) RaulDaSilva(3) 4 — 61
(Jeremy Gask) *hmpd s: hld up in rr: effrt on outer over 2f out: sn rdn and nt qckn: wknd over 1f out* **5/2**[1]

5-21 **7** *2* **Sunley Pride**[79] 1166 3-8-12 **76**.. SamHitchcott 7 — 56
(Mick Channon) *chsng ldrs whn hmpd over 4f out: rdn in 5th over 2f out: sn btn* **20/1**

2-44 **8** *2 ¾* **Backtrade (IRE)**[21] 2611 3-8-6 **70**................................ DavidProbert 3 — 41
(Andrew Balding) *fractious coming out on to crse: wnt sharply lft s: hld up in last: no real prog* **16/1**

01 **9** *10* **Furbelow**[51] 1705 3-9-4 **82**... RyanMoore 1 — 21
(Jeremy Noseda) *hld up in tch: wknd qckly 2f out: eased and t.o* **11/4**[2]

1m 11.96s (-1.14) **Going Correction** -0.10s/f (Stan) — **9** Ran SP% **113.8**

Speed ratings (Par 101): **103,102,97,95,92 92,89,85,72**

toteswingers: 1&2 £7.60, 1&3 £6.00, 2&3 £5.00. CSF £72.76 CT £397.03 TOTE £17.20: £6.10, £1.50, £1.10; EX 91.00 Trifecta £187.00 Pool: £566.24 - 2.24 winning units..

Owner Ahmad Al Shaikh **Bred** Wood Hall Stud Limited **Trained** Hambleton, N Yorks

FOCUS

This fair 3yo sprint proved to be a very messy contest with a fair amount of scrimmaging. In the end it produced a close finish with the first two clear. The market leaders disappointed, but a clear personal best from the winner.

Gabbiano Official explanation: jockey said gelding suffered interference at start

Furbelow Official explanation: jockey said saddle slipped

T/Plt: £312.30 to a £1 stake. Pool £74,814.19. 174.85 winning tickets. T/Qpdt: £67.40 to a £1 stake. Pool £4,706.73. 51.61 winning tickets. JN

2822 RIPON (R-H)

Wednesday, June 20

OFFICIAL GOING: Good (8.0)

Wind: Almost nil Weather: Overcast

3285 SUNDOWN SKY APPRENTICE CLASSIFIED (S) STKS — 6f

6:50 (6:50) (Class 6) 3-4-Y-O — £1,940 (£577; £288; £144) Stalls High

Form — RPR

0065 **1** **Another Citizen (IRE)**[2] 3211 4-9-7 65............................(b) PaulMcGiff 1 — 67
(Tim Easterby) *mde all: edgd lft over 2f out: 3 l clr over 1f out: drvn out: hld on towards fin* **4/1**[3]

00-5 **2** *½* **Slenningford**[36] 2139 3-9-0 60.. KevinStott 6 — 63
(Ollie Pears) *chsd ldrs: kpt on ins fnl f: jst hld* **16/1**

0-00 **3** *1 ¼* **Fayr Fall (IRE)**[33] 2256 3-9-0 68... GaryMahon 3 — 59
(Tim Easterby) *t.k.h towards rr: hdwy over 2f out: chsng ldrs over 1f out: kpt on same pce last 100yds* **3/1**[1]

6424 **4** *4* **Finefrenzyrolling (IRE)**[23] 2551 4-9-7 58......................(p) JoeyHaynes 4 — 48
(Mrs K Burke) *trckd ldrs: t.k.h: edgd rt over 1f out: one pce* **5/1**

14 **5** *½* **Superplex**[82] 1110 3-9-5 67..(p) MatthewMcGhee 2 — 50
(John Quinn) *chsd ldrs: effrt over 2f out: one pce* **9/2**

1-60 **6** *8* **Guava**[60] 1531 3-9-0 64.. RobJFitzpatrick 8 — 19
(David O'Meara) *chsd ldrs: lost pl over 2f out* **7/2**[2]

0406 **7** *14* **Script**[36] 2139 3-9-0 45.. MichaelKenny 5
(Alan Berry) *swvd rt s: sn chsng ldrs on outer: lost pl wl over 1f out: eased fnl f* **66/1**

00-0 **8** *6* **Hereselle (IRE)**[26] 2436 4-9-7 43.................................. DanielleMooney 7
(Michael Chapman) *rrd and swvd rt s: t.k.h: sn trcking ldrs: lost pl over 3f out: sn bhd: eased ins fnl f* **66/1**

1m 13.57s (0.57) **Going Correction** +0.05s/f (Good)

WFA 3 from 4yo 7lb — **8** Ran SP% **110.9**

Speed ratings (Par 101): **98,97,95,90,89 79,60,52**

toteswingers: 1&2 £5.80, 1&3 £2.90, 2&3 £12.30. CSF £59.59 TOTE £3.90: £1.10, £5.60, £1.70; EX 57.40.There was no bid for the winner.

Owner Middleham Park Racing V & Partners **Bred** Sandro Garavelli **Trained** Great Habton, N Yorks

■ Stewards' Enquiry : Gary Mahon caution: careless riding.

FOCUS

This seller for apprentices saw the principals come clear.

3286 CHARLIE WALLER MEMORIAL MEDIAN AUCTION MAIDEN STKS — 5f

7:20 (7:22) (Class 5) 2-Y-O — £2,587 (£770; £384; £192) Stalls High

Form — RPR

04 **1** **Rat Catcher (IRE)**[23] 2537 2-9-3 0.................................(b¹) DavidAllan 4 — 77
(Tim Easterby) *mde all: drvn 2 l clr ins fnl f: edgd rt: jst hld on* **13/2**[2]

2 *hd* **Antonio Gramsci** 2-9-3 0.. GrahamGibbons 9 — 78+
(David Barron) *dwlt: drvn to sn chse ldrs: lost pl over 3f out: gd hdwy over 1f out: styd on wl towards fin: jst hld* **11/8**[1]

3 *2 ¼* **Findog** 2-9-3 0.. GrahamLee 10 — 71+
(Ollie Pears) *swvd lft s: in rr: swtchd rt and hdwy appr fnl f: kpt on wl* **12/1**

020 **4** *1 ½* **Mount Seymour (IRE)**[37] 2123 2-9-0 0.................... DeclanCannon(3) 2 — 63
(Nigel Tinkler) *chsd wnr: over 2f out: kpt on same pce appr fnl f* **8/1**

0 **5** *1 ¼* **Tumblewind**[18] 2686 2-8-12 0.. RussKennemore 3 — 53
(Richard Whitaker) *mid-div: hdwy over 2f out: swtchd rt over 1f out: sn fdd* **16/1**

0 **6** *1 ¾* **Archie Stevens**[14] 2822 2-9-3 0.................................... StephenCraine 8 — 52
(Tom Dascombe) *s.i.s: hdwy to chse ldrs over 2f out: wknd over 1f out* **8/1**

0 **7** *2 ¼* **Supercruiser (IRE)**[30] 2349 2-9-3 0.................................... TomEaves 5 — 44
(Nigel Tinkler) *t.k.h: mid-div: effrt over 2f out: wknd over 1f out* **40/1**

04 **8** *1 ½* **Colours Of Nature**[11] 2912 2-9-3 0................................. MickyFenton 6 — 38
(Eric Alston) *sn outpcd and in rr: hdwy on outer over 2f out: hung lft and lost pl over 1f out* **12/1**

40 **9** *8* **Betty Boo (IRE)**[29] 2376 2-8-12 0........................... RobbieFitzpatrick 11 — 5
(Shaun Harris) *chsd ldrs: lost pl over 2f out: eased whn bhd* **16/1**

00 **10** *3* **Bronte Belle**[18] 2686 2-8-12 0.. AndrewElliott 7
(Jedd O'Keeffe) *led to post: chsd ldrs: lost pl 2f out: sn bhd* **25/1**

430 **11** *1 ½* **Hellolini**[26] 2437 2-8-12 0... RobertWinston 1 — 53+
(Robin Bastiman) *chsd ldrs: sddle slipped: heavily eased appr fnl f* **15/2**[3]

1m 1.22s (0.52) **Going Correction** +0.05s/f (Good) — **11** Ran SP% **122.9**

Speed ratings (Par 93): **97,96,93,90,88 85,82,79,67,62 59**

toteswingers: 1&2 £2.70, 1&3 £14.40, 2&3 £10.30. CSF £16.48 TOTE £6.50: £3.00, £1.10, £5.70; EX 20.20.

Owner Trevor Hemmings **Bred** Gleadhill House Stud Ltd **Trained** Great Habton, N Yorks

FOCUS

A weak 2yo maiden, but the second and third caught the eye.

NOTEBOOK

Rat Catcher(IRE) was equipped with first-time blinkers and got off the mark at the third time of asking, handing his yard a quickfire double. He got across early and bagged the stands' rail, which ultimately proved a winning move. Had the penny dropped with the runner-up earlier he would have come out second-best, but his previous experience was just enough to see him prevail. (op 11-2 tchd 7-1)

Antonio Gramsci ◆ was starting off in a winnable-looking race and was heavily backed. He lost out by getting behind early and then running distinctly green, but it's testament to his ability that he managed to only just lose out in the circumstances. Compensation surely awaits in the coming weeks on a stiffer track. (op 7-2)

Findog, whose dam was a multiple winner in Italy, showed up nicely from the rails draw on this debut and looks sure to come on for the experience. A stiffer test may also suit ideally. (tchd 11-1 and 14-1)

Mount Seymour(IRE) was well held, but this was better again from him back on a sounder surface. (op 17-2 tchd 7-1)

Hellolini Official explanation: jockey said saddle slipped

3287 RIPON-RACES.CO.UK H'CAP — 1m 1f 170y

7:50 (7:51) (Class 4) (0-85,83) 4-Y-O+ — £4,528 (£1,347; £673; £336) Stalls Low

Form — RPR

0224 **1** **Brockfield**[11] 2926 6-8-9 **71**... RobertWinston 5 — 81
(Mel Brittain) *trckd ldng pair: led wl over 1f out: hung rt: jst hld on* **7/1**

-630 **2** *nk* **Muffin McLeay (IRE)**[21] 2606 4-9-6 **82**.............................. LeeNewman 7 — 92+
(David Barron) *trckd ldrs: effrt over 2f out: nt clr run on inner and swtchd lft 1f out: styd on strly clsng stages: jst hld* **4/1**[2]

5413 **3** *1 ¼* **Maven**[12] 2884 4-9-1 **77**... DavidAllan 4 — 83
(Tim Easterby) *led: hdd wl over 1f out: kpt on same pce* **13/2**

4-35 **4** *2 ½* **Desert Romance (IRE)**[18] 2720 6-9-6 **82**........................ DanielTudhope 6 — 83
(David O'Meara) *w ldr: drvn over 2f out: one pce over 1f out* **11/4**[1]

-004 **5** *nk* **Royal Trooper (IRE)**[11] 2921 6-9-0 **76**.......................... FrederikTylicki 1 76
(James Given) *drvn to chse ldrs: sn hmpd lost pl: sme hdwy 4f out: one pce fnl 2f* **7/1**
5054 **6** *4* **Mazovian (USA)**[9] 2981 4-7-10 **65**.............................. EvaMoscrop(7) 3 57
(Michael Chapman) *trckd ldrs: t.k.h: lost pl over 7f out and sn detached in last: kpt on fnl f* **50/1**
-U36 **7** *2* **Law To Himself (IRE)**[33] 2241 5-8-8 **70**............................ TomEaves 8 58
(Alan Swinbank) *in rr: effrt over 3f out: nvr nr ldrs* **16/1**
0-00 **8** *3 1/4* **City Of The Kings (IRE)**[22] 2590 7-9-7 **83**..................... GrahamLee 2 64
(Ollie Pears) *s.v.s: drvn and sme hdwy 3f out: wknd over 1f out* **6/1**[3]
5-20 **9** *1/2* **New Hampshire (USA)**[35] 2176 4-9-7 **83**.................... StephenCraine 9 63
(Tony Coyle) *chsd ldrs: drvn 4f out: wknd over 1f out* **14/1**

2m 2.63s (-2.77) **Going Correction** -0.15s/f (Firm) **9** Ran SP% **113.8**
Speed ratings (Par 105): **105,104,103,101,101 98,96,94,93**
toteswingers: 1&2 £9.00, 1&3 £3.70, 12&3 £11.70. CSF £34.59 CT £190.65 TOTE £6.40: £2.90, £1.50, £1.60; EX 51.80.
Owner Mel Brittain **Bred** Cheveley Park Stud Ltd **Trained** Warthill, N Yorks

FOCUS
An open-looking handicap. There was a solid pace on the form looks straightforward.
City Of The Kings(IRE) Official explanation: jockey said gelding missed the break

3288 WELLS MEMORIAL CHALLENGE TROPHY H'CAP 6f
8:20 (8:24) (Class 3) (0-95,83) 3-Y-O **£6,931** (£2,074; £1,037; £519; £258) **Stalls** High

Form RPR
6031 **1** **I'm So Glad**[9] 2987 3-9-6 **83** 6ex.................................... MatthewDavies 8 93
(Mick Channon) *mde all: styd on strly to forge clr fnl f: eased cl home* **4/1**[2]
1503 **2** *2 3/4* **Rusty Rocket (IRE)**[11] 2914 3-9-2 **79**........................ PaulMulrennan 2 79
(Paul Green) *w ldrs on outer: drvn over 2f out: chsd wnr over 1f out: kpt on same pce* **8/1**
4013 **3** *hd* **Wicked Wench**[9] 2986 3-9-4 **81**.................................... TonyCulhane 7 80
(Jo Hughes) *hld up on ins: effrt over 2f out: checked over 1f out: kpt on same pce ins fnl f* **10/1**
-243 **4** *nk* **Personal Touch**[41] 1998 3-9-3 **80**................................. BarryMcHugh 6 78
(Richard Fahey) *w ldrs: drvn over 2f out: one pce over 1f out* **2/1**[1]
-032 **5** *10* **Profile Star (IRE)**[20] 2616 3-9-3 **80**........................... GrahamGibbons 4 46
(David Barron) *stdd s: sn trcking ldrs: edgd lft over 1f out: sn wknd: eased fnl 50yds* **9/2**[3]
-100 **6** *1 1/4* **Marford Missile (IRE)**[27] 2416 3-9-3 **80**...................... StephenCraine 3 42
(Tom Dascombe) *in rr: effrt over 2f out: sn wknd: bhd whn eased towards fin* **33/1**

1m 12.81s (-0.19) **Going Correction** +0.05s/f (Good) **6** Ran SP% **94.7**
Speed ratings (Par 103): **103,99,99,98,85 83**
toteswingers: 1&2 £5.40, 1&3 £6.40, 2&3 £2.40. CSF £23.30 CT £150.92 TOTE £3.60: £1.60, £2.70; EX 20.80.
Owner Chris Wright & The Hon Mrs J M Corbett **Bred** Stratford Place Stud **Trained** West Ilsley, Berks

FOCUS
This looked a really tight sprint handicap, but most were in trouble before the final furlong.

NOTEBOOK
I'm So Glad readily made most to follow up her Windsor success nine days earlier. She was faced with quicker ground again and went under a penalty, but she coped without fuss. She could have been called the winner 1f out and is clearly improving fast. (tchd 9-2)
Rusty Rocket(IRE), somewhat free to post, gave her all wide of runners and posted another solid effort, confirming her Nottingham form in April with the fourth. She rates the benchmark. (op 15-2 tchd 17-2)
Wicked Wench stalked the leaders, but lacked an immediate gear change when asked to pick up and looked to find the track sharp enough. She remains in good heart. (tchd 9-1 and 11-1)
Personal Touch, well backed off a 4lb higher mark, always looked to be going a stride too quick despite lying up early with the winner. He was coming back towards the finish and clearly found it too sharp. (tchd 9-4)

3289 SIS LIVE MAIDEN STKS 6f
8:50 (8:51) (Class 5) 3-Y-O **£2,587** (£770; £384; £192) **Stalls** High

Form RPR
06 **1** **Planetex (IRE)**[11] 2918 3-9-3 0....................................... BarryMcHugh 7 69+
(John Quinn) *led over 1f: w ldr: led 1f out: drvn out* **16/1**
00- **2** *1 1/4* **Majestic Manannan (IRE)**[312] 5058 3-9-3 0............... AdrianNicholls 6 63
(David Nicholls) *t.k.h: w ldr: led over 4f out: edgd rt wl over 1f out: hdd 1f out: kpt on same pce* **28/1**
2 **3** *hd* **Legal Bond**[40] 2036 3-9-3 0.. TomEaves 5 64+
(Bryan Smart) *mid-div: hdwy over 2f out: bdly hmpd wl over 1f out: swtchd rt appr fnl f: styd on wl towards fin* **11/4**[2]
4 *1* **Thats Molly (IRE)** 3-8-12 0....................................... GrahamGibbons 8 54+
(Eric Alston) *s.i.s: in rr: hdwy 2f out: swtchd lft over 1f out: kpt on ins fnl f* **17/2**
6000 **5** *2 1/2* **Essexvale (IRE)**[7] 3028 3-8-12 45..................................(p) GrahamLee 1 46?
(Robert Johnson) *mid-div: hdwy on outer over 2f out: hung rt: one pce over 1f out* **50/1**
02 **6** *1/2* **Compton Time**[16] 2774 3-9-3 0.. PaulMulrennan 3 49
(Michael Dods) *chsd ldrs: effrt 2f out: edgd lft: one pce* **9/4**[1]
6 **7** *32* **Quan (IRE)**[11] 2927 3-9-3 0.. PJMcDonald 9
(Alan Swinbank) *s.i.s: swtchd wd after 1f: hung rt: lost pl over 2f out: sn eased: t.o* **10/1**
00-0 **8** *6* **Ruskins View (IRE)**[56] 1596 3-8-5 26.................. MatthewHopkins(7) 10
(Alan Berry) *chsd ldrs: lost pl over 3f out: bhd whn hmpd wl over 1f out: eased: t.o* **200/1**
00 **9** *13* **High Meadow Prince**[22] 2592 3-9-3 0......................... PatrickMathers 11
(Ron Barr) *sn outpcd and in rr: bhd whn hmpd wl over 1f out: eased: t.o* **125/1**
0402 **F** **Warrick Brown**[19] 2680 3-9-3 69.. DavidAllan 4
(Tim Easterby) *chsd ldrs: fell wl over 1f out: fatally injured* **3/1**[3]

1m 14.47s (1.47) **Going Correction** +0.05s/f (Good) **10** Ran SP% **114.6**
Speed ratings (Par 99): **92,90,90,88,85 84,42,34,16,**
toteswingers: 1&2 £26.80, 1&3 £6.40, 2&3 £9.50. CSF £356.70 TOTE £22.30: £5.30, £8.00, £1.30; EX 340.00.
Owner Ross Harmon **Bred** Mrs Diane Williams **Trained** Settrington, N Yorks

FOCUS
An ordinary 3yo sprint maiden and a dramatic event.
Quan(IRE) Official explanation: jockey said gelding hung right

3290 FOSSGATE H'CAP 1m 4f 10y
9:20 (9:20) (Class 5) (0-75,75) 4-Y-O+ **£2,911** (£866; £432; £216) **Stalls** Low

Form RPR
06-1 **1** **Bright Applause**[22] 2593 4-8-10 **64**.............................. BarryMcHugh 2 75
(Tracy Waggott) *trckd ldrs: led over 1f out: fnd ex nr fin* **9/2**[2]
4-00 **2** *1/2* **Fossgate**[16] 2751 11-8-12 **66**... GrahamLee 1 76
(James Bethell) *in rr: hdwy and swtchd ins over 3f out: chal last 100yds: no ex towards fin* **6/1**[3]
0-55 **3** *4* **Skyfire**[18] 2687 5-8-10 **64**... MichaelStainton 9 68
(Nick Kent) *trckd ldrs: led 2f out: edgd rt and hdd over 1f out: one pce* **20/1**
0300 **4** *shd* **Mazij**[8] 3015 4-8-13 **70**... AdamBeschizza(3) 3 74
(Peter Hiatt) *mid-div: lost pl 6f out: styd on wl appr fnl f* **40/1**
0-26 **5** *1/2* **Come Here Yew (IRE)**[15] 2792 4-8-11 **70**.................... NeilFarley(5) 12 73
(Declan Carroll) *mid-div: drvn and outpcd 6f out: sn lost pl: styd on over 1f out: keeping on fin* **17/2**
2-30 **6** *nk* **Tobrata**[7] 3022 6-8-6 **60**.. DuranFentiman 6 62
(Mel Brittain) *in rr: styd on over 1f out: keeping on fin: nvr nr ldrs* **40/1**
3-22 **7** *1 1/4* **Chatterer (IRE)**[34] 2199 4-9-7 **75**................................. TadhgO'Shea 13 75
(Marcus Tregoning) *t.k.h in rr: hdwy over 6f out: chsng ldrs over 3f out: hung rt and one pce over 1f out* **7/2**[1]
0002 **8** *1 1/2* **Hail Bold Chief (USA)**[7] 3029 5-8-9 **63**....................... PJMcDonald 11 61
(Alan Swinbank) *hld up in rr: effrt 4f out: one pce fnl 2f* **6/1**[3]
36-4 **9** *nse* **King's Counsel (IRE)**[26] 2440 6-9-0 **68**..................(v) DanielTudhope 5 66
(David O'Meara) *led: hdd 2f out: fdd appr fnl f* **8/1**
-043 **10** *9* **Bavarian Nordic (USA)**[32] 2260 7-8-2 **56**...................(v) PaulQuinn 8 39
(Richard Whitaker) *sn w ldr: n.m.r over 1f out: sn wknd: heavily eased towards fin* **12/1**
336- **11** *3 1/2* **Folk Tune (IRE)**[29] 4856 9-8-8 **62**..................................... TomEaves 4 40
(John Quinn) *t.k.h: in tch: drvn 6f out: lost pl over 2f out: sn bhd* **33/1**
-000 **12** *33* **Sally Friday (IRE)**[32] 2260 4-8-6 **60**.........................(t) JamesSullivan 10
(Edwin Tuer) *trckd ldrs: t.k.h: hmpd and lost pl over 8f out: in rr whn wd bnd over 4f out: t.o over 2f out: eased: t.o* **25/1**

2m 35.36s (-1.34) **Going Correction** -0.15s/f (Firm) **12** Ran SP% **114.7**
Speed ratings (Par 103): **98,97,95,94,94 94,93,92,92,86 84,62**
toteswingers: 1&2 £2.50, 1&3 £28.10, 2&3 £35.10. CSF £28.50 CT £480.81 TOTE £6.10: £1.90, £1.70, £6.70; EX 40.20.
Owner Littlethorpe Park Racing **Bred** Old Mill Stud **Trained** Spennymoor, Co Durham

FOCUS
This modest handicap was run at a decent pace and the first pair came clear in a driving finish.
T/Plt: £589.50 to a £1 stake. Pool £78,150.92. 96.77 winning tickets. T/Qpdt: £120.70 to a £1 stake. Pool £6,677.88. 40.92 winning tickets. WG

3265 ASCOT (R-H)
Thursday, June 21

OFFICIAL GOING: Good to soft (stands' side 8.4, centre 8.4, farside 8.6, round 7.2)
Rail on Round course moved out 3yds from 9f to bend turning into home straight adding 9yd to 1m 2f race and 12yds to1m 4f &2m 4f races.
Wind: showers Weather: light, half against

3291 NORFOLK STKS (GROUP 2) 5f
2:30 (2:30) (Class 1) 2-Y-O
£42,532 (£16,125; £8,070; £4,020; £2,017; £1,012) **Stalls** Centre

Form RPR
1 **1** **Reckless Abandon**[33] 2261 2-9-1 0.................................. AdamKirby 12 107+
(Clive Cox) *unf: scope: racd in centre gp: chsd ldr: led overall over 2f out: rdn and hung bdly lft over 1f out: hdd briefly ins fnl f: r.o gamely on stands' side towards fin* **4/1**[2]
1 **2** *3/4* **Gale Force Ten**[11] 2958 2-9-1 0.. JPO'Brien 2 104
(A P O'Brien, Ire) *w'like: racd on far-side: chsd ldrs: led gp 2f out: rdn and hung lft over 1f out: led overall briefly and edgd rt ins fnl f: r.o u.p but hld cl home: fin 1st of 6 in gp* **8/1**
2 **3** *3/4* **Ian's Dream (USA)**[20] 2663 2-9-1 0................................. FrankieDettori 1 101
(Jeremy Noseda) *ponied to s: racd on far-side: hld up: hdwy over 2f out: chalng over 1f out and edgd lft: ev ch whn r.o u.p and carried rt ins fnl f: hld cl home: fin 2nd of 6 in gp* **16/1**
1 **4** *hd* **Morawij**[28] 2415 2-9-1 0... NeilCallan 8 101+
(Roger Varian) *w'like: scope: str: lw: racd in centre gp: hld up: rdn and hdwy over 1f out: r.o and tried to chal ins fnl f: one pce cl home: fin 2nd of 5 in gp* **14/1**
1 **5** *3/4* **Ahern**[19] 2715 2-9-1 0.. JohnnyMurtagh 5 101+
(David Barron) *str: lw: squeezed out and s.i.s: racd in rr on far-side: pushed along over 2f out: hdwy to chse ldrs over 1f out: kpt on towards fin: nt gng pce to chal: fin 3rd of 6 in gp* **5/1**[3]
511 **6** *1/2* **Cay Verde**[26] 2512 2-9-1 0.. CraigAWilliams 10 96
(Mick Channon) *lw: racd in centre gp: chsd ldrs: effrt 2f out: no ex fnl 100yds: fin 3rd of 5 in gp* **11/4**[1]
04 **7** *2 1/2* **Ocean Applause**[21] 2638 2-9-1 0.. BrettDoyle 9 87
(John Ryan) *racd in centre gp: pushed along early: racd in rr: rdn 2f out: kpt on and edgd rt over 1f out: nt gng pce to chal: fin 4th of 5 in gp* **100/1**
12 **8** *2 3/4* **Mister Marc (IRE)**[17] 2779 2-9-1 0.................................... RyanMoore 3 77
(Richard Hannon) *racd on far-side: disp 2nd tl rdn over 2f out: nt qckn: fdd and eased fnl 100yds: fin 4th of 6 in gp* **7/1**
115 **9** *nk* **Storm Moon (USA)**[21] 2638 2-9-1 0........................ SilvestreDeSousa 11 76
(Mark Johnston) *racd in centre gp: displayed plenty of pce and led overall: rdn and hdd over 2f out: wknd over 1f out: fin 5th of 5 in gp* **25/1**
221 **10** *1 3/4* **Annunciation**[24] 2556 2-9-1 0... RichardHughes 4 70
(Richard Hannon) *angular: led far-side gp tl rdn and hdd 2f out: wknd ent fnl f: fin 5th of 6 in gp* **12/1**
321 **11** *3 3/4* **Jubilee Brig**[15] 2808 2-9-1 0... TomQueally 7 56
(Gary Moore) *unf: racd on far-side: disp 2nd tl rdn over 2f out: wknd over 1f out: fin 6th of 6 in gp* **33/1**

1m 1.41s (0.91) **Going Correction** +0.30s/f (Good) **11** Ran SP% **115.0**
Speed ratings (Par 105): **104,102,101,101,100 99,95,90,90,87 81**
toteswingers:1&2:£7.60, 2&3:£21.00, 1&3:£10.30 CSF £34.66 CT £467.69 TOTE £5.40: £1.80, £2.30, £3.20; EX 47.70 Trifecta £929.50 Pool: £12950.71 - 10.31 winning units..
Owner Miss J Deadman & S Barrow **Bred** Car Colston Hall Stud **Trained** Lambourn, Berks
■ Stewards' Enquiry : Adam Kirby 21 day ban: used whip above permitted level (5th demeanour within 6mths) (Jul 6-14, Jul 16-27)

FOCUS
The course endured 8mm of overnight rain which eased the official going description to good to soft. A going stick reading of 7.7 dictated it would be notably harder work on the round course. This looked a strong Norfolk Stakes with the field having amassed 11 previous wins between them, despite only one having prevailed in Pattern company. It proved something of a messy race, though, as the field split into two groups and again they shunned the near side. The winner could improve on this while the sixth probably sets the level, if fractionally below his best.

NOTEBOOK

Reckless Abandon would have no doubt scored with more authority but for hanging right over to the stands' rail from the furlong marker. Clive Cox's colt posted a decent time when making a successful debut at Doncaster last month and would have won by further that day as well had he not drifted left late on. He's not the biggest, but is a real speedball and quickened smartly in between the final two furlongs. That he held on at the finish dictates he must have had a deal in hand and jockey Adam Kirby later said "he's still a big baby", so he's given the benefit of doubt as to his temperament at present. His next outing will reveal more on that front, though, and no doubt the Group 1 Nunthorpe against older horses at York in August will be at the back of his trainer's mind, a race that is attractive due to the weight-for-age allowance. Cox afterwards hinted the horse could go for the Molecomb Stakes at Glorious Goodwood, but while that test would suit, it would mean dropping in class and that's often a path the placed horses in this event follow, not the winner. Despite his speed, there is every chance on breeding another furlong will suit ideally this year, so he should have plenty of options. (op 9-2 tchd 5-1 in places)

Gale Force Ten finished strongly on the far side and, while flattered by his proximity to the winner, there is little doubt he can build on this back over another furlong. His trainer nominated the Railway Stakes back over 6f at the Curragh for him later this month. (op 15-2 tchd 7-1)

Ian's Dream(USA) ♦ was just held on his debut on quick ground at Haydock 20 days earlier and hails from a yard that has won with a 2-y-o maiden at this meeting in the past. Ponied to the start, he made his challenge nearest to the far rail and turned in a huge effort. Reverting to quicker ground should prove ideal and he's one to follow. (op 20-1)

Morawij worked hard to justify favouritism on his debut at Haydock over 6f last month and there was live chance he would find this too sharp. He ran a blinder down the centre, though, and clearly takes after his speedy dam. He's a powerful colt and there should be more heard of him this summer. The July Stakes back up in trip at Newmarket next month could be a suitable target. Official explanation: jockey said colt became unbalanced shortly before line (op 16-1)

Ahern ♦ won a race with a decent history of previous winners when scoring in style at Musselburgh on his debut 19 days earlier. He was slow to break that day and lost ground again here, but it wasn't his fault as he got squeezed up. There was a lot to like about his finishing effort, suggesting he will relish another furlong and he may well turn out to be the best of these down the line. (tchd 6-1)

Cay Verde won his maiden impressively over C&D two runs back, the form of which was well franked when the runner-up that day Hototo landed the Windsor Castle here on the opening day, and he set the standard on his Listed success at the Curragh last time out. He was unsurprisingly popular, but held every chance and can have no excuses. (op 5-2 tchd 3-1 in places)

Ocean Applause finished fourth behind Sir Prancealot in the National Stakes at Sandown last time and probably ran right up to that level again. He's clearly useful and should go and win a maiden without much fuss.

Mister Marc(IRE)\n\x\x pushed subsequent Coventry winner Dawn Approach in this company at Naas last time, and this strong colt seemed likely to cope with dropping back to 5f on this stiff track. However, he was never going the pace. (tchd 8-1)

Annunciation was closing on today's winner when they met at Doncaster last month and hosed up at Windsor next time. The pick of Richard Hughes, he proved easy to back and ultimately went off too quick for his own good. (op 11-1 tchd 14-1)

Jubilee Brig, a Polytrack winner, showed up early but ultimately found it far too hot.

3292 RIBBLESDALE STKS (GROUP 2) (FILLIES) — 1m 4f

3:05 (3:07) (Class 1) 3-Y-O

£77,091 (£29,227; £14,627; £7,286; £3,656; £1,835) **Stalls** Low

Form / RPR

1 **1** **Princess Highway (USA)**[36] 2187 3-8-12 101 PatSmullen 12 — 117+
(D K Weld, Ire) *w'like: scope: lw: stdd after s: hld up in midfield: hdwy 4f out: rdn to chse ldr and edgd rt 2f out: led over 1f out: sn clr and in command r.o wl: rdn out: readily* **17/2**

-413 **2** 6 **The Fugue**[20] 2658 3-8-12 111 WilliamBuick 4 — 107
(John Gosden) *hld up in midfield: swtchd lft and effrt over 4f out: rdn to chse ldrs 2f out: outpcd by wnr and btn whn swtchd lft and chal for 2nd over 1f out: no ch w wnr but battled on to go 2nd last stride* **5/2**[1]

1-22 **3** shd **Shirocco Star**[20] 2658 3-8-12 112 DarryllHolland 14 — 107+
(Hughie Morrison) *swtg: t.k.h early: chsd ldr tl led 8f out: increased gallop after: clr over 4f out: rdn and hdd over 1f out: sn btn and no ch w wnr: duelling for 2nd and battled on v gamely fnl f: lost 2nd last stride* **7/1**

5-44 **4** ¾ **Salford Art (IRE)**[36] 2178 3-8-12 96 PaulHanagan 3 — 106
(David Elsworth) *hld up in midfield: lost pl 5f out: 12th and wl bhd wl over 2f out: hdwy u.p over 1f out: styd on strly fnl f: no ch w wnr* **100/1**

220 **5** 3 **Twirl (IRE)**[20] 2658 3-8-12 103 RyanMoore 7 — 101
(A P O'Brien, Ire) *chsd ldr: rdn 3f out: 5th and struggling to qckn whn swtchd lft over 2f out: outpcd and no ch w wnr wl over 1f out: plugged on* **10/1**

114 **6** 2¾ **Vow**[20] 2658 3-8-12 109 JohnnyMurtagh 2 — 97
(William Haggas) *led tl 8f out: chsd ldrs after: rdn to chse wnr 3f out tl 2f out: sn outpcd and btn: wl hld whn wandered over 1f out: fdd fnl f* **11/2**[2]

1-10 **7** 2¾ **Kailani**[20] 2658 3-8-12 106 MickaelBarzalona 10 — 92
(Mahmood Al Zarooni) *s.i.s: rdn along early: racd in last pair: swtchd lft and effrt over 3f out: 11th and no imp over 2f out: plugged on but no ch* **13/2**[3]

12-2 **8** 5 **Hazel Lavery (IRE)**[46] 1887 3-8-12 95 MichaelHills 1 — 84
(Charles Hills) *chsd ldrs: rdn and struggling 3f out: sn wknd and no ch fnl 2f* **22/1**

3-10 **9** 1½ **Inchina**[43] 1973 3-8-12 80 JamesDoyle 5 — 82
(Roger Charlton) *in tch in midfield: rdn and struggling over 3f out: wknd and wl btn fnl 2f* **66/1**

1-20 **10** ½ **Colima (IRE)**[20] 2658 3-8-12 98 (p) JimCrowley 8 — 81
(Ralph Beckett) *in tch in midfield: rdn and no rspnse over 3f out: sn outpcd and wl btn fnl 2f* **28/1**

1 **11** 12 **Pink Damsel (IRE)**[34] 2249 3-8-12 86 JamieSpencer 6 — 62
(Roger Varian) *w'like: lw: t.k.h: hld up in midfield: rdn and effrt over 3f out: drvn and wknd over 2f out: wl bhd and eased fnl f* **14/1**

41 **12** 42 **Momentary**[34] 2232 3-8-12 105 HayleyTurner 11
(Michael Bell) *t.k.h early: hld up in midfield: stmbld and lost pl over 8f out: towards rr after: rdn and lost tch over 3f out: t.o and virtually p.u fr over 1f out* **10/1**

0 **13** nk **Chella Thriller (SPA)**[14] 2849 3-8-12 0 MartinHarley 13
(Alastair Lidderdale) *w'like: stdd s: a bhd: lost tch 4f out: t.o and virtually p.u fr over 1f out* **200/1**

4-61 **14** 8 **Dinvar Diva**[21] 2633 3-8-12 83 RichardHughes 9
(John Gosden) *t.k.h: hld up in midfield tl hdwy to chse ldr over 7f out: clr w ldr over 4f out: rdn and wknd over 2f out: fdd 2f out: wl bhd and heavily eased fnl f: t.o* **66/1**

2m 33.67s (1.17) **Going Correction** +0.40s/f (Good) **14** Ran SP% **117.4**
Speed ratings (Par 108): **112,108,107,107,105 103,101,98,97,97 89,61,60,55**
toteswingers:1&2:£4.40, 2&3:£4.70, 1&3:£12.40 CSF £28.30 CT £161.45 TOTE £9.20: £2.50, £1.60, £2.80; EX 22.30 Trifecta £118.30 Pool: £14085.51 - 88.05 winning units..
Owner Moyglare Stud Farm **Bred** Moyglare Stud **Trained** The Curragh, Co Kildare

FOCUS

This year's Ribblesdale looked a stronger race than is often the case, and the Epsom Oaks form was well represented. The early fractions didn't seem strong, and there was a bit of trouble in the pack, but the time compared well with the King George V Handicap. The winner was unexposed and rates the leading 1m4f winner now, giving the second and third a much bigger beating than Was did in the Oaks.

NOTEBOOK

Princess Highway(USA), whose dam won this race for same trainer in 2002, beat the subsequent Epsom Oaks winner Was in the Blue Wind Stakes at Naas on her previous start and showed that performance was no fluke with an authoritative victory. Reported to be a late-developing type, Pat Smullen dropped his filly into a chasing position before striking for home on turning in and the filly saw it out well. The logical next step is the Irish Oaks, where she'll presumably come up against Was once again. (op 9-1 tchd 8-1 and 10-1 in places)

The Fugue ran close to her Oaks form, this time getting the better of the enterprisingly ridden third. Some thought the Gosden filly was unlucky at Epsom and she duly reversed form with Hughie Morrison's runner despite being briefly tightened for room in the straight. She may be better suited by quicker ground and she could be aimed at the Yorkshire Oaks. (op 9-4 tchd 11-4 in places)

Shirocco Star enjoyed the run of the race and quickened the tempo at what looked the right time. Considering the way she seemed to enjoy front-running duties, the German Oaks might be made for her, as Dusseldorf is a fairly tight track. (tchd 8-1)

Salford Art(IRE) put up an extraordinary performance, passing eight horses from the home bend after getting behind. Presumably, at a slightly lower level, she'll be of some interest over further. (op 66-1)

Twirl(IRE) was readily beaten by The Fugue in the Musidora and finished behind plenty of these in the Oaks, so her task was always going to be hard. She had nothing to offer off the bridle. (op 12-1 tchd 9-1 and 14-1 in places)

Vow was always nicely positioned but was left behind when the pace increased. One would imagine she'll benefit from a break after some hard races this spring. (tchd 6-1 and 13-2 in places)

Kailani proved disappointing in the Oaks after being ridden out the back and pretty much lost all chance here when emerging from the stalls slowly. Mickeal Barzalona reported afterward that the filly hung right. Official explanation: jockey said filly hung right (op 7-1 tchd 8-1)

Pink Damsel(IRE), a 600,000gns Galileo filly, won a Newmarket maiden five weeks previously but found this an altogether different task, especially after taking a grip early. (tchd 12-1)

Momentary got first run on Shirocco Star when winning at Newbury and obviously should have made a bigger impact than she did here, but this run was too poor to be true. Hayley Turner wasn't hard on her mount some way from home and the rider later reported her mount stumbled approaching Swinley Bottom. Official explanation: jockey said filly stumbled approaching Swinley Bottom (tchd 9-1)

3293 GOLD CUP (BRITISH CHAMPIONS SERIES) (GROUP 1) — 2m 4f

3:45 (3:46) (Class 1) 4-Y-O+

£198,485 (£75,250; £37,660; £18,760; £9,415; £4,725) **Stalls** Low

Form / RPR

33-1 **1** **Colour Vision (FR)**[50] 1750 4-9-0 117 FrankieDettori 5 — 118+
(Saeed Bin Suroor) *chsd ldr for 5f: remained prom: rdn to chal 2f out: led and edgd rt over 1f out: hdd narrowly and edgd lft into rival 150yds out: gamely plld out more to regain ld fnl 75yds: in command last strides* **6/1**

-211 **2** ½ **Opinion Poll (IRE)**[21] 2639 6-9-2 116 MickaelBarzalona 3 — 117+
(Mahmood Al Zarooni) *lw: broke wl: sn stdd: hld up: hdwy 2f out: rdn over 1f out: r.o to nose in front 150yds out: sn bmpd twice: hdd fnl 75yds: hld last strides* **5/1**[3]

31-2 **3** nk **Saddler's Rock (IRE)**[13] 2903 4-9-0 114 (t) JohnnyMurtagh 4 — 117+
(John M Oxx, Ire) *trckd ldrs: pushed along 3f out: edgd lft wl over 1f out: clsd and edgd rt briefly bhd ldrs jst ins fnl f: r.o cl home* **9/2**[2]

2133 **4** 1 **Gulf Of Naples (IRE)**[26] 2506 4-9-0 107 SilvestreDeSousa 6 — 116?
(Mark Johnston) *sn led at stdy pce: grad increased tempo fr over 4f out: pressed 3f out: sn rdn: hdd over 1f out: stl ch ins fnl f tl no ex fnl 75yds* **25/1**

65-6 **5** 3 **Askar Tau (FR)**[21] 2639 7-9-2 110 (v) GeorgeBaker 7 — 113
(Marcus Tregoning) *hld up in rr: rdn over 2f out: styd on u.p fr over 1f out: unable to trble ldrs* **40/1**

34-3 **6** 1 **Nehaam**[33] 2267 6-9-2 110 PaulHanagan 9 — 112
(John Gosden) *racd keenly: trckd ldrs: wnt 2nd after 5f: chalng fr 3 out: sn rdn: no ex ent fnl f: sn no ch* **33/1**

41-1 **7** 2½ **Fame And Glory**[32] 2318 6-9-2 120 JamieSpencer 1 — 110
(A P O'Brien, Ire) *hld up in midfield on inner: plld out and tried to make an effrt over 2f out: failed to pick-up: no imp whn sltly intimidated wl over 1f out: one pce* **4/5**[1]

5-30 **8** 3 **Caucus**[34] 2253 5-9-2 104 WilliamBuick 8 — 107
(John Gosden) *racd keenly: hld up: impr to trck ldrs after 5f: rdn over 2f out: sn wknd* **66/1**

2-35 **9** 48 **Bridge Of Gold (USA)**[34] 2228 6-9-2 102 RyanMoore 2 — 59
(Mikael Magnusson) *hld up: pushed along over 2f out: sn lft bhd and eased: t.o* **66/1**

4m 42.05s (17.25) **Going Correction** +0.40s/f (Good)
WFA 4 from 5yo+ 2lb **9** Ran SP% **116.9**
Speed ratings (Par 117): **81,80,80,80,79 78,77,76,57**
toteswingers:1&2:£3.80, 2&3:£3.50, 1&3:£3.00 CSF £34.51 CT £148.05 TOTE £7.20: £1.60, £1.60, £1.50; EX 32.50 Trifecta £113.70 Pool: £29556.26 - 192.28 winning units..
Owner Godolphin **Bred** Capricorn Stud **Trained** Newmarket, Suffolk

FOCUS

Thanks to the great Yeats's four-timer from 2006-2009, the Gold Cup has rightly reclaimed it's position as the feature race of the entire meeting, and with last year's winner Fame And Glory bidding to go halfway to emulating his former stablemate, it was another fascinating affair. There was just an ordinary pace early on, though, with riders looking mindful of the deteriorating surface. Most therefore took time to settle and it did develop into something of a dash for home half a mile out. It saw a tight finish between the principals and it's hard to rate the form too highly, with the first three all rated below their recent efforts. Colur Vision was entitled to win on his Kempton form.

NOTEBOOK

Colour Vision(FR) progressed rapidly last season and who won tidily at Kempton in the Sagaro Stakes last month (switched to Kempton's Polytrack due to unraceable ground here), the form of which had been well franked by the runner-up Red Cadeaux. He had ground to make up with Fame And Glory on their previous meeting here on Champions Day last year, but that came in his 3-y-o campaign and his comeback win advertised he was still improving. He showed a definite turn of foot too at Kempton, but the rain coming saw him easy to back and he momentarily looked in trouble when the pace lifted seriously turning for home. His brave attitude got him home from thereon, and he was a rightful winner, but no doubt he impeded runner-up Opinion Poll as he drifted left nearing the finish and gave him a bump. He's clearly the real deal now in the Cup division and should relish a return to quicker ground. A rematch with Fame And Glory would be something to savour and he deserves the chance to confirm his authority over that rival. Perhaps it will come in the Goodwood Cup next month. (tchd 13-2 and 7-1 in places)

Opinion Poll(IRE), impressive at Sandown on his British return 21 days earlier, gave Godolphin a 1-2 by filling the same spot as last year. Like Fame And Glory, he too came from well back and got hampered when the winner drifted into him. It wasn't enough for the placings to be reversed in the stewards' enquiry, however. It makes sense for him to now renew rivalry with Colour Vision in the Goodwood Cup, a race he won narrowly last year, although connections may opt to keep him back for York in August, a meeting at which he also won at in 2011. (op 11-2 tchd 6- in places)

Saddler's Rock(IRE) looked a natural candidate for this when beating Opinion Poll in the Doncaster Cup over 2m2f last September and, as with Colour Vision, looked sure to improve further from three to four. He wasn't disgraced on his return on bad ground over 1m6f earlier this month and proved popular back up in distance. The 4-y-o had every chance, but proving free off the early gallop wouldn't have helped his finishing effort. It is likely he needs a sounder surface, so the best of him has probably still to be seen and he helps to make the Cup division very competitive. (tchd 5-1 in places)
Gulf Of Naples(IRE) arrived with plenty to find, but the ground turned in his favour and being allowed to dictate from the front really suited this dour stayer. He didn't give up lightly in the home straight and posted by far his best effort to date. Mark Johnston also trained Colour Vision for the same owner last season and his 4-y-o has a similarly lightly raced profile as that rival did at this stage last season, despite already being the same age.
Askar Tau(FR), a winner over 2m at this venue, was well behind Opinion Poll on his return 21 days earlier. He kept on dourly from well out the back and took a step back in the right direction, running close to his fifth in this race last year.
Nehaam was not far behind the first pair when signing off last term over 2m here on Champion's Day. He raced handily, but his unproven stamina gave way in the home straight and ultimately the ground went against him.
Fame And Glory was beaten before the final furlong and ran flat. He travelled powerfully into contention, but had made his move much earlier when successful 12 months earlier and, on such ground, he was given enough to do from out the back. Official explanation: trainer said horse was unsuited by the slow early pace (op 5-6 tchd 10-11 and evens in places)
Caucus gave himself no chance of lasting home by refusing to settle.
Bridge Of Gold(USA) was also keen and got predictably outclassed.

3294 BRITANNIA STKS (HERITAGE H'CAP) (C&G) 1m (S)

4:25 (4:26) (Class 2) (0-105,98) 3-Y-O

£62,250 (£18,640; £9,320; £4,660; £2,330; £1,170) **Stalls** Centre

Form RPR

6-11 **1** **Fast Or Free**^{12} [2930] 3-8-10 **87** ... RyanMoore 6 103+
(William Haggas) *racd far side: chsd ldr tl rdn to ld 2f out: kpt on wl u.p and in command fnl f: rdn out* **6/1**^{1}

2503 **2** *1 1/4* **Mister Music**^{12} [2916] 3-9-4 **95** ... JimmyFortune 7 108
(Richard Hannon) *racd far side: stdd s: hld up in rr: swtchd rt and hdwy on far rail 2f out: chsd wnr over 1f out: kpt on u.p but no imp on wnr fnl f* **50/1**

-161 **3** *1 3/4* **Bronze Angel (IRE)**^{33} [2263] 3-9-0 **91** ... (p) HayleyTurner 17 100+
(Marcus Tregoning) *racd in centre tl gps merged 3f out: hld up in tch: hdwy gng wl over 2f out: rdn to chse ldng pair over 1f out: edgd rt and kpt on ins fnl f* **20/1**

235- **4** *2 1/4* **Compton**^{281} [6055] 3-9-1 **92** ... WilliamBuick 3 96
(Ralph Beckett) *racd far side: in tch in midfield: effrt and rdn 2f out: hdwy to chse ldrs and drvn over 1f out: no imp and one pce ins fnl f* **40/1**

1- **5** *1 1/2* **Piri Wango (IRE)**^{50} [1760] 3-9-6 **97** ... FrankieDettori 8 97
(G M Lyons, Ire) *str: racd far side: overall ldr tl rdn and hdd over 2f out: btn ent fnl f: wknd fnl 150yds* **12/1**

4-14 **6** *hd* **Kahruman (USA)**^{21} [2641] 3-9-7 **98** ... PaulHanagan 2 98
(William Haggas) *racd far side: t.k.h: hld up towards rr: rdn and hdwy 2f out: drvn and chsd ldrs over 1f out: no imp and btn 1f out: plugged on* **25/1**

2-10 **7** *4* **Born To Surprise**^{63} [1470] 3-9-1 **92** ... JamieSpencer 5 83
(Michael Bell) *lw: racd far side: stdd s: hld up in rr: hdwy and nt clr run 2f out: swtchd lft and hdwy over 1f out: plugged on fnl f: nvr trbld ldrs* **10/1**^{3}

0360 **8** *3/4* **Swing Alone (IRE)**^{83} [1127] 3-8-10 **87** ... NeilCallan 20 76
(Gay Kelleway) *racd in centre tl gps merged 3f out: in tch in midfield: rdn and unable qck jst over 2f out: drvn and plugged on fnl f: no threat to ldrs* **66/1**

0-01 **9** *2* **Hamza (IRE)**^{26} [2490] 3-8-12 **89** ... (b) AmyRyan 22 73
(Kevin Ryan) *racd in centre tl gps merged 3f out: led gp and prom overall: rdn over 2f out: wknd u.p over 1f out* **40/1**

1626 **10** *3/4* **Van Ellis**^{12} [2910] 3-9-5 **96** ... SilvestreDeSousa 11 79
(Mark Johnston) *racd far side: chsd ldrs: rdn over 2f out: no ex and btn over 1f out: wknd fnl f* **25/1**

1-62 **11** *hd* **Trader Jack**^{26} [2477] 3-9-0 **91** ... JamesDoyle 15 73
(Roger Charlton) *lw: racd far side: hld up in tch towards rr: rdn and effrt 3f out: no imp u.p 2f out: wknd over 1f out* **11/1**

-356 **12** *nk* **Graphic (IRE)**^{15} [2819] 3-9-3 **94** ... GeorgeBaker 12 75
(Richard Hannon) *racd far side: in tch in midfield: rdn and unable qck over 2f out: wknd over 1f out: nt pushed after* **50/1**

40-0 **13** *1/2* **Moon Pearl (USA)**^{41} [2022] 3-9-1 **95** ... (b^{1}) HarryBentley$^{(3)}$ 24 75
(Ralph Beckett) *racd in centre tl gps merged 3f out: hld up in rr: rdn and effrt over 2f out: no imp 2f out: plugged on but nvr trbld ldrs* **50/1**

3-30 **14** *nk* **Democretes**^{33} [2276] 3-8-11 **88** ... RichardHughes 16 68
(Richard Hannon) *racd in centre tl gps merged 3f out: swtchd lft s: hld up in rr: rdn and hdwy 3f out: no imp u.p over 1f out: wl hld fnl f* **20/1**

10 **15** *nk* **Mississippi**^{33} [2263] 3-8-13 **90** ... MartinDwyer 13 69
(Brian Meehan) *racd far side: in tch in midfield: effrt u.p over 2f out: no imp 2f out: wknd over 1f out* **25/1**

-335 **16** *shd* **Tidentime (USA)**^{26} [2485] 3-9-1 **92** ... MartinHarley 9 71
(Mick Channon) *racd far side: hld up in tch towards rr: rdn and struggling 3f out: no threat to ldrs but plugged on fnl f* **40/1**

55-1 **17** *nk* **Forest Row**^{61} [1512] 3-8-11 **88** ... JohnFahy 4 66
(Clive Cox) *racd far side: in tch: rdn and unable qck over 2f out: wknd wl over 1f out* **16/1**

253 **18** *1 1/2* **Prince Alzain (USA)**^{20} [2660] 3-9-0 **91** ... EddieAhern 25 66+
(Gerard Butler) *racd in centre tl gps merged 3f out: in tch in midfield: rdn and struggling over 2f out: wknd over 1f out* **14/1**

3-34 **19** *1 1/2* **Frog Hollow**^{26} [2485] 3-8-13 **90** ... (b^{1}) JimCrowley 31 61+
(Ralph Beckett) *lw: racd in centre tl gps merged 3f out: towards rr: rdn and effrt over 2f out: no imp: wl btn over 1f out* **8/1**^{2}

1001 **20** *hd* **Chapter Seven**^{12} [2916] 3-9-1 **92** ... RobertWinston 18 63+
(Richard Fahey) *racd in centre tl gps merged 3f out: a towards rr: rdn and struggling 1/2-way: n.d* **12/1**

-262 **21** *1 1/2* **Lucky Henry**^{26} [2485] 3-8-11 **88** ... PaulMulrennan 14 55
(Clive Cox) *racd far side: chsd ldrs: rdn and struggling 3f out: wknd u.p wl over 1f out* **20/1**

-540 **22** *3/4* **Lord Ofthe Shadows (IRE)**^{26} [2485] 3-9-0 **94** ... SeanLevey$^{(3)}$ 26 60+
(Richard Hannon) *lw: racd in centre tl gps merged 3f out: racd keenly: chsd ldrs tl rdn and wknd over 2f out: bhd over 1f out* **33/1**

-100 **23** *3 3/4* **Apostle (IRE)**^{12} [2930] 3-8-12 **89** ... MickaelBarzalona 19 46
(Michael Bell) *racd in centre tl gps merged 3f out: in tch: rdn and struggling over 2f out: wknd 2f out* **33/1**

310- **24** *8* **Nawwaar (USA)**^{243} [7026] 3-8-12 **89** ... TadhgO'Shea 23 27
(John Dunlop) *racd in centre tl gps merged 3f out: in tch tl rdn and wknd 3f out: t.o and eased fnl f* **25/1**

0-21 **25** *6* **Come On Blue Chip (IRE)**^{105} [841] 3-9-0 **91** ... (b) AdamKirby 28 16
(Paul D'Arcy) *racd in centre tl gps merged 3f out: in tch in midfield: rdn and struggling 3f out: bhd 2f out: eased fnl f: t.o* **33/1**

4-20 **26** *10* **Evervescent (IRE)**^{42} [1996] 3-8-10 **87** ... GrahamGibbons 33
(J S Moore) *racd in centre tl gps merged 3f out: in tch towards rr: rdn and btn 3f out: t.o and eased fnl f* **50/1**

5033 **27** *3/4* **Switzerland (IRE)**^{26} [2485] 3-9-4 **95** ... JoeFanning 27
(Mark Johnston) *lw: racd in centre tl gps merged 3f out: a bhd: lost tch over 2f out: t.o and eased fnl f* **16/1**

32-3 **28** *hd* **Leqqaa (USA)**^{75} [1216] 3-9-4 **95** ... IanMongan 21
(Mark Johnston) *racd in centre tl gps merged 3f out: in tch tl rdn and wknd 3f out: t.o and eased fnl f* **33/1**

4-64 **29** *3/4* **Red Seventy**^{47} [1845] 3-9-4 **95** ... PatDobbs 29
(Richard Hannon) *racd in centre tl gps merged 3f out: hld up in rr: rdn and btn 3f out: t.o and eased fnl f* **66/1**

1m 42.08s (1.28) **Going Correction** +0.30s/f (Good) **29** Ran SP% **136.2**
Speed ratings (Par 105): **105,103,102,99,98 98,94,93,91,90 90,90,89,89,88 88,88,87,85,85 83,83,79,71,65 55,54,54,53**
toteswingers:1&2:£79.80, 2&3:£181.40, 1&3:£24.30 CSF £320.86 CT £5735.12 TOTE £6.60: £1.80, £11.30, £5.60, £15.30; EX 321.60 Trifecta £8318.00 Part won. Pool: £11240.60 - 0.70 winning units..
Owner Ian and Christine Beard **Bred** Usk Valley Stud **Trained** Newmarket, Suffolk

FOCUS
A mammoth field as usual, but the top weight was rated 7lb lower than the ceiling rating, and six of the first seven home were drawn in stall ten or lower. Those who stayed in the near-side bunch early never really had a hope. The winner is progressive with the second more exposed, and the bare form is perhaps not as strong as usual for the race.

NOTEBOOK
Fast Or Free ◆ has come quite a way in a short space of time and should be able to run in another handicap before connections think about edging him up in class. His sire got better with age, so this gelding has all the attributes to be able to handle himself in Group company at some stage, although it remains to see how he'd handle genuinely fast ground. (op 7-1 tchd 15-2 in places)
Mister Music ◆, who had plenty of experience on his side, showed improved form when dropped back to 1m on his previous outing and confirmed that level here after keeping close to the far rail. He was clear of the remainder on that side and ran well trying to give 8lb away. (op 40-1)
Bronze Angel(IRE) ◆ ran a huge race as he had no company for much of the final stages and travelled on the bridle for longer than the winner. The cheekpieces have had a positive effect and he will clearly be interesting in another big-field handicap, possibly the totesport Mile, a race the stable landed in 2011. (op 18-1)
Compton, gelded since his last outing, ran a cracker on this seasonal debut without cheekpieces on, not quite getting home after being prominent. He won first time out last season and clearly goes well fresh.
Piri Wango(IRE), whose three starts had all been on the AW at Dundalk, shaped like a non-stayer in this company. He has plenty of size about him, however, and should continue to improve faced with realistic tasks. (op 14-1 tchd 16-1 in places)
Kahruman(USA), the winner's stablemate, took a while to get going but kept on from mid-pack on his side and wasn't disgraced under top weight.
Born To Surprise travelled really strongly towards the rear of the far-side group and probably had a bit too much to do from where he started, especially as he encountered a bit of trouble in running. He is one to take from the race. (op 12-1)
Swing Alone(IRE), a non-runner the previous day, kept on plugging away towards the centre of the course on his first outing after being gelded. He'll no doubt get further. (op 50-1)
Trader Jack was on the 'right side' but never looked to be travelling that strongly. (op 10-1)
Frog Hollow's run is easy to forgive on account of the draw. (tchd 9-1 in places)
Chapter Seven raced in the near-side group but was struggling from an early stage, so doesn't really have an obvious excuse.

3295 TERCENTENARY STKS (GROUP 3) 1m 2f

5:00 (5:00) (Class 1) 3-Y-O

£39,697 (£15,050; £7,532; £3,752; £1,883; £945) **Stalls** Low

Form RPR

5-24 **1** **Energizer (GER)**^{24} [2568] 3-9-0 111 ... ^{1} ADeVries 9 113
(J Hirschberger, Germany) *lw: hld up: hdwy on outer 2f out: led over 1f out: r.o ins fnl f: in command fnl 110yds* **15/2**

-142 **2** *2 1/2* **Stipulate**^{21} [2641] 3-9-0 108 ... IanMongan 4 108
(Sir Henry Cecil) *racd keenly: trckd ldrs: wnt 2nd over 4f out: led over 2f out: hdd over 1f out: no imp on wnr fnl 110yds* **11/1**

-114 **3** *2 1/2* **Rewarded**^{33} [2269] 3-9-0 90 ... KirstyMilczarek 2 103
(James Toller) *lw: chsd ldrs: lost pl over 3f out: rdn and outpcd over 2f out: rallied ent fnl f: sn swtchd lft: styd on to take 3rd last strides: nt gng pce to chal* **7/1**

21 **4** *nk* **Mukhadram**^{33} [2280] 3-9-0 90 ... PaulHanagan 3 102
(William Haggas) *lw: midfield: hdwy 2f out: chalng over 1f out: no ex fnl 75yds: lost 3rd last strides* **13/2**^{3}

1-3 **5** *1 1/4* **Tales Of Grimm (USA)**^{21} [2641] 3-9-0 99 ... RyanMoore 10 100
(Sir Michael Stoute) *s.i.s: hld up: pushed along over 2f out: hdwy and styd on over 1f out to chse ldrs: no further imp whn carried lft sltly wl ins fnl f: one pce towards fin* **7/1**

-216 **6** *shd* **Goldoni (IRE)**^{40} [2080] 3-9-0 100 ... DavidProbert 7 100
(Andrew Balding) *lw: racd keenly: prom: rdn 2f out: sn lost pl: kpt on same pce and no imp fnl f* **20/1**

-412 **7** *nk* **Grandeur (IRE)**^{19} [2701] 3-9-0 99 ... FrankieDettori 6 99
(Jeremy Noseda) *hld up: hdwy over 4f out: chsd ldrs over 3f out: ch over 2f out: edgd rt over 1f out: no ex ins fnl f: fdd* **9/2**^{2}

1-30 **8** *5* **Cavaleiro (IRE)**^{19} [2705] 3-9-0 95 ... HayleyTurner 1 89
(Marcus Tregoning) *swtg: chsd ldr to 4f out: rdn over 2f out: sn wknd* **16/1**

-261 **9** *2 1/2* **Wrotham Heath**^{19} [2701] 3-9-0 95 ... TomQueally 11 84
(Sir Henry Cecil) *lw: led: abt 5 l clr over 7f out: rdn and hdd over 2f out: wknd over 1f out* **4/1**^{1}

1-26 **10** *81* **Crius (IRE)**^{25} [2524] 3-9-4 110 ... RichardHughes 8
(Richard Hannon) *plld hrd: hld up: swtchd rt and racd on wd outside over 7f out: a in rr: lost tch over 3f out: t.o* **16/1**

2m 10.03s (2.63) **Going Correction** +0.40s/f (Good) **10** Ran SP% **113.1**
Speed ratings (Par 109): **105,103,101,100,99 99,99,95,93,28**
toteswingers:1&2:£16.70, 2&3:£14.80, 1&3:£11.40 CSF £84.03 CT £599.82 TOTE £8.00: £2.40, £3.70, £2.60; EX 102.40 Trifecta £572.60 Pool: £14965.55 - 19.34 winning units..
Owner Gestut Schlenderhan **Bred** G Baron Von Ullmann **Trained** Germany
■ The first German-trained winner at Royal Ascot.

FOCUS
This 3-y-o contest was only upgraded to Group 3 status in 2011 and it looked a wide-open race this year. There was a strong pace on and it saw a host of chances in the home straight, but the top-rated horse in the race ultimately ran out a clear-cut winner. The standard is ordinary for the grade, with the runner-up the best guide.

NOTEBOOK
Energizer(GER) finished fourth behind Caspar Netscher in the German 2000 Guineas and was up in trip for this British debut. He got lucky with the ground deteriorating and was given a confident ride. He timed his challenge perfectly and was well on top nearing the business end, with the application of first-time hood aiding his cause. He's clearly a cut above this class and should have more to offer in international races over the trip. He became the first German-trained winner at Royal Ascot. (op 7-1 tchd 8-1)
Stipulate ◆, his powerful owner's second string, was just touched off over 1m at Sandown last time out and he made a bold bid on this foray into Group company. Had he been held onto longer back over this longer distance he may well have given the winner more to think about as he ideally does want quicker ground. With a return to sounder surface in mind, he looks a sure-fire future winner in Pattern company. (op 10-1 tchd 12-1)
Rewarded, rated 90, would have gone closer in his bid to make it 3-3 since resuming this year with a better passage at Newbury last time out. He got a nice trip through the race and stayed on well to grab third near the line past the easing-off fourth. A drop into Listed company looks on the cards and he helps to set the level here. (op 6-1)
Mukhadram, another officially rated 90, was taking a steep rise in class having comfortably won his maiden at Newmarket over 1m last month and attracted support to hand his trainer a quick double. He ran a big race, travelling sweetly into content, but failed to see out the extra distance on this ground. The son of Shamardal would surely have been third had Paul Hanagan been harder on him late on, and it wouldn't surprise were he to prove the best of these in due course. (op 8-1)
Tales Of Grimm(USA) ran close to his last-time-out form over 1m with the runner-up, despite not looking in love with this ground, and looks an improver. (op 5-1)
Goldoni(IRE) could have settled better early and wasn't disgraced back on turf, but this level looks beyond him at present. (op 25-1)
Grandeur(IRE) was produced with his chance from 2f out but he struggled to see it out on this ground from thereon. Look out for him back on a faster surface. (op 11-2 tchd 4-1)
Cavaleiro(IRE) was down in class having finished ninth in the Derby on his previous outing. He never threatened and needs his sights lowering even further. (op 20-1 tchd 14-1)
Wrotham Heath beat Grandeur despite not enjoying the course at Epsom last time out and was expected to handle this ground. Somewhat surprisingly he went hard from the front in this better class, however, and was done with shortly after turning in. (tchd 9-2 and 5-1 in places)
Crius(IRE) Official explanation: jockey said colt hung left

3296 KING GEORGE V STKS (H'CAP) 1m 4f
5:35 (5:35) (Class 2) (0-105,105) 3-Y-O

£34,237 (£10,252; £5,126; £2,563; £1,281; £643) **Stalls** Low

Form / RPR

2551 **1** **Fennell Bay (IRE)**[5] 3157 3-8-1 **85** 4ex .... JoeFanning 17 94+
(Mark Johnston) *t.k.h: in tch: n.m.r and shuffled bk 3f out: swtchd lft and rallied on outer 2f out: chal 1f out: styd on wl u.p to ld last strides* **12/1**

-041 **2** *nk* **Handsome Man (IRE)**[33] 2281 3-7-11 **84** .... HarryBentley(3) 7 92
(Saeed Bin Suroor) *chsd ldrs: chsd ldr wl over 2f out: rdn and ev ch wl over 1f out: led but hrd pressed 1f out: kpt on wl tl hdd and no ex last strides* **14/1**

-135 **3** *nk* **Rougemont (IRE)**[40] 2080 3-9-7 **105** .... RichardHughes 16 113
(Richard Hannon) *hld up towards rr: hdwy over 4f out: rdn and effrt to chse ldrs over 2f out: drvn and ev ch over 1f out: kpt on wl tl no ex cl home* **25/1**

32-1 **4** *1 1/2* **Anomaly**[35] 2196 3-8-9 **93** .... SilvestreDeSousa 14 99
(Mahmood Al Zarooni) *lw: led tl over 7f out: chsd ldr tl led again 3f out: hrd pressed and drvn wl over 1f out: hdd 1f out: no ex and btn fnl 100yds* **8/1**[3]

4-11 **5** *nse* **Pilgrims Rest (IRE)**[24] 2552 3-8-0 **84** .... KieranO'Neill 5 90+
(Richard Hannon) *chsd ldrs: swtchd lft and rdn to chal between horses wl over 1f out: ev ch after tl no ex 1f out: outpcd and btn fnl 100yds* **16/1**

6 *nk* **Moldowney**[48] 1836 3-8-2 **86** .... WayneLordan 15 91
(T Stack, Ire) *leggy: stdd s: hld up in tch in rr: nt clr run 3f out: swtchd lft and effrt 2f out: jostling match w rival and no hdwy over 1f out: edgd rt but styd on wl fnl f: nt rch ldrs* **16/1**

-116 **7** *1 1/4* **Sparkling Portrait**[19] 2718 3-8-9 **93** .... PaulHanagan 22 101+
(Richard Fahey) *lw: hld up in tch: nt clr run 3f out: effrt whn clipped heels: stmbld bdly and rdr lost iron 2f out: no hdwy and pushed rt over 1f out: rdr fnlly rcvrd iron and rdn ent fnl f: styd on wl: nt rcvr* **10/1**

11-4 **8** *1/2* **Misdemeanour (IRE)**[26] 2477 3-8-0 **84** .... JimmyQuinn 3 86
(Richard Hannon) *in tch: nt clr run 3f out: rdn and effrt on inner jst over 2f out: no ex ent fnl f: wknd fnl 100yds* **33/1**

211 **9** *1* **Nicholascopernicus (IRE)**[7] 3072 3-8-0 **84** 4ex .... NickyMackay 8 85
(Ed Walker) *chsd ldrs: rdn and effrt over 2f out: stl chsng ldrs but styng on same pce whn nt clr run over 1f out: wknd ins fnl f* **11/2**[2]

5-24 **10** *1/2* **Uriah Heep (FR)**[41] 2026 3-8-7 **91** ow1 .... RyanMoore 10 91
(Sir Michael Stoute) *lw: in tch: rdn: nt qckn and hung rt over 2f out: stl racing awkwardly and no prog over 1f out: plugged on u.p but no threat to ldrs fnl f* **16/1**

5-12 **11** *1* **Gabrial The Great (IRE)**[43] 1978 3-8-0 **84** .... FrannyNorton 12 82+
(Michael Bell) *t.k.h: hld up in tch: nt clr run over 2f out: sltly hmpd 2f out: trying to rally and carried rt over 1f out: styd on fnl f but no threat to ldrs* **7/2**[1]

1103 **12** *2* **Samba King**[13] 2897 3-8-9 **93** .... MickaelBarzalona 11 88
(Mahmood Al Zarooni) *styd wd: chsd ldr tl led over 7f out: hdd 3f out: wknd u.p jst over 1f out* **20/1**

0-21 **13** *1 1/2* **Niceofyoutotellme**[72] 1270 3-8-1 **85** .... MartinLane 21 78
(Ralph Beckett) *hld up in tch: n.m.r but rdn and effrt 2f out: no ex u.p over 1f out: wknd ins fnl f* **11/1**

-120 **14** *nse* **Commitment**[19] 2718 3-7-12 **87** .... DarrenEgan(5) 4 80
(Luca Cumani) *hld up in tch in midfield: n.m.r wl over 1f out: rdn and effrt whn hung rt wl over 1f out: no prog and btn 1f out* **14/1**

1151 **15** *1 3/4* **Prussian**[17] 2772 3-8-4 **88** .... MartinDwyer 2 78
(Mark Johnston) *in tch towards rr: rdn and effrt on inner whn hmpd over 1f out: no prog and sn wknd* **25/1**

3211 **16** *nk* **Rocktherunway (IRE)**[19] 2716 3-8-2 **86** .... CathyGannon 1 75
(Michael Dods) *lw: s.i.s: a in rr: rdn wl over 2f out: no imp and nvr trbld ldrs* **25/1**

0-03 **17** *1* **Ghost Protocol (IRE)**[26] 2477 3-8-4 **88** .... HayleyTurner 9 76
(David Simcock) *stdd after s: hld up in tch in rr: rdn and effrt whn sltly hmpd 2f out: no imp after: wknd fnl f* **25/1**

2-34 **18** *6* **Open Water (FR)**[19] 2701 3-8-2 **86** .... DavidProbert 20 64
(Andrew Balding) *in tch in midfield: rdn and struggling over 2f out: wknd over 1f out* **16/1**

2m 35.59s (3.09) **Going Correction** +0.40s/f (Good) **18** Ran SP% **133.8**
Speed ratings (Par 105): **105,104,104,103,103 103,102,102,101,101 100,99,98,98,97 96,96,92**
toteswingers:1&2:£47.00, 2&3:£77.40, 1&3:£57.00 CSF £168.66 CT £4163.00 TOTE £15.30: £3.40, £3.00, £5.50, £2.50; EX 354.10 Trifecta £6508.80 Pool: £15304.65 - 1.74 winning units..
Owner Sheikh Hamdan Bin Mohammed Al Maktoum **Bred** J R Wills **Trained** Middleham Moor, N Yorks

FOCUS
A really difficult contest to work out, with so many runners open to improvement now switching to handicaps and/or up in trip. The early gallop didn't appear frenetic, which resulted in a rough race. The race lacked a bit of its usual class but the form looks sound overall Fennell Bay improved again tackling 1m4f for the first time.
NOTEBOOK
Fennell Bay(IRE) had won all of his four races at about 1m, but his breeding suggested he could be interesting at this trip (half-sister Rising Cross was a Group 2 winner at 1m6f and finished second in the 2006 Epsom Oaks) and he duly improved for the extra distance, swooping late around runners to get up close to the line under a 4lb penalty. There could be more to come and he can remain in handicaps for the time being. (tchd 14-1)
Handsome Man(IRE) was never going to have any issues with the distance having won over it at Newmarket in mid-May and was narrowly denied by the winner in the dying strides. He can win a valuable handicap as long as he isn't punished for this. (tchd 16-1)
Rougemont(IRE) ◆, whose participation gave the weights a slightly uneven look, ran a cracker from off the pace and having raced wide before being worn down. There is every chance he ran close to his official rating and he obviously emerges the best horse at the weights.
Anomaly, making his handicap debut, didn't look an obvious candidate to improve for this distance on pedigree (his siblings had proved to be above average from 1m-1m2f) but it's difficult to argue he didn't get home, although he was ideally placed turning in. Like the third, he was giving the first two weight.
Pilgrims Rest(IRE), previously unbeaten in handicaps, didn't aid his chance by racing freely just behind the leaders.
Moldowney looked difficult to assess on his first try in handicaps after running at Dundalk twice this year, but got tapped for speed when the pace quickened and couldn't get to the leaders. (tchd 20-1)
Sparkling Portrait ◆ was the unlucky horse of the race, as he still had something to give when stumbling badly after clipping heels 2f out - the jockey did extremely well not to come off. Once Paul Hanagan had recovered his equilibrium, the colt ran on really strongly and was closing with every stride. Official explanation: jockey said colt clipped heels 2f out (op 14-1)
Misdemeanour(IRE) wasn't disgraced up in distance but may want better ground. (op 25-1)
Nicholascopernicus(IRE) had been in tremendous form recently and sneaked in at the bottom of the weights after taking a Newbury handicap a week previously with any amount to spare. Conditions appeared to have come right for him, but although he was squeezed up a couple of times in the home straight, one felt he finished in about the right place on the day. (op 9-2 tchd 6-1 and 13-2 in places)
Uriah Heep(FR), representing a stable with a decent record in this contest, continually found trouble inside the final 2f, and is a little better than his final position suggests. (tchd 20-1 in places)
Gabrial The Great(IRE) took a ferocious hold for quite some time behind a wall of horses, so wasn't in the best place as things turned out. He can be given another chance, especially as his mark won't be touched, but he'll need to settle much better. (op 6-1)
T/Jkpt: Not won. T/Plt: £1,505.80 to a £1 stake. Pool of £533,513.84 - 258.63 winning tickets. T/Qpdt: £203.70 to a £1 stake. Pool of £29,728.20 - 107.97 winning tickets. DO

2783 LEICESTER (R-H)
Thursday, June 21
3297 Meeting Abandoned - Unraceable

3285 RIPON (R-H)
Thursday, June 21
OFFICIAL GOING: Soft (heavy in places) changing to heavy after race 5 (4.35)
Wind: Virtually nil Weather: Heavy rain

3303 BRITISH STALLION STUDS SUPPORTING BRITISH RACING EBF MAIDEN STKS 6f
2:10 (2:10) (Class 5) 2-Y-O **£3,557** (£1,058; £529; £264) **Stalls** High

Form / RPR

2 **1** **Bircham (IRE)**[15] 2822 2-9-3 0 .... AhmedAjtebi 9 85
(Mahmood Al Zarooni) *chsd clr ldr: hdwy and cl up 2f out: led over 1f out and sn rdn clr: edgd lft and styd on wl* **11/10**[1]

05 **2** *5* **Deepest Blue**[28] 2420 2-9-3 0 .... GrahamLee 6 69
(Jamie Osborne) *chsd ldng pair: rdn along 2f out: styd on ent fnl f: tk 2nd towards fin* **20/1**

33 **3** *1 1/2* **Opt Out**[34] 2224 2-9-3 0 .... AdrianNicholls 7 65
(Mark Johnston) *led and sn clr: rdn along and jnd 2f out: hdd over 1f out: wknd ins fnl f* **7/1**[3]

0 **4** *1 1/4* **Vino Collapso (IRE)**[19] 2686 2-9-3 0 .... JamesSullivan 8 61
(James Given) *towards rr: hdwy over 2f out: rdn wl over 1f out: kpt on fnl f: nrst fin* **66/1**

5 *nk* **Pour La Victoire (IRE)** 2-9-3 0 .... PhillipMakin 11 60
(Nigel Tinkler) *t.k.h: chsd ldrs: rdn along over 2f out: sn no imp* **100/1**

6 *3 1/2* **Red Cobra (IRE)** 2-9-3 0 .... DuranFentiman 4 49+
(Tim Easterby) *towards rr and hmpd after 1f: sme hdwy 2f out: sn rdn and n.d* **33/1**

7 *5* **Medicoe** 2-9-3 0 .... LukeMorris 3 38+
(Sir Mark Prescott Bt) *wnt rt s: midfield: pushed along and green on outer 1/2-way: sn outpcd* **11/4**[2]

8 *5* **Nifty Nadine (IRE)** 2-8-9 0 .... DeclanCannon(3) 10 14
(Nigel Tinkler) *chsd ldrs: rdn along 1/2-way: sn wknd* **100/1**

9 *12* **Honest Boy** 2-9-3 0 .... TedDurcan 2
(Saeed Bin Suroor) *wnt rt s: green and sn pushed along: a in rr* **15/2**

10 *7* **Smooth Handle** 2-9-3 0 .... RichardKingscote 5
(Tom Dascombe) *sn outpcd and a bhd* **16/1**

1m 18.34s (5.34) **Going Correction** +0.75s/f (Yiel) **10** Ran SP% **115.6**
Speed ratings (Par 93): **94,87,85,83,83 78,71,65,49,39**
toteswingers:1&2:£6.30, 2&3:£10.90, 1&3:£2.40 CSF £30.50 TOTE £2.20: £1.10, £4.60, £2.10; EX 20.50.
Owner Godolphin **Bred** Stowell Park Stud **Trained** Newmarket, Suffolk

FOCUS
An uncompetitive 2yo maiden won in clear-cut fashion.
NOTEBOOK
Bircham(IRE), runner-up to another Godolphin inmate, subsequent Chesham winner Tha'ir, on his debut over the C&D two weeks earlier, kept tabs on the leader. His inexperience showed in front but he came right away. (op 10-11 tchd 6-5)
Deepest Blue, who showed improvement when fifth in a race working out well on his second start at Salisbury, stayed on really well in the closing stages to snatch second spot. He looks a likely nursery type. (tchd 22-1)
Opt Out, beaten at odds-on on his second start and his turf debut at Hamilton, showed speed and may be worth dropping back to the minimum trip. (op 15-2 tchd 13-2)
Vino Collapso(IRE), a half-brother to two winners, fared much better than on his debut and will be suited by 7f.

Medicoe, soon struggling to keep up, will need to improve markedly if he is to figure on his second start. (op 7-2)
Smooth Handle Official explanation: trainer said colt was unsuited by the soft (heavy in places) ground

3304 SIS LIVE CLAIMING STKS 6f
2:45 (2:45) (Class 5) 3-Y-O+ **£2,587** (£770; £384; £192) **Stalls** High

Form RPR
3504 **1** **Tajneed (IRE)**[15] 2825 9-9-0 88 AdrianNicholls 6 87
(David Nicholls) *cl up: led 2f out and sn rdn: drvn ent fnl f: hdd last 100yds: rallied gamely to ld on line* **13/8**[1]
5100 **2** *nse* **Arganil (USA)**[6] 3128 7-9-5 91 (p) PhillipMakin 4 92
(Kevin Ryan) *hld up: hdwy 1/2-way: chsd ldng pair 2f out: rdn to chse ldr wnr over 1f out: chal ent fnl f: sn drvn and slt ld last 100yds: hdd and no ex on line* **7/2**[3]
-016 **3** *5* **Ballista (IRE)**[19] 2697 4-9-8 82 StephenCraine 2 80
(Tom Dascombe) *led: rdn along and hdd 2f out: sn drvn and grad wknd ent fnl f* **10/1**
3611 **4** *3 3/4* **Zomerlust**[38] 2120 10-8-12 74 (v) MichaelO'Connell 7 59
(John Quinn) *trckd ldng pair: hdwy on rails 1/2-way: rdn along over 2f out and sn wknd* **13/2**
0460 **5** *1 3/4* **Fathsta (IRE)**[8] 3049 7-9-8 86 GrahamLee 5 64
(David Simcock) *dwlt: sn rdn along: a in rr* **3/1**[2]
0-03 **6** *43* **Chandigarh (IRE)**[10] 2972 3-7-10 75 ow1 (b) RyanPowell(3) 1
(Paul Fitzsimons) *chsd ldrs on outer: rdn along 1/2-way: sn wknd and bhd* **50/1**

1m 16.73s (3.73) **Going Correction** +0.75s/f (Yiel)
WFA 3 from 4yo+ 7lb **6** Ran SP% **109.7**
Speed ratings (Par 103): **105,104,98,93,90 33**
toteswingers:1&2:£1.60, 2&3:£4.50, 1&3:£3.20 CSF £7.20 TOTE £2.60: £1.90, £2.00; EX 8.70.
Owner Middleham Park Racing LIII & Partner **Bred** R Hodgins **Trained** Sessay, N Yorks

FOCUS
The first two stood out on official ratings in this good-class claimer. It's hard to be confident about the form.

3305 KEVAN JON OCCASION & BRIDAL WEAR H'CAP 1m 4f 10y
3:20 (3:21) (Class 4) (0-85,82) 3-Y-O **£4,528** (£1,347; £673; £336) **Stalls** Low

Form RPR
0064 **1** **Choisan (IRE)**[19] 2716 3-9-2 75 DuranFentiman 1 82
(Tim Easterby) *mde most: rdn along over 3f out: jnd 2f out and sn drvn: hdd wl ins fnl f: rallied gamely to ld again nr fin* **11/1**
16-1 **2** *hd* **Gassin Golf**[8] 3033 3-9-9 82 6ex LukeMorris 5 89
(Sir Mark Prescott Bt) *hld up in rr: tk clsr order 1/2-way: niggled along and stmbld over 3f out: rdn to chal 2f out: drvn over 1f out: slt ld wl ins fnl f: hdd and no ex nr fin* **1/2**[1]
3450 **3** *3* **Torero**[19] 2716 3-8-9 68 PhillipMakin 2 70
(Kevin Ryan) *trckd ldng pair: rdn along over 3f out: drvn over 2f out: sn one pce* **18/1**
2133 **4** *1 3/4* **Party Line**[13] 2889 3-9-1 74 AdrianNicholls 4 73
(Mark Johnston) *trckd wnr: effrt and cl up 4f out: rdn along wl over 2f out: sn drvn and one pce* **7/1**[3]
5-05 **5** *10* **Bohemian Rhapsody (IRE)**[12] 2942 3-9-4 77 GrahamLee 3 60
(J W Hills) *trckd ldng pair: rdn along over 3f out: wknd over 2f out* **6/1**[2]

2m 46.72s (10.02) **Going Correction** +0.75s/f (Yiel) **5** Ran SP% **107.0**
Speed ratings (Par 101): **96,95,93,92,86**
CSF £16.57 TOTE £16.90: £6.10, £1.02; EX 20.50.
Owner Croft, Taylor & Hebdon **Bred** David A Cahill **Trained** Great Habton, N Yorks

FOCUS
This was a true test in the conditions, and the game winner is rated to his 2yo best.
Bohemian Rhapsody(IRE) Official explanation: jockey said colt hung left throughout

3306 LADIES DAY H'CAP 1m 1f
4:00 (4:00) (Class 3) (0-90,90) 4-Y-O+ **£6,931** (£2,074; £1,037; £519; £258) **Stalls** Low

Form RPR
-622 **1** **Lieutenant Kojak**[13] 2899 4-8-2 71 oh1 LukeMorris 1 80
(Peter Charalambous) *dwlt and sn pushed along in rr: niggled along 1/2-way: hdwy over 3f out: rdn to chse ldrs whn n.m.r 2f out: sn swtchd lft and drvn to ld ent fnl f: kpt on gamely towards fin* **9/4**[1]
-000 **2** *1/2* **Las Verglas Star (IRE)**[12] 2911 4-9-1 84 TonyHamilton 6 92
(Richard Fahey) *t.k.h early: hld up in rr: hdwy over 3f out: swtchd to outer and rdn 2f out: drvn to chal ent fnl f and ev ch tl no ex towards fin* **13/2**
0430 **3** *2 1/4* **Jonny Lesters Hair (IRE)**[5] 3167 7-8-11 80 DuranFentiman 4 83
(Tim Easterby) *led and sn clr: rdn along wl over 2f out: sn jnd and drvn over 1f out: hdd ent fnl f: kpt on same pce* **7/2**[2]
1205 **4** *nk* **Colour Guard**[5] 3164 4-9-7 90 AdrianNicholls 5 92
(Mark Johnston) *chsd clr ldr: tk clsr order 3f out: chal 2f out: sn rdn and ev ch: drvn and edgd lft ent fnl f: sn wknd* **5/1**[3]
0-50 **5** *7* **Crown Counsel (IRE)**[82] 1128 4-9-4 87 GrahamLee 2 74
(Mark Johnston) *hld up in tch: hdwy 3f out: rdn over 2f out: sn wknd* **14/1**
-000 **6** *2 3/4* **Pravda Street**[12] 2910 7-8-10 82 DaleSwift(3) 3 63
(Brian Ellison) *in tch: rdn along 4f out: wknd wl over 2f out* **6/1**
110- **7** *12* **So Wise (USA)**[208] 7558 4-8-12 81 DanielTudhope 7 35
(David O'Meara) *chsd ldng pair: rdn along over 3f out: wknd over 2f out* **10/1**

1m 59.73s (5.03) **Going Correction** +0.75s/f (Yiel) **7** Ran SP% **113.0**
Speed ratings (Par 107): **107,106,104,104,98 95,84**
toteswingers:1&2:£3.70, 2&3:£5.10, 1&3:£2.40 CSF £16.95 TOTE £3.00: £1.80, £3.60; EX 12.80.
Owner P Charalambous **Bred** Cheveley Park Stud Ltd **Trained** Newmarket, Suffolk

FOCUS
A competitive handicap run at a strong pace. There are doubts over most of this field, but the winner is rated up a length on his Newmarket latest.

NOTEBOOK
Lieutenant Kojak, a shade unlucky from a 4lb lower mark at Newmarket, made it hard work for himself with a tardy start. Flat out once in line for home and forced to switch to find racing room, he showed a good attitude. He's progressing nicely. (op 7-2)
Las Verglas Star(IRE), who sat off the strong pace, has slipped 4lb down the ratings this year. He had hinted at a return to form at Chester on his previous start and confirmed it with a bold effort. (tchd 11-2)
Jonny Lesters Hair(IRE), who likes it round here, had them at full stretch at the halfway mark. He proved game but could not contain the first two. (op 4-1 tchd 9-2)
Colour Guard, a winner three times at Southwell in the winter, had run moderately on his turf debut at York just five days earlier. This was better but he is 15lb higher than his last Fibresand success. (op 9-2)
Pravda Street, yet to prove he stays this far, continues off the boil but as a result he is slipping down the ratings. (op 5-1 tchd 13-2)

3307 BEAUMONT ROBINSON LADIES' DERBY H'CAP (LADY AMATEUR RIDERS) (DIV I) 1m 4f 10y
4:35 (4:35) (Class 6) (0-65,70) 4-Y-O+ **£2,495** (£774; £386; £193) **Stalls** Low

Form RPR
30-1 **1** **Sula Two**[7] 3073 5-10-13 70 6ex MissSBrotherton 5 83
(Ron Hodges) *trckd ldrs on inner: smooth hdwy 4f out: led wl over 2f out: rdn clr over 1f out: styd on* **2/1**[1]
5-64 **2** *3 1/4* **Aegean Destiny**[7] 3061 5-9-13 59 MissBeckyBrisbourne(3) 1 65
(John Mackie) *hld up in tch: hdwy on wd outside 3f out: rdn 2f out: chsd wnr over 1f out: no imp wl ins fnl f* **9/1**
/5-6 **3** *6* **Lava Steps (USA)**[13] 1580 6-8-11 45 (b) MissAliceMills(5) 3 41
(David O'Meara) *led: rdn along 3f out: hdd wl over 2f out: drvn and kpt on same pce fnl f* **50/1**
0/0- **4** *3 1/4* **Endeavor**[12] 1794 7-8-11 45 MissRobynGray(5) 4 36
(Dianne Sayer) *bhd: hdwy on wd outside wl over 2f out: sn rdn and styd on fnl f: nrst fin* **50/1**
-051 **5** *hd* **Silver Tigress**[7] 3061 4-9-7 53 MissCWalton(3) 6 44
(George Moore) *hld up towards rr: stdy hdwy 5f out: rdn to chse ldrs over 2f out: sn no imp* **5/1**[2]
2100 **6** *nk* **Hunters Belt (IRE)**[2] 3253 8-10-2 64 MissRSmith(5) 9 54
(Noel Wilson) *hld up in rr: sme hdwy fnl 3f: nvr a factor* **18/1**
2332 **7** *2 1/2* **Shy**[17] 2755 7-10-0 62 MissPhillipaTutty(5) 2 48
(Karen Tutty) *a towards rr* **9/1**
-363 **8** *4 1/2* **Zaplamation (IRE)**[8] 3022 7-10-2 62 MissJRRichards(3) 8 41
(John Quinn) *chsd ldrs: rdn along 3f out: wknd over 2f out* **11/2**[3]
5-03 **9** *3 1/4* **Cool Baranca (GER)**[6] 3116 6-9-6 49 MissECSayer 10 23
(Dianne Sayer) *prom on outer: pushed along 4f out: rdn 3f out: sn wknd* **8/1**
-035 **10** *16* **Tigerino (IRE)**[12] 2925 4-9-4 47 MrsAdeleMulrennan 7
(Chris Fairhurst) *chsd ldrs: rdn along over 5f out: sn lost pl and bhd* **22/1**
0032 **11** *14* **Coax**[20] 2669 4-10-0 62 MrsFreyaBrewer(5) 12
(Patrick Holmes) *t.k.h early: chsd ldr: rdn along over 5f out: sn wknd* **14/1**

2m 46.88s (10.18) **Going Correction** +0.75s/f (Yiel) **11** Ran SP% **116.7**
Speed ratings (Par 101): **96,93,89,87,87 87,85,82,80,69 60**
CSF £20.50 CT £673.94 TOTE £3.10: £1.10, £3.10, £13.90; EX 24.50.
Owner Richard Prince **Bred** D R Tucker **Trained** Charlton Mackrell, Somerset

FOCUS
Part one of a modest lady amateur riders' handicap. They went a good gallop and came home strung out. The winner was value for extra and could still be well handicapped.
Cool Baranca(GER) Official explanation: trainer had no explanation for the poor form shown

3308 FORTY YEARS OF EXCELLENCE NAGS HEAD PICKHILL H'CAP 5f
5:10 (5:14) (Class 5) (0-75,74) 3-Y-O+ **£2,911** (£866; £432; £216) **Stalls** High

Form RPR
1344 **1** **El McGlynn (IRE)**[19] 2691 3-7-13 58 HannahNunn(7) 6 69
(Peter Salmon) *cl up: led after 1 1/2f: rdn wl over 1f out: styd on wl fnl f* **20/1**
1223 **2** *2* **First In Command (IRE)**[7] 3065 7-9-8 73 (t) MarkCoumbe(5) 4 79
(Daniel Mark Loughnane) *in tch: hdwy to chse ldrs 1/2-way: rdn wl over 1f out: kpt on same pce fnl f* **7/2**[2]
6405 **3** *shd* **Captain Scooby**[5] 3159 6-9-11 74 DeclanCannon(3) 8 79
(Richard Guest) *sn outpcd and bhd: swtchd wd and hdwy 2f out: sn rdn and styd on fnl f: nrst fin* **9/4**[1]
5300 **4** *4* **Wicked Wilma (IRE)**[6] 3113 8-9-10 70 GrahamLee 9 61
(Alan Berry) *led 1 1/2f: cl up: rdn 2f out: sn drvn and wknd 1f out* **5/1**[3]
1026 **5** *4 1/2* **Chosen One (IRE)**[6] 3109 7-8-9 55 JamesSullivan 7 30
(Ruth Carr) *chsd ldng pair: rdn along over 2f out: sn wknd* **13/2**
50-3 **6** *1/2* **Lady Del Sol**[46] 1881 4-8-9 60 DeanHeslop(5) 1 33
(Marjorie Fife) *chsd ldrs on outer: rdn along 1/2-way: sn btn* **6/1**
0440 **7** *18* **Ever Roses**[34] 2244 4-8-12 58 (v) PJMcDonald 3
(Paul Midgley) *chsd ldrs: hmpd and squeezed out after 1f: bhd after* **13/2**

1m 3.98s (3.28) **Going Correction** +0.75s/f (Yiel)
WFA 3 from 4yo+ 6lb **7** Ran SP% **115.4**
Speed ratings (Par 103): **103,99,99,93,86 85,56**
toteswingers:1&2:£6.60, 2&3:£2.10, 1&3:£8.20 CSF £89.83 CT £225.43 TOTE £25.30: £8.70, £1.60; EX 75.20.
Owner Leods Contracts Limited **Bred** Michael Lyons Jnr **Trained** Kirk Deighton, W Yorks

FOCUS
The ground was changed to heavy, but at last the rain had relented ahead of this modest sprint handicap. Not easy form to fathom, but the winner's best since he was a 2yo at face value.

3309 RACING AGAIN ON MONDAY 9TH JULY H'CAP 1m
5:40 (5:41) (Class 6) (0-65,66) 4-Y-O+ **£2,587** (£770; £384; £192) **Stalls** Low

Form RPR
1-52 **1** **Eastward Ho**[8] 3021 4-9-6 62 TonyHamilton 8 71
(Jason Ward) *led: rdn along 2f out: hdd and drvn over 1f out: rallied to ld again last 75yds* **6/4**[1]
/00- **2** *nk* **Petrocelli**[421] 1615 5-8-9 51 GrahamLee 9 59
(Wilf Storey) *trckd ldng pair: hdwy over 3f out: cl up 2f out: rdn to ld over 1f out: drvn ins fnl f: hdd and no ex last 75yds* **16/1**
5001 **3** *6* **Ela Gonda Mou**[7] 3081 5-9-10 66 6ex MichaelO'Connell 5 60
(Peter Charalambous) *dwlt: t.k.h and sn trcking ldrs on inner: pushed along 3f out: n.m.r and swtchd lft 2f out: sn rdn and one pce appr fnl f* **5/2**[2]
2-20 **4** *2 1/4* **Cathcart Castle**[19] 2692 4-8-13 55 DuranFentiman 7 44
(Simon West) *t.k.h: hld up in tch: effrt 5f out: rdn along over 2f out: sn one pce* **10/1**
-604 **5** *2* **My Mate Jake (IRE)**[15] 2821 4-9-2 63 ShaneBKelly(5) 11 47
(James Given) *chsd ldrs: rdn along 3f out: drvn over 2f out and sn btn* **5/1**[3]
-005 **6** *3 3/4* **Viking Dancer**[8] 3032 5-8-3 45 JamesSullivan 12 21
(Ruth Carr) *cl up: effrt 3f out and cl up: rdn to dispute ld over 2f out and ev ch tl drvn and wknd over 1f out* **11/1**

1m 49.8s (8.40) **Going Correction** +1.075s/f (Soft) **6** Ran SP% **108.5**
Speed ratings (Par 101): **101,100,94,92,90 86**
toteswingers:1&2:£3.10, 2&3:£5.20, 1&3:£1.50 CSF £23.78 CT £49.36 TOTE £2.20: £1.20, £3.80; EX 23.40.
Owner Miss Vivian Pratt **Bred** H & V Pratt **Trained** Middleham, N Yorks

FOCUS
A depleted field for this modest handicap, run in bad ground, and pretty weak form.

3310 BEAUMONT ROBINSON LADIES' DERBY H'CAP (LADY AMATEUR RIDERS) (DIV II) 1m 4f 10y
6:10 (6:10) (Class 6) (0-65,65) 4-Y-0+ £2,495 (£774; £386; £193) Stalls Low

Form RPR

/0-0 **1** **Shaloo Diamond**[45] 1913 7-10-7 **65** MissADeniel 2 77+
(Richard Whitaker) *stdd s: hld up in rr: stdy hdwy over 4f out: trckd ldrs gng wl over 2f out: shkn up to ld jst over 1f out: rdn clr ins fnl f: styd on* **17/2**

0-61 **2** *3* **Politbureau**[20] 2669 5-9-9 **53** MissSBrotherton 12 57
(Michael Easterby) *a.p: cl up 1/2-way: led 4f out: rdn over 2f out: hdd appr fnl f: kpt on same pce* **2/1**[1]

500- **3** *6* **Ritsi**[14] 7145 9-8-11 **46** oh1 (t) MissAliceMills(5) 9 40
(Marjorie Fife) *hld up in rr: gd hdwy on outer 4f out: chsd ldrs 2f out: sn rdn and one pce appr fnl f* **16/1**

6-02 **4** *1 ½* **Graceful Act**[16] 2794 4-9-13 **62** MissVBarr(5) 1 54
(Ron Barr) *in tch: hdwy to chse ldrs 4f out: rdn and cl up over 2f out: drvn and wknd over 1f out* **12/1**

000/ **5** *2 ¼* **Imperial Royale (IRE)**[39] 664 11-8-13 **48** oh1 ow2 MissKMargarson(5) 7 36
(Patrick Clinton) *prom on outer: cl up 1/2-way: effrt and ev ch 3f out: sn rdn and wknd wl over 1f out* **50/1**

-005 **6** *hd* **Damascus Symphony**[14] 2842 4-9-13 **60** MissCWalton(3) 5 48
(James Bethell) *hld up: hdwy and in tch 3f out: rdn over 2f out: n.d* **15/2**[3]

600 **7** *nse* **Mystified (IRE)**[6] 3116 9-8-13 **46** MissWGibson(3) 8 34
(Alan Berry) *led: rdn along 5f out: hdd 4f out: grad wknd* **33/1**

20-4 **8** *10* **Monthly Medal**[12] 2922 9-9-9 **58** (t) MissSMDoolan(5) 11 30
(Wilf Storey) *t.k.h: chsd ldrs on outer: rdn along wl over 3f out: sn wknd* **8/1**

30-0 **9** *2 ¼* **Donna Elvira**[20] 2670 5-9-0 **47** MissHCuthbert(3) 4 15
(Edwin Tuer) *bhd fr 1/2-way* **12/1**

4300 **10** *nk* **Polurrian (IRE)**[17] 2751 5-10-1 **64** MrsFreyaBrewer(5) 10 32
(David O'Meara) *a towards rr* **5/1**[2]

3/0- **11** *9* **Front Rank (IRE)**[19] 1519 12-9-2 **46** oh1 MissECSayer 6
(Dianne Sayer) *chsd ldrs: rdn along 1/2-way: sn lost pl and bhd fnl 3f* **28/1**

2m 53.37s (16.67) **Going Correction** +1.075s/f (Soft) 11 Ran SP% **113.0**
Speed ratings (Par 101): **87,85,81,80,78 78,78,71,70,69 63**
toteswingers:1&2:£4.10, 2&3:£7.60, 1&3:£19.00 CSF £24.36 CT £268.64 TOTE £11.80: £3.10, £1.30, £2.60; EX 34.00.
Owner The Barflys **Bred** Hellwood Stud Farm **Trained** Scarcroft, W Yorks

FOCUS
Division two of this low-grade lady amateur riders' handicap. They seemed to go a good pace and the winner came from last. He handled the ground better than most, and the form is rated around the runner-up.
Damascus Symphony Official explanation: jockey said filly stumbled on bend approaching home straight
T/Plt: £22.90 to a £1 stake. Pool of £55,618.35 - 1,769.88 winning tickets. T/Qpdt: £10.60 to a £1 stake. Pool of £3,586.21 - 248.78 winning tickets. JR

3216 WARWICK (L-H)
Thursday, June 21

OFFICIAL GOING: Soft (5.9)
Wind: moderate behind Weather: cloudy

3311 COMMSCOPE IPATCH FOR ENERGY CLAIMING STKS 1m 22y
2:20 (2:20) (Class 5) 3-Y-0+ £2,264 (£673; £336; £168) Stalls Low

Form RPR

4040 **1** **Nezami (IRE)**[12] 2924 7-8-11 63 (b) NedCurtis(7) 6 70
(Paul Midgley) *racd keenly: sn led: brought field over to stands' side over 2f out: sn rdn: jst hld on* **5/1**

-105 **2** *hd* **Abidhabidubai**[21] 2636 4-8-13 77 KevinLundie(7) 1 72
(John Quinn) *midfield: pushed along over 3f out: chsd wnr 2f out: edgd rt and r.o u.p ins fnl f: jst hld* **9/4**[1]

-305 **3** *7* **Fu Fic Fas**[8] 3048 3-8-1 55 (t) RaulDaSilva(3) 8 47
(Paul Fitzsimons) *in tch: rdn over 3f out: styd on one pce 2f: nvr trbld first two* **20/1**

0- **4** *3 ¼* **Before Bruce**[33] 7766 5-9-6 0 (t) FergusSweeney 5 48
(Brendan Powell) *s.s: in rr: rdn over 2f out: mod late hdwy* **80/1**

0501 **5** *1* **Son Vida (IRE)**[100] 886 4-9-2 75 NatashaEaton(7) 4 49
(Alan Bailey) *led early: trckd ldr: styd towards far side in st: rdn and lost 2nd 2f out: wknd ins fnl f* **3/1**[3]

-600 **6** *9* **Crown Dependency (IRE)**[20] 2660 3-9-1 92 (b[1]) DaneO'Neill 7 28
(Richard Hannon) *t.k.h early: trckd ldrs: rdn over 2f out: fnd little and grad wknd* **5/2**[2]

000- **7** *2* **Letham Cottage**[215] 7493 3-9-1 42 ShaneKelly 3 23
(Brian Meehan) *a towards rr: shkn up and no hdwy over 2f out* **33/1**

1m 44.25s (3.25) **Going Correction** +0.50s/f (Yiel)
WFA 3 from 4yo+ 10lb 7 Ran SP% **109.9**
Speed ratings (Par 103): **103,102,95,92,91 82,80**
toteswingers:1&2:£4.00, 2&3:£3.90, 1&3:£4.10 CSF £15.32 TOTE £4.50: £1.90, £1.60; EX 20.40.
Owner R Wardlaw **Bred** Falah Ithnein **Trained** Westow, N Yorks

FOCUS
A moderate yet interesting claimer, with the race revolving around Crown Dependency. Shaky form and not a race to be too positive about.

3312 LMG SMARTSPACE MAIDEN FILLIES' STKS 6f
2:55 (2:56) (Class 5) 3-Y-0+ £2,264 (£673; £336; £168) Stalls Low

Form RPR

1 **Minalisa** 3-9-0 0 ChrisCatlin 3 79+
(Rae Guest) *hld up: rdn and gd hdwy over 1f out: sn led: pushed clr fnl f* **14/1**

03 **2** *3* **Gladiatrix**[13] 2871 3-9-0 0 JamesMillman 6 69
(Rod Millman) *s.s: towards rr: pushed along and hdwy over 2f out: led narrowly over 1f out: sn hdd: one pce ins fnl f* **14/1**

4 **3** *2 ¾* **Funcheon Vale (IRE)**[13] 2871 3-9-0 0 RobertHavlin 11 60
(Hughie Morrison) *trckd ldrs: ev ch over 1f out: one pce ins fnl f* **16/1**

3 **4** *2* **If So**[40] 2085 3-9-0 0 JackMitchell 10 54
(James Fanshawe) *trckd ldrs: n.m.r over 1f out: kpt on same pce fnl f* **9/2**[2]

046 **5** *3* **Missus Mills (IRE)**[9] 3012 3-9-0 0 PatCosgrave 12 44
(George Baker) *led: rdn over 2f out: hdd over 1f out: one pce fnl f* **9/1**

0-0 **6** *nse* **Too Ambitious**[12] 2918 3-8-7 0 JackDuern(7) 15 44
(Reg Hollinshead) *prom: rdn 2f out: wknd ins fnl f* **100/1**

640 **7** *2 ¼* **Aarti (IRE)**[31] 2344 3-9-0 72 LiamJones 4 37
(William Haggas) *chsd ldrs early: sn racing in midfield: pushed along fnl 3f: no imp on ldrs* **6/4**[1]

35- **8** *1 ¾* **Dahab Gold (IRE)**[188] 7784 3-9-0 0 TomMcLaughlin 16 31
(Jane Chapple-Hyam) *trckd ldrs: rdn over 2f out: btn over 1f out: eased towards fin* **16/1**

9 *½* **Consenting** 3-9-0 0 FergusSweeney 14 30
(Roger Charlton) *s.s and racd on outer: hung rt bnd over 2f out: a towards rr* **14/1**

10 *nse* **Havin' A Good Time (IRE)** 3-9-0 0 AndreaAtzeni 1 29
(Roger Varian) *racd keenly: chsd ldrs: rdn over 1f out: sn wknd* **6/1**[3]

00- **11** *nk* **Silent Mistress**[252] 6820 3-9-0 0 TomEaves 5 29
(J R Jenkins) *broke wl: sn in rr: struggling over 3f out* **100/1**

1m 14.48s (2.68) **Going Correction** +0.50s/f (Yiel)
WFA 3 from 4yo+ 7lb 11 Ran SP% **116.2**
Speed ratings (Par 100): **102,98,94,91,87 87,84,82,81,81 81**
toteswingers:1&2:£16.00, 2&3:£22.90, 1&3:£40.20 CSF £192.69 TOTE £18.50: £5.80, £3.70, £5.40; EX 141.00.
Owner C J Mills **Bred** C J Mills **Trained** Newmarket, Suffolk

FOCUS
There was little worthwhile form to go on for this fillies' maiden, but the time was fair and the first two could rate higher.
Aarti(IRE) Official explanation: trainer's rep said filly never travelled
Consenting Official explanation: jockey said filly hung right

3313 ROYCE COMMUNICATIONS PRESTIGE BUSINESSPARTNER E B F MAIDEN FILLIES' STKS 5f
3:30 (3:30) (Class 5) 2-Y-0 £3,234 (£962; £481; £240) Stalls Low

Form RPR

1 **Columella** 2-9-0 0 LiamJones 3 74+
(William Haggas) *wnt sltly rt s: sn pushed along and chsd ldrs: wnt 2nd wl over 1f out: led 100yds out: comf* **7/4**[2]

6 **2** *1 ¾* **Mrs Warren**[63] 1466 2-9-0 0 WilliamCarson 1 68
(Charles Hills) *led: pushed along appr fnl f: hdd 100yds out: no ex* **6/4**[1]

3 *6* **Derrochadora (IRE)** 2-9-0 0 ShaneKelly 5 46
(Robert Cowell) *wnt sltly rt leaving stalls: racd in tch in last: rdn over 2f out: sn one pce: wnt modest 3rd cl home* **12/1**

64 **4** *¾* **Summer Isles**[13] 2892 2-9-0 0 TomMcLaughlin 4 43
(Ed Dunlop) *trckd ldr: rdn and lost 2nd wl over 1f out: sn wknd* **3/1**[3]

1m 2.79s (3.19) **Going Correction** +0.50s/f (Yiel) 4 Ran SP% **109.1**
Speed ratings (Par 90): **94,91,81,80**
CSF £4.80 TOTE £2.40; EX 4.20.
Owner Wood Hall Stud Limited **Bred** Wood Hall Stud Limited **Trained** Newmarket, Suffolk

FOCUS
Quite an interesting maiden despite the small field size, run at a decent pace, with the front two pulling a long way clear.

NOTEBOOK
Columella, a half-sister to five winners including very smart 6f 2yo Memory, looked green early on but ultimately ran out a convincing winner. She did not look overly happy on the ground and was the first to be niggled, but she kept responding to pressure. This was a decent debut. (op 6-4 tchd 15-8)
Mrs Warren, who looked green when finishing in midfield in a Newmarket maiden in April, knew a lot more this time and looked the likeliest winner for much of the contest. She may have been out in front too long on this testing ground and should be capable of landing a similar contest. (op 2-1)
Derrochadora(IRE), a half-sister to winning sprinter Alis Aquilae, showed a bit of pace early but could not quicken, and should come on for this. (tchd 11-1)
Summer Isles, who had run well in a couple of 6f Newmarket maidens, found this ground against her but this was still slightly disappointing. She may be seen to better effect over further. (tchd 11-4 and 10-3)

3314 COMMSCOPE SOLUTIONS YOUR TRUSTED ADVISORS H'CAP 7f 26y
4:10 (4:11) (Class 5) (0-70,70) 3-Y-0+ £2,385 (£704; £352) Stalls Low

Form RPR

4051 **1** **Best Trip (IRE)**[24] 2538 5-9-5 **61** BarryMcHugh 9 77+
(Brian Ellison) *hld up in tch: gd hdwy over 2f out: led against stands' rail over 1f out: pushed along fnl f: comf* **4/1**[2]

6432 **2** *2 ½* **Mata Hari Blue**[6] 3103 6-9-13 **69** (t) RussKennemore 10 78
(John Holt) *s.s: in rr: sltly short of room bnd 3f out: sn rdn and clsd: wnt 2nd over 1f out: no imp on wnr fnl f* **9/2**[3]

1622 **3** *3* **Lindoro**[8] 3037 7-9-11 **70** PaulPickard(3) 8 71+
(Brian Ellison) *trckd ldrs: wnt 2nd over 2f out: sn rdn: kpt on one pce* **7/2**[1]

-560 **4** *1 ¼* **Prince Of Passion (CAN)**[24] 2549 4-9-4 **60** RobbieFitzpatrick 6 58
(Derek Shaw) *towards rr: hdwy 3f out: styd on u.p fnl 2f: jockey stopped riding for a few strides at 1/2f pole: nt rch ldrs* **28/1**

2005 **5** *½* **Satwa Laird**[3] 3229 6-9-13 **69** LiamKeniry 11 66
(Conor Dore) *towards rr: rdn and hdwy 3f out: nt clr run and swtchd lft over 1f out: styd on ins fnl f: nt trble ldrs* **9/1**

2030 **6** *½* **Ghostwing**[23] 2572 5-9-8 **67** (v) SophieDoyle(3) 4 62
(Ronald Harris) *led: rdn 2f out: sn hdd: wknd fnl f* **14/1**

0-42 **7** *1 ¾* **Light Burst (USA)**[23] 2583 3-8-12 **63** RoystonFfrench 5 51
(Ismail Mohammed) *chsd ldrs: rdn 3f out: wknd ent fnl f* **17/2**

4434 **8** *5* **Tahnee Mara (IRE)**[16] 2795 3-8-13 **64** TomEaves 3 39
(Kevin Ryan) *trckd ldrs: rdn over 2f out: edgd rt and grad wknd* **6/1**

5025 **9** *6* **Perfect Ch'l (IRE)**[15] 2811 5-9-8 **67** (v) RaulDaSilva(3) 7 29
(Ian Wood) *pushed along early to r cl up: lost 2nd over 2f out: sn wknd* **12/1**

0-55 **10** *23* **Norwood Lane**[138] 429 3-8-7 **58** (p) FergusSweeney 2
(Peter Hedger) *midfield: rdn 3f out: sn wknd: t.o* **25/1**

1m 27.53s (2.93) **Going Correction** +0.50s/f (Yiel)
WFA 3 from 4yo+ 9lb 10 Ran SP% **116.9**
Speed ratings (Par 103): **103,100,96,95,94 94,92,86,79,53**
toteswingers:1&2:£4.90, 2&3:£3.70, 1&3:£2.70 CSF £22.47 CT £69.05 TOTE £6.80: £2.20, £1.60, £2.60; EX 26.30.
Owner Koo's Racing Club **Bred** Limetree Stud **Trained** Norton, N Yorks

FOCUS
It started to rain heavily before this handicap, that was run at a decent pace with plenty keen to lead, and the field were strung out at the finish. The winner looks capable of getting closer to his old form.

Perfect Ch'l(IRE) Official explanation: trainer said mare had a breathing problem

3315 PTC SYSTEMS H'CAP 7f 26y

4:45 (4:47) (Class 6) (0-60,60) 3-Y-O £1,617 (£481; £240; £120) Stalls Low

Form				RPR
6002	1		**Rockme Cockney**[18] 2733 3-9-1 57............................(p) RaulDaSilva(3) 3 (Jeremy Gask) *led: pushed along over 1f out: sn jnd: rdn fnl f: hld on wl* 10/3[1]	64
-026	2	nk	**Marah Music**[14] 2862 3-9-4 57............................ SebSanders 1 (Peter Makin) *trckd ldrs: effrt over 1f out: sn chal wnr: ev ch thrght fnl f: jst hld* 6/1	63
4460	3	1 ¼	**Arte Del Calcio**[16] 2787 3-9-0 60............................ GeorgeDowning(7) 2 (Tony Carroll) *towards rr: hdwy 2f out: chsd ldrs 1f out: swtchd rt fnl 75yds: kpt on* 10/1	63
0-06	4	2 ¾	**Elusive Island (USA)**[8] 3028 3-9-3 56............................(v[1]) DavidNolan 5 (Ann Duffield) *racd keenly bhd ldrs: rdn over 2f out: kpt on one pce fnl f* 20/1	52
3543	5	1 ¼	**Kashmiri Star**[16] 2803 3-9-0 53............................ PatCosgrave 9 (Michael Quinn) *trckd ldr: rdn over 2f out: lost 2nd over 1f out: one pce fnl f* 11/2[3]	46
-054	6	2 ¼	**Moody Dancer**[16] 2803 3-9-7 60............................ TomEaves 7 (William Muir) *midfield: dropped to rr over 2f out: sn rdn: swtchd lft over 1f out: kpt on same pce* 8/1	47
5106	7	¾	**Skyeron**[8] 3048 3-9-0 53............................ LiamJones 10 (Mark Brisbourne) *chsd ldrs: rdn over 2f out: wknd over 1f out* 13/2	38
006-	8	2 ¼	**Justine Time (IRE)**[257] 6695 3-8-13 52............................ BarryMcHugh 11 (Julie Camacho) *hld up towards rr: rdn 3f out: no imp on ldrs over 1f out* 20/1	31
0-23	9	hd	**Green Mountain (IRE)**[8] 3052 3-8-4 46............................(t) AdamBeschizza(3) 4 (Philip McBride) *s.s: sn chsd along in rr: rdn and sme hdwy over 2f out: wknd fnl f* 5/1[2]	24

1m 28.51s (3.91) **Going Correction** +0.50s/f (Yiel) 9 Ran SP% 112.5
Speed ratings (Par 97): **97,96,95,92,90 88,87,84,84**
toteswingers:1&2:£3.70, 2&3:£10.10, 1&3:£5.60 CSF £22.50 CT £155.41 TOTE £4.00: £1.40, £1.70, £2.90; EX 15.30.
Owner The Kathryn Stud **Bred** The Kathryn Stud Ltd **Trained** Sutton Veny, Wilts

FOCUS
Not the strongest of races but again the pace was solid enough on this testing ground, although few were able to close from behind. The winner is rated to her latest Nottingham form.

3316 ANIXTER IP ASSURED H'CAP 1m 6f 213y

5:20 (5:20) (Class 5) (0-75,75) 4-Y-O+ £2,264 (£673; £336; £168) Stalls Low

Form				RPR
4-02	1		**Ponte Di Rosa**[7] 3086 4-7-13 56 oh4............................ DominicFox(3) 5 (Michael Appleby) *trckd ldr tl led 4f out: drifted lft u.p fnl 2f but r.o wl: eased nr fin* 18/1	69+
0/21	2	2 ¼	**Our Folly**[6] 3102 4-8-7 61 6ex............................(t) FergusSweeney 3 (Stuart Kittow) *in tch: shkn up 4f out: wnt 2nd 2f out: kpt on: no imp on wnr fnl f* 7/2[2]	68
3-51	3	hd	**Handles For Forks (IRE)**[4] 3180 4-8-9 68............................ CharlesBishop(5) 6 (Mick Channon) *hld up: stdy hdwy 6f out: chsng ldrs whn sltly hmpd bnd wl over 2f out: sn rdn and unable qck: kpt on same pce* 9/4[1]	76+
30-	4	6	**Kahsabelle (FR)**[37] 5966 7-8-10 64............................ ChrisCatlin 2 (Venetia Williams) *chsd ldrs: pushed along 6f out: wknd over 4f out: plugged on past btn rivals fnl f* 28/1	63
4651	5	1 ¼	**Achalas (IRE)**[9] 3015 4-9-7 75 6ex............................(b) StevieDonohoe 7 (Heather Main) *s.s: hld up and racd keenly: stdy hdwy 4f out: rdn over 2f out: one pce* 8/1	72
0253	6	2 ¼	**Not Til Monday (IRE)**[10] 2976 6-9-1 69............................(v) TomEaves 1 (J R Jenkins) *led at stdy pce: rdn and hdd 4f out: wknd 3f out* 6/1	63
0-03	7	2 ½	**Devoted (IRE)**[17] 2755 4-9-2 70............................(p) SebSanders 4 (Ralph Beckett) *prom: chsd wnr 3f out to 2f out: sn wknd u.p* 9/2[3]	61
252-	8	58	**Schism**[59] 6891 4-9-7 75............................(b) DaneO'Neill 8 (Jonjo O'Neill) *in rr: sn shkn up and nvr gng wl: lost tch over 5f out: t.o* 12/1	
0-	9	29	**Bold Identity (IRE)**[62] 2649 6-9-3 71............................ RobertHavlin 9 (Richard Phillips) *in tch tl wknd over 5f out: t.o* 50/1	

3m 26.32s (7.32) **Going Correction** +0.50s/f (Yiel) 9 Ran SP% 114.9
Speed ratings (Par 103): **100,98,98,95,94 93,92,61,45**
toteswingers:1&2:£12.60, 2&3:£2.10, 1&3:£4.60 CSF £79.90 CT £201.63 TOTE £16.30: £3.60, £1.70, £1.80; EX 79.70.
Owner Reed, Mould, Gorley & Spershott **Bred** The Woodhaven Stud **Trained** Danethorpe, Notts

FOCUS
A moderate yet competitive staying handicap with a number of the runners having recently won on soft ground, run at a muddling gallop. The winner built on her Yarmouth form despite being 4lb out of the handicap.

3317 COMMSCOPE SOLUTIONS CUSTOMERS ARE KINGS APPRENTICE TRAINING SERIES H'CAP (E. INITIATIVE) (DIV I) 1m 22y

5:50 (5:51) (Class 6) (0-60,60) 4-Y-O+ £1,704 (£503; £251) Stalls Low

Form				RPR
1150	1		**Join Up**[14] 2858 6-9-1 56............................ RachealKneller 10 (Mark Brisbourne) *hld up: gd hdwy 2f out: led ent fnl f: r.o wl* 6/1[2]	67
224-	2	2 ¼	**Know No Fear**[216] 7455 7-8-12 56............................(p) NedCurtis(3) 1 (Alastair Lidderdale) *hld up: hdwy after 2f: sn trcking ldrs: led 2f out: sn edgd rt: hdd ent fnl f: one pce* 7/1	62
4525	3	3 ¾	**So Is She (IRE)**[16] 2804 4-8-3 51............................(be) RobertTart(7) 7 (Alan Bailey) *in tch: effrt 2f out: sn chsng ldrs: kpt on same pce fnl f* 7/1	48
4403	4	shd	**Georgebernardshaw (IRE)**[2] 3257 7-9-5 60............................ NoraLooby 4 (Richard Guest) *s.s: sn in tch: chsng ldrs whn nt clr run 2f out: styd on same pce u.p* 3/1[1]	57
5545	5	2	**Gazboolou**[14] 2858 8-8-8 49............................(t) NicoleNordblad 2 (Henry Candy) *hld up in rr: nt clr run over 2f out tl swtchd lft over 1f out: r.o fnl f: nt rch ldrs* 13/2[3]	45
6544	6	4 ½	**Princess Gail**[84] 1095 4-8-8 49............................ JackDuern 6 (Mark Brisbourne) *hld up: rdn over 2f out: nt qckn* 11/1	31
1044	7	½	**Rigid**[12] 2937 5-8-12 53............................ GeorgeDowning 8 (Tony Carroll) *sddle slipped on way to post: led 1f: chsd ldrs: rdn over 2f out: wknd over 1f out* 11/1	34
0500	8	3 ½	**Bertie Blu Boy**[44] 1961 4-8-5 46............................ DannyBrock 9 (Paul Green) *in tch on outer: effrt over 2f out: wknd over 1f out* 20/1	19
5416	9	10	**Sky Diamond (IRE)**[16] 2804 4-8-13 54............................(b) JoshBaudains 5 (John Mackie) *sn pressing ldr: rdn 3f out: led over 2f out: sn hdd: wknd qckly: t.o* 7/1	
000-	10	10	**Mistress Shy**[351] 3726 5-8-2 46 oh1............................ NoelGarbutt(3) 3 (Michael Appleby) *racd keenly: led after 1f tl hdd over 2f out: wknd qckly: t.o* 50/1	

1m 45.77s (4.77) **Going Correction** +0.50s/f (Yiel) 10 Ran SP% 113.5
Speed ratings (Par 101): **96,93,90,89,87 83,82,79,69,59**
toteswingers:1&2:£6.60, 2&3:£8.60, 1&3:£5.20 CSF £46.25 CT £305.66 TOTE £5.60: £1.50, £2.30, £2.90; EX 43.40.
Owner P R Kirk **Bred** A S Reid **Trained** Great Ness, Shropshire
■ Stewards' Enquiry : Nora Looby seven-day ban: used whip contrary to race conditions (Jul 5-11)

FOCUS
This apprentice handicap was another truly run affair and, despite there being plenty in contention approaching the final furlong, the field were strung out crossing the line. It was the slower division and the form is not the most solid.
Mistress Shy Official explanation: trainer said mare was unsuited by the soft ground

3318 COMMSCOPE SOLUTIONS CUSTOMERS ARE KINGS APPRENTICE TRAINING SERIES H'CAP (E. INITIATIVE) (DIV II) 1m 22y

6:20 (6:20) (Class 6) (0-60,58) 4-Y-O+ £1,704 (£503; £251) Stalls Low

Form				RPR
2430	1		**Polar Auroras**[5] 3153 4-9-1 54............................(t) GeorgeDowning 8 (Tony Carroll) *s.s: hld up in rr: gd hdwy over 2f out: led gng wl over 1f out: rdn out* 6/1	64
0410	2	3	**Titan Diamond (IRE)**[30] 2366 4-8-10 49............................ RachealKneller 9 (Mark Usher) *chsd ldrs tl lost pl 4f out: clsd again 2f out: wnt 2nd 1f out: no imp on wnr* 11/2[3]	52
0364	3	nk	**Rapid Water**[8] 3043 6-9-2 58............................ WilliamTwiston-Davies(3) 3 (Pat Eddery) *in tch: clsd to chse ldrs 3f out: styd towards ins in st: kpt on same pce fnl f* 4/1[2]	60
6505	4	2 ½	**Whats For Pudding (IRE)**[6] 3115 4-8-11 50............................ JasonHart 1 (Declan Carroll) *led: rdn over 2f out: hdd over 1f out: one pce* 10/3[1]	47
4-35	5	1 ¾	**Diddums**[9] 3006 6-8-10 56............................ SemiraPashai(7) 7 (Alastair Lidderdale) *dwlt: in rr: nudged along and hdwy 2f out: nvr trbld ldrs* 12/1	49
0015	6	10	**Hilbre Court (USA)**[29] 2401 7-8-6 45............................(v) DannyBrock 2 (Brian Baugh) *sn pushed along: chsd ldrs: rdn 3f out: wknd 2f out* 7/1	15
-500	7	2 ¼	**Alexs Rainbow (USA)**[24] 2555 4-9-1 54............................ IanBurns 5 (Peter Hiatt) *trckd ldr: rdn over 2f out: wknd over 1f out* 15/2	18
5-00	8	4 ½	**Ayaarah (IRE)**[148] 296 4-8-8 52............................(b) EvaMoscrop(5) 10 (William Knight) *racd keenly: hld up in midfield: pushed along and wknd over 2f out* 16/1	
0560	9	12	**Ellielusive (IRE)**[12] 2915 5-8-8 47............................ JackDuern 4 (Mark Brisbourne) *v.s.a: in rr: rdn over 3f out: sn lost tch: t.o* 28/1	

1m 44.89s (3.89) **Going Correction** +0.50s/f (Yiel) 9 Ran SP% 114.0
Speed ratings (Par 101): **100,97,96,94,92 82,80,75,63**
toteswingers:1&2:£4.10, 2&3:£6.40, 1&3:£7.80 CSF £38.39 CT £147.73 TOTE £5.60: £2.80, £1.90, £1.50; EX 47.10.
Owner Balding, Davenport, Hayman, Prestwich **Bred** P Balding **Trained** Cropthorne, Worcs

FOCUS
Plenty of pace on for division two of this apprentice handicap and it was no surprise to see the finishers dominate. Again there were few solid coming into this.
Alexs Rainbow(USA) Official explanation: jockey said filly stopped quickly
Ellielusive(IRE) Official explanation: jockey said mare was slowly away and stopped quickly
T/Plt: £127.20 to a £1 stake. Pool of £34,188.74 - 196.08 winning tickets. T/Qpdt: £12.50 to a £1 stake. Pool of £3,618.93 - 214.12 winning tickets. RL

3319 - 3321a (Foreign Racing) - See Raceform Interactive

3089 LEOPARDSTOWN (L-H)

Thursday, June 21

OFFICIAL GOING: Soft changing to heavy after race 3 (6:55)

3322a GLENCAIRN STKS (LISTED RACE) 1m

7:30 (7:35) 3-Y-O+ £21,666 (£6,333; £3,000; £1,000)

			RPR
1		**Takar (IRE)**[26] 2514 3-9-2 105............................(t) JohnnyMurtagh 2 (John M Oxx, Ire) *trckd ldrs in 3rd: swtchd lft to chal and led 1f out: sn asserted and styd on wl: easily* 4/7[1]	107+
2	4 ¼	**Soul Custody (CAN)**[26] 2515 5-9-6 93............................ FranBerry 3 (M J Grassick, Ire) *disp ld: rdn to ld early st: sn strly pressed and hdd 1f out: no ch w wnr fnl f: kpt on one pce* 25/1	91
3	½	**Bible Black (IRE)**[25] 2524 3-9-2 97............................ GaryCarroll 4 (G M Lyons, Ire) *hld up in rr racing keenly: rdn ent st and stl 5th over 1f out: kpt on u.p into 3rd fnl f: no ch w easy wnr* 14/1	94+
4	1 ½	**Simla Sunset (IRE)**[17] 2777 6-9-6 89............................(p) ChrisHayes 7 (P J Prendergast, Ire) *led or disp ld: rdn and hdd early st: no ex ins fnl f* 8/1[3]	86
5	1	**Akeed Wafi (IRE)**[67] 1401 3-8-13 102............................ NGMcCullagh 5 (John M Oxx, Ire) *racd in 4th: rdn early st and no imp over 1f out: kpt on one pce* 5/2[2]	85

1m 50.12s (8.92) **Going Correction** +1.20s/f (Soft)
WFA 3 from 4yo+ 10lb 5 Ran SP% 113.8
Speed ratings: **103,98,98,96,95**
CSF £17.38 TOTE £1.50: £1.20, £4.90; DF 12.70.
Owner H H Aga Khan **Bred** His Highness The Aga Khan's Studs S C **Trained** Currabeg, Co Kildare

FOCUS
The blot on his copybook after a disappointing effort in the Irish 2000 Guineas was put behind Takar with a most decisive victory here.

NOTEBOOK
Takar(IRE) ◆ had to switch to the inside to get a run in the straight but when seeing daylight and asked for his effort he quickened well and drew right away inside the last furlong. It wasn't the strongest of contests but he couldn't have done it more emphatically and this sort of ground seems to be what he wants. (op 8/13 tchd 4/6)
Soul Custody(CAN) is one that could be interesting as the season goes on. She raced towards the front and found a bit when challenged but eventually the winner was far too good. She's likely to progress a bit further on better ground.
Bible Black(IRE) was struggling a bit in last place before turning out of the back straight and staying on to reasonable effect. He could be a horse that will be difficult to place this season.
Simla Sunset(IRE) was also ridden positively and had every chance if she was good enough when in front turning in. She just wasn't good enough. (op 12/1)
Akeed Wafi(IRE) floundered in the conditions in the straight but he will be seen in a better light on better ground.. (op 9/4 tchd 11/4)

3323 - 3325a (Foreign Racing) - See Raceform Interactive

3291 **ASCOT** (R-H)

Friday, June 22

OFFICIAL GOING: Soft (standside 8.1, centre, 8.1, farside 8.1, round 5.9)

Rail on Round course on inside line and distances as advertised.

3326 ALBANY STKS (GROUP 3) (FILLIES) 6f

2:30 (2:36) (Class 1) 2-Y-O

£34,026 (£12,900; £6,456; £3,216; £1,614; £810) **Stalls** Centre

Form RPR

1 **1** **Newfangled (USA)**[14] 2892 2-8-12 0 .... WilliamBuick 12 105+
(John Gosden) *w'like: racd keenly: displayed plenty of pce: mde all: shkn up over 1f out: sn over 3 l clr: r.o wl and in command fnl f: pushed out towards fin* **7/4**[1]

1 **2** 2 ½ **Agent Allison**[11] 2977 2-8-12 0 .... JamieSpencer 18 96+
(Peter Chapple-Hyam) *str: lw: hld up: rdn and hdwy over 1f out: r.o ins fnl f: unable to go pce of wnr: snatched 2nd post* **6/1**[2]

01 **3** shd **Premier Steps (IRE)**[42] 2019 2-8-12 0 .... RichardKingscote 10 95
(Tom Dascombe) *in tch: rdn and nt qckn 2f out: kpt on to take 2nd ins fnl f: no ch w wnr: lost 2nd post* **25/1**

1 **4** 1 ¾ **Amazonas (IRE)**[17] 2797 2-8-12 0 .... JohnnyMurtagh 3 90
(Ed Dunlop) *leggy: hld up: pushed along over 2f out: hdwy over 1f out: styd on towards fin: nt pce to mount serious chal* **14/1**

3 **5** ½ **The Gold Cheongsam (IRE)**[27] 2480 2-8-12 0 .... FrankieDettori 1 89
(Jeremy Noseda) *hld up: impr into midfield over 3f out: prog 2f out: wnt 2nd over 1f out: no ch w wnr: lost 2nd ins fnl f: no ex fnl 75yds* **6/1**[2]

5 **6** ½ **Becky Lou (USA)**[36] 2193 2-8-12 0 .... KierenFallon 19 87
(Jeremy Noseda) *leggy: s.i.s: in rr: rdn over 2f out: hdwy over 1f out: kpt on ins fnl f: one pce fnl 75yds: nt pce to mount serious chal* **33/1**

04 **7** 2 ¼ **Ana Emaratiya**[22] 2631 2-8-12 0 .... AmyRyan 11 80
(Kevin Ryan) *trckd ldrs: rdn to take 2nd over 2f out: unable to go w wnr and lost 2nd over 1f out: wknd fnl 100yds* **100/1**

61 **8** 3 ½ **Mary's Daughter**[17] 2783 2-8-12 0 .... PaulHanagan 15 70
(Richard Fahey) *w'like: trckd ldrs: pushed along 3f out: outpcd over 2f out: dropped away fnl f* **28/1**

1 **9** nk **Light Up My Life (IRE)**[27] 2499 2-8-12 0 .... JimmyFortune 17 69
(Richard Hannon) *w'like: leggy: hld up: rdn over 2f out: outpcd after* **25/1**

116 **10** 1 ½ **Judy In Disguise**[23] 2603 2-8-12 0 .... TomQueally 7 64
(Bill Turner) *leggy: racd in cl 2nd pl: rdn and lost 2nd over 2f out: wknd over 1f out* **20/1**

2 **11** 2 **Equitania**[42] 2019 2-8-12 0 .... RyanMoore 9 58
(Richard Hannon) *w'like: racd keenly in midfield: pushed along and outpcd wl over 1f out: bhd after* **20/1**

4 **12** 1 ¼ **Shafaani**[17] 2797 2-8-12 0 .... MartinDwyer 14 55
(Clive Brittain) *w'like: scope: dwlt: bhd: outpcd 3f out: nvr on terms* **100/1**

1213 **13** 1 **All On Red (IRE)**[20] 2715 2-8-12 0 .... StevieDonohoe 6 52
(Tobias B P Coles) *w'like: hld up: impr into midfield over 3f out: rdn over 2f out: no imp over 1f out: outpcd and bhd fnl f* **25/1**

10 **14** 3 ¼ **Tassel**[47] 1891 2-8-12 0 .... RichardHughes 5 42
(Richard Hannon) *lw: trckd ldrs: pushed along over 2f out: sn wknd* **12/1**[3]

1m 16.78s (2.28) **Going Correction** +0.525s/f (Yiel) **14** Ran SP% **108.7**
Speed ratings (Par 100): **105,101,101,99,98 97,94,90,89,87 85,83,82,77**
Swingers:1&2:£2.10, 2&3:£32.20, 1&3:£13.40 CSF £7.85 CT £161.21 TOTE £2.60: £1.30, £2.20, £7.00; EX 10.00 Trifecta £122.60 Pool: £6,595.72 - 39.78 winning units..

Owner H R H Princess Haya Of Jordan **Bred** Darley **Trained** Newmarket, Suffolk

FOCUS

The ground was officially soft on this fourth day of the meeting. The jockeys reported that the ground was riding as described, although there was a stiff headwind. There were three non-runners and Kosika was withdrawn having refused to enter the stalls, while there was a nasty incident when Sendmylovetorose appeared to panic and rear over backwards in the stalls, but thankfully seemed to avoid serious injury. This Group 3 has proved a decent pointer to the Cherry Hinton at Newmarket, with three of the last ten winners following up in that race. The majority of winners, though, failed to go on as 3yos, the exception being last year's scorer Samitar, who recently took the Irish 1,000 Guineas. The field raced up the centre of the track but there was only one in it from an early stage. Newfangled is likely to rate 110+ in time, and the second built on her debut.

NOTEBOOK

Newfangled(USA) ◆ impressed when taking a 6f Newmarket maiden on soft ground on her debut and looked an exciting prospect. She was very keen and soon showed in front racing into a headwind, but when her rider asked her to go over 2f out, she opened up a clear advantage and the race was over. She got a little tired near the finish and the bit slipped through her mouth, but this was still the sort of performance that suggests she is a top-notcher. She will be aimed at the Lowther and Cheveley Park now, and was quoted as long as 16/1 for the 1000 Guineas, which might prove value providing she gets the trip, with her pedigree offering encouragement on that count. (tchd 15-8, 2-1 in places)

Agent Allison bolted up in a Pontefract maiden auction on her debut on good ground but she was held up at the back here before making good late headway, by which time the race was over. She is clearly a decent sort and perhaps the Cherry Hinton will be next for her, although connections are looking to step up in distance. (op 13-2 tchd 7-1)

Premier Steps(IRE), a half-sister to five winners, had made an encouraging debut against colts in a race that worked out well and then scored over 5f here next time (beating Equitania). The soft ground was no problem and she went in pursuit of the winner, which might have cost her the runner-up spot in the end. There is more to come from her.

Amazonas(IRE), the winner of a Yarmouth maiden on fast ground on her debut, appeared to handle the ground but like the runner-up came from a long way back and just picked up the pieces as others tired. (op 16-1)

The Gold Cheongsam(IRE) ran well when third against colts on her debut and moved into contention at halfway. However, she had no more to offer and faded in the last furlong. (op 8-1)

Becky Lou(USA) ◆ finished a close fifth after a slow start on her debut and the form has worked out reasonably well. She handled this step up and showed enough to suggest she will be winning her share of races.

Ana Emaratiya made her debut when slowly away in a York Listed race behind the subsequent Queen Mary winner, but was then beaten on fast ground over this trip last time. She has clearly been held in high regard and went some way to justifying that opinion here, if not lasting home having been close to the pace early.

Mary's Daughter showed up early before fading. (op 25-1 tchd 33-1)

Light Up My Life(IRE) saw plenty of daylight on the outside of the pack.

Tassel had made a winning debut before finishing lame when a well-beaten odds-on favourite next time. She was a market drifter and after showing up just behind the leaders early, faded right away. She may have physical problems that are holding her back. (op 10-1)

3327 KING EDWARD VII STKS (GROUP 2) (C&G) 1m 4f

3:05 (3:08) (Class 1) 3-Y-O **£85,065** (£32,250; £16,140; £8,040; £4,035) **Stalls** Low

Form RPR

1-51 **1** **Thomas Chippendale (IRE)**[14] 2897 3-8-12 96 .... JohnnyMurtagh 5 116
(Sir Henry Cecil) *lw: in tch: rdn to chal whn pushed lft and sltly hmpd over 1f out: rallied jst ins fnl f: led fnl 50yds: pushed out towards fin* **9/2**[3]

-112 **2** ½ **Noble Mission**[34] 2275 3-8-12 110 .... TomQueally 2 115
(Sir Henry Cecil) *in tch: swtchd lft and trying to chal between horses whn squeezed out and hmpd over 1f out: rallied and rdn to ld 1f out: pricked ears and sn drvn: kpt on tl hdd and no ex fnl 50yds* **4/1**[2]

-214 **3** nk **Thought Worthy (USA)**[20] 2705 3-8-12 106 .... WilliamBuick 7 114
(John Gosden) *lw: chsd ldrs: jnd ldr over 3f out: rdn to ld over 2f out: hrd pressed whn hung lft and bmpd rivals over 1f out: hdd 1f out: one pce u.p after* **8/1**

3-13 **4** 9 **Astrology (IRE)**[20] 2705 3-8-12 115 .... RyanMoore 6 100
(A P O'Brien, Ire) *lw: led and set stdy gallop: jnd and qcknd 3f out: drvn and hdd over 1f out: btn ent fnl f: fdd* **8/11**[1]

4-1 **5** 14 **Initiator**[25] 2560 3-8-12 84 .... RichardHughes 1 78
(Jeremy Noseda) *heavily restrained leaving stalls: t.k.h: hld up in detached last: clsd and in tch 4f out: rdn 3f out: sn outpcd and wl btn after* **25/1**

2m 35.41s (2.91) **Going Correction** +0.35s/f (Good) **5** Ran SP% **111.0**
Speed ratings (Par 111): **104,103,103,97,88**
CSF £22.04 TOTE £5.80: £1.90, £1.60; EX 22.00.

Owner Sir Robert Ogden **Bred** Premier Bloodstock **Trained** Newmarket, Suffolk
■ A 1-2 for Sir Henry Cecil.

FOCUS

Only five runners - the smallest field since the race was staged at York in 2005 - and they included the third and fourth from the Derby, but that pair did nothing to advertise Camelot's Epsom form. It rates a below-average renewal but the first pair are progressive.

NOTEBOOK

Thomas Chippendale(IRE) tends to race keenly, and he did so again, but that didn't stop him coping with this significant rise in class, following up a 1m2f handicap win gained off just 86. His juvenile maiden success had been well advertised by the runner-up Went The Day Well (Grade 3 winner and fourth in Kentucky Derby), and Sir Henry Cecil's colt has himself progressed to a smart level despite still being immature. There ought to be more to come provided he goes the right way mentally, and his trainer has one eye on the St Leger. (op 6-1)

Noble Mission, upped to this trip for the first time, reversed Newmarket form with Thought Worthy on 5lb better terms. He was badly bumped by the third in the closing stages, but it didn't cost him and he basically wasn't quite good enough. Like his winning stablemate, he still has a lot of growing up to do. (tchd 9-2)

Thought Worthy(USA), from whom a bit better could have been expected, considering the ground and track looked more suitable than he faced at Epsom, and he was well placed, but he didn't do enough, hanging left when tired late on. Perhaps his recent exertions have taken the edge off him, but it seems probable that he just wasn't quite up to it. He has a little way to go if he's to further emulate his brother Lucarno (runner-up in this race after fourth in the Derby) by winning the St Leger. (op 13-2)

Astrology(IRE) set the pace, as he had in the Derby, and appeared to go steady early on, but he was beaten at the top of the straight. Clearly he didn't run his race, but it's hard to blame the ground considering he'd won the Dee Stakes on soft and he might be best swerved in the short term. Official explanation: trainer said colt ran flat (op 4-5 tchd 4-6)

Initiator was a clear-cut winner of a Windsor maiden (1m2f, good to firm) on his reappearance, but he refused to settle in this better class under vastly different conditions.

3328 CORONATION STKS (BRITISH CHAMPIONS SERIES) (GROUP 1) (FILLIES) 1m (R)

3:45 (3:45) (Class 1) 3-Y-O

£154,534 (£58,587; £29,321; £14,606; £7,330; £3,678) **Stalls** Low

Form RPR

5-16 **1** **Fallen For You**[41] 2078 3-9-0 108 .... WilliamBuick 11 118
(John Gosden) *lw: hld up: swtchd lft arnd the field and hdwy 2f out: led over 1f out: sn edgd rt: r.o wl to draw clr and in command ins fnl f* **12/1**

-423 **2** 3 ¼ **Starscope**[35] 2232 3-9-0 104 .... JimmyFortune 5 110
(John Gosden) *lw: racd keenly in midfield: hdwy on outer whn sltly intimidated 2f out: effrt whn n.m.r briefly over 1f out but unable to go w wnr: wnt 2nd jst ins fnl f: kpt on: no imp* **11/1**

10 **3** 2 ¼ **Irish History (IRE)**[22] 2641 3-9-0 94 .... MickaelBarzalona 1 105
(Mahmood Al Zarooni) *lw: trckd ldrs: effrt and wandered 2f out: chalng over 1f out: sn unable to go w wnr: styd on same pce ins fnl f* **11/1**

-001 **4** 2 **Samitar**[26] 2527 3-9-0 112 .... MartinHarley 4 100
(Mick Channon) *lw: mostly disp 2nd: effrt to chal over 1f out: nt qckn: one pce ins fnl f* **9/2**[3]

1-4 **5** nse **Bugie D'Amore**[19] 2742 3-9-0 103 ....(t) MaximeGuyon 9 100
(A De Royer-Dupre, France) *w'like: hld up: hdwy 2f out: chsd ldrs over 1f out: kpt on u.p but no imp* **14/1**

1011 **6** 5 **Laugh Out Loud**[19] 2742 3-9-0 111 .... FrankieDettori 6 89
(Mick Channon) *mostly disp 2nd tl effrt to chal over 2f out: wknd over 1f out* **7/2**[2]

3-10 **7** ¾ **Intense Pink**[20] 2713 3-9-0 90 .... ChrisCatlin 3 87
(Chris Wall) *midfield: pushed along over 2f out: wknd wl over 1f out* **33/1**

0114 **8** 3 ¼ **Homecoming Queen (IRE)**[26] 2527 3-9-0 119 .... JPO'Brien 2 80
(A P O'Brien, Ire) *led: pushed along over 2f out: rdn and hdd over 1f out: sn wknd* **9/4**[1]

26-0 **9** 12 **Russelliana**[65] 1454 3-9-0 103 .... RyanMoore 10 52
(Sir Michael Stoute) *hld up: pushed along over 2f out: sn lft bhd* **33/1**

1- **10** 30 **Cardigan (IRE)**[273] 6291 3-9-0 88 .... PaulHanagan 7
(William Haggas) *hld up in rr: struggling over 2f out: sn lft bhd: t.o* **12/1**

1m 42.95s (2.25) **Going Correction** +0.525s/f (Yiel) **10** Ran SP% **115.8**
Speed ratings (Par 110): **109,105,103,101,101 96,95,92,80,50**
Swingers:1&2:£12.80, 2&3:£15.70, 1&3:£16.10 CSF £135.30 CT £1524.30 TOTE £13.90: £3.60, £3.20, £2.60; EX 141.30 Trifecta £2032.30 Pool: £18,840.00 - 6.86 winning units..

Owner Normandie Stud Ltd **Bred** Normandie Stud Ltd **Trained** Newmarket, Suffolk
■ A 1-2 for John Gosden.

FOCUS

The roll of honour for this Group 1 is littered with Classic winners who followed up in this, including the likes of Russian Rhythm, Attraction and Ghanaati in the last ten years, but it has also proved a pointer to future events, with three of the last four winners going on to beat older rivals at the highest level later in the season. This year's line-up was pretty much up to standard, with the winners of the Newmarket and Irish Guineas re-opposing, although some of the interest was lost with the withdrawal of Maybe. The pace was fairly sound but there were several in line early in the straight before the winner asserted. Fallen For You is entitled to rate the best 3yo miling filly.

NOTEBOOK

Fallen For You, a dual winner at up to this trip on fast ground and Polytrack, but beaten in all three previous tries in Group company (although only narrowly once), had never encountered soft ground previously. However, she was the pick of stable jockey William Buick, and produced a strong run around the outside of her field to score going away. She did hang across her rivals once in front but was the winner on merit. Presumably races such as the Falmouth will be under consideration now. (op 14-1 tchd 16-1)

Starscope has looked quirky at times, notably when playing up ahead of a below-par run over 1m2f at Newbury last time, but she had earlier finished runner-up in the 1000 Guineas. Dropped in trip, she travelled well in mid-division before making her move off the turn but did not have the speed of her stablemate, although she was done no favours by that filly in the closing stages. (op 8-1)

Irish History(IRE), closely rated to the same owner's Group-class 1m-1m3f performer Echo Of Light, made a winning debut over 1m at Windsor but was keen and ran into traffic problems on her second start. Up in class and with the ground an unknown, she was never far away and stuck on well under pressure, like the first two racing wide of the rail in the straight. (tchd 12-1)

Samitar ◆ won the Albany Stakes at this meeting last year on just her second start and went close in the Fillies' Mile. Back to form when taking the Irish 1000 Guineas on her previous outing, she was always close to the pace and did best of those to race prominently, so can probably be given extra credit. (tchd 5-1 in places)

Bugie D'Amore beat a subsequent dual winner in a Group 3 in Italy when trained there in 2011 but had finished fourth to Laugh Out Loud on her debut for this yard last time. She came from well back to reverse placings with that filly and is open to further progress. (op 16-1)

Laugh Out Loud had won four of her six previous starts and improved from her turf debut in the 1000 Guineas, taking a Listed race from a subsequent winner and a Group 2 at Chantilly with today's fifth in fourth. She was another to race close to the leader and paid for her early efforts in the straight. (op 4-1)

Intense Pink ◆ bolted up in a 6f Pontefract maiden on he reappearance when the time was very good in the conditions, and ran a creditable race back on this ground, having been well beaten in a Listed race on fast. She should be up to winning a Pattern race.

Homecoming Queen(IRE) is well suited by soft ground and ran away with the 1000 Guineas when there was cut. However, she was beaten by Samitar in the Irish version on good ground and, after making the running, faded pretty quickly. Joseph O'Brien, subsequently reported that the filly lost her action. Official explanation: jockey said filly lost its action (op 5-2)

3329 WOLFERTON H'CAP (LISTED RACE) 1m 2f

4:25 (4:25) (Class 1) (0-110,108) 4-Y-O+

£31,190 (£11,825; £5,918; £2,948; £1,479; £742) **Stalls** Low

Form RPR

4-11 **1** **Gatewood**[21] 2655 4-8-11 **98** .... WilliamBuick 8 109+
(John Gosden) *in tch: pushed lft and hmpd after 1f: settled in midfield after: swtchd lft and effrt over 2f out: hdwy u.p over 1f out: chal fnl 150yds: drvn and styd on wl to ld fnl 50yds* **3/1**[1]

-444 **2** *nk* **Black Spirit (USA)**[21] 2655 5-8-13 **100** .... (t) AdamKirby 12 110
(Clive Cox) *hld up in last quartet: effrt and rdn 2f out: swtchd lft and hdwy wl over 1f out: drvn and styd on wl ins fnl f: wnt 2nd last strides and clsng on wnr at fin* **20/1**

42-3 **3** *hd* **Mijhaar**[36] 2211 4-9-1 **102** .... NeilCallan 2 112+
(Roger Varian) *lw: t.k.h: chsd ldrs: rdn and qcknd to ld over 1f out: drvn ent fnl f: battled on gamely tl hdd and lost 2 pls fnl 50yds* **9/2**[2]

1121 **4** *¾* **Qaraaba**[14] 2884 5-9-0 **101** .... GeorgeBaker 14 109
(Seamus Durack) *taken down early: stdd and dropped in bhd after s: hld up in rr: rdn and effrt on outer 2f out: styd on wl ins fnl f: nvr quite gng pce to rch ldrs* **9/2**[2]

5-13 **5** *nk* **Retrieve (AUS)**[27] 2478 5-9-7 **108** .... FrankieDettori 3 116
(Saeed Bin Suroor) *t.k.h: hld up in tch: rdn and effrt 2f out: hdwy u.p to chse ldr ent fnl f tl fnl 150yds: styd on same pce after* **14/1**

01-0 **6** *nk* **Kirthill (IRE)**[37] 2176 4-8-13 **100** .... RyanMoore 4 107
(Luca Cumani) *hld up in tch in midfield: rdn and effrt 2f out: hdwy and edgd rt and hdwy over 1f out: kpt on wl u.p ins fnl f: nt rch ldrs* **9/1**[3]

0230 **7** *1 ¾* **Sirvino**[18] 2773 7-8-11 **98** .... RichardHughes 9 101
(David Barron) *hld up in midfield: effrt and n.m.r briefly 2f out: swtchd lft and rdn over 1f out: styd on same pce fnl f* **12/1**

46-4 **8** *2 ¼* **Opera Gal (IRE)**[27] 2478 5-8-10 **97** .... DavidProbert 11 96
(Andrew Balding) *racd keenly: chsd ldr tl over 7f out: wnt 2nd again 5f out tl over 1f out: wknd ins fnl f* **33/1**

9 *¾* **Hyper (USA)**[35] 5-8-13 **100** .... (v[1]) JohnnyMurtagh 15 97
(Chad C Brown, U.S.A) *rangy: stdd and dropped in after s: bhd: rdn and hung lft bnd over 2f out: sn outpcd and looked wl btn: rallied over 1f out: kpt on but no threat to ldrs fnl f* **25/1**

01-3 **10** *2* **Con Artist (IRE)**[18] 2773 5-9-1 **102** .... SilvestreDeSousa 7 95
(Saeed Bin Suroor) *led: rdn and qcknd over 2f out: drvn and hdd 2f out: btn 1f out: wknd ins fnl f* **16/1**

106- **11** *1 ¼* **French Navy**[244] 7027 4-9-7 **108** .... MickaelBarzalona 10 99
(Mahmood Al Zarooni) *stdd s: t.k.h: hld up towards rr: hdwy 5f out: chsd ldrs and rdn ent fnl 2f: no ex and btn ent fnl f: fdd* **9/1**[3]

14-0 **12** *9* **Beachfire**[41] 2081 5-9-4 **105** .... (b) PaulHanagan 1 78
(John Gosden) *plld hrd: hld up in towards rr: rdn and no rspnse over 2f out: sn wl btn* **20/1**

4302 **13** *3 ¼* **Ottoman Empire (FR)**[21] 2655 6-9-1 **102** .... JamesDoyle 6 68
(David Simcock) *lw: pushed along to go prom after s: edgd lft after 1f: chsd ldr over 7f out tl 5f out: rdn and btn 2f out: sn wknd* **25/1**

2m 8.0s (0.60) **Going Correction** +0.35s/f (Good) **13** Ran SP% **121.8**
Speed ratings (Par 111): **111,110,110,110,109 109,108,106,105,104 103,95,93**
Swingers:1&2:£18.10, 2&3:£25.40, 1&3:£3.10 CSF £73.22 CT £277.12 TOTE £4.20: £1.90, £6.30, £2.30; EX 96.40 Trifecta £518.30 Pool: £13,848.63 - 19.77 winning units..
Owner George Strawbridge **Bred** George Strawbridge **Trained** Newmarket, Suffolk

FOCUS

A high-quality handicap and a strong pace set it up for the closers. Rock-solid handicap form, with the winner continuing to progress.

NOTEBOOK

Gatewood made it 3-3 for the season, defying a 7lb rise and a mark 12lb higher than at the beginning of the campaign. He was just about ideally placed by a rider enjoying a most impressive Royal Ascot, being waited with off the decent gallop before challenging out wide, well away from the possibly slow rail. He shapes as though he may improve again for 1m4f and is one of six John Gosden-trained horses currently entered in the Group 2 Princess of Wales's Stakes at the Newmarket July meeting, but that sort of company will be a lot tougher. (op 11-4 tchd 10-3, 7-2 in places and 5-2 in a place)

Black Spirit(USA) ran well from an unhelpful draw at Epsom on his previous start and he finished strongly here from well back. He reportedly returned with a nasty cut on a hind leg, but could go to York for the John Smith's Cup. (op 25-1)

Mijhaar ◆ managed only third but there's little doubt he's well handicapped. He was free to post, and in the race itself, and fared best of those handy, as well as best of those towards the possibly unfavoured inside rail after edging right under pressure. It remains to be seen if he'll settle well enough to fulfil his potential, but there's a nice prize in him if he does, and maybe he'll be one for the John Smith's Cup at York. (op 7-2 tchd 5-1 in places)

Qaraaba, taken to post early, raced last for much of the way after being dropped in from her wide draw, and she just got going too late. She reportedly may now look for black-type in fillies-only events. (op 7-1)

Retrieve(AUS) was second best of those handy. This was a smart effort under joint-top weight.

Kirthill(IRE) was going on at the finish and his effort may want marking up a touch as he ended up towards the possibly unfavoured inside rail. (op 12-1 tchd 14-1)

Sirvino stayed on past beaten horses, but he was never a threat. (op 14-1 tchd 16-1)

Opera Gal(IRE) paid for chasing the hot pace and couldn't reverse recent form with the similarly ridden Retrieve.

Hyper(USA) is a prolific winner in relatively minor company in the US, but he was up slightly in trip and it's doubtful this ground would have been suitable for his British debut. (op 22-1 tchd 20-1, 33-1 in a place)

Beachfire, last year's winner off 7lb lower, was much too keen this time. (tchd 22-1)

3330 QUEEN'S VASE (GROUP 3) 2m

5:00 (5:00) (Class 1) 3-Y-O

£34,026 (£12,900; £6,456; £3,216; £1,614; £810) **Stalls** Low

Form RPR

0-1 **1** **Estimate (IRE)**[47] 1893 3-8-12 86 .... RyanMoore 8 106
(Sir Michael Stoute) *w'like: scope: str: hld up in midfield: hdwy over 3f out: led 2f out: sn edgd rt: styd on wl to draw clr ins fnl f* **3/1**[1]

-453 **2** *5* **Athens (IRE)**[26] 2524 3-9-1 104 .... JPO'Brien 12 103
(A P O'Brien, Ire) *w'like: scope: hld up: nt clr run over 2f out: hdwy sn after: rdn and hung rt whn chsd wnr over 1f out: no imp fnl f* **11/2**[3]

1110 **3** *1 ½* **Ed De Gas**[41] 2080 3-9-1 97 .... ChrisCatlin 10 101
(Rae Guest) *hld up: rdn and hdwy 2f out: wnt 3rd chsng ldrs over 1f out: kpt on u.p but no imp ins fnl f* **8/1**

4 **4** *2* **Macbeth (IRE)**[14] 2901 3-9-1 98 .... JohnnyMurtagh 6 99
(K J Condon, Ire) *w'like: trckd ldrs: moved upsides 3f out: led over 2f out: sn hdd: carried rt sltly wl over 1f out: kpt on same pce appr fnl f* **6/1**

2150 **5** *½* **Minimise Risk**[20] 2705 3-9-1 101 .... JamieSpencer 4 98
(Andrew Balding) *trckd ldrs: effrt over 2f out: carried rt sltly wl over 1f out: nt qckn: one pce fnl f* **13/2**

2-63 **6** *5* **Perennial**[28] 2445 3-9-1 97 .... MichaelHills 2 92
(Charles Hills) *lw: midfield: effrt over 2f out: nt clr run wl over 1f out: sn u.p and unable to pick-up: wl btn fnl f* **12/1**

31 **7** *½* **Yazdi (IRE)**[48] 1867 3-9-1 90 .... FrankieDettori 9 92
(Brian Meehan) *chsd ldr: led narrowly 3f out: hdd over 2f out: carried rt sltly whn wkng wl over 1f out* **9/2**[2]

-310 **8** *6* **Singalat**[9] 3042 3-9-1 80 .... JimCrowley 1 84
(James Given) *led: pushed along over 3f out: sn hdd: rdn and wknd over 1f out* **50/1**

3231 **9** *3 ¼* **Somemothersdohavem**[8] 3087 3-9-1 66 .... (p) AdamKirby 5 81?
(John Ryan) *sluggish s: in rr: struggling 3f out: lft bhd fnl 2f: nvr on terms* **50/1**

-412 **10** *4 ½* **Flying Trader (USA)**[29] 2427 3-9-1 79 .... RichardHughes 7 75
(Jane Chapple-Hyam) *b: hld up: struggling 3f out: lft bhd fnl 2f: nvr on terms* **33/1**

3m 34.05s (5.05) **Going Correction** +0.35s/f (Good) **10** Ran SP% **111.9**
Speed ratings (Par 109): **101,98,97,96,96 94,93,90,89,86**
Swingers:1&2:£4.00, 2&3:£7.80, 1&3:£5.10 CSF £18.34 CT £115.59 TOTE £3.70: £1.50, £2.20, £2.80; EX 17.00 Trifecta £245.30 Pool: £16,646.45 - 50.20 winning units..
Owner The Queen **Bred** His Highness The Aga Khan's Studs S C **Trained** Newmarket, Suffolk

FOCUS

A 2m race for 3yos at this meeting should theoretically provide pointers to the following season's Gold Cup, but only two of the last ten winners even took part the following year, with Patkai (runner-up) doing best. To be fair Mahler did go on to finish second in the St Leger and third in the Melbourne Cup in 2007, but otherwise it has rarely proved a useful guide to future staying events. This year's running had a field of mixed abilities, with official ratings beforehand ranging from 66-104. This was a tough test in the conditions for these young stayers, but the only filly in the race really appreciated conditions and provided a Royal winner at the meeting. The form makes a fair bit of sense amongst the first six.

NOTEBOOK

Estimate(IRE) ◆, a half-sister to three smart performers, including the Ascot Gold Cup winner Enzeli, was a good winner of a maiden on her second start over 1m4f at Salisbury. She handled cut that day and relished it and the longer trip here, powering away once hitting the front. This strong stayer could well make up into a Park Hill filly and the Cup races may be on her agenda next year if she progresses sufficiently. (tchd 11-4, 7-2 in a place and 10-3 in places)

Athens(IRE), a winner at up to 1m2f who handles soft ground, had been beaten in all four tries at Group level but coped well with the big step up in trip, if no match for the winner. (op 5-1 tchd 9-2)

Ed De Gas had won his first three starts before being well held in the Lingfield Derby trial. He had bolted up on his only try on turf (soft going) and ran well having been held up, if not able to stay with the winner. (op 10-1)

Macbeth(IRE) stays 1m4f and had been placed in Listed company on heavy ground. Stepping up in distance but not bred to stay, he weakened after being in the first three for most of the journey and keen early. A drop back to middle-distances looks likely. (op 7-1 tchd 8-1)

Minimise Risk, a winner on soft on his reappearance but beaten in the Chester Vase and Derby since, appeared to travel well in the wake of the leaders but, after not getting much room early in the straight, failed to pick up and probably did not last the trip. (op 5-1)

Perennial, placed in Group and Listed company, was taking a big step up in trip but had never raced on a soft surface and was one of the first to come under the pump. (op 10-1 tchd 14-1)

Yazdi(IRE), an easy winner over 1m4f on easy ground at Thirsk, was taking a big step up in trip and grade and was found out after racing close to the pace. (tchd 5-1 in a place)

Singalat winner of a fast ground Chester handicap in May off 76, had a lot to find and dropped away after making much of the running. (tchd 66-1)

3331 BUCKINGHAM PALACE STKS (H'CAP) 7f

5:35 (5:40) (Class 2) (0-105,105) 3-Y-O+

£46,687 (£13,980; £6,990; £3,495; £1,747; £877) **Stalls** Centre

Form RPR

2-50 **1** **Eton Forever (IRE)**[27] 2472 5-9-8 **103** .... NeilCallan 11 115
(Roger Varian) *racd far side: in tch in midfield: rdn and qcknd to ld gp and led overall jst over 1f out: styd on strly: rdn out* **14/1**

66-0 **2** *1 ¾* **Jamesie (IRE)**[18] 2778 4-8-11 **92** .... JohnnyMurtagh 23 99
(David Marnane, Ire) *racd nr side: stdd s: hld up towards rr: rdn and effrt: pressed gp ldrs and ch overall 1f out: outpcd by wnr on far side but kpt on to go 2nd ins fnl f: 1st of 10 in gp* **16/1**

20-0 **3** *½* **Atlantic Sport (USA)**[14] 2896 7-8-11 **92** .... MartinHarley 32 98
(Mick Channon) *racd nr side: hld up towards rr: swtchd rt and effrt wl over 1f out: hdwy to chse gp ldrs and nt clr run jst ins fnl f: swtchd rt and styd on wl fnl 100yds: 2nd of 10 in gp* **20/1**

5131 **4** *¾* **Global Village (IRE)**[41] 2068 7-8-13 **94** .... KierenFallon 25 98
(Brian Ellison) *racd nr side: in tch: pushed along 3f out: rdn and hdwy to ld gp and pressing overall ldrs 2f out: edgd lft over 1f out: outpcd by wnr on far side and one pce fnl f: 3rd of 10 in gp* **4/1**[1]

510- **5** 1 **Decent Fella (IRE)**[265] 6521 6-9-1 **96**......................(vt) JimmyFortune 28 97
(Andrew Balding) *racd nr side: in tch: rdn to press gp ldr and ch overall 2f out: unable qck 1f out: styd on same pce fnl f: 4th of 10 in gp* **16/1**

0-52 **6** shd **Directorship**[22] 2642 6-8-11 **92**.......................... FergusSweeney 18 93+
(Patrick Chamings) *racd far side: stdd s: t.k.h: hld up in rr: hdwy on far rail over 2f out: nt clr run and swtchd lft over 1f out: styd on u.p fnl f: no threat to wnr: 2nd of 13 in gp* **20/1**

0020 **7** 1 **Belgian Bill**[2] 3268 4-9-1 **99**..............................(t) SeanLevey(3) 2 97
(George Baker) *racd far side: in tch: rdn and effrt to ld overall wl over 1f out: sn hdd and unable qck: outpcd by wnr and plugged on same pce fnl f: 3rd of 13 in gp* **14/1**

-101 **8** ¾ **Tariq Too**[13] 2919 5-9-0 **98**................................ HarryBentley(3) 9 94
(Amy Weaver) *swtg: racd far side: hld up towards rr: hdwy on far rail 2f out: drvn and pressed ldrs over 1f out: no ex and btn whn edgd lft 1f out: outpcd fnl 150yds: 4th of 13 in gp* **16/1**

-501 **9** 1 **Emilio Largo**[24] 2590 4-8-11 **92**.............................. TomQueally 19 86
(Sir Henry Cecil) *racd nr side: in tch: rdn and effrt to press ldrs 2f out: unable qck ent fnl f: btn whn carried lft and short of room ent fnl f: wknd ins fnl f: 5th of 10 in gp* **8/1**[2]

3003 **10** nk **Mia's Boy**[10] 3004 8-8-13 **94**.................................... AndreaAtzeni 3 87
(Chris Dwyer) *racd far side: hld up in midfield: rdn and effrt 2f out: edgd lft and no imp ent fnl f: plugged on same pce after: 5th of 13 in gp* **16/1**

5211 **11** nk **Imperial Djay (IRE)**[13] 2910 7-9-2 **97**........................ PJMcDonald 6 89
(Ruth Carr) *racd far side: hld up towards rr: rdn and effrt 2f out: no ch w wnr but kpt on u.p fnl f: 6th of 13 in gp* **12/1**[3]

06-0 **12** 2 **Imperial Guest**[41] 2068 6-8-11 **95**........................ AshleyHamblett(3) 29 81
(George Margarson) *lw: racd nr side: chsd ldrs: rdn and pressed ldrs 2f out: no ex and btn whn nt clr run and hmpd jst over 1f out: no threat to ldrs fnl f: 6th of 10 in gp* **20/1**

0415 **13** 1 **Bronze Prince**[29] 2409 5-9-3 **98**................................ JimCrowley 10 82
(Michael Attwater) *racd far side: stdd s: in tch: rdn and effrt to press ldrs wl over 1f out: no ex and btn 1f out: wknd ins fnl f: 7th of 13 in gp* **28/1**

03-0 **14** ½ **Castles In The Air**[76] 1220 7-9-0 **95**........................ RichardHughes 24 77
(Richard Fahey) *racd nr side: stdd s: hld up in rr: rdn and effrt on stands' rail 2f out: no imp whn nt clr run over 1f out: n.d fnl f: 7th of 10 in gp* **20/1**

10-0 **15** ½ **Valencha**[21] 2654 5-8-10 **91**...................................... DarryllHolland 15 72
(Hughie Morrison) *racd far side: stdd s: t.k.h and racd v awkwardly: hld up in rr: rdn and effrt jst over 2f out: drvn and wknd over 1f out: 8th of 13 in gp* **33/1**

-620 **16** 4½ **Louis The Pious**[13] 2919 4-9-0 **95**..........................(b[1]) PhillipMakin 22 64
(Kevin Ryan) *racd nr side: broke fast: crossed to stands' rail and overall ldr after 1f: hdd 3f out: wknd wl over 1f out: 8th of 10 in gp* **40/1**

2003 **17** 1¾ **Advanced**[16] 2825 9-9-0 **95**.. AmyRyan 8 59
(Kevin Ryan) *racd far side: chsd gp ldr tl led overall 3f out: rdn and hdd wl over 1f out: sn wknd: 9th of 13 in gp* **50/1**

5403 **18** 1½ **Docofthebay (IRE)**[8] 3078 8-8-10 **91**..........................(b) LukeMorris 13 51
(Scott Dixon) *racd far side: hld up in rr: rdn and effrt 2f out: sn no imp and wknd over 1f out: 10th of 13 in gp* **16/1**

1050 **19** 5 **Thunderball**[5] 3183 6-8-11 **92**..............................(p) RussKennemore 1 39
(Scott Dixon) *b: racd far side: chsd ldrs: rdn to press overall ldr 3f out: sn struggling: wknd wl over 1f out: 11th of 13 in gp* **33/1**

-402 **20** 2½ **Spectacle Du Mars (FR)**[59] 1593 5-9-10 **105**.......... GregoryBenoist 26 45
(X Nakkachdji, France) *racd nr side: overall ldr for 1f: chsd ldrs after tl wknd 2f out: bhd fnl f: 9th of 10 in gp* **50/1**

11 **21** ¾ **Primaeval**[29] 2409 6-9-5 **100**..............................(v) HayleyTurner 17 38
(James Fanshawe) *racd far side: in tch: rdn and no rspnse 2f out: sn wknd: bhd fnl f: 12th of 13 in gp* **8/1**[2]

1050 **22** 12 **The Rectifier (USA)**[113] 757 5-9-7 **102**..................(t) FrankieDettori 4
(Jim Boyle) *racd far side: led gp and prom overall: lost pl qckly over 2f out: t.o fnl f: 13th of 13 in gp* **50/1**

-133 **23** 10 **Gossamer Seed (IRE)**[5] 3196 4-9-9 **104**........................(t) JPO'Brien 30
(John Joseph Murphy, Ire) *racd nr side: in tch tl 3f out: sn lost pl and bhd: t.o and eased fnl f: 10th of 10 in gp* **16/1**

1m 29.68s (2.08) **Going Correction** +0.525s/f (Yiel) **23** Ran SP% **135.2**
Speed ratings (Par 109): **109,107,106,105,104 104,103,102,101,100 100,98,97,96,95 90,88,87,81,78 77,63,52**
Swingers:1&2:£77.90, 2&3:£99.30, 1&3:£70.80 CSF £207.16 CT £4533.84 TOTE £17.90: £3.50, £3.90, £8.00, £1.60; EX 303.60 Trifecta £7084.50 Pool: £12,637.24 - 1.32 winning units..
Owner H R H Sultan Ahmad Shah **Bred** Mrs Brid Cosgrove **Trained** Newmarket, Suffolk
■ Stewards' Enquiry : Kieren Fallon two-day ban: careless riding (Jul 8-9)

FOCUS
A competitive and high-class handicap. They split into two groups, with the winner on the far side and the next four home stands' side. The winner rates a 5lb personal best.

NOTEBOOK
Eton Forever(IRE) ◆, who raced far side, produced a really smart performance to win so readily considering the next four finishers were positioned stands' side. He hadn't gone on as expected since taking the 2011 Spring Cup in similar fashion (only fifth in this year's Lincoln), but in fairness he got no sort of run at Chester on his most recent start and this was only the 11th outing of his career. It was undoubtedly his best effort to date and looked the performance of a future Group horse. (op 12-1)
Jamesie(IRE) ◆ showed himself on a decent mark by faring best of the group who raced stands' side. He's an obvious one for the Bunbury Cup. (tchd 14-1)
Atlantic Sport(USA) hasn't won since 2008 and was only 13th in this race last year, but he was on a good mark judged on his best form and left behind a dismal reappearance, despite not getting the clearest of runs. (op 25-1 tchd 28-1)
Global Village(IRE) was 5-10 since joining this trainer, including the C&D Victoria Cup last time, and he had conditions to suit, but it seems a further 6lb rise found him out. (op 5-1 tchd 11-2 in places)
Decent Fella(IRE), fourth in this race last year from 6lb lower, ran well after 265 days off, although he did win on his 2011 reappearance so is not sure to find significant improvement next time.
Directorship was second best of those on the far side and would have been closer with a clearer run, but he was basically beaten by a better-handicapped rival.
Belgian Bill, 12th in the Hunt Cup two days earlier, tends to find little off the bridle and again didn't do enough. He probably needs to be produced as late as possible.
Tariq Too, up 7lb for winning at Doncaster last time, was the only runner to make a move against the far rail and that may not have been the best ground, albeit that's where the winner ended up once the race was in safe keeping. (op 14-1)
Emilio Largo was a winner over 1m on fast ground (off 2lb lower) on his previous start, but he has won on soft and a bit better could have been expected. (tchd 9-1, 10-1 in a place)
Primaeval had won his last two starts, the most recent on turf, but that came on fast going off 8lb lower and he struggled this time. (tchd 7-1, 10-1 in a place)
T/Jkpt: £137,563.10 to a £1 stake. Pool: £545,843.73 - 2.50 winning tickets. T/Plt: £257.60 to a £1 stake. Pool: £550,305.25 - 1,559.41 winning tickets. T/Qpdt: £68.70 to a £1 stake. Pool: £26,952.70 - 289.96 winning tickets. SP

[2614] AYR (L-H)
Friday, June 22

OFFICIAL GOING: Good to firm (good in places; 9.1)
Wind: Breezy, half against Weather: Overcast

3332 COLLEGE GROUP APPRENTICE H'CAP — 1m
6:40 (6:40) (Class 6) (0-55,55) 4-Y-0+ **£1,940** (£577; £288; £144) **Stalls** Low

Form RPR
0-33 **1** **Cheeky Wee Red**[22] 2621 4-8-12 **48**..............................(p) LauraBarry 9 60
(Richard Fahey) *t.k.h: hld up in tch on outside: pushed along and hdwy to chse (clr) ldr over 1f out: led wl ins fnl f: kpt on strly* **11/2**

0 **2** 2 **Tazaamun (IRE)**[24] 2588 4-9-0 **55**............................ DavidBergin(5) 4 63
(David O'Meara) *t.k.h: pressed ldr: led after 3f: rdn clr and hung lft 2f out: hdd wl ins fnl f: eased and nrly ct for 2nd cl home* **10/3**[1]

4540 **3** nse **Sweet Vera**[18] 1919 7-8-3 **46**...................................... JordanUys(7) 11 53
(Shaun Harris) *hld up: pushed along over 2f out: hung lft and hdwy over 1f out: styd on fnl f: nrst fin* **33/1**

-005 **4** 5 **Glenluji**[23] 2600 7-9-5 **55**... ConorHarrison 2 51
(Jim Goldie) *prom: pushed along whn nt clr run over 3f out: no imp fr 2f out* **9/2**[3]

40-3 **5** nk **Bridge Valley**[17] 2791 5-8-13 **49**..............................(b) DavidSimmonson 8 44
(Jason Ward) *plld hrd in midfield: shkn up over 2f out: no imp fr over 1f out* **7/1**

0355 **6** 1 **Crocodile Bay (IRE)**[9] 3053 9-8-10 **46**....................(p) SophieSilvester 10 39
(Richard Guest) *t.k.h: hld up: rdn over 2f out: nvr able to chal* **14/1**

/0-4 **7** 1½ **Shamo Hill Theatre**[22] 2621 5-8-10 **46** oh1........................ NedCurtis 1 35
(Paul Midgley) *prom: lost pl and pushed along over 2f out: n.d after* **4/1**[2]

0-40 **8** 1½ **Shunkawakhan (IRE)**[22] 2621 9-8-5 **46** oh1..............(tp) RossSmith(5) 5 32
(Linda Perratt) *cl up: chsd (clr) ldr over 3f out to over 1f out: sn wknd* **20/1**

600- **9** 14 **Number One Guy**[24] 7370 5-8-7 **48**................................ EvaMoscrop(5) 6
(Philip Kirby) *s.i.s: t.k.h in rr: struggling 3f out: sn btn* **16/1**

0-50 **10** 7 **Naafetha (IRE)**[23] 2600 4-8-13 **54**............................ BTTreanor(5) 3
(George Foster) *led 3f: cl up tl rdn and wknd over 2f out* **16/1**

1m 41.76s (-2.04) **Going Correction** -0.275s/f (Firm) **10** Ran SP% **115.3**
Speed ratings (Par 101): **99,97,96,91,91 90,89,87,73,66**
toteswingers:1&2:£6.30, 2&3:£21.80, 1&3:£21.80 CSF £23.86 CT £562.25 TOTE £4.60: £1.60, £1.50, £12.30; EX 32.50.
Owner Eildon Hill Racing **Bred** Thoroughbred Farms Ltd **Trained** Musley Bank, N Yorks

FOCUS
A moderate but well-run apprentice handicap and a convincing winner, who improved again.
Glenluji Official explanation: jockey said gelding suffered interference in running

3333 SCOTTISH SUN MAIDEN STKS — 7f 50y
7:10 (7:10) (Class 5) 3-Y-0+ **£2,587** (£770; £384; £192) **Stalls** High

Form RPR
3-22 **1** **Sir Fredlot (IRE)**[38] 2147 3-9-3 78.............................. RobertWinston 11 75
(Charles Hills) *prom on outside: hdwy to chal over 2f out: sn rdn: hung lft and led over 1f out: hld on fnl f* **11/4**[2]

-352 **2** ¾ **Tortoni (IRE)**[20] 2689 3-9-3 75.................................. DanielTudhope 2 73
(Kevin Ryan) *led to 1f: chsd ldr: effrt and rdn over 1f out: hung lft: kpt on ins fnl f: hld nr fin* **10/3**[3]

432 **3** ½ **Gladsome**[9] 3024 4-9-7 0... MichaelStainton 4 69
(Jason Ward) *dwlt: hld up: rdn and hdwy on outside over 1f out: kpt on ins fnl f: nt gng pce of first two* **14/1**

202 **4** 2¾ **Vital Calling**[14] 2881 3-9-3 77.................................. GrahamGibbons 3 64
(David Barron) *t.k.h: in tch: rdn along 3f out: rallied over 1f out: kpt on same pce ins fnl f* **9/4**[1]

03 **5** 8 **Muhdiq (USA)**[27] 2496 3-9-3 0... LeeNewman 8 42
(Brian Meehan) *plld hrd: led after 1f to over 1f out: sn rdn and wknd* **5/1**

0-05 **6** 1 **Time To Excel**[21] 2673 3-9-3 47................................ PaulMulrennan 1 40
(Michael Dods) *hld up in tch: shkn up and outpcd over 2f out: n.d after* **33/1**

5-05 **7** 5 **Face East (USA)**[22] 2618 4-9-5 41.......................... MatthewHopkins(7) 6 29
(Alan Berry) *cl up tl rdn and wknd wl over 1f out* **100/1**

8 ¾ **Laybach (IRE)**[22] 8-9-12 0... GrahamLee 5 27
(Jim Goldie) *missed break: bhd: outpcd after 3f: nvr on terms* **20/1**

9 10 **Destiny Awaits (IRE)** 3-9-3 0...................................... JamesSullivan 7
(Ian Semple) *bhd and sn pushed along: struggling 1/2-way: nvr on terms* **50/1**

00F **10** nk **Dragon Spirit (IRE)**[13] 2927 3-8-10 0.............................. RossSmith(7) 9
(Linda Perratt) *s.i.s: bhd: short lived effrt over 2f out: sn btn* **100/1**

1m 31.99s (-1.41) **Going Correction** -0.275s/f (Firm)
WFA 3 from 4yo+ 9lb **10** Ran SP% **115.5**
Speed ratings (Par 103): **97,96,95,92,83 82,76,75,64,63**
toteswingers:1&2:£1.60, 2&3:£5.80, 1&3:£6.70 CSF £11.82 TOTE £2.80: £1.60, £1.20, £2.30; EX 13.80.
Owner Rupert Williams & P Winkworth **Bred** Churchtown House Stud **Trained** Lambourn, Berks

FOCUS
A fairly modest maiden and a hard fought victory. The first two set the standard.
Dragon Spirit(IRE) Official explanation: jockey said gelding hung right on bend

3334 IOMART GROUP PLC H'CAP — 7f 50y
7:45 (7:45) (Class 4) (0-85,84) 4-Y-0+ **£4,851** (£1,443; £721; £360) **Stalls** High

Form RPR
0054 **1** **Able Master (IRE)**[14] 2896 6-9-0 **77**.............................. DanielTudhope 11 93
(David O'Meara) *mde all: rdn and qcknd clr over 2f out: styd on wl: unchal* **6/1**[3]

0066 **2** 3½ **Blues Jazz**[9] 3027 6-8-11 **79**.................................... GarryWhillans(5) 7 85
(Ian Semple) *hld up: pushed along 3f out: hdwy on ins to chse (clr) wnr ins fnl f: kpt on: no imp* **7/1**

-004 **3** 2 **Orbit The Moon (IRE)**[23] 2597 4-9-3 **80**....................(t) PaulMulrennan 4 80
(Michael Dods) *prom: effrt and rdn over 2f out: kpt on same pce fnl f* **8/1**

-040 **4** 1 **Polar Annie**[23] 2597 7-9-0 **77**.. GrahamLee 12 74
(Jim Goldie) *chsd wnr: rdn over 2f out: no ex and lost 2nd ins fnl f* **16/1**

553- **5** 2¾ **Frognal (IRE)**[177] 7895 6-9-0 **77**................................(bt) SaleemGolam 10 67
(Richard Guest) *hld up: rdn over 2f out: hdwy over 1f out: nvr able to chal* **33/1**

-431 **6** nk **Fieldgunner Kirkup (GER)**[13] 2924 4-8-9 **77**.................... LMcNiff(5) 9 66
(David Barron) *dwlt: hld up on outside: rdn over 2f out: kpt on fnl f: no imp* **11/2**[2]

-050 **7** 1¼ **Ted's Brother (IRE)**[22] 2632 4-8-6 **72**........................ DeclanCannon(3) 6 58
(Richard Guest) *t.k.h: hld up in tch: outpcd over 2f out: n.d after* **8/1**

3120 **8** 3/4 **St Oswald**[5] 3185 4-8-7 **77**..(v) NatashaEaton(7) 13 61
(Alan Bailey) *prom: rdn over 2f out: wknd over 1f out* **12/1**

0-06 **9** 3/4 **Sabratha (IRE)**[23] 2598 4-8-3 **66**.. JamesSullivan 1 48
(Linda Perratt) *chsd ldrs tl rdn and wknd over 1f out* **25/1**

0021 **10** 3/4 **Frequency**[15] 2838 5-9-2 **79**..(b) RobertWinston 2 59
(Keith Dalgleish) *t.k.h: in tch: nt clr run briefly over 2f out: sn rdn: wknd over 1f out* **12/1**

00-0 **11** 3/4 **Namwahjobo (IRE)**[48] 1863 4-8-12 **75**.. LeeNewman 5 53
(Jim Goldie) *bhd: rdn over 3f out: nvr on terms* **16/1**

0253 **12** 2 1/2 **Celtic Sultan (IRE)**[23] 2597 8-9-7 **84**.. MickyFenton 8 55
(Paul Midgley) *dwlt: plld hrd in rr: shkn up 2f out: nvr on terms* **7/2**[1]

1m 30.51s (-2.89) **Going Correction** -0.275s/f (Firm) **12** Ran SP% **120.6**
Speed ratings (Par 105): **105,101,98,97,94 94,92,91,90,90 89,86**
toteswingers:1&2:£16.70, 2&3:£4.10, 1&3:£0.00 CSF £48.60 CT £350.90 TOTE £6.30: £2.00, £2.30, £3.30; EX 48.60.
Owner Direct Racing Club **Bred** Scuderia Miami Di Sandro Guerra And Co **Trained** Nawton, N Yorks

FOCUS
The winner took advantage of his old form and this rating could underestimate him.
Celtic Sultan(IRE) Official explanation: jockey said gelding missed the break

3335 BURNS SUPPER AT WESTERN HOUSE HOTEL H'CAP 1m
8:15 (8:15) (Class 5) (0-75,75) 4-Y-0+ **£2,587** (£770; £384; £192) **Stalls** Low

Form RPR

0051 **1** **Oratory (IRE)**[18] 2753 6-9-7 **75**.. MickyFenton 9 86+
(Paul Midgley) *hld up in tch on outside: hdwy over 1f out: led ins fnl f: pushed out* **5/1**[3]

5040 **2** 1 **Elijah Pepper (USA)**[21] 2675 7-9-0 **68**.. GrahamGibbons 7 75
(David Barron) *s.i.s: sn pushed along in rr: rdn 3f out: hdwy on outside over 1f out: styd on to go 2nd towards fin: no ch w wnr* **9/1**

-011 **3** 3/4 **Cono Zur (FR)**[27] 2491 5-9-7 **75**.. JamesSullivan 10 80
(Ruth Carr) *led: rdn over 2f out: hdd ins fnl f: kpt on same pce* **9/2**[2]

5223 **4** nk **Save The Bees**[20] 2696 4-8-12 **71**.. NeilFarley(5) 5 75
(Declan Carroll) *prom: rdn along over 2f out: edgd lft over 1f out: kpt on ins fnl f* **7/2**[1]

-054 **5** 3 1/4 **Daring Dream (GER)**[13] 2924 7-9-3 **71**.. GrahamLee 8 68
(Jim Goldie) *t.k.h: hld up towards rr: rdn whn n.m.r briefly over 2f out: styd on fnl f: nvr able to chal* **5/1**[3]

-121 **6** 1 1/4 **Violent Velocity (IRE)**[65] 1436 9-8-13 **74**.. KevinLundie(7) 2 68
(John Quinn) *in tch: rdn over 2f out: n.m.r over 1f out: sn outpcd* **14/1**

4101 **7** 3/4 **Spavento (IRE)**[15] 2840 6-8-11 **65**.. DavidAllan 4 57
(Eric Alston) *hld up: rdn and outpcd over 2f out: n.d after* **7/1**

3064 **8** 1/2 **Master Of Dance (IRE)**[4] 3215 5-8-13 **67**..(p) PaulMulrennan 1 58
(Keith Dalgleish) *trckd ldrs tl rdn and wknd fnl f* **10/1**

0-35 **9** nse **North Central (USA)**[9] 3027 5-8-11 **65**.. DanielTudhope 3 56
(Jim Goldie) *chsd ldr: rdn and ev ch over 2f out: wknd ins fnl f* **25/1**

1m 41.25s (-2.55) **Going Correction** -0.275s/f (Firm) **9** Ran SP% **115.8**
Speed ratings (Par 103): **101,100,99,98,95 94,93,93,93**
toteswingers:1&2:£8.30, 2&3:£17.30, 1&3:£17.30 CSF £49.28 CT £217.32 TOTE £7.20: £1.60, £3.70, £2.50; EX 53.40.
Owner The Unique Partnership **Bred** Lynch Bages Ltd & Samac Ltd **Trained** Westow, N Yorks

FOCUS
A fair handicap, run at an even pace and a brave winner, who was value for a bit extra.
Daring Dream(GER) Official explanation: jockey said gelding hung left throughout
Spavento(IRE) Official explanation: jockey said mare suffered interference on the bend

3336 BARCLAYS H'CAP 6f
8:50 (8:51) (Class 3) (0-90,89) 3-Y-0+ **£7,439** (£2,213; £1,106; £553) **Stalls** Low

Form RPR

6313 **1** **Head Space (IRE)**[5] 3183 4-9-7 **82**.. JamesSullivan 12 99+
(Ruth Carr) *confidently rdn in rr: plld out over 1f out: qcknd to ld ins fnl f: readily: j. winning line* **9/4**[1]

1302 **2** 2 1/4 **Crimson Knot (IRE)**[9] 3027 4-8-7 **75**.. MatthewHopkins(7) 9 83
(Alan Berry) *chsd ldrs: rdn to ld over 1f out: hdd ins fnl f: no ch w wnr* **14/1**

2300 **3** 1 3/4 **Rothesay Chancer**[20] 2717 4-9-3 **78**.. GrahamLee 11 80
(Jim Goldie) *hld up: rdn and hdwy over 1f out: kpt on fnl f: nvr able to chal* **10/1**

-066 **4** 3/4 **Barney McGrew (IRE)**[9] 3049 9-9-7 **82**.. PaulMulrennan 5 82
(Michael Dods) *t.k.h: led to over 1f out: sn no ex* **9/1**

0-06 **5** hd **Roker Park (IRE)**[16] 2825 7-9-12 **87**..(p) DanielTudhope 6 86
(David O'Meara) *cl up: rdn and ev ch over 2f out: one pce fr over 1f out* **4/1**[2]

1323 **6** 1/2 **Green Park (IRE)**[3] 3255 9-8-12 **78**..(b) NeilFarley(5) 7 75
(Declan Carroll) *t.k.h: trckd ldrs tl wknd over 1f out* **11/2**[3]

0-03 **7** 1/2 **Mortitia**[25] 2554 4-9-13 **88**.. RobertWinston 10 84
(Brian Meehan) *in tch: rdn along over 2f out: no ex over 1f out* **14/1**

0600 **8** 3 **Crown Choice**[20] 2697 7-9-10 **85**.. MickyFenton 8 71
(Paul Midgley) *dwlt: t.k.h bhd ldng gp: rdn and edgd lft over 1f out: n.d* **20/1**

6300 **9** nk **Five Star Junior (USA)**[95] 962 6-9-7 **87**.. LMcNiff(5) 3 72
(Linda Stubbs) *dwlt: hld up: rdn 2f out: sn outpcd* **9/1**

60-0 **10** 3 1/4 **Ryan Style (IRE)**[27] 2482 6-9-2 **77**.. GrahamGibbons 2 52
(Lisa Williamson) *prom tl rdn and wknd wl over 1f out* **25/1**

5-00 **11** 8 **Wildcat Wizard (USA)**[60] 1558 6-9-10 **85**.. AdrianNicholls 4 34
(David Nicholls) *hld up: struggling 2f out: sn btn: eased whn no ch* **20/1**

1m 13.06s (0.66) **Going Correction** +0.25s/f (Good) **11** Ran SP% **121.9**
Speed ratings (Par 107): **105,102,99,98,98 97,97,93,92,88 77**
toteswingers:1&2:£77.90, 2&3:£99.30, 1&3:£70.80 CSF £37.31 CT £243.17 TOTE £3.40: £1.50, £2.70, £3.50; EX 40.50.
Owner The Bottom Liners & Mrs R Carr **Bred** Castlemartin Stud And Skymarc Farm **Trained** Huby, N Yorks

FOCUS
Not the strongest of sprint handicaps for the grade but a smart performance. The winner ran as well as ever for his rider's claim.

NOTEBOOK
Head Space(IRE) ◆ made it two wins from his last three starts. He was switched off at the tail of the field and only needed to have the reins shaken at him as he shot clear in a matter of strides. He benefited from the strong early pace but is clearly a rapidly improving sort. He was rated as high as 90 when trained in Ireland and likely to be back up to somewhere near that figure once he's reassessed. He could reappear at Carlisle next week under a penalty. (tchd 2-1 and 5-2)
Crimson Knot(IRE) is a useful yardstick and she ran yet another sound race in defeat. She may have preferred softer ground and is one to keep an eye on if returning to Hamilton, a track that suits her well.
Rothesay Chancer stayed on to grab third but never threatened to get seriously involved. She was in great form at this stage 12 months ago and is unlikely to have to wait too long before getting her head in front again.
Barney McGrew(IRE) ran better than his finishing position suggests. He was keen and went off quicker than ideal. (tchd 10-1)
Roker Park(IRE) was another to run better than his finishing positions suggested. He also went off quicker than ideal and should be given another chance. (tchd 9-2 in places)
Green Park(IRE) has been in decent form since the blinkers were reapplied but was probably too keen early this time. (tchd 6-1)

3337 DOMINOS PIZZA H'CAP 1m 5f 13y
9:20 (9:20) (Class 5) (0-75,75) 4-Y-0+ **£2,587** (£770; £384; £192) **Stalls** Low

Form RPR

6-01 **1** **Callisto Moon**[20] 2698 8-8-13 **67**..(p) DanielTudhope 5 73
(Jo Hughes) *led: rdn 3f out: hdd over 1f out: rallied to ld ins fnl f: gamely* **6/1**

-610 **2** 1/2 **Fourth Generation (IRE)**[29] 2419 5-9-7 **75**.. RobertWinston 2 80
(Alan Swinbank) *hld up: smooth hdwy to ld over 1f out: sn rdn: hdd ins fnl f: keeping on same pce whn rdr got whip tangled in reins* **11/4**[1]

3304 **3** 1/2 **Sohcahtoa (IRE)**[16] 2827 6-8-11 **70**.. LMcNiff(5) 3 74
(David Barron) *chsd ldrs: drvn and outpcd over 2f out: rallied appr fnl f: kpt on fin* **7/2**[2]

40-6 **4** 1/2 **Forrest Flyer (IRE)**[28] 2457 8-8-12 **66**.. GrahamLee 6 69
(Jim Goldie) *hld up in tch: effrt over 2f out: sn outpcd: styd on ins fnl f: nt gng pce to chal* **4/1**[3]

035- **5** 1 3/4 **Ryton Runner (IRE)**[16] 7002 4-9-6 **74**.. PaulMulrennan 7 75
(Lucinda Russell) *hld up: pushed along whn hung lft and outpcd over 2f out: kpt on ins fnl f: no imp* **14/1**

2040 **6** hd **Chookie Hamilton**[7] 3114 8-9-1 **74**..(p) GarryWhillans(5) 1 74
(Ian Semple) *trckd ldrs: drvn along 3f out: no ex over 1f out* **8/1**

5-55 **7** 4 1/2 **Hawdyerwheesht**[22] 2620 4-8-7 **61**.. LeeNewman 4 55
(Jim Goldie) *chsd wnr: drvn 3f out: wknd over 1f out* **7/1**

2m 54.74s (0.74) **Going Correction** -0.275s/f (Firm) **7** Ran SP% **113.5**
Speed ratings (Par 103): **86,85,85,85,84 83,81**
toteswingers:1&2:£3.80, 2&3:£3.50, 1&3:£6.20 CSF £22.49 TOTE £5.30: £2.30, £2.50; EX 17.60.
Owner B Bedford & Mrs Gill White **Bred** Barton Stud **Trained** Lambourn, Berks

FOCUS
A fair staying handicap, run at a strong pace and an ultra tough display from the veteran Callisto Moon. There was a bunch finish and it's hard to be positive about this.
T/Plt: £232.60 to a £1 stake. Pool of £54,974.98 - 172.50 winning tickets. T/Qpdt: £73.40 to a £1 stake. Pool of £3,877.39 - 39.07 winning tickets. RY

3103 GOODWOOD (R-H)
Friday, June 22

OFFICIAL GOING: Good (7.5)
First 2f of Mile course moved out 5yds. Top bend out 3yds increasing distances on that course by 7yds.
Wind: strong against Weather: cloudy

3338 THREE FRIDAY NIGHTS APPRENTICE H'CAP 1m 1f 192y
6:15 (6:15) (Class 5) (0-75,74) 3-Y-0 **£3,234** (£962; £481; £240) **Stalls** Low

Form RPR

2103 **1** **Take Two**[14] 2866 3-9-2 **74**.. WilliamTwiston-Davies(5) 6 80+
(John O'Shea) *dwlt: bhd: smooth hdwy over 4f out: led travelling wl over 1f out: rdn 3 l clr ent fnl f: hld on by the narrowest of margins* **4/1**[2]

0020 **2** nse **Musically**[3] 3246 3-8-4 **57**.. CharlesBishop 4 60
(Mick Channon) *hld up: rdn over 2f out: little imp tl gd run ent fnl f: stl 2 l down 120yds out: str burst to fin: jst failed* **9/1**

1-33 **3** 2 1/2 **Feisty Champion (IRE)**[19] 2733 3-9-5 **72**.. BrendanPowell 5 70
(J W Hills) *cl up: rdn and ev ch 2f out: nt gng pce of wnr sn after: no ex whn lost 2nd ins fnl f* **7/4**[1]

1140 **4** 2 1/2 **Whipcrackaway (IRE)**[14] 2889 3-9-0 **74**.. NoraRichardson(7) 2 67
(Peter Hedger) *cl up tl dropped to last trio 6f out: hdwy over 3f out: rdn whn swtchd rt 2f out: kpt on same pce fnl f* **11/2**[3]

3-55 **5** 1 3/4 **Dutch Master**[41] 2089 3-8-11 **71**.. JoeyHaynes(7) 9 61
(Andrew Balding) *trckd ldrs: rdn over 2f out: nt quite pce to chal: no ex ins fnl f* **12/1**

4242 **6** 5 **Santadelacruze**[29] 2425 3-9-1 **68**.. JamieJones 3 48
(Gary Moore) *trckd ldrs: squeezed up rails to ld 4f out: rdn and hdd wl over 1f out: wknd fnl f* **11/1**

3033 **7** 2 3/4 **Attain**[22] 2626 3-8-13 **71**.. ShirleyTeasdale(5) 7 45
(Julia Feilden) *trckd ldr: rdn and ev ch 3f out: wknd over 1f out* **7/1**

00-0 **8** 17 **Jambobo**[36] 2196 3-7-11 **55** oh10..(p) NoelGarbutt(5) 1
(William Knight) *led tl 4f out: wknd 2f out* **50/1**

2m 17.39s (9.29) **Going Correction** +0.625s/f (Yiel) **8** Ran SP% **112.2**
Speed ratings (Par 99): **87,86,84,82,81 77,75,61**
toteswingers:1&2:£6.90, 2&3:£3.80, 1&3:£2.40 CSF £37.73 CT £82.78 TOTE £5.60: £1.80, £1.50, £1.60; EX 39.60.
Owner S P Bloodstock **Bred** Steven & Petra Wallace **Trained** Elton, Gloucs

FOCUS
There was strong headwind into the runners in the straight, and after a drying day the going was changed to good. They went a steady pace in this apprentice handicap and it was a race of changing fortunes in the closing stages. The placed horses set the level.

3339 GORDON'S MAIDEN AUCTION FILLIES' STKS 6f
6:50 (6:51) (Class 4) 2-Y-0 **£3,881** (£1,155; £577; £288) **Stalls** High

Form RPR

52 **1** **Momalorka**[10] 3010 2-8-6 0.. KellyHarrison 13 75+
(William Haggas) *broke wl: mde all: kpt on gamely fnl f: hld on wl towards fin* **9/2**[2]

2 nk **Miss You Too** 2-9-0 0.. MatthewDavies 15 82+
(Mick Channon) *trckd wnr: rdn 2f out: kpt on wl fnl 120yds: hld nring fin* **18/1**

2 **3** 1 **Botanica (IRE)**[13] 2938 2-9-0 0.. RichardHughes 7 79
(Richard Hannon) *mid-div: swtchd lft and tk clsr order 3f out: sn rdn: kpt on ins fnl f but nvr getting there* **11/10**[1]

4 2 1/2 **Ziggy's Secret** 2-9-1 0.. IanMongan 9 74+
(Lucy Wadham) *trckd ldrs: rdn over 2f out: kpt on same pce fnl f: eased nr fin: jst hung on for 4th* **16/1**

4 **5** shd **Mystical Moment**[16] 2812 2-9-0 0.. KieranO'Neill 5 73+
(Richard Hannon) *towards rr: swtchd rt and hdwy 3f out: sn rdn: kpt on wl ins fnl f: nrly snatched 4th* **7/1**

6 1 1/2 **Sound Of Guns** 2-8-11 0.. MartinLane 3 64
(Ed Walker) *hld up: hdwy over 2f out: rdn to chse ldrs sn after: fdd ins fnl f* **11/2**[3]

7 *shd* **Our Sweet Art** 2-8-5 0 .... DarrenEgan(5) 12 62
(John Best) *towards rr: sme late hdwy: nvr threatened ldrs* **66/1**

40 8 *3 ½* **Lobelia**[27] 2499 2-8-6 0 .... JoeFanning 2 48
(Brian Meehan) *trckd ldrs: rdn over 2f out: wknd ent fnl f* **100/1**

9 *1* **Starlight Symphony (IRE)** 2-8-10 0 .... CathyGannon 14 49
(Eve Johnson Houghton) *chsd ldrs: rdn and ev ch over 2f out: wknd jst over 1f out* **40/1**

0 10 *2 ¼* **Lady Bonanova (IRE)**[27] 2499 2-8-3 0 .... JemmaMarshall(5) 4 40
(Pat Phelan) *trckd ldrs: rdn over 2f out: wknd ent fnl f* **33/1**

62 11 *8* **Alexandrakollontai (IRE)**[23] 2609 2-8-8 0 .... LiamKeniry 6 16
(J S Moore) *in tch: rdn over 3f out: sn chsng ldrs: squeezed out 2f out: wknd over 1f out* **33/1**

0 12 *4 ½* **We Are City**[27] 2499 2-8-12 0 .... StevieDonohoe 11 7
(Michael Bell) *trckd ldrs: rdn over 2f out: wknd over 1f out* **14/1**

13 *7* **Kimvara** 2-8-10 0 .... RichardThomas 10
(Joseph Tuite) *mid-div: hmpd 3f out and stmbld: sn in rr: wknd over 1f out* **100/1**

1m 15.19s (2.99) **Going Correction** +0.525s/f (Yiel) **13** Ran SP% **123.3**
Speed ratings (Par 92): **101,100,99,95,95 93,93,89,87,84 74,68,58**
toteswingers:1&2:£11.50, 2&3:£6.10, 1&3:£2.40 CSF £80.78 TOTE £5.70: £2.00, £2.80, £1.20; EX 32.30.

Owner The Duchess Syndicate **Bred** J A And Mrs M A Knox **Trained** Newmarket, Suffolk

FOCUS
A decent fillies' maiden in which the third looks the best guide to the level. The field converged towards the stands' rail and the winner scored in gritty style under a prominent ride.

NOTEBOOK
Momalorka had been beaten less than 3l in a pair of maidens at Newbury and Salisbury and had solid form claims. Always well positioned near the stands' rail, she put in a brave effort to get off the mark on her third attempt. She cost just £800 as a yearling but has achieved decent form at this early stage of her career and has also run well on fast and testing turf. (op 5-1 tchd 4-1)

Miss You Too ◆, a sister to Group 3-placed 7f 2-y-o winner Vitruvian Man, tracked the winner for most of the way before delivering a sustained challenge but she was just held. This was a very promising debut by a Montjeu filly who is bred to stay a lot further than this in time. (op 20-1)

Botanica(IRE) had decent form claims on her strong finishing second behind her stablemate City Image in a 5f Windsor fillies' maiden on debut. Strong in the market, she got a bit trapped behind rivals against the near rail before finishing well for a close third stepped up to 6f. She was not an unlucky loser but this was still a decent second run from a £28,000 half-sister to five winners. (tchd 6-5 and 11-8 in a place)

Ziggy's Secret, a 32,000gns half-sister to 7f AW winner Cheers out of an unraced half-sister to Italian 1m2f Group 1 winner Imperial Dancer, looked inexperienced but she shaped with plenty of promise on her debut and would have finished a bit closer if not eased in the closing stages.

Mystical Moment ◆, a 4l fourth in a 6f Kempton fillies' maiden on debut, had to be switched a couple of times before finishing fast from some way back. This was an eyecatching second run by a Dutch Art filly who is a first foal of a 1m winner. Official explanation: jockey said filly ran green (op 10-1)

Sound Of Guns attracted support and travelled well through the pack, but she couldn't match the finishing kick of the first two and faded in the closing stages. This was a decent start by an Acclamation half-sister to placed runners in US and Italy. (op 15-2)

Kimvara Official explanation: jockey said filly ran green

3340 ROTHSCHILD'S MAIDEN FILLIES' STKS 1m 1f
7:20 (7:22) (Class 5) 3-Y-O+ £2,911 (£866; £432; £216) Stalls Low

Form RPR

0- 1 **Valiant Girl**[265] 6529 3-9-0 0 .... JamesDoyle 16 84+
(Roger Charlton) *mid-div: nt clrest of runs tl swtchd to centre for gd hdwy over 1f out: qcknd up wl to chal fnl 170yds: led nring fin* **13/2**

2 *hd* **Infinite Hope (USA)** 3-9-0 0 .... KirstyMilczarek 17 82+
(Luca Cumani) *s.i.s: rcvring whn nt clr run and dropped bk to rr after 1f: hdwy into midfield 4f out: r.o wl to ld fnl 150yds: drew clr w wnr: hdd nring fin* **20/1**

4423 3 *4 ½* **Gold Show**[8] 3070 3-9-0 86 .... MatthewDavies 13 73
(Mick Channon) *trckd ldr: led wl over 2f out: sn rdn: hdd fnl 150yds: nt gng pce of ldng pair* **9/4**[1]

0-42 4 *1 ¾* **Santarini (IRE)**[14] 2891 3-9-0 72 .... RichardHughes 7 69
(Richard Hannon) *trckd ldrs: moved upsides travelling best jst over 1f out: rdn ins fnl f: nt qckn* **4/1**[2]

0 5 *3* **Miss Dashwood**[19] 2734 3-9-0 0 .... StevieDonohoe 6 62+
(James Fanshawe) *mid-div: nt clr run over 2f out tl swtchd lft over 1f out: styd on fnl f but nvr a danger* **12/1**

6 *shd* **Mariet** 3-9-0 0 .... LiamKeniry 8 62+
(Andrew Balding) *s.i.s: towards rr: styd on fr over 1f out: nvr trbld ldrs* **66/1**

06-0 7 *1 ¼* **Layali Dubai (USA)**[36] 2196 3-9-0 67 .... RichardMullen 14 59
(Saeed Bin Suroor) *trckd ldrs: rdn over 2f out: fdd ins fnl f* **14/1**

8 *¾* **Not Now Katie** 3-9-0 0 .... SamHitchcott 5 58
(Chris Gordon) *hld up towards rr: hdwy into midfield whn nt clr run and swtchd lft over 2f out: sn rdn: no further imp* **50/1**

0-5 9 *1 ¼* **Heyaaraat (IRE)**[18] 2757 3-9-0 0 .... ChrisCatlin 9 55
(Charles Hills) *mid-div: hdwy 3f out: sn rdn: wknd fnl f* **14/1**

3- 10 *2* **Morrow**[248] 6934 3-9-0 0 .... AhmedAjtebi 3 51
(Mahmood Al Zarooni) *mid-div: hdwy 3f out: sn rdn to chse ldrs: wknd fnl f* **9/2**[3]

0 11 *1 ½* **Riviera Romance**[32] 2344 3-9-0 0 .... SebSanders 12 47
(J W Hills) *trckd ldrs: rdn over 2f out: wknd fnl f* **50/1**

00 12 *hd* **Luna Rosa (IRE)**[14] 2891 3-9-0 0 .... JohnFahy 10 47
(Clive Cox) *stdd s after being short of room: a towards rr* **66/1**

63- 13 *2 ¼* **Brief Chat (USA)**[239] 7125 3-9-0 0 .... JoeFanning 11 42
(Amanda Perrett) *in tch: rdn 3f out: nt gng pce to cl: wknd ent fnl f* **16/1**

00 14 *37* **Doyle's Dream**[29] 2422 3-9-0 0 .... JamieGoldstein 4
(Michael Madgwick) *racd freely: led tl wl over 2f out: sn wknd: t.o* **100/1**

00 15 *hd* **Ebtisama (USA)**[14] 2891 3-8-7 0 .... KatiaScallan(7) 2
(Marcus Tregoning) *mid-div tl over 3f out: sn wl bhd and eased: t.o* **50/1**

2m 0.5s (4.20) **Going Correction** +0.625s/f (Yiel) **15** Ran SP% **123.8**
Speed ratings (Par 100): **106,105,101,100,97 97,96,95,94,92 91,91,89,56,56**
toteswingers:1&2:£40.10, 2&3:£15.40, 1&3:£6.90 CSF £136.99 TOTE £6.80: £2.10, £5.60, £1.70; EX 159.60.

Owner A E Oppenheimer **Bred** Hascombe And Valiant Studs **Trained** Beckhampton, Wilts

FOCUS
An interesting fillies' maiden. The pace was just fair but the first two pulled clear of the two main contenders and the form could be useful.

3341 CAPITAL FM H'CAP 1m 6f
7:55 (7:56) (Class 3) (0-95,93) 4-Y-O+
£7,470 (£1,677; £1,677; £559; £279; £140) Stalls Low

Form RPR

-312 1 **Lady Rosamunde**[28] 2447 4-8-2 81 .... (p) KatiaScallan(7) 3 89
(Marcus Tregoning) *in tch: hdwy 4f out: rdn over 2f out: led and edgd lft briefly over 1f out: styd on wl: pushed out* **4/1**[2]

0-01 2 *1 ½* **Life And Soul (IRE)**[27] 2479 5-9-5 91 .... HayleyTurner 6 97
(Amanda Perrett) *prom: led after 2f: rdn over 2f out: hdd over 1f out: styd on but a being hld by wnr ins fnl f* **6/1**[3]

12-2 2 *dht* **Tmaam (USA)**[9] 3036 4-9-4 90 .... JoeFanning 11 96
(Mark Johnston) *mid-div: rdn and hdwy over 2f out: chsng ldng pair whn swtchd rt over 1f out: styd on but a being hld by wnr* **2/1**[1]

212 4 *1 ¼* **O Ma Lad (IRE)**[15] 2857 4-8-8 80 .... JamesDoyle 5 84
(Sylvester Kirk) *hld up in last trio: hdwy over 3f out: rdn over 2f out: styng on at same pce whn carried sltly rt over 1f out* **17/2**

0-56 5 *7* **Woolfall Treasure**[27] 2479 7-9-4 90 .... (v) RichardMullen 10 84
(Gary Moore) *pushed into ld: hdd after 2f: trckd ldr: rdn 3f out but nvr quite ev ch: wknd fnl f* **12/1**

10-0 6 *3 ½* **Samsons Son**[47] 1890 8-9-2 88 .... JimmyFortune 8 77
(Alan King) *hld up in last pair: effrt chsng ldrs over 2f out: wknd jst over 1f out* **14/1**

0-06 7 *1 ¼* **Jehanbux (USA)**[32] 2346 4-9-0 86 .... RichardHughes 9 74
(Richard Hannon) *stdd s: in last: rdn over 3f out: nvr any imp: wknd over 1f out* **12/1**

1115 8 *5* **Chabada (JPN)**[27] 2474 4-8-13 85 .... JimCrowley 2 66
(Ian Williams) *trckd ldrs: rdn over 3f out: wknd 2f out* **8/1**

14- 9 *1 ¾* **Colloquial**[266] 6499 11-9-7 93 .... (v) FergusSweeney 7 71
(Henry Candy) *trckd ldrs: rdn 3f out: wknd 2f out* **20/1**

3m 9.61s (6.01) **Going Correction** +0.625s/f (Yiel) **9** Ran SP% **116.1**
Speed ratings (Par 107): **107,106,106,105,101 99,98,95,94**
PL: Life and Soul £1.50, Tmaam £1.40 EX: Lady Rosamunde/LAS £10.70, LR/T £8.00, CSF: LR/LAS £14.21, LR/T £6.23, TRICAST: LR/LAS/T £30.61, LR/T/LAS £23.48. toteswingers:1&2:£6.00, 2&2:£2.50, 1&2:£2.10 TOTE £5.70: £1.70.

Owner Mr And Mrs A E Pakenham **Bred** Mr & Mrs A E Pakenham **Trained** Lambourn, Berks

FOCUS
A decent staying handicap and the form looks straightforward rated through the runner-up. The pace was fair and the first four pulled clear.

NOTEBOOK
Lady Rosamunde travelled well into contention before forging her way to a decisive victory on her first run at 1m6f. She can carry her head a bit high, but she looks a resolute galloper who has progressed as she has moved up in trip and she now has a record of 3-9. There should be scope for further improvement and her versatility regarding ground is a useful asset. (op 5-1 tchd 6-1)
Life And Soul(IRE) took advantage of a drop in the weights when holding off smart hurdler Grumeti in a 1m4f handicap here last time. He went into unknown territory stepped up to 1m6f, but put in a brave front-running effort off 5lb higher than last time. (tchd 5-1)
Tmaam(USA) ◆ got a bit tapped for speed before staying on well on his first try at 1m6f. He is not the most fluent of travellers but he has form figures of 222 in 1m4f/1m6f handicaps on fast and slow ground since his 1m4f Bath maiden win in September, and this very lightly raced 4-y-o still has potential for further progress. (tchd 5-1)
O Ma Lad(IRE) kept battling but he couldn't pose a big threat back up in trip. He is a willing type but has a bit of work to do to defy a mark 10lb higher than his 1m4f Catterick win two runs back. (op 10-1)
Woolfall Treasure, the winner of this race in 2010, faded some way out. (op 11-1 tchd 9-1)
Chabada(JPN) improved her record to 3-4 when completing an AW hat-trick off 3lb lower over 1m6f at Wolverhampton in March but she has not done much back on turf on her last two starts. (op 7-1)

3342 PETER SEWELL FILLIES' H'CAP 7f
8:25 (8:26) (Class 4) (0-85,85) 3-Y-O+ £5,175 (£1,540; £769; £384) Stalls Low

Form RPR

-031 1 **Russian Rave**[18] 2766 6-9-10 81 .... JamesDoyle 10 92
(Jonathan Portman) *little slowly away: hld up in last: hdwy jst over 2f out: sn rdn: led ins fnl f: kpt on strly* **11/4**[1]

-043 2 *2 ½* **Wahylah (IRE)**[8] 3085 3-9-0 80 .... SebSanders 8 81
(Clive Brittain) *cl up: hdwy to ld 2f out: sn rdn: hdd ins fnl f: kpt on but sn hld by wnr* **11/2**

13-4 3 *½* **Ma Quillet**[58] 1609 4-8-12 69 .... FergusSweeney 6 72+
(Henry Candy) *cl up: rdn whn sltly outpcd over 2f out: styd on fnl f* **12/1**

0-26 4 *¾* **Camache Queen (IRE)**[25] 2558 4-9-9 80 .... CathyGannon 2 81
(Denis Coakley) *racd keenly: trckd ldr: rdn jst over 2f out: kpt on same pce fnl f* **6/1**

12-1 5 *¾* **Delft**[24] 2583 3-8-12 78 .... JimmyFortune 9 74
(Jeremy Noseda) *led: rdn over 2f out: sn hdd: no ex ins fnl f* **10/3**[2]

-005 6 *1 ¼* **Rougette**[15] 2855 4-9-3 74 .... JimCrowley 5 69
(Charles Hills) *hld up in last pair: rdn over 2f out: nvr gng pce to get involved* **12/1**

2511 7 *29* **Abi Scarlet (IRE)**[30] 2400 3-9-5 85 .... DarryllHolland 11
(Hughie Morrison) *prom: pushed along 4f out: rdn 3f out: wknd 2f out* **4/1**[3]

1m 30.73s (3.73) **Going Correction** +0.625s/f (Yiel)
WFA 3 from 4yo+ 9lb **7** Ran SP% **114.8**
Speed ratings (Par 102): **103,100,99,98,97 96,63**
toteswingers:1&2:£4.40, 2&3:£4.70, 1&3:£6.60 CSF £18.39 CT £154.08 TOTE £3.50: £2.20, £3.30; EX 22.00.

Owner The Traditionalists **Bred** P A & M J Reditt & Morton Bloodstock **Trained** Compton, Berks

FOCUS
There were a number of non-runners in this 7f handicap but the well-backed winner completed a double with something in hand and the form looks solid rated around the placed horses.
Abi Scarlet(IRE) Official explanation: jockey said filly never travelled

3343 GOODWOOD FARM SHOP H'CAP 6f
9:00 (9:01) (Class 5) (0-75,75) 3-Y-O £3,408 (£1,006; £503) Stalls High

Form RPR

0-60 1 **Alice's Dancer (IRE)**[27] 2503 3-9-4 72 ....[1] StevieDonohoe 4 86
(William Muir) *s.i.s: in last but in tch: swtchd rt over 2f out: sn rdn and hdwy: led over 1f out: drifted rt: r.o strly to draw clr: comf* **9/1**

3-33 2 *6* **School Fees**[52] 1723 3-9-4 75 .... SeanLevey(3) 8 70
(Henry Candy) *trckd ldrs: rdn to ld over 1f out: sn hdd: kpt on but nt pce of wnr* **85/40**[1]

4625 3 *4 ½* **Le King Beau (USA)**[7] 3108 3-9-1 69 .... SamHitchcott 5 49
(John Bridger) *led: rdn over 2f out: hdd over 1f out: no ex fnl f* **10/1**

-455 **4** *shd* **Amphora**[27] 2503 3-8-12 **66** JimmyFortune 2 46
(Andrew Balding) *trckd ldrs: rdn over 2f out: kpt on same pce fnl f* **4/1**[2]
5050 **5** *2 1/2* **Tinzapeas**[5] 3184 3-9-0 **68** MatthewDavies 12 40
(Mick Channon) *prom: rdn over 2f out: fdd fnl f* **5/1**[3]
4651 **6** *1 3/4* **Maria Montez**[23] 2610 3-8-6 **60** MartinLane 7 26
(J W Hills) *chsd ldrs: rdn over 2f out: wknd over 1f out* **12/1**
65-0 **7** *2 1/2* **Caterina**[15] 2846 3-9-2 **70** KieranO'Neill 10 28
(Richard Hannon) *s.i.s: in last pair but in tch: effrt over 2f out: wknd over 1f out* **20/1**
300 **8** *1* **Red Ramesses (IRE)**[42] 2041 3-9-2 **70** JimCrowley 11 25
(John Best) *trckd ldrs: rdn over 2f out: wknd over 1f out* **9/1**
03-5 **9** *9* **Poseidon Grey (IRE)**[21] 2649 3-9-2 **70** (b[1]) AdamKirby 3
(Clive Cox) *prom: rdn over 2f out: wknd over 1f out* **9/1**

1m 15.36s (3.16) **Going Correction** +0.525s/f (Yiel) **9** Ran SP% **120.2**
Speed ratings (Par 99): **99,91,85,84,81 79,75,74,62**
toteswingers:1&2:£7.90, 2&3:£7.00, 1&3:£20.50 CSF £29.73 CT £204.90 TOTE £12.40: £3.30, £1.60, £3.30; EX 40.70.
Owner Perspicacious Punters Racing Club **Bred** Rathasker Stud **Trained** Lambourn, Berks

FOCUS
There was a runaway winner in this sprint handicap but the form is hard to read and so is rated slightly cautiously.
T/Plt: £13.60 to a £1 stake. Pool of £54046.95 - 2895.91 winning tickets. T/Qpdt: £6.20 to a £1 stake. Pool of £3854.57 - 457.06 winning tickets. TM

2929 NEWMARKET (R-H)
Friday, June 22

OFFICIAL GOING: Good to soft changing to soft after race 2 (6.25)
Wind: Strong half-behind Weather: Raining

3344 POPTELECOM.CO.UK 50% OFF BROADBAND APPRENTICE H'CAP 1m
5:50 (5:51) (Class 5) (0-70,70) 4-Y-O+ **£2,587** (£770; £384; £192) **Stalls** High

Form RPR
-003 **1** **Rough Rock (IRE)**[15] 2847 7-9-3 **68** JoshCrane(5) 7 77
(Chris Dwyer) *racd stands' side: a.p: led 1f out: pushed out* **7/1**[3]
0016 **2** *2* **Hail Promenader (IRE)**[7] 3099 6-9-7 **67** (p) MatthewLawson 5 71
(Anthony Carson) *overall ldr stands' side: hdd over 2f out: sn rdn: edgd rt over 1f out: styd on: 2nd of 11 in gp* **10/1**
1222 **3** *1/2* **Douze Points (IRE)**[7] 3099 6-9-10 **70** TobyAtkinson 4 73
(John Butler) *racd stands' side: hld up: hdwy over 1f out: sn rdn: styd on same pce ins fnl f: 3rd of 11 in gp* **9/2**[1]
042- **4** *1 1/2* **Beauchamp Zorro**[256] 6754 4-9-3 **63** AmyScott 1 63
(Henry Candy) *racd stands' side: s.i.s: sn prom: led overall over 2f out: hung lft over 1f out: sn rdn and hdd: no ex ins fnl f: 4th of 11 in gp* **10/1**
400 **5** *1 3/4* **Rufus Stone (USA)**[16] 2826 4-8-11 **62** (p) LewisWalsh(5) 3 58
(Jane Chapple-Hyam) *racd stands' side: prom: pushed along over 5f out: hmpd over 1f out: styd on same pce: 5th of 11 in gp* **22/1**
1650 **6** *nk* **Muhandis (IRE)**[25] 2549 4-9-2 **65** (b) JackDuern(3) 6 60
(Nick Littmoden) *racd stands' side: prom: rdn over 2f out: wknd ins fnl f: 6th of 11 in gp* **14/1**
0-20 **7** *3 1/2* **Tenavon**[37] 2170 4-8-12 **58** DavidKenny 14 45
(William Knight) *racd far side: s.i.s: sn chsng ldrs: led that gp over 2f out: rdn and hung rt over 1f out: wknd ins fnl f: 1st of 3 in gp* **10/1**
3431 **8** *1 1/2* **Hierarch (IRE)**[21] 2652 5-8-12 **65** SiobhanMiller(7) 2 51
(David Simcock) *racd stands' side: s.i.s: hld up: hdwy over 2f out: hung lft over 1f out: wknd and eased ins fnl f: 7th of 11 in gp* **11/2**[2]
0023 **9** *1 1/2* **Marvo**[30] 2392 8-9-0 **67** (b) RobJFitzpatrick(7) 11 47
(Mark H Tompkins) *racd alone in centre tl jnd stands' side over 3f out: prom: rdn and wknd over 1f out: 8th of 11 in gp* **14/1**
00/- **10** *6* **Cavendish Road (IRE)**[609] 7063 6-9-0 **65** (t) ThomasBrown(5) 15 31
(Nicky Vaughan) *racd far side: chsd ldr: led that gp over 3f out: hung rt and hdd over 2f out: wknd over 1f out: 2nd of 3 that side* **28/1**
6-00 **11** *19* **Darcey**[17] 2801 6-8-13 **64** HayleyBurton(5) 10
(Amy Weaver) *racd stands' side: prom: rdn over 3f out: wknd over 2f out: t.o: 9th of 11 in gp* **16/1**
200/ **12** *1 1/4* **King's Sabre**[618] 6853 6-9-0 **60** NathanAlison 16
(John Spearing) *racd far side: led that gp over 4f: wknd over 2f out: eased: t.o: last of 3 in gp* **16/1**
0000 **13** *2 1/2* **Final Drive (IRE)**[14] 2899 6-8-13 **62** (t) IanBurns(3) 12
(John Butler) *racd stands' side: dwlt: hld up: a in rr: wknd over 2f out: t.o: 10th of 11 in gp* **16/1**
1656 **U** **Inpursuitoffreedom**[44] 1980 5-9-1 **64** DannyBrock(3) 8
(Philip McBride) *racd stands' side: hld up: stmbld and uns rdr over 4f out* **7/1**[3]

1m 41.46s (1.46) **Going Correction** +0.275s/f (Good) **14** Ran SP% **124.6**
Speed ratings (Par 103): **103,101,100,99,97 96,93,91,90,84 65,64,61,**
toteswingers:1&2:£22.10, 2&3:£7.10, 1&3:£3.00 CSF £78.18 CT £359.46 TOTE £7.80: £2.20, £4.80, £2.10; EX 92.80 Trifecta £236.60 Part won. Pool of £319.80 - 0.72 winning units..
Owner M M Foulger **Bred** Mrs B Stroomer **Trained** Six Mile Bottom, Cambs

FOCUS
The official going description was amended from good before racing, and the opener was run in heavy rain. The winning rider described the ground as "soft." This was a modest apprentice handicap. They split into two groups, with three on the far side and the rest racing towards the stands' side, plus Marvo who was isolated towards the centre. It was dominated by those in the larger group, and the first three home were the topweights. The time was five seconds slower than standard but was the best on the card. Straightforward form.
Final Drive(IRE) Official explanation: jockey said gelding never travelled

3345 RACE YOUR WAY TO POPTELECOM.CO.UK CLASSIFIED STKS 1m 4f
6:25 (6:26) (Class 5) 3-Y-O **£2,587** (£770; £384; £192) **Stalls** Centre

Form RPR
0412 **1** **Dovils Date**[8] 3072 3-9-0 68 JamesMillman 1 76+
(Rod Millman) *s.i.s: hld up: hdwy over 2f out: chsd wnr over 1f out: sn rdn: hung lft and styd on to ld wl ins fnl f* **7/2**[1]
4553 **2** *1 1/2* **Harry Buckle**[23] 2605 3-8-11 68 RaulDaSilva(3) 7 74
(Philip McBride) *led: clr over 4f out: rdn over 1f out: hung lft and hdd wl ins fnl f* **13/2**[3]
5-00 **3** *2* **Gallipot**[15] 2848 3-9-0 68 NickyMackay 6 70
(John Gosden) *hld up: hdwy over 3f out: rdn and outpcd over 1f out: styd on ins fnl f* **10/1**
2104 **4** *nk* **Key Gold**[8] 3087 3-9-0 70 DaneO'Neill 11 70
(Mark Johnston) *hld up: hdwy over 1f out: r.o: nt rch ldrs* **8/1**
-042 **5** *1* **Third Half**[9] 3031 3-9-0 70 StephenCraine 3 68
(Tom Dascombe) *hld up: hdwy over 3f out: chsd ldr over 2f out tl rdn over 1f out: no ex ins fnl f* **5/1**[2]
4020 **6** *1 1/4* **Thecornishcockney**[17] 2787 3-9-0 67 [1] PatCosgrave 10 66
(John Ryan) *hld up: hdwy over 3f out: rdn over 1f out: wknd ins fnl f* **25/1**
0-06 **7** *8* **Attwaal (IRE)**[41] 2095 3-9-0 66 JackMitchell 9 54
(Roger Varian) *chsd ldr tl rdn over 2f out: wknd over 1f out* **16/1**
60-1 **8** *4* **Mixora (USA)**[17] 2794 3-9-0 67 PatDobbs 12 47
(Sir Henry Cecil) *chsd ldrs: rdn over 2f out: wknd over 1f out* **16/1**
-164 **9** *1/2* **Rapid Heat Lad (IRE)**[27] 2471 3-9-0 67 TonyCulhane 8 46
(Reg Hollinshead) *hld up: rdn over 3f out: a in rr* **16/1**
2-56 **10** *7* **Aleksandar**[20] 2716 3-9-0 68 J-PGuillambert 5 35
(Luca Cumani) *prom: rdn over 4f out: wknd over 2f out* **5/1**[2]
00-6 **11** *15* **Angelic Note (IRE)**[15] 2849 3-9-0 68 MartinDwyer 2
(Brian Meehan) *prom: rdn over 5f out: wkng whn hung lft over 2f out: t.o* **33/1**
445 **12** *2 1/4* **Joe The Coat**[31] 2368 3-9-0 70 TedDurcan 4
(Mark H Tompkins) *hld up: rdn 1/2-way: wknd 4f out: t.o* **12/1**

2m 36.4s (3.50) **Going Correction** +0.275s/f (Good) **12** Ran SP% **121.2**
Speed ratings (Par 99): **99,98,96,96,95 94,89,86,86,81 71,70**
toteswingers:1&2:£3.70, 2&3:£21.00, 1&3:£8.60 CSF £26.55 TOTE £5.20: £2.00, £2.80, £4.40; EX 37.10 TRIFECTA Not won..
Owner Always Hopeful Partnership **Bred** Cranford Stud **Trained** Kentisbeare, Devon

FOCUS
A typically tight knit classified stakes, and probably a decent race for the grade with some big stables represented. The winner probably didn't have to improve on his Newbury form.
Joe The Coat Official explanation: jockey said gelding never travelled

3346 NGK SPARK PLUGS MAIDEN STKS 6f
7:00 (7:00) (Class 5) 2-Y-O **£3,234** (£962; £481; £240) **Stalls** High

Form RPR
3 **1** **Boomshackerlacker (IRE)**[21] 2648 2-9-3 0 PatCosgrave 8 79+
(George Baker) *trckd ldrs: racd keenly: shkn up over 2f out: rdn to ld wl ins fnl f: r.o* **11/2**[3]
2 *3/4* **Whipper Snapper (IRE)** 2-8-12 0 DavidKenny(5) 12 77
(William Knight) *mid-div: hdwy over 2f out: led over 1f out: rdn: edgd lft and hdd wl ins fnl f* **25/1**
3 *shd* **Bravo Youmzain (IRE)** 2-9-3 0 TedDurcan 3 77+
(Marco Botti) *s.i.s: hld up: hdwy: hung lft and nt clr run over 1f out: r.o* **10/1**
4 *3/4* **Darkening (IRE)** 2-9-3 0 SilvestreDeSousa 4 74
(Mahmood Al Zarooni) *chsd ldrs: hung lft and ev ch wl over 1f out: sn rdn and hung rt: styd on* **13/2**
5 *nk* **Emperatriz** 2-8-12 0 AmirQuinn 7 68+
(John Holt) *hld up: shkn up over 2f out: r.o ins fnl f: nt rch ldrs* **66/1**
6 **6** *1 1/2* **Aussie Reigns (IRE)**[14] 2888 2-9-3 0 ShaneKelly 11 69
(William Knight) *w ldr tl led over 2f out: rdn and hdd over 1f out: no ex ins fnl f* **33/1**
7 *nk* **Lawmans Thunder** 2-9-3 0 MickaelBarzalona 13 68
(Mahmood Al Zarooni) *prom: pushed along 1/2-way: rdn and ev ch over 1f out: no ex ins fnl f* **11/2**[3]
8 *nk* **Mission Approved** 2-9-3 0 RyanMoore 2 68+
(Sir Michael Stoute) *chsd ldrs: rdn and ev ch over 1f out: edgd lft and no ex fnl f* **5/2**[1]
9 *6* **Sharjah (IRE)** 2-9-3 0 JamieSpencer 10 49+
(Noel Quinlan) *led over 3f: sn rdn: wknd over 1f out* **4/1**[2]
10 *1/2* **Romanoff (IRE)** 2-9-3 0 J-PGuillambert 1 48
(Luca Cumani) *wnt rt s: sn pushed along in rr: wknd over 2f out* **16/1**
11 *2 1/2* **Whipper's Boy (IRE)** 2-9-3 0 MartinDwyer 9 40+
(Brian Meehan) *s.s: a wl bhd* **25/1**

1m 16.06s (3.56) **Going Correction** +0.45s/f (Yiel) **11** Ran SP% **119.8**
Speed ratings (Par 93): **94,93,92,91,91 89,89,88,80,80 76**
toteswingers:1&2:£15.70, 2&3:£42.60, 1&3:£14.70 CSF £139.98 TOTE £5.80: £1.90, £3.70, £3.10; EX 193.50 TRIFECTA Not won..
Owner PJL Racing **Bred** Miss Elaine Marie Smith **Trained** Whitsbury, Hants
■ Stewards' Enquiry : Pat Cosgrave two-day ban: used whip above permitted level (Jul 6,8)

FOCUS
Following some heavy showers there was another going change, to soft, with the result that Pearl Secret, who would have been favourite, was taken out of this race. Subsequent Group 2 winner Byron was the best winner of this maiden in the past decade. There were half a dozen in line heading to the furlong pole and the form looks likely to prove fairly ordinary. Only two of the field had run before so there was little to go on.

NOTEBOOK
Boomshackerlacker(IRE), one of only two with prior experience, had only been third of five on his debut at Brighton. Showing the benefit of that outing, he displayed a willing attitude to assert in the latter stages. He looks a nursery type. (op 5-1)
Whipper Snapper(IRE) is a brother to the very useful sprinter Gramercy. After taking a narrow lead he edged over to the far rail and could not hold on, but this obviously represents a pleasing initial effort. (op 20-1)
Bravo Youmzain(IRE) ◆, out of a decent sprinter, is a half-brother to a US Grade 2 winner and his sales price more than doubled to 90,000gns as a 2yo. He ran on nicely after encountering a bit of a troubled passage, and has improvement in him. (tchd 12-1)
Darkening(IRE), in the Godolphin second colours, is a 160,000gns foal who holds a Derby entry. He wandered both ways when the pressure was on, looking decidedly green, but clearly has ability. (op 7-1)
Emperatriz, the sole filly in the field and modestly bred, was running on adjacent to the rail in the latter stages. (op 50-1)
Aussie Reigns(IRE), the other to have run before, had been last of six at Goodwood. He stepped up on that and only faded out of the frame inside the last. (tchd 25-1)
Lawmans Thunder, out of a half-sister to the Cheveley Park Stakes winner Hooray, is another who was in there pitching when the race took shape. (op 13-2)
Mission Approved ◆ was a little disappointing, failing to pick up towards the stands' side of the group, but he is sure to improve for better ground and a longer trip. A half-brother to Supreme Novice Hurdle winner Cinders And Ashes, he's out of a smart half-sister to St Leger winner Brian Boru. (op 2-1)
Sharjah(IRE), reportedly the paddock pick, dropped away after showing pace and may not have acted on the ground.

3347 DANWOOD H'CAP 1m
7:30 (7:31) (Class 5) (0-75,74) 3-Y-O **£2,587** (£770; £384; £192) **Stalls** High

Form RPR
-402 **1** **Negin**[16] 2820 3-9-3 **70** WilliamBuick 12 81
(Ed Dunlop) *hld up: hdwy on bit over 2f out: shkn up to ld over 1f out: rdn and hung rt ins fnl f: styd on wl* **7/2**[2]
5350 **2** *3 1/4* **Tharawal (IRE)**[25] 2543 3-9-4 **74** SimonPearce(3) 2 77
(Terry Clement) *a.p: rdn and ev ch over 1f out: styd on same pce ins fnl f* **20/1**

01-0 **3** *nse* **Afnoon (USA)**[36] 2194 3-9-4 **71** TadhgO'Shea 11 74
(John Dunlop) *hld up: hdwy over 2f out: rdn and ev ch over 1f out: edgd rt and styd on same pce ins fnl f* **7/1**[3]

1400 **4** *½* **Roedean (IRE)**[19] 2733 3-8-7 **65** (tp) LauraPike(5) 7 67
(William Stone) *hld up: hdwy over 2f out: rdn over 1f out: styd on same pce ins fnl f* **20/1**

46-3 **5** *3 ½* **Gold Sceptre (FR)**[25] 2557 3-9-5 **72** RyanMoore 3 66
(Richard Hannon) *led: rdn over 2f out: edgd rt and hdd over 1f out: hmpd sn after: wknd ins fnl f* **3/1**[1]

350- **6** *5* **Excellent Jem**[241] 7080 3-9-3 **70** PatCosgrave 16 52
(Jane Chapple-Hyam) *trckd ldr: racd keenly: rdn over 1f out: wknd fnl f* **7/1**[3]

30-0 **7** *2 ½* **Croquembouche (IRE)**[29] 2428 3-9-7 **74** DaneO'Neill 5 51
(Ed de Giles) *hld up in tch: rdn over 2f out: wknd over 1f out* **14/1**

1-05 **8** *1 ¾* **Brimstone Hill (IRE)**[32] 2331 3-9-7 **74** WilliamCarson 13 47
(Anthony Carson) *hld up: rdn over 2f out: wknd over 1f out* **10/1**

6423 **9** *2 ¾* **Casa Bex**[9] 3048 3-8-7 **63** (vt) RaulDaSilva(3) 9 29
(Philip McBride) *chsd ldrs: rdn over 2f out: wknd over 1f out* **9/1**

-240 **10** *2 ¾* **Widyaan (IRE)**[14] 2898 3-9-3 **70** (b) NickyMackay 10 30
(John Gosden) *s.s: hdwy over 4f out: rdn over 2f out: sn wknd* **8/1**

040 **11** *3 ¼* **Cutting It Fine (IRE)**[114] 737 3-8-12 **65** ShaneKelly 8 17
(Jeremy Noseda) *pushed along in rr early: rdn over 3f out: sn wknd* **20/1**

1m 44.14s (4.14) **Going Correction** +0.45s/f (Yiel) **11** Ran SP% **123.4**
Speed ratings (Par 99): **97,93,93,93,89 84,82,80,77,74 71**
toteswingers:1&2:£31.10, 2&3:£21.40, 1&3:£3.10 CSF £77.97 CT £470.15 TOTE £4.90: £2.20, £8.60, £2.60; EX 129.70 Trifecta £398.70 Pool: £700.43 - 1.30 winning units..
Owner Mohammed Jaber **Bred** Sir Thomas Pilkington **Trained** Newmarket, Suffolk

FOCUS
An ordinary handicap run at a fair pace. The winner did it well but this form is limited.
Casa Bex Official explanation: trainer said gelding was unsuited by the soft ground

3348 WALKER TRANSPORT H'CAP 7f
8:05 (8:06) (Class 3) (0-95,95) 3-Y-0+ **£7,762** (£2,310; £1,154; £577) **Stalls** High

Form RPR

03-0 **1** **Fulbright**[48] 1858 3-9-2 **92** SilvestreDeSousa 6 100
(Mark Johnston) *racd stands' side tl gps merged over 4f out: prom: outpcd 4f out: hdwy over 2f out: led over 1f out: edgd lft: rdn out* **10/1**

0-22 **2** *1* **Gouray Girl (IRE)**[42] 2023 5-9-5 **86** DaneO'Neill 16 94
(Henry Candy) *racd centre tl gps merged over 4f out: hld up: hdwy over 2f out: rdn: edgd rt and ev ch over 1f out: styd on same pce* **9/2**[1]

1245 **3** *¾* **Mr Red Clubs (IRE)**[34] 2277 3-9-5 **95** ShaneKelly 12 98
(Tim Pitt) *racd centre tl gps merged over 4f out: hmpd s: sn prom: rdn and nt clr run over 1f out: swtchd lft: styd on u.p* **7/1**[3]

51-4 **4** *2 ¼* **Yair Hill (IRE)**[29] 2409 4-9-6 **87** TedDurcan 9 87
(John Dunlop) *racd centre tl gps merged over 4f out: hld up: nt clr run and swtchd lft over 1f out: styd on ins fnl f: nt rch ldrs* **9/2**[1]

-015 **5** *hd* **My Son Max**[14] 2896 4-9-0 **81** PatCosgrave 4 80
(P J O'Gorman) *racd stands' side tl gps merged over 4f out: s.i.s and hmpd s: hld up: rdn over 1f out: r.o ins fnl f: nrst fin* **12/1**

1140 **6** *1 ½* **Forceful Appeal (USA)**[21] 2657 4-9-7 **88** MickaelBarzalona 15 83
(Simon Dow) *racd centre tl gps merged over 4f out: mid-div: hdwy 1/2-way: rdn: hung rt and ev ch over 1f out: wknd ins fnl f* **8/1**

4/30 **7** *3 ¼* **Cape Rock**[25] 2545 7-8-11 **78** JamieSpencer 1 65
(William Knight) *racd on stands' side tl gps merged over 4f out: overall ldr tl rdn and edgd rt over 1f out: wknd ins fnl f* **12/1**

2155 **8** *3 ¾* **Masai Moon**[27] 2482 8-8-11 **78** JamesMillman 8 54
(Rod Millman) *racd centre tl gps merged over 4f out: chsd ldrs: rdn over 2f out: wknd over 1f out* **16/1**

4-00 **9** *½* **Mubtadi**[14] 2896 4-8-11 **78** (t) RoystonFfrench 2 53
(Ismail Mohammed) *racd stands' side tl gps merged over 4f out: s.i.s and hmpd s: hld up: rdn over 2f out: a in rr* **33/1**

-010 **10** *1 ¾* **Cruiser**[27] 2500 4-9-4 **85** MartinDwyer 11 55
(William Muir) *racd centre tl gps merged over 4f out: chsd ldrs: rdn and hmpd over 1f out: sn wknd* **12/1**

55-0 **11** *2 ¼* **Al Khan (IRE)**[48] 1858 3-9-1 **91** WilliamBuick 7 52
(Peter Chapple-Hyam) *racd stands' side tl gps merged over 4f out: chsd ldr tl rdn over 2f out: wknd over 1f out* **14/1**

400 **12** *20* **Azrael**[7] 3128 4-9-2 **83** TomQueally 10
(Alan McCabe) *racd centre tl gps merged over 4f out: edgd lft s: chsd ldrs: rdn over 2f out: sn wknd: t.o* **25/1**

-010 **13** *7* **Paramour**[5] 3183 5-9-4 **85** LiamJones 13
(Alan Bailey) *racd centre and led that gp tl gps merged over 4f out: chsd ldrs: rdn over 2f out: sn wknd: t.o* **11/2**[2]

1m 27.52s (1.82) **Going Correction** +0.45s/f (Yiel)
WFA 3 from 4yo+ 9lb **13** Ran SP% **126.9**
Speed ratings (Par 107): **107,105,105,102,102 100,96,92,91,89 87,64,56**
toteswingers:1&2:£9.50, 2&3:£3.80, 1&3:£26.90 CSF £58.00 CT £362.64 TOTE £14.70: £4.30, £1.90, £1.70; EX 108.00 TRIFECTA Not won..
Owner Sheikh Hamdan Bin Mohammed Al Maktoum **Bred** R F And S D Knipe **Trained** Middleham Moor, N Yorks

FOCUS
Following three non-runners the topweight in this decent handicap was running off 7lb below than the race maximum. Initially they divided into two groups, with five of them on the stands' side, but they soon merged again. The pace was sound and the form is rated around the runner-up.

NOTEBOOK
Fulbright came from off the gallop near the stands' rail to win fairly comfortably in the end. This was his first victory since taking the Listed Woodcote Stakes at Epsom in 2011 and the handicapper had proved reluctant to drop him. He had shown little on his reppearance but the step back up in trip and softer ground seemed to suit. (op 14-1)
Gouray Girl(IRE) had her ground and has now finished runner-up on her last three starts. Equally effective at 6f, she is not handicapped out of things but is without a win since October 2010.
Mr Red Clubs(IRE) delivered his challenge widest out on the course after having to be switched. A progressive type, he had gone up 4lb after a good effort in a Listed event last time. (op 11-2 tchd 5-1)
Yair Hill(IRE) ◆ had to wait for a run before staying on nicely. He should be close to peaking now and a handicap at this trip should come his way. The trainer's representative reported that the gelding was unsuited by the soft ground. Official explanation: trainer's rep said gelding was unsuited by the soft ground (op 13-2)
My Son Max, another doing some decent late work, had taken a hefty bump leaving the stalls. He is worth another chance at a mile. (op 10-1)
Forceful Appeal(USA) has been held three times from this mark now since racking up a Polytrack hat-trick at the beginning of the year. (op 7-1 tchd 17-2)
Paramour dropped right away and has been well beaten twice now since his C&D win earlier this month. (tchd 6-1)

3349 POPTELECOM.CO.UK INTERNATIONAL SAVER MAIDEN STKS 1m 2f
8:40 (8:42) (Class 5) 3-Y-0 **£3,234** (£962; £481; £240) **Stalls** Centre

Form RPR

1 **Proofreader** 3-9-3 0 WilliamBuick 11 90+
(John Gosden) *hld up: hdwy over 3f out: rdn to ld over 1f out: styd on wl: eased nr fin* **6/1**[3]

2 *1 ¾* **Awake My Soul (IRE)** 3-9-3 0 KierenFallon 13 86
(Luca Cumani) *hld up: hdwy 6f out: rdn and ev ch over 1f out: styd on same pce ins fnl f* **7/1**

2 **3** *1 ¼* **Suegioo (FR)**[36] 2196 3-9-3 0 AndreaAtzeni 4 83+
(Marco Botti) *chsd ldrs: outpcd 3f out: rallied over 1f out: r.o* **4/1**[2]

0- **4** *shd* **Blazing Speed**[241] 7083 3-9-3 0 JackMitchell 14 83
(James Fanshawe) *hld up: hdwy over 2f out: rdn and edgd lft over 1f out: styd on same pce* **18/1**

4 **5** *2* **Dr Yes (FR)**[15] 2856 3-9-3 0 TomQueally 3 79+
(Sir Henry Cecil) *chsd ldrs: hmpd over 2f out: sn lost pl: swtchd lft and styd on ins fnl f* **7/4**[1]

53 **6** *¾* **Trend Is My Friend (USA)**[34] 2279 3-9-3 0 PatDobbs 16 77
(Amanda Perrett) *trckd ldrs: racd keenly: ev ch over 1f out: sn rdn: no ex fnl f* **14/1**

7 *1 ½* **City Of Canton (IRE)** 3-9-0 0 PatrickHills(3) 9 74+
(Luca Cumani) *hld up: rdn over 2f out: styd on ins fnl f: nvr trbld ldrs* **40/1**

2-0 **8** *nk* **Moshaagib (USA)**[36] 2197 3-9-3 0 TadhgO'Shea 8 74
(John Gosden) *chsd ldr: rdn to ld 2f out: sn hdd: wknd fnl f* **10/1**

05 **9** *2* **Chapelle du Roi (USA)**[36] 2197 3-9-3 0 TedDurcan 15 70
(David Lanigan) *led at stdy pce tl qcknd over 3f out: rdn and hung lft over 2f out: sn hdd: wknd fnl f* **14/1**

0- **10** *¾* **Harlestone Wood**[238] 7134 3-9-3 0 DaneO'Neill 1 68
(John Dunlop) *mid-div: outpcd fr over 2f out* **16/1**

00 **11** *5* **Confluence**[15] 2848 3-8-12 0 PatCosgrave 5 53
(Clifford Lines) *hld up: hdwy over 2f out: wknd and eased over 1f out* **66/1**

0 **12** *¾* **Al Qatari (USA)**[36] 2196 3-9-3 0 LiamJones 10 57
(William Haggas) *sn pushed along in rr: rdn over 3f out: sn lost tch* **33/1**

13 *¾* **Cometography (IRE)** 3-9-3 0 RoystonFfrench 6 55
(Ismail Mohammed) *sn pushed along and a in rr* **50/1**

0 **14** *15* **Bashaash (USA)**[62] 1532 3-8-12 0 TomMcLaughlin 2 20
(Ed Dunlop) *hld up: rdn over 3f out: wknd over 2f out: t.o* **66/1**

2m 11.41s (5.91) **Going Correction** +0.45s/f (Yiel) **14** Ran SP% **127.0**
Speed ratings (Par 99): **94,92,91,91,89 89,88,87,86,85 81,81,80,68**
toteswingers:1&2:£8.30, 2&3:£6.80, 1&3:£3.00 CSF £49.47 TOTE £7.50: £1.80, £1.70, £1.80; EX 43.00 Trifecta £112.20 Pool: £727.57 - 4.80 winning units..
Owner H R H Princess Haya Of Jordan **Bred** Darley **Trained** Newmarket, Suffolk

FOCUS
Probably a reasonable maiden, but one that was run at a steady gallop, and it was something of a messy race. The first two look above-average.
Chapelle du Roi(USA) Official explanation: jockey said colt hung badly left
Confluence Official explanation: jockey said filly ran too free

3350 POPTELECOM.CO.UK BUSINESS BROADBAND H'CAP 5f
9:10 (9:11) (Class 5) (0-75,75) 3-Y-0 **£2,587** (£770; £384; £192) **Stalls** High

Form RPR

1-41 **1** **Lupin Pooter**[22] 2615 3-9-4 **72** JamieSpencer 1 83+
(David Barron) *hld up: hdwy to ld and hung lft 1f out: rdn out* **5/4**[1]

2435 **2** *1 ¼* **Ring For Baileys**[4] 3234 3-8-8 **65** RaulDaSilva(3) 8 71
(Chris Dwyer) *chsd ldrs: led over 1f out: sn hdd: styd on same pce ins fnl f* **6/1**[3]

4521 **3** *1 ½* **Millibar (IRE)**[14] 2871 3-8-13 **67** (p) TomMcLaughlin 2 68
(Nick Littmoden) *prom: edgd lft and outpcd over 1f out: r.o towards fin* **14/1**

5026 **4** *¾* **Ghazeer (IRE)**[30] 2388 3-8-2 **56** oh1 (v[1]) SilvestreDeSousa 3 54
(Derek Shaw) *hld up: rdn over 1f out: r.o: nt trble ldrs* **20/1**

2425 **5** *hd* **Welease Bwian (IRE)**[11] 2986 3-8-13 **67** (v[1]) WilliamCarson 5 64
(Stuart Williams) *hld up in tch: swtchd lft 2f out: rdn over 1f out: no ex ins fnl f* **9/1**

0511 **6** *¾* **Cats Eyes**[16] 2816 3-9-7 **75** ShaneKelly 4 69
(Robert Cowell) *chsd ldrs: rdn over 1f out: hmpd sn after: no ex* **3/1**[2]

-250 **7** *1 ½* **Christopher Chua (IRE)**[28] 2443 3-8-7 **66** ow2 DavidKenny(5) 6 53
(Simon Dow) *trckd ldrs: plld hrd: led wl over 1f out: sn rdn and hdd: wknd ins fnl f* **28/1**

5113 **8** *4* **Laura's Bairn**[7] 3118 3-9-3 **71** (v) KierenFallon 7 46
(J R Jenkins) *led: rdn and hdd wl over 1f out: hmpd and wknd 1f out: eased* **7/1**

1m 1.07s (1.97) **Going Correction** +0.45s/f (Yiel) **8** Ran SP% **121.1**
Speed ratings (Par 99): **102,100,97,96,96 94,92,86**
toteswingers:1&2:£2.40, 2&3:£10.60, 1&3:£4.50 CSF £10.29 CT £77.57 TOTE £2.20: £1.10, £1.90, £2.60; EX 9.60 Trifecta £88.10 Pool: £704.16 - 5.91 winning units..
Owner Liam & Dermot Kelly **Bred** John Starbuck **Trained** Maunby, N Yorks
■ Stewards' Enquiry : David Kenny two-day ban: weighed-in 2lb heavy (Jul 6,8)
Jamie Spencer caution: careless riding.

FOCUS
An ordinary sprint handicap but the winner looks likely to do better.
T/Plt: £3,568.00 to a £1 stake. Pool of £50,833.00 - 10.40 winning tickets. T/Qpdt: £546.80 to a £1 stake. Pool of £3,857.52 - 5.22 winning tickets. CR

2790 REDCAR (L-H)
Friday, June 22

OFFICIAL GOING: Good to soft changing to soft after race 1 (2.10)
Wind: Moderate half behind Weather: Cloudy

3351 BUY YOUR TICKETS ON-LINE @ REDCARRACING.CO.UK (S) STKS 7f
2:10 (2:10) (Class 6) 2-Y-0 **£1,617** (£481; £240; £120) **Stalls** Centre

Form RPR

6214 **1** **Mad Jazz**[7] 3126 2-8-7 0 ShaneBKelly(5) 3 62
(Tony Coyle) *trckd ldrs: pushed along over 2f out: hdwy wl over 1f out: sn rdn and styd on ins fnl f to ld last 75yds* **11/10**[1]

2512 **2** *¾* **Tiger Sunset (IRE)**[8] 3084 2-9-0 0 (p) RyanPowell(3) 8 65
(J S Moore) *trckd ldr: hdwy to ld 2f out: sn clr and hung bdly rt to stands' rail: rdn over 1f out: hdd & wknd last 75yds* **9/2**[2]

3 1 3/4 **Tricky Madam** 2-8-6 0 PatrickMathers 6 50
(Tim Easterby) *dwlt and towards rr: hdwy to trck ldrs 1/2-way: rdn along 2f out: kpt on same pce appr fnl f* **11/1**

00 4 1 **Kendal Princess (IRE)**[17] 2790 2-8-6 0 AndrewElliott 5 47
(David O'Meara) *t.k.h: led: rdn along 3f out: hdd 2f out and grad wknd* **18/1**

0 5 nk **Princess Hollow**[11] 2977 2-8-6 0 BarryMcHugh 1 47
(Tony Coyle) *hld up in rr: swtchd lft to outer and sme hdwy over 2f out: sn rdn and n.d* **14/1**

6 2 1/4 **Chant (IRE)** 2-8-11 0 TomEaves 7 46
(Ann Duffield) *hld up in tch: hdwy to chse ldrs 3f out: sn pushed along and wknd 2f out* **6/1**[3]

0034 7 18 **Zero Rated (IRE)**[9] 3019 2-8-6 0 (p) DuranFentiman 4
(Tim Easterby) *chsd ldrs: rdn along 1/2-way: sn outpcd* **10/1**

1m 28.76s (4.26) **Going Correction** +0.425s/f (Yiel) 7 Ran SP% **109.4**
Speed ratings (Par 91): **92,91,89,88,87 85,64**
Swingers:1&2:£1.60, 2&3:£1.90, 1&3:£5.00 CSF £5.55 TOTE £2.40: £1.20, £1.60; EX 5.30.No bid for the winner.
Owner Paul Inman & Tony Coyle **Bred** Usk Valley Stud **Trained** Norton, N Yorks
■ Stewards' Enquiry : Ryan Powell two-day ban: used whip above permitted level (Jul 6,8)

FOCUS

A modest selling stakes for juveniles that was run at an honest gallop. The winner is a trier and the second is progressing steadily.

NOTEBOOK

Mad Jazz won a similar contest over 5f at Catterick on good to soft on her third start in April, before a below par display over the same trip in a better class York seller on soft ground this month, and she has appreciated this step up to 7f in defying her 6lb penalty. In fact, she only got on top late in the contest and her breeding suggests a further step up in trip is an option, which could bring about more improvement. There was no bid at the subsequent auction. (op 6-5)
Tiger Sunset(IRE) skipped a couple of lengths clear of the field 2f out, only to hang to the near-side rail. He was caught well inside the final furlong and better ground may enable him to see the 7f trip out better. (op 4-1)
Tricky Madam came home well into third on debut, after a tardy start, and can build on this display at a similar level. (op 12-1)
Kendal Princess(IRE) raced prominently for the first 5f. (op 16-1 tchd 20-1)

3352 REDCAR RACECOURSE FOR YOUR WEDDING VENUE MAIDEN STKS 1m 2f
2:45 (2:45) (Class 5) 3-Y-0+ **£1,940** (£577; £288; £144) **Stalls** Low

Form RPR

532 1 **Star Deal (IRE)**[24] 2592 3-9-0 73 AndrewElliott 11 78
(Alan Swinbank) *trckd ldr: tk cl order 3f out: led over 2f out: sn rdn clr: drvn ins fnl f: kpt on* **5/2**[2]

6-5 2 nk **Adeste**[35] 2249 3-8-9 0 JimmyQuinn 6 72
(Noel Quinlan) *trckd ldrs: hdwy to chse ldng pair over 2f out: rdn to chse wnr over 1f out: drvn ins fnl f and styd on: jst hld* **5/4**[1]

5 3 4 1/2 **Echo Of Footsteps**[22] 2633 3-8-9 0 TonyHamilton 5 63
(Michael Herrington) *trckd ldrs: effrt 3f out and sn pushed along: rdn 2f out and kpt on same pce* **7/1**[3]

4 8 **Albillanbaz (IRE)** 3-9-0 0 MichaelO'Connell 7 52
(John Quinn) *midfield: hdwy and in tch 1/2-way: hdwy to chse ldrs whn sltly hmpd and swtchd rt 3f out: rdn along over 2f out: sn one pce* **8/1**

-020 5 1 **Master Chipper**[8] 3066 3-9-0 67 (b[1]) TomEaves 10 50
(Michael Dods) *led: rdn along 3f out: hdd jst over 2f out and grad wknd* **16/1**

03 6 3 3/4 **Airmyles**[17] 2794 4-9-7 0 ShaneBKelly[(5)] 1 43
(Tracy Waggott) *midfield: hdwy and in tch 1/2-way: chsd ldrs over 2f out: sn rdn and wknd* **20/1**

5 7 10 **Mr Flintstone**[13] 2927 3-9-0 0 DavidNolan 8 23
(Tim Walford) *a towards rr* **66/1**

30/ 8 1 **Spokesperson (USA)**[718] 3735 4-9-12 0 (v[1]) PatrickMathers 4 21
(Frederick Watson) *a in rr* **66/1**

0- 9 29 **Misty Eyes**[261] 6630 3-8-9 0 DuranFentiman 13
(Geoffrey Harker) *chsd ldng pair: rdn along over 4f out: sn wknd* **66/1**

10 nk **Showmehow** 4-9-7 0 PaddyAspell 2
(Ray Craggs) *s.i.s: a in rr* **66/1**

11 3 3/4 **Wotsitgotodowithu (IRE)**[23] 4-9-12 0 BarryMcHugh 3
(Noel Wilson) *s.i.s: a in rr* **20/1**

2m 15.0s (7.90) **Going Correction** +0.70s/f (Yiel)
WFA 3 from 4yo 12lb 11 Ran SP% **118.0**
Speed ratings (Par 103): **96,95,92,85,84 81,73,73,49,49 46**
Swingers:1&2:£2.00, 2&3:£2.50, 1&3:£4.60 CSF £5.66 TOTE £3.00: £1.10, £1.40, £1.70; EX 7.30.
Owner G H Bell **Bred** Wiji Bloodstock & Marco Bozzi **Trained** Melsonby, N Yorks

FOCUS

A pretty modest maiden for 3-y-os and up. They finished strung out off a solid gallop under attritional ground conditions and the third looks the best guide to the level. The ground was officially changed to soft after the race.

3353 WIN A VIP DAY OUT @ REDCARRACING.CO.UK H'CAP 1m 2f
3:20 (3:23) (Class 5) (0-70,69) 4-Y-0+ **£1,940** (£577; £288; £144) **Stalls** Low

Form RPR

-000 1 **Gala Casino Star (IRE)**[29] 2414 7-8-13 **68** (v) JordanNason[(7)] 7 81
(Geoffrey Harker) *trckd ldrs: hdwy to chse ldr over 4f out: led over 3f out: oushecd clr 2f out: styd on wl* **8/1**

0 2 3 3/4 **Snooker (GER)**[73] 1276 6-8-12 **60** TonyHamilton 4 66
(Rose Dobbin) *in tch: hdwy to trck ldrs over 4f out: effrt 3f out: rdn to chse wnr wl over 1f out: drvn and no imp fnl f* **40/1**

6- 3 3/4 **Xclaim**[299] 5511 4-9-5 **67** MichaelO'Connell 14 71
(Micky Hammond) *towards rr: gd hdwy on inner 3f out: rdn to chse ldrs over 2f out: swtchd rt over 1f out: styd on ins fnl f: nrst fin* **22/1**

33-0 4 1 1/2 **Pinotage**[24] 2588 4-8-13 **64** DaleSwift[(3)] 2 65
(Peter Niven) *trckd kldr on inner: rdn along over 3f out: drvn 2f out: kpt on same pce* **9/2**[2]

6-41 5 6 **Al Furat (USA)**[17] 2792 4-9-0 **67** ShaneBKelly[(5)] 5 56
(Ron Barr) *s.i.s and bhd: pushed along and hdwy on inner 3f out: rdn 2f out: nvr nr ldrs* **2/1**[1]

3243 6 9 **Free Art**[9] 3031 4-9-7 **69** DuranFentiman 8 40
(Geoffrey Harker) *midfield: rdn along and 4f out: nvr a factor* **5/1**[3]

3330 7 2 **Coral Sands (IRE)**[24] 2593 4-8-8 **56** AndrewElliott 13 23
(Alan Swinbank) *prom: pushed along 4f out: rdn over 3f out and sn wknd* **17/2**

5050 8 10 **Downtown Boy (IRE)**[9] 3029 4-8-2 **50** oh3 PatrickMathers 3
(Ray Craggs) *led: rdn along overc 4f out: hdd over 3f out and sn wknd* **20/1**

440 9 21 **Border Bandit (USA)**[34] 2287 4-9-1 **63** PaddyAspell 12
(Tracy Waggott) *a in rr: bhd fnl 3f* **22/1**

0502 10 9 **Media Stars**[21] 2670 7-8-2 **53** (p) DominicFox[(3)] 11
(Robert Johnson) *in tch: rdn along 4f out: sn wknd and bhd* **18/1**

103- 11 2 **Pattern Mark**[324] 4673 6-8-11 **59** TomEaves 9
(Ollie Pears) *dwlt: a in rr: bhd fnl 3f* **16/1**

2m 13.18s (6.08) **Going Correction** +0.70s/f (Yiel) 11 Ran SP% **116.9**
Speed ratings (Par 103): **103,100,99,98,93 86,84,76,59,52 51**
Swingers:1&2:£22.80, 2&3:£51.50, 1&3:£19.80 CSF £297.33 CT £6568.87 TOTE £10.20: £3.00, £11.90, £7.60; EX 677.90.
Owner Mrs Tracy Nason **Bred** Glashare House Stud **Trained** Thirkleby, N Yorks

FOCUS

A below-average handicap for older horses. The form is rated around the winner, third and fourth.
Al Furat(USA) Official explanation: trainer said gelding was unsuited by the soft ground

3354 ANDERSON BARROWCLIFF H'CAP (QUALIFIER FOR THE JOHN SMITH'S STRAIGHT-MILE CHAMPIONSHIP) 1m
4:00 (4:00) (Class 3) (0-95,85) 3-Y-0+ **£3,881** (£1,155; £577; £288) **Stalls** Centre

Form RPR

2500 1 **Kiwi Bay**[14] 2882 7-10-0 **85** TomEaves 3 90
(Michael Dods) *t.k.h: trckd ldr: effrt to chal 2f out: rdn over 1f out: drvn ins fnl f: edgd lft: led nr line* **7/4**[1]

36-2 2 hd **Next Edition (IRE)**[27] 2510 4-9-6 **82** ShaneBKelly[(5)] 6 86
(Philip Kirby) *set stdy pce: qcknd 3f out: jnd 2f out and sn rdn: drvn ins fnl f: hdd and no ex nr line* **2/1**[2]

-660 3 3/4 **Merchant Of Medici**[6] 3167 5-9-5 **76** BarryMcHugh 5 78
(Micky Hammond) *hld up: hdwy to chse ldng pair 2f out: rdn over 1f out: kpt on fnl f* **5/1**

1-24 4 4 1/2 **Springheel Jake**[16] 2824 3-8-7 **77** DaleSwift[(3)] 4 69
(Ann Duffield) *chsd ldng pair: rdn along wl over 2f out: sn outpcd* **7/2**[3]

1m 41.6s (3.60) **Going Correction** +0.55s/f (Yiel)
WFA 3 from 4yo+ 10lb 4 Ran SP% **108.6**
Speed ratings (Par 107): **104,103,103,98**
CSF £5.55 TOTE £2.50; EX 5.20.
Owner Kiwi Racing **Bred** Templeton Stud **Trained** Denton, Co Durham

FOCUS

A fair handicap for 3-y-os and up, despite the disappointingly small field after three runners were taken out in the morning. The gallop appeared quite sedate early on but the form looks reasonable, rated around the placed horses.

NOTEBOOK

Kiwi Bay was competing off a rating only 1lb higher than when recording his third C&D success last October, and 4lb lower than his peak career-winning mark on good to soft ground here in October 2010. He did well to get on top close home considering the race was not run to suit. He will reportedly be back for more, at this his favourite hunting ground, in the final of this straight-mile handicap series. (op 15-8 tchd 13-8)
Next Edition(IRE) was headed on the line at York last month over this trip (big field, good to firm), and suffered a similar fate here, after very nearly managing to make all at his own tempo. A drop back to 7f on soft ground may be an option worth exploring. (op 5-2)
Merchant Of Medici ran sixth in the same York race as Next Edition last month and was weighted to get much closer to that rival. He duly did so, and is currently competing off a feasible mark. (op 4-1 tchd 6-1)
Springheel Jake didn't appear to appreciate this step up to 1m on soft ground. (tchd 3-1 and 4-1)

3355 SUMMER WEDDING FAYRE HERE ON 29TH JULY CLASSIFIED CLAIMING STKS 1m 2f
4:35 (4:36) (Class 6) 3-Y-0+ **£1,704** (£503; £251) **Stalls** Low

Form RPR

-435 1 **Elizabeth Coffee (IRE)**[13] 2909 4-9-7 73 GeorgeDowning[(7)] 5 67
(Ian Williams) *s.i.s and hld up in rr: stdy hdwy over 3f out: chsd ldrs 2f out: rdn to ld wl over 1f out: drvn out* **6/4**[1]

060- 2 1/2 **Scarlet Prince**[256] 6760 3-8-7 54 DaleSwift[(3)] 8 60
(Tony Coyle) *hld up: hdwy wl over 2f out: chsd ldrs and swtchd lft 1f out: sn rdn to chal and ev ch tl drvn and nt qckn nr fin* **14/1**

0/-0 3 1 1/4 **Uncle Brit**[7] 3116 6-9-6 60 TomEaves 4 56
(Malcolm Jefferson) *trckd ldng pair: hdwy 4f out: led wl over 2f out and sn rdn and hdd wl over 1f out: ev ch tl one pce ins fnl f* **25/1**

2022 4 1 3/4 **Eijaaz (IRE)**[14] 2874 11-9-2 59 (p) DuranFentiman 3 48
(Geoffrey Harker) *hld up in rr: hdwy over 3f out: chsd ldrs wl over 1f out: rdn and ch jst ins fnl f: sn drvn and one pce* **4/1**[3]

3100 5 6 **Crunched**[13] 2936 5-9-4 75 (b) JimmyQuinn 6 38
(Tim Pitt) *cl up: led 4f out: rdn along and hdd wl over 2f out: sn wknd* **6/1**

2-53 6 11 **Sinatramania**[17] 2792 5-9-8 56 PatrickMathers 11 20
(Tracy Waggott) *trcaked ldrs: hdwy over 3f out: rdn over 2f out and sn btn* **7/2**[2]

-630 7 35 **Norton Girl**[24] 2588 4-8-11 44 ShaneBKelly[(5)] 9
(Tracy Waggott) *sn led: rdn along and hdd 4f out: sn wknd* **25/1**

2m 14.4s (7.30) **Going Correction** +0.70s/f (Yiel)
WFA 3 from 4yo+ 12lb 7 Ran SP% **110.9**
Speed ratings (Par 101): **98,97,96,95,90 81,53**
Swingers:1&2:£4.30, 2&3:£16.70, 1&3:£5.60 CSF £23.11 TOTE £2.30: £2.00, £6.60; EX 17.50.
Owner Dr Marwan Koukash **Bred** David Carey **Trained** Portway, Worcs

FOCUS

A fair claimer run at an honest gallop but the form is rated cautiously.

3356 FOLLOW REDCARRACING ON FACEBOOK & TWITTER H'CAP 1m
5:10 (5:11) (Class 5) (0-70,69) 3-Y-0+ **£1,940** (£577; £288; £144) **Stalls** Centre

Form RPR

6-66 1 **Izzet**[4] 3215 4-8-11 **52** PatrickMathers 4 63
(Ron Barr) *hld up towards rr: stdy hdwy on wd outside over 3f out: jnd ldrs over 2f out and edgd rt over 1f out: led 1f out: styd on strly* **11/1**

6-03 2 3 1/4 **Gadobout Dancer**[9] 3021 5-8-11 **52** BarryMcHugh 5 55
(Tony Coyle) *midfield: hdwy 1/2-way: rdn to chse ldr 2f out: drvn and ev ch over 1f out: kpt on same pce fnl f* **10/1**

0-23 3 hd **Broctune Papa Gio**[25] 2535 5-9-4 **64** ShaneBKelly[(5)] 10 67
(Keith Reveley) *trckd ldrs: hdwy 1/2-way: led wl over 2f out: rdn wl over 1f out: hdd and drvn 1f out: kpt on same pce* **3/1**[1]

-003 4 1 **Iceblast**[7] 3115 4-9-5 **60** DavidNolan 2 61
(Michael Easterby) *in tch: hdwy to trck ldrs 1/2-way: effrt over 2f out: rdn wl over 1f out: sn one pce* **12/1**

-003 5 3 1/2 **Triple Eight (IRE)**[13] 2922 4-9-12 **67** (p) MichaelO'Connell 6 60
(Philip Kirby) *towards rr: gd hdwy to chse ldrs wl over 2f out: sn rdn and hung bdly lft wl over 1f out: kpt on same pce fnl f* **6/1**[3]

-006 6 2 3/4 **Kieron's Rock (IRE)**[17] 2788 3-7-10 **50** DominicFox[(3)] 17 34
(Jedd O'Keeffe) *led: rdn along 1/2-way: hdd wl over 2f out and grad wknd* **16/1**

1243 **7** *nse* **Pelican Rock (IRE)**[13] 2283 3-8-8 **59**.........................(t) DuranFentiman 1 43
(Andrew Crook) *chsd ldrs: hdwy and cl up 3f out: rdn along and hld whn hmpd 1 1/2f out: one pce after* **12/1**

-000 **8** *2 1/2* **Benidorm**[17] 2796 4-8-9 **50**..(p) TonyHamilton 9 30
(John Wainwright) *nvr bttr than midfield* **40/1**

215 **9** *nk* **Outlaw Torn (IRE)**[17] 2786 3-8-1 **59**.............................(e) JasonHart(7) 8 37
(Richard Guest) *a towards rr* **17/2**

-232 **10** *6* **What's The Point**[28] 2455 4-9-12 **67**.................................(p) TomEaves 3 33
(Ollie Pears) *chsd ldrs: rdn along 3f out: sn wknd* **5/1**[2]

00-0 **11** *16* **Stillington**[42] 2048 6-8-10 **51** oh3 ow1...................... RobbieFitzpatrick 14
(Mel Brittain) *chsd ldrs: rdn along 1/2-way: sn lost pl and bhd* **33/1**

060- **12** *6* **Minne Wa Wa**[268] 6458 3-8-3 **57**.................................. RyanPowell(3) 12
(David Brown) *chsd ldr 3f: rdn along 1/2-way: sn lost pl and bhd* **25/1**

550- **13** *14* **Northgate Lodge (USA)**[223] 7400 7-8-9 **50** oh3........... JimmyQuinn 13
(Mel Brittain) *a in rr: bhd fr 1/2-way* **33/1**

1m 41.74s (3.74) **Going Correction** +0.55s/f (Yiel)
WFA 3 from 4yo+ 10lb **13** Ran SP% **117.3**
Speed ratings (Par 103): **103,99,99,98,95 92,92,89,89,83 67,61,47**
Swingers:1&2:£14.70, 2&3:£8.50, 1&3:£8.90 CSF £110.43 CT £417.01 TOTE £10.90: £4.00, £2.90, £1.20; EX 110.60.
Owner A Suddes **Bred** Paulyn Limited **Trained** Seamer, N Yorks
■ Stewards' Enquiry : Patrick Mathers one-day ban: careless riding (Jul 6)

FOCUS
A moderate handicap but a sound gallop and the form is rated through the runner-up to her latest mark.
What's The Point Official explanation: trainer's rep said gelding finished distressed
Northgate Lodge(USA) Official explanation: jockey said gelding never travelled

3357 COME RACING TOMORROW ON LADIES' DAY MAIDEN H'CAP 5f
5:45 (5:46) (Class 5) (0-70,69) 3-Y-0+ **£1,940** (£577; £288; £144) **Stalls** Centre

Form RPR

04-0 **1** **Baltic Bomber (IRE)**[65] 1441 3-8-10 **57**.................... MichaelO'Connell 8 66
(John Quinn) *a cl up: led 2f out: rdn ent fnl f: kpt on wl* **5/2**[1]

0620 **2** *1* **Ambitious Icarus**[9] 3050 3-8-13 **60**.......................(e[1]) RobbieFitzpatrick 1 65
(Richard Guest) *towards rr: hdwy 2f out: rdn to chse wnr ins fnl f: kpt on* **5/1**[3]

060- **3** *1 1/4* **Toffee Nose**[300] 5490 5-8-4 **50** oh5............................. ShaneBKelly(5) 11 51
(Ron Barr) *prom on outer: effrt 2f out and ev ch tl rdn and one pce ent fnl f* **14/1**

3/5- **4** *1/2* **Moorhouse Girl**[415] 1813 5-9-11 **69**.................................... DaleSwift(3) 6 68
(David Brown) *cl up: rdn over 1f out: wknd fnl f* **11/2**

4060 **5** *1 1/4* **Script**[2] 3285 3-8-3 **50** oh5...................................... PatrickMathers 7 44
(Alan Berry) *dwlt: sn chsng ldrs: rdn along 2f out and sn one pce* **33/1**

405- **6** *3 1/4* **Trust Fund Babe (IRE)**[276] 6232 3-8-12 **59**................ DuranFentiman 4 42
(Tim Easterby) *chsd ldrs: rdn along 2f out: sn wknd* **8/1**

546- **7** *2* **Kara's Vision**[297] 5590 3-8-6 **53**...................................... AndrewElliott 10 28
(Robert Cowell) *dwlt: a towards rr* **4/1**[2]

5-00 **8** *1* **Never In (IRE)**[20] 2695 3-8-3 **50** oh5................................ JimmyQuinn 2 22
(Alan Berry) *s.i.s: a in rr* **25/1**

4-00 **9** *1 1/4* **Cried For You (IRE)**[48] 1843 3-8-8 **55**............................... TomEaves 5 22
(Tim Easterby) *led: rdn along 1/2-way: sn hdd & wknd* **10/1**

1m 1.12s (2.52) **Going Correction** +0.55s/f (Yiel)
WFA 3 from 4yo+ 6lb **9** Ran SP% **114.3**
Speed ratings (Par 103): **101,99,97,96,94 89,86,84,82**
Swingers:1&2:£77.90, 2&3:£99.30, 1&3:£70.80 CSF £14.88 CT £143.30 TOTE £2.40: £1.10, £3.80, £7.60; EX 20.00.
Owner The New Century Partnership **Bred** D And Mrs D Veitch **Trained** Settrington, N Yorks

FOCUS
A modest maiden handicap with few offering solid form and the third racing from out of the handicap.
Never In(IRE) Official explanation: jockey said filly reared as stalls opened
T/Plt: £155.50 to a £1 stake. Pool: £37,957.30 - 178.19 winning tickets. T/Qpdt: £142.30 to a £1 stake. Pool: £2,500.80 - 13.00 winning tickets. JR

3358 - 3360a (Foreign Racing) - See Raceform Interactive

3170 LIMERICK (R-H)
Friday, June 22

OFFICIAL GOING: Soft (good to soft in places)

3361a MARTIN MOLONY STKS (LISTED RACE) 1m 3f 70y
7:05 (7:05) 3-Y-0+ **£21,666** (£6,333; £3,000; £1,000)

RPR

1 **Tannery (IRE)**[14] 2901 3-8-10 102.................................... WayneLordan 5 106+
(David Wachman, Ire) *w.w: clsd 3f out: chal and led fr 1f out: styd on wl* **11/1**

2 *3* **Backbench Blues (IRE)**[14] 2901 3-8-13 107................. FranBerry 6 104+
(Mrs John Harrington, Ire) *sn trckd ldrs: cl up and almost on terms fr over 4f out: led and wandered under 2f out: hdd fr 1f out and sn wandered abt again: kpt on same pce* **6/4**[1]

3 *nk* **Defining Year (IRE)**[12] 2961 4-9-6 103............................ ShaneFoley 1 100
(M Halford, Ire) *prom: 4th 3f out: chal fr 2f out: sn sltly impeded: no imp and kpt on same pce ins fnl f* **5/1**[3]

4 *1 1/4* **Rising Wind (IRE)**[12] 2964 4-9-6 87................................... ChrisHayes 2 95+
(Kevin Prendergast, Ire) *in rr: no imp u.p fr 2f out: kpt on wl wout threatening fnl f* **25/1**

5 *nk* **Offer (IRE)**[33] 2317 3-8-10 .... CO'Donoghue 4 98
(A P O'Brien, Ire) *sn prom: rdn to ld 3f out: hdd fr 2f out: no imp and kpt on same pce fr 1f out* **7/2**[2]

6 *2 1/2* **Aklan (IRE)**[14] 2901 3-8-10 .... BenCurtis 3 94
(John M Oxx, Ire) *w.w: 6th fr 3f out: kpt on same pce u.p fr 1 1/2f out* **7/1**

7 *7 1/2* **Tower Rock (IRE)**[14] 2901 3-8-10 108................. SeamieHeffernan 8 81
(A P O'Brien, Ire) *sn led: hdd fr 3f out: no ex fr 2f out* **7/1**

8 *10* **Frontier (GER)**[14] 2901 3-8-10 87..............................(b[1]) DavidMcCabe 7 64
(A P O'Brien, Ire) *sn trckd ldrs: rdn and wknd fr 4f out* **25/1**

2m 37.48s (157.48)
WFA 3 from 4yo+ 13lb **8** Ran SP% **119.9**
CSF £29.46 TOTE £32.80: £4.00, £1.02, £1.02; DF 35.60.
Owner Mrs D P Magnier **Bred** Grange Stud **Trained** Goolds Cross, Co Tipperary

FOCUS
Considering her progression since, it is hard to fathom how Tannery was beaten off a mark of 75 in a Leopardstown handicap a matter of weeks ago. It's equally clear, though, how much better she is with cut in the ground. Weak form for a Listed race, rated around the winner and fourth.

NOTEBOOK
Tannery(IRE) was slowest away, which probably suited her, as she made up her ground travelling well in the straight. When asked to go and win her race she quickened up well. Her trainer won't mind a wet summer for this filly as she's smart when conditions are in her favour. (op 10/1 tchd 12/1)
Backbench Blues(IRE) had little chance with the winner but certainly did himself no favours with his antics in the straight as he interfered with at least two of his rivals as he hung both left and right away from the whip. (op 11/8 tchd 13/8)
Defining Year(IRE) ran a straightforward race by comparison to the runner-up, but just wasn't quite good enough. He almost got to the front in the straight but the winner's turn of foot was just too much for him and the runner-up also bumped him. It wouldn't have been the oddest outcome had the stewards promoted him to second. He just falls short at this level though. (op 9/2)
Rising Wind(IRE) did her best work when the race was over. (op 20/1)
Offer(IRE) seemed to go quite hard towards the front and just didn't get home. (op 9/2 tchd 5/1)

3362 - 3366a (Foreign Racing) - See Raceform Interactive

2907 MAISONS-LAFFITTE (R-H)
Friday, June 22

OFFICIAL GOING: Turf: very soft

3367a PRIX LA MOSKOWA (LISTED RACE) (4YO+) (TURF) 1m 7f 110y
2:55 (12:00) 4-Y-0+ **£21,666** (£8,666; £6,500; £4,333; £2,166)

RPR

1 **Inside Man (IRE)**[36] 6-8-11 0..................................(b) AnthonyCrastus 4 106
(E Lellouche, France) **22/5**[2]

2 *hd* **Tac De Boistron (FR)**[26] 2534 5-9-1 0.........................(p) ThierryJarnet 3 109
(A Lyon, France) **2/1**[1]

3 *1 1/4* **Lone Ranger (FR)**[29] 4-8-11 0............................ ChristopheSoumillon 6 104
(A De Royer-Dupre, France) **2/1**[1]

4 *shd* **Aaim To Prosper (IRE)**[22] 2639 8-8-11 0...................... LouisBeuzelin 8 104
(Brian Meehan) *settled midfield: racing on outside: sent to ld bef 1/2-way: stl led 2 1/2f out: rdn and u.p 2f out: hdd 1 1/2f out: r.o u.str ride fnl f: lost 3rd cl home* **21/1**

5 *2* **Lacateno**[27] 5-9-1 0.. JohanVictoire 1 106
(W Hickst, Germany) **7/1**[3]

6 *4* **Affaire D'Etat (FR)**[14] 4-8-11 0.................................(p) ThierryThulliez 2 97
(P Demercastel, France) **25/1**

7 *3/4* **Mandali (FR)**[465] 860 8-8-11 0.. GaetanMasure 7 96
(J-P Gallorini, France) **26/1**

8 *snk* **Night Serenade (IRE)**[25] 5-8-11 0...............................(p) FabriceVeron 5 96
(H-A Pantall, France) **12/1**

3m 26.3s (206.30) **8** Ran SP% **117.5**
WIN (incl. 1 euro stake): 5.40. PLACES: 1.40, 1.20, 1.30. DF: 8.30. SF: 19.70.
Owner Mme Francis Teboul **Bred** F Teboul & E Lellouche **Trained** Lamorlaye, France

3326 ASCOT (R-H)
Saturday, June 23

OFFICIAL GOING: Straight course - good to soft changing to good after race 1 (2.30); round course - good to soft (good in places)
Rail on Round course on inside line and distances as advertised.
Wind: Medium, against Weather: Sunny spells

3368 CHESHAM STKS (LISTED RACE) 7f
2:30 (2:33) (Class 1) 2-Y-0
£31,190 (£11,825; £5,918; £2,948; £1,479; £742) **Stalls** Centre

Form RPR

41 **1** **Tha'Ir (IRE)**[17] 2822 2-9-3 0... FrankieDettori 7 99+
(Saeed Bin Suroor) *t.k.h: hld up in tch towards rr: stl plenty to do and nt clr run 2f out: rdn and gd hdwy over 1f out: led 1f out: r.o strly and drew clr: rdn out* **9/2**[3]

231 **2** *2 1/4* **Cruck Realta**[11] 3010 2-8-12 0...................................... MatthewDavies 3 88
(Mick Channon) *leggy: stdd and stmbld s: t.k.h: chsd ldrs: rdn to chse ldr 2f out: led and drvn over 1f out: hdd 1f out: outpcd by wnr but battled on for 2nd fnl f* **33/1**

1 **3** *nk* **Lovely Pass (IRE)**[28] 2492 2-8-12 0......................... SilvestreDeSousa 2 87
(Mahmood Al Zarooni) *leggy: stdd s: t.k.h: hld up in tch: effrt and rdn 2f out: chal over 1f out: drvn and unable qck 1f out: outpcd by wnr but kpt on battling for 2nd fnl f* **11/1**

4 *2 3/4* **Move To Strike (IRE)**[47] 1942 2-9-3 0............................. KevinManning 8 85
(J S Bolger, Ire) *unf: scope: lw: broke wl: t.k.h: grad stdd bk and hld up in tch: swtchd lft and effrt 2f out: hdwy to chse ldrs over 1f out: edgd lft 1f out: sn wknd ins fnl f* **2/1**[1]

0121 **5** *nk* **Chilworth Icon**[21] 2702 2-9-6 0.. MartinHarley 4 87
(Mick Channon) *lw: t.k.h: hld up in tch: rdn and effrt 2f out: drvn and chsd ldrs over 1f out: no ex 1f out: wknd ins fnl f* **14/1**

5 **6** *1 3/4* **The Sixties**[12] 2983 2-9-3 0.. JamesDoyle 5 80
(Mick Channon) *w'like: str: sn led and set stdy gallop: rdn and qcknd 3f out: hdd over 1f out: wknd ent fnl f* **66/1**

4 **7** *nk* **Frege (USA)**[16] 2844 2-8-12 0... KierenFallon 9 74
(Brian Meehan) *ponied to s: t.k.h: sn chsd ldr tl 2f out: sn outpcd u.p and n.m.r over 1f out: plugged on but no threat to wnr fnl f* **50/1**

1 **8** *shd* **Jalaa (IRE)**[18] 2784 2-9-3 0.. PaulHanagan 6 80
(Richard Hannon) *hld up in tch: n.m.r ent fnl 2f: drvn an unable qck wl over 1f out: outpcd and btn over 1f out: plugged on same pce after* **11/4**[2]

0 **9** *1* **Zanetto**[28] 2480 2-9-3 0.. DavidProbert 14 76+
(Andrew Balding) *plld hrd: chsd ldr: rdn and struggling ent fnl 2f: outpcd and btn over 1f out: plugged on same pce and wl hld fnl f* **33/1**

1 **10** *nk* **Pasaka Boy**[11] 3009 2-9-3 0... LeeNewman 12 75
(Jonathan Portman) *leggy: in tch: pushed along 1/2-way: rdn and no imp over 2f out: plugged on same pce u.p and n.d fnl 2f* **33/1**

2421 **11** *3* **Hillbilly Boy (IRE)**[34] 2308 2-9-3 0............................ RichardHughes 16 68
(Bill Turner) *in tch: rdn and struggling 3f out: wknd wl over 1f out* **16/1**

11 *dht* **Downright Dizzie** 2-8-12 0... LeonnaMayor 15 63
(Alastair Lidderdale) *leggy: hld up in tch: outpcd and struggling whn hung rt ent fnl 2f: no threat to ldrs fnl 2f* **250/1**

13 *2* **St Paul De Vence (IRE)** 2-9-3 0... StevieDonohoe 1 62
(Paul Cole) *rn green and sn outpcd and pushed along in rr: wl bhd 1/2-way: styd on fnl f: n.d* **50/1**

1533 **14** *2 ¼* **Effie B**[23] 2638 2-8-12 0.. WilliamBuick 11 52
(Mick Channon) *a towards rr: rdn and struggling whn pushed rt over 2f out: hung rt and lost tch 2f out* **22/1**

1m 30.01s (2.41) **Going Correction** +0.175s/f (Good) **14** Ran SP% **118.0**
Speed ratings (Par 101): **93,90,90,86,86 84,84,84,83,82 79,79,76,74**
toteswingers: 1&2 £25.50, 1&3 £6.20, 2&3 £46.00 CSF £152.00 CT £1548.00 TOTE £5.30: £1.90, £8.70, £2.20; EX 168.80 Trifecta £1151.00 Pool: £14,911.34 - 9.58 winning units..
Owner Godolphin **Bred** Lodge Park Stud **Trained** Newmarket, Suffolk

FOCUS
Jockeys in the first variously described the ground as "nearly good", "good to soft" and "dead". It was certainly drying out, depite one downpour before racing, and after this race the official description was amended to good. The early pace was very modest and several took a tug, with the lack of a true gallop contributing to a modest time, four seconds outside standard. The Chesham is confined to the progeny of sires who won at 1m2f or further, so tends to attract more late-maturing types than the other 2yo events at the meeting. The majority of recent winners have not amounted to a great deal but last year's scorer, the filly Maybe, has bucked that trend by making her mark at Group 1 level. This year's edition appeared to lack something in the way of depth, and is rated at the bottom end of the recent race averages, but was still par for the grade.

NOTEBOOK
Tha'Ir(IRE) was giving his sire New Approach his third 2yo winner of the week, following Dawn Approach in the Coventry Stakes and Newfangled in the Albany. The colt's Ripon win looked even better in the light of runner-up Bircham, who races in the same colours, going in by five lengths next time. Settled two-thirds of the way down the field, he made fluent progress before quickening up nicely to assert. He looks a nice prospect and is likely to step up in grade now, with the Vintage Stakes at Glorious Goodwood perhaps next for him. He will need to improve on this bare form, but ought to progress again. (op 11-2)

Cruck Realta's trainer ran four, all of them by first-season sire Sixties Icon. This filly did best of them, racing prominently all the way after nodding leaving the stalls and fighting on to the line, if no threat late on to the winner. She got the extra furlong well and her Salisbury win had been boosted when runner-up Momalorka won at Goodwood on Friday night

Lovely Pass(IRE) was carrying the second Godolphin colours. She issued her challenge earlier than the winner but could not prevent him skating past. Notably green when making a winning debut at Lingfield, she edged both ways here late on, but is clearly a useful filly with more to offer when back against her own sex. (op 9-1)

Move To Strike(IRE), from the same yard as Dawn Approach, had won by 9l on his second start but the next three home that day have all been beaten since. He was one of those who pulled for their heads early, before he managed to find some cover further back in the field. After improving on the stands' side of the bunch he briefly posed a threat, but hung to his right under pressure and lacked a change of pace. His jockey described him as big and raw, and in need of more time. (tchd 9-4)

Chilworth Icon, another of the Channon four, was conceding a 3lb penalty for his win in the Listed Woodcote Stakes at Epsom. After racing keenly early, his measure was taken when things hotted up but he stuck on for fifth. This trip looks as far as he wants to go at this stage. (tchd 16-1 in places)

The Sixties, another of the Channon team, ran well from the front and this was a big step up on his Windsor debut. However, his proximity doesn't enhance this form.

Frege(USA) had been fourth in a Lingfield maiden auction first time and she wasn't up to this much stiffer task, pulling early in common with several others. She got the seventh furlong well enough. (tchd 66-1)

Jalaa(IRE)'s trainer won this in both 2008 and 2009 and this well regarded Leicester maiden winner was his choice from a large number of possibles this time. The colt didn't settle until he was reined back, then found himself short of room when he needed to pick up. His response when in the clear was lacking and he has something to prove now. (op 5-2 tchd 2-1 and 3-1 in places)

Zanetto wasn't discredited and will have prospects back in ordinary company. (op 66-1)

Pasaka Boy won the other division of the Salisbury maiden won by Cruck Realta, albeit in a slower time, but he wasn't up to this level. (tchd 40-1)

3369 HARDWICKE STKS (GROUP 2) 1m 4f

3:05 (3:06) (Class 1) 4-Y-0+

£113,420 (£43,000; £21,520; £10,720; £5,380; £2,700) **Stalls** Low

Form RPR

32-1 **1** **Sea Moon**[28] 2481 4-9-0 121.. RyanMoore 3 125+
(Sir Michael Stoute) *midfield: hdwy 3f out: led 2f out: edgd rt over 1f out: sn qcknd clr: stretched out nicely and in command thrght fnl f* **3/1**[1]

1-33 **2** *3 ¼* **Dunaden (FR)**[20] 2744 6-9-0 117................. Christophe-PatriceLemaire 6 122+
(M Delzangles, France) *trckd ldrs: lost pl over 3f out: outpcd over 2f out: rdn and styng on whn nt clr run and hmpd over 1f out: prog thrght fnl f and tk 2nd fnl 110yds: nt rch wnr* **9/2**[3]

-212 **3** *¾* **Red Cadeaux**[21] 2703 6-9-0 116................................. TomMcLaughlin 8 119
(Ed Dunlop) *lw: hld up: pushed along over 3f out: hdwy over 2f out: rdn and styd on over 1f out: wnt 2nd briefly ins fnl f: no imp on wnr: kpt on but hld towards fin* **9/1**

-111 **4** *3 ½* **Aiken**[20] 2744 4-9-0 113... WilliamBuick 7 113
(John Gosden) *midfield: hdwy on outer 4f out: led 3f out: rdn and hdd 2f out: outpcd by wnr over 1f out: lost 2nd jst ins fnl f: no ex fnl 110yds* **4/1**[2]

0-33 **5** *1 ¼* **Jakkalberry (IRE)**[84] 1149 6-9-0 119......................(t) SilvestreDeSousa 5 111
(Marco Botti) *hld up in midfield: hdwy on inner 3f out: chsd ldrs over 2f out: kpt on u.p over 1f out: one pce and no imp fnl f* **16/1**

2-62 **6** *4 ½* **Fiorente (IRE)**[28] 2478 4-9-0 108.....................................(p) JamesDoyle 2 104
(Sir Michael Stoute) *trckd ldrs: effrt over 2f out: nt qckn wl over 1f out: no ex and fdd ins fnl f* **25/1**

1-63 **7** *4 ½* **Hunter's Light (IRE)**[23] 2640 4-9-0 110........................ FrankieDettori 11 97
(Saeed Bin Suroor) *racd keenly: midfield: hdwy over 3f out: chsd ldrs over 2f out: wknd u.p 1f out* **22/1**

-215 **8** *3* **Allied Powers (IRE)**[20] 2744 7-9-0 110........................... TomQueally 10 92
(Michael Bell) *hld up: pushed along briefly over 7f out: rdn over 3f out: past btn horses over 1f out: nvr on terms w ldrs* **100/1**

312 **9** *4* **Calico Cat**[28] 2506 4-9-0 108... PaulHanagan 12 85
(Alastair Lidderdale) *in rr: rdn 3f out: nvr able to get on terms* **66/1**

5-24 **10** *11* **Quest For Peace (IRE)**[21] 2703 4-9-0 114....................... KierenFallon 9 68
(Luca Cumani) *trckd ldrs: pushed along 5f out: wknd over 3f out* **16/1**

120- **11** *13* **Testosterone (IRE)**[265] 6567 4-8-11 115.................... JohnnyMurtagh 13 44
(Ed Dunlop) *led: hdd 3f out: wknd qckly over 2f out: eased whn wl btn over 1f out* **20/1**

43-1 **12** *26* **Memphis Tennessee (IRE)**[43] 2027 4-9-0 117.................. JPO'Brien 1
(A P O'Brien, Ire) *lw: prom: pushed along 4f out: wknd qckly over 3f out: eased whn wl btn fnl 2f: t.o* **11/2**

2m 29.6s (-2.90) **Going Correction** +0.175s/f (Good) **12** Ran SP% **115.8**
Speed ratings (Par 115): **116,113,113,111,110 107,104,102,99,92 83,66**
toteswingers: 1&2 £3.30, 1&3 £6.50, 2&3 £7.30 CSF £14.86 CT £108.12 TOTE £4.10: £1.70, £2.00, £2.20; EX 19.10 Trifecta £65.40 Pool: £18,911.34 - 213.73 winning units..
Owner K Abdulla **Bred** Juddmonte Farms Ltd **Trained** Newmarket, Suffolk

FOCUS
Even with the absence of Masked Marvel, this was the largest Hardwicke field in decades and a fascinating renewal as well. The race has proved a pointer to the King George VI And Queen Elizabeth Stakes with Doyen in 2004 and Harbinger in 2010 successfully returning here the following month. They appeared to go just a reasonable pace and a few took a grip as a result, but the winner could hardly have been more impressive. The time was good and Sea Moon is a well above-average winner of the race. Dunaden and Red Cadeaux are rated pretty much to their Australia/Hong Kong form.

NOTEBOOK
Sea Moon ◆, whose stable had won this three times between 2006 and 2011, was impressive when winning the Great Voltigeur last August before finishing third in the St Leger and runner-up to St Nicholas Abbey in the Breeders' Cup Turf. He did make heavy weather of winning a four-runner Listed event at Goodwood on his return last month, but this performance suggested that run was badly needed and he was different gear here. Although keen in the middle of the field early on, the turn of foot he produced down the outside to take himself to the front over a furlong from home and then put the race to bed in a matter of strides was the mark of a high-class colt. This was just his eighth career start, so there is every reason to believe he can get better still and the King George back here next month looks the obvious next step, a race his trainer has taken twice in the past three years and five times in all. He could also enter the Arc picture. (op 10-3 tchd 7-2)

Dunaden(FR), winner of the Melbourne Cup and Honk Kong Vase on his last two starts of 2011, finished just over 3l behind Aiken in the Grand Prix de Chantilly but that race wasn't really run to suit him. Although the pace here was more to his liking, he didn't enjoy much luck as he lost his prominent position when caught behind the weakening Memphis Tennessee on the home bend, but was staying on again when squeezed out between Hunter's Light and Red Cadeaux over a furlong from home. He may not have beaten the winner with a clear run, but would have been a lot closer. (op 11-2 tchd 4-1, 6-1 in places)

Red Cadeaux has become more renowned for the races in which he has gone down with all guns blazing rather than races he was won, but he showed he could do it at this level when winning the Yorkshire Cup last month. Held up early, he became a little outpaced approaching the home turn, but stayed on powerfully down the outside once into the straight to record yet another brave effort in defeat. (tchd 10-1)

Aiken was bidding for his seventh straight win and proved himself up to this class when winning the Grand Prix de Chantilly earlier this month, but he rather had the run of the race there. He tried to take the race by the scruff of the neck with a sweeping move around the outside turning for home and found himself in front, but he was firmly put in his place once the winner was unleashed. (tchd 10-3)

Jakkalberry(IRE), a former Group 1 winner in Italy, ran his best race on his third start for his new trainer when third behind Cirrus Des Aigles and St Nicholas Abbey in the Dubai Sheema Classic. He did have to take evasive action to avoid the weakening Testosterone when trying to make ground against the inside rail after turning in, but it made little difference to his finishing position. Perhaps the run was just needed. (op 10-1 tchd 9-1)

Fiorente(IRE), the winner's stablemate, hasn't quite reached the heights that had seemed likely so far this season and was tried in cheekpieces. Nothing was travelling better turning for home and he was close enough if good enough, but he didn't find much off the bridle. (op 20-1)

Hunter's Light(IRE) took a grip early and though close enough starting up the home straight, his earlier exertions then took their toll. Although 3-3 in Listed company, he is now 0-6 at Group level. (op 25-1 tchd 20-1)

Allied Powers(IRE) finished around 6l behind Aiken in the Grand Prix de Chantilly and made little impression from the back of the field. (op 66-1)

Quest For Peace(IRE) had around 5l to find with Red Cadeaux on Coronation Cup running and dropped right out after racing handily to the start of the home turn. His rider reported that the colt suffered interference in running. Official explanation: jockey said colt suffered interference in running (op 20-1)

Testosterone(IRE) developed into a high-class filly for Pascal Bary last season, winning twice at Group level before chasing home Galikova in the Vermeille, but she hadn't been seen since a moderate effort in the Arc. Picked up for 1,200,000gns in November, she made much of the running before blowing up coming to the last 2f, but has joined a yard that knows the time of day with fillies and mares so it would be little surprise to see her leave this form well behind in due course. Her rider reported that the filly ran too free. Official explanation: jockey said filly ran too free

Memphis Tennessee(IRE), in the frame in both the Epsom Derby and Irish Derby last year, was having his first start since when comfortably beating three rivals in the Ormonde last month, but having raced prominently for a long way he dropped right out on the home turn and something must have been amiss. (tchd 6-1 and 7-1 in places)

3370 DIAMOND JUBILEE STKS (BRITISH CHAMPIONS SERIES & GLOBAL SPRINT CHALLENGE) (GROUP 1) 6f

3:45 (3:46) (Class 1) 3-Y-0+

£283,550 (£107,500; £53,800; £26,800; £13,450; £6,750) **Stalls** Centre

Form RPR

1- **1** **Black Caviar (AUS)**[42] 2098 6-9-1 132.............................. LukeNolen 15 122+
(Peter G Moody, Australia) *str: chsd ldng pair: wnt 2nd 2f out: rdn to ld over 1f out: pushed along hands and heels and in command ins fnl f: pressed and rdr stopped riding towards fin: hrd pressed and pushed along again cl home: hld on* **1/6**[1]

15-1 **2** *hd* **Moonlight Cloud**[21] 2728 4-9-1 118................................ ThierryJarnet 5 120
(F Head, France) *hld up in tch in midfield: swtchd lft and effrt u.p over 1f out: hrd drvn and styd on to press wnr eased wnr wl ins fnl f: r.o to go 2nd cl home: jst hld* **5/1**[2]

1-40 **3** *nk* **Restiadargent (FR)**[38] 2179 3-8-8 110......................... MaximeGuyon 11 117
(H-A Pantall, France) *hld up in tch in midfield: rdn and effrt over 1f out: styd on u.p to chse wnr fnl 100yds: pressing eased wnr wl ins fnl f: r.o cl home* **40/1**

/106 **4** *¾* **Soul (AUS)**[38] 2179 5-9-4 111... FrankieDettori 8 119
(Saeed Bin Suroor) *lw: chsd ldr tl led over 2f out: rdn 2f out: hdd over 1f out: hrd drvn and styd on same pce after: lost 2 pls fnl 100yds* **33/1**

00-3 **5** *¾* **Society Rock (IRE)**[38] 2179 5-9-4 117....................... JohnnyMurtagh 13 117+
(James Fanshawe) *restless in stalls: v.s.a: bhd in last trio: rdn and stl plenty to do over 2f out: swtchd lft and hdwy over 1f out: r.o wl ins fnl f: nt rch ldrs* **8/1**[3]

2115 **6** *hd* **Krypton Factor**[34] 2326 4-9-4 124...................................(b) KierenFallon 4 116
(F Nass, Bahrain) *str: in tch: rdn and unable qck 2f out: rallied u.p ins fnl f: styd on fnl 100yds: nvr quite gng pce to rch ldrs* **16/1**

-000 **7** *nk* **Sirius Prospect (USA)**[38] 2179 4-9-4 107......................(b[1]) ShaneKelly 1 115
(Dean Ivory) *stdd and dropped in bhd after s: hld up towards rr: rdn and effrt over 1f out: swtchd rt and hdwy 1f out: styd on fnl 100yds: nvr quite pce to chal ldrs* **50/1**

4-45 **8** *1 ¼* **Royal Rock**[21] 2710 8-9-4 110.. TedDurcan 14 111
(Chris Wall) *taken down early: stdd s: hld up in rr: swtchd lft and effrt 2f out: no imp and hung rt over 1f out: hdwy jst ins fnl f: styd on fnl 100yds but nvr gng pce to threaten ldrs* **66/1**

1422 **9** *½* **Es Que Love (IRE)**[14] 2931 3-8-11 107...................... SilvestreDeSousa 7 108
(Mark Johnston) *chsd ldrs: rdn ent fnl 2f: drvn and unable qck over 1f out: edgd lft and btn 1f out: wknd ins fnl f* **50/1**

1-61 **10** *1 ½* **Pastoral Player**[21] 2710 5-9-4 112................................ DarryllHolland 10 105
(Hughie Morrison) *taken down early: awkward leaving stalls: hld up towards rr: rdn and effrt over 1f out: drvn and no imp 1f out: nvr threatened ldrs* **20/1**

0-04 **11** *½* **Genki (IRE)**[26] 2559 8-9-4 111.......................................(b) GeorgeBaker 2 103
(Roger Charlton) *stdd s: hld up in rr: hdwy towards centre 2f out: drvn and sme hdwy over 1f out: no ex 1f out and wknd ins fnl f* **50/1**

3-12 **12** *1 ¾* **The Cheka (IRE)**[38] 2179 6-9-4 111...............................(p) TomQueally 6 98
(Eve Johnson Houghton) *dwlt: sn pushed along and rcvrd to r in midfield: rdn and lost pl 2f out: drvn and no prog over 1f out: wknd ins fnl f* **25/1**

0222 **13** *7* **Jimmy Styles**[28] 2513 8-9-4 105...............................(p) RichardHughes 9 75
(Clive Cox) *chsd ldrs: rdn and unable qck ent fnl 2f: btn over 1f out: wknd fnl f* **50/1**

0-44 **14** *1* **Bogart**[21] 2712 3-8-11 110... PhillipMakin 12 70
(Kevin Ryan) *led tl rdn and hdd over 2f out: sn struggling u.p: btn over 1f out: wknd fnl f* **66/1**

1m 14.1s (-0.40) **Going Correction** +0.175s/f (Good)
WFA 3 from 4yo+ 7lb **14** Ran SP% **144.2**
Speed ratings (Par 117): **109,108,108,107,106 106,105,104,103,101 100,98,89,87**
toteswingers: 1&2 £1.60, 1&3 £8.40, 2&3 £57.20 CSF £2.30 CT £33.11 TOTE £1.20: £1.10, £1.60, £10.50; EX 3.40 Trifecta £66.10 Pool: £5,637.91 - 600.22 winning units..
Owner G J Wilkie, Mrs K J Wilkie et al **Bred** R Jamieson **Trained** Australia

■ Stewards' Enquiry : Maxime Guyon four-day ban: used whip above permitted level (Jul 8-11)

FOCUS

Another name change for this event, which had become the Golden Jubilee Stakes in 2002, at the same time receiving Group 1 status. Unusually there were no runners from Tuesday's King's Stand Stakes, which had supplied four of the last nine winners. Only four of this field had a top-level success to their name, in what looked an ordinary renewal. The time was 11lb slower than that for the Wokingham. Black Caviar is rated around 10lb off her best Australian form, with Moonlight Cloud close to her best. No filly or mare had won since 1988, when Posada took what was in those days the Group 3 Cork And Orrery Stakes, but they filled the first three places here.

NOTEBOOK

Black Caviar(AUS) arrived unbeaten in 21 starts in her home country, eleven of them at the top level, but faced the biggest challenge of her career. On all known figures she looked set to win easily, but there were inevitably minor doubts, among them the prospect (unrealised)of soft ground and a draw nearest the stands' side. The biggest factor, though, was whether she would run her race after travelling halfway round the world. Things looked to be going according to the script as she took the lead moving smoothly, but she needed a couple of taps from Luke Nolen and did not pull away from her pursuers as expected. Deep inside the last Nolen stopped riding, just as the second and third bore down on her, but he realised his mistake with four strides to go and, shaken up, the mare scrambled home. There were suggestions that the jockey had mistaken the winning post, but he later said that he had underestimated the stiffness of Ascot's 6f, hinting that she was tiring and that he wanted to win without knocking her about. It was nearly a calamitous error. This bare form is limited, with no more than two and a half lengths between the first seven, and she won't be troubling Frankel's position as the world's top-rated horse. Even so she was more superior to this opposition than the margin suggests despite being clearly below par, and she remains a phenomenal sprinter. Her connections deserve huge credit for their enterprise in taking up the challenge, but she will head back to Australia now and won't run in the July Cup. She as found to have sustained some soft issue injuries, but is likely to race on. (tchd 1-5 in places and 2-9 in a place)

Moonlight Cloud got over from stall 5 to race near the stands' fence and was closing hand over fist on the favourite, but the line just beat her. She would have been a fortunate winner in the circumstances, but this confirms her as a high-class sprinter. This was only her second run at the bare 6f - she was hampered in the British Champions Sprint here in the autumn - and she will be suited by the extra half-furlong of the Prix Maurice de Gheest at Deauville in August. She won that race in soft ground last season. (op 11-2)

Restiadargent(FR) looked better than the bare facts when seventh in the Duke Of York Stakes and she confirmed that impression with a big run in her first Group One. Switched out from behind the winner inside the final furlong, she was running on at the death but just lost second late on. She will reoppose Moonlight Cloud in the Maurice de Gheest and quite probably has improvement in her. (tchd 50-1)

Soul(AUS) proved best of the 'British' contingent, as well as the leading male. He showed bright pace to lead but could not sustain it in the final furlong. He wasn't beaten far, but is perhaps not quite up to this level. (op 50-1)

Society Rock(IRE) fell out of the stalls before flying home from the rear and was only beaten around two lengths, less than the ground he forfeited at the start. The winner last year and runner-up to Starspangledbanner, another with Aussie connections, in 2010, he reserves his best efforts for this event. Official explanation: jockey said horse was slowly away (op 10-1)

Krypton Factor, adding to the race's international flavour, was the Bahrain-based winner of the Dubai Golden Shaheen at Meydan in March, where Soul was last. Connections had been concerned by the likelihood of easy ground but he was allowed to take his chance in the drying conditions and ran respectably. (op 20-1)

Sirius Prospect(USA) had not fired this year but this was his best run of the campaign, with the first-time hood and blinkers a likely factor. A successful second half of the season can be anticipated.

Royal Rock generally runs creditably at Ascot and this was no exception, but he is always likely to come up short in this company. (tchd 50-1)

Es Que Love(IRE) began the season winning a Pontefract handicap off 85 and has made great strides, for all that he was comfortably held in the end. (tchd 66-1)

Pastoral Player's last two wins have come at 7f and he lacked the required pace here.

Bogart runs like a horse ready for a drop back to the minimum. Philip Makin reported that the colt hung right throughout. Official explanation: jockey said colt hung right throughout

3371 WOKINGHAM STKS (HERITAGE H'CAP) 6f

4:25 (4:25) (Class 2) (0-110,108) 3-Y-O+

£77,812 (£23,300; £11,650; £5,825; £2,912; £1,462) **Stalls** Centre

Form RPR

-500 **1** **Dandy Boy (ITY)**[28] 2516 6-9-8 106.................................... PatDobbs 15 117
(David Marnane, Ire) *racd on far side: hld up: hdwy 2f out: swtchd lft over 1f out: r.o ins fnl f: led overall fnl 150yds: in command towards fin: 1st of 15 in gp* **33/1**

-004 **2** *1 ¼* **Waffle (IRE)**[38] 2177 6-9-2 100... FranBerry 23 107
(David Barron) *lw: racd on stands' side: hld up: hdwy over 1f out: swtchd rt ins fnl f: r.o to ld gp fnl 75yds: nt rch wnr: 1st of 13 in gp* **11/1**[3]

04-0 **3** *½* **Hawkeyethenoo (IRE)**[42] 2068 6-9-4 102....................... GrahamLee 16 107+
(Jim Goldie) *racd on far side: hld up: effrt whn bmpd over 1f out: hdwy sn after: r.o fnl 100yds: gng on at fin: 2nd of 15 in gp* **9/2**[1]

0-35 **4** *shd* **Morache Music**[6] 3190 4-9-7 105.. SebSanders 6 110
(Peter Makin) *racd on far side: hld up: hdwy 2f out: nt clr run and swtchd lft over 1f out: r.o to chal ent fnl f: no imp on wnr and run flattened out towards fin: fin 3rd of 15 in gp* **20/1**

00-0 **5** *nk* **Dungannon**[48] 1885 5-8-13 97.. WilliamBuick 11 101
(Andrew Balding) *racd on far side: midfield: effrt 2f out: bmpd over 1f out: sn chalng: styd on same pce wl ins fnl f: fin 4th of 15 in gp* **33/1**

1-21 **6** *shd* **Maarek**[48] 1885 5-9-10 108.. JPO'Brien 9 112
(David Peter Nagle, Ire) *racd on far side: midfield: hdwy 2f out: bmpd over 1f out: sn chalng: styd on same pce wl ins fnl f: styd on same pce towards fin: fin 5th of 15 in gp* **8/1**[2]

5652 **7** *¾* **Scarf (AUS)**[14] 2919 5-9-4 102................................. SilvestreDeSousa 24 103
(Saeed Bin Suroor) *racd stands' side: a.p: chalng over 1f out: kpt on but nt quite pce of ldrs: fin 2nd of 13 in gp* **12/1**

1041 **8** *hd* **Palace Moon**[35] 2268 7-9-7 105.....................................(t) TomQueally 18 106
(William Knight) *racd stands' side: a.p: chalng over 1f out: led gp ins fnl f: hdd fnl 75yds: hld towards fin: fin 3rd of 13 in gp* **33/1**

2135 **9** *nse* **Alben Star (IRE)**[48] 1885 4-9-0 98................................ PaulHanagan 14 99
(Richard Fahey) *lw: racd on far side: prom: led gp over 1f out: hdd fnl 15yds: kpt on same pce towards fin: fin joint 6th of 15 in gp* **20/1**

21-5 **9** *dht* **Lightning Cloud (IRE)**[42] 2068 4-8-11 95........................ PhillipMakin 4 96
(Kevin Ryan) *racd on far side: midfield: hdwy over 2f out: chalng over 1f out: nt qckn ins fnl f: no ex fnl 75yds: fin joint 6th of 15 in gp* **15/2**[1]

-636 **11** *shd* **Elusivity (IRE)**[28] 2486 4-9-9 107.................................. FrankieDettori 21 107
(Brian Meehan) *racd on stands' side: midfield: hdwy to chse ldrs over 1f out: one pce fnl 75yds: fin 4th of 13 in gp* **20/1**

3120 **12** *¾* **Secret Witness**[28] 2507 6-9-7 105...............................(b) JamesDoyle 30 103
(Ronald Harris) *racd stands' side: led gp: rdn over 1f out: hdd ins fnl f: sn hung rt: no ex towards fin: fin 5th of 13 in gp* **50/1**

5-33 **13** *½* **Mac's Power (IRE)**[35] 2268 6-9-0 98............................(t) KierenFallon 31 94
(James Fanshawe) *racd stands' side: hld up: nt clr run 2f out: hdwy ins fnl f: styd on: nt pce to get to ldrs: fin 6th of 13 in gp* **11/1**[3]

13-2 **14** *hd* **Gordon Lord Byron (IRE)**[19] 2777 4-9-6 104.......... RichardHughes 29 100+
(T Hogan, Ire) *racd stands' side: trckd ldrs: rdn over 1f out: nt clr run fnl 110yds: eased towards fin: 7th of 13 in gp* **20/1**

6-16 **15** *¾* **Seal Rock**[48] 1885 4-9-1 99.. DaneO'Neill 25 92
(Henry Candy) *racdd stands' side: trckd ldrs: rdn over 1f out: outpcd ins fnl f: no imp after: fin 8th of 13 in gp* **20/1**

0-02 **16** *1 ¼* **Pabusar**[35] 2268 4-9-6 104.. GeorgeBaker 26 93
(Ralph Beckett) *racd stands' side: trckd ldrs: rdn over 1f out: btn ins fnl f: fin 9th of 13 in gp* **33/1**

3151 **17** *½* **Lui Rei (ITY)**[21] 2707 6-8-11 102 5ex...................... GeorgeDowning(7) 28 90
(Robert Cowell) *s.i.s: racd stands' side: in rr: styd on ins fnl f: nvr rchd chalng position: fin 10th of 13 in gp* **25/1**

-110 **18** *shd* **Oasis Dancer**[91] 1033 5-9-7 105....................................... JimCrowley 17 92
(Ralph Beckett) *racd on far side: midfield: hdwy over 2f out: chalng over 1f out: nt qckn ins fnl f: no ex fnl 100yds: fin 8th of 15 in gp* **50/1**

5534 **19** *hd* **Medicean Man**[4] 3238 6-9-2 103..........................(p) RaulDaSilva(3) 19 90
(Jeremy Gask) *racd stands' side: effrt and chsd ldrs over 1f out: fdd fnl 100yds: fin 11th of 13 in gp* **12/1**

40-0 **20** *½* **Gramercy (IRE)**[37] 2208 5-9-1 99.............................. JohnnyMurtagh 20 84
(Kevin Ryan) *racd on stands' side: midfield: pushed along and outpcd over 2f out: eased whn btn ins fnl f: fin 12th of 13th in gp* **25/1**

0-33 **21** *1 ¼* **King Of Jazz (IRE)**[42] 2068 4-9-0 98............................ HayleyTurner 27 79
(Michael Bell) *racd stands' side: hld up: outpcd over 1f out: nvr able to trble ldrs: fin 13th of 13 in gp* **14/1**

0-02 **22** *1 ¼* **Desert Law (IRE)**[21] 2704 4-8-13 97................................ JimmyFortune 3 74
(Andrew Balding) *lw: racd on far side: in tch: rdn over 1f out: no imp: eased whn wl btn fnl 75yds: fin 9th of 15 in gp* **16/1**

050 **23** *1* **Sir Reginald**[141] 420 4-9-2 100... TedDurcan 13 74
(Richard Fahey) *racd on far side: hld up: outpcd fnl 2f: fin 10th of 15 in gp* **100/1**

-150 **24** *hd* **New Planet (IRE)**[38] 2177 4-9-0 98............................ MichaelO'Connell 8 71
(John Quinn) *racd on far side: chsd ldrs: rdn 2f out: wknd over 1f out: fin 11th of 15 in gp* **40/1**

0004 **25** *hd* **High Standing (USA)**[14] 2931 7-9-2 100........................(p) RyanMoore 1 73
(Jeremy Gask) *racd on far side: midfield: rdn over 1f out: nvr able to get to ldrs: fin 12th of 15 in gp* **14/1**

50-0 **26** *nk* **Joe Packet**[83] 1157 5-9-0 98.. LeeNewman 2 70
(Jonathan Portman) *racd on far side: chse ldr: led gp 2f out: hdd over 1f out: wknd ins fnl f: fin 13th of 15 in gp* **66/1**

0013 **27** *8* **Colonel Mak**[48] 1885 5-9-2 105.. LMcNiff(5) 5 51
(David Barron) *racd on far side: led overall: hdd 2f out: wknd over 1f out: fin 14th of 15 in gp* **14/1**

0-60 **28** *16* **Pepper Lane**[21] 2713 5-9-2 100...................................... DanielTudhope 7
(David O'Meara) *missed break: bhd on far side: wl adrift over 1f out: fin 15th of 15 in gp* **33/1**

1m 13.87s (-0.63) **Going Correction** +0.175s/f (Good) **28** Ran SP% **140.6**
Speed ratings (Par 109): **111,109,108,108,108 108,107,106,106,106 106,105,104,104,103 101,101,101,100,100 98,96,95,95,95**
toteswingers: 1&2 £277.00, 1&3 £48.10, 2&3 £145.40 CSF £322.16 CT £7408.81 TOTE £66.50: £13.10, £3.70, £7.20, £8.00; EX 1897.80 Trifecta £46255.30 Pool: £162,518.76 - 2.60 winning units..
Owner Malih Lahej Al Basti **Bred** Az Ag Rz Emiliana Srl **Trained** Bansha, Co Tipperary

FOCUS

The annual spin of the roulette wheel that is the Wokingham and the field unsurprisingly soon split into two, with 15 going far side and 13 coming stands' side. Although there didn't seem to be that much between the two groups, the far-side were always just ahead and five of the first six home raced on that flank. The winning time was 0.23 seconds faster than Black Caviar took to win the Diamond Jubilee. The finish was dominated by horses who have shown some of their best form here previously. Dandy Boy rates better than ever.

NOTEBOOK

Dandy Boy(ITY) does most of his racing over further and prefers better ground, but a strongly run race over this trip proved ideal and the ground had obviously dried up just enough. He was well back in the far-side group early, but produced a smart turn of speed to thread his way through and hit the front well inside the last furlong. He can win a Pattern race on this evidence. (tchd 50-1 in places)

Waffle(IRE) had been beaten 22 times since a successful racecourse debut, but he was off the same mark as when narrowly beaten by Deacon Blues in this last year. Held up in the nearside group, he fairly flew home to beat the others on his side comfortably, only to find that one horse had gone clear on the far side. He has all the talent in the world and it must be so frustrating that he just cannot hit the bullseye.

Hawkeyethenoo(IRE) ◆ didn't run badly in the Victoria Cup here on last month's reappearance, but he has appeared to need 7f these days and looks better on a quicker surface. Under the circumstances he ran a blinder in the far-side group, especially as he received quite a bump over a furlong out yet stayed on really well to grab third. He has the ability to win another decent handicap. (op 25-1)

Morache Music was a stone higher than when winning over C&D on easy ground last August, but he had run really well in a Salisbury Listed event six days earlier when meeting traffic problems. Another to finish well on the far side, this was a decent effort turned out quickly and his trainer nominated a race for him at Maisons-Laffitte early next month.

Dungannon was just 2lb higher than when beating Medicean Man over 5f here last August, but ran poorly when behind five of these on last month's Newmarket return. This was much better as he was another to receive a bump over a furlong from home, yet stayed on well. He seems to like this track and is entitled to step up again from this.
Maarek, bidding for a hat-trick off a 6lb higher mark, had five of these behind when winning at Newmarket last time but could probably have done with the ground staying soft. He caused problems for a couple when switched out to challenge over a furlong out, but finished in good style. He is on a stiff mark now and looks worth a try in Listed company. (tchd 15-2 and 9-1)
Scarf(AUS) has done all his racing over further since joining Godolphin and this was his first start over 6f since winning over it in Australia more than a year ago. He was always handy in the nearside group and kept on to finish second on his side, but he is already due to go up 6lb so things are about to get harder. (op 14-1 tchd 16-1 in a place)
Palace Moon was put up 5lb for last month's Newbury success which put him on the same mark as when third in this two years ago. He was always up there in the nearside group, but would probably have preferred the ground to have dried out even more.
Lightning Cloud(IRE) has gained all five career wins over 7f and ran a fine race when fifth of 24 in the Victoria Cup here last month on his return from a 248-day absence. He managed to creep into this race at the last minute as first reserve, but lacked the speed to put in an effective challenge in the far-side group over this shorter trip. (op 8-1 tchd 9-1 in places)
Alben Star(IRE), very progressive on Polytrack during the winter, ran creditably behind a couple of these on his return to turf at Newmarket last month and ran well enough in the far-side group here to suggest he can win a decent sprint handicap on grass. (op 8-1 tchd 9-1 in places)
Secret Witness made much of the running in the nearside group, but is on a very stiff mark now, 11lb higher than when winning at York last month
Mac's Power(IRE) won the race on the stands' side, though only eighth overall, in this race last year and was 2lb lower here, but he never saw much daylight in the nearside group this time and by the time he did it was too late. He hasn't won since October 2010. (op 12-1)
Gordon Lord Byron(IRE) Official explanation: jockey said gelding was denied a clear run
Medicean Man, a triple course winner, ran a cracker when fourth in the King's Stand four days earlier, but saw plenty of daylight in the nearside group here and didn't pick up. Perhaps this came too soon and he remains above his highest winning mark. (op 14-1 tchd 10-1)
Desert Law(IRE) was off the same mark as when narrowly beaten in the Investec Dash at Epsom on Derby day and therefore 5lb well in compared to his revised rating, but his trainer was worried about this stiffer test in the ground and his fears were borne out.
Pepper Lane lost all chance at the start. Official explanation: jockey said mare reared in stalls

3372 DUKE OF EDINBURGH H'CAP — 1m 4f

5:00 (5:00) (Class 2) (0-105,103) 3-Y-O+

£43,575 (£13,048; £6,524; £3,262; £1,631; £819) **Stalls** Low

Form				RPR
1061	**1**		**Camborne**[14] 2921 4-9-4 **97**....(p) WilliamBuick 12	108+
			(John Gosden) *stdd after 1f: hld up in rr: stl last 3f out: effrt and nt clr run 2f out: stl plenty to do and swtchd lft wl over 1f out: edgd rt but str run after to ld ins fnl f: edgd bk lft briefly 100yds out: sn clr* **11/2**[1]	
	2	*2 ½*	**Hammerfest**[26] 5-9-3 **96**.... GeraldMosse 2	103
			(J E Hammond, France) *travelled strly: chsd ldrs: stl gng wl and trcking ldrs over 2f out: rdn and qcknd to ld jst over 1f out: hdd and immediately outpcd by wnr ins fnl f: hld on for 2nd towards fin* **8/1**[3]	
/0-5	**3**	*½*	**Harrison's Cave**[27] 2526 4-9-1 **94**.... JPO'Brien 10	100
			(A P O'Brien, Ire) *swtg: stdd s: hld up in rr: effrt and nt clr run jst over 2f out tl rdn and hdwy over 1f out: pushed rt 1f out: outpcd by wnr fnl f but kpt on to press for 2nd towards fin* **12/1**	
-630	**4**	*1 ½*	**Alkimos (IRE)**[114] 755 4-9-8 **101**.... SilvestreDeSousa 5	105
			(Saeed Bin Suroor) *hld up in midfield: stuck bhd horses and shuffled bk 4f out: edging rt and effrt over 1f out: drvn and chsd ldrs 1f out: kpt on but no threat to wnr* **20/1**	
63-4	**5**	*1 ¼*	**Cill Rialaig**[28] 2481 7-9-5 **98**.... DarryllHolland 21	100
			(Hughie Morrison) *chsd ldrs: wnt 2nd 3f out: rdn to ld over 1f out: hdd jst over 1f out: sn outpcd and btn fnl f: plugged on* **11/1**	
U-10	**6**	*4*	**Right Step**[38] 2176 5-9-3 **96**.... DaneO'Neill 14	91
			(Alan Jarvis) *lw: hld up towards rr: rdn and hdwy on outer 2f out: keeping on but stl plenty to do whn pushed lft wl over 1f out: plugged on but no threat to ldrs fnl f* **33/1**	
1644	**7**	*nk*	**Eternal Heart (IRE)**[15] 2903 4-9-10 **103**.... JoeFanning 8	98
			(Mark Johnston) *led: rdn and hdd over 2f out: drvn and stl chsng ldrs over 1f out: btn 1f out: wknd fnl f* **20/1**	
3-14	**8**	*1*	**Mulaqen**[14] 2933 4-9-3 **96**.... PaulHanagan 1	89
			(Marcus Tregoning) *chsd ldrs: swtchd out lft and effrt ent fnl 2f: stl chsng ldrs but unable qck over 1f out: wknd ent fnl f* **10/1**	
-135	**9**	*nk*	**Midsummer Sun**[35] 2278 4-9-5 **98**.... TomQueally 13	91
			(Sir Henry Cecil) *t.k.h early: hld up in midfield: hdwy to chse ldrs 3f out: drvn and chsd ldr over 1f out: no ex ent fnl f: wknd qckly ins fnl f* **14/1**	
50-2	**10**	*½*	**Harlestone Times (IRE)**[35] 2278 5-9-7 **100**.... TedDurcan 18	92
			(John Dunlop) *stdd and dropped in bhd after s: sn pushed along in rr: rdn and effrt on inner wl over 1f out: no real imp: nvr trbld ldrs* **25/1**	
6-03	**11**	*1 ¼*	**Spanish Duke (IRE)**[21] 2706 5-9-4 **97**.... EddieAhern 11	87
			(John Dunlop) *b.hind: t.k.h early: hld up in midfield: effrt u.p jst over 2f out: drvn and no ex over 1f out: wknd ent fnl f* **14/1**	
1135	**12**	*2 ¼*	**Ithoughtitwasover (IRE)**[14] 2933 4-9-9 **102**.... JohnnyMurtagh 3	88
			(Mark Johnston) *in tch in midfield: rdn and effrt jst over 2f out: drvn and no ex over 1f out: wknd ent fnl f* **8/1**[3]	
1-02	**13**	*4*	**Anatolian**[14] 2933 4-9-10 **103**.... FrankieDettori 22	83
			(Mahmood Al Zarooni) *lw: hld up towards rr: rdn on outer 3f out: hdwy u.p over 2f out: btn over 1f out: sn wknd* **13/2**[2]	
1661	**14**	*2 ¾*	**Licence To Till (USA)**[14] 2911 5-9-2 **95**.... RyanMoore 6	71
			(Mark Johnston) *lw: chsd ldrs: rdn and unable qck jsut over 2f out: stl in tch but struggling whn short of room over 1f out: sn wknd* **16/1**	
-124	**15**	*2*	**Stand To Reason (IRE)**[14] 2911 4-9-1 **94**.... JimmyFortune 7	66
			(Mikael Magnusson) *lw: in tch: rdn and effrt on outer over 2f out: stl plenty to do and keeping on same pce whn nt clr run and hmpd over 1f out: sn wknd* **12/1**	
15-0	**16**	*4 ½*	**Classic Vintage (USA)**[14] 2933 6-9-2 **95**....(b) JimCrowley 4	60
			(Amanda Perrett) *in tch in midfield: rdn and struggling 3f out: wknd u.p 2f out: bhd and eased ins fnl f* **33/1**	
	17	*2 ½*	**Clearwater Bay (IRE)**[636] 6404 5-9-6 **99**.... JamesDoyle 9	60
			(Gary Moore) *broke okay in midfield: sn bustled along and dropped to rr after 2f out: a towards rr after: rdn and struggling 3f out: lost tch wl over 1f out: eased ins fnl f* **33/1**	
52/	**18**	*8*	**Bobbyscot (IRE)**[762] 2367 5-9-6 **99**.... GeorgeBaker 17	47
			(Gary Moore) *chsd ldr tl 3f out: sn lost pl: bhd over 1f out: eased fnl f: t.o* **50/1**	

2m 31.47s (-1.03) **Going Correction** +0.175s/f (Good) **18** Ran SP% **127.1**
Speed ratings (Par 109): **110,108,108,107,106 103,103,102,102,102 101,99,97,95,93 90,89,83**
toteswingers: 1&2 £10.30, 1&3 £11.90, 2&3 £22.60 CSF £45.05 CT £527.83 TOTE £6.70: £2.20, £1.90, £2.80, £4.70; EX 32.10 Trifecta £420.80 Pool: £14,121.73 - 24.83 winning units..
Owner H R H Princess Haya Of Jordan **Bred** Southill Stud **Trained** Newmarket, Suffolk

FOCUS
A competitive edition of this hot handicap, and strong form. The pace was solid and three of the first four came from the rear. The progressive winner was impressive.
NOTEBOOK
Camborne was still virtually last turning in, and William Buick was looking for a run for some time before angling him out. Once in the clear the quirky gelding produced a sharp turn of foot to sweep to the front, before veering both ways with the race in the bag. Having only his sixth race, and defying a rise of nearly a stone for his Doncaster win, he is surely a Group performer in the making but is obviously not straightforward and it may be that the smaller fields in pattern races won't play to his strengths. It will be fascinating to see where he goes next. (op 5-1 tchd 6-1 in places and 13-2 in a place)
Hammerfest, a French raider, raced more prominently than the others in the frame, leading after being switched off the fence but soon left trailing by the winner. A handicap debutant who stays further, he goes well in easy ground too and his trainer's runners in this country are always worthy of respect. (op 7-1)
Harrison's Cave's trainer Aidan O'Brien does not run many in the handicaps at this meeting and his Chester Cup fifth ran a big race, travelling well in the pack before running on. He gets further than this. (op 10-1)
Alkimos(IRE), runner-up in the Tercentenary Stakes at the meeting for Luca Cumani last year, has been gelded since his Dubai campaign in the spring. He was looking for room on the home turn but ran on without reaching the principals. (tchd 22-1)
Cill Rialaig, the 2010 winner, made a bold attempt to supplement that off 7lb higher this time round, but after striking the front she was soon swallowed up. This was a good effort. (op 12-1 tchd 10-1)
Right Step, back up in trip, ran on down the outside for sixth, if not as quickly as the winner whom he had been upsides entering the final two furlongs.
Eternal Heart(IRE) helped set the pace and stuck on without being able to enhance his trainer's fine record in this race. He was unbeaten at this trip previously but his best form has come over further.
Mulaqen ran respectably, but has twice been held from this sort of mark now since his comfortable win at York. (op 12-1)
Midsummer Sun had excuses on his last two starts and it all appeared to be in place for a big run here. He was well positioned turning in, but was soon under pressure and he eventually faded right out of it. (op 12-1)
Harlestone Times(IRE) finds this trip insufficient and was staying on steadily. (tchd 33-1)
Spanish Duke(IRE) again raced rather keenly and didn't quite see it out. (op 12-1 tchd 16-1 in places)
Anatolian, the shorter priced of the Godolphin pair, had three of these behind when narrowly beaten at Newmarket, but was well held off a 7lb higher mark. A wide draw made things difficult for him. (op 8-1)
Stand To Reason(IRE), tackling this trip for the first time, would have finished a bit closer had he not been hampered. (tchd 14-1)

3373 QUEEN ALEXANDRA STKS (CONDITIONS RACE) — 2m 5f 159y

5:35 (5:37) (Class 2) 4-Y-O+

£34,237 (£10,252; £5,126; £2,563; £1,281; £643) **Stalls** Low

Form				RPR
50-1	**1**		**Simenon (IRE)**[4] 3241 5-9-2 95.... RyanMoore 16	104+
			(W P Mullins, Ire) *hld up: hdwy on inner over 4f out: nt clr run over 2f out: sn swtchd lft: styd on to ld over 1f out: sn edgd rt: drew clr and in command ins fnl f: won gng away* **11/4**[1]	
/00-	**2**	*7*	**Shahwardi (FR)**[10] 6-9-2 92.... GeraldMosse 11	96
			(A De Royer-Dupre, France) *midfield: hdwy over 3f out: rdn to chse wnr over 1f out: kpt on but no ch ins fnl f: eased whn wl hld towards fin* **33/1**	
6200	**3**	*1 ½*	**Romeo Montague**[14] 2932 4-9-0 86.... JohnnyMurtagh 3	95
			(Ed Dunlop) *midfield: hdwy over 4f out: styd on to ld ent fnl 2f: sn hdd: unable to go w front two over 1f out: sn edgd rt: styd on but no imp ins fnl f* **66/1**	
3-24	**4**	*nk*	**Zuider Zee (GER)**[23] 2639 5-9-2 108.... WilliamBuick 13	94
			(John Gosden) *lw: midfield: pushed along and hdwy over 2f out: rdn to chse ldrs over 1f out: styd on u.p but no imp thrght fnl f* **4/1**[3]	
00-0	**5**	*2 ¼*	**Elyaadi**[4] 3241 8-8-11 90.... FranBerry 6	87
			(John Queally, Ire) *hld up: in last pl to 10f out: rdn and hdwy on outer 2f out: kpt on fr over 1f out: changed legs ins fnl 75yds: no imp on ldrs* **33/1**	
01-0	**6**	*5*	**Seaside Sizzler**[21] 2706 5-9-2 88....(bt) JimCrowley 4	87
			(Ralph Beckett) *midfield: hdwy over 5f out: chsng ldrs but nt qckning whn n.m.r over 1f out: one pce: no imp ins fnl f and dropped away* **50/1**	
2-62	**7**	*5*	**Riptide**[61] 1559 6-9-2 75....(v) JamieGoldstein 15	82
			(Michael Scudamore) *s.i.s: chsd ldr after 1f: pushed along over 4f out: sn lost 2nd: rdn and sl cl up over 2f out: wknd over 1f out* **100/1**	
60-2	**8**	*7*	**Overturn (IRE)**[45] 1974 8-9-2 112.... EddieAhern 19	75
			(Donald McCain) *led: rdn over 2f out: hdd ent fnl 2f: wknd over 1f out: eased whn btn fnl f* **3/1**[2]	
0-00	**9**	*nk*	**Bernie The Bolt (IRE)**[35] 2278 6-9-2 91.... TomQueally 18	75
			(Andrew Balding) *in tch: rdn and outpcd over 2f out: no imp after* **14/1**	
5-	**10**	*nse*	**Scotsbrook Cloud**[23] 4753 7-9-2 0.... JamesDoyle 2	75
			(David Evans) *hld up: rdn over 2f out: nvr able to get to ldrs* **100/1**	
-101	**11**	*2 ¾*	**Kangaroo Court (IRE)**[30] 2423 8-9-2 80.... DarryllHolland 12	72
			(Emma Lavelle) *trckd ldrs: rdn over 3f out: wknd over 1f out* **33/1**	
441-	**12**	*1 ½*	**Petara Bay (IRE)**[329] 4532 8-9-2 108.... JimmyFortune 7	70
			(Robert Mills) *hld up: hdwy on inner 4f out: rdn over 2f out: chsng ldrs whn n.m.r over 1f out: sn drifted rt and no imp: wknd btn fnl f* **12/1**	
-311	**13**	*8*	**Cloudy Spirit**[37] 2214 7-8-11 82.... TonyCulhane 1	57
			(Reg Hollinshead) *lw: midfield: pushed along over 4f out: wknd over 2f out* **16/1**	
	14	*32*	**American Trilogy (IRE)**[42] 1359 8-9-2 90.... JPO'Brien 8	30
			(Paul Nicholls) *chsd ldrs tl rdn and wknd over 3f out: t.o* **14/1**	
	15	*4 ½*	**Golden Sunbird (IRE)**[39] 2155 8-8-11 0....(t) KierenFallon 5	21
			(Paul Nolan, Ire) *hld up in midfield: impr to chse ldrs over 8f out: wknd 4f out: t.o* **33/1**	
0-13	**16**	*7*	**Dawn Twister (GER)**[42] 2066 5-9-5 100.... PaulHanagan 10	22
			(Lucy Wadham) *trckd ldrs: pushed along over 4f out: rdn over 2f out: wknd over 1f out: t.o* **40/1**	
10-0	**17**	*33*	**Swingkeel (IRE)**[14] 2933 7-9-5 99....(p) TedDurcan 9	
			(John Dunlop) *hld up: pushed along over 7f out: lft bhd fnl 4f: t.o* **20/1**	
60-5	**18**	*¾*	**Dalhaan (USA)**[27] 963 7-9-2 65....(t) TomMcLaughlin 14	
			(Luke Dace) *hld up: struggling 4f out: sn lft bhd: t.o* **200/1**	

4m 48.67s (-0.73) **Going Correction** +0.175s/f (Good)
WFA 4 from 5yo+ 2lb **18** Ran SP% **123.5**
Speed ratings (Par 109): **108,105,104,104,103 102,100,97,97,97 96,96,93,81,79 77,65,65**
toteswingers: 1&2 £22.80, 1&3 £55.10, 2&3 £242.70 CSF £107.95 CT £4974.52 TOTE £3.80: £1.70, £9.40, £16.00; EX 135.40 Trifecta £6380.30 Pool: £21,828.40 - 2.53 winning units..
Owner Wicklow Bloodstock Limited **Bred** Max Morris **Trained** Muine Beag, Co Carlow

FOCUS
The longest Flat race run under rules in Britain featuring a wide range of abilities under both codes. Despite a fair pace, there were still several in with a chance starting up the home straight. Simenon did not need to match his Ascot Stakes figure with his main market rivals not at their best.

NOTEBOOK

Simenon(IRE) showed his wellbeing when winning the Ascot Stakes impressively earlier in the week and this was just as emphatic. Having travelled smoothly into contention starting the turn for home, there was a moment when he was stuck in a pocket coming to the last 2f, but once seeing daylight he quickened up smartly to put daylight between himself and the rest and emulate Baddam, who won both races six years earlier. There should be plenty more big races to be won with him on the Flat and over hurdles, with the Goodwood Cup a reported target. (tchd 3-1 in places)

Shahwardi(FR), having his sixth start back with his original trainer after a spell with Jeremy Gask, travelled particularly well and despite getting hampered on the home bend, was still on the bridle when produced with his effort 2f out, but he could do nothing about the winner. The trip wasn't a problem. (tchd 40-1)

Romeo Montaguedidn't seem to stay in one previous try over further than 1m4f, so this effort was something of a revelation. He was in front over a furlong from home, but only on sufferance until the winner was unleashed. He has looked a weak finisher over middle distances and campaigning him as a stayer may be the way forward. (op 50-1)

Zuider Zee(GER) seemed to stay 2m well enough when dead-heating for fourth behind Opinion Poll in the Henry II at Sandown last time, but although staying on down the outside from the home bend over this longer trip, never looked like getting to the front. (op 9-2 tchd 5-1 in a place)

Elyaadi, runner-up to Swingkeel in this last year, finished around 18l behind Simenon in the Ascot Handicap earlier in the week and was meeting him on the same terms. Held up right out the back early, she stayed on down the wide outside over the last half-mile, but could never get to the leaders.

Seaside Sizzler was entitled to need his Epsom reappearance earlier this month and was only narrowly beaten over just short of this trip at Goodwood last July. He didn't run at all badly and a staying handicap back off his proper mark can be found.

Riptide was only just beaten over a similar trip at Pontefract last time, but that was off a mark of 73 and it was his limitless stamina that enabled him to stay in this race for so long.

Overturn(IRE), high class over hurdles and smart on the Flat, looked as good as ever when only finding only one too strong in his attempt to win his second consecutive Chester Cup last month. Despite enjoying the run of the race out in front here, he didn't get home and it seemed that this extreme test of stamina was too much even for him. (tchd 10-3 and 7-2 in places)

Petara Bay(IRE) had never raced beyond 2m before and was having his first start since winning at Goodwood last July, but he can go well fresh. He wasn't totally out of it when short of room over 2f out, but it looked doubtful that he would have seen his race out even with a clear run. (tchd 14-1 in a place)

Swingkeel(IRE), last year's winner and third the year before, was hunted around at the back as usual, but his rider wasn't happy almost a mile from home and this wasn't to be his day. Official explanation: jockey said gelding had no more to give

T/Jkpt: Not won. T/Plt: £508.40 to a £1 stake. Pool: £532,589.75. 764.68 winning tickets. T/Qpdt: £58.30 to a £1 stake. Pool: £31,293.25. 397.05 winning tickets. SP

3332 AYR (L-H)

Saturday, June 23

OFFICIAL GOING: Good (8.9) changing to good to soft after race 5 (4.05)

Bottom bend moved out 2m from inner line.

Wind: Fresh, half against Weather: Overcast

3374 SCOTTISH SUN MISS SCOTLAND H'CAP — 5f

1:55 (1:55) (Class 3) (0-95,93) 3-Y-O+ **£9,703** (£2,887; £1,443; £721) **Stalls** Centre

Form				RPR
1211	1		**Bosun Breese**[18] 2793 7-9-5 **86** .... GrahamGibbons 9 (David Barron) *mde all: rdn over 1f out: kpt on wl fnl f: eased nr fin* **11/2**[2]	98
0402	2	1 1/4	**Hazelrigg (IRE)**[8] 3127 7-9-6 **87** ....(be) DavidAllan 1 (Tim Easterby) *cl up: shkn up and ev ch ins fnl f: sn rdn and carried hd high: no ex last 75yds* **5/1**[1]	94
2115	3	hd	**Jack Dexter**[23] 2616 3-8-9 **82** .... PJMcDonald 3 (Jim Goldie) *bhd and sn outpcd: drvn 1/2-way: hdwy over 1f out: styd on wl towards fin* **11/2**[2]	86
3666	4	1	**Tax Free (IRE)**[21] 2717 10-9-12 **93** .... AdrianNicholls 4 (David Nicholls) *chsd ldng gp: effrt and rdn 2f out: styd on u.p ins fnl f* **8/1**	96
0-12	5	1 1/4	**Kingsgate Choice (IRE)**[20] 2731 5-9-9 **90** .... LukeMorris 8 (Ed de Giles) *t.k.h: trckd ldrs tl rdn and nt qckn over 1f out* **6/1**[3]	88
0-55	6	nse	**Doctor Parkes**[37] 2208 6-9-10 **91** .... RobertWinston 2 (Eric Alston) *hld up bhd ldng gp: effrt on outside over 1f out: no imp ins fnl f* **7/1**	89
0110	7	3/4	**Dancing Freddy (IRE)**[21] 2717 5-9-10 **91** ....(tp) SaleemGolam 10 (Richard Guest) *dwlt: sn in tch: drvn 2f out: sn one pce* **16/1**	86
4202	8	3	**Bronze Beau**[9] 3065 5-9-2 **83** ....(t) JamesSullivan 12 (Linda Stubbs) *cl up tl rdn and wknd over 1f out* **20/1**	68
0100	9	nk	**Partner (IRE)**[6] 3183 6-9-11 **92** ....(b) PaulMulrennan 14 (Kevin Ryan) *hld up towards nr side of gp: rdn over 2f out: wknd wl over 1f out* **10/1**	75
-050	10	1/2	**Dickie's Lad (IRE)**[21] 2704 4-9-12 **93** ....(t) AmyRyan 11 (Kevin Ryan) *hld up bhd ldrs on nr side of gp: struggling over 2f out: sn btn* **15/2**	75

1m 0.01s (0.61) **Going Correction** +0.30s/f (Good)

WFA 3 from 4yo+ 6lb **10 Ran SP% 116.8**

Speed ratings (Par 107): **107,105,104,103,101 101,99,95,94,93**

toteswingers: 1&2 £6.70, 1&3 £7.00, 2&3 £2.00 CSF £33.25 CT £163.57 TOTE £6.80: £1.60, £2.30, £2.50; EX 21.10 Trifecta £169.90 Pool: £583.50 - 2.54 winning units..

Owner Harrowgate Bloodstock Ltd **Bred** Lady Lonsdale **Trained** Maunby, N Yorks

FOCUS

Overnight rain meant the ground had eased to good following the previous evening's meeting, but the concensus of the jockeys who rode in the first was that it was riding on the slow side. This opening sprint was just over 2 secs slower than standard, which backs that view up. The winner confirmed that he is better than ever.

NOTEBOOK

Bosun Breese may have been one of the oldest in the line-up but he has looked better than ever this season and made it four wins from five starts this term with what has to go down as a career-best effort. He showed loads of early speed and kept rolling out in front to win nicely and he looks set to contest some of the top 5f handicaps this season. (op 5-1)

Hazelrigg(IRE) had every chance having tracked the leader throughout but he's a quirky sort and never really looked like going past the leader. He's in good form but his losing run stretches back the best part of two years now.

Jack Dexter ◆ would ideally want slower ground over this trip and he flew home having been outpaced at the back early on. He'll probably be seen to better effect over 6f and is clearly still a horse with a progressive profile. (tchd 6-1)

Tax Free(IRE) is at the opposite end of his career and he ran well enough but is clearly vulnerable to better treated/younger rivals in handicap company.

Kingsgate Choice(IRE) had a fair bit to find on these terms and wasn't disgraced, especially as he would probably prefer slightly quicker conditions. (op 15-2)

Doctor Parkes ran reasonably and has now slipped to within a couple of pounds of his last winning mark. (op 15-2)

3375 SCOTTISH SUN/E.B.F. LAND O'BURNS FILLIES' STKS (LISTED RACE) — 5f

2:25 (2:25) (Class 1) 3-Y-O+

£22,684 (£8,600; £4,304; £2,144; £1,076; £540) **Stalls** Centre

Form				RPR
03-3	1		**Angels Will Fall (IRE)**[26] 2559 3-8-11 106 .... RobertWinston 3 (Charles Hills) *s.i.s: t.k.h in rr: hdwy on outside of gp to ld ins fnl f: drvn and hld on wl* **7/2**[1]	103
0-02	2	hd	**My Girl Anna (IRE)**[6] 3196 5-9-3 89 .... GrahamGibbons 5 (Muredach Kelly, Ire) *hld up in tch: nt clr run briefly 2f out: smooth hdwy over 1f out: effrt and rdn ins fnl f: r.o fin: jst hld* **15/2**	104
2-01	3	1/2	**Excelette (IRE)**[22] 2664 3-9-1 101 .... RoystonFfrench 1 (Bryan Smart) *chsd ldrs: effrt and rdn over 1f out: ev ch ins fnl f: kpt on: hld nr fin* **13/2**	104
0-15	4	2 1/4	**Duchess Dora (IRE)**[22] 2664 5-9-3 101 .... PaulMulrennan 8 (John Quinn) *led to ins fnl f: kpt on same pce* **10/1**	94
-U04	5	1 1/4	**Astrophysical Jet**[24] 2602 5-9-3 92 .... DavidAllan 7 (Ed McMahon) *chsd ldrs: drvn along wl over 1f out: kpt on same pce fnl f* **14/1**	90
-620	6	1 1/2	**Sioux Rising (IRE)**[21] 2713 6-9-3 97 .... TonyHamilton 6 (Richard Fahey) *hld up: swtchd to nr side of gp and effrt 2f out: no imp fnl f* **16/1**	84
0133	7	1 1/4	**Wicked Wench**[3] 3288 3-8-11 81 .... FrannyNorton 15 (Jo Hughes) *trckd ldr tl rdn and wknd over 1f out* **33/1**	78
20-5	8	1	**Albany Rose (IRE)**[28] 2507 4-9-3 87 .... RyanClark 9 (Rae Guest) *chsd ldrs: drvn 1/2-way: wknd over 1f out* **14/1**	76
0-33	9	1 1/4	**Ladies Are Forever**[21] 2713 4-9-3 107 .... DaleSwift 12 (Geoffrey Oldroyd) *prom: drvn along 1/2-way: wknd wl over 1f out* **9/2**[3]	72
66-4	10	1 1/4	**Celerina (IRE)**[28] 2507 5-9-3 95 ....(b[1]) WayneLordan 14 (T Stack, Ire) *hld up: drvn along over 2f out: wknd over 1f out* **4/1**[2]	67

59.41s (0.01) **Going Correction** +0.30s/f (Good)

WFA 3 from 4yo+ 6lb **10 Ran SP% 116.7**

Speed ratings (Par 108): **111,110,109,106,104 101,99,98,96,94**

toteswingers: 1&2 £7.20, 1&3 £6.80, 2&3 £5.00 CSF £30.19 TOTE £4.20: £1.60, £2.80, £2.50; EX 33.90 Trifecta £222.50 Pool: £688.72 - 2.29 winning units..

Owner Mrs E O'Leary **Bred** Islanmore Stud **Trained** Lambourn, Berks

FOCUS

A competitive Listed race with four of the field rated 100+, some of whom hold Group-race entries, and the time was slightly quicker than the handicap 30 mins earlier. There is no reason why the form shouldn't work out, although it has been rated slightly positively.

NOTEBOOK

Angels Will Fall(IRE) ◆ brought some excellent juvenile form to the table and, having shaped well at Windsor on her reappearance, she confirmed herself a really progressive filly by picking up nicely to win this, having travelled in eye-catching style on the outside of the field. She holds a July Cup entry so connections clearly think she can make her mark in Group company this year and, if she can progress in the manner of last year's winner Margot Did, then she will be winning more races this season. (tchd 4-1)

My Girl Anna(IRE) ◆ belied her official mark to run a blinder in second. She is rated 17lb inferior to the winner and was conceding allowances to that rival yet still went mighty close to a first Listed success. She has gone close twice in Listed company now and this strong traveller looks capable of winning one of these.

Excelette(IRE) ran well having never been far away and conditions might not have been ideal for her given she is so well suited by a sound surface. (op 7-1)

Duchess Dora(IRE) was ridden positively but she only set things up for those in behind and she wasn't quite at her best. (tchd 9-1)

Ladies Are Forever was a disappointment and couldn't land a blow from off the pace. (op 4-1)

Celerina(IRE), for whom maybe the first-time blinkers didn't work, although it's hard to be sure. Official explanation: trainer's rep said mare ran too keenly in the first-time blinkers (op 9-2)

3376 SCOTTISH SUN ON SUNDAY H'CAP — 1m

2:55 (2:55) (Class 2) (0-100,90) 3-Y-O

£15,562 (£4,660; £2,330; £1,165; £582; £292) **Stalls** Low

Form				RPR
-101	1		**Ardmay (IRE)**[9] 3063 3-9-0 **83** .... AmyRyan 3 (Kevin Ryan) *in tch: rdn and effrt over 2f out: led appr fnl f: kpt on strly: veered rt cl home* **9/1**	92
-351	2	1 3/4	**Satanic Beat (IRE)**[22] 2678 3-8-13 **82** .... PaulMulrennan 4 (Jedd O'Keeffe) *led: rdn and hdd appr fnl f: kpt on u.p fnl f* **8/1**[3]	86
1021	3	hd	**Basseterre (IRE)**[29] 2452 3-8-13 **82** .... RobertWinston 8 (Charles Hills) *t.k.h: hld up: smooth hdwy on outside over 2f out: rdn and ev ch appr fnl f: kpt on same pce last 100yds* **7/2**[2]	86
-046	4	2	**Just Fabulous**[15] 2897 3-9-0 **83** .... PJMcDonald 5 (George Moore) *hld up towards rr: nt clr run over 2f out: rdn and hdwy over 1f out: kpt on fnl f* **11/1**	82
1-60	5	2 1/2	**Assizes**[14] 2916 3-9-2 **85** .... WayneLordan 10 (Mark Johnston) *hld up in tch on outside: rdn and outpcd 2f out: no imp fnl f* **25/1**	78
-611	6	2 1/4	**Xinbama (IRE)**[30] 2416 3-8-10 **79** .... FrannyNorton 1 (J W Hills) *hld up: rdn over 2f out: n.m.r over 1f out: no imp ins fnl f* **16/1**	67
5011	7	nse	**Stellar Express (IRE)**[17] 2820 3-9-3 **86** .... LukeMorris 6 (Michael Appleby) *bhd: rdn over 3f out: kpt on fnl f: nvr on terms* **9/1**	74
3-20	8	1/2	**Lady Layla**[19] 2752 3-8-10 **79** .... RoystonFfrench 7 (Bryan Smart) *in tch: hdwy and cl up over 2f out: wknd over 1f out* **16/1**	66
31-1	9	1 1/2	**Baccarat (IRE)**[38] 2182 3-9-1 **84** .... TonyHamilton 2 (Richard Fahey) *t.k.h early: trckd ldrs: rdn over 2f out: wknd over 1f out* **13/8**[1]	67
2-50	10	25	**Abishena (IRE)**[28] 2485 3-9-7 **90** .... AdrianNicholls 9 (Mark Johnston) *trckd ldr: rdn over 2f out: wknd over 1f out* **33/1**	

1m 42.75s (-1.05) **Going Correction** -0.05s/f (Good) **10 Ran SP% 118.3**

Speed ratings (Par 105): **103,101,101,99,96 94,94,93,92,67**

toteswingers: 1&2 £16.90, 1&3 £9.20, 2&3 £11.90 CSF £80.09 CT £310.43 TOTE £13.50: £3.70, £3.50, £1.30; EX 79.60 Trifecta £681.50 Part won. Pool: £921.04 - 0.65 winning units..

Owner A C Henson **Bred** Tom Kelly **Trained** Hambleton, N Yorks

FOCUS

A decent handicap run at a sound gallop but a disappointing favourite. The form is still decent amongst the principals.

NOTEBOOK

Ardmay(IRE), who, barring a blip at York last month (when a long way behind Baccarat), had looked most progressive this season. This was his first try at a mile, he saw it out strongly and there is plenty of stamina on the dam's side of his pedigree, raising the prospect that he could get further in time. (op 10-1)

Satanic Beat(IRE) set a reasonable pace and he deserves credit for keeping on so well. He was racing off a career-high mark so ran very well and he'll be a very dangerous rival in races where he can boss things from the front. (op 9-1)
Basseterre(IRE) caught the eye with the way he travelled on the outside of the field but he lacked the gears to go with the winner in the closing stages. His impressive Haydock win came on quicker ground, and it may be that he is a better horse on that kind of surface. Either way, it's still relatively early days for him. (tchd 4-1)
Just Fabulous, whom the drop back to 1m seemed to suit,o kept on well from off the pace despite having been a bit keen early. Perhaps a strong pace on a stiffer track would bring the best out in her. (tchd 12-1)
Stellar Express(IRE) Official explanation: jockey said filly never travelled
Baccarat(IRE) looked to be in a good position just behind the pace around the inside, but he didn't pick up when shaken up and dropped away tamely. This clearly wasn't him but he has questions to answer now. Official explanation: trainer's rep had no explanation for the poor form shown (op 6-4)

3377 STV APPEAL H'CAP 1m 5f 13y
3:30 (3:30) (Class 3) (0-95,92) 4-Y-O+ £9,703 (£2,887; £1,443; £721) Stalls Low

Form RPR
32-3 **1** **Reem Star**[16] 2863 4-8-8 **79**.......... AmyRyan 2 90
(Kevin Ryan) *trckd ldr: led over 2f out: drvn out fnl f* **11/2**[2]
-023 **2** 2 ½ **Cape Rising (IRE)**[19] 2751 5-8-4 **75**.......... RoystonFfrench 6 82
(Alan Swinbank) *led to over 2f out: rdn and rallied over 1f out: kpt on fnl f: nt pce of wnr* **6/1**[3]
2-01 **3** 2 **Blue Destination**[8] 3114 4-8-10 **81**.......... PaulMulrennan 7 85
(John Quinn) *in tch: hdwy and rdn over 2f out: kpt on same pce fnl f* **7/1**
5003 **4** nk **The Bells O Peover**[12] 2978 4-8-9 **80**..........(v) WayneLordan 9 84
(Mark Johnston) *cl up: rdn and ev ch over 2f out: carried hd high and edgd lft over 1f out: one pce* **11/2**[2]
24-0 **5** ½ **Bollin Greta**[10] 3036 7-8-13 **84**..........(t) DavidAllan 4 87
(Tim Easterby) *rrd s: hld up: rdn and hdwy 2f out: kpt on fnl f: no imp* **9/1**
24-1 **6** 1 ¾ **Amazing King (IRE)**[29] 2457 8-8-12 **83**.......... PJMcDonald 10 83
(Philip Kirby) *hld up: rdn over 2f out: nvr able to chal* **9/1**
5/ **7** ½ **Beidh Tine Anseo (IRE)**[27] 6493 6-8-11 **82**..........(p) RobertWinston 8 81
(Lucinda Russell) *in tch: rdn along over 2f out: outpcd over 1f out* **25/1**
60-0 **8** ½ **Tepmokea (IRE)**[36] 2253 6-9-4 **92**.......... MichaelMetcalfe(3) 11 91
(Mrs K Burke) *trckd ldrs: rdn over 2f out: edgd lft and wknd over 1f out* **5/1**[1]
6-00 **9** 3 **Bowdler's Magic**[14] 2936 5-8-9 **80**.......... AdrianNicholls 12 74
(Mark Johnston) *s.i.s: rdn on outside over 3f out: nvr able to chal* **16/1**
-000 **10** hd **Tenhoo**[19] 2751 6-8-2 **73** oh1.......... LukeMorris 3 67
(Eric Alston) *hld up towards rr: struggling 3f out: sn btn* **20/1**
/00- **11** 2 ¼ **Sea Change (IRE)**[280] 6171 5-8-2 **73**.......... JamesSullivan 1 64
(Jim Goldie) *hld up on ins: struggling over 2f out: sn btn* **40/1**
024- **12** 14 **Gordonsville**[174] 7544 9-8-12 **83**.......... SaleemGolam 5 53
(Jim Goldie) *hld up in midfield: struggling over 3f out: sn btn: t.o* **16/1**

2m 57.73s (3.73) **Going Correction** +0.30s/f (Good) **12** Ran SP% **117.0**
Speed ratings (Par 107): **100,98,97,97,96 95,95,95,93,93 91,83**
toteswingers: 1&2 £2.90, 1&3 £7.00, 2&3 £2.50 CSF £37.06 CT £235.79 TOTE £5.80: £2.10, £2.30, £2.00; EX 36.00 Trifecta £111.80 Pool: £1,056.36 - 6.99 winning units..
Owner Ahmed Ali **Bred** Newsells Park Stud **Trained** Hambleton, N Yorks

FOCUS
Another competitive handicap run at what looked an even gallop, although it did prove difficult to get in a blow from off the pace. The front three home were never that far off the pace but the form looks pretty sound.

NOTEBOOK
Reem Star has done most of her racing on Polytrack but she has been a consistent filly on that surface and she proved herself just as effective on easy turf here. She slipped into the lead over 2f out and got a break on her rivals that she was able to maintain throughout the closing stages. She clearly doesn't lack for stamina and could easily have more to offer on turf. (op 13-2)
Cape Rising(IRE) is lightly raced for a 5-y-o but she looks all about stamina and she kept on rolling despite being headed well over a furlong out. Not fully exposed, there are more races to be won with her. (op 5-1)
Blue Destination had every chance and kept on well enough without quite having the gears to challenge the winner.
The Bells O Peover did best of those to come from off the pace but could never get in a blow and he probably needs slightly further. (op 5-1)
Bollin Greta Official explanation: jockey said mare reared as gates opened
Tepmokea(IRE), for whom there appeared to be no excuses, sat close to the pace but failed to pick up when the race began to unfold in the straight. (tchd 11-2)

3378 SUN SPORT/E.B.F. MAIDEN STKS 6f
4:05 (4:06) (Class 5) 2-Y-O £3,881 (£1,155; £577; £288) Stalls Centre

Form RPR
1 **Tickle Time (IRE)** 2-9-3 0.......... GrahamGibbons 4 87+
(David Barron) *cl up: led over 1f out: rdn and kpt on wl fnl f* **7/2**[3]
2 1 ¼ **Elnadancer (IRE)** 2-9-3 0.......... PJMcDonald 2 82
(Alan Swinbank) *dwlt: hld up bhd ldng gp: effrt and rdn 2f out: styd on to take 2nd wl ins fnl f: nt rch wnr* **20/1**
3 ¾ **Nordikhab (IRE)** 2-9-3 0.......... PaulMulrennan 5 80
(Kevin Ryan) *led centre tl rdn and hdd over 1f out: kpt on same pce ins fnl f* **17/2**
02 **4** 4 ½ **Bonnie Lesley (IRE)**[8] 3110 2-8-12 0.......... DavidAllan 1 61
(Keith Dalgleish) *trckd ldrs: rdn over 2f out: edgd lft and wknd over 1f out* **12/1**
22 **5** 3 **Lucky Beggar (IRE)**[38] 2163 2-9-3 0.......... RobertWinston 9 57
(Charles Hills) *t.k.h: w ldrs: swtchd to stands' side and overall ldr over 4f out: hdd over 1f out: wknd* **11/4**[2]
6 2 **Corton Lad** 2-9-3 0.......... RoystonFfrench 8 51
(Keith Dalgleish) *dwlt: bhd and outpcd: sme late hdwy: nvr on terms* **50/1**
3 **7** ¾ **Sugar Blaze**[29] 2456 2-8-12 0.......... SaleemGolam 7 44
(Jim Goldie) *hld up bhd ldng gp: struggling over 2f out: sn btn* **33/1**
452 **8** 6 **Star Of Rohm**[9] 3074 2-9-3 0.......... LukeMorris 3 31
(Michael Bell) *chsd ldrs tl rdn and wknd over 2f out* **13/8**[1]

1m 15.01s (2.61) **Going Correction** +0.30s/f (Good) **8** Ran SP% **114.9**
Speed ratings (Par 93): **94,92,91,85,81 78,77,69**
toteswingers: 1&2 £13.60, 1&3 £3.80, 2&3 £14.30 CSF £66.94 TOTE £5.30: £2.00, £5.30, £2.20; EX 110.70.
Owner Miss N J Barron **Bred** Pier House Stud **Trained** Maunby, N Yorks

FOCUS
Quite a surprising result because Lucky Beggar and Star Of Rohm set quite a useful standard on form yet the first three home were all gelded debutants. They finished clear and the form seems sound.

NOTEBOOK
Tickle Time(IRE), for whom there had been a lot of market support, justified the money in good style, moving through to take up the lead over a furlong out and never really looking in any danger thereafter. Clearly held in high regard by a stable in blistering form this month, he looks above average. (op 3-1 tchd 4-1)
Elnadancer(IRE) was sent off an apparently unfancied 20-1 chance, but he clearly has a lot of ability and he kept on really well just behind the winner. He is bred to want further than this in time so connections will surely be delighted with this first run. (op 14-1 tchd 22-1)
Nordikhab(IRE) ◆ showed good speed to take them along down the middle of the course and he shouldn't be long in getting off the mark if building on this. (tchd 8-1 and 9-1)
Bonnie Lesley(IRE), who had finished a long way behind today's favourite at Ripon, easily reversed that form without ever threatening the front three. (op 11-1)
Lucky Beggar(IRE)'s rider steered the colt away from his rivals over to the stands' rail but it proved a fruitless venture as the group in the centre ended up dominating. Official explanation: jockey said colt ran too free (op 3-1)
Star Of Rohm ran a shocker, easily his worst race so far, and maybe the easing ground went against him as he was hard under the pump a long way out. Official explanation: trainer's rep said colt was unsuited by the good to soft ground (op 2-1 tchd 6-4)

3379 WEATHERSEAL H'CAP 6f
4:40 (4:42) (Class 4) (0-80,80) 3-Y-O £6,145 (£1,828; £913; £456) Stalls Centre

Form RPR
-311 **1** **Show Flower**[22] 2649 3-9-4 **77**.......... PaulMulrennan 3 87
(Mick Channon) *prom: hdwy to ld appr fnl f: rdn out* **4/1**[3]
-546 **2** 1 ¼ **Discression**[23] 2616 3-9-1 **74**.......... AmyRyan 1 80
(Kevin Ryan) *chsd ldrs: ev ch and rdn 2f out: kpt on fnl f: nt rch wnr* **17/2**
410- **3** nse **Dutch Heritage**[260] 6670 3-8-11 **70**.......... TonyHamilton 2 76
(Richard Fahey) *dwlt: bhd and sn pushed along: hdwy over 1f out: kpt on fnl f: nrst fin* **8/1**
0-00 **4** 1 ¼ **West Leake Hare (IRE)**[10] 3041 3-8-11 **70**..........(b[1]) RobertWinston 5 72
(Charles Hills) *t.k.h: cl up: led 2f out to appr fnl f: kpt on same pce last 100yds* **12/1**
0041 **5** 3 ½ **Rock Canyon (IRE)**[10] 3028 3-8-5 **64**..........(p) RoystonFfrench 7 55
(Linda Perratt) *chsd ldrs tl rdn and wknd over 1f out* **20/1**
4-10 **6** 2 ¾ **Lisiere (IRE)**[38] 2182 3-9-5 **78**.......... LukeMorris 6 60
(Mrs K Burke) *dwlt: sn pushed along bhd ldng gp: drvn over 2f out: sn btn* **8/1**
5603 **7** 8 **Dubai Sunshine (IRE)**[36] 2229 3-9-0 **80**.......... WilliamTwiston-Davies(7) 8 36
(Michael Bell) *hld up in tch: struggling over 2f out: sn btn* **9/4**[1]
1-41 **8** 16 **Takealookatmenow (IRE)**[17] 2824 3-9-0 **73**.......... AdrianNicholls 4
(David Nicholls) *led to 2f out: rdr looked down and sn eased* **7/2**[2]

1m 13.84s (1.44) **Going Correction** +0.30s/f (Good) **8** Ran SP% **118.2**
Speed ratings (Par 101): **102,100,100,98,93 90,79,58**
toteswingers: 1&2 £7.10, 1&3 £5.90, 2&3 £10.00 CSF £38.85 CT £221.61 TOTE £4.80: £1.80, £2.60, £2.10; EX 51.10.
Owner Jaber Abdullah **Bred** Maywood Stud **Trained** West Ilsley, Berks

FOCUS
A competitive little handicap run at a good clip. The form looks sound enough.
Dubai Sunshine(IRE) Official explanation: jockey said gelding never travelled
Takealookatmenow(IRE) Official explanation: jockey said filly lost its action

3380 PEOPLES FORD H'CAP 1m 2f
5:15 (5:15) (Class 4) (0-85,85) 4-Y-O+ £6,145 (£1,828; £913; £456) Stalls Low

Form RPR
0-00 **1** **Cool Macavity (IRE)**[23] 2642 4-9-2 **80**.......... RobertWinston 6 91
(Charles Hills) *t.k.h: hld up: hdwy on outside to ld over 1f out: rdn and hld on wl fnl f* **10/1**
60-5 **2** nk **Red Inca**[24] 2606 4-8-7 **71**.......... AmyRyan 9 81
(Brian Ellison) *hld up in tch: hdwy to ld briefly wl over 1f out: sn rdn and styd upsides: kpt on fnl f: hld nr fin* **7/2**[1]
-004 **3** 5 **Shamdarley (IRE)**[21] 2720 4-9-4 **82**.......... PaulMulrennan 2 82+
(Michael Dods) *t.k.h: hld up in tch: effrt whn n.m.r over 2f out to over 1f out: styng on whn lft 3rd ins fnl f: no imp* **7/2**[1]
1222 **4** 1 **The Lock Master (IRE)**[10] 3022 5-8-3 **67**.......... LukeMorris 4 65
(Michael Appleby) *trckd ldrs: rdn along 3f out: outpcd fnl f* **8/1**[3]
3 **5** 2 ¾ **Charpoy (USA)**[21] 2720 4-9-4 **82**..........(p) TonyHamilton 5 77
(Ian Semple) *cl up: led over 2f out to wl over 1f out: sn no ex: hld whn hmpd ins fnl f* **6/1**[2]
4-01 **6** ¾ **Full Toss**[23] 2620 6-8-11 **75**.......... SaleemGolam 3 66
(Jim Goldie) *led to over 2f out: rdn and wknd over 1f out* **8/1**[3]
2502 **7** nse **Santefisio**[24] 2597 6-9-7 **85**..........(p) DavidAllan 1 76
(Keith Dalgleish) *s.i.s: t.k.h in rr: effrt on ins 2f out: wknd appr fnl f* **8/1**[3]
5-41 **8** 3 ¾ **Oneofapear (IRE)**[36] 2241 6-9-5 **83**.......... PJMcDonald 8 73
(Alan Swinbank) *prom: rdn and edgd lft over 2f out: sn wknd: btn whn hmpd ins fnl f* **6/1**[2]
000 **U** **King Of Windsor (IRE)**[95] 978 5-8-11 **75**.......... RoystonFfrench 10 79
(Keith Dalgleish) *hld up: rdn and hdwy over 1f out: cl 3rd and styng on whn stmbld bdly and uns rdr ins fnl f* **20/1**

2m 13.88s (1.88) **Going Correction** +0.30s/f (Good) **9** Ran SP% **120.2**
Speed ratings (Par 105): **104,103,99,98,96 96,96,93,**
toteswingers: 1&2 £9.50, 1&3 £10.90, 2&3 £3.90 CSF £46.92 CT £152.19 TOTE £15.30: £4.90, £1.70, £1.40; EX 59.20.
Owner Triermore Stud **Bred** C O P Hanbury **Trained** Lambourn, Berks

FOCUS
A competitive race run at an even tempo and the field grouped up entering the final two furlongs as the closers made their moves. The winner built on his better latest run.
T/Plt: £295.90 to a £1 stake. Pool:£85,318.22 - 210.42 winning tickets T/Qpdt: £112.10 to a £1 stake. Pool:£3,725.69 - 24.58 winning tickets RY

3061 HAYDOCK (L-H)
Saturday, June 23

OFFICIAL GOING: Soft (good to soft in places; 7.6)
All races on Inner home straight and distances on Round course increased by 1yd.
Wind: Strong, half against Weather: overcast, very windy, rain race 3 onwards

3381 CHRISTIE BUCKET COLLECTORS ARMY MAIDEN STKS 5f
6:50 (6:53) (Class 5) 2-Y-O £2,911 (£866; £432; £216) Stalls Centre

Form RPR
1 **Secret Look** 2-9-3 0.......... FrannyNorton 11 80+
(Ed McMahon) *trckd ldrs: led jst ins fnl f: drvn out* **4/1**[2]
2 1 ¼ **Red Explorer (USA)** 2-9-3 0.......... MichaelHills 13 76+
(Charles Hills) *s.i.s: hdwy stands' side over 2f out: styd on to take 2nd last 50yds* **11/4**[1]
3 1 **Mitchell** 2-8-12 0.......... DeanHeslop(5) 6 72+
(David Barron) *edgd lft s: in rr: hdwy over 2f out: kpt on same pce fnl f* **15/2**[3]

05 **4** ½ **Millie N Aire**[10] 3034 2-8-12 0 RussKennemore 12 65
(Danielle McCormick) *led: hdd jst ins fnl f: wknd towards fin* **8/1**

0 **5** *nk* **Max The Machine**[6] 3182 2-9-0 0 DaleSwift(3) 2 69+
(Derek Shaw) *chsd ldrs: upsides over 1f out: kpt on same pce* **14/1**

0 **6** *nse* **Charlie Em**[8] 3110 2-8-12 0 DavidNolan 8 64+
(Richard Fahey) *in rr: kpt on fnl f* **14/1**

7 5 **Fidget** 2-8-12 0 MartinHarley 3 46
(David Brown) *chsd ldrs: wknd over 1f out* **11/1**

8 2 **Strange Angel (IRE)** 2-8-9 0 RyanClark(3) 9 39+
(Tom Tate) *chsd ldrs: wknd 2f out* **10/1**

4 **9** *shd* **Oh Boy Oh Boy**[36] 2224 2-9-3 0 PaddyAspell 7 43
(James Moffatt) *chsd ldrs: drvn and outpcd over 2f out: lost pl over 1f out* **28/1**

5 **10** 1 **Pacquiao (IRE)**[15] 2873 2-9-3 0 WilliamCarson 4 40
(John Quinn) *bmpd s: in rr: bhd fnl 2f* **8/1**

1m 3.31s (2.51) **Going Correction** +0.475s/f (Yiel) **10** Ran SP% **114.9**
Speed ratings (Par 93): **98,96,94,93,93 93,85,81,81,80**
toteswingers: 1&2 £2.30, 1&3 £6.70, 2&3 £5.70 CSF £15.13 TOTE £5.20: £1.70, £1.60, £2.90; EX 14.40 Trifecta £55.50 Pool 408.82 - 5.45 winning unuts..
Owner S L Edwards **Bred** S L Edwards **Trained** Lichfield, Staffs

FOCUS
Probably an ordinary juvenile maiden but the first three all made nice starts.

NOTEBOOK
Secret Look was never far away and knuckled down well inside the final furlong to make a winning debut. He evidently handles easy ground well and, from a yard whose juveniles often come on markedly for a run, is entitled to improve a deal for the debut experience, so his future bodes well. (op 5-1)
Red Explorer(USA) ◆, who cost 130,000gns and was well backed, showed up nicely and posted a decent debut effort. He's in good hands and will hold strong claims next time out (op 3-1)
Mitchell, speedily bred, did his best work towards the finish on his debut. He looks sure to appreciate another furlong and has a future. (tchd 7-1)
Millie N Aire tried to make this a test back down in trip and, running close to her previous level, she helps to set the standard of this form. (op 12-1)

3382 CHRISTIE H'CAP (BETFAIR SPRINT FLAT SERIES QUALIFIER) 5f
7:20 (7:25) (Class 5) (0-75,74) 3-Y-0+ £3,234 (£962; £481; £240) Stalls Centre

Form RPR
2232 **1** **First In Command (IRE)**[2] 3308 7-9-6 73 (t) ShaneBKelly(5) 10 82
(Daniel Mark Loughnane) *trckd ldrs: led 1f out: edgd lft: drvn out* **5/1**[3]

0365 **2** *nk* **Fair Passion**[16] 2861 5-9-7 69 FrannyNorton 7 77
(Derek Shaw) *hmpd s: in rr: stands' side: hdwy 2f out: hung rt then lft: kpt on wl ins fnl f* **12/1**

135- **3** 1 **Jamaican Bolt (IRE)**[320] 4855 4-9-9 74 DaleSwift(3) 8 78+
(Geoffrey Oldroyd) *chsd ldrs: edgd lft and kpt on same pce fnl f* **9/4**[1]

0331 **4** 1 **Avonvalley**[12] 2971 5-8-12 60 RobbieFitzpatrick 6 61
(Peter Grayson) *s.s and wnt rt s: in rr: hdwy over 1f out: edgd lft: kpt on ins fnl f* **10/1**

3430 **5** 1 **Sally's Swansong**[4] 3256 6-8-2 55 oh5 (p) NeilFarley(5) 13 52
(Eric Alston) *in rr: sn drvn along: kpt on fnl 2f: nvr threatened ldrs* **10/1**

-034 **6** 1 ¼ **Ballarina**[8] 3109 6-8-2 57 JasonHart(7) 3 50
(Eric Alston) *set off to r alone far side: overall ldr: hdd 1f out: sn wknd* **16/1**

-331 **7** *shd* **Red Roar (IRE)**[5] 3211 5-9-9 71 6ex PaddyAspell 9 63
(Alan Berry) *reluctant and led to post after unseating rdr: chsd ldrs: outpcd over 2f out: kpt on fnl f* **6/1**

0503 **8** 3 **Absa Lutte (IRE)**[5] 3211 9-9-5 67 StephenCraine 4 48
(Michael Mullineaux) *in rr: nvr a factor* **25/1**

11-0 **9** 1 ¼ **Cool In The Shade**[18] 2793 4-9-2 71 (b) NedCurtis(7) 5 48
(Paul Midgley) *walked rdrkless to post: led centre gp: chsd overall ldr: edgd lft and wknd over 1f out* **9/2**[2]

546/ **10** 6 **Hyde Lea Flyer**[852] 668 7-8-5 56 oh6 ow1 RyanClark(3) 11 11
(Barry Leavy) *s.i.s: in rr: bhd fnl 2f* **22/1**

1m 2.78s (1.98) **Going Correction** +0.475s/f (Yiel) **10** Ran SP% **119.9**
Speed ratings (Par 103): **103,102,100,99,97 95,95,90,88,79**
toteswingers: 1&2 £12.00, 1&3 £3.50, 2&3 £9.90 CSF £65.26 CT £173.79 TOTE £6.90: £2.00, £4.10, £1.40; EX 74.90 TRIFECTA Not won..
Owner Mrs C Loughnane **Bred** Peter And Mrs McCutcheon **Trained** Baldwin's Gate, Staffs

FOCUS
A modest sprint handicap but a slight improvement from the winner with the second showing her best turf form.
Fair Passion Official explanation: jockey sasid mare hung left and right-handed

3383 CHRISTIE CHARITABLE FUND H'CAP 1m
7:50 (7:51) (Class 4) (0-85,82) 3-Y-0 £5,175 (£1,540; £769; £384) Stalls Low

Form RPR
112 **1** **Trail Blaze (IRE)**[9] 3064 3-9-6 81 PatCosgrave 2 91
(Kevin Ryan) *mde all: qckd 4f out: edgd rt 1f out: hld on towards fin* **11/4**[1]

1 **2** ½ **Prophesy (IRE)**[46] 1953 3-8-9 77 JasonHart(7) 4 85
(Declan Carroll) *chsd ldrs: drvn over 3f out: wnt 2nd over 1f out: kpt on: jst hld* **12/1**

2251 **3** 3 ¾ **Lady Loch**[18] 2785 3-9-3 78 (b) DavidNolan 5 77
(Richard Fahey) *chsd ldrs: drvn: hung rt bnd over 5f out: lost pl over 2f out: kpt on fnl f: tk 3rd nr line* **9/2**[3]

-313 **4** *nk* **Annie Walker (IRE)**[5] 3214 3-8-10 71 PaulQuinn 3 70
(David Nicholls) *trckd ldrs: drvn over 3f out: kpt on ins fnl f* **8/1**

4160 **5** *nk* **Masters Blazing**[30] 2408 3-9-0 75 (p) BrettDoyle 9 73
(John Ryan) *hld up in rr: effrt over 3f out: hdwy on ins 1f out: kpt on* **9/1**

1- **6** ¾ **Kiz Kulesi**[248] 6953 3-9-7 82 AhmedAjtebi 1 78
(Mahmood Al Zarooni) *chsd ldrs: 2nd and hung rt over 2f out: one pce appr fnl f* **7/2**[2]

-550 **7** 1 ½ **Bountiful Girl**[26] 2539 3-8-6 72 ShaneBKelly(5) 7 65
(Richard Fahey) *hld up in rr: drvn 4f out: nvr a factor* **15/2**

3413 **8** *nse* **On The Hoof**[29] 2459 3-8-12 73 JamesSullivan 10 66
(Michael Easterby) *stdd s: hld up towards rr: sme hdwy 3f out: wknd over 1f out* **14/1**

1m 44.1s (0.40) **Going Correction** +0.10s/f (Good) **8** Ran SP% **114.3**
Speed ratings (Par 101): **102,101,97,97,97 96,94,94**
toteswingers: 1&2 £5.80, 1&3 £2.00, 2&3 £11.10 CSF £36.53 CT £143.72 TOTE £3.60: £1.60, £3.90, £1.80; EX 25.80 Trifecta £54.40 Pool 224.46 - 3.05 winning units..
Owner Mr & Mrs Julian And Rosie Richer **Bred** Edmond Kent **Trained** Hambleton, N Yorks

FOCUS
A fair 3-y-o handicap but the winner can do better and the second recorded a personal-best.

3384 ABACUS SECURITIES 10TH YEAR ANNIVERSARY MAIDEN STKS 1m
8:20 (8:21) (Class 5) 3-Y-0+ £2,911 (£866; £432; £216) Stalls Low

Form RPR
6-62 **1** **Kaafel (IRE)**[32] 2380 3-9-2 79 MichaelHills 9 85
(Charles Hills) *mde all: shkn up over 1f out: hld on wl towards fin* **1/2**[1]

2 ¾ **Mean It (IRE)** 3-9-2 0 MickyFenton 6 83+
(Tom Tate) *t.k.h: sn trcking wnr: rdn over 1f out: rallied ins fnl f: a jst hld* **7/2**[2]

6 **3** 16 **One For The Girls**[22] 2665 3-9-2 0 RussKennemore 4 46
(Nicky Vaughan) *stdd s: hld up: effrt 4f out: outpcd over 2f out: kpt on to take modest 3rd nr fin* **33/1**

0 **4** 1 ¼ **Dream On Paddy**[15] 2881 3-8-13 0 DaleSwift(3) 5 44
(Ian McInnes) *chsd ldrs: drvn and 3rd over 3f out: hung lft over 2f out: wknd towards fin* **11/1**

6-0 **5** 2 ½ **Silent Ambition**[71] 1363 3-8-8 0 RyanClark(3) 3 33
(Mark Brisbourne) *chsd ldrs: drvn over 3f out: wknd over 2f out* **20/1**

6 3 ½ **Mountain Summit** 3-8-6 0 ShaneBKelly(5) 8 25
(Richard Fahey) *s.i.s: in rr: drvn 6f out: bhd fnl 3f* **9/1**[3]

/ **P** **Advocacy (USA)** 7-9-12 0 DavidNolan 1
(Roy Brotherton) *s.i.s: towards rr: p.u over 4f out* **100/1**

1m 44.96s (1.26) **Going Correction** +0.10s/f (Good)
WFA 3 from 4yo+ 10lb **7** Ran SP% **115.9**
Speed ratings (Par 103): **97,96,80,79,76 73,**
toteswingers: 1&2 £1.30, 1&3 £3.80, 2&3 £2.30 CSF £2.60 TOTE £1.40: £1.10, £2.40; EX 2.20 Trifecta £10.30 Pool 301.15 - 21.48 winning units..
Owner Hamdan Al Maktoum **Bred** Shadwell Estate Company Limited **Trained** Lambourn, Berks

FOCUS
An ordinary maiden in which the first pair came a long way clear. The winner is rated close to form but a race with little depth.

3385 CHRISTIE CHARITY RACEDAY H'CAP 1m
8:50 (8:50) (Class 4) (0-85,87) 4-Y-0+ £5,175 (£1,540; £769; £384) Stalls Low

Form RPR
00-6 **1** **Venutius**[28] 2491 5-9-0 78 FrannyNorton 7 89
(Ed McMahon) *trckd ldrs: drvn over 3f out: outpcd over 2f out: 2nd and styd on wl fnl 100yds: led nr fin* **10/1**

510- **2** *nk* **Epernay**[199] 7651 5-8-5 72 (vt) RyanClark(3) 4 82
(Ian Williams) *trckd ldrs: smooth hdwy over 3f out: effrt and hung lft 2f out: sn led: hdd nr fin* **10/1**

6211 **3** 2 ¾ **Postscript (IRE)**[10] 3037 4-8-8 79 GeorgeDowning(7) 9 83
(Ian Williams) *trckd ldrs: drvn over 3f out: edgd lft over 1f out: hung bdly rt ins fnl f: kpt on to take 3rd nr fin* **7/2**[3]

0603 **4** *nk* **Dolphin Rock**[7] 3167 5-8-12 76 LeeNewman 3 79
(David Barron) *led: increased pce over 3f out: hdd wl over 1f out: one pce* **15/8**[1]

-006 **5** 5 **Chiswick Bey (IRE)**[15] 2882 4-9-2 85 ShaneBKelly(5) 6 77
(Richard Fahey) *in last: shkn up after 2f: sn outpcd: hdwy on ins 4f out: outpcd over 3f out: lost pl over 1f out* **15/2**

4452 **6** *shd* **Illustrious Prince (IRE)**[15] 2896 5-8-8 77 NeilFarley(5) 1 68
(Declan Carroll) *trckd ldr: t.k.h: effrt over 3f out: wknd over 1f out* **10/3**[2]

1m 43.33s (-0.37) **Going Correction** +0.10s/f (Good) **6** Ran SP% **110.0**
Speed ratings (Par 105): **105,104,101,101,96 96**
toteswingers: 1&2 £13.70, 1&3 £5.20, 2&3 £6.30 CSF £91.94 CT £394.78 TOTE £11.00: £3.50, £5.20; EX 117.60 Trifecta £181.90 Part won. Pool 245.85 - 0.62 winning units..
Owner Dr Hugh Jones **Bred** Mrs F S Williams **Trained** Lichfield, Staffs

FOCUS
Not a bad handicap and soundly run. The winner can build on this from what is now a fair mark, while the second and third both hung in the claosing stages.

3386 MADNESS IN CONCERT HERE 6TH JULY H'CAP 1m 2f 95y
9:20 (9:21) (Class 5) (0-75,75) 4-Y-0+ £2,911 (£866; £432; £108; £108) Stalls High

Form RPR
5004 **1** **Amazing Blue Sky**[4] 3253 6-9-7 75 JamesSullivan 3 82
(Ruth Carr) *sn led: increased pce over 4f out: narrowly hdd 2f out: styd on gamely to regain ld last 100yds: kpt on wl* **6/4**[1]

0021 **2** 1 ¼ **Mighty Clarets (IRE)**[19] 2765 5-8-10 64 MartinHarley 4 69
(Barry Leavy) *led early: trckd ldr: narrow ld 2f out: hdd ins fnl f: no ex* **9/2**[3]

0-03 **3** 4 **Ampleforth**[159] 192 4-9-3 74 RyanClark(3) 8 71
(Ian Williams) *trckd ldrs: effrt over 3f out: edgd rt over 1f out: one pce* **11/2**

1055 **4** ½ **Vanilla Rum**[15] 2899 5-8-13 67 (b) FrannyNorton 9 63
(John Mackie) *trckd ldrs: drvn 4f out: outpcd over 2f out: kpt on fnl f* **4/1**[2]

1330 **4** *dht* **Mount Abora (IRE)**[14] 2915 5-8-6 67 GeorgeDowning(7) 2 63
(Ian Williams) *hld up in rr: hdwy over 3f out: sn drvn: one pce fnl 2f* **11/1**

4-00 **6** 5 **Tartan Gunna**[18] 2792 6-9-1 72 DaleSwift(3) 6 59
(James Given) *dwlt: hld up in rr: effrt outside 4f out: wknd over 1f out* **9/1**

2m 16.83s (1.33) **Going Correction** +0.10s/f (Good) **6** Ran SP% **111.9**
Speed ratings (Par 103): **98,97,93,93,93 89**
toteswingers: 1&2 £1.60, 1&3 £2.90, 2&3 £2.40 CSF £8.47 CT £27.49 TOTE £2.40: £1.60, £1.90; EX 8.10 Trifecta £10.70 Pool 354.92 - 24.41 winning units..
Owner Graham Scruton **Bred** Hong Kong Breeders Club **Trained** Huby, N Yorks

FOCUS
A modest handicap with the winner down in grade and rated back to his Beverley winning mark, while the runner-up sets the standard.
T/Plt: £88.40 to a £1 stake. Pool: £75,406.39. 622.60 winning tickets. T/Qpdt: £60.00 to a £1 stake. Pool: £4,062.38. 50.10 winning tickets. WG

[3150] LINGFIELD (L-H)
Saturday, June 23

OFFICIAL GOING: Turf course - good to firm (good in places; 8.2); all-weather - standard
Wind: Fresh, half behind Weather: Fine but cloudy

3387 HERBIE'S MAIDEN AUCTION STKS 7f
6:35 (6:38) (Class 6) 2-Y-0 £2,181 (£644; £322) Stalls High

Form RPR
5 **1** **Beau Select (IRE)**[16] 2852 2-8-11 0 AndreaAtzeni 7 69
(Robert Eddery) *racd against rail: w ldrs: shkn up to chal 1f out: led ins fnl f: rdn out* **7/2**[2]

05 **2** *nk* **Poetic Verse**[31] 2384 2-8-4 0 .... DavidProbert 2 61
(Rod Millman) *led 2f: pressed ldr: rdn to ld again 2f out: hdd ins fnl f: styd on but jst hld* **8/1**

04 **3** *2 ¾* **Bix (IRE)**[24] 2609 2-9-1 0 .... ShaneKelly 8 65
(Brian Meehan) *s.i.s: trckd ldrs: rdn 2f out: nt qckn over 1f out: styd on to take 3rd ins fnl f* **6/1**

0 **4** *¾* **Spithead**[11] 3009 2-8-10 0 .... LiamJones 6 58
(William Haggas) *racd against rail: trckd ldrs: outpcd 2f out: reminders 1f out: kpt on* **12/1**

5 *nk* **Choral Prince (IRE)** 2-9-0 0 .... RichardHughes 9 61+
(Mike Murphy) *dwlt: hld up in last pair: prog over 2f out: plld out over 1f out: shkn up and one pce* **4/1**[3]

40 **6** *1* **Frosted Off**[16] 2844 2-8-12 0 .... CathyGannon 5 57
(John Spearing) *taken down early: led after 2f: rdn and hdd 2f out: wknd fnl f* **33/1**

7 *2 ¼* **Runninglikethewind (IRE)** 2-8-13 0 .... SebSanders 4 51
(Chris Wall) *got loose in paddock: free to post: wnt lft s: in tch but rn green: plld out and effrt 2f out: hanging lft and wknd over 1f out* **9/4**[1]

0 **8** *¾* **Mick Dundee (IRE)**[30] 2415 2-9-1 0 .... DaneO'Neill 3 51
(J W Hills) *sltly hmpd s: hld up in last pair: effrt on outer over 2f out: lost tch over 1f out* **25/1**

00 **9** *13* **Gowertonian (IRE)**[25] 2579 2-8-4 0 .... DarrenEgan(5) 1 11
(Ronald Harris) *s.s: in tch on wd outside: rdn 3f out: wknd 2f out: t.o* **66/1**

1m 22.94s (-0.36) **Going Correction** -0.325s/f (Firm) **9** Ran SP% **114.4**
Speed ratings (Par 91): **89,88,85,84,84 83,80,79,64**
toteswingers: 1&2 £5.10, 1&3 £4.60, 2&3 £3.90 CSF £30.54 TOTE £4.20: £1.80, £1.70, £2.40; EX 22.30.
Owner Ms Trisha Keane **Bred** Denis McDonnell **Trained** Newmarket, Suffolk

FOCUS
This was an unremarkable maiden but it should yield a few winners at a realistic level. The rail was the place to be.

NOTEBOOK
Beau Select(IRE), determined to grab the stands' rail, was also aided by the faster ground and longer trip this time. He won a shade more comfortably than the margin might suggest and shouldn't get too tough a mark in nurseries. (op 3-1 tchd 11-4)
Poetic Verse raced a little further from the stands' rail than the winner, but not so wide that it will have been a disdvantage. This trip looks ideal at present and, though now qualified for nurseries, she might yet sneak a maiden. (op 15-2 tchd 7-1)
Bix(IRE), who has improved with racing, is creeping closer to the winner's enclosure. He is worth keeping at this longer trip. (op 9-2)
Spithead was a bit unlucky to lose a prominent position against the stands' rail and from then on was always fighting a losing battle. He cost only 3,000gns, but this half-brother to winners at 5f and 7f never stopped battling and is worth checking out next time. (op 10-1)
Choral Prince(IRE), a 15,000GBP half-bother to a 1m4f winner, wasn't helped by having to make his effort in the middle. He will reach his peak over longer trips as he matures. (op 7-1)
Frosted Off ran his best race yet but needs to switch to nurseries now he is qualified. Official explanation: jockey said pin had slipped through leather of left stirrup and caused gelding to ease prematurely.
Runninglikethewind(IRE) was getting worked up beforehand and probably didn't run his race. A 12,000gns yearling who has several winners in the family, he attracted plenty of support and can do better. (op 11-4)

3388 PREMIER CONSULTING H'CAP 7f 140y
7:05 (7:08) (Class 5) (0-75,74) 3-Y-O+ **£3,067** (£905; £453) **Stalls** Centre

Form RPR

1-66 **1** **Strathnaver**[25] 2583 3-9-1 **71** .... SilvestreDeSousa 8 82
(Ed Dunlop) *trckd ldrs: prog to go 2nd bhd clr ldr 2f out: rdn and clsd over 1f out: led last 75yds: won gng away* **4/1**[2]

3000 **2** *1 ½* **Calypso Cay**[14] 2926 4-8-5 **56** oh1 ow1 .... MatthewLawson(5) 5 65
(Peter Salmon) *racd freely: led: clr and crossed to nr side rail after 2f: stl clr 2f out: tired and collared last 75yds* **25/1**

1223 **3** *4* **Mayo Lad (IRE)**[15] 2898 3-9-4 **74** .... RichardHughes 2 71
(Richard Hannon) *moved to s in awkard fashion: s.s: hld up in last trio: effrt on outer over 2f out: styd on fr over 1f out to take 3rd nr fin* **13/8**[1]

0055 **4** *nk* **Amethyst Dawn (IRE)**[6] 3192 6-9-10 **70** .... GeorgeBaker 3 68
(Andrew Reid) *prom: chsd clr ldr 3f out to 2f out: one pce after* **28/1**

004- **5** *nk* **Bajan Bear**[246] 6997 4-9-11 **71** .... DaneO'Neill 9 69
(Michael Blanshard) *trckd ldrs: effrt over 2f out: rdn and no imp on ldrs over 1f out: kpt on* **14/1**

005 **6** *2 ½* **Soweto Star (IRE)**[12] 2975 4-9-7 **72** .... DarrenEgan(5) 4 63
(John Best) *stdd s: hld up wl in rr: stdy prog wl over 2f out: rdn and no hdwy over 1f out: fdd* **7/1**[3]

6445 **7** *½* **Rock Anthem (IRE)**[63] 1530 8-9-8 **68** .... PatDobbs 10 58
(Mike Murphy) *hld up in rr: jst pushed along 2f out: styd on fnl f: nvr involved* **16/1**

5500 **8** *½* **Cativo Cavallino**[38] 2173 9-9-8 **68** .... RichardThomas 7 57
(John E Long) *nvr beyond midfield: rdn and no prog over 2f out: wl btn after* **33/1**

-055 **9** *1* **Isingy Red (FR)**[26] 2546 4-9-3 **63** .... FergusSweeney 11 49
(Jim Boyle) *in tch in midfield: rdn and no prog over 2f out: n.d after* **10/1**

66 **10** *10* **Bold Ring**[58] 1626 6-8-11 **60** .... SophieDoyle(3) 13 21
(Eric Wheeler) *trckd ldrs tl wknd qckly over 2f out* **20/1**

3300 **11** *1 ½* **Irons On Fire (USA)**[11] 3007 4-9-2 **62** .... AmirQuinn 12 20
(Lee Carter) *stdd s: hld up wl in rr: no prog 3f out: eased whn no ch over 1f out* **28/1**

3000 **12** *½* **Tiradito (USA)**[51] 1769 5-9-10 **70** .... (p) ShaneKelly 6 26
(Michael Attwater) *chsd clr ldr to 3f out: wknd qckly* **28/1**

0000 **13** *27* **Ensnare**[11] 3006 7-8-11 **57** .... StevieDonohoe 1
(Willie Musson) *sn t.o* **50/1**

1m 29.07s (-3.23) **Going Correction** -0.325s/f (Firm)
WFA 3 from 4yo+ 10lb **13** Ran SP% **116.1**
Speed ratings (Par 103): **103,101,97,97,96 94,93,93,92,82 80,80,53**
toteswingers: 1&2 £37.80, 1&3 £2.50, 2&3 £20.50 CSF £103.77 CT £231.57 TOTE £4.90: £1.30, £8.00, £1.10; EX 125.80.
Owner St Albans Bloodstock LLP **Bred** Mrs C R Philipson & Mrs H G Lascelles **Trained** Newmarket, Suffolk

FOCUS
As in the previous race, racing prominently within three horse-widths of the stands' rail appeared to be the perfect strategy. They went a decent gallop.
Rock Anthem(IRE) Official explanation: jockey said gelding was denied a clear run
Bold Ring Official explanation: trainer said mare was unsuited by the good to firm (good in places) ground
Irons On Fire(USA) Official explanation: trainer's rep said gelding was unsuited by the good to firm (good in places) ground
Ensnare Official explanation: trainer said gelding did not come down the hill

3389 PREMIER FINANCIAL SERVICES MAIDEN STKS 6f
7:35 (7:39) (Class 5) 3-Y-O+ **£3,067** (£905; £453) **Stalls** High

Form RPR

00 **1** **Modern Tutor**[14] 2941 3-9-0 0 .... PatDobbs 11 87
(Sir Michael Stoute) *prom: chsd ldr 2f out: shkn up briefly and clsd to ld 1f out: edgd rt but won decisively* **16/1**

222- **2** *2 ¾* **Signor Sassi**[292] 5786 3-9-0 79 .... NeilCallan 7 78
(Roger Varian) *led and sn crossed to nr side rail: rdn and hdd 1f out: hld whn hmpd ins fnl f* **1/1**[1]

5 **3** *1* **Avalanche**[29] 2461 3-8-11 0 .... PatrickHills(3) 12 75+
(Luca Cumani) *chsd ldrs: rdn over 2f out: kpt on to take 3rd 1f out: n.d* **25/1**

0320 **4** *2 ¾* **Standing Strong (IRE)**[7] 3157 4-9-7 78 .... StevieDonohoe 5 68
(Robert Mills) *in tch: rdn and sme prog 2f out: nt on terms w ldrs over 1f out: one pce* **9/4**[2]

-UR0 **5** *½* **Aurens (IRE)**[7] 3155 3-9-0 0 ....[1] AmirQuinn 10 64
(Gary Moore) *s.v.s: ct up at bk of field after 2f: urged along and styd on wl fnl 2f: nrst fin* **33/1**

05 **6** *½* **Common Cents**[42] 2065 3-8-9 0 .... DarrenEgan(5) 8 63
(Ronald Harris) *dwlt: mostly chsd ldr to 2f out: fdd* **14/1**

00 **7** *1 ½* **Highway Warrior**[42] 2095 3-8-10 0 ow1 .... JamieGoldstein 4 54
(Zoe Davison) *prom on outer: rdn over 2f out: fdd* **200/1**

5 **8** *2* **River Pageant**[28] 2501 3-8-9 0 .... SilvestreDeSousa 14 47
(Eve Johnson Houghton) *t.k.h at rr of main gp: pushed along and sme prog 2f out: no hdwy fnl f* **8/1**[3]

6006 **9** *½* **Luisa Tetrazzini (IRE)**[9] 3082 6-8-9 49 .... RichardOld(7) 2 47
(Terry Clement) *dwlt: in tch and racd wdst of all: rdn over 2f out: wknd over 1f out* **200/1**

0-00 **10** *3 ¼* **A B Celebration**[15] 2886 4-9-2 38 .... KieranO'Neill 15 37
(John Bridger) *cl up against rail to 1/2-way: wknd over 2f out* **200/1**

11 *1* **Barnacle** 3-9-0 0 .... JohnFahy 13 36
(Pat Eddery) *dwlt: rn green and detached in rr: nvr a factor* **50/1**

0-5 **12** *nk* **Two Sugars**[7] 3155 4-9-7 0 .... CathyGannon 6 37
(Louise Best) *chsd ldrs over 3f: wknd* **50/1**

13 *nse* **Rupeetoups** 4-9-7 0 .... DaneO'Neill 9 37
(Henry Candy) *a wl in rr: detached fr main gp by 1/2-way: nvr a factor* **33/1**

5-0 **14** *hd* **Spellmaker**[9] 3079 3-9-0 0 .... FergusSweeney 1 35
(Tony Newcombe) *t.k.h early: hld up wl in rr: no ch sn after 1/2-way* **100/1**

1m 9.41s (-1.79) **Going Correction** -0.325s/f (Firm)
WFA 3 from 4yo+ 7lb **14** Ran SP% **120.6**
Speed ratings (Par 103): **98,94,93,89,88 88,86,83,82,78 77,76,76,76**
toteswingers: 1&2 £5.00, 1&3 £26.80, 2&3 £6.60 CSF £32.01 TOTE £18.40: £4.50, £1.10, £6.50; EX 41.50.
Owner Lady Rothschild **Bred** Kincorth Investments Inc **Trained** Newmarket, Suffolk
■ Stewards' Enquiry : Pat Dobbs two-day ban: careless riding (Jul 8-9)

FOCUS
This was a routine maiden, but the first three have potential.
Aurens(IRE) Official explanation: jockey said gelding missed the break

3390 CGGVERITAS H'CAP 5f
8:05 (8:07) (Class 5) (0-70,70) 3-Y-O+ **£3,067** (£905; £453) **Stalls** High

Form RPR

3425 **1** **Steelcut**[28] 2476 8-9-10 **68** .... (p) GrahamLee 10 77
(Mark Buckley) *trckd ldng pair: shkn up over 1f out: produced between rivals fnl f: drvn and r.o to ld last strides* **7/1**[3]

-300 **2** *nk* **Wooden King (IRE)**[28] 2494 7-9-12 **70** .... TomMcLaughlin 8 78
(Malcolm Saunders) *pressed ldr: led over 1f out gng wl: drvn fnl f: hdd last strides* **7/1**[3]

25-0 **3** *1* **Rebecca Romero**[32] 2369 5-9-10 **68** .... RichardHughes 4 72
(Denis Coakley) *hld up in rr: prog 2f out: rdn and styd on fnl f to take 3rd nr fin* **4/1**[2]

-000 **4** *nk* **Miss Polly Plum**[102] 887 5-8-10 **54** .... (p) AndreaAtzeni 11 57
(Chris Dwyer) *led against rail: rdn and hdd over 1f out: one pce* **7/1**[3]

605 **5** *1* **Temple Road (IRE)**[24] 2611 4-8-13 **57** .... DaneO'Neill 1 57+
(Milton Bradley) *racd wd: towards rr: sme prog 2f out: styd on fnl f: nvr able to chal* **22/1**

4425 **6** *1 ½* **The Strig**[11] 2994 5-9-6 **64** .... (v) DavidProbert 7 58
(Stuart Williams) *nt gng wl in rr: drvn and struggling 1/2-way: styd on fr over 1f out* **7/1**[3]

4000 **7** *nse* **Roodee Queen**[15] 2870 4-9-12 **70** .... (p) CathyGannon 5 64
(Milton Bradley) *chsd ldrs: drvn 2f out: styd in tch tl fdd fnl f* **10/1**

3035 **8** *shd* **Pharoh Jake**[51] 1787 4-8-7 **51** oh5 .... KieranO'Neill 3 45
(John Bridger) *racd on outer: chsd ldrs: no prog over 1f out: fdd* **40/1**

3600 **9** *½* **Bobby's Doll**[9] 3085 5-9-7 **65** .... GeorgeBaker 6 57
(Terry Clement) *hld up in last: stl there over 1f out: taken to outer fnl f: running on at fin: nvr involved* **12/1**

2223 **10** *nk* **Picansort**[101] 890 5-9-2 **60** .... ShaneKelly 12 51
(Peter Crate) *trckd ldrs against rail: nt qckn 2f out: fdd fnl f* **7/2**[1]

6600 **11** *3 ½* **Itum**[17] 2815 5-8-4 **51** oh2 .... (v[1]) DominicFox(3) 13 29
(Christine Dunnett) *rousted along and early reminder: nvr gng wl and a in rr* **40/1**

57.08s (-1.12) **Going Correction** -0.325s/f (Firm) **11** Ran SP% **118.2**
Speed ratings (Par 103): **95,94,92,92,90 88,88,88,87,86 81**
toteswingers: 1&2 £14.30, 1&3 £7.20, 2&3 £7.50 CSF £54.68 CT £227.51 TOTE £9.80: £3.20, £2.30, £1.80; EX 38.60.
Owner Potters Hill Racing **Bred** Mrs B Skinner **Trained** Castle Bytham, Lincs

FOCUS
This race followed the pattern of the previous three, with a front-runner on the rail having to hold off challengers two and three horses wider, in this case unsuccessfully.
Rebecca Romero Official explanation: jockey said mare hung left

3391 PREMIER ADMINISTRATION (S) STKS 1m 4f (P)
8:35 (8:36) (Class 6) 3-Y-O **£2,181** (£644; £322) **Stalls** Low

Form RPR

036 **1** **Madame St Clair (IRE)**[9] 3083 3-8-8 59 ow1 .... ShaneKelly 1 66
(Brian Meehan) *trckd ldrs: wnt 2nd 5f out: led 2f out: drvn clr* **10/3**[2]

1000 **2** *5* **Natasha Rostova**[10] 3042 3-8-12 63 .... DavidProbert 7 62
(Andrew Balding) *in tch: pushed along 5f out: drvn and only 6th 3f out: styd on after: tk 2nd ins fnl f: no ch w wnr* **3/1**[1]

004 **3** *3 ¾* **Aiaam Al Wafa (IRE)**[10] 3048 3-8-12 63 .... (p) SilvestreDeSousa 2 56
(Phil McEntee) *hld up towards rr: prog to go 3rd over 3f out: drvn over 2f out: wnt 2nd briefly 1f out: one pce* **8/1**

-660 **4** 2 3/4 **Maccabees**[7] 3142 3-8-12 59 JamesMillman 3 52
(Rod Millman) *prog to trck ldr after 4f: led over 6f out: drvn and hdd 2f out: wknd* **10/3**[2]
0604 **5** 5 **Armiger**[16] 2845 3-8-12 46 DaneO'Neill 8 44
(William Muir) *hld up in last pair: pushed along 5f out: lost tch w ldrs over 3f out: nvr on terms* **25/1**
0-00 **6** 2 1/2 **Delishuss**[18] 2787 3-8-2 41 ow2 (p) JoshBaudains(7) 4 37
(Dominic Ffrench Davis) *led 2f: lost pl rapidly over 5f out: sn bhd* **50/1**
00 **7** nse **The Way To Be (IRE)**[15] 2895 3-8-12 0 [1] EddieAhern 9 40
(Gerard Butler) *s.i.s: detached in last and nt gng wl: nvr a factor* **16/1**
-000 **8** hd **Cato Minor**[7] 3142 3-8-12 50 (v[1]) GrahamLee 6 39
(Amanda Perrett) *prog to go prom after 3f: drvn and wknd over 3f out* **20/1**
53-4 **9** 3 3/4 **Red Hermes (IRE)**[33] 2340 3-8-7 47 LiamJones 5 28
(Mark H Tompkins) *prog to ld after 2f: hdd over 6f out: lost pl 5f out: wknd 3f out* **5/1**[3]

2m 32.86s (-0.14) **Going Correction** +0.025s/f (Slow) **9** Ran SP% **115.4**
Speed ratings (Par 97): **101,97,95,93,90 88,88,88,85**
toteswingers: 1&2 £1.40, 1&3 £4.90, 2&3 £7.90 CSF £13.45 TOTE £5.30: £2.00, £1.30, £2.00; EX 15.80.The winner was sold to Roger Curtis for 7,400gns. Maccabees was claimed by Mr Roger Curtis for £6,000.
Owner Astor Syndicate **Bred** Carlingford Breeding Syndicate **Trained** Manton, Wilts
FOCUS
The first two were dropping in grade, giving this seller a slightly above-average look. The pace was good for the first 2f, then medium.

3392 PREMIER ACTUARIAL H'CAP 1m 2f (P)
9:05 (9:06) (Class 6) (0-60,58) 4-Y-0+ **£2,181** (£644; £322) **Stalls** Low

Form RPR
1245 **1** **Lord Of The Storm**[16] 2851 4-9-1 52 KierenFox 1 65
(Bill Turner) *trckd ldrs: got through on inner to ld wl over 1f out: sn rdn clr: in n.d fnl f* **4/1**[2]
32 **2** 4 1/2 **Wind Star**[29] 2463 9-9-7 58 (p) GeorgeBaker 12 62+
(Brendan Powell) *hld up wl in rr: gng wl enough but plenty to do whn prog 2f out: r.o to take 2nd ins fnl f: no ch of catching wnr* **9/2**[3]
6-02 **3** 1/2 **Camera Shy (IRE)**[18] 2804 8-9-3 57 AshleyHamblett(3) 13 60+
(Kevin Morgan) *slowest away and pushed along to rch midfield on outer: effrt 3f out: nt qckn over 2f out: styd on fr over 1f out to take 3rd nr fin* **7/2**[1]
2006 **4** nk **Warden Bond**[7] 3153 4-9-4 55 (p) MartinLane 8 57
(William Stone) *trckd ldrs: cl up 2f out: nt qckn sn after: rdn to chse wnr jst over 1f out to ins fnl f: one pce* **22/1**
35-0 **5** 3 1/2 **Formidable Guest**[32] 2371 8-9-6 57 IanMongan 11 52
(Jamie Poulton) *dwlt: hld up in last pair: prog on wd outside 3f out: nt on terms 2f out: plugged on* **9/1**
4060 **6** 1/2 **Arctic Mirage**[7] 3153 4-9-4 55 FergusSweeney 4 49
(Michael Blanshard) *hld up in midfield: effrt but outpcd over 2f out: kpt on same pce after* **20/1**
6052 **7** shd **Diamond Twister (USA)**[50] 1831 6-8-3 45 (t) LeonnaMayor(5) 2 39
(Lisa Williamson) *dwlt: hld up in last pair: bhd 2f out: taken to outer and r.o fnl f: no ch* **16/1**
4036 **8** 1/2 **Iguacu**[31] 2391 8-9-1 52 (p) SilvestreDeSousa 9 45
(Richard Price) *pressed ldng pair on outer to jst over 2f out: sn btn* **8/1**
0-60 **9** hd **Daddyow**[54] 1722 4-8-11 55 RichardOld(7) 6 48
(Terry Clement) *pressed ldr: rdn to chal over 2f out: chsd wnr briefly over 1f out: wknd* **50/1**
5/45 **10** 1 1/4 **Mutanaker**[20] 2735 5-9-7 58 (p) LiamKeniry 3 48
(Ed de Giles) *led at stdy pce: tried to kick on over 2f out: hdd & wknd wl over 1f out* **16/1**
0-00 **11** hd **Harry Lime**[16] 2851 4-8-12 49 AndreaAtzeni 5 39
(Chris Dwyer) *towards rr: shkn up 3f out: no prog and btn over 2f out* **25/1**
2263 **12** 3 3/4 **Cahala Dancer (IRE)**[7] 3152 4-8-11 53 MarkCoumbe(5) 7 35
(Roger Teal) *wl in tch in midfield: rdn over 2f out: sn wknd* **17/2**
2/00 **13** 12 **Rosaria**[17] 2814 4-9-6 57 EddieAhern 10 15
(Harry Dunlop) *hld up towards rr: wknd over 2f out: t.o* **50/1**

2m 7.6s (1.00) **Going Correction** +0.025s/f (Slow) **13** Ran SP% **120.7**
Speed ratings (Par 101): **97,93,93,92,89 89,89,89,88,87 87,84,75**
toteswingers: 1&2 £4.80, 1&3 £4.10, 2&3 £2.30 CSF £21.17 CT £69.79 TOTE £4.90: £1.70, £1.90, £2.00; EX 16.70.
Owner Mrs M S Teversham **Bred** Mrs Monica Teversham **Trained** Sigwells, Somerset
FOCUS
This was an uncompetitive race, with few of the runners in top form, and run at a modest pace.
T/Plt: £13.80 to a £1 stake. Pool: £82,654.80. 4,341.28 winning tickets. T/Qpdt: £6.40 to a £1 stake. Pool: £4,636.13. 529.90 winning tickets. JN

3344 NEWMARKET (R-H)
Saturday, June 23

OFFICIAL GOING: Good to soft (7.4)
Home straight bend movement increased distance of 1m 5f race by about 6m.
Wind: Fresh, half-behind Weather: Cloudy with sunny spells

3393 CASINO AT BET365 H'CAP 7f
2:05 (2:05) (Class 4) (0-85,85) 3-Y-O **£6,469** (£1,925; £962; £481) **Stalls** Low

Form RPR
-660 **1** **Campanology**[14] 2930 3-9-4 85 SeanLevey(3) 16 96
(Richard Hannon) *a.p: rdn and edgd rt over 1f out: styd on to ld wl ins fnl f* **15/2**
4-44 **2** 1/2 **Amadeus Wolfe Tone (IRE)**[9] 3063 3-9-1 79 (p) JamieSpencer 7 89
(Jamie Osborne) *hld up in tch: nt clr run over 2f out: rdn over 1f out: led ins fnl f: sn hdd: styd on* **4/1**[1]
-255 **3** 3/4 **Johnno**[30] 2428 3-9-0 78 MichaelHills 1 86
(J W Hills) *sn led: rdn over 1f out: hdd ins fnl f: kpt on* **7/1**[3]
4-10 **4** 1/2 **Obliterеight (IRE)**[17] 2813 3-9-2 80 AdamKirby 6 86
(William Knight) *hld up: rdn over 2f out: hdwy over 1f out: styd on* **14/1**
10 **5** 3/4 **Dutch Old Master**[22] 2660 3-9-2 80 RichardMullen 10 84+
(Gary Moore) *hld up: hdwy over 1f out: sn rdn: r.o: nt rch ldrs* **8/1**
0-00 **6** 1/2 **Elusive Flame**[28] 2490 3-9-4 82 LiamKeniry 4 85
(David Elsworth) *chsd ldr: rdn over 1f out: no ex ins fnl f* **33/1**
-403 **7** 1 **Responsive**[16] 2854 3-9-6 84 RobertHavlin 9 84
(Hughie Morrison) *s.i.s: hld up: rdn over 1f out: r.o towards fin: nvr nrr* **25/1**
015 **8** 2 1/4 **Hometown Glory**[28] 2490 3-9-2 80 MartinDwyer 3 74
(Brian Meehan) *hld up in tch: rdn over 1f out: wknd ins fnl f* **16/1**

-532 **9** 3 **Periphery (USA)**[43] 2042 3-9-2 80 (t) MickaelBarzalona 5 66
(Mahmood Al Zarooni) *sn pushed along in rr: nvr on terms* **12/1**
0-10 **10** nse **Equation Of Time**[91] 1032 3-9-4 82 TonyCulhane 8 68
(Willie Musson) *hld up: bhd 1/2-way: nvr nrr* **28/1**
31 **11** hd **Unex Annigoni (IRE)**[15] 2881 3-9-2 80 (t) NickyMackay 15 65
(John Gosden) *chsd ldrs: rdn and ev ch over 1f out: wknd fnl f* **11/2**[2]
01-0 **12** nk **Afaal (USA)**[28] 2490 3-9-3 81 TadhgO'Shea 12 65
(William Haggas) *chsd ldrs: rdn over 2f out: wknd over 1f out* **14/1**
4-04 **13** shd **Sir Glanton (IRE)**[12] 2975 3-9-4 82 IanMongan 14 66
(Amanda Perrett) *chsd ldrs tl rdn and wknd over 1f out* **25/1**
0604 **14** 1 **Cravat**[7] 3160 3-9-0 78 J-PGuillambert 13 59
(Mark Johnston) *sn pushed along and prom: rdn over 2f out: sn wknd* **16/1**

1m 26.19s (0.49) **Going Correction** +0.10s/f (Good) **14** Ran SP% **117.6**
Speed ratings (Par 101): **101,100,99,99,98 97,96,93,90,90 90,89,89,88**
toteswingers:1&2:£6.80, 1&3:£11.30, 2&3:£8.20 CSF £34.94 CT £229.19 TOTE £10.70: £3.50, £1.10, £3.00; EX 50.80 Trifecta £472.80 Part won. Pool: £639.02 - 0.82 winning units..
Owner Andrew Tinkler **Bred** A H Bennett **Trained** East Everleigh, Wilts
■ Stewards' Enquiry : Sean Levey two-day ban: used whip above permitted level (Jul 8-9)
Jamie Spencer two-day ban: used whip above permitted level (Jul 8-9)
FOCUS
The going was changed to Good to soft following 5mm of rain during the meeting the previous evening. The jockeys reported it was riding 'dead'. A decent 3yo handicap in which recent winners have been near the top of the weights. Richard Hannon had trained two of the previous three winners and improved his record. The form looks solid, with the winner back to his 2yo form.

3394 BET365.COM H'CAP 6f
2:40 (2:40) (Class 4) (0-85,85) 3-Y-0+ **£6,469** (£1,925; £962; £481) **Stalls** Low

Form RPR
3112 **1** **Trojan Rocket (IRE)**[29] 2466 4-9-2 75 MickaelBarzalona 10 84+
(Michael Wigham) *hld up: rdn over 1f out: str run to ld post* **3/1**[1]
0000 **2** hd **Button Moon (IRE)**[10] 3049 4-9-4 77 (p) CathyGannon 1 84
(Ian Wood) *led: rdn over 1f out: hdd post* **20/1**
2-41 **3** shd **Crew Cut (IRE)**[15] 2870 4-9-4 77 IanMongan 14 83+
(Jeremy Gask) *a.p: rdn and swtchd lft over 1f out: r.o wl* **9/2**[2]
-100 **4** shd **Rafaaf (IRE)**[29] 2444 4-9-4 77 AndreaAtzeni 3 83
(Robert Eddery) *chsd ldr to 1/2-way: remained handy: rdn and ev ch fr over 1f out: r.o* **11/1**
-004 **5** 3/4 **Quasi Congaree (GER)**[15] 2870 6-9-9 82 (t) NeilCallan 6 86
(Ian Wood) *chsd ldrs: rdn over 1f out: r.o* **11/2**
3165 **6** nse **Caldercruix (USA)**[11] 3004 5-9-4 82 (v) DavidKenny(5) 8 85
(James Evans) *chsd ldrs: rdn and ev ch over 1f out: edgd rt ins fnl f: r.o* **10/1**
21-0 **7** 3/4 **Expose**[16] 2853 4-9-9 82 JamieSpencer 4 83
(William Haggas) *trckd ldrs: plld hrd: rdn and ev ch over 1f out: styd on same pce ins fnl f* **5/1**[3]
4-04 **8** 1 **Lujeanie**[149] 311 6-9-8 81 MartinLane 9 79
(Dean Ivory) *s.i.s: hld up: rdn over 2f out: nvr trbld ldrs* **16/1**
0-00 **9** 1/2 **Mr David (USA)**[21] 2697 5-9-12 85 (p) MartinDwyer 12 81
(Jamie Osborne) *hld up: rdn over 2f out: nt trble ldrs* **13/2**

1m 14.42s (1.92) **Going Correction** +0.10s/f (Good) **9** Ran SP% **116.6**
Speed ratings (Par 105): **91,90,90,90,89 89,88,87,86**
toteswingers:1&2:£6.80, 1&3:£11.30, 2&3:£8.20 CSF £67.09 CT £271.34 TOTE £5.10: £1.70, £4.80, £1.50; EX 81.30 Trifecta £524.80 Pool: £744.69 - 1.05 winning units..
Owner G D J Linder **Bred** J G F Fox **Trained** Newmarket, Suffolk
FOCUS
Another good sprint handicap whose best recent winner was Zidane. However, the field was reduced by nearly a half by withdrawals and the early pace was modest for a sprint, resulting in a blanket finish. The winner possibly has a bit more to offer.

3395 MOBILE AT BET365 E B F FILLIES' H'CAP 1m
3:10 (3:10) (Class 4) (0-85,82) 3-Y-0+ **£6,469** (£1,925; £962; £481) **Stalls** Low

Form RPR
1- **1** **Punita (USA)**[291] 5814 3-9-0 78 MickaelBarzalona 10 91+
(Mahmood Al Zarooni) *trckd ldrs: plld hrd: rdn over 1f out: led ins fnl f: r.o* **5/2**[1]
1-2 **2** 1 1/2 **Ariyfa (IRE)**[171] 36 4-9-11 79 AdamKirby 6 87
(Noel Quinlan) *sn led: rdn over 1f out: hdd and unable qck ins fnl f* **11/2**[2]
3-13 **3** 1 3/4 **Parley (USA)**[19] 2752 3-9-2 80 J-PGuillambert 1 82
(Mark Johnston) *chsd ldr: rdn over 2f out: edgd lft over 1f out: styd on same pce ins fnl f* **9/1**
-031 **4** 1/2 **Fenella Fudge**[10] 3021 4-8-13 67 MartinDwyer 11 70+
(Derek Shaw) *hld up: hdwy over 1f out: nt rch ldrs* **6/1**[3]
2611 **5** 2 1/2 **Methayel (IRE)**[16] 2859 4-9-9 77 NeilCallan 2 74
(Clive Brittain) *chsd ldrs: rdn over 2f out: no ex fnl f* **13/2**
0-41 **6** 2 **Tea Cup**[19] 2757 3-8-13 80 SeanLevey(3) 8 70
(Richard Hannon) *hld up: rdn over 2f out: nvr trbld ldrs* **6/1**[3]
50-5 **7** nk **Saskia's Dream**[9] 3085 4-9-7 75 (p) JimmyQuinn 9 67
(Jane Chapple-Hyam) *prom: racd keenly: rdn and wknd over 1f out* **15/2**
-223 **8** 22 **Princess Lexi (IRE)**[113] 761 5-8-9 68 DavidKenny(5) 4
(William Knight) *hld up: rdn over 2f out: sn wknd* **16/1**

1m 40.35s (0.35) **Going Correction** +0.10s/f (Good)
WFA 3 from 4yo+ 10lb **8** Ran SP% **113.5**
Speed ratings (Par 102): **102,100,98,98,95 93,93,71**
toteswingers:1&2:£2.10, 1&3:£9.80, 2&3:£16.10 CSF £15.99 CT £105.09 TOTE £3.40: £1.70, £1.60, £2.80; EX 17.50 Trifecta £153.90 Pool: £705.23 - 3.39 winning units..
Owner Godolphin **Bred** Darley **Trained** Newmarket, Suffolk
FOCUS
This fair fillies' handicap was won by the subsequent Group 3 winner I'm a Dreamer in 2010, but was weakened by four defectors, a couple of which would have been near the head of the market. This time they raced close to the stands' rail and the time was comparatively the best of the day. A nice step up from the winner with the second up a length on her winter AW form.

3396 BET365 H'CAP 5f
3:40 (3:40) (Class 2) (0-105,92) 3-Y-O
£12,450 (£3,728; £1,864; £932; £466; £234) **Stalls** Low

Form RPR
31-2 **1** **Annie Beach (IRE)**[36] 2256 3-9-0 85 JamieSpencer 1 92+
(David Barron) *mde all: qcknd and hung lft fr over 1f out: r.o* **3/1**[1]
6230 **2** 3/4 **Lupo D'Oro (IRE)**[33] 2347 3-8-3 74 KieranO'Neill 8 78
(John Best) *hld up: hdwy over 1f out: r.o: nt rch wnr* **16/1**
6-36 **3** nk **Heeraat (IRE)**[21] 2714 3-9-2 87 TadhgO'Shea 9 90
(William Haggas) *chsd ldrs: rdn to go 2nd and edgd rt over 1f out: hung lft ins fnl f: r.o* **13/2**
212 **4** 1/2 **Miliika**[12] 2986 3-8-12 83 ChrisCatlin 2 84
(Rae Guest) *prom: rdn over 1f out: styd on* **7/2**[2]

2112 **5** *2* **Bartolomeu**[35] [2276] 3-9-7 **92** AdamKirby 6 86
(Marco Botti) *hld up in tch: rdn over 1f out: styd on same pce ins fnl f* **7/2**[2]

0001 **6** *2 1/4* **Muaamara**[8] [3108] 3-9-6 **91** SamHitchcott 3 77
(Mick Channon) *hmpd s: hld up: rdn over 1f out: n.d* **10/1**

60-1 **7** *8* **Tioman Pearl**[47] [1941] 3-9-2 **87** NeilCallan 5 44
(Roger Varian) *chsd wnr: pushed along 1/2-way: rdn whn hmpd and wknd over 1f out* **11/2**[3]

59.82s (0.72) **Going Correction** +0.10s/f (Good) **7** Ran SP% **113.1**
Speed ratings (Par 105): **98,96,96,95,92 88,75**
toteswingers:1&2:£2.10, 1&3:£9.80, 2&3:£16.10 CSF £47.91 CT £288.57 TOTE £4.50: £2.40, £7.20; EX 55.70 Trifecta £444.50 Pool: £871.03 - 1.45 winning units..
Owner Mrs Christine Barron **Bred** D And Mrs D Veitch **Trained** Maunby, N Yorks

FOCUS
This good sprint for 3-y-os has been won by the likes of Moorhouse Lad and Green Manalishi in recent years, but this did not look the strongest renewal with the top weight 13lb below the race ceiling. The runner-up limits the form to an extent.

NOTEBOOK
Annie Beach(IRE), 10lb higher than when touched off at York, showed good pace in front and Jamie Spencer won the race when kicking clear running down the hill. She drifted left when meeting the rising ground but did enough to hold on. A similarly positive ride next time may prove the best way to ride her. (op 4-1)
Lupo D'Oro(IRE) was held up at the back and ran another good race on ground he handles, staying on to close down the winner all the way to the line. He has now been placed ten times but has still yet to win, although he clearly has his share of ability. (op 14-1)
Heeraat(IRE) showed up throughout and kept plugging away, despite having raced quite keenly early on. (op 8-1)
Miliika tracked the winner throughout but could not go with her down the hill before staying on late. She handles this ground but her win was gained on her sole start on fast going. (tchd 3-1)
Bartolomeu, whose form has been on Polytrack and fast turf, was held up and never landed a blow on this soft surface, even though his pedigree suggested he would handle the ground. (op 9-2)
Muaamara was hampered by Tioman Pearl leaving the stalls, effectively ending her chance. (op 8-1)
Tioman Pearl raised 18lb for his runaway success on soft ground on his handicap debut, rather pitched as the stalls opened and bumped into Muaamara. He then raced too freely and dropped away when the winner kicked. (op 4-1 tchd 6-1)

3397 BET365 MAIDEN STKS 7f
4:15 (4:21) (Class 5) 2-Y-O **£3,234** (£962; £481; £240) **Stalls** Low

Form RPR

1 **Chesterfield (IRE)** 2-9-3 0 MickaelBarzalona 2 83+
(Mahmood Al Zarooni) *sn pushed along and prom: rdn over 1f out: r.o to ld wl ins fnl f: sn clr* **2/1**[1]

2 *1 3/4* **Top Joker** 2-8-12 0 AntiocoMurgia(5) 3 78
(Mahmood Al Zarooni) *dwlt: hld up: hdwy over 2f out: rdn to ld over 1f out: hdd and unable qck wl ins fnl f* **15/2**

3 *1* **Yellow Mountain (IRE)** 2-9-3 0 AdamKirby 4 75
(Marco Botti) *chsd ldrs: led 2f out: rdn and hdd over 1f out: styd on same pce ins fnl f* **6/1**[2]

4 *3/4* **Harry Bosch** 2-9-3 0 MartinDwyer 6 73
(Brian Meehan) *disp ld over 4f: sn rdn: styd on same pce ins fnl f* **20/1**

5 *2 1/4* **Makafeh** 2-9-3 0 J-PGuillambert 7 68
(Luca Cumani) *s.i.s: sn w ldrs: rdn over 2f out: wknd ins fnl f* **14/1**

6 *5* **Tropical Song** 2-9-3 0 RobertHavlin 5 55
(John Gosden) *disp ld over 4f: rdn: hung lft and wknd over 1f out* **13/2**[3]

7 *8* **Royal Challis** 2-9-3 0 KieranO'Neill 9 35
(Richard Hannon) *disp ld tl rdn over 2f out: wknd over 1f out* **8/1**

8 *2 1/4* **High Force (IRE)** 2-9-3 0 JamieSpencer 10 30
(Mahmood Al Zarooni) *disp ld over 4f: sn wknd* **11/1**

1m 28.82s (3.12) **Going Correction** +0.10s/f (Good) **8** Ran SP% **103.6**
Speed ratings (Par 93): **86,84,82,82,79 73,64,62**
toteswingers:1&2:£4.10, 1&3:£3.50, 2&3:£5.80 CSF £13.92 TOTE £2.50: £1.10, £2.40, £1.70; EX 16.70.
Owner Godolphin **Bred** Darley **Trained** Newmarket, Suffolk

FOCUS
A juvenile maiden that has produced subsequent Group 2 winner Silver Grecian and Listed performers Unnefer and Coup De Ville in recent seasons. Only one of the runners (Shebebi) had previous experience but he reared up and broke out of the stalls and was withdrawn. The pace looked fairly steady early, with six of them racing abreast until past halfway. The form is rated to the mid-point of the race averages.

NOTEBOOK
Chesterfield(IRE), out of a Listed winner and tracing to an Irish 1000 Guineas heroine, was held up at the back and looked in trouble going into the Dip when also short of room. However, on meeting the rising ground he really responded to his rider's urgings and powered home to score ultimately in comfortable fashion. He looks sure to have learnt plenty from this. (op 3-1)
Top Joker ◆Out of an Australian mare, made a fine debut considering he was least fancied of the three Godolphin runners. He looked as if he might prevail entering the last furlong, only to be run down by his stable companion. He moved well to post and should be winning before too long. (op 9-1 tchd 7-1)
Yellow Mountain(IRE), whose pedigree suggests middle-distances will suit in due course, came through from off the pace and looked the most likely winner 2f out, but tired up the hill. He looks to need a little more time but better can be expected in due course. (op 5-1)
Harry Bosch ◆ cost 78,000GBP and is related to winners at various trips. He was never far away and stuck to his guns up the hill. The yard's juveniles often benefit considerably from a run, so this was encouraging. (op 16-1 tchd 14-1)
Makafeh, a 190,000gns first foal who is related to several high-class performers, was keen early racing up with the pace and did well to finish as close as he did. Better can be expected with this under his belt. (op 10-1 tchd 16-1)
Tropical Song, a brother to the useful Tropical Beat, was close up early but was soon on the retreat when the pace quickened. (op 5-1)
Royal Challis showed up with the leaders early but probably did too much and finished up well behind. (tchd 7-1)
High Force(IRE), like the seventh, showed up with the leaders early but both probably did too much. (tchd 10-1)

3398 BET365.COM MAIDEN STKS (DIV I) 1m
4:50 (4:51) (Class 5) 3-Y-O **£3,234** (£962; £481; £240) **Stalls** Low

Form RPR

0-0 **1** **Bassara (IRE)**[65] [1472] 3-8-12 0 ChrisCatlin 5 79+
(Chris Wall) *chsd ldrs: shkn up to ld 1f out: styd on wl* **8/1**

2 *1 3/4* **Estebsaal (IRE)** 3-9-3 0 AdamKirby 8 80+
(John Dunlop) *hld up: hdwy over 2f out: rdn over 1f out: r.o to 2nd towards fin: nt rch wnr* **16/1**

2- **3** *3/4* **Moodhill**[239] [7134] 3-9-3 0 TadhgO'Shea 3 78
(Charles Hills) *led: rdn and hung lft over 1f out: sn hdd: styd on same pce: lost 2nd towards fin* **7/2**[3]

62-2 **4** *3 1/2* **Jack Of Diamonds (IRE)**[70] [1377] 3-9-3 76 JackMitchell 4 70
(Roger Teal) *chsd ldrs: rdn and edgd lft over 1f out: no ex fnl f* **10/3**[2]

0 **5** *nse* **Zain Glory**[37] [2197] 3-9-3 0 [1] MartinDwyer 9 70
(Gerard Butler) *hld up: plld hrd: hdwy and hung lft to r alone 1/2-way: outpcd over 2f out: styd on ins fnl f* **33/1**

50- **6** *hd* **Twin Shadow (IRE)**[249] [6935] 3-8-12 0 NeilCallan 11 64+
(James Fanshawe) *mid-div: hdwy over 2f out: sn rdn: styd on* **14/1**

7 *4 1/2* **Asia Minor (IRE)** 3-8-12 0 KirstyMilczarek 12 54
(Terry Clement) *chsd ldrs tl wknd over 1f out* **66/1**

0 **8** *2* **Regalo Rosado**[26] [2542] 3-8-12 0 KieranO'Neill 1 49
(Mike Murphy) *s.i.s: hld up: racd keenly: bhd 3f out: nvr nrr* **22/1**

9 *hd* **Keeping Time** 3-9-3 0 IanMongan 6 54
(Sir Henry Cecil) *dwlt: hdwy over 3f out: rdn over 2f out: sn edgd lft: wknd wl over 1f out* **3/1**[1]

0- **10** *nk* **Princess Of Rock**[315] [5048] 3-8-12 0 SamHitchcott 13 48
(Mick Channon) *chsd ldr tl rdn and wknd over 1f out* **33/1**

3- **11** *4 1/2* **Champagne Reefing (USA)**[246] [7000] 3-9-3 0 JimmyQuinn 2 43
(Jane Chapple-Hyam) *mid-div: hdwy over 2f out: rdn: hung lft and wknd over 1f out* **11/1**

1m 42.65s (2.65) **Going Correction** +0.10s/f (Good) **11** Ran SP% **114.0**
Speed ratings (Par 99): **90,88,87,84,83 83,79,77,77,76 72**
CSF £117.79 TOTE £9.00: £3.00, £5.40, £1.90; EX 167.60.
Owner Ms Aida Fustoq **Bred** Deerfield Farm **Trained** Newmarket, Suffolk

FOCUS
The first division of a maiden whose best recent winner was Multidimensional, and the majority of these had limited experience. They raced up the centre until drifting to the far rail in the closing stages and the time was 2.3secs slower than the earlier fillies' handicap. The form is rated around the third.
Zain Glory Official explanation: jockey said colt hung left

3399 BET365.COM MAIDEN STKS (DIV II) 1m
5:25 (5:27) (Class 5) 3-Y-O **£3,234** (£962; £481; £240) **Stalls** Low

Form RPR

3-43 **1** **Touch Gold (IRE)**[26] [2552] 3-9-3 75 IanMongan 5 88
(Sir Henry Cecil) *mde all: rdn over 1f out: jst hld on* **11/4**[1]

2 *nk* **Marshgate Lane (USA)** 3-9-3 0 MickaelBarzalona 1 87
(Mahmood Al Zarooni) *mid-div: hdwy over 2f out: rdn to chse wnr over 1f out: r.o* **4/1**[3]

6- **3** *5* **Alraased (USA)**[239] [7133] 3-9-3 0 AdamKirby 3 76
(John Dunlop) *a.p: rdn over 2f out: no ex ins fnl f* **4/1**[3]

4 *5* **Afraah (USA)** 3-8-12 0 TadhgO'Shea 2 59+
(Roger Varian) *chsd ldr tl rdn over 1f out: wknd ins fnl f* **7/2**[2]

05 **5** *2 3/4* **Mankini (IRE)**[18] [2799] 3-9-3 0 J-PGuillambert 11 58+
(Luca Cumani) *hld up: shkn up over 2f out: nvr nr to chal* **16/1**

6 *1* **Caption** 3-8-12 0 RichardMullen 7 50+
(Sir Michael Stoute) *stmbld s: sn prom: rdn over 2f out: wknd over 1f out* **7/1**

0 **7** *6* **Virginia Galilei (IRE)**[25] [2584] 3-8-12 0 ChrisCatlin 4 37
(David Lanigan) *s.i.s: hld up: nvr on terms* **50/1**

8 *2 1/4* **Sandy Lane (IRE)** 3-9-3 0 DaraghO'Donohoe 9 36
(Amy Weaver) *s.s: hld up: a in rr* **50/1**

9 *2 1/4* **Shahrazad (IRE)** 3-8-12 0 JamieMackay 8 26
(Patrick Gilligan) *s.s: rn green and a in rr* **66/1**

0-0 **10** *5* **Karistar (IRE)**[30] [2430] 3-8-12 0 JimmyQuinn 13 15
(Tom Keddy) *hld up: drvn along over 3f out: sn wknd* **66/1**

006- **11** *1/2* **Hawkino (IRE)**[240] [7117] 3-9-3 47 MartinLane 6 19
(Derek Shaw) *prom over 4f* **150/1**

1m 41.21s (1.21) **Going Correction** +0.10s/f (Good) **11** Ran SP% **114.8**
Speed ratings (Par 99): **97,96,91,86,83 82,76,74,72,67 66**
CSF £13.44 TOTE £3.90: £1.60, £2.10, £1.30; EX 11.40.
Owner H E Sheikh Sultan Bin Khalifa Al Nahyan **Bred** Runnymede Farm Inc **Trained** Newmarket, Suffolk

FOCUS
The second division of this maiden was run 1.44secs faster than the first leg and they came straight up the centre of the track. There were several with good pedigrees and this looked the stronger of the two divisions. The form is rated around the third, with an 8lb personal best from the winner.

3400 POKER AT BET365 H'CAP 1m 5f
5:55 (6:00) (Class 5) (0-75,75) 4-Y-O+ **£3,234** (£962; £481; £240) **Stalls** Centre

Form RPR

510- **1** **Kian's Delight**[18] [6279] 4-8-7 **61** MickaelBarzalona 6 77+
(Peter Bowen) *prom: lost pl over 7f out: hdwy over 3f out: led over 1f out: rdn out* **9/2**[1]

30-4 **2** *3 3/4* **Dawn Gale (IRE)**[21] [2708] 4-9-7 **75** RobertHavlin 5 86
(Hughie Morrison) *hld up in tch: led over 2f out: rdn and hdd over 1f out: styd on same pce ins fnl f* **12/1**

64-0 **3** *3 3/4* **Sohar**[26] [2561] 4-9-7 **75** KirstyMilczarek 11 80
(James Toller) *chsd ldrs: rdn over 3f out: no ex fnl f* **33/1**

-004 **4** *nk* **Odin (IRE)**[15] [2899] 4-9-2 **70** MarcHalford 13 75
(David Elsworth) *hld up: hdwy over 3f out: rdn over 1f out: styd on: nt trble ldrs* **14/1**

24-0 **5** *3/4* **Castlemorris King**[28] [2502] 4-8-6 **65** MarkCoumbe(5) 12 68
(Michael Attwater) *prom: rdn over 3f out: no ex fnl f* **20/1**

10-2 **6** *1/2* **Kayaan**[15] [2260] 5-8-13 **67** JimmyQuinn 7 70
(Pam Sly) *s.i.s: hld up: plld hrd: rdn over 2f out: styd on u.p: nt trble ldrs* **8/1**[3]

-022 **7** *3 3/4* **Dubai Glory**[6] [3187] 4-9-7 **75** ChrisCatlin 15 72
(Sheena West) *chsd ldr after 2f tl over 4f out: sn rdn: wknd fnl f* **9/2**[1]

2-23 **8** *1* **Sugar Hiccup (IRE)**[14] [2909] 4-9-5 **73** JamieSpencer 4 70
(David Simcock) *chsd ldr 2f: remained handy: wnt 2nd again over 4f out: led over 3f out: rdn and hdd over 2f out: wknd and eased fnl f* **5/1**[2]

-005 **9** *1 1/2* **Mollyow (IRE)**[9] [3086] 4-7-13 **56** oh11 DominicFox(3) 9 49
(Terry Clement) *led: rdn and hdd over 3f out: wknd over 1f out* **50/1**

40-1 **10** *1 3/4* **Maoi Chinn Tire (IRE)**[21] [2378] 5-9-0 **68** SeanQuinlan 2 59
(Jennie Candlish) *hld up: hdwy over 3f out: rdn and wknd over 1f out* **14/1**

1100 **11** *3 1/4* **Admirable Duque (IRE)**[26] [2561] 6-8-12 **73** (b) JoshBaudains(7) 14 59
(Dominic Ffrench Davis) *s.i.s: hld up: hdwy over 5f out: rdn and wknd over 1f out* **16/1**

-U05 **12** *15* **Who Loves Ya Baby**[10] [3043] 4-7-11 **56** oh8 RosieJessop(5) 1 19
(Peter Charalambous) *hld up: a in rr: rdn over 3f out: sn wknd: t.o* **33/1**

301/ **13** *24* **Giant Sequoia (USA)**[263] [4769] 8-8-13 **67** DaraghO'Donohoe 3
(Barney Curley) *hld up: a in rr: wknd over 3f out: t.o* **33/1**

14-4 **14** *47* **Armoise**[23] 2637 4-9-7 **75**....................(t) AdamKirby 8
(Marco Botti) *prom: lost pl over 8f out: rdn and wknd over 3f out: t.o* **5/1**[2]

2m 47.03s (3.03) **Going Correction** +0.10s/f (Good) **14** Ran SP% **123.3**
Speed ratings (Par 103): **94,91,89,89,88 88,86,85,84,83 81,72,57,28**
toteswingers:1&2:£11.80, 1&3:£24.90, 2&3:£82.90 CSF £57.54 TOTE £4.70: £2.10, £3.40, £9.60; EX 72.40.
Owner Yeh Man Partnership **Bred** Mrs J M Quy **Trained** Little Newcastle, Pembrokes

FOCUS
A fair but competitive staying handicap with five fillies at the head of the weights. It was sound run and they went right over to the far side in the straight. The winner has more to offer and the winner produced a personal best.
Armoise Official explanation: trainer's rep said filly had a breathing problem
T/Plt: £146.60 to a £1 stake. Pool:£89,954.92 - 447.82 winning tickets T/Qpdt: £26.20 to a £1 stake. Pool:£4,700.60 - 132.60 winning tickets CR

3351 REDCAR (L-H)
Saturday, June 23

OFFICIAL GOING: Soft (7.2)
Wind: Fresh, across Weather: Cloudy

3401 BRITISH STALLION STUDS E B F MARKET CROSS JEWELLERS MAIDEN STKS 7f
2:15 (2:15) (Class 5) 2-Y-0 **£2,975** (£885; £442; £221) **Stalls** Centre

Form RPR

3 **1** **Shrewd**[15] 2888 2-8-10 0....................IanBurns(7) 7 80+
(Michael Bell) *trckd ldrs: effrt and n.m.r wl over 1f out: sn swtchd lft and hdwy to join ldr 1f out: rdn to ld ins fnl f: styd on wl* **15/8**[1]

2 *1 ¼* **Royal Skies (IRE)** 2-9-3 0....................MichaelStainton 2 77+
(Mark Johnston) *cl up: led wl over 2f out: rdn over 1f out: edgd lft and jnd 1f out: hdd and one pce ins fnl f* **9/2**[3]

3 *4 ½* **Beat The Tide** 2-9-0 0....................LeeTopliss(3) 6 66+
(Michael Dods) *trckd ldrs: hdwy over 2f out: sn rdn and styd on same pce fnl f* **16/1**

4 *½* **Miss Perfect** 2-8-12 0....................DavidNolan 4 59+
(John Quinn) *in tch: hdwy 1/2-way: rdn over 2f out: styd on to chse ldng pair over 1f out: one pce fnl f* **16/1**

5 *1 ¾* **Dark Ocean (IRE)** 2-9-3 0....................AndrewElliott 1 60
(Jedd O'Keeffe) *towards rr: hdwy over 2f out: rdn: rn green and swvd bdly lft wl over 1f out: kpt on fnl f: nrst fin* **50/1**

632 **6** *3 ½* **Finaz**[7] 3168 2-9-3 0....................MickyFenton 9 51
(Paul Midgley) *led: pushed along over 3f out: hdd wl over 2f out: sn rdn and grad wknd* **3/1**[2]

7 *2 ½* **Shillito** 2-9-3 0....................BarryMcHugh 11 45
(Tony Coyle) *chsd ldrs: rdn along wl over 2f out: grad wknd* **16/1**

8 *2 ¼* **Surround Sound** 2-8-12 0....................AdamCarter(5) 8 39
(Tim Easterby) *dwlt: hdwy and in tch 1/2-way: sn rdn along and wknd over 2f out* **40/1**

9 *10* **Navajo Nights** 2-9-3 0....................TomEaves 10 14
(Bryan Smart) *t.k.h: chsd ldrs on outer: pushed along 3f out: sn rdn and wknd over 2f out* **10/1**

10 *1 ¾* **Lady Niramax** 2-8-12 0....................PaulQuinn 12
(David Nicholls) *wnt rt s and s.i.s: a in rr* **40/1**

11 *2* **Heliconia** 2-8-12 0....................PatCosgrave 3
(Sir Mark Prescott Bt) *dwlt: a in rr* **14/1**

00 **12** *5* **Bollin Billy**[17] 2822 2-9-3 0....................DuranFentiman 5
(Tim Easterby) *chsd ldrs: rdn along after 2f: sn lost pl and bhd* **50/1**

1m 29.09s (4.59) **Going Correction** +0.325s/f (Good) **12** Ran SP% **120.2**
Speed ratings (Par 93): **86,84,79,78,76 72,70,67,56,54 51,46**
toteswingers: 1&2 £3.00, 1&3 £15.50, 2&3 £11.50 CSF £10.30 TOTE £3.10: £1.10, £1.50, £6.40; EX 13.90.
Owner Sheikh Marwan Al Maktoum **Bred** Darley **Trained** Newmarket, Suffolk

FOCUS
Little form to go on, but this looked a decent enough maiden that was run at a solid pace in the testing conditions, with the front two coming a long way clear. The form looks up to the recent solid average.

NOTEBOOK
Shrewd, who finished third at Goodwood over 6f (good to soft) on his debut showed the benefit of that experience and he responded willingly to his riders urgings to win going away. He was driven before the 3f pole but, showed a decent attitude and looks as though he will improve over further in time. (op 2-1)
Royal Skies(IRE), an 80,000 euros yearling and half-brother to four French winners over 1m4f plus, ran a race full of promise on his debut. His breeding suggests he will be better over further, but he was travelling best 2f from home and should be more than capable of landing a similar contest, having finished some way clear of the third. (op 4-1)
Beat The Tide, a half-brother to a 1m winner and a 2m2f hurdle scorer, stayed on well for pressure and looks to want further. His yard is adept is improving its juveniles. (tchd 18-1)
Miss Perfect, whose trainer won this last year with subsequent Group 2 winner Red Duke, was held up early and stayed on well enough for pressure and can be expected to come on a good deal for this. (op 12-1)
Dark Ocean(IRE) pulled hard early and was noticed making good progress late on, this was an encouraging debut.
Finaz, who was running further than 6f for the first time, was up with the pace early before folding tamely, and this was a disappointing effort. (op 5-1)

3402 KATE FEARNLEY & CHIC HATS FASHION SHOW H'CAP 1m 6f 19y
2:45 (2:45) (Class 6) (0-60,60) 4-Y-0+ **£1,617** (£481; £240; £120) **Stalls** Low

Form RPR

-002 **1** **Tarantella Lady**[19] 2775 4-9-7 **60**....................(v) AndrewElliott 4 70
(George Moore) *trckd ldrs on inner: pushed along and lost pl 1/2-way: in rr and rdn along over 4f out: hdwy on wd outside 3f out: rdn to chse ldrs 2f out: styd on u.p to ld last 100yds* **13/2**[3]

32-2 **2** *2* **Falcun**[23] 2635 5-9-5 **58**....................(v) TomEaves 2 65
(Micky Hammond) *s.i.s and sn rdn along in rr: hdwy 1/2-way: trckd ldrs over 5f out: effrt 3f out and sn rdn: led wl over 1f out: drvn ent fnl f: hdd and no ex last 100yds* **7/2**[1]

5-63 **3** *3* **Shirls Son Sam**[23] 2635 4-8-11 **50**....................KellyHarrison 1 53
(Chris Fairhurst) *hld up in rr: smooth hdwy on outer to trck ldrs over 6f out: led 4f out: rdn along over 2f out: hdd wl over 1f out: sn drvn and kpt on same pce* **5/1**[2]

0/0- **4** *1* **French Seventyfive**[31] 3450 5-8-0 **46** oh1....................(p) GemmaTutty(7) 6 47
(Tim Walford) *hld up in rr: hdwy 4f out: pushed along 3f out: rdn and styd on fnl 2f: nrst fin* **14/1**

200- **5** *6* **Word Of Warning**[233] 4856 8-9-1 **54**....................DavidNolan 8 47
(Martin Todhunter) *hld up towards rr: smooth hdwy over 4f out: trckd ldng trio 3f out gng wl: effrt 2f out: sn rdn and btn* **14/1**

0-05 **6** *13* **Brook Star (IRE)**[9] 3081 4-8-10 **52**....................LeeTopliss(3) 15 27
(Michael Dods) *hld up in tch: hdwy to chse ldrs over 3f out: sn rdn and wknd 2f out* **15/2**

0-65 **7** *4 ½* **Operateur (IRE)**[25] 2593 4-9-2 **55**....................PatrickMathers 14 24
(Ben Haslam) *prom: chsd ldng pair 1/2-way: rdn along over 4f out: drvn 3f out and sn wknd* **8/1**

3-25 **8** *30* **Commander Veejay**[10] 3029 4-8-13 **52**....................(b) BarryMcHugh 12
(Brian Rothwell) *led: rdn along over 4f out: sn hdd & wknd* **14/1**

23-0 **9** *11* **Stormy Morning**[17] 2827 6-9-1 **59**....................(p) ShaneBKelly(5) 9
(Philip Kirby) *in tch: rdn along over 5f out: sn wknd and bhd* **9/1**

5324 **10** *12* **Needwood Park**[22] 2670 4-9-1 **54**....................PaddyAspell 13
(Ray Craggs) *prom: rdn along over 6f out: sn wknd* **7/1**

3m 16.26s (11.56) **Going Correction** +0.875s/f (Soft) **10** Ran SP% **117.6**
Speed ratings (Par 101): **101,99,98,97,94 86,84,67,60,53**
toteswingers: 1&2 £3.10, 1&3 £2.40, 2&3 £1.90 CSF £29.78 CT £125.21 TOTE £5.00: £2.80, £1.10, £2.60; EX 15.70.
Owner David Parker **Bred** Whatton Manor Stud **Trained** Middleham Moor, N Yorks

FOCUS
A moderate staying handicap with few of the runners coming here in form. It was run at a muddling pace and the field were well strung out at the finish. The form is rated through the runner-up.
Needwood Park Official explanation: trainer said gelding was unsuited by the soft ground

3403 H JARVIS 134TH ANNIVERSARY H'CAP 7f
3:20 (3:22) (Class 3) (0-90,87) 4-Y-0+ **£3,881** (£1,155; £577; £288) **Stalls** Centre

Form RPR

0-34 **1** **Dubai Hills**[8] 3128 6-9-7 **87**....................TomEaves 4 95
(Bryan Smart) *chsd clr ldr: tk clsr order over 2f out: led wl over 1f out and sn rdn: drvn ins fnl f and kpt on wl* **9/4**[1]

6610 **2** *1 ¾* **Polish World (USA)**[8] 3128 8-9-6 **86**....................MickyFenton 2 89
(Paul Midgley) *led and sn clr: rdn along over 2f out: hdd wl over 1f out: rallied and n.m.r ins fnl f: sn swtchd lft and kpt on wl towards fin* **8/1**

3600 **3** *nse* **Aerodynamic (IRE)**[7] 3167 5-8-8 **74**....................PaddyAspell 5 77
(Michael Easterby) *hld up in rr: hdwy 2f out: rdn over 1f out: kpt on fnl f* **8/1**

6053 **4** *½* **Redvers (IRE)**[15] 2896 4-9-5 **85**....................(b) PatCosgrave 6 87
(Ed Vaughan) *plld hrd early: trckd ldrs: hdwy over 2f out: chal over 1f out: sn rdn and edgd rt: ev ch tl drvn and wknd last 150yds* **5/1**[3]

0453 **5** *1 ¼* **Tevez**[12] 2975 7-9-1 **81**....................(p) BarryMcHugh 7 79
(Des Donovan) *hld up in rr: hdwy to chse ldrs over 2f out: rdn wl over 1f out: styng on whn n.m.r 1f out: sn swtchd lft and no imp* **7/2**[2]

-006 **6** *2 ¾* **Space War**[8] 3128 5-9-3 **83**....................DavidNolan 8 74
(Michael Easterby) *hld up in tch: hdwy to chse ldrs wl over 2f out: sn rdn and wknd over 1f out* **7/1**

1000 **7** *hd* **Mujaadel (USA)**[21] 2697 7-8-2 **75**....................ShirleyTeasdale(7) 3 65
(David Nicholls) *chsd ldrs: rdn along over 2f out: grad wknd* **16/1**

1m 29.22s (4.72) **Going Correction** +0.325s/f (Good) **7** Ran SP% **110.3**
Speed ratings (Par 107): **86,84,83,83,81 78,78**
toteswingers: 1&2 £2.70, 1&3 £3.80, 2&3 £12.80 CSF £19.23 CT £112.27 TOTE £2.90: £1.70, £4.30; EX 21.30.
Owner Mrs F Denniff **Bred** A S Denniff **Trained** Hambleton, N Yorks

FOCUS
This looked a competitive handicap despite the small field, that was run at a sound pace, although the field finished well grouped.

NOTEBOOK
Dubai Hills looked on a handy enough marked judged on his two runs this season at York, and he ran out a convincing winner. Settled nicely behind the strong early pace, he took up the running a furlong out and stayed on well. His only previous win on turf came on heavy (Sept 2008) so had no problems with the ground and remains in good heart. (op 5-2)
Polish World(USA), who finished second in this race last season off a 12lb lower mark, set a frantic early pace and one would have expected him to drop away once headed at the 2f pole, but he battled backed bravely into second. He has not won off such a mark before and this was a fine effort on ground softer than ideal. (op 15-2 tchd 17-2)
Aerodynamic(IRE) looked outpaced early but stayed on well enough into third, suggesting further would suit. (op 7-1)
Redvers(IRE) pulled too hard early and came with a dangerous run but could not sustain his challenged, and paid for his early exertions. (op 7-2)
Tevez, who goes well on soft and was running off his last winning mark, travelled kindly but could not quicken as well as the principals, although was staying on well enough. (op 9-2)
Space War was going as well as any 2f out, but lacked the pace over this trip. (op 9-1)

3404 SUMMER WEDDING FAYRE HERE ON 29TH JULY H'CAP 5f
3:55 (3:56) (Class 4) (0-85,81) 3-Y-0 **£2,587** (£770; £384) **Stalls** Centre

Form RPR

4236 **1** **Phoenix Clubs (IRE)**[36] 2256 3-8-5 **65**....................BarryMcHugh 6 74
(Paul Midgley) *cl up: chal over 1f out and sn rdn: drvn ins fnl f: led last 75yds* **1/1**[1]

122 **2** *¾* **Wild Sauce**[23] 2615 3-8-10 **70**....................(b) TomEaves 3 76
(Bryan Smart) *cl up: led over 1f out: sn rdn and edgd lft ins fnl f: hdd and no ex last 75yds* **5/4**[2]

244- **3** *5* **Sunrise Dance**[191] 7765 3-9-0 **77**....................LeeTopliss(3) 4 65
(Robert Johnson) *slt ld: rdn 2f out: hdd over 1f out: wknd fnl f* **6/1**[3]

1m 0.25s (1.65) **Going Correction** +0.325s/f (Good) **3** Ran SP% **108.7**
Speed ratings (Par 101): **99,97,89**
CSF £2.62 TOTE £1.80; EX 3.10.
Owner Williams, Lindley, Turton, Bate **Bred** Mark & Pippa Hackett **Trained** Westow, N Yorks

FOCUS
Only three went to post for this sprint handicap, that was run at a sound pace and produced an exciting finish.

3405 LADIES' AND GENTS EVENING - 25TH AUGUST CLAIMING STKS 7f
4:30 (4:30) (Class 5) 3-Y-0+ **£1,940** (£577; £288; £144) **Stalls** Centre

Form RPR

0-50 **1** **King Pin**[14] 2922 7-8-13 55....................(p) BarryMcHugh 8 65
(Tracy Waggott) *hld up in tch: hdwy 1/2-way: rdn to ld over 2f out: drvn and kpt on wl fnl f* **5/1**[3]

0000 **2** *1 ¼* **Light From Mars**[30] 2417 7-9-6 85....................JustinNewman(5) 4 74
(John Quinn) *a.p: effrt over 2f out: rdn to chse wnr over 1f out: drvn and one pce fnl f* **9/4**[2]

-030 **3** *2 ¼* **Rasselas (IRE)**[18] 2791 5-8-8 60....................(v[1]) ShirleyTeasdale(7) 9 58
(David Nicholls) *chsd ldrs: rdn along 2f out: drvn and one pce ent fnl f* **15/2**

5402 **4** *1 1/4* **River Ardeche**[26] 2536 7-8-12 64 .... RossAtkinson(3) 13 55
(Tracy Waggott) *led: rdn along and hdd over 2f out: sn drvn and grad wknd* **6/1**

0-00 **5** *24* **King Laertis (IRE)**[10] 3025 3-8-0 40 .... DeclanCannon(3) 7
(Tracy Waggott) *a in rr: rdn 1/2-way: outpcd and bhd fr over 2f out* **50/1**

2525 **P** **Tarooq (USA)**[105] 868 6-9-11 89 .... MickyFenton 10
(Stuart Williams) *cl up: disp ld 1/2-way: rdn and lost pl qckly over 2f out: sn eased and bhd: p.u ins fnl f: dismntd* **15/8**[1]

1m 27.93s (3.43) **Going Correction** +0.325s/f (Good)
WFA 3 from 4yo+ 9lb **6** Ran SP% **110.2**
Speed ratings (Par 103): **93,91,89,87,60**
toteswingers: 1&2 £2.00, 1&3 £3.00, 2&3 £5.60 CSF £16.05 TOTE £5.20: £2.70, £1.60; EX 21.40.

Owner H Conlon **Bred** Cheveley Park Stud Ltd **Trained** Spennymoor, Co Durham

FOCUS
Only six stood their ground from the 13 declared for this moderate claimer, that was run at a steady pace, with the front four well grouped passing the post.

Tarooq(USA) Official explanation: jockey said gelding lost its action but returned sound

3406 CAPTURE LE COEUR PHOTOGRAPHY MEDIAN AUCTION MAIDEN STKS 6f

5:05 (5:08) (Class 5) 3-5-Y-O **£1,940** (£577; £288; £144) **Stalls** Centre

Form RPR

0 **1** **Military Green (FR)**[15] 2881 3-9-3 0 .... DuranFentiman 6 56
(Tim Easterby) *in rr: pushed along 1/2-way: hdwy wl over 1f out: sn rdn and styd on to ld ins fnl f: drvn out* **6/1**[3]

0-03 **2** *1 1/4* **Isle Of Ellis (IRE)**[10] 3026 5-9-3 46 ....(v) ShirleyTeasdale(7) 4 54
(Ron Barr) *trckd ldrs: effrt 2f out and sn ev ch: rdn over 1f out: kpt on u.p ins fnl f* **5/1**[2]

00 **3** *hd* **Kapunda**[35] 2262 4-9-10 0 .... AndrewElliott 5 53
(Jedd O'Keeffe) *led: rdn along over 2f out: drvn over 1f out: hdd and one pce ins fnl f* **14/1**

40 **4** *2* **Mon Duchess**[14] 2918 4-9-5 0 .... BarryMcHugh 1 42
(Lawrence Mullaney) *cl up: rdn along over 2f out: drvn over 1f out and sn one pce* **3/1**[1]

0-00 **5** *nk* **Queen's Princess**[24] 2601 4-9-0 31 .... AdamCarter(5) 7 41
(John Wainwright) *chsd ldrs: rdn along 2f out: sn edgd lft and one pce* **66/1**

05 **6** *3* **Majestic Angel (IRE)**[14] 2918 3-8-12 0 .... MickyFenton 10 30
(Brian Rothwell) *in tch: rdn along 2f out: sn drvn and wknd over 1f out* **12/1**

7 *2 1/2* **Artillery Train (IRE)** 3-8-10 0 .... IanBurns(7) 11 26
(Tim Etherington) *s.i.s: a bhd* **16/1**

1m 15.85s (4.05) **Going Correction** +0.325s/f (Good)
WFA 3 from 4yo+ 7lb **7** Ran SP% **77.7**
Speed ratings (Par 103): **86,84,84,81,81 77,73**
toteswingers: 1&2 £4.30, 1&3 £5.50, 2&3 £6.60 CSF £15.48 TOTE £4.40: £2.70, £1.60; EX 22.10.

Owner Habton Farms **Bred** Gestut Ittlingen **Trained** Great Habton, N Yorks

FOCUS
This moderate median auction maiden had plenty of interest taken out of it, with the withdrawal of the favourite Vanity´s Girl, who refused to enter the stalls. It was run at a steady pace with plenty in contention entering the final furlong. The form looks modest.

3407 WIN A VIP DAY OUT @ REDCARRACING.CO.UK H'CAP 5f

5:40 (5:45) (Class 6) (0-60,58) 3-Y-O **£1,704** (£503; £251) **Stalls** Centre

Form RPR

-000 **1** **Elusive Bonus (IRE)**[26] 2540 3-8-7 **51** .... DavidBergin(7) 1 72
(David O'Meara) *wnt rt s: mde most: clr wl over 1f out: r.o strly* **12/1**

3506 **2** *7* **One Kool Dude**[20] 2730 3-9-0 **58** .... IanBurns(7) 3 54
(Michael Bell) *hmpd s: in tch: rdn along over 2f out: styd on u.p fnl f: no ch w wnr* **15/2**

-524 **3** *nse* **Red Shadow**[16] 2862 3-8-12 **54** .... GarryWhillans(5) 5 50
(Alan Brown) *dwlt: towards rr: hdwy on wd outside 2f out: rdn and styd on fnl f* **11/2**[3]

630 **4** *nk* **Dartrix**[35] 2262 3-9-3 **57** .... LeeTopliss(3) 9 52
(Michael Dods) *dwlt and in rr: swtchd rt and hdwy wl over 1f out: sn rdn and styd on fnl f: nrst fin* **7/2**[1]

-060 **5** *1 3/4* **Dazzlin Bluebell (IRE)**[4] 3256 3-8-12 **49** ....(b[1]) BarryMcHugh 11 37
(Tim Easterby) *prom: rdn along 2f out: sn wknd* **7/1**

524 **6** *2 3/4* **Imperial Legend (IRE)**[14] 2918 3-8-13 **57** .... ShirleyTeasdale(7) 13 35
(David Nicholls) *trckd ldrs: hdwy over 2f out: chsd wnr over 1f out: sn rdn and wknd fnl f* **9/2**[2]

610- **7** *1/2* **Wake Up Sioux (IRE)**[243] 7059 3-9-5 **56** .... AndrewElliott 4 33
(David C Griffiths) *cl up: rdn along 2f out: sn wknd* **15/2**

0-44 **8** *1/2* **Pavers Star**[21] 2695 3-8-8 **45** .... DuranFentiman 6 20
(Noel Wilson) *prom: rdn along 1/2-way: sn wknd* **16/1**

0-00 **9** *3* **Majestic Bounty**[15] 2881 3-8-8 **45** .... KellyHarrison 8 9
(Chris Fairhurst) *a in rr* **25/1**

0005 **10** *1/2* **First Fast Now (IRE)**[5] 3218 3-9-0 **58** .... EvaMoscrop(7) 15 20
(Nigel Tinkler) *a in rr* **15/2**

1m 0.56s (1.96) **Going Correction** +0.325s/f (Good) **10** Ran SP% **121.0**
Speed ratings (Par 97): **97,85,85,85,82 78,77,76,71,70**
toteswingers: 1&2 £16.20, 1&3 £16.20, 2&3 £14.00 CSF £102.58 CT £435.58 TOTE £9.40: £4.60, £3.50, £2.40; EX 51.30.

Owner The Three County Partnership **Bred** T Jones **Trained** Nawton, N Yorks

■ Stewards' Enquiry : David Bergin two-day ban: careless riding (Jul 8-9)

FOCUS
A moderate yet competitive looking apprentice sprint handicap, run at a decent pace that saw a most impressive winner, who made nearly all.

Elusive Bonus(IRE) Official explanation: trainer's rep said, regarding apparent improvement in form, that the filly was suited by the drop back 5f.

First Fast Now(IRE) Official explanation: trainer said filly became upset in stalls and cut its mouth

T/Plt: £465.60 to a £1 stake. Pool £43,041.50. 67.48 winning tickets. T/Qpdt: £225.20 to a £1 stake. Pool £2,374.40. 7.80 winning tickets. JR

3408 - 3414a (Foreign Racing) - See Raceform Interactive

[2977]PONTEFRACT (L-H)

Sunday, June 24

OFFICIAL GOING: Soft changing to soft (heavy in places) after race 3 (3.10)
False rail in place over last 6furlongs, about 15ft from the inside rail.
Wind: Fresh, half- behind Weather: overcast, breezy

3415 BRITISH STALLION STUDS E B F TOTEPLACEPOT MAIDEN FILLIES' STKS 6f

2:10 (2:14) (Class 5) 2-Y-O **£3,881** (£1,155; £577; £288) **Stalls** Low

Form RPR

303 **1** **Fantacise**[11] 3034 2-9-0 0 ....(b[1]) RobertWinston 1 75
(Brian Meehan) *w ldrs: drvn to ld 2f out: styd on fnl f* **9/4**[1]

365 **2** *2* **Inchy Coo**[9] 3123 2-9-0 0 .... GrahamGibbons 2 69
(Tim Easterby) *led: hdd 2f out: kpt on same pce fnl f* **10/1**

3 *1 3/4* **Bondesire** 2-9-0 0 .... DanielTudhope 8 64+
(David O'Meara) *dwlt: hdwy over 2f out: hmpd and swtchd rt over 1f out: hung lft and kpt on same pce* **16/1**

64 **4** *2 1/4* **Art Mistress (IRE)**[15] 2917 2-9-0 0 .... KierenFallon 5 57
(Tim Easterby) *w ldrs: hung lft over 1f out: wknd towards fin* **5/2**[2]

5 *2 3/4* **Skidby Mill (IRE)** 2-9-0 0 .... MichaelO'Connell 10 49+
(John Quinn) *in rr: hdwy 2f out: nvr nr ldrs* **12/1**

46 **6** *9* **Tussie Mussie**[22] 2686 2-9-0 0 .... JoeFanning 12 22
(Mark Johnston) *chsd ldrs on outer: lost pl wl over 1f out* **8/1**[3]

7 *2 1/2* **Vida Eterna (IRE)** 2-9-0 0 .... TomEaves 9 14
(Ollie Pears) *a towards rr* **33/1**

3 **8** *1* **Balinka**[9] 3126 2-9-0 0 .... PJMcDonald 11 11
(Mel Brittain) *chsd ldrs: wknd over 1f out* **10/1**

60 **9** *3 1/4* **Strasbourg Place**[29] 2508 2-9-0 0 .... PhillipMakin 6
(Nigel Tinkler) *mid-div: lost pl 2f out* **50/1**

10 *shd* **Chloe's Dream (IRE)** 2-9-0 0 .... SilvestreDeSousa 4
(Ann Duffield) *dwlt: sn chsng ldrs: wknd wl over 1f out: sn eased* **20/1**

40 **11** *29* **Lincolnrose (IRE)**[19] 2783 2-9-0 0 ....(p) AdrianNicholls 7
(Alan McCabe) *chsd ldrs: drvn 3f out: sn lost pl: wl bhd whn eased: t.o* **33/1**

1m 24.2s (7.30) **Going Correction** +0.975s/f (Soft) **11** Ran SP% **114.8**
Speed ratings (Par 90): **90,87,85,82,78 66,63,61,57,57 18**
Tote Swingers:1&2:£4.80, 2&3:£19.40, 1&3:£8.50 CSF £23.82 TOTE £2.90: £1.50, £3.70, £4.70; EX 26.00 Trifecta £196.40 Pool 607.78 - 2.29 winning units..

Owner T G & Mrs M E Holdcroft **Bred** Bearstone Stud **Trained** Manton, Wilts

FOCUS
This fillies' maiden had been won by some nice sorts in recent years. The high-class Nannina took it in 2005, whilst a couple of subsequent winners have gone on to score in Listed company. This looked very hard work in the ground, however, and few ever got into it. The winner is rated to her pre-race mark with the second back to her debut level.

NOTEBOOK
Fantacise's best two performances from three previous starts came with give in the ground and she seemed to cope with these conditions better than her rivals, racing closest to the inside rail in a handy position and finding plenty once sent to the front over a furlong out. The first-time blinkers may have helped also, but the ground was probably the key and it remains to be seen how much longer the going remains in her favour. (tchd 2-1)
Inchy Coo had twice disappointed following a promising debut, but was trying an extra furlong here and this was better. Soon bowling along on front, she started to hang about in the centre of the track whilst the winner challenged up the inner, but she never looked in much danger of losing second. She is more exposed than most, but with the nurseries just around the corner she will have a few more options. (op 11-1)
Bondesire ◆ stayed on nicely from the back of the field as the race progressed and fared best of the four newcomers. She showed signs of greenness before the start and during the race, but this 4,000GBP half-sister to five winners obviously has ability and is one to note. (op 25-1)
Art Mistress(IRE) was an eyecatcher on her second start at Doncaster and that form has since been advertise by the third winning next time and then finishing second in the Chesham. However, her rider wasn't happy from a long way out and all she could do was keep plugging on. Perhaps even this was an insufficient test and she may be one for staying nurseries in the autumn. (op 3-1)
Skidby Mill(IRE) ◆ did well to stay on into fifth and finish a long way clear for the rest. A 23,000GBP 2-y-o and half-brother to the winning sprinter Diamond Vine, she can be expected to step forward from this. (op 11-1 tchd 10-1)
Chloe's Dream(IRE) Official explanation: jockey said filly had no more to give

3416 TOTEEXACTA FILLIES' H'CAP 1m 4y

2:40 (2:40) (Class 5) (0-70,70) 3-Y-O+ **£2,911** (£866; £432; £216) **Stalls** Low

Form RPR

2440 **1** **Dansili Dutch (IRE)**[27] 2540 3-8-5 **57** .... FrannyNorton 6 73
(Andrew Crook) *hld up in rr: hdwy over 2f out: led over 1f out: forged clr* **20/1**

5-60 **2** *6* **Miss Ella Jade**[23] 2673 3-7-13 **51** oh2 .... PaulQuinn 11 55
(Richard Whitaker) *in rr: hdwy 3f out: kpt on to take 2nd towards fin* **40/1**

0-12 **3** *nk* **Kathlatino**[25] 2598 5-9-2 **58** .... KellyHarrison 8 63
(Micky Hammond) *in rr: hdwy over 3f out: led over 2f out: hdd over 1f out: one pce and wknd ins fnl f* **6/1**[3]

0-22 **4** *3 1/4* **Silly Gilly (IRE)**[17] 2840 8-9-3 **64** .... ShaneBKelly(5) 5 63
(Ron Barr) *chsd ldrs: rdn 3f out: one pce over 1f out* **4/1**[1]

3100 **5** *2 1/4* **Woteva**[15] 2922 6-9-2 **65** ....(p) EvaMoscrop(7) 10 59
(Nigel Tinkler) *mid-div: effrt over 3f out: c stands' side 2f out: kpt on one pce* **9/1**

-000 **6** *8* **Goldenveil (IRE)**[15] 2915 4-9-4 **60** ....(b) PaulHanagan 1 38
(Richard Fahey) *awkward s: w ldr: led after 2f: hdd over 2f out: lost pl over 1f out* **9/2**[2]

3106 **7** *3 3/4* **Wiseman's Diamond (USA)**[23] 2675 7-9-10 **66** ....(b) MickyFenton 9 37
(Paul Midgley) *chsd ldrs: upsides over 2f out: lost pl over 1f out* **13/2**

F046 **8** *17* **American Lover (FR)**[43] 2091 5-8-9 **51** .... PaddyAspell 13
(John Wainwright) *chsd ldrs: lost pl over 2f out: sn bhd* **20/1**

105 **9** *1* **Hawaiian Storm**[5] 3252 3-9-1 **70** .... MichaelMetcalfe(3) 3
(Mrs K Burke) *hld up in rr: smooth hdwy to join ldrs over 2f out: wknd over 1f out* **6/1**[3]

2-00 **10** *7* **Song Of The Siren**[22] 2696 4-10-0 **70** ....(v) DanielTudhope 7
(David O'Meara) *chsd ldrs: lost pl 4f out: sn bhd* **20/1**

-651 **11** *11* **Lady Advocate (IRE)**[11] 3025 3-8-9 **61** ....(b) DuranFentiman 12
(Tim Easterby) *led 2f: reminders 4f out: lost pl over 2f out: sn bhd* **10/1**

1m 53.1s (7.20) **Going Correction** +0.975s/f (Soft)
WFA 3 from 4yo+ 10lb **11** Ran SP% **115.9**
Speed ratings (Par 100): **103,97,96,93,91 83,79,62,61,54 43**
Tote Swingers:1&2:£58.50, 2&3:£35.30, 1&3:£14.70 CSF £619.42 CT £5378.82 TOTE £27.90: £6.10, £15.00, £1.50; EX 1111.20 TRIFECTA Not won..

Owner Mrs Christine Hopper **Bred** Castlefarm Stud **Trained** Middleham Moor, N Yorks

FOCUS
An ordinary fillies' handicap and again conditions took their toll with the field finishing well spread out. The first two home occupied the last two places at halfway, suggesting the leaders went off too quick.

3417 TOTEQUADPOT H'CAP — 1m 2f 6y
3:10 (3:10) (Class 3) (0-90,89) 3-Y-0+

£8,715 (£2,609; £1,304; £652; £326; £163) **Stalls** Low

Form — RPR

2201 **1** **Edmaaj (IRE)**[8] 3167 4-9-5 **80**........ DanielTudhope 1 92+
(David O'Meara) *trckd ldr: led 2f out: styd on wl fnl f* **7/4**[1]

-200 **2** *1 3/4* **New Hampshire (USA)**[4] 3287 4-9-5 **83**........ LeeTopliss(3) 5 91
(Tony Coyle) *led: increased pce over 3f out: hdd 2f out: styd on same pce fnl f* **20/1**

1-0 **3** *nk* **Tamarrud**[11] 3042 3-8-3 **76**........ SilvestreDeSousa 4 83+
(Saeed Bin Suroor) *t.k.h in rr: hdwy to trck ldrs 7f out: wnt 3rd over 2f out: kpt on same pce fnl f* **7/2**[2]

1340 **4** *1 3/4* **Calaf**[15] 2911 4-9-8 **83**........ PaulHanagan 8 87+
(Richard Fahey) *t.k.h in rr: effrt over 2f out: kpt on same pce ins fnl f* **10/1**[3]

542 **5** *6* **Robemaker**[15] 2911 4-10-0 **89**........ WilliamBuick 10 81
(John Gosden) *trckd ldrs: t.k.h: stdd and dropped to rr after 2f: hdwy 4f out: hung lft over 1f out: wl hld whn eased towards fin* **7/2**[2]

-106 **6** *7* **Blades Lad**[22] 2701 3-8-1 **74**........ PatrickMathers 6 52
(Richard Fahey) *t.k.h in mid-div: effrt over 2f out: one pce whn sddle slipped over 1f out: sn eased* **16/1**

0303 **7** *2 3/4* **Oceanway (USA)**[15] 2911 4-10-0 **89**........ JoeFanning 9 61
(Mark Johnston) *chsd ldrs: lost pl over 2f out* **11/1**

03-0 **8** *26* **Brocklebank (IRE)**[29] 2490 3-8-13 **86**........ PhillipMakin 2
(Kevin Ryan) *trckd ldrs: drvn over 3f out: lost pl over 2f out: bhd whn eased: t.o* **28/1**

2m 21.56s (7.86) **Going Correction** +0.975s/f (Soft)
WFA 3 from 4yo+ 12lb — **8** Ran SP% **112.3**
Speed ratings (Par 107): **107,105,105,103,99 93,91,70**
Tote Swingers:1&2:£8.60, 2&3:£9.90, 1&3:£2.40 CSF £39.21 CT £111.37 TOTE £2.90: £1.60, £4.00, £1.70; EX 34.70 Trifecta £225.10 Pool 827.63 - 2.72 winning units..

Owner K Nicholson **Bred** Airlie Stud **Trained** Nawton, N Yorks

FOCUS
Whilst the leaders went off too quick in the preceding contest, they got the fractions just right here as the first two were up front throughout and an injection of pace from the pair turning in proved too much for those in behind.

NOTEBOOK
Edmaaj(IRE) ◆ was 6lb higher than when beating 16 rivals at York eight day earlier, but his ability to handle the ground wasn't in doubt and he benefited from a handy ride to hit the front passing the 2f pole and keep on finding. The extra furlong wasn't a problem and he seemed to win this with a little bit in hand, so the hat-trick must be on. (op 9-4)

New Hampshire(USA) had twice been thrashed in handicaps since finishing second of four behind Jet Away in a Ripon conditions event, but the return to a soft surface brought about a return to form and, having set the pace, only the winner was able to get the better of him. (op 16-1)

Tamarrud ◆ was making his turf debut on his third outing. He was keen enough in midfield early before coming through to challenge over a furlong out, but he showed signs of inexperience and couldn't go through with it. He still has a bit of scope and could be interesting on better ground. (op 9-2 tchd 5-1)

Calaf, who finished behind Robemaker and Oceanway at Chester last time, was heavily restrained in last place early, but although he stayed on to reverse the form with the aforementioned pair, he never looked like winning. (op 11-1 tchd 9-1)

Robemaker gained his only win in 13 previous starts in soft ground, but when switched wide to make an effort off the final bend he didn't find very much off the bridle. The trainer's representative reported that the colt was unsuited by the ground. Official explanation: ttrainer's rep said colt was unsuited by the soft (heavy in places) ground (op 11-4)

Blades Lad, twice well beaten in handicaps on quicker ground after winning a soft-ground Ripon maiden on his reappearance, pulled hard early and was going nowhere turning in.

3418 TOTEPOOL PONTEFRACT CASTLE STKS (LISTED RACE) — 1m 4f 8y
3:40 (3:40) (Class 1) 4-Y-0+ **£18,714** (£7,095; £3,550; £1,768) **Stalls** Low

Form — RPR

22-4 **1** **Brown Panther**[44] 2027 4-9-1 115........ KierenFallon 2 117
(Tom Dascombe) *trckd ldr: t.k.h: led over 3 f out: wnt clr 2f out: eased towards fin* **85/40**[2]

46-4 **2** *7* **Lost In The Moment (IRE)**[43] 2081 5-9-1 111.....(p) SilvestreDeSousa 1 106
(Saeed Bin Suroor) *hld up in last: outpcd and reminders over 3f out: hdwy over 2f out: chsd wnr over 1f out: no imp* **11/4**[3]

4-11 **3** *4* **Jet Away**[29] 2478 5-9-4 114........ TomQueally 3 102
(Sir Henry Cecil) *dwlt: hld up: jnd ldrs 5f out: drvn over 3f out: wknd over 1f out* **2/1**[1]

4652 **4** *18* **Glen's Diamond**[37] 2254 4-9-1 113........ TonyHamilton 5 71
(Richard Fahey) *led: hdd over 3f out: wknd over 2f out: bhd whn eased over 1f out* **6/1**

2m 49.0s (8.20) **Going Correction** +0.975s/f (Soft) — **4** Ran SP% **106.3**
Speed ratings (Par 111): **111,106,103,91**
CSF £7.81 TOTE £3.10; EX 10.00.

Owner A Black & Owen Promotions Limited **Bred** Owen Promotions Ltd **Trained** Malpas, Cheshire

FOCUS
The joint-smallest field in eight runnings of this contest and they didn't go much of a pace.

NOTEBOOK
Brown Panther was so progressive last year and his second in the St Leger was just about the best form on show here, but his poor effort when last of four in the Ormonde on his reappearance placed a major question mark against him. He was keen enough in second place early, but his rider's decision to play his cards over 3f from home proved the right one and it wasn't long before he had established a big advantage. He is just as good on a faster surface and looks ready for a return to Group company now. (op 2-1 tchd 9-4)

Lost In The Moment(IRE) ran some cracking races in defeat last year, including when beaten a head by Opinion Poll in the Goodwood Cup and when sixth in the Melbourne Cup. He was always going to find 1m2f on the Lingfield Polytrack an inadequate test on his return and being held up in a steadily run race in a small field here wasn't ideal either. Having got outpaced in last place half a mile from home, his stamina eventually kicked in and he ground out second place, but was never in the same parish as the winner. A return to 2m looks much needed. (op 5-2)

Jet Away was bidding for a hat-trick having proved himself up to this class when winning at Goodwood last time, but conceding 3lb to three rivals with Group-race form was never going to be easy, especially over a trip beyond his best. Although he moved up to join issue around half a mile out, he was in trouble before reaching the start of the home bend and his stamina patently deserted him in these conditions. (op 9-4 tchd 15-8)

Glen's Diamond ran the race of his life when splitting Red Cadeaux and Harris Tweed (both rated 9lb higher than him) in the Yorkshire Cup last time, but despite getting the run of the race out in front he was easily picked off over 3f from home and stopped to nothing. The ground was the likely reason. (op 11-2 tchd 5-1)

3419 TOTEPOOL.COM PONTEFRACT CUP (H'CAP) — 2m 1f 216y
4:10 (4:10) (Class 4) (0-85,81) 4-Y-0+ **£5,175** (£1,540; £769; £384) **Stalls** Low

Form — RPR

6-42 **1** **Orsippus (USA)**[18] 2827 6-9-3 **75**........ KierenFallon 1 85
(Michael Smith) *trckd ldrs: drvn to ld over 3f out: clr over 1f out: eased towards fin* **2/1**[1]

163- **2** *4 1/2* **French Hollow**[260] 6707 7-9-8 **80**........ PaulHanagan 3 86
(Tim Fitzgerald) *t.k.h in rr: hdwy 6f out: wnt 2nd over 2f out: kpt on same pce* **9/1**

3411 **3** *nk* **Blackstone Vegas**[13] 2978 6-8-9 **67**........ JoeFanning 11 72
(Derek Shaw) *hld up in rr: hdwy 6f out: chsng ldrs 4f out: wnt 3rd 1f out: kpt on same pce* **5/1**[2]

5500 **4** *1/2* **My Arch**[13] 2978 10-9-0 **75**........ DaleSwift(3) 9 80
(Ollie Pears) *trckd ldrs: drvn 5f out: outpcd over 2f out: kpt on fnl f* **15/2**

0306 **5** *6* **Descaro (USA)**[13] 2978 6-8-9 **67**........(v) SilvestreDeSousa 10 66
(David O'Meara) *hld up towards rr: hdwy over 2f out: wknd fnl f* **9/1**

2311 **6** *3* **Veloce (IRE)**[21] 2732 4-9-1 **81**........(v) GeorgeDowning(7) 8 77
(Ian Williams) *trckd ldrs: drvn to chal 3f out: wknd fnl f* **7/1**[3]

0-10 **7** *32* **Mr Crystal (FR)**[31] 2214 8-8-9 **72**........ ShaneBKelly(5) 5 36
(Micky Hammond) *hld up in mid-div: trckd ldrs 10f out: drvn 5f out: lost pl over 3f out: bhd whn eased* **7/1**[3]

0-00 **8** *1 3/4* **Wells Lyrical (IRE)**[13] 2978 7-9-4 **76**........ TomEaves 6 38
(Bryan Smart) *set stdy pce: increased gallop 8f out: drvn 6f out: hdd over 3f out: lost pl over 2f out: sn bhd: eased* **20/1**

4m 26.42s (30.22) **Going Correction** +0.975s/f (Soft)
WFA 4 from 5yo+ 1lb — **8** Ran SP% **111.5**
Speed ratings (Par 105): **71,69,68,68,65 64,50,49**
Tote Swingers:1&2:£4.30, 2&3:£6.40, 1&3:£2.90 CSF £19.85 CT £76.18 TOTE £2.20: £1.40, £2.80, £1.80; EX 21.00 Trifecta £57.30 Pool 555.79 - 7.17 winning units..

Owner Mrs Sandra Smith **Bred** Stephen H Batchelder & Gainesway Farm **Trained** Kirkheaton, Northumberland

FOCUS
The ground was changed to Soft, heavy in places and they seemed to go a sensible pace in this staying event given the conditions.

3420 BET TOTEPOOL ON ALL UK RACING MAIDEN STKS — 1m 4f 8y
4:40 (4:40) (Class 5) 3-Y-0 **£2,911** (£866; £432; £216) **Stalls** Low

Form — RPR

32 **1** **Swnymor (IRE)**[11] 3035 3-9-3 0........ WilliamBuick 1 91+
(William Haggas) *trckd ldr: shkn up to ld over 1f out: wandered: drvn out* **6/4**[2]

02 **2** *1 3/4* **Mashaari (IRE)**[16] 2895 3-9-3 0........ PaulHanagan 6 88+
(John Gosden) *led: increased pce over 4f out: drvn over 3f out: hdd over 1f out: kpt on same pce* **1/1**[1]

00 **3** *27* **Joyful Motive**[11] 3035 3-9-3 0........ MickyFenton 4 45
(Tom Tate) *trckd ldrs: pushed along 6f out: 3rd and outpcd over 4f out: no ch w 1st 2* **66/1**

4 *4 1/2* **Crystal Monarch (IRE)** 3-9-3 0........ TomQueally 5 38
(Sir Henry Cecil) *s.v.s: hdwy to chse ldrs after 2f: drvn over 5f out: sn outpcd: wknd over 1f out* **6/1**[3]

2m 50.42s (9.62) **Going Correction** +0.975s/f (Soft) — **4** Ran SP% **105.8**
Speed ratings (Par 99): **106,104,86,83**
CSF £3.21 TOTE £1.70; EX 3.10.

Owner Roberts Green Savidge Whittal-Williams **Bred** Easton Park Stud **Trained** Newmarket, Suffolk

FOCUS
Just four runners, but this only ever concerned the two market leaders.

3421 BET TOTEPOOL ON ALL IRISH RACING H'CAP — 6f
5:10 (5:11) (Class 5) (0-75,74) 3-Y-0 **£2,911** (£866; £432; £216) **Stalls** Low

Form — RPR

-600 **1** **Byronic Hero**[19] 2785 3-9-5 **72**........(b1) TonyHamilton 5 84
(Jedd O'Keeffe) *s.s: reminders after s: hdwy on ins to join ldrs over 3f out: led over 2f out: wnt clr over 1f out: drvn out* **10/1**

0-13 **2** *4 1/2* **Dream Walker (FR)**[11] 3050 3-8-11 **64**........ PatrickMathers 1 63
(Ian McInnes) *chsd ldrs: drvn over 3f out: sn outpcd: hdwy over 1f out: tk 2nd last 75yds* **6/4**[1]

30-0 **3** *nk* **Anton Chigurh**[36] 2273 3-9-7 **74**........ RichardKingscote 12 72
(Tom Dascombe) *hld up in rr: hdwy over 1f out: kpt on to take 3rd clsng stages* **6/1**[3]

10-0 **4** *1 1/2* **Commanche**[10] 3063 3-9-3 **70**........ TomEaves 2 63
(Bryan Smart) *w ldr: led after 2f: hdd over 2f out: kpt on same pce fnl f* **7/2**[2]

3 **5** *9* **Speedy Yaki (IRE)**[34] 2342 3-9-5 **72**........(t) PaulHanagan 8 38
(Daniel Mark Loughnane) *chsd ldrs: lost pl over 2f out* **9/1**

6-60 **6** *1/2* **Only A Round (IRE)**[34] 2341 3-7-11 **55** oh10........ NeilFarley(5) 7 20
(Micky Hammond) *led 2f: lost pl over 1f out* **50/1**

00-2 **7** *3 1/2* **Premier Choice**[30] 2460 3-8-10 **63**........ KierenFallon 13 17
(Tim Easterby) *trckd ldrs: t.k.h: drvn and lost pl over 3f out* **7/1**

643 **8** *14* **Dolly Diva**[23] 2680 3-8-11 **64**........ MickyFenton 3
(Paul Midgley) *t.k.h: trckd ldrs: drvn over 3f out: lost pl over 2f out: eased whn bhd* **12/1**

1m 21.9s (5.00) **Going Correction** +0.975s/f (Soft) — **8** Ran SP% **117.8**
Speed ratings (Par 99): **105,99,98,96,84 83,79,60**
Tote Swingers:1&2:£5.40, 2&3:£2.30, 1&3:£9.40 CSF £26.32 CT £104.07 TOTE £14.20: £2.80, £1.60, £2.10; EX 56.60 Trifecta £172.00 Pool 837.19 - 3.60 winning units..

Owner Highbeck Racing **Bred** Kevin Daniel Crabb **Trained** Middleham Moor, N Yorks

FOCUS
A modest sprint handicap and the first four pulled well clear of the others.

Premier Choice Official explanation: trainer said gelding was unsuited by the soft (heavy in places) ground

Dolly Diva Official explanation: trainer said filly was unsuited by the soft (heavy in places) ground

T/Plt: £203.10 to a £1 stake. Pool £80,052.13. 287.59 winning tickets T/Qpdt: £21.10 to a £1 stake. Pool £4,787.03. 167.40 winning tickets WG

3422 - (Foreign Racing) - See Raceform Interactive

2570 SAINT-CLOUD (L-H)

Sunday, June 24

OFFICIAL GOING: Turf: good to soft

3423a ABU DHABI PRIX DE MALLERET (GROUP 2) (3YO FILLIES) (TURF) 1m 4f

1:30 (12:00) 3-Y-O **£71,250** (£27,500; £13,125 ; £8,750 ; £4,375)

RPR

1 **Yellow And Green**[21] 2741 3 -8-110 ThierryThulliez 6 108+
(N Clement, France) *hld up at rr: rdn 2 1/2f out: qcknd wl on outside: chal for ld 1 1/2f out: tk ld 1f out: r.o wl under hands and heels ride: comf* **2/1**[1]

2 1 1/2 **Mandistana (FR)**[21] 2741 3 -8 110 Christophe-PatriceLemaire 1 105
(A De Royer-Dupre, France) *settled 5th on rail: slipped through opening on rail over 2f out: tk ld 1 1/2f out: hdd 1f out: r.o wl: no ch w wnr* **5/2**[2]

3 2 **Nobilis**[22] 3 -8-110 MaximeGuyon 5 102
(A Fabre, France) *racd 2nd for first 2f: settled 3rd on rail: short of room 2 1/2f out: had to be stdd 2f out: relegated to rr of field: r.o strly ent fnl f: got up for 3rd cl home* **7/1**

4 snk **Bassamba (FR)**[42] 2111 3 -8-110 (b) Francois-XavierBertras 4 102
(F Rohaut, France) *racd in 4th on outside: rdn 2 1/2f out: wnt 3rd and threatened briefly 1 1/2f out: no ex ins fnl f: lost 3rd cl home* **7/2**[3]

5 2 1/2 **Makana (FR)**[30] 3 -8-110 GeraldMosse 2 98
(A De Royer-Dupre, France) *racd in 3rd for 2f: wnt 2nd down bk st: chal for ld 2 1/2f out: led briefly 2f out: hdd 1 1/2f: styd on at one pce fnl f* **8/1**

6 dist **Darayya (IRE)**[29] 3 -8-110 FreddyDiFede 3
(A De Royer-Dupre, France) *led fr s: rdn 2 1/2f out: hdd 2f out: sn fdd: eased fnl 1 1/2f* **16/1**

2m 32.0s (-8.40) **6**Ran SP% **113.6**

WIN (incl. 1 euro stake): 2.40. PLACES: 1.30, 1.80. SF: 8.50.

Owner Comte Andre de Ganay **Bred** Newsells Park Stud **Trained** Chantilly, France

NOTEBOOK

Yellow And Green, runner-up in the Prix de Royaumont last time out, where she had Mandistana one place behind her, settled at the back of the field and came with a sweeping run to lead a furlong out. Breaking her maiden in a Group 2 race, she's improving with racing and the Prix Vermeille will be her big autumn target.

3424a GRAND PRIX DE SAINT-CLOUD (GROUP 1) (4YO+) (TURF) 1m 4f

2:40 (12:00) 4-Y-O+ **£190,466** (£76,200; £38,100 ; £19,033)

RPR

1 **Meandre (FR)**[13] 2989 4 -9-20 MaximeGuyon 5 122+
(A Fabre, France) *hld up in 3rd under restraint: qcknd wl on outside 2f out: chal for ld 1 1/2f out: tk ld 1f out: r.o wl under hands and heels ride: comf* **8/1**

2 1 1/4 **Shareta (IRE)**[27] 2570 4 -8-130 Christophe-PatriceLemaire 4 117
(A De Royer-Dupre, France) *led fr s: set gd pce: led field wd into st: chal for ld 2 1/2f out: hdd 2f out: rallied and r.o wl to regain ld 1 1/2f out: chal and hdd 1f out: r.o wl fnl f: no threat to wnr* **5/1**[3]

3 1 1/2 **Galikova (FR)**[266] 6567 4 -8-130 OlivierPeslier 3 115+
(F Head, France) *hld up at rr: rdn 2f out: nt pce to go w ldrs 2f out: styd on fnl f: tk 3rd 50yds out* **10/3**[2]

4 1/2 **Danedream (GER)**[35] 2322 4 -8-130 AStarke 1 114
(P Schiergen, Germany) *settled in cl 2nd on ins: chal for ld 2 1/2f out: led 2f out: unable qck whn chal and hdd 1 1/2f out: styd on at one pce: lost 3rd 50yds out* **4/5**[1]

2m 31.5s (-8.90) **4**Ran SP% **106.4**

WIN (incl. 1 euro stake): 6.90. PLACES: 3.70, 2.20. SF: 16.60.

Owner Rothschild Family **Bred** Famille Rothschild **Trained** Chantilly, France

FOCUS

Despite the absence of Cirrus Des Aigles, who was withdrawn on the eve of the race due to a slight leg inflammation, and the lack of a British raider, this looked a strong renewal. However, with Danedream disappointing and Galikova in need of the run this isn't form to get carried away with. The four remaining runners raced on ground described as good, good to soft in places. They went an average gallop and it turned into a sprint 2f out. The front-running runner-up has been rated to her best. The winner does well in small fields.

NOTEBOOK

Meandre(FR), winner of the Grand Prix De Paris last season prior to finishing sixth in the Arc, carried high hopes coming into his four-year-old career. Before this victory he had failed to live up to them, being readily outpaced in the Jockey Club Stakes at Newmarket and when dropped to 1m2f in Group 3 company at Longchamp 13 days ago. He showed no signs of that here though, quickening smartly to get the better of the pacesetting Shareta on the soundest surface he had encountered this season. Presumably he will be aimed at the Arc and he's likely to be at the forefront of the older horse challenge. Connections believe he is a horse who takes a few races to get fit and should continue to improve with racing.

Shareta(IRE), also without a victory in two starts this season, had the run of the race out in front but was readily brushed aside by the winner. Her prominent style of racing often gives her a tactical advantage when racing in France, but the truth is she is short of top class, although she'll be seen at her best when the ground is firmer than this.

Galikova(FR) had by her trainer's own admission taken time to come to hand this year. Settled in rear, she couldn't quicken with the front pair - looking short of race fitness - but did show she retained all of her ability by running on to take third. She looks set to have a good summer/autumn with last year's rival Golden Lilac appearing better over shorter. A repeat victory in the Vermeille looks likely.

Danedream(GER), last year's Arc heroine (beat all three of today's rivals in that race), was unsuited by the lack of a true gallop, but she still ran poorly considering she wouldn't have minded the ground and came here on the back of winning a Group 2 at Baden-Baden. There's no doubting she's very good, however she is yet to convince that her Arc victory doesn't overrate her, and it would seem unlikely she'll be up to going close this year.

HANOVER (L-H)

Sunday, June 24

OFFICIAL GOING: Turf: good

3425a GROSSER PREIS DER VGH VERSICHERUNGEN (GROUP 3) (3YO+) (TURF) 1m

4:15 (12:00) 3-Y-O+

£26,666 (£9,166; £4,583 ; £2,500 ; £1,666 ; £1,250)

RPR

1 **Empire Storm (GER)**[40] 2160 5 -9-00 EPodroza 2 109
(A Wohler, Germany) *mde all: rdn and skipped clr on turn into st: kpt on wl under hands and heels to maintain advantage ins fnl f: readily* **66/10**[3]

2 3 1/2 **Amarillo (IRE)**[27] 2568 3 -8-60 FilipMinarik 1 101
(P Schiergen, Germany) *trckd ldr in 3rd on inner: rdn and wnt 2nd on turn into st: kpt on wout matching wnr thrght fnl 1 1/2f* **7/10**[1]

3 7 **Nafar (GER)**[38] 2222 4 -8-110 ShaneKelly 3 82
(W Hickst, Germany) *midfield: rdn on turn into st: wnt 3rd over 1 1/2f out: outpcd by ldng duo over 1f out: plugged on* **237/10**

4 1/2 **Ganimed**[42] 4 -8-110 EFrank 6 81
(M G Mintchev, Germany) *hld up in last: rdn over 2 1/2f out: outpcd by ldng duo over 1f out: plugged on* **27/1**

5 11 **Final Destination (FR)**[37] 2259 3 -8-60 StefanieHofer 4 58
(Mario Hofer, Germany) *hld up in last pair: rdn over 2 1/2f out: outpcd and btn 1 1/2f out: nvr a factor* **106/10**

6 12 **Alianthus (GER)**[29] 2521 7 -9-60 ADeVries 5 37
(J Hirschberger, Germany) *trckd ldr in 2nd on outer: rdn on turn into st: no rspnse and qckly btn: fdd: eased and dropped to last ins fnl f* **11/10**[2]

1m 44.84s (104.84)

WFA 3 from 4yo+ 10lb **6**Ran SP% **135.8**

WIN (incl. 10 euro stake): 76. PLACES: 16, 11. SF: 192.

Owner Frau M Sohl **Bred** Hannes K Gutschow **Trained** Germany

2967 SAN SIRO (R-H)

Sunday, June 24

OFFICIAL GOING: Turf: good

3426a PREMIO MARIO INCISA DELLA ROCCHETTA (GROUP 3) (3YO FILLIES) (TURF) 1m 2f

5:00 (12:00) 3-Y-O **£23,333** (£10,266; £5,600 ; £2,800)

RPR

1 **Faciascura**[105] 3 -8-110 CColombi 7 100
(S Botti, Italy) *mde most: pushed up to ld after 1 1/2f: over 2 l clr and stl gng wl 4f out: rdn and strly pressed over 2f out: fnd more and kpt on gamely to go clr again ins fnl f: drvn out* **89/10**

2 1 **Delicatezza** 3 -8-110 NicolaPinna 6 98
(E Botti, Italy) *led 1 1/2f: hdd and trckd ldr in 2nd: rdn 3f out: sustained chal fr over 2f out: no ex and hld ins fnl 150yds: almost ct for 2nd post* **43/5**

3 hd **Aquila D'Oriente (ITY)**[29] 2522 3 -8-110 CristianDemuro 2 98
(S Botti, Italy) *hld up in last: rdn to improve 3f out: kpt on thrght fnl 2 1/2f: wnt 3rd post: gng on at fin* **2/1**[2]

4 nse **Etoile D'Argent (ITY)**[56] 1699 3 -8-110 CFiocchi 1 98
(G Mosconi, Italy) *midfield: rdn over 2 1/2f out: sustained chal fr over 2f out: no ex and hld ins fnl 150yds: ct for 3rd post* **151/10**

5 3/4 **Gala Sakhee**[252] 6904 3 -8-110 DarioVargiu 4 96
(B Grizzetti, Italy) *hld up in last pair: rdn over 2 1/2f out: edgd rt u.p: kpt on one pce ins fnl 1 1/2f* **25/1**

6 nk **Wasimah (GER)**[28] 2531 3 -9-20 LManiezzi 5 101
(H J Groschel, Germany) *hld up in last trio: rdn 3f out: keeping on whn short of room and forced to check wl ins fnl f: nt rcvr and eased fnl strides* **4/5**[1]

7 8 **Freezy (IRE)**[29] 2522 3 -8-110 FabioBranca 3 80
(S Botti, Italy) *midfield: rdn and brief effrt 3f out: no ex and btn over 1 1/2f out: qckly eased and coasted home ins fnl f* **78/10**[3]

2m 1.8s (-4.90) **7**Ran SP% **130.8**

WIN (incl. 1 euro stake): 9.88. PLACES: 4.45, 4.92. DF: 39.03.

Owner Scud. Rencati **Bred** Az. Agricola Francesca **Trained** Italy

3427a-3428a (Foreign Racing) See RI

3096 CHEPSTOW (L-H)

Monday, June 25

OFFICIAL GOING: Heavy changing to soft after race 5 (4.30)

Wind: mild breeze across Weather: sunny with cloudy periods

3429 FREEBETS.CO.UK FREE BETS H'CAP 1m 2f 36y

2:30 (2:30) (Class 5) (0-75,72) 4-Y-O+ **£2,264** (£673; £336 ; £168) **Stalls** Low

Form RPR

6-02 1 **James Pollard (IRE)**[17] 2867 7 -8-967 (t) AliceHaynes(7) 1 75
(Bernard Llewellyn) *trckd ldrs: led over 2f out: sn rdn and hrd pressed: hld on gamely fnl f* **4/1**[2]

2610 2 shd **Hamilton Hill**[8] 3187 5 -8-765 KatiaScallan(7) 8 73
(Dai Burchell) *hld up: hdwy to chal 3f out: rdn for str chal over 2f out: ev ch thrght fnl f: kpt on* **6/4**[1]

10-0 3 3 1/4 **Sweet World**[20] 2389 8 -8-1263 MartinLane 3 64
(Bernard Llewellyn) *trckd ldr: led over 3f out tl rdn over 2f out: kpt on same pce* **8/1**

20-3 4 4 **Taste The Wine (IRE)**[10] 3101 6 -8-462 DanielMuscutt(7) 5 55
(Bernard Llewellyn) *hld up: hdwy over 3f out: sn rdn: disp 3rd over 2f out: fdd ins fnl f* **11/1**

5-02 5 3 **Tijori (IRE)**[10] 3101 4 -9-065 DavidProbert 2 52
(Bernard Llewellyn) *led tl over 3f out: sn rdn: wknd fnl f* **13/2**

254- **6** *7* **Miss Exhibitionist**[22] 6311 4-9-6 **71** .... FergusSweeney 7 44
(Alan King) *in tch: effrt over 3f out: nvr gng pce to chal: wknd over 1f out* **11/2**[3]

2m 19.05s (8.45) **Going Correction** +0.775s/f (Yiel) **6** Ran SP% **108.2**
Speed ratings (Par 103): **97,96,94,91,88 83**
toteswingers 1&2 £2.20, 2&3 £2.70, 1&3 £4.70 CSF £9.66 CT £36.77 TOTE £4.50: £2.10, £2.10; EX 12.50.
Owner B J Llewellyn **Bred** Gainsborough Stud Management Ltd **Trained** Fochriw, Caerphilly
■ Stewards' Enquiry : Alice Haynes caution: careless riding.

FOCUS
A tight finish and a career-best for the winner, whose trainer was responsible for over half the field. Modest form, with a small personal best from the winner.

3430 WEATHERBYS BANK MEDIAN AUCTION MAIDEN STKS 1m 4f 23y
3:00 (3:00) (Class 5) 3-5-Y-O **£2,264** (£673; £336; £168) **Stalls** Low

Form RPR
1 **Asker (IRE)**[250] 4-9-6 0 .... (b) KatiaScallan(7) 5 87
(Marcus Tregoning) *dwlt: last of 5 but sn in tch: pushed along over 5f out: rdn 4f out: no imp tl str run over 1f out: led ent fnl f: hung rt: styd on wl: comf* **11/4**[2]
33-6 **2** *6* **Villa Royale**[11] 3069 3-8-8 71 .... (p) JamesDoyle 3 72
(Harry Dunlop) *trckd ldr: led over 3f out: rdn and chal sn after: hdd ent fnl f: kpt on same pce* **4/1**[3]
4242 **3** *1 ½* **Cyrus Sod**[13] 3003 3-8-13 76 .... (p) JamieSpencer 7 75
(Ed Dunlop) *trckd ldrs: chal 3f out: sn rdn: kpt on tl no ex fnl 100yds* **4/5**[1]
00 **4** *8* **Bold Duke**[12] 3035 4-9-10 0 .... RaulDaSilva(3) 8 62
(Edward Bevan) *hld up bhd ldrs: rdn over 3f out: wknd over 1f out* **100/1**
0406 **5** *9* **Bashama**[17] 2872 4-9-8 49 .... DavidProbert 2 42
(Nikki Evans) *led tl rdn over 3f out: wknd 2f out* **25/1**

2m 47.2s (8.20) **Going Correction** +0.775s/f (Yiel)
WFA 3 from 4yo+ 14lb **5** Ran SP% **107.1**
Speed ratings (Par 103): **103,99,98,92,86**
CSF £12.91 TOTE £4.10: £2.00, £2.50; EX 12.20.
Owner Nurlan Bizakov **Bred** Roncon Churchtown Bloodstock & Lane Ltd **Trained** Lambourn, Berks

FOCUS
There was a fair enough pace on in this modest maiden and it saw changing fortunes in the home straight. The winner is clearly both above-average and far from straightforward.

3431 WEATHERBYS BLOODSTOCK INSURANCE MAIDEN STKS 1m 14y
3:30 (3:30) (Class 5) 3-Y-0+ **£2,264** (£673; £336; £168) **Stalls** Centre

Form RPR
2- **1** **Hallings Comet**[248] 6993 3-9-2 0 .... DavidProbert 3 75+
(Andrew Balding) *mde all: drew clr over 1f out: wl in control whn rdn fnl f* **8/13**[1]
0-4 **2** *10* **Before Bruce**[4] 3311 5-9-7 0 .... (t) BrendanPowell(5) 5 54
(Brendan Powell) *outpcd 6f out: sn lost tch: stdy prog fr over 2f out: styd on to go 2nd ent fnl f: nvr any ch w wnr* **16/1**[3]
00- **3** *5* **Grande Illusion**[280] 6216 3-9-2 0 .... MartinLane 6 41
(J W Hills) *outpcd and bhd 6f out: stdy prog fr over 2f out: styd on to go 3rd ins fnl f: nvr a threat* **20/1**
2-40 **4** *4* **Journalistic (USA)**[14] 2980 3-8-9 77 .... (v[1]) KatiaScallan(7) 2 31
(Marcus Tregoning) *racd keenly trcking wnr: rdn over 2f out: wknd over 1f out: sn dropped to 4th* **2/1**[2]
50- **5** *15* **River Valley**[325] 4761 3-9-2 0 .... ChrisCatlin 4
(Dai Burchell) *outpcd 6f out: nvr any danger* **50/1**
0 **6** *14* **Silver Threepence**[18] 2864 4-9-4 0 .... RaulDaSilva(3) 1
(Roy Brotherton) *s.i.s: sn chsng wnr: rdn 3f out: wknd over 2f out: t.o* **100/1**

1m 41.08s (4.88) **Going Correction** +0.425s/f (Yiel)
WFA 3 from 4yo+ 10lb **6** Ran SP% **108.8**
Speed ratings (Par 103): **92,82,77,73,58 44**
toteswingers 1&2 £1.70, 2&3 £3.60, 1&3 £2.30 CSF £11.16 TOTE £1.70: £1.10, £5.90; EX 8.60.
Owner Lord Blyth **Bred** Lord Blyth **Trained** Kingsclere, Hants

FOCUS
One-way traffic in this weak maiden, which was run in a slow time with the winner perhaps having done too much early.
Silver Threepence Official explanation: jockey said filly ran green

3432 FREEBETS.CO.UK FREE MOBILE BETTING CLASSIFIED STKS 1m 14y
4:00 (4:00) (Class 5) 3-Y-O **£2,264** (£673; £336; £168) **Stalls** Centre

Form RPR
656- **1** **Viscount Vert (IRE)**[303] 5475 3-9-0 70 .... [1] DavidProbert 2 75
(Andrew Balding) *trckd ldrs: hdwy to ld ent fnl f: shkn up ins fnl f: readily* **9/4**[1]
5443 **2** *2* **Nevaeh**[21] 2757 3-8-11 67 .... (v[1]) SeanLevey(3) 4 70
(Pat Eddery) *little slowly away: trckd ldrs: led over 2f out: rdn whn hdd ent fnl f: kpt on same pce* **5/1**[2]
20-0 **3** *6* **Siouxperhero (IRE)**[41] 2150 3-9-0 68 .... JamesDoyle 1 56
(William Muir) *prom for 3f: trckd ldrs: rdn wl over 2f out: wknd fnl f* **9/4**[1]
4015 **4** *hd* **Devote Myself (IRE)**[8] 3186 3-9-0 70 .... PadraigBeggy 3 56
(David Evans) *led: rdn and hdd over 2f out: wknd fnl f* **9/4**[1]

1m 40.29s (4.09) **Going Correction** +0.425s/f (Yiel) **4** Ran SP% **109.0**
Speed ratings (Par 99): **96,94,88,87**
CSF £12.80 TOTE £3.60; EX 10.90.
Owner Martin & Valerie Slade & Partner **Bred** Scuderia San Pancrazio Sas **Trained** Kingsclere, Hants

FOCUS
A typically tight 3-y-o classified stakes. It was run at a sound pace and the first pair drew clear from the furlong marker. Pretty limited form, and unconvincing.
Viscount Vert(IRE) Official explanation: trainer said, regarding apparent improvement in form, that the gelding had strengthened up over the winter.

3433 FREEBETS.CO.UK H'CAP 7f 16y
4:30 (4:30) (Class 5) (0-70,66) 3-Y-O **£2,264** (£673; £336; £168) **Stalls** Centre

Form RPR
-052 **1** **Rocky Reef**[13] 3014 3-9-6 **65** .... (v) DavidProbert 5 79
(Andrew Balding) *trckd ldrs: led over 1f out: pushed clr: comf* **4/6**[1]
0-00 **2** *7* **Bajan Hero**[13] 3014 3-8-9 **54** .... KirstyMilczarek 2 50
(David Evans) *led for over 1f: trckd ldrs: rdn 3f out: kpt on same pce fnl 2f: regained 2nd towards fin: no ch w wnr* **10/1**
4-00 **3** *½* **Sir Dylan**[21] 2756 3-9-1 **60** .... (p) MarcHalford 4 57
(Ronald Harris) *bmpd leaving stalls: prom: led over 3f out: rdn whn hdd over 1f out: hld whn veered rt ent fnl f: no ex and lost 2nd towards fin* **12/1**
-400 **4** *3 ¾* **Doc Hill**[18] 2862 3-7-13 **47** oh2 .... SimonPearce(3) 1 32
(Michael Blanshard) *trckd ldrs: rdn over 2f out: fdd ins fnl f* **7/1**[3]
42-0 **5** *17* **Frederickthegreat**[67] 1486 3-9-7 **66** .... (tp) DarryllHolland 3
(Hughie Morrison) *bmpd leaving stalls: prom: led after 1f: hdd over 3f out: sn rdn: hld fr over 2f out: wknd over 1f out* **4/1**[2]

1m 27.47s (4.27) **Going Correction** +0.425s/f (Yiel) **5** Ran SP% **109.3**
Speed ratings (Par 99): **92,84,83,79,59**
CSF £8.00 TOTE £1.50: £1.10, £2.80; EX 9.60.
Owner Kingsclere Racing CLub **Bred** Gary Sanderson **Trained** Kingsclere, Hants

FOCUS
This weak 3-y-o handicap was run at a solid pace and the form is straightforward enough. The winner beat the second slightly further than he had at Salisbury.
Sir Dylan Official explanation: jockey said gelding ducked right towards paddock

3434 FREE BETS WITH FREEBETS.CO.UK H'CAP 6f 16y
5:00 (5:01) (Class 5) (0-70,70) 3-Y-0+ **£2,264** (£673; £336; £168) **Stalls** Centre

Form RPR
-012 **1** **Full Shilling (IRE)**[11] 3075 4-9-10 **66** .... JamesDoyle 8 75
(John Spearing) *hld up: nt best of runs 2f out: swtchd rt and squeezed through gap for hdwy over 1f out: r.o to ld ins fnl f: drifted lft: rdn out* **5/1**[2]
364 **2** *nk* **Gracie's Games**[19] 2815 6-8-9 **58** .... (v) JacobButterfield(7) 3 66
(Richard Price) *reluctant at s: hld up: hdwy over 1f out: str chal thrght fnl f: carried lft: kpt on* **8/1**[3]
0452 **3** *1* **Bermondsey Bob (IRE)**[6] 3245 6-8-12 **61** .... WilliamTwiston-Davies(7) 6 66
(John Spearing) *led: rdn over 1f out: hdd ins fnl f: carried lft: no ex* **5/1**[2]
0304 **4** *2* **Olynard (IRE)**[28] 2555 6-8-12 **54** .... JimmyQuinn 1 52
(Michael Mullineaux) *in tch: rdn to chse ldrs 2f out: kpt on same pce fnl f* **25/1**
5502 **5** *½* **Mucky Molly**[9] 3151 4-8-9 **51** oh2 .... KirstyMilczarek 5 48
(Olivia Maylam) *chsd ldrs: rdn 3f out: kpt on same pce fnl f* **18/1**
5005 **6** *1 ¼* **Jack My Boy (IRE)**[7] 3225 5-9-11 **70** .... (v) RichardEvans(3) 10 63
(David Evans) *trckd ldr: rdn and ev ch 2f out: no ex ent fnl f* **5/1**[2]
221 **7** *1* **Caramelita**[14] 2973 5-10-0 **70** .... (v) JamieGoldstein 7 60
(J R Jenkins) *trckd ldrs: rdn over 2f out: wknd fnl f* **8/1**[3]
6551 **8** *2 ¾* **Dancing Welcome**[11] 3075 6-10-0 **70** .... (b) MartinLane 2 51
(Milton Bradley) *prom: rdn over 2f out: wknd over 1f out* **10/1**
4022 **9** *½* **Sarangoo**[13] 3016 4-9-6 **62** .... TomMcLaughlin 9 41
(Malcolm Saunders) *in tch: rdn over 2f out: wknd fnl f* **9/2**[1]
0023 **10** *¾* **Kyllachy Storm**[10] 3103 8-8-6 **55** .... RyanTate(7) 4 32
(Ron Hodges) *rrd leaving stalls: in tch: rdn 3f out: wknd wl over 1f out* **12/1**

1m 14.05s (2.05) **Going Correction** +0.425s/f (Yiel) **10** Ran SP% **116.3**
Speed ratings (Par 103): **103,102,101,98,97 96,94,91,90,89**
toteswingers 1&2 £10.10, 2&3 £12.50, 1&3 £4.90 CSF £44.58 CT £215.79 TOTE £4.20: £2.10, £3.70, £2.30; EX 53.70.
Owner Not The Full Shilling Syndicate **Bred** Michael Dalton **Trained** Kinnersley, Worcs
■ Stewards' Enquiry : James Doyle two-day ban: careless riding (Jul 9-10)

FOCUS
A wide-open sprint handicap. It was run at a strong pace and the first two were both given waiting rides. The winner recorded a length personal best.

3435 FREEBETTINGTIPS.COM FREE BETTING TIPS H'CAP 5f 16y
5:30 (5:30) (Class 6) (0-60,59) 3-Y-0+ **£1,617** (£481; £240; £120) **Stalls** Centre

Form RPR
0003 **1** **Spic 'n Span**[14] 2971 7-8-11 **46** .... (v) MarcHalford 4 53
(Ronald Harris) *mde all: clr over 1f out: drifted lft fnl f: kpt on: drvn out* **16/1**
0-06 **2** *½* **Superior Edge**[16] 2943 5-9-10 **59** .... (p) MartinLane 10 64
(Christopher Mason) *mid-div: rdn over 3f out: stdy prog fr wl over 1f out: r.o ins fnl f: clsng on wnr at fin* **10/1**
44-4 **3** *¾* **The Jailer**[24] 2647 9-8-12 **54** .... WilliamTwiston-Davies(7) 9 56
(John O'Shea) *trckd ldrs: rdn over 2f out: nt pce to chal: styd on fnl f: nt pce to get involved* **14/1**
06-6 **4** *nk* **Crimson Queen**[140] 445 5-9-9 **58** .... (b) ChrisCatlin 7 59
(Roy Brotherton) *prom: rdn to chse wnr fr 2f out tl no ex fnl 120yds* **20/1**
-603 **5** *nk* **Red Rhythm**[10] 3098 5-9-1 **50** .... PadraigBeggy 3 50
(David Evans) *sn chsng ldrs: rdn over 2f out: kpt on same pce* **6/1**
6455 **6** *¾* **Two Turtle Doves (IRE)**[6] 3256 6-9-9 **58** .... JimmyQuinn 11 55
(Michael Mullineaux) *towards rr: rdn over 3f out: styd on fr over 1f out: nvr trbld ldrs* **7/2**[1]
2102 **7** *nk* **Seventeen Seventy**[7] 3218 3-9-4 **59** .... AmirQuinn 5 53
(Alan Coogan) *s.i.s: outpcd in rr over 3f out: plenty to find whn styng on fr over 1f out: (apart fr stalls) nrst fin* **9/2**[2]
05-0 **8** *1* **Depden (IRE)**[11] 3076 4-8-5 **45** .... MatthewLawson(5) 6 38
(Richard Price) *towards rr and outpcd over 3f out: sme late prog: nvr a factor* **33/1**
6322 **9** *2* **Bookiesindex Boy**[14] 2971 8-8-13 **48** .... JamieGoldstein 2 34
(J R Jenkins) *chsd ldrs: rdn 3f out: wknd ins fnl f* **5/1**[3]
2543 **10** *¾* **Yanza**[11] 3076 6-8-12 **52** .... LauraPike(5) 1 35
(Pam Ford) *prom tl rdn over 3f out: sn btn* **8/1**

1m 2.42s (3.12) **Going Correction** +0.425s/f (Yiel)
WFA 3 from 4yo+ 6lb **10** Ran SP% **111.8**
Speed ratings (Par 101): **92,91,90,89,89 87,87,85,82,81**
toteswingers 1&2 £2.20, 2&3 £2.70, 1&3 £4.70 CSF £159.37 CT £2319.48 TOTE £23.30: £6.40, £3.30, £3.70; EX 258.60.
Owner P Nurcombe **Bred** C A Cyzer **Trained** Earlswood, Monmouths

FOCUS
There was a strong pace on here and the runners were spread across the track late on. Pretty modest form.
Seventeen Seventy Official explanation: jockey said gelding was slowly away
T/Plt: £142.40 to a £1 stake. Pool: £56,851.00 - 291.32 winning tickets. T/Qpdt: £18.10 to a £1 stake. Pool: £4,660.00 - 189.76 winning tickets. IM

[3250] THIRSK (L-H)

Monday, June 25

OFFICIAL GOING: Good to soft (8.5)

Wind: light 1/2 behind Weather: overcast

3436 SUMMER JAZZ EVENING AT THIRSK RACES MAIDEN AUCTION STKS 6f

6:20 (6:22) (Class 6) 2-Y-O **£2,045** (£603; £302) **Stalls** High

Form RPR

1 **Lady Moonlight (IRE)** 2-8-12 0 GrahamLee 13 70+
(Ann Duffield) *dwlt: in rr: hdwy stands' rail over 2f out: led jst jst fnl f: r.o* **20/1**

00 2 1 1/2 **Penny Garcia**[16] 2917 2-8-12 0 DuranFentiman 7 65
(Tim Easterby) *chsd ldrs: led over 1f out: hdd and no ex ins fnl f* **14/1**

0 3 1 1/4 **Teetotal (IRE)**[11] 3074 2-9-3 0 KellyHarrison 14 66
(Nigel Tinkler) *dwlt: bhd: gd hdwy over 1f out: fin wl* **66/1**

2240 4 1 1/4 **Out Of The Blocks**[10] 3112 2-8-12 0 ShaneBKelly(5) 12 63
(Ruth Carr) *dwlt: in rr: hdwy over 2f out: kpt on fnl f* **13/2**[2]

5 5 1 1/2 **Sleepy Haven (IRE)**[28] 2537 2-9-3 0 GrahamGibbons 11 58
(David Barron) *chsd ldrs: drvn over 2f out: kpt on same pce over 1f out* **12/1**

6 1/2 **Garmelow Girl** 2-8-12 0 PhillipMakin 1 52+
(Kevin Ryan) *dwlt: bhd: hdwy over 1f out: styd on ins fnl f* **16/1**

7 nk **Dr Phibes (IRE)** 2-9-3 0 PJMcDonald 8 56
(Alan Swinbank) *dwlt: in rr: kpt on fnl 2f: nvr nr ldrs* **16/1**

8 1 1/4 **Grand Jipeck (IRE)** 2-9-3 0 (t) PatrickMathers 10 52
(Ian McInnes) *chsd ldrs: edgd lft and wknd jst ins fnl f* **66/1**

04 9 nk **Relight My Fire**[42] 2123 2-9-3 0 DavidNolan 6 51
(Tim Easterby) *chsd ldrs on outer: wknd over 1f out* **7/1**[3]

4 10 1 **Marabout (IRE)**[16] 2923 2-9-3 0 PaulMulrennan 4 48
(Mel Brittain) *chsd ldrs: edgd rt and wknd jst ins fnl f* **15/2**

663 11 4 **Moss Quito (IRE)**[10] 3110 2-9-3 0 DanielTudhope 9 36
(David O'Meara) *led: hdd over 1f out: wkng whn hmpd jst ins fnl f: eased towards fin* **9/4**[1]

12 2 3/4 **Passionate Poet** 2-8-10 0 DavidSimmonson(7) 2 28
(Michael Easterby) *dwlt: swtchd rt after s: hdwy over 2f out: wknd 1f out: eased towards fin* **25/1**

00 13 3 3/4 **Poetic Star**[16] 2923 2-9-3 0 TonyHamilton 3 16
(Ben Haslam) *s.i.s: a bhd* **100/1**

14 3 1/4 **Secret Empress** 2-8-12 0 TomEaves 5
(Bryan Smart) *chsd ldrs on outer: wknd and edgd rt 2f out* **8/1**

1m 15.96s (3.26) **Going Correction** +0.50s/f (Yiel) **14** Ran SP% **118.2**

Speed ratings (Par 91): **98,96,94,92,90 90,89,87,87,86 80,77,72,67**

toteswingers:1&2 £51.70, 2&3 £132.40, 1&3 £115.20 CSF £264.22 TOTE £28.60: £7.80, £6.10, £12.50; EX 760.00.

Owner M Wynne **Bred** Sean Madigan **Trained** Constable Burton, N Yorks

FOCUS

Rail moved out 3-4 yards on both bends adding about 12yds to races of 7f and 1m and 17yds to races in excess of 1m. This did not look the strongest of maidens, that was run at a sound enough pace, with plenty in contention a furlong out. High draws dominated and this is modest form.

NOTEBOOK

Lady Moonlight(IRE), a half-sister to 5f 2yo winner King's Approach, was picked up for 6,000euros as a yearling but ran out a convincing winner to give her stable it's first 2yo winner of the season. Nicely berthed in stall 13, she showed good early pace to sit just behind the pace and benefited from a nice run up the stands rail, picking up impressively. While the form does not look the strongest, this was an encouraging debut. (op 16-1)

Penny Garcia, whose latest run over 7f on good to soft at Doncaster came in a better race than this, could not match the pace of the winner over this shorter trip, but stayed on well in second and will be of interest in nurseries, possibly back over 7f.

Teetotal(IRE) showed little on his debut at Nottingham, but ran much better here, making good progress inside the final furlong. It certainly helped that he raced up the stands rail but, over a trip shorter than ideal, this was a promising effort. (op 100-1)

Out Of The Blocks, the most experienced runner in the field, kept responding to pressure but could never get competitive and will find it easier in nurseries. (op 6-1 tchd 7-1)

Dr Phibes(IRE), a first foal whose dam was placed at 9.4f-1m6f, was noted making decent progress over this inadequate trip, and one can expect him to step up on this. (op 14-1)

Grand Jipeck(IRE) looked a nice type and travelled well before fading, and can be expected to come on for this.

Marabout(IRE) showed good pace to get across from his low draw, but raced too keenly, and paid for those early exertions. (op 10-1)

Moss Quito(IRE), who had suggested that the step up to this 6f would suit after three runs over 5f, got out alertly and helped set the pace but found little for pressure, dropping tamely away. (op 11-4)

3437 YORKSHIRE OUTDOORS ADVENTURE EXPERIENCES H'CAP 2m

6:50 (6:50) (Class 5) (0-70,67) 4-Y-O+ **£2,328** (£693; £346; £173) **Stalls** Low

Form RPR

0-24 1 **Nay Secret**[16] 2925 4-7-11 48 NeilFarley(5) 3 55
(Jim Goldie) *mid-div: styd on fnl 2f: led ins fnl f: hld on towards fin* **11/2**[3]

56-3 2 nk **Bijou Dan**[17] 2874 11-8-9 55 PJMcDonald 8 62
(George Moore) *mid-div: sn drvn along: styd on fnl 2f: wnt 2nd last 75yds: no ex nr fin* **7/1**

-250 3 1 3/4 **Dan's Heir**[16] 2925 10-8-0 49 (p) DominicFox(3) 6 54
(Wilf Storey) *chsd ldrs: drvn and outpcd over 3f out: styd on same pce ins fnl f* **10/1**

0006 4 1 3/4 **Amir Pasha (UAE)**[11] 3061 7-8-7 53 (p) TomEaves 2 56
(Micky Hammond) *trckd ldrs: t.k.h: wnt 2nd 2f out: wknd towards fin* **18/1**

-305 5 nk **Mohawk Ridge**[19] 2827 6-9-4 67 (p) LeeTopliss(3) 5 70+
(Michael Dods) *t.k.h: trckd ldrs: wnt 2nd over 6f out: led 3f out: 4 l clr 2f out: hdd ins fnl f: wknd towards fin* **7/2**[1]

0440 6 4 1/2 **Bocamix (FR)**[14] 2978 6-9-4 64 (t) DanielTudhope 4 61
(Andrew Crook) *hld up in rr: kpt on fnl 2f: nvr a factor* **8/1**

16-3 7 1 1/4 **Strikemaster (IRE)**[23] 2698 6-9-0 60 (t) DuranFentiman 9 56
(Lee James) *half-rrd s: in rr: drvn 7f out: nvr on terms* **9/2**[2]

5006 8 1/2 **Grey Command (USA)**[6] 3253 7-9-1 61 PaulMulrennan 10 56
(Mel Brittain) *hld up in rr: drvn 3f out: nvr on terms* **9/1**

5-63 9 4 **Lava Steps (USA)**[4] 3307 6-8-2 48 oh3 (b) PatrickMathers 7 38
(David O'Meara) *led: t.k.h: clr after 3f tl 4f out: hdd 3f out: wknd over 1f out* **17/2**

3m 40.88s (12.58) **Going Correction** +0.60s/f (Yiel) **9** Ran SP% **114.3**

Speed ratings (Par 103): **92,91,90,90,89 87,87,86,84**

toteswingers:1&2 £7.40, 2&3 £12.30, 1&3 £11.60 CSF £43.11 CT £373.68 TOTE £7.70: £2.70, £2.70, £3.60; EX 55.60.

Owner Mrs M Craig **Bred** Fiona Gordon And Fortune Racing **Trained** Uplawmoor, E Renfrews

FOCUS

A competitive staying handicap, run at a sound pace, with five nearly in a line half a furlong out. Modest form, rated around the third.

3438 YORKSHIRE RACING SUMMER FESTIVAL 21ST-29TH JULY MAIDEN STKS 5f

7:20 (7:21) (Class 5) 3-4-Y-O **£2,328** (£693; £346; £173) **Stalls** High

Form RPR

2 1 **Miss Complex**[17] 2871 3-8-12 0 LeeNewman 8 68+
(Brian Meehan) *wnt rt s: chsd ldrs: swtchd stands' side rail jst ins fnl f: styd on to ld fnl strides* **7/4**[1]

6253 2 hd **Elegant Girl (IRE)**[16] 2928 3-8-12 65 (p) DuranFentiman 3 67
(Tim Easterby) *w ldrs: led jst ins fnl f: hdd and no ex nr fin* **3/1**[2]

04- 3 3 **Marmalade Moon**[238] 7194 3-8-12 0 PaulMulrennan 4 56
(Robert Cowell) *w ldrs: led after 1f: hdd jst ins fnl f: kpt on same pce* **20/1**

3-42 4 1 1/2 **How Sweet It Is (IRE)**[116] 750 3-8-12 60 GrahamGibbons 1 51
(James Bethell) *chsd ldrs: rdn 2f out: one pce* **8/1**

56 5 1 1/4 **John Coffey (IRE)**[30] 2470 3-9-3 0 AdrianNicholls 6 51
(David Nicholls) *led 1f: chsd ldrs: one pce fnl 2f* **6/1**[3]

000- 6 2 **Peteron**[282] 6156 4-9-9 40 PaddyAspell 2 46
(Colin Teague) *chsd ldrs on outer: drvn and edgd lft over 2f out: sn wknd* **100/1**

06 7 1/2 **New Lease Of Life**[23] 2695 3-9-3 0 GrahamLee 5 42
(Jim Goldie) *outpcd in rr: kpt on fnl 2f: nvr a factor* **10/1**

5 8 1 **Well Bank (IRE)**[17] 2881 3-8-12 0 ShaneBKelly(5) 9 39
(Colin Teague) *hmpd s: outpcd in rr: kpt on fnl f: nvr on terms* **8/1**

1m 1.9s (2.30) **Going Correction** +0.50s/f (Yiel)

WFA 3 from 4yo 6lb **8** Ran SP% **112.7**

Speed ratings (Par 103): **101,100,95,93,91 88,87,85**

toteswingers:1&2 £1.70, 2&3 £16.10, 1&3 £6.90 CSF £6.77 TOTE £2.60: £1.20, £1.40, £3.60; EX 4.90.

Owner Miss E J Tanner **Bred** D J Weston **Trained** Manton, Wilts

FOCUS

An average-looking maiden, run at a steady pace, with the front two pulling clear inside the final furlong. The winner is rated to her Bath debut, with the sixth limiting the form.

3439 MARKET CROSS JEWELLERS H'CAP 7f

7:50 (7:50) (Class 4) (0-80,79) 4-Y-O+ **£4,140** (£1,232; £615; £307) **Stalls** Low

Form RPR

3-02 1 **Ingleby Exceed (IRE)**[8] 3185 4-9-3 75 DanielTudhope 1 85
(David O'Meara) *chsd ldrs: edgd rt 2f out: wnt 2nd 1f out: styd on to ld post* **11/8**[1]

0-42 2 nse **Mingun Bell (USA)**[26] 2608 5-9-6 78 PhillipMakin 6 88
(Ed de Giles) *trckd ldr: chal over 2f out: led over 1f out: hdd post* **9/2**[2]

0060 3 2 3/4 **Glenridding**[23] 2697 8-9-0 75 DaleSwift(3) 3 78
(James Given) *led: hdd over 1f out: one pce* **14/1**

0000 4 2 1/4 **Day Of The Eagle (IRE)**[9] 3167 6-8-10 68 PaddyAspell 5 65
(Michael Easterby) *in rr after 1f: hdwy on ins over 2f out: kpt on same pce* **33/1**

556- 5 2 1/4 **Nasharra (IRE)**[292] 5820 4-9-3 75 GrahamLee 2 65
(Kevin Ryan) *chsd ldrs: drvn over 2f out: fdd fnl f* **25/1**

-354 6 1 **Defence Council (IRE)**[9] 3169 4-9-6 78 PaulMulrennan 10 66
(Mel Brittain) *chsd ldrs: checked 2f out: fdd fnl f* **13/2**[3]

-000 7 3/4 **Switchback**[9] 3167 4-8-8 73 DavidSimmonson(7) 9 59
(Michael Easterby) *mid-div: outpcd over 2f out: kpt on fnl f* **50/1**

4045 8 2 3/4 **Icy Blue**[8] 3185 4-8-12 70 (v[1]) TomEaves 8 48
(Richard Whitaker) *sn drvn in rr: sme hdwy on outside over 2f out: sn wknd* **15/2**

0112 9 1 **George Benjamin**[13] 3011 5-9-7 79 AdrianNicholls 4 55
(Christopher Kellett) *sn chsng ldrs on inner: effrt 3f out: wknd over 1f out* **12/1**

0050 10 3 1/2 **Dozy Joe**[30] 2500 4-9-5 77 TonyHamilton 7 43
(Ian Wood) *mid-div: drvn over 3f out: lost pl 2f out* **9/1**

1m 30.46s (3.26) **Going Correction** +0.60s/f (Yiel) **10** Ran SP% **118.5**

Speed ratings (Par 105): **105,104,101,99,96 95,94,91,90,86**

toteswingers:1&2 £3.40, 2&3 £10.70, 1&3 £7.30 CSF £7.46 CT £63.35 TOTE £2.70: £1.10, £1.80, £2.80; EX 10.00.

Owner Dave Scott **Bred** Dave Scott **Trained** Nawton, N Yorks

FOCUS

The was a fair handicap run at a sound pace, with the first three home always filling the front three positions, with the front two pulling a long way clear. The winner posted a small peraonal best.

3440 LADIES' DAY SATURDAY 8TH SEPTEMBER BOOK NOW H'CAP 1m 4f

8:20 (8:20) (Class 6) (0-60,60) 4-Y-O+ **£1,940** (£577; £288; £144) **Stalls** Low

Form RPR

0333 1 **Asterales**[9] 3143 5-9-1 54 TonyHamilton 9 63
(Jo Hughes) *chsd ldrs: led over 1f out: all out* **9/1**

0403 2 shd **Sartingo (IRE)**[7] 3236 5-9-7 60 PJMcDonald 4 69
(Alan Swinbank) *trckd ldrs: swtchd rt over 2f out: styd on fnl f: jst failed* **4/1**[1]

0430 3 1 **Bavarian Nordic (USA)**[5] 3290 7-8-12 56 (v) ShaneBKelly(5) 14 63
(Richard Whitaker) *in rr: gd hdwy on ins over 3f out: sn chsng ldrs: styd on same pce ins fnl f* **9/1**

-306 4 1/2 **Tobrata**[5] 3290 6-9-6 59 PaulMulrennan 7 65
(Mel Brittain) *led: hdd over 1f out: kpt on same pce last 100yds* **7/1**

400- 5 5 **Highland Love**[26] 6698 7-8-9 48 (p) GrahamLee 12 46
(Jedd O'Keeffe) *chsd ldrs: drvn over 3f out: wknd appr fnl f* **9/1**

6-05 6 3/4 **Ferney Boy**[21] 2775 6-8-9 48 DuranFentiman 6 45+
(Chris Fairhurst) *mid-div: hdwy over 3f out: one pce fnl 2f* **14/1**

-440 7 2 3/4 **Magic Haze**[111] 811 6-8-12 51 (v[1]) KellyHarrison 5 44
(Sally Hall) *mid-div: hdwy over 2f out: edgd lft over 1f out: nvr trbld ldrs* **25/1**

00/- 8 4 1/2 **Acknowledgement**[562] 7840 10-8-8 52 (bt) GarryWhillans(5) 15 37
(Philip Kirby) *swtchd lft s: in rr: sme hdwy whn hmpd over 2f out: nvr on terms* **6/1**[2]

-020 9 6 **Srimenanti**[18] 1952 4-8-7 46 oh1 (p) BarryMcHugh 8 22
(Brian Rothwell) *sn chsng ldrs: wknd 2f out* **40/1**

130/ 10 hd **Prairie Hawk (USA)**[640] 6328 7-9-0 53 TomEaves 1 28
(Brian Rothwell) *in rr: sme hdwy over 2f out: nvr on terms* **50/1**

000- 11 1 1/2 **Thoroughly Red (IRE)**[254] 6877 7-9-4 60 DaleSwift(3) 16 33
(Suzzanne France) *in rr: effrt and swtchd outside over 2f out: sn wknd* **40/1**

/26- 12 1/2 **Sea Cliff (IRE)**[192] 859 8-9-0 53 LeeNewman 2 25
(Andrew Crook) *chsd ldrs: wknd over 1f out: eased ins fnl f* **50/1**

0-04 13 1 1/2 **Goodlukin Lucy**[12] 3029 5-9-0 53 DanielTudhope 13 23
(Dianne Sayer) *chsd ldrs: effrt and swtchd rt over 2f out: sn wknd* **13/2**[3]

0-01 **14** *nk* **Idealism**[24] 2670 5-8-12 51 PhillipMakin 10 20
(Micky Hammond) *t.k.h in rr: effrt on outer whn hmpd over 2f out: sn wknd* **16/1**

460- **15** *hd* **Marino Prince (FR)**[11] 7112 7-8-5 51 GemmaTutty(7) 3 20
(Joanne Foster) *in rr: bhd fnl 3f* **22/1**

2m 44.41s (8.21) **Going Correction** +0.60s/f (Yiel) 15 Ran SP% **119.7**
Speed ratings (Par 101): **96,95,95,94,91 91,89,86,82,82 81,80,79,79,79**
toteswingers:1&2 £7.30, 2&3 £5.60, 1&3 £19.10 CSF £41.57 CT £340.45 TOTE £11.60: £4.10, £2.20, £4.20; EX 54.90.
Owner G Sheehy **Bred** Miss Nicola Gilbert **Trained** Lambourn, Berks
■ Stewards' Enquiry : Daniel Tudhope two-day ban: careless riding (Jul 9-10)

FOCUS
A moderate yet competitive middle distance handicap run at a steady pace where again it paid to race prominently, with the front four pulling a long way clear. Pretty straightforward form.
Sea Cliff(IRE) Official explanation: trainer said gelding had a breathing problem

3441 THIRSK £30K SUMMER CUP SATURDAY 4TH AUGUST CONDITIONS STKS 5f
8:50 (8:50) (Class 4) 3-Y-0+ **£4,140** (£1,232; £615; £307) **Stalls** High

Form RPR
1320 **1** **Magical Macey (USA)**[30] 2507 5-9-0 101 (b) GrahamGibbons 1 101+
(David Barron) *mde all: styd on strly fnl 2f: v easily* **11/8**[2]

5246 **2** *3 ½* **Borderlescott**[8] 3196 10-9-0 105 DanielTudhope 4 87
(Robin Bastiman) *chsd wnr: swtchd lft 2f out: sn rdn: kpt on same pce* **10/11**[1]

-460 **3** *2 ¼* **Jamesway (IRE)**[10] 3127 4-9-0 82 TonyHamilton 3 79
(Richard Fahey) *trckd ldrs on ins: t.k.h: rdn over 1f out: no imp* **8/1**[3]

4616 **4** *2 ¾* **Rio's Girl**[14] 2982 5-8-9 57 BarryMcHugh 2 64?
(Tony Coyle) *chsd ldrs on outside: drvn 2f out: wknd fnl f* **100/1**

1m 0.97s (1.37) **Going Correction** +0.50s/f (Yiel) 4 Ran SP% **106.6**
Speed ratings (Par 105): **109,103,99,95**
CSF £2.89 TOTE £2.30, EX 3.10.
Owner K J Alderson **Bred** Silver Springs Stud Farm Inc & Mrs J Costelloe **Trained** Maunby, N Yorks

FOCUS
Despite the small field, the presence of dual Nunthorpe winner Borderlescott added real interest to this conditions stakes, that was run at a steady pace with the field well strung out at the line. The winner got an easy lead and did not need to improve.

3442 GO RACING AT BEVERLEY TOMORROW H'CAP 6f
9:20 (9:21) (Class 6) (0-60,60) 3-Y-0+ **£2,045** (£603; £302) **Stalls** High

Form RPR
0444 **1** **Novalist**[14] 2973 4-9-4 52 (b) DanielTudhope 4 60
(Robin Bastiman) *overall ldr far side: kpt on wl fnl f: hld on towards fin: 1st of 9 that gp* **14/1**

00-0 **2** *nk* **Ingleby Angel (IRE)**[8] 3184 3-8-9 50 DuranFentiman 17 55
(David O'Meara) *s.s: racd stands' side: gd hdwy on rail 2f out: styd on wl ins fnl f: tk 2nd on line: 1st of 10 that gp* **33/1**

0-23 **3** *hd* **Besty**[6] 3256 5-9-10 58 PhillipMakin 1 64
(Paul Midgley) *racd far side: chsd ldrs: no ex clsng stages: 2nd of 9 that gp* **9/1**

0006 **4** *hd* **Lizzie (IRE)**[12] 3026 4-9-11 59 (b) GrahamGibbons 5 64
(Tim Easterby) *plunged s: racd far side: sn chsng ldrs: no ex fnl 75yds: 3rd of 9 that gp* **17/2**[3]

5-05 **5** *¾* **Glenlini**[10] 3113 6-9-5 53 GrahamLee 10 56
(Jim Goldie) *racd stands' side: in rr: hdwy on ins over 1f out: styd on towards fin: 2nd of 10 that gp* **20/1**

-065 **6** *nk* **Charles Parnell (IRE)**[47] 1987 9-8-13 47 AdrianNicholls 7 49
(Simon Griffiths) *s.i.s: racd far side: hdwy 2f out: kpt on ins fnl f: 4th of 9 that gp* **50/1**

4035 **7** *½* **Anjomarba (IRE)**[9] 3151 5-9-10 58 TomEaves 3 58
(Conor Dore) *racd far side: chsd ldrs: kpt on same pce fnl f: 5th of 9 that gp* **25/1**

-613 **8** *¾* **Made In The Shade**[31] 2460 3-8-8 56 DanielleMooney(7) 8 52
(Paul Midgley) *racd far side: chsd ldrs: one pce appr fnl f: 6th of 9 that gp* **33/1**

0004 **9** *½* **Cross Of Lorraine (IRE)**[7] 3209 9-9-10 58 (p) TonyHamilton 9 54
(Chris Grant) *racd far side: towards rr: kpt on fnl 2f: nvr a threat: 7th of 9 that gp* **25/1**

3222 **10** *nse* **Fama Mac**[7] 3211 5-9-6 54 PaulMulrennan 12 50+
(Neville Bycroft) *racd stands' side: w ldrs: led that gp 2f out: hung lft and one pce: 3rd of 10 that gp* **3/1**[1]

3020 **11** *3 ½* **Beachwood Bay**[21] 2760 4-9-3 58 NedCurtis(7) 18 43
(Jo Hughes) *racd stands' side: prom: effrt over 2f out: wknd fnl f: 4th of 10 that gp* **16/1**

653 **12** *nk* **Mark Anthony (IRE)**[14] 2981 5-9-0 53 (p) LMcNiff(5) 6 37
(Shaun Harris) *racd far side: chsd ldrs: wknd over 1f out: 8th of 9 that gp* **16/1**

221 **13** *1* **Gracie's Gift (IRE)**[33] 2406 10-9-0 51 (v) DeclanCannon(3) 19 32
(Richard Guest) *racd stands' side: chsd ldrs: wknd over 1f out: 5th of 10 that gp* **8/1**[2]

-346 **14** *nk* **Majestic Breeze (IRE)**[25] 2615 3-8-8 49 BarryMcHugh 15 27
(Brian Ellison) *racd stands' side: mid-div: effrt over 2f out: wknd over 1f out: 6th of 10 that gp* **12/1**

-400 **15** *hd* **Fairy Mist (IRE)**[12] 3032 5-8-10 47 (bt1) LeeTopliss(3) 16 26
(Brian Rothwell) *led stands' side: hung lft and hdd 2f out: sn wknd: 7th of 10 that gp* **25/1**

505- **16** *½* **Ypres**[192] 7778 3-9-5 60 MichaelStainton 20 36
(Jason Ward) *racd stands' side: chsd ldrs on inner: wknd over 1f out: 8th of 10 that gp* **25/1**

2363 **17** *2 ½* **Pilgrim Dancer (IRE)**[125] 640 5-9-7 55 PJMcDonald 11 25
(Tony Coyle) *racd stands' side: mid-div: lost pl 2f out: 9th of 10 that gp* **33/1**

2413 **18** *3 ½* **Trending (IRE)**[21] 2762 3-8-12 56 (b) RaulDaSilva(3) 14 12
(Jeremy Gask) *racd stands' side: in tch on outer: lost pl 2f out: last of 10 that gp* **10/1**

6-34 **19** *20* **Bond Blade**[111] 813 4-9-5 56 DaleSwift(3) 2
(Suzzanne France) *rrd s: a detached last far side: virtually p.u fnl f: t.o: last of 9 that gp* **40/1**

1m 16.36s (3.66) **Going Correction** +0.50s/f (Yiel)
WFA 3 from 4yo+ 7lb 19 Ran SP% **125.2**
Speed ratings (Par 101): **95,94,94,94,93 92,92,91,90,90 85,85,83,83,83 82,79,74,47**
toteswingers:1&2 £91.50, 2&3 £51.60, 1&3 £19.60 CSF £423.47 CT £4456.70 TOTE £17.80: £4.30, £8.20, £3.30, £2.50; EX 596.60.
Owner Ms M Austerfield **Bred** Whitsbury Manor Stud **Trained** Cowthorpe, N Yorks

FOCUS
A moderate yet competitive sprint handicap that split into two even groups from the start. The far side group had the advantage, with eight of the first ten home racing that side. The winner is rated back to something like last year's form.
Fama Mac Official explanation: jockey said gelding hung left throughout
Fairy Mist(IRE) Official explanation: jockey said gelding hung left throughout
T/Plt: £682.50 to a £1 stake. Pool £54,345.75 - 58.12 winning units. T/Qpdt: £9.10 to a £1 stake. Pool £5,299.03 - 429.06 winning units WG

3222 WINDSOR (R-H)
Monday, June 25

OFFICIAL GOING: Good (good to soft in places; 7.3)
Wind: Light, behind Weather: Fine

3443 DAVISBAKERYCARIBBEAN.COM FILLIES' H'CAP 1m 2f 7y
6:10 (6:11) (Class 5) (0-70,70) 3-Y-0+ **£2,264** (£673; £336; £168) **Stalls** Centre

Form RPR
350- **1** **Livia's Dream (IRE)**[271] 6458 3-9-0 68 WilliamBuick 7 77
(Ed Walker) *hld up in last pair: prog on wd outside over 3f out: rdn to chal over 1f out: edgd rt but led last 100yds: drvn out* **9/2**[1]

11-0 **2** *nk* **Bernisdale**[33] 2389 4-9-9 65 KierenFox 10 73
(John Flint) *trckd ldrs: rdn 3f out: prog on outer to ld over 1f out: hrd pressed and carried rt fnl f: hdd last 100yds* **33/1**

5-24 **3** *3* **Idyllic Star (IRE)**[11] 3080 3-8-13 67 LiamKeniry 11 69
(J S Moore) *hld up towards rr gng wl: prog 3f out: drvn and styd on to take 3rd fnl f: ldng pair already gone* **16/1**

4U03 **4** *4 ½* **Tweet Lady**[13] 3002 3-8-13 67 JamesMillman 1 60
(Rod Millman) *pressed ldng pair: led 3f out and kicked on: rdn over 2f out against rail: hdd and btn over 1f out* **10/1**

3266 **5** *1* **Gabrial's Lexi (IRE)**[73] 1364 3-8-9 63 SilvestreDeSousa 4 54+
(Ian Williams) *hld up in midfield: prog over 2f out: trying to cl whn n.m.r over 1f out: sn btn* **14/1**

-006 **6** *4 ½* **Larkrise Star**[12] 3039 5-9-8 64 ShaneKelly 14 46+
(Dean Ivory) *hld up in midfield: gng wl whn trying to cl on ldrs over 2f out: nowhere to go and then squeezed and stmbld over 1f out: eased* **11/1**

0-20 **7** *hd* **If I Were A Boy (IRE)**[7] 3222 5-9-7 70 (p) JoshBaudains(7) 3 52
(Dominic Ffrench Davis) *mde most to 3f out: losing pl whn n.m.r briefly over 1f out* **22/1**

0564 **8** *nk* **Al Aqabah (IRE)**[9] 3154 7-9-8 64 (b) RyanMoore 5 45+
(Brian Gubby) *trckd ldrs: rdn on inner wl over 2f out: hld whn n.m.r against rail over 1f out: eased* **6/1**[2]

-043 **9** *nse* **Chrissycross (IRE)**[10] 3122 3-8-4 63 (p) MarkCoumbe(5) 13 44
(Roger Teal) *pushed along in rr after 3f: swtchd out wd and drvn 3f out: modest late prog* **12/1**

006 **10** *2 ¾* **Rocquaine (IRE)**[22] 2734 3-8-0 54 LukeMorris 9 29
(David Evans) *mostly in midfield: rdn over 3f out: wknd 2f out* **20/1**

-540 **11** *2 ¼* **Shannon Spree**[9] 3142 3-8-13 67 (b1) RichardHughes 15 38
(Richard Hannon) *racd alone early: trckd ldrs on outer fr 7f out: shkn up wl over 2f out: wknd over 1f out* **17/2**[3]

0-56 **12** *1 ½* **Lily Potts**[21] 2768 3-8-11 65 DaneO'Neill 8 33
(Chris Down) *pressed ldr to 3f out: wknd 2f out: eased over 1f out* **20/1**

5-06 **13** *34* **Golden Waters**[25] 2637 5-9-13 69 SebSanders 6
(Eve Johnson Houghton) *trckd ldrs: rdn on inner 3f out: wknd qckly over 2f out: eased and t.o* **9/2**[1]

0-04 **14** *15* **Cloud Illusions (USA)**[40] 2161 4-9-11 67 TadhgO'Shea 2
(Heather Main) *a last: rdn and wknd 4f out: t.o* **33/1**

2m 9.7s (1.00) **Going Correction** +0.225s/f (Good)
WFA 3 from 4yo+ 12lb 14 Ran SP% **118.6**
Speed ratings (Par 100): **105,104,102,98,97 94,94,93,93,91 89,88,61,49**
toteswingers:1&2 £50.30, 2&3 £47.80, 1&3 £15.90 CSF £170.91 CT £2168.85 TOTE £4.80: £2.80, £9.50, £6.70; EX 142.30 Trifecta £424.90 Part won. Pool £574.21 - 0.30 winning units..
Owner Mrs Olivia Hoare **Bred** Mount Coote Stud And M H Dixon **Trained** Newmarket, Suffolk

FOCUS
Inner of straight dolled out 17yds at 6f and 7yds at Winning Post. Top bend dolled out 10yds from normal inner configuration adding 42yds to race distances of 1m and over. The pace appeared sound in what was a moderate fillies' handicap, and the time was relatively good. The winner built on last year's debut form.
Al Aqabah(IRE) Official explanation: jockey said mare suffered interference in running
Shannon Spree Official explanation: jockey said filly suffered interference in running
Golden Waters Official explanation: trainer said mare was unsuited by the good (good to soft places) ground

3444 SKYBET MOBILE FOR IPHONE & ANDROID MAIDEN AUCTION STKS 6f
6:40 (6:42) (Class 5) 2-Y-0 **£2,264** (£673; £336; £168) **Stalls** Low

Form RPR
6 **1** **Front Page News**[30] 2499 2-8-6 0 AndreaAtzeni 11 75+
(Robert Eddery) *pressed ldrs and racd on outer: led wl over 1f out gng strly: edgd rt after: shkn up and styd on wl fnl f* **7/2**[3]

23 **2** *2* **Boleyn**[13] 3009 2-8-4 0 KieranO'Neill 14 67
(Richard Hannon) *hld up in midfield: prog on outer over 2f out: rdn to chse wnr jst over 1f out: styd on but nvr able to chal* **10/3**[2]

0 **3** *2 ¼* **Branson (IRE)**[13] 3010 2-9-2 0 RyanMoore 13 72+
(Richard Hannon) *hld up in midfield gng wl: pushed along and sme prog 2f out: shkn up and styd on to take 3rd ins fnl f: nvr nrr* **16/1**

35 **4** *1 ¼* **Wordsaplenty (IRE)**[9] 3140 2-8-1 0 RyanPowell(3) 2 57
(J S Moore) *pressed ldr: upsides wl over 1f out: fdd* **25/1**

5 *nk* **Blackdown Spirit** 2-8-13 0 JamesMillman 1 65
(Rod Millman) *racd against nr side rail: led to wl over 1f out: fdd* **33/1**

6 *nse* **Fit For A King (IRE)** 2-9-2 0 LukeMorris 15 67+
(John Best) *dwlt: wl in rr and pushed along: rdn and styd on fnl 2f: nrest at fin* **33/1**

5 **7** *¾* **Why So Fast (IRE)**[7] 3223 2-8-3 0 HarryBentley(3) 3 62+
(Stuart Williams) *trckd ldrs towards nr side: gng wl 2f out: stuck bhd rivals fr over 1f out and lost all ch* **12/1**

8 *½* **Swift Cedar (IRE)** 2-8-11 0 KierenFallon 12 59+
(Alan Jarvis) *s.s: wl in rr and rn green: effrt on wd outside 2f out: pushed along and kpt on* **15/2**

9 *shd* **Aint Got A Scooby (IRE)** 2-8-9 0 JohnFahy 6 57
(Clive Cox) *chsd ldrs against nr side rail: cl enough 2f out: hld whn n.m.r over 1f out* **16/1**

10 *nse* **Imperial Oak** 2-8-9 0 SilvestreDeSousa 10 56
(Eve Johnson Houghton) *slowest away: rn green in rr: nvr really a factor: kpt on fnl f* **50/1**

33 **11** *1* **Red Adair (IRE)**[13] 3010 2-9-2 0.......................... RichardHughes 8 60
(Richard Hannon) *broke w ldrs but lost pl over 4f out and sn pushed along: effrt 2f out: nvr gng pce to threaten* **3/1**[1]

12 *1* **Ropehanger** 2-8-4 0.......................... KierenFox 7 45
(Lee Carter) *pressed ldrs to 2f out: wknd qckly fnl f* **66/1**

13 *½* **Fossa** 2-8-11 0.......................... ShaneKelly 9 51
(Dean Ivory) *s.i.s: a in rr: hung lft and almost on far side sn after 1/2-way: kpt on nr fin* **25/1**

0 **14** *12* **Karl Marx (IRE)**[13] 3010 2-8-11 0.......................... DaneO'Neill 5 15
(Mark Usher) *nvr gng wl: a in rr: t.o* **100/1**

1m 14.15s (1.15) **Going Correction** +0.05s/f (Good) **14** Ran SP% **119.5**
Speed ratings (Par 93): **94,91,88,86,86 86,85,84,84,84 83,81,81,65**
toteswingers:1&2 £21.20, 2&3 £7.60, 1&3 £2.00 CSF £14.54 TOTE £4.20: £1.40, £2.30, £3.60; EX 16.30 Trifecta £88.30 Pool £626.94 - 5.25 winning units..
Owner Gurnett,Rayment,Anderson & Lammin **Bred** Helen Plumbly And Wendy Balding **Trained** Newmarket, Suffolk

FOCUS
Just an ordinary juvenile maiden, but a race that should provide winners none the less. The winner built on her debut effort.

NOTEBOOK
Front Page News played up a bit beforehand, unshipping her rider when presented to the stalls, but she travelled strongly into contention and the result never looked in doubt once taking over. She'd shaped with plenty of promise on debut at Newbury (in season) and should have more to offer. (op 5-2)
Boleyn ran another solid race from her wide draw. Whether it be a maiden or nursery, there's a race in her. (tchd 7-2)
Branson(IRE) was another drawn wide who couldn't really go the gallop early (half-brother to a 1m2f/triple bumper winner). He finished nicely, stepping up markedly on his debut effort, and should relish 7f. (op 20-1)
Wordsaplenty(IRE) showed pace and can pick up a race when dropping in grade.
Blackdown Spirit, half-brother to a pair of 6f winners, knew his job and showed enough to suggest he'll be capable of winning a small race.
Fit For A King(IRE), half-brother to a French 1m7f winner, is thought to be above average by his trainer, but he was drawn wide and fared quite well considering. (op 40-1)
Why So Fast(IRE) ran to a similar level as on last week's debut and would have been closer with a better run through. Official explanation: jockey said filly was denied a clear run (op 16-1)
Swift Cedar(IRE), whose dam was placed over 1m, wasn't the best away and got behind. He tried to close out wide and should benefit from an extra furlong. (op 14-1)
Red Adair(IRE) was below par, soon losing his place and finding little. Perhaps he is more of a nursery type now. (op 7-2 tchd 4-1)

3445 LOVE TRAVEL LOVE TRAILFINDERS H'CAP 6f
7:10 (7:19) (Class 4) (0-85,85) 3-Y-O **£4,851** (£1,443; £721; £360) **Stalls** Low

Form RPR
31-0 **1** **Duke Of Firenze**[63] 1565 3-9-2 **80**.......................... RyanMoore 2 93+
(Sir Michael Stoute) *w.w in mdifield: prog and plld off rail 2f out: led over 1f out: drvn and r.o wl* **10/3**[1]

0-40 **2** *1 ¾* **Jack Who's He (IRE)**[50] 1892 3-9-5 **83**.......................... RichardThomas 7 90
(David Evans) *towards rr: rdn and prog on outer fr 2f out: chsd wnr jst over 1f out: styd on but nvr able to chal* **20/1**

3-1 **3** *2 ½* **Fast Finian (IRE)**[12] 3041 3-8-9 **73**.......................... JimCrowley 3 72
(Paul D'Arcy) *trckd ldrs: tried to chal 2f out but sn outpcd: wnt 3rd 1f out: no imp* **15/2**[3]

-226 **4** *½* **Royal Reyah**[16] 2914 3-8-12 **76**.......................... FergusSweeney 5 73
(Stuart Kittow) *towards rr: rdn over 2f out: taken to outer over 1f out: styd on to press for 3rd nr fin* **16/1**

1 **5** *3 ¾* **Sir Pedro**[37] 2262 3-9-7 **85**.......................... MichaelHills 8 70
(Charles Hills) *prom: chsd ldr 1/2-way: chal 2f out: wknd fnl f: eased* **10/3**[1]

5044 **6** *1 ¼* **Mister Musicmaster**[21] 2764 3-9-0 **78**..........(b[1]) JamesMillman 4 59
(Rod Millman) *led: clr over 3f out: hdd & wknd over 1f out* **20/1**

-000 **7** *1 ¼* **Marygold**[35] 2347 3-8-13 **77**.......................... KierenFox 11 54
(Lee Carter) *in tch on outer: effrt 2f out: wknd qckly over 1f out* **66/1**

10-0 **8** *1 ¼* **Gung Ho Jack**[68] 1457 3-9-3 **81**.......................... LukeMorris 6 54
(John Best) *s.i.s: sn pushed along: a in last trio: no ch over 1f out* **33/1**

50-0 **9** *2 ¼* **Wise Venture (IRE)**[30] 2485 3-9-4 **82**.......................... KierenFallon 12 48
(Alan Jarvis) *a in last trio: shkn up and no prog over 2f out* **9/1**

1100 **10** *2 ½* **Dishy Guru**[23] 2714 3-9-1 **79**.......................... LiamKeniry 9 37
(Michael Blanshard) *a in last trio: shkn up and no prog 2f out* **40/1**

41-0 **P** **Heyward Girl (IRE)**[68] 1457 3-9-3 **81**.......................... AndreaAtzeni 1
(Robert Eddery) *chsd ldr to 1/2-way: wknd rapidly 2f out: t.o whn p.u and dismntd nr fin* **9/2**[2]

1m 13.06s (0.06) **Going Correction** +0.05s/f (Good) **11** Ran SP% **108.4**
Speed ratings (Par 101): **101,98,95,94,89 88,86,84,81,78**
toteswingers:1&2 £18.50, 2&3 £25.50, 1&3 £4.10 CSF £63.28 CT £349.84 TOTE £4.80: £1.50, £4.60, £1.60; EX 80.00 Trifecta £317.50 Part won. Pool £429.17 - 0.20 winning units..
Owner Cheveley Park Stud **Bred** Cheveley Park Stud Ltd **Trained** Newmarket, Suffolk
■ Bella Ophelia was withdrawn (8/1, broke out of the stalls). R4 applies, deduct 10p in the £.

FOCUS
There was a false start to this sprint handicap, with Bella Ophelia bursting out of her gate and being forced to withdraw. Several of the runners took quite a while to pull up, among them Fast Finian and Sir Pedro. The pace was decent. The form is rated around the second.

3446 SEE THE WORLD WITH TRAILFINDERS H'CAP 1m 67y
7:40 (7:44) (Class 4) (0-85,82) 3-Y-O **£4,851** (£1,443; £721; £360) **Stalls** Low

Form RPR
5250 **1** **Ocean Tempest**[16] 2930 3-9-4 **79**..........................(p) BrettDoyle 6 85
(John Ryan) *led at gd pce but hdd after 2f: led again over 2f out: hrd rdn and jnd fnl f: styd on wl nr fin* **11/2**[2]

-626 **2** *hd* **Presburg (IRE)**[45] 2021 3-9-7 **82**.......................... LiamKeniry 7 87
(Joseph Tuite) *hld up in 6th: prog over 2f out: chal over 1f out: hrd rdn and w wnr fnl f: nt qckn last strides* **12/1**

621- **3** *1* **Restaurateur (IRE)**[215] 7521 3-9-1 **76**.......................... DavidProbert 2 79
(Andrew Balding) *trckd ldrs in 5th: taken to outer and prog over 2f out: drvn to chal 1f out: no ex last 50yds* **7/1**

-410 **4** *1 ½* **Dixie's Dream (IRE)**[16] 2930 3-9-2 **80**.......................... SeanLevey(3) 8 80
(Richard Hannon) *hld up in 8th: taken to outer and prog 2f out: drvn to chal 1f out: fdd last 100yds* **11/1**

4226 **5** *5* **Tight Lipped (IRE)**[32] 2428 3-9-1 **76**.......................... LukeMorris 11 64
(James Eustace) *trckd ldng trio: cl up 2f out: wknd jst over 1f out* **16/1**

4-00 **6** *1 ½* **Poetic Lord**[17] 2897 3-9-4 **79**.......................... RichardHughes 5 64
(Richard Hannon) *trckd ldng pair: nt qckn 2f out: wknd over 1f out* **9/1**

3-63 **7** *8* **Strident Force**[41] 2145 3-8-12 **73**.......................... RyanMoore 9 39
(Sir Michael Stoute) *dismntd and inspected bef s: led after 2f at str pce: hdd over 2f out against rail: wknd and eased* **4/1**[1]

00- **8** *5* **Cockney Dancer**[276] 6296 3-9-5 **80**.......................... MichaelHills 3 35
(Charles Hills) *hld up in 7th: pushed along and no prog over 2f out: wknd rapidly and eased over 1f out* **6/1**[3]

11 **9** *19* **Dellbuoy**[17] 2898 3-9-7 **82**.......................... IanMongan 10
(Pat Phelan) *hld up in last pair: effrt on outer 4f out: no prog over 2f out: wl btn whn lost action over 1f out and virtually p.u* **4/1**[1]

1120 **10** *1 ½* **Oratorian (IRE)**[124] 659 3-9-5 **80**.......................... JamesDoyle 1
(Sylvester Kirk) *hld up in last pair: shkn up and no prog over 2f out: wknd over 1f out: virtually p.u* **40/1**

1m 46.22s (1.52) **Going Correction** +0.225s/f (Good) **10** Ran SP% **116.5**
Speed ratings (Par 101): **101,100,99,98,93 91,83,78,59,58**
toteswingers:1&2 £15.40, 2&3 £29.30, 1&3 £11.90 CSF £69.33 CT £469.64 TOTE £7.90: £2.00, £5.20, £2.70; EX 132.90 Trifecta £599.70 Part won. Pool £810.49 - 0.20 winning units..
Owner W McLuskey & C Little **Bred** Old Mill Stud Ltd And Oomswell Ltd **Trained** Newmarket, Suffolk

FOCUS
The pace was quite strong and the front four pulled clear. The form appears pretty sound.
Strident Force Official explanation: jockey said gelding lost two shoes
Cockney Dancer Official explanation: trainer's rep said filly lost its action and hung left

3447 TRAILFINDERS TRAVEL EXPERTS MAIDEN STKS 1m 67y
8:10 (8:12) (Class 5) 3-Y-O **£2,264** (£673; £336; £168) **Stalls** Low

Form RPR
5 **1** **Cannizaro House (IRE)**[27] 2585 3-9-3 0.......................... FergusSweeney 7 83
(Terry Clement) *wl in tch: prog over 3f out: led over 2f out: clr over 1f out: rdn out* **6/1**[3]

60 **2** *3 ¾* **Cool Sky**[27] 2584 3-9-3 0.......................... JimCrowley 5 74
(William Knight) *trckd ldrs: gng wl 3f out: pushed along over 2f out and sn outpcd: shkn up over 1f out: styd on to take 2nd last strides* **12/1**

2 **3** *nk* **Barkis**[20] 2800 3-9-3 0.......................... KierenFallon 8 74
(Luca Cumani) *trckd ldng pair: shkn up after 1/2-way: chal over 2f out but sn outpcd: chsd wnr after and no imp: lost 2nd last strides* **5/4**[1]

0-4 **4** *3* **Cayuga**[54] 1754 3-9-3 0.......................... RyanMoore 10 67
(Sir Michael Stoute) *towards rr: pumped along 4f out: outpcd fr 3f out: kpt on to take 4th over 1f out: no imp after* **5/2**[2]

0 **5** *4* **London Silver**[65] 1512 3-9-3 0.......................... DaneO'Neill 9 58
(Henry Candy) *in tch in midfield: pushed along over 3f out: no imp 2f out: fdd* **40/1**

00 **6** *hd* **Little Miss Mayhem (IRE)**[26] 2601 3-8-12 0.......... MircoMimmocchi 6 52
(Philip McBride) *wl in rr: pushed along fnl 3f on outer: nvr on terms* **80/1**

34 **7** *2 ½* **Admiralty**[18] 2865 3-9-3 0.......................... JamieSpencer 12 51
(Ismail Mohammed) *led to over 2f out: sn wknd* **13/2**

00- **8** *shd* **Feb Thirtyfirst**[201] 7650 3-9-3 0.......................... IanMongan 14 51
(Sheena West) *pressed ldr to over 3f out: wknd sn after* **66/1**

0 **9** *hd* **Kaypea**[35] 2344 3-8-12 0.......................... HayleyTurner 4 46
(Simon Dow) *a towards rr: shkn up and no prog 3f out* **66/1**

10 *16* **Otto Nicolai** 3-9-3 0.......................... LiamKeniry 11 14
(J S Moore) *a in rr: lost tch sn after 1/2-way: t.o* **66/1**

P **La Troisieme** 3-8-12 0..........................(b[1]) ShaneKelly 13
(Dean Ivory) *s.s: sn t.o: over a f bhd whn p.u over 2f out* **100/1**

1m 46.13s (1.43) **Going Correction** +0.225s/f (Good) **11** Ran SP% **117.5**
Speed ratings (Par 99): **101,97,96,93,89 89,87,87,86,70**
toteswingers:1&2 £12.00, 2&3 £4.30, 1&3 £3.90 CSF £70.76 TOTE £10.50: £2.10, £2.90, £1.10; EX 103.20 Trifecta £447.50 Pool £846.68 - 1.40 winning units..
Owner Miss S Hickland **Bred** Pier House Stud **Trained** Newmarket, Suffolk

FOCUS
Quite an ordinary maiden, but the well backed winner was no fluke and the form makes sense.

3448 CITIBANK SUPPORTING CLIC SARGENT H'CAP 1m 3f 135y
8:40 (8:42) (Class 5) (0-75,74) 3-Y-O **£2,264** (£673; £336; £168) **Stalls** Centre

Form RPR
2-00 **1** **Scarlet Whispers**[22] 2733 3-9-5 **72**.......................... MickyFenton 12 79
(Pam Sly) *led after 1f: mde rest: urged along over 3f out: styd on wl whn pressed fr over 1f out* **50/1**

3334 **2** *1 ¼* **Viola Da Gamba (IRE)**[26] 2613 3-8-10 **63**.......................... JimCrowley 8 68
(William Knight) *trckd ldng pair: chsd wnr 3f out: drvn and tried to cl over 1f out: kpt on same pce* **20/1**

0206 **3** *nk* **Thecornishcockney**[3] 3345 3-9-0 **67**.......................... BrettDoyle 9 71
(John Ryan) *hld up in last quartet: prog on wd outside fr 3f out: drvn to dispute 2nd over 1f out: nt qckn* **20/1**

-201 **4** *hd* **Burnham**[7] 3228 3-9-3 **70** 6ex.......................... RichardHughes 4 74+
(Hughie Morrison) *hld up in 10th: pushed along 3f out: sme prog 2f out: drvn and styd on wl fnl f: nrly snatched 3rd* **5/2**[1]

1265 **5** *¾* **Sheila's Buddy**[18] 2860 3-9-4 **71**.......................... LiamKeniry 14 74
(J S Moore) *t.k.h: hld up in 8th: prog on outer over 2f out: drvn to dispute 2nd over 1f out: one pce after* **20/1**

1625 **6** *¾* **Gabrial's King (IRE)**[23] 2716 3-9-2 **69**.......................... JamieSpencer 2 71+
(Ian Williams) *hld up in last quartet: prog on outer fr 3f out: chsd ldrs over 1f out but hanging: nt qckn* **13/2**[3]

0-60 **7** *2 ¼* **Just When**[39] 2196 3-8-7 **67**.......................... DanielMuscutt(7) 3 65
(Andrew Balding) *hld up in last pair: stl wl in rr and pushed along 2f out: rdn and kpt on after: no ch* **16/1**

1-40 **8** *3 ¼* **Instrumentalist (IRE)**[31] 2449 3-9-7 **74**.......................... LukeMorris 5 66
(John Best) *hld up in 9th: rdn 3f out: no imp and wl btn 2f out: wknd* **16/1**

-005 **9** *1 ¾* **Cappielow Park**[26] 2605 3-9-3 **70**.......................... WilliamCarson 15 59
(William Jarvis) *trckd ldrs in 5th: rdn over 3f out: wknd 2f out* **14/1**

0-03 **10** *1 ¼* **Alvitude (USA)**[28] 2560 3-9-4 **71**.......................... JamesDoyle 11 58
(Roger Charlton) *trckd ldrs disputing 6th: rdn 3f out: fading whn short of room briefly 2f out* **9/2**[2]

-054 **11** *2 ½* **Mizbah**[21] 2772 3-9-6 **73**.......................... SilvestreDeSousa 7 56
(Saeed Bin Suroor) *trckd ldrs disputing 6th: shkn up and no prog 3f out: lost pl over 2f out: eased over 1f out* **15/2**

3205 **12** *shd* **Kudoz**[26] 2613 3-9-5 **72**..........................(t) JohnFahy 1 55
(Clive Cox) *trckd ldng trio: rdn 3f out: wknd over 2f out* **20/1**

43-0 **13** *¾* **Mr Churchill (IRE)**[32] 2408 3-9-5 **72**.......................... AhmedAjtebi 13 53
(Mahmood Al Zarooni) *led 1f: chsd wnr to 3f out: wknd 2f out: eased* **14/1**

304 **14** *37* **Kashgar**[37] 2287 3-9-6 **73**.......................... HayleyTurner 6
(Michael Bell) *dwlt: t.k.h: hld up last: no prog 3f out: sn wknd: virtually p.u* **20/1**

2m 33.07s (3.57) **Going Correction** +0.225s/f (Good) **14** Ran SP% **122.7**
Speed ratings (Par 99): **97,96,95,95,95 94,93,91,90,89 87,87,86,62**
toteswingers:1&2 £126.50, 2&3 £126.50, 1&3 £126.50 CSF £815.51 CT £18739.01 TOTE £74.60: £15.30, £7.00, £5.80; EX 857.80 TRIFECTA Not won..
Owner G A Libson **Bred** Miss K Rausing & Mr & Mrs A E Pakenham **Trained** Thorney, Cambs
■ Stewards' Enquiry : Daniel Muscutt two-day ban: used whip above permitted level (Jul 9-10)

FOCUS
A clean sweep for outsiders, with the front pair benefiting from prominent rides. The pace was ordinary and it was a bit of a muddling race. The winner is rated up 3lb on his previous best.
Alvitude(USA) Official explanation: jockey said gelding was denied a clear run
T/Jkpt: Not won. T/Plt: £6,240.50 to a £1 stake. Pool £113,269.65 - 13.25 winning units. T/Qpdt: £1,726.90 to a £1 stake. Pool £8,868.30 - 3.80 winning units. JN

3229 WOLVERHAMPTON (A.W) (L-H)
Monday, June 25

OFFICIAL GOING: Standard
Wind: Light across Weather: Overcast

3449 HORIZONS RESTAURANT AMATEUR RIDERS' (S) STKS 1m 4f 50y(P)
2:15 (2:15) (Class 6) 4-Y-O+ **£1,646** (£506; £253) **Stalls** Low

Form RPR
4103 **1** **Rub Of The Relic (IRE)**[27] 2588 7-10-10 57.............(v) MissHDukes(7) 4 63
(Paul Midgley) *led: hdd 3f out: led again over 2f out: rdn ins fnl f: jst hld on* **7/1**
-156 **2** *hd* **Maid Of Meft**[52] 1822 5-10-9 63................................ MissWGibson(3) 12 58+
(Paul Midgley) *s.i.s: hld up: hdwy over 5f out: outpcd over 2f out: r.o wl ins fnl f: jst failed* **11/2**[3]
04- **3** *nk* **Cordillera**[21] 3478 4-10-2 0.. MrNSlatter(5) 6 52
(Donald McCain) *chsd ldrs: rdn over 1f out: r.o* **28/1**
00-0 **4** *½* **Runaway Tiger (IRE)**[7] 3216 4-10-5 60.........(v[1]) MissLucySaunders(7) 7 56
(Paul D'Arcy) *chsd wnr tl led 3f out: hdd over 2f out: sn rdn: r.o* **66/1**
0626 **5** *¾* **Spartan King (IRE)**[13] 2997 4-10-12 56........................ MrJHodson(5) 8 60+
(Ian Williams) *stdd s: hld up: hdwy over 1f out: sn rdn: r.o* **17/2**
2034 **6** *nk* **Overrule (USA)**[23] 2694 8-10-10 70................(p) MissFrancesHarper(7) 9 60
(Jason Ward) *chsd ldrs: rdn over 1f out: styd on* **3/1**[1]
-016 **7** *shd* **William's Way**[7] 3216 10-11-0 56.................................(tp) MrCMartin(3) 2 60
(Ian Wood) *s.i.s: hld up: hdwy 6f out: rdn over 1f out: r.o* **7/1**
-145 **8** *1 ¾* **Dew Reward (IRE)**[17] 2874 4-10-12 58.......................... PhilipPrince(5) 5 57
(Bill Turner) *chsd ldrs: rdn over 2f out: sn outpcd: r.o ins fnl f* **20/1**
2004 **9** *¾* **Polly Holder (IRE)**[7] 3216 4-10-0 56.........................(p) MrsRWilson(7) 11 46
(Paul D'Arcy) *hld up: hdwy over 5f out: outpcd over 2f out: r.o ins fnl f* **8/1**
2323 **10** *½* **Kames Park (IRE)**[114] 786 10-10-5 66.............................. MrsAGuest(7) 1 50
(Richard Guest) *s.s: hld up: r.o ins fnl f: nvr nr to chal* **9/2**[2]
11 *6* **Marineside (FR)**[22] 5-10-7 60.................................... MrMJMcIntyre(5) 3 40
(Kim Bailey) *prom: lost pl over 6f out: wknd over 3f out* **66/1**
2m 45.81s (4.71) **Going Correction** 0.0s/f (Stan) **11** Ran SP% **116.4**
Speed ratings (Par 101): **84,83,83,83,82 82,82,81,80,80 76**
toteswingers 1&2 £7.40, 2&3 £19.70, 1&3 £18.40 CSF £43.44 TOTE £8.70: £3.20, £1.80, £4.70; EX 61.90 TRIFECTA Not won..There was no bid for the winner.
Owner O R Dukes **Bred** M J Wiley **Trained** Westow, N Yorks
■ The first winner under rules for Harriet Dukes.

FOCUS
An ordinary race, but a one-two for trainer Paul Midgley. The winner is rated in line with his recent best while the fifth is rated close to form.
Kames Park(IRE) Official explanation: jockey said, regarding running and riding, that her orders were to settle in rear and make her move around the field as the gelding is reluctant to come between horses, it was slow out of the stalls and as a result was further back than she had intended, she had to wait to make her effort until the home straight, having been carried wide on the final bend.

3450 MIRROR PUNTERS CLUB H'CAP 5f 20y(P)
2:45 (2:46) (Class 5) (0-75,78) 3-Y-O **£2,264** (£673; £336; £168) **Stalls** Low

Form RPR
6531 **1** **Electric Qatar**[7] 3234 3-9-10 **78** 6ex.......................... RichardKingscote 1 84+
(Tom Dascombe) *hld up: hdwy over 1f out: swtchd rt ins fnl f: r.o to ld towards fin: readily* **5/6**[1]
6626 **2** *½* **Kyanight (IRE)**[17] 2869 3-9-2 **70**.. AdamKirby 5 74
(Clive Cox) *chsd ldrs: rdn over 1f out: led ins fnl f: hdd towards fin* **6/1**[2]
5342 **3** *½* **Economic Crisis (IRE)**[5] 3276 3-8-2 **56** oh2...................... PaulQuinn 2 58
(Alan Berry) *awkward leaving stalls: sn pushed along in rr: rdn and hdwy over 1f out: r.o: nt rch ldrs* **12/1**
4-40 **4** *1 ½* **Little China**[34] 2375 3-9-5 **73**.. WilliamCarson 4 70
(William Muir) *in rr: drvn along 1/2-way: r.o u.p ins fnl f: nrst fin* **13/2**[3]
0653 **5** *nk* **Gran Canaria Queen**[12] 3028 3-8-0 **57** oh6 ow1...(v) DeclanCannon(3) 6 53
(Ian Semple) *chsd ldr tl led over 1f out: rdn and hung lft ins fnl f: sn hdd: styd on same pce* **33/1**
4516 **6** *¾* **My Name Is Sam**[21] 2762 3-8-6 **60**................................(b) LukeMorris 7 53
(Ronald Harris) *chsd ldrs: rdn and hung lft 1/2-way: sn outpcd: kpt on ins fnl f* **20/1**
1650 **7** *2 ¼* **Bookiesindexdotnet**[7] 3234 3-9-7 **75**..........................(t) FrannyNorton 3 60
(J R Jenkins) *led: hdd over 1f out: hmpd and no ex ins fnl f* **10/1**
0-50 **8** *2 ¼* **Star Kingdom (IRE)**[56] 1709 3-8-6 **60**............................ PaulHanagan 8 37
(Robert Mills) *hld up: effrt 1/2-way: rdn and wknd over 1f out* **25/1**
-534 **9** *1 ½* **Saint Boniface**[135] 524 3-8-12 **66**.................................. PatCosgrave 9 37
(Peter Makin) *s.i.s: hld up: rdn 1/2-way: a in rr* **22/1**
1m 1.79s (-0.51) **Going Correction** 0.0s/f (Stan) **9** Ran SP% **114.9**
Speed ratings (Par 99): **104,103,102,100,99 98,94,91,88**
toteswingers 1&2 £2.70, 2&3 £6.90, 1&3 £3.10 CSF £5.55 CT £35.32 TOTE £1.90: £1.10, £1.50, £2.90; EX 6.30 Trifecta £62.50 Pool: £754.37 - 8.93 winning units..
Owner A Black & M Owen **Bred** Miss Nicola Kent **Trained** Malpas, Cheshire
■ Stewards' Enquiry : Declan Cannon two-day ban: careless riding (Jul 9-10)

FOCUS
An ordinary handicap that was a virtual replay of one here the week before. The winner confirmed his recent effort while the runner-up ran her best race since her juvenile debut.
My Name Is Sam Official explanation: jockey said gelding hung badly left-handed

3451 STEAMERBOT.COM STEAMERS AND DRIFTERS BETFAIR BOT CLAIMING STKS 5f 216y(P)
3:15 (3:16) (Class 5) 3-Y-O **£2,264** (£673; £336; £168) **Stalls** Low

Form RPR
-000 **1** **Aubrietia**[18] 2862 3-8-0 43...(b[1]) NickyMackay 2 60
(Ed Vaughan) *chsd ldr tl led wl over 2f out: rdn and hdd 1f out: rallied to ld nr fin* **20/1**
0242 **2** *nk* **Marinus (IRE)**[20] 2786 3-8-2 62...................................... SophieDoyle(3) 3 64
(Sylvester Kirk) *chsd ldrs: led 1f out: sn rdn: rdr dropped reins wl ins fnl f: hdd nr fin* **7/2**[2]
504 **3** *4* **Miserere Mei (IRE)**[7] 3218 3-7-13 48.....................(e) DeclanCannon(3) 6 48
(Richard Guest) *hld up: hdwy over 2f out: rdn over 1f out: hung lft ins fnl f: styd on same pce* **16/1**
1454 **4** *1 ¾* **Tiablo (IRE)**[13] 3005 3-8-0 61... JamieMackay 8 41
(David Evans) *chsd ldrs: rdn over 1f out: edgd lft and wknd fnl f* **12/1**
-003 **5** *¾* **Fayr Fall (IRE)**[5] 3285 3-8-11 68.. PaulHanagan 4 49
(Tim Easterby) *sn pushed along in rr: hdwy u.p over 1f out: nvr nrr* **9/4**[1]
-050 **6** *1 ¼* **Aquasulis (IRE)**[8] 3188 3-8-6 70...................................... FrannyNorton 10 40
(David Evans) *led: hdd wl over 2f out: sn rdn: wknd fnl f* **5/1**[3]
3-00 **7** *1 ¼* **Mae Rose Cottage (IRE)**[11] 3083 3-8-4 57.......................... JoeFanning 5 34
(Barney Curley) *prom: rdn over 2f out: wknd over 1f out* **16/1**
41-0 **8** *nk* **Fifteentwo**[20] 2795 3-9-5 68.. AdrianNicholls 7 48
(David Nicholls) *stdd s: hld up: plld hrd: nvr nr to chal* **10/1**
3336 **9** *hd* **Faraway**[28] 2547 3-8-5 61..(b) LukeMorris 9 34
(Ronald Harris) *mid-div: drvn along over 2f out: wknd over 1f out* **10/1**
0500 **10** *12* **Barbarella Blue (IRE)**[7] 3214 3-8-0 62.............................. PaulQuinn 1
(Alan Berry) *sn pushed along in rr: bhd fr 1/2-way* **66/1**
1m 13.91s (-1.09) **Going Correction** 0.0s/f (Stan) **10** Ran SP% **113.6**
Speed ratings (Par 99): **107,106,101,98,97 96,94,94,93,77**
toteswingers 1&2 £16.60, 2&3 £9.50, 1&3 £51.00 CSF £86.80 TOTE £26.60: £6.50, £1.50, £4.50; EX 150.60 TRIFECTA Not won..
Owner C J Murfitt **Bred** C J Murfitt **Trained** Newmarket, Suffolk

FOCUS
Low-grade form rated through the runner-up.
Fayr Fall(IRE) Official explanation: jockey said gelding never travelled

3452 BRITISH STALLION STUDS SUPPORTING BRITISH RACING E B F MAIDEN STKS 5f 216y(P)
3:45 (3:46) (Class 5) 2-Y-O **£3,137** (£933; £466; £233) **Stalls** Low

Form RPR
0 **1** **Claude Greenwood**[18] 2844 2-9-3 0................................ MartinHarley 1 75
(Sylvester Kirk) *mde all: rdn over 1f out: edgd rt: styd on* **33/1**
54 **2** *1 ¼* **Club House (IRE)**[16] 2934 2-9-3 0................................. PaulHanagan 4 71
(Robert Mills) *a.p: pushed along over 2f out: rdn to chse wnr over 1f out: styd on same pce ins fnl f* **5/6**[1]
3 *2 ¾* **Lars Krister (IRE)** 2-8-10 0..............................(tp) NicoleNordblad(7) 5 63
(Hans Adielsson) *chsd wnr tl nt clr run over 1f out: hung lft and no ex ins fnl f* **33/1**
4 *2 ½* **Miako (USA)** 2-9-3 0... AdamKirby 2 56
(Marco Botti) *chsd ldrs: shkn up over 2f out: wknd and eased fnl f* **9/4**[2]
0 **5** *5* **Smooth Handle**[4] 3303 2-9-3 0................................ RichardKingscote 7 40
(Tom Dascombe) *chsd ldrs: pushed along 1/2-way: rdn and wknd over 2f out* **12/1**
6 *4 ½* **Kingsville** 2-9-3 0.. JoeFanning 6 27
(Mark Johnston) *sn outpcd* **7/1**[3]
7 *hd* **Borough Boy (IRE)** 2-9-0 0.. DaleSwift(3) 3 26
(Derek Shaw) *racd keenly: w ldrs tl wknd over 2f out* **28/1**
1m 16.24s (1.24) **Going Correction** 0.0s/f (Stan) **7** Ran SP% **114.8**
Speed ratings (Par 93): **91,89,85,82,75 69,69**
toteswingers 1&2 £5.60, 2&3 £7.40, 1&3 £15.90 CSF £62.26 TOTE £24.00: £6.40, £1.10; EX 69.60.
Owner Miss Amanda Rawding **Bred** Mrs J A Rawding **Trained** Upper Lambourn, Berks

FOCUS
This didn't look a strong maiden, and the early gallop was steady. The runner-up was probably a shade below form.

NOTEBOOK
Claude Greenwood showed some ability on his debut, but this was still a big jump up. He broke well this time, was up there the whole way on the rail, and held off the favourite well. He's bred to get better as he steps up in trip (dam won at up to 1m2f) so he could be interesting for nurseries over 7f.
Club House(IRE) had posted sound enough efforts in defeat on his first two starts and was the one to beat here, but he got trapped wider than ideal, raced keenly off the steady pace and ultimately paid the price. (op 11-10)
Lars Krister(IRE), wearing a tongue-tie and cheekpieces, did best of the newcomers, mixing it with the winner until hanging left and being seen off in the closing stages. He should come on for this and his pedigree (half-brother to several winners, including Sgt Schultz, who was at his best on Polytrack) suggests a longer distance is going to suit him as he gets older. (op 28-1)
Miako(USA), whose sales price went up from 20,000gns as a yearling to 65,000GBP as a 2-y-o, didn't shape badly and should benefit from the outing. (op 11-4 tchd 2-1)
Smooth Handle, who apparently couldn't cope with the testing ground on his debut at Ripon, again struggled to go the pace and he was also caught wide. (op 17-2)
Kingsville ran green throughout. The latter is out of an unraced half-sister to top-class miler Soviet Song, and better can be expected in time. (op 5-1 tchd 8-1)

3453 DOWNLOAD OUR IPHONE APP MEDIAN AUCTION MAIDEN STKS 1m 141y(P)
4:15 (4:15) (Class 6) 3-Y-O **£1,704** (£503; £251) **Stalls** Low

Form RPR
3- **1** **Mugazala (IRE)**[324] 4804 3-8-12 0.................................. PaulHanagan 5 81+
(Ed Dunlop) *hld up: racd keenly: hdwy over 3f out: shkn up to ld over 1f out: sn clr: easily* **1/5**[1]
20 **2** *8* **Queen Cassiopeia**[22] 2734 3-8-12 0.............................. HayleyTurner 2 63
(J R Jenkins) *chsd ldr tl led over 2f out: pushed along and hdd over 1f out: sn outpcd* **6/1**[2]
0 **3** *3* **Kodiac Island**[18] 2865 3-8-12 0.. FrannyNorton 3 56
(Ed McMahon) *led: pushed along and hdd over 2f out: no ex fr over 1f out* **12/1**[3]
0 **4** *7* **Shakespeare Dancer**[47] 1989 3-8-7 0................................ DavidKenny(5) 1 40
(James Evans) *prom tl wknd over 2f out* **66/1**
0 **5** *3 ¼* **Austerity Boy**[17] 2881 3-9-3 0... EddieAhern 4 38
(Des Donovan) *chsd ldrs: pushed along over 3f out: sn wknd* **20/1**
1m 52.36s (1.86) **Going Correction** 0.0s/f (Stan) **5** Ran SP% **111.6**
Speed ratings (Par 97): **91,83,81,75,72**
CSF £2.03 TOTE £1.20: £1.02, £1.70; EX 2.00.
Owner Hamdan Al Maktoum **Bred** Shadwell Estate Company Limited **Trained** Newmarket, Suffolk

FOCUS
A modest maiden for 3-y-os in which the runner-up is the best guide rated close to her Southwell debut figure.

3454 TIPSTERSUITE.COM TIPSTER BOT SOFTWARE FOR BETFAIR H'CAP 1m 141y(P)
4:45 (4:46) (Class 6) (0-65,65) 3-Y-O+ **£1,704** (£503; £251) **Stalls** Low

Form RPR
0-34 **1** **Grey Seal (IRE)**[28] 2542 3-9-3 **65**...................................... HayleyTurner 6 76+
(James Fanshawe) *chsd ldrs: shkn up to ld ins fnl f: r.o* **7/4**[1]
-000 **2** *1 ¾* **Top Frock (IRE)**[12] 3044 3-9-1 **63**..............................(b) AdamKirby 5 67
(Clive Cox) *chsd ldr 3f: remained handy: rdn over 1f out: styd on: wnt 2nd nr fin* **14/1**

2-15 **3** *nk* **Ishikawa (IRE)**[52] 1829 4-9-13 **64** PaulHanagan 11 69+
(Alan King) *hld up: swtchd rt and hdwy over 1f out: r.o wl: wnt 3rd post: nt rch ldrs* **7/2**[2]

0000 **4** *nk* **Moral Issue**[23] 2692 4-9-11 **65** DaleSwift(3) 4 69
(Ian McInnes) *led 5f: led again over 2f out: rdn over 1f out: hdd and unable qck ins fnl f* **9/1**[3]

0601 **5** *2* **Mr Chocolate Drop (IRE)**[18] 2858 8-9-12 **63** (t) RussKennemore 1 62
(Mandy Rowland) *hld up: plld hrd: hdwy over 1f out: sn rdn: edgd rt: styd on* **16/1**

00-0 **6** *hd* **Connishka**[16] 2935 3-8-4 **52** FrannyNorton 3 50
(Alan Bailey) *hld up: hdwy over 1f out: r.o: nrst fin* **25/1**

1065 **7** *1* **Just Five (IRE)**[12] 3039 6-9-7 **65** (v) GeorgeDowning(7) 7 62
(John Weymes) *hld up: rdn over 1f out: styd on ins fnl f: nvr trbld ldrs* **10/1**

0066 **8** *hd* **John Potts**[11] 3081 7-10-0 **65** WilliamCarson 2 61
(Brian Baugh) *chsd ldrs: rdn over 2f out: wknd ins fnl f* **12/1**

5000 **9** *1* **Bertie Blu Boy**[4] 3317 4-8-9 **46** JoeFanning 9 40
(Paul Green) *hld up: hdwy over 2f out: rdn over 1f out: wknd fnl f* **33/1**

-500 **10** *½* **Remix (IRE)**[12] 3044 3-9-1 **63** EddieAhern 10 55
(J W Hills) *prom: rdn over 1f out: wknd fnl f* **16/1**

0000 **11** *3 ¾* **Justcallmehandsome**[18] 2858 10-8-10 **52** (v) AmyScott(5) 12 36
(Dominic Ffrench Davis) *s.i.s: hld up: nvr on terms* **33/1**

6000 **12** *9* **Breakheart (IRE)**[12] 3039 5-9-13 **64** MichaelStainton 8 27
(Paul Howling) *dwlt: hdwy over 6f out: chsd ldr over 5f out tl led over 3f out: rdn and hdd over 2f out: wknd over 1f out* **40/1**

1m 50.29s (-0.21) **Going Correction** 0.0s/f (Stan)
WFA 3 from 4yo+ 11lb 12 Ran SP% **116.0**
Speed ratings (Par 101): **100,98,98,97,96 95,95,94,94,93 90,82**
toteswingers 1&2 £6.50, 2&3 £8.60, 1&3 £2.60 CSF £27.05 CT £81.45 TOTE £3.50: £1.20, £4.90, £1.40; EX 26.30 Trifecta £211.10 Pool: £1,078.61 - 3.78 winning units..
Owner Lord Vestey **Bred** Ms E Flynn **Trained** Newmarket, Suffolk

FOCUS
Just a modest handicap, but there were one or two less exposed sorts in the line-up and it looks fair form for the grade. The winner looks an improver, while the fourth sets the level, backed up by the placed horses.

3455 BOOK HOSPITALITY AT WOLVERHAMPTON RACECOURSE H'CAP (DIV I) 7f 32y(P)
5:15 (5:15) (Class 6) (0-60,60) 3-Y-O+ **£1,704** (£503; £251) **Stalls** High

Form RPR

0-00 **1** **Conry (IRE)**[35] 2355 6-9-12 **60** StephenCraine 9 68
(Daniel Mark Loughnane) *hld up in tch: led over 1f out: rdn and edgd lft ins fnl f: styd on u.p* **16/1**

0-03 **2** *½* **Mudhish (IRE)**[18] 2858 7-9-12 **60** (b) EddieAhern 8 66
(Clive Brittain) *hld up: hdwy over 1f out: r.o to go 2nd post: nt rch wnr* **9/2**[2]

32 **3** *nk* **Basle**[18] 2845 5-9-9 **57** (t) PaulHanagan 1 63
(Gay Kelleway) *hld up: hdwy over 1f out: sn rdn and ev ch: styd on* **3/1**[1]

3556 **4** *¾* **Crocodile Bay (IRE)**[3] 3332 9-8-9 **46** oh1 (p) DeclanCannon(3) 3 50
(Richard Guest) *chsd ldrs: rdn and ev ch over 1f out: styd on same pce ins fnl f* **14/1**

1050 **5** *5* **Lisselton Cross**[13] 3006 4-9-4 **52** (v) AdamKirby 2 42
(Martin Bosley) *prom: rdn over 1f out: no ex fnl f* **11/1**

4 **6** *4* **Yes Mam (IRE)**[95] 995 4-8-12 **46** oh1 FrannyNorton 6 25
(Tom Tate) *led: rdn and hdd over 1f out: wknd ins fnl f* **9/2**[2]

0053 **7** *¾* **Big Sylv (IRE)**[7] 3218 3-8-7 **50** JoeFanning 11 24
(James Unett) *hld up: rdn over 1f out: nvr trbld ldrs* **9/1**

P-40 **8** *½* **Imjin River (IRE)**[12] 3052 5-9-5 **58** AshleyMorgan(5) 10 34
(William Stone) *prom: rdn over 1f out: wknd fnl f* **33/1**

4540 **9** *6* **Julier Pass (IRE)**[21] 2749 3-9-3 **60** RussKennemore 7 17
(Hugh McWilliams) *chsd ldrs: rdn over 2f out: wknd over 1f out: eased* **16/1**

0060 **10** *1 ¼* **Kyncraighe (IRE)**[13] 3007 4-8-7 **46** (tp) JemmaMarshall(5) 12
(Joseph Tuite) *s.s: a bhd* **40/1**

0004 **11** *15* **Dhhamaan (IRE)**[6] 3254 7-9-2 **55** (b) LMcNiff(5) 5
(Ruth Carr) *w ldr tl pushed along 3f out: wknd over 2f out: t.o* **5/1**[3]

1m 29.34s (-0.26) **Going Correction** 0.0s/f (Stan)
WFA 3 from 4yo+ 9lb 11 Ran SP% **120.2**
Speed ratings (Par 101): **101,100,100,99,93 88,88,87,80,79 62**
toteswingers 1&2 £18.00, 2&3 £4.60, 1&3 £10.20 CSF £88.58 CT £289.59 TOTE £35.40: £4.70, £2.20, £1.40; EX 136.60 Trifecta £142.60 Pool: £657.42 - 3.41 winning units..
Owner T Birchall & Mrs C Loughnane **Bred** Shay White **Trained** Baldwin's Gate, Staffs

FOCUS
A moderate handicap but pretty ordinary form rated around the placed horses.
Conry(IRE) Official explanation: trainer said, regarding apparent improvement in form, that the yard was coming back in to form.
Yes Mam(IRE) Official explanation: jockey said filly lost its action
Julier Pass(IRE) Official explanation: jockey said gelding lost its action home straight
Dhhamaan(IRE) Official explanation: jockey said gelding had no more to give

3456 BOOK HOSPITALITY AT WOLVERHAMPTON RACECOURSE H'CAP (DIV II) 7f 32y(P)
5:45 (5:46) (Class 6) (0-60,60) 3-Y-O+ **£1,704** (£503; £251) **Stalls** High

Form RPR

00-0 **1** **Sir Mozart (IRE)**[159] 13 9-9-12 **60** JoeFanning 12 77
(Barney Curley) *mid-div: hdwy to chse ldr 5f out: led over 2f out: pushed clr fr over 1f out: easily* **9/2**[2]

5600 **2** *8* **Bold Diva**[35] 2350 7-8-6 **47** (v) GeorgeDowning(7) 6 42
(Tony Carroll) *hld up: hdwy over 1f out: rdn to go 2nd ins fnl f: no ch w wnr* **8/1**

640- **3** *¾* **Forzarzi (IRE)**[350] 3902 8-8-12 **46** oh1 RussKennemore 3 39
(Hugh McWilliams) *hld up: rdn over 1f out: r.o ins fnl f: nvr nrr* **20/1**

-106 **4** *hd* **July Days (IRE)**[110] 828 6-9-10 **58** WilliamCarson 5 51
(Brian Baugh) *chsd ldrs: rdn over 2f out: styd on same pce fnl f* **6/1**

0000 **5** *2* **See The Storm**[12] 3026 4-8-5 **46** oh1 MatthewMcGhee(7) 8 33
(Lisa Williamson) *prom: rdn over 1f out: wknd fnl f* **25/1**

0350 **6** *nk* **Fortunate Bid (IRE)**[40] 2170 6-9-9 **57** (p) MichaelO'Connell 4 44
(Linda Stubbs) *hld up: rdn over 2f out: nvr nrr* **4/1**[1]

00-0 **7** *½* **Stilettoesinthemud (IRE)**[30] 2476 4-9-7 **55** J-PGuillambert 10 40
(James Given) *chsd ldrs: rdn over 2f out: wknd fnl f* **20/1**

0600 **8** *nk* **Marksbury**[12] 3053 5-9-4 **59** JackDuern(7) 11 43
(Mark Brisbourne) *hld up: rdn over 2f out: n.d* **14/1**

0530 **9** *1 ¾* **Royal Box**[6] 3249 5-9-4 **52** (p) FrannyNorton 7 32
(David Evans) *prom: rdn 1/2-way: wknd over 1f out* **11/2**[3]

0-00 **10** *1 ¾* **Champagne Valley**[42] 2131 3-8-6 **49** AndrewElliott 9 21
(Sharon Watt) *hld up: rdn and wknd over 2f out* **40/1**

6002 **11** *1 ½* **Little Perisher**[35] 2350 5-9-3 **51** (p) MichaelStainton 1 22
(Paul Howling) *led: rdn and hdd over 2f out: wknd over 1f out* **11/1**

-000 **12** *½* **Great Nicanor (IRE)**[12] 3032 3-8-9 **55** DeclanCannon(3) 2 22
(Ian Semple) *chsd ldrs: rdn over 2f out: n.m.r sn after: wknd over 1f out* **8/1**

1m 28.75s (-0.85) **Going Correction** 0.0s/f (Stan)
WFA 3 from 4yo+ 9lb 12 Ran SP% **120.9**
Speed ratings (Par 101): **104,94,94,93,91 91,90,90,88,86 84,83**
toteswingers 1&2 £11.70, 2&3 £39.10, 1&3 £27.30 CSF £39.13 CT £676.58 TOTE £8.10: £2.90, £3.90, £5.70; EX 42.90 TRIFECTA Not won..
Owner Curley Leisure **Bred** Western Bloodstock **Trained** Newmarket, Suffolk

FOCUS
The quicker of the two divisions by 0.59sec and the winner is rated back to his best previous turf form, although could be worth more at face value.
Fortunate Bid(IRE) Official explanation: jockey said gelding never travelled
T/Plt: £78.60 to a £1 stake. Pool: £55,999.00 - 519.85 winning tickets. T/Qpdt: £7.10 to a £1 stake. Pool: £5,864.00 - 604.53 winning tickets. CR

3018 BEVERLEY (R-H)
Tuesday, June 26

OFFICIAL GOING: Good to soft (6.2)
Wind: Light half behind Weather: Fine & dry

3457 IN LOVING MEMORY OF LES PREEN MAIDEN AUCTION STKS 7f 100y
2:30 (2:30) (Class 6) 2-Y-O **£1,617** (£481; £240; £120) **Stalls** Low

Form RPR

1 **Arthurs Secret** 2-9-3 0 MichaelO'Connell 1 83+
(John Quinn) *trckd ldrs: hdwy 2f out: led ent fnl f: sn rdn clr: styd on strly* **9/2**[3]

033 **2** *8* **Yorkshire Icon**[17] 2923 2-8-11 0 GrahamLee 5 58
(Ann Duffield) *towards rr: pushed along 1/2-way: rdn and outpcd over 2f out: styd on appr fnl f: tk 2nd towards fin* **2/1**[1]

222 **3** *1 ¼* **Throwing Roses**[15] 2977 2-8-4 0 JamesSullivan 6 48
(Ollie Pears) *plld hrd: led: rdn 2f out: hdd ent fnl f: one pce* **9/4**[2]

6 **4** *10* **Tiger Prince (IRE)**[11] 3112 2-9-1 0 PaddyAspell 3 36
(Ann Duffield) *chsd ldng pair: rdn over 2f out: sn drvn and wknd* **8/1**

0 **5** *½* **Cielo Rojo (IRE)**[12] 3062 2-9-1 0 TonyHamilton 4 34
(Richard Fahey) *chsd ldrs: rdn along 3f out: sn drvn and wknd* **10/1**

005 **6** *1* **Valetto (IRE)**[7] 3251 2-8-13 0 (b) DanielTudhope 7 30
(Tim Easterby) *chsd ldr: rdn along wl over 2f out: sn drvn and wknd* **33/1**

7 *1* **Santa Fe Stinger** 2-8-4 0 DuranFentiman 8 19
(Tim Easterby) *a bhd* **16/1**

0 **8** *3 ¾* **Double Happiness**[21] 2790 2-8-5 0 ow1 BarryMcHugh 9 11
(Brian Rothwell) *t.k.h: chsd ldrs: rdn along 1/2-way: sn wknd* **66/1**

1m 37.59s (3.79) **Going Correction** +0.525s/f (Yiel) 8 Ran SP% **112.8**
Speed ratings (Par 91): **99,89,88,77,76 75,74,69**
toteswingers 1&2 £3.00, 1&3 £2.40, 2&3 £2.30 CSF £13.52 TOTE £4.80: £1.10, £1.30, £1.30; EX 22.80.
Owner E A Brook **Bred** Howard Barton Stud **Trained** Settrington, N Yorks

FOCUS
Inside rail around bottom bend in narrow position adding about 19yds to all races except 5f races. An ordinary maiden, but an impressive debut winner who could be useful. The third was below form.

NOTEBOOK
Arthurs Secret cost £21,000 and is related to a couple of AW winners. His trainer had already struck with a couple of first-time-out winners this season, and he the way he powered clear suggests there ought to be more to come once handicapping. (op 7-1)
Yorkshire Icon, up 1 1/2f in trip, was dropped out but got too far back and never stood a chance of reaching the winner (op 13-8 tchd 6-4)
Throwing Roses, runner-up on each of her previous three starts, boiled over before the start and pulled hard in front, actually doing well to last as long as she did. (op 7-4 tchd 13-8)
Tiger Prince(IRE) is bred for a longer trip and faster ground, and should do better in handicaps following another run. (tchd 9-1)

3458 ST JOHN AMBULANCE CLAIMING STKS 1m 4f 16y
3:00 (3:01) (Class 6) 3-Y-O+ **£1,617** (£481; £240; £120) **Stalls** Low

Form RPR

4-4 **1** **Just Lille (IRE)**[86] 1159 9-9-8 **88** (p) GrahamLee 2 88
(Ann Duffield) *trckd ldng pair: pushed along wl over 2f out: hdwy over 1f out: rdn to ld jst ins fnl f: styd on strly* **11/10**[1]

2450 **2** *4* **Halla San**[10] 3163 10-9-8 **80** TonyHamilton 5 82
(Richard Fahey) *dwlt and sn pushed along in rr: hdwy to trck ldrs 6f out: rdn to ld over 2f out: hdd over 1f out: drvn and rallied to have ev ch ent fnl f: kpt on same pce* **6/4**[2]

3-00 **3** *1 ¼* **Kinyras (IRE)**[39] 2253 4-9-6 **83** DavidSimmonson(7) 1 85
(Michael Easterby) *hld up in rr: hdwy on outer over 2f out: rdn to ld over 1f out: drvn and hdd jst ins fnl f: one pce* **9/2**[3]

06-0 **4** *30* **Chlodan**[8] 3236 5-9-3 **52** JamesSullivan 6 27
(Michael Easterby) *led: rdn along 3f out: sn hdd & wknd* **40/1**

00-0 **5** *6* **Iberian Rock**[36] 2341 3-8-1 **50** (p) JimmyQuinn 4 15
(Alan Brown) *prom: chsd ldr after 3f: rdn along wl over 3f out: sn outpcd and bhd* **50/1**

2m 46.1s (6.30) **Going Correction** +0.525s/f (Yiel)
WFA 3 from 4yo+ 14lb 5 Ran SP% **110.2**
Speed ratings (Par 101): **100,97,96,76,72**
CSF £3.03 TOTE £1.80: £1.10, £1.50; EX 3.60.
Owner Middleham Park Racing XLVI **Bred** Sweetmans Bloodstock **Trained** Constable Burton, N Yorks

FOCUS
A fair claimer on paper, but it has been rated cautiously.

3459 REMEMBER JOHN "MOTHER" HUBBARD H'CAP 1m 1f 207y
3:30 (3:31) (Class 4) (0-80,77) 4-Y-O+ **£4,528** (£1,347; £673; £336) **Stalls** Low

Form RPR

-030 **1** **Pintrada**[33] 2419 4-9-0 **70** GrahamLee 1 80+
(James Bethell) *t.k.h: hld up in rr: hdwy and nt clr run over 1f out: effrt and squeezed through ins fnl f: swtchd to inner and drvn last 100yds: styd on to ld on line* **6/1**[3]

0-03 **2** *shd* **King Of The Celts (IRE)**[24] 2687 4-9-1 **71** TomEaves 2 79
(Tim Easterby) *pushed along and sn led: set stdy pce: qcknd wl over 2f out: rdn wl over 1f out: drvn ins fnl f: edgd lft and hdd on line* **7/1**

0604 **3** 3 1/2 **Count Bertoni (IRE)**[21] 2792 5-9-1 **71**.......................... DanielTudhope 6 72
(David O'Meara) *led early: cl up: trckd ldng pair and keen after 2f: effrt on inner and nt clr run wl over 1f out: swtchd lft and rdn ent fnl f: sn drvn and one pce* **6/1**[3]

2-00 **4** 2 **Gold Rules**[22] 2751 5-8-12 **68**.......................... GrahamGibbons 5 65
(Michael Easterby) *t.k.h: trckd ldrs: effrt on outer over 2f out: rdn wl over 1f out and sn one pce* **4/1**[2]

2134 **5** 2 3/4 **Carragold**[10] 3167 6-9-7 **77**.......................... DuranFentiman 3 68
(Mel Brittain) *t.k.h: trckd ldrs: effrt on outer 3f out: rdn 2f out: sn rdn and wknd* **6/5**[1]

2m 11.76s (4.76) **Going Correction** +0.525s/f (Yiel) 5 Ran SP% **106.5**
Speed ratings (Par 105): **101,100,98,96,94**
CSF £39.64 TOTE £7.40: £3.50, £4.40; EX 42.30.
Owner Scotyork Partnership I **Bred** Carmel Stud **Trained** Middleham Moor, N Yorks

FOCUS
The front pair pulled clear late on in what was a modest handicap. The pace was steady. The winner is rated back to his 3yo level and was value for a bit extra.
Carragold Official explanation: trainer said gelding was found to be coughing

3460 ARDENT FINANCIAL PLANNING H'CAP 7f 100y
4:00 (4:01) (Class 5) (0-70,70) 3-Y-0+ **£2,264** (£673; £336; £168) **Stalls** Low

Form RPR

30-1 **1** **Eeny Mac (IRE)**[24] 2692 5-8-12 **54**.......................... MichaelO'Connell 5 67
(Neville Bycroft) *mde all: rdn clr 2f out: drvn and hung bdly lft ins fnl f: kpt on* **11/4**[1]

4025 **2** 3/4 **Hayek**[29] 2535 5-9-1 **62**..........................(b) AdamCarter(5) 11 74
(Tim Easterby) *s.i.s and bhd: hdwy 3f out: rdn 2f out: swtchd lft to outer and drvn over 1f out: str run ent fnl f: ch whn hung bdly rt wl ins fnl f: sltly hmpd: nt rcvr* **13/2**[3]

2033 **3** 2 1/2 **Striker Torres (IRE)**[8] 3229 6-9-12 **68**..........................(v) GrahamLee 8 73
(Ian McInnes) *hld up in rr: hdwy on inner 2f out: rdn over 1f out: styd on fnl f: nrst fin* **17/2**

-030 **4** 1 **More Bottle (IRE)**[19] 2840 3-7-11 **51**.......................... DominicFox(3) 4 50+
(Tom Tate) *in tch: hdwy wl over 2f out: swtchd lft and rdn to chse ldrs over 1f out: drvn and one pce fnl f* **16/1**

1220 **5** 2 3/4 **Bonnie Prince Blue**[13] 3021 9-8-13 **58**.......................... DaleSwift(3) 2 53
(Ian McInnes) *in rr: hdwy 2f out: rdn wl over 1f out: styd on fnl f: nrst fin* **25/1**

0034 **6** 1 **Iceblast**[4] 3356 4-9-3 **59**..........................(b) GrahamGibbons 12 52
(Michael Easterby) *trckd ldrs: hdwy wl over 2f out: rdn wl over 1f out: grad wknd* **13/2**[3]

5604 **7** 3/4 **Meandmyshadow**[13] 3021 4-9-7 **63**.......................... TomEaves 9 54
(Alan Brown) *chsd wnr: rdn 2f out: drvn over 1f out: grad wknd* **20/1**

-300 **8** 3/4 **Loyal Master (IRE)**[18] 2883 3-9-5 **70**..........................(t) JimmyQuinn 7 56
(David C Griffiths) *a towards rr* **5/1**[2]

-030 **9** hd **So Cheeky**[13] 3025 3-7-11 **55**.......................... HannahNunn(7) 3 41
(Peter Salmon) *chsd ldrs on inner: rdn along 3f out: sn wknd* **16/1**

30-0 **10** 7 **Boy The Bell**[151] 329 5-8-13 **62**.......................... JacobButterfield(7) 13 33
(Ollie Pears) *midfield: rdn along 3f out: sn wknd* **22/1**

-065 **11** 18 **Strong Man**[8] 3215 4-9-7 **63**..........................(b) PaddyAspell 1
(Michael Easterby) *dwlt: t.k.h and rapid hdwy on inner to chse ldrs after 1f: rdn along wl over 2f out: sn wknd* **12/1**

0-24 **12** 4 **Carnival Dream**[29] 2536 7-8-9 **51** oh5.......................... RussKennemore 10
(Hugh McWilliams) *a towards rr* **28/1**

1m 36.93s (3.13) **Going Correction** +0.525s/f (Yiel)
WFA 3 from 4yo+ 9lb 12 Ran SP% **116.4**
Speed ratings (Par 103): **103,102,99,98,95 93,93,92,91,83 63,58**
toteswingers 1&2 £4.60, 1&3 £3.40, 2&3 £9.80 CSF £18.51 CT £137.44 TOTE £3.60: £1.50, £3.00, £3.20; EX 22.70.
Owner Mrs J Dickinson **Bred** Kenneth Heelan **Trained** Brandsby, N Yorks
■ Stewards' Enquiry : Michael O'Connell two-day ban: careless riding (Jul 10-11)

FOCUS
A well run handicap, and solid enough form for the level, the winner confirming his latest win here with a game success.
Loyal Master(IRE) Official explanation: trainer said gelding had been struck into

3461 RACING UK ON SKY 432 MEDIAN AUCTION MAIDEN STKS 1m 100y
4:30 (4:30) (Class 5) 3-Y-O **£2,385** (£704; £352) **Stalls** Low

Form RPR

3 **1** **Voice From Above (IRE)**[12] 3079 3-8-12 **0**.......................... DanielTudhope 1 69
(Patrick Holmes) *trckd ldrs: smooth hdwy on inner to ld wl over 1f out: sn rdn and styd on strly fnl f* **11/4**[2]

0-20 **2** 1 1/4 **Cufflink**[17] 2941 3-8-12 **77**.......................... RichardKingscote 2 66
(Rae Guest) *hld up in rr: hdwy over 2f out: swtchd rt to inner over 1f out: sn rdn and n.m.r: swtchd lft to chse wnr ent fnl f: sn drive: edgd lft and no imp* **1/1**[1]

6-4 **3** 1 1/2 **Yojojo (IRE)**[46] 2030 3-8-12 **0**.......................... GrahamLee 5 63
(Gay Kelleway) *trckd ldrs: hdwy on outer wl over 2f out: rdn and ch whn sltly hmpd over 1f out: drvn and one pce ins fnl f* **17/2**

0 **4** 4 **Revelette (IRE)**[67] 1501 3-8-12 **0**.......................... WilliamCarson 4 53
(Charles Hills) *t.k.h and led early: trckd clr ldr: tk clsr order 3f out: swtchd lft and rdn wl over 1f out: sn one pce* **7/2**[3]

6-55 **5** 9 **Landaho**[19] 2843 3-8-12 **40**.......................... RussKennemore 3 33
(Hugh McWilliams) *led after 1f and sn clr: rdn along and wandered wl over 2f out: hdd & wknd qckly wl over 1f out* **125/1**

1m 53.71s (6.11) **Going Correction** +0.525s/f (Yiel) 5 Ran SP% **110.2**
Speed ratings (Par 99): **90,88,87,83,74**
CSF £5.94 TOTE £3.00: £1.20, £1.20; EX 5.50.
Owner Foulrice Park Racing Limited **Bred** Mrs L Vaughan **Trained** Brandsby, N. Yorks
■ Stewards' Enquiry : William Carson one-day ban: careless riding (Jul 10)

FOCUS
A moderate maiden, contested solely by fillies and run in a slow time. The favourite disappointed and the winner built on her debut promise.

3462 STARS OF THE FUTURE APPRENTICE H'CAP (DIV I) 5f
5:00 (5:00) (Class 6) (0-55,55) 3-Y-0+ **£1,617** (£481; £240; £120) **Stalls** Low

Form RPR

0604 **1** **Tenancy (IRE)**[34] 2401 8-8-5 **47**..........................(b) JordanUys(7) 4 58
(Shaun Harris) *qckly away: mde all: rdn ent fnl f and kpt on wl* **10/1**

4420 **2** 2 **Drumpellier (IRE)**[8] 3209 5-8-10 **50**.......................... DavidBergin(5) 9 54
(Simon West) *in tch: hdwy to chse ldrs wl over 1f out: sn rdn and styd on fnl f: nrst fin* **9/2**[2]

0102 **3** 1/2 **Dotty Darroch**[13] 3018 4-9-6 **55**.......................... ConorHarrison 1 57+
(Robin Bastiman) *rrd s and in rr: swtchd to wd outside 1/2-way: sn rdn: styd on fnl f: nrst fin* **11/2**[3]

5000 **4** shd **Grand Stitch (USA)**[104] 904 6-8-7 **49**.......................... MichaelKenny(7) 3 51
(Declan Carroll) *chsd wnr: rdn over 1f out: edgd lft and one pce fnl f* **9/1**

0505 **5** 1/2 **Spirit Of Coniston**[32] 2436 9-9-5 **54**.......................... NedCurtis 5 54
(Paul Midgley) *chsd ldrs: rdn along over 1f out: kpt on same pce fnl f* **15/2**

-005 **6** 1 **Queen's Princess**[3] 3406 4-8-11 **46** oh1..........................(p) ThomasBrown 7 43
(John Wainwright) *chsd ldrs rdn wl over 1f out: n.m.r and wknd ins fnl f* **25/1**

0424 **7** 3/4 **Balti's Sister (IRE)**[9] 3184 3-9-0 **55**..........................(b[1]) DavidSimmonson 6 47
(Michael Easterby) *dwlt and towards rr: hdwy to chse ldrs wl over 1f out: rdn and n.m.r appr fnl f: sn no imp* **7/2**[1]

2000 **8** 3/4 **Sleights Boy (IRE)**[36] 2350 4-9-2 **51**.......................... LauraBarry 2 42+
(Ian McInnes) *chsd ldrs: rdn along and lost pl 1/2-way: sme hdwy appr fnl f: n.d* **11/2**[3]

000 **9** 20 **Busy Bimbo (IRE)**[26] 2615 3-8-5 **51**..........................(p) MatthewHopkins(5) 10
(Alan Berry) *a in rr* **25/1**

-066 **U** **Boga (IRE)**[21] 2791 5-8-11 **46** oh1..........................(p) GemmaTutty 8
(Karen Tutty) *chsd ldrs: rdn along and wkng whn stmbld bdly and uns rdr jst ins fnl 2f* **14/1**

1m 5.82s (2.32) **Going Correction** +0.525s/f (Yiel)
WFA 3 from 4yo+ 6lb 10 Ran SP% **116.4**
Speed ratings (Par 101): **102,98,98,97,97 95,94,93,61,**
toteswingers 1&2 £9.70, 1&3 £10.30, 2&3 £5.50 CSF £54.54 CT £280.79 TOTE £13.70: £3.30, £2.40, £1.30; EX 66.00.
Owner The Moorhouse Partnership **Bred** G A E And J Smith Bloodstock Ltd **Trained** Carburton, Notts
■ The first winner for Jordan Uys.

FOCUS
A weak handicap, confined to apprentice riders, but the faster division. The form is set around the second.
Balti's Sister(IRE) Official explanation: jockey said filly missed the break

3463 STARS OF THE FUTURE APPRENTICE H'CAP (DIV II) 5f
5:30 (5:31) (Class 6) (0-55,57) 3-Y-0+ **£1,617** (£481; £240; £120) **Stalls** Low

Form RPR

0001 **1** **Elusive Bonus (IRE)**[3] 3407 3-8-11 **57** 6ex.......................... DavidBergin(5) 4 62
(David O'Meara) *mde most: rdn over 1f out: edgd lft ins fnl f: hld on wl* **5/6**[1]

-430 **2** hd **Brunswick Vale (IRE)**[27] 2595 3-8-10 **51**..........................(b) NedCurtis 2 55
(Paul Midgley) *chsd ldrs on inner: rdn along and n.m.r 1f out: sn swtchd lft and drvn: styd on and ev ch last 100yds: no ex nr fin* **11/1**

5500 **3** 1/2 **Blue Noodles**[13] 3026 6-8-6 **46**..........................(p) EvaMoscrop(5) 5 51
(John Wainwright) *towards rr: hdwy 2f out: sn rdn: styd on strly fnl f: nrst fin* **12/1**

36-5 **4** 1 1/4 **See Vermont**[15] 2971 4-9-0 **49**.......................... ConorHarrison 9 49
(Robin Bastiman) *in tch: hdwy on outer 1/2-way: chsd wnr wl over 1f out: sn rdn and one pce fnl f* **9/1**[3]

-000 **5** 1 1/2 **Never In (IRE)**[4] 3357 3-8-0 **46** oh1.......................... MatthewHopkins(5) 10 39
(Alan Berry) *chsd ldrs on outer: hdwy to chse wnr 2f out: sn rdn and wknd ent fnl f* **50/1**

0261 **6** 4 **Sophie's Beau (USA)**[13] 3018 5-9-1 **53**..........................(b) JacobButterfield(3) 8 33
(Michael Chapman) *sltly hmpd s: in tch: hdwy to chse ldrs 1/2-way: rdn and edgd rt 1f out: sn wknd* **7/2**[2]

000- **7** 6 **Media Jury**[300] 5620 5-9-6 **55**..........................(v) ThomasBrown 3 14
(John Wainwright) *prom: rdn along 2f out: sn wknd* **20/1**

0000 **8** 1/2 **Morermaloke**[13] 3053 4-8-12 **47**.......................... LauraBarry 7
(Ian McInnes) *in tch: rdn along 2f out: sn wknd* **20/1**

00-0 **9** 4 1/2 **Saxby (IRE)**[21] 2791 5-8-6 **46** oh1.......................... KevinLundie(5) 1
(Alan Lockwood) *rrd s: a in rr* **40/1**

1m 6.76s (3.26) **Going Correction** +0.525s/f (Yiel)
WFA 3 from 4yo+ 6lb 9 Ran SP% **116.7**
Speed ratings (Par 101): **94,93,92,90,88 82,72,71,64**
toteswingers 1&2 £4.00, 1&3 £3.60, 2&3 £5.20 CSF £11.09 CT £70.26 TOTE £1.80: £1.10, £2.30, £3.10; EX 12.60.
Owner The Three County Partnership **Bred** T Jones **Trained** Nawton, N Yorks
■ Stewards' Enquiry : Conor Harrison 20-day ban: used whip above permitted level (Jul 10-14,16-30)
David Bergin two-day ban: used whip above permitted level (tbn)

FOCUS
The quicker division. As in division one, little featured from off the pace and they raced more centre-field. Pretty limited, with few in form.
T/Plt: £27.20 to a £1 stake. Pool: £53440.41- 1431.94 winning tickets T/Qpdt: £17.70 to a £1 stake. Pool: £2866.16 - 119.62 winning tickets JR

3243 BRIGHTON (L-H)

Tuesday, June 26

OFFICIAL GOING: Good (good to soft in places; 7.0)
Wind: Moderate, half against Weather: Race 1 - fine; Rest - sea fret

3464 THORLEY TAVERNS AND CRABBIE'S GINGER BEER H'CAP 5f 59y
2:15 (2:15) (Class 6) (0-65,65) 3-Y-0+ **£1,617** (£481; £240; £120) **Stalls** Centre

Form RPR

30 **1** **Scommettitrice (IRE)**[15] 2971 4-8-7 **45** oh1..........................(p) AndreaAtzeni 3 53
(David Evans) *chsd ldr: rdn to ld ins fnl f: jst hld on* **15/2**

45-5 **2** hd **Dear Maurice**[92] 1050 8-9-12 **65**..........................(t) MartinLane 6 71
(Tobias B P Coles) *hld up in 5th: rdn and hdwy 2f out: r.o wl fnl f: tk 2nd and clsng on wnr nr fin* **13/2**

0-00 **3** nk **Cape Royal**[31] 2494 12-9-12 **65**..........................(tp) CathyGannon 1 70
(Milton Bradley) *led: hrd rdn and hdd ins fnl f: kpt on wl* **14/1**

-600 **4** 3 **Atlantic Cycle (IRE)**[17] 2943 5-9-4 **57**..........................(tp) LukeMorris 8 52
(Milton Bradley) *chsd ldrs: rdn over 2f out: one pce appr fnl f* **11/2**[3]

5005 **5** 3/4 **Simple Rhythm**[7] 3243 6-8-4 **45** oh1..........................(v) RyanPowell(3) 5 38
(John Ryan) *prom tl no ex 1f out* **12/1**

5454 **6** 3/4 **Imaginary Diva**[7] 3243 6-9-6 **59**.......................... TomQueally 7 49
(George Margarson) *hld up in 6th: rdn and no imp fnl 2f* **9/4**[1]

04-0 **7** 1 3/4 **Stonecrabstomorrow (IRE)**[35] 2360 9-9-6 **64**.......................... MarkCoumbe(5) 2 47
(Michael Attwater) *s.i.s: a bhd* **3/1**[2]

1m 3.25s (0.95) **Going Correction** +0.125s/f (Good) 7 Ran SP% **110.6**
Speed ratings (Par 101): **97,96,96,91,90 89,86**
toteswingers 1&2 £5.00, 1&3 £12.10, 2&3 £6.30 CSF £50.66 CT £634.75 TOTE £8.70: £4.40, £2.10; EX 48.10 Trifecta £232.40 Pool: £634.55 - 2.02 winning units..
Owner Out Of Bounds Racing Club **Bred** L Mulryan **Trained** Pandy, Monmouths

FOCUS
Rail moved out 3m from 4.5f to 3.5f adding 8yds to all distances. This was a moderate sprint handicap, and they raced stands' side in the straight.

Dear Maurice Official explanation: trainer said gelding finished distressed
Stonecrabstomorrow(IRE) Official explanation: jockey said gelding never travelled

3465 NORTH ROAD TIMBER ANNIVERSARY MEDIAN AUCTION MAIDEN STKS 5f 213y

2:45 (2:45) (Class 5) 2-Y-O **£2,264** (£673; £336; £168) **Stalls** Centre

Form RPR
422 **1** **Kicken Off (IRE)**[7] 3244 2-9-3 .... AdamKirby 1 70+
(Phil McEntee) *mde all: rdn and swvd rt 1f out: veered lft ins fnl f: drvn out* **4/9**[1]
40 **2** *nk* **Must Be Me**[32] 2437 2-8-12 .... CathyGannon 5 64
(Eve Johnson Houghton) *hld up in 4th: effrt 2f out: lft 2nd 1f out: clsd on wnr: hld fnl 50yds* **5/1**[3]
4 **3** *1 3/4* **Petite Georgia (IRE)**[28] 2579 2-8-12 .... PatCosgrave 3 60
(George Baker) *chsd wnr: rdn whn hmpd and lost 2nd 1f out: kpt on same pce* **9/2**[2]
46 **4** *4* **Black Eider**[61] 1629 2-8-12 .... LukeMorris 4 46
(John Spearing) *dwlt: in rr: hdwy into 3rd 2f out: no ex appr fnl f* **22/1**
06 **5** *9* **Cernanova (IRE)**[28] 2579 2-8-12 .... MartinLane 2 18
(Hugo Palmer) *free to post: plld hrd in 3rd: rdn and wknd 2f out* **22/1**
1m 12.07s (1.87) **Going Correction** +0.125s/f (Good) **5** Ran SP% **112.8**
Speed ratings (Par 93): **92,91,89,83,71**
CSF £3.34 TOTE £1.40: £1.10, £2.40; EX 2.60.
Owner M M Racing **Bred** Moygaddy Stud **Trained** Newmarket, Suffolk

FOCUS
A modest juvenile maiden. The idling winner was probably below form.

NOTEBOOK
Kicken Off(IRE), runner-up here on his last two outings, won despite wandering badly under pressure. He only made his debut on June 6 and was already having the fourth start of his career, so clearly he's a tough colt, and he should be competitive in nurseries in due course, provided he is not always so wayward. (op 1-3)
Must Be Me was possibly a bit flattered to finish so close to the wandering winner, but she showed enough to suggest she can win a small race. (op 8-1)
Petite Georgia(IRE), who ran to a moderate level on her debut, was held when hampered by the winner in the closing stages, but she otherwise might have finished a little closer. (op 6-1)

3466 PIPE CENTER H'CAP (DIV I) 5f 213y

3:15 (3:15) (Class 6) (0-60,60) 3-Y-O+ **£1,617** (£481; £240; £120) **Stalls** Centre

Form RPR
3114 **1** **Clear Spring (IRE)**[7] 3249 4-9-11 **59** .... NickyMackay 4 71+
(John Spearing) *hdwy to chse ldrs 3f out: led 1f out: rdn out: readily* **15/8**[1]
6044 **2** *3/4* **Perfect Honour (IRE)**[13] 3020 6-8-12 **46** oh1 ....(p) DavidProbert 7 54
(Des Donovan) *led: rdn and hdd 1f out: kpt on* **12/1**
0503 **3** *hd* **Homeboy (IRE)**[7] 3245 4-9-2 **57** .... KatiaScallan(7) 2 64
(Marcus Tregoning) *mid-div: hdwy 2f out: kpt on wl nr fin* **4/1**[2]
630 **4** *4* **Toms River Tess (IRE)**[15] 2971 4-8-9 **46** oh1 .... SimonPearce(3) 3 40
(Zoe Davison) *prom: rdn over 2f out: one pce* **33/1**
50-5 **5** *1 1/4* **Ridgeway Sapphire**[12] 3075 5-9-0 **48** ....(v) HayleyTurner 1 38
(Mark Usher) *towards rr: squeezed on rail over 4f out: effrt 2f out: nvr able to chal* **17/2**
3004 **6** *shd* **Memphis Man**[26] 2617 9-9-6 **54** .... PadraigBeggy 5 44
(David Evans) *chsd ldrs: outpcd fnl 2f* **12/1**
0046 **7** *nk* **Microlight**[10] 3151 4-8-13 **47** ....(v) RichardThomas 8 36
(John E Long) *mid-div on outer: rdn over 2f out: sn btn* **16/1**
-020 **8** *3/4* **Amber Heights**[41] 2170 4-9-12 **60** .... FergusSweeney 10 47
(Henry Candy) *hld up in rr: rdn and sme hdwy 2f out: sn wknd: b.b.v* **6/1**[3]
2020 **9** *1 3/4* **Flaxen Lake**[10] 3151 5-9-4 **52** ....(p) LukeMorris 9 33
(Milton Bradley) *towards rr: rdn 4f out: struggling fnl 3f* **12/1**
-000 **10** *62* **Invincible Beauty (IRE)**[10] 3152 3-8-9 **50** ....(b1) JimCrowley 6
(Seamus Durack) *prom tl lost action 2f out: qckly lost pl and virtually p.u* **16/1**
1m 10.83s (0.63) **Going Correction** +0.125s/f (Good)
WFA 3 from 4yo+ 7lb **10** Ran SP% **117.4**
Speed ratings (Par 101): **100,99,98,93,91 91,91,90,87,5**
toteswingers 1&2 £7.70, 1&3 £2.40, 2&3 £8.00 CSF £26.89 CT £85.54 TOTE £2.40: £1.70, £3.60, £2.00; EX 37.80 Trifecta £229.80 Pool: £695.69 - 2.24 winning units..
Owner H James **Bred** Rocal Bloodstock **Trained** Kinnersley, Worcs

FOCUS
A moderate handicap run in a time 0.27 seconds faster than the second leg.
Amber Heights Official explanation: trainer's rep said filly had bled from the nose
Invincible Beauty(IRE) Official explanation: vet said filly had been struck into

3467 PIPE CENTER H'CAP (DIV II) 5f 213y

3:45 (3:45) (Class 6) (0-60,60) 3-Y-O+ **£1,617** (£481; £240; £120) **Stalls** Centre

Form RPR
0332 **1** **Ooi Long**[13] 3050 3-8-7 **53** ....(t) TobyAtkinson(5) 1 64+
(Mark Rimmer) *chsd ldrs: led 2f out: rdn out* **9/2**
3-06 **2** *1 3/4* **Amba**[32] 2466 6-9-12 **60** .... TomQueally 3 67
(Des Donovan) *led tl 2f out: kpt on u.p: hld by wnr fnl f* **11/4**[1]
0401 **3** *1/2* **Whiteoak Lady (IRE)**[7] 3245 7-9-5 **53** 6ex........(p) AndreaAtzeni 5 58
(David Evans) *towards rr: hdwy and hung lft over 1f out: styd on fnl f* **3/1**[2]
3005 **4** *2* **Sherjawy (IRE)**[14] 3008 8-9-7 **55** .... KirstyMilczarek 2 54
(Zoe Davison) *prom: rdn to chal 2f out: one pce* **10/1**
5000 **5** *1 1/4* **Replicator**[14] 3008 7-8-9 **46** oh1 ....(e) RyanClark(3) 7 41
(Patrick Gilligan) *prom tl outpcd fnl 2f* **16/1**
0003 **6** *1 3/4* **Colourbearer (IRE)**[7] 3243 5-9-8 **56** ....(tp) LukeMorris 8 45
(Milton Bradley) *dwlt: sn in tch: hrd rdn and btn over 2f out* **10/3**[3]
0-00 **7** *6* **Prophet In A Dream**[26] 2627 4-9-0 **48** .... CathyGannon 4 18
(Paddy Butler) *chsd ldrs tl wknd over 2f out* **25/1**
0000 **8** *2 3/4* **Litotes**[15] 2971 4-8-12 **46** oh1 ....(v) JohnFahy 6
(Michael Attwater) *dwlt: in rr: mod effrt on rail 2f out: sn wknd* **50/1**
1m 11.1s (0.90) **Going Correction** +0.125s/f (Good)
WFA 3 from 4yo+ 7lb **8** Ran SP% **113.7**
Speed ratings (Par 101): **99,96,96,93,91 89,81,77**
toteswingers 1&2 £4.60, 1&3 £3.40, 2&3 £9.80 CSF £17.09 CT £42.28 TOTE £4.70: £1.40, £1.30, £1.40; EX 22.80 Trifecta £88.60 Pool: £625.03 - 5.21 winning units..
Owner Clive Dennett **Bred** Clive Dennett **Trained** Newmarket, Suffolk

FOCUS
The time was 0.27 seconds slower than the first division.

3468 WOLSELEY UK H'CAP 1m 3f 196y

4:15 (4:16) (Class 6) (0-65,65) 4-Y-O+ **£1,617** (£481; £240; £120) **Stalls** Centre

Form RPR
34-6 **1** **Bouggatti**[19] 2857 4-9-7 **65** .... SebSanders 6 76
(Lady Herries) *trckd ldr: led 6f out: hld on wl fnl f: drvn out* **9/2**[2]
1-03 **2** *1* **Shouda (IRE)**[14] 2997 6-9-0 **58** ....[1] TomQueally 5 67
(Barney Curley) *dwlt: hld up in rr: hdwy 2f out: chsd wnr fnl f: kpt on u.p* **4/1**[1]
0012 **3** *6* **Ryedale Lass**[10] 3137 4-9-5 **63** .... LiamKeniry 9 63
(Joseph Tuite) *hld up towards rr: hdwy 3f out: chsd wnr 2f out tl 1f out: wknd fnl f* **9/2**[2]
0225 **4** *3 1/4* **Crimson Monarch (USA)**[10] 3143 8-8-4 **48** .... ChrisCatlin 1 43
(Peter Hiatt) *prom tl wknd over 1f out* **13/2**
-314 **5** *4 1/2* **King's Road**[47] 2009 7-9-3 **61** ....(t) GeorgeBaker 3 48
(Anabel K Murphy) *hld up in rr of midfield: gng wl whn hdwy 2f out: wknd over 1f out* **11/2**[3]
6062 **6** *6* **Royal Defence (IRE)**[14] 2997 6-8-12 **56** .... PatCosgrave 7 34
(Michael Quinn) *led tl 6f out: 6th and wkng whn hmpd over 1f out* **10/1**
4-03 **7** *5* **My Sister**[12] 3081 5-8-2 **46** oh1 .... DavidProbert 4 16
(Mark Usher) *hld up towards rr: hdwy and rdn 4f out: wknd over 2f out* **12/1**
4-30 **8** *3 3/4* **Penang Cinta**[35] 2364 9-9-0 **58** .... PadraigBeggy 2 22
(David Evans) *prom: rdn 4f out: sn lost pl* **14/1**
052- **9** *29* **Galloping Queen (IRE)**[225] 6968 4-8-8 **52** ....(t) SamHitchcott 8
(Sheena West) *chsd ldrs on outer: wknd 5f out: sn bhd* **14/1**
2m 33.88s (1.18) **Going Correction** +0.125s/f (Good) **9** Ran SP% **115.2**
Speed ratings (Par 101): **101,100,96,94,91 87,83,81,62**
toteswingers 1&2 £3.60, 1&3 £4.90, 2&3 £3.90 CSF £22.81 CT £85.14 TOTE £6.10: £2.30, £1.90, £2.00; EX 22.30 Trifecta £75.80 Pool: £847.08 - 8.26 winning units..
Owner Lady Sarah Clutton **Bred** Chippenham Lodge Stud **Trained** Patching, W Sussex

FOCUS
A moderate handicap.

3469 3663 FIRST FOR FOOD SERVICE H'CAP 1m 1f 209y

4:45 (4:47) (Class 6) (0-65,65) 3-Y-O+ **£2,264** (£673; £336; £168) **Stalls** Centre

Form RPR
22 **1** **Wind Star**[3] 3392 9-9-8 **58** ....(p) SebSanders 10 65+
(Brendan Powell) *hld up in rr: gd hdwy over 1f out: r.o to ld fnl 30yds* **11/2**[2]
-003 **2** *1* **Welsh Nayber**[14] 2999 3-9-0 **62** ....(b) JimCrowley 1 67
(Amanda Perrett) *led: rdn 4 l ahd 2f out: hdd and no ex fnl 30yds* **11/2**[2]
-060 **3** *nk* **Ben Croy**[7] 3246 3-7-12 **46** oh1 ....(t1) CathyGannon 4 51
(Brian Meehan) *in tch: lost pl 5f out: rallied 2f out: styd on wl fnl f* **25/1**
2104 **4** *1 1/2* **Ostentation**[15] 2985 5-9-9 **64** ....(b) LeonnaMayor(5) 2 66
(Alastair Lidderdale) *hld up in rr: gd hdwy on rail to chse clr ldr 2f out: no ex and lost 2nd ins fnl f* **11/1**
-066 **5** *1 3/4* **Tigertoo (IRE)**[21] 2787 3-8-4 **52** .... AndreaAtzeni 8 50
(Stuart Williams) *prom tl wknd 1f out* **8/1**[3]
0031 **6** *1 1/4* **Renegotiate**[7] 3246 3-9-3 **65** 6ex .... DavidProbert 6 61
(Andrew Balding) *hld up towards rr: mod effrt over 2f out: unable to chal* **2/1**[1]
4545 **7** *hd* **Anginola (IRE)**[7] 3246 3-9-1 **63** .... PadraigBeggy 5 58
(David Evans) *in tch: rdn over 3f out: wknd over 2f out* **20/1**
-033 **8** *5* **Border Abby**[10] 3137 4-9-2 **52** .... ChrisCatlin 7 37
(Rae Guest) *t.k.h towards rr: sme hdwy over 2f out: wknd wl over 1f out* **8/1**[3]
0040 **9** *shd* **Vertibes**[13] 3047 4-8-11 **54** ....(v1) KatiaScallan(7) 9 39
(Marcus Tregoning) *chsd ldrs on outer: wknd over 2f out: sn bhd* **14/1**
4-20 **10** *7* **Lithograph (USA)**[36] 2341 3-8-7 **55** .... JoeFanning 3 26
(Mark Johnston) *w ldr tl wknd over 2f out* **14/1**
2m 6.07s (2.47) **Going Correction** +0.125s/f (Good)
WFA 3 from 4yo+ 12lb **10** Ran SP% **116.6**
Speed ratings (Par 101): **95,94,93,92,91 90,90,86,86,80**
toteswingers 1&2 £5.00, 1&3 £20.00, 2&3 £23.40 CSF £35.85 CT £699.91 TOTE £4.80: £1.70, £1.70, £8.60; EX 26.60 Trifecta £530.80 Pool: £918.19 - 1.28 winning units..
Owner Paul Frank Barry **Bred** Mrs N F M Sampson **Trained** Upper Lambourn, Berks

FOCUS
Another moderate contest.
Renegotiate Official explanation: jockey said gelding never travelled

3470 BRIGHTON AND HOVE STREAMLINE TAXIS H'CAP 7f 214y

5:15 (5:15) (Class 6) (0-55,58) 3-Y-O+ **£1,617** (£481; £240; £120) **Stalls** Centre

Form RPR
0-11 **1** **Toga Tiger (IRE)**[7] 3247 5-9-9 **58** 6ex .... RaulDaSilva(3) 12 81+
(Jeremy Gask) *in tch: led 2f out: sn clr: easily* **8/11**[1]
4015 **2** *3* **Waspy**[10] 3141 3-8-6 **48** ....(t) KirstyMilczarek 15 57
(George Baker) *towards rr: hdwy over 2f out: styd on to take 2nd ins fnl f* **16/1**
0250 **3** *1 1/4* **Director's Dream (IRE)**[19] 2851 4-8-13 **50** .... TobyAtkinson(5) 14 58
(Mark Rimmer) *mid-div: effrt and hrd rdn over 2f out: styd on same pce* **25/1**
060 **4** *1 1/4* **Tawseef (IRE)**[110] 831 4-9-6 **52** .... GeorgeBaker 16 57
(Roy Brotherton) *chsd ldrs on outer: rdn and nt qckn 2f out: kpt on fnl f* **25/1**
2520 **5** *1/2* **Putin (IRE)**[7] 3247 4-8-12 **49** ....(bt) LeonnaMayor(5) 5 53
(Phil McEntee) *led tl 2f out: sn outpcd by wnr: wknd and lost 2nd ins fnl f* **16/1**
4433 **6** *2 1/4* **Avon Supreme**[13] 3051 4-9-3 **49** .... ShaneKelly 13 48
(Gay Kelleway) *chsd ldrs: pushed along 4f out: one pce* **10/1**[3]
060 **7** *3/4* **Wyebridge**[18] 2891 3-8-10 **52** .... FergusSweeney 11 47
(Gary Moore) *mid-div: lost pl and in rr 5f out: styd on fnl 2f: gng on at fin* **28/1**
5353 **8** *2* **Warbond**[26] 2627 4-9-7 **53** .... JamieGoldstein 8 45
(Michael Madgwick) *towards rr tl rdn and styd on fnl 2f* **8/1**[2]
6056 **9** *1/2* **Inquisitress**[10] 3152 8-9-1 **47** ....(v) KieranO'Neill 6 38
(John Bridger) *dwlt: bhd: rdn and sme hdwy 2f out: unable to chal* **16/1**
-355 **10** *3 1/4* **Diddums**[5] 3318 6-9-1 **54** ....(p) KatiaScallan(7) 4 38
(Alastair Lidderdale) *dwlt: sn in rr of midfield: n.m.r on rail over 4f out: no prog fnl 3f* **12/1**
-350 **11** *2 3/4* **Men Don't Cry (IRE)**[21] 2802 3-8-13 **55** .... LiamKeniry 1 31
(Ed de Giles) *chsd ldrs tl hrd rdn and wknd over 2f out* **25/1**
0-00 **12** *3 1/4* **Johnny Splash (IRE)**[10] 3151 3-8-9 **51** ....(v) JoeFanning 10 19
(Roger Teal) *chsd ldrs tl wknd over 2f out* **40/1**
500- **13** *4* **The Wonga Coup (IRE)**[364] 3476 5-9-1 **47** .... IanMongan 2
(Pat Phelan) *a bhd* **33/1**
-505 **14** *7* **Trove (IRE)**[31] 2495 3-8-4 **46** oh1 .... CathyGannon 9
(Mark Hoad) *chsd ldr tl wknd over 2f out* **50/1**
0006 **15** *1* **Choisirez (IRE)**[7] 3246 3-8-4 **46** oh1 ....(v) AndreaAtzeni 3
(David Evans) *chsd ldrs: n.m.r and lost pl over 4f out: bhd fnl 3f* **20/1**

0604 **16** *hd* **Gay Gallivanter**[21] 2804 4-9-0 **46** oh1............................(p) PatCosgrave 7
(Michael Quinn) *mid-div: rdn whn n.m.r over 4f out: sn bhd* **25/1**

1m 36.62s (0.62) **Going Correction** +0.125s/f (Good)
WFA 3 from 4yo+ 10lb **16** Ran SP% **134.4**
Speed ratings (Par 101): **101,98,96,95,95 92,92,90,89,86 83,80,76,69,68 68**
toteswingers 1&2 £7.90, 1&3 £13.20, 2&3 £57.80 CSF £14.29 CT £228.11 TOTE £1.80: £1.10, £4.00, £5.00, £4.40; EX 11.10 Trifecta £499.90 Part won. Pool: £675.62 - 0.20 winning units..
Owner For Sale **Bred** Daniel Spaight **Trained** Sutton Veny, Wilts

FOCUS
A well-handicapped winner.
Diddums Official explanation: jockey said gelding suffered interference in running
Choisirez(IRE) Official explanation: jockey said filly suffered interference in runing

3471 BRASSERIE ITALIAN AT BRIGHTON MARINA H'CAP 6f 209y
5:45 (5:45) (Class 5) (0-75,75) 3-Y-0+ **£2,264** (£673; £336; £168) **Stalls** Centre

Form RPR
3-63 **1** **Paperetto**[25] 2652 4-8-2 **56**.. DanielCremin(7) 6 70
(Robert Mills) *chsd ldr: led 2f out: rdn clr fnl f* **14/1**
30-3 **2** *4 ½* **Patavium Prince (IRE)**[14] 3007 9-9-11 **72**...................... IanMongan 11 74
(Jo Crowley) *in tch: effrt over 2f out: kpt on u.p fnl f: jst snatched 2nd* **10/1**
0314 **3** *nse* **Cheylesmore (IRE)**[7] 3245 4-9-12 **73**.............................(v) ShaneKelly 2 75
(Michael Wigham) *led tl 2f out: kpt on same pce* **3/1**[1]
6540 **4** *1* **Lutine Charlie (IRE)**[7] 3247 5-9-0 **61**.............................. AndreaAtzeni 7 60
(David Evans) *chsd ldrs: rdn and one pce fnl 2f* **33/1**
2002 **5** *½* **Hawk Moth (IRE)**[8] 3229 4-9-6 **67**................................. CathyGannon 10 65
(John Spearing) *towards rr: effrt in centre 2f out: styd on same pce* **13/2**[2]
5234 **6** *9* **Fonterutoli (IRE)**[11] 3099 5-8-9 **56**.............................(v[1]) RobertHavlin 3 29
(Roger Ingram) *towards rr: sme hdwy and hrd rdn over 2f out: sn wknd* **9/1**
51-0 **7** *2* **Micky P**[20] 2811 5-9-2 **63**..(v) SaleemGolam 5 31
(Stuart Williams) *bhd: passed btn horses fnl 2f: n.d* **20/1**
3-50 **8** *2* **My Learned Friend (IRE)**[27] 2608 8-9-12 **73**................. DavidProbert 1 36
(Andrew Balding) *mid-div on rail: effrt and hrd rdn over 2f out: sn wknd* **7/1**[3]
1-53 **9** *5* **Four Richer**[8] 3230 3-9-5 **75**.......................................(b) FergusSweeney 8 21
(Jamie Osborne) *towards rr on outer: hrd rdn 3f out: sn wknd* **10/1**
-045 **10** *8* **Long Lost Love**[11] 3111 3-8-7 **63**.. JoeFanning 4
(Mark Johnston) *prom tl wknd 3f out* **3/1**[1]

1m 23.36s (0.26) **Going Correction** +0.125s/f (Good)
WFA 3 from 4yo+ 9lb **10** Ran SP% **118.4**
Speed ratings (Par 103): **103,97,97,96,96 85,83,81,75,66**
toteswingers 1&2 £20.70, 1&3 £9.20, 2&3 £7.70 CSF £148.04 CT £548.60 TOTE £23.60: £5.50, £3.10, £2.00; EX 98.10 Trifecta £371.00 Pool: £802.34 - 1.60 winning units..
Owner Mrs B B Mills **Bred** New England Stud Farm Ltd **Trained** Headley, Surrey
■ Daniel Cremin's first winner.

FOCUS
A modest handicap.
T/Plt: £150.40 to a £1 stake. Pool: £66108.23 - 320.71 winning tickets T/Qpdt: £9.80 to a £1 stake. Pool: £8182.04 - 613.21 winning tickets LM

3067 NEWBURY (L-H)
Tuesday, June 26

OFFICIAL GOING: Good to soft (good in places; 6.3)
Wind: medium, half against Weather: dry, muggy

3472 PUMP TECHNOLOGY APPRENTICE H'CAP 1m 3f 5y
6:20 (6:20) (Class 5) (0-70,70) 4-Y-0+ **£2,587** (£770; £384; £192) **Stalls** Centre

Form RPR
6-00 **1** **Beat Route**[57] 1706 5-8-11 **60**.................................... NicoleNordblad(3) 1 69
(Michael Attwater) *t.k.h: chsd ldr for 2f: chsd ldrs after: rdn 3f out: hdwy to chse ldr over 1f out: led ins fnl f: r.o wl and drew clr fnl 100yds* **13/2**
1451 **2** *2 ¼* **Eagle Nebula**[15] 2984 8-9-7 **70**... IanBurns(3) 2 75
(Brett Johnson) *chsd ldng trio: clsd on ldrs 3f out: rdn to ld jst over 2f out: drvn and hdd ins fnl f: no ex and outpcd by wnr fnl 100yds* **7/2**[2]
11-0 **3** *¾* **Librettela**[57] 1706 4-9-2 **67**.................................... MichaelJMMurphy(5) 7 71
(Alan Jarvis) *styd wd early: led: rdn 3f out: hdd over 2f out: stl chsng ldrs and swtchd rt wl over 1f out: styd on same pce fnl f* **14/1**
3240 **4** *2 ½* **Mister Fizz**[31] 2502 4-9-5 **68**.. JoshBaudains(3) 4 68
(Edward Bevan) *chsd ldr: rdn and chal 3f out: unable qck u.p over 1f out: outpcd and btn 1f out: plugged on same pce fnl f* **12/1**
5511 **5** *1 ¾* **Isdaal**[17] 2915 5-9-4 **69**.. MichaelJMurphy(5) 6 65
(Kevin Morgan) *hld up in last pair: swtchd lft and hdwy on bit 3f out: rdn to chse ldr 2f out: no ex over 1f out: wknd ins fnl f* **3/1**[1]
-603 **6** *¾* **Rather Cool**[13] 3043 4-8-6 **52** oh2 ow1.............................. JamesRogers 8 47
(John Bridger) *racd in midfield: clsd on ldrs 3f out: unable qck u.p 2f out: wknd fnl f* **9/1**
1-60 **7** *hd* **Mons Calpe (IRE)**[8] 3222 6-9-4 **67**.............................. DarylByrne(3) 5 62
(Paul Cole) *dwlt: hld up in last trio: effrt on inner 3f out: chsd ldrs and unable qck u.p 2f out: wknd ent fnl f* **4/1**[3]
6004 **8** *6* **Khamseen**[14] 3001 5-9-2 **65**...................................... GeorgeDowning(3) 3 49
(Karen George) *stdd s: hld up in last pair: clsd on ldrs 3f out: wknd u.p over 1f out* **9/1**

2m 27.02s (5.82) **Going Correction** +0.125s/f (Good) **8** Ran SP% **114.9**
Speed ratings (Par 103): **83,81,80,79,77 77,77,72**
toteswingers 1&2 £3.60, 1&3 £12.90, 2&3 £11.50 CSF £29.67 CT £308.70 TOTE £8.80: £2.30, £1.20, £3.10; EX 50.70 Trifecta £381.50 Pool: £577.52 - 1.12 winning units..
Owner Canisbay Bloodstock **Bred** Canisbay Bloodstock Ltd **Trained** Epsom, Surrey

FOCUS
Rail movement on bend between 1m and 5f on Round course added 10ydm to races on Round course. A fair apprentice handicap, run only at a modest pace. The winner produced his best turf form.

3473 PEGASUS PUMPS LTD MAIDEN AUCTION FILLIES' STKS 6f 8y
6:55 (6:55) (Class 4) 2-Y-0 **£3,557** (£1,058; £529; £264) **Stalls** Centre

Form RPR
1 **Maureen (IRE)** 2-8-8 0... RichardHughes 4 86+
(Richard Hannon) *a travelling strly: hld up in tch: hdwy to join ldrs on bit 2f out: led over 1f out: readily cruised clr ins fnl f: nt extended* **11/10**[1]
4 **2** *2 ½* **Annecdote**[31] 2499 2-8-4 0... LukeMorris 2 68
(Jonathan Portman) *restless in stalls: chsd ldr: rdn wl over 2f out: led 2f out: hdd over 1f out: easily brushed aside by wnr ins fnl f: kpt on u.p to hold 2nd* **2/1**[2]
5 **3** *hd* **Haatefina**[14] 3009 2-8-6 0.. SilvestreDeSousa 7 69
(Mark Usher) *sn niggled along in last pair: rdn 1/2-way: hdwy to chse ldng trio and swtchd lft jst ins fnl f: kpt on and pressing for 2nd cl home: no ch w wnr* **20/1**
4 *2* **Martinas Delight (USA)** 2-8-7 0 ow1............................ KierenFallon 3 64
(Alan Jarvis) *s.i.s: rn green and flashing tail early: bhd: hdwy after 2f out: ev ch and rdn 2f out: outpcd by wnr and btn jst ins fnl f: wknd fnl 50yds* **25/1**
5 *10* **Lady Calantha** 2-8-8 0... RyanMoore 5 35
(Richard Hannon) *t.k.h: chsd ldrs: rdn wl over 1f out: unable qck and sn struggling: wknd ent fnl f* **16/1**
6 *½* **Magical Rose (IRE)** 2-8-8 0....................................... FrannyNorton 6 34
(Paul D'Arcy) *in tch: rdn and effrt ent fnl 2f: wknd u.p ent fnl f* **7/1**[3]
4 **7** *1 ¾* **Moonlit Dancer (IRE)**[13] 3040 2-8-8 0.............................. MartinLane 1 29
(J W Hills) *led tl rdn and hdd 2f out: wknd u.p jst over 1f out* **11/1**

1m 16.31s (3.31) **Going Correction** +0.40s/f (Good) **7** Ran SP% **116.3**
Speed ratings (Par 92): **93,89,89,86,73 72,70**
toteswingers 1&2 £1.10, 1&3 £6.10, 2&3 £7.20 CSF £3.60 TOTE £2.10: £1.20, £1.50; EX 4.80.
Owner Ahmad Alkhallafi **Bred** C McEvoy **Trained** East Everleigh, Wilts

FOCUS
Probably not the strongest of juvenile fillies' events for the track, but the winner hacked up and was value for two extra lengths.

NOTEBOOK
Maureen(IRE) barely broke sweat. The daughter of Holy Roman Emperor had attracted solid support throughout the day and it was clear from an early stage that she knew her job. She was covered up behind the leaders and arrived on the scene full of running. Youngsters from this yard invariably improve considerably for experience and it's likely that a step up grade will follow. (op 5-4 tchd 11-8 in a place)
Annecdote stuck on creditably for minor honours. (tchd 11-4)
Haatefina never threatened the winner but has clearly got ability. (op 18-1)
Martinas Delight(USA) pulled well clear of the remainder and showed enough on debut to suggest she has a future. She lost two positions in the final furlong but is entitled to improve. (tchd 28-1)
Lady Calantha, a stable companion of the winner, was disappointing and will need to step up considerably if she's to make an impact. (op 12-1)
Moonlit Dancer(IRE) Official explanation: trainer said filly had choked

3474 PUMPMATIC PUMP STATIONS BY PUMP TECHNOLOGY MAIDEN FILLIES' STKS 7f (S)
7:25 (7:27) (Class 4) 2-Y-0 **£3,557** (£1,058; £529; £264) **Stalls** Centre

Form RPR
1 **Just The Judge (IRE)** 2-9-0 0.. MichaelHills 9 85+
(Charles Hills) *stdd s: hld up in last trio: hdwy 2f out: rdn and chal 1f out: led ins fnl f: r.o wl* **11/4**[1]
2 *¾* **Pompeia** 2-9-0 0.. JimCrowley 6 82+
(Ralph Beckett) *chsd ldrs: rdn and edgd rt over 1f out: drvn and ev ch 1f out: chsd wnr and kpt on fnl 75yds* **16/1**
4 **3** *1 ¾* **Califante**[9] 3182 2-9-0 0... RichardHughes 4 78
(Richard Hannon) *led tl 1/2-way: chsd ldrs after tl rdn to ld over 1f out: drvn 1f out: hdd ins fnl f: no ex and wknd fnl 50yds* **3/1**[2]
2 **4** *1* **Strictly Silca**[13] 3034 2-9-0 0... MartinHarley 2 76
(Mick Channon) *hld up in tch: swtchd lft and effrt 2f out: drvn and ev ch over 1f out: no ex 1f out: wknd ins fnl f* **11/4**[1]
5 *1 ¾* **Color Shades** 2-9-0 0... AdamKirby 12 71+
(Clive Cox) *chsd ldrs: wnt 2nd 3f out tl rdn and unable qck whn short of room 2f out: styd on same pce fnl f* **16/1**
6 *3 ¾* **Lady Marmelo (IRE)** 2-9-0 0.. MatthewDavies 3 62
(Mick Channon) *hld in last trio: rdn ent fnl 2f: edgd lft and outpcd wl over 1f out: sn wknd* **40/1**
7 *1 ¼* **Ottauquechee (IRE)** 2-8-11 0...................................... SeanLevey(3) 11 59
(Richard Hannon) *t.k.h early: in tch: rdn and unable qck ust over 2f out: wknd over 1f out* **33/1**
8 *½* **Upper Echelon** 2-9-0 0... SilvestreDeSousa 10 57
(Mark Johnston) *chsd ldr tl led 1/2-way: rdn and edgd rt 2f out: hdd over 1f out: sn outpcd and btn: wknd fnl f* **7/1**[3]
9 *2 ½* **Equitissa (IRE)** 2-9-0 0.. RyanMoore 1 51
(Richard Hannon) *hld up in tch in last trio: rdn 2f out: sn outpcd and btn: wknd over 1f out* **20/1**

1m 29.56s (3.86) **Going Correction** +0.40s/f (Good) **9** Ran SP% **112.7**
Speed ratings (Par 92): **93,92,90,89,87 82,81,80,77**
toteswingers 1&2 £14.90, 1&3 £4.30, 2&3 £10.00 CSF £44.48 TOTE £3.20: £1.10, £3.80, £1.30; EX 57.90 Trifecta £659.30 Part won. Pool: £890.94 - 0.30 winning units..
Owner Sangster Family & Matthew Green **Bred** Mrs J Dempsey **Trained** Lambourn, Berks

FOCUS
An interesting renewal of this juvenile fillies' maiden and a really likeable performance from the winner, who looks to have improvement in her.

NOTEBOOK
Just The Judge(IRE) stayed on powerfully to win without being knocked around. The Charles Hills-trained newcomer was the subject of substantial support prior to the off and she duly obliged, despite signs of greenness. She really pointed her toe when launched with her effort and should be even better once tackling a firmer surface. She holds an entry in the Group 1 Moyglare Stud Stakes in Ireland later in the year and is clearly highly regarded. She looks a filly worth following on this evidence. (op 9-2)
Pompeia should be all about middle-distances and the fact that she got so close here, in such a steadily run affair, suggests she's another above average recruit. She came to win her race at the furlong pole but was unsurprisingly outpaced by the speedier bred winner. She shouldn't have any trouble getting off the mark next time. (op 14-1 tchd 11-1)
Califante performed with credit. (op 5-2)
Strictly Silca had her limitations exposed. (op 5-2)

3475 JUNG PUMPEN & PUMP TECHNOLOGY H'CAP 1m 7y(R)
8:00 (8:00) (Class 5) (0-70,70) 3-Y-0 **£2,587** (£770; £384; £192) **Stalls** Centre

Form RPR
20-2 **1** **Hilali (IRE)**[21] 1589 3-9-5 **68**.. GeorgeBaker 1 79
(Gary Brown) *stdd after s: hld up towards rr: hdwy 3f out: swtchd rt over 2f out: rdn to ld 1f out: r.o strly and drew clr fnl f: readily* **28/1**
0466 **2** *6* **Darnathean**[14] 3002 3-9-4 **67**......................................(e[1]) FrannyNorton 11 64
(Paul D'Arcy) *taken down early: racd keenly: chsd ldr: drvn and chalng over 2f out: nt qckn u.p wl over 1f out: outpcd by wnr fnl f: plugged on to go 2nd wl ins fnl f* **25/1**
11-0 **3** *¾* **Elegant Flight**[56] 1733 3-9-4 **67**.....................................(v) KierenFallon 9 62
(Alan Jarvis) *t.k.h: midfield early: hdwy to chse ldrs over 6f out: rdn to ld edgd lft over 2f out: hdd 1f out: outpcd by wnr and sn btn: lost 2nd wl ins fnl f* **20/1**

1 **4** 1/2 **Shena's Dream (IRE)**[25] 2680 3-9-4 **67** RyanMoore 10 61+
(William Haggas) *fly-jmpd leaving stalls and slowly away: bhd: prog 1/2-way: swtchd rt and effrt wl over 2f out: 6th and no imp over 1f out: no threat to wnr but kpt on fnl 100yds* **5/4**[1]

-200 **5** 1/2 **Shot In The Dark (IRE)**[17] 2942 3-9-5 **68** LiamKeniry 4 61
(Andrew Balding) *led tl hdd and rdn over 2f out: styd pressing ldrs tl no ex ent fnl f: outpcd by wnr and plugged on same pce fnl f* **12/1**

-004 **6** nse **Netley Marsh**[22] 2756 3-8-13 **65** (b[1]) SeanLevey(3) 5 58
(Richard Hannon) *in tch: rdn and effrt wl over 2f out: chsd ldrs and drvn wl over 1f out: outpcd by wnr and btn ins fnl f: plugged on same pce* **14/1**

030- **7** 8 **Royale Ransom**[222] 7444 3-9-2 **65** MartinHarley 2 39
(Sylvester Kirk) *stdd s: hld up in rr: clsd 3f out: rdn and fnd little 2f out: sn wknd* **66/1**

1000 **8** 3 1/4 **Three Bards (IRE)**[15] 2980 3-9-5 **68** (b[1]) SilvestreDeSousa 3 35
(Mark Johnston) *chsd ldrs: rdn and unable qck 3f out: wknd wl over 1f out: bhd fnl f* **14/1**

0-10 **9** 8 **Golden Jubilee (USA)**[22] 2756 3-9-3 **66** RichardHughes 12 15
(Richard Hannon) *a towards rr: rdn and effrt over 3f out: wl btn over 1f out: bhd and eased ins fnl f* **9/1**[3]

5-43 **10** 16 **Raffinn**[35] 2382 3-9-4 **67** JamesDoyle 6
(Sylvester Kirk) *t.k.h: in tch in midfield: rdn 3f out: sn struggling: wknd 2f out: wl bhd and eased fnl f: t.o* **3/1**[2]

065 **11** 9 **Wildomar**[21] 2800 3-9-7 **70** WilliamBuick 7
(Jeremy Noseda) *in tch in midfield on outer: rdn and wandered u.p 3f out: wknd 2f out: wl bhd and eased fnl f: t.o* **12/1**

1m 40.42s (1.72) **Going Correction** +0.125s/f (Good) **11** Ran SP% **121.7**
Speed ratings (Par 99): **96,90,89,88,88 88,80,76,68,52 43**
toteswingers 1&2 £53.40, 1&3 £21.30, 2&3 £74.30 CSF £588.09 CT £13641.99 TOTE £57.20: £9.40, £7.60, £4.50; EX 476.40 TRIFECTA Not won..
Owner Gary Brown **Bred** Shadwell Estate Company Limited **Trained** Lambourn, Berks

FOCUS
A modest 3yo handicap, run at a steady pace. A surprise win but it seems no fluke.
Raffinn Official explanation: jockey said gelding lost its action
Wildomar Official explanation: jockey said colt stopped quickly

3476 ENJOY JUNIOR RUGBY WITH TADLEY TIGERS FILLIES' H'CAP 1m 2f 6y
8:35 (8:35) (Class 4) (0-85,82) 3-Y-0 **£4,075** (£1,212; £606; £303) **Stalls** Centre

Form RPR

0-1 **1** **Khione**[23] 2734 3-9-6 **81** KierenFallon 7 91+
(Luca Cumani) *hld up in last quartet: rdn and effrt 2f out: hdwy u.p over 1f out: led ins fnl f: edgd lft but styd on wl and pushed out after* **15/8**[1]

02-1 **2** 1 1/2 **Varnish**[40] 2200 3-9-0 **75** RichardHughes 3 82
(Richard Hannon) *chsd ldrs: rdn and pressed ldrs 2f out: drvn over 1f out: kpt on fnl 100yds: wnt 2nd cl home* **16/1**

-266 **3** nk **Little Dutch Girl**[18] 2889 3-8-12 **73** (b) AdamKirby 6 79
(Clive Cox) *rdn along leaving stalls: chsd ldr tl rdn to ld over 2f out: hdd over 1f out: kpt on u.p tl no ex ins fnl f: lost 2nd cl home* **14/1**

3132 **4** 2 1/2 **Dutch Diamond**[12] 3080 3-9-0 **75** WilliamBuick 2 76
(John Gosden) *chsd ldrs: rdn to chal over 2f out: drvn to ld over 1f out: hdd ins fnl f: no ex and wknd towards fin* **9/2**[2]

1 **5** hd **Selfsame (USA)**[18] 2891 3-8-13 **74** JimCrowley 8 75
(Amanda Perrett) *dropped in bhd after s: clsd and wl in tch 3f out: swtchd rt 2f out: sn rdn unable qck and edgd lft: plugged on same pce fnl f* **5/1**[3]

2-14 **6** 3 1/2 **Shestheman**[40] 2201 3-9-7 **82** TedDurcan 5 76
(David Lanigan) *hld up in last quartet: rdn and effrt over 2f out: no imp 2f out: wknd over 1f out* **9/2**[2]

035 **7** 1 3/4 **Junior Diary (USA)**[22] 2768 3-8-12 **73** MartinDwyer 1 63
(Brian Meehan) *led tl hdd and rdn over 2f out: wknd over 1f out* **33/1**

54-1 **8** 27 **Amber Silk (IRE)**[32] 2448 3-9-6 **81** MichaelHills 4 17
(Charles Hills) *in tch in last quartet: rdn over 2f out: sn struggling and btn 2f out: eased fnl f: t.o* **8/1**

2m 9.78s (0.98) **Going Correction** +0.125s/f (Good) **8** Ran SP% **114.4**
Speed ratings (Par 98): **101,99,99,97,97 94,93,71**
toteswingers 1&2 £4.80, 1&3 £7.30, 2&3 £25.70 CSF £35.69 CT £328.54 TOTE £3.30: £1.20, £2.20, £2.90; EX 19.80 Trifecta £520.40 Part won. Pool: £703.36 - 0.10 winning units..
Owner Aston House Stud **Bred** Aston House Stud **Trained** Newmarket, Suffolk

FOCUS
A decent 3yo fillies' handicap, run at a strong pace and won in authoritaative fashion. The winner looks sure to do better.
Varnish Official explanation: jockey said filly hung right throughout
Amber Silk(IRE) Official explanation: jockey said filly lost its action

3477 OPTIMA CONSULTING ENGINEERS H'CAP 5f 34y
9:05 (9:05) (Class 5) (0-70,70) 3-Y-0+ **£2,587** (£770; £384; £192) **Stalls** Centre

Form RPR

-425 **1** **Cruise Tothelimit (IRE)**[21] 2789 4-8-13 **62** GeorgeDowning(5) 7 74
(Ian Williams) *chsd ldrs: rdn and effrt to ld 2f out: clr w rival 1f out: r.o wl and asserted fnl 75yds* **10/3**[2]

1444 **2** 3/4 **Rylee Mooch**[21] 2789 4-9-9 **70** (e) DeclanCannon(3) 12 79
(Richard Guest) *in tch: rdn and effrt to press wnr wl over 1f out: ev ch and clr w wnr 1f out: no ex and btn fnl 75yds* **14/1**

-204 **3** 2 3/4 **Speightowns Kid (USA)**[35] 2369 4-9-11 **69** AdamKirby 11 68
(Matthew Salaman) *towards rr: rdn and hdwy 2f out: sltly hmpd and swtchd rt over 1f out: styd on fnl f: wnt 3rd wl ins fnl f: no threat to ldng pair* **9/1**

4303 **4** 3/4 **Even Bolder**[14] 3008 9-9-4 **62** GeorgeBaker 5 58
(Eric Wheeler) *stdd s: hld up towards rr: hdwy 2f out: chsd ldrs and unable qck u.p over 1f out: styd on same pce fnl f* **10/1**

3022 **5** nk **Whitecrest**[14] 2994 4-9-12 **70** CathyGannon 2 65
(John Spearing) *fly-jmpd and awkward leaving stalls: chsd ldr utnil led 1/2-way: sn rdn and hdd 2f out: outpcd and btn 1f out: plugged on* **5/2**[1]

0166 **6** 1 3/4 **Flashbang**[31] 2493 4-9-1 **64** (t) DuilioDaSilva(5) 13 53
(Paul Cole) *hld up in midfield: hdwy and edging lft 2f out: rdn and chsd ldng pair 1f out: no imp: wknd and lost 3 pls fnl 100yds* **20/1**

-000 **7** 2 1/2 **Brandywell Boy (IRE)**[14] 3008 9-8-1 **52** oh1 ow1..(b) JoshBaudains(7) 6 32
(Dominic Ffrench Davis) *chsd ldrs: rdn 1/2-way: sn struggling: wknd over 1f out: no ch fnl f* **14/1**

2060 **8** nse **Not My Choice (IRE)**[29] 2546 7-9-4 **62** (t) TomMcLaughlin 8 42
(Paul Howling) *in tch in midfield: u.p and struggling 1/2-way: wknd over 1f out: no ch fnl f* **33/1**

2046 **9** 3 1/2 **Royal Envoy (IRE)**[41] 2170 9-8-7 **51** MichaelStainton 10 18
(Paul Howling) *a towards rr: rdn and struggling 1/2-way: no threat to ldrs fnl 2f* **40/1**

020- **10** 5 **Adaeze (IRE)**[271] 6479 4-8-11 **55** LeeNewman 3
(Jonathan Portman) *sltly hmpd s: sn rcvrd and racd in midfield: rdn and wknd 2f out: bhd fnl f* **33/1**

-502 **11** 9 **Madame Kintyre**[17] 2943 4-9-6 **64** (b) JamesMillman 4
(Rod Millman) *a bhd: lost tch 2f out: eased ins fnl f* **6/1**[3]

2300 **12** 19 **Love You Louis**[21] 2789 6-9-12 **70** (p) RichardHughes 1
(J R Jenkins) *racd along towards far side: led tl 1/2-way: sn rdn and btn: eased fr over 1f out: t.o* **17/2**

1m 2.96s (1.56) **Going Correction** +0.40s/f (Good) **12** Ran SP% **122.0**
Speed ratings (Par 103): **103,101,97,96,95 92,88,88,83,75 60,30**
toteswingers 1&2 £14.20, 1&3 £7.20, 2&3 £10.90 CSF £48.94 CT £397.84 TOTE £4.70: £1.70, £4.90, £3.40; EX 55.30 Trifecta £511.00 Part won. Pool: £690.65 - 0.94 winning units..
Owner Odysian Ltd T/A Cruise Nightspot **Bred** D And Mrs D Veitch **Trained** Portway, Worcs

FOCUS
A fair sprint handicap, run at a strong pace. The winner was well in on his 2yo best and the runner-up is consistent.
Adaeze(IRE) Official explanation: trainer said filly was unsuited by the good to soft (good in places) ground
Madame Kintyre Official explanation: jockey said filly slipped on leaving stalls and never travelled
Love You Louis Official explanation: jockey said gelding moved poorly
T/Jkpt: Not won. T/Plt: £2,190.00 to a £1 stake. Pool: £78602.66 - 26.2 winning tickets T/Qpdt: £262.20 to a £1 stake. Pool: £5882.34 - 16.6 winning tickets SP

3478 - 3482a (Foreign Racing) - See Raceform Interactive

3137 BATH (L-H)
Wednesday, June 27

OFFICIAL GOING: Good to soft (good in places)
Wind: Mild breeze half across Weather: Cloudy, humid

3483 BET IN-PLAY AT BETVICTOR.COM H'CAP 1m 3f 144y
6:10 (6:11) (Class 6) (0-60,60) 3-Y-0 **£1,704** (£503; £251) **Stalls** Low

Form RPR

0503 **1** **The Quarterjack**[11] 3142 3-8-12 **54** RaulDaSilva(3) 5 69
(Ron Hodges) *trckd ldr: rdn 3f out: led ent fnl f: styd on strly* **6/1**[2]

654- **2** 2 3/4 **Alborz (IRE)**[259] 6807 3-9-7 **60** ShaneKelly 11 70
(Tim Vaughan) *led: rdn over 2f out: hdd ent fnl f: kpt on but no ex* **12/1**

60-4 **3** 3 3/4 **Isobella**[27] 2625 3-9-1 **54** (p) RobertHavlin 2 58
(Hughie Morrison) *mid-div: rdn over 3f out: styd on fr over 1f out: wnt 3rd ins fnl f: nvr trbld ldng pair* **16/1**

-040 **4** 1 1/4 **Kaiser Wilhelm (IRE)**[13] 3087 3-9-1 **54** PatCosgrave 3 56
(Paul Cole) *mid-div: pushed along over 5f out: rdn over 3f out: styd on fnl 2f: nvr threatened* **18/1**

66-3 **5** 2 **Capriska**[37] 2340 3-8-13 **52** MartinHarley 6 51
(Willie Musson) *mid-div: rdn and hdwy 3f out: styd on same pce fnl 2f* **9/2**[1]

5040 **6** 6 **Roughlyn**[43] 2144 3-9-1 **54** (p) SamHitchcott 13 43
(Lisa Williamson) *trckd ldr: rdn over 3f out: fdd fnl f* **66/1**

0-63 **7** 3 **Choral Bee**[42] 2162 3-9-4 **57** DaneO'Neill 4 41
(Henry Candy) *trckd ldr tl rdn over 3f out: wknd ent fnl f* **8/1**[3]

6023 **8** 3/4 **Looks Like Rain**[20] 2850 3-8-10 **56** IanBurns(7) 12 39
(Michael Bell) *pushed along over 4f out: swtchd rt on bnd over 3f out: nvr bttr than mid-div* **8/1**[3]

0-43 **9** 7 **Manbaa (USA)**[29] 2578 3-8-12 **51** PaulHanagan 10 22
(John Dunlop) *stmbld leaving stalls: towards rr: pushed along over 5f out: c wd and sme prog over 3f out: no further prog fnl 2f* **11/1**

0-04 **10** 1/2 **Cash Injection**[11] 3142 3-8-12 **51** (t) TomMcLaughlin 14 21
(Karen George) *trckd ldrs: rdn over 3f out: wknd 2f out* **20/1**

0-00 **11** 1 **Hurricane Emerald (IRE)**[21] 2818 3-9-6 **59** SilvestreDeSousa 1 28
(Mark Johnston) *mid-div: rdn over 3f out: nvr any imp: wknd over 1f out* **16/1**

2030 **12** 3/4 **Green Legacy (USA)**[20] 2850 3-9-4 **57** (v[1]) PatDobbs 16 24
(Amanda Perrett) *s.i.s: a towards rr* **25/1**

3160 **13** 1 1/2 **Like Clockwork**[13] 3087 3-9-5 **58** MichaelHills 15 23
(Mark H Tompkins) *hld up towards rr: u.p whn carried wd on bnd over 3f out: no imp after: eased whn btn over 1f out* **17/2**

-255 **14** 3 3/4 **Lady Romanza (IRE)**[49] 1982 3-9-5 **58** CathyGannon 7 17
(Brendan Powell) *in tch: rdn over 3f out: wknd over 2f out* **14/1**

0-00 **15** 50 **Lady Ocarina**[30] 2560 3-9-0 **53** MartinLane 8
(John Dunlop) *s.i.s: sn pushed into midfield: dropped to rr over 5f out: t.o fnl 2f* **40/1**

05-0 **16** 26 **Silent Energy (IRE)**[53] 1853 3-8-11 **55** DarrenEgan(5) 9
(Ronald Harris) *s.i.s: nvr travelling in detached last: t.o fnl 2f* **40/1**

2m 32.21s (1.61) **Going Correction** +0.05s/f (Good) **16** Ran SP% **119.9**
Speed ratings (Par 97): **96,94,91,90,89 85,83,83,78,78 77,76,75,73,40 22**
toteswingers: 1&2 £23.00, 1&3 £28.50, 2&3 £35.30. CSF £70.83 CT £1107.27 TOTE £8.60: £1.70, £3.50, £4.30, £4.60; EX 137.20.
Owner P E Axon **Bred** Cheveley Park Stud Ltd **Trained** Charlton Mackrell, Somerset

FOCUS
Rail realignment added 12yds to distance of races utilising bottom bend. An extremely moderate 3yo handicap, run at a fair pace.
Manbaa(USA) Official explanation: jockey said filly stumbled leaving stalls

3484 BETVICTOR ON YOUR MOBILE MAIDEN STKS 1m 3f 144y
6:40 (6:41) (Class 5) 3-Y-0+ **£2,264** (£673; £336; £168) **Stalls** Low

Form RPR

4-22 **1** **Mysterious Man (IRE)**[39] 2266 3-8-13 83 DavidProbert 4 80
(Andrew Balding) *trckd ldrs: rdn over 2f out: led jst over 1f out: styd on: rdn out* **1/1**[1]

4-55 **2** 2 1/4 **Linkable**[30] 2557 3-8-13 71 MichaelHills 8 76
(Charles Hills) *prom: led over 4f out: rdn 3f out: hdd jst over 1f out: kpt on same pce* **9/1**[3]

43-2 **3** 1 **Mawaqeet (USA)**[34] 2430 3-8-13 83 PaulHanagan 6 74
(Sir Michael Stoute) *hld up towards rr of midfield: pushed along and hdwy over 3f out: sn rdn: styd on fnl f* **2/1**[2]

63-0 **4** 5 **Danehill Dante (IRE)**[58] 1706 4-9-13 71 DaneO'Neill 10 66
(Alan King) *led tl over 4f out: trckd ldr: rdn 3f out: styd on same pce fnl 2f* **25/1**

5 nk **Benartic (IRE)**[95] 8-9-13 0 TomQueally 11 66
(Harry Dunlop) *s.i.s: sn chsng ldrs: swtchd rt for effrt whn rdn 3f out: no ex fnl f* **50/1**

0 **6** 2 1/2 **Regal Diva**[23] 2768 4-9-8 0 ShaneKelly 3 56
(Reg Hollinshead) *mid-div: rdn 3f out: nvr any imp on ldrs* **100/1**

06 **7** 1 1/4 **Taigan (FR)**[14] 3035 5-9-13 0 FrannyNorton 2 59+
(Ian Williams) *towards rr: sme late prog: nvr a factor* **40/1**

-05 **8** *1* **Rhossili Bay**[28] 2612 3-8-8 0 .... MartinHarley 1 53
(Alastair Lidderdale) *hld up towards rr: hdwy on inner fr 4f out: rdn 3f out: wknd jst over 1f out* **100/1**

03- **9** *12* **Rishikesh**[377] 3080 4-9-13 0 .... HayleyTurner 9 38
(Michael Bell) *s.i.s: sn mid-div: rdn over 3f out: wknd over 1f out* **12/1**

00 **10** *16* **Imagery**[9] 3227 3-8-8 0 .... DarrenEgan(5) 12 12
(Ronald Harris) *trckd ldrs early: lost pl after 2f: dropped to rr 4f out: t.o* **150/1**

5 **11** *33* **Madrilene (USA)**[135] 546 4-9-8 0 .... SilvestreDeSousa 7
(Mark Johnston) *in tch: reminders 5f out: wknd 3f out: t.o* **20/1**

12 *55* **Castle Legend**[33] 7-9-8 0 .... JamesRogers(5) 5
(David Lewis) *sn struggling: a last: t.o* **150/1**

2m 32.86s (2.26) **Going Correction** +0.05s/f (Good)
WFA 3 from 4yo+ 14lb **12** Ran SP% **117.3**
Speed ratings (Par 103): **94,92,91,88,88 86,85,85,77,66 44,7**
toteswingers: 1&2 £4.00, 1&3 £1.10, 2&3 £3.40. CSF £10.89 TOTE £2.40: £1.10, £2.60, £1.10; EX 9.70.
Owner Mr & Mrs R Gorell/Mr & Mrs P Pausewang **Bred** Barronstown Stud **Trained** Kingsclere, Hants

FOCUS
There weren't too many that could be fancied for this maiden.

3485 BEST PRICES AT BETVICTOR.COM H'CAP 1m 5y
7:10 (7:11) (Class 5) (0-70,70) 4-Y-0+ **£2,264** (£673; £336; £168) **Stalls** Low

Form RPR

3411 **1** **Woolston Ferry (IRE)**[26] 2675 6-9-2 **65** .... FergusSweeney 3 74+
(Henry Candy) *mid-div: rdn and hdwy fr 2f out: led ent fnl f: r.o wl* **7/2**[1]

5005 **2** *2 ¼* **Ocean Legend (IRE)**[14] 3045 7-9-7 **70** .... KirstyMilczarek 5 74
(Tony Carroll) *trckd ldrs: rdn and ev ch ent fnl f: kpt on but sn hld by wnr* **14/1**

3400 **3** *shd* **Prince Namid**[11] 3152 10-7-11 **51** oh1 .... DarrenEgan(5) 9 55
(Jonathen de Giles) *hld up towards rr: c wd over 3f out: rdn and hdwy 2f out: styd on wl fnl f: wnt 3rd fnl strides* **40/1**

6-00 **4** *shd* **Blue Maisey**[20] 2847 4-9-2 **65** .... SebSanders 1 68
(Peter Makin) *led: rdn over 2f out: edgd rt over 1f out: hdd ent fnl f: no ex* **16/1**

-614 **5** *1 ½* **Bold Cross (IRE)**[23] 2767 9-8-12 **64** .... MatthewCosham(3) 10 64
(Edward Bevan) *mid-div: rdn over 2f out: hdwy whn nt clr run and swtchd rt ent fnl f: styd on* **10/1**

0330 **6** *¾* **Catchanova (IRE)**[14] 3039 5-9-5 **68** .... TomQueally 6 66
(Eve Johnson Houghton) *mid-div rdn over 2f out: sn chsng ldrs: one pce fnl f* **8/1**

0-00 **7** *¾* **Cobbs Quay**[19] 2886 4-8-13 **62** .... SilvestreDeSousa 2 58
(Daniel Kubler) *trckd ldrs: rdn wl over 2f out: fdd ins fnl f* **7/1**[3]

3-05 **8** *¾* **Frozen Over**[20] 2847 4-9-1 **64** .... LiamKeniry 15 59
(Stuart Kittow) *towards rr of midfield: rdn over 2f out: styd on ins fnl f: nvr a threat* **12/1**

36-3 **9** *½* **Cool Hand Jake**[14] 3039 6-9-1 **64** .... PatDobbs 4 58
(Jamie Osborne) *hld up towards rr: rdn over 2f out: no imp tl hdwy ent fnl f: styng on whn short of room on rails fnl 75yds* **8/1**

2004 **10** *2 ¼* **Bedibyes**[15] 3006 4-8-5 **54** .... FrannyNorton 8 42
(Richard Mitchell) *pushed along and squeezed up early: in tch: rdn wl over 2f out: fdd fnl f* **25/1**

424 **11** *½* **Cheers**[34] 2421 4-9-3 **66** .... FrankieMcDonald 11 53
(Oliver Sherwood) *trckd ldrs: rdn wl over 2f out: styng on at same pce whn squeezed out ent fnl f: eased after* **6/1**[2]

60-0 **12** *3* **Bidable**[29] 2574 8-9-0 **66** .... RaulDaSilva(3) 14 46
(Bryn Palling) *mid-div: rdn wl over 2f out: wknd over 1f out* **40/1**

605 **13** *2 ¾* **Call Me April**[35] 2387 4-8-5 **54** .... TadhgO'Shea 13 28
(Karen George) *mid-div: rdn over 3f out: wknd over 1f out* **20/1**

60-0 **14** *5* **Mr Udagawa**[41] 2207 6-9-3 **66** ....(p) MartinLane 12 29
(Bernard Llewellyn) *sn pushed along: chsd ldr tl rdn over 3f out: wknd 2f out* **40/1**

02- **15** *½* **Fire King**[316] 5136 6-9-2 **65** ....(p) DaneO'Neill 7 26
(Natalie Lloyd-Beavis) *a towards rr* **16/1**

1m 42.38s (1.58) **Going Correction** +0.05s/f (Good) **15** Ran SP% **122.4**
Speed ratings (Par 103): **94,91,91,91,90 89,88,87,87,85 84,81,78,73,73**
toteswingers: 1&2 £10.40, 1&3 £41.40, 2&3 £89.00. CSF £52.53 CT £1712.18 TOTE £3.40: £1.50, £6.40, £17.40; EX 65.50.
Owner Ms L Burns **Bred** Tim Taylor **Trained** Kingston Warren, Oxon
■ Stewards' Enquiry : Matthew Cosham one-day ban: careless riding (Jul 11)

FOCUS
A fair handicap, run at a decent pace.

3486 SOLSBURY SOLUTIONS H'CAP 5f 11y
7:40 (7:40) (Class 4) (0-85,85) 3-Y-0 **£4,075** (£1,212; £606; £303) **Stalls** Centre

Form RPR

031- **1** **Jwala**[198] 7736 3-9-3 **81** .... ShaneKelly 5 92
(Robert Cowell) *broke wl: mde all: kpt on gamely: rdn out* **9/2**[2]

0-24 **2** *½* **Place In My Heart**[19] 2893 3-9-2 **85** .... DavidKenny(5) 3 94
(George Baker) *chsd wnr: rdn over 2f out: kpt on towards fin but a being hld* **5/1**[3]

2230 **3** *2* **Ashpan Sam**[20] 2853 3-8-10 **74** .... CathyGannon 7 76
(John Spearing) *chsd wnr tl rdn over 2f out: kpt on same pce* **9/1**

1556 **4** *1 ¾* **Red Senor (IRE)**[16] 2986 3-8-12 **76** .... WilliamCarson 2 72
(Charles Hills) *chsd ldrs: rdn over 2f out: kpt on same pce* **8/1**

3355 **5** *1* **Signifer (IRE)**[18] 2914 3-9-5 **83** .... MartinHarley 6 75
(Mick Channon) *chsd ldrs: rdn over 2f out: nt pce to get on terms: no ex fnl 100yds* **7/1**

21-1 **6** *3* **Blanc De Chine (IRE)**[33] 2443 3-8-13 **77** .... SebSanders 8 58
(Peter Makin) *hld up in last pair but wl in tch: rdn over 2f out: nvr threatened: wknd fnl 120yds* **9/4**[1]

1005 **7** *1* **Heartsong (IRE)**[19] 2870 3-8-11 **80** .... DarrenEgan(5) 1 58
(John Gallagher) *s.i.s: in last pair but wl in tch: rdn over 2f out: nvr threatened: wknd fnl 120yds* **7/1**

1m 1.98s (-0.52) **Going Correction** +0.05s/f (Good) **7** Ran SP% **111.7**
Speed ratings (Par 101): **106,105,102,99,97 92,91**
toteswingers: 1&2 £3.20, 1&3 £11.00, 2&3 £8.10. CSF £25.68 CT £188.62 TOTE £6.40: £3.00, £2.50; EX 28.60.
Owner Manor Farm Stud & Miss S Hoare **Bred** Manor Farm Stud (rutland) **Trained** Six Mile Bottom, Cambs
■ Stewards' Enquiry : William Carson two-day ban: used whip with excessive force (Jul 11-12)

FOCUS
A decent sprint.

Blanc De Chine(IRE) Official explanation: trainer said, regasrding running, that the filly was unsuited by being settled in off a relatively slow early pace and would prefer faster ground

3487 BETVICTOR ON YOUR MOBILE IRISH E B F MAIDEN FILLIES' STKS 5f 161y
8:10 (8:10) (Class 5) 2-Y-0 **£3,234** (£962; £481; £240) **Stalls** Centre

Form RPR

1 **Redressthebalance (IRE)** 2-9-0 0 .... RichardThomas 5 72+
(Ralph Beckett) *prom: rdn and looked hld over 1f out: rallied fnl 75yds: led nring fin* **9/4**[2]

2 *¾* **Smart Daisy K** 2-9-0 0 .... ShaneKelly 11 70+
(Reg Hollinshead) *led: rdn 1 1/2 l clr over 1f out: no ex whn hdd nring fin* **14/1**

30 **3** *2 ½* **Cio Cio San (IRE)**[32] 2499 2-9-0 0 .... PatDobbs 8 62+
(Richard Hannon) *sn pushed along in tch: rdn over 1f out: r.o ins fnl f: nvr a threat* **7/4**[1]

4 *2 ½* **Silver Arny** 2-8-9 0 .... DavidKenny(5) 4 54
(Brendan Powell) *in tch: rdn over 2f out: wnt 3rd ent fnl f tl no ex fnl 75yds* **33/1**

5 *1 ¼* **Kunzea (IRE)** 2-9-0 0 .... MartinHarley 9 50
(Mick Channon) *s.i.s: in rr: styd on fnl f: nvr gng pce to get involved* **9/2**[3]

44 **6** *1 ¾* **Spray Tan**[37] 2338 2-9-0 0 .... KirstyMilczarek 1 44
(Tony Carroll) *t.k.h: trckd ldrs: rdn over 2f out: fdd fnl f* **14/1**

0 **7** *2* **Our Golden Girl**[21] 2812 2-9-0 0 .... DavidProbert 6 43+
(Mark Usher) *in tch: rdn over 2f out: hung lft and wknd jst over 1f out* **14/1**

5 **8** *2 ¾* **Pearl Of Phoenix**[13] 3084 2-9-0 0 .... TadhgO'Shea 10 29
(Jo Hughes) *chsd ldrs: rdn over 2f out: wknd ent fnl f* **40/1**

9 *8* **Katy Spirit (IRE)** 2-9-0 0 .... FergusSweeney 7 4
(Michael Blanshard) *bucked leaving stalls: mid-div: rdn over 2f out: sn wknd* **14/1**

1m 12.76s (1.56) **Going Correction** +0.05s/f (Good) **9** Ran SP% **117.4**
Speed ratings (Par 90): **91,90,86,83,81 79,76,73,62**
toteswingers: 1&2 £7.40, 1&3 £2.70, 2&3 £5.40. CSF £34.54 TOTE £4.20: £1.90, £2.90, £1.10; EX 37.40.
Owner R A Pegum **Bred** Kevin Walsh **Trained** Kimpton, Hants

FOCUS
An interesting juvenile fillies' maiden.

NOTEBOOK
Redressthebalance(IRE) got back up to beat Smart Daisy K, who had looked sure to collect. The Ralph Beckett-trained newcomer showed bright speed from the stalls but, headed at halfway, looked set to play only a minor role in the finish. However, she stayed on powerfully and won with a bit in hand. A 25,000gns purchase, she is entitled to improve both physically and mentally for this and ought to have no problem getting either 6f or 7f this season. (op 7-2 tchd 4-1)
Smart Daisy K appeared to have the race in the bag before the combination of greenness and the uphill finish caught her out. This was a really promising debut effort and compensation surely awaits. (op 12-1)
Cio Cio San(IRE) finished her race and she could well prove the best of these in time. She was all at sea in the early stages but fairly rattled home when it was too late. She'll be hard to beat next time. (op 15-8 tchd 13-8)
Silver Arny ran well for a long way before getting tired. (tchd 28-1)

3488 IN-PLAY EURO BETTING AT BETVICTOR.COM CLASSIFIED STKS 5f 161y
8:40 (8:40) (Class 5) 3-Y-0 **£2,264** (£673; £336; £168) **Stalls** Centre

Form RPR

5213 **1** **Millibar (IRE)**[5] 3350 3-9-0 67 ....(p) TomMcLaughlin 4 75
(Nick Littmoden) *trckd ldrs: nt clr run 2f out tl jst over 1f out: qcknd up wl to ld sn after: r.o: kpt up to work: readily* **9/4**[1]

10-2 **2** *2 ½* **Courtland Avenue (IRE)**[51] 1941 3-9-0 69 .... RichardKingscote 5 67
(Jonathan Portman) *disp ld tl rdn into clr ld 2f out: hdd jst ins fnl f: nt pce of wnr* **7/2**[3]

4554 **3** *2* **Amphora**[5] 3343 3-9-0 66 .... DavidProbert 6 60
(Andrew Balding) *trckd ldrs: rdn for str chal jst over 1f out: kpt on same pce fnl 140yds* **11/4**[2]

6-16 **4** *nk* **Pettochside**[72] 1412 3-9-0 70 .... WilliamCarson 2 59
(Stuart Williams) *t.k.h: in last pair: swtchd rt over 1f out: sn rdn: nt pce to chal* **8/1**

10-0 **5** *6* **Idols Eye**[13] 3071 3-9-0 69 ....(t) FergusSweeney 8 39
(Martyn Meade) *disp ld tl rdn 2f out: wknd ent fnl f* **22/1**

13-4 **6** *2 ½* **Topflight Princess**[16] 2987 3-9-0 70 .... PatCosgrave 7 30
(Jeremy Gask) *in last pair: rdn over 2f out: cl enough whn stmbld jst over 1f out: sn hld and eased: nt rcvr* **6/1**

1m 11.9s (0.70) **Going Correction** +0.05s/f (Good) **6** Ran SP% **109.4**
Speed ratings (Par 99): **97,93,91,90,82 79**
toteswingers: 1&2 £1.60, 1&3 £1.60, 2&3 £1.80. CSF £9.83 TOTE £2.70: £2.00, £2.50; EX 8.60.
Owner Mrs Linda Francis **Bred** Martin Francis **Trained** Newmarket, Suffolk

FOCUS
A modest classified event.

Topflight Princess Official explanation: jockey said filly lost its action

3489 BETVICTOR FOR EURO 2012 H'CAP 5f 161y
9:10 (9:12) (Class 6) (0-60,59) 3-Y-0 **£1,704** (£503; £251) **Stalls** Centre

Form RPR

1020 **1** **Seventeen Seventy**[2] 3435 3-9-7 **59** .... FrankieMcDonald 15 69
(Alan Coogan) *mid-div: reminder after 1f: rdn 3f out: hdwy over 2f out: led over 1f out: kpt on: rdn out* **8/1**

0533 **2** *½* **One Last Dream**[11] 3141 3-8-8 **46** .... RichardKingscote 14 54
(Ron Hodges) *trckd ldrs: rdn to ld briefly over 1f out: kpt on ins fnl f* **9/2**[1]

6636 **3** *nk* **Represent (IRE)**[30] 2540 3-9-6 **58** .... MatthewDavies 9 65
(Mick Channon) *mid-div: hdwy u.p 3f out: kpt on to chse ldrs ent fnl f* **5/1**[2]

6304 **4** *4* **Bitter Lemon**[23] 2762 3-8-8 **53** .... IanBurns(7) 16 46
(Tony Newcombe) *towards rr: rdn and hdwy fr over 2f out: wnt 4th over 1f out: drifted lft: kpt on same pce* **18/1**

06-0 **5** *½* **Gypsy Rider**[36] 2367 3-8-13 **56** .... DarrenEgan(5) 2 48
(Bryn Palling) *towards rr: rdn 3f out: no imp tl r.o wl fnl f* **33/1**

5226 **6** *1 ¼* **First Rebellion**[9] 3218 3-8-8 **46** .... DavidProbert 3 33
(Tony Carroll) *chsd ldrs: rdn 3f out: kpt on same pce fnl 2f* **11/2**[3]

00-0 **7** *1* **La Sonadora**[22] 2803 3-8-9 **47** ....(b[1]) WilliamCarson 8 31
(John Spearing) *hld up towards rr: swtchd rt and hdwy over 2f out: sn rdn: kpt on same pce over 1f out* **50/1**

624 **8** *shd* **Copper Falls**[11] 3141 3-9-2 **54** .... KirstyMilczarek 1 38
(Brendan Powell) *in tch: rdn over 2f out: keeping on at same pce whn jockey lost whip ins fnl f* **12/1**

-503 **9** *4 ½* **Enthrall (IRE)**[22] 2786 3-8-7 **45** .... CathyGannon 11 13
(Denis Coakley) *prom tl rdn 3f out: wknd over 1f out* **8/1**

44-4 **10** *nk* **Selinda**[28] 2595 3-8-8 **51** .... CharlesBishop(5) 13 18
(Mick Channon) *towards rr: hung rt u.p 2f out: little imp* **18/1**

0-00 **11** *nse* **Imperial Elegance**[32] 2501 3-8-7 **45** MartinHarley 17 12
(Mick Channon) *a towards rr* **40/1**
0-04 **11** *dht* **Madame Feu**[42] 2166 3-9-5 **57** DaneO'Neill 5 24
(Henry Candy) *nvr bttr than mid-div* **10/1**
0164 **13** *nk* **Russian Bullet**[30] 2547 3-9-7 **59** FergusSweeney 6 25
(Jamie Osborne) *led: rdn whn hdd briefly over 2f out: hdd over 1f out: wknd* **16/1**
0-00 **14** *3/4* **Peg Peg**[15] 3014 3-8-0 **45** NoelGarbutt(7) 4 9
(Nerys Dutfield) *s.i.s: a in rr* **66/1**
005 **15** *1* **Ishi**[34] 2422 3-9-2 **54** JamesMillman 7 14
(Rod Millman) *prom: led briefly over 2f out: sn rdn: wknd over 1f out* **25/1**
60-0 **16** *9* **Our Monica (IRE)**[13] 3076 3-8-7 **45** FrannyNorton 10
(Ian Williams) *mid-div tl wknd over 2f out:* **18/1**
0000 **17** *21* **Exkaliber**[24] 2730 3-8-9 **50** (b[1]) RaulDaSilva(3) 12
(Jeremy Gask) *chsd ldrs tl over 2f out* **33/1**
1m 11.98s (0.78) **Going Correction** +0.05s/f (Good) **17** Ran SP% **126.5**
Speed ratings (Par 97): **96,95,94,89,88 87,85,85,79,79 79,79,78,77,76 64,36**
toteswingers: 1&2 £13.00, 1&3 £10.70, 2&3 £8.00. CSF £42.89 CT £208.03 TOTE £11.80: £2.50, £1.80, £1.40, £4.80; EX 46.80.
Owner A B Coogan **Bred** Leydens Farm Stud **Trained** Soham, Cambs
FOCUS
A competitive, if modest handicap, run at a furious pace. High draws dominated.
First Rebellion Official explanation: jockey said gelding hung right
T/Plt: £120.00 to a £1 stake. Pool: £69,792.09 - 424.36 winning tickets. T/Qpdt: £16.70 to a £1 stake. Pool: £5,392.66 - 237.73 winning tickets. TM

3208 CARLISLE (R-H)
Wednesday, June 27

OFFICIAL GOING: Soft (6.9)
Wind: Breezy, half Weather: Overcast, showers

3490 APD 25 YEAR ANNIVERSARY MAIDEN AUCTION STKS 5f
2:00 (2:00) (Class 5) 2-Y-O **£2,264** (£673; £336; £168) **Stalls** Low

Form RPR
40 **1** **Blue Lotus (IRE)**[39] 2261 2-8-11 0 DanielTudhope 3 77+
(Tim Easterby) *t.k.h early: trckd ldrs: effrt and rdn over 1f out: led ins fnl f: drvn out* **4/1**[3]
2 **2** *hd* **Boom And Bloom (IRE)**[27] 2631 2-8-11 0 TonyHamilton 7 76
(Richard Fahey) *cl up: effrt and ev ch over 1f out: kpt on ins fnl f: hld towards fin* **2/1**[1]
224 **3** *1/2* **Mandy Lexi (IRE)**[14] 3034 2-8-11 0 TomEaves 2 74
(Bryan Smart) *led: rdn 2f out: hdd ins fnl f: kpt on: hld nr fin* **7/2**[2]
60 **4** *2* **Al Khisa (IRE)**[33] 2450 2-8-8 0 AmyRyan 4 64
(Kevin Ryan) *hld up: pushed along 1/2-way: hdwy over 1f out: kpt on fnl f: nvr able to chal* **40/1**
5 **5** *nk* **Grievous Angel (IRE)**[12] 3110 2-8-9 0 ow1 GrahamLee 1 64
(Ann Duffield) *s.i.s: bhd on ins: drvn and outpcd over 2f out: styd on fnl f: nvr rchd ldrs* **8/1**
2 **6** *2 3/4* **Cracking Choice (IRE)**[33] 2456 2-8-11 0 PaulMulrennan 6 58
(Michael Dods) *chsd ldng gp: effrt and rdn over 2f out: wknd over 1f out* **5/1**
45 **7** *3/4* **Lucy Bee**[44] 2135 2-8-4 0 JoeFanning 8 47
(Keith Dalgleish) *prom on outside tl rdn and wknd wl over 1f out* **25/1**
0 **8** *1 3/4* **Cromwell Rose (IRE)**[9] 3208 2-8-4 0 JamesSullivan 5 40
(John Weymes) *hld up in tch: rdn over 2f out: wknd over 1f out* **66/1**
1m 5.75s (4.95) **Going Correction** +0.80s/f (Soft) **8** Ran SP% **111.1**
Speed ratings (Par 93): **92,91,90,87,87 82,81,78**
toteswingers 1&2 £2.90, 1&3 £3.50, 2&3 £1.70 CSF £11.65 TOTE £3.70: £1.10, £1.50, £1.70; EX 15.10.
Owner C H Stevens **Bred** Peter And Jackie Grimes **Trained** Great Habton, N Yorks
FOCUS
Old stable bend moved out 2yds adding 3yds to races of 7f and further. Following an inch of rain since teatime the previous day, the ground was officially Soft all round. The winning time for the juveniles in the opener was 5.75 seconds outside standard.
NOTEBOOK
Blue Lotus(IRE) had finished behind the subsequent Windsor Castle and Norfolk Stakes winners in each of his first two starts and found this a bit easier. Always handy, he proved game in getting on top of the leader well inside the last furlong and looks just the type for nurseries. The way he saw his race out suggests he will get another furlong without much problem.
Boom And Bloom(IRE) finished just ahead of a subsequent winner when runner-up on last month's Newcastle debut over a furlong further. She ran just as well here considering she raced wider than the winner and third, yet only just failed. A return to 6f looks in order. (op 9-4)
Mandy Lexi(IRE) hadn't built on her narrow debut defeat over this trip at Chester in two subsequent starts over 6f, but made a bold bid to make all against the inside rail and wasn't worn down until late. A return to an easier 5f may help, but she has had more chances than anything else in this field and nurseries look the way forward with her. (op 3-1 tchd 11-4)
Al Khisa(IRE) didn't build on a reasonably promising Beverley debut at Haydock last time, but this was better considering she was off the bridle at the back of the field from an early stage yet stayed on late.
Grievous Angel(IRE) caught the eye on her Musselburgh debut 12 days earlier and did so again, staying on late without being knocked about. (op 10-1)
Cracking Choice(IRE) was probably not helped by seeing plenty of daylight on the wide outside, though his trainer had expressed fears beforehand over the ground.

3491 EDINBURGH WOOLLEN MILL/EUROPEAN BREEDERS' FUND MAIDEN STKS 5f 193y
2:30 (2:30) (Class 5) 2-Y-O **£3,234** (£962; £481; £240) **Stalls** Low

Form RPR
022 **1** **Secret Destination**[35] 2402 2-8-9 0 DaleSwift(3) 1 74
(Brian Ellison) *mde all: rdn and edgd lft over 1f out: kpt on wl fnl f* **7/4**[1]
2 *1 1/4* **Rocky Two (IRE)** 2-9-3 0 PaulMulrennan 6 75+
(Michael Dods) *dwlt: rn green in rr: hdwy on outside over 2f out: styd on to chse wnr towards fin: nt rch wnr* **9/2**[2]
3 **3** *1 1/4* **Dark Opal (IRE)**[23] 2747 2-8-12 0 ChrisCatlin 4 66
(John Weymes) *trckd ldrs: wnt 2nd over 2f out: sn rdn and ev ch: one pce ins fnl f: lost 2nd towards fin* **12/1**
4 *6* **Bachotheque (IRE)** 2-9-3 0 DanielTudhope 3 53+
(Tim Easterby) *dwlt: hld up: shkn up and hdwy over 2f out: outpcd fnl f* **16/1**
0 **5** *1* **Marhaba Malayeen (IRE)**[11] 3168 2-9-3 0 PhillipMakin 2 50
(Kevin Ryan) *trckd wnr to over 2f out: sn rdn: wknd over 1f out* **9/1**[3]
03 **6** *7* **Team Challenge**[9] 3208 2-9-3 0 TomEaves 7 28
(Tim Easterby) *trckd ldrs tl rdn and wknd wl over 1f out* **9/1**[3]
04 **7** *10* **Baltic Prince (IRE)**[9] 3217 2-9-3 0 PJMcDonald 8
(Paul Green) *prom: rdn over 2f out: sn lost pl* **28/1**
8 *9* **Gambino (IRE)** 2-9-3 0 AndrewElliott 5
(Hugh McWilliams) *s.i.s: bhd and pushed along: no ch fr 1/2-way* **66/1**
0 **9** *hd* **Birdy Boy (USA)**[41] 2213 2-9-3 0 JoeFanning 9
(Mark Johnston) *prom on outside tl rdn and wknd over 2f out* **9/2**[2]
1m 18.73s (5.03) **Going Correction** +0.80s/f (Soft) **9** Ran SP% **111.2**
Speed ratings (Par 93): **98,96,94,86,85 76,62,50,50**
toteswingers 1&2 £2.60, 1&3 £5.80, 2&3 £9.70 CSF £8.84 TOTE £2.70: £1.50, £1.30, £3.10; EX 10.00.
Owner Brian Ellison **Bred** Jtz International **Trained** Norton, N Yorks
FOCUS
This looked hard work for these 2yos and previous experience proved the key.
NOTEBOOK
Secret Destination had probably came up against fair sorts when runner-up in a couple of Fibresand maidens and utilised her streetwise qualities to make all the running from the rails draw and keep on gamely, despite hanging away to her left late. She obviously appreciates a testing surface and should make her mark in nurseries where those conditions prevail. (op 9-4 tchd 13-8)
Rocky Two(IRE) ◆, unlike the winner, had no experience to draw upon, though he was backed earlier in the day. Having been outpaced at the back of the field early, he made relentless late progress down the centre of the track to grab an encouraging runner-up spot. A 26,000euros colt of out a 1m3f Flat/2m1f hurdle winner, he should improve for further as his pedigree suggests. (op 4-1)
Dark Opal(IRE) showed some ability when a well-held third of seven over 5f on very different ground here earlier this month and did well here too, as she tried to serve it up to the winner from a long way out. (op 11-1)
Bachotheque(IRE), a 10,000gns half-brother to a multiple winning plater, took a keen grip early and ended up a well-beaten fourth, but he did manage to get himself into a challenging position passing the 2f pole, so obviously possesses some ability. (op 10-1)
Marhaba Malayeen(IRE), beaten a very long way on his York debut 11 days earlier, dropped away after showing prominently early and still has a bit to prove. (op 10-1 tchd 8-1)
Team Challenge showed no ill-effects from his unfortunate Doncaster debut when third of 13 over C&D nine days earlier, but he proved friendless in the market here and ended up well beaten. (op 13-2)
Birdy Boy(USA), a well-beaten ninth of 13 on last month's York debut, attracted support but although he saw plenty of daylight on the wide outside early and is bred to need further than this, he was still bitterly disappointing. (op 13-2)

3492 LLOYD LTD CARLISLE BELL CONSOLATION RACE (H'CAP) 7f 200y
3:00 (3:02) (Class 4) (0-85,79) 3-Y-O+ **£5,175** (£1,540; £769; £384) **Stalls** Low

Form RPR
-350 **1** **Lady Chaparral**[23] 2751 5-9-9 **77** [1] TomEaves 11 87
(Michael Dods) *hld up in tch: hdwy to ld 2f out: rdn and styd on wl fnl f* **5/1**[3]
6053 **2** *1* **Lockantanks**[10] 3185 5-9-10 **78** GrahamLee 5 86
(Michael Appleby) *cl up: swtchd to centre and ev ch 2f out: sn rdn: kpt on fnl f: hld towards fin* **7/2**[1]
3560 **3** *3/4* **Moheebb (IRE)**[7] 3274 8-9-4 **72** PJMcDonald 7 78
(Ruth Carr) *hld up in midfield: effrt and rdn 2f out: kpt on ins fnl f: nt pce to chal* **9/2**[2]
-605 **4** *2 1/2* **Silver Rime (FR)**[7] 3274 7-9-7 **75** PhillipMakin 6 76
(Linda Perratt) *hld up: hdwy to chse ldrs over 1f out: sn rdn: kpt on same pce fnl f* **16/1**
244- **5** *6* **Ravi River (IRE)**[21] 7557 8-9-5 **73** PaddyAspell 8 60
(Alistair Whillans) *hld up: drvn over 2f out: kpt on fnl f: nvr able to chal* **66/1**
0003 **6** *shd* **Mangham (IRE)**[9] 3215 7-7-12 **57** (p) NeilFarley(5) 4 43
(George Foster) *dwlt: sn prom: rdn over 2f out: edgd rt and wknd over 1f out* **22/1**
-000 **7** *2 3/4* **Cool Marble (IRE)**[11] 3167 5-9-9 **77** (p) ChrisCatlin 9 57
(Jeremy Gask) *hld up: drvn along over 2f out: nvr able to chal* **10/1**
-054 **8** *3/4* **Chookie Royale**[14] 3027 4-9-7 **75** (p) RobertWinston 10 53
(Keith Dalgleish) *hld up: drvn along over 2f out: btn over 1f out* **12/1**
6135 **9** *1* **Call Of Duty (IRE)**[9] 3213 7-8-8 **62** TonyHamilton 1 38
(Dianne Sayer) *led: styd alone far rail and hdd 2f out: sn wknd* **22/1**
310 **10** *6* **Icelander (USA)**[39] 2269 3-8-13 **77** JoeFanning 3 37
(Mark Johnston) *trckd ldr: rdn over 2f out: sn struggling* **12/1**
1m 45.87s (5.87) **Going Correction** +0.80s/f (Soft)
WFA 3 from 4yo+ 10lb **10** Ran SP% **97.6**
Speed ratings (Par 105): **102,101,100,97,91 91,88,88,87,81**
toteswingers 1&2 £3.40, 1&3 £4.50, 2&3 £3.00 CSF £16.05 CT £51.89 TOTE £4.70: £1.50, £1.70, £1.50; EX 19.00.
Owner Geoff & Sandra Turnbull **Bred** Geoff & Sandra Turnbull **Trained** Denton, Co Durham
FOCUS
A race for those just outside the top 17 who made it into the Carlisle Bell itself, but not a bad little handicap in its own right. The field was reduced by one when Sound Advice was withdrawn after rearing in the stalls. In a race run at a solid tempo, most of the principals came from off the pace, but the most noticeable aspect to this race was that the majority came out into the centre of the track up the final straight.

3493 LLOYD MOTOR GROUP CARLISLE BELL (H'CAP) 7f 200y
3:30 (3:30) (Class 4) (0-85,87) 3-Y-O+ **£14,231** (£4,235; £2,116; £1,058) **Stalls** Low

Form RPR
2261 **1** **Levitate**[10] 3185 4-9-3 **87** 6ex (v) WilliamTwiston-Davies(7) 15 95
(Alan McCabe) *hld up: hdwy stands' rail over 2f out: rdn and edgd rt over 1f out: swtchd lft and styd on wl ins fnl f: led post* **18/1**
6124 **2** *shd* **Toto Skyllachy**[29] 2590 7-9-8 **85** DanielTudhope 17 93
(David O'Meara) *chsd ldrs: led stands' rail over 2f out: sn rdn: kpt on wl fnl f: hdd post* **14/1**
0230 **3** *nk* **Silvery Moon (IRE)**[19] 2882 5-9-5 **82** PaulMulrennan 12 89
(Tim Easterby) *trckd ldrs: effrt over 2f out: drvn and sltly outpcd over 1f out: rallied fnl f: kpt on: hld nr fin* **10/1**[3]
3310 **4** *6* **Solar Spirit (IRE)**[10] 3183 7-9-1 **83** ShaneBKelly(5) 8 76
(Tracy Waggott) *hld up in tch: hdwy and cl up wl over 1f out: sn rdn: wknd ins fnl f* **33/1**
-121 **5** *1/2* **Barwick**[22] 2801 4-9-5 **82** ChrisCatlin 4 74+
(Mark H Tompkins) *hld up: rdn along over 2f out: styd on fnl f: nvr able to chal* **11/4**[1]
0310 **6** *3/4* **Fazza**[32] 2473 5-8-13 **81** LMcNiff(5) 2 71+
(Edwin Tuer) *s.i.s: hld up: rdn over 2f out: sme late hdwy: nvr rchd ldrs* **10/1**[3]
0043 **7** *nk* **Karaka Jack**[11] 3157 5-9-6 **83** AdrianNicholls 6 73
(David Nicholls) *in tch: drvn along over 3f out: btn over 1f out* **10/1**[3]
6001 **8** *1* **Sam Nombulist**[12] 3128 4-9-8 **85** (v) RobertWinston 16 72
(Richard Whitaker) *hld up on outside: rdn and carried hd high over 2f out: sn n.d* **11/1**

3500 **9** ½ **West End Lad**[28] 2606 9-9-4 **81**..............................(b) RussKennemore 5 67
(Roy Bowring) *hld up towards rr: drvn along over 3f out: nvr able to chal* **66/1**

-160 **10** 2½ **Staff Sergeant**[11] 3164 5-9-5 **82**.............................. GrahamLee 1 62
(Jim Goldie) *towards rr: pushed along over 3f out: nvr on terms* **12/1**

-354 **11** ¾ **Desert Romance (IRE)**[7] 3287 6-8-12 **82**..................(v) DavidBergin(7) 3 61
(David O'Meara) *cl up: ev ch and styd alone far rail over 2f out: sn wknd* **14/1**

-003 **12** 2 **King Of Eden (IRE)**[27] 2632 6-8-9 **79**.............................. JasonHart(7) 10 53
(Eric Alston) *s.i.s: hld up: rdn over 3f out: btn fnl 2f* **25/1**

0-60 **13** 1 **Pleasant Day (IRE)**[40] 2257 5-9-0 **80**..........................(b) LeeTopliss(3) 7 52
(Richard Fahey) *trckd ldrs tl rdn and wknd over 2f out* **8/1**[2]

40-1 **14** 3½ **Amaze**[21] 2826 4-9-5 **82**.............................. BarryMcHugh 13 46
(Brian Ellison) *hld up towards rr: effrt u.p 3f out: wknd 2f out* **16/1**

3001 **15** 1¾ **Miami Gator (IRE)**[7] 3274 5-8-13 **83** 6ex..............(v) ConorHarrison(7) 9 43
(Mrs K Burke) *led to over 2f out: sn rdn and wknd* **14/1**

1m 44.77s (4.77) **Going Correction** +0.80s/f (Soft) 15 Ran SP% **120.5**
Speed ratings (Par 105): **108,107,107,101,101 100,100,99,98,96 95,93,92,88,87**
toteswingers 1&2 £12.10, 1&3 £32.50, 2&3 £29.60 CSF £245.87 CT £1626.47 TOTE £20.80: £6.00, £5.20, £4.00; EX 214.00.
Owner Charles Wentworth **Bred** Cheveley Park Stud Ltd **Trained** Averham Park, Notts

FOCUS
A fascinating renewal of the Carlisle Bell, but tactics played their part. This time the principals came right over to the stands' rail and again the one horse who stayed on the inside, Desert Romance, ended up well beaten. The winning time was 1.1 seconds faster than the consolation race.

3494 TOTEPOOL.COM CUMBERLAND PLATE (H'CAP) 1m 3f 107y
4:05 (4:05) (Class 4) (0-85,85) 3-Y-O+ **£14,231** (£4,235; £2,116; £1,058) **Stalls** High

Form RPR

021- **1** **Lexi's Boy (IRE)**[60] 3474 4-9-4 **80**.............................. GrahamLee 6 96+
(Donald McCain) *mde all: rdn over 2f out: styd on strly fnl f* **9/4**[1]

6341 **2** 1¾ **Rio's Rosanna (IRE)**[12] 3129 5-9-9 **85**.............................. AmyRyan 7 95
(Richard Whitaker) *hld up in midfield: hdwy over 3f out: rdr dropped whip and chsd wnr ins fnl f: r.o* **9/1**[3]

1-50 **3** nk **Union Island (IRE)**[81] 751 6-9-1 **80**.............................. DaleSwift(3) 3 89
(Brian Ellison) *chsd ldrs: effrt and wnt 2nd over 3f out to ins fnl f: hld towards fin* **33/1**

6302 **4** 4½ **Muffin McLeay (IRE)**[7] 3287 4-9-6 **82**.............................. LeeNewman 2 84+
(David Barron) *hld up in tch: stdy hdwy over 3f out: rdn 2f out: sn one pce* **11/2**[2]

1345 **5** 2 **Tres Coronas (IRE)**[18] 2911 5-9-9 **85**.............................. TomEaves 5 83
(David Barron) *hld up: rdn over 3f out: hdwy over 1f out: no imp fnl f* **14/1**

-320 **6** 1 **Eltheeb**[23] 2773 5-9-7 **83**.............................. DanielTudhope 10 80+
(David O'Meara) *hld up: effrt on outside over 2f out: no imp appr fnl f* **10/1**

5-01 **7** hd **Dark Dune (IRE)**[26] 2676 4-9-2 **78**.............................. JamesSullivan 1 74
(Tim Easterby) *hld upf: rdn and hdwy over 2f out: btn ins fnl f* **40/1**

4-05 **8** 5 **Bollin Greta**[4] 3377 7-9-8 **84**.............................. PaulMulrennan 12 72
(Tim Easterby) *midfield: pushed along whn nt clr run briefly over 3f out and over 2f out: rallied over 1f out: no imp* **22/1**

5-20 **9** 5 **Lucky Windmill**[27] 2620 5-9-2 **78**.............................. AndrewElliott 8 57
(Alan Swinbank) *restless in stalls: dwlt: hld up: rdn over 3f out: btn fnl 2f* **28/1**

-562 **10** 1¾ **Hong Kong Island (IRE)**[11] 3163 5-9-3 **84**.............................. ShaneBKelly(5) 14 60
(Micky Hammond) *in tch tl rdn and wknd over 2f out* **10/1**

3163 **11** 1¾ **Veiled Applause**[11] 3163 9-9-6 **82**.............................. MichaelO'Connell 9 55
(John Quinn) *in tch: rdn over 3f out: wknd fnl 2f* **25/1**

0550 **12** ½ **Smokey Oakey (IRE)**[12] 3125 8-9-4 **80**.............................. ChrisCatlin 4 53
(Mark H Tompkins) *hld up: drvn along over 3f out: nvr on terms* **20/1**

-002 **13** 4 **King Kurt (IRE)**[26] 2676 4-9-4 **80**.............................. PhillipMakin 11 46
(Kevin Ryan) *trckd ldrs tl rdn and wknd over 2f out* **22/1**

-126 **14** 5 **Mica Mika (IRE)**[14] 3036 4-9-6 **85**.............................. LeeTopliss(3) 15 42
(Richard Fahey) *hld up in tch: struggling over 3f out: sn btn* **12/1**

3066 **15** 1½ **Northside Prince (IRE)**[23] 2773 6-9-9 **85**.............................. PJMcDonald 13 40
(Alan Swinbank) *hld up: rdn over 3f out: sn struggling* **25/1**

/431 **16** 2¼ **Hawkeshead**[19] 2877 5-9-2 **78**.............................. JoeFanning 16 29
(Ian Williams) *chsd wnr to over 3f out: sn rdn: wknd over 2f out* **28/1**

4221 **17** 27 **Entihaa**[8] 3253 4-9-5 **81** 6ex.............................. RobertWinston 17
(Alan Swinbank) *hld up: struggling 4f out: btn and eased fnl 2f* **14/1**

2m 30.57s (7.47) **Going Correction** +0.80s/f (Soft) 17 Ran SP% **128.8**
Speed ratings (Par 105): **104,102,102,99,97 97,96,93,89,88 87,86,83,80,79 77,57**
toteswingers 1&2 £5.60, 1&3 £48.80, 2&3 £66.40 CSF £19.85 CT £573.37 TOTE £3.20: £1.10, £2.10, £12.40, £1.70; EX 26.30.
Owner T G Leslie **Bred** R S Cockerill (farms) Ltd & Peter Dodd **Trained** Cholmondeley, Cheshire

FOCUS
This looked a competitive handicap beforehand, but the result wasn't in much doubt from some way out and the winner proved different class. This time the whole field came over to the stands' rail.
Bollin Greta Official explanation: jockey said mare ran too free

3495 BRITISH STALLION STUDS SUPPORTING BRITISH RACING E B F FILLIES' H'CAP 6f 192y
4:35 (4:35) (Class 4) (0-80,78) 3-Y-O+ **£5,175** (£1,540; £769; £384) **Stalls** Low

Form RPR

1102 **1** **No Poppy (IRE)**[8] 3252 4-9-9 **78**.............................. AdamCarter(5) 5 89+
(Tim Easterby) *hld up in tch: hdwy to ld over 2f out: sn rdn: pricked ears ins fnl f: comf* **5/2**[1]

-426 **2** 1½ **Last Supper**[19] 2881 3-8-8 **67**.............................. AndrewElliott 9 71
(James Bethell) *led to over 2f out: rdn and rallied over 1f out: kpt on fnl f: nt rch wnr* **14/1**

-032 **3** 1½ **Ursula (IRE)**[44] 2120 6-9-2 **66**.............................. RobertWinston 8 69
(Mrs K Burke) *plld hrd: cl up: rdn over 2f out: outpcd over 1f out: styd on ins fnl f* **8/1**

4126 **4** nse **Dubious Escapade (IRE)**[22] 2785 3-8-11 **70**.............................. GrahamLee 7 70
(Ann Duffield) *t.k.h: cl up: effrt and ev ch over 2f out: one pce fnl f* **11/4**[2]

0-41 **5** nk **Emeralds Spirit (IRE)**[8] 3254 5-9-3 **67** 6ex.............................. PaulMulrennan 4 69
(John Weymes) *t.k.h: cl up: rdn over 2f out: kpt on same pce fnl f* **7/2**[3]

6002 **6** 6 **Dolly Royal (IRE)**[9] 3209 7-8-4 **59** oh14..................(p) ShaneBKelly(5) 1 46
(Robert Johnson) *dwlt: bhd and sn pushed along: outpcd 1/2-way: n.d after* **33/1**

5312 **7** shd **Cut The Cackle (IRE)**[8] 3249 6-9-0 **64**..................(bt) SaleemGolam 2 50
(Richard Guest) *t.k.h: hld up in tch: outpcd over 3f out: sn n.d* **10/1**

6510 **8** 5 **Hold The Star**[9] 3230 6-8-4 **59**.............................. AnnStokell(5) 3 32
(Ann Stokell) *towards rr: struggling 1/2-way: sn btn* **33/1**

1m 33.94s (6.84) **Going Correction** +0.80s/f (Soft)
WFA 3 from 4yo+ 9lb 8 Ran SP% **110.2**
Speed ratings (Par 102): **92,90,88,88,88 81,81,75**
toteswingers 1&2 £5.00, 1&3 £4.30, 2&3 £8.10 CSF £34.97 CT £226.71 TOTE £3.80: £1.20, £4.60, £2.50; EX 27.90.
Owner Exors Of The Late Mrs P M Easterby **Bred** Michael O'Mahony **Trained** Great Habton, N Yorks

FOCUS
A fair fillies' handicap and again they ended up towards the stands' side.
Emeralds Spirit(IRE) Official explanation: jockey said mare ran too free
Hold The Star Official explanation: trainer said mare was unsuited by the soft ground

3496 BET ON EURO 2012 AT TOTEPOOL.COM H'CAP 5f
5:05 (5:06) (Class 4) (0-85,82) 3-Y-O+ **£4,075** (£1,212; £606; £303) **Stalls** Low

Form RPR

0511 **1** **Best Trip (IRE)**[6] 3314 5-9-0 **68** 6ex.............................. BarryMcHugh 9 86
(Brian Ellison) *t.k.h: trckd ldrs: nt clr run over 2f out tl swtchd rt and led 1f out: qcknd clr: readily* **11/8**[1]

3006 **2** 3½ **Haajes**[12] 3127 8-9-9 **77**.............................. MickyFenton 6 81
(Paul Midgley) *hld up: rdn along 1/2-way: hdwy to chse (clr) wnr ins fnl f: r.o: no imp* **6/1**[3]

5333 **3** ½ **Jack Luey**[11] 3159 5-9-9 **77**.............................. DanielTudhope 5 79
(Lawrence Mullaney) *chsd ldrs: effrt and rdn 2f out: kpt on same pce ins fnl f* **9/2**[2]

0111 **4** shd **Pitkin**[9] 3209 4-9-5 **73** 6ex..............................(b) PaulMulrennan 3 75
(Michael Easterby) *pressed ldr: rdn and led briefly appr fnl f: kpt on same pce* **6/1**[3]

1000 **5** 2 **Mandalay King (IRE)**[11] 3169 7-9-5 **76**..........................(p) JulieBurke(3) 1 71
(Marjorie Fife) *bhd and sn outpcd: hdwy over 1f out: nvr able to chal* **20/1**

003 **6** 1¼ **Comptonspirit**[25] 2693 8-9-1 **74**.............................. NeilFarley(5) 2 64
(Brian Baugh) *hld up in tch on outside: rdn and edgd rt 2f out: sn outpcd* **25/1**

3310 **7** ¾ **Red Roar (IRE)**[4] 3382 5-9-3 **71** 6ex.............................. GrahamLee 8 58
(Alan Berry) *chsd ldng gp: rdn over 2f out: wknd over 1f out* **8/1**

-000 **8** 7 **Amenable (IRE)**[25] 2707 5-10-0 **82**.............................. AdrianNicholls 4 44
(David Nicholls) *led tl blkd and hdd appr fnl f: sn wknd* **20/1**

20-0 **9** 3¾ **Berberana (IRE)**[123] 715 4-9-12 **80**.............................. RobertWinston 7 29
(Jeremy Gask) *chsd ldrs: drvn over 2f out: wknd wl over 1f out* **20/1**

1m 4.32s (3.52) **Going Correction** +0.80s/f (Soft) 9 Ran SP% **118.1**
Speed ratings (Par 105): **103,97,96,96,93 91,90,78,72**
toteswingers 1&2 £3.40, 1&3 £2.60, 2&3 £5.80 CSF £9.53 CT £30.91 TOTE £2.50: £1.10, £1.90, £1.50; EX 14.30.
Owner Koo's Racing Club **Bred** Limetree Stud **Trained** Norton, N Yorks

FOCUS
Again they came stands' side. This was a decent sprint handicap with three in-form runners at the foot of the handicap, all of whom were carrying penalties, and one of them bolted up.
T/Jkpt: Not won. T/Plt: £22.40 to a £1 stake. Pool: £63224.76 - 2058.8 winning tickets T/Qpdt: £14.30 to a £1 stake. Pool: £4156.6 - 214.2 winning tickets RY

3278 KEMPTON (A.W) (R-H)
Wednesday, June 27

OFFICIAL GOING: Standard
Wind: Light, behind Weather: Overcast, humid

3497 WIN BIG WITH BETDAQ MULTIPLES APPRENTICE H'CAP 1m (P)
6:20 (7:26) (Class 6) (0-60,60) 4-Y-O+ **£1,617** (£481; £240; £120) **Stalls** Low

Form RPR

3-14 **1** **Shaunas Spirit (IRE)**[157] 264 4-8-10 **56**.............................. PaulBooth(7) 5 66
(Dean Ivory) *t.k.h: trckd ldng pair: clsd to ld jst over 2f out and sn clr: pushed along and wandered but nvr in serious danger after* **5/1**[1]

0003 **2** 1¼ **Blue Deer (IRE)**[11] 3153 4-9-7 **60**..........................(v[1]) CharlesBishop 13 66
(Lee Carter) *trckd ldr: chal gng strly 3f out: nt qckn as wnr breezed by jst over 2f out: chsng after: narrowed gap nr fin* **5/1**[1]

-000 **3** 3¼ **Gee Major**[27] 2627 5-8-4 **46**..............................(p) JackDuern(3) 1 45
(Nicky Vaughan) *led to jst over 2f out: one pce in 3rd fr wl over 1f out* **16/1**

2260 **4** 3 **Jackie Love (IRE)**[11] 3152 4-8-9 **48**..............................(v) RosieJessop 11 40
(Olivia Maylam) *hld up towards rr: effrt on wd outside over 3f out: tk 4th over 1f out: no threat* **16/1**

506 **5** 2¼ **Abriachan**[14] 3053 5-9-5 **58**.............................. TobyAtkinson 7 44+
(Noel Quinlan) *hld up towards rr: hmpd 4f out: nt on terms after: styd on fr over 1f out* **10/1**

432 **6** ½ **Do More Business (IRE)**[36] 2365 5-9-1 **54**.............. MatthewLawson 4 39+
(Alison Batchelor) *hld up and sn last: sltly hmpd 4f out: nt on terms after: styd on fr over 1f out* **6/1**[3]

5-0 **7** shd **Chasin' Rainbows**[159] 225 4-8-8 **52**.............................. ThomasBrown(5) 14 37+
(Sylvester Kirk) *hld up in rr: nt on terms after melee 4f out: n.d fnl 2f* **40/1**

00-1 **8** nk **Carpentras**[33] 2463 4-9-0 **53**.............................. JustinNewman 10 37
(Dr Jon Scargill) *chsd ldrs: pushed along bef 1/2-way: rdn in 4th over 3f out: wknd over 1f out* **12/1**

0050 **9** 2¼ **Dinner Date**[51] 1919 10-9-3 **59**.............................. DannyBrock(3) 2 38+
(Tom Keddy) *dwlt: sn in midfield: hmpd 4f out: nt on terms after: wknd over 1f out* **7/1**

45-0 **10** 4 **Scarborough Lily**[33] 2464 4-9-6 **59**..............................(b) AshleyMorgan 6 29+
(Ed Vaughan) *hld up in midfield: bdly hmpd 4f out and rdr nrly off: nt rcvr* **10/1**

1006 **11** 41 **Holyfield Warrior (IRE)**[36] 2366 8-8-12 **51**.............................. NathanAlison 3 +
(Michael Attwater) *dwlt: hld up towards rr: hmpd 4f out and rdr nrly off: lost irons and sn t.o* **20/1**

0042 **U** **Volcanic Jack (IRE)**[11] 3152 4-8-11 **53**.............................. GeorgeDowning(3) 8
(Tony Carroll) *trckd ldng pair tl stmbld and uns rdr 4f out* **11/2**[2]

1m 39.55s (-0.25) **Going Correction** -0.025s/f (Stan) 12 Ran SP% **120.3**
Speed ratings (Par 101): **100,98,95,92,90 89,89,89,87,83 42,**
toteswingers: 1&2 £3.30, 1&3 £14.10, 2&3 £16.90. CSF £29.86 CT £386.36 TOTE £3.30: £1.50, £2.20, £7.80; EX 22.90 Trifecta £316.20 Pool: £1,504.30 - 3.52 winning units..
Owner John Connolly & Cynthia Smith **Bred** Miss Breda Wright **Trained** Radlett, Herts
■ Paul Booth's first winner.

FOCUS
A moderate handicap for older horses and restricted to apprentice riders. They appeared to go a relatively steady gallop until turning for home and those who raced prominently were favoured by how this race was run, particularly in avoiding the problems caused in behind by Volcanic Jack unseating his jockey turning for home. The winning time was nearly three seconds slower than standard.

Dinner Date Official explanation: jockey said gelding lost a front shoe
Scarborough Lily Official explanation: jockey said filly suffered interference in running
Holyfield Warrior(IRE) Official explanation: jockey said gelding suffered interference in running

3498 BACK OR LAY AT BETDAQ.COM H'CAP 2m (P)
6:50 (7:26) (Class 6) (0-65,65) 4-Y-0+ £1,617 (£481; £240; £120) Stalls Low

Form RPR
0-01 **1** **Waterford Star (IRE)**[13] 3086 4-8-11 55.....................(v) JamieSpencer 7 68
(Ian Williams) *sn trckd ldr: led 6f out: drvn on 4f out: wandered u.p fnl 2f but hld on wl* **16/5**[2]
1-26 **2** 1 1/4 **Grandad Mac**[49] 1984 4-9-3 61..................... RichardHughes 5 73
(Jane Chapple-Hyam) *hld up in last trio: prog over 3f out: chsd wnr over 1f out: tried to cl fnl f: no imp last 100yds* **5/2**[1]
351 **3** 8 **Reillys Daughter**[7] 3283 4-9-5 63 6ex.............................. IanMongan 10 65
(Laura Mongan) *racd wd: trckd ldrs: chsd wnr jst over 4f out: sn rdn: lost 2nd and wknd over 1f out* **13/2**
0 **4** 1 3/4 **Terra Bleu (IRE)**[11] 3143 5-7-13 46 oh1.....................(p) RyanPowell(3) 2 46
(Brendan Powell) *chsd ldng pair to 6f out: dropped to rr u.p 4f out: plugged on fnl 2f* **50/1**
4145 **5** 4 1/2 **Delagoa Bay (IRE)**[19] 2872 4-8-11 55............................... SeanLevey 9 50
(Sylvester Kirk) *hld up in last: rdn once pce lifted over 3f out: no prog* **11/1**
0343 **6** 1 **Bengal Tiger**[36] 2371 6-8-2 51....................................... NathanAlison(5) 1 44
(Tony Carroll) *led to 6f out: lost 2nd jst over 4f out: wknd over 2f out* **9/1**
0030 **7** 1 1/4 **Inside Knowledge (USA)**[7] 3283 6-8-8 52..................... LukeMorris 11 44
(Garry Woodward) *t.k.h: hld up in last trio: rdn once pce lifted over 3f out: no prog* **14/1**
1160 **8** 12 **Steady Gaze**[20] 2863 7-9-7 65... AmirQuinn 4 42
(Richard Rowe) *trckd ldrs: rdn in 4th over 3f out: wknd qckly over 2f out: virtually p.u* **7/2**[3]

3m 28.45s (-1.65) **Going Correction** -0.025s/f (Stan) 8 Ran SP% **114.9**
Speed ratings (Par 101): **103,102,98,97,95 94,94,88**
toteswingers: 1&2 £2.30, 1&3 £4.00, 2&3 £2.50. CSF £11.72 CT £47.55 TOTE £5.00: £1.60, £1.70, £1.80; EX 11.40 Trifecta £41.70 Pool: £4,269.56 - 75.59 winning units..
Owner R S Brookhouse **Bred** Denis McDonnell **Trained** Portway, Worcs

FOCUS
A modest staying handicap for older horses. They went an honest gallop for the majority of the journey. The winning time was respectable for the grade.

3499 BETDAQ MOBILE APPS MAIDEN STKS 7f (P)
7:20 (7:32) (Class 5) 2-Y-0 £2,264 (£673; £336; £168) Stalls Low

Form RPR
1 **Snowboarder (USA)** 2-9-3 0.................................. MickaelBarzalona 8 84+
(Mahmood Al Zarooni) *trckd ldr after 2f: shkn up 2f out: clsd to ld jst over 1f out: in command whn veered lft nr fin* **3/1**[1]
2 1 3/4 **Tobacco Road (IRE)** 2-9-3 0.................................. RichardHughes 10 79+
(Richard Hannon) *t.k.h: racd wd early: prog to chse ldng pair over 4f out: effrt over 2f out: chsd wnr fnl f: styd on but no imp* **8/1**
55 **3** 2 3/4 **Mowhoob**[13] 3062 2-9-3 0.. WilliamBuick 13 72
(John Gosden) *led after 2f: kicked on over 2f out: rdn and one tail flash over 1f out: sn hdd and one pce* **9/2**[3]
4 hd **Yarroom (IRE)** 2-9-3 0... AndreaAtzeni 3 71+
(Roger Varian) *t.k.h: trckd ldrs: taken to outer 4f out: outpcd in 4th 2f out: styd on fnl f: nrly snatched 3rd* **4/1**[2]
5 6 **Buxted's Choice (IRE)** 2-9-3 0................................ StevieDonohoe 12 56+
(Robert Mills) *dwlt: wl in rr: sme prog into midfield over 2f out: outpcd wl over 1f out: fdd* **50/1**
6 nk **Zain Spirit (USA)** 2-9-3 0.. EddieAhern 6 55+
(Gerard Butler) *dwlt: hld up in rr: prog into midfield over 2f out gng wl: pushed along over 1f out: wknd* **14/1**
7 1 3/4 **Perseverent Pete (USA)** 2-9-3 0.................................... IanMongan 1 51
(Christine Dunnett) *chsd ldrs over 4f: wknd* **125/1**
8 2 **Gabrial The Boss (USA)** 2-9-3 0.............................. JamieSpencer 11 45
(David Simcock) *s.i.s: rn green in last pair: nvr a factor* **25/1**
9 2 1/4 **Compton Silver** 2-9-3 0.. JimCrowley 2 40
(Hans Adielsson) *led 2f: trckd ldrs tl wknd 2f out* **16/1**
10 nk **Salutation (IRE)** 2-9-3 0.. KierenFallon 9 39
(Mark Johnston) *rn green in last pair: urged along 4f out: nvr a factor* **4/1**[2]
00 **11** 1/2 **Shearian**[34] 2420 2-9-3 0... MartinDwyer 4 37
(Brian Meehan) *chsd ldrs: lost pl and rdn 1/2-way: wl in rr fnl 2f* **50/1**

1m 26.63s (0.63) **Going Correction** -0.025s/f (Stan) 11 Ran SP% **115.4**
Speed ratings (Par 93): **95,93,89,89,82 82,80,78,75,75 74**
toteswingers: 1&2 £2.20, 1&3 £2.00, 2&3 £9.90. CSF £26.82 TOTE £3.10: £1.20, £2.70, £1.60; EX 19.60 Trifecta £40.10 Pool: £2,298.99 - 42.32 winning units..
Owner Godolphin **Bred** Fares Farm Llc **Trained** Newmarket, Suffolk

FOCUS
Very little worthwhile form on offer. This juvenile maiden looked likely to go to one of the intriguing debutants on show from one of the leading stables, and so it proved. The gallop was respectable and the time was just over two seconds slower than standard.

NOTEBOOK
Snowboarder(USA) was reportedly the pick of the paddock. The American bred is from the first crop of Raven's Pass and is out of an unraced half-sister to the very well-related Munnings, a triple Grade 2 winner in the USA. He cost $190,000 as a foal. He did well to get a fair position from a wider than ideal draw. He tracked the leader in the home straight, before asserting just over 1f out, and was well on top by the line, despite veering to his left through inexperience near the line. He looks a nice future 1m2f prospect in the making. (op 5-2)
Tobacco Road(IRE) did well despite racing keenly from a wide draw on debut. He is bred to stay middle-distances at the very least, being by Westerner out of a half-sister to a German Derby winner. He will be of interest over further later this term, possibly one of the few 1m2f juvenile contests. (tchd 15-2 and 9-1)
Mowhoob set the form standard prior to this contest. He achieved an RPR of 67 on debut at Yarmouth, and returned to a similar level here on this third career start. He may become of interest in modest nursery handicaps later this season. (op 4-1)
Yarroom(IRE) came home strongly into fourth once the penny dropped. The half-brother to Saamidd (high-class 2yo in 2010) will benefit from this experience and looks potentially useful at up to 1m this term. (op 7-2)
Buxted's Choice(IRE) showed a modicum of promise (op 66-1)
Zain Spirit(USA) showed a modicum of promise. (op 16-1)

3500 BETDAQ CASINO GAMES FILLIES' H'CAP 6f (P)
7:50 (7:58) (Class 4) (0-80,80) 3-Y-0+ £4,075 (£1,212; £606; £303) Stalls Low

Form RPR
-112 **1** **Athenian (IRE)**[19] 2893 3-9-3 76... LukeMorris 1 85
(Sir Mark Prescott Bt) *mde all: set stdy pce: kicked on fr 1/2-way: drvn and hrd pressed fnl f: hld on wl* **5/2**[2]
1-22 **2** 3/4 **Rivas Rhapsody (IRE)**[10] 3192 4-9-8 74.................... RichardHughes 5 83
(Ian Wood) *hld up in midfield: prog over 2f out: rdn to chse wnr over 1f out: styd on and pressed fnl f but a hld* **6/4**[1]
5533 **3** 1 1/2 **Red Larkspur (IRE)**[19] 2894 3-9-5 78.............................. JamesDoyle 2 80
(Roger Teal) *trckd wnr: rdn over 2f out: lost 2nd over 1f out: kpt on same pce after* **11/2**[3]
-061 **4** nk **Piddie's Power**[32] 2493 5-10-0 80....................................... SeanLevey 9 83
(Ed McMahon) *taken down early: hld up in 7th in steadily run contest: prog on inner 2f out: wnt 4th over 1f out: styd on but nvr able to threaten* **16/1**
506 **5** 2 1/4 **Judas Jo (FR)**[9] 3234 3-9-3 76.. WilliamBuick 8 70
(Gay Kelleway) *hld up in last in steadily run r: tried to make prog 2f out: rchd 5th 1f out: no ch w ldrs* **33/1**
3-06 **6** 3 1/4 **Drift And Dream**[32] 2494 5-9-7 73....................................... TedDurcan 6 59
(Chris Wall) *hld up in midfield: wd in st: nt qckn over 2f out: wl btn over 1f out* **9/1**
30-0 **7** 2 **Celtic Sixpence (IRE)**[38] 2310 4-9-12 78.......................... AdamKirby 3 57
(Noel Quinlan) *awkward s: sn chsd ldrs: rdn over 2f out: wknd over 1f out* **25/1**
32 **8** 5 **Black Baccara**[21] 2809 5-9-2 71..................................(be) RyanClark(3) 4 34
(Phil McEntee) *t.k.h: trckd ldng pair: rdn and fnd nil 2f out: wknd* **20/1**

1m 12.58s (-0.52) **Going Correction** -0.025s/f (Stan)
WFA 3 from 4yo+ 7lb 8 Ran SP% **111.4**
Speed ratings (Par 102): **102,101,99,98,95 91,88,81**
toteswingers: 1&2 £1.60, 1&3 £4.00, 2&3 £2.80. CSF £6.18 CT £16.17 TOTE £3.80: £1.30, £1.10, £1.70; EX 7.90 Trifecta £25.00 Pool: £3,026.28 - 89.53 winning units..
Owner Axom (XXXI) **Bred** Keatly Overseas Ltd **Trained** Newmarket, Suffolk

FOCUS
A fair fillies' handicap for 3yos and up. They went steady enough early but the winning time was the pick of the evening so far, being just over one second slower than standard.

3501 BRITISH STALLION STUDS SUPPORTING BRITISH RACING E B F NOVICE STKS 6f (P)
8:20 (8:20) (Class 5) 2-Y-0 £3,234 (£962) Stalls Low

Form RPR
321 **1** **Janoub Nibras (IRE)**[14] 3040 2-9-5 0......................... RichardHughes 1 86
(Richard Hannon) *mde all: jst pushed along whn pressed over 1f out: rdn more urgently fnl f: jst hld on* **1/7**[1]
1340 **2** shd **Woodland Mill (IRE)**[28] 2603 2-9-0 0............................... DavidNolan 2 81
(Richard Fahey) *trckd wnr: shkn up to chal 2f out: persistent threat after: jst hld last strides* **9/2**[2]

1m 14.61s (1.51) **Going Correction** -0.025s/f (Stan) 2 Ran SP% **105.7**
Speed ratings (Par 93): **88,87**
TOTE £1.10.
Owner Saeed H Altayer **Bred** Rathbarry Stud **Trained** East Everleigh, Wilts

FOCUS
A very disappointing turn out for this fair juvenile novice stakes, but this turned out to be a compelling match. The winning time was just over three seconds slower than standard, which is the slowest comparative time of the evening but respectable in the circumstances. There was little between the pair on pre-race marks and the form is straightforward.

NOTEBOOK
Janoub Nibras(IRE) set the fractions and was ridden confidently up the home straight. He was a comfortable C&D maiden winner this month, but only just followed up. He is capable of further success this term under these conditions, or back on a decent turf surface over this trip. (op 1-6)
Woodland Mill(IRE) was stepping up in trip, having won the first juvenile contest of the season over 1f shorter in March. She ran well in Listed company at York on her penultimate start and she brought that A-game to the table here, serving up a real treat for those in attendance by nearly upsetting the applecart. (tchd 5-1)

3502 RACING PLUS OUT EVERY SATURDAY H'CAP 1m 4f (P)
8:50 (8:51) (Class 4) (0-85,85) 4-Y-0+ £4,075 (£1,212; £606; £303) Stalls Centre

Form RPR
30-0 **1** **Incendo**[25] 2706 6-9-4 82..(t) EddieAhern 4 93+
(James Fanshawe) *hld up in midfield disputing 6th: smooth prog fr over 3f out: trckd ldr over 1f out and stl on bit: eased ahd last 100yds: cheekily* **11/1**
00-0 **2** 1/2 **Australia Day (IRE)**[37] 2346 9-9-7 85.......................... MartinDwyer 11 93
(Paul Webber) *trckd ldr: led 5f out: injected pce and sn had field spread: drvn over 2f out: hdd last 100yds: kpt on wl but no ch* **25/1**
1251 **3** 2 **Sand Skier**[7] 3278 5-9-2 80.. WilliamBuick 6 85
(Hans Adielsson) *trckd ldng pair: wnt clr 3rd 4f out: drvn over 2f out: styd on but nvr able to chal* **7/2**[1]
0-34 **4** 3/4 **Communicator**[25] 2706 4-9-7 85.................................. RichardHughes 3 89
(Andrew Balding) *trckd ldng pair: shkn up to chse ldr over 4f out: drvn over 2f out: one pce and lost 2nd over 1f out* **5/1**[3]
3-15 **5** hd **Art Scholar (IRE)**[144] 427 5-9-6 84................................ LukeMorris 14 87
(Michael Appleby) *hld up towards rr: rdn and sme prog fr 4f out: rchd 6th over 2f out but nt on terms: kpt on: nrst fin* **12/1**
5401 **6** 1/2 **Mataaleb**[20] 2863 5-9-6 84... DaraghO'Donohoe 9 87+
(Lydia Pearce) *stdd s: hld up in last trio: stl there 2f out whn r had long since unfolded: rdn and styd on wl after: hopeless task* **10/1**
14-5 **7** 1/2 **Planetoid (IRE)**[30] 2561 4-9-7 85...................................... TedDurcan 13 87
(David Lanigan) *racd wd: trckd ldrs disputing 6th: rdn to go 4th over 3f out: no imp fr 2f out: kpt on one pce* **8/1**
3563 **8** 2 1/4 **Borug (USA)**[26] 2655 4-9-5 83...(p) KierenFallon 1 81+
(James Tate) *t.k.h: hld up in midfield disputing 6th: trapped bhd wkng rival 4f out and dropped to rr: tried to rally on inner 2f out: nvr able to rcvr* **4/1**[2]
6/00 **9** 1 **Toughness Danon**[13] 2706 6-8-13 82..................... BrendanPowell(5) 10 79
(Brendan Powell) *hld up in last trio: rdn over 3f out: kpt on fnl 2f but n.d* **66/1**
20/- **10** nk **Cotillion**[105] 6926 6-9-7 85.. JamieSpencer 12 81
(Ian Williams) *hld up in last: effrt on outer 3f out but ldrs wl beyond recall: kpt on one pce fnl 2f* **11/1**
35-4 **11** 1/2 **Ellemujie**[164] 187 7-9-3 84... PatrickHills(3) 8 79+
(Dean Ivory) *hld up towards rr: hmpd and lost pl wl over 3f out: sn rdn: nvr able to land a blow* **14/1**
300- **12** 9 **Trovare (USA)**[228] 7139 5-9-2 80....................................... IanMongan 5 61
(Amanda Perrett) *trckd ldng pair tl wknd rapidly fr 4f out* **40/1**
0-40 **13** 8 **Kyllachy Spirit**[42] 2180 4-9-4 82....................................... JimCrowley 7 50
(William Knight) *hld up towards rr: rdn on outer wl over 3f out: no prog over 2f out: wknd* **16/1**

520- **14** 1 1/4 **Wayward Glance**[28] 6988 4-8-12 **83**.......................... AprilKitchener(7) 2 49
(Jim Best) *led to 5f out: sn dropped out* **50/1**

2m 32.64s (-1.86) **Going Correction** -0.025s/f (Stan) **14** Ran SP% **125.7**
Speed ratings (Par 105): **105,104,103,102,102 102,102,100,99,99 99,93,88,87**
toteswingers: 1&2 £8.90, 1&3 £10.20, 2&3 £29.00. CSF £273.30 CT £1177.60 TOTE £17.90: £3.60, £8.20, £1.80; EX 248.50 TRIFECTA Not won..
Owner Andrew & Julia Turner **Bred** London Thoroughbred Services Ltd **Trained** Newmarket, Suffolk

FOCUS
A decent middle-distance handicap for older horses. They went an honest gallop and recorded the best comparative time of the evening so far.
Incendo Official explanation: trainer's rep said, regarding apparent improvement in form, that the gelding was better suited by the flat all-weather track rather than the undulations of Epsom.
Ellemujie Official explanation: jockey said gelding was denied a clear run
Trovare(USA) Official explanation: jockey said gelding suffered interference in running

3503 OLLY MURS LIVE AT KEMPTON 17.08.12 H'CAP (LONDON MILE QUALIFIER) 1m (P)
9:20 (9:20) (Class 4) (0-85,85) 3-Y-0+ **£4,075** (£1,212; £606; £303) **Stalls** Low

Form RPR
-021 **1** **Ibtahaj**[27] 2626 3-9-4 **85**.......................... MickaelBarzalona 13 102+
(Saeed Bin Suroor) *won battle for ld bef end of 1f: mde rest: stretched clr fr over 2f out: 5 l up whn veered rt 100yds out: unchal* **9/4**[1]

41-4 **2** 3 **Eurystheus (IRE)**[34] 2408 3-8-12 **79**.......................... RichardHughes 3 86+
(Richard Hannon) *trckd ldrs: rdn over 2f out: prog to go 2nd jst ins fnl f: styd on but no ch w wnr* **11/4**[2]

3 2 1/4 **Saoi (USA)**[673] 5400 5-9-5 **76**..........................[1] JamieSpencer 7 80
(William Knight) *chsd wnr after 1f to 5f out: styd pressing for pls fr over 2f out: one pce fnl f* **18/1**

3033 **4** 3/4 **Incendiary (IRE)**[19] 2883 3-8-9 **76**.......................... JamesDoyle 8 76
(Hugo Palmer) *prom: rdn to chse wnr jst over 2f out: no imp: lost 2nd and fdd jst ins fnl f* **8/1**[3]

5-06 **5** 1 **Emkanaat**[14] 3045 4-9-5 **76**.......................... AndreaAtzeni 4 76
(Roger Varian) *hld up towards rr: rdn 3f out: styd on fnl 2f: nrst fin but no ch* **20/1**

5265 **6** 1 3/4 **Kakapuka**[28] 2608 5-9-9 **80**.......................... LukeMorris 2 76
(Anabel K Murphy) *led 100yds: sn settled in 7th: rdn over 2f out: no real imp after* **25/1**

4-03 **7** 1 **Ezdeyaad (USA)**[14] 3045 8-9-1 **79**.......................... MichaelJMurphy(7) 1 73
(Ed Walker) *hld up towards rr: rdn wl over 2f out: one pce and no ch w ldrs* **14/1**

-400 **8** 1 1/2 **Islesman**[14] 3045 4-9-4 **75**..........................(p) WilliamBuick 5 65+
(Heather Main) *hld up in last pair: sme prog 2f out: shkn up over 1f out: kpt on but nvr in it* **12/1**

0-00 **9** 3/4 **Uncle Fred**[56] 1752 7-9-5 **76**.......................... GeorgeBaker 6 64+
(Patrick Chamings) *slowest away: hld up in last: stl there 3f out: passed sme toiling rivals fnl 2f but nvr in it* **20/1**

0003 **10** 1 3/4 **Standpoint**[16] 2985 6-9-0 **74**..........................(p) RyanPowell(3) 9 58
(Conor Dore) *chsd ldrs: rdn in 6th 3f out: sn wknd* **50/1**

-005 **11** 3 **Perfect Cracker**[32] 2500 4-10-0 **85**.......................... AdamKirby 12 63
(Clive Cox) *hld up wl in rr: rdn 3f out: no great prog and nvr figured* **9/1**

1066 **12** nk **Chatterati (USA)**[14] 3031 3-8-10 **77**.......................... KierenFallon 14 52
(Mark Johnston) *chsd wnr 5f out to jst over 2f out: wknd rapidly* **40/1**

33-1 **13** 1/2 **Cool Rhythm**[15] 3012 4-9-8 **79**.......................... JimCrowley 10 55
(Ralph Beckett) *a wl in rr: struggling over 2f out* **14/1**

1m 37.92s (-1.88) **Going Correction** -0.025s/f (Stan)
WFA 3 from 4yo+ 10lb **13** Ran SP% **122.6**
Speed ratings (Par 105): **108,105,102,102,101 99,98,96,96,94 91,90,90**
toteswingers: 1&2 £1.70, 1&3 £12.70, 2&3 £21.90. CSF £7.82 CT £94.84 TOTE £3.80: £1.30, £1.10, £5.90; EX 8.50 Trifecta £292.10 Part won. Pool: £394.80 - 0.92 winning units..
Owner Godolphin **Bred** Newsells Park Stud **Trained** Newmarket, Suffolk

FOCUS
A decent handicap for 3yos and up. The winning time was only one second slower than standard off a pretty vigorous pace.
T/Plt: £14.50 to a £1 stake. Pool: £60,238.98 - 3,030.14 winning tickets. T/Qpdt: £4.40 to a £1 stake. Pool: £4,287.30 - 720.53 winning tickets. JN

3187 SALISBURY (R-H)
Wednesday, June 27

OFFICIAL GOING: Good (good to soft in places; 7.9)
Wind: Almost nil Weather: Overcast, light rain race 1

3504 BRITISH STALLION STUDS E B F ASHBRITTLE STUD MAIDEN FILLIES' STKS 5f
2:20 (2:20) (Class 4) 2-Y-0 **£4,237** (£1,260; £630; £315) **Stalls** Centre

Form RPR
6 **1** **Jollification (IRE)**[39] 2282 2-9-0 0.......................... PatCosgrave 3 83
(George Baker) *mde virtually all: narrow ld most of way: shkn up 2f out: jst maintained ld to line* **10/1**

2 hd **City Girl (IRE)** 2-9-0 0.......................... JimCrowley 2 82+
(Ralph Beckett) *w wnr thrght: shkn up 2f out: str chal fnl f: r.o* **13/8**[1]

3 3 **Contradict** 2-9-0 0.......................... RyanMoore 7 71+
(Sir Michael Stoute) *dwlt: in rr of main gp tl hdwy into 3rd over 1f out: no imp on first 2* **5/2**[2]

4 1/2 **Red Four** 2-9-0 0.......................... WilliamBuick 8 70+
(George Baker) *chsd ldrs: rdn 2f out: one pce* **12/1**

5 8 **Everleigh** 2-9-0 0.......................... RichardHughes 6 41+
(Richard Hannon) *carried lft s: outpcd: a trailing* **11/2**[3]

6 nk **Hayyona** 2-9-0 0.......................... MartinDwyer 4 40
(Mick Channon) *wnt lft s: in tch tl wknd 2f out* **15/2**

1m 2.01s (1.01) **Going Correction** +0.025s/f (Good) **6** Ran SP% **110.6**
Speed ratings (Par 92): **92,91,86,86,73 72**
toteswingers 1&2 £3.00, 1&3 £4.40, 2&3 £1.60 CSF £26.06 TOTE £16.50: £3.10, £1.90; EX 33.40 Trifecta £111.10 Pool: £570.52 - 3.80 winning units..
Owner Mr & Mrs J Pittam **Bred** Tinnakill Bloodstock & P Lawlor **Trained** Whitsbury, Hants

FOCUS
Rail up straight 20ft off permanent far side rail. Two on the main contenders, both previously raced, came out during the morning, meaning this looked less competitive as a result.

NOTEBOOK
Jollification(IRE) was the only runner left with experience and that may well have counted in a contest where a few ran green. Quickly away, she battled on nicely but it remains to be seen what she beat. (op 8-1)
City Girl(IRE) ◆, a half-sister to 2yo AW winner Echo Ridge, was by far the most professional of the newcomers and showed good pace. She can go one better soon if kept at a similar level. (op 9-4 tchd 6-4)
Contradict, from the first crop of Raven's Pass, raced keenly before keeping on for a never dangerous third. One would imagine better can be expected on her next outing. (op 3-1)
Red Four, a half-sister to two French winners, showed speed but didn't see it out. However, it was still a good start to her career. (op 8-1)
Everleigh was really slowly into stride and never had a hope of being involved in the finish. (op 9-2 tchd 6-1)
Hayyona, who cost 130,000gns as a foal and then 145,000gns as a yearling, is a half-sister to the Group 2 level performer Shimraan but will need to come on a ton for this to be dangerous next time. (op 6-1 tchd 17-2 in a place)

3505 BEGBIES TRAYNOR GROUP MAIDEN STKS (DIV I) 6f
2:50 (2:50) (Class 5) 2-Y-0 **£2,911** (£866; £432; £216) **Stalls** Low

Form RPR
26 **1** **Ask Dad**[8] 3242 2-9-3 0.......................... RichardHughes 6 82
(Richard Hannon) *pressed ldr: led 2f out: drvn to hold on fnl f* **8/13**[1]

2 nk **Ashaadd (IRE)** 2-9-3 0.......................... AndreaAtzeni 7 81+
(Roger Varian) *trckd ldrs: rdn to chse wnr fnl f: r.o: clsng nr fin: jst hld* **7/1**[3]

3 **3** 1 1/4 **Shahdaroba (IRE)**[42] 2164 2-9-3 0.......................... JamesMillman 2 77
(Rod Millman) *led: hdd and hrd rdn 2f out: one pce* **10/1**

6 **4** 3/4 **Ferjaan**[18] 2934 2-9-3 0.......................... PaulHanagan 5 75
(John Gosden) *trckd ldrs: rdn and one pce fnl 2f* **6/1**[2]

5 3 **Nenge Mboko** 2-9-3 0.......................... PatCosgrave 8 66
(George Baker) *chsd ldrs: rdn over 2f out: no ex over 1f out* **50/1**

6 hd **Signature Dish (IRE)** 2-8-12 0.......................... DavidProbert 4 61+
(Andrew Balding) *s.s: sn in midfield: rdn and outpcd over 3f out: kpt on fr over 1f out* **16/1**

7 5 **Foie Gras** 2-9-3 0.......................... MartinDwyer 9 51
(William Muir) *stdd in rr s: rdn over 3f out: nvr trbld ldrs* **33/1**

0 **8** 2 3/4 **My Sweet Lord**[13] 3074 2-9-0 0.......................... HarryBentley(3) 1 42
(Mark Usher) *bhd: rdn over 3f out: nvr nr ldrs* **50/1**

9 1/2 **Jawinski (IRE)** 2-9-3 0.......................... PadraigBeggy 11 41
(David Evans) *mid-div: rdn and outpcd over 3f out: wknd 2f out* **66/1**

10 shd **Digress** 2-9-3 0.......................... RyanMoore 3 40
(Sir Michael Stoute) *s.s: rdn over 3f out: a bhd* **10/1**

1m 16.05s (1.25) **Going Correction** +0.025s/f (Good) **10** Ran SP% **121.1**
Speed ratings (Par 93): **92,91,89,88,84 84,78,74,73,73**
toteswingers 1&2 £2.00, 1&3 £2.70, 2&3 £8.90 CSF £5.85 TOTE £1.60: £1.10, £1.70, £2.00; EX 6.50 Trifecta £36.20.
Owner Andrew Tinkler **Bred** Wallace Holmes & Partners **Trained** East Everleigh, Wilts

FOCUS
The winner was the standout on form and just about got the job done.

NOTEBOOK
Ask Dad, sixth in the Listed Windsor Castle Stakes at Royal Ascot the previous week, got the job done for those who backed him heavily, winning narrowly from a newcomer. One would imagine he'll find things tough now, whatever route connections take with him. (op 8-11 tchd 4-7 and 4-5 in a place)
Ashaadd(IRE) ◆, who cost 110,000gns as a yearling, posted a most pleasing debut and pushed Ask Dad all the way to the line. Presuming he doesn't go backwards, a maiden ought to be a formality. (tchd 15-2)
Shahdaroba(IRE) ◆ finished third to Sir Prancealot on his previous start back in mid-May, and at least ran up to that level from the front. He's another who has a maiden victory in his scope. (op 12-1)
Ferjaan ran to a modest level on debut but probably improved a little bit here. He looked all set to get into a place in the final stages but due to a bit of crowding never could quite get there. (op 7-1)
Nenge Mboko, a half-brother to Group 3-winning sprinter Ringmoor Down among others, showed ability on the outside of the field before weakening.
Signature Dish(IRE) never threatened to get her head to the front but got the idea late on and finished well. (op 14-1)
Foie Gras ran freely in behind and will need to learn to settle.
Digress, whose dam's siblings include Main Aim and Home Affairs, got squeezed out soon after leaving the stalls and couldn't get involved. (op 15-2)

3506 BEGBIES TRAYNOR GROUP MAIDEN STKS (DIV II) 6f
3:20 (3:20) (Class 5) 2-Y-0 **£2,911** (£866; £432; £216) **Stalls** Low

Form RPR
1 **Verdane** 2-9-3 .... JamesDoyle 8 79
(David Evans) *hld up in midfield: j. path over 3f out: hdwy 2f out: r.o to ld fnl 50yds: hurdled winning line* **50/1**

32 **2** 1/2 **Echion (IRE)**[23] 2763 2-9-3 .... RichardHughes 1 77
(Richard Hannon) *prom: slt ld 2f out: rdn and hdd fnl 50yds* **3/1**[2]

24 **3** 3/4 **Bairam**[23] 2763 2-9-3 .... PaulHanagan 2 75
(Brian Meehan) *led tl 2f out: styd w ldrs: nt qckn fnl 75yds* **7/2**[3]

4 1 1/2 **Related** 2-9-3 .... AdamKirby 4 71+
(Clive Cox) *chsd ldrs: pushed along 3f out: cl 4th and jst hld whn squeezed out wl ins fnl f* **6/4**[1]

5 1 1/2 **Herbalist** 2-9-3 .... DaneO'Neill 3 66
(Henry Candy) *dwlt: sn in midfield: rdn 3f out: styd on fnl f* **16/1**

0 **6** 1 1/4 **Silverrica (IRE)**[11] 3140 2-8-12 .... TomMcLaughlin 5 57
(Malcolm Saunders) *plld hrd: pressed ldrs 4f: btn whn n.m.r and swtchd rt over 1f out* **66/1**

7 3 1/2 **Elounta** 2-8-7 .... DarrenEgan(5) 9 47
(John Best) *hld up towards rr: rdn 3f out: nvr trbld ldrs* **33/1**

8 1/2 **Eton Rambler (USA)** 2-9-3 .... PatCosgrave 10 50
(George Baker) *s.s: bhd tl sme late hdwy* **20/1**

9 13 **Panther Patrol (IRE)** 2-9-3 .... TomQueally 6 11
(Eve Johnson Houghton) *s.i.s: a towards rr: no ch fnl 2f: lame* **20/1**

10 3/4 **Elvin** 2-9-3 .... JimCrowley 7 9
(Amanda Perrett) *in rr of midfield: rdn 3f out: n.d after* **12/1**

11 11 **Crafty Wonder (IRE)** 2-9-3 .... PadraigBeggy 11
(David Evans) *v.s.a: a wl bhd* **66/1**

1m 15.55s (0.75) **Going Correction** +0.025s/f (Good) **11** Ran SP% **118.2**
Speed ratings (Par 93): **96,95,94,92,90 88,84,83,66,65 50**
toteswingers 1&2 £12.10, 1&3 £32.50, 2&3 £29.60 CSF £189.85 TOTE £61.50: £11.80, £1.20, £1.10; EX 207.40 Trifecta £604.10 Part won. Pool: £816.45 - 0.40 winning units..
Owner Wayne Clifford **Bred** Mrs S Clifford **Trained** Pandy, Monmouths

FOCUS
An ordinary event, which looked the weaker of the two divisions despite the time being quicker.

NOTEBOOK
Verdane won at long odds but there appeared no fluke about the result, indeed, he had enough enthusiasm left to hurdle the mark across the course denoting the winning line. A horse with a bit of size, he should keep progressing.
Echion(IRE) finished in front of Bairam last time, and confirmed that form narrowly over a furlong further. There wasn't a great deal between them at the end. (op 11-4 tchd 5-2)
Bairam was ridden prominently but didn't quite get home. (op 4-1 tchd 9-2)
Related, a half-brother to most notably Wootton Bassett, attracted plenty of market interest and shaped nicely before being squeezed out towards the end when held. (op 13-8 tchd 7-4)

Herbalist sat in midfield before staying on nicely in the final stages.
Silverrica(IRE) showed early pace but didn't get home.
Panther Patrol(IRE) Official explanation: jockey said colt lost its action; vet said colt returned lame right-hind

3507 SMITH & WILLIAMSON MAIDEN FILLIES' STKS 6f 212y
3:50 (3:52) (Class 5) 3-Y-O £2,911 (£866; £432; £216) Stalls Centre

Form				RPR
2-22	1		**Riot Of Colour**[39] 2273 3-9-0 87 JimCrowley 7 (Ralph Beckett) *hld up in 5th: led over 1f out: edgd rt: drvn out* **8/11**[1]	86
6-4	2	¾	**Dalkova**[24] 2734 3-9-0 RichardHughes 5 (Richard Hannon) *settled in midfield: rdn 3f out: hdwy over 1f out: r.o to press wnr fnl 50yds: jst hld* **16/1**	84
56	3	1	**Bunraku**[47] 2030 3-9-0 MichaelHills 10 (Charles Hills) *prom: led over 2f out tl over 1f out: nt qckn fnl f* **15/2**[3]	81
43	4	1 ½	**Stirring Ballad**[12] 3107 3-9-0 DavidProbert 1 (Andrew Balding) *led tl over 2f out: no ex fnl f* **13/2**[2]	77
0-	5	¾	**Catherine Laboure (IRE)**[364] 3520 3-9-0 TomQueally 3 (Eve Johnson Houghton) *mid-div: swtchd wd into centre and effrt over 2f out: one pce appr fnl f* **40/1**	75
	6	2 ½	**Enrol** 3-9-0 RyanMoore 14 (Sir Michael Stoute) *hld up towards rr: rdn and hdwy over 2f out: no imp appr fnl f* **10/1**	68
06-	7	6	**Zaahya (IRE)**[319] 5029 3-9-0 PaulHanagan 2 (John Dunlop) *chsd ldrs tl wknd 2f out* **16/1**	52
5-0	8	¾	**Cha Ching (IRE)**[43] 2145 3-9-0 SebSanders 11 (J W Hills) *towards rr: rdn 3f out: nvr rchd ldrs* **50/1**	50
0-	9	nk	**Your Word**[252] 6950 3-9-0 AdamKirby 4 (Clive Cox) *t.k.h: w ldrs tl wknd 2f out* **33/1**	49
6	10	5	**Precision Five**[20] 2865 3-9-0 (p) PatCosgrave 6 (Jeremy Gask) *stdd s: plld hrd in rr: rdn 3f out: n.d* **100/1**	36
6	11	4	**Mrs Bridges**[16] 2974 3-9-0 RobertHavlin 9 (Roger Ingram) *mid-div tl wknd over 2f out* **150/1**	25
60-	12	3	**Ice Missile**[336] 4427 3-9-0 JamesDoyle 8 (Sylvester Kirk) *rdn 4f out: a bhd* **40/1**	17
	13	9	**User Name (USA)** 3-9-0 WilliamBuick 12 (Mikael Magnusson) *outpcd: sn wl bhd* **25/1**	

1m 28.14s (-0.46) **Going Correction** +0.025s/f (Good) **13 Ran SP% 119.1**
Speed ratings (Par 96): **103,102,101,99,98 95,88,87,87,81 77,73,63**
toteswingers 1&2 £4.70, 1&3 £3.10, 2&3 £11.40 CSF £14.19 TOTE £1.70: £1.10, £4.10, £2.70; EX 14.60 Trifecta £36.80 Pool: £839.03 - 16.38 winning units..
Owner The Eclipse Partnership **Bred** Car Colston Hall Stud **Trained** Kimpton, Hants

FOCUS
It's probably fair to assume there were no stars lurking in this considering the race type for the time of year. The early gallop didn't look strong.
User Name(USA) Official explanation: jockey said filly ran green

3508 MOLSON COORS NOEL CANNON MEMORIAL TROPHY H'CAP 1m
4:25 (4:26) (Class 2) (0-100,95) 3-Y-O+
£9,960 (£2,982; £1,491; £745; £372; £187) Stalls Low

Form				RPR
313	1		**Trade Commissioner (IRE)**[18] 2932 4-9-5 86 WilliamBuick 9 (John Gosden) *hld up in 6th: hdwy to ld wl over 1f out: sn qcknd clr: easily* **5/2**[1]	109+
1651	2	4 ½	**Shamaal Nibras (USA)**[11] 3160 3-9-3 94 RichardHughes 6 (Richard Hannon) *towards rr: rdn and hdwy over 1f out: chsd wnr ins fnl f: no imp* **9/1**	103+
-045	3	1 ¼	**Vainglory (USA)**[19] 2882 8-9-3 89 LauraPike(5) 8 (David Simcock) *bhd: rdn and hdwy fnl 2f: fin wl* **16/1**	96
01-0	4	¾	**Uppercut**[43] 2151 4-9-0 81 FergusSweeney 13 (Stuart Kittow) *chsd ldrs: rdn to chal over 2f out: one pce* **20/1**	86
0025	5	¾	**Shavansky**[18] 2932 8-9-5 86 JamesMillman 10 (Rod Millman) *dwlt: bhd: rdn 3f out: hdwy over 1f out: nt rch ldrs* **10/1**	89
2106	6	1 ¼	**George Guru**[27] 2642 5-9-5 91 MarkCoumbe(5) 2 (Michael Attwater) *prom: rdn to chal 2f out: wknd over 1f out* **20/1**	91
-155	7	2	**Norse Blues**[26] 2657 4-9-9 90 JamesDoyle 5 (Sylvester Kirk) *chsd ldr: led over 2f out tl wl over 1f out: sn wknd* **6/1**[3]	86
006	8	nk	**Fantasy Gladiator**[11] 3157 6-8-13 80 (p) JimCrowley 4 (Robert Cowell) *in tch tl wknd wl over 1f out* **22/1**	75
012	9	2	**Roserrow**[21] 2813 3-8-10 87 DavidProbert 7 (Andrew Balding) *bhd: drvn along 3f out: nvr trbld ldrs* **11/1**	76
0643	10	1 ½	**First Post (IRE)**[14] 3037 5-9-1 82 DaneO'Neill 11 (Derek Haydn Jones) *mid-div: hrd rdn over 2f out: sn btn* **14/1**	69
0010	11	¾	**Shifting Star (IRE)**[15] 3004 7-9-7 88 SeanLevey 3 (John Bridger) *mid-div: rdn 3f out: fdd fnl 2f* **40/1**	73
3132	12	1 ¾	**Mawaakef (IRE)**[26] 2657 4-10-0 95 RyanMoore 1 (J R Jenkins) *led tl over 2f out: wknd over 1f out* **9/2**[2]	76
0-00	13	1 ¼	**Leviathan**[11] 3157 5-9-3 84 (p) TomQueally 12 (Tony Newcombe) *t.k.h: sn stdd towards rr: rdn 3f out: n.d after* **14/1**	62

1m 42.17s (-1.33) **Going Correction** +0.025s/f (Good)
WFA 3 from 4yo+ 10lb **13 Ran SP% 124.0**
Speed ratings (Par 109): **107,102,101,100,99 98,96,96,94,92 91,90,88**
toteswingers 1&2 £5.10, 1&3 £10.50, 2&3 £22.10 CSF £25.26 CT £315.05 TOTE £3.60: £1.70, £3.70, £5.60; EX 15.50 Trifecta £169.80 Pool: £963.97 - 4.20 winning units..
Owner Lady Rothschild **Bred** Kincorth Investments Inc **Trained** Newmarket, Suffolk

FOCUS
A strong-looking handicap prior to the off, but it was won with ease by the unexposed winner.

NOTEBOOK
Trade Commissioner(IRE) ◆ was by far the most interesting of these despite easing in distance. Dropped into a chasing position, it was clear he'd take some stopping about 2f out if finding for pressure, and that he did without ever being subjected to a hard time. He's bred to be pretty good, so even after a hefty rise he'll presumably get for this, he should be given plenty of respect in a big handicap over 1m-1m2f if connections keep to that type of race. (op 9-4 tchd 11-4)
Shamaal Nibras(USA) ◆, up 6lb for his 7f victory at Sandown, beat the rest nicely but time will surely tell he bumped into a well-handicapped rival here. It was a fine effort against older horses and he remains of some interest.
Vainglory(USA), second in this last year off a 1lb higher mark, came home strongly from an unpromising position to get into third. It's fair to say he doesn't get his head to front that often because his mark stays high through consistency.
Uppercut is a consistent performer at a fair level and there is no reason to think he didn't run up to somewhere close to his best. (tchd 22-1)
Norse Blues reversed Epsom form with Mawaakef but was well beaten after racing up with the lead. (op 8-1)
Mawaakef(IRE) dropped out quickly after having the run of the race. (op 6-1)

3509 ASHBRITTLE STUD BIBURY CUP STKS (H'CAP) 1m 4f
4:55 (4:55) (Class 3) (0-95,87) 3-Y-O £7,762 (£2,310; £1,154; £577) Stalls Low

Form				RPR
521	1		**Rule Book (IRE)**[11] 3161 3-9-3 83 RichardHughes 1 (Richard Hannon) *chsd ldng pair: rdn 3f out: wnt 2nd 2f out: styd on to ld nr fin* **13/2**	95
0-41	2	hd	**Rye House (IRE)**[44] 2129 3-9-2 82 RyanMoore 3 (Sir Michael Stoute) *hld up in 5th: hdwy 5f out: led wl over 2f out and qcknd 3 l clr: hrd rdn ins fnl f: hdd nr fin* **6/5**[1]	93+
5116	3	4	**Last Shadow**[32] 2484 3-9-2 82 MartinDwyer 2 (William Muir) *stdd in rr s: rdn 3f out: styd on to take 3rd 1f out: nt trble first 2* **7/1**	87
6-02	4	2 ½	**Al Saham**[14] 3042 3-9-7 87 MickaelBarzalona 6 (Saeed Bin Suroor) *hld up in 4th: rdn 3f out: one pce* **9/2**[2]	88
0-52	5	2 ½	**Moon Trip**[25] 2716 3-8-11 77 KierenFallon 5 (Mark Johnston) *led tl wl over 2f out: wknd over 1f out* **6/1**[3]	74
1-30	6	½	**Cherry Street**[49] 1978 3-9-4 84 DavidProbert 8 (Andrew Balding) *plld hrd: chsd ldr: rdn 3f out: wknd 2f out* **12/1**	80

2m 38.78s (0.78) **Going Correction** +0.025s/f (Good) **6 Ran SP% 111.4**
Speed ratings (Par 103): **98,97,95,93,91 91**
toteswingers 1&2 £2.00, 1&3 £4.30, 2&3 £2.40 CSF £14.65 CT £54.09 TOTE £5.60: £1.50, £1.60; EX 14.30 Trifecta £103.20 Pool: £818.93 - 5.87 winning units..
Owner Andrew Tinkler **Bred** Joseph Heavey **Trained** East Everleigh, Wilts

FOCUS
Not many runners and the early gallop was far from frenetic. It steadily increased from roughly 5f out.

NOTEBOOK
Rule Book(IRE) ◆, making his handicap debut, got caught a little flat-footed at one stage, but his rider kept pressing his mount to go after the leader and eventually won a shade comfortably despite getting up close to the line - Richard Hughes put his whip down a few yards from the line. The colt's dam never won a race but she was out of Sweetness Herself, a very useful type at up to 2m, so another furlong or two might be within the winner's scope. (op 7-1)
Rye House(IRE) ◆ was sent to the front plenty early enough, although Ryan Moore was no doubt wary that he didn't want a sprint to develop. Things looked good once the pair got to the front, but they didn't go right away as seemed likely and were worn down late on. A step up in distance will no doubt bring about some more improvement. (op 5-4 tchd 11-10)
Last Shadow ran pretty well without causing the front two many problems. He can develop in a nice handicapper but may need to ease down the weight a little to have an obvious winning chance against similar types. One would imagine he'll be a horse to watch at the back-end of the season when the ground becomes properly soft again. (op 15-2)
Al Saham was one-paced at the end. (op 5-1 tchd 11-2)
Moon Trip dropped away tamely after leading. (op 13-2 tchd 7-1)

3510 NEW FOREST FARM MACHINERY/JOHN DEERE FILLIES' H'CAP 6f
5:25 (5:25) (Class 5) (0-70,69) 3-Y-O £2,587 (£770; £384; £192) Stalls Low

Form				RPR
3311	1		**Dark Ages (IRE)**[15] 3005 3-9-6 68 (t) JimCrowley 9 (Paul Burgoyne) *hld up in 6th: led over 1f out: rdn clr: readily* **10/3**[1]	76
5025	2	2 ¾	**Ocean Myth**[19] 2869 3-9-3 65 NickyMackay 4 (Jonathan Portman) *chsd ldrs: led briefly wl over 1f out: chsd wnr after: nt qckn* **9/1**	64
2303	3	hd	**Hey Fiddle Fiddle (IRE)**[19] 2869 3-9-0 62 (b) WilliamCarson 13 (Charles Hills) *prom: led over 2f out tl wl over 1f out: one pce fnl f* **8/1**	60
0-00	4	½	**Red Mischief (IRE)**[47] 2045 3-9-6 68 JamesDoyle 14 (Harry Dunlop) *chsd ldrs: outpcd 2f out: r.o again ins fnl f* **16/1**	65
0-00	5	¾	**Pindrop**[14] 3044 3-8-9 57 JohnFahy 5 (Clive Cox) *bhd: pshd along 4f out: rdn and hdwy fr over 1f out: nrst fin* **22/1**	51
43-0	6	1 ½	**Iced Opal**[72] 1412 3-9-7 69 LiamKeniry 3 (Michael Blanshard) *towards rr: rdn and hdwy over 1f out: nt rch ldrs* **14/1**	59
2006	7	1 ½	**Lana (IRE)**[103] 917 3-8-8 56 (v) KirstyMilczarek 11 (David Evans) *t.k.h: bhd tl rdn and styd on fnl 2f* **18/1**	41
041-	8	2 ½	**Miriam's Song**[224] 7435 3-9-2 64 FergusSweeney 1 (Stuart Kittow) *chsd ldrs tl wknd 2f out* **15/2**[3]	41
-040	9	¾	**Tenderly Place**[14] 3050 3-8-4 55 (t) HarryBentley(3) 12 (William Knight) *stdd s: t.k.h towards rr: pshd wd after 1f: mod effrt 3f out: nt trble ldrs* **11/1**	29
4544	10	2	**Tiablo (IRE)**[2] 3451 3-8-13 61 PadraigBeggy 10 (David Evans) *mid-div: hrd rdn 3f out: outpcd fnl 2f* **14/1**	29
36-5	11	1 ½	**Rode Two Destiny (IRE)**[19] 2871 3-8-12 60 (p) SebSanders 6 (Peter Makin) *led tl over 2f out: sn wknd* **14/1**	23
423	12	17	**Catflap (IRE)**[58] 1705 3-9-2 64 RyanMoore 2 (Derek Haydn Jones) *t.k.h: settled in rr: rdn 3f out: eased 2f out* **4/1**[2]	

1m 16.12s (1.32) **Going Correction** +0.025s/f (Good) **12 Ran SP% 119.8**
Speed ratings (Par 96): **92,88,88,87,86 84,82,79,78,75 73,50**
toteswingers 1&2 £7.10, 1&3 £6.30, 2&3 £12.40 CSF £34.10 CT £230.81 TOTE £2.60: £1.10, £3.60, £2.80; EX 36.00 Trifecta £452.10 Part won. Pool: £611.07 - 0.84 winning units..
Owner Mrs Helen Adams **Bred** G W Robinson **Trained** Shepton Montague, Somerset

FOCUS
Nothing more than a modest contest.

3511 CATHEDRAL HOTEL SALISBURY H'CAP (FOR GENTLEMAN AMATEUR RIDERS) 6f 212y
5:55 (5:55) (Class 6) (0-65,65) 4-Y-O+ £1,871 (£580; £290; £145) Stalls Centre

Form				RPR
0-14	1		**Takitwo**[14] 3053 9-10-7 58 MrJHarding(7) 10 (Jonathan Portman) *hld up in 5th: led over 1f out: pushed out: comf* **10/1**	68
-600	2	1 ½	**George Thisby**[19] 2886 6-11-1 62 (p) MrPMillman(3) 4 (Rod Millman) *prom: rdn 3f out: nt qckn ins fnl f* **10/1**	68
3643	3	1 ¼	**Rapid Water**[6] 3318 6-10-8 57 MatthewStanley(5) 11 (Pat Eddery) *led over 1f: chsd ldr after: led again over 2f out: hrd rdn and hdd over 1f out: one pce* **7/2**[1]	60
60	4	nk	**Bold Ring**[4] 3388 6-10-13 60 MrCMartin(3) 7 (Eric Wheeler) *mid-div: rdn and hdwy 2f out: styd on same pce fnl f* **16/1**	62
0000	5	¾	**Northern Spy (USA)**[19] 2886 8-10-7 56 MrJCoffill-Brown(5) 9 (Simon Dow) *mid-div: rdn and hdwy 2f out: kpt on same pce appr fnl f* **11/2**[2]	56
05-0	6	1 ¼	**Gallego**[19] 2867 10-10-11 58 MrMPrice(3) 6 (Richard Price) *s.s: wl bhd tl r.o fnl 2f* **7/1**[3]	54
-204	7	2	**Arachnophobia (IRE)**[51] 1934 6-10-6 57 (v) MrZBaker(7) 14 (Martin Bosley) *hld up in midfield: rdn and no hdwy fnl 2f* **18/1**	48
5461	8	2 ½	**Silvee**[15] 3007 5-11-2 60 MrRBirkett 2 (John Bridger) *towards rr: hrd rdn 2f out: n.d* **8/1**	44

0545 **9** *2* **Forty Proof (IRE)**[30] 2551 4-10-8 **52**....................(vt) MrFWindsorClive 13 31
(David Evans) *towards rr: rdn 3f out: nvr trbld ldrs* **25/1**
001 **10** *½* **Irie Ute**[37] 2350 4-10-7 **58**.. MrNicholasMeek(7) 1 35
(Sylvester Kirk) *chsd ldrs tl wknd wl over 2f out* **16/1**
1000 **11** *6* **May's Boy**[14] 3039 4-10-12 **63**...........................(p) MrEdwardSibbick(7) 5 24
(Mark Usher) *mid-div: outpcd 3f out: sn struggling* **16/1**
4030 **12** *12* **National Hope (IRE)**[21] 2811 4-10-11 **62**...................(t) MrATJones(7) 12
(George Baker) *rrd s: hdwy to ld over 5f out: hdd & wknd over 2f out* **16/1**
0-43 **13** *15* **Annes Rocket (IRE)**[34] 2421 7-10-11 **62**.......................(p) MrPHarty(7) 3
(Jimmy Fox) *a bhd* **8/1**

1m 30.18s (1.58) **Going Correction** +0.025s/f (Good) **13** Ran SP% **123.1**
Speed ratings (Par 101): **91,89,87,87,86 85,82,80,77,77 70,56,39**
toteswingers 1&2 £16.20, 1&3 £3.90, 2&3 £8.40 CSF £109.67 CT £443.03 TOTE £12.10: £3.00, £2.80, £1.30; EX 54.00 TRIFECTA Not won..
Owner P D Cundell **Bred** Roden House Stud **Trained** Compton, Berks
■ A first winner under rules on only his second ride for James Harding.
■ Stewards' Enquiry : Matthew Stanley two-day ban: used whip above permitted level (tbn)

FOCUS
Not a race to get too carried away with.
T/Plt: £11.00 to a £1 stake. Pool: £55126.14 - 3639.27 winning tickets T/Qpdt: £3.30 to a £1 stake. Pool: £3352.70 - 735.40 winning tickets LM

3512 - 3518a (Foreign Racing) - See Raceform Interactive

3271 HAMILTON (R-H)

Thursday, June 28

OFFICIAL GOING: Soft (7.4)
Wind: Fresh, half behind Weather: Cloudy, bright

3519 ROGANO GLASGOW LADY AMATEUR RIDERS' H'CAP 1m 5f 9y
6:50 (6:51) (Class 6) (0-65,65) 4-Y-0+ **£2,634** (£810; £405) **Stalls** Low

Form RPR
330/ **1** **Livvy Inn (USA)**[204] 4630 7-9-4 **51**.................................. MissCWalton(3) 9 64
(Lucinda Russell) *hld up: stdy hdwy over 3f out: led over 1f out: pushed clr fnl f* **18/1**
3-20 **2** *5* **Hi Dancer**[51] 1952 9-9-10 **54**.. MissJCoward 2 60
(Ben Haslam) *led: rdn and hdd over 1f out: kpt on same pce fnl f* **4/1**[2]
0-40 **3** *2* **Terenzium (IRE)**[22] 2827 10-9-1 **50**............................(p) MissRSmith(5) 6 53
(Micky Hammond) *t.k.h early: prom: hdwy to chse ldr 1/2-way: effrt over 2f out: one pce appr fnl f* **4/1**[2]
0/60 **4** *11* **Sydney Cove (IRE)**[4] 3029 6-8-13 **46** oh1..........(p) MissJRRichards(3) 3 32
(Iain Jardine) *s.i.s: hld up: stdy hdwy over 3f out: outpcd 2f out: n.d after* **25/1**
3331 **5** *1* **Asterales**[3] 3440 5-10-2 **60** 6ex.. MissEJJones 4 45
(Jo Hughes) *chsd ldrs: rdn and outpcd over 3f out: n.d after* **85/40**[1]
06-3 **6** *1 ¾* **Stags Leap (IRE)**[13] 3114 5-10-7 **65**...........................(p) MissECSayer 8 47
(Dianne Sayer) *unruly in preliminaries: prom tl rdn and outpcd over 3f out: n.d after* **4/1**[2]
/0-0 **7** *14* **Front Rank (IRE)**[7] 3310 12-8-11 **46** oh1.............(p) MissRobynGray(5) 5 7
(Dianne Sayer) *chsd ldrs: outpcd over 3f out: hung lft and sn wknd* **33/1**
604- **8** *4* **Grand Diamond (IRE)**[238] 6385 8-9-5 **56**..................... MrsICGoldie(7) 1 11
(Jim Goldie) *in tch tl rdn and wknd fr 3f out* **16/1**[3]

3m 1.74s (7.84) **Going Correction** +0.575s/f (Yiel) **8** Ran SP% **109.9**
Speed ratings (Par 101): **98,94,93,86,86 85,76,74**
toteswingers: 1&2 £6.90, 1&3 £10.90, 2&3 £3.40 CSF £81.86 CT £329.04 TOTE £17.60: £6.30, £1.10, £1.30; EX 51.10 TRIFECTA Not won..
Owner Mrs Elizabeth Ferguson **Bred** Camelia Casby **Trained** Arlary, Perth & Kinross

FOCUS
Races on Round course run over approximately 25yds less than advertised. All races on the round course were run over a distance 25 yards less than advertised. After 2mm of rain during the day the going was soft, with the going stick reading 7.4. A moderate staying lady amateur riders' handicap, with three previous winners of the race in the line-up. It was run at a steady pace with the field well strung out crossing the line. The winner recordeed a personal-best with the second setting the level.

3520 TAGGARTS MOTOR GROUP MAIDEN AUCTION STKS 6f 5y
7:20 (7:21) (Class 5) 2-Y-0 **£3,234** (£962; £481; £240) **Stalls** High

Form RPR
2 **1** **Red Joker (IRE)**[19] 2923 2-8-13 0................................ PaulMulrennan 3 66
(Alan Swinbank) *mde all: rdn over 1f out: edgd rt ins fnl f: kpt on wl* **4/1**[3]
00 **2** *¾* **Amelia Jay**[21] 2837 2-8-4 0.. JoeFanning 4 55
(Danielle McCormick) *dwlt: in tch: effrt on outside over 1f out: edgd rt and chsd wnr ins fnl f: kpt on: hld nr fin* **80/1**
5 **3** *1 ¼* **Red Paladin (IRE)**[42] 2213 2-9-1 0.................................. PhillipMakin 2 62
(Kevin Ryan) *chsd ldrs: rdn and ev ch over 1f out: kpt on same pce last 100yds* **85/40**[2]
622 **4** *5* **Pastoral Prey**[21] 2837 2-8-9 0.. AdrianNicholls 6 41
(George Foster) *t.k.h: cl up: rdn over 2f out: outpcd over 1f out: edgd rt and sn no imp* **8/1**
42 **5** *2 ¼* **Gold Beau (FR)**[8] 3271 2-8-11 0...................................... GrahamLee 5 36
(Linda Stubbs) *t.k.h: cl up: rdn over 2f out: wknd over 1f out* **5/4**[1]

1m 15.66s (3.46) **Going Correction** +0.30s/f (Good) **5** Ran SP% **108.8**
Speed ratings (Par 93): **88,87,85,78,75**
toteswingers: 1&2 £32.20 CSF £99.69 TOTE £5.30: £3.20, £6.10; EX 43.60.
Owner Chris Tremewan **Bred** Christopher Maye **Trained** Melsonby, N Yorks

FOCUS
This maiden was run at a steady pace with the front three drawing clear late on. The form looks modest but the winner has more to offer.

NOTEBOOK
Red Joker(IRE), for whom Paul Mulrennan was a late jockey switch, ran well when runner-up at Newcastle on his debut (6f, soft) and had clearly learnt from that. He stayed on well for pressure to give his stable their first 2yo winner of the season. There is plenty of stamina on his dam's side and improvement should come over further. (op 10-3)
Amelia Jay, well held in two 6f maidens, showed much more here but may have benefited from racing away from the rails. Slowly away and green early, she had to be niggled to stay in contention before hanging to the centre of the track when driven. She stayed on well enough for pressure, clearly acted on easier ground and is now qualified for a mark.
Red Paladin(IRE) was dropping in class, having finished fifth in a Class 3 York maiden on his debut. He looked dangerous inside the final 2f before tiring in the testing conditions. (op 11-4)
Pastoral Prey, for whom Adrian Nicholls was a late jockey change, had proved progressive in his three starts but found little here and paid for doing too much early. (op 13-2)
Gold Beau(FR) was well supported in the market but raced too freely and weakened late on ground that was softer than ideal. Official explanation: trainer said gelding was unsuited by the soft ground (op 11-8 tchd 6-4)

3521 IRN BRU OPEN MAIDEN STKS 1m 1f 36y
7:50 (7:50) (Class 5) 3-4-Y-0 **£3,234** (£962; £481; £240) **Stalls** Low

Form RPR
0-64 **1** **Supreme Luxury (IRE)**[21] 2860 3-8-10 72 ow1................ PhillipMakin 3 74+
(Kevin Ryan) *trckd ldrs: smooth hdwy to ld over 2f out: shkn up and sn clr: eased ins fnl f* **15/8**[1]
2 *3* **Madame Blavatsky (FR)**[18] 4-8-13 0..................... GeorgeChaloner(7) 9 61
(Karen McLintock) *hld up: rdn over 3f out: hdwy on outside to chse (clr) wnr appr fnl f: kpt on: no imp* **33/1**
443 **3** *7* **Outback (IRE)**[8] 3273 3-9-0 70...(p) GrahamLee 8 51
(Ann Duffield) *in tch: rdn over 3f out: no imp fr 2f out* **10/3**[3]
04 **4** *1 ¾* **Artistic Dawn (IRE)**[28] 2633 3-8-9 0.............................. PaulMulrennan 4 42
(John Weymes) *led to over 2f out: sn rdn: wknd over 1f out* **9/1**
5 *10* **Centrifugal (IRE)** 3-9-0 0.. JoeFanning 7 25
(Mark Johnston) *hld up in tch: effrt and pushed along over 3f out: wknd fr 2f out* **12/5**[2]
6 *1 ½* **Giveherachance** 3-8-9 0.. PatrickMathers 2 17
(Ann Duffield) *hld up in tch: rdn over 3f out: wknd over 2f out* **28/1**
00 **7** *13* **Oasis Love (IRE)**[30] 2592 3-9-0 0................................... AdrianNicholls 5
(Mark Johnston) *cl up tl rdn and wknd over 3f out: t.o* **16/1**
0 **8** *40* **Lochluichart (IRE)**[8] 3273 3-8-11 0................................... LeeTopliss(3) 6
(Ian Semple) *dwlt: hld up: rdn over 3f out: sn lost tch: t.o* **40/1**

2m 4.01s (4.31) **Going Correction** +0.575s/f (Yiel)
WFA 3 from 4yo 11lb **8** Ran SP% **112.0**
Speed ratings (Par 103): **103,100,94,92,83 82,70,35**
toteswingers: 1&2 £5.60, 1&3 £1.90, 2&3 £11.60 CSF £65.88 TOTE £2.30: £1.10, £7.70, £1.40; EX 61.60 Trifecta £155.70 Pool: £736.79 - 3.50 winning units..
Owner Mubarak Al Naemi **Bred** Mrs E Alberti **Trained** Hambleton, N Yorks

FOCUS
A moderate looking maiden run at a sound pace with the field well strung out crossing the line. An easy winner but some doubt over what she achieved here and she looks the best guide to previous form.
Artistic Dawn(IRE) Official explanation: jockey said filly hung left throughout

3522 E B F CAPTAIN J.C. STEWART FILLIES' H'CAP 1m 65y
8:20 (8:20) (Class 3) (0-95,87) 3-Y-0+ **£7,762** (£2,310; £1,154; £577) **Stalls** Low

Form RPR
4103 **1** **Madam Macie (IRE)**[9] 3252 5-10-0 **87**.......................... DanielTudhope 5 98
(David O'Meara) *chsd ldr: led after 2f: brought main gp centre ent st: pushed clr fr over 2f out: eased ins fnl f* **11/4**[2]
1060 **2** *8* **She's A Character**[11] 3185 5-9-0 **80**........................ GeorgeChaloner(7) 2 73
(Richard Fahey) *in tch: hdwy to chse (clr) wnr over 2f out: no imp fr over 1f out* **11/1**
0600 **3** *3 ¼* **What's Up (IRE)**[8] 3270 3-9-4 **87**......................................(p) PhillipMakin 7 70
(Kevin Ryan) *in tch: rdn and outpcd over 3f out: rallied over 1f out: nvr able to chal* **9/1**
0404 **4** *4* **Polar Annie**[6] 3334 7-9-4 **77**.. GrahamLee 1 53
(Jim Goldie) *led 2f: cl up: styd alone towards far rail ent st: rdn and wknd fr 2f out* **6/1**[3]
-133 **5** *1 ¼* **Parley (USA)**[5] 3395 3-8-11 **80**.. JoeFanning 4 51
(Mark Johnston) *chsd ldrs: rdn over 2f out: wknd wl over 1f out* **13/8**[1]
0020 **6** *13* **Hot Rod Mamma (IRE)**[12] 3163 5-9-11 **87**.................... LeeTopliss(3) 3 30
(Dianne Sayer) *t.k.h: hld up: struggling 3f out: sn btn: eased whn no ch fnl f* **6/1**[3]

1m 51.49s (3.09) **Going Correction** +0.575s/f (Yiel)
WFA 3 from 4yo+ 10lb **6** Ran SP% **111.7**
Speed ratings (Par 104): **107,99,95,91,90 77**
toteswingers: 1&2 £5.60, 1&3 £3.60, 2&3 £11.20 CSF £30.16 TOTE £3.00: £1.70, £3.90; EX 27.10.
Owner Direct Racing Club **Bred** Michael McGlynn **Trained** Nawton, N Yorks

FOCUS
A decent fillies handicap run at a sound pace, with the majority of the field racing up the centre of the track, with the winner pulling a long way clear. Not form to take literally, although the winner could rate higher at face value.

NOTEBOOK
Madam Macie(IRE) returned to form when third at Thirsk last time, having disappointed at York on her penultimate start, and she won in fine style. Unable to get to the front from the start, her jockey bided his time before taking up the running 6f out. The top-weight had stamina to prove over this trip on the testing ground but she put those doubts emphatically to bed, to win in the style of an improving sort. She will be due a hefty rise after this but, looks a decent type if able to dominate. (op 7-2)
She's A Character, who was 10lb better off for finishing 13l behind the winner at Carlisle earlier in the month (1m, good to firm), won the battle for second but was ultimately well beaten. This was a better effort after three poor runs, and she will be interesting if returning to Doncaster, where all three career wins have come. (op 12-1)
What's Up(IRE) has been highly tried by connections and was last seen in the Sandringham Handicap. She was driven a long way home, before staying on well enough for pressure although things do not look easy off her current mark. (op 10-1 tchd 11-1)
Polar Annie was the only runner to remain up the far side and did not truly see out the 1m trip but, showed a bit more here than of late, and is dropping to a feasible looking mark. (op 5-1 tchd 13-2)
Parley(USA), 9lb better off for finishing 10l behind the winner at Carlisle, had been in decent form but could not pick up in the conditions, and looks to require better ground. (op 15-8 tchd 6-4)

3523 KILBRYDE HOSPICE (S) STKS 5f 4y
8:50 (8:51) (Class 5) 3-Y-0+ **£2,385** (£704; £352) **Stalls** High

Form RPR
0-15 **1** **Fol Hollow (IRE)**[9] 3255 7-9-9 78................................... AdrianNicholls 1 66
(David Nicholls) *cl up: led over 2f out: drvn out ins fnl f* **11/8**[1]
0020 **2** *¾* **Distant Sun (USA)**[13] 3109 8-9-4 55..................................(p) PhillipMakin 2 58
(Linda Perratt) *cl up on outside: effrt and ev ch over 1f out: kpt on ins fnl f* **22/1**
4540 **3** *nse* **Sharp Shoes**[24] 2749 5-9-4 57..(p) GrahamLee 3 58
(Ann Duffield) *trckd ldrs: effrt and rdn over 1f out: kpt on fnl f* **7/1**
6054 **4** *3* **Angelo Poliziano**[8] 3276 6-9-4 70.............................(b) PaulMulrennan 6 47
(George Foster) *led to over 2f out: rallied: outpcd appr fnl f* **6/1**[3]
200 **5** *3* **Northern Bolt**[17] 2981 7-9-4 67...................................... PatrickMathers 5 36
(Ian McInnes) *s.i.s: bhd and drvn along thrght: nvr rchd ldrs* **2/1**[2]
5600 **6** *½* **Andrasta**[15] 3026 7-8-6 44.. MatthewHopkins(7) 4 29
(Alan Berry) *hld up in tch: drvn and outpcd over 2f out: sn btn* **40/1**

1m 1.43s (1.43) **Going Correction** +0.30s/f (Good) **6** Ran SP% **109.0**
Speed ratings (Par 103): **100,98,98,93,89 88**
toteswingers: 1&2 £5.70, 1&3 £1.10, 2&3 £9.80 CSF £28.74 TOTE £2.60: £1.60, £4.80; EX 18.10.There was no bid for the winner.

Owner Middleham Park Racing Iii **Bred** Dan O'Brien **Trained** Sessay, N Yorks

FOCUS

An uncompetitive looking seller, run at a decent pace, with the front three well grouped passing the post. The form is rated negatively through the runner-up.

3524 PATERSONS OF GREENOAKHILL H'CAP 6f 5y

9:20 (9:21) (Class 4) (0-85,83) 3-Y-O+ **£5,175** (£1,540; £769; £384) **Stalls** High

Form				RPR
5051	1		**Klynch**[12] 3169 6-10-0 **82**....(b) JamesSullivan 4	98
			(Ruth Carr) *hld up bhd ldrs: hdwy to ld over 1f out: rdn clr fnl f* **5/2**[2]	
6053	2	4 ½	**Rio Cobolo (IRE)**[8] 3272 6-9-1 **69**....(v) AdrianNicholls 3	72
			(David Nicholls) *cl up: led over 2f out to over 1f out: kpt on fnl f: no ch w wnr* **16/1**	
0541	3	2	**Able Master (IRE)**[6] 3334 6-10-1 **83** 6ex.... DanielTudhope 2	80
			(David O'Meara) *in tch: rdn over 2f out: hdwy over 1f out: no imp ins fnl f* **9/4**[1]	
0665	4	2	**Jeannie Galloway (IRE)**[24] 2752 5-9-13 **81**.... PaulMulrennan 7	72
			(Keith Dalgleish) *led to over 2f out: rdn and no ex over 1f out* **9/2**[3]	
3022	5	½	**Crimson Knot (IRE)**[6] 3336 4-9-0 **75**.... MatthewHopkins(7) 1	64
			(Alan Berry) *in tch on outside: rdn over 2f out: btn fnl f* **6/1**	
-003	6	14	**Ballinargh Girl (IRE)**[21] 2841 4-9-2 **70**.... JoeFanning 8	17
			(Danielle McCormick) *in tch: struggling over 2f out: sn lost tch* **9/1**	
0000	7	2 ¼	**Oil Strike**[15] 3027 5-9-2 **77**.... DavidSimmonson(7) 5	17
			(Michael Easterby) *cl up tl rdn and wknd qckly appr fnl f* **25/1**	

1m 13.13s (0.93) **Going Correction** +0.30s/f (Good) **7** Ran SP% **111.5**

Speed ratings (Par 105): **105,99,96,93,93 74,71**

toteswingers: 1&2 £6.80, 1&3 £1.80, 2&3 £6.30 CSF £37.56 CT £98.16 TOTE £3.20: £1.70, £4.30; EX 30.70 Trifecta £159.10 Pool: £546.17 - 2.54 winning units..

Owner Douglas Renton **Bred** J C S Wilson Bloodstock **Trained** Huby, N Yorks

FOCUS

A competitive handicap run at a sound pace with yet another wide margin winner. The winner is rated to the best of last year's form.

Ballinargh Girl(IRE) Official explanation: jockey said filly hung left

3525 DONNA MORTIMER BALLANTYNE CHARITABLE TRUST H'CAP 1m 65y

9:50 (9:50) (Class 5) (0-75,74) 3-Y-O+ **£3,408** (£1,006; £503) **Stalls** Low

Form				RPR
4412	1		**Peter Anders**[20] 2883 3-9-3 **73**.... JoeFanning 6	80+
			(Mark Johnston) *w ldr: led over 1f out: qcknd clr ins fnl f: readily* **11/8**[1]	
0406	2	2 ½	**Botham (USA)**[10] 3213 8-9-9 **69**.... GrahamLee 7	72
			(Jim Goldie) *in tch: rdn over 2f out: chsd (clr) wnr ins fnl f: kpt on: no imp* **4/1**[2]	
-000	3	1 ¼	**Kalk Bay (IRE)**[24] 2753 5-9-7 **74**.... DavidSimmonson(7) 3	74
			(Michael Easterby) *led at stdy pce: rdn and hdd over 1f out: kpt on same pce fnl f* **9/2**[3]	
-500	4	½	**High Resolution**[10] 3213 5-9-6 **66**.... JamesSullivan 8	65
			(Linda Perratt) *hld up in tch: effrt and rdn 2f out: no imp fnl f* **17/2**	
0052	5	6	**Khandaq (USA)**[8] 3277 5-9-0 **60**.... PaulMulrennan 5	45
			(Keith Dalgleish) *trckd ldrs: effrt and rdn over 1f out: wknd ent fnl f* **9/2**[3]	

1m 55.98s (7.58) **Going Correction** +0.575s/f (Yiel)

WFA 3 from 4yo+ 10lb **5** Ran SP% **109.0**

Speed ratings (Par 103): **85,82,81,80,74**

toteswingers: 1&2 £5.00 CSF £6.94 TOTE £2.20: £1.30, £2.10; EX 6.80 Trifecta £20.80 Pool: £444.42 - 15.80 winning units..

Owner Newsells Park Stud **Bred** Newsells Park Stud **Trained** Middleham Moor, N Yorks

FOCUS

This handicap was run at a steady pace with the field racing up the centre of the course. The runner-up sets the standard rated close to his best.

T/Plt: £284.20 to a £1 stake. Pool: £74,429.80. 191.15 winning tickets. T/Qpdt: £25.10 to a £1 stake. Pool: £7,225.62. 212.65 winning tickets. RY

2783 LEICESTER (R-H)

Thursday, June 28

3526 Meeting Abandoned - waterlogged

2922 NEWCASTLE (L-H)

Thursday, June 28

OFFICIAL GOING: Heavy (5.0)

Racing abandoned after Race 4 (3:30); torrential rain.

Wind: light behind Weather: cloudy, outbreaks of rain

3532 BETFRED "THE BONUS KING" NOVICE STKS 6f

2:00 (2:03) (Class 5) 2-Y-O **£2,264** (£673; £336) **Stalls** Centre

Form				RPR
41	1		**Jubilee Games**[56] 1795 2-8-13 0.... LeeTopliss(3) 4	77
			(Richard Fahey) *trckd ldr: rdn and outpcd over 2f out: kpt on as ldr faltered: led fnl 100yds* **4/1**[2]	
120	2	4	**New Pearl (IRE)**[9] 3240 2-9-5 0.... RobertWinston 2	68
			(David Brown) *led: pushed arnd 3 l clr 2f out: rdn appr fnl f: sn wknd: hung lft ins fnl f: hdd fnl 100yds* **1/2**[1]	
	3	22	**Titus Titan (IRE)** 2-9-0 0.... BarryMcHugh 3	
			(Brian Ellison) *s.i.s: sn trckd ldr: pushed along over 2f out: wknd* **10/1**[3]	

1m 25.36s (10.76) **Going Correction** +1.10s/f (Soft) **3** Ran SP% **95.8**

Speed ratings (Par 93): **72,66,37**

CSF £5.35 TOTE £3.60; EX 4.40.

Owner Lets Go Racing 1 **Bred** P And Mrs A G Venner **Trained** Musley Bank, N Yorks

■ Somethingboutmary was withdrawn (17/2, ref to ent stalls). Deduct 10p in the under R4).

FOCUS

Entire running rail on Round course from Winning Post to junction of Straight moved to provide 3yds of fresh ground not raced on this season. After some heavy showers on ground already described as heavy the meeting had to survive a noon inspection. A depleted field for this 2yo novice event. The leader went very steady in the ground to halfway. Not form to pay too much attention to given the deep condtions.

NOTEBOOK

Jubilee Games, off the mark at the second attempt in soft ground over 5f at Musselburgh, looked second best for much of the race. With the favourite emptying badly, he won going away and this decent type is likely to improve again. (op 3-1 tchd 11-4)

New Pearl(IRE), who made a good impression when winning first time at Newmarket, has since been turned over at 1/6 at Pontefract and finished down the field in the Coventry. He set his own pace and looked to have put it to bed when sent about four lengths clear 2f out. His stride shortened markedly entering the final furlong and, hanging badly left, he stopped to almost nothing. He presumably has a problem. (op 8-13 tchd 4-6 and 4-9)

Titus Titan(IRE), fitted with a cross noseband, was left a long way behind. It was a tough introduction. (op 8-1)

3533 BETFRED MOBILE SPORTS MEDIAN AUCTION MAIDEN STKS 6f

2:30 (2:33) (Class 5) 2-Y-O **£2,264** (£673; £336; £168) **Stalls** Centre

Form				RPR
	1		**Unsinkable (IRE)** 2-9-3 0.... TonyHamilton 4	80+
			(Richard Fahey) *led trio up centre: overall ldr 2f out: pushed clr fnl f: comf* **5/4**[1]	
	2	4	**Vegas Belle** 2-8-12 0.... TomEaves 3	60+
			(Ollie Pears) *dwlt: hld up in tch in centre: hdwy over 2f out: rdn to chal over 1f out: kpt on but sn no ch w wnr fnl f* **7/1**	
	3	8	**Angels Calling** 2-8-12 0.... RobertWinston 2	36+
			(Mrs K Burke) *sn swtchd to trck ldr stands' side: rdn 2f out: sn no imp: wnt poor 3rd ins fnl f* **9/2**[3]	
6	4	2	**Notional Demand**[12] 3168 2-9-3 0.... DanielTudhope 1	35
			(Tim Easterby) *racd centre: trckd ldr: rdn over 2f out: wknd over 1f out* **9/1**	
053	5	18	**Tiger's Home**[12] 3150 2-8-12 0.... GrahamLee 5	
			(Julia Feilden) *racd stands' side: led: hdd 2f out: sn wknd and eased* **11/4**[2]	

1m 22.19s (7.59) **Going Correction** +1.10s/f (Soft) **5** Ran SP% **111.8**

Speed ratings (Par 93): **93,87,77,74,50**

CSF £10.65 TOTE £1.90: £1.40, £2.10; EX 11.20.

Owner Penman Bond Partnership **Bred** Stephanie Hanly **Trained** Musley Bank, N Yorks

FOCUS

Previous form was thin on the ground in this median auction maiden juvenile event. Three raced up the centre, in the end the other two opted to go stands' side. It's very hard to be sure about this given the bad ground.

NOTEBOOK

Unsinkable(IRE), who changed hands for 75,000euros as a yearling, is a robust newcomer. He gave a problem or two at the stalls, but jumped out smartly and was always dominating the other pair up the centre. A powerful mover, he took this in fine style and is clearly useful. (op 7-4)

Vegas Belle, from a small but shrewd stable going through a lean spell, was the only one to make a race of it with the favourite. The first foal of a 1m4f winner, she will improve and will surely find a race. (op 11-2)

Angels Calling, who got loose in the paddock on her debut, was switched to race stands' side after a furlong. She kept on to claim a modest third spot but what she achived is open to doubt. (tchd 11-2)

Notional Demand, well beaten first time, tired noticeably late on and will need more time yet. (op 10-1 tchd 8-1)

Tiger's Home, having her fourth start and already rated 61, was blanketed for stalls entry. Taken to race against the stands' side rail, she was in trouble a long way from home and eventually completed in her own time. Conditions were probably just too demanding. (op 5-2 tchd 9-4)

3534 BETFRED SEATON DELAVAL H'CAP 1m 3y(S)

3:00 (3:02) (Class 2) (0-105,96) 4-Y-O+

£9,835 (£2,945; £1,472; £736; £368; £184) **Stalls** Centre

Form				RPR
6-21	1		**Swiftly Done (IRE)**[20] 2882 5-9-1 **90**.... DanielTudhope 4	100+
			(Declan Carroll) *hld up in rr: pushed along and hdwy over 2f out: kpt on wl: led post* **6/1**[3]	
112	2	nse	**Prince Of Sorrento**[12] 3157 5-9-0 **89**.... StevieDonohoe 8	99
			(Lee Carter) *trckd ldrs: led over 2f out: rdn 2f out: sn strly pressed: kpt on: hdd post* **3/1**[1]	
1230	3	1 ¾	**Memory Cloth**[19] 2911 5-9-7 **96**.... BarryMcHugh 6	102
			(Brian Ellison) *midfield: hdwy 3f out: rdn to chal 2f out: kpt on tl no ex fnl 100yds* **7/2**[2]	
6636	4	5	**Extraterrestrial**[12] 3164 8-8-12 **90**.... LeeTopliss(3) 2	85
			(Richard Fahey) *hld up in midfield: hdwy over 2f out: sn rdn: plugged on* **16/1**	
5344	5	8	**Dubai Dynamo**[12] 3164 7-9-3 **92**.... PJMcDonald 5	68
			(Ruth Carr) *trckd ldrs: rdn over 2f out: wknd over 1f out* **9/1**	
0160	6	4	**Viva Ronaldo (IRE)**[19] 2910 6-8-13 **88**.... TonyHamilton 11	55
			(Richard Fahey) *hld up: rdn over 3f out: sn btn* **20/1**	
2054	7	7	**Colour Guard**[7] 3306 4-9-1 **90**.... FrannyNorton 7	41
			(Mark Johnston) *prom: wknd over 2f out* **9/1**	
446	8	3	**Suits Me**[22] 2810 9-9-2 **91**.... TomEaves 1	35
			(David Barron) *led: rdn whn hdd over 2f out: wknd* **10/1**	
/5-0	9	7	**Fighter Boy (IRE)**[12] 3164 5-9-6 **95**.... PaddyAspell 10	23
			(Michael Easterby) *hld up in midfield: rdn over 2f out: sn wknd* **50/1**	
1510	10	3 ½	**Al Muheer (IRE)**[33] 2489 7-9-1 **90**....(b) JamesSullivan 9	10
			(Ruth Carr) *hld up: a bhd* **16/1**	
20-0	11	62	**Prince Of Dance**[125] 694 6-8-8 **83**.... RobertWinston 3	
			(Tom Tate) *trckd ldr: wknd qckly 3f out: eased* **16/1**	

1m 50.27s (6.87) **Going Correction** +1.10s/f (Soft) **11** Ran SP% **115.0**

Speed ratings (Par 109): **109,108,107,102,94 90,83,80,73,69 7**

toteswingers 1&2 £3.40, 1&3 £5.40, 2&3 £3.10 CSF £23.67 CT £72.62 TOTE £6.70: £1.70, £1.70, £1.70; EX 27.10 Trifecta £96.00 Pool: £615.18 - 4.74 winning units..

Owner D Watts, Miss C King, J Syme & M Syme **Bred** Joe Fogarty **Trained** Sledmere, E Yorks

FOCUS

What looked beforehand a highly competitive handicap. The pacesetter kicked for home at the halfway mark and as a result they came home well strung out with only the first three seriously involved in the finish. The winner was not ideally sorted by the ground and may be capable of a bit better.

NOTEBOOK

Swiftly Done(IRE), who has a progressive profile, was asked to race from a mark 5lb higher than his hard gained Doncaster success. Forced to sit off the pace, after being hampered leaving the stalls he still looked to have plenty of work to do when taking third spot over a furlong out. He ran on with real determination to get up on the line. The Cambridgeshire is his back-end target. (tchd 11-2)

Prince Of Sorrento, winner of four of his last six starts, was hoisted 5lb after finishing runner-up to subsequent Royal Ascot winner Fennell Bay at Sandown. He went on with over 2f left to run and, edging slightly left in the closing stages, was nailed on the line. He doesn't fully appreciate conditions as testing as this and probably hit the front plenty soon enough. Trouble is that he will go up in the ratings again. (op 10-3)

Memory Cloth, a winner from a stone lower mark in the mud at Ripon in April, didn't see out 1m2f on his latest start. He took on the runner-up but came up short, though clear of the remainder. (tchd 10-3)

Extraterrestrial runs the odd decent race these days but his losing run stretches back 14 runs now.

3535 BETFRED "BONUS KING BINGO" H'CAP 2m 19y
3:30 (3:30) (Class 4) (0-80,79) 4-Y-0+ **£4,075** (£1,212; £606; £303) **Stalls** Low

Form RPR
4120 **1** **Pokfulham (IRE)**[13] 3129 6-9-2 **74**..............................(v) DanielTudhope 1 83
(Jim Goldie) *led: rdn over 2f out: strly pressed appr fnl f: hdd fnl 100yds: rallied to ld again nr fin* **6/1**
4/6- **2** *nse* **Rock Relief (IRE)**[32] 7536 6-8-2 **60** oh9........................ FrannyNorton 6 68
(Chris Grant) *trckd ldr: rdn 5f out: chal appr fnl f: led narrowly fnl 100yds: kpt on: hdd nr fin* **9/2**[2]
-056 **3** *9* **Bollin Felix**[13] 3129 8-8-12 **77**............................(p) RachelRichardson(7) 5 74
(Tim Easterby) *hld up: hdwy to trck ldr over 5f out: rdn over 3f out: wknd over 1f out* **5/1**[3]
0-00 **4** *35* **Hollins**[42] 2214 8-9-4 **76**.. PJMcDonald 4 31
(Micky Hammond) *midfield: rdn 5f out: sn btn* **14/1**
55-6 **5** *3* **John Forbes**[64] 1598 10-8-8 **66**....................................... BarryMcHugh 8 18
(Brian Ellison) *midfield: pushed along and lost pl over 5f out: sn btn* **9/2**[2]
0-51 **6** *35* **Boston Blue**[28] 2623 5-9-3 **75**.. GrahamLee 7
(Tony Carroll) *hld up in rr: a bhd* **9/2**[2]
2160 **7** *dist* **Boss's Destination**[19] 2936 5-9-7 **79**........................... RobertWinston 2
(Alan Swinbank) *trckd ldr: wknd over 4f out: eased over 2f out* **4/1**[1]

3m 56.48s (17.08) **Going Correction** +1.20s/f (Soft) **7** Ran SP% **112.2**
Speed ratings (Par 105): **105,104,100,82,81 63,**
toteswingers 1&2 £4.20, 1&3 £5.10, 2&3 £7.20 CSF £31.53 CT £143.16 TOTE £4.70: £1.70, £3.50; EX 28.40 Trifecta £139.90 Pool: £514.42 - 2.72 winning units..
Owner Ambrose Turnbull **Bred** Killian Farm **Trained** Uplawmoor, E Renfrews

FOCUS
They went a sound gallop in the very testing underfoot conditions and just the first three home got seriously involved once in line for home. A small personal best from the winner.
Boston Blue Official explanation: jockey said gelding never travelled
Boss's Destination Official explanation: jockey said gelding never travelled and stopped quickly

3536 BETFRED MOBILE CASINO H'CAP 1m 2f 32y
() (Class 6) (0-55,) 4-Y-0+ £

3537 BETFRED STILL TREBLE ODDS ON LUCKY 15'S H'CAP 1m 2f 32y
() (Class 5) (0-75,) 4-Y-0+ £

3538 BETFRED BONUS BINGO H'CAP 7f
() (Class 5) (0-75,) 3-Y-0 £

T/Plt: £39.30 to a £1 stake. Pool: £52,122.98 - 968.00 winning tickets T/Qpdt: £4.30 to a £1 stake. Pool: £5,034.94 - 885.06 winning tickets AS

3311 WARWICK (L-H)
Thursday, June 28

OFFICIAL GOING: Good to soft changing to soft after race 1 (2:10)
Wind: almost nil Weather: very muggy

3539 WEATHERBYS BANK MAIDEN STKS 7f 26y
2:10 (2:18) (Class 5) 3-Y-0+ **£2,264** (£673; £336; £168) **Stalls** Low

Form RPR
06- **1** **Malih**[262] 6743 3-9-3 0.. FergusSweeney 9 72
(Jamie Osborne) *mde all: rdn over 1f out: pressed 1f out: drvn to assert cl home* **5/1**[2]
60 **2** *2* **Tunnager Grove**[16] 3012 3-9-3 0....................................... RobertHavlin 1 66+
(Hughie Morrison) *towards rr: hdwy over 2f out: rdn to chse ldrs 1f out: chsd wnr in vain fnl 100yds* **16/1**
0 **3** *1 ¾* **Aureolin Gulf**[139] 499 3-9-3 0..................................... RussKennemore 2 61
(Reg Hollinshead) *t.k.h: in tch: rdn over 2f out: drvn and effrt over 1f out: no ex fnl 100yds* **66/1**
02 **4** *2* **Indigo Iris (IRE)**[12] 3155 3-9-3 0.................................. RichardHughes 4 59+
(Richard Hannon) *in tch: urged along 2f out: rdn and effrt over 1f: sn nt clr run: drvn and unable to cl on ldrs ins fnl f* **10/11**[1]
0- **5** *¾* **Salutary**[342] 4292 3-9-3 0.. SebSanders 12 54
(Jane Chapple-Hyam) *in tch: drvn and pressed wnr over 1f out: wknd ins fnl f* **16/1**
0-0 **6** *nk* **Dark Orchid**[19] 2935 3-8-12 0.. DaneO'Neill 6 48
(Peter Chapple-Hyam) *midfield: rdn along 2f out: no immediate hdwy: plugged on past btn horses ins fnl f: could improve* **16/1**
64 **7** *1* **Duke Of Destiny (IRE)**[17] 2974 3-9-3 0.......................... GeorgeBaker 7 50
(Ed Walker) *in tch: on outer: hdwy over 2f out: rdn and no imp 1f out: lost shoe* **9/1**
00 **8** *15* **Blackthorn Stick (IRE)**[12] 3155 3-9-3 0.......................... ChrisCatlin 11 10
(John Butler) *cl up: pushed along and briefly short of room over 2f out: wknd dramatically 2f out* **150/1**
9 *1 ¼* **I Stand Corrected** 3-8-12 0.. JamesDoyle 13
(Ed Walker) *in rr: niggled early: no ch fnl 2f* **8/1**[3]
06 **10** *12* **Linton Hill (IRE)**[29] 2612 3-9-3 0.................................. TomMcLaughlin 8
(Murty McGrath) *in rr: outpcd and struggling 3f out: t.o* **150/1**
11 *4* **Ellen Dean** 4-9-7 0... TomQueally 10
(Eve Johnson Houghton) *slow away and a in last: clueless and sn unable to keep up: t.o* **40/1**

1m 29.55s (4.95) **Going Correction** +0.50s/f (Yiel)
WFA 3 from 4yo 9lb **11** Ran SP% **113.1**
Speed ratings (Par 103): **91,88,86,84,83 83,82,64,63,49 45**
toteswingers 1&2 £8.40, 1&3 £50.70, 2&3 £50.70 CSF £72.67 TOTE £5.10: £1.20, £4.40, £20.10; EX 93.90.
Owner Wedgewood Estates **Bred** Wedgewood Estates **Trained** Upper Lambourn, Berks
■ Bypass was withdrawn (12/1, unruly in stalls). Deduct 5p in the £ under R4).

FOCUS
Back straight rail moved out 2m, Home bend moved in 1.5m and distances on Round course increased by 20yds. Few got into what was quite a modest 3yo plus maiden. The field came stands' side in the straight, a pattern that continued throughout the afternoon. Prominent runners were favoured. The winner probably did not need to improve much on his 2yo form.
Indigo Iris(IRE) Official explanation: trainer's rep said colt was unsuited by the soft ground
Duke Of Destiny(IRE) Official explanation: vet said gelding lost a front shoe
Ellen Dean Official explanation: jockey said filly never travelled

3540 ROUTEONE H'CAP 5f
2:40 (2:41) (Class 5) (0-70,64) 3-Y-0 **£2,385** (£704; £352) **Stalls** Low

Form RPR
0264 **1** **Ghazeer (IRE)**[6] 3350 3-8-12 **55**..............................(v) SilvestreDeSousa 8 62
(Derek Shaw) *chsd ldr: rdn to ld over 1f out: hung lft 1f out: organised and drvn to assert fnl 100yds* **11/4**[2]
3304 **2** *1 ½* **Middleton Flyer (IRE)**[28] 2615 3-8-12 **62**........................ NedCurtis(7) 6 63
(Paul Midgley) *led: rdn and hdd over 1f out: ev ch tl drvn and no ex ins fnl f* **10/3**[3]
3421 **3** *shd* **Celestial Dawn**[12] 3141 3-9-5 **62**.. ChrisCatlin 7 63+
(John Weymes) *hld up: pushed along 2f out: rdn and hdwy against stands' rail over 1f out: kpt on to press for 2nd cl home* **15/8**[1]
5043 **4** *3* **Miserere Mei (IRE)**[3] 3451 3-8-5 **48**..................................(e) JohnFahy 1 38
(Richard Guest) *in tch: pushed along over 1f out: effrt 1f out: no ex ins fnl f* **13/2**
2330 **5** *2 ¼* **Chicarito**[43] 2166 3-9-1 **58**...(p) TomQueally 3 40
(John Gallagher) *t.k.h: anchored in rr: rdn and no ex 2f out* **8/1**

1m 2.7s (3.10) **Going Correction** +0.45s/f (Yiel) **5** Ran SP% **109.0**
Speed ratings (Par 99): **93,90,90,85,82**
CSF £11.82 TOTE £4.50: £2.10, £2.50; EX 14.10.
Owner Philip Derbyshire & Martyn Elvin **Bred** Holborn Trust Co **Trained** Sproxton, Leics

FOCUS
Moderate sprinting form and it again paid to race prominently. A personal best for the winner.

3541 ALI CAMPBELL LIVE HERE 21ST AUGUST H'CAP (BETFAIR SPRINT FLAT SERIES QUALIFIER) 6f
3:10 (3:10) (Class 4) (0-80,80) 3-Y-0+ **£5,175** (£1,540; £769; £384) **Stalls** Low

Form RPR
-300 **1** **Perfect Pastime**[52] 1936 4-9-11 **77**..................................(p) TomQueally 5 86
(Jim Boyle) *cl up: rdn to ld over 1f out: drvn and strly pressed fr 1f out: hld on wl u.p* **12/1**
3264 **2** *hd* **Midnight Rider (IRE)**[19] 2940 4-9-12 **78**......................... GeorgeBaker 13 86
(Chris Wall) *hld up: smoothly weaved way through field to chse ldrs on bit 1f out: sn pushed along and chalng for ld: drifted lft and unable to get by cl home* **4/1**[1]
-413 **3** *3 ½* **Lady Bayside**[19] 2940 4-9-5 **71**..................................... TomMcLaughlin 7 68
(Malcolm Saunders) *in tch: niggled along and effrt 2f out: drvn and ev ch fnl f: no ch w ldng pair fnl 75yds* **4/1**[1]
4040 **4** *1 ¾* **Lost In Paris (IRE)**[26] 2717 6-9-12 **78**..............................(p) DavidAllan 9 69
(Tim Easterby) *wl away and sn led: rdn 2f out: hdd & wknd 1f out* **16/1**
0060 **5** *½* **Night Trade (IRE)**[12] 3139 5-9-3 **74**............................(p) DarrenEgan(5) 2 64
(Ronald Harris) *hld up: drvn and effrt in centre of crse 1f out: sn no ex and btn* **7/1**
-411 **6** *½* **Cardinal**[12] 3159 7-9-8 **74**.. JamesDoyle 15 62+
(Robert Cowell) *in tch: rdn and hdwy 2f out: effrt and nt clr run 1f out: sn one pce* **9/2**[2]
0016 **7** *2 ¾* **Jungle Bay**[19] 2913 5-9-8 **74**..(p) RichardHughes 12 53
(Jane Chapple-Hyam) *cl up: effrt 2f out: drvn and wknd 1f out: nt clr run whn btn ins fnl f* **13/2**[3]
-020 **8** *1 ¼* **Forest Edge (IRE)**[31] 2557 3-8-11 **70**............................. RobertHavlin 10 45
(David Evans) *in rr: rdn over 2f out: sn no imp and btn* **40/1**
0-30 **9** *¾* **Great Charm (IRE)**[10] 3226 7-9-8 **74**........................ SilvestreDeSousa 4 47
(Daniel Kubler) *in rr: rdn along over 1f out: effrt 1f out: no ex fnl 100yds* **18/1**
0306 **10** *nse* **Ghostwing**[7] 3314 5-8-12 **67**..(v) SophieDoyle(3) 3 40
(Ronald Harris) *in tch: brief effrt and carried hd high over 1f out: wknd and sn btn fnl f* **16/1**
-036 **11** *1* **Alpha Delta Whisky**[21] 2853 4-9-1 **67**........................ FergusSweeney 11 36
(John Gallagher) *in tch: drvn and effrt over 1f out: no ex and wknd qckly ins fnl f* **20/1**

1m 13.73s (1.93) **Going Correction** +0.45s/f (Yiel)
WFA 3 from 4yo+ 7lb **11** Ran SP% **115.9**
Speed ratings (Par 105): **105,104,100,97,97 96,92,91,90,90 88**
wingers 1&2 £13.80, 2&3 £3.20, 1&3 £16.60 CSF £58.70 CT £234.65 TOTE £19.10: £6.40, £1.80, £1.30; EX 59.50.
Owner Country Friends **Bred** R G & T E Levin **Trained** Epsom, Surrey

FOCUS
Two drew clear in what had looked quite a competitive sprint, run in the best time on the card. A small personal best from the winner.
Great Charm(IRE) Official explanation: jockey said gelding had no more to give

3542 WEATHERBYS BLOODSTOCK INSURANCE ETERNAL STKS (LISTED RACE) 7f 26y
3:40 (3:43) (Class 1) 3-Y-0
£18,714 (£7,095; £3,550; £1,768; £887; £445) **Stalls** Low

Form RPR
3-20 **1** **Radio Gaga**[53] 1884 3-8-12 98...................................... RichardMullen 13 100
(Ed McMahon) *cl up: pushed along to ld 2f out: drvn clr ins fnl f: hld on wl* **11/2**[2]
0-40 **2** *½* **Switcher (IRE)**[8] 3270 3-8-12 98..........................(v[1]) RichardKingscote 6 99
(Tom Dascombe) *in tch: urged along on inner over 2f out: nt clr run over 1f out: kpt on nicely to chse wnr ins fnl f* **16/1**
0405 **3** *3 ½* **Roger Sez (IRE)**[12] 3165 3-9-6 97...............................(p) DavidAllan 5 97
(Tim Easterby) *in rr and drvn along early: struggling and u.str.p 3f out: kpt on past btn horses fnl f* **33/1**
-101 **4** *½* **Appealing (IRE)**[14] 3085 3-8-12 88..................................... AdamKirby 2 88
(Marco Botti) *cl up: drvn along 2f out: wknd and nt pce of ldrs fnl f* **9/1**
-131 **5** *hd* **Charlotte Rosina**[20] 2893 3-8-12 86................................ SebSanders 8 87
(Roger Teal) *led: drvn and hdd 2f out: ev ch tl wknd ins fnl f* **20/1**
21-0 **6** *¾* **Diala (IRE)**[53] 1884 3-8-12 90.. EddieAhern 3 90+
(William Haggas) *t.k.h: in tch: short of room and bdly hmpd whn asked for effrt 2f out: sn lost pl: pushed along and plugged on past btn horses ins fnl f: nvr able to trble ldrs: had more to give* **15/8**[1]
3-41 **7** *½* **Poisson D'Or**[19] 2935 3-8-12 79..................................... JamesDoyle 11 84
(Rae Guest) *in rr: pushed along over 2f out: sn one pce* **14/1**
1-53 **8** *1 ½* **Free Verse**[20] 2890 3-8-12 85.................................... RichardHughes 10 80
(Richard Hannon) *cl up: urged along over 2f out: drvn and no imp fnl f* **8/1**
0-00 **9** *1 ½* **Queens Revenge**[12] 3165 3-8-12 88............................... PaulHanagan 9 76
(Tim Easterby) *a in rr: drvn and no imp fnl 2f* **50/1**
-100 **10** *1 ¼* **Intense Pink**[6] 3328 3-8-12 90.. DaneO'Neill 12 72
(Chris Wall) *cl up: urged along over 2f out: drvn and btn over 1f out* **10/1**

2310 **11** ¾ **Emman Bee (IRE)**[33] 2503 3-8-12 77 .... FergusSweeney 7 70
(John Gallagher) *in tch: urged along over 3f out: struggling and btn fnl 2f* **66/1**

5-60 **12** *18* **Sunday Times**[53] 1884 3-8-12 103 .... RobertHavlin 14 22
(Peter Chapple-Hyam) *hld up: brief effrt over 2f out: sn rdn w little responce: eased and btn: t.o* **13/2**[3]

4040 **13** *5* **Kickingthelilly**[8] 3270 3-8-12 81 .... ChrisCatlin 1 8
(Rae Guest) *in rr and outpcd: t.o fnl 3f* **50/1**

1m 26.58s (1.98) **Going Correction** +0.50s/f (Yiel) **13** Ran SP% **119.4**
Speed ratings (Par 107): **108,107,103,102,102 101,101,99,97,96 95,74,69**
toteswingers 1&2 £38.40, 1&3 £9.70, 2&3 £20.10 CSF £85.42 TOTE £6.80: £1.50, £5.30, £8.90; EX 107.80.
Owner Multiplex Racing **Bred** Mickley Stud **Trained** Lichfield, Staffs

FOCUS
The pace was steady. An open Listed contest, although not particularly strong form for the grade. It has been rated around the winner's Fred Darling second and the runner-up's French Group 3 form.

NOTEBOOK
Radio Gaga, runner-up in the Fred Darling prior to finishing well beaten in the Guineas, was nicely placed throughout and never in any danger once taken to the front. This has proven her best distance so far. (op 6-1 tchd 13-2)
Switcher(IRE), beaten 14l in last week's Sandringham at Royal Ascot, finished a lot closer to the winner than she had done in the Fred Darling, clearly being helped by a first-time visor. (tchd 18-1)
Roger Sez(IRE), saddled with an 8lb penalty for a Group 3 win last season, emerges as the best horse at the weights, but will remain difficult to place. (op 40-1)
Appealing(IRE) won a Yarmouth handicap off 82 the time before, so this represents a marked step forward. (op 8-1)
Charlotte Rosina was another with a bit to do at the weights, but her last win had received a boost the previous evening and she ran well from the front until her stamina gave way. (tchd 22-1)
Diala(IRE) disappointed when tipped as a lively outsider for the Guineas and was solid at the head of the market on this drop in grade, but she'd raced keenly and lost all chance when squeezed out with 2f to run. She tried to stay on afterwards and is probably worth one more chance. Official explanation: trainer's rep said filly was unsuited by the soft ground (op 11-4)
Poisson D'Or, a 79-rated Newmarket maiden winner, ran about as well as could have been expected on this marked rise in grade. (op 11-1)
Sunday Times made her move wide at the wrong time and took a further step in the wrong direction. Official explanation: trainer's rep said filly was unsuited by the soft ground (op 5-1 tchd 15-2)

3543 SUPPORT YOUR LOCAL LONDIS CONVENIENCE STORE H'CAP 1m 2f 188y
4:10 (4:13) (Class 5) (0-70,70) 3-Y-O £2,264 (£673; £336; £168) **Stalls** Low

Form RPR
-661 **1** **April Ciel**[12] 3142 3-8-10 **64** .... DarrenEgan(5) 12 71
(Ronald Harris) *mde all: drvn 2f out: strly pressed ins fnl f: hld on wl and in command fnl strides* **5/1**[3]

0-50 **2** ¾ **Underwritten**[20] 2898 3-9-6 **69** .... (v[1]) JimmyFortune 4 75
(Andrew Balding) *cl up: rdn and hdd and carried hd high 2f out: drvn and chsd wnr ins fnl f: nt quite rch wnr* **16/1**

00-0 **3** *1 ¼* **Dangerous To Know**[25] 2734 3-8-2 **51** oh1 .... AndreaAtzeni 5 55
(Hughie Morrison) *in tch: urged along over 2f out: drvn and ev ch over 1f out: no ex fnl f* **16/1**

6000 **4** *3 ¼* **Hyson**[50] 1976 3-9-5 **68** .... (p) RussKennemore 3 66+
(Reg Hollinshead) *hld up on inner: nt clr run 3f out: lost pl and dropped to rr 2f out: wildly drvn and kpt on ins fnl 2f: hung lft fnl f* **14/1**

-000 **5** *1 ¾* **Mcvicar**[40] 2269 3-9-3 **66** .... MatthewDavies 1 61+
(Mick Channon) *unruly and reluctant to load into stalls: in rr: drvn over 2f out: nt clr run over 1f out: plugged on one pce: no threat* **7/2**[1]

3012 **6** *1 ¾* **Temuco (IRE)**[11] 3193 3-8-10 **62** .... MatthewCosham(3) 11 54+
(David Evans) *slow away: stl in rr and drvn 3f out: kpt on one pce ins fnl 2f but nvr a threat* **8/1**

-561 **7** *nk* **Curly Come Home**[14] 3088 3-9-5 **68** .... SebSanders 2 59
(Chris Wall) *midfield: rdn 3f out: hdwy 2f out: effrt over 1f out: wknd ins fnl f* **4/1**[2]

0060 **8** *14* **Opus (IRE)**[13] 3122 3-8-10 **59** .... (t) EddieAhern 10 25
(Amanda Perrett) *hld up: urged along 3f out: ev ch 2f out whn taken stands' side rail: eased over 1f out and sn btn* **33/1**

-202 **9** *1 ¼* **Queen's Estate (GER)**[11] 3186 3-9-7 **70** .... SilvestreDeSousa 13 34
(Mark Johnston) *cl up: wknd u.p 3f out: btn fnl 2f* **6/1**

6600 **10** *10* **Bridal Medic**[14] 3066 3-8-2 **51** oh1 .... KieranO'Neill 15
(John Mackie) *cl up: rdn over 2f out: sn toiling and t.o* **33/1**

-000 **11** *9* **Can Do Les (IRE)**[23] 407 3-8-3 **52** oh3 ow1 .... RichardThomas 6
(Richard Phillips) *a in rr: btn fnl 3f* **66/1**

30-0 **12** *6* **Frosty Secret**[25] 2734 3-9-2 **65** .... RichardHughes 7
(Jane Chapple-Hyam) *hld up: lost pl 4f out: btn fnl 2f* **20/1**

0-00 **13** *47* **Marhoona (USA)**[24] 2756 3-9-0 **63** .... (t) PaulHanagan 9
(John Dunlop) *midfield: lost pl and dropped last 4f out: sn hopelessly t.o* **25/1**

2m 26.74s (5.64) **Going Correction** +0.50s/f (Yiel) **13** Ran SP% **118.7**
Speed ratings (Par 99): **99,98,97,95,93 92,92,82,81,74 67,63,28**
toteswingers 1&2 £16.80, 1&3 £21.90, 2&3 £47.70 CSF £76.13 CT £1200.83 TOTE £7.30: £2.40, £4.60, £3.60; EX 104.60.
Owner Paul & Ann de Weck **Bred** Paul And Ann De Weck **Trained** Earlswood, Monmouths
■ Stewards' Enquiry : Jimmy Fortune two-day ban: used whip above permitted level (Jul 12,16)

FOCUS
Few got into this from off the pace, continuing the trend set earlier in the afternoon. Another step forward from the winner.

3544 DTZ & MUCKLOW ANNIVERSARY APPRENTICE H'CAP 1m 22y
4:40 (4:41) (Class 5) (0-70,70) 4-Y-O+ £2,264 (£673; £336; £168) **Stalls** Low

Form RPR
24-2 **1** **Know No Fear**[7] 3317 7-8-10 **56** .... (p) AmyScott 9 67
(Alastair Lidderdale) *chsd ldr tl led 3f out: rdn clr over 1f out: nicely* **8/1**

0055 **2** *3 ½* **Satwa Laird**[7] 3314 6-9-9 **69** .... DavidKenny 2 72
(Conor Dore) *cl up: drvn 2f out: ev ch over 1f out: plugged on to take 2nd ins fnl f: no ch w wnr* **20/1**

1501 **3** *2* **Join Up**[7] 3317 6-8-13 **62** 6ex .... RachealKneller(3) 1 60
(Mark Brisbourne) *cl up: rdn to chse wnr 2f out: ev ch 1f out: wknd and jst hld on to modest 3rd* **7/2**[1]

-240 **4** *shd* **Signora Frasi (IRE)**[20] 2867 7-8-10 **59** .... IanBurns(3) 6 57+
(Tony Newcombe) *in rr: plenty to do and drvn 2f out: kpt on wl towards centre of trck ins fnl f: nrly grabbed 3rd* **14/1**

30-4 **5** ¾ **Justbookie Dot Com (IRE)**[90] 1117 4-9-7 **70**(v)
WilliamTwiston-Davies(3) 7 66
(David Evans) *in tch: rdn and lost pl 3f out: hanging and racing awkwardly whn btn over 1f out* **18/1**

0533 **6** *2* **Jalors (IRE)**[20] 2867 4-9-3 **63** .... DarrenEgan 4 55
(Ronald Harris) *in rr: rdn and plenty to do over 2f out: plugged on and hmpd over 1f out: one pce* **9/2**[2]

511 **7** *2 ¼* **Jake The Snake (IRE)**[13] 3103 11-9-10 **70** .... BrendanPowell 11 57
(Tony Carroll) *slow away and last tl 3f out: hdwy on bit 2f out: sn rdn along and swtchd lft: unable to cl after* **7/1**[3]

-203 **8** ¾ **First Class Favour (IRE)**[9] 3254 4-9-6 **66** .... AdamCarter 8 51
(Tim Easterby) *led tl hdd 3f out: sn drvn and grad wknd* **8/1**

0544 **9** *3 ½* **Shared Moment (IRE)**[13] 3096 6-8-8 **57** .... (v) NatashaEaton(3) 3 34
(John Gallagher) *in tch: drvn 2f out: sn wknd and no further imp* **25/1**

3500 **10** *nk* **Menadati (USA)**[48] 2051 4-9-3 **63** .... CharlesBishop 13 39
(Peter Hiatt) *in tch: effrt over 3f out: drvn and wknd fnl 2f* **16/1**

3054 **11** *16* **Big Bay (USA)**[34] 2463 6-8-3 **53** ow1 .... LewisWalsh(5) 5
(Jane Chapple-Hyam) *midfield: drvn along and struggling whn bdly hmpd over 1f out: sn eased rt off* **7/1**[3]

000 **12** *3* **Craniac**[14] 3079 5-8-5 **51** oh6 .... (bt[1]) JamesRogers 10
(Frank Sheridan) *a in rr: t.o* **66/1**

036/ **13** *19* **Cheers Big Ears (IRE)**[787] 1782 6-8-5 **51** oh1 .... MatthewLawson 12
(Richard Price) *a in rr: t.o* **20/1**

1m 45.01s (4.01) **Going Correction** +0.50s/f (Yiel) **13** Ran SP% **120.3**
Speed ratings (Par 103): **99,95,93,93,92 90,88,87,84,83 67,64,45**
toteswingers 1&2 £27.00, 1&3 £7.50, 2&3 £15.90 CSF £163.79 CT £688.43 TOTE £8.20: £3.00, £6.30, £1.70; EX 149.60.
Owner C S J Beek **Bred** B Bargh **Trained** Lambourn, Berks

FOCUS
Yet again racing prominently was an advantage in this low-grade handicap. The winner turned around C&D form with the third.
T/Jkpt: Not won. T/Plt: £3,313.40 to a £1 stake. Pool: £59,686.62 - 13.15 winning tickets T/Qpdt: £107.30 to a £1 stake. Pool: £4,803.2 - 33.1 winning tickets CS

3082 YARMOUTH (L-H)
Thursday, June 28

OFFICIAL GOING: Good to firm (7.6)
Wind: light to medium half against Weather: sunny

3545 BET IN-PLAY AT BETVICTOR.COM MAIDEN STKS 6f 3y
2:20 (2:20) (Class 5) 2-Y-O £2,264 (£673; £336; £168) **Stalls** Low

Form RPR
1 **Rocky Ground (IRE)** 2-9-3 0 .... NeilCallan 1 88+
(Roger Varian) *a travelling wl: chsd ldrs tl led over 2f out: clr over 1f out: pushed along and r.o wl fnl f: comf* **6/4**[1]

2 *4* **A Certain Romance** 2-9-3 0 .... WilliamBuick 9 76+
(Peter Chapple-Hyam) *chsd ldrs: chsd wnr ent fnl 2f: rdn and styd on same pce and wl hld fnl f* **15/8**[2]

3 *1 ¾* **Echo Of Silence (FR)** 2-9-3 0 .... JamieSpencer 10 70+
(Marco Botti) *stdd s: hld up in tch: hdwy into midfield after 2f: rdn and chsd ldng pair over 1f out: kpt on but no ch w wnr* **13/2**[3]

4 *3 ¼* **Bartack (IRE)** 2-9-3 0 .... KierenFallon 6 61+
(Luca Cumani) *in tch in midfield: pushed along after 2f out: outpcd by ldng pair 2f out: no ch but plugged on fnl f* **14/1**

05 **5** *1 ½* **Santo Prince (USA)**[14] 3067 2-9-3 0 .... HayleyTurner 3 56
(Michael Bell) *stdd s: bhd: rdn 1/2-way: sme hdwy past btn horses over 1f out: nvr trbld ldrs* **9/1**

0 **6** ¾ **Plexolini**[12] 3140 2-9-3 0 .... TadhgO'Shea 8 54
(Jo Hughes) *racd keenly: sn led: hdd over 2f out: edging lft and wknd over 1f out: fdd fnl f* **28/1**

7 *½* **The Obvious Choice** 2-9-0 0 .... HarryBentley(3) 7 52
(Stuart Williams) *a towards rr: rdn and outpcd ent fnl 2f: plugged on but no ch fnl f* **40/1**

8 *1* **Likelikelikelikeit** 2-8-12 0 .... TedDurcan 2 44
(Mark H Tompkins) *a bhd: rdn and struggling 1/2-way: no ch whn swtchd lft wl over 1f out: plugged on fnl f* **66/1**

0 **9** *nk* **Whitford (IRE)**[19] 2934 2-9-3 0 .... CathyGannon 5 48
(Chris Dwyer) *in tch in midfield: rdn and struggling over 2f out: wl btn over 1f out* **125/1**

6 **10** *33* **Marvelous Miss (IRE)**[12] 3150 2-8-13 0 ow1 .... IanMongan 4
(Christine Dunnett) *racd keenly: chsd ldr tl over 2f out: sn lost pl: wl bhd and virtually p.u ins fnl f: t.o* **125/1**

1m 14.19s (-0.21) **Going Correction** +0.025s/f (Good) **10** Ran SP% **113.7**
Speed ratings (Par 93): **102,96,94,90,88 87,86,85,84,40**
toteswingers 1&2 £1.70, 1&3 £2.90, 2&3 £3.50 CSF £4.21 TOTE £2.70: £1.20, £1.70, £1.40; EX 6.10.
Owner Clipper Logistics **Bred** Messrs Mark Hanly & James Hanly **Trained** Newmarket, Suffolk

FOCUS
Back straight and bottom bend dolled out 3m adding 5m to all races on Round course. This has gone to some decent types in recent years and Rocky Ground looks useful. It's not clear how much depth to the race there was with some in behind given easier introductions.

NOTEBOOK
Rocky Ground(IRE) ◆, who cost £105,000 as a yearling, ran like a horse that knew his job first-time-out, and came right away from his rivals once Neil Callan pressed on. Connections have him entered in a few sales races this season, so it'll be interesting to see in what direction they go with their colt, because he looks up to winning a conditions event before graduating to something better. (op 2-1)
A Certain Romance, a 40,000gns Invincible Spirit colt, wore a sheepskin noseband for his debut and was firmly put in his place. His pedigree suggests he'll get further. (op 7-4 tchd 13-8)
Echo Of Silence(FR), whose sales price increased to 120,000euros as a 2yo from 50,000 as a yearling, travelled nicely for a long way but took a while to get going when asked to quicken. There's little doubt he'll be mentally sharper next time. (op 9-1)
Bartack(IRE), who cost 78,000gns as a yearling, is an Acclamation half-brother to Italian 1m1f 2yo winner Vankook. Reported to be coltish in the paddock, he needed riding along for some time but got the idea late on and finished off well. Kieren Fallon reported that the colt ran green. Official explanation: jockey said colt ran green (op 11-1)
Santo Prince(USA) probably set the standard of those with experience but never made the slightest impression. (op 15-2)
Marvelous Miss(IRE) Official explanation: jockey said filly ran green

3546 BETVICTOR ON YOUR MOBILE H'CAP 6f 3y
2:50 (2:54) (Class 6) (0-65,65) 4-Y-O+ £1,617 (£481; £240; £120) **Stalls** Low

Form RPR
2-02 **1** **Amosite**[33] 2493 6-9-3 **61** .... (p) HayleyTurner 5 69
(J R Jenkins) *mde all: rdn over 1f out: hrd pressed ins fnl f: hld on v gamely* **18/1**

0460 **2** *nse* **Mister Green (FR)**[52] 1919 6-8-13 **57**....................(t[1]) MickaelBarzalona 8 65
(David Flood) *stdd s: hld up in tch in rr: swtchd lft and hdwy 2f out: str chal ins fnl f: jst hld* **16/1**

0006 **3** *1* **Green Warrior**[24] 2749 4-8-2 **49**................................(e) DeclanCannon[(3)] 3 54
(Richard Guest) *taken down early: chsd ldrs: rdn and edgd rt jst over 1f out: styd on same pce u.p fnl f* **80/1**

1022 **4** *1* **Yankee Storm**[15] 3053 7-9-0 **58**.......................................(b) JimmyQuinn 9 59
(Michael Wigham) *stdd s: t.k.h: hld up in midfield: hdwy 2f out: rdn to chse ldrs and edgd rt 1f out: styd on same pce ins fnl f* **13/2[2]**

36-1 **5** *1 ½* **Running Mate (IRE)**[99] 986 5-9-2 **60**................................(t) IanMongan 1 57
(Jo Crowley) *taken down early: t.k.h: hld up in tch: rdn and effrt on far side over 1f out: no ex 1f out: wknd ins fnl f* **9/1**

05-5 **6** *hd* **Dream Catcher (FR)**[35] 2421 4-9-7 **65**............................. WilliamBuick 6 61
(Henry Candy) *chsd ldrs: rdn and nt qckn over 1f out: wknd ins fnl f: b.b.v* **7/4[1]**

4351 **7** *2* **Danzoe (IRE)**[12] 3151 5-9-4 **62**.. KirstyMilczarek 4 52
(Christine Dunnett) *hld up towards rr: hdwy 2f out: drvn and chsd ldrs ent fnl f: no ex and wknd fnl 100yds* **16/1**

-154 **8** *1* **Les Verguettes (IRE)**[14] 3075 4-9-2 **60**............................. TedDurcan 13 46
(Chris Wall) *in tch in midfield: lost pl and bhd whn rdn 2f out: styd on ins fnl f: no threat to ldrs* **9/1**

3400 **9** *1 ¾* **Silver Linnet (IRE)**[19] 2943 5-8-12 **61**....................(p) TobyAtkinson[(5)] 14 42
(John Butler) *stdd s: hld up towards rr: rdn and effrt 2f out: no imp 1f out: wknd ins fnl f* **33/1**

0005 **10** *hd* **Rasteau (IRE)**[15] 3051 4-7-9 **46** oh1.............................. NoelGarbutt[(7)] 11 26
(Tom Keddy) *sn bustled along towards rr: plugged on fr over 1f out: nvr trbld ldrs* **66/1**

003- **11** *nk* **Elusive Hawk (IRE)**[254] 6939 8-9-7 **65**........................... MickyFenton 16 44
(Barney Curley) *in tch: rdn and short-lived effrt 2f out: sn wknd* **8/1[3]**

04-6 **12** *8* **Thalia Grace**[168] 126 5-8-0 **47**....................................[1] HarryBentley[(3)] 12
(William Knight) *taken down early: chsd ldrs tl wknd 2f out: bhd fnl f* **20/1**

132- **13** *1* **Excellent Aim**[183] 7896 5-9-1 **59**....................................(t) JamieSpencer 7
(George Margarson) *chsd ldrs tl over 2f out: sn struggling: bhd and eased ins fnl f* **10/1**

1m 14.36s (-0.04) **Going Correction** +0.025s/f (Good) 13 Ran SP% **117.4**
Speed ratings (Par 101): **101,100,99,98,96 96,93,92,89,89 89,78,77**
toteswingers 1&2 £34.10, 1&3 £64.60, 2&3 £60.80 CSF £266.27 CT £20216.47 TOTE £26.50: £4.90, £5.30, £10.30; EX 289.90.
Owner Mrs Claire Goddard **Bred** Richard Kent **Trained** Royston, Herts

FOCUS
A moderate sprint in which quite a few of the runners came into this off the back off a good run. Unconvincing form given the profiles of the principals, and the first three came down the centre.
Yankee Storm Official explanation: jockey said gelding suffered interference shortly after start
Dream Catcher(FR) Official explanation: trainer's rep said following scope gelding was found to have bled
Excellent Aim Official explanation: jockey said gelding had no more to give

3547 BETVICTOR FOR BEST PRICES H'CAP (DIV I) 7f 3y

3:20 (3:22) (Class 6) (0-65,65) 3-Y-O **£1,617** (£481; £240; £120) **Stalls** Low

Form RPR

043 **1** **Charity Box**[14] 3082 3-9-7 **65**.. TedDurcan 9 76+
(Chris Wall) *chsd ldrs tl led over 5f out: mde rest: rdn over 1f out: in command and kpt on wl fnl f* **5/1[2]**

6-03 **2** *1 ¾* **Princess Maya**[78] 1313 3-9-2 **60**.. IanMongan 7 66
(Jo Crowley) *in tch in midfield: effrt u.p over 1f out: drvn ins fnl f and chsd wnr fnl 75yds: styd on* **6/1[3]**

3500 **3** *¾* **Love Grows Wild (USA)**[23] 2803 3-8-8 **52**..............(v[1]) HayleyTurner 11 56
(Michael Bell) *in tch: chsd wnr over 2f out: rdn and nt qckn over 1f out: styd on same pce fnl f: lost 2nd fnl 75yds* **16/1**

35-3 **4** *½* **Gold Falcon (IRE)**[121] 730 3-9-6 **64**.................................... MartinLane 6 67
(David Simcock) *stdd s: t.k.h: hld up towards rr: hdwy to chse ldrs and rdn 2f out: hung rt over 1f out: edgd bk lft and styd on same pce ins fnl f* **10/1**

-000 **5** *¾* **Amis Reunis**[21] 2846 3-9-4 **62**.. WilliamCarson 8 63
(Anthony Carson) *chsd ldrs: effrt u.p over 2f out: drvn and chsd ldng pair over 1f out: no imp: one pce and lost 2 pls ins fnl f* **6/1[3]**

0-50 **6** *2 ¼* **Symphony Star (IRE)**[37] 2379 3-9-1 **59**..........................(p) LukeMorris 4 54
(Paul D'Arcy) *led tl over 5f out: chsd ldr tl rdn and unable qck over 2f out: plugged on same pce but no threat to ldrs fr over 1f out* **10/1**

0-15 **7** *nk* **Atlantis Crossing (IRE)**[42] 2206 3-9-3 **61**......................... PatCosgrave 5 55
(Jim Boyle) *restless in stalls: hld up in tch: swtchd lft and effrt over 2f out: drvn and chsd ldrs over 1f out: btn 1f out: wknd ins fnl f* **13/2**

500 **8** *¾* **July Specialists**[55] 1825 3-8-1 **48** oh1 ow2................ DeclanCannon[(3)] 1 40
(Richard Guest) *in tch towards rr: rdn and effrt 2f out: plugged on steadily fnl f: nvr trbld ldrs* **66/1**

-020 **9** *10* **Artful Lady (IRE)**[31] 2548 3-8-2 **49**................................ RyanPowell[(3)] 12 14
(George Margarson) *in tch in midfield: struggling u.p wl over 1f out: sn wknd* **22/1**

0-61 **10** *6* **Sarah Berry**[15] 3050 3-9-0 **58**.. CathyGannon 3
(Chris Dwyer) *t.k.h: chsd ldrs: rdn and fnd little ent fnl 2f: hung lft and wknd over 1f out: bhd and eased ins fnl f* **7/2[1]**

0050 **11** *2* **Gone To Ground**[16] 3005 3-8-2 **46** oh1........................(p) JamieMackay 2
(Michael Squance) *a towards rr: rdn and struggling 1/2-way: lost tch wl over 1f out* **66/1**

650 **12** *27* **Give Us A Belle (IRE)**[54] 1843 3-8-10 **54**..............(tp) KirstyMilczarek 10
(Christine Dunnett) *a in rr: rdn and lost tch over 2f out: t.o and eased fnl f* **33/1**

1m 27.3s (0.70) **Going Correction** +0.025s/f (Good) 12 Ran SP% **115.1**
Speed ratings (Par 97): **97,95,94,93,92 90,89,88,77,70 68,37**
toteswingers 1&2 £6.20, 1&3 £13.00, 2&3 £16.00 CSF £33.03 CT £442.58 TOTE £7.10: £2.30, £3.10, £4.00; EX 29.10.
Owner John E Sims **Bred** Farmers Hill Stud **Trained** Newmarket, Suffolk

FOCUS
A modest handicap run in a similar time to division II. The winner is rated up 9lb and is likely to do better, with the second close to his 2yo debut form.
Sarah Berry Official explanation: jockey said filly ran too free
Give Us A Belle(IRE) Official explanation: trainer said gelding was unsuited by the good to firm ground

3548 BETVICTOR FOR BEST PRICES H'CAP (DIV II) 7f 3y

3:50 (3:52) (Class 6) (0-65,65) 3-Y-O **£1,617** (£481; £240; £120) **Stalls** Low

Form RPR

-002 **1** **Multi Bene**[10] 3230 3-9-4 **62**... KierenFallon 7 70+
(Tom Dascombe) *squeezed for room and hmpd sn after s: in tch: rdn over 2f out: chsd ldr over 1f out: led fnl 75yds: styd on wl and gng away at fin* **15/8[1]**

-654 **2** *½* **Intomist (IRE)**[14] 3071 3-8-11 **60**.................................... NathanAlison[(5)] 1 67
(Jim Boyle) *swtchd rt s: led: rdn over 1f out: hdd and no ex fnl 75yds* **12/1**

1100 **3** *2 ¼* **One More Roman (IRE)**[9] 3248 3-9-6 **64**.......................(bt) NeilCallan 12 65
(Gay Kelleway) *t.k.h: hld up in tch in rr: rdn and hdwy over 1f out: kpt on but no imp ins fnl f* **20/1**

5435 **4** *2 ½* **Kashmiri Star**[7] 3315 3-8-10 **54** ow1................................ PatCosgrave 3 48
(Michael Quinn) *chsd ldr tl over 1f out: sn unable qck u.p: wknd ins fnl f* **13/2[3]**

-055 **5** *3 ¾* **Cambridge Duchess**[29] 2610 3-8-11 **55**........................ WilliamCarson 8 39
(Stuart Williams) *hmpd sn after s: in tch: rdn and unable qck ent fnl 2f: edgd lft u.p and wknd over 1f out* **9/1**

0001 **6** *1 ½* **Aubrietia**[3] 3451 3-8-7 **51** 6ex..(b) NickyMackay 9 31
(Ed Vaughan) *hmpd s: plld v hrd: in tch: rdn and fnd little 2f out: wknd over 1f out* **7/2[2]**

2150 **7** *½* **Outlaw Torn (IRE)**[6] 3356 3-8-12 **59**......................(e) DeclanCannon[(3)] 4 37
(Richard Guest) *stdd s: hld up in last pair: rdn and effrt over 1f out: no imp and no threat to ldrs fnl f* **8/1**

5060 **8** *1 ¾* **Canning Vale**[28] 2625 3-8-2 **46** oh1................................... JimmyQuinn 10 20
(Julia Feilden) *in tch towards rr: rdn and no rspnse over 2f out: sn struggling: no ch 1f out* **50/1**

000- **9** *¾* **Awesome Rock (IRE)**[180] 7937 3-7-13 **46** oh1............. RyanPowell[(3)] 2 18
(Louise Best) *wnt rt s: t.k.h: hld up in tch: rdn jst over 2f out: sn struggling and wknd 2f out* **40/1**

240 **10** *7* **Chart**[64] 1600 3-8-11 **58**.. HarryBentley[(3)] 11 11
(William Jarvis) *chsd ldrs tl over 2f out: sn struggling u.p: wknd 2f out* **20/1**

-000 **11** *6* **Brailsford (IRE)**[10] 3229 3-9-7 **65**................................(v[1]) JamieSpencer 6
(Ismail Mohammed) *stdd s: hld up in rr: rdn and effrt ent fnl 2f: unbalanced wl over 1f out: sn eased and wl btn* **22/1**

1m 27.35s (0.75) **Going Correction** +0.025s/f (Good) 11 Ran SP% **117.4**
Speed ratings (Par 97): **96,95,92,90,85 84,83,81,80,72 65**
toteswingers 1&2 £7.50, 1&3 £5.40, 2&3 £21.60 CSF £24.20 CT £359.60 TOTE £2.80: £1.50, £2.70, £6.80; EX 20.00.
Owner Mrs Richards & Mrs Brazier **Bred** Mickley Stud **Trained** Malpas, Cheshire
■ Stewards' Enquiry : Nathan Alison four-day ban: careless riding (Jul 12,16-18)

FOCUS
The winning time was 5/100ths of a second slower than the first division. The runner-up is perhaps the key to the form.
Brailsford(IRE) Official explanation: jockey said colt lost its action

3549 BEST PRICES AT BETVICTOR.COM H'CAP 7f 3y

4:20 (4:22) (Class 5) (0-70,70) 4-Y-O+ **£2,264** (£673; £336; £168) **Stalls** Low

Form RPR

0303 **1** **Comrade Bond**[22] 2815 4-9-7 **70**.. TedDurcan 1 81
(Mark H Tompkins) *racd centre to far side: hld up in tch: hdwy over 2f out: rdn to ld overall over 1f out: kpt on wl u.p fnl f* **8/1[3]**

313 **2** *½* **First Class**[34] 2466 4-8-6 **55**... LukeMorris 5 65
(Rae Guest) *racd centre to nr side: in tch in midfield: rdn 3f out: kpt on u.p to chse wnr ins fnl f: styd on wl* **9/2[2]**

013- **3** *1 ¼* **Forks**[196] 7767 5-9-1 **69**.. AntiocoMurgia[(5)] 6 76
(Jane Chapple-Hyam) *racd nr side: in tch: rdn and effrt 2f out: chsd wnr over 1f out: lost 2nd and styd on same pce fnl f* **17/2**

0/60 **4** *¾* **Marster Parkes**[80] 1250 4-8-11 **60**.................................. JamieSpencer 13 65
(John Quinn) *racd nr side: stdd s: hld up towards rr: swtchd lft and effrt over 1f out: kpt on u.p fnl f* **20/1**

0031 **5** *nse* **Rough Rock (IRE)**[6] 3344 7-9-5 **68**................................. CathyGannon 12 72+
(Chris Dwyer) *racd nr side: hld up towards rr: hdwy to chse ldrs and gng wl whn nt clr run and snatched up 2f out: swtchd lft over 1f out: kpt on fnl f: unable to chal* **3/1[1]**

00-0 **6** *2 ¼* **Primo Lady**[33] 2493 4-9-1 **70** ow1..........................(v) MichaelJMurphy[(7)] 3 69
(Gay Kelleway) *racd centre to far side: led gp and chsd overall ldr tl over 1f out wknd fnl f* **40/1**

3011 **7** *½* **Spin Again (IRE)**[15] 3052 7-9-2 **65**................................. PatCosgrave 11 62
(John Ryan) *racd nr side: in tch: rdn and effrt to chse ldrs over 1f out: no ex 1f out: wknd ins fnl f* **9/2[2]**

2000 **8** *1 ½* **Mishrif (USA)**[36] 2399 6-9-7 **70**.......................................(b) KierenFallon 9 63
(J R Jenkins) *racd nr side: overall ldr tl rdn and hdd over 1f out: btn whn hmpd 1f out: wknd ins fnl f* **12/1**

-060 **9** *11* **Ellies Image**[10] 3215 5-8-11 **60**...................................... WilliamCarson 2 23
(Brian Baugh) *racd centre to far side: sn rdn along and a struggling in rr: wl bhd fnl f* **33/1**

-410 **10** *4* **Proper Charlie**[44] 2146 4-9-5 **68**.................................... WilliamBuick 10 20
(William Knight) *racd nr side: stdd s: hld up in rr: rdn and effrt 2f out: sn btn: bhd fnl f* **9/1**

046- **11** *20* **Joyful Sound (IRE)**[317] 5134 4-8-10 **59**............................. MartinLane 8
(Natalie Lloyd-Beavis) *racd nr side: hld up in rr: lost tch 2f out: virtually p.u ins fnl f: t.o* **66/1**

45-2 **12** *nk* **Tiberius Claudius (IRE)**[34] 2461 4-9-4 **67**......................... NeilCallan 7
(George Margarson) *racd nr side: stdd s: t.k.h: hld up in midfield: rdn and btn over 2f out: virtually p.u ins fnl f: t.o* **25/1**

1m 26.82s (0.22) **Going Correction** +0.025s/f (Good) 12 Ran SP% **116.2**
Speed ratings (Par 103): **99,98,97,96,96 93,92,91,78,74 51,50**
CSF £40.69 CT £317.66 TOTE £10.00: £2.90, £1.50, £2.60; EX 63.50.
Owner Raceworld **Bred** Misses Wright, Lightower And King **Trained** Newmarket, Suffolk

FOCUS
A fair contest, in which at one stage there were three different groups. The first three all raced down the centre at times, but the form is sound amongst them.
Rough Rock(IRE) Official explanation: jockey said gelding was denied a clear run
Mishrif(USA) Official explanation: jockey said gelding ran too free
Proper Charlie Official explanation: jockey said gelding ran too free
Joyful Sound(IRE) Official explanation: jockey said gelding stumbled
Tiberius Claudius(IRE) Official explanation: jockey said gelding lost its action

3550 IN-PLAY EURO BETTING AT BETVICTOR.COM FILLIES' H'CAP 1m 1f

4:50 (4:50) (Class 4) (0-85,85) 4-Y-O+ **£4,075** (£1,212; £606; £303) **Stalls** Low

Form RPR

5-21 **1** **Laverre (IRE)**[27] 2679 5-8-8 **72**.. HayleyTurner 10 80
(Lucy Wadham) *chsd ldr: rdn to ld over 1f out: asserting whn edgd lft ins fnl f: r.o wl under hands and heels after* **4/1[2]**

1-10 **2** *1 ½* **Silken Thoughts**[41] 2248 4-9-7 **85**.................................... CathyGannon 8 90+
(John Berry) *stdd s: t.k.h: hld up in last pair: swtchd rt and nt clr run over 2f out: hdwy over 1f out: r.o wl to go 2nd towards fin* **5/1[3]**

1636 **3** *nk* **Sail Home**[14] 3073 5-8-5 **69**... JimmyQuinn 9 73
(Julia Feilden) *led: rdn and hdd over 1f out: unable qck whn sltly hmpd ins fnl f: styd on same pce after and lost 2nd towards fin* **14/1**

0-30 **4** 1 ¼ **Our Gal**[20] 2884 4-9-2 **80** MickaelBarzalona 6 81
(Noel Quinlan) *t.k.h: hld up in tch: rdn and effrt over 2f out: nt clr run over 1f out: hdwy u.p 1f out: kpt on but no threat to wnr* **10/1**

2125 **5** *nk* **Viking Rose (IRE)**[24] 2766 4-8-6 **70** LukeMorris 2 71
(James Eustace) *chsd ldng pair: rdn 3f out: outpcd and drvn over 1f out: plugged on same pce and hld fnl f* **7/1**

5321 **6** 3 ¼ **Strawberrymystique**[98] 1000 4-8-9 **73** JamieSpencer 1 66
(Marco Botti) *t.k.h: chsd ldrs: rdn and effrt 2f out: nt qckn u.p over 1f out: btn and eased fnl 75yds* **2/1**[1]

-103 **7** *nse* **Ssafa**[21] 2859 4-8-8 **72** WilliamBuick 4 65
(J W Hills) *hld up in last pair: swtchd lft 3f out: rdn and effrt over 2f out: no ex u.p over 1f out: wknd ins fnl f* **20/1**

30-0 **8** 1 ¾ **Obligada (IRE)**[20] 2882 4-9-5 **83** NeilCallan 3 72
(Tobias B P Coles) *t.k.h: hld up in tch: rdn and effrt over 2f out: wknd 1f out* **14/1**

30-0 **9** 33 **Zennor**[90] 1114 5-8-13 **77** IanMongan 5
(George Margarson) *in tch in midfield: rdn and struggling over 2f out: wknd over 1f out: virtually p.u fnl f: t.o* **14/1**

1m 54.66s (-1.14) **Going Correction** -0.275s/f (Firm) **9** Ran SP% **116.4**
Speed ratings (Par 102): **94,92,92,91,91 88,88,86,57**
CSF £24.57 CT £217.58 TOTE £5.10: £1.30, £1.70, £3.60; EX 27.60.

Owner Mr And Mrs A E Pakenham **Bred** Kilnamoragh Stud **Trained** Newmarket, Suffolk

FOCUS
This looked the classiest event of the day using official figures as a guide, but was still just an ordinary fillies' handicap. A clear personal best from the winner but the runner-up was unlucky.

3551 BETVICTOR FOR EURO 2012 MEDIAN AUCTION MAIDEN STKS 1m 2f 21y
5:20 (5:22) (Class 6) 3-Y-O £1,617 (£481; £240; £120) Stalls Low

Form RPR

0 **1** **Educate**[12] 3161 3-9-3 0 TadhgO'Shea 5 81
(Ismail Mohammed) *chsd ldrs: rdn to chal over 2f out: led over 1f out: r.o wl and drew clr fnl f: comf* **10/3**[2]

-434 **2** 6 **La Pampita (IRE)**[14] 3070 3-8-12 74 WilliamBuick 7 64
(William Knight) *taken down early: led: rdn and hdd over 1f out: btn jst ins fnl f: no ch w wnr after* **13/8**[1]

0002 **3** 4 ½ **Thecornishcowboy**[10] 3228 3-9-3 49 (t) JimmyQuinn 6 60
(John Ryan) *in tch: effrt u.p over 2f out: outpcd and btn 2f out: modest 3rd 1f out* **20/1**

0 **4** ½ **Cellist**[21] 2856 3-9-3 0 KierenFallon 10 59
(William Haggas) *chsd ldr: rdn 4f out: lost 2nd over 3f out: 3rd and wknd wl over 1f out* **7/2**[3]

52 **5** 1 ¼ **Broadway Babe (IRE)**[37] 2368 3-8-12 0 LukeMorris 9 52
(Harry Dunlop) *chsd ldrs: rdn 5f out: hung lft fr 4f out: wknd wl over 1f out* **5/1**

0 **6** 10 **Merchants Return**[40] 2279 3-9-3 0 DaraghO'Donohoe 8 37
(Lydia Pearce) *a in rr: rdn 5f out: lost tch 3f out* **100/1**

0 **7** *nse* **Omega Omega**[21] 2848 3-8-12 0 BrettDoyle 1 31
(Julia Feilden) *a in rr: rdn and struggling 3f out: bhd over 1f out* **28/1**

00-0 **8** 31 **Fine Finale**[16] 3002 3-8-12 40 (b) HarryPoulton(5) 3
(Michael Squance) *in tch: rdn 5f out: lost tch 3f out: t.o* **200/1**

9 1 ¼ **Roman Eglenovich** 3-9-3 0 IanMongan 4
(George Margarson) *s.i.s: sn rdn and lost tch immediately: t.o thrght* **40/1**

2m 6.66s (-3.84) **Going Correction** -0.275s/f (Firm) **9** Ran SP% **112.2**
Speed ratings (Par 97): **104,99,95,95,94 86,86,61,60**
toteswingers 1&2 £2.90, 1&3 £6.40, 2&3 £2.70 CSF £8.58 TOTE £5.90: £1.70, £1.10, £3.00; EX 9.00.

Owner Sultan Ali **Bred** Lady Legard **Trained** Newmarket, Suffolk

■ The first winner in Britain for former Dubai-based Ismail Mohammed.

FOCUS
Not many winners are likely to emerge from this contest in the short-term. The winner did it well and the moderate third is the best guide.

3552 INJURED JOCKEYS FUND H'CAP 1m 6f 17y
5:50 (5:50) (Class 5) (0-70,70) 4-Y-O+ £2,264 (£673; £336; £168) Stalls High

Form RPR

0-00 **1** **Marhaba Malyoon (IRE)**[20] 2899 4-9-7 **70** JamieSpencer 3 80+
(David Simcock) *stdd s: hld up in rr: swtchd rt 2f out: rdn to ld and edgd lft jst over 1f out: sn rdn clr: r.o wl* **7/1**

0646 **2** 3 **Brouhaha**[34] 2454 8-9-4 **67** KierenFallon 5 72
(Tom Dascombe) *dwlt: racd in midfield: clsd on ldrs 5f out: rdn and chsng ldrs whn nt clr run over 1f out: hdwy to chse wnr ins fnl f: no imp* **6/1**

-520 **3** *nk* **Lyric Poet (USA)**[135] 555 5-9-1 **64** (tp) WilliamCarson 4 69
(Anthony Carson) *stdd s: hld up in last pair: clsd on ldrs 5f out: chsng ldrs whn nt clr run and hmpd wl over 1f out: swtchd rt and hdwy jst over 1f out: styd on but no threat to wnr* **5/1**[3]

4026 **4** ¾ **Cotton Grass**[14] 3086 4-8-11 **60** TedDurcan 7 64
(Mark H Tompkins) *chsd ldrs tl rdn to ld wl over 2f out: drvn and hdd jst over 1f out: sn outpcd and btn: one pce and lost 2 pls fnl 150yds* **10/3**[1]

-000 **5** 5 **Rose Of Sarratt (IRE)**[19] 2925 4-8-11 **60** MartinLane 2 57
(Rae Guest) *chsd ldr: rdn and ev ch wl over 2f out: no ex and btn ent fnl f: wknd fnl f* **9/1**

5-02 **6** 4 **Young Jackie**[15] 3047 4-8-2 **51** oh4 CathyGannon 1 42
(George Margarson) *chsd ldrs: rdn and effrt over 2f out: stl pressing ldrs but unable qck whn pushed rt and hmpd over 1f out: wknd 1f out* **6/1**

00-1 **7** 1 **Sommersturm (GER)**[162] 105 8-9-5 **68** MickyFenton 6 58
(Barney Curley) *led tl wl over 2f out: sn dropped out: bhd over 1f out* **4/1**[2]

3m 7.3s (-0.30) **Going Correction** -0.275s/f (Firm) **7** Ran SP% **110.8**
Speed ratings (Par 103): **89,87,87,86,83 81,80**
toteswingers 1&2 £6.40, 1&3 £5.10, 2&3 £4.60 CSF £44.66 TOTE £8.50: £4.20, £2.40; EX 47.50.

Owner Ahmad Al Shaikh **Bred** Mrs Clodagh McStay **Trained** Newmarket, Suffolk

FOCUS
An interesting race that contained a few runners capable of showing good form. The winner's first real form since his 2yo debut.

Marhaba Malyoon(IRE) Official explanation: trainer's rep said, regarding apparent improvement in form, that the gelding settled better and appreciated the good to firm ground.

Sommersturm(GER) Official explanation: jockey said gelding moved poorly

T/Plt: £964.70 to a £1 stake. Pool: £66147.18 - 50.05 winning tickets T/Qpdt: £43.90 to a £1 stake. Pool: £5575.14 - 93.97 winning tickets SP

3553 - (Foreign Racing) - See Raceform Interactive

2909 CHESTER (L-H)
Friday, June 29

OFFICIAL GOING: Good (7.4)
Wind: Strong, half behind Weather: Cloudy

3554 TETLEY'S BITTER MAIDEN FILLIES' STKS 7f 2y
6:15 (6:17) (Class 4) 2-Y-O £4,528 (£1,347; £673; £336) Stalls Low

Form RPR

2 **1** **Savanna La Mar (USA)**[9] 3282 2-9-0 0 ChrisCatlin 1 81
(Sir Mark Prescott Bt) *mde all: rdn over 1f out: r.o wl to draw clr fnl f* **8/13**[1]

32 **2** 3 ½ **Lady Margaeux (IRE)**[11] 3208 2-9-0 0 DanielTudhope 4 72
(David O'Meara) *trckd ldrs: wnt 2nd 2f out: swtchd rt over 1f out: no imp on wnr fnl f* **8/1**[2]

4 **3** 2 ¾ **Pira Palace (IRE)**[32] 2541 2-9-0 0 RichardMullen 8 65
(Sir Michael Stoute) *in rr: sltly hmpd after 1f: pushed along over 3f out: effrt to chse ldrs over 2f out: styd on to take 3rd wl ins fnl f: nt trble front two* **12/1**[3]

40 **4** ¾ **Tough Lady (IRE)**[14] 3123 2-9-0 0 FrannyNorton 5 64
(Mark Johnston) *chsd ldrs: wnt 2nd after 2f and pressed wnr: rdn over 2f out: lost 2nd over 1f out: sn outpcd and no threat after* **14/1**

4404 **5** 15 **Windsor Rose (IRE)**[10] 3251 2-9-0 0 (p) TomMcLaughlin 2 26
(Mark Brisbourne) *racd keenly: in 2nd pl for 2f: chsd ldrs after: pushed along over 3f out: wknd over 2f out: wl bhd fnl f* **50/1**

0 **6** 1 ¾ **Her Royal Empress**[43] 2193 2-9-0 0 RichardKingscote 6 22
(James Unett) *racd keenly: hld up: lugged rt after 1f: pushed along over 3f out: struggling and lft bhd 2f out: nvr a threat* **40/1**

1m 28.17s (1.67) **Going Correction** +0.075s/f (Good) **6** Ran SP% **91.8**
Speed ratings (Par 92): **93,89,85,85,67 65**
Tote Swingers: 1&2 £1.10, 1&3 £1.50, 2&3 £2.10 CSF £3.13 TOTE £1.20: £1.10, £2.50; EX 2.80.

Owner Miss K Rausing **Bred** Kirsten Rausing **Trained** Newmarket, Suffolk

FOCUS
Rail from 6f to 1.5f moved out 3yds adding 10yds to 5f races, 7f +13yds, 1m 2f 75y +14yds, 1m 3f 79y +19yds, 1m 4f 66y +20yds. There was just 3mm of rain in the previous 24 hours and the going was good. A decent fillies' maiden won in professional style by the hot favourite. Singapura (5/1) was removed from the stalls and withdrawn, while Oriental Romance (14/1) got worked up at the start and was also taken out of the race. Deduct 20p in the £ under R4. The winner took a small step forward and has more to offer.

NOTEBOOK
Savanna La Mar(USA) set a fair standard on her strong finishing close second behind a Mark Johnston-trained newcomer in a 7f Kempton fillies' maiden on debut. She set a decent pace and showed a willing attitude to forge clear for a comfortable success. The first European runner for US sire Curlin, she is a powerful long-striding filly who looks potentially useful and represents the same connections who won this race with subsequent Listed winner Kinetica last year. (op 8-11 tchd 4-7)

Lady Margaeux(IRE), placed in 6f maidens on fast and slow ground at Redcar and Carlisle, looked uncomfortable on the sharp track but she deserves credit for battling on for a clear second stepped up to 7f. She is still learning and has scope for quite a bit of further improvement, particularly back on a more galloping track.

Pira Palace(IRE) who was under pressure some way out, plugged on for third but was beaten a bit further than she was in a 6f Kempton maiden on debut. (op 11-1)

Tough Lady(IRE) gave the winner something to think about for a long way but she was a spent force just after the final turn on her first try at 7f. (op 12-1)

3555 TRAFFORD CENTRE FASHION FLUTTER H'CAP 7f 122y
6:50 (6:52) (Class 5) (0-70,70) 3-Y-O £4,043 (£1,203; £601; £300) Stalls Low

Form RPR

-164 **1** **Lolita Lebron (IRE)**[27] 2689 3-9-7 **70** [1] DanielTudhope 2 76
(Lawrence Mullaney) *trckd ldrs: wnt 2nd over 2f out: led under 2f out: sn rdn: kpt on wl and a doing enough towards fin* **7/1**

4503 **2** ½ **Ferdy (IRE)**[22] 2843 3-7-13 **51** oh6 SophieDoyle(3) 15 56
(Paul Green) *trckd ldrs: effrt over 2f out: sn chalng: wnt 2nd over 1f out: unable to go w wnr and edgd lft ent fnl f: r.o cl home but a hld* **50/1**

0-00 **3** ¾ **Jay Kay**[32] 2540 3-8-5 **54** ChrisCatlin 4 57
(Danielle McCormick) *hld up: gd hdwy on outer over 2f out: r.o ins fnl f: gng on at fin* **25/1**

3453 **4** 1 ¾ **Chester Aristocrat**[14] 3111 3-8-13 **69** JasonHart(7) 7 68+
(Eric Alston) *bmpd s: hld up: hdwy on wd outer over 3f out: chsd ldrs 2f out: styd on same pce and no further imp fnl 75yds* **9/2**[2]

041 **5** ¾ **Ptolemy**[25] 2774 3-9-3 **66** GrahamGibbons 6 63+
(David Barron) *n.m.r and hmpd s: midfield: hdwy for press to chse ldrs over 1f out: kpt on ins fnl f: allowed to coast home towards fin* **5/1**[3]

61-0 **6** *shd* **Taro Tywod (IRE)**[18] 2981 3-9-4 **67** (p) DavidNolan 12 63
(Ann Duffield) *in tch: effrt 2f out: rdn whn chsng ldrs over 1f out: no ex fnl 75yds* **20/1**

0-00 **7** ½ **Minty Jones**[22] 2862 3-8-6 **55** (b[1]) JimmyQuinn 5 50
(Michael Mullineaux) *bhd: swtchd rt over 1f out: styd on ins fnl f: unable to rch ldrs* **66/1**

-605 **8** *nk* **Alabanda (IRE)**[11] 3214 3-9-0 **63** PJMcDonald 13 57
(Tim Easterby) *midfield: effrt to chse ldrs 2f out: one pce fnl 100yds* **16/1**

1305 **9** ½ **My New Angel (IRE)**[16] 3025 3-8-2 **51** oh5 (b) FrannyNorton 3 47
(Paul Green) *midfield: nt clr run over 2f out: rdn and hdwy whn swtchd lft 1f out: nt clr run fnl 100yds and allowed to coast home* **25/1**

-455 **10** *hd* **Al's Memory (IRE)**[26] 2733 3-9-7 **70** StephenCraine 11 63
(David Evans) *midfield: rdn 2f out: no hdwy fnl f* **11/1**

4351 **11** 3 ½ **Double Cee**[9] 3275 3-8-13 **65** 6ex LeeTopliss(3) 9 49+
(Richard Fahey) *bhd: hmpd after 1f: sn pushed along briefly: rdn over 1f out: nvr able to get on terms w ldrs* **10/3**[1]

-400 **12** 11 **Not Bad For A Boy (IRE)**[15] 3063 3-9-5 **68** SeanLevey 1 24
(Barry Leavy) *led: rdn and hdd under 2f out: sn wknd* **20/1**

1135 **13** 3 ¾ **First Bid**[16] 3041 3-9-7 **70** (b) RichardMullen 8 17
(James Given) *in tch: rdn over 1f out: sn wknd* **14/1**

6323 **14** 10 **Pendle Lady (IRE)**[17] 3014 3-8-11 **60** TomMcLaughlin 17
(Mark Brisbourne) *hld up: pushed along 4f out: nvr a threat* **16/1**

600- **15** 2 ½ **Monumental Man**[239] 7251 3-8-11 **60** FergusSweeney 16
(James Unett) *chsd ldr: rdn over 3f out: wknd qckly 2f out* **50/1**

3-00 **16** 1 ¼ **Zammy**[43] 2205 3-8-4 **60** IanBurns(7) 14
(Michael Wigham) *hld up: pushed along 4f out: nvr a threat* **33/1**

30-0 **17** 4 ½ **Theresnoneedfordat (IRE)**[24] 2785 3-9-6 **69** (b[1]) MartinHarley 10
(Stuart Williams) *trckd ldrs tl rdn and wknd qckly over 2f out* **33/1**

1m 34.94s (1.14) **Going Correction** +0.075s/f (Good) **17** Ran SP% **125.7**
Speed ratings (Par 99): **97,96,95,94,93 93,92,92,91,91 88,77,73,63,60 59,55**
Tote Swingers: 1&2 £33.60, 1&3 £223.40, 2&3 £155.20 CSF £340.16 TOTE £6.90: £1.70, £7.20, £6.90, £1.10; EX 494.30.

Owner Ian Buckley **Bred** Epona Bloodstock Ltd **Trained** Great Habton, N Yorks

FOCUS

They went a fast pace in this minor handicap but not many got into it from behind. Not many showed their best in this big field and there are one or two doubts over the form. The winner is rated up 4lb on his recent form.

Minty Jones Official explanation: jockey said colt hung right throughout

My New Angel(IRE) Official explanation: jockey said filly was denied a clear run

3556 BRITISH STALLION STUDS SUPPORTING EBF FILLIES' H'CAP 1m 2f 75y

7:25 (7:25) (Class 3) (0-90,85) 3-Y-O+ £9,703 (£2,887; £1,443; £721) Stalls High

Form RPR

0-33 1 **Al Baidaa**[39] 2344 3-8-10 79 ChrisCatlin 6 87
(Roger Varian) chsd ldr: rdn to ld narrowly 1f out and carried hd high: hung lft wl ins fnl f: gamely plld out more fnl strides **13/2**

23-5 2 ½ **Kenyan Cat**[16] 3038 5-9-11 82 SeanLevey 5 89
(Ed McMahon) in tch: pushed along 3f out: effrt to chse ldrs 2f out: nt qckn over 1f out: styd on ins fnl f: tk 2nd fnl strides **3/1**[1]

-566 3 hd **El Torbellino (IRE)**[21] 2884 4-9-7 78 DanielTudhope 1 85
(David O'Meara) led: rdn and hdd narrowly 1f out: bmpd whn stl chalng wl ins fnl f: no ex and lost 2nd fnl strides **4/1**[3]

-200 4 4 ½ **Fork Handles**[25] 2773 4-10-0 85 (v[1]) MartinHarley 7 83
(Mick Channon) hld up: rdn over 2f out: swtchd rt over 1f out: kpt on ins fnl f: no imp on ldrs **12/1**

-055 5 2 ¾ **Antigua Sunrise (IRE)**[13] 3163 6-9-1 75 LeeTopliss(3) 2 68
(Richard Fahey) hld up: u.p over 3f out: outpcd over 2f out: nvr a threat **7/2**[2]

1305 6 1 ¾ **Danube River**[31] 2589 3-8-3 72 FrannyNorton 3 61
(Mark Johnston) racd keenly: prom tl rdn and wknd over 1f out **8/1**

11 7 11 **Reyamour**[20] 2909 4-10-0 85 FergusSweeney 8 52
(Alan King) in tch: pushed along over 2f out: sn wknd **13/2**

2m 10.46s (-0.74) **Going Correction** +0.075s/f (Good)
WFA 3 from 4yo+ 12lb 7 Ran SP% **112.7**
Speed ratings (Par 104): **105,104,104,100,98 97,88**
Tote Swingers: 1&2 £5.20, 1&3 £4.70, 2&3 £3.90 CSF £25.50 CT £87.24 TOTE £7.40: £1.90, £2.60; EX 31.50.

Owner Saif Ali **Bred** Serpentine Bloodstock Ltd **Trained** Newmarket, Suffolk

FOCUS

There was a tight three-way finish in this decent fillies' handicap which was run at just a fair pace. The form looks sound enough, rated around the second.

NOTEBOOK

Al Baidaa, third behind subsequent Group 1 Coronation Stakes-placed Irish History in a Windsor maiden last month, was not very strong in the market on her handicap debut but she raced up with the pace and showed a good attitude to just prevail stepped up to 1m2f. A half-sister to 1m2f Group 3 winner Prince Siegfried, she is a big type who still showed signs of inexperience here and has potential for further improvement. (op 7-1 tchd 11-2)

Kenyan Cat hit a brief flat spot when the pace increased but she stayed on well out wide and was just held in a creditable attempt to make it 3-3 at this track. She has been knocking on the door off marks in the low 80s on her last four runs and is an admirably consistent mare who is effective on fast and slow turf. (op 11-4 tchd 10-3 and 7-2 in a place)

El Torbellino(IRE) had faded in three runs this season but she bounced back with a bold bid and can be marked up a bit because she received a few bumps from the winner in the closing stages. (op 5-1 tchd 11-2)

Fork Handles couldn't find any spark with a first-time visor tried and has been below form in three runs since a close call off 5lb higher at Kempton in March. (op 11-1)

Antigua Sunrise(IRE) who is in foal to Pastoral Pursuits, had done some encouraging late work in 1m4f handicaps on her last two runs but she looked short of pace back at 1m2f on a sharp track. (op 9-2)

Danube River put a big dent in her chance by taking a strong hold and had nothing left turning in. (tchd 9-1)

3557 STOBART MANAGEMENT DEVELOPMENT PROGRAM H'CAP 7f 2y

7:55 (7:59) (Class 4) (0-85,84) 4-Y-O+ £4,851 (£1,443; £721; £360) Stalls Low

Form RPR

0030 1 **King Of Eden (IRE)**[2] 3493 6-9-2 79 JimmyQuinn 4 89
(Eric Alston) midfield: plld off rail and hdwy over 1f out: r.o to ld wl ins fnl f: pushed out whn in command towards fin **13/2**[3]

2222 2 ½ **My Kingdom (IRE)**[11] 3221 6-9-5 82 (t) MartinHarley 12 91
(Ian Williams) midfield on outer: hdwy 2f out: wnt 2nd 1f out: chalng ins fnl f: hld by wnr cl home **6/1**[2]

0163 3 ½ **Ballista (IRE)**[8] 3304 4-9-5 82 RichardKingscote 3 90
(Tom Dascombe) led: rdn over 1f out: hdd wl ins fnl f: no ex cl home **5/1**[1]

3520 4 3 **Beckermet (IRE)**[14] 3128 10-9-5 82 PJMcDonald 6 82+
(Ruth Carr) trckd ldrs: nt clr run 2f out: lost pl and swtchd rt over 1f out: sn rdn: kpt on ins fnl f: nt knocked abt fnl 75yds **5/1**[1]

3236 5 ½ **Green Park (IRE)**[7] 3336 9-8-10 80 (b) JasonHart(7) 8 78
(Declan Carroll) hld up in midfield: rdn over 1f out: hdwy over 1f out: styd on ins fnl f: nt trble ldrs **12/1**

6201 6 1 **Tamareen (IRE)**[34] 2489 4-9-6 83 FrannyNorton 10 79
(Richard Fahey) chsd ldrs: wnt 2nd 2f out: rdn over 1f out: sn lost 2nd: wknd fnl 100yds **10/1**

40-0 7 3 ¾ **Fireback**[27] 2707 5-9-7 84 (t) FergusSweeney 5 69
(Daniel Kubler) broke loose and rn rdrless bef r: awkward s: in rr: nvr able to get to ldrs **25/1**

0-00 8 ¾ **Rulesn'regulations**[21] 2870 6-9-5 82 (b) TomMcLaughlin 1 65
(Matthew Salaman) prom: rdn over 1f out: wknd fnl f **14/1**

0340 9 1 ½ **Legal Eagle (IRE)**[22] 2841 7-8-10 73 (p) GrahamGibbons 2 52
(Paul Green) prom: chsd ldr over 5f out tl rdn 2f out: wknd over 1f out **20/1**

0546 10 3 **Lucky Numbers (IRE)**[13] 3169 6-9-2 79 DavidNolan 7 50
(David O'Meara) restless in stalls: awkward s: a in rr: nvr on terms **10/1**

0603 11 5 **Glenridding**[4] 3439 8-8-12 75 RichardMullen 9 33
(James Given) midfield: niggled along: rdn over 2f out: sn wknd **10/1**

-304 12 26 **Dasho**[32] 2545 4-8-12 75 (t) ChrisCatlin 11
(Gay Kelleway) s.i.s: hld up: toiling fnl 2f: nvr on terms **16/1**

1m 26.11s (-0.39) **Going Correction** +0.075s/f (Good) 12 Ran SP% **117.1**
Speed ratings (Par 105): **105,104,103,100,99 98,94,93,91,88 82,53**
Tote Swingers: 1&2 £6.50, 1&3 £5.90, 2&3 £5.80 CSF £44.68 CT £215.98 TOTE £7.80: £2.50, £2.00, £1.80; EX 59.40.

Owner The Grumpy Old Geezers **Bred** Gainsborough Stud Management Ltd **Trained** Longton, Lancs

FOCUS

A decent handicap run at a good pace. The winner's best form since last summer.

Lucky Numbers(IRE) Official explanation: jockey said gelding was slowly away

3558 EDMUNDSON ELECTRICAL H'CAP 1m 2f 75y

8:25 (8:26) (Class 5) (0-75,75) 3-Y-O £4,043 (£1,203; £601; £300) Stalls High

Form RPR

40-1 1 **Clon Brulee (IRE)**[15] 3066 3-9-5 73 GrahamGibbons 6 82+
(David Barron) chsd ldrs: rdn and carried lft sltly whn chalng over 1f out: sn led: r.o ins fnl f: eased down towards fin **7/2**[1]

324 2 ½ **Angel Gabrial (IRE)**[21] 2866 3-9-7 75 MartinHarley 10 82+
(Ian Williams) hld up: nt clr run over 1f out: prog ent fnl f: running on whn swtchd lft wl ins fnl f: fin strly **12/1**

2300 3 1 ¼ **Green Mitas (ITY)**[22] 2860 3-7-12 59 IanBurns(7) 13 63
(Frank Sheridan) sn prom on outer: led jst over 2f out: rdn and edgd lft over 1f out: sn hdd: outpcd by wnr ins fnl f: no ex fnl 100yds **50/1**

0-54 4 ½ **District Attorney (IRE)**[16] 3031 3-8-13 67 PJMcDonald 4 70
(William Haggas) midfield: pushed along over 2f out: rdn and hdwy over 1f out: styd on ins fnl f: nt pce to get to ldrs **15/2**[3]

3035 5 nk **Chelsea Mick**[18] 2980 3-8-8 69 JoshBaudains(7) 7 71
(John Mackie) midfield: outpcd over 2f out: styd on u.p ins fnl f: no imp towards fin **16/1**

0425 6 1 ¼ **Third Half**[7] 3345 3-9-2 70 RichardKingscote 11 70+
(Tom Dascombe) s.i.s: hld up: sltly hmpd wl over 7f out: effrt and swtchd rt over 1f out: styd on ins fnl f: nt rch ldrs **5/1**[2]

-630 7 6 **Night Flash (GER)**[22] 2860 3-9-2 70 RichardMullen 2 58
(James Given) chsd ldrs: rdn over 2f out: wknd jst over 1f out **25/1**

-321 8 1 ¼ **My Guardian Angel**[12] 3186 3-9-7 75 6ex ChrisCatlin 9 60
(Mark H Tompkins) midfield: rdn 3f out: wknd wl over 1f out **8/1**

0-36 9 ½ **Ventura Spirit**[13] 3156 3-8-10 67 LeeTopliss(3) 3 51+
(Richard Fahey) hld up: n.m.r wl over 7f out: rdn over 2f out: nt clr run over 1f out: eased whn no imp wl ins fnl f **15/2**[3]

-503 10 5 **Ghalaa (IRE)**[28] 2671 3-8-7 61 FrannyNorton 1 35
(Mark Johnston) led: hdd jst over 2f out: rdn whn n.m.r over 1f out: wknd fnl f **12/1**

0321 11 1 ¼ **Silvas Romana (IRE)**[14] 3120 3-9-7 75 TomMcLaughlin 5 47
(Mark Brisbourne) chsd ldr to 4f out: rdn and wknd over 2f out **5/1**[2]

2m 12.62s (1.42) **Going Correction** +0.075s/f (Good) 11 Ran SP% **117.3**
Speed ratings (Par 99): **97,96,95,95,94 93,89,88,87,83 82**
Tote Swingers: 1&2 £10.80, 1&3 £55.30, 2&3 £66.90 CSF £47.21 CT £1787.54 TOTE £3.60: £2.50, £4.30, £18.30; EX 47.20.

Owner Ms Colette Twomey **Bred** Collette Twomey **Trained** Maunby, N Yorks

FOCUS

A gamble was landed in this competitive handicap which was run at a fair pace. The form seems sound enough overall.

3559 TRAFFORD CENTRE HIGH HEELS COMPETITION H'CAP 7f 122y

9:00 (9:00) (Class 5) (0-70,70) 4-Y-O+ £4,043 (£1,203; £601; £300) Stalls Low

Form RPR

0252 1 **Hayek**[3] 3460 5-8-8 62 (b) AdamCarter(5) 8 72
(Tim Easterby) dwlt: in rr: hdwy on inner over 1f out: r.o ins fnl f: led towards fin **9/2**[2]

2122 2 ½ **Goldstorm**[22] 2858 4-8-10 59 (p) GrahamGibbons 5 68
(Brian Baugh) bmpd early: prom: rdn 2f out: r.o to ld ins fnl f: hdd and hld towards fin **6/1**[3]

5306 3 ½ **Chosen Character (IRE)**[27] 2696 4-9-6 69 (vt) RichardKingscote 4 76
(Tom Dascombe) midfield: rdn and hdwy over 1f out: r.o ins fnl f: gng on towards fin **4/1**[1]

4422 4 ½ **Cyflymder (IRE)**[44] 2173 6-9-2 65 FrannyNorton 14 71
(David C Griffiths) rdn leaving stalls: led: crossed over to rail bef first bnd: rdn over 1f out: hdd ins fnl f: no ex towards fin **8/1**

-504 5 3 ¼ **Clumber Place**[10] 3257 6-9-0 63 RichardMullen 12 61
(James Given) hld up: rdn 3f out: r.o ins fnl f: nt pce to rch ldrs **25/1**

6000 6 nk **Marksbury**[4] 3456 5-8-1 53 SophieDoyle(3) 3 50
(Mark Brisbourne) in tch: rdn over 1f out: styd on same pce ins fnl f **40/1**

6005 7 1 ¼ **Flipping**[10] 3257 5-9-4 67 KellyHarrison 1 61
(Eric Alston) chsd ldrs: rdn over 1f out: one pce ins fnl f **14/1**

0552 8 nk **Satwa Laird**[1] 3544 6-9-1 69 DavidKenny(5) 9 62
(Conor Dore) n.m.r s: in rr: nt clr run over 1f out: styd on ins fnl f: nt trble ldrs **16/1**

6160 9 1 **McCool Bannanas**[62] 1659 4-9-2 65 TomMcLaughlin 2 56
(James Unett) hld up: rdn 2f out: no imp fnl f **16/1**

0040 10 2 ¾ **Methaaly (IRE)**[15] 3065 9-8-8 57 (be) JimmyQuinn 6 41
(Michael Mullineaux) midfield tl rdn and wknd 2f out **33/1**

3321 11 ½ **Viking Warrior (IRE)**[21] 2879 5-9-4 70 LeeTopliss(3) 15 53
(Michael Dods) chsd ldr tl rdn over 1f out: wknd ins fnl f **15/2**

5446 12 hd **Princess Gail**[8] 3317 4-7-9 51 oh2 IanBurns(7) 7 33
(Mark Brisbourne) bmpd early: prom: pushed along 3f out: wknd over 1f out **40/1**

5013 13 9 **Join Up**[1] 3544 6-8-2 56 RachealKneller(5) 10 16
(Mark Brisbourne) midfield tl rdn and wknd over 2f out **10/1**

306- 14 22 **Crucis Abbey (IRE)**[286] 6179 4-8-6 55 ow1 ChrisCatlin 11
(Mark Brisbourne) hld up: struggling over 2f out: nvr on terms **25/1**

1m 34.38s (0.58) **Going Correction** +0.075s/f (Good) 14 Ran SP% **120.4**
Speed ratings (Par 103): **100,99,99,98,95 94,93,92,89 89,88,79,57**
Tote Swingers: 1&2 £7.50, 2&3 £5.20 CSF £29.92 CT £117.97 TOTE £5.50: £2.50, £3.20, £1.40; EX 40.10.

Owner Numac Engineering Ltd **Bred** Cranford Stud **Trained** Great Habton, N Yorks

■ Stewards' Enquiry : Adam Carter one-day ban: careless riding (Jul 16)

FOCUS

The first four pulled clear in this handicap and the winner came from a long way back. The pace was sound and the form is rated around the fourth.

Satwa Laird Official explanation: jockey said gelding was slowly away

Join Up Official explanation: vet said gelding finished lame

T/Jkpt: Not won. T/Plt: £113.70 to a £1 stake. Pool: £83,742.87 - 537.45 winning tickets. T/Qpdt: £17.20 to a £1 stake. Pool: £6,305.27 - 270.20 winning tickets. DO

^{3180}DONCASTER (L-H)

Friday, June 29

OFFICIAL GOING: Good (good to soft in places on round course)

Wind: Fresh against Weather: Cloudy

3560 CWU LEGAL SERVICES E B F MAIDEN FILLIES' STKS 6f

2:00 (2:03) (Class 5) 2-Y-O **£3,169** (£943; £471; £235) **Stalls** High

Form RPR

1 **Badr Al Badoor (IRE)** 2-9-0 0 HayleyTurner 8 83+
(James Fanshawe) *hld up: stdy hdwy 1/2-way: chal wl over 1f out: led ent fnl f: rdn and kpt on wl towards fin* **8/1**

2 ½ **Diaminda (IRE)** 2-9-0 0 JimCrowley 15 81+
(Alan Jarvis) *towards rr: gd hdwy on outer over 2f out: rdn to chal and edgd lft jst ins fnl f: ev ch tl no ex towards fin* **40/1**

3 1 ¾ **Pearl Sea (IRE)** 2-9-0 0 JamieSpencer 3 76+
(David Brown) *stdd s and sn in rr: pushed along 1/2-way: gd hdwy on wd outside 2f out: rdn to chse ldrs over 1f out: no imp on ldng pair ins fnl f* **4/1^{3}**

4 4 **March** 2-9-0 0 AdamKirby 16 63
(Marco Botti) *hld up in tch: gd hdwy over 2f out: chal wl over 1f out and ev ch tl rdn and one pce ent fnl f* **7/2^{2}**

5 1 **Dixie Sky (USA)** 2-9-0 0 TomQueally 11 60+
(Noel Quinlan) *chsd ldrs: rdn along 2f out: wknd appr fnl f* **28/1**

6 nk **Palladius** 2-9-0 0 PaulMulrennan 10 59+
(Kevin Ryan) *led: rdn along 2f out: drvn and hdd ent fnl f: sn wknd* **50/1**

7 hd **Dusky Queen (IRE)** 2-9-0 0 DavidNolan 7 59
(Richard Fahey) *midfield: hdwy to chse ldrs 2f out: rdn and no imp appr fnl f* **25/1**

8 3 **Take The Lead** 2-9-0 0 KieranO'Neill 9 50
(Richard Hannon) *a in midfield* **20/1**

9 ¾ **Jubilee Dancer** 2-8-11 0 DaleSwift$^{(3)}$ 12 48
(Geoffrey Oldroyd) *dwlt: a in rr* **80/1**

U3 **10** ½ **Panama Cat (USA)**^{21} 2873 2-9-0 0 PhillipMakin 13 46
(Kevin Ryan) *chsd ldrs: rdn along over 2f out: sn wknd* **14/1**

43 **11** 1 ½ **Ighraa (IRE)**^{24} 2783 2-9-0 0 KierenFallon 4 42
(Brian Meehan) *prom: rdn along over 2f out: grad wknd* **6/1**

2 **12** ½ **Desert Sunrise**^{34} 2492 2-9-0 0 RyanMoore 2 40
(Sir Michael Stoute) *trckd ldrs: effrt 2f out: sn rdn and wknd wl over 1f out* **3/1^{1}**

0 **13** 3 ¼ **Una Bella Cosa**^{9} 3282 2-9-0 0 IPoullis 14 30
(Alan McCabe) *prom: rdn along 1/2-way: sn wknd* **100/1**

1m 14.67s (1.07) **Going Correction** +0.175s/f (Good) **13** Ran SP% **118.0**

Speed ratings (Par 90): **99,98,96,90,89 88,88,84,83,83 81,80,76**

toteswingers 1&2 £26.50, 2&3 £57.10, 1&3 £8.20 CSF £295.13 TOTE £10.30: £2.90, £14.30, £2.20; EX 262.70 TRIFECTA Not won..

Owner Mohamed Obaida **Bred** Con Harrington **Trained** Newmarket, Suffolk

FOCUS

This fillies' maiden was dominated by newcomers and winners will come out of it. The first three came clear and the form looks sound. The time was 3.47sec outside the standard.

NOTEBOOK

Badr Al Badoor(IRE) knew her job first time, travelling smoothly and just needing pushing out for a cosy success. Her trainer's first 2yo runner of the year, and Hayley Turner's only ride at the meeting, she is related to some very useful performers and looks a decent sprinting juvenile. She may not want the ground much faster than this. (op 11-1 tchd 15-2)

Diaminda(IRE) raced on the opposite flank of the group to the winner and picked up to pose a threat entering the last, but was held late on. This half-sister to Golden Jubilee Stakes winner Fayr Jag should be winning before too long. (tchd 50-1)

Pearl Sea(IRE) ◆ took a bit of time to find her feet, but was running on from the back of the field on the far side in the latter stages. A half-sister to Listed juvenile winner Vladimir, she looks sure to win a maiden. (op 7-1)

March showed promise. The yard's juveniles have not really been firing, but this one can win when they are. The vet reported that March lost a front shoe. Official explanation: vet said filly lost a front shoe (op 9-2 tchd 11-2)

Dixie Sky(USA), a close relative of smart filly Sander Camillo, hinted that she will benefit from a seventh furlong. (op 33-1 tchd 25-1)

Palladius showed decent speed against the headwind but faded once headed. (op 28-1)

Dusky Queen(IRE), a 90,000euros half-sister to the Sweet Solera Stakes winner Albabilia, was one of the first off the bridle but did stick on. (op 28-1)

Ighraa(IRE) had the most experience of these, but lacks scope and isn't progressing. (op 13-2 tchd 11-2)

Desert Sunrise was runner-up to the Chesham third Lovely Pass on her debut, but this half-sister to Middle Park winner Primo Valentino patently failed to match that form. Perhaps the dead ground didn't suit. (op 2-1)

3561 MG LAW EDUCATION AND SOCIAL CARE LAW MAIDEN STKS 6f

2:30 (2:33) (Class 5) 3-Y-O+ **£2,264** (£673; £336; £168) **Stalls** High

Form RPR

2402 **1** **Uprise**^{11} 3234 3-9-3 73 RyanMoore 6 79
(Sir Michael Stoute) *trckd ldrs: hdwy and cl up over 2f out: rdn to ld wl over 1f out: hdd 1f out and sn drvn: rallied u.p to ld again last 50yds* **4/7^{1}**

434 **2** ½ **Art Form**^{22} 2864 3-8-12 75 (t) KierenFallon 1 72
(Alan McCabe) *hld up in tch: smooth hdwy wl over 2f out: rdn to ld 1f out: hdd and no ex last 50yds* **9/4^{2}**

0 **3** 6 **First Voice (IRE)**^{38} 2381 3-9-3 0 RoystonFfrench 3 58
(James Given) *led: rdn along over 2f out: hdd wl over 1f out: sn drvn and one pce* **28/1**

4 hd **Charmel's Delight** 3-8-9 0 DaleSwift$^{(3)}$ 7 52
(Geoffrey Oldroyd) *s.i.s and in rr: hdwy over 2f out: sn rdn and kpt on same pce* **20/1**

0 **5** 4 **Artillery Train (IRE)**^{6} 3406 3-8-10 0 IanBurns$^{(7)}$ 8 44
(Tim Etherington) *prom: rdn along wl over 2f out: sn drvn and wknd fnl 2f* **33/1**

6 2 ¼ **Mexican Mick** 3-9-3 0 MichaelO'Connell 9 37
(Ian Williams) *s.i.s: a in rr* **10/1^{3}**

7 nse **China Excels**^{94} 5-9-10 0 JimCrowley 4 39
(Sue Smith) *s.i.s: sn chsng ldrs: cl up 1/2-way: rdn wl over 2f out and sn wknd* **25/1**

00 **8** 10 **One Bid Too Many (USA)**^{32} 2543 3-8-9 0 JulieBurke$^{(3)}$ 2
(Derek Shaw) *prom: rdn along 1/2-way: sn wknd* **66/1**

1m 15.71s (2.11) **Going Correction** +0.175s/f (Good)

WFA 3 from 4yo+ 7lb **8** Ran SP% **120.0**

Speed ratings (Par 103): **92,91,83,83,77 74,74,61**

toteswingers 1&2 £1.30, 2&3 £8.50, 1&3 £7.50 CSF £2.05 TOTE £1.70: £1.02, £1.10, £6.60; EX 2.00 Trifecta £20.70 Pool: £1434.36 - 51.20 winning units..

Owner Cheveley Park Stud **Bred** Cheveley Park Stud Ltd **Trained** Newmarket, Suffolk

FOCUS

High-class sprinter Medicean Man won this in 2009. Just two counted on paper in what looked a very modest event, and they had the race between them in the final furlong and a half. The time was over a second slower than the earlier juvenile fillies' maiden and this is not form to treat too positively. The winner rates a small personal best.

3562 TRADE UNION CONGRESS NOVICE STKS 7f

3:00 (3:02) (Class 5) 2-Y-O **£2,264** (£673; £336; £168) **Stalls** High

Form RPR

1 **1** **Maxentius (IRE)**^{30} 2609 2-9-2 0 WilliamBuick 4 95+
(Peter Chapple-Hyam) *hld up in rr: nt clr run 2f out: qcknd up along inner rail to chal ent fnl f: sn led: cleverly* **7/4^{1}**

01 **2** 2 ½ **Silver Ridge (IRE)**^{18} 2983 2-9-2 0 JimCrowley 2 86+
(Ralph Beckett) *set stdy pce: qcknd 3f out: pushed along wl over 1f out: rdn and hung lft appr fnl f: sn hdd and kpt on same pce* **10/3^{3}**

1 **3** 1 ½ **Dashing David (IRE)**^{23} 2817 2-9-5 0 PatDobbs 1 85
(Richard Hannon) *trckd ldng pair: pushed along over 2f out: rdn over 1f out and sn one pce* **11/4^{2}**

1 **4** nk **London Citizen (USA)**^{38} 2370 2-9-2 0 LukeMorris 3 81
(Mrs K Burke) *trckd ldr: effrt and cl up 2f out: sn rdn and one pce appr fnl f* **4/1**

1m 31.19s (4.89) **Going Correction** +0.175s/f (Good) **4** Ran SP% **106.1**

Speed ratings (Par 93): **79,76,74,74**

CSF £7.35 TOTE £2.30; EX 7.00.

Owner Tony Elliott **Bred** Barronstown Stud **Trained** Newmarket, Suffolk

FOCUS

An interesting little event contested by four last-time-out maiden winners. The winner impressed but the form has been rated conservatively as this hasn't proved the strongest novice race in recent years.

NOTEBOOK

Maxentius(IRE) ◆, successful at Folkestone on his debut, followed up in impressive style and looks a nice prospect. Held up in last and finding cover from the wind, it looked for a few seconds that he wasn't going to get out, but then the runner-up moved off the fence and he cruised through for a really easy win. A very fluent mover, he will probably be at his best on a sound surface and there is stamina on his dam's side, which suggests he will get further. He's well worth a crack at a stakes race. (old market op 9-4 new market op 15-8 tchd 2-1)

Silver Ridge(IRE), the most experienced of the four, proved no match for the easy winner but stuck on for second. He'd have preferred genuine soft ground. (old market op 10-3 tchd 4-1 new market tchd 3-1)

Dashing David(IRE), whose trainer had won two of the last three runnings of this, was conceding 3lb to his rivals. Up a quarter of a mile in trip, he could never land a blow but didn't seem to fail for lack of stamina. (old market tchd 15-8 new market op 5-2)

London Citizen(USA)'s initial success came over 6f on the Kempton Polytrack and this different test in better grade found him out. (old market op 4-1 new market tchd 7-2)

3563 SIMPSON MILLAR LEGAL SERVICES H'CAP 1m (R)

3:35 (3:36) (Class 3) (0-95,92) 3-Y-O **£7,439** (£2,213; £1,106; £553) **Stalls** Low

Form RPR

12-6 **1** **Chil The Kite**^{20} 2930 3-9-0 85 RyanMoore 9 95+
(Hughie Morrison) *hld up in rr: gd hdwy on outer wl over 2f out: led jst over 1f out: sn rdn and hung rt ins fnl f: kpt on* **7/4^{1}**

312- **2** 1 ¾ **Jake's Destiny (IRE)**^{223} 7483 3-9-2 87 LiamKeniry 3 93
(George Baker) *t.k.h early: hld up in tch: hdwy on inner over 2f out: rdn over 1f out: styd on fnl f* **33/1**

0005 **3** ¾ **Ghostwriting (USA)**^{23} 2813 3-8-11 82 WilliamBuick 5 86
(John Gosden) *trckd ldng pair: hdwy 3f out: rdn to ld 2f out: hdd appr fnl f and kpt on same pce* **15/2^{3}**

3-32 **4** 1 ¼ **Van Der Art**^{44} 2182 3-9-7 92 KierenFallon 7 93
(Alan Jarvis) *hld up towards rr: swtchd wd and hdwy 2f out: sn rdn and kpt on fnl f* **11/4^{2}**

-110 **5** 2 ¼ **Grey Mirage**^{20} 2916 3-9-4 89 AdamKirby 6 85
(Marco Botti) *trckd ldr: cl up 3f out: rdn 2f out and ev ch: drvn and wknd appr fnl f* **9/1**

4-25 **6** ¾ **Sardanapalus**^{28} 2678 3-8-4 78 JulieBurke$^{(3)}$ 1 72
(Kevin Ryan) *hld up: a in rr* **11/1**

2140 **7** ½ **Nameitwhatyoulike**^{13} 3165 3-8-12 83 PhillipMakin 8 76
(Michael Easterby) *led: rdn along 3f out: hdd 2f out grad wknd* **9/1**

0110 **8** 6 **Stellar Express (IRE)**^{6} 3376 3-9-1 86 LukeMorris 4 65
(Michael Appleby) *chsd ldrs: rdn along 3f out: sn wknd* **16/1**

1m 39.85s (0.15) **Going Correction** +0.175s/f (Good) **8** Ran SP% **112.0**

Speed ratings (Par 103): **106,104,103,102,100 99,98,92**

toteswingers 1&2 £10.30, 2&3 £15.10, 1&3 £3.90 CSF £59.16 CT £350.59 TOTE £2.30: £1.10, £4.80, £2.30; EX 55.50 Trifecta £199.40 Pool: £1544.60 - 5.73 winning units..

Owner Hazel Lawrence & Graham Doyle **Bred** Whitsbury Manor Stud & Pigeon House Stud **Trained** East Ilsley, Berks

FOCUS

A decent handicap. They went a brisk gallop and those who raced up with the pace paid for it late on. The winner should do better still.

NOTEBOOK

Chil The Kite's reappearance sixth had been franked when the winner Fast Or Free followed up in the Britannia. He swept through from the back of the field to win well, but is not straightforward and drifted to his right as he assumed control. There could be more improvement in him. (op 15-8)

Jake's Destiny(IRE), off the track for seven months, ran on up the inside after needing to be switched. This was a pleasing turf debut, and judging by his action faster ground will suit him. (op 22-1)

Ghostwriting(USA) has dropped to 3lb below the mark off which he won a nursery at this track last September, but he had done better at Kempton last time and this was another fair effort. A winning opportunity should be found for him. (op 6-1)

Van Der Art went up 8lb for her York second but she continues on the upgrade. Ending up taking the winner's route down the centre of the track, she was not stopping at the end of this longer trip. (op 4-1)

Grey Mirage ran better than he had when last over C&D on his previous start but has not gone on as expected from his Esher Cup win. He was not helped by racing up with the pace here, and his rider also reported that the colt's saddle slipped. Official explanation: jockey said saddle slipped (op 7-1)

Sardanapalus merely stayed on past beaten rivals. (op 10-1 tchd 12-1)

3564 PRESERVE ACCESS TO JUSTICE H'CAP 1m 6f 132y

4:10 (4:11) (Class 4) (0-85,85) 4-Y-O+ **£4,204** (£1,251; £625; £312) **Stalls** Low

Form RPR

-203 **1** **Getabuzz**^{20} 2921 4-8-13 77 DavidAllan 1 87+
(Tim Easterby) *hld up: gd hdwy on inner 3f out: led 2f out: rdn over 1f out: kpt on wl* **15/2^{3}**

-105 **2** 1 ¾ **Royal Swain (IRE)**[16] 3036 6-8-12 **76**.......................... RobertWinston 3 82
(Alan Swinbank) *hld up in tch: hdwy 3f out: chsd ldrs 2f out: rdn to chse wnr ent fnl f: no imp towards fin* **9/1**

-034 **3** ½ **Purification (IRE)**[16] 3036 4-9-7 **85**..............................(b) WilliamBuick 9 90
(John Gosden) *t.k.h: led after 1f: rdn along and hdd 2f out: swtchd rt and drvn over 1f out: kpt on same pce* **9/2**[1]

3-44 **4** *nse* **Jonny Delta**[14] 3114 5-8-9 **73**... KierenFallon 6 78
(Jim Goldie) *hld up: hdwy wl over 3f out: rdn to chse ldrs 2f out: kpt on u.p fnl f* **7/1**[2]

22 **5** ¾ **Luggers Hall (IRE)**[21] 2887 4-9-0 **78**.......................... TomQueally 12 82
(Tony Carroll) *hld up towards rr: hdwy over 3f out: rdn 2f out and sn chsng ldrs: no imp fnl f* **8/1**

2322 **6** *shd* **Favorite Girl (GER)**[12] 3180 4-8-4 **68**.............................. LukeMorris 10 72+
(Michael Appleby) *hld up towards rr: hdwy over 3f out: rdn 2f out: kpt on appr fnl f: nrst fin* **7/1**[2]

0006 **7** 1 **Red Jade**[13] 3163 7-8-9 **73**......................................(p) MichaelO'Connell 7 76
(Mrs K Burke) *trckd ldng pair: hdwy and cl up 4f out: rdn along 3f out: wknd fnl 2f* **9/1**

-146 **8** *shd* **Bradbury (IRE)**[23] 2827 4-8-5 **69**..............................(p) AndrewElliott 13 72
(James Bethell) *trckd ldrs: effrt over 3f out: sn rdn along and wknd over 2f out* **20/1**

3406 **9** *nk* **Embsay Crag**[25] 2751 6-8-2 **66**.. KellyHarrison 5 68
(Kate Walton) *t.k.h: cl up: rdn along over 3f out: drvn 2f out: wkng whn n.m.r appr fnl f* **20/1**

0-05 **10** *nk* **Harvey's Hope**[28] 2666 6-8-6 **70**.................................. RoystonFfrench 2 72
(Keith Reveley) *hld up: a towards rr* **16/1**

-005 **11** 1 **Activate**[14] 3114 5-9-5 **83**.. PhillipMakin 11 84
(Kevin Ryan) *a towards rr* **9/1**

0/0- **12** 1 **Liberate**[259] 4423 9-9-5 **83**... AdamKirby 4 82
(Anabel K Murphy) *a towards rr* **50/1**

12-0 **13** 3 **Singzak**[48] 2093 4-8-8 **72**... PaddyAspell 8 67
(Michael Easterby) *t.k.h: led 1f: trckd ldng pair: rdn along over 3f out: sn wknd* **33/1**

3m 15.75s (8.35) **Going Correction** +0.175s/f (Good) **13** Ran SP% **116.4**
Speed ratings (Par 105): **84,83,82,82,82 82,81,81,81,81 80,80,78**
toteswingers 1&2 £12.90, 2&3 £7.20, 1&3 £6.50 CSF £68.05 CT £341.19 TOTE £10.40: £3.30, £3.10, £2.00; EX 64.40 Trifecta £327.00 Pool: £1430.53 - 3.23 winning units..
Owner Langham Hall Stud Three **Bred** Peter Botham **Trained** Great Habton, N Yorks

FOCUS
A fair handicap, but it was run at a steady pace and they finished in a heap behind the winner. Consequently there are one or two doubts over the form. The level is set around the runner-up.

3565 COMMUNICATION WORKERS UNION HUMANITARIAN AID EBF MAIDEN FILLIES' STKS 1m 2f 60y
4:45 (4:46) (Class 5) 3-Y-0+ **£3,557** (£1,058; £529; £264) **Stalls** Low

Form RPR

6 **1** **Emirates Queen**[39] 2344 3-8-12 0.................................... KierenFallon 3 90+
(Luca Cumani) *led to s: hld up in midfield: hdwy whn n.m.r 3f out: swtchd to outer and str run fr over 1f out to ld last 100yds: readily* **11/4**[1]

2 1 ¾ **Seal Of Approval** 3-8-12 0... PatDobbs 5 85+
(James Fanshawe) *hld up towards rr: stdy hdwy on outer wl over 2f out: rdn to ld ent fnl f: hdd and no ex last 100yds* **50/1**

45 **3** 3 **Ghusoon**[22] 2849 3-8-12 0... NickyMackay 12 79
(John Gosden) *trckd ldrs: hdwy 3f out: chal 2f out: sn rdn to ld and edgd lft wl over 1f out: hdd ent fnl f: one pce* **33/1**

5 **4** 1 ¼ **Missouri Belle**[15] 3079 3-8-12 0.. WilliamBuick 6 77
(John Gosden) *hld up in tch: hdwy 3f out: rdn to chse ldrs 2f out: one pce appr fnl f* **12/1**

4-5 **5** ½ **Miracle Maid**[54] 1887 3-8-12 0.. AdamKirby 7 76
(Clive Cox) *trckd ldr: effrt 3f out: sn rdn along: drvn and edgd rt wl over 1f out: one pce after* **11/2**

3- **6** 4 ½ **Shada (IRE)**[308] 5445 3-8-12 0.. RyanMoore 8 67
(Sir Michael Stoute) *trckd ldng pair: pushed along 3f out: rdn over 2f out: sn wknd and btn whn hmpd over 1f out* **3/1**[2]

5 **7** 2 ½ **Bobs Her Uncle**[23] 2826 3-8-12 0..................................... AndrewElliott 4 63
(James Bethell) *chsd ldng pair: pushed along over 4f out: rdn and n.m.r 3f out: sn swtchd rt: drvn whn n.m.r over 2f out: sn wknd* **40/1**

2-02 **8** 1 **Coplow**[15] 3070 3-8-12 81.. KieranO'Neill 11 61
(Richard Hannon) *led: pushed along over 3f out: rdn over 2f out: sn hdd & wknd* **7/2**[3]

0- **9** 1 ½ **Simply**[251] 7025 3-8-12 0.. RobertWinston 2 58
(Eve Johnson Houghton) *hld up: a towards rr* **100/1**

10 ¾ **Symposia** 3-8-12 0.. TomQueally 1 57
(Sir Henry Cecil) *a in rr* **8/1**

11 62 **Connie Carlton** 3-8-12 0.. JamieMackay 9
(David Thompson) *t.k.h early: a in rr: outpcd and wl bhd fnl 3f* **200/1**

2m 11.07s (1.67) **Going Correction** +0.175s/f (Good) **11** Ran SP% **116.9**
Speed ratings (Par 100): **100,98,96,95,94 91,89,88,87,86 37**
toteswingers 1&2 £29.70, 2&3 £40.80, 1&3 £14.30 CSF £148.84 TOTE £4.10: £1.50, £11.10, £6.70; EX 153.10 Trifecta £1507.40 Part won. Pool: £2033.48 - 0.64 winning units..
Owner Sheikh Mohammed Obaid Al Maktoum **Bred** Darley **Trained** Newmarket, Suffolk

FOCUS
A fascinating maiden contested by some well-bred fillies. Decent form, even with the eighth below par. The winner was a bit better than the bare form.

3566 THE GMB - BRITAIN'S GENERAL UNION H'CAP (DIV I) 6f
5:20 (5:21) (Class 5) (0-70,70) 3-Y-0 **£2,264** (£673; £336; £168) **Stalls** High

Form RPR

42-3 **1** **Duke Of Aricabeau (IRE)**[12] 3184 3-9-2 **65**.............. RobertWinston 10 73
(Mrs K Burke) *trckd ldrs: hdwy to chse ldr wl over 1f out: swtchd lft and rdn to ld ent fnl f: sn drvn and edgd rt: jst hld on* **5/2**[2]

-531 **2** *nse* **Picture Dealer**[17] 2996 3-9-7 **70**.. TomQueally 2 85+
(Gary Moore) *hld up in rr: nt clr run 2f out and again over 1f out: gd hdwy on inner rail ent fnl f: styng on whn swtchd lft 75yds out: fin strly: jst failed* **15/8**[1]

3-00 **3** 1 **Sir Windsorlot (IRE)**[31] 2591 3-8-9 **58**..................(t) MichaelO'Connell 6 63
(John Quinn) *hld up in tch: hdwy on inner to chse ldng pair over 1f out: swtchd lft and drvn ins fnl f: styd on wl towards fin* **8/1**

3651 **4** ¾ **New Decade**[11] 3218 3-9-2 **65** 6ex....................................... LukeMorris 9 68
(Milton Bradley) *led: rdn clr 2f out: drvn and hdd ent fnl f: kpt on same pce* **7/1**

6202 **5** 4 ½ **Ambitious Icarus**[7] 3357 3-8-11 **60**.......................(e) RobbieFitzpatrick 4 48
(Richard Guest) *plld hrd: chsd ldrs: rdn along over 2f out: no imp* **16/1**

600- **6** ¾ **Simpson Millar**[256] 6912 3-8-3 **52**.................................. KellyHarrison 3 38
(Noel Wilson) *in tch on outer: hdwy to chse ldrs 2f out: sn rdn and one pce* **100/1**

000 **7** ½ **Perfect Policy**[41] 2262 3-8-6 **55**..................................(b[1]) NickyMackay 1 39
(Ralph Beckett) *chsd ldrs on outer: rdn along wl over 1f out: sn one pce* **25/1**

345 **8** 11 **Compton Prince**[59] 1723 3-9-6 **69**.. AdamKirby 8 18
(Clive Cox) *chsd ldr: rdn along 1/2-way: sn wknd* **13/2**[3]

60-6 **9** 2 ¼ **Irrational**[57] 1798 3-8-13 **62**.. RoystonFfrench 7
(Bryan Smart) *dwlt: sn chsng ldrs: rdn along wl over 2f out and sn wknd* **11/1**

1m 16.15s (2.55) **Going Correction** +0.175s/f (Good) **9** Ran SP% **119.4**
Speed ratings (Par 99): **90,89,88,87,81 80,79,65,62**
toteswingers 1&2 £2.70, 2&3 £4.80, 1&3 CSF £7.90 CT £32.43 TOTE £2.80: £1.20, £1.50, £2.20; EX 11.80 Trifecta £112.10 Pool: £2680.59 - 17.69 winning units..
Owner McMahon Thoroughbreds Ltd **Bred** Castleton Lyons & Kilboy Estate **Trained** Middleham Moor, N Yorks

FOCUS
Division one of an ordinary sprint handicap for 3yos, and reasonable form for the grade. They went steadily until halfway and the time was 1.37sec slower than the second division. A small personal best from the winner, but the runner-up should have won.

3567 THE GMB - BRITAIN'S GENERAL UNION H'CAP (DIV II) 6f
5:50 (5:53) (Class 5) (0-70,70) 3-Y-0 **£2,264** (£673; £336; £168) **Stalls** High

Form RPR

-101 **1** **Johnny Cavagin**[32] 2540 3-8-12 **61**..............................(t) RobertWinston 8 77
(Richard Guest) *trckd ldrs: smooth hdwy and nt clr run 2f out and again over 1f out: squeezed through to ld ent fnl f: sn clr* **4/1**[3]

-132 **2** 4 **Dream Walker (FR)**[5] 3421 3-9-1 **64**.......................... RoystonFfrench 5 67
(Ian McInnes) *cl up: rdn wl over 1f out and ev ch tl drvn and one pce ent fnl f* **5/2**[1]

2-12 **3** 2 ¾ **Untold Melody**[42] 2244 3-9-5 **68**..................................... PhillipMakin 10 62
(Kevin Ryan) *cl up: led over 2f out: rdn over 1f out: hdd ent fnl f: sn one pce* **10/3**[2]

0021 **4** *nk* **Medam**[22] 2862 3-7-10 **52**.. ShirleyTeasdale[(7)] 2 45
(Shaun Harris) *trckd ldrs on outer: cl up 1/2-way: effrt 2f out: rdn and ev ch over 1f out: one pce ent fnl f* **10/1**

-050 **5** 2 ¼ **Magic Bounty**[21] 2878 3-8-6 **55**..................................... KellyHarrison 11 41
(Tim Easterby) *chsd ldrs: hdwy and cl up over 2f out: sn rdn and ev ch tl wknd appr fnl f* **12/1**

4-33 **6** 2 ½ **Conowen**[64] 1622 3-9-5 **68**.. PatDobbs 7 46
(William Jarvis) *a towards rr* **8/1**

-600 **7** 1 ¼ **Tallula (IRE)**[12] 3184 3-8-2 **51** oh6................................ JamieMackay 6 25
(Micky Hammond) *led: rdn along and hdd 1/2-way: grad wknd* **100/1**

P-06 **8** ¾ **Especially Red (IRE)**[14] 3118 3-9-2 **65**.......................... PaddyAspell 4 37
(Lisa Williamson) *dwlt: in tch on outer: rdn along wl over 2f out and sn wknd* **66/1**

3-60 **9** 14 **Knight Vision**[38] 2375 3-9-2 **65**... AdamKirby 1
(David Nicholls) *in tch on outer: reminders 1/2-way: sn wknd* **8/1**

1m 14.78s (1.18) **Going Correction** +0.175s/f (Good) **9** Ran SP% **113.1**
Speed ratings (Par 99): **99,93,90,89,86 83,81,80,61**
toteswingers: 1&2 £4.20, 2&3 £3.00, 1&3 £3.70 CSF £14.07 CT £35.85 TOTE £4.10: £1.50, £1.40, £1.60; EX 14.20 Trifecta £32.50 Pool: £1820.55 - 41.42 winning units..
Owner A Bell **Bred** A Bell **Trained** Stainforth, S Yorks

FOCUS
This was run in a time 1.37sec quicker than the previous division. The form seems sound enough with the winner much improved.
Especially Red(IRE) Official explanation: jockey said saddle slipped
T/Plt: £328.90 to a £1 stake. Pool of £73599.46 - 163.32 winning tickets. T/Qpdt: £33.40 to a £1 stake. Pool of £7558.69 - 167.38 winning tickets. JR

2970 FOLKESTONE (R-H)
Friday, June 29

OFFICIAL GOING: Good to firm (round course 8.5; straight course: far side 7.7; stands' side 8.6)
Wind: strong across Weather: bright and breezy

3568 FGS PLANT BRITISH STALLION STUDS EBF MAIDEN FILLIES' STKS 6f
2:20 (2:21) (Class 5) 3-Y-0+ **£3,234** (£962; £481; £240) **Stalls** High

Form RPR

3-5 **1** **Byton**[49] 2042 3-8-12 0.. DaneO'Neill 6 79
(Henry Candy) *racd against stands' rail: w ldr tl led 1/2-way: mde rest: rdn and asserted over 1f out: r.o wl: comf* **85/40**[2]

4-30 **2** 1 ½ **Al Janadeirya**[42] 2251 4-9-5 70.................................... RichardHughes 2 76
(Peter Chapple-Hyam) *hld in tch: hdwy to chse ldrs 1/2-way: effrt to press wnr and edgd lft 2f out: unable qck over 1f out: one pce after* **4/1**[3]

0- **3** ½ **Macchiara**[286] 6169 3-8-12 0..[1] SebSanders 7 73
(Rae Guest) *s.i.s: sn bustled along in rr: hdwy and swtchd rt over 2f out: edging bk lft over 1f out: kpt on wl ins fnl f* **25/1**

2 **4** *nk* **Palmette**[15] 3082 3-8-12 0.. RobertHavlin 1 72
(John Gosden) *chsd ldrs: rdn whn short of room and hmpd 2f out: stl chsng ldrs and drvn over 1f out: kpt on same pce* **11/10**[1]

53 **5** ½ **Charming (IRE)**[11] 3235 3-8-12 0.................................. KirstyMilczarek 4 70
(Olivia Maylam) *t.k.h: hld up wl in tch: swtchd rt and effrt 2f out: kpt on same pce u.p fnl f* **8/1**

4044 **6** 13 **Miakora**[35] 2461 4-9-5 46.. PatCosgrave 3 30
(Michael Quinn) *in tch towards rr: rdn and struggling 2f out: wknd over 1f out: wl btn and eased ins fnl f* **66/1**

5 **7** ¾ **Bazron (IRE)**[18] 2974 4-9-2 0..................................... AdamBeschizza[(3)] 8 28
(Des Donovan) *chsd ldrs: rdn over 2f out: struggling whn sltly hmpd wl over 1f out: sn wknd* **33/1**

00-0 **8** ½ **Pink Belini**[167] 182 3-8-12 46...(t) DavidProbert 5 24
(Alan McCabe) *hld tl 1/2-way: struggling whn sltly hmpd and flashed tail u.p wl over 1f out: sn wknd* **100/1**

1m 11.09s (-1.61) **Going Correction** -0.275s/f (Firm)
WFA 3 from 4yo 7lb **8** Ran SP% **120.0**
Speed ratings (Par 100): **99,97,96,95,95 77,76,76**
totewingers: 1&2 £3.10, 2&3 £7.40, 1&3 £8.80 CSF £11.54 TOTE £3.30: £1.10, £1.40, £5.40; EX 14.80.
Owner Major M G Wyatt **Bred** Mrs Sheila Oakes **Trained** Kingston Warren, Oxon

FOCUS
A modest fillies' maiden which was sound run. The form is rated through the runner-up.

Macchiara Official explanation: jockey said gates flicked back as stalls opened

3569 FGS ACCESS MEDIAN AUCTION MAIDEN STKS 7f (S)
2:50 (2:50) (Class 6) 2-Y-O **£1,704** (£503; £251) **Stalls** High

Form RPR
03 **1** **Senafe**[18] 2977 2-8-12 0 SebSanders 1 82+
(Marco Botti) *mde all and grad crossed towards stands' rail: in command and pushed clr over 1f out: comf* **14/1**
23 **2** *4* **Super Simon (IRE)**[15] 3074 2-9-3 0 NeilCallan 2 77
(Paul D'Arcy) *chsd ldrs: rdn 4f out: drvn fr 1/2-way: chsd clr wnr 1f out: no imp* **2/1**[2]
56 **3** *1 3/4* **The Sixties**[6] 3368 2-9-3 0 MatthewDavies 5 72
(Mick Channon) *chsd wnr: rdn and fnd little over 1f out: 3rd and wl hld fnl f* **7/4**[1]
4 *13* **Rio Cato** 2-8-12 0 ShaneKelly 7 33
(Ed Dunlop) *s.i.s: rn green and sn pushed along in rr: no ch w ldrs 2f out: swtchd rt and sme hdwy over 1f out: kpt on* **20/1**
5 *2 1/4* **Double Jeopardy** 2-9-3 0 RobertHavlin 6 32
(Dr Jon Scargill) *stdd s: rn green and bhd: switching rt and sme hdwy over 3f out: outpcd and wl btn 2f out* **66/1**
40 **6** *9* **Lawful**[22] 2844 2-9-3 0 (b[1]) GeorgeBaker 3 9
(Paul Fitzsimons) *hld up in tch: hdwy to chse ldng trio 3f out: rdn and btn 2f out: sn fdd: eased fnl f: t.o* **25/1**
0 **7** *4* **Diva Cavallina**[9] 3282 2-8-12 0 JohnFahy 9
(Alan McCabe) *chsd ldrs: rdn and struggling 1/2-way: wl bhd fnl 2f: t.o* **50/1**
8 *1 1/2* **Age Of Bronze** 2-9-3 0 RichardHughes 4
(Richard Hannon) *dwlt: a towards rr: lost tch over 2f out: t.o* **7/1**[3]

1m 25.1s (-2.20) **Going Correction** -0.275s/f (Firm) **8** Ran SP% **100.9**
Speed ratings (Par 91): **101,96,94,79,77 66,62,60**
toteswingers: 1&2 £2.60, 1&3 £3.60, 2&3 £1.20 CSF £32.43 TOTE £14.60: £2.90, £1.10, £1.10; EX 37.40.
Owner Mubarak Al Naemi **Bred** Mrs M L Parry **Trained** Newmarket, Suffolk
■ Overcoat was withdrawn on vet's advice (6/1, deduct 10p in the £ under R4).

FOCUS
A fair juvenile maiden for the grade.

NOTEBOOK
Senafe reportedly looked a nice individual in the paddock beforehand. She was the second consecutive winner on the card sired by Byron, and Seb Sanders did well to bag the near stands' rail from a low draw. She progressed from her modest Newmarket debut (6f, good to firm) in May over the same trip at Pontefract this month, but she has found significant improvement for this step up to 7f. This was a good performance to make all, winning going away at the end. She looks a decent prospect at up to 1m this term. (op 16-1)
Super Simon(IRE) arrived with very solid form credentials, but was rousted quite early in the contest and never seemed comfortable in the race. The combination of faster ground than he has raced on thus far, on an undulating track, resulted in a below-par display. He is one to keep faith with over this trip on a more conventional course, and on good ground or slightly easier. (tchd 5-2)
The Sixties ran sixth in the Chesham Stakes at Royal Ascot over this trip on good to soft ground last week. He gives this form some substance, but doesn't appear to appreciate this 7f trip. A drop back to 6f, possibly even 5f, on easier ground may suit. (op 15-8 tchd 2-1 and 6-4)
Rio Cato started slowly and raced green, but will know more next time. (tchd 25-1)

3570 GDS RECRUITMENT GOING NATIONAL CLAIMING STKS 6f
3:20 (3:20) (Class 5) 3-Y-O+ **£2,385** (£704; £352) **Stalls** High

Form RPR
3624 **1** **Sandbetweenourtoes (IRE)**[11] 3229 3-8-8 74 (tp) ShaneKelly 2 76
(Brian Meehan) *racd against stands' rail: mde virtually all: rdn 2f out: kpt on and in command fnl 100yds* **13/2**
1-13 **2** *1 1/4* **Aye Aye Digby (IRE)**[34] 2482 7-9-8 78 GeorgeBaker 1 81
(Patrick Chamings) *w wnr: pushed along over 1f out: rdn and fnd little ins fnl f: btn fnl 100yds* **5/2**[2]
5150 **3** *nk* **Beat The Bell**[16] 3045 7-8-11 79 (p) LeonnaMayor(5) 4 74
(Jamie Osborne) *t.k.h: sn pressing ldrs: rdn and ev ch 2f out: drvn and unable qck over 1f out: one pce after* **9/2**[3]
0064 **4** *2* **Haadeeth**[26] 2731 5-8-12 78 MatthewCosham(3) 3 67
(David Evans) *taken down early: t.k.h: in tch: rdn and effrt 2f out: no ex and btn ins fnl f* **7/1**
6003 **5** *1 3/4* **Silenzio**[17] 3016 4-9-1 73 RichardHughes 5 61
(Richard Hannon) *bustled along leaving stalls: in tch: rdn and effrt 2f out: unable qck u.p and btn 1f out* **7/4**[1]

1m 11.17s (-1.53) **Going Correction** -0.275s/f (Firm)
WFA 3 from 4yo+ 7lb **5** Ran SP% **109.0**
Speed ratings (Par 103): **99,97,96,94,91**
CSF £22.32 TOTE £7.20: £4.80, £1.10; EX 22.10.Sandbetweenourtoes was claimed by R Curtis for £8000.
Owner Trelawny II **Bred** Barouche Stud Ireland Ltd **Trained** Manton, Wilts

FOCUS
A decent claimer. They went an honest gallop but the time was relatively modest. The winner rates a small personal best, but had the advantage of the rail.

3571 FGS PLANT FOLKESTONE HAMMER (A H'CAP) 6f
3:55 (3:56) (Class 4) (0-85,85) 3-Y-O+ **£9,703** (£2,887; £1,443; £721) **Stalls** High

Form RPR
61 **1** **Poole Harbour (IRE)**[32] 2543 3-9-3 85 RichardHughes 12 95+
(Richard Hannon) *taken down early: in tch: hdwy to chse ldr 2f out: swtchd rt and rdn to chal over 1f out: carried rt and sustained chal fnl f to ld last strides* **5/2**[1]
4-50 **2** *hd* **Fair Value (IRE)**[32] 2558 4-9-7 82 SebSanders 11 93
(Simon Dow) *led and racd against stands' rail: rdn 2f out: clr w wnr over 1f out: kpt edging rt u.p fnl f: hdd last strides* **9/1**
-005 **3** *4* **Flynn's Boy**[16] 3049 4-8-13 74 RobertHavlin 2 72+
(Rae Guest) *hld up in rr: swtchd rt and hdwy wl over 1f out: hdwy u.p to chse clr ldng pair 1f out: no imp* **14/1**
301 **4** *1/2* **Close To The Edge (IRE)**[29] 2636 4-9-5 80 ShaneKelly 6 77
(Alan McCabe) *in tch in midfield: shuffled bk and sltly hmpd wl over 1f out: rallied u.p and pressing for 3rd 1f out: kpt on but no ch w ldrs* **14/1**
0-64 **5** *1 3/4* **Yurituni**[34] 2487 5-8-13 79 (v) AmyScott(5) 13 70
(Eve Johnson Houghton) *in tch: rdn and effrt 2f out: outpcd and btn over 1f out: one pce and wl hld fnl f* **20/1**
-322 **6** *1 3/4* **Arctic Lynx (IRE)**[43] 2195 5-9-9 84 DavidProbert 10 69+
(John Best) *stdd s: hld up in rr: effrt but stl plenty to do whn swtchd rt and nt clr run wl over 1f out: plugged on: no ch* **9/2**[2]
0403 **7** *1 1/4* **We Have A Dream**[11] 3225 7-9-8 83 MartinDwyer 9 64
(William Muir) *chsd ldrs: rdn 1/2-way: outpcd u.p and btn over 1f out: fdd fnl f* **7/1**[3]
0-60 **8** *1* **Bless You**[21] 2890 4-9-5 80 DaneO'Neill 5 58
(Henry Candy) *in tch: rdn and struggling ent fnl 2f: wknd over 1f out* **8/1**
0266 **9** *1* **Piscean (USA)**[17] 3004 7-9-9 84 GeorgeBaker 7 59
(Tom Keddy) *stdd and dropped in bhd: a bhd* **10/1**
0000 **10** *1/2* **Ginger Ted (IRE)**[13] 3169 5-8-10 74 (v[1]) RyanClark(3) 3 47
(Stuart Williams) *sn rdn along: struggling u.p over 2f out: wknd wl over 1f out* **28/1**
-345 **11** *6* **Lunar Deity**[25] 2764 3-8-12 80 NeilCallan 1 32
(Eve Johnson Houghton) *chsd ldrs: wknd u.p over 2f out: bhd whn sltly hmpd wl over 1f out: bhd fnl f* **10/1**

1m 10.28s (-2.42) **Going Correction** -0.275s/f (Firm)
WFA 3 from 4yo+ 7lb **11** Ran SP% **120.1**
Speed ratings (Par 105): **105,104,99,98,96 94,92,91,89,89 81**
toteswingers 1&2 £9.30, 2&3 £27.70, 1&3 £10.50 CSF £26.46 CT £275.60 TOTE £3.40: £1.50, £3.80, £4.80; EX 30.50.
Owner The Heffer Syndicate **Bred** Lisieux Stud **Trained** East Everleigh, Wilts

FOCUS
A fair sprint handicap but few got involved. The winner built on his latest AW win.
Piscean(USA) Official explanation: trainer's rep said gelding made a noise

3572 HOMELEIGH TIMBER AND BUILDING SUPPLIES H'CAP 1m 7f 92y
4:30 (4:30) (Class 5) (0-75,75) 4-Y-O+ **£2,385** (£704; £352) **Stalls** High

Form RPR
-112 **1** **Alfraamsey**[9] 3283 4-8-10 64 RichardHughes 2 75+
(Sheena West) *in tch: hdwy to ld over 7f out: mde rest: rdn 2f out: in command fr over 1f out: eased cl home* **6/4**[1]
0650 **2** *3/4* **Saborido (USA)**[18] 2978 6-9-7 75 GeorgeBaker 8 83
(Amanda Perrett) *hld up in tch: hdwy to chse ldr 8f out tl 7f out: rdn and chsd wnr again over 2f out: kpt on u.p but a hld* **15/2**
-000 **3** *9* **Hidden Valley**[36] 2412 4-9-2 70 (v) DavidProbert 1 66
(Andrew Balding) *led for 3f: chsd ldrs after: rdn and outpcd over 2f out: wnt 3rd over 1f out: no imp and wl btn fnl f* **4/1**[2]
036/ **4** *3/4* **Clowance House**[25] 5870 6-9-0 75 (t) WilliamTwiston-Davies(7) 6 70
(Barry Brennan) *hld up in rr: hdwy on outer 4f out: c centre over 2f out: sn rdn and no real prog: wl btn but plugged on fnl f* **13/2**
355- **5** *2* **Dr Finley (IRE)**[204] 7674 5-8-7 64 SimonPearce(3) 3 57
(Lydia Pearce) *t.k.h: hld up in tch towards rr: rdn and struggling 3f out: sn outpcd and wl btn 2f out: plugged on fnl f* **12/1**
/50- **6** *2* **Lombok**[35] 6469 6-8-6 63 (b) AdamBeschizza(3) 5 53
(Gary Moore) *dwlt and pushed along early: in tch: rdn and effrt over 3f out: wknd over 2f out* **33/1**
00/6 **7** *5* **Princely Hero (IRE)**[26] 1890 8-8-13 67 (tp) SamHitchcott 4 51
(Chris Gordon) *chsd ldr tl led after 3f: hdd over 7f out: sn rdn: lost pl over 5f out: bhd fnl 2f* **33/1**
623- **8** *7* **Native Colony**[257] 6891 4-9-6 74 (p) NeilCallan 7 49
(Roger Varian) *chsd ldrs tl wnt 2nd 7f out tl over 2f out: 3rd and wkng u.p 2f out: sn fdd* **11/2**[3]

3m 22.97s (-6.73) **Going Correction** -0.35s/f (Firm) course record **8** Ran SP% **114.1**
Speed ratings (Par 103): **103,102,97,97,96 95,92,88**
toteswingers 1&2 £3.20, 2&3 £6.10, 1&3 £2.60 CSF £13.60 CT £36.73 TOTE £2.00: £1.10, £2.30, £1.80; EX 12.20.
Owner Tapestry Partnership **Bred** G Hedley & Mike Channon Bloodstock Limited **Trained** Falmer, E Sussex

FOCUS
A fair staying handicap but muddling form. The winner is rated a bit closer to his old best.

3573 BSS MAIDSTONE H'CAP 1m 4f
5:05 (5:05) (Class 6) (0-60,59) 4-Y-O+ **£2,045** (£603; £302) **Stalls** High

Form RPR
6320 **1** **Rodrigo De Freitas (IRE)**[15] 3086 5-9-3 55 (v) PatCosgrave 2 62
(Jim Boyle) *chsd ldrs: rdn and effrt to chse ldr 2f out: drvn and chal over 1f out: led ins fnl f: r.o wl* **9/1**
1200 **2** *1 1/2* **El Libertador (USA)**[37] 2396 6-9-0 52 (b) RichardHughes 1 57
(Eric Wheeler) *stdd after s: hld up in rr: rdn and hdwy over 1f out: rdn and r.o to chse wnr fnl 75yds: kpt on but nvr looked like chalng wnr* **15/2**
0053 **3** *1* **Taqaat (USA)**[16] 3047 4-9-6 58 NeilCallan 8 61
(Tim McCarthy) *awkward leaving stalls: sn led: hung lft to paddock exit and hdd briefly over 9f out: rdn and hung lft wl over 1f out: hdd and no ex ins fnl f* **7/1**
1/51 **4** *1 1/2* **Pindar (GER)**[13] 3137 8-9-0 52 DaraghO'Donohoe 9 53
(Barney Curley) *t.k.h: chsd ldrs: hmpd bnd over 9f out: hdwy to chse ldr 7f out: rdn and unable qck over 2f out: outpcd and btn 1f out* **7/4**[1]
5534 **5** *1/2* **Barbirolli**[17] 2997 10-8-4 45 AdamBeschizza(3) 5 45
(William Stone) *pushed along in last trio early: hdwy to chse ldrs 6f out: unable qck u.p over 2f out: plugged on but no threat to wnr fnl f* **22/1**
0/3- **6** *1 1/4* **Screaming Brave**[26] 355 6-9-2 59 (t) HarryPoulton(5) 4 57
(Sheena West) *hld up in last trio: effrt on outer over 2f out: hung lft and no imp over 1f out: nvr trbld ldrs* **9/2**[3]
0326 **7** *1 1/4* **Gower Rules (IRE)**[11] 3222 4-8-12 57 WilliamTwiston-Davies(7) 6 53
(John Bridger) *in tch: lost pl over 5f out: rdn and no prog over 2f out: one pce and wl hld fnl 2f* **7/2**[2]
-000 **8** *4 1/2* **Disturbia (IRE)**[13] 3137 4-8-7 45 KirstyMilczarek 7 34
(Olivia Maylam) *chsd ldrs: lost pl 4f out: bhd and rdn over 2f out: wknd 2f out* **25/1**

2m 38.88s (-2.02) **Going Correction** -0.35s/f (Firm) **8** Ran SP% **119.2**
Speed ratings (Par 101): **92,91,90,89,89 88,87,84**
toteswingers 1&2 £5.50, 2&3 £5.30, 1&3 £7.9 CSF £76.84 CT £508.14 TOTE £9.90: £2.30, £1.80, £3.60; EX 46.70.
Owner The Rodrigo De Freitas Partnership **Bred** Castlemartin Stud And Skymarc Farm **Trained** Epsom, Surrey

FOCUS
A moderate middle-distance handicap, and unconvincing form. The winner is rated to his best of the past year.

3574 FGS ACCESS H'CAP 1m 1f 149y
5:40 (5:40) (Class 5) (0-75,78) 3-Y-O+ **£2,385** (£704; £352) **Stalls** Centre

Form RPR
2200 **1** **Franco Is My Name**[76] 1374 6-9-11 72 (p) DaneO'Neill 7 85
(Peter Hedger) *hld up in last trio: hdwy to chse ldrs over 2f out: rdn to ld over 1f out: in command and idling fnl f: pushed out* **12/1**
04-1 **2** *3 3/4* **Watheeq (USA)**[35] 2449 3-8-12 71 NeilCallan 5 76+
(Roger Varian) *chsd ldrs: effrt on outer to chse ldr over 3f out: rdn to ld 2f out: drvn and hdd over 1f out: sn btn and plugged on same pce after* **8/13**[1]

4022 **3** 4½ **Whitby Jet (IRE)**[24] 2792 4-9-7 **75**................ WilliamTwiston-Davies(7) 4 71
(Ed Vaughan) *bhd: hdwy over 3f out: swtchd rt and effrt 2f out: chsd ldng pair over 1f out: no imp* **4/1**[2]
5424 **4** 6 **Emperor Vespasian**[17] 3002 3-8-11 **70**....................(b[1]) DavidProbert 3 53
(Andrew Balding) *chsd ldrs: 3rd and unable qck u.p over 2f out: wknd over 1f out* **14/1**
-610 **5** 7 **Understory (USA)**[29] 2637 5-9-8 **74**........................... MarkCoumbe(5) 9 42
(Tim McCarthy) *pressed ldr tl led 7f out: rdn and hdd 2f out: sn wknd* **16/1**
43-3 **6** 25 **Foxhaven**[18] 2984 10-10-0 **75**...(v) GeorgeBaker 6
(Patrick Chamings) *hld up in last pair: shkn up and no rspnse 3f out: sn lost tch: t.o and eased ins fnl f* **11/1**[3]
-040 **7** 18 **Audacious**[24] 2801 4-9-13 **74**.. PatCosgrave 2
(Michael Quinn) *led tl 7f out: rdn and struggling whn squeezed for room and hmpd over 3f out: sn bhd: t.o* **33/1**

2m 0.43s (-4.47) **Going Correction** -0.35s/f (Firm)
WFA 3 from 4yo+ 12lb 7 Ran SP% **113.4**
Speed ratings (Par 103): **103,100,96,91,86 66,51**
toteswingers 1&2 £2.90, 2&3 £1.90, 1&3 £3.80 CSF £19.72 CT £37.82 TOTE £13.10: £4.60, £1.10; EX 28.80.
Owner P C F Racing Ltd **Bred** J J Whelan **Trained** Dogmersfield, Hampshire
■ Stewards' Enquiry : Neil Callan two-day ban: careless riding (Jul 16-17)

FOCUS
A fair handicap which was strong run. The winner rates an 8lb turf best.
Foxhaven Official explanation: jockey said gelding never travelled
T/Plt: £116.60 to a £1 stake. Pool of £54750.41 - 342.61 winning tickets. T/Qpdt: £45.80 to a £1 stake. Pool of £5961 - 52 - 96.32 winning tickets. SP

3109 MUSSELBURGH (R-H)
Friday, June 29

OFFICIAL GOING: Soft (good to soft in places) changing to soft after race 1 (2.10)
Wind: Fresh, half against Weather: Cloudy, bright

3575 INVESTEC WEALTH & INVESTMENT EDINBURGH H'CAP 1m
2:10 (2:10) (Class 6) (0-65,65) 3-Y-O **£1,940** (£577; £288; £144) **Stalls** Low

Form RPR
-414 **1** **Fine Altomis**[22] 2843 3-9-2 **60**.. TomEaves 4 74
(Michael Dods) *mde all: rdn 2f out: sn clr: styd on wl fnl f: unchal* **2/1**[1]
1606 **2** 4½ **Daddy Warbucks (IRE)**[27] 2689 3-9-7 **65**.................... AdrianNicholls 9 69
(David Nicholls) *t.k.h early: chsd wnr thrght: rdn over 2f out: no imp fr over 1f out* **5/2**[2]
-450 **3** 8 **Divine Success (IRE)**[39] 2340 3-8-8 **52**...................(b[1]) TonyHamilton 6 37
(Richard Fahey) *t.k.h early: trckd ldrs tl rdn and outpcd fr 2f out* **12/1**
2004 **4** shd **Athletic**[44] 2162 3-8-13 **57**... GrahamLee 8 42
(Andrew Reid) *hld up in tch: stdy hdwy 1/2-way: rdn and edgd rt over 2f out: wknd fnl f* **11/2**
0-00 **5** 5 **Captain Baldwin**[14] 3111 3-7-11 **46** oh1.......................... NeilFarley(5) 7 20
(Jim Goldie) *s.i.s: bhd and sn pushed along: drvn over 3f out: sme hdwy over 1f out: nvr on terms* **25/1**
5-00 **6** 19 **Tresabella**[15] 3083 3-7-13 **46** oh1.................................... DominicFox(3) 5
(Michael Appleby) *hld up bhd ldng gp: drvn and struggling over 3f out: sn btn: t.o* **33/1**
1405 **7** ½ **Hikma (USA)**[22] 2840 3-9-4 **62**.. JoeFanning 1
(Mark Johnston) *dwlt: chsd ldng gp: drvn and outpcd wl over 2f out: sn btn: t.o* **9/2**[3]

1m 48.02s (6.82) **Going Correction** +0.80s/f (Soft) 7 Ran SP% **110.0**
Speed ratings (Par 97): **97,92,84,84,79 60,59**
toteswingers 1&2 £2.90, 2&3 £7.90, 1&3 £4.40 CSF £6.58 CT £39.32 TOTE £4.10: £3.20, £1.90; EX 7.20.
Owner Steve Catchpole & Keith Hanson **Bred** Aston House Stud **Trained** Denton, Co Durham

FOCUS
A weak handicap in which the pace was honest. A step up from the winner on his penultimate Redcar win.
Tresabella Official explanation: jockey said filly hung left throughout
Hikma(USA) Official explanation: trainer said, regarding running, that in his opinion the filly had not run poorly

3576 STEADFAST E B F MAIDEN STKS 5f
2:40 (2:40) (Class 5) 2-Y-O **£3,234** (£962; £481; £240) **Stalls** High

Form RPR
1 **Strictly Ballroom (IRE)** 2-8-12 0.................................... JoeFanning 3 77+
(Mark Johnston) *dwlt: hld up in tch on outside: hdwy to ld over 1f out: rdn out fnl f* **9/4**[1]
2 2 **Megamunch (IRE)** 2-9-3 0.. TomEaves 6 75+
(Linda Stubbs) *prom: effrt and pushed along 2f out: chsd wnr ins fnl f: kpt on: nt gng pce to chal* **8/1**
0320 **3** 7 **Princess In Exile**[29] 2631 2-8-12 0.................................. LeeNewman 4 45
(George Foster) *led tl rdn and hdd over 1f out: sn edgd rt: wknd ins fnl f* **10/3**[2]
4300 **4** 2 **Hellolini**[9] 3286 2-8-12 0... TonyHamilton 5 37
(Robin Bastiman) *dwlt: sn trcking ldrs: rdn over 2f out: wknd over 1f out* **7/2**[3]
50 **5** 2¼ **Jordanstown**[36] 2415 2-9-3 0.. GrahamLee 1 34
(Kevin Ryan) *s.i.s: bhd and pushed along: nvr able to chal* **7/2**[3]
460 **6** 8 **Maggies Gem (IRE)**[39] 2338 2-8-12 0.........................(b[1]) MickyFenton 2
(Paul Midgley) *trckd ldr: rdn over 2f out: hung rt and sn wknd* **40/1**

1m 4.0s (3.60) **Going Correction** +0.725s/f (Yiel) 6 Ran SP% **111.8**
Speed ratings (Par 93): **100,96,85,82,78 66**
toteswingers 1&2 £8.50, 2&3 £1.10, 1&3 £4.10 CSF £20.44 TOTE £2.50: £1.40, £4.70; EX 17.30.
Owner Gerry Ryan **Bred** W Maxwell Ervine **Trained** Middleham Moor, N Yorks

FOCUS
After the first race the official going was changed to Soft. Only a modest maiden, but the form should hold up as it was dominated by the two newcomers who pulled well clear of the rest. The form is rated in line with the race averages.

NOTEBOOK
Strictly Ballroom(IRE), a speedily-bred daughter of Choisir, made a tidy winning debut to justify market support. Despite being slowly away, she travelled well through the race and picked up nicely inside the final furlong to record a comfortable success. She can only improve. (op 3-1 tchd 2-1)
Megamunch(IRE) ran a blinder on his debut. He lengthened clear of the third and chased the winner hard inside the final furlong, shaping as though he would appreciate a stiffer test. (tchd 7-1)
Princess In Exile set the standard on her previous placed efforts and had conditions in her favour. She paid the price for racing too freely in the early stages and was ultimately well beaten by the front two. (op 3-1 tchd 7-2)
Hellolini hasn't progressed since finishing third in a Redcar maiden in testing conditions on her second start. (op 3-1)
Jordanstown Official explanation: trainer's rep said colt was unsuited by the soft ground

3577 TURCAN CONNELL H'CAP 1m 4f 100y
3:10 (3:10) (Class 6) (0-65,65) 4-Y-0+ **£1,940** (£577; £288; £144) **Stalls** Low

Form RPR
3/-3 **1** **Dispol Diva**[11] 3222 6-8-2 **46**...(v) DuranFentiman 1 66
(Paul Midgley) *t.k.h: cl up: led gng wl 3f out: pushed wl clr fr 2f out: easily* **2/1**[2]
50-2 **2** 17 **Oddsmaker (IRE)**[14] 3116 11-9-2 **60**.................................(t) TomEaves 2 54
(Maurice Barnes) *led after 1f to 3f out: plugged on same pce fnl 2f* **15/8**[1]
0353 **3** 5 **Cadgers Brig**[22] 2842 4-9-6 **64**..(p) JoeFanning 6 50
(Keith Dalgleish) *prom: effrt and rdn over 3f out: carried hd high and no imp fr 2f out* **4/1**[3]
64-0 **4** 6 **Grand Art (IRE)**[20] 366 8-8-13 **57**.................................... LeeNewman 4 34
(Noel Wilson) *hld up: drvn and edgd lft 3f out: sn no imp* **20/1**
5-53 **5** 5 **Wind Shuffle (GER)**[16] 3029 9-8-10 **54**.......................... TonyHamilton 3 23
(Richard Fahey) *prom: drvn along 3f out: sn struggling: btn fnl 2f* **15/2**
006 **6** 6 **Rock Of Deauville (IRE)**[28] 2666 5-9-7 **65**....................(p) GrahamLee 5 25
(Julie Camacho) *hld up: drvn along over 3f out: sn outpcd: n.d after* **14/1**
10/0 **7** 8 **Isitcozimcool (IRE)**[15] 3061 7-8-3 **47**............................ JamesSullivan 8
(Barry Murtagh) *t.k.h: led 1f: cl up tl rdn and wknd over 3f out* **50/1**
-005 **8** 4½ **Decadence**[23] 2823 4-7-13 **46** oh1............................... DeclanCannon(3) 7
(Nigel Tinkler) *hld up in tch: struggling over 3f out: sn btn* **25/1**

2m 56.03s (14.03) **Going Correction** +1.275s/f (Soft) 8 Ran SP% **117.1**
Speed ratings (Par 101): **104,92,89,85,82 78,72,69**
toteswingers 1&2 £1.10, 2&3 £2.70, 1&3 £2.40 CSF £6.20 CT £12.91 TOTE £2.00: £1.20, £1.10, £2.50; EX 7.20.
Owner The French Bred Syndicate **Bred** P C Hunt **Trained** Westow, N Yorks

FOCUS
A modest handicap that was run at a sound gallop. The winner was most impressive but there were some wide margins on this card. He is rated back to something like her 3yo best.

3578 INVESTEC WEALTH & INVESTMENT H'CAP 5f
3:45 (3:45) (Class 4) (0-80,77) 3-Y-0+ **£6,469** (£1,925; £962; £481) **Stalls** High

Form RPR
0350 **1** **The Nifty Fox**[16] 3027 8-9-2 **67**......................................(p) JamesSullivan 6 76
(Tim Easterby) *chsd ldng gp: rdn and hdwy over 1f out: led wl ins fnl f: hld on wl* **5/1**
63-1 **2** nk **Oldjoesaid**[21] 2875 8-9-11 **76**.. MickyFenton 1 84
(Paul Midgley) *sn pushed along in rr: rdn and hdwy over 1f out: styd on fnl f: tk 2nd cl home* **4/1**[2]
2004 **3** hd **Come On Dave (IRE)**[21] 2875 3-8-6 **63**........................ AdrianNicholls 3 68
(David Nicholls) *led: rdn over 1f out: edgd lft: hdd wl ins fnl f: hld nr fin* **12/1**
1113 **4** 4½ **Sandwith**[14] 3113 9-8-11 **67**..(p) LMcNiff(5) 7 58
(George Foster) *prom tl rdn and outpcd appr fnl f* **12/1**
0-41 **5** ½ **Liberty Island (IRE)**[14] 3109 7-9-10 **75**......................(p) DuranFentiman 5 64
(Ian Semple) *chsd ldrs tl hung rt and wknd over 1f out* **9/2**[3]
0600 **6** 2 **Blown It (USA)**[25] 2750 6-9-1 **66**... JoeFanning 2 48
(Keith Dalgleish) *bhd: rdn 1/2-way: kpt on fnl f: nvr able to chal* **22/1**
2241 **7** ¾ **Da'Quonde (IRE)**[14] 3113 4-9-7 **77**.............................. JustinNewman(5) 8 56
(Bryan Smart) *dwlt: sn chsng ldrs: rdn 1/2-way: wknd over 1f out* **2/1**[1]
0002 **8** 14 **Missile Attack (IRE)**[14] 3113 4-8-7 **58** oh5.....................(p) TomEaves 4
(Ian Semple) *in tch on outside: drvn along 1/2-way: sn struggling: t.o* **28/1**

1m 3.39s (2.99) **Going Correction** +0.725s/f (Yiel)
WFA 3 from 4yo+ 6lb 8 Ran SP% **111.4**
Speed ratings (Par 105): **105,104,104,97,96 93,91,69**
toteswingers 1&2 £5.70, 2&3 £3.80, 1&3 £8.30 CSF £23.91 CT £219.93 TOTE £6.10: £2.20, £1.40, £2.90; EX 25.80.
Owner Roy Peebles **Bred** Mrs Norma Peebles **Trained** Great Habton, N Yorks

FOCUS
A decent sprint handicap which was run at a strong gallop, with the first three pulling clear inside the final furlong. The winner finally took advantage of a reduced mark.
Da'Quonde(IRE) Official explanation: trainer's rep said filly ran flat

3579 BRUCE STEVENSON INSURANCE BROKERS H'CAP 2m
4:20 (4:20) (Class 6) (0-65,63) 4-Y-0+ **£2,587** (£770; £384; £192) **Stalls** Low

Form RPR
-203 **1** **Spruzzo**[23] 2827 6-8-13 **55**.. DuranFentiman 1 66
(Chris Fairhurst) *mde all: qcknd clr after 5f: rdn over 3f out: styd on wl to draw clr fr over 1f out* **10/3**[2]
0-63 **2** 16 **Old Boy Ted**[15] 3086 4-8-5 **47**.. JoeFanning 9 49
(Mark H Tompkins) *hld up in tch: hdwy to chse wnr over 5f out: rdn and c wd over 2f out: no ex over 1f out* **15/2**
-545 **3** 2¾ **Lady Gargoyle**[9] 3277 4-7-12 **45**..................................... NeilFarley(5) 4 34
(Jim Goldie) *s.i.s: bhd: rdn and hdwy over 3f out: kpt on: nvr able to chal* **20/1**
0/0- **4** 1¾ **Hoar Frost**[27] 4602 7-8-1 **50**...(p) GemmaTutty(7) 7 36
(Karen Tutty) *hld up: drvn along 1/2-way: hdwy over 2f out: nt gng pce to chal* **50/1**
00-0 **5** 13 **Ballade De La Mer**[30] 2599 6-8-3 **45**..........................(p) JamesSullivan 8 16
(George Foster) *bhd: struggling 1/2-way: nvr on terms* **33/1**
-021 **6** 2½ **Ponte Di Rosa**[8] 3316 4-9-1 **60** 6ex.............................. DominicFox(3) 3 28
(Michael Appleby) *prom: stdy hdwy over 6f out: sn drvn along: wknd wl over 2f out* **5/4**[1]
501- **7** 15 **Illustration (IRE)**[5] 7077 4-9-1 **62**............................(b[1]) LucyAlexander(5) 6 12
(Barry Murtagh) *hld up in tch: drvn and outpcd over 6f out: n.d after* **25/1**
0001 **8** 31 **Vittachi**[30] 2599 5-9-7 **63**.. TomEaves 2
(Alistair Whillans) *chsd wnr to over 5f out: wknd over 4f out: t.o* **11/2**[3]
53/6 **9** 6 **Veloso (FR)**[21] 2874 10-9-6 **62**... LeeNewman 5
(Noel Wilson) *chsd ldrs to 1/2-way: sn lost pl: struggling last 4f* **14/1**

3m 48.84s (15.34) **Going Correction** +1.00s/f (Soft) 9 Ran SP% **114.8**
Speed ratings (Par 101): **101,93,91,90,84 83,75,60,57**
toteswingers 1&2 £3.50, 2&3 £14.80, 1&3 £8.90 CSF £26.64 CT £429.87 TOTE £3.30: £1.50, £1.80, £6.20; EX 29.70.
Owner 980 Racing **Bred** C And Mrs Wilson **Trained** Middleham Moor, N Yorks

FOCUS
A modest handicap that turned into a real slog up the straight in the testing conditions. They finished at some wide intervals and it's doubtful this form should be taken too literally.
Ponte Di Rosa Official explanation: trainer had no explanation for the poor form shown

Vittachi Official explanation: trainer had no explanation for the poor form shown

3580 BOOGIE IN THE MORNING MAIDEN STKS 7f 30y
4:55 (4:55) (Class 5) 3-Y-O+ **£2,726** (£805; £402) **Stalls** Low

Form RPR
5- **1** **Safe House (IRE)**^{254} [6950] 3-8-12 0 JoeFanning 3 70
(Mark Johnston) *led 1f: pressed ldr: chal over 2f out: sn rdn: led wl ins fnl f: styd on wl* **4/7**^{1}
3203 **2** *nk* **Henry Bee**^{25} [2774] 3-9-3 72 (p) TonyHamilton 1 74
(Richard Fahey) *led after 1f: jnd and rdn over 2f out: hdd wl ins fnl f: r.o: hld cl home* **2/1**^{2}
0 **3** *10* **Stormont Bridge**^{9} [3273] 4-9-7 0 (t) LucyAlexander$^{(5)}$ 4 51
(Maurice Barnes) *in tch: effrt over 3f out: outpcd by first two fr 2f out* **40/1**
0 **4** *8* **Laybach (IRE)**^{7} [3333] 8-9-12 0 GrahamLee 6 30
(Jim Goldie) *hld up: pushed along and outpcd over 3f out: n.d after* **12/1**^{3}
00F0 **5** *2 1/4* **Dragon Spirit (IRE)**^{7} [3333] 3-8-12 0 (p) LMcNiff$^{(5)}$ 5 21
(Linda Perratt) *prom tl rdn and wknd over 2f out* **33/1**
0/ **6** *29* **Heart Beat Song**^{640} [6442] 4-9-5 0 MatthewHopkins$^{(7)}$ 2
(Alan Berry) *plld hrd: chsd ldrs tl wknd over 2f out* **66/1**

1m 37.3s (8.30) **Going Correction** +1.275s/f (Soft)
WFA 3 from 4yo+ 9lb **6 Ran SP% 111.6**
Speed ratings (Par 103): **103,102,91,82,79 46**
toteswingers 1&2 £1.10, 2&3 £5.00, 1&3 £3.30 CSF £1.88 TOTE £1.60: £1.02, £2.00; EX 1.90.
Owner Sheikh Hamdan Bin Mohammed Al Maktoum **Bred** Darley **Trained** Middleham Moor, N Yorks

FOCUS
Little strength in depth to this weak maiden and as the betting suggested the two market leaders dominated. the runner-up sets the standard.

3581 ISLE OF SKYE WHISKY H'CAP 7f 30y
5:30 (5:30) (Class 5) (0-70,70) 4-Y-O+ **£3,234** (£962; £481; £240) **Stalls** Low

Form RPR
-331 **1** **Cheeky Wee Red**^{7} [3332] 4-8-2 51 oh3 PatrickMathers 4 59
(Richard Fahey) *prom: rdn over 2f out: hdwy to ld wl ins fnl f: r.o wl* **5/1**^{3}
6040 **2** *1 1/4* **Spread Boy (IRE)**^{16} [3026] 5-7-13 51 oh6 DominicFox$^{(3)}$ 9 56
(Alan Berry) *led: carried lft by loose horse after 1f: rdn over 2f out: hdd and no ex wl ins fnl f* **80/1**
3041 **3** *3 1/2* **Jupiter Fidius**^{14} [3115] 5-8-4 60 (p) GemmaTutty$^{(7)}$ 3 55
(Karen Tutty) *bhd: rdn over 3f out: styd on wl fnl f: nvr able to chal* **3/1**^{1}
-060 **4** *nse* **Sabratha (IRE)**^{7} [3334] 4-8-12 66 LMcNiff$^{(5)}$ 1 61
(Linda Perratt) *t.k.h: trckd ldrs: rdn and outpcd over 2f out: kpt on same pce fnl f* **8/1**
0554 **5** *hd* **Amethyst Dawn (IRE)**^{6} [3388] 6-9-7 70 GrahamLee 6 65
(Andrew Reid) *chsd ldr: rdn over 2f out: edgd lft and kpt on same pce fnl f* **4/1**^{2}
0-40 **6** *5* **Shamo Hill Theatre**^{7} [3332] 5-8-2 51 oh6 (p) DuranFentiman 7 32
(Paul Midgley) *hld up: drvn and outpcd over 2f out: edgd rt: btn over 1f out* **20/1**
6066 **7** *3/4* **Chookie Avon**^{20} [2924] 5-9-3 66 (p) JoeFanning 8 45
(Keith Dalgleish) *chsd ldrs: drvn over 2f out: wknd appr fnl f* **13/2**
4-22 **U** **Goninodaethat**^{14} [3115] 4-8-0 54 NeilFarley$^{(5)}$ 5
(Jim Goldie) *uns rdr sn after s* **3/1**^{1}

1m 37.36s (8.36) **Going Correction** +1.275s/f (Soft) **8 Ran SP% 117.1**
Speed ratings (Par 103): **103,101,97,97,97 91,90,**
totesswingers 1&2 £22.70, 2&3 £22.50, 1&3 £3.40 CSF £255.36 CT £1419.56 TOTE £4.30: £1.20, £7.40, £2.50; EX 204.10.
Owner Eildon Hill Racing **Bred** Thoroughbred Farms Ltd **Trained** Musley Bank, N Yorks

FOCUS
A fair handicap run at a strong pace where it proved advantageous to race handy, and not many got into it. There was drama at the start when Neil Farley was unshipped from Goninodaethat shortly after the stalls had opened. It's doubtful this is form to take too literally.
Goninodaethat Official explanation: jockey said he lost right iron as stalls opened
T/Plt: £47.00 to a £1 stake. Pool of £40953.98 - 635.20 winning tickets. T/Qpdt: £8.40 to a £1 stake. Pool of £3626.18 - 317.24 winning tickets. RY

3532 NEWCASTLE (L-H)
Friday, June 29
3582 Meeting Abandoned - waterlogged

3393 NEWMARKET (R-H)
Friday, June 29
OFFICIAL GOING: Good (good to firm in places; 8.0)
Wind: Cloudy with sunny spells Weather: Blustery

3589 POPTELECOM.CO.UK 0843 FREE DIVERT TO MOBILE H'CAP 1m
5:55 (5:55) (Class 5) (0-75,73) 3-Y-O+ **£2,587** (£770; £384; £192) **Stalls** High

Form RPR
06-2 **1** **Daruband**^{32} [2549] 4-10-0 73 (v) FrankieDettori 5 83
(Alan McCabe) *hld up in tch: nt clr run over 1f out: rdn to ld ins fnl f: edgd lft: r.o* **7/1**^{3}
2234 **2** *1 1/2* **Save The Bees**^{7} [3335] 4-9-12 71 JamieSpencer 10 78
(Declan Carroll) *chsd ldrs: led over 2f out: rdn over 1f out: hdd ins fnl f: styd on same pce* **3/1**^{1}
5043 **3** *1 1/4* **Climaxfortackle (IRE)**^{11} [3220] 4-9-2 61 (v) SilvestreDeSousa 11 65
(Derek Shaw) *hld up: swtchd rt and hdwy over 1f out: rdn and edgd lft ins fnl f: r.o* **16/1**
4004 **4** *3/4* **Roedean (IRE)**^{7} [3347] 3-8-5 65 (tp) LauraPike$^{(5)}$ 3 65
(William Stone) *mid-div: hdwy over 1f out: sn rdn: r.o* **14/1**
6P/3 **5** *1* **Sacrilege**^{21} [2899] 7-9-8 67 (v) IanMongan 8 67
(Daniel O'Brien) *a.p: rdn over 2f out: styd on same pce fnl f* **17/2**
1002 **6** *3/4* **Patriotic (IRE)**^{24} [2801] 4-9-12 71 MichaelHills 13 69
(Chris Dwyer) *hld up: hdwy over 2f out: rdn over 1f out: no ex ins fnl f* **6/1**^{2}
04-2 **7** *hd* **Enriching (USA)**^{114} [655] 4-8-10 55 MartinLane 7 53
(Lydia Pearce) *w ldr tl led over 5f out: rdn and hdd over 2f out: no ex ins fnl f* **25/1**
4021 **8** *2 1/2* **Speedi Mouse**^{15} [3083] 3-9-0 69 CathyGannon 1 59
(Philip McBride) *prom: rdn over 2f out: wknd fnl f* **6/1**^{2}
0546 **9** *nk* **Mazovian (USA)**^{9} [3287] 4-8-11 63 DannyBrock$^{(7)}$ 2 54
(Michael Chapman) *led: hdd over 5f out: remained w ldr tl rdn over 2f out: wknd fnl f* **25/1**
6400 **10** *5* **Petsas Pleasure**^{27} [2692] 6-9-1 60 PaulHanagan 12 40
(Ollie Pears) *hld up: rdn over 2f out: nvr on terms* **12/1**
00-0 **11** *1 1/4* **Bassett Road (IRE)**^{53} [1936] 4-9-6 65 StevieDonohoe 4 42
(Willie Musson) *hld up: a in rr: bhd fnl 3f* **33/1**
3335 **12** *2 1/2* **Hereford Boy**^{37} [2399] 8-9-10 69 (v) MickaelBarzalona 9 40
(Dean Ivory) *s.i.s: hld up: rdn over 2f out: wknd over 1f out* **9/1**
41-0 **13** *14* **Chalk And Cheese (USA)**^{18} [2975] 3-9-4 73 (v^{1}) SaleemGolam 6 10
(Stuart Williams) *s.i.s: plld hrd and sn prom: wknd over 2f out: t.o* **33/1**

1m 41.02s (1.02) **Going Correction** +0.125s/f (Good)
WFA 3 from 4yo+ 10lb **13 Ran SP% 120.4**
Speed ratings (Par 103): **99,97,96,95,94 93,93,91,90,85 84,82,68**
Tote Swingers: 1&2 £6.50, 1&3 £5.90, 2&3 £5.80 CSF £27.30 CT £339.94 TOTE £7.30: £2.70, £1.50, £4.60; EX 29.90 TRIFECTA Not won..
Owner Mrs June Bownes **Bred** Mickley Stud **Trained** Averham Park, Notts

FOCUS
Stands side track used with stalls on stands' side except 10f &12f: Centre. There was a stiff crosswind blowing from the stands' side and they went steadily in this first race until picking it up in the last 3f. An ordinary handicap. The form looks pretty straightforward with a step up from the winner.

3590 GET YOUR 0800 NUMBER FROM POPTELECOM.CO.UK EBF MAIDEN FILLIES' STKS 6f
6:30 (6:33) (Class 4) 2-Y-O **£4,528** (£1,347; £673; £336) **Stalls** High

Form RPR
1 **Reyaadah** 2-9-0 0 PaulHanagan 14 83+
(Charles Hills) *a.p: shkn up over 2f out: rdn to ld wl ins fnl f: r.o* **11/4**^{2}
2 *1* **Pearl Bell (IRE)** 2-9-0 0 JamieSpencer 10 80+
(Brian Meehan) *chsd ldrs: led wl over 2f out: shkn up and hung rt over 1f out: rdn and hdd wl ins fnl f: styd on same pce* **25/1**
3 *3/4* **Nargys (IRE)** 2-9-0 0 J-PGuillambert 13 78+
(Luca Cumani) *chsd ldrs: rdn over 1f out: r.o* **33/1**
4 *1/2* **El Manati (IRE)** 2-9-0 0 MartinDwyer 2 77+
(James Tate) *s.i.s: hld up: hdwy and hung lft fr over 1f out: styd on* **66/1**
5 *3/4* **Invincible Cara (IRE)** 2-9-0 0 JimmyFortune 12 74+
(John Dunlop) *dwlt: hld up: hdwy over 1f out: r.o* **33/1**
3 **6** *3/4* **Testamatta**^{42} [2245] 2-9-0 0 RyanMoore 15 72
(Marco Botti) *hld up: rdn and r.o ins fnl f: nt rch ldrs* **8/1**
7 *2* **Olympic Jule** 2-9-0 0 JamesDoyle 8 66+
(John Dunlop) *prom: rdn and ev ch over 2f out: no ex fnl f* **50/1**
2 **8** *1/2* **Sugar House (USA)**^{23} [2812] 2-9-0 0 MickaelBarzalona 1 65
(Mahmood Al Zarooni) *prom: rdn over 2f out: hung lft: hmpd and lost pl over 1f out: n.d after* **15/8**^{1}
3 **8** *dht* **Summer Dream (IRE)**^{21} [2892] 2-9-0 0 TedDurcan 7 65
(Marco Botti) *chsd ldrs: nt clr run and hmpd over 1f out: n.d after* **9/2**^{3}
10 *nse* **El Mirage (IRE)** 2-9-0 0 MichaelHills 6 64
(Dean Ivory) *s.i.s: hld up: pushed along over 2f out: styd on ins fnl f: nvr nrr* **28/1**
11 *1 1/2* **Astrosapphire** 2-9-0 0 DarryllHolland 5 60
(Mark H Tompkins) *prom: shkn up over 2f out: outpcd fr over 1f out* **100/1**
12 *1 1/4* **Perpetual Glory** 2-9-0 0 IanMongan 9 56
(Sir Henry Cecil) *s.i.s: hld up: pushed along over 2f out: nvr on terms* **20/1**
13 *nk* **Iris Blue** 2-9-0 0 WilliamBuick 11 55
(John Gosden) *hld up: hung lft fr over 1f out: n.d* **10/1**
54 **14** *8* **Lilly May (IRE)**^{16} [3046] 2-8-9 0 LeonnaMayor$^{(5)}$ 3 31
(Phil McEntee) *w ldr over 4f: hmpd and wknd over 1f out* **66/1**
15 *1* **On The Bias (USA)** 2-9-0 0 FrankieDettori 4 28
(Brian Meehan) *led: hdd wl over 2f out: hung rt and wknd over 1f out* **18/1**

1m 14.7s (2.20) **Going Correction** +0.125s/f (Good) **15 Ran SP% 129.0**
Speed ratings (Par 92): **90,88,87,87,86 85,82,81,81,81 79,77,77,66,65**
Tote Swingers: 1&2 £25.30, 1&3 £44.10, 2&3 £74.70 CSF £82.41 TOTE £4.40: £1.80, £9.00, £12.00; EX 131.40 Trifecta £1041.50 Part won. Pool: £1,407.43 - 0.10 winning units..
Owner Hamdan Al Maktoum **Bred** Shadwell Estate Company Limited **Trained** Lambourn, Berks

FOCUS
Juvenile maidens on this track usually hold plenty of interest. The best recent winner of this one was subsequent Classic victor Russian Rhythm, while in 2011 Discourse got the better of a close finish with Gamilati and both went on to win Group races on their next starts. A number of major yards were represented and it looked a race likely to throw up its share of future winners. The early pace was steady and those racing closer to the far side from high draws dominated.

NOTEBOOK
Reyaadah ◆, the second foal of a half-sister to several winners including the high-class Muhtathir, was well backed earlier in the day and had clearly been showing ability prior to this debut. However, after being keen early she was being niggled soon after halfway, but once she got the idea, picked up really well and was pulling away at the finish. She should be better for the outing and it will be interesting to see where she goes next. (op 7-2 tchd 4-1)
Pearl Bell(IRE) ◆, a £25,000 half-sister to a couple of winners at various trips including Inventor, was noisy and green in the paddock beforehand but showed clear ability in the race and looked the likely winner, only to be run out of it up the hill. She is entered in a couple of sales races and one of those could be the target, with a maiden to be picked up beforehand.
Nargys(IRE) ◆, a 125,000euros daughter of a 7f winner who is related to Listed performers from the family of One So Wonderful, showed good ability on this debut, having never been far away. She has a fair bit of size about her and, from a yard not noted for first-time out juvenile winners, looks sure to be better for the experience.
El Manati(IRE) ◆, a 40,000gns half-sister to the sprinter Kelly's Eye and a middle-distance winner. She raced on the outside of the field, away from the pace, for much of the way, but picked up really well to mount a challenge despite drifting across the track. She showed good speed and should be able to build on this. (op 80-1)
Invincible Cara(IRE) ◆, a home-bred half-sister to a number of winners including the Group-class Elusive Pimpernel and Palavicini, is bred to win races as a juvenile, but possibly over further. She missed the break but was noted keeping on nicely to finish on the heels of the placed horses. Her siblings both made their debuts on this track and she looks set to follow their lead by picking up a race before long.
Testamatta had shown fair promise when third in a fast-ground maiden over C&D in May and the runner-up and fourth had scored since. She tracked the winner but could not pick up as well as that rival. (tchd 15-2)
Olympic Jule, a half-sister to a number of winners including the smart Golden Desert, performed encouragingly on this debut.
Sugar House(USA) disappointed but had excuses, as she got involved in scrimmaging running down the hill as Lilly May weakened. \n\x\x Out of a multiple 6f-1m stakes winner (including Grade 1) on dirt in the US, she had made a promising debut over 6f on Polytrack early in the month and was probably the worst sufferer, struggling to keep her balance down the hill. (op 9-4 tchd 5-2)

Summer Dream(IRE) disappointed but had excuses, as she got involved in scrimmaging running down the hill as Lilly May weakened. Out of a sister to 2000 Guineas third Olympian Odyssey, had made a promising debut behind subsequent impressive Albany winner Newfangled over C&D on soft and can be given another chance. Marco Botti reported that the filly was unsuited by the good, good to firm in places ground. Official explanation: trainer said filly was unsuited by the good (good to firm places) ground (op 9-4 tchd 5-2)

El Mirage(IRE), a 97,000gns first foal of a juvenile winner who was a half-sister to Coventry Stakes victor Helvellyn, missed the break slightly and then raced towards the outside, finishing just behind more experienced rivals. (op 25-1)

3591 POPTELECOM.CO.UK MOBILE OFFERS CLAIMING STKS 1m

7:05 (7:05) (Class 5) 3-Y-O **£2,587** (£770; £384; £192) **Stalls** High

Form RPR

0420 **1** **Purple Affair (IRE)**[27] 2689 3-8-11 67 JamieSpencer 7 71
(J S Moore) *mde all far side: clr fr over 4f out tl rdn and hung rt over 1f out: styd on u.p* **7/2**[3]

-100 **2** *1 3/4* **Vivid Blue**[15] 3085 3-9-0 74 (b[1]) RyanMoore 5 70
(William Haggas) *racd far side: prom: chsd wnr over 2f out: sn rdn: hung rt and ev ch over 1f out: nt run on: 2nd of 5 in gp* **11/4**[2]

0-60 **3** *9* **Surrey Dream (IRE)**[46] 2128 3-9-3 64 JamesDoyle 3 51
(Roger Teal) *racd far side: prom: chsd wnr over 3f out tl rdn over 2f out: sn hung rt: wknd fnl f: 3rd of 5 in gp* **16/1**

22-1 **4** *9* **Purple 'n Gold (IRE)**[16] 3048 3-8-11 75 (b[1]) FrankieDettori 1 24
(George Baker) *racd alone stands' side: up w the pce tl rdn over 1f out: wknd and eased fnl f* **10/11**[1]

0 **5** *14* **Secret Jubilee**[20] 2935 3-8-2 0 ow1 RaulDaSilva(3) 6
(Philip McBride) *racd far side: chsd wnr over 4f: sn rdn: wknd wl over 2f out: t.o: 4th of 5 in gp* **25/1**

-600 **6** *14* **Fen Flyer**[16] 3050 3-8-9 35 (b) SaleemGolam 4
(Chris Dwyer) *dwlt: racd far side: a last: lost tch fr over 3f out: t.o: last of 5 in gp* **100/1**

1m 40.6s (0.60) **Going Correction** +0.125s/f (Good) **6** Ran SP% **112.0**
Speed ratings (Par 99): **102,100,91,82,68 54**
Tote Swingers: 1&2 £1.50, 1&3 £4.60, 2&3 £5.80 CSF £13.45 TOTE £4.00: £2.00, £1.40; EX 12.10.
Owner Mrs Teresa Kennedy **Bred** Fintan Walsh **Trained** Upper Lambourn, Berks

FOCUS
The usual mix of abilities among the runners in this claimer and a somewhat unsatisfactory race, although the time was faster than the opening handicap. Weakish form, rated around the winner.

Purple 'n Gold(IRE) Official explanation: jockey said gelding hung right
Secret Jubilee Official explanation: jockey said filly ran green

3592 POPTELECOM.CO.UK FIXED PRICES FOR 2 YEARS H'CAP 1m 5f

7:35 (7:36) (Class 4) (0-80,80) 3-Y-O **£4,528** (£1,347; £673; £336) **Stalls** Centre

Form RPR

2-40 **1** **Mubaraza (IRE)**[36] 2429 3-9-6 79 PaulHanagan 12 90
(John Dunlop) *hld up: pushed along 6f out: hung lft fr over 3f out: hdwy u.p over 2f out: led ins fnl f: drvn out* **9/1**

5232 **2** *1* **Cheviot Quest (IRE)**[15] 3087 3-8-0 62 HarryBentley(3) 5 71
(William Jarvis) *a.p: rdn to ld and hung lft fr over 1f out: hdd and unable qck ins fnl f* **14/1**

0221 **3** *2 1/4* **Bathwick Street**[23] 2818 3-8-8 67 CathyGannon 7 73
(David Evans) *chsd ldr over 3f: remained handy: rdn over 3f out: edgd lft over 1f out: styd on same pce fnl f* **9/1**

3121 **4** *1* **Lady Kashaan (IRE)**[11] 3212 3-8-6 65 6ex AndrewElliott 10 69
(Alan Swinbank) *hld up: hdwy over 4f out: led over 3f out: rdn and hdd over 1f out: no ex ins fnl f* **10/3**[1]

6-32 **5** *2 3/4* **Bayan (IRE)**[27] 2708 3-9-7 80 (b[1]) KierenFallon 1 80
(Brian Meehan) *prom: lost pl and swtchd lft wl over 3f out: rdn over 1f out: no ex fnl f* **7/2**[2]

-314 **6** *7* **Cape Savannah**[16] 3042 3-9-6 79 MartinLane 8 69
(David Simcock) *prom: rdn over 3f out: wknd over 1f out: eased* **12/1**

0-03 **7** *nk* **Dollar Bill**[36] 2427 3-8-11 70 (p) JimmyFortune 9 59
(Andrew Balding) *prom: chsd ldr over 9f out tl rdn over 3f out: wknd over 1f out* **16/1**

223 **8** *6* **Pistol (IRE)**[27] 2708 3-9-7 80 RyanMoore 6 60
(Sir Michael Stoute) *s.i.s: hld up: rdn over 3f out: wknd over 2f out* **4/1**[3]

5131 **9** *16* **Quiet Appeal (IRE)**[30] 2605 3-8-4 63 SilvestreDeSousa 4 19
(Mark Johnston) *led over 9f: wknd 2f out: t.o* **16/1**

2310 **10** *20* **Somemothersdohavem**[7] 3330 3-8-12 71 (p) StevieDonohoe 11
(John Ryan) *dwlt: hld up: rdn and wknd over 3f out: t.o* **20/1**

0043 **11** *39* **Aiaam Al Wafa (IRE)**[6] 3391 3-8-0 64 ow1 (p) LeonnaMayor(5) 3
(Phil McEntee) *hld up: swtchd to r alone far side over 8f out: bhd fnl 5f: t.o* **66/1**

2m 43.3s (-0.70) **Going Correction** +0.125s/f (Good) **11** Ran SP% **117.7**
Speed ratings (Par 101): **107,106,105,104,102 98,98,94,84,72 48**
Tote Swingers: 1&2 £14.40, 1&3 £23.20, 2&3 £17.90 CSF £127.91 CT £1171.86 TOTE £10.20: £2.60, £3.70, £3.90; EX 164.10 Trifecta £527.60 Pool: £798.56 - 1.12 winning units..
Owner Hamdan Al Maktoum **Bred** Shadwell Estate Company Limited **Trained** Arundel, W Sussex

FOCUS
A fair staying handicap for 3yos in which they looked to go a good pace and were racing seriously from a long way out. A step up from the winner on his good reappearance run.

3593 POPTELECOM.CO.UK FREE ROUTER WITH BROADBAND EBF FILLIES' CONDITIONS STKS 6f

8:05 (8:06) (Class 3) 3-Y-O+ **£7,762** (£2,310; £1,154; £577) **Stalls** High

Form RPR

10-0 **1** **La Fortunata**[34] 2507 5-8-7 86 CharlesBishop(5) 1 94
(Mike Murphy) *mde all: set stdy pce tl qcknd over 1f out: sn rdn: styd on wl* **16/1**

6206 **2** *1 1/2* **Sioux Rising (IRE)**[6] 3375 6-8-12 97 PaulHanagan 5 89
(Richard Fahey) *prom: pushed along over 2f out: rdn and edgd rt ins fnl f: styd on to go 2nd towards fin* **5/1**

-122 **3** *1/2* **Moretta Blanche**[14] 3105 5-8-12 85 (t) JimCrowley 6 88
(Ralph Beckett) *hld up: hdwy 2f out: rdn to chse wnr over 1f out: styd on same pce ins fnl f: lost 2nd towards fin* **7/2**[3]

4-03 **4** *2* **Ultrasonic (USA)**[13] 3158 3-8-8 93 RyanMoore 7 84
(Sir Michael Stoute) *racd keenly: trckd wnr: pushed along 2f out: nt clr run over 1f out: styd on same pce* **3/1**[2]

321- **5** *nk* **Pearl Diva (IRE)**[358] 3767 3-8-8 93 WilliamBuick 4 81
(Peter Chapple-Hyam) *chsd ldrs: pushed along over 2f out: no ex ins fnl f* **7/1**

1-23 **6** *2 1/2* **Catfish (IRE)**[27] 2704 4-8-12 91 MickaelBarzalona 2 72
(Brian Meehan) *rrd s: hld up: rdn and hung lft fr over 2f out: nvr trbld ldrs* **9/4**[1]

1m 12.32s (-0.18) **Going Correction** +0.125s/f (Good)
WFA 3 from 4yo+ 7lb **6** Ran SP% **113.0**
Speed ratings (Par 104): **106,104,103,100,100 96**
Tote Swingers: 1&2 £9.10, 1&3 £4.00, 2&3 £3.10 CSF £91.63 TOTE £21.40: £5.50, £2.60; EX 79.80.
Owner James Patton **Bred** James Patton **Trained** Westoning, Beds

FOCUS
A good, competitive fillies' conditions stakes, but rather muddling form. The time was considerably faster than the earlier juvenile contest and the race is rated around the winner and third.

NOTEBOOK

La Fortunata is best when making the running and got a relatively uncontested lead here. The drying ground was also in her favour and she kept finding for pressure and was always holding the challengers up the hill. Connections will look for small-field races for her on fast ground, and will aim for black type with her should a suitable opportunity arise. Official explanation: trainer said, regarding apparent improvement in form, that the mare had come on for its first run of the season and appreciated an easy lead. (op 14-1)

Sioux Rising(IRE) had the highest official rating and showed something of a return to form after a couple of below-par efforts since earning black type at Nottingham in May. She doesn't win very often but is effective at both this trip and 7f. (op 11-2 tchd 9-2)

Moretta Blanche, whose handler had trained three of the five previous winners, ran her race but after having her chance inside the last 2f could not find any more. In-foal to Authorized, she had the lowest official rating in the race, so probably ran as well as could be expected. (op 4-1)

Ultrasonic(USA) had run well when third in a 5f Listed race last time and the return to this trip should have suited, but she backed out of it up the hill. Faster ground and a Flat track might suit her best. (op 10-3 tchd 7-2 and 4-1)

Pearl Diva(IRE) had not been seen since winning her maiden almost a year ago. She showed up well if a little free early and paid for it late on. She was not given a hard time once her chance had gone and should be better for the outing. (op 5-1 tchd 15-2)

Catfish(IRE) was the disappointment. Ponied to the start, she took a while to load and then half-reared as the gates opened, missing the break. She was held up but could not pick up once asked to improve, hanging right running down the hill. She stays this trip but a return to a sharp 5f will be in her favour. Brian Meehan reported that the filly was in season. Official explanation: trainer said filly was in season (tchd 5-2)

3594 CLUTTERBUCKS RESTAURANT AT WHEATSHEAF EXNING H'CAP 1m 2f

8:40 (8:41) (Class 4) (0-80,80) 3-Y-O+ **£4,357** (£1,304; £652; £326; £163; £81) **Stalls** Centre

Form RPR

542- **1** **Greek War (IRE)**[289] 6059 3-9-0 78 MickaelBarzalona 13 95+
(Mahmood Al Zarooni) *hld up: racd centre turning for home: swtchd to r stands' side over 6f out: hdwy over 2f out: rdn to ld overall over 1f out: r.o wl: readily* **9/2**[1]

000 **2** *6* **Daring Indian**[69] 1513 4-9-5 71 KierenFallon 6 76
(Tom Dascombe) *hld up in tch: racd centre turning for home: led thatr gp over 2f out: rdn: hung rt and ev ch over 1f out: styd on same pce: 1st of 11 in gp* **20/1**

2353 **3** *2 1/2* **Red Shuttle**[43] 2199 5-9-6 72 (t) JamieSpencer 5 72
(Noel Quinlan) *s.i.s: hld up: racd centre turning for home: hdwy 3f out: rdn over 1f out: no ex fnl f: wnt 3rd nr fin: 2nd of 11 in gp* **8/1**[3]

15-0 **4** *shd* **Antarctic (IRE)**[22] 2857 4-9-10 76 (b[1]) WilliamBuick 12 76
(John Gosden) *hld up: racd centre turning for home: hdwy over 3f out: rdn and ev ch over 1f out: wknd ins fnl f: lost 3rd nr fin: 3rd of 11 in gp* **10/1**

0016 **5** *3/4* **Amoya (GER)**[24] 2801 5-10-0 80 MircoMimmocchi 1 78
(Philip McBride) *overall ldr: styd stands' side turning for home: rdn over 2f out: edgd lft and hdd over 1f out: wknd ins fnl f: 2nd of 3 in gp* **33/1**

5111 **6** *1* **St Ignatius**[16] 3038 5-9-11 77 (p) DarryllHolland 16 73
(Alan Bailey) *prom: racd centre turning for home: rdn over 2f out: wknd fnl f: 4th of 11 in gp* **12/1**

146 **7** *1* **Main Line**[23] 2813 3-9-0 78 TedDurcan 14 72
(David Lanigan) *hld up: racd centre turning for home: hdwy over 3f out: rdn and wknd over 1f out: 5th of 11 in gp* **9/2**[1]

3240 **8** *1 3/4* **Layline (IRE)**[27] 2706 5-9-11 77 JimCrowley 15 68
(Gay Kelleway) *s.s: hld up: racd centre turning for home: rdn over 2f out: n.d: 6th of 11 in gp* **12/1**

0203 **9** *nk* **Good Boy Jackson**[16] 3038 4-9-12 78 NeilCallan 4 68
(Kevin Ryan) *chsd ldrs: wnt centre turning for home and led that gp tl rdn and hdd over 2f out: wknd over 1f out: 7th of 11 in gp* **9/1**

2200 **10** *1 3/4* **Hurricane Hymnbook (USA)**[40] 1418 7-9-4 70 StevieDonohoe 7 57
(Willie Musson) *hld up: racd centre turning for home: bhd 3f out: nvr nrr: 8th of 11 in gp* **33/1**

0250 **11** *1 1/4* **Mcbirney (USA)**[9] 3278 5-9-3 76 LouisSteward(7) 3 60
(Paul D'Arcy) *prom: chsd ldr stands' side turning for home tl rdn over 2f out: wknd over 1f out: last of 3 in gp* **28/1**

1-45 **12** *6* **Top Diktat**[11] 3226 4-10-0 80 RyanMoore 2 52+
(Sir Michael Stoute) *hld up in tch: racd centre over 7f out: rdn over 3f out: wknd 2f out: 9th of 11 in gp* **11/2**[2]

040- **13** *1 1/2* **Fremont (IRE)**[275] 6439 5-9-10 76 MichaelHills 10 45
(Hugo Palmer) *hld up: racd centre turning for home: hdwy over 3f out: rdn and wknd over 2f out: 10th of 11 in gp* **8/1**[3]

00-3 **14** *41* **Allanit (GER)**[157] 276 8-9-0 66 DaraghO'Donohoe 11
(Barney Curley) *prom: racd centre turning for home: chsd ldr tl rdn over 3f out: wknd over 2f out: t.o: last of 11 in gp* **40/1**

2m 5.01s (-0.49) **Going Correction** +0.125s/f (Good)
WFA 3 from 4yo+ 12lb **14** Ran SP% **125.0**
Speed ratings (Par 105): **106,101,99,99,98 97,96,95,95,93 92,88,86,54**
Tote Swingers: 1&2 £19.60, 1&3 £3.60, 2&3 £45.40 CSF £103.09 CT £722.82 TOTE £5.80: £2.50, £5.90, £2.80; EX 162.20 Trifecta £640.40 Part won. Pool: £865.47 - 0.40 winning units..
Owner Godolphin **Bred** Darley **Trained** Newmarket, Suffolk

FOCUS
A big field for this fair handicap and a competitive race on paper. They went a good gallop, if not quite as fast as the other race round the turn, but it resulted in a runaway winner. The form seems sound enough.

Main Line Official explanation: trainer said colt was unsuited by the good (good to firm places) ground

3595 POPTELECOM.CO.UK FREE WEEKEND CALLS ON BROADBAND H'CAP 5f

9:10 (9:10) (Class 4) (0-85,84) 3-Y-O+ **£4,528** (£1,347; £673; £336) **Stalls** High

Form RPR

1-00 **1** **Le Toreador**[14] 3127 7-9-12 84 (tp) NeilCallan 3 93
(Kevin Ryan) *chsd ldr: rdn 1/2-way: led over 1f out: jst hld on* **15/2**[3]

0413 **2** 3/4 **Showboating (IRE)**[42] 2251 4 -9-375..........................(tp) FrankieDettori 9 81
(Alan McCabe) *chsd ldrs: outpcd 3f out: rallied 1f out: r.o to go 2nd wl ins fnl f: nt rch wnr* **3/1**[2]

0052 **3** 1 1/4 **Whozthecat (IRE)**[10] 3255 5 -9-779..................................(v) RyanMoore 4 81
(Declan Carroll) *chsd ldrs: outpcd 1/2-way: rallied fnl f: r.o* **1/1**[1]

4355 **4** 1 3/4 **Estonia**[38] 2369 5 -8-1169.. CathyGannon 2 64
(Michael Squance) *chsd ldrs: rdn 1/2-way: styd on same pce ins fnl f* **16/1**

-00 **5** 6 **Bertoliver**[35] 2439 8 -9-779..(b[1]) JamesDoyle 1 53
(Stuart Williams) *led: clr 1/2-way: rdn and hdd over 1f out: wknd ins fnl f* **20/1**

5-00 **6** 4 **Swendab (IRE)**[13] 3139 4 -9-577...................................(v) DarryllHolland 7 36
(John O'Shea) *sn pushed along and prom: wknd 2f out* **8/1**

1650 **7** 1 1/2 **Sulis Minerva (IRE)**[20] 2940 5 -9-577............................... KieranO'Neill 6 31
(Jeremy Gask) *s.s: outpcd* **14/1**

59.05s (-0.05) **Going Correction** +0.125s/f (Good) **7**Ran SP% **115.2**
Speed ratings (Par 105): **105,103,101,99,89 83,80**
Tote Swingers: 1&2 £2.80, 1&3 £2.40, 2&3 £1.30 CSF £30.67 CT £41.57 TOTE £7.20 : £3.20, £1.80; EX 23.00 Trifecta £68.30 Pool: £924.52 - 10.01 winning units.
Owner Guy Reed **Bred** G Reed **Trained** Hambleton, N Yorks

FOCUS
Not surprisingly they went a good pace in this sprint handicap. The winner is rated back to his best.
Le Toreador Official explanation: trainer's rep said, regarding apparent improvement in form, that the gelding benefited from the re-application of a tongue strap.
T/Plt: £3,356.20 to a £1 stake. Pool: £79,768.43 - 17.35 winning tickets. T/Qpdt: £343.90 to a £1 stake. Pool: £7,251.26 - 15.60 w. tickets CR

3596a-3602a (Foreign Racing) See RI

HAMBURG (R-H)
Friday, June 29

OFFICIAL GOING: Turf: soft

3603a GROSSER PREIS DER JUNGHEINRICH GABELSTAPLER (FLIEGER TROPHY) (GROUP 3) (3YO+) (TURF) 6f
6:25 (12:00) 3-Y-0+
£26,666 (£9,166; £4,583 ; £2,500 ; £1,666 ; £1,250)

RPR

1 **Govinda (USA)**[22] 5 -9-00.. EPedroza 10 104
(A Wohler, Germany) *mde all: broke sharply and got across fr wd draw to ld: rdn over 1 1/2f out: extended advantage ins fnl f: unchal* **92/10**

2 2 **Tertio Bloom (SWE)**[10] 7 -9-00.................. LennartHammer-Hansen 2 98
(Fabricio Borges, Sweden) *midfield on inner: rdn over 2f out: r.o to go 2nd post: no ch w wnr* **87/10**

3 nse **Ferro Sensation (GER)**[22] 6 -9-00... ADeVries 3 97
(J Pubben, Holland) *trckd ldr on outer: rdn over 2f out: outpcd by wnr ins fnl f: kpt on: ct for 2nd post* **241/10**

4 1 1/2 **Smooth Operator (GER)**[27] 2728 6 -9-40..................(b) StefanieHofer 1 97
(Mario Hofer, Germany) *trckd ldr on inner: rdn 2f out: kpt on one pce ins fnl 1 1/2f* **66/10**

5 hd **Exhibition (IRE)**[24] 7 -9-20.. THellier 4 94
(Francisco Castro, Sweden) *hld up in last: rdn to improve over 1 1/2f out: r.o to go 5th cl home: gng on at fin: nvr able to chal* **129/10**

6 hd **Amico Fritz (GER)**[30] 2325 6 -9-00................................. FabriceVeron 6 91
(H-A Pantall, France) *midfield: rdn over 2f out: kpt on one pce ins fnl 1 1/2f: ct for 5th last strides* **3/1**[1]

7 3 **Walero (GER)**[22] 6 -9-00... KClijmans 5 82
(Uwe Ostmann, Germany) *hld up in last gp: rdn over 2f out: outpcd over 1 1/2f out: plugged on* **31/5**

8 1 **Calrissian (GER)**[24] 8 -9-00.. AStarke 7 79
(Fredrik Reuterskiold, Sweden) *hld up in last pair: rdn over 1 1/2f out: edgd rt u.p: kpt on one pce* **13/2**

9 4 **Exciting Life (IRE)**[22] 4 -9-00... FilipMinarik 9 66
(P Schiergen, Germany) *midfield: rdn and struggling to maintain position over 2 1/2f out: no ex and btn 1 1/2f out: fdd* **61/10**[3]

10 2 **The Call (FR)**[22] 3 -8-70.. AndreBest 8 59
(Uwe Ostmann, Germany) *midfield on outer: rdn 2 1/2f out: no ex and btn over 1f out: fdd and dropped to last ins fnl f* **4/1**[2]

1m 10.82s (-1.87)
WFA 3 from 4yo+ 7lb **10**Ran SP% **130.8**
WIN (incl. 10 euro stake): 102. PLACES: 30, 38, 60. SF: 1,080
Owner Stall Konigsforst **Bred** F N Sahadi **Trained** Germany

[3554]CHESTER (L-H)
Saturday, June 30

OFFICIAL GOING: Good (7.5)
Wind: Moderate, half behind Weather: Sunshine and showers

3604 LINDE MATERIAL HANDLING NOVICE STKS 5f 16y
2:10 (2:11) (Class 4) 2-Y-0 **£4,528** (£1,347; £673 ; £336) **Stalls** Low

Form RPR

2210 **1** **Annunciation**[9] 3291 2 -9-599... RyanMoore 1 97
(Richard Hannon) *racd keenly: mde all: strly pressed fr over 1f out: r.o and plld out more towards fin* **4/5**[1]

0313 **2** 1 **Lady Ibrox**[11] 3250 2 -9-072.. MichaelO'Connell 3 88
(Alan Brown) *chsd ldrs: effrt on inner over 1f out to chal wnr strly: no ex towards fin* **12/1**

3331 **3** 1 3/4 **Faithfilly (IRE)**[15] 3117 2 -9-086............................... RichardKingscote 2 82
(Ed Walker) *pressed wnr: rdn and lost 2nd over 1f out: nt qckn: styd on same pce ins fnl f* **2/1**[2]

06 **4** 3 1/2 **Archie Stevens**[10] 3286 2 -8-110............................... RossAtkinson(3) 5 69
(Tom Dascombe) *s.i.s: pushed along and outpcd early: clsd over 2f out: outpcd over 1f out: no ch after* **28/1**

5123 **5** 9 **Just Past Andover (IRE)**[10] 2345 2 -8-983..................(t) JakePayne(7) 4 39
(Bill Turner) *s.i.s: racd keenly: sn chsd ldrs: pushed along over 2f out: wknd over 1f out* **10/1**[3]

105 **6** 67 **Lothian Countess**[30] 2630 2 -8-1168.............................. FrannyNorton 6
(George Foster) *upset in stalls: sat down whn gate opened s: completely missed break: a t.o* **33/1**

1m 1.85s (0.85) **Going Correction** +0.125s/f (Good) **6**Ran SP% **112.1**
Speed ratings (Par 95): **98,96,93,88,73**
toteswingers 1&2 £3.40, 2&3 £22.00, 1&3 £1.02 CSF £12.06 TOTE £1.70 : £1.10 , £3.20 ; EX 11.40.
Owner Middleham Park Racing XXXIX & James Pak **Bred** Abingdon & Witney College **Trained** East Everleigh, Wilts

FOCUS
Rail from 6f to 1.5f moved out 3yds adding 10yds to 5f races, 7f +13yds, 1m 2f 75y +14yds, 1m 3f 79y +19yds, 1m 4f 66y +20yds. The form is rated to the mid-point of the race averages, based on the fourth and time.

NOTEBOOK
Annunciation appeared to take this with a bit more in hand than the winning margin suggests, giving away at least 5lb to all rivals. Quick ground is reported to suit him best and connections feel he could be a Group horse when conditions are in his favour. Maybe the Molecomb could be the right contest for him. (op 10-11 tchd Evens)
Lady Ibrox threw down a strong challenge to Annunciation close to the inside rail after tracking him, but couldn't get to the front. She looks more than capable of winning in novice company. (op 8-1)
Faithfilly(IRE) shed her maiden tag in soft ground on her previous outing but didn't get home here after mixing it with the Ryan Moore-ridden colt in front early. (op 9-4 tchd 15-8)
Archie Stevens had been well beaten on both previous outings and was comfortably held again. That said, this effort wasn't without promise if heading towards handicaps now. (tchd 25-1)
Just Past Andover (IRE)who finished second in the Lily Agnes here back in May, raced with the choke out for a while before being outpaced. (op 9-1)
Lothian Countess proved troublesome to load into the stalls and finally emerged from them, when they opened, after her rivals were long gone. Official explanation: jockey said filly sat down in stalls and was slowly away (op 28-1)

3605 ASSEMBLY TECHNIQUES 25TH ANNIVERSARY H'CAP 1m 4f 66y
2:40 (2:40) (Class 4) (0-85,84) 3-Y-0 **£5,175** (£1,540; £769 ; £384) **Stalls** Low

Form RPR

3134 **1** **Naseem Alyasmeen (IRE)**[17] 3033 3 -8-1275................ PatCosgrave 2 89
(Mick Channon) *hld up: hdwy on outer over 3f out: led over 2f out: drew clr 1f out: styd on wl and in command ins fnl f* **7/1**[3]

0311 **2** 4 1/2 **Courtesy Call (IRE)**[23] 2843 3 -8-972................................. JoeFanning 4 79
(Mark Johnston) *led: hdd over 2f out: one pce and no ch fnl f* **8/1**

-045 **3** 1 1/4 **Arley Hall**[22] 2885 3 -8-467... FrannyNorton 7 72
(Richard Fahey) *s.i.s: in rr: sn niggled along: hdwy on outer 2f out: chsd clr front two wl over 1f out: styd on u.p ins fnl f wout threatening* **12/1**

312 **4** 10 **Gabrial The Hero (USA)**[17] 3033 3 -9-784..................... CathyGannon 8 73
(David Simcock) *v s.i.s: in rr: plld hrd: rdn wl over 1f out: plugged on to take 4th 1f out: nvr able to trble ldrs* **4/1**[2]

3220 **5** 3 **Hallmark Star**[28] 2718 3 -9-683...[1] ShaneKelly 6 67
(Gerard Butler) *w ldr: rdn 4f out: lost pl 3f out: wknd wl over 1f out* **12/1**

3-05 **6** 3 3/4 **Zenaat**[23] 2848 3 -9-077... RyanMoore 1 55
(Sir Michael Stoute) *trckd ldrs: rdn and outpcd over 2f out: wl btn over 1f out* **17/2**

1-03 **7** 2 1/4 **Rayvin Black**[43] 2258 3 -9-380... TedDurcan 5 55
(Mark H Tompkins) *trckd ldrs: rdn and outpcd over 2f out: wl btn over 1f out* **2/1**[1]

-201 **8** 7 **Hyperlink (IRE)**[15] 3104 3 -9-077.. AmyRyan 3 40
(Mark Johnston) *racd keenly: prom on outer: chalng 3f out: rdn and outpcd over 2f out: wknd wl over 1f out* **7/1**[3]

2m 37.99s (-0.51) **Going Correction** +0.125s/f (Good) **8**Ran SP% **115.4**
Speed ratings (Par 101): **106,103,102,95,93 91,89,84**
toteswingers 1&2 £3.40, 2&3 £5.70, 1&3 £6.30 CSF £61.48 CT £661.91 TOTE £10.30 : £2.50 , £3.40, £4.70 ; EX 48.00 .
Owner Jaber Abdullah **Bred** Patrick Byrnes **Trained** West Ilsley, Berks

FOCUS
A decent affair run at what looked an sensible pace. The winner's improvement had seemed to stall but this was another step forward.
Rayvin Black Official explanation: jockey said colt stopped quickly

3606 CES MIDSUMMER MAIDEN STKS 1m 2f 75y
3:10 (3:11) (Class 4) 3-Y-0+ **£5,175** (£1,540; £769 ; £384) **Stalls** High

Form RPR

0-3 **1** **Sun Central (IRE)**[42] 2266 3 -9-10..................................... ShaneKelly 8 91+
(William Haggas) *chsd ldrs: wnt 2nd over 6f out: led wl over 1f out: r.o wl to stretch clr fnl 75yds: readily* **6/5**[1]

-034 **2** 3 1/2 **Energize (FR)**[15] 3107 3 -9-172.. RyanMoore 4 84
(Richard Hannon) *chsd ldrs: rdn over 2f out: wnt 2nd 1f out: tried to chal ins fnl f: no ex fnl 75yds* **6/1**

-35 **3** 1 **Devine Guest (IRE)**[16] 3069 3 -8-100................................ PatCosgrave 5 77
(Mick Channon) *led: hdd 7f out: trckd ldrs after: effrt 2f out: nt qckn over 1f out: styd on same pce fnl 75yds* **4/1**[2]

32-0 **4** 2 1/2 **Almaas (USA)**[41] 2313 3 -9-184.. TedDurcan 7 77
(Saeed Bin Suroor) *chsd ldr: led 7f out: rdn and hdd wl over 1f out: wknd fnl 150yds* **5/1**[3]

05 **5** 7 **Zain Glory**[7] 3398 3 -9-10.. FrannyNorton 3 63
(Gerard Butler) *missed break: bhd: pushed along over 3f out: prog u.p over 2f out: nvr able to trble ldrs* **10/1**

0 **6** 11 **Miss Mohawk (IRE)**[30] 2633 3 -8-100....................... MichaelO'Connell 1 36
(Alan Brown) *s.i.s: in rr: pushed along over 3f out: lft bhd over 2f out* **50/1**

0 **7** 2 3/4 **Monicker**[17] 3035 3 -8-100... JoeFanning 2 31
(Mark Johnston) *s.i.s: midfield: hdwy 4f out: rdn and wknd over 2f out* **16/1**

0 **8** 36 **Awaywithefairies**[40] 2335 3 -8-100.................................... CathyGannon 6
(Richard Ford) *bhd: struggling 5f out: lost tch 3f out: t.o* **40/1**

2m 11.93s (0.73) **Going Correction** +0.125s/f (Good) **8**Ran SP% **115.8**
Speed ratings (Par 105): **102,99,98,96,90 82,79,51**
toteswingers 1&2 £2.30, 2&3 £4.80, 1&3 £1.40 CSF £9.20 TOTE £2.90 : £1.10 , £1.80 , £1.40 ; EX 10.30 .
Owner Lael Stable **Bred** Lael Stables **Trained** Newmarket, Suffolk

FOCUS
Only four of these made serious appeal and they duly came away from the remainder at the end. An improved effort from the winner, who is likely to do better.

3607 KATHLEEN CORBETT MEMORIAL H'CAP 7f 2y
3:45 (3:49) (Class 2) (0-100,96) 3-Y-0 **£12,602** (£3,772; £1,886 ; £944 ; £470) **Stalls** Low

Form RPR

6260 **1** **Van Ellis**[9] 3294 3 -9-796.. JoeFanning 9 105+
(Mark Johnston) *midfield: hdwy over 1f out: sn led: r.o and in command fnl 75yds* **7/1**[3]

1-40 **2** 2 **Kimbali (IRE)**[42] 2276 3-8-9 **84** .... TedDurcan 6 88
(Richard Fahey) *hld up: hdwy 2f out: rdn and styd on ins fnl f: tk 2nd towards fin: nt rch wnr* **9/1**

-311 **3** *nk* **All Or Nothin (IRE)**[19] 2979 3-8-8 **83** .... MichaelO'Connell 3 86
(John Quinn) *trckd ldrs: led wl over 1f out: sn hdd: stl ch ins fnl f: outpcd fnl 75yds* **9/2**[2]

255- **4** ¾ **Red Art (IRE)**[252] 7026 3-9-7 **96** .... RyanMoore 2 97
(Charles Hills) *hld up: rdn and hdwy on inner over 1f out: styd on ins fnl f: no further imp towards fin* **4/1**[1]

12 **5** *nk* **Well Painted (IRE)**[21] 2916 3-9-5 **94** .... ShaneKelly 8 96+
(William Haggas) *hld up: hdwy whn nt clr run over 1f out: rdn and nt qckn ins fnl f: eased fnl 75yds* **9/2**[2]

5032 **6** 2 ¾ **Rusty Rocket (IRE)**[10] 3288 3-8-4 **79** .... CathyGannon 1 72
(Paul Green) *led: rdn hdd wl over 1f out: wknd fnl 100yds* **12/1**

0501 **7** 5 **Shamrocked (IRE)**[16] 3071 3-8-2 **77** oh1 .... FrannyNorton 5 56
(Mick Channon) *chsd ldrs: rdn over 1f out: wknd ins fnl f* **14/1**

0433 **8** 1 ¾ **Zakreet**[21] 2930 3-8-4 **79** ....(b) AmyRyan 10 54
(Kevin Ryan) *midfield: hdwy to chse ldrs 4f out: rdn over 2f out: sn wknd* **15/2**

1-01 **9** 4 **Decision By One**[36] 2451 3-8-6 **81** ....(t) RichardKingscote 4 45
(Tom Dascombe) *racd keenly: chsd ldr tl wl over 1f out: sn wknd* **8/1**

1m 26.25s (-0.25) **Going Correction** +0.125s/f (Good) **9** Ran SP% **116.1**
Speed ratings (Par 105): **106,103,103,102,102 99,93,91,86**
toteswingers 1&2 £15.30, 2&3 £6.50, 1&3 £7.90 CSF £68.26 CT £317.51 TOTE £7.90: £2.60, £3.10, £1.30; EX 59.00.
Owner Sheikh Hamdan Bin Mohammed Al Maktoum **Bred** D A Yardy **Trained** Middleham Moor, N Yorks

FOCUS
It paid to come off the pace in this decent handicap, which was sound run. The winner improved again.

NOTEBOOK
Van Ellis, beaten around 14l in the Britannia at Royal Ascot, surged to the front when the gap opened up perfectly for him and found enough to hang on. He's proved to be an admirable and hardy type in only his first season of racing. (op 6-1)
Kimbali(IRE), given a break since about the middle of May, was forced to make his challenge reasonably wide but didn't have any obvious excuses considering he was at least upsides Van Ellis when the tempo increased.
All Or Nothin(IRE), a previous course winner over nearly a furlong less in May, was chasing a hat-trick back up to 7f and ran right up to his best after finding no trouble. He's far from exposed but the handicapper might have his measure for the time being, although he can go back down in trip again. (op 5-1)
Red Art(IRE), who won the opening novice event on this card 12 months previously, got caught one-paced as the field turned in, losing a bit of ground, but stayed on resolutely towards the stands' rail. (op 9-2)
Well Painted(IRE) ◆ was unexposed and had the subsequent Britannia runner-up behind him last time when tried over 1m. Down in trip, he met traffic for most of the home straight, possibly while hanging, and is better than his fifth place suggests. Shane Kelly reported that the gelding was denied a clear run. Official explanation: jockey said gelding was denied a clear run (op 4-1 tchd 7-2)
Rusty Rocket(IRE) Official explanation: jockey said colt hung right-handed
Decision By One pulled much too hard early to have a lot left for the final couple of furlongs. Richard Kingscote reported that the colt hung right handed. Official explanation: jockey said colt hung right-handed (op 17-2 tchd 9-1)

3608 AGA ITOTAL CONTROL H'CAP — 5f 16y
4:15 (4:16) (Class 3) (0-90,86) 3-Y-O **£8,191** (£2,451; £1,225; £613; £305) **Stalls** Low

Form RPR

4212 **1** **Silvanus (IRE)**[15] 3109 7-9-4 **78** .... RussKennemore 6 92
(Paul Midgley) *mde all: kicked clr fr 2f out: r.o wl and in command ins fnl f* **12/1**

2365 **2** 2 **Green Park (IRE)**[1] 3557 9-8-12 **79** ....(b) JasonHart(7) 4 86
(Declan Carroll) *chsd ldrs: rdn to take 2nd 1f out: styd on u.p: no imp on wnr* **7/1**

5125 **3** 1 ½ **Diman Waters (IRE)**[16] 3065 5-9-2 **76** .... PatCosgrave 1 78
(Eric Alston) *midfield: rdn and hdwy over 1f out: styd on ins fnl f: nt rch ldrs* **4/1**[1]

3302 **4** ½ **Church Music (IRE)**[23] 2853 3-9-3 **83** ....(p) FrannyNorton 2 81
(Michael Scudamore) *chsd ldrs: pushed along to take 2nd 2f out: nt gng pce of wnr: lost 2nd 1f out: no ex fnl 75yds* **13/2**

5311 **5** 1 ¼ **Electric Qatar**[5] 3450 3-9-6 **86** 6ex .... RichardKingscote 3 79
(Tom Dascombe) *dwlt: towards rr: nt clr run over 2f out: prog ins fnl f: styd on: nt rch ldrs* **5/1**[3]

3503 **6** ½ **Jedward (IRE)**[14] 3169 5-9-6 **80** .... TedDurcan 5 74
(Richard Fahey) *midfield: pushed along 4f out: kpt on ins fnl f: nt gng pce to chal* **9/2**[2]

3400 **7** 5 **Legal Eagle (IRE)**[1] 3557 7-8-13 **73** ....(p) SeanQuinlan 13 49
(Paul Green) *in rr: pushed along and outpcd over 2f out: n.m.r and hmpd over 1f out: kpt on ins fnl f: nt trble ldrs* **40/1**

-500 **8** 3 **Living It Large (FR)**[28] 2704 5-9-12 **86** .... JoeFanning 10 51
(Ed de Giles) *racd keenly: trckd ldrs: rdn over 2f out: wknd over 1f out* **12/1**

3060 **9** ½ **Hamoody (USA)**[13] 3183 8-8-12 **79** .... ShirleyTeasdale(7) 8 42
(David Nicholls) *missed break: hld up in rr: rdn and swtchd lft over 1f out: nvr a threat* **16/1**

-003 **10** 1 **Tyfos**[29] 2674 7-9-9 **83** .... ShaneKelly 7 42
(Brian Baugh) *chsd ldrs tl rdn and wknd over 2f out* **12/1**

003 **11** 2 ¼ **Crimea (IRE)**[23] 2861 6-9-6 **80** .... MichaelO'Connell 11 31
(David Nicholls) *w wnr tl pushed along over 2f out: wknd over 1f out* **33/1**

2413 **U** **Beau Mistral (IRE)**[12] 3234 3-8-13 **79** .... CathyGannon 9
(Paul Green) *rrd and uns rdr s* **20/1**

1m 0.71s (-0.29) **Going Correction** +0.125s/f (Good)
WFA 3 from 4yo+ 6lb **12** Ran SP% **119.8**
Speed ratings (Par 107): **107,103,101,100,98 97,89,85,84,82 79,**
toteswingers 1&2 £34.90, 2&3 £9.40, 1&3 £14.00 CSF £92.83 CT £409.33 TOTE £10.90: £4.00, £2.30, £1.30; EX 81.00.
Owner Colin Alton **Bred** Barronstown Stud And Mrs T Stack **Trained** Westow, N Yorks

FOCUS
A strong race but a great ride by Russ Kennemore won the day. A clear personal best from the winner despite his age.

NOTEBOOK
Silvanus(IRE) had never won going left-handed previously but brushed that statistic readily aside as he strode clear. Connections feel that he is only starting to show what they see at home on the course now, so presumably the gelding has a bit more scope to improve, although one does have the suspicion plenty of praise goes to the jockey for this win. (op 9-1)
Green Park(IRE), fifth the previous night here over about 7f, was handily placed from a low draw but was never going to get to the winner. That said, it was a fine effort within 24hrs of his last one. (op 6-1)
Diman Waters(IRE), who has good Chester form, sat in midfield moving well before making late headway. He remains in good heart. (op 5-1)
Church Music(IRE), who'd run well at this course in May, stayed on from a chasing position but was another who simply couldn't get involved when the winner got away. (op 7-1)
Electric Qatar was ridden in a similar way to the third, and for his two recent victories. He can be given another chance on turf or the AW considering nothing got involved here from off the gallop. (tchd 11-2)
Jedward(IRE) shaped nicely at York last time over 6f but proved to be one paced here once in the clear towards the centre of the course. (op 6-1)
Hamoody(USA) is on a career-low mark, which may get reduced again after he was slow to leave the stalls here - possibly distracted by Beau Mistral's antics next to him. While he may not be as good as he once was, it can only be a matter of time before he sparks back into life. (op 14-1)
Crimea(IRE) Official explanation: jockey said gelding was unsuited by being rushed along from wide draw

3609 RAYMOND CORBETT MEMORIAL CLAIMING STKS — 1m 2f 75y
4:50 (4:50) (Class 5) 3-Y-O+ **£4,043** (£1,203; £601; £300) **Stalls** High

Form RPR

4-41 **1** **Just Lille (IRE)**[4] 3458 9-8-12 88 ....(p) JoeFanning 2 74
(Ann Duffield) *chsd ldr tl wl over 7f out: remained handy: swtchd lft over 1f out: sn chalng: r.o to ld wl ins fnl f: in control cl home* **2/1**[1]

0-00 **2** ½ **Reflect (IRE)**[43] 2248 4-9-3 85 ....(t) RyanMoore 1 78
(Richard Hannon) *led: hdd wl over 7f out: chsd ldr tl rdn to regain ld over 1f out: hdd wl ins fnl f: hld cl home* **9/4**[2]

1050 **3** ½ **Mirrored**[26] 2773 6-9-4 87 .... FrannyNorton 6 78
(Tim Easterby) *hld up: hdwy 2f out: nt clr run and snatched up over 1f out: in clr sn after: r.o and clsd towards fin* **3/1**[3]

4140 **4** 1 ¾ **Sir Boss (IRE)**[14] 3163 7-9-3 75 .... CathyGannon 3 73
(Michael Mullineaux) *s.i.s: hld up in rr: effrt over 1f out: styd on ins fnl f: nt gng pce to get to ldrs* **14/1**

2 **5** 5 **Offbeat Safaris (IRE)**[19] 2984 4-9-3 0 .... RichardKingscote 5 63
(Brendan Powell) *s.i.s: trckd ldrs: rdn and failed to pick-up over 1f out: wknd fnl 150yds* **10/1**

0402 **6** 3 **Amazing Star (IRE)**[21] 2913 7-9-3 75 .... ShaneKelly 7 57
(Declan Carroll) *s.i.s: hld up: rdn over 1f out: outpcd fnl f: nvr a threat* **16/1**

2055 **7** *hd* **Zenarinda**[21] 2915 5-8-7 61 .... HarryPoulton(5) 8 52
(Mark H Tompkins) *plld hrd: prom: led wl over 7f out: rdn and hdd over 1f out: wknd ins fnl f* **33/1**

2m 12.52s (1.32) **Going Correction** +0.125s/f (Good)
WFA 3 from 4yo+ 12lb **7** Ran SP% **113.7**
Speed ratings (Par 103): **99,98,98,96,92 90,90**
toteswingers 1&2 £1.60, 2&3 £9.00, 1&3 £1.70 CSF £6.70 TOTE £3.30: £2.20, £3.30; EX 5.50.
Owner Middleham Park Racing XLVI **Bred** Sweetmans Bloodstock **Trained** Constable Burton, N Yorks

■ Stewards' Enquiry : Joe Fanning three-day ban: careless riding (Jul 16-18)

FOCUS
Some of these had a bit to prove for one reason or another, and the early gallop was poor, resulting in unreliable form. The race is rated around the fourth.

3610 CRUISE NIGHTSPOT H'CAP — 1m 3f 79y
5:25 (5:25) (Class 4) (0-85,82) 4-Y-O+ **£5,175** (£1,540; £769; £384) **Stalls** Low

Form RPR

1 **Solaras Exhibition (IRE)**[25] 6198 4-8-12 **73** .... RyanMoore 9 85+
(Tim Vaughan) *hld up: hdwy on outer over 2f out: swtchd rt over 1f out: r.o to ld wl ins fnl f: in command towards fin* **7/2**[1]

2002 **2** 1 ¾ **New Hampshire (USA)**[6] 3417 4-9-5 **80** ....(p) MichaelO'Connell 5 89
(Tony Coyle) *led for 2f: remained prom: led over 3f out: kicked 3 l clr 2f out: hdd wl ins fnl f: no ex towards fin* **13/2**

535 **3** ½ **Noble Alan (GER)**[28] 2708 9-9-2 **82** .... PaddyAspell(5) 3 90
(Nicky Richards) *midfield: hdwy whn nt clr run 3f out: effrt on inner 2f out: nt qckn jst ins fnl f: styd on towards fin* **13/2**

4325 **4** 2 ¼ **Kathleen Frances**[13] 3187 5-8-13 **74** .... TedDurcan 4 78
(Mark H Tompkins) *midfield: hdwy 3f out: rdn to chse ldr over 1f out: no imp: lost 2nd ins fnl f: no ex fnl 100yds* **5/1**[3]

0000 **5** 3 ¼ **Tenhoo**[7] 3377 6-8-9 **70** .... RichardKingscote 2 68
(Eric Alston) *trckd ldrs: rdn to chse ldr over 2f out: lost 2nd over 1f out: wknd fnl f* **20/1**

2-24 **6** 5 **Woop Woop (IRE)**[36] 2447 4-8-10 **74** .... RyanPowell(3) 7 63
(Ian Williams) *s.i.s: hld up: struggling over 2f out: kpt on into midfield over 1f out: no imp on ldrs* **9/1**

-600 **7** 11 **Unknown Rebel (IRE)**[31] 2606 4-9-1 **76** ....(p) AmyRyan 6 45
(Kevin Ryan) *prom tl rdn and wknd over 3f out* **11/1**

4060 **8** 11 **Smart Step**[12] 3213 4-8-4 **65** .... JoeFanning 11 15
(Mark Johnston) *hld up: u.p over 2f out: nvr on terms* **33/1**

243/ **9** 2 **Clerk's Choice (IRE)**[43] 6571 6-8-13 **79** .... BrendanPowell(5) 1 25
(Oliver Sherwood) *hld up: u.p fr 6f out: nvr a threat* **9/2**[2]

5555 **10** 14 **Uphold**[14] 3162 5-9-5 **80** ....(vt) ShaneKelly 8
(Gay Kelleway) *prom: led after 2f: hdd over 3f out: wknd over 2f out: sn eased* **20/1**

-050 **11** 2 ½ **Look Left**[17] 3038 4-8-13 **74** .... CathyGannon 10
(David Simcock) *in tch tl rdn and wknd over 2f out* **16/1**

2m 24.68s (-0.12) **Going Correction** +0.125s/f (Good) **11** Ran SP% **120.4**
Speed ratings (Par 105): **105,103,103,101,99 95,87,79,78,68 66**
toteswingers 1&2 £5.60, 2&3 £16.80, 1&3 £16.80 CSF £26.31 CT £145.39 TOTE £3.50: £2.60, £2.30, £3.30; EX 26.20.
Owner C Davies **Bred** John Skehan **Trained** Aberthin, Vale of Glamorgan

FOCUS
A few horses better known for their recent exploits over jumps lined up for this among some established Flat performers. The pace was sound and the form is rated around the runner-up.

Clerk's Choice(IRE) Official explanation: jockey said gelding never travelled
Uphold Official explanation: trainer's rep said gelding was unsuited by the good ground

T/Plt: £66.50 to a £1 stake. Pool of £69954.54 - 767.04 winning tickets. T/Qpdt: £8.80 to a £1 stake. Pool of £4142 -70 - 345.02 winning tickets. DO

3560 DONCASTER (L-H)

Saturday, June 30

OFFICIAL GOING: Good (good to soft in places; 8.1)

Wind: Moderate against Weather: Cloudy with showers

3611 QUADRO SERVICES PRECAST CONCRETE & MODULAR INSTALLATION MAIDEN STKS 7f

6:05 (6:05) (Class 5) 2-Y-O **£2,911** (£866; £432; £216) **Stalls** High

Form RPR

1 **Azrur (IRE)** 2-9-3 0 JamieSpencer 13 77+
(Michael Bell) *hld up and bhd: smooth hdwy 3f out: trckd ldrs 2f out: swtchd lft and effrt over 1f out: led ins fnl f: readily* **4/1**[2]

2 ½ **French Press (IRE)** 2-9-3 0 RobertWinston 6 75+
(David Brown) *in tch: hdwy over 2f out: rdn to chse ldrs over 1f out: styd on ins fnl f* **33/1**

4 3 shd **Specialty (IRE)**[24] 2822 2-8-12 0 MickyFenton 5 70
(Pam Sly) *led: rdn along 2f out: drvn ent fnl f: sn hdd: kpt on gamely u.p towards fin* **9/2**[3]

2 4 nk **Bornean (IRE)**[29] 2648 2-9-3 0 SilvestreDeSousa 3 74
(Mahmood Al Zarooni) *t.k.h early: trckd ldrs: hdwy and cl up 2f out: sn rdn and styd on to ld briefly ins fnl f: sn hdd: no ex nr line* **2/1**[1]

5 3½ **Constans (IRE)** 2-9-3 0 AdamKirby 16 65+
(Clive Cox) *dwlt and towards rr: pushed along 1/2-way: hdwy wl over 2f out: rdn wl over 1f out: kpt on fnl f: nrst fin* **10/1**

6 2¾ **Thatchmaster (USA)** 2-9-3 0 AhmedAjtebi 4 58
(Mahmood Al Zarooni) *dwlt: hdwy and in tch after 2f: cl up over 2f out: rdn to chal wl over 1f out and ev ch tl wknd ent fnl f* **15/2**

0 7 2½ **Sekumkum (IRE)**[21] 2934 2-9-0 0 (b[1]) MatthewCosham(3) 8 51
(Marco Botti) *prom: rdn along 2f out: grad wknd appr fnl f* **33/1**

8 5 **Order Of Service** 2-9-3 0 RichardMullen 11 38
(David Brown) *nvr bttr than midfield* **25/1**

9 shd **Byron's Dream** 2-8-12 0 JustinNewman(5) 10 38
(Jedd O'Keeffe) *dwlt: sn in tch: chsd ldrs 1/2-way: rdn along wl over 2f out and grad wknd* **66/1**

30 10 ¾ **Mickstathetricksta**[13] 3182 2-9-3 0 GrahamLee 17 36
(Scott Dixon) *midfield on outer: pushed along 3f out: n.d* **14/1**

0 11 ¾ **Hazza The Jazza**[13] 3182 2-9-3 0 RobbieFitzpatrick 1 34
(Richard Guest) *s.i.s: a towards rr* **40/1**

4 12 ½ **Complicator**[14] 3168 2-9-3 0 IPoullis 14 33
(Alan McCabe) *in tch: pushed along wl over 2f out: n.d* **12/1**

6 13 ½ **Spivey Cove**[22] 2880 2-9-3 0 RichardThomas 2 31
(Ed McMahon) *t.k.h: sn chsng ldrs: cl up 1/2-way: rdn along wl over 2f out and sn wknd* **25/1**

14 nk **Good Speech (IRE)** 2-8-12 0 RoystonFfrench 7 26
(Tom Tate) *chsd ldrs 3f: sn lost pl and bhd* **33/1**

15 3 **Azzurra Leonessa (IRE)** 2-8-12 0 PJMcDonald 15 18
(Ben Haslam) *nvr bttr than midfield* **66/1**

16 2½ **Captain's Dream (IRE)** 2-9-3 0 AndrewElliott 9 16
(Jedd O'Keeffe) *midfield: pushed along 1/2-way: sn wknd* **50/1**

1m 29.64s (3.34) **Going Correction** +0.15s/f (Good) **16** Ran SP% **130.6**
Speed ratings (Par 93): **86,85,85,84,80 77,74,69,69,68 67,66,66,65,62 59**
toteswingers 1&2 £35.80, 2&3 £45.20, 1&3 £6.60 CSF £147.68 TOTE £5.30: £1.70, £13.40, £1.90; EX 272.10 TRIFECTA Not won..
Owner Saleh Al Homaizi & Imad Al Sagar **Bred** Kildaragh Stud **Trained** Newmarket, Suffolk

FOCUS

On a breezy night with squally showers the ground was described by Jamie Spencer after the opening 2-y-o maiden as 'on the easy side of good, heading towards good to soft'. Previous form was thin on the ground and the first two home were newcomers. The form can't be rated any higher at this stage but the winner should do a good bit better.

NOTEBOOK

Azrur(IRE) ◆, who cost 110,000gns as a yearling, is quite a tall, athletic type. Reported on the lazy side at home, he was lit up on his debut and his rider was keen to settle him in behind. He made good ground towards the outer and was firmly in command at the line. A mile will suit him even better and he looks a useful prospect. (op 7-1)

French Press(IRE), whose dam has bred three winners including one Group 3 winner at two, ran much better than expected judging by his SP on his debut. He stuck to his task in willing fashion and should soon go one better.

Specialty(IRE), first foal of the stable's 1000 Guineas winner Speciosa, showed the benefit of her first outing. She showed bags of toe to take them along and will improve again. (op 4-1 tchd 5-1)

Bornean(IRE), who split two subsequent winners when runner-up first time at Brighton, is not that big and looked very dull in his coat. He weakened noticeably towards the finish and will appreciate a less stiff task and better ground. Official explanation: jockey said, regarding running, that the colt was running green and had no more to give latter stages. (op 5-2)

Constans(IRE) ◆, a close-coupled newcomer, cost 155,000euros as a yearling. He stayed on from an unpromising position and can be expected to improve a good deal for this first run. (op 8-1)

Thatchmaster(USA), first foal of a Ribblesdale winner, matched strides with the leader but tired appreciably in the closing stages. He is by Street Cry whose offspring shine on Polytrack. (op 7-1 tchd 8-1)

Spivey Cove Official explanation: jockey said colt ran too free

3612 PTL OCCUPATIONAL HYGIENE ASBESTOS SURVEYS H'CAP 6f

6:40 (6:41) (Class 4) (0-85,85) 3-Y-O+ **£5,175** (£1,540; £769; £384) **Stalls** High

Form RPR

0004 1 **Johannes (IRE)**[17] 3049 9-9-5 83 GeorgeChaloner(7) 6 95
(Richard Fahey) *hld up in tch: hdwy wl over 1f out: squeezed through to chal ent fnl f: sn rdn and kpt on wl to ld last 100yds* **8/1**

3546 2 ½ **Defence Council (IRE)**[5] 3439 4-9-7 78 SilvestreDeSousa 10 88
(Mel Brittain) *hld up in tch: hdwy 2f out: rdn to ld ent fnl f: drvn and hdd last 100yds: no ex* **7/1**[3]

0030 3 2¾ **Sutton Veny (IRE)**[28] 2707 6-10-0 85 JamieSpencer 11 86
(Jeremy Gask) *hld up and bhd: hdwy 2f out: nt clr run over 1f out: styd on ins fnl f: nt rch front pair* **10/1**

0062 4 nk **Haajes**[3] 3496 8-9-6 77 RoystonFfrench 7 77
(Paul Midgley) *prom: effrt and cl up 2f out: rdn and ev ch over 1f out: drvn and one pce ins fnl f* **12/1**

5500 5 1¼ **Courageous (IRE)**[28] 2704 6-9-5 81 (t) NeilFarley(5) 5 77
(Milton Bradley) *led: rdn along wl over 1f out: drvn and hdd ent fnl f: sn wknd* **25/1**

-001 6 nk **Main Beach**[25] 2791 5-9-1 72 (t) MickyFenton 2 67
(Paul Midgley) *s.i.s and bhd: hdwy on wd outside over 2f out: rdn to chse ldrs wl over 1f out: sn drvn and one pce* **7/1**[3]

0260 7 nk **Little Jimmy Odsox (IRE)**[14] 3169 4-9-6 77 (p) DavidAllan 3 71
(Tim Easterby) *dwlt: sn rdn along into midfield: effrt over 2f out: rdn to chal and ev ch over 1f out: wknd ent fnl f* **8/1**

0-6 8 ¾ **Azzurra Du Caprio (IRE)**[40] 2337 4-9-13 84 PJMcDonald 12 76
(Ben Haslam) *a towards rr* **12/1**

000 9 3 **Star Rover (IRE)**[35] 2488 5-9-6 80 (v) MatthewCosham(3) 9 62
(David Evans) *chsd ldrs: rdn along 2f out: sn wknd* **28/1**

1140 10 1 **Alive And Kicking**[24] 2825 4-9-6 77 GrahamGibbons 13 56
(James Bethell) *t.k.h: prom: cl up 1/2-way: rdn along 2f out and sn wknd* **5/1**[2]

42 11 ¾ **Paradise Spectre**[12] 3225 5-9-4 75 MartinHarley 14 52
(Mrs K Burke) *chsd ldrs: rdn along over 2f out: sn btn* **4/1**[1]

0642 12 1½ **Tabaret**[25] 2793 9-8-11 68 (p) TomEaves 4 40
(Richard Whitaker) *trckd ldrs: cl up 1/2-way: effrt and ev ch 2f out: sn rdn and wknd appr fnl f* **12/1**

1m 13.67s (0.07) **Going Correction** +0.15s/f (Good) **12** Ran SP% **123.4**
Speed ratings (Par 105): **105,104,100,100,98 98,97,96,92,91 90,88**
toteswingers 1&2 £13.10, 2&3 £6.40, 1&3 £19.70 CSF £65.76 CT £581.18 TOTE £11.00: £3.40, £2.80, £4.10; EX 97.40 TRIFECTA Not won..
Owner John Nicholls Ltd/David Kilburn **Bred** Blue Bloodstock Limited **Trained** Musley Bank, N Yorks

FOCUS

They raced in one group towards the centre in this fair but competitive sprint handicap. Straightforward form.

3613 SANDRA GILKS H'CAP 5f 140y

7:15 (7:17) (Class 4) (0-85,82) 3-Y-O **£5,175** (£1,540; £769; £384) **Stalls** High

Form RPR

-141 1 **Khubala (IRE)**[26] 2764 3-9-2 77 (b) SilvestreDeSousa 12 90
(Ed Dunlop) *hld up in rr: hdwy and nt clr run over 1f out: sn swtchd rt and rdn: qcknd to ld ins fnl f: edgd lft and kpt on wl towards fin* **11/2**[2]

-031 2 ½ **Goldream**[12] 3235 3-9-3 78 KierenFallon 11 89
(Luca Cumani) *hld up towards rr: hdwy 2f out: nt clr run over 1f out: rdn and squeezed through to chal whn hung bdly lft ins fnl f: kpt on* **2/1**[1]

-004 3 1¾ **West Leake Hare (IRE)**[7] 3379 3-8-7 68 (p) HayleyTurner 4 73
(Charles Hills) *chsd ldrs: hdwy and cl up over 2f out: rdn to ld over 1f out: drvn and hdd ins fnl f: kpt on same pce* **11/2**[2]

3030 4 ½ **Whisky Bravo**[19] 2979 3-9-0 75 JamieSpencer 6 78
(David Brown) *dwlt and bhd: hdwy wl over 1f out: sn swtchd rt and rdn: styd on fnl f: nrst fin* **14/1**

3535 5 nk **Waseem Faris (IRE)**[19] 2979 3-9-2 77 MartinHarley 1 79
(Mick Channon) *dwlt and towards rr: hdwy 2f out: sn rdn and kpt on same pce appr fnl f* **11/1**

2-03 6 1¾ **O'Gorman**[28] 2714 3-9-7 82 PhillipMakin 2 78
(Kevin Ryan) *in tch: gd hdwy on wd outside 2f out: rdn to chal over 1f out and ev ch tl drvn and wknd ins fnl f* **9/1**

5P-0 7 ¾ **Almond Branches**[24] 2824 3-8-10 71 PJMcDonald 7 65
(George Moore) *chsd ldrs: hdwy and cl up 2f out: sn rdn and hld whn hmpd ins fnl f* **50/1**

-001 8 4 **Bop It**[16] 3065 3-9-7 82 TomEaves 10 62
(Bryan Smart) *in tch: hdwy to chse ldrs on outer over 2f out: sn rdn and wknd over 1f out* **13/2**[3]

3210 9 nk **Available (IRE)**[24] 2824 3-8-13 74 FrannyNorton 8 53
(John Mackie) *hld up in tch: rdn along over 2f out: sn wknd* **20/1**

-504 10 1¼ **Cockney Fire**[19] 2986 3-8-8 72 MatthewCosham(3) 5 47
(David Evans) *cl up: led 1/2-way: rdn wl over 1f out: sn hdd & wknd* **25/1**

0 11 3 **Bahama Spirit (IRE)**[22] 2893 3-9-2 77 GrahamLee 9 42
(Jeremy Gask) *chsd ldrs: rdn along over 2f out: drvn and btn whn hmpd appr fnl f* **14/1**

00-5 12 1¾ **Roy's Legacy**[157] 295 3-7-9 63 oh3 ShirleyTeasdale(7) 13 22
(Shaun Harris) *chsd ldrs on wd outside: rdn along over 2f out: sn wknd* **50/1**

31-6 13 9 **Taffe**[157] 295 3-9-6 81 MickyFenton 3
(James Given) *led: rdn along and hdd 1/2-way: wknd qckly* **25/1**

1m 8.7s (-0.10) **Going Correction** +0.15s/f (Good) **13** Ran SP% **125.5**
Speed ratings (Par 101): **106,105,103,102,101 99,98,93,92,91 87,84,72**
toteswingers 1&2 £2.70, 2&3 £5.40, 1&3 £7.10 CSF £16.79 CT £68.93 TOTE £6.70: £2.30, £1.50, £2.70; EX 13.70 Trifecta £46.50 Pool: £365.95 - 5.82 winning units..
Owner Miss P Araci **Bred** James F Hanly **Trained** Newmarket, Suffolk

FOCUS

This fair handicap was run over the Portland Handicap trip. The complexion changed dramatically late on. Decent form for the grade, and it looks sound.

3614 DERBYSHIRE AGGREGATES H'CAP 1m 6f 132y

7:45 (7:49) (Class 3) (0-95,88) 3-Y-O **£8,409** (£2,502; £1,250; £625) **Stalls** Low

Form RPR

514 1 **Suraj**[42] 2281 3-9-7 88 HayleyTurner 2 102+
(Michael Bell) *hld up in rr: swtchd outside and smooth hdwy wl over 2f out: rdn to ld wl over 1f out: clr ent fnl f: styd on strly* **15/8**[1]

1-23 2 6 **Beyond Conceit (IRE)**[35] 2484 3-9-6 87 JamieSpencer 4 92
(Tom Tate) *trckd ldng pair: hdwy 3f out: led briefly 2f out: sn rdn and hdd wl over 1f out: drvn and kpt on fnl f: no ch w wnr* **7/2**[2]

6-01 3 1¾ **Bute Hall**[29] 2668 3-8-13 80 JoeFanning 5 82
(Mark Johnston) *hld up in rr: hdwy 3f out: chsd ldrs over 2f out: sn rdn and cl up tl drvn and one pce appr fnl f* **5/1**[3]

2-04 4 6 **Badea**[17] 3035 3-8-7 74 ow1 KierenFallon 3 68
(Richard Fahey) *hld up: hdwy on inner to chse ldrs over 3f out: sn rdn and wknd 2f out* **14/1**

-241 5 5 **Spanish Wedding**[22] 2889 3-9-2 83 (b) MartinHarley 6 70
(Marco Botti) *trckd ldr: hdwy to ld wl over 2f out: sn rdn and hdd 2f out: sn wknd* **5/1**[3]

2-1 6 18 **Tajriba (IRE)**[53] 1957 3-9-1 82 SilvestreDeSousa 1 45
(Saeed Bin Suroor) *led: pushed along and qcknd 4f out: rdn 3f out: sn hdd & wknd* **6/1**

3m 8.73s (1.33) **Going Correction** +0.15s/f (Good) **6** Ran SP% **111.3**
Speed ratings (Par 103): **102,98,97,94,92 82**
toteswingers 1&2 £1.10, 2&3 £4.20, 1&3 £3.10 CSF £8.45 TOTE £2.90: £1.60, £2.00; EX 9.40.
Owner Lady Bamford **Bred** Lady Bamford **Trained** Newmarket, Suffolk

FOCUS

A decent stayers' handicap. The pace was steady until the final half-mile. The improved winner could make a smart stayer and the form is rated around the runner-up.

NOTEBOOK

Suraj, a wide margin winner of a maiden in soft ground over 1m4f here in April, came fourth on his handicap bow on a much quicker surface at Newmarket next time. Anchored in last and forced to switch to make his final effort, he came right away to score in tremendous fashion. There is even better to come from this promising young stayer. (op 7-4 tchd 2-1)

Beyond Conceit(IRE), like the winner a son of Galileo, had been put up 8lb after finishing runner-up over 1m2f on his reappearance here in April. He travelled strongly but was made to look one-paced by the winner. (op 9-2)
Bute Hall, much improved when opening his account in a dubious maiden at Newcastle, made his handicap debut from a mark of 80. He finished clear third-best but, like the runner-up, was no match for the winner. (op 9-2 tchd 4-1)
Badea, making his handicap bow on his seventh start, is already looking fully exposed. Kieren Fallon reported that he hung left-handed. Official explanation: jockey said gelding hung badly left (tchd 12-1)
Spanish Wedding, blinkered for the first time when opening his account from a 7lb lower mark over 1m4f at Goodwood, stopped to nothing after hitting the front halfway up the home straight. (tchd 9-2)
Tajriba(IRE), the only filly in the line-up, set her own pace on her handicap bow. A Southwell all-weather maiden winner over 1m3f, she stopped to nothing when headed and was eased right off in the final furlong.

3615 MULTIFAB METALS ENGINEERING & FABRICATION H'CAP — 1m (R)
8:15 (8:17) (Class 4) (0-80,80) 4-Y-0+ — **£5,175** (£1,540; £769; £384) **Stalls** Low

Form			Horse	RPR
521	1		**Eastward Ho**[9] 3309 4-8-8 **67** ow1 .... TonyHamilton 5 (Jason Ward) *trckd ldng pair: hdwy on inner over 2f out: led wl over 1f out and sn rdn: drvn and edgd rt ins fnl f: hld on wl* **12/1**	78
4025	2	nk	**Anderiego (IRE)**[14] 3169 4-9-5 **78** .... DanielTudhope 15 (David O'Meara) *hld up in rr: hdwy on outer over 2f out: rdn over 1f out: str run ent fnl f and ev ch tl drvn and no ex towards fin* **6/1**[3]	88
0532	3	1	**Lockantanks**[3] 3492 5-9-5 **78** .... CathyGannon 2 (Michael Appleby) *hld up in rr: hdwy 3f out: effrt to chse ldrs 2f out: rdn to chal appr fnl f: ev ch tl drvn and no ex last 100yds* **3/1**[2]	86
5-05	4	1 ¼	**My Single Malt (IRE)**[35] 2491 4-9-1 **74** .... GrahamLee 4 (Julie Camacho) *in tch: hdwy to chse ldrs 3f out: cl up 2f out: rdn wl over 1f out: ev ch tl drvn and one pce wl ins fnl f* **12/1**	79
2353	5	2 ¼	**Batgirl**[13] 3192 5-8-11 **70** .... JamieSpencer 14 (John Berry) *hld up: hdwy over 2f out: rdn to chse ldrs over 1f out: no imp fnl f* **12/1**	70
6-00	6	2 ¼	**Dubai Bay (FR)**[82] 1249 4-8-10 **69** .... MickyFenton 7 (Paul Midgley) *led: rdn along 3f out: drvn 2f out: sn hdd and grad wknd* **33/1**	63
4526	7	½	**Illustrious Prince (IRE)**[7] 3385 5-8-13 **77** .... NeilFarley(5) 9 (Declan Carroll) *in tch: hdwy on outer over 3f out: rdn 2f out: sn wknd* **14/1**	70
0210	8	15	**Musnad (USA)**[14] 3167 4-9-3 **76** .... BarryMcHugh 16 (Brian Ellison) *hld up: a in rr* **7/1**	35
6201	9	½	**Steel Stockholder**[11] 3257 6-8-9 **68** ow1 .... RobertWinston 8 (Mel Brittain) *chsd ldr: cl up 3f out: sn rdn and wknd over 2f out* **22/1**	26
0-32	10	5	**Rustic Deacon**[14] 3167 5-9-5 **78** .... KierenFallon 10 (Willie Musson) *trckd ldrs: effrt 3f out: rdn over 2f out: sn btn* **2/1**[1]	24
230-	11	35	**Fairlie Dinkum**[252] 7024 4-9-1 **74** .... FrannyNorton 13 (Andrew Crook) *in tch: pushed along 1/2-way: sn wknd* **50/1**	

1m 39.78s (0.08) **Going Correction** +0.15s/f (Good) — **11** Ran SP% **124.1**
Speed ratings (Par 105): **105,104,103,102,100 97,97,82,81,76 41**
toteswingers 1&2 £16.40, 2&3 £6.10, 1&3 £6.20 CSF £85.64 CT £285.90 TOTE £13.60: £3.00, £2.50, £1.70; EX 124.70 Trifecta £340.00 Pool: £464.08 - 1.01 winning units..
Owner Miss Vivian Pratt **Bred** H & V Pratt **Trained** Middleham, N Yorks
■ Stewards' Enquiry : Cathy Gannon six-day ban: used whip above permitted level an in incorrect place (Jul 14-19)

FOCUS
A depleted field but nine horses still bang in contention a furlong out and a tight three-way finish. The winner posted a 3lb personal best.
Fairlie Dinkum Official explanation: jockey said filly lost its action

3616 ALTRAD BEAVER 84 HIRE & SALES FILLIES' H'CAP — 1m 2f 60y
8:45 (8:47) (Class 5) (0-70,70) 3-Y-0+ — **£2,911** (£866; £432; £216) **Stalls** Low

Form			Horse	RPR
4401	1		**Dansili Dutch (IRE)**[6] 3416 3-8-9 **63** 6ex .... FrannyNorton 12 (Andrew Crook) *hld up: hdwy on outer over 3f out: rdn to ld ent fnl f: sn drvn: hdd and no ex last 100yds* **13/2**[3]	71
5104	2	3	**Jane Lachatte (IRE)**[18] 3003 3-9-0 **68** .... DanielTudhope 5 (Stuart Williams) *in tch on inner: hdwy over 3f out: rdn 2f out: styd on and ev ch appr fnl f: sn drvn and kpt on same pce* **10/1**	70
064-	3	nk	**Darling Lexi (IRE)**[312] 5342 3-8-10 **64** .... KierenFallon 2 (Richard Fahey) *t.k.h: chsd ldng pair: hdwy to ld over 3f out: rdn 2f out: drvn and hdd ent fnl f: sn wknd* **6/1**[2]	65
0202	4	nk	**Musically**[8] 3338 3-8-5 **59** .... SamHitchcott 10 (Mick Channon) *hld up in rr: gd hdwy over 3f out: chsd ldrs 2f out: sn rdn and ev ch tl drvn and wknd ins fnl f* **7/1**	60
132-	5	2 ¼	**Stylistickhill (IRE)**[210] 7632 4-9-6 **62** .... (t) GrahamLee 3 (Scott Dixon) *midfield: hdwy wl over 2f out: sn rdn and no imp appr fnl f* **8/1**	59
15	6	1 ½	**Exclusive Dancer**[26] 2772 3-9-2 **70** .... PJMcDonald 16 (George Moore) *chsd ldrs: rdn along 3f out: drvn 2f out and grad wknd* **11/1**	64
3040	7	2 ¼	**Sangar**[21] 2915 4-9-7 **66** .... DaleSwift(3) 1 (Ollie Pears) *hld up towards rr: hdwy over 3f out: rdn to chse ldrs 2f out: drvn and wknd appr fnl f* **7/1**	55
0553	8	6	**Maybeagrey**[16] 3066 3-8-9 **63** .... DuranFentiman 13 (Tim Easterby) *led 2f: cl up: rdn along 3f out: sn wknd* **17/2**	41
0463	9	8	**Merrjanah**[16] 3073 4-8-10 **52** oh2 .... SilvestreDeSousa 9 (John Wainwright) *chsd ldrs: rdn along 3f out: sn wknd* **22/1**	15
0	10	15	**Nakuru Breeze (IRE)**[30] 2633 3-8-9 **63** ow2 .... [1] RobertWinston 15 (David Thompson) *cl up: led after 2f: rdn along and hdd over 3f out: wknd wl over 2f out* **33/1**	
0-32	D		**Circle Of Angels**[12] 3220 4-9-3 **59** .... JamieSpencer 4 (Ian Williams) *dwlt and hld up in rr: hdwy on wd outside 2f out: rdn over 1f out: styd on to chal ins fnl f: edgd lft: led last 100yds* **7/2**[1]	68
5403	F		**Sweet Vera**[8] 3332 7-8-3 **52** oh6 .... ShirleyTeasdale(7) 7 (Shaun Harris) *chsd ldrs on inner: rdn along whn fell and fatally injured over 3f out* **20/1**	

2m 10.73s (1.33) **Going Correction** +0.15s/f (Good)
WFA 3 from 4yo+ 12lb — **12** Ran SP% **126.0**
Speed ratings (Par 100): **99,97,96,96,94 93,91,87,80,68 100,**
toteswingers 1&2 £4.70, 2&3 £34.10, 1&3 £12.50 CSF £26.94 CT £219.24 TOTE £4.30: £1.80, £2.80, £4.10; EX 25.90 Trifecta £345.80 Pool: £579.52 - 1.24 winning units..
Owner Mrs Christine Hopper **Bred** Castlefarm Stud **Trained** Middleham Moor, N Yorks
■ Stewards' Enquiry : Daniel TudhopeM one-day ban: careless riding (Jul 17)

FOCUS
A steady pace to past halfway in this fillies' handicap. They chose to come up the middle in the home straight. Ordinary fillies' form.

Nakuru Breeze(IRE) Official explanation: jockey said filly ran too free and had no more to give
T/Jkpt: Part won. £63,713.70 to a £1 stake. Pool of £89,737.63 - 0.50 winning units. T/Plt: £105.50 to a £1 stake. Pool of £109,505.26 - 757.42 winning units. T/Qpdt: £14.50 to a £1 stake. Pool of £7431.69 - 376.69 winning units. JR

3387 LINGFIELD (L-H)
Saturday, June 30

OFFICIAL GOING: Turf course - good to firm (8.2); all-weather - standard
Wind: Fresh, behind Weather: Fine but cloudy

3617 BRITISH STALLION STUDS SUPPORTING BRITISH RACING E B F MAIDEN STKS — 5f
6:20 (6:21) (Class 5) 2-Y-0 — **£4,090** (£1,207; £604) **Stalls** High

Form			Horse	RPR
	1		**Normal Equilibrium** 2-9-0 0 .... HarryBentley(3) 2 (Roger Varian) *green in preliminaries: hld up in 4th: prog on outer to press ldng pair over 1f out: shkn up to ld ins fnl f: drifted lft nr fin* **11/10**[1]	78+
2	2	½	**Royal Aspiration (IRE)**[12] 3223 2-9-3 0 .... KirstyMilczarek 4 (William Haggas) *pressed ldr: shkn up over 1f out: upsides ins fnl f: outpcd by wnr last 100yds* **2/1**[2]	74
	3	¾	**Just Charlie** 2-9-3 0 .... DaneO'Neill 7 (Henry Candy) *racd towards nr side rail: led: rdn and hrd pressed over 1f out: hdd and one pce ins fnl f* **20/1**[3]	71
446	4	1 ½	**Jimmy Elder**[14] 3140 2-8-10 64 .... WilliamTwiston-Davies(7) 3 (Richard Hannon) *pressed ldng pair: shkn up over 2f out: lost 3rd over 1f out and nt qckn: kpt on* **20/1**[3]	66
	5	3 ½	**Mystical Man** 2-9-3 0 .... ChrisCatlin 5 (James Tate) *t.k.h: hld up in detached last pair and rn green: pushed along fr 2f out and lost no grnd* **33/1**	53
	6	nk	**Man In The Arena** 2-9-3 0 .... JohnFahy 1 (Dr Jon Scargill) *outpcd in last pair: pushed along 1/2-way: nvr on terms but lost no further grnd* **100/1**	52

58.22s (0.02) **Going Correction** -0.15s/f (Firm) — **6** Ran SP% **94.4**
Speed ratings (Par 93): **93,92,91,88,83 82**
toteswingers 1&2 £1.10, 2&3 £2.80, 1&3 £4.50 CSF £2.16 TOTE £1.80: £1.10, £1.50; EX 2.40.
Owner Qatar Racing Limited **Bred** D R Tucker **Trained** Newmarket, Suffolk

FOCUS
A fair juvenile maiden, rated on the mid point of the race averages. There was no hanging about on ground officially described as Good to firm and it appeared to be riding on the quick side.

NOTEBOOK
Normal Equilibrium reportedly looked a nice individual in the paddock beforehand. He is reportedly a sharp and mature sort at home who work wells. He cost 85,000 GBP in April and the money for him in the market spoke volumes. He did it very nicely in the race itself from an unhelpful low draw which meant he had to make his challenge against a decent marker with previous experience up the middle of the track. He is blessed with plenty of speed and quickened past his rivals inside the final furlong in comfortable fashion. He is bred to be a smart sprinter, being a brother to Group 3 winning sprinter Elnawin out a useful sprinting dam, and he is a very nice prospect at up to 6f on a quick surface. (op 10-11)
Royal Aspiration(IRE) gives the form real substance in second and appears to have reproduced the level of form displayed on his debut in a Windsor maiden (5f, good to soft - RPR 77) this month. He can win a similar contest, possibly over 6f. (op 11-4)
Just Charlie reportedly looked well and produced a good debut run. He is by Piccolo and appears to have inherited his modest but very well-related dam's sprinting genes. He can win a similar contest over this trip on similar ground. (op 25-1 tchd 28-1)
Jimmy Elder will do better in modest nursery handicaps this term. (op 14-1)
Mystical Man was slowly away and never got into this on debut. (op 66-1)

3618 TFL ONLINE "JABBA TRAINER" H'CAP — 5f
6:50 (6:50) (Class 5) (0-75,75) 3-Y-0+ — **£3,067** (£905; £453) **Stalls** High

Form			Horse	RPR
5034	1		**Lady Gibraltar**[24] 2816 3-8-9 **71** .... (v) MichaelJMMurphy(7) 7 (Alan Jarvis) *trckd ldrs: prog to ld over 1f out: shkn up and styd on wl* **14/1**	82
3126	2	1 ¾	**Clear Praise (USA)**[18] 2994 5-9-10 **73** .... SebSanders 12 (Simon Dow) *taken down early and steadily to post: mde most against nr side rail to over 1f out: kpt on but no ch w wnr* **7/1**[3]	79
0101	3	1 ¾	**Billy Red**[18] 2994 8-9-12 **75** .... (b) FergusSweeney 3 (J R Jenkins) *nt that wl away: prog on outer to chse ldrs 1/2-way: kpt on to take 3rd nr fin: nvr able to chal* **14/1**	75
1152	4	nk	**Howyadoingnotsobad (IRE)**[35] 2494 4-9-5 **73** .... DavidKenny(5) 4 (Karen George) *taken down early and steadily to post: pressed ldrs and racd towards outer: rdn 2f out and on terms: one pce over 1f out* **5/1**[2]	72
5660	5	¾	**Dreams Of Glory**[14] 3139 4-8-7 **59** .... SimonPearce(3) 10 (Ron Hodges) *mostly in midfield: rdn and outpcd sn after 1/2-way: kpt on fnl f: nrst fin* **9/1**	55
0656	6	hd	**Mawjoodah**[12] 3230 4-8-7 **56** .... ChrisCatlin 14 (Brian Ellison) *towards rr: outpcd by 1/2-way: hrd rdn and styd on fr over 1f out: nrst fin* **7/1**[3]	52
5400	7	1 ¾	**Intercept (IRE)**[10] 3281 4-9-10 **73** .... (t) RobertHavlin 8 (John Gosden) *hld up in rr: rdn and nt qckn 2f out: nvr on terms* **4/1**[1]	62
0-05	8	hd	**Jameela Girl**[52] 1990 4-9-8 **74** .... HarryBentley(3) 5 (Robert Cowell) *nvr beyond midfield: outpcd and rdn sn after 1/2-way: no imp after* **20/1**	62
0122	9	1 ½	**Mary's Pet**[19] 2973 5-8-13 **62** .... (p) AmirQuinn 1 (Lee Carter) *sn wl in rr on outer: nvr a factor* **14/1**	45
-113	10	1 ¼	**Jimmy Ryan (IRE)**[120] 763 11-9-6 **69** .... (t) J-PGuillambert 2 (Tim McCarthy) *walked to post early: sn wl in rr on outer: shkn up 1/2-way: no prog* **20/1**	48
0004	11	11	**Miss Polly Plum**[7] 3390 5-8-7 **56** oh2 .... (p) AndreaAtzeni 11 (Chris Dwyer) *w ldr to 2f out: wknd rapidly and eased fnl f* **5/1**[2]	

57.01s (-1.19) **Going Correction** -0.15s/f (Firm)
WFA 3 from 4yo+ 6lb — **11** Ran SP% **117.9**
Speed ratings (Par 103): **103,100,97,96,95 95,92,92,89,87 70**
toteswingers 1&2 £16.30, 2&3 £14.20, 1&3 £28.10 CSF £108.97 CT £1422.10 TOTE £22.30: £5.80, £2.60, £4.20; EX 194.10.
Owner Buckingham Flooring **Bred** Netherfield House Stud **Trained** Twyford, Bucks

FOCUS
A fair sprint handicap for 3yos and up. The gallop appeared particularly strong and the winning time nearly broke standard. The winner rates a 6lb personal best.

Miss Polly Plum Official explanation: jockey said mare moved poorly throughout

3619 BRITISH ARMED FORCES DAY 2012 FILLIES' H'CAP 7f

7:25 (7:26) (Class 5) (0-75,75) 3-Y-O **£3,067** (£905; £453) **Stalls** High

Form RPR

3500 **1** **Serene Oasis (IRE)**[12] 3214 3-8-12 **66**....................(v[1]) MatthewDavies 2 76
(Mick Channon) *pressed ldrs: rdn to ld towards outer wl over 1f out: drvn and kpt on fnl f* **33/1**

506- **2** *1* **Miss Cap Estel**[255] 6950 3-9-4 **72**.................................. JimmyFortune 5 79
(Andrew Balding) *trckd ldrs: rdn over 2f out: styd on fr over 1f out to snatch 2nd last stride* **7/1**[3]

-043 **3** *nse* **Little Rainbow**[26] 2759 3-8-8 **62**.. JohnFahy 4 69
(Clive Cox) *s.i.s: wl in rr: prog on wd outside fr 3f out: drvn to chse wnr jst over 1f out: kpt on but hld fnl f: lost 2nd post* **14/1**

224- **4** *2* **Gifted Dancer**[264] 6742 3-9-2 **70**... DaneO'Neill 7 72
(Henry Candy) *hld up wl in rr: pushed along over 2f out: styd on steadily fr over 1f out: nvr rchd ldrs* **9/2**[1]

3541 **5** *nse* **Tenbridge**[23] 2846 3-9-4 **72**..(p) AndreaAtzeni 3 74
(Derek Haydn Jones) *settled wl in rr: rdn and prog on outer fr over 2f out: chsd ldrs 1f out: no imp last 100yds* **8/1**

2064 **6** *2* **Alkadi (IRE)**[12] 3230 3-9-4 **72**.. MartinLane 10 68
(Mark Johnston) *mde most against nr side rail to wl over 1f out: wknd fnl f* **7/1**[3]

6106 **7** *2 1/4* **Boudoir (IRE)**[17] 3041 3-8-12 **73**.................. WilliamTwiston-Davies(7) 6 63
(Richard Hannon) *w ldr over 4f: wknd quite qckly over 1f out* **11/1**

3640 **8** *1 1/4* **Fine Painting (IRE)**[23] 2846 3-9-0 **68**............................. TomQueally 11 55
(Gary Moore) *hld up wl in rr: shkn up and no prog over 2f out: taken towards outer over 1f out: nvr a factor* **12/1**

-300 **9** *3/4* **Symphony Time (IRE)**[22] 2894 3-9-2 **70**................. MickaelBarzalona 1 55
(Brian Meehan) *chsd ldrs: rdn and stl in tch over 2f out: wknd qckly over 1f out* **16/1**

-055 **10** *2 1/2* **More Than Words (IRE)**[16] 3071 3-9-3 **71**................. RichardHughes 8 49
(Richard Hannon) *trckd ldrs: rdn over 2f out: wknd wl over 1f out* **5/1**[2]

-030 **11** *6* **Sangrail**[16] 3083 3-8-8 **62**.. MartinDwyer 12 24
(William Muir) *chsd ldrs against nr side rail: wknd 2f out* **16/1**

2-60 **12** *6* **Toffee Tart**[52] 1985 3-9-7 **75**.. SebSanders 13 21
(J W Hills) *hld up in rr against rail: rdn over 2f out: sn wknd and bhd* **12/1**

0-00 **13** *nse* **Zingana**[23] 2846 3-9-4 **72**...(b[1]) FergusSweeney 9 17
(Eve Johnson Houghton) *a in last and sn detached fr rest: wl bhd fnl 2f* **25/1**

1m 22.87s (-0.43) **Going Correction** -0.15s/f (Firm) **13** Ran SP% **119.9**
Speed ratings (Par 96): **96,94,94,92,92 90,87,86,85,82 75,68,68**
toteswingers 1&2 £56.40, 2&3 £89.10, 1&3 £117.20 CSF £251.67 CT £2169.27 TOTE £49.50: £7.00, £2.50, £4.00; EX 20.30.
Owner Doric Racing **Bred** Round Hill Stud **Trained** West Ilsley, Berks

FOCUS
A fair fillies' handicap for 3yos.The gallop was respectable at best and the winning time was nearly two seconds slower than standard. The winner returned to form in the visor.

3620 SURREY ROYAL BRITISH LEGION (S) STKS 1m 4f (P)

8:00 (8:00) (Class 6) 3-Y-0+ **£2,181** (£644; £322) **Stalls** Low

Form RPR

2564 **1** **Kiss A Prince**[17] 3047 6-9-13 74.............................(p) RichardHughes 13 71+
(Dean Ivory) *stdd s: hld up wl in rr: prog 4f out: trckd ldr over 2f out: cruised alongside over 1f out: pushed into ld last 100yds and sn clr* **7/4**[1]

40-0 **2** *1 3/4* **Locum**[42] 2260 7-9-8 54.. DarryllHolland 7 56
(Mark H Tompkins) *trckd ldrs: wnt 2nd over 4f out: led 3f out: hrd rdn and jnd over 1f out: hdd last 100yds and no ch w wnr* **6/1**[3]

1450 **3** *1 3/4* **Dew Reward (IRE)**[5] 3449 4-9-13 58.................................. AndreaAtzeni 8 58
(Bill Turner) *settled in midfield: rdn 5f out: responded to press and prog to go 3rd over 2f out: styd on but nvr able to chal* **14/1**

00 **4** *10* **Soldier Spy**[14] 3155 3-8-8 0...(b[1]) RobertHavlin 6 37
(Mark Usher) *hld up wl in rr: prog fr 3f out: only 8th 2f out: styd on to take remote 4th post* **25/1**

0 **5** *shd* **Head Office**[10] 3279 3-7-12 0... NathanAlison(5) 4 32
(Pat Phelan) *v awkward s: wl bhd in last early: prog fr rr on outer over 3f out: chsd clr ldng trio fnl f tl lost 4th post* **50/1**

0231 **6** *4 1/2* **Oneiric**[23] 2851 4-9-1 61.. IanBurns(7) 1 30
(Brett Johnson) *chsd ldrs: rdn 5f out: outpcd and btn over 2f out* **3/1**[2]

445/ **7** *7* **Beggar's Opera (IRE)**[214] 7876 5-9-8 74...............(bt) MattieBatchelor 9 19
(Jim Best) *chsd ldr: jinked rt over 9f out: drvn and lost 2nd over 4f out: sn wknd* **7/1**

-600 **8** *3/4* **Daddyow**[7] 3392 4-9-8 50... GeorgeBaker 12 17
(Terry Clement) *hld up in last pair and wl off the pce early: prog over 3f out: rchd remote 6th over 1f out: sn wknd* **20/1**

-040 **9** *1/2* **Shek O Lad**[26] 2771 3-8-1 45............................(v[1]) MichaelJMMurphy(7) 3 17
(Alan Jarvis) *led at gd pce and sn 4 l clr: hdd & wknd 3f out* **33/1**

0200 **10** *25* **Always Ends Well (IRE)**[10] 3275 3-8-3 56........................ MartinLane 2
(Mark Johnston) *chsd ldrs: rdn and wknd 5f out: t.o* **11/1**

0- **11** *1/2* **Murmur (IRE)**[296] 5854 3-8-3 0.............................. FrankieMcDonald 10
(Paul Fitzsimons) *a towards rr: wknd over 4f out: t.o* **40/1**

-046 **12** *5* **You Got The Love**[18] 2999 3-8-1 43 ow1.................(t) RaulDaSilva(3) 11
(Jeremy Gask) *prom on outer: forced wd over 9f out and lost pl: reminders and wnt prom again over 7f out: wknd over 3f out: t.o* **33/1**

2m 34.71s (1.71) **Going Correction** +0.175s/f (Slow)
WFA 3 from 4yo+ 14lb **12** Ran SP% **122.0**
Speed ratings (Par 101): **101,99,98,92,91 88,84,83,83,66 66,63**
toteswingers 1&2 £3.80, 2&3 £14.90, 1&3 £7.30 CSF £12.09 TOTE £2.80: £1.20, £2.20, £3.90; EX 15.60.There was no bid for the winner.
Owner Radlett Racing **Bred** Baroness, Magnusson, Myriade, Redmyre **Trained** Radlett, Herts
■ Stewards' Enquiry : Nathan Alison four-day ban: failed to ride out for 4th (Jul 19-20,22-23)

FOCUS
A weak seller, rated around the second and third. They went a solid enough gallop.

3621 POPPY SHOP - POPPYSHOP.ORG.UK H'CAP 1m 4f (P)

8:30 (8:30) (Class 6) (0-65,65) 3-Y-O **£2,181** (£644; £322) **Stalls** Low

Form RPR

5243 **1** **Fleur De La Vie (IRE)**[16] 3087 3-8-13 **60**.................. HarryBentley(3) 11 72
(Ralph Beckett) *trckd ldr 2f: styd prom: wnt 2nd again 3f out: led 2f out gng wl: shkn up and r.o wl fnl f* **6/1**

4411 **2** *3/4* **Bridgehampton**[40] 2333 3-9-7 **65**.. RichardHughes 7 76
(Michael Bell) *hld up in last trio: prog over 3f out: rdn 2f out: chsd wnr jst over 1f out: r.o but a hld* **13/8**[1]

-241 **3** *2* **Astroscarlet**[23] 2850 3-9-0 **58**.. DarryllHolland 14 66
(Mark H Tompkins) *hld up wl in rr: prog on outer over 3f out: rdn to try to chal in cl 3rd 2f out: one pce after* **9/2**[2]

0-22 **4** *6* **Seven Veils (IRE)**[12] 3233 3-9-7 **65**...................................... ChrisCatlin 5 63
(Sir Mark Prescott Bt) *sn prom: trckd ldng pair 7f out: led over 3f out: hdd 2f out: wknd qckly fnl f* **5/1**[3]

0504 **5** *5* **Rano Pano (USA)**[12] 3232 3-8-8 **52**.............................. AndreaAtzeni 13 42
(Brian Ellison) *t.k.h: hld up in last trio: prog on wd outside over 3f out: drvn and cl enough over 2f out: sn wknd* **25/1**

0120 **6** *8* **Daring Damsel (IRE)**[33] 2544 3-9-7 **65**.....................(b) StevieDonohoe 3 43
(Paul Cole) *trckd ldrs: rdn over 3f out: wknd over 2f out* **25/1**

-001 **7** *4 1/2* **Autarch (USA)**[30] 2624 3-9-7 **65**.. MartinDwyer 2 35
(Amanda Perrett) *nvr beyond midfield: dropped to rr and lost tch over 3f out: no ch after* **16/1**

0004 **8** *2 1/4* **Capitol Gain (IRE)**[12] 3228 3-9-6 **64**................................. TomQueally 1 31
(Brian Meehan) *hld up in rr: rdn and lost tch over 3f out: no ch after* **16/1**

2454 **9** *3 1/2* **Dalmo**[16] 3088 3-9-2 **60**.. GeorgeBaker 12 21
(Gary Moore) *chsd ldr after 2f: led 4f out to over 3f out: wknd rapidly* **14/1**

606 **10** *3/4* **Scarlett Fever**[18] 3001 3-8-6 **57**...................................(p) KatiaScallan(7) 6 17
(Marcus Tregoning) *s.s: t.k.h: hld up in last trio: lost tch over 3f out: sn bhd* **33/1**

40-0 **11** *1* **Beacon Lady**[23] 2850 3-8-4 **48**... MartinLane 10
(William Knight) *led to 4f out: wknd rapidly* **50/1**

2m 32.91s (-0.09) **Going Correction** +0.175s/f (Slow) **11** Ran SP% **118.3**
Speed ratings (Par 97): **107,106,105,101,97 92,89,88,85,85 84**
toteswingers 1&2 £4.20, 2&3 £3.10, 1&3 £5.80 CSF £15.64 CT £49.49 TOTE £8.80: £2.60, £1.10, £2.20; EX 20.30.
Owner Prime Of Life 3 **Bred** Edward & Scarlet Leatham **Trained** Kimpton, Hants

FOCUS
A modest middle-distance handicap for 3yos but an interesting race for the grade. A clear personal best from the winner. The gallop was respectable at best.

3622 LINGFIELD MARRIOTT HOTEL & COUNTRY CLUB MEDIAN AUCTION MAIDEN STKS 1m 2f (P)

9:00 (9:06) (Class 6) 3-4-Y-O **£2,181** (£644; £322) **Stalls** Low

Form RPR

22- **1** **Bold Cuffs**[191] 7855 3-9-2 0.. ChrisCatlin 12 68+
(Sir Mark Prescott Bt) *t.k.h: prom: trckd ldr 1/2-way: shkn up over 2f out: led jst over 1f out: hrd pressed after: drvn out* **9/4**[2]

2 *nk* **Altaria** 3-8-11 0.. TomQueally 8 62+
(Amanda Perrett) *led at mod pce for 2f: trckd ldr to 1/2-way: pushed along over 2f out: at least 2 l bhd ldng pair over 1f out: r.o wl nr fin: jst failed* **9/2**[3]

62 **3** *hd* **Elegant Ophelia**[17] 3048 3-8-11 0..............................(t) DarryllHolland 2 62
(Dean Ivory) *led after 2f at ordinary pce: kicked on 3f out: hdd jst over 1f out: battled on wl but jst hld and lost 2nd last strides* **14/1**

6-34 **4** *3* **Exning Halt**[22] 2883 3-9-2 73.. GeorgeBaker 11 61+
(James Fanshawe) *hld up in last pair: prog 3f out but only 6th over 2f out: chsd clr ldng trio wl over 1f out: styd on but no ch* **11/8**[1]

000 **5** *5* **Flamborough Breeze**[17] 3044 3-8-8 65.................... HarryBentley(3) 10 46
(Ed Vaughan) *rn wout declared tongue-strap: s.s: hld up last: stl there 2f out: kpt on fr over 1f out* **14/1**

0 **6** *1 3/4* **Any Given Dream (IRE)**[39] 2368 3-9-2 0............................ MartinLane 4 48+
(David Simcock) *hld up in midfield: outpcd 3f out: jst pushed along and n.d after* **20/1**

7 *nk* **Comedy House**[27] 4-10-0 0.. JamieGoldstein 3 47
(Michael Madgwick) *hld up in rr: outpcd in last pair 3f out: no ch after: kpt on fnl f* **40/1**

0- **8** *hd* **Time For A Tiger**[264] 6745 3-8-11 0.................................... DaneO'Neill 9 42
(Henry Candy) *trckd ldrs: outpcd over 2f out: wknd over 1f out* **28/1**

-000 **9** *3* **Chater Garden (IRE)**[23] 2845 3-8-9 45................. MichaelJMMurphy(7) 5 41
(Alan Jarvis) *hld up in midfield: outpcd 3f out: n.d after: wknd fnl f* **50/1**

00 **10** *6* **Bonbon Bonnie**[23] 2865 4-9-2 0.. DannyBrock(7) 1 24
(Phil McEntee) *hld up in midfield: outpcd 3f out: no ch after: wknd over 1f out* **50/1**

2m 10.08s (3.48) **Going Correction** +0.175s/f (Slow)
WFA 3 from 4yo 12lb **10** Ran SP% **119.0**
Speed ratings (Par 101): **93,92,92,90,86 84,84,84,82,77**
toteswingers 1&2 £3.10, 2&3 £7.20, 1&3 £4.40 CSF £12.49 TOTE £3.70: £1.40, £1.50, £3.00; EX 11.80.
Owner Fawzi Abdulla Nass **Bred** Aislabie Bloodstock Ltd **Trained** Newmarket, Suffolk

FOCUS
A modest maiden at best. The gallop was slow early on and the tempo eventually increased down the back straight. The winning time was significantly the worst comparative time of the evening. Messy and dubious form, limited by the third.
T/Plt: £100.40 to a £1 stake. Pool of £78,478.08 - 570.59 winning units. T/Qpdt: £31.00 to a £1 stake. Pool of Pool - £5,811.10 - 138.40 winning units. JN

3532 NEWCASTLE (L-H)

Saturday, June 30

OFFICIAL GOING: Heavy
Wind: Fairly strong, half against Weather: Cloudy, showers

3623 BETFRED MOBILE LOTTO CHIPCHASE STKS (GROUP 3) 6f

2:15 (2:15) (Class 1) 3-Y-O+

£31,190 (£11,825; £5,918; £2,948; £1,479; £742) **Stalls** High

Form RPR

-216 **1** **Maarek**[7] 3371 5-9-3 108.. GrahamLee 7 113+
(David Peter Nagle, Ire) *in tch: squeezed through against stands' rail 2f out: hdwy to ld ins fnl f: edgd lft: kpt on wl* **11/4**[1]

0-10 **2** *2* **Boastful (IRE)**[29] 2654 4-9-0 100....................................... JimCrowley 9 104
(Mrs K Burke) *led against stands' rail: rdn and qcknd over 1f out: hdd ins fnl f: kpt on same pce* **25/1**

0026 **3** *3* **Regal Parade**[35] 2505 8-9-3 107.. LukeMorris 2 98
(Milton Bradley) *hld up in tch: hdwy to chse ldrs over 2f out: sn rdn: kpt on same pce fnl f* **16/1**

-044 **4** *5* **Eton Rifles (IRE)**[13] 3190 7-9-3 109........................... DanielTudhope 1 83
(Stuart Williams) *stdd s and swtchd to stands' rail over 4f out: hld up: n.m.r over 3f out: effrt and swtchd lft over 1f out: sn rdn: no imp fnl f* **10/3**[2]

3110 **5** *3 3/4* **Mayson**[45] 2179 4-9-7 110... TonyHamilton 8 76
(Richard Fahey) *cl up: drvn along whn edgd rt: hmpd and lost pl wl over 1f out: n.d after* **7/1**[3]

0-12 **6** *15* **Our Jonathan**[13] 3190 5-9-3 112.. JamieSpencer 3 27
(Kevin Ryan) *hld up: pushed along over 3f out: swtchd lft and hdwy over 2f out: sn rdn: wknd over 1f out: eased whn btn ins fnl f* **11/4**[1]

-032 **7** *2 1/4* **Doncaster Rover (USA)**[14] 3166 6-9-3 105................ RobertWinston 6 20
(David Brown) *in tch: drvn along thrght: rdn and wknd over 2f out* **8/1**
6155 **8** *2 3/4* **Confessional**[28] 2704 5-9-3 104..(be) DavidAllan 5 12
(Tim Easterby) *trckd ldrs: effrt and drvn over 2f out: wknd over 1f out: eased whn btn* **16/1**
44-3 **9** *60* **Sunrise Dance**[7] 3404 3-8-7 74.. TomEaves 4
(Robert Johnson) *cl up 2f: sn lost pl and detached: t.o* **100/1**

1m 19.15s (4.55) **Going Correction** +1.025s/f (Soft)
WFA 3 from 4yo+ 7lb **9** Ran SP% **116.6**
Speed ratings (Par 113): **110,107,103,96,91 71,68,65,**
Tote Swingers: 1&2 £27.60, 1&3 £11.20, 2&3 £25.90 CSF £74.14 TOTE £3.80: £1.40, £4.60, £4.00; EX 93.70 Trifecta £672.60 Part won. Pool: £909.96 - 0.60 winning units..
Owner Lisbunny Syndicate **Bred** New England Stud & P J & P M Vela **Trained** Fethard, Co Tipperary

FOCUS
Despite around 40mm of rain falling on Thursday, the course passed a morning inspection. The entire running rail on the round course from the winning line to 3.5f (junction of straight) was moved to allow a minimum of 3yds of fresh ground that had previously not been raced on this season. Those who rode in the opener all concurred the ground was heavy, with Tom Eaves suggesting "it couldn't get any worse". As a result the form of this meeting should be treated with caution. The first two raced on the rail more or less throughout. The first two set the standard.

NOTEBOOK
Maarek had finished sixth from a mark of 108 in the Wokingham a week earlier and relished the return to testing conditions on this first try at Group level. Despite getting into a barging match with Mayson, he had enough in hand to win well, and is clearly smart when conditions are in his favour. The Haydock Sprint Cup is a viable aim. (op 3-1)
Boastful(IRE) won a Listed race over 1m at Goodwood in May (soft ground) and the forward ride against the rail in testing conditions played to her strengths at this distance, resulting in a career best. (op 20-1 tchd 28-1)
Regal Parade filled the same position as last year, bouncing back from a poor effort at York on this first start since leaving David Nicholls. (op 14-1)
Eton Rifles(IRE) should have enjoyed conditions and he travelled well, but couldn't pick up once forced to switch. (op 7-2)
Mayson, conceding weight all round, wouldn't have enjoyed ground this testing and he was already struggling when coming off worse in a barging match with the winner. (tchd 15-2)
Our Jonathan has handled testing going well in the past, but he struggled to pick up out of this ground. (tchd 3-1)

3624 BETFRED MOBILE SPORTS H'CAP 6f
2:45 (2:45) (Class 2) (0-100,91) 3-Y-0+

£12,450 (£3,728; £1,864; £932; £466; £234) **Stalls** High

Form RPR
0300 **1** **Fast Shot**[15] 3128 4-9-9 86.. DavidAllan 15 95
(Tim Easterby) *trckd ldrs: rdn over 2f out: hdwy to ld ins fnl f: drvn out* **8/1**[3]
4013 **2** *1* **Misplaced Fortune**[30] 2636 7-9-9 89.............................. DaleSwift(3) 14 95
(Nigel Tinkler) *hld up: hdwy over 2f out: chsd ldrs fnl f: kpt on to take 2nd last stride* **16/1**
-111 **3** *shd* **Powerful Presence (IRE)**[28] 2697 6-9-13 90........... DanielTudhope 12 96
(David O'Meara) *led against stands' rail: rdn over 2f out: rallied: hdd ins fnl f: kpt on: lost 2nd last stride* **7/2**[1]
3003 **4** *4 1/2* **Rothesay Chancer**[8] 3336 4-9-0 77............................... PJMcDonald 13 69
(Jim Goldie) *hld up in midfield stands' rail: rdn over 2f out: kpt on fnl f: no imp* **12/1**
0052 **5** *2 1/4* **Mass Rally (IRE)**[13] 3183 5-10-0 91.........................(b[1]) PaulMulrennan 9 76
(Michael Dods) *hld up in last: smooth hdwy stands' rail and in tch whn nt clr run and swtchd lft appr fnl f: sn no imp* **16/1**
0006 **6** *2* **Cheveton**[16] 3078 8-9-7 84.. JimCrowley 10 63
(Richard Price) *prom: effrt and rdn over 2f out: wknd ins fnl f* **7/1**[2]
5041 **7** *1 1/4* **Tajneed (IRE)**[9] 3304 9-9-10 87.................................. AdrianNicholls 8 63
(David Nicholls) *chsd ldrs: drvn and outpcd over 2f out: n.d after* **9/1**
1300 **8** *6* **Arctic Feeling (IRE)**[28] 2704 4-9-2 86........................... LauraBarry(7) 1 44
(Richard Fahey) *chsd centre ldrs: swtchd to outer of stands' side gp after 2f: effrt over 2f out: wknd over 1f out* **40/1**
-000 **9** *3 3/4* **Valery Borzov (IRE)**[45] 2177 8-9-10 90........................(v) LeeTopliss(3) 4 36
(Richard Fahey) *led centre trio: lft alone after 2f: cl up tl wknd wl over 1f out* **14/1**
6250 **10** *2 3/4* **Baby Strange**[18] 3004 8-9-10 87..................................... TonyHamilton 2 25
(Derek Shaw) *hld up in midfield on outside of stands' side gp: effrt over 2f out: wknd over 1f out* **12/1**
0255 **11** *1 1/4* **Grissom (IRE)**[21] 2919 6-9-9 91..................................... AdamCarter(5) 6 25
(Tim Easterby) *dwlt: sn trckd ldrs: rdn and wknd over 1f out* **10/1**
3402 **12** *8* **Mon Brav**[16] 3078 5-9-6 83.. BarryMcHugh 3
(Brian Ellison) *chsd centre ldr: swtchd to stands' side and towards rr that gp after 2f: rdn and wknd over 2f out* **9/1**
2660 **13** *1 3/4* **I'll Be Good**[35] 2509 3-8-2 79.. NoelGarbutt(7) 5
(Robert Johnson) *dwlt: sn cl up: hung lft into centre over 2f out: sn wknd* **25/1**
-000 **14** *21* **Marvellous Value (IRE)**[13] 3183 7-9-10 87...................... TomEaves 11
(Michael Dods) *plld hrd: hld up: struggling wl over 2f out: sn btn: t.o* **14/1**
1002 **15** *1 3/4* **Arganil (USA)**[9] 3304 7-9-13 90......................................(p) GrahamLee 7
(Kevin Ryan) *sn pushed along in rr: struggling fr 1/2-way: nvr on terms: t.o* **16/1**

1m 20.79s (6.19) **Going Correction** +1.225s/f (Soft)
WFA 3 from 4yo+ 7lb **15** Ran SP% **127.6**
Speed ratings (Par 109): **107,105,105,99,96 93,92,84,79,75 73,63,60,32,30**
Tote Swingers: 1&2 £70.10, 1&3 £5.60, 2&3 £13.30 CSF £136.85 CT £430.54 TOTE £10.30: £3.60, £5.50, £1.60; EX 193.50 TRIFECTA Not won..
Owner Ontoawinner & Partners **Bred** Whitsbury Manor Stud & Pigeon House Stud **Trained** Great Habton, N Yorks
■ Stewards' Enquiry : Daniel Tudhope one-day ban: failed to ride to draw (Jul 16)

FOCUS
Nearer the stands' rail the better in this, with the first quartet occupying the top four stalls. A length best from the winner.

NOTEBOOK
Fast Shot, whose yard is in cracking form at present, ultimately had to switch off the rail to launch his winning run, but he'd raced against it for 4f, and stayed on best for his second win of the season. These conditions suit well. Official explanation: trainer said, regarding apparent improvement in form, that the gelding appreciated the better draw. (op 12-1)
Misplaced Fortune did really well considering these conditions would have been much softer than ideal, although he was still unable to reverse form from earlier in the season with the winner.
Powerful Presence(IRE), up 3lb but down 1f in trip in this bid for a four-timer, soon bagged the lead on the stands' rail, and given his extra stamina, it was slightly surprising he couldn't hold on. (op 5-1)
Rothesay Chancer had the rail, but couldn't obtain a forward position, and was never getting there. (op 14-1)
Mass Rally(IRE) made good headway near the rail, but was always likely to encounter trouble in running. (op 12-1)
Valery Borzov(IRE) stayed centre-track to no avail. (op 12-1)

3625 JOHN SMITH'S NORTHUMBERLAND PLATE (HERITAGE H'CAP) 2m 19y
3:20 (3:22) (Class 2) 3-Y-0+

£86,226 (£25,956; £12,978; £6,468; £3,248; £1,638) **Stalls** Low

Form RPR
0U-1 **1** **Ile De Re (FR)**[52] 1974 6-9-3 101.. JimCrowley 9 107
(Donald McCain) *t.k.h early: hld up in midfield on outside: hdwy to chse ldr 1 1/2-way: led 5f out: drvn over 3f out: kpt on gamely fr 2f out* **5/2**[1]
0-31 **2** *1/2* **Crackentorp**[14] 3163 7-9-0 98 5ex.................................. DavidAllan 6 104
(Tim Easterby) *t.k.h early: cl up: effrt and rdn 3f out: styd on u.p to take 2nd towards fin* **16/1**
062- **3** *1/2* **Icon Dream (IRE)**[336] 4532 5-9-0 98................................... GrahamLee 8 103
(Jim Goldie) *in tch: hdwy to chse wnr over 2f out: ev ch gng wl over 2f out: sn rdn: kpt on fnl f: no ex and lost 2nd towards fin* **20/1**
63-2 **4** *2* **French Hollow**[6] 3419 7-7-7 82 oh2................................ NeilFarley(5) 14 85+
(Tim Fitzgerald) *hld up: rdn and hdwy on outside 2f out: styd on strly fnl f: nvr able to chal* **20/1**
0300 **5** *3 1/2* **Montaff**[28] 2709 6-8-7 91.. SamHitchcott 12 89
(Mick Channon) *t.k.h: hld up on ins: rdn and hdwy over 2f out: no imp fr over 1f out* **8/1**
4-23 **6** *2 3/4* **High Office**[21] 2933 6-8-6 90... BarryMcHugh 13 85
(Richard Fahey) *hld up towards rr: rdn and hdwy over 3f out: sn rdn: no imp fr 2f out* **20/1**
00-3 **7** *1/2* **The Betchworth Kid**[15] 3125 7-8-13 97......................... JamieSpencer 3 92
(Alan King) *sn drvn along in midfield: hdwy and prom over 3f out: sn rdn: btn ins fnl f* **12/1**
41-0 **8** *14* **Petara Bay (IRE)**[7] 3373 8-9-10 108................................... TomEaves 5 86
(Robert Mills) *hld up in midfield: hdwy and prom over 3f out: wknd fr 2f out* **33/1**
3-00 **9** *1 3/4* **Merchant Of Dubai**[15] 3125 7-8-6 93............................ PaulPickard(3) 4 69
(Jim Goldie) *in tch: lost pl over 4f out: sn struggling: n.d after* **28/1**
4502 **10** *1* **Halla San**[4] 3458 10-7-12 82... JamesSullivan 10 56
(Richard Fahey) *hld up: rdn on outside whn hmpd bnd wl over 3f out: sn btn* **40/1**
1334 **11** *22* **Gulf Of Naples (IRE)**[9] 3293 4-9-9 107.................. SilvestreDeSousa 17 55
(Mark Johnston) *dwlt: bhd on ins: rdn over 4f out: wknd over 3f out: eased whn no ch fnl f* **8/1**
00-0 **12** *63* **Trovare (USA)**[3] 3502 5-7-7 82 oh2.............................. DarrenEgan(5) 19
(Amanda Perrett) *hld up: struggling over 5f out: lost tch and eased over 2f out* **66/1**
014- **13** *29* **Motivado**[280] 6333 4-8-12 96.. LukeMorris 1
(Sir Mark Prescott Bt) *reluctant to enter stalls: cl up tl rdn and wknd wl over 3f out: eased whn no ch fnl 2f* **5/1**[2]
-320 **14** *12* **Lexington Bay (IRE)**[14] 3163 4-8-4 88....................... PatrickMathers 16
(Richard Fahey) *hld up towards rr: drvn along 5f out: wknd over 3f out: eased whn no ch fnl 2f* **10/1**
2-33 **15** *5* **Palazzo Bianco**[28] 2709 4-8-2 86.................................... NickyMackay 7
(John Gosden) *chsd ldrs: drvn and outpcd over 5f out: wknd wl over 3f out: eased whn no ch fnl 2f* **7/1**[3]
1-21 **16** *16* **Figaro**[36] 2447 4-8-6 90... KellyHarrison 2
(William Haggas) *led: rdn and hdd 5f out: wknd wl over 3f out: eased whn no ch fnl 2f* **16/1**

3m 53.94s (14.54) **Going Correction** +1.225s/f (Soft) **16** Ran SP% **133.1**
Speed ratings (Par 109): **112,111,111,110,108 107,107,100,99,98 87,56,41,35,33 25**
Tote Swingers: 1&2 £13.00, 1&3 £18.60, 2&3 £38.10 CSF £48.03 CT £724.85 TOTE £3.70: £1.10, £4.10, £4.80, £3.50; EX 61.50 Trifecta £1240.00 Pool: £6,954.39 - 4.15 winning units..
Owner D Mead **Bred** R Moser & Haras De S A Aga Khan Scea **Trained** Cholmondeley, Cheshire
■ Stewards' Enquiry : David Allan two-day ban: used whip above permitted level (Jul 16-17)
Jim Crowley two-day ban: used whip above permitted level (Jul 16-17)

FOCUS
Not quite as open as usual, with the ground ruling out a few. Understandably the pace was quite steady. Ile De Re stepped up on his Chester Cup win, with the third the best guide to the form.

NOTEBOOK
Ile De Re(FR) completed the prestigious Chester Cup/Northumberland Plate double in gritty fashion, benefiting from a fine ride by Jim Crowley, who wisely moved him prominent down the back. Although up 8lb for his Chester victory, these conditions weren't a problem, and with stamina assured, it was no surprise to see him repel all challengers. He's a smart staying handicapper when conditions are in his favour and he can rank higher yet when returning to hurdles later in the year. (op 3-1)
Crackentorp, well beaten in this in 2010, has yet to win beyond 1m4f on the Flat, but he came into the race following a recent win at his beloved York and, having held a prominent position throughout, stuck on really well to record a career best. His trainer is in cracking form at present.
Icon Dream(IRE), seventh from the same mark last year, had been off 11 months, but has gone well fresh in the past, and he ran right up to his best on this first start for Jim Goldie.
French Hollow, runner-up over 2m2f at Pontefract six days earlier, did best of those coming from off the pace, running really well considering he was 2lb wrong. (op 16-1)
Montaff was 1llb lower than when runner-up in 2011, but he hasn't been able to match that form since, and the ground was testing enough for him. (op 10-1)
High Office was never involved, but did plug on late. (tchd 25-1)
Gulf Of Naples(IRE) was always likely to find this coming too soon after his huge effort in the Gold Cup. He was never able to get into the race following a slow start and is due to race off 6lb higher in future. (op 7-1)
Motivado, making his seasonal reappearance, floundered once under pressure. He's a fine, big sort who surely has more to offer this season on a faster surface. (op 7-1 tchd 15-2)
Lexington Bay(IRE) was beaten before the straight. (op 9-1 tchd 11-1)
Palazzo Bianco wouldn't have liked the ground and was duly tailed off. Official explanation: trainer's rep said colt was unsuited by the heavy ground (tchd 15-2)
Figaro has looked progressive, but he had major stamina doubts trying this trip for the first time, especially on such testing ground, and he was quickly beaten once headed. He can be given another chance.

3626 BETFRED BONUS KING BINGO H'CAP 7f
3:55 (3:55) (Class 2) (0-105,98) 3-Y-0+

£12,450 (£3,728; £1,864; £932; £466; £234) **Stalls** High

Form RPR
2303 **1** **Memory Cloth**[2] 3534 5-9-9 96.. DaleSwift(3) 11 104
(Brian Ellison) *mde all against stands' rail: rdn 2f out: hld on wl fnl f* **6/4**[1]
1440 **2** *1/2* **Brae Hill (IRE)**[10] 3268 6-10-0 98..................................... TonyHamilton 9 104
(Richard Fahey) *dwlt: hld up last: hdwy whn nt clr run and swtchd to wd outside over 1f out: chsd wnr ins fnl f: kpt on* **10/1**

-065 **3** 1 1/2 **Roker Park (IRE)**[8] 3336 7-9-1 **85** ... DanielTudhope 8 87
(David O'Meara) *in tch against stands' rail: effrt and rdn over 1f out: kpt on ins fnl f* **12/1**

4316 **4** 1/2 **Fieldgunner Kirkup (GER)**[8] 3334 4-8-9 **79** oh2... GrahamGibbons 7 80
(David Barron) *trckd ldrs: effrt and rdn to chse wnr appr fnl f to ins fnl f: one pce* **11/1**

3030 **5** 5 **Prime Exhibit**[21] 2919 7-9-1 **85** ... SamHitchcott 6 73
(Milton Bradley) *t.k.h: hld up bhd ldng gp: hdwy and prom over 2f out: rdn and wknd over 1f out* **20/1**

5100 **6** 1 3/4 **Al Muheer (IRE)**[2] 3534 7-9-6 **90** ...(b) JamesSullivan 4 73
(Ruth Carr) *t.k.h: prom: hdwy to chse wnr over 2f out to appr fnl f: sn btn* **25/1**

5005 **7** 2 1/4 **Alejandro (IRE)**[29] 2660 3-8-8 **90** ... LeeTopliss(3) 2 68
(Richard Fahey) *hld up: rdn along over 2f out: btn appr fnl f* **18/1**

4200 **8** 7 **Osteopathic Remedy (IRE)**[21] 2910 8-9-5 **89**... PaulMulrennan 10 48
(Michael Dods) *t.k.h: trckd ldrs: n.m.r and lost pl over 2f out: n.d after* **7/1**

-341 **9** 30 **Dubai Hills**[7] 3403 6-9-7 **91** ... TomEaves 5
(Bryan Smart) *trckd wnr to over 2f out: sn rdn and wknd: eased whn btn fnl f* **6/1**[2]

3-01 **10** 6 **Fulbright**[8] 3348 3-9-3 **96** ... AdrianNicholls 3
(Mark Johnston) *hld up bhd ldng gp: drvn along over 2f out: wknd wl over 1f out: lost tch and eased ins fnl f* **13/2**[3]

0-00 **11** 31 **Gramercy (IRE)**[7] 3371 5-9-13 **97** ... JimCrowley 1
(Kevin Ryan) *in tch on wd outside tl rdn and wknd over 2f out: sn eased* **25/1**

1m 36.15s (8.35) **Going Correction** +1.425s/f (Soft)
WFA 3 from 4yo+ 9lb **11** Ran SP% **123.0**
Speed ratings (Par 109): **109,108,106,106,100 98,95,87,53,46 11**
Tote Swingers: 1&2 £4.40, 1&3 £7.70, 2&3 £9.70 CSF £18.33 CT £135.39 TOTE £2.40: £1.10, £3.20, £3.20; EX 21.50 Trifecta £321.90 Pool: £913.58 - 2.10 winning units..
Owner Racing Management & Training Ltd **Bred** Darley **Trained** Norton, N Yorks

FOCUS
A decent handicap, although the stands' rail again had a big say on the outcome. A small personal best from the winner with the second the besty guide.

NOTEBOOK
Memory Cloth handles testing ground well and was always going to take some passing once in front on the favoured stands' rail. He had little in hand of the runner-up, who had to challenge widest of all, at the line, though, and he may even be able to cope with 6f when conditions are soft. (op 5-2)
Brae Hill(IRE) returned to form following a couple of quiet efforts, and was probably best on the day, doing all his work away from the favoured stands' rail. He still nearly got up, and will likely remain dangerous in big handicaps when on song. (op 8-1)
Roker Park(IRE) was never far from the rail and is now back on his last winning mark.
Fieldgunner Kirkup(GER) was soon prominent and ran well from 2lb wrong on ground he looked to handle. (op 9-1 tchd 12-1)
Prime Exhibit Official explanation: jockey said gelding ran too free
Osteopathic Remedy(IRE) refused to settle. Official explanation: jockey said gelding ran too free and was denied a clear run (op 11-2)
Dubai Hills should have handled conditions but stopped quickly. Official explanation: trainer's rep said gelding was unsuited by the heavy ground (op 13-2 tchd 5-1)
Fulbright wouldn't have been suited by the heavy ground. Official explanation: trainer's rep had no explanation for the poor form shown (op 8-1)

3627 BETFRED/IRISH STALLION FARMS E B F MAIDEN STKS 5f
4:25 (4:25) (Class 4) 2-Y-O **£5,369** (£1,597; £798; £399) **Stalls** High

Form RPR

1 **Slipstream Angel (IRE)** 2-8-12 0 ... TonyHamilton 3 69+
(Richard Fahey) *trckd ldrs: wnt 2nd over 2f out: rdn along over 1f out: 4 l down ins fnl f: styd on strly to ld cl home* **4/1**[3]

333 **2** 1/2 **Opt Out**[9] 3303 2-9-3 72 ... AdrianNicholls 4 72
(Mark Johnston) *led: rdn and qcknd 4 l clr over 1f out: stride shortened last 100yds: hdd cl home* **6/4**[1]

3 6 **Red Gift (IRE)** 2-9-3 0 ... BarryMcHugh 1 50
(Brian Ellison) *s.i.s: rn green in last pl: rdn and hdwy over 1f out: no ch w first two* **7/1**

05 **4** 4 1/2 **Max The Machine**[7] 3381 2-9-0 0 ... DaleSwift(3) 2 34
(Derek Shaw) *chsd wnr to 1/2-way: sn rdn: wknd over 1f out* **13/8**[2]

1m 8.51s (7.41) **Going Correction** +1.425s/f (Soft) **4** Ran SP% **110.6**
Speed ratings (Par 95): **97,96,86,79**
CSF £10.60 TOTE £4.10; EX 10.10.
Owner Darras Partnership **Bred** J & J Waldron **Trained** Musley Bank, N Yorks

FOCUS
Modest form and in-running carnage for punters, Opt Out, who pulled clear over 1f out (done at 1.01 on Betfair), tying up in the final half furlong and being claimed by newcomer Slipstream Angel. Not a race to take too literally.

NOTEBOOK
Slipstream Angel(IRE) looked beaten over 1f out, hitting 999-1 in running on Betfair, but she is a sister to a 1m winner, and her stamina kicked in late. She travelled well until becoming outpaced, but got a second wind and should benefit greatly from 6f. Handicaps will be her thing. (op 9-2)
Opt Out was soon in front on the favoured stands' rail and the race looked done as readily went clear (hit 1.01 in running on Betfair), but he got very tired and is now 0-4. Faster ground will probably help and he can probably pick up a minor maiden at one of the lesser tracks, for all that he's exposed. (op 7-4)
Red Gift(IRE), related to winners from 5f-1m1f, was slowly away and green, so soon had no chance of winning, but at least he was going on, albeit slowly, at the end of his race. (op 11-2)
Max The Machine raced one off the rail but should still have done better. At least this should help him get a lowly provisional mark for nurseries. Official explanation: jockey said colt hung right (op 15-8 tchd 6-4 and 7-4)

3628 BETFRED HAT TRICK HEAVEN ON EUROS H'CAP 1m 2f 32y
4:55 (4:55) (Class 4) (0-85,82) 3-Y-O+ **£5,175** (£1,540; £769; £384)

Form RPR

-503 **1** **Union Island (IRE)**[3] 3494 6-9-9 **80** ... DaleSwift(3) 8 89
(Brian Ellison) *trckd ldr: led over 2f out: sn rdn: edgd lft over 1f out: hdd last 50yds: rallied gamely to regain ld cl home* **9/4**[2]

0-52 **2** shd **Red Inca**[7] 3380 4-9-7 **75** ... BarryMcHugh 7 84
(Brian Ellison) *t.k.h: hld up: stdy hdwy over 4f out: effrt and rdn 2f out: led last 50yds: ct cl home* **13/8**[1]

0041 **3** 7 **Amazing Blue Sky**[7] 3386 6-9-11 **79** ... JamesSullivan 6 74
(Ruth Carr) *t.k.h: led to over 2f out: sn outpcd: rallied appr fnl f: sn no imp* **11/2**

1334 **4** 19 **Party Line**[9] 3305 3-8-7 **73** ...(b[1]) AdrianNicholls 3 30
(Mark Johnston) *t.k.h: hld up: hdwy to chse ldrs 4f out: rdn and wknd over 2f out* **5/1**[3]

-000 **5** 4 **Tiger Webb**[14] 3163 4-8-10 **71** ... DavidSimmonson(7) 10 20
(Michael Easterby) *t.k.h: trckd ldrs: lost pl after 4f: rdn and struggling fr 3f out* **28/1**

04-0 **6** 72 **Waltz Darling (IRE)**[15] 3128 4-9-4 **75** ... LeeTopliss(3) 1
(Richard Fahey) *t.k.h: trckd ldrs tl rdn and wknd over 3f out: t.o* **12/1**

1-06 **7** 26 **Valantino Oyster (IRE)**[21] 2926 5-8-10 **64** oh2... PatrickMathers 11
(Tracy Waggott) *hld up in tch: struggling 5f out: lost tch wl over 3f out: t.o* **25/1**

2m 27.3s (15.40) **Going Correction** +1.625s/f (Heav)
WFA 3 from 4yo+ 12lb **7** Ran SP% **115.9**
Speed ratings (Par 105): **103,102,97,82,78 21,**
Tote Swingers: 1&2 £3.00, 1&3 £2.80, 2&3 £3.40 CSF £6.51 CT £16.53 TOTE £3.50: £2.40, £2.20; EX 8.20.
Owner Union Of Friends **Bred** Barouche Stud Ireland Ltd **Trained** Norton, N Yorks
■ Stewards' Enquiry : Barry McHugh two-day ban: used whip above permitted level (Jul 16-17)

FOCUS
The front pair, both Brian Ellison-trained, drew clear in what was an ordinary handicap. A punishing finish between stablemates, whom the form is rated around.

3629 BETFRED "THE BONUS KING" H'CAP 1m (R)
5:30 (5:30) (Class 4) (0-85,82) 3-Y-O **£5,175** (£1,540; £769; £384)

Form RPR

-032 **1** **Indepub**[32] 2589 3-9-0 **78** ... JulieBurke(3) 5 86
(Kevin Ryan) *mde all at stdy pce: shkn up and qcknd clr over 2f out: styd on wl fnl f: unchal* **13/2**[3]

-201 **2** 2 1/4 **Fire Ship**[23] 2854 3-9-7 **82** ... JimCrowley 1 85
(William Knight) *t.k.h: chsd wnr: rdn over 2f out: kpt on same pce fnl f* **7/4**[1]

-430 **3** 3/4 **Mr Spiggott (IRE)**[35] 2477 3-9-7 **82** ... SamHitchcott 6 83
(Mick Channon) *hld up in tch: effrt and rdn over 2f out: no imp fnl f* **7/4**[1]

-451 **4** 2 1/4 **Hi There (IRE)**[15] 3111 3-8-6 **67** ... PatrickMathers 3 63
(Richard Fahey) *t.k.h: trckd ldrs: drvn over 2f out: edgd lft and no ex over 1f out* **7/2**[2]

2m 3.3s (18.00) **Going Correction** +1.625s/f (Heav) **4** Ran SP% **108.3**
Speed ratings (Par 101): **75,72,72,69**
CSF £17.92 TOTE £6.40; EX 16.30.
Owner D W Barker **Bred** Mrs Deborah O'Brien **Trained** Hambleton, N Yorks

FOCUS
Half of the eight originally declared came out and not form to read much into. The winner enjoyed an easy lead.
T/Plt: £588.00 to a £1 stake. Pool: £164,760.00 - 204.53 winning tickets. T/Qpdt: £54.80 to a £1 stake. Pool: £10,079.00 - 136.10 winning tickets. RY

3589 NEWMARKET (R-H)
Saturday, June 30

OFFICIAL GOING: Good to firm (8.4)
Wind: Fresh, half-behind Weather: Cloudy

3630 £150,000 TATTERSALLS MILLIONS 3-Y-O CUP 1m 2f
2:00 (2:02) (Class 2) 3-Y-O
£81,150 (£36,885; £14,760; £7,365; £4,440; £2,955) **Stalls** Centre

Form RPR

31 **1** **Michelangelo**[36] 2445 3-9-3 99 ... WilliamBuick 4 110
(John Gosden) *dwlt: hld up: hdwy over 3f out: led over 2f out: rdn and hung rt fr over 1f out: styd on wl* **5/6**[1]

3-13 **2** 2 3/4 **Cameron Highland (IRE)**[66] 1604 3-9-3 90... FrankieDettori 3 105
(Roger Varian) *chsd ldrs: led over 3f out: hdd over 2f out: rdn over 1f out: styd on same pce ins fnl f* **7/2**[2]

-200 **3** 8 **Miblish**[11] 3239 3-9-3 97 ...(t) TomQueally 1 89
(Clive Brittain) *hld up in tch: rdn over 2f out: styd on same pce fr over 1f out* **8/1**[3]

0330 **4** 1 **Switzerland (IRE)**[9] 3294 3-9-3 94 ... KierenFallon 6 87
(Mark Johnston) *hld up: hdwy over 2f out: rdn and edgd lft over 1f out: nt trble ldrs* **11/1**

002 **5** 1 1/4 **Viewpoint (IRE)**[35] 2496 3-9-3 78 ... RichardHughes 7 84
(Richard Hannon) *prom: reminder over 5f out: hmpd over 3f out: sn rdn: outpcd fnl 2f* **25/1**

3221 **6** 3/4 **Perfect Delight**[16] 3070 3-8-12 83 ... JohnFahy 12 78
(Clive Cox) *chsd ldrs: rdn over 2f out: wknd over 1f out* **14/1**

0-03 **7** 7 **Dance With Me (IRE)**[21] 2941 3-9-3 75... KirstyMilczarek 11 69
(Andrew Balding) *s.s: hld up: plld hrd: hdwy 4f out: rdn and wknd wl over 1f out* **50/1**

66 **8** 2 1/4 **Divine Pamina (IRE)**[22] 2891 3-8-12 0... DarryllHolland 2 59
(Jim Boyle) *led: hdd over 8f out: chsd ldrs: edgd lft over 3f out: sn rdn: wknd 2f out* **100/1**

2000 **9** 3 **Cape Safari (IRE)**[14] 3163 3-8-12 78...(v[1]) HayleyTurner 13 53
(Alan Bailey) *prom: led over 8f out: hdd over 3f out: sn rdn: wknd wl over 1f out* **40/1**

0 **10** 15 **Hoonose**[54] 1922 3-9-3 0 ... RaulDaSilva 9 28
(Pat Eddery) *prom: rdn over 3f out: wknd 2f out: t.o* **150/1**

5-10 **11** 32 **Forest Row**[9] 3294 3-9-3 88 ... AdamKirby 5
(Clive Cox) *hld up: bhd fnl 3f: t.o* **14/1**

-504 **U** **No Dominion (IRE)**[16] 3083 3-9-3 62... PaulHanagan 8
(James Given) *hld up: hmpd and uns rdr over 3f out* **150/1**

2m 4.14s (-1.36) **Going Correction** 0.0s/f (Good) **12** Ran SP% **120.1**
Speed ratings (Par 105): **105,102,96,95,94 94,88,86,84,72 46,**
Tote Swingers: 1&2 £2.20, 1&3 £2.90, 2&3 £5.00 CSF £3.67 TOTE £1.90: £1.10, £1.50, £2.50; EX 4.10 Trifecta £13.70 Pool: £1,263.59 - 68.06 winning units..
Owner B E Nielsen **Bred** Denford Stud And Balmerino Bloodstock **Trained** Newmarket, Suffolk

FOCUS
Stands side track used with stalls on stands side except 10f &12f: Centre. Solid 3-y-o form, albeit this was not the strongest of renewals. The first two finished clear.

NOTEBOOK
Michelangelo looked to have a cracking opportunity on this slight drop back in trip and he followed up his Listed win at Goodwood last month, landing some decent bets in the process. William Buick was intent on covering him up early, after he made another tardy start, and he sat well back. He was thus forced to make his challenge nearing the far side when scything through the pack, but it worked out as he got a clear passage and Buick asked for everything nearing the final furlong. He drifted right and took time to master the runner-up, but probably hit the front plenty soon enough. It's also likely that a longer trip is his optimum and this progressive colt now looks well worth his place in Group company. He's entered in the Princess Of Wales Stakes over 1m4f back here next month, but could well take in a trial for the St Leger instead. (op 8-11 tchd 10-11 and evens in a place)

Cameron Highland(IRE), whose yard took this last year, was having his first outing since getting bogged down on heavy ground at Epsom in May. He was scratched from Royal Ascot last week, where he was due to wear a first-time hood. In contrast to the winner he was given a positive ride and although he couldn't fend off the winner when that one made his move, he went down with all guns blazing. This ground was more like it for him and the best of him has likely still to be seen. (op 9-2)
Miblish, not disgraced in the Group 1 St James's Palace Stakes last week, got a nice tow through the race more towards the near side. He failed to threaten the first pair, but posted another sound effort up in trip and deserves to get his head back in front.
Switzerland(IRE) showed his Royal Ascot effort nine days earlier to be all wrong, but it's hard to gauge whether he truly stayed this longer trip. (op 12-1 tchd 14-1)
Hoonose Official explanation: jockey said gelding ran green

3631 ACD PROJECTS SUPPORTING THE ANIMAL HEALTH TRUST EMPRESS STKS (LISTED RACE) (FILLIES) 6f

2:30 (2:37) (Class 1) 2-Y-O

£13,043 (£4,945; £2,474; £1,232; £618; £310) **Stalls** Low

Form				RPR
1	**1**		**City Image (IRE)**^{21} [2938] 2-8-12 0 ... RichardHughes 3 (Richard Hannon) *hld up: pushed along 1/2-way: hdwy over 1f out: rdn to ld and hmpd wl ins fnl f: r.o wl: readily* **3/1^{2}**	96+
1	**2**	*1 1/4*	**Sandreamer (IRE)**^{43} [2245] 2-8-12 0 ... MartinHarley 1 (Mick Channon) *trckd ldrs: rdn to ld and hung lft fr over 1f out: hdd and bmpd wnr wl ins fnl f: styd on same pce* **2/1^{1}**	92+
1600	**3**	*3 1/4*	**Baileys Jubilee**^{10} [3269] 2-8-12 92 ... KierenFallon 4 (Mark Johnston) *chsd ldrs: led wl over 1f out: shkn up: hmpd and hdd sn after: no ex ins fnl f* **11/2**	82
2	**4**	*1/2*	**Hasanan**^{15} [3117] 2-8-12 0 ... BrettDoyle 5 (Clive Brittain) *hld up: racd keenly: hung lft over 2f out: sn rdn: styd on: nt trble ldrs* **16/1**	81
41	**5**	*2 3/4*	**Tipping Over (IRE)**^{21} [2929] 2-8-12 0 ... MichaelHills 9 (Hugo Palmer) *chsd ldr tl led over 2f out: rdn and hdd wl over 1f out: wknd ins fnl f* **9/2^{3}**	72
3310	**6**	*2 1/4*	**Sylvia Pankhurst (IRE)**^{31} [2603] 2-8-12 65 ... DarryllHolland 8 (David C Griffiths) *led over 3f: sn rdn: wknd over 1f out* **100/1**	66
311	**7**	*10*	**Bridge Night**^{14} [3138] 2-8-12 89 ... WilliamBuick 6 (Eve Johnson Houghton) *hmpd s: plld hrd and sn prom: rdn over 1f out: sn wknd and eased* **5/1**	36

1m 12.51s (0.01) **Going Correction** 0.0s/f (Good) **7 Ran SP% 115.4**
Speed ratings (Par 98): **99,97,93,92,88 85,72**
Tote Swingers: 1&2 £1.90, 1&3 £3.60, 2&3 £2.90 CSF £9.65 TOTE £4.00: £2.20, £2.00; EX 8.80 Trifecta £45.00 Pool: £1,362.09 - 22.39 winning units..
Owner P A Byrne **Bred** Patrick Byrnes **Trained** East Everleigh, Wilts
■ Stewards' Enquiry : Martin Harley one-day ban: careless riding (Jul 16)
Richard Hughes caution: careless riding.

FOCUS
A host of unexposed juvenile fillies lined up in this Listed contest and two once-raced maiden winners fought it out inside the final furlong. Howecer this race is usually weak for the grade and the form is rated on a par with the race averages.

NOTEBOOK
City Image(IRE) readily added to her soft-ground 5f Windsor maiden success 21 days earlier and looks a filly of real potential. She did her best work towards the finish last time so it wasnt surprising that she enjoyed this stiffer test and Richard Hughes didnt have to fully extend her near the finish. She's in the right hands to keep improving this year and stepping up again into Group company is the natural progression for her. She is in the Super Sprint at Newbury next month, but the Cherry Hinton back here looks favourite for her next outing. (op 5-2)
Sandreamer(IRE) beat two subsequent winners when landing her maiden on the Rowley Mile in May. She held every chance after travelling strongly on the near side, but has to rate as somewhat unfortunate as she initially got into a barging match with the third and then drifted into the winner somewhat nearing the finish. That looked down to inexperience and she should be well up to winning in this grade. (op 5-2 tchd 11-4)
Baileys Jubilee was better than the bare form at Royal Ascot ten days earlier and met support on this step up a furlong. She had her chance, but failed to see it out up the rising finish like the first pair and this is probably as good as she is. (op 13-2)
Hasanan caught the eye running on with promise late in the day on this move up to 6f. She ought to have no trouble winning a maiden in the coming weeks. (tchd 20-1)
Tipping Over(IRE) looked progressive when winning her maiden over C&D 21 days previously. She was found out in this much better contest, but remains a useful prospect and should enjoy getting back on some easier ground. (tchd 5-1)
Bridge Night failed to settle and looked a non-stayer over this extra furlong. Official explanation: trainer's rep said filly was unsuited by the good to firm ground (op 9-2)

3632 BETFAIR SUPPORTS THE ANIMAL HEALTH TRUST FRED ARCHER STKS (LISTED RACE) 1m 4f

3:00 (3:07) (Class 1) 4-Y-O+

£18,714 (£7,095; £3,550; £1,768; £887; £445) **Stalls** Centre

Form				RPR
0-00	**1**		**Polygon (USA)**^{28} [2711] 4-8-9 95 ... (b^{1}) WilliamBuick 1 (John Gosden) *led over 2f: chsd ldr tl led again over 2f out: rdn and hdd over 1f out: rallied to ld wl ins fnl f* **33/1**	105
0-32	**2**	*1/2*	**Dandino**^{35} [2481] 5-9-0 110 ... HayleyTurner 5 (James Fanshawe) *chsd ldrs: led over 1f out: sn rdn: hdd wl ins fnl f* **4/7^{1}**	109
0404	**3**	*4 1/2*	**Barbican**^{35} [2506] 4-9-3 105 ... RichardHughes 2 (Alan Bailey) *hld up: rdn over 2f out: styd on to go 3rd nr fin: nt trble ldrs* **4/1^{2}**	105
14-3	**4**	*nk*	**Berling (IRE)**^{35} [2481] 5-9-0 99 ... TomQueally 7 (John Dunlop) *hld up: hdwy over 3f out: rdn over 1f out: no ex ins fnl f: lost 3rd nr fin* **7/1^{3}**	102
166-	**5**	*3*	**Zafarana**^{247} [7129] 4-8-9 88 ... KierenFallon 6 (Roger Varian) *plld hrd and prom: led over 9f out: rdn and hdd over 2f out: wknd ins fnl f* **25/1**	92
-022	**6**	*1 1/4*	**Proud Chieftain**^{15} [3121] 4-9-0 85 ... DarryllHolland 8 (Clifford Lines) *prom: rdn over 2f out: hung lft over 1f out: wknd ins fnl f* **22/1**	95
1-00	**7**	*11*	**Khawlah (IRE)**^{28} [2711] 4-8-9 110 ... FrankieDettori 3 (Saeed Bin Suroor) *hld up: rdn over 2f out: wknd over 1f out* **14/1**	72

2m 30.01s (-2.89) **Going Correction** 0.0s/f (Good) **7 Ran SP% 114.0**
Speed ratings (Par 111): **109,108,105,105,103 102,95**
Tote Swingers: 1&2 £8.30, 1&3 £12.90, 2&3 £1.60 CSF £52.98 TOTE £25.60: £6.40, £1.30; EX 73.40 Trifecta £373.00 Pool: £2,263.27 - 4.49 winning units..
Owner Lady Rothschild **Bred** Carwell Equities Ltd **Trained** Newmarket, Suffolk

FOCUS
There was a turn up in this Listed event. This is below-par form off a muddling pace. The winner is only rated back to her bset, with the second disappointing.

NOTEBOOK
Polygon(USA) sprung back to life under a very strong ride from the bang in-form William Buick. She had bombed out in two previous outings since resuming this year, but her top trainer continues to churn out the winners and the application of headgear evidently worked the oracle. She showed real guts to get the better of Dandino throughout the final furlong and, while there is always a worry about how a horse will react to second-time headgear, this was a case of job done as she now has some all important winning black type. Official explanation: trainer said, regarding apparent improvement in form, that the filly showed more interest with the application of blinkers.
Dandino, all the rage, would have enjoyed more of a test no doubt and it was his first outing on this course, but it has to be considered a disappointment he failed to master a rival rated 15lb inferior to him. (op 4-6 tchd 8-15 and 8-11 in a place)
Barbican tracked Dandino and Polygon through the race and moved stands' side with his effort from 2f out, but was unable to seriously challenge. His optimum trip is something of an unknown at present. (op 11-2 tchd 6-1)
Berling(IRE) is another that would have appreciated a stronger gallop, but he still ran close to his last-time-out form with Dandino. (op 6-1 tchd 15-2)

3633 JOHN SUNLEY MEMORIAL CRITERION STKS (GROUP 3) 7f

3:35 (3:36) (Class 1) 3-Y-O+

£31,190 (£11,825; £5,918; £2,948; £1,479; £742) **Stalls** Low

Form				RPR
-501	**1**		**Libranno**^{13} [3190] 4-9-3 109 ... RichardHughes 8 (Richard Hannon) *mde all: set stdy pce tl qcknd over 2f out: rdn over 1f out: r.o* **10/3^{2}**	111
1-40	**2**	*1/2*	**Edinburgh Knight (IRE)**^{10} [3268] 5-9-3 104 ... WilliamBuick 5 (Paul D'Arcy) *hld up: hdwy over 2f out: rdn and ev ch fr over 1f out: unable qck nr fin* **4/1^{3}**	110
2-32	**3**	*1/2*	**Majestic Myles (IRE)**^{28} [2710] 4-9-3 108 ... TomQueally 3 (Richard Fahey) *trckd ldrs: plld hrd: rdn over 1f out: r.o* **4/1^{3}**	109
2200	**4**	*nk*	**Bannock (IRE)**^{10} [3265] 3-8-8 107 ... KierenFallon 1 (Mark Johnston) *chsd ldrs: shkn up over 2f out: rdn over 1f out: r.o* **11/1**	105
63-5	**5**	*2 1/2*	**Hoof It**^{45} [2179] 5-9-3 118 ... FrankieDettori 6 (Michael Easterby) *plld hrd: trckd wnr tl shkn up over 1f out: styd on same pce* **6/4^{1}**	101
4602	**6**	*6*	**Mister Green (FR)**^{2} [3546] 6-9-3 57 ... (t) MickaelBarzalona 4 (David Flood) *hld up: rdn over 2f out: sn wknd* **125/1**	85?
5660	**7**	*3 3/4*	**Sos Brillante (CHI)**^{13} [3190] 7-9-0 74 ... (p) MartinHarley 2 (Terry Clement) *hld up: rdn over 2f out: sn wknd* **150/1**	72

1m 24.66s (-1.04) **Going Correction** 0.0s/f (Good)
WFA 3 from 4yo+ 9lb **7 Ran SP% 112.9**
Speed ratings (Par 113): **105,104,103,103,100 93,89**
Tote Swingers: 1&2 £3.20, 1&3 £2.60, 2&3 £2.50 CSF £16.57 TOTE £4.90: £2.30, £2.10; EX 18.80 Trifecta £67.20 Pool: £1,620.47 - 17.84 winning units..
Owner Mcdowell Racing **Bred** O McDowell **Trained** East Everleigh, Wilts

FOCUS
A steadily run Group 3 and a blanket finish. Hoof It was clearly below his sprint best and Libranno is rated similarly to when winning last year.

NOTEBOOK
Libranno followed up his win in the race last year. He had gamely opened his account for the campaign at Salisbury over 6f 13 days earlier and was well fancied to go in again back here. He was gifted the early lead and was therefore able to set his own fractions, which he does enjoy. That meant Richard Hughes had something left in the tank when strongly challenged when the dash for home developed and he was nicely on top at the line. His form figures here now read 1141 and another crack at the July Cup back here next month now looks on the cards. (op 11-4 tchd 7-2)
Edinburgh Knight(IRE), only 17th in the Hunt Cup ten days earlier, was making his debut in this class (has won in Listed company) and he ran a big race in defeat, only just failing. A stronger pace would have probably seen him back to winning ways and he's clearly up to this sort of level, but 7f is his optimum distance. (op 9-2)
Majestic Myles(IRE) rates the best guide for this form. He didn't settle that well off the uneven pace and this ultra-consistent 4-y-o fully deserves to get his head back in front. (op 7-2 tchd 10-3)
Bannock(IRE), the sole 3-y-o, came under pressure a fair way out but stuck bravely to his task and this was much more like it again. He is tricky to place, however.
Hoof It, again well backed, flopped at York on his return in May and was having his first outing over further than 6f since finishing last in a handicap at Doncaster in 2010. He tried to come between the first pair nearing the final furlong, but the effort proved short-lived and he did shape like a non-stayer. He's not one to write off as he does seem at his best when racing in big fields off a searching pace. (op 15-8 tchd 2-1 in places)

3634 GRAND HOTEL LIENZ TYROL MAIDEN STKS 7f

4:05 (4:06) (Class 5) 2-Y-O **£3,234** (£962; £481; £240) **Stalls** Low

Form				RPR
333	**1**		**Luhaif**^{16} [3062] 2-9-3 81 ... MartinHarley 1 (Mick Channon) *racd stands' side: mde all: rdn and hung lft over 2f out: r.o wl* **12/1**	89
0	**2**	*6*	**Noble Bull (IRE)**^{19} [2983] 2-9-3 0 ... DarryllHolland 8 (Charles Hills) *racd stands' side: chsd ldrs: rdn over 1f out: sn hung lft: styd on same pce* **66/1**	73
	3	*nk*	**Hoarding (USA)** 2-9-3 0 ... SaleemGolam 2 (John Gosden) *racd stands' side: s.i.s: hld up: hdwy over 1f out: r.o: nt trble ldrs* **7/1**	73+
	4	*1*	**Glory City (IRE)** 2-9-3 0 ... SebSanders 7 (Marco Botti) *racd stands' side: chsd wnr: rdn and hung lft over 2f out: hmpd 1f out: no ex* **33/1**	70+
	5	*1 1/4*	**Disclaimer** 2-9-3 0 ... TomQueally 12 (Sir Henry Cecil) *racd centre: chsd ldr over 4f: sn rdn: styd on same pce fr over 1f out* **11/4^{2}**	67+
	6	*1 1/4*	**Estifzaaz (IRE)** 2-9-3 0 ... TadhgO'Shea 14 (Charles Hills) *racd centre: chsd ldrs: led that gp over 2f out: sn rdn and hung rt: no ex fnl f* **2/1^{1}**	64+
4	**7**	*3/4*	**Quintilian (IRE)**^{22} [2880] 2-9-3 0 ... MickaelBarzalona 15 (Mahmood Al Zarooni) *racd alone far side: up w the pce: rdn and hung rt and jnd centre over 2f out: sn rdn: wknd ins fnl f* **5/1^{3}**	62+
	8	*1 1/4*	**Blue Wave (IRE)** 2-8-12 0 ... AntiocoMurgia$^{(5)}$ 6 (Mahmood Al Zarooni) *racd centre: hld up: hdwy u.p over 1f out: wknd ins fnl f* **20/1**	58+
	9	*1 1/2*	**Khudoua** 2-9-3 0 ... MarcHalford 10 (John Gosden) *racd centre: hld up: hdwy over 1f out: wknd ins fnl f* **40/1**	54+
	10	*nse*	**Inaad (IRE)** 2-9-3 0 ... FrankieDettori 4 (Saeed Bin Suroor) *racd stands' side: hld up: wnt towards centre 1/2-way: nvr trbld ldrs* **7/1**	54
	11	*3 1/4*	**Intibaah** 2-9-3 0 ... KierenFallon 13 (Brian Meehan) *racd centre: led centre over 4f: sn hung rt: wknd over 1f out* **25/1**	46

0 **12** *19* **Grace Of Hearts**44 2193 2-8-12 0 PaoloSirigu 9
(Robert Eddery) *racd stands' side: plld hrd and prom: rdn over 2f out: wknd over 1f out: t.o* **33/1**

13 *2 ¾* **Hawsies Dream** 2-8-12 0 HayleyTurner 3
(Alan Bailey) *racd stands' side: hld up: wknd 2f out: t.o* **66/1**

14 *1* **Royal Caper** 2-9-3 0 BrettDoyle 11
(John Ryan) *racd centre: s.i.s: a in rr: lost tch over 2f out: t.o* **80/1**

1m 26.2s (0.50) **Going Correction** 0.0s/f (Good) 14 Ran SP% 130.5
Speed ratings (Par 93): **97,90,89,88,87 85,84,83,81,81 78,56,53,52**
Tote Swingers: 1&2 £46.00, 1&3 £9.60, 2&3 £41.00 CSF £667.46 TOTE £17.00: £3.30, £11.20, £2.30; EX 622.80 TRIFECTA Not won..
Owner Sheikh Mohammed Bin Khalifa Al Maktoum **Bred** T R G Vestey **Trained** West Ilsley, Berks

FOCUS
The runners spread across the track early on which dictated a messy race, however, and previous experience told. The principals all stayed stands' side.

NOTEBOOK
Luhaif broke his duck at the fourth time of asking. He had finished third on his three previous outings and shown a good level of form, but it was surprising that he disposed of this field in such a comfortable manner. He was no doubt in the right place near the stands' rail, though, and he clearly likes quick ground. His breeding suggests further will suit at three, so another furlong this year should be within his compass, and his trainer afterwards put the improvement down to a change of tactics. (op 16-1)
Noble Bull(IRE) stayed stands' side and, without threatening the winner, stayed on nicely up the rising finish to register a much-improved effort. This ground was obviously more to his liking, as was the extra furlong and he shouldn't be long in getting off the mark.
Hoarding(USA), another that kept stands' side, was settled right out the back early on. He moved nicely but was green under pressure and shaped as though a more positive ride would have seen him go closer. His rider's kindness is sure to pay off soon. (tchd 6-1)
Glory City(IRE) ◆, related to numerous winners at up to 1m4f, proved distinctly green when put under pressure. He still showed plenty, though, and, granted the normal improvement, should soon be winning. (op 40-1)
Disclaimer raced nearer the far side and lacked a turn of foot. He has plenty of stamina in his pedigree, however, and already looks to want 1m. (op 2-1 tchd 3-1)
Estifzaaz(IRE), stablemate of the runner-up, looked a player down the centre 2f out. He flattened out markedly from the furlong marker, though, and a drop to 6f may help. (op 7-2 tchd 9-2)
Inaad(IRE) Official explanation: jockey said colt ran too free

3635 FEE CLUB H'CAP 1m 2f
4:40 (4:42) (Class 2) (0-100,100) 3-Y-0+ **£12,938** (£3,850; £1,924; £962) **Stalls** Centre

Form RPR

1-02 **1** **Area Fifty One**14 3164 4-9-6 92 DavidNolan 10 106
(Richard Fahey) *chsd ldr tl led over 2f out: rdn clr fnl f* **5/1**2

-043 **2** *4* **Unex El Greco**29 2657 4-9-3 89 TonyCulhane 3 95
(John Gosden) *hld up: hdwy over 1f out: sn rdn: r.o to go 2nd post: nt trble wnr* **8/1**3

6610 **3** *nk* **Licence To Till (USA)**7 3372 5-9-9 95 KierenFallon 15 100
(Mark Johnston) *a.p: chsd ldr 2f out: sn rdn: edgd lft ins fnl f: styd on same pce: lost 2nd post* **14/1**

0-00 **4** *1 ¾* **Qushchi**21 2933 4-9-7 93 DarryllHolland 13 95
(William Jarvis) *a.p: rdn over 1f out: styd on same pce fnl f* **16/1**

-121 **5** *1 ¾* **Media Hype**43 2257 5-9-5 91 PhillipMakin 8 89+
(Mrs K Burke) *hld up: nt clr run over 2f out: r.o ins fnl f: nvr nrr* **2/1**1

3430 **6** *1* **Start Right**91 1130 5-10-0 100 FrankieDettori 1 96
(Saeed Bin Suroor) *hld up: rdn over 2f out: r.o ins fnl f: nvr nrr* **12/1**

60-0 **7** *nk* **Dangerous Midge (USA)**14 3178 6-9-11 100 PatrickHills(3) 9 95
(Brian Meehan) *mid-div: hdwy over 2f out: sn rdn: wknd ins fnl f* **33/1**

1-10 **8** *½* **War Poet**21 2911 5-9-7 93 (v1) MickaelBarzalona 4 87
(David O'Meara) *hld up: rdn over 2f out: n.d* **10/1**

03-0 **9** *½* **Classic Punch (IRE)**21 2933 9-10-0 100 BrettDoyle 11 93
(David Elsworth) *led over 7f: wknd ins fnl f* **22/1**

02-0 **10** *5* **Fadhaa (IRE)**43 2248 4-8-12 84 TadhgO'Shea 5 67
(Charles Hills) *hld up: rdn over 2f out: wknd over 1f out* **17/2**

/225 **11** *2 ½* **King's Warrior (FR)**28 2706 5-9-5 91 RichardHughes 14 69
(Peter Chapple-Hyam) *s.i.s: hld up and a in rr: rdn and wknd over 2f out* **10/1**

0106 **12** *5* **Resurge (IRE)**21 2911 7-9-8 94 (b1) SebSanders 2 62
(Stuart Kittow) *hld up: a in rr: rdn over 2f out: sn wknd* **25/1**

12-0 **13** *17* **Pivotman**29 2655 4-9-7 93 (t) TomQueally 6 27
(Amanda Perrett) *mid-div: hdwy 1/2-way: rdn over 2f out: wknd over 1f out: t.o* **16/1**

2m 3.25s (-2.25) **Going Correction** 0.0s/f (Good) 13 Ran SP% 127.1
Speed ratings (Par 109): **109,105,105,104,102 101,101,101,100,96 94,90,77**
Tote Swingers: 1&2 £8.80, 1&3 £16.50, 2&3 £20.70 CSF £46.97 CT £548.53 TOTE £6.30: £2.30, £3.00, £3.00; EX 61.90 Trifecta £774.30 Pool: £42,555.66 - 40.67 winning units..
Owner Dr Marwan Koukash **Bred** Carmel Stud **Trained** Musley Bank, N Yorks

FOCUS
A good handicap which was well run, and pretty solid form. The winner built on his latest personal best.

NOTEBOOK
Area Fifty One set sail for home nearing the final furlong and ran out a clear-cut winner, going one better than his close second at York a fortnight earlier. He got the run of the race just off the leader, but was in front plenty soon enough and there was plenty to like about his attitude. It rates a career-best and he's obviously versatile regards ground. A return to York for the ultra-competitive John Smith's Cup is now firmly on the cards. (op 9-2 tchd 11-2)
Unex El Greco fared best of those coming from off the pace and ran another slid race for his bang in-form yard. He can be ridden more positively now connections know he gets this trip, and his turn is not looking far off. (op 7-1)
Licence To Till(USA) raced upsides the winner for a long way and this showed his flop at Royal Ascot last time to be all wrong. He helps set a decent level. (op 12-1)
Qushchi came home widest of all down the middle of the track. This trip is really too sharp for her and she wasn't disgraced. (op 14-1)
Media Hype was racing off an 8lb higher mark yet was again gambled on to make it four wins from his last five outings. He found himself get well back and by the time he was out in the clear it was all too late. He's better than this. Official explanation: trainer's rep said horse was unsuited by the good to firm ground (op 3-1)

3636 BEDFORD LODGE SUPPORTING THE ANIMAL HEALTH TRUST E B F FILLIES' H'CAP 1m
5:15 (5:16) (Class 3) (0-95,88) 3-Y-0+ **£8,409** (£2,502; £1,250; £625) **Stalls** Low

Form RPR

-140 **1** **Moone's My Name**29 2657 4-10-0 88 RichardHughes 9 101
(Ralph Beckett) *a.p: pushed along over 2f out: swtchd rt and chsd ldr over 1f out: rdn to ld 1f out: edgd lft: styd on u.p* **11/4**2

-112 **2** *hd* **Love Your Looks**33 2539 4-9-8 82 TonyCulhane 12 95
(Mike Murphy) *a.p: chsd ldr 6f out tl led over 2f out: rdn and hdd 1f out: r.o u.p* **7/1**

0311 **3** *4 ½* **Russian Rave**8 3342 6-9-12 86 DarryllHolland 1 88
(Jonathan Portman) *hld up: hdwy over 1f out: sn rdn: styd on same pce ins fnl f* **13/2**

10-0 **4** *nk* **Whimsical (IRE)**24 2820 3-8-10 80 SeanLevey 11 80
(Richard Hannon) *chsd ldrs: rdn over 1f out: no ex ins fnl f* **25/1**

-500 **5** *5* **Abishena (IRE)**7 3376 3-9-1 85 MichaelStainton 6 73
(Mark Johnston) *prom: rdn over 2f out: wknd over 1f out* **25/1**

640- **6** *nk* **Tuscania**245 7168 4-9-11 85 1 TadhgO'Shea 8 74
(Lucy Wadham) *hld up: racd keenly: rdn and hung lft over 1f out: sn wknd* **18/1**

4-05 **7** *1 ½* **Diverting**30 2642 4-9-9 86 RyanClark(3) 4 72
(William Jarvis) *hld up: rdn over 2f out: wknd over 1f out* **9/2**3

6-05 **8** *3 ¾* **Dreamwriter (USA)**22 2890 3-9-4 88 KieranO'Neill 3 63
(Richard Hannon) *sn led: rdn and hdd over 2f out: wknd over 1f out* **20/1**

13- **9** *15* **Ihsas (USA)**276 6466 3-9-3 87 FrankieDettori 7 28
(Saeed Bin Suroor) *hld up: racd keenly: hdwy 3f out: wknd wl over 1f out: eased t.o* **5/2**1

1m 38.83s (-1.17) **Going Correction** 0.0s/f (Good)
WFA 3 from 4yo+ 10lb 9 Ran SP% 117.0
Speed ratings (Par 104): **105,104,100,100,95 94,93,89,74**
Tote Swingers: 1&2 £4.70, 1&3 £4.20, 2&3 £3.90 CSF £22.01 CT £113.00 TOTE £3.40: £1.30, £1.70, £2.40; EX 24.40 Trifecta £103.60 Pool: £2,795.95 - 19.97 winning units..
Owner McDonagh Murphy And Nixon **Bred** Baroness Bloodstock & Tweenhills Stud **Trained** Kimpton, Hants

FOCUS
A decent fillies' handicap, run at average pace and the first pair came nicely clear. The winner is rated up 5lb.

NOTEBOOK
Moone's My Name bounced back to her best and, not for the first time in her career, completed the task in gutsy fashion. She cruised into the lead under Richard Hughes and looked set for a comfortable success, but ultimately had to work very hard to fend off the renewed challenge of the runner-up. There must be a chance she can nick a Listed race before the year is out, but perhaps the Totesport Mile Handicap at Glorious Goodwood would be ideal next time out. Official explanation: trainer's rep said, regarding apparent improvment in form, that, on its previous run at Epsom, the filly likes to be prominent but was unable to do so being drawn 17 of 17, (op 7-2 tchd 4-1 in a place)
Love Your Looks arrived in top form and she made a really bold bid once more back down a furlong in trip. There was a great deal to admire about the way she came back at the winner once headed and this was her best effort to date in defeat. (op 6-1)
Russian Rave, bidding for a hat-trick, was another coming here at the top of her game and raced off a 5lb higher mark. She took time to settle out the back and allowed the two ahead of her first run, but stayed on willingly. She too gives this form a decent look. (op 7-1 tchd 15-2)
Whimsical(IRE) ran an awful lot more encouragingly again on this second run back from her break. She got the trip and can build on this. (op 33-1)
Ihsas(USA), a sister to Rio De La Plata, looked as though she may have got in lightly off 87 on this belated return. The longer trip seemed sure to suit and she was well backed, but ultimately ran a tame race. She's a big filly and may still be weak, but this leaves her with a lot to prove. (op 3-1 tchd 9-4)
T/Plt: £72.10 to a £1 stake. Pool: £120,893.00 - 1,222.43 winning tickets. T/Qpdt: £29.40 to a £1 stake. Pool: £5,672.00 - 142.30 winning tickets. CR

3443 WINDSOR (R-H)
Saturday, June 30

OFFICIAL GOING: Good (good to firm in places; 8.4)
Wind: medium, behind Weather: light cloud, bright spells

3637 BETFRED HOME OF THE BIG WINNERS MAIDEN STKS (DIV I) 6f
2:25 (2:25) (Class 5) 2-Y-O **£2,911** (£866; £432; £216) **Stalls** Low

Form RPR

1 **I'm Back (IRE)** 2-9-3 0 IanMongan 5 79+
(Saeed Bin Suroor) *squeezed for room leaving stalls: sn chsng ldrs: swtchd lft and effrt over 1f out: r.o wl under hands and heels riding fnl f to ld last strides* **13/2**

3 **2** *hd* **Bold Prediction (IRE)**13 3191 2-9-3 0 PatDobbs 2 78
(Richard Hannon) *led for 1f: w ldr tl led again 3f out: hrd pressed and drvn over 1f out: battled on gamely tl hdd and no ex last strides* **7/2**1

6 **3** *¾* **It's Taboo**16 3074 2-8-12 0 DavidProbert 1 71
(Mark Usher) *in tch in midfield: hdwy to chse ldr 3f out: ev ch and drvn over 1f out: no ex and one pce fnl 100yds* **10/1**

0 **4** *nk* **Fils Anges (IRE)**71 1499 2-8-10 0 IanBurns(7) 7 76
(Michael Bell) *t.k.h: hld up in tch in midfield: edgd rt and hdwy over 2f out: swtchd rt and trying to chal against stands' rail 1f out: n.m.r ins fnl f: no ex u.p fnl 100yds* **7/2**1

5 *2 ½* **Shamaheart (IRE)** 2-9-3 0 DaneO'Neill 9 67
(Richard Hannon) *in tch: swtchd lft and effrt 2f out: sn outpcd and btn over 1f out: styd on same pce after* **8/1**

6 *3 ½* **Blessington (IRE)** 2-9-3 0 RobertHavlin 8 62+
(John Gosden) *v.s.a: clsd and in tch in rr after 2f: effrt whn squeezed out and bdly hmpd over 2f out: sn swtchd lft: no ch after but kpt on steadily fnl f* **6/1**3

3263 **7** *1 ¾* **Strong Conviction**22 2868 2-9-3 78 MatthewDavies 10 52
(Mick Channon) *wnt lft and racing v awkwardly leaving stalls: rdn along in rr early: hdwy to chse ldrs 3f out: wknd over 1f out* **5/1**2

8 *5* **Royal Guinevere** 2-8-12 0 JamesDoyle 6 32
(Dean Ivory) *in tch: rdn and struggling 2f out: wknd over 1f out: wl btn and eased wl ins fnl f* **25/1**

5 **9** *5* **Persian Marvel (IRE)**15 3117 2-9-3 0 StephenCraine 3 22
(Jim Boyle) *in tch in midfield tl lost pl and bhd whn sltly hmpd jst over 2f out: sn lost tch* **50/1**

10 *16* **Pal Of The Cat** 2-9-3 0 AmirQuinn 4
(Brian Gubby) *t.k.h: dashed up to ld after 1f: hdd 3f out: sn lost pl: t.o and eased fnl f* **40/1**

1m 12.61s (-0.39) **Going Correction** -0.30s/f (Firm) 10 Ran SP% 117.2
Speed ratings (Par 93): **90,89,88,88,85 80,78,71,64,43**
toteswingers 1&2 £3.90, 2&3 £8.30, 1&3 £17.50 CSF £29.29 TOTE £8.90: £2.50, £2.10, £3.30; EX 23.40.
Owner Godolphin **Bred** Darley **Trained** Newmarket, Suffolk
■ Stewards' Enquiry : Ian Burns two-day ban: careless riding (Jul 16-17)

FOCUS
Inner of straight dolled out 4yds at 6f down to the intersection then reducing to full width at Winning Post. Top bend dolled out 3yds from normal inner configuration adding 12yds to race distances of 1m and over. The ground had been watered with good to firm included in the description and the jockeys reported that it was lovely ground. The first division a fair maiden and it resulted in a close finish. It's doubtful the form matched the race averages.

NOTEBOOK
I'm Back(IRE) ◆, the first foal of a winning daughter of Cape Verdi, made a good start to his career, overcoming being short of room at the start by picking up well when ridden and getting to the front close home. There should be more to come with this behind him. (op 7-1 tchd 15-2)
Bold Prediction(IRE), whose handler had trained two of the previous three winners of this contest, went close to giving him another success. He built on his debut run here but, after getting the better of the filly in the latter stages, was caught near the line. He should be capable of winning a similar contest. (op 10-3 tchd 3-1)
It's Taboo ◆ built considerably on her Nottingham debut here and was only just run out of it late, holding a good pitch on the rail and only losing out to a couple of colts from major yards near the finish. She should be winning her maiden before long if going on from this. (op 14-1)
Fils Anges(IRE), well beaten in Englishman's Newbury maiden on his debut back in April, was having his first run since. He looked a big threat when getting a gap on the rail over a furlong out but couldn't pick up from that point. (tchd 9-2)
Shamaheart(IRE), the stable second string, made an encouraging debut, finishing not far behind those in the frame. He had to switch around a couple of fading rivals around 2f out and was not given a hard time once his chance had gone. He can be expected to build on this, possibly over another furlong. (op 17-2 tchd 9-1)
Blessington(IRE), a half-brother to Listed winner Excelette, missed the break and only ran on late. He should be better for the experience. (op 8-1)
Strong Conviction, the most experienced runner in the line-up, went left and lost ground leaving the stalls but was up with the leaders by the elbow. It was no surprise he paid for those early exertions later in the contest. Nurseries look the best way forward with him. (op 9-2)

3638 BETFRED HOME OF THE BIG WINNERS MAIDEN STKS (DIV II) 6f
2:55 (2:56) (Class 5) 2-Y-O **£2,911** (£866; £432; £216) **Stalls** Low

Form				RPR
0	**1**		**Secret Sign**[43] 2231 2-9-3 0 MartinLane 9 (Brian Meehan) *chsd ldrs: rdn to chal ent fnl f: led fnl 100yds: r.o wl* **20/1**	72
052	**2**	*1*	**Deepest Blue**[9] 3303 2-9-3 0 JamesDoyle 4 (Jamie Osborne) *pressed ldr: u.p and ev ch whn carried lft 1f out: no ex and one pce fnl 100yds* **11/2**	69
0	**3**	*shd*	**Blazing Knight (IRE)**[42] 2261 2-9-3 0 GeorgeBaker 6 (Ralph Beckett) *led: hrd pressed and hung rt u.p 1f out: hdd fnl 100yds: one pce after* **11/4**[2]	69
02	**4**	*½*	**Carlton Blue (IRE)**[25] 2784 2-9-3 0 ChrisCatlin 2 (Paul Cole) *t.k.h: chsd ldng trio: effrt and hung lft over 1f out: kpt on but nvr quite gng pce to chal fnl f* **5/2**[1]	67
50	**5**	*3*	**Royal Mizar (SPA)**[16] 3067 2-8-12 0 LeonnaMayor(5) 1 (Alastair Lidderdale) *stdd s: t.k.h: hld up in last pair: hdwy over 2f out: rdn and edgd lft over 1f out: no imp after* **33/1**	58
	6	*3*	**Linguine (FR)** 2-9-3 0 MartinDwyer 7 (Charles Hills) *stdd s: hld up in tch: rdn and struggling whn hung lft over 2f out: wknd 2f out* **5/1**[3]	49
	7	*4 ½*	**Lisa's Legacy** 2-9-3 0 PatDobbs 8 (Richard Hannon) *a bhd: rdn after 2f: lost tch over 2f out* **7/1**	36
	8	*¾*	**Picc Of Burgau** 2-8-9 0 HarryBentley(3) 3 (Joseph Tuite) *dwlt: sn in tch in midfield: rdn and struggling 1/2-way: bhd fnl 2f* **18/1**	28
	9	*14*	**Swift Code (IRE)** 2-9-3 0 J-PGuillambert 5 (Nigel Tinkler) *dwlt: sn in tch in midfield: rdn and struggling 1/2-way: sn wknd* **40/1**	

1m 12.65s (-0.35) **Going Correction** -0.30s/f (Firm) **9** Ran SP% **115.2**
Speed ratings (Par 93): **90,88,88,87,83 79,73,72,54**
toteswingers 1&2 £6.60, 2&3 £18.30, 1&3 £10.10 CSF £123.72 TOTE £23.90: £5.10, £1.60, £1.10; EX 136.10.
Owner Trelawny II **Bred** Whitsbury Manor Stud **Trained** Manton, Wilts

FOCUS
The second leg of the juvenile maiden was run fractionally slower than the first division. Just a fair race, rated through the second and fourth.

NOTEBOOK
Secret Sign, well beaten in a maiden that has produced five subsequent winners, added to that total in good fashion, despite still looking a bit green. He jumped well from the outside stall and was never far away, but took a while to assert and can be expected to be more street-wise next time.
Deepest Blue was always in the leading group and had every chance. He helps set the standard but might be better off contesting nurseries in future. (op 5-1 tchd 6-1)
Blazing Knight(IRE) was another to improve on his debut effort and made the running nearest the rail, but could not find the extra required late on. There should be more to come. (tchd 5-2)
Carlton Blue(IRE) built on his debut effort when second in a Leicester maiden but, after tracking the pace never looked like picking up sufficiently to land a blow. He might need a stiffer track but now qualifies for a handicap mark. The representative of the trainer reported that the colt had been struck into behind. Official explanation: trainer's rep said colt had been struck into behind (op 3-1)
Royal Mizar(SPA) was again slowly away but did make ground to chase the leaders before his effort flattened out. He has ability and could be of interest once he learns to break more quickly. (op 20-1)
Linguine(FR), a 52,000euros half-brother to an AW winner, was keen under restraint early and made very little impression in the latter stages. He was reasonably well supported beforehand, so better must have been expected. (op 7-1 tchd 8-1)

3639 BETFRED MOBILE CASINO H'CAP 6f
3:30 (3:30) (Class 2) (0-100,99) 3-Y-O **£12,938** (£3,850; £1,924; £962) **Stalls** Low

Form				RPR
0202	**1**		**Mezzotint (IRE)**[10] 3284 3-8-5 **83** AndreaAtzeni 8 (Marco Botti) *chsd ldrs: rdn over 1f out: ev ch 1f out: led wl ins fnl f: styd on wl* **5/1**[3]	95
512	**2**	*nk*	**Nassau Storm**[17] 3049 3-7-13 **80** HarryBentley(3) 2 (William Knight) *t.k.h: hld up wl in tch: rdn and effrt to chse ldr wl over 1f out: drvn to ld ins fnl f: hdd and no ex wl ins fnl f* **9/2**[2]	91
-101	**3**	*1 ¼*	**Sholaan (IRE)**[14] 3165 3-9-7 **99** (b) LiamJones 4 (William Haggas) *dwlt: sn rcvrd to ld: rdn over 1f out: hdd ins fnl f: no ex and btn fnl 100yds* **6/4**[1]	106
1566	**4**	*2*	**Fanrouge (IRE)**[28] 2712 3-8-11 **89** TomMcLaughlin 3 (Malcolm Saunders) *in tch in midfield: rdn over 2f out: swtchd lft and drvn over 1f out: no imp fnl f* **28/1**	90
1-60	**5**	*hd*	**Intransigent**[14] 3165 3-8-9 **87** DavidProbert 5 (Andrew Balding) *chsd ldr tl wl over 1f out: edging lft and unable qck ent fnl f: wknd fnl 150yds* **8/1**	87
0-20	**6**	*1 ¾*	**Silverheels (IRE)**[42] 2277 3-9-6 **98** PatDobbs 7 (Paul Cole) *in tch in midfield on outer: rdn over 2f out: drvn and no prog over 1f out: wknd ins fnl f* **12/1**	93
10-	**7**	*¾*	**Miss Azeza**[303] 5656 3-8-10 **88** MartinLane 6 (David Simcock) *stdd s: hld up in rr: rdn and effrt over 1f out: no prog and btn 1f out: wknd fnl f* **14/1**	80
1362	**8**	*3 ½*	**Bella Ophelia (IRE)**[22] 2894 3-8-4 **82** ow2 ChrisCatlin 1 (Hughie Morrison) *taken down early: towards rr: rdn and no rspnse 2f out: wknd over 1f out* **17/2**	63

1m 10.26s (-2.74) **Going Correction** -0.30s/f (Firm) **8** Ran SP% **114.3**
Speed ratings (Par 105): **106,105,103,101,101 98,97,93**
toteswingers 1&2 £6.90, 2&3 £1.50, 1&3 £2.50 CSF £27.67 CT £49.58 TOTE £6.40: £2.20, £1.90, £1.10; EX 28.10.
Owner Gianni Paladini **Bred** David Barry **Trained** Newmarket, Suffolk

FOCUS
A decent 3-y-o sprint handicap and a good finish. The time was fair and the winner matched his AW latest.

NOTEBOOK
Mezzotint(IRE) ◆, who looked unlucky not to score at Kempton the previous time, is arguably better on Polytrack but has a lower rating on turf and took full advantage. He had to race three wide from his outside draw, but kept finding under pressure and proved too strong for the runner-up late on. He is in good form and could be worth keeping on-side. (op 13-2 tchd 7-1)
Nassau Storm narrowly beaten on just his second turf start last time, looked the most likely winner when coming between the leaders over a furlong out, but could not find enough to get past the winner. He is already proven at 7f on Polytrack and might be worth a try at that trip on turf. (op 7-2)
Sholaan(IRE) had been raised 12lb for bolting up in a valuable York handicap in first-time blinkers on his previous start but was still favourite to follow up. However, after missing the break slightly he rushed up to lead and that may have cost him in the latter stages. He was not beaten far and can be given another chance. (op 15-8 tchd 11-8)
Fanrouge(IRE) chased the pace but could not pick up in the closing stages. She is 4-4 at Bath and has never won anywhere else, so when and where to back her is pretty straightforward. (op 25-1)
Intransigent, whose sole success was on his only try on both Polytrack and at 5f. He showed good speed before fading here and a drop back to the minimum looks worth trying again. (op 9-1 tchd 15-2)
Silverheels(IRE), dropping in trip and grade, was struggling to go the pace from around the halfway mark and has not lived up to his juvenile form, although his yard is struggling at present. (op 11-1)

3640 BETFRED THE BONUS KING STKS (REGISTERED AS THE MIDSUMMER STAKES) (LISTED RACE) 1m 67y
4:00 (4:01) (Class 1) 3-Y-O+ **£18,714** (£7,095; £3,550; £1,768; £887) **Stalls** Low

Form				RPR
135-	**1**		**Thistle Bird**[273] 6530 4-8-13 95 [1] JamesDoyle 1 (Roger Charlton) *chsd ldng pair: swtchd rt and effrt on stands' rail 2f out: ev ch 1f out: led ins fnl f: hung lft after: kpt on* **6/1**[3]	109
5503	**2**	*½*	**Coupe De Ville (IRE)**[21] 2951 3-8-8 112 PatDobbs 4 (Richard Hannon) *chsd ldr: rdn to ld over 1f out: edgd rt u.p 1f out: hdd ins fnl f: carried bdly lft and one pce after* **6/5**[1]	111
-301	**3**	*4 ½*	**Highland Knight (IRE)**[29] 2657 5-9-4 104 (t) DavidProbert 2 (Andrew Balding) *led: rdn and hdd over 1f out: struggling and swtchd lft over 1f out: btn 1f out: wknd fnl f* **7/4**[2]	103
05-6	**4**	*2 ½*	**Loving Spirit**[54] 1924 4-9-4 90 RobertHavlin 3 (James Toller) *stdd s: hld up in last pair: rdn and effrt over 1f out: no imp and btn 1f out: wknd* **12/1**	97
0500	**5**	*10*	**The Rectifier (USA)**[8] 3331 5-9-4 100 (t) JimmyFortune 5 (Jim Boyle) *s.i.s: in tch in last pair: rdn and effrt to press ldrs 3f out: wknd over 1f out: bhd and eased ins fnl f* **12/1**	74

1m 41.25s (-3.45) **Going Correction** -0.225s/f (Firm)
WFA 3 from 4yo+ 10lb **5** Ran SP% **111.5**
Speed ratings (Par 111): **108,107,103,100,90**
CSF £14.02 TOTE £5.20: £2.10, £1.40; EX 11.90.
Owner Lady Rothschild **Bred** The Rt Hon Lord Rothschild **Trained** Beckhampton, Wilts
■ Stewards' Enquiry : James Doyle four-day ban: careless riding (Jul 16-19)
Pat Dobbs one-day ban: careless riding (Jul 16); two-day ban: used whip above permitted level (Jul 17-18)

FOCUS
A good Listed contest whose best recent winner was the subsequent Jacques Le Marois and Prix du Moulin scorer Librettist. As is often the case there was only a small field, but it produced a good finish and there was a stewards' enquiry as the first two came close as they drew clear of the rest. The winner built on last year's C&D win.

NOTEBOOK
Thistle Bird, the winner of a C&D handicap last season, was dropping in trip for this reappearance and was fitted with a hood for the first time. She got a good lead into the race and came through on the inside of the favourite, but then carried that rival across the course in the last furlong. She was going away a little at the finish and that probably made the difference. (op 9-2)
Coupe De Ville(IRE), a four-time winner as a juvenile, including at this level, never gave the leader much rope and went on going into the last 2f. This was a drop in grade for him, having contested Group races on all three starts this year, but he was carried across the course by the winner in the closing stages and deserves another chance at this level. Connections might step him up in trip now. (op 6-4 tchd 11-10)
Highland Knight(IRE), stepping up in grade after his all-the-way win in a handicap at Epsom, set off in front again but was taken on by the runner-up over 2f out and could not respond. He had a bit to find with that rival so probably ran his race. David Probert reported that the gelding hung left. Official explanation: jockey said gelding hung left (op 2-1)
Loving Spirit had a lot to do on the ratings and was in the rear throughout. (op 9-1)
The Rectifier(USA), winner of this race in 2010 and touched off last year, missed the break and did plenty of work to get into a challenging position at the course intersection before dropping away. (op 9-1 tchd 8-1)

3641 BETFRED STILL TREBLE ODDS ON LUCKY 15'S H'CAP 6f
4:35 (4:38) (Class 2) (0-105,102) 3-Y-O+
£18,675 (£5,592; £2,796; £1,398; £699; £351) **Stalls** Low

Form				RPR
05-5	**1**		**Rex Imperator**[14] 3158 3-9-3 **98** GeorgeBaker 12 (Roger Charlton) *in tch: smooth hdwy to join ldrs on bit over 1f out: shkn up to ld ins fnl f: nudged along and wnt clr fnl 100yds: easily* **14/1**	109+
0200	**2**	*2*	**Shropshire (IRE)**[21] 2931 4-9-6 **94** MartinDwyer 6 (Charles Hills) *stdd s: t.k.h: hld up in midfield: rdn and effrt 2f out: styd on u.p fnl f to snatch 2nd last strides: no ch w wnr* **14/1**	101
05-0	**3**	*hd*	**Zero Money (IRE)**[177] 50 6-9-10 **98** (b) JamesDoyle 4 (Roger Charlton) *chsd ldrs: rdn to ld over 1f out: hung lft u.p and hdd ins fnl f: sn brushed aside and one pce: lost 2nd last strides* **7/1**[3]	104
0-00	**4**	*¾*	**Joe Packet**[7] 3371 5-9-7 **95** MatthewDavies 1 (Jonathan Portman) *in tch in midfield: hdwy u.p over 1f out: swtchd rt 1f out: kpt on u.p: no ch w wnr* **12/1**	99
1510	**5**	*1 ¼*	**Lui Rei (ITY)**[7] 3371 6-9-7 **102** WilliamTwiston-Davies(7) 7 (Robert Cowell) *bhd: rdn and hdwy over 1f out: swtchd rt and styd on ins fnl f: no ch w wnr* **12/1**	102

0-40 **6** ½ **Lexi's Hero (IRE)**[35] 2507 4 -9-10**98**........................(p) StephenCraine 15 96
(Kevin Ryan) *led and crossed towards stands' rail: drvn and hdd over 1f out: pushed lft ent fnl f: wandered u.p and btn 1f out: wknd fnl 100yds* **14/1**

040 **7** ½ **Swiss Cross**[16] 3078 5 -9-6**94**....................................(bt) DavidProbert 13 91
(Phil McEntee) *switching rt and hmpd sn after s: chsd ldrs: rdn and unable qck over 1f out: wknd ins fnl f* **25/1**

0210 **8** 3 **Pearl Ice**[21] 2931 4 -9-7**98**... HarryBentley(3) 10 85
(David Barron) *in tch in midfield: effrt u.p and unable qck wl over 1f out: wknd fnl f* **9/2**[1]

2-00 **9** ½ **Barnet Fair**[28] 2717 4 -8-12**89**...................................... DeclanCannon(3) 5 75
(Richard Guest) *hld up towards rr: effrt and drvn over 1f out: plugged on same pce fnl f: nvr trbld ldrs* **8/1**

0000 **10** 2 ¾ **Nasri**[28] 2717 6 -9-2**90**... JimmyFortune 14 67
(Milton Bradley) *slipped and awkward leaving stalls: slowly away: a in rr: rdn 2f out: nvr trbld ldrs* **12/1**

000 **11** *shd* **Vocational (USA)**[22] 2890 3 -9-3**98**................................. IanMongan 16 72
(Mark Johnston) *racd keenly: chsd ldr tl unable qck 2f out: wknd ent fnl f* **25/1**

-600 **12** ½ **Kakatosi**[37] 2409 5 -8-9**90**...(v) DanielMuscutt(7) 8 65
(Andrew Balding) *hld up in rr: nvr a factor* **33/1**

0-30 **13** *nk* **Piazza San Pietro**[16] 3078 6 -9-4**92**................................... DaneO'Neill 3 66
(Zoe Davison) *in tch in midfield: u.p and struggling over 2f out: wknd over 1f out* **20/1**

00-4 **14** 3 ¼ **Lutine Bell**[42] 2268 5 -9-3**91**... PatDobbs 9 54
(Mike Murphy) *v.s.a: a bhd* **13/2**[2]

-330 **15** *shd* **King Of Jazz (IRE)**[7] 3371 4 -9-9**97**.................................. MartinLane 2 60
(Michael Bell) *in tch in midfield: rdn and struggling over 2f out: wknd wl over 1f out* **7/1**[3]

110- **16** 54 **Ajjaadd (USA)**[273] 6522 6 -9-2**90**................................. J-PGuillambert 11
(Ted Powell) *in tch in midfield: rdn 2f out: sn btn and bhd: virtually p.u fnl f: t.o: burst blood vessel* **25/1**

1m 10.33s (-2.67) **Going Correction** -0.30s/f (Firm)
WFA 3 from 4yo+ 7lb **16**Ran SP% **129.9**
Speed ratings (Par 109): **105,102,102,101,99 98,98,94,93,89 89,88,88,84,84 12**
toteswingers 1&2 £69.30, 2&3 £12.50, 1&3 £18.80 CSF £196.20 CT £1580.83 TOTE £15.30 : £4.10, £3.60 , £2.90 , £2.80 ; EX 134.80 .
Owner Michael Pescod **Bred** Christopher J Mason **Trained** Beckhampton, Wilts
■ Stewards' Enquiry : Stephen Craine one-day ban: careless riding (Jul 16)

FOCUS
A big field for this valuable and competitive sprint handicap. The form makes sense, rated around the second.

NOTEBOOK
Rex Imperator ◆, who travelled well throughout, came away to score in the style of an improving performer. A 3-y-o having just his second run of the season, he scored in the manner of a potential Group performer and it would be no surprise if he was raised in class next time, although the Stewards' Cup could come under consideration after this. (op 16-1)
Shropshire(IRE) had disappointed somewhat since being narrowly beaten by the subsequent Group 3 winner Maarek at Newmarket in May. However, the re-fitted hood seemed to help and he ran on well late to snatch second. (op 10-1)
Zero Money (IRE)improved in the second half of last season but was returning from a break since disappointing in Dubai during January. This was more like his form and he had his chance, despite going left under pressure and being caught for second close home. He should be able to build on this. (op 10-1)
Joe Packet goes well on this track and the return here helped produce his best effort of the season, aided by a drop in the weights.
Lui Rei (ITY)did not run as badly as his finishing position suggests in the Wokingham and ran on late to grab fifth. He has won at Goodwood and is another who might be heading to the Stewards' Cup.
Lexi's Hero (IRE) whose trainer had won two of the three previous renewals, had an outside stall and made a bold bid from the front, but got tired and wandered once headed inside the last quarter-mile.
Swiss Cross, with blinkers back on along with the tongue tie, showed up well until tiring. He seemingly reserves his best for really sharp or downhill tracks. (op 28-1 tchd 33-1)
Pearl Ice who disappointed last time when turned out quickly after scoring at Ripon, again went off favourite but failed to make an impression. Possibly that quick reappearance has taken the edge off him, although he might prefer softer ground. Freshening him up for something like the Great St Wilfrid might be an option. (op 4-1 tchd 10-3)
Barnet Fair's rider reported that the gelding ran flat. Official explanation: jockey said gelding ran flat (op 17-2 tchd 9-1)
Nasri lost his chance with a tardy start. (op 20-1)
Lutine Bell lost his chance with a very slow start. (op 8-1 tchd 6-1)
Ajjaadd(USA)'s trainer reported that the gelding bled from the nose. Official explanation: trainer said gelding bled from the nose (op 28-1)

3642 BETFRED MOBILE SPORTS H'CAP 1m 3f 135y
5:05 (5:05) (Class 2) (0-100,96) 3-Y-O+ **£12,938** (£3,850; £1,924 ; £962) **Stalls** Centre

Form RPR

-010 **1** **Vasily**[21] 2933 4 -9-5**87**.. AndreaAtzeni 10 97
(Robert Eddery) *t.k.h: chsd ldrs tl led 7f out: mde rest: rdn 2f out: styd on wl fnl f: rdn out* **6/1**

1-0 **2** 1 ½ **Rawaki (IRE)**[43] 2248 4 -9-1**83**... JimmyFortune 2 91
(Andrew Balding) *led tl 8f out: chsd ldrs after: rdn to chse wnr jst over 1f out: nt qckn u.p and styd on same pce fnl f* **10/3**[1]

32-2 **3** 1 **A Boy Named Suzi**[28] 2706 4 -9-10**92**............................. JamesDoyle 5 98+
(James Eustace) *in tch in midfield shuffled bk and switching lft 2f out: hdwy u.p over 1f out: chsd ldrs and styd on same pce ins fnl f* **9/2**[2]

12-3 **4** *nk* **Robin Hoods Bay**[43] 2248 4 -9-5**87**.................................. RobertHavlin 6 92+
(Ed Vaughan) *stdd s: hld up in last pair: hdwy over 2f out: drvn to chse ldrs over 1f out: no ex and one pce ins fnl f* **5/1**[3]

5630 **5** 2 **Borug (USA)**[3] 3502 4 -9-1**83**...(p) MartinLane 8 85
(James Tate) *s.i.s: hld up in rr: swtchd lft and effrt u.p wl over 1f out: plugged on fnl f: no threat to ldrs* **11/1**

02-0 **6** 1 **Warlu Way**[43] 2253 5 -9-10**92**... MichaelHills 12 92
(John Dunlop) *t.k.h: hld up towards rr: hdwy 7f out: chsd ldr over 4f out tl over 1f out: sn wknd* **14/1**

00-0 **7** 5 **Rock A Doodle Doo (IRE)**[5] 1882 5 -9-10**92**............. MartinDwyer 11 84
(William Jarvis) *in tch in midfield: effrt u.p on outer over 2f out: wknd ent fnl f* **9/1**

2300 **8** 1 ¼ **Sirvino**[8] 3329 7 -9-9**96**.. LMcNiff(5) 4 86
(David Barron) *in tch in midfield: rdn and unable qck over 2f out: wknd over 1f out* **5/1**[3]

10-0 **9** ¾ **Becausewecan (USA)**[11] 3241 6 -9-9**91**............................ IanMongan 1 79
(Mark Johnston) *chsd ldr tl led 8f out: hdd 7f out: chsd wnr tl over 4f out: lost pl u.p over 3f out: wknd and bhd over 1f out* **16/1**

2m 29.51s (0.01) **Going Correction** -0.225s/f (Firm) **9**Ran SP% **119.8**
Speed ratings (Par 109): **90,89,88,88,86 86,82,81,81**
toteswingers 1&2 £8.50, 2&3 £4.20, 1&3 £16.10 CSF £27.39 CT £101.06 TOTE £9.60 : £2.60 , £1.30, £1.70 ; EX 36.00 .
Owner Owen O'Brien & David Bannon **Bred** Cheveley Park Stud Ltd **Trained** Newmarket, Suffolk

FOCUS
Decent prizemoney resulted in another good, competitive handicap but they went very steady early on. The winner rates up 5lb on his C&D win last month.

NOTEBOOK
Vasily ◆ is well suited by fast ground and repeated his C&D success in May off a 6lb higher mark. He went on after the two previous leaders had gone steadily and wound up the pace from the intersection, finding plenty for pressure. He looks to be on the upgrade and can score again this summer. (op 8-1 tchd 17-2)
Rawaki(IRE), having just his third start, was a well-backed favourite on this step up in trip. He led early but was then settled just off the pace before coming through again. He ran on well for pressure but bumped into an improver and can win on turf before long. (op 9-2 tchd 3-1)
A Boy Named Suzi, narrowly beaten on both his previous starts, was held up off the pace before being produced over a furlong out but could not get to the principals. He has yet to win on turf but surely his turn is not far away. (op 11-2)
Robin Hoods Bay, having just his fourth start on turf, came through looking a big danger but his effort flattened out in the last furlong. It might be that he is better at 1m2f on turf. (op 9-2)
Borug(USA) missed the break and only ran on past beaten rivals. (op 8-1)
Warlu Way was much too keen for his own good and paid for it in the last 2f. (tchd 12-1)
Sirvino was bidding to repeat his 2011 success but ran below par for no obvious reason. (op 9-2)

3643 BETFRED MOBILE FILLIES' H'CAP 1m 67y
5:35 (5:35) (Class 5) (0-75,76) 3-Y-O+ **£2,911** (£866; £432 ; £216) **Stalls** Low

Form RPR

1-60 **1** **Forgive**[16] 3080 3 -9-2**73**.. PatDobbs 1 82
(Richard Hannon) *chsd ldrs tl led 2f out: sn rdn: kpt on wl fnl f: rdn out* **16/1**

21-4 **2** *nk* **Rhagori**[42] 2272 3 -9-2**73**.. MartinLane 8 81+
(Ralph Beckett) *hld up in tch towards rr: rdn and effrt 2f out: hdwy and swtchd lft over 1f out: styd on wl to press wnr fnl 50yds: nvr quite getting to wnr* **11/4**[1]

0012 **3** 1 ½ **Choral Festival**[12] 3226 6 -10-1**76**.............................. JamieGoldstein 13 83
(John Bridger) *in tch in midfield: swtchd lft and effrt over 2f out: chsd wnr 1f out: no ex and one pce fnl 100yds* **8/1**

-400 **4** 1 ½ **Amy Dorrit**[23] 2846 3 -8-12**69**...(p) RobertHavlin 5 71
(John Gosden) *hld up in last pair: rdn 2f out: switching lft and hdwy over 1f out: styd on fnl f: nvr trbld ldrs* **20/1**

-415 **5** ½ **Al Jabreiah**[39] 2379 3 -8-12**69**... LiamJones 11 69
(William Haggas) *in tch: rdn and chsd ldrs 2f out: drvn and unable qck over 1f out: one pce fnl f* **7/1**[3]

10-0 **6** *hd* **Feelthedifference**[43] 2246 3 -9-1**72**.................................. IanMongan 14 72
(Sir Henry Cecil) *t.k.h: hld up in tch in midfield: hdwy over 2f out: no ex u.p over 1f out: one pce after* **9/1**

-205 **7** 3 ¾ **Candycakes (IRE)**[24] 2820 3 -9-2**73**............................... JimmyFortune 3 64
(Michael Bell) *hld up in midfield: hmpd and shuffled bk 5f out: effrt and nt clr run over 2f out: swtchd lft and sme hdwy over 1f out: n.d* **10/1**

6-1 **8** 1 **Rugosa**[31] 2601 3 -9-4**75**... MichaelHills 10 64
(Charles Hills) *chsd ldr tl led 3f out: hdd 2f out: sn rdn and no ex: btn 1f out: wl btn and eased fnl 100yds* **6/1**[2]

4-43 **9** *hd* **Travelling**[37] 2425 3 -8-11**68**...(b[1]) MartinDwyer 9 57
(Marco Botti) *sn bhd: rdn 5f out: styd on past btn horses fnl f: n.d* **14/1**

5061 **10** ¾ **Zing Wing**[24] 2811 4 -9-3**69**... DuilioDaSilva(5) 6 58
(Paul Cole) *led tl 3f out: rdn and lost pl over 2f out: wknd wl over 1f out: bhd fnl f* **18/1**

1-56 **11** 2 **Operettist**[27] 2733 3 -9-3**74**.. DavidProbert 4 56
(Richard Hannon) *in tch in midfield: rdn and struggling over 2f out: wknd wl over 1f out* **8/1**

6-20 **12** 1 ¾ **Barathea Dancer (IRE)**[30] 2637 4 -9-13**74**...................... JamesDoyle 7 54
(Roger Teal) *t.k.h: chsd ldrs: struggling u.p 3f out: wknd wl over 1f out* **12/1**

-005 **13** 5 **Cockney Rhyme**[15] 3120 3 -9-1**72**.............................. StevieDonohoe 12 39
(Heather Main) *in tch in midfield: rdn and wknd over 2f out: bhd fnl f* **33/1**

1m 42.82s (-1.88) **Going Correction** -0.225s/f (Firm)
WFA 3 from 4yo+ 10lb **13**Ran SP% **128.0**
Speed ratings (Par 100): **100,99,98,96,96 96,92,91,91,90 88,86,81**
toteswingers 1&2 £17.70, 2&3 £13.00, 1&3 £21.30 CSF £63.94 CT £420.99 TOTE £22.30 : £4.50, £1.50 , £3.00 ; EX 131.00 .
Owner Highclere Thoroughbred Racing-Spearmint **Bred** The Athenians And Cheveley Park Stud Ltd **Trained** East Everleigh, Wilts

FOCUS
Just a fair but tightly knit fillies' handicap. Pretty sound form.
Forgive Official explanation: trainer said, regarding apparent improvement in form, that the filly appreciated the better ground and more positive ride.
Rugosa Official explanation: jockey said filly lost a front shoe
Travelling Official explanation: jockey said filly was denied a clear run
Cockney Rhyme Official explanation: jockey said filly lost its action
T/Jkpt: T/Plt: £75.70 to a £1 stake. Pool of £76595.88 - 738.10 winning tickets. T/Qpdt: £15.00 to a £1 stake. Pool of £5705.25 -279.75 winning tickets. SP

3644a & 3646a - (Foreign Racing) - See Raceform Interactive

3596 CURRAGH (R-H)
Saturday, June 30

OFFICIAL GOING: Soft to heavy (heavy in places)
A new slot for the Irish Derby as the last race of an early-evening Saturday card.

3645a DUBAI DUTY FREE MILLENNIUM MILLIONAIRE EUROPEAN BREEDERS FUND FILLIES H'CAP (PREMIER HANDICAP) 7f
4:10 (4:11) 3-Y-O+
£27,625 (£8,708; £4,125 ; £1,375 ; £791 ; £458)

RPR

1 **Rock On Ciara (IRE)**[14] 3175 6 -8-8**72**........................... ShaneFoley 12 88+
(Joseph G Murphy, Ire) *trckd ldrs on outer: 4th 2f out: smooth hdwy to ld 1f out and styd on wl: easily* **8/1**

2 4 ¼ **Redoutable (IRE)**[45] 2185 3 -8-6**79**.................................. ChrisHayes 2 80
(Kevin Prendergast, Ire) *trckd ldrs on far rail: hdwy to ld 2f out: rdn and hdd 1f out: kpt on same pce but no ch w easy wnr* **16/1**

3 ¾ **New Magic (IRE)**[14] 3175 5-9-12 90 (t) NGMcCullagh 14 92
(Dermot Anthony McLoughlin, Ire) *towards rr: rdn and hdwy on outer over 1f out: wnt 3rd ins fnl f: kpt on same pce u.p but no ch w easy wnr* **11/1**

4 *hd* **Imaginationrunwild (IRE)**[13] 3195 3-8-9 82 GaryCarroll 13 80
(A Oliver, Ire) *hld up in rr of mid-div: sme hdwy to go 9th over 1f out: kpt on ins fnl f to go 4th* **16/1**

5 *2* **Duchess Of Foxland (IRE)**[76] 1402 5-9-8 89 EmmetMcNamara(3) 15 85
(Mark L Fagan, Ire) *hld up in rr: hdwy into 8th 1f out: kpt on ins fnl f wout troubling ldrs* **12/1**

6 *1* **Colour Of Love (IRE)**[24] 2829 4-9-6 84 (b) WayneLordan 3 77
(W McCreery, Ire) *in rr of mid-div: hdwy into 6th over 2f out: sn rdn and no imp in 3rd 1f out: no ex fnl f* **14/1**

7 *2 ¼* **Angel Bright (IRE)**[13] 3201 3-8-1 79 (b) LeighRoche(5) 10 63
(D K Weld, Ire) *chsd ldrs: 5th 1/2-way: rdn and no imp in 4th over 1f out: no ex ins fnl f* **12/1**

8 *1 ¼* **Ondeafears (IRE)**[44] 2217 5-8-11 82 MarcMonaghan(7) 6 65
(M Halford, Ire) *trckd ldrs and t.k.h: 4th 1/2-way: rdn 2f out and no ex in 6th 1f out* **5/1[2]**

9 *hd* **Simla Sunset (IRE)**[9] 3322 6-9-6 89 (p) RonanWhelan(5) 5 72
(P J Prendergast, Ire) *prom: led briefly 3f out: sn hdd and rdn in 5th 1f out: no ex* **14/1**

10 *10* **Suzette De Bavay (IRE)**[14] 3175 3-8-9 82 CO'Donoghue 1 35
(A Oliver, Ire) *chsd ldrs: towards rr fr 1/2-way* **16/1**

11 *6 ½* **Rubina (IRE)**[16] 3092 3-9-10 97 (tp) JohnnyMurtagh 4 32
(John M Oxx, Ire) *prom racing keenly: 3rd 1/2-way: no ex fr 2f out: wknd* **10/1**

12 *shd* **Janey Muddles (IRE)**[34] 2527 3-9-7 94 (t) KevinManning 11 29
(J S Bolger, Ire) *slowly away and a towards rr* **16/1**

13 *4 ¾* **Hopes N Dreams (IRE)**[23] 2841 4-9-4 82 PatSmullen 9
(Kevin Ryan) *dwlt: mid-div: no threat fr 2f out: wknd* **7/1[3]**

14 *2 ¼* **One Fine Day (IRE)**[9] 3323 3-9-1 88 FranBerry 7
(Mrs John Harrington, Ire) *trckd ldrs: rdn in 8th 1/2-way: no threat fr over 2f out: wknd* **5/2[1]**

15 *8 ½* **Clara Zetkin**[103] 960 4-8-6 70 (b[1]) FergalLynch 8
(James J Hartnett, Ire) *led: hdd 3f out and sn wknd* **25/1**

1m 30.58s (-0.22) **Going Correction** +0.20s/f (Good)
WFA 3 from 4yo+ 9lb **15** Ran SP% **142.4**
Speed ratings: **109,104,103,103,100 99,97,95,95,83 76,76,71,68,58**
CSF £152.83 CT £1510.39 TOTE £7.50: £2.40, £5.30, £3.70; DF 160.20.
Owner Miss Ciara McGee **Bred** Paget Bloodstock **Trained** Fethard, Co Tipperary

FOCUS

A competitive handicap turned into a procession. The third and fourth set the standard.

NOTEBOOK

Rock On Ciara(IRE) travelled like a dream for Shane Foley in the centre of the track and found every bit as much as she threatened to from over a furlong out and ended up storming clear. It was a most decisive success, which the handicapper is likely to punish, but the way she has progressed this season and the consistency she has shown may mean she's not far off a filly that can try and earn some black type, particularly if getting this sort of ground.

Redoutable(IRE) has come down a little bit in the handicap since winning a big-field maiden here in March and is undoubtedly at the right end. She was just unfortunate to come up against a mare in tremendous form. She tracked the pace towards the far side and found a bit when asked for her effort, but the winner just had too much. It was quite a smart effort without being good enough on the day.

New Magic(IRE) did little wrong. Happy to sit just off the pace, she was unable to match the kick of the winner but came home well. (op 10/1)

Imaginationrunwild(IRE) had a lot to do past halfway and wasn't making much headway but she certainly came home at a rate of knots from just over a furlong out. (op 14/1)

Duchess Of Foxland(IRE) has come down considerably in the ratings, so much so that handicaps like this are now an option and, while she wasn't a factor, she came home to pretty good effect. She may well win a nice handicap off a mark such as this.

Colour Of Love(IRE)'s effort petered out inside the last furlong. (op 14/1 tchd 16/1)

One Fine Day(IRE) ran no race whatsoever and was beaten shortly after halfway. Official explanation: jockey said filly ran flat (op 9/2)

3647a DUBAI DUTY FREE FINEST SURPRISE H'CAP (PREMIER HANDICAP) 1m

5:20 (5:20) 3-Y-0+

£30,000 (£9,500; £4,500; £1,500; £1,000; £500)

RPR

1 **Bold Thady Quill (IRE)**[13] 3199 5-8-9 81 (p) ShaneFoley 4 95
(K J Condon, Ire) *in rr of mid-div: rdn and hdwy into 6th 2f out: wnt 2nd over 1f out and sn chal: kpt on best to ld fnl 100yds* **6/1[2]**

2 ¾ **Spa's Dancer (IRE)**[19] 2975 5-9-3 89 LiamKeniry 9 101+
(Ed de Giles) *a.p: led over 3f out and travelling best: rdn over 1f out and sn edgd lft: hdd and no ex fnl 100yds* **7/1[3]**

3 *3 ½* **Gunner Lindley (IRE)**[13] 3199 5-9-4 90 (b[1]) NGMcCullagh 12 94
(Reginald Roberts, Ire) *trckd ldrs: 3rd 1/2-way: rdn 2f out and no imp fr 1f out: kpt on one pce* **9/1**

4 ½ **Potomac (IRE)**[13] 3199 4-8-11 83 ChrisHayes 2 86
(A Oliver, Ire) *trckd ldrs: 5th 1/2-way: rdn and no imp 2f out: kpt on one pce fnl f wout troubling ldrs* **4/1[1]**

5 *3 ¾* **Prince Jock (USA)**[29] 2657 5-8-9 81 CO'Donoghue 8 76
(John Patrick Shanahan, Ire) *led: hdd over 3f out and sn drvn along: dropped to 4th u.p over 1f out: no ex* **12/1**

6 *2* **Waydownsouth (IRE)**[13] 3199 5-9-2 88 DannyGrant 13 78
(Patrick J Flynn, Ire) *towards rr on outer: rdn and sme hdwy 3f out: 8th 2f out: no imp fr over 1f out: kpt on one pce* **16/1**

7 ¾ **Castle Bar Sling (USA)**[13] 3199 7-8-13 85 WayneLordan 1 73
(T J O'Mara, Ire) *in rr of mid-div: 11th 1/2-way: rdn in 7th 2f out: sn no imp u.p* **16/1**

8 *8 ½* **Akasaka (IRE)**[57] 1837 5-9-1 87 FranBerry 6 55
(Edward Lynam, Ire) *chsd ldrs: 6th 1/2-way: pushed along in 4th 2f out and sn no ex: wknd* **14/1**

9 *2 ½* **Brown Butterfly**[26] 2778 4-8-7 82 SamJames(3) 5 45
(Kevin Prendergast, Ire) *trckd ldrs: 4th 1/2-way: rdn and no ex over 2f out: wknd* **11/1**

10 *5 ½* **Barack (IRE)**[16] 3094 6-9-11 97 (bt) BenCurtis 10 47
(Francis Ennis, Ire) *chsd ldrs: no ex fr over 2f out: wknd* **9/1**

11 *14* **Super Say (IRE)**[13] 3199 6-9-8 94 JPO'Brien 14 12
(A Oliver, Ire) *chsd ldrs: rdn along fr 3f out and no ex 2f out: eased whn btn fnl f* **14/1**

12 *3 ¼* **Taameer**[293] 5977 6-9-12 98 PatSmullen 7 8
(D K Weld, Ire) *a towards rr: nvr a factor* **16/1**

13 *7 ½* **Indian Landing (IRE)**[13] 3201 4-8-6 78 MichaelHussey 11
(Tracey Collins, Ire) *chsd ldrs: 7th 1/2-way: rdn 3f out and sn no ex: wknd* **6/1[2]**

14 *13* **Bancnuanaheireann (IRE)**[20] 2961 5-9-6 92 KevinManning 3
(J S Bolger, Ire) *a towards rr: nvr a factor: eased whn btn fnl f* **14/1**

1m 46.17s (0.17) **Going Correction** +0.20s/f (Good) **14** Ran SP% **134.7**
Speed ratings: **107,106,102,102,98 96,95,87,84,79 65,62,54,41**
CSF £53.87 CT £409.06 TOTE £6.10: £1.90, £2.80, £2.70; DF 35.50.
Owner Mrs Pauline Condon **Bred** Iona Equine **Trained** The Curragh , Co Kildare

FOCUS

It looked a competitive handicap but very few horses got into it and in the end it was almost presented to the winner. The third, fourth and fifth have been rated close to their previous form.

NOTEBOOK

Bold Thady Quill(IRE)'s enjoying something of a new lease of life and seems at home in most ground conditions. He was patiently ridden by Shane Foley and was just about the only horse able to make ground through the field, showing a willing attitude. That and running straight to the line were the winning elements. More handicaps like this are his immediate future. (op 6/1 tchd 13/2)

Spa's Dancer(IRE) was handy the whole way, travelling strongly, but when he got to the front and was asked to go and win his race he started to drift left and continued to do so. Whether it was a case of him floundering in the ground or a question of resolution, the outcome was the same. (op 6/1)

Gunner Lindley(IRE) raced as prominently as most and, while he kept going well enough, he was no match for the two in front of him who drew away inside the last. (op 7/1)

Potomac(IRE) was in a good position tracking the pace on the inner but was off the bridle plenty far enough out. He did keep on well enough at the same pace, but never looked like threatening. (op 13/2)

Prince Jock(USA) helped set a pretty reasonable gallop in the conditions. He paid for it in the end but didn't do badly. (op 11/1)

Castle Bar Sling(USA) did some reasonable late work but never threatened. Official explanation: jockey said gelding lost its action in this race

Indian Landing(IRE) Official explanation: trainer said gelding scoped badly post-race

3648a PADDY POWER SPRINT (PREMIER H'CAP) 6f 63y

5:55 (5:55) 3-Y-0+

£42,500 (£13,458; £6,375; £2,125; £1,416; £708)

RPR

1 **An Saighdiur (IRE)**[41] 2316 5-7-13 80 oh5 MACleere(5) 8 88
(Andrew Slattery, Ire) *a.p: disp ld after 1/2-way and led over 2f out: rdn and styd on wl ins fnl f* **20/1**

2 *1 ½* **Arctic (IRE)**[15] 3131 5-10-0 104 (t) MichaelHussey 4 107
(Tracey Collins, Ire) *a.p: led or disp ld: hdd over 2f out: sn rdn and no imp on wnr ins fnl f: kpt on same pce* **8/1**

3 ½ **Gordon Lord Byron (IRE)**[7] 3371 4-10-0 104 FranBerry 7 105
(T Hogan, Ire) *towards rr: 12th 1/2-way: sme hdwy between horses in 8th over 1f out: kpt on u.p ins fnl f wout troubling wnr* **5/1[1]**

4 ¾ **Bubbly Bellini (IRE)**[8] 3360 5-8-1 80 (p) IJBrennan(3) 9 79
(Adrian McGuinness, Ire) *chsd ldrs: 5th 1/2-way: rdn in 6th over 1f out: kpt on same pce u.p ins fnl f* **8/1**

5 *1* **Oor Jock (IRE)**[28] 2704 4-8-7 88 RonanWhelan(5) 3 84
(John Patrick Shanahan, Ire) *chsd ldrs on outer: 7th 1/2-way: 3rd 2f out: rdn and no imp fr 1f out: no ex ins fnl f* **25/1**

6 ¾ **Flameoftheforest (IRE)**[21] 2913 5-8-7 83 (p) LiamKeniry 10 76+
(Ed de Giles) *towards rr: nt clr run 2f out: 11th over 1f out: kpt on ins fnl f: nt rch ldrs* **7/1[3]**

7 *nk* **Invincible Ridge (IRE)**[17] 3055 4-8-6 87 (t) LeighRoche(5) 2 79
(D J Bunyan, Ire) *trckd ldrs on outer: 4th 1/2-way: rdn 2f out and no imp fr over 1f out: no ex ins fnl f* **20/1**

8 *nk* **Farmleigh House (IRE)**[84] 1226 5-8-4 80 NGMcCullagh 12 71+
(W J Martin, Ire) *towards rr: nvr a factor: sme hdwy into 9th 1f out: kpt on one pce ins fnl f* **16/1**

9 ¾ **Seanie (IRE)**[17] 3055 3-8-11 94 FergalLynch 6 81+
(David Marnane, Ire) *in rr of mid-div racing keenly: sme hdwy on outer after 1/2-way: 7th 1f out: no ex ins fnl f* **6/1[2]**

10 *nk* **Battleroftheboyne (IRE)**[7] 3408 3-7-13 87 oh6 ConorHoban(5) 1 73+
(Michael Mulvany, Ire) *mid-div on outer: rdn and 5th briefly 1f out: no ex ins fnl f* **10/1**

11 ¾ **Bertiewhittle**[13] 3183 4-9-0 90 (b[1]) JPO'Brien 14 76+
(David Barron) *mid-div on stands' side: 8th 1/2-way: no ex fr over 1f out* **6/1[2]**

12 *3 ¼* **Bajan Tryst (USA)**[28] 2717 6-9-12 102 PatSmullen 13 77+
(Kevin Ryan) *a towards rr: nvr a factor* **10/1**

13 *2* **Luisant**[15] 3131 9-9-2 92 CO'Donoghue 5 61
(J A Nash, Ire) *trckd ldrs: 6th 1/2-way: no ex under 2f out* **16/1**

14 *3 ¾* **Knock Stars (IRE)**[7] 3410 4-8-9 85 (p) ChrisHayes 11 42
(Patrick Martin, Ire) *trckd ldrs on stands' side: 3rd 1/2-way: no ex under 2f out: wknd* **12/1**

1m 19.46s (0.36) **Going Correction** +0.375s/f (Good)
WFA 3 from 4yo+ 7lb **14** Ran SP% **131.0**
Speed ratings: **109,107,106,105,104 103,102,102,101,100 99,95,92,87**
CSF £182.72 CT £955.81 TOTE £30.20: £6.20, £2.90, £2.10; DF 429.50.
Owner Men Of Forty Eight Syndicate **Bred** S Ross **Trained** Thurles, Co Tipperary

FOCUS

A horse that made his reputation on the Polytrack over the winter finally showed that he can be as good on turf, even on ground as bad as this. The first four set the standard.

NOTEBOOK

An Saighdiur(IRE) was keen enough early on and one doubted whether he would last home, but he got there strongly inside the final furlong and, while it took him a good few strides to shake off the runner-up, he was the one finishing the stronger. One imagines he's opened up these premier sprint handicaps for himself now, although what will be left for him on his favourite surface at Dundalk is another matter. (op 25/1)

Arctic(IRE) is coming back to the form he showed as a juvenile and the prevalence of soft ground has had a fair bit to do with it. He was positively ridden and, while the winner travelled more strongly, he responded gamely when headed. Eventually the concession of two stone on this ground proved too much for him.

Gordon Lord Byron(IRE) does handle plenty of ease in the ground but he could never really get into this contest. He kept on well enough but was unable to threaten the front two. (op 5/1 tchd 4/1)

Bubbly Bellini(IRE) fared well in what was his biggest test in attempting to complete a quick four-timer. He did come off the bridle early enough but to his credit he found a bit for pressure. His effort wasn't quite good enough but it probably sits well in comparison with any of his previous wins. (op 9/1)

Oor Jock(IRE) was ridden quite patiently. He was brought with a reasonable looking challenge over a furlong out but he just seemed to flounder a little bit on the ground when let down. (op 20/1)

Farmleigh House(IRE) couldn't get on terms. (op 16/1 tchd 20/1)

Seanie(IRE) did some late work but never really threatened in a race that not many managed to get into. (op 13/2 tchd 11/2)

Luisant Official explanation: trainer said gelding was found to be lame behind post-race

3649a DUBAI DUTY FREE FULL OF SURPRISES RAILWAY STKS (GROUP 2) 6f

6:30 (6:30) 2-Y-O

£47,625 (£15,041; £7,125; £2,375; £1,458; £791)

RPR

1 **Probably (IRE)**[14] 3171 2-9-3 .... WJLee 1 105
(David Wachman, Ire) *trckd ldrs on outer in 3rd: 2nd and rdn 2f out: edgd lft u.p and led 100yds out: kpt on best* **7/1**[3]

2 1 ¾ **Cristoforo Colombo (USA)**[11] 3240 2-9-3 .... JPO'Brien 3 99
(A P O'Brien, Ire) *trckd ldrs in 4th: qcknd between horses to ld 1f out: sn strly pressed and hdd 100yds out: no ex* **11/10**[1]

3 2 **Tiger Stripes**[17] 3054 2-9-3 .... ChrisHayes 6 93
(A Oliver, Ire) *led: drvn along 2f out and hdd 1f out: no ex in 3rd fnl f: kpt on one pce* **25/1**

4 ¾ **Ayaar (IRE)**[16] 3067 2-9-3 .... PatSmullen 4 91
(Mick Channon) *dwlt and settled in rr: wnt 4th on outer 2f out: sn rdn and kpt on same pce ins fnl f* **20/1**

5 5 ½ **Pedro The Great (USA)**[9] 3319 2-9-3 .... SeamieHeffernan 7 75
(A P O'Brien, Ire) *trckd ldr on stands' rail: 2nd 1/2-way: rdn and no ex under 2f out: wknd* **6/4**[2]

6 nk **Almanack**[43] 2300 2-9-3 ....(t) WayneLordan 5 74
(T Stack, Ire) *chsd ldrs in 5th: no ex fr wl over 1f out* **14/1**

1m 17.24s (1.74) **Going Correction** +0.375s/f (Good) **6** Ran SP% **115.4**
Speed ratings: **95,92,90,89,81 81**
CSF £15.87 TOTE £6.00: £1.70, £1.02; DF 18.70.
Owner Michael Tabor **Bred** Michael Lowry **Trained** Goolds Cross, Co Tipperary
■ Stewards' Enquiry : Chris Hayes three-day ban: careless riding (Jul 14-16)

FOCUS
The value of the form of this race will become more apparent over time but it's hard to imagine that the ground didn't play at least some part in it. It's been rated an average renewal, with the runner-up well below his Coventry form.

NOTEBOOK
Probably(IRE) handled the ground the best but in fairness he looks like a colt that will be be equally good on better going. He ground out the win, having coped with the testing conditions better than the runner-up, who emptied quickly inside the final furlong. Probably beat a subsequent winner over 7f on better ground last time and looks a genuine and progressive colt, and one with a bit of size and frame-filling to do, which indicates that he should do better with time. Whatever the merits of the performance, he's certainly a colt to look forward to. (op 8/1)
Cristoforo Colombo(USA) seemed to handle the ground reasonably well and looked to have made a race-winning move when switching to the stands' rail and leading inside the final furlong, but he ran out gas. Combined with a hard race at Ascot less than two weeks previously it may just have all happened too quickly. (op 1/1 tchd 5/4)
Tiger Stripes ran a huge race on paper and won't have difficulty winning a maiden on this evidence. He was positively ridden and kept going at the same pace when headed. He wasn't good enough but more than justified the decision to run him. (op 40/1)
Ayaar(IRE) couldn't find any extra inside the final furlong or so and was a shade keen early on which didn't help.
Pedro The Great(USA) was expected to handle the ground much better than his stable companion but he dropped right out inside the final furlong. (op 6/4 tchd 13/8)
Almanack never featured on his first effort on turf. (op 12/1)

3650a WOODIES D.I.Y. SAPPHIRE STKS (GROUP 3) 5f

7:00 (7:00) 3-Y-O+

£31,250 (£9,895; £4,687; £1,562; £1,041; £520)

RPR

1 **Definightly**[13] 3190 6-9-7 ....(b) JohnnyMurtagh 5 110
(Roger Charlton) *trckd ldr in 2nd: rdn over 1f out: kpt on u.p to ld cl home* **13/8**[1]

2 ½ **Judge 'n Jury**[15] 3127 8-9-7 ....(t) DarrenEgan 8 108+
(Ronald Harris) *led: rdn and drifted rt 1f out: kpt on u.p: hdd cl home* **10/1**

3 ¾ **Katla (IRE)**[16] 3092 4-9-4 97.. WJLee 1 102+
(J F Grogan, Ire) *towards rr: 6th over 1f out: kpt on wl ins fnl f: nt rch first 2* **20/1**

4 ¾ **Secret Witness**[7] 3371 6-9-7 ....(b) LukeMorris 9 103+
(Ronald Harris) *chsd ldrs: drvn along in 5th 2f out: no imp u.p and edgd rt ins fnl f: kpt on one pce* **10/1**

5 2 **Tiddliwinks**[35] 2513 6-9-12 .... PatSmullen 3 100
(Kevin Ryan) *settled in rr: hdwy into 3rd under 2f out: sn rdn and no ex ins fnl f* **9/2**[3]

6 ¾ **Mirza**[13] 3196 5-9-7 .... FranBerry 4 93
(Rae Guest) *trckd ldrs: 3rd 1/2-way: rdn in 4th under 2f out: no imp whn short of room and checked 100yds out* **11/4**[2]

7 4 ½ **Santo Padre (IRE)**[13] 3196 8-9-7 106.............................. FergalLynch 7 77
(David Marnane, Ire) *chsd ldrs and a towards rr: no threat fr wl over 1f out* **9/1**

8 10 **Empowering (IRE)**[16] 3091 4-9-4 100................................... JPO'Brien 6 38
(A P O'Brien, Ire) *a towards rr: no ex under 2f out and eased whn btn fnl f* **14/1**

1m 2.13s (-0.77) **Going Correction** +0.375s/f (Good) **8** Ran SP% **122.6**
Speed ratings: **103,102,101,99,96 95,88,72**
CSF £21.40 TOTE £2.30: £1.20, £2.00, £4.30; DF 28.60.
Owner S Emmet And Miss R Emmet **Bred** S Emmet And Miss R Emmet **Trained** Beckhampton, Wilts
■ Stewards' Enquiry : Luke Morris one-day ban: careless riding (Jul 14)
W J Lee one-day ban: careless riding (Jul 14)

FOCUS
This was won in a good time, but it was difficult to make up ground. It's been rated around the third to her 5f form.

NOTEBOOK
Definightly hadn't managed to win for 19 months despite going close on several occasions and any bad luck that might have been involved in any of those defeats was certainly expunged here. He raced handily but couldn't cope with the turn of foot shown by the runner-up, and no matter how uncomplicated this horse was and no matter how straight he ran to the line, there's no way he would have caught the runner-up had that horse kept even a reasonably straight course. Connections will take it though, and the horse probably deserved a change of luck. (op 15/8 tchd 6/4)
Judge 'n Jury, racing on ground which should have suited him more than most, certainly quickened up well, but the way he drifted to his right into the whip would have made one wonder whether something was hurting him. In the end it was an opportunity lost. (op 10/1 tchd 9/1)
Katla(IRE) fared best of the home brigade and did well overall. She was ridden for a finishing kick and came home well but couldn't make any real impression on the two leaders.
Secret Witness showed speed but just wasn't good enough. He kept his place but couldn't make an impression on the leaders. (op 8/1)
Tiddliwinks is a horse that has never really been at home on soft ground and did seem to flounder on it when asked for his effort over a furlong out. (op 5/1)
Mirza did his best in pursuit of the leaders early on but didn't look at home on the ground. (op 3/1 tchd 7/2)

3651a DUBAI DUTY FREE IRISH DERBY (GROUP 1) (ENTIRE COLTS & FILLIES) 1m 4f

7:40 (7:41) 3-Y-O **£604,166** (£197,916; £93,750; £31,250; £20,833)

RPR

1 **Camelot**[28] 2705 3-9-0 124.. JPO'Brien 3 119+
(A P O'Brien, Ire) *settled in 4th: clsr appr st and smooth hdwy to chal early st: jinked lft and led under 2f out: rdn out and kpt on wl fnl f* **1/5**[1]

2 2 **Born To Sea (IRE)**[11] 3239 3-9-0 112......................(b[1]) JohnnyMurtagh 2 116
(John M Oxx, Ire) *settled in rr: clsr in 4th ent st: wnt 2nd under 2f out: sn rdn and tried to chal: no imp on wnr ins fnl f: kpt on same pce* **8/1**[2]

3 9 **Light Heavy (IRE)**[48] 2102 3-9-0 109.........................(tp) KevinManning 7 101
(J S Bolger, Ire) *chsd ldr in 3rd: clsr after 1/2-way and rdn in 2nd ent st: no imp u.p in 3rd over 1f out: no ex* **10/1**[3]

4 7 ½ **Akeed Mofeed**[279] 6391 3-9-0 112.................................. WilliamBuick 5 91
(John M Oxx, Ire) *chsd ldr in 2nd: hdwy to ld appr st: rdn and hdd under 2f out: no ex in 4th over 1f out: wknd* **11/1**

5 33 **Astrology (IRE)**[8] 3327 3-9-0 115.............................. SeamieHeffernan 4 37
(A P O'Brien, Ire) *led: 4 l advantage 1/2-way: drvn along and hdd appr st: sn no ex and wknd* **14/1**

2m 43.96s (5.46) **Going Correction** +0.825s/f (Soft) **5** Ran SP% **118.5**
Speed ratings: **114,112,106,101,79**
Pick Six: Not won. CSF £3.31 TOTE £1.10: £1.02, £1.70; DF 3.30.
Owner Derrick Smith **Bred** Sheikh Abdulla Bin Isa Al-Khalifa **Trained** Ballydoyle, Co Tipperary

FOCUS
The smallest field since 1912 (Imperial Monarch and Speaking Of Which taken out because of the ground), as well as the shortest-priced favourite since Orby in 1907 - it was an historic Irish Derby in many ways. With the third and fourth failing to give their running, and the winner apparently unsuited by the ground, the form of the race hangs on the performance of the runner-up. Camelot is rated at the mid point of the race averages.

NOTEBOOK
Camelot travelled really well throughout the race, but when asked to go a bit quicker and eventually deal with the one challenge which emerged he really floundered in the conditions, rolling around and labouring quite significantly. It was a tribute to the horse's considerable ability that he was able to overcome that and deal with a runner-up who only really laid the faintest of gloves on him. Lips are tight, but if the Triple Crown isn't being ruled out then it looks a probable target. There are variables there about whether the horse will come back to 1m2f, the most obvious of which is what the future plan is for So You Think, but the Triple Crown allure might just be too powerful to ignore. To sum up, though, it is to the credit of connections that they let the horse run as it would have been a total damp squib without him in it. As said, they had little to gain and a considerable amount to lose. (op 2/11 tchd 1/4)
Born To Sea(IRE) saw out the trip a lot better than many people imagined. Johnny Murtagh did a terrific job in switching him off at the back of the field and he saw his race out well. The winner was just too good. At this stage it's safe to say that the runner-up is not good enough to win at proper Group 1 level, but he's a very good horse and it might just be time to lower his sights a little. (op 10/1)
Light Heavy(IRE) was floundering completely from the turn into the straight.
Akeed Mofeed was fresh and a little bit keen early on, too, and he faded quite quickly once coming under pressure in the straight. (op 10/1 tchd 12/1)
Astrology(IRE) was ridden more as a pacemaker here than he was at Epsom. However, the hard race he had that day seemed to have taken its toll at Ascot, and the quick turnaround here meant he faced a very difficult task. (op 16/1)
T/Jkpt: Not won. T/Plt: @131.70. Pool of @27,840.25 - 158.45 winning units. II

3603 HAMBURG (R-H)

Saturday, June 30

OFFICIAL GOING: Turf: soft

3652a GROSSER PREIS DER MERCEDES-BENZ NIEDERLASSUNG HAMBURG (LISTED RACE) (4YO+ FILLIES & MARES) (TURF) 1m 3f

3:20 (12:00) 4-Y-O+ **£10,000** (£4,166; £1,666; £833)

RPR

1 **Temida (IRE)**[45] 2191 4-9-4 0... FilipMinarik 5 109
(M G Mintchev, Germany) **6/4**[1]

2 2 **Lana Jolie (GER)**[45] 2191 4-8-9 0... EPedroza 3 96
(A Wohler, Germany) **71/10**

3 hd **Hot Blood (IRE)**[20] 2965 4-9-0 0.. AStarke 8 101
(P Schiergen, Germany) **49/10**[2]

4 1 ¾ **Labrice**[258] 4-9-2 0 ow2.. THellier 2 100
(P Harley, Germany) **32/5**

5 2 **Salve Haya (IRE)** 4-8-9 0... JBojko 4 89
(W Hickst, Germany) **5/1**[3]

6 hd **Serenity Star**[25] 4-9-0 0... FabriceVeron 1 94
(H-A Pantall, France) **91/10**

7 2 ½ **Albaraka**[279] 6395 4-8-11 0... JimmyQuinn 6 87
(Sir Mark Prescott Bt) *s.i.s: qckly rcvrd and circled field to be prom on outer: led briefly over 6f out: 4th and rdn 2 1/2f out: kpt on one pce tl no ex and fdd ins fnl f* **32/5**

8 8 **Baisse**[33] 4-9-2 0.. APietsch 7 77
(R Dzubasz, Germany) **104/10**

2m 22.31s (-2.39) **8** Ran SP% **131.7**
WIN (incl. 10 euro stake): 25. PLACES: 13, 18, 15. SF: 234.
Owner Litex Commerce Ad **Bred** Anne & Gerard Corry **Trained** Germany

3653a FRANZ GUNTHER VON GAERTNER-GEDACHTNISRENNEN (HAMBURGER STUTENMEILE) (GROUP 3) (3YO+ FILLIES & MARES) 1m

4:20 (12:00) 3-Y-O+

£26,666 (£9,166; £4,583; £2,500; £1,666; £1,250)

RPR

1 **Cherry Danon (IRE)**[27] 2746 3-8-6 0... AStarke 8 106
(P Schiergen, Germany) *prom thrght: rdn over 2f out: r.o to chal over 1f out: led ins fnl 100yds: drvn out* **21/10**[1]

2 1 ¼ **Survey (GER)**[27] 2746 3-8-8 0.. StefanieHofer 4 105
(Mario Hofer, Germany) *led: rdn 2f out: strly pressed fr over 1f out: hdd ins fnl 100yds: kpt on* **107/10**

3 1 1/4 **Lady Jacamira (GER)** 3-8-6 0 .... NRichter 10 100+
(R Dzubasz, Germany) *hld up in last trio on inner: rdn 2 1/2f out: r.o to go 3rd cl home: nvr able to chal* **142/10**

4 nk **Cerveza**[28] 2728 4-9-0 0 .... LouisBeuzelin 7 99
(F Poulsen, France) *hld up towards rr: prog into midfield 2 1/2f out: rdn 2f out: hung rt u.p: r.o to go 3rd jst ins fnl f: no ex and dropped to 4th cl home* **116/10**

5 nk **Paraisa**[27] 2746 3-8-6 0 .... JBojko 2 99
(A Wohler, Germany) *midfield: rdn over 2f out: r.o to go 5th ins fnl f: nt pce to chal* **135/10**

6 2 **Molly Filia (GER)**[27] 2746 3-8-6 0 .... WPanov 11 94
(Uwe Ostmann, Germany) *rrd as stalls opened and missed break: hld up in last: rdn over 2f out: r.o to go 6th post: nvr able to chal* **41/1**

7 hd **Wolkenburg (GER)**[33] 4-9-0 0 .... FilipMinarik 6 94
(P Schiergen, Germany) *trckd ldr in 2nd on outer: rdn to chal over 2f out: outpcd ins fnl f: fdd and ct for 6th post* **23/1**

8 1/2 **Dessau (GER)**[27] 2746 3-8-6 0 .... DavyBonilla 13 93
(W Hickst, Germany) *t.k.h: hld up towards rr on outer: prog into midfield over 3f out: rdn over 2f out: edgd rt: kpt on one pce ins fnl 1 1/2f* **71/10**

9 1 1/2 **Dalarna (GER)**[33] 4-9-2 0 .... APietsch 3 91
(W Hickst, Germany) *trckd ldr in 3rd on inner: rdn 2f out: kpt on tl no ex and wknd ins fnl f* **7/1**[3]

10 nk **Jardina (GER)**[33] 4-9-2 0 .... MrDennisSchiergen 1 90
(P Schiergen, Germany) *midfield on inner: rdn 2 1/2f out: kpt on one pce tl no ex and fdd ins fnl f* **202/10**

11 1 3/4 **Chica Loca (FR)**[48] 2109 3-8-6 0 .... SHellyn 9 84
(M Figge, Germany) *t.k.h: midfield: rdn and lost pl over 2f out: plugged on* **43/10**[2]

12 1 1/4 **Street Secret (USA)**[25] 2805 4-9-0 0 .... FabriceVeron 12 81
(Mme Pia Brandt, France) *hld up in last trio on outer: rdn over 2 1/2f out: outpcd over 1 1/2f out: hung rt u.p and sn btn: eased ins fnl f* **169/10**

13 5 **Gooseberry Fool**[315] 5296 3-8-6 0 .... JimmyQuinn 5 70
(Sir Mark Prescott Bt) *s.i.s: hld up towards rr on inner: rdn over 2f out: no prog and nt given hrd time whn btn* **164/10**

14 12 **Sun Of Jamaica**[258] 6904 3-8-6 0 .... AndreBest 14 42
(Mario Hofer, Germany) *midfield on outer: rdn and lost position rapidly over 2f out: qckly btn and dropped to detached last: eased* **44/1**

1m 39.38s (99.38)
WFA 3 from 4yo 10lb **14** Ran SP% **130.8**
WIN (incl. 10 euro stake): 31. PLACES: 15, 23, 32. SF: 201.
Owner Gestut Brummerhof **Bred** Ken Lynch **Trained** Germany

2159 JAGERSRO (R-H)
Saturday, June 30

OFFICIAL GOING: Dirt: standard

3654a PRIAMHANDICAP (H'CAP) (3YO+) (DIRT) 1m 143y(D)
5:46 (12:00) 3-Y-0+ **£3,745** (£1,872; £898; £599; £374)

RPR

1 **Amazing Tiger (GER)**[293] 5981 6-9-6 0 .... FJohansson 8 80
(Peter Jardby, Sweden) **228/10**

2 hd **Po Po Poker Face (IRE)**[275] 5-10-1 0 .... ElioneChaves 7 89
(Ms K Stenefeldt, Sweden) **67/10**

3 1 3/4 **Energia Carioca (BRZ)**[119] 789 5-9-11 0 .... RafaelSchistl 3 81
(Fabricio Borges, Sweden) **11/2**[3]

4 3 **Loveinthesand (IRE)**[727] 3708 5-9-0 0 .... Per-AndersGraberg 11 63
(Johan Reuterskiold, Sweden) **69/10**

5 3 1/2 **Smart Endeavour (USA)**[31] 6-9-11 0 .... DannyPatil 9 67
(Peter Jardby, Sweden) **102/10**

6 1 3/4 **Highway (IRE)**[46] 2160 9-9-13 0 .... ManuelMartinez 4 65
(Francisco Castro, Sweden) **18/1**

7 nk **Gladtoseeme (USA)**[275] 5-9-8 0 .... JacobJohansen 6 60
(Fredrik Reuterskiold, Sweden) **23/5**[2]

8 7 **Nightjar (USA)**[275] 7-9-11 0 .... OliverWilson(4) 1 51
(Elisabeth Gautier, Sweden) **214/10**

9 1 1/2 **Hurricane Spirit (IRE)**[17] 3039 8-8-7 0 .... NicoleNordblad(7) 5 33
(Hans Adielsson) *dwlt: pushed along to chse ldng gp: cl 5th and travelling wl 1/2-way: outpcd: shkn up and lost pl over 2 1/2f out: wknd appr fnl 1 1/2f* **8/5**[1]

10 nk **Saddle The Storm** 5-9-4 0 .... (p) NikolajStott 2 37
(Birgitte Nielsen, Denmark) **149/10**

1m 47.3s (107.30) **10** Ran SP% **126.5**
PARI-MUTUEL (all including 1sek stake): WIN 23.80; PLACE 4.24, 1.85, 2.58; SF 126.44.
Owner Peter Jardby, Wiveka & Andersson Bo **Bred** Gestut Karlshof **Trained** Sweden

3655a VOTERLOPNING 2012 (CONDITIONS) (3YO) (DIRT) 1m 143y(D)
6:57 (12:00) 3-Y-0

£25,889 (£11,909; £5,177; £3,624; £2,588; £1,553)

RPR

1 **Bomar (IRE)**[16] 3-9-4 0 .... FJohansson 3
(Wido Neuroth, Norway) **19/20**[1]

2 1 3/4 **Holly Martins**[23] 2860 3-9-4 0 .... ElioneChaves 8
(Hans Adielsson) *broke wl and led on outside: swtchd to ins rail after 1f: qcknd 2l clr over 2f out: sn rdn: hdd 1 1/2f out: kpt on at same pce fnl f* **83/10**

3 1 3/4 **Funinthesand (IRE)**[16] 3-9-4 0 .... (p) EspenSki 2
(Wido Neuroth, Norway) **68/10**[3]

4 1 1/4 **Sir Freddie (USA)** 3-9-4 0 .... JacobJohansen 1
(Fredrik Reuterskiold, Sweden) **14/5**[2]

5 12 **Altalus (SWE)** 3-9-4 0 .... (b) ManuelMartinez 7
(Christer Hederud, Sweden) **206/10**

6 2 3/4 **Proud Cash Flow (USA)**[16] 3-9-4 0 .... (b) Per-AndersGraberg 4
(Niels Petersen, Norway) **44/5**

7 7 1/2 **T Bag (IRE)** 3-9-4 0 .... RafaelSchistl 6
(Wido Neuroth, Norway) **157/10**

8 nk **Attila (SWE)** 3-9-4 0 .... (b) FabienneDeGeer 5
(Christer Andersson, Sweden) **25/1**

1m 47.0s (107.00) **8** Ran SP% **125.8**
PARI-MUTUEL (all including 1sek stake): WIN 1.95; PLACE 1.31, 2.02, 2.33; SF 16.64.
Owner Bo Tommy Nygard **Bred** Peter Reynolds & Robert Dore **Trained** Norway

2989 LONGCHAMP (R-H)
Saturday, June 30

OFFICIAL GOING: Turf: good

3656a PRIX DAPHNIS (GROUP 3) (3YO COLTS & GELDINGS) (TURF) 1m 1f 55y
12:30 (12:00) 3-Y-0 **£33,333** (£13,333; £10,000; £6,666; £3,333)

RPR

1 **So Beautiful (FR)**[61] 2931 3-8-11 0 .... ThierryJarnet 5 112
(Mlle S-V Tarrou, France) *hld up in rr: swtchd to outside early in st: rdn over 2f out: qcknd wl: tk ld 1f out: r.o wl: comf* **15/2**

2 1 1/2 **Mainsail**[24] 2836 3-8-11 0 .... MaximeGuyon 2 109
(P Bary, France) *settled in 4th: relegated to 5th bef st: rdn 2f out: no room to chal: relegated to last: qcknd wl 1f out whn fnd daylight: r.o wl fnl 150yds: nvr rchd ldr* **1/1**[1]

3 1 1/4 **Abtaal (USA)**[56] 1856 3-9-1 0 .... ChristopheSoumillon 6 110
(J-C Rouget, France) *prom on outside fr s: settled in 3rd: rdn 2 1/2f out: r.o wl to ld 1 1/2f out: hdd 1f out: no ex fnl 100yds: styd on* **23/10**[2]

4 nse **Lunayir (FR)**[27] 2743 3-8-11 0 .... Christophe-PatriceLemaire 4 106
(A De Royer-Dupre, France) *settled in 3rd on rail: wnt 2nd bef st: rdn 2f out: r.o: nt qckn fnl 1 1/2f: styd on fnl f* **53/10**[3]

5 2 **Mustaheel (IRE)**[21] 2951 3-8-11 0 .... (p) Francois-XavierBertras 3 102
(F Rohaut, France) *settled in 4th: qcknd wl to chal over 1 1/2f out: effrt short-lived: fdd fnl f* **14/1**

6 1 3/4 **Tifongo (FR)**[27] 2743 3-8-11 0 .... OlivierPeslier 1 98
(H-A Pantall, France) *led on ins on settling: stl in front ent st: rdn over 1 1/2f out: hdd 1 1/2f out: nt qckn: fdd fnl f* **16/1**

1m 57.19s (1.89) **6** Ran SP% **120.5**
WIN (incl. 1 euro stake): 8.50. PLACES: 2.40, 1.30. SF: 19.10.
Owner Mlle S-V Tarrou **Bred** S C E A Haras De Manneville **Trained** France

NOTEBOOK

So Beautiful(FR), coltish and a bit of a handful for his two handlers beforehand, appreciated the step up in trip and picked up well from off the pace to secure his first win in Group company. The Prix Guillaume d'Ornano at Deauville could well be a suitable race for him next.

Abtaal(USA), having his first run since finishing eighth in the Guineas at Newmarket, didn't convince with his stamina over this longer trip, although he was giving 4lb all round.

3657a PRIX DE LA PORTE MAILLOT (GROUP 3) (3YO+) (TURF) 7f
1:30 (12:00) 3-Y-0+ **£33,333** (£13,333; £10,000; £6,666; £3,333)

RPR

1 **Mashoora (IRE)**[27] 2742 3-8-7 0 .... ChristopheSoumillon 6 111
(J-C Rouget, France) *settled in 4th: shkn up 2f out: r.o wl u.p fnl f: tk ld 100yds out: u.p to hold advantage to line* **6/5**[1]

2 1/2 **Shamalgan (FR)**[13] 3205 5-9-2 0 .... GregoryBenoist 5 113
(X Nakkachdji, France) *led fr s: set gd pce: stl in front and gng wl 1f out: hdd 100yds out: r.o wl* **10/1**

3 3/4 **Kendam (FR)**[28] 2728 3-8-7 0 .... MaximeGuyon 8 108
(H-A Pantall, France) *settled in midfield: rdn and swtchd towards outside over 1f out: r.o wl fnl 150yds: tk 3rd cl home* **38/1**

4 snk **American Devil (FR)**[50] 2064 3-8-7 0 .... RonanThomas 4 108
(J Van Handenhove, France) *settled in 3rd on rail: ev ch ent fnl 1 1/2f: r.o u.p fnl 150yds: nt rch ldrs: lost 3rd cl home* **11/1**

5 1/2 **Sulle Orme (FR)**[58] 1809 4-9-2 0 .... JulienAuge 2 109
(C Ferland, France) *racd towards rr of field: u.p 1 1/2f out: r.o wl fnl 150yds: nt rch ldrs* **13/1**

6 hd **Nova Hawk**[28] 2728 4-8-13 0 .... Christophe-PatriceLemaire 7 106
(Rod Collet, France) *settled in 3rd fr s: wnt 2nd bef st: rdn over 1 1/2f out: r.o: no ex fnl 150yds: styd on* **83/10**[3]

7 1/2 **So Long Malpic (FR)**[28] 2728 5-8-13 0 .... OlivierPeslier 10 104
(T Lemer, France) *hld up in rr: swtchd to wd outside in st: picked up and r.o fnl 1 1/2f wout threatening ldrs* **4/1**[2]

8 hd **Ch'Tio Bilote (FR)**[13] 3205 4-9-2 0 .... GaetanMasure 1 107
(J-P Gallorini, France) *settled in 5th on ins: rdn but fnd no ex fr 1 1/2f out: styd on u.p fnl 150yds* **25/1**

9 snk **Myasun (FR)**[31] 5-9-2 0 .... JohanVictoire 9 106
(C Baillet, France) *settled towards rr: swtchd towards outside early in st: r.o wl u.p 1f out: styd on one pce fnl 100yds* **12/1**

10 8 **Konig Concorde (GER)**[23] 7-9-5 0 .... UmbertoRispoli 3 88
(C Sprengel, Germany) *settled towards rr: shkn up early in st: fnd no ex: sn wknd: eased fnl f* **45/1**

1m 20.19s (-0.51)
WFA 3 from 4yo+ 9lb **10** Ran SP% **117.1**
WIN (incl. 1 euro stake): 2.20. PLACES: 1.40, 2.10, 6.50. DF: 8.80. SF: 12.10.
Owner Hamdan Al Maktoum **Bred** Grangecon Stud **Trained** Pau, France

NOTEBOOK

Mashoora(IRE), winner of the Prix Imprudence earlier in the year and runner-up in the Prix de Sandringham last time out, got back to winning ways on this drop in class. She has options at Deauville, including the Prix Rothschild over 1m, and the Maurice de Gheest over 6 1/2f, so connections will have to decide which way they want to go with her trip-wise.

3504 SALISBURY (R-H)
Sunday, July 1

OFFICIAL GOING: Straight course - good to firm (good in places); loop section - good (8.4)

Wind: mild breeze against Weather: cloudy with sunny periods

3658 WILTSHIRE COMMUNITY FOUNDATION E B F BLAGRAVE MAIDEN STKS 6f 212y
2:05 (2:06) (Class 4) 2-Y-0 **£4,398** (£1,309; £654; £327) **Stalls** Centre

Form RPR

1 **Here Comes When (IRE)** 2-9-3 0 .... JamieSpencer 4 76+
(Andrew Balding) *dwlt: in last pair: swtchd lft and hdwy over 1f out: r.o wl fnl f: led fnl 100yds* **11/4**[1]

3 2 3/4 **Red Refraction (IRE)**[20] 2983 2-9-3 0 .... DaneO'Neill 1 74
(Richard Hannon) *led: rdn whn hdd over 2f out: rallied to ld again over 1f out: kpt on: hdd fnl 100yds* **7/1**[3]

03 3 3/4 **Freeport**[25] 2822 2-9-3 0 .... DarryllHolland 2 72+
(Brian Meehan) *t.k.h early: trckd ldrs: rdn 3f out: no imp tl swtchd lft over 1f out: r.o fnl 120yds: wnt 3rd nr fin* **8/1**

0 **4** ½ **Secret Beau**[20] [2983] 2-9-3 0 JamesDoyle 3 71
(George Baker) *pressed ldr: led over 2f out tl rdn and hdd over 1f out: no ex fnl 120yds* **25/1**

5 1½ **Stiff Upper Lip (IRE)** 2-9-3 0 JimCrowley 8 67+
(Richard Hannon) *in tch: rdn over 2f out: kpt on same pce* **14/1**

3 **6** 8 **Sejalaat (IRE)**[22] [2934] 2-9-3 0 TadhgO'Shea 5 46
(John Dunlop) *trckd ldrs: rdn over 2f out: keeping on at same pce whn bdly hmpd over 1f out: wknd fnl f* **5/1**[2]

7 64 **Stockholm** 2-9-3 0 JamesMillman 6
(Rod Millman) *s.i.s: racd green: a last: outpcd 1/2-way: t.o* **66/1**

1m 29.7s (1.10) **Going Correction** +0.15s/f (Good) **7** Ran SP% **78.9**
Speed ratings (Par 96): **99,98,97,96,95 85,12**
toteswingers:1&2 £2.30, 2&3 £3.30, 1&3 £2.80 CSF £9.61 TOTE £2.50: £1.90, £2.70; EX 9.20.
Owner Mrs Fitri Hay **Bred** Old Carhue & Graeng Bloodstock **Trained** Kingsclere, Hants
■ Stewards' Enquiry : Jamie Spencer one-day ban: careless riding (Jul 16)

FOCUS
Not much previous form to go on and the favourite One Word More was withdrawn at the start after becoming unruly in the stalls. The winner was quite impressive in running down the runner-up, who had a soft lead.

NOTEBOOK
Here Comes When(IRE), a 170,000 euros yearling half-brother to a couple of winners, wasn't the quickest away but was given time to find his stride and powered home wide of rivals to win under hands and heels. There should be a lot more to come, although it's worth noting he flashed his tail quite a bit. (tchd 3-1)
Red Refraction(IRE), who ran to a modest level on debut, was pretty much left alone to lead early before staying on well. The 7f trip didn't appear to be a problem. (tchd 13-2 and 15-2)
Freeport finished third to subsequent Royal Ascot winner Tha'Ir at Ripon last time, so clearly has ability, but never really got competitive here after getting outpaced once the tempo lifted. (op 15-2)
Secret Beau finished nearly 5l behind Red Refraction last time, but got a bit closer to that rival here even after being squeezed up a little late on, so is at least progressing. (op 28-1 tchd 33-1)
Stiff Upper Lip(IRE) ◆, who cost 38,000gns as a yearling, is a half-brother to three winners and caught the eye on his debut considering the ground he made up in the final furlong. (op 16-1)
Sejalaat(IRE) is a nice big type but didn't find much off the bridle when his jockey asked for more. He was hampered late on but that incident made little difference. (op 11-2 tchd 6-1)

3659 K J PIKE & SONS LTD H'CAP — 1m 1f 198y
2:35 (2:35) (Class 5) (0-70,70) 4-Y-0+ **£2,911** (£866; £432; £216) **Stalls** Low

Form RPR

0044 **1** **Odin (IRE)**[8] [3400] 4-9-7 **70** MarcHalford 3 79
(David Elsworth) *mid-div: hdwy 3f out: sn rdn: led 2f out: hung bdly rt jst over 1f out: kpt on: drvn rt out: jst hld on* **5/1**[2]

2303 **2** nse **Hurakan (IRE)**[11] [3278] 6-8-6 **62** (p) DanielMuscutt(7) 1 71
(Richard Price) *trckd ldrs: pushed along over 4f out: rdn over 2f out: sn swtchd lft: styd on to chse wnr jst ins fnl f: kpt on: jst failed* **4/1**[1]

-P45 **3** 3½ **South Cape**[23] [2867] 9-9-2 **65** JamesDoyle 2 73+
(Gary Moore) *mid-div: rdn and hdwy over 2f out: chsng wnr whn v bdly hmpd jst over 1f out: kpt on but no ch after* **13/2**[3]

2431 **4** 2¾ **Bennelong**[19] [2997] 6-9-7 **70** AmirQuinn 4 66
(Richard Rowe) *hld up in rr: hdwy over 2f out: sn rdn: wnt 4th ent fnl f: styd on same pce* **9/1**

34-0 **5** 4 **Hawridge Song**[44] [2233] 4-9-5 **68** JamesMillman 10 56
(Rod Millman) *in tch: rdn 3f out: kpt on same pce fnl 2f* **14/1**

3000 **6** 3½ **Beggers Belief**[23] [2867] 4-8-6 **55** (b) HayleyTurner 12 36
(Eric Wheeler) *s.i.s: sn pushed along towards rr: styd on fnl 2f: nvr trbld ldrs* **20/1**

400- **7** ½ **Tenessee**[272] [6592] 5-9-7 **70** FergusSweeney 9 50
(Jamie Osborne) *trckd ldrs: effrt over 2f out: wknd jst over 1f out* **14/1**

3/1- **8** 3 **Cyril The Squirrel**[513] [425] 8-9-4 **67** TomMcLaughlin 6 41
(Karen George) *mid-div: rdn 3f out: wknd over 1f out* **10/1**

1450 **9** ½ **Thundering Home**[44] [2237] 5-8-6 **60** ow1 DavidKenny(5) 11 33
(Richard Mitchell) *hld up towards rr: rdn 3f out: nvr any imp* **33/1**

0410 **10** ¾ **Shirataki (IRE)**[13] [3222] 4-9-0 **63** LukeMorris 13 35
(Peter Hiatt) *trckd ldr: rdn over 2f out: wknd fnl f* **8/1**

0606 **11** 3¼ **Arctic Mirage**[8] [3392] 4-8-0 **52** (b) RyanPowell(3) 5 17
(Michael Blanshard) *rdn wl over 2f out: a towards rr* **25/1**

4302 **12** nk **Midas Moment**[24] [2859] 4-9-7 **70** GeorgeBaker 8 35
(William Muir) *led: rdn and hdd 2f out: sn wknd* **7/1**

2m 8.77s (-1.13) **Going Correction** -0.025s/f (Good) **12** Ran SP% **117.6**
Speed ratings (Par 103): **103,102,100,97,94 91,91,89,88,88 85,85**
toteswingers: 1&2 £4.50, 2&3 £6.40, 1&3 £6.70 CSF £24.41 CT £132.83 TOTE £6.20: £2.20, £1.70, £2.40; EX 28.30.
Owner J C Smith **Bred** Littleton Stud **Trained** Newmarket, Suffolk
■ Stewards' Enquiry : Amir Quinn two-day ban: careless riding (Jul 16-17)
Marc Halford four-day ban: careless riding (Jul 16-19)

FOCUS
A fair handicap that produced a dramatic finish.

3660 K J PIKE & SONS LTD SENIORS' SPRINT H'CAP — 5f
3:05 (3:06) (Class 4) (0-80,79) 6-Y-0+ **£5,175** (£1,540; £769; £384) **Stalls** Low

Form RPR

3002 **1** **Wooden King (IRE)**[8] [3390] 7-9-1 **73** (p) TomMcLaughlin 11 81
(Malcolm Saunders) *a.p: led jst over 1f out: hld on wl whn pressed towards fin: rdn out* **5/1**[3]

1345 **2** nk **The Wee Chief (IRE)**[50] [2071] 6-8-11 **69** DaneO'Neill 1 76
(Jimmy Fox) *hld up: hdwy fr 2f out: cl 3rd ent fnl f where nt best of runs: r.o strly fnl 170yds: jst hld* **11/2**

4301 **3** 1¾ **Triple Dream**[36] [2494] 7-9-1 **73** (tp) LukeMorris 3 74
(Milton Bradley) *trckd ldrs: rdn whn swtchd lft over 1f out: kpt on same pce* **9/2**[2]

-560 **4** nse **Bateleur**[12] [3245] 8-8-3 **61** CathyGannon 2 62
(Mick Channon) *hld up: rdn and stdy prog fr 2f out: kpt on but nvr getting there: jst failed to snatch 3rd* **20/1**

-324 **5** 1¼ **Wreningham**[87] [1204] 7-8-6 **64** (v[1]) TadhgO'Shea 10 60
(Pat Eddery) *sn pushed into ld: rdn 2f out: hdd jst over 1f out: fdd fnl 120yds* **12/1**

1220 **6** ¾ **Efistorm**[15] [3139] 11-9-3 **75** HayleyTurner 9 68
(Joseph Tuite) *mid-div: pushed along over 3f out: rdn over 2f out: nt pce to get involved* **9/1**

25-3 **7** nk **Osiris Way**[40] [2369] 10-9-4 **76** GeorgeBaker 6 68
(Patrick Chamings) *trckd ldrs early: in tch: swtchd lft and rdn 2f out: no imp* **7/2**[1]

020- **8** 2½ **Invincible Lad (IRE)**[289] [6112] 8-9-5 **77** JamieSpencer 8 60
(Milton Bradley) *trckd ldrs: rdn over 1f out: wknd fnl f* **7/1**

-600 **9** 12 **Alfresco**[36] [2482] 8-8-7 **65** (b) LiamKeniry 5
(John Best) *in tch: rdn over 2f out: wknd over 1f out* **14/1**

1m 1.4s (0.40) **Going Correction** +0.15s/f (Good) **9** Ran SP% **114.1**
Speed ratings: **102,101,98,98,96 95,94,90,71**
toteswingers:1&2 £4.80, 2&3 £5.80, 1&3 £3.80 CSF £32.18 CT £132.49 TOTE £6.60: £2.10, £1.80, £1.20; EX 39.40.
Owner Pat Hancock **Bred** Terence E Connelly **Trained** Green Ore, Somerset

FOCUS
Fast and furious stuff for sprinters aged six and upwards.

3661 H S LESTER MEMORIAL H'CAP — 1m 6f 21y
3:40 (3:40) (Class 4) (0-85,84) 4-Y-0+ **£5,175** (£1,540; £769; £384) **Stalls** Far side

Form RPR

10-6 **1** **Western Prize**[43] [2278] 4-9-4 **81** JimCrowley 3 90+
(Ralph Beckett) *in tch: tk clsr order 6f out: led 2f out: sn rdn: styd on wl and in command fnl f* **15/8**[1]

4-44 **2** 1¼ **Gosbeck**[14] [3187] 4-9-5 **82** DaneO'Neill 12 88
(Henry Candy) *mid-div: rdn and hdwy wl over 2f out: styd on to chse wnr ins fnl f: a being readily hld* **9/2**[3]

302 **3** ½ **Wild Desert (FR)**[38] [2412] 7-9-3 **83** MatthewCosham(3) 6 88
(Charlie Longsdon) *trckd ldrs: wnt 2nd 7f out: rdn to ld 3f out: hdd over 1f out: styd on same pce* **20/1**

5-53 **4** hd **Anton Dolin (IRE)**[34] [2561] 4-9-3 **80** RichardMullen 9 85
(John Dunlop) *hld up towards rr: rdn 3f out: no imp tl styd on wl fnl f* **12/1**

1-01 **5** ½ **Lily In Pink**[27] [2755] 4-9-7 **84** JamesDoyle 10 88
(Jonathan Portman) *in tch: rdn to chse ldrs 3f out: styd on same pce fnl 2f* **8/1**

-506 **6** 2½ **Sherman McCoy**[38] [2423] 6-9-1 **78** JamesMillman 11 79
(Rod Millman) *led tl rdn 3f out: kpt chsng ldrs tl no ex fnl 100yds* **8/1**

020- **7** ¾ **Markington**[331] [4463] 9-8-7 **70** (t) LiamKeniry 13 70
(Anthony Honeyball) *hld up towards rr: sme late prog: nvr threatened ldrs* **40/1**

0/44 **8** shd **Swinging Hawk (GER)**[29] [2709] 6-9-5 **82** JamieSpencer 8 82
(Ian Williams) *mid-div: rdn and hdwy 3f out: sn chsng ldrs: fdd ent fnl f* **7/2**[2]

0/0 **9** nk **Balerina (FR)**[55] [1940] 5-9-2 **79** (b) FergusSweeney 4 78
(Alan King) *trckd ldr tl 7f out: rdn over 3f out: nt pce to get bk on terms: fdd ent fnl f* **40/1**

105- **10** 16 **Bollin Judith**[54] [7102] 6-9-7 **84** (vt[1]) MattieBatchelor 1 61
(Jim Best) *hld up in rr: pushed along over 4f out: rdn 3f out: nvr any imp: wknd over 1f out* **33/1**

3m 6.83s (-0.57) **Going Correction** -0.025s/f (Good) **10** Ran SP% **117.7**
Speed ratings (Par 105): **100,99,99,98,98 97,96,96,96,87**
toteswingers:1&2 £3.00, 2&3 £13.80, 1&3 £7.60 CSF £10.11 CT £125.24 TOTE £3.70: £1.70, £2.40, £4.20; EX 13.30.
Owner J C Smith **Bred** Littleton Stud **Trained** Kimpton, Hants

FOCUS
As usual a flag start over this distance, and the leaders set a respectable gallop.

3662 K J PIKE & SONS LTD AUCTION STKS (CONDITIONS RACE) — 6f
4:15 (4:15) (Class 3) 2-Y-0 **£7,439** (£2,213; £1,106; £553) **Stalls** Low

Form RPR

2312 **1** **Cruck Realta**[8] [3368] 2-7-12 92 CathyGannon 4 77
(Mick Channon) *squeezed up and bmpd s: sn rcvrd to chse ldrs: rdn 3f out: kpt on to wear down ldr ins fnl f: led towards fin* **4/7**[1]

14 **2** ½ **Ask The Guru**[29] [2688] 2-8-11 0 JimCrowley 3 89
(Ralph Beckett) *led: rdn wl over 1f out: kpt on: hdd towards fin* **5/1**[2]

4135 **3** 2 **Ishi Honest**[16] [3097] 2-7-6 80 NoelGarbutt(7) 1 71
(Mark Usher) *trckd ldr: rdn over 2f out: kpt on same pce fnl f* **8/1**

32 **4** 1¼ **The Black Jacobin**[29] [2688] 2-8-3 0 LukeMorris 5 71
(J S Moore) *trckd ldr: rdn over 2f out: kpt on same pce fnl f* **6/1**[3]

5 2 **Pinarius (IRE)** 2-8-6 0 HayleyTurner 2 68+
(Brian Meehan) *s.i.s and wnt lft s: cl up tl outpcd 3f out: nvr threatened* **20/1**

1m 16.19s (1.39) **Going Correction** +0.15s/f (Good) **5** Ran SP% **110.5**
Speed ratings (Par 98): **96,95,92,91,88**
CSF £3.87 TOTE £1.80: £1.10, £1.50; EX 4.00.
Owner Anne & Steve Fisher **Bred** Wansdyke Farms Limited **Trained** West Ilsley, Berks

FOCUS
A difficult contest to assess. The winner has been rated a bit below her Chesham form, while the runner-up has improved.

NOTEBOOK
Cruck Realta, who finished runner-up in the Chesham Stakes eight days previously, wasn't at her best but nosed to the front close to the line. There is little doubt she will be better once up in trip again but she was getting lots of weight from the second here. (op 8-15 tchd 4-6 in places)
Ask The Guru finished behind The Black Jacobin when they met last time but easily reversed that form, possibly due to the less-demanding course. Ralph Beckett's colt is one to keep an eye on for a sprint nursery unless this line of form affords him a high handicap mark. (op 7-1)
Ishi Honest ran below par in heavy ground last time but did better here carrying a featherweight. (op 9-1)
The Black Jacobin raced a bit keen for a while, like the runner-up, before finding only the one pace. (op 13-2 tchd 7-1)
Pinarius(IRE), a 24,000GBP yearling, is a half-brother to winners and shaped as though this experience was needed up against some useful juveniles. (op 14-1)

3663 GOLDRING SECURITY SERVICES MAIDEN STKS (DIV I) — 1m 1f 198y
4:50 (4:51) (Class 5) 3-Y-0+ **£2,911** (£866; £432; £216) **Stalls** Low

Form RPR

2 **1** **Hippy Hippy Shake**[24] [2848] 3-8-9 0 KierenFallon 5 84+
(Luca Cumani) *trckd ldrs: led 3f out: sn pushed clr: styd on wl: readily* **6/4**[1]

2 **2** 3½ **Sir Quintin (IRE)**[15] [3161] 3-9-0 0 HayleyTurner 6 82+
(Andrew Balding) *trckd ldrs: squeezed out whn trying to mount chal 3f out: sn rdn: styd on same pce and a being hld by wnr* **15/8**[2]

22-3 **3** 2½ **Pulverize (USA)**[33] [2584] 3-9-0 85 TadhgO'Shea 1 77
(Sir Michael Stoute) *trckd ldrs: rdn to dispute 2nd fr over 2f out tl no ex ins fnl f* **11/4**[3]

0-0 **4** 7 **Cape Joy (IRE)**[34] [2553] 3-8-9 0 DaneO'Neill 3 58
(Richard Hannon) *led: rn wd on bnd 6f out: hdd 3f out: sn rdn: wknd ent fnl f* **16/1**

00 **5** 4 **Moonshine Ruby**[27] [2768] 6-9-6 0 LukeMorris 2 50
(Peter Hiatt) *hld up in tch: rdn wl over 2f out: nvr threatened: wknd fnl f* **100/1**

6 ¾ **Dei Amore (IRE)** 3-8-9 0 JamesDoyle 4 49
(Jonathan Portman) *awkward leaving stalls: a towards rr* **25/1**

0/ 7 2 3/4 **Gavi**[1381] 6084 6-9-11 0 TomMcLaughlin 8 48
(Karen George) *hld up in tch: effrt wl over 2f out: nt pce to chal: wknd fnl f* 50/1

6 8 29 **Alfie Joe**[19] 3005 3-8-7 0 RyanWhile(7) 9
(Ron Hodges) *in tch on outer tl wknd 3f out: t.o* 66/1

2m 10.77s (0.87) **Going Correction** -0.025s/f (Good)
WFA 3 from 6yo 11lb 8 Ran SP% **115.6**
Speed ratings (Par 103): **95,92,90,84,81 80,78,55**
toteswingers:1&2 £1.50, 2&3 £1.60, 1&3 £1.60 CSF £4.59 TOTE £2.20: £1.10, £1.10, £1.50; EX 4.20.

Owner Helena Springfield Ltd **Bred** Meon Valley Stud **Trained** Newmarket, Suffolk

FOCUS
Three dominated the market and those rivals came home in betting order, nicely clear of the fourth.

3664 GOLDRING SECURITY SERVICES MAIDEN STKS (DIV II) 1m 1f 198y
5:20 (5:20) (Class 5) 3-Y-0+ £2,911 (£866; £432; £216) **Stalls** Low

Form RPR

3- 1 **Gospel Choir**[324] 5013 3-9-0 0 RichardMullen 2 86+
(Sir Michael Stoute) *trckd ldrs: rdn whn sltly outpcd over 2f out: str run ins fnl f: led fnl stride* 4/7[1]

0 2 hd **Checkpoint**[15] 3161 3-9-0 0 IanMongan 4 85+
(Sir Henry Cecil) *t.k.h: in tch: swtchd out after 1f: rdn to ld jst over 2f out: kpt on: hdd fnl stride* 9/2[2]

3460 3 5 **Dynastic**[17] 3072 3-9-0 73 JimCrowley 7 75
(Richard Hannon) *sn led: rdn whn hdd over 2f out: kpt on same pce fnl f* 8/1[3]

00 4 4 1/2 **Carmen's Concerto**[24] 2849 3-8-9 0 HayleyTurner 3 61
(Andrew Balding) *trckd ldrs: chal briefly 3f out: sn rdn: one pce fnl 2f* 25/1

0- 5 hd **Mabel's Song**[265] 6744 3-8-9 0 DaneO'Neill 1 61
(Henry Candy) *trckd ldrs: rdn 3f out: one pce fnl 2f* 20/1

00 6 3/4 **Runway Girl (IRE)**[11] 3279 3-8-9 0 JamesDoyle 6 59
(Roger Charlton) *hld up towards rr: rdn 3f out: kpt on fnl 2f but no imp on ldrs* 25/1

6 7 3 1/4 **Chemistry Master**[17] 3079 4-9-11 0 RobertWinston 8 58
(Jeremy Gask) *hld up in last: rdn 3f out: nvr any real imp* 11/1

0-0 8 17 **Phantom Ranch**[13] 3227 3-9-0 0 DarryllHolland 5 24
(Hughie Morrison) *in tch: carried lft after 1f: rdn over 3f out: wknd wl over 1f out* 20/1

2m 11.68s (1.78) **Going Correction** -0.025s/f (Good)
WFA 3 from 4yo 11lb 8 Ran SP% **118.5**
Speed ratings (Par 103): **91,90,86,83,83 82,79,66**
toteswingers:1&2 £1.70, 2&3 £2.80, 1&3 £2.30 CSF £3.31 TOTE £1.60: £1.02, £1.80, £2.00; EX 4.00.

Owner Cheveley Park Stud **Bred** Cheveley Park Stud Ltd **Trained** Newmarket, Suffolk

FOCUS
The second division of the maiden produced a thrilling finish.

3665 CGA RACING EXCELLENCE APPRENTICE H'CAP (WHIPS SHALL BE CARRIED BUT NOT USED) 1m
5:50 (5:52) (Class 6) (0-60,59) 3-Y-0 £2,070 (£616; £307; £153) **Stalls** Low

Form RPR

4015 1 **Archina (IRE)**[26] 2802 3-8-11 **54** ThomasBrown(3) 10 61
(Andrew Balding) *trckd ldrs: led over 3f out: kpt on gamely: hld on wl whn chal ins fnl f* 9/2[2]

4644 2 1/2 **La Confession**[12] 3246 3-8-6 **49** NoelGarbutt(3) 13 55
(Rae Guest) *towards rr: hdwy fr over 2f out: str chal thrght fnl f: hld towards fin* 10/1

0-04 3 2 1/4 **Tazweed (IRE)**[24] 2850 3-8-6 **53** JeanVanOvermeire(7) 7 54
(Roger Varian) *mid-div: hdwy to chse ldrs 3f out: styd on same pce fnl f* 8/1[3]

-604 4 nse **Saint Irene**[19] 3014 3-9-1 **55** JoshBaudains 11 56
(Michael Blanshard) *towards rr: swtchd lft 3f out: hdwy sn after: styd on same pce fnl f* 9/1

0000 5 1 3/4 **Here Comes Jeanie**[31] 2628 3-8-5 **45** NatashaEaton 8 42
(Michael Madgwick) *in tch: pushed along over 2f out: kpt on same pce* 66/1

-030 6 1 **Authoritarian**[26] 2802 3-8-11 **58** MeganWhitehead(7) 2 52
(Richard Hannon) *sn prom: led 4f out tl over 3f out: chsd ldrs: fdd ins fnl f* 14/1

-651 7 3/4 **Lady Percy (IRE)**[14] 3193 3-9-0 **59** DanielMuscutt(5) 1 52
(Mark Usher) *in tch: effrt over 2f out: sn edgd lft: fdd fnl f* 15/8[1]

4320 8 1 1/4 **Stag Hill (IRE)**[97] 1046 3-9-1 **55** WilliamTwiston-Davies 5 45
(Sylvester Kirk) *towards rr: pushed along and hdwy fr 3f out: one pce fnl 2f* 10/1

00-0 9 6 **Plum Bay**[17] 3071 3-9-0 **57** AliceHaynes(3) 9 33
(David Elsworth) *a towards rr* 20/1

00-0 10 7 **Glaze**[24] 2864 3-8-10 **57** ow2 ChristianSewell(7) 6 17
(Hughie Morrison) *s.i.s: sn prom: wknd 2f out* 16/1

6-10 11 3/4 **Kingscombe (USA)**[26] 2788 3-9-2 **59** RyanWhile(3) 4 17
(Pat Eddery) *unsettled in stalls: led over 5f out tl 4f out: wknd over 2f out* 12/1

040 12 3 **Jacasa Too**[19] 3014 3-7-13 **46** (p) JoeyHaynes(7) 12
(Rod Millman) *unsettled in stalls: chsd ldrs tl wknd over 2f out* 40/1

00-0 13 26 **Refreshestheparts (USA)**[40] 2367 3-9-1 **55** IanBurns 3
(George Baker) *racd keenly: led for 3f: wknd over 2f out* 33/1

1m 45.0s (1.50) **Going Correction** +0.15s/f (Good) 13 Ran SP% **124.1**
Speed ratings (Par 98): **98,97,95,95,93 92,91,90,84,77 76,73,47**
toteswingers:1&2 £3.00, 2&3 £13.10, 1&3 £8.00 CSF £49.66 CT £372.12 TOTE £5.60: £1.90, £2.80, £3.10; EX 59.00.

Owner Dr Philip Brown **Bred** Good Breeding **Trained** Kingsclere, Hants

FOCUS
As is always the case for contests of this type, the form is unlikely to be reliable. The fourth is probably the best guide.

Saint Irene Official explanation: jockey said saddle slipped

Lady Percy(IRE) Official explanation: jockey said filly was unsuited by the good to firm (good in places) ground

T/Plt: £12.40 to a £1 stake. Pool £81,079.77 - 4,768.07 winning units. T/Qpdt: £4.10 to a £1 stake. Pool £4,006.75 - 715.00 winning units. TM

3637 WINDSOR (R-H)
Sunday, July 1

OFFICIAL GOING: Good to firm (good in places; 9.0)
Wind: Moderate, behind Weather: Sunshine and showers

3666 BETFRED MOBILE SPORTS MAIDEN FILLIES' STKS 1m 67y
2:15 (2:16) (Class 5) 3-5-Y-0 £2,911 (£866; £432; £216) **Stalls** Low

Form RPR

5-4 1 **Keene Dancer**[45] 2204 3-8-10 0 RyanMoore 1 80+
(Sir Michael Stoute) *s.i.s and rousted into midfield: rdn and prog wl over 2f out: chal over 1f out: drvn ahd last 150yds* 9/4[1]

03 2 1 **Four Leaves (IRE)**[11] 3279 3-8-10 0 AndreaAtzeni 8 77
(Marco Botti) *pressed ldr: led wl over 1f out: edgd lft and hdd last 150yds: one pce* 10/1

3 1 1/2 **Tonle Sap (IRE)** 3-8-10 0 JohnFahy 2 73
(Clive Cox) *mostly trckd ldng pair: shkn up over 2f out: styd on fr over 1f out: nvr quite able to chal* 40/1

4 3 **Eponastone (IRE)** 3-8-10 0 [1] SilvestreDeSousa 11 66
(Gerard Butler) *difficult to load into stalls: dwlt: mostly last tl prog over 2f out: shkn up over 1f out: styd on to take 4th nr fin* 50/1

0 5 1 **Natural Bloom (IRE)**[24] 2849 3-8-10 0 TomQueally 4 64
(Sir Henry Cecil) *trckd ldrs: pushed along 3f out: nvr on terms but kpt on steadily fr over 1f out* 16/1

6 1/2 **Mama Quilla (USA)** 3-8-10 0 JimmyFortune 5 63+
(William Haggas) *hld up in midfield: pushed along over 2f out: kpt on steadily fr over 1f out* 12/1

40- 7 nse **Pearl War (USA)**[248] 7124 3-8-7 0 HarryBentley(3) 7 63
(William Haggas) *led: rdn and edgd lft fr 2f out: hdd & wknd wl over 1f out* 9/2[3]

4233 8 1/2 **Gold Show**[9] 3340 3-8-10 76 ChrisCatlin 6 62
(Mick Channon) *hld up in midfield: pushed along fr over 2f out: nvr on terms but kpt on steadily* 3/1[2]

0-0 9 2 1/4 **Sweet Liberta (IRE)**[14] 3189 3-8-10 0 DavidProbert 10 56
(Andrew Balding) *a towards rr: rdn and no prog wl over 2f out* 22/1

05 10 1 1/2 **Poly Pomona**[22] 2935 3-8-10 0 RichardHughes 12 53
(Richard Hannon) *trckd ldng trio: pushed along and steadily wknd fnl 2f* 12/1

4-0 11 1 3/4 **Present Day**[23] 2891 3-8-10 0 TedDurcan 14 49
(Clive Cox) *trapped out wd towards rr: shkn up and no prog 3f out: sn btn* 25/1

-6 12 3/4 **Bubbly Bounty**[26] 2799 3-8-10 0 LiamJones 9 47
(Alan Bailey) *a in last trio: shkn up and no prog 3f out* 50/1

5 13 1 1/4 **Rowan Rhapsody**[19] 2996 3-8-10 0 JoeFanning 13 44
(Jim Boyle) *racd wd in midfield: wknd over 2f out* 80/1

1m 43.69s (-1.01) **Going Correction** -0.225s/f (Firm) 13 Ran SP% **120.1**
Speed ratings (Par 100): **96,95,93,90,89 89,88,88,86,84 82,82,80**
toteswingers: 1&2 £10.70, 2&3 £74.20, 1&3 £29.60 CSF £24.76 TOTE £3.50: £1.60, £3.60, £17.90; EX 28.80 Trifecta £239.40 Part won. Pool £323.59 - 0.10 winning units..

Owner Newsells Park Stud **Bred** Newsells Park Stud **Trained** Newmarket, Suffolk

FOCUS
Inner of straight dolled out 4yds at 6f down to the intersection then reducing to full width at Winning Post. Top bend dolled out 3yds from normal inner configuration adding 12yds to race distances of 1m and over. Andrea Atzeni was of the opinion that the ground had dried out a little from Saturday, and the opening time was just 1.61sec below standard. A fair fillies' maiden. The pace was modest until quickening with 3f to run.

3667 BETFRED MOBILE CASINO H'CAP 1m 67y
2:45 (2:45) (Class 3) (0-90,90) 3-Y-0+ £8,409 (£2,502; £1,250; £625) **Stalls** Low

Form RPR

11- 1 **Asatir (USA)**[232] 7390 3-9-4 **89** SilvestreDeSousa 2 98+
(Saeed Bin Suroor) *chsd ldr: rdn over 3f out: responded wl to chal 2f out: led jst over 1f out: styd on wl* 7/2[1]

6-21 2 hd **Razorbill (USA)**[17] 3079 3-9-0 **85** MichaelHills 8 93+
(Charles Hills) *hld up in midfield: prog on outer over 2f out: rdn to chal over 1f out: jst hld ins fnl f* 5/1[3]

-505 3 1 1/2 **Crown Counsel (IRE)**[10] 3306 4-9-9 **85** JoeFanning 1 92
(Mark Johnston) *led at gd pce: rdn wl over 2f out: hdd and one pce jst over 1f out* 14/1

-500 4 1 1/4 **Chapter And Verse (IRE)**[31] 2642 6-9-3 **79** RichardHughes 3 83
(Mike Murphy) *hld up but sn in midfield: prog and cl up 2f out: nt qckn over 1f out: one pce after* 10/1

3-22 5 1 1/4 **Juvenal (IRE)**[19] 3012 3-8-5 **76** KieranO'Neill 11 75
(Richard Hannon) *hld up towards rr: prog fr 3f out: chsd ldrs wl over 1f out: no hdwy after* 16/1

-100 6 nk **Push Me (IRE)**[44] 2250 5-9-0 **76** MichaelO'Connell 10 77
(Jamie Poulton) *a in midfield: no imp on ldrs over 2f out: n.d over 1f out* 25/1

0312 7 nk **Oriental Scot**[29] 2720 5-9-13 **89** TomQueally 7 89
(William Jarvis) *shoved along in rr early and nt gng wl: effrt 3f out: no imp on ldrs fnl 2f* 15/2

-231 8 1/2 **Ree's Rascal (IRE)**[36] 2500 4-9-6 **82** RyanMoore 4 81
(Jim Boyle) *prom: rdn 3f out: wknd fr 2f out* 9/2[2]

9 3/4 **Silver Sycamore (USA)**[95] 1077 3-9-5 **90** TedDurcan 12 85
(David Lanigan) *restrained into last fr wd draw: pushed along over 2f out: kpt on but nvr remotely involved* 20/1

1636 10 3/4 **Verse Of Love**[17] 3064 3-8-5 **76** AndreaAtzeni 13 69
(David Evans) *wl in rr: effrt on outer 3f out: no prog 2f out: fdd* 16/1

003 11 hd **Yojimbo (IRE)**[36] 2500 4-9-4 **80** ChrisCatlin 5 75
(Mick Channon) *trckd ldrs: rdn wl over 2f out: wknd wl over 1f out* 12/1

-061 12 1 **Starwatch**[16] 3105 5-9-13 **89** SeanLevey 9 82
(John Bridger) *in tch in midfield: lost pl 1/2-way: struggling in rr fnl 2f* 12/1

1m 41.33s (-3.37) **Going Correction** -0.225s/f (Firm)
WFA 3 from 4yo+ 9lb 12 Ran SP% **120.4**
Speed ratings (Par 107): **107,106,105,104,102 102,102,101,100,100 100,99**
toteswingers:1&2 £3.30, 2&3 £17.90, 1&3 £12.20 CSF £20.72 CT £226.46 TOTE £3.90: £2.20, £2.10, £3.20; EX 11.50 Trifecta £183.50 Pool £436.57 - 1.76 winning units..

Owner Godolphin **Bred** Robert Raphaelson **Trained** Newmarket, Suffolk

FOCUS
This reasonable handicap was run at what looked a brisk pace in a quick time compared with the previous maiden and 0.67sec faster than standard. Not many became involved from the back and a low draw proved to be an asset. The first two are progressive types with more to offer.

NOTEBOOK

Asatir(USA) retained his unbeaten record with a likeable performance, coming under pressure a good way out but finding plenty to fend off the runner-up. He clearly goes well fresh and it would be interesting if he takes up either of his forthcoming entries under a penalty. (tchd 4-1)

Razorbill(USA) ran a big race on this handicap debut, caught wider than the other principals and rallying close home. He should remain competitive. (tchd 4-1)

Crown Counsel(IRE) came in for support and he ran well from the front out of stall one. He had not been at his best for some time and had dropped to his last winning mark. (tchd 12-1)

Chapter And Verse(IRE) has come down a long way in the weights and showed a return to form with the decent gallop suiting. His losing run dates back to September 2010, and he hasn't won on turf since a year before that, but he is certainly well handicapped now. (op 11-1)

Juvenal(IRE) proved consistent in maiden company without getting his reward and he ran respectably on this first handicap venture.

Push Me(IRE) was racing off her correct mark and this was a fair effort on drier ground than ideal. (tchd 28-1)

Oriental Scot went up a further 4lb for his Musselburgh second and never figured from the rear, but he was closing at the end. (op 17-2 tchd 9-1)

Ree's Rascal(IRE) had been running consistently well but he was found wanting off a career-high mark.

3668 OSSIE & HUTCH MEMORIAL H'CAP — 1m 2f 7y

3:15 (3:15) (Class 3) (0-90,88) 3-Y-O **£8,409** (£2,502; £1,250; £625) **Stalls** Centre

Form / RPR

0-24 **1** **Stature (IRE)**[29] 2718 3-9-0 **81** ... JimmyFortune 1 — 91
(Andrew Balding) *mde all: drvn over 2f out: hrd pressed fr over 1f out: hld on wl* **13/2**[3]

-015 **2** *nk* **Beaufort Twelve**[16] 3124 3-9-4 **88** ... HarryBentley(3) 2 — 97
(William Jarvis) *trckd wnr after 3f: chal fr 3f out: upsides fnl f: nt qckn nr fin* **5/1**[2]

1-50 **3** *3 3/4* **Jungle Beat (IRE)**[23] 2897 3-9-5 **86** ...(b[1]) NickyMackay 3 — 88
(John Gosden) *hld up in tch: clsd to chal 3f out: nt qckn 2f out: hld after: fdd ins fnl f* **8/1**

0-1 **4** *3/4* **Inthar (USA)**[33] 2584 3-9-5 **86** ... SilvestreDeSousa 5 — 86
(Saeed Bin Suroor) *trckd ldrs: rdn and nt qckn over 2f out: no imp after: fdd over 1f out* **5/1**[2]

61 **5** *1 1/4* **Glittering Gold**[32] 2612 3-9-4 **85** ... RyanMoore 6 — 83
(Sir Michael Stoute) *hld up in last pair: effrt on outer over 3f out: rdn and no imp over 2f out: wl hld after* **2/1**[1]

4-16 **6** *2 1/2* **Morant Bay (IRE)**[44] 2232 3-9-2 **83** ... TomQueally 4 — 76
(Sir Henry Cecil) *chsd wnr 3f: styd prom tl wknd jst over 2f out* **16/1**

1-15 **7** *1/2* **Freddy Q (IRE)**[16] 3106 3-9-5 **86** ... RichardHughes 8 — 78
(Richard Hannon) *hld up in last: shoved along over 2f out: one pce and no prog fnl 2f* **5/1**[2]

2m 6.2s (-2.50) **Going Correction** -0.225s/f (Firm) **7** Ran SP% **113.7**

Speed ratings (Par 104): **101,100,97,97,96 94,93**

toteswingers:1&2 £6.40, 2&3 £4.90, 1&3 £9.50 CSF £37.97 CT £262.88 TOTE £8.00: £3.70, £1.90; EX 51.90 Trifecta £367.80 Pool £626.37 - 1.26 winning units..

Owner N Botica **Bred** Barronstown Stud **Trained** Kingsclere, Hants

FOCUS

This decent 3yo handicap was run during a shower. The pace was ordinary and it paid to race prominently. The first two finished clear. There was only 7lb between the runners.

NOTEBOOK

Stature(IRE) was the only maiden in the field. He did it under a good ride from the front, grabbing the rail in the straight and finding plenty to hold off the runner-up. Effective on easy ground too, he won't mind a return to 1m4f. (op 8-1)

Beaufort Twelve put in a sustained challenge but could not get past a tough opponent. The topweight has kept his best efforts for a sound surface although one of his two well-beaten runs on easy ground did come in the Craven Stakes. (tchd 11-2)

Jungle Beat(IRE) did not look wholly straightforward in the first-time blinkers and was readily held in third. He is able, but his application is lacking. (op 13-2 tchd 6-1)

Inthar(USA)'s trainer won this event when it was last staged two years ago but this colt lacked the pace to mount an effective challenge. He looks in need of 1m4f, the trip over which his dam won the Ribblesdale. (op 9-2 tchd 11-2)

Glittering Gold, a maiden winner at Folkestone, failed to threaten on this handicap debut, but attempted to come down the outside from the back and lacked the required pace over this sharper trip. (op 5-2)

Morant Bay(IRE), the sole filly, was making her handicap debut. This was her first run on a sound surface and she faded after racing close to the pace. (op 12-1)

Freddy Q(IRE) settled reasonably well this time but was always at the back of the field. (op 9-2)

3669 BRITISH STALLION STUDS / BETFRED MOBILE E B F FILLIES' CONDITIONS STKS — 5f 10y

3:50 (3:50) (Class 2) 2-Y-O

£9,337 (£2,796; £1,398; £699; £349; £175) **Stalls** High

Form / RPR

42 **1** **Three Crowns**[25] 2808 2-8-9 0 ... SilvestreDeSousa 3 — 82
(Ian Wood) *trckd ldrs: rdn 2f out: wnt 2nd 1f out: sustained chal to ld post* **11/1**

210 **2** *nse* **Miss Diva**[11] 3269 2-8-12 90 ... RichardHughes 6 — 85
(Richard Hannon) *w ldr: shkn up to ld over 1f out: rdn fnl f: styd on but hdd post* **2/1**[2]

043 **3** *1* **Shrimpton**[16] 3123 2-8-9 0 ... ChrisCatlin 4 — 78
(Mick Channon) *pushed along in last 1/2-way: gd prog over 1f out to chse ldng pair fnl f: no imp last 75yds* **16/1**

0 **4** *2 1/4* **Seraphima**[73] 1466 2-8-9 0 ... LiamJones 2 — 70
(Alan Bailey) *t.k.h: cl up bhd ldng pair: hanging and nt qckn over 1f out: sn btn* **22/1**

1 **5** *1/2* **Columella**[10] 3313 2-8-12 0 ... RyanMoore 1 — 71
(William Haggas) *mde most: rdn 2f out: hanging and hdd over 1f out: fdd* **5/4**[1]

440 **6** *2 3/4* **Excel Yourself (IRE)**[11] 3269 2-8-9 81 ... MartinDwyer 5 — 58
(James Tate) *s.i.s: trckd ldrs and cl up after 2f: nt qckn over 1f out: wknd* **11/2**[3]

051 **7** *1 1/2* **Harleys Rocket**[15] 3150 2-8-9 69 ... KirstyMilczarek 7 — 53
(Brendan Powell) *racd on outer: in tch: edgd lft fr 1/2-way: wknd over 1f out* **33/1**

59.71s (-0.59) **Going Correction** -0.225s/f (Firm) **7** Ran SP% **114.7**

Speed ratings (Par 97): **95,94,93,89,88 84,82**

toteswingers:1&2 £3.90, 2&3 £5.70, 1&3 £6.80 CSF £33.65 TOTE £10.50: £3.30, £1.70; EX 45.00.

Owner C R Lambourne, M Forbes, D Losse **Bred** Miss Jacqueline Goodearl **Trained** Upper Lambourn, Berks

FOCUS

A good little conditions event. The best recent winner of this was Lady Darshaan in 2009, who went on to finish second in the Fillies' Mile. The form has been given the benefit of the doubt and the third can prove the key.

NOTEBOOK

Three Crowns responded to pressure to lead on the line. Getting off the mark after two promising efforts in maidens, finishing fourth to Miss Diva in the first of them, this tough filly should get another furlong if required. She could be worth a crack at a Listed race. (op 10-1 tchd 12-1)

Miss Diva, winner of her maiden over C&D before finishing in mid-division in the Queen Mary, had 6lb in hand on BHA figures. The better ground suited and she travelled best before getting to the front, but could not quite hold on. (tchd 15-8)

Shrimpton's connections won this with Betty Fontaine a year ago. Back against her own sex, she came from the rear down the outside and looks in need of further.

Seraphima had not been seen since her debut in April and looked a difficult ride, proving very keen early and hanging in the second half of the contest. This was a reasonable run in the circumstances. (tchd 25-1)

Columellahas changed ownership since her winning debut at Warwick recently, but remains with the same trainer. She needed bustling along to claim the rail and her efforts eventually told. Her debut win came in soft ground and while she probably handled this surface, the sharper test seemed against her. (op 6-4 tchd 13-8)

Excel Yourself(IRE) actually finished a nose in front of Miss Diva in the Queen Mary but looks flattered by that now. (op 5-1)

Harleys Rocket was trapped wide and didn't help matters by hanging left too. Official explanation: jockey said filly hung left (op 25-1)

3670 BETFRED STILL TREBLE ODDS ON LUCKY 15'S H'CAP — 5f 10y

4:25 (4:25) (Class 5) (0-70,68) 3-Y-O **£2,911** (£866; £432; £216) **Stalls** Low

Form / RPR

03-3 **1** **Million Faces**[22] 2918 3-9-5 **66** ... ChrisCatlin 1 — 79+
(Rae Guest) *slowest away: off the pce in last pair: prog u.p on outer fr 1/2-way: wnt 2nd 1f out: sustained effrt to ld last 50yds* **3/1**[1]

060 **2** *nk* **Irish Girls Spirit (IRE)**[57] 1843 3-8-2 **49** ... PaulQuinn 5 — 61
(Paul Midgley) *chsd ldng pair: shkn up 1/2-way: clsd to ld and edgd lft over 1f out: styd on but hdd last 50yds* **12/1**

4352 **3** *3* **Ring For Baileys**[9] 3350 3-9-4 **68** ... RaulDaSilva(3) 3 — 70
(Chris Dwyer) *trckd ldrs in 4th: looking for room and swtchd lft over 1f out: one pce fnl f* **10/3**[2]

0506 **4** *1/2* **Aquasulis (IRE)**[6] 3451 3-9-3 **64** ... TomQueally 4 — 64+
(David Evans) *chsd ldrs in 5th: rdn and nt qckn whn hmpd over 1f out: styd on again nr fin* **16/1**

0054 **5** *nk* **Hannibal Hayes (USA)**[16] 3118 3-8-13 **60** ... RichardHughes 7 — 59
(Jeremy Noseda) *in tch towards rr: shkn up 2f out: short of room over 1f out: kpt on one pce after* **4/1**[3]

6253 **6** *3/4* **Le King Beau (USA)**[9] 3343 3-9-7 **68** ... SeanLevey 8 — 64
(John Bridger) *in tch in rr: drvn and hld whn bmpd over 1f out: one pce after* **17/2**

-620 **7** *1/2* **Monty Fay (IRE)**[16] 3098 3-8-9 **56** ...(t) AndreaAtzeni 2 — 50
(Derek Haydn Jones) *w ldr to 2f out: fdd over 1f out* **6/1**

-140 **8** *1 3/4* **Pucon**[39] 2397 3-9-2 **63** ... JimmyFortune 6 — 51
(Roger Teal) *mde most tl hdd over 1f out: wknd* **12/1**

1050 **9** *1/2* **Flying Kitty**[33] 2582 3-8-4 **51** ... KieranO'Neill 9 — 37
(John Bridger) *dwlt: a in last pair: rdn and no prog over 2f out: eased whn no ch ins fnl f* **25/1**

59.05s (-1.25) **Going Correction** -0.225s/f (Firm) **9** Ran SP% **118.0**

Speed ratings (Par 100): **101,100,95,94,94 93,92,89,88**

toteswingers:1&2 £10.80, 2&3 £9.80, 1&3 £2.80 CSF £40.83 CT £128.79 TOTE £5.20: £2.00, £4.60, £1.50; EX 62.90 Trifecta £119.00 Pool 789.62 - 4.91 winning units..

Owner C J Mills **Bred** C J Mills **Trained** Newmarket, Suffolk

■ Stewards' Enquiry : Raul Da Silva three-day ban: careless riding (Jul 16-18)

FOCUS

Just a modest sprint handicap, but the first two, who finished clear, were unexposed handicap debutantes. The time was 0.66sec quicker than the preceding 2yo event.

3671 BETFRED HOME OF THE BIG WINNERS H'CAP — 1m 67y

5:00 (5:00) (Class 5) (0-70,73) 3-Y-O **£2,911** (£866; £324; £324) **Stalls** Low

Form / RPR

-640 **1** **Titus Bolt (IRE)**[19] 3002 3-8-7 **56** ...(v[1]) JoeFanning 4 — 62
(Jim Boyle) *hld up in rr: prog sn after 1/2-way: rdn to ld over 2f out: hrd pressed after: hld on wl nr fin* **7/1**[3]

1363 **2** *nk* **Lady Sylvia**[14] 3193 3-9-1 **64** ... TedDurcan 6 — 69
(Joseph Tuite) *trckd ldrs: rdn to chal 2f out: w wnr fnl f tl nt qckn last 75yds* **9/1**

0-03 **3** *1 3/4* **Highland Duke (IRE)**[34] 2553 3-9-7 **70** ... AdamKirby 2 — 71
(Clive Cox) *trckd ldrs: rdn and nt qckn over 2f out: styd on fr over 1f out: nvr able to chal* **9/4**[1]

5-05 **3** *dht* **Flavius Victor (IRE)**[14] 3184 3-9-2 **65** ... RichardHughes 8 — 66
(Richard Hannon) *awkward s and slowest away: rdn in last pair 3f out: prog on outer 2f out: styd on same pce fnl f* **7/2**[2]

20-6 **5** *nk* **Scarlet Belle**[27] 2757 3-8-9 **65** ... KatiaScallan(7) 5 — 65
(Marcus Tregoning) *towards rr: effrt on wd outside over 2f out: kpt on same pce fr over 1f out: nvr able to chal* **12/1**

-013 **6** *3/4* **The New Black (IRE)**[18] 3044 3-9-4 **67** ...(v) JimmyFortune 11 — 66
(Gay Kelleway) *wl in tch: prog to chal over 2f out: nt qckn over 1f out: one pce after* **8/1**

0-30 **7** *1 1/4* **Acer Diamonds (IRE)**[23] 2898 3-9-7 **70** ... SilvestreDeSousa 9 — 66
(Julia Feilden) *led 1f: chsd ldr to 5f out: lost pl sn after: renewed effrt over 2f out: one pce over 1f out* **8/1**

2200 **8** *2 1/4* **Imtithal (IRE)**[38] 2431 3-9-6 **69** ...(b[1]) MartinDwyer 12 — 60
(James Tate) *rousted along early then t.k.h and prom: wnt 2nd 5f out: lft in ld jst over 3f out: fnd nil and hdd over 2f out: wknd* **33/1**

5430 **9** *6* **Bondi Mist (IRE)**[13] 3228 3-8-11 **60** ... NickyMackay 3 — 37
(Jonathan Portman) *towards rr: rdn and no prog over 2f out: eased whn btn fnl f* **14/1**

-450 **U** **Mitie Mouse**[13] 3234 3-9-4 **67** ... TomQueally 10
(Mike Murphy) *t.k.h: led after 1f: jst in front whn jinked rt and uns rdr jst over 3f out* **25/1**

1m 43.22s (-1.48) **Going Correction** -0.225s/f (Firm) **10** Ran SP% **118.9**

Speed ratings (Par 100): **98,97,95,95,95 94,93,91,85**, PL: Highland Duke 0.60, Flavius Victor 0.90. toteswingers:1&2 £7.10, 2&HD £2.60, 1&FV £2.90, 2&FV £3.00, 1&HD £2.10. CSF £69.74 TOTE £10.00: £2.60, £2.50; EX 99.40 TRIFECTA TRIFECTA: 1,2 &HD £179.10 - 1.74 winning units; 1,2 &FV £227.50 - 1.37 winning u27 Owner.

FOCUS

A modest handicap rather lacking in progressive types.

T/Plt: £180.60 to a £1 stake. Pool £98,843.48 - 399.52 winning units. T/Qpdt: £44.60 to a £1 stake. Pool £5,996.74 - 99.30 winning units. JN

3672 - 3673a (Foreign Racing) - See Raceform Interactive

3644 CURRAGH (R-H)

Sunday, July 1

OFFICIAL GOING: Soft to heavy

3674a GRANGECON STUD STKS (GROUP 3) (FILLIES) 6f
3:10 (3:11) 2-Y-O **£28,437** (£8,312; £3,937; £1,312)

RPR

1 **Sendmylovetorose**[22] 2944 2-9-0 .... CO'Donoghue 3 104+
(A Oliver, Ire) *cl up and disp early: led after 1/2-way and extended advantage ent fnl f: kpt on wl ins fnl f: readily* **9/2**[3]

2 1 1/4 **True Verdict (IRE)**[27] 2780 2-9-0 .... WayneLordan 2 100
(David Wachman, Ire) *settled towards rr: hdwy on outer fr over 2f out to go 2nd 1f out: no ch w wnr ins fnl f* **11/8**[1]

3 4 **Slope**[25] 2828 2-9-0 .... WJLee 8 88
(David Wachman, Ire) *chsd ldrs: swtchd and rdn in mod 4th under 2f out: kpt on into 3rd fnl f* **11/1**

4 9 **Katchy Lady**[16] 3130 2-9-0 ....(b[1]) ChrisHayes 7 61
(P J Prendergast, Ire) *bhd: pushed along bef 1/2-way and kpt on wl ins fnl f wout ever threatening* **14/1**

5 1/2 **Boston Rocker (IRE)**[18] 3054 2-9-0 .... ShaneFoley 6 60
(Edward Lynam, Ire) *hmpd s: settled in 5th and rdn after 1/2-way: no imp fr bef 2f out* **10/1**

6 1 **Scent Of Roses (IRE)**[14] 3194 2-9-0 .... PatSmullen 5 57
(D K Weld, Ire) *edgd lft s and lost grnd: settled in rr: sme hdwy over 2f out: sn no imp fr over 2f out* **10/3**[2]

7 11 **Calissa (IRE)**[25] 2828 2-9-0 .... FranBerry 4 24
(Mrs John Harrington, Ire) *broke wl to dispute: rdn over 3f out and sn wknd* **11/1**

1m 16.92s (1.42) **Going Correction** +0.475s/f (Yiel) 7 Ran SP% **115.8**
Speed ratings: **101,99,94,82,81 80,65**
CSF £11.44 TOTE £4.20: £1.20, £1.50; DF 9.30.
Owner John Gildea **Bred** Silfield Bloodstock **Trained** Caledon, Co Tyrone

FOCUS
The winner was very impressive when taking her maiden and stepped up on that to win this in good style. She's one to take seriously when stepped up in grade. The runner-up brought solid form to the table and the race looks solid for the grade.

NOTEBOOK
Sendmylovetorose won under an assertive ride from Colm O'Donoghue. She is clearly a bright prospect, and her trainer, one of the up-and-coming forces in Irish racing, is hopeful that she will be similarly effective on good ground.
True Verdict(IRE), attempting to give David Wachman a third successive winner in this contest following Meow in 2010 and Experience last year, appeared to have plenty going for her. Runner-up to the Richard Hannon-trained Sky Lantern in a Listed race at Naas on her second outing, she had to settle for second for the third time, failing to make much impression on the winner.
Slope needs her sights lowering.
Katchy Lady was well beaten.
Boston Rocker(IRE) was hampered coming out of the stalls but soon recovered.
Scent Of Roses(IRE) failed to improve from a recent Cork debut.
Calissa(IRE) was unable to reproduce her previous Fairyhouse running relative to Slope.

3675a FRIARSTOWN STUD INTERNATIONAL STKS (GROUP 3) 1m 2f
3:45 (3:45) 3-Y-O+ **£32,520** (£9,520; £4,520; £1,520)

RPR

1 **Famous Name**[35] 2525 7-9-12 115........ PatSmullen 3 117
(D K Weld, Ire) *settled in 2nd: niggled into st and clsd sn travelling wl to ld over 1f out: wnt clr ins fnl f: easily* **4/7**[1]

2 3 3/4 **Defining Year (IRE)**[9] 3361 4-9-12 103........ ShaneFoley 4 106
(M Halford, Ire) *led: pushed along and qcknd pce 3f out: hdd over 1f out and no ch w wnr: kpt on* **7/1**

3 3 1/4 **Native Khan (FR)**[371] 3442 4-9-9 115........ JohnnyMurtagh 5 100
(John M Oxx, Ire) *t.k.h: cl up 3rd: pushed along bef st and sn no imp on two principals* **5/1**[2]

4 nk **Windsor Palace (IRE)**[12] 3237 7-9-12 106........(b) JPO'Brien 6 102
(A P O'Brien, Ire) *edgd lft and lost grnd s: settled in rr: wnt 3rd on outer 3f out: sn pushed along and no imp fr over 2f out* **6/1**[3]

5 2 **Sweet Lightning**[21] 2961 7-9-9 101........(t) NGMcCullagh 2 95
(Thomas Carmody, Ire) *settled in 4th: pushed along 3f out and sn struggling: wknd over 2f out* **14/1**

2m 14.49s (0.19) **Going Correction** +0.35s/f (Good) 5 Ran SP% **113.8**
Speed ratings: **113,110,107,107,105**
CSF £5.59 TOTE £1.60: £1.10, £2.90; DF 5.90.
Owner K Abdulla **Bred** Juddmonte Farms Ltd **Trained** The Curragh, Co Kildare

FOCUS
A third victory for Famous Name in this contest. The front-running runner-up sets the standard, while the winner has been rated in line with his recent best.

NOTEBOOK
Famous Name obliged again to bring his tally to 17 wins from 34 starts. Though best known for his exploits at Leopardstown, the scene of 11 victories, he is also proving a notable Curragh performer with five wins at the venue, as well as two seconds at Group 1 level in the Tattersalls Gold Cup. Many less admirable, less accomplished horses have won a Group 1 race in the European Pattern, and the splendidly durable 7yo, a credit to the Rosewell House team, will get another crack at the Bayerisches Zuchtrennen, the 1m2f Munich event in which he was second to Durban Thunder last year.
Defining Year(IRE) is a solid Listed-standard type, consistently placed in that sphere, but without a win since landing the Madrid Handicap at this venue at the beginning of last season.
Native Khan(FR) might well have been a worthy opponent for Famous Name on better ground, but last season's 2,000 Guineas third and Derby fifth was all at sea in the conditions on his first run since last year's Irish Derby. He should be a notable addition to the Oxx squad when he gets his favoured conditions.
Windsor Palace(IRE) will never capture the headlines in the way that happened when he upstaged St Nicholas Abbey in the Mooresbridge Stakes.
Sweet Lightning, a default second when Famous Name won at odds of 1-5 at Leopardstown in May, was unable to make any impact.

3676a BARCLAYS BANK IRELAND PRETTY POLLY STKS (GROUP 1) (F&M) 1m 2f
4:20 (4:20) 3-Y-O+ **£95,000** (£30,083; £14,250; £4,750)

RPR

1 **Izzi Top**[45] 2209 4-9-9 .... WilliamBuick 1 118+
(John Gosden) *trckd ldr in 2nd: clsd travelling bttr to ld over 1f out and kpt on wl: comf* **6/4**[2]

2 1 1/4 **Sapphire (IRE)**[14] 3197 4-9-9 113........ PatSmullen 2 115
(D K Weld, Ire) *broke wl to ld: 2 l clr 5f out: niggled 3f out and sn pressed: hdd over 1f out and sn no ex; kpt on* **10/11**[1]

3 1/2 **I'm A Dreamer (IRE)**[31] 2640 5-9-9 .... JohnnyMurtagh 5 114
(David Simcock) *t.k.h in cl 3rd: pushed along into st and hrd rdn fr 2f out: kpt on wl ins fnl f wout ever threatening* **12/1**

4 1/2 **Up (IRE)**[14] 3203 3-8-12 111........ CO'Donoghue 7 113
(A P O'Brien, Ire) *w.w in rr: pushed along under 3f out and styd on u.p ins fnl f* **8/1**[3]

2m 15.05s (0.75) **Going Correction** +0.35s/f (Good)
WFA 3 from 4yo+ 11lb 4 Ran SP% **111.2**
Speed ratings: **111,110,109,109**
CSF £3.35 TOTE £2.10; DF 2.60.
Owner Helena Springfield Ltd **Bred** Meon Valley Stud **Trained** Newmarket, Suffolk

FOCUS
Having been responsible for all three of the 3yos declared on Friday, Aidan O'Brien withdrew the two Group 1 winners among them, the Oaks winner Was and last season's Moyglare winner Maybe, to give this event a somewhat threadbare appearance. The winner continues on the up, while the runner-up handles this sort of ground and is a good guide to the level. The third and fourth have been rated to their best.

NOTEBOOK
Izzi Top is a daughter of the top-class Zee Zee Top, who was third to Hanami in this event in 2003 before winning the Prix de l'Opera later that season. The Longchamp Group 1 could also figure on the agenda for the Pivotal filly, who is now unbeaten in four races since finishing third to Dancing Rain in last season's Oaks.
Sapphire(IRE) was sent off favourite in what the market correctly identified as a match. She set out to make all and Pat Smullen tried to raise the tempo from 2f down, but Izzi Top soon had the measure of the Cork Group 3 winner.
I'm A Dreamer(IRE) finished a little closer to the winner than was the case in the Group 2 Betfred Middleton Stakes at York in May, but she is possibly flattered by that detail.
Up(IRE) was the sole runner for the Classic generation. She excelled herself when second in the Poule d'Essai des Pouliches but was soundly beaten in the Prix de Diane and could make no impression under a restrained ride here, though she was not beaten far.

3678a AT THE RACES CURRAGH CUP (GROUP 3) 1m 6f
5:25 (5:25) 3-Y-O+
£31,250 (£9,895; £4,687; £1,562; £1,041; £520)

RPR

1 **Hartani (IRE)**[38] 2432 3-8-10 95........ JohnnyMurtagh 4 114+
(John M Oxx, Ire) *chsd ldr in 2nd: 4th 6f out: clsd into st to ld over 2f out: edgd rt u.p and r.o wl fnl f: comf* **5/2**[2]

2 5 1/2 **Midnight Soprano (IRE)**[23] 2903 5-9-8 104........ ChrisHayes 6 103
(P D Deegan, Ire) *hld up in tch: swtchd to chal over 2f out: no imp on wnr ent fnl f* **2/1**[1]

3 3/4 **Offer (IRE)**[9] 3361 3-8-10 100........(b[1]) CO'Donoghue 3 105
(A P O'Brien, Ire) *cl up: 3rd 6f out: outpcd over 2f out and kpt on fnl f* **11/2**[3]

4 3 1/2 **Father Of Science (IRE)**[53] 1976 3-8-10 .... SeamieHeffernan 7 100
(A P O'Brien, Ire) *hld up in rr: clsd over 3f out and kpt on wout ever threatening st* **11/2**[3]

5 7 1/2 **Goldplated (IRE)**[12] 3262 4-9-8 94........ KevinManning 2 89
(John Joseph Murphy, Ire) *hld up: rdn and sme hdwy over 3f out: wknd under 2f out* **33/1**

6 shd **Sense Of Purpose (IRE)**[297] 5850 5-9-11 104........ PatSmullen 5 89
(D K Weld, Ire) *attempted to make all: narrow ld 5f out: hdd 3f out and sn no ex: kpt on fnl f* **8/1**

7 1/2 **Macbeth (IRE)**[9] 3330 3-8-10 98........(p) ShaneFoley 1 89
(K J Condon, Ire) *trckd ldr in 2nd: hdwy to dispute under 4f out: rdn and wknd fr over 2f out* **15/2**

3m 12.72s (3.32) **Going Correction** +0.575s/f (Yiel)
WFA 3 from 4yo+ 15lb 7 Ran SP% **118.5**
Speed ratings: **113,109,109,107,103 103,102**
CSF £8.42 TOTE £3.70: £2.50, £3.30; DF 5.90.
Owner H H Aga Khan **Bred** His Highness The Aga Khan's Studs S C **Trained** Currabeg, Co Kildare

FOCUS
A comprehensive win in this test of stamina. The sprint from the turn-in probably didn't suit the runner-up, but the winner showed class to come clear, and the form looks solid for the grade.

NOTEBOOK
Hartani(IRE) has the potential to mature into a smart staying type. John Oxx views the Shirocco colt as a possible St Leger candidate. As of now, the Curragh all-aged version may represent a more agreeable assignment than the prospect of taking on a putative history-maker in the original of the species.
Midnight Soprano(IRE) is enjoying a splendid season. Defeat at this level takes no lustre from a campaign that has seen her progress from a mark of 81 to her current 104. She had won five races in a row, one of them at the back-end of last season, and is clearly not out of place at Pattern level at this stage.
Offer(IRE) got within half a length of Hartani first time out in a Tipperary maiden in May. He has not made the same degree of progress, but there should be more races to be won with him.
Father Of Science(IRE) found himself racing in isolation on the inside on the approach to the straight and was ultimately well beaten, but finished clear of the remainder.
Sense Of Purpose(IRE), who looked a progressive staying type last season, can be excused a first run of the season on ground that would have been far from ideal.

3677 - 3679a (Foreign Racing) - See Raceform Interactive

3203 CHANTILLY (R-H)

Sunday, July 1

OFFICIAL GOING: Turf: good

3680a PRIX DU BOIS (GROUP 3) (2YO) (TURF) 5f
1:00 (12:00) 2-Y-O **£33,333** (£13,333; £10,000; £6,666; £3,333)

RPR

1 **Snowday (FR)**[22] 2-8-11 0........ OlivierPeslier 2 106
(C Laffon-Parias, France) *amongst ldrs fr s: tk ld 2f out: sn wnt clr: given a couple of reminders whn chal on outside by eventual runner-up 150yds out: r.o wl: readily* **9/1**

2 1 **To My Valentine (FR)**[23] 2907 2-8-8 0........ Christophe-PatriceLemaire 8 99
(F-H Graffard, France) *towards rr: swtchd to wd outside 2f out: r.o strly to threaten ldr 150yds out: a being hld* **14/1**

3 shd **Sage Melody (FR)**[39] 2-8-8 0........ ThierryJarnet 5 99
(P Demercastel, France) *racd cl up bhd ldrs: qcknd wl ent fnl 1 1/2f: wnt 2nd 1f out: r.o wl: lost 2nd 50yds out* **14/1**

4 1 **El Trastolillo (IRE)**[23] 2907 2-8-11 0........ MaximeGuyon 4 98
(P Bary, France) *slowly away: mde gd prog on outside 1 1/2f out: r.o strly fnl f: clst at fin* **3/1**[2]

5 1 1/2 **Bungle Inthejungle**[12] 3242 2-8-11 0 .... MatthewDavies 9 93
(Mick Channon) *amongst ldrs fr s: u.p 1 1/2f out: no ex: styd on one pce fnl f* **13/2**[3]

6 *hd* **Perrecalla (FR)**[23] 2907 2-8-8 0 .... RonanThomas 3 89
(P Van De Poele, France) *prom on ins rail fr s: unable qck 2f out: styd u.p fnl f* **10/1**

7 2 **Hairy Rocket**[11] 3269 2-8-8 0 .... PatDobbs 1 82
(Richard Hannon) *amongst early ldrs: rdn but unable qck 2f out: grad fdd* **13/8**[1]

8 1 1/4 **T'Choupi Chop (FR)**[30] 2-8-11 0 .... IoritzMendizabal 6 81
(A De Watrigant, France) *cl up bhd ldrs fr s: rdn and wknd 1 1/2f out* **10/1**

9 8 **Surely Speightful (USA)**[29] 2702 2-8-8 0 .... StephanePasquier 7 49
(Kevin Ryan) *unsettled in stalls: sn bhd: rdn at 1/2-way: no ex: wl bhd fnl 1 1/2f* **16/1**

59.31s (1.01) **Going Correction** +0.025s/f (Good) **9** Ran SP% **123.8**
Speed ratings: **92,90,90,88,86 85,82,80,67**
WIN (incl. 1 euro stake): 11.80. PLACES: 3.50, 3.20, 4.10. DF: 41.40. SF: 118.90.
Owner Wertheimer & Frere **Bred** Wertheimer Et Frere **Trained** Chantilly, France

NOTEBOOK
Snowday(FR) is a nice size for a 2yo and won nicely after staying towards the far rail. He ought to do well as a juvenile.
El Trastolillo(IRE) wasn't best away and took an age to get going.
Bungle Inthejungle showed speed away from the winner and wasn't disgraced after such a bold show at Royal Ascot.
Hairy Rocket raced upsides Snowday early but found little. Supplemented for this, perhaps she found this coming too quickly after her Queen Mary effort.
Surely Speightful(USA) never got involved and finished tailed off.

3681a PRIX JEAN PRAT (GROUP 1) (3YO COLTS & FILLIES) (TURF) 1m
2:40 (12:00) 3-Y-O **£190,466** (£76,200; £38,100; £19,033; £9,533)

RPR

1 **Aesop's Fables (USA)**[29] 2728 3-9-2 0 .... MaximeGuyon 5 118
(A Fabre, France) *settled in 4th: rdn over 1 1/2f out: no immediate rspnse: given reminders: picked up ent fnl f: qcknd wl 100yds out: tk ld 50yds out: r.o wl* **12/1**

2 1 **Gregorian (IRE)**[12] 3239 3-9-2 0 .... MickaelBarzalona 4 115
(John Gosden) *settled in 2nd: rdn and chal for ld 2f out: tk ld 1 1/2f out: r.o wl ins fnl f: hdd 50yds out: r.o* **5/1**[3]

3 2 **Coup De Theatre (FR)**[22] 2951 3-9-2 0..... Christophe-PatriceLemaire 8 110
(P Van De Poele, France) *covered up in 3rd on rail: swtchd away fr rail over 1f out: qcknd wl: r.o wout threatening ldrs* **50/1**

4 *hd* **Xanadou (IRE)**[22] 2951 3-9-2 0 .... ChristopheSoumillon 7 110
(J-C Rouget, France) *hld up towards rr: rdn 1 1/2f out: r.o wl fnl f: nt rch ldrs* **7/2**[2]

5 3/4 **Sofast (FR)**[28] 2743 3-9-2 0 .... OlivierPeslier 6 108
(F Head, France) *hld up in midfield on outside: shkn up 1 1/2f out: nt qckn: styd on fnl f* **11/2**

6 *snk* **Caspar Netscher**[34] 2568 3-9-2 0 .... ShaneKelly 2 108
(Alan McCabe) *settled in midfield on rail: ev ch 2f out: rdn 1 1/2f out: nt pce to chal ldrs: styd on u.p fnl f* **8/1**

7 *snk* **French Fifteen (FR)**[28] 2743 3-9-2 0 .... ThierryThulliez 3 107+
(N Clement, France) *hld up in rr: wl in rr ent st: shkn up and qckning on outside whn taking false step over 1f out: lost momentum: rallied and r.o ins fnl f* **13/8**[1]

8 1 **Arnold Lane (IRE)**[12] 3239 3-9-2 0 .... MartinHarley 1 105?
(Mick Channon) *broke fast to ld: rdn and hdd 1 1/2f out: styd on u.p bef wkng fnl 150yds* **33/1**

1m 37.59s (-0.41) **Going Correction** +0.025s/f (Good) **8** Ran SP% **116.1**
Speed ratings: **103,102,100,99,99 98,98,97**
WIN (incl. 1 euro stake): 11.10. PLACES: 3.30, 2.90, 6.70. DF: 28.00. SF: 65.10.
Owner Godolphin SNC **Bred** Darley Stud Management Co Ltd **Trained** Chantilly, France

FOCUS
A good looking Group 1, run a at decent clip thanks to the early exertions of Arnold Lane, and in the end it paid to race handy to the pace. The runner-up, third, fourth and fifth have all been rated close to their recent form.

NOTEBOOK
Aesop's Fables(USA) was up in trip having finished third last time out behind Moonlight Cloud over 7f. He was one of the first off the bridle in the home straight, but kept finding for pressure and won a shade cosily in the end, quickening away well in the final 100 yards. He is versatile ground-wise and there is no reason to think he won't keep improving.
Gregorian(IRE), third in the St James's Palace, ran another blinder under a good ride from Mickael Barzalona, who kept his mount close to the early pace which allowed him to get first run. Just swamped by the winner in the closing stages, he perhaps doesn't have the same scope as some of these, but in an open looking division he can win races.
Coup De Theatre(FR) has struggled since beating subsequent French Guineas winner Lucayan earlier in the year, but returned to form here at huge odds and was another who benefited from racing close to the pace.
Xanadou(IRE) won the main trial for this, the Prix Paul de Moussac, but gave away all chance by missing the break. He was unable to make up enough ground to reach the winner, but was staying on to some effect and can win races at this level.
Sofast(FR) hasn't quite looked up to this level in his starts this year and so it proved here as he never really got involved.
Caspar Netscher won the German 2000 Guineas, but had no excuses here and the suspicion remains that he is found out by a truly run mile. A drop back in trip for something like the July Cup may suit.
French Fifteen(FR) was the major disappointment of the race. Held up in rear, he never got any nearer and was well beaten when stumbling at the furlong maker. That is two poor efforts in a row after his good second in the 2000 Guineas behind Camelot and he needs to bounce back.

3682a PRIX CHLOE (GROUP 3) (3YO FILLIES) (TURF) 1m 1f
3:15 (12:00) 3-Y-O **£33,333** (£13,333; £10,000; £6,666; £3,333)

RPR

1 **Ridasiyna (FR)**[23] 2908 3-8-11 0 .... Christophe-PatriceLemaire 13 111+
(M Delzangles, France) *prom thrght: rdn over 2f out: led jst ins fnl f: sn wl in command: pushed out* **5/4**[1]

2 2 **Romantica**[34] 3-8-11 0 .... MaximeGuyon 4 106+
(A Fabre, France) *midfield: rdn 2f out: swtchd rt and r.o to go 2nd ins fnl f: no ch w wnr* **8/1**[2]

3 1 1/4 **Rock Me Baby**[28] 2742 3-8-11 0 .... OlivierPeslier 9 103
(X Thomas-Demeaulte, France) *prom on outer: rdn 2f out: wnt 3rd 1 1/2f out: kpt on* **10/1**[3]

4 1 1/4 **Dark Orchid (USA)**[28] 2742 3-8-11 0 .... Pierre-CharlesBoudot 5 100
(A Fabre, France) *hld up in last gp on inner: short of room and had to wait for gap over 1 1/2f out: in the clr and rdn over 1f out: r.o to go 4th post* **18/1**

5 *hd* **Regatta (FR)**[26] 2806 3-8-11 0 .... AnthonyCrastus 7 100
(E Lellouche, France) *trckd ldr in clr 2nd: led 2f out: rdn over 1 1/2f out: hdd jst ins fnl f: fdd and dropped to 5th post* **25/1**

6 3/4 **Preferential**[30] 3-8-11 0 .... JohanVictoire 10 98
(Mme C Head-Maarek, France) *hld up in last gp: rdn over 2f out: plugged on down wd outside ins fnl 1 1/2f: wnt 6th post: nt pce to chal* **12/1**

7 *hd* **Gathering (USA)**[38] 2410 3-8-11 0 ....(p) MickaelBarzalona 8 98
(John Gosden) *prom: rdn and reminders over 1 1/2f out: outpcd and fdd ins fnl f: dropped to 7th post* **10/1**[3]

8 3 **Crecy**[35] 2532 3-8-11 0 .... IoritzMendizabal 14 92
(Y Fouin, France) *hld up towards rr on outer: rdn to improve 2f out: kpt on tl no ex and fdd ins fnl f* **16/1**

9 4 **Icebreaking (IRE)**[36] 2522 3-8-11 0 .... GeraldMosse 3 83
(L Riccardi, Italy) *prom on outer: lost pl over 1 1/2f out: fdd: nvr put under any sort of press by jockey* **33/1**

10 2 **Lily America (FR)**[28] 2742 3-8-11 0 .... ThierryJarnet 6 79
(F Rohaut, France) *midfield on outer: rdn and qckly lost pl 2f out: sn no ex and btn: eased ins fnl f* **10/1**[3]

11 **Poupee Flash (USA)**[28] 2742 3-8-11 0 .... StephanePasquier 1
(P Bary, France) *midfield on inner: rdn over 2f out: lost pl and btn 1 1/2f out: sn eased* **12/1**

12 **Parisham (FR)**[23] 2908 3-8-11 0 ....(b[1]) GregoryBenoist 11
(M Delzangles, France) *led: hdd 2f out: immediately btn and eased* **33/1**

13 **Mikkwa (USA)**[31] 3-8-11 0 .... ChristopheSoumillon 2
(E Lellouche, France) *nvr out of last: rdn and reminders over 3f out: sn btn: heavily ins fnl 1 1/2f* **12/1**

1m 49.68s (-1.42) **Going Correction** +0.025s/f (Good) **13** Ran SP% **126.8**
Speed ratings: **107,105,104,103,102 102,101,99,95,93 93,93,93**
WIN (incl. 1 euro stake): 2.00 (Ridasiyna coupled with Parisham). PLACES: 1.30, 2.30, 2.10. DF: 6.50. SF: 7.50.
Owner H H Aga Khan **Bred** Hh The Aga Khans Studs Sc **Trained** France

NOTEBOOK
Ridasiyna(FR), unbeaten coming into this, was nicely placed close up and won in the manner of a filly who should hold her own at a higher level.
Romantica, a daughter of Banks Hill, came from out of the pack but could never quite get to the winner. This was only her third start, so there should be more improvement to come.
Rock Me Baby finished in the same position in a Group 2 on her previous start, so gives the form a decent look.

3652 HAMBURG (R-H)
Sunday, July 1

OFFICIAL GOING: Turf: good

3683a SPARDA 143 DEUTSCHES DERBY (GROUP 1) (3YO COLTS & FILLIES) (TURF) 1m 4f
4:40 (4:46) 3-Y-O **£250,000** (£83,333; £50,000; £25,000; £8,333)

RPR

1 **Pastorius (GER)**[34] 2568 3-9-2 0 .... THellier 15 113
(Mario Hofer, Germany) *hld up in last trio on outer: rdn over 2f out: edgd lft u.p and ended up alone on stands' side rail: r.o strly to ld last strides* **25/1**

2 1/2 **Novellist (IRE)**[21] 2966 3-9-2 0 .... EPedroza 8 112
(A Wohler, Germany) *settled towards rr: rdn to improve over 2f out: r.o to chal wl ins fnl f: led briefly ins fnl 75yds: hdd last strides* **4/6**[1]

3 *shd* **Girolamo (GER)**[21] 2966 3-9-2 0 .... AStarke 6 112
(P Schiergen, Germany) *towards rr: prog into midfield 2 1/2f out: rdn 2f out: r.o to chal over 1f out: led jst ins fnl f: hdd ins fnl 75yds: dropped to 3rd last strides* **20/1**

4 1 **Baltic Rock (IRE)**[14] 3202 3-9-2 0 .... GHind 10 110
(J D Hillis, Germany) *midfield on outer: rdn over 2 1/2f out: carried hd high u.p: r.o to chal ins fnl f: no ex and dropped to 4th cl home* **12/1**

5 1 1/4 **Black Arrow (IRE)**[34] 2569 3-9-2 0 .... FrankieDettori 9 108
(A Wohler, Germany) *trckd ldrs: rdn to chal over 2f out: sn led: kpt on tl hdd jst ins fnl f: fdd* **5/1**[2]

6 3 1/2 **Andolini (GER)**[21] 2966 3-9-2 0 .... JBojko 14 103
(A Wohler, Germany) *dropped in fr wd draw and hld up in last gp: rdn to improve over 2f out: plugged on to go 6th post: nt pce to chal* **33/1**

7 *hd* **Salon Soldier (GER)**[34] 2569 3-9-2 0 .... FilipMinarik 7 102
(P Schiergen, Germany) *midfield: swtchd ins to rail and prog to trck ldrs over 3f out: rdn and effrt to chal 2f out: stl ev ch jst over 1f out: no ex and fdd ins fnl f: ct for 6th post* **14/1**

8 *nk* **Nostro Amico (GER)**[28] 3-9-2 0 .... AndreBest 11 102
(Mario Hofer, Germany) *dropped in fr wd draw and hld up in last pair on inner: prog into midfield over 4f out: rdn 2f out: kpt on one pce ins fnl 1 1/2f* **40/1**

9 1/2 **Anakin Skywalker (GER)**[43] 2296 3-9-2 0 .... DPorcu 13 101
(P Vovcenko, Germany) *slowly away: dropped in fr wd draw and hld up in last: stl in rr and rdn over 2f out: plugged on to go 9th ins fnl f: nt pce to chal* **66/1**

10 *hd* **Feuerblitz (GER)**[42] 2324 3-9-2 0 .... RobertHavlin 5 101
(M Figge, Germany) *prom early: sn settled in midfield: rdn over 2f out: lost momentum whn short of room and forced to check over 1 1/2f out: sn outpcd: plugged on* **8/1**[3]

11 8 **Macao (IRE)**[259] 6901 3-9-2 0 .... APietsch 1 88
(R Dzubasz, Germany) *pushed along and reminder to go forward early: trckd ldr in 2nd tl led after 1st bnd: rdn and hdd 2f out: steadily fdd ins fnl 1 1/2f: eased cl home* **66/1**

12 3 **Milord (GER)**[43] 2296 3-9-2 0 .... ADeVries 3 83
(J Hirschberger, Germany) *prom on outer: rdn 2 1/2f out: no ex and btn 1f out: eased ins fnl f* **33/1**

13 20 **Russian Song (GER)**[14] 3202 3-9-2 0 .... EFrank 2 51
(A Wohler, Germany) *midfield on inner: rdn and lost pl rapidly over 2 1/2f out: sn btn and eased: t.o* **40/1**

14 10 **Mano Diao**[21] 2966 3-9-2 0 .... FJohansson 4 35
(Mario Hofer, Germany) *led tl m v wd on 1st bnd: rcvrd and trckd ldr in 2nd: lost pl and dropped to rr on turn into st: sn detached in last and eased: t.o* **25/1**

2m 32.23s (-2.32) **14** Ran SP% **128.3**
WIN (incl. 10 euro stake): 321. PLACES: 49, 16, 25. SF: 726.
Owner Stall Antanando **Bred** Franz Prinz Von Auersperg & Florian Haffa **Trained** Germany

NOTEBOOK
Pastorius(GER) gave both his trainer Mario Hofer and jockey Terry Hellier their first success in the race after many near misses. He came with a strong run on the wide outside to get up, and might run next in the Grosser Preis von Baden. Official explanation: gave both his trainer Mario Hofer and jockey Terry Hellier their first success in the race after many near misses. He came with a strong run on the wide outside to get up, and might run next in the Grosser Preis von Baden.
Novellist(IRE) had every chance down the centre of the track but the jinx on favourites in this Classic continues.

3426 SAN SIRO (R-H)
Sunday, July 1

OFFICIAL GOING: Turf: good

3684a PREMIO PRIMI PASSI (GROUP 3) (2YO) (TURF) — 6f
6:00 (12:00) 2-Y-O **£23,333** (£10,266; £5,600; £2,800)

RPR

1 **Chilworth Icon**[8] 3368 2-8-11 0 .... SamHitchcott 5 101
(Mick Channon) *midfield: rdn 3f out: short of room and had to wait for gap 2f out: sn in the clr and r.o to chal between rivals over 1f out: led ins fnl f: drvn out* **10/9**[1]

2 *nk* **Tiger Day** 2-8-11 0 .... DarioVargiu 1 100
(B Grizzetti, Italy) *led on rail: rdn and strly pressed over 1f out: hdd ins fnl f: kpt on* **8/5**[2]

3 *1 1/4* **Cloud (IRE)**[29] 2-8-11 0 .... CristianDemuro 6 96
(L Riccardi, Italy) *hld up in tch on rail: cut through field to chal over 1f out: rdn and kpt on wout matching front pair ins fnl f* **105/10**

4 *2* **Spirit Dream (ITY)**[29] 2-8-11 0 .... UmbertoRispoli 7 90
(F Saggiomo, Italy) *hld up towards rr on outer: rdn over 2 1/2f out: outpcd by ldng trio over 1f out: plugged on to go 4th cl home* **152/10**

5 *1/2* **Freetown (USA)**[29] 2-8-11 0 .... FabioBranca 4 89
(S Botti, Italy) *prom on outer: rdn to chal 2f out: stl ev ch over 1f out: no ex and fdd ins fnl f: dropped to 5th cl home* **3/1**[3]

6 *5* **Ici La Cote (IRE)**[29] 2-8-11 0 .... GArena 2 74
(B Grizzetti, Italy) *trckd ldr: rdn over 2f out: outpcd over 1f out: fdd: eased whn btn* **32/1**

7 *10* **Rollingarab (ITY)** 2-8-11 0 .... CColombi 8 44
(Sergio Dettori, Italy) *restrained in midfield: rdn and outpcd 2f out: sn btn and eased* **72/1**

8 *3* **Valle Nordica** 2-8-11 0 .... PierantonioConvertino 3 35
(B Grizzetti, Italy) *prom: rdn and lost pl over 2f out: dropped to last and btn over 1f out: eased* **8/5**[2]

1m 11.6s (-0.20) 8 Ran SP% **168.6**
WIN (incl. 1 euro stake): 2.11. PLACES: 1.20, 1.21, 1.66. DF: 2.54.
Owner 7Rus **Bred** Norman Court Stud **Trained** West Ilsley, Berks

NOTEBOOK
Chilworth Icon almost certainly stepped up on his previous efforts to take this Group 3 event, although it's hard to know by how much. Too keen in the Chesham last time, the drop back to 6f proved no problem, and he got up late having had his challenged delayed.

FFOS LAS (L-H)
Monday, July 2

3685 Meeting Abandoned - waterlogged

3415 PONTEFRACT (L-H)
Monday, July 2

OFFICIAL GOING: Good (good to soft in places) changing to good to soft after race 4 (4:00) changing to soft after race 5 (4:30)
Wind: moderate across Weather: Cloudy

3692 TIM EASTERBY RACING PARTNERSHIPS LADIES' H'CAP (LADY AMATEUR RIDERS) (DIV I) — 1m 2f 6y
2:30 (2:30) (Class 5) (0-75,75) 3-Y-0+ **£2,183** (£677; £338; £169) **Stalls** Low

Form RPR

0000 **1** **Pertuis (IRE)**[17] 3129 6-8-11 **56** oh1 .... MissRSmith(5) 11 66
(Micky Hammond) *hld up towards rr: stdy hdwy 4f out: trckd ldrs wl over 1f out: effrt and nt clr run appr fnl f: sn swtchd rt and rdn: styd on wl to ld last 100yds* **40/1**

0-01 **2** *1 1/4* **Shaloo Diamond**[11] 3310 7-10-6 **74** .... MissADeniel 4 81
(Richard Whitaker) *hld up in rr: smooth hdwy over 3f out: rdn to chse ldrs over 1f out: edgd lft 1f out: chal and ev ch ins fnl f: kpt on same pce* **8/1**

2400 **3** *hd* **Flag Of Glory**[52] 2043 5-9-1 **62** .... MissMEdden(7) 5 69
(Peter Hiatt) *led: rdn clr wl over 1f out: hdd last 100yds: no ex towards fin* **20/1**

0061 **4** *1 1/4* **Cosmic Moon**[23] 2926 4-8-13 **60** .... MissKMabon(7) 3 64
(Richard Fahey) *hld up in rr: hdwy 3f out: swtchd to outer wl over 1f out: styd on to chse ldng trio over 1f out: sn rdn and edgd lft: kpt on same pce fnl f* **7/2**[1]

1404 **5** *3 1/4* **Sir Boss (IRE)**[2] 3609 7-10-4 **75** .... MissMMullineaux(3) 12 73
(Michael Mullineaux) *hld up in tch: hdwy to trck ldrs 4f out: rdn to chse ldr 2f out: wknd ent fnl f* **8/1**

3061 **6** *1 1/2* **Falcon's Reign (FR)**[20] 3002 3-9-3 **71** .... MissCWalton(3) 2 66
(Michael Appleby) *chsd ldrs on inner: rdn along 2f out: wknd ent fnl f* **9/2**[2]

0326 **7** *2 1/4* **Scamperdale**[30] 2687 10-10-1 **69** .... (p) MissSBrotherton 7 59
(Brian Baugh) *hld up towards rr: hdwy on inner over 3f out: rdn 2f out: n.d* **12/1**

-634 **8** *4 1/2* **Tribal Myth (IRE)**[30] 2687 5-9-4 **65** .... MissLSutcliffe(7) 8 46
(Kevin Ryan) *in tch: effrt 3f out: rdn along over 2f out: sn wknd* **8/1**

0102 **9** *10* **Jack Dawkins (USA)**[40] 2403 7-9-13 **70** .... MissJRRichards(3) 6 31
(David Nicholls) *prom: rdn along 3f out: wknd 2f out* **9/1**

3630 **10** *22* **Pilgrim Dancer (IRE)**[7] 3442 5-8-11 **56** oh1 .... MissHDukes(5) 10
(Tony Coyle) *t.k.h: prom: rdn along 3f out: sn wknd* **40/1**

4402 **U** **Strike Force**[16] 3154 8-9-11 **68** .... (t) MissALHutchinson(3) 1
(Alison Hutchinson) *towards rr: plld hrd and sddle slipped after 1f: swtchd wd and prom tl wknd over 4f out: bhd whn uns rdr over 2f out* **13/2**[3]

2m 20.73s (7.03) **Going Correction** +0.55s/f (Yiel)
WFA 3 from 4yo+ 11lb 11 Ran SP% **114.4**
Speed ratings (Par 103): **93,92,91,90,88 87,85,81,73,56**
toteswingers 1&2 £46.70, 1&3 £131.10, 2&3 £27.30 CSF £321.62 CT £6461.48 TOTE £55.30: £10.70, £2.50, £5.90; EX 398.30 TRIFECTA Not won..
Owner Derek Gennard **Bred** Killeen Castle Stud **Trained** Middleham Moor, N Yorks

FOCUS
False rail for last 6f approximately 15ft from inside rail. Ground on the soft side and it deteriorated throughout the afternoon. A fair lady riders' handicap, run at an unusually steady pace, and something of an upset. It has been rated through the third to his winter AW form.
Pertuis(IRE) Official explanation: trainer had no explanation for the apparent improvement in form
Scamperdale Official explanation: jockey said gelding was denied a clear run
Strike Force Official explanation: jockey said saddle slipped

3693 TIM EASTERBY RACING PARTNERSHIPS LADIES' H'CAP (LADY AMATEUR RIDERS) (DIV II) — 1m 2f 6y
3:00 (3:02) (Class 5) (0-75,74) 3-Y-0+ **£2,183** (£677; £338; £169) **Stalls** Low

Form RPR

1031 **1** **Rub Of The Relic (IRE)**[7] 3449 7-9-4 **62** 6ex .... (v) MissHDukes(5) 2 72
(Paul Midgley) *trckd ldng pair: hdwy over 2f out: rdn to chal over 1f out: led ent fnl f: kpt on* **13/2**[3]

-302 **2** *3/4* **Entrance**[31] 2653 4-8-11 **55** .... MissSBirkett(5) 9 63
(Julia Feilden) *hld up in rr: stdy hdwy over 3f out: trckd ldrs and nt clr run over 1f out: swtchd rt and rdn ent fnl f: kpt on* **10/1**

-251 **3** *5* **Moody Tunes**[24] 2886 9-10-2 **74** .... MissALMurphy(5) 6 72
(Tom Dascombe) *led: rdn along 2f out: hdd ent fnl f: sn one pce* **5/1**[2]

3320 **4** *1* **Shy**[11] 3307 7-9-4 **62** .... (b) MissPhillipaTutty(5) 11 58
(Karen Tutty) *hld up and bhd: stdy hdwy 4f out: chsd ldrs 2f out: swtchd rt and rdn over 1f out: kpt on same pce* **9/1**

-004 **5** *shd* **Gold Rules**[6] 3459 5-9-10 **68** .... (t) MissJoannaMason(5) 8 64
(Michael Easterby) *cl up: rdn along 2f out: drvn and wknd over 1f out* **15/2**

0-R4 **6** *6* **That'll Do Nicely (IRE)**[17] 3116 9-9-12 **68** .... MissJRRichards(3) 3 52
(Nicky Richards) *towards rr: hdwy 4f out: chsd ldrs 2f out: sn rdn and wknd* **10/1**

0-00 **7** *4 1/2* **Mr Perceptive (IRE)**[28] 2751 4-9-12 **70** .... MissRSmith(5) 12 45
(Micky Hammond) *a in rr* **18/1**

2040 **8** *1* **Ailsa Craig (IRE)**[30] 2687 6-10-6 **73** .... MissSBrotherton 7 46
(Edwin Tuer) *hld up in tch: hdwy to chse ldrs wl over 2f out: rdn wl over 1f out: sn btn* **4/1**[1]

0-00 **9** *13* **Umverti**[19] 3022 7-9-2 **55** oh2 .... (v[1]) MissADeniel 5
(Joanne Foster) *prom: rdn along over 4f out: sn wknd* **22/1**

0346 **10** *1 3/4* **Overrule (USA)**[7] 3449 8-9-10 **70** .... (p) MissFrancesHarper(7) 1
(Jason Ward) *a towards rr* **9/1**

-024 **11** *25* **Graceful Act**[11] 3310 4-9-2 **60** .... MissVBarr(5) 4
(Ron Barr) *chsd ldrs: rdn along 3f out: sn wknd* **14/1**

2m 20.08s (6.38) **Going Correction** +0.55s/f (Yiel) 11 Ran SP% **116.2**
Speed ratings (Par 103): **96,95,91,90,90 85,82,81,70,69 49**
toteswingers 1&2 £9.40, 1&3 £6.20, 2&3 £5.10 CSF £69.05 CT £353.18 TOTE £7.20: £3.10, £3.00, £1.50; EX 84.10 Trifecta £203.30 Pool £838.31 - 3.05 winning units..
Owner O R Dukes **Bred** M J Wiley **Trained** Westow, N Yorks
■ Stewards' Enquiry : Miss Joanna Mason two-day ban: used whip above permitted level (tbn)

FOCUS
The second division of this lady riders' handicap appeared to be run at a much sounder pace. The runner-up is the best guide to the level.
Graceful Act Official explanation: jockey said filly never travelled

3694 PAT BRILLY - A LIFETIME IN RACING FILLIES' H'CAP — 1m 4y
3:30 (3:31) (Class 5) (0-70,70) 3-Y-0+ **£2,264** (£673; £336; £168) **Stalls** Low

Form RPR

602 **1** **Miss Ella Jade**[8] 3416 3-8-0 **51** oh2 .... PaulQuinn 2 60
(Richard Whitaker) *hld up in rr: hdwy on inner wl over 2f out: rdn to chse ldng pair over 1f out: styd on wl fnl f to ld nr fin* **13/2**

120 **2** *nk* **Frosty Berry**[46] 2194 3-9-2 **67** .... AdamKirby 6 75
(Marco Botti) *hld up in rr: hdwy 3f out: chsd clr ldr 1 1/2f out: sn rdn and styd on to ld ins fnl f: hdd and no ex nr fin* **9/2**[2]

05-5 **3** *2* **Tamara Bay**[31] 2679 4-9-1 **57** .... PJMcDonald 3 63
(John Davies) *led: rdn clr 2f out: drvn over 1f out: hdd ins fnl f: wknd last 100yds* **7/1**

5054 **4** *15* **Whats For Pudding (IRE)**[11] 3318 4-8-4 **51** oh4 .... NeilFarley(5) 1 22
(Declan Carroll) *chsd ldng trio on inner: hdwy 3f out: rdn 2f out and sn wknd* **9/1**

1005 **5** *1 1/2* **Woteva**[8] 3416 6-9-2 **65** .... (p) EvaMoscrop(7) 10 33
(Nigel Tinkler) *midfield: hdwy on wd outside 1/2-way: rdn to chse ldrs over 2f out: sn drvn and btn* **14/1**

-032 **6** *6* **Gadobout Dancer**[10] 3356 5-8-10 **52** .... BarryMcHugh 5
(Tony Coyle) *hld up: hdwy to chse ldrs 1/2-way: rdn along 3f out: wknd 2f out* **3/1**[1]

00-0 **7** *1 1/2* **Totally Trusted**[25] 2858 4-8-9 **51** oh2 .... PaulMulrennan 8
(Scott Dixon) *a in rr* **28/1**

1442 **8** *2 3/4* **Indian Giver**[14] 3215 4-9-1 **60** .... PaulPickard(3) 9
(Hugh McWilliams) *cl up: rdn along 3f out: drvn 2f out and sn wknd* **6/1**[3]

5-55 **9** *1* **Arrow Lake (FR)**[25] 2846 3-8-11 **62** .... ChrisCatlin 7
(Noel Quinlan) *dwlt: rapid hdwy to chse ldrs after 1f: rdn along over 3f out: sn wknd* **25/1**

-606 **10** *7* **Guava**[12] 3285 3-8-3 **61** .... DavidBergin(7) 12
(David O'Meara) *chsd ldrs: rdn along 3f out: sn wknd* **25/1**

10-0 **11** *70* **Lady Sledmere (IRE)**[84] 1249 4-10-0 **70** .... MickyFenton 4
(Paul Midgley) *cl up: rdn along 4f out: wknd qckly: bhd and eased fnl 2f* **20/1**

1m 50.14s (4.24) **Going Correction** +0.55s/f (Yiel)
WFA 3 from 4yo+ 9lb 11 Ran SP% **115.9**
Speed ratings (Par 100): **100,99,97,82,81 75,73,70,69,62**
toteswingers 1&2 £5.60, 1&3 £8.50, 2&3 £8.70 CSF £33.41 CT £212.44 TOTE £7.00: £2.70, £2.20, £2.60; EX 42.40 Trifecta £512.80 Part won. Pool £693.04 - 0.73 winning units..
Owner Mark Preston **Bred** Hellwood Stud Farm **Trained** Scarcroft, W Yorks
■ Stewards' Enquiry : David Bergin three-day ban: careless riding (Jul 16-18)

FOCUS
A fair handicap, run in steadily deteriorating conditions. The winner was confirming her latest C&D effort was no fluke, while the runner-up has been rated as running a small personal best.
Gadobout Dancer Official explanation: trainer said mare became upset in preliminaries; jockey said mare suffered interference first bend

Lady Sledmere(IRE) Official explanation: trainer said filly had a breathing problem

3695 SPINDRIFTER CONDITIONS STKS 6f
4:00 (4:01) (Class 2) 2-Y-O **£7,762** (£2,310; £1,154; £577) **Stalls** Low

Form RPR
14 **1** **Euxton Hall (IRE)**[30] 3702 2-8-12 0 TonyHamilton 1 91+
(Richard Fahey) *cl up on inner: led 2f out: rdn wl over 1f out: drvn ins fnl f: kpt on wl towards fin* **8/11**[1]
31 **2** ¾ **Royal Rascal**[16] 3168 2-8-7 0 DavidAllan 3 84
(Tim Easterby) *cl up: effrt to chal wl over 1f out: sn rdn and ev ch tl drvn ins fnl f and no ex last 75yds* **2/1**[2]
4130 **3** *shd* **Top Notch Tonto (IRE)**[13] 3242 2-8-12 79 PatrickMathers 4 89
(Ian McInnes) *in rr and pushed along after 1f: hdwy over 2f out: rdn to chse ldng pair and edgd lft over 1f out: drvn and styd on strly ins fnl f: nrst fin* **12/1**
321 **4** *28* **Mazeppa**[17] 3112 2-8-12 75 TomEaves 2 5
(Keith Dalgleish) *sn led: rdn along and hdd 2f out: sn wknd* **8/1**[3]

1m 22.05s (5.15) **Going Correction** +0.55s/f (Yiel) **4** Ran SP% **110.0**
Speed ratings (Par 100): **87,86,85,48**
CSF £2.50 TOTE £1.70; EX 2.00.
Owner David W Armstrong **Bred** B Scholer **Trained** Musley Bank, N Yorks

FOCUS
The ground was changed to good to soft following this race. A decent renewal of this conditions race, despite the small field. The winner has been rated to his pre-race level.

NOTEBOOK
Euxton Hall(IRE) bounced back from a somewhat disappointing effort in Listed company last time. The ground at Pontefract was testing enough and that makes his performance even more impressive, as he was in front and there to be shot at as they turned into the straight. Successful on good to soft ground at Haydock on debut, he clearly acts with ease underfoot but should be equally effective on a quicker surface. This represented a drop in class from his Woodcote Stakes run but it's likely he'll be aimed towards pattern company for the remainder of the season, with his confidence sure to be buoyed. (op 4-5)
Royal Rascal had run away with a race on soft ground at York and conditions were very much in her favour here. She may not have been able to follow up, despite her allowances, but it's likely that this represented a significant step forward. She was pushed along at a relatively early stage but kept finding for pressure. Connections ought to be able to pick up another race before too long, especially against her own sex. (op 9-4 tchd 5-2)
Top Notch Tonto(IRE), who stayed on well in the closing stages, was unquestionably the eyecatcher of the race. A creditable 12th in the Windsor Castle, this was the first time he'd tackled 6f and the way he finished off his race suggests he'll get even further, in keeping with his breeding. (op 10-1 tchd 14-1)
Mazeppa, winner of a 7f Musselburgh maiden, was beaten a long, long way and ran as if something was amiss. (op 7-1 tchd 17-2)

3696 BRITISH STALLION STUDS E.B.F./ PARK SUITE FILLIES' H'CAP 6f
4:30 (4:30) (Class 3) (0-90,90) 3-Y-0+
£8,092 (£2,423; £1,211; £605; £302; £152) **Stalls** Low

Form RPR
-230 **1** **Spinatrix**[13] 3255 4-9-1 80 (p) LeeTopliss(3) 1 88
(Michael Dods) *dwlt: rdn along on inner to ld after 1f: jnd over 1f out: drvn ins fnl f: kpt on gamely towards fin* **9/2**[2]
2034 **2** ½ **Bouncy Bouncy (IRE)**[16] 3159 5-9-1 77 (t) HayleyTurner 7 83
(Michael Bell) *dwlt and hld up in rr: hdwy on inner 2f out: rdn to chal over 1f out: drvn and ev ch ins fnl f: no ex last 50yds* **14/1**
0432 **3** ¾ **Wahylah (IRE)**[10] 3342 3-8-12 80 SebSanders 2 82
(Clive Brittain) *towards rr: hdwy over 2f out: effrt and n.m.r wl over 1f out: rdn to chal ent fnl f: ev ch tl drvn and one pce last 75yds* **10/3**[1]
6600 **4** 3 ¼ **Coolminx (IRE)**[15] 3183 5-9-2 85 LauraBarry(7) 4 79
(Richard Fahey) *led early: sn hdd and chsd ldrs: rdn along 1/2-way: sn lost pl and bhd 2f out: rallied and styd on fnl f* **8/1**[3]
-602 **5** 3 ¾ **Song Of Parkes**[37] 2476 5-8-9 71 oh1 DavidAllan 8 53
(Eric Alston) *cl up: rdn along 2f out: drvn and wknd over 1f out* **9/1**
-264 **6** 1 ½ **Camache Queen (IRE)**[10] 3342 4-9-3 79 EddieAhern 3 56
(Denis Coakley) *trckd ldrs gng wl: effrt wl over 1f out: rdn appr fnl f and sn btn* **9/2**[2]
4613 **7** 2 **Avonrose**[14] 3221 5-8-9 71 oh1 (v) PaulMulrennan 6 41
(Derek Shaw) *chsd ldrs on outer: rdn along 2f out: grad wknd* **14/1**
0311 **8** 21 **I'm So Glad**[12] 3288 3-9-8 90 MatthewDavies 5
(Mick Channon) *hld up: hdwy to chse ldrs 2f out: sn rdn and btn* **9/2**[2]

1m 21.46s (4.56) **Going Correction** +0.55s/f (Yiel)
WFA 3 from 4yo+ 6lb **8** Ran SP% **112.1**
Speed ratings (Par 104): **91,90,89,85,80 78,75,47**
toteswingers 1&2 £10.00, 1&3 £4.00, 2&3 £9.10 CSF £60.86 CT £234.78 TOTE £4.90: £1.90, £2.50, £1.10; EX 105.40 Trifecta £385.20 Pool £1,150.55 - 2.21 winning units..
Owner Mrs J W Hutchinson & Mrs P A Knox **Bred** T K & Mrs P A Knox **Trained** Denton, Co Durham

FOCUS
The ground was changed to soft following this contest. A decent fillies' handicap, run at a fair pace. The runner-up has been rated as running a small personal best, with the third in line with her recent 7f form.

NOTEBOOK
Spinatrix made virtually all of the running. She had been rather disappointing when finishing down the field at Thirsk last time, but was allowed her own way out in front and that proved crucial. She hasn't always been the best of starters and again lost ground as the gates opened. However, she was punched through to the lead on the inside rail and kept on bravely to fend off her only two challengers in the straight. She relishes ease underfoot and will surely continue to make an impact while the wet spell continues. (tchd early 7-1 in a place)
Bouncy Bouncy(IRE) sacrificed valuable ground at the start and did well to finish as close as she did. It's likely she'd have gone even closer with a better start but she was always being held on the run-in. She's probably high enough in the weights. (op 12-1)
Wahylah(IRE) had questions to answer on this ground but, well backed beforehand, performed well. She was a bit short of room when launched with her effort but it's unlikely that it made any difference. (op 9-2)
Coolminx(IRE) made up significant ground from an unpromising position. She was badly outpaced throughout and may benefit from a return to 7f. (op 7-1)
Camache Queen(IRE) Official explanation: trainer's rep said filly was unsuited by the soft ground
I'm So Glad Official explanation: trainer's rep said filly was unsuited by the soft ground

3697 WAYNE CONWAY MEMORIAL H'CAP 1m 4f 8y
5:00 (5:01) (Class 5) (0-70,69) 3-Y-O **£2,264** (£673; £336; £168) **Stalls** Low

Form RPR
4623 **1** **Mr Snoozy**[19] 3023 3-8-8 56 DuranFentiman 4 70
(Tim Walford) *towards rr and rn in snatches: pushed along and hdwy on inner over 3f out: led wl over 1f out and sn rdn: drvn ins fnl f: kpt on wl towards fin* **11/1**
0452 **2** *1* **Jennifer J**[18] 3088 3-9-3 65 PaulMulrennan 1 77
(Mark H Tompkins) *a cl up: led briefly over 2f out: sn rdn along and hdd wl over 1f out: drvn to chal and ev ch ins fnl f: no ex last 100yds* **3/1**[1]
-551 **3** *2* **Flashman**[28] 2771 3-9-1 66 LeeTopliss(3) 3 75+
(Richard Fahey) *trckd ldrs: effrt 3f out and sn rdn along: styd on appr fnl f: no imp towards fin* **7/1**[3]
-000 **4** 2 ¼ **Brasingaman Espee**[19] 3023 3-7-13 50 oh5 JulieBurke(3) 12 55
(George Moore) *hld up towards rr: stdy hdwy over 3f out: rdn to chse ldng pair over 1f out: ch ent fnl f: sn wknd* **66/1**
3-06 **5** 2 ½ **Margo Channing**[31] 2679 3-8-4 52 PJMcDonald 5 53
(Micky Hammond) *chsd ldrs: rdn along over 2f out: sn one pce* **18/1**
-003 **6** *2* **Saffa Hill (IRE)**[28] 2772 3-9-7 69 DavidAllan 10 67
(Tim Easterby) *in rr: pushed along 1/2-way: hdwy 3f out: kpt on fnl 2f: n.d* **15/2**
0-06 **7** *14* **Hard Road**[30] 2708 3-8-11 59 ChrisCatlin 6 35
(Chris Wall) *sn rdn along towards rr: sme hdwy on outer and in tch over 4f out: sn drvn and wknd 3f out* **12/1**
4054 **8** *10* **Tallevu (IRE)**[21] 2980 3-9-3 65 RichardKingscote 2 25
(Tom Dascombe) *trckd ldrs: pushed along 3f out: rdn 2f out and sn wknd* **4/1**[2]
2342 **9** *18* **Rosie's Lady (IRE)**[14] 3212 3-8-7 55 TomEaves 8
(David O'Meara) *led: rdn along over 3f out: hdd over 2f out and wknd qckly* **8/1**
0-60 **10** ½ **Isolde's Return**[24] 2877 3-7-13 50 oh5 DeclanCannon(3) 9
(George Moore) *sn rdn along and bhd thrght* **100/1**
00-6 **11** 2 ½ **Astonished Harry (GER)**[19] 3023 3-8-5 53 HayleyTurner 7
(Reg Hollinshead) *chsd ldrs on outer: rdn along 4f out: sn wknd* **20/1**

2m 46.93s (6.13) **Going Correction** +0.55s/f (Yiel) **11** Ran SP% **108.9**
Speed ratings (Par 100): **101,100,99,97,95 94,85,78,66,66 64**
toteswingers 1&2 £7.20, 1&3 £10.30, 2&3 £3.90 CSF £38.53 CT £216.19 TOTE £14.50: £3.60, £1.60, £1.90; EX 51.70 Trifecta £316.10 Pool £657.92 - 1.54 winning units..
Owner T W Heseltine **Bred** J W Mursell **Trained** Sheriff Hutton, N Yorks

FOCUS
A fair 3yo handicap, run at a steady pace in worsening conditions. The form could be okay, with the runner-up likely to improve for a greater test of stamina.

3698 WILFRED UNDERWOOD AND PHILIP UNDERWOOD MEMORIAL CLASSIFIED STKS 6f
5:30 (5:30) (Class 5) 3-Y-O **£2,264** (£673; £336; £168) **Stalls** Low

Form RPR
1-00 **1** **Indego Blues**[26] 2824 3-9-0 73 AdrianNicholls 6 81
(David Nicholls) *mde all: rdn and qcknd clr 2f out: styd on wl* **15/2**[3]
1 **2** 1 ¾ **Minalisa**[11] 3312 3-9-0 75 ChrisCatlin 4 75
(Rae Guest) *in tch: hdwy to chse wnr over 2f out: rdn wl over 1f out: no imp* **2/5**[1]
-210 **3** 1 ¼ **Sunley Pride**[12] 3284 3-9-0 75 MartinHarley 2 71
(Mick Channon) *chsd wnr: rdn along over 2f out: sn one pce* **9/2**[2]
4353 **4** *25* **Scrooby Doo**[17] 3109 3-8-7 67 JordanUys(7) 3
(Scott Dixon) *swvd bdly lft and almost uns rdr s: lost many l and a bhd* **14/1**

1m 22.56s (5.66) **Going Correction** +0.55s/f (Yiel) **4** Ran SP% **108.0**
Speed ratings (Par 100): **84,81,80,46**
CSF £11.47 TOTE £5.10; EX 9.70.
Owner Pinnacle Indesatchel Partnership **Bred** Bearstone Stud **Trained** Sessay, N Yorks
■ Stewards' Enquiry : Jordan Uys five-day ban: used whip when out of contention (Aug 3-7)

FOCUS
A small-field classified contest, run in testing conditions. The winner has been rated to his best in what was a messy race.
Scrooby Doo Official explanation: jockey said filly missed the break

3699 ANNUAL BADGE HOLDER DAY H'CAP 1m 4y
6:00 (6:00) (Class 5) (0-75,75) 3-Y-O+ **£2,264** (£673; £336; £168) **Stalls** Low

Form RPR
506 **1** **Vito Volterra (IRE)**[15] 3185 5-9-12 73 AdrianNicholls 2 85+
(Michael Smith) *mde all: rdn clr 2f out: drvn and kpt on wl fnl f* **9/4**[1]
035- **2** 3 ¼ **Honoured (IRE)**[93] 7564 5-8-2 56 oh4 (t) ShirleyTeasdale(7) 4 61
(Michael Appleby) *in tch: hdwy on inner 3f out: rdn along 2f out: swtchd rt and drvn over 1f out: styd on ins fnl f: nt rch wnr* **33/1**
1-05 **3** 1 ¼ **Change The Subject (USA)**[48] 2142 4-9-11 72 (t) HayleyTurner 1 74
(Peter Salmon) *dwlt and towards rr: hdwy on inner over 2f out: rdn to chse ldrs over 1f out: jkpt on same pce* **5/1**[2]
040- **4** *5* **Tukitinyasok (IRE)**[303] 5733 5-8-13 60 (p) TonyHamilton 7 50
(Clive Mulhall) *chsd wnr: rdn along 2f out: drvn wl over 1f out and grad wknd* **20/1**
6603 **5** ¾ **Merchant Of Medici**[10] 3354 5-9-9 75 GarryWhillans(5) 9 63
(Micky Hammond) *dwlt and hld up in rr: hdwy 1/2-way: rdn to chse ldrs 2f out: sn btn* **5/1**[2]
1040 **6** *10* **Tapis Libre**[17] 3129 4-9-9 70 PaulMulrennan 11 35
(Michael Easterby) *chsd ldrs: rdn along 3f out: sn wknd* **9/1**
3451 **7** *1* **Copperwood**[14] 3215 7-9-10 71 AdamKirby 10 34
(Mark Johnston) *chsd ldng pair: rdn along over 2f out: sn wknd* **13/2**[3]
02 **8** *14* **Iulus**[28] 2765 4-9-3 64 (e[1]) MichaelO'Connell 8
(John Quinn) *hld up: effrt 3f out: sn rdn and wknd* **15/2**
6043 **9** *58* **Count Bertoni (IRE)**[6] 3459 5-9-10 71 (b) TomEaves 12
(David O'Meara) *sn chsng ldrs: rdn along over 3f out: wknd qckly* **15/2**

1m 51.67s (5.77) **Going Correction** +0.55s/f (Yiel)
WFA 3 from 4yo+ 9lb **9** Ran SP% **118.7**
Speed ratings (Par 103): **93,89,88,83,82 72,71,57,**
toteswingers 1&2 £22.70, 1&3 £4.60, 2&3 £13.30 CSF £89.74 CT £321.43 TOTE £3.00: £1.20, £6.00, £1.80; EX 97.00 Trifecta £519.90 Part won. Pool £702.68 - 0.10 winning units..
Owner Ace Racing **Bred** O McElroy **Trained** Kirkheaton, Northumberland

FOCUS
A fair handicap run at a steady pace. The runner-up ran his best race since his 3yo days on his first start for his new yard, while the third has been rated close to his 3yo turf form.
Count Bertoni(IRE) Official explanation: jockey said gelding stopped quickly

T/Plt: £437.70 to a £1 stake. Pool: £75169.93 - 125.35 winning tickets T/Qpdt: £34.60 to a £1 stake. Pool: £7505.90 - 160.30 winning tickets JR

3666 WINDSOR (R-H)

Monday, July 2

OFFICIAL GOING: Good (good to firm in places) changing to good after race 1 (6:40)

Wind: Almost nil Weather: Raining before meeting; overcast with drizzle

3700 BETFRED HOME OF BIG WINNERS FILLIES' MEDIAN AUCTION MAIDEN STKS 5f 10y

6:40 (6:40) (Class 5) 2-Y-O £2,264 (£673; £336; £168) **Stalls** Low

Form RPR

22 **1** **Hoyam**[12] 3269 2-9-0 0 JamieSpencer 4 79+
(Michael Bell) *hld up bhd ldrs: weaving arnd looking for a passage fr 2f out: fnd way through to ld ins fnl f: pushed out* **1/5**[1]

5 **2** *1 1/4* **Dusty Storm (IRE)**[44] 2282 2-9-0 0 FrannyNorton 10 71
(Ed McMahon) *t.k.h: hld up bhd ldrs on outer: prog to chal 1f out: styd on but no real ch w wnr* **11/1**

3 *nk* **Clean Blow (USA)** 2-9-0 0 RichardMullen 7 69
(David Brown) *mde most against nr side rail: hdd and one pce ins fnl f* **6/1**[2]

62 **4** *1 1/4* **Hot Secret**[14] 3217 2-9-0 0 JimmyFortune 1 65
(Andrew Balding) *s.i.s: hld up in tch: prog to chse ldr wl over 1f out: no ex ins fnl f* **8/1**[3]

60 **5** *8* **Little Miss Zuri (IRE)**[13] 3242 2-9-0 0 LiamKeniry 5 36
(Sylvester Kirk) *t.k.h: trckd ldr to wl over 1f out: wknd qckly fnl f* **33/1**

6 *3 1/2* **Our Three Graces (IRE)** 2-8-11 0 HarryBentley(3) 3 24
(Gary Moore) *dwlt: mostly in last pair: wknd wl over 1f out* **20/1**

0 **7** *1 3/4* **Jackpot**[13] 3242 2-9-0 0 KirstyMilczarek 2 17
(Brendan Powell) *a in last pair: wknd wl over 1f out* **50/1**

43 **8** *13* **Sand And Deliver**[23] 2938 2-9-0 0 IanMongan 9
(Peter Crate) *t.k.h: trckd ldr to 2f out: wknd rapidly: heavily eased fnl f* **8/1**[3]

1m 0.56s (0.26) **Going Correction** -0.05s/f (Good) **8** Ran SP% **137.8**

Speed ratings (Par 91): **95,93,92,90,77 72,69,48**

toteswingers 1&2 £2.70, 1&3 £2.00, 2&3 £11.00 CSF £6.55 TOTE £1.30: £1.02, £4.50, £1.80; EX 7.50 Trifecta £42.10 Pool £11,165.42 - 195.86 winning units..

Owner Ahmad Al Shaikh **Bred** Brook Stud Bloodstock Ltd **Trained** Newmarket, Suffolk

FOCUS

Inner of straight dolled out 4yds at 6f then reducing to full width of course at Winning Post. Top bend dolled out 3yds from normal inner configuration adding 12yds to race distances of 1m and over. With the ground easing it was interesting to see where the riders elected to go in this modest opening fillies' juvenile maiden, but they clearly didn't feel it was too bad as they shunned the far side. It was run at a decent pace. The fifth and the time of the race help put the form in perspective.

NOTEBOOK

Hoyam rates value for further than the winning margin. Michael Bell's filly was nigh on impossible to oppose on the strength of her second in the Queen Mary at Royal Ascot 12 days earlier and indeed the strength of her second over C&D in May entitled her to be the clear favourite. Jamie Spencer was determined to find cover, but she pulled hard and covered plenty of ground in attempting to get a run when things became tight from 2f out. Such was her superiority, however, she quickened smartly and was well on top at the finish. There is a lot of speed in her pedigree, but her dam has produced a 6f 2yo winner and stepping up a furlong now looks her best option. The Cherry Hinton at Newmarket later this month may suit, but there is also the Princess Margaret Stakes back at Ascot, and that looks favourite considering her proven liking for the course.

Dusty Storm(IRE) improved a good bit on her Thirsk debut in May and deserves credit as she was drawn widest of all. There should be a small maiden to be won with her. (op 14-1)

Clean Blow(USA), whose dam won a 6f Group 3, met support and knew her job, leading on the stands' rail. She paid for her exertions late on, but this was a promising start and she should be well up to winning. (op 10-1)

Hot Secret posted a solid effort on this third outing and ought to find her feet when the nurseries kick off later this month. (op 5-1)

Sand And Deliver got warm and edgy down at the start. Something clearly wasn't right with her.

3701 BETFRED STILL TREBLE ODDS ON LUCKY 15'S (S) STKS 6f

7:10 (7:10) (Class 6) 3-Y-0+ £1,617 (£481; £240; £120) **Stalls** Low

Form RPR

0300 **1** **National Hope (IRE)**[5] 3511 4-8-11 62 (tp) PatCosgrave 8 65
(George Baker) *disp ld at gd pce and racd against nr side rail: hrd rdn to gain upper hand over 1f out: styd on wl* **6/1**[3]

-000 **2** *2 1/4* **Pose (IRE)**[16] 3151 5-8-11 52 (t) DaneO'Neill 6 58
(Roger Ingram) *trckd ldng trio: effrt 2f out: styd on to take 2nd ins fnl f: no imp on wnr* **20/1**

0350 **3** *1/2* **Anjomarba (IRE)**[7] 3442 5-8-11 58 (b[1]) KirstyMilczarek 7 56
(Conor Dore) *t.k.h: trckd ldng pair: rdn 2f out: no imp and lost 3rd over 1f out: kpt on* **5/1**[2]

0046 **4** *1/2* **Memphis Man**[6] 3466 9-8-13 54 MatthewCosham(3) 1 60
(David Evans) *settled wl in rr and wl off the pce: pushed along 2f out: styd on fr over 1f out: nrst fin* **9/1**

0-00 **5** *1/2* **Mandianna (IRE)**[124] 734 3-8-5 53 JohnFahy 4 51
(Jo Crowley) *mostly in midfield and off the pce: styd on against rail fr over 1f out: nrst fin* **20/1**

-520 **6** *1 1/2* **Scarlet Rocks (IRE)**[37] 2503 4-8-11 64 (p) DavidProbert 10 48
(David Evans) *disp ld at gd pce: rdn and nt qckn over 1f out: wknd ins fnl f* **13/8**[1]

4000 **7** *1 1/4* **Griffin Point (IRE)**[23] 2943 5-8-11 53 JimCrowley 5 44
(William Muir) *nvr bttr than midfield and a off the pce: rdn over 2f out: no prog* **20/1**

306 **8** *1 3/4* **Divine Rule (IRE)**[25] 2845 4-9-0 52 (b) CharlotteJenner(7) 9 49
(Laura Mongan) *s.i.s: a towards rr: swtchd lft jst over 3f out: no prog* **25/1**

0-00 **9** *1 1/2* **Baltic Flyer (IRE)**[17] 3118 3-8-5 59 PaoloSirigu 11 32
(Robert Eddery) *stmbld s: wl off the pce in last pair: bmpd jst over 3f out: no prog* **16/1**

4205 **10** *12* **Sugar Prince (IRE)**[96] 1072 3-8-10 70 JamieSpencer 2
(Tim Pitt) *s.s: a in last pair and wl off the pce: eased whn no ch over 1f out* **7/1**

1m 12.68s (-0.32) **Going Correction** -0.05s/f (Good)

WFA 3 from 4yo+ 6lb **10** Ran SP% **115.6**

Speed ratings (Par 101): **100,97,96,95,95 93,91,89,87,71**

toteswingers 1&2 £42.40, 1&3 £8.30, 2&3 £20.60 CSF £120.22 TOTE £7.40: £2.30, £6.60, £2.10; EX 139.90 Trifecta £1750.90 Pool £2,886.73 - 1.22 winning units..The winner was bought in £5,000. Scarlet Rocks was claimed by Mr J. Darby for £5,000.

Owner Bowditch, Knox & Partners **Bred** Oghill House Stud & Jimmy Hyland **Trained** Whitsbury, Hants

FOCUS

They went hard early up front in this seller. It has been rated around the winner to this year's form.

3702 BETFRED MOBILE CASINO MAIDEN STKS 6f

7:40 (7:40) (Class 5) 3-4-Y-O £2,264 (£673; £336; £168) **Stalls** Low

Form RPR

04 **1** **Nocturn**[37] 2501 3-9-3 0 WilliamBuick 11 78+
(Jeremy Noseda) *w ldrs: upsides 2f out: hanging and nt qckn wl over 1f out: stl hanging but galvanized and r.o to ld last 100yds: sn clr* **7/4**[1]

U0-0 **2** *2* **Blue Tiger**[59] 1824 3-9-3 67 (t) MickaelBarzalona 8 72
(Saeed Bin Suroor) *awkward s: wl in rr early: prog on outer over 3f out: led wl over 1f out: hdd and outpcd last 100yds: stmbld and uns rdr after fin* **16/1**

3 *2 1/4* **Angelito** 3-9-3 0 FrannyNorton 5 65+
(Ed McMahon) *hld up bhd ldrs: pushed along 2f out: styd on to take 3rd 1f out: no imp on ldng pair* **15/2**[3]

4-4 **4** *2 1/2* **Norlander**[39] 2422 3-8-12 0 JimCrowley 12 52
(Ralph Beckett) *pressed ldrs: cl enough 2f out: fdd 1f out* **16/1**

65-0 **5** *3/4* **Generalyse**[46] 2205 3-9-3 71 PatDobbs 6 54
(Ben De Haan) *hld up in midfield: gng wl 1/2-way: pushed along and outpcd fr over 1f out* **10/1**

43 **6** *3/4* **Funcheon Vale (IRE)**[11] 3312 3-8-12 0 DarryllHolland 1 47
(Hughie Morrison) *taken down early: prom: cl up 2f out: fdd over 1f out* **9/1**

60 **7** *nk* **Monzino (USA)**[19] 3024 4-9-4 0 LeonnaMayor(5) 13 53
(Michael Chapman) *dwlt: rcvrd on outer and in tch in midfield 1/2-way: fdd over 1f out* **200/1**

42-5 **8** *2 1/4* **Dark Don (IRE)**[35] 2542 3-9-3 72 RobertWinston 14 44
(Charles Hills) *mde most: tk field down centre fr 1/2-way: hdd & wknd wl over 1f out* **10/3**[2]

3 **9** *2 1/4* **Exceedexpectations (IRE)**[21] 2974 3-9-3 0 JamieSpencer 3 37+
(Michael Bell) *broke wl but restrained into last pair: shuffled along 2f out: passed sme tiring rivals fnl f: nvr remotely involved* **8/1**

5-0 **10** *1* **Triple Salchow**[89] 1182 3-8-12 0 TedDurcan 2 28
(Alastair Lidderdale) *in tch in midfield: pushed along over 2f out: wknd over 1f out* **100/1**

0-0 **11** *hd* **Tijuca (IRE)**[21] 2974 3-8-12 0 LiamKeniry 7 28
(Ed de Giles) *hld up in midfield: pushed along and lost pl fr over 2f out: n.d after* **200/1**

0 **12** *nk* **Rupeetoups**[9] 3389 4-9-9 0 DaneO'Neill 9 34
(Henry Candy) *taken down early: in tch in midfield: shkn up 2f out: steadily wknd* **100/1**

0 **13** *2* **Barnacle**[9] 3389 3-9-3 0 IanMongan 10 25
(Pat Eddery) *sn rdn in last pair: nvr a factor* **66/1**

0- **14** *7* **Waldstein**[251] 7080 3-9-3 0 ShaneKelly 4
(Dean Ivory) *v free to post: in tch to 1/2-way: sn wknd* **150/1**

1m 12.96s (-0.04) **Going Correction** -0.05s/f (Good)

WFA 3 from 4yo 6lb **14** Ran SP% **118.3**

Speed ratings (Par 103): **98,95,92,89,88 87,86,83,80,79 79,78,75,66**

toteswingers 1&2 £6.60, 1&3 £6.90, 2&3 £35.00 CSF £34.33 TOTE £2.80: £1.30, £3.00, £2.80; EX 26.80 Trifecta £269.40 Pool £2,505.31 - 6.88 winning units..

Owner Miss Yvonne Jacques **Bred** J Ellis **Trained** Newmarket, Suffolk

FOCUS

Little strength in depth to this sprint maiden and the first pair dominated from the furlong marker. The rain looked to be getting into the ground at last and the riders mainly ignored the stands' side this time. The form is unconvincing with the form choice only finishing eighth.

Dark Don(IRE) Official explanation: jockey said colt hung left

Exceedexpectations(IRE) Official explanation: jockey said gelding ran too free to post and early on in race

3703 BETFRED THE BONUS KING H'CAP 1m 2f 7y

8:10 (8:10) (Class 4) (0-80,80) 3-Y-0+ £4,204 (£1,251; £625; £312) **Stalls** Centre

Form RPR

032- **1** **Blue Surf**[310] 5475 3-9-3 **80** PatDobbs 6 90
(Amanda Perrett) *prog to trck ldng trio after 3f: rdn to chse new ldr 2f out: styd on to ld last 150yds* **9/1**

10-4 **2** *1 1/4* **Destiny Of Dreams**[73] 1491 4-9-13 **79** DaneO'Neill 9 86
(Jo Crowley) *hld up in midfield: smooth prog over 3f out: led main gp over 2f out and sn overall ldr: drvn and hdd last 150yds: one pce* **14/1**

0123 **3** *3/4* **Choral Festival**[2] 3643 6-9-10 **76** KieranO'Neill 4 82
(John Bridger) *hld up in midfield: prog over 2f out: hanging u.p but styd on to take 3rd nr fin* **11/2**[3]

2201 **4** *nk* **Royal Etiquette (IRE)**[14] 3222 5-8-9 **66** LeonnaMayor(5) 13 71
(Lawney Hill) *hld up wl in rr: prog on wd outside over 3f out: chsd ldng pair u.p over 1f out: kpt on but lost 3rd nr fin* **12/1**

-200 **5** *2 1/2* **If I Were A Boy (IRE)**[7] 3443 5-9-2 **68** (p) JamesDoyle 1 68
(Dominic Ffrench Davis) *mde most: one of two styng nr side 3f out: lost overall ld arnd 2f out: one pce* **33/1**

5-53 **6** *hd* **Drummond**[49] 2126 3-8-10 **73** JohnFahy 10 73
(Clive Cox) *trckd ldr: styd nr side 3f out and nt clr run against rail w only one rival to pass: swtchd lft and one pce fnl 2f* **9/1**

1-03 **7** *1 3/4* **Keepax**[23] 2942 3-8-13 **76** TedDurcan 3 72
(Chris Wall) *trckd ldrs: rdn over 3f out: tried to chal over 2f out: wknd over 1f out* **4/1**[2]

-022 **8** *1/2* **Urban Space**[14] 3222 6-9-7 **73** JamieSpencer 2 68
(John Flint) *a in midfield: rdn and no prog over 2f out* **7/2**[1]

1105 **9** *1/2* **Indian Art (IRE)**[20] 3011 6-9-12 **78** JimmyFortune 5 72
(Sylvester Kirk) *restrained into last pair: nvr a factor: modest late prog* **28/1**

6-00 **10** *2 1/2* **Mahadee (IRE)**[14] 3226 7-9-6 **72** (p) LiamKeniry 7 61
(Ed de Giles) *hld up wl in rr: shkn up and no prog over 2f out: no ch after* **50/1**

1116 **11** *3/4* **St Ignatius**[3] 3594 5-9-4 **77** (p) NatashaEaton(7) 8 65
(Alan Bailey) *trckd ldng pair: on terms whn c alone towards centre 3f out: lost pl qckly fnl 2f* **10/1**

000/ **12** *12* **Encompassing (IRE)**[351] 6343 5-9-12 **78** (t) NeilCallan 14 42
(Sophie Leech) *restrained into last pair: rdn and sme prog 3f out: wknd 2f out: t.o* **66/1**

0035 **13** *1/2* **Aciano (IRE)**[32] 2623 4-9-6 **72** ShaneKelly 12 35
(Brendan Powell) *wl in tch tl wknd u.p fr 3f out: t.o* **33/1**

102- **14** *18* **On Khee**[96] 5328 5-10-0 **80** JimCrowley 11
(David Pipe) *a towards rr: reminder and wknd over 2f out: eased and wl t.o* **10/1**

2m 6.93s (-1.77) **Going Correction** -0.05s/f (Good)
WFA 3 from 4yo+ 11lb **14** Ran SP% **122.9**
Speed ratings (Par 105): **105,104,103,103,101 101,99,99,98,96 96,86,86,71**
toteswingers 1&2 £28.80, 2&3 £23.10, 1&3 £13.40 CSF £126.21 TOTE £11.40: £3.40, £5.20, £2.70; EX 234.60 Trifecta £1348.50 Part won. Pool £1,822.33 - 0.50 winning units..
Owner The Green Dot Partnership **Bred** Star Pointe Ltd,Brosnan And Williamson **Trained** Pulborough, W Sussex

FOCUS
An open handicap. It developed into a messy race down the home straight with most of the riders taking time to cross over to the far side. The form looks solid enough, though, rated through the runner-up, third and fourth.
On Khee Official explanation: jockey said mare was slowly away and slipped on bend

3704 BETFRED MOBILE FILLIES' H'CAP 1m 3f 135y
8:40 (8:40) (Class 5) (0-70,69) 3-Y-O+ **£2,264** (£673; £336; £168) **Stalls** Centre

Form RPR

1-02 **1** **Bernisdale**[7] 3443 4-9-10 **65** JamieSpencer 4 72
(John Flint) *mde all: urged along leaving stalls to assert: hrd rdn fnl 2f: fought off chairs gamely* **7/2**[2]

506- **2** *3/4* **Ironically (IRE)**[278] 6443 3-8-9 **63** TedDurcan 1 69
(David Lanigan) *hld up in 8th: prog 3f out: nt clr run briefly over 2f out: styd on to chse wnr 1f out and looked real threat: hld whn short of room nr fin* **11/1**

-501 **3** *1 1/4* **Zowaina**[14] 3233 3-9-1 **69** NeilCallan 8 73
(Roger Varian) *prom: chsd wnr 2f out and cl enough: hrd rdn and one pce over 1f out* **5/2**[1]

33-2 **4** *6* **Suzi's A Class Act**[18] 3077 4-9-12 **67** (p) JamesDoyle 11 61
(James Eustace) *mostly chsd wnr to 3f out: wknd over 1f out* **7/1**

4002 **5** *3 1/4* **Painted Tail (IRE)**[14] 3213 5-9-12 **67** RobertWinston 6 55
(Alan Swinbank) *hld up in 7th: shkn up and effrt over 3f out: no imp on ldrs 2f out: fdd* **4/1**[3]

6 *1* **Vakiyla (FR)**[134] 4-10-0 **69** WilliamBuick 3 56
(David Simcock) *hld up in last pair: shkn up over 3f out: limited prog over 2f out: no ch over 1f out* **14/1**

3004 **7** *6* **Mazij**[12] 3290 4-9-13 **68** JimCrowley 10 44
(Peter Hiatt) *trckd ldrs and sn in 5th: rdn and wl on terms over 2f out: wknd wl over 1f out* **14/1**

00-0 **8** *6* **Swift Winged**[25] 2848 3-8-1 **55** NickyMackay 9 21
(Hughie Morrison) *hld up in 6th and quite keen early: wknd wl over 2f out* **20/1**

5-05 **9** *nse* **Formidable Guest**[9] 3392 8-8-12 **53** IanMongan 7 27
(Jamie Poulton) *trckd ldng trio: chsd wnr 3f out to 2f out: wknd rapidly* **25/1**

6036 **10** *16* **Rather Cool**[6] 3472 4-8-12 **53** oh4 KieranO'Neill 2
(John Bridger) *dwlt: mostly in last pair: wknd 3f out: t.o* **25/1**

2m 28.82s (-0.68) **Going Correction** -0.05s/f (Good)
WFA 3 from 4yo+ 13lb **10** Ran SP% **117.4**
Speed ratings (Par 100): **100,99,98,94,92 91,87,83,83,73**
toteswingers 1&2 £11.00, 1&3 £1.50, 2&3 £10.70 CSF £40.64 TOTE £5.10: £1.70, £3.40, £1.30; EX 40.70 TRIFECTA Pool £884.33 - 2.34 winning units..
Owner Roderick James **Bred** Evelyn Duchess Of Sutherland **Trained** Kenfig Hill, Bridgend

FOCUS
The principals came nicely clear in this fillies' handicap and again the main action was on the far side. The winner was well in at the weights and ran to a similar level as the previous week over 1m2f.
Mazij Official explanation: trainer said filly was unsuited by the good ground
Formidable Guest Official explanation: trainer's rep said mare was unsuited by the good ground

3705 BETFRED MOBILE SPORTS H'CAP 1m 67y
9:10 (9:10) (Class 5) (0-70,76) 3-Y-O+ **£2,264** (£673; £336; £168) **Stalls** Low

Form RPR

56-1 **1** **Viscount Vert (IRE)**[7] 3432 3-9-11 **76** 6ex DavidProbert 5 84+
(Andrew Balding) *trckd ldng trio: shkn up and effrt 2f out: chsd ldr over 1f out: drvn to ld last 150yds: styd on wl* **11/4**[1]

0535 **2** *1* **My Lord**[82] 1307 4-9-9 **65** IanMongan 8 71
(Luke Dace) *trckd ldr to 1/2-way: styd cl up: rdn to ld 2f out: hdd and one pce last 150yds* **18/1**

0400 **3** *2 1/4* **Calypso Magic (IRE)**[25] 2847 4-9-9 **65** (t) KirstyMilczarek 6 66
(Olivia Maylam) *taken down early: led to 3f out: styd in centre after: kpt on fr over 1f out: unable to chal* **25/1**

4450 **4** *1 1/2* **Rock Anthem (IRE)**[9] 3388 8-9-12 **68** PatDobbs 4 65
(Mike Murphy) *dwlt: hld up: last tl prog jst over 2f out: chsd ldrs over 1f out: rdn and kpt on same pce after* **9/1**

0215 **5** *1 1/2* **Lightning Spirit**[13] 3247 4-9-1 **57** (p) JamesDoyle 10 51
(Gary Moore) *hld up in rr: prog towards far rail over 2f out: one pce fr over 1f out* **13/2**

0400 **6** *1 1/2* **Kings 'n Dreams**[14] 3225 5-9-10 **66** NickyMackay 14 56
(Dean Ivory) *t.k.h: prom: trckd ldr 1/2-way: led 3f out to 2f out: wknd fnl f* **12/1**

0002 **7** *1 1/2* **Last Destination (IRE)**[19] 3032 4-9-1 **57** JimmyFortune 9 44
(Nigel Tinkler) *a in midfield: rdn over 2f out: no prog over 1f out: fdd* **5/1**[2]

536- **8** *1/2* **I'm Harry**[226] 7494 3-9-3 **68** PatCosgrave 3 54
(George Baker) *hld up in midfield: rdn over 2f out: no prog: wknd fnl f* **6/1**[3]

1040 **9** *hd* **Byrd In Hand (IRE)**[18] 3073 5-9-4 **60** KieranO'Neill 2 45
(John Bridger) *hld up in rr: prog and styd in centre 3f out: wknd over 1f out* **7/1**

200- **10** *nk* **Play The Blues (IRE)**[373] 3412 5-9-6 **65** (t[1]) RyanPowell(3) 11 50
(Roger Curtis) *t.k.h and racd wd: in tch: effrt and on terms 3f out: wknd 2f out* **50/1**

032 **11** *4 1/2* **West Leake (IRE)**[34] 2586 6-9-4 **60** LiamKeniry 13 34
(Paul Burgoyne) *sltly awkward s: t.k.h: trckd ldrs: wl there over 2f out: wknd qckly* **14/1**

1m 44.38s (-0.32) **Going Correction** -0.05s/f (Good)
WFA 3 from 4yo+ 9lb **11** Ran SP% **118.9**
Speed ratings (Par 103): **99,98,95,94,92 91,89,89,89,88 84**
toteswingers 1&2 £13.60, 2&3 £111.10, 1&3 £25.10 CSF £58.84 TOTE £3.30: £1.50, £5.30, £5.70; EX 70.40 TRIFECTA Not won..
Owner Martin & Valerie Slade & Partner **Bred** Scuderia San Pancrazio Sas **Trained** Kingsclere, Hants

FOCUS
This moderate handicap looked a tight affair on paper, but the first pair had it to themselves in the final furlong. The runner-up has been rated to his best since his 2yo season, with the fourth close to this year's form.
West Leake(IRE) Official explanation: jockey said gelding ran too free
T/Jkpt: £6,993.30 to a £1 stake. Pool: £261,019.34 - 26.50 winning tickets T/Plt: £230.40 to a £1 stake. Pool: £14,6272.88 - 463.26 winning tickets T/Qpdt: £29.40 to a £1 stake. Pool: £1,2202.18 - 306.45 winning tickets JN

3449 WOLVERHAMPTON (A.W) (L-H)
Monday, July 2

OFFICIAL GOING: Standard
Wind: Light behind Weather: Raining

3706 BET TOTEPLACEPOT TEXT TOTE TO 89660 H'CAP 5f 216y(P)
2:15 (2:16) (Class 6) (0-65,64) 3-Y-O **£1,704** (£503; £251) **Stalls** Low

Form RPR

3460 **1** **Majestic Breeze (IRE)**[7] 3442 3-8-6 **49** SilvestreDeSousa 2 54
(Brian Ellison) *a.p: chsd ldr 2f out: rdn and r.o to ld post* **10/1**

205 **2** *nse* **Kyllachy Dancer**[27] 2795 3-9-1 **58** (v) MichaelO'Connell 9 63
(John Quinn) *chsd ldrs: rdn to ld over 1f out: hung rt: hdd post* **13/2**

0-46 **3** *1* **Hadrians Rule (IRE)**[68] 1595 3-9-0 **57** JamesSullivan 10 61+
(Tim Easterby) *a.p: rdn and ev ch fr over 1f out: sn carried rt: hmpd ins fnl f: unable qck nr fin* **4/1**[2]

2554 **4** *2* **Samba Night (IRE)**[19] 3050 3-9-5 **62** (v) LukeMorris 7 57
(James Eustace) *mid-div: sn pushed along: rdn over 2f out: styd on u.p ins fnl f: nt trble ldrs* **5/1**[3]

0-30 **5** *3/4* **Lazeez (USA)**[32] 2628 3-9-1 **58** (b[1]) MartinDwyer 5 51
(Clive Brittain) *s.i.s: outpcd: r.o ins fnl f: nvr nrr* **14/1**

31- **6** *2 3/4* **Compton Ashdown**[242] 7248 3-9-0 **64** NicoleNordblad(7) 4 48
(Hans Adielsson) *chsd ldr 4f: rdn: hung lft and no ex fnl f* **6/1**

000 **7** *1 1/4* **Compton Crofter**[25] 2864 3-9-0 **57** (t) JamesDoyle 3 37
(Hans Adielsson) *sn pushed along towards rr: styd on fr over 1f out: nvr trbld ldrs* **20/1**

46-0 **8** *1 1/4* **Kara's Vision**[10] 3357 3-8-9 **52** LiamKeniry 6 28
(Robert Cowell) *hld up: rdn over 2f out: sme hdwy u.p over 1f out: hung lft and wknd fnl f* **33/1**

-003 **9** *5* **Yes It's The Boy (USA)**[20] 2996 3-9-4 **61** (b[1]) NeilCallan 1 21
(Ed Walker) *led: racd keenly: rdn and hdd over 1f out: wknd ins fnl f* **11/4**[1]

-060 **10** *2 1/2* **Angel Kiss (IRE)**[12] 3275 3-8-2 **45** KellyHarrison 8
(Colin Teague) *sn outpcd: lost tch fr 1/2-way* **100/1**

1m 14.5s (-0.50) **Going Correction** -0.075s/f (Stan) **10** Ran SP% **115.4**
Speed ratings (Par 98): **100,99,98,95,94 91,89,87,81,77**
toteswingers 1&2 £9.60, 1&3 £6.90, 2&3 £4.90 CSF £71.51 CT £311.42 TOTE £11.40: £2.40, £2.70, £1.40; EX 98.60.
Owner Koo's Racing Club **Bred** Yvonne & Gerard Kennedy **Trained** Norton, N Yorks
■ Stewards' Enquiry : Michael O'Connell four-day ban: careless riding (Jul 16-19)

FOCUS
A moderate sprint handicap in which the leaders may have gone off too quickly. The winner appeared to want it more than the second and third, and the runner-up has been rated close to his 2yo debut form.

3707 BET TOTEPOOL TEXT TOTE TO 89660 (S) STKS 5f 20y(P)
2:45 (2:45) (Class 6) 3-Y-O+ **£1,704** (£503; £251) **Stalls** Low

Form RPR

P-00 **1** **Jack Smudge**[18] 3076 4-9-4 72 (b) GrahamLee 4 72
(James Given) *led 1f: chsd ldr: rdn to ld ins fnl f: r.o* **16/1**

030 **2** *1/2* **Crimea (IRE)**[2] 3608 6-9-4 80 AdrianNicholls 1 70+
(David Nicholls) *hld up: hdwy over 1f out: rdn to chse wnr wl ins fnl f: r.o* **4/5**[1]

2002 **3** *1 1/4* **Falasteen (IRE)**[25] 2838 5-9-4 76 (b) SilvestreDeSousa 2 65
(Patrick Morris) *plld hrd and prom: rdn and nt clr run ins fnl f: r.o* **7/2**[2]

0060 **4** *1 1/4* **Lucky Art (USA)**[13] 3256 6-8-13 61 DavidKenny(5) 7 61
(Conor Dore) *led 4f out: rdn 1/2-way: hdd and no ex ins fnl f* **25/1**

0652 **5** *3/4* **Loyal Royal (IRE)**[42] 2352 9-9-4 57 (bt) LiamKeniry 5 58
(Milton Bradley) *trckd ldrs: plld hrd: rdn over 1f out: styd on same pce* **16/1**

0436 **6** *1 3/4* **Mother Jones**[27] 2789 4-9-1 67 MatthewCosham(3) 6 52
(David Evans) *s.i.s: hdwy over 3f out: rdn over 1f out: wknd fnl f* **5/1**[3]

0006 **7** *hd* **Speedyfix**[21] 2971 5-9-4 52 (vt) TomMcLaughlin 8 51
(Christine Dunnett) *s.i.s: rdn and hung lft over 1f out: nvr on terms* **66/1**

-560 **8** *4 1/2* **Matsunosuke**[16] 3159 10-9-4 82 JoeFanning 9 35
(Dr Richard Newland) *prom tl wknd wl over 1f out* **11/1**

1m 1.93s (-0.37) **Going Correction** -0.075s/f (Stan) **8** Ran SP% **119.9**
Speed ratings (Par 101): **99,98,96,94,93 90,89,82**
toteswingers 1&2 £4.50, 1&3 £7.50, 2&3 £1.80 CSF £30.98 TOTE £12.80: £3.40, £1.10, £1.60; EX 41.90.The winner was bought in for 6,500gns. Crimea was subject to a friendly claim of £6,000. Falasteen was subject to a friendly claim of £6,000.
Owner Danethorpe Racing Partnership **Bred** P And Mrs A G Venner **Trained** Willoughton, Lincs

FOCUS
A weak seller. It's been rated around the fourth to this year's form.

3708 BRITISH STALLION STUDS SUPPORTING BRITISH RACING E B F MAIDEN STKS 7f 32y(P)
3:15 (3:16) (Class 5) 2-Y-O **£3,137** (£933; £466; £233) **Stalls** High

Form RPR

02 **1** **Oasis Cannes**[17] 3112 2-9-3 0 LukeMorris 3 75+
(Sir Mark Prescott Bt) *chsd ldr: rdn over 1f out: r.o to ld wl ins fnl f* **2/5**[1]

46 **2** *1 1/4* **Kalicamix**[23] 2929 2-9-3 0 PhillipMakin 6 72
(Paul Cole) *led: rdn over 1f out: hdd and unable qck ins fnl f* **7/1**[3]

4 **3** *7* **Aseela (IRE)**[27] 2784 2-8-12 0 MartinDwyer 5 50
(Clive Brittain) *sn prom: rdn over 2f out: wknd over 1f out* **5/1**[2]

4 *1/2* **Just A Pound (IRE)** 2-9-3 0 J-PGuillambert 4 54
(Jo Hughes) *s.i.s: effrt 1/2-way: outpcd fr over 2f out* **50/1**

6 **5** *5* **Kingsville**[7] 3452 2-9-3 0 JoeFanning 2 41
(Mark Johnston) *chsd ldrs: rdn 1/2-way: wknd over 1f out* **22/1**

6 *14* **Bitter Ale** 2-9-3 0 IPoullis 1 7
(Alan McCabe) *s.i.s and wnt lft s: a bhd: lost tch fr 1/2-way* **50/1**

1m 30.32s (0.72) **Going Correction** -0.075s/f (Stan) **6** Ran SP% **108.9**
Speed ratings (Par 94): **92,90,82,82,76 60**
toteswingers 1&2 £1.30, 1&3 £1.20, 2&3 £1.90 CSF £3.39 TOTE £2.00: £1.10, £1.70; EX 3.60.
Owner J L C Pearce **Bred** J L C Pearce **Trained** Newmarket, Suffolk

FOCUS
An uncompetitive maiden. The runner-up helps set the level.

NOTEBOOK

Oasis Cannes had narrowly been beaten over this trip at Musselburgh on his second start and went one better to enhance his sire's decent record on this track. It took him a long time to wear down the runner-up, but he was well on top at the line, and should appreciate further, just as the dam's side of his pedigree would suggest. (op 4-7)

Kalicamix made a bold bid to make all and ensured the favourite had to work hard to collar him. He finished a long way clear of the rest and an ordinary maiden can be found, while nurseries are also now a possibility. (op 11-2 tchd 15-2)

Aseela(IRE) showed ability on last month's Leicester debut and is bred to have relished this extra furlong, but she was still made to look one-paced by the front pair and may need an even stiffer test. (tchd 4-1)

Just A Pound(IRE), out of a seven-time winner at up to 1m2f including three on Polytrack, cost just 500GBP and looked green on this debut. (op 33-1)

Kingsville was always outpaced on his debut over 6f here seven days earlier and is bred to have appreciated this extra furlong, but he dropped away disappointingly and has plenty to prove. (op 14-1)

3709 WORLD HORSE WELFARE CELEBRATES 85 YEARS APPRENTICE CLAIMING STKS — 7f 32y(P)

3:45 (3:46) (Class 6) 4-Y-0+ — **£1,704** (£503; £251) **Stalls** High

Form — RPR

1200 **1** **St Oswald**[10] 3334 4-8-9 77 ....(v) RobertTart(7) 2 — 81
(Alan Bailey) *chsd ldr tl led over 2f out: pushed out* **11/2**[3]

0100 **2** *1 1/4* **Bawaardi (IRE)**[33] 2597 6-8-7 77 .... DannyBrock(3) 4 — 72
(David Evans) *prom: pushed along 1/2-way: rdn to chse wnr over 1f out: edgd rt: styd on same pce towards fin* **6/4**[1]

3000 **3** *3 1/4* **Qeethaara (USA)**[19] 3039 8-8-8 72 ....(p) JackDuern(3) 8 — 64
(Mark Brisbourne) *chsd ldrs: shkn up over 2f out: no ex fnl f* **16/1**

2443 **4** *2 1/4* **Unlimited**[23] 2939 10-8-12 67 .... ShaneBKelly 7 — 59+
(Tony Carroll) *hld up and bhd: rdn over 1f out: r.o to go 4th nr fin: nvr nr to chal* **9/1**

0/10 **5** *1* **Ansells Pride (IRE)**[31] 2652 9-8-7 60 .... JakePayne(3) 5 — 54
(Bill Turner) *led: rdn and hdd over 2f out: wknd ins fnl f* **16/1**

000- **6** *hd* **Buaiteoir (FR)**[376] 3285 6-8-7 84 .... IanBurns(3) 6 — 54
(Amy Weaver) *hld up: hdwy over 2f out: rdn over 1f out: wknd ins fnl f* **7/2**[2]

234- **7** *8* **Clearing House**[387] 2922 7-8-3 63 .... BradleyBosley(7) 1 — 32
(John Ryan) *prom tl rdn and wknd over 2f out* **28/1**

8 *21* **Tata Corner (IRE)**[10] 6-8-10 0 .... AdamCarter 9
(Owen Brennan) *s.s: outpcd: t.o* **250/1**

/40- **9** *4* **Atlantic Story (USA)**[478] 844 10-9-5 98 ....(bt) DavidSimmonson(5) 3
(Michael Easterby) *s.i.s: hld up: a in rr: wknd 3f out: eased over 1f out: t.o* **9/1**

1m 29.12s (-0.48) **Going Correction** -0.075s/f (Stan) — **9** Ran SP% **113.2**

Speed ratings (Par 101): **99,97,93,91,90 89,80,56,52**

toteswingers 1&2 £2.50, 2&3 £5.30, 1&3 £9.60 CSF £13.81 TOTE £5.30: £1.70, £1.40, £5.00; EX 15.00.

Owner Richard Jeffrey **Bred** Paul Hearson Bloodstock **Trained** Newmarket, Suffolk

FOCUS

An interesting claimer, in that the pair most favoured by the weights were both returning from lengthy absences. The second and third have not been at their best recently and the fourth was making up ground from a hopeless position, so muddling form.

Atlantic Story(USA) Official explanation: jockey said gelding lost its action

3710 RACING POST FORM WITH TOTEPOOL MOBILE MEDIAN AUCTION MAIDEN STKS — 1m 4f 50y(P)

4:15 (4:20) (Class 6) 3-4-Y-O — **£1,704** (£503; £251) **Stalls** Low

Form — RPR

04 **1** **Cellist**[4] 3551 3-9-0 0 .... LiamJones 5 — 74
(William Haggas) *chsd ldr over 2f: remained handy: pushed along 6f out: drvn to ld over 2f out: sn clr: styd on wl* **8/11**[1]

06 **2** *19* **Card Sweep**[24] 2895 3-9-0 0 ....(p) RoystonFfrench 6 — 44
(Ismail Mohammed) *prom: chsd ldr over 9f out: rdn over 3f out: hmpd over 2f out: sn wknd* **9/4**[2]

5303 **3** *2 1/4* **Angel Cake (IRE)**[14] 3233 3-8-9 45 ....(p) SilvestreDeSousa 3 — 35
(Phil McEntee) *led: rdn over 3f out: hdd & wknd over 2f out* **8/1**[3]

0 **4** *59* **Vital Merlin**[40] 2387 3-9-0 0 .... RussKennemore 1
(Nicky Vaughan) *s.s: a in rr: lost tch fnl 5f: t.o* **40/1**

0 **5** *34* **Flaming Telepath**[58] 1866 4-9-8 0 .... TomMcLaughlin 4
(Christine Dunnett) *sn outpcd: t.o fnl 7f* **66/1**

0 **P** **Barnacre**[14] 3232 3-9-0 0 .... GrahamLee 2
(Richard Ford) *got loose prior to the s: prom: pushed along 6f out: wknd 5f out: t.o whn p.u and dismntd over 3f out* **14/1**

2m 38.62s (-2.48) **Going Correction** -0.075s/f (Stan)

WFA 3 from 4yo 13lb — **6** Ran SP% **110.4**

Speed ratings (Par 101): **105,92,90,51,28**

toteswingers 1&2 £1.40, 1&3 £1.40, 2&3 £1.50 CSF £2.43 TOTE £2.00: £1.40, £1.10; EX 2.90.

Owner The Royal Ascot Racing Club **Bred** Jonathan Shack & Gawain Barnard **Trained** Newmarket, Suffolk

FOCUS

A shocking middle-distance maiden. The time was okay judged on the following handicap, and it's been rated around that for now.

3711 TOTEPOOL MOBILE TEXT TOTE TO 89660 H'CAP — 1m 4f 50y(P)

4:45 (4:45) (Class 4) (0-80,80) 3-Y-O — **£4,204** (£1,251; £625; £312) **Stalls** Low

Form — RPR

3-02 **1** **Venegazzu (IRE)**[32] 2634 3-8-12 71 ....(v[1]) RobertHavlin 8 — 80
(Peter Chapple-Hyam) *a.p: chsd ldr over 3f out: rdn to ld wl over 1f out: styd on* **5/1**

001 **2** *2 1/4* **Sondeduro**[24] 2866 3-9-4 77 .... FergusSweeney 7 — 82
(Jamie Osborne) *hld up: reminders over 4f out: hdwy over 2f out: styd on u.p to go 2nd ins fnl f: nt rch wnr* **3/1**[1]

5001 **3** *1 1/4* **Tingo In The Tale (IRE)**[20] 3003 3-9-2 75 .... JamesDoyle 6 — 78
(David Arbuthnot) *hld up: hdwy u.p over 1f out: styd on to go 3rd post: nt trble ldrs* **12/1**

-160 **4** *hd* **Ukrainian (IRE)**[30] 2718 3-9-2 75 .... JoeFanning 5 — 78
(Mark Johnston) *chsd ldr tl rdn over 3f out: remained handy: styd on same pce ins fnl f: lost 3rd post* **7/2**[2]

1400 **5** *2 3/4* **Cool Hand Luke (IRE)**[27] 2788 3-8-8 67 ....(v[1]) SilvestreDeSousa 3 — 65
(Tom Dascombe) *led: rdn and hdd wl over 1f out: rdn dropped whip ent fnl f: no ex* **16/1**

105 **6** *3 3/4* **Bob's World**[37] 2484 3-9-7 80 .... SeanQuinlan 4 — 72
(Jennie Candlish) *hld up in tch: rdn over 4f out: wknd over 1f out* **4/1**[3]

-250 **7** *8* **Cape Samba**[35] 2544 3-8-12 71 ....(v) RoystonFfrench 1 — 50
(Ismail Mohammed) *chsd ldrs: rdn over 4f out: wknd 3f out* **22/1**

100 **8** *16* **Ogaritmo**[39] 2431 3-9-1 74 .... JimmyQuinn 2 — 28
(Marco Botti) *hld up: a in rr: rdn over 5f out: wknd over 3f out: t.o* **8/1**

2m 37.49s (-3.61) **Going Correction** -0.075s/f (Stan) — **8** Ran SP% **112.9**

Speed ratings (Par 102): **109,107,106,106,104 102,96,86**

toteswingers 1&2 £3.50, 1&3 £4.60, 2&3 £6.80 CSF £19.86 CT £167.73 TOTE £7.90: £2.50, £1.10, £2.90; EX 25.70.

Owner Eledy Srl **Bred** Pat And Mrs O'Donovan **Trained** Newmarket, Suffolk

FOCUS

A fair middle-distance handicap for 3yos in which the winning time was 1.13 seconds quicker than the maiden. Solid enough form rated through the runner-up, third and fourth.

Ogaritmo Official explanation: jockey said filly had no more to give

3712 DOWNLOAD OUR IPHONE APP H'CAP (DIV I) — 1m 141y(P)

5:15 (5:16) (Class 6) (0-60,60) 3-Y-O+ — **£1,704** (£503; £251) **Stalls** Low

Form — RPR

/00- **1** **Noble Jack (IRE)**[248] 7153 6-9-13 59 .... J-PGuillambert 13 — 73+
(Jo Hughes) *s.i.s: hld up: hdwy over 1f out: led and edgd lft ins fnl f: r.o: readily* **9/2**[1]

0460 **2** *2* **American Lover (FR)**[8] 3416 5-9-1 47 .... PaddyAspell 8 — 54
(John Wainwright) *mid-div: hdwy 1/2-way: rdn over 1f out: styd on same pce ins fnl f: wnt 2nd nr fin* **16/1**

5050 **3** *nk* **Poppy Golightly**[116] 837 5-8-8 47 .... JasonHart(7) 12 — 53
(Declan Carroll) *chsd ldr tl led 1/2-way: rdn over 1f out: hdd and no ex ins fnl f* **14/1**

000 **4** *2 1/4* **Miss Socialite**[24] 2891 3-8-10 52 .... FergusSweeney 5 — 52
(Jeremy Gask) *s.i.s: hld up: r.o ins fnl f: nvr nrr* **20/1**

0000 **5** *1/2* **Stamp Duty (IRE)**[38] 2438 4-9-3 52 .... DaleSwift(3) 11 — 52
(Suzzanne France) *mid-div: hdwy over 5f out: rdn over 1f out: no ex ins fnl f* **14/1**

-550 **6** *nse* **Mighty Motive**[29] 2733 3-8-9 58 .... JoshBaudains(7) 2 — 57
(John Mackie) *prom: pushed along over 2f out: no ex ins fnl f* **15/2**

3506 **7** *1* **Fortunate Bid (IRE)**[7] 3456 6-9-11 57 ....(p) JamesSullivan 7 — 55
(Linda Stubbs) *hld up: racd keenly: hdwy over 1f out: sn rdn: wknd ins fnl f* **13/2**[2]

0240 **8** *nk* **Kielty's Folly**[25] 2847 8-9-9 60 .... JamesRogers(5) 10 — 57
(Brian Baugh) *chsd ldrs: rdn over 1f out: wknd ins fnl f* **7/1**[3]

0002 **9** *1 1/2* **Danceyourselfdizzy (IRE)**[19] 3051 4-8-7 46 .... DannyBrock(7) 9 — 39
(Phil McEntee) *sn pushed along and prom: rdn over 1f out: wknd fnl f* **10/1**

2600 **10** *4 1/2* **Petomic (IRE)**[14] 3236 7-9-9 55 ....(p) StephenCraine 6 — 38
(Daniel Mark Loughnane) *hld up in tch: rdn over 2f out: wknd over 1f out* **8/1**

0000 **11** *7* **Ensnare**[9] 3388 7-9-9 55 .... StevieDonohoe 4 — 22
(Willie Musson) *sn pushed along in rr: wknd 3f out* **14/1**

3-00 **12** *3 3/4* **Tigerbill**[56] 1907 4-9-6 52 ....(t) RussKennemore 1
(Nicky Vaughan) *led: hdd over 4f out: chsd ldr tl rdn over 2f out: wknd over 1f out* **14/1**

0-06 **13** *3/4* **Hal Of A Lover**[12] 3277 4-9-0 46 oh1 ....(v[1]) SilvestreDeSousa 3
(Lisa Williamson) *hld up: rdn over 5f out: wknd over 3f out* **33/1**

1m 49.79s (-0.71) **Going Correction** -0.075s/f (Stan)

WFA 3 from 4yo+ 10lb — **13** Ran SP% **116.2**

Speed ratings (Par 101): **100,98,97,95,95 95,94,94,92,88 82,79,78**

toteswingers 1&2 £20.20, 1&3 £14.80, 2&3 £35.80 CSF £77.00 CT £934.42 TOTE £4.40: £1.20, £5.90, £4.90; EX 107.50.

Owner P J Hanly **Bred** Team Hogdala **Trained** Lambourn, Berks

FOCUS

A moderate handicap. The winner had dropped to a good mark and the race has been rated through the runner-up to his C&D April form.

3713 DOWNLOAD OUR IPHONE APP H'CAP (DIV II) — 1m 141y(P)

5:45 (5:46) (Class 6) (0-60,60) 3-Y-O+ — **£1,704** (£503; £251) **Stalls** Low

Form — RPR

-013 **1** **Footstepsofspring (FR)**[34] 2586 5-9-10 56 .... TonyCulhane 8 — 66
(Willie Musson) *hld up: hdwy over 2f out: led and hung lft 1f: drvn out* **9/4**[1]

0064 **2** *1/2* **Warden Bond**[9] 3392 4-9-8 54 ....(p) SilvestreDeSousa 6 — 63+
(William Stone) *hld up: hdwy over 1f out: rdn to chse wnr ins fnl f: r.o* **5/1**[2]

5600 **3** *2 1/2* **Godwit**[38] 2464 4-8-7 46 oh1 .... JoshBaudains(7) 3 — 49
(Eugene Stanford) *a.p: chsd ldr over 2f out: rdn and ev ch over 1f out: hung lft and no ex ins fnl f* **50/1**

6444 **4** *nk* **Just Timmy Marcus**[14] 3231 6-9-7 53 ....(b) TomMcLaughlin 12 — 56
(Brian Baugh) *hld up: hdwy over 1f out: r.o: nt trble ldrs* **14/1**

-100 **5** *1 1/2* **One Of Twins**[30] 2692 4-9-6 59 .... DavidSimmonson(7) 9 — 58
(Michael Easterby) *hld up: hdwy over 3f out: rdn over 1f out: styd on same pce ins fnl f* **11/1**

4102 **6** *1 1/2* **Titan Diamond (IRE)**[11] 3318 4-8-11 48 .... RachealKneller(5) 2 — 44
(Mark Usher) *chsd ldrs: rdn over 1f out: wknd ins fnl f* **10/1**

005- **7** *1 1/4* **Crystal Sky (IRE)**[248] 7144 4-9-9 55 .... FergusSweeney 4 — 48
(Natalie Lloyd-Beavis) *hld up: rdn over 1f out: styd on ins fnl f: nrst fin* **50/1**

-000 **8** *shd* **Abdul Malik**[18] 3066 3-8-8 50 ....(e[1]) JoeFanning 7 — 42
(Kate Walton) *led: rdn and hdd 1f out: hmpd and wknd sn after* **20/1**

2645 **9** *nk* **Ma Kellys (IRE)**[18] 3066 3-8-10 57 .... ShaneBKelly(5) 10 — 52
(Micky Hammond) *s.i.s: hdwy to chse ldr over 7f out tl rdn over 2f out: btn whn hmpd and eased ins fnl f* **11/2**[3]

0-60 **10** *nk* **My Vindication (USA)**[13] 3247 4-9-12 58 .... GrahamLee 1 — 49
(Gay Kelleway) *chsd ldrs: hmpd over 7f out: nt clr run over 2f out: rdn over 1f out: wknd ins fnl f* **25/1**

0-05 **11** *3 1/2* **Duneen Dream (USA)**[48] 1014 7-9-1 47 .... J-PGuillambert 11 — 30
(Nikki Evans) *mid-div: hdwy over 3f out: sn rdn: wknd wl over 1f out* **25/1**

-065 **12** *1* **Jimmy The Lollipop (IRE)**[18] 1082 3-9-4 60 ....(vt[1]) StevieDonohoe 5 — 40
(Ian Williams) *hld up: rdn and wknd over 2f out* **13/2**

1m 49.91s (-0.59) **Going Correction** -0.075s/f (Stan)

WFA 3 from 4yo+ 10lb — **12** Ran SP% **116.6**

Speed ratings (Par 101): **99,98,96,96,94 93,92,92,91,91 88,87**

toteswingers 1&2 £3.30, 1&3 £31.80, 2&3 £46.10 CSF £11.76 CT £433.79 TOTE £4.00: £1.50, £2.10, £18.30; EX 14.50.

Owner Le Printemps Partnership **Bred** S R L Unitrade **Trained** Newmarket, Suffolk

FOCUS

The winning time for this leg was 0.12 seconds slower than the first division and it saw another well-backed winner, who has been rated 3lb higher than his previous C&D win.

T/Plt: £27.60 to a £1 stake. Pool: £63432.77 - 1675.66 winning tickets T/Qpdt: £3.40 to a £1 stake. Pool: £6623.92 - 1406.14 winning tickets CR

3017 COMPIEGNE (L-H)

Monday, July 2

OFFICIAL GOING: Turf: soft

3714a PRIX DU MONT SAINT-JEAN (MAIDEN) (UNRACED 2YO COLTS & GELDINGS) (TURF) 7f

1:50 (12:00) 2-Y-O **£10,000** (£4,000; £3,000; £2,000; £1,000)

RPR

1 **Kapstadt (FR)** 2-9-2 0 GeraldMosse 4 79
(F Doumen, France) **92/10**

2 1 3/4 **Bertimont (FR)** 2-9-2 0 GregoryBenoist 1 75
(C Lerner, France) **58/10**[3]

3 3/4 **Star System (IRE)** 2-9-2 0 OlivierPeslier 5 73
(F Head, France) **2/1**[1]

4 1/2 **Abonito (GER)** 2-9-2 0 UmbertoRispoli 2 72
(J-P Carvalho, Germany) **15/2**

5 3/4 **Gold Knight (FR)** 2-8-13 0 PaulineProd'homme(3) 13 70
(D Prod'Homme, France) **25/1**

6 3 1/2 **Crackos (FR)** 2-9-2 0 Pierre-CharlesBoudot 11 61
(F Belmont, France) **34/1**

7 shd **Yallah Habibi (FR)** 2-9-2 0 DavidBreux 8 61
(Mme L Audon, France) **45/1**

8 1 1/2 **Zeus De Cerisy (FR)** 2-9-2 0 DavyBonilla 12 57
(Mme L Audon, France) **48/1**

9 2 **Gaelic Style (FR)** 2-9-2 0 TheoBachelot 7 52
(J Bertran De Balanda, France) **21/1**

10 3/4 **Le Deluge (FR)** 2-9-2 0 ChristopheSoumillon 9 50
(John Best) *s.i.s: racd in midfield: plld hrd: swtchd towards rail 2f out: short of room over 1f out: had to be stdd and lost all ch: eased fnl 150yds* **9/2**[2]

0 **Back To Capri (IRE)** 2-9-2 0 ThierryThulliez 3
(G Collet, France) **14/1**

0 **Alanlad (FR)** 2-9-2 0 ThomasHuet 6
(P Demercastel, France) **14/1**

1m 28.79s (88.79) **12** Ran SP% **116.6**
WIN (incl. 1 euro stake): 10.20. PLACES: 2.70, 1.90, 1.50. DF: 38.70. SF: 85.20.
Owner Peter Hans Vogt **Bred** C Barel **Trained** Bouce, France

3715 - 3716a (Foreign Racing) - See Raceform Interactive

3464 BRIGHTON (L-H)

Tuesday, July 3

OFFICIAL GOING: Good to soft changing to soft after race 1 (2.15)
Wind: virtually nil Weather: sea mist (poor visibility)

3717 HARDINGS CATERING H'CAP (DIV I) 5f 213y

2:15 (2:15) (Class 6) (0-55,55) 3-Y-O+ **£1,617** (£481; £240; £120) **Stalls** Centre

Form RPR

301 **1** **Scommettitrice (IRE)**[7] 3464 4-9-1 **51** 6ex (p) AndreaAtzeni 9 58
(David Evans) *in tch in midfield: rdn and hdwy over 1f out: styd on wl fnl f to ld fnl 50yds: jst hld on* **15/2**

5000 **2** nse **Captainrisk (IRE)**[17] 3152 6-9-0 **50** (v) SebSanders 13 57+
(Christine Dunnett) *bhd: nt clr run 2f out: hdwy but stl plenty to do jst over 1f out: str run ins fnl f: jst failed* **17/2**

6041 **3** 1/2 **Tenancy (IRE)**[7] 3462 8-8-4 **47** (b) ShirleyTeasdale(7) 1 52
(Shaun Harris) *led: styd off stands' rail fr 3f out: hrd pressed and drvn 1f out: kpt on wl tl hdd and no ex fnl 50yds* **9/4**[1]

0350 **4** nk **Pharoh Jake**[10] 3390 4-8-10 **46** KieranO'Neill 2 50
(John Bridger) *chsd ldr: drvn and ev ch 1f out: unable qck ins fnl f: one pce towards fin* **10/1**

-400 **5** 1/2 **Imjin River (IRE)**[8] 3455 5-9-0 **55** AshleyMorgan(5) 5 57
(William Stone) *taken down early: in tch: effrt to chse ldrs over 1f out: styd on same pce ins fnl f* **12/1**

6-04 **6** 2 3/4 **Louphole**[21] 3007 10-9-5 **55** DaneO'Neill 3 49
(J R Jenkins) *s.i.s: bhd: hdwy 1/2-way: chsd ldrs and drvn 1f out: btn ins fnl f: wknd fnl 100yds* **7/1**[3]

-000 **7** 1 **Botanist**[17] 3153 5-9-2 **52** (be[1]) LukeMorris 7 42
(Milton Bradley) *in tch: rdn and effrt over 1f out: no ex and edgd lft ins fnl f: wknd fnl 100yds* **25/1**

054 **8** 12 **Majestic South**[21] 2996 3-8-13 **55** MartinHarley 11
(Mick Channon) *sn bustled along to chse ldrs: struggling u.p 2f out: wknd over 1f out: fdd fnl f* **7/2**[2]

3565 **9** 4 1/2 **Grand Honour (IRE)**[21] 3007 6-8-10 **46** oh1 JimmyQuinn 10
(Paul Howling) *in tch in midfield: rdn over 1f out: sn btn and fdd fnl f* **20/1**

04-0 **10** 3 3/4 **Hawaiian Freeze**[82] 1337 3-8-4 **46** NickyMackay 4
(John Stimpson) *sn rdn along: chsd ldrs: struggling over 2f out: wknd over 1f out: wl btn and eased fnl f* **50/1**

1m 13.64s (3.44) **Going Correction** +0.45s/f (Yiel)
WFA 3 from 4yo+ 6lb **10** Ran SP% **115.1**
Speed ratings (Par 101): **95,94,94,93,93 89,88,72,66,61**
toteswingers 1&2 £12.20, 2&3 £5.20, 1&3 £3.80 CSF £66.90 CT £193.51 TOTE £7.30: £2.10, £2.60, £2.20; EX 67.50 Trifecta £432.40 Part won. Pool: £584.45 - 0.63 winning units..
Owner Out Of Bounds Racing Club **Bred** L Mulryan **Trained** Pandy, Monmouths

FOCUS
All races on Inner and distances as advertised. Runners came centre to stands' side in the first division of what was a moderate handicap. The time was similar to division II and the winner showed her best form since she was a 2yo.

3718 HARDINGS CATERING H'CAP (DIV II) 5f 213y

2:45 (2:45) (Class 6) (0-55,55) 3-Y-O+ **£1,617** (£481; £240; £120) **Stalls** Centre

Form RPR

5025 **1** **Mucky Molly**[8] 3434 4-8-13 **49** NeilCallan 9 58
(Olivia Maylam) *in tch: swtchd lft and effrt over 1f out: drvn to ld ins fnl f: kpt on wl* **7/2**[2]

4013 **2** 3/4 **Whiteoak Lady (IRE)**[7] 3467 7-9-4 **54** (p) AndreaAtzeni 5 61
(David Evans) *in tch: rdn and effrt over 1f out: pressed wnr fnl 100yds: kpt on but no imp towards fin* **3/1**[1]

0442 **3** nk **Perfect Honour (IRE)**[7] 3466 6-8-10 **46** oh1 (p) DavidProbert 11 52
(Des Donovan) *taken down early: chsd ldrs: wnt 2nd 4f out: ev ch and drvn over 1f out: styd on same pce fnl 100yds* **4/1**[3]

0460 **4** nk **Microlight**[7] 3466 4-8-11 **47** RichardThomas 12 52+
(John E Long) *sn pushed along: in tch: lost pl and bhd 1/2-way: swtchd lft and hdwy ins fnl f: styd on wl: nt rch ldrs* **14/1**

0-34 **5** 1 1/4 **Trade Centre**[29] 2760 7-9-0 **50** LukeMorris 8 51
(Milton Bradley) *in tch: swtchd lft and hdwy u.p 2f out: no ex and one pce ins fnl f* **5/1**

020 **6** 2 1/4 **Jemimaville (IRE)**[61] 1768 5-8-10 **46** oh1 WilliamCarson 10 40
(Giles Bravery) *stdd s: hld up towards rr: swtchd lft and hdwy 2f out: drvn and no ex 1f out: wknd ins fnl f* **28/1**

5300 **7** 1 **White Shift (IRE)**[131] 665 6-8-10 **46** JimmyQuinn 1 37
(Paul Howling) *led: rdn over 1f out: hdd ins fnl f: sn wknd* **22/1**

-046 **8** 8 **Athaakeel (IRE)**[144] 498 6-9-3 **53** (b) CathyGannon 2 18
(Ronald Harris) *taken down early: chsd ldr for 2f: lost pl over 2f out: bhd over 1f out* **8/1**

450- **9** 1/2 **London Avenue (IRE)**[235] 7366 4-9-0 **50** (b[1]) PaddyAspell 7 13
(Neil Mulholland) *hld up in last trio: hdwy over 2f out: chsd ldrs and rdn wl over 1f out: fnd little and sn btn: fdd fnl f* **20/1**

1m 13.58s (3.38) **Going Correction** +0.45s/f (Yiel)
WFA 3 from 4yo+ 6lb **9** Ran SP% **114.2**
Speed ratings (Par 101): **95,94,93,93,91 88,87,76,75**
toteswingers 1&2 £3.00, 2&3 £3.50, 1&3 £2.80 CSF £13.83 CT £42.80 TOTE £4.30: £1.10, £1.60, £1.60; EX 13.80 Trifecta £27.70 Pool: £822.14 - 21.91 winning units..
Owner P Sweeting **Bred** Paul Sweeting **Trained** Epsom, Surrey

FOCUS
This was run in a time 0.06secs quicker than division one. Pretty straightforward form.
Microlight Official explanation: jockey said gelding was denied a clear run

3719 3663 FIRST FOR FOOD SERVICE H'CAP 6f 209y

3:15 (3:15) (Class 5) (0-70,72) 3-Y-O **£2,264** (£673; £336; £168) **Stalls** Centre

Form RPR

4412 **1** **Subtle Knife**[20] 3044 3-9-3 **65** WilliamCarson 6 75
(Giles Bravery) *in tch: swtchd lft and effrt to ld over 1f out: clr whn hung bdly lft fnl 100yds: r.o* **8/1**

6614 **2** 1 1/4 **Mr Fickle (IRE)**[17] 3151 3-9-5 **67** GeorgeBaker 11 74
(Gary Moore) *bhd: pushed along 3f out: hdwy u.p over 1f out: chsd wnr ins fnl f: kpt on* **13/8**[1]

234- **3** hd **Alice Rose (IRE)**[252] 7081 3-9-5 **67** NickyMackay 9 73
(Rae Guest) *in tch: hdwy and bmpd over 2f out: chsd ldng pair ins fnl f: kpt on same pce* **7/1**[3]

-500 **4** 3 1/4 **Star Kingdom (IRE)**[8] 3450 3-8-5 **60** DanielCremin(7) 2 58
(Robert Mills) *detached in last: hdwy 1/2-way: rdn and chsd wnr jst over 1f out tl ins fnl f: wknd fnl 100yds* **33/1**

0262 **5** 1 3/4 **Marah Music**[12] 3315 3-8-11 **59** (p) SebSanders 8 52
(Peter Makin) *led tl 4f out: pressed ldr tl led again 3f out: hdd over 1f out: wknd fnl f* **9/2**[2]

00-0 **6** 2 1/4 **King's Ciel**[16] 3193 3-8-9 **57** (v[1]) LiamKeniry 4 45
(George Baker) *w ldr tl led 4f out: hdd over 2f out: wknd u.p over 1f out* **33/1**

4613 **7** 7 **Esprit Danseur**[34] 2610 3-9-3 **65** PatCosgrave 12 34
(Jim Boyle) *in tch: drvn and chsd ldrs over 1f out: btn 1f: eased ins fnl f* **7/1**[3]

00 **8** 9 **Fight (IRE)**[30] 2733 3-8-12 **60** DaneO'Neill 3
(Jeremy Gask) *dwlt: sn rdn along and rcvrd to r in midfield: wknd over 1f out* **22/1**

0064 **9** 2 1/2 **Tidy Affair (IRE)**[18] 3122 3-9-7 **69** ShaneKelly 7
(Murty McGrath) *bhd: lost tch 2f out* **10/1**

-003 **10** 8 **Sir Dylan**[8] 3433 3-8-12 **60** (b[1]) MarcHalford 5
(Ronald Harris) *chsd ldrs tl 1/2-way: sn bhd: eased fr over 1f out* **33/1**

1m 26.22s (3.12) **Going Correction** +0.45s/f (Yiel) **10** Ran SP% **114.7**
Speed ratings (Par 100): **100,98,98,94,92 90,82,71,68,59**
toteswingers 1&2 £3.90, 2&3 £3.60, 1&3 £6.50 CSF £20.29 CT £95.43 TOTE £13.00: £3.60, £1.30, £2.40; EX 27.10 Trifecta £227.80 Pool: £1019.02 - 3.31 winning units..
Owner D B Clark & Russel Grant **Bred** Mrs F Bravery **Trained** Newmarket, Suffolk
■ Stewards' Enquiry : Seb Sanders one-day ban: careless riding (Jul 17)

FOCUS
A modest race, but solid enough form for the grade, with the front trio drawing a little way clear late on. They again headed stands' side.
Sir Dylan Official explanation: jockey said gelding hung badly right

3720 CATERING SERVICES INTERNATIONAL LTD MAIDEN STKS 1m 1f 209y

3:45 (3:45) (Class 5) 3-Y-O+ **£2,264** (£673; £336; £168) **Stalls** Centre

Form RPR

0-2 **1** **Palus San Marco (IRE)**[73] 1518 3-9-1 0 RobertHavlin 3 76
(Peter Chapple-Hyam) *in tch: rdn and effrt 3f out: kpt on u.p and ev ch 1f out: styd on to ld cl home* **7/4**[2]

00- **2** hd **Kampai**[294] 6020 4-9-4 0 AdamBeschizza(3) 7 71
(Julia Feilden) *hld up in tch: rdn and effrt wl over 2f out: styd on to ld 1f out: kpt on wl tl hdd cl home* **50/1**

32 **3** 1/2 **Scottish Vespers (IRE)**[41] 2393 3-9-1 0 WilliamBuick 1 75
(Sir Michael Stoute) *pressed ldr: rdn to ld 4f out: hdd 2f out: awkward hd carriage and wandering lft and rt u.p but ev ch after: nt qckn fnl 100yds* **4/5**[1]

5-4 **4** 2 1/4 **Schoolmaster**[89] 1206 4-9-12 0 WilliamCarson 8 70
(Giles Bravery) *t.k.h: chsd ldrs: effrt to chse ldr over 3f out: led 2f out: sn rdn: hdd 1f out: hung lft u.p: wknd fnl 100yds* **10/1**[3]

54 **5** 9 **Authentication**[133] 642 3-9-1 0 MircoDemuro 4 55
(Mark Johnston) *led tl 4f out: hmpd over 3f out: 5th and btn over 1f out: wknd fnl f* **20/1**

6 11 **Ice Apple** 4-9-7 0 RichardThomas 6 25
(John E Long) *detached in last: nvr on terms* **66/1**

00 **7** 6 **Riviera Romance**[11] 3340 3-8-11 0 ow1 SebSanders 5 14
(J W Hills) *hld up in tch: rdn over 3f out: wknd 2f out: bhd and eased ins fnl f* **66/1**

2m 8.85s (5.25) **Going Correction** +0.45s/f (Yiel)
WFA 3 from 4yo 11lb **7** Ran SP% **110.7**
Speed ratings (Par 103): **97,96,96,94,87 78,73**
toteswingers 1&2 £12.80, 2&3 £13.80, 1&3 £1.10 CSF £71.30 TOTE £4.00: £1.30, £24.30; EX 130.80 Trifecta £242.00 Pool: £1369.51 - 4.18 winning units..
Owner Eledy Srl **Bred** J & L Young / Darlacher Ltd **Trained** Newmarket, Suffolk
■ Stewards' Enquiry : Robert Havlin caution: careless riding

FOCUS
Hard to get excited about the worth of this form, which is rated around the winner. Having made their way to the stands' rail, the principals ultimately drifted back nearer the far side.

3721 3663 FIRST FOR FOOD SERVICES H'CAP — 1m 1f 209y
4:15 (4:16) (Class 6) (0-55,55) 4-Y-0+ — **£1,617** (£481; £240; £120) **Stalls** Centre

Form — RPR

604 **1** **Tawseef (IRE)**[7] 3470 4-8-13 **52** — IanMongan 4 — 67
(Roy Brotherton) *in tch: rdn to chse ldr 2f out: chal and drew clr w ldr over 1f out: led ins fnl f: styd on wl* **7/1**[3]

0635 **2** *2 ½* **Cantor**[27] 2814 4-9-2 **55** — WilliamCarson 13 — 65
(Giles Bravery) *chsd ldr tl led after 2f: rdn 2f out: clr w wnr over 1f out: hdd and no ex ins fnl f* **8/1**

5306 **3** *9* **Market Puzzle (IRE)**[25] 2886 5-8-12 **51** — KierenFallon 7 — 43
(Mark Brisbourne) *hld up towards rr: gd hdwy to chse ldr 4f out tl 2f out: wknd u.p jst over 1f out: hld on for modest 3rd cl home* **5/1**[2]

3361 **4** *nk* **Tinkerbell Will**[20] 3043 5-8-13 **52** — RichardThomas 12 — 43
(John E Long) *towards rr: pushed along 6f out: hdwy and swtchd lft over 2f out: 5th and no prog over 1f out: plugged on and pressing for modest 3rd cl home* **4/1**[1]

00 **5** *½* **Chasin' Rainbows**[6] 3497 4-8-13 **52** — LiamKeniry 16 — 42
(Sylvester Kirk) *t.k.h: hld up in tch: chsd ldrs and rdn over 2f out: 4th and wl btn over 1f out: plugged on and pressing for modest 3rd cl home* **25/1**

23 **6** *¾* **Laconicos (IRE)**[21] 2998 10-8-10 **54** — (t) LauraPike(5) 9 — 43
(William Stone) *hld up in tch: hdwy to chse ldrs 4f out: rdn and btn 2f out: 6th and wl hld over 1f out* **8/1**

0-40 **7** *7* **Cottonfields (USA)**[17] 3153 6-8-11 **50** — StevieDonohoe 15 — 25
(Heather Main) *dwlt: steadily rcvrd to chse ldrs after 2f: rdn and lost pl over 3f out: wl btn 2f out: plugged on past btn horses fnl f* **25/1**

36/2 **8** *nse* **Devon Diva**[21] 2998 6-8-3 **49** — JoshBaudains(7) 1 — 24
(David Bridgwater) *chsd ldrs: rdn over 2f out: wknd wl over 1f out* **11/1**

3550 **9** *½* **Diddums**[7] 3470 6-8-7 **53** — KatiaScallan(7) 10 — 27
(Alastair Lidderdale) *hld up in rr: rdn and sme hdwy 3f out: no prog 2f out: sn wknd* **16/1**

6040 **10** *2 ¼* **Gay Gallivanter**[7] 3470 4-8-7 **46** oh1 — (p) AndreaAtzeni 3 — 15
(Michael Quinn) *in tch: rdn and struggling over 2f out: wknd over 1f out: fdd fnl f* **33/1**

030/ **11** *2 ¼* **Celebrian**[763] 2619 5-8-13 **52** — PatCosgrave 8 — 17
(George Baker) *hld up in tch: drvn and no prog over 2f out: wknd wl over 1f out: wl btn and eased wl ins fnl f* **8/1**

1405 **12** *½* **Satwa Ballerina**[21] 2997 4-8-6 **50** — TobyAtkinson(5) 2 — 14
(Mark Rimmer) *hld up towards rr: rdn and no prog whn hung lft over 3f out: lost tch 2f out* **9/1**

0600 **13** *1* **Kyncraighe (IRE)**[8] 3455 4-8-3 **47** ow1 — JemmaMarshall(5) 6 — 9
(Joseph Tuite) *hld up towards rr: rdn and short-lived effrt over 2f out: sn wknd* **50/1**

-000 **14** *25* **Avec Moi**[22] 2973 5-8-4 **46** oh1 — DominicFox(3) 11
(Christine Dunnett) *led for 2f: chsd ldr tl 4f out: sn bhd: t.o* **66/1**

2m 7.72s (4.12) **Going Correction** +0.45s/f (Yiel) — **14** Ran SP% **120.8**
Speed ratings (Par 101): **101,99,91,91,91 90,84,84,84,82 80,80,79,59**
toteswingers 1&2 £13.70, 2&3 £8.20, 1&3 £8.50 CSF £59.47 CT £311.21 TOTE £6.50: £2.00, £3.00, £2.20; EX 78.60 Trifecta £599.40 Pool: £1093.57 - 1.35 winning units..
Owner Millend Racing Club **Bred** Shadwell Estate Company Limited **Trained** Elmley Castle, Worcs

FOCUS
This had looked competitive, but the front pair drew quite a way clear, with the time 1.13secs quicker than the previous maiden. The front pair were as near as could be to the stands' rail. A 5lb best from the winner.

3722 JANES SOLICITORS JUBILEE H'CAP — 1m 3f 196y
4:45 (4:46) (Class 5) (0-70,70) 3-Y-0+ — **£2,264** (£673; £336; £168) **Stalls** Centre

Form — RPR

-032 **1** **Shouda (IRE)**[7] 3468 6-9-2 **58** — TomQueally 9 — 67
(Barney Curley) *hld up in last pair: rdn and effrt over 2f out: hdwy over 1f out: led fnl f: sn in command and pushed out after* **13/8**[1]

1044 **2** *1 ¾* **Ostentation**[7] 3469 5-9-8 **64** — (b) KierenFallon 4 — 70
(Alastair Lidderdale) *t.k.h: hld up in tch: rdn to ld over 1f out: hdd and no ex fnl 100yds* **7/1**

6-30 **3** *1 ½* **The Calling Curlew**[19] 3077 4-9-4 **65** — AmyScott(5) 8 — 69
(Henry Candy) *chsd ldrs: wnt 2nd 7f out tl 2f out: hld hd high u.p and styd on same pce fnl f* **5/1**[3]

0000 **4** *½* **Unex Renoir**[17] 3154 4-9-6 **62** — (b) NeilCallan 3 — 65
(Michael Attwater) *sn led: rdn and edgd lft over 2f out: hdd over 1f out: wandered u.p 1f out: wknd ins fnl f* **10/1**

-024 **5** *6* **Filun**[33] 2623 7-10-0 **70** — JohnFahy 1 — 63
(Anthony Middleton) *in tch: rdn and effrt over 2f out: wknd ent fnl f* **10/1**

-204 **6** *½* **Haymarket**[36] 2544 3-9-0 **69** — MircoDemuro 7 — 61
(Mark Johnston) *chsd ldr tl 7f out: lost pl and rdn wl over 2f out: wknd over 1f out* **3/1**[2]

2m 39.97s (7.27) **Going Correction** +0.55s/f (Yiel)
WFA 3 from 4yo+ 13lb — **6** Ran SP% **110.4**
Speed ratings (Par 103): **97,95,94,94,90 90**
toteswingers 1&2 £2.30, 2&3 £3.80, 1&3 £2.20 CSF £13.04 CT £42.88 TOTE £2.50: £1.70, £1.90; EX 10.00 Trifecta £34.20 Pool: £1266.95 - 27.34 winning units..
Owner Curley Leisure **Bred** Gestut Schlenderhan **Trained** Newmarket, Suffolk

FOCUS
The pace was steady and the field this time came up the centre. Changing fortunes late. The winner ran to his C&D latest.

3723 BULMERS VINTAGE RESERVE H'CAP — 7f 214y
5:15 (5:15) (Class 5) (0-70,69) 4-Y-0+ — **£2,264** (£673; £336; £168) **Stalls** Centre

Form — RPR

4-21 **1** **Know No Fear**[5] 3544 7-8-5 **58** — (p) LeonnaMayor(5) 8 — 69
(Alastair Lidderdale) *prom in main gp: chsd ldr 3f out: rdn to ld over 2f out: kpt on wl fnl f* **6/4**[1]

6530 **2** *1 ½* **Mark Anthony (IRE)**[8] 3442 5-7-12 **53** — ShirleyTeasdale(7) 10 — 60
(Shaun Harris) *led and sn clr: rdn and hdd over 2f out: 4th and looked wkng ins fnl f: battled on gamely to go 2nd cl home* **16/1**

4326 **3** *nk* **Do More Business (IRE)**[6] 3497 5-8-3 **54** — RyanPowell(3) 1 — 60
(Alison Batchelor) *racd off the pce in midfield: effrt u.p to chse ldrs over 1f out: chsd wnr ins fnl f: no imp and lost 2nd cl home* **8/1**

0053 **4** *1 ½* **Nibani (IRE)**[22] 2988 5-9-0 **69** — SemiraPashai(7) 3 — 72
(Alastair Lidderdale) *rdr fiddling w iron leaving stalls: racd off the pce in rr of main gp: pushed along and hdwy 2f out: kpt on fnl f* **14/1**

-631 **5** *½* **Paperetto**[7] 3471 4-8-7 **62** 6ex — DanielCremin(7) 5 — 64
(Robert Mills) *prom in main gp: chsd clr ldr 4f out tl 3f out: chsd wnr jst over 1f out tl ins fnl f: wknd towards fin* **7/2**[2]

0232 **6** *1 ¼* **Potentiale (IRE)**[25] 2886 8-8-8 **63** — (v) Leah-AnneAvery(7) 6 — 62
(J W Hills) *sn outpcd and niggled along in last pair: sme hdwy 3f out: kpt on fnl f: nvr trbld ldrs* **10/1**

630- **7** *3 ¾* **No Larking (IRE)**[231] 7425 4-9-3 **65** — DaneO'Neill 4 — 55
(Henry Candy) *chsd ldr tl 4f out: wknd u.p 2f out* **5/1**[3]

0504 **8** *8* **Rainsborough**[33] 2627 5-7-11 **50** oh5 — (p) DarrenEgan(5) 7 — 22
(Peter Hedger) *sn wl bhd: rdn and effrt 3f out: wknd 2f out: wl bhd fnl f* **28/1**

-005 **9** *2 ¼* **Guilded Warrior**[21] 3000 9-9-0 **62** — IanMongan 2 — 29
(Paddy Butler) *prom in main gp: rdn and wknd 2f out* **33/1**

1m 39.67s (3.67) **Going Correction** +0.55s/f (Yiel) — **9** Ran SP% **118.0**
Speed ratings (Par 103): **103,101,101,99,99 97,94,86,83**
toteswingers 1&2 £7.30, 2&3 £13.50, 1&3 £6.80 CSF £30.43 CT £155.54 TOTE £2.10: £1.10, £5.30, £2.70; EX 24.70 Trifecta £138.50 Pool: £1288.25 - 6.88 winning units..
Owner C S J Beek **Bred** B Bargh **Trained** Lambourn, Berks

FOCUS
The runners again came more centre-field. Few got into this, which was well run, and the form is rated through the third.

3724 HARDINGS CATERING SERVICES H'CAP — 5f 59y
5:45 (5:45) (Class 5) (0-70,70) 3-Y-0+ — **£2,264** (£673; £336; £168) **Stalls** Centre

Form — RPR

4256 **1** **The Strig**[10] 3390 5-9-5 **63** — WilliamCarson 1 — 73
(Stuart Williams) *stdd and dropped into last pair after 1f: styd on ins rail 3f out: hdwy to chse ldr over 1f out: led ins fnl f: drvn out* **12/1**

0225 **2** *1 ½* **Whitecrest**[7] 3477 4-9-5 **70** — WilliamTwiston-Davies(7) 4 — 75
(John Spearing) *in tch: rdn to chse ldrs over 1f out: kpt on u.p to go 2nd towards fin* **5/2**[1]

-003 **3** *nk* **Cape Royal**[7] 3464 12-9-7 **65** — (tp) CathyGannon 7 — 69
(Milton Bradley) *chsd ldrs: c to r against stands' rail over 2f out: pressed ldrs u.p over 1f out: kpt on same pce fnl f* **16/1**

3121 **4** *½* **Big Wave (IRE)**[19] 3076 4-9-11 **69** — NeilCallan 9 — 71+
(Alison Hutchinson) *racd keenly: sn led: rdn over 1f out: hdd ins fnl f: no ex and lost 2 pls towards fin* **5/2**[1]

0445 **5** *nk* **Welsh Inlet (IRE)**[16] 3188 4-9-10 **68** — SeanLevey 8 — 69
(John Bridger) *chsd ldrs: unable qck u.p wl over 1f out: styd on same pce ins fnl f* **9/1**[3]

0000 **6** *½* **Roodee Queen**[10] 3390 4-9-5 **68** — (b) DarrenEgan(5) 6 — 67
(Milton Bradley) *t.k.h: in tch: effrt u.p 2f out: no imp and styd on same pce fnl f* **16/1**

-000 **7** *2* **Johnny Splash (IRE)**[7] 3470 3-8-2 **51** — (p[1]) NickyMackay 3 — 41
(Roger Teal) *in tch in midfield: effrt u.p over 1f out: wknd ins fnl f* **22/1**

4-00 **8** *nk* **Stonecrabstomorrow (IRE)**[7] 3464 9-9-1 **64** — MarkCoumbe(5) 2 — 55
(Michael Attwater) *s.i.s: in tch in rr: effrt u.p 2f out: drvn and styd on same pce fr over 1f out* **16/1**

341 **9** *5* **Amazing Win (IRE)**[15] 3210 4-9-2 **65** — CharlesBishop(5) 5 — 39
(Mick Channon) *in tch in last quartet: rdn and unable qck over 1f out: wknd ins fnl f* **4/1**[2]

1m 4.71s (2.41) **Going Correction** +0.55s/f (Yiel)
WFA 3 from 4yo+ 5lb — **9** Ran SP% **116.8**
Speed ratings (Par 103): **102,99,99,98,97 97,93,93,85**
toteswingers 1&2 £8.10, 2&3 £9.80, 1&3 £15.10 CSF £42.76 CT £501.24 TOTE £14.70: £3.10, £1.30, £4.30; EX 53.20 Trifecta £496.40 Pool: £1207.65 - 1.80 winning units..
Owner Brian Piper & David Cobill **Bred** Old Mill Stud **Trained** Newmarket, Suffolk

FOCUS
A typical sprint handicap for the course. The runners were spread across the track. Hard to know how literally to take the form, with the winner staying on the inside.
T/Plt: £57.50 to a £1 stake. Pool of £85615.02 - 1085.84 winning tickets. T/Qpdt: £33.70 to a £1 stake. Pool of £5852.52 - 128.17 winning tickets. SP

3519 HAMILTON (R-H)
Tuesday, July 3

OFFICIAL GOING: Soft (heavy in places)
Wind: Breezy, half against Weather: Overcast

3725 TOM JONES LIVE THIS FRIDAY MAIDEN STKS — 6f 5y
2:30 (2:34) (Class 5) 2-Y-0 — **£3,408** (£1,006; £503) **Stalls** High

Form — RPR

1 **Luck (IRE)** 2-9-3 0 — PhillipMakin 2 — 83+
(Kevin Ryan) *w ldr: led gng wl over 1f out: pushed clr fnl f: readily* **11/10**[1]

05 **2** *7* **Sandy's Row (USA)**[33] 2631 2-8-12 0 — JoeFanning 4 — 57+
(Mark Johnston) *led: rdn over 2f out: hdd over 1f out: sn outpcd by wnr* **5/2**[2]

6 **3** *3 ¼* **Corton Lad**[10] 3378 2-9-3 0 — TomEaves 3 — 52
(Keith Dalgleish) *reluctant to enter stalls: dwlt: sn outpcd and drvn along: sme late hdwy: nvr on terms* **11/1**

6 **4** *2* **Flighty Clarets (IRE)**[27] 2822 2-8-12 0 — TonyHamilton 1 — 41
(Richard Fahey) *hung rt thrght: plld hrd early: outpcd and rdn after 2f: no imp fr 2f out* **4/1**[3]

5 *40* **Salvatore Fury (IRE)** 2-9-3 0 — PaulMulrennan 5
(Keith Dalgleish) *s.s: a wl bhd* **16/1**

1m 15.65s (3.45) **Going Correction** +0.45s/f (Yiel) — **5** Ran SP% **110.4**
Speed ratings (Par 94): **95,85,81,78,25**
CSF £4.11 TOTE £2.10: £1.10, £1.60; EX 4.30.
Owner Liam Sheridan **Bred** Clody E Norton & Robert Norton **Trained** Hambleton, N Yorks

FOCUS
Races on Round course reduced in distance by about 25yds. After 2.8mm of overnight rain on already testing ground, conditions were described by jockeys as 'pretty testing, bordering on heavy'. The second and third have been rated to their pre-race marks.

NOTEBOOK
Luck(IRE), from a stable with a strong hand in the juvenile division, is an attractive, close-coupled type. Out of a mare who won over 7f at two, his sales price increased each time when offered as a foal, a yearling and then at the breeze-ups when he made 45,000gns. He carried plenty of market confidence and certainly knew his job. He stretched clear when nudged along and looks at least useful. (op 6-5 tchd Evens)
Sandy's Row(USA), whose dam took both the Lowther and the Cherry Hinton, had shown improved form on her second start. She jumped out smartly and made the running, but it was clear some way from home that she was just the hare. She is a daughter of Street Cry whose progeny excel on the Polytrack surface. (op 11-4 tchd 3-1)
Corton Lad, having his second start, gave serious problems behind the stalls. Soon outpaced, he kept on to claim a modest third spot. He will appreciate further, but will need to mend his way at the stalls. (op 14-1 tchd 16-1)
Flighty Clarets(IRE), whose dam took the John Smith's Cup in these colours, was edgy in the stalls. Very keen early before soon being outpaced, she tired late on and will need plenty more time. (op 7-2)

Salvatore Fury(IRE) started slowly and, always detached in last, was allowed to complete in his own time. (op 14-1)

3726 SCOTTISH RACING CLAIMING STKS 5f 4y
3:00 (3:00) (Class 6) 3-5-Y-O £2,045 (£603; £302) Stalls Centre

Form RPR
0306 1 **No Hubris (USA)**[14] 3255 5-9-4 77 (b) DaleSwift(3) 2 80
(Ruth Carr) *wnt rt s: t.k.h early: mde all: rdn 2f out: kpt on wl fnl f* 9/4[3]
-004 2 ½ **Love Delta (USA)**[26] 2861 5-9-6 83 AmyRyan 4 77
(Kevin Ryan) *chsd wnr: effrt and rdn 2f out: kpt on ins fnl f: hld towards fin* 7/4[2]
210 3 3 **Frequency**[11] 3334 5-9-12 77 (b) JoeFanning 3 73
(Keith Dalgleish) *stdd bhd ldrs: rdn wl over 1f out: no imp fnl f* 13/8[1]
0605 4 1 ¼ **Script**[11] 3357 3-7-12 45 MatthewHopkins(7) 1 50
(Alan Berry) *t.k.h: chsd ldrs tl edgd rt and wknd over 1f out* 66/1

1m 1.98s (1.98) **Going Correction** +0.45s/f (Yiel)
WFA 3 from 4yo+ 5lb 4 Ran SP% 106.7
Speed ratings (Par 101): **102,101,96,94**
CSF £6.39 TOTE £4.20; EX 6.70.
Owner The Bottom Liners & Mrs R Carr **Bred** Brereton C Jones **Trained** Huby, N Yorks
■ Stewards' Enquiry : Dale Swift two-day ban: used whip in incorrect place (Jul 17-18)

FOCUS
A Class 6 claimer, but in quality terms the strongest race on the card. Again they raced towards the centre, avoiding the stands' rail. The winner has been rated close to this year's handicap form.

3727 RACING UK SKY 432 H'CAP 1m 65y
3:30 (3:31) (Class 5) (0-70,66) 3-Y-O £3,234 (£962; £481; £240) Stalls Low

Form RPR
-041 1 **King Of Paradise (IRE)**[20] 3032 3-9-0 64 JasonHart(7) 4 75+
(Eric Alston) *t.k.h early: prom: hdwy to ld over 1f out: rdn and edgd rt: kpt on wl fnl f* 3/1[2]
3202 2 1 ½ **Only Orsenfoolsies**[32] 2671 3-9-7 64 PJMcDonald 3 71
(Micky Hammond) *t.k.h early: trckd ldrs: effrt and chsd wnr over 1f out: kpt on fnl f: hld towards fin* 9/2[3]
4141 3 3 ¼ **Fine Altomis**[4] 3575 3-9-9 66 6ex TomEaves 1 66
(Michael Dods) *led: rdn over 2f out: hdd over 1f out: hung lft and no ex ins fnl f* 1/1[1]
-005 4 3 ¾ **Captain Baldwin**[4] 3575 3-7-11 45 (v) NeilFarley(5) 5 36
(Jim Goldie) *hld up: drvn along 4f out: plugged on fr over 1f out: nvr able to chal* 33/1
45-0 5 nk **Catramis**[20] 3025 3-8-10 56 DaleSwift(3) 2 46
(Geoffrey Oldroyd) *dwlt: hld up: drvn along over 3f out: no imp fnl 2f* 16/1
5000 6 26 **Barbarella Blue (IRE)**[8] 3451 3-8-2 52 MatthewHopkins(7) 6
(Alan Berry) *hld up in tch on outside: struggling over 4f out: sn btn: t.o* 100/1
-441 7 2 **Always Eager**[78] 1424 3-9-7 64 JoeFanning 7
(Mark Johnston) *chsd ldr to over 3f out: sn rdn and wknd: t.o* 12/1

1m 52.21s (3.81) **Going Correction** +0.50s/f (Yiel) 7 Ran SP% 110.7
Speed ratings (Par 100): **100,98,95,91,91 65,63**
toteswingers 1&2 £2.30, 2&3 £1.60, 1&3 £1.40 CSF £15.70 TOTE £3.30: £1.10, £2.60; EX 15.20.
Owner P G Buist **Bred** Sandro Garavelli **Trained** Longton, Lancs

FOCUS
Races on the round course were run over 25 yards less than the advertised distances and again they made their way home up the centre in the home straight.

3728 STEPS AND PETER ANDRE LIVE THIS SATURDAY H'CAP 1m 3f 16y
4:00 (4:00) (Class 5) (0-75,75) 3-Y-O+ £3,881 (£1,155; £577; £288) Stalls Low

Form RPR
-304 1 **Alsahil (USA)**[32] 2676 6-9-4 70 GarryWhillans(5) 4 80
(Micky Hammond) *t.k.h early: chsd ldr: hdwy to ld over 1f out: hung rt: kpt on strly fnl f* 10/1
0005 2 4 **Tenhoo**[3] 3610 6-9-2 70 JasonHart(7) 5 73
(Eric Alston) *hld up in tch: pushed along briefly 1/2-way: effrt over 2f out: edgd rt and chsd wnr fnl f: r.o same pce* 5/1[3]
6-00 3 6 **Never Perfect (IRE)**[22] 2980 3-8-12 71 MickyFenton 2 63
(Tom Tate) *t.k.h: led: 4 l clr after 3f: rdn over 2f out: wandered and hdd over 1f out: sn btn* 13/8[1]
0056 4 2 **Damascus Symphony**[12] 3310 4-8-10 57 GrahamLee 6 45
(James Bethell) *hld up: drvn and outpcd over 4f out: rallied over 1f out: nvr able to chal* 13/2
3-26 5 3 ¼ **Croftamie**[26] 2848 3-9-2 75 JoeFanning 3 58
(Mark Johnston) *chsd ldng pair tl rdn and wknd over 3f out* 9/2[2]
-135 6 5 **Joshua The First**[46] 2229 3-9-0 73 TomEaves 1 47
(Keith Dalgleish) *t.k.h early: hld up in tch: struggling over 3f out: sn btn* 7/1

2m 30.26s (4.66) **Going Correction** +0.50s/f (Yiel)
WFA 3 from 4yo+ 12lb 6 Ran SP% 107.9
Speed ratings (Par 103): **103,100,95,94,91 88**
toteswingers 1&2 £7.70, 2&3 £2.10, 1&3 £3.20 CSF £52.96 TOTE £9.70: £3.60, £2.60; EX 61.80.
Owner R D Bickenson **Bred** Shadwell Farm LLC **Trained** Middleham Moor, N Yorks

FOCUS
They went a very strong gallop and only the first three home were ever seriously involved.

3729 JOHN SMITH'S FAIR FRIDAY H'CAP 1m 4f 17y
4:30 (4:30) (Class 6) (0-65,63) 3-Y-O £1,940 (£577; £288; £144) Stalls Low

Form RPR
-360 1 **Madam Lilibet (IRE)**[20] 3023 3-8-3 45 PaulQuinn 3 59
(Sharon Watt) *hld up: stdy hdwy over 4f out: effrt over 2f out: blkd and led ins fnl f: kpt on wl* 50/1
3304 2 ½ **Luctor Emergo (IRE)**[13] 3275 3-8-11 53 TomEaves 5 66
(Keith Dalgleish) *chsd ldrs: rdn over 3f out: led over 1f out: hung rt and hdd ins fnl f: edgd lft and kpt on same pce towards fin* 7/1
00-0 3 2 **Solar View (IRE)**[28] 2787 3-8-5 47 ChrisCatlin 4 57
(Sir Mark Prescott Bt) *led: rdn 4f out: hung lft and hdd over 1f out: kpt on same pce fnl f* 6/4[1]
1303 4 8 **Za'Lan (USA)**[21] 3003 3-9-7 63 JoeFanning 6 60
(Mark Johnston) *w ldr: rdn over 3f out: wknd over 1f out* 3/1[2]
6-60 5 2 **Altnaharra**[49] 2141 3-8-7 49 (p) PJMcDonald 1 43
(Jim Goldie) *prom: lost pl over 5f out: sn rdn: no imp fr 2f out* 8/1
6004 6 2 **Oops Caroline (IRE)**[20] 3023 3-8-8 50 (b) PaulMulrennan 2 41
(David O'Meara) *hld up in tch: stdy hdwy 1/2-way: rdn and hung rt over 3f out: sn btn* 13/2[3]
4-06 7 20 **Hunting Gonk**[16] 3186 3-9-7 63 GrahamLee 7 22
(James Given) *prom: lost pl 1/2-way: lost tch fnl 4f* 12/1

2m 44.81s (6.21) **Going Correction** +0.50s/f (Yiel) 7 Ran SP% 111.6
Speed ratings (Par 98): **99,98,97,92,90 89,76**
toteswingers 1&2 £21.70, 2&3 £2.60, 1&3 £12.80 CSF £340.36 TOTE £47.20: £5.80, £3.90; EX 199.60.
Owner D H Montgomerie **Bred** Mrs Clodagh McStay **Trained** Brompton-on-Swale, N Yorks

FOCUS
A weak 3yo stayers' handicap and a shock winner.

3730 FOLLOW @HAMILTONPARKRC ON TWITTER H'CAP 5f 4y
5:00 (5:00) (Class 5) (0-75,75) 3-Y-O+ £3,234 (£962; £481; £240) Stalls Centre

Form RPR
35-3 1 **Jamaican Bolt (IRE)**[10] 3382 4-9-9 75 DaleSwift(3) 1 94+
(Geoffrey Oldroyd) *t.k.h early: mde all: qcknd clr whn drifted lft ins fnl f: eased nr fin: readily* 11/4[2]
3004 2 3 ¼ **Wicked Wilma (IRE)**[12] 3308 8-8-11 67 MatthewHopkins(7) 9 72
(Alan Berry) *t.k.h: cl up: effrt and rdn over 1f out: kpt on fnl f: no ch w wnr* 14/1
0202 3 1 **Distant Sun (USA)**[5] 3523 8-8-7 56 oh1 (p) BarryMcHugh 8 57
(Linda Perratt) *trckd ldrs: drvn 1/2-way: edgd rt over 1f out: kpt on ins fnl f* 10/1
0651 4 1 **Another Citizen (IRE)**[13] 3285 4-9-2 65 (b) DavidAllan 4 63
(Tim Easterby) *cl up: effrt and drvn 2f out: one pce fnl f* 7/1
005 5 nk **Northern Bolt**[5] 3523 7-9-4 67 (b) PatrickMathers 2 64
(Ian McInnes) *in tch: sn drvn along: rallied 2f out: no imp fnl f* 16/1
-233 6 1 ¾ **Besty**[8] 3442 5-8-8 57 MickyFenton 5 47
(Paul Midgley) *dwlt: bhd and outpcd: hdwy over 1f out: nvr able to chal* 2/1[1]
140- 7 2 **Tongalooma**[251] 7104 6-9-5 68 GrahamLee 6 51
(James Moffatt) *cl up tl rdn and wknd ent fnl f* 13/2[3]
10-0 8 4 ½ **Wake Up Sioux (IRE)**[10] 3407 3-7-11 56 oh1 NeilFarley(5) 3 21
(David C Griffiths) *chsd ldng gp: drvn over 2f out: wknd over 1f out* 25/1
5004 9 4 ½ **Cayman Fox**[18] 3113 7-8-7 56 oh1 (p) PJMcDonald 7
(Linda Perratt) *dwlt: sn chsd ldng gp: struggling over 2f out: sn btn* 20/1

1m 1.83s (1.83) **Going Correction** +0.45s/f (Yiel)
WFA 3 from 4yo+ 5lb 9 Ran SP% 116.1
Speed ratings (Par 103): **103,97,96,94,94 91,88,80,73**
toteswingers 1&2 £8.30, 2&3 £11.80, 1&3 £4.00 CSF £41.01 CT £342.22 TOTE £4.00: £1.20, £3.80, £2.50; EX 36.70.
Owner R C Bond **Bred** Swordlestown Stud **Trained** Brawby, N Yorks

FOCUS
What beforehand looked a competitive sprint handicap turned out to be a one-horse race.

3731 FAMILY NIGHT WITH REGGIE YATES NEXT SATURDAY H'CAP 6f 5y
5:30 (5:32) (Class 6) (0-65,65) 3-Y-O+ £2,045 (£603; £302) Stalls Centre

Form RPR
-22 1 **Sovereign Street**[13] 3272 4-10-0 65 PaulMulrennan 8 76
(Ann Duffield) *t.k.h: in tch: smooth hdwy to ld 2f out: rdn and r.o strly fnl f* 9/2[2]
6120 2 1 ¾ **Alpha Tauri (USA)**[33] 2617 6-8-13 50 (t) RobbieFitzpatrick 1 56
(David C Griffiths) *t.k.h: hld up: smooth hdwy over 2f out: rdn and ev ch over 1f out: kpt on same pce wl ins fnl f* 16/1
0415 3 1 ¾ **Rock Canyon (IRE)**[10] 3379 3-9-2 64 (p) ShaneBKelly(5) 3 64
(Linda Perratt) *dwlt: bhd: rdn and hdwy over 2f out: kpt on fnl f: nt rch first two* 13/2[3]
0402 4 ¾ **Spread Boy (IRE)**[4] 3581 5-8-2 46 oh1 MatthewHopkins(7) 6 44
(Alan Berry) *led to 2f out: sn drvn: kpt on ins fnl f* 8/1
/1-2 5 ¾ **Bid For Gold**[20] 3026 8-9-12 63 TonyHamilton 12 58
(Jedd O'Keeffe) *hld up: rdn and hdwy over 2f out: kpt on fnl f: no imp* 7/1
0026 6 ¾ **Dolly Royal (IRE)**[6] 3495 7-8-11 48 (p) MichaelO'Connell 9 41
(Robert Johnson) *towards rr: drvn and outpcd over 2f out: styd on fnl f: nvr able to chal* 15/2
-065 7 shd **Reason To Believe (IRE)**[24] 2924 4-9-11 62 (p) PhillipMakin 13 54
(Ben Haslam) *hld up: rdn and hdwy over 2f out: no imp over 1f out* 3/1[1]
000- 8 1 ¼ **Carrie's Magic**[228] 7463 5-8-13 55 GarryWhillans(5) 10 43
(Alistair Whillans) *cl up: rdn over 2f out: edgd lft and wknd over 1f out* 12/1
0000 9 shd **Sleights Boy (IRE)**[7] 3462 4-9-0 51 (v) PatrickMathers 2 39
(Ian McInnes) *prom tl rdn and wknd 2f out* 33/1
406- 10 5 **Findhornbay**[237] 7337 3-9-4 61 JoeFanning 4 33
(Keith Dalgleish) *trckd ldrs: rdn over 2f out: wknd wl over 1f out* 20/1
003 11 6 **Kapunda**[10] 3406 4-8-11 48 AndrewElliott 5
(Jedd O'Keeffe) *cl up tl rdn and wknd over 2f out* 16/1

1m 15.58s (3.38) **Going Correction** +0.45s/f (Yiel)
WFA 3 from 4yo+ 6lb 11 Ran SP% 119.1
Speed ratings (Par 101): **95,92,90,89,88 87,87,85,85,78 70**
toteswingers 1&2 £7.30, 2&3 £13.50, 1&3 £6.80 CSF £75.22 CT £481.49 TOTE £6.10: £2.70, £7.00, £3.10; EX 92.30.
Owner Evelyn Duchess Of Sutherland **Bred** Evelyn Duchess Of Sutherland **Trained** Constable Burton, N Yorks
■ Stewards' Enquiry : Shane B Kelly one-day ban: careless riding (Jul 17)

FOCUS
A modest, but wide-open sprint handicap and the first two pulled clear.
Kapunda Official explanation: trainer said gelding was unsuited by the soft (heavy in places) ground
T/Plt: £1,690.80 to a £1 stake. Pool of £50747.97 - 21.91 winning tickets. T/Qpdt: £264.60 to a £1 stake. Pool of £4183.89 - 11.70 winning tickets RY

3497 KEMPTON (A.W) (R-H)
Tuesday, July 3

OFFICIAL GOING: Standard
Wind: Half behind, moderate becoming light Weather: Overcast and drizzly, rain mid meeting

3732 BETFAIR CLASSIFIED STKS 6f (P)
6:20 (6:22) (Class 6) 3-Y-O £1,617 (£481; £240; £120) Stalls Low

Form RPR
30-0 1 **Take A Note**[36] 2542 3-9-0 60 JimCrowley 8 75
(Patrick Chamings) *hld up towards rr: prog on outer over 2f out: rdn to ld over 1f out: styd on wl* 4/1[2]
0623 2 1 **Taizong (IRE)**[18] 3108 3-9-0 65 StevieDonohoe 5 72
(Ian Williams) *trckd ldrs: prog on outer over 2f out: chal wl over 1f out but edgd lft: styd on but readily hld by wnr* 2/1[1]

5-00 **3** 2 1/4 **Caterina**[11] 3343 3-9-0 65 ....(b[1]) PatDobbs 6 65
(Richard Hannon) *hld up in last trio: hanging and nt qckn over 2f out: stl same pl over 1f out: r.o fnl f to take 3rd nr fin* **22/1**

6305 **4** 3/4 **Langley Vale**[18] 3118 3-9-0 64 .... SebSanders 3 62
(Roger Teal) *plld hrd early: trckd ldng pair: tried to chal on inner wl over 1f out: edgd lft and outpcd by ldng pair after: lost 3rd nr fin* **8/1**

006- **5** *hd* **Kinglami**[237] 7330 3-9-0 65 .... AmirQuinn 11 62
(Brian Gubby) *hld up in midfield: effrt 2f out: nt pce to hold pl and squeezed out over 1f out: kpt on* **14/1**

2500 **6** 2 **Christopher Chua (IRE)**[11] 3350 3-9-0 61 .... DarryllHolland 2 55
(Simon Dow) *dwlt: t.k.h in midfield: effrt 2f out: fdd fnl f* **9/1**

4366 **7** 2 1/2 **Glennten**[18] 3098 3-9-0 65 .... LiamKeniry 9 47
(Sylvester Kirk) *trckd ldr: led over 2f out to over 1f out: wknd qckly* **12/1**

0-60 **8** 2 1/2 **Wordismybond**[19] 3071 3-9-0 63 ....(p) WilliamBuick 4 39
(Peter Makin) *t.k.h early: hld up in last: lost tch w main bunch over 2f out: nvr on terms after* **6/1[3]**

35-0 **9** *nse* **Dahab Gold (IRE)**[12] 3312 3-9-0 60 .... TomMcLaughlin 12 39
(Jane Chapple-Hyam) *racd freely: led to over 2f out: wknd qckly* **25/1**

040- **10** *48* **Copp The Lot (USA)**[314] 5367 3-9-0 62 ....[1] ShaneKelly 1
(Dean Ivory) *difficult to load into stalls: chsd ldrs 2f: dropped rt away: sn t.o* **12/1**

1m 12.29s (-0.81) **Going Correction** -0.075s/f (Stan) **10** Ran SP% **119.0**
Speed ratings (Par 98): **102,100,97,96,96 93,90,87,87,23**
toteswingers:1&2 £2.30, 2&3 £10.20, 1&3 £12.30 CSF £12.66 TOTE £3.70: £1.70, £1.20, £6.60; EX 15.30 Trifecta £149.20 Pool £614.98 - 3.05 winning units..
Owner The Foxford House Partnership **Bred** P J L Wright **Trained** Baughurst, Hants
■ Stewards' Enquiry : Stevie Donohoe one-day ban: careless riding (Jul 17)

FOCUS
A moderate sprint, but the first two were relatively unexposed. The pace was set by Dahab Gold and the time was over a second quicker than the following juvenile maiden.
Christopher Chua(IRE) Official explanation: jockey said gelding suffered interference in running

3733 BETFAIR MEDIAN AUCTION MAIDEN STKS 6f (P)
6:50 (6:51) (Class 6) 2-Y-O **£1,617** (£481; £240; £120) **Stalls** Low

Form RPR

3 **1** **Glass Office**[40] 2415 2-9-3 0 .... JamieSpencer 1 82+
(David Simcock) *led 1f: trckd ldr: led over 2f out: pushed along over 1f out: readily asserted: eased nr fin* **4/11[1]**

0 **2** 1 3/4 **Secret Symphony**[46] 2231 2-9-3 0 .... JamesDoyle 2 73+
(Sylvester Kirk) *trckd ldrs: chsd wnr jst over 2f out and sn clr of rest: styd on wl but no ch to chal* **10/1[3]**

5 **3** 4 **Typhon (USA)**[20] 3040 2-9-3 0 .... TedDurcan 5 64+
(David Lanigan) *trckd ldrs: hanging and outpcd fr over 2f out: pushed along and styd on to take 3rd ins fnl f while stl hanging* **12/1**

00 **4** 2 1/4 **Marguerite St Just**[13] 3282 2-8-12 0 .... SebSanders 11 49
(Olivia Maylam) *led after 1f to over 2f out: sn outpcd by ldng pair: fdd and lost 3rd ins fnl f* **33/1**

5 *hd* **Dashing Storm** 2-8-12 0 .... LukeMorris 7 48
(Jeremy Gask) *s.s: rn green in midfield: effrt fr 1/2-way: hung lft whn pressing for a pl over 1f out: one pce* **50/1**

00 **6** 1 3/4 **Harrogate Fair**[38] 2508 2-9-3 0 .... AndreaAtzeni 3 48
(Michael Squance) *hld up in midfield: pushed along and effrt whn trapped bhd rivals 2f out to over 1f out: fdd whn in the clr fnl f* **33/1**

54 **7** 1/2 **Standing Bear (IRE)**[22] 2983 2-8-12 0 .... DuilioDaSilva(5) 6 47
(Paul Cole) *pushed along in last trio after 2f: effrt on inner over 2f out: sn outpcd* **20/1**

50 **8** 7 **Magic Channel (USA)**[26] 2844 2-9-3 0 .... PatDobbs 9 26
(Richard Hannon) *restless stalls: chsd ldrs on outer to 1/2-way: wknd qckly* **14/1**

63 **9** 1 1/2 **Classic Art**[18] 3117 2-9-3 0 .... EddieAhern 10 21
(Roger Teal) *sn pushed along in last pair: a bhd* **7/1[2]**

10 1 1/4 **Dancing Chief (IRE)** 2-9-3 0 .... DarryllHolland 4 17
(Alan Jarvis) *s.s: rn green in last pair: a bhd* **33/1**

1m 13.31s (0.21) **Going Correction** -0.075s/f (Stan) **10** Ran SP% **124.8**
Speed ratings (Par 92): **95,92,87,84,84 81,81,71,69,68**
toteswingers:1&2 £2.50, 2&3 £10.10, 1&3 £2.30 CSF £5.39 TOTE £1.40: £1.02, £3.20, £1.90; EX 5.00 Trifecta £34.20 Pool £922.82 - 19.92 winning units..
Owner Mrs Fitri Hay **Bred** Bloomsbury Stud **Trained** Newmarket, Suffolk
■ Stewards' Enquiry : Ted Durcan interference to Marguerite St Just by Typhon ins fnl f. No action taken.

FOCUS
An uncompetitive maiden. The time was just over a second slower than the opening Class 6 classified contest for 3yos. It's doubtful the winner had to improve to win. The fourth and the sixth help set the level.

NOTEBOOK
Glass Office didn't require a particularly hard ride to readily see off the quietly fancied runner-up, with the pair clear. The winner had shaped well in a good Haydock maiden (6f, good to firm) on his debut and is evidently useful. (op 2-5)
Secret Symphony hinted at ability on his debut at Newbury and this represents good progression. He went well for a long way but just found a fair sort too good. (op 12-1)
Typhon(USA), who shaped okay over C&D on his recent debut, showed ability out wider than ideal, but he looked a bit awkward under pressure, wanting to hang right. Official explanation: jockey said colt hung right (tchd 11-1)
Marguerite St Just improved on her first two performances, doing well to hang on for fourth having started from the widest stall. (tchd 40-1)
Dashing Storm, a half-sister to, among others, decent 6f winner Intoxicating, out of a 7f winner, showed ability on this debut. She seemed to be a bit short of room at the start and ran green, but kept on.
Harrogate Fair ◆ travelled enthusiastically and might have been a bit closer had he not been short of room late on. He could make an okay sprinter in time. (op 40-1)

3734 BETFAIR SUPPORTING GRASSROOTS RACING H'CAP 2m (P)
7:20 (7:20) (Class 6) (0-65,65) 4-Y-O+ **£1,617** (£481; £240; £120) **Stalls** Low

Form RPR

-011 **1** **Waterford Star (IRE)**[6] 3498 4-9-3 61 6ex ....(v) JamieSpencer 1 72
(Ian Williams) *led at stdy pce to over 10f out: trckd ldr: rdn 3f out: led 2f out: drvn and grad drew clr* **1/1[1]**

5042 **2** 4 **Galiotto (IRE)**[30] 1791 6-9-1 59 ....(v) GeorgeBaker 2 65
(Gary Moore) *trckd ldrs: rdn 3f out: kpt on to take 2nd over 1f out: only able to keep on at one pce* **11/2[2]**

0-10 **3** 1 1/2 **Jacob McCandles**[84] 1269 5-9-7 65 .... KierenFallon 9 69
(Shaun Lycett) *t.k.h: racd wd: hld up in midfield: rdn 3f out: plugged on quite slowly to take 3rd ins fnl f* **12/1**

-051 **4** 1 **Kadouchski (FR)**[22] 2976 8-8-10 61 .... HannahNunn(7) 7 64
(John Berry) *t.k.h: hld up in last pair: pushed along over 3f out: plugged on fnl 2f: nvr a threat* **10/1**

6144 **5** 4 1/2 **Talbot Green**[19] 3086 4-9-4 62 .... MartinDwyer 3 60
(William Muir) *led over 10f out and dictated varied pce: rdn 3f out: hdd 2f out: lost 2nd and wknd over 1f out* **6/1[3]**

4-00 **6** 8 **Wily Fox**[15] 3222 5-9-6 64 .... LukeMorris 8 52
(James Eustace) *hld up in rr: rdn 4f out: struggling and nt on terms over 2f out: no ch after* **9/1**

1460 **7** 10 **Blue Cossack (IRE)**[13] 3283 4-9-2 60 .... DavidProbert 6 36
(Mark Usher) *trckd ldrs: rdn 4f out: wknd 3f out: sn bhd* **20/1**

05/0 **8** 11 **Ildiko (USA)**[20] 3043 5-8-3 47 oh1 ow1 .... RichardThomas 5 10
(Dr Jeremy Naylor) *awkward s: a in last pair: wknd 3f out: t.o* **100/1**

3m 29.97s (-0.13) **Going Correction** -0.075s/f (Stan) **8** Ran SP% **112.2**
Speed ratings (Par 101): **97,95,94,93,91 87,82,77**
toteswingers:1&2 £2.00, 2&3 £10.30, 1&3 £4.30 CSF £6.47 CT £39.09 TOTF £2.00: £1.10, £1.50, £3.40; EX 5.00 Trifecta £22.70 Pool £608.72 - 19.79 winning units..
Owner R S Brookhouse **Bred** Denis McDonnell **Trained** Portway, Worcs

FOCUS
The gallop seemed a bit muddling and this probably isn't a race to be positive about, but the winner took another small step forward.
Ildiko(USA) Official explanation: trainer said mare bled from the nose

3735 OLLY MURS 17.08.12 MAIDEN STKS 1m (P)
7:50 (7:51) (Class 5) 3-Y-O+ **£2,264** (£673; £336; £168) **Stalls** Low

Form RPR

45- **1** **Coco Rouge (IRE)**[414] 2157 4-9-7 0 ....[1] HayleyTurner 3 73
(James Fanshawe) *trckd ldr: led briefly 2f out: pressed new ldr after: styd on wl to ld last 50yds* **6/1[2]**

2 1/2 **Eltifaat (IRE)** 3-9-3 0 .... TadhgO'Shea 14 75+
(Sir Michael Stoute) *slowest away: sn rcvrd to trck ldrs on outer: prog to ld wl over 1f out: rdn fnl f: worn down last 50yds* **12/1**

0 **3** 1 3/4 **Positively**[19] 3070 3-8-12 0 .... WilliamBuick 6 66
(Sir Michael Stoute) *hld up in midfield: shkn up and nt qckn jst over 2f out: styd on fr over 1f out to take 3rd ins fnl f: nvr able to chal* **10/11[1]**

4 1 1/2 **Iz She** 4-9-7 0 .... DarryllHolland 9 64
(William Knight) *sn hld up towards rr: pushed along fr over 2f out: styd on steadily to take 4th nr fin* **66/1**

5 1 3/4 **Sir Palomides (USA)** 3-9-3 0 .... KierenFallon 12 63
(William Haggas) *s.i.s: sn prom on outer: chal jst over 2f out: nt qckn over 1f out: fdd fnl f* **7/1[3]**

6 *shd* **Narcissist (IRE)** 3-9-3 0 .... GeorgeBaker 7 63+
(Ed Dunlop) *hld up towards rr: pushed along over 2f out: styd on steadily fr over 1f out: nrst fin* **20/1**

30- **7** 1 3/4 **Tribouley**[202] 7750 4-9-7 0 .... ShaneKelly 1 56
(Dean Ivory) *led to 2f out: wknd fnl f* **50/1**

04- **8** *shd* **Lone Foot Laddie (IRE)**[305] 5672 3-9-3 0 ....[1] LiamKeniry 13 59
(Sylvester Kirk) *wl away but sn restrained into last quartet: pushed along over 2f out: reminder over 1f out: styd on* **25/1**

00 **9** *shd* **Imperial Wave (IRE)**[30] 2734 3-8-12 0 .... TedDurcan 4 54+
(David Lanigan) *in tch in midfield: no imp on ldrs 2f out: fdd* **33/1**

10 3/4 **Cool As Cash** 3-9-3 0 .... NeilCallan 2 57+
(Paul D'Arcy) *trckd ldrs: pushed along and cl up whn stmbld bdly jst over 2f out: nt rcvr* **20/1**

00 **11** 1 1/2 **Geeaitch**[36] 2543 3-9-3 0 .... WilliamCarson 8 53
(Anthony Carson) *hld up and sn in last quartet: edgd lft towards nr side in st: nvr a factor* **125/1**

0- **12** 1 **Garzoni**[279] 6440 3-8-12 0 .... LukeMorris 11 46+
(Sir Mark Prescott Bt) *plld hrd: hld up in last quartet: rdn wl over 2f out: no real prog* **28/1**

03- **13** 3/4 **Monopoli**[265] 6805 3-8-12 0 .... JimCrowley 10 44
(Ralph Beckett) *hld up and sn in last quartet: brief effrt on inner over 2f out: sn no prog* **7/1[3]**

14 1 1/4 **Medeeba** 3-9-3 0 .... JamieGoldstein 5 47
(Zoe Davison) *trckd ldrs: pushed along over 3f out: wknd over 2f out* **125/1**

1m 41.27s (1.47) **Going Correction** -0.075s/f (Stan)
WFA 3 from 4yo 9lb **14** Ran SP% **124.2**
Speed ratings (Par 103): **89,88,86,85,83 83,81,81,81,80 79,78,77,76**
toteswingers:1&2 £12.40, 2&3 £4.40, 1&3 £4.10 CSF £69.83 TOTE £5.80: £2.90, £2.50, £1.80; EX 35.00 Trifecta £226.40 Pool £397.85 - 1.30 winning units..
Owner Carivalis, Eady & Swinburn **Bred** Roundhill Stud & C & M Murphy **Trained** Newmarket, Suffolk

FOCUS
The bare form doesn't look anything special (time 2.08 seconds slower than following Class 5 handicap), but an interesting maiden nonetheless and the runner-up shaped like much the best horse in the race. The winner was up a length from last year's debut form.
Cool As Cash Official explanation: jockey said gelding clipped heels

3736 BETFAIR.COM H'CAP (LONDON MILE QUALIFIER) 1m (P)
8:20 (8:20) (Class 5) (0-75,74) 3-Y-O **£2,264** (£673; £336; £168) **Stalls** Low

Form RPR

-140 **1** **Jumeirah Palm Star**[38] 2503 3-9-5 72 .... PatDobbs 6 79
(Richard Hannon) *trckd ldng pair in r where it paid to be prom: wnt 2nd jst over 2f out: styd on to ld last 75yds* **14/1**

-166 **2** *hd* **Enery (IRE)**[38] 2471 3-9-7 74 .... MickaelBarzalona 4 80
(Mark Johnston) *trckd ldrs on outer: rdn over 2f out: styd on fr over 1f out to take 2nd last strides* **8/1**

-245 **3** 1/2 **Gunner Will (IRE)**[21] 3001 3-9-5 72 .... JamieSpencer 5 77
(Jamie Osborne) *led: increased pce fr 1/2-way: drvn for home over 2f out: collared last 75yds* **16/1**

-520 **4** *hd* **Daliance (IRE)**[40] 2428 3-9-6 73 .... RichardKingscote 1 78+
(Tom Dascombe) *hld up bhd ldrs: rdn over 2f out: styd on fr over 1f out: clsng on ldrs fin: too much to do* **11/4[1]**

-403 **5** 1 1/4 **Halling Dancer**[19] 3071 3-9-6 73 .... SebSanders 10 75
(Lee Carter) *trckd ldr to jst over 2f out: nt qckn: one pce fr over 1f out* **12/1**

014- **6** 1 1/4 **Fresa**[333] 4760 3-9-4 71 .... LukeMorris 3 70+
(Sir Mark Prescott Bt) *rn in snatches in midfield: effrt u.p 2f out: no prog over 1f out* **9/2[3]**

4-32 **7** *nk* **The Noble Ord**[52] 2089 3-9-6 73 .... JamesDoyle 2 71
(Sylvester Kirk) *hld up towards rr: rdn on inner over 2f out: one pce and nvr on terms w ldrs* **15/2**

1425 **8** 2 **Berlusca (IRE)**[19] 3063 3-9-4 71 .... ShaneKelly 14 65+
(Mark Brisbourne) *stdd s: tk fierce hold early in last trio: sme modest prog under sympathetic handling fnl f* **8/1**

5-06 **9** 1 **Superciliary**[19] 3071 3-9-0 67 .... JimCrowley 7 58
(Ralph Beckett) *a towards rr: struggling once pce lifted over 2f out: n.d after* **16/1**

60-5 **10** *nk* **Supreme Rock**[164] 249 3-8-10 **63**................................. PatCosgrave 11 56
(Jim Boyle) *hld up in rr: shkn up over 2f out: n.d after* **25/1**
1-03 **11** *1 ½* **Amoralist**[25] 2898 3-9-7 **74**................................. WilliamBuick 9 61
(Ed Dunlop) *t.k.h: hld up in last trio: rdn and no rspnse over 2f out: wl btn after* **4/1**[2]
06-0 **12** *nk* **Greatest Dancer (IRE)**[19] 3071 3-9-5 **72**.....................(b) TedDurcan 13 58
(Jamie Osborne) *t.k.h: hld up in last trio: rdn and no prog over 2f out: wl btn after* **66/1**

1m 39.19s (-0.61) **Going Correction** -0.075s/f (Stan) **12** Ran SP% **130.3**
Speed ratings (Par 100): **100,99,99,99,97 96,96,94,93,93 91,91**
toteswingers:1&2 £26.60, 2&3 £41.90, 1&3 £30.70 CSF £133.60 CT £1861.80 TOTE £27.70: £5.50, £2.20, £7.20; EX 152.20 TRIFECTA Not won..
Owner Hamed Rashed Bin Ghadayer **Bred** Plantation Stud **Trained** East Everleigh, Wilts
■ Stewards' Enquiry : Pat Dobbs three-day ban: careless riding (Jul 19,20,22); two-day ban: used whip above permitted level (Jul 23-24)

FOCUS
The time was over two seconds quicker than the preceding maiden, yet it was still steadily run and it proved difficult to make up significant ground. The winner is rated up 4lb on her Lingfield win.
Berlusca(IRE) Official explanation: jockey said, regarding running and riding, that his orders were to do the best he could from a wide draw and, having opted to settle in, the pace slowed and the gelding then ran free early stages, he would have preferred to have been in a better position when turning into the straight as it could only stay on one pace when asked for an effort inside 2f mark.

3737 BETFAIR H'CAP 1m 3f (P)
8:50 (8:50) (Class 4) (0-80,79) 3-Y-O **£4,528** (£1,347; £673; £336) **Stalls** Low

Form RPR
-412 **1** **Ruscello (IRE)**[29] 2772 3-9-5 **77**....................................... WilliamBuick 2 86+
(Ed Walker) *hld up in midfield: hmpd by wkng ldr on inner over 2f out: prog fnl 2f: sustained effrt u.p to ld last 75yds* **6/1**[2]
335- **2** *nk* **Yours Ever**[206] 7709 3-8-13 **71**................................. LukeMorris 5 79+
(Sir Mark Prescott Bt) *trckd ldrs: lost pl and drvn over 4f out: rallied over 2f out: drvn ahd narrowly 1f out: hdd last 75yds: styd on* **20/1**
2-24 **3** *½* **Debating Society (IRE)**[57] 1938 3-9-3 **75**......................... PatDobbs 1 82
(Sir Michael Stoute) *trckd ldng pair: clsd to chal over 2f out: upsides over 1f out tl ins fnl f: kpt on* **7/1**[3]
-162 **4** *¾* **Hurricane In Dubai (IRE)**[25] 2866 3-9-3 **75**..................... EddieAhern 6 81
(Denis Coakley) *hld up in midfield: effrt over 2f out: drvn and cl enough 1f out: nt qckn fnl f* **7/1**[3]
403 **5** *1* **Sound Hearts (USA)**[26] 2849 3-9-5 **77**............................. NeilCallan 9 81
(Roger Varian) *hld upin last trio: effrt over 2f out: clsd on ldrs over 1f out: nt qckn after* **14/1**
-433 **6** *nk* **Corsetry (USA)**[22] 2980 3-9-3 **75**.................................. TomQueally 7 79
(Sir Henry Cecil) *hld up in last: looking for room over 2f out: prog on wd outside over 1f out: nt qckn fnl f* **9/1**
41- **7** *3 ¾* **Saytara (IRE)**[266] 6776 3-9-7 **79**............................ MickaelBarzalona 8 76
(Saeed Bin Suroor) *hld up: racd wd in last trio: prog 5f out: drvn to ld over 2f out: hdd & wknd 1f out* **1/1**[1]
-515 **8** *9* **Ballyheigue (IRE)**[40] 2427 3-9-7 **79**..............................(b) ShaneKelly 4 60
(Brian Meehan) *led at gd pce: drew clr 1/2-way: wknd and hdd over 2f out* **20/1**
05-0 **9** *17* **Turned To Gold (IRE)**[45] 2271 3-9-1 **73**........................... JimCrowley 3 23
(Alan Jarvis) *chsd clr ldr to wl over 2f out: wknd rapidly: t.o* **40/1**

2m 17.92s (-3.98) **Going Correction** -0.075s/f (Stan) **9** Ran SP% **117.9**
Speed ratings (Par 102): **111,110,110,109,109 108,106,99,87**
toteswingers:1&2 £3.60, 2&3 £22.90, 1&3 £8.30 CSF £117.83 CT £863.34 TOTE £7.30: £1.20, £5.10, £2.20; EX 111.20 Trifecta £337.60 Pool £579.52 - 1.27 winning units..
Owner Laurence A Bellman **Bred** Ballymacoll Stud Farm Ltd **Trained** Newmarket, Suffolk

FOCUS
A bunch finish, but still quite good-looking form, and this was the only race on the card that saw the winning time dip under standard. The winner continued his progress.

3738 BETFAIR BRINGS YOU BETTER VALUE H'CAP 7f (P)
9:20 (9:22) (Class 5) (0-70,70) 3-Y-O+ **£2,264** (£673; £336; £84; £84) **Stalls** Low

Form RPR
42-1 **1** **Eager To Bow (IRE)**[178] 91 6-9-11 **67**............................ JimCrowley 7 76
(Patrick Chamings) *hld up in midfield: prog on inner over 2f out: led over 1f out: hung lft after: hld on* **5/1**[2]
5033 **2** *hd* **Homeboy (IRE)**[7] 3466 4-8-13 **62**................................... KatiaScallan(7) 1 70
(Marcus Tregoning) *hld up in rr: rapid prog arnd field to go prom 3f out: rdn to chse wnr 1f out: edgd lft: nvr quite got there* **9/1**[3]
40-6 **3** *1 ¼* **Paphos**[27] 2811 5-9-7 **63**..(v) SaleemGolam 11 68
(Stuart Williams) *slowest away: t.k.h and hld up in last trio: shkn up over 2f out: prog wl over 1f out: styd on wl to take 3rd nr fin* **33/1**
2212 **4** *½* **Dvinsky (USA)**[21] 3006 11-9-9 **65**...........................(b) TomMcLaughlin 12 68
(Paul Howling) *pushed along fr wd draw to chse ldr: drvn and lost 2nd 2f out: kpt plugging away but a hld* **12/1**
0-01 **4** *dht* **Sir Mozart (IRE)**[8] 3456 9-9-10 **66** 6ex.............................. TomQueally 8 69
(Barney Curley) *settled to trck ldrs: shkn up and nt qckn over 2f out: styd on fr over 1f out: edgd lft and nvr able to chal* **1/1**[1]
-062 **6** *nse* **Amba**[7] 3467 6-9-1 **60**.. AdamBeschizza(3) 9 63
(Des Donovan) *disruptive gng to post: rousted along to ld: drvn over 2f out: hdd over 1f out: plugged on one pce after* **10/1**
6-00 **7** *1 ¼* **Victorian Number (FR)**[15] 3222 4-8-6 **55**..................... AliceHaynes(7) 3 55
(Geoffrey Deacon) *hld up towards rr: effrt on inner over 2f out: kpt on same pce: nvr able to chal* **66/1**
1030 **8** *1 ¼* **Gallantry**[17] 3154 10-9-5 **61**... JimmyQuinn 5 57
(Paul Howling) *hld up wl in rr: pushed along over 2f out: kpt on fr over 1f out: nvr a threat* **20/1**
-400 **9** *1 ¼* **Orpen'Arry (IRE)**[38] 2500 4-10-0 **70**..............................(t) SeanLevey 13 63
(Jimmy Fox) *nvr bttr than midfield fr wd draw: drvn over 2f out: sn btn* **25/1**
3000 **10** *3 ¼* **Irons On Fire (USA)**[10] 3388 4-9-6 **62**............................... AmirQuinn 4 46
(Lee Carter) *prom tl wknd over 2f out* **50/1**
6000 **11** *½* **Ace Of Spies (IRE)**[21] 3006 7-9-6 **62**............................ HayleyTurner 10 45
(Conor Dore) *prom: shkn up and nt qckn over 2f out: sn lost pl and wknd* **16/1**
22-0 **12** *shd* **Leelu**[41] 2399 6-9-9 **65**... JamesDoyle 6 48
(David Arbuthnot) *t.k.h: hld up towards rr: urged along over 2f out: wknd over 1f out* **16/1**

1m 25.92s (-0.08) **Going Correction** -0.075s/f (Stan) **12** Ran SP% **120.2**
Speed ratings (Par 103): **97,96,95,94,94 94,93,91,90,86 86,86**
toteswingers:1&2 £7.50, 2&3 £8.30, 1&3 £20.20 CSF £47.41 CT £1386.68 TOTE £5.20: £1.60, £2.80, £6.20; EX 37.60 Trifecta £436.60 Part won. Pool £590.00 - 0.63 winning units..
Owner Mrs J E L Wright **Bred** Stone Ridge Farm **Trained** Baughurst, Hants

FOCUS
The pace appeared modest in this weak handicap, and runner-up Homeboy looked by some margin the best horse in the race at the weights. The form is rated through the third and fourth.
Leelu Official explanation: jockey said mare missed the break
T/Plt: £59.90 to a £1 stake. Pool £60,620.18 - 738.19 winning units. T/Qpdt: £67.80 to a £1 stake. Pool £4,664.76 - 50.90 winning units. JN

3739 - 3745a (Foreign Racing) - See Raceform Interactive

3683 HAMBURG (R-H)
Tuesday, July 3

OFFICIAL GOING: Turf: good

3746a IDEE HANSA-PREIS (GROUP 2 (3YO+) (TURF) 1m 4f
6:00 (12:00) 3-Y-O+
£33,333 (£12,916; £5,416; £3,333; £2,083; £1,250)

RPR
1 **Ovambo Queen (GER)**[44] 2322 5-9-3 0.............................. FilipMinarik 7 112
(Dr A Bolte, Germany) *trckd ldr in 2nd on outer: rdn 2 1/2f out: r.o to chal over 1 1/2f out: sustained battle w runner-up thrght fnl f: got up to ld post: jst prevailed* **12/5**[3]
2 *nse* **Waldpark (GER)**[51] 2106 4-9-6 0... EPedroza 6 115
(A Wohler, Germany) *midfield on inner: rdn over 2f out: r.o to chal over 1 1/2f out: sn led: sustained battle w wnr thrght fnl f: hdd post: jst denied* **7/5**[1]
3 *2 ½* **Atempo (GER)**[65] 1700 4-9-6 0... ADeVries 3 111
(J Hirschberger, Germany) *hld up in last pair: rdn and outpcd over 2 1/2f out: stern reminders over 2f out: plugged on u.p to go 3rd wl ins fnl f: nt pce to chal* **23/10**[2]
4 *1* **Baschar**[47] 5-9-6 0.. VSchulepov 4 109
(M G Mintchev, Germany) *stdd and settled in midfield on outer: rdn over 2 1/2f out: outpcd over 1 1/2f out: plugged on to go 4th cl home* **166/10**
5 *¾* **Lindenthaler (GER)**[44] 2322 4-9-6 0....................................... AStarke 1 108
(P Schiergen, Germany) *led: rdn to extend advantage over 2 1/2f out: strly pressed fr over 1 1/2f out: sn hdd: no ex and fdd ins fnl f* **13/1**
6 *½* **Silvaner (GER)**[44] 2322 4-9-6 0.. THellier 5 107
(P Schiergen, Germany) *trckd ldr in 3rd on inner: rdn to chal over 1 1/2f out: kpt on tl no ex and fdd ins fnl f* **6/1**
7 *3* **Kasumi (GER)**[48] 2191 5-9-3 0... APietsch 2 100
(R Dzubasz, Germany) *hld up in last: rdn over 2 1/2f out: sn outpcd: plugged on: n.d* **33/1**

2m 35.96s (1.41) **7** Ran SP% **131.4**
WIN (incl. 10 euro stake): 34. PLACES: 12, 12, 12. SF: 78.
Owner Dr H H Leimbach **Bred** Gestut Rietberg **Trained** Germany

2873 CATTERICK (L-H)
Wednesday, July 4

OFFICIAL GOING: Good to soft (soft in places) changing to soft after race 3 (3:20)
Wind: Light behind Weather: Cloudy

3747 BRITISH STALLION STUDS SUPPORTING BRITISH RACING E B F MAIDEN FILLIES' STKS 5f
2:20 (2:21) (Class 5) 2-Y-O **£3,169** (£943; £471; £235) **Stalls** Low

Form RPR
05 **1** **Our Diane (IRE)**[25] 2912 2-9-0 0................................. DanielTudhope 12 77
(David O'Meara) *led stands' side gp: overall ldr jst ins fnl 2f: rdn and styd on strly fnl f* **15/2**
00 **2** *2* **Red Highlites (IRE)**[36] 2587 2-9-0 0.............................(p) GrahamLee 10 70
(Ann Duffield) *chsd wnr stands' side: hdwy 2f out: rdn over 1f out: no imp ins fnl f: 2nd of 4 in gp* **28/1**
33 **3** *¾* **Dream Maker (IRE)**[30] 2770 2-9-0 0....................... RichardKingscote 1 67+
(Tom Dascombe) *chsd ldrs far side: rdn along 2f out: kpt on u.p fnl f: 1st of 9 in gp* **5/1**[3]
2243 **4** *1 ¾* **Mandy Lexi (IRE)**[7] 3490 2-9-0 76....................................... TomEaves 4 61
(Bryan Smart) *cl up far side: rdn along over 2f out: drvn wl over 1f out: sn wknd: 2nd of 9 in gp* **2/1**[1]
0 **5** *3 ¼* **Ena Sharples**[36] 2587 2-9-0 0.. AdrianNicholls 11 49+
(David Nicholls) *bhd far side far side: rdn along 2f out: styd on strly appr fnl f: nrst fin: 3rd of 9 in gp* **40/1**
424 **6** *¾* **Therapeutic**[19] 3110 2-9-0 69.................................... SilvestreDeSousa 3 47
(Scott Dixon) *overall ldr far side: rdn along 2f out: sn hdd: wknd over 1f out: 4th of 9 in gp* **3/1**[2]
7 *2 ¾* **Tussy Marx** 2-9-0 0... GrahamGibbons 2 37
(David Barron) *racd far side: bhd: rdn along on inner 1/2-way: sme late hdwy: 5th of 9 in gp* **9/1**
26 **8** *1 ¼* **Cymeriad**[26] 2873 2-8-7 0.. DavidSimmonson(7) 7 32
(Michael Easterby) *chsd ldrs far side: rdn along over 2f out: sn wknd: 6th of 9 in gp* **40/1**
044 **9** *¾* **Shirley's Pride**[18] 3150 2-9-0 56................................. RussKennemore 9 30
(John Holt) *chsd ldrs far side: rdn along 2f out: grad wknd: 7th of 9 in gp* **40/1**
10 *1 ¼* **Shesnotforturning (IRE)** 2-9-0 0.................................. PhillipMakin 5 25
(Ben Haslam) *sltly hmpd s: a towards rr far side: 8th of 9 in gp* **50/1**
0 **11** *2* **Pink Cadillac (IRE)**[16] 3208 2-9-0 0.............................. PJMcDonald 14 18
(Ben Haslam) *chsd ldng pair stands' side: rdn along 2f out: sn one pce: 3rd of 4 in gp* **66/1**
0 **12** *hd* **Strange Angel (IRE)**[11] 3381 2-9-0 0.............................. MickyFenton 6 17
(Tom Tate) *in midfield on far side: rdn along at 1/2-way: sn outpcd: last of 9 in gp* **28/1**
0 **13** *12* **Poppy's Purse**[30] 2770 2-9-0 0...................................... PaulMulrennan 13
(Ollie Pears) *s.i.s: a bhd stands' side: last of 4 in gp* **66/1**

1m 0.98s (1.18) **Going Correction** +0.025s/f (Good) **13** Ran SP% **115.9**
Speed ratings (Par 91): **91,87,86,83,78 77,73,71,69,67 64,64,45**
toteswingers 1&2 £18.90, 1&3 £4.70, 2&3 £13.20 CSF £197.20 TOTE £8.50: £2.80, £6.70, £1.50; EX 110.70 TRIFECTA Not won..
Owner Middleham Park Racing Xii **Bred** Simba Holdings **Trained** Nawton, N Yorks

FOCUS
There was a difference of opinion in this opening maiden, with the field splitting, and two of the four runners to come stands' side led them home. The runner-up is possibly the best guide to the form, while the fourth was below his best.

NOTEBOOK
Our Diane(IRE) didn't get home in soft ground at Chester the time before (not helped by wide draw), but conditions were slightly better here and she had the run of things, leading her small group against the stands' rail. Nurseries will presumably be the next step. (op 5-1)

Red Highlites(IRE), in the same ownership as the winner, improved markedly on her previous efforts, benefiting from the fitting of first-time cheekpieces and perhaps the softer ground as well. (tchd 25-1)

Dream Maker(IRE), having her first experience of soft ground, did best of those who stayed far side without being able to improve on her previous efforts. (op 6-1)

Mandy Lexi(IRE) looked solid, with conditions no problem, but she found disappointingly little having raced up on the pace far side. Now 0-5, she's left with a bit to prove. (op 7-4, tchd 9-4 in a place)

Ena Sharples showed more than on debut, staying on late on the far side. (op 50-1)

Therapeutic was another to disappoint, leading early on the far side, and looking at how she faded it's possible she went too fast. Her best run came on fast ground. (op 9-2)

Tussy Marx, half-sister to a pair of 5f winners, as well as a winning hurdler, looked in need of the experience and should progress. (op 10-1 tchd 11-1)

3748 YORKSHIRE-OUTDOORS.CO.UK MEDIAN AUCTION MAIDEN STKS 5f 212y

2:50 (2:50) (Class 5) 2-Y-O £2,264 (£673; £336; £168) Stalls Low

Form			Horse	Jockey	RPR
	1		**Strange Magic (IRE)** 2-8-12 0 (Richard Fahey) *s.i.s: hdwy on inner to chse ldrs after 1f: styd far side and led 2f out: pushed clr over 1f out: styd on strly: comf* **4/1[3]**	TonyHamilton 1	74+
6	2	3	**Red Cobra (IRE)**[13] 3303 2-9-3 0 (Tim Easterby) *trckd ldrs: styd far side and sn chsng wnr home st: rdn wl over 1f out: no imp fnl f* **7/1**	DavidAllan 5	70+
522	3	2 1/4	**Deepest Blue**[4] 3638 2-9-3 0 (Jamie Osborne) *led: wd st to stands' rail: hdd and rdn 2f out: drvn and one pce appr fnl f* **11/8[1]**	GrahamLee 3	63
252	4	8	**Perfect Words (IRE)**[70] 1594 2-9-3 63 (Marjorie Fife) *chsd ldr: wd st towards stands' rail: rdn along 2f out: grad wknd* **12/1**	BarryMcHugh 4	39
02	5	3 3/4	**Old Man Clegg**[19] 3126 2-9-3 0 (Michael Easterby) *in tch: wd st towards stands' rail: rdn along 2f out: sn outpcd* **7/2[2]**	PhillipMakin 10	28
3	6	1 3/4	**Derrochadora (IRE)**[13] 3313 2-8-12 0 (Robert Cowell) *in rr: wd st to stands' rail: a outpcd* **16/1**	PaulMulrennan 8	18
4034	7	nk	**Jamnean**[29] 2790 2-8-12 55 (John Holt) *chsd ldng pair on outer: wd st twards stands' rail: rdn along 2f out: sn wknd* **25/1**	RussKennemore 6	17
00	8	2 1/4	**Hi Candy (IRE)**[16] 3208 2-8-12 0 (Ben Haslam) *chsd ldrs: lost pl after 2f and rr whn wd st to stands' rail: sn bhd* **66/1**	PJMcDonald 9	

1m 16.02s (2.42) **Going Correction** +0.275s/f (Good) 8 Ran SP% **115.7**
Speed ratings (Par 94): **94,90,87,76,71 69,68,65**
toteswingers 1&2 £4.90, 1&3 £2.10, 2&3 £3.00 CSF £32.33 TOTE £4.50: £1.40, £1.50, £1.10; EX 41.00 Trifecta £269.70 Pool: £1,210.21 - 3.32 winning units..

Owner Middleham Park Racing LX **Bred** J Cullinan **Trained** Musley Bank, N Yorks

FOCUS

There was again a split in the straight, although in contrast to the opener the only two who elected to stick to the inside rail came out on top. Those coming stands' side have all been rated below form, and perhaps the runner-up is the best guide.

NOTEBOOK

Strange Magic(IRE), a half-sister to 2yo winners at 6f and 1m, wasn't best away but showed good mid-race speed to close and never looked like being caught once in front. She clearly knew her job, but should have more to offer and is an obvious type for nurseries. (op 5-1 tchd 7-2)

Red Cobra(IRE) came in for support and duly improved on his initial effort, reversing form with Deepest Blue in the process. He never looked like reeling in the winner but can progress again upped to 7f. (op 10-1)

Deepest Blue came stands' side and pulled clear of his group, but never quite looked on terms with the winner. He's proving consistent, if a little vulnerable. Official explanation: trainer said that the colt had a breathing problem (op 5-4 tchd 6-4)

Perfect Words(IRE), runner-up in a course seller last time, was below par on this first start since leaving Mick Channon and probably requires a drop back down in grade. (op 8-1)

Old Man Clegg, runner-up in a competitive seller at York the time before, was never involved and looks more a type for nurseries.

3749 FOLLOW US ON TWITTER @CATTERICKRACES H'CAP 7f

3:20 (3:20) (Class 4) (0-80,77) 3-Y-O+ £4,075 (£1,212; £606; £303) Stalls Centre

Form			Horse	Jockey	RPR
0664	1		**Dr Red Eye**[32] 2696 4-9-3 66 (p) (Scott Dixon) *cl up: led over 2f out: rdn clr wl over 1f out: eased towards fin* **7/2[2]**	SilvestreDeSousa 11	87
-1	2	6	**Miss Ellany (IRE)**[21] 3024 3-9-6 77 (David O'Meara) *trckd ldng pair on inner: swtchd rt and hdwy to chse wnr wl over 1f out: sn rdn and no imp fnl f* **6/5[1]**	DanielTudhope 1	79
0042	3	nk	**No Quarter (IRE)**[15] 3257 5-8-10 59 (Tracy Waggott) *hld up towards rr: hdwy wl over 2f out: rdn wl over 1f out: kpt on fnl f: nrst fin* **14/1**	FrannyNorton 6	64
4322	4	2 1/4	**Mata Hari Blue**[13] 3314 6-9-8 71 (t) (John Holt) *in rr: hdwy 2f out: sn rdn and kpt on appr fnl f: nrst fin* **11/2[3]**	RussKennemore 3	70
5045	5	1 3/4	**Clumber Place**[5] 3559 6-8-13 62 (James Given) *prom: rdn along 3f out: drvn 2f out and sn one pce* **10/1**	PaulMulrennan 7	56
0000	6	nk	**Switchback**[9] 3439 4-9-3 73 (Michael Easterby) *towards rr: sme hdwy over 3f out: sn rdn and n.d* **66/1**	DavidSimmonson(7) 2	66
0-0	7	1	**Nufoudh (IRE)**[37] 2538 8-8-13 62 (Tracy Waggott) *led: pushed along and hdd over 2f out: sn rdn and wknd appr fnl f* **25/1**	JoeFanning 8	53
0306	8	1 1/2	**Boundaries**[32] 2719 4-9-7 70 (v) (Tim Easterby) *s.i.s: a in rr* **22/1**	DavidAllan 10	57
-020	9	1 1/2	**Bay Of Fires (IRE)**[19] 3115 4-8-13 69 (David O'Meara) *chsd ldrs: rdn along 1/2-way: sn wknd* **25/1**	DavidBergin(7) 4	52
600-	10	9	**Desert Creek (IRE)**[292] 6113 6-10-0 77 (David Nicholls) *dwlt: a bhd* **20/1**	AdrianNicholls 5	37

1m 29.54s (2.54) **Going Correction** +0.525s/f (Yiel)
WFA 3 from 4yo+ 8lb 10 Ran SP% **117.1**
Speed ratings (Par 105): **106,99,98,96,94 93,92,91,89,79**
toteswingers 1&2 £2.00, 1&3 £5.40, 2&3 £4.50 CSF £7.53 CT £51.76 TOTE £3.60: £1.50, £1.10, £3.80; EX 11.70 Trifecta £87.30 Pool: £1,169.08 - 9.90 winning units..

Owner The Red Eye Partnership **Bred** G E Amey **Trained** Babworth, Notts

FOCUS

The entire field stayed far side in the straight this time, a pattern that continued throughout the remainder of the afternoon, and little got into the race from off the pace. The winner was close to his best AW form.

3750 RACING AGAIN NEXT WEDNESDAY H'CAP 1m 7f 177y

3:50 (3:51) (Class 5) (0-75,69) 4-Y-O+ £2,264 (£673; £336; £168) Stalls Low

Form			Horse	Jockey	RPR
3055	1		**Mohawk Ridge**[9] 3437 6-9-2 67 (p) (Michael Dods) *a.p: cl up 1/2-way: led over 3f out: rdn clr 2f out: styd on* **6/4[1]**	LeeTopliss(3) 3	75+
6-32	2	2 1/2	**Bijou Dan**[9] 3437 11-8-7 55 (George Moore) *hld up in rr: hdwy 3f out: rdn to chse ldrs 2f out: drvn and one pce fnl f* **11/2[3]**	PJMcDonald 4	59
625	3	nk	**Anna's Arch (IRE)**[17] 3181 5-9-2 69 (Alan Swinbank) *trckd ldrs: hdwy over 3f out: rdn along 2f out: drvn and one pce fnl f* **7/1**	GarryWhillans(5) 7	72
2503	4	3 1/2	**Dan's Heir**[9] 3437 10-7-13 50 oh1 (p) (Wilf Storey) *prom: rdn along over 3f out: drvn over 2f out: sn wknd* **9/1**	DominicFox(3) 1	49
3065	5	3/4	**Descaro (USA)**[10] 3419 6-9-5 67 (v) (David O'Meara) *trckd ldrs on inner: rdn along over 3f out: sn one pce* **9/2[2]**	SilvestreDeSousa 2	65
1400	6	12	**Zefooha (FR)**[17] 3180 8-9-6 68 (p) (Tim Walford) *led: rdn along and hdd over 3f out: wknd over 2f out* **14/1**	GrahamGibbons 5	52
-034	F		**Incitement**[26] 2877 4-9-6 68 (Andrew Crook) *hld up in rr: effrt and pushed along whn slipped and fell home turn: fatally injured* **9/1**	DanielTudhope 6	

3m 42.76s (10.76) **Going Correction** +0.525s/f (Yiel) 7 Ran SP% **112.7**
Speed ratings (Par 103): **94,92,92,90,90 84,**
toteswingers 1&2 £2.00, 1&3 £2.60, 2&3 £4.70 CSF £9.76 TOTE £3.00: £1.40, £2.10; EX 11.60.
Owner Doug Graham **Bred** Old Mill Stud Ltd And Oomswell Ltd **Trained** Denton, Co Durham

FOCUS

Ordinary form for the grade. The winner rates a small personal best with the second and fourth close to their marks.

3751 GO RACING IN YORKSHIRE CLASSIFIED STKS 7f

4:20 (4:22) (Class 6) 3-Y-O+ £2,045 (£603; £302) Stalls Centre

Form			Horse	Jockey	RPR
-254	1		**Dora's Sister (IRE)**[19] 3111 3-8-12 63 (John Quinn) *hld up in tch: hdwy 3f out: led 1 1/2f out: sn rdn and edgd lft ins fnl f: drvn and hld on towards fin* **1/1[1]**	MichaelO'Connell 11	68+
03-0	2	nk	**Eastlands Lad (IRE)**[63] 1757 3-8-12 63 (Micky Hammond) *trckd ldrs on inner: hdwy 1/2-way: cl up over 2f out: rdn and ev ch over 1f out: drvn ins fnl f: kpt on: jst hld* **16/1**	PJMcDonald 4	67
00-5	3	3	**Logans Legend (IRE)**[29] 2791 4-9-6 57 (p) (Lawrence Mullaney) *chsd ldrs: hdwy 1/2-way: cl up over 3f out: sn rdn and kpt on same pce appr fnl f* **12/1**	DanielTudhope 5	62
0-30	4	1	**Oakbrook**[27] 2862 3-8-12 44 (Ann Duffield) *t.k.h early: cl up: led over 2f out: rdn and hdd 1 1/2f out: sn drvn and wknd fnl f* **40/1**	PaulMulrennan 2	56
0-52	5	4 1/2	**Slenningford**[14] 3285 3-8-5 63 (Ollie Pears) *bhd: hdwy wl over 1f out: rdn and kpt on fnl f: nrst fin* **17/2**	JacobButterfield(7) 9	44
-204	6	shd	**Cathcart Castle**[13] 3309 4-9-6 53 (Simon West) *led 2f: cl up: rdn along over 2f out: sn wknd* **20/1**	DuranFentiman 3	47
2430	7	15	**Pelican Rock (IRE)**[12] 3356 3-8-9 58 (t) (Andrew Crook) *chsd ldrs on outer: rdn along 3f out: wknd over 2f out* **7/1[3]**	GaryBartley(3) 7	
-000	8	7	**Nearly A Gift (IRE)**[34] 2615 3-8-12 65 (Tim Easterby) *cl up: slt ld after 3f tl rdn and hdd over 2f out: sn wknd* **11/2[2]**	DavidAllan 1	
06-5	9	10	**Rosa Luxemburg**[21] 3024 4-8-13 23 (p) (Lawrence Mullaney) *virtually ref to r: lost many l s: a wl bhd* **200/1**	GaryMahon(7) 10	

1m 31.77s (4.77) **Going Correction** +0.525s/f (Yiel)
WFA 3 from 4yo+ 8lb 9 Ran SP% **109.7**
Speed ratings (Par 101): **93,92,89,88,82 82,65,57,46**
toteswingers 1&2 £5.30, 1&3 £3.50, 2&3 £16.60 CSF £17.51 TOTE £2.10: £1.10, £5.70, £3.50; EX 16.30 Trifecta £205.70 Pool: £978.76 - 3.52 winning units..
Owner The Clay Family **Bred** Glending Bloodstock **Trained** Settrington, N Yorks
■ Stewards' Enquiry : Gary Mahon five-day ban: used whip when out of contention (19, 20, 21, 22 July)

FOCUS

Few could be given a chance in this classified event. A weak race, and slowly run. The winner did not need to match her best.
Pelican Rock(IRE) Official explanation: jockey said that the gelding ran flat
Nearly A Gift(IRE) Official explanation: trainer's representative said that the filly had a breathing problem

3752 AUGUST 17TH IS LADIES' EVENING H'CAP (DIV I) 1m 3f 214y

4:50 (4:50) (Class 6) (0-65,65) 4-Y-O+ £2,045 (£603; £302) Stalls Low

Form			Horse	Jockey	RPR
655-	1		**Tinseltown**[20] 1216 6-8-2 46 (p) (Brian Rothwell) *mde all: rdn clr over 2f out: kpt on wl* **2/1[1]**	JoeFanning 8	59+
0-60	2	3 1/4	**Jan Smuts (IRE)**[28] 2823 4-7-13 46 oh1 (tp) (Wilf Storey) *hld up towards rr: hdwy 3f out: rdn 2f out: drvn and styd on fnl f: tk 2nd towards fin* **66/1**	DominicFox(3) 4	51
0064	3	3/4	**Amir Pasha (UAE)**[9] 3437 7-8-9 53 (p) (Micky Hammond) *sn trcking wnr: effrt over 2f out and sn rdn: drvn over 1f out and kpt on same pce: lost 2nd towards fin* **6/1[3]**	TomEaves 10	57
-200	4	9	**Arizona High**[28] 2823 4-8-4 48 (v[1]) (Andrew Crook) *hld up in tch: hdwy 4f out: rdn along and in tch over 2f out: sn drvn and imp* **40/1**	DuranFentiman 9	38
1101	5	2 1/2	**Harare**[14] 3277 11-8-12 63 (v) (Karen Tutty) *bhd: pushed along 1/2-way: rdn 3f out: sme late hdwy* **12/1**	GemmaTutty(7) 1	49
4032	6	1 1/4	**Sartingo (IRE)**[9] 3440 5-9-2 60 (Alan Swinbank) *trckd ldrs: effrt to chse ldng pair 4f out: rdn along 3f out: wknd fnl 2f* **11/5[2]**	PaulMulrennan 7	44
-612	7	3/4	**Politbureau**[13] 3310 5-8-13 57 (Michael Easterby) *prom: pushed along 4f out: rdn 3f out and sn wknd* **7/1**	PaddyAspell 3	39
060-	8	6	**Gumnd (IRE)**[331] 4866 5-8-10 54 (Chris Grant) *chsd ldrs: rdn along and lost pl 1/2-way: sn bhd* **28/1**	TonyHamilton 6	27
060-	9	8	**Leaving Alone (USA)**[347] 4326 5-8-6 50 (Edwin Tuer) *hld up: a bhd* **12/1**	BarryMcHugh 5	

2m 44.71s (5.81) **Going Correction** +0.525s/f (Yiel) 9 Ran SP% **114.1**
Speed ratings (Par 101): **101,98,98,92,90 89,89,85,80**
toteswingers 1&2 £8.80, 1&3 £4.00, 2&3 £25.20 CSF £140.74 CT £690.59 TOTE £3.00: £1.10, £12.00, £1.30; EX 143.60 Trifecta £649.10 Part won. Pool: £877.29 - 0.63 winning units..

Owner Tony Arnott **Bred** Biddestone Stud **Trained** Norton, N Yorks

FOCUS

The first division of quite a weak handicap, 1.37secs quicker than division two. The winner was well in on his recent Flat form and could well do better on the Flat.

Sartingo(IRE) Official explanation: jockey said that the gelding ran flat

3753 AUGUST 17TH IS LADIES' EVENING H'CAP (DIV II) 1m 3f 214y

5:20 (5:20) (Class 6) (0-65,64) 4-Y-O+ £2,045 (£603; £302) Stalls Low

Form				RPR
50	1		**Operateur (IRE)**[11] 3402 4-8-9 52 ... PhillipMakin 2	62

(Ben Haslam) *trckd ldr: hdwy to ld 1/2-way: rdn clr wl over 1f out: drvn out* **6/1**

0224 **2** 2 1/4 **Eijaaz (IRE)**[12] 3355 11-9-2 59 ... (p) SilvestreDeSousa 7 — 65
(Geoffrey Harker) *hld up towards rr: stdy hdwy 3f out: rdn to chse ldrs wl over 1f out: drvn to chse wnr ins fnl f: no imp towards fin* **9/4**[1]

145/ **3** 1 1/4 **Gulf Coast**[682] 5333 7-8-10 53 ... (p) GrahamGibbons 4 — 57
(Tim Walford) *chsd ldng pair: rdn along 2f out and sn chsng wnr: drvn and one pce ent fnl f* **11/2**[3]

0320 **4** 1/2 **Coax**[13] 3307 4-9-5 62 ... LeeNewman 1 — 65
(Patrick Holmes) *chsd ldrs: rdn along 3f out: drvn wl over 1f out: kpt on u.p* **8/1**

60/0 **5** 7 **Aggravation**[16] 3213 10-8-13 56 ... TonyHamilton 9 — 48
(Chris Grant) *hld up towards rr: sme hdwy over 2f out: sn rdn and n.d* **22/1**

0053 **6** 10 **Goodness**[16] 3213 4-9-7 64 ... (v) DanielTudhope 3 — 40
(David O'Meara) *led to 1/2-way: trckd wnr: pushed along 4f out: rdn 3f out: wknd over 2f out* **5/2**[2]

000- **7** 1 1/4 **Mainland (USA)**[253] 7077 6-8-7 50 ... PJMcDonald 6 — 24
(Robert Johnson) *chsd ldrs: rdn along over 3f out: wknd over 2f out* **28/1**

00-0 **8** 11 **Zoom In**[29] 2796 4-8-2 45 ... DuranFentiman 8
(Lee James) *hld up: a in rr* **50/1**

0- **9** 4 **Erycina (IRE)**[160] 7357 4-7-12 46 ... NeilFarley(5) 5
(Noel Wilson) *a in rr: rdn along 1/2-way: sn bhd* **28/1**

2m 46.08s (7.18) **Going Correction** +0.525s/f (Yiel) **9 Ran SP% 113.3**

Speed ratings (Par 101): **97,95,94,94,89 83,82,74,72**

toteswingers 1&2 £3.60, 1&3 £5.70, 2&3 £3.20 CSF £18.80 CT £77.84 TOTE £5.80: £1.50, £1.10, £1.30; EX 27.90 Trifecta £119.60 Pool: £807.16 - 4.99 winning units..

Owner Mrs Alison Royston & Mrs C Barclay **Bred** Razza Pallorsi **Trained** Middleham Moor, N Yorks

FOCUS

The time was 1.37secs slower than division one. The pace increased throughout, with Goodness and then the winner forcing the tempo. The runner-up is a decent guide.

Operateur(IRE) Official explanation: trainer said, regarding the apparent improvement in form, that the gelding benefitted from the drop back in trip

T/Plt: £34.20 to a £1 stake. Pool: £71123.03 - 1514.29 winning tickets T/Qpdt: £4.80 to a £1 stake. Pool: £6323.86 - 967.36 winning tickets JR

3429 CHEPSTOW (L-H)

Wednesday, July 4

3754 Meeting Abandoned - Waterlogged

3732 KEMPTON (A.W) (R-H)

Wednesday, July 4

OFFICIAL GOING: Standard

Wind: Moderate, behind Weather: Fine becoming cloudy

3761 WIN BIG WITH BETDAQ MULTIPLES APPRENTICE H'CAP 6f (P)

5:50 (5:52) (Class 5) (0-75,73) 4-Y-O+ £2,264 (£673; £336; £168) Stalls Low

Form — RPR

1666 **1** **Flashbang**[8] 3477 4-9-1 67 ... (t) AshleyMorgan 5 — 76
(Paul Cole) *disp ld: narrow advantage fr over 1f out: hld on wl nr fin* **5/1**[3]

2043 **2** 1/2 **Speightowns Kid (USA)**[8] 3477 4-9-4 73 ... IanBurns(3) 4 — 80
(Matthew Salaman) *disp ld: narrowly hdd over 1f out: same small deficit thrght fnl f: jst hld* **6/5**[1]

0406 **3** hd **Blueberry Fizz (IRE)**[23] 2973 4-7-12 55 ... (v) BradleyBosley(5) 1 — 62
(John Ryan) *awkward s and pushed up to chse ldng pair: tried to chal fnl 2f: bmpd along vigorously and jst hld* **8/1**

165 **4** 3/4 **Perlachy**[128] 718 8-9-1 67 ... (v) DarrenEgan 7 — 71
(Ronald Harris) *hld up in last: rdn over 2f out: styd on fnl 2f: nrst fin but nvr quite able to chal* **10/1**

0056 **5** 1 **Chevise (IRE)**[100] 1049 4-9-7 73 ... DavidKenny 2 — 74
(Steve Woodman) *hld up in 5th: rdn over 2f out: clsd on ldrs and looked a threat 1f out: fdd last 150yds* **12/1**

2060 **6** 1 3/4 **Hinton Admiral**[25] 2940 8-9-1 70 ... JackDuern(3) 6 — 66
(Conor Dore) *s.i.s: hld up in last pair: rdn over 2f out: one pce and nvr on terms* **9/2**[2]

1100 **7** 2 **Punching**[28] 2809 8-9-2 68 ... MatthewLawson 9 — 57
(Conor Dore) *chsd ldng pair: rdn over 2f out: wknd over 1f out* **25/1**

4060 **8** 8 **Elhamri**[22] 3008 8-8-9 64 ... NoelGarbutt(3) 3 — 28
(Conor Dore) *awkward to load into stalls: sn in rr: dropped to last over 2f out: sn bhd* **25/1**

1m 12.68s (-0.42) **Going Correction** -0.125s/f (Stan) **8 Ran SP% 115.9**

Speed ratings (Par 103): **97,96,96,95,93 91,88,78**

toteswingers 1&2 £2.50, 1&3 £6.20, 2&3 £3.30 CSF £11.57 CT £45.70 TOTE £6.70: £1.70, £1.30, £2.00; EX 15.40 Trifecta £129.90 Pool: £656.65 - 3.74 winning units..

Owner A H Robinson **Bred** D J Weston **Trained** Whatcombe, Oxon

FOCUS

A modest apprentices' handicap in which Flashbang and Speightowns Kid finished one-two despite taking each other on for the lead, suggesting they didn't go quick, and the time was 0.57 seconds slower than following Class 5 handicap for 3yos. The winner matched her May Lingfield win.

Chevise(IRE) Official explanation: jockey said that the filly was slowly away

3762 TIME ORDER CARDS IN RACING PLUS H'CAP (BETFAIR SPRINT FLAT SERIES QUALIFIER) 6f (P)

6:20 (6:20) (Class 5) (0-75,75) 3-Y-O £3,234 (£962; £481; £240) Stalls Low

Form — RPR

4-45 **1** **Impel (IRE)**[79] 1412 3-9-7 75 ... PatDobbs 10 — 84
(Richard Hannon) *hld up in last trio: prog jst over 2f out: r.o to ld ins fnl f: drvn out* **6/1**[2]

5543 **2** 3/4 **Ghost Train (IRE)**[32] 2689 3-8-12 66 ... NeilCallan 11 — 72
(Mark Johnston) *pushed up to ld fr wd draw: drvn over 2f out: hdd ins fnl f: kpt on* **8/1**

5-05 **3** 1 **Generalyse**[2] 3702 3-9-3 71 ... AdamKirby 2 — 74
(Ben De Haan) *dwlt: hld up in midfield on inner: prog 2f out: tried to cl on ldr 1f out: styd on same pce* **20/1**

201 **4** 1/2 **Bint Alzain (IRE)**[21] 3044 3-9-4 75 ... RaulDaSilva(3) 12 — 78+
(Gerard Butler) *hld up in last pair fr wd draw: looking for room 2f out: hanging lft over 1f out: jst pushed along and styd on steadily to take 4th ins fnl f: nvr nr to chal* **7/1**[3]

2536 **5** 1/2 **Le King Beau (USA)**[3] 3670 3-9-0 68 ... (v[1]) SeanLevey 3 — 68
(John Bridger) *t.k.h: trckd ldng trio: rdn to cl fr 2f out: ch 1f out: nt qckn* **20/1**

2013 **6** 1/2 **Dressed In Lace**[21] 3041 3-9-4 72 ... IanMongan 9 — 70
(Jo Crowley) *racd wd: chsd ldrs in 5th: rdn over 2f out: kpt on same pce fr over 1f out: nvr able to chal* **11/1**

5221 **7** 2 3/4 **Dancheur (IRE)**[29] 2795 3-9-7 75 ... MartinHarley 6 — 64
(Mrs K Burke) *t.k.h: hld up in midfield: rdn and nt qckn 2f out: fdd fnl f* **6/4**[1]

-404 **8** nk **Little China**[9] 3450 3-9-5 73 ... MartinDwyer 8 — 61
(William Muir) *racd wd in midfield: rdn and no prog over 2f out: n.d over 1f out* **25/1**

065 **9** 1/2 **Judas Jo (FR)**[7] 3500 3-9-6 74 ... WilliamBuick 7 — 61
(Gay Kelleway) *s.s: mostly in last: drvn on outer over 2f out: no great prog* **16/1**

2055 **10** 3/4 **Adranian (IRE)**[42] 2400 3-9-7 75 ... (v) KirstyMilczarek 1 — 59
(David C Griffiths) *t.k.h: cl up bhd ldng pair: chsd ldr briefly over 2f out: wknd over 1f out* **20/1**

4-00 **11** 1/2 **Poetry Writer**[30] 2756 3-8-11 65 ... FergusSweeney 4 — 48
(Michael Blanshard) *mostly chsd ldr to over 2f out: sn wknd* **33/1**

1m 12.11s (-0.99) **Going Correction** -0.125s/f (Stan) **11 Ran SP% 113.2**

Speed ratings (Par 100): **101,100,98,98,97 96,93,92,91,90 90**

toteswingers 1&2 £5.90, 1&3 £21.30, 2&3 £20.70 CSF £46.04 CT £913.31 TOTE £6.10: £3.00, £2.40, £5.70; EX 56.10 Trifecta £302.80 Part won. Pool: £409.26 - 0.10 winning units..

Owner Miss Yvonne Jacques **Bred** Richard McDonnell **Trained** East Everleigh, Wilts

FOCUS

A modest sprint handicap with the favourite disappointing. The form is rated around the third.

Bint Alzain(IRE) Official explanation: jockey said that the filly was denied a clear run

3763 BACK OR LAY AT BETDAQ.COM MAIDEN STKS 1m 4f (P)

6:50 (6:51) (Class 5) 3-Y-O+ £2,264 (£673; £336; £168) Stalls Centre

Form — RPR

-322 **1** **Muntasir (IRE)**[23] 2980 3-8-13 82 ... FrankieDettori 4 — 92
(Saeed Bin Suroor) *trckd ldng pair: wnt 2nd over 3f out: led over 2f out and sn swept 6 l clr: rdn out* **6/5**[1]

0-0 **2** 2 3/4 **Galleon**[46] 2266 3-8-13 0 ... PatDobbs 7 — 88
(Sir Michael Stoute) *dwlt: pushed along in 7th after 4f: reminders 1/2-way: gd prog over 2f out: chsd clr wnr over 1f out: styd on wl but no ch to threaten* **8/1**

43 **3** 11 **Regal Aura**[21] 3035 3-8-8 0 ... WilliamBuick 8 — 65
(John Gosden) *led: gng strly 4f out: rdn and hdd over 2f out whn clr of rest: folded tamely* **7/1**[3]

2 **4** 6 **Presume**[36] 2584 3-8-8 0 ... NeilCallan 11 — 56
(Sir Michael Stoute) *trckd ldrs: rdn over 3f out: lft bhd over 2f out: wl btn after* **9/4**[2]

5 1 3/4 **Murphy (IRE)**[290] 10-9-12 0 ... (t) GeorgeBaker 2 — 58
(Nick Gifford) *dwlt and stdd s: hld up in last: wl bhd whn shkn up to make prog 3f out: styd on steadily after: no ch but nt disgracd* **100/1**

0 **6** 16 **Dee Ee Williams (IRE)**[16] 3227 9-9-12 0 ... JimCrowley 9 — 32
(Nick Gifford) *dwlt: pushed along in last trio: wl bhd 3f out: passed a few stragglers late on: t.o* **33/1**

00 **7** nk **Reigns Of Glory (IRE)**[32] 2708 3-8-13 0 ... SeanLevey 10 — 32
(Richard Hannon) *t.k.h: trckd ldrs tl wknd qckly fr 3f out: t.o* **25/1**

05 **8** 1 1/2 **Bryer (IRE)**[47] 2226 3-8-13 0 ... MircoDemuro 1 — 30
(Mark Johnston) *chsd ldr: drvn and lost 2nd over 3f out: wknd rapidly over 2f out: eased and t.o* **33/1**

9 2 1/4 **Autumnus (IRE)** 3-8-13 0 ... RoystonFfrench 6 — 26
(Ismail Mohammed) *s.s: rn green in last trio: a bhd: t.o* **33/1**

10 4 **Clu Agus Cail (IRE)**[31] 7-9-4 0 ... (t) RyanPowell(3) 5 — 15
(Alison Batchelor) *sn pushed along in 8th: couldn't keep up fr 1/2-way: no ch fnl 3f: t.o* **100/1**

00 **11** 11 **Soho Spirit**[36] 2585 3-8-8 0 ... (b[1]) KirstyMilczarek 3
(James Toller) *chsd ldrs tl wknd rapidly over 3f out: t.o* **100/1**

2m 30.96s (-3.54) **Going Correction** -0.125s/f (Stan)

WFA 3 from 7yo+ 13lb **11 Ran SP% 115.5**

Speed ratings (Par 103): **106,104,96,92,91 81,80,79,78,75 68**

toteswingers 1&2 £1.90, 2&3 £5.10, 1&3 £3.40 CSF £11.17 TOTE £2.10: £1.02, £2.10, £2.50; EX 10.50 Trifecta £32.40 Pool: £977.48 - 22.32 winning units..

Owner Godolphin **Bred** Darley **Trained** Newmarket, Suffolk

FOCUS

They finished strung out in this ordinary maiden, with Regal Aura setting a decent pace before fading. The winner was the clear form pick.

3764 BETDAQ MOBILE APPS/BRITISH STALLION STUDS E B F MAIDEN FILLIES' STKS 7f (P)

7:25 (7:26) (Class 5) 2-Y-O £3,234 (£962; £481; £240) Stalls Low

Form — RPR

0 **1** **Roz**[22] 3009 2-9-0 0 ... JimCrowley 7 — 81+
(Harry Dunlop) *trckd ldr: led 3f out: gng clr whn drifted lft wl over 1f out: r.o wl* **40/1**

0 **2** 3 1/2 **Blue Nova**[47] 2245 2-9-0 0 ... WilliamBuick 2 — 72
(Jeremy Noseda) *chsd ldng pair: rdn as wnr skipped clr over 2f out: wnt 2nd over 1f out: no imp* **15/8**[1]

00 **3** 3/4 **Wittgenstein (IRE)**[14] 3282 2-9-0 0 ... FrankieDettori 9 — 70
(Brian Meehan) *led to 3f out: sn rdn: lost 2nd and one pce over 1f out* **8/1**

4 4 1/2 **Poetic Belle** 2-9-0 0 ... KierenFallon 6 — 58+
(Alan Jarvis) *t.k.h: hld up towards rr: outpcd over 2f out: rdn and kpt on to take modest 4th fnl f* **16/1**

5 hd **Woodlandsway** 2-9-0 0 ... PatDobbs 5 — 58+
(Richard Hannon) *racd wd: chsd ldrs: rdn over 3f out: sn outpcd: kpt on fnl f* **7/2**[2]

0 **6** 1 1/4 **Heliconia**[11] 3401 2-9-0 0 ... LukeMorris 4 — 54+
(Sir Mark Prescott Bt) *in tch: pushed along by 1/2-way: rdn and outpcd over 2f out: kpt on fnl f* **40/1**

0 **7** ½ **Alpine Mysteries (IRE)**[14] 3282 2-9-0 0 .... TedDurcan 8 53+
(John Dunlop) *hld up in last pair: outpcd and pushed along over 2f out: n.d after: kpt on* **33/1**

3 **8** *nse* **Something Magic**[37] 2541 2-9-0 0 .... LiamKeniry 10 53
(Sylvester Kirk) *awkward to load into stalls: hld up in last pair: shkn up and outpcd over 2f out: no ch after* **6/1**[3]

2 **9** *shd* **Sadiigah**[21] 3040 2-9-0 0 .... TomQueally 3 53
(Clive Brittain) *chsd ldng trio: outpcd over 2f out: fdd fnl f* **6/1**[3]

10 *5* **Rosia Bay** 2-9-0 0 .... MichaelHills 1 40
(Charles Hills) *wl in rr: brief effrt on inner over 2f out: sn wknd* **16/1**

1m 26.87s (0.87) **Going Correction** -0.125s/f (Stan) **10** Ran SP% **116.3**
Speed ratings (Par 91): **90,86,85,80,79 78,77,77,77,71**
toteswingers 1&2 £10.70, 2&3 £3.50, 1&3 £49.00 CSF £113.91 TOTE £29.00: £6.40, £1.10, £2.40; EX 244.20 TRIFECTA Not won..
Owner Mrs Mary-Anne Parker **Bred** Darley **Trained** Lambourn, Berks

FOCUS
The pace looked steady, courtesy of Wittgenstein, who had been well held on her first two starts, and the time was slow. This is probably muddling form, but the winner did it well.

NOTEBOOK
Roz showed nothing on her debut over 6f at Salisbury, but she was clearly helped by the longer trip and sounder surface this time, as well as being handily placed. We should learn more about her next time. (op 33-1)
Blue Nova had been off for 47 days since showing ability over 6f on her debut at Newmarket. She was well backed to improve, but the winner got first run and she never looked like mustering the required pace. It's likely she can do better off a truer gallop, but similarly she doesn't look anything out of the ordinary. (op 9-4)
Wittgenstein(IRE) had the run of the race and looks flattered. (op 12-1)
Poetic Belle fared best of the newcomers and could win a similar race granted normal improvement.
Woodlandsway, who is out of a 5f winner, was nicely backed for this debut but she ran to just an ordinary level, not helped by being caught wide.
Heliconia didn't show anything on her debut (7f, soft) but she hinted at ability this time, going on at the finish, and can do a lot better in due course. (op 50-1)
Alpine Mysteries(IRE), like on her debut over C&D, hinted at ability with minor late progress. She should improve given time.
Sadiigah, runner-up over 6f here on her debut, found nothing after travelling well. (op 5-1)
Rosia Bay Official explanation: jockey said the filly would not face the kickback

3765 BETDAY CASINO GAMES H'CAP 2m (P)
8:00 (8:00) (Class 3) (0-90,90) 4-Y-0+ **£6,663** (£1,982; £990; £495) **Stalls** Low

Form RPR

0-04 **1** **Rumh (GER)**[16] 3219 4-9-7 **90** .... FrankieDettori 6 103
(Saeed Bin Suroor) *hld up tl prog to ld after 4f: mde rest: drew rt away fr over 2f out: rdn over 1f out: eased last 100yds* **9/2**[2]

3-00 **2** *7* **Late Telegraph (IRE)**[25] 2933 4-9-5 **88** .... TomQueally 3 91
(Sir Henry Cecil) *trckd ldng pair after 4f: rdn over 3f out: wnt 2nd jst over 2f out: kpt on but no ch w wnr* **3/1**[1]

1150 **3** *1¾* **Chabada (JPN)**[12] 3341 4-9-4 **87** .... JimCrowley 8 88
(Ian Williams) *trckd ldng trio after 4f: rdn over 3f out: kpt on to take modest 3rd fnl f* **7/1**

164- **4** *¾* **Spensley (IRE)**[237] 7347 6-9-7 **90** .... KierenFallon 2 90
(James Fanshawe) *tended to run in snatches: hld up in 7th: rdn over 3f out: plugged on to take modest 4th fnl f* **13/2**

-260 **5** *1¾* **Iron Condor**[39] 2504 5-8-4 **73** .... LukeMorris 4 71
(James Eustace) *pushed along early: sn in midfield: drvn over 3f out: outpcd along w rest by wnr over 2f out: no ch after* **6/1**

0034 **6** *1¾* **The Bells O Peover**[11] 3377 4-8-10 **79** ....(v) MircoDemuro 5 75
(Mark Johnston) *led 4f: chsd wnr to jst over 2f out: wknd fnl f* **12/1**

203- **7** *¾* **Sirius Superstar**[370] 3550 4-8-11 **80** .... JimmyFortune 1 75
(Andrew Balding) *hld up in 6th: rdn over 3f out: no prog: wknd ins fnl f* **11/2**[3]

504/ **8** *52* **Moose Moran (USA)**[134] 6506 5-9-7 **90** ....(t) KirstyMilczarek 7 23
(Olivia Maylam) *a in last pair: wknd 4f out: t.o over 2f out: virtually p.u fnl f* **40/1**

0 **9** *2¾* **Clearwater Bay (IRE)**[11] 3372 5-9-7 **90** .... GeorgeBaker 9 19
(Gary Moore) *a in last pair: rdn 6f out: wknd 4f out: sn wl t.o* **14/1**

3m 23.9s (-6.20) **Going Correction** -0.125s/f (Stan) **9** Ran SP% **115.5**
Speed ratings (Par 107): **110,106,105,105,104 103,103,77,75**
toteswingers 1&2 £3.40, 2&3 £7.90, 1&3 £8.80 CSF £18.41 CT £92.82 TOTE £3.60: £1.20, £1.40, £2.60; EX 20.60 Trifecta £153.00 Pool: £481.93 - 2.33 winning units..
Owner Godolphin **Bred** Stiftung Gestut Fahrhof **Trained** Newmarket, Suffolk

FOCUS
Superb stuff from Frankie Dettori, who seized the initiative in this modestly run race by sending Rumh to the front after a few furlongs, and his mount was allowed a totally uncontested lead while still going an ordinary pace. The other jockeys hardly excelled themselves, and what had looked an interesting staying handicap has to be treated with caution. The winner rated back to her standout 3yo effort.

NOTEBOOK
Rumh(GER) was chucked in if back to her best - she was a 6l Listed winner over 1m2f last year - and her speed was an asset. She was allowed an easy lead and her stamina for this trip was not severely tested. (op 7-2)
Late Telegraph(IRE), upped in trip, readily won the separate race for second and will be worth another try at the distance. (op 7-2 tchd 4-1)
Chabada(JPN) was back on what may be her favoured surface, but the race did not unfold to suit. She made all for her latest win (over 1m6f), but didn't go to the front over this slightly longer trip. (op 6-1)
Spensley(IRE), a four-time course winner over 1m3f-1m4f, was worth a try over this distance, but he hadn't been seen for 237 days and the steady pace gave him no chance. (op 5-1 tchd 7-1)
Iron Condor didn't run to his best, but can be given another chance. (op 7-1 tchd 9-2)

3766 LEONARD CURTIS H'CAP 1m 4f (P)
8:35 (8:37) (Class 3) (0-95,95) 4-Y-0+ **£6,663** (£1,982; £990; £495) **Stalls** Centre

Form RPR

0-00 **1** **Rock A Doodle Doo (IRE)**[4] 3642 5-9-4 **92** .... MartinDwyer 2 103
(William Jarvis) *hld up disputing 7th: prog out wd over 2f out: drvn to ld over 1f out: edgd rt fnl f but r.o wl* **11/2**[3]

242- **2** *1½* **Roxy Flyer (IRE)**[251] 7129 5-9-6 **94** .... PatDobbs 9 102
(Amanda Perrett) *trckd ldrs: plld out wd and prog over 2f out: c to chal wl over 1f out: chsd wnr after: r.o but hld whn impeded ins fnl f* **15/2**

-155 **3** *2¼* **Art Scholar (IRE)**[7] 3502 5-8-10 **84** .... KierenFallon 8 89
(Michael Appleby) *hld up in midfield disputing 7th: prog wl over 2f out: chal wl over 1f out but ldng pair sn wnt past: one pce after* **5/1**[2]

1-10 **4** *1½* **Old Hundred (IRE)**[34] 2639 5-9-7 **95** ....(v) HayleyTurner 11 97+
(James Fanshawe) *sarted v slowly: urged along in last pair early: stl last over 2f out: prog on inner after: tk 4th ins fnl f: no ch* **9/2**[1]

-000 **5** *1½* **Bowdler's Magic**[11] 3377 5-8-4 **78** .... MircoDemuro 1 78
(Mark Johnston) *settled in last quartet: rdn and prog over 2f out but in laboured fashion: one pce fr over 1f out* **16/1**

3510 **6** *2* **Ramona Chase**[33] 2655 7-8-8 **87** ....(t) MarkCoumbe(5) 6 84
(Michael Attwater) *a abt same pl: rdn over 3f out: tried to cl on ldrs 2f out: fdd fnl f* **14/1**

5-03 **7** ½ **Nave (USA)**[26] 2887 5-8-2 **76** .... MartinLane 3 72
(David Simcock) *disp ld 3f: trckd ldr after: led 3f out and tried to kick on: hdd & wknd over 1f out* **13/2**

-646 **8** ½ **All The Winds (GER)**[25] 2921 7-8-6 **83** .... RyanPowell(3) 4 78
(Shaun Lycett) *s.v.s: hld up in last pair: t.k.h at 1/2-way: taken wd and rdn 2f out: sme late prog whn r all over* **12/1**

11/0 **9** *3½* **Ascalon**[18] 3163 8-8-7 **84** .... RaulDaSilva(3) 10 74
(Pat Eddery) *disp ld 3f: pushed along 5f out: wknd u.p 2f out* **25/1**

52/0 **10** *4* **Bobbyscot (IRE)**[11] 3372 5-9-2 **90** .... GeorgeBaker 5 73
(Gary Moore) *hld up in last quartet: shkn up 3f out: no prog 2f out: wl btn after* **20/1**

2334 **11** *6* **Big Creek (IRE)**[58] 1939 5-8-5 **79** .... ChrisCatlin 7 53
(Jeremy Noseda) *trckd ldrs: prog on outer to go prom over 5f out: drvn over 3f out: wkng whn short of room briefly 2f out* **10/1**

11-0 **12** *2¾* **Covert Decree**[79] 1421 4-8-10 **84** .... WilliamBuick 12 53
(Clive Cox) *plld hrd: led after 3f: hdd 3f out: wknd 2f out and eased* **12/1**

2m 30.6s (-3.90) **Going Correction** -0.125s/f (Stan) **12** Ran SP% **121.0**
Speed ratings (Par 107): **108,107,105,104,103 102,101,101,99,96 92,90**
toteswingers 1&2 £5.50, 2&3 £4.60, 1&3 £4.50 CSF £47.57 CT £224.20 TOTE £7.40: £2.80, £2.80, £1.90; EX 46.50 Trifecta £383.70 Part won. Pool: £518.55 - 0.50 winning units..
Owner The Doodle Doo Partnership **Bred** Mrs A S O'Brien And Lars Pearson **Trained** Newmarket, Suffolk

■ Stewards' Enquiry : Martin Dwyer one-day ban: careless riding (18 July)

FOCUS
The pace seemed fair enough, even if it slowed a bit down the back straight. Sound form.

NOTEBOOK
Rock A Doodle Doo(IRE) looked awkward under pressure, not fully extending his head and drifting right, and may have had more in reserve than the official margin suggests. The winner, who progressed to a decent level last year, was improving on his first two efforts of the season and is now 4-5 on Polytrack. (op 8-1)
Roxy Flyer(IRE) was carried right by the winner in the closing stages, but it made no difference to the result. This was her first start for 251 days and it should put her spot on for Glorious Goodwood - she's gained her two wins to date at that course. (op 13-2 tchd 6-1)
Art Scholar(IRE) travelled nicely and was given every chance, but he wasn't good enough. (op 7-2)
Old Hundred(IRE) ideally wants further than this (winner over 2m here on penultimate start), and having missed the break he was hopelessly placed turning into the straight. Official explanation: jockey said that the gelding was slowly away (op 6-1 tchd 13-2)
Bowdler's Magic is another who wants more of a test. (op 25-1)
All The Winds(GER) Official explanation: jockey said that the gelding missed the break
Ascalon Official explanation: jockey said the horse had no more to give
Covert Decree Official explanation: jockey said that the filly ran too freely

3767 IRISH NIGHT AT KEMPTON 11.07.12 H'CAP (LONDON MILE QUALIFIER) 1m (P)
9:05 (9:06) (Class 4) (0-85,91) 3-Y-0+ **£4,075** (£1,212; £606; £303) **Stalls** Low

Form RPR

3013 **1** **Hefner (IRE)**[18] 3156 3-9-1 **81** .... PatDobbs 5 89
(Richard Hannon) *trckd ldr: led over 2f out: rdn and hdd over 1f out: rallied fnl f to ld last 75yds* **14/1**[3]

0211 **2** ½ **Ibtahaj**[7] 3503 3-9-11 **91** 6ex .... FrankieDettori 7 99+
(Saeed Bin Suroor) *slowest away: t.k.h and sn in midfield: gd prog over 2f out to ld over 1f out: edgd rt and hdd last 75yds: nt qckn* **1/3**[1]

0100 **3** *2¼* **Cruiser**[12] 3348 4-10-0 **85** .... MartinDwyer 8 89
(William Muir) *chsd ldrs in 5th: drvn over 2f out: styd on to take 3rd fnl f: n.d to ldng pair* **33/1**

0155 **4** *¾* **My Son Max**[12] 3348 4-9-10 **81** .... WilliamBuick 9 84
(P J O'Gorman) *t.k.h: hld up in last quartet: rdn over 2f out: styd on fr over 1f out to take 4th last strides* **14/1**[3]

5 *hd* **Elwazeer (USA)**[39] 2516 4-9-5 **76** ....(b) TomQueally 10 78
(David Peter Nagle, Ire) *hld up in last quartet: stdy prog over 2f out: coaxed along to cl on ldrs over 1f out: rdn and fnd nil sn after* **20/1**

0500 **6** ½ **Dozy Joe**[9] 3439 4-9-9 **80** .... LukeMorris 4 81
(Ian Wood) *a in midfield: rdn sn after 1/2-way: struggling after but kpt on fr over 1f out* **66/1**

3013 **7** *shd* **Snow Trooper**[16] 3226 4-9-7 **78** .... ShaneKelly 12 81+
(Dean Ivory) *trckd ldng pair: shkn up and nt qckn over 2f out: sn lost pl then hmpd wl over 1f out: one pce after* **20/1**

0-06 **8** ½ **Rossetti**[16] 3229 4-9-2 **73** .... KierenFallon 3 73
(James Fanshawe) *trckd ldrs on inner: drvn to try to chal 2f out: nt qckn over 1f out: fdd fnl f* **16/1**

-100 **9** *2¾* **Ashva (USA)**[26] 2882 4-10-0 **85** ....(bt[1]) AdamKirby 1 78
(Michael Dods) *hld up in 6th: effrt on inner over 2f out but sn lost pl: shkn up and wl btn over 1f out: eased ins fnl f* **14/1**[3]

5056 **10** *3¼* **Prince Of Burma (IRE)**[41] 2417 4-10-0 **85** ....(b) IanMongan 6 71
(Jeremy Gask) *wl in rr: rdn and no great prog over 2f out* **11/1**[2]

5201 **11** *nk* **Megalala (IRE)**[23] 2985 11-9-12 **83** .... KieranO'Neill 11 68
(John Bridger) *led to over 2f out: sn wknd* **25/1**

33-1 **12** *36* **All Nighter (IRE)**[29] 182 3-8-12 **78** .... HayleyTurner 2
(Jamie Snowden) *a in last quartet: wknd over 3f uot: wl t.o* **40/1**

1m 38.33s (-1.47) **Going Correction** -0.125s/f (Stan)
WFA 3 from 4yo+ 9lb **12** Ran SP% **129.5**
Speed ratings (Par 105): **102,101,99,98,98 97,97,97,94,91 90,54**
toteswingers 1&2 £2.40, 2&3 £10.50, 1&3 £64.10 CSF £19.73 CT £237.98 TOTE £20.40: £4.50, £1.10, £8.90; EX 48.20 Trifecta £877.70 Part won. Pool of £1186.16 - 0.30 winning units..
Owner Mrs J Wood **Bred** Denis A McCarthy **Trained** East Everleigh, Wilts

FOCUS
The main story of this contest was the favourite's tough trip and it undoubtedly cost him the race. The winner is rated up a length.
T/Jkpt: Not won. T/Plt: £79.40 to a £1 stake. Pool of £100281 - 46, 921.17 winning tickets.
T/Qpdt: £12.40 to a £1 stake. Pool of £10101.71 -599.54 winning tickets. JN

3746 HAMBURG (R-H)

Wednesday, July 4

OFFICIAL GOING: Turf: good to soft

3768a HAMBURG-DRESDEN-POKAL (LANGER HAMBURGER) (LISTED RACE) (4YO+) (TURF) 2m

4:15 (12:00) 4-Y-0+ **£10,000** (£4,166; £1,666; £833)

RPR

1 **Tres Rock Danon (FR)**[24] 2965 6-9-0 0 APietsch 3 109
(W Hickst, Germany) **1/1**[1]

2 ½ **Tidespring (IRE)**[26] 4-8-10 0 FabriceVeron 4 104+
(H-A Pantall, France) **42/10**

3 1¾ **Flamingo Fantasy (GER)**[39] 7-9-0 0 AStarke 6 106
(S Smrczek, Germany) **43/5**

4 2 **Altano (GER)**[38] 2534 6-9-2 0 EPedroza 1 106
(A Wohler, Germany) **37/10**[3]

5 3½ **All My Heart**[24] 2965 4-8-10 0 JimmyQuinn 2 96
(Sir Mark Prescott Bt) *racd keenly and restrained towards rr: last at 1/2-way: tk clsr order fr 4f out: 3rd and nt qckn whn rdn over 2f out: wknd u.p fnl f* **128/10**

6 7 **Slight Advantage (IRE)**[24] 2965 4-8-10 0 JBojko 5 88
(A Wohler, Germany) **33/10**[2]

3m 26.83s (206.83) **6 Ran SP% 131.4**
WIN (incl. 10 euro stake): 20. PLACES: 15, 21. SF: 152.
Owner Stall D'Angelo **Bred** Chevotel De La Hauquerie & Morton Bloodstock **Trained** Germany

2701 EPSOM (L-H)

Thursday, July 5

OFFICIAL GOING: Good (good to soft in places; overall: 7.7; straight: far side 8.0; stands' side 8.4)
Wind: medium, across Weather: bright, light cloud

3769 DOWNLOAD EPSOM'S ANDROID OR IPHONE APP NOW H'CAP 1m 4f 10y

6:05 (6:05) (Class 5) (0-75,75) 4-Y-0+ **£2,587** (£770; £384; £192) **Stalls** Centre

Form RPR

-120 **1** **Colinca's Lad (IRE)**[60] 1882 10-9-1 **74** RosieJessop(5) 5 82
(Peter Charalambous) *mde all: sn clr: rdn over 2f out: tiring but kpt on gamely fnl f: a gng to hold on* **6/1**

25-1 **2** ¾ **Reggie Perrin**[43] 2395 4-8-2 **61** (v) JemmaMarshall(5) 6 67
(Pat Phelan) *chsd ldng pair: rdn and clsd on wnr fr 2f out: kpt on to go 2nd wl ins fnl f: nvr quite getting to wnr* **15/2**

5110 **3** nk **Steely**[17] 3222 4-9-1 **69** GeorgeBaker 4 75
(Gary Moore) *taken down early: chsd clr wnr: clsd over 3f out: rdn and hld hd high over 1f out: 2 l down 1f out: one pce fnl f and lost 2nd wl ins fnl f* **13/2**

-002 **4** 10 **Shesha Bear**[23] 3015 7-9-7 **75** (p) LeeNewman 3 65
(Jonathan Portman) *sn in midfield but wl off the pce: pushed along 8f out: rdn and no imp 3f out: n.d* **3/1**[1]

-513 **5** shd **Handles For Forks (IRE)**[14] 3316 4-8-13 **72** CharlesBishop(5) 2 62
(Mick Channon) *stdd s: hld up wl off the pce in last trio: rdn over 3f out: no imp: n.d* **4/1**[2]

0-65 **6** 1 **Kings Troop**[23] 3015 6-8-11 **72** WilliamTwiston-Davies(7) 7 60
(Alan King) *stdd after s: hld up wl off the pce in last trio: rdn 3f out: no imp: n.d* **5/1**[3]

1243 **7** ¾ **Mediterranean Sea (IRE)**[93] 1175 6-9-2 **75** ShaneBKelly(5) 1 62
(J R Jenkins) *stdd s: hld up wl of fthe pce in rr: pushed along 6f out: rdn and no prog 4f out: n.d* **10/1**

2m 38.3s (-0.60) **Going Correction** +0.05s/f (Good) **7 Ran SP% 110.1**
Speed ratings (Par 103): **104,103,103,96,96 95,95**
Tote Swingers: 1&2 £11.10, 1&3 £8.00, 2&3 £9.00 CSF £45.33 CT £281.71 TOTE £6.40: £3.60, £2.80; EX 78.60.
Owner P Charalambous **Bred** Peter Charles **Trained** Newmarket, Suffolk

FOCUS
Course at normal configuration and all distances as advertised. An ultra-competitive handicap on paper but the front three in the market disappointed. The winner is rated up 4lb.

3770 BRITISH STALLION STUDS SUPPORTING BRITISH RACING E B F MEDIAN AUCTION MAIDEN STKS 7f

6:35 (6:35) (Class 5) 2-Y-0 **£3,881** (£1,155; £577; £288) **Stalls** Low

Form RPR

234 **1** **Well Acquainted (IRE)**[44] 2376 2-9-3 75 AdamKirby 1 82
(Clive Cox) *mde all: jnd and rdn 2f out: forged ahd u.p ins fnl f: r.o gamely: edgd rt cl home* **4/1**[3]

2 **2** 1 **Martial Art (IRE)**[18] 3191 2-9-3 0 DavidProbert 3 80
(Andrew Balding) *chsd wnr: hdwy to join wnr ent fnl 2f: drvn over 1f out: no ex and btn fnl 100yds* **9/4**[2]

2 **3** 1 **Rising Legend**[48] 2247 2-9-3 0 PatDobbs 6 77+
(Richard Hannon) *awkward leaving stalls: in tch: hdwy to chse ldrs 5f out: rdn over 2f out: edgd rt and outpcd u.p over 1f out: rallied and styd on wl fnl 100yds* **2/1**[1]

5 **4** 1½ **Athman (IRE)**[18] 3182 2-9-3 0 MickaelBarzalona 2 73
(Mahmood Al Zarooni) *chsd ldrs: swtchd rt and clsd on ldng pair 3f out: unable qck 2f out: edgd lft u.p and one pce fr over 1f out* **4/1**[3]

40 **5** 8 **Warrant Officer**[18] 3182 2-9-3 0 MatthewDavies 5 53
(Mick Channon) *in tch: rdn and outpcd 3f out: wknd 2f out* **40/1**

0 **6** 5 **Secretori**[19] 3140 2-9-3 0 ShaneKelly 4 41+
(Matthew Salaman) *dropped to rr over 5f out: rdn and no hdwy 3f out: lost tch 2f out* **20/1**

1m 23.64s (0.34) **Going Correction** +0.05s/f (Good) **6 Ran SP% 111.3**
Speed ratings (Par 94): **100,98,97,96,86 81**
Tote Swingers: 1&2 £2.40, 1&3 £2.40, 2&3 £1.10 CSF £13.19 TOTE £3.70: £1.90, £2.00; EX 13.80.
Owner The Orienteers **Bred** Stunning Rose Syndicate **Trained** Lambourn, Berks

FOCUS
An interesting juvenile maiden. Improvement from the winner with the second rated tentatively to his debut mark.

NOTEBOOK
Well Acquainted(IRE) made all and showed great determination in the final furlong. He lined up officially rated 75 after three first-four efforts, the best of which arguably came in the Brocklesby, and may well be raised a little after this first attempt over 7f. His future is surely in nurseries. (op 11-2)
Martial Art(IRE), beaten just a short head over 6f at Salisbury on his only previous start, was always second. He appears to have improved slightly on this second outing and, although he is no superstar, should win a similar event. (op 13-8)
Rising Legend, runner-up on his 6f Newmarket debut in mid May, was slowest away. He made up much of the ground in the first couple of furlongs, racing in fourth at the top of the hill, but struggled for pace in the home straight. He was staying on at the finish, suggesting he will handle 1m in due course, but did not step forward significantly from his first outing. (op 9-4)
Athman(IRE) met traffic problems when fifth at Doncaster on his debut and had problems with the cambers this time. He seemed to become unbalanced on a couple of occasions and was treading water in the closing stages. (op 5-1)
Warrant Officer had not shown a great deal in two previous outings and was never closer than fifth here. (tchd 33-1 and 50-1)
Secretori, stepping up markedly in trip after a 5f debut seventh at Bath, was in rear throughout. (op 25-1)

3771 TRY TOTEQUICKPICK IF YOU'RE FEELING LUCKY H'CAP 6f

7:10 (7:11) (Class 3) (0-95,94) 3-Y-0+ **£6,663** (£1,982; £990; £495) **Stalls** High

Form RPR

0024 **1** **Sacrosanctus**[23] 3004 4-9-4 **84** MircoDemuro 1 92
(Scott Dixon) *led: rdn ent fnl 2f: hdd over 1f out: sn ld again: styd on wl fnl f: rdn out* **6/1**[3]

400 **2** 1 **Swiss Cross**[5] 3641 5-10-0 **94** (t) DavidProbert 2 99
(Phil McEntee) *racd keenly: chsd ldrs: rdn ent fnl 2f: kpt on u.p ins fnl f: wnt 2nd last stride* **11/2**[2]

1024 **3** shd **Taajub (IRE)**[33] 2704 5-9-12 **92** IanMongan 4 96
(Peter Crate) *racd keenly: chsd wnr: chal 2f out: rdn to ld over 1f out: sn hdd and unable qck ins fnl f: one pce fnl 100yds: lost 2nd last stride* **9/1**

-003 **4** nk **Sohraab**[20] 3127 8-9-10 **90** DarryllHolland 11 94
(Hughie Morrison) *broke wl: sn struggling to go pce and dropped to midfield after 2f out: swtchd rt and effrt over 2f out: styd on wl ins fnl f* **8/1**

1-22 **5** ½ **Seeking Magic**[40] 2488 4-9-7 **87** (t) AdamKirby 6 91+
(Clive Cox) *taken down early: racd keenly: in tch: rdn and edgd lft 2f out: swtchd rt and rallied ins fnl f: kpt on* **9/2**[1]

0000 **6** ¾ **Mac Gille Eoin**[40] 2487 8-9-0 **80** NeilCallan 7 80
(John Gallagher) *chsd ldrs: rdn and unable qck whn edgd lft u.p 2f out: styd on same pce fnl f* **12/1**

0-63 **7** shd **Baldemar**[33] 2707 7-8-12 **83** ShaneBKelly(5) 10 82+
(Richard Fahey) *broke fast but awkwardly: sn pushed along and losing pl: in last trio at 1/2-way: hdwy 1f out: styd on fnl 100yds: no threat to ldrs* **9/2**[1]

1141 **8** 2 **Italian Tom (IRE)**[17] 3225 5-9-3 **88** DarrenEgan(5) 5 81
(Ronald Harris) *sn off the pce in last pair: effrt on inner over 2f out: swtchd rt over 1f out: kpt on but nvr trbld ldrs* **8/1**

0400 **9** hd **Tagula Night (IRE)**[22] 3049 6-9-4 **84** (b) ShaneKelly 3 76
(Dean Ivory) *in tch in midfield: rdn: outpcd and edgd lft 2f out: styd on same pce and no threat to ldrs after* **16/1**

6030 **10** 2 **Diamond Charlie (IRE)**[33] 2704 4-9-5 **85** SebSanders 9 71
(Simon Dow) *t.k.h: in tch: effrt on inner and rdn 3f out: sme hdwy whn nt clr run and hmpd over 1f out: n.d after* **20/1**

4-00 **11** 4 **Golden Desert (IRE)**[15] 3268 8-9-7 **87** HayleyTurner 12 60
(Simon Dow) *a bhd: struggling fr 1/2-way* **33/1**

1m 9.11s (-0.29) **Going Correction** +0.05s/f (Good) **11 Ran SP% 119.5**
Speed ratings (Par 107): **103,101,101,101,100 99,99,96,96,93 88**
Tote Swingers: 1&2 £6.90, 1&3 £9.00, 2&3 £10.80 CSF £39.72 CT £244.56 TOTE £7.20: £2.60, £2.30, £3.20; EX 42.60.
Owner Paul J Dixon **Bred** Worksop Manor Stud **Trained** Babworth, Notts

FOCUS
A decent handicap, with the top weight rated 94, and it looked highly competitive on paper. Racing prominently seemed an advantage. The winner rates a personal best.

NOTEBOOK
Sacrosanctus, second off a 1lb lower mark here two outings back, was always in the first two. In the lead at halfway, he was headed at the 2f pole, but fought back gamely. He handles this tricky track really well. (op 7-1)
Swiss Cross, a winner here in June 2011, also figured among the leaders from the outset. He battled away all the way to the line, posting a decent effort under top weight. (tchd 5-1)
Taajub(IRE), fourth in the Derby-day 'Dash' here on his latest start, was third early on and in the lead at the 2f marker. He could not quite maintain the gallop in the closing stages, but ran creditably all the same. (op 8-1)
Sohraab was 3lb higher than when third as favourite at York last time and, judged on this showing, could now be in the grip of the handicapper. He was one of the few to make late ground, but never seriously threatened to overhaul the principals.
Seeking Magic had made the first three on each of his eight previous outings and was unlucky not to do at least as well here. He chased the pace from the start and was just beginning to launch a challenge when getting stuck in a pocket. He had nowhere to go entering the final furlong, but kept plugging away, despite the traffic problems. (op 6-1)
Mac Gille Eoin Official explanation: jockey said horse hung left
Baldemar lined up with a 3-5 record at this course, but never threatened to improve his stats. Towards the rear early on, his home straight move proved too little too late. Official explanation: jockey said gelding stumbled at start (tchd 11-2)

3772 BELTANE ASSET MANAGEMENT H'CAP 7f

7:45 (7:48) (Class 4) (0-85,88) 3-Y-0+ **£4,075** (£1,212; £606; £303) **Stalls** Low

Form RPR

0511 **1** **Klynch**[7] 3524 6-10-3 **88** 6ex (b) JamesSullivan 4 98
(Ruth Carr) *chsd ldrs: wnt 2nd 4f out: rdn to ld over 1f out: in command fnl f: r.o wl* **11/2**[2]

4-21 **2** 1¾ **Henry Allingham**[24] 2974 3-8-12 **77** NeilCallan 5 79
(Roger Varian) *t.k.h: chsd ldrs: rdn and edgd lft over 2f out: kpt on same pce fnl f: wnt 2nd last stride* **3/1**[1]

-000 **3** nse **The Guru Of Gloom (IRE)**[36] 2608 4-9-9 **80** MartinDwyer 1 85
(William Muir) *t.k.h: hld up wl in tch: chsng ldrs and n.m.r over 1f out: rdn and hdwy 1f out: chsd wnr ins fnl f: no imp: lost 2nd last stride* **33/1**

3244 **4** 1¼ **Corporal Maddox**[15] 3281 5-10-0 **85** HayleyTurner 8 86
(Jamie Osborne) *sn pushed along: in tch in midfield: rdn and unable qck whn short of room and swtchd rt over 2f out: hdwy over 1f out: kpt on but no threat to wnr* **6/1**[3]

2140 **5** ½ **April Fool**[38] 2545 8-9-6 **82** (b) DarrenEgan(5) 3 82
(Ronald Harris) *chsd ldr tl led over 5f out: hdd and drvn over 1f out: no ex: lost 2nd and wknd fnl 100yds* **10/1**

34-0 **6** 1 1/4 **Rondeau (GR)**[15] 3281 7-9-12 **83** GeorgeBaker 9 80
(Patrick Chamings) *taken down early: stdd after s: hld up in last pair: rdn and hdwy over 1f out: no imp ins fnl f* **11/1**

0000 **7** 1 3/4 **The Tichborne (IRE)**[15] 3281 4-8-13 **70** (v[1]) DavidProbert 2 62
(Roger Teal) *led tl over 5f out: chsd ldrs after: rdn 2f out: nt qckning and short of room jst over 1f out: wknd ins fnl f* **12/1**

1-04 **8** shd **Konstantin (IRE)**[41] 2444 4-9-1 **79** KatiaScallan(7) 11 71
(Marcus Tregoning) *styd wd: in tch in midfield: outpcd 1/2-way: rallied and edgd lft over 1f out: no imp ins fnl f* **17/2**

2-05 **9** 3/4 **Ellie In The Pink (IRE)**[95] 1156 4-9-6 **77** DarryllHolland 6 67
(Alan Jarvis) *squeezed for room leaving stalls: a towards rr: rdn and effrt 3f out: no imp: nvr trbld ldrs* **15/2**

0500 **10** 3 1/2 **Space Station**[41] 2444 6-9-7 **78** (b) SebSanders 7 58
(Simon Dow) *a in rr: rdn 3f out: edgd lft u.p and no hdwy over 1f out: n.d* **8/1**

1m 22.71s (-0.59) **Going Correction** +0.05s/f (Good)
WFA 3 from 4yo+ 8lb **10** Ran SP% **116.1**
Speed ratings (Par 105): **105,103,102,101,100 99,97,97,96,92**
Tote Swingers: 1&2 £2.60, 1&3 £56.20, 2&3 £21.20 CSF £22.25 CT £499.29 TOTE £7.10: £2.40, £1.90, £6.10; EX 24.60.
Owner Douglas Renton **Bred** J C S Wilson Bloodstock **Trained** Huby, N Yorks

FOCUS
Another fair handicap, this one featuring a penalised top weight rated 88. The winner rates better than ever.
Ellie In The Pink(IRE) Official explanation: jockey said filly was unsuited by the ground

3773 E B F ARTHUR BUDGETT MEMORIAL MAIDEN FILLIES' STKS 1m 4f 10y
8:20 (8:15) (Class 4) 3-4-Y-O **£4,528** (£1,347; £673; £336) **Stalls** Centre

Form RPR
034 **1** **Amaraja (GER)**[15] 3279 3-8-10 70 IanMongan 5 85+
(Sir Henry Cecil) *led for 1f: in tch after: rdn to chal 3f out: led wl over 1f out: edgd lft u.p ent fnl f: styd on wl* **8/1**

00 **2** 1 1/2 **Bite Of The Cherry**[48] 2249 3-8-10 0 HayleyTurner 3 83
(Michael Bell) *chsd ldr tl led after 1f: rdn and hrd pressed 3f out: hdd 2f out: unable qck and unbalanced ent fnl f: one pce after* **6/1**[3]

0-2 **3** 1 1/2 **Rose Season**[20] 3100 3-8-10 0 NeilCallan 2 80
(Roger Varian) *t.k.h: dwlt: sn rcvrd and chsd ldr over 9f out tl 8f out: rdn and chal 3f out: unable qck and sltly hmpd over 1f out: wknd ins fnl f* **4/1**[2]

2 **4** 1 **Infinitum**[49] 2204 3-8-10 0 MickaelBarzalona 4 79+
(John Gosden) *in tch in last pair: pushed along 6f out: rdn and outpcd over 3f out: rallied and styd on 1f out: no threat to wnr and nt pushed towards fin* **8/11**[1]

44 **5** 3 **Jorum**[31] 2768 3-8-10 0 DarryllHolland 6 74
(Sir Henry Cecil) *in tch: chsd ldr 8f out but sn pushed along: rdn 6f out: lost 2nd and immediately outpcd 3f out: wl hld over 1f out* **16/1**

00 **6** 39 **Raving Monsun**[15] 3279 3-8-10 0 SebSanders 1
(Marco Botti) *s.i.s: hld up in tch in last pair: rdn over 3f out: sn struggling and lost tch: eased fnl f: t.o* **33/1**

2m 39.26s (0.36) **Going Correction** +0.05s/f (Good) **6** Ran SP% **112.1**
Speed ratings (Par 102): **100,99,98,97,95 69**
Tote Swingers: 1&2 £2.50, 1&3 £5.50, 2&3 £2.60 CSF £52.65 TOTE £8.10: £3.60, £2.30; EX 60.60.
Owner Niarchos Family **Bred** The Niarchos Family **Trained** Newmarket, Suffolk

FOCUS
A fascinating fillies' maiden. The favourite was the clear form pick and proved disappointing, but the winner is getting her act together.

3774 WILL YOUNG LIVE AT EPSOM 12/7/12 H'CAP (BETFAIR 10 FURLONG FLAT SERIES QUALIFIER) 1m 2f 18y
8:50 (8:53) (Class 4) (0-80,79) 3-Y-O+ **£4,075** (£1,212; £606; £303) **Stalls** Low

Form RPR
-042 **1** **John Biscuit (IRE)**[15] 3278 4-9-11 **76** DavidProbert 8 86
(Andrew Balding) *taken down early: hld up in tch: rdn and effrt 2f out: hdwy to ld 1f out: r.o strly: readily* **7/2**[1]

6263 **2** 2 1/2 **Hip Hip Hooray**[16] 3247 6-8-6 **62** DarrenEgan(5) 4 67
(Luke Dace) *stdd after s: hld up in tch in rr: rdn and hdwy over 1f out: r.o wl to go 2nd fnl 100yds: no threat to wnr* **20/1**

0032 **3** 3/4 **Tidal Way (IRE)**[20] 3122 3-8-12 **74** HayleyTurner 6 78
(Mick Channon) *in tch: rdn and effrt to chse ldrs 3f out: styd on same pce u.p fr over 1f out* **7/2**[1]

345- **4** 3/4 **Ethics Girl (IRE)**[269] 6749 6-9-11 **76** (t) NeilCallan 1 78
(John Berry) *chsd ldng pair: drvn and unable qck 3f out: rallied and hdwy over 1f out: kpt on but no threat to wnr ins fnl f* **14/1**

6145 **5** nk **Bloodsweatandtears**[28] 2857 4-9-4 **74** (b) DavidKenny(5) 10 75
(William Knight) *sn chsng ldr: rdn and qcknd ahd w rival over 3f out: led over 2f out: drvn and hdd 1f out: fdd fnl 100yds* **16/1**

-333 **6** nk **Feisty Champion (IRE)**[13] 3338 3-8-9 **71** SebSanders 7 74+
(J W Hills) *in tch: rdn: outpcd and lost pl 3f out: rallied over 1f out: styng on but no threat to wnr whn nt clr run and swtchd rt wl ins fnl f* **5/1**[3]

3130 **7** hd **Eshaab (USA)**[24] 2980 3-9-2 **78** [1] GeorgeBaker 5 78
(Ed Dunlop) *hld up in tch in last trio: rdn and hdwy towards inner over 2f out: edgd lft and kpt on fnl f: no threat to wnr* **8/1**

6622 **8** 2 1/2 **Super Duplex**[29] 2814 5-9-2 **67** IanMongan 11 62
(Pat Phelan) *in tch: hdwy to press ldrs 5f out: rdn to ld over 3f out: hdd over 2f out: drvn and stl pressing ldr tl no ex ent fnl f: wknd and btn whn n.m.r and eased wl ins fnl f* **10/1**

025 **9** 5 **Viewpoint (IRE)**[5] 3630 3-9-2 **78** PatDobbs 12 63
(Richard Hannon) *s.i.s: hld up in tch in last pair: rdn and effrt over 2f out: no prog 2f out: wknd ent fnl f* **9/2**[2]

4645 **10** 14 **Salient**[20] 3105 8-8-13 **64** J-PGuillambert 3 21
(Michael Attwater) *led tl hdd and rdn over 3f out: wknd and dropped to rr over 1f out: eased fnl f* **25/1**

2m 10.54s (0.84) **Going Correction** +0.05s/f (Good)
WFA 3 from 4yo+ 11lb **10** Ran SP% **120.7**
Speed ratings (Par 105): **98,96,95,94,94 94,94,92,88,76**
Tote Swingers: 1&2 £13.10, 1&3 £2.50, 2&3 £15.70 CSF £79.89 CT £269.08 TOTE £4.70: £2.00, £4.70, £1.90; EX 120.20.
Owner Dr Philip Brown **Bred** Dr Philip J Brown **Trained** Kingsclere, Hants

FOCUS
A competitive finale, even if not quite the standard of the five preceding events. In contrast to those races hold-up horses became involved. The third and fourth are the best guides.
T/Plt: £1,383.80 to a £1 stake. Pool: £72,889.48 - 38.45 winning tickets. T/Qpdt: £135.40 to a £1 stake. Pool: £8,526.81 - 46.60 winning tickets. SP

3381 HAYDOCK (L-H)
Thursday, July 5
OFFICIAL GOING: Soft (good to soft in places; 7.9)
Wind: Virtually nil Weather: Cloudy, sunny periods

3775 GLASS TIMES H'CAP 1m 2f 95y
2:20 (2:22) (Class 5) (0-70,70) 3-Y-O+ **£2,264** (£673; £336; £168) **Stalls** High

Form RPR
5522 **1** **Brockwell**[21] 3066 3-9-3 **70** RichardKingscote 15 83+
(Tom Dascombe) *hld up in tch: pushed along and hdwy over 2f out: rdn to chal ent fnl f: drvn and styd on to ld last 50yds* **3/1**[1]

-553 **2** nk **Skyfire**[15] 3290 5-9-6 **62** MichaelStainton 5 74
(Nick Kent) *led: pushed along 3f out: rdn wl over 1f out: jnd ent fnl f and sn drvn: hdd and no ex last 50yds* **8/1**[3]

-000 **3** 5 **Equity Card (FR)**[23] 3002 3-8-11 **64** JoeFanning 6 67
(Mark Johnston) *trckd ldrs: hdwy 3f out: rdn to chse ldr over 2f out: drvn and one pce appr fnl f* **33/1**

02 **4** 2 1/4 **Snooker (GER)**[13] 3353 6-9-5 **61** TonyHamilton 12 59
(Rose Dobbin) *hld up: hdwy over 3f out: rdn 2f out: styd on appr fnl f* **20/1**

0212 **5** shd **Mighty Clarets (IRE)**[12] 3386 5-9-10 **66** SeanLevey 7 64
(Barry Leavy) *trckd ldng pair: effrt 3f out: rdn along 2f out: sn drvn and one pce appr fnl f* **9/1**

0236 **6** nk **Dazzling Valentine**[26] 2915 4-9-10 **66** LiamJones 2 63
(Alan Bailey) *chsd ldrs: rdn along wl over 2f out: drvn and one pce fr wl over 1f out* **20/1**

-504 **7** 1/2 **Now My Sun**[21] 3066 3-9-1 **68** MartinHarley 9 65
(Mrs K Burke) *s.i.s and bhd: stdy hdwy 3f out: rdn and styd on fnl 2f: nrst fin* **9/2**[2]

032- **8** 1/2 **Phase Shift**[356] 4071 4-8-13 **58** PaulPickard(3) 4 54
(Brian Ellison) *dwlt: a towards rr* **16/1**

1-15 **9** 1 **Rockweiller**[22] 3022 5-9-9 **65** (v) RobertWinston 14 59
(Steve Gollings) *cl up: effrt to dispute ld 3f out: rdn over 2f out and grad wknd* **14/1**

2665 **10** hd **Gabrial's Lexi (IRE)**[10] 3443 3-8-10 **63** MichaelO'Connell 13 56
(Ian Williams) *in tch: rdn along 3f out: sn drvn and wknd over 2f out* **12/1**

1010 **11** nk **Spavento (IRE)**[13] 3335 6-9-9 **65** DavidAllan 10 58
(Eric Alston) *hld up: hdwy over 3f out: rdn along and in tch 2f out: sn drvn and no imp* **16/1**

6000 **12** 5 **Petomic (IRE)**[3] 3712 7-9-5 **61** (be[1]) FrannyNorton 1 44
(Daniel Mark Loughnane) *a towards rr* **40/1**

6-14 **13** 3/4 **Kian's Joy**[22] 3025 3-7-13 **52** JimmyQuinn 8 34
(Jedd O'Keeffe) *t.k.h early: chsd ldrs: rdn along over 3f out and sn wknd* **14/1**

0333 **14** 2 1/2 **Striker Torres (IRE)**[9] 3460 6-9-12 **68** (v) GrahamLee 16 45
(Ian McInnes) *hld up: a in rr* **16/1**

1-26 **15** nk **A Little Bit Dusty**[17] 3231 4-9-6 **69** JackDuern(7) 3 45
(Reg Hollinshead) *midfield on inner whn n.m.r and hmpd after 3f: rdn along 4f out: sn wknd* **40/1**

2m 14.57s (-0.93) **Going Correction** 0.0s/f (Good)
WFA 3 from 4yo+ 11lb **15** Ran SP% **120.3**
Speed ratings (Par 103): **103,102,98,96,96 96,96,95,95,94 94,90,90,88,87**
toteswingers 1&2 £6.50, 1&3 £22.80, 2&3 £78.60 CSF £24.39 CT £667.18 TOTE £4.40: £1.60, £3.40, £11.50; EX 30.40 Trifecta £486.00 Part won. Pool £656.82 - 0.64 winning units..
Owner South Wind Racing 3 **Bred** South Wind Bloodstock **Trained** Malpas, Cheshire

FOCUS
All races on Inner home straight and distances on Round course increased by about 7yds. The runners in the opener made for the nearside rail once into the straight. The front pair pulled clear. Race times suggested the ground wasn't riding that bad. The form is rated around the runner-up.
Rockweiller Official explanation: jockey said horse hung left-handed
Striker Torres(IRE) Official explanation: trainer said gelding was unsuited by the soft (good to soft places) ground
A Little Bit Dusty Official explanation: jockey said gelding suffered interference in running

3776 FIT SHOW EVERYONE'S GOING E B F MAIDEN FILLIES' STKS 6f
2:50 (2:53) (Class 5) 2-Y-O **£3,234** (£962; £481; £240) **Stalls** High

Form RPR
2 **1** **Mollyvator (IRE)**[40] 2508 2-9-0 0 MartinHarley 8 78+
(Mrs K Burke) *trckd ldrs: hdwy over 2f out: rdn to ld appr fnl f: sn clr: comf* **10/11**[1]

5 **2** 4 **Emperatriz**[13] 3346 2-9-0 0 RussKennemore 3 66
(John Holt) *trckd ldrs: hdwy over 2f out: sn rdn and styd on fnl f: no ch w wnr* **5/1**[2]

3652 **3** 3/4 **Inchy Coo**[11] 3415 2-9-0 67 (p) DavidAllan 5 64
(Tim Easterby) *led: rdn along 2f out: drvn and hdd appr fnl f: kpt on same pce* **6/1**[3]

40 **4** 2 **Mixed Message (IRE)**[22] 3034 2-9-0 0 RichardMullen 12 58
(Ed McMahon) *in tch: hdwy to chse ldrs over 2f out: sn rdn and no imp ent fnl f* **9/1**

0 **5** 2 3/4 **Autumn Shadow (IRE)**[41] 2450 2-9-0 0 TonyHamilton 9 50+
(Richard Fahey) *chsd ldrs: rdn along over 2f out: sn one pce* **20/1**

6 1 3/4 **La Danza** 2-9-0 0 LiamJones 6 44
(Alan Bailey) *chsd ldrs: rdn along over 2f out: sn wknd* **18/1**

7 1 **Ceekay's Girl** 2-8-11 0 MichaelMetcalfe(3) 11 41
(Mrs K Burke) *dwlt: green and sn outpcd in rr* **25/1**

8 6 **Noosa Sound** 2-9-0 0 PJMcDonald 1 23
(John Davies) *wnt lft s: green and sn rdn along: a outpcd and bhd* **50/1**

002 **9** 3 **Amelia Jay**[7] 3520 2-9-0 0 JoeFanning 2 14
(Danielle McCormick) *prom: rdn along over 2f out: sn wknd* **18/1**

1m 16.08s (2.28) **Going Correction** +0.35s/f (Good) **9** Ran SP% **114.4**
Speed ratings (Par 91): **98,92,91,89,85 83,81,73,69**
toteswingers 1&2 £2.50, 1&3 £2.10, 2&3 £4.00 CSF £5.34 TOTE £2.00: £1.10, £1.70, £1.50; EX 6.30 Trifecta £19.70 Pool £1,266.73 - 47.37 winning units..
Owner David & Yvonne Blunt **Bred** T Whitehead **Trained** Middleham Moor, N Yorks

FOCUS
Probably not a great deal of depth to this fillies' maiden but the winner impressed. The third helps set a solid level.

NOTEBOOK
Mollyvator(IRE) showed plenty of ability when runner-up over this trip on her York debut in May, but that race had yet to produce a winner until now. She didn't seem to be travelling that well coming to the last 2f, but once in front she powered right away from these rivals. Despite there being plenty of speed on the dam's side of her pedigree, her sire's influence suggests she will improve for further. (op 6-5)

Emperatriz showed ability when fifth of 11 on last month's Newmarket debut and did so again having raced widest. She had no chance with the winner, but has an ordinary race in her on this evidence. (op 9-2)
Inchy Coo improved for the step up to this trip when runner-up at Pontefract last time and tried to make all again, but was put in her place from over a furlong out. She is beginning to look exposed and nurseries may be her best option now. (op 5-1)
Mixed Message(IRE) didn't get the best of runs over C&D last month, but had no excuses this time. She may be another for whom nurseries may be the best move. (op 14-1)
Autumn Shadow(IRE), green and outpaced when well beaten on her debut over C&D in May, showed a bit more here but will need to improve again if she is to win a race. (tchd 22-1)

3777 DISTINCTION DOORS E B F MAIDEN STKS 6f
3:20 (3:20) (Class 5) 2-Y-O **£3,234** (£962; £481; £240) **Stalls** High

Form RPR
4 **1** **Yourartisonfire**[21] 3074 2-9-0 0 MichaelMetcalfe(3) 4 81+
(Mrs K Burke) *trckd ldrs: effrt and n.m.r 2f out: swtchd lft to outer and rdn to chal over 1f out: led ins fnl f: sn edgd rt: styd on wl towards fin* **6/4**[1]
4 **2** 2 ¼ **Mayaasem**[34] 2663 2-9-3 0 TadhgO'Shea 2 72
(Charles Hills) *trckd ldng pair: hdwy and cl up 2f out: rdn to take slt ld over 1f out: green and hdd ins fnl f: kpt on same pce* **4/1**[3]
3 1 ¼ **Loch Moy** 2-9-3 0 TonyHamilton 1 68+
(Richard Fahey) *wnt lft s: sn cl up: led briefly 2f out: sn rdn: rn green and edgd lft: hdd over 1f out: kpt on same pce* **9/4**[2]
033 **4** 1 ¼ **Capo Rosso (IRE)**[15] 3271 2-9-3 72 RichardKingscote 3 65
(Tom Dascombe) *led: rdn along over 2f out: sn hdd and one pce* **4/1**[3]
1m 17.6s (3.80) **Going Correction** +0.525s/f (Yiel) 4 Ran SP% **110.8**
Speed ratings (Par 94): **95,92,90,88**
CSF £7.73 TOTE £2.40; EX 8.80.
Owner J O'Shea, W Rooney & Ontoawinner **Bred** J A And Mrs M A Knox **Trained** Middleham Moor, N Yorks

FOCUS
Just the four runners and a modest pace resulted in a time 1.52 seconds slower than the fillies' maiden. A few of these still have more to offer, however. The second and fourth set the level.

NOTEBOOK
Yourartisonfire finished an encouraging fourth of 14 on his Nottingham debut last month and duly built on that, but this was by no means straightforward. Not only did he have to come from last in a steadily run race, he was also forced to switch left and come right around his three rivals in order to get a run, but he was comfortably on top at the line. There should be more to come. (op 15-8 tchd 2-1)
Mayaasem finished just behind a subsequent winner when fourth of seven on his debut here last month and shaped then as though he would be suited by this extra furlong. He was keen enough early and came off the bridle over 2f from home, but stuck on well enough if unable to match the finishing pace of the winner.
Loch Moy, a 50,000gns half-brother to five winners at up to 1m4f, raced enthusiastically behind the leader before getting outpaced in the sprint to the line. He should improve plenty. (op 5-2 tchd 11-4)
Capo Rosso(IRE), having his fourth start, tried to make his experience count from the front but found these unexposed rivals too good late on. He looks destined for nurseries. (op 7-2 tchd 10-3)

3778 TUFFX GLASS H'CAP (BETFAIR SPRINT FLAT SERIES QUALIFIER) 6f
3:50 (3:51) (Class 4) (0-80,79) 3-Y-O+ **£5,175** (£1,540; £769; £384) **Stalls** High

Form RPR
3441 **1** **El McGlynn (IRE)**[14] 3308 3-7-13 **65** HannahNunn(7) 6 73
(Peter Salmon) *mde all: rdn jst ins fnl f: kpt on wl* **50/1**
4055 **2** 1 **Emiratesdotcom**[19] 3139 6-9-8 **75** RichardKingscote 11 80
(Milton Bradley) *hld up in rr: hdwy wl over 1f out: rdn and styd on strly fnl f* **16/1**
0-66 **3** shd **Rash Judgement**[19] 3159 7-9-6 **73** FergusSweeney 4 77
(Stuart Kittow) *midfield: hdwy 2f out: rdn over 1f out: styd on ins fnl f: nrst fin* **50/1**
0/00 **4** nk **Loukoumi**[34] 2675 4-8-9 **62** (b[1]) TomEaves 5 65
(Tim Easterby) *in tch: hdwy to chse ldrs wl over 1f out: drvn and kpt on fnl f* **80/1**
1-2 **5** nk **Magic Secret**[26] 2940 4-9-9 **79** RaulDaSilva(3) 13 85+
(Jeremy Gask) *hld up: hdwy wl over 1f out: nt clr run 1f out: n.m.r and swtchd rt last 100yds: nrst fin* **3/1**[2]
11-6 **6** ½ **Hills Of Dakota**[28] 2841 4-9-6 **73** GrahamGibbons 15 74
(David Barron) *trckd ldrs: effrt 2f out: sn rdn and kpt on same pce fnl f* **7/1**[3]
0231 **7** nse **Barkston Ash**[15] 3272 4-9-1 **75** JasonHart(7) 7 76
(Eric Alston) *chsd ldrs: rdn wl over 1f out: drvn and one pce ins fnl f* **10/1**
0532 **8** nse **Rio Cobolo (IRE)**[7] 3524 6-9-1 **68** (v) AdrianNicholls 10 69
(David Nicholls) *chsd ldr on stands' rail: rdn over 1f out: drvn and wknd ins fnl f* **20/1**
4251 **9** 1 **Steelcut**[12] 3390 8-9-5 **72** (p) GrahamLee 12 69
(Mark Buckley) *hld up: hdwy to chse ldrs 1/2-way: rdn 2f out: kpt on same pce* **33/1**
5111 **10** 4 ½ **Best Trip (IRE)**[8] 3496 5-9-7 **74** 6ex BarryMcHugh 3 57
(Brian Ellison) *chsd ldrs: rdn along 2f out: drvn and wknd over 1f out* **9/4**[1]
5462 **11** nk **Defence Council (IRE)**[5] 3612 4-9-11 **78** RobertWinston 9 60
(Mel Brittain) *hld up: a towards rr* **15/2**
4053 **12** 2 **Master Of Disguise**[24] 2982 6-9-9 **76** (t) DuranFentiman 8 52
(Brian Baugh) *chsd ldrs: rdn wl over 1f out: grad wknd* **50/1**
0000 **13** 5 **Mr Optimistic**[27] 2876 4-9-1 **71** (p) LeeTopliss(3) 2 31
(Richard Fahey) *in tch: rdn along 3f out: wknd over 2f out* **50/1**
6001 **14** 2 ¼ **Byronic Hero**[11] 3421 3-9-5 **78** 6ex (b) TonyHamilton 14 30
(Jedd O'Keeffe) *s.i.s: a bhd* **12/1**
0600 **15** ¾ **Divine Call**[15] 3281 5-9-6 **73** (p) JoeFanning 1 23
(Milton Bradley) *racd alone far side: prom: rdn along 1/2-way: sn wknd* **25/1**
1m 16.13s (2.33) **Going Correction** +0.525s/f (Yiel)
WFA 3 from 4yo+ 6lb 15 Ran SP% **123.3**
Speed ratings (Par 105): **105,103,103,103,102 102,102,101,100,94 94,91,84,81,80**
toteswingers 1&2 £142.70, 1&3 £131.20, 2&3 £50.80 CSF £691.09 CT £33704.12 TOTE £65.80: £14.70, £6.00, £12.00; EX 519.60 TRIFECTA Not won..
Owner Leods Contracts Limited **Bred** Michael Lyons Jnr **Trained** Kirk Deighton, W Yorks

FOCUS
A competitive sprint handicap containing a handful of horses facing an imminent rise in their marks. All bar one of the runners raced centre-to-stands' side. Improvement from the winner and no fluke against this pretty solid field. The form is rated around the third and fourth.
Magic Secret ◆ Official explanation: jockey said gelding was denied a clear run
Best Trip(IRE) Official explanation: jockey said gelding ran flat
Defence Council(IRE) Official explanation: jockey said gelding was denied a clear run

3779 SELECTA SYSTEMS H'CAP 1m
4:20 (4:20) (Class 3) (0-95,95) 3-Y-O+ **£7,115** (£2,117; £1,058; £529) **Stalls** Low

Form RPR
0603 **1** **Don't Call Me (IRE)**[15] 3268 5-9-12 **93** (t) AdrianNicholls 10 103
(David Nicholls) *hld up in rr: niggled along after 3f: hdwy on outer 3f out: chsd ldrs and swtchd rt ent fnl f: sn rdn and styd on wl fnl f to ld last 75yds* **3/1**[2]
-430 **2** 1 ½ **Lord Aeryn (IRE)**[20] 3128 5-9-0 **88** GeorgeChaloner(7) 7 95
(Richard Fahey) *trckd ldrs: hdwy 3f out: effrt to chal 2f out: sn rdn to ld over 1f out: hung bdly lft ent fnl f: hdd and no ex last 75yds* **9/2**[3]
-605 **3** 1 ¼ **Assizes**[12] 3376 3-8-6 **82** FrannyNorton 1 84
(Mark Johnston) *led: rdn along wl over 2f out: drvn and hdd over 1f out: kpt on u.p fnl f* **8/1**
3400 **4** 2 **Kinloch Castle**[40] 2477 3-8-5 **81** JoeFanning 4 79
(Mark Johnston) *chsd ldrs: hdwy over 3f out: rdn along over 2f out: kpt on same pce* **5/2**[1]
00-0 **5** 5 **Rakaan (IRE)**[26] 2910 5-10-0 **95** GrahamLee 2 83
(Jamie Osborne) *hld up towards rr: hdwy 3f out: rdn 2f out: no imp* **20/1**
0300 **6** ¾ **Eastern Hills**[43] 2405 7-8-3 **77** (p) GemmaTutty(7) 9 63
(Alan McCabe) *trckd ldng pair: rdn along 4f out: wknd 3f out* **40/1**
02-0 **7** ¾ **Alakhan (IRE)**[22] 3036 6-9-4 **85** MichaelO'Connell 3 70
(Ian Williams) *hld up: effrt and sme hdwy 3f out: sn rdn and btn* **5/1**
0066 **8** hd **Space War**[12] 3403 5-8-7 **81** DavidSimmonson(7) 5 65
(Michael Easterby) *dwlt: sn chsng ldr: cl up 1/2-way: rdn along 3f out and sn wknd* **14/1**
1m 43.59s (-0.11) **Going Correction** +0.175s/f (Good)
WFA 3 from 5yo+ 9lb 8 Ran SP% **113.4**
Speed ratings (Par 107): **107,105,104,102,97 96,95,95**
toteswingers 1&2 £3.30, 1&3 £4.20, 2&3 £6.10 CSF £16.65 CT £96.41 TOTE £4.30: £1.10, £1.80, £2.20; EX 19.10 Trifecta £64.00 Pool £958.69 - 11.07 winning units..
Owner Matt & Lauren Morgan **Bred** Darley **Trained** Sessay, N Yorks

FOCUS
This had been won by a 3yo six times in seven previous runnings, but the older horses came to the fore this time. Again they came over to the stands' rail in the straight. The first two were closely matched on last autumn's Ayr form. The winner rates a length personal best.

NOTEBOOK
Don't Call Me(IRE) was 2lb higher than when third in the Royal Hunt Cup and the softening ground would have been ideal for him. However, he raced in snatches throughout and was being ridden along in last place turning for home. Having made up his ground coming to the last 2f, he followed the runner-up by hanging away to his left in the closing stages yet still managed to force his way to the front where it mattered. This was the highest mark he has won off.
Lord Aeryn(IRE) raced keenly in a handy position early, but had put himself in with every chance when hanging right over to the far rail inside the last furlong and getting run out of it. He is without a win since his reappearance last season and may need quicker ground. (op 5-1 tchd 11-2)
Assizes, winner of his only start at two but unplaced in three handicaps this term, was representing a stable that had won the previous three runnings of this with a 3yo. He had the run of the race out in front, but despite his two older rivals trying to hang their chances away he couldn't capitalise once headed inside the last furlong. (op 7-1 tchd 13-2)
Kinloch Castle held a decent position throughout, but didn't find much off the bridle and hasn't built on his promising Musselburgh reappearance. (op 3-1)
Rakaan(IRE) never offered a threat and hasn't shown much in an abbreviated campaign since winning at Meydan early last year. (op 25-1 tchd 16-1)
Eastern Hills gradually lost his prominent early position, and though a five-time winner on Fibresand in the meantime, his last success on turf came off 20lb lower. (op 33-1)

3780 RESIDENCE 9 FILLIES' H'CAP 1m
4:50 (4:51) (Class 5) (0-75,72) 3-Y-O+ **£2,264** (£673; £336; £168) **Stalls** Low

Form RPR
1362 **1** **Magic Destiny**[17] 3214 3-8-13 **72** MichaelMetcalfe(3) 1 83
(Mrs K Burke) *hld up towards rr: hdwy 3f out: cl up 2f out: shkn up to ld 1 1/2f out: rdn clr ent fnl f* **11/8**[1]
-022 **2** 4 **Bella Noir**[22] 3030 5-9-3 **71** (p) ConorHarrison(7) 2 75
(Mrs K Burke) *trckd ldng pair: hdwy to ld 3df out: rdn over 2f out and sn jnd: hdd 1 1/2f out: kpt on same pce* **13/2**
0314 **3** 2 ¼ **Fenella Fudge**[12] 3395 4-9-6 **67** GrahamGibbons 4 66
(Derek Shaw) *dwlt and in rr: hdwy on inner over 2f out: rdn to chse ldng pair wl over 1f out: sn no imp* **11/4**[2]
640- **4** ¾ **Elbow Beach**[80] 3-9-2 **72** JamesMillman 3 67
(Rod Millman) *t.k.h: cl up: rdn along over 3f out: sn wknd* **25/1**
-651 **5** 1 ½ **Ken's Girl**[20] 3096 8-9-11 **72** FergusSweeney 6 66
(Stuart Kittow) *led: rdn along 4f out: hdd 3f out: grad wknd* **3/1**[3]
1m 45.01s (1.31) **Going Correction** +0.175s/f (Good)
WFA 3 from 4yo+ 9lb 5 Ran SP% **111.0**
Speed ratings (Par 100): **100,96,93,93,91**
CSF £10.86 TOTE £2.60: £2.10, £2.80; EX 7.10.
Owner Ray Bailey **Bred** Ray Bailey **Trained** Middleham Moor, N Yorks

FOCUS
An ordinary fillies' handicap and again they came stands' side. It resulted in a 1-2 for the Elaine Burke yard and a treble for the stable on the day. The winner may not have needed to improve much.
Ken's Girl Official explanation: jockey said mare ran flat

3781 RITEC CLEARSHIELD H'CAP 1m 6f
5:20 (5:22) (Class 5) (0-70,70) 3-Y-O **£2,264** (£673; £336; £168) **Stalls** Low

Form RPR
-566 **1** **Byron Blue (IRE)**[21] 3087 3-9-2 **65** GrahamLee 7 76
(Jamie Osborne) *trckd ldrs: hdwy 4f out: led wl over 2f out: rdn appr fnl f: styd on strly* **5/1**[3]
1545 **2** 6 **Juno The Muffinman (IRE)**[22] 3033 3-9-7 **70** (v) RichardKingscote 6 73
(Tom Dascombe) *v.s.a and lost many l s: sn jnd field: hdwy over 3f out: rdn to chse ldrs whn hung bdly lft over 1f out: drvn and kpt on* **3/1**[2]
1044 **3** 3 ¼ **Key Gold**[13] 3345 3-9-7 **70** JoeFanning 5 68
(Mark Johnston) *trckd ldrs: hdwy 3f out: rdn and ev ch over 2f out tl drvn and one pce appr fnl f* **11/4**[1]
040 **4** ½ **Eanans Bay (IRE)**[57] 1981 3-8-7 **56** PaulMulrennan 9 54
(Mark H Tompkins) *midfield: hdwy over 4f out: rdn over 2f out: styd on u.p appr fnl f: nrst fin* **11/1**
0-04 **5** 3 ¼ **Lord Nandi**[18] 3181 3-9-1 **64** EddieAhern 3 57
(Sir Henry Cecil) *midfield: hdwy 3f out: rdn along wl over 2f out: n.d* **12/1**
6426 **6** 5 **Micquus (IRE)**[28] 2850 3-8-4 **53** (v) FrannyNorton 8 39
(Andrew Balding) *led: rdn along wl over 3f out: hdd wl over 2f out: grad wknd* **15/2**
0300 **7** 3 ¼ **So Cheeky**[9] 3460 3-8-6 **55** AdrianNicholls 4 37
(Peter Salmon) *dwlt: a bhd* **25/1**

0-50 **8** *40* **Bells Of Berlin**[17] 3233 3-8-3 **52** ow1............................(vt) TadhgO'Shea 2
(Alan McCabe) *rn wout tongue strap: chsd ldr: rdn along over 3f out: sn wknd* **50/1**

20-0 **9** *1 ¼* **Bedlam**[52] 2118 3-8-13 **62**..(p) DavidAllan 1
(Tim Easterby) *a towards rr: bhd fnl 4f* **25/1**

0434 **10** *4* **Dropzone (USA)**[18] 3186 3-9-4 **67**..............................(b[1]) JimmyQuinn 10
(Marco Botti) *prom: rdn along over 3f out: sn wknd* **10/1**

3m 3.09s (1.09) **Going Correction** +0.175s/f (Good) **10** Ran SP% **114.9**
Speed ratings (Par 100): **103,99,97,97,95 92,90,68,67,65**
toteswingers 1&2 £3.70, 1&3 £3.90, 2&3 £3.00 CSF £19.66 CT £49.03 TOTE £7.30: £1.90, £1.20, £2.00; EX 24.30 Trifecta £76.20 Pool £1,250.25 - 12.14 winning units..
Owner Mr & Mrs I H Bendelow **Bred** San Gabriel Investments **Trained** Upper Lambourn, Berks

FOCUS
A modest staying handicap for 3yos and it developed into quite a test. This time the runners came out into the centre of the track in the home straight rather than all the way over. The winner built on his latest effort but there were doubts over what else showed their form.
Micquus(IRE) Official explanation: jockey said gelding ran too freely
T/Plt: £1,644.90 to a £1 stake. Pool: £64444.27 - 28.60 winning tickets T/Qpdt: £452.40 to a £1 stake. Pool: £4096.12 - 6.70 winning tickets JR

3472 NEWBURY (L-H)
Thursday, July 5

OFFICIAL GOING: Good to soft
Wind: light across Weather: quite cloudy with a few sunny periods

3782 UFTON ADVENTURE APPRENTICE H'CAP — 1m 3f 5y
6:20 (6:22) (Class 5) (0-70,70) 4-Y-0+ **£2,264** (£673; £336; £168) **Stalls** Centre

Form RPR

5445 **1** **Shades Of Grey**[24] 2976 5-9-1 **66**.................................... RyanTate(5) 12 79
(Clive Cox) *cl up: hdwy to ld 3f out: pushed clr 2f out: edgd rt but in n.d fnl 100yds* **5/1[2]**

5005 **2** *3 ½* **Redinessence (IRE)**[19] 3137 4-8-5 **51** oh4........................... AmyScott 9 58
(Willie Musson) *towards rr: rdn over 3f out: swtchd rt and kpt on fr over 1f out: wnt 2nd wl ins fnl f: no ch w wnr* **28/1**

-031 **3** *1* **Matavia Bay (IRE)**[29] 2821 4-9-1 **66**................. MichaelJMMurphy(5) 10 71
(Alan Jarvis) *t.k.h: a.p: rdn and press wnr 3f out: ev ch tl no ex 1f out: lost 2nd wl ins fnl f* **13/2[3]**

42/0 **4** *2 ¼* **Gordon Flash**[27] 2867 5-9-0 **60**.................................... MatthewLawson 5 61
(Charles Hills) *hld up: rdn 4f out: swtchd rt over 2f out: kpt on one pce fnl f: nvr posed a threat* **7/1**

4512 **5** *3* **Eagle Nebula**[9] 3472 8-9-3 **70**.................................. AccursioRomeo(7) 8 66
(Brett Johnson) *t.k.h in midfield: dropped to rr 7f out: hdwy and nt asked for effrt 3f out: urged along 2f out: sn one pce and no hope of catching ldrs* **8/1**

00-0 **6** *1 ¾* **Transfer**[21] 3073 7-8-7 **58**... DanielMuscutt(5) 2 50
(Richard Price) *hld up: rdn and sme hdwy 3f out: effrt to chse ldrs 2f out: wknd fnl f* **20/1**

-001 **7** *2* **Beat Route**[9] 3472 5-9-3 **66** 6ex........................... NicoleNordblad(3) 11 55
(Michael Attwater) *in tch: hdwy on outer over 3f out: drvn and one pce fnl 2f* **3/1[1]**

6040 **8** *2* **Yes Chef**[24] 2975 5-9-7 **67**.. BrendanPowell 13 52
(Chris Gordon) *t.k.h: sn crossed over to ld and grabbed rail: qckd pce 5f out: rdn and hdd 3f out: wknd qckly after* **12/1**

3260 **9** *shd* **Gower Rules (IRE)**[6] 3573 4-8-10 **56**.................................. DavidKenny 4 41
(John Bridger) *cl up: rdn 4f out: wknd fnl 2f* **16/1**

-400 **10** *3 ¼* **Cottonfields (USA)**[2] 3721 6-8-2 **53** oh1 ow2..........(p) AliceHaynes(5) 7 32
(Heather Main) *unruly s and reluctant to load: towards rr: rdn and no imp 3f out* **16/1**

5250 **11** *½* **Black Coffee**[75] 1533 7-9-0 **63**...............................(b) RachealKneller(3) 1 41
(Mark Brisbourne) *slow away: t.k.h in rr: pushed along over 4f out: sn btn and drifted rt and ended up against stands' side rail* **12/1**

2m 28.28s (7.08) **Going Correction** +0.575s/f (Yiel) **11** Ran SP% **114.0**
Speed ratings (Par 103): **97,94,93,92,89 88,87,85,85,83 82**
Tote Swingers: 1&2 £32.40, 1&3 £6.70, 2&3 £28.40 CSF £129.35 CT £914.14 TOTE £5.90: £2.30, £12.40, £2.70; EX 199.50 TRIFECTA Not won..
Owner Dr and Mrs John Merrington **Bred** Theakston Stud **Trained** Lambourn, Berks
■ Stewards' Enquiry : Alice Haynes two-day ban: weighed in 2lb heavy (Jul 19-20)

FOCUS
The rail has been moved out from the 8f to the 5f pole on the round course, so the round course distances are 21m longer. A modest middle-distance handicap restricted to apprentice jockeys. They went a respectable gallop at best and the winning time was over 11 seconds slower than standard, which suggests the official description of good to soft ground is accurate but it is riding more soft than good. The winner took a slight step up on her recent form.

3783 UFTON COURT EDUCATIONAL TRUST E B F MAIDEN FILLIES' STKS — 6f 8y
6:50 (6:51) (Class 4) 2-Y-0 **£4,398** (£1,309; £654; £327) **Stalls** Centre

Form RPR

1 **Ollie Olga (USA)** 2-9-0 0.. MartinHarley 4 79+
(Mick Channon) *hld up: hdwy over 2f out: qckn up nicely to ld ins fnl f: sprinted clr: impressive* **12/1**

04 **2** *1 ¼* **Bountybeamadam**[23] 3010 2-9-0 0.................................. PatCosgrave 3 75
(George Baker) *broke wl and sn led: urged along 2f out: strly pressed 1f out: hdd ins fnl f: nt pce of wnr* **12/1**

0 **3** *½* **Cut No Ice (IRE)**[30] 2783 2-9-0 0.. ChrisCatlin 5 74
(Paul Cole) *in tch: chsd ldr 3f out: pushed along and ev ch 2f out: remained pressing ldrs tl no ex fnl 100yds* **14/1**

20 **4** *1 ¼* **Equitania**[13] 3326 2-9-0 0.. RichardHughes 10 70
(Richard Hannon) *cl up: rdn ins fnl 2f: drvn to chse ldrs over 1f out: drifted rt and wknd 1f out: no ex fnl 100yds* **5/6[1]**

5 *2* **Sinaadi (IRE)** 2-9-0 0.. JamesDoyle 1 64
(Clive Brittain) *midfield: pushed along to chse ldrs 2f out: hrd drvn and wknd ins fnl f* **40/1**

6 *3 ½* **Velvetina (IRE)** 2-9-0 0.. JimmyFortune 7 57+
(John Dunlop) *broke slowly and rn v green thrght: stl last over 2f out: pushed along and hdwy 2f out: wandering and stl green but kpt on fr 1f out: should improve* **25/1**

7 *¾* **Dali's Lover (IRE)** 2-9-0 0..................................... SilvestreDeSousa 11 51+
(Charles Hills) *slow away: a in rr: rdn and effrt ins fnl 2f: plugged on one pce: nvr a threat* **7/1[2]**

8 *½* **Burlesque Star (IRE)** 2-9-0 0.. DaneO'Neill 6 50
(Harry Dunlop) *t.k.h: midfield: pushed along over 2f out: wknd ins fnl 2f* **28/1**

9 *3 ¼* **Spicy (IRE)** 2-9-0 0.. WilliamBuick 8 42
(Marco Botti) *in tch: rdn 3f out: drvn and lost pl 2f out: sn btn: eased ins fnl f* **10/1[3]**

10 *21* **Casta Diamante** 2-9-0 0.. JimCrowley 9
(Ralph Beckett) *slow away: rdn and brief effrt 3f out: wknd 2f out: eased and t.o ins fnl f* **10/1[3]**

1m 16.57s (3.57) **Going Correction** +0.425s/f (Yiel) **10** Ran SP% **117.0**
Speed ratings (Par 93): **93,91,90,89,86 81,80,80,75,47**
Tote Swingers: 1&2 £9.20, 1&3 £16.60, 2&3 £22.00 CSF £143.23 TOTE £13.80: £3.10, £3.30, £3.70; EX 117.90 TRIFECTA Not won..
Owner Nick & Olga Dhandsa & John & Zoe Webster **Bred** Greenwood Lodge Farm Inc **Trained** West Ilsley, Berks

FOCUS
Probably no more than a fair juvenile maiden contest for fillies, but a nice start from the winner. They went a sensible gallop and the winning time was over five seconds slower than standard, which suggested the straight course was riding on the soft side of good to soft.

NOTEBOOK
Ollie Olga(USA) was held up out the back, before being noted travelling well 2f out and coming through the lead horses about 1f from home to make a nice winning debut. The American-bred filly cost 46,000gns as a foal and is out of a well-related dam who placed up to 1m1f in France and is a half-sister to high-class 1m-1m2f winner Await The Dawn. She was an early foal who appears to have a nice mix of speed and stamina. She should go on from here at up to 1m this term. (op 9-1)
Bountybeamadam deserves credit for sticking to her task to reach second after attempting to make all. She could be interesting in a fillies' nursery handicap over this trip, or 7f, on similar ground later this season. (op 11-1 tchd 14-1)
Cut No Ice(IRE) has progressed from her modest debut over 5f on similar ground at Leicester. She is another to note in fillies' nursery handicap company under similar conditions later this term. (op 22-1)
Equitania ran well over 5f on soft ground at Ascot on debut in May but went the wrong way at the Royal meeting over this trip on similar ground. This was a better display but slightly disappointing all the same, and her future also lies in handicaps. (op 11-10 tchd 6-5 and 6-4)
Sinaadi(IRE) may be one to take out of this contest. She stuck on into fifth once the penny dropped. She cost 65,000gns as a yearling and is out of a well-related dam who is an influence for stamina. A step up to 1m may suit this filly later in the year. (op 33-1)
Velvetina(IRE) Official explanation: jockey said filly ran green

3784 UFTON ADVENTURE CONDITIONS STKS — 7f (S)
7:25 (7:25) (Class 4) 3-Y-0+ **£3,921** (£1,174; £587; £293) **Stalls** Centre

Form RPR

6520 **1** **Scarf (AUS)**[12] 3371 5-9-2 **108**................................ SilvestreDeSousa 3 113
(Saeed Bin Suroor) *mde all: racd in centre of crse tl trckd over to stands' side rail 4f out: pressed over 2f out: drvn along and asserted 1f out* **11/8[2]**

-206 **2** *4 ½* **Silverheels (IRE)**[5] 3639 3-8-5 **98**.. ChrisCatlin 2 94
(Paul Cole) *t.k.h in 3rd: rdn and wnt 2nd over 2f out: pressing wnr ins fnl 2f tl readily brushed aside 1f out* **16/1**

0030 **3** *10* **Mia's Boy**[13] 3331 8-9-2 **94**.. AndreaAtzeni 1 73
(Chris Dwyer) *hld up: last: rdn 3f out: sn no ch w ldng pair: wnt modest 3rd ins fnl 2f* **10/1[3]**

4-30 **4** *19* **Bronterre**[61] 1856 3-8-8 **110**.. RichardHughes 4 19
(Richard Hannon) *anchored leaving stalls and taken stands' side: chsd wnr 4f out: urged along and lost pl 3f out: dropped away tamely over 2f out: eased fnl f* **10/11[1]**

1m 30.13s (4.43) **Going Correction** +0.425s/f (Yiel)
WFA 3 from 4yo+ 8lb **4** Ran SP% **109.5**
Speed ratings (Par 105): **91,85,74,52**
CSF £16.44 TOTE £2.10; EX 12.50.
Owner Godolphin **Bred** Woodlands Stud NSW **Trained** Newmarket, Suffolk

FOCUS
A fair conditions stakes. The winning time was over seven seconds slower than standard, which equates to soft ground in this grade, but they went a dawdle early on and the time may not prove an accurate guide. With the favourite disappointing the winner had little to beat.
Bronterre Official explanation: trainer's rep said, regarding running, that the colt moved poorly on the good to soft ground.

3785 BETFAIR FILLIES' H'CAP — 7f (S)
8:00 (8:15) (Class 4) (0-80,80) 3-Y-0+ **£4,075** (£1,212; £606; £303) **Stalls** Centre

Form RPR

2302 **1** **My Sharona**[28] 2846 3-9-5 **79**.. JamesDoyle 8 87
(Sylvester Kirk) *midfield: hdwy 2f out: drvn to ld ins fnl f: drvn out and hld on wl* **11/2[3]**

-416 **2** *1 ½* **Tea Cup**[12] 3395 3-9-4 **78**.. RichardHughes 6 82
(Richard Hannon) *hld up: hdwy 2f out: pushed along and kpt on fr over 1f out: wnt 2nd fnl 25yds: no ch w wnr* **10/1**

10 **3** *hd* **Savanna Days (IRE)**[47] 2263 3-9-6 **80**............................. MartinHarley 5 83
(Mick Channon) *in tch: pushed along to ld 2f out: hdd ins fnl f and hanging lft: lost 2nd fnl 25yds* **7/2[2]**

1-63 **4** *½* **No Compromise**[20] 3120 3-9-0 **74**...............................(b[1]) JimmyFortune 7 76
(Hughie Morrison) *cl up: pushed along and pressed ldrs over 2f out: ev ch u.str.p 1f out: wknd fnl 100yds* **8/1**

2404 **5** *1 ½* **Shes Rosie**[31] 2766 4-9-1 **67**.. RussKennemore 2 68
(John O'Shea) *in tch: hdd 2f out: drvn and wknd 1f out: sn hanging lft and btn* **20/1**

02-3 **6** *1 ½* **Baheeja**[27] 2891 3-8-12 **72**... AndreaAtzeni 12 66
(Roger Varian) *in tch: drvn 2f out: sn wknd: btn ins fnl f* **5/2[1]**

0-06 **7** *4* **Imelda Mayhem**[27] 2894 3-9-5 **79**.. LiamKeniry 11 62
(J S Moore) *in rr: pushed along over 2f out: wknd and btn fnl f* **33/1**

106- **8** *5* **Supreme Spirit (IRE)**[229] 7486 5-9-11 **77**......................... WilliamBuick 3 50
(Peter Makin) *in rr of midfield: pushed along and effrt ins fnl 3f: rdn and no imp over 1f out* **28/1**

4432 **9** *1 ½* **Nevaeh**[10] 3432 3-8-4 **67**..(v) RaulDaSilva(3) 10 33
(Pat Eddery) *hld up: swtchd rt over 3f out: drvn 2f out: no imp fnl f* **20/1**

04 **10** *3* **Ziefhd**[20] 3108 3-9-4 **78**.. SilvestreDeSousa 13 36
(Paul Cole) *midfield: rdn and wknd 2f out: nvr really on terms* **33/1**

3-43 **11** *8* **Ma Quillet**[13] 3342 4-8-11 **68**.. AmyScott(5) 1
(Henry Candy) *in tch: drvn ins fnl 3f: lost pl 2f out: dropped rt away and eased fnl f* **8/1**

-040 **12** *13* **Cloud Illusions (USA)**[10] 3443 4-8-8 **67**............................ JakePayne(7) 9
(Heather Main) *rousted early: cl up: drvn over 2f out: sn wknd: t.o* **80/1**

1m 28.19s (2.49) **Going Correction** +0.425s/f (Yiel)
WFA 3 from 4yo+ 8lb **12** Ran SP% **117.6**
Speed ratings (Par 102): **102,100,100,99,97 96,91,85,84,80 71,56**
Tote Swingers: 1&2 £8.00, 1&3 £5.00, 2&3 £5.10 CSF £53.03 CT £221.27 TOTE £5.90: £2.10, £3.00, £1.60; EX 62.30 Trifecta £227.80 Pool: £418.69 - 1.36 winning units..
Owner Verano Quartet II **Bred** Seaton Partnership **Trained** Upper Lambourn, Berks

The Form Book Flat, Raceform Ltd, Compton, RG20 6NL

FOCUS
A fair fillies' handicap for 3yos and up. They went a sensible gallop. The form is rated around the third.

3786 UFTON COURT EDUCATIONAL TRUST MAIDEN STKS 1m 4f 5y
8:35 (8:35) (Class 5) 3-Y-O+ **£2,587** (£770; £384; £192) **Stalls** Centre

Form RPR

2 **1** **Guarantee**[17] 3227 3-9-1 0 SilvestreDeSousa 7 87+
(William Haggas) *midfield: hdwy to trck ldrs over 3f out: repeatedly stooped in run 2f out: swtchd rt and strly drvn 1f out: carried hd high u.p but surged home to ld fnl strides* **10/3**[2]

0-0 **2** *nk* **Harlestone Wood**[13] 3349 3-9-1 0 DaneO'Neill 10 84
(John Dunlop) *in tch: hdwy to press ldrs over 3f out: urged along 2f out: drvn to ld fnl 100yds: overwhelmed fnl strides* **28/1**

3-22 **3** *1 ¾* **Bank Bonus**[20] 3106 3-9-1 80 [1] JimmyFortune 1 81
(Andrew Balding) *cl up on inner: pushed along over 2f out: drvn and one pce 2f out: kpt on to press for pls ins fnl f: wnt 3rd post* **7/2**[3]

4063 **4** *shd* **Black Mascara (IRE)**[27] 2895 3-8-10 80 RichardHughes 2 76
(Richard Hannon) *in tch: pushed along to ld on inner 3f out: drvn and strly pressed fnl 2f: hdd ins fnl f: no ex fnl 50yds and lost 3rd post* **5/1**

0-4 **5** *½* **Top Billing**[19] 3161 3-9-1 0 WilliamBuick 9 80
(John Gosden) *t.k.h in tch: hdwy to press ldrs over 2f out: drvn along 1f out: ev ch and duelling for ld tl no ex fnl 75yds* **5/2**[1]

0 **6** *4* **Not Now Katie**[13] 3340 3-8-10 0 LiamKeniry 8 69
(Chris Gordon) *in rr: hdwy 4f out: drvn to chse ldrs 2f out: grad fdd fr 1f out* **50/1**

7 *6* **Sanctioned** 3-9-1 0 JamesDoyle 5 64
(Roger Charlton) *slow away and a towards rr: sme late prog past btn horses* **12/1**

4 **8** *3* **Crystal Monarch (IRE)**[11] 3420 3-9-1 0 PatCosgrave 3 59
(Sir Henry Cecil) *slow away: in rr: hdwy 3f out: bustled along and swtchd rt over 2f out: carried hd high and no imp fnl f* **20/1**

3 **9** *2 ½* **Native Eight (USA)**[18] 3181 3-9-1 0 MartinHarley 12 55
(Ian Williams) *prom: drvn ins fnl 3f: wknd fnl 2f* **50/1**

06- **10** *nse* **Mahayogin (USA)**[27] 6096 4-10-0 0 (tp) ChrisCatlin 6 55
(Charlie Mann) *sn led: rdn and hdd 3f out: sn wknd: dropped rt away* **66/1**

46 **11** *2 ½* **Moonglow**[19] 3161 3-8-10 0 NickyMackay 4 46
(John Gosden) *hld up: nvr a factor: btn fnl 3f* **20/1**

00 **12** *14* **Roman Around**[17] 3232 3-8-10 0 JimCrowley 11 24
(William Knight) *midfield: hdwy on outer over 3f out: drvn and wknd fnl 2f: t.o* **100/1**

2m 44.82s (9.32) **Going Correction** +0.575s/f (Yiel)
WFA 3 from 4yo 13lb **12** Ran SP% **117.6**
Speed ratings (Par 103): **91,90,89,89,89 86,82,80,78,78 77,67**
Tote Swingers: 1&2 £19.70, 1&3 £2.80, 2&3 £31.60 CSF £97.62 TOTE £4.10: £1.40, £7.20, £1.60; EX 88.60 Trifecta £366.20 Pool: £536.21 - 1.08 winning units..
Owner Highclere Thoroughbred Racing-Authorized **Bred** Highbury Stud Ltd **Trained** Newmarket, Suffolk

FOCUS
A decent maiden. The gallop appeared sedate and the winner was very keen early in the contest down the back straight. He rates better than the bare form, which looks sound enough.

3787 UFTON ADVENTURE H'CAP 1m 4f 5y
9:05 (9:10) (Class 4) (0-85,85) 3-Y-O **£4,075** (£1,212; £606; £303) **Stalls** Centre

Form RPR

1-06 **1** **Moidore**[22] 3042 3-8-12 **76** JamesDoyle 4 86
(Roger Charlton) *mde virtually all: drew clr w one rival 3f out: drvn and strly pressed for ld 2f out: battled on gamely: gained upper hand fnl 25yds* **2/1**[2]

1-40 **2** *nk* **Misdemeanour (IRE)**[14] 3296 3-9-5 **83** RichardHughes 2 93
(Richard Hannon) *cl up: pushed along to chse wnr 3f out: drew clr of remainder and duelled for ld fr 2f out tl no ex fnl 25yds* **11/8**[1]

-600 **3** *10* **Just When**[10] 3448 3-8-0 **67** (v[1]) SimonPearce(3) 8 61
(Andrew Balding) *in tch: pushed along 4f out: lost pl u.str.p 3f out: one pce fnl 2f: wnt modest 3rd ins fnl f* **10/1**

3-10 **4** *¾* **Paloma's Prince (IRE)**[42] 2408 3-9-0 **78** PatCosgrave 1 70
(Jim Boyle) *cl up: drvn 4f out: outpcd by ldng pair 3f out: wknd fnl 2f* **6/1**

2-05 **5** *9* **Position**[22] 3042 3-9-4 **82** (t) ChrisCatlin 6 60
(Sir Mark Prescott Bt) *rn wout declared tongue tie: hld up: drvn and no hdwy over 3f out: one pce fnl 2f* **5/1**[3]

0-00 **6** *3 ¼* **Wise Venture (IRE)**[10] 3445 3-9-4 **82** DaneO'Neill 3 55
(Alan Jarvis) *in tch: pushed along ins fnl 4f: lost pl and btn fnl 3f* **20/1**

2m 41.75s (6.25) **Going Correction** +0.575s/f (Yiel) **6** Ran SP% **120.2**
Speed ratings (Par 102): **102,101,95,94,88 86**
Tote Swingers: 1&2 £1.30, 1&3 £5.30, 2&3 £3.70 CSF £5.67 CT £21.11 TOTE £2.80: £1.70, £1.60; EX 6.70 Trifecta £30.80 Pool: £297.65 - 7.15 winning units..
Owner The Queen **Bred** The Queen **Trained** Beckhampton, Wilts
■ Ultimate Destiny was withdrawn (5/2, broke loose & bridle broke bef s). Deduct 25p in the £ under R4.

FOCUS
A decent middle-distance handicap, confined to 3yos. They went a sensible gallop in the testing conditions and the first two came clear in a stirring duel. A step up from the winner.
Position Official explanation: trainer's rep said he had been unable to fit tongue strap and the gelding ran without
T/Plt: £218.40 to a £1 stake. Pool: £74,066.99 - 247.53 winning tickets. T/Qpdt: £11.00 to a £1 stake. Pool: £6,628.32 - 444.52 winning tickets. CS

3545 YARMOUTH (L-H)
Thursday, July 5

OFFICIAL GOING: Good to firm (watered; 7.7)
Wind: Light across Weather: Cloudy with sunny spells

3788 BRITISH STALLION STUDS/BHEST E B F MAIDEN STKS 6f 3y
2:10 (2:10) (Class 5) 2-Y-O **£3,234** (£962; £481; £240) **Stalls** Low

Form RPR

52 **1** **Hasopop (IRE)**[27] 2880 2-9-3 0 AndreaAtzeni 5 83+
(Marco Botti) *a.p: rdn to ld ins fnl f: r.o* **5/1**[3]

0 **2** *½* **Ajmany (IRE)**[16] 3242 2-9-3 0 KierenFallon 7 81
(Luca Cumani) *w ldr: rdn and ev ch ins fnl f: styd on* **10/11**[1]

040 **3** *1* **Ocean Applause**[14] 3291 2-9-3 95 BrettDoyle 2 78
(John Ryan) *led over 3f: rdn and ev ch ins fnl f: styd on same pce* **11/4**[2]

4 *2 ¾* **Hasbah (IRE)** 2-8-12 0 JamieSpencer 6 65+
(Peter Chapple-Hyam) *hld up: racd keenly: hdwy to ld over 2f out: rdn and hdd ins fnl f: no ex* **9/1**

6 **5** *2 ¾* **Meet Me Halfway**[45] 2343 2-8-12 0 TedDurcan 4 57+
(Chris Wall) *prom: rdn over 1f out: sn wknd* **16/1**

0 **6** *¾* **Vinifera (USA)**[22] 3040 2-8-12 0 TomQueally 8 54
(Clive Brittain) *edgd rt s: sn prom: rdn over 1f out: edgd lft and wknd fnl f* **33/1**

0 **7** *nk* **Likelikelikelikeit**[7] 3545 2-8-7 0 HarryPoulton(5) 3 53
(Mark H Tompkins) *chsd ldrs: lost pl over 4f out: rdn over 2f out: sn wknd* **50/1**

00 **8** *¾* **Whitford (IRE)**[7] 3545 2-9-3 0 SaleemGolam 1 56
(Chris Dwyer) *hld up: rdn and hung lft over 2f out: sn wknd* **100/1**

1m 15.45s (1.05) **Going Correction** -0.15s/f (Firm) **8** Ran SP% **117.5**
Speed ratings (Par 94): **87,86,85,81,77 76,76,75**
toteswingers 1&2 £2.20, 2&3 £1.70, 1&3 £2.40 CSF £10.24 TOTE £4.70: £1.20, £1.40, £1.10; EX 11.00.
Owner Giuliano Manfredini **Bred** B Kennedy **Trained** Newmarket, Suffolk

FOCUS
Back straight and bottom bend dolled out 3m adding 5m to all races on Round course. One of the jockeys reported afterwards the going rode firm. Quite an interesting maiden, although the early pace didn't appear strong. The time was slow but the first two improved.

NOTEBOOK
Hasopop(IRE) gained his first success after taking a little while to get organised and hit top gear. A robust type, he's the sort who could go close in some valuable nurseries. The trainer feels his colt will get further. (op 9-2 tchd 4-1)
Ajmany(IRE), who made his debut at Royal Ascot, looked to appreciate this extra furlong but shaped as though another may not go amiss in due course. (op 5-6 tchd 11-10)
Ocean Applause finished a close seventh in the Norfolk Stakes recently, so was the form pick, but he didn't get home as well as the first two after racing prominently. Considering he had the run of the race, one can only conclude he was below his best, possibly due to the ground. (op 7-2)
Hasbah(IRE), a half-sister to Listed-placed Samminder, was a little keen on her debut and couldn't sustain her effort after hitting the front. She wasn't given a hard time once held and won't be long in winning if building on this. (op 11-1)
Meet Me Halfway seemed to be making a bit of late headway up in distance, suggesting she has ability. (op 22-1)

3789 YARMOUTH STADIUM (S) STKS 6f 3y
2:40 (2:41) (Class 6) 2-Y-O **£1,617** (£481; £240; £120) **Stalls** Low

Form RPR

0 **1** **Senora Lobo (IRE)**[17] 3208 2-8-6 0 RoystonFfrench 7 57
(Lisa Williamson) *chsd ldr tl led over 4f out: rdn over 1f out: r.o u.p* **9/2**[3]

44 **2** *¾* **Smiling Shark (USA)**[24] 2970 2-8-11 0 TomQueally 4 60
(Robert Cowell) *led: hdd over 4f out: ev ch fr over 2f out: rdn over 1f out: styd on same pce towards fin* **13/8**[1]

620 **3** *2* **Strawberry Duck (IRE)**[17] 3224 2-8-6 55 KirstyMilczarek 1 49
(Amy Weaver) *a.p: racd keenly: rdn over 2f out: styd on same pce fnl f* **7/1**

4 *1 ¾* **Cotton Dancer (IRE)**[29] 2828 2-8-6 0 WilliamCarson 6 44
(David Peter Nagle, Ire) *prom: rdn over 2f out: styd on same pce appr fnl f* **11/1**

06 **5** *½* **Madam Moreton**[16] 3244 2-8-3 0 RyanPowell(3) 5 42
(George Margarson) *prom: rdn over 1f out: styd on same pce* **50/1**

06 **6** *hd* **Iffley Fields**[17] 3224 2-8-11 0 CathyGannon 2 46+
(David Evans) *sn drvn along and outpcd* **9/4**[2]

1m 15.3s (0.90) **Going Correction** -0.15s/f (Firm) **6** Ran SP% **109.8**
Speed ratings (Par 92): **88,87,84,82,81 81**
toteswingers 1&2 £2.10, 1&3 £3.40, 2&3 £2.10 CSF £11.74 TOTE £3.40: £2.50, £1.50; EX 12.30.There was no bid for the winner. Smiling Shark was claimed by Mr Claes Bjorling for £5,000.
Owner Mrs Lisa Williamson **Bred** Mrs G P Booth **Trained** Saighton, Cheshire

FOCUS
Not much form to go on, especially when the likely favourite was withdrawn earlier in the afternoon. Typical selling form, the third helping with the level.

NOTEBOOK
Senora Lobo(IRE), eased in company after shaping with promise in a Carlisle maiden on debut, jumped smartly from the stalls and made a lot of the running. She didn't set a searing test of speed, so may have been well positioned in an ordinarily run contest, although one couldn't fault the heart she showed to hang on. (tchd 4-1)
Smiling Shark(USA), up in trip and down in grade, took a strong hold chasing the leader and couldn't force his way to the front when given the chance. (op 6-4 tchd 7-4)
Strawberry Duck(IRE) was another to race prominently, so her position may flatter her a little. (op 6-1)
Cotton Dancer(IRE), who had been well beaten in a couple of Irish maidens, was pushed along quite early and made no real impression. (tchd 12-1)
Iffley Fields was being hard ridden almost from the start and never featured. Official explanation: jockey said gelding never travelled (op 11-4 tchd 3-1)

3790 WATERAID CHARITY H'CAP 7f 3y
3:10 (3:15) (Class 5) (0-75,74) 3-Y-O+ **£2,264** (£673; £336; £168) **Stalls** Low

Form RPR

0-60 **1** **Mrs Greeley**[31] 2766 4-9-13 **73** TedDurcan 8 83
(Eve Johnson Houghton) *hld up: hdwy over 2f out: rdn over 1f out: r.o to ld towards fin* **16/1**

50-6 **2** *½* **Excellent Jem**[13] 3347 3-9-0 **68** KierenFallon 9 74
(Jane Chapple-Hyam) *a.p: pushed along over 2f out: rdn over 1f out: r.o* **18/1**

132 **3** *hd* **First Class**[7] 3549 4-8-10 **56** ow1 TomQueally 15 64
(Rae Guest) *hld up: hdwy over 1f out: sn rdn: r.o* **9/2**[2]

0053 **4** *shd* **Flynn's Boy**[6] 3571 4-10-0 **74** RobertHavlin 5 82
(Rae Guest) *a.p: rdn over 1f out: led ins fnl f: hdd towards fin* **6/1**[3]

0016 **5** *1 ¾* **Main Beach**[5] 3612 5-9-12 **72** MickyFenton 6 75
(Paul Midgley) *s.i.s and hmpd s: hld up: hdwy over 1f out: sn rdn: r.o* **10/1**

0-03 **6** *1* **Anton Chigurh**[11] 3421 3-9-6 **74** StephenCraine 14 71
(Tom Dascombe) *hld up: hdwy over 2f out: rdn over 1f out: styd on same pce ins fnl f* **22/1**

00 **7** *½* **Gabrial's Gift (IRE)**[40] 2490 3-9-5 **73** JamieSpencer 7 69
(David Simcock) *chsd ldr: rdn over 1f out: edgd rt and no ex ins fnl f* **25/1**

0401 **8** *½* **Spirit Of Gondree (IRE)**[19] 3153 4-9-3 **63** (b) CathyGannon 2 61
(Milton Bradley) *led: rdn over 1f out: hdd and no ex ins fnl f* **28/1**

-141 **9** *2 ¼* **Takitwo**[8] 3511 9-9-4 **64** 6ex LiamKeniry 11 56
(Jonathan Portman) *sn pushed along in rr: nvr trbld ldrs* **25/1**

-016 **10** *1 ½* **My Own Way Home**[18] 3192 4-9-3 **63** KirstyMilczarek 1 50
(David Evans) *chsd ldrs: rdn 1/2-way: wknd over 1f out* **33/1**

0110 **11** *1* **Spin Again (IRE)**[7] 3549 7-9-5 **65**................................ StevieDonohoe 13 50
(John Ryan) *prom: rdn over 2f out: wknd over 1f out* **22/1**

0315 **12** *½* **Rough Rock (IRE)**[7] 3549 7-9-6 **73**................................ JoshCrane(7) 12 56
(Chris Dwyer) *hld up: hmpd after 1f: nvr on terms* **10/1**

6523 **13** *1 ½* **Great Expectations**[20] 3105 4-9-13 **73**.......................... FrederikTylicki 3 52
(J R Jenkins) *chsd ldrs: rdn over 2f out: wknd wl over 1f out* **11/4**[1]

-050 **14** *¾* **Brimstone Hill (IRE)**[13] 3347 3-9-4 **72**.......................... WilliamCarson 4 46
(Anthony Carson) *s.i.s: sn mid-div: rdn and wknd over 2f out* **50/1**

6542 **15** *15* **Intomist (IRE)**[7] 3548 3-8-1 **60**.................................. NathanAlison(5) 10
(Jim Boyle) *sn pushed along towards rr: bhd fr 1/2-way* **16/1**

1m 24.93s (-1.67) **Going Correction** -0.15s/f (Firm)
WFA 3 from 4yo+ 8lb **15** Ran SP% **119.1**
Speed ratings (Par 103): **103,102,102,102,100 98,98,97,95,93 92,91,90,89,72**
toteswingers 1&2 £40.10, 1&3 £17.50, 2&3 £16.40 CSF £248.32 CT £1549.56 TOTE £19.30: £5.00, £6.80, £2.10; EX 364.50.

Owner Mrs Romilla Arber **Bred** Minster Stud **Trained** Blewbury, Oxon

FOCUS
Probably just a modest contest, although the pace wasn't too bad thanks to Spirit Of Gondree.
My Own Way Home Official explanation: trainer's rep said filly was not suited by the track
Intomist(IRE) Official explanation: jockey said colt lost its action

3791 NORFOLK CHAMBER OF COMMERCE H'CAP 5f 43y
3:40 (3:46) (Class 6) (0-60,60) 3-Y-O+ **£1,617** (£481; £240; £120) **Stalls** Low

Form RPR

602 **1** **Irish Girls Spirit (IRE)**[4] 3670 3-8-8 **49**.............................. MickyFenton 7 60+
(Paul Midgley) *racd centre: led 2f: chsd ldfers: rdn to ld ins fnl f: styd on* **11/4**[1]

5062 **2** *½* **One Kool Dude**[12] 3407 3-9-3 **58**................................(v) JamieSpencer 12 67
(Michael Bell) *racd centre: mid-div: hdwy 1/2-way: rdn over 1f out: edgd lft ins fnl f: r.o: 2nd of 11 in gp* **15/2**

-512 **3** *¾* **Autocracy**[16] 3243 5-9-9 **59**..(bt) TomQueally 5 68
(Daniel Kubler) *racd centre: chsd ldrs: rdn to ld over 1f out: hdd and unable qck ins fnl f: 3rd of 11 in gp* **12/1**

4-43 **4** *1* **The Jailer**[10] 3435 9-9-1 **54**.. RyanPowell(3) 2 59
(John O'Shea) *racd centre: a.p: rdn over 1f out: styd on same pce ins fnl f: 4th of 11 in gp* **16/1**

0055 **5** *½* **Simple Rhythm**[9] 3464 6-8-3 **46** oh1......................(v) BradleyBosley(7) 11 49+
(John Ryan) *racd centre: sn pushed along in rr: hdwy 1/2-way: rdn over 1f out: styd on same pce ins fnl f: 5th of 11 in gp* **33/1**

0-00 **6** *¾* **Crabbies Ginger**[35] 2617 4-8-10 **46**.......................... RoystonFfrench 10 47
(Lisa Williamson) *racd centre: sn outpcd: r.o u.p ins fnl f: nvr nrr: 6th of 11 in gp* **80/1**

20-0 **7** *hd* **Adaeze (IRE)**[9] 3477 4-9-5 **55**.. StephenCraine 3 55
(Jonathan Portman) *racd centre: prom: rdn over 1f out: styd on same pce fnl f: 7th of 11 in gp* **22/1**

-060 **8** *nse* **Arch Walker (IRE)**[16] 3256 5-9-10 **60**......................(b) WilliamCarson 14 60
(John Weymes) *racd stands' side: chsd ldr tl led that gp 2f out: rdn and edgd lft over 1f out: styd on same pce: 1st of 3 in gp* **6/1**[2]

1600 **9** *1 ¼* **Canadian Danehill (IRE)**[114] 887 10-9-5 **58**.....(p) AdamBeschizza(3) 1 53
(Robert Cowell) *racd centre: chsd ldrs: lost pl over 3f out: rdn and edgd rt over 1f out: n.d after: 8th of 11 in gp* **25/1**

3321 **10** *hd* **Ooi Long**[9] 3467 3-8-13 **59** 6ex..................................(t) TobyAtkinson(5) 8 51+
(Mark Rimmer) *s.s: racd centre: outpcd: nvr nrr: 9th of 11 in gp* **7/1**[3]

5450 **11** *1 ½* **Forty Proof (IRE)**[8] 3511 4-9-2 **52**..........................(p) KirstyMilczarek 13 41
(David Evans) *racd stands' side: outpcd: 2nd of 3 in gp* **20/1**

6055 **12** *¾* **Temple Road (IRE)**[12] 3390 4-9-6 **56**.............................. CathyGannon 9 42
(Milton Bradley) *racd centre: chsd ldrs: led 3f out: rdn and hdd over 1f out: wknd ins fnl f: 10th of 11 in gp* **9/1**

6004 **13** *3 ½* **Atlantic Cycle (IRE)**[9] 3464 5-9-7 **57**..........................(tp) NickyMackay 4 31
(Milton Bradley) *racd centre: chsd ldrs: rdn 1/2-way: wknd over 1f out: last of 11 in gp* **18/1**

0040 **14** *6* **Miss Polly Plum**[5] 3618 5-9-4 **54**..............................(b[1]) SaleemGolam 15
(Chris Dwyer) *led stands' side 3f: sn wknd: last of 3 in gp* **22/1**

1m 2.5s (-0.20) **Going Correction** -0.15s/f (Firm)
WFA 3 from 4yo+ 5lb **14** Ran SP% **115.5**
Speed ratings (Par 101): **95,94,93,91,90 89,89,89,87,86 84,83,77,67**
CSF £19.16 CT £218.94 TOTE £3.90: £1.70, £2.40, £2.80; EX 24.50.
Owner Sheard, Banks, Jackson & Johnson **Bred** Seamus McMullan **Trained** Westow, N Yorks

FOCUS
A moderate contest where it paid to race centre to far side of the track. The winner was well in after her improved Windsor effort and can do better still. The runner-up was back to form.
Ooi Long Official explanation: jockey said gelding was slowly away
Atlantic Cycle(IRE) Official explanation: trainer's rep said mare lost a front shoe

3792 GUIDE DOGS FOR BLIND H'CAP 1m 1f
4:10 (4:12) (Class 4) (0-80,85) 3-Y-O **£3,969** (£1,188; £594; £297; £148) **Stalls** Low

Form RPR

-431 **1** **Touch Gold (IRE)**[12] 3399 3-9-5 **77**................................ TomQueally 8 92
(Sir Henry Cecil) *mde all: pushed clr fr over 1f out: styd on wl* **9/2**[2]

454 **2** *5* **Sarmatian Knight (IRE)**[38] 2560 3-8-12 **70**.................. StevieDonohoe 11 74
(Ian Williams) *prom: chsd wnr over 7f out: rdn over 2f out: outpcd fr over 1f out* **16/1**

-346 **3** *2 ¼* **Disposition**[21] 3070 3-9-6 **78**.. RobertHavlin 4 79+
(John Gosden) *hld up: hmpd wl over 1f out: r.o ins fnl f: wnt 3rd post: nvr able to chal* **16/1**

23-3 **4** *nk* **Fulney**[32] 2734 3-9-5 **77**.. CathyGannon 7 75
(James Eustace) *hld up: plld hrd: hdwy over 2f out: rdn over 1f out: styd on same pce fr over 1f out: lost 3rd post* **9/1**

55-0 **5** *½* **Operation Tracer**[32] 2733 3-8-6 **64**.............................. RoystonFfrench 5 62
(Michael Bell) *hld up: rdn over 2f out: r.o ins fnl f: nrst fin* **40/1**

1031 **6** *hd* **Take Two**[13] 3338 3-9-6 **78**.. JamieSpencer 6 75
(John O'Shea) *s.i.s: hld up: rdn over 2f out: hdwy over 1f out: nt trble ldrs* **9/1**

-360 **7** *shd* **Yaa Salam**[26] 2942 3-9-4 **76**......................................(vt) AhmedAjtebi 2 76+
(Mahmood Al Zarooni) *hld up: hmpd wl over 1f out: r.o ins fnl f: nvr nrr* **20/1**

3-62 **8** *¾* **Strada Facendo (USA)**[21] 3063 3-9-7 **79**...................... KierenFallon 9 74
(Luca Cumani) *prom: rdn over 1f out: no ex fnl f* **3/1**[1]

-630 **9** *nk* **Strident Force**[10] 3446 3-9-1 **73**................................. TedDurcan 3 67
(Sir Michael Stoute) *prom: rdn over 1f out: no ex* **16/1**

2501 **10** *9* **Ocean Tempest**[10] 3446 3-9-13 **85** 6ex..........................(p) BrettDoyle 10 60
(John Ryan) *chsd ldrs: rdn over 1f out: wknd and eased fnl f* **7/1**

303 **11** *¾* **California English (IRE)**[29] 2813 3-9-1 **76**............ AdamBeschizza(3) 1 49
(Marco Botti) *chsd ldrs: rdn over 2f out: sn wknd* **13/2**[3]

1m 52.0s (-3.80) **Going Correction** -0.35s/f (Firm) course record **11** Ran SP% **113.9**
Speed ratings (Par 102): **102,97,95,95,94 94,94,93,93,85 84**
toteswingers 1&2 £18.10, 1&3 £13.10, 2&3 £28.80 CSF £71.62 CT £1065.44 TOTE £4.40: £1.50, £6.30, £4.30; EX 91.80.

Owner H E Sheikh Sultan Bin Khalifa Al Nahyan **Bred** Runnymede Farm Inc **Trained** Newmarket, Suffolk

FOCUS
This produced a very useful-looking winner but there was trouble in behind for a few. The winner improved again, with the form rated around the second.

3793 E.A.C.H. CHARITY H'CAP 1m 2f 21y
4:40 (4:40) (Class 5) (0-70,70) 3-Y-O+ **£2,264** (£673; £336; £168) **Stalls** Low

Form RPR

0-13 **1** **Tis Rock 'N' Roll (USA)**[28] 2860 3-9-2 **69**........................ TedDurcan 1 83+
(David Lanigan) *a.p: nt clr run over 2f out: rdn to ld ins fnl f: r.o* **6/1**[3]

0-20 **2** *1 ¼* **Landesherr (GER)**[27] 2260 5-9-4 **60**............................(t) FrederikTylicki 7 69
(Steve Gollings) *chsd ldrs: led over 2f out: sn rdn: hdd over 1f out: styd on* **12/1**

3663 **3** *½* **Silver Alliance**[27] 2886 4-9-7 **66**.............................. AdamBeschizza(3) 10 74
(Julia Feilden) *hld up: hdwy over 2f out: rdn to ld over 1f out: hdd and unable qck ins fnl f* **14/1**

4605 **4** *3 ½* **Rogue Reporter (IRE)**[17] 3228 3-8-11 **64**.................... SaleemGolam 9 65
(Stuart Williams) *hld up: rdn over 1f out: r.o ins fnl f: nt rch ldrs* **16/1**

6 **5** *1 ¼* **Amistress**[42] 2414 4-9-11 **67**.. CathyGannon 2 66
(Eve Johnson Houghton) *hld up: plld hrd: hdwy u.p over 1f out: nt trble ldrs* **9/1**

0401 **6** *1* **Five Hearts**[22] 3047 4-8-10 **52**......................................(b) TomQueally 5 49
(Mark H Tompkins) *s.i.s: hld up: plld hrd: hdwy over 1f out: rdn and hung lft ins fnl f: no ex* **11/1**

6-02 **7** *3 ½* **Tin Pan Alley**[30] 2799 4-10-0 **70**................................ RobertHavlin 4 60
(Giles Bravery) *hld up in tch: rdn over 2f out: wknd over 1f out* **4/1**[2]

0-50 **8** *2 ¼* **Heyaaraat (IRE)**[13] 3340 3-8-12 **65**............................ WilliamCarson 6 50
(Charles Hills) *hld up in tch: rdn over 2f out: sn wknd* **16/1**

4005 **9** *3 ¼* **Rufus Stone (USA)**[13] 3344 4-8-13 **62**......................(p) LewisWalsh(7) 8 41
(Jane Chapple-Hyam) *chsd ldr tl rdn over 3f out: wknd over 1f out* **33/1**

0000 **10** *2* **Goal (IRE)**[18] 3180 4-9-11 **67**.................................. RobbieFitzpatrick 12 42
(Charles Smith) *led: clr 7f out tl rdn and hdd over 2f out: wknd over 1f out* **66/1**

304 **11** *5* **Mount Abora (IRE)**[12] 3386 5-9-9 **65**.............................. JamieSpencer 11 30
(Ian Williams) *s.i.s: hld up: a in rr: wknd over 2f out* **8/1**

6-53 **12** *¾* **Porcini**[51] 2144 3-9-3 **70**.. KierenFallon 3 33
(Philip McBride) *hld up: a in rr: pushed along over 3f out: rdn and wknd over 2f out* **3/1**[1]

2m 6.18s (-4.32) **Going Correction** -0.35s/f (Firm)
WFA 3 from 4yo+ 11lb **12** Ran SP% **119.3**
Speed ratings (Par 103): **103,102,101,98,97 97,94,92,89,88 84,83**
toteswingers 1&2 £14.50, 1&3 £11.60, 2&3 £23.40 CSF £76.60 CT £975.82 TOTE £7.00: £2.30, £2.80, £4.80; EX 80.80.

Owner Catesby W Clay **Bred** Runnymede Farm Inc **Trained** Upper Lambourn, Berks

FOCUS
Goal, who ran over 1m6f last time, ensured this wasn't run at a false pace, meaning the form ought to be reliable in the coming weeks. A fair step up from the winner, who was value for a bit extra.
Rufus Stone(USA) Official explanation: trainer said gelding was unsuited by the good to firm ground

3794 INJURED JOCKEYS FUND "HANDS AND HEELS" APPRENTICE SERIES H'CAP (RACING EXCELLENCE INITIATIVE) 1m 3f 101y
5:10 (5:10) (Class 6) (0-65,65) 4-Y-O+ **£1,617** (£481; £240; £120) **Stalls** Low

Form RPR

3412 **1** **The Ducking Stool**[17] 3216 5-9-1 **56**.......................... ShirleyTeasdale 8 66+
(Julia Feilden) *chsd ldr tl led 9f out: shkn up over 2f out: pushed out* **3/1**[1]

0-02 **2** *¾* **Locum**[5] 3620 7-8-8 **54**.. RobJFitzpatrick(5) 9 63
(Mark H Tompkins) *hld up: hdwy over 3f out: chsd wnr over 2f out: sn pushed along: styd on* **11/2**[3]

3 *7* **Rio Silver (IRE)**[98] 1102 4-8-6 **47**.................................... IanBurns 1 44
(Shaun Harris) *prom: pushd along over 3f out: styd on same pce fr over 1f out* **13/2**

-023 **4** *hd* **Camera Shy (IRE)**[12] 3392 8-9-2 **57**.......................... MichaelJMurphy 4 54
(Kevin Morgan) *s.s: hld up: hdwy over 1f out: nvr nrr* **6/1**

0264 **5** *1* **Cotton Grass**[7] 3552 4-9-5 **60**.. NoelGarbutt 7 55
(Mark H Tompkins) *hld up: hdwy over 1f out: nt rch ldrs* **11/1**

0004 **6** *2 ¼* **Magicalmysterytour (IRE)**[20] 3129 9-9-7 **65**.............. LewisWalsh(3) 2 56
(Willie Musson) *prom: chsd wnr over 5f out tl pushed along over 2f out: wknd over 1f out* **4/1**[2]

0406 **7** *1 ¾* **Thank You Joy**[22] 3047 4-9-0 **55**..................................(v) LauraBarry 6 43
(J R Jenkins) *prom: pushed along over 2f out: wknd over 1f out* **28/1**

0442 **8** *2 ¼* **Ostentation**[2] 3722 5-9-4 **64**................................(p) Leah-AnneAvery(5) 5 48
(Alastair Lidderdale) *hld up: pushed along over 2f out: n.d* **6/1**

004 **9** *5* **Ivan The Terrible (IRE)**[74] 924 4-8-8 **49**...................... JoshBaudains 3 25
(Richard Guest) *led 3f: chsd wnr tl over 5f out: pushed along over 3f out: wknd over 1f out* **50/1**

2m 26.89s (-1.81) **Going Correction** -0.35s/f (Firm) **9** Ran SP% **116.0**
Speed ratings (Par 101): **92,91,86,86,85 83,82,80,77**
toteswingers 1&2 £3.70, 1&3 £3.90, 2&3 £3.00 CSF £19.87 CT £99.71 TOTE £4.30: £1.60, £2.00, £2.50; EX 20.50.

Owner Mrs S McGuiness **Bred** Cheveley Park Stud Ltd **Trained** Exning, Suffolk

FOCUS
Nothing more than a moderate affair. The winner was less exposed than most and the runner-up sets the standard.

Ivan The Terrible(IRE) Official explanation: jockey said gelding lost its action

T/Jkpt: Not won. T/Plt: £42.20 to a £1 stake. Pool: £81797.81 - 1414.07 winning tickets T/Qpdt: £40.80 to a £1 stake. Pool: £6016.15 - 108.97 winning tickets CR

3795 - 3801a (Foreign Racing) - See Raceform Interactive

3768 HAMBURG (R-H)
Thursday, July 5

OFFICIAL GOING: Turf: good to soft

3802a GROSSER PREIS VON LOTTO HAMBURG (HAMBURGER STUTEN-PREIS) (GROUP 3) (3YO FILLIES) (TURF) 1m 3f
5:55 (5:56) 3-Y-O

£26,666 (£9,166; £4,583; £2,500; £1,666; £1,250)

RPR
1 **Salomina (GER)**[32] 3-9-2 0 AStarke 3 99
(P Schiergen, Germany) *stdd s and sn settled towards rr: rdn to improve 2 1/2f out: r.o u.p to chal ins fnl f: led on hd bob post: jst prevailed* **2/1**[2]
2 *shd* **Caitania (IRE)**[20] 3-9-2 0 ADeVries 1 99
(C Sprengel, Germany) *midfield: rdn over 2 1/2f out: led over 1 1/2f out: strly pressed ins fnl f: kpt on but nailed on hd bob post: jst denied* **181/10**
3 *1* **Wilddrossel (GER)**[40] 2522 3-9-2 0 EFrank 5 97
(Markus Klug, Germany) *prom: rdn over 3f out: outpcd on turn into st: rallied and r.o strly u.p to go 3rd ins fnl f* **51/10**[3]
4 *1* **Monami (GER)**[39] 2531 3-9-2 0 EPedroza 9 95
(A Wohler, Germany) *hld up in tch on outer: rdn over 2 1/2f out: r.o to go 4th ins fnl f: styd on* **11/10**[1]
5 *1* **Lady Of Budysin (GER)**[32] 2746 3-9-2 0 MSuerland 8 93
(Andreas Lowe, Germany) *hld up in last: rdn over 2 1/2f out: r.o to go 5th ins fnl f: styd on* **94/10**
6 *2* **Ilena (GER)**[32] 2746 3-9-2 0 JBojko 7 90
(Dr A Bolte, Germany) *sn trcking ldr in 2nd on outer: led briefly over 2f out: rdn and hdd over 1 1/2f out: kpt on tl no ex and fdd ins fnl f* **102/10**
7 *7* **Goldschatzchen (GER)** 3-9-2 0 APietsch 4 77
(W Hickst, Germany) *sn led: rdn and hdd over 2f out: wknd* **135/10**
8 *shd* **Kolosseum (GER)**[38] 2569 3-9-2 0 FilipMinarik 2 77
(W Figge, Germany) *hld up towards rr on inner: rdn and outpcd over 2f out: sn btn: eased and dropped to last ins fnl f* **34/1**

2m 20.61s (-4.09) 8 Ran SP% **130.9**
WIN (incl. 10 euro stake): 30. PLACES: 17, 34, 17. SF: 406.
Owner Gestut Bona **Bred** Gestut Bona **Trained** Germany

3457 BEVERLEY (R-H)
Friday, July 6

3803 Meeting Abandoned - waterlogged

3611 DONCASTER (L-H)
Friday, July 6

OFFICIAL GOING: Soft (heavy in places) changing to heavy after race 1 (2.00)
SOFT (Heavy in places) changing to HEAVY after Race 1 (2.00).
Wind: Virtually nil Weather: Heavy rain

3809 CARDSAVE LAURAN BINKS & ROSE GLYNN MAIDEN STKS 7f
2:00 (2:01) (Class 5) 3-Y-O **£2,264** (£673; £336; £168) **Stalls** High

Form RPR
2-3 1 **Moodhill**[13] 3398 3-9-3 0 MichaelHills 8 80
(Charles Hills) *mde all: rdn over 1f out: styd on* **11/4**[1]
3662 2 *1* **Pashan Garh**[22] 3071 3-9-3 74 JoeFanning 3 77
(Pat Eddery) *cl up: effrt 2f out: sn rdn and ev ch tl one pce ins fnl f* **5/1**[2]
3 *6* **The Baronet** 3-9-3 0 LukeMorris 5 62+
(Sir Mark Prescott Bt) *dwlt: bhd and green: sn pushed along: hdwy 2f out: styd on fnl f: nrst fin* **16/1**
50 4 *1 1/4* **Well Bank (IRE)**[11] 3438 3-9-3 0 PaulMulrennan 1 59
(Colin Teague) *in tch: rdn along and outpcd over 2f out: styd on fnl f* **50/1**
40 5 *hd* **Thereabouts (USA)**[22] 3079 3-9-3 0 MartinHarley 4 58
(Marco Botti) *chsd ldrs: rdn along wl over 2f out: grad wknd* **16/1**
30 6 *4* **Asian Trader**[41] 2470 3-9-3 0 JamieSpencer 2 48
(William Haggas) *trckd ldrs: hdwy 3f out: rdn wl over 1f out and sn wknd* **7/1**[3]
2400 7 *10* **Widyaan (IRE)**[14] 3347 3-9-3 70 RobertHavlin 7 22
(John Gosden) *racd alone on stands' rail: prom: rdn along 3f out: sn outpcd* **8/1**
03 8 *4* **First Voice (IRE)**[7] 3561 3-9-3 0 RoystonFfrench 10 11
(James Given) *chsd ldng pair: rdn along 3f out: wknd over 2f out* **40/1**
9 *21* **Doting** 3-9-3 0 RussKennemore 11
(Peter Salmon) *s.i.s: a bhd* **50/1**

1m 30.79s (4.49) **Going Correction** +0.725s/f (Yiel) 9 Ran SP% **85.1**
Speed ratings (Par 100): **103,101,95,93,93 88,77,72,48**
toteswingers: 1&2 £1.70, 1&3 £4.40, 2&3 £9.90. CSF £7.93 TOTE £2.70: £1.10, £1.50, £3.70; EX 7.30.
Owner Hamdan Al Maktoum **Bred** Shadwell Estate Company Limited **Trained** Lambourn, Berks

FOCUS
After 25mm of rain in the morning, the going was soft, heavy in places. Racing went ahead after passing a noon inspection, but there were numerous non-runners on the day. There was drama before the race when favourite Niger reared in the stalls, putting both legs over the sides, and had to be withdrawn (7/4F, deduct 35p in the £ under R4). An average maiden run at a decent pace in the conditions, with the field well strung out crossing the line. Michael Hills, the winning jockey, described the ground as "bottomless". The winner was the form pick in this ordinary maiden.

3810 CARDSAVE ADAM COLEMAN & MOLLY WOODS CLAIMING STKS 1m (S)
2:30 (2:31) (Class 5) 4-Y-O+ **£2,264** (£673; £336; £168) **Stalls** High

Form RPR
0240 1 **Kay Gee Be (IRE)**[35] 2657 8-8-12 85 ShaneBKelly(5) 1 85
(Richard Fahey) *cl up: led 3f out: rdn 2f out: clr ins fnl f: styd on strly* **7/4**[1]
-501 2 *5* **King Pin**[13] 3405 7-8-12 64 (p) BarryMcHugh 7 68
(Tracy Waggott) *hld up: hdwy wl over 2f out: rdn to chse wnr wl over 1f out: drvn and no imp ent fnl f* **8/1**
1052 3 *4* **Abidhabidubai**[15] 3311 4-8-10 76 MichaelO'Connell 9 57
(John Quinn) *led 1f: cl up: effrt and ev ch 3f out: sn rdn and wknd fnl 2f* **2/1**[2]
100- 4 *4* **High Five Society**[307] 5733 8-8-8 70 (b) MarkCoumbe(5) 3 51
(Roy Bowring) *trckd ldrs: hdwy 1/2-way: rdn along wl over 2f out: sn btn* **25/1**
0401 5 *31* **Nezami (IRE)**[15] 3311 7-8-5 67 ow3 (b) NedCurtis(7) 2
(Paul Midgley) *plld hrd: cl up: led after 1f: pushed along and hdd 3f out: wknd qckly* **5/1**[3]

1m 46.7s (7.40) **Going Correction** +0.725s/f (Yiel) 5 Ran SP% **101.3**
Speed ratings (Par 103): **92,87,83,79,48**
toteswinger: 1&2 £6.70. CSF £12.60 TOTE £2.20: £1.40, £2.80; EX 10.40.
Owner G H Leatham & M A Leatham **Bred** Pursuit Of Truth Syndicate **Trained** Musley Bank, N Yorks

FOCUS
The going was changed to heavy all round before the second race, and there were four non-runners because of the ground. West End Land bolted to post before the race and had to be withdrawn (6/1, deduct 10p in the £ under R4). A decent claimer run at a steady pace with the field coming up the stands rail with the winner pulling a long way clear. He did not need to be at his best, with the form rated around the runner-up.

3811 PARK HILL HOSPITAL MAIDEN FILLIES' STKS 7f
3:00 (3:05) (Class 5) 3-Y-O+ **£2,264** (£673; £336; £168) **Stalls** High

Form RPR
563 1 **Bunraku**[9] 3507 3-8-12 0 MichaelHills 12 84
(Charles Hills) *cl up: led 1/2-way: rdn clr wl over 1f out: styd on strly* **4/1**[3]
34 2 *5* **Catwalk (IRE)**[46] 2332 3-8-12 0 RyanMoore 5 71
(James Fanshawe) *hld up: hdwy over 2f out: rdn wl over 1f out: styd on to chse wnr ins fnl f: sn no imp* **7/2**[2]
6 3 *1 3/4* **Shore Performer (IRE)**[27] 2935 3-8-12 0 KellyHarrison 4 66
(William Haggas) *hld up in tch: hdwy to trck ldng pair 3f out: rdn to chse wnr 2f out: sn drvn and kpt on same pce* **5/1**
4 *1 1/4* **Urban Daydream (IRE)** 3-8-12 0 JamieSpencer 10 63
(Roger Varian) *prom: effrt and ch over 2f out: sn rdn and wknd over 1f out* **7/2**[2]
0 5 *2 1/4* **Malindi**[28] 2881 3-8-12 0 PaulMulrennan 8 57
(James Given) *chsd ldrs: rdn along wl over 2f out: grad wknd* **25/1**
32 6 *4 1/2* **Raheeba**[21] 3107 3-8-12 0 JoeFanning 14 46
(Mark Johnston) *trckd ldrs: hdwy 3f out: rdn over 2f out: sn btn* **3/1**[1]
0- 7 *2 1/4* **Toothache**[399] 2673 4-9-6 0 KirstyMilczarek 1 43
(Garry Woodward) *slt ld to 1/2-way: rdn along and hung bdly lft 2f out: grad wknd* **50/1**
8 *8* **Vera Richardson (IRE)** 3-8-12 0 TomEaves 11 19
(Michael Dods) *chsd ldrs to 1/2-way: sn wknd* **20/1**
9 *17* **The Nifty Notion** 3-8-12 0 DavidAllan 6
(Lawrence Mullaney) *s.i.s: sn rdn along: a bhd* **50/1**
10 *2 1/4* **Miss Matiz**[395] 5-9-3 0 PaulPickard(3) 7
(Alan Kirtley) *s.i.s: a bhd* **50/1**

1m 31.23s (4.93) **Going Correction** +0.725s/f (Yiel)
WFA 3 from 4yo+ 8lb 10 Ran SP% **120.6**
Speed ratings (Par 100): **100,94,92,90,88 83,80,71,52,49**
toteswingers: 1&2 £2.80, 1&3 £5.80, 2&3 £5.50. CSF £18.25 TOTE £5.30: £2.10, £2.10, £2.70; EX 17.70.
Owner K Abdulla **Bred** Juddmonte Farms Ltd **Trained** Lambourn, Berks

FOCUS
This maiden fillies' stakes was run at a solid pace with very few able to get competitive, but was the slowest of the three C&D races. Ordinary form, with the favourite disappointing.

3812 CARDSAVE LEIGHA EDWARDS & LAUREN HOE H'CAP 7f
3:35 (3:38) (Class 3) (0-90,88) 3-Y-O+ **£6,792** (£2,021; £1,010; £505) **Stalls** High

Form RPR
5204 1 **Beckermet (IRE)**[7] 3557 10-9-8 82 JamesSullivan 10 93
(Ruth Carr) *cl up: led 3f out: rdn wl over 1f out: kpt on strly fnl f* **15/2**
1-13 2 *3* **Green Howard**[21] 3128 4-9-9 83 SilvestreDeSousa 3 86
(Robin Bastiman) *racd wd to 1/2-way: chsd ldrs: niggled along 1/2-way: hdwy 2f out: sn rdn and chal over 1f out: drvn and one pce fnl f* **7/4**[1]
0-00 3 *3/4* **Shesastar**[41] 2489 4-9-11 85 GrahamGibbons 8 86
(David Barron) *racd wd 3f: hld up towards rr: hdwy over 2f out: rdn over 1f out: kpt on fnl f: nrst fin* **7/1**
-601 4 *1 3/4* **Duster**[25] 2975 5-9-12 86 RyanMoore 1 83
(Hughie Morrison) *racd wd to 1/2-way: chsd ldrs: effrt over 2f out: sn rdn and wknd appr fnl f* **9/2**[3]
6102 5 *4* **Polish World (USA)**[13] 3403 8-9-12 86 MickyFenton 12 72
(Paul Midgley) *led: pushed along and hdd 3f out: wknd over 2f out* **16/1**
-222 6 *2 3/4* **Gouray Girl (IRE)**[14] 3348 5-9-11 88 HarryBentley(3) 5 67
(Henry Candy) *racd wd 3f: hld up: hdwy to chse ldrs 3f out: rdn over 2f out: wknd over 1f out* **3/1**[2]
-006 7 *7* **Point North (IRE)**[23] 3037 5-9-3 77 PaulMulrennan 4 38
(John Balding) *s.i.s: sn chsng ldrs: rdn along 3f out and sn wknd* **14/1**

1m 29.99s (3.69) **Going Correction** +0.725s/f (Yiel) 7 Ran SP% **116.4**
Speed ratings (Par 107): **107,103,102,100,96 93,85**
toteswingers: 1&2 £4.00, 1&3 £6.60, 2&3 £3.70. CSF £21.81 CT £98.54 TOTE £9.70: £3.40, £1.90; EX 25.40.
Owner Shopping, Shoes & Champers Partnership **Bred** Fritz Von Ball Moss **Trained** Huby, N Yorks

FOCUS
Six non-runners took some of the interest out of this handicap, with the seven-strong field splitting into two groups early before coming home up the centre of the course. The winner handled the ground better than most and this rates his best effort for three years.

NOTEBOOK
Beckermet(IRE) has enjoyed a resurgence of form this season and ran out a convincing winner here off a mark 6lb above his last success. He was suited by racing in the stands'-side group, but showed a willing attitude to draw clear inside the final furlong on ground that suited. (tchd 7-1 and 8-1)
Green Howard, who was Silvestre de Sousa's only ride of the day at the track, did best of those taken to the far side. He has never won on anything more testing than good to soft, but stayed on well enough, suggesting he will remain competitive off this career-high mark once the ground improves. (op 9-4)
Shesastar ran a strange sort of race. She was taken to the far side early, before switching to the stands' side at the 3f pole and was the last to make her move. She picked up well enough, although was never going to catch the winner. The was a more encouraging effort after two poor runs. (op 9-2)
Duster, for whom Ryan Moore was a late jockey change, had appreciated the drop back to 7f (soft) when a game winner at Folkestone last time, but could not pick up as well in these conditions off a 3lb higher mark. He was not helped by racing towards the far side and floundered late on in the heavy ground. (op 5-1)

Gouray Girl(IRE), runner-up on her last three starts, all on soft ground, was another who raced far side but faded tamely and clearly did not give her running. (op 10-3 tchd 7-2)

3813 CARDSAVE LAURA HORNE & JANE CARDWELL FILLIES' H'CAP 1m 4f
4:10 (4:11) (Class 4) (0-85,83) 3-Y-O+ **£4,204** (£1,251; £625; £312) **Stalls** Low

Form RPR
603 1 **Require**[32] 2768 3-8-9 77 KirstyMilczarek 4 93+
(Luca Cumani) *trckd ldr: hdwy 3f out: effrt to ld 2f out: sn rdn: styd on strly fnl f* **13/8**[1]
4133 2 2 1/2 **Maven**[16] 3287 4-9-8 77 DavidAllan 1 88
(Tim Easterby) *t.k.h: hld up: hdwy 3f out: rdn to chse wnr over 1f out: drvn and one pce fnl f* **4/1**[3]
0025 3 5 **Finity Run (GER)**[28] 2877 3-8-3 71 JoeFanning 5 74
(Mark Johnston) *set stdy pce: pushed along and qcknd over 3f out: rdn over 2f out and sn hdd: drvn and wknd over 1f out* **12/1**
0-11 4 2 1/2 **Sula Two**[15] 3307 5-9-5 77 HarryBentley(3) 12 76
(Ron Hodges) *trckd ldr: hdwy and cl up 3f out: rdn over 2f out: sn drvn and wknd* **7/4**[2]
5-04 5 24 **Jaaryah (IRE)**[27] 2909 4-10-0 83 TomEaves 6 44
(Roger Varian) *t.k.h: hld up in rr: effrt over 3f out: sn rdn and btn: bhd and eased wl over 1f out* **9/1**

2m 46.13s (11.23) **Going Correction** +1.075s/f (Soft)
WFA 3 from 4yo+ 13lb 5 Ran SP% **112.2**
Speed ratings (Par 102): **105,103,100,98,82**
toteswinger: 1&2 £5.50. CSF £8.67 TOTE £3.10: £2.10, £1.80; EX 11.00.
Owner Duke Of Devonshire **Bred** The Duke Of Devonshire **Trained** Newmarket, Suffolk

FOCUS
Seven were taken out because of the ground. This fillies' handicap, the first race of the afternoon on the round course, was run at a steady pace with the winner staying on strongly to win impressively. She rates a clear personal best.

3814 SUE FELTON HAPPY 60TH BIRTHDAY H'CAP 1m 4f
4:45 (4:46) (Class 5) (0-70,70) 4-Y-O+ **£2,264** (£673; £336) **Stalls** Low

Form RPR
4620 1 **Kingaroo (IRE)**[19] 3180 6-8-2 51 oh1 LukeMorris 4 58
(Garry Woodward) *set stdy pce: qcknd 4f out: rdn along 2f out: drvn appr fnl f: kpt on gamely* **11/4**[3]
-002 2 1 3/4 **Fossgate**[16] 3290 11-9-4 70 HarryBentley(3) 11 74
(James Bethell) *hld up: hdwy 3f out: rdn to chse wnr wl over 1f out: drvn and ev ch tl no ex wl ins fnl f* **15/8**[2]
-636 3 1/2 **Korngold**[24] 3015 4-9-2 65 (b[1]) RyanMoore 7 68
(John Dunlop) *trckd wnr: hdwy 3f out: rdn 2f out: sn drvn and one pce* **11/10**[1]

2m 49.4s (14.50) **Going Correction** +1.075s/f (Soft) 3 Ran SP% **109.1**
Speed ratings (Par 103): **94,92,92**
CSF £7.59 TOTE £3.60; EX 6.00.
Owner J Pownall **Bred** Kevin Walsh **Trained** Bolham, Notts

FOCUS
Only three of the 11 declared runners went to post for this handicap which was run at a modest pace, suiting the leader who made all under a fine ride. Shaky form.

3815 BJS FILLIES' H'CAP 5f
5:15 (5:15) (Class 4) (0-80,79) 4-Y-O+ **£4,204** (£1,251; £625; £312) **Stalls** High

Form RPR
-210 1 **Breezolini**[23] 3027 4-9-0 72 RobertWinston 2 80
(Geoffrey Harker) *chsd ldrs: rdn along 1/2-way: hdwy to ld over 1f out: drvn ins fnl f and kpt on wl* **15/8**[1]
6316 2 1 **Pivotal Prospect**[18] 3211 4-8-5 63 ow1 RoystonFfrench 5 67
(Tracy Waggott) *cl up: effrt to chal 2f out: rdn and ev ch ent fnl f: sn drvn: carried hd high and no ex last 100yds* **4/1**
0500 3 1 3/4 **Style And Panache (IRE)**[20] 3139 4-8-12 70 RyanMoore 6 68
(David Evans) *led: rdn along 2f: drvn and hdd wl over 1f out: kpt on same pce* **3/1**[3]
6500 4 3/4 **Sulis Minerva (IRE)**[7] 3595 5-9-5 77 EddieAhern 3 72
(Jeremy Gask) *s.i.s: hdwy to join field after 1f: effrt and ch wl over 1f out: sn rdn and one pce fnl f* **16/1**
-600 5 nk **Beauty Pageant (IRE)**[31] 2793 5-9-0 79 WilliamTwiston-Davies(7) 1 73
(Ed McMahon) *cl up: rdn 2f out: sn drvn and wknd* **11/4**[2]

1m 3.37s (2.87) **Going Correction** +0.725s/f (Yiel) 5 Ran SP% **112.3**
Speed ratings (Par 102): **106,104,101,100,99**
CSF £9.91 TOTE £3.20: £2.00, £2.60; EX 15.00.
Owner Northumbria Leisure Ltd **Bred** Hellwood Stud Farm **Trained** Thirkleby, N Yorks

FOCUS
A competitive sprint handicap despite the small field size, run at a steady pace, with the runners well grouped entering the final furlong. Modest fillies' form.
Sulis Minerva(IRE) Official explanation: jockey said mare was slowly away
T/Jkpt: £3,043.70 to a £1 stake. Pool: £60,016.86 - 14.00 winning tickets. T/Plt: £65.20 to a £1 stake. Pool: £82,525.63 - 922.63 winning tickets. T/Qpdt: £38.60 to a £1 stake. Pool: £6,059.08 - 116.00 winning tickets. JR

3775 HAYDOCK (L-H)
Friday, July 6
3816 Meeting Abandoned - waterlogged

3156 SANDOWN (R-H)
Friday, July 6
OFFICIAL GOING: Good changing to good to soft after race 3 (3.15)
Wind: Light, across Weather: Overcast becoming brighter

3822 BLUEFIN H'CAP 5f 6y
2:20 (2:24) (Class 4) (0-85,85) 3-Y-O+ **£4,204** (£1,251; £625; £312) **Stalls** Low

Form RPR
-100 1 **Jarrow (IRE)**[23] 3027 5-9-5 78 RichardKingscote 2 88
(Milton Bradley) *trckd ldng pair far side: rdn to go 2nd wl over 1f out: led gp and overall ldr last 150yds: styd on wl* **6/1**[2]
0-55 2 1 **Picabo (IRE)**[41] 2494 4-8-13 72 [1] DaneO'Neill 9 78
(Henry Candy) *hld up in rr far side: prog 2f out: r.o to take 2nd last 100yds: a hld* **16/1**
-142 3 1 **Ray Of Joy**[19] 3188 6-9-8 81 RichardHughes 5 83
(J R Jenkins) *chsd ldng trio far side but racd towards centre: rdn and styd on to take 3rd last strides* **10/1**
046 4 nk **Ganas (IRE)**[18] 3225 4-9-9 82 WilliamBuick 12 83+
(Clive Cox) *led nr side quintet and overall ldr: could nvr grab rail: stl in front whn drifted to centre 1f out: sn hdd and btn* **13/2**[3]
2004 5 hd **West Coast Dream**[19] 3188 5-9-9 82 IanMongan 13 83+
(Roy Brotherton) *pressed overall ldr of nr side gp: drvn over 1f out: no ex ins fnl f* **33/1**
-040 6 3/4 **Lujeanie**[13] 3394 6-9-6 79 (p) JimmyFortune 4 77
(Dean Ivory) *towards rr far side: rdn and sme prog wl over 1f out: kpt on but nvr able to threaten* **12/1**
2500 7 nk **Elna Bright**[34] 2707 7-9-10 83 JimmyQuinn 14 80+
(Peter Crate) *sn bdly out of tch in last of nr side gp: pushed along 2f out: stl last 1f out: fin strly* **25/1**
1004 8 nse **Rafaaf (IRE)**[13] 3394 4-9-5 78 AndreaAtzeni 10 75+
(Robert Eddery) *dwlt: chsd ldng trio nr side but nt on terms: wnt 3rd in gp over 1f out: tried to cl but one pce* **10/1**
0200 9 1 1/4 **Ertikaan**[28] 2870 5-9-5 83 (p) DarrenEgan(5) 7 75
(Ronald Harris) *racd in far side gp but on the outer of it: nvr on terms w ldrs* **16/1**
502 10 1 **Fair Value (IRE)**[7] 3571 4-9-9 82 SebSanders 6 71
(Simon Dow) *trckd ldr far side: led gp 1/2-way: drvn and hdd last 150yds: wknd rapidly nr fin* **11/2**[1]
3-12 11 3/4 **Oldjoesaid**[7] 3578 8-9-3 76 NeilCallan 8 62
(Paul Midgley) *racd far side but towards middle: nvr on terms w ldrs: struggling over 1f out* **8/1**
463- 12 3/4 **Foxtrot India (IRE)**[314] 5492 3-9-4 85 RaulDaSilva(3) 11 66
(Jeremy Gask) *dwlt: chsd ldng pair nr side: no imp over 1f out: sn wknd* **33/1**
5005 13 2 3/4 **Courageous (IRE)**[6] 3612 6-9-8 81 (t) KierenFallon 3 54
(Milton Bradley) *led far side gp to 1/2-way: wknd over 1f out* **6/1**[2]
5 14 3 1/4 **Rowe Park**[62] 1849 9-9-9 85 AdamBeschizza(3) 1 47
(Linda Jewell) *dwlt: racd far side: a struggling: plld out wd 2f out: no prog* **25/1**

1m 1.68s (0.08) **Going Correction** +0.15s/f (Good)
WFA 3 from 4yo+ 5lb 14 Ran SP% **119.6**
Speed ratings (Par 105): **105,103,101,101,101 99,99,99,97,95 94,93,88,83**
toteswingers: 1&2 £30.20, 1&3 £20.90, 2&3 £42.20. CSF £93.42 CT £971.23 TOTE £8.60: £3.50, £4.50, £2.50; EX 197.30 TRIFECTA Not won..
Owner Dab Hand Racing **Bred** Derek Veitch **Trained** Sedbury, Gloucs

FOCUS
Rail dolled out up to 4yds from 7f to Winning Post adding 5yds to distances on Round course. Far side rail moved in 3yds on Sprint track. They split into two groups in this fair sprint handicap, with nine on the far side and five on the other flank. The smaller group held the call in the first part of the race, but in the end the first three came from the bigger group. The winner is rated back to form with the second to her best since last summer.
Elna Bright ◆ Official explanation: jockey said, regarding runing and riding, that his orders were to pop out, sit on the gelding and allow it to go its own pace, he was tapping it on the shoulder and trying to keep in touch and it would probably been better suited by faster ground.

3823 MOBILE BETTING AT CORAL.CO.UK DRAGON STKS (LISTED RACE) 5f 6y
2:50 (2:55) (Class 1) 2-Y-O **£13,043** (£4,945; £2,474; £1,232; £618) **Stalls** Low

Form RPR
14 1 **Morawij**[15] 3291 2-9-2 0 NeilCallan 5 101+
(Roger Varian) *trckd ldr: led 2f out: in command fnl f: rdn out* **4/11**[1]
5106 2 2 1/4 **Lasilia (IRE)**[16] 3269 2-8-11 91 RichardHughes 3 88
(Kevin Ryan) *hld up in last: prog to chse wnr wl over 1f out: hung lft and no imp fnl f* **5/1**[2]
2641 3 3/4 **Botanic Garden**[27] 2912 2-9-2 81 RichardMullen 2 90
(David Brown) *hld up in 4th: rdn to chse ldng pair over 1f out: kpt on same pce* **10/1**[3]
01 4 10 **Star Breaker**[19] 3191 2-9-2 0 JamesDoyle 6 54
(Sylvester Kirk) *racd wd: chsd ldng pair to 1/2-way: wknd qckly: t.o* **11/1**
5 7 **Nation (USA)** 2-8-12 0 ow1 (t) SebSanders 1 25
(Garry Woodward) *fractious preliminaries: ponied to s: led to 2f out: wkng rapidly whn hmpd over 1f out: t.o* **100/1**

1m 2.75s (1.15) **Going Correction** +0.15s/f (Good) 5 Ran SP% **108.4**
Speed ratings (Par 102): **96,92,91,75,64**
toteswinger: 1&2 £2.70. CSF £2.46 TOTE £1.40: £1.10, £1.70; EX 2.20.
Owner Sheikh Ahmed Al Maktoum **Bred** Dunchurch Lodge Stud Co **Trained** Newmarket, Suffolk

FOCUS
The smart Zebedee, successful two years ago, stands out among recent winners of this Listed event. This is not strong form overall for the grade, the race lacking depth, but it makes sense with the first two to their Aacot marks.

NOTEBOOK
Morawij rates an up-to-scratch winner. This powerfully built colt could not find cover and raced keenly, but once in front he ran on strongly to pull clear. A Gimcrack entry, he will get 6f but may be kept to shorter for now with the Molecomb Stakes a possibility. (op 2-5 tchd 4-9 in a place)
Lasilia(IRE) was also in action at Ascot, finishing sixth of 27 to Ceiling Kitty in the Queen Mary. Coming from the rear, she was held by the favourite when edging to her left late on. Last year's runner-up Kohala went on to win the St Hugh's Stakes next time, and that Listed race for fillies at Newbury next month could be suitable for Lasilia. (op 9-2)
Botanic Garden had the ground come right and he ran respectably in this better grade after taking quite a tug towards the rail. (op 9-1)
Star Breaker was inconvenienced by the drop back in trip and was the first in trouble. (op 14-1 tchd 10-1)
Nation(USA) is the first foal of a juvenile sprint winner in the USA. Her trainer's first runner at Sandown, she was green in the preliminaries and needed to be ponied to the start. She showed bright pace in the race, but was already back-tracking when she was tightened up on the rail. She will have learned from this and, while evidently not straightforward, has the ability to win in a lesser grade.

3824 BET AT CORAL.CO.UK IRISH STALLION FARMS E B F MAIDEN STKS 7f 16y
3:25 (3:26) (Class 5) 2-Y-O **£3,881** (£1,155; £577; £288) **Stalls** Low

Form RPR
0 1 **Hot Diggity (FR)**[41] 2480 2-9-3 0 JamesDoyle 4 81
(Peter Chapple-Hyam) *trckd ldng trio: shkn up wl over 2f out: prog to ld overall nr side over 1f out: hld on wl nr fin* **12/1**
6 2 1/2 **Tropical Song**[13] 3397 2-9-3 0 WilliamBuick 7 80
(John Gosden) *hld up in 7th: prog 2f out: chsd wnr ins fnl f and sn chalng: nt qckn nr fin* **9/1**

4 **3** 2 ½ **Harry Bosch**[13] 3397 2-9-3 0 .... NeilCallan 8 74
(Brian Meehan) *chsd ldrs disputing 5th: clsd fr over 2f out: tried to chal 1f out: one pce* **11/4**[2]

0 **4** 2 ¾ **Al Muntazah (IRE)**[22] 3074 2-8-12 0 .... DarrenEgan(5) 1 67
(Ronald Harris) *uns rdr gng to post: led at gd pce: styd alone far side in st: stl in front whn sed to come across to nr side 2f out: hdd over 1f out: wknd and eased ins fnl f* **14/1**

5 *nk* **Persian Wave** 2-9-3 0 .... MartinDwyer 10 66
(James Tate) *settled in last trio: wl adrift over 2f out: stl only modest 9th whn shkn up over 1f out: fin wl: nrly snatched 4th* **40/1**

6 *nk* **Labienus** 2-9-3 0 .... TedDurcan 2 65+
(David Lanigan) *rn green in last trio: wl adrift over 2f out: pushed along and styd on steadily fr over 1f out* **28/1**

4 **7** 1 ½ **Royal Prize**[21] 3119 2-9-3 0 .... JimCrowley 3 61
(Ralph Beckett) *trckd ldr: led main gp nr side over 3f out to wl over 2f out: wknd over 1f out* **20/1**

8 *hd* **Caramack** 2-9-3 0 .... RichardHughes 6 61+
(Richard Hannon) *trckd ldrs disputing 5th: effrt over 2f out: cl up but hld whn sltly hmpd over 1f out: wknd* **7/2**[3]

2 **9** *nk* **Royal Skies (IRE)**[13] 3401 2-9-3 0 .... KierenFallon 5 60
(Mark Johnston) *trckd ldng pair: led main gp nr side wl over 2f out to over 1f out: wknd* **9/4**[1]

10 *21* **Firmdecisions (IRE)** 2-9-3 0 .... IanMongan 9 8
(Brett Johnson) *a in last trio: wknd over 2f out: t.o* **50/1**

1m 32.33s (2.83) **Going Correction** +0.275s/f (Good) **10** Ran SP% **116.6**
Speed ratings (Par 94): **94,93,90,87,87 86,85,84,84,60**
toteswingers: 1&2 £18.50, 1&3 £3.80, 2&3 £6.30. CSF £109.55 TOTE £17.50: £3.90, £2.60, £1.10; EX 142.10 Trifecta £845.00 Pool: £1,484.52 - 1.30 winning units..
Owner The Horse Players Two **Bred** S El Alami **Trained** Newmarket, Suffolk
■ Stewards' Enquiry : Darren Egan one-day ban: careless riding (Jul 20)

FOCUS
This maiden has been won by subsequent Group winners Mister Monet, Zacinto, Scintillo and (last year) Talwar. This edition perhaps lacked a star, but there were some promising performances nonetheless. The whole field came to the stands' side on entering the straight, other than leader Al Muntazah who tacked over from the two pole. Those with previous experience dominated. The form is leargely rated around the time and race averages.

NOTEBOOK
Hot Diggity(FR) duly stepped up on what he had shown on his debut at Goodwood. He displayed a gutsy attitude to fend off the runner-up and the extra furlong clearly suited. His trainer has been enjoying a good season with his 2yos and it will be interesting to see where this one figures among them. (op 11-1 tchd 14-1)
Tropical Song endured a bit of a troubled passage before coming with what looked a race-winning challenge, but he could not get past a brave opponent. This was a considerable improvement on his debut effort at Newbury and a maiden should be his before long.
Harry Bosch ran respectably without perhaps improving much on his debut effort. (op 5-2)
Al Muntazah(IRE) was still in with every chance when linking up with the main group, but the unconventional line he'd taken told in the latter stages. He had also run loose briefly before the start after unshipping his rider, and all things considered this was a decent effort. A well built individual, he is still weak but is well capable of making his mark before long. (op 16-1)
Persian Wave was in rear for much of the contest before picking up well when it was all over. Out of a 6f-7f winner, he was first home of the four newcomers. (op 50-1)
Labienus ◆ ran green at the back of the field, but was another coming home nicely This 105,000gns yearling is a half-brother to three winners and should be adding to the family tally in the near future. (op 33-1)
Caramack is a half-brother to Superlative Stakes winner Hatta Fort and his sales price more than trebled when he was resold as a 2yo. He was hampered by the fourth heading to the final furlong and was not knocked about from there, giving the impression that he can better this. (op 9-2)
Royal Skies(IRE) was somewhat keen and didn't get home. (tchd 2-1)

3825 AMBANT GALA STKS (LISTED RACE) 1m 2f 7y
4:00 (4:00) (Class 1) 3-Y-O+
£18,714 (£7,095; £3,550; £1,768; £887; £445) **Stalls** Low

Form RPR

4-42 **1** **Afsare**[54] 2106 5-9-5 113 .... KierenFallon 9 116
(Luca Cumani) *trckd ldr: led main gp on far side in st: overall ldr over 1f out and clr of rest on that side: styd on wl* **2/1**[1]

1130 **2** 2 ¼ **Songcraft (IRE)**[97] 1149 4-9-5 115 .... FrankieDettori 6 112
(Saeed Bin Suroor) *trckd ldng pair: chsd wnr on far side in st: rdn and no imp 2f out: kpt on to take 2nd nr fin* **11/4**[2]

-236 **3** *nk* **Cai Shen (IRE)**[16] 3268 4-9-5 105 .... RichardHughes 7 111
(Richard Hannon) *led: c alone to nr side in st: lost ld over 1f out: pipped for 2nd nr fin* **7/2**[3]

3-45 **4** 3 ½ **Cill Rialaig**[13] 3372 7-9-0 97 .... JimmyFortune 8 99
(Hughie Morrison) *hld up in 4th: rdn and effrt over 2f out: no prog and btn wl over 1f out* **13/2**

24-6 **5** ¾ **Tazahum (USA)**[78] 1471 4-9-5 112 .... TadhgO'Shea 3 103
(Sir Michael Stoute) *t.k.h: hld up in last: effrt 3f out: rdn and no prog 2f out: wl btn after* **7/1**

0-40 **6** *37* **Biondetti (USA)**[118] 878 4-9-5 109 .... MickaelBarzalona 2
(Mahmood Al Zarooni) *unsuitable grnd* **16/1**

2m 12.42s (1.92) **Going Correction** +0.275s/f (Good)
WFA 3 from 4yo+ 11lb **6** Ran SP% **113.9**
Speed ratings (Par 111): **103,101,100,98,97 67**
toteswingers: 1&2 £1.20, 1&3 £1.70, 2&3 £3.50. CSF £7.96 TOTE £3.40: £1.70, £2.10; EX 8.20 Trifecta £19.90 Pool: £1,331.89 - 49.51 winning units..
Owner Sheikh Mohammed Obaid Al Maktoum **Bred** Darley **Trained** Newmarket, Suffolk

FOCUS
The ground was officially amended to Good to soft before this event. This is often a strong Listed race and proved so again, despite the withdrawals. The pace was just modest and again there was a difference of opinion among the jockeys with all except Richard Hughes on Cai Shen sticking to the inside in the home straight. Afsare rates a length personal best.

NOTEBOOK
Afsare was second to Eclipse runner Crackerjack King in the Group 1 Premio Presidente Della Repubblica in Rome last time and he took advantage of a drop in class. His rider wanted to lead on him, but reined back when Cai Shen went on, only to effectively be left in front turning into the straight. The gelding ran on strongly for a deserved victory, his first win since taking the Listed Hampton Court Stakes at Royal Ascot two years ago. He's capable of winning at a higher level. (op 13-8 tchd 6-4)
Songcraft(IRE) was officially best in on BHA figures. Last seen when eighth of ten in the Dubai Sheema Classic when a visor was tried, he ran his race but the winner proved much too strong. He won't mind a return to 1m4f. (op 7-2)
Cai Shen(IRE) ran a fine race from stall one in the Royal Hunt Cup and has previous placed form at this level. Richard Hughes opted to come over to the stands' side and the colt ran on willingly up the straight despite having nothing to race with. He was second best on merit. (tchd 5-1)
Cill Rialaig had not run over this short since the spring of 2010. She has run at this level eight times now without managing a victory, although she did win a Listed bumper on her second raceourse appearance. (op 8-1)
Tazahum(USA), behind Afsare on his seasonal reappearance in the Earl Of Sefton back in April, failed to settle and was well beaten. He'd won both his previous starts at Sandown. (op 15-2 tchd 6-1)
Biondetti(USA) was clearly well below par on this first start since the Dubai Carnival. (tchd 14-1)

3826 TEXT CORAL TO 65559 FOR MOBILE BETTING H'CAP 1m 2f 7y
4:35 (4:37) (Class 3) (0-95,93) 3-Y-O+ **£6,792** (£2,021; £1,010; £505) **Stalls** Low

Form RPR

21- **1** **Encke (USA)**[279] 6529 3-9-0 90 .... MickaelBarzalona 5 99+
(Mahmood Al Zarooni) *hld up in 6th tl quick move to chse ldr after 4f: pushed along 1/2-way: responded to press to ld over 2f out: drvn and fnd enough to hold on fnl f* **2/1**[1]

0-12 **2** ½ **Ginger Jack**[16] 3274 5-9-3 82 .... JimmyFortune 10 90
(Geoffrey Harker) *handy: rdn over 2f out: prog to chse wnr wl over 1f out: kpt on wl fnl f: a jst hld* **20/1**

0-01 **3** *nk* **Tropical Beat**[30] 2810 4-9-12 91 .... WilliamBuick 6 98
(John Gosden) *hld up in last pair: effrt whn chopped off over 2f out: taken out wd and prog over 1f out: drvn and r.o fnl f: nrst fin* **11/2**[3]

-042 **4** ½ **Fattsota**[46] 2346 4-9-12 91 .... SebSanders 2 97
(Marco Botti) *trckd ldrs on inner: effrt whn nowhere to go over 2f out: prog over 1f out: drvn and styng on whn nt clr run ins fnl f: kpt on* **8/1**

0050 **5** *1* **Lyssio (GER)**[27] 2933 5-9-8 87 .... KierenFallon 1 91
(Michael Attwater) *trckd ldr 4f: lost pl over 2f out: drvn and styd on again fr over 1f out: nvr able to chal* **33/1**

2240 **6** 3 ¾ **Tinshu (IRE)**[20] 3164 6-9-8 87 .... (p) DaneO'Neill 4 84
(Derek Haydn Jones) *trckd ldrs: rdn over 2f out: no prog over 1f out: wknd fnl f* **33/1**

-001 **7** *hd* **Cool Macavity (IRE)**[13] 3380 4-9-1 85 .... MatthewLawson(5) 14 82
(Charles Hills) *s.i.s: hld up in last: effrt whn nt clr run wl over 1f out: no ch after: styd on fnl f* **14/1**

3611 **8** *3* **Chain Of Events**[21] 3121 5-9-5 84 .... HayleyTurner 8 75
(Sarah Humphrey) *led to over 2f out: wknd wl over 1f out* **15/2**

-102 **9** *nse* **Silken Thoughts**[8] 3550 4-9-6 85 .... TomQueally 11 75
(John Berry) *hld up in last trio: prog on outer 3f out: no hdwy 2f out: sn wknd* **9/2**[2]

2-60 **10** *nk* **Roayh (USA)**[35] 2657 4-10-0 93 .... FrankieDettori 3 83
(Saeed Bin Suroor) *hld up in last quartet: shkn up and no prog over 2f out: sn btn* **14/1**

2m 11.37s (0.87) **Going Correction** +0.275s/f (Good)
WFA 3 from 4yo+ 11lb **10** Ran SP% **113.8**
Speed ratings (Par 107): **107,106,106,105,105 102,102,99,99,99**
toteswingers: 1&2 £6.40, 1&3 £4.40, 2&3 £1.6.80 CSF £48.07 CT £189.69 TOTE £3.10: £1.60, £3.20, £2.40; EX 34.00 Trifecta £166.00 Pool: £2,377.01 - 10.59 winning units..
Owner Godolphin **Bred** Darley **Trained** Newmarket, Suffolk

FOCUS
A decent handicap run at a solid pace, and in a time around a second faster than the previous Listed race. This time, all the field remained on the far side in the home straight. The well treated Encke looks sure to do better and the second is in his best form since he was a 2yo.

NOTEBOOK
Encke(USA) had been supplemented at a cost of £20,000 for last autumn's Racing Post Trophy, only to miss the race following a setback. Not seen since, he looked potentially thrown in off 90. He didn't win easily, needing to be stoked along in second place turning in, but did find plenty for pressure and can step up considerably on this when given the chance to tackle 1m4f on quicker ground. He holds a Great Voltigeur entry, but that rise in grade could prove a little beyond him at this stage of his career. (tchd 9-4)
Ginger Jack took some persuading to enter the stalls but ran a cracker, rallying towards the finish. Trip and ground did not seem ideal for him on paper, but he belied those concerns and remains well treated on his old form.
Tropical Beat was 6lb higher on this return to turf. His off-putting head carriage was again in evidence, but he ran on down the outer after the gap he'd been going for closed. (op 6-1)
Fattsota didn't enjoy the best of runs, but still ran creditably on this drop back in trip. His current mark may not be beyond him. (tchd 7-1)
Lyssio(GER) travelled strongly but could not quicken up when let down. He is relatively unexposed and is very well treated on his best form.
Cool Macavity(IRE) was 5lb higher here, but officially 2lb ahead of the handicapper. He made late progress without ever threatening. (op 12-1 tchd 10-1)
Chain Of Events was seeking a C&D hat-trick, but was a stone higher than for his initial victory. (op 8-1)
Silken Thoughts managed only a short-lived effort down the outside. (op 5-1)

3827 FOLLOW @CORAL ON TWITTER H'CAP 1m 6f
5:05 (5:06) (Class 4) (0-85,84) 3-Y-O+ **£4,204** (£1,251; £625; £312) **Stalls** Low

Form RPR

-321 **1** **Rosairlie (IRE)**[30] 2827 4-9-0 70 .... PJMcDonald 5 80
(Micky Hammond) *trckd ldrs: prog to ld 2f out: drvn and styd on wl* **5/1**[2]

5300 **2** *1* **Dunhoy (IRE)**[30] 2810 4-9-9 79 .... DaneO'Neill 9 87
(Tony Newcombe) *trckd ldrs: looking for room over 2f out and eased to outer: drvn and r.o fr over 1f out: tk 2nd last 150yds: clsd on wnr but nvr able to chal* **16/1**

1-33 **3** 3 ½ **Knightly Escapade**[27] 2936 4-9-9 79 .... JimmyFortune 2 82
(John Dunlop) *hld up: t.k.h whn pce slackened after 2f: smooth prog 3f out: trckd ldr wl over 1f out: sn rdn and nt qckn: lost 2nd last 150yds and wknd* **11/4**[1]

22-6 **4** *nk* **Money Money Money**[29] 2863 6-9-6 76 .... JamesMillman 10 79
(Rod Millman) *stdd s: hld up in last: effrt on outer 3f out: nt qckn 2f out: styd on fnl f* **8/1**

-342 **5** 1 ¾ **Mohanad (IRE)**[20] 3162 6-9-9 79 .... RichardHughes 4 80
(Sheena West) *trckd ldr to 1/2-way: trckd new ldr 5f out: rdn to ld over 2f out to 2f out: wknd fnl f* **11/2**[3]

4016 **6** 3 ½ **Mataaleb**[9] 3502 5-10-0 84 .... FrankieDettori 14 80
(Lydia Pearce) *hld up: t.k.h whn pce slackened after 2f: effrt 3f out: shkn up and wknd 2f out* **5/1**[2]

-043 **7** 2 ½ **Tasfeya**[19] 3187 4-9-5 75 .... AmirQuinn 3 67
(Lee Carter) *trckd ldng pair: t.k.h after pce slackened after 2f: plld way to ld 1/2-way: hdd & wknd over 2f out* **10/1**

-302 **8** *7* **Bounty Seeker (USA)**[37] 2613 3-8-3 74 .... MartinLane 6 56
(Mark Johnston) *won battle for ld and stdd pce after 2f: hdd 1/2-way: wknd over 2f out* **15/2**

3m 11.37s (6.87) **Going Correction** +0.275s/f (Good)
WFA 3 from 4yo+ 15lb **8** Ran SP% **113.2**
Speed ratings (Par 105): **91,90,88,88,87 85,83,79**
toteswingers: 1&2 £9.50, 1&3 £3.40, 2&3 £8.60. CSF £76.67 CT £261.02 TOTE £5.60: £1.70, £4.60, £1.50; EX 76.00 Trifecta £156.70 Pool: £2,061.27 - 9.73 winning units..
Owner The Bay Horse Masham **Bred** Airlie Stud **Trained** Middleham Moor, N Yorks

FOCUS
Half the field for this ordinary stayers' handicap were absentees for various reasons. The pace was not especially strong. It's doubtful Rosairlie had to improve on her Ripon form but she is probably still on the upgrade.
T/Plt: £41.70 to a £1 stake. Pool: £99,226.46 - 1,733.58 winning tickets. T/Qpdt: £7.40 to a £1 stake. Pool: £7,533.85 - 743.53 winning tickets. JN

3539 WARWICK (L-H)
Friday, July 6
3828 Meeting Abandoned - waterlogged

3835 - 3841a (Foreign Racing) - See Raceform Interactive

3457 BEVERLEY (R-H)
Saturday, July 7
OFFICIAL GOING: Soft (heavy in places; 6.0)
Wind: Light behind Weather: Sunny periods

3842 AWARD-WINNING COACHMAN CARAVANS MAIDEN AUCTION STKS 7f 100y
1:55 (1:55) (Class 6) 2-Y-O £2,181 (£644; £322) Stalls Low

Form RPR
0332 1 **Yorkshire Icon**[11] 3457 2-8-10 0.................................(p) PaulMulrennan 5 66
(Ann Duffield) *trckd ldrs: hdwy and cl up after 2f: chal 2f out: rdn to ld ent fnl f: sn drvn and edgd rt: styd on* **2/1**[1]
64 2 ¾ **Notional Demand**[9] 3533 2-8-9 0.............................. GrahamGibbons 11 63
(Tim Easterby) *t.k.h: sn led: rdn along and jnd 2f out: drvn and hdd ent fnl f: sn n.m.r: kpt on* **18/1**
0 3 5 **Surround Sound**[14] 3401 2-8-9 0.............................. DavidAllan 1 51
(Tim Easterby) *hld up towards rr: hdwy 3f out: rdn to chse ldrs wl over 1f out: kpt on same pce* **14/1**
05 4 nk **Princess Hollow**[15] 3351 2-8-5 0 ow1............................ BarryMcHugh 9 47
(Tony Coyle) *chsd ldrs: rdn along over 2f out: drvn wl over 1f out: sn one pce* **12/1**
6 5 ¾ **Trymyluck**[20] 3182 2-8-8 0 ow3.. MickyFenton 3 48
(Pam Sly) *hld up towards rr: sme hdwy over 2f out: swtchd lft and rdn wl over 1f out: n.d* **5/2**[2]
6 hd **By A Wiska** 2-8-13 0.. PaddyAspell 8 53
(Ann Duffield) *prom: rdn along wl over 2f out: grad wknd* **12/1**
7 7 **French Revolution** 2-8-12 0.. AndrewElliott 4 35
(Jedd O'Keeffe) *s.i.s: a bhd* **25/1**
6 8 7 **Naughtybychoice**[19] 3208 2-8-7 0.................................. IJBrennan(3) 12 17
(Ollie Pears) *hld up in tch: effrt wl over 2f out: sn rdn and wknd* **4/1**[3]
1m 37.87s (4.07) **Going Correction** +0.35s/f (Good) 8 Ran SP% **113.1**
Speed ratings (Par 92): **90,89,83,83,82 82,74,66**
toteswingers 1&2 £13.50, 2&3 £20.80, 1&3 £9.50 CSF £38.47 TOTE £3.30: £1.10, £5.00, £4.00; EX 40.10.
Owner Middleham Park Racing XXIX **Bred** G Hedley & Mike Channon Bloodstock Limited **Trained** Constable Burton, N Yorks

FOCUS
Rail at normal configuration and distances as advertised. The early pace was ordinary and it paid to be handy. Low-grade form with just modest improvement from the winner.

NOTEBOOK
Yorkshire Icon, wearing cheekpieces for the first time, certainly wasn't winning out of turn and maybe the headgear and prominent ride made all the difference. No doubt he'll do okay in some 7f-1m nurseries. (tchd 9-4)
Notional Demand hadn't shown a great deal previously, which does cause some concern for the level here - recorded RPRs of 20 and 35. The easy lead helped up in distance. (op 25-1)
Surround Sound was soundly beaten on his debut but showed much more here after finding some early trouble. (tchd 12-1)
Princess Hollow, whose jockey put up 1lb overweight, came wide of runners turning in before being steered back towards the far-side rail. (op 11-1)
Trymyluck, whose jockey put up 3lb overweight, never looked completely comfortable around here, especially after some early scrimmaging and then being tightened up heading into the home straight. (op 3-1)
By A Wiska, a 13,000gns yearling half-brother to two winners, didn't shape too badly but appeared green in the final 2f. (tchd 16-1)
Naughtybychoice offered little off the bridle late on up in trip. (op 10-3)

3843 ELTHERINGTON STKS (H'CAP) 7f 100y
2:30 (2:30) (Class 5) (0-75,75) 4-Y-O+ £3,234 (£962; £481; £240) Stalls Low

Form RPR
2030 1 **First Class Favour (IRE)**[9] 3544 4-8-9 63.......................... DavidAllan 9 73
(Tim Easterby) *cl up: led after 2f: jnd and rdn along 2f out: hdd jst ins fnl f: drvn and rallied to ld again last 100yds: styd on wl* **5/2**[2]
-342 2 ¾ **Horatio Carter**[18] 3254 7-9-0 68.................................. DanielTudhope 8 76
(David O'Meara) *led 2f: cl up: effrt 2f out: sn rdn and slt advantage jst ins fnl f: drvn: hdd and no ex last 100yds* **13/8**[1]
-001 3 4 **Conry (IRE)**[12] 3455 6-9-7 75...................................... StephenCraine 1 73
(Daniel Mark Loughnane) *t.k.h: trckd ldrs: hdwy over 2f out and sn rdn: kpt on same pce u.p fnl f* **7/1**
3204 4 1 **Standing Strong (IRE)**[14] 3389 4-9-7 75...................... StevieDonohoe 5 71
(Robert Mills) *sn trcking ldng pair 2f out: rdn along over 2f out: wknd over 1f out* **4/1**[3]
0-35 5 shd **Brave Battle**[18] 3254 4-8-3 60................................... DeclanCannon(3) 2 55
(Ron Barr) *t.k.h: chsd ldrs: rdn along wl over 2f out: sn wknd* **7/1**
1m 35.78s (1.98) **Going Correction** +0.35s/f (Good) 5 Ran SP% **111.7**
Speed ratings (Par 103): **102,101,96,95,95**
CSF £7.12 TOTE £3.30: £2.00, £1.30; EX 7.20.
Owner S A Heley **Bred** Oghill House Stud **Trained** Great Habton, N Yorks

FOCUS
It's best to presume this wasn't anything better than a modest contest, but the form is straightforward. The first two home were pretty much the first two throughout.

3844 BRITISH STALLION STUDS EBF LEISURE FURNISHINGS MAIDEN STKS 5f
3:00 (3:02) (Class 5) 2-Y-O £3,234 (£962; £481; £240) Stalls Low

Form RPR
1 **Diggory Delvet** 2-8-13 0.. BarryMcHugh 4 75+
(Richard Fahey) *trckd ldrs: n.m.r and sltly outpcd 1/2-way: pushed along and hdwy wl over 1f out: rdn to ld ent fnl f: styd on strly* **5/1**[3]
06 2 3½ **Showtime Girl (IRE)**[28] 2912 2-8-12 0................................ DavidAllan 6 60
(Tim Easterby) *cl up: led after 1f: rdn over 1f out: drvn and hdd ent fnl f: kpt on same pce* **15/2**
0 3 3¾ **Edith Anne**[22] 3126 2-8-12 0... MickyFenton 14 47
(Paul Midgley) *in tch on wd outside: hdwy 2f out: sn rdn and kpt on same pce fnl f* **33/1**
0 4 nk **Purple Day**[24] 3046 2-9-3 0.. PaulMulrennan 11 51
(Pam Sly) *chsd ldr: rdn wl over 1f out: grad wknd* **12/1**
3502 5 5 **Blue Clumber**[38] 2603 2-8-5 84.............................. ShirleyTeasdale(7) 3 28
(Shaun Harris) *led 1f: trckd ldrs: effrt 2f out: sn rdn: edgd lft and wknd* **10/3**[1]
0 6 ¾ **Grand Jipeck (IRE)**[12] 3436 2-9-3 0..............................(t) FrederikTylicki 8 30
(Ian McInnes) *chsd ldrs: rdn along 2f out: wknd wl over 1f out* **12/1**
0 7 4½ **Grey Destiny**[22] 3123 2-9-3 0.. RobertWinston 12 14
(Mel Brittain) *in tch: rdn to chse ldrs 1/2-way: wknd wl over 1f out* **16/1**
8 ½ **Joeluke** 2-8-6 0... NedCurtis(7) 10 8
(Paul Midgley) *s.i.s and bhd: rdn along and hung bdly lft 2f out* **16/1**
9 3¾ **Armada Bay (IRE)** 2-8-13 0... TomEaves 5
(Bryan Smart) *dwlt: green and a in rr* **4/1**[2]
0204 10 hd **Mount Seymour (IRE)**[17] 3286 2-9-3 68........................ KellyHarrison 1
(Nigel Tinkler) *hld up: a in rr* **10/1**
00 11 20 **Chiming Hart**[37] 2631 2-8-12 0...................................... GrahamGibbons 2
(Tim Easterby) *dwlt: sn chsng ldrs: rdn along over 2f out: wknd qckly* **11/1**
1m 5.32s (1.82) **Going Correction** +0.35s/f (Good) 11 Ran SP% **119.0**
Speed ratings (Par 94): **99,93,87,86,78 77,70,69,63,63 31**
toteswingers 1&2 £7.00, 2&3 £24.50, 1&3 £37.10 CSF £42.99 TOTE £8.60: £2.60, £2.40, £9.40; EX 56.80.
Owner D W Barker **Bred** E Cantillon **Trained** Musley Bank, N Yorks
■ Stewards' Enquiry : Shirley Teasdale one-day ban: careless riding (Jul 22)

FOCUS
With the favourite running poorly, this didn't take a lot of winning. Diggory Delvet did it well and the next two will prove the key to the form.

NOTEBOOK
Diggory Delvet ◆, whose dam is a half-sister to 1m4f-1m6f Listed winner Art Eyes, made a fairly impressive debut. Never far away early, he got outpaced about 3f out but came home really strongly once the penny had dropped and edged clear while still looking green. Another furlong won't go amiss. (op 6-1)
Showtime Girl(IRE) had shown a moderate level of ability in two previous starts, so gives the form a marker. The return to a prominent racing style could have helped. (op 10-1)
Edith Anne had no change of gear whatsoever towards the centre of the track and must want a return further. (op 28-1)
Purple Day, gelded since his first outing, showed up for a while but couldn't quicken. (op 11-1 tchd 10-1)
Blue Clumber set a high standard if reproducing her Hilary Needler effort, but she fell a long way short of that performance even after breaking smartly. Shirley Teasdale reported that the filly hung left-handed. Official explanation: jockey said filly hung left-handed (tchd 11-4 and 7-2)
Armada Bay(IRE) didn't show a tremendous amount of promise on debut but must be thought capable of better judged on his starting price. (tchd 9-2)
Mount Seymour(IRE) Official explanation: trainer said gelding was unsuited by the soft (heavy in places) ground
Chiming Hart Official explanation: trainer's rep said filly finished distressed

3845 COACHMAN CARAVANS QUALITY H'CAP 5f
3:35 (3:36) (Class 4) (0-85,84) 3-Y-O+ £5,175 (£1,154; £1,154; £384) Stalls Low

Form RPR
4053 1 **Captain Scooby**[16] 3308 6-9-0 75............................... DeclanCannon(3) 3 82
(Richard Guest) *towards rr and pushed along 1/2-way: hdwy wl over 1f out: rdn ins fnl f: squeezed through last 50yds: led nr line* **7/1**[3]
1624 2 hd **Noodles Blue Boy**[36] 2674 6-9-7 82................................. IJBrennan(3) 4 88
(Ollie Pears) *trckd ldrs on inner: effrt over 1f out: rdn to chal ins fnl f: drvn to ld nr fin: hdd nr line* **6/1**[2]
2410 2 dht **Bond Fastrac**[21] 3169 5-9-5 80.. DaleSwift(3) 11 86
(Geoffrey Oldroyd) *towards rr: pushed along 2f out: swtchd to outer and rdn over 1f out: str run ins fnl f: jst failed* **14/1**
0510 4 hd **Caranbola**[21] 3169 6-9-7 79.. RobertWinston 6 84
(Mel Brittain) *cl up: led 2f out: sn rdn: drvn ins fnl f: edgd lft and hdd last 50yds: no ex* **7/1**[3]
6-03 5 2¼ **Another Wise Kid (IRE)**[47] 2337 4-9-11 83..................... MickyFenton 7 80
(Paul Midgley) *trckd ldrs: hdwy on outer over 1f out: rdn ent fnl f and ev ch tl drvn and no ex last 100yds* **6/1**[2]
2020 6 1¼ **Bronze Beau**[14] 3374 5-9-11 83.................................(t) KirstyMilczarek 10 76
(Linda Stubbs) *cl up: rdn wl over 1f out: ev ch tl drvn and wknd ins fnl f* **22/1**
1114 7 ½ **Pitkin**[10] 3496 4-9-1 73.. PaulMulrennan 5 64
(Michael Easterby) *trckd ldrs: effrt 2f out: rdn over 1f out: drvn whn n.m.r ins fnl f: one pce after* **8/1**
6040 8 2¼ **Meandmyshadow**[11] 3460 4-8-7 65 oh4............................ AndrewElliott 12 48
(Alan Brown) *a towards rr* **20/1**
0523 9 ½ **Whozthecat (IRE)**[8] 3595 5-9-8 80..............................(v) DanielTudhope 8 61
(Declan Carroll) *led: rdn along and hdd 2f out: cl up tl drvn and wknd ent fnl f* **11/4**[1]
0000 10 24 **Marine Commando**[23] 3078 4-9-5 84.................(b[1]) GeorgeChaloner(7) 9
(Richard Fahey) *rrd and plunged and lost many l s: a wl bhd* **8/1**
1m 4.96s (1.46) **Going Correction** +0.35s/f (Good) 10 Ran SP% **118.2**
CSF £50.60 CT £322.64 TOTE £7.80: £2.30; £27 Owner Trifecta £Mrs Alison Guest Bred Hellwood Stud Farm & Paul Davies (h'Gate).
■ Stewards' Enquiry : I J Brennan two-day ban: used whip above permitted level (Jul 22-23)

FOCUS
The leaders set a strong gallop in the easy ground, so it wasn't a surprise to see finishers dominate in the final stages. The time was modest compared with the latter maiden.
Whozthecat(IRE) Official explanation: jockey said gelding ran flat
Marine Commando Official explanation: jockey said gelding reared as stalls opened

3846 C.G.I. H'CAP 1m 100y
4:10 (4:10) (Class 5) (0-75,75) 3-Y-O £3,234 (£962; £481; £240) Stalls Low

Form RPR
-550 1 **Foursquare Funtime**[32] 2787 3-8-8 64 ow2.............. GrahamGibbons 3 68
(Reg Hollinshead) *trckd ldr: hdwy and cl up 2f out: rdn to chal wl over 1f out: led ent fnl f: sn clr* **7/1**
1020 2 3¼ **Captivity**[30] 2860 3-9-5 73.. FrederikTylicki 4 71
(Mark Johnston) *led: rdn along and jnd 2f out: drvn and hdd ent fnl f: kpt on same pce* **3/1**[3]

440 **3** 1 3/4 **Light Zabeel (USA)**[50] 2249 3-9-7 **75** TomEaves 2 69
(Mick Channon) *trckd ldng pair: effrt over 2f out and sn rdn: drvn over 1f out and sn one pce* **5/2**[2]
0522 **4** nse **It's A Privilege**[25] 3001 3-9-3 **71** (b) RichardKingscote 1 65
(Ralph Beckett) *rrd s: hld up in rr: effrt and hdwy over 2f out: rdn wl over 1f out: sn drlven and no imp* **5/4**[1]
1m 51.95s (4.35) **Going Correction** +0.35s/f (Good) **4** Ran SP% **110.5**
Speed ratings (Par 100): **92,88,87,86**
CSF £26.37 TOTE £9.50; EX 36.00.
Owner Tim Kelly **Bred** Mr & Mrs W Hodge **Trained** Upper Longdon, Staffs
■ Stewards' Enquiry : Graham Gibbons three-day ban: weighed in 2lb heavy (Jul 22-24)
FOCUS
This can't be form taken too seriously, considering it was a small field and the going was unseasonably soft. The winner is rated to his AW best.
Foursquare Funtime Official explanation: trainer's rep had no explanation regarding apparent improvement in form.

3847 POWERPART FILLIES' H'CAP 1m 1f 207y
4:45 (4:45) (Class 5) (0-70,70) 3-Y-O £2,911 (£866; £432; £216) Stalls Low

Form RPR
005 **1** **Guiletta (IRE)**[29] 2891 3-8-13 **65** RyanClark(3) 1 72
(Rae Guest) *hld up in rr: hdwy on wd outside 3f out: chsd ldrs over 2f out: rdn to ld wl over 1f out: drvn and edgd lft and rt ins fnl f: kpt on wl towards fin* **3/1**[1]
-005 **2** 1 **Napoleon's Muse (IRE)**[23] 3080 3-9-7 **70** RichardKingscote 2 75
(Ralph Beckett) *trckd ldrs: hdwy 3f out: cl up whn bmpd over 2f out: sn led: rdn and hdd wl over 1f out: drvn and ev ch ins fnl f: no ex last 100yds* **5/1**
3123 **3** nk **Mistress Of Rome**[23] 3080 3-9-6 **69** (b[1]) PaulMulrennan 3 73
(Michael Dods) *trckd ldrs: effrt over 2f out: sn rdn and n.m.r wl over 1f out: swtchd lft and drvn to chse ldng pair ins fnl f: kpt on* **4/1**[2]
40-0 **4** 3 **Baileys Over Ice**[20] 3184 3-8-9 **58** J-PGuillambert 8 56
(James Given) *hld up in rr: hdwy wl over 2f out: rdn wl over 1f out: kpt on appr fnl f nrst fin:* **10/1**
0660 **5** nk **Chatterati (USA)**[10] 3503 3-8-12 **61** FrederikTylicki 5 58
(Mark Johnston) *hld up towards rr: hdwy over 3f out: rdn to chse ldrs 2f out: drvn and one pce appr fnl f* **14/1**
0-36 **6** 15 **Neige D'Antan**[23] 3066 3-7-13 **53** (b[1]) RosieJessop(5) 6 20
(Sir Mark Prescott Bt) *dwlt and in rr: rapid hdwy to join ldrs after 1 1/2f: cl up: rdn to ld wl over 2f out whn hung bdly rt and hdd 2f out: sn wknd* **9/2**[3]
6510 **7** 10 **Lady Advocate (IRE)**[13] 3416 3-8-12 **61** (b) DavidAllan 4
(Tim Easterby) *led 2f: trckd ldng pair: hdwy and cl up 3f out: disp ld and rdn 2f out: sn wknd and eased fnl f* **10/1**
0035 **8** 1 1/2 **Inffiraaj (IRE)**[23] 3083 3-8-7 **61** CharlesBishop(5) 7
(Mick Channon) *cl up: led after 2f: rdn along 3f out: sn hdd & wknd qckly* **15/2**
2m 12.41s (5.41) **Going Correction** +0.35s/f (Good) **8** Ran SP% **116.5**
Speed ratings (Par 97): **92,91,90,88,88 76,68,67**
toteswingers 1&2 £3.60, 2&3 £2.80, 1&3 £3.00 CSF £18.61 CT £60.51 TOTE £4.20: £1.40, £1.90, £1.90; EX 23.50.
Owner The Hornets **Bred** The Hornets **Trained** Newmarket, Suffolk
FOCUS
An honest pace ensured a fair degree of stamina was required to get home in this. Modest form, with a 6lb personal best from the winner.
Guiletta(IRE) ◆ Official explanation: trainer said, regarding apparent improvement in form, that the filly benefited from a step up in trip and a weaker race.

3848 COACHMAN MAIDEN STKS 5f
5:20 (5:23) (Class 5) 3-Y-O+ £2,911 (£866; £432; £216) Stalls Low

Form RPR
2032 **1** **Henry Bee**[8] 3580 3-9-3 72 FrederikTylicki 14 78
(Richard Fahey) *chsd ldng pair: rdn over 1f out: styd on u.p ent fnl f to ld last 100yds* **9/4**[2]
3423 **2** 1 1/4 **Economic Crisis (IRE)**[12] 3450 3-8-12 57 PaddyAspell 6 68
(Alan Berry) *cl up: led after 2f: rdn over 1f out: hdd and one pce last 100yds* **10/1**
23 **3** 1 1/4 **Legal Bond**[17] 3289 3-9-3 0 TomEaves 4 69
(Bryan Smart) *chsd ldrs: rdn along wl over 1f out: kpt on ins fnl f* **7/4**[1]
2532 **4** 2 **Elegant Girl (IRE)**[12] 3438 3-8-12 65 (b[1]) DavidAllan 8 56
(Tim Easterby) *chsd ldrs: rdn along 2f out: kpt on same pce appr fnl f* **7/2**[3]
4302 **5** 2 1/2 **Brunswick Vale (IRE)**[11] 3463 3-8-5 53 (b) NedCurtis(7) 2 47
(Paul Midgley) *towards rr and pushed along after 1f: hdwy 2f out: sn rdn and n.d* **10/1**
0-06 **6** 3/4 **Too Ambitious**[16] 3312 3-8-5 46 JackDuern(7) 11 45
(Reg Hollinshead) *led 2f: cl up: rdn along over 2f out: drvn and wknd appr fnl f* **33/1**
4 **7** 3/4 **Charmel's Delight**[8] 3561 3-8-9 0 DaleSwift(3) 9 42
(Geoffrey Oldroyd) *s.i.s: a in rr* **14/1**
00-6 **8** 3 1/2 **Peteron**[12] 3438 4-9-8 48 PaulMulrennan 15 36
(Colin Teague) *in tch on wd outside: rdn along 1/2-way: sn outpcd* **40/1**
9 3 3/4 **Pilarcita** 3-8-9 0 IJBrennan(3) 7 16
(Ollie Pears) *midfield: rdn along wl over 1f out: grad wknd* **33/1**
0-0 **10** 1 1/2 **Red All Over (IRE)**[42] 2470 3-8-12 0 BarryMcHugh 12
(Alan Berry) *a in rr* **66/1**
/030 **11** 11 **Beaux Yeux**[19] 3235 6-8-12 42 (be) AnnStokell(5) 1
(Ann Stokell) *s.i.s: a bhd* **80/1**
1m 4.85s (1.35) **Going Correction** +0.35s/f (Good)
WFA 3 from 4yo+ 5lb **11** Ran SP% **125.3**
Speed ratings (Par 103): **103,101,99,95,91 90,89,83,77,75 57**
toteswingers 1&2 £5.40, 2&3 £5.80, 1&3 £1.90 CSF £26.31 TOTE £3.20: £1.30, £1.90, £1.30; EX 27.40.
Owner Wildcard Racing Syndicate X2 **Bred** T M M Partnership **Trained** Musley Bank, N Yorks
FOCUS
It's very unlikely that the winner is really up to his official mark, considering he's been beaten off similar ones in handicaps, although the winning time was quicker than the 0-85 handicap over the same distance earlier in the day. The winner did not need to improve.
T/Plt: £1,453.50 to a £1 stake. Pool of £76758.48 - 38.55 winning tickets. T/Qpdt: £236.30 to a £1 stake. Pool of £4823.78 - 15.10 winning tickets. JR

3490 CARLISLE (R-H)
Saturday, July 7
3849 Meeting Abandoned - waterlogged

3775 HAYDOCK (L-H)
Saturday, July 7
OFFICIAL GOING: Heavy (soft in places) changing to soft after race 1 (2.20)
Wind: light to medium, behind Weather: dry, bright spells and light cloud

3855 BET365 H'CAP 7f
2:20 (2:27) (Class 2) (0-105,100) 3-Y-O+ £12,938 (£3,850; £1,924; £962) Stalls Low

Form RPR
0-03 **1** **Atlantic Sport (USA)**[15] 3331 7-9-7 **94** MartinHarley 5 101
(Mick Channon) *hld up in tch: clsd to trck ldrs 2f out: swtchd rt and effrt over 1f out: styd on u.p to ld fnl 100yds: hld on wl towards fin* **4/1**[2]
1006 **2** hd **Al Muheer (IRE)**[7] 3626 7-9-2 **89** (b) JamesSullivan 3 95
(Ruth Carr) *stdd s: t.k.h: hld up in rr: hdwy over 1f out: drvn and str chal fnl 75yds: hld towards fin* **7/1**
2110 **3** 1 1/2 **Imperial Djay (IRE)**[15] 3331 7-9-10 **97** PJMcDonald 7 100
(Ruth Carr) *stdd s: hld up in last pair: smooth hdwy to join ldrs 2f out: rdn and unable qck over 1f out: stl ev ch tl no ex and outpcd fnl 100yds* **7/1**
1032 **4** 1/2 **Esprit De Midas**[22] 3128 6-9-7 **94** (b) ShaneKelly 1 95
(Dean Ivory) *t.k.h: chsd ldrs tl jnd ldr ent fnl 2f: drvn to ld narrowly over 1f out: hdd fnl 100yds: wknd towards fin* **3/1**[1]
6200 **5** 1 1/4 **Louis The Pious**[15] 3331 4-9-7 **94** (p) PhillipMakin 2 92
(Kevin Ryan) *led: jnd and rdn 2f out: hdd over 1f out: drvn and styd pressing ldrs tl wknd fnl 100yds* **9/1**
3/50 **6** 5 **Fair Trade**[17] 3268 5-9-13 **100** GrahamLee 4 85
(Hughie Morrison) *t.k.h: hld up in tch: rdn and effrt 3f out: sn struggling: wknd over 1f out* **10/1**
3445 **7** 3 1/4 **Dubai Dynamo**[9] 3534 7-9-3 **90** SebSanders 8 67
(Ruth Carr) *chsd ldr tl ent fnl 2f: sn struggling u.p: wknd over 1f out* **5/1**[3]
0330 **8** 1 **Clockmaker (IRE)**[22] 3128 6-9-2 **89** DuranFentiman 6 63
(Tim Easterby) *taken down early: awkward leaving stalls: sn rcvrd and in tch: hdwy to chse ldrs 5f out: rdn and effrt 1/2-way: wknd over 1f out* **10/1**
1m 29.58s (-1.12) **Going Correction** +0.075s/f (Good) **8** Ran SP% **114.8**
Speed ratings (Par 109): **109,108,107,106,105 99,95,94**
toteswingers 1&2 £6.20, 2&3 £6.40, 1&3 £7.60 CSF £32.05 CT £190.76 TOTE £4.80: £1.30, £2.60, £2.20; EX 39.50 Trifecta £234.10 Pool: £885.96 - 2.80 winning units..
Owner M Channon **Bred** Gainsborough Farm Llc **Trained** West Ilsley, Berks
■ Stewards' Enquiry : Martin Harley two-day ban: used whip above permitted level (Jul 22-23)
FOCUS
All races on Outer Home straight and distances on Round course increased by circa 37yds. Ordinary form for the grade, those coming from off the pace rising to the fore late. The winner has come down a lot in the weights and is rated a length off last year's best.
NOTEBOOK
Atlantic Sport(USA) hadn't won since his 3yo days (2008), and had still to win a handicap coming into the race, but he'd finished a fine third in the Buckingham Palace the time before and just held on. These conditions are no problem for him and he could run well in next week's Bunbury Cup. (tchd 7-2)
Al Muheer(IRE) raced against a strong track bias at Newcastle the time before, and this was a truer reflection of his capabilities. He came from a little further back than the winner, but still had ample time to get up (in front soon after the line). (op 12-1 tchd 14-1)
Imperial Djay(IRE), around 5l behind the winner at Royal Ascot (raced opposite sides), ran well enough to suggest he might be able to defy this career-high mark. (op 5-1 tchd 9-2)
Esprit De Midas travelled best but couldn't quicken and failed to reproduce the form of his recent York second. (op 11-4 tchd 5-2)
Louis The Pious was readily swept aside and remains below his best. (op 12-1 tchd 16-1)
Fair Trade was loaded early into the stalls and quickly beaten once under pressure. (op 11-1 tchd 12-1)

3856 BET365 LANCASHIRE OAKS (GROUP 2) (F&M) 1m 3f 200y
2:55 (2:55) (Class 1) 3-Y-O+
£45,368 (£17,200; £8,608; £4,288; £2,152; £1,080) Stalls High

Form RPR
5-11 **1** **Great Heavens**[23] 3069 3-8-6 98 RobertHavlin 3 115+
(John Gosden) *mde all: rdn and drew clr fr 2f out: in total command 1f out: eased towards fin: impressive* **11/4**[1]
5-21 **2** 5 **Shimmering Surf (IRE)**[35] 2711 5-9-5 107 GeorgeBaker 7 105
(Roger Varian) *chsd wnr thrght: rdn and unable qck w wnr 2f out: wl hld after but kpt on for 2nd* **7/1**
-621 **3** 1 1/4 **Set To Music (IRE)**[19] 3219 4-9-5 105 JamieSpencer 5 103
(Michael Bell) *stdd after s: hld up in last pair: hdwy on outer 3f out: chsd ldng pair and edgd lft u.p ent fnl 2f: no ch w wnr and plugged on same pce after* **3/1**[2]
026 **4** 1/2 **Myplacelater**[19] 3219 5-9-5 107 DavidNolan 9 102
(Richard Fahey) *stdd s: hld up in rr: rdn and hdwy 2f out: wnt 4th ins fnl f: kpt on but no ch w wnr* **28/1**
20-0 **5** 2 1/4 **Testosterone (IRE)**[14] 3369 4-9-5 115 GrahamLee 4 98
(Ed Dunlop) *t.k.h: hld up in tch: rdn and chsd ldrs 3f out: sn struggling and outpcd 2f out: wl btn after* **6/1**[3]
3160 **6** 2 **Good Morning Star (IRE)**[35] 2718 3-8-6 88 JoeFanning 1 95
(Mark Johnston) *chsd ldng pair tl over 3f out: 4th and wkng 2f out: wl btn after* **40/1**
4-04 **7** 7 **Mohedian Lady (IRE)**[35] 2711 4-9-5 103 KierenFallon 6 84
(Luca Cumani) *t.k.h: hld up in tch: rdn over 3f out: sn struggling and wl btn fnl 2f* **17/2**
-444 **8** nk **Salford Art (IRE)**[16] 3292 3-8-6 108 SilvestreDeSousa 8 84
(David Elsworth) *in tch in midfield tl dropped to rr 5f out: sn lost tch u.p and bhd fnl 3f* **8/1**
4-10 **9** 3/4 **Aquamarine (JPN)**[40] 2570 4-9-5 110 SebSanders 2 82
(M Delzangles, France) *t.k.h: hld up in tch: rdn ent fnl 3f: sn struggling and wl btn 2f out: bhd and eased fnl f* **8/1**
2m 32.3s (-1.50) **Going Correction** +0.075s/f (Good)
WFA 3 from 4yo+ 13lb **9** Ran SP% **117.1**
Speed ratings (Par 115): **108,104,103,103,102 100,96,95,95**
toteswingers 1&2 £5.00, 2&3 £2.80, 1&3 £1.80 CSF £22.96 TOTE £3.80: £1.50, £2.30, £1.50; EX 28.00 Trifecta £36.40 Pool: £1348.46 - 27.41 winning units..
Owner Lady Rothschild **Bred** Kincorth Investments Inc **Trained** Newmarket, Suffolk
FOCUS
This looked open beforehand, but the market principals came to the fore late and the form looks good, with the placed runners running right up to their earlier course meeting in June. Great Heavens' effort is up there with the better 1m4f 3yo fillies' form. The winning time was 1.09secs quicker than the following handicap.

NOTEBOOK

Great Heavens ◆ became the first 3yo to win since 2006, impressively drawing clear from the front. A sister to Nathaniel, she'd already shown in winning her maiden and a Listed race at Newbury that soft ground suits well, and the step up to 1m4f brought about a career-best by some way. Improving all the time, she'll surely step into Group 1 company now, with her very much appealing as a type for races such as the Yorkshire Oaks and Prix Vermeille. (op 3-1)
Shimmering Surf(IRE) has rediscovered her best form of late and confirmed last month's C&D form with the third, simply proving no match for the classy winner. (op 8-1)
Set To Music(IRE) had won easily at Warwick in Listed company since her course defeat by the runner-up, and again ran well without suggesting she's quite up to winning a Group 2. Official explanation: jockey said filly hung left and suffered interference in running (op 7-2)
Myplacelater made late gains having been dropped in as usual, getting closer to Set To Music than she had done at Warwick. (op 25-1)
Testosterone(IRE) is beginning to look very expensive having been purchased for 1,200,000gns out of Pascal Bary's yard last year. Her dam won up to 1m7f and this effort pointed to her needing further. (op 5-1)
Mohedian Lady(IRE) was disappointing, failing to pick up and perhaps finding the ground too soft. (op 11-1 tchd 12-1)
Aquamarine(JPN) put in another poor effort and is clearly not firing at present. (op 7-1 tchd 9-1)

3857 BET365 OLD NEWTON CUP (HERITAGE H'CAP) 1m 3f 200y

3:25 (3:26) (Class 2) 4-Y-0+

£62,250 (£18,640; £9,320; £4,660; £2,330; £1,170) **Stalls** High

Form RPR

-311 **1** **Number Theory**[24] 3036 4-8-6 **92** ow1 RussKennemore 19 101
(John Holt) *in tch: hdwy to chse ldrs 4f out: chsd ldr 2f out: sn rdn and ev ch: drvn to ld 1f out: forged ahd ins fnl f: styd on and a gng to hold runner-up* **8/1**[3]

-101 **2** *nk* **Quiz Mistress**[20] 3187 4-8-4 **90** NickyMackay 7 98
(Hughie Morrison) *hld up towards rr: rdn and hdwy over 1f out: barging match w rivals 1f out: chsd wnr wl ins fnl f: gng on wl towards fin but nvr quite getting to wnr* **12/1**

0-00 **3** *1 ¼* **Tepmokea (IRE)**[14] 3377 6-8-4 **90** CathyGannon 9 96
(Mrs K Burke) *led: rdn ent fnl 3f: hrd pressed and drvn over 1f out: hdd 1f out: no ex and btn fnl 100yds: lost 2nd wl ins fnl f* **33/1**

36/5 **4** *1 ¼* **Dreamspeed (IRE)**[49] 2267 5-8-13 **99** LiamKeniry 15 103
(Andrew Balding) *t.k.h: chsd ldrs: wnt 2nd over 3f out tl 2f out: drvn and edgd rt 1f out: styd on same pce fnl f* **40/1**

-100 **5** *hd* **War Poet**[7] 3635 5-8-6 **92** (v) PJMcDonald 16 96
(David O'Meara) *stdd s: hld up in rr: rdn over 3f out: hdwy on outer over 2f out: styng on chsng ldrs whn edgd lft and barging match w rivals 1f out: kpt on same pce ins fnl f* **16/1**

21-1 **6** *1* **Lexi's Boy (IRE)**[10] 3494 4-8-4 **90** ChrisCatlin 2 92
(Donald McCain) *in tch: rdn to chse ldrs 5f out: stl chsng ldrs but unable qck u.p 2f out plugged on same pce and no threat to wnr after* **2/1**[1]

0-06 **7** *shd* **Kiama Bay (IRE)**[59] 1974 6-8-9 **95** MichaelO'Connell 11 97
(John Quinn) *in tch: rdn and effrt over 2f out: styd on same pce u.p fr over 1f out* **16/1**

3030 **8** *1 ½* **Hurricane Higgins (IRE)**[22] 3125 4-8-10 **96** JoeFanning 10 96
(Mark Johnston) *in tch in midfield: lost pl and n.m.r 3f out: rdn and tried to rally over 1f out: styd on same pce fnl f* **33/1**

2150 **9** *¾* **Allied Powers (IRE)**[14] 3369 7-9-3 **110** ThomasGarner(7) 14 109
(Michael Bell) *hld up in tch in midfield: rdn and hdwy 3f out: chsng ldrs and plugging on whn squeezed for room 1f out: no imp and hld after* **20/1**

-023 **10** *3 ¼* **Hillview Boy (IRE)**[21] 3164 8-8-8 **94** ow1 GrahamLee 3 87
(Jim Goldie) *hld up in rr: switching out rt and effrt over 1f out: no imp: nvr trbld ldrs* **14/1**

-106 **11** *1 ¾* **Deauville Flyer**[22] 3125 6-8-4 **90** (p) DuranFentiman 6 81
(Tim Easterby) *chsd ldrs: rdn and struggling to qckn 3f out: wknd over 1f out* **25/1**

1-51 **12** *3 ½* **Franciscan**[42] 2504 4-8-5 **91** KierenFallon 5 76
(Luca Cumani) *in tch in midfield: rdn and no imp 3f out: wknd over 1f out* **4/1**[2]

0-00 **13** *7* **Becausewecan (USA)**[7] 3642 6-8-4 **90** AdrianNicholls 8 64
(Mark Johnston) *bustled along leaving stalls: sn pressing ldr tl rdn over 3f out: sn dropped out: bhd and eased ins fnl f* **40/1**

2-22 **14** *8* **Tmaam (USA)**[15] 3341 4-8-6 **92** SilvestreDeSousa 13 53
(Mark Johnston) *in tch in midfield tl dropped to rr and rdn 5f out: lost tch 2f out: wl bhd and eased fnl f* **11/1**

6-11 **15** *6* **Easy Terms**[50] 2253 5-8-10 **96** JamesSullivan 17 47
(Edwin Tuer) *hld up towards rr: rdn and no hdwy over 2f out: wknd wl over 1f out: bhd and eased fnl f* **12/1**

2m 33.39s (-0.41) **Going Correction** +0.075s/f (Good) **17 Ran SP% 126.0**
Speed ratings (Par 109): **104,103,102,102,102 101,101,100,99,97 96,94,89,84,80**
toteswingers 1&2 £16.50, 2&3 £197.00, 1&3 £76.30 CSF £96.81 CT £3021.89 TOTE £10.00: £3.10, £3.80, £10.10; EX 131.00 Trifecta £4262.80 Pool: £57893.92 - 10.05 winning units..
Owner Mohan Fonseka **Bred** R Haim **Trained** Peckleton, Leics

FOCUS

Traditionally a hot middle-distance handicap and it again looked hugely competitive. Solid handicap form. The pace appeared reasonable, yet three of the first four home were prominent throughout. The winning time was 1.09secs slower than the previous Group 2.

NOTEBOOK

Number Theory continued his progression with a third C&D victory since May, defying a further 5lb rise. He travelled strongly and saw it out well, albeit there's a case to be made for the runner-up being a tad unfortunate. His rating will likely be nudging 100 following this, and it would be no surprise to see him return to 1m6f (staying on sixth sole previous attempt) for a crack at the Ebor. (op 9-1)
Quiz Mistress would probably have won on another day, doing best of those to come from off the pace despite being short of room racing into the final 3f and then getting into a bumping match with Allied Powers. She still produced a late run to just miss out, and clearly remains on the up. Placed at up to 2m, she'd be fancied to reverse form with the winner were they to clash again in the Ebor.
Tepmokea(IRE) was back on his last winning mark and left behind a couple of modest efforts in holding on for third.
Dreamspeed(IRE) missed all of 2011 and offered little on his reappearance in Listed company, but he'd been gelded subsequently and, despite taking a while to settle, ran to a level more in keeping with his old ability. He should come on again.
War Poet was running on late, not getting the best of trips, but never looked a threat. (op 14-1)
Lexi's Boy(IRE), up 10lb for his Cumberland Plate victory, couldn't get to the front, as is his want. He used up some juice in improving his position down the back, but couldn't quicken and was always being held. A tough horse who likes to dominate his rivals, he can have this form ignored. (op 5-2 tchd 11-4 in a place)
Kiama Bay(IRE) took a step back in the right direction and ought to be capable of winning from this mark. (op 12-1)
Hurricane Higgins(IRE) needs faster ground and a longer trip.
Allied Powers(IRE) was in the process of running well until things got a little rough and he was squeezed for room.
Franciscan, up 4lb for his last-gasp York win, seems best suited by faster ground and can be given another chance if lining up in the Ebor. (op 11-2)
Tmaam(USA) was never well placed and one of the first beaten. (op 14-1)
Easy Terms, a winner of six of her last seven, was beaten too far for the 4lb rise to be blamed. Official explanation: jockey said mare ran flat (op 10-1)

3858 MOBILE AT BET365.COM NURSERY 7f

4:00 (4:01) (Class 4) (0-85,85) 2-Y-0 **£5,175** (£1,540; £769; £384) **Stalls** Low

Form RPR

612 **1** **Rated**[50] 2238 2-8-11 **75** MartinHarley 6 77
(Mick Channon) *stdd s: t.k.h: hld up in tch in rr: clsd 3f out: swtchd rt and effrt over 1f out: drvn to ld fnl 100yds: kpt on wl* **4/1**[2]

3201 **2** *hd* **Steer By The Stars (IRE)**[17] 3271 2-8-12 **76** JoeFanning 8 77
(Mark Johnston) *chsd ldrs: rdn over 2f out: drvn and ev ch ins fnl f: kpt on wl but hld towards fin* **9/4**[1]

563 **3** *1 ¼* **It's Only Business**[18] 3244 2-8-1 **65** CathyGannon 7 64
(Bill Turner) *led: rdn 2f out: drvn over 1f out and led again 1f out: hdd fnl 100yds: no ex and btn whn eased cl home* **7/1**

036 **4** *¾* **Bayan Kasirga (IRE)**[17] 3282 2-8-5 **69** PatrickMathers 9 65
(Richard Fahey) *t.k.h: in tch: rdn and effrt 3f out: chsd ldrs u.p 1f out: styd on same pce fnl f* **8/1**

504 **5** *nk* **Walter White (IRE)**[22] 3097 2-8-7 **71** LiamKeniry 10 67
(Andrew Balding) *t.k.h: in tch: hdwy to chse ldr 5f out: led 2f out and sn rdn: hdd 1f out: stl pressing ldrs but struggling whn short of room fnl 100yds: eased cl home* **9/2**[3]

2404 **6** *hd* **Out Of The Blocks**[12] 3436 2-8-1 **65** JamesSullivan 5 60
(Ruth Carr) *in tch: rdn 3f out: swtchd lft and hdwy u.p to chse ldrs 1f out: sn no imp: wknd towards fin* **10/1**

000 **7** *3 ¼* **Delores Rocket**[24] 3034 2-7-13 **66** JulieBurke(3) 1 53
(Kevin Ryan) *chsd ldr tl 5f out: rdn over 2f out: drvn and stl chsng ldrs over 1f out: wknd ins fnl f* **9/1**

620 **8** *3 ¾* **Alexandrakollontai (IRE)**[15] 3339 2-7-5 **62** oh2 NoelGarbutt(7) 3 39
(J S Moore) *dwlt: sn pushed along in rr: wknd wl over 1f out* **25/1**

1m 32.86s (2.16) **Going Correction** +0.075s/f (Good) **8 Ran SP% 115.5**
Speed ratings (Par 96): **90,89,88,87,87 86,83,78**
toteswingers 1&2 £1.10, 2&3 £5.70, 1&3 £5.10 CSF £13.60 CT £60.23 TOTE £4.70: £1.70, £1.40, £1.90; EX 9.50.
Owner M Channon **Bred** Mike Channon Bloodstock Ltd **Trained** West Ilsley, Berks

FOCUS

The first nursery of the season. The ratings shown are provisional. It looked open on paper and that's the way it played out, but the form makes a lot of sense. The pace was quite a steady one.

NOTEBOOK

Rated, gelded since finishing a 9l second in a 6f novice event at Newcastle in May, did well considering how keenly he'd raced, clearly needing every yard of the 7f trip. A more truly run race will suit and he looks to have more to offer. (op 9-2 tchd 7-2)
Steer By The Stars(IRE), off the mark at the fourth attempt in maidens, was up 1f in trip for this nursery debut and had her chance. (tchd 5-2 in a place)
It's Only Business didn't quite see it out on this step up to 7f, despite his dam being a 1m4f winner. It's possible the soft ground was to blame. (op 13-2)
Bayan Kasirga(IRE) couldn't quicken and would have appreciated a stronger pace to aim at. (op 10-1 tchd 11-1)
Walter White(IRE) wanted to get on with it, and his rider allowed him to close right up turning in, but he was always likely to fade late on as a result. He can be given another chance. (op 13-2)

3859 BET365.COM H'CAP 1m 3f 200y

4:35 (4:36) (Class 2) (0-100,92) 3-Y-0 **£12,938** (£3,850; £1,924; £962) **Stalls** High

Form RPR

-120 **1** **Gabrial The Great (IRE)**[16] 3296 3-8-13 **84** JamieSpencer 4 94+
(Michael Bell) *stdd s: hld up in last pair: clsd 6f out: trckd ldrs and gng best 2f out: rdn to ld over 1f out: edgd lft and 2 l clr 1f out: kpt on and a doing enough ins fnl f* **5/6**[1]

122- **2** *1 ¾* **Repeater**[252] 7167 3-9-7 **92** ChrisCatlin 1 99+
(Sir Mark Prescott Bt) *stdd s: t.k.h: hld up in rr: clsd 6f out: rdn and effrt over 1f out: hdwy u.p and chsd wnr ins fnl f: no imp fnl 100yds* **7/2**[2]

0641 **3** *4 ½* **Choisan (IRE)**[16] 3305 3-8-9 **80** DuranFentiman 6 80
(Tim Easterby) *led: stdd gallop 6f out: jnd and rdn 3f out: hdd and outpcd by wnr over 1f out: wknd fnl 150yds* **10/1**

-013 **4** *3* **Bute Hall**[7] 3614 3-8-9 **80** JoeFanning 2 75
(Mark Johnston) *chsd ldng pair tl wnt 2nd over 7f out: jnd ldr 3f out: rdn and edging lft 2f out: outpcd by wnr over 1f out and btn 1f out: sn wknd* **7/1**[3]

3231 **5** *5* **Fleeting Image**[35] 2708 3-8-0 **78** (p) NatashaEaton(7) 3 65
(Alan Bailey) *chsd ldr tl over 7f out: dropped to rr and rdn over 2f out: wknd over 1f out* **8/1**

2m 35.82s (2.02) **Going Correction** +0.075s/f (Good) **5 Ran SP% 109.5**
Speed ratings (Par 106): **96,94,91,89,86**
CSF £3.93 TOTE £1.70: £1.10, £1.90; EX 3.90.
Owner Dr Marwan Koukash **Bred** Sarl Elevage Du Haras De Bourgeauville **Trained** Newmarket, Suffolk

FOCUS

Not as competitive as it could have been, with the defection of both Proofreader and Willie Wag Tail, but still a decent 3yo handicap. The pace appeared quite brisk early (steadied at halfway) and the front pair drew clear. The winner may be capable of better and the second ran to his 2yo best.

NOTEBOOK

Gabrial The Great(IRE) was backed into favourite for the King George V handicap at Royal Ascot, a race which went pretty disastrously for him, but things went much smoother here and he won with a bit in hand. He appears to have his quirks and doesn't do much in front, but clearly has plenty of ability and could be the type for a race like the Melrose, as he looks to have plenty of stamina. (tchd evens in a place)
Repeater, off for 252 days and gelded, was a bit keen and would have preferred faster ground, so this has to go down as a fair effort conceding 8lb to the winner. He too could be a Melrose type. (op 10-3 tchd 4-1)
Choisan(IRE), up 5lb for his all-the-way Ripon win, kept going once headed but wasn't good enough against stronger company. (op 9-1)
Bute Hall moved well to a point, but finished quite weakly and may have found the race coming too soon. (tchd 8-1)
Fleeting Image could have been expected to finish closer looking at some of her earlier form.

3860 BET365.COM CONDITIONS STKS 6f

5:10 (5:10) (Class 3) 3-Y-0+ **£8,092** (£2,423; £1,211; £605) **Stalls** High

Form RPR

1350 **1** **Alben Star (IRE)**[14] 3371 4-8-11 **97** JamieSpencer 2 92
(Richard Fahey) *taken down early: stdd s: hld up in rr: wnt 3rd 1/2-way: swtchd lft and effrt 2f out: rdn to ld 1f out: drvn and styd on wl fnl f* **11/8**[2]

-354 **2** 3/4 **Morache Music**[14] 3371 4-8-11 106 SebSanders 1 90
(Peter Makin) *chsd ldrs tl wnt 2nd over 4f out: clsd to press ldr over 1f out: drvn and ev ch 1f out: no ex and btn wl ins fnl f* **5/6**[1]

6600 **3** 1 1/4 **Sos Brillante (CHI)**[7] 3633 7-8-6 74 FrankieMcDonald 4 81
(Terry Clement) *chsd ldr tl over 4f out: rdn and dropped to last 1/2-way: looked wl hld 2f out: rallied ins fnl f: styd on wl to go 3rd cl home* **50/1**

5005 **4** nk **Inxile (IRE)**[20] 3196 7-9-10 110 (p) AdrianNicholls 3 98
(David Nicholls) *taken down early and led to s: led and sn clr: rdn over 1f out: hdd 1f out: no ex and btn fnl 100yds: lost 3rd cl home* **8/1**[3]

1m 14.17s (0.37) **Going Correction** +0.30s/f (Good) **4** Ran SP% **109.7**
Speed ratings (Par 107): **109,108,106,105**
CSF £2.92 TOTE £2.10; EX 2.80.
Owner J K Shannon & M A Scaife **Bred** Rathasker Stud **Trained** Musley Bank, N Yorks
■ Stewards' Enquiry : Jamie Spencer two-day ban: careless riding (Jul 22-23)

FOCUS
This was left looking a match following the defection of Doncaster Rover, and they went a strong gallop. The close-up placing of the 74-rated Sos Brillante holds the form down, with the winner rated 9lb off his turf best and the second 20lb off his Wokingham run.

NOTEBOOK
Alben Star(IRE) was right there until the closing stages in the Wokingham, ultimately finishing behind Morache Music, and being 7lb worse off at the weights looked to make things tough, but Jamie Spencer was probably the right jockey booking, and he always just looked to be coming out on top. He should remain competitive in top sprint handicaps, and the Stewards' Cup is the plan. (op 7-4)
Morache Music had his chance and this reverse shouldn't be held against him as his better efforts have come in double-figure fields. He remains a very useful handicap sprinter. (tchd 4-5)
Sos Brillante(CHI), rated just 74, shouldn't be held to mark down the form too much, as becoming outpaced when she did probably worked in her favour, with the principals making their move plenty soon enough and finishing quite tired. (op 25-1)
Inxile(IRE) faced a very stiff task conceding 13lb to the pair at the head of the market, and he did little more than tee it up for them. (op 6-1)

3861 CASINO AT BET365.COM H'CAP 5f
5:40 (5:42) (Class 4) (0-85,85) 3-Y-O **£5,175** (£1,540; £769; £384) **Stalls** High

Form RPR

51-0 **1** **Tango Sky (IRE)**[26] 2986 3-8-6 75 (p) JamesRogers(5) 1 82
(Ralph Beckett) *bmpd s and slowly away: grad rcvrd and chsd ldr after 2f: rdn to ld ent fnl f: kpt on wl u.p* **11/2**

3024 **2** 1 **Church Music (IRE)**[7] 3608 3-9-4 82 (p) DarryllHolland 8 85
(Michael Scudamore) *chsd ldr for 2f: styd in tch: rdn and hdwy whn swtchd rt 1f out: kpt on to go 2nd nr fin* **7/2**[2]

0050 **3** 1/2 **Heartsong (IRE)**[10] 3486 3-9-0 78 FrankieMcDonald 9 79
(John Gallagher) *chsd ldrs: rdn 2f out: kpt on u.p fnl f* **11/1**

6600 **4** hd **I'll Be Good**[7] 3624 3-8-12 76 GrahamLee 4 76
(Robert Johnson) *chsd ldrs: rdn and effrt over 1f out: chsd wnr ins fnl f: no imp and lost 2 pls nr fin* **9/2**[3]

-122 **5** 2 **Sonko (IRE)**[28] 2914 3-9-7 85 (p) JamieSpencer 3 78
(Tim Pitt) *led: rdn and pressed over 1f out: hdd ent fnl f: drvn and btn ins fnl f: edgd lft and wknd towards fin* **9/4**[1]

0-10 **6** 24 **Tioman Pearl**[14] 3396 3-9-7 85 AndreaAtzeni 6
(Roger Varian) *hld up in tch: rdn 2f out: sn btn: wl btn and virtually p.u ins fnl f: t.o* **9/2**[3]

1m 1.83s (1.03) **Going Correction** +0.30s/f (Good) **6** Ran SP% **113.1**
Speed ratings (Par 102): **103,101,100,100,97 58**
toteswingers 1&2 £9.50, 2&3 £9.60, 1&3 £16.60 CSF £25.11 CT £202.25 TOTE £9.30: £4.20, £1.70; EX 36.60.
Owner A W A Partnership **Bred** L Mulryan **Trained** Kimpton, Hants

FOCUS
A competitive 3yo sprint handicap that was run at a fast pace. The winner rates a 6lb personal best.
T/Plt: £137.40 to a £1 stake. Pool of £137,464.56 - 730.13 winning units. T/Qpdt: 40.60 to a £1 stake. Pool of £7,479.84 - 136.00 winning units. SP

2783 LEICESTER (R-H)
Saturday, July 7
3862 Meeting Abandoned - waterlogged

3074 NOTTINGHAM (L-H)
Saturday, July 7
3869 Meeting Abandoned - waterlogged

3822 SANDOWN (R-H)
Saturday, July 7

OFFICIAL GOING: Good to soft (soft in places; sprint 6.9 (stands' side 6.7) round 7.2 (home str: stands' side 7.7, far side 7.0) changing to good to soft after race 4 (3.10)
Wind: Moderate, half behind Weather: Cloudy

3876 BET ON MOVE WITH CORAL.CO.UK MOBILE H'CAP 7f 16y
1:30 (1:31) (Class 3) (0-95,93) 3-Y-O
£8,092 (£2,423; £1,211; £605; £302; £152) **Stalls** Low

Form RPR

2553 **1** **Johnno**[14] 3393 3-8-7 79 MartinLane 7 89
(J W Hills) *mde all: led field to nr side in st: rdn 2f out: styd on wl: virtually unchal* **3/1**[2]

0521 **2** 2 **Rocky Reef**[12] 3433 3-8-2 74 oh2 (v) DavidProbert 13 79
(Andrew Balding) *pressed wnr: tried to grab nr side rail in st but nt gng pce to do so: lost pl over 2f out: styd on to take 2nd again ins fnl f* **5/1**

412 **3** 1 1/2 **Dutch Supreme**[17] 3281 3-9-3 89 TedDurcan 15 90+
(David Lanigan) *hld up in 4th: shkn up and nt qckn over 2f out: kpt on to take 3rd nr fin* **9/4**[1]

0-06 **4** 1/2 **North Star Boy (IRE)**[51] 2212 3-9-4 90 RichardHughes 6 90
(Richard Hannon) *t.k.h: hld up in 3rd: chsd wnr over 2f out: rdn and no imp wl over 1f out: fdd fnl f* **9/1**

0-11 **5** 1 1/4 **Ivor's Princess**[20] 3192 3-8-11 83 (b) SeanLevey 14 79
(Rod Millman) *hld up in last: rdn and no prog wl over 2f out: taken wd over 1f out: wl btn after* **7/1**

22-2 **6** 2 1/4 **Signor Sassi**[14] 3389 3-8-7 79 NeilCallan 10 69
(Roger Varian) *t.k.h: hld up in 5th: prog to dispute 2nd over 2f out: wknd over 1f out* **9/2**[3]

1m 29.86s (0.36) **Going Correction** +0.10s/f (Good) **6** Ran SP% **113.1**
Speed ratings (Par 104): **101,98,97,96,95 92**
toteswingers: 1&2 £3.30, 2&3 £2.70, 1&3 £2.0 CSF £18.31 CT £38.38 TOTE £4.10: £2.20, £2.40; EX 18.40 Trifecta £79.90 Pool: £745.88 - 6.90 winning units..
Owner Gary And Linnet Woodward **Bred** Gestut Sohrenhof **Trained** Upper Lambourn, Berks

FOCUS
The ground had eased from the previous day and was described as good to soft, soft in places on both the sprint and round courses, although the winning time of the first race (2.86sec outside standard) suggested it wasn't too bad. The GoingStick read 6.9 (Stands' side 6.7) on the sprint track, and 7.2 (Home Straight: Stands' side 7.7, Far side 7.0) on the Round course. The far-side rail was 3yds in on the Sprint course, while the Round course was at its innermost configuration. All distances were as advertised. The opening race of the card was decimated by non-runners, with ten of the original 16 due to line up withdrawn, at least officially because of the change in the going since the declaration stage. They came stands' side in the straight. The first two were pretty much the front pair throughout and the winner is rated similarly to Newmarket.

NOTEBOOK
Johnno put up a good effort in defeat on easy ground at Newmarket last time, and off just a 1lb higher mark, was clearly a big player in this company. Being handed an uncontested lead made things simple for him, and he won easily in the end. He has plenty of size about him and his trainer expects him to make an even better 4yo. (op 10-3)
Rocky Reef, who bolted up in a weak race at Chepstow last time, confirming his liking for plenty of cut in the ground, was effectively 9lb higher here and put up a perfectly sound effort in defeat. (op 9-2 tchd 11-2)
Dutch Supreme was interesting on his turf debut, but he still looked a little green and, in a race in which the places didn't change much throughout, he was given a bit to do. He should improve with more experience. (op 5-2 tchd 11-4 in places)
North Star Boy(IRE) started the year off a stiff mark and has struggled. The longer trip here didn't prove the answer. (op 16-1)
Ivor's Princess has improved for the fitting of blinkers this year, winning both previous starts, but she was 11lb higher than for her latest win and, with Sean Levey having lost his claim, she was effectively a stone higher. Being held up at the tail of the field in a race dominated from the front didn't help either. (op 11-2 tchd 15-2)
Signor Sassi had his stamina to prove over this longer trip so it didn't help that he completely failed to settle early on. (op 5-1)

3877 CORAL CHARGE (REGISTERED AS THE SPRINT STKS) (GROUP 3) 5f 6y
2:05 (2:05) (Class 1) 3-Y-O+
£31,190 (£11,825; £5,918; £2,948; £1,479; £742) **Stalls** Low

Form RPR

2630 **1** **Caledonia Lady**[18] 3238 3-8-9 102 HayleyTurner 9 105+
(Jo Hughes) *a gng wl: hld up in midfield against rail: prog but trbld run through fr over 1f out: burst through wl ins fnl f to ld post* **10/1**

1550 **2** nse **Confessional**[7] 3623 5-9-3 102 (be) EddieAhern 8 110
(Tim Easterby) *hld up in midfield: shkn up on outer 2f out: gd prog 1f out: r.o to ld last 25yds: hdd post* **25/1**

1312 **3** 1/2 **Free Zone**[21] 3158 3-8-12 104 RoystonFfrench 7 106+
(Bryan Smart) *trckd ldng pair on outer: chal over 1f out: rdn to ld last 150yds: hdd and outpcd fnl 25yds* **16/1**

4325 **4** 1/2 **Spirit Quartz (IRE)**[18] 3238 4-9-3 107 FrankieDettori 2 106
(Robert Cowell) *racd against rail: trckd ldng trio: rdn to chal fnl f: nrly upsides 150yds out: one pce* **7/2**[1]

0-60 **5** hd **Dinkum Diamond (IRE)**[18] 3238 4-9-3 103 DaneO'Neill 12 106
(Henry Candy) *settled in midfield: rdn and in trble 2f out: effrt and nt clr run briefly jst over 1f out: styd on fnl f: nrst fin* **33/1**

1-02 **6** nk **Elnawin**[40] 2559 6-9-3 110 RichardHughes 6 104
(Richard Hannon) *pressed ldr: rdn to ld over 1f out: hdd and no ex last 150yds* **13/2**[3]

6360 **7** 3/4 **Elusivity (IRE)**[14] 3371 4-9-3 106 (b[1]) WilliamBuick 1 102
(Brian Meehan) *hld up: hmpd on inner after 100yds and dropped to last trio: taken to wd outside and effrt wl over 1f out: styd on fnl f: nrst fin* **13/2**[3]

5340 **8** hd **Medicean Man**[14] 3371 6-9-3 109 (p) JimmyQuinn 14 101+
(Jeremy Gask) *nt wl away: hld up in last quartet and swtchd to rail: prog whn nt clr run over 1f out: styng on but no ch whn short of room nr fin* **20/1**

-154 **9** 1/2 **Duchess Dora (IRE)**[14] 3375 5-9-0 100 TomQueally 5 96
(John Quinn) *chsd ldrs: rdn 2f out: nt qckn towards outer over 1f out: fdd ins fnl f* **20/1**

-556 **10** hd **Night Carnation**[18] 3238 4-9-0 103 JimmyFortune 4 95
(Andrew Balding) *trckd ldrs disputing 5th: rdn over 1f out: nt qckn and no prog: fdd ins fnl f* **9/2**[2]

1012 **11** 2 3/4 **Judge 'n Jury**[7] 3650 8-9-3 105 (t) LukeMorris 3 89
(Ronald Harris) *racd against rail: led to over 1f out: sing to lose pl whn rdr dropped whip sn after* **13/2**[3]

5-50 **12** 10 **Triple Aspect (IRE)**[43] 2446 6-9-3 100 NeilCallan 10 53
(Jeremy Gask) *nt that wl away: a in last trio: t.o* **50/1**

-300 **13** 6 **Humidor (IRE)**[135] 681 5-9-3 105 (t) PatCosgrave 11 31
(George Baker) *dwlt and n.m.r s: hmpd after 1f: a bhd: t.o* **25/1**

1m 1.33s (-0.27) **Going Correction** +0.225s/f (Good)
WFA 3 from 4yo+ 5lb **13** Ran SP% **117.5**
Speed ratings (Par 113): **111,110,110,109,109 108,107,107,106,105 101,85,75**
toteswingers 1&2 £50.80, 2&3 £62.00, 1&3 £14.00 CSF £243.01 TOTE £12.30: £3.10, £8.20, £3.80; EX 232.30 TRIFECTA Not won..
Owner Isla & Colin Cage **Bred** Mrs I M Cage And C J Cage **Trained** Lambourn, Berks

FOCUS
Far side rail moved in 3yds on Sprint track. The previous six winners of this sprint had been drawn in one of the bottom three stalls, but with Judge 'N Jury going off at quite a rate, that proved less significant, and those that benefited were those ridden with a bit of patience. This looked below standard for the grade, and it was a messy race too.

NOTEBOOK
Caledonia Lady was behind three of these in the King's Stand, but she was finishing well that day and this track promised to suit. Staying on from mid-pack, she faced a wall of horses a furlong out, and was denied racing room until a gap appeared well inside the last, at which point she quickened up well to edge ahead. She takes her racing well, a bit of cut suits her and she's the sort who could keep progressing and end up in the Abbaye in the autumn. (op 9-1 tchd 11-1)
Confessional, back over his ideal trip, stayed on strongly up the centre of the track and just came up short. He's suited by plenty of cut in the ground and could be the type to pick up a similar race abroad. (tchd 28-1)
Free Zone ◆, who chased home the exciting Pearl Secret here last time, did best of those who raced in the front rank. A progressive 3yo, there should be more to come from him. (tchd 14-1)

Spirit Quartz(IRE) looked to be have the race run to suit as he had a nice sit on the rail in behind the trailblazing leader, but he just couldn't pick up sufficiently when it mattered. (op 9-2)

Dinkum Diamond(IRE) had shown very little in his previous two starts this season but this was more encouraging as he rallied well after getting outpaced.

Elnawin eventually paid for racing up with the strong pace. (op 7-1 tchd 6-1)

Elusivity(IRE), who was blinkered for the first time, was chopped for room more than once early on and got shuffled back. He finished well and shouldn't be judged too harshly on this bare form, although he just doesn't win very often. Official explanation: jockey said gelding suffered interference shortly after start (op 15-2)

Medicean Man got no run in the closing stages and finished without having been asked for everything. Official explanation: jockey said gelding was denied a clear run (op 16-1)

Night Carnation, last year's winner, was disappointing, despite appearing to have the ground to suit. (tchd 5-1)

Judge 'n Jury looked to have his ideal conditions and, given his antics at the Curragh, a right-handed rail to race against looked sure to help, but he just went off too quick and simply set things up the closers. His rider said the gelding ran flat. Official explanation: jockey said gelding ran flat (tchd 6-1 and 7-1)

Humidor(IRE) Official explanation: jockey said gelding suffered interference shortly after start

3878 CORAL CHALLENGE (H'CAP) — 1m 14y

2:40 (2:40) (Class 2) 3-Y-O+

£43,575 (£13,048; £6,524; £3,262; £1,631; £819) **Stalls** Low

Form — RPR

3131 **1** **Trade Commissioner (IRE)**[10] 3508 4-9-6 **98** .... WilliamBuick 1 107+
(John Gosden) *settled in 7th: pushed along and stdy prog fr 2f out: shkn up to ld jst ins fnl f: sn in command: rdn out* **2/1**[1]

0453 **2** ¾ **Vainglory (USA)**[10] 3508 8-8-11 **89** .... MartinLane 9 97
(David Simcock) *hld up in rr: rdn 3f out: no prog tl over 1f out: styd on strly to take 2nd last 75yds and cl on wnr: no real threat* **25/1**

2122 **3** 1½ **Spa's Dancer (IRE)**[7] 3647 5-9-2 **94** .... TomQueally 4 98
(Ed de Giles) *pressed ldng pair: rdn to chse ldr 2f out to 1f out: kpt on same pce* **9/1**[3]

1-30 **4** nse **Con Artist (IRE)**[15] 3329 5-9-10 **102** .... FrankieDettori 15 106+
(Saeed Bin Suroor) *shkn up fr wd draw to show gd spd and chse ldr: led over 2f out: hdd and one pce jst ins fnl f* **11/1**

050 **5** hd **Albaqaa**[17] 3268 7-9-1 **93** .... KieranO'Neill 17 97+
(P J O'Gorman) *s.s: hld up in last trio: gng wl but stl there 2f out: no prog tl fnl f: fin wl* **25/1**

-010 **6** 1½ **Fulbright**[7] 3626 3-8-9 **96** .... LukeMorris 10 96
(Mark Johnston) *chsd ldrs disputing 4th: rdn over 2f out: stl cl up jst over 1f out: fdd* **25/1**

004 **7** hd **Field Of Dream**[17] 3268 5-9-7 **99** .... (v[1]) RyanMoore 2 99
(Jamie Osborne) *hld up towards rr: effrt over 2f out: sme prog over 1f out but nvr gng pce to threaten: one pce fnl f* **12/1**

-410 **8** hd **Captain Bertie (IRE)**[17] 3268 4-9-1 **93** .... MichaelHills 13 92
(Charles Hills) *chsd ldrs in 6th: rdn over 2f out: no prog over 1f out: one pce* **11/2**[2]

-245 **9** ½ **Kyllachy Star**[28] 2910 6-8-12 **90** .... TonyHamilton 8 88
(Richard Fahey) *chsd ldrs disputing 4th: rdn and nt qckn over 2f out: steadily lost pl* **20/1**

-020 **10** 1¾ **Classic Colori (IRE)**[21] 3164 5-8-11 **89** .... RichardHughes 11 83
(David O'Meara) *hld up towards rr: effrt over 2f out: no prog over 1f out: fdd fnl f* **10/1**

3-04 **11** ¾ **Deire Na Sli (IRE)**[36] 2657 4-8-5 **88** .... (b) DarrenEgan[(5)] 7 80
(Martyn Meade) *hld up in midfield: rdn over 2f out: wandering and fnd nil: sn btn* **25/1**

-334 **12** 3¾ **Stage Attraction (IRE)**[21] 3157 4-8-9 **87** .... DavidProbert 14 71
(Andrew Balding) *led at gd pce fr wd draw: hdd over 2f out: wknd over 1f out* **11/1**

3304 **13** 3½ **Switzerland (IRE)**[7] 3630 3-8-7 **94** .... (b[1]) MircoDemuro 12 70
(Mark Johnston) *dwlt: hld up in last trio: styd alone far side briefly ent st but sn jnd rest: no prog* **25/1**

-526 **14** 5 **Directorship**[15] 3331 6-9-0 **92** .... FergusSweeney 6 56
(Patrick Chamings) *t.k.h: hld up in last trio: shkn up and no prog over 2f out: wknd and eased over 1f out: b.b.v* **10/1**

1m 42.22s (-1.08) **Going Correction** +0.10s/f (Good)
WFA 3 from 4yo+ 9lb — **14** Ran SP% **125.3**
Speed ratings (Par 109): **109,108,106,106,106 105,104,104,104,102 101,97,94,89**
toteswingers 1&2 £15.70, 2&3 £32.70, 1&3 £3.80 CSF £70.34 CT £373.40 TOTE £3.10: £1.80, £6.50, £2.60; EX 69.10 Trifecta £297.90 Pool: £3293.36 - 8.18 winning units..
Owner Lady Rothschild **Bred** Kincorth Investments Inc **Trained** Newmarket, Suffolk

■ Stewards' Enquiry : Michael Hills four-day ban: failed to ride out for 6th (Jul 22-25)

FOCUS

A good quality handicap run at a sound gallop, and won by a most progressive sort in Trade Commissioner, who is fast improving into a Group horse. Solid form.

NOTEBOOK

Trade Commissioner(IRE), given a patient ride, defied a 12lb rise for his win at Salisbury ten days earlier, and, despite being by Montjeu, confirmed that he doesn't lack speed, travelling well before putting the race to bed. On this evidence he's going to be running in pattern company sooner rather than later, but he holds an entry in the valuable Betfred Mile at Goodwood, which gives connections another option short-term. (op 5-2)

Vainglory(USA) had a nice pull in the weights and made up five lengths on his deficit to Trade Commissioner at Salisbury, but it wasn't enough to see him reverse the form.

Spa's Dancer(IRE), whose course form now reads 4213413, remains progressive and posted another sound effort having been raised 5lb for his latest Curragh defeat. (op 17-2 tchd 10-1)

Con Artist(IRE), like the third, was up there the whole way, but had to have a bit more use made of him early to get a prominent position from his wide draw. He didn't have a problem with the drop back to a mile. (op 12-1)

Albaqaa, out the back early, didn't get the clearest of runs early in the straight and then hung right under pressure, but he finished well. He won at Newmarket's July meeting and at Glorious Goodwood last summer, and he's one to keep in mind. (op 33-1)

Fulbright didn't get home upped in distance to a mile for the first time. (op 28-1 tchd 33-1)

Field Of Dream, who ran so well in the Hunt Cup, never really got competitive in the first-time visor. (op 11-1)

Captain Bertie(IRE) was expected to appreciate getting back on a softish surface, but he was disappointing (rider received four-day ban for easing up in the closing stages, possibly missing out on sixth place). (op 8-1)

Stage Attraction(IRE) had plenty of use made of him early and curled up with 2f to run. He could be worth a try back over 7f. (op 12-1)

Directorship Official explanation: trainer said gelding bled from the nose

3879 CORAL DISTAFF (LISTED RACE) (FILLIES) — 1m 14y

3:10 (3:10) (Class 1) 3-Y-O

£18,714 (£7,095; £3,550; £1,768; £887; £445) **Stalls** Low

Form — RPR

-100 **1** **Falls Of Lora (IRE)**[17] 3270 3-9-4 102 .... FrankieDettori 6 108
(Mahmood Al Zarooni) *hld up in last pair in strly run contest: stdy prog over 2f out: chsd ldr over 1f out: rdn and narrow ld jst ins fnl f: hld on* **14/1**

5-23 **2** hd **Ladys First**[17] 3270 3-8-12 95 .... PaulHanagan 2 101
(Richard Fahey) *trckd ldng trio: prog to ld wl over 1f out: narrowly hdd jst ins fnl f: fought on wl: jst hld* **5/1**[3]

24-0 **3** shd **Bana Wu**[91] 1215 3-8-12 102 .... DavidProbert 11 101
(Andrew Balding) *stdd s: hld up in last pair: taken wd and prog over 1f out: hrd rdn to chal ins fnl f: nt qckn nr fin* **20/1**

4232 **4** 3¼ **Starscope**[15] 3328 3-8-12 110 .... WilliamBuick 7 94
(John Gosden) *hld up disputing 6th: prog on outer 2f out: cajoled along and nt qckn 2f out: brief effrt again over 1f out: wl hld in 4th fnl f* **1/1**[1]

-000 **5** 2¼ **Fillionaire**[17] 3270 3-8-12 90 .... SamHitchcott 9 88
(Mick Channon) *chsd ldrs in 5th: first one rdn 3f out: responded and on terms 2f out: sn outpcd: n.d fnl f* **50/1**

5302 **6** 7 **Arsaadi (IRE)**[17] 3270 3-8-12 100 .... (b) RichardHughes 10 72
(William Haggas) *racd wd early: sn disp 2nd: chal over 2f out: swept aside over 1f out: wknd* **7/2**[2]

12- **7** 1½ **Kunooz (IRE)**[308] 5698 3-8-12 90 .... MickaelBarzalona 3 69
(Mahmood Al Zarooni) *nt that wl away but sn pushed up to chse ldr: lost pl and wknd 2f out* **14/1**

-246 **8** 4 **Way Too Hot**[17] 3270 3-8-12 93 .... (p) NeilCallan 5 60
(Clive Cox) *plld hrd: hld up disputing 6th: wknd 2f out* **25/1**

30-0 **9** hd **Kinetica**[17] 3270 3-9-1 98 .... (b[1]) LukeMorris 1 62
(Sir Mark Prescott Bt) *racd v freely: led at str pce: hdd & wknd qckly wl over 1f out* **20/1**

1m 43.46s (0.16) **Going Correction** +0.10s/f (Good) — **9** Ran SP% **117.6**
Speed ratings (Par 105): **103,102,102,99,97 90,88,84,84**
toteswingers 1&2 £10.10, 2&3 £12.50, 1&3 £20.50 CSF £79.45 TOTE £14.40: £3.00, £1.70, £4.40; EX 102.20 Trifecta £2136.30 Part won. Pool: £2886.99 - 0.10 winning units..
Owner Godolphin **Bred** Darley **Trained** Newmarket, Suffolk

FOCUS

The leaders seemed to go for home a long way out here and that set things up for those ridden more patiently. The favourite disappointed and this is ordinary fillies' form for the grade. Falls Of Lora is up 4lb on her Dubai best.

NOTEBOOK

Falls Of Lora(IRE), for whom the ground was a question mark, handled it well, and the way the race was run also played to her strengths, as she stays further than this. She's not been the most consistent in her career so far, but is not short of ability when things drop right, and defying a 6lb penalty was no mean feat. She deserves another go in Group company now. (op 16-1)

Ladys First comprehensively reversed Sandringham Handicap form with Arsaadi, who was one of those who had too much use made of her, and posted a solid effort. That said, she came into the race rated 95 and it's questionable whether she's improved more than five or six pounds. (op 13-2)

Bana Wu, a bit disappointing on the Polytrack last time out, ran a better race back on turf on her return from a three-month break. She helps set the level. (op 16-1 tchd 25-1 in a place)

Starscope looked to have been found a good opportunity to go one better than in the 1000 Guineas and Coronation Stakes, especially as she had the ground in her favour, but she laid an egg. She can get worked up beforehand but seemed well enough behaved this time, and although a little keen early on in the race, she was brought to have every chance in the straight and simply didn't go through with her effort. She looks one to oppose in the win market in future. (op 10-11 tchd 11-10 in places)

Fillionaire, out with the washing at Ascot, outran her odds here and could yet do better back on a sound surface.

Arsaadi(IRE), who improved for the fitting of blinkers at Ascot, dropped out after having too much use made of her. (op 11-2)

Kinetica was another who kicked on plenty soon enough and ended up paying the price. (op 16-1)

3880 CORAL-ECLIPSE (BRITISH CHAMPIONS SERIES) (GROUP 1) — 1m 2f 7y

3:45 (3:47) (Class 1) 3-Y-O+

£241,584 (£91,590; £45,837; £22,833; £11,459; £5,751) **Stalls** Low

Form — RPR

115- **1** **Nathaniel (IRE)**[266] 6861 4-9-7 126 .... WilliamBuick 4 127
(John Gosden) *trckd ldr: led over 3f out and committed for home: drvn and hrd pressed over 1f out: nrly jnd ins fnl f: r.o gamely and asserted last 100yds* **7/2**[2]

1-13 **2** ½ **Farhh**[17] 3267 4-9-7 118 .... FrankieDettori 10 126
(Saeed Bin Suroor) *hld up in rr: shkn up and prog on outer fr over 2f out: chsd wnr over 1f out: edgd rt but str chal and nrly upsides ins fnl f: nt qckn last 100yds* **11/4**[1]

0-23 **3** 2¾ **Twice Over**[70] 1677 7-9-7 119 .... TomQueally 7 120
(Sir Henry Cecil) *hld up towards rr: prog over 2f out: rdn and styd on wl to take 3rd fnl f: nvr able to chal* **16/1**

2-10 **4** 5 **Cityscape**[62] 1902 6-9-7 125 .... JamesDoyle 3 110
(Roger Charlton) *trckd ldrs: wnt 2nd wl over 2f out and gng strly: btn off over 1f out: wknd fnl f* **6/1**

10-1 **5** 3¼ **Crackerjack King (IRE)**[55] 2106 4-9-7 118 .... RyanMoore 5 104
(Marco Botti) *trckd ldrs: shkn up and effrt 3f out: cl enough in 3rd 2f out: sn wknd* **11/2**[3]

3-16 **6** 7 **Bonfire**[35] 2705 3-8-10 115 .... JimmyFortune 6 90
(Andrew Balding) *t.k.h: hld up in 6th: dropped to last pair over 4f out: rdn and lost tch over 2f out: bhd after* **13/2**

-165 **7** ½ **Sri Putra**[17] 3267 6-9-7 116 .... NeilCallan 9 89
(Roger Varian) *hld up in last: lft bhd fr 3f out: no ch after* **40/1**

3-41 **8** 14 **Monterosso**[98] 1150 5-9-7 127 .... (t) MickaelBarzalona 8 61
(Mahmood Al Zarooni) *chsd ldrs: pushed along 4f out: wknd over 2f out: t.o* **8/1**

1236 **9** 17 **City Style (USA)**[17] 3267 6-9-7 116 .... AhmedAjtebi 1 27
(Mahmood Al Zarooni) *sn led: hdd over 3f out: wknd and eased: t.o* **33/1**

2m 6.94s (-3.56) **Going Correction** +0.10s/f (Good)
WFA 3 from 4yo+ 11lb — **9** Ran SP% **114.3**
Speed ratings (Par 117): **118,117,115,111,108 103,102,91,78**
toteswingers 1&2 £2.70, 2&3 £8.10, 1&3 £7.00 CSF £13.39 CT £132.16 TOTE £4.80: £1.90, £1.10, £2.70; EX 14.50 Trifecta £144.70 Pool: £8235.16 - 42.10 winning units..
Owner Lady Rothschild & Newsells Park Stud **Bred** Kincorth Investments Inc **Trained** Newmarket, Suffolk

FOCUS

The ground was changed to good to soft all round. The defection and subsequent retirement to stud of So You Think robbed the race of its star attraction, and in his absence it appeared to lack some quality, despite five individual Group 1 winners (one was from Italy and two from Dubai) lining up. The winning time was very good, though, and the form has been rated up to scratch for the race. Nathaniel looks a big player for the top middle-distance races now and Farhh looks well up to winning an ordinary Group 1.

NOTEBOOK

Nathaniel(IRE) hadn't been seen since finishing fifth in last year's Champion Stakes and John Gosden had got his excuses out beforehand, explaining that the colt had had an interrupted preparation and wouldn't be cherry-ripe, but with this being an excellent opportunity to add a 1m2f Group 1 to the CV, and with the King George only a fortnight away, it was hard to imagine that the colt wouldn't be at least very close to his best. Given a prominent ride, once he hit the front in the straight it was always going to take a good one to beat him, as he stays 1m4f really well, and while strongly pressed by Farhh close home, he was always holding him off. Shortened up to a best price 7-2 for the King George, he'll probably need to step up on this to repeat last year's success in that race, as the competition promises to be hotter at Ascot, and it's not like he had an easy race here. Relatively unexposed after only eight starts, his trainer will have to decide whether to give him two hard races now or give him a break with the big autumn prizes in mind. Coral go a best price 10-1 for the Arc and, having missed the race last year, that will surely be his big target this time around. (tchd 9-2)

Farhh, who was unlucky in running in the Prince of Wales's Stakes, was supplemented into the race and had the ground in his favour. The concern beforehand was about how he would handle the start - he'd got upset, reared and lost ground at the start at Ascot, and as a 2yo he was due to take on Frankel in a conditions race at Doncaster but was withdrawn having been unruly in the stalls. He was loaded last and, although slightly agitated, got away on terms this time, and had no real excuse in the race itself, although he did race wider than the winner for much of the way. He needs some dig in the ground, so is likely to go where conditions are suitable. The Irish Champion Stakes could be a suitable race for him later in the season, although connections are considering dropping him back to a mile. (op 5-2 tchd 9-4)

Twice Over, who won this race two years ago, hadn't been at his best earlier this season and, as a 7yo now, his best days are probably behind him, but he put up a good effort in defeat here, staying on for a clear third. He's likely to remain hard to place, though. (op 14-1)

Cityscape, impressive winner of the Dubai Duty Free earlier in the year, was racing over 1m2f for the first time and had his stamina to prove. After travelling as well as anything into contention, he failed the test miserably, dropping right out of contention on the climb to the line. It's probably a case of back to a mile for him now. (op 5-1)

Crackerjack King(IRE)'s only previous defeat came in last year's French Derby when he didn't travel over well and the ground was the softest he'd encountered. Some of his form, including last year's Italian Derby win, where he had subsequent Arc winner Danedream 4 1/2l back in third, read well, but his new trainer had warned that he didn't want the ground to ease any further and perhaps conditions were just too testing for him. He might not be quite up to this standard but he deserves another chance on better ground. (op 7-1 tchd 9-2)

Bonfire was the only representative of the Classic generation in the race. However, while three 3yos had won in the previous ten years, they all came into the race with a Group 1 win under their belts. So far the current crop of 3yos haven't looked up to much (Camelot being the best of an average bunch), and Bonfire, who promised to be much happier back on this more conventional track having failed to handle Epsom, did little to alter that view, albeit he didn't help his cause by taking a keen hold through the early stages of the race and reportedly returned lame on his near hind. (op 8-1 tchd 17-2 in a places)

Sri Putra finished behind Farhh at Ascot and was ultimately outclassed once again. (op 33-1 tchd 50-1)

Monterosso, the Dubai World Cup winner, was expected to need the race, but he was the first under pressure and was being eased with over 2f to run. Presumably the King George was his major target, but it's hard to see him being seriously involved at Ascot on the back of this tame effort. (op 11-1)

3881 CORAL MARATHON (REGISTERED AS THE ESHER STKS) (LISTED RACE) 2m 78y

4:20 (4:20) (Class 1) 4-Y-0+

£18,714 (£7,095; £3,550; £1,768; £887; £445) **Stalls** Centre

Form RPR

-201 **1** **Cavalryman**[42] 2506 6-9-3 113.. FrankieDettori 3 117
(Saeed Bin Suroor) *hld up in 6th: prog fr 3f out to ld over 1f out: sn swept clr: v decisive* **3/1**[1]

6-04 **2** *4 1/2* **Aaim To Prosper (IRE)**[15] 3367 8-9-0 103.......................... NeilCallan 1 109
(Brian Meehan) *trckd ldng pair: drvn and one pce 3f out: kpt on u.p fr over 1f out to win battle for 2nd* **10/1**

20-3 **3** *shd* **Chiberta King**[37] 2639 6-9-0 108..................................(p) JimmyFortune 2 109
(Andrew Balding) *trckd ldng trio: rdn and one pce 3f out: styd on u.p to battle for 2nd ins fnl f* **7/2**[2]

5-65 **4** *nk* **Askar Tau (FR)**[16] 3293 7-9-0 110....................................(v) RyanMoore 9 109
(Marcus Tregoning) *dwlt: humoured in detached last: cajoled along 3f out: prog 2f out: r.o to press for 2nd nr fin* **5/1**[3]

1-13 **5** *nk* **Thimaar (USA)**[66] 1750 4-9-0 105.............................. PaulHanagan 8 108
(John Gosden) *sn led: tried to kick on wl over 3f out but jnd over 2f out: hdd over 1f out and no ch w wnr after: lost pls last 100yds* **7/2**[2]

6524 **6** *2 1/2* **Glen's Diamond**[13] 3418 4-9-0 113................................ TonyHamilton 7 105
(Richard Fahey) *hld up in 5th: rdn and struggling 3f out: n.d after: kpt on fnl f* **8/1**

0155 **7** *3/4* **Electrolyser (IRE)**[50] 2254 7-9-3 109................................ TomQueally 6 107
(Clive Cox) *sn trckd ldr: chal and upsides wl over 2f out tl wnr wnt by over 1f out: wknd fnl f* **12/1**

3m 39.19s (0.49) **Going Correction** +0.10s/f (Good) **7** Ran SP% **114.0**
Speed ratings (Par 111): **102,99,99,99,99 98,97**
toteswingers 1&2 £4.70, 2&3 £5.10, 1&3 £2.70 CSF £32.68 TOTE £3.30: £2.20, £4.50; EX 31.30 Trifecta £126.30 Pool: £3338.55 - 19.56 winning units..
Owner Godolphin **Bred** Darley **Trained** Newmarket, Suffolk

FOCUS

This looked quite an open race but the winner did it easily in the end. This rates his best effort for two years. Not the strongest form for the grade.

NOTEBOOK

Cavalryman, who enjoyed a confidence-boosting win at York last time out, built on that back over 2m, quickening up well from off the pace to put the race to bed with a furlong to run. He has plenty of back-class, and now he's developed into a stayer he has the potential to rise up the ladder in this rather weak division. His trainer suggested he could head to the Goodwood Cup next, or perhaps Deauville. (tchd 11-4)

Aaim To Prosper(IRE), beaten a nose by Chiberta King in this race last year, reversed those placings, but the pair almost ran to the pound again. He will remain vulnerable to something a little less exposed. (op 9-1 tchd 11-1)

Chiberta King couldn't quite confirm last year's form with Aaim To Prosper but basically looks to have run to the same level. (tchd 4-1)

Askar Tau(FR) was detached in last for much of the race but stayed on well up the straight to narrowly miss out on a place. He wants quicker ground ideally. (op 11-2 tchd 6-1)

Thimaar(USA) enjoyed a pretty easy time of it in front but he's another who might ideally have preferred a sounder surface. He can be given another chance. (tchd 4-1 in a place)

Glen's Diamond, up in trip having run a shocker at Pontefract last time out, shaped better, but remains below his best. (op 17-2 tchd 9-1)

Electrolyser(IRE) is at his best when dominating, and with Thimaar bossing it in front he was denied his favoured role. (op 14-1 tchd 16-1)

3882 TEXT CORAL TO 65559 FOR MOBILE BETTING H'CAP 1m 2f 7y

4:55 (4:55) (Class 4) (0-85,85) 3-Y-0 **£6,469** (£1,925; £962; £481) **Stalls** Low

Form RPR

536 **1** **Trend Is My Friend (USA)**[15] 3349 3-8-12 **76**.................. EddieAhern 7 85
(Amanda Perrett) *prom in chsng gp: rdn wl over 2f out: clsd w others over 1f out: drvn ahd ins fnl f* **20/1**

3-11 **2** *1* **Sabhan (IRE)**[38] 2604 3-8-9 **73**... JimCrowley 1 80
(Geoffrey Harker) *hld up in 7th: prog on outer over 2f out: drvn and clsd to ld briefly 150yds out: one pce nr fin* **8/1**

01-3 **3** *nk* **Goodwood Atlantis (IRE)**[44] 2408 3-9-0 **78**.................... TedDurcan 11 85
(John Dunlop) *mostly in 8th: nt gng wl fr 1/2-way: struggling 3f out: sed to run on 2f out: swtchd three times fr over 1f out: styd on wl and nrly snatched 2nd* **13/2**[3]

-043 **4** *1 3/4* **Scrupul (IRE)**[17] 3280 3-8-11 **75**...................................... WilliamBuick 6 78
(Luca Cumani) *led at gd pce: fought off chalr 2f out and looked in command: wknd and hdd last 150yds* **9/1**

2212 **5** *4* **Traveller's Tales**[25] 3013 3-9-4 **82**................................. RichardHughes 4 77
(Richard Hannon) *trckd ldrs: rdn wl over 2f out: clsd w others over 1f out: wknd ins fnl f* **9/1**

01- **6** *1/2* **Dandy (GER)**[289] 6267 3-9-7 **85**..................................... JimmyFortune 12 79
(Andrew Balding) *hld up in last: pushed along and wl off the pce over 2f out: kpt on steadily fr over 1f out: nvr in it* **12/1**

0464 **7** *4 1/2* **Just Fabulous**[14] 3376 3-9-4 **82**....................................... TomQueally 10 67
(George Moore) *trckd ldrs: rdn wl over 2f out: no prog over 1f out: wknd* **8/1**

0-52 **8** *1 1/2* **Oojooba**[22] 3120 3-9-3 **81**.. NeilCallan 8 63
(Roger Varian) *trckd ldr: chal 3f out and clr of rest: btn off 2f out: wknd over 1f out* **11/4**[1]

-213 **9** *21* **Fortieth And Fifth (IRE)**[39] 2589 3-9-2 **80**..................... HayleyTurner 2 20
(Michael Bell) *nt that wl away: rcvrd to go 3rd after 4f: wknd over 2f out: t.o* **10/3**[2]

2m 10.36s (-0.14) **Going Correction** +0.10s/f (Good) **9** Ran SP% **117.8**
Speed ratings (Par 102): **104,103,102,101,98 97,94,93,76**
toteswingers 1&2 £17.00, 2&3 £6.50, 1&3 £17.90 CSF £173.09 CT £1170.73 TOTE £28.10: £5.40, £2.70, £2.20; EX 173.60 Trifecta £803.20 Pool: £2626.89 - 2.42 winning units..
Owner D Gorton **Bred** Brookdale Thoroughbreds LLC **Trained** Pulborough, W Sussex

FOCUS

Some interesting, unexposed horses lined up for this 3yo handicap, and this is decent form for the grade. The winner was a surprise improver, but it seemed no fluke.

Fortieth And Fifth(IRE) Official explanation: trainer's rep had no explanation for the poor form shown

T/Jkpt: Not won. T/Plt: £1,360.70 to a £1 stake. Pool of £223417.30 - 119.86 winning tickets. T/Qpdt: £71.40 to a £1 stake. Pool of £16474.3, - 170.60 winning tickets. JN

3883 - 3885a (Foreign Racing) - See Raceform Interactive

OVREVOLL (R-H)

Saturday, July 7

OFFICIAL GOING: Turf: soft

3886a WALTER NILSENS MINNELOP (GROUP 3) (3YO+) (TURF) 1m 4f

6:40 (12:00) 3-Y-0+ **£64,585** (£21,528; £10,764; £6,458; £4,305)

RPR

1 **Sir Lando**[32] 2807 5-9-6 0.. FJohansson 7 114+
(Wido Neuroth, Norway) *hld up in midfield: tk clsr order on rail 1/2-way to trck ldr gng wl: led under 2f out: shkn up and qcknd clr fnl f: easily* **11/10**[1]

2 *7* **Without Fear (FR)**[32] 2807 4-9-4 0............................... JacobJohansen 9 101
(Arnfinn Lund, Norway) *hld up towards rr: hdwy to trck ldrs over 4f out: 5th and rdn along 2f out: styd on to go 2nd appr fnl f: kpt on but no ch w wnr* **5/2**[2]

3 *1* **Bank Of Burden (USA)**[32] 2807 5-9-6 0............(b) Per-AndersGraberg 5 101
(Niels Petersen, Norway) *settled towards rr: hdwy into midfield 4f out: 3rd and ev ch 2f out: sn rdn: kpt on at one pce fnl f* **56/10**[3]

4 *1 1/2* **Touch Of Hawk (FR)**[32] 2807 6-9-4 0.................................... EspenSki 3 97
(Wido Neuroth, Norway) *chsd ldrs: 4th and ev ch over 2f out: nt qckn u.p: one pce fnl f* **16/1**

5 *1 1/2* **Boxing Day**[32] 2807 5-9-4 0.. ShaneKarlsson 8 95
(Bent Olsen, Denmark) *midfield: chsd ldrs fr 1/2-way: rdn and nt qckn ins fnl 2f* **236/10**

6 *11* **Weald**[265] 6900 7-9-4 0.. DannyPatil 11 77
(Hans-Inge Larsen, Sweden) *hld up: short-lived effrt on ins 2 1/2f out: sn rdn and no imp 1 1/2f out: wknd ins fnl f* **129/10**

7 *nse* **Alnitak (USA)**[335] 4842 11-9-4 0.. RafaelSchistl 10 77
(Bent Olsen, Denmark) *hld up in rr: last 3f out: mod late prog: nvr threatened ldrs* **198/10**

8 *2* **Palermo (GER)**[13] 6-9-4 0.. CarlosLopez 2 74
(Cathrine Erichsen, Norway) *led: rdn and hdd under 2f out: wknd u.p fnl 1 1/2f* **32/1**

9 *1/2* **Dramatic Act**[396] 4-9-4 0.. SaraSlot 4 73
(Arne O Karlsen, Norway) *trckd ldr: lost pl 4f out: sn wl btn* **137/10**

10 *1/2* **Mulan (GER)**[282] 5-9-4 0.. MartinRodriguez 6 72
(Elisabeth Gautier, Sweden) *chsd ldng gp: rdn and wknd over 2f out* **36/1**

2m 37.4s (3.30) **10** Ran SP% **125.8**
PARI-MUTUEL (all including 1krone stakes): WIN 2.10; PLACE 1.21, 1.13, 1.33; DF 4.68.
Owner Stall Perlen **Bred** Stowell Hill Ltd **Trained** Norway

[3374]AYR (L-H)

Sunday, July 8

OFFICIAL GOING: Soft (8.2)

Wind: Breezy, half against Weather: Overcast

3887 SADIE SAWERS MEMORIAL MEDIAN AUCTION MAIDEN STKS 7f 50y

2:00 (2:01) (Class 5) 2-Y-0 **£3,169** (£943; £471; £235) **Stalls** High

Form				RPR
2	1		**Elnadancer (IRE)**[15] 3378 2-9-3 0 ... RobertWinston 4 (Alan Swinbank) *t.k.h early: trckd ldr: led over 2f out: sn rdn along: kpt on strly fnl f: comf* **9/4**[2]	84+
	2	1 ¼	**Simply Shining (IRE)** 2-8-12 0 ... TonyHamilton 6 (Richard Fahey) *stdd s: t.k.h in tch: rdn over 2f out: styd on fnl f to take 2nd towards fin: nt rch wnr* **7/1**[3]	76+
	3	¾	**Burning Blaze** 2-9-3 0 ... PhillipMakin 5 (Kevin Ryan) *t.k.h: trckd ldrs on outside: rdn to chal over 1f out: kpt on same pce ins fnl f: lost 2nd towards fin* **10/11**[1]	79+
	4	3	**Hunting Rights (USA)** 2-9-3 0 ... JoeFanning 3 (Mark Johnston) *led at stdy gallop: rdn and hdd over 2f out: outpcd fnl f* **12/1**	72
	5	7	**Zadig (USA)** 2-8-12 0 ... GrahamGibbons 1 (Garry Woodward) *trckd ldrs tl rdn and wknd over 2f out* **16/1**	49

1m 37.59s (4.19) **Going Correction** +0.30s/f (Good) **5** Ran SP% **109.2**

Speed ratings (Par 94): **88,86,85,82,74**

toteswingers: 1&2 £6.70 CSF £16.70 TOTE £2.70: £1.10, £2.60; EX 12.50.

Owner S S Anderson **Bred** Freedom Partnership **Trained** Melsonby, N Yorks

FOCUS

Home bend dolled out 4m from inner line, straights moved out 2m from inner line adding 12yds to 7f &1m races and 17yds to 1m 5f race. Probably a decent little maiden and worth rating positively, despite the slow time.

NOTEBOOK

Elnadancer(IRE) had run well on his debut and set a good standard for the newcomers to match with that experience under his belt. He won well in the end, seeing off the strong challenge of the well-fancied favourite, and looks the type that might win a decent 7f or 1m nursery in the coming weeks. (op 13-8)

Simply Shining(IRE) shaped with encouragement and was really warming to her task at the finish. She'll come on for this and will get a mile in time. (op 6-1)

Burning Blaze ◆, who cost 75,000gns earlier this year, travelled best of all, but when push came to shove the more experienced winner saw him off. He showed more than enough to suggest he has a future. (op 6-4)

Hunting Rights(USA), who is out of a half-sister to US 1m Grade 1 winner Mr Sydney, weakened after making much of the running. His stable is struggling for winners at the moment but he showed enough to suggest he'll be all right in time. (op 10-1)

Zadig(USA), who was ponied to the start, is a sister to US stakes-placed winners Rio Tricky and Got Tobe Rio. This was probably a tough maiden in which to make her debut and she will face easier opportunities down the road. (op 22-1 tchd 25-1)

3888 BET ON BRITISH GP AT TOTEPOOL.COM H'CAP 7f 50y

2:30 (2:30) (Class 5) (0-70,65) 3-Y-0+ **£2,522** (£750; £375; £187) **Stalls** High

Form				RPR
-22U	1		**Goninodaethat**[9] 3581 4-9-3 54 ... GrahamLee 6 (Jim Goldie) *chsd ldrs: wnt 2nd after 3f: rdn to ld over 1f out: styd on wl* **3/1**[2]	62
0604	2	1 ¼	**Sabratha (IRE)**[9] 3581 4-9-12 63 ... PhillipMakin 9 (Linda Perratt) *dwlt: hld up: hdwy wl over 1f out: styd on to take 2nd nr fin: nt rch wnr* **15/2**	68
-415	3	shd	**Emeralds Spirit (IRE)**[11] 3495 5-10-0 65 ... PaulMulrennan 4 (John Weymes) *led: rdn and hdd over 1f out: kpt on same pce fnl f: lost 2nd nr fin* **5/2**[1]	69
020-	4	hd	**Let's Face Facts**[256] 7099 5-8-11 53 ... NeilFarley(5) 3 (Jim Goldie) *in tch: drvn and outpcd wl over 2f out: rallied on outside over 1f out: kpt on fnl f* **25/1**	57
0-40	5	1	**Monthly Medal**[17] 3310 9-9-6 57 ...(t) JamesSullivan 8 (Wilf Storey) *hld up: rdn and hdwy over 1f out: kpt on fnl f: no ex towards fin* **11/1**	58
0640	6	3 ¼	**Master Of Dance (IRE)**[16] 3335 5-10-0 65 ...(p) JoeFanning 7 (Keith Dalgleish) *chsd ldrs: effrt and drvn over 2f out: wknd ent fnl f* **5/1**[3]	57
4024	7	1 ½	**Spread Boy (IRE)**[5] 3731 5-9-0 51 ... TomEaves 2 (Alan Berry) *cl up tl rdn and wknd wl over 1f out* **12/1**	39
40-0	8	1 ¾	**Berbice (IRE)**[23] 3115 7-9-8 62 ... JulieBurke(3) 1 (Linda Perratt) *s.s: hld up: stdy hdwy against far rail whn n.m.r 2f out: sn rdn and outpcd* **22/1**	46
-540	9	12	**Rutterkin (USA)**[20] 3210 4-8-12 56 ... MatthewHopkins(7) 10 (Alan Berry) *hld up in tch on outside: struggling over 2f out: sn btn* **33/1**	
505/	10	11	**Jebel Tara**[910] 114 7-9-4 55 ... LeeNewman 5 (Ian Semple) *anticipated s and missed break: towards rr: struggling wl over 2f out: sn btn* **25/1**	

1m 34.95s (1.55) **Going Correction** +0.30s/f (Good) **10** Ran SP% **113.0**

Speed ratings (Par 103): **103,101,101,101,100 96,94,92,78,66**

toteswingers: 1&2 £5.20, 1&3 £2.60, 2&3 £4.50 CSF £23.37 CT £64.12 TOTE £3.70: £1.60, £1.90, £1.50; EX 12.90 Trifecta £102.80 Pool: £412.93 - 2.97 winning units..

Owner Jim Goldie Racing Club **Bred** W G H Barrons **Trained** Uplawmoor, E Renfrews

FOCUS

Modest handicap form.

Jebel Tara Official explanation: jockey said gelding anticipated the start and missed the break

3889 BET ON WIMBLEDON FINAL AT TOTEPOOL.COM H'CAP 1m

3:00 (3:00) (Class 6) (0-60,58) 4-Y-0+ **£1,908** (£563; £281) **Stalls** Low

Form				RPR
02	1		**Tazaamun (IRE)**[16] 3332 4-9-5 56 ... PaulMulrennan 12 (David O'Meara) *prom: smooth hdwy over 2f out: led and rdn 1f out: hung lft ins fnl f: hld on towards fin* **11/4**[1]	64
0036	2	hd	**Mangham (IRE)**[11] 3492 7-8-12 54 ...(p) NeilFarley(5) 2 (George Foster) *s.i.s: hld up: hdwy on ins over 2f out: effrt over 1f out: chsd wnr wl ins fnl f: r.o: jst hld* **8/1**	61
4234	3	1 ¼	**Kyllachykov (IRE)**[25] 3051 4-8-11 48 ... RobertWinston 5 (Robin Bastiman) *hld up on outside: rdn and hdwy over 2f out: edgd lft ins fnl f: hld towards fin* **10/3**[2]	52
460-	4	½	**Spin A Wish**[236] 7424 4-8-8 45 ... AmyRyan 13 (Richard Whitaker) *led: rdn over 2f out: hdd 1f out: one pce whn hmpd wl ins fnl f* **25/1**	50
0006	5	¾	**Goldenveil (IRE)**[14] 3416 4-9-1 57 ...(b) ShaneBKelly(5) 11 (Richard Fahey) *dwlt: t.k.h in rr: n.m.r over 2f out: effrt and edgd lft wl over 1f out: r.o fnl f: nrst fin* **5/1**[3]	58
00-6	6	nse	**Catcher Of Dreams (IRE)**[101] 884 6-8-1 45 ....(p) MatthewHopkins(7) 9 (George Foster) *cl up: rdn 2f out: one pce whn hmpd ins fnl f* **100/1**	48
0054	7	2 ¼	**Glenluji**[16] 3332 7-9-3 54 ... GrahamLee 4 (Jim Goldie) *prom: drvn over 2f out: no ex fr over 1f out* **10/1**	50
00-2	8	1 ¼	**Petrocelli**[17] 3309 5-9-3 54 ... JamesSullivan 1 (Wilf Storey) *hld up in midfield: nt clr run 3f out: effrt 2f out: sn outpcd* **6/1**	47
-500	9	hd	**Henrys Gift (IRE)**[25] 3032 4-8-10 47 ...(p) TomEaves 3 (Michael Dods) *plld hrd in midfield: struggling over 2f out: n.d after* **20/1**	40
-050	10	11	**Face East (USA)**[16] 3333 4-8-8 45 ... TonyHamilton 6 (Alan Berry) *dwlt: bhd: struggling over 2f out: sn btn* **100/1**	12
-400	11	2	**Shunkawakhan (IRE)**[16] 3332 9-8-8 45 ...(tp) PJMcDonald 14 (Linda Perratt) *cl up: lost pl over 2f out: sn struggling* **33/1**	
6000	12	23	**Tinzo (IRE)**[33] 2796 4-8-5 45 ... JulieBurke(3) 7 (Alan Berry) *s.s: bhd: struggling 3f out: sn btn: t.o* **100/1**	

1m 46.69s (2.89) **Going Correction** +0.30s/f (Good) **12** Ran SP% **115.4**

Speed ratings (Par 101): **97,96,95,95,94 94,92,90,90,79 77,54**

toteswingers: 1&2 £5.70, 1&3 £2.90, 2&3 £7.40 CSF £23.33 CT £75.48 TOTE £4.10: £1.20, £3.40, £1.10; EX 27.70 Trifecta £96.70 Pool: £1,077.78 - 8.24 winning units..

Owner Patterns And Profiles 1 **Bred** Darley **Trained** Nawton, N Yorks

FOCUS

There was a decent pace on here thanks to a contested lead.

Tinzo(IRE) Official explanation: jockey said gelding missed the break

3890 YOUR FAVOURITE POOL BETS AT TOTEPOOL.COM H'CAP 1m

3:30 (3:30) (Class 4) (0-85,85) 3-Y-0+ **£5,175** (£1,540; £769; £384) **Stalls** Low

Form				RPR
2303	1		**Silvery Moon (IRE)**[11] 3493 5-9-12 83 ... DavidAllan 4 (Tim Easterby) *plld hrd: prom: rdn to ld over 2f out: edgd lft over 1f out: hld on wl fnl f* **2/1**[1]	92
12	2	1 ¼	**Prophesy (IRE)**[15] 3383 3-8-9 80 ... NeilFarley(5) 8 (Declan Carroll) *trckd ldrs on outside: rdn and ev ch over 2f out: kpt on fnl f: nt rch wnr* **4/1**[2]	84
360-	3	hd	**Star Surprise**[127] 793 4-10-0 85 ... HayleyTurner 2 (Michael Bell) *led to over 2f out: sn rdn and rallied: kpt on same pce fnl f* **6/1**	91
1301	4	¾	**Le Chat D'Or**[29] 2922 4-9-1 72 ...(t) TomEaves 1 (Michael Dods) *t.k.h: prom: rdn and outpcd wl over 1f out: kpt on ins fnl f* **9/2**[3]	76
6054	5	shd	**Silver Rime (FR)**[11] 3492 7-9-2 73 ... PhillipMakin 9 (Linda Perratt) *hld up: rdn and hdwy on outside wl over 1f out: kpt on fnl f: no imp* **16/1**	77
0662	6	shd	**Blues Jazz**[16] 3334 6-9-3 79 ... GarryWhillans(5) 7 (Ian Semple) *hld up in tch: rdn over 2f out: effrt over 1f out: nvr able to chal* **12/1**	82
0065	7	2 ¼	**Chiswick Bey (IRE)**[15] 3385 4-9-6 82 ...(b[1]) ShaneBKelly(5) 3 (Richard Fahey) *t.k.h: hld up: rdn and edgd rt over 2f out: no imp fr over 1f out* **20/1**	80
-010	8	2 ½	**Northern Fling**[39] 2597 8-9-2 73 ... GrahamLee 6 (Jim Goldie) *hld up: effrt over 2f out: btn appr fnl f* **18/1**	66
1-00	9	14	**Master Of Ages (IRE)**[36] 2714 3-8-9 75 ... JoeFanning 5 (Mark Johnston) *w ldr tl rdn and wknd over 2f out* **20/1**	33

1m 45.12s (1.32) **Going Correction** +0.30s/f (Good)

WFA 3 from 4yo+ 9lb **9** Ran SP% **114.2**

Speed ratings (Par 105): **105,103,103,102,102 102,100,97,83**

toteswingers: 1&2 £2.90, 1&3 £3.60, 2&3 £5.40 CSF £9.67 CT £38.88 TOTE £3.90: £1.50, £1.60, £2.60; EX 11.30 Trifecta £53.50 Pool: £873.08 - 12.06 winning units..

Owner R J Swinbourne **Bred** Colin Kennedy **Trained** Great Habton, N Yorks

FOCUS

A fair handicap and the form looks solid enough.

3891 TOTEPOOL.COM SPORTS, GAMES, BINGO & MORE H'CAP 1m 5f 13y

4:00 (4:08) (Class 5) (0-70,68) 3-Y-0+ **£2,911** (£866; £432; £216) **Stalls** Low

Form				RPR
3-03	1		**The Oil Magnate**[21] 3180 7-10-0 68 ... TomEaves 5 (Michael Dods) *t.k.h: hld up in tch: smooth hdwy over 2f out: led and pricked ears wl over 1f out: sn clr: eased nr fin* **2/1**[1]	80+
3534	2	3	**Pandorica**[22] 3143 4-9-5 59 ...(p) RobertWinston 4 (Bernard Llewellyn) *cl up: rdn and led over 2f out: hdd wl over 1f out: edgd lft: kpt on: no ch w wnr* **15/2**	64
4303	3	1 ¼	**Bavarian Nordic (USA)**[13] 3440 7-9-3 57 ...(v) AmyRyan 8 (Richard Whitaker) *hld up: rdn and outpcd over 2f out: rallied over 1f out: kpt on: nvr able to chal* **4/1**[2]	60
246-	4	3 ½	**A Southside Boy (GER)**[316] 5489 4-8-9 49 oh4 ... GrahamLee 3 (Jim Goldie) *t.k.h: prom: rdn and outpcd over 2f out: plugged on fnl f: n.d* **28/1**	47
3034	5	1 ½	**Za'Lan (USA)**[5] 3729 3-8-9 63 ... PhillipMakin 2 (Mark Johnston) *led: rdn and hdd over 2f out: no ex over 1f out* **13/2**[3]	59
U360	6	7	**Law To Himself (IRE)**[18] 3287 5-10-0 68 ... PJMcDonald 7 (Alan Swinbank) *hld up: rdn along and outpcd wl over 2f out: sn btn* **4/1**[2]	53
1310	7	3	**Quiet Appeal (IRE)**[9] 3592 3-8-9 63 ... JoeFanning 1 (Mark Johnston) *t.k.h: trckd ldrs tl rdn and wknd over 2f out* **7/1**	44

3m 3.41s (9.41) **Going Correction** +0.30s/f (Good)

WFA 3 from 4yo+ 14lb **7** Ran SP% **114.4**

Speed ratings (Par 103): **83,81,80,78,77 73,71**

toteswingers: 1&2 £4.00, 1&3 £2.00, 2&3 £5.30 CSF £17.90 CT £54.71 TOTE £2.90: £1.90, £4.00; EX 10.70 Trifecta £34.40 Pool: £757.83 - 16.26 winning units..

Owner Smith & Allan Racing **Bred** Wheelersland Stud **Trained** Denton, Co Durham

FOCUS

This proved a simple task for The Oil Magnate, as he cruised up going much better than anything else and quickened clear when the button was pressed.

3892 LILIAN FLYNN "ALL THE BEST" MEMORIAL H'CAP 6f

4:30 (4:31) (Class 6) (0-60,60) 3-Y-0 **£1,908** (£563; £281) **Stalls** Centre

Form				RPR
4240	1		**Balti's Sister (IRE)**[12] 3462 3-9-2 55 ... PaulMulrennan 1 (Michael Easterby) *w ldr: led over 2f out: sn rdn: styd on wl fnl f* **11/4**[1]	64
6054	2	2 ¾	**Script**[5] 3726 3-8-0 46 oh1 ... MatthewHopkins(7) 7 (Alan Berry) *in tch: effrt over 2f out: edgd lft ins fnl f: styd on to take 2nd towards fin: no ch w wnr* **22/1**	46
00-6	3	½	**Simpson Millar**[9] 3566 3-8-6 50 ... NeilFarley(5) 4 (Noel Wilson) *hung lft thrght: prom: sn drvn along: rallied 2f out: kpt on ins fnl f* **20/1**	48

The Form Book Flat, Raceform Ltd, Compton, RG20 6NL

6304 **4** *shd* **Dartrix**[15] 3407 3 -9-4**57**.. TomEaves 6 55
(Michael Dods) *cl up: effrt and ev ch over 2f out: sn rdn: no ex and lost two pls towards fin* **4/1**[3]
3-06 **5** *3 1/4* **Dylan's Dream (IRE)**[20] 3210 3 -8-11**50**.............................. DavidAllan 3 38
(Tim Easterby) *led to over 2f out: rdn and wknd over 1f out* **12/1**
060 **6** *3 3/4* **New Lease Of Life**[13] 3438 3 -9-6**59**.................................. GrahamLee 8 35
(Jim Goldie) *hld up: outpcd 1/2-way: n.d after* **6/1**
6535 **7** *nse* **Gran Canaria Queen**[13] 3450 3 -8-11**50**....................(v) BarryMcHugh 2 26
(Ian Semple) *stdd s: t.k.h in rr: rdn over 2f out: sn btn* **13/2**
0-06 **8** *16* **Rock Of Monet**[25] 3050 3 -9-7**60**.............................(v) HayleyTurner 5
(Michael Bell) *prom tl rdn and wknd fr 2f out: t.o* **7/2**[2]

1m 14.6s (2.20)**Going Correction** +0.30s/f (Good) **8**Ran SP% **113.3**
Speed ratings (Par 98): **97,93,92,92,88 83,83,61**
toteswingers: 1&2 £7.90, 1&3 £8.40, 2&3 £12.60 CSF £61.96 CT £1009.24 TOTE £3.60 : £1.30 , £6.10, £5.30 ; EX 66.80 Trifecta £535.10 Part won. Pool: £723.11 - 0.40 winning units.
Owner Steve Hull & David Swales **Bred** P Monaghan, J Collins & G Dillon **Trained** Sheriff Hutton, N Yorks

FOCUS
They came up the middle of the track in this moderate sprint handicap.
Rock Of Monet Official explanation: trainer's rep had no explanation for the poor form shown

3893 DEAL OR NO DEAL AT TOTEPOOL.COM AMATEUR RIDERS' H'CAP 5f
5:00 (5:00) (Class 6) (0-60,60) 4-Y-0+ **£1,844** (£567; £283)**Stalls** Centre

Form RPR
0460 **1** **Ryedane (IRE)**[19] 3257 10 -10-6**57**..........................(b) MrWEasterby(5) 4 65
(Tim Easterby) *prom: rdn over 1f out: led ins fnl f: edgd lft: kpt on wl towards fin* **13/2**[3]
0020 **2** *3/4* **Missile Attack (IRE)**[9] 3578 4 -10-1**52**......................(p) MrJHamilton(5) 3 57
(Ian Semple) *led: rdn and edgd lft over 1f out: hdd ins fnl f: r.o* **20/1**
2023 **3** *nk* **Distant Sun (USA)**[7] 3730 8 -10-11**57**...............(p) MrsAdeleMulrennan 5 61
(Linda Perratt) *trckd ldrs: rdn over 1f out: kpt on ins fnl f* **9/1**
-250 **4** *hd* **Foreign Rhythm (IRE)**[41] 2538 7 -10-9**60**....................... MissVBarr(5) 1 63
(Ron Barr) *dwlt: sn in tch: hdwy to chal over 1f out to ent fnl f: edgd rt: one pce fnl 100yds* **15/2**
5003 **5** *nse* **Blue Noodles**[12] 3463 6 -9-8**47**......................................(p) MrAFrench(7) 7 50
(John Wainwright) *in tch: outpcd over 2f out: rallied fnl f: r.o* **7/1**
60-3 **6** *1/2* **Toffee Nose**[16] 3357 5 -10-1**47**................................. MissSBrotherton 12 48
(Ron Barr) *pressed ldr: pushed along 2f out: kpt on ins fnl f* **5/1**[2]
4556 **7** *3/4* **Two Turtle Doves (IRE)**[13] 3435 6 -10-7**56**......... MissMMullineaux(3) 9 55
(Michael Mullineaux) *hld up: pushed along over 2f out: kpt on fnl f: nvr able to chal* **9/2**[1]
5536 **8** *1 1/4* **Amno Dancer (IRE)**[31] 2839 5 -9-11**48**.......................(b) MrNSlatter(5) 8 42
(Ian Semple) *t.k.h: hld up in tch: pushed along 2f out: no imp fnl f* **16/1**
055 **9** *1 1/2* **Glenlini**[13] 3442 6 -10-0**53**.. MrsICGoldie(7) 2 42
(Jim Goldie) *hld up: effrt and edgd lft 2f out: wknd fnl f* **5/1**[2]
6006 **10** *1 1/2* **Andrasta**[10] 3523 7 -9-9**46** oh1...................................... MissHDukes(5) 11 29
(Alan Berry) *hld up: pushed along over 2f out: n.d after* **28/1**

1m 2.44s (3.04)**Going Correction** +0.30s/f (Good) **10**Ran SP% **113.2**
Speed ratings (Par 101): **87,85,85,85,84 84,82,80,78,76**
toteswingers: 1&2 £20.30, 1&3 £12.20, 2&3 £18.90 CSF £122.48 CT £1161.62 TOTE £7.80 : £2.20, £5.10 , £2.40 ; EX 161.80 Trifecta £294.30 Pool: £632.35 - 1.59 winning units.
Owner Habton Farms **Bred** Tally-Ho Stud **Trained** Great Habton, N Yorks

FOCUS
Not strong form.
T/Jkpt: £909.00 to a £1 stake. Pool: £17,304.96. 27.50 winning tickets. T/Plt: £28.80 to a £1 stake. Pool: £94,051.08. 2,381.98 winning tickets. T/Qpdt: £9.70 to a £1 stake. Pool: £7,000.93. 529.20 winning tickets.RY

3894a-3899a (Foreign Racing) See Raceform Interactive

3366 MAISONS-LAFFITTE (R-H)
Sunday, July 8

OFFICIAL GOING: Turf: good to soft

3900a PRIX MESSIDOR (GROUP 3) (3YO+) (TURF) 1m (S)
1:30 (12:00) 3-Y-0+ **£33,333** (£13,333; £10,000 ; £6,666 ; £3,333)

RPR
1 **Tin Horse (IRE)**[42] 2533 4 -9-10....................................... ThierryJarnet 3 117
(D Guillemin, France) *racd 4th: relegated to last on rail bhd Moonwalk In Paris over 2 1/2f out: shkn up and swtchd away fr rail 2f out: qckndwl to chal 1 1/2f out: tk ld 1f out: r.o wl whn reminders ins fnl f: wnt clr 50yds out* **15/8**[1]
2 *2* **Prince D'Alienor (IRE)**[42] 4 -9-10............................(p) GregoryBenoist 7 112
(X Nakkachdji, France) *hld up at rr: swtchd to wd outside 2 1/2f out: qcknd wl to ld 1 1/2f out: hdd 1f out: r.o: clr 2nd* **8/1**
3 *2 1/2* **Moonwalk In Paris (FR)**[31] 3205 4 -9-5**0**........... ChristopheSoumillon 6 110
(J-C Rouget, France) *hld up towards rr: swtchd to stands' rail 2f out: r.o wl: ev ch over 1f out: fnd no ex u.p fnl 150yds: styd on one pce* **9/4**[2]
4 *2* **Stand My Ground (IRE)**[38] 1745 5 -9-10.. Christophe-PatriceLemaire 2 102
(Mme Pia Brandt, France) *led fr s: set gd pce: hdd 1 1/2f out: rdn but fnd no ex: styd on one pce* **16/1**
5 *2 1/2* **Vagabond Shoes (IRE)**[31] 3205 5 -9-5**0**......................... OlivierPeslier 5 100
(Y Durepaire, Spain) *cl up on outside fr s: rdn 2f out: no ex: styd on one pce fnl 1 1/2f* **9/2**[3]
6 *10* **Pisco Sour (USA)**[120] 879 4 -9-10.......................... MickaelBarzalona 4 73
(Saeed Bin Suroor) *racd cl up between ldrs fr s: rdn 3f out: no ex: grad wknd* **6/1**

1m 35.45s (-6.85)
WFA 3 from 4yo+ 9lb **6**Ran SP% **115.0**
WIN (incl. 1 euro stake): 3.70. PLACES: 1.90, 2.50. SF: 22.50 .
Owner Marquesa De Moratalla **Bred** Marquesa De Moratalla **Trained** France

NOTEBOOK
Tin Horse (IRE)gained his first win since last term's French Guineas. The grey son of Sakhee was delivered perfectly at the furlong pole by Thierry Jarnet, who is enjoying a vintage spell in the saddle. He doesn't like testing ground, but got away with these conditions. The Jacques Le Marois at Deauville may be next.
Prince D'Alienor (IRE)briefly looked a big danger and, although no match for the winner, was clear second best having progressed from giving weight away in a conditions race at Lyon Parilly last time.
Pisco Sour (USA) having his first run since the Dubai Carnival, produced a tame effort.

3901a PRIX DE RIS-ORANGIS (GROUP 3) (3YO+) (TURF) 6f (S)
2:40 (12:00) 3-Y-0+ **£33,333** (£13,333; £10,000 ; £6,666 ; £3,333)

RPR
1 **Lockwood**[54] 3 -8-8**0**.. Pierre-CharlesBoudot 9 110
(A Fabre, France) *hld towards rr of field on outside: qcknd wl 1 1/2f out: chal for ld 150yds fr home: r.o strly u.p to ld 50yds out: comf* **11/2**[3]
2 *3/4* **Gammarth (FR)**[36] 2728 4 -9-0**0**.......................... ChristopheSoumillon 4 109
(H-A Pantall, France) *racd towards rr tl 1/2-way: clsd on ldrs 1 1/2f out whn swtchd towards stands' rail: qcknd to ld u.p 150yds out: chal and hdd 50yds out: r.o* **12/1**
3 *1 1/4* **Marchand D'Or (FR)**[250] 7221 9 -9-4**0**............................... DavyBonilla 7 109
(M Delzangles, France) *hld up in rr: swtchd to outside over 1f out: r.o wl fnl f: nt rch ldrs: tk 3rd cl home* **6/1**
4 *hd* **Boomerang Bob (IRE)**[8] 3265 3 -8-8**0**........................... SebSanders 2 103
(J W Hills) *prom fr s: rdn and r.o wl ent fnl f: ev ch 100yds out: no ex fnl 50yds: lost 3rd cl home* **5/1**[2]
5 *1 3/4* **Noble Hachy**[35] 2745 3 -8-9**0**....................................... CristianDemuro 1 99
(L Riccardi, Italy) *amongst ldrs fr s: r.o wl to ld 1 1/2f out: hdd 150yds out: no ex fnl 100yds* **5/1**[2]
6 *hd* **Chopouest (FR)**[13] 5 -9-0**0**.. FredericSpanu 6 98
(T Castanheira, France) *sn prom: tk ld after 1f: u.p and hdd 1 1/2f out: no ex ins fnl f* **14/1**
7 *3/4* **Fred Lalloupet**[36] 2728 5 -9-0**0**....................................... GregoryBenoist 8 96
(D Smaga, France) *prom on outside fr s: rdn but no rspnse fr 1 1/2f out: nt hrd rdn fnl 150yds* **4/1**[1]
8 *hd* **Rosendhal (IRE)**[16] 3366 5 -9-0**0**........................(b) StephanePasquier 3 95
(G Botti, Italy) *racd front rnk on stands' rail: rdn 2f out: no ex: styd on one pce fnl f* **11/2**[3]
9 *6* **Nordic Truce (USA)**[36] 2728 5 -9-0**0**.............................. UmbertoRispoli 5 76
(P Schiergen, Germany) *racd midfield: u.p over 2 1/2f out: fnd no ex: wknd* **10/1**

1m 11.21s (-2.19)
WFA 3 from 4yo+ 6lb **9**Ran SP% **121.8**
WIN (incl. 1 euro stake): 5.70. PLACES: 2.40, 2.70, 3.20. DF: 24.00. SF: 51.20 .
Owner Godolphin SNC **Bred** Darley Stud Manaagement Company Ltd **Trained** Chantilly, France

NOTEBOOK
Lockwood was making only his fifth career start and was dropping back to sprint distances for the first time. He benefited from racing off the pace and quickened up well.
Gammarth(FR) justified the supplementary fee paid to enter him.
Marchand D'Or (FR)made a satisfactory reappearance.
Boomerang Bob (IRE)was right in the four-horse firing line a furlong from home and was only denied third by a head. The Phoenix Stakes in Ireland in August could suit him.

3887 AYR (L-H)
Monday, July 9

OFFICIAL GOING: Soft (heavy in places; 8.2)
Wind: Light, across Weather: Overcast

3902 IRISH STALLION FARMS E B F MAIDEN STKS 5f
2:00 (2:01) (Class 5) 2-Y-0 **£3,234** (£962; £481 ; £240) **Stalls** High

Form RPR
2 **1** **Megamunch (IRE)**[10] 3576 2 -9-3**0**..................................... TomEaves 3 73
(Linda Stubbs) *cl up: rdn along 2f out: rallied to ld wl ins fnl f: kpt on wl* **5/4**[1]
3332 **2** *3/4* **Opt Out**[9] 3627 2 -9-3**70**.. JoeFanning 5 70
(Mark Johnston) *led: rdn over 1f out: hdd and no ex wl ins fnl f* **11/8**[2]
3 *3 1/4* **Municipal (IRE)** 2 -9-3**0**.. PaulMulrennan 2 59
(Michael Dods) *cl up: pushed along and outpcd wl over 1f out: kpt on ins fnl f: nt rch first two* **11/2**[3]
4 *13* **Princess Cayan (IRE)**2 -8-12**0**....................................... PhillipMakin 4 7
(Linda Perratt) *s.s: a wl bhd* **25/1**

1m 4.47s (5.07)**Going Correction** +0.65s/f (Yiel) **4**Ran SP% **105.8**
Speed ratings (Par 94): **85,83,78,57**
CSF £3.13 TOTE £2.40 ; EX 2.70 .
Owner P & L Partners **Bred** Ardrums House Stud **Trained** Norton, N Yorks

FOCUS
Home bend out 4m from inner line and straight out 2m from inner line. 12yds added to races between 7f and 10f and 18yds to others race on Round course. Following 8mm of rain since the previous day's meeting, the ground had eased to soft, heavy in places. This was an uncompetitive four-runner maiden. The winner did not need to improve.

NOTEBOOK
Megamunch(IRE) showed plenty of ability and pulled a long way clear of the rest when second of six in a soft-ground Musselburgh maiden on his debut ten days earlier. He came off the bridle well over a furlong from home here and looked held, but he stuck at it and wore down the leader near the line. On this evidence another furlong wouldn't be a problem. (op 11-10)
Opt Out had been run down late after trying to make all in his last three starts and tried the same tactics here with the stands' rail to help, but again after looking likely to win he was collared close to the line. It would be interesting to see if he could last home on a faster surface over a sharp 5f and nurseries remain a possibility, but he remains vulnerable to an improver. (op 6-4)
Municipal(IRE) is a 48,000gns half-brother to three winners at up to 1m4f (two of them in Pattern company), but his dam is a half-sister to Pipalong so there is speed in his pedigree. He had a problem keeping up with his two more experienced rivals at around halfway, but wasn't losing any more ground on them inside the last furlong and was by no means knocked about. Plenty of improvement can be expected. (op 6-1 tchd 13-2)
Princess Cayan (IRE) an 11,500euros half-sister to three winners at up to 1m1f, walked out of the stalls and found it all too much. (op 22-1)

3903 ISLE OF SKYE 8YO BLENDED WHISKY H'CAP 5f
2:30 (2:31) (Class 3) (0-95,91) 3-Y-0+ **£6,663** (£1,982; £743 ; £743) **Stalls** High

Form RPR
0100 **1** **Mayoman (IRE)**[24] 3127 7 -9-7**86**...................................(v) DavidNolan 8 94
(David O'Meara) *trckd ldrs: rdn to ld appr fnl f: jnd whn lft jst in front cl home: all out* **14/1**
0624 **2** *hd* **Haajes**[9] 3612 8 -8-6**78** ow1... NedCurtis(7) 4 85
(Paul Midgley) *in tch: drvn and outpcd 1/2-way: gd hdwy fnl f: keeping on strly whn lft 2nd cl home: jst hld* **4/1**[3]
3131 **3** *nk* **Head Space (IRE)**[7] 3336 4 -9-12**91**........................... JamesSullivan 9 100+
(Ruth Carr) *hld up: rdn and hdwy over 1f out: chal and looked likely wnr whn shied bdly, stmbld and nrly uns rdr appr winning line: nt rcvr* **3/1**[2]

0225 **3** *dht* **Crimson Knot (IRE)**[11] 3524 4-8-12 **77** .... TomEaves 3 83
(Alan Berry) *chsd ldrs: n.m.r and outpcd wl over 1f out: rallied ins fnl f: kpt on fin* **20/1**

2450 **5** *3/4* **Foxy Music**[24] 3127 8-9-12 **91** .... GrahamGibbons 5 94
(Eric Alston) *led to appr fnl f: rdn and kpt on same pce last 100yds* **12/1**

4022 **6** *1/2* **Hazelrigg (IRE)**[16] 3374 7-9-9 **88** ....[1] DavidAllan 2 89
(Tim Easterby) *hld up: rdn over 2f out: kpt on fnl f: nvr able to chal* **11/4**[1]

6002 **7** *1* **What About You (IRE)**[32] 2861 4-8-12 **77** .... FrederikTylicki 7 75
(Richard Fahey) *dwlt: hld up in tch: rdn over 2f out: edgd lft and no ex fr over 1f out* **16/1**

1000 **8** *hd* **Go Go Green (IRE)**[23] 3169 6-8-5 **75** .... NeilFarley(5) 1 72
(Jim Goldie) *dwlt: bhd: rdn over 2f out: nvr able to chal* **25/1**

0034 **9** *1/2* **Rothesay Chancer**[9] 3624 4-8-11 **76** .... GrahamLee 6 71
(Jim Goldie) *cl up: rdn over 2f out: wknd ent fnl f* **15/2**

1m 1.76s (2.36) **Going Correction** +0.65s/f (Yiel) **9 Ran SP% 112.3**
Speed ratings (Par 107): **107,106,106,106,105 104,102,102,101**PL: Headspace £0.90 Crimson Knot £1.50 TRICAST: Mayoman/H/HS £108.20 M/H/CK £565.84 TRIFECTA: M/H/HS £151.80 - 2.61 w/u. M/H/CK Part won. £396.40 - 0.03 w/u. £517.86 carried forward: toteswingers 1&2 £12.10, M&HS £4.40, H&HS £1.90. M&CK £12.50, H&CK£4.90 CSF £27 CT £Owner TOTE £Tom Tuohy: £Bred, £James Cosgrove, £Trained, £Nawton, N Yorks .

FOCUS
A decent sprint handicap which turned out to be a dramatic contest. The form seems sound if limited.

NOTEBOOK
Mayoman(IRE) was always close to the pace before taking it up inside the final furlong, but would have been just caught by Head Space had it not been for his rival's antics and he can be considered fortunate. This was still a good effort, but his form for his new yard this season has a very uneven look to it.
Haajes's ten wins have all come over 5f and he is 0-28 over further, so the return to the minimum trip on ground he likes was always going to make him interesting. However, he wasn't travelling at all well for a long way and it wasn't until he was switched to the stands' rail that he really began to motor, but the line was always going to beat him. (tchd 9-2)
Crimson Knot(IRE) was another to finish well after switching to her right. She may be better over 6f these days, but isn't the easiest to win with. (op 22-1)
Head Space(IRE) came into this in fine form and was put up 9lb for his win here last month when he jumped the winning line, and that particular issue became very significant this time. Having unseated his rider going to post, he was held up early but appeared to have been produced with a well-timed challenge when putting on the brakes as he spotted the mown section of the turf marking the winning line and almost sent his rider over this head. He had to be content with dead-heating for third rather than winning this outright and this was one that got away. Official explanation: jockey said gelding shied at the winning line causing it to stumble (op 22-1)
Foxy Music has plenty of decent form on soft ground and set the pace until the winner collared him entering the last, but he is still 7lb higher than when winning at Chester last September. (op 11-1)
Hazelrigg(IRE) came into this on a losing run of 18, yet had been nudged up in the weights again following a couple of recent second placings. Tried in a first-time hood, he plugged on late but not for the first time didn't appear to be giving everything. (op 3-1 tchd 10-3)

3904 BET MOBILE AT BETVICTOR.COM H'CAP — 2m 1f 105y
3:00 (3:00) (Class 5) (0-70,66) 3-Y-0+ — **£2,264** (£673; £336; £168) **Stalls** Low

Form — RPR

0/-0 **1** **Acknowledgement**[14] 3440 10-8-4 **49** ....(b) EvaMoscrop(7) 4 63
(Philip Kirby) *t.k.h: hld up: effrt whn bdly hmpd bnd over 3f out: swtchd wd and hdwy to chse ldr over 2f out: led ins fnl f: r.o wl* **12/1**

2-44 **2** *1 1/2* **Lady Bluesky**[22] 3180 9-9-9 **61** .... PaulMulrennan 6 72
(Alistair Whillans) *prom: wnt 2nd 1/2-way: led 4f out: rdn clr over 2f out: hdd ins fnl f: kpt on* **11/4**[1]

-241 **3** *14* **Nay Secret**[14] 3437 4-8-8 **51** .... NeilFarley(5) 2 33
(Jim Goldie) *hld up towards rr: rdn and hdwy wl over 3f out: outpcd fr 2f out* **11/2**

2031 **4** *1 1/4* **Spruzzo**[10] 3579 6-9-13 **65** .... PhillipMakin 1 44
(Chris Fairhurst) *prom: rdn and hdwy to chse ldr over 3f out to over 2f out: sn outpcd* **7/2**[2]

30/1 **5** *3* **Livvy Inn (USA)**[11] 3519 7-9-7 **59** .... JoeFanning 9 32
(Lucinda Russell) *hld up: rdn over 3f out: drifted lft and wknd over 2f out* **4/1**[3]

0-64 **6** *2 1/2* **Forrest Flyer (IRE)**[17] 3337 8-9-13 **65** .... GrahamLee 5 32
(Jim Goldie) *chsd ldr to 1/2-way: sn drvn along: rallied: wknd over 2f out* **6/1**

0-22 **7** *52* **Oddsmaker (IRE)**[10] 3577 11-9-8 **60** ....(t) TomEaves 8
(Maurice Barnes) *t.k.h: led to 4f out: lost tch fr 3f out: t.o* **18/1**

4m 7.51s (7.81) **Going Correction** +0.65s/f (Yiel) **7 Ran SP% 111.5**
Speed ratings (Par 103): **107,106,99,99,97 96,72**
toteswingers 1&2 £7.20, 2&3 £2.90, 1&3 £10.30 CSF £42.84 CT £201.35 TOTE £15.90: £4.00, £1.50; EX 64.70 Trifecta £496.60 Pool: £686.74 - 1.02 winning units..
Owner Skip Racing Limited **Bred** The Woodhaven Stud **Trained** Castleton, N Yorks

FOCUS
A modest handicap and quite a test of stamina test in the ground. The winner's first real Flat form since 2006
Spruzzo Official explanation: jockey said gelding never travelled
Forrest Flyer(IRE) Official explanation: jockey said gelding never travelled

3905 BEST ODDS AT BETVICTOR.COM H'CAP — 6f
3:30 (3:31) (Class 5) (0-75,74) 4-Y-0+ — **£2,264** (£673; £336; £168) **Stalls** High

Form — RPR

3501 **1** **The Nifty Fox**[10] 3578 8-9-4 **71** ....(p) JamesSullivan 6 84
(Tim Easterby) *t.k.h: prom: nt clr run over 2f out: effrt over 1f out: swtchd lft and led ins fnl f: edgd rt: sn clr* **5/2**[2]

0200 **2** *3 1/4* **Saxonette**[24] 3109 4-8-4 **57** ....(p) PJMcDonald 3 60
(Linda Perratt) *led tl rdn and hdd ins fnl f: kpt on: no ch w wnr* **25/1**

0-00 **3** *1* **Namwahjobo (IRE)**[17] 3334 4-9-5 **72** ....(v[1]) LeeNewman 1 71
(Jim Goldie) *cl up: rdn along 2f out: kpt on same pce ins fnl f* **6/1**[3]

0-00 **4** *3/4* **Ryan Style (IRE)**[17] 3336 6-9-7 **74** ....(v[1]) TomEaves 7 71
(Lisa Williamson) *prom against stands' rail: nt clr run over 2f out tl ins fnl f: sn rdn and one pce* **10/1**

0-50 **5** *2 1/2* **Midnight Dynamo**[24] 3109 5-8-12 **65** .... GrahamLee 5 54
(Jim Goldie) *bhd and sn pushed along: kpt on fnl f: nvr able to chal* **15/2**

0540 **6** *3* **Chookie Royale**[12] 3492 4-9-6 **73** .... JoeFanning 2 52
(Keith Dalgleish) *bhd on outside: sn pushed along: effrt over 2f out: btn fnl f* **9/4**[1]

0233 **7** *1 3/4* **Distant Sun (USA)**[1] 3893 8-8-1 **57** ....(p) JulieBurke(3) 4 31
(Linda Perratt) *chsd ldrs: rdn over 2f out: wknd ins fnl f* **15/2**

1m 16.43s (4.03) **Going Correction** +0.65s/f (Yiel) **7 Ran SP% 110.1**
Speed ratings (Par 103): **99,94,93,92,89 85,82**
toteswingers 1&2 £6.90, 2&3 £13.60, 1&3 £3.60 CSF £52.05 TOTE £3.70: £1.80, £7.70; EX 54.70.
Owner Roy Peebles **Bred** Mrs Norma Peebles **Trained** Great Habton, N Yorks

FOCUS
An ordinary sprint handicap. The winner is rated to his best form since last summer.

3906 MONEY BACK ON THE OPEN AT BETVICTOR.COM H'CAP — 1m 2f
4:00 (4:01) (Class 4) (0-85,79) 3-Y-0+ — **£4,204** (£1,251; £625; £312) **Stalls** Low

Form — RPR

0001 **1** **Gala Casino Star (IRE)**[17] 3353 7-9-3 **75** ....(v) JordanNason(7) 7 84
(Geoffrey Harker) *t.k.h: trckd ldrs: smooth hdwy to ld over 2f out: sn pushed along: idled ins fnl f: r.o* **5/1**[3]

-41 **2** *3/4* **Another For Joe**[26] 3031 4-9-6 **71** .... GrahamLee 3 77
(Jim Goldie) *trckd ldrs: rdn over 2f out: chsd wnr over 1f out: kpt on ins fnl f* **6/1**

0413 **3** *1/2* **Amazing Blue Sky**[9] 3628 6-9-11 **79** .... DaleSwift(3) 4 84
(Ruth Carr) *led at ordinary gallop: rdn and hdd over 2f out: rallied: kpt on ins fnl f* **4/1**[2]

5004 **4** *8* **High Resolution**[11] 3525 5-8-11 **62** .... TomEaves 1 51
(Linda Perratt) *s.i.s: hld up: hdwy and prom over 2f out: wknd appr fnl f* **18/1**

5500 **5** *9* **Bountiful Girl**[16] 3383 3-8-7 **69** .... FrederikTylicki 2 40
(Richard Fahey) *hld up in tch: drvn along over 3f out: wknd over 2f out* **11/4**[1]

002 **6** *5* **Euston Square**[26] 3038 6-9-5 **75** .... GarryWhillans(5) 6 36
(Alistair Whillans) *s.i.s: hld up: rdn over 3f out: wknd over 2f out* **4/1**[2]

1335 **7** *27* **Parley (USA)**[11] 3522 3-9-3 **79** .... JoeFanning 5
(Mark Johnston) *chsd ldr tl wknd 3f out: t.o* **8/1**

2m 17.44s (5.44) **Going Correction** +0.65s/f (Yiel)
WFA 3 from 4yo+ 11lb **7 Ran SP% 114.0**
Speed ratings (Par 105): **104,103,103,96,89 85,63**
toteswingers 1&2 £6.00, 2&3 £3.70, 1&3 £4.10 CSF £34.19 TOTE £5.90: £3.40, £3.40; EX 47.20.
Owner Mrs Tracy Nason **Bred** Glashare House Stud **Trained** Thirkleby, N Yorks

FOCUS
A fair handicap and the pace looked sensible in the conditions. The winner's best turf form since 2009.
Euston Square Official explanation: jockey said gelding never travelled

3907 PLAY CASINO AT BETVICTOR.COM H'CAP — 1m 2f
4:30 (4:31) (Class 6) (0-60,57) 3-Y-0+ — **£1,617** (£481; £240; £120) **Stalls** Low

Form — RPR

3042 **1** **Luctor Emergo (IRE)**[6] 3729 3-8-13 **53** ....(p) JoeFanning 4 63
(Keith Dalgleish) *led 1f: cl up: led over 3f out: rdn and clr over 1f out: kpt on fnl f: hung rt nr fin* **9/4**[1]

-550 **2** *nk* **Hawdyerwheesht**[17] 3337 4-10-0 **57** .... GrahamLee 10 66
(Jim Goldie) *hld up on outside: stdy hdwy over 3f out: effrt and chsd wnr over 1f out: edgd lft ins fnl f: styd on: hmpd nr fin* **8/1**[3]

0-32 **3** *7* **Schmooze (IRE)**[19] 3275 3-8-13 **53** .... FrederikTylicki 1 48
(Linda Perratt) *hld up: rdn and hdwy over 2f out: kpt on fnl f: no ch w first two* **10/1**

-03 **4** *1 1/4* **Uncle Brit**[17] 3355 6-9-8 **51** .... TomEaves 2 44
(Malcolm Jefferson) *t.k.h: prom: hdwy 3f out: rdn and no ex over 1f out* **18/1**

4033 **5** *7* **No Time To Cry**[26] 3025 3-8-10 **53** ....(p) DaleSwift(3) 8 32
(Ann Duffield) *cl up: rdn over 3f out: wknd fr 2f out* **10/1**

0300 **6** *3 1/4* **Monsieur Pontaven**[26] 3047 5-9-6 **49** .... MichaelO'Connell 6 21
(Robin Bastiman) *hld up on outside: hdwy and in tch wl over 2f out: sn rdn: wknd 2f out* **12/1**

0466 **7** *12* **Deep Applause**[26] 3032 4-9-5 **51** ....(b) LeeTopliss(3) 3
(Michael Dods) *hld up: rdn over 3f out: wknd over 2f out* **20/1**

0520 **8** *9* **Diamond Twister (USA)**[16] 3392 6-9-2 **45** ....(t) AmyRyan 5
(Lisa Williamson) *hld up: rdn and struggling over 4f out: sn btn* **25/1**

0-03 **9** *5* **Critical Point**[19] 3275 3-8-5 **45** .... LukeMorris 9
(Sir Mark Prescott Bt) *prom: sn drvn along: struggling over 4f out: btn fnl 3f* **5/2**[2]

-040 **10** *14* **Dynamic Drive (IRE)**[19] 3277 5-9-3 **51** ....(b[1]) GarryWhillans(5) 11
(Barry Murtagh) *led after 1f to after 3f: cl up tl wknd over 3f out* **33/1**

44-0 **11** *4 1/2* **Purkab**[21] 3215 4-9-1 **49** ....(v[1]) NeilFarley(5) 7
(Jim Goldie) *s.i.s: hdwy to ld after 3f: hdd over 3f out: sn wknd* **50/1**

2m 17.91s (5.91) **Going Correction** +0.65s/f (Yiel)
WFA 3 from 4yo+ 11lb **11 Ran SP% 115.1**
Speed ratings (Par 101): **102,101,96,95,89 86,77,70,66,54 51**
toteswingers 1&2 £5.10, 2&3 £7.50, 1&3 £6.00 CSF £19.38 CT £149.89 TOTE £3.80: £1.50, £2.90, £2.50; EX 25.00 Trifecta £123.30 Pool: £979.05 - 5.87 winning units..
Owner Gordon McDowall **Bred** Kilnamoragh Stud **Trained** Carluke, S Lanarks

FOCUS
A moderate handicap, but they seemed to go a fair pace and the winning time was only around half a second slower than the preceding Class 4 handicap. The first two pulled clear. The winner was well in and rates a small personal best.
Critical Point Official explanation: jockey said gelding never travelled

3908 BET AT BETVICTOR.COM APPRENTICE H'CAP — 7f 50y
5:00 (5:01) (Class 6) (0-65,61) 3-Y-0 — **£1,704** (£503; £251) **Stalls** High

Form — RPR

46-0 **1** **Oddysey (IRE)**[34] 2795 3-9-10 **60** .... LeeTopliss 6 77
(Michael Dods) *hld up in tch: rdn and hdwy 2f out: led 1f out: drvn out* **15/2**

50-0 **2** *2 1/4* **Lord Franklin**[19] 3275 3-8-6 **47** ow1 .... NedCurtis(5) 2 58
(Eric Alston) *t.k.h: led: edgd rt and hdd 1f out: edgd lft: kpt on same pce* **12/1**

5221 **3** *1 3/4* **Mick Slates (IRE)**[22] 3184 3-9-4 **57** .... NeilFarley(3) 3 64
(Declan Carroll) *trckd ldrs: effrt and rdn over 2f out: kpt on same pce fnl f* **3/1**[2]

1522 **4** *4* **Regal Acclaim (IRE)**[22] 3184 3-9-5 **58** .... AdamCarter(3) 4 54
(Tim Easterby) *cl up: rdn along and effrt over 2f out: drifted lft and wknd over 1f out: eased whn hld ins fnl f* **6/4**[1]

2401 **5** *2 1/2* **Balti's Sister (IRE)**[1] 3892 3-9-6 **61** 6ex .... DavidSimmonson(5) 5 51
(Michael Easterby) *prom: effrt over 2f out: sn rdn: wknd over 1f out* **7/1**

5040 **6** *19* **Madam Bonny (IRE)**[19] 3275 3-8-10 **46** .... JulieBurke 7
(Jim Goldie) *hld up: rdn over 2f out: sn struggling: t.o* **28/1**

304 **U** **Oakbrook**[5] 3751 3-8-9 **45** .... AmyRyan 1
(Ann Duffield) *chsng ldrs whn stmbld and uns rdr after 2f* **6/1**[3]

1m 38.3s (4.90) **Going Correction** +0.65s/f (Yiel) **7 Ran SP% 114.7**
Speed ratings (Par 98): **98,95,93,88,86 64,**
toteswingers: 1&2 £9.70, 2&3 £5.60, 1&3 £4.00 CSF £88.27 CT £328.99 TOTE £8.60: £3.70, £8.10; EX 107.50 Trifecta £927.70 Part won. Pool of £1253.71 - 0.20 winning units..
Owner Pearson, Lowthian & Coburn **Bred** Darling Smile Syndicate **Trained** Denton, Co Durham
■ Stewards' Enquiry : Ned Curtis seven-day ban: careless riding (Jul 23-29)

The Form Book Flat, Raceform Ltd, Compton, RG20 6NL

FOCUS
A moderate apprentice handicap and a rough race. The winner is rated around his early 2yo form.
T/Plt: £101.40 to a £1 stake. Pool of £87455.86 - 629.01 winning tickets. T/Qpdt: £32.80 to a £1 stake. Pool of £7775.13 - 175.40 winning tickets. RY

[3303]RIPON (R-H)
Monday, July 9

OFFICIAL GOING: Soft (7.2)
Wind: light 1/2 against Weather: overcast

3909 RACING AGAIN SATURDAY 21ST JULY MAIDEN AUCTION FILLIES' STKS — 6f
6:50 (6:53) (Class 5) 2-Y-O **£2,587** (£770; £384; £192) **Stalls** High

Form RPR
002 **1** **Penny Garcia**[14] 3436 2-8-4 66 .... DuranFentiman 2 69
(Tim Easterby) *chsd ldrs: led over 1f out: hdd ins fnl f: rallied to ld post* **3/1**[2]
3 **2** *nse* **Bondesire**[15] 3415 2-8-4 0 .... SilvestreDeSousa 4 69+
(David O'Meara) *mid-div: hdwy on outside over 2f out: led last 75yds: hdd post* **5/2**[1]
3 *2 1/4* **Krupskaya (FR)** 2-8-7 0 .... MartinLane 5 65
(Mrs K Burke) *s.i.s: hdwy on outside over 2f out: styd on same pce fnl f* **18/1**
06 **4** *nk* **Charlie Em**[16] 3381 2-8-8 0 ow1 .... TonyHamilton 8 65
(Richard Fahey) *chsd ldrs: kpt on one pce fnl f* **7/1**
55 **5** *1* **Grievous Angel (IRE)**[12] 3490 2-8-10 0 .... PaulMulrennan 11 64
(Ann Duffield) *led: hdd over 1f out: kpt on same pce* **13/2**[3]
6 **6** *8* **Lucky Prize**[28] 2977 2-8-4 0 .... PatrickMathers 1 34
(Mel Brittain) *swvd rt s: chsd ldrs: wknd over 1f out* **50/1**
23 **7** *1 3/4* **Napinda**[33] 2808 2-8-5 0 ow1 .... ChrisCatlin 6 30
(Des Donovan) *chsd ldrs: lost pl over 1f out* **25/1**
0 **8** *1/2* **Nifty Nadine (IRE)**[18] 3303 2-8-4 0 .... KellyHarrison 9 27
(Nigel Tinkler) *in rr: hdwy over 3f out: lost pl over 1f out* **100/1**
0 **9** *1 1/4* **Vida Eterna (IRE)**[15] 3415 2-8-13 0 .... PhillipMakin 10 33
(Ollie Pears) *chsd ldrs: wknd 2f out* **40/1**
10 *2 1/4* **Juhaina (IRE)** 2-8-7 0 .... FrannyNorton 3 20
(Ann Duffield) *sn outpcd in rr: bhd fnl 4f* **18/1**

1m 17.67s (4.67) **Going Correction** +0.75s/f (Yiel) **10 Ran SP% 99.2**
Speed ratings (Par 91): **98,97,94,94,93 82,80,79,77,74**
toteswingers: 1&2 £2.10, 2&3 £9.80, 1&3 £7.10 CSF £7.78 TOTE £3.00: £1.10, £1.40, £4.60; EX 8.20.
Owner Jim & Helen Bowers **Bred** J Bowers **Trained** Great Habton, N Yorks
■ Throwing Roses was withdrawn (9/2, unruly in stalls). Deduct 15p in the £ under R4.

FOCUS
Rail on bend from back straight to home straight moved out 2m adding 6yds to races on Round course. The market principals came to the fore in what looked a very ordinary contest. The winner took a minor step forward.

NOTEBOOK
Penny Garcia has improved with each run and just about found this enough of a stamina test, getting back up to deny what had seemed a likely victory for the runner-up. She is an obvious type for nurseries, with her likely to be as effective from 6f-7f. (op 11-4 tchd 10-3)
Bondesire confirmed the promise of her debut third in similar conditions, picking up well only to get run out of it by a more experienced filly. She looks capable of gaining compensation before stepping into nurseries. (op 3-1)
Krupskaya(FR), whose dam is a half-sister to a Listed 6f winner, is bred to go on soft ground and she shaped with a deal of promise following a slow start. (op 20-1 tchd 16-1)
Charlie Em looks in need of an extra furlong and now has the option of nurseries. (tchd 15-2)
Grievous Angel(IRE) should benefit from an extra furlong and now has the option of nurseries (op 17-2)

3910 FOLLOW @ATTHERACES ON TWITTER H'CAP — 1m 4f 10y
7:20 (7:21) (Class 4) (0-80,79) 3-Y-O **£4,528** (£1,347; £673; £336) **Stalls** Low

Form RPR
-001 **1** **Scarlet Whispers**[14] 3448 3-9-4 76 .... MickyFenton 5 84
(Pam Sly) *led: qcknd over 4f out: chal over 2f out: hld on gamely nr fin* **4/1**[3]
-325 **2** *nk* **Bayan (IRE)**[10] 3592 3-9-7 79 .... RobertWinston 1 86
(Brian Meehan) *sn trcking ldrs: hdwy over 4f out: chal over 2f out: no ex towards fin* **6/4**[1]
5530 **3** *2 1/4* **Maybeagrey**[9] 3610 3-8-4 62 .... DuranFentiman 2 65
(Tim Easterby) *racd in last: effrt on ins 3f out: chsng ldrs over 2f out: swtchd lft jst ins fnl f: kpt on one pce* **9/1**
0453 **4** *10* **Arley Hall**[9] 3605 3-8-8 66 .... TonyHamilton 4 53
(Richard Fahey) *trckd ldrs: chal over 2f out: wknd over 1f out* **3/1**[2]
0003 **5** *19* **Equity Card (FR)**[4] 3775 3-8-6 64 .... SilvestreDeSousa 3 21
(Mark Johnston) *chsd ldrs: effrt over 4f out: losing pl whn sltly hmpd over 3f out: sn bhd* **5/1**

2m 43.2s (6.50) **Going Correction** +0.425s/f (Yiel) **5 Ran SP% 111.7**
Speed ratings (Par 102): **95,94,93,86,73**
CSF £10.67 TOTE £3.60: £1.40, £1.10; EX 12.10.
Owner G A Libson **Bred** Miss K Rausing & Mr & Mrs A E Pakenham **Trained** Thorney, Cambs

FOCUS
The pace was steady in this fair handicap and the front two had it between them for the final 2f. The winner continued her improvement.

3911 RIPON CATHEDRAL CELEBRATION H'CAP — 1m
7:50 (7:50) (Class 3) (0-90,90) 3-Y-O+ **£6,663** (£1,982; £990; £495) **Stalls** Low

Form RPR
3512 **1** **Satanic Beat (IRE)**[16] 3376 3-8-11 82 .... PaulMulrennan 3 91
(Jedd O'Keeffe) *trckd ldrs: led 2f out: hld on gamely* **7/2**[2]
4450 **2** *nk* **Dubai Dynamo**[2] 3855 7-10-0 90 .... PJMcDonald 4 100
(Ruth Carr) *hld up: hdwy over 4f out: upsides over 1f out: no ex towards fin* **13/2**
0062 **3** *1 3/4* **Al Muheer (IRE)**[2] 3855 7-9-13 89 .... (b) JamesSullivan 2 95
(Ruth Carr) *hld up in rr: hdwy on ins over 3f out: nt clr run over 2f out: chal jst ins fnl f: edgd rt and wknd towards fin* **3/1**[1]
-225 **4** *2 1/4* **Sam Sharp (USA)**[23] 3157 6-9-8 84 .... SilvestreDeSousa 7 85
(Ian Williams) *towards rr: hdwy on ins 4f out: chsng ldrs over 2f out: one pce over 1f out* **9/2**[3]
0010 **5** *4* **Miami Gator (IRE)**[12] 3493 5-8-12 81 .... (v) ConorHarrison(7) 6 73
(Mrs K Burke) *led: hdd 2f out: hung rt and wknd appr fnl f* **16/1**
2244 **6** *6* **Honeymead (IRE)**[20] 3252 4-9-6 87 .... ShaneBKelly(5) 1 65
(Richard Fahey) *trckd ldrs: effrt over 3f out: wknd over 1f out* **7/2**[2]
-030 **7** *7* **Koo And The Gang (IRE)**[23] 3167 5-8-11 73 .... BarryMcHugh 9 35
(Brian Ellison) *chsd ldrs: lost pl over 2f out* **20/1**
5-60 **8** *3* **Beaumont's Party (IRE)**[72] 1654 5-9-13 89 .... TonyHamilton 8 44
(Chris Grant) *sn trcking ldrs: drvn 4f out: sn lost pl and bhd* **28/1**

1m 43.3s (1.90) **Going Correction** +0.425s/f (Yiel)
WFA 3 from 4yo+ 9lb **8 Ran SP% 115.1**
Speed ratings (Par 107): **107,106,104,102,98 92,85,82**
toteswingers: 1&2 £6.10, 2&3 £4.70, 1&3 £2.90 CSF £26.61 CT £75.25 TOTE £4.30: £1.40, £2.30, £1.30; EX 28.30.
Owner Caron & Paul Chapman **Bred** Patrick Gleeson **Trained** Middleham Moor, N Yorks

FOCUS
There was plenty of pace on in this and the form looks solid. The winner rates a length personal best.

NOTEBOOK
Satanic Beat(IRE), who came into the race in good form but was unproven on soft ground, took another step forward with a battling win, handling the conditions well. He shouldn't go up much and can rate higher still. (op 9-2)
Dubai Dynamo ran poorly just two days earlier, behind stablemate Al Muheer, but he takes his racing well and bounced back to form at a course he likes, trying hard but not being able to get past. (op 11-2 tchd 5-1)
Al Muheer(IRE), another reappearing quickly, had to wait for a run, but had his chance switching inside, perhaps finding his stamina stretched. (op 10-3 tchd 7-2)
Sam Sharp(USA) handles the ground but didn't get going in time and remains without a win in 14 months. (tchd 4-1)
Miami Gator(IRE) was forced into going too hard, with plenty of competition for the lead. (op 14-1)
Honeymead(IRE), who chased the pace, found little and took a further step backwards. (op 9-2)

3912 SUMMER SPRINT TROPHY H'CAP — 6f
8:20 (8:23) (Class 3) (0-90,87) 3-Y-O **£6,931** (£2,074; £1,037; £519; £258) **Stalls** High

Form RPR
1121 **1** **Athenian (IRE)**[12] 3500 3-9-1 81 .... ChrisCatlin 8 89
(Sir Mark Prescott Bt) *chsd ldrs: effrt over 2f out: styd on to ld last 100yds: kpt on wl* **3/1**[1]
5205 **2** *1* **Tip Top Gorgeous (IRE)**[23] 3160 3-8-12 78 .... SilvestreDeSousa 9 83
(David O'Meara) *gave problems gng to s: led: hdd ins fnl f: no ex* **12/1**
2-31 **3** *1/2* **Sujet Bellagio**[166] 298 3-8-9 75 .... RobertWinston 7 78
(Brian Meehan) *dwlt: towards rr: hdwy and edgd lft over 1f out: kpt on wl to take 3rd last 100yds* **20/1**
0-04 **4** *4* **Commanche**[15] 3421 3-8-2 68 .... JamesSullivan 10 58
(Bryan Smart) *chsd ldrs on inner: drvn over 3f out: nt clr run on inner 2f out: wl outpcd appr fnl f* **8/1**
3024 **5** *1* **Chooseday (IRE)**[28] 2979 3-9-0 80 .... (p) PhillipMakin 5 67
(Kevin Ryan) *gave problems in stalls: hld up in mid-div: effrt over 2f out: wknd appr fnl f* **17/2**
2-31 **6** *nk* **Duke Of Aricabeau (IRE)**[10] 3566 3-8-4 70 .... MartinLane 4 56
(Mrs K Burke) *trckd ldrs: t.k.h: effrt over 2f out: wknd appr fnl f* **10/1**
10-3 **7** *1 1/2* **Dutch Heritage**[16] 3379 3-8-4 70 .... PatrickMathers 3 51
(Richard Fahey) *dwlt: sn detached in last and drvn along: kpt on fnl f: nvr on terms* **4/1**[2]
-021 **8** *nk* **Kyleakin Lass**[28] 2986 3-9-7 87 .... TonyHamilton 1 67
(Ian Wood) *in tch on outer: effrt over 2f out: wknd over 1f out* **8/1**
0306 **9** *nse* **See Clearly**[33] 2824 3-8-4 70 .... (p) DuranFentiman 2 50
(Tim Easterby) *chsd ldrs: wknd rapidly last 150yds* **16/1**
-410 **10** *14* **Takealookatmenow (IRE)**[16] 3379 3-8-7 73 .... AdrianNicholls 6
(David Nicholls) *trckd ldr: t.k.h: lost pl over 1f out: heavily eased ins fnl f* **15/2**[3]

1m 16.81s (3.81) **Going Correction** +0.75s/f (Yiel) **10 Ran SP% 116.9**
Speed ratings (Par 104): **104,102,102,96,95 94,92,92,92,73**
toteswingers: 1&2 £5.50, 2&3 £75.40, 1&3 £7.30 CSF £40.58 CT £491.81 TOTE £3.20: £1.70, £3.40, £4.40; EX 48.10.
Owner Axom (XXXI) **Bred** Keatly Overseas Ltd **Trained** Newmarket, Suffolk

FOCUS
A competitive sprint handicap in which three runners finished clear. They all raced stands' side. The winner continues to progress, with the second setting the standard.

NOTEBOOK
Athenian(IRE) ◆ defied her latest rise in the weights - this time 5lb - to improve her record to 4-5 this season. She rather got the run of the race when defeating another progressive filly at Kempton last time, but this victory was well earned and there was a lot to like about how strongly she travelled through the race. (op 5-2)
Tip Top Gorgeous(IRE) had to be walked some of the way to the start but she did nothing wrong in the race, showing speed towards the rail and keeping on well. The drop in trip and easy ground suited her. (op 16-1 tchd 10-1)
Sujet Bellagio, absent since winning a maiden (6f, Polytrack) in January, made an encouraging return, keeping on well to finish clear of the others. (op 16-1)
Commanche just didn't pick up well enough. (op 14-1)
Chooseday(IRE) played up in the stalls. (op 11-1 tchd 12-1 and 8-1)
Dutch Heritage, who had shaped nicely enough on his return, didn't travel at all after starting slowly, but he did make late headway. It wouldn't surprise to see him on a stiffer course next time and/or tried in headgear. (tchd 9-2)
Kyleakin Lass was 6lb higher than when winning over 5f at Windsor on her previous start, and she didn't see her race out over this longer trip after being stuck wide with little cover. It's probably worth excusing this performance. (tchd 7-1)

3913 SIS LIVE MAIDEN STKS — 1m
8:50 (8:54) (Class 5) 3-Y-O+ **£2,587** (£770; £384; £192) **Stalls** Low

Form RPR
6- **1** **The Tiger**[453] 1311 4-9-12 0 .... TomMcLaughlin 4 81
(Ed Dunlop) *s.i.s: sn mid-div: hdwy on ins 4f out: chsd ldrs over 1f out: r.o to ld last 50yds* **12/1**[3]
3-36 **2** *1 1/4* **Cathedral**[32] 2856 3-9-3 79 .... RobertWinston 10 76
(Brian Meehan) *trckd ldrs: swtchd lft 4f out: drvn to ld over 1f out: hdd and no ex wl ins fnl f* **2/5**[1]
50 **3** *7* **Naburn**[26] 3035 4-9-7 0 .... GarryWhillans(5) 18 62
(Alan Swinbank) *dwlt: hld up towards rr: hdwy over 2f out: styd on to take 3rd last 100yds* **20/1**
4 *shd* **Quiet Route (IRE)** 3-9-3 0 .... BarryMcHugh 7 60
(Brian Ellison) *in rr: swtchd lft 3f out: styd on to take 4th last 100yds* **28/1**
0- **5** *4 1/2* **Dubawi Island (FR)**[285] 6463 3-9-3 0 .... (b[1]) PaulMulrennan 5 49
(James Tate) *trckd ldrs: led over 4f out: hdd over 1f out: wknd fnl 100yds* **14/1**
0- **6** *1 1/2* **Morna's Glory**[252] 7197 3-8-12 0 .... MichaelStainton 17 41
(Jason Ward) *chsd ldrs: chal 4f out: wknd last 150yds* **80/1**
7 *7* **Nowdoro** 3-9-0 0 .... PaulPickard(3) 14 30
(Julie Camacho) *in rr: bhd and drvn 4f out: kpt on fnl 2f: nvr a factor* **40/1**

8 1 ¾ **Horatian (USA)** 4-9-12 0 WilliamCarson 12 28
(Anthony Carson) *s.s: bhd and drvn along: sme hdwy over 2f out: nvr on terms* **33/1**
9 4 **Icing Sugar**[46] 4-9-7 0 PatrickMathers 13 14
(Mike Sowersby) *mid-div: sn drvn along: nvr a factor* **100/1**
5 10 ½ **Centrifugal (IRE)**[11] 3521 3-9-3 0 SilvestreDeSousa 11 15
(Mark Johnston) *reluctant to load: chsd ldrs: drvn to chal 4f out: wknd 2f out* **13/2[2]**
0 11 2 **Connie Carlton**[10] 3565 3-8-12 0 AndrewElliott 2
(David Thompson) *led: hdd over 4f out: wknd over 2f out* **100/1**
60- 12 1 ½ **Upton Crystal**[326] 5212 4-9-7 0 JamesSullivan 16
(Michael Easterby) *mid-div: edgd lft and lost pl 3f out* **50/1**
06/ 13 1 **Moorgate Lad**[644] 6624 5-9-12 0 ChrisCatlin 8
(Garry Woodward) *t.k.h in mid-div: drvn 3f out: sn wknd* **40/1**
14 15 **Shavalley (USA)** 3-8-12 0 AdrianNicholls 9
(David Nicholls) *s.i.s: wl bhd and drvn 4f out* **28/1**
600 15 12 **Monzino (USA)**[7] 3702 4-9-5 0 GerardGalligan(7) 6
(Michael Chapman) *s.i.s: sn mid-div: wknd over 3f out: sn bhd* **80/1**
0 16 9 **Libby's Lad**[31] 2881 3-9-3 0 DavidNolan 3
(David C Griffiths) *chsd ldrs: eased and lost pl over 3f out: sn bhd: virtually p.u* **100/1**

1m 45.61s (4.21) **Going Correction** +0.425s/f (Yiel)
WFA 3 from 4yo+ 9lb 16 Ran SP% **126.0**
Speed ratings (Par 103): **95,93,86,86,82 80,73,71,67,67 65,63,62,47,35 26**
toteswingers 1&2 £3.10, 2&3 £6.50, 1&3 £12.20 CSF £16.70 TOTE £11.00: £2.10, £1.10, £4.30; EX 26.50.
Owner J R Weatherby **Bred** Preston Lodge Stud **Trained** Newmarket, Suffolk

FOCUS
This didn't look a strong maiden, but there are at least a couple to be interested in with the future in mind. The first two came clear and the time was reasonable.
Quiet Route(IRE) ◆ Official explanation: jockey said, regarding runing and riding, that his orders were to finish in the best position he could, the gelding was slightly outpaced early stages and continued to stay on past tired horses closing stages.
Dubawi Island(FR) Official explanation: jockey said gelding hung right-handed
Libby's Lad Official explanation: jockey said gelding lost its action

3914 YORKSHIRE RACING SUMMER FESTIVAL COMING SOON H'CAP 1m
9:20 (9:22) (Class 5) (0-70,70) 3-Y-0+ **£2,911** (£866; £432; £216) **Stalls** Low

Form RPR
3422 1 **Horatio Carter**[2] 3843 7-9-12 68 TomEaves 2 77
(David O'Meara) *trckd ldrs: led over 1f out: rdn and hld on wl* **10/3[1]**
-661 2 1 ¼ **Izzet**[17] 3356 4-9-2 58 PatrickMathers 6 63
(Ron Barr) *mid-div: hdwy over 3f out: chsd wnr fnl f: no real imp* **5/1[2]**
0450 3 ½ **Icy Blue**[14] 3439 4-9-11 67 TonyHamilton 4 73+
(Richard Whitaker) *s.i.s: hdwy on ins over 2f out: nt clr run over 1f out: r.o ins fnl f* **5/1[2]**
5520 4 nse **Satwa Laird**[10] 3559 6-9-9 70 DavidKenny(5) 3 74
(Conor Dore) *s.i.s: sn mid-div: edgd lft 3f out: kpt on fnl f* **16/1**
05/0 5 1 ¼ **Consider Yourself (USA)**[159] 374 5-9-11 67 WilliamCarson 12 68
(Anthony Carson) *swtchd rt after s: led: hdd over 1f out: wknd ins fnl f* **50/1**
000 6 1 ¼ **Thatcherite (IRE)**[21] 3230 4-9-13 69 (t) StephenCraine 1 67
(Tony Coyle) *in tch: effrt on ins over 2f out: one pce over 1f out* **16/1**
030- 7 nk **Dandarrell**[275] 6698 5-8-9 51 PaulMulrennan 5 48+
(Julie Camacho) *in rr: hdwy over 1f out: gng on at fin* **33/1**
4400 8 ½ **Collateral Damage (IRE)**[22] 3185 9-9-10 66 (t) DavidAllan 14 62
(Tim Easterby) *s.i.s: in rr: swtchd ins and nt clr run over 2f out: swtchd rt over 1f out: kpt on: nvr a factor* **8/1[3]**
03-0 9 3 **Pattern Mark**[17] 3353 6-8-9 58 JacobButterfield(7) 10 47
(Ollie Pears) *in rr: kpt on fnl 2f: nvr a factor* **33/1**
0000 10 ¾ **Bertie Blu Boy**[14] 3454 4-8-9 51 oh6 SilvestreDeSousa 15 39
(Paul Green) *sn chsng ldrs on outer: 2nd over 5f out tl over 2f out: wknd over 1f out* **50/1**
0035 11 2 ¼ **Triple Eight (IRE)**[17] 3356 4-9-10 66 (b) MichaelO'Connell 8 48
(Philip Kirby) *sn chsng ldrs: drvn over 3f out: edgd lft over 2f out: wknd over 1f out* **17/2**
1060 12 ½ **Wiseman's Diamond (USA)**[15] 3416 7-9-9 65 (b) MickyFenton 11 46
(Paul Midgley) *mid-div: effrt over 3f out: wknd 2f out* **9/1**
-600 13 nk **Keys Of Cyprus**[20] 3254 10-9-3 66 ShirleyTeasdale(7) 13 47
(David Nicholls) *t.k.h: sn trcking ldrs: wknd 2f out* **25/1**
0004 14 ½ **Fine Kingdom**[47] 2404 3-8-0 51 oh1 JamesSullivan 9 28
(Brian Ellison) *trckd ldrs: lost pl over 3f out* **33/1**
5460 15 1 **Mazovian (USA)**[10] 3589 4-9-3 59 RussKennemore 7 36
(Michael Chapman) *sn chsng ldrs: swtchd lft 4f out: lost pl 3f out* **28/1**

1m 46.09s (4.69) **Going Correction** +0.425s/f (Yiel)
WFA 3 from 4yo+ 9lb 15 Ran SP% **119.9**
Speed ratings (Par 103): **93,91,91,91,89 88,88,87,84,84 81,81,81,80,79**
toteswingers 1&2 £5.70, 2&3 £7.70, 1&3 £7.70 CSF £17.42 CT £83.15 TOTE £3.70: £2.20, £2.30, £2.00; EX 17.20.
Owner Trendy Ladies **Bred** Mrs T Brudenell **Trained** Nawton, N Yorks

FOCUS
An interesting little handicap and pretty straightforward form, rated around the fourth.
Bertie Blu Boy Official explanation: jockey said gelding had no more to give
T/Jkpt: Not won. T/Plt: £12.30 to a £1 stake. Pool of £96354.48 - 5706.33 winning tickets.
T/Qpdt: £3.80 to a £1 stake. Pool of £7327.67 - 1410.25 winning tickets. WG

3700 WINDSOR (R-H)
Monday, July 9

OFFICIAL GOING: Soft (6.2)
Wind: Almost nil Weather: Overcast with showers

3915 DAVISBAKERYCARIBBEAN.COM APPRENTICE H'CAP 6f
6:10 (6:11) (Class 5) (0-75,75) 4-Y-0+ **£2,264** (£673; £336; £168) **Stalls** Low

Form RPR
5-56 1 **Dream Catcher (FR)**[11] 3546 4-8-11 65 AmyScott(3) 3 74
(Henry Candy) *pressed ldrs: rdn over 2f out and looked in trble: rallied to ld 1f out: pushed out firmly fnl 100yds* **4/1[2]**
0035 2 ¾ **Silenzio**[10] 3570 4-9-2 72 WilliamTwiston-Davies(5) 8 78
(Richard Hannon) *dwlt: in tch in rr: prog and grabbed far side rail fr 2f out: chal over 1f out: pressed wnr fnl f: nt qckn* **11/2[3]**
4026 3 ¾ **Rambo Will**[30] 2940 4-9-3 71 DarrenEgan(3) 11 75
(J R Jenkins) *disp ld: narrow advantage briefly over 1f out: one pce fnl f* **6/1**
04 4 ¾ **Bold Ring**[12] 3511 6-8-1 59 JoeyHaynes(7) 4 61
(Eric Wheeler) *in tch: effrt over 2f out: rdn whn nt clr run briefly over 1f out: styd on fnl f: nvr able to chal* **16/1**
5003 5 2 **Style And Panache (IRE)**[3] 3815 4-9-0 70 (p) NathanSweeney(5) 5 65
(David Evans) *chsd ldrs: rdn and cl up 2f out: no ex over 1f out: one pce* **10/1**
2206 6 3 ½ **Efistorm**[8] 3660 11-9-10 75 SophieDoyle 9 59
(Joseph Tuite) *pressed ldrs to 1/2-way: lost pl and sn rdn: nvr on terms after* **16/1**
1042 7 1 ¼ **Interakt**[23] 3159 5-9-10 75 HarryBentley 10 55
(Joseph Tuite) *disp ld to over 1f out: wknd rapidly* **10/3[1]**
-006 8 ½ **Swendab (IRE)**[10] 3595 4-9-10 75 RyanPowell 2 53
(John O'Shea) *s.i.s: a in rr and sn rdn: nvr a factor* **25/1**
0111 9 ½ **Valmina**[23] 3139 5-9-5 75 (t) ThomasGarner(5) 1 52
(Tony Carroll) *hld up in rr but in tch: rdn 2f out: sn wknd* **7/1**
4302 10 ½ **Nubar Boy**[41] 2572 5-9-7 72 (v) MatthewCosham 6 47
(David Evans) *s.v.s: a in last pair and struggling* **14/1**

1m 15.59s (2.59) **Going Correction** +0.525s/f (Yiel) 10 Ran SP% **116.6**
Speed ratings (Par 103): **103,102,101,100,97 92,91,90,89,89**
toteswingers 1&2 £4.80, 2&3 £7.30, 1&3 £5.40 CSF £26.37 CT £133.85 TOTE £3.70: £1.20, £2.40, £2.20; EX 26.50 Trifecta £96.50 Pool: £546.72 - 4.19 winning uits..
Owner Miss N M Haine **Bred** Daniel Cherdo **Trained** Kingston Warren, Oxon

FOCUS
Inner of straight dolled out 9yds at 6f and 1yd at winning post. The top bend was dolled out 7yds from its normal inner configuration adding 28yds to race distances of 1m+. A fair handicap run at a solid pace in the conditions and they finished up on the far side. Straightforward form.

3916 E B F MACDONALD HOTEL WINDSOR MAIDEN STKS 6f
6:40 (6:41) (Class 5) 2-Y-O **£3,299** (£981; £490; £245) **Stalls** Low

Form RPR
30 1 **King Dragon (IRE)**[20] 3240 2-9-3 0 ShaneKelly 4 89+
(Brian Meehan) *trckd clr ldng pair: clsd over 2f out: led wl over 1f out: drvn and styd on wl* **9/2[3]**
2 2 **Dominate** 2-9-3 0 RyanMoore 6 83+
(Richard Hannon) *squeezed out sn after s: rn green in last: prog fr 1/2-way: rdn to chse wnr jst over 1f out: styd on but no imp last 100yds* **11/1**
2 3 5 **Whipper Snapper (IRE)**[17] 3346 2-9-3 0 JimCrowley 2 68
(William Knight) *trckd ldrs: prog to go 2nd over 1f out and cl enough to chal: sn btn: fdd fnl f* **11/4[2]**
4 2 ¼ **Dance With Dragons (IRE)** 2-9-3 0 StevieDonohoe 11 61
(Paul Cole) *rousted along early to go prom: rdn and outpcd fr 1/2-way: kpt on to take 4th nr fin* **25/1**
0220 5 nk **Fletcher Christian**[20] 3242 2-9-3 77 NeilCallan 10 60
(John Gallagher) *led and clr w one rival: hdd & wknd wl over 1f out* **16/1**
6 1 ¾ **Derwent (USA)** 2-9-3 0 EddieAhern 1 55+
(Roger Charlton) *settled in rr: last 1/2-way: pushed along over 2f out: kpt on steadily fnl f: bttr for experience* **7/1**
7 ½ **The Art Of Racing (IRE)** 2-9-3 0 RichardHughes 8 54
(Richard Hannon) *wl in tch: no prog over 2f out: wknd over 1f out* **9/4[1]**
5240 8 1 ¼ **Marvelino**[20] 3242 2-9-3 75 DarryllHolland 9 50
(Pat Eddery) *pressed ldr and clr of rest: wknd jst over 2f out* **25/1**
9 2 ½ **Bobby Two Shoes** 2-9-3 0 IanMongan 12 42
(Brett Johnson) *a in rr: outpcd bef 1/2-way: nvr on terms after* **200/1**
10 7 **Muskat Link** 2-9-3 0 DaneO'Neill 7 21
(Henry Candy) *a wl in rr: wl bhd fnl 2f* **33/1**
11 11 **Xerxes (IRE)** 2-8-12 0 MichaelHills 5
(Hugo Palmer) *chsd ldrs to 1/2-way: wknd rapidly: t.o* **33/1**

1m 16.36s (3.36) **Going Correction** +0.525s/f (Yiel) 11 Ran SP% **116.4**
Speed ratings (Par 94): **98,95,88,85,85 82,82,80,77,67 53**
toteswingers: 1&2 £8.80, 2&3 £4.60, 1&3 £2.30 CSF £49.06 TOTE £4.50: £1.50, £2.60, £1.60; EX 34.40 Trifecta £84.60 Pool: £424.60 - 3.71 winning units..
Owner Trelawny II **Bred** A Brosnan **Trained** Manton, Wilts

FOCUS
An interesting maiden featuring several newcomers of note. The pace was honest and the first two ultimately finished clear. The winner built on his debut effort.

NOTEBOOK
King Dragon(IRE) was outclassed in the Coventry but set the standard on his debut third at Newmarket and built on that promise with a decisive win. Happy to track the lead, he was ridden 2f out but showed a professional attitude and ran on strongly all the way to the line. He handled the conditions well and should stay an extra furlong. (op 7-2)
Dominate, the apparent second string of Richard Hannon, made a highly encouraging debut and fared best of the debutants. He was given a patient ride, making his challenge further out from the rail than the winner, and shaped very much as though he would improve significantly for the experience. He should have no trouble winning a maiden. (tchd 12-1)
Whipper Snapper(IRE) looked a threat entering the final furlong but was left behind by the front two. He's now been placed on his both starts but didn't really build on the promise of his debut second at Newmarket. (tchd 3-1)
Dance With Dragons(IRE) needed the experience but did some good late work. This was a pleasing debut. (op 33-1)
Fletcher Christian didn't last home after making much of the running over this longer trip. (op 20-1 tchd 14-1)
Derwent(USA), the first juvenile runner of the season for Roger Charlton, had an eyecatching pedigree being a half-brother to several winners, including high-class winning 2yo Three Valleys. This was only a fair start but he should improve. (op 8-1)
The Art Of Racing(IRE), an 87,000GBP Acclamation newcomer, is bred to be a speedy juvenile and was made favourite on this debut. He'll have to improve to justify his Gimcrack entry but may be suited by better ground. (op 5-2)
Xerxes(IRE) Official explanation: trainer said filly lost a left-fore shoe

3917 JANE DE WARDENER MEMORIAL H'CAP 1m 67y
7:10 (7:10) (Class 4) (0-85,82) 3-Y-O **£4,204** (£1,251; £625; £312) **Stalls** Low

Form RPR
1425 1 **Takeitfromalady (IRE)**[23] 3156 3-9-7 82 (b) JimCrowley 2 90+
(Ralph Beckett) *hld up in rr: prog over 3f out: trckd ldng pair and trapped bhd them over 1f out: swtchd to rail and gap appeared ins fnl f: led last 100yds: drvn clr* **11/4[2]**
-223 2 1 ¼ **Sir Mike**[24] 3106 3-9-6 81 IanMongan 5 86
(Amanda Perrett) *trckd ldr after 3f: rdn to ld over 2f out: hdd and outpcd last 100yds* **8/1**
1122 3 nse **Love Tale**[24] 3108 3-9-1 76 FergusSweeney 8 81
(Mark Rimell) *hld up in last: pushed along 1/2-way: gd prog on outer over 2f out: clsd on ldrs fnl f: one pce last 100yds* **22/1**
1066 4 3 ¼ **Fourth Of June (IRE)**[28] 2975 3-9-3 78 GeorgeBaker 9 75
(Ed Dunlop) *led to over 2f out: chsd ldr tl fdd fnl f* **16/1**

1-42 **5** *3* **Eurystheus (IRE)**[12] 3503 3 -9-580 .... RichardHughes 3 73
(Richard Hannon) *trckd ldrs: effrt against far rail over 2f out: cl up but hld whn hmpd 1f out: eased* **5/2**[1]

0006 **6** *9* **Venetian View (IRE)**[9] 3280 3 -9-176 ....(v[1]) TomQueally 7 46
(Gary Moore) *nvr gng wl and sn pushed along: struggling 3f out* **33/1**

5-50 **7** *3* **Monymusk**[42] 2557 3 -8-1172 .... DaneO'Neill 1 35
(David Elsworth) *trckd ldrs: cl enough over 2f out: wknd qckly over 1f out* **20/1**

514- **8** *10* **Sugarformyhoney (IRE)**[310] 5698 3 -9-681 .... RyanMoore 6 21
(Richard Hannon) *t.k.h: trckd ldr 3f: styd cl up tl wknd 2f out: bmpd over 1f out: eased* **12/1**

6-11 **U** **Viscount Vert (IRE)**[7] 3705 3 -9-580 6ex .... DavidProbert 4 84
(Andrew Balding) *towards rr: rdn wl over 2f out: prog whn swtchd rt and bmpd rival over 1f out: styng on in 4th but hld whn sddle slipped and uns rdr 100yds out* **10/3**[3]

1m 49.15s (4.45) **Going Correction** +0.625s/f (Yiel) **9**Ran SP% **115.1**
Speed ratings (Par 102): **102,100,100,97,94 85,82,72,**
toteswingers: 1&2 £5.90, 2&3 £14.80, 1&3 £20.40 CSF £24.12 CT £402.47 TOTE £3.40 : £1.40 , £1.70, £5.20 ; EX 20.60 Trifecta £348.30 Pool: £ 784.53 - 1.66 winning units.

Owner R Roberts **Bred** Sean Collins **Trained** Kimpton, Hants

■ Stewards' Enquiry : Jim Crowley two-day ban: careless riding (Jul 23-24)

FOCUS
A decent handicap but it was a rough race. The winner rates a 4lb personal best and the second is progressing too.

Sugarformyhoney(IRE) Official explanation: jockey said filly hit a soft patch and became unbalanced

3918 STOWE FAMILY LAW LLP MAIDEN FILLIES' STKS 1m 67y
7:40 (7:41) (Class 5) 3-4-Y-O **£2,264** (£673; £336 ; £168) **Stalls** Low

Form RPR

0-4 **1** **Proximity**[30] 2941 3 -9-00 .... RyanMoore 2 78+
(Sir Michael Stoute) *mde all: rdn over 2f out: clr over 1f out: styd on wl* **3/1**[2]

00 **2** *3 3/4* **Virginia Galilei (IRE)**[6] 3399 3 -9-00 .... TedDurcan 8 70+
(David Lanigan) *hld up towards rr: jst pushed along over 2f out: plld off rail and prog over 1f out: r.o to take 2nd last strides: do bttr* **33/1**

65 **3** *nk* **Waveguide (IRE)**[22] 3189 3 -9-00 .... FergusSweeney 7 69
(David Simcock) *trckd ldrs: rdn to chse wnr over 1f out: no imp: lost 2nd last strides* **18/1**

0-4 **4** *2 1/4* **All Time**[31] 2891 4 -9-90 .... TomQueally 14 66
(Sir Henry Cecil) *trckd ldrs: rdn over 2f out: no imp over 1f out: wl hld after* **2/1**[1]

0-0 **5** *1 1/2* **Garzoni**[6] 3735 3 -8-90 .... RosieJessop[(5)] 1 61+
(Sir Mark Prescott Bt) *s.i.s: rn green in last pair: prog on wd outside 3f out: rdn and no hdwy fnl 2f and stl green* **40/1**

5 **6** *3* **We Used To Wait (USA)**[5] 3070 3 -9-00 .... RobertHavlin 5 54
(Peter Chapple-Hyam) *trckd ldrs: rdn over 2f out: wknd over 1f out* **14/1**

5 **7** *1 1/2* **Hummingbird**[30] 2941 3 -9-00 .... RichardHughes 9 50
(William Haggas) *chsd wnr: shkn up 3f out: no imp 2f out: lost 2nd over 1f out and wknd* **5/1**[3]

8 *nk* **Divea** 3 -9-00 .... MichaelHills 10 50
(Charles Hills) *t.k.h: hld up in last: pushed along and rchd 8th over 2f out: no further prog* **7/1**

0 **9** *9* **Queen Hermione (IRE)**[91] 3227 4 -9-90 ....(p) LiamKeniry 12 31
(Linda Jewell) *a towards rr: wknd 3f out: wl bhd fnl 2f* **200/1**

-000 **10** *12* **Lady Ocarina**[12] 3483 3 -9-048 ....(b[1]) DaneO'Neill 11
(John Dunlop) *v s.i.s: sn in tch: rdn and wknd over 3f out: eased and t.o* **100/1**

1m 50.31s (5.61) **Going Correction** +0.625s/f (Yiel)
WFA 3 from 4yo 9lb **10**Ran SP% **106.3**
Speed ratings (Par 100): **96,92,91,89,88 85,83,83,74,62**
toteswingers: 1&2 £18.40, 2&3 £27.80, 1&3 £5.70 CSF £81.85 TOTE £2.90 : £1.50 , £7.30 , £4.30; EX 113.30 TRIFECTA Not won.

Owner K Abdulla **Bred** Juddmonte Farms Ltd **Trained** Newmarket, Suffolk

■ Treasured Dream was withdrawn (8/1, burst out of stalls). Deduct 10p in the £ under R4.

FOCUS
This didn't look a strong maiden but the winner did it the hard way from the front and deserves credit. The pre-race standard was not great, but the form has been given a bit of a chance with improvement from the first two.

3919 BUILDING MANAGEMENT SOLUTIONS INTEGRATORS H'CAP 5f 10y
8:10 (8:11) (Class 4) (0-85,82) 3-Y-0+ **£4,204** (£1,251; £625 ; £312) **Stalls** Low

Form RPR

0045 **1** **West Coast Dream**[3] 3822 5 -9-1282 .... IanMongan 2 93
(Roy Brotherton) *mde all: racd nr side 1st 2f: rdn clr over 1f out: unchal* **11/10**[1]

-000 **2** *4 1/2* **Macdillon**[32] 2853 6 -9-171 .... LiamKeniry 3 66
(Stuart Kittow) *hld up: prog to go 2nd wl over 1f out: sn rdn and no imp on wnr* **9/2**[2]

-002 **3** *2 1/4* **Knocker Knowles (IRE)**[28] 2987 3 -9-075 .... CathyGannon 5 60
(David Evans) *chsd ldr of gp which wnt far side: outpcd wl over 1f out: plugged on* **11/2**

0644 **4** *2* **Haadeeth**[10] 3570 5 -9-477 .... MatthewCosham[(3)] 1 57
(David Evans) *taken down early: rousted along early: chsd wnr and styd nr side 1st 2f: drvn and wknd wl over 1f out* **18/1**

000 **5** *1 1/4* **Star Rover (IRE)**[9] 3612 5 -9-378 .... NathanSweeney[(5)] 6 53
(David Evans) *sn detached in last: jst pushed along over 1f out: tk modest 5th nr fin: nvr involved* **10/1**

1013 **6** *2* **Billy Red**[9] 3618 8 -9-575 ....(b) FergusSweeney 4 43
(J R Jenkins) *led gp who wnt far side: losing pl whn sltly hmpd 2f out and dropped out* **5/1**[3]

1m 2.46s (2.16) **Going Correction** +0.525s/f (Yiel)
WFA 3 from 5yo+ 5lb **6**Ran SP% **112.2**
Speed ratings (Par 105): **103,95,92,89,87 83**
toteswingers: 1&2 £1.90, 2&3 £4.70, 1&3 £2.40 CSF £6.37 TOTE £2.20 : £1.40 , £2.80 ; EX 7.20 TRIFECTA Not won.

Owner Miss Emma Byrd **Bred** Eurostrait Ltd **Trained** Elmley Castle, Worcs

FOCUS
A moderate sprint handicap and despite the small field they split into two groups before joining at halfway where they raced up the far rail. It's doubtful this was a personal best from the winner despite the size of the margin.

3920 ALEXANDER DEVINE CHILDREN'S HOSPICE SERVICE H'CAP 1m 2f 7y
8:40 (8:40) (Class 5) (0-75,75) 3-Y-0+ **£2,264** (£673; £336 ; £168) **Stalls** High

Form RPR

0334 **1** **Incendiary (IRE)**[12] 3503 3 -9-375 .... MichaelHills 3 83
(Hugo Palmer) *trckd ldrs: lost pl 3f out: renewed effrt and weaved through fr over 1f out: styd on wl to ld last strides* **5/1**[1]

54-5 **2** *hd* **Rysbrack (USA)**[21] 3227 6 -9-1374 .... JimmyFortune 10 81
(Paul Webber) *trckd ldr to 3f out: hrd rdn 2f out: r.o fr over 1f out: led ins fnl f: hdd last strides* **5/1**[1]

-626 **3** *1/2* **Graylyn Valentino**[79] 1519 3 -8-263 .... HarryBentley[(3)] 7 69
(Robin Dickin) *prom: styd on outer fnl 3f: rdn over 2f out: c to chal over 1f out: nt qckn ins fnl f* **14/1**

0066 **4** *1/2* **Larkrise Star**[14] 3443 5 -9-364 .... ShaneKelly 4 69
(Dean Ivory) *hld up in rr: prog fr 1/2-way: grabbed far rail and drvn to ld 2f out: hdd and one pce ins fnl f* **6/1**[3]

4-30 **5** *1 1/2* **Red Lover**[31] 2899 4 -10-075 .... RyanMoore 1 77
(Ed Dunlop) *dwlt: hld up in rr: tried to make prog fr over 3f out: chsd ldrs 2f out: kpt on but nvr able to chal* **6/1**[3]

1404 **6** *1 3/4* **Whipcrackaway (IRE)**[17] 3338 3 -9-173 .... NeilCallan 5 80+
(Peter Hedger) *hld up in midfield: rdn 3f out: prog u.p against far rail 2f out: chalng whn hmpd 100yds out: nt rcvr and eased* **11/2**[2]

2300 **7** *3/4* **Macy Anne (IRE)**[12] 3193 3 -7-1259 ow2 .... RyanPowell[(3)] 12 56
(Robert Mills) *trckd ldrs: prog to ld 3f out: hdd 2f out: wknd fnl f* **50/1**

1265 **8** *1 1/4* **Cairanne**[26] 3047 4 -8-557 .... DarrenEgan[(5)] 6 52
(Tom Keddy) *taken down early: led to 3f out: styd cl up tl wknd over 1f out* **10/1**

0126 **9** *nk* **Temuco (IRE)**[11] 3543 3 -8-1068 .... CathyGannon 2 62
(David Evans) *trckd ldrs: rdn over 2f out: nt qckn wl over 1f out: wknd fnl f* **8/1**

62-0 **10** *13* **Vergrigio (IRE)**[27] 3014 3 -7-1360 .... SimonPearce[(3)] 9 28
(David Pipe) *hld up in last and detached: lost tch 4f out: wl bhd after* **40/1**

0-00 **11** *18* **Alshazah**[22] 3187 4 -9-1071 .... JamesMillman 13
(Rod Millman) *hld up wl in rr: lost tch 4f out: wl bhd after: t.o* **16/1**

04-0 **12** *37* **Songburst**[39] 2637 4 -9-1374 .... KieranO'Neill 8
(Richard Hannon) *t.k.h: hld up in last trio: lost tch 4f out: wl bhd after: wl t.o* **28/1**

2m 15.62s (6.92) **Going Correction** +0.625s/f (Yiel)
WFA 3 from 4yo+ 11lb **12**Ran SP% **117.9**
Speed ratings (Par 103): **97,96,96,96,94 93,92,91,91,81 66,37**
toteswingers: 1&2 £7.70, 2&3 £19.60, 1&3 £9.70 CSF £28.93 CT £332.13 TOTE £6.90 : £2.10 , £2.90, £7.00 ; EX 36.30 TRIFECTA Not won.

Owner Derek Iceton **Bred** Limestone & Tara Studs **Trained** Newmarket, Suffolk

■ Stewards' Enquiry : Jimmy Fortune two-day ban: used whip above permitted level (Jul 23-24)
Michael Hills one-day ban: careless riding (Jul 26)

FOCUS
A fair handicap and again there was trouble in the closing stages as the field tightened up against the far rail. The sixth has been rated as finishing second and the winner improved for the trip.
T/Plt: £187.90 to a £1 stake. Pool of £116216.87 - 451.44 winning tickets. T/Qpdt: £49.10 to a £1 stake. Pool of £7585.40 - 114.26 w. tickets JN 3921a-3927a (Foreign Racing) See RI

3680 CHANTILLY (R-H)
Monday, July 9

OFFICIAL GOING: Turf: soft; polytrack: standard

3928a PRIX DU SOLEIL DE BRETAGNE (MAIDEN) (UNRACED 2YO COLTS & GELDINGS) (TURF) 6f
1:20 (12:00) 2-Y-0 **£10,000** (£4,000; £3,000 ; £2,000 ; £1,000)

RPR

1 **Bontoni (FR)** 2 -9-20 .... FabriceVeron 1 80
(H-A Pantall, France) **98/10**

2 *1 1/2* **Thats Notall Folks (IRE)**2 -9-20 .... Christophe-PatriceLemaire 7 76
(F-H Graffard, France) **5/1**[3]

3 *snk* **Lewamy (IRE)** 2 -9-20 .... ChristopheSoumillon 4 75
(John Best) *broke wl: racd cl up bhd ldrs: wnt 2nd after 2 1/2f: rdn and chal for ld 1 1/2f out: shared ld for a few strides 250yds out: nt qckn: r.o u.p fnl f: lost 2nd cl home* **3/1**[2]

4 *2* **Chaparral Ridge (FR)**2 -8-100 .... AntoineCoutier[(6)] 2 69
(F Chappet, France) **21/1**

5 *5* **Strix** 2 -9-20 .... StephanePasquier 6 54
(P Bary, France) **2/1**[1]

6 *snk* **Sparks Fly (FR)**2 -9-20 .... UmbertoRispoli 5 54
(S Kobayashi, France) **22/1**

7 *6* **Crazy Beloved (IRE)**2 -9-20 .... OlivierPeslier 3 36
(Robert Collet, France) **3/1**[2]

1m 15.53s (4.13) **7**Ran SP% **118.2**
WIN (incl. 1 euro stake): 10.80. PLACES: 4.20, 3.10. SF: 62.80
Owner Guy Heald **Bred** Appapays Racing Club **Trained** France

3692 PONTEFRACT (L-H)
Tuesday, July 10
3929 Meeting Abandoned - waterlogged

2400 SOUTHWELL (L-H)
Tuesday, July 10

OFFICIAL GOING: Standard
Wind: Moderate, behind. Weather: Overcast and raining

3936 BET TOTEPLACEPOT AT TOTEPOOL.COM NURSERY 5f (F)
6:05 (6:05) (Class 6) (0-65,65) 2-Y-O £1,617 (£481; £240; £120) **Stalls** High

Form				RPR
456	1		**La Sylphe**[46] 2437 2-9-5 **63** GrahamGibbons 5 (David Barron) *qckly away: mde all: rdn over 1f out: styd on strly* **2/1**[2]	68
400	2	2 1/4	**Lincolnrose (IRE)**[16] 3415 2-8-9 **60** WilliamTwiston-Davies(7) 1 (Alan McCabe) *chsd ldrs on outer: pushed along 2f out: sn rdn and styd on ins fnl f to take 2nd nr fin* **8/1**	57
2600	3	3/4	**Stripped Bear (IRE)**[50] 2338 2-8-12 **56** RichardKingscote 6 (Tom Dascombe) *chsd wnr: rdn over 1f out: drvn and one pce fnl f: lost 2nd nr fin* **7/1**	50
3544	4	nse	**Crystal Cove**[32] 2873 2-9-1 **59** DavidAllan 2 (Tim Easterby) *chsd ldng pair: rdn along 2f out: no imp appr fnl f* **13/8**[1]	53
0533	5	12	**Dil Laney (IRE)**[21] 3251 2-9-7 **65** (b[1]) SilvestreDeSousa 4 (David O'Meara) *dwlt: sn rdn along in rr: bhd fnl 2f* **13/2**[3]	16

58.99s (-0.71) **Going Correction** -0.35s/f (Stan) **5** Ran SP% **108.4**
Speed ratings (Par 92): **91,87,86,86,66**
CSF £16.27 TOTE £8.60: £2.20, £4.50; EX 25.30.
Owner M Dalby **Bred** Denis Barry **Trained** Maunby, N Yorks

FOCUS
A modest nursery run at a decent gallop with the wind behind the runners. The winner raced in the centre of the track throughout. Straightforward form.

NOTEBOOK
La Sylphe ◆, with the headgear left off, showed bags of foot and turned in an improved display to win in comfortable fashion on this AW and nursery debut. This wasn't a strong race but she's open to further progress and will be of interest after reassessment. (tchd 9-4)
Lincolnrose(IRE), well beaten on her last two starts, returned to the form of her debut run on this AW and nursery debut with the cheekpieces left off. She'll be suited by the step up to 6f and she should be able to pick up a small event at some point. (op 13-2 tchd 11-2)
Stripped Bear(IRE) had disappointed since running encouragingly on her debut but she appreciated the switch back to Fibresand and wasn't disgraced on this nursery debut. The step up to 6f may suit better but her record suggests she wouldn't be certain to build on this next time. (tchd 13-2 and 15-2)
Crystal Cove attracted plenty of support on this nursery debut but, although not disgraced, failed to reverse debut C&D placings with Stripped Bear. However he's another that will benefit from a step up in distance and he isn't one to write off just yet. (op 2-1 tchd 9-4)
Dil Laney(IRE) hadn't been in much form and was soundly beaten after a tardy start on this nursery and AW debut in the first-time blinkers. He has plenty to prove at present. (op 11-2)

3937 E B F RON BROOKS TOYOTA 50TH ANNIVERSARY MAIDEN STKS 5f (F)
6:35 (6:36) (Class 5) 2-Y-O £3,408 (£1,006; £503) **Stalls** High

Form				RPR
	1		**Dutch Masterpiece** 2-9-3 0 GeorgeBaker 4 (Gary Moore) *led to s: trckd ldrs: smooth hdwy to ld over 1f out: sn pushed clr: comf* **11/4**[1]	80+
054	2	2 1/4	**Max The Machine**[10] 3627 2-9-0 68 DaleSwift(3) 1 (Derek Shaw) *chsd ldrs on outer: rdn along wl over 1f out: styd on to chse wnr ent fnl f: sn no imp* **10/1**	69
62	3	5	**Mrs Warren**[19] 3313 2-8-12 0 RobertWinston 3 (Charles Hills) *led: rdn along 2f out: hdd over 1f out: sn drvn and wknd fnl f* **3/1**[2]	46
	4	1 1/2	**Ingleby Symphony (IRE)** 2-8-12 0 BarryMcHugh 5 (Richard Fahey) *rn green and sn outpcd in rr: rdn along 1/2-way: hdwy on wd outside wl over 1f out: styd on fnl f: nrest at fin* **28/1**	41
	5	1	**Queen Flush (IRE)** 2-8-12 0 AdrianNicholls 9 (David Nicholls) *cl up: rdn along 2f out: sn drvn and wknd* **11/4**[1]	37
53	6	9	**Miss Starry Eyed**[27] 3046 2-8-12 0 SilvestreDeSousa 10 (Derek Shaw) *racd nr stands' rail: chsd ldrs: rdn along over 2f out: sn wknd* **28/1**	5
4	7	1/2	**Masai King (IRE)**[25] 3123 2-9-3 0 DarryllHolland 6 (Robin Bastiman) *dwlt: sn rdn along: a towards rr* **5/1**[3]	8
65	8	4 1/2	**Kingsville**[8] 3708 2-9-3 0 JoeFanning 8 (Mark Johnston) *sn rdn along in rr: a outpcd and bhd* **33/1**	
00	9	13	**Karl Marx (IRE)**[15] 3444 2-8-12 0 (p) LeeNewnes(5) 2 (Mark Usher) *dwlt: a outpcd and bhd* **100/1**	

58.65s (-1.05) **Going Correction** -0.35s/f (Stan) **9** Ran SP% **114.9**
Speed ratings (Par 94): **94,90,82,80,78 64,63,56,35**
Tote Swingers 1&2 £6.00, 2&3 £4.00, 1&3 CSF £29.38 TOTE £3.80: £1.30, £3.60, £1.40; EX 29.50 Trifecta £148.70 Pool £570.82 - 2.84 winning units..
Owner R A Green **Bred** Bumble Bloodstock Ltd **Trained** Lower Beeding, W Sussex

FOCUS
No more than a fair maiden but the winner did it in style and looks a useful prospect. The gallop was sound throughout and the winner came down the centre. It will be a surprise if he can't progress to the mid 80s at least. The runner-up is rated to his mark.

NOTEBOOK
Dutch Masterpiece ◆, a 67,000euro scopey half-brother to triple 6f-7f Fibresand winner Beachwood Bay, had bolted and was withdrawn before his intended debut last month but he was led to the start this time and created a favourable impression with the way he travelled and quickened in the race itself. His trainer doesn't have too many debut scorers but this one is open to plenty of improvement, will be at least as good over 6f and is the type to hold his own in stronger company. (op 2-1 tchd 15-8)
Max The Machine, bogged down in testing ground at Newcastle on his previous start, returned to form on this Fibresand debut against one that could turn out to be very useful. He's had a few chances but will be worth keeping an eye on when switched to ordinary nursery company. (tchd 12-1)
Mrs Warren had shown modest form on both turf runs but failed to build on those efforts on this Fibresand debut. She's likely to remain vulnerable to the better types in this grade but may do better back on turf in nurseries. (tchd 7-2)
Ingleby Symphony(IRE), who has plenty of stamina on the dam's side of his pedigree, was too green to do himself justice on this racecourse debut over a trip that looked on the short side but showed he has ability. He'll be one to look out for granted a much stiffer test once qualified for a nursery mark. (tchd 25-1 and 33-1)
Queen Flush(IRE), who cost 30,000GBP, attracted plenty of support and showed up well for a long way on this racecourse debut. She should be better for this experience and will be worth another chance in ordinary company. (op 7-2)
Masai King(IRE) had shown ability (albeit at a moderate level) on his debut at York but he failed to build on that and looked anything but happy on the Fibresand surface. He'll be of more interest back on turf when stepped up in trip and once qualified for a nursery mark. (op 7-1)

3938 BOOK TICKETS ONLINE AT SOUTHWELL-RACECOURSE.CO.UK CLAIMING STKS 1m (F)
7:05 (7:05) (Class 6) 3-Y-O £1,704 (£503; £251) **Stalls** Low

Form				RPR
6062	1		**Daddy Warbucks (IRE)**[11] 3575 3-9-5 70 AdrianNicholls 2 (David Nicholls) *mde all: rdn 2f out: sn jnd: drvn ins fnl f and kpt on wl* **7/4**[1]	73
1300	2	1/2	**Smart Affair**[27] 3048 3-8-2 48 (v[1]) LukeMorris 6 (Alan Bailey) *midfield: hdwy on inner to chse ldrs 3f out: effrt to chal wl over 1f out: sn rdn and ev ch tl drvn and no ex last 100yds* **16/1**	55
0456	3	3 3/4	**Adili (IRE)**[18] 2118 3-9-5 65 BarryMcHugh 7 (Brian Ellison) *bhd and rdn along 1/2-way: hdwy wl over 1f out: drvn and styd on fnl f: nrst fin* **16/1**	63
2-05	4	1 1/4	**Fredrickthegreat**[15] 3433 3-9-1 64 (t) DarryllHolland 8 (Hughie Morrison) *in tch: pushed along and wd st: rdn 2f out: kpt on one pce u.p fnl f* **9/1**	57
514	5	3/4	**Final Delivery**[21] 3248 3-9-1 68 (p) PatCosgrave 4 (George Baker) *chsd ldng pair: rdn along over 2f out: drvn wl over 1f out and grad wknd* **6/1**[3]	55
-603	6	1 1/2	**Surrey Dream (IRE)**[11] 3591 3-8-11 62 GrahamLee 5 (Roger Teal) *towards rr: rdn along 1/2-way: styd on u.p fnl 2f: nrst fin* **10/1**	47
-430	7	2 1/4	**Raffinn**[14] 3475 3-9-2 66 LiamKeniry 10 (Sylvester Kirk) *cl up: rdn along over 2f out: sn wknd* **8/1**	47
-530	8	6	**Four Richer**[14] 3471 3-9-5 75 (b) GeorgeBaker 9 (Jamie Osborne) *chsd ldrs: rdn along over 2f out: sn drvn and wknd* **4/1**[2]	36
-646	9	2	**High Five Prince (IRE)**[28] 3014 3-8-0 45 NicoleNordblad(7) 3 (Mark Usher) *dwlt: a in rr: bhd fnl 3f* **40/1**	20
2000	10	26	**Always Ends Well (IRE)**[10] 3620 3-8-0 54 SilvestreDeSousa 1 (Mark Johnston) *chsd ldrs on inner: rdn along and lost pl bef 1/2-way: bhd fnl 3f* **20/1**	

1m 42.88s (-0.82) **Going Correction** -0.15s/f (Stan) **10** Ran SP% **119.8**
Speed ratings (Par 98): **98,97,93,92,91 90,88,82,80,54**
Tote Swingers 1&2 £5.10, 2&3 £38.20, 1&3 £14.30 CSF £35.37 TOTE £3.00: £1.10, £3.50, £10.20; EX 40.00 Trifecta £177.40 Pool £273.40 - 1.14 winning units..
Owner Martin Love **Bred** Edmond Kent **Trained** Sessay, N Yorks

FOCUS
An ordinary event of its type. The gallop was fair and the first two, who pulled clear, edged from the centre towards the far side in the closing stages.

3939 YOUR FAVOURITE POOL BETS AT TOTEPOOL.COM MAIDEN H'CAP 1m (F)
7:35 (7:36) (Class 6) (0-60,60) 3-Y-O+ £1,704 (£503; £251) **Stalls** Low

Form				RPR
00-0	1		**Kung Hei Fat Choy (USA)**[49] 2382 3-9-2 **59** (b[1]) GrahamLee 10 (James Given) *trckd ldrs on outer: smooth hdwy to ld over 2f out: rdn clr over 1f out: styd on strly* **8/1**	77
-506	2	7	**Symphony Star (IRE)**[12] 3547 3-8-13 **56** [1] LukeMorris 2 (Paul D'Arcy) *chsd ldrs on inner: hdwy 3f out: rdn to chse wnr wl over 1f out: drvn and no imp fnl f* **14/1**	58
4-04	3	2	**Tony Hollis**[25] 3098 4-9-5 **53** JamesMillman 7 (Rod Millman) *prom: led 1/2-way: rdn along and hdd 3f out: sn drvn and kpt on same pce* **8/1**	52
0/	4	4	**Glendaragh (IRE)**[354] 4304 4-9-9 **57** SilvestreDeSousa 8 (David O'Meara) *led to 1/2-way: cl up: rdn to ld again 3f out: hdd over 2f out and sn drvn: grad wknd* **13/2**[3]	47
5-33	5	2 1/4	**Trusting (IRE)**[21] 3246 3-9-2 **59** CathyGannon 9 (Eve Johnson Houghton) *in tch: hdwy to chse ldrs 3f out: rdn along over 2f out: sn no imp* **9/2**[1]	42
3300	6	8	**Coral Sands (IRE)**[18] 3353 4-9-6 **54** RobertWinston 14 (Alan Swinbank) *midfield: hdwy over 3f out: sn rdn and n.d* **11/2**[2]	28
2050	7	shd	**Tooley Woods (IRE)**[37] 2733 3-8-10 **60** WilliamTwiston-Davies(7) 12 (Alan McCabe) *dwlt and in rr: sme hdwy 3f out: sn rdn along and nvr a factor* **33/1**	24
0-00	8	1 1/2	**Cookieshake**[31] 2937 4-9-2 **50** WilliamCarson 4 (Peter Hiatt) *in tch: rdn along over 3f out: sn wknd* **25/1**	
5-40	9	13	**Snow Ridge**[150] 522 4-9-5 **53** (b) RichardThomas 13 (Ralph Beckett) *sn rdn along: a in rr* **9/1**	
3300	10	8	**Vena Amoris (USA)**[52] 2283 3-9-3 **60** JoeFanning 1 (Mark Johnston) *a towards rr: bhd fnl 3f* **18/1**	
054	11	49	**Alpha Arion (IRE)**[32] 2881 3-9-1 **58** DavidAllan 3 (Tim Easterby) *cl up whn stmbld and lost action after 2 1/2f: sn lost pl and bhd: virtually p.u fnl 3f* **9/2**[1]	
/066	12	19	**Jessica Ashton**[28] 3011 4-9-2 **50** (b) PatCosgrave 5 (Stuart Kittow) *dwlt and in rr whn swtchd to outer after 2f: sn outpcd and bhd: eased fnl 2f* **50/1**	

1m 42.35s (-1.35) **Going Correction** -0.15s/f (Stan)
WFA 3 from 4yo 9lb **12** Ran SP% **118.0**
Speed ratings (Par 101): **100,93,91,87,84 76,76,75,62,54 5,**
Tote Swingers 1&2 £23.60, 2&3 £17.10, 1&3 £18.00 CSF £111.97 CT £944.39 TOTE £8.30: £3.30, £2.90, £3.00; EX 120.90 TRIFECTA Not won..
Owner Danethorpe Racing Partnership **Bred** Gilgai Farm **Trained** Willoughton, Lincs

FOCUS
A moderate handicap in which the gallop was a reasonable one. The wide-margin winner came down the centre in the straight.
Kung Hei Fat Choy(USA) ◆ Official explanation: trainer said, regarding apparent improvement in form, that the gelding had matured since its last run and had also benefited from the application of the first-time blinkers.
Coral Sands(IRE) Official explanation: jockey said gelding hung left on bend
Alpha Arion(IRE) Official explanation: jockey said gelding lost its action

3940 TOTEPOOL.COM SPORTS, GAMES, BINGO & MORE FILLIES' H'CAP 7f (F)
8:05 (8:06) (Class 5) (0-75,75) 3-Y-O+ £2,264 (£673; £336; £168) **Stalls** Low

Form				RPR
0323	1		**Ursula (IRE)**[13] 3495 6-9-2 **66** MichaelMetcalfe(3) 11 (Mrs K Burke) *chsd ldrs on outer: hdwy to chal 2f out: rdn over 1f out: drvn ins fnl f: kpt on to ld nr fin* **12/1**	74
4340	2	hd	**Tahnee Mara (IRE)**[19] 3314 3-8-8 **63** AmyRyan 10 (Kevin Ryan) *prom: hdwy to ld 3f out: jnd 2f out and sn rdn: drvn ent fnl f: hdd and no ex towards fin* **8/1**	67

3134 **3** *2 3/4* **Annie Walker (IRE)**[17] 3383 3-9-1 **70**............................ AdrianNicholls 2 67
(David Nicholls) *led: rdn along and hdd 3f out: cl up tl drvn and one pce appr fnl f* **5/1**[3]

14 **4** *1/2* **Sweetnessandlight**[39] 2679 3-8-8 **63**.......................... MichaelStainton 7 59+
(Jason Ward) *awkward s and sn pushed along in rr: rdn and hdwy 3f out: drvn to chse ldrs over 1f out: kpt on fnl f: nrst fin* **5/2**[1]

5100 **5** *5* **Hold The Star**[13] 3495 6-8-5 **57**.. AnnStokell(5) 3 42
(Ann Stokell) *chsd ldrs: rdn along 3f out: grad wknd fnl 2f* **40/1**

0066 **6** *1 3/4* **Basantee**[21] 3252 3-8-10 **65**.. RichardKingscote 5 42
(Tom Dascombe) *chsd ldrs: rdn along 3f out: sn wknd* **7/1**

-200 **7** *1 3/4* **Barathea Dancer (IRE)**[10] 3643 4-9-11 **72**...................... KierenFallon 6 48
(Roger Teal) *a towards rr* **12/1**

5-1 **8** *13* **Safe House (IRE)**[11] 3580 3-9-6 **75**.................................. JoeFanning 1 13
(Mark Johnston) *chsd ldrs on inner: rdn along 1/2-way: sn wknd* **4/1**[2]

250 **9** *hd* **Piece Of Cake**[33] 2865 3-8-9 **64**.................................... RobertWinston 9
(Charles Hills) *in tch: rdn along 1/2-way: sn wknd* **11/1**

1m 28.85s (-1.45) **Going Correction** -0.15s/f (Stan)
WFA 3 from 4yo+ 8lb **9** Ran SP% **115.0**
Speed ratings (Par 100): **102,101,98,98,92 90,88,73,73**
Tote Swingers 1&2 £10.70, 2&3 £9.30, 1&3 £5.10 CSF £103.25 CT £550.73 TOTE £20.20: £3.40, £3.30, £1.90; EX 113.10 Trifecta £196.50 Pool £366.62 - 1.38 winning units..
Owner Mrs Elaine M Burke **Bred** Rathbarry Stud **Trained** Middleham Moor, N Yorks

FOCUS
An ordinary fillies' handicap in which the gallop was sound but another race on the card that proved difficult to make ground from off the pace. The winner came down the centre.
Safe House(IRE) Official explanation: jockey said filly never travelled

3941 DEAL OR NO DEAL AT TOTEPOOL.COM H'CAP 6f (F)
8:35 (8:36) (Class 5) (0-70,68) 3-Y-0+ **£2,264** (£673; £336; £168) **Stalls** Low

Form RPR

21-0 **1** **Salik Tag (USA)**[80] 1520 4-9-9 **65**................................(t) AdrianNicholls 6 76
(David Nicholls) *dwlt and sn bustled along to join ldrs: sn cl up: rdn to chal 2f out: led over 1f out: drvn out* **8/1**

602 **2** *3/4* **Tunnager Grove**[12] 3539 3-9-6 **68**.................................. DarryllHolland 3 76
(Hughie Morrison) *trckd ldrs on inner: hdwy wl over 2f out: chal wl over 1f out and sn rdn: drvn and ev ch ins fnl f: no ex last 75yds* **5/1**[3]

1141 **3** *1 1/4* **Clear Spring (IRE)**[14] 3466 4-9-8 **64**.............................. NickyMackay 8 69
(John Spearing) *cl up on outer: effrt 2f out: sn rdn and ev ch tl drvn and one pce ins fnl f* **5/2**[1]

210 **4** *1/2* **Gracie's Gift (IRE)**[15] 3442 10-8-9 **51**....................(v) SilvestreDeSousa 7 54
(Richard Guest) *in rr: hdwy 2f out: sn rdn and styd on fnl f: nrest at fin* **7/1**

1000 **5** *1 3/4* **Punching**[6] 3761 8-9-12 **68**.. HayleyTurner 1 65
(Conor Dore) *led: rdn along over 2f out: drvn and hdd over 1f out: grad wknd* **8/1**

0200 **6** *1* **Beachwood Bay**[15] 3442 4-9-1 **64**................ WilliamTwiston-Davies(7) 2 58
(Jo Hughes) *hld up on inner: hdwy over 2f out: sn rdn and no imp appr fnl f* **10/3**[2]

0000 **7** *1/2* **Ace Of Spies (IRE)**[7] 3738 7-9-6 **62**................................... LukeMorris 5 55
(Conor Dore) *chsd ldrs: rdn along over 2f out: sn drvn and wknd* **20/1**

0600 **8** *1/2* **Elhamri**[6] 3761 8-9-8 **64**... KirstyMilczarek 4 55
(Conor Dore) *chsd ldrs: rdn along over 2f out: wknd over 1f out* **20/1**

/406 **9** *3 1/2* **Amber Moon**[33] 2859 7-8-3 **50** oh4 ow1........................(b) AnnStokell(5) 9 30
(Ann Stokell) *a towards rr* **66/1**

1m 15.37s (-1.13) **Going Correction** -0.15s/f (Stan)
WFA 3 from 4yo+ 6lb **9** Ran SP% **114.1**
Speed ratings (Par 103): **101,100,98,97,95 94,93,92,88**
Tote Swingers 1&2 £8.50, 2&3 £3.40, 1&3 £6.60 CSF £45.90 CT £129.46 TOTE £11.60: £4.00, £2.40, £1.10; EX 74.30 TRIFECTA Not won..
Owner Malih Lahej Al Basti **Bred** Lantern Hill Farm Llc **Trained** Sessay, N Yorks

FOCUS
A modest handicap run at a decent gallop and it again paid to race right up with the pace. The gallop was sound and the winner came down the centre.

3942 MIRROR PUNTERS CLUB H'CAP 1m 6f (F)
9:05 (9:05) (Class 6) (0-65,63) 4-Y-0+ **£1,704** (£503; £251) **Stalls** Low

Form RPR

5000 **1** **Omid**[26] 3086 4-8-10 **52**..(vt[1]) LukeMorris 3 63
(Nicky Vaughan) *trckd ldrs: hdwy 4f out: rdn to chse ldr 3f out: led wl over 1f out: sn clr and styd on strly* **10/1**

0060 **2** *9* **Yas Marina (USA)**[36] 2775 4-8-4 **46**....................(b[1]) SilvestreDeSousa 1 44
(David O'Meara) *led and set str pce: sn clr: rdn along 3f out: drvn 2f out: sn hdd and one pce* **9/2**[2]

00-6 **3** *6* **Astragal**[36] 2755 4-8-12 **54**... KierenFallon 5 44
(Shaun Lycett) *in tch: hdwy 6f out: rdn to chse ldr over 5f out: drvn along 3f out: sn wknd* **8/1**

0504 **4** *3* **Lucas Pitt**[42] 2575 5-8-4 **46**..(v) WilliamCarson 4 32
(Michael Scudamore) *chsd ldrs: rdn along over 5f out: sn drvn and outpcd fr over 3f out* **9/2**[2]

1036 **5** *7* **Carnac (IRE)**[23] 3180 6-9-0 **63**....................(p) WilliamTwiston-Davies(7) 7 39
(Alan McCabe) *sn pushed along in rr: rdn 1/2-way: nvr a factor* **2/1**[1]

-000 **6** *10* **Cozy Tiger (USA)**[24] 3162 7-9-6 **62**.............................. StevieDonohoe 8 24
(Willie Musson) *hld up: rdn along in rr 6f out: nvr a factor* **5/1**[3]

00-3 **7** *46* **Ritsi**[16] 3310 9-8-0 **45**..(t) JulieBurke(3) 2
(Marjorie Fife) *chsd clr ldr: rdn along 1/2-way: sn wknd and wl bhd fnl 3f* **20/1**

3m 6.57s (-1.73) **Going Correction** -0.15s/f (Stan) **7** Ran SP% **111.3**
Speed ratings (Par 101): **98,92,89,87,83 78,51**
Tote Swingers 1&2 £8.50, 2&3 £5.80, 1&3 £13.70 CSF £51.10 CT £370.28 TOTE £9.60: £3.50, £3.00; EX 51.40 Trifecta £183.60 Pool £307.75 - 1.24 winning units..
Owner Andrew Tinkler **Bred** Silfield Bloodstock **Trained** Stoke Heath, Shropshire

FOCUS
A modest handicap but one that didn't take as much winning as seemed likely with three of the market leaders under-performing. The gallop was sound and the winner came down the centre.
Omid Official explanation: trainer said, regarding apparent improvement in form, that the gelding benefited for the first-time visor.
Carnac(IRE) Official explanation: jockey said gelding ran flat
T/Plt: £647.00 to a £1 stake. Pool £72,821.95. 82.16 winning tickets. T/Qpdt: £130.80 to a £1 stake. Pool £7,371.36. 41.70 winning tickets. JR

3706 WOLVERHAMPTON (A.W) (L-H)
Tuesday, July 10

OFFICIAL GOING: Standard
Wind: Light across Weather: Showers

3943 WOLVERHAMPTON-RACECOURSE.CO.UK H'CAP 5f 216y(P)
2:15 (2:17) (Class 6) (0-60,60) 3-Y-0+ **£1,704** (£503; £251) **Stalls** Low

Form RPR

2422 **1** **Marinus (IRE)**[15] 3451 3-8-10 **60**................................ ThomasBrown(7) 2 68
(Sylvester Kirk) *a.p: hmpd 5f out: shkn up to ld over 1f out: edgd lft ins fnl f: rdn out* **3/1**[1]

4063 **2** *shd* **Blueberry Fizz (IRE)**[6] 3761 4-9-4 **55**.................(v) DaraghO'Donohoe 10 63
(John Ryan) *outpcd: hung lft and r.o wl ins fnl f: jst failed* **12/1**

-300 **3** *1/2* **Glastonberry**[24] 3151 4-9-6 **57**.. JamieSpencer 8 64
(Geoffrey Deacon) *hld up: nt clr run over 1f out: swtchd lft and r.o wl ins fnl f: hmpd towards fin* **10/1**

2040 **4** *1/2* **Arachnophobia (IRE)**[13] 3511 6-9-9 **60**..........................(v) LukeMorris 1 65
(Martin Bosley) *sn pushed along in mid-div: hdwy u.p over 1f out: r.o: hmpd towards fin* **16/1**

1521 **5** *1 1/2* **Almaty Express**[50] 2352 10-9-9 **60**..............................(b) DarryllHolland 5 60
(John Weymes) *chsd ldrs: wnt 2nd 1/2-way: led wl over 1f out: sn rdn and hdd: edgd lft and styd on same pce ins fnl f* **6/1**[3]

6566 **6** *1* **Mawjoodah**[10] 3618 4-9-9 **60**... BarryMcHugh 4 57
(Brian Ellison) *hld up: hdwy over 2f out: rdn whn hmpd ins fnl f: no ex* **5/1**[2]

5363 **7** *1 1/2* **Insolenceofoffice (IRE)**[22] 3210 4-9-3 **59**.........................(p) LMcNiff(5) 3 51
(Richard Ford) *prom: rdn over 1f out: styd on same pce* **17/2**

4000 **8** *3/4* **Silver Linnet (IRE)**[12] 3546 5-9-6 **57**............................(p) TomQueally 11 47
(John Butler) *hld up: hdwy over 1f out: sn rdn: styd on same pce fnl f* **22/1**

0460 **9** *1 1/2* **Athaakeel (IRE)**[7] 3718 6-8-13 **53**.................................. SophieDoyle(3) 6 38
(Ronald Harris) *prom: rdn 1/2-way: wknd over 1f out* **33/1**

3503 **10** *3/4* **Anjomarba (IRE)**[8] 3701 5-9-2 **53**............................(b) KirstyMilczarek 13 36
(Conor Dore) *chsd ldr to 1/2-way: sn rdn: wknd over 1f out* **14/1**

3500 **11** *nk* **Men Don't Cry (IRE)**[14] 3470 3-9-3 **60**............................... LiamKeniry 12 41
(Ed de Giles) *broke wl: sn lost pl: drvn along 1/2-way: n.d after* **14/1**

0-60 **12** *6* **Yungaburra (IRE)**[55] 2171 8-9-2 **53**................................(t) DavidProbert 7 15
(David C Griffiths) *sn pushed along in rr: bhd fr 1/2-way* **14/1**

0060 **13** *3 1/4* **Spanish Acclaim**[34] 2815 5-9-2 **53**.................................(v[1]) AmyRyan 9
(Ruth Carr) *led: clr 5f out: hdd & wknd wl over 1f out* **12/1**

1m 14.65s (-0.35) **Going Correction** -0.05s/f (Stan)
WFA 3 from 4yo+ 6lb **13** Ran SP% **124.1**
Speed ratings (Par 101): **100,99,99,98,96 95,93,92,90,89 88,80,76**
toteswingers: 1&2 £8.40, 2&3 £17.10, 1&3 £8.60 CSF £42.63 CT £345.36 TOTE £3.50: £1.40, £4.20, £5.00; EX 48.00.
Owner Dennis Potter **Bred** M H Dixon **Trained** Upper Lambourn, Berks
■ Stewards' Enquiry : Daragh O'Donohoe three-day ban: careless riding (Jul 24-26)

FOCUS
They went hard up front early in this low-grade handicap, Spanish Acclaim tearing off in the first-time visor, and the race set up for the closers. The time was 0.86secs slower than the following claimer.

3944 DOWNLOAD OUR IPHONE APP CLASSIFIED CLAIMING STKS 5f 216y(P)
2:45 (2:50) (Class 6) 3-Y-0+ **£1,704** (£503; £251) **Stalls** Low

Form RPR

5243 **1** **Restless Bay (IRE)**[22] 3231 4-9-0 70............................(v) JimCrowley 11 73
(Reg Hollinshead) *hld up: hdwy over 1f out: rdn to ld nr fin* **5/2**[1]

6514 **2** *hd* **Another Citizen (IRE)**[7] 3730 4-8-12 65....................(b) RichardMullen 6 70
(Tim Easterby) *sn pushed along to chse ldr: led over 2f out: rdn over 1f out: hdd nr fin* **11/1**

6420 **3** *1 1/2* **Tabaret**[10] 3612 9-9-4 68..(p) AmyRyan 8 71
(Richard Whitaker) *a.p: rdn over 2f out: styd on* **9/1**

45 **4** *nk* **Superplex**[20] 3285 3-8-2 67..(p) LukeMorris 2 59
(John Quinn) *a.p: rdn over 2f out: hung lft fr over 1f out: styd on* **7/1**[2]

063 **5** *2 3/4* **Strictly Pink (IRE)**[64] 1934 4-8-7 64............................... RobertTart(7) 3 57
(Alan Bailey) *mid-div: rdn over 1f out: styd on ins fnl f: nt trble ldrs* **12/1**

3235 **6** *nk* **Waabel**[21] 3245 5-8-11 70............................(t) WilliamTwiston-Davies(7) 10 60
(Richard Guest) *mid-div: rdn over 1f out: styd on ins fnl f: nt rch ldrs* **7/1**[2]

3060 **7** *1/2* **Boundaries**[6] 3749 4-8-12 70..(b[1]) TedDurcan 13 53
(Tim Easterby) *in rr: rdn over 1f out: r.o ins fnl f: nvr nrr* **8/1**[3]

2066 **8** *2 1/2* **Efistorm**[1] 3915 11-8-11 67.. HarryBentley(3) 1 47
(Joseph Tuite) *hld up: rdn over 1f out: nvr on terms* **9/1**

065 **9** *1* **One Way Or Another (AUS)**[22] 3231 9-8-6 65..........(bt) AndreaAtzeni 9 36
(David Evans) *hld up: nvr nrr* **11/1**

5030 **10** *nk* **Absa Lutte (IRE)**[17] 3382 9-8-12 65.................................. JimmyQuinn 7 41
(Michael Mullineaux) *mid-div: rdn over 2f out: wknd over 1f out* **28/1**

0465 **11** *nse* **Missus Mills (IRE)**[19] 3312 3-8-4 64........................(p) KirstyMilczarek 5 38
(George Baker) *chsd ldrs: rdn over 2f out: wknd fnl f* **16/1**

1352 **12** *3 1/2* **Chjimes (IRE)**[28] 3008 8-8-10 66.................................(b) JamieSpencer 4 27
(Conor Dore) *led over 3f: sn rdn: wknd fnl f* **12/1**

1m 13.79s (-1.21) **Going Correction** -0.05s/f (Stan)
WFA 3 from 4yo+ 6lb **12** Ran SP% **126.1**
Speed ratings (Par 101): **106,105,103,103,99 99,98,95,93,93 93,88**
toteswingers 1&2 £8.70, 2&3 £22.60, 1&3 £7.00 CSF £34.08 TOTE £4.20: £1.80, £4.80, £3.50; EX 45.40.
Owner John L Marriott **Bred** Grangemore Stud **Trained** Upper Longdon, Staffs

FOCUS
A competitive claimer, with 6lb separating the entire field on ratings, and the pace was fair. The time was 0.86secs quicker than the preceeding handicap.
Boundaries Official explanation: jockey said gelding would not face the first-time blinkers

3945 CONNOLLY'S RED MILLS HORSE FEEDS H'CAP 1m 4f 50y(P)
3:15 (3:16) (Class 5) (0-75,77) 3-Y-0+ **£2,264** (£673; £336; £168) **Stalls** Low

Form RPR

1662 **1** **Enery (IRE)**[7] 3736 3-9-0 **74**... MircoDemuro 2 84
(Mark Johnston) *a.p: pushed along over 3f out: rdn to chse ldr over 1f out: styd on to ld ins fnl f: jst hld on* **12/1**

0540 **2** *nk* **Mizbah**[15] 3448 3-8-12 **72**.. JamieSpencer 3 82
(Saeed Bin Suroor) *hld up: hdwy over 1f out: rdn to chse wnr and hung lft ins fnl f: r.o* **6/1**[3]

-021 **3** *2 3/4* **Venegazzu (IRE)**[8] 3711 3-9-3 **77** 6ex...........................(v) RobertHavlin 6 82
(Peter Chapple-Hyam) *trckd ldrs: rdn over 1f out: styd on same pce ins fnl f* **9/4**[1]

-062 **4** *hd* **Flying Power**[21] 3253 4-10-0 **75**........................ PaddyAspell 1 80
(John Norton) *led over 10f out: pushed clr 2f out: rdn over 1f out: hdd and no ex ins fnl f* **20/1**

35-2 **5** *3 ½* **Yours Ever**[7] 3737 3-8-11 **71**........................ LukeMorris 5 70
(Sir Mark Prescott Bt) *led: hdd over 10f out: chsd ldr: rdn over 2f out: lost 2nd over 1f out: sn hung lft: wknd ins fnl f* **11/4[2]**

-055 **6** *3 ¾* **Bohemian Rhapsody (IRE)**[19] 3305 3-9-1 **75**........................ SebSanders 9 68
(J W Hills) *hld up: drvn along over 2f out: nvr trbld ldrs* **17/2**

130 **7** *1 ¾* **Rei D'Oro (USA)**[32] 2889 3-9-0 **74**........................ MartinLane 4 65
(David Simcock) *hld up: hdwy u.p over 2f out: wknd over 1f out* **8/1**

1046 **8** *1 ¾* **Sir Boss (IRE)**[8] 3692 7-10-0 **75**........................ TomQueally 8 63
(Michael Mullineaux) *hld up: rdn over 2f out: sn wknd* **25/1**

504- **9** *84* **Muzo (USA)**[416] 2312 6-10-0 **75**........................ AndreaAtzeni 7
(Chris Dwyer) *chsd ldrs: rdn over 3f out: wknd wl over 2f out: t.o* **50/1**

2m 38.69s (-2.41) **Going Correction** -0.05s/f (Stan)
WFA 3 from 4yo+ 13lb **9** Ran SP% **111.6**
Speed ratings (Par 103): **106,105,103,103,101 99,97,96,40**
toteswingers 1&2 £11.60, 2&3 £3.70, 1&3 £5.40 CSF £77.26 CT £218.76 TOTE £9.50: £2.80, £1.10, £2.00; EX 98.70.
Owner Sheikh Hamdan Bin Mohammed Al Maktoum **Bred** Ceka Ireland Limited **Trained** Middleham Moor, N Yorks

FOCUS
Fair form for the grade, with the 3yos dominating. The pace was quite ordinary.
Muzo(USA) Official explanation: vet said gelding finished lame right-fore

3946 HAPPY 60TH BIRTHDAY PAUL FREEMAN MEDIAN AUCTION MAIDEN STKS 1m 1f 103y(P)
3:45 (3:46) (Class 6) 3-4-Y-O **£1,704** (£503; £251) **Stalls** Low

Form RPR

0 **1** **Maria's Choice (IRE)**[33] 2856 3-9-3 0........................ RichardMullen 6 85
(Sir Michael Stoute) *chsd ldrs: pushed along over 2f out: rdn over 1f out: edgd lft and styd on to ld wl ins fnl f* **11/8[1]**

4342 **2** *1* **La Pampita (IRE)**[12] 3551 3-8-12 74........................[1] JimCrowley 2 78
(William Knight) *chsd ldr tl led over 2f out: rdn and hdd wl ins fnl f* **11/4[2]**

3 **3** *5* **Christingle**[48] 2387 3-8-12 0........................ LiamJones 5 68
(William Haggas) *prom: pushed along over 5f out: styd on same pce fr over 1f out* **4/1[3]**

6605 **4** *6* **Arctic Galaxy (CAN)**[26] 3088 3-8-10 62....... WilliamTwiston-Davies(7) 7 60
(John Gosden) *hld up: hdwy 1/2-way: nt clr run and lost pl over 2f out: n.d after* **11/1**

0 **5** *1 ¼* **Sandy Lane (IRE)**[17] 3399 3-9-3 0........................ DaraghO'Donohoe 1 57
(Amy Weaver) *trckd ldrs: racd keenly: rdn and wknd over 1f out* **40/1**

2063 **6** *1 ¼* **Thecornishcockney**[15] 3448 3-9-3 68........................(p[1]) StevieDonohoe 4 55
(John Ryan) *s.i.s: hld up: nvr on terms* **6/1**

0 **7** *6* **Spanish Trail**[23] 3189 3-8-12 0........................ TomMcLaughlin 8 37
(Christopher Kellett) *hld up: a in rr* **200/1**

00/ **8** *10* **Super Smile (IRE)**[673] 5808 4-9-8 0........................ LukeMorris 9 16
(Michael Appleby) *hld up: rdn over 2f out: sn wknd: t.o* **50/1**

000 **9** *4 ½* **Bonbon Bonnie**[10] 3622 4-9-1 32........................ DannyBrock(7) 3
(Phil McEntee) *led: racd keenly: rdn and hdd over 2f out: wknd over 1f out: t.o* **200/1**

10 *3 ¾* **Legal Pursuit** 3-9-0 0........................ MatthewCosham(3) 10
(Edward Bevan) *s.i.s: hld up: a in rr: t.o* **80/1**

2m 2.13s (0.43) **Going Correction** -0.05s/f (Stan)
WFA 3 from 4yo 10lb **10** Ran SP% **118.0**
Speed ratings (Par 101): **96,95,90,85,84 83,77,68,64,61**
toteswingers: 1&2 £1.80, 2&3 £3.90, 1&3 £2.90 CSF £5.38 TOTE £1.80: £1.10, £1.70, £1.60; EX 6.80.
Owner Athos Christodoulou **Bred** A Christodoulou **Trained** Newmarket, Suffolk

FOCUS
An ordinary maiden lacking depth, but a winner that can rate higher.
Sandy Lane(IRE) Official explanation: vet said gelding was struck into left-hind

3947 HOLIDAY INN WOLVERHAMPTON (S) STKS 1m 141y(P)
4:15 (4:15) (Class 6) 3-Y-0+ **£1,704** (£503; £251) **Stalls** Low

Form RPR

0350 **1** **Aciano (IRE)**[8] 3703 4-9-8 72........................(t) SebSanders 2 73
(Brendan Powell) *sn pushed along and prom: rdn over 1f out: led ins fnl f: jst hld on* **9/2[3]**

00/0 **2** *nk* **Encompassing (IRE)**[8] 3703 5-9-8 78........................(t) JamieSpencer 6 72
(Sophie Leech) *s.i.s and hmpd s: hld up: rdn over 1f out: r.o wl ins fnl f: jst failed* **8/1**

00-6 **3** *2 ¼* **Buaiteoir (FR)**[8] 3709 6-9-1 84........................ IanBurns(7) 9 67
(Amy Weaver) *hld up: hdwy over 1f out: swtchd lft ent fnl f: sn ev ch: no ex towards fin* **9/2[3]**

6003 **4** *1* **Nant Saeson (IRE)**[99] 1167 3-8-12 61........................ PaddyAspell 5 64
(John Wainwright) *hld up: rdn over 2f out: r.o ins fnl f: nvr nrr* **5/2[1]**

00-4 **5** *hd* **Resuscitator (USA)**[42] 2580 5-9-8 70........................(v) DarryllHolland 8 64
(Linda Stubbs) *led over 7f out: rdn over 1f out: hdd and no ex ins fnl f* **4/1[2]**

-206 **6** *1 ½* **Pearl Opera**[21] 3247 4-9-3 55........................(v[1]) TadhgO'Shea 7 56
(Denis Coakley) *trckd ldrs: plld hrd: rdn and hung lft fr over 1f out: no ex fnl f* **10/1**

0-00 **7** *10* **Jambobo**[18] 3338 3-8-7 25........................(b[1]) DavidKenny(5) 10 37
(William Knight) *hld up: hdwy over 3f out: sn rdn: wknd over 1f out* **100/1**

40 **8** *3* **Aragorn Rouge**[22] 3230 4-9-9 67........................ AdamCarter(5) 12 37
(John Wainwright) *prom: n.m.r and wknd over 2f out* **18/1**

245- **9** *4 ½* **Dougie Boy**[35] 4646 3-8-5 60........................ JakePayne(7) 3 19
(Bill Turner) *led 1f: chsd ldrs: drvn along 1/2-way: wknd over 2f out* **33/1**

1m 50.66s (0.16) **Going Correction** -0.05s/f (Stan)
WFA 3 from 4yo+ 10lb **9** Ran SP% **114.3**
Speed ratings (Par 101): **97,96,94,93,93 92,83,80,76**
toteswingers: 1&2 £5.60, 2&3 £7.60, 1&3 £4.10 CSF £39.75 TOTE £3.10: £1.60, £2.80, £1.70; EX 33.30.There was no bid for the winner. Nant Saeson was claimed by J. J. Quinn for £6000.
Owner Mrs Sheila Tucker **Bred** Miss Sarah Thompson **Trained** Upper Lambourn, Berks

FOCUS
The pace was relentless in this seller and it was no surprise to see the closers have their way late on.

3948 MIRROR PUNTERS CLUB MAIDEN AUCTION STKS 7f 32y(P)
4:45 (4:48) (Class 5) 2-Y-0 **£2,264** (£673; £336; £168) **Stalls** High

Form RPR

1 **Purr Along** 2-8-7 0........................ MartinDwyer 12 80+
(William Muir) *a.p: chsd ldr 1/2-way: led over 2f out: shkn up over 1f out: r.o wl: readily* **16/1**

2 *5* **Jumeirah Moon** 2-8-12 0........................ MartinLane 3 71+
(David Simcock) *a.p: pushed along over 2f out: rdn to chse wnr fnl f: no imp* **8/1[3]**

6 **3** *3* **Chant (IRE)**[18] 3351 2-8-12 0........................ FrannyNorton 11 63
(Ann Duffield) *mid-div: hdwy over 2f out: rdn over 1f out: nt clr run ins fnl f: styd on to go 3rd post: nt trble ldrs* **14/1**

4 *shd* **Poor Duke (IRE)** 2-8-11 0........................ FergusSweeney 5 62
(Jamie Osborne) *hld up: hdwy over 2f out: edgd lft fnl f: styd on* **12/1**

04 **5** *3 ¾* **Spithead**[17] 3387 2-8-9 0........................ LiamJones 6 51
(William Haggas) *led: rdn and hdd over 2f out: wknd fnl f* **9/4[1]**

0 **6** *3 ¾* **Eliya**[26] 3084 2-8-4 0........................ TadhgO'Shea 1 37
(Jo Hughes) *chsd ldr to 1/2-way: rdn over 2f out: wknd over 1f out* **66/1**

7 *½* **Caramel Sundae** 2-8-6 0........................ AndreaAtzeni 10 30
(Marco Botti) *s.s: nvr nrr* **4/1[2]**

4 **8** *5* **Rio Cato**[11] 3569 2-8-7 0 ow1........................ ShaneKelly 2 26
(Ed Dunlop) *hld up: drvn along 1/2-way: n.d* **8/1[3]**

9 *2* **Chamtille (IRE)** 2-8-5 0........................ DavidProbert 4 19
(Derek Haydn Jones) *sn pushed along in rr: bhd fr 1/2-way* **28/1**

0 **10** *¾* **Synphonic Air (IRE)**[40] 2631 2-8-5 0........................ WilliamCarson 8 18
(John Weymes) *sn outpcd* **14/1**

64 **11** *nk* **Tiger Prince (IRE)**[14] 3457 2-8-13 0........................ PaddyAspell 7 25
(Ann Duffield) *chsd ldrs tl rdn and wknd over 2f out* **17/2**

5 **12** *dist* **Double Jeopardy**[11] 3569 2-8-10 0........................ RobertHavlin 9
(Dr Jon Scargill) *mid-div: hung rt thrght: wknd 1/2-way: t.o* **33/1**

1m 29.13s (-0.47) **Going Correction** -0.05s/f (Stan) **12** Ran SP% **118.3**
Speed ratings (Par 94): **100,94,90,90,86 82,81,75,73,72 72,**
toteswingers: 1&2 £18.90, 2&3 £19.70, 1&3 £33.80 CSF £136.55 TOTE £23.60: £6.50, £3.30, £6.30; EX 191.80.
Owner Muir Racing Partnership - Manchester **Bred** Moyns Park Estate And Stud Ltd **Trained** Lambourn, Berks

FOCUS
A modest juvenile maiden run at a decent gallop. The winner impressed and could do a good deal better.

NOTEBOOK
Purr Along, a half-sister to numerous useful winners over further, won with quite a bit in hand. A daughter of Mount Nelson, she looks to have a good bit of scope, and it will be interesting to see what sort of mark she's given with nurseries in mind, although it would be no surprise to see her head straight into pattern company given the regard in which she's seemingly held by her trainer. (op 18-1 tchd 20-1)
Jumeirah Moon, whose dam was a 5f 2yo winner, travelled well into the straight and stayed on without troubling the winner. He's already gelded but should improve. (tchd 13-2)
Chant(IRE), a well-beaten sixth in a 7f seller on debut, had clearly improved for the experience and he should find his level once handicapping after another run. (tchd 16-1)
Poor Duke(IRE), whose dam is a half sister to a 10.6f AW/2m1f hurdles winner, showed some ability but shouldn't be good enough to win a maiden. (op 16-1)
Spithead went plenty quick enough in front and it was no surprise to see him stop in the straight. Nurseries are now an option, but he's clearly fairly limited. (op 2-1)
Caramel Sundae, closely related to 6f-1m5f Listed winner High Heel Sneakers, completely blew the start and was given an educational ride thereafter. She should leave this behind in time. Official explanation: jockey said filly was slowly away (op 5-1)
Double Jeopardy Official explanation: jockey said gelding hung badly right-handed

3949 FOLLOW US ON TWITTER @WOLVESRACES H'CAP (DIV I) 7f 32y(P)
5:15 (5:17) (Class 6) (0-60,60) 3-Y-0+ **£1,704** (£503; £251) **Stalls** High

Form RPR

5404 **1** **Lutine Charlie (IRE)**[14] 3471 5-9-11 **59**........................ AndreaAtzeni 3 67
(David Evans) *a.p: led 1f out: rdn out* **6/1[3]**

0546 **2** *½* **Moody Dancer**[19] 3315 3-9-4 **60**........................ MartinDwyer 9 63
(William Muir) *hld up in tch: shkn up and swtchd lft over 1f out: sn rdn: r.o* **11/2[2]**

5455 **3** *½* **Gazboolou**[19] 3317 8-9-3 **51**........................(t) FergusSweeney 7 56
(Henry Candy) *a.p: chsd ldr 1/2-way: rdn over 1f out: r.o* **11/2[2]**

4000 **4** *1 ¼* **Whitstable Native**[68] 1768 4-9-2 **50**........................ TadhgO'Shea 11 52
(Joseph Tuite) *s.s: hld up: hdwy over 1f out: sn rdn and edgd lft: r.o: nrst fin* **18/1**

23 **5** *nk* **Basle**[15] 3455 5-9-9 **57**........................(t) ShaneKelly 6 58
(Gay Kelleway) *s.i.s: hld up: hdwy over 2f out: shkn up over 1f out: styd on: nt rch ldrs* **4/1[1]**

1064 **6** *nk* **July Days (IRE)**[15] 3456 6-9-9 **57**........................ WilliamCarson 10 57
(Brian Baugh) *chsd ldr tl led over 4f out: rdn and hdd 1f out: styd on same pce* **12/1**

-010 **7** *nk* **Sairaam (IRE)**[36] 2766 6-9-2 **53**........................ HarryBentley(3) 8 52
(Charles Smith) *prom: rdn over 1f out: styd on same pce fnl f* **9/1**

4660 **8** *2* **Petrarchan**[25] 3099 4-8-13 **52**........................(t) DarrenEgan(5) 2 46
(Milton Bradley) *hld up: rdn over 1f out: nvr trbld ldrs* **12/1**

0010 **9** *1* **Irie Ute**[13] 3511 4-9-10 **58**........................ DaneO'Neill 12 49
(Sylvester Kirk) *s.i.s: hld up: hdwy 1/2-way: rdn over 2f out: wknd fnl f* **10/1**

0600 **10** *1 ¾* **Not My Choice (IRE)**[14] 3477 7-9-12 **60**........................(t) MichaelStainton 5 46
(Paul Howling) *s.i.s: hld up: shkn up over 2f out: a in rr* **14/1**

0000 **11** *1 ¼* **Sermons Mount (USA)**[56] 2146 6-9-12 **60**........................ TomMcLaughlin 1 43
(Paul Howling) *hld up: rdn over 1f out: a in rr* **28/1**

00-0 **12** *6* **Lucky Mellor**[51] 670 5-9-7 **60**........................(t) ShaneBKelly(5) 4 27
(Barry Murtagh) *led: hdd over 4f out: rdn over 2f out: wknd over 1f out* **66/1**

1m 30.08s (0.48) **Going Correction** -0.05s/f (Stan)
WFA 3 from 4yo+ 8lb **12** Ran SP% **116.4**
Speed ratings (Par 101): **95,94,93,92,92 91,91,89,87,85 84,77**
toteswingers: 1&2 £6.70, 2&3 £5.20, 1&3 £7.40 CSF £38.22 CT £196.29 TOTE £7.60: £2.60, £2.90, £1.50; EX 39.60.
Owner Jason Tucker **Bred** Patrice O'Connell **Trained** Pandy, Monmouths

FOCUS
The first division of a moderate handicap. The pace was steady enough and the time was 0.84secs slower than the second leg.

3950 FOLLOW US ON TWITTER @WOLVESRACES H'CAP (DIV II) 7f 32y(P)
5:45 (5:47) (Class 6) (0-60,60) 3-Y-0+ **£1,704** (£503; £251) **Stalls** High

Form RPR

0035 **1** **Fayr Fall (IRE)**[15] 3451 3-9-4 **60**........................(b[1]) TedDurcan 5 71
(Tim Easterby) *a.p: led over 1f out: shkn up: styd on wl* **9/2[1]**

213 **2** *1 ¼* **Jonnie Skull (IRE)**[21] 3249 6-9-2 **57**........................(vt) DannyBrock(7) 4 68
(Phil McEntee) *chsd ldrs: nt clr run over 2f out: rdn to chse wnr fnl f: edgd lft: styd on* **7/1**

0006 **3** *2 ½* **Marksbury**[11] 3559 5-9-3 **58**........................ JackDuern(7) 6 62
(Mark Brisbourne) *hld up: pushed along 1/2-way: hdwy over 1f out: nt trble ldrs* **20/1**

0-60 **4** 3 **Thane Of Cawdor (IRE)**32 2883 3-9-4 **60**.................. JamieSpencer 12 53+
(Tom Tate) *s.i.s: in rr: reminder over 4f out: styd on u.p ins fnl f: nvr nrr* **15/2**

3510 **5** 3/4 **Compton Target (IRE)**23 3193 3-8-11 **58**..................(t) DarrenEgan(5) 8 49
(Milton Bradley) *hld up: hdwy over 1f out: wknd fnl f* **10/1**

4301 **6** 1 3/4 **Polar Auroras**19 3318 4-9-11 **59**..................(t) DavidProbert 11 48
(Tony Carroll) *hld up: rdn over 1f out: n.d* **9/1**

2003 **7** 1/2 **Huzzah (IRE)**24 3151 7-9-12 **60**.................. MichaelStainton 1 48
(Paul Howling) *mid-div: rdn and wknd over 1f out* **5/1**2

2400 **8** nse **Kielty's Folly**8 3712 8-9-12 **60**..................(p) SaleemGolam 10 48
(Brian Baugh) *chsd ldrs: led over 2f out tl over 1f out: wknd ins fnl f* **20/1**

0440 **9** 7 **Smoky Cloud (IRE)**21 3245 5-9-8 **56**.................. DaneO'Neill 7 25
(Tony Newcombe) *chsd ldr 6f out: rdn and ev ch over 2f out: wknd fnl f* **11/1**

-033 **10** 2 1/2 **Welsh Royale**28 3000 3-9-3 **59**.................. MartinDwyer 9 18
(William Muir) *s.i.s: hld up: rdn: over 2f out: n.d* **14/1**

5-00 **11** 6 **Cha Ching (IRE)**13 3507 3-9-2 **58**.................. SebSanders 3
(J W Hills) *s.i.s: sn drvn along and prom: wknd over 1f out* **12/1**

-230 **12** 15 **Cadmium Loch**29 2981 4-9-12 **60**..................(p) RussKennemore 2
(Reg Hollinshead) *led over 4f: wknd and eased over 1f out* **6/1**3

1m 29.24s (-0.36) **Going Correction** -0.05s/f (Stan)
WFA 3 from 4yo+ 8lb **12** Ran SP% **124.7**
Speed ratings (Par 101): **100,98,95,92,91 89,88,88,80,77 71,53**
toteswingers: 1&2 £11.50, 2&3 £35.90, 1&3 £25.80 CSF £37.83 CT £581.97 TOTE £4.90: £2.30, £2.70, £8.30; EX 67.50.
Owner Reality Partnerships **Bred** M Sinanan **Trained** Great Habton, N Yorks

FOCUS
This looked stronger than division one and the time was 0.84secs quicker.
T/Jkpt: Not won. T/Plt: £157.10 to a £1 stake. Pool of £107377.28 - 498.67 winning tickets.
T/Qpdt: £29.50 to a £1 stake. Pool of £9242.71 - 231.60 winning tickets. CR

3747 CATTERICK (L-H)
Wednesday, July 11

OFFICIAL GOING: Soft (heavy in places; 6.4) - meeting abandoned after 3.50 (race 4) following heavy rain
Wind: Light, against Weather: Sunny periods and showers

3951 YORKSHIRE-OUTDOORS.CO.UK CLAIMING STKS 5f
2:20 (2:20) (Class 6) 2-Y-O £1,704 (£503; £251) Stalls Low

Form RPR
261 **1** **Jamesbo's Girl**22 3251 2-8-11 75.................. AdrianNicholls 4 75
(David Nicholls) *wnt rt s: sn pushed along in rr: rdn after 1 1/2f: swtchd rt and gd hdwy 1/2-way: led 2f out: rdn clr over 1f out: edgd rt ins fnl f: styd on strly* **4/7**1

00 **2** 7 **Charlemagne Diva**26 3110 2-8-7 0.................. JamesSullivan 3 45
(Ann Duffield) *slt ld: rdn along 1/2-way: hdd 2f out: sn drvn and kpt on same pce* **14/1**

3240 **3** 3/4 **Fly Fisher (IRE)**26 3126 2-8-13 0..................(p) TonyHamilton 2 48
(Richard Fahey) *cl up: rdn 2f out: sn drvn and one pce* **11/4**2

002 **4** 6 **Sulky Sheila (IRE)**28 3019 2-8-8 0.................. DavidAllan 1 22
(Tim Easterby) *cl up on inner: rdn along 1/2-way: sn outpcd* **9/1**3

1m 3.06s (3.26) **Going Correction** +0.525s/f (Yiel) **4** Ran SP% **107.0**
Speed ratings (Par 92): **94,82,81,72**
CSF £8.55 TOTE £1.70; EX 9.50.Jamesbo's Girl was claimed by Mr R. A. Fahey for £10,000.
Owner Pinnacle Jamesbo's Partnership **Bred** Lady Juliet Tadgell **Trained** Sessay, N Yorks

FOCUS
The winner proved much too good in this juvenile claimer. They went an honest gallop on ground officially described as soft, heavy in places. The winning time was over four seconds slower than standard and appeared to confirm that as an accurate description.

NOTEBOOK
Jamesbo's Girl stayed on strongly to record a 7l success in a Thirsk seller (6f, good to soft) last month on her third start and she repeated the dose here with an emphatic success on softer ground over the minimum trip. She drifted slightly to her right when stretching clear inside the final furlong. She was duly claimed by Richard Fahey for £10,000, and may be able to pay her way in nursery handicaps at up to 7f this term. (tchd 8-13)
Charlemagne Diva should qualify for a lowly handicap mark after this slightly more promising third career start. (op 16-1 tchd 12-1)
Fly Fisher(IRE) is going the wrong way currently and failed to reproduce his respectable maiden form from the spring in first-time cheekpieces. (op 3-1)
Sulky Sheila(IRE) is already exposed as very modest and ran poorly. (op 8-1)

3952 BOOK TICKETS ON-LINE AT CATTERICKBRIDGE.CO.UK H'CAP 7f
2:50 (2:51) (Class 5) (0-75,75) 3-Y-O £2,264 (£673; £336; £168) Stalls Centre

Form RPR
2213 **1** **Mick Slates (IRE)**2 3908 3-7-12 **57**.................. NeilFarley(5) 1 67
(Declan Carroll) *dwlt: hdwy on inner to trck ldrs after 2f: effrt over 2f out: rdn to chal over 1f out: kpt on wl to ld last 100yds* **9/2**1

001 **2** nk **Serene Oasis (IRE)**11 3619 3-9-2 **70**..................(v) SamHitchcott 8 79
(Mick Channon) *midfield: hdwy on outer to trck ldrs 4f out: effrt over 2f out: rdn to ld 1 1/2f out: drvn ins fnl f: hdd and no ex last 100yds* **15/2**3

143 **3** 7 **Boots And Spurs**48 2416 3-9-4 **75**..................(v) MichaelMetcalfe(3) 12 66
(Mrs K Burke) *hld up in rr hdwy on inner 3f out: rdn 2f out: kpt on appr fnl f* **9/1**

-006 **4** 1 1/4 **La Salida**24 3184 3-8-7 **61** ow1.................. GrahamGibbons 9 49
(David Barron) *slt ld 3f: cl up: rdn along and wd st: sn drvn and wknd* **11/1**

1264 **5** 1 1/4 **Dubious Escapade (IRE)**14 3495 3-9-2 **70**.................. GrahamLee 2 55
(Ann Duffield) *chsd ldrs on inner: led 4f out: rdn over 2f out: hdd 1 1/2f out and grad wknd* **6/1**2

01-3 **6** 2 3/4 **Lucky Money**30 2987 3-9-6 **74**.................. LukeMorris 5 51
(Sir Mark Prescott Bt) *dwlt and towards rr: hdwy to chse ldrs 1/2-way: rdn along over 2f out: sn wknd* **6/1**2

3522 **7** nk **Tortoni (IRE)**19 3333 3-9-7 **75**.................. PhillipMakin 6 52
(Kevin Ryan) *cl up: rdn along wl over 2f out: sn wknd* **9/1**

0-30 **8** 6 **Ebony Clarets**27 3063 3-8-12 **66**.................. TonyHamilton 7 27
(Richard Fahey) *chsd ldrs: n.m.r after 2f: rdn along and lost pl 1/2-way: wd st and bhd* **22/1**

5300 **9** 5 **Darrow (IRE)**38 2733 3-8-11 **65**..................1 PJMcDonald 4 13
(Noel Quinlan) *midfield: pushed along and lost pl 4f out: sn bhd* **11/1**

216 **10** 2 1/2 **Liliargh (IRE)**23 3214 3-9-6 **74**.................. DanielTudhope 3 15
(Ben Haslam) *midfield: lost pl 1/2-way: wd st and sn bhd* **11/1**

-005 **11** 4 **King Laertis (IRE)**18 3405 3-8-2 **56** oh11.................. FrannyNorton 11
(Tracy Waggott) *dwlt: a in rr: bhd and wd st* **150/1**

3-35 **12** 3 **Zaffy (IRE)**44 2540 3-8-3 **57**.................. DuranFentiman 10
(Tim Easterby) *chsd ldrs on outer: rdn along and lost pl 1/2-way: bhd and wd st* **14/1**

1m 32.01s (5.01) **Going Correction** +0.725s/f (Yiel) **12** Ran SP% **115.2**
Speed ratings (Par 100): **100,99,91,90,88 85,85,78,72,69 65,61**
toteswingers: 1&2 £7.00, 1&3 £5.40, 2&3 £14.60 CSF £36.43 CT £295.20 TOTE £5.80: £2.10, £4.00, £2.00; EX 35.50.
Owner Ormskirk **Bred** Peter McCutcheon **Trained** Sledmere, E Yorks

FOCUS
A fair handicap for 3yos. They went a solid gallop and the winning time was over eight seconds slower than standard. The first three horses home raced up the far side in the home straight.

3953 PIN POINT RECRUITMENT TURMERIC H'CAP 1m 7f 177y
3:20 (3:20) (Class 4) (0-85,81) 3-Y-O+ £4,075 (£1,212; £606; £303) Stalls Low

Form RPR
10-1 **1** **Kian's Delight**18 3400 4-9-4 **71**.................. LukeMorris 10 80
(Peter Bowen) *trckd ldrs: hdwy and cl up 4f out: led 2f out: sn jnd and rdn: drvn ins fnl f: kpt on gamely* **9/4**1

0-13 **2** 3/4 **Herostatus**22 3253 5-9-13 **80**.................. DanielTudhope 2 88
(David O'Meara) *trckd ldng pair: hdwy to chse wnr 2f out: rdn to chal over 1f out: drvn and ev ch ins fnl f: no ex towards fin* **9/1**

0-05 **3** 8 **Beat The Shower**22 3253 6-9-4 **71**.................. GrahamLee 7 70
(Peter Niven) *hld up in midfield: stdy hdwy over 3f out: rdn to chse ldng pair 2f out: sn drvn and kpt on same pce* **15/2**

1052 **4** 1 **Royal Swain (IRE)**12 3564 6-9-10 **77**.................. RobertWinston 1 74
(Alan Swinbank) *hld up in tch: hdwy 3f out: rdn to chse ldrs 2f out: drvn and no imp appr fnl f* **9/2**2

0563 **5** 2 **Bollin Felix**13 3535 8-9-9 **76**..................(b) DavidAllan 9 71
(Tim Easterby) *in rr and pushed along early: hld up: hdwy 4f out: effrt on inner over 2f out: sn rdn and kpt on: nt rch ldrs* **15/2**

0-02 **6** hd **L Frank Baum (IRE)**65 1905 5-9-2 **76**.................. RobertWilliams(7) 3 71
(Bernard Llewellyn) *hld up in rr: stdy hdwy 5f out: rdn and in tch over 2f out: sn drvn and n.d* **11/1**

0050 **7** 3/4 **Activate**12 3564 5-10-0 **81**..................(t) PaulMulrennan 5 75
(Kevin Ryan) *hld up and bhd: hdwy 4f out: rdn to chse ldrs wl over 1f out: sn no imp* **6/1**3

43-0 **8** 8 **Jeu De Roseau (IRE)**92 1272 8-9-1 **68**.................. TonyHamilton 4 52
(Chris Grant) *chsd ldrs: rdn along over 4f out: sn wknd* **25/1**

00/- **9** 4 1/2 **Toledo Gold (IRE)**55 7062 6-8-9 **62** oh2..................(t) PJMcDonald 6 41
(Maurice Barnes) *led: rdn along over 3f out: hdd 2f out: sn wknd* **66/1**

4212 **10** 72 **Focail Maith**161 374 4-10-0 **81**..................(p) GrahamGibbons 8
(Tim Pitt) *chsd ldr: rdn along 4f out: wknd 3f out: bhd and eased over 1f out* **14/1**

3m 48.55s (16.55) **Going Correction** +1.10s/f (Soft) **10** Ran SP% **117.1**
Speed ratings (Par 105): **102,101,97,97,96 96,95,91,89,53**
toteswingers: 1&2 £6.20, 1&3 £11.50, 2&3 £4.10 CSF £23.81 CT £132.70 TOTE £5.10: £1.50, £4.30, £3.40; EX 18.80.
Owner Yeh Man Partnership **Bred** Mrs J M Quy **Trained** Little Newcastle, Pembrokes

FOCUS
A decent staying handicap. The winning time was over 24 seconds slower than standard on what was very testing ground.

3954 TURFTV.CO.UK H'CAP 5f 212y
3:50 (3:55) (Class 5) (0-75,75) 3-Y-O £2,264 (£673; £336; £168) Stalls Low

Form RPR
-106 **1** **Lisiere (IRE)**18 3379 3-9-4 **75**..................(b1) MichaelMetcalfe(3) 6 83
(Mrs K Burke) *chsd ldrs on outer: hdwy to ld 3f out and wd st to stands' rail: rdn 2f out: drvn over 1f out: styd on wl* **7/1**

-563 **2** 1 1/2 **Blue Shoes (IRE)**43 2591 3-8-8 **62**.................. DavidAllan 8 65
(Tim Easterby) *cl up: disp ld 1/2-way: wd st: rdn 2f out and ev ch tl drvn ins fnl f and wknd last 75yds* **4/1**2

505 **3** 1 1/4 **Tinzapeas**19 3343 3-8-11 **65**..................(v1) SamHitchcott 2 64
(Mick Channon) *led: rdn along and hdd 3f out: wd st: drvn 2f out and ev ch tl one pce ins fnl f* **11/1**

4213 **4** 3/4 **Celestial Dawn**13 3540 3-8-8 **62**.................. LukeMorris 5 59
(John Weymes) *chsd ldrs: wd st and rdn 2f out: drvn over 1f out and no imp* **8/1**

4-01 **5** hd **Baltic Bomber (IRE)**19 3357 3-8-6 **60**.................. BarryMcHugh 1 56
(John Quinn) *in tch: wd st: hdwy to chse ldrs 2f out: sn rdn and ev ch tl drvn and wknd jst ins fnl f* **7/2**1

-123 **6** 1/2 **Untold Melody**12 3567 3-8-13 **67**.................. PhillipMakin 3 62
(Kevin Ryan) *cl up: rdn along and wd st: drvn 2f out: sn btn* **9/2**3

1-06 **7** 1 1/2 **Taro Tywod (IRE)**12 3555 3-8-12 **66**..................(p) PaulMulrennan 4 56
(Ann Duffield) *a towards rr* **5/1**

3534 **R** **Scrooby Doo**9 3698 3-8-13 **67**.................. GrahamLee 7
(Scott Dixon) *ref to r: tk no part* **25/1**

1m 22.39s (8.79) **Going Correction** +1.475s/f (Soft) **8** Ran SP% **112.9**
Speed ratings (Par 100): **100,98,96,95,95 94,92,**
toteswingers: 1&2 £7.30, 1&3 £23.30, 2&3 £12.20 CSF £34.14 CT £305.87 TOTE £9.40: £3.60, £1.10, £1.90; EX 38.00.
Owner David & Yvonne Blunt **Bred** Swordlestown Stud **Trained** Middleham Moor, N Yorks

FOCUS
A fair 3yo sprint handicap. There was a deluge of rain prior to, and during, this contest. The winning time was over 10 seconds slower than standard. Racing was abandoned on safety grounds after this contest.

3955 YORKSHIRE RACING SUMMER FESTIVAL H'CAP (DIV I) 7f
() (Class 6) (0-65,) 3-Y-O+ £

3956 YORKSHIRE RACING SUMMER FESTIVAL H'CAP (DIV II) 7f
() (Class 6) (0-65,) 3-Y-O+ £

3957 RACING AGAIN WEDNESDAY 18TH JULY MEDIAN AUCTION MAIDEN STKS 1m 3f 214y
() (Class 5) 3-4-Y-O £

T/Plt: £27.60 to a £1 stake. Pool: £54,734.22. 1,444.66 winning tickets. T/Qpdt: £8.00 to a £1 stake. Pool: £3,823.50. 352.45 winning tickets. JR

3761 KEMPTON (A.W) (R-H)

Wednesday, July 11

OFFICIAL GOING: Standard

Wind: Moderate, half against Weather: Mostly fine

3958 WIN BIG WITH BETDAQ MULTIPLES APPRENTICE H'CAP 7f (P)

6:20 (8:19) (Class 5) (0-70,70) 4-Y-0+ £2,264 (£673; £336; £168) Stalls Low

Form				RPR
3141	1		**Lady Mango (IRE)**[37] 2760 4-9-2 **63** DarrenEgan 8 (Ronald Harris) *settled off the pce in midfield: rdn and prog over 2f out: chsd ldr over 1f out: kpt on to ld last 50yds* **7/1**	73
364	2	hd	**Perfect Mission**[28] 3045 4-9-3 **69** (v) DanielMuscutt(5) 7 (Andrew Balding) *pressed ldr: led 3f out: 2 l clr 2f out: kpt on but hdd last 50yds: only one of early ldrs to fin in first six* **11/2**[2]	78
0-63	3	nk	**Paphos**[8] 3738 5-9-2 **63** (v) DavidKenny 1 (Stuart Williams) *slowly away and urged along: off the pce in midfield: rdn and prog over 2f out: wnt 3rd jst over 1f out: styd on: jst hld* **6/1**[3]	71
0025	4	3 ¾	**Hawk Moth (IRE)**[15] 3471 4-9-4 **68** WilliamTwiston-Davies(3) 3 (John Spearing) *dwlt: hld up in last pair: rdn wl over 2f out: swtchd lft wl over 1f out: kpt on u.p: nrst fin* **9/2**[1]	66
2223	5	hd	**Douze Points (IRE)**[19] 3344 6-9-5 **66** TobyAtkinson 9 (John Butler) *towards rr: urged along bef 1/2-way: effrt on inner over 2f out: kpt on same pce: nvr a threat* **8/1**	64
0000	6	1 ¾	**May's Boy**[14] 3511 4-9-2 **66** (p) RachealKneller(3) 5 (Mark Usher) *settled off the pce in midfield: rdn wl over 2f out and no prog: plugged on fr over 1f out* **25/1**	59
4010	7	½	**Spirit Of Gondree (IRE)**[6] 3790 4-8-11 **63** (b) RyanWhile(5) 2 (Milton Bradley) *pressed ldr to over 2f out: wknd and lost 2nd over 1f out* **6/1**[3]	55
2124	8	1	**Dvinsky (USA)**[8] 3738 11-8-13 **65** (b) RyanTate(5) 11 (Paul Howling) *pressed ldrs to 3f out: steadily wknd fnl 2f* **12/1**	54
00	9	1 ¼	**Local Singer (IRE)**[23] 3230 4-9-2 **63** CharlesBishop 10 (Paul Howling) *wl in rr: rdn bef 1/2-way: nvr a factor* **18/1**	49
0020	10	3 ½	**Beautiful Lando (FR)**[23] 3229 4-8-13 **63** (b) JakePayne(3) 13 (Heather Main) *stdd s and dropped in fr wd draw: mostly in last pair: no prog over 2f out* **28/1**	39
0250	11	3 ¼	**Perfect Ch'l (IRE)**[20] 3314 5-9-5 **66** (v) JamieJones 4 (Ian Wood) *mde most to 3f out: wknd qckly* **16/1**	33
030-	12	7	**Aultcharn (FR)**[394] 2995 5-9-6 **70** (t) NicoleNordblad(3) 14 (Hans Adielsson) *w ldrs to 3f out: wknd rapidly: t.o* **12/1**	18

1m 25.86s (-0.14) **Going Correction** -0.025s/f (Stan) 12 Ran SP% **119.6**

Speed ratings (Par 103): **99,98,98,94,93 91,91,90,88,84 81,73**

toteswingers: 1&2 £4.90, 1&3 £8.80, 2&3 £5.30 CSF £45.72 CT £253.19 TOTE £9.10: £2.30, £2.20, £2.30; EX 45.10 Trifecta £118.30 Pool: £468.63 - 2.93 winning units..

Owner L Scadding & Mrs S Peachey-Scadding **Bred** Mount Coote Stud **Trained** Earlswood, Monmouths

FOCUS

A fair apprentice handicap, run at a strong pace. The winner continued his fine run, with the next two close to their bests.

3959 BETDAQ MOBILE APPS/IRISH STALLION FARMS E B F MAIDEN FILLIES' STKS 6f (P)

6:50 (8:19) (Class 5) 2-Y-0 £3,169 (£943; £471; £235) Stalls Low

Form				RPR
	1		**Hoodna (IRE)** 2-9-0 0 FrankieDettori 12 (Saeed Bin Suroor) *trckd ldr after 1f: shkn up to ld wl over 1f out: pushed out fnl f: readily* **2/1**[1]	81+
4	2	2	**Nardin**[21] 3282 2-9-0 0 TadhgO'Shea 7 (Ed Dunlop) *trckd ldrs on outer: brought to chal 2f out: nt qckn whn reminder over 1f out: pushed along and styd on to take 2nd last 75yds* **11/2**[3]	73
4	3	½	**March**[12] 3560 2-9-0 0 MartinHarley 8 (Marco Botti) *led: shkn up and hdd wl over 1f out: no ch w wnr fnl f: lost 2nd last 75yds* **5/2**[2]	72
5	4	nse	**Everleigh**[14] 3504 2-9-0 0 PatDobbs 1 (Richard Hannon) *chsd ldr 1f: styd cl up: rdn and nt qckn over 2f out: kpt on again fnl f* **16/1**	71
50	5	hd	**This Is Nice (IRE)**[54] 2252 2-9-0 0 JimCrowley 4 (Tom Dascombe) *chsd ldrs: pushed along bef 1/2-way: outpcd and rdn over 2f out: styd on wl again fnl f* **6/1**	73+
	6	5	**Icon Dance** 2-9-0 0 JohnFahy 6 (Ben De Haan) *stdd s: hld up towards rr: sed taking t.k.h after 2f: pushed along over 2f out: nvr on terms but nt disgracd* **66/1**	56
0	7	10	**Iris Blue**[12] 3590 2-9-0 0 TedDurcan 2 (John Gosden) *nvr beyond midfield: effrt wl over 2f out: sn outpcd: wknd wl over 1f out* **9/1**	26
	8	1	**Bugsy's Babe** 2-9-0 0 KirstyMilczarek 9 (George Baker) *s.v.s: ct up at bk of field over 3f out: wknd over 2f out: sn bhd* **40/1**	23+
	9	1 ¾	**Actonetaketwo** 2-8-7 0 RyanWhile(7) 3 (Bill Turner) *a towards rr: wknd u.p over 2f out: wl bhd after* **40/1**	18

1m 13.85s (0.75) **Going Correction** -0.025s/f (Stan) 9 Ran SP% **113.8**

Speed ratings (Par 91): **94,91,90,90,90 83,70,69,66**

toteswingers: 1&2 £2.50, 1&3 £1.50, 2&3 £2.40 CSF £13.19 TOTE £2.60: £1.20, £1.90, £1.20; EX 14.00 Trifecta £26.30 Pool: £765.19 - 21.53 winning units..

Owner Godolphin **Bred** Petra Bloodstock Agency Ltd **Trained** Newmarket, Suffolk

FOCUS

An intriguing juvenile maiden. The winner should improve on this and the second is the best guide.

NOTEBOOK

Hoodna(IRE) overcame a lack of experience to win readily and enhance Saeed Bin Suroor's excellent record at the track. The daughter of Invincible Spirit was certainly not without support on this her debut and, having raced handily throughout, picked up in the style of a smart recruit to win going away. The 160,000euros purchase looks sure to come on considerably for the outing and is an exciting prospect. (op 5-2 tchd 7-4)

Nardin had run with promise on her only previous start here last month and again ran well, snatching second on the post. The Royal Applause filly had looked dangerous approaching the 2f pole but was unable to go with the winner late on. She clearly has ability and was probably unfortunate to bump into an above average type. (op 5-1)

March gives further substance to the form with her having shaped pleasing at Doncaster on debut. She travelled well here but could only manage the one-pace. She did well to hang onto a place and looks to be crying out for an extra furlong. (op 9-4 tchd 11-4)

Everleigh stepped up considerably on what she'd achieved at Salisbury. A win shouldn't be too far away.

This Is Nice(IRE), considered good enough to run in Listed company at York, has now qualified for nurseries and should be able to pick up a race, especially over further. (tchd 15-2)

3960 BACK OR LAY AT BETDAQ.COM H'CAP 6f (P)

7:20 (8:19) (Class 4) (0-80,80) 3-Y-0+ £4,075 (£1,212; £606; £303) Stalls Low

Form				RPR
-300	1		**Noverre To Go (IRE)**[24] 3188 6-9-10 **80** JamesDoyle 7 (Ronald Harris) *trckd ldrs: clsd gng wl fr 2f out: led jst over 1f out: sn drvn and grad asserted* **9/1**	92
4-01	2	½	**Avonmore Star**[41] 2629 4-9-8 **78** RichardHughes 3 (Richard Hannon) *hld up in midfield: clsd on ldrs over 2f out: looking for room and edgd rt over 1f out: styd on fnl f to take 2nd last 75yds* **9/1**	88
-000	3	½	**Peace Seeker**[26] 3139 4-9-5 **76** FrankieDettori 5 (Anthony Carson) *led to over 3f out: pressed ldr: led again wl over 1f out to jst over 1f out: one pce* **11/2**[2]	83
035	4	¾	**Sole Danser (IRE)**[21] 3281 4-9-2 **72** SilvestreDeSousa 12 (Milton Bradley) *hmpd s: swtchd to inner fr wdst draw and hld up in last trio: prog 2f out: nt clr run over 1f out: styd on to take 4th nr fin* **11/1**	80+
6626	5	¾	**Street Power (USA)**[21] 3281 7-9-7 **77** JimCrowley 4 (Jeremy Gask) *hld up wl in rr: rdn and prog jst over 2f out: clsd on ldrs 1f out: effrt fizzled out* **4/1**[1]	81
0664	6	¾	**Barney McGrew (IRE)**[19] 3336 9-9-10 **80** TomEaves 2 (Michael Dods) *trckd ldrs: on inner: effrt 2f out: nt qckn over 1f out: one pce after* **8/1**[3]	81
014	7	2	**Close To The Edge (IRE)**[12] 3571 4-9-3 **80** WilliamTwiston-Davies(7) 10 (Alan McCabe) *racd wd: pressed ldrs: drvn and steadily outpcd fr over 2f out: nt on terms after* **14/1**	75
0002	8	¾	**Button Moon (IRE)**[18] 3394 4-9-3 **73** (p) CathyGannon 9 (Ian Wood) *pressed ldr: led over 3f out to wl over 1f out: wknd fnl f* **16/1**	65
0605	9	1	**Night Trade (IRE)**[13] 3541 5-8-12 **73** DarrenEgan(5) 8 (Ronald Harris) *racd wd in rr: brought v wd in st: no prog 2f out: kpt on fnl f* **20/1**	62
4120	10	½	**Black Cadillac (IRE)**[50] 2369 4-9-3 **73** JimmyFortune 6 (Andrew Balding) *a towards rr: rdn in last pair over 2f out: struggling after* **4/1**[1]	61
0006	11	nk	**Mac Gille Eoin**[6] 3771 8-9-10 **80** NeilCallan 11 (John Gallagher) *reluctant to enter stalls: wnt lft s: pushed up into midfield: rdn and no rspnse over 2f out: sn btn* **16/1**	67
1006	12	nk	**Marford Missile (IRE)**[21] 3288 3-9-2 **78** StephenCraine 1 (Tom Dascombe) *pushed along in midfield on inner bef 1/2-way: no prog 2f out: wknd qckly fnl f* **20/1**	63

1m 11.85s (-1.25) **Going Correction** -0.025s/f (Stan)

WFA 3 from 4yo+ 6lb 12 Ran SP% **122.8**

Speed ratings (Par 105): **107,106,105,104,103 102,100,99,97,97 96,96**

toteswingers: 1&2 £10.90, 1&3 £19.50, 2&3 £4.80 CSF £90.82 CT £493.10 TOTE £10.10: £2.90, £3.00, £2.20; EX 105.10 Trifecta £580.80 Part won. Pool: £784.92 - 0.75 winning units..

Owner Robert & Nina Bailey **Bred** Gestut Gorlsdorf **Trained** Earlswood, Monmouths

FOCUS

A decent sprint handicap which was well run. Pretty solid form, rated on the positive side.

Night Trade(IRE) Official explanation: jockey said that the mare hung left

Black Cadillac(IRE) Official explanation: jockey said that the gelding was never travelling

3961 BETDAQ CASINO GAMES H'CAP 2m (P)

7:50 (8:19) (Class 5) (0-75,74) 4-Y-0+ £2,264 (£673; £336; £168) Stalls Low

Form				RPR
0-00	1		**Trovare (USA)**[11] 3625 5-9-7 **74** JimCrowley 8 (Amanda Perrett) *trckd ldrs early: in tch in midfield after: stoked up over 2f out: prog on outer to ld jst over 1f out: styd on wl and sn clr* **7/1**	82
060	2	4 ½	**Lady of Burgundy**[23] 3222 6-8-12 **65** DavidProbert 1 (Mark Usher) *t.k.h: hld up last: allowed others to crack on w it fr 5f out: gd prog over 2f out to cl on ldrs over 1f out: wnr sn wnt by: one pce after* **8/1**	68
4610	3	1 ¼	**Frederick William**[49] 2396 4-9-3 **70** (p) LiamKeniry 7 (Chris Gordon) *prom early: steadily lost pl but gng wl enough: in last pair 4f out: prog over 2f out: kpt on same pce fr over 1f out* **16/1**	72
4-20	4	½	**Emrani (USA)**[30] 2978 5-9-7 **74** (b) TomEaves 6 (Donald McCain) *prom: drvn over 4f out: disp 2nd over 2f out to over 1f out: wknd* **15/2**	75
2605	5	2 ½	**Iron Condor**[7] 3765 5-9-6 **73** RichardHughes 4 (James Eustace) *hld up tl quick move to ld after 5f: reminder over 6f out: stepped it up fr over 4f out: rdn 3 l clr 2f out: wknd and hdd jst over 1f out* **7/2**[1]	71
50-6	6	2	**Lombok**[12] 3572 6-8-7 **67** ow1 WilliamTwiston-Davies(7) 5 (Gary Moore) *dwlt: hld up in last pair: prog 7f out to go prom 5f out: rdn to dispute 2nd over 2f out to over 1f out: wknd* **20/1**	63
0456	7	6	**Action Front (USA)**[32] 2936 4-9-0 **67** SilvestreDeSousa 2 (Derek Shaw) *in tch: rdn over 3f out: wknd 2f out* **9/2**[2]	55
1-34	8	2 ¼	**Decana**[26] 3102 4-9-0 **67** DarryllHolland 9 (Hughie Morrison) *mostly in rr: struggling over 2f out: sn btn* **13/2**	53
4-25	9	10	**Phonic (IRE)**[21] 3283 5-8-10 **63** TedDurcan 3 (John Dunlop) *led 5f: chsd ldr to over 2f out: wknd rapidly* **6/1**[3]	37

3m 28.0s (-2.10) **Going Correction** -0.025s/f (Stan) 9 Ran SP% **114.0**

Speed ratings (Par 103): **104,101,101,100,99 98,95,94,89**

toteswingers: 1&2 £13.30, 1&3 £24.80, 2&3 £3.50 CSF £60.71 CT £861.06 TOTE £6.10: £3.10, £3.00, £4.50; EX 68.60 Trifecta £681.20 Part won. Pool: £920.66 - 0.65 winning units..

Owner John Connolly **Bred** James Heyward **Trained** Pulborough, W Sussex

FOCUS

A fair staying handicap run at an ordinary pace for the most part. The winner's first form since last summer.

Iron Condor Official explanation: jockey said the gelding hung on the bend

Decana Official explanation: jockey said that filly ran flat

3962 COYLE RECRUITMENT H'CAP 1m 3f (P)

8:20 (8:20) (Class 4) (0-80,80) 3-Y-0+ £4,075 (£1,212; £606; £303) Stalls Low

Form				RPR
5-21	1		**Silent Moment (USA)**[21] 3279 3-9-1 **79** FrankieDettori 14 (Saeed Bin Suroor) *trckd ldng trio: prog to ld jst over 2f out: shkn up and sn clr: eased last 100yds* **7/4**[1]	95+
006-	2	4	**Huff And Puff**[258] 7120 5-9-11 **77** NeilCallan 1 (Amanda Perrett) *trckd ldng pair: rdn over 2f out: kpt on u.p to take 2nd jst over 1f out: no ch w wnr* **7/2**[2]	83
2005	3	3 ¾	**If I Were A Boy (IRE)**[9] 3703 5-9-1 **67** (p) JamesDoyle 12 (Dominic Ffrench Davis) *trckd ldr: rdn over 3f out: led wl over 2f out to jst over 2f out: no ch w wnr: lost 2nd jst over 1f out* **16/1**	67

5150 **4** ¾ **Ballyheigue (IRE)**[8] 3737 3-9-1 **79**................................(p) WilliamBuick 2 77
(Brian Meehan) *chsd ldng quartet: rdn 3f out: wl outpcd over 2f out: kpt on to press for 4th nr fin* **10/1**

4-00 **5** ¾ **Twice Bitten**[32] 2921 4-10-0 **80**.. LiamKeniry 3 77+
(James Toller) *settled in midfield disputing 7th: rdn to cl on ldrs 3f out: outpcd over 2f out: n.d after: kpt on* **9/1**[3]

0100 **6** 4½ **Sedgwick**[26] 3129 10-8-7 **66**..................................... ShirleyTeasdale(7) 9 55
(Shaun Harris) *chsd ldng quartet: rdn to try to cl 3f out: wl outpcd over 2f out: nvr on terms* **33/1**

/00- **7** 1½ **Lastofthemohicans (FR)**[290] 6375 5-9-12 **78**...........(t) RichardHughes 6 64
(Paul Webber) *hld up in rr: hmpd on inner after 2f: lost tch in last trio over 4f out: jst pushed along after and passed a few stragglers* **16/1**

6-32 **8** 1¾ **Officer In Command (USA)**[42] 2044 6-9-4 **70**............(p) SebSanders 7 53
(Paul Rich) *hld up in rr: lost tch in last trio over 4f out: no ch after* **12/1**

0203 **9** ¾ **Mafi (IRE)**[25] 3154 4-9-4 **70**... IanMongan 11 52
(Mark Hoad) *settled in midfield disputing 7th: rdn to cl on ldng gp over 3f out: wknd over 2f out* **14/1**

555 **10** *hd* **Saint Helena (IRE)**[34] 2863 4-9-6 **72**........................ SilvestreDeSousa 4 53
(Harry Dunlop) *led at str pce to wl over 2f out: wknd and eased* **16/1**

/00- **11** 8 **Farleigh House (USA)**[53] 3366 8-9-0 **73**.... WilliamTwiston-Davies(7) 10 40
(Neil King) *hld up in rr: rdn on outer to cl on main gp over 3f out: wknd over 2f out* **40/1**

106/ **12** 11 **Curacao**[695] 5144 6-9-9 **75**.. JimCrowley 8 22
(Amanda Perrett) *a in last pair and nvr gng wl: lost tch over 4f out: t.o* **14/1**

2m 18.49s (-3.41) **Going Correction** -0.025s/f (Stan)
WFA 3 from 4yo+ 12lb **12** Ran SP% **121.7**
Speed ratings (Par 105): **111,108,105,104,104 101,99,98,98,97 92,84**
toteswingers: 1&2 £2.90, 1&3 £9.40, 2&3 £16.20 CSF £7.50 CT £76.51 TOTE £2.80: £1.80, £1.50, £5.30; EX 9.90 Trifecta £82.10 Pool: £728.05 - 6.56 winning units..
Owner Godolphin **Bred** Darley **Trained** Newmarket, Suffolk

FOCUS
A useful middle-distance handicap, turned into a procession by the lightly-raced Silent Moment, who was backing up last month's course win. It was sound run and the winner is value for extra.
Sedgwick Official explanation: trainer said the gelding lost a left hind shoe
Saint Helena(IRE) Official explanation: jockey said that the filly hung left

3963 QUINN LONDON H'CAP (LONDON MILE QUALIFIER) 1m (P)
8:50 (8:51) (Class 4) (0-85,85) 3-Y-O+ **£4,075** (£1,212; £606; £303) **Stalls** Low

Form RPR

-124 **1** **Famous Poet (IRE)**[40] 2660 3-9-5 **85**............................. FrankieDettori 2 95+
(Saeed Bin Suroor) *trckd ldng pair: pushed along over 2f out: produced between ldng pair to ld 1f out: sn in command: readily* **7/4**[1]

144 **2** 1½ **Great Shot**[23] 3226 4-9-3 **74**.. JamesDoyle 6 81
(Sylvester Kirk) *racd freely: led: rdn 2f out: hdd 1f out: kpt on but no ch w wnr* **12/1**[3]

0043 **3** *nk* **Shamdarley (IRE)**[18] 3380 4-9-9 **80**.................................... TomEaves 9 86
(Michael Dods) *hld up in midfield: rdn and prog fr 2f out: styd on fnl f to take 3rd nr fin* **16/1**

2656 **4** ½ **Kakapuka**[14] 3503 5-9-7 **78**... GeorgeBaker 12 83
(Anabel K Murphy) *trckd ldr: rdn to chal 2f out: nt qckn jst over 1f out: one pce after* **40/1**

110 **5** ¾ **Dellbuoy**[16] 3446 3-9-2 **82**.. IanMongan 3 83
(Pat Phelan) *trckd ldrs: rdn over 2f out: kpt on fnl f: nt pce to threaten* **12/1**[3]

6-00 **6** 1¼ **Camberley Two**[32] 2932 4-9-5 **83**................. WilliamTwiston-Davies(7) 8 84
(Roger Charlton) *t.k.h early: trckd ldng pair: rdn and nt qckn 2f out: fdd fnl f* **20/1**

5006 **7** 3 **Dozy Joe**[7] 3767 4-9-8 **79**... NeilCallan 1 73
(Ian Wood) *wl in rr: first one to be rdn 3f out: sme prog on outer over 1f out: n.d* **40/1**

1/ **8** *nk* **Morning Charm (USA)**[704] 4844 4-9-9 **80**..................... WilliamBuick 11 73+
(John Gosden) *s.i.s: sn rcvrd into midfield: shkn up and no prog over 2f out: wl btn over 1f out* **2/1**[2]

4006 **9** 1¼ **Right Result (IRE)**[30] 2979 3-9-5 **85**................................ TedDurcan 4 73
(James Bethell) *t.k.h: trckd ldrs: rdn and nt qckn over 2f out: fdd fnl f* **40/1**

0100 **10** ½ **Sinfonico (IRE)**[25] 3157 4-9-13 **84**..........................(be) RichardHughes 7 73
(Richard Hannon) *didn't wear declared blinkers: hld up in last trio: shkn up over 2f out: no real prog* **12/1**[3]

606- **11** 2¼ **Buckland (IRE)**[363] 4011 4-8-9 **73**.......................(b) NicoleNordblad(7) 10 57
(Hans Adielsson) *hld up in last trio: effrt on inner over 2f out: sn no prog* **50/1**

-322 **12** 3 **Russian Ice**[132] 746 4-9-7 **78**... ShaneKelly 14 55
(Dean Ivory) *hld up in last trio and racd on outer: shkn up over 2f out: no prog* **25/1**

12-1 **13** 9 **Rio Grande**[111] 994 3-9-5 **85**.................................(p) SilvestreDeSousa 5 39
(Ann Duffield) *rrd s and slowest away: a towards rr: btn 2f out: eased* **16/1**

1m 39.13s (-0.67) **Going Correction** -0.025s/f (Stan)
WFA 3 from 4yo+ 9lb **13** Ran SP% **122.4**
Speed ratings (Par 105): **102,100,100,99,98 97,94,94,93,92 90,87,78**
toteswingers: 1&2 £6.70, 1&3 £7.30, 2&3 £25.70 CSF £23.16 CT £281.06 TOTE £2.80: £1.30, £3.40, £4.80; EX 26.80 Trifecta £425.70 Pool: £1,133.49 - 1.97 winning units..
Owner Godolphin **Bred** Hadi Al Tajir **Trained** Newmarket, Suffolk

FOCUS
A decent handicap. It was not strong run but the form makes enough sense among the principals.
Rio Grande Official explanation: jockey said that the gelding was slow away, and then ran too free

3964 THAMES MATERIALS H'CAP 1m (P)
9:20 (9:20) (Class 6) (0-58,57) 3-Y-O+ **£1,617** (£481; £240; £120) **Stalls** Low

Form RPR

5065 **1** **Abriachan**[14] 3497 5-9-6 **57**.. RichardHughes 1 65
(Noel Quinlan) *hld up in rr: smooth prog fr over 2f out: waited tl unleashed ins fnl f: sn led and in control* **7/2**[2]

-000 **2** ½ **Victorian Number (FR)**[8] 3738 4-8-11 **55**.................. AliceHaynes(7) 14 62
(Geoffrey Deacon) *led: shkn up 2f out: styd on but hdd and outpcd ins fnl f* **16/1**

2664 **3** ¾ **Storm Runner (IRE)**[28] 3052 4-9-6 **57**............................. SebSanders 9 62
(George Margarson) *trckd ldrs: rdn 2f out: cl up over 1f out: styd on to take 3rd nr fin* **8/1**

3263 **4** *shd* **Do More Business (IRE)**[8] 3723 5-9-3 **54**......................(p) IanMongan 6 59
(Alison Batchelor) *hld up in last pair: prog fr 2f out w hd to one side: r.o to press for 3rd nr fin* **5/1**[3]

5604 **5** *hd* **Prince Of Passion (CAN)**[20] 3314 4-9-4 **55**...................... NeilCallan 10 59
(Derek Shaw) *s.i.s: hld up towards rr: rdn on outer 2f out: styd on fr over 1f out to press for a pl nr fin* **8/1**

0000 **6** 1¼ **High On The Hog (IRE)**[22] 3247 4-9-6 **57**..............(p) TomMcLaughlin 3 58
(Paul Howling) *t.k.h: trckd ldng pair: chsd ldr 2f out to 1f out: fdd* **25/1**

016 **7** ¾ **Querido (GER)**[43] 2586 8-8-12 **56**.............(tp) WilliamTwiston-Davies(7) 8 56
(Paddy Butler) *dwlt: t.k.h: hld up in last pair: effrt on inner 2f out: kpt on but n.d* **16/1**

2155 **8** 2¼ **Lightning Spirit**[9] 3705 4-9-6 **57**....................................(p) GeorgeBaker 7 52
(Gary Moore) *t.k.h: hld up in midfield: effrt whn nt clr run over 1f out: no prog fnl f* **10/3**[1]

4-00 **9** 1½ **Wishformore (IRE)**[76] 1635 5-9-4 **55**......................... JamieGoldstein 11 46
(Zoe Davison) *trckd ldng trio: rdn 2f out: wknd over 1f out* **16/1**

000 **10** 1¼ **Perfect Outlook**[33] 2891 4-9-6 **57**....................................... TomEaves 13 45
(Jeremy Gask) *chsd ldr to 2f out: sn wknd* **10/1**

00/0 **11** 12 **King's Sabre**[19] 3344 6-9-2 **53**..(p) KellyHarrison 4 14
(John Spearing) *slowest away: tk fierce hold: racd wd in rr: prog over 3f out: wknd qckly 2f out: t.o* **28/1**

1m 40.7s (0.90) **Going Correction** -0.025s/f (Stan) **11** Ran SP% **118.2**
Speed ratings (Par 101): **94,93,92,92,92 91,90,88,86,85 73**
toteswingers: 1&2 £19.60, 1&3 £5.90, 2&3 £28.00 CSF £58.92 CT £433.53 TOTE £2.30: £1.40, £5.80, £2.40; EX 86.10 TRIFECTA Not won..
Owner Thomas Mann **Bred** Plantation Stud **Trained** Newmarket, Suffolk

FOCUS
A modest handicap, run at a fair pace. Doubts over most of thse, with the fourth the best guide.
Lightning Spirit Official explanation: jockey said that the filly was denied a clear run
T/Jkpt: Not won. T/Plt: £184.40 to a £1 stake. Pool £85,499.37. 338.40 winning tickets. T/Qpdt: £118.70 to a £1 stake. Pool: £6,353.42. 39.60 winning tickets. JN

3617 LINGFIELD (L-H)
Wednesday, July 11

OFFICIAL GOING: Turf course - good to soft (soft in places; 6.0) changing to soft after 2.30 (race 2); aw course - standard
Wind: Medium, half behind Weather: Bright, dry for now

3965 LINGFIELD PARK MARRIOTT HOTEL & COUNTRY CLUB H'CAP (DIV I) (TURF) 1m 1f
2:00 (2:01) (Class 6) (0-60,60) 3-Y-O **£1,704** (£503; £251) **Stalls** Low

Form RPR

4603 **1** **Arte Del Calcio**[20] 3315 3-9-2 **60**........................... BrendanPowell(5) 6 66
(Tony Carroll) *hld up in tch: trcking ldrs and gng wl 4f out: effrt and rdn to chse ldng pair over 1f out: led ins fnl f: styd on: rdn out* **9/2**[3]

0030 **2** ½ **Vexillum (IRE)**[22] 3246 3-9-3 **56**....................................... MartinHarley 9 61
(Mick Channon) *in tch in last quartet: rdn over 3f out: hrd drvn over 2f out: styd on to chse ldng pair 1f out: chsd wnr wl ins fnl f: kpt on* **11/4**[1]

0600 **3** ¾ **Wyebridge**[15] 3470 3-8-11 **50**.. FergusSweeney 8 53
(Gary Moore) *in tch in last pair but sn niggled along: unbalanced on downhill run 4f out: rdn and swtchd rt over 2f out: styd on wl ins fnl f: nt rch ldrs* **10/1**

-060 **4** ¾ **Winter Dress**[23] 3228 3-9-4 **60**..................................(v[1]) HarryBentley(3) 7 61
(Roger Teal) *sn pressing ldr: rdn to ld 2f out: hrd drvn ent fnl f: hdd ins fnl f: wknd wl ins fnl f* **6/1**

000 **5** 1¼ **Ececheira**[24] 3189 3-8-9 **48**.. TedDurcan 1 47
(Dean Ivory) *t.k.h: chsd ldrs: rdn 3f out: sn outpcd and looked hld over 1f out: rallied ins fnl f: styng on but no threat to ldrs whn swtchd lft towards fin* **25/1**

-005 **6** 1¼ **Desert Red (IRE)**[51] 2353 3-8-13 **52**.................................. EddieAhern 4 48
(Michael Bell) *chsd ldrs: flashed tail 4f out: rdn and unable qck over 2f out: wknd ent fnl f* **4/1**[2]

600 **7** 2¼ **Goodie Goodie**[37] 2768 3-8-11 **50**..............................(t) RichardHughes 2 41
(Sylvester Kirk) *sn led: rdn 3f out: hdd 2f out: struggling and btn over 1f out: wknd fnl f* **12/1**

00-0 **8** 1¼ **Feb Thirtyfirst**[16] 3447 3-9-4 **57**... IanMongan 12 45
(Sheena West) *in tch on outer: rdn and unable qck 3f out: wknd over 1f out* **10/1**

05-0 **9** ½ **Retromania (IRE)**[63] 1979 3-8-10 **54**............................ DarrenEgan(5) 10 41
(John Best) *hld up in last pair: pushed along 6f out: drvn and no prog 3f out: n.d* **20/1**

1m 59.74s (3.14) **Going Correction** +0.30s/f (Good) **9** Ran SP% **113.6**
Speed ratings (Par 98): **98,97,96,96,95 94,92,90,90**
toteswingers: 1&2 £3.20, 1&3 £9.60, 2&3 £7.90 CSF £16.96 CT £115.30 TOTE £5.00: £1.80, £1.40, £3.00; EX 19.30.
Owner K F Coleman **Bred** Lordship Stud **Trained** Cropthorne, Worcs

FOCUS
This was a poor handicap with the nine remaining runners all maidens coming into it.

3966 LINGFIELD PARK MARRIOTT HOTEL & COUNTRY CLUB H'CAP (DIV II) (TURF) 1m 1f
2:30 (2:34) (Class 6) (0-60,60) 3-Y-O **£1,704** (£503; £251) **Stalls** Low

Form RPR

0340 **1** **Eightfold**[44] 2544 3-9-7 **60**..(t) GeorgeBaker 7 66
(Seamus Durack) *hld up wl off the pce in last pair: swtchd rt and hdwy over 2f out: styd on wl u.p ins fnl f: led last strides* **7/2**[1]

0306 **2** *hd* **Authoritarian**[10] 3665 3-9-5 **58**....................................... RichardHughes 9 63
(Richard Hannon) *racd off the pce in midfield: reminder 6f out: drvn over 2f out: styd on u.p fr over 1f out: chsd wnr ins fnl f: ev ch wl ins fnl f: kpt on* **8/1**

-546 **3** *hd* **Joyful Spirit (IRE)**[41] 2624 3-9-4 **57**..................................(b) TedDurcan 5 62
(John Dunlop) *racd keenly: led and sn clr: rdn over 2f out: drvn and coming bk to rivals 1f out: hdd last strides* **6/1**

5-02 **4** *nk* **Hollywood All Star (IRE)**[22] 3246 3-8-12 **51**............... RaulDaSilva(3) 12 55
(William Muir) *racd wl off the pce in last quartet: rdn 3f out: stl plenty to do but hdwy over 1f out: styd on wl fnl 100yds* **8/1**

-502 **5** ½ **Coup De Grace (IRE)**[27] 3068 3-9-7 **60**............................ JimCrowley 6 63
(Amanda Perrett) *chsd ldrs but wl off the pce: rdn 3f out: kpt on and grad clsd on ldr: pressing ldr wl ins fnl f: kpt on* **5/1**[3]

023 **6** 1½ **Thecornishcowboy**[13] 3551 3-9-0 **53**.............................(t) JimmyQuinn 2 53
(John Ryan) *chsd ldrs: chsd clr wnr u.p over 2f out: grad clsng on ldr 1f out: lost 2nd and plugged on same pce ins fnl f* **10/1**

2025 **7** 5 **Musically**[11] 3616 3-9-6 **59**... MartinHarley 14 48
(Mick Channon) *hld up wl off the pce in last quartet: effrt u.p wl over 2f out: plugged on but nvr on terms* **4/1**[2]

-000 **8** ½ **Invincible Dream (IRE)**[23] 3228 3-9-3 **56**............................. IanMongan 1 44
(Pat Phelan) *racd wl off the pce in midfield: rdn and no rspnse 3f out: nvr trbld ldrs* **20/1**

5000 **9** *26* **Findeln**[27] 3083 3-9-7 **60** .... NeilCallan 4
(Eve Johnson Houghton) *squeezed for room sn after s: sn pushed along and rcvrd to chse ldr after 2f: rdn and lost 2nd over 2f out: sn wknd: t.o and eased ins fnl f* **33/1**

000 **10** *5* **Fleeting Indian (IRE)**[151] 523 3-8-10 **49** .... LiamKeniry 11
(Linda Jewell) *hld up off the pce in midfield: rdn 3f out: sn struggling and btn 2f out: wknd: t.o and eased ins fnl f* **50/1**

-200 **11** *3 ½* **Lithograph (USA)**[15] 3469 3-8-11 **50** .... SilvestreDeSousa 13
(Mark Johnston) *a wl off the pce towards rr: rdn and btn wl over 2f out: wl bhd ins fnl f* **25/1**

00-3 **12** *2* **Grande Illusion**[16] 3431 3-9-1 **54** .... SebSanders 8
(J W Hills) *chsd ldr for 2f: chsd ldrs but off the pce: rdn and wknd 3f out: t.o and eased fnl f* **22/1**

2m 2.79s (6.19) **Going Correction** +0.45s/f (Yiel) **12** Ran SP% **122.3**
Speed ratings (Par 98): **90,89,89,89,88 87,83,82,59,55 52,50**
toteswingers: 1&2 £7.60, 1&3 £6.60, 2&3 £11.10 CSF £30.87 CT £168.69 TOTE £5.50: £2.30, £3.80, £1.90; EX 50.60.
Owner Miss Sam Beddoes **Bred** Avington Manor Stud **Trained** Baydon, Wilts
■ Stewards' Enquiry : Richard Hughes two-day ban: use of whip (25-26 July)

FOCUS
This race was preceded by a downpour, thunder and lightning. Again this lot were all maidens coming into the race. The early pace was very solid in the conditions, thanks to the eventual third, and the winning time being over three seconds slower than the first division was more down to the deterioration in the ground.
Authoritarian Official explanation: jockey said that the filly had hung left throughout
Thecornishcowboy Official explanation: jockey said that the gelding had lost a shoe

3967 BLACKBERRY LANE (S) STKS (TURF) — 1m 2f
3:00 (3:01) (Class 6) 3-Y-O+ **£1,704** (£503; £251) **Stalls** Low

Form RPR

13/6 **1** **King's Masque**[30] 2984 6-9-6 74 .... MartinLane 6 — 62
(Bernard Llewellyn) *hld up wl in tch towards rr: effrt and rdn jst over 2f out: pressed ldrs 1f out: styd on wl fnl 100yds to ld last stride* **9/2**[2]

040 **2** *shd* **Mount Abora (IRE)**[6] 3793 5-9-0 65 .... WilliamTwiston-Davies(7) 5 — 63
(Ian Williams) *hld up wl in tch in last pair: hdwy to chse ldrs and gng wl 2f out: rdn ro ld over 1f out: edgd lft and bmpd rival 1f out: kpt on u.p: hdd last stride* **3/1**[1]

40/1 **3** *¾* **Reaction**[20] 2392 6-9-7 64 ....(p) HarryPoulton(5) 7 — 66
(Sheena West) *chsd ldrs: wnt 2nd 1/2-way: rdn to ld over 2f out: hdd over 1f out stl ev ch whn bmpd 1f out: pushed lft jst ins fnl f: styd on same pce after* **5/1**[3]

6/0- **4** *½* **Goodwood Starlight (IRE)**[38] 3538 7-9-6 76 ....(t) GeorgeBaker 4 — 59
(Jim Best) *chsd ldrs: effrt u.p to press ldrs 2f out: styd on same pce fnl f* **14/1**

0230 **5** *4 ½* **Marvo**[19] 3344 8-9-12 65 ....(b) EddieAhern 1 — 60
(Mark H Tompkins) *t.k.h: trckd ldr tl 1/2-way: styd handy: rdn and effrt 1f out: one pce and looked hld whn squeezed out and bdly hmpd ins fnl f: lost any ch and eased after* **10/1**

-600 **6** *25* **My Vindication (USA)**[9] 3713 4-9-6 58 .... NeilCallan 3
(Gay Kelleway) *led: rdn and hdd over 2f out: wknd wl over 1f out: wl bhd and eased ins fnl f* **12/1**

2m 20.29s (9.79) **Going Correction** +0.60s/f (Yiel)
WFA 3 from 4yo+ 11lb **6** Ran SP% **83.3**
Speed ratings (Par 101): **84,83,83,82,79 59**
toteswingers: 1&2 £1.70, 1&3 £2.00, 2&3 £2.10 CSF £9.95 TOTE £3.70: £2.50, £1.10; EX 11.90.There was no bid for the winner. Mount Abora was claimed by Mrs L. J. Mongan for £6,000.
Owner B J Llewellyn **Bred** Deerfield Farm **Trained** Fochriw, Caerphilly
■ Rock Band was withdrawn (2/1F; not enter stalls). Deduct 30p in the £ under R4.
■ Stewards' Enquiry : William Twiston-Davies four-day ban: careless riding (25-28 July)

FOCUS
This was a poor seller, especially following the late withdrawal of the favourite Rock Band. With little covering the front four at the line, the form looks moderate.

3968 BRITANIACREST RECYCLING FILLIES' H'CAP (TURF) — 1m 3f 106y
3:30 (3:30) (Class 5) (0-70,70) 3-Y-O+ **£2,385** (£704; £352) **Stalls** High

Form RPR

0-00 **1** **Astra Hall**[34] 2856 3-7-12 **52** oh1 .... NickyMackay 6 — 71
(Ralph Beckett) *chsd ldrs: rdn and chal 2f out: clr w ldr over 1f out: drvn to ld ent fnl f: asserted fnl 100yds: eased cl home* **4/1**[3]

-003 **2** *1 ½* **Gallipot**[19] 3345 3-9-0 **68** .... WilliamBuick 11 — 84
(John Gosden) *chsd ldrs: wnt 2nd 8f out: rdn to chal 3f out: led 2f out and drew clr w wnr over 1f out: hdd ent fnl f: one pce and btn fnl 100yds* **9/4**[1]

-062 **3** *7* **News Show**[51] 2333 3-8-11 **65** .... MartinLane 9 — 69
(David Simcock) *in tch: rdn and effrt over 2f out: outpcd by ldng pair 2f out: modest 3rd and plugged on same pce fr over 1f out* **17/2**

000- **4** *2* **Panettone (IRE)**[238] 7431 3-8-11 **65** .... NeilCallan 3 — 66
(Roger Varian) *t.k.h: chsd ldr tl 8f out: styd chsng ldrs: rdn and unable qck over 2f out: outpcd 2f out and wl hld after* **10/1**

06-2 **5** *hd* **Ironically (IRE)**[9] 3704 3-8-9 **63** .... TedDurcan 5 — 63
(David Lanigan) *hld up in tch in last quartet: hdwy over 3f out: no ex u.p 2f out: sn outpcd and wl btn* **7/2**[2]

3603 **6** *1 ½* **Beauchamp Castle**[27] 3068 3-8-5 **66** ....(bt) NicoleNordblad(7) 7 — 64+
(Hans Adielsson) *stdd s: hld up in rr: lost tch on downhill run 4f out: virtually t.o and rdn 3f out: styd on fnl f: n.d* **16/1**

6/6- **7** *nk* **Lindsay's Dream**[20] 314 6-8-11 **53** oh1 ow1 .... JamieGoldstein 8 — 50
(Zoe Davison) *in tch in midfield: effrt over 3f out: rdn and no ex ent fnl 2f: sn wknd* **50/1**

0-66 **8** *2* **Broughtons Swinger**[23] 3220 5-9-8 **64** .... RichardHughes 4 — 58
(Willie Musson) *hld up in tch in last quartet: rdn and effrt 3f out: btn ent fnl 2f: sn wknd* **16/1**

4666 **9** *5* **Rythmic**[44] 2539 3-9-2 **70** .... SilvestreDeSousa 1 — 55
(Mark Johnston) *led: rdn and hrd pressed 3f out: wknd 2f out: sn bhd* **9/1**

4000 **10** *30* **Castalian Spring (IRE)**[144] 619 3-7-12 **52** oh7 .... JimmyQuinn 2
(Terry Clement) *hld up in tch: lost tch over 3f out: sn eased: t.o* **66/1**

2m 40.84s (9.34) **Going Correction** +0.75s/f (Yiel)
WFA 3 from 5yo+ 12lb **10** Ran SP% **117.8**
Speed ratings (Par 100): **96,94,89,88,88 87,86,85,81,60**
toteswingers: 1&2 £4.20, 1&3 £9.40, 2&3 £3.50 CSF £13.55 CT £72.93 TOTE £6.90: £2.20, £1.80, £2.60; EX 22.00.
Owner G B Balding **Bred** Miss B Swire **Trained** Kimpton, Hants

FOCUS
A modest fillies' handicap which would have been quite a test in the conditions, but the first two pulled well clear and both can rate higher.
Astra Hall Official explanation: trainer's representative said, regarding the apparent improvement of form, that it was the filly's first time in a handicap
Beauchamp Castle Official explanation: jockey said that the filly did not handle the track
Castalian Spring(IRE) Official explanation: trainer said that the filly was not suited by the soft going

3969 FOLLOW US ON TWITTER @LINGFIELDPARK H'CAP (TURF) — 2m
4:00 (4:01) (Class 6) (0-60,59) 4-Y-O+ **£1,704** (£503; £251) **Stalls** Low

Form RPR

4503 **1** **Dew Reward (IRE)**[11] 3620 4-9-4 **56** .... CathyGannon 8 — 67
(Bill Turner) *in tch: chsd ldr over 3f out: rdn to ld ent fnl 2f: kpt on and a holding runner-up fnl f* **10/1**

0050 **2** *nk* **Mollyow (IRE)**[18] 3400 4-8-9 **47** ow1 .... RichardHughes 6 — 58
(Terry Clement) *hld up in tch: hdwy 5f out: rdn to chal 2f out: ev ch after: kpt on wl but a jst hld fnl f* **5/1**[3]

0/23 **3** *4 ½* **Tae Kwon Do (USA)**[43] 2575 6-8-10 **48** ....(t) DavidProbert 11 — 53+
(Tim Vaughan) *hld up in tch: hdwy to trck ldrs gng wl 4f out: effrt and chsd ldng pair 2f out: unable qck over 1f out: outpcd and btn fnl f* **11/2**

006- **4** *14* **On Alert**[285] 6504 4-8-3 **46** ow1 ....(t) MatthewLawson(5) 2 — 34
(Seamus Durack) *hld up in last pair: struggling over 4f out: no ch but styd on past btn horses fnl 2f* **14/1**

-632 **5** *3 ¼* **Old Boy Ted**[12] 3579 4-8-11 **49** .... EddieAhern 3 — 34
(Mark H Tompkins) *in tch: pushed along 5f out: 6th and wknd over 3f out* **4/1**[2]

0360 **6** *¾* **Rather Cool**[9] 3704 4-8-11 **49** ....(t) KieranO'Neill 10 — 33
(John Bridger) *chsd ldrs: wnt 2nd over 5f out: sn rdn: btn over 2f out: sn wknd* **16/1**

0-42 **7** *1 ½* **Before Bruce**[16] 3431 5-9-2 **59** ....(t) BrendanPowell(5) 9 — 41
(Brendan Powell) *hld up in tch in last trio: rdn over 5f out: wknd 4f out* **14/1**

-015 **8** *½* **Tallulah Mai**[24] 3180 5-9-2 **54** .... WilliamBuick 7 — 35
(Matthew Salaman) *chsd ldr: styd wd in bk st: led 6f out: rdn and hdd ent fnl 2f: sn btn: fdd* **5/2**[1]

630 **9** *48* **Kavaloti (IRE)**[27] 3086 8-9-3 **55** ....(b) GeorgeBaker 1
(Gary Moore) *hld up in last pair: lost tch 4f out: t.o fnl 3f* **12/1**

0/ **10** *9* **Ashmolian (IRE)**[692] 546 9-8-7 **45** .... NickyMackay 5
(Zoe Davison) *led tl 6f out: sn dropped out and t.o fnl 3f* **33/1**

0/00 **11** *2 ¾* **Sahara Sunshine**[34] 2851 7-8-7 **45** ....(tp) LiamKeniry 4
(Laura Mongan) *chsd ldrs tl 6f out: t.o fnl 3f* **50/1**

3m 48.87s (14.07) **Going Correction** +0.90s/f (Soft) **11** Ran SP% **121.5**
Speed ratings (Par 101): **100,99,97,90,88 88,87,87,63,59 57**
toteswingers: 1&2 £12.40, 1&3 £8.30, 2&3 £7.10 CSF £61.47 TOTE £10.60: £3.20, £1.50, £1.50; EX 98.50.
Owner Mrs Derien Tucker **Bred** Tim Hyde Jnr **Trained** Sigwells, Somerset

FOCUS
A real test of stamina in the conditions for this moderate staying handicap. The front three pulled miles clear of the rest.
Before Bruce Official explanation: trainer's representative said that the gelding was unsuited by the soft going

3970 MARKEL SPECIALTY NURSERY — 5f (P)
4:30 (4:32) (Class 5) (0-75,75) 2-Y-O **£2,385** (£704; £352) **Stalls** High

Form RPR

0343 **1** **Windforpower (IRE)**[25] 3140 2-8-13 **67** ....(p) JamesDoyle 5 — 70+
(Ronald Harris) *chsd ldr: jnd ldr 3f out: rdn to ld 2f out: hung lft 1f out: hanging bdly and hdd fnl 100yds: rallied to ld again last strides* **3/1**[2]

551 **2** *hd* **Bheleyf (IRE)**[41] 2622 2-9-3 **74** .... HarryBentley(3) 4 — 76
(Joseph Tuite) *t.k.h: hld up in tch: rdn and effrt over 1f out: str chal whn lft in ld fnl 100yds: hdd and no ex last strides* **4/1**[3]

232 **3** *1 ½* **Boleyn**[16] 3444 2-9-2 **70** .... RichardHughes 3 — 67
(Richard Hannon) *led: hdd 2f out: sn rdn: stl pressing wnr 1f out: no ex and one pce fnl 100yds* **1/1**[1]

354 **4** *1* **Wordsaplenty (IRE)**[16] 3444 2-8-7 **61** .... LiamKeniry 2 — 54
(J S Moore) *awkward leaving stalls: in tch: racd awkwardly bnd 2f out: swtchd rt and outpcd ent fnl f: styd on same pce* **6/1**

1m 1.35s (2.55) **Going Correction** +0.25s/f (Slow) **4** Ran SP% **109.3**
Speed ratings (Par 94): **89,88,86,84**
CSF £13.99 TOTE £4.90; EX 17.10.
Owner Anthony Cooke **Bred** Tally-Ho Stud **Trained** Earlswood, Monmouths

FOCUS
A tight little Polytrack nursery. The quartet were all fairly familiar with each other and the form looks straightforward, if limited.

NOTEBOOK
Windforpower(IRE) had only progressed slowly at a modest level, but his dam won over this C&D. Ridden to poke his head in front on the home bend, he started to hesitate and hang inside the last furlong, but his rider was having none of it and made him stick his neck out where it mattered. He doesn't look straightforward, even with the headgear. (tchd 4-1)
Bheleyf(IRE) put her experience to good use when beating the newcomers Boleyn and Wordsaplenty in a maiden over this trip at Brighton in May and managed to confirm the form. She ran on well when switched out wide for her effort over a furlong out, but could never quite get up. (op 9-2 tchd 10-3)
Boleyn had twice been placed over 6f since running Bheleyf to a head on her Brighton debut. Soon in front, she battled away against the inside rail after being headed by the winner over 2f out, but looks in need of a return to a stiffer test. Her rider reported that the filly suffered interference in running. Official explanation: jockey said that the filly suffered interference in running (tchd 10-11 and 11-10)
Wordsaplenty(IRE) had finished behind at least one of today's rivals in each of her previous three starts and maintained that sequence, though she was running on out wide at the line and wasn't beaten far. (tchd 11-2)

3971 MIRROR PUNTERS CLUB MAIDEN AUCTION STKS — 6f (P)
5:00 (5:03) (Class 6) 2-Y-O **£1,704** (£503; £251) **Stalls** Low

Form RPR

35 **1** **Stupenda**[29] 3010 2-8-4 0 .... TadhgO'Shea 2 — 62
(Denis Coakley) *hld up in tch: hdwy to chse ldr wl over 1f out: ev ch 1f out: led wl ins fnl f: kpt on* **11/1**

2 *nk* **Solvanna** 2-8-8 0 ow1 .... EddieAhern 8 — 65+
(Heather Main) *wnt lft s: in tch towards rr: rdn on outer over 2f out: swtchd lft and str run 1f out: ev ch wl ins fnl f: r.o* **20/1**

0 **3** *½* **Our Sweet Art**[19] 3339 2-8-10 0 .... LiamJones 7 — 66
(John Best) *in tch in midfield: hdwy u.p over 1f out: ev ch fnl 100yds: unable qck cl home* **8/1**

20 **4** *shd* **Jet Acclaim (IRE)**[35] 2812 2-8-4 0 .... NickyMackay 3 — 59
(Marco Botti) *sn led: rdn and hrd pressed wl over 1f out: hdd wl ins fnl f: no ex* **5/1**[3]

3 **5** *hd* **Bay Laurel (IRE)**[28] 3040 2-8-10 0 .... WilliamBuick 6 — 68+
(Harry Dunlop) *squeezed for room sn after s: bhd: nt clr run 2f out: stl last 1f out: in the clr and str run fnl 150yds: nvr quite getting to ldrs* **2/1**[1]

6 shd **Ovett** 2-8-9 0 AmirQuinn 10 63
(Gary Moore) *in tch towards rr: rdn over 3f out: hdwy u.p on inner over 1f out: ev ch ins fnl f: one pce fnl 75yds* **8/1**

005 7 1 3/4 **Proventi**[35] 2817 2-8-5 0 DannyBrock(7) 9 61
(Alan McCabe) *t.k.h: hld up in tch in rr: rdn and hdwy over 1f out: styd on same pce ins fnl f* **66/1**

50 8 1/2 **Why So Fast (IRE)**[16] 3444 2-8-4 0 HarryBentley(3) 4 55+
(Stuart Williams) *chsd ldrs: j. imaginary object and nrly uns rdr 5f out: stl pressing ldr after tl 2f out: wknd ins fnl f* **4/1**[2]

0 9 1 1/4 **Kalahari Breeze (IRE)**[51] 2343 2-8-7 0 MartinHarley 11 51
(William Muir) *in tch in midfield: effrt u.p over 1f out: wknd ins fnl f* **16/1**

00 10 1 1/4 **Grace Of Hearts**[11] 3634 2-8-4 0 PaoloSirigu 5 44
(Robert Eddery) *wnt lft s: in tch: pushed wd bnd 2f out: wknd 1f out* **25/1**

11 1 1/2 **Sarahmanda** 2-8-4 0 SilvestreDeSousa 1 40
(Peter Makin) *chsd ldrs: rn green and hung rt bnd 2f out: btn ent fnl f: wknd* **20/1**

1m 14.51s (2.61) **Going Correction** +0.25s/f (Slow) **11** Ran SP% **121.3**
Speed ratings (Par 92): **92,91,90,90,90 90,88,87,85,84 82**
toteswingers: 1&2 £32.10, 1&3 £12.20, 2&3 £26.70 CSF £215.95 TOTE £14.60: £2.80, £7.40, £2.40; EX 219.90.

Owner Finders Keepers Partnership **Bred** Mr & Mrs James Went **Trained** West Ilsley, Berks

■ Stewards' Enquiry : William Buick two-day ban: careless riding (25-26 July)

FOCUS
The principals finished in a heap in this maiden, but there were still some interesting performances. The bare form is just modest, though.

NOTEBOOK
Stupenda hadn't got home (though she did show ability) in her first two starts over this trip, but this easier 6f helped her. It almost seemed too sharp as she had to be stoked along at halfway, but she stuck at it and forged her way to the front well inside the last. Nurseries look the way forward with her now. (tchd 10-1 and 12-1)

Solvanna, a 7,500gns filly out of a dual 1m2f winner, was slow to break and found herself at the back of the field, but she weaved her way through once into the straight and finished strongly. She should improve, especially when put over further. (op 16-1)

Our Sweet Art showed some ability when seventh of 13 on last month's Goodwood debut and improved on that here with a staying-on effort to grab third. She can win a modest maiden. (op 5-1 tchd 17-2)

Jet Acclaim(IRE) had the run of the race out in front and wasn't worn down until late. She now gets a mark. (op 9-2 tchd 13-2)

Bay Laurel(IRE) showed plenty of promise when third of eight on last month's Kempton debut and was probably unlucky not to go two better here. She found herself in a poor position when squeezed out just after the start and was last passing the 2f pole, but she then flew home down the wide outside. She can be considered the best horse on the day. Official explanation: jockey said that the filly was denied a clear run (op 3-1 tchd 15-8)

Ovett, a 14,000gns yearling but retained for just 900GBP as a 2yo, is a half-brother to a 1m winner and a 3m winner over hurdles. He was having to be pumped along from a long way out, but ran on well against the inside rail and obviously possesses ability. (op 9-1 tchd 10-1)

Why So Fast(IRE) would have finished better than seventh of 14 on her second start at Windsor with more luck and considering she fly-jumped after a furlong here and almost lost her rider, she did well to stay in the action for so long. She also now gets a mark and could be interesting for a nursery. Official explanation: jockey said that the filly jumped and became unbalanced about five furlongs out (tchd 9-2)

3972 LADBROKES GAME ON! MEDIAN AUCTION MAIDEN STKS 6f (P)
5:30 (5:32) (Class 6) 3-4-Y-O £1,704 (£503; £251)

Form RPR

2-24 1 **Jack Of Diamonds (IRE)**[18] 3398 3-9-3 75 RichardHughes 6 76
(Roger Teal) *chsd ldrs: rdn and effrt wl over 1f out: led over 1f out: r.o wl and in command wl ins fnl f* **1/1**[1]

6 2 1 1/4 **Ginger Monkey (IRE)**[168] 298 3-9-3 0 JimmyFortune 5 72
(Peter Chapple-Hyam) *t.k.h: hld up in tch: rdn and effrt to chal over 1f out: drew clr w wnr ins fnl f: a hld: outpcd fnl 75yds* **11/4**[2]

0020 3 4 **King's Future**[44] 2548 3-9-3 58 CathyGannon 8 59
(Lee Carter) *led: rdn and hdd over 1f out: unable qck 1f out: sn outpcd by ldng pair and wl hld fnl f* **25/1**

40-0 4 1/2 **Bahri Sheen (IRE)**[119] 896 4-9-9 63 GeorgeBaker 2 58
(John Best) *in tch in midfield: rdn and effrt over 1f out: outpcd and no ch w ldng pair ins fnl f: kpt on to press for 3rd cl home* **25/1**

30 5 4 1/2 **Exceedexpectations (IRE)**[9] 3702 3-9-3 0 MartinLane 4 43
(Michael Bell) *chsd ldr tl wl over 1f out: btn ent fnl f: wknd* **18/1**

-342 6 1 **Mister Mackenzie**[159] 394 3-9-3 66 LiamJones 12 40
(John Best) *t.k.h: hld up towards rr: effrt u.p over 2f out: plugged on fnl f: no ch w ldrs* **6/1**[3]

500- 7 hd **Style Margi (IRE)**[281] 6617 4-9-4 63 LiamKeniry 11 35
(Ed de Giles) *chsd ldrs: rdn and unable qck 2f out: wknd over 1f out* **40/1**

6-50 8 nk **Rode Two Destiny (IRE)**[14] 3510 3-8-12 55 (b[1]) SebSanders 9 33
(Peter Makin) *in tch in midfield on outer: rdn and unable qck 2f out: wknd over 1f out* **33/1**

9 1 1/2 **Venetias Dream (IRE)** 3-8-12 0 SaleemGolam 10 28
(Stuart Williams) *hld up in rr: n.d* **66/1**

0 10 2 3/4 **Snowy Valley**[71] 1723 3-9-0 0 RaulDaSilva(3) 3 25
(Simon Earle) *a in rr: n.d* **33/1**

60 11 3/4 **Mrs Bridges**[14] 3507 3-8-12 0 FergusSweeney 7 17
(Roger Ingram) *hld up in tch towards rr: rdn and wknd 2f out* **100/1**

0 12 5 **Consenting**[20] 3312 3-8-12 0 JamesDoyle 1
(Roger Charlton) *t.k.h: hld up in tch towards rr: struggling whn rn green and lost tch wl over 1f out* **12/1**

1m 12.15s (0.25) **Going Correction** +0.25s/f (Slow) **12** Ran SP% **122.4**
WFA 3 from 4yo 6lb
Speed ratings (Par 101): **108,106,101,100,94 93,92,92,90,86 85,79**
toteswingers: 1&2 £1.90, 1&3 £8.70, 2&3 £14.50 CSF £3.56 TOTE £2.10: £1.20, £1.30, £6.30; EX 5.20.

Owner Inside Track Racing Club **Bred** Gigginstown House Stud **Trained** Ashtead, Surrey

FOCUS
With lightning around, it was decided not to use the stalls and have a 'flip' start. Perfectly understandably though it was, it was far from ideal for a 6f sprint and the draw numbers had only a spiritual connection with reality. The right horses still came to the fore, though, with the two market leaders pulling clear of the rest.

T/Plt: £145.40 to a £1 stake. Pool: £61,706.59. 309.67 winning tickets. T/Qpdt: £34.40 to a £1 stake. Pool £4,228.25. 90.80 winning tickets. SP

[3788]YARMOUTH (L-H)
Wednesday, July 11

OFFICIAL GOING: Soft (good to soft in places; 6.7) changing to soft after 3.40 (race 4)
Wind: Light, across Weather: Sunshine and showers

3973 CASINO AT BET365.COM MEDIAN AUCTION MAIDEN STKS 5f 43y
2:10 (2:12) (Class 6) 2-Y-O £1,617 (£481; £240; £120) Stalls Low

Form RPR

223 1 **Uncomplicated**[34] 2852 2-8-12 73 PatCosgrave 5 76
(Jim Boyle) *chsd ldrs tl led over 1f out: rdn and edgd lft ins fnl f: jst hld on* **2/1**[1]

563 2 nse **The Sixties**[12] 3569 2-9-3 79 MatthewDavies 7 81
(Mick Channon) *led over 3f: sn rdn: edgd lft ins fnl f: styd on* **2/1**[1]

0 3 1 3/4 **Medicoe**[20] 3303 2-9-3 0 ChrisCatlin 10 75+
(Sir Mark Prescott Bt) *chsd ldrs: pushed along 1/2-way: edgd lft ins fnl f: styd on* **9/1**[2]

4 3 **Oscars Journey** 2-9-3 0 FrederikTylicki 8 64
(J R Jenkins) *prom: shkn up over 1f out: styd on same pce* **20/1**

5 1 1/4 **Whatwehavewehold** 2-9-3 0 AndreaAtzeni 3 59
(Des Donovan) *chsd ldrs: rdn over 1f out: wknd fnl f* **20/1**

5 6 3/4 **Mystical Man**[11] 3617 2-9-3 0 MartinDwyer 1 57
(James Tate) *chsd ldrs: pushed along 1/2-way: wknd over 1f out* **10/1**[3]

0 7 2 **Holding Fast (IRE)**[33] 2873 2-9-3 0 StevieDonohoe 6 49
(Tobias B P Coles) *prom tl wknd over 1f out* **100/1**

00 8 2 3/4 **The Manx Missile**[34] 2852 2-9-3 0 JamieSpencer 4 39
(Michael Bell) *s.i.s: hld up: rdn 1/2-way: sn wknd* **16/1**

9 3/4 **Southern Sapphire** 2-9-3 0 TomEaves 9 37
(Linda Stubbs) *hld up: plld hrd: wknd 2f out* **10/1**[3]

1m 3.56s (0.86) **Going Correction** +0.05s/f (Good) **9** Ran SP% **111.2**
Speed ratings (Par 92): **95,94,92,87,85 84,80,76,75**
toteswingers: 1&2 £1.20, 1&3 £3.00, 2&3 £4.30 CSF £5.14 TOTE £3.70: £1.30, £1.40, £1.90; EX 7.20 Trifecta £20.30 Pool: £700.71 - 25.52 winning units..

Owner The Vine Associates **Bred** Miss J Staughton And Mrs O Staughton **Trained** Epsom, Surrey

FOCUS
The time of this opening race suggested the ground wasn't too soft on the straight course. Fair form, limited by those down the field.

NOTEBOOK
Uncomplicated, the only filly in the line-up, showed a fine attitude to just hold off the runner-up's persistent challenge. The winner hadn't progressed from a close second on her debut at Windsor, although she wasn't helped by racing wide at Sandown on her previous start and this was a fair effort. (op 5-2 tchd 11-4)

The Sixties didn't match the form he showed in the Chesham when a beaten favourite at Folkestone (7f, good to firm) last time, and he again failed to really build on his Royal Ascot performance, even though he was just held. He's clearly up to winning, however. (op 15-8 tchd 7-4 and 9-4)

Medicoe ◆ couldn't justify a short price on his debut over 6f at Ripon, when never going the pace, but this was better. He ran on after getting outpaced and should come on again for the run. (tchd 7-1 and 10-1)

Oscars Journey, a half-brother to a 1m winner, out of a smart 6f-1m performer (Listed winner) for these connections, showed plenty of ability on his debut and could be a fair type in the making. (tchd 22-1)

Whatwehavewehold shaped okay, faring second best of the newcomers. (op 16-1)

Southern Sapphire Official explanation: jockey said that the gelding was unsuited by the soft, good to soft in places ground.

3974 BET365.COM (S) STKS 1m 3f 101y
2:40 (2:40) (Class 6) 3-4-Y-O £1,617 (£481; £240; £120) Stalls Low

Form RPR

-405 1 **Emperors Waltz (IRE)**[28] 3023 3-8-9 54 ChrisCatlin 1 59
(Rae Guest) *chsd ldr tl led over 2f out: rdn over 1f out: styd on wl* **10/3**[2]

3-40 2 3 1/4 **Red Hermes (IRE)**[18] 3391 3-8-9 47 PaulHanagan 6 53
(Mark H Tompkins) *a.p: rdn to chse wnr over 1f out: styd on same pce ins fnl f* **6/1**[3]

0050 3 6 **Cappielow Park**[16] 3448 3-9-0 68 RyanMoore 4 48
(William Jarvis) *s.i.s: hld up: hdwy over 3f out: rdn over 2f out: edgd lft: styd on same pce: wnt 3rd ins fnl f* **5/6**[1]

-030 4 1 1/2 **Shomberg**[23] 3233 3-9-0 54 (b[1]) KierenFallon 3 46
(Mark H Tompkins) *led: rdn and hdd over 2f out: wknd fnl f* **9/1**

-000 5 25 **Harry Lime**[18] 3392 4-9-5 46 JoshCrane(7) 5
(Chris Dwyer) *s.s: hld up: wknd 3f out: t.o* **25/1**

0-00 6 6 **Verona Bay (FR)**[33] 2895 3-8-11 26 (b[1]) AdamBeschizza(3) 2
(Julia Feilden) *chsd ldrs: pushed along over 4f out: rdn and wknd 3f out: t.o* **100/1**

2m 30.72s (2.02) **Going Correction** +0.05s/f (Good)
WFA 3 from 4yo 12lb **6** Ran SP% **106.8**
Speed ratings (Par 101): **94,91,87,86,68 63**
toteswingers: 1&2 £2.20, 1&3 £1.10, 2&3 £1.70 CSF £20.54 TOTE £4.90: £1.80, £2.40; EX 23.00.There was no bid for the winner.

Owner Hirschfeld, Alexander, Murphy & Guest **Bred** Speers Bloodstock Ltd **Trained** Newmarket, Suffolk

FOCUS
A weak seller.

3975 BET365.COM MEDIAN AUCTION MAIDEN STKS 1m 3y
3:10 (3:11) (Class 5) 3-Y-O £2,264 (£673; £336; £168) Stalls Low

Form RPR

1 **Nadema Rose (IRE)** 3-8-9 0 DominicFox(3) 10 70
(Anthony Carson) *hld up: hdwy over 2f out: r.o to ld wl ins fnl f* **100/1**

2 1 1/4 **Medici Music** 3-9-3 0 KierenFallon 5 72
(Luca Cumani) *hld up in tch: led over 1f out: rdn and hdd wl ins fnl f* **11/2**[2]

000 3 3 **Confluence**[19] 3349 3-8-12 60 PatCosgrave 2 60
(Clifford Lines) *chsd ldr tl led over 2f out: rdn and hdd over 1f out: no ex ins fnl f* **10/1**[3]

4 hd **Balcary Bay** 3-9-3 0 AndreaAtzeni 1 65
(James Eustace) *prom: rdn over 2f out: styd on same pce ins fnl f* **33/1**

5 3 1/4 **Lea Valley** 3-8-9 0 AdamBeschizza(3) 6 52
(Julia Feilden) *prom: pushed along over 4f out: wknd fnl f* **25/1**

2 6 21 **Medhyaar**[32] 2935 3-8-12 0 PaulHanagan 8
(William Haggas) *dwlt: hld up: rdn over 3f out: wknd over 1f out: bhd whn hmpd ins fnl f* **4/11**[1]

06 **7** 1 3/4 **Pont Menai**[36] 2800 3-9-3 0.............................(v[1]) FrederikTylicki 7
(J R Jenkins) *led over 5f: sn wknd* **100/1**
P- **P** **High Miswaki (FR)**[301] 6059 3-9-3 0........................ JamieSpencer 3
(Jeremy Noseda) *hld up: pushed along over 3f out: hdwy over 1f out: disputing 5th and btn whn broke down and p.u ins fnl f* **12/1**
1m 41.61s (1.01) **Going Correction** +0.05s/f (Good) **8** Ran SP% **114.2**
Speed ratings (Par 100): **96,94,91,91,88 67,65,**
toteswingers: 1&2 £16.80, 1&3 £16.80, 2&3 £9.40 CSF £570.55 TOTE £107.60: £29.50, £2.80, £4.00; EX 177.50 TRIFECTA Not won..
Owner W H Carson **Bred** Keogh Family & Virgivia Kraft Payson **Trained** Newmarket, Suffolk

FOCUS
This looked a pretty modest maiden, with the favourite flopping.
Medhyaar Official explanation: jockey said that the filly was never travelling

3976 BET365.COM H'CAP 1m 3y
3:40 (3:40) (Class 5) (0-75,74) 3-Y-0+ £2,264 (£673; £336; £168) Stalls Low

Form RPR
0162 **1** **Hail Promenader (IRE)**[19] 3344 6-9-7 **67**..................(p) PaulHanagan 5 76
(Anthony Carson) *chsd ldrs: led 3f out: rdn over 1f out: styd on wl* **4/1**[3]
0026 **2** 2 3/4 **Patriotic (IRE)**[12] 3589 4-9-10 **70**........................ RyanMoore 6 73
(Chris Dwyer) *hld up: bhd 1/2-way: hdwy u.p over 1f out: styd on to go 2nd towards fin: no ch w wnr* **9/4**[2]
3350 **3** 1 1/4 **Hereford Boy**[12] 3589 8-9-8 **68**..........................(v) RobertHavlin 2 68
(Dean Ivory) *s.i.s: hld up: hdwy over 3f out: chsd wnr over 2f out: rdn over 1f out: no ex ins fnl f: lost 2nd towards fin* **10/1**
-341 **4** 13 **Grey Seal (IRE)**[16] 3454 3-9-3 **72**........................ HayleyTurner 3 40
(James Fanshawe) *chsd ldrs tl wknd over 1f out* **2/1**[1]
0-30 **5** 11 **Allanit (GER)**[12] 3594 8-9-0 **60**........................ TomQueally 1
(Barney Curley) *w ldr 5f: wknd over 2f out* **25/1**
3-64 **6** 4 **Saslong**[21] 3273 3-9-0 **69**........................ MircoDemuro 4
(Mark Johnston) *led 5f: wknd 2f out* **6/1**
1m 40.4s (-0.20) **Going Correction** +0.05s/f (Good)
WFA 3 from 4yo+ 9lb **6** Ran SP% **111.3**
Speed ratings (Par 103): **103,100,99,86,75 71**
toteswingers: 1&2 £1.70, 1&3 £3.20, 2&3 £6.10 CSF £13.20 CT £78.32 TOTE £6.40: £2.80, £1.90; EX 15.60 Trifecta £73.30 Pool: £649.06 - 6.55 winning units..
Owner Athos Racing **Bred** Rathbarry Stud **Trained** Newmarket, Suffolk

FOCUS
This race was run in a heavy downpour, but the winning time suggested the ground had yet to get testing. It wasn't much of a race, however.

3977 BET365 H'CAP 7f 3y
4:10 (4:10) (Class 3) (0-90,90) 3-Y-0+ £6,490 (£1,942; £971; £486; £242) Stalls Low

Form RPR
3031 **1** **Comrade Bond**[13] 3549 4-8-12 **74**........................ RyanMoore 12 81
(Mark H Tompkins) *prom: rdn over 1f out: r.o to ld post* **15/2**
-100 **2** nk **Born To Surprise**[20] 3294 3-9-6 **90**........................ JamieSpencer 11 93+
(Michael Bell) *stdd s: hld up: racd keenly: hdwy to ld 2f out: rdn and hung lft ins fnl f: hdd post* **2/1**[1]
00-0 **3** 3/4 **Master Mylo (IRE)**[28] 3049 5-9-6 **82**........................ FrederikTylicki 3 86
(Robert Cowell) *led 5f: sn rdn: styd on* **40/1**
3150 **4** shd **Rough Rock (IRE)**[6] 3790 7-8-11 **73**........................ AndreaAtzeni 5 77
(Chris Dwyer) *chsd ldr 5f: sn rdn: styd on u.p* **16/1**
5-64 **5** 1/2 **Loving Spirit**[11] 3640 4-10-0 **90**........................ RobertHavlin 6 93
(James Toller) *chsd ldrs: rdn over 1f out: styd on* **15/2**
-300 **6** 3 1/4 **The Confessor**[53] 2268 5-9-12 **88**........................ DaneO'Neill 10 82
(Henry Candy) *hld up: hdwy over 1f out: no ex ins fnl f* **4/1**[2]
3546 **7** 1/2 **Hadaj**[46] 2477 3-9-4 **88**..........................(b[1]) TomQueally 7 77
(Clive Brittain) *prom: rdn over 1f out: hung lft and no ex fnl f* **9/1**
-445 **8** nk **Solar Deity (IRE)**[53] 2263 3-9-2 **86**..................(b[1]) PatCosgrave 9 75
(Marco Botti) *hld up in tch: rdn over 1f out: no ex fnl f* **7/1**[3]
6040 **9** 13 **Cravat**[18] 3393 3-8-6 **76**........................ MircoDemuro 14 30
(Mark Johnston) *hld up: rdn 1/2-way: wknd and eased over 2f out* **16/1**
1m 27.45s (0.85) **Going Correction** +0.30s/f (Good)
WFA 3 from 4yo+ 8lb **9** Ran SP% **113.6**
Speed ratings (Par 107): **107,106,105,105,105 101,100,100,85**
toteswingers: 1&2 £4.50, 1&3 £20.50, 2&3 £11.40 CSF £22.47 CT £567.71 TOTE £10.70: £2.20, £1.90, £8.40; EX 30.40 Trifecta £436.40 Pool: £589.82 - 0.65 winning units..
Owner Raceworld **Bred** Misses Wright, Lightowler And King **Trained** Newmarket, Suffolk

FOCUS
A decent handicap.

NOTEBOOK
Comrade Bond, more sensibly ridden than the winner, can be considered a little flattered, but he was defying a mark 4lb higher than when winning over C&D on quicker ground last time and is clearly on the up. (tchd 7-1 and 8-1)
Born To Surprise ◆ looked much the best horse on the day, but he was sent to the front far too soon and didn't see his race out after edging left. It was a complete contrast to way he was ridden by the same jockey at Royal Ascot, when he got going too late in the Britannia. There's surely more to come from a horse who once held a 2000 Guineas entry, and a return to better ground might help. (op 3-1)
Master Mylo(IRE) has gained his last two wins over 1m and he was going on at the finish. (op 28-1)
Rough Rock(IRE), a six-time course winner, had conditions to suit and ran a lot better than when hampered under a 7lb claimer here last time. He's due to be eased 1lb. (op 14-1)
Loving Spirit was eased in grade but had no easy task under top weight. (op 6-1)
The Confessor is nearly always picked off when sitting handy and it was no surprise to see him ridden with more patience than is often the case, and the change in run style looked as though it might pay off for some of the way as he travelled well. However, he was denied a clear run and his effort flattened out before he could get going. (op 7-2)

3978 MOBILE AT BET365.COM FILLIES' H'CAP 1m 1f
4:40 (4:41) (Class 5) (0-70,70) 3-Y-0+ £2,264 (£673; £336; £168) Stalls Low

Form RPR
0-00 **1** **Al Karlovyyh (IRE)**[43] 2585 3-7-11 **52**........................ RyanPowell(3) 1 58
(Clive Brittain) *chsd ldr tl led 7f out: rdn over 1f out: edgd lft ins fnl f: styd on* **28/1**
5-04 **2** 3/4 **Saaboog**[41] 2628 3-8-12 **64**........................ MartinDwyer 8 69
(James Tate) *hld up: plld hrd: hdwy over 2f out: rdn over 1f out: n.m.r ins fnl f: styd on* **10/1**
2050 **3** nk **Candycakes (IRE)**[11] 3643 3-9-4 **70**........................ JamieSpencer 6 74
(Michael Bell) *sn pushed along to chse ldrs: shkn up over 3f out: hrd rdn and ev ch over 1f out: unable qck towards fin* **3/1**[2]
2503 **4** nk **Director's Dream (IRE)**[15] 3470 4-8-9 **51** oh2...........(t) FrederikTylicki 7 55
(Mark Rimmer) *hld up: rdn and hung lft fr over 2f out: hdwy over 1f out: styd on u.p* **5/1**
6-03 **5** shd **Darling Grace**[27] 3083 3-8-11 **63**........................ RyanMoore 4 66
(William Haggas) *broke wl: sn stdd and lost pl: hdwy over 2f out: rdn over 1f out: styd on: nvr able to chal* **9/4**[1]
6-06 **6** 12 **Exopuntia**[139] 676 6-8-6 **51** oh1........................ AdamBeschizza(3) 3 29
(Julia Feilden) *plld hrd and prom: rdn over 2f out: wknd over 1f out* **12/1**
300 **7** 3 1/2 **Secrets Away (IRE)**[24] 3189 3-8-13 **65**........................ AndreaAtzeni 9 34
(Marco Botti) *led 2f: remained w wnr tl rdn over 2f out: wknd over 1f out* **4/1**[3]
1m 59.52s (3.72) **Going Correction** +0.40s/f (Good)
WFA 3 from 4yo+ 10lb **7** Ran SP% **112.7**
Speed ratings (Par 100): **99,98,98,97,97 87,83**
toteswingers: 1&2 £13.90, 1&3 £11.00, 2&3 £3.90 CSF £260.50 CT £1094.76 TOTE £40.10: £6.60, £3.50; EX 260.30 Trifecta £421.30 Pool: £569.32 - 0.71 winning units..
Owner C E Brittain **Bred** Rabbah Bloodstock Limited **Trained** Newmarket, Suffolk

FOCUS
The going was changed to soft all over. They finished in a bunch in this fillies' handicap and it doesn't look strong form.
Al Karlovyyh(IRE) Official explanation: trainer's representative said, regarding the apparent improvement of form, that the filly benefited from being given more time and from the soft ground

3979 POKER AT BET365.COM H'CAP 1m 6f 17y
5:10 (5:10) (Class 5) (0-70,67) 4-Y-0+ £2,264 (£673; £336; £168) Stalls High

Form RPR
303 **1** **Stock Hill Fair**[29] 3001 4-9-7 **67**........................ KierenFallon 1 79
(Brendan Powell) *a.p: chsd ldr over 5f out: led over 3f out: styd on wl* **11/2**[3]
-262 **2** 3 1/2 **Grandad Mac**[14] 3498 4-9-4 **64**........................ RyanMoore 4 71
(Jane Chapple-Hyam) *hld up in tch: chsd wnr over 2f out: sn ev ch: rdn over 1f out: no ex ins fnl f* **3/1**[2]
3-24 **3** 3/4 **Suzi's A Class Act**[9] 3704 4-9-7 **67**..................(p) AndreaAtzeni 3 73
(James Eustace) *chsd ldrs: rdn over 2f out: styd on same pce fnl f* **9/1**
55-1 **4** 8 **Tinseltown**[7] 3752 6-8-6 **52** 6ex..................(p) PaulHanagan 2 47
(Brian Rothwell) *led over 10f: sn rdn: wknd fnl f* **11/10**[1]
4304 **5** 12 **Broughton Sands**[23] 3222 4-9-6 **66**........................ StevieDonohoe 5 44
(Willie Musson) *hld up: a in rr: bhd fnl 3f* **10/1**
0-10 **6** 43 **Sommersturm (GER)**[13] 3552 8-9-2 **62**........................ TomQueally 6
(Barney Curley) *chsd ldr over 8f: sn wknd: t.o* **25/1**
3m 13.36s (5.76) **Going Correction** +0.50s/f (Yiel) **6** Ran SP% **110.9**
Speed ratings (Par 103): **103,101,100,96,89 64**
toteswingers: 1&2 £2.70, 1&3 £3.00, 2&3 £2.00 CSF £21.66 TOTE £6.80: £2.10, £1.20; EX 22.80.
Owner Mrs M Fairbairn, E Gadsden & P Dean **Bred** Mrs M Fairbairn And E Gadsden **Trained** Upper Lambourn, Berks

FOCUS
This looked a proper test despite the small field.
T/Plt: £1,511.60 to a £1 stake. Pool: £55,910.77. 27.00 winning tickets. T/Qpdt: £222.20 to a £1 stake. Pool: £4,295.49. 14.30 winning tickets. CR

3980 - 3982a (Foreign Racing) - See Raceform Interactive

3512 NAAS (L-H)
Wednesday, July 11

OFFICIAL GOING: Heavy

3983a IRISH STALLION FARMS EUROPEAN BREEDERS FUND BROWNSTOWN STKS (GROUP 3) (FILLIES) 7f
7:30 (7:30) 3-Y-0+ £41,979 (£12,270; £5,812; £1,937)

RPR
1 **Marvada (IRE)**[27] 3091 4-9-7 101........................ ShaneFoley 5 106+
(K J Condon, Ire) *racd in 2nd: pushed along to cl on ldr 2f out: kpt on wl to assert fnl 100yds* **3/1**[2]
2 3/4 **Caprella**[6] 3795 3-8-13 82........................ ChrisHayes 4 101
(P D Deegan, Ire) *tried to make all: qckнd 2f out: kpt on wl: only hdd fnl 100yds* **25/1**
3 3/4 **After (IRE)**[27] 3092 3-9-0 108 ow1........................ JPO'Brien 1 99+
(A P O'Brien, Ire) *disp 3rd: pushed along to cl over 1f out: nvr quite on terms: no ex fnl 50yds* **11/10**[1]
4 1 1/4 **Bulbul (IRE)**[46] 2513 3-8-13 97........................ DeclanMcDonogh 2 96+
(Kevin Prendergast, Ire) *hld up in rr: kpt on: nvr nrr* **9/2**
5 3 3/4 **Singing Bird (IRE)**[27] 3091 3-8-13 96........................ WayneLordan 3 85+
(David Wachman, Ire) *disp 3rd tl wkng appr fnl f* **7/2**[3]
1m 32.96s (5.46)
WFA 3 from 4yo 8lb **5** Ran SP% **116.9**
CSF £52.20 TOTE £4.30: £1.60, £4.80; DF 40.20.
Owner Zinlo Syndicate **Bred** Irish National Stud **Trained** The Curragh , Co Kildare

FOCUS
The only non 3-y-o in the race displayed her battling qualities to beat the younger generation.

NOTEBOOK
Marvada(IRE) didn't look the most likely winner halfway up the straight but responded well when challenging between horses inside the last furlong. She should continue to be a standing dish in races like this.
Caprella has always been highly thought-of by her trainer and went some way towards showing why. She benefited from a very good tactical ride from Chris Hayes, who kicked her on early in the straight. He appeared to have caught the opposition napping, but his filly was not good enough.
After(IRE) had her chance but didn't pick up under pressure.
Bulbul(IRE) was held up in last place and came over to the stands' side in the straight. She ended up staying on at one pace but never looked like threatening.
Singing Bird(IRE) found little from over a furlong out. She had looked progressive on her last run, so this was probably too bad to be true.

3984 - 3986a (Foreign Racing) - See Raceform Interactive

3900 MAISONS-LAFFITTE (R-H)
Wednesday, July 11

OFFICIAL GOING: Turf: good

3987a PRIX AMANDINE (LISTED RACE) (3YO FILLIES) (TURF) 7f (S)
2:05 (12:00) 3-Y-O £22,916 (£9,166; £6,875; £4,583; £2,291)

RPR
1 **Barbayam**[39] 2728 3-8-11 0........................ OlivierPeslier 6 109
(F Head, France) **32/5**[3]
2 3 **Carnoustie (FR)**[64] 1970 3-8-11 0........................ ThierryThulliez 8 101
(N Clement, France) **53/10**[2]

3 snk **Reech Band**[20] 3365 3-8-11 0 IoritzMendizabal 4 101
(D De Watrigant, France) **10/1**
4 3 **Royal Fortune (IRE)**[26] 3-8-11 0 Christophe-PatriceLemaire 11 92
(F-H Graffard, France) **27/1**
5 2 **Night Garden (USA)**[29] 3-8-11 0 Pierre-CharlesBoudot 10 87
(A Fabre, France) **13/2**
6 3/4 **Villeneuve**[21] 3270 3-8-11 0 StephanePasquier 3 85
(William Muir) *trckd ldrs: 5th 1/2-way: rdn and lost pl over 2 1/2f out: kpt on u.p fnl f: nt pce to chal* **20/1**
7 snk **Irish Cliff (IRE)**[20] 3365 3-8-11 0 ChristopheSoumillon 5 85
(M Delcher-Sanchez, Spain) **5/2**[1]
8 nk **Switcher (IRE)**[13] 3542 3-8-11 0 (b) RichardKingscote 12 84
(Tom Dascombe) *dwlt: swtchd fr wd outside draw to ins and settled towards rr: shkn up over 2f out and no imp: rdn and kpt on at one pce fnl f: nvr plcd to chal* **10/1**
9 4 **Ruby's Day**[19] 3-8-11 0 ThomasHuet 2 73
(E J O'Neill, France) **29/1**
10 2 **Jellicle (IRE)**[45] 3-8-11 0 FabriceVeron 9 68
(H-A Pantall, France) **25/1**
0 **Ma Victoryan (FR)**[19] 3-8-11 0 AurelienLemaitre 1
(C Baillet, France) **12/1**
0 **Rosina Bella (IRE)**[38] 3-8-11 0 APolli 7
(P L Giannotti, Italy) **75/1**

1m 24.0s (-4.00) **12** Ran SP% **114.0**
WIN (incl. 1 euro stake): 7.40. PLACES: 2.60, 2.00, 2.70. DF: 20.90. SF: 49.40..
Owner Wertheimer & Frere **Bred** Wertheimer & Frere **Trained** France

3809 DONCASTER (L-H)

Thursday, July 12

OFFICIAL GOING: Soft (good to soft in places) changing to good to soft after race 2 (2.40)

Wind: Virtually nil Weather: Sunny with cloudy periods

3988 AMATEUR JOCKEYS ASSOCIATION H'CAP (FOR AMATEUR RIDERS) 2m 110y

2:05 (2:05) (Class 6) (0-65,65) 4-Y-0+ **£1,559** (£483; £241; £121) **Stalls** Low

Form RPR
335 **1** **Jamarjo (IRE)**[28] 3077 5-11-0 **65** MrSWalker 5 79+
(Steve Gollings) *trckd ldrs: smooth hdwy 3f out: led wl over 1f out: clr ent fnl f: comf* **11/2**[2]
-403 **2** 6 **Terenzium (IRE)**[14] 3519 10-9-7 **49** (p) MissRSmith(5) 12 52
(Micky Hammond) *hld up towards rr: stdy hdwy on inner 4f out: rdn to chse ldrs wl over 1f out: styd on ins fnl f: tk 2nd nr line* **7/1**
26-2 **3** nk **Finellas Fortune**[40] 2698 7-10-5 **56** MissSBrotherton 2 59
(George Moore) *trckd ldng pair: hdwy to ld over 4f out: rdn along wl over 2f out: hdd wl over 1f out: sn one pce: lost 2nd nr line* **6/1**[3]
/0-4 **4** 1 1/4 **French Seventyfive**[19] 3402 5-9-6 **46** oh1 (p) MrNdeBoinville(3) 10 47
(Tim Walford) *trckd ldrs: hdwy 5f out: rdn along over 3f out: kpt on same pce fnl 2f* **10/1**
0021 **5** 2 **Tarantella Lady**[19] 3402 4-10-7 **63** (v) MrMGarnett(5) 8 62
(George Moore) *hld up towards rr: hdwy on outer 3f out: rdn and styd on appr fnl f: nrst fin* **7/2**[1]
0-30 **6** 3 1/2 **Ritsi**[2] 3942 9-9-2 **46** oh1 (t) MissNHayes(7) 3 41
(Marjorie Fife) *towards rr: hdwy 1/2-way: chsd ldrs 4f out: rdn along 3f out: sn no imp* **16/1**
304/ **7** 2 1/4 **Border Tale**[40] 2765 12-9-4 **48** ow2 (v) MissRebeccaSparkes(7) 15 41
(James Moffatt) *led: jnd 1/2-way: rdn along and hdd over 4f out: drvn 3f out: grad wknd* **25/1**
-250 **8** 2 1/4 **Commander Veejay**[19] 3402 4-9-6 **50** (p) MissJMcLernon(7) 1 40
(Brian Rothwell) *in rr tl styd on fnl 3f: n.d* **40/1**
-440 **9** 3 **Cardi King**[29] 3043 4-9-13 **53** (t) MrCMartin(3) 11 40
(Ian Wood) *hld up in midfield: stdy hdwy 1/2-way: trckd ldrs 5f out: rdn along 3f out and sn wknd* **14/1**
4-65 **10** 3 1/2 **Marina's Ocean**[41] 2669 8-9-12 **49** oh1 ow3 (b) MrFWindsorClive 13 32
(Roy Bowring) *hld up towards rr: hdwy over 6f out: chsd ldrs over 4f out: rdn along 3f out: wknd fnl 2f* **28/1**
5034 **11** 2 **Dan's Heir**[8] 3750 10-9-7 **49** (t) MissSMDoolan(5) 6 30
(Wilf Storey) *hld up: a towards rr* **12/1**
-400 **12** nk **Bollistick**[28] 3061 6-9-8 **48** MissMMullineaux(3) 7 29
(Michael Mullineaux) *midfield: pushed along bef 1/2-way: sn lost pl and bhd* **20/1**
400- **13** 1 1/2 **Grethel (IRE)**[225] 6236 8-9-4 **46** oh1 MissVBarr(5) 14 25
(Alan Berry) *chsd ldrs: rdn along over 5f out: sn wknd* **50/1**
0060 **14** 3 1/4 **Munaawib**[36] 2827 4-9-4 **46** oh1 MrARawlinson(5) 16 21
(David C Griffiths) *a in rr* **33/1**
0-04 **15** 13 **Runaway Tiger (IRE)**[17] 3449 4-9-5 **49** (v) MissLucySaunders(7) 9 10
(Paul D'Arcy) *t.k.h: cl up: disp ld 1/2-way: rdn along over 4f out: sn wknd* **28/1**

3m 46.13s (5.73) **Going Correction** +0.275s/f (Good) **15** Ran SP% **116.6**
Speed ratings (Par 101): **97,94,94,93,92 90,89,88,87,85 84,84,83,82,76**
Tote Swingers: 1&2 £7.30, 1&3 £5.80, 2&3 £8.60 CSF £38.35 CT £240.17 TOTE £6.30: £2.10, £2.40, £2.20; EX 46.70.
Owner Northern Bloodstock Racing **Bred** Frank Dunne **Trained** Scamblesby, Lincs

FOCUS
Following a dry night and breezy morning, the ground was changed to soft, good to soft in places. Mainly exposed sorts in a modest handicap but an easy winner who is value for extra with the placed horses rated close to recent marks.
Dan's Heir Official explanation: trainer said gelding resented its tongue-strap

3989 LSL LAND AND NEW HOMES MAIDEN STKS 6f

2:40 (2:40) (Class 5) 2-Y-0 **£2,264** (£673; £336; £168) **Stalls** High

Form RPR
2 **1** **A Certain Romance**[14] 3545 2-9-3 0 SilvestreDeSousa 6 75
(Peter Chapple-Hyam) *prom on stands' rail: hdwy to ld 2f out: rdn over 1f out: hdd ent fnl f: drvn and rallied to ld again last 40yds* **8/11**[1]
2 nk **Burning Dawn (USA)** 2-8-12 0 RobertWinston 7 69+
(David Brown) *hld up: trckd wnr 1/2-way: hdwy 2f out: rdn to ld ent fnl f: green: hdd and no ex last 40yds* **4/1**[2]
0 **3** 1 3/4 **Shillito**[19] 3401 2-9-3 0 BarryMcHugh 4 69
(Tony Coyle) *led: rdn along and hdd 2f out: drvn over 1f out: kpt on same pce fnl f* **10/1**
4 nk **Bond Club** 2-9-0 0 DaleSwift(3) 5 68
(Geoffrey Oldroyd) *in rr: hdwy 1/2-way: rdn to chse ldrs over 2f out: one pce appr fnl f* **14/1**
0 **5** 1/2 **Makinson Lane (IRE)**[43] 2594 2-9-3 0 TonyHamilton 2 66
(Richard Fahey) *t.k.h: chsd ldrs: hdwy over 2f out: sn rdn and one pce appr fnl f* **9/1**[3]
04 **6** 5 **Vino Collapso (IRE)**[21] 3303 2-9-3 0 JamesSullivan 3 51
(James Given) *chsd ldng pair: pushed along 1/2-way: sn rdn and wknd* **16/1**
00 **7** 3 3/4 **If You Can (IRE)**[28] 3062 2-9-3 0 DavidAllan 1 41
(Tim Easterby) *racd wd: prom: rdn along wl over 2f out: sn wknd* **50/1**

1m 15.4s (1.80) **Going Correction** +0.10s/f (Good) **7** Ran SP% **111.5**
Speed ratings (Par 94): **92,91,89,88,88 81,76**
Tote Swingers: 1&2 £1.50, 1&3 £2.70, 2&3 £3.80 CSF £3.60 TOTE £1.70: £1.60, £1.90; EX 3.60.

Owner Joseph Barton **Bred** Peter Gleeson And Irish National Stud **Trained** Newmarket, Suffolk

FOCUS
Not the strongest of maidens for the track but a race that could throw up winners in due course. The third to fifth will govern the level of the form in time. The gallop was fair and the first two raced closest to the stands' rail. The ground was changed to good to soft after this race.

NOTEBOOK
A Certain Romance confirmed debut promise in these much softer conditions, in the process showing a good attitude under pressure in the closing stages. He'll be even better suited by the step up to 7f and appeals as the sort to win again. (op 5-6 tchd 8-13)
Burning Dawn(USA) ◆, who cost 80,000gns and is the third foal of a half-sister to a US Grade 3 winner, attracted support and showed more than enough on this racecourse debut against more experienced rivals to suggest she should be able to pick up a similar event at the very least. Her pedigree suggests a quicker surface shouldn't inconvenience. (op 7-1)
Shillito stepped up a fair way on his debut effort and, although likely to remain vulnerable to the more progressive types in this grade, he may do better over further in ordinary nurseries. (op 7-1)
Bond Club, the second foal of a half-sister to a couple of useful sprinters, showed ability at a modest level on this racecourse debut and is entitled to improve for the experience. (op 12-1)
Makinson Lane(IRE) stepped up on the form shown on his debut but he's going to have to settle much better than he did here if he is to progress. He's more a nursery type. (op 8-1 tchd 10-1)

3990 CROWNHOTEL-BAWTRY.COM MAIDEN STKS 6f

3:15 (3:15) (Class 5) 3-Y-0+ **£2,264** (£673; £336; £168) **Stalls** High

Form RPR
0-3 **1** **Macchiara**[13] 3568 3-8-12 0 SilvestreDeSousa 4 75
(Rae Guest) *t.k.h: cl up: led after 2f: rdn over 1f out: styd on wl u.p fnl f* **7/2**[2]
52 **2** 1 1/4 **Pearl Nation (USA)**[24] 3235 3-9-3 0 FrederikTylicki 2 76
(Brian Baugh) *prom: hdwy to chse wnr over 1f out and sn ev ch: drvn ins fnl f and kpt on same pce* **3/1**[1]
6 **3** hd **Mexican Mick**[13] 3561 3-9-3 0 MichaelO'Connell 3 75+
(Ian Williams) *dwlt and towards rr: hdwy over 2f out: rdn wl over 1f out: styd on fnl f: nrst fin* **25/1**
4 **4** 1 **Evanescent (IRE)**[89] 1377 3-9-3 0 IPoullis 9 72
(Alan McCabe) *chsd ldrs: hdwy over 2f out: rdn wl over 1f out: kpt on same pce fnl f* **33/1**
5 3/4 **Transfix** 3-8-12 0 AmyRyan 5 64+
(Ed Vaughan) *dwlt and in rr: hdwy 1/2-way: swtchd to wd outside and effrt to chse ldrs 2f out: sn rdn and one pce fnl f* **5/1**
0- **6** nk **Black Douglas**[308] 5863 3-9-3 0 TomEaves 1 68
(William Jarvis) *in tch: hdwy to trck ldrs wl over 2f out: sn prom: rdn and ev ch wl over 1f out: wknd appr fnl f* **12/1**
7 4 **Choice Pearl (USA)**[104] 1121 3-8-12 0 RobertWinston 10 51
(Tobias B P Coles) *in tch: hdwy to chse ldrs over 2f out: sn rdn and wknd wl over 1f out:* **10/1**
4 **8** shd **Thats Molly (IRE)**[22] 3289 3-8-12 0 DuranFentiman 7 50
(Eric Alston) *prom: rdn along wl over 2f out: sn wknd* **4/1**[3]
9 6 **Red Baron (IRE)** 3-9-3 0 DavidAllan 8 36
(Eric Alston) *led 2f: rdn along 1/2-way: sn wknd* **12/1**
0 **10** 2 1/4 **Kuraanda**[58] 2139 3-8-12 0 PaddyAspell 11 24
(John Wainwright) *a in rr* **100/1**

1m 14.76s (1.16) **Going Correction** +0.10s/f (Good) **10** Ran SP% **116.1**
Speed ratings (Par 103): **96,94,94,92,91 91,86,85,77,74**
Tote Swingers: 1&2 £2.50, 1&3 £11.40, 2&3 £8.90 CSF £14.18 TOTE £4.80: £1.90, £1.40, £4.80; EX 13.70.
Owner Mrs Linda P Fish **Bred** Horizon Bloodstock Limited **Trained** Newmarket, Suffolk

FOCUS
A modest maiden in which the gallop was ordinary. The winner is rated in line with hier Folkestone form while the second ran close to his AW mark.

3991 TERRY BELLAS MEMORIAL FILLIES' H'CAP 1m (R)

3:45 (3:46) (Class 4) (0-85,84) 3-Y-0+ **£4,204** (£1,251; £625; £312) **Stalls** High

Form RPR
3621 **1** **Magic Destiny**[7] 3780 3-8-10 **78** 6ex MichaelMetcalfe(3) 4 83+
(Mrs K Burke) *mde all: qcknd clr over 2f out: rdn over 1f out: edgd lft fnl f: kpt on* **13/8**[1]
40-6 **2** 1/2 **Tuscania**[12] 3636 4-10-0 **84** FrederikTylicki 2 88
(Lucy Wadham) *trckd ldrs: hdwy over 2f out: rdn wl over 1f out: kpt on u.p fnl f* **14/1**
1021 **3** shd **No Poppy (IRE)**[15] 3495 4-9-9 **84** AdamCarter(5) 3 88
(Tim Easterby) *trckd wnr: effrt over 2f out: rdn wl over 1f out: edgd lft fnl f: sn n.m.r and one pce: lost 2nd nr line* **5/1**[3]
0602 **4** 4 1/2 **She's A Character**[14] 3522 5-9-3 **78** ShaneBKelly(5) 8 72
(Richard Fahey) *hld up in rr: pushed along over 3f out: sn rdn along and outpcd: sme late hdwy* **11/2**
4021 **5** 11 **Negin**[20] 3347 3-8-13 **78** PaulMulrennan 5 44
(Ed Dunlop) *t.k.h: chsd ldng pair: effrt 3f out: rdn over 2f out and sn wknd* **2/1**[2]

1m 41.47s (1.77) **Going Correction** +0.275s/f (Good)
WFA 3 from 4yo+ 9lb **5** Ran SP% **110.1**
Speed ratings (Par 102): **102,101,101,96,85**
CSF £21.83 TOTE £2.50: £1.10, £4.90; EX 24.10.
Owner Ray Bailey **Bred** Ray Bailey **Trained** Middleham Moor, N Yorks

FOCUS
A useful handicap on paper but a steady pace means it's best not to take these bare facts at face value. The winner is value for more than the official margin with the third the best guide to the level.

Negin Official explanation: trainer's rep said filly boiled over in preliminaries

3992 YORKSHIRE RADIO H'CAP 1m 4f
4:20 (4:20) (Class 4) (0-80,79) 3-Y-0+ £4,204 (£1,251; £625; £312) Stalls Low

Form RPR
2224 1 **The Lock Master (IRE)**[19] 3380 5-9-2 67 SilvestreDeSousa 5 75
(Michael Appleby) *trckd ldrs: hdwy to ld 3f out: rdn 2f out: drvn ins fnl f: hld on wl* 12/1
-012 2 hd **Shaloo Diamond**[10] 3692 7-9-9 74 RobertWinston 7 81
(Richard Whitaker) *awkward s: hld up in rr: gd hdwy on outer wl over 2f out: chal and ev ch over 1f out: drvn ins fnl f: no ex towards fin* 7/1[3]
0011 3 ¾ **Ultimate Destiny**[27] 3122 3-8-12 76 RichardKingscote 6 82
(Ralph Beckett) *led: pushed along and hdd 3f out: rdn 2f out: drvn and one pce ins fnl f* 9/4[1]
0022 4 1 **Fossgate**[6] 3814 11-9-5 70 AmyRyan 1 74
(James Bethell) *hld up: hdwy to trck ldng pair 1/2-way: effrt to chal 3f out: rdn 2f out and ev ch tl one pce ins fnl f* 14/1
2-44 5 ¾ **Ashiri (IRE)**[53] 2312 4-10-0 79 DavidAllan 2 82
(David Simcock) *plld hrd early: hld up: hdwy over 3f out: rdn 2f out: chsd ldrs: kpt on same pce fnl f* 7/2[2]
0045 6 hd **Royal Trooper (IRE)**[22] 3287 6-9-10 75 FrederikTylicki 3 78
(James Given) *trckd ldrs: effrt 3f out: rdn along 2f out: drvn and kpt on same pce appr fnl f* 7/2[2]
3226 7 4 ½ **Favorite Girl (GER)**[13] 3564 4-9-5 70 TomEaves 4 66
(Michael Appleby) *hld up: hdwy to chse ldrs 3f out: rdn 2f out: wknd over 1f out* 10/1

2m 37.96s (3.06) **Going Correction** +0.275s/f (Good)
WFA 3 from 4yo+ 13lb 7 Ran SP% 111.2
Speed ratings (Par 105): **100,99,99,98,98 98,95**
Tote Swingers: 1&2 £7.80, 1&3 £5.50, 2&3 £2.80 CSF £85.59 TOTE £16.70: £5.50, £3.50; EX 51.80.
Owner K G Kitchen **Bred** Patrick F Kelly **Trained** Danethorpe, Notts

FOCUS
A fair handicap but one run at just a steady gallop and the form may not be entirely reliable, although the placed horses were close to previous marks.

3993 YORKSHIRE RACING SUMMER FESTIVAL 21ST-29TH JULY H'CAP 5f
4:50 (4:50) (Class 5) (0-75,74) 3-Y-0+ £2,264 (£673; £336; £168) Stalls High

Form RPR
0502 1 **Sir Geoffrey (IRE)**[31] 2982 6-9-6 68 (p) RobertWinston 2 79
(Scott Dixon) *in tch: hdwy on wd outside over 2f out: rdn over 1f out: led ins fnl f: kpt on wl* 9/1
0606 2 2 **Waking Warrior**[47] 2475 4-9-6 71 (tp) JulieBurke(3) 7 75
(Kevin Ryan) *dwlt and towards rr: hdwy 2f out: rdn over 1f out: styd on wl fnl f* 6/1[3]
-440 3 nk **Just For Mary**[53] 2314 8-9-4 66 (bt) StephenCraine 12 69
(Daniel Mark Loughnane) *s.i.s: sn rdn along and outpcd in rr: hdwy over 1f out: drvn and styd on strly ins fnl f: nrst fin* 12/1
4442 4 nk **Rylee Mooch**[16] 3477 4-9-9 74 (e) DeclanCannon(3) 11 76
(Richard Guest) *trckd ldrs: hdwy to chal over 1f out: sn rdn and ev ch tl one pce ins fnl f* 11/2[2]
0000 5 1 **Oil Strike**[14] 3524 5-9-4 73 DavidSimmonson(7) 4 71
(Michael Easterby) *led: jnd and rdn wl over 1f out: drvn and hdd ins fnl f: wknd towards fin* 16/1
642 6 shd **Gracie's Games**[17] 3434 6-8-5 60 (v) JacobButterfield(7) 9 58
(Richard Price) *towards rr: hdwy wl over 1f out: sn rdn and no imp fnl f* 11/2[2]
0604 7 ¾ **Lucky Art (USA)**[10] 3707 6-8-13 61 PaulMulrennan 1 56
(Conor Dore) *prom on wd outside: rdn along 2f out: sn wknd* 25/1
-500 8 2 ¼ **Liberty Ship**[58] 2140 7-9-3 65 (t) RoystonFfrench 3 52
(Mark Buckley) *dwlt and towards rr: sme hdwy 2f out: sn rdn and n.d* 12/1
-440 9 ½ **Mango Music**[22] 3272 9-9-5 67 (p) FrederikTylicki 6 52
(David Thompson) *a towards rr* 20/1
-151 10 nk **Fol Hollow (IRE)**[14] 3523 7-9-11 73 AdrianNicholls 13 57
(David Nicholls) *prom: rdn along wl over 1f out: wknd and lost action ent fnl f: sn eased* 9/2[1]
-522 11 shd **Befortyfour**[40] 2693 7-9-11 73 RobbieFitzpatrick 8 57
(Charles Smith) *chsd ldrs: rdn along over 2f out: grad wknd* 10/1
-003 12 ¾ **Black Annis Bower**[34] 2875 4-9-5 67 JamesSullivan 10 48
(Michael Easterby) *chsd ldrs: rdn along over 2f out: sn wknd* 12/1

1m 0.56s (0.06) **Going Correction** +0.10s/f (Good) 12 Ran SP% 119.9
Speed ratings (Par 103): **103,99,99,98,97 97,95,92,91,91 90,89**
Tote Swingers: 1&2 £10.90, 1&3 £23.50, 2&3 £15.80 CSF £62.92 CT £672.52 TOTE £10.30: £3.00, £2.00, £5.40; EX 63.30.
Owner Dixon, Howlett & The Chrystal Maze Ptn **Bred** P Rabbitte **Trained** Babworth, Notts
■ Stewards' Enquiry : Declan Cannon two-day ban: used whip above permitted level (Jul 26-27)

FOCUS
Exposed performers in a fair handicap. The gallop was a decent one and the leaders tied up in the closing stages. The winner is rated to last year's best turf form with the second and fourth helping to back up the level.
Fol Hollow(IRE) Official explanation: jockey said gelding lost its action

3994 DANWOOD H'CAP 7f
5:25 (5:25) (Class 5) (0-75,75) 3-Y-0+ £2,264 (£673; £336; £168) Stalls High

Form RPR
-036 1 **Anton Chigurh**[7] 3790 3-9-4 73 RichardKingscote 5 85
(Tom Dascombe) *trckd ldrs: smooth hdwy 2f out: led over 1f out: rdn clr ins fnl f: kpt on strly* 9/2[2]
6003 2 3 **Aerodynamic (IRE)**[19] 3403 5-9-13 74 PaddyAspell 10 81
(Michael Easterby) *hld up in rr: swtchd wd and gd hdwy over 2f out: rdn to chse ldrs over 1f out: styd on ins fnl f: no imp on wnr* 8/1[3]
66 3 ½ **Majuro (IRE)**[132] 765 8-10-0 75 RobbieFitzpatrick 6 81
(Charles Smith) *led: rdn 2f out: hdd over 1f out: drvn and one pce fnl f* 33/1
0-50 4 2 ¼ **Two Sugars**[19] 3389 4-8-9 56 oh1 AdrianNicholls 1 56
(Louise Best) *in tch on wd outside: hdwy to chse ldrs 2f out: rdn wl over 1f out: edgd rt and one pce appr fnl f* 50/1
621 5 3 ½ **Red Trump (IRE)**[143] 638 3-8-13 68 RobertWinston 7 55
(Charles Hills) *in tch: hdwy to chse ldrs over 2f out: rdn wl over 1f out and sn no imp* 8/1[3]
6641 6 ½ **Dr Red Eye**[8] 3749 4-9-11 72 6ex (p) SilvestreDeSousa 12 61
(Scott Dixon) *chsd ldrs: effrt 2f out: sn rdn and one pce* 13/8[1]
0055 7 4 ½ **Woteva**[10] 3694 6-8-8 62 (p) ShirleyTeasdale(7) 4 39
(Nigel Tinkler) *chsd ldrs: rdn along 2f out: grad wknd* 14/1
5032 8 5 **Bartley**[24] 3210 3-8-8 63 (p) TomEaves 3 23
(Bryan Smart) *hld up: hdwy to chse ldrs whn n.m.r jst over 2f out: sn rdn and wknd* 16/1
1004 9 3 ½ **Just The Tonic**[23] 3255 5-9-7 71 JulieBurke(3) 9 25
(Marjorie Fife) *chsd ldrs: rdn along 1/2-way: sn wknd* 20/1
0064 10 1 **Lizzie (IRE)**[17] 3442 4-8-13 60 (b) DavidAllan 13
(Tim Easterby) *in tch: rdn along and lost pl 1/2-way: sn bhd* 10/1
03-0 11 hd **Elusive Hawk (IRE)**[14] 3546 8-9-1 62 DaraghO'Donohoe 8
(Barney Curley) *prom: pushed along 3f out: sn rdn and wknd 2f out* 33/1
6006 12 ½ **Dancing Maite**[28] 3075 7-8-9 61 MarkCoumbe(5) 2
(Roy Bowring) *cl up: rdn along 3f out: sn wknd* 33/1
4006 13 1 ¼ **Kings 'n Dreams**[10] 3705 5-9-5 66 (b) MichaelO'Connell 11
(Dean Ivory) *a in rr* 25/1

1m 26.56s (0.26) **Going Correction** +0.10s/f (Good)
WFA 3 from 4yo+ 8lb 13 Ran SP% 119.5
Speed ratings (Par 103): **102,98,98,95,91 90,85,80,76,74 74,74,72**
Tote Swingers: 1&2 £6.60, 1&3 £29.60, 2&3 £28.00 CSF £37.01 CT £1072.25 TOTE £4.00: £1.50, £3.10, £9.60; EX 40.80.
Owner Panarea Racing **Bred** Mr & Mrs G Middlebrook **Trained** Malpas, Cheshire

FOCUS
A fair handicap run at a reasonable pace and the form looks straightforward and sound, rated around the placed horses.
Dr Red Eye Official explanation: jockey said gelding had no more to give
Kings 'n Dreams Official explanation: trainer';s rep said gelding bled from the nose
T/Plt: £121.20 to a £1 stake. Pool: £77,187.20 - 464.67 winning tickets. T/Qpdt: £64.30 to a £1 stake. Pool: £5,169.00 - 59.42 winning tickets. JR

3769 EPSOM (L-H)
Thursday, July 12

OFFICIAL GOING: Soft (overall 7.0; home straight - stands' side 7.6, far side 7.3)
Wind: Blustery Weather: Persistent rain

3995 DOWNLOAD EPSOM'S ANDROID OR IPHONE APP NOW APPRENTICE H'CAP 1m 2f 18y
6:15 (6:16) (Class 5) (0-75,80) 4-Y-0+ £3,234 (£962; £481; £240) Stalls Low

Form RPR
6352 1 **Cantor**[9] 3721 4-8-5 56 oh1 AdamBeschizza 5 69
(Giles Bravery) *pushed up to ld after 2f: mde rest and mostly pushed along: drew clr fr over 2f out: styd on wl* 11/4[2]
5-06 2 6 **Hawaana (IRE)**[154] 480 7-9-5 73 DarrenEgan(3) 4 74
(Gay Kelleway) *hld up in 4th: prog to chse wnr wl over 1f out: styd on but no imp* 7/2[3]
0032 3 7 **Blue Deer (IRE)**[15] 3497 4-8-11 69 AaronChave(7) 9 56
(Lee Carter) *trckd ldng pair: wnt 2nd over 5f out to wl over 1f out: wknd* 6/1
1201 4 3 **Colinca's Lad (IRE)**[7] 3769 10-9-12 80 6ex RosieJessop(3) 8 61
(Peter Charalambous) *set off in front but hdd after 2f: sltly hmpd over 6f out: lost 2nd over 5f out: wknd 2f out* 11/8[1]
5-40 5 22 **Saharia (IRE)**[176] 205 5-9-1 66 (p) KierenFox 3
(Michael Attwater) *a last: wknd 3f out: t.o* 16/1

2m 16.21s (6.51) **Going Correction** +0.625s/f (Yiel) 5 Ran SP% 111.2
Speed ratings (Par 103): **98,93,87,85,67**
CSF £12.64 TOTE £3.30: £1.30, £2.20; EX 11.50 Trifecta £17.80 Pool: £176.61 - 7.31 winning units..
Owner Jim Tew **Bred** Cheveley Park Stud Ltd **Trained** Newmarket, Suffolk

FOCUS
The rail was dolled out up to eight yards from 1m to 5f and up to five yards from 5f to the winning post adding approximately ten yards to race distances. It was raining heavily and the going was changed to soft. The winner scored with plenty of authority under an aggressive ride in this apprentice handicap and they finished strung out. The winner looks to have improved but the form is not easy to assess.

3996 SUTTON MAIDEN AUCTION STKS 6f
6:45 (6:47) (Class 5) 2-Y-0 £3,234 (£962; £481; £240) Stalls High

Form RPR
52 1 **Hipster**[30] 3009 2-8-13 0 (p) JimCrowley 9 82
(Ralph Beckett) *disp ld and clr w two others: grabbed nr side rail in st: hrd rdn over 1f out: narrow advantage ins fnl f: hld on* 6/4[1]
5 2 nk **Nenge Mboko**[15] 3505 2-8-13 0 PatCosgrave 8 81+
(George Baker) *disp clr ld w two others: stl upsides 1f out: jst hld last 100yds* 17/2
0 3 5 **Aint Got A Scooby (IRE)**[17] 3444 2-8-9 0 EddieAhern 1 62
(Clive Cox) *chsd clr ldrs: 4th st: shkn up over 2f out: kpt on to take 3rd ins fnl f* 8/1
026 4 1 **Cappadocia (IRE)**[35] 2852 2-8-13 71 MatthewDavies 7 63
(Mick Channon) *disp ld and clr w two others: wdst of the trio in st: wknd 2f out: lost 3rd ins fnl f* 5/1[2]
0 5 ½ **Frans Hals**[26] 3140 2-8-11 0 KieranO'Neill 12 60+
(Dominic Ffrench Davis) *chsd clr ldrs: 5th: st: shkn up 2f out: kpt on fnl f: n.d* 8/1
00 6 1 **We Are City**[20] 3339 2-8-11 0 DaneO'Neill 4 57
(Michael Bell) *chsd clr ldrs: 6th st: pushed along and no imp over 2f out* 33/1
0 7 1 **Perseverent Pete (USA)**[15] 3499 2-8-13 0 IanMongan 5 56+
(Christine Dunnett) *a towards rr: 7th st: pushed along firmly over 2f out: no prog* 80/1
6 8 2 **Fit For A King (IRE)**[17] 3444 2-8-8 0 DarrenEgan(5) 10 50
(John Best) *a in rr: 8th st: pushed along and no prog over 2f out* 13/2[3]
06 9 3 ¾ **Epsom Flyer**[30] 3009 2-8-4 0 JemmaMarshall(5) 6 34
(Pat Phelan) *stdd s: wl detached in last tl passed one rival fnl f: nvr remotely involved* 25/1
5 10 10 **Lady Calantha**[16] 3473 2-8-10 0 ow2 RichardHughes 13
(Richard Hannon) *restless stalls: dwlt: racd wd in rr: 9th st: no ch 2f out: eased* 20/1

1m 12.7s (3.30) **Going Correction** +0.625s/f (Yiel) 10 Ran SP% 115.5
Speed ratings (Par 94): **103,102,95,94,93 92,91,88,83,70**
Tote Swingers: 1&2 £3.20, 1&3 £3.80, 2&3 £11.50 CSF £14.29 TOTE £2.50: £1.20, £3.00, £2.60; EX 19.90 Trifecta £144.20 Pool: £516.51 - 2.65 winning units..
Owner R Roberts **Bred** Cheveley Park Stud Ltd **Trained** Kimpton, Hants

FOCUS
This maiden auction was weakened by some withdrawals and not many got into it, but the favourite showed a good attitude to beat the clear second. The time was good and there are reasons to be positive about the form.

NOTEBOOK

Hipster set the standard on his close second in a 6f soft-ground maiden at Salisbury last time. He travelled well up with the pace and showed fighting spirit to hold off the persistent runner-up with cheekpieces applied on his third attempt. He did have the advantage of the stands' rail in the straight but there was a lot to like about this display from a first foal of a well-related 6f 2-y-o winner. He is open to more progress and should stay a bit further than this. (op 5-4 tchd 13-8)

Nenge Mboko was always prominent and gave the winner plenty to think about in an improved second run. He should continue to progress and is a half-brother to stacks of winners, notably Group 3-winning sprinter Ringmoor Down. (op 11-1 tchd 8-1)

Aint Got A Scooby(IRE) showed some promise, staying on well to snatch third on his second start. (op 10-1 tchd 12-1)

Cappadocia(IRE) ran well for a long way before fading stepped back up to 6f. His four-race profile is a bit patchy and an opening mark of 71 looks high enough but he showed a decent cruising speed in these arduous conditions and should be able to find an opening, possibly back at 5f. (op 6-1)

Frans Hals did a bit of late work from some way back. A half-brother to a winning miler, he should be more competitive in nurseries over longer trips.

Fit For A King(IRE) didn't get the best of runs but he was laboured in his attempt to build on his debut sixth at Windsor and may have had a problem with the ground and track. (tchd 6-1)

3997 SPARKS CHARITY "RACING FOR RESEARCH" H'CAP 1m 4f 10y

7:20 (7:21) (Class 4) (0-80,80) 4-Y-O+ £5,175 (£1,540; £769; £384) Stalls Centre

Form				RPR
6221	1		**Lieutenant Kojak**[21] 3306 4-9-2 **75**.................. EddieAhern 11 (Peter Charalambous) *trckd ldr 2f: wnt 2nd again over 5f out: grabbed nr side rail in st: rdn to ld over 1f out: hld on wl nr fin* **7/2**[3]	83
3254	2	hd	**Kathleen Frances**[12] 3610 5-9-1 **74**.................. RichardHughes 10 (Mark H Tompkins) *hld up in rr: prog 1/2-way: wnt 3rd 5f out: smooth effrt to ld over 2f out but didn't go to nr side rail: rdn and hdd over 1f out: w wnr fnl f: jst hld* **5/2**[1]	81
50-0	3	3 ¾	**Significant Move**[35] 2857 5-9-4 **77**..................(t) IanMongan 5 (Stuart Kittow) *s.i.s: hld up in rr: prog and 4th st: wnt 3rd and cl enough over 2f out: hanging and btn over 1f out: jst hld on for 3rd* **9/1**	78
5-12	4	hd	**Reggie Perrin**[7] 3769 4-8-2 **61**..................(v) CathyGannon 7 (Pat Phelan) *in tch: pushed along 1/2-way: sn struggling: rdn and poor 6th st: styd on fr over 2f out to press for 3rd fnl f* **3/1**[2]	62+
-033	5	6	**Ampleforth**[19] 3386 4-8-11 **73**.................. RyanClark[(3)] 4 (Ian Williams) *chsd ldrs: pushed along after 4f: lost pl 5f out: rdn and effrt again in 5th st: pressed for 3rd 1f out: nt clr run and eased last 100yds* **8/1**	70
5550	6	9	**Uphold**[12] 3610 5-9-4 **77**..................(vt) ShaneKelly 2 (Gay Kelleway) *led: rdn and hdd over 2f out: wknd qckly* **16/1**	54
212-	7	26	**Tanjung Agas (IRE)**[11] 1349 4-8-6 **65**..................(b) JimmyQuinn 9 (Christopher Kellett) *a in rr: wknd 1/2-way: last and t.o st* **66/1**	
2603	8	9	**Battleoftrafalgar**[21] 3015 5-8-10 **69**..................(b) KierenFox 3 (Michael Attwater) *chsd ldr after 2f to over 5f out: 7th and wkng whn styd far side in st: wl t.o* **11/1**	
0-00	L		**Gunslinger (FR)**[25] 3187 7-9-1 **79**.................. DavidKenny[(5)] 1 (Michael Scudamore) *ref to r: tk no part* **20/1**	

2m 49.68s (10.78) **Going Correction** +0.80s/f (Soft) **9** Ran SP% **117.4**

Speed ratings (Par 105): **96,95,93,93,89 83,65,59,**

Tote Swingers: 1&2 £2.40, 1&3 £4.60, 2&3 £5.40 CSF £12.93 CT £72.41 TOTE £4.40: £1.80, £1.50, £2.40; EX 11.70 Trifecta £74.40 Pool: £515.42 - 5.12 winning units..

Owner P Charalambous **Bred** Cheveley Park Stud Ltd **Trained** Newmarket, Suffolk

FOCUS

There was an exciting finish between two of the three market leaders in this middle-distance handicap which was run at a fair pace. Most of the runners again converged to the near rail and the first two pulled clear. The third looks the best guide to the level.

3998 WALTON H'CAP 1m 2f 18y

7:55 (7:58) (Class 5) (0-75,75) 3-Y-O £3,234 (£962; £481; £240) Stalls Low

Form				RPR
1043	1		**Jane Lachatte (IRE)**[12] 3616 3-8-13 **67**.................. DaneO'Neill 6 (Stuart Williams) *hld up in tch: prog and cl 5th st: wnt 2nd 2f out on outer: led over 1f out: rdn and styd on wl* **3/1**[1]	79+
0005	2	1 ¼	**Mcvicar**[14] 3543 3-8-10 **64**.................. MatthewDavies 2 (Mick Channon) *led: c to nr side rail in st: drvn and hdd over 1f out: styd on but a hld after* **7/2**[3]	73
2010	3	11	**Hyperlink (IRE)**[12] 3605 3-9-7 **75**.................. MircoDemuro 1 (Mark Johnston) *cl up: trckd ldr over 4f out: tried to chal over 2f out: lost 2nd and wknd sn after* **6/1**	62
6164	4	2	**Ermyn Flyer**[35] 2846 3-8-1 **60**.................. JemmaMarshall[(5)] 10 (Pat Phelan) *hld up in rr and racd wd: 6th st: shkn up over 2f out: sn lft bhd* **7/1**	43
0430	5	4 ½	**Chrissycross (IRE)**[17] 3443 3-8-4 **61**..................(b) HarryBentley[(3)] 3 (Roger Teal) *mostly chsd ldr to over 4f out: cl 4th but rdn st: sn lost pl: wknd 2f out* **12/1**	35
0342	6	2 ¼	**Energize (FR)**[12] 3606 3-9-7 **75**..................(t) RichardHughes 8 (Richard Hannon) *hld up in tch: prog and cl 3rd st: c to nr side rail bhd ldr over 2f out: wknd wl over 1f out: eased* **10/3**[2]	45
000	7	hd	**Wasabi (IRE)**[25] 3189 3-8-4 **58**.................. CathyGannon 9 (John Berry) *hld up in rr: 7th and rdn st: sn btn* **16/1**	27
000-	8	27	**The Ploughman**[288] 6462 3-7-11 **56** oh11.................. DarrenEgan[(5)] 4 (John Bridger) *prom to 1/2-way: sn wknd: t.o last st* **66/1**	

2m 17.83s (8.13) **Going Correction** +0.80s/f (Soft) **8** Ran SP% **112.2**

Speed ratings (Par 100): **99,98,89,87,84 82,82,60**

Tote Swingers: 1&2 £3.00, 1&3 £4.40, 2&3 £4.00 CSF £13.15 CT £56.68 TOTE £4.20: £1.70, £1.30, £2.10; EX 16.00 Trifecta £65.50 Pool: £672.64 - 7.59 winning units..

Owner S P Tindall **Bred** Simon Tindall **Trained** Newmarket, Suffolk

FOCUS

The first two pulled a long way clear in this handicap and the winner can be marked up because she raced a bit away from the favoured stands' rail. Not form to be too positive about though, with the runner-up to this year's form the best guide.

Energize(FR) Official explanation: jockey said colt lost its action

3999 TRY TOTEQUICKPICK IF YOU'RE FEELING LUCKY H'CAP 1m 114y

8:30 (8:30) (Class 4) (0-85,83) 3-Y-O+ £5,175 (£1,540; £769; £384) Stalls Low

Form				RPR
31-6	1		**May Be Some Time**[44] 2574 4-8-12 **67**..................(t) FergusSweeney 2 (Stuart Kittow) *hld up in last pair: prog and cl 6th st: hdwy on outer to ld over 1f out: edgd rt towards rail: drvn out* **6/1**	79
6-24	2	1 ¼	**Benzanno (IRE)**[78] 1606 3-8-7 **72**..................[1] DavidProbert 3 (Andrew Balding) *hld up in tch: cl 5th st: prog against rail 2f out: wnt 2nd 1f out: sltly checked sn after: styd on but no imp on wnr* **11/2**[3]	80+
030	3	2 ½	**Yojimbo (IRE)**[11] 3667 4-9-11 **80**.................. MatthewDavies 1 (Mick Channon) *trckd ldrs: cl 4th st: led 3f out to over 1f out: n.m.r and lost 2nd 1f out: one pce* **3/1**[2]	83
2-21	4	9	**Henry Clay**[185] 107 3-8-13 **78**.................. MircoDemuro 4 (Mark Johnston) *led to 5f out: cl 2nd st: on terms w ldrs to 2f out: wknd over 1f out* **11/4**[1]	60
0-40	5	2 ¼	**Right Divine (IRE)**[33] 2930 3-8-13 **78**.................. ShaneKelly 8 (Brian Meehan) *trckd ldr 3f: 3rd st: lost pl 3f out: rdn and wknd 2f out* **20/1**	55
6220	6	6	**Super Duplex**[7] 3774 5-8-12 **67**.................. IanMongan 9 (Pat Phelan) *cl up: led 5f out to 3f out: racd awkwardly and sn wknd* **7/1**	31
0000	7	2 ¾	**Pat's Legacy (USA)**[24] 3226 6-9-7 **76**.................. J-PGuillambert 6 (Jo Hughes) *s.i.s: hld up in last pair: last and struggling st: sn bhd* **17/2**	33
0000	8	14	**Lowther**[26] 3157 7-9-7 **83**..................(p) AccursioRomeo[(7)] 5 (Brett Johnson) *t.k.h: hld up towards rr: awkward downhill and struggling in 7th st: sn bhd: t.o* **20/1**	

1m 51.97s (5.87) **Going Correction** +0.80s/f (Soft)

WFA 3 from 4yo+ 10lb **8** Ran SP% **113.9**

Speed ratings (Par 105): **105,103,101,93,91 86,83,71**

Tote Swingers: 1&2 £3.30, 1&3 £1.80, 2&3 £2.50 CSF £38.41 CT £111.33 TOTE £8.30: £1.80, £1.90, £1.10; EX 24.90 Trifecta £212.50 Part won. Pool: £287.23 - 0.59 winning units..

Owner Dr G S Plastow **Bred** D R Tucker **Trained** Blackborough, Devon

FOCUS

They went a good pace in this handicap. The winner stayed on strongly to score under a hold-up ride but the second looked a bit unlucky. Both are rated as having run personal bests.

4000 RAZORLIGHT LIVE 19.7.12 H'CAP (BETFAIR SPRINT FLAT SERIES QUALIFIER) 6f

9:00 (9:00) (Class 4) (0-80,78) 3-Y-O+ £5,175 (£1,540; £769; £384) Stalls High

Form				RPR
4610	1		**Silvee**[15] 3511 5-8-7 **59** oh2.................. KieranO'Neill 4 (John Bridger) *wl in tch: cl 6th st: rdn and prog on outer 2f out: styd on wl to ld last 100yds* **17/2**	69
3510	2	1 ½	**Danzoe (IRE)**[14] 3546 5-8-9 **61**.................. KierenFox 3 (Christine Dunnett) *in tch in rr: cl 6th st: prog on outer over 2f out: led over 1f out: hdd and one pce last 100yds* **20/1**	66
-132	3	1 ¼	**Aye Aye Digby (IRE)**[13] 3570 7-9-12 **78**.................. GeorgeBaker 2 (Patrick Chamings) *led 1f: cl 3rd st: shkn up and nt qckn 2f out: styd on to take 3rd ins fnl f* **9/4**[1]	79
-645	4	¾	**Yurituni**[13] 3571 5-9-12 **78**..................(v) CathyGannon 7 (Eve Johnson Houghton) *disp ld after 1f: narrow ld over 2f out to over 1f out: one pce* **16/1**	77
0604	5	1	**Mambo Spirit (IRE)**[26] 3139 8-9-4 **70**.................. DaneO'Neill 10 (Tony Newcombe) *in tch: cl 4th st: rdn over 2f out: no prog over 1f out* **7/1**	65
3214	6	1 ½	**Cocohatchee**[24] 3225 4-9-4 **70**.................. IanMongan 11 (Pat Phelan) *disp ld after 1f to over 2f out: hanging and fdd over 1f out* **5/2**[2]	61
1310	7	nk	**Hopes N Dreams (IRE)**[12] 3645 4-9-5 **78**.................. KevinStott[(7)] 9 (Kevin Ryan) *stmbld s then veered bdly lft and rdr nrly off: t.o after tl kpt on fnl 2f* **9/2**[3]	68+

1m 13.32s (3.92) **Going Correction** +0.80s/f (Soft)

WFA 3 from 4yo+ 6lb **7** Ran SP% **111.2**

Speed ratings (Par 105): **105,103,101,100,99 97,96**

Tote Swingers: 1&2 £12.00, 1&3 £3.80, 2&3 £9.30 CSF £138.35 CT £494.62 TOTE £8.30: £3.70, £6.40; EX 78.80 Trifecta £231.60 Part won. Pool: £313.09 - 0.22 winning units..

Owner Mr & Mrs K Finch **Bred** Mr And Mrs K Finch **Trained** Liphook, Hants

FOCUS

They went a good pace in the conditions in this sprint handicap but not a race to rate too positively with conditions deteriorating.

T/Plt: £1,153.70 to a £1 stake. Pool: £77,758.05 - 49.20 winning units. T/Qpdt: £165.50 to a £1 stake. Pool: £6,420.16 - 28.70 winning units. JN

3568 FOLKESTONE (R-H)

Thursday, July 12

OFFICIAL GOING: Good to firm changing to good after race 1 (6.00) then soft after race 3 (7.05)

Wind: meduim across Weather: rain

4001 LADBROKES.COM MEDIAN AUCTION MAIDEN STKS 7f (S)

6:00 (6:01) (Class 6) 3-Y-O £1,704 (£503; £251) Stalls High

Form				RPR
434	1		**Stirring Ballad**[15] 3507 3-8-12 76.................. LiamKeniry 9 (Andrew Balding) *hld up in tch: trcking ldrs and gng wl whn nt clr run and hmpd over 1f out: swtchd rt ins fnl f: qcknd to ld wl ins fnl f: comf* **11/4**[2]	76+
53	2	¾	**Avalanche**[19] 3389 3-9-0 0.................. PatrickHills[(3)] 4 (Luca Cumani) *chsd ldrs: rdn and ev ch over 1f out: styd on but outpcd by wnr ins fnl f* **5/1**[3]	75
43	3	nk	**Engrossing**[30] 3012 3-9-3 74.................. PatDobbs 11 (Richard Hannon) *hld up in tch: hdwy over 2f out: rdn to ld and edgd lft over 1f out: hdd and outpcd by wnr wl ins fnl f* **11/8**[1]	74
53-	4	1 ¼	**Typography**[246] 7329 3-9-3 0.................. MartinLane 8 (William Muir) *w ldr: rdn and ev ch over 1f out: outpcd ins fnl f* **9/1**	71
0-00	5	5	**Strategic Action (IRE)**[26] 3152 3-9-3 49..................(p) JohnFahy 12 (Linda Jewell) *hld up in tch towards rr: swtchd rt and effrt to chse ldrs over 1f out: wknd fnl f* **200/1**	57
0	6	1 ¼	**Made Of More**[58] 2147 3-9-3 0.................. RobertHavlin 3 (Roger Ingram) *led tl hdd and hmpd wl over 1f out: wknd fnl f* **150/1**	57
	7	1	**Neat Little Rows (IRE)** 3-8-12 0.................. MartinHarley 2 (Marco Botti) *dwlt: sn in tch: hdwy and chsng ldrs 2f out: wknd ent fnl f* **16/1**	46
0	8	3	**Dame Shirley**[54] 2273 3-8-12 0.................. SebSanders 5 (J W Hills) *in tch in midfield: rdn and effrt 2f out: wknd over 1f out* **20/1**	38
00	9	2 ¾	**Kaypea**[17] 3447 3-8-12 0.................. HayleyTurner 1 (Simon Dow) *stdd s: sn dropped in bhd: t.k.h: hld up in tch in rr: rdn and wknd 2f out* **40/1**	31
60	10	3 ½	**Precision Five**[15] 3507 3-8-12 0..................(p) LiamJones 7 (Jeremy Gask) *t.k.h: in tch and rn green in midfield: swtchd rt over 2f out: wknd 2f out* **66/1**	21
4-0	11	66	**Elmora**[70] 1793 3-8-12 0.................. LeeNewman 6 (Sylvester Kirk) *t.k.h: chsd ldrs tl lost pl qckly 1/2-way: t.o and virtually p.u fnl f: dismntd immediately after fin* **33/1**	

1m 26.58s (-0.72) **Going Correction** -0.05s/f (Good) **11** Ran SP% **114.1**

Speed ratings (Par 98): **102,101,100,99,93 92,91,87,84,80 5**

Tote Swingers: 1&2 £4.90, 1&3 £5.60, 2&3 £5.70 CSF £15.60 TOTE £4.10: £1.20, £1.70, £1.30; EX 13.20.

Owner George Strawbridge **Bred** George Strawbridge **Trained** Kingsclere, Hants
FOCUS
A fair 3yo maiden rated around the placed horses. The official going description of good to firm was changed to good after this race due to persistent rain.

4002 BRITISH STALLION STUDS SUPPORTING BRITISH RACING E B F MAIDEN FILLIES' STKS 5f
6:30 (6:30) (Class 5) 2-Y-O **£3,234** (£962; £481; £240) **Stalls** High

Form RPR
53 **1** **Snow Angel (IRE)**[39] 2729 2-9-0 0 SebSanders 1 74
(J W Hills) *mde all: sn crossed to r against stands' rail: rdn over 1f out: r.o wl fnl f* **6/1**
2 *1* **Jubilant Queen** 2-9-0 0 JohnFahy 7 70
(Clive Cox) *t.k.h: trckd ldrs against stands' rail: rdn and effrt to chse wnr over 1f out: r.o but no imp on wnr fnl f* **4/1**[3]
0 **3** *3 ½* **Glossy Posse**[34] 2892 2-9-0 0 PatDobbs 4 58
(Richard Hannon) *chsd ldr: rdn and effrt 2f out: outpcd by ldng pair and btn 1f out: kpt on to hold 3rd after* **9/1**
4 *½* **Naalatt (IRE)** 2-8-9 0 AntiocoMurgia(5) 8 56+
(Mahmood Al Zarooni) *s.i.s: niggled along in last trio: rdn and hdwy over 2f out: chsd ldrs over 1f out: outpcd and btn 1f out: kpt on* **17/2**
5 *½* **Tregereth (IRE)** 2-9-0 0 LeeNewman 9 54+
(Jonathan Portman) *dwlt: in tch in midfield: rdn and outpcd wl over 1f out: rallied and kpt on ins fnl f: no threat to ldrs* **40/1**
6 *¾* **Bint Youmzain (IRE)** 2-9-0 0 MartinHarley 10 56+
(Mick Channon) *v.s.a: bhd: rdn and styng on but stl plenty to do whn nt clr run and hmpd 1f out: kpt on but no threat to ldrs fnl 100yds* **11/4**[1]
7 *2* **Idle Curiosity (IRE)** 2-9-0 0 HayleyTurner 2 44
(Jim Boyle) *chsd wnr tl over 1f out: sn wknd u.p* **14/1**
00 **8** *3* **Jackpot**[10] 3700 2-8-9 0 BrendanPowell(5) 6 34
(Brendan Powell) *in tch: rdn and fnd little over 1f out: sn wknd* **66/1**
9 *1 ½* **Breezily (USA)** 2-9-0 0 MickaelBarzalona 5 28+
(Mahmood Al Zarooni) *in tch in last trio: rdn over 2f out: no prog and wknd over 1f out* **7/2**[2]

1m 0.3s (0.30) **Going Correction** +0.025s/f (Good) **9** Ran SP% **114.3**
Speed ratings (Par 91): **98,96,90,90,89 88,84,80,77**
Tote Swingers: 1&2 £4.90, 1&3 £5.60, 2&3 £5.70 CSF £29.90 TOTE £8.00: £2.10, £1.80, £2.10; EX 45.30.
Owner Richard Tufft & Partners **Bred** Barronstown Stud **Trained** Upper Lambourn, Berks
FOCUS
The state of the ground was in flux owing to persistent rain. A fair juvenile fillies' maiden in which the form is rated around recent renewals and a decent time.
NOTEBOOK
Snow Angel(IRE) had produced very respectable form in two 5f maidens on good ground at Windsor and Nottingham since May. In fact, her latest about 2l third of five at the latter track last month looks significantly better in the light of the winner Alhebayeb's Group 2 success at Newmarket's July meeting. She likes to race prominently and was quick to grab the favoured stands' rail from a poor draw. She was asked a serious question at around the furlong pole and the outcome was in little doubt with 100 yards to go. She looks a nice sprinter in the making. (op 7-1)
Jubilant Queen produced a good debut performance and looks one to note in similar contests going forward, probably over at least 6f this term. (op 7-2 tchd 10-3)
Glossy Posse has progressed markedly from her very modest Newmarket debut run over 6f on soft ground last month. She can go well in a similar contest back over 6f, possibly further, on decent ground in the near future. (op 10-1)
Naalatt(IRE) raced up the middle of the track and will know more next time. (op 8-1 tchd 10-1)
Tregereth(IRE) produced a perfectly respectable fifth on debut. (tchd 33-1)
Bint Youmzain(IRE) reportedly looked well but was slow away and struggled to make up the deficit. Official explanation: jockey said filly missed the break (tchd 3-1)
Breezily(USA) proved disappointing. (op 9-2 tchd 10-3)

4003 SHEPHERD NEAME SPITFIRE ALE SUPPORTING SSAFA H'CAP 5f
7:05 (7:05) (Class 5) (0-70,69) 3-Y-0+ **£2,385** (£704; £352) **Stalls** High

Form RPR
535 **1** **Charming (IRE)**[13] 3568 3-9-4 66 SebSanders 9 74
(Olivia Maylam) *chsd ldrs: rdn to chal ent fnl f: led fnl 100yds: pressed cl home but a gng to hold on* **5/1**[2]
5-52 **2** *nk* **Dear Maurice**[16] 3464 8-9-9 66 (t) MartinLane 7 75
(Tobias B P Coles) *in tch in midfield: rdn 3f out: hdwy u.p over 1f out: styd on wl u.p fnl 100yds: wnt 2nd last stride* **8/1**
3034 **3** *shd* **Even Bolder**[16] 3477 9-9-3 60 LiamJones 11 68
(Eric Wheeler) *in tch: swtchd rt and effrt to chse ldrs ent fnl f: wnt 2nd wl ins fnl f: styd on: lost 2nd last stride* **13/2**[3]
3000 **4** *1 ½* **Love You Louis**[16] 3477 6-9-12 69 PatDobbs 13 72
(J R Jenkins) *led: rdn and hrd pressed ent fnl f: hdd fnl 100yds: no ex* **5/1**[2]
5604 **5** *nk* **Bateleur**[11] 3660 8-8-13 61 CharlesBishop(5) 1 63+
(Mick Channon) *stdd and swtchd lft after s: bhd: hdwy ent fnl f: r.o wl fnl f: nt rch ldrs* **9/1**
0005 **6** *½* **See The Storm**[17] 3456 4-8-0 50 oh5 (v[1]) NatashaEaton(7) 8 50
(Lisa Williamson) *towards rr: swtchd rt and hdwy 1f out: styd on fnl f: nt rch ldrs* **20/1**
60-0 **7** *1* **Monessa (IRE)**[23] 3245 3-8-11 59 (t) JohnFahy 12 54
(Linda Jewell) *in tch towards rr: rdn and swtchd rt over 1f out: kpt on same pce ins fnl f* **33/1**
040- **8** *½* **Roman Myst (IRE)**[287] 6474 3-9-0 62 LiamKeniry 2 55
(Sylvester Kirk) *bhd: rdn and no prog 2f out: styd on fnl f but no threat to ldrs* **22/1**
400- **9** *1 ½* **Indian Shuffle (IRE)**[311] 5781 4-9-12 69 LeeNewman 6 58
(Jonathan Portman) *in tch in midfield: rdn and unable qck 2f out: wknd ent fnl f* **20/1**
1214 **10** *1 ½* **Big Wave (IRE)**[9] 3724 4-9-12 69 RobertHavlin 10 53
(Alison Hutchinson) *chsd ldr: rdn and unable qck over 1f out: btn 1f out: wknd* **11/4**[1]
1450 **11** *½* **Court Applause (IRE)**[37] 2789 4-9-4 61 MartinDwyer 5 43
(William Muir) *a towards rr: rdn and no prog wl over 1f out: wknd ent fnl f* **16/1**

1m 0.11s (0.11) **Going Correction** +0.10s/f (Good)
WFA 3 from 4yo+ 5lb **11** Ran SP% **117.1**
Speed ratings (Par 103): **103,102,102,99,99 98,97,96,93,91 90**
Tote Swingers: 1&2 £7.00, 1&3 £3.90, 2&3 £6.50 CSF £41.76 CT £264.74 TOTE £5.40: £1.90, £2.50, £1.90; EX 55.20.
Owner Mrs V A Ward **Bred** Rabbah Bloodstock Limited **Trained** Epsom, Surrey

FOCUS
A modest sprint handicap for 3yos and up but the form looks reasonable, rated around the placed horses. The ground was officially changed to soft after this race, but the winning time was under one second slower than standard.

4004 CLAYDON HORSE EXERCISERS H'CAP 1m 7f 92y
7:40 (7:40) (Class 6) (0-60,60) 4-Y-0+ **£1,704** (£503; £251) **Stalls** High

Form RPR
000- **1** **Green To Gold (IRE)**[147] 7496 7-9-2 55 (b) LiamKeniry 2 66+
(Don Cantillon) *in tch and a travelling strly: stl tanking along and hdwy to chse ldr 3f out: led over 2f out and sn rdn clr: pushed along and in n.d after: eased wl ins fnl f* **5/1**[2]
030- **2** *3* **Hi Note**[189] 6926 4-8-3 49 MartinLeonard(7) 1 54
(Sheena West) *in tch: chsd ldr 8f out: led 7f out: hdd over 2f out and immediately outpcdand no ch w wnr: styd on to hold 2nd fnl 2f* **10/1**
504 **3** *1* **Big Time Billy (IRE)**[27] 3100 6-9-7 60 LukeMorris 6 64
(Mike Hammond) *in tch in midfield: rdn and effrt 4f out: hrd drvn to go 3rd 2f out: no ch w wnr and plugged on same pce after* **5/2**[1]
0502 **4** *½* **Mollyow (IRE)**[1] 3969 4-8-7 46 MartinLane 8 49
(Terry Clement) *hld up in last pair: hdwy 5f out: rdn and effrt over 2f out: 5th and plugged on same pce fnl 2f* **5/2**[1]
60-3 **5** *1 ½* **Maggie Aron**[27] 3102 6-8-13 52 PatDobbs 5 53
(Tim Vaughan) *stdd s: hld up in rr: swtchd lft and effrt over 2f out: modest 4th and rdn 2f out: kpt on but no ch w wnr* **15/2**[3]
42/6 **6** *7* **Cubism**[28] 3077 6-9-1 54 (t) KirstyMilczarek 9 46
(Brendan Powell) *chsd ldrs: wnt 2nd 10f out tl led 8f out: hdd 7f out: styd chsng ldr tl 3f out: wknd 2f out* **12/1**
/6-0 **7** *12* **Plug In Baby**[24] 3216 4-8-7 46 HayleyTurner 3 22
(Nick Mitchell) *hld up in tch towards rr: rdn 4f out: wknd 3f out: sn lost tch* **25/1**
63-0 **8** *1 ¾* **Appointment**[21] 2348 7-8-10 49 ow2 JamieGoldstein 11 23
(Zoe Davison) *in tch: rdn over 3f out: sn struggling and wknd wl over 2f out* **40/1**
4 **9** *21* **Perfect Buttons (IRE)**[34] 2872 6-8-7 46 oh1 (v[1]) JohnFahy 10
(Tim Vaughan) *led tl 10f out: styd handy: rdn over 5f out: wknd over 3f out: wl bhd fnl 2f* **25/1**
/000 **10** *59* **Rosaria**[19] 3392 4-8-10 49 (v[1]) MickaelBarzalona 7
(Harry Dunlop) *chsd ldrs tl 7f out: sn lost pl: wl t.o fnl 3f* **33/1**

3m 31.5s (1.80) **Going Correction** +0.175s/f (Good) **10** Ran SP% **115.4**
Speed ratings (Par 101): **102,100,99,98,99 95,88,87,76,45**
Tote Swingers: 1&2 £7.40, 1&3 £2.90, 2&3 £2.70 CSF £50.51 CT £153.47 TOTE £4.80: £1.60, £3.50, £2.20; EX 51.10.
Owner Sir Alex Ferguson & Sotirios Hassiakos **Bred** Dominic O'Neill And Julie White **Trained** Newmarket, Suffolk
FOCUS
A modest staying handicap for older horses. The ground was changed to soft prior to this race and the winning time was nearly 10secs slower than standard. The runner-up is rated close to form and looks the best guide.
Green To Gold(IRE) Official explanation: trainer said, regarding apparent improvement in form, that the gelding had benefited from a break and its confidence improved by a change in training routine.

4005 LADBROKECASINO.COM H'CAP 1m 4f
8:15 (8:15) (Class 5) (0-70,70) 3-Y-0 **£2,385** (£704; £352) **Stalls** High

Form RPR
5-00 **1** **Dont Take Me Alive**[26] 3142 3-9-1 64 (p) JohnFahy 8 71
(Clive Cox) *chsd ldrs: rdn to chal over 1f out: led 1f out: r.o wl and forged ahd fnl 75yds* **13/2**
064 **2** *1* **Petaluma**[27] 3104 3-9-7 70 MartinHarley 4 75
(Mick Channon) *chsd ldr: jnd ldr 3f out: rdn to ld ent fnl 2f: drvn and hdd 1f out: no ex and btn fnl 75yds* **13/8**[1]
5610 **3** *6* **Curly Come Home**[14] 3543 3-9-5 68 SebSanders 3 64
(Chris Wall) *t.k.h: hld up in rr: clsd on ldrs 3f out: rdn to chse ldng pair over 1f out: no ex and btn 1f out: wknd fnl f* **7/4**[2]
00-0 **4** *2* **Letham Cottage**[21] 3311 3-8-2 51 oh6 (b[1]) MartinLane 7 44?
(Brian Meehan) *led: rdn and hdd ent fnl 2f: wknd u.p over 1f out* **28/1**
0040 **5** *nk* **Morlotti**[26] 3161 3-9-3 66 KirstyMilczarek 6 58
(Luca Cumani) *hld up in last pair: clsd on ldrs 3f out: rdn ent fnl 2f: sn btn and wknd wl over 1f out* **5/1**[3]

2m 44.18s (3.28) **Going Correction** +0.25s/f (Good) **5** Ran SP% **107.9**
Speed ratings (Par 100): **99,98,94,93,92**
CSF £16.89 TOTE £3.50: £2.60, £1.40; EX 18.20.
Owner Tim Bostwick **Bred** Larry Stratton And Plantation Stud **Trained** Lambourn, Berks
FOCUS
A fair middle-distance handicap for 3-y-os. They went a respectable gallop on soft ground and steps forward from the first two.

4006 KMFM KENT'S LOCAL RADIO STATION FILLIES' H'CAP 1m 1f 149y
8:45 (8:45) (Class 5) (0-70,67) 3-Y-0+ **£2,385** (£704; £352) **Stalls** Centre

Form RPR
1225 **1** **Our Phylli Vera (IRE)**[25] 3193 3-9-0 64 MickaelBarzalona 11 72+
(Harry Dunlop) *hld up in last pair: clsd on ldrs over 2f out: rdn to ld 1f out: wnt clr ins fnl f: eased cl home* **5/4**[1]
00-0 **2** *1* **Kittens**[90] 1357 3-8-6 56 MartinDwyer 10 61
(William Muir) *in tch in midfield: clsd on ldrs: chsd ldr 2f out: rdn to ld over 1f out: hdd 1f out: no ex and sn outpcd by wnr: kpt on* **12/1**
5003 **3** *1 ½* **Love Grows Wild (USA)**[14] 3547 3-8-2 52 (v) HayleyTurner 5 54
(Michael Bell) *chsd ldrs: rdn and effrt on inner 2f out: no ex and styd on same pce fnl f* **7/2**[2]
-000 **4** *5* **Imperial Elegance**[15] 3489 3-7-12 48 oh3 NickyMackay 9 40
(Mick Channon) *in tch in midfield: rdn 3f out: outpcd and btn wl over 1f out: plugged on to go 4th ins fnl f* **33/1**
00-6 **5** *1 ¼* **Velvet Star (IRE)**[44] 2577 3-8-3 53 (t) MartinLane 2 42
(Paul Cole) *racd freely: led: hung lft over 2f out: rdn and hdd over 1f out: sn wknd* **6/1**[3]
4030 **6** *¾* **Hubood**[87] 1425 4-9-1 54 JamieGoldstein 4 41
(Zoe Davison) *awkward s and rdr adjsting iron sn after: in tch in last pair: effrt and rdn jst over 2f out: wknd wl over 1f out* **12/1**
000 **7** *2 ¼* **Luna Rosa (IRE)**[20] 3340 3-8-4 54 JohnFahy 7 37
(Clive Cox) *taken down early: t.k.h: chsd ldr tl 2f out: sn wknd* **13/2**

2m 8.36s (3.46) **Going Correction** +0.325s/f (Good)
WFA 3 from 4yo+ 11lb **7** Ran SP% **112.6**
Speed ratings (Par 100): **99,98,97,93,92 91,89**
Tote Swingers: 1&2 £3.20, 1&3 £1.40, 2&3 £3.60 CSF £17.58 CT £42.78 TOTE £2.30: £1.30, £6.10; EX 13.30.
Owner Kieron Drake & Simon Withers **Bred** Awbeg Stud **Trained** Lambourn, Berks

FOCUS
A modest fillies' handicap for 3-y-os and up. The winning time was very respectable for the grade on soft ground and the winner is value for a little further.
Velvet Star(IRE) Official explanation: jockey said filly hung badly left
T/Plt: £19.90 to a £1 stake. Pool: £74,176.00 - 2,714.06 winning units. T/Qpdt: £7.90 to a £1 stake. Pool: £6,087.00 - 568.44 winning units. SP

3630 NEWMARKET (R-H)
Thursday, July 12

OFFICIAL GOING: Soft (6.2)
Wind: Light behind Weather: Cloudy with sunny spells

4007 BAHRAIN TROPHY (GROUP 3) 1m 5f
1:20 (1:20) (Class 1) 3-Y-O
£31,190 (£11,825; £5,918; £2,948; £1,479; £742) **Stalls** Centre

Form				RPR
221	1		**Shantaram**34 3-9-0 104 ... WilliamBuick 3 (John Gosden) *hld up in tch: ld 2f out: rdn and hung rt over 1f out: styd on wl* **9/4**2	104
1341	2	3 1/4	**Naseem Alyasmeen (IRE)**12 3-8-11 84 ... MartinHarley 5 (Mick Channon) *hld up: pushed along over 4f out: hdwy over 2f out: rdn to chse wnr over 1f out: styd on same pce ins fnl f* **20/1**	96
1606	3	2 3/4	**Good Morning Star (IRE)**5 3-8-11 88 ... JoeFanning 1 (Mark Johnston) *led: shkn up over 3f out: rdn and hdd 2f out: no ex fnl f* **20/1**	92
1143	4	hd	**Rewarded**21 3-9-0 101 ... KirstyMilczarek 4 (James Toller) *hld up: plld hrd: hdwy over 2f out: sn rdn: edgd lft over 1f out: no ex fnl f* **10/3**3	95
11	5	5	**Valiant**27 3-9-0 95 ... RyanMoore 2 (William Haggas) *chsd ldr 2f: remained handy: pushed along over 4f out: hrd rdn over 2f out: wknd over 1f out* **15/8**1	87
310	6	3/4	**Yazdi (IRE)**20 3-9-0 90 ... KierenFallon 6 (Brian Meehan) *prom: chsd ldr 11f out: rdn over 2f out: wknd over 1f out* **8/1**	86

2m 53.07s (9.07) **Going Correction** +0.30s/f (Good) **6** Ran SP% **109.3**
Speed ratings (Par 110): **84,82,80,80,77 76**
Tote Swingers: 1&2 £4.20, 1&3 £5.70, 2&3 £10.70 CSF £37.77 TOTE £2.90: £1.80, £5.20; EX 34.30.
Owner Lady Bamford **Bred** Lady Bamford **Trained** Newmarket, Suffolk

FOCUS
The far side of the track was in use for the first time this summer. Stalls on Far Side except 10f, 12f, 13f: Centre. Rail realignment around bend added 18metres to races beyond a mile.They raced centre-field. A race that has proven most informative as a St Leger trial in recent years, Masked Marvel going on to land the Doncaster feature last season, and before that Kite Wood and Corsica (winners of this in 2009 and 2010 respectively) going on to hit the frame. The pace was modest enough (time over 13secs slower than standard) and the form is ordinary for the level on the face of it, but it would be a surprise were Shantaram not to rank higher, his rider feeling the penny has only just dropped. As it is he is rated 7lb off his Lingfield form here, with the race rated around the third.

NOTEBOOK
Shantaram, runner-up to Derby second Main Sequence in the Lingfield Derby Trial, was not at his best when scrambling home at odds of 1-8 in a 1m4f maiden here last time (said to have disliked the soft ground), but he travelled well throughout on this step back up in grade and the way he pulled clear close home very much suggests he'll relish the extra 11/2f of the St Leger, a race for which his trainer also has Michelangelo, who is currently half the odds at 8-1, amongst others. There's a class gap to bridge, obviously, and he'll likely be tested again in the Great Voltigeur first, but he's clearly going the right way. (op 2-1)
Naseem Alyasmeen(IRE), progressive in handicaps and having her ninth start of the year, was quite keen, but that didn't stop her putting in a career-best by some way. She'll presumably be sent in search of some winning black type now back at shorter. (op 16-1)
Good Morning Star(IRE), beaten 11l by the impressive Great Heavens at Haydock just five days earlier, recorded her best effort since springing a 50-1 shock in the Cheshire Oaks, although it's clear she had the run of the race. (op 25-1)
Rewarded, third in a 1m2f Group 3 at Royal Ascot, is proven on soft ground, but he took a while to settle and didn't get home. (op 7-2 tchd 3-1)
Valiant had looked most progressive in winning a maiden and then handicap at 1m2f, appearing in need of further on the latter occasion, but he didn't respond to pressure this time, being beaten before stamina became an issue, and it's probable the ground was to blame. (op 2-1)
Yazdi(IRE) didn't get home over 2m in the Queen's Vase, and his finishing effort was again somewhat disappointing. It's likely the son of Galileo needs better ground. (tchd 15-2)

4008 TNT JULY STKS (GROUP 2) (C&G) 6f
1:50 (1:50) (Class 1) 2-Y-O
£34,026 (£12,900; £6,456; £3,216; £1,614; £810) **Stalls** Low

Form				RPR
12	1		**Alhebayeb (IRE)**23 2-8-12 0 ... PaulHanagan 7 (Richard Hannon) *chsd ldrs: rdn to ld and edgd rt over 1f out: hdd ins fnl f: rallied to ld fnl 50yds* **9/2**3	105
23	2	nk	**Lewisham**25 2-8-12 0 ... JamesDoyle 6 (Noel Quinlan) *s.i.s: hld up: hdwy and carried rt over 1f out: rdn and r.o wl ins fnl f: wnt 2nd post: nt quite rch wnr* **25/1**	104
15	3	shd	**Ahern**21 2-8-12 0 ... JamieSpencer 5 (David Barron) *chsd ldr: pushed along over 2f out: n.m.r and outpcd over 1f out: rallied to ld ins fnl f: sn hdd and unable qck* **9/4**2	104
12	4	2 1/4	**Gale Force Ten**21 2-8-12 0 ... RyanMoore 1 (A P O'Brien, Ire) *chsd ldrs: rdn and hung rt over 1f out: no ex ins fnl f* **15/8**1	97
2151	5	nse	**Chilworth Icon**11 2-8-12 95 ... MartinHarley 2 (Mick Channon) *plld hrd and prom: rdn and nt clr run over 1f out: styd on same pce fnl f* **9/1**	97
210	6	3/4	**Smoothtalkinrascal (IRE)**23 2-8-12 92 ... ShaneKelly 8 (Brian Meehan) *rrd s: hld up: hdwy over 1f out: sn rdn and hung lft: no ex ins fnl f* **10/1**	95
1120	7	1 1/4	**Heavy Metal**23 2-8-12 95 ... JoeFanning 3 (Mark Johnston) *led: qcknd over 2f out: rdn and hdd over 1f out: no ex ins fnl f* **16/1**	91

1m 14.39s (1.89) **Going Correction** +0.30s/f (Good) **7** Ran SP% **112.6**
Speed ratings (Par 106): **99,98,98,95,95 94,92**
Tote Swingers: 1&2 £8.00, 1&3 £2.40, 2&3 £11.80 CSF £92.45 TOTE £4.80: £2.40, £6.40; EX 92.90 Trifecta £246.50 Pool: £2,892.18 - 8.68 winning units..
Owner Hamdan Al Maktoum **Bred** Yeomanstown Stud **Trained** East Everleigh, Wilts
■ Stewards' Enquiry : Ryan Moore two-day ban: careless riding (Jul 26-27)

FOCUS
The early pace was steady (time a fraction slower than the later fillies' maiden) and the runners again came centre-field. A weal renewal with the finish compressed, although the form could be rated up to 4lb higher. The winner is up 6lb on his Ascot figure.

NOTEBOOK
Alhebayeb(IRE), the Windsor Castle runner-up, promised to be suited by the extra furlong and held on well, improving on his Ascot form. Clearly effective on the softer ground, he should get 7f, but probably just lacks the class to make it at the top level. The Vintage Stakes and Gimcrack will no doubt be considered. (tchd 4-1)
Lewisham had run to a similar level when placing in 6f maidens at Newcastle and Doncaster, so it's hard to explain where this sudden improvement came from. He travelled well and may have won but for being carried right (albeit on to the possibly favoured stands' rail), just failing to get up. He should go one better, although wouldn't be the first to disappoint back in a maiden following a big run in a Group race. The Molecomb is apparently being considered. (op 33-1)
Ahern, who lost all chance when squeezed out early in the Norfolk, picked up well to challenge, looking the winner, but couldn't see it out. An easier 6f in the Richmond Stakes at Glorious Goodwood should suit. (op 2-1)
Gale Force Ten was unable to confirm Norfolk form with Ahern, taking a good grip early on this return to 6f and then drifting right under pressure. This clearly wasn't his best. (op 2-1 tchd 7-4)
Chilworth Icon found this tougher than the Group 3 he won in Italy last time, proving unable to quicken having raced keenly.
Smoothtalkinrascal(IRE) blew the start when rearing, but likely wouldn't have been good enough anyway. (op 12-1)
Heavy Metal, midfield in the Coventry, would have found this ground soft enough and was readily brushed aside. (op 20-1)

4009 GOLDSMITHS H'CAP 1m 2f
2:25 (2:25) (Class 2) (0-105,93) 3-Y-O
£31,125 (£9,320; £4,660; £2,330; £1,165; £585) **Stalls** Centre

Form				RPR
-241	1		**Stature (IRE)**11 3-9-1 87 6ex ... RyanMoore 14 (Andrew Balding) *chsd ldr tl led wl over 1f out: sn rdn: styd on u.p* **12/1**	98
1252	2	1 3/4	**Silver Blaze**27 3-9-5 91 ... PJMcDonald 12 (Alan Swinbank) *chsd ldrs: rdn and nt clr run over 1f out: styd on u.p to go 2nd post* **12/1**	98
1030	3	hd	**Samba King**21 3-9-7 93 ... AhmedAjtebi 9 (Mahmood Al Zarooni) *chsd ldrs: rdn and ev ch wl over 1f out: styd on same pce ins fnl f: lost 2nd post* **16/1**	100
-115	4	1/2	**Pilgrims Rest (IRE)**21 3-9-0 86 ... RichardHughes 3 (Richard Hannon) *hld up: hdwy over 4f out: rdn over 1f out: styd on u.p* **8/1**	92+
-620	5	1	**Trader Jack**21 3-9-4 90 ... JamesDoyle 6 (Roger Charlton) *hld up in tch: plld hrd: rdn over 2f out: styd on* **14/1**	94
112	6	nk	**Hajras (IRE)**54 3-9-4 90 ... PaulHanagan 5 (Mark Johnston) *hld up: pushed along over 3f out: hdwy and nt clr run over 1f out: styd on: nt rch ldrs* **7/1**3	93+
-212	7	nk	**Razorbill (USA)**11 3-8-13 85 ... MichaelHills 11 (Charles Hills) *hld up: hdwy over 2f out: rdn and ev ch wl over 1f out: no ex ins fnl f* **8/1**	87
-030	8	3/4	**Ghost Protocol (IRE)**21 3-9-2 88 ... (p) JamieSpencer 4 (David Simcock) *s.i.s: hld up: swtchd rt over 1f out: nt clr run sn after: styd on u.p ins fnl f: nvr nrr* **20/1**	89
210	9	1 1/2	**Zaina (IRE)**49 3-8-13 85 ... FrankieDettori 7 (Gerard Butler) *hld up: hdwy over 4f out: rdn over 1f out: wknd ins fnl f* **20/1**	83
421	10	3/4	**Nabucco**24 3-9-2 88 ... WilliamBuick 1 (John Gosden) *hld up: hdwy u.p and hung rt over 2f out: wknd fnl f* **3/1**1	84
5511	11	1 1/2	**Fennell Bay (IRE)**21 3-9-5 91 ... JoeFanning 13 (Mark Johnston) *prom: nt clr run 2f out: sn rdn: wknd fnl f* **8/1**	84
1510	12	3/4	**Prussian**21 3-9-1 87 ... KierenFallon 10 (Mark Johnston) *led: rdn and hdd over 1f out: wknd fnl f* **33/1**	79
42-1	13	1 1/4	**Greek War (IRE)**13 3-9-6 92 ... MickaelBarzalona 2 (Mahmood Al Zarooni) *hld up: swtchd rt over 3f out: sn rdn and hung lft: wknd over 1f out: eased* **13/2**2	81

2m 9.11s (3.61) **Going Correction** +0.30s/f (Good) **13** Ran SP% **124.6**
Speed ratings (Par 106): **97,95,95,95,94 94,93,93,91,91 90,89,88**
Tote Swingers: 1&2 £41.10, 1&3 £43.50, 2&3 £34.90 CSF £150.73 CT £2334.18 TOTE £12.60: £4.30, £4.70, £5.60; EX 272.40 TRIFECTA Not won..
Owner N Botica **Bred** Barronstown Stud **Trained** Kingsclere, Hants

FOCUS
Traditionally a competitive handicap and this year looked no exception, even though the top weight was 12lb below the race ceiling. The form was probably only ordinary for the grade, but looks sound enough. The pace was fair and all the action unfolded down the centre of the track, but it was a big advantage to race close to the pace.

NOTEBOOK
Stature(IRE) has improved plenty since the hood was fitted and made light of a penalty for his narrow Windsor success 11 days earlier. He was plenty keen enough early, but crucially got a nice lead from Prussian until that one dropped away from the 3f pole. Having forged his way to the front over a furlong out, he pulled nicely clear and on this evidence can go on to better things. He seems equally effective on both fast and soft ground. (op 16-1)
Silver Blaze was put up 4lb after chasing home Valiant (fifth in the opener) at York last time and ran another cracker in defeat. Another to be handy from the off, he had to be switched over a furlong out but it didn't affect his final placing. His only win so far came on Fibresand, but he will surely win a nice handicap on turf before too long. (tchd 16-1)
Samba King started off the season with two soft-ground wins over this trip, but hadn't been so good since including when around 9l behind Fennell Bay in the King George V Handicap at Royal Ascot. Mickael Barzalona deserted him for Greek War, but as it turned out he fared much the best of the Godolphin pair and had worked his way to the front over 3f from home before the winner collared him approaching the last. He clearly relishes these conditions. (op 20-1)
Pilgrims Rest(IRE) finished around 2l behind Fennell Bay at Royal Ascot when bidding for a hat-trick and enjoyed a 4lb pull. He had every chance inside the last furlong here and ran his race with few apparent excuses. (op 11-1)
Trader Jack had questions to answer following a tame effort in the Britannia, but this was much better, especially as he pulled fiercely early and those trying to come from off this pace were at a disadvantage. He looks well worth persevering with over this trip.
Hajras(IRE) was up another 6lb having lost his unbeaten record when second in the London Gold Cup at Newbury last time, though that was still decent form. Another to be at a disadvantage in trying to come from off the pace, he was stopped in his run on a couple of occasions inside the last 2f and can be rated a bit closer. Unraced at two, this was only his fourth start and he still has scope. (op 13-2 tchd 6-1)
Razorbill(USA), stepping up around 2f in trip, pulled hard at the back early and an effort coming to the last 2f came to little. His stamina remains unproven and he is already due to go up 4lb.
Ghost Protocol(IRE) had cheekpieces on for the first time, but he was at a disadvantage in trying to come from the back of the field and was never getting there. (tchd 22-1)
Zaina(IRE) found the step up into Listed company too much for her at Goodwood in May and this was more realistic. She wasn't helped by getting short of room over a furlong out when trying to get closer towards the far side and she is still unexposed. (op 25-1)

Nabucco, who only made his debut in May, was making his handicap debut after beating a subsequent winner in a Windsor maiden. Dropped to the rear of the field early, he found very little when asked to get closer over 3f from home and is surely better than this. Official explanation: trainer had no explanation for the poor form shown (op 7-2 tchd 4-1 in places)
Greek War(IRE) was put up a stone after bolting up over C&D on his handicap debut/seasonal reappearance last month. He wasn't travelling at all well at the back of the field from before halfway and switching him to race alone against the stands' rail made no difference. This was too bad to be true. (op 7-1 tchd 8-1 in a place)

4010 PRINCESS OF WALES'S GOLDSMITHS STKS (GROUP 2) 1m 4f

3:00 (3:00) (Class 1) 3-Y-O+

£61,898 (£23,467; £11,744; £5,850; £2,936; £1,473) **Stalls** Centre

Form				RPR
-626	**1**		**Fiorente (IRE)**[19] 3369 4-9-2 108 ... RyanMoore 6 (Sir Michael Stoute) *a.p: wnt centre over 7f out: rdn to ld and hung rt fr over 1f out: styd on u.p* **11/2**[3]	120
6244	**2**	2 ¾	**Joshua Tree (IRE)**[32] 2968 5-9-2 112 ... (t) AndreaAtzeni 2 (Marco Botti) *chsd ldr tl styd stands' side to r alone over 7f out: remained handy: rdn over 2f out: led wl over 1f out: sn hdd: hung lft ins fnl f: styd on same pce* **20/1**	116
2123	**3**	1 ½	**Red Cadeaux**[19] 3369 6-9-5 116 ... TomMcLaughlin 7 (Ed Dunlop) *chsd ldrs: wnt centre over 7f out: rdn to chse ldr over 3f out: hung lft over 2f out: ev ch over 1f out: styd on same pce ins fnl f* **5/2**[2]	117
3-13	**4**	7	**Harris Tweed**[55] 2254 5-9-2 115 ... LiamJones 8 (William Haggas) *led: wnt centre over 7f out: shkn up over 3f out: rdn and hdd wl over 1f out: sn hung rt: wknd fnl f* **2/1**[1]	102
15-0	**5**	1 ¾	**Sea Of Heartbreak (IRE)**[56] 2209 5-8-13 108 ... JamesDoyle 3 (Roger Charlton) *hld up: wnt centre over 7f out: rdn over 2f out: wknd over 1f out* **25/1**	97
10-4	**6**	3 ¾	**Modun (IRE)**[133] 759 5-9-2 110 ... FrankieDettori 1 (Saeed Bin Suroor) *hld up: wnt centre over 7f out: pushed along over 4f out: rdn and wknd over 2f out* **7/1**	94
-322	**7**	25	**Dandino**[12] 3632 5-9-2 107 ... RichardHughes 5 (James Fanshawe) *prom: lft chsng ldr whn wnt centre over 7f out: reminder over 5f out: rdn over 3f out: wknd 2f out: eased: t.o* **6/1**	54

2m 33.76s (0.86) **Going Correction** +0.30s/f (Good) **7 Ran SP% 112.7**
Speed ratings (Par 115): **109,107,106,101,100 97,81**
Tote Swingers: 1&2 £8.70, 1&3 £3.20, 2&3 £6.60 CSF £94.43 TOTE £6.90: £3.20, £4.80; EX 72.00 Trifecta £409.40 Pool: £5,132.24 - 9.24 winning units..
Owner Ballymacoll Stud **Bred** Ballymacoll Stud Farm Ltd **Trained** Newmarket, Suffolk

FOCUS
A race lacking depth and hard to know what to make of the form, with the runners finishing dotted all over the track and the first two pulling clear towards the possibly favoured stands' side. The winner has been rated up 10lb. Liam Jones cranked up the tempo a long way out aboard Harris Tweed, teeing it up for the others, and it proved a thorough test at the distance. The time was 6.56secs outside standard. Sir Michael Stoute improved his already impressive record in the race, making it five wins in the last eight years.

NOTEBOOK
Fiorente(IRE) got his career back on track with this strong, staying performance. He had been disappointing this season, but minus the cheekpieces tried in the Hardwicke (actually fared better than the bare result), he travelled smoothest of all and knuckled down better than he has in the past. The soft ground was a concern, but it's possible this late-maturing type is now just beginning to come good, and he very shaped as though 1m6f would be within range. Although a beating of Joshua Tree doesn't leap off the page, he could be one to keep on side, with further progress likely. (op 8-1 tchd 5-1)
Joshua Tree(IRE) was taken to race alone against the stands' rail and it was a move that paid off, racing on what was probably the best ground. He's been well travelled over the past ten months and is clearly still capable of running to a fairly high level. The new Arlington St Leger is his aim. (op 14-1)
Red Cadeaux has been running well against some of the best older middle-distance performers around of late, as well as bumping into Gold Cup winner Colour Vision earlier in the season, so on the face of it he was disappointing back in a less-competitive race. He did have a 3lb penalty to deal with, though, and ended up against the far rail from over 2f out (probably slowest ground), so shouldn't have this held against him. The Melbourne Cup remains the aim. (op 15-8)
Harris Tweed bypassed another crack at the Hardwicke for this, and the ground looked in his favour, but Liam Jones did too much too soon and he didn't get home. He can be given another chance. (op 9-4)
Sea Of Heartbreak(IRE) showed more than on her reappearance at York, although was still well held. She remains below last season's best. (op 20-1)
Modun(IRE) had been off since Meydan in March, missing an engagement at Newbury in April due to soft ground, and it's likely his performance here can be put down to the going. (op 10-1)
Dandino was disappointing when turned over at 4-7 here last time, and he ran poorly back up in grade faced with softer ground, finding little. (op 15-2 tchd 11-2)

4011 THREE CHIMNEYS E B F MAIDEN FILLIES' STKS 6f

3:35 (3:35) (Class 4) 2-Y-O **£6,469** (£1,925; £962; £481) **Stalls** Low

Form				RPR
	1		**Certify (USA)** 2-9-0 0 ... MickaelBarzalona 10 (Mahmood Al Zarooni) *racd centre: hld up: hdwy over 2f out: rdn to ld ins fnl f: r.o wl* **10/1**	98+
3	**2**	3	**Pearl Sea (IRE)**[13] 3560 2-9-0 0 ... JamieSpencer 19 (David Brown) *racd far side: led that gp tl over 4f out: chsd ldr: jnd centre gp over 3f out: rdn to ld and hung rt over 1f out: hdd and unable qck ins fnl f* **5/1**[2]	89
	3	2 ¾	**Shuruq (USA)** 2-9-0 0 ... FrankieDettori 11 (Saeed Bin Suroor) *racd centre: chsd ldrs: rdn over 1f out: styd on same pce fnl f* **11/4**[1]	81+
	4	nk	**Supernova Heights (IRE)** 2-9-0 0 ... KierenFallon 2 (Brian Meehan) *racd stands' side: chsd ldr: rdn and ev ch over 1f out: no ex ins fnl f* **10/1**	80+
4	**5**	2 ¼	**Royal Steps (IRE)**[84] 1466 2-9-0 0 ... MartinDwyer 12 (James Tate) *racd centre: hld up: hdwy over 1f out: styd on: nt trble ldrs* **20/1**	73
	6	½	**Lady Vermeer** 2-9-0 0 ... JimCrowley 14 (Ralph Beckett) *racd centre: overall ldr tl over 4f out: remained handy: shkn up over 1f out: wknd ins fnl f* **8/1**[3]	72+
24	**7**	1 ½	**Hasanan**[12] 3631 2-9-0 0 ... BrettDoyle 16 (Clive Brittain) *racd far side: s.i.s: plld hrd and sn trcking ldr: overall ldr over 4f out: jnd centre over 3f out: rdn and hdd over 2f out: wknd fnl f* **12/1**	67
4	**8**	nse	**Ziggy's Secret**[20] 3339 2-9-0 0 ... IanMongan 1 (Lucy Wadham) *racd stands' side: led that gp: overall ldr over 2f out: rdn and hdd over 1f out: wknd fnl f* **20/1**	67
	9	nk	**Emerald Sea** 2-9-0 0 ... TedDurcan 8 (Chris Wall) *racd centre: s.i.s: hld up: styd on ins fnl f: nvr nrr* **50/1**	67+
	10	½	**Lizzie Tudor** 2-9-0 0 ... WilliamBuick 6 (Andrew Balding) *racd centre: prom: rdn over 2f out: wknd over 1f out* **20/1**	65+
	11	1	**Mandeville (IRE)** 2-9-0 0 ... RichardHughes 20 (Richard Hannon) *racd far side: hld up: jnd centre over 3f out: rdn over 1f out: n.d* **16/1**	62
	12	1	**Tequila Sunrise** 2-9-0 0 ... MichaelHills 3 (Charles Hills) *s.i.s: racd stands' side: hld up: effrt over 1f out: sn wknd* **16/1**	59+
	13	¾	**New Fforest** 2-9-0 0 ... TomQueally 15 (Andrew Balding) *racd centre: chsd ldrs: effrt and nt clr run over 1f out: wknd ins fnl f* **12/1**	56
2	**14**	2 ¾	**Not Now Blondie**[29] 3046 2-9-0 0 ... AndreaAtzeni 4 (Chris Dwyer) *racd stands' side: chsd ldrs tl wknd over 1f out* **50/1**	48
	15	1 ¼	**Three Choirs (IRE)** 2-9-0 0 ... RyanMoore 9 (Richard Hannon) *racd centre: hld up: rdn and wknd over 2f out* **10/1**	44
	16	17	**Anna Law (IRE)** 2-9-0 0 ... JamesDoyle 13 (Charles Hills) *racd centre: plld hrd and prom: wknd over 2f out* **33/1**	
0	**17**	10	**Hawsies Dream**[12] 3634 2-9-0 0 ... GrahamGibbons 5 (Alan Bailey) *racd centre: hld up: wknd over 2f out* **200/1**	

1m 14.34s (1.84) **Going Correction** +0.30s/f (Good) **17 Ran SP% 130.5**
Speed ratings (Par 93): **99,95,91,90,87 87,85,85,84,84 82,81,80,76,75 52,39**
Tote Swingers: 1&2 £4.80, 1&3 £8.00, 2&3 £7.80 CSF £59.18 TOTE £14.10: £4.70, £2.30, £1.90; EX 74.70 Trifecta £266.30 Pool: £1,052.13 - 2.92 winning units..
Owner Godolphin **Bred** Hurstland Farm Inc Et Al **Trained** Newmarket, Suffolk

FOCUS
This maiden has been won by some nice fillies over the years including the Group-class Fantasia four years ago. There were plenty of interesting types lining up for this year's renewal, some with attractive pedigrees and a few already with solid form on the board, although the race was weakened by the withdrawal of the likely favourite Fleeting Smile. The form has still been rated very positively. The field split into three early, with four racing against the stands' rail and three up the far rail, whilst the largest group came up the middle. The three groups eventually merged and raced centre-to-stands' side. The time was 0.05 seconds faster than the colts in the July Stakes.

NOTEBOOK
Certify(USA), an $80,000 half-sister to a Grade 1 winning juvenile in the US, took this in great style and impressed with the way she moved into contention from the middle of the field and quickened clear after hitting the front over a furlong from home. It was a decent effort to record a faster time than the earlier Group 2 and she looks a very nice prospect. (op 11-1)
Pearl Sea(IRE) had the benefit of previous experience and very much caught the eye when third of 13 on last month's Doncaster debut. She was always handy and had every chance, but was dazzled by the winner's turn of foot. An ordinary maiden should be hers. (tchd 11-2 in a place)
Shuruq(USA), whose dam took the 2007 Challenge Stakes, represented last year's winning stable. She came through to hold every chance a furlong from home before her effort flattened out, and normal improvement should see her off the mark. (tchd 9-4 in places)
Supernova Heights(IRE), a half-sister to five winners over a variety of trips including the Group 3 winners Greek Renaissance and Side Saddle, showed good speed towards the nearside of the track until fading well inside the last. Better can be expected with this run under her belt. (op 12-1)
Royal Steps(IRE) showed plenty of promise on her debut when fourth of eight on the Rowley Mile in April and the form of that race has worked out well. She was noted doing some solid late work and there should be a race in her before too long. (op 16-1)
Lady Vermeer, a 32,000gns half-sister to two winners at 7f to 1m from the family of Orientor and Yeast, ran well for a long way in the centre group and can only improve for the experience. (op 11-1)
Hasanan had the edge in experience on her rivals and ran well when fourth of seven in a C&D Listed contest 12 days earlier. She showed up for a fair way, but the drop in trip may not have been ideal and she lacks the scope of many of these. (op 10-1)
Ziggy's Secret showed plenty of ability when fourth of 13 on her Goodwood debut last month and displayed decent speed against the stands' rail for a long way here. She can win races, but may need her sights lowering. (op 16-1)
Emerald Sea, out of a Canadian stakes winner from the family of the 1,000 Guineas winner Ravinella, was noted making some late progress and, as her stable was just 4-106 with 2yo newcomers in the past ten years, this was an encouraging debut.

4012 PORTLAND PLACE PROPERTIES CONDITIONS STKS 1m

4:05 (4:06) (Class 3) 3-Y-O

£9,337 (£2,796; £1,398; £699; £349; £175) **Stalls** Low

Form				RPR
-210	**1**		**Sovereign Debt (IRE)**[22] 3265 3-8-12 104 ... JamieSpencer 4 (Michael Bell) *hld up: swtchd rt over 2f out: hdwy and hung lft over 1f out: rdn to ld ins fnl f: r.o wl* **11/8**[1]	108+
214	**2**	2	**Mukhadram**[21] 3295 3-8-12 101 ... PaulHanagan 2 (William Haggas) *chsd ldrs: led 2f out: sn rdn: hdd and unable qck ins fnl f* **5/2**[2]	103+
0460	**3**	1 ¾	**Saigon**[23] 3239 3-9-6 107 ... KirstyMilczarek 5 (James Toller) *hld up: hdwy over 2f out: rdn over 1f out: styd on same pce* **9/1**	107
1300	**4**	½	**Eastern Sun (IRE)**[22] 3265 3-9-3 98 ... WilliamBuick 8 (John Gosden) *chsd clr ldr: tk clsr order over 3f out: led over 2f out: sn rdn and hdd: hung lft and no ex fnl f* **10/1**	103
5032	**5**	6	**Mister Music**[21] 3294 3-9-1 100 ... RyanMoore 1 (Richard Hannon) *hld up: rdn over 2f out: wknd over 1f out* **6/1**[3]	87
-260	**6**	3	**Crius (IRE)**[21] 3295 3-9-6 101 ... RichardHughes 6 (Richard Hannon) *led: racd keenly: clr tl over 3f out: hdd over 2f out: wknd and eased over 1f out* **12/1**	85

1m 41.6s (1.60) **Going Correction** +0.30s/f (Good) **6 Ran SP% 111.7**
Speed ratings (Par 104): **104,102,100,99,93 90**
Tote Swingers: 1&2 £1.70, 1&3 £2.10, 2&3 £3.60 CSF £4.92 TOTE £2.20: £1.40, £2.10; EX 4.30 Trifecta £25.10 Pool: £1,012.86 - 29.75 winning units..
Owner Lawrie Inman **Bred** Yeomanstown Stud **Trained** Newmarket, Suffolk

FOCUS
The defection of Gabrial left this looking a match, and the race played out the way the market suggested it would. In contrast to the earlier races, they raced far side. The form is Listed class, and makes sense.

NOTEBOOK
Sovereign Debt(IRE) endured a troubled passage in the Jersey (would likely have gone close) and simply possessed too much speed for his main market rival on this return to 1m. His change of pace will remain an asset and he looks capable of winning at Listed/Group 3 level. (op 15-8 after 9-4 in a place and 2-1 in places)
Mukhadram improved a good deal on his maiden form when fourth, not quite getting home, in a 1m2f Group 3 at Royal Ascot, and he had every opportunity on this drop in grade. It's likely a step back up in trip on better ground will prove his optimum conditions. (op 9-4)
Saigon, beaten just over 4l in a below-average running of the St James's Palace, stayed on well close home and runs like a horse worth trying at 1m2f. This was a good effort considering he was conceding 8lb to the front pair. (op 15-2 tchd 10-1)
Eastern Sun(IRE), conceding 5lb to the front pair, has had limitations exposed and shall remain difficult to place off his current rating. (op 11-1 tchd 12-1)

Mister Music didn't look good enough beforehand and was duly well held. (op 11-2 tchd 13-2)

4013 EGERTON HOUSE STABLES H'CAP 5f

4:40 (4:40) (Class 3) (0-90,90) 3-Y-0+ **£9,703** (£2,887; £1,443; £721) **Stalls** Low

Form RPR

5036 **1** **Jedward (IRE)**[12] 3608 5-9-2 **80** PaulHanagan 2 93
(Richard Fahey) *chsd ldrs: led over 3f out: rdn over 1f out: jst hld on* **13/2**[3]

5100 **2** *hd* **Pearl Blue (IRE)**[25] 3183 4-9-6 **84** GeorgeBaker 1 96+
(Chris Wall) *hld up: hdwy over 1f out: swtchd lft and r.o wl ins fnl f: jst failed* **5/1**[1]

00-5 **3** *3 1/4* **Edge Closer**[54] 2268 8-9-9 **87** SeanLevey 13 87+
(Tony Carroll) *chsd ldrs: rdn over 1f out: edgd rt and no ex wl ins fnl f* **10/1**

1100 **4** *nk* **Dancing Freddy (IRE)**[19] 3374 5-9-12 **90** (tp) SaleemGolam 4 89
(Richard Guest) *hld up in tch: rdn over 1f out: styd on same pce ins fnl f* **25/1**

-000 **5** *shd* **Medici Time**[27] 3127 7-9-3 **81** KierenFallon 19 80+
(Tim Easterby) *hld up: rdn 1/2-way: styd on ins fnl f: nt trble ldrs* **10/1**

0013 **6** *3/4* **Solemn**[25] 3188 7-9-12 **90** (b) RyanMoore 12 86
(Milton Bradley) *led: hdd over 3f out: rdn over 1f out: no ex ins fnl f* **9/1**

4132 **6** *dht* **Showboating (IRE)**[13] 3595 4-8-13 **77** (tp) FrankieDettori 9 73+
(Alan McCabe) *hld up: rdn over 1f out: r.o ins fnl f: nvr nrr* **11/2**[2]

01 **8** *1/2* **Rocket Rob (IRE)**[26] 3139 6-8-8 **72** StevieDonohoe 17 66
(Willie Musson) *hld up: r.o ins fnl f: nrst fin* **14/1**

116 **9** *3/4* **Cardinal**[14] 3541 7-8-10 **74** ShaneKelly 20 66
(Robert Cowell) *mid-div: hdwy 2f out: sn rdn: no ex ins fnl f* **10/1**

-100 **10** *3/4* **Long Awaited (IRE)**[27] 3127 4-9-9 **87** GrahamGibbons 5 76
(David Barron) *prom: rdn over 1f out: wknd ins fnl f* **10/1**

000- **11** *1 3/4* **Quality Art (USA)**[297] 6217 4-9-8 **86** J-PGuillambert 10 69
(Richard Guest) *chsd ldrs: rdn over 1f out: wknd ins fnl f* **50/1**

315 **12** *1/2* **Gorgeous Goblin (IRE)**[43] 2602 5-8-13 **77** (t) JamieSpencer 15 58
(David C Griffiths) *s.i.s: hld up: nvr on terms* **25/1**

-001 **13** *nk* **Le Toreador**[13] 3595 7-9-11 **89** (tp) PhillipMakin 16 69
(Kevin Ryan) *chsd ldrs: rdn 1/2-way: wknd ins fnl f* **16/1**

3015 **14** *2 1/4* **Taurus Twins**[27] 3127 6-9-10 **88** (b) TomQueally 3 60
(Richard Price) *chsd ldrs: drvn along 1/2-way: wknd fnl f* **16/1**

005 **15** *1/2* **Bertoliver**[13] 3595 8-8-13 **77** WilliamBuick 14 47
(Stuart Williams) *chsd ldrs: rdn 1/2-way: wknd and esed ins fnl f* **33/1**

59.71s (0.61) **Going Correction** +0.30s/f (Good) **15 Ran SP% 122.8**
Speed ratings (Par 107): **107,106,101,101,100 99,99,98,97,96 93,92,92,88,87**
Tote Swingers: 1&2 £9.50, 1&3 £19.60, 2&3 £19.40 CSF £38.03 CT £339.71 TOTE £7.80: £3.10, £2.60, £4.30; EX 51.20 TRIFECTA Not won..
Owner Dr Marwan Koukash **Bred** Halmex Ltd **Trained** Musley Bank, N Yorks

FOCUS
A competitive sprint handicap, but those drawn towards the nearside were at a major advantage with stall 2 beating stall 1. A clear personal best from the winner.

NOTEBOOK
Jedward(IRE) was without a win since her second start at three when trained by Charles O'Brien, but she loves to get her toe in so conditions were in her favour and her narrow defeat by Klynch at York two starts back is looking decent form now. However, it was bagging the stands' rail in front from her low draw that proved to be the key and she kept on finding just enough to last home by the skin of her teeth. She is entered in the DBS August HIT sales. (op 8-1)
Pearl Blue(IRE) was back down to the minimum trip after not getting home over 6f in her previous two starts and also likes to get her toe in. Held up towards the nearside, she finished strongly on meeting the rising ground and would have got there in another stride. (tchd 13-2 in a place)
Edge Closer, lightly raced in the past two seasons and without a win since August 2008, had exclusively raced over 6f in all 30 of his previous outings, but he tried something new on his second start for the yard. Considering he raced out towards the centre of the track, away from the front pair, it was some effort to put himself in with every chance and he will be of real interest back up in trip if he can be kept sound. (tchd 12-1)
Dancing Freddy(IRE) had found life much tougher off similar marks since winning twice on fast ground in May and although this was better, he was in the right place in racing prominently from a low draw.
Medici Time has dropped to a mark 3lb lower than winning over C&D just over a year ago and did well to finish where he did, as he was being shoved along to stay in touch at halfway. (op 14-1)
Solemn showed up for a while before fading and remains 7lb higher than when winning on testing ground at Sandown two starts ago. (op 5-1)
Showboating(IRE), beaten just under a length by Le Toreador (poorly drawn here) over C&D 13 days earlier and 3lb better off, stayed on late against the stands' rail and will be suited by a return to 6f. (op 5-1)
Rocket Rob(IRE), up 2lb after dead-heating at Bath last time, gave himself plenty to do from his high draw and his finishing effort was too little too late. He has gained all his turf wins on quicker ground. (tchd 12-1)
Cardinal was thwarted in his bid for a hat-trick off this mark at Warwick last time and can probably be excused this on account of the highest draw.
T/Jkpt: Not won. T/Plt: £2,395.60 to a £1 stake. Pool: £137,041.89 - 41.76 winning tickets.
T/Qpdt: £260.80 to a £1 stake. Pool: £12,546.81 - 35.60 winning tickets. CR

3539 WARWICK (L-H)

Thursday, July 12

4014 Meeting Abandoned - waterlogged

4020 - 4034a (Foreign Racing) - See Raceform Interactive

3429 CHEPSTOW (L-H)

Friday, July 13

4035 Meeting Abandoned - waterlogged

3604 CHESTER (L-H)

Friday, July 13

OFFICIAL GOING: Good to soft (soft in places; 6.6) changing to soft after race 2 (6.30pm)
Wind: Nil Weather: Heavy rain

4042 CHESHIRE OAKS H'CAP (FOR LADY AMATEUR RIDERS) 7f 122y

6:00 (6:01) (Class 5) (0-75,75) 4-Y-0+ **£3,951** (£1,215; £607) **Stalls** Low

Form RPR

4224 **1** **Cyflymder (IRE)**[14] 3559 6-9-11 **65** MissSBrotherton 13 73
(David C Griffiths) *chsd ldr tl over 5f out: remained prom: wnt 2nd again over 2f out: r.o for press to ld fnl 100yds: kpt on wl towards fin* **9/1**[3]

-054 **2** *nk* **My Single Malt (IRE)**[13] 3615 4-9-13 **72** MissLWilson(5) 6 79
(Julie Camacho) *chsd ldrs: rdn over 2f out: r.o to chal ins fnl 100yds: jst hld* **11/2**[1]

2521 **3** *3/4* **Hayek**[14] 3559 5-9-12 **66** (b) MissJCoward 14 71+
(Tim Easterby) *swtchd lft s: hld up: nt clr run and plenty to do over 1f out: sn mde prog: rdn and hung lft ins fnl f: fin strly* **13/2**[2]

6030 **4** *1/2* **Glenridding**[14] 3557 8-10-6 **74** MissEJJones 8 79
(James Given) *led: pushed along and kicked on over 2f out: rdn over 1f out: hdd fnl 100yds: eased whn no ex towards fin: sn lost 3rd pl* **14/1**

0240 **5** *4* **Spread Boy (IRE)**[5] 3888 5-9-2 **56** oh5 MissJRRichards 15 50
(Alan Berry) *midfield early: wnt prom over 5f out: rdn over 2f out: nt qckn: styd on same pce fnl f* **100/1**

6000 **6** *nk* **Keys Of Cyprus**[4] 3914 10-9-12 **66** MrsAdeleMulrennan 2 59
(David Nicholls) *midfield: hdwy over 1f out: styd on ins fnl f: nvr able to rch ldrs* **16/1**

-355 **7** *2 1/4* **Brave Battle**[6] 3843 4-9-1 **60** MissRSmith(5) 3 48
(Ron Barr) *midfield: rdn over 2f out: kpt on fnl f: nvr able to trble ldrs* **16/1**

5015 **8** *1* **Son Vida (IRE)**[22] 3311 4-10-4 **72** MissMMullineaux 10 57
(Alan Bailey) *in tch: lost pl 5f out: pushed along and sme hdwy into midfield over 3f out: no imp on ldrs: plugged on at one pce fnl f* **25/1**

0-45 **9** *1 1/2* **Justbookie Dot Com (IRE)**[15] 3544 4-10-0 **68** (v) MissHayleyMoore 9 50
(David Evans) *hld up: hdwy into midfield over 4f out: chsng ldrs on inner whn bdly hmpd and nrly uns rdr over 2f out: sn rdn and lost pl: wknd fnl f* **22/1**

-224 **10** *hd* **Silly Gilly (IRE)**[19] 3416 8-9-4 **63** MissVBarr(5) 12 44
(Ron Barr) *prom: rdn 2f out: sn wknd* **16/1**

0063 **11** *3 1/2* **Marksbury**[3] 3950 5-9-2 **56** oh5 (p) MissBeckyBrisbourne 11 28
(Mark Brisbourne) *hld up: hdwy into midfield 3f out: no imp on ldrs: wknd fnl f* **22/1**

0530 **12** *1 1/2* **Ra Junior (USA)**[41] 2692 6-9-2 **56** oh4 MissWGibson 4 25
(Paul Midgley) *hld up: u.p over 2f out: nvr a threat* **20/1**

0154 **13** *3/4* **Ibiza Sunset (IRE)**[31] 3016 4-9-12 **71** MissSKerswell(5) 5 38
(Brendan Powell) *hld up: hmpd jst after s: pushed along and hdwy 4f out: nvr trbld ldrs: wknd over 1f out* **10/1**

2001 **14** *3 1/4* **St Oswald**[11] 3709 4-10-6 **74** (v) MissLMasterton 1 33
(Alan Bailey) *hld up: struggling over 2f out: nvr on terms* **13/2**[2]

5260 **D** *6* **Illustrious Prince (IRE)**[13] 3615 5-10-7 **75** (v) MissAZetterholm 7
(Declan Carroll) *midfield early: wnt prom 5f out: rdn and wknd over 2f out: fin last: disqualified: jockey weighed-in light* **11/2**[1]

1m 42.41s (8.61) **Going Correction** +1.10s/f (Soft) **15 Ran SP% 119.1**
Speed ratings (Par 103): **100,99,98,98,94 94,91,90,89,89 85,84,83,80,74**
Tote Swingers 1&2 £10.20, 2&3 £6.10, 1&3 £5.80 CSF £52.89 CT £358.65 TOTE £13.50: £4.40, £2.70, £1.90; EX 70.30 Trifecta £377.80 Part won. Pool 510.65 - 0.10 winning units..
Owner Steve Young **Bred** Miss Laura G F Ferguson **Trained** Bawtry, S Yorks
■ Stewards' Enquiry : Miss E J Jones seven-day ban: failed to take all reasonable and permissable measures to finish third (tba)
Miss A Zetterholm one-day ban: weighed in 2lb light (tba)
Miss L Wilson four-day ban: careless riding (tba)

FOCUS
Rail between 6f and 1.5f moved out 3yds with a drop in at that point and consequently 10yds added to races of 5f, 13yds to races between 6f and 8f, 14yds to 10f race and 20yds to 12f race. A competitive looking renewal of this fair handicap, run at a strong pace. It paid to race handily. The winner rates up a length on recent form.

4043 IRVINGS SOLICITORS H'CAP 7f 2y

6:30 (6:30) (Class 5) (0-70,70) 3-Y-0+ **£3,881** (£1,155; £577; £288) **Stalls** Low

Form RPR

0004 **1** **Day Of The Eagle (IRE)**[18] 3439 6-9-10 **66** PaddyAspell 6 76
(Michael Easterby) *hld up: rdn and hdwy over 1f out: r.o ins fnl f: led towards fin* **16/1**

0332 **2** *1/2* **Homeboy (IRE)**[10] 3738 4-9-2 **58** JimCrowley 7 66
(Marcus Tregoning) *midfield: hdwy over 3f out: chsd ldrs over 2f out: led ent fnl f: hdd towards fin* **7/1**[3]

3210 **3** *1 1/2* **Viking Warrior (IRE)**[14] 3559 5-10-0 **70** TomEaves 3 74
(Michael Dods) *chsd ldrs: lost pl over 4f out: rdn to cl and chse ldrs over 1f out: swtchd rt ent fnl f: styd on and tried to chal sn after: outpcd by front two towards fin* **7/2**[2]

2010 **4** *3* **Steel Stockholder**[13] 3615 6-9-4 **67** RobertDodsworth(7) 4 63
(Mel Brittain) *hld up: pushed along and gd hdwy over 3f out: chalng fr over 2f out: no ex fnl 75yds* **16/1**

5032 **5** *1 1/2* **Ferdy (IRE)**[14] 3555 3-8-2 **52** FrannyNorton 10 41
(Paul Green) *w ldr: led over 5f out: rdn 2f out: hdd ent fnl f: wknd fnl 75yds* **10/1**

4000 **6** *3* **Legal Eagle (IRE)**[13] 3608 7-10-0 **70** (p) CathyGannon 2 54
(Paul Green) *midfield: rdn and outpcd over 2f out: kpt on ins fnl f: no imp on ldrs* **14/1**

0646 **7** *3 3/4* **Hoppy's Flyer (FR)**[35] 2879 4-9-4 **60** MickyFenton 12 34
(Paul Midgley) *hld up: hdwy over 3f out: rdn to chse ldrs 2f out: one pce over 1f out: eased whn wl btn ins fnl f* **20/1**

0400 **8** *1/2* **Methaaly (IRE)**[14] 3559 9-8-13 **55** (be) SeanQuinlan 5 27
(Michael Mullineaux) *hld up: struggling over 2f out: nvr a threat* **33/1**

0052 **9** *3 1/2* **Ocean Legend (IRE)**[16] 3485 7-10-0 **70** JoeFanning 8 33
(Tony Carroll) *chsd ldrs: ev ch 2f out: sn u.p: wknd 1f out* **9/1**

0021 **10** *2 3/4* **Rockme Cockney**[22] 3315 3-8-7 **60** (p) RaulDaSilva(3) 1 13
(Jeremy Gask) *led: hdd over 5f out: remained handy: rdn over 2f out: sn wknd: eased whn wl btn over 1f out* **9/4**[1]

1-00 **11** *24* **Chalk And Cheese (USA)**[14] 3589 3-8-13 **70** HannahNunn(7) 9
(Stuart Williams) *s.s: a wl bhd* **40/1**

0-00 **12** *20* **Theresnoneedfordat (IRE)**[14] 3555 3-9-0 **64**..........(b) SaleemGolam 14
(Stuart Williams) *unruly gng to post: in tch: gd hdwy to press ldr over 5f out: rdn over 3f out: wknd qckly over 2f out: t.o* **66/1**

1m 33.83s (7.33) **Going Correction** +1.10s/f (Soft)
WFA 3 from 4yo+ 8lb **12** Ran SP% **114.6**
Speed ratings (Par 103): **102,101,99,96,94 91,86,86,82,79 51,28**
Tote Swingers 1&2 £8.30, 2&3 £4.90, 1&3 £9.20 CSF £116.14 TOTE £13.30: £4.10, £3.10, £1.90; EX 87.80 Trifecta £520.60 Pool 914.60 - 1.30 winning units..
Owner S Hull, J Bryan & S Hollings **Bred** Swersky & Associates **Trained** Sheriff Hutton, N Yorks
■ Stewards' Enquiry : Jim Crowley two-day ban: used whip above permitted level (Jul 27-28)

FOCUS
The ground was changed to soft after this race. A fair handicap, run at a furious pace. The winner had come down a long way in the weights and will still be potentially well weighted after this.
Rockme Cockney Official explanation: trainer's rep said filly was unsuited by the good to soft (soft in places) ground

4044 IG MARKETS H'CAP 5f 16y
7:05 (7:06) (Class 3) (0-95,94) 3-Y-O **£8,821** (£2,640; £1,320; £660; £329) **Stalls** Low

Form RPR
413U **1** **Beau Mistral (IRE)**[13] 3608 3-8-6 **79**................................ CathyGannon 3 87
(Paul Green) *chsd ldrs: rdn over 1f out: r.o to ld wl ins fnl f: all out and jst hld on* **13/2**

036 **2** *shd* **O'Gorman**[13] 3613 3-8-4 **80**.. JulieBurke(3) 4 88+
(Kevin Ryan) *dwlt: outpcd in rr: rdn and hdwy over 1f out: r.o ins fnl f: finshed strly: jst denied* **11/4**[1]

5355 **3** *½* **Waseem Faris (IRE)**[13] 3613 3-8-0 **76**........................... RaulDaSilva(3) 8 82
(Mick Channon) *sn chsd ldrs: nt clr run over 1f out: sn burst through gap to ld: hdd wl ins fnl f: no ex towards fin* **7/1**

4540 **4** *1 ¾* **Pale Orchid (IRE)**[27] 3165 3-8-12 **85**.................................. JimCrowley 5 85
(David Evans) *hld up: n.m.r after 100yds: hdwy and effrt on outer over 1f out: one pce fnl 100yds* **9/1**

40-4 **5** *½* **Kool Henry (IRE)**[83] 1524 3-8-13 **86**.............................. DanielTudhope 2 84
(David O'Meara) *broke wl: lost pl after 1f: sn in rr: pushed along over 1f out: kpt on ins fnl f: no imp on ldrs* **5/1**[3]

4411 **6** *5* **El McGlynn (IRE)**[8] 3778 3-7-9 **75** 6ex......................... HannahNunn(7) 7 55
(Peter Salmon) *w ldr: rdn and pushed rt by rival over 1f out: wknd ent fnl f* **13/2**

1225 **7** *8* **Sonko (IRE)**[6] 3861 3-8-12 **85**.......................................(p) FrannyNorton 6 36
(Tim Pitt) *showed gd spd to ld: rdn and hdd over 1f out: sn wknd* **4/1**[2]

1m 5.92s (4.92) **Going Correction** +1.10s/f (Soft) **7** Ran SP% **112.5**
Speed ratings (Par 104): **104,103,103,100,99 91,78**
Tote Swingers 1&2 £3.70, 2&3 £5.20, 1&3 £7.00 CSF £23.89 CT £127.77 TOTE £6.00: £3.70, £1.50; EX 23.30 Trifecta £347.60 Pool 587.25 - 1.25 winning units..
Owner The Winsor Not Group **Bred** John McEnery **Trained** Lydiate, Merseyside

FOCUS
A decent sprint handicap, run at a furious pace, and a thrilling finish. The winner looks better than ever.

NOTEBOOK
Beau Mistral(IRE) just got the verdict. The 3yo, who had unseated at the start here last time, picked up well down the outside to gain a second course victory. She was forced to mount her challenge wider than was probably ideal but she clearly appreciates these conditions and was able to defy an 8lb higher mark than when successful over C&D last month. She is clearly progressive but will need to improve again if she's to add to her tally. (op 11-2 tchd 7-1)
O'Gorman, for howm things didn't go accordingly to plan on leaving the stalls, has to be considered an unlucky loser. His sire, Sleeping Indian, had a decent record with cut in the ground and he deserves plenty of credit for getting so close having been detached in the early stages. He would surely have scored had he not crossed the line with his head to one side and this was a definite step forward on what he'd achieved in his three previous runs this term. He should be given the chance to atone. (op 4-1, tchd 9-2 in a place)
Waseem Faris(IRE) wasn't beaten far and was another to perform well. He hasn't been able to add to his Bath maiden victory but is slipping to a handy mark. He would probably have preferred quicker ground. (op 8-1)
El McGlynn(IRE), a recent Haydock winner, went off too quickly. (op 9-2)
Sonko(IRE) went off too quickly. Official explanation: jockey said filly had no more to give (tchd 7-2)

4045 TETLEY'S BITTER CONDITIONS STKS 5f 16y
7:40 (7:44) (Class 2) 2-Y-O **£8,191** (£2,451; £1,225; £613) **Stalls** Low

Form RPR
3132 **1** **Lady Ibrox**[13] 3604 2-8-9 88... DaleSwift 2 87
(Alan Brown) *disp ld: def advantage over 2f out: abt 3 l clr ins fnl f: a doing enough whn advantage reduced towards fin* **15/8**[2]

142 **2** *¾* **Ask The Guru**[12] 3662 2-9-0 0.. JimCrowley 4 89
(Ralph Beckett) *chsd ldrs: rdn and outpcd over 2f out: kpt on to take 2nd over 1f out: abt 3 l down ins fnl f: styd on to cl towards fin: nvr able to chal wnr* **10/11**[1]

041 **3** *5* **Rat Catcher (IRE)**[23] 3286 2-8-11 79................................(p) TomEaves 1 68
(Tim Easterby) *disp ld tl over 2f out: sn unable to go w wnr: outpcd and lost 2nd over 1f out: no imp after* **6/1**[3]

6 **4** *4 ½* **Annie Besant**[51] 2402 2-8-6 0.. FrannyNorton 3 47
(David C Griffiths) *in rr: outpcd over 2f out: lft bhd over 1f out* **20/1**

1m 6.76s (5.76) **Going Correction** +1.175s/f (Soft) **4** Ran SP% **106.2**
Speed ratings (Par 100): **100,98,90,83**
CSF £3.84 TOTE £3.10; EX 4.20.
Owner Rangers Racing **Bred** D Simpson **Trained** Yedingham, N Yorks

FOCUS
Only a small field for this juvenile conditions event but they went a decent pace throughout. The first two were clear and the winner is progressing really well.

NOTEBOOK
Lady Ibrox had finished second at this course last time but, appearing to benefit from a more positive ride, she had just enough in reserve to fend off the late challenge of the odds-on favourite. A winner on fast ground at Carlisle last month, she looks to be improving and is clearly versatile in terms of ground. This wouldn't have done her nursery mark much good but she remains open to improvement and would have to be considered if lining up a race where she might be able to dominate. (tchd 7-4 and 2-1)
Ask The Guru was doing all his best work in the closing stages and will surely appreciate a return to 6f. He is by the same sire as the winner but didn't appear as at home on this testing surface. (op 5-6 tchd Evens)
Rat Catcher(IRE) looked to have something to find with the principals and, while running creditably, was firmly put in his place. He had won in first-time blinkers last time at Ripon but had only cheekpieces fitted here. It's too early to give up on him but he's clearly got his limitations. (op 13-2 tchd 5-1)
Annie Besant was always in the rear but wasn't entirely disgraced. A drop down in class will surely be necessary however. (op 22-1 tchd 16-1)

4046 MORSON GROUP/XCHANGING H'CAP 1m 2f 75y
8:10 (8:10) (Class 4) (0-85,83) 3-Y-O **£5,175** (£1,540; £769; £384) **Stalls** High

Form
-063 **1** **Paddyfrommenlo (IRE)**[35] 2898 3-8-12 **74**.................... FrannyNorton 5 84+
(J W Hills) *racd keenly: w ldr tl 7f out: racd in cl 2nd tl led 2f out: rdn and jnd jst over 1f out: gamely plld out ex fnl stride* **8/1**

6624 **2** *shd* **Deepsand (IRE)**[29] 3064 3-8-13 **75**.................................... DavidAllan 3 84
(Tim Easterby) *hld up: hdwy on outer 2f out: drew level and str chal fr jst over 1f out: hld fnl stride* **10/3**[2]

-615 **3** *9* **Cosmic Halo**[30] 3031 3-8-4 **66**.. PatrickMathers 6 58
(Richard Fahey) *trckd ldrs: effrt over 2f out: outpcd over 1f out: kpt on to take 3rd wl ins fnl f: no ch w front pair* **16/1**

-210 **4** *1* **Niceofyoutotellme**[22] 3296 3-9-7 **83**................................... JimCrowley 2 73
(Ralph Beckett) *hld up: hdwy 2f out: rdn to chse ldrs over 1f out: sn outpcd: no ex wl ins fnl f* **11/8**[1]

2150 **5** *1 ¾* **Priestley's Reward (IRE)**[41] 2716 3-8-10 **72**..............(v) CathyGannon 7 58
(Mrs K Burke) *in rr: pushed along briefly wl over 7f out: u.p over 2f out: wknd over 1f out* **20/1**

0323 **6** *12* **Tidal Way (IRE)**[8] 3774 3-8-12 **74**................................. MatthewDavies 9 38
(Mick Channon) *led: pushed along 3f out: hdd 2f out: rdn and wknd over 1f out* **5/1**[3]

-256 **7** *5* **Sardanapalus**[14] 3563 3-8-11 **76**.................................... JulieBurke(3) 4 30
(Kevin Ryan) *trckd ldrs: rdn and lost pl 2f out: sn wknd* **12/1**

2m 22.34s (11.14) **Going Correction** +1.175s/f (Soft) **7** Ran SP% **111.3**
Speed ratings (Par 102): **102,101,94,93,92 82,78**
Tote 1&2 £4.10, 2&3 £10.20, 1&3 £16.40 CSF £32.84 CT £405.15 TOTE £12.50: £4.40, £1.60; EX 25.80 Trifecta £284.40 Part won. Pool 384.41 - 0.50 winning units..
Owner Pat McDonagh **Bred** Pierce Molony **Trained** Upper Lambourn, Berks

FOCUS
A decent 3yo handicap with the first two clear. The favourite disappointed and with the ground testing it's hard to pin down what the form is worth.
Tidal Way(IRE) Official explanation: trainer's rep had no explanation for the poor form shown

4047 BETTOR.COM NURSERY 6f 18y
8:40 (8:43) (Class 4) (0-85,83) 2-Y-O **£4,851** (£1,443; £721; £360) **Stalls** Low

Form RPR
243 **1** **Bairam**[16] 3506 2-8-12 **74**... TadhgO'Shea 1 79
(Brian Meehan) *mde all: kicked on over 2f out: rdn whn edgd rt over 1f out: styd on to pull out more towards fin* **5/2**[1]

4210 **2** *1 ¾* **Hillbilly Boy (IRE)**[20] 3368 2-9-0 **83**................................ RyanWhile(7) 7 83
(Bill Turner) *w ldr tl outpcd over 3f out: wnt 2nd 2f out: rallied on inner to cl on wnr over 1f out: no ex fnl 75yds* **6/1**

3106 **3** *nk* **Sylvia Pankhurst (IRE)**[13] 3631 2-8-7 **69**...................... FrannyNorton 6 68+
(David C Griffiths) *bhd: outpcd over 3f out: nt clr run and checked over 1f out: sn rdn: styd on to take 3rd wl ins fnl f: gng on at fin but nvr gng to trble front two* **25/1**

410 **4** *1* **Party Royal**[24] 3240 2-9-5 **81**... JoeFanning 3 77
(Mark Johnston) *chsd ldrs: outpcd over 3f out: tried to get on terms w ldrs over 1f out: styd on same pce and no imp ins fnl f* **9/2**[3]

1 **5** *¾* **Slipstream Angel (IRE)**[13] 3627 2-8-4 **66**.................... PatrickMathers 5 65+
(Richard Fahey) *s.i.s and squeezed out whn n.m.r shortly after s: bhd and outpcd: styd on ins fnl f: nvr gng pce to get competitive* **5/2**[1]

220 **6** *3 ¾* **Pearl Noir**[24] 3242 2-8-11 **73**.. JimCrowley 2 55
(Scott Dixon) *racd keenly: chsd ldrs: moved upsides 3 wd over 4f out: unable to go w wnr over 2f out: sn lost 2nd: wknd over 1f out* **4/1**[2]

1m 21.52s (7.72) **Going Correction** +1.175s/f (Soft) **6** Ran SP% **113.5**
Speed ratings (Par 96): **95,92,92,90,89 84**
Tote 1&2 £3.30, 2&3 £10.40, 1&3 £8.70 CSF £18.28 TOTE £4.30: £2.00, £2.50; EX 19.00.
Owner Hamdan Al Maktoum **Bred** Shadwell Estate Company Limited **Trained** Manton, Wilts

FOCUS
A decent nursery, run at a strong pace. The runner-up is a pretty solid marker.

NOTEBOOK
Bairam justified solid market support with a dominant display. The gelded son of Hateef was given an aggressive ride and, having committed for home at halfway, kept on strongly to win a shade more cosily than the bare result suggests. He had excuses when disappointing on soft ground at Leicester (missed break) and clearly handled these conditions, despite his US pedigree. He showed more than enough pace to suggest that he wouldn't be inconvenienced by a return to the minimum trip, especially on a stiffer track. (op 9-2)
Hillbilly Boy(IRE) was considered good enough to run in the Chesham Stakes at Royal Ascot but this is much more his level. He stuck on gamely for pressure but is always likely to be vulnerable to improving type. (tchd 5-1 and 13-2)
Sylvia Pankhurst(IRE) is another that's been highly tried but she has her limitations based on this evidence. She was staying on at the finish but was flattered by her proximity to the winner. (tchd 22-1 and 33-1)
Slipstream Angel(IRE) was very easy to back and the writing was on the wall from an early stage. She was flat to the boards throughout and appeared ill at ease on this tight track. A step up in trip will surely follow. (op 13-8 tchd 11-4)
Pearl Noir Official explanation: jockey said clot slipped leaving stalls and then ran too freely

4048 CHESHIRE OAKS BEST DRESSED COUPLE H'CAP 1m 4f 66y
9:10 (9:10) (Class 5) (0-75,72) 3-Y-O+ **£3,881** (£1,155; £577; £288) **Stalls** Low

Form RPR
0515 **1** **Silver Tigress**[22] 3307 4-9-1 **59**...................................... PJMcDonald 1 67
(George Moore) *in tch: plld off rail 2f out: led 1f out: kpt on wl towards fin* **7/1**

3064 **2** *½* **Tobrata**[18] 3440 6-8-8 **59**... RobertDodsworth(7) 7 66
(Mel Brittain) *prom: w ldr 3f out and gng wl: led over 1f out: sn rdn and hdd: continued to chal: hld towards fin* **16/1**

3344 **3** *1 ¾* **Party Line**[13] 3628 3-9-1 **72**.. JoeFanning 10 76
(Mark Johnston) *hld up: bmpd over 2f out: rdn and hdwy over 1f out: styd on ins fnl f: no imp on front two* **11/4**[2]

3-13 **4** *¾* **Hydrant**[28] 3129 6-9-11 **72**.. AdamBeschizza(3) 6 75
(Peter Salmon) *led: hdd after 2f: remained prom: pushed along over 3f out: outpcd over 1f out: styd on and lugged lft wl ins fnl f* **9/4**[1]

0052 **5** *½* **Tenhoo**[10] 3728 6-9-1 **66**... JasonHart(7) 5 68
(Eric Alston) *stdd s: hld up: nt clr run and bmpd over 2f out: effrt and hdwy to chse ldrs over 1f out: one pce fnl 100yds* **4/1**[3]

6-40 **6** *½* **King's Counsel (IRE)**[23] 3290 6-9-9 **67**......................(v) DanielTudhope 8 69
(David O'Meara) *w ldr: led after 2f: rdn 2f out: hdd over 1f out: wknd fnl 100yds* **10/1**

-036 **7** *14* **Avison (IRE)**[30] [3029] 4-9-1 **59**........................ PatrickMathers 2 40
(Richard Fahey) *racd keenly: in tch tl wknd 2f out* **11/1**
2m 55.64s (17.14) **Going Correction** +1.25s/f (Soft)
WFA 3 from 4yo+ 13lb **7** Ran SP% **113.2**
Speed ratings (Par 103): **92,91,90,90,89 89,80**
Tote 1&2 £9.30, 2&3 £5.30, 1&3 £7.50 CSF £100.83 CT £379.56 TOTE £8.90: £2.10, £4.00; EX 73.10 Trifecta £156.50 Pool 516.19 - 2.44 winning units..
Owner A Crute & Partners **Bred** Mrs J M F Dibben & Mrs Amanda Brudenell **Trained** Middleham Moor, N Yorks
FOCUS
A fair handicap, but run at only a steady pace and muddling form.
T/Plt: £283.00 to a 1 stake Pool £99,787.21. 257.39 winning tickets T/Qpdt: £58.70 to a 1 stake. Pool £8,361.52. 105.3 winning tickets DO

3725 HAMILTON (R-H)
Friday, July 13
4049 Meeting Abandoned - waterlogged

3782 NEWBURY (L-H)
Friday, July 13
OFFICIAL GOING: Soft (heavy in places; 5.5)
Wind: Moderate ahead Weather: Patchy rain

4055 HIGHCLERE THOROUGHBRED RACING E B F MAIDEN FILLIES' STKS 6f 8y
1:40 (1:40) (Class 4) 2-Y-O **£4,560** (£1,357; £678; £339) **Stalls** Centre

Form RPR
1 **Amberley Heights (IRE)** 2-9-0 0........................ RichardHughes 8 76+
(Richard Hannon) *hld up in rr: hdwy: swtchd lft and hdwy ins fnl 2f and sn hit over hd w opponent's whip: drvn and qcknd to chse ldr ins fnl f: kpt on wl to ld fnl 25yds* **2/1**[1]
63 **2** *nk* **It's Taboo**[13] [3637] 2-9-0 0........................ DavidProbert 3 75
(Mark Usher) *led: pushed along fr 2f out: kpt on wl fnl f: hdd and outpcd fnl 25yds* **4/1**[2]
3 *1 3/4* **Elegant In Silk (USA)** 2-9-0 0........................ EddieAhern 9 70+
(William Haggas) *trckd ldrs: wnt 2nd 2f out: pushed along over 1f out: styd on same pce into 3rd ins fnl f* **7/1**
4 *3/4* **Sorella Bella (IRE)** 2-9-0 0........................ SamHitchcott 6 68+
(Mick Channon) *chsd ldrs: drvn and outpcd over 1f out: styd on wl again fnl 120yds* **7/1**
5 *3* **Linda's Icon** 2-9-0 0........................ ChrisCatlin 1 59
(Mick Channon) *sn rdn along and bdly outpcd fr 4f out: styd on appr fnl f: r.o strly ins fnl f: gng on cl home* **11/1**
5 **6** *nse* **Jathabah (IRE)**[23] [3282] 2-9-0 0........................ SebSanders 4 58
(Clive Brittain) *chsd ldr: chal over 2f out: wknd appr fnl f* **5/1**[3]
7 *2 1/2* **Byroness** 2-9-0 0........................ StevieDonohoe 7 51
(Heather Main) *in rr: rdn 2f out: a outpcd* **100/1**
0 **8** *1* **Michael's Song (IRE)**[48] [2499] 2-9-0 0........................ PatCosgrave 2 48
(Mick Channon) *chsd ldrs: rdn over 2f out: sn btn* **25/1**
9 *1 1/2* **Girl Of Cadiz** 2-9-0 0........................ PatDobbs 5 43
(Richard Hannon) *in rr: hdwy to get in tch 3f out: wknd 2f out* **16/1**
1m 21.02s (8.02) **Going Correction** +0.95s/f (Soft) **9** Ran SP% **114.1**
Speed ratings (Par 93): **84,83,81,80,76 76,72,71,69**
Tote Swingers: 1&2 £3.00, 1&3 £3.50, 2&3 £4.30 CSF £9.71 TOTE £3.00: £2.10, £1.30, £1.80; EX 9.50.
Owner Ms Elaine Chivers **Bred** Tinnakill Bloodstock & Alan Byrne **Trained** East Everleigh, Wilts
FOCUS
Rail moved out between 8f and 5f on Round course and races on Round course run over approximately 32m further than advertised. The going was soft, heavy in places. A fillies' maiden which was won by subsequent Prix Morny winner Silca's Sister in 2005. This didn't the strongest edition, but the first four pulled clear and the favourite scored from some way back on her debut to provide Richard Hannon with a third win in this race in the last five years. The form is rated cautiously given the conditions.
NOTEBOOK
Amberley Heights(IRE) was slowly away and took a while to find her rhythm but she found a surging run to overhaul an experienced rival on her debut. A 37,000gns half-sister to six winners including French/US 7f-1m1f (Listed) scorer Green Lady, she could improve significantly for the experience and holds entries in several valuable sales races. (op 5-2)
It's Taboo, a close third in a 6f Windsor maiden on her second start last time, made a bold bid near the stands' rail on this switch to soft ground but she was just run down in the closing stages. She looks an uncomplicated type and is related to four 5f-7f winners. (op 7-2)
Elegant In Silk(USA) travelled well near the pace for a long way before keeping on in a promising debut run. A 50,000gns purchase in April, she is a half-sister to winners in Japan, US and Argentina and could take some stopping in a similar race next time.
Sorella Bella(IRE), a 15,000euro half-sister to decent winners Thrust Control (6f-1m) and Whitby Jet (1m), ran green and didn't get the best of runs but she stayed on well in an encouraging debut run. She should improve next time. (tchd 6-1)
Linda's Icon was detached for most of the way but she caught the eye finishing well on her debut. She should know a lot more next time and is a Sixties Icon first foal of a tough winning sprinter. (op 10-1)
Jathabah(IRE) showed promise when a staying-on fifth of 14 in a 7f Kempton maiden on her debut last month but this Singspiel sister to a 1m-1m2f winner looked tapped for speed when the pace increased on this drop back to 6f. (op 11-2)

4056 HIGHCLERE THOROUGHBRED RACING E B F MAIDEN STKS 7f (S)
2:15 (2:15) (Class 4) 2-Y-O **£4,560** (£1,357; £678; £339) **Stalls** Centre

Form RPR
1 **Montiridge (IRE)** 2-9-3 0........................ RichardHughes 10 91+
(Richard Hannon) *in tch: hdwy 2f out: trckd ldr over 1f out: drvn to ld fnl 140yds: readily* **7/2**[2]
2 **2** *1 1/2* **One Word More (IRE)**[29] [3067] 2-9-3 0........................ WilliamCarson 6 86
(Charles Hills) *trckd ldrs: led ins fnl 2f: drvn appr fnl f: hdd and nt pce of wnr fnl 140yds* **11/4**[1]
3 *5* **Pythagorean** 2-9-3 0........................ GeorgeBaker 7 74+
(Roger Charlton) *s.i.s: in rr and t.k.h: pushed along and hdwy fr 2f out: green but styd on wl fnl f but nvr any ch w ldng duo* **6/1**[3]
434 **4** *3 3/4* **Ayaar (IRE)**[13] [3649] 2-9-3 0........................ SamHitchcott 9 64
(Mick Channon) *chsd ldrs: rdn over 2f out whn chsng ldng duo: no imp: wknd and lost 3rd ins fnl f* **7/2**[2]
6 **5** *2 1/2* **Linguine (FR)**[13] [3638] 2-9-3 0........................ DavidProbert 12 58+
(Charles Hills) *s.i.s: sn in mid-div: rdn over 2f out: styd on same pce* **28/1**
6 *2* **Colmar Kid (IRE)** 2-9-3 0........................ PatDobbs 1 53
(Richard Hannon) *in tch and rdn along 3f out: no imp on ldrs and kpt on same pce* **8/1**
462 **7** *1* **Kalicamix**[11] [3708] 2-9-3 0........................ ChrisCatlin 8 51
(Paul Cole) *led tl hdd ins fnl 2f: sn btn* **16/1**
8 *shd* **Gracious George (IRE)** 2-9-3 0........................ SeanLevey 5 50
(Jimmy Fox) *chsd ldrs: rdn 3f out: wknd ins fnl 2f* **150/1**
9 *3/4* **Imperial Spirit** 2-9-3 0........................ PatCosgrave 3 49+
(Mick Channon) *s.i.s: sn in mid-div: rdn 3f out: wkng whn hmpd and green jst ins fnl 2f* **50/1**
10 *4* **Banovallum** 2-9-3 0........................ LiamKeniry 13 39
(Sylvester Kirk) *s.i.s: in rr: rdn along: hung lft and green 3f out: no ch after* **40/1**
0 **11** *2 1/4* **Downright Dizzie**[20] [3368] 2-8-7 0........................ LeonnaMayor(5) 4 28
(Alastair Lidderdale) *chsd ldr over 3f: wknd qckly over 2f out* **25/1**
5 **12** *24* **Buxted's Choice (IRE)**[16] [3499] 2-9-3 0........................ StevieDonohoe 2
(Robert Mills) *plld hrd in tch tl wknd qckly 1/2-way* **40/1**
1m 31.81s (6.11) **Going Correction** +0.95s/f (Soft) **12** Ran SP% **117.2**
Speed ratings (Par 96): **103,101,95,91,88 86,85,84,84,79 76,49**
Tote Swingers: 1&2 £3.00, 1&3 £5.20, 2&3 £4.30 CSF £12.67 TOTE £4.80: £2.10, £1.60, £2.10; EX 14.20.
Owner M Clarke,J Jeffries,R Ambrose,B Reilly **Bred** Century Bloodstock **Trained** East Everleigh, Wilts
FOCUS
It was raining heavily. A useful maiden which was won by dual subsequent Group 2/3 winner Emerald Commander in 2009, and subsequent Dante second Ektihaam won a division of this contest last year. The pace was decent and a well-backed newcomer scored in good style from the experienced second who finished clear of the rest. The winner looks a pattern-class colt in the making.
NOTEBOOK
Montiridge(IRE) who was heavily backed in the morning, travelled well in the pack before cruising into the slipstream of the breakaway second and forging ahead in an impressive debut performance. A £55,000 yearling who is out of a German 1,000 Guineas runner-up, he looks another potentially smart 2yo for Richard Hannon and this Ramonti colt should stay a bit further than this in time. (op 11-4 tchd 4-1)
One Word More(IRE) made a promising debut when second in a C&D maiden last month. He was withdrawn after getting unruly in the stalls at Salisbury last time but he looked much more relaxed at the start here. Tucked away behind the leaders, he quickened away from most of his rivals approaching the furlong pole but he couldn't shake off a useful newcomer and was run down. This was another big run from a half-brother to useful four-time 5f winner Archers Road. He adds substance to the form and should be able to gain compensation next time. (op 3-1 tchd 7-2)
Pythagorean showed signs of inexperience before staying on strongly from some way back. This was a promising debut from a scopey Oasis Dream colt who is out of a 1m4f winning sister to Oaks second Flight Of Fancy. (op 13-2)
Ayaar(IRE) had strong claims on his 20-1 fourth of six in a Group 2 on testing ground in Ireland last month but he was probably flattered by his proximity in that steadily run 6.5f race and he couldn't sustain his effort back at 7f in maiden company. (op 4-1)
Linguine(FR) ran green before plugging on late on his second start. He should continue to improve and is a half-brother to a 7f winner on Fibresand. (op 33-1)
Colmar Kid(IRE) was a market springer in the morning but he looked very inexperienced before doing some late work from a long way back. (op 9-1)

4057 SHARES IN ISHI AMY @ CHRISBEEKRACING.COM FILLIES' H'CAP 1m 2f 6y
2:50 (2:50) (Class 4) (0-80,80) 3-Y-O **£4,075** (£1,212; £606; £303) **Stalls** Centre

Form RPR
4234 **1** **Play Street**[49] [2448] 3-8-0 **62**........................ HarryBentley(3) 3 79
(Jonathan Portman) *mde all: drvn and qcknd clr fr 2f out: styd on strly: unchal* **10/1**
2-12 **2** *4 1/2* **Varnish**[17] [3476] 3-9-5 **78**........................ RichardHughes 5 86
(Richard Hannon) *racd in 2nd tl over 5f out: chsd wnr again fr over 3f out: rdn and no imp fr 2f out but styd on wl for clr 2nd* **7/2**[2]
-120 **3** *8* **The Giving Tree (IRE)**[41] [2701] 3-9-7 **80**........................ PatDobbs 7 72
(Sylvester Kirk) *in rr: hdwy fr 3f out: rdn to chse ldng duo over 2f out but nvr any ch and sn lft in wl hld 3rd* **9/2**[3]
64-4 **4** *7* **Darling Lexi (IRE)**[13] [3616] 3-8-4 **63**........................ WilliamCarson 8 41
(Richard Fahey) *in rr: rdn and sme hdwy over 3f out: nvr on terms and no ch fr over 2f out* **11/1**
441 **5** *8* **Anya**[31] [3001] 3-9-0 **73**........................ DaneO'Neill 1 35
(Ed Walker) *chsd wnr tl rdn over 3f out: sn btn* **7/2**[2]
13 **6** *9* **Secret Quest**[37] [2820] 3-9-7 **80**........................ GeorgeBaker 2 24
(James Fanshawe) *trckd ldrs: wnt 3rd over 5f out tl rdn over 3f out and sn dropped away* **2/1**[1]
2m 18.32s (9.52) **Going Correction** +0.95s/f (Soft) **6** Ran SP% **113.4**
Speed ratings (Par 99): **99,95,89,83,77 69**
Tote Swingers: 1&2 £4.20, 1&3 £5.80, 2&3 £3.10 CSF £45.02 CT £181.16 TOTE £13.10: £4.90, £2.10; EX 49.70.
Owner Anthony Boswood **Bred** The Hon Mrs R Pease **Trained** Compton, Berks
FOCUS
An interesting handicap involving several unexposed improvers. The favourite was disappointing but a market springer put in a dominant front-running performance. The form is rated around the runner-up.
Secret Quest Official explanation: trainer's rep had no explanation for the poor form shown

4058 ROSE BOWL STKS - SPONSORED BY COMPTON BEAUCHAMP ESTATES LTD (LISTED RACE) 6f 8y
3:25 (3:25) (Class 1) 2-Y-O
£13,043 (£4,945; £2,474; £1,232; £618; £310) **Stalls** Centre

Form RPR
510 **1** **Master Of War**[24] [3240] 2-9-0 90........................ PatDobbs 4 95+
(Richard Hannon) *trckd ldr: slt ld 2f out sn hrd pressed: drvn to assert jst ins fnl f: edgd rt and styd on strly clsng stages* **7/2**[3]
31 **2** *1 3/4* **Boomshackerlacker (IRE)**[21] [3346] 2-9-0 0........................ PatCosgrave 2 90
(George Baker) *in tch: hdwy 3f out: chal fr 2f out tl jst ins fnl f whn outpcd by wnr: hung rt but hld on wl for 2nd clsng stages* **8/1**
2130 **3** *nk* **All On Red (IRE)**[21] [3326] 2-8-9 82........................ StevieDonohoe 1 84
(Tobias B P Coles) *stdd towards rr but in tch: rdn over 2f out: styd on wl fnl f to cl on 2nd cl home but no imp on wnr* **20/1**
141 **4** *shd* **Euxton Hall (IRE)**[11] [3695] 2-9-0 0........................ DavidNolan 5 89
(Richard Fahey) *led tl rdn and hdd 2f out: styd on same pce and edgd lft ins fnl f* **3/1**[2]

20 **5** *2* **Living Desert**[24] 3240 2-9-0 0 .... KirstyMilczarek 6 83
(James Toller) *rrd stalls and s.i.s: sn chsng ldrs: drvn and hung lft ins fnl 2f: wkng whn bmpd ins fnl f* **9/1**

21 **6** *1 ½* **Rhamnus**[36] 2852 2-9-0 0 .... RichardHughes 3 78
(Richard Hannon) *unruly in stalls: in rr: gd hdwy 3f out: rdn and btn 2f out* **6/4**[1]

1m 20.41s (7.41) **Going Correction** +0.95s/f (Soft) **6** Ran SP% **113.1**
Speed ratings (Par 102): **88,85,85,85,82 80**
Tote Swingers: 1&2 £4.90, 1&3 £6.10, 2&3 £4.50 CSF £30.30 TOTE £4.50: £2.00, £3.20; EX 29.90.
Owner M S Al Shahi **Bred** R J Cornelius **Trained** East Everleigh, Wilts

FOCUS
A Listed sprint which has produced a couple of subsequent Group 2 winners in recent seasons (Deportivo and Assertive), and Caspar Netscher has been a multiple Group winner since finishing second in this race last year. However, this didn't look a particularly strong renewal. The hot favourite was disappointing but his stablemate delivered. The third is perhaps the best guide.

NOTEBOOK
Master Of War had fair claims on the form of his Haydock win and respectable ninth in the Coventry Stakes last time. Always well positioned near the steady pace, he handled the conditions well and scored with authority to provide Richard Hannon with a fifth win in this race in the last nine years. A Compton Place colt, he has improved with each of his four runs and seems equally effective on fast and slow ground. (op 9-2)
Boomshackerlacker(IRE) beat a majority of unraced rivals in a 6f soft-ground Newmarket maiden on his second start last month. He had quite a bit to find stepped up to Listed company but he travelled well for a long way and showed a good attitude to hang on for second in another improved effort. He is learning to settle better with practice and has scope for further progress.
All On Red(IRE) battled well to snatch third from off the pace. She has had her limitations exposed in Listed/Group company since winning a maiden and novice event on slow ground in the spring but she looks a tough filly who is very effective on testing ground. (op 16-1)
Euxton Hall(IRE) added to his Haydock maiden win when landing the odds in a Pontefract conditions event 11 days earlier. He had solid form claims and was allowed to dictate but he had no answer when the challengers loomed up and may have been inconvenienced by the taxing conditions. (op 7-2 tchd 4-1)
Living Desert found life tough in the Coventry Stakes last time and his effort flattened out and he hung left in this Listed event. Official explanation: jockey said colt reared as stalls opened (op 14-1)
Rhamnus was just held in a fast-ground Newmarket maiden on debut before hammering his rivals on soft ground at Sandown last time. He was strong favourite but he compromised his chance by racing freely off the steady early pace and found a very limited response. Official explanation: jockey said colt became unsettled in stalls. (op 6-5)

4059 CHRISBEEKRACING.COM H'CAP — 5f 34y
4:00 (4:00) (Class 5) (0-70,70) 3-Y-O+ **£2,587** (£770; £384; £192) **Stalls** Centre

Form RPR

0031 **1** **Festival Dance**[24] 3243 4-9-1 **62** .... HarryBentley(3) 3 71
(Ron Hodges) *trckd ldrs: chal 2f out: slt ld appr fnl f: pushed out fnl 120yds* **7/1**[3]

0000 **2** *1* **Griffin Point (IRE)**[11] 3701 5-8-9 **53** .... (b[1]) StevieDonohoe 4 58
(William Muir) *led: jnd and rdn 2f out: narrowly hdd appr fnl f: outpcd by wnr fnl 120yds* **25/1**

3504 **3** *¾* **Pharoh Jake**[10] 3717 4-8-7 **51** oh5 .... SamHitchcott 5 54
(John Bridger) *chsd ldrs: rdn and kpt on in 3rd fr over 2f out: kpt on clsng stages but a hld by ldng duo* **25/1**

2252 **4** *3* **Whitecrest**[10] 3724 4-9-5 **70** .... WilliamTwiston-Davies(7) 2 62
(John Spearing) *chsd ldrs: rdn over 2f out: sn one pce* **5/2**[1]

0501 **5** *1* **Catalinas Diamond (IRE)**[31] 3006 4-9-5 **63** .... (t) GeorgeBaker 9 51
(Pat Murphy) *wnt rt s: in rr: sme hdwy 2f out: sn one pce* **7/1**[3]

0033 **6** *2* **Cape Royal**[10] 3724 12-9-7 **65** .... (tp) PatDobbs 6 46
(Milton Bradley) *in rr: pushed along 1/2-way: styd on same pce fr over 1f out* **9/1**

4455 **7** *1 ¾* **Welsh Inlet (IRE)**[10] 3724 4-9-10 **68** .... SeanLevey 7 43
(John Bridger) *in tch whn rdn 1/2-way: sn outpcd* **12/1**

3452 **8** *1 ¾* **The Wee Chief (IRE)**[12] 3660 6-9-11 **69** .... DaneO'Neill 13 38
(Jimmy Fox) *bmpd s: sme hdwy 1/2-way: sn shkn up and btn* **4/1**[2]

5020 **9** *½* **Madame Kintyre**[17] 3477 4-9-6 **64** .... JamesMillman 1 31
(Rod Millman) *in tch: rdn 1/2-way and sn wknd* **8/1**

0036 **10** *29* **Colourbearer (IRE)**[17] 3467 5-8-12 **56** .... (bt[1]) WilliamCarson 11
(Milton Bradley) *bmpd s: bhd: racd alone stands' side: no ch fr 1/2-way: t.o* **10/1**

1m 6.22s (4.82) **Going Correction** +0.95s/f (Soft)
WFA 3 from 4yo+ 5lb **10** Ran SP% **119.2**
Speed ratings (Par 103): **99,97,96,91,89 86,83,81,80,33**
Tote Swingers: 1&2 £32.10, 1&3 £13.30, 2&3 £26.60 CSF £166.69 TOTE £7.40: £2.70, £8.70, £4.90; EX 217.90.
Owner Mrs M Watt A Midgley & K Meredith **Bred** M Watt & Exors Of The Late Miss J John **Trained** Charlton Mackrell, Somerset

FOCUS
An ordinary sprint handicap. Most of the runners raced down the centre of the track and the hold-up performers couldn't get involved. The winner built on her Brighton victory.

4060 OAKLEY COACHBUILDERS H'CAP — 1m 2f 6y
4:35 (4:35) (Class 3) (0-95,94) 3-Y-O+ **£6,536** (£1,957; £978; £489; £244; £122) **Stalls** Centre

Form RPR

0-34 **1** **Little Rocky**[34] 2932 4-9-6 **86** .... DaneO'Neill 5 97
(David Simcock) *sn led: hung rt to stands' side ins fnl 2f: drvn out fnl f* **9/4**[2]

2220 **2** *1* **Troopingthecolour**[27] 3163 6-9-7 **94** .... (t) WilliamTwiston-Davies(7) 4 101
(Steve Gollings) *in tch: drvn and hdwy over 2f out: styd on to chse wnr fnl f but no imp* **2/1**[1]

1- **3** *6* **War Singer (USA)**[80] 5-9-13 **93** .... (t) EddieAhern 3 88
(David Pipe) *trckd ldrs 5f out: drvn to chse wnr ins fnl 2f: wknd into 3rd fnl f* **8/1**

1-00 **4** *4* **Sandbanks Sizzler (IRE)**[34] 2932 4-8-11 **82** .... (t[1]) JamesRogers(5) 1 69
(Ralph Beckett) *sn chsng ldrs and hmpd on ins after 2f: chsd wnr over 3f out: hrd rdn over 2f out: sn btn* **8/1**

-154 **5** *4 ½* **Aldwick Bay (IRE)**[28] 3121 4-9-4 **84** .... RichardHughes 2 62
(Richard Hannon) *stdd in rr: pushed along and brief effrt over 2f out: sn btn* **9/2**[3]

0 **6** *41* **Provisional**[97] 1213 4-9-5 **85** .... FergusSweeney 6
(Martyn Meade) *chsd wnr: rdn 3f out: sn btn: eased whn no ch fnl f* **16/1**

2m 19.37s (10.57) **Going Correction** +0.95s/f (Soft) **6** Ran SP% **110.4**
Speed ratings (Par 107): **95,94,89,86,82 49**
Tote Swingers: 1&2 £1.80, 1&3 £2.90, 2&3 £3.40 CSF £6.90 TOTE £3.10: £1.80, £1.40; EX 5.70.

Owner C J Murfitt **Bred** C J Murfitt **Trained** Newmarket, Suffolk
■ Stewards' Enquiry : Dane O'Neill two-day ban: careless riding (Jul 27-28)

FOCUS
The two market leaders pulled clear in this steadily run handicap. The winner reversed Newmarket form with the second but it's hard to be too positive about this race.

NOTEBOOK
Little Rocky set the pace and battled bravely to record a second win despite hanging right towards the stands' rail. He has been very consistent on good and slower ground in handicaps since his Hamilton maiden win in May last year and should continue to run well but this was not a strong race for the grade and things will be tougher off a higher mark next time. (tchd 2-1)
Troopingthecolour didn't quite get home over 1m4f at York last time but he quickly got back near his best with a good run returned to his optimum trip. He has finished runner-up four times this season but he is edging up the weights without winning. (op 5-2)
War Singer(USA) had a record of 5-8 in minor company on the Flat in France for Jean-Claude Rouget but he didn't really progress in four hurdles runs for this yard during the winter/spring and his promising effort petered out on this switch back to the Flat after 80 days off. (op 9-1 tchd 13-2)
Sandbanks Sizzler(IRE) ended last season with a runaway win in a 1m2f Epsom maiden but he has shown little with and without equipment in three handicaps this year. (op 13-2 tchd 9-1)
Aldwick Bay(IRE) didn't find much when the pace increased and was well beaten. He is not easy to predict but he is suited by chasing a stronger pace and could bounce back if things go his way next time. (op 4-1 tchd 7-2)

4061 CHRIS BEEK RACING APPRENTICE H'CAP — 1m 3f 5y
5:10 (5:10) (Class 5) (0-75,75) 4-Y-O+ **£2,587** (£770; £384; £192) **Stalls** Centre

Form RPR

4451 **1** **Shades Of Grey**[8] 3782 5-9-2 **72** 6ex .... RyanTate(5) 13 86
(Clive Cox) *in rr: rdn and hdwy over 2f out: kpt on to ld 1f out: drvn clr fnl f* **9/4**[1]

013- **2** *5* **Dancing Primo**[280] 6676 6-9-2 **72** .... MatthewHopkins(5) 8 77
(Mark Brisbourne) *in tch: hdwy over 3f out: led 2f out: sn rdn: hdd 1f out: sn outpcd by wnr but kpt on for clr 2nd* **11/1**

3611 **3** *5* **Bute Street**[27] 3143 7-8-10 **64** .... PhilipPrince(3) 9 60
(Ron Hodges) *chsd ldrs: drvn and ev ch fr over 2f out: wknd over 1f out* **13/2**[2]

-211 **4** *2 ½* **Know No Fear**[10] 3723 7-8-12 **70** 6ex .... (p) SemiraPashai(7) 11 62
(Alastair Lidderdale) *t.k.h and sn led: styd far side turning into home st but kpt ld and jnd main gp 3f out: hdd 2f out: wknd appr fnl f* **10/1**

61/ **5** *½* **Jolly Roger (IRE)**[17] 6571 5-9-3 **75** .... AidenBlakemore(7) 6 66
(Tony Carroll) *in rr: pushed along and styd on fr over 2f out: nvr rchd ldrs* **13/2**[2]

0534 **6** *2 ¾* **Nibani (IRE)**[10] 3723 5-8-11 **69** .... (p) Leah-AnneAvery(7) 3 55
(Alastair Lidderdale) *s.i.s: in rr: sme hdwy 3f out: nvr gng pce to rch ldrs* **14/1**

-244 **7** *nk* **Henry San (IRE)**[29] 3077 5-8-10 **66** .... DanielCremin(5) 2 51
(Alan King) *in tch: hdwy 4f out: in tch 3f out: wknd fr 2f out* **8/1**[3]

5500 **8** *2 ½* **Diddums**[10] 3721 6-8-0 **56** oh4 .... RobertTart(5) 5 37
(Alastair Lidderdale) *in rr: mod prog 3f out: nvr a threat* **33/1**

5 **9** *4 ½* **Belleau (IRE)**[39] 2755 4-8-10 **61** .... NoelGarbutt 4 34
(Matt Sheppard) *mid-div: pushed along 4f out: wknd fr 3f out* **33/1**

3-36 **10** *2 ½* **Foxhaven**[14] 3574 10-9-7 **72** .... (v) ThomasBrown 12 40
(Patrick Chamings) *chsd ldrs: wknd qckly over 2f out* **10/1**

002- **11** *5* **Wordiness**[267] 6969 4-9-0 **65** .... ThomasGarner 7 24
(Seamus Durack) *bhd most of way* **20/1**

1000 **12** *31* **Admirable Duque (IRE)**[20] 3400 6-9-5 **70** .... SophieSilvester 1
(Dominic Ffrench Davis) *chsd ldrs over 6f: t.o* **20/1**

0005 **13** *1 ¼* **Polly Adler**[86] 1443 5-7-12 **56** oh7 .... (v) JeanVanOvermeire(7) 10
(Alastair Lidderdale) *chsd ldr to 4f out: wknd qckly over 3f out: t.o* **50/1**

2m 32.86s (11.66) **Going Correction** +0.95s/f (Soft) **13** Ran SP% **119.1**
Speed ratings (Par 103): **95,91,87,85,85 83,83,81,78,76 72,50,49**
Tote Swingers: 1&2 £6.50, 1&3 £4.70, 2&3 £7.20 CSF £26.24 CT £145.64 TOTE £3.00: £1.30, £3.70, £2.30; EX 30.00.
Owner Dr and Mrs John Merrington **Bred** Theakston Stud **Trained** Lambourn, Berks

FOCUS
They went a steady pace in this apprentice handicap, run in bad ground. The well-backed favourite scored in style under a waiting ride and rates another personal best. They finished strung out.
T/Plt: £353.00 to a £1 stake. Pool: £54,852.00 - 113.42 winning tickets. T/Qpdt: £227.50 to a £1 stake. Pool: £4,152.00 - 13.50 winning tickets. ST

4007 NEWMARKET (R-H)
Friday, July 13

OFFICIAL GOING: Soft (overall 6.0, stands side 6.2; centre 6.2; far side 5.8)
Wind: Light across Weather: Overcast

4062 PIPER-HEIDSIECK E B F FILLIES' H'CAP — 7f
1:20 (1:20) (Class 2) (0-100,99) 3-Y-O
£12,450 (£3,728; £1,864; £932; £466; £234) **Stalls** Low

Form RPR

-530 **1** **Free Verse**[15] 3542 3-8-3 **86** ow1 .... BrendanPowell(5) 2 100
(Richard Hannon) *hld up in tch: n.m.r and led over 1f out: rdn clr ins fnl f* **8/1**

-221 **2** *4 ½* **Riot Of Colour**[16] 3507 3-8-6 **84** .... RichardKingscote 11 86
(Ralph Beckett) *hld up in tch: racd keenly: rdn and ev ch over 1f out: hung lft ins fnl f: wkng whn hung rt towards fin* **4/1**[1]

03 **3** *1 ½* **Savanna Days (IRE)**[8] 3785 3-8-2 **80** .... TadhgO'Shea 15 78
(Mick Channon) *hld up: hdwy 1/2-way: rdn over 2f out: ev ch over 1f out: hmpd and wknd ins fnl f: edgd rt nr fin* **7/1**[3]

2522 **4** *½* **Tartiflette**[27] 3160 3-8-6 **84** .... LukeMorris 8 81
(Ed McMahon) *s.i.s: hld up: hdwy and nt clr run over 1f out: r.o ins fnl f: nvr trbld ldrs* **9/2**[2]

4030 **5** *nk* **Responsive**[20] 3393 3-8-4 **82** .... (b[1]) KieranO'Neill 14 78
(Hughie Morrison) *trckd ldrs: plld hrd: led over 2f out: rdn and hdd over 1f out: wknd ins fnl f: n.m.r towards fin* **16/1**

6-30 **6** *1 ½* **Hello Glory**[23] 3270 3-9-1 **93** .... JamieSpencer 1 85
(David Simcock) *chsd ldrs: rdn over 2f out: edgd rt and ev ch over 1f out: wknd ins fnl f* **10/1**

360- **7** *2 ½* **Illaunglass (IRE)**[342] 4803 3-9-7 **99** .... RyanMoore 7 85
(Jeremy Noseda) *prom: outpcd 3f out: n.d after* **10/1**

4323 **8** *shd* **Wahylah (IRE)**[11] 3696 3-8-2 **80** .... SilvestreDeSousa 10 66
(Clive Brittain) *hld up: hdwy over 2f out: rdn and wknd over 1f out* **12/1**

1-0 **9** *7* **Cardigan (IRE)**[21] 3328 3-8-10 **88** .... PaulHanagan 4 55
(William Haggas) *led over 4f: hmpd and wknd over 1f out* **10/1**

4053 **10** *6* **Roger Sez (IRE)**[15] 3542 3-9-5 **97** .... (p) TedDurcan 3 49
(Tim Easterby) *chsd ldrs: lost pl 4f out: rdn and wknd 2f out: eased ins fnl f* **9/1**

5110 **11** *21* **Abi Scarlet (IRE)**[21] 3342 3-8-8 **86** ow1 .... DarryllHolland 6
(Hughie Morrison) *chsd ldrs: pushed along over 4f out: wknd 3f out: eased: t.o* **40/1**

1m 27.58s (1.88) **Going Correction** +0.425s/f (Yiel) **11** Ran SP% **115.1**
Speed ratings (Par 103): **106,100,99,98,98 96,93,93,85,78 54**
Tote Swingers: 1&2 £8.10, 1&3 £9.80, 2&3 £6.20 CSF £39.09 CT £241.22 TOTE £9.60: £3.10, £2.10, £2.70; EX 53.10 Trifecta £585.20 Part won. Pool: £790.81 - 0.10 winning units..
Owner The Queen **Bred** The Queen **Trained** East Everleigh, Wilts

FOCUS
Following 18mm of rain overnight the ground was described as soft (GoingStick 6.0; Stands' side 6.2; Centre 6.2; Far side 5.8). The far side course was used, and the re-positioning of the bend into the home straight increased the distance of the 1m2f race by 18m. Jockey Brendan Powell described the ground "on the soft side of good, but no worse". They didn't go much of an early gallop in this fillies' handicap, and they headed towards the stands' side rail, which had proved an advantage the previous day. Decent form, with a clear personal best from the winner.

NOTEBOOK
Free Verse, whose rider put up 1lb overweight, got a nice lead into the race on the rail, quickened well between horses when the gap came, and ran on strongly up the hill to win well. The drop in grade suited her (eighth in Listed company last time) and clearly she's very much at home when the ground is testing. If she continues to progress she might still grab a bit of black type when conditions allow. (op 9-1)
Riot Of Colour didn't have the benefit of the rail like the winner, but she was comprehensively beaten into second in the end. Consistent in maiden company, this was probably a little step up. (op 9-2 tchd 5-1)
Savanna Days(IRE) had the worst of the draw and was stuck out wide for much of the race. She didn't do badly in the circumstances and, as another consistent type, helps set a level for the form. (op 15-2 tchd 8-1)
Tartiflette again didn't really have the race run to suit and was finishing all too late. A stronger pace will suit her, but it remains open to question how much she really wants it. (tchd 5-1)
Responsive is another who could have done with them going quicker early as she was a bit keen out wide in the first-time blinkers, but this trip might just stretch her on ground this soft anyway. (op 12-1)
Hello Glory raced close to the leader, one off the rail, and had no real excuse. She looks handicapped up to her very best. (op 11-1)
Illaunglass(IRE), off the track since disappointing in the Sweet Solera last August, is entitled to come on for this. (tchd 9-1)
Wahylah(IRE) should appreciate getting back on a faster ground. (op 14-1 tchd 16-1)
Roger Sez(IRE) Official explanation: jockey said filly never travelled

4063 BETFRED "THE BONUS KING" STKS (HERITAGE H'CAP) 6f

1:50 (1:53) (Class 2) (0-105,101) 3-Y-O

£62,250 (£18,640; £9,320; £4,660; £2,330; £1,170) **Stalls** Low

Form RPR

0106 **1** **Fulbright**[6] 3878 3-9-2 **96** .... SilvestreDeSousa 3 107
(Mark Johnston) *chsd stands' side ldrs: led and overall ldr over 1f out: kpt on strly fnl f: 1st of 7 in gp* **10/1**

-242 **2** *3/4* **Place In My Heart**[16] 3486 3-8-9 **89** .... MickaelBarzalona 6 98
(George Baker) *chsd stands' side ldrs: drvn and edgd lft 2f out: chsd wnr fnl f: kpt on: hld towards fin: 2nd of 7 in gp* **10/1**

0-50 **3** *1 1/4* **Gatepost (IRE)**[86] 1457 3-9-1 **95** .... JamieSpencer 1 100
(Richard Fahey) *disp ld stands' side to over 1f out: hung lft: kpt on same pce ins fnl f: 3rd of 7 in gp* **14/1**

0206 **4** *1 3/4* **Big Note (IRE)**[42] 2659 3-9-0 **94** .... JimmyFortune 13 93
(Andrew Balding) *prom centre: rdn and effrt over 2f out: kpt on same pce ins fnl f: 1st of 9 in gp* **22/1**

2453 **5** *3/4* **Mr Red Clubs (IRE)**[21] 3348 3-9-1 **95** .... ShaneKelly 20 92
(Tim Pitt) *chsd centre ldrs: rdn and ev ch over 1f out: outpcd fnl f: 2nd of 9 in gp* **14/1**

1-5 **6** *2* **Piri Wango (IRE)**[22] 3294 3-9-3 **97** .... FrankieDettori 5 88+
(G M Lyons, Ire) *t.k.h: hld up stands' side: rdn and outpcd over 2f out: kpt on fnl f: nvr able to chal: 4th of 7 in gp* **4/1**[1]

1423 **7** *nse* **Glen Moss (IRE)**[27] 3165 3-8-10 **90** .... MichaelHills 7 80
(Charles Hills) *disp ld stands' side to over 1f out: edgd lft and sn btn: 5th of 7 in gp* **6/1**[3]

-210 **8** *1* **Mince**[41] 2713 3-9-1 **95** .... JamesDoyle 4 82
(Roger Charlton) *hld up stands' side: drvn over 2f out: no imp fr over 1f out: 6th of 7 in gp* **9/2**[2]

-106 **9** *3/4* **Accession (IRE)**[55] 2276 3-9-1 **95** ....(b[1]) WilliamBuick 18 80
(Clive Cox) *prom centre: rdn along over 2f out: no ex fr over 1f out: 3rd of 9 in gp* **10/1**

0016 **10** *4 1/2* **Muaamara**[20] 3396 3-8-11 **91** .... MartinHarley 17 61+
(Mick Channon) *dwlt: bhd centre: rdn and hdwy wl over 1f out: nvr able to chal: 4th of 9 in gp* **20/1**

-030 **11** *1 1/4* **Semayyel (IRE)**[23] 3270 3-8-12 **92** ....(b[1]) NeilCallan 14 58
(Clive Brittain) *t.k.h: led and overall ldr centre: hdd over 1f out: sn btn: 5th of 9 in gp* **33/1**

100- **12** *1/2* **Diamondhead (IRE)**[265] 7026 3-8-13 **93** .... MartinDwyer 12 58
(Brian Meehan) *in tch centre: drvn and outpcd over 2f out: sn btn: 6th of 9 in gp* **25/1**

1520 **13** *3/4* **Dam Beautiful**[27] 3165 3-8-13 **93** .... TomEaves 15 55
(Kevin Ryan) *midfield centre: hung lft and outpcd over 2f out: n.d after: 7th of 9 in gp* **40/1**

0-40 **14** *1 1/4* **Rebellious Guest**[23] 3265 3-9-5 **99** .... TomQueally 10 57
(George Margarson) *hld up centre: drvn along 1/2-way: btn fnl 2f: 8th of 9 in gp* **9/1**

5026 **15** *hd* **Last Bid**[27] 3165 3-9-0 **94** .... TedDurcan 19 52
(Tim Easterby) *midfield centre: drvn wl over 2f out: sn struggling: last of 9 in gp* **50/1**

-004 **16** *25* **Bayleyf (IRE)**[27] 3158 3-9-2 **96** .... LukeMorris 9
(John Best) *prom stands' side tl rdn: edgd lft and wknd over 2f out: lost tch over 1f out: eased: last of 7 in gp* **33/1**

1m 13.68s (1.18) **Going Correction** +0.425s/f (Yiel) **16** Ran SP% **126.3**
Speed ratings (Par 106): **109,108,106,104,103 100,100,98,97,91 90,89,88,86,86 53**
Tote Swingers: 1&2 £19.60, 1&3 £28.60, 2&3 £33.90 CSF £102.11 CT £918.21 TOTE £11.70: £3.50, £2.80, £3.30, £5.40; EX 171.10 Trifecta £837.10 Part won. Pool: £1,131.26 - 0.10 winning units..
Owner Sheikh Hamdan Bin Mohammed Al Maktoum **Bred** R F And S D Knipe **Trained** Middleham Moor, N Yorks

FOCUS
The winning time was 3.48 seconds above standard, suggesting the ground wasn't as soft as expected. A valuable prize for this competitive handicap, with the top-weight 6lb below the ceiling, and it's feasible Group race sprinters can emerge, such as Total Gallery who won this before winning the Prix de L'Abbaye. The form has been taken at face value. The large field split into two groups leaving the stalls. The majority raced centre-field, somewhat surprisingly after the winner of the first came down the stands' rail. Only seven runners followed that route. The groups merged after about 2 1/2f. Indeed the first, second, third and sixth home were amongst the stands' side group.

NOTEBOOK
Fulbright, racing closest to the stands' rail, showed a good turn of foot from 2f out, and this previous course winner was in command thereafter. He came up against a well handicapped horse at Sandown last time and looked to enjoy the return to sprinting. However, one must question whether a track bias proved the defining edge. The winner is still quoted at 33-1 for the Betfred Mile at Glorious Goodwood by the sponsors. (op 12-1)
Place In My Heart, a lightly-raced filly, put in a career-best performance. She had stamina doubts coming into the race, but saw the trip out well and may head to a sprint handicap at Glorious Goodwood (entered for the Stewards' Cup). She will appreciate better ground. (op 12-1 tchd 9-1)
Gatepost(IRE) disputed the lead on the stands' side and showed a much improved effort. He has plenty of ability and it appears the gelding operation and change of stable has worked well. Official explanation: jockey said gelding hung left throughout (tchd 16-1)
Big Note(IRE), a strong puller, settled well in this bigger field. Racing prominently in the centre-field group, he came under pressure 2f out but to his credit battled on well to keep fourth. Forget his run at Epsom where he didn't handle the course, this was an improved effort wearing the hood and he could pop up in a big-race handicap before the end of the season. (op 20-1 tchd 25-1)
Mr Red Clubs(IRE), a five-time winner on the AW during the winter, came with his challenge far side at the 2f pole and led briefly. He didn't get home afterwards, but his performance can be upgraded as he raced on the unfavoured side of the track. (op 12-1)
Piri Wango(IRE), a dual winner on the Polytrack at Dundalk, wasn't beaten far in the Britannia. He got outpaced and ran on well, but was never going to get any nearer to the front. He is unexposed after only five starts and looks to have more to offer in handicaps, possibly over 7f. (op 7-1)
Glen Moss(IRE), well-backed, has been most consistent in three turf starts this term. He disputed the lead on the stands' side, but had no more to give when push came to shove inside the final furlong. His best runs to date have been on better ground. (op 8-1)
Mince was fancied to improve on her trainer's good record (2-3) in the race. She had been progressive in winning on the Rowley Mile previously, but has now run twice below that form. A 25lb hike from when first winning in handicaps looks to have stopped any more progress for now, but she is in safe hands. (op 7-2)
Bayleyf(IRE) Official explanation: jockey said colt stopped quickly

4064 IRISH THOROUGHBRED MARKETING CHERRY HINTON STKS (GROUP 2) (FILLIES) 6f

2:25 (2:25) (Class 1) 2-Y-O

£34,026 (£12,900; £6,456; £3,216; £1,614; £810) **Stalls** Low

Form RPR

1 **1** **Sendmylovetorose**[12] 3674 2-8-12 0........................ CO'Donoghue 7 105+
(A Oliver, Ire) *hld up: hdwy and hung lft over 2f out: sn rdn: led and edgd rt ins fnl f: styd on u.p* **2/1**[1]

1 **2** *nk* **Maureen (IRE)**[17] 3473 2-8-12 0........................ JimmyFortune 1 105+
(Richard Hannon) *s.i.s: hld up: nt clr run fr over 2f out tl r.o ins fnl f: nt quite rch wnr* **5/1**[3]

115 **3** *1 1/4* **Jadanna (IRE)**[23] 3269 2-8-12 **94** .... FrankieDettori 8 100
(James Given) *chsd ldr tl led over 1f out: rdn and hdd ins fnl f: styd on same pce* **8/1**

013 **4** *1 1/4* **Premier Steps (IRE)**[21] 3326 2-8-12 **99** .... RichardKingscote 10 96
(Tom Dascombe) *a.p: rdn and hung lft over 1f out: styd on same pce ins fnl f* **8/1**

3031 **5** *2 1/4* **Fantacise**[19] 3415 2-8-12 **78** ....(b) KierenFallon 6 90
(Brian Meehan) *chsd ldrs: pushed along 1/2-way: rdn over 1f out: no ex fnl f* **20/1**

11 **6** *1/2* **City Image (IRE)**[13] 3631 2-8-12 0........................ RyanMoore 3 88
(Richard Hannon) *hld up in tch: lost pl over 3f out: nt clr run and swtchd lft over 2f out: rdn and hung lft over 1f out: no ex ins fnl f* **7/2**[2]

41 **7** *5* **Mandy Layla (IRE)**[36] 2837 2-8-12 **77** .... TomEaves 5 73
(Bryan Smart) *sn led: rdn and hdd over 1f out: wknd ins fnl f* **33/1**

430 **8** *1/2* **Threes Grand**[23] 3269 2-8-12 **84** .... TomQueally 9 72
(Scott Dixon) *prom: rdn over 2f out: edgd lft and wknd fnl f* **40/1**

13 **9** *5* **Lovely Pass (IRE)**[20] 3368 2-8-12 0........................ SilvestreDeSousa 11 57
(Mahmood Al Zarooni) *s.i.s: hld up: rdn and hung lft over 2f out: sn wknd* **8/1**

50 **10** *1/2* **Masarah (IRE)**[23] 3269 2-8-12 0........................ MartinDwyer 12 55
(Clive Brittain) *hdwy over 4f out: rdn and wknd over 2f out* **100/1**

1m 14.53s (2.03) **Going Correction** +0.425s/f (Yiel) **10** Ran SP% **116.7**
Speed ratings (Par 103): **103,102,100,99,96 95,88,88,81,80**
Tote Swingers: 1&2 £3.30, 1&3 £3.60, 2&3 £7.00 CSF £11.83 TOTE £3.10: £1.40, £2.60, £1.40; EX 14.10 Trifecta £72.80 Pool: £7,043.63 - 71.52 winning units..
Owner John Gildea **Bred** Silfield Bloodstock **Trained** Caledon, Co Tyrone
■ Stewards' Enquiry : Jimmy Fortune caution: careless riding.

FOCUS
There seemed to be a decent pace on early. Sectional times suggest they went a little slower than the 3yo handicappers in the previous race through the first half, before finishing more strongly. The winning time was 0.85sec slower. As is often the case this race brought together a number of strands of early juvenile form, including the Queen Mary, Albany and Chesham from Royal Ascot. The form has been rated a little more positively than it might have been.

NOTEBOOK
Sendmylovetorose, winner of a Group 3 in testing ground at the Curragh last time out, is very much at home in these sorts of conditions and gets credit for winning despite racing away from the favoured rail, and she quickened away well as they hit the rising ground. That said, the runner-up had a nightmare run, and she was fortunate to collect. This has not been a good guide to the 1000 Guineas, with just two winners (Sayyedati and Attraction) going on to take the first fillies' Classic since the 1972 winner Mysterious, and there won't be many takers of the 33-1 available about the winner. She has still to prove she can go on quicker ground and is not entered in the Lowther, but she could apparently be supplemented for the Phoenix Stakes. (op 9-4)
Maureen(IRE) ◆, who impressed when winning easily on her debut, was an unlucky loser. Brought over to race on the favoured stands' rail, she was held up out the back and her rider was clearly hoping for a run up the rail, but the gap never came and he was forced to switch. Her path was blocked more than once and by the time she'd found a way through the winner had flown. She looked the best filly in the field, and her trainer, who clearly holds her in some regard, is now considering the Prix Morny for her, which would mean skipping the Lowther. (op 13-2)
Jadanna(IRE), fifth in the Queen Mary, raced freely early on but bagged a nice position tracking the leader. The sixth furlong just found her out in the end and dropping back to 5f should see her to best effect. We know she handles quicker ground as well, so she should get plenty of opportunities to add to her tally. The Molecomb was mentioned, and that looks a suitable race for her. (tchd 15-2)
Premier Steps(IRE), who was third in the Albany, got a little outpaced at halfway but she kept on well for pressure. She's yet to be tried on anything other than soft ground, so will have something to prove if the rain ever stops falling. (op 11-2)
Fantacise came into the race rated 75 following four starts, so had a bit to prove in this grade, but she's by Pivotal and these conditions suit her. She did have the rail to help for much of the race, however. (op 22-1 tchd 25-1)
City Image(IRE) couldn't pick up and despite being a winner in soft ground on her debut, these conditions are not really what she wants at this level. (op 4-1)
Mandy Layla(IRE), taking a big step up in class from a Hamilton maiden, got to the favoured stands' rail first and made the running. She didn't get home, though, and perhaps a combination of the softer ground and rise in grade found her out.

Lovely Pass(IRE) lost several lengths with a slow start and then carried her head awkwardly and hung badly left while racing on the outside of the field. She doesn't look at all straightforward. (op 9-1 tchd 10-1)

4065 ETIHAD AIRWAYS FALMOUTH STKS (BRITISH CHAMPIONS SERIES) (GROUP 1) (F&M) 1m

3:00 (3:01) (Class 1) 3-Y-0+

£90,736 (£34,400; £17,216; £8,576; £4,304; £2,160) **Stalls** Low

Form RPR

1-12 **1** **Giofra**[75] 1696 4-9-5 115 (t) ChristopheSoumillon 10 118+
(A De Royer-Dupre, France) *hld up in tch on ins: effrt and hdwy over 2f out: rdn to ld ins fnl f: kpt on wl* **10/1**

110- **2** ½ **Elusive Kate (USA)**[252] 7281 3-8-10 116 FrankieDettori 4 115
(John Gosden) *cl up: led and qcknd over 2f out: rdn and edgd lft over 1f out: hdd ins fnl f: kpt on: hld nr fin* **25/1**

3 **3** ¾ **Siyouma (IRE)**[46] 2570 4-9-5 109 GeraldMosse 11 115+
(F Doumen, France) *hld up on ins: rdn and effrt over 2f out: hung lft over 1f out: kpt on to pull clr of remainder fnl f: r.o fin* **33/1**

103 **4** 3 ¾ **Irish History (IRE)**[21] 3328 3-8-10 106 MickaelBarzalona 6 105+
(Mahmood Al Zarooni) *t.k.h: hld up in tch: rdn and outpcd 2f out: styd on fnl f: nt pce of first three* **16/1**

1-35 **5** nk **Maybe (IRE)**[42] 2658 3-8-10 110 RyanMoore 9 104
(A P O'Brien, Ire) *hld up in tch on outside: rdn over 2f out: effrt and edgd lft wl over 1f out: sn outpcd* **5/1[2]**

4434 **6** 2 ¾ **Barefoot Lady (IRE)**[23] 3266 4-9-5 108 PaulHanagan 3 99
(Richard Fahey) *hld up towards rr on outside: drvn and outpcd over 2f out: n.d after* **50/1**

6-31 **7** 1 ½ **Alanza (IRE)**[29] 3091 4-9-5 109 JohnnyMurtagh 1 96
(John M Oxx, Ire) *stdd and wnt rt s: hld up on outside: rdn and outpcd 2f out: sme late hdwy: nvr rchd ldrs* **16/1**

1-53 **8** ½ **Lay Time**[23] 3266 4-9-5 110 JimmyFortune 5 95
(Andrew Balding) *dwlt: sn led at stdy pce: swtchd to far rail over 6f out: rdn and hdd over 2f out: wknd over 1f out* **10/1**

13-1 **9** ½ **Golden Lilac (IRE)**[47] 2533 4-9-5 120 MaximeGuyon 2 94
(A Fabre, France) *in tch on outside tl rdn and outpcd 2f out: edgd lft and sn wknd: eased whn no ch ins fnl f* **10/11[1]**

0-21 **10** 9 **Joviality**[23] 3266 4-9-5 113 WilliamBuick 8 73
(John Gosden) *t.k.h: early ldr: cl up tl rdn and wknd 2f out: sn hung lft: eased whn no ch fnl f* **8/1[3]**

1m 42.14s (2.14) **Going Correction** +0.425s/f (Yiel)
WFA 3 from 4yo+ 9lb **10** Ran SP% **118.9**
Speed ratings (Par 117): **106,105,104,101,100 97,96,95,95,86**
Tote Swingers: 1&2 £11.10, 1&3 £31.90, 2&3 £49.80 CSF £230.63 TOTE £7.00: £1.70, £4.50, £6.50; EX 100.70 Trifecta £3592.00 Pool: £11,067.42 - 2.28 winning units..
Owner Haras De La Perelle **Bred** Haras De La Perelle **Trained** Chantilly, France

FOCUS

The ninth edition of this race since being granted Group 1 status, and it appeared to revolve around three-time Group 1 winner Golden Lilac, who looked potentially different class to the rest, but she was disappointing, and it's hard to rate the form that highly. However, it was just about an up-to-scratch renewal, and the first two are rated to form.

NOTEBOOK

Giofra, one of two other French challengers in the line-up, came in a little under the radar, but she'd impressed when beating colts in the Prix d'Harcourt earlier in the year and didn't run at all badly in the Prix Ganay last time. With the whole field heading to the far side this time, she raced in mid-division on the rail and picked up well once switched to challenge. Her stamina came into play up the hill and she ground it out well. The Nassau Stakes could be next on her agenda and the longer trip ought to suit her there, while her trainer hopes she'll make up into an Arc filly by the autumn. (op 9-1 tchd 12-1)

Elusive Kate(USA) ◆ comes out of the race with plenty of credit, as she was conceding race-fitness to the rest of the field and she's known to prefer a sound surface. While she was suited by racing prominently in a race lacking a little bit of early pace, she raced away from the far rail and all things considered this was hugely encouraging. She has clearly trained on and all the big mile races will be open to her now. The Matron Stakes was mentioned, although she could also go back to Deauville, where she won twice at two.

Siyouma(IRE) might not have been ideally placed out the back considering the lack of early pace, but she did race on the far rail which was probably an advantage. Having never run over a trip as short as this before, the concern was whether she'd have the required speed and while she was keeping on well at the finish, the ground clearly helped on that score. The Prix de l'Opera on Arc weekend was mentioned as a long-range target.

Irish History(IRE), placed in the Coronation Stakes last time out, backed that up with another solid effort in defeat. She still looks quite green, and didn't settle that well early, so there's probably better to come from her. (op 20-1)

Maybe(IRE) had a bit to prove dropped back in trip having been a little disappointing in the Oaks. Although a winner on soft at two, she's probably more effective on a decent surface and she deserves another shot to prove she's still of Group 1 ability. (op 13-2 tchd 9-2)

Barefoot Lady(IRE) is exposed as not quite up to this level. (op 66-1)

Alanza(IRE) never looked comfortable on the ground and should be a different proposition back on a fast surface. (tchd 20-1)

Lay Time was able to dictate an ordinary early gallop on the seemingly favoured far rail, but she wasn't good enough to take advantage on this ground. Official explanation: trainer said filly was unsuited by the soft ground (op 11-1 tchd 12-1)

Golden Lilac(IRE) looked to have been found a good opportunity to notch her seventh win from eight starts, but she proved desperately disappointing, failing to pick up at all and weakening right out. Clearly this was not her true running, and the ground, which her trainer had expressed concerns about beforehand, was surely the reason. Official explanation: trainer said filly was unsuited by the soft ground (op 5-6 tchd 4-5 and evens in a place)

Joviality doesn't want the ground this soft and, after racing keenly in the front rank, she dropped right out. Official explanation: trainer said filly was unsuited by the soft ground (op 12-1)

4066 WEATHERBYS E B F MAIDEN STKS 7f

3:35 (3:38) (Class 4) 2-Y-0

£6,469 (£1,925; £962; £481) **Stalls** Low

Form RPR

1 **Ghurair (USA)** 2-9-3 0 PaulHanagan 2 91+
(John Gosden) *s.i.s: hdwy over 4f out: shkn up to ld over 1f out: rn green: pushed out* **3/1[1]**

2 1 ½ **Improvisation (IRE)** 2-9-3 0 MickaelBarzalona 3 86+
(Mahmood Al Zarooni) *a.p: pushed along and hung lft over 2f out: rdn to chse wnr ins fnl f: styd on* **7/1**

3 1 ¼ **Dundonnell (USA)** 2-9-3 0 JamesDoyle 6 82+
(Roger Charlton) *chsd ldrs: rdn over 1f out: styd on same pce ins fnl f* **10/1**

4 1 ¾ **Afonso De Sousa (USA)**[13] 3644 2-9-3 0 JPO'Brien 1 78
(A P O'Brien, Ire) *led: rdn and edgd rt over 1f out: sn hdd: no ex ins fnl f* **7/2[2]**

5 ¾ **Mirsaale** 2-9-3 0 NeilCallan 14 76+
(James Tate) *hld up: hdwy u.p over 2f out: styd on: nt rch ldrs* **50/1**

6 ½ **Contributer (IRE)** 2-9-3 0 WilliamBuick 18 75+
(Ed Dunlop) *s.i.s: hld up: hdwy over 2f out: rdn over 1f out: nt trble ldrs* **16/1**

7 shd **No Jet Lag (USA)** 2-9-3 0 TedDurcan 12 75+
(David Lanigan) *hld up: rdn over 2f out: hung lft over 1f out: r.o: nvr nrr* **40/1**

8 8 **Elhaame (IRE)** 2-9-3 0 KierenFallon 16 56+
(Luca Cumani) *prom: pushed along over 4f out: wknd over 1f out* **20/1**

0 **9** 1 ½ **Khudoua**[13] 3634 2-9-3 0 TadhgO'Shea 15 56+
(John Gosden) *s.i.s: hld up: styd on fr over 1f out: nrst fin* **33/1**

10 2 **Evangelist** 2-9-3 0 RyanMoore 13 46
(Sir Michael Stoute) *sn pushed along in mid-div: wknd over 2f out* **16/1**

11 hd **Progenitor (IRE)** 2-9-3 0 JimmyFortune 17 45
(David Lanigan) *hld up: nvr on terms* **50/1**

12 shd **Star Of Missouri** 2-9-3 0 TomQueally 9 45
(Mark H Tompkins) *sn pushed along in rr: n.d* **66/1**

13 shd **Grilletto (USA)** 2-9-3 0 MartinDwyer 4 45
(James Tate) *prom: rdn over 2f out: wknd wl over 1f out* **50/1**

14 ½ **Day In Day Out** 2-9-3 0 RichardThomas 10 44
(Ralph Beckett) *prom over 4f* **33/1**

15 2 ¼ **Gravitational (IRE)** 2-9-3 0 TomMcLaughlin 20 38
(Ed Dunlop) *stdd s: sn swtchd rt: hld up: a in rr* **50/1**

3 **16** shd **Requested**[42] 2662 2-9-3 0 SilvestreDeSousa 7 38
(Mahmood Al Zarooni) *chsd ldr: pushed along and ev ch 2f out: hmpd and wknd sn after* **4/1[3]**

17 2 **Abraq** 2-9-3 0 JamieSpencer 8 33
(Ed Dunlop) *s.i.s: a in rr* **25/1**

0 **18** 11 **Royal Caper**[13] 3634 2-9-3 0 BrettDoyle 11 5
(John Ryan) *prom: rdn over 2f out: sn wknd: t.o* **200/1**

1m 28.79s (3.09) **Going Correction** +0.425s/f (Yiel) **18** Ran SP% **127.3**
Speed ratings (Par 96): **99,97,95,93,93 92,92,83,81,79 78,78,78,78,75 75,73,60**
Tote Swingers: 1&2 £7.60, 1&3 £8.70, 2&3 £13.30 CSF £22.95 TOTE £4.20: £1.80, £3.20, £3.10; EX 34.50 Trifecta £209.40 Pool: £1,307.41 - 4.62 winning units..
Owner Hamdan Al Maktoum **Bred** Kirsten Rausing **Trained** Newmarket, Suffolk

FOCUS

Often a strong maiden that can unearth Group-class horses, and it'll be no surprise if one or two of these prove up to running in Pattern company in time. The time was fast and form is rated positively. The race should throw up plenty of winners.

NOTEBOOK

Ghurair(USA), who cost 180,000gns and is out of a daughter of dual Champion Stakes winner Alborada, was well backed and impressed in winning first time up. He travelled smoothly through the race and quickened up well, and while it's worth remembering that he benefited from racing on the favoured stands' rail, he was noticeably green and should come on for the race. (op 7-2 tchd 9-2 in a place)

Improvisation(IRE), like the winner, was drawn low and was able to benefit from racing near the stands' rail. He looked like he was in the process of weakening out of things 2f out, but he kept battling away and this 200,000gns purchase looks like he'll stay well next year (dam got 1m4f and related to smart middle-distance stayer Self Defense). (op 10-1)

Dundonnell(USA) ◆, who is out of an unraced sister to top-class sprinter/sire Danehill, really took the eye and impressed in the way he travelled through the race. He was at a disadvantage in racing further away from the favoured rail than his main rivals, so gets extra credit, and faster ground ought to suit him in future. He looks a useful prospect. (op 9-1 tchd 11-1)

Afonso De Sousa(USA), who holds entries in the Phoenix, Gimcrack and National Stakes, is a half-brother to four winners including Kentucky Derby/Preakness winner Big Brown. One of just four in the race who had the benefit of previous experience, he was wisely sent on from the start, but for some reason he was kept away from the favoured stands' rail and he began to wander with a furlong and a half to run. His sire Henrythenavigator preferred a sound surface and it might be the case with him as well. (tchd 9-2)

Mirsaale managed to get over to the stands' rail from stall 14 and that proved a great move by Neil Callan. Keeping on well at the finish, he's bred to come into his own over middle distances next year.

Contributer(IRE) ◆, who was drawn in stall 18, can possibly have his effort upgraded as he was stuck on the wide outside throughout. Out of a French 1m2f Group 3 winner and from a stable whose juveniles are rarely fired up first time, he ought to come on quite a bit for this. (op 12-1 tchd 20-1 in a place)

No Jet Lag(USA) is by Breeders' Cup Turf winner Johar, but there's plenty of speed on the dam's side of his pedigree. He was keeping on well at the end and finished eight lengths clear of the rest. (op 50-1)

Elhaame(IRE) came under pressure some way out. (tchd 22-1)

Khudoua was out the back early but who made some headway out wide late on. He still looked green and will be of far more interest once eligible for handicaps after one more outing.

Requested, who was up there for a long way, weakened quickly after Afonso De Sousa cut across him just inside the final 2f. Perhaps the ground wasn't to his liking. Official explanation: jockey said colt had no more to give (tchd 7-2 and 9-2)

4067 EQUINEFX.COM MAIDEN STKS 1m 2f

4:10 (4:12) (Class 4) 3-Y-O

£6,469 (£1,925; £962; £481) **Stalls** Centre

Form RPR

2 **1** **Marshgate Lane (USA)**[20] 3399 3-9-3 0 MickaelBarzalona 15 92+
(Mahmood Al Zarooni) *hld up: stdy hdwy on outside 3f out: effrt and chsd ldr over 1f out: rdn and styd on wl fnl f to ld nr fin* **7/2[1]**

2 **2** hd **Ruwaiyan (USA)**[29] 3079 3-9-3 0 SilvestreDeSousa 9 89
(Mahmood Al Zarooni) *t.k.h: w ldr: led and rdn over 1f out: edgd lft ins fnl f: hdd nr fin* **9/1**

30- **3** 1 ¾ **Big Johnny D (IRE)**[314] 5697 3-9-3 0 TedDurcan 11 86
(John Dunlop) *plld hrd: hld up bhd ldng gp: hdwy to chse ldrs over 2f out: rdn and edgd lft over 1f out: kpt on ins fnl f: nt rch first two* **15/2**

2205 **4** 2 ¼ **Hallmark Star**[13] 3605 3-9-3 79 FrankieDettori 12 81
(Gerard Butler) *chsd ldrs: drvn and outpcd over 2f out: kpt on ins fnl f* **13/2[3]**

2 **5** ½ **Awake My Soul (IRE)**[21] 3349 3-9-3 0 KierenFallon 5 80+
(Luca Cumani) *in tch: rdn and outpcd wl over 2f out: styd on fnl f: nvr able to chal* **4/1[2]**

0-23 **6** ¾ **Rose Season**[8] 3773 3-8-12 0 NeilCallan 2 74
(Roger Varian) *mde most tl rdn and hdd over 1f out: outpcd fnl f* **14/1**

7 1 ½ **Leo Luna** 3-9-3 0 RyanMoore 7 76+
(Sir Michael Stoute) *s.i.s: rn green in rr: pushed along and effrt wl over 2f out: no imp: bttr for r* **7/2[1]**

2-00 **8** 41 **Moshaagib (USA)**[21] 3349 3-9-3 75 (p) PaulHanagan 6
(John Gosden) *hld up bhd ldng gp: struggling wl over 3f out: sn lost tch: t.o* **14/1**

9 ¾ **Red Protector (IRE)** 3-9-3 0 MartinDwyer 8
(Amy Weaver) *s.i.s: hld up: struggling over 3f out: sn btn: t.o* **66/1**

-60 **10** 8 **Bubbly Bounty**[12] 3666 3-8-12 0 LiamJones 10
(Alan Bailey) *in tch on outside: stdy hdwy over 4f out: rdn and wknd 3f out: t.o* **200/1**

0 **11** *2* **Keeping Time**[20] 3398 3-9-3 0 TomQueally 1
(Sir Henry Cecil) *s.i.s: t.k.h and sn in tch: struggling wl over 3f out: sn btn: t.o* **22/1**

2m 10.85s (5.35) **Going Correction** +0.425s/f (Yiel) **11** Ran SP% **119.2**
Speed ratings (Par 102): **95,94,93,91,91 90,89,56,56,49 48**
Tote Swingers: 1&2 £6.80, 1&3 £8.70, 2&3 £13.10 CSF £36.13 TOTE £5.20: £2.30, £3.00, £2.80; EX 24.60 Trifecta £1,742.89 - 1.55 winning units..
Owner Godolphin **Bred** Edmund A Gann **Trained** Newmarket, Suffolk
■ Stewards' Enquiry : Silvestre De Sousa two-day ban: used whip in incorrect place (Jul 27-28)

FOCUS
Not a maiden which usually throws up a superstar. Manifest was the possible exception, runner-up in 2009 before subsequently winning the Yorkshire Cup. The form is decent and it looked an up-to-scratch renewal.

4068 NEWMARKET HISTORIC HOME OF RACING H'CAP 1m
5:20 (5:22) (Class 3) (0-90,90) 3-Y-O+ **£9,703** (£2,887; £1,443; £721) **Stalls** Low

Form RPR
221 **1** **Jack's Revenge (IRE)**[25] 3226 4-9-5 **81** (bt) RyanMoore 14 93
(George Baker) *racd centre: hld up: hdwy over 2f out: rdn and hung lft fr over 1f out: led wl ins fnl f: sn clr* **7/1**

2-1 **2** *2 1/2* **Hallings Comet**[18] 3431 3-8-11 **82** JimmyFortune 9 87
(Andrew Balding) *led centre and overall ldr 5f: rdn over 1f out: ev ch wl ins fnl f: styd on same pce: 2nd of 8 in gp* **9/2**[2]

1-22 **3** *nk* **Ariyfa (IRE)**[20] 3395 4-9-6 **82** SilvestreDeSousa 4 88
(Noel Quinlan) *racd stands' side: led that gp: overall ldr 3f out: rdn over 1f out: hdd and no ex wl ins fnl f: 1st of 4 in gp* **5/1**[3]

1-42 **4** *1 1/4* **Jawhar (IRE)**[36] 2855 4-9-1 **77** PaulHanagan 12 80
(William Haggas) *racd centre: a.p: chsd ldr of that gp 3f out: rdn over 1f out: styd on same pce fnl f: 3rd of 8 in gp* **8/1**

6305 **5** *1* **Borug (USA)**[13] 3642 4-9-6 **82** (p) MartinDwyer 3 83
(James Tate) *racd stands' side: s.i.s: hld up: r.o ins fnl f: nrst fin: 2nd of 4 in gp* **11/1**

6262 **6** *1 1/4* **Presburg (IRE)**[18] 3446 3-8-13 **84** KierenFallon 10 80
(Joseph Tuite) *racd centre: hld up: hdwy over 2f out: rdn over 1f out: no ex: 4th of 8 in gp* **8/1**

-000 **7** *3 1/4* **Mubtadi**[21] 3348 4-8-13 **75** (v[1]) NeilCallan 1 65
(Ismail Mohammed) *racd stands' side: chsd ldr: swtchd lft 2f out: sn rdn: wknd ins fnl f: 3rd of 4 in gp* **25/1**

533- **8** *3 1/4* **Voodoo Prince**[230] 7558 4-9-11 **87** JamieSpencer 13 70
(Ed Dunlop) *racd centre: stdd s: hld up: hdwy over 1f out: wknd ins fnl f: 5th of 8 in gp* **8/1**

1215 **9** *hd* **Barwick**[16] 3493 4-9-6 **82** TedDurcan 5 65
(Mark H Tompkins) *racd stands' side: prom: rdn over 1f out: wknd and eased ins fnl f: last of 4 in gp* **7/2**[1]

-050 **10** *6* **Focail Eile**[171] 280 7-8-5 **74** GeorgeanBuckell(7) 15 43
(Tim Pitt) *racd centre: chsd ldrs: rdn over 2f out: wknd over 1f out: 6th of 8 in gp* **25/1**

0-0 **11** *15* **Cockney Dancer**[18] 3446 3-8-8 **79** ow1 DarryllHolland 11 11
(Charles Hills) *racd centre: chsd ldr tl over 5f out: rdn over 2f out: wknd over 1f out: eased: t.o: 7th of 8 in gp* **33/1**

2210 **12** *11* **Diplomatic (IRE)**[30] 3045 7-8-9 **71** oh9 LukeMorris 6
(Michael Squance) *racd centre: prom: pushed along and lost pl 6f out: rdn and wknd over 2f out: t.o* **40/1**

1m 42.64s (2.64) **Going Correction** +0.425s/f (Yiel)
WFA 3 from 4yo+ 9lb **12** Ran SP% **124.3**
Speed ratings (Par 107): **103,100,100,98,97 96,93,90,90,84 69,58**
Tote Swingers: 1&2 £4.80, 1&3 £5.70, 2&3 £4.10 CSF £39.13 CT £180.83 TOTE £5.00: £1.60, £2.10, £2.60; EX 18.90 Trifecta £108.20 Pool: £947.73 - 6.47 winning units..
Owner PJL Racing **Bred** Con Marnane **Trained** Whitsbury, Hants

FOCUS
A competitive handicap on paper, but the winner proved to be a step ahead of his rivals. There was a difference of opinion where the best ground was. A group of four on the stands' side emerged, but the majority raced centre-field, possibly the drying ground evening out any bias beforehand. The winner stepped up again on his Windsor form.

NOTEBOOK
Jack's Revenge(IRE), up 3lb for winning in good style at Windsor last month, took this stronger race with an authoritative performance under a good ride. He tanked through the race down the centre, but showed awkward tendencies before he hit the front where Ryan Moore became unbalanced, and was intelligently produced between rivals 1f out to keep the horse's concentration. Once clear he hung across the track, but won going away. He is improving with every run with the combination of tongue-tie and blinkers clearly working, and there is more to come from a guaranteed higher mark if he can be kept straight. (op 5-1)

Hallings Comet performed with credit on his handicap debut. It was guesswork whether an opening mark of 82 was fair, but that now looks granted. He led the centre group, was headed by the winner and Jawhar, but battled on bravely to stay on again for second. The stable continues in good form and it would be a surprise if he can't improve again now we know how well he stays a mile. (tchd 5-1)

Ariyfa(IRE), 3lb higher than when second last time out, led the stands' side at a good pace and looked to hold the aces 1f out, but was brushed aside by a rival who is clearly ahead of his mark and one who is unexposed. The Cape Cross filly is admirably consistent and will surely win more races on better ground. (op 13-2)

Jawhar(IRE) was keen to post, but settled better during the race. Always handily placed, he challenged for the lead 2f out but had no more to give. The gelding is unexposed and, if more relaxed before racing, he can win off a similar mark. (op 13-2 tchd 6-1)

Borug(USA) battled on well under pressure from some way out and enjoyed the stiff finish, and would ideally prefer further judged on this. (op 12-1 tchd 10-1)

Presburg(IRE) found the one-pace after travelling powerfully in the centre-field group. Perhaps the ground was too soft and a return to the AW can yield another victory. (op 9-1 tchd 12-1)

Mubtadi raced with exuberance sporting a first-time visor, but weakened inside the final furlong. A drop to 7f can prove a good move. (op 33-1)

Voodoo Prince isn't one to give up on. He was looked after by his jockey on this seasonal debut and needs much further anyway. (op 14-1 tchd 16-1)

Barwick raced in the stands' side group, but could never land a blow. This wasn't his true running and can be given another chance. (op 9-2)

Cockney Dancer Official explanation: trainer said filly was unsuited by the soft ground

T/Jkpt: Part won. £92,212.10 to a £1 stake. Pool: £129,876.00 - 0.50 winning tickets. T/Plt: £1,119.80 to a £1 stake. Pool: £181,066.00 - 118.03 winning tickets. T/Qpdt: £89.60 to a £1 stake. Pool: £10,468.00 - 86.38 winning tickets. CR

3163 YORK (L-H)
Friday, July 13

OFFICIAL GOING: Good to soft (soft in places; 7.0)
Wind: Moderate half against Weather: cloudy

4069 CAKEMARK E B F MAIDEN STKS 7f
2:05 (2:06) (Class 3) 2-Y-O **£6,469** (£1,925; £962; £481) **Stalls** Low

Form RPR
2 **1** **Miss You Too**[21] 3339 2-8-12 0 MatthewDavies 1 80+
(Mick Channon) *t.k.h early: trckd ldrs: hdwy to ld wl over 2f out and sn hung bdly lft to far rail: sn clr: easily* **4/5**[1]

0 **2** *4* **Woody Bay**[34] 2934 2-9-3 0 GrahamLee 2 71
(James Given) *set stdy pce: qckned 1/2-way: rdn and hdd wl over 2f out: kpt on same pce* **9/2**[2]

4 **3** *3* **Montcliffe**[23] 3271 2-9-3 0 TonyHamilton 3 63
(Richard Fahey) *dwlt: plld hrd in rr early: hdwy 3f out: rdn over 2f out and sn no imp* **9/2**[2]

0 **4** *nk* **Order Of Service**[13] 3611 2-9-3 0 RichardMullen 4 62
(David Brown) *trckd ldr: effrt 3f out: sn rdn and wknd over 2f out* **16/1**

5 *1* **Inovate (IRE)** 2-9-3 0 DavidAllan 5 61+
(Tim Easterby) *cl up: pushed along 1/2-way: rdn wl over 2f out: sn wknd* **7/1**[3]

1m 31.37s (6.07) **Going Correction** +0.475s/f (Yiel) **5** Ran SP% **110.3**
Speed ratings (Par 98): **84,79,76,75,74**
CSF £4.79 TOTE £1.60: £1.10, £2.10; EX 5.40.
Owner Prime Oak Buildings Ltd **Bred** Plantation Stud & Amarvilas Bloodstock **Trained** West Ilsley, Berks

FOCUS
Home bend rail moved in from 9f to entrance to Home straight reducing distances of races of 1m+ by 27yds. After three relatively dry days the ground had dried up slightly and was described as 'bit dead, tacky but not to bad' by the riders in the opener. One filly against four colts in this juvenile maiden. They swung wide once in line for home and at first raced up the centre. The winner can probably rate 90+ in time.

NOTEBOOK
Miss You Too, closely related to Irish Derby winner Grey Swallow, had finished runner-up over 6f on her debut at Goodwood. Stepping up in trip, she was very keen to post and gave problems behind the stalls. Refusing to settle, she hung badly left in front and ended up against the far side rail. She had plenty in hand, but her temperament is under suspicion and it remains to be seen how much she progresses. (op 8-13 tchd 4-7)
Woody Bay, whose dam was a Group 1 winner in the USA, made the running but was readily brushed aside by the filly. This was a step up on his debut effort and he should improve again. (op 8-1)
Montcliffe, another to race freely, appeared to find the extra furlong a problem, especially in this ground. (op 4-1 tchd 5-1)
Order Of Service has shown little in two starts now. (tchd 20-1)
Inovate(IRE), out of an unraced mare, will need more time yet. (op 10-1 tchd 12-1)

4070 TYREGIANT.COM SUMMER STKS (GROUP 3) 6f
2:35 (2:35) (Class 1) 3-Y-O+ **£32,560** (£12,314; £6,154; £3,074) **Stalls** Centre

Form RPR
1 **Gracia Directa (GER)**[47] 2530 4-9-2 87 RobertWinston 11 106
(D Moser, Germany) *cl up: led 2f out: rdn over 1f out: drvn and edgd rt ins fnl f: hld on wl* **14/1**

2062 **2** *1/2* **Sioux Rising (IRE)**[14] 3593 6-9-2 94 TonyHamilton 8 104
(Richard Fahey) *hmpd s and bhd: hdwy 2f out: rdn wl over 1f out: styd on strly ins fnl f: ev ch whn edgd lft and no ex nr fin* **33/1**

1-21 **3** *1/2* **Hallelujah**[35] 2890 4-9-2 89 MartinLane 9 102
(James Fanshawe) *wnt lft s: in tch whn n.m.r: lost pl and rr after 1f: pushed along and hdwy on outer 1/2-way: rdn to chse ldrs wl over 1f out: drvn to chal ent fnl f: ev ch tl no ex last 50yds* **11/1**

-102 **4** *4* **Boastful (IRE)**[13] 3623 4-9-2 104 GrahamLee 2 90
(Mrs K Burke) *cl up on outer: rdn and ev ch 2f out: drvn and sltly outpcd over 1f out: kpt on fnl f* **13/2**[3]

-022 **5** *1 3/4* **My Girl Anna (IRE)**[20] 3375 5-9-2 100 GrahamGibbons 1 84
(Muredach Kelly, Ire) *cl up: chal 2f out and ev ch: rdn and wknd ent fnl f* **9/1**

-201 **6** *1 3/4* **Radio Gaga**[15] 3542 3-8-10 98 RichardMullen 3 78
(Ed McMahon) *chsd ldrs: rdn along 1/2-way: kpt on one pce u.p fnl 2f* **6/1**[2]

112 **7** *4 1/2* **Sentaril**[23] 3265 3-8-10 108 KellyHarrison 4 64
(William Haggas) *chsd ldrs: rdn along over 2f out: sn wandered and wknd* **13/8**[1]

21-5 **8** *4* **Pearl Diva (IRE)**[14] 3593 3-8-10 90 RobertHavlin 7 51
(Peter Chapple-Hyam) *wnt rt s: a towards rr* **50/1**

5036 **9** *6* **Lady Gorgeous**[23] 3265 3-8-10 102 MatthewDavies 12 32
(Mick Channon) *trckd ldrs: rdn along wl over 2f out: sn wknd* **12/1**

0000 **10** *nk* **Margot Did (IRE)**[24] 3238 4-9-2 111 HayleyTurner 10 31
(Michael Bell) *led: rdn along and hdd 2f out: sn wknd* **10/1**

-614 **11** *3 3/4* **Inetrobil (IRE)**[29] 3092 3-8-10 100 (b) PhillipMakin 5 19
(Kevin Ryan) *wnt rt s: in tch: rdn along wl over 2f out: sn wknd* **18/1**

1m 14.1s (2.20) **Going Correction** +0.60s/f (Yiel)
WFA 3 from 4yo+ 6lb **11** Ran SP% **117.7**
Speed ratings (Par 113): **109,108,107,102,100 97,91,86,78,77 72**
Tote Swingers: 1&2 £43.70, 1&3 £12.30, 2&3 £39.10 CSF £394.63 TOTE £15.70: £3.70, £6.70, £2.70; EX 592.00 TRIFECTA Not won..
Owner Rennstall Directa **Bred** Gestut Directa **Trained** Germany

FOCUS
A group 3 sprint for fillies and mares. Not easy to pin down with a few disappointments, with the runner-up probably the best guide.

NOTEBOOK
Gracia Directa(GER), German trained, followed up a handicap success with victory in a Listed event at Hoppegarten. She travelled very strongly and in the end did just enough. The ground was not a problem. (op 12-1 tchd 11-1)
Sioux Rising(IRE), who is in foal, has recorded all her three career wins at Pontefract. She went down with flying colours after taking a bump at the start, but her time on the racecourse is running out.
Hallelujah, who came into this with a progressive profile, made her effort towards the stands' side. She likes soft ground and should continue on the upgrade. (tchd 10-1)
Boastful(IRE), possibly flattered by racing against the stands'-side rail at Newcastle, showed bags of toe racing towards the outer. This is as good as she is. (tchd 15-2)
My Girl Anna(IRE), runner-up on her last two starts in Listed company in Ireland, travelled strongly but, in the end, seemed to find the sixth furlong in this ground beyond her. (op 11-1)
Radio Gaga was putting in her best work at the finish and she really needs the extra furlong. (op 8-1)

Sentaril, runner-up in the Group 3 Jersey at Royal Ascot, was already in trouble when involved in some buffeting. This was not her true running and her rider reported that she ran flat. Official explanation: jockey said filly ran flat (tchd 7-4)
Margot Did(IRE), the 2011 Nunthorpe winner here, dropped right away and looks to have lost her form totally. (op 11-1)

4071 HAYLIN NURSERY 5f
3:10 (3:10) (Class 3) (0-95,81) 2-Y-O **£7,439** (£2,213; £1,106; £553) **Stalls** Centre

Form				RPR
1254	**1**		**Mayfield Girl (IRE)**[24] 3250 2-9-5 **79** RobertWinston 1 (Mel Brittain) *prom: hdwy to ld 1/2-way: rdn over 1f out: kpt on gamely fnl f* **8/1**	81
401	**2**	¾	**Blue Lotus (IRE)**[16] 3490 2-9-4 **78** DavidAllan 5 (Tim Easterby) *trckd ldr: hdwy 2f out: rdn to chse wnr ins fnl f: sn edgd rt and kpt on* **5/1**[3]	77
5632	**3**	*hd*	**The Sixties**[2] 3973 2-9-5 **79** MatthewDavies 8 (Mick Channon) *prom on outer: effrt 2f out: sn rdn: edgd lft ins fnl f: kpt on* **7/2**[2]	78
665	**4**	½	**Bispham Green**[35] 2880 2-8-12 **72** TonyHamilton 6 (Richard Fahey) *in tch: rdn along and outpcd wl over 2f out: styd on u.p appr fnl f* **14/1**	69+
5041	**5**	2 ¼	**Lucky Lodge**[39] 2770 2-9-1 **75** PaulMulrennan 7 (Mel Brittain) *led to 1/2-way: rdn along wl over 1f out: hld whn n.m.r and squeezed out ins fnl f* **16/1**	64
5212	**6**	3 ½	**Forray**[24] 3250 2-9-7 **81** RichardMullen 2 (Ed McMahon) *dwlt: rapid hdwy and cl up after 2f: effrt to chal wl over 1f out: ev ch whn rdn and hung rt 1f out: sn wknd* **15/8**[1]	62
001	**7**	1	**Starbotton**[28] 3110 2-9-1 **75** GrahamLee 3 (James Bethell) *a in rr: rdn along and outpcd fnl 2f* **13/2**	47

1m 3.18s (3.88) **Going Correction** +0.60s/f (Yiel) **7** Ran SP% **110.7**
Speed ratings (Par 98): **92,90,90,89,86 80,78**
Tote Swingers: 1&2 £5.70, 1&3 £4.90, 2&3 £3.60 CSF £44.01 CT £157.87 TOTE £9.40: £3.60, £2.80; EX 47.70.
Owner Mel Brittain **Bred** Mark Commins **Trained** Warthill, N Yorks

FOCUS
A competitive nursery. Straightforward form, with a decent effort from the winner.

NOTEBOOK
Mayfield Girl(IRE), runner-up in a Listed race over 5f here in May, put two sub-standard efforts behind her, hanging on in very game fashion. No doubt it will be more of the same for her. (op 15-2)
Blue Lotus(IRE), who overcame a six-week absence to get off the mark at Carlisle, found plenty for pressure. He will be suited by a stiffer track or a step up to 6f. (op 4-1)
The Sixties must be very tough. After a good sixth in the 7f Chesham, he went under by a nose in a maiden auction over this trip at Yarmouth just two days earlier. Six might prove the happy medium. (tchd 3-1)
Bispham Green, who showed precious little in three starts in maiden company, shaped much better and is another who will be suited by 6f. (op 16-1)
Lucky Lodge, a stablemate of the winner, showed plenty of toe but was well held when running out of racing room near the line.
Forray, a maiden winner in soft ground at Leicester, had shown improved form when runner-up to a useful type in a novice event at Thirsk. After missing a beat at the start he showed ahead, but hung badly right and was eased in the closing stages. On this occasion he looked anything but straightforward. Official explanation: jockey said colt hung right (op 9-4 tchd 5-2)

4072 CARAVAN CHAIRMAN'S CHARITY CUP (H'CAP) 1m 4f
3:45 (3:47) (Class 2) (0-100,100) 3-Y-O+ **£11,450** (£3,407; £1,702; £851) **Stalls** Low

Form				RPR
-050	**1**		**Bollin Greta**[16] 3494 7-8-11 **83** oh1 DavidAllan 10 (Tim Easterby) *hld up in rr: stdy hdwy over 3f out: rdn to chse ldrs over 1f out: styd on ins fnl f to ld last 75yds* **16/1**	92
2-23	**2**	*nk*	**A Boy Named Suzi**[13] 3642 4-9-6 **92** GrahamLee 15 (James Eustace) *hld up towards rr: stdy hdwy over 3f out: rdn to chse ldrs over 1f out: sn chal: led briefly ins fnl f: drvn and hdd last 75yds: no ex* **14/1**	100
3412	**3**	¾	**Rio's Rosanna (IRE)**[16] 3494 5-9-2 **88** AmyRyan 7 (Richard Whitaker) *trckd ldrs: hdwy and cl up 4f out: led wl over 2f out: rdn over 1f out: drvn and hdd ins fnl f: kpt on same pce* **7/2**[1]	95
1-50	**4**	2	**The Fun Crusher**[58] 2180 4-8-11 **83** oh4 GrahamGibbons 3 (Tim Easterby) *in tch: hdwy to chse ldrs 3f out: rdn to chal wl over 1f out and ev ch tl drvn and one pce fnl f* **10/1**	87
2011	**5**	*hd*	**Edmaaj (IRE)**[19] 3417 4-9-0 **86** DanielTudhope 2 (David O'Meara) *midfield: hdwy to chse ldrs 3f out: rdn over 2f out: drvn and one pce appr fnl f* **9/2**[3]	89
6-50	**6**	5	**Scrapper Smith (IRE)**[27] 3163 6-8-11 **88** GarryWhillans(5) 11 (Alistair Whillans) *hld up in rr: hdwy on inner over 3f out: rdn to chse ldrs 2f out: sn no imp* **9/1**	83
0-00	**7**	1 ½	**Demolition**[27] 3163 8-8-13 **88** GaryBartley(3) 14 (Noel Wilson) *sn trcking ldr: hdwy to ld over 4f out: rdn along over 3f out: hdd wl over 2f out: sn drvn and grad wknd* **22/1**	81
0	**8**	½	**Astral Thunder (ARG)**[161] 421 5-9-9 **100** TobyAtkinson(5) 9 (Marco Botti) *midfield on outer: pushed along and outpcd over 4f out: styng on u.p whn n.m.r 2f out: nvr a factor* **50/1**	92
4-31	**9**	3 ¾	**Cardinal Walter (IRE)**[30] 3035 3-8-0 **85** MartinLane 6 (David Simcock) *hld up towards rr: hdwy on inner 4f out: rdn and in tch 3f out: wknd 2f out* **4/1**[2]	71
0004	**10**	2 ¼	**Askaud (IRE)**[35] 2884 4-9-0 **86** HayleyTurner 12 (Scott Dixon) *a towards rr* **20/1**	69
5100	**11**	2	**Persian Peril**[28] 3125 8-9-1 **87** RobertWinston 16 (Alan Swinbank) *hld up towards rr: hdwy on outer over 3f out: rdn and in tch over 2f out: sn wknd* **40/1**	66
0062	**12**	4 ½	**Bridle Belle**[28] 3125 4-9-1 **87** TonyHamilton 1 (Richard Fahey) *midfield: rdn along over 3f out: sn wknd* **7/1**	59
-003	**13**	11	**Kinyras (IRE)**[17] 3458 4-8-11 **83** oh3 PaulMulrennan 5 (Michael Easterby) *prom: rdn along over 4f out: sn wknd* **40/1**	38
/444	**14**	½	**Steuben (GER)**[30] 3038 6-8-13 **85** DaraghO'Donohoe 13 (Barney Curley) *led after 1f: rdn along and hdd over 4f out: sn wknd* **33/1**	39

2m 34.27s (1.07) **Going Correction** +0.325s/f (Good)
WFA 3 from 4yo+ 13lb **14** Ran SP% **123.4**
Speed ratings (Par 109): **109,108,108,106,106 103,102,102,99,98 96,93,86,86**
Tote Swingers: 1&2 £25.90, 1&3 £15.40, 2&3 £5.50 CSF £211.58 CT £977.46 TOTE £23.30: £5.20, £2.70, £1.60; EX 348.60.
Owner Habton Farms **Bred** Sir Neil & Exors Of Late Lady Westbrook **Trained** Great Habton, N Yorks

FOCUS
A competitive handicap run at a sound pace and the first five finished clear. Pretty solid form.

NOTEBOOK
Bollin Greta, too keen on her previous start at Carlisle, her second outing in four days, recorded her first success for 14 months, making it six wins from 37 career starts. She stays further and, settled in the rear, showed pluck and courage to squeeze through between horses. Her trainer's horses are in fine form. (tchd 18-1)
A Boy Named Suzi, whose two wins have been on the AW, showed he is equally effective on turf and the soft ground was not a problem. He made his effort down the outside, but in the end was held at bay by a most determined winner. (op 11-1)
Rio's Rosanna(IRE) took an apprentice handicap here two outings ago from a 12lb lower mark and went up another 3lb after finishing runner-up in the Cumberland Plate. She too is all heart, but is high enough in the weights now. (op 11-2)
The Fun Crusher, absent since the May meeting here, was having just his fourth career start. There may be even better to come. (op 14-1)
Edmaaj(IRE), ridden to stay this extended trip, found another 6lb rise too much. (op 5-1 tchd 11-2)
Astral Thunder(ARG) Official explanation: jockey said horse was denied a clear run
Cardinal Walter(IRE), who accounted for a subsequent winner when opening his account at the third attempt at Haydock, looked possibly leniently treated off a mark of 85 on his handicap bow. He made a forward move once in line for home, but was soon under pressure and going nowhere. He must be given another chance. (op 10-3)

4073 RACING PLUS 31.20 ON SATURDAY H'CAP 5f
4:20 (4:25) (Class 2) (0-105,103) 3-Y-O+ **£11,450** (£3,407; £1,702; £851) **Stalls** Centre

Form				RPR
0226	**1**		**Hazelrigg (IRE)**[4] 3903 7-8-11 **88** DavidAllan 8 (Tim Easterby) *qckly away and led to 1/2-way: cl up: led again ins fnl f: kpt on* **6/1**[3]	95
2004	**2**	*hd*	**Secret Witness**[13] 3650 6-9-12 **103** (b) HayleyTurner 2 (Ronald Harris) *in rr: hdwy 2f out: rdn over 1f out: styd on to chal ins fnl f: ev ch tl no ex nr line* **9/2**[2]	109
-305	**3**	1 ¾	**Steps (IRE)**[29] 3078 4-9-0 **91** (b[1]) AndreaAtzeni 10 (Roger Varian) *cl up: effrt to ld over 1f out: sn rdn and hdd ins fnl f: one pce* **8/1**	91
5105	**4**	*hd*	**Lui Rei (ITY)**[13] 3641 6-9-10 **101** RobertWinston 7 (Robert Cowell) *chsd ldrs: rdn along wl over 1f out: kpt on same pce u.p fnl f* **9/1**	100
01-0	**5**	2 ¾	**Verinco**[57] 2208 6-9-1 **97** (v) JustinNewman(5) 4 (Bryan Smart) *cl up: led 1/2-way: rdn and hdd over 1f out: grad wknd* **12/1**	86
20-0	**6**	½	**Kaldoun Kingdom (IRE)**[58] 2177 7-9-5 **96** BarryMcHugh 1 (Richard Fahey) *outpcd and bhd tl sme late hdwy* **9/1**	83+
5-31	**7**	*hd*	**Jamaican Bolt (IRE)**[10] 3730 4-8-7 **84** 6ex RichardMullen 5 (Geoffrey Oldroyd) *chsd ldrs: rdn along 2f out: sn wknd* **7/2**[1]	71
-000	**8**	*nse*	**Ancient Cross**[48] 2507 8-9-6 **97** (t) PaulMulrennan 6 (Michael Easterby) *in tch: hdwy to chse ldrs 2f out: sn rdn and wknd appr fnl f* **7/1**	83
6440	**9**	8	**Racy**[28] 3127 5-9-1 **92** PhillipMakin 9 (Kevin Ryan) *blind removed late and s.i.s: a in rr* **8/1**	50

1m 1.13s (1.83) **Going Correction** +0.60s/f (Yiel) **9** Ran SP% **117.1**
Speed ratings (Par 109): **109,108,105,105,101 100,100,99,87**
Tote Swingers: 1&2 £5.50, 1&3 £5.70, 2&3 £5.30 CSF £33.66 CT £221.12 TOTE £7.80: £2.40, £1.80, £2.70; EX 34.10.
Owner The Senators **Bred** Rathbarry Stud **Trained** Great Habton, N Yorks

FOCUS
A tight sprint handicap with five horses almost abreast a furlong out. The winner is rated back to his best.

NOTEBOOK
Hazelrigg(IRE), who failed by a whisker from a 1lb lower mark over this C&D three outings ago, never fired in a first-time hood at Ayr four days earlier. With the hood retained, he flew out the traps and under a very good ride was persuaded to do just enough. He has something of a mind of his own. (op 8-1 tchd 11-2)
Secret Witness, a winner over this C&D in May from a 9lb lower mark, finished runner-up under a penalty next day when five of these, including the winner, were behind him. Fourth in a Group 3 in Ireland on his previous start, after a real set to he came off just second best. He is a credit to his trainer. (op 13-2)
Steps(IRE), in first-time blinkers, raced wide towards the stands' side. He travelled strongly, but looked to be saving a bit for himself in the closing stages. (op 5-1)
Lui Rei(ITY), a winner at Epsom on Derby day from a 4lb lower mark, stuck on in willing fashion towards the stands' side, but he looks rated to the limit now. (op 10-1 tchd 11-1)
Verinco, a winner three times in 2011, improving a stone and a half, was having his first outing since his reappearance in May. He showed bags of toe and should be spot on next time. (tchd 14-1)
Kaldoun Kingdom(IRE), a regular here, is without a win since March 2010. (op 10-1)
Jamaican Bolt(IRE), a clear-cut winner at Hamilton, was in effect just 6lb higher. Raised 10lb, this lightly-raced sort possibly found this coming too soon. Whatever he will have more on his plate in future. (tchd 10-3 and 4-1)
Racy, whose one success was in his maiden at two, lost all chance when the blind was left on as the stalls opened. Official explanation: jockey said gelding dropped its head in stalls causing it to be slowly away as he had difficulty removing blindfold (tchd 15-2)

4074 KEN HODGSON MEMORIAL STKS (CONDITIONS RACE) 1m 208y
4:55 (4:55) (Class 3) 3-Y-O+ **£7,439** (£2,213; £829; £829) **Stalls** Low

Form				RPR
0-00	**1**		**Dubai Prince (IRE)**[125] 877 4-9-5 112 AhmedAjtebi 2 (Mahmood Al Zarooni) *trckd ldng pair: led wl over 2f out: rdn clr over 1f out: edgd rt and styd on* **5/2**[2]	107+
2315	**2**	4 ½	**Fury**[26] 3205 4-9-5 107 GrahamGibbons 1 (William Haggas) *t.k.h: trckd ldr: hdwy to chal over 3f out: sn rdn and one pce fr wl over 1f out* **1/1**[1]	98
2-25	**3**	2 ½	**Invisible Man**[23] 3268 6-9-0 107 (b) AntiocoMurgia(5) 3 (Saeed Bin Suroor) *hld up in rr: hdwy 3f out: rdn along over 2f out: sn one pce* **4/1**[3]	92
0022	**3**	*dht*	**New Hampshire (USA)**[13] 3610 4-9-2 84 LeeTopliss(3) 4 (Tony Coyle) *set stdy pce: qcknd over 4f out: rdn along over 3f out: hdd wl over 2f out and sn wknd* **10/1**	92

1m 53.5s (1.50) **Going Correction** +0.325s/f (Good) **4** Ran SP% **107.7**
Speed ratings (Par 107): **106,102,99,99**
CSF £5.42 TOTE £3.40; EX 5.00.
Owner Godolphin **Bred** Mrs Eithne Hamilton **Trained** Newmarket, Suffolk

FOCUS
This Class 3 event was run at just a steady pace. Muddling form and the winner didn't need to be at his best.

NOTEBOOK
Dubai Prince(IRE), a Group 3 winner in Ireland at two, had shown little in two starts at Meydan earlier in the year. He edged right when he hit the front, but won easing down in the end. Hopefully this will have put him back on the right track. (op 11-4)

Fury, who has rekindled his career this year after being gelded, had taken a Listed handicap over a mile here in May from a mark of 104. He raced keenly due to the lack of real pace and in the end proved no match. (tchd 10-11 and 6-5)
Invisible Man, without a success since taking the 2010 Royal Hunt Cup from a mark of 95, had finished fifth in the same contest this time from 107. He is better suited by big fields and an end-to-end gallop. Here he never looked comfortable. (op 17-2)
New Hampshire(USA), rated just 84, set his own pace. He kept on to dead-heat for third and connections will be hoping that the form is not taken at face value. (op 17-2)

4075 LIVWELL APPRENTICE H'CAP — 7f
5:30 (5:30) (Class 3) (0-95,90) 3-Y-O — **£7,439** (£2,213; £829; £829) **Stalls** Low

Form — RPR

1131 **1** **Dutch Rose (IRE)**[25] 3214 3-8-6 **79** ... DavidBergin(7) 1 — 90
(David O'Meara) *hld up: hdwy 1/2-way: led wl over 1f out: rdn and edgd rt ins fnl f: kpt on* **11/4**[2]

10-0 **2** ¾ **Miss Azeza**[13] 3639 3-9-1 **86** ... AliceHaynes(5) 7 — 95
(David Simcock) *hld up in rr: hdwy wl over 2f out: rdn over 1f out: chsd wnr ins fnl f: kpt on* **20/1**

1121 **3** 3¾ **Trail Blaze (IRE)**[20] 3383 3-9-5 **85** ... AmyRyan 3 — 84
(Kevin Ryan) *chsd ldr: hdwy and cl up over 2f out: sn rdn and ev ch tl one pce fnl f* **5/2**[1]

0-05 **3** dht **Princess Of Orange**[35] 2894 3-8-12 **81** ... JamieJones(3) 6 — 80
(Rae Guest) *hld up in tch: hdwy 3f out: rdn to chse ldrs wl over 1f out: kpt on same pce fnl f* **11/1**

01- **5** ¾ **Dakota Canyon (IRE)**[263] 7052 3-8-5 **78** ... EireannCagney(7) 5 — 75
(Richard Fahey) *hld up in rr: hdwy over 2f out: rdn over 1f out: no imp fnl f* **16/1**

2434 **6** 6 **Personal Touch**[23] 3288 3-8-13 **79** ... LeeTopliss 4 — 60
(Richard Fahey) *chsd ldng pair: rdn along wl over 2f out: sn wknd* **5/1**[3]

3350 **7** ½ **Tidentime (USA)**[22] 3294 3-9-7 **90** ... CharlesBishop(3) 2 — 69
(Mick Channon) *chsd ldrs: rdn along wl over 2f out: sn wknd* **6/1**

0604 **8** 1 **Boris Grigoriev (IRE)**[27] 3165 3-8-13 **84** ... DavidSimmonson(5) 8 — 61
(Michael Easterby) *led: rdn along wl over 2f out: hdd wl over 1f out and sn wknd* **12/1**

1m 27.42s (2.12) **Going Correction** +0.475s/f (Yiel) — **8** Ran SP% **112.9**
Speed ratings (Par 104): **106,105,100,100,100 93,92,91**
PL: Trail Blaze £0.70 Princess Of Orange £1.10. Tricast: DR,MA,TB £76.55 DR,MA,POO £262.06. Toteswinger: 2-3 £5.20 2-5 £7.00 2-6 £12.20 3-6 £1.00 5-6 £3.80. CSF £52.49 TOTE £3.60: £1.60, £5.50; EX 68.60.
Owner Favourites Racing XXIV **Bred** Joseph Kennedy **Trained** Nawton, N Yorks

FOCUS
A competitive 3yo apprentice handicap which was quite strong run. The winner may not need to have improved.

NOTEBOOK
Dutch Rose(IRE) has been a revelation since joining this yard. Her win at Carlisle, her third in four previous starts this time, has been advertised by the runner-up since. Due to race from a 3lb higher mark in future, she did just enough in the end. She can turn out without a penalty from her revised mark until next Friday. (op 3-1 tchd 10-3)
Miss Azeza, dropped 2lb after finishing well beaten on her handicap debut on her reappearance, was stepping up to 7f for the first time. Under a confident ride, she moved up looking a real threat but, in the end, the winning combination proved just the stronger. She deserves to go one better.
Trail Blaze(IRE), winner of three of his previous four starts this time, had a 4lb increase to overcome. He didn't make the running this time and, in the end, came up well short. (op 9-4)
Princess Of Orange, fitted with a hood for the second time, didn't improve for the step up in distance. (op 9-4)
Dakota Canyon(IRE), who accounted for six subsequent winners when winning on his second start at Leicester in October, made his handicap debut from a mark of 78. After a tardy start and soon being pushed along, he put in some solid late work. He will improve for the outing and is crying out for a mile plus. (op 12-1)
T/Plt: £1,153.80 to a £1 stake. Pool: £85,308.00 - 53.97 winning tickets. T/Qpdt: £63.80 to a £1 stake. Pool: £5,687.00 - 65.92 winning tickets. JR

4042 CHESTER (L-H)
Saturday, July 14

OFFICIAL GOING: Soft (6.2)
Wind: Light, half against Weather: Sunny spells

4076 WIN VW UP! ON EASYSIX AT CHESTERBET MAIDEN AUCTION STKS — 5f 16y
2:15 (2:15) (Class 5) 2-Y-O — **£3,881** (£1,155; £577; £288) **Stalls** Low

Form — RPR

22 **1** **Boom And Bloom (IRE)**[17] 3490 2-8-8 0 ... FrederikTylicki 3 — 76
(Richard Fahey) *racd in cl 2nd pl tl over 3f out: rdn and chsd ldr over 1f out: styd on to ld fnl 75yds* **10/11**[1]

2434 **2** hd **Mandy Lexi (IRE)**[10] 3747 2-8-8 72 ... FrannyNorton 4 — 75
(Patrick Morris) *led: rdn over 1f out: hdd fnl 75yds: hld after* **2/1**[2]

054 **3** 3 **Millie N Aire**[21] 3381 2-8-4 66 ... PJMcDonald 6 — 60
(Danielle McCormick) *chsd ldrs: wnt 2nd over 3f out: rdn whn lost 2nd and outpcd over 1f out: styd on same pce and no imp ins fnl f* **6/1**[3]

0 **4** 4½ **Eyeline**[27] 3182 2-8-9 0 ... RussKennemore 7 — 49
(Reg Hollinshead) *s.i.s: in rr: pushed along on outer over 2f out: outpcd over 1f out: n.d after* **11/1**

1m 6.28s (5.28) **Going Correction** +0.875s/f (Soft) — **4** Ran SP% **108.3**
Speed ratings (Par 94): **92,91,86,79**
CSF £2.98 TOTE £2.00; EX 2.30.
Owner Mrs Mary McDonald **Bred** Keatly Overseas Ltd **Trained** Musley Bank, N Yorks

FOCUS
The rail has been moved out three yards between the 6f and 1.5f point, adding 24 yards to all races up to an extended 1m2f (20 yards 5f and 7f), and 46 yards to the extended 1m6f contest. A fair juvenile maiden auction stakes. They went a respectable gallop on ground officially described as soft and the form looks straightforward.

NOTEBOOK
Boom And Bloom(IRE) produced a similar level of form when second on her first two starts over 6f on good to firm at Nottingham (RPR 78) in May, and this 5f trip on soft ground at Carlisle last month. A reproduction of that level of display was good enough to go one better on this occasion. She was representing the in-form Richard Fahey yard and benefited from a strong ride under Freddie Tylicki, who now has a 31% strike-rate when riding for this stable at this venue since 2008. She should continue to pay her way in decent nursery handicaps, possibly at up to 7f, this term. (op 5-6 tchd 4-5)
Mandy Lexi(IRE) finished a close third behind the winner under similar conditions at Carlisle on her penultimate start last month (RPR 75). She reproduced a comparative level of form here and looks likely to remain competitive in average nursery handicaps at up to 6f. (op 9-4)
Millie N Aire showed bright speed once again before fading over 1f out. She may be able to pick up a modest nursery over a sharp 5f on decent ground later this term. (op 11-2 tchd 5-1)
Eyeline failed to go on from his modest Doncaster debut last month, after a slow start. (op 12-1 tchd 10-1)

4077 LAST CHANCE TO BET EASY SIX H'CAP — 6f 18y
2:50 (2:50) (Class 3) (0-90,90) 3-Y-O+ — **£9,703** (£2,887; £1,443; £721) **Stalls** Low

Form — RPR

-00P **1** **Elusive Prince**[56] 2284 4-9-8 **88** ... (b[1]) FrannyNorton 2 — 101
(David Barron) *mde all: rdn over 1f out: edgd lft towards fin: kpt on wl* **10/1**

2444 **2** 1½ **Corporal Maddox**[9] 3772 5-9-4 **84** ... GeorgeBaker 3 — 92
(Jamie Osborne) *hld up in tch: clsd 3f out: chse wnr travelling wl over 2f out: effrt over 1f out: no imp ins fnl f* **5/2**[1]

3000 **3** 5 **Arctic Feeling (IRE)**[14] 3624 4-8-11 **84** ... LauraBarry(7) 14 — 76
(Richard Fahey) *in rr: niggled along 4f out: swtchd lft and hdwy over 1f out: kpt on to take 3rd wl ins fnl f: nt trble front two* **14/1**

0020 **4** 2 **Arganil (USA)**[14] 3624 7-9-9 **89** ... (p) DavidNolan 6 — 74
(Kevin Ryan) *in rr: hdwy on inner over 2f out: rdn to chse ldrs over 1f out but no imp: no ex wl ins fnl f* **16/1**

4620 **5** 2 **Defence Council (IRE)**[9] 3778 4-9-2 **82** ... FrederikTylicki 7 — 61
(Mel Brittain) *in tch: effrt 2f out: no imp on ldrs: btn over 1f out: dropped away ins fnl f* **7/1**[2]

4540 **6** 5 **Parisian Pyramid (IRE)**[50] 2446 6-9-3 **90** ... GeorgeChaloner(7) 5 — 53
(Patrick Morris) *chsd wnr tl rdn over 2f out: wknd over 1f out* **5/2**[1]

-630 **7** nk **Baldemar**[9] 3771 7-9-2 **82** ... LiamJones 11 — 44
(Richard Fahey) *chsd ldrs: outpcd over 2f out: wknd over 1f out* **8/1**[3]

-002 **8** 7 **Fred Willetts (IRE)**[49] 2487 4-9-7 **87** ... (v) StephenCraine 9 — 27
(Tony Coyle) *hld up: rdn over 2f out: nvr a threat* **7/1**[2]

1m 17.91s (4.11) **Going Correction** +0.875s/f (Soft) — **8** Ran SP% **114.9**
Speed ratings (Par 107): **107,105,98,95,93 86,85,76**
toteswingers 1&2 £5.80, 1&3 £10.90, 2&3 £4.30 CSF £35.53 CT £359.31 TOTE £6.40: £3.30, £1.80, £4.80; EX 41.00.
Owner Bridge Extraction Systems Ltd **Bred** Usk Valley Stud **Trained** Maunby, N Yorks

FOCUS
A decent sprint handicap for 3-y-os and up. They went a solid gallop throughout on soft ground and this rates a personal-best from the winner with the second in line with recent marks.

NOTEBOOK
Elusive Prince broke well from a good low draw, sporting first-time blinkers, and never saw another rival on this return from an eight-week break since pulling up after reportedly hurting his head in the stalls at Thirsk in May. Franny Norton got on board the gelding when his original mount was declared a non-runner in the morning. He was competing off a 3lb higher rating than when last successful over this trip on good to soft ground at Ripon last August. He is versatile as regards ground and, provided the headgear continues to have the desired effect, he looks capable of further success over this trip this term. (op 8-1)
Corporal Maddox has been running well over 7f and this drop back to 6f from a good low draw on soft ground looked suitable for a horse with decent placed course form. He travelled notably well behind the front-running winner rounding the bend for home, but could not get to grips with him up the home straight. He should remain competitive at up to 7f off this sort of mark. (tchd 9-4 after early 3-1 in a place)
Arctic Feeling(IRE), five lengths back in third, will benefit from a dry spell of weather. (op 11-1)
Arganil(USA) enjoys these conditions on more conventional tracks. (op 10-1)
Parisian Pyramid(IRE) disappointed returning from a seven-week break, and probably needed this first start for new trainer Patrick Morris after leaving Kevin Ryan. (op 7-2 tchd 4-1)
Baldemar tried in vain to keep tabs on the leader from a poor draw. (op 7-1)

4078 CHESTERBET CITY PLATE (LISTED RACE) — 7f 2y
3:25 (3:25) (Class 1) 3-Y-O+
£19,848 (£7,525; £3,766; £1,876; £941; £472) **Stalls** Low

Form — RPR

-323 **1** **Majestic Myles (IRE)**[14] 3633 4-9-2 108 ... FrederikTylicki 6 — 114
(Richard Fahey) *mde all: rdn over 1f out: r.o wl to draw clr and edgd rt ins fnl f* **7/2**[2]

-450 **2** 4½ **Royal Rock**[21] 3370 8-9-2 110 ... GeorgeBaker 2 — 102
(Chris Wall) *in tch: rdn to take 2nd 1f out: no ch w wnr ins fnl f* **11/2**[3]

-126 **3** 1¾ **Our Jonathan**[14] 3623 5-9-2 110 ... FrannyNorton 7 — 98
(Kevin Ryan) *v awkward s and slowly away: sn swtchd lft: in rr: u.p over 2f out: rdn and hdwy over 1f out: kpt on ins fnl f: nvr able to chal* **3/1**[1]

0320 **4** nk **Doncaster Rover (USA)**[14] 3623 6-9-2 105 ... (p) RobertWinston 3 — 97
(David Brown) *hld up: rdn 2f out: kpt on u.p ins fnl f: nvr able to trble ldrs* **7/1**

24-0 **5** ½ **I Love Me**[24] 3266 4-8-11 107 ... KirstyMilczarek 1 — 91
(Andrew Balding) *racd keenly in 2nd pl to 5f out: remained handy: chsd wnr over 2f out: no imp and outpcd whn lost 2nd u.p 1f out: no ex wl ins fnl f* **3/1**[1]

1103 **6** 3½ **Imperial Djay (IRE)**[7] 3855 7-9-2 97 ... PJMcDonald 5 — 87
(Ruth Carr) *hld up: pushed along 2f out: no imp whn n.m.r and checked over 1f out: sn swtchd lft and outpcd: nvr a threat* **6/1**

3104 **7** 4½ **Solar Spirit (IRE)**[17] 3493 7-9-2 83 ... PaulPickard 4 — 75
(Tracy Waggott) *chsd ldrs: wnt 2nd 5f out: pushed along and lost 2nd over 2f out: wknd over 1f out* **40/1**

1m 30.52s (4.02) **Going Correction** +0.875s/f (Soft) — **7** Ran SP% **116.8**
Speed ratings (Par 111): **112,106,104,104,103 99,94**
toteswingers 1&2 £4.70, 1&3 £2.60, 2&3 £2.90 CSF £23.74 TOTE £4.50: £2.30, £4.00; EX 18.60.
Owner James Gaffney **Bred** Arctic Tack Stud **Trained** Musley Bank, N Yorks

FOCUS
A decent Listed contest and a pattern was emerging on this card, in that it was very difficult to make up ground on a surface described as "very dead and tacky" by one of the jockeys. The winner is rated to his best and is probably the only one to show his true form.

NOTEBOOK
Majestic Myles(IRE) had won this contest last year on good ground from an always handy position. He made all his own running on this occasion in emphatic style, after a quick break from the gates on a soft surface, with the state of the ground the one legitimate concern for form students beforehand. He had run well in Group 3 company on good to firm ground at Newmarket the previous month, and a race of that stature looks well within his compass this year over this 7f trip. (op 4-1 tchd 9-2)
Royal Rock ran on well to finish eighth of 14 in the Group 1 Diamond Jubilee Stakes at Royal Ascot last month, and he had already won over 7f at Lingfield on good ground much earlier in his career. He gives plenty of substance to this form and may be able to pick up a similar contest back over 6f on better ground. (op 9-2 tchd 6-1)
Our Jonathan missed the break and duly took his medicine by racing in behind the pack on the rail. He always looked likely to struggle to play a significant role from that moment onwards and did well to come round the field to finish third in the circumstances. (op 5-2 tchd 9-4)
Doncaster Rover(USA) was wearing first-time cheekpieces and kept on into a never-nearer fourth from a poor position. (op 15-2 tchd 8-1)

I Love Me finished fourth in the Group 1 Coronation Stakes at Royal Ascot last season. She raced keenly on this course and ran some way below that level of form on this second subsequent start. She will benefit from a return to better ground on a more conventional track at up to 1m. (op 9-2)

4079 HAVE IT EACHWAY AT CHESTERBET H'CAP 1m 6f 91y
4:00 (4:01) (Class 3) (0-95,87) 3-Y-O **£8,409** (£2,502; £1,250; £625) **Stalls** Low

Form RPR

21 **1** **Monshak (IRE)**[29] 3100 3-9-1 **81** GeorgeBaker 5 90+
(Sir Michael Stoute) *hld up: pushed along 4f out: hdwy 2f out: effrt over 1f out: styd on to ld wl ins fnl f: pushed out whn in control towards fin* **9/4**[2]

2113 **2** *1* **Ruacana**[42] 2718 3-9-7 **87** PJMcDonald 4 94
(Michael Bell) *prom: rdn and outpcd by ldrs over 3f out: rallied to take 2nd over 2f out: styd on for press to ld briefly ins fnl f: hld towards fin* **9/2**[3]

3100 **3** *2* **Singalat**[22] 3330 3-9-0 **80** FrederikTylicki 1 84
(James Given) *led: pressed 3f out: sn pushed along: rdn and edgd rt ent st over 1f out: hdd ins fnl f: no ex fnl 75yds* **9/1**

6-12 **4** *21* **Gassin Golf**[23] 3305 3-9-6 **86** RobertWinston 6 63
(Sir Mark Prescott Bt) *s.i.s: hld up: racd keenly: hdwy to take 2nd after 5f: rdn to chal 3f out: lost 2nd over 2f out: sn wknd* **13/8**[1]

2-20 **5** *34* **Maastricht (IRE)**[42] 2718 3-9-1 **81** AdrianNicholls 7 14
(Mark Johnston) *prom: niggled along and lost pl wl over 7f out: pushed along 5f out: struggling after: lost tch over 2f out: t.o* **13/2**

3m 20.18s (13.18) **Going Correction** +1.00s/f (Soft) 5 Ran SP% **110.4**
Speed ratings (Par 104): **102,101,100,88,68**
CSF £12.41 TOTE £3.60: £1.40, £2.00; EX 8.60.

Owner Nurlan Bizakov **Bred** Ecurie Des Monceaux **Trained** Newmarket, Suffolk

FOCUS
A decent staying handicap for 3-y-os. They went a respectable gallop at best on the prevailing soft ground and the third probably provides the key to the form.

NOTEBOOK
Monshak(IRE) ◆ finished 3l second of five behind Great Heavens, who won the Group 2 Lancashire Oaks the previous week, on her debut over an extended 1m3f at Yarmouth in May, and won her maiden over 1m4f on soft ground at Chepstow last month. She looked a potential blot on the handicap here off an initial mark of 81, provided she handled this course and an extended 2f longer trip. She rallied to win her maiden which gave hope on that score. She duly became the first horse on the card to come from a held-up position to win and clearly has bundles of stamina, with this sort of ground possibly important to her, but she looks of interest for a work up through the ranks at up to 2m. (tchd 2-1 and 5-2)
Ruacana was returning from a six-week break and ran on well to finish second. He got this longer trip well after posting some good 1m4f displays this term. He should be up to winning a similar contest on better ground over this trip from a fair mark. (op 7-2)
Singalat appeared likely to be another all-the-way winner on this card, after setting his own tempo on the lead. He got tired up the home straight on this ground, drifting to his right, but stuck to his task gamely enough. A drop back to 1m4f on good to firm ground looks his ideal scenario. (op 13-2)
Gassin Golf didn't look to cope with the testing conditions. Official explanation: trainer's rep said gelding was unsuited by the soft ground (op 9-4 tchd 6-4 and 5-2)

4080 BET CHESTERBET YANKEE H'CAP 1m 2f 75y
4:35 (4:35) (Class 4) (0-80,81) 4-Y-O+ **£5,175** (£1,540; £769; £384) **Stalls** High

Form RPR

2004 **1** **Fork Handles**[15] 3556 4-9-7 **80** (v) GeorgeBaker 2 88
(Mick Channon) *mde all: gng strly over 2 l clr over 2f out: rdn over 1f out: kpt on gamely towards fin* **11/4**[1]

6-11 **2** *1 1/4* **Bright Applause**[24] 3290 4-8-11 **70** FrederikTylicki 3 76
(Tracy Waggott) *handy: pushed along to chse wnr 2f out: no imp tl styd on towards fin: unable to chal* **3/1**[2]

2125 **3** *2* **Mighty Clarets (IRE)**[9] 3775 5-8-6 **65** KirstyMilczarek 8 67
(Barry Leavy) *hld up: pushed along over 3f out: hdwy on outer 2f out: rdn to chse ldrs over 1f out: styd on same pce ins fnl f* **15/2**

0-65 **4** *1 1/4* **Robert The Painter (IRE)**[28] 3167 4-9-4 **77** DavidNolan 6 80
(David O'Meara) *hld up: pushed along over 3f out: n.m.r and hmpd 2f out: plugged on at one pce fnl f: no imp* **7/2**[3]

0406 **5** *8* **Tapis Libre**[12] 3699 4-8-8 **70** RossAtkinson(3) 7 55
(Michael Easterby) *prom: rdn over 4f out: wknd 3f out* **16/1**

2241 **6** *5* **Brockfield**[24] 3287 6-9-2 **75** RobertWinston 11 50
(Mel Brittain) *hld up: plld hrd: hdwy to go prom after 2f: rdn whn chalng 3f out: wknd over 1f out: eased whn wl btn ins fnl f* **4/1**

2m 22.03s (10.83) **Going Correction** +1.00s/f (Soft) 6 Ran SP% **111.5**
Speed ratings (Par 105): **96,95,93,92,86 82**
toteswingers 1&2 £2.60, 1&3 £2.30, 2&3 £2.90 CSF £11.14 CT £51.42 TOTE £3.30: £1.80, £1.50; EX 11.50.

Owner Dr Marwan Koukash **Bred** Mike Channon Bloodstock Ltd **Trained** West Ilsley, Berks

FOCUS
A fair handicap for older horses. The form is ordinary with the third and fourth helping to set the standard.
Brockfield Official explanation: trainer's rep said gelding was unsuited by the track

4081 PICK A PATENT AT CHESTERBET H'CAP 6f 18y
5:10 (5:13) (Class 4) (0-80,80) 3-Y-O **£5,175** (£1,540; £769; £384) **Stalls** Low

Form RPR

1010 **1** **Towbee**[57] 2256 3-8-11 **77** DavidSimmonson(7) 7 87
(Michael Easterby) *s.i.s: hld up: hdwy 2f out: rdn and hung lft 1f out: r.o ins fnl f to ld towards fin* **11/1**

1-01 **2** *1* **Tango Sky (IRE)**[7] 3861 3-9-1 **79** (p) JamesRogers(5) 2 86
(Ralph Beckett) *led: rdn over 1f out: hdd and no answer to wnr towards fin* **15/8**[1]

3111 **3** *1 1/2* **Dark Ages (IRE)**[17] 3510 3-8-11 **75** (t) DavidKenny(5) 10 77
(Paul Burgoyne) *in rr: hdwy on inner over 1f out: styd on u.p ins fnl f: nt quite pce of front two fnl 100yds* **10/1**

2153 **4** *2* **Half A Billion (IRE)**[33] 2979 3-9-4 **77** PJMcDonald 5 73
(Michael Dods) *chsd ldrs: wnt 2nd over 2f out: rdn and nt qckn over 1f out: sn hmpd: styd on same pce and no imp ins fnl f* **9/2**[2]

3620 **5** *hd* **Bella Ophelia (IRE)**[14] 3639 3-9-7 **80** GeorgeBaker 6 75
(Hughie Morrison) *chsd ldrs: rdn and nt qckn over 1f out: styd on same pce ins fnl f: no imp on ldrs fnl 100yds* **5/1**[3]

0326 **6** *28* **Rusty Rocket (IRE)**[14] 3607 3-9-6 **79** RobertWinston 8
(Paul Green) *towards rr: u.p over 2f out: forced wd whn bhd and no ch ent st wl over 1f out: nvr a threat* **9/2**[2]

0550 **7** *13* **Adranian (IRE)**[10] 3762 3-9-0 **73** (v) AdrianNicholls 4
(David C Griffiths) *pressed ldr tl rdn over 2f out: sn wknd: c wd and eased whn btn ent st wl over 1f out* **33/1**

-600 **R** **Blodwen Abbey**[61] 2136 3-8-4 **63** LiamJones 3
(James Unett) *ref to r* **12/1**

1m 20.3s (6.50) **Going Correction** +1.00s/f (Soft) 8 Ran SP% **115.9**
Speed ratings (Par 102): **96,94,92,90,89 52,35,**
toteswingers 1&2 £7.50, 1&3 £10.50, 2&3 £3.30 CSF £32.56 CT £222.85 TOTE £20.80: £5.60, £2.60, £5.20; EX 49.90.

Owner Mrs A Jarvis **Bred** Mrs A Jarvis **Trained** Sheriff Hutton, N Yorks

FOCUS
A fair sprint handicap for 3-y-os. They went a contested gallop and this time the first and third came from off the pace. The latter is rated to her recent personal-best.
Tango Sky(IRE) Official explanation: jockey said gelding hung right-handed
Rusty Rocket(IRE) Official explanation: jockey said colt hung right-handed
Adranian(IRE) Official explanation: jockey said gelding hung right-handed

4082 FIND A FORECAST AT CHESTERBET APPRENTICE H'CAP 7f 122y
5:45 (5:45) (Class 4) (0-80,79) 3-Y-O **£5,175** (£1,540; £769; £384) **Stalls** Low

Form RPR

2123 **1** **Our Boy Jack (IRE)**[28] 3160 3-9-2 **79** LauraBarry(5) 10 88+
(Richard Fahey) *hld up: hdwy over 2f out: led over 1f out: edgd rt wl ins fnl f: jst hld on* **7/2**[1]

2-1 **2** *hd* **Gaul Wood (IRE)**[178] 204 3-9-6 **78** RossAtkinson 2 88+
(Tom Dascombe) *in tch: pushed along over 3f out: effrt on inner whn nt clr run and hmpd 2f out: swtchd lft over 1f out: r.o strly ins fnl f: jst failed* **7/1**

4250 **3** *2* **Berlusca (IRE)**[11] 3736 3-8-13 **71** KierenFox 11 73
(Mark Brisbourne) *in rr: niggled along over 4f out: hdwy wl over 3f out: rdn over 2f out: chalng whn edgd lft over 1f out: nt qckn: lugged lft ins fnl f: styd on same pce towards fin* **20/1**

630 **4** *5* **Running Reef (IRE)**[24] 3274 3-8-11 **69** PaulPickard 6 59
(Tracy Waggott) *led: hdd over 5f out: regained ld 4f out: rdn and hdd over 1f out: no ex fnl 150yds* **22/1**

1641 **5** *2 3/4* **Lolita Lebron (IRE)**[15] 3555 3-9-1 **73** MichaelMetcalfe 9 56
(Lawrence Mullaney) *sn bmpd: trckd ldrs: pushed along over 3f out: rdn and outpcd 2f out: wl btn fnl f* **11/2**[3]

5010 **6** *3/4* **Shamrocked (IRE)**[14] 3607 3-9-4 **76** CharlesBishop 12 60
(Mick Channon) *sn bmpd: prom: led over 5f out: hdd 4f out: rdn 2f out: ev ch whn n.m.r and hmpd over 1f out: sn lost pl and wknd* **8/1**

3003 **7** *3/4* **Green Mitas (ITY)**[15] 3558 3-7-11 **60** oh1 NatashaEaton(5) 7 39
(Frank Sheridan) *midfield: pushed along over 2f out: sn outpcd: wl btn fnl f* **14/1**

4000 **8** *3 3/4* **Not Bad For A Boy (IRE)**[15] 3555 3-8-5 **63** ow1 JamesRogers 4 33
(Barry Leavy) *prom: lost pl over 4f out: nvr on terms w ldrs after* **28/1**

9 *12* **Eternal Gift (FR)**[67] 3-9-7 **79** JamieJones 3 19
(Rae Guest) *hld up: struggling 3f out: nvr a threat* **11/1**

-630 **10** *1 3/4* **Border Revia (IRE)**[24] 3274 3-9-0 **77** (p) GeorgeChaloner(5) 5 12
(Richard Fahey) *rrd s and slowly away: nvr gng wl: a bhd* **8/1**

4534 **P** **Chester Aristocrat**[15] 3555 3-8-5 **68** JasonHart(5) 8
(Eric Alston) *racd v keenly: handy: sn bmpd and lost pl: p.u after nrly 1f* **4/1**[2]

1m 41.29s (7.49) **Going Correction** +1.00s/f (Soft) 11 Ran SP% **119.9**
Speed ratings (Par 102): **102,101,99,94,92 91,90,86,74,73**
toteswingers 1&2 £7.00, 1&3 £14.90, 2&3 £24.10 CSF £28.04 CT £443.93 TOTE £4.60: £1.80, £2.70, £6.30; EX 31.10.

Owner Middleham Park Racing XXXVI **Bred** Mrs Ian Fox **Trained** Musley Bank, N Yorks

FOCUS
A fair 3-y-o handicap for apprentice riders. They appeared to go off too quickly in this contest on soft ground and the first three came from off the pace and finished clear. The winner is rated to form while the second looked unlucky.
Eternal Gift(FR) Official explanation: jockey said colt never travelled
T/Plt: £31.40 to a £1 stake. Pool: £70,485.20 to a £1 stake - 1,634.89 winning tickets T/Qpdt: £8.40 to a £1 stake. Pool: £4,073.88 - 358.06 winning tickets DO

3725 HAMILTON (R-H)
Saturday, July 14

OFFICIAL GOING: Heavy (soft in places 7.1)
Wind: Almost nil Weather: Overcast

4083 BOOK NOW FOR LADIES NIGHT MAIDEN AUCTION STKS 5f 4y
5:40 (5:41) (Class 5) 2-Y-O **£3,408** (£1,006; £503) **Stalls** High

Form RPR

450 **1** **Lucy Bee**[17] 3490 2-8-5 54 AndrewMullen 1 57
(Keith Dalgleish) *prom: pushed along over 2f out: hdwy and swtchd rt over 1f out: led wl ins fnl f: edgd lft: r.o* **7/1**[3]

35 **2** *1/2* **Twilight Pearl**[77] 1671 2-8-6 0 JamesSullivan 4 56
(Tim Easterby) *chsd ldr: pushed along 1/2-way: rdn and sltly outpcd over 1f out: styd on to take 2nd nr fin* **5/4**[1]

002 **3** *3/4* **Red Highlites (IRE)**[10] 3747 2-8-8 70 (p) PaddyAspell 6 55
(Ann Duffield) *t.k.h: led: rdn over 1f out: hdd and no ex wl ins fnl f* **11/8**[2]

00 **4** *1* **Beadle**[37] 2837 2-8-13 0 AndrewElliott 5 57
(Richard Fahey) *trckd ldrs: n.m.r over 1f out: sn rdn: kpt on same pce ins fnl f* **12/1**

4 **5** *17* **Princess Cayan (IRE)**[5] 3902 2-8-0 0 ShirleyTeasdale(7) 3
(Linda Perratt) *dwlt: bhd and sn outpcd: lost tch fr 1/2-way: t.o* **20/1**

1m 4.05s (4.05) **Going Correction** +0.625s/f (Yiel) 5 Ran SP% **111.5**
Speed ratings (Par 94): **92,91,90,88,61**
CSF £16.64 TOTE £7.50: £2.70, £1.30; EX 18.90.

Owner Mrs Lucille Bone **Bred** Sandy Bone **Trained** Carluke, S Lanarks
■ Stewards' Enquiry : Andrew Mullen one-day ban: careless riding (Jul 28)

FOCUS
The rail had been moved to give fresh ground, meaning that all races beyond 6f were approximately 25 yards longer than the official distances. The stalls were placed on the stands' side for the opening race, otherwise for the remaining 5f and 6f races they were in the middle. The form is weak with the runner-up the best guide.

NOTEBOOK
Lucy Bee had shown only poor form hitherto but she showed some improvement faced with a greater test of stamina than previously, getting up late having looked an unlikely winner when seemingly struggling and pushed along in rear at halfway. She's rather blown her handicap mark with this win but there's every chance of a bit more progress at 6f. (op 15-2)
Twilight Pearl ran well back from a three-month break, but looked a bit tapped for speed at this minimum trip even on this stiff track and is almost certainly ready for a step up to 6f. (op 7-4)
Red Highlites(IRE) had the best form and travelled like the best horse in the race for a long way but was found out by conditions and the uphill finish, being headed close home. She's unlikely to find another maiden auction as weak as this and might need dropping into a claimer to open her account, but faster ground will at least play to her strengths. (op 5-4)

Beadle shaped with some encouragement without being given a hard time on his first run since leaving Keith Dalgleish, and his shrewd new trainer has almost certainly left something to work now he is eligible for nurseries. (op 17-2)

Princess Cayan(IRE) didn't show much again but still looked very inexperienced and clearly isn't one for the short term.

4084 BULMERS H'CAP 5f 4y

6:10 (6:10) (Class 6) (0-65,63) 3-Y-O **£2,587** (£770; £384; £192) **Stalls** Centre

Form				RPR
4232	**1**		**Economic Crisis (IRE)**[7] 3848 3-9-1 **57**.......... PaddyAspell 1 (Alan Berry) *fly j. s: t.k.h and sn cl up: led gng wl over 1f out: rdn clr fnl f* **3/1**[3]	68
621	**2**	*2 ¼*	**Lord Buffhead**[71] 1817 3-8-12 **57**.......... DeclanCannon(3) 3 (Richard Guest) *led: rdn and hdd over 1f out: edgd rt ins fnl f: kpt on: nt pce of wnr* **2/1**[1]	60
0005	**3**	*1 ½*	**Essexvale (IRE)**[24] 3289 3-7-10 **45**..........(p) EvaMoscrop(7) 4 (Robert Johnson) *in tch: pushed along and outpcd over 1f out: edgd rt: styd on fnl f: nvr able to chal* **16/1**	43
4153	**4**	*nk*	**Rock Canyon (IRE)**[11] 3731 3-9-2 **63**..........(p) LMcNiff(5) 5 (Linda Perratt) *s.i.s: sn drvn and outpcd: hdwy over 1f out: kpt on fnl f: nrst fin* **5/2**[2]	59
0-50	**5**	*1*	**Roy's Legacy**[14] 3613 3-8-9 **58**.......... ShirleyTeasdale(7) 6 (Shaun Harris) *trckd ldrs: rdn and edgd rt over 1f out: outpcd fnl f* **15/2**	51
0F05	**6**	*5*	**Dragon Spirit (IRE)**[15] 3580 3-8-3 **45**..........(p) JamesSullivan 2 (Linda Perratt) *in tch: pushed along over 2f out: wknd wl over 1f out* **16/1**	20

1m 2.77s (2.77) **Going Correction** +0.625s/f (Yiel) **6** Ran SP% **110.4**

Speed ratings (Par 98): **102,98,96,95,93 85**

toteswingers 1&2 £1.70, 1&3 £4.40, 2&3 £6.50 CSF £9.11 TOTE £3.50: £2.00, £1.50; EX 7.80.

Owner Mr & Mrs T Blane **Bred** Philip Hore Jnr **Trained** Cockerham, Lancs

FOCUS

A very weak handicap in which only one of the runners had a mark within 6lb of the rating ceiling. The field were soon strung out and the first two dominated, and they set the level.

4085 JOHN SMITH'S EXTRA SMOOTH H'CAP 6f 5y

6:40 (6:40) (Class 5) (0-70,70) 3-Y-O+ **£3,881** (£1,155; £577; £288) **Stalls** Centre

Form				RPR
6-40	**1**		**Sparking**[35] 2943 5-9-3 **61**.......... RichardKingscote 5 (Tom Dascombe) *t.k.h: cl up: led over 1f out: rdn and r.o wl fnl f* **7/2**[1]	72
0455	**2**	*1 ½*	**Soopacal (IRE)**[26] 3209 7-8-8 **55** ow1.......... DaleSwift(3) 9 (Brian Ellison) *chsd ldrs: rdn over 2f out: edgd rt and chsd wnr fnl f: kpt on* **7/2**[1]	61
0413	**3**	*1 ¼*	**Tenancy (IRE)**[11] 3717 8-8-2 **53**..........(b) ShirleyTeasdale(7) 3 (Shaun Harris) *led tl rdn and hdd over 1f out: kpt on same pce ins fnl f* **7/1**[3]	55
2356	**4**	*1 ½*	**Waabel**[4] 3944 5-9-12 **70**..........(t) StephenCraine 4 (Richard Guest) *hld up bhd ldng gp: rdn and hdwy over 1f out: kpt on ins fnl f: nvr able to chal* **9/1**	68
3120	**5**	*¾*	**Cut The Cackle (IRE)**[17] 3495 6-9-2 **65**..........(bt) LMcNiff(5) 2 (Richard Guest) *dwlt: sn in tch: rdn and edgd rt 2f out: no ex fnl f* **9/2**[2]	61
0040	**6**	*2 ¾*	**Cross Of Lorraine (IRE)**[19] 3442 9-8-8 **57**..........(p) GarryWhillans(5) 8 (Chris Grant) *dwlt: bhd: outpcd after 2f: sme late hdwy: nvr on terms* **7/2**[1]	44
3100	**7**	*3*	**Red Roar (IRE)**[17] 3496 5-9-4 **69**.......... MatthewHopkins(7) 1 (Alan Berry) *t.k.h: prom tl rdn and wknd fr 2f out* **8/1**	47

1m 15.49s (3.29) **Going Correction** +0.625s/f (Yiel) **7** Ran SP% **118.5**

Speed ratings (Par 103): **103,101,99,97,96 92,88**

toteswingers 1&2 £3.20, 1&3 £5.50, 2&3 £5.00 CSF £16.75 CT £82.21 TOTE £5.00: £3.30, £2.20; EX 11.90.

Owner P Bamford **Bred** Dandy's Farm **Trained** Malpas, Cheshire

FOCUS

A very modest handicap run at an ordinary gallop for a sprint and with hardly any of the field in top form it's not form to be dwelling on. The form looks sound rated around the first two.

Cross Of Lorraine(IRE) Official explanation: jockey said gelding never travelled

4086 JOHN SMITH'S SCOTTISH STEWARDS' CUP (H'CAP) 6f 5y

7:15 (7:16) (Class 2) (0-105,104) 3-Y-O+

£21,787 (£6,524; £3,262; £1,631; £815; £409) **Stalls** High

Form				RPR
2550	**1**		**Grissom (IRE)**[14] 3624 6-8-12 **90**.......... AndrewElliott 1 (Tim Easterby) *hld up in tch: hdwy on far side of gp to ld ins fnl f: kpt on strly* **14/1**	98
0653	**2**	*¾*	**Roker Park (IRE)**[14] 3626 7-8-0 **85**.......... DavidBergin(7) 14 (David O'Meara) *hld up in tch: hdwy on nr side of gp to ld briefly ent fnl f: kpt on: hld towards fin* **9/2**[1]	91
0525	**3**	*½*	**Mass Rally (IRE)**[14] 3624 5-8-13 **91**..........(b) PaulMulrennan 4 (Michael Dods) *hld up: smooth hdwy nr side of gp to chse ldrs ent fnl f: sn rdn and kpt on same pce* **10/1**	95
5111	**4**	*hd*	**Klynch**[9] 3772 6-9-3 **95** 6ex..........(b) JamesSullivan 6 (Ruth Carr) *dwlt: bhd: hdwy into midfield whn nt clr run briefly 2f out: rdn and styd on wl fnl f: nrst fin* **6/1**[2]	99
0500	**5**	*2*	**Thunderball**[22] 3331 6-8-10 **91**..........(p) DeclanCannon(3) 5 (Scott Dixon) *in tch: effrt and drvn over 2f out: kpt on same pce fnl f* **16/1**	89
3001	**6**	*nse*	**Fast Shot**[14] 3624 4-9-0 **92**.......... PaddyAspell 16 (Tim Easterby) *disp ld on nr side of gp to over 1f out: no ex fnl f* **13/2**[3]	90
0130	**7**	*1 ¾*	**Colonel Mak**[21] 3371 5-9-7 **104**.......... LMcNiff(5) 8 (David Barron) *cl up: effrt and rdn 2f out: wknd ins fnl f* **9/1**	96
0030	**8**	*1*	**Advanced**[22] 3331 9-8-9 **94**.......... PaulMcGiff(7) 3 (Kevin Ryan) *prom on far side of gp: drvn over 2f out: wknd over 1f out* **16/1**	83
0000	**9**	*½*	**Valery Borzov (IRE)**[14] 3624 8-8-5 **88** ow1..........(v) ShaneBKelly(5) 7 (Richard Fahey) *sn pushed along towards rr: drvn and effrt 2f out: sn no imp* **15/2**	76
0016	**10**	*½*	**Damika (IRE)**[27] 3183 9-8-10 **88**..........(v) MichaelStainton 12 (David Brown) *mde most to ent fnl f: sn btn* **12/1**	74
100	**11**	*8*	**Masked Dance (IRE)**[30] 3078 5-8-0 **85** oh1..........(p) JordanUys(7) 2 (Scott Dixon) *in tch on outside of gp: rdn over 2f out: wknd wl over 1f out* **33/1**	47
1500	**12**	*1 ¾*	**New Planet (IRE)**[21] 3371 4-9-3 **95**.......... MichaelO'Connell 11 (John Quinn) *cl up tl rdn and wknd over 2f out* **9/1**	52
4030	**13**	*4 ½*	**Docofthebay (IRE)**[22] 3331 8-8-8 **89**..........(b) DaleSwift(3) 13 (Scott Dixon) *prom tl rdn and wknd over 1f out: b.b.v* **14/1**	33

1m 14.98s (2.78) **Going Correction** +0.70s/f (Yiel) **13** Ran SP% **122.4**

Speed ratings (Par 109): **109,108,107,107,104 104,102,100,100,99 88,86,80**

toteswingers 1&2 £16.90, 1&3 £15.70, 2&3 £6.20 CSF £77.75 CT £704.57 TOTE £20.40: £6.20, £1.90, £3.40; EX 109.10.

Owner Jim & Helen Bowers **Bred** Michael McGlynn **Trained** Great Habton, N Yorks

■ Stewards' Enquiry : James Sullivan two-day ban: careless riding (Jul 28-29)

FOCUS

Not the race it has been in past years with a good majority of the field in or approaching the veteran stage. The pace was a strong one and the first four all came from behind. The form makes sense rated around the placed horses.

NOTEBOOK

Grissom(IRE) hails from a stable in cracking form and maintained his unbeaten record here in good style, having to wait for a passage as the runners rather bunched towards the far side but shooting clear once it came. He won back-to-back handicaps last year and would have to merit consideration if turned out quickly with his yard firing as it is, not least as he is just as effective at 7f. Official explanation: trainer's rep said, regarding apparent improvement in form, that the gelding had benefited from being ridden more patiently.

Roker Park(IRE) had plenty in his favour coming here in form off a 6lb lower mark than when third in this race last year and other than getting to the front a bit sooner than might have been ideal he needs no excuses. A good effort.

Mass Rally(IRE) is clearly well handicapped given how strongly he travelled, on the bridle for much longer than anything else, but he hasn't won since 2009 and it was clear why, finding very little once finally cajoled for his effort.

Klynch was trying to defy a career-high mark but though out of the places this run shouldn't be taken as evidence it is beyond him (down 3lb after this anyway) as he was impeded at the start and then didn't get a run as he began his challenge. He finished with a flourish and looks in great heart still. (op 5-1)

Thunderball had the race run to suit but looks to be paying the price right now for his early-season wins and despite that couldn't get competitive. (op 22-1)

Fast Shot had conditions in his favour but faced a tougher task off a 5lb higher mark than he has raced off before without the benefit of a favourable draw like he had at Newcastle last time. He wasn't up to it without being discredited. (tchd 5-1)

Colonel Mak did best of those that cut out the strong pace and needs his effort upgrading. (op 8-1)

Damika(IRE) was still a length or so in front entering the last but couldn't sustain his effort. He effectively set the race up for the others. (op 16-1)

Docofthebay(IRE) Official explanation: trainer's rep said gelding bled from the nose

4087 GLASGOW STKS RACEDAY NEXT THURSDAY (S) H'CAP 6f 5y

7:50 (7:50) (Class 6) (0-65,64) 3-5-Y-O **£2,215** (£654; £327) **Stalls** Centre

Form				RPR
000	**1**		**Lothair (IRE)**[26] 3235 3-8-4 **48** ow1.......... AndrewElliott 10 (Alan Swinbank) *w ldr: led 1/2-way: edgd rt u.p and hrd pressed ins fnl f: hld on wl* **10/1**	54
0500	**2**	*nk*	**Face East (USA)**[6] 3889 4-8-8 **46** ow1..........(b[1]) PaddyAspell 9 (Alan Berry) *hld up: rdn and hdwy over 1f out: disp ld ins fnl f: edgd rt: hld cl home* **40/1**	51
0003	**3**	*2 ¼*	**Red Scintilla**[26] 3209 5-8-10 **48**..........(p) AndrewMullen 7 (Nigel Tinkler) *prom: outpcd over 3f out: rallied and edgd rt over 1f out: kpt on: nt pce of first two* **13/2**	46
0434	**4**	*1*	**Miserere Mei (IRE)**[16] 3540 3-8-1 **48** ow1..........(e) DeclanCannon(3) 6 (Richard Guest) *hld up in tch: smooth hdwy over 2f out: rdn appr fnl f: sn one pce* **9/1**	43
4605	**5**	*1 ½*	**Weetentherty**[24] 3272 5-8-9 **52**..........(p) ShaneBKelly(5) 4 (Linda Perratt) *dwlt: bhd and sn drvn along: rdn and hdwy 2f out: sn rdn and carried hd high: no imp fnl f* **15/2**	43
5302	**6**	*hd*	**Mark Anthony (IRE)**[11] 3723 5-8-8 **53**.......... ShirleyTeasdale(7) 2 (Shaun Harris) *led to 1/2-way: drvn and outpcd over 1f out: n.d after* **11/4**[1]	43
-064	**7**	*2 ½*	**Elusive Island (USA)**[23] 3315 3-8-8 **52** ow1..........(v) PaulMulrennan 1 (Ann Duffield) *t.k.h: cl up tl rdn and wknd over 1f out* **5/1**[2]	34
0154	**8**	*8*	**Qubuh (IRE)**[37] 2838 4-9-12 **64**.......... JamesSullivan 3 (Linda Stubbs) *in tch: rdn and outpcd over 3f out: n.d after* **11/2**[3]	22
6630	**9**	*5*	**Nine Before Ten (IRE)**[25] 3256 4-9-8 **60**.......... RobbieFitzpatrick 11 (Charles Smith) *awkward s: sn cl up: rdn and wknd wl over 1f out* **9/1**	
405-	**10**	*8*	**Come To Mind**[259] 7157 3-7-10 **47** ow2.......... MatthewHopkins(7) 5 (Alan Berry) *missed break: a bhd and outpcd* **50/1**	

1m 17.4s (5.20) **Going Correction** +0.70s/f (Yiel)

WFA 3 from 4yo+ 6lb **10** Ran SP% **117.3**

Speed ratings (Par 101): **93,92,89,88,86 86,82,72,65,54**

toteswingers 1&2 £60.60, 1&3 £8.70, 2&3 £38.10 CSF £331.80 CT £1899.20 TOTE £9.20: £2.00, £14.60, £2.10; EX 249.30.There was no bid for the winner.

Owner Mrs J Porter **Bred** Lynch Bages Ltd & Samac Ltd **Trained** Melsonby, N Yorks

FOCUS

A much weaker race than the rating band implies with only two of the runners having marks higher than 53. The pace seemed a solid one and the winner's effort is worth upgrading in view of where the the in-form others that were upsides him early eventually finished. The form looks limited and shaky with the third the best guide.

Lothair(IRE) ◆ Official explanation: trainer's rep said, regarding apparent improvement in form, that the gelding had benefited from being dropped in class.

Qubuh(IRE) Official explanation: jockey said gelding never travelled

4088 JOHN SMITH'S H'CAP 1m 3f 16y

8:20 (8:20) (Class 5) (0-75,72) 3-Y-O+ **£3,881** (£1,155; £577; £288) **Stalls** Low

Form				RPR
2020	**1**		**Queen's Estate (GER)**[16] 3543 3-9-0 **70**.......... JoeFanning 2 (Mark Johnston) *set stdy pce: mde virtually all: rdn and qcknd over 1f out: drew clr fnl f* **4/1**[2]	82
002	**2**	*3 ¼*	**Daring Indian**[15] 3594 4-9-13 **71**.......... RichardKingscote 3 (Tom Dascombe) *t.k.h early: trckd ldrs: effrt over 1f out: sn chsng wnr: no imp fnl f* **2/1**[1]	77
045	**3**	*1 ½*	**Nolecce**[37] 2051 5-8-13 **60**..........(p) DeclanCannon(3) 1 (Richard Guest) *in tch: stdy hdwy over 2f out: effrt and edgd lft over 1f out: one pce fnl f* **10/1**	63
0555	**4**	*4 ½*	**Antigua Sunrise (IRE)**[15] 3556 6-9-9 **72**.......... ShaneBKelly(5) 5 (Richard Fahey) *trckd ldrs: rdn over 2f out: hung rt and wknd over 1f out* **2/1**[1]	67
111-	**5**	*1 ¼*	**Sky High Diver (IRE)**[211] 7779 4-9-7 **70**.......... GarryWhillans(5) 4 (Alan Swinbank) *w ldr: rdn over 2f out: hung lft and wknd over 1f out* **9/2**[3]	63

2m 40.49s (14.89) **Going Correction** +0.70s/f (Yiel)

WFA 3 from 4yo+ 12lb **5** Ran SP% **113.9**

Speed ratings (Par 103): **73,70,69,66,65**

CSF £12.89 TOTE £4.30: £3.20, £1.60; EX 17.60.

Owner J C Daley **Bred** Gestut Gorlsdorf **Trained** Middleham Moor, N Yorks

FOCUS

A tactcal affair in which the gallop didn't increase until 3f out. The form is best rated through the runner-up to his latest form.

Queen's Estate(GER) Official explanation: trainer had no explanation for the apparent improvement in form

Antigua Sunrise(IRE) Official explanation: jockey said mare hung right from 4f out

4089 TURFTV IN YOUR BETTING SHOP H'CAP — 1m 65y

8:50 (8:50) (Class 5) (0-70,68) 3-Y-O+ — £3,881 (£1,155; £577; £288) Stalls Low

Form — RPR

4000 **1** — **Collateral Damage (IRE)**[5] 3914 9-9-7 66 ....(t) JamesSullivan 5 — 73
(Tim Easterby) *chsd ldr: pushed along over 2f out: hdwy to ld last 100yds: kpt on wl* — **3/1**[1]

6406 **2** *1 1/2* **Master Of Dance (IRE)**[6] 3888 5-9-6 65 ....(p) JoeFanning 6 — 68
(Keith Dalgleish) *hld up: pushed along and hdwy over 1f out: styd on wl fnl f: tk 2nd cl home* — **7/2**[2]

4034 **3** *nse* **Georgebernardshaw (IRE)**[23] 3317 7-8-13 61........ DeclanCannon(3) 3 — 64
(Richard Guest) *led: rdn and qcknd over 2f out: edgd rt and hdd last 100yds: kpt on same pce: lost 2nd cl home* — **9/2**[3]

0044 **4** *1 1/4* **High Resolution**[5] 3906 5-8-12 62................................ ShaneBKelly(5) 8 — 62
(Linda Perratt) *s.i.s: hld up in tch: hdwy and prom over 2f out: sn rdn: kpt on same pce fnl f* — **9/2**[3]

003- **5** *1 1/2* **Christmas Light**[264] 7061 5-9-3 65.................................... DaleSwift(3) 7 — 62
(Brian Ellison) *t.k.h early: chsd ldrs: effrt and rdn over 2f out: kpt on same pce fnl f* — **6/1**

1534 **6** *nk* **Brown Pete (IRE)**[25] 3247 4-9-2 61...........................(e) StephenCraine 2 — 57
(Richard Guest) *hld up in tch: effrt and pushed along over 2f out: no ex over 1f out* — **9/2**[3]

0000 **7** *2 1/4* **Goal (IRE)**[9] 3793 4-9-6 65... RobbieFitzpatrick 1 — 56
(Charles Smith) *s.i.s: t.k.h in rr: rdn over 2f out: nvr able to chal* — **20/1**

1m 55.13s (6.73) **Going Correction** +0.70s/f (Yiel) — 7 Ran SP% **120.8**
Speed ratings (Par 103): **94,92,92,91,89 89,87**
toteswingers 1&2 £5.00, 1&3 £4.60, 2&3 £4.90 CSF £14.91 CT £47.82 TOTE £4.00: £2.20, £2.30; EX 18.40.
Owner Middleham Park Racing XXV & Partners **Bred** Minch Bloodstock And Castletown Stud **Trained** Great Habton, N Yorks

FOCUS
Very ordinary fare once again in the finale with the field soon well strung out despite there being no more than a fair gallop. The form is rated thriough the third to this year's level.
T/Plt: £206.40 to a £1 stake. Pool: £81816.24 - 289.32 winning tickets T/Qpdt: £56.10 to a £1 stake. Pool: £7967.39 - 105.00 winning tickets RY

4055 NEWBURY (L-H)

Saturday, July 14

OFFICIAL GOING: Heavy (soft in places; 5.5)
Wind: half-across Weather: overcast

4090 SHARES IN DOWNRIGHT DIZZIE @ CHRISBEEKRACING.COM CONDITIONS STKS — 7f (S)

2:00 (2:00) (Class 4) 2-Y-O — £4,668 (£1,398; £699; £349) Stalls Centre

Form — RPR

31 **1** — **Shrewd**[21] 3401 2-8-6 .... IanBurns(7) 1 — 85
(Michael Bell) *disp 3rd: hdwy to chse ldr over 2f out: sn chalng: led over 1f out: drvn out* — **13/8**[1]

505 **2** *6* **Royal Mizar (SPA)**[14] 3638 2-8-5 63......................... LeonnaMayor(5) 5 — 67
(Alastair Lidderdale) *racd in 3rd: hdwy to take narrow ld 3f out: jnd 2f out: hdd wl over 1f out: one pce* — **22/1**

23 **3** *1* **Rising Legend**[9] 3770 2-8-10 .... SeanLevey 4 — 65
(Richard Hannon) *chsd ldr: rdn 4f out: styd in tch tl outpcd by ldng duo over 1f out* — **9/4**[3]

1 **4** *18* **Strictly Ballroom (IRE)**[15] 3576 2-8-8 .... SilvestreDeSousa 2 — 18
(Mark Johnston) *t.k.h: led: hdd 3f out: wknd over 2f out* — **15/8**[2]

1m 35.64s (9.94) **Going Correction** +1.05s/f (Soft) — 4 Ran SP% **108.0**
Speed ratings (Par 96): **85,78,77,56**
CSF £22.07 TOTE £2.90; EX 25.40.
Owner Sheikh Marwan Al Maktoum **Bred** Darley **Trained** Newmarket, Suffolk

FOCUS
Rail moved out between 8f and 5f on Round course and races on Round course run over approximately 32m further than advertised. An opener run on ground officially described as heavy, soft in places, the four runners all brought to race towards the stands' rail. It's hard to be sure what this form's worth.

NOTEBOOK
Shrewd is clearly heading in the right direction, following up his Redcar maiden win in clear-cut fashion in the end, forging clear inside the last. Whether testing ground is vital to him remains to be seen (raced only on softer than good so far) but he'll stay 1m and will be worth his place in something better. (op 7-4 tchd 15-8 and 2-1 in a place)
Royal Mizar(SPA) has clearly bettered his previous form, though by quite how much isn't that easy to ascertain. He looked a threat to the winner until just fading late on over this longer trip. Immediate prospects will clearly depend to some extent on how the handicapper interprets the form (only rated 63 coming into the race). (op 14-1)
Rising Legend looked very promising on his debut but hasn't really built on that since. He was rather laboured on the testing ground, coming off the bridle over 3f out and well held in third before plugging on late. (op 3-1)
Strictly Ballroom(IRE) had made a winning debut in the mud at Musselburgh (5f) so this was most disappointing, particularly as a Lowther entry suggests she's well regarded. She backed out of things very tamely in the final 2f and she can't have been right. (op 13-8)

4091 CHRISBEEKRACING.COM E B F FILLIES' STKS (H'CAP) — 1m (S)

2:35 (2:35) (Class 3) (0-95,86) 3-Y-O+ — £8,092 (£2,423; £1,211; £605; £302; £152) Stalls Centre

Form — RPR

-304 **1** — **Our Gal**[16] 3550 4-9-6 78.. ChrisCatlin 6 — 85
(Noel Quinlan) *chsd ldrs: led 2f out: hdd 1f out: styd pressing ldr: led again as ldr lost momentum fnl 120yds: hld on all out* — **15/2**

3113 **2** *hd* **Russian Rave**[14] 3636 6-10-0 86................................... LeeNewman 5 — 94
(Jonathan Portman) *hld up in rr: hdwy over 2f out: led 1f out: slt ld whn rdr mistk winning line 120yds out and lost momentum: rallied clsng stages: nt rcvr* — **9/2**[2]

10-2 **3** *2 1/2* **Epernay**[21] 3385 5-9-4 76...(vt) StevieDonohoe 1 — 76
(Ian Williams) *in rr but in tch: rdn 2f out: styd on to take 3rd ins fnl f: no imp on ldng duo* — **11/4**[1]

1-04 **4** *4 1/2* **Emmuska**[29] 3120 3-8-9 76.. KieranO'Neill 2 — 64
(Richard Hannon) *chsd ldr: rdn and ev ch fr over 2f out: wknd ins fnl f* **7/1**

3-1 **5** *2 1/2* **Mugazala (IRE)**[19] 3453 3-8-13 80.. TadhgO'Shea 7 — 62
(Ed Dunlop) *in rr: rdn along 3f out: a outpcd* — **9/2**[2]

0-03 **6** *6* **Hurricane Lady (IRE)**[37] 2855 4-9-0 77.................... DarrenEgan(5) 4 — 47
(Mike Murphy) *t.k.h: led: rdn and hdd 2f out: sn btn* — **6/1**[3]

5005 **7** *18* **Abishena (IRE)**[14] 3636 3-8-13 80............................ SilvestreDeSousa 3
(Mark Johnston) *chsd ldrs: rdn 3f out: sn btn* — **9/1**

1m 46.67s (6.97) **Going Correction** +1.05s/f (Soft)
WFA 3 from 4yo+ 9lb — 7 Ran SP% **111.6**
Speed ratings (Par 104): **107,106,104,99,97 91,73**
toteswingers 1&2 £7.50, 1&3 £2.80, 2&3 £1.60 CSF £38.76 TOTE £9.10: £3.40, £2.60; EX 46.50.
Owner G Wilding **Bred** G Wilding **Trained** Newmarket, Suffolk
■ Stewards' Enquiry : Lee Newman 28-day ban: failed to ride out on mare that would have won (Jul 28-Aug 24)

FOCUS
A fair fillies' event which was run at a pretty sedate pace until around 3f out. They came up the centre of the course this time and the runner-up is rated as a narrow winner.

NOTEBOOK
Our Gal had plenty of solid efforts to her name in handicaps since her Yarmouth maiden success around a year ago and finally got her head back in front. She is a reliable sort who clearly goes well in the mud and should continue to give a good account. (op 6-1)
Russian Rave may have won had Lee Newman not briefly stopped riding half a furlong out, his mount holding a narrow advantage at the time. The rider appeared to mistake the half-furlong pole for the winning post and the error cost him a 28-day ban. The mare is a winner without a penalty and can gain compensation if reappearing before the handicapper has his say. (op 4-1 tchd 5-1)
Epernay is another with a pretty consistent record, certainly when the ground is on the soft side, and there's little reason to doubt she gave her running, the 4lb she went up for finishing second at Haydock just seeming to catch her out in the end. (op 7-2)
Emmuska has quickly come back down to the mark she won off on her final juvenile start. She's not in quite the same form at present but it's possible testing ground doesn't suit her and she's not one to give up on back on a quicker surface or the all-weather. (op 6-1)
Mugazala(IRE) looked to have the potential for better still after just two starts and is surely worth another chance as the heavy ground is a ready excuse, struggling even before the race began in earnest. (op 11-2)
Hurricane Lady(IRE) is proven in the mud but failed to build on last month's Sandown third. (op 5-1 tchd 7-1)
Abishena(IRE) has simply been very disappointing so far this season. (op 11-1)

4092 CHRISBEEKRACING.COM STKS (REGISTERED AS THE HACKWOOD STAKES) (GROUP 3) — 6f 8y

3:10 (3:10) (Class 1) 3-Y-O+

£31,190 (£11,825; £5,918; £2,948; £1,479; £742) Stalls Centre

Form — RPR

1064 **1** — **Soul (AUS)**[21] 3370 5-9-4 115.................................. SilvestreDeSousa 5 — 120
(Saeed Bin Suroor) *trckd ldr: led 2f out: styd on strly fnl f* — **3/1**[2]

1-20 **2** *4* **Firebeam**[42] 2728 4-9-4 111.. EddieAhern 1 — 108
(William Haggas) *t.k.h: trckd ldrs: drvn to take 2nd 1f out: sn no imp on wnr* — **5/1**[3]

2161 **3** *1 1/4* **Maarek**[14] 3623 5-9-8 112.. CO'Donoghue 8 — 108
(David Peter Nagle, Ire) *in rr: rdn: edgd lft and rt 2f out: styd on to take 3rd fnl f: no imp on ldng duo* — **9/4**[1]

3542 **4** *1* **Morache Music**[7] 3860 4-9-4 105................................(v[1]) SebSanders 3 — 101
(Peter Makin) *in rr: rdn 3f out: styd on fr over 1f out: nvr gng pce to rch ldrs* — **20/1**

-026 **5** *nk* **Elnawin**[7] 3877 6-9-4 109... SeanLevey 7 — 100
(Richard Hannon) *chsd ldrs: wnt 2nd ins fnl 2f: no imp on wnr: wknd ins fnl f* — **16/1**

0263 **6** *1 3/4* **Regal Parade**[14] 3623 8-9-4 107................................... WilliamCarson 9 — 95
(Milton Bradley) *in rr and rdn along: struggling to go pce fr 1/2-way but sme late prog* — **12/1**

-231 **7** *2 1/4* **Definightly**[14] 3650 6-9-8 107...................................(b) FergusSweeney 4 — 92
(Roger Charlton) *led: hdd 2f out: btn sn after* — **9/1**

0116 **8** *6* **Mirza**[14] 3650 5-9-4 105... DavidProbert 2 — 70
(Rae Guest) *s.i.s: sn prom: rdn and wknd 2f out* — **12/1**

1100 **9** *3/4* **Oasis Dancer**[21] 3371 5-9-4 102.. JimCrowley 6 — 68
(Ralph Beckett) *chsd ldrs tl rdn and wknd 2f out* — **20/1**

1m 17.22s (4.22) **Going Correction** +1.05s/f (Soft) — 9 Ran SP% **113.2**
Speed ratings (Par 113): **113,107,106,104,104 101,98,90,89**
toteswingers 1&2 £4.50, 1&3 £2.10, 2&3 £3.40 CSF £18.06 TOTE £3.50: £1.30, £2.30, £1.40; EX 17.80.
Owner Godolphin **Bred** Woodlands Stud **Trained** Newmarket, Suffolk

FOCUS
A one-sided Group 3 in the end with the winner backing up his Royal Ascot effort, while the rest are rated at least 5lb off.

NOTEBOOK
Soul(AUS) backed up his fine fourth in the Diamond Jubilee with a ready success. This was impressive and gives hope he may be even more competitive at a higher level another day. He'll also probably stay 7f, which will increase options still further. (tchd 5-2)
Firebeam is a strong traveller who was never going to have any difficulty with the drop back to sprinting and he wasted no time putting a below-par run in France behind him. He's up to winning at least a Listed race at some stage. (op 13-2)
Maarek wasn't disgraced in the end but never looked like adding to the Group 3 he'd landed under similar conditions at Newcastle last month. (tchd 2-1)
Morache Music was another who wasn't far off his best without ever threatening a serious blow, the first-time visor not really having the desired effect as he was just about the first off the bridle. (tchd 25-1)
Elnawin is in a bit better form than this bare result implies, chasing the winner approaching the final furlong before the testing conditions found him out late on. All his ability remains intact at the age of six. (op 12-1)
Regal Parade has yet to come close to his best in a couple of starts for his new yard and was never a threat. (tchd 14-1)
Definightly had been consistent this year and might have been expected to do better with the ground in his favour, even allowing for a penalty from his recent Curragh success, but was rather keen early. (op 8-1)
Mirza had excuses at the Curragh last time but no obvious one on this occasion, particularly as he goes so well in the mud. (op 14-1)
Oasis Dancer is in better form than this suggests, travelling well for a long way but soon floundering on the ground once push came to shove in the final 2f. (tchd 25-1)

4093 WEATHERBYS SUPER SPRINT — 5f 34y

3:50 (3:50) (Class 2) 2-Y-O

£122,925 (£52,275; £24,600; £14,750; £9,825; £7,375) Stalls Centre

Form — RPR

611 **1** — **Body And Soul (IRE)**[25] 3250 2-7-12 85.................... DuranFentiman 21 — 89+
(Tim Easterby) *chsd ldrs: led over 1f out: hld on all out* — **9/2**[1]

120 **2** *nk* **Satsuma**[24] 3269 2-8-0 91.. NickyMackay 2 — 90
(David Brown) *racd far side: chsd ldr tl tk advantage over 2f out whn upsides w main gp: rdn and str chal thrght fnl f: jst failed* — **8/1**

521 **3** *nse* **Momalorka**[22] 3339 2-7-12 78 .... KellyHarrison 16 88+
(William Haggas) *in rr: drvn and gd hdwy over 1f out: fin strly fnl f: nt quite get up* **16/1**

3420 **4** *1 1/2* **Top Boy**[25] 3240 2-9-1 90 .... WilliamCarson 8 99
(Derek Shaw) *in tch: chsd ldrs fr 2f out: kpt on fr ins fnl f* **50/1**

110 **5** *shd* **Madam Mojito (USA)**[24] 3269 2-8-1 87 .... JimmyQuinn 25 85
(John Quinn) *in tch: rdn 1/2-way: styd on ins fnl f: gng on cl home* **25/1**

3211 **6** *nse* **Hototo**[25] 3242 2-8-13 102 .... PhillipMakin 13 97
(Kevin Ryan) *chsd ldrs: rdn over 2f out: styd on same pce ins fnl f* **5/1**[2]

4110 **7** *1/2* **Lyric Ace (IRE)**[25] 3242 2-8-9 95 .... SeanLevey 1 91
(Richard Hannon) *racd w sole opponent far side and led: hdd over 2f out: styd front rnk tl one pce ins fnl f* **7/1**[3]

3402 **8** *nk* **Woodland Mill (IRE)**[17] 3501 2-8-3 80 .... KieranO'Neill 18 84
(Richard Fahey) *in tch: rdn 2f out: styd on fnl f* **40/1**

2130 **9** *nse* **Liber**[25] 3242 2-8-11 98 .... ChrisCatlin 5 92
(Sir Mark Prescott Bt) *chsd ldrs: slt ld fr 2f out tl hdd over 1f out: sn one pce* **11/1**

22 **10** *shd* **Royal Aspiration (IRE)**[14] 3617 2-8-10 .... JimCrowley 22 90
(William Haggas) *settled in mid-div: hdwy 2f out: r.o fnl f: nt rchd ldrs* **25/1**

33 **11** *3/4* **Shahdaroba (IRE)**[17] 3505 2-8-9 .... JamesMillman 4 87
(Rod Millman) *mid-div: rdn 2f out: styd on fnl f* **40/1**

154 **12** *1* **Tatlisu (IRE)**[42] 2715 2-8-5 82 ....(v[1]) PatrickMathers 6 79
(Richard Fahey) *slt ld tl hdd 2f out: wknd fnl f* **28/1**

5325 **13** *1 1/2* **Vestibule**[39] 2783 2-7-12 74 .... DarrenEgan 10 67
(Eve Johnson Houghton) *chsd ldrs: rdn 2f out: wknd fnl f* **50/1**

210 **14** *1/2* **Pay Freeze (IRE)**[25] 3242 2-8-3 92 .... SamHitchcott 17 70
(Mick Channon) *in tch: rdn and hung lft ins fnl 2f: nvr rchd ldrs* **8/1**

2400 **15** *2* **Marvelino**[5] 3916 2-8-7 75 ow2 .... EddieAhern 14 67
(Pat Eddery) *wnt rt and bmpd s: chsd ldrs tl 1/2-way* **100/1**

3 **16** *shd* **Ceelo**[54] 2330 2-8-13 .... DarryllHolland 15 72
(Richard Hannon) *bmpd s and outpcd: sme late hdwy* **25/1**

6 **17** *1 3/4* **Palladius**[15] 3560 2-8-0 .... JulieBurke 3 53
(Kevin Ryan) *chsd ldrs over 3f* **50/1**

411 **18** *3/4* **Jubilee Games**[16] 3532 2-8-3 .... RyanPowell 20 53
(Richard Fahey) *chsd ldrs over 3f* **14/1**

324 **19** *1 1/2* **The Black Jacobin**[13] 3662 2-8-1 82 .... FrankieMcDonald 11 46
(J S Moore) *outpcd most of way* **66/1**

61 **20** *5* **Knight Charm**[26] 3217 2-8-7 .... JohnFahy 19 34
(Eve Johnson Houghton) *bmpd s: outpcd after* **25/1**

15 **21** *1 1/4* **Rhagori Aur**[42] 2715 2-8-2 .... SilvestreDeSousa 23 24
(Bryan Smart) *sn outpcd* **25/1**

6552 **22** *8* **Ouzinkie (IRE)**[28] 3140 2-8-8 75 .... CO'Donoghue 24
(Mick Channon) *s.i.s: outpcd* **66/1**

1m 6.55s (5.15) **Going Correction** +1.05s/f (Soft) **22** Ran SP% **127.9**
Speed ratings (Par 100): **100,99,99,97,96 96,96,95,95,95 94,92,90,89,86 85,83,81,79,71 69,56**
toteswingers 1&2 £5.60, 1&3 £14.60, 2&3 £49.80 CSF £34.63 TOTE £4.60: £2.40, £3.70, £7.00; EX 58.30 Trifecta £1715.30 Part won. Pool: £2,318.02 - 0.20 winning units..
Owner C H Stevens **Bred** Michael Downey & Roalso Ltd **Trained** Great Habton, N Yorks
■ Stewards' Enquiry : Kelly Harrison four-day ban: used whip above permitted level (Jul 28-310

FOCUS
This valuable sales event was fast and furious and it ended being dominated by three fillies at the bottom of the weights. The runner-up was one of only two who stayed towards the far side, the main group more centre to near side, and it would be hard to argue that any part of the track conveyed an advantage. The form looks straightforward with the first two and five of the next seven home fitting in on previous form.

NOTEBOOK
Body And Soul(IRE) has now won all three starts since her debut and provided her yard with a third win in this contest, always in the firing line and finding plenty under pressure to just shade the verdict. She's reportedly likely to go hunting more big prizes, with a step up to 6f in the DBS sales race at York next on the agenda. That will demand more but it's doubtful we've seen the best of her yet. (tchd 4-1)
Satsuma wasn't beaten that far in the Queen Mary but probably stepped up a little on that form. She showed bags of speed and was just edged out by one on the opposite side. (tchd 10-1)
Momalorka ◆ ran an extraordinary race. Her Goodwood maiden win had come over 6f and she was badly outpaced over this shorter trip, still having only a couple behind her 2f out before storming home. A return to further will suit and she has the potential for better still judged on this.
Top Boy made no impact in the Coventry, but had been runner-up in the National Stakes prior to that and produced a useful effort under his big weight. He'd be a good thing in a maiden. (op 33-1)
Madam Mojito(USA) had been just behind Satsuma in the Queen Mary and ran to a very similar level here. She's clearly fairly useful but there's no obvious indication she'll prove capable of much better.
Hototo probably wasn't far off his Windsor Castle form under his big weight. He was in the firing line from the off but found no extra late on under these testing conditions. (op 11-2 tchd 6-1)
Lyric Ace(IRE) showed his Ascot running to be all wrong but looks only useful and no better at this stage, after being upsides the runner-up for a long way towards the far side. (op 6-1)
Woodland Mill(IRE) had a bit to find and ran as well as could be expected.
Liber showed his customary speed but seems to have found his level for the time being, fading late on. (op 12-1)
Royal Aspiration(IRE) wasn't beaten far. This was a step up on his pair of seconds in maiden company and repeat of this will see him break his duck soon back down at that level.
Pay Freeze(IRE) has been a little disappointing since his York maiden win, but shouldn't be written off until he's had another try over 6f plus. He was never able to go the pace here. (op 10-1)

4094 CALICO CAT AT CHRISBEEKRACING.COM STKS (REGISTERED AS THE STEVENTON STAKES) (LISTED RACE) 1m 2f 6y
4:20 (4:20) (Class 1) 3-Y-O+
£18,714 (£7,095; £3,550; £1,768; £887; £445) **Stalls** Centre

Form RPR

-624 **1** **Poet**[33] 2989 7-9-4 110 .... EddieAhern 7 113
(Clive Cox) *led tl hdd over 2f out: rallied gamely to ld again ins fnl f: drvn out* **3/1**[3]

06-0 **2** *1 3/4* **French Navy**[22] 3329 4-9-4 106 .... AhmedAjtebi 1 111
(Mahmood Al Zarooni) *hld up in rr: hdwy 3f out: led over 2f out: 2 l clr over 1f out: hdd ins fnl f and fnd no ex* **7/1**

-135 **3** *2 3/4* **Retrieve (AUS)**[22] 3329 5-9-4 108 .... SilvestreDeSousa 6 104
(Saeed Bin Suroor) *chsd ldrs: rdn and lost position over 2f out: rallied fnl f to take 3rd last strides: no imp on ldng duo* **11/4**[2]

1123 **4** *nk* **Expense Claim (IRE)**[35] 2920 3-8-7 97 .... DavidProbert 3 103
(Andrew Balding) *chsd ldr tl over 3f out: styd chsng ldng duo but no imp fnl 2f: wknd and lost 3rd last strides* **6/1**

1214 **5** *4 1/2* **Qaraaba**[22] 3329 5-8-13 102 .... FergusSweeney 4 89
(Seamus Durack) *hld up in rr: rdn and hdwy over 2f out: sn disputing 3rd but nvr on terms w ldrs: wknd fnl f* **9/4**[1]

0616 **6** *11* **Falcon's Reign (FR)**[12] 3692 3-8-7 71 .... DarrenEgan 5 72?
(Michael Appleby) *in rr: rdn and sme hdwy over 3f out: wknd wl over 2f out* **150/1**

0 **7** *17* **Hyper (USA)**[22] 3329 5-9-4 95 ....(v) JimCrowley 2 38
(Jim Boyle) *racd on outer: rdn and btn 3f out* **25/1**

2m 18.71s (9.91) **Going Correction** +1.275s/f (Soft)
WFA 3 from 4yo+ 11lb **7** Ran SP% **113.7**
Speed ratings (Par 111): **111,109,107,107,103 94,81**
toteswingers 1&2 £5.40, 1&3 £1.60, 2&3 £4.00 CSF £23.66 TOTE £3.50: £2.40, £3.30; EX 37.30.
Owner H E Sheikh Sultan Bin Khalifa Al Nahyan **Bred** Meon Valley Stud **Trained** Lambourn, Berks

FOCUS
Probably not the strongest of Listed races, with a few presumably failing to cope with the testing conditions. The winner is rated a bit off his best with the fourth and sixth close to their marks.

NOTEBOOK
Poet has always revelled in the mud and rallied when headed to regain the initiative inside the last. He's been a good servant over the years, winning a couple of Group 3s and three Listed events, and will now reportedly be retired to stud. (op 7-2 tchd 4-1)
French Navy bettered his reappearance, this probably pretty close to the level he showed when landing a Goodwood Group 3 last autumn, though he was rather worried out of it having briefly looked likely to take the winner's measure approaching the final furlong. (op 8-1)
Retrieve(AUS) had run a blinder under a big weight in the Wolferton but wasn't in the same form here. He was rather laboured on the heavy ground, plugging on to be nearest at the finish. (op 5-2)
Expense Claim(IRE) had a bit to find at this level and ran close to his best. He's likeable but perhaps won't prove the easiest to place. (tchd 15-2)
Qaraaba probably remains in a bit better form than the bare result suggest, tiring late on under conditions which probably stretched her stamina. Listed races among her own sex will likely provide easier opportunities. (tchd 2-1)

4095 GT EXHIBITIONS CONDITIONS STKS 7f (S)
4:55 (4:55) (Class 3) 3-Y-O
£8,092 (£2,423; £1,211; £605; £302) **Stalls** Centre

Form RPR

13-0 **1** **Ewell Place (IRE)**[24] 3265 3-8-9 98 .... StevieDonohoe 4 96
(Robert Mills) *t.k.h: trckd ldrs: rdn 2f out: drvn and styd on to ld fnl 120yds: hld on wl clsng stages* **6/1**[2]

2062 **2** *nk* **Silverheels (IRE)**[9] 3784 3-8-9 95 .... ChrisCatlin 5 95
(Paul Cole) *in tch: hdwy to chse ldrs 1/2-way: rdn 2f out: str chal fnl 120yds: no ex cl home* **15/2**[3]

-100 **3** *1* **Arnold Lane (IRE)**[13] 3681 3-8-9 97 .... SamHitchcott 3 93
(Mick Channon) *chsd ldrs: rdn and outpcd 2f out: rallied to press ldrs fnl 120yds: one pce and edgd rt clsng stages* **6/4**[1]

-315 **4** *1* **Producer**[24] 3265 3-9-5 107 .... SeanLevey 1 100
(Richard Hannon) *trckd ldr: led ins fnl 3f: rdn fnl f: hdd and no ex fnl 120yds: btn whn bmpd cl home* **6/4**[1]

-064 **5** *15* **North Star Boy (IRE)**[7] 3876 3-8-9 88 .... KieranO'Neill 2 51
(Richard Hannon) *led tl hdd ins fnl 3f: wknd qckly over 2f out* **14/1**

1m 33.53s (7.83) **Going Correction** +1.275s/f (Soft) **5** Ran SP% **112.7**
Speed ratings (Par 104): **106,105,104,103,86**
CSF £45.14 TOTE £10.70: £4.50, £1.90; EX 62.30.
Owner Brendan Kerr, Mrs B B Mills **Bred** Peter & Hugh McCutcheon **Trained** Headley, Surrey

FOCUS
A useful conditions event. With a small field on testing ground it was predictable the gallop wouldn't be strong, the race effectively not beginning in earnest until the final 2f with four still in with every chance 100yds out. The form looks muddling with the runner-up raising doubts based on this year's previous form.

NOTEBOOK
Ewell Place(IRE) had found the Jersey too much on his reappearance but was firmly back on the up here, keeping on strongly considering he was keen enough in the first half of the contest. He clearly handles the mud well and will be worth his place back up in class. (op 11-2 tchd 8-1)
Silverheels(IRE) has proved hard to win with but there's no knocking his consistency. This is about as well as he's ever run. (op 11-2)
Arnold Lane(IRE) was always going to find this easier than the Group 1s he'd tackled the last twice, though the tactical nature of the contest seemed to find him out to some extent back down at 7f. He was tapped for speed just under 2f out and keptg on without ever looking like getting there. (op 7-4 tchd 11-8)
Producer's four career wins have all come at Epsom, though this was a decent effort conceding 10lb all round, giving best only late on. (op 9-4)
North Star Boy(IRE) was soon done with once headed, beaten too far out to put this down to lack of stamina. (op 9-1, tchd 16-1 in a place)

4096 CHRISBEEKRACING.COM IT STARTED WITH STARGAZY H'CAP 2m
5:30 (5:30) (Class 4) (0-80,80) 4-Y-O+
£5,175 (£1,540; £769; £384) **Stalls** Centre

Form RPR

0-10 **1** **Kleitomachos (IRE)**[68] 1940 4-9-4 **77** .... SilvestreDeSousa 4 86
(Stuart Kittow) *chsd ldrs: led over 2f out: sn drvn: styd on strly fnl f* **15/2**

3-34 **2** *1 1/2* **Hawridge Star (IRE)**[28] 3162 10-9-0 **73** .... SeanLevey 9 80
(Stuart Kittow) *hld up in rr: hdwy 3f out: rdn over 2f out: styd on to chse ldrs sn after: styd on same pce* **9/2**[2]

-001 **3** *1 3/4* **Sansili**[23] 2575 5-7-11 **61** oh1 ....(tp) DarrenEgan(5) 6 66
(Peter Bowen) *in tch: rdn 3f out: styd on to take one pce 3rd ins fnl f* **3/1**[1]

1-35 **4** *10* **Blazing Field**[51] 2412 4-9-6 **79** .... JohnFahy 5 72
(Clive Cox) *led 1f: styd chsng ldr tl led over 3f out: hdd over 2f out: wknd appr fnl f* **3/1**[1]

5135 **5** *shd* **Handles For Forks (IRE)**[9] 3769 4-8-12 **71** .... SamHitchcott 11 64
(Mick Channon) *in rr: rdn and sme prog over 2f out but nvr on terms: sn no ch w ldrs* **10/1**

/00- **6** *1/2* **Raslan**[87] 4423 9-8-11 **70** ....(bt) SebSanders 8 62
(David Pipe) *drvn to ld after 1f: rdn along 4f out: hdd over 3f out: wknd fr 2f out* **20/1**

-542 **7** *6* **Sunny Future (IRE)**[29] 3102 6-8-6 **65** .... WilliamCarson 7 50
(Malcolm Saunders) *in tch: rdn and wknd fr 3f out* **7/1**[3]

3425 **8** *dist* **Mohanad (IRE)**[8] 3827 6-9-5 **78** .... EddieAhern 2
(Sheena West) *chsd ldrs tl wknd 3f out: t.o* **9/1**

3m 55.61s (23.61) **Going Correction** +1.275s/f (Soft) **8** Ran SP% **116.3**
Speed ratings (Par 105): **91,90,89,84,84 84,81,**
toteswingers 1&2 £4.30, 1&3 £7.70, 2&3 £7.90 CSF £41.83 CT £124.75 TOTE £9.10: £2.90, £1.70, £2.00; EX 46.90.
Owner Eric Gadsden **Bred** Carrigbeg Stud Co Ltd **Trained** Blackborough, Devon

FOCUS
There was a fair level of form in this handicap with the placed horses setting the level. A steady pace wasn't wound up until early in the straight but they still finished well strung out under the conditions.
Mohanad(IRE) Official explanation: trainer said gelding was unsuited by the heavy (soft in places) ground
T/Plt: £557.40 to a £1 stake. Pool: £96335.80 - 126.16 winning tickets T/Qpdt: £64.30 to a £1 stake. Pool: £5689.56 - 65.40 winning tickets ST

4062 NEWMARKET (R-H)

Saturday, July 14

OFFICIAL GOING: Heavy (overall 5.6; stands' side 5.8; centre 5.9; far side 5.4)

Wind: Light, across Weather: Showers

4097 32RED CASINO H'CAP 1m

1:40 (1:43) (Class 2) (0-100,95) 3-Y-O

£12,450 (£3,728; £1,864; £932; £466; £234) **Stalls** High

Form RPR

5010 **1** **Ocean Tempest**[9] 3792 3-8-8 **82**........(p) BrettDoyle 5 89
(John Ryan) *led: hdd over 6f out: chsd ldrs: rdn to ld over 1f out: edgd lft: all out* **33/1**

2012 **2** *nse* **Fire Ship**[14] 3629 3-8-5 **82**........HarryBentley(3) 2 89
(William Knight) *s.i.s: sn prom: led over 6f out: rdn and hdd wl over 1f out: rallied ins fnl f: jst failed* **10/1**

12-2 **3** *nk* **Jake's Destiny (IRE)**[15] 3563 3-9-1 **89**........PatCosgrave 8 95
(George Baker) *chsd ldrs: led wl over 1f out: sn rdn and hdd: r.o* **16/1**

0010 **4** *4 1/2* **Chapter Seven**[23] 3294 3-9-4 **92**........PaulHanagan 10 88+
(Richard Fahey) *s.i.s: hld up: rdn over 3f out: edgd lft and styd on ins fnl f: nvr nrr* **15/2**

1011 **5** *1/2* **Ardmay (IRE)**[21] 3376 3-9-0 **88**........GrahamLee 11 83
(Kevin Ryan) *chsd ldrs: rdn over 2f out: no ex fnl f* **9/2**[2]

2-51 **6** *6* **Andalieb**[36] 2883 3-8-6 **80** ow1........WilliamBuick 9 61
(David Simcock) *hld up: hdwy over 2f out: rdn and wknd over 1f out* **6/1**[3]

35-4 **7** *5* **Compton**[23] 3294 3-9-4 **92**........JimmyFortune 1 62
(Ralph Beckett) *plld hrd and prom: rdn over 2f out: wknd over 1f out* **9/2**[2]

1 **8** *2 1/2* **Sir John Hawkwood (IRE)**[61] 2125 3-9-4 **92**........RyanMoore 4 56
(Sir Michael Stoute) *hld up: pushed along 1/2-way: rdn and wknd over 1f out* **15/8**[1]

1m 45.54s (5.54) **Going Correction** +0.85s/f (Soft) 8 Ran SP% **115.1**

Speed ratings (Par 106): **106,105,105,101,100 94,89,87**

toteswingers: 1&2 £21.50, 1&3 £26.10, 2&3 £8.80 CSF £324.06 CT £5402.30 TOTE £42.80: £6.30, £2.40, £3.60; EX 279.60 Trifecta £1089.30 Pool: £1,962.85 - 1.33 winning units..

Owner W McLuskey & C Little **Bred** Old Mill Stud Ltd And Oomswell Ltd **Trained** Newmarket, Suffolk

FOCUS

Once again the far side course was used, and the re-positioning of the bend into the home straight increased the distance of the 1m4f race by 18m. There was 20mm of rain since 10.00 the previous night, and the ground, officially changed to heavy (GoingStick stands' side 5.9; middle 5.9; far side 5.4) just before the first race, proved to be very testing, with the winning time 9.14sec slower than the RP standard. They went steady early on before Fire Ship moved to the front and picked the pace up, and it proved difficult to challenge from behind. Small personal bests from the first three.

NOTEBOOK

Ocean Tempest, who was the rag of the field, likes to be up with the pace, and that was the place to be in this ground. Finding plenty for pressure, he defied what had looked a pretty stiff mark by the slimmest of margins, and he's likely to find things tricky off an even higher revised mark. Official explanation: trainer said, regarding apparent improvement in form, that the gelding appeared better suited by the heavy ground and reduction in trip. (op 40-1)

Fire Ship rallied strongly, having looked to be dropping back to third place, and gave the winner's 1.01 backers a big fright. Very much at home in these conditions, he ran right up to his best in defeat. (op 9-1 tchd 17-2)

Jake's Destiny(IRE) had only run on turf once before, and that was on good ground, so these conditions were an unknown for him. He coped with them well, but did benefit from racing handily. That said, he remains unexposed and open to further improvement. (tchd 20-1)

Chapter Seven who was held up at the back of the field, was the only one to make up ground from off the pace. He does have winning form on soft so may not have been as inconvenienced as some by conditions, but he was given too much to do in a race dominated by those up front. (op 8-1)

Ardmay(IRE) was the only one who couldn't maintain his position having raced up with the pace, but he had raced a touch keenly early, and presumably that cost him later on. (op 11-2)

Andalieb, whose rider put up 1lb overweight, sweated up beforehand, was keen early on and never really threatened from off the pace. (op 5-1)

Compton, who was the subject of good support, was another who proved hard to settle off the sedate early gallop. Fourth in the Britannia last time, he's capable of a lot better than this, and can be given another chance on better ground. (op 10-1)

Sir John Hawkwood(IRE) won easily on his debut but never gave his supporters much hope here. He shouldn't be judged too harshly considering the conditions and his lack of experience. (op 6-4)

4098 32RED.COM SUPERLATIVE STKS (GROUP 2) 7f

2:10 (2:15) (Class 1) 2-Y-O

£34,026 (£12,900; £6,456; £3,216; £1,614; £810) **Stalls** High

Form RPR

12 **1** **Olympic Glory (IRE)**[25] 3240 2-9-0 0........RichardHughes 10 110+
(Richard Hannon) *hld up in tch: shkn up to ld over 1f out: rdn and edgd lft ins fnl f: jst hld on* **6/4**[1]

311 **2** *hd* **Birdman (IRE)**[29] 3097 2-9-0 89........MartinLane 7 110
(David Simcock) *s.i.s: hld up: pushed along and nt clr run over 2f out: hdwy u.p and edgd lft over 1f out: r.o wl ins fnl f: jst failed* **7/1**

11 **3** *1 3/4* **Maxentius (IRE)**[15] 3562 2-9-0 0........WilliamBuick 11 105+
(Peter Chapple-Hyam) *hld up: hdwy 3f out: led wl over 1f out: sn rdn and hdd: styd on same pce ins fnl f* **3/1**[2]

315 **4** *shd* **Artigiano (USA)**[25] 3240 2-9-0 102........FrankieDettori 3 105
(Mahmood Al Zarooni) *chsd ldrs: rdn: ev ch and hung lft over 1f out: no ex wl ins fnl f* **4/1**[3]

403 **5** *7* **Ocean Applause**[9] 3788 2-9-0 90........BrettDoyle 2 87
(John Ryan) *hld up: hdwy 2f out: rdn: edgd lft and wknd over 1f out* **33/1**

14 **6** *1 1/4* **London Citizen (USA)**[15] 3562 2-9-0 82........LukeMorris 5 84
(Mrs K Burke) *chsd ldrs tl rdn and wknd over 1f out* **40/1**

3331 **7** *shd* **Luhaif**[14] 3634 2-9-0 90........MartinHarley 8 84
(Mick Channon) *led: hdd over 5f out: led again over 4f out: rdn and hdd wl over 1f out: wknd sn after* **16/1**

1 **8** *6* **Operation Chariot (IRE)**[29] 3119 2-9-0 0........JimmyFortune 4 69
(Andrew Balding) *prom: rdn over 2f out: wknd over 1f out* **12/1**

001 **9** *3 1/2* **Glory Awaits (IRE)**[30] 3062 2-9-0 87........GrahamLee 1 60
(Kevin Ryan) *chsd ldrs: led over 5f out: hdd over 4f out: rdn and wknd over 1f out* **25/1**

1m 32.19s (6.49) **Going Correction** +0.975s/f (Soft) 9 Ran SP% **120.3**

Speed ratings (Par 106): **101,100,98,98,90 89,89,82,78**

toteswingers 1&2 £3.40, 1&3 £2.20, 2&3 £5.40 CSF £13.52 TOTE £2.40: £1.10, £2.20, £1.80; EX 16.10 Trifecta £53.90 Pool: £4,623.65 - 63.39 winning units..

Owner Mrs J Wood **Bred** Denis McDonnell **Trained** East Everleigh, Wilts

FOCUS

A race which held Listed status as recently as 2002, but was swiftly raised again four years later following successive wins from Dubawi and Horatio Nelson. The quality appeared to take a dip after that, but this looked a reasonable renewal on paper. Olympic Glory is rated a little below his Coventry form in victory, but was value for a bit extra. Most of them raced down the centre initially, leaving Luhaif on his own near the far rail, but the runners were spread across the track by the two pole and the winner ended up against the rail. It was hard work for these juveniles in the ground and those that raced on the pace dropped away.

NOTEBOOK

Olympic Glory(IRE), the clear form pick on his Coventry Stakes second, paid a compliment to Dawn Approach who beat him at Ascot. Raised in trip, he picked up well to open up a decisive lead, then showed a plucky attitude as he began to tire in the ground and the runner-up closed him down. Richard Hughes felt the colt had just blown up, having missed a bit of work earlier in the week. He was below his best in victory, with the bare form limited, but it's likely that the margin underplays his superiority and there's surely more to come from him back on a sound surface. Three of the last four winners next carried a penalty in Goodwood's Vintage Stakes, with King Torus, another from the Hannon yard, winning both races in 2010. It would be no surprise to see Olympic Glory go there. (op 7-4 tchd 2-1)

Birdman(IRE) won a novice race in conditions officially described as heavy at Chepstow latest, but was withdrawn from Thursday's July Stakes here as the ground (soft then) was considered unsuitable. Held up after a slightly slow start, he was still just about last passing the two pole but picked up well towards the outer and was clawing back the winner with every stride close home. He may be flattered by this but this was still an improved run from this tough colt, who'll get a mile. (op 9-1)

Maxentius(IRE) arrived unbeaten in two and was the subject of glowing reports from his trainer, who won this race with subsequent Derby winner Dr Devious in 1991. After making a rapid forward move against the far rail, his effort flattened out, but he kept going to shade third. He reportedly became upset and coltish in the preliminaries, which cannot have helped his performance, and while he handled the ground better than some he is likely to be best suited by a sound surface. It is much too soon to write him off. (op 9-4 tchd 2-1)

Artigiano(USA) was expected to be suited by the extra furlong, but after holding every chance he was floundering inside the last as his stamina quickly emptied in the ground. He still finished about a length and a half closer to Olympic Glory than he had in the Coventry. (op 6-1 tchd 13-2, 7-1 in a place)

Ocean Applause, a useful maiden whose connections won this three years ago with Silver Grecian, failed to get home in the conditions.

London Citizen(USA), prominently ridden, faded to finish further adrift of Maxentius than he had at Doncaster. (op 66-1)

Luhaif, whose easy C&D win had been on good to firm, raced alone through the early stahes and ultimately dropped away. (tchd 14-1)

Operation Chariot(IRE) made a winning debut in deep ground, but that may have been a weak race. (tchd 10-1)

Glory Awaits(IRE), who had Luhaif behind when winning at Haydock, dropped right away. (op 33-1 tchd 22-1)

4099 32RED BUNBURY CUP (H'CAP) 7f

2:40 (2:42) (Class 2) 3-Y-O+

£31,125 (£9,320; £4,660; £2,330; £1,165; £585) **Stalls** High

Form RPR

-260 **1** **Bonnie Brae**[24] 3268 5-9-9 **99**........RyanMoore 12 108
(David Elsworth) *racd far side: mid-div: hdwy over 2f out: chsd ldr and edgd rt over 1f out: rdn to ld ins fnl f: r.o wl* **13/2**[2]

4100 **2** *2* **Captain Bertie (IRE)**[7] 3878 4-9-3 **93**........MichaelHills 11 97
(Charles Hills) *racd far side: led that gp: overall ldr 3f out: rdn over 1f out: hdd and unable qck ins fnl f: 2nd of 10 in gp* **7/1**[3]

1-00 **3** *3/4* **Captain Ramius (IRE)**[170] 315 6-9-10 **100**........PatCosgrave 2 102
(Kevin Ryan) *racd stands' side: overall ldr 4f: continued to ld that gp: rdn over 1f out: styd on: 1st of 5 in gp* **20/1**

500 **4** *2 3/4* **Sir Reginald**[21] 3371 4-9-5 **95**........PaulHanagan 14 90
(Richard Fahey) *racd far side: s.i.s: hld up: rdn over 2f out: styd on ins fnl f: nvr nrr: 3rd of 10 in gp* **50/1**

10-5 **5** *nk* **Decent Fella (IRE)**[22] 3331 6-9-6 **96**........(vt) JimmyFortune 4 90
(Andrew Balding) *racd stands' side: prom: chsd ldr over 2f out: rdn over 1f out: styd on: 2nd of 5 in gp* **9/1**

6-02 **6** *1 3/4* **Jamesie (IRE)**[22] 3331 4-9-5 **95**........PatDobbs 1 84
(David Marnane, Ire) *racd stands' side: s.i.s: hld up: hdwy over 1f out: sn rdn and edgd lft: styd on: nt trble ldrs: 3rd of 5 in gp* **13/2**[2]

-160 **7** *3/4* **Seal Rock**[21] 3371 4-9-8 **98**........DaneO'Neill 15 85
(Henry Candy) *racd far side: mid-div: hdwy 1/2-way: rdn over 2f out: wknd fnl f: 4th of 10 in gp* **12/1**

3300 **8** *1 3/4* **King Of Jazz (IRE)**[14] 3641 4-9-6 **96**........(v[1]) LukeMorris 13 79
(Michael Bell) *racd far side: chsd ldr tl rdn and wknd over 1f out: 5th of 10 in gp* **20/1**

1320 **9** *2 1/4* **Mawaakef (IRE)**[17] 3508 4-9-5 **95**........FrankieDettori 10 72
(J R Jenkins) *racd far side: chsd ldrs: rdn over 2f out: wknd over 1f out: eased ins fnl f: 6th of 10 in gp* **10/1**

-000 **10** *2 1/4* **Gramercy (IRE)**[14] 3626 5-9-4 **94**........GrahamLee 8 65
(Kevin Ryan) *racd far side: hld up: rdn over 2f out: nvr on terms: 7th of 10 in gp* **33/1**

-031 **11** *6* **Atlantic Sport (USA)**[7] 3855 7-9-8 **98**........MartinHarley 16 54
(Mick Channon) *racd far side: hld up: a in rr: 8th of 10 in gp* **17/2**

0200 **12** *3/4* **Belgian Bill**[22] 3331 4-9-9 **99**........(t) RichardHughes 3 53
(George Baker) *racd stands' side: s.i.s: hld up: n.d: eased ins fnl f: 4th of 5 in gp* **6/1**[1]

-000 **13** *2* **Stevie Thunder**[24] 3268 7-9-0 **93**........RyanClark(3) 9 41
(Ian Williams) *racd far side: prom: rdn over 2f out: wknd over 1f out: 9th of 10 in gp* **8/1**

4-03 **14** *40* **Citrus Star (USA)**[51] 2409 5-9-3 **93**........WilliamBuick 6
(Chris Wall) *racd stands' side: chsd ldr over 4f: sn wknd and eased: t.o: last of 5 in gp* **20/1**

0-05 **15** *11* **Rakaan (IRE)**[9] 3779 5-9-2 **92**........ShaneKelly 19
(Jamie Osborne) *racd far side: hld up: a in rr: bhd fr 1/2-way: eased: t.o: last of 10 in gp* **33/1**

1m 30.91s (5.21) **Going Correction** +0.975s/f (Soft) 15 Ran SP% **124.0**

Speed ratings (Par 109): **109,106,105,102,102 100,99,97,94,92 85,84,82,36,24**

toteswingers: 1&2 £13.10, 1&3 £29.50, 2&3 £38.00 CSF £47.96 CT £905.83 TOTE £7.40: £2.70, £3.20, £8.60; EX 50.60 Trifecta £1945.80 Pool: £68,076.70 - 25.89 winning units..

Owner Mrs T A Foreman **Bred** Rosyground Stud **Trained** Newmarket, Suffolk

■ Stewards' Enquiry : Luke Morris one-day ban: careless riding (Jul 28)

FOCUS

Perhaps not the strength in depth of some years, but nevertheless the race was run at a sound enough gallop and the winner deserves credit for coming from midfield to run down front-runners on both sides of the track who had benefited from uncontested leads. The field split into two groups, with five heading to the stands' rail and the larger bunch racing on the far side. The first two came from the far side but there didn't look to be a bias. Five of the previous nine winners had made all, at least on their side of the track, and so both the runner-up and third followed a pattern for success in the race. It's hard to rate the form too positively given the conditions.

NOTEBOOK
Bonnie Brae, given that the testing conditions made making up ground from behind even more difficult, did really well to come through and score. She clearly relishes these conditions, though, as she showed at Doncaster last back-end, and at Ascot on her reappearance, and she should be up to picking up some black type later this season when conditions allow. She's entered in the big heritage handicap at Ascot next Saturday but the worry would be that the race comes a bit soon. (op 11-2 tchd 7-1)
Captain Bertie(IRE) was eighth to Trade Commissioner in a 1m handicap at Sandown which is beginning to look like hot form, and he stepped up on that effort under a more positive ride down in trip. He was in the right place given the conditions, though. (op 9-1)
Captain Ramius(IRE), given a break since running at Meydan in January, has made all to win on more than one occasion in the past, and his style of running was an asset in this ground. He put up a good effort to see off his rivals on the stands' side. (op 28-1 tchd 16-1)
Sir Reginald was a little keen early on under restraint, but he stayed on well once they hit the rising ground. He probably doesn't want conditions as testing as this, and he's on a fair mark based on his best form, so should remain of interest for similar races.
Decent Fella(IRE), fourth in the Buckingham Palace Stakes, reversed form with Jamesie, who finished second at Royal Ascot, but both were always playing catch-up on the stands' side. (op 10-1 tchd 11-1)
Jamesie(IRE), runner-up in the Buckingham Place, was never in it. (tchd 7-1)
Seal Rock didn't get home on his one and only previous try over 7f, but he didn't run badly this time considering the very testing conditions. He can be given another try over the distance on better ground.
King Of Jazz(IRE), who was well beaten in this race last year, was visored for the first time. He didn't get home in the end, and while he ran well on soft ground in the Victoria Cup at Ascot earlier this year (one place behind Bonnie Brae), these conditions were far more testing. (op 16-1)
Mawaakef(IRE) has made the running in the past, but for some reason Dettori chose not to take advantage of that, but was happy to sit among the leading bunch on the far side. In truth the gelding simply looks held off his current mark. (op 11-1)
Gramercy(IRE) struggled to get involved from off the pace on the far side.
Atlantic Sport(USA) struggled to get involved from off the pace on the far side. (op 15-2)
Belgian Bill was held up last of five on the stands' side which was of no use to him, and he could also do with quicker ground. He was reported to have lost his action at halfway. Official explanation: jockey said colt lost its action from halfway (op 8-1)
Stevie Thunder was disappointing, but these were extreme conditions and he probably needs a longer trip anyway. (op 10-1)

4100 DARLEY JULY CUP (BRITISH CHAMPIONS SERIES AND GLOBAL SPRINT CHALLENGE) (GROUP 1) 6f

3:20 (3:21) (Class 1) 3-Y-O+

£256,329 (£97,180; £48,635; £24,227; £12,158; £6,102) **Stalls** High

Form RPR

1105 **1** **Mayson**[14] 3623 4-9-5 110 PaulHanagan 11 121
(Richard Fahey) *w ldr tl led 5f out: shkn up over 1f out: edgd rt and rdn clr fnl f* **20/1**

-120 **2** *5* **The Cheka (IRE)**[21] 3370 6-9-5 111 (v[1]) JimmyFortune 10 106
(Eve Johnson Houghton) *a.p: chsd wnr over 2f out: rdn over 1f out: no ex ins fnl f* **14/1**

0-35 **3** *1* **Society Rock (IRE)**[21] 3370 5-9-5 117 RyanMoore 12 103
(James Fanshawe) *chsd ldrs: rdn over 1f out: styd on same pce* **7/2**[1]

5/10 **4** *2 1/4* **Ortensia (AUS)**[25] 3238 7-9-2 115 WilliamBuick 8 93
(Paul Messara, Australia) *prom: rdn over 1f out: wknd ins fnl f* **7/1**

4-03 **5** *nse* **Hawkeyethenoo (IRE)**[21] 3371 6-9-5 103 GrahamLee 3 96+
(Jim Goldie) *hld up: rdn over 1f out: styd on ins fnl f: nrst fin* **16/1**

0000 **6** *3 1/4* **Sirius Prospect (USA)**[21] 3370 4-9-5 112 (b) ShaneKelly 13 86
(Dean Ivory) *s.i.s: hld up: rdn over 2f out: nvr on terms* **14/1**

2561 **7** *3/4* **Fire Lily (IRE)**[30] 3092 3-8-10 110 WayneLordan 6 81
(David Wachman, Ire) *mid-div: hdwy u.p over 2f out: wknd over 1f out* **11/2**[3]

10-0 **8** *2* **Strong Suit (USA)**[25] 3237 4-9-5 123 RichardHughes 2 78
(Richard Hannon) *hld up: rdn over 2f out: wknd over 1f out* **8/1**

5001 **9** *3* **Dandy Boy (ITY)**[21] 3371 6-9-5 113 PatDobbs 15 69
(David Marnane, Ire) *s.i.s: hld up: a in rr* **8/1**

-040 **10** *5* **Genki (IRE)**[21] 3370 8-9-5 109 (v) JamesDoyle 9 54
(Roger Charlton) *dwlt: hld up: rdn over 2f out: a in rr* **25/1**

0 **11** *3 1/4* **Sepoy (AUS)**[105] 1147 4-9-5 123 FrankieDettori 4 44
(Mahmood Al Zarooni) *prom: rdn over 2f out: wknd wl over 1f out* **9/2**[2]

3-30 **12** *9* **Reply (IRE)**[24] 3265 3-8-13 111 (v[1]) JPO'Brien 14 17
(A P O'Brien, Ire) *racd alone towards far side: led: hdd 5f out: chsd wnr tl rdn over 2f out: wknd and eased over 1f out* **16/1**

1m 15.9s (3.40) **Going Correction** +0.975s/f (Soft)
WFA 3 from 4yo+ 6lb **12** Ran SP% **124.2**
Speed ratings (Par 117): **116,109,108,105,104 100,99,96,92,86 81,69**
toteswingers 1&2 £35.40, 1&3 £14.40, 2&3 £10.10 CSF £286.82 CT £1230.84 TOTE £32.30: £8.20, £4.90, £1.60; EX 183.70 Trifecta £1125.90 Pool: £7,242.25 - 4.75 winning units..
Owner David W Armstrong **Bred** Highfield Farm Llp **Trained** Musley Bank, N Yorks

FOCUS
Run in desperate conditions, this has to go down as an unsatisfactory edition of the July Cup, with an outsider making virtually all to win virtually unchallenged. The form cannot be treated literally, although Mayson's effort could clearly be rated higher. It looked a weak renewal on paper too, attracting none of the principals from Black Caviar's Diamond Jubilee Stakes or from the King's Stand Stakes whose runner-up, Bated Breath, was the ante-post favourite but was withdrawn on the day because of the ground. Excelebration was not declared and other notable absentees were Power and Hoof It. Only three of the field had won at the top level, two of those in Australia. Eleven of the last 13 winners had run at Royal Ascot, the exceptions both trained by Hughie Morrison, but the nine runners who'd seen action at the Royal meeting were all eclipsed this time. At first the the field split into three groups, with five racing down the centre of the track, another six nearer the stands' side, and Reply isolated near the far rail. The groups merged in the second half of the race, but the first three home, drawn 11, 10 and 12, came from the five down the middle.

NOTEBOOK
Mayson, taken to post early, showed bright pace down the centre and had all his rivals in trouble heading down to the two pole, keeping up the gallop to win emphatically. Successful twice on the Rowley Mile in the spring, he came here on the back of two below-par efforts, becoming upset in the stalls at York then failing to act at all in near unraceable ground at Newcastle. Bad though they were, these conditions cannot have been quite as bad and he simply handled them better than the opposition. For all that this seemed to fall in his lap, he is a tough and likeable colt, and clearly a very smart sprinter. He's in the Nunthorpe and would have a chance if the ground is still soft at York next month. The Haydock Sprint Cup must also come into consideration, while the Abbaye has been mentioned too. Longer term, this win has surely secured a stallion career for the son of Invincible Spirit. Official explanation: trainer said, regarding apparent improvement in form, that the gelding had been hampered on heavy ground on its previous run. (op 25-1 tchd 28-1)
The Cheka(IRE) has been reinvented as a sprinter this season and it has been fully justified with this Group 1 second to back up a Listed win at Doncaster and a second in the Group 2 Duke Of York Stakes. Tried in different headgear after finishing well back in the Diamond Jubilee, he chased Mayson all the way and held on for the runner-up spot as he tired in the final furlong. His target is Ascot's British Champions Sprint in October. (op 12-1)
Society Rock(IRE), the 2011 Golden Jubilee winner, missed the break badly before finishing fast for fifth in the event this year, and had a rug for stalls entry now. He became upset once installed but broke well enough and ran respectably, always chasing the pace near the centre, to finish four places closer than he had behind Starspangledbanner two years ago. The Ascot race, which the Fanshawe yard won with Deacon Blues last year, looks the obvious aim for him. (op 3-1)
Ortensia(AUS) disappointed in the King's Stand after getting worked up beforehand, but was much more relaxed here. She had been working well on the July course too, but this ground was a serious concern. Ponied early to the start, she ran creditably, doing best of those who raced towards the stands' side, but was not at her best in the conditions. The Nunthorpe could be next for her. (op 10-1)
Hawkeyethenoo(IRE), the Wokingham third and Graham Lee's first ride in a Group 1, ran on from the back and nearly grabbed fourth place. This was a fine run from a gelding who had never previously contested a Listed race, let alone one at this level, and who gained his first win off a mark of just 51. (tchd 20-1)
Sirius Prospect(USA), seventh in the Diamond Jubilee, played up in the stalls, seemingly being set off by Society Rock alongside him. Well positioned in the centre of the track as it turned out, he ran reasonably well without ever threatening the leaders. (op 12-1)
Fire Lily(IRE) was one of only two representatives of the younger generation here, both Irish trained. The Ballyogan Stakes winner did the better of them, but was comfortably held after racing prominently towards the near side. (op 6-1)
Strong Suit(USA)'s connections paid a fee of £30,000 to supplement him, but were worried about the ground and their fears proved justified. Tackling 6f and soft (or worse) for the first time since finishing a 9l second to Dream Ahead in the 2010 Middle Park Stakes, he raced nearest to the stands' side and never looked like picking up. Now 0-6 in Group 1s, that's two below-par runs this season and he has something to prove now, but this effort can be safely written off. (op 14-1)
Dandy Boy(ITY), another supplementary entry, never threatened after missing the break. Last year's Wokingham scorer Deacon Blues developed into a top sprinter afterwards and Dandy Boy may be worth another chance. The representative of David Marnane reported that horse was unsuited by the heavy ground. Official explanation: trainer's rep said horse was unsuited by the heavy ground (tchd 9-1)
Genki(IRE), who would have been second string to Bated Breath, was slowest away and is regularly found wanting at this level in any case. Official explanation: jockey said gelding was slowly away (op 20-1)
Sepoy(AUS) avoided Black Caviar in Australia and took four Grade 1s at this trip for Peter Snowden, winning all bar two of his 12 runs in that country, but he did not act on the ground on this first start since March. It's likely to have been his only run for Mahmood Al Zarooni, as the colt is set for a stud career in Australia now. Perhaps Godolphin would have been better represented by Diamond Jubilee fourth Soul, an easy winner at Newbury earlier in the day. (op 11-2 tchd 6-1)
Reply(IRE) came here on the back of a run in the Jersey Stakes, a route taken by two previous July Cup winners from Ballydoyle, Mozart and Stravinsky. Visored for the first time, the Irish Guineas third raced alone on the far side from his high draw and was one of the first beaten on this drop back in trip. (op 14-1)

4101 ROSSDALES E B F CONDITIONS STKS 6f

3:55 (3:56) (Class 2) 2-Y-O **£9,703** (£2,887; £1,443) **Stalls** High

Form RPR

521 **1** **Hasopop (IRE)**[9] 3788 2-9-1 85 RyanMoore 1 96+
(Marco Botti) *trckd ldr: shkn up to ld over 1f out: edgd rt: r.o wl* **7/2**[2]

21 **2** *7* **Bircham (IRE)**[23] 3303 2-9-1 0 FrankieDettori 3 79
(Mahmood Al Zarooni) *set stdy pce tl qcknd over 2f out: rdn and hdd over 1f out: sn hung lft: wknd ins fnl f* **1/4**[1]

5 **3** *8* **Hajam**[57] 2247 2-8-13 0 MartinLane 7 49
(James Tate) *prom tl wknd over 1f out* **12/1**[3]

1m 18.65s (6.15) **Going Correction** +0.975s/f (Soft) **3** Ran SP% **109.9**
Speed ratings (Par 100): **98,88,78**
CSF £5.23 TOTE £3.90; EX 4.50.
Owner Giuliano Manfredini **Bred** B Kennedy **Trained** Newmarket, Suffolk

FOCUS
Two of the previous three winners went on to win in Group company, but the race was decimated by non-runners this time and the form is hard to quantify. The winner could do no moer than thrash the favourite.

NOTEBOOK
Hasopop(IRE) was far more professional than the favourite and got the job done in no-nonsense style, staying on strongly up the hill in the manner of a colt who'll be suited by another furlong. It remains to be seen what he actually achieved, but he's clearly versatile ground wise and has the right attitude, so he deserves his chance to prove himself in better company. (tchd 3-1)
Bircham(IRE) was sent off a short price to build on his easy Ripon success in soft ground, and he was allowed to dictate a steady pace, but he's not as big as the winner and, once eyeballed, he soon wanted no part of it and hung left. The ground is clearly a plausible excuse, but he has something to prove now. (op 1-3)
Hajam, who has a fast-ground pedigree, looked ill at ease on this testing surface and was soon seen off by the front two. (op 8-1)

4102 EARL OF EUSTON NURSERY 7f

4:30 (4:30) (Class 2) 2-Y-O **£9,703** (£2,887; £1,443; £721) **Stalls** High

Form RPR

031 **1** **Senafe**[15] 3569 2-9-0 **79** MircoDemuro 7 82
(Marco Botti) *led: rdn and hdd ins fnl f: rallied to ld post* **8/1**

021 **2** *shd* **Oasis Cannes**[12] 3708 2-8-13 **78** LukeMorris 1 81
(Sir Mark Prescott Bt) *chsd wnr: rdn and hung lft over 1f out: r.o* **7/2**[3]

521 **3** *hd* **Kimberella**[27] 3182 2-9-7 **86** FrankieDettori 2 88+
(Michael Bell) *hld up: plld hrd: hdwy over 2f out: swtchd lft over 1f out: rdn to ld ins fnl f: hdd post* **5/2**[1]

322 **4** *18* **Echion (IRE)**[17] 3506 2-8-10 **75** RichardHughes 5 32
(Richard Hannon) *hld up: rdn over 2f out: wknd over 1f out* **3/1**[2]

006 **5** *nk* **Getaway Car**[31] 3046 2-7-12 **63** (p) JamieMackay 9 20
(Gerard Butler) *prom: rdn over 2f out: wknd over 1f out* **10/1**

510 **6** *3/4* **Tommy's Secret**[25] 3242 2-9-1 **80** BrettDoyle 6 35
(Jane Chapple-Hyam) *hld up: rdn over 2f out: wknd over 1f out* **12/1**

6121 **7** *27* **Rated**[7] 3858 2-8-13 **78** MartinHarley 8
(Mick Channon) *chsd ldrs: rdn over 2f out: wknd over 1f out: eased: t.o* **6/1**

1m 32.54s (6.84) **Going Correction** +0.975s/f (Soft) **7** Ran SP% **118.0**
Speed ratings (Par 100): **99,98,98,78,77 76,46**
toteswingers 1&2 £5.60, 1&3 £4.60, 2&3 £2.70 CSF £37.64 CT £92.10 TOTE £8.40: £3.40, £2.80; EX 51.10 Trifecta £177.00 Pool: £1,720.08 - 7.18 winning units..
Owner Mubarak Al Naemi **Bred** Mrs M L Parry **Trained** Newmarket, Suffolk
■ Stewards' Enquiry : Mirco Demuro two-day ban: used whip above permitted level (Jul 28-29)

FOCUS
Not for the first time on the card it paid to race handily. The winning time was only 0.35sec slower than that recorded in the Group 2 Superlative Stakes earlier. The fifrst three finished miles clear, but the winner is rated just to the bare form of her maiden win.

NOTEBOOK
Senafe, the only filly in the line-up, was soon sent to the front and, although headed by the third on the climb to the line, rallied bravely to edge ahead again close home. An all-the-way winner on fast ground at Folkestone last time, she coped with these very different conditions admirably. Given the stamina on the dam's side of her pedigree, she's likely to get further in time. (tchd 7-1)

Oasis Cannes was never far off the lead and stayed on strongly up the hill. She was in front a few yards past the line and a mile probably can't come soon enough for her. (tchd 11-2 in a place)
Kimberella, who was stepping up from 6f, did well considering it was a day when making ground up from off the pace was difficult. She came through to lead on the climb to the line, only to weaken close home and lose out narrowly, probably as a result of having been keen early. She's got more than enough ability to win something similar and should be kept on side. (tchd 11-4 in places)
Echion(IRE), beaten a country mile in fourth, found this longer trip on heavy ground far too much of a test of stamina. (op 7-2 tchd 9-2)
Getaway Car didn't look at all comfortable on the ground. (tchd 9-1)
Tommy's Secret, who was taking a big step up in trip, was never travelling.
Rated, who won on soft ground just a week earlier, dropped out quickly once pressure was applied. (op 11-2)

4103 CELEBRATING NEWMARKET - HISTORIC HOME OF HORSE RACING H'CAP — 1m 4f

5:05 (5:05) (Class 3) (0-90,90) 3-Y-O+ **£9,703** (£2,887; £1,443; £721) **Stalls** Centre

Form / RPR

1521 **1** **John Louis**35 2932 4-9-4 **83** .... RaulDaSilva(3) 17 — 94
(Philip McBride) *mde all: rdn over 1f out: jst hld on* **11/2**2

4-03 **2** ½ **Sohar**21 3400 4-8-13 **75** .... MircoDemuro 5 — 85
(James Toller) *a.p: chsd wnr over 4f out: rdn and ev ch over 2f out: hung rt over 1f out: styd on* **20/1**

-344 **3** 3 **Communicator**17 3502 4-9-8 **84** .... JimmyFortune 8 — 90
(Andrew Balding) *a.p: rdn and ev ch over 2f out: styd on same pce fnl f* **6/1**3

1F4 **4** 2 **Star Date (IRE)**24 3280 3-8-3 **83** .... LukeMorris 2 — 86
(Gerard Butler) *plld hrd and sn prom: rdn over 2f out: sn outpcd: styd on ins fnl f* **9/1**

01 **5** 2½ **Educate**16 3551 3-8-7 **82** .... TadhgO'Shea 1 — 81+
(Ismail Mohammed) *hld up: plld hrd: hdwy over 3f out: hung rt over 1f out: sn rdn and swvd lft: wknd fnl f* **13/2**

-603 **6** 7 **Mountain Range (IRE)**29 3121 4-9-7 **83** .... RyanMoore 11 — 72
(John Dunlop) *hld up: effrt over 2f out: wknd fnl f* **15/2**

/224 **7** 12 **Local Hero (GER)**29 3125 5-9-12 **88** ....(p) WilliamBuick 14 — 59
(Steve Gollings) *hld up: hdwy u.p over 3f out: wknd wl over 2f out* **5/2**1

0-05 **8** 7 **Blimey O'Riley (IRE)**33 2978 7-8-11 **73** .... MichaelHills 16 — 33
(Mark H Tompkins) *hld up: a in rr: rdn over 3f out: sn wknd: t.o* **14/1**

1-00 **9** 4½ **Snow Hill**35 2921 4-9-0 **76** .... MartinHarley 4 — 29
(Chris Wall) *hld up: rdn over 4f out: wknd over 2f out: t.o* **12/1**

/400 **10** 72 **Eye Of The Tiger (GER)**31 3036 7-9-8 **84** .... TomQueally 9 —
(Barney Curley) *chsd wnr tl rdn and wknd over 4f out: t.o* **14/1**

2m 42.32s (9.42) **Going Correction** +0.975s/f (Soft)
WFA 3 from 4yo+ 13lb — 10 Ran SP% **119.1**
Speed ratings (Par 107): **107,106,104,103,101 97,89,84,81,33**
toteswingers 1&2 £23.20, 1&3 £4.80, 2&3 £15.90 CSF £110.19 CT £689.36 TOTE £5.70: £2.20, £5.50, £2.20; EX 122.50 Trifecta £603.70 Pool: £1,974.28 - 2.42 winning units..
Owner Four Winds Racing **Bred** Wood Farm Stud (Waresley) **Trained** Newmarket, Suffolk

FOCUS

A fair handicap run on the worst of the ground. Considering the conditions the pace, set by the winner, was reasonable, and nothing became involved from off the gallop. They raced down the middle of the track in the long home straight. The winner produced another personal best.

NOTEBOOK

John Louis, considering the pace he'd set, maintained the gallop remarkably well, although the runner-up was cutting into his lead late on. A winner off 6lb lower over 1m2f here last month, he improved again for the longer trip but may need some time to get over this hard-earned success. His trainer mentioned the Ebor, but he would struggle to get in there even after being reassessed. (tchd 9-2)
Sohar was never far from the lead and she was closing on the winner close home after hanging over to the stands-side rail. She remains a maiden, but is still lightly raced and a winning opportunity should come.
Communicator is running solidly this term without quite finding that winning spark. He is well handicapped, currently 4lb lower than when fourth for Michael Bell in a warm King George V Handicap last season, but gives the impression he does not put it all in. (op 7-1 tchd 15-2)
Star Date(IRE) ◆, who was keen early, did not drop away as he seemed likely to and the stiffer test was justified. He took a bad fall at Epsom on Derby day but his confidence has obviously not been affected too adversely and he is capable of finding more improvement, perhaps over even further. (op 11-1)
Educate looked interesting on this handicap debut, but the son of Echo Of Light took time to settle, then ducked both ways when the pressure was on and looked far from straightforward. If his quirks can be ironed out he can step forward from this. (tchd 6-1)
Mountain Range(IRE)'s trainer won this two years ago with Times Up, who went on to land that season's November Handicap. The gelding made only a short-lived forward move from the back but did finish clear of the remainder. (op 7-1 tchd 8-1)
Local Hero(GER), who ended up with topweight following withdrawals, was expected to be suited by the drop back in trip, but he failed to handle the conditions and was in trouble with over three to run. The trainer's representative reported that the gelding was unsuited by the heavy ground.
Official explanation: trainer's rep said gelding was unsuited by the heavy ground (op 3-1 tchd 10-3 in a place)
T/Plt: £2,609.00 to a £1 stake. Pool: £184,064.66, 51.50 winning tickets. T/Qpdt: £180.80 to a £1 stake. Pool: £11,642.06. 47.65 winning tickets. CR

3658 SALISBURY (R-H)

Saturday, July 14

4104 Meeting Abandoned - waterlogged

4069 YORK (L-H)

Saturday, July 14

OFFICIAL GOING: Good (good to soft in places) (overall 7.3; stands' side 6.8; centre 7.0; far side; 7.1)
Wind: Moderate, half against Weather: Overcast, light showers

4110 JOHN SMITH'S RACING STKS (H'CAP) — 1m

1:55 (1:55) (Class 3) (0-95,93) 3-Y-O+ **£9,703** (£2,887; £1,443; £721) **Stalls** Low

Form / RPR

0252 **1** **Anderiego (IRE)**14 3615 4-9-1 **80** .... KierenFallon 5 — 92
(David O'Meara) *mid-div: drvn 4f out: nt clr run and swtchd rt over 2f out: styd on down outside to ld jst ins fnl f: drvn out* **13/2**3

2611 **2** 2½ **Levitate**17 3493 4-9-4 **90** ....(v) WilliamTwiston-Davies(7) 10 — 96
(Alan McCabe) *s.i.s: in rr: hdwy on outside over 1f out: styd on to take 2nd nr fin* **7/1**

3031 **3** ¾ **Silvery Moon (IRE)**6 3890 5-9-10 **89** 6ex .... DavidAllan 8 — 93
(Tim Easterby) *chsd ldrs: drvn and outpcd over 3f out: rallied over 1f out: kpt on same pce last 150yds* **11/2**1

5061 **4** hd **Vito Volterra (IRE)**12 3699 5-9-1 **80** .... AndrewMullen 2 — 84
(Michael Smith) *led: qcknd pce over 4f out: hdd jst ins fnl f: kpt on same pce* **12/1**

1242 **5** 1½ **Toto Skyllachy**17 3493 7-9-8 **87** .... DanielTudhope 4 — 87
(David O'Meara) *in tch: effrt over 2f out: edgd lft and kpt on same pce fnl f* **6/1**2

-122 **6** ½ **Ginger Jack**8 3826 5-9-5 **84** .... PaulMulrennan 11 — 83
(Geoffrey Harker) *chsd ldrs: drvn over 3f out: one pce appr fnl f* **6/1**2

2-00 **7** 2¼ **Common Touch (IRE)**24 3268 4-9-11 **93** .... LeeTopliss(3) 6 — 87
(Richard Fahey) *mid-div: hdwy over 2f out: one pce* **14/1**

0025 **8** ¾ **Majestic Dream (IRE)**29 3128 4-9-0 **79** .... JamesSullivan 7 — 71
(Michael Easterby) *in rr and sn drvn along: kpt on fnl 2f: nvr a factor* **22/1**

6053 **9** 1½ **Assizes**9 3779 3-8-7 **81** .... JoeFanning 12 — 68
(Mark Johnston) *in rr: drvn 4f out: kpt on fnl f: nvr on terms* **12/1**

005- **10** 6 **Tiger Reigns**151 6150 6-9-12 **91** .... TomEaves 9 — 66
(Michael Dods) *t.k.h in rr: sme hdwy over 3f out: lost pl over 1f out* **16/1**

0511 **11** 1¾ **Oratory (IRE)**22 3335 6-9-3 **82** .... MickyFenton 1 — 53
(Paul Midgley) *dwlt: hdwy on ins 4f out: hung lft and wknd 2f out* **8/1**

5-00 **12** ¾ **Fighter Boy (IRE)**16 3534 5-9-9 **88** .... PaddyAspell 3 — 57
(Michael Easterby) *trckd ldrs: lost pl wl over 1f out* **25/1**

1m 38.04s (-0.96) **Going Correction** -0.075s/f (Good)
WFA 3 from 4yo+ 9lb — 12 Ran SP% **117.0**
Speed ratings (Par 107): **101,98,97,97,96 95,93,92,91,85 83,82**
toteswingers: 1&2 £7.80, 1&3 £8.70, 2&3 £5.00 CSF £50.85 CT £272.74 TOTE £7.60: £2.70, £2.60, £2.30; EX 64.00 Trifecta £156.80 Pool: £981.39 - 4.63 winning units..
Owner Ebor Racing Club **Bred** Gerrardstown House Stud **Trained** Nawton, N Yorks

FOCUS

After a dry night the going had changed to good, good to soft in places and, as with the previous day, rail movement meant that all races over 1m-plus were actually staged over a distance 27 yards shorter than advertised. The pace, set by Vito Volterra, looked a solid one (backed up by a time less than a second above standard) and the field came down the middle of the track up the straight. The form looks solid rated around the first four.

NOTEBOOK

Anderiego(IRE) was switched towards the stands' side to get a clear run having been caught in a pocket, and he powered clear in the final furlong to score in quite impressive style. He had shown his best form for David O'Meara when narrowly beaten at Doncaster last time and he took another step forward to go one better in this hotter race. Given the way he travelled and quickened once in the clear, a rise in the weights may not prevent him going in again. (op 6-1)
Levitate, chasing a hat-trick, finished strongly from off the pace having been under pressure from some way out. He is clearly still in great form but on this evidence a stiffer track would suit better. (tchd 13-2)
Silvery Moon(IRE), who was closely matched with Levitate on Carlisle Bell form, kept on well towards the far side and has run right up to form. (op 6-1)
Vito Volterra(IRE) deserves a lot of credit for sticking on so gamely having set what looked a strong pace and he probably bettered his latest Pontefract win off this 7lb higher mark. (tchd 14-1)
Toto Skyllachy looked a major player entering the final furlong but his effort petered out somewhat in the closing stages. He probably needs to take another step forward to overcome this career-high mark.
Ginger Jack probably hasn't run as well as at Sandown last week despite drying conditions being in his favour.
Oratory(IRE) Official explanation: jockey said gelding hung right in straight

4111 JOHN SMITH'S SILVER CUP (H'CAP) (LISTED RACE) — 1m 6f

2:25 (2:26) (Class 1) (0-110,108) 3-Y-O+ **£19,536** (£7,388; £3,692; £1,844) **Stalls** Low

Form / RPR

04-1 **1** **Mount Athos (IRE)**56 2278 5-10-0 **108** .... KierenFallon 1 — 119+
(Luca Cumani) *t.k.h early: hld up in tch: hdwy 3f out: led wl over 1f out: sn rdn clr: comf* **5/1**2

3-41 **2** 4 **High Jinx (IRE)**35 2933 4-9-6 **100** .... RobertHavlin 9 — 105+
(James Fanshawe) *hld up towards rr: hdwy on wd outside over 3f out: sn rdn along: styd on to chse wnr ins fnl f: no imp* **5/1**2

60-0 **3** nk **Lyric Street (IRE)**57 2253 4-9-0 **94** oh1 .... PaulMulrennan 14 — 99
(Ed Dunlop) *trckd ldrs: smooth hdwy over 4f out: led 3f out: rdn over 2f out: hdd over 1f out: kpt on same pce* **20/1**

4560 **4** 1¼ **Blue Bajan (IRE)**44 2639 10-9-6 **100** .... GrahamGibbons 15 — 103
(David O'Meara) *hld up towards rr: stdy hdwy 4f out: rdn to chse ldrs over 2f out: styng on u.p whn n.m.r and swtchd rt ent fnl f: nrst fin* **16/1**

05 **5** 2 **Western Pearl**25 3241 5-9-0 **94** oh4 .... MartinDwyer 6 — 94
(William Knight) *trckd ldrs: hdwy 4f out: disp ld 3f out: rdn 2f out and ev ch: sn drvn and wkng whn edgd lft over 1f out* **16/1**

5141 **6** 2¼ **Suraj**14 3614 3-8-2 **97** .... HayleyTurner 5 — 94
(Michael Bell) *dwlt and hld up in rr: t.k.h and swtchd to outer 1/2-way: hdwy on wd outside over 3f out: rdn along wl over 2f out: kpt on same pce* **11/4**1

-060 **7** 1 **Kiama Bay (IRE)**7 3857 6-9-0 **94** .... MichaelO'Connell 16 — 90
(John Quinn) *in tch: hdwy 5f out: rdn to chal 3f out: drvn and one pce fnl 2f* **14/1**

14-0 **8** 2½ **Motivado**14 3625 4-9-1 **95** .... TomEaves 10 — 87
(Sir Mark Prescott Bt) *hld up and bhd: gd hdwy on inner over 3f out: rdn to chal and ev ch 2f out: sn drvn and grad wknd* **12/1**3

-312 **9** 9 **Crackentorp**14 3625 7-9-7 **101** .... DavidAllan 13 — 81
(Tim Easterby) *cl up: led briefly over 3f out: sn rdn along and wknd 2f out* **5/1**2

230/ **10** ¾ **Stormy Weather (FR)**140 7293 6-9-0 **94** oh4 .... BarryMcHugh 8 — 73
(Brian Ellison) *a in rr* **25/1**

11-0 **11** 17 **Never Can Tell (IRE)**66 1974 5-9-2 **96** .... TonyHamilton 3 — 51
(Jamie Osborne) *trckd ldr: pushed along 4f out: rdn 3f out: sn wknd* **14/1**

-003 **12** 14 **Tepmokea (IRE)**7 3857 6-9-0 **94** oh2 .... NeilCallan 2 — 29
(Mrs K Burke) *set stdy pce: pushed along over 4f out: hdd over 3f out and sn wknd* **16/1**

3m 2.15s (1.95) **Going Correction** -0.075s/f (Good)
WFA 3 from 4yo+ 15lb — 12 Ran SP% **123.9**
Speed ratings (Par 111): **91,88,88,87,86 85,84,83,78,77 68,60**
toteswingers: 1&2 £6.20, 1&3 £28.30, 2&3 £28.80 CSF £31.77 CT £477.39 TOTE £6.00: £2.50, £1.90, £7.80; EX 40.30 Trifecta £1143.60 Part won. Pool: £1,545.47 - 0.74 winning units..
Owner Dr Marwan Koukash **Bred** David Magnier And Cobra Bloodstock **Trained** Newmarket, Suffolk

FOCUS

Strong staying handicap form with the runner-up and third helping to set the level.

NOTEBOOK

Mount Athos(IRE) ◆ absolutely bolted up off top weight and looks a stayer going places. Despite not enjoying a strong pace to run at, Mount Athos put this race to bed with a lethal turn of foot entering the final furlong and the Ebor seems an obvious target now. Given his preference for a quicker surface, however, connections may well have one eye on a trip to Australia for the Melbourne Cup. (op 13-2)

High Jinx(IRE), stepping up to this trip for the first time, stuck on well having come from off the pace and he is a horse on the upgrade and still unexposed over staying trips. (op 9-2)

Lyric Street(IRE) threw down a big challenge entering the final two furlongs but his effort flattened out in the closing stages. This was a definite step forward from his seasonal return and he continues to shape like a horse with more to offer. There is probably a race in him off this sort of mark. (op 16-1)

Blue Bajan(IRE), entering the veteran stages of his career now, ran another solid race but he is clearly vulnerable to progressive young stayers nowadays. (op 28-1)

Suraj couldn't make any headway from off the pace and looked in trouble a long way out. (op 7-2)

Crackentorp dropped away tamely at the business end and clearly did not run to anything like his best. Official explanation: jockey said gelding ran flat (op 7-1)

4112 53RD JOHN SMITH'S CUP (HERITAGE H'CAP) 1m 2f 88y

3:00 (3:00) (Class 2) 3-Y-0+ **£97,035** (£28,875; £14,430; £7,215) **Stalls** Low

Form RPR

2250 **1** **King's Warrior (FR)**[14] 3635 5-8-9 **91** .... RobertHavlin 19 106
(Peter Chapple-Hyam) *hld up towards rr: smooth hdwy to trck ldrs over 2f out: shkn up to ld over 1f out: forged clr* **33/1**

0-23 **2** *4 ½* **Mid Mon Lady (IRE)**[26] 3219 7-9-4 **100** .... TomEaves 15 107
(Sir Mark Prescott Bt) *in rr: hdwy and swtchd outer over 2f out: hung lft: styd on same pce fnl f* **22/1**

1215 **3** *hd* **Media Hype**[14] 3635 5-8-9 **91** .... GrahamGibbons 2 97+
(Mrs K Burke) *in tch: drvn over 3f out: sn outpcd: nt clr run and swtchd rt over 1f out: styd on towards fin* **9/2**[2]

1240 **4** *hd* **Stand To Reason (IRE)**[21] 3372 4-8-12 **94** .... (p) HayleyTurner 9 100
(Mikael Magnusson) *w ldrs: led over 3f out: hdd over 1f out: styd on same pce* **20/1**

021 **5** *hd* **Area Fifty One**[14] 3635 4-8-10 **97** 5ex .... ShaneBKelly(5) 10 103
(Richard Fahey) *trckd ldrs: effrt 3f out: n.m.r and stmbld over 2f out: styd on same pce over 1f out* **9/2**[2]

-020 **6** *1 ½* **Tameen**[39] 2805 4-8-8 **90** ....[1] PaulMulrennan 22 93
(Ed Dunlop) *hld up in rr: effrt on outer 3f out: kpt on fnl f* **50/1**

6304 **7** *1 ¼* **Alkimos (IRE)**[21] 3372 4-9-5 **101** .... RichardMullen 6 101
(Saeed Bin Suroor) *in rr: hdwy 3f out: nt clr run and swtchd stands' side 2f out: kpt on fnl f* **10/1**[3]

3031 **8** *2 ¼* **Memory Cloth**[14] 3626 5-9-2 **101** 5ex .... DaleSwift(3) 1 97
(Brian Ellison) *rr-div: hdwy 4f out: chal over 2f out: fdd over 1f out* **18/1**

0230 **9** *1 ¾* **Hillview Boy (IRE)**[7] 3857 8-8-11 **93** .... LiamKeniry 12 86
(Jim Goldie) *in tch: hdwy to chse ldrs over 2f out: wknd fnl 100yds* **28/1**

-000 **10** *nk* **Nanton (USA)**[118] 10-9-2 **98** .... BarryMcHugh 11 90
(Jim Goldie) *in rr: hdwy over 3f out: fdd over 1f out* **50/1**

4541 **11** *nk* **Navajo Chief**[28] 3164 5-9-2 **105** .... MichaelJMMurphy(7) 20 97
(Alan Jarvis) *trckd ldrs: upsides over 3f out: fdd over 1f out* **12/1**

-000 **12** *½* **Take It To The Max**[28] 3157 5-8-10 **92** .... TonyHamilton 3 83
(Richard Fahey) *mid-div: effrt over 3f out: one pce fnl 2f* **50/1**

00-5 **13** *1 ½* **Kings Gambit (SAF)**[63] 2081 8-9-9 **105** .... MickyFenton 8 93
(Tom Tate) *trckd ldrs: upsides over 2f out: wknd over 1f out* **33/1**

6103 **14** *21* **Licence To Till (USA)**[14] 3635 5-8-13 **95** .... JoeFanning 4 43
(Mark Johnston) *s.i.s: sme hdwy on inner over 4f out: lost pl 3f out: sn bhd: t.o* **16/1**

2-33 **15** *1 ½* **Mijhaar**[22] 3329 4-9-6 **102** ....[1] NeilCallan 7 47+
(Roger Varian) *towards rr: sme hdwy whn stmbld bdly 3f out: nt rcvr: eased over 1f out: t.o* **7/2**[1]

-106 **16** *11* **Right Step**[21] 3372 5-9-0 **96** .... MichaelO'Connell 21 20
(Alan Jarvis) *in tch: chsng ldrs over 3f out: wknd 2f out: bhd: t.o* **33/1**

/506 **17** *17* **Fair Trade**[7] 3855 5-9-3 **106** .... WilliamTwiston-Davies(7) 5
(Hughie Morrison) *led: hdd over 3f out: sn lost pl and bhd: t.o* **50/1**

2-00 **18** *58* **Pivotman**[14] 3635 4-8-11 **93** .... (t) MartinDwyer 17
(Amanda Perrett) *w ldrs: lost pl over 3f out: sn bhd: virtually p.u: hopelessly t.o* **33/1**

2m 8.28s (-4.22) **Going Correction** -0.075s/f (Good) **18** Ran SP% **118.7**

Speed ratings (Par 109): **113,109,109,109,108 107,106,104,103,103 103,102,101,84,83 74,61,14**

toteswingers: 1&2 £179.20, 1&3 £41.30, 2&3 £24.40 CSF £521.84 CT £2894.17 TOTE £46.40: £6.00, £5.30, £1.70, £4.10; EX 1371.70 TRIFECTA Not won..

Owner Paul Hancock **Bred** Sunny Days Limited **Trained** Newmarket, Suffolk

FOCUS

A typically competitive renewal and the pace looked strong. The finish mostly concerned horses that came from off the pace, but there was a notable incident up the straight when favourite Mijhaar appeared to clip heels with the weakening Fair Trade. Nevertheless, the form looks solid rated around the runner-up and fifth.

NOTEBOOK

King's Warrior(FR) had looked a big handicap winner in waiting when second on his first two starts of the season and although he hasn't been able to reproduce that form on quicker ground since, this turned out to be his day as he strode clear in the closing stages despite carrying his head quite high. His profile suggests he's a better horse on easy ground so there was just enough juice in the turf here and he showed just what he's capable of on his day. Official explanation: trainer's rep said, regarding apparent improvement in form, that the gelding was better suited by the softer ground.

Mid Mon Lady(IRE) is on a long losing run that stretches back to the sumer of 2010 but she showed quality handicap form when only just beaten in the Zetland Gold Cup at Redcar on first start for Sir Mark Prescott and this was right up there with her best efforts. (op 20-1)

Media Hype was the strongest finisher from off the pace having not had the clearest of runs. Still relatively lightly-raced and definitely with a progressive profile, he looks like he'll do better again over further. (op 6-1)

Stand To Reason(IRE) did best of those to race close to the pace and deserves real credit for doing so. This is something close to a career best from this colt and the first-time cheekpieces may have played their part. (op 18-1)

Area Fifty One had every chance but just lacked the zest in the finish that he showed at Newmarket. (op 5-1)

Mijhaar appeared to clip heels and very nearly came down 3f out. He lost all chance at that moment but was still travelling strongly at the time and remains a horse of significant promise. Official explanation: jockey said colt clipped heels

Right Step Official explanation: jockey said gelding was unsuited by the good (good to soft places) ground

4113 JOHN SMITH'S CITY WALLS STKS (LISTED RACE) 5f

3:35 (3:36) (Class 1) 3-Y-0+ **£19,536** (£7,388; £3,692; £1,844) **Stalls** Centre

Form RPR

2030 **1** **Hamish McGonagall**[25] 3238 7-9-0 110 .... DavidAllan 3 116
(Tim Easterby) *qckly away: led 1f: cl up tl led again 1/2-way: rdn over 1f out: styd on strly* **5/1**[1]

-020 **2** *1 ½* **Pabusar**[21] 3371 4-9-0 103 .... RobertHavlin 15 111
(Ralph Beckett) *in tch: hdwy 2f out: rdn to chal and ev ch whn edgd lft ins fnl f: nt qckn last 100yds* **10/1**[3]

4200 **3** *¾* **Monsieur Joe (IRE)**[25] 3238 5-9-0 108 .... RichardMullen 2 108
(Robert Cowell) *trckd ldrs: hdwy 2f out: rdn to chse wnr over 1f out: drvn and one pce fnl f* **16/1**

0000 **4** *1* **Prohibit**[25] 3238 7-9-0 111 .... (v[1]) NeilCallan 5 104
(Robert Cowell) *chsd ldrs: rdn along wl over 1f out: drvn and edgd lft ent fnl f: one pce after* **12/1**

3201 **5** *2 ¼* **Magical Macey (USA)**[19] 3441 5-9-0 101 .... (b) GrahamGibbons 6 96
(David Barron) *cl up: slt ld after 1f: hdd 1/2-way: cl up tl rdn wl over 1f out and grad wknd* **15/2**[2]

1-20 **6** *2* **Ponty Acclaim (IRE)**[25] 3238 3-8-4 105 .... BarryMcHugh 14 82
(Tim Easterby) *hld up: swtchd rt and hdwy 2f out: rdn wl over 1f out: sn no imp* **10/1**[3]

-020 **7** *¾* **Stepper Point**[25] 3238 3-8-9 109 .... MartinDwyer 1 84
(William Muir) *chsd ldrs: hdwy 1/2-way: rdn wl over 1f out and sn wkd* **14/1**

6301 **8** *½* **Caledonia Lady**[7] 3877 3-8-11 105 .... HayleyTurner 9 85
(Jo Hughes) *dwlt and in rr: effrt and sme hdwy 2f out: sn rdn and n.d* **5/1**[1]

5502 **9** *½* **Confessional**[7] 3877 5-9-0 106 .... (be) PaulMulrennan 12 83
(Tim Easterby) *a towards rr* **10/1**[3]

20-0 **10** *nk* **Breathless Kiss (USA)**[35] 2931 5-8-9 94 .... (b) AmyRyan 10 77
(Kevin Ryan) *dwlt: a towards rr* **28/1**

20-0 **11** *1 ½* **Masamah (IRE)**[49] 2486 6-9-0 113 .... KierenFallon 8 76
(Kevin Ryan) *dwlt and in rr: swtchd wd and sme hdwy 2f out: sn rdn and nvr a factor* **5/1**[1]

1540 **12** *nk* **Duchess Dora (IRE)**[7] 3877 5-8-9 100 .... (v[1]) MichaelO'Connell 4 70
(John Quinn) *chsd ldrs: rdn along over 2f out: sn wknd* **16/1**

13 *6* **Josephine Blanche (GER)**[48] 2530 4-8-9 78 .... LiamKeniry 7 49
(D Moser, Germany) *prom: rdn along 1/2-way: sddle slipped and sn wknd: eased over 1f out* **22/1**

59.41s (0.11) **Going Correction** +0.30s/f (Good)

WFA 3 from 4yo+ 5lb **13** Ran SP% **123.0**

Speed ratings (Par 111): **111,108,107,105,102 99,97,97,96,95 93,92,83**

toteswingers 1&2 £13.60, 1&3 £22.80, 2&3 £32.20 CSF £57.08 TOTE £5.30: £2.20, £3.10, £5.30; EX 82.90 Trifecta £1595.60 Part won. Pool: £2,156.33 - 0.49 winning units..

Owner Reality Partnerships I **Bred** J P Coggan And Whitsbury Manor Stud **Trained** Great Habton, N Yorks

FOCUS

A wide open sprint but not many got in a blow from behind the speed and quite a few of these proved disappointing. The winner is rated to last year's Nunthorpe best with a small personal-best from the runner-up.

NOTEBOOK

Hamish McGonagall was always on the front end having broken fast and he found plenty to come home strongly and see off Pabusar, who looked a major threat a furlong out. The winner, who had a leading chance on ratings, loves this track and he found this much more to his liking than the King's Stand Stakes last time. The Nunthorpe, in which he was only beaten three-parts of a length in last season, will surely be on the agenda again. (tchd 9-2)

Pabusar, dropping back to 5f, made what looked a threatening move onto the quarters of the leader but his challenge flattened out in the final furlong where the winner went away again. (op 16-1)

Monsieur Joe(IRE) raced close to the speed but just couldn't see his race out as well as the winner. Given he is rated 2lb inferior to that rival, he has probably run to something approaching his best. (tchd 14-1)

Prohibit hasn't been at his best this season but this was a step in the right direction in the first-time visor. He was only beaten just over a length in the Nunthorpe last season and if connections can coax him back to that sort of form he'll be a player in this season's renewal. (tchd 14-1)

Magical Macey(USA) couldn't dominate this opposition in the manner he had been doing in handicaps, but he was far from disgraced and deserves another crack at this level. (op 8-1)

Caledonia Lady was disappointing, unable to land a blow from off the pace. (op 11-2)

Masamah(IRE) also failed to get competitive from off the pace. Official explanation: jockey said gelding hung left (tchd 9-2)

Josephine Blanche(GER) Official explanation: jockey said saddle slipped

4114 JOHN SMITH'S MEDIAN AUCTION MAIDEN STKS 6f

4:10 (4:10) (Class 3) 2-Y-0 **£7,439** (£2,213; £1,106; £553) **Stalls** Centre

Form RPR

1 **Blaine** 2-9-3 0 .... AmyRyan 4 85+
(Kevin Ryan) *mde virtually all: shkn up over 2f out: hung lft ins fnl f: hld on wl towards fin* **7/2**[2]

4 **2** *½* **Bachotheque (IRE)**[17] 3491 2-9-3 0 .... DavidAllan 8 82
(Tim Easterby) *hld up towards rr: hdwy to trck ldrs 3f out: styd on to take 2nd last 50yds: no ex* **14/1**

3 *1 ½* **Garswood** 2-9-3 0 .... TonyHamilton 12 77+
(Richard Fahey) *trckd ldrs travelling strly: shkn up over 1f out: kpt on same pce last 150yds: will improve* **9/4**[1]

0433 **4** *5* **Shrimpton**[13] 3669 2-8-12 81 .... IanMongan 1 57
(Mick Channon) *mid-div: hdwy and swtchd lft over 1f out: kpt on one pce* **5/1**[3]

60 **5** *6* **Spivey Cove**[14] 3611 2-9-3 0 .... RichardMullen 13 44+
(Ed McMahon) *swtchd lft after s: t.k.h in rr: effrt over 2f out: nvr nr ldrs* **40/1**

6 *¾* **Grandorio (IRE)** 2-9-3 0 .... GrahamGibbons 6 43+
(David O'Meara) *mid-div: drvn and outpcd over 2f out: grad wknd* **20/1**

7 *4 ½* **New Rich** 2-9-3 0 .... TomEaves 5 28+
(Michael Dods) *w ldrs: wknd over 1f out* **9/1**

50 **8** *1* **Sandsend (IRE)**[29] 3123 2-9-3 0 .... BarryMcHugh 9 25
(Richard Fahey) *trckd ldrs: t.k.h: wknd over 1f out* **25/1**

0 **9** *7* **Salutation (IRE)**[17] 3499 2-9-3 0 .... JoeFanning 11 4
(Mark Johnston) *chsd ldrs: drvn over 2f out: sn lost pl* **18/1**

0 **10** *1 ¾* **Romanoff (IRE)**[22] 3346 2-9-3 0 .... KierenFallon 7
(Luca Cumani) *hld up in rr: bhd whn eased fnl f* **6/1**

05 **11** *1* **Loki's Strike**[26] 3208 2-9-3 0 .... NeilCallan 3
(Mrs K Burke) *a in rr* **20/1**

12 *6* **Blazeofenchantment (USA)** 2-9-3 0 .... MickyFenton 10
(Paul Midgley) *s.i.s: sn detached in last* **25/1**

13 2 1/4 **Portside Blue** 2 -9-0[0] .... LeeTopliss(3) 2
(Tony Coyle) *dwlt: in rr: sme hdwy over 2f out: sn wknd* **50/1**

1m 14.42s (2.52)**Going Correction** +0.30s/f (Good) 13Ran SP% **127.5**
Speed ratings (Par 98): **95,94,92,85,77 76,70,69,60,57 56,48,45**
toteswingers 1&2 £8.90, 1&3 £4.00, 2&3 £8.10 CSF £50.18 TOTE £5.50 : £2.20 , £4.40 , £1.40 ; EX 92.60 .
Owner Matt & Lauren Morgan **Bred** Toby Barker **Trained** Hambleton, N Yorks

FOCUS
This looks quite useful maiden form with the front three finishing clear of the 81-rated Shrimpton, who set the standard from those to have raced. The form could be rated higher through that one and the sixth.

NOTEBOOK
Blaine ◆, who cost £100,000 at the sales in April, has clearly been showing connections plenty at home given his Gimcrack Stakes entry and he looks a juvenile with a bright future on the back of this. He travelled smoothly on the front end throughout and, although he showed signs of greenness when hanging to his left in the final furlong, he had enough in the locker to hold on to his his lead. He is a half-brother to the stable's smart juvenile winner Bogart and could be just as good. (op 13-2)
Bachotheque(IRE) took a big step forward from his mildly encouraging Carlisle debut, finishing strongly and shaping like he'll soon be winning, especially granted a slightly stiffer test of stamina. (op 12-1 tchd 16-1 in a place)
Garswood was the buzz horse beforehand and although beaten, there was plenty of promise in this first run. He couldn't quicken with Blaine, but kept plugging away to close on that rival in the final half furlong and he will clearly not be long in winning. Like the winner he has a Gimcrack entry. 5-2 tchd 2-1)
Shrimpton couldn't get in a blow but kept on in a manner that suggests she hasn't run significantly below par, which augurs well for the strength of the form. She looks more of a nursery type, and would probably appreciate another furlong. (op 13-2)
Romanoff(IRE) Official explanation: jockey said colt moved poorly throughout

4115 JOHN SMITH'S STAYERS' H'CAP — 2m 88y
4:45 (4:46) (Class 3) (0-95,100) 4-Y-0+ **£8,409** (£2,502; £1,250 ; £625) **Stalls** Low

Form				RPR
-340	**1**		**Very Good Day** (FR)[31] 3036 5 -8-11[85] .... NeilCallan 9 (Mick Channon) *mid-div: hdwy stands' side 3f out: chal 2f out: styd on wl to ld last 100yds: drvn out* **8/1**	95
2-31	**2**	2 1/4	**Reem Star**[21] 3377 4 -8-11[85] .... AmyRyan 1 (Kevin Ryan) *led 1f: trckd ldrs: led 4f out: hdd and no ex ins fnl f* **8/1**	92
2031	**3**	3	**Getabuzz**[15] 3564 4 -8-8[82] .... DavidAllan 10 (Tim Easterby) *in rr: hdwy over 3f out: chal over 2f out: wknd fnl 100yds* **15/2**	85+
-421	**4**	2	**Orsippus (USA)**[20] 3419 6 -8-8[82] .... KierenFallon 6 (Michael Smith) *hld up in mid-div: drvn over 3f out: one pce fnl 2f* **4/1**[1]	83+
1260	**5**	1/2	**Mica Mika (IRE)**[7] 3494 4 -8-11[85] .... TonyHamilton 12 (Richard Fahey) *in rr: hdwy 4f out: one pce fnl 2f* **12/1**	85
/440	**6**	nk	**Swinging Hawk (GER)**[3] 3661 6 -8-6[80] ....(t) MartinDwyer 13 (Ian Williams) *sn detached in last: sme hdwy over 3f out: styd on fnl 2f: nvr on terms* **14/1**	80
-132	**7**	nse	**Herostatus**[3] 3953 5 -8-7[81] ow1 .... GrahamGibbons 5 (David O'Meara) *chsd ldrs: wknd over 1f out* **6/1**[2]	81
-444	**8**	1	**Jonny Delta**[15] 3564 5 -7-11[76] oh3 .... NeilFarley(5) 8 (Jim Goldie) *hld up: effrt over 3f out: wknd 2f out* **11/1**	75
-041	**9**	21	**Rumh (GER)**[10] 3765 4 -9-12[100] .... RichardMullen 4 (Saeed Bin Suroor) *trckd ldrs: drvn and lost pl over 2f out: eased whn bhd: t.o* **6/1**[2]	74
3	**10**	2 1/2	**Bruslini (FR)**[58] 2214 7 -8-6[80] .... BarryMcHugh 3 (Brian Ellison) *led after 1f: hdd after 5f: reluctant and lost pl 9f out: bhd fnl 6f: t.o 3f out* **7/1**[3]	51
0060	**11**	1 3/4	**Red Jade**[15] 3564 7 -7-13[76] oh4 ....(v) DominicFox(3) 11 (Mrs K Burke) *w ldrs: led after 5f: hdd 4f out: sn wknd: eased whn bhd: t.o* **25/1**	44

3m 34.05s (-0.45)**Going Correction** -0.075s/f (Good) 11Ran SP% **121.6**
Speed ratings (Par 107): **98,96,95,94,94 93,93,93,82,81 80**
toteswingers 1&2 £15.10, 1&3 £13.70, 2&3 £16.60 CSF £73.08 CT £510.12 TOTE £11.40 : £3.30, £3.60 , £2.00 ; EX 141.70 .
Owner Dr Marwan Koukash **Bred** Darley Stud Management Co Ltd **Trained** West Ilsley, Berks

FOCUS
Solid staying handicap form with so many in-form runners. A small personal-best from the runner-up backed up by the third.

NOTEBOOK
Very Good Day (FR) relished the step back up in trip. He had only tried 2m twice before and both of those runs had been on soft ground, so he is unexposed under these conditions and the son of Sinndar took a marked step forward, staying on strongly in the closing stages and relishing every yard of the trip. He is in the Ebor, but he needs to go up further in the weights to stand any chance of getting in that race. (op 11-1)
Reem Star, who is wonderfully consistent, went down fighting and has to have posted a career-best effort despite being beaten. Like the winner, she is unexposed over this trip on a sound surface and just found that rival a bit better handicapped on the day. (tchd 9-1)
Getabuzz looks to be getting better and his trainer is of the opinion he'll be a much better horse next year when he has filled his big frame. (tchd 8-1)
Orsippus(USA) kept on in the closing stages but lacked the gears to get into contention in the straight. He looks more of a grinder, so more testing conditions would probably help him. (op 9-2 tchd 7-2)
Mica Mika (IRE) was another who didn't really pick up when shaken up but kept plugging away. (tchd 14-1)
Rumh(GER) dropped away like a stone through water when push came to shove and something must have been amiss. (op 7-1 tchd 8-1)

4116 JOHN SMITH'S STKS (NURSERY H'CAP) — 6f
5:20 (5:21) (Class 2) 2-Y-0 **£9,703** (£2,887; £1,443 ; £721) **Stalls** Centre

Form				RPR
312	**1**		**Royal Rascal**[12] 3695 2 -8-13[78] .... DavidAllan 8 (Tim Easterby) *w ldrs: led over 2f out: drvn clr 1f out: kpt on wl* **7/4**[1]	91+
025	**2**	2 1/4	**Old Man Clegg**[10] 3748 2 -7-12[66] .... DominicFox(3) 3 (Michael Easterby) *sltly hmpd s: sn outpcd in rr: last whn stmbld over 3f out: hdwy over 1f out: styd on wl to go 2nd last 50yds* **20/1**	71
31	**3**	2	**Dream Scenario**[42] 2686 2 -8-7[77] .... NeilFarley(5) 4 (Mel Brittain) *n.m.r s: hdwy over 2f out: sn chsng ldrs: one pce appr fnl f* **9/2**[3]	76+
10	**4**	1 1/4	**Projectisle (IRE)**[24] 3269 2 -8-11[76] .... AmyRyan 9 (Kevin Ryan) *chsd ldrs: wnt 2nd jst ins fnl f: wknd last 50yds* **13/2**	71
3210	**5**	2 1/4	**Polski Max**[25] 3242 2 -9-4[86] .... LeeTopliss(3) 2 (Richard Fahey) *wnt rt s: led tl over 2f out: wknd appr fnl f* **7/2**[2]	75
413	**6**	4	**Hiddon Coin (IRE)**[44] 2630 2 -8-11[76] .... KierenFallon 1 (David O'Meara) *w ldrs: wknd appr fnl f* **8/1**	53
304	**7**	6	**Symboline**[26] 3223 2 -8-3[68] .... HayleyTurner 6 (Mick Channon) *chsd ldrs: lost pl over 2f out: bhd whn eased ins fnl f* **20/1**	27
0310	**8**	2 1/2	**Vanessa**[29] 3126 2 -8-2[70] ow2 .... AdamBeschizza(3) 7 (Jim Goldie) *chsd ldrs: lost pl over 2f out: eased ins fnl f* **33/1**	21
300	**9**	15	**Mickstathetricksta**[14] 3611 2 -8-10[75] .... NeilCallan 5 (Scott Dixon) *n.m.r s: sn outpcd: bhd whn eased over 1f out: t.o* **20/1**	

1m 15.35s (3.45)**Going Correction** +0.30s/f (Good) 9Ran SP% **118.4**
Speed ratings (Par 100): **89,86,83,81,78 73,65,62,42**
toteswingers 1&2 £7.90, 1&3 £3.10, 2&3 £17.20 CSF £45.25 CT £144.19 TOTE £2.70 : £1.30 , £3.60, £1.80 ; EX 43.70 .
Owner C H Stevens **Bred** Habton Farms **Trained** Great Habton, N Yorks

FOCUS
A fair handicap and solid form worth being positive about.

NOTEBOOK
Royal Rascal looked potentially well handicapped even before her Pontefract conqueror ran well in Listed company yesterday, and this improving filly absolutely bolted up here. She could have been called the winner a long way out as she travelled all over her rivals before moving smoothly clear once asked to quicken. Her maiden win, which also came at this track, was on soft ground, so she proved here that she is just as effective on a sound surface and a Lowther Stakes entry suggests connections don't think she'll be hanging around at this sort of level for too long. (op 2-1)
Old Man Clegg found things happening all too quickly through the first three quarters of the race, but he finished better than anything and looks to be crying out for a step up in trip. He could be very well handicapped. (op 16-1)
Dream Scenario stuck to her task well enough but doesn't strike as having a great deal in hand of her mark.
Projectisle(IRE) got tired in the closing stages having tried to keep tabs on the easy winner. (op 17-2)
Polski Max was anchored by a big weight and he dropped away in the closing stages. (op 9-2)
Mickstathetricksta Official explanation: jockey said colt moved poorly throughout
T/Jkpt: Not won. T/Plt: £1,138.70 to a £1 stake. Pool: £212,705.69. 136.35 winning tickets. T/Qpdt: £123.10 Pool: £9,927.53 59.65 w. tkts WG

4117a, 4119a, 4122a-4129a (Foreign Racing)

3656 LONGCHAMP (R-H)
Saturday, July 14

OFFICIAL GOING: Turf: soft

4118a PRIX ROLAND DE CHAMBURE (LISTED RACE) (2YO) (TURF) — 7f
4:00 (12:00) 2-Y-0 **£22,916** (£9,166; £6,875 ; £4,583 ; £2,291)

			RPR
1		**Zenji (USA)**[36] 2 -9-0[0] .... Pierre-CharlesBoudot 2 (A Fabre, France) **42/10**[3]	100
2	2	**Sir Patrick Moore (FR)**[32] 3017 2 -9-0[0] .... ChristopheSoumillon 6 (Harry Dunlop) *broke wl: racd in cl 2nd or 3rd bef st: rdn 2f out: short of room over 1 1/2f out whn shkn up to chal between horses: pushed his way through: qckndclr 1f out: u.p 100yds out: hdd 75yds out: styd on* **6/4**[1]	95
3	4	**Kamran (FR)**[32] 3017 2 -9-0[0] .... OlivierPeslier 5 (F Head, France) **2/1**[2]	85
4	nk	**Cucuma (FR)**[36] 2907 2 -8-10[0] .... StephanePasquier 1 (P Bary, France) **73/10**	80
5	1 3/4	**Blissful Thinking**[25] 2 -9-0[0] .... Christophe-PatriceLemaire 3 (F-H Graffard, France) **14/1**	80
6	9	**Hidden Talent**[22] 2 -9-0[0] .... ThomasHuet 4 (E J O'Neill, France) **14/1**	57

1m 24.41s (3.71) 6Ran SP% **117.9**
WIN (incl. 1 euro stake): 5.20. PLACES: 1.90, 1.60. SF: 16.70 .
Owner Mme Andre Fabre **Bred** Ecurie Peregrine SAS **Trained** Chantilly, France

NOTEBOOK
Sir Patrick Moore (FR) the winner of a conditions stakes at Compiegne last time on heavy, ran well on this step up in grade having not got the best of runs. He confirmed previous form with the third on worse terms.

4120a PRIX MAURICE DE NIEUIL (GROUP 2) (4YO+) (TURF) — 1m 6f
6:15 (12:00) 4-Y-0+ **£61,750** (£23,833; £11,375 ; £7,583 ; £3,791)

			RPR
1		**Tac De Boistron (FR)**[32] 3367 5 -8-13[0] .... ChristopheSoumillon 6 (A Lyon, France) *settled in 3rd: relegated to 4th on rail over 1 1/2f out: unable to chal on ins: swtchd away fr rail and r.o strly under hrd ride fnl 100yds to get up fnl strides* **3/1**[2]	109+
2	shd	**Vadamar (FR)**[34] 2968 4 -8-13[0] .... Christophe-PatriceLemaire 4 (M Delzangles, France) *settled in clr 2nd: lft in front whn ldr broke down 2f out: wnt clr: r.o wl fnl 100yds: ct fnl strides* **11/10**[1]	109
3	1 3/4	**Shahwardi (FR)**[21] 3373 6 -8-13[0] .... GeraldMosse 5 (A De Royer-Dupre, France) *hld up towards rr: rdn over 1 1/2f out: wnt 2nd u.p 1f out: r.o wl: lost 2nd 25yds out* **10/1**	106
4	nk	**Miss Lago (IRE)**[48] 2534 4 -8-9[0] ....(p) GregoryBenoist 8 (E Lellouche, France) *hld up at rr of field: qcknd wl on outside 2f out: r.o wl fnl f but nt rch ldrs: wnt 4th 50yds out* **12/1**	102
5	1 1/2	**Los Cristianos (FR)**[49] 6 -8-13[0] .... MaximeGuyon 3 (A Couetil, France) *settled in midfield: qcknd wl over 1 1/2f out: wnt 2nd u.p 1f out: running on whn had to be stdd 100yds out: relegated to 5th: r.o again fnl 50yds* **12/1**	104
6	1 1/2	**Brigantin (USA)**[76] 1697 5 -8-13[0] .... Pierre-CharlesBoudot 1 (A Fabre, France) *settled towards rr: dropped bk to rr of field bef st: r.o u.p fnl 1 1/2f wout threatening* **5/1**[3]	102
P		**War Is War (IRE)**[48] 3178 4 -8-13[0] .... ThomasHuet 7 (E J O'Neill, France) *led fr s: clr ent st: rdn 2 1/2f out: broke down bdly whn stl in front 2f out* **14/1**	

3m 4.85s (184.85) 7Ran SP% **120.4**
WIN (incl. 1 euro stake): 3.70. PLACES: 1.30, 1.20, 1.60. DF: 3.20. SF: 9.60 .
Owner A Lyon **Bred** Mme J-P Reverseau **Trained** France

NOTEBOOK
Tac De Boistron (FR) made up a huge amount of ground after being locked on the rail land the spoils in the shadow of the post. A confirmed stayer over much further, he would have been long odds in running to reel in Vadamar. His rider appeared to be sitting in the perfect spot to deliver his run until the leader War Is War broke down badly, but then he picked up under strong pressure to just get there. He needs soft ground so ground conditions will determine where he goes next.

Vadamar(FR), a Group 2 winner over 1m4f,. set out to make the best of his way home on the former Aga Khan colt when the leader broke down but was just collared.

4121a JUDDMONTE GRAND PRIX DE PARIS (GROUP 1) (3YO COLTS & FILLIES) (TURF) 1m 4f

6:50 (12:00) 3-Y-O **£285,700** (£114,300; £57,150; £28,550; £14,300)

RPR

1 **Imperial Monarch (IRE)**[41] 2743 3-9-2 0............................ JPO'Brien 1 118+
(A P O'Brien, Ire) *led after 1f: hld clr ld ent st: r.o wl but wandered off st line u.p fnl 1 1/2f: strly chal fnl 50yds: jst hld on* **6/5**[1]

2 *hd* **Last Train**[42] 3-9-2 0.. MaximeGuyon 2 117
(A Fabre, France) *settled in 3rd: chsd ldr 2f out: wnt 2nd 1f out: r.o wl u.p fnl 100yds: jst failed* **9/1**

3 *½* **Saint Baudolino (IRE)**[41] 2743 3-9-2 0.................... MickaelBarzalona 8 116
(A Fabre, France) *racd towards rr: qcknd wl 2f out: r.o wl u.p fnl f: clst at fin* **4/1**[2]

4 *¾* **Main Sequence (USA)**[42] 2705 3-9-2 0............................ TedDurcan 4 116+
(David Lanigan) *settled in midfield: rdn 2f out: short of room on ins: swtchd away fr rail 1 1/2f out: r.o strly: had to be stdd: swtchd to chal between horses 50yds out: short of room and stdd: unlucky* **5/1**[3]

5 *snk* **Top Trip**[41] 2743 3-9-2 0.. ThomasHuet 7 115
(F Doumen, France) *hld up at rr of field: swtchd to outside in st: r.o wl fnl 1 1/2f: clst at fin* **11/1**

6 *5* **Hard Dream (IRE)**[41] 2743 3-9-2 0.......................... StephanePasquier 6 107
(F Rohaut, France) *racd in 2nd on settling: rdn to chal early in st: wknd u.p fnl 1 1/2f* **14/1**

7 *snk* **Albion**[41] 2743 3-9-2 0... Pierre-CharlesBoudot 5 106
(A Fabre, France) *a towards rr of field: rdn early in st: running on whn suffered interference 1f out: styd on* **33/1**

8 *12* **Nutello (USA)**[41] 2743 3-9-2 0.. OlivierPeslier 3 87
(C Laffon-Parias, France) *prom fr s then settled in midfield: rdn early in st: nt qckn: wknd* **16/1**

9 *5* **Lidari (FR)**[29] 3179 3-9-2 0.......................... Christophe-PatriceLemaire 9 79
(J-C Rouget, France) *settled in 4th: rdn early in st: no ex: wknd* **16/1**

2m 35.47s (5.07) **9** Ran SP% **121.8**
WIN (incl. 1 euro stake): 2.80. PLACES: 1.50, 2.70, 1.60. DF: 25.20. SF: 33.40.
Owner Mrs John Magnier **Bred** David Magnier And Cobra Bloodstock **Trained** Ballydoyle, Co Tipperary

FOCUS
A rather steady early pace, followed by a sprint to the line and a bunch finish did nothing to alter the consensus view that, apart from perhaps Camelot, this year's 3-y-o colts are nothing much. The third and fourth are rated to their frame efforts in earlier Classics.

NOTEBOOK
Imperial Monarch(IRE) having enjoyed an uncontested lead, had a bit left in the tank when the second and third came to challenge, and the impression left was that, despite the narrow margin, he actually won a shade cosily, although he had to survive a pointless and endless stewards' inquiry before his victory was confirmed. While he made the running here, that was probably just a pragmatic decision due to the lack of another obvious front-runner in the line-up, and he could well be seen to even better effect when held up off a stronger pace. Stamina is his forte and, while he carries his head a shade high, there's nothing wrong with his attitude, as he showed here in the closing stages. In a normal year he'd look an obvious candidate for the St Leger, but with stablemate Camelot chasing the Triple Crown it wouldn't be a surprise to see him rerouted, just as he was from the Irish Derby. The Great Voltigeur looks a suitable race, although he'd have a penalty to carry at York, and the Prix Niel was mentioned by Aidan O'Brien, perhaps as a stepping stone to the Arc, for which he's an unappealing top price of 20-1 with Ladbrokes. The Irish Champion Stakes, for which the stable lacks a strong candidate at the moment, might be an opportunity to grab a 1m2f Group 1, though, and it's easy to see a Ballydoyle train, a la Team Sky, making it a real test and peeling off one by one for him up the straight at Leopardstown.
Last Train, whose trainer had sent out three of the previous six winners of the race, is a half-brother to Powerscourt, but looked to have plenty on his plate upped to this company from conditions races. However, he'd been shaping as though in need of this longer distance and, having bagged a nice position on the rail tracking the leader, he was always well positioned to provide the biggest challenge. This was still a big jump for him, though, and there should be better to come.
Saint Baudolino(IRE) has a good turn of foot, but he was given plenty to do in a race run at a fairly sedate early pace, as he was held up out the back. He picked up well in the straight to get within half a length of the winner, but it was asking too much to get by him. This trip probably stretches him a little and his ability to quicken will be more effective back over 1m2f.
Main Sequence(USA), the Derby runner-up, was held up on the rail and didn't get much of a clear run early in the straight, and again just inside the last (the reason for the lengthy inquiry), when he wasn't quick enough to take a gap between the winner and runner-up. His rider had to ease off, and it's possible that with an uninterrupted passage he'd have been second at best, but probably third. The Voltigeur and St Leger appeal as suitable races for him next.
Top Trip, in last place turning in, lacked the turn of pace of Saint Baudolino, but stayed on well nonetheless in race not run to suit. Quietly progressive, he should do better off a stronger all-round gallop.
Hard Dream(IRE), who had a nice trip to the outer of the winner, was unable to pick up in the straight.
Albion was beginning to stay on when hampered a furlong out and shapes like a stayer.
Nutello(USA), who was weakening when hampered, couldn't confirm his shock 50-1 third placing in the Prix du Jockey Club, highlighting what a nonsense of a race that was.
Lidari(FR) was taking a big step up in class and dropped out quickly at the top of the straight.

3425 HANOVER (L-H)

Sunday, July 15

OFFICIAL GOING: Turf: good to soft

4130a GROSSER PREIS VOM AUDI ZENTRUM HANNOVER (EX MEILEN-TROPHY) (GROUP 2) (3YO+) (TURF) 1m

3:40 (12:00) 3-Y-O+

£33,333 (£12,916; £5,416; £3,333; £2,083; £1,250)

RPR

1 **Sir Oscar (GER)**[38] 5-9-2 0.. ADeVries 108
(T Potters, Germany) *hld up in rr: last but in tch 1/2-way: rdn and hdwy 2f out: 3rd and hrd rdn 1 1/2f out: r.o wl u.p fnl f: led cl home* **91/10**

2 *nk* **Worthadd (IRE)**[26] 3237 5-9-2 0............................ Jean-BernardEyquem 108
(Sir Mark Prescott Bt) *led: shkn up 2 1/2f out: hrd rdn and edgd lft over 1f out: r.o u.p fnl f: edgd rt 100yds out: ct cl home* **13/10**[1]

3 *¾* **Amarillo (IRE)**[21] 3425 3-8-7 0.. FilipMinarik 104
(P Schiergen, Germany) *trckd ldrs on rail: cl 5th 1/2-way: gd prog to press ldr ins fnl 2f: sn hrd rdn and nt qckn 1 1/2f out: swtchd outside runner-up ent fnl f: kpt on u.p* **3/1**[2]

4 *nk* **Neatico (GER)**[59] 2222 5-9-2 0................................ MrDennisSchiergen 105
(P Schiergen, Germany) *hld up towards rr: hdwy u.p 2f out: 6th whn briefly short of room and swtchd ins over 1f out: styd on u.p fnl f: nt pce to chal* **173/10**

5 *3* **Energia Dust (BRZ)**[46] 4-9-2 0.. SHellyn 98
(Fabricio Borges, Sweden) *racd in midfield: scrubbed along to hold pl 1/2-way: outpcd and dropped to next to last 2 1/2f out: styd on u.p fr 1 1/2f out: wnt 5th ins fnl f: effrt flattened out last 100yds* **48/1**

6 *½* **Empire Storm (GER)**[21] 3425 5-9-2 0.. JBojko 97
(A Wohler, Germany) *trckd ldng gp towards outside: 4th and scrubbed along to hold pl over 2f out: sn rdn and nt qckn 1 1/2f out: kpt on at one pce fnl f* **39/10**

7 *6* **Sandagiyr (FR)**[106] 1143 4-9-2 0................................. SilvestreDeSousa 83
(Saeed Bin Suroor) *dwlt: chsd up to get on terms: settled in midfield: 5th and scrubbed along 2 1/2f out: sn hrd rdn and no imp: wknd fnl f* **37/10**[3]

8 *4 ½* **Ganimed**[21] 3425 4-9-2 0.. APietsch 73
(M G Mintchev, Germany) *midfield: wnt 2nd 1/2-way: 3rd whn rdn and nt qckn 2 1/2f out: wknd fnl 1 1/2f* **45/1**

9 *16* **Gereon (GER)**[36] 4-9-2 0... DPorcu 36
(C Zschache, Germany) *racd freely and chsd ldrs towards outside: 3rd and pushed along 3f out: sn hrd rdn and nt qckn: wknd qckly fnl 2f: detached last whn eased fnl f: t.o* **221/10**

1m 41.28s (101.28)
WFA 3 from 4yo+ 9lb **9** Ran SP% **134.1**
PARI-MUTUEL (incl. 10 euro stake): WIN: 101; PLACE: 17, 15, 14; SF: 836.
Owner Frau Angelika Muntwyler **Bred** Benedikt Fassbender **Trained** Germany

NOTEBOOK
Worthadd(IRE) tried to make every yard but was just run out of it close home. The Woodbine Mile was mentioned as his next possible target.

3899 HOLLYWOOD PARK (L-H)

Sunday, July 15

OFFICIAL GOING: Turf: firm

4131a AMERICAN OAKS STKS (GRADE 1) (3YO FILLIES) (TURF) 1m 2f

12:40 (12:49) 3-Y-O **£135,483** (£45,161; £27,096; £13,548; £4,516)

RPR

1 **Lady Of Shamrock (USA)**[36] 3-8-9 0.................................. MESmith 2 105
(John W Sadler, U.S.A) *w.w towards rr: trckd ldng quartet on rail over 2f out: pressed ldr 1 1/2f out: qcknd through gap on rail to ld appr fnl 110yds: sn clr: cosily* **6/4**[1]

2 *1 ¼* **My Gi Gi (USA)**[36] 3-8-9 0.. JTalamo 4 102
(Peter Eurton, U.S.A) *settled towards rr in tch: outside wnr trcking ldng quartet over 2f out: briefly short of room and swtchd ins 1 1/2f out: r.o wl fnl f: tk 2nd 50yds out: nt rch wnr* **61/10**

3 *1 ½* **Best Present Ever (USA)**[42] 3-8-9 0................................. VEspinoza 3 99
(J Eric Kruljac, U.S.A) *trckd ldng pair in share of 3rd: hdwy on rail to ld narrowly 2 1/2f out: rdn 1 1/2f out: nt qckn and hdd appr fnl 110yds: wknd and lost 2nd 50yds fr home* **102/10**

4 *1 ¼* **Miss Cato**[31] 3069 3-8-9 0.. GKGomez 7 97
(Rae Guest) *t.k.h early: sn trcking ldr: three off the rail (outside Best Present Ever and Nayarra) and one of four virtually in line 2 1/2f out: rdn and nt qckn 1 1/2f out: kpt on at one pce fnl f* **51/10**[3]

5 *½* **Stormy Lucy (USA)**[36] 3-8-9 0... EFlores 1 96
(Frank Lucarelli, U.S.A) *midfield early: dropped towards rr 4f out: rdn and nt qckn 2f out: kpt on at one pce fnl f* **27/1**

6 *1* **Left A Message (USA)**[28] 3-8-9 0.............................. YuichiFukunaga 6 94
(Thomas F Proctor, U.S.A) *a towards rr: bhd and detached fr main gp 1/2-way: tk clsr order 3 1/2f out: sn rdn: no imp fnl 2f* **171/10**

7 *hd* **Nayarra (IRE)**[44] 2658 3-8-9 0... CNakatani 8 93
(Mick Channon) *broke wl and led: cut ins to set stdy gallop on rail: pressed and responded over 4f out: hdd 2 1/2f out but styd w ldrs (outside Best Present Ever): rdn and nt qckn 1 1/2f out: wknd ins fnl f* **124/10**

8 *1 ½* **Colonial Flag (USA)**[28] 3-8-9 0.. RMaragh 9 90
(Michael Matz, U.S.A) *chsd ldrs: cl up on outside of three ldrs over 2f out: rdn and wknd fr 1 1/2f out* **31/10**[2]

2m 3.19s (123.19) **8** Ran SP% **120.4**
PARI-MUTUEL (all including $2 stakes): WIN 5.00; PLACE (1-2) 3.00, 5.60; SHOW (1-2-3) 2.20, 3.40, 4.20; DF 13.60; SF 21.80.
Owner Hronis Racing Llc **Bred** Grovendale Sales **Trained** USA

NOTEBOOK
Miss Cato was always well placed close to the leader, who was setting a steady pace, and so can't have too many excuses.
Nayarra(IRE) couldn't take advantage of an uncontested lead and being allowed to set a fairly steady pace. Dropping back to a mile might help.

3902 AYR (L-H)

Monday, July 16

OFFICIAL GOING: Good (9.2)
Wind: Almost nil Weather: Overcast

4132 OPEN LOST BOYS OFFER AT BETVICTOR.COM MEDIAN AUCTION MAIDEN STKS 6f

2:05 (2:07) (Class 4) 2-Y-O **£2,264** (£673; £336; £168) **Stalls** Centre

Form RPR

1 **Parisian Prince (IRE)** 2-9-3 0.................................... GrahamGibbons 9 78+
(David Barron) *dwlt and wnt sltly rt s: chsd ldng gp: effrt and hdwy over 1f out: qcknd to ld ins fnl f: edgd rt: styd on wl* **4/1**[3]

2 *¾* **Majestic Moon (IRE)** 2-9-3 0... TonyHamilton 4 76+
(Richard Fahey) *dwlt: t.k.h and sn chsng ldrs: hdwy to ld over 1f out: hdd ins fnl f: kpt on: hld towards fin* **9/4**[1]

0236 **3** *2 ½* **Red Style (IRE)**[31] 3110 2-9-3 70...................................... MickyFenton 3 67
(Paul Midgley) *led tl rdn and hdd over 1f out: rallied: no ex ins fnl f* **8/1**

03 **4** *3 ½* **Teetotal (IRE)**[21] 3436 2-9-3 0... KellyHarrison 2 58
(Nigel Tinkler) *plld hrd: trckd ldrs: effrt and ev ch over 1f out: sn rdn: wknd ins fnl f* **4/1**[3]

5 *3 ½* **Alex Zara** 2-8-12 0... GrahamLee 1 41
(Jim Goldie) *s.i.s: bhd and outpcd: sme hdwy fnl f: nvr able to chal* **22/1**

53 **6** 1 1/4 **Red Paladin (IRE)**[18] 3520 2-9-3 0.................................... PhillipMakin 8 42
(Kevin Ryan) *edgy in preliminaries: w ldr tl rdn and wknd appr fnl f* **7/2**[2]

0 **7** 1/2 **Lady Niramax**[23] 3401 2-8-12 0.................................... AdrianNicholls 5 36
(David Nicholls) *dwlt: sn in tch: struggling over 3f out: sn btn* **50/1**

8 2 1/2 **Foolbythepool** 2-9-3 0.................................... TomEaves 6 33+
(Keith Dalgleish) *dwlt: bhd and sn outpcd: no ch fr 1/2-way* **20/1**

1m 12.82s (0.42) **Going Correction** +0.10s/f (Good) 8 Ran SP% **115.2**
Speed ratings (Par 96): **101,100,96,92,87 85,85,81**
toteswingers 1&2 £2.60, 1&3 £5.60, 2&3 £4.20 CSF £13.26 TOTE £3.80: £1.70, £1.60, £1.20; EX 14.30.
Owner Raymond Miquel **Bred** Kenneth Heelan **Trained** Maunby, N Yorks

FOCUS
Home bend out 6m from inner line and straight out 4m from inner line. 18yds added to races between 7f and 10f and 30yds to others race on Round course. Straightforward maiden form. The first pair should both improve.

NOTEBOOK
Parisian Prince(IRE) certainly wasn't without support on his debut and he won with a bit more in hand than the official winning margin suggests. The son of Chineur was held up towards the rear early and, having shown definite signs of greenness, was doing all his best work late on. He had to be hard ridden to get the job done but was clearly the best on the day. It's difficult to say what this £20,000 purchase achieved but he lacks nothing for size and scope so should be capable of much better, especially once tackling an extra furlong. (op 13-2)
Majestic Moon(IRE) ◆, half-brother to smart stablemate Majestic Myles, ran with real promise, despite coming up short. He, like the winner, showed a lack of experience through the early stages and was keen enough. A maiden win in similar company shouldn't be too long in coming (op 5-2 tchd 85-40)
Red Style(IRE), the most exposed of these, ran well but was ultimately no match for the principals. He brought a rating of 70 into this contest and his future lies in handicaps. However, it's likely he's got very little to work with in terms of his rating and is always likely to prove vulnerable to an improver. (op 7-1)
Teetotal(IRE) was by no means knocked around once his chance had gone and could be of interest in a low-grade nursery.
Red Paladin(IRE) fell in a hole under pressure and disappointed. Official explanation: jockey said the colt hung left throughout (op 11-4)

4133 BET MOBILE AT BETVICTOR.COM H'CAP 6f
2:35 (2:36) (Class 4) (0-85,84) 3-Y-0+ **£4,075** (£1,212; £606; £303) **Stalls** Centre

Form RPR

2301 **1** **Spinatrix**[14] 3696 4-9-9 **84**.................................... (p) LeeTopliss(3) 9 94
(Michael Dods) *dwlt: hdwy to ld after 1f: rdn over 1f out: hrd pressed fnl f: hld on gamely* **11/2**[3]

5011 **2** hd **The Nifty Fox**[7] 3905 8-8-5 **77** 6ex.................................... (p) KierenFallon 10 86
(Tim Easterby) *t.k.h: hld up bhd ldng gp: effrt and hdwy over 1f out: disp ld over 1f out: kpt on: hld cl home* **3/1**[1]

2253 **3** 1 1/4 **Crimson Knot (IRE)**[7] 3903 4-9-5 **77**.................................... TomEaves 7 82
(Alan Berry) *prom: effrt and ev ch over 1f out: sn rdn: kpt on same pce ins fnl f* **15/2**

003P **4** 2 **Toby Tyler**[30] 3169 6-9-6 **78**.................................... (v) MickyFenton 14 77
(Paul Midgley) *hld up: rdn and hdwy over 1f out: hung lft but kpt on ins fnl f: nvr able to chal* **20/1**

03-0 **5** nk **Bonnie Charlie**[27] 3255 6-9-8 **80**.................................... PaulQuinn 6 78+
(David Nicholls) *dwlt: t.k.h in rr: stdy hdwy gng wl over 1f out: shkn up ins fnl f: no imp fnl 100yds* **18/1**

5521 **6** 1/2 **Rasaman (IRE)**[29] 3183 8-9-8 **80**.................................... GrahamLee 1 76+
(Jim Goldie) *rdr slow to remove blindfold and wnt bdly rt s: sn t.o: plenty to do over 1f out: rapid hdwy fnl f: fin wl* **13/2**

3061 **7** 1 1/4 **No Hubris (USA)**[13] 3726 5-9-7 **79**.................................... (b) JamesSullivan 8 71
(Ruth Carr) *t.k.h: led 1f: cl up tl rdn and no ex appr fnl f* **16/1**

0000 **8** hd **Amenable (IRE)**[19] 3496 5-9-8 **80**.................................... AdrianNicholls 12 71
(David Nicholls) *cl up: rdn and ev ch over 1f out: wknd ins fnl f* **28/1**

0000 **9** 1 **Go Go Green (IRE)**[7] 3903 6-8-12 **75**.................................... NeilFarley(5) 13 63
(Jim Goldie) *dwlt: hld up: rdn and effrt over 1f out: no imp fnl f* **25/1**

1534 **10** 3 1/2 **Rock Canyon (IRE)**[2] 4084 3-7-13 **65** oh2.................................... (p) JulieBurke(3) 5 42
(Linda Perratt) *prom tl rdn and wknd over 1f out* **25/1**

1-66 **11** 3 **Hills Of Dakota**[11] 3778 4-9-0 **72**.................................... GrahamGibbons 4 39
(David Barron) *prom: rdn over 2f out: sn wknd* **10/3**[2]

321- **12** nse **Galilee Chapel (IRE)**[283] 6662 3-8-4 **67**.................................... AmyRyan 2 34
(Alistair Whillans) *cl up: rdn over 2f out: wknd over 1f out* **25/1**

021/ **13** 1 1/2 **Jinky**[630] 7119 4-9-8 **80**.................................... PhillipMakin 11 42
(Linda Perratt) *cl up tl rdn and wknd fr 2f out* **22/1**

1m 12.18s (-0.22) **Going Correction** +0.10s/f (Good)
WFA 3 from 4yo+ 5lb 13 Ran SP% **123.8**
Speed ratings (Par 105): **105,104,103,100,100 99,97,97,96,91 87,87,85**
toteswingers 1&2 £4.90, 1&3 £8.80, 2&3 £6.80 CSF £20.84 CT £130.34 TOTE £5.90: £1.70, £2.20, £3.40; EX 37.60.
Owner Mrs J W Hutchinson & Mrs P A Knox **Bred** T K & Mrs P A Knox **Trained** Denton, Co Durham
■ Stewards' Enquiry : Paul Quinn 14-day-ban: failed to take all reasonable and permissible measures to obtain the best possible placing (30 July- 12 Aug)

FOCUS
A fair sprint handicap. Pretty straightforward form.
Bonnie Charlie Official explanation: jockey said, regarding the running and riding, that his instructions were to hold the gelding up, travel away, keep him balanced and finish as close as possible but not to use his whip; trainer's representative confirmed these instructions but added that the rider had not ridden the gelding vigorously enough with hands and heels throughout the race

4134 BEST ODDS AT BETVICTOR.COM H'CAP 7f 50y
3:05 (3:06) (Class 6) (0-65,65) 3-Y-0+ **£1,704** (£503; £251) **Stalls** High

Form RPR

4062 **1** **Master Of Dance (IRE)**[2] 4089 5-9-9 **65**.................................... (p) LMcNiff(5) 4 74
(Keith Dalgleish) *hld up: gd hdwy on outside to ld appr fnl f: rdn and r.o wl* **5/1**[2]

6-01 **2** 3/4 **Oddysey (IRE)**[7] 3908 3-8-13 **60**.................................... LeeTopliss(3) 11 61
(Michael Dods) *s.i.s: hld up: gd hdwy on outside over 1f out: chsd wnr wl ins fnl f: r.o* **85/40**[1]

20-4 **3** 1/2 **Let's Face Facts**[8] 3888 5-8-9 **53**.................................... (v[1]) JasonHart(7) 9 58
(Jim Goldie) *in tch: rdn and hdwy over 1f out: kpt on ins fnl f* **14/1**

4040 **4** 1 **Orwellian**[31] 3111 3-8-11 **55**.................................... TomEaves 7 55+
(Bryan Smart) *t.k.h: hld up: rdn and hdwy over 1f out: kpt on ins fnl f* **14/1**

0544 **5** 1/2 **Whats For Pudding (IRE)**[14] 3694 4-8-5 **47**.................................... NeilFarley(5) 13 48
(Declan Carroll) *pressed ldr: led over 3f out to appr fnl f: kpt on same pce last 100yds* **16/1**

066U **6** 1 1/4 **Boga (IRE)**[20] 3462 5-8-9 **46** oh1.................................... (p) JimmyQuinn 1 43
(Karen Tutty) *missed break: bhd: nt clr run over 2f out: rdn and hdwy over 1f out: kpt on fnl f: nvr able to chal* **50/1**

6042 **7** 4 **Sabratha (IRE)**[8] 3888 4-9-12 **63**.................................... PhillipMakin 3 49
(Linda Perratt) *hld up: rdn over 1f out: nvr able to chal* **8/1**

0660 **8** nk **Chookie Avon**[17] 3581 5-9-13 **64**.................................... (p) GrahamGibbons 5 50+
(Keith Dalgleish) *hld up: effrt whn n.m.r wl over 1f out: nvr able to chal* **16/1**

00 **9** 2 **Berbice (IRE)**[8] 3888 7-9-11 **62**.................................... KierenFallon 2 42
(Linda Perratt) *hld up in tch: rdn and hdwy over 1f out: wknd ins fnl f* **18/1**

006 **10** 1 **Dubai Bay (FR)**[16] 3615 4-10-0 **65**.................................... MickyFenton 6 42
(Paul Midgley) *t.k.h: chsd ldrs: rdn over 2f out: wknd over 1f out* **6/1**[3]

-350 **11** 2 3/4 **North Central (USA)**[24] 3335 5-9-11 **62**.................................... (p) GrahamLee 8 32
(Jim Goldie) *prom: rdn and outpcd whn nt clr run over 1f out: sn btn* **18/1**

0056 **12** 1 1/4 **Viking Dancer**[25] 3309 5-8-9 **46** oh1.................................... (b[1]) JamesSullivan 14 13
(Ruth Carr) *midfield on outside: rdn and edgd lft over 2f out: sn btn* **40/1**

-000 **13** 3/4 **Cara's Request (AUS)**[38] 2879 7-9-9 **60**.................................... AdrianNicholls 10 25
(David Nicholls) *led to over 3f out: rdn and wknd wl over 1f out* **25/1**

05/0 **14** 7 **Jebel Tara**[8] 3888 7-9-4 **55**.................................... (b) LeeNewman 12
(Ian Semple) *dwlt: t.k.h and sn prom: rdn over 2f out: wknd wl over 1f out* **66/1**

1m 31.23s (-2.17) **Going Correction** -0.25s/f (Firm)
WFA 3 from 4yo+ 7lb 14 Ran SP% **119.4**
Speed ratings (Par 101): **102,101,100,99,98 97,92,92,90,89 85,84,83,75**
toteswingers 1&2 £3.90, 1&3 £9.50, 2&3 £6.60 CSF £15.36 CT £146.94 TOTE £6.00: £2.50, £1.70, £4.00; EX 22.20.
Owner Gordon McDowall **Bred** Mick McGinn **Trained** Carluke, S Lanarks

FOCUS
A moderate handicap, run at a solid pace. The winner is rated back to his best form of the past year. The second was 9lb off last week's C&D win.
Boga(IRE) Official explanation: jockey said the mare was slowly away
Chookie Avon Official explanation: jockey said that the gelding was denied a clear run

4135 WATCH LIVE RACING AT BETVICTOR.COM H'CAP 7f 50y
3:35 (3:35) (Class 4) (0-85,85) 3-Y-0+ **£4,075** (£1,212; £606; £303) **Stalls** High

Form RPR

0301 **1** **King Of Eden (IRE)**[17] 3557 6-9-9 **82**.................................... JimmyQuinn 5 93
(Eric Alston) *hld up: effrt and gd hdwy to ld over 1f out: sn clr: readily* **11/2**

0545 **2** 4 1/2 **Silver Rime (FR)**[8] 3890 7-9-0 **73**.................................... GrahamLee 3 74+
(Linda Perratt) *hld up: nt clr run over 2f out: sn swtchd rt: hdwy to chse (clr) wnr ins fnl f: no imp* **10/1**

3164 **3** 1 1/4 **Fieldgunner Kirkup (GER)**[16] 3626 4-9-4 **77**.................................... GrahamGibbons 1 72
(David Barron) *t.k.h: effrt over 2f out: chsd wnr over 1f out to ins fnl f: one pce* **5/1**[3]

-402 **4** 3/4 **Kimbali (IRE)**[16] 3607 3-9-0 **85**.................................... ShaneBKelly(5) 6 76
(Richard Fahey) *dwlt: hld up: stdy hdwy whn rdn and swtchd lft over 1f out: edgd lft: kpt on fnl f: nvr nr ldrs* **11/4**[1]

0545 **5** 1/2 **Daring Dream (GER)**[24] 3335 7-8-11 **70**.................................... JamesSullivan 4 62
(Jim Goldie) *t.k.h: hld up in tch: hdwy and cl up 1/2-way: outpcd and hung lft 2f out: kpt on fnl f* **12/1**

2260 **6** 3/4 **Dance The Rain**[32] 3064 3-8-13 **79**.................................... TomEaves 8 67
(Bryan Smart) *led to over 1f out: sn drvn and outpcd ins fnl f* **11/2**

0043 **7** hd **Orbit The Moon (IRE)**[24] 3334 4-9-4 **80**.................................... (t) LeeTopliss(3) 7 70
(Michael Dods) *cl up: rdn and hung lft over 2f out: no ex over 1f out* **9/2**[2]

56-5 **8** 12 **Nasharra (IRE)**[21] 3439 4-9-0 **73**.................................... PhillipMakin 2 30
(Kevin Ryan) *t.k.h: prom tl rdn and wknd over 2f out* **22/1**

1m 30.5s (-2.90) **Going Correction** -0.25s/f (Firm)
WFA 3 from 4yo+ 7lb 8 Ran SP% **113.4**
Speed ratings (Par 105): **106,100,99,98,98 97,96,83**
toteswingers 1&2 £11.00, 1&3 £4.70, 2&3 £9.10 CSF £57.08 CT £292.35 TOTE £7.30: £2.40, £2.80, £1.30; EX 58.40.
Owner The Grumpy Old Geezers **Bred** Gainsborough Stud Management Ltd **Trained** Longton, Lancs

FOCUS
A good handicap but an ordinary time. The winner impressed and the second sets the standard.
Kimbali(IRE) Official explanation: jockey said the gelding missed the break

4136 POLYFLOR H'CAP 1m
4:05 (4:05) (Class 2) (0-100,88) 3-Y-0+
£9,960 (£2,982; £1,491; £745; £372; £187) **Stalls** Low

Form RPR

4502 **1** **Dubai Dynamo**[7] 3911 7-10-0 **88**.................................... PJMcDonald 9 101
(Ruth Carr) *hld up in tch: smooth hdwy to ld over 1f out: sn rdn and edgd lft: drew clr ins fnl f* **3/1**[1]

0430 **2** 5 **Karaka Jack**[19] 3493 5-9-8 **82**.................................... AdrianNicholls 6 84
(David Nicholls) *hld up: rdn and hdwy over 2f out: styd on fnl f: tk 2nd towards fin: no ch w wnr* **7/1**

120 **3** 1/2 **Oriental Scot**[15] 3667 5-10-0 **88**.................................... TomEaves 4 88
(William Jarvis) *t.k.h: hld up: hdwy to chse wnr over 1f out: sn rdn and one pce: lost 2nd towards fin* **15/2**

0010 **4** 1 3/4 **Sam Nombulist**[19] 3493 4-9-11 **85**.................................... (v) AmyRyan 1 81
(Richard Whitaker) *led: clr after 3f: rdn: hung lft and hdd over 1f out: sn outpcd: n.d after* **9/1**

0321 **5** 3 1/4 **Indepub**[16] 3629 3-8-11 **82**.................................... (p) JulieBurke(3) 3 69
(Kevin Ryan) *dwlt: hld up in tch: rdn and outpcd over 2f out: rallied fnl f: no imp* **8/1**

1600 **6** 1/2 **Staff Sergeant**[19] 3493 5-9-6 **80**.................................... GrahamLee 8 68
(Jim Goldie) *chsd ldr: rdn over 2f out: edgd lft and wknd wl over 1f out* **9/1**

4-06 **7** 1 1/2 **Dhaular Dhar (IRE)**[51] 2473 10-8-13 **80**.................................... JasonHart(7) 5 64
(Jim Goldie) *rdr slow to remove blindfold and missed break: hld up: rdn and effrt over 2f out: no imp fnl f* **25/1**

6364 **8** 1/2 **Extraterrestrial**[18] 3534 8-9-9 **88**.................................... ShaneBKelly(5) 7 71
(Richard Fahey) *hld up: drvn along over 2f out: nvr able to chal* **13/2**[3]

0100 **9** 10 **Paramour**[24] 3348 5-9-10 **84**.................................... (p) GrahamGibbons 10 44
(Alan Bailey) *prom tl rdn and outpcd over 2f out: sn wknd* **12/1**

0540 **10** 4 **Colour Guard**[18] 3534 4-9-13 **87**.................................... KierenFallon 2 38
(Mark Johnston) *trckd ldrs: rdn over 3f out: wknd wl over 2f out* **6/1**[2]

1m 39.98s (-3.82) **Going Correction** -0.25s/f (Firm)
WFA 3 from 4yo+ 8lb 10 Ran SP% **119.5**
Speed ratings (Par 109): **109,104,103,101,98 98,96,96,86,82**
toteswingers 1&2 £4.80, 1&3 £5.40, 2&3 £5.70 CSF £24.76 TOTE £4.30: £1.60, £3.00, £2.70; EX 25.10.
Owner The Bottom Liners **Bred** T K & Mrs P A Knox **Trained** Huby, N Yorks
■ Stewards' Enquiry : Adrian Nicholls one-day ban: careless riding (30 Jul)

FOCUS
A solid handicap for the class, run in a good time. The winner is rated back to his 2010 best.

NOTEBOOK

Dubai Dynamo made light of top weight and continued the excellent form of his yard. He had caught the eye when a close second on soft ground at Ripon last time and, having been well backed throughout the day, duly confirmed that confidence with a superb performance. Having his 15th start of the campaign, he raced handily throughout and, having loomed up on the bridle, needed only a few shakes of the reins as he powered clear. Effective at either 7f or 1m, he's clearly at the top of his game right now and is likely to be force to be reckoned with if turned out under a penalty at Ascot this weekend. (op 5-2)

Karaka Jack is a likeable sort and he ran yet another solid race. The 5yo knuckled down well for pressure in the straight and is certainly one to bear in mind for the remainder of the summer on drying ground. He was just 1lb higher than when winning at Doncaster earlier in the year and is unlikely to be put up much for this. (op 8-1)

Oriental Scot was done for toe by both the winner and runner-up and may appreciate a stiffer test these days. All of his four wins have come over this trip, but he's not getting any younger and has a middle-distance pedigree. (tchd 8-1)

Sam Nombulist kept on pluckily having gone off quickly. A winner of soft ground over 7f at York on his penultimate start, he may still be fairly treated. (op 16-1)

Dhaular Dhar(IRE) sacrificed valuable ground at the start but wasn't entirely disgraced. This was a hot enough race and he is entitled to sharpen up after a 51-day absence. (tchd 28-1)

4137 BETVICTOR AT THE OPEN CHAMPIONSHIP H'CAP 1m 2f

4:35 (4:35) (Class 5) (0-70,70) 3-Y-O+ £2,264 (£673; £336; £168) Stalls Low

Form				RPR
6635	1		**Royal Straight**[31] 3116 7-9-8 64 (t) TomEaves 6 — (Linda Perratt) *hld up in last: smooth hdwy over 2f out: rdn to ld ins fnl f: hld on wl* 14/1	74
-323	2	1	**Schmooze (IRE)**[7] 3907 3-8-1 53 JamesSullivan 4 — (Linda Perratt) *hld up: nt clr run over 2f out to over 1f out: chsd wnr ins fnl f: r.o* 6/1	61
0311	3	½	**Rub Of The Relic (IRE)**[14] 3693 7-9-5 66 (v) LMcNiff(5) 1 — (Paul Midgley) *led at stdy pce: rdn over 2f out: hdd ins fnl f: kpt on same pce* 11/2[3]	73
3056	4	4	**Danube River**[17] 3556 3-9-4 70 KierenFallon 2 — (Mark Johnston) *t.k.h: cl up: rdn over 2f out: wknd ins fnl f* 7/2[2]	69
5502	5	1 ½	**Hawdyerwheesht**[7] 3907 4-9-1 57 (vp[1]) GrahamLee 9 — (Jim Goldie) *t.k.h: in tch: hdwy and cl up over 2f out: wknd fnl f* 7/4[1]	53
0353	6	1	**Retreat Content (IRE)**[37] 2926 4-9-2 58 PhillipMakin 3 — (Linda Perratt) *trckd ldrs tl rdn and wknd over 1f out* 8/1	52
4-00	7	1 ¼	**Purkab**[7] 3907 4-8-4 51 oh2 NeilFarley(5) 8 — (Jim Goldie) *s.i.s: hld up: rdn over 2f out: nvr able to chal* 28/1	43
0400	8	2	**Dynamic Drive (IRE)**[7] 3907 5-8-9 51 (tp) PJMcDonald 5 — (Barry Murtagh) *trckd ldrs tl rdn and wknd over 2f out* 22/1	39

2m 10.58s (-1.42) **Going Correction** -0.25s/f (Firm)
WFA 3 from 4yo+ 10lb 8 Ran SP% 113.8
Speed ratings (Par 103): **95,94,93,90,89 88,87,86**
toteswingers 1&2 £6.60, 1&3 £7.70, 2&3 £3.70 CSF £93.80 CT £523.20 TOTE £10.10: £2.20, £2.20, £1.60; EX 75.20.
Owner Ken McGarrity **Bred** Brook Stud Bloodstock & Leydens Farm Stud **Trained** East Kilbride, S Lanarks

FOCUS

A fair handicap, run at a decent pace. The winner is rated back to his reappearance form.
Retreat Content(IRE) Official explanation: jockey said that the gelding hung right in the straight

4138 BET NOW AT BETVICTOR.COM APPRENTICE H'CAP 1m 5f 13y

5:05 (5:05) (Class 6) (0-65,63) 3-Y-O+ £1,704 (£503; £251) Stalls Low

Form				RPR
-442	1		**Lady Bluesky**[7] 3904 9-9-12 61 JasonHart 5 — (Alistair Whillans) *hld up: rn wd first bnd after 1f: hdwy to ld over 3f out: sn kicked clr: kpt on wl: unchal* 8/11[1]	70+
1015	2	2 ½	**Harare**[12] 3752 11-9-11 63 (v) GemmaTutty(3) 6 — (Karen Tutty) *hld up: carried wd first bnd after 1f: rdn over 3f out: hdwy 2f out: chsd wnr ins fnl f: no imp* 9/1[3]	68
3533	3	2 ¼	**Cadgers Brig**[17] 3577 4-9-5 61 (p) PaulHainey(7) 4 — (Keith Dalgleish) *in tch: pushed along 1/2-way: hdwy over 3f out: chsd wnr over 1f out to ins fnl f: one pce* 9/2[2]	63
-540	4	2	**Toshi (USA)**[31] 3116 10-8-12 47 GeorgeChaloner 8 — (Jim Goldie) *hld up: rdn along over 2f out: no imp wl over 1f out* 9/1[3]	46
6-06	5	nk	**Stanley Rigby**[48] 2593 6-9-8 60 LauraBarry(3) 1 — (Richard Fahey) *prom: pushed along over 2f out: edgd lft and no ex over 1f out* 12/1	58
-056	6	13	**Brook Star (IRE)**[23] 3402 4-8-12 50 (b[1]) DavidSimmonson(3) 7 — (Michael Dods) *chsd ldrs: ev ch over 3f out: sn rdn: wknd over 1f out* 18/1	29
0-00	7	6	**Rare Coincidence**[22] 2599 11-8-5 45 (p) MatthewHopkins(5) 3 — (Alan Berry) *led: clr after 3f: rdn and hdd over 3f out: sn wknd* 40/1	15
/32-	8	18	**Rhyton (IRE)**[48] 4633 5-9-13 62 (p) HarryChalloner 2 — (Brian Storey) *t.k.h: chsd ldr tl wknd fr 4f out* 25/1	

2m 53.71s (-0.29) **Going Correction** -0.25s/f (Firm) 8 Ran SP% 115.3
Speed ratings (Par 101): **90,88,87,85,85 77,73,62**
toteswingers 1&2 £2.70, 1&3 £1.70, 2&3 £3.60 CSF £8.49 CT £19.45 TOTE £2.20: £1.30, £1.90, £1.60; EX 8.70.
Owner Mrs S Harrow Mrs L M Whillans **Bred** C E Whiteley **Trained** Newmill-On-Slitrig, Borders

FOCUS

A modest apprentice riders' handicap, run at a good pace. The winner was well in and is rated close to her old best.
T/Jkpt: Part won. £160,619.40 to a £1 stake. Pool: £226,224.55 - 0.50 winning tickets. T/Plt: £63.60 to a £1 stake. Pool: £85991.35 - 986.88 winning tickets T/Qpdt: £17.90 to a £1 stake. Pool: £5795.59 - 238.56 winning tickets RY

3936 SOUTHWELL (L-H)

Monday, July 16

OFFICIAL GOING: Standard

Wind: light across Weather: raining and very overcast; 16 degrees

4139 LADBROKES GAME ON! NURSERY 6f (F)

2:15 (2:15) (Class 6) (0-65,65) 2-Y-O £1,940 (£577; £288; £144) Stalls Low

Form				RPR
466	1		**Tussie Mussie**[22] 3415 2-9-2 60 SilvestreDeSousa 4 — (Mark Johnston) *cl up: led gng wl after 2f: strly drvn fnl f: hld on gamely* 11/4[1]	65+
040	2	½	**Relight My Fire**[21] 3436 2-9-2 60 DuranFentiman 3 — (Tim Easterby) *drvn along: sltly outpcd after 2f: wnt 2nd over 1f out: sustained effrt fnl f: a jst hld* 11/4[1]	63+
6003	3	10	**Stripped Bear (IRE)**[6] 3936 2-8-12 56 RichardKingscote 1 — (Tom Dascombe) *mounted outside paddock: led 2f: rdn 2f out: pressed wnr tl fdd bdly over 1f out* 6/1	30
4002	4	1 ½	**Lincolnrose (IRE)**[6] 3936 2-8-9 60 WilliamTwiston-Davies(7) 7 — (Alan McCabe) *mounted outside paddock: last away: forced to r wd 1/2-way: rdn 2f out: wknd wl over 1f out* 7/2[2]	29
006	5	1 ¼	**Hitherto**[37] 2923 2-9-7 65 PaulMulrennan 6 — (David Barron) *towards rr: rdn and struggling wl over 1f out* 5/1[3]	30
004	6	1 ½	**Kendal Princess (IRE)**[24] 3351 2-8-3 47 AndrewElliott 5 — (David O'Meara) *prom: rdn 1/2-way: lost tch wl over 1f out: edgd rt ins fnl f* 12/1	7

1m 17.17s (0.67) **Going Correction** -0.05s/f (Stan) 6 Ran SP% 114.2
Speed ratings (Par 92): **93,92,79,77,75 73**
toteswingers 1&2 £1.80, 1&3 £2.80, 2&3 £2.40 CSF £10.82 TOTE £3.10: £1.60, £2.80; EX 13.90.
Owner Inner Circle Thoroughbreds - Carpe Diem **Bred** Mrs Mary Taylor **Trained** Middleham Moor, N Yorks

FOCUS

This was a poor nursery and it only concerned the front pair from some way out. Both acted well on the surface and the form could have been rated up to 10lb higher.

NOTEBOOK

Tussie Mussie, one of four in this race making both their AW and nursery debuts, hadn't built on her promising York debut in two starts since, but found a weak race in which to break her duck. Sent to the front before halfway, she kept on finding enough to hold off her only conceivable danger and had no problem with the surface, but this looks moderate form. (op 7-2)

Relight My Fire was needing to be ridden along to keep in touch from the start, but emerged to throw down the only challenge to the winner from over a furlong out. He looks modest, but on this evidence he may appreciate another furlong. (tchd 7-2)

Stripped Bear(IRE) managed to reverse previous course form with Lincolnrose over this extra furlong, but she was still made to look slow over the last 2f. (op 5-1)

Lincolnrose(IRE) raced widest of the sextet, but that was no excuse for this moderate effort. (op 3-1)

4140 LADBROKES MOBILE MAIDEN AUCTION STKS 7f (F)

2:45 (2:47) (Class 5) 2-Y-O £2,587 (£770; £384; £192) Stalls Low

Form				RPR
2356	1		**Poetic Princess**[41] 2790 2-8-4 67 FrannyNorton 4 — (Jo Hughes) *mounted outside paddock: mde virtually all: rdn over 1f out: outbattled rival ins fnl f: bit in hand* 10/3[2]	62
043	2	½	**Bix (IRE)**[23] 3387 2-9-0 61 (b[1]) PaulHanagan 2 — (Brian Meehan) *immediately drvn: swtchd fr rails to r outside after 1f: jnd wnr 4f out and c clr w her 2f out: ev ch after: drvn but declined to overtake fnl f* 15/8[1]	71+
660	3	10	**Brazilian Clown (IRE)**[56] 2334 2-8-11 70 RichardKingscote 3 — (Tom Dascombe) *last at 1/2-way: rdn whn hmpd over 3f out: wl btn 4th 2f out: plugged on into 3rd over 1f out* 11/2	42
60	4	2 ¼	**Naughtybychoice**[9] 3842 2-8-10 0 PaulMulrennan 7 — (Ollie Pears) *cl up: rdn 3f out: wl btn 3rd 2f out tl over 1f out* 22/1	35
	5	6	**Bougaloo** 2-8-3 0 DannyBrock(7) 1 — (Alan McCabe) *rrd and s.v.s: drvn to catch up after 2f: unbalanced and hmpd rival bnd over 3f out: struggling after* 11/1	19
	6	2 ¾	**Lexington Blue** 2-8-10 0 SilvestreDeSousa 6 — (David O'Meara) *prom tl rdn and wknd wl over 2f out: eased over 1f out: t.o* 7/2[3]	12

1m 30.81s (0.51) **Going Correction** -0.05s/f (Stan) 6 Ran SP% 108.1
Speed ratings (Par 94): **95,94,83,80,73 70**
toteswingers 1&2 £1.80, 1&3 £2.10, 2&3 £2.40 CSF £9.24 TOTE £3.80: £1.70, £1.40; EX 8.60.
Owner Isla & Colin Cage **Bred** Paul Blows And Jenny Hall **Trained** Lambourn, Berks

FOCUS

This was a moderate maiden and, as in the opener, the first two pulled a long way clear of the rest. The winner is the key to the form.

NOTEBOOK

Poetic Princess had been placed four times from six previous starts including twice on Polytrack, but is by a sire with a 20% strike-rate on Fibresand. However, it was her will to win that proved the key and, having made the majority of the running, she wanted it that much more than the runner-up. She stayed the extra furlong well, but she lacks scope and will need to find improvement from somewhere if taking the nursery route. (op 7-2 tchd 11-4)

Bix(IRE), blinkered for the first time on this AW debut, missed the break slightly and was soon taken out widest away from the kickback. He was just about in front at halfway, but when it came down to a battle in the straight he spent more time hanging into the winner than applying himself and, despite every assistance from the saddle, seemed perfectly content to finish second. (op 9-4)

Brazilian Clown(IRE), gelded after appearing to regress in three starts on turf, got into a bumping match with Bougaloo on the home bend, but even without it he would still have finished a distant third. (op 4-1 tchd 6-1)

Lexington Blue, retained for 9,000GBP as a yearling, is a brother to a winner at up to 1m on the continent and a half-brother to two other winners at up to 1m. He showed up early, but dropped out worryingly tamely. Official explanation: jockey said that the gelding had no more to give (op 5-1)

4141 @LADBROKESNEWS CLASSIFIED CLAIMING STKS 7f (F)

3:15 (3:15) (Class 6) 3-Y-O+ £2,045 (£603; £302) Stalls Low

Form				RPR
2060	1		**Flying Pickets (IRE)**[28] 3229 3-8-7 69 (be) WilliamTwiston-Davies(7) 3 — (Alan McCabe) *rdn to chse ldrs: effrt 3f out: drvn upsides ldr 2f out: prevailed fnl stride* 6/1	71
256-	2	nse	**Elusive Warrior (USA)**[223] 7648 9-8-4 56 NoraLooby(7) 6 — (Alan McCabe) *mounted outside paddock and taken down early: led: jnd 2f out: pushed along and battled for ld through fnl f: jst pipped* 33/1	63
4015	3	shd	**Nezami (IRE)**[10] 3810 7-8-8 67 (b) RussKennemore 9 — (Paul Midgley) *drvn along to chse ldrs: chal between ldng pair over 1f out: ev ch fnl 150yds: jst hld* 6/1	60
2000	4	2 ¼	**Upper Lambourn (IRE)**[39] 2861 4-8-7 74 ow2 DaleSwift(7) 1 — (Brian Ellison) *bhd: hdwy over 2f out: rdn to take 4th over 1f out: nvr able to chal* 5/1[2]	60
0000	5	6	**Vogarth**[65] 2092 8-8-1 39 (b) DannyBrock(7) 7 — (Michael Chapman) *t.k.h: prom for 5f: sn lost pl* 300/1	37
00-0	6	2 ¼	**My Gacho (IRE)**[26] 3281 10-9-4 75 (v) AndrewMullen 4 — (David Nicholls) *prom: rdn 3f out: lost tch over 2f out* 16/1	41
4106	7	1	**Bold Marc (IRE)**[54] 2405 10-8-8 72 (p) MichaelMetcalfe(3) 10 — (Mrs K Burke) *prom tl rdn and lost pl over 2f out* 11/2[3]	32
-000	8	24	**Song Of The Siren**[22] 3416 4-8-13 66 (v) SilvestreDeSousa 5 — (David O'Meara) *racd wd in rr: struggling after 2f: t.o fnl 3f* 16/1	

0150 **9** *4 ½* **Son Vida (IRE)**[3] 4042 4-8-13 75 DarrylHolland 2
(Alan Bailey) *nvr travelling and drvn along in rr: t.o fnl 3f* **13/8**[1]
1m 29.57s (-0.73) **Going Correction** -0.05s/f (Stan)
WFA 3 from 4yo+ 7lb 9 Ran SP% **113.8**
Speed ratings (Par 101): **102,101,101,99,92 89,88,61,56**
toteswingers 1&2 £11.00, 1&3 £4.70, 2&3 £9.10 CSF £169.87 TOTE £10.60: £1.80, £4.10, £1.10; EX 68.80 Trifecta £473.90 Part won. Pool: 640.46 - 0.39 winning units..Upper Lambourn was claimed by Mr C. N. Kellett for £3,000.
Owner Tariq Al Nisf **Bred** Richard Frayne **Trained** Averham Park, Notts
FOCUS
A thrilling three-way finish to this modest classified claimer, but with a couple of the market leaders flopping badly the form may not amount to much. The runner-up is the best guide. It resulted in a 1-2 for trainer Alan McCabe.
Son Vida(IRE) Official explanation: jockey said the gelding hung badly left throughout

4142 LADBROKES H'CAP 1m (F)
3:45 (3:45) (Class 5) (0-70,69) 3-Y-O+ £2,587 (£770; £384; £192) Stalls Low

Form RPR
40-3 **1** **For What (USA)**[66] 2044 4-9-13 68 TedDurcan 3 87+
(David Lanigan) *trckd ldrs: drvn on inner 3f out: led 2f out and immediately shot clr: heavily eased ins fnl f* **85/40**[1]
-034 **2** *3 ½* **Uncle Brit**[7] 3907 6-8-10 51 PaulHanagan 10 55
(Malcolm Jefferson) *chsd ldrs: rdn and effrt over 2f out: racd awkwardly but tk 2nd 120yds out: flattered by proximity to wnr* **9/2**[2]
645 **3** *hd* **Sir George (IRE)**[45] 2675 7-10-0 69 PaulMulrennan 9 73
(Ollie Pears) *trckd ldrs gng wl: effrt over 2f out and sn chsng wnr vainly: lost 2nd 120yds out: one pce* **7/1**
3050 **4** *2 ¼* **My New Angel (IRE)**[17] 3555 3-8-1 50 (b) FrannyNorton 12 46
(Paul Green) *detached in last pair early: effrt 1/2-way: rdn and styd on same pce fnl 2f: nvr looked like chalng* **9/1**
/20- **5** *5* **Opus Dei**[353] 4517 5-9-11 69 GaryBartley(3) 7 56
(Noel Wilson) *led after 2f: drvn over 3f out: hdd 2f out and lost pl qckly* **25/1**
4060 **6** *10* **Amber Moon**[6] 3941 7-8-4 50 oh5 (b) AnnStokell(5) 8 14
(Ann Stokell) *led 2f: prom tl rdn and lost pl 3f out: t.o* **80/1**
0650 **7** *nk* **Just Five (IRE)**[21] 3454 6-9-8 63 (v) DarrylHolland 11 26
(John Weymes) *detached in last pair on outer: effrt 1/2-way: rdn and fdd over 2f out: t.o* **16/1**
2-50 **8** *nk* **Dream Win**[46] 2632 6-9-11 69 DaleSwift(3) 6 31
(Brian Ellison) *sn rdn: chsd ldrs tl rdn and wknd 3f out: t.o* **11/2**[3]
0156 **9** *4* **Hilbre Court (USA)**[25] 3318 7-8-12 53 (v) DuranFentiman 2
(Brian Baugh) *drvn along and nvr wnt a yard: t.o after 3f* **25/1**
2206 **10** *8* **D'Urberville**[30] 3154 5-9-12 67 FrederikTylicki 5
(J R Jenkins) *mounted outside paddock: prom tl drvn and hmpd and lost pl over 3f out* **15/2**
1m 42.91s (-0.79) **Going Correction** -0.05s/f (Stan)
WFA 3 from 4yo+ 8lb 10 Ran SP% **114.6**
Speed ratings (Par 103): **101,97,97,95,90 80,79,79,75,67**
toteswingers 1&2 £3.60, 1&3 £4.60, 2&3 £4.40 CSF £10.94 CT £56.67 TOTE £2.90: £1.10, £1.90, £2.70; EX 17.40 Trifecta £23.00 Pool: 915.36 - 29.39 winning units..
Owner Niarchos Family **Bred** Flaxman Holdings Limited **Trained** Upper Lambourn, Berks
FOCUS
An ordinary handicap, but the winner won pulling a cart. This wasn't a fluke, but there's a doubt over him repeating this elsewhere, though.

4143 MEMBERSHIP AVAILABLE AT SOUTHWELL GOLF CLUB H'CAP 6f (F)
4:15 (4:15) (Class 5) (0-70,70) 3-Y-O+ £2,587 (£770; £384; £192) Stalls Low

Form RPR
4600 **1** **Mazovian (USA)**[7] 3914 4-9-4 69 DannyBrock(7) 9 79
(Michael Chapman) *missed break: sn prom: led over 2f out: urged along and styd on gamely ins fnl f* **10/1**
5000 **2** *1 ½* **Dunmore Boy (IRE)**[49] 2538 4-9-3 61 (p) PaulHanagan 4 66
(Richard Fahey) *led 1f: sn rdn and outpcd in rr-div: drvn and rallied over 1f out: kpt on to go 2nd cl home: nt rch wnr* **13/2**[3]
4005 **3** *¾* **Imjin River (IRE)**[13] 3717 5-8-7 56 AshleyMorgan(5) 5 59
(William Stone) *taken down early: bhd: hdwy over 1f out: wnt 2nd ins fnl f: nt rch wnr: lost 2nd clsng stages* **16/1**
326 **4** *¾* **Reve Du Jour (IRE)**[42] 2764 3-9-0 70 WilliamTwiston-Davies(7) 7 69
(Alan McCabe) *taken down early: led at brisk pce after 1f: rdn and hdd over 2f out: nt qckn over 1f out and hung rt and lost two pls after* **7/2**[2]
0005 **5** *2 ¾* **Punching**[6] 3941 8-9-8 66 KirstyMilczarek 8 58
(Conor Dore) *prom: urged along and ev ch over 2f out: no ex over 1f out* **9/1**
6022 **6** *2* **Tunnager Grove**[6] 3941 3-9-5 68 DarrylHolland 1 52
(Hughie Morrison) *pressed ldrs tl rdn and wknd over 2f out* **5/4**[1]
1-46 **7** *4* **Katy's Secret**[130] 834 5-9-8 69 RyanPowell(3) 3 41
(William Jarvis) *missed break: bhd: effrt wd into st: sn struggling* **7/1**
0/04 **8** *30* **Gypsy Jazz (IRE)**[37] 2939 5-8-3 52 ow1 (tp) AnnStokell(5) 2
(Ann Stokell) *struggling 1/2-way: t.o and eased over 1f out* **50/1**
1m 16.0s (-0.50) **Going Correction** -0.05s/f (Stan)
WFA 3 from 4yo+ 5lb 8 Ran SP% **119.4**
Speed ratings (Par 103): **101,99,98,97,93 90,85,45**
toteswingers 1&2 £9.70, 1&3 £12.80, 2&3 £13.30 CSF £75.96 CT £1051.90 TOTE £6.40: £2.00, £2.60, £3.60; EX 97.00 TRIFECTA Not won..
Owner Mrs M Chapman **Bred** Darley **Trained** Market Rasen, Lincs
FOCUS
An ordinary sprint handicap, run at a solid pace. The winner is rated back to his winter best.
Punching Official explanation: vet said the gelding was struck into
Tunnager Grove Official explanation: jockey said that the gelding was never travelling

4144 PLAY GOLF AT SOUTHWELL GOLF CLUB MAIDEN STKS 5f (F)
4:45 (4:46) (Class 5) 3-Y-O £2,587 (£770; £384; £192) Stalls High

Form RPR
1 **With Compliments** 3-9-3 0 PaulMulrennan 1 83
(Kevin Ryan) *prom: led 2f out: rdn and kpt on wl fnl f: cosily* **9/1**
2 *¾* **Silken Express (IRE)** 3-8-12 0 TedDurcan 3 75
(Robert Cowell) *s.s: sn rcvrd to press ldrs: drvn and tried to chal over 1f out: rn green and hld fnl 100yds* **13/8**[1]
00-2 **3** *2 ¼* **Majestic Manannan (IRE)**[26] 3289 3-9-3 60 AndrewMullen 7 72
(David Nicholls) *w ldr: rdn and ev ch over 1f out: kpt on same pce* **4/1**[2]
04-3 **4** *8* **Marmalade Moon**[21] 3438 3-8-12 59 FrannyNorton 2 38
(Robert Cowell) *led 3f: sn floundering and hanging rt: poor 4th 1f out* **13/2**[3]
05 **5** *3 ¼* **Artillery Train (IRE)**[17] 3561 3-8-10 0 WilliamTwiston-Davies(7) 8 32
(Tim Etherington) *midfield: outpcd fr 1/2-way: rn green and wandering after* **66/1**
0 **6** *1* **Pilarcita**[9] 3848 3-8-9 0 DaleSwift(3) 10 23
(Ollie Pears) *s.s: nvr on terms: hung lft over 1f out* **66/1**
00 **7** *shd* **Hoonose**[16] 3630 3-9-3 0 RussKennemore 11 28
(Pat Eddery) *drvn and sn t.o: wnt lft but fin strly ins fnl f: promising* **16/1**
00-6 **8** *1 ½* **Ottavino (IRE)**[52] 2461 3-8-10 37 LewisWalsh(7) 9 22
(Jane Chapple-Hyam) *missed break: bmpd along and sn lost tch: t.o* **40/1**
50 **9** *1* **River Pageant**[23] 3389 3-8-12 0 JohnFahy 4
(Eve Johnson Houghton) *missed break: chsd ldrs tl 1/2-way: rdn and sn fdd: t.o* **13/2**[3]
10 *1* **Byron's Gem** 3-8-12 0 FrederikTylicki 12
(J R Jenkins) *missed break: sn t.o* **10/1**
0- **11** *1 ¾* **Jack Barker**[352] 4557 3-9-3 0 DanielTudhope 6
(Robin Bastiman) *chsd ldrs tl 1/2-way: t.o* **25/1**
58.68s (-1.02) **Going Correction** -0.20s/f (Stan) 11 Ran SP% **119.0**
Speed ratings (Par 100): **100,98,95,82,77 75,75,73,71,69 67**
toteswingers 1&2 £4.70, 1&3 £7.60, 2&3 £3.20 CSF £23.90 TOTE £13.70: £3.70, £1.10, £1.80; EX 34.10 Trifecta £411.00 Pool: 710.93 - 1.28 winning units..
Owner Guy Reed **Bred** G Reed **Trained** Hambleton, N Yorks
FOCUS
Very few ever got into this modest 3yo sprint maiden and the front pair were newcomers. The time was good for the grade and the firfst three finished clear, so the form could be a bit better than the average.

4145 FOLLOW US ON TWITTER @SOUTHWELL_RACES H'CAP 1m 6f (F)
5:15 (5:15) (Class 6) (0-65,63) 4-Y-O+ £2,045 (£603; £302) Stalls Low

Form RPR
2242 **1** **Three White Socks (IRE)**[30] 2925 5-9-3 62 DaleSwift(3) 9 71
(Brian Ellison) *pushed along after 3f: towards rr: effrt 4f out: clsd to ld wl over 1f out: in command ins fnl f* **13/8**[2]
0001 **2** *1 ¾* **Omid**[6] 3942 4-9-2 58 6ex (vt) TedDurcan 8 65
(Nicky Vaughan) *chsd ldrs: pushed along after 4f: wnt 2nd 6f out: hrd drvn and ev ch 2f out: wl hld ins fnl f* **5/4**[1]
3/60 **3** *6* **Veloso (FR)**[17] 3579 10-8-11 56 ow2 GaryBartley(3) 6 55
(Noel Wilson) *led 3f: led again 10f out: drvn and hdd wl over 1f out: sn btn* **20/1**
-056 **4** *14* **Ferney Boy**[21] 3440 6-8-5 47 DuranFentiman 5 26
(Chris Fairhurst) *trckd ldrs: 4th and rdn 3f out: fdd qckly: t.o* **20/1**
3543 **5** *1 ¾* **Dream Catcher (SWE)**[26] 3283 9-9-5 61 (p) GeorgeBaker 1 38
(Jonjo O'Neill) *chsd ldrs: drvn 6f out: sn struggling: t.o fnl 3f* **8/1**[3]
0365 **6** *hd* **Carnac (IRE)**[6] 3942 6-9-0 63 (p) NoraLooby(7) 3 39
(Alan McCabe) *rdn and nvr travelling in last pl: lost tch 5f out: t.o fnl 3f* **16/1**
0/03 **7** *34* **Adorabella (IRE)**[28] 3216 9-8-7 49 (t) KirstyMilczarek 2
(Paul Rich) *led after 3f tl hdd 10f out: rdn and stopped to nil 6f out: sn t.o* **20/1**
3m 8.05s (-0.25) **Going Correction** -0.05s/f (Stan) 7 Ran SP% **113.8**
Speed ratings (Par 101): **98,97,93,85,84 84,65**
toteswingers 1&2 £1.20, 1&3 £6.80, 2&3 £7.70 CSF £3.87 CT £21.53 TOTE £3.20: £1.80, £1.20; EX 4.90 Trifecta £177.70 Pool: 922.11 - 3.84 winning units..
Owner Racing Management & Training Ltd **Bred** Hippodromos Y Caballos S A **Trained** Norton, N Yorks
FOCUS
A demanding test of stamina and the two market leaders dominated. A weak race with the winner rated back to his best.
Carnac(IRE) Official explanation: jockey said that the gelding hung right throughout
T/Plt: £421.90 to £1 stake. Pool: £61738.45 - 106.80 winning tickets T/Qpdt: £87.10 to a £1 stake. Pool: £4646.24 - 39.46 winning tickets IM

3915 WINDSOR (R-H)
Monday, July 16

OFFICIAL GOING: Heavy (soft in places; 5.6)
Wind: Moderate, behind Weather: Overcast with drizzle

4146 DAVISBAKERYCARIBBEAN.COM APPRENTICE H'CAP 5f 10y
6:10 (6:10) (Class 5) (0-75,70) 3-Y-O+ £2,264 (£673; £336; £168) Stalls Low

Form RPR
0220 **1** **Sarangoo**[21] 3434 4-9-5 61 (p) MatthewLawson 8 70
(Malcolm Saunders) *settled wl off the pce: prog to go 4th wl over 1f out: rdn and clsd on ldrs after: led last 100yds: won gng away* **13/2**[3]
4251 **2** *1 ¼* **Cruise Tothelimit (IRE)**[20] 3477 4-9-12 68 CharlesBishop 5 73+
(Ian Williams) *led at str pce and sn clr w two rivals: fought them off ins fnl f: hdd and no ex last 100yds* **7/4**[1]
60-6 **3** *1* **Belle Bayardo (IRE)**[48] 2572 4-9-11 67 DarrenEgan 1 68
(Ronald Harris) *outpcd and pushed along in rr over 3f out: styd on fr over 1f out: tk 3rd last strides* **7/1**
0343 **4** *1 ¼* **Even Bolder**[4] 4003 9-8-12 60 JoeyHaynes(6) 6 56
(Eric Wheeler) *pressed ldng pair and sn clr of rest: wnt 2nd jst over 1f out and tried to chal: wknd ins fnl f* **5/1**[2]
1345 **5** *½* **Invigilator**[33] 3018 4-8-9 51 oh1 JamesRogers 2 46
(Derek Shaw) *sn outpcd in rr: rdn bef 1/2-way: kpt on fr over 1f out: nrst fin* **11/1**
0035 **6** *1 ¼* **Style And Panache (IRE)**[7] 3915 4-9-10 68 (p) NathanSweeney(2) 3 58
(David Evans) *pressed ldr and sn clr in ldng trio: lost 2nd jst over 1f out: wknd* **8/1**
4550 **7** *4 ½* **Welsh Inlet (IRE)**[3] 4059 4-9-7 67 ThomasBrown(4) 9 41
(John Bridger) *chsd ldng trio but sn outpcd by them: wknd wl over 1f out* **10/1**
360- **8** *15* **One Cool Chick**[229] 7588 4-8-12 58 NoelGarbutt(4) 4
(John Bridger) *free to post: awkward s: a off the pce in rr: wknd 1/2-way: t.o* **33/1**
1m 3.19s (2.89) **Going Correction** +0.675s/f (Yiel) 8 Ran SP% **110.3**
Speed ratings (Par 103): **103,101,99,97,96 94,87,63**
toteswingers:1&2 £3.30, 2&3 £3.90, 1&3 £9.70 CSF £16.99 CT £77.02 TOTE £6.10: £1.50, £1.30, £2.50; EX 20.80 Trifecta £79.00 Pool £687.07 - 6.43 winning units..
Owner Chris Scott **Bred** M S Saunders And Chris Scott **Trained** Green Ore, Somerset
FOCUS
Inner of straight dolled out 9yds at 6f then reducing to 1yd at Winning Post. Top bend at normal inner configuration. The inner of the straight was dolled out nine yards at 6f and one yard at the winning post, but the top bend was at its normal configuration. They raced middle to far side and the pace looked a bit too strong. The winner is rated to her best.

The Form Book Flat, Raceform Ltd, Compton, RG20 6NL

Sarangoo Official explanation: trainer said, regarding the apparent improvement of form, that the filly appreciated the faster pace over five furlongs in this race

4147 DAVIS WEST INDIAN BAKERY (S) STKS 1m 3f 135y
6:40 (6:41) (Class 5) 3-4-Y-O £2,264 (£673; £336; £168) **Stalls** Centre

Form RPR
5450 **1** **Anginola (IRE)**[20] 3469 3-8-9 60 SeanLevey 4 60
(David Evans) *t.k.h: sn hld up bhd ldrs: prog to ld 2f out: sn rdn: styd on to draw clr fnl f* **6/1**[2]
4051 **2** *3 ½* **Emperors Waltz (IRE)**[5] 3974 3-8-9 54 ChrisCatlin 8 54
(Rae Guest) *mostly trckd ldr: led 3f out gng strly: rdn and hdd 2f out: one pce fnl f* **4/5**[1]
4050 **3** *½* **Satwa Ballerina**[13] 3721 4-9-2 49 (b) TobyAtkinson(5) 9 53
(Mark Rimmer) *hld up in last pair: styd alone nr side fr 3f out: at least on terms w far side 2f out: fdd fnl f* **14/1**
0-05 **4** *3 ½* **Ladram Bay (IRE)**[42] 2765 3-8-1 41 HarryBentley(3) 7 42
(Jonathan Portman) *prom: rdn over 3f out: nt qckn 2f out: fdd fnl f* **22/1**
30-5 **5** *1 ½* **Bussa**[102] 1205 4-9-7 67 RichardHughes 3 45
(David Evans) *hld up in tch: rdn over 3f out: tried to cl on ldrs over 1f out: wknd fnl f* **13/2**[3]
0-00 **6** *5* **Swift Winged**[14] 3704 3-8-4 51 NickyMackay 6 31
(Hughie Morrison) *led at mod pce: rdn and hdd 3f out: wknd 2f out* **8/1**
004 **7** *8* **Soldier Spy**[16] 3620 3-8-9 46 (b) RobertHavlin 1 23
(Mark Usher) *t.k.h: hld up in last: wknd over 2f out* **20/1**

2m 47.36s (17.86) **Going Correction** +0.675s/f (Yiel)
WFA 3 from 4yo 12lb 7 Ran SP% **110.1**
Speed ratings (Par 103): **67,64,64,62,61 57,52**
toteswingers:1&2 £1.90, 2&3 £4.10, 1&3 £9.90 CSF £10.37 TOTE £6.30: £2.10, £1.20; EX 14.50 Trifecta £148.80 Pool £551.08 - 2.74 winning units..There was no bid for the winner.
Owner Mrs E Evans **Bred** T C Clarke **Trained** Pandy, Monmouths

FOCUS
They went no pace in this weak seller and the time was by some margin the slowest of 176 races over C&D since 2005. Satwa Ballerina raced alone stands' side (the others went far side) and her proximity suggests she may not have been at a disadvantage as far as the ground was concerned. Dubious form with the winner only having to run to something like her latest.

4148 EBF DAVISBAKERYCARIBBEAN.COM MAIDEN STKS 5f 10y
7:10 (7:10) (Class 5) 2-Y-O £3,234 (£962; £481; £240) **Stalls** Low

Form RPR
225 **1** **Lucky Beggar (IRE)**[23] 3378 2-9-3 79 MichaelHills 4 88+
(Charles Hills) *mde all: pushed clr over 1f out: v comf* **13/8**[2]
4 **2** *6* **Kodatish (IRE)**[30] 3140 2-8-12 0 DarrenEgan(5) 5 65
(Ronald Harris) *dwlt: in tch: rdn 2f out: sn outpcd: kpt on to take modest 2nd fnl f* **4/1**[3]
320 **3** *2 ½* **Dust Whirl**[60] 2213 2-9-3 0 RichardHughes 9 56
(Richard Hannon) *chsd wnr: rdn 2f out: sn lft bhd: wknd and lost 2nd fnl f* **11/8**[1]
0 **4** *2 ¼* **Pal Of The Cat**[16] 3637 2-9-0 0 [1] AdamBeschizza(3) 3 48
(Brian Gubby) *pushed along early and racd awkwardly: styd alone nr side fr 3f out: nt on terms over 1f out* **20/1**
0 **5** *3 ¾* **Borough Boy (IRE)**[21] 3452 2-9-3 0 NeilCallan 10 35
(Derek Shaw) *dwlt: in tch: rdn over 2f out: wkng whn veered bdly lft over 1f out* **25/1**

1m 3.65s (3.35) **Going Correction** +0.675s/f (Yiel) 5 Ran SP% **108.8**
Speed ratings (Par 94): **100,90,86,82,76**
CSF £8.19 TOTE £2.70: £1.80, £1.70; EX 8.60 Trifecta £7.30 Pool £544.50 - 54.83 winning units..
Owner Hon Mrs Corbett, C Wright, Mrs B W Hills **Bred** Mrs Cherry Faeste **Trained** Lambourn, Berks

FOCUS
The favourite again ran below form and this was an uncompetitive maiden, but it was still a useful effort from the winner. He raced up the middle and was followed by all bar Pal Of The Cat, who stuck to the stands' rail.

NOTEBOOK
Lucky Beggar(IRE) sustained a strong run to the line, clearly handling the ground well. He was reported to have run too freely when below form over 6f at Ayr last time, so the drop in trip was in his favour, and he confirmed earlier promise. (tchd 6-4 and 2-1)
Kodatish(IRE) went some way to confirming the ability he showed when a close fourth on his debut (5f, good), but he was no match at all for the winner. (op 9-2 tchd 7-2)
Dust Whirl was reported to have run flat when a beaten favourite at York on his previous start, but it's difficult to excuse this performance. He appeared to handle soft ground when shaping well on his debut at Newbury, but this time he was beaten a long way out. (tchd 6-4)
Pal Of The Cat hadn't shown anything over 6f here on his debut and, tried in a hood this time, looked a bit awkward through the early stages. (op 14-1)

4149 SKYBET EBF MAIDEN STKS 6f
7:40 (7:44) (Class 5) 2-Y-O £3,299 (£981; £490; £245) **Stalls** Low

Form RPR
2 **1** **Ashaadd (IRE)**[19] 3505 2-9-3 0 NeilCallan 3 89+
(Roger Varian) *mde all: pushed along and drew rt away fr 2f out: eased nr fin* **5/6**[1]
02 **2** *6* **Ronaldinho (IRE)**[35] 2983 2-9-3 0 RichardHughes 6 69
(Richard Hannon) *in tch: pushed along 1/2-way: rdn and prog to go 2nd over 1f out: kpt on but no ch* **5/2**[2]
06 **3** *1 ½* **Secretori**[11] 3770 2-8-12 0 DarrenEgan(5) 1 65
(Matthew Salaman) *t.k.h: cl up: disp 2nd jst over 2f out to over 1f out: one pce* **20/1**
4 *1 ¾* **Emell** 2-9-3 0 KieranO'Neill 7 59+
(Richard Hannon) *in tch in rr: prog 1/2-way: shkn up to dispute 2nd jst over 2f out to over 1f out: fdd* **12/1**
5 *hd* **Hot Mustard** 2-9-3 0 HayleyTurner 8 59+
(Michael Bell) *s.s: rousted along in detached last: sme prog over 2f out: one pce over 1f out* **7/1**[3]
0 **6** *3* **Foie Gras**[19] 3505 2-9-3 0 MartinDwyer 10 51
(William Muir) *chsd wnr to jst over 2f out: steadily wknd* **16/1**
0 **7** *5* **Casta Diamante**[11] 3783 2-8-12 0 RichardThomas 11 30
(Ralph Beckett) *chsd ldrs to over 2f out: sn wknd* **25/1**
0 **8** *shd* **Firmdecisions (IRE)**[10] 3824 2-9-3 0 SeanLevey 2 34
(Brett Johnson) *chsd ldrs: rdn and wknd sn after 1/2-way* **40/1**

1m 17.64s (4.64) **Going Correction** +0.675s/f (Yiel) 8 Ran SP% **120.2**
Speed ratings (Par 94): **96,88,86,83,83 79,72,72**
toteswingers:1&2 £1.10, 2&3 £9.30, 1&3 £2.70 CSF £3.19 TOTE £1.80: £1.10, £1.10, £6.80; EX 3.50 Trifecta £40.00 Pool £1,063.12 - 19.65 winning units..
Owner Sheikh Ahmed Al Maktoum **Bred** Socrates Partnership **Trained** Newmarket, Suffolk

FOCUS
They raced up the middle of the track. There was a taking performance from Ashaadd, who built on his debut promise, and the runner-up helps give the form some substance.

NOTEBOOK
Ashaadd(IRE) ◆ is not a big horse, but he had shaped well on his debut at Salisbury (6f, good), cruising through the race before finding only a decent sort with previous experience too strong, and the third and fifth from that maiden have since run to a useful level in defeat. Once again he travelled like an above-average type and proved too good for this lot. Whether he can improve enough in the long term to deal with later-maturing types remains to be seen, but he's a fast horse and might be worth his place in pattern company. He's in the Gimcrack. (tchd 8-11)
Ronaldinho(IRE) was on and off the bridle, but he was essentially outclassed by a smart-looking type. He's out of a 1m4f winner and might want a bit further. (op 7-2 tchd 4-1)
Secretori struggled over 7f at Epsom last time, but he'd shaped okay on his debut and confirmed that promise here. He now has the option of nurseries. (op 16-1)
Emell, a stablemate of the runner-up, is a half-brother to a 7f winner, out of a 7f-1m (including Listed) winner. He shaped as though he'd come on a good deal for the run. (op 14-1 tchd 11-1)
Hot Mustard, a 55,000gns purchase, is a half-brother to Horseradish, a decent 6f-7f winner for these connections. He missed the break and needed pressure almost immediately, but his rider was persistent and the horse showed ability. This might have woken him up. (op 11-2)

4150 SKYBET FILLIES' H'CAP 1m 67y
8:10 (8:10) (Class 4) (0-80,80) 3-Y-O+ £4,204 (£1,251; £625; £312) **Stalls** Low

Form RPR
5-41 **1** **Keene Dancer**[15] 3666 3-9-4 78 RyanMoore 6 88
(Sir Michael Stoute) *wl in tch in midfield: pushed along 3f out: rdn and prog wl over 1f out: led ins fnl f: styd on strly* **7/2**[1]
1233 **2** *2 ¼* **Choral Festival**[14] 3703 6-9-10 76 KieranO'Neill 7 83
(John Bridger) *towards rr: pushed along 1/2-way: prog 3f out: drvn to ld jst over 1f out to ins fnl f: outpcd* **9/2**[2]
02-0 **3** *¾* **On Khee**[14] 3703 5-9-10 79 SimonPearce(3) 5 84
(David Pipe) *s.i.s: hld up in last pair: prog over 2f out: looking for room over 1f out: styd on to take 3rd ins wl fnl f* **33/1**
5631 **4** *½* **Bunraku**[10] 3811 3-9-6 80 MichaelHills 11 82
(Charles Hills) *prom: rdn to chal wl over 2f out: upsides over 1f out: one pce* **5/1**[3]
0222 **5** *nk* **Bella Noir**[11] 3780 5-9-1 70 (p) MichaelMetcalfe(3) 9 73
(Mrs K Burke) *led 1f: trckd ldr: chal and upsides over 3f out to over 1f out: one pce* **9/1**
1006 **6** *½* **Push Me (IRE)**[15] 3667 5-9-7 73 NeilCallan 3 75
(Jamie Poulton) *wl in tch in midfield: rdn over 2f out: chsd ldrs over 1f out: kpt on one pce* **13/2**
0253 **7** *1* **Junket**[79] 1652 5-9-4 70 SeanLevey 12 70
(Dr Jon Scargill) *racd wd in midfield: rdn over 3f out: tried to cl on ldrs 2f out: no imp after* **9/1**
5545 **8** *nk* **Amethyst Dawn (IRE)**[17] 3581 6-9-2 68 WilliamBuick 1 67
(Andrew Reid) *cl up: rdn wl over 2f out: nt qckn over 1f out: fdd* **12/1**
4162 **9** *1 ¼* **Tea Cup**[11] 3785 3-9-4 78 RichardHughes 10 72
(Richard Hannon) *taken down early: led after 1f: jnd over 3f out: hdd & wknd jst over 1f out* **11/2**
0600 **10** *20* **Smarty Time**[30] 3152 5-8-6 61 oh11 RyanPowell(3) 2
(John Bridger) *hld up and sn in last pair: wknd 3f out: t.o* **80/1**

1m 49.94s (5.24) **Going Correction** +0.675s/f (Yiel)
WFA 3 from 5yo+ 8lb 10 Ran SP% **117.7**
Speed ratings (Par 102): **100,97,97,96,96 95,94,94,93,73**
toteswingers:1&2 £4.50, 2&3 £74.20, 1&3 £24.50 CSF £19.28 CT £447.42 TOTE £4.50: £2.20, £1.50, £12.30; EX 26.80 Trifecta £588.70 Part won. Pool £795.58 - 0.20 winning units..
Owner Newsells Park Stud **Bred** Newsells Park Stud **Trained** Newmarket, Suffolk

FOCUS
Again, they raced up the middle in the straight. This looks just fair form (runner-up not obviously well handicapped), but the lightly raced winner is going the right way. The second sets the standard.

4151 SKYBET H'CAP 1m 3f 135y
8:40 (8:40) (Class 4) (0-85,84) 3-Y-O £4,204 (£1,251; £625; £312) **Stalls** Centre

Form RPR
1163 **1** **Last Shadow**[19] 3509 3-9-5 82 MartinDwyer 3 92
(William Muir) *hld up in 5th: prog against nr side rail to ld over 2f out: sn rdn: edgd lft and jnd 2f out: styd on wl to assert fnl f* **7/2**[3]
321 **2** *1 ½* **Swnymor (IRE)**[22] 3420 3-9-7 84 WilliamBuick 1 91
(William Haggas) *trckd ldng pair: brought to chal gng strly 2f out: drvn over 1f out: nt qckn and hld ins fnl f* **11/4**[2]
-104 **3** *8* **Paloma's Prince (IRE)**[11] 3787 3-9-0 77 (p) PatCosgrave 5 70
(Jim Boyle) *won battle for ld: rdn and hdd over 2f out: carried lft sn after: wknd over 1f out* **14/1**
1 **4** *3* **Minoan Dancer (IRE)**[39] 2849 3-9-3 80 RyanMoore 2 68
(Sir Michael Stoute) *hld up in last: prog to go 4th 3f out: tried to cl on ldrs 2f out: sn wknd* **15/8**[1]
-005 **5** *28* **Humungosaur**[38] 2889 3-9-0 77 RichardHughes 4 18
(Richard Hannon) *trckd ldng trio: shkn up 1/2-way: rdn and wknd qckly over 3f out: t.o* **8/1**
10 **6** *16* **Modernism**[106] 1160 3-9-2 79 NeilCallan 7
(Mark Johnston) *pressed ldr but unable to ld: drvn wl over 3f out: fnd nil and wknd qckly: t.o* **17/2**

2m 38.26s (8.76) **Going Correction** +0.675s/f (Yiel) 6 Ran SP% **112.0**
Speed ratings (Par 102): **97,96,90,88,70 59**
toteswingers:1&2 £2.70, 2&3 £7.90, 1&3 £6.80 CSF £13.44 TOTE £3.80: £1.80, £2.10; EX 17.90.
Owner M J Caddy **Bred** Newsells Park Stud **Trained** Lambourn, Berks

FOCUS
Most of these failed to stay and/or handle the ground, but the front two finished a long way clear and look to have run to a useful enough level. A clear personal best from the winner.
T/Plt: £18.10 to a £1 stake. Pool £89,658.31 - 3,601.96 winning units. T/Qpdt: £8.10 to a £1 stake. Pool £6,194.48 - 563.03 winning units. JN

[3943] WOLVERHAMPTON (A.W) (L-H)
Monday, July 16

OFFICIAL GOING: Standard
Wind: Light behind Weather: Raining

4152 A.B.F. THE SOLDIERS CHARITY MAIDEN AUCTION STKS 5f 216y(P)
6:00 (6:02) (Class 5) 2-Y-O £2,264 (£673; £336; £168) **Stalls** Low

Form RPR
334 **1** **Capo Rosso (IRE)**[11] 3777 2-8-11 70 RichardKingscote 8 81+
(Tom Dascombe) *chsd ldrs: pushed along over 2f out: led over 1f out: r.o wl* **3/1**[3]

2 2¾ **Living The Life (IRE)** 2-8-6 0 ow2 .... FergusSweeney 11 68+
(Jamie Osborne) *s.i.s: hld up: hdwy over 1f out: rdn to go 2nd and hung lft ins fnl f: no ch w wnr* **5/2**[1]

03 **3** 6 **Branson (IRE)**[21] 3444 2-8-13 0 .... PatDobbs 2 58
(Richard Hannon) *chsd ldrs: nt clr run and swtchd lft over 1f out: sn rdn: wknd fnl f* **11/4**[2]

4246 **4** hd **Therapeutic**[12] 3747 2-8-4 65 .... SilvestreDeSousa 4 47
(Scott Dixon) *led 1f: led again over 3f out: rdn and hdd over 1f out: wknd ins fnl f* **9/2**

230 **5** ½ **Napinda**[7] 3909 2-8-4 0 .... DavidProbert 10 46+
(Des Donovan) *prom: rdn over 2f out: wknd over 1f out* **18/1**

660 **6** 3½ **Schottische**[33] 3034 2-8-4 0 .... (b[1]) FrankieMcDonald 5 35
(Derek Haydn Jones) *sn outpcd: nvr nrr* **80/1**

7 3 **Bear Totem (IRE)** 2-8-9 0 .... J-PGuillambert 6 31
(Jo Hughes) *sn outpcd* **25/1**

60 **8** 3 **Marvelous Miss (IRE)**[18] 3545 2-8-1 0 .... DominicFox(3) 7 17
(Christine Dunnett) *chsd ldr tl led 5f out: hdd over 3f out: rdn and wknd over 1f out* **200/1**

30 **9** 8 **Simply Dreaming**[60] 2193 2-8-4 0 .... JamieMackay 1
(Michael Squance) *chsd ldrs: rdn over 3f out: wknd over 2f out* **33/1**

10 68 **Cerys** 2-8-4 0 .... AndreaAtzeni 3
(Derek Haydn Jones) *s.s: outpcd: t.o* **40/1**

1m 14.09s (-0.91) **Going Correction** -0.10s/f (Stan) 10 Ran SP% **114.6**
Speed ratings (Par 94): **102,98,90,90,89 84,80,76,66,**
toteswingers:1&2 £2.50, 2&3 £3.00, 1&3 £2.20 CSF £10.41 TOTE £4.20: £1.20, £1.50, £1.10; EX 16.00.
Owner Deva Racing Red Clubs Partnership **Bred** Michael Wiley **Trained** Malpas, Cheshire

FOCUS
Only two or three could be given a chance in this modest juvenile maiden and those towards the head of the market duly dominated. The time and the sixth offer perspective.

NOTEBOOK
Capo Rosso(IRE) was expected to benefit from the switch to Polytrack on this AW debut and his pace/previous experience was a deciding factor in his victory over the runner-up. He's the right type for ordinary sprint nurseries. (tchd 7-2)
Living The Life(IRE), a daughter of 2,000 Guineas winner Footstepsinthesand who is a half-sister to two winners in Italy, is a fine looker and was gambled throughout the day, but she was slowly away from her wide draw, ran green, and couldn't match the more streetwise winner. Her rider was putting up 2lb overweight, but it didn't affect the result, and she should improve enough to win a standard maiden. (op 11-4 tchd 3-1 and 9-4)
Branson(IRE) looked in need of a step up to 7f when third on his previous start at Windsor and, having travelled well, he was badly outpaced down the straight once forced to switch. He's now qualified for nurseries and should win upped to 7f or even 1m (half-brother to 1m2f Flat/triple bumper winner). (op 5-2)
Therapeutic took them along but was readily brushed aside and this exposed sort may need a drop in grade to get off the mark. (tchd 11-2)

4153 FREEBETS.CO.UK H'CAP — 1m 5f 194y(P)
6:30 (6:32) (Class 6) (0-65,65) 3-Y-O — **£1,704** (£503; £251) **Stalls** Low

Form — RPR

000- **1** **Up Ten Down Two (IRE)**[283] 6667 3-8-6 **50** .... (t) AndreaAtzeni 6 67
(Michael Easterby) *a.p: led over 2f out: shkn up over 1f out: styd on wl: eased nr fin* **22/1**

0-03 **2** 1¾ **Solar View (IRE)**[13] 3729 3-8-3 **47** .... LukeMorris 2 62
(Sir Mark Prescott Bt) *chsd ldrs: shkn up 7f out: rdn over 4f out: chsd wnr over 1f out: styd on* **7/2**[2]

2413 **3** 9 **Astroscarlet**[16] 3621 3-9-1 **59** .... EddieAhern 4 61
(Mark H Tompkins) *hld up: hdwy 6f out: rdn over 2f out: styd on same pce* **5/2**[1]

6650 **4** 2¼ **Gabrial's Lexi (IRE)**[11] 3775 3-9-2 **60** .... StevieDonohoe 8 59
(Ian Williams) *hmpd sn after s: hld up: hdwy u.p over 1f out: nvr trbld ldrs* **14/1**

0-40 **5** 4 **Onertother**[39] 2856 3-9-2 **60** .... SamHitchcott 7 54
(Joseph Tuite) *hld up: hdwy on outer over 2f out: wknd over 1f out* **17/2**

0002 **6** 1¾ **Natasha Rostova**[23] 3391 3-9-5 **63** .... DavidProbert 10 54
(Andrew Balding) *s.i.s: hld up: hdwy and hmpd wl over 3f out: sn rdn: nt clr run over 2f out: sn wknd* **17/2**

-060 **7** 2¼ **Hard Road**[14] 3697 3-8-12 **56** ow1 .... SebSanders 13 44
(Chris Wall) *chsd ldrs: reminders over 4f out: led 3f out: hdd over 2f out: rdn and wknd over 1f out* **7/1**[3]

0-60 **8** 13 **Angelic Note (IRE)**[24] 3345 3-9-7 **65** .... (b[1]) ShaneKelly 11 35
(Brian Meehan) *sn chsng ldr: rdn over 2f out: wknd over 1f out: t.o* **33/1**

0665 **9** ½ **Tigertoo (IRE)**[20] 3469 3-8-6 **50** .... WilliamCarson 3 19
(Stuart Williams) *hld up: hdwy 3f out: rdn and wknd wl over 1f out: t.o* **18/1**

-225 **10** ½ **Mexican Wave**[48] 2578 3-8-2 **46** .... (v[1]) SilvestreDeSousa 5 14
(Michael Bell) *led 11f: rdn and wknd wl over 1f out: t.o* **16/1**

2-50 **11** 8 **Istan Star (USA)**[56] 2340 3-8-7 **51** .... RoystonFfrench 9
(Julie Camacho) *sn pushed along in rr: drvn along over 8f out: a in rr: lost tch fnl 4f: t.o* **80/1**

4200 **12** 5 **Rocco Breeze (IRE)**[48] 2577 3-8-8 **52** ow2 .... MircoMimmocchi 12
(Philip McBride) *hld up: a in rr: bhd fnl 4f: t.o* **25/1**

505 **13** 2¼ **Plumbago Blue**[67] 2008 3-9-2 **60** .... TomQueally 1
(John Butler) *mid-div: pushed along and wknd over 5f out: t.o* **28/1**

3m 0.83s (-5.17) **Going Correction** -0.10s/f (Stan) 13 Ran SP% **118.0**
Speed ratings (Par 98): **110,109,103,102,100 99,98,90,90,90 85,82,81**
toteswingers:1&2 £26.10, 2&3 £2.60, 1&3 £15.70 CSF £92.96 CT £270.09 TOTE £50.50: £8.10, £2.20, £1.10; EX 196.00.
Owner B Delaney,A Duke & Backup Technology **Bred** Ammerland Verwaltung Gmbh **Trained** Sheriff Hutton, N Yorks

FOCUS
Fair form for the grade with the front pair, both capable of ranking higher, drawing well clear. The time was good and the form is rated at something like face value.
Gabrial's Lexi(IRE) Official explanation: jockey said that the filly suffered interference at the start

4154 SOLDIERSCHARITY.ORG (S) STKS — 5f 20y(P)
7:00 (7:01) (Class 6) 3-4-Y-O — **£1,704** (£503; £251) **Stalls** Low

Form — RPR

0563 **1** **Ice Trooper**[105] 1169 4-9-4 65 .... (p) DarryllHolland 4 61
(Linda Stubbs) *sn led: hdd over 3f out: chsd ldr: rdn over 1f out: r.o u.p to ld wl ins fnl f: edgd rt towards fin* **7/2**[2]

0202 **2** nk **Missile Attack (IRE)**[8] 3893 4-9-4 55 .... (p) RoystonFfrench 8 60
(Ian Semple) *chsd ldr: led over 3f out: shkn up over 1f out: rdn and hdd wl ins fnl f: r.o* **11/1**

4366 **3** hd **Mother Jones**[14] 3707 4-8-11 66 .... WilliamTwiston-Davies(7) 9 59
(David Evans) *s.s: hld up: hdwy and nt clr run over 1f out: rdn ins fnl f: r.o* **11/2**[3]

5064 **4** shd **Aquasulis (IRE)**[15] 3670 3-8-9 63 .... SilvestreDeSousa 2 53
(David Evans) *chsd ldrs: rdn over 1f out: r.o* **5/2**[1]

0214 **5** ½ **Medam**[17] 3567 3-8-7 52 .... ShirleyTeasdale(7) 1 56+
(Shaun Harris) *hld up in tch: rdn over 1f out: r.o* **7/1**

3360 **6** 3½ **Faraway**[21] 3451 3-9-0 58 .... (b) LukeMorris 7 44
(Ronald Harris) *sn pushed along in rr: drvn along 1/2-way: styd on ins fnl f: nt pce to chal* **15/2**

-006 **7** nk **Love Club**[123] 910 4-9-4 43 .... WilliamCarson 3 43
(Brian Baugh) *chsd ldrs: rdn over 1f out: no ex fnl f* **40/1**

26-5 **8** 2¼ **I'm Still The Man (IRE)**[193] 42 3-8-7 58 .... RyanWhile(7) 6 34
(Bill Turner) *chsd ldrs: rdn over 1f out: wknd fnl f* **16/1**

60 **9** 1¾ **Alfie Joe**[15] 3663 3-8-7 0 .... PhilipPrince(7) 5 28
(Ron Hodges) *sn pushed along in rr: wknd 1/2-way* **50/1**

10 19 **Love To Tara** 3-8-9 0 .... ShaneKelly 10
(Robert Cowell) *sn pushed along in rr: wknd 3f out* **16/1**

1m 1.91s (-0.39) **Going Correction** -0.10s/f (Stan)
WFA 3 from 4yo 4lb 10 Ran SP% **114.9**
Speed ratings (Par 101): **99,98,98,98,97 91,91,87,84,54**
toteswingers: 1&2 £3.90, 2&3 £7.80, 1&3 £5.70 CSF £41.16 TOTE £4.50: £1.10, £3.80, £2.80; EX 35.50.There was no bid for the winner.
Owner J P Hames **Bred** Low Ground Stud **Trained** Norton, N Yorks

FOCUS
An open seller, with little to separate five of these at the line. The runner-up looks the most likely guide.

4155 NEAL WOOD THIRD ANNIVERSARY MEMORIAL H'CAP — 7f 32y(P)
7:30 (7:35) (Class 5) (0-75,75) 3-Y-O+ — **£2,264** (£673; £336; £168) **Stalls** High

Form — RPR

-065 **1** **Emkanaat**[19] 3503 4-9-9 **75** .... AndreaAtzeni 7 85
(Roger Varian) *mde virtually all: shkn up over 1f out: r.o: readily* **4/1**[1]

06-0 **2** 1½ **Buckland (IRE)**[5] 3963 4-9-0 **73** .... NicoleNordblad(7) 3 79
(Hans Adielsson) *led early: chsd ldrs: pushed along to go 2nd over 1f out: r.o* **16/1**

5025 **3** 1½ **Spinning Ridge (IRE)**[31] 3099 7-9-5 **71** .... (b) LukeMorris 4 73
(Ronald Harris) *plld hrd and prom: rdn over 1f out: r.o* **20/1**

1100 **4** hd **Spin Again (IRE)**[11] 3790 7-9-6 **72** .... StevieDonohoe 10 73
(John Ryan) *chsd wnr 6f out tl rdn over 1f out: styd on* **22/1**

4660 **5** ¾ **I Confess**[41] 2792 7-9-2 **75** .... (b) JordanNason(7) 6 74
(Geoffrey Harker) *prom: racd keenly: rdn over 1f out: nt trble ldrs* **9/1**

4-26 **6** ¾ **Levi Draper**[49] 2543 3-9-2 **75** .... SilvestreDeSousa 8 70
(James Fanshawe) *hld up: rdn over 1f out: hung lft ins fnl f: nvr trbld ldrs* **4/1**[1]

0254 **7** nse **Hawk Moth (IRE)**[5] 3958 4-9-2 **68** .... SamHitchcott 1 65
(John Spearing) *s.i.s: sn pushed along and prom: rdn over 1f out: no ex fnl f* **6/1**[3]

-450 **8** 1 **Justbookie Dot Com (IRE)**[3] 4042 4-8-13 **72**(v) WilliamTwiston-Davies(7) 12 67
(David Evans) *hld up: rdn over 1f out: nvr nrr* **14/1**

6241 **9** 1¾ **Sandbetweenourtoes (IRE)**[17] 3570 3-9-2 **75** .... PaulHanagan 5 63
(Roger Curtis) *rn wout declared tongue strap: hld up: rdn over 2f out: n.d* **9/2**[2]

0601 **10** 1 **Pick A Little**[40] 2809 4-9-2 **71** .... RyanClark(3) 2 58
(Brian Ellison) *hld up: rdn over 2f out: nvr on terms* **10/1**

-410 **11** 3¼ **Stevie Gee (IRE)**[51] 2476 8-9-4 **70** .... RussKennemore 11 48
(Mark Buckley) *hld up: rdn over 2f out: a in rr* **20/1**

1m 29.4s (-0.20) **Going Correction** -0.10s/f (Stan)
WFA 3 from 4yo+ 7lb 11 Ran SP% **118.0**
Speed ratings (Par 103): **97,95,93,93,92 91,91,90,88,87 83**
toteswingers:1&2 £20.90, 2&3 £88.90, 1&3 £26.30 CSF £66.82 CT £1151.37 TOTE £4.20: £1.40, £7.70, £3.70; EX 93.30.
Owner Michael Hill **Bred** C J Mills **Trained** Newmarket, Suffolk

FOCUS
Few got into this from off the pace. The winner's best form since his maiden win last year.
Stevie Gee(IRE) Official explanation: jockey said that the gelding hung right-handed throughout

4156 FREEBETS.CO.UK FREE BETS CLASSIFIED CLAIMING STKS — 1m 4f 50y(P)
8:00 (8:04) (Class 6) 3-Y-O+ — **£1,704** (£503; £251) **Stalls** Low

Form — RPR

-605 **1** **Honest Deal**[37] 2926 4-9-8 60 .... RobertWinston 1 64
(Alan Swinbank) *mde all: pushed clr 2f out: styd on wl* **3/1**[2]

-364 **2** 2¼ **White Deer (USA)**[73] 1829 8-9-2 55 .... (v) SilvestreDeSousa 8 55
(Geoffrey Harker) *hld up: hdwy over 2f out: nt clr run wl over 1f out: rdn to go 2nd 1f out: no ch w wnr* **11/8**[1]

2254 **3** 1¾ **Crimson Monarch (USA)**[20] 3468 8-9-1 47 .... WilliamCarson 10 51
(Peter Hiatt) *hld up: hdwy over 1f out: sn rdn: styd on same pce ins fnl f* **8/1**

0040 **4** 5 **Port Hill**[33] 3043 5-9-2 45 .... ShaneKelly 5 44
(Mark Brisbourne) *chsd ldrs: rdn over 2f out: wknd over 1f out* **12/1**

006- **5** hd **Layla's Boy**[15] 7195 5-9-3 53 .... (bt) StephenCraine 9 45
(John Mackie) *prom: chsd wnr over 9f out: rdn over 2f out: wknd fnl f* **25/1**

05-5 **6** ¾ **Catchy Tune (IRE)**[24] 472 3-8-8 51 .... (p) MichaelStainton 6 46
(Graeme McPherson) *chsd wnr tl over 9f out: remained handy: rdn over 2f out: wknd over 1f out* **11/1**

4644 **7** 3¼ **Guga (IRE)**[45] 2669 6-9-1 50 .... (v) FrannyNorton 11 36
(John Mackie) *hld up: hdwy over 3f out: wknd over 1f out* **7/1**[3]

/-00 **8** 55 **Weet In Nerja**[185] 153 6-9-3 35 .... (tp) LiamKeniry 3
(Ken Wingrove) *hld up: a in rr: wknd over 3f out: t.o* **200/1**

105/ **9** 129 **Elaala (USA)**[807] 2163 10-9-6 48 .... SebSanders 4
(Trevor Wall) *mid-div: rdn and wknd over 5f out: t.o* **25/1**

00-0 **P** **Indycisive**[40] 2438 4-8-8 39 .... (v[1]) WilliamTwiston-Davies(7) 7
(Simon West) *s.i.s: in rr and pushed along over 6f out: sn reluctant and plld himself up* **66/1**

2m 40.21s (-0.89) **Going Correction** -0.10s/f (Stan)
WFA 3 from 4yo+ 12lb 10 Ran SP% **116.4**
Speed ratings (Par 101): **98,96,95,92,91 91,89,52, ,**
toteswingers:1&2 £2.10, 2&3 £3.10, 1&3 £4.40 CSF £7.29 TOTE £3.30: £1.10, £1.30, £2.20; EX 9.20.
Owner Guy Reed **Bred** G Reed **Trained** Melsonby, N Yorks

FOCUS
The market leaders came to the fore in this weak claimer. There was little between the front two at the weights. Front-runners did well on the card and the winner had a fairly easy lead. He was still a stone off his 3yo level.

4157 HOLIDAY INN WOLVERHAMPTON MEDIAN AUCTION MAIDEN STKS 1m 1f 103y (P)
8:30 (8:32) (Class 6) 3-4-Y-0 **£1,704** (£503; £251) **Stalls** Low

Form RPR
0 **1** **Nimble Thimble (USA)**[77] 1704 3 -8-120........................ TomQueally 13 71+
(Roger Charlton) *hld up: hdwy over 2f out: led over 1f out: r.o wl: readily* **13/2**
2 *2 1/2* **Fly Solo** 3 -9-30... RobertWinston 5 68
(Alan Swinbank) *chsd ldrs: rdn and ev ch over 1f out: styd on same pce ins fnl f* **7/1**
3 *1 1/2* **Sauvage L'Il** 4 -9-70.. SilvestreDeSousa 12 60
(Ed Dunlop) *s.s: hld up: hdwy over 2f out: r.o to go 3rd nr fin: nt rch ldrs* **16/1**
0-30 **4** *nk* **Edraaq**[38] 2895 3 -9-368..(t) PaulHanagan 1 64
(Brian Meehan) *led: racd keenly: rdn and hdd over 1f out: no ex ins fnl f* **7/4**[1]
6 **5** *shd* **Mariet**[24] 3340 3 -8-120.. DavidProbert 7 59
(Andrew Balding) *a.p: rdn over 3f out: hung lft ins fnl f: styd on* **4/1**[2]
6 *hd* **Broughtons Pearl** 3 -8-120.. JamieMackay 3 58
(Willie Musson) *s.s: hld up: hdwy over 1f out: r.o* **40/1**
60 **7** *3/4* **Chemistry Master**[15] 3664 4 -9-120.................................. LukeMorris 8 62
(Jeremy Gask) *prom: rdn over 3f out: wknd ins fnl f* **10/1**
04 **8** *1 1/2* **Sir Lexington (IRE)**[45] 2665 3 -9-30....................................... PatDobbs 6 59
(Richard Hannon) *chsd ldr: reminder over 3f out: rdn over 1f out: wknd ins fnl f* **6/1**[3]
0 **9** *2 1/4* **Destiny Awaits (IRE)**[24] 3333 3 -9-00............................. DaleSwift(3) 4 54
(Ian Semple) *mid-div: rdn over 2f out: n.d* **66/1**
60-0 **10** *5* **Upton Crystal**[7] 3913 4 -9-70... DavidNolan 10 38
(Michael Easterby) *hld up: racd keenly: pushed along over 3f out: wknd over 2f out* **50/1**
04 **11** *1 1/2* **Shakespeare Dancer**[21] 3453 3 -8-120.......................... FergusSweeney 9 35
(James Evans) *prom: rdn over 2f out: wknd 2f out* **80/1**
05 **12** *20* **Flaming Telepath**[14] 3710 4 -9-70.......................................(p) SebSanders 2
(Christine Dunnett) *sn pushed along in rr: wknd over 3f out: t.o* **100/1**

2m 1.96s (0.26) **Going Correction** -0.10s/f (Stan)
WFA 3 from 4yo 9lb **12**Ran SP% **119.6**
Speed ratings (Par 101): **94,91,90,90,90 89,89,87,85,81 80,62**
toteswingers:1&2 £11.00, 2&3 £9.10, 1&3 £15.50 CSF £51.25 TOTE £11.00 : £2.50 , £1.10 , £4.90; EX 71.70 .
Owner K Abdulla **Bred** Juddmonte Farms Inc **Trained** Beckhampton, Wilts

FOCUS
No more than a modest maiden. The favourite set just a modest standard and this form is muddling. The winner is rated value for a bit extra.

4158 FREE BETTING WITH FREEBETS.CO.UK H'CAP 1m 141y (P)
9:00 (9:03) (Class 6) (0-60,60) 3-Y-0+ **£1,704** (£503; £251) **Stalls** Low

Form RPR
00-5 **1** **Mac Tiernan (IRE)**[96] 1310 5 -9-252.................................. LiamKeniry 8 63
(Ed de Giles) *a.p: led over 2f out: rdn over 1f out: hung rt ins fnl f: jst hld on* **9/2**[3]
0131 **2** *hd* **Footstepsofspring (FR)**[14] 3713 5 -9-1060................ JamieMackay 12 71
(Willie Musson) *hld up: hdwy over 3f out: chsd wnr 2f out: sn rdn and ev ch: edgd rt ins fnl f: r.o* **4/1**[2]
0642 **3** *1 1/4* **Warden Bond**[14] 3713 4 -9-757.............................(p) SilvestreDeSousa 13 65
(William Stone) *a.p: rdn over 1f out: hung rt ins fnl f: r.o* **7/2**[1]
0002 **4** *1* **Victorian Number (FR)**[5] 3964 4 -8-1053................ AliceHaynes(7) 6 59
(Geoffrey Deacon) *got loose prior to the s: hld up in tch: racd keenly: rdn over 1f out: r.o* **10/1**
1005 **5** *7* **One Of Twins**[14] 3713 4 -9-757.......................................(b) PaulMulrennan 3 47
(Michael Easterby) *dwlt: hld up: styd on ins fnl f: nvr nrr* **6/1**
6643 **6** *shd* **Storm Runner (IRE)**[5] 3964 4 -9-757................................ SebSanders 2 46
(George Margarson) *hld up: hdwy over 2f out: sn rdn: nvr trbld ldrs* **13/2**
2046 **7** *3/4* **Cathcart Castle**[12] 3751 4 -9-252.....................................(p) TomQueally 5 40
(Simon West) *hld up: rdn over 3f out: swtchd lft over 1f out: n.d* **14/1**
46/0 **8** *3* **Hyde Lea Flyer**[23] 3382 7 -9-858.................................. KirstyMilczarek 4 39
(Barry Leavy) *led: rdn and hdd over 2f out: wknd over 1f out* **25/1**
10-0 **9** *3 3/4* **Diamond Sunrise (IRE)**[17] 2600 4 -8-1352................. GaryBartley(3) 10 24
(Noel Wilson) *chsd ldr: rdn and ev ch over 2f out: wknd over 1f out* **50/1**
006/ **10** *5* **Head Down**[760] 3131 6 -9-252..(p) LukeMorris 9 13
(Martin Bosley) *s.i.s: hld up: drvn along 1/2-way:wknd over 2f out* **25/1**
4600 **11** *hd* **Valley Tiger**[84] 1561 4 -9-959.......................................[1] PaulHanagan 11 19
(Patrick Morris) *s.i.s: hld up: wknd over 2f out* **20/1**
34-0 **12** *5* **Clearing House**[14] 3709 7 -9-259.............................. BradleyBosley(7) 7
(John Ryan) *chsd ldrs: rdn over 2f out: sn wknd* **33/1**
05-0 **13** *1* **Crystal Sky (IRE)**[14] 3713 4 -9-252.................................. FergusSweeney 1
(Natalie Lloyd-Beavis) *prom: racd keenly: rdn and wknd over 2f out* **25/1**

1m 48.61s (-1.89)**Going Correction** -0.10s/f (Stan) **13**Ran SP% **125.0**
Speed ratings (Par 101): **104,103,102,101,95 95,94,92,88,84 84,79,78**
toteswingers:1&2 £7.10, 2&3 £3.80, 1&3 £7.10 CSF £21.98 CT £73.42 TOTE £3.10 : £1.10 , £2.80, £2.80 ; EX 41.80 .
Owner T Gould **Bred** Paul Kiernan **Trained** Ledbury, H'fords
■ Stewards' Enquiry : Liam Keniry four-day ban: use of whip (30, 31 Jul, 2, 3 Aug)

FOCUS
Another race dominated by the market principals, the front four pulling clear. The pace was fairly decent. The form is rated through the third.
T/Plt: £182.20 to a £1 stake. Pool £72,471.98 - 290.31 winning units T/Qpdt: £73.50 to a £1 stake. Pool £4,720.83 - 47.50 winning units. CR

4020 DUNDALK (A.W) (L-H)
Monday, July 16

OFFICIAL GOING: Standard

4161a IRISH STALLION FARMS EUROPEAN BREEDERS FUND MAIDEN 7f (P)
2:25 (2:27) 2-Y-O **£6,037** (£1,400; £612 ; £350)

RPR
1 **Mars (IRE)** 2 -9-5.. JPO'Brien 10 95+
(A P O'Brien, Ire) *sn led: almost jnd 2f out: pushed along and edgd clr ent fnl f: kpt on wl: easily* **4/7**[1]
2 *4 3/4* **The Ferryman (IRE)**2 -9-5..................................... SeamieHeffernan 6 81+
(A P O'Brien, Ire) *hld up in tch: pushed along in 4th 3f out: styd on under hands and heels to go 2nd ins fnl f: no ch w wnr* **14/1**
3 *2 3/4* **My Rules (IRE)**[17] 3921 2 -9-0... NGMcCullagh 3 68+
(P D Deegan, Ire) *trckd wnr in 2nd: pushed along to cl 2f out: sn struggling to stay on terms and wknd ins fnl f* **12/1**
4 *2 1/4* **Estinaad (USA)** 2 -9-0.. DeclanMcDonogh 8 62
(Kevin Prendergast, Ire) *hld up in tch: disp 4th after 1/2-way: no imp over 2f out: kpt on one pce* **5/1**[2]
5 *1/2* **Beluckyformammy (IRE)**[23] 3409 2 -8-11.......... AndrewPThornton(3) 4 61
(S Donohoe, Ire) *cl up: 3rd 3f out and sn no ex* **33/1**
6 *3/4* **Forty One Phases (IRE)**2 -9-5.................................. MichaelHussey 5 64
(David Wachman, Ire) *bhd: clsd into 6th under 3f out and kpt on one pce fnl f* **20/1**
7 *nk* **Peggy's Leg (USA)**2 -9-0... FranBerry 9 58
(Mrs John Harrington, Ire) *hld up towards rr: kpt on fr 2f out* **7/1**[3]
8 *1* **Maudlin Magdalen (IRE)**[17] 3596 2 -9-0.................................. BenCurtis 1 56
(Donal Kinsella, Ire) *hld up towards rr: n.d fr 1/2-way* **33/1**
9 *4 1/2* **Rain God (USA)**2 -9-5.. CO'Donoghue 2 49
(A P O'Brien, Ire) *dwlt and in rr: nvr a threat* **9/1**
10 *shd* **Highest Office** 2 -9-5.. GaryCarroll 11 49
(G M Lyons, Ire) *t.k.h on outer: no imp fr 1/2-way* **25/1**
11 *2 1/2* **Speak Slowly**[64] 2099 2 -9-0.. WayneLordan 7 37
(T Stack, Ire) *in rr: n.d fr 1/2-way* **20/1**

1m 25.13s (85.13) **11**Ran SP% **136.4**
CSF £13.26 TOTE £1.60 : £1.02 , £3.00 , £3.80 ; DF 10.20 .
Owner Michael Tabor & Derrick Smith & Mrs John Magnier **Bred** Massarra Syndicate **Trained** Ballydoyle, Co Tipperary

FOCUS
A winning debut for a highly touted newcomer. The third deserves credit for trying to mix it with the winner and is the best guide to the level.

NOTEBOOK
Mars(IRE) ◆, already at the summit of some ante-post lists for the 2013 Investec Derby before being seen in public, the beautifully bred son of Galileo enhanced his position (10-1 favourite from 12s with Boylesports) with a thoroughly professional display. He knew his job pretty well in the early stages, breaking smartly and soon dictating matters. He got into a nice rhythm and gradually increased the tempo, stretching right away in the closing stages. Only time will tell what he beat and the runner-up certainly wasn't given a hard time but, as debuts go they don't get much more taking than this. He didn't look overly big in the parade ring beforehand and still looks to have plenty of growing to do, so one would imagine he will improve as the season goes on. The winning jockey was full of praise and it's likely Mars will develop into a genuine Group 1 performer, particularly next season when he fills out.
The Ferryman (IRE)could also turn out to be quite useful. He travelled well through the race and wasn't given a hard time once the winner had kicked clear. He will improve for this and it would be a surprise if he didn't open his account next time.
My Rules (IRE)hinted that there was some ability there in a Roscommon maiden and proved it here. She put it up to the winner 2f out and, while she was easily brushed aside, showed enough to suggest there are races to be won with her.
Estinaad(USA) ran well enough and travelled nicely but couldn't land a blow at the business end. She should improve and may need further.
Peggy's Leg (USA)is entered in the Moyglare Stakes and, while that may be wishful thinking, she did keep on well enough from an unpromising position and will know much more next time.

4159a-4160a & 4162a-4171a - (Foreign Racing) - See Raceform Interactive

3842 BEVERLEY (R-H)
Tuesday, July 17

OFFICIAL GOING: Good to firm (good in places; 8.1)
Wind: light 1/2 against Weather: fine, becoming overcast, light rain race 4 onwards

4172 BEVERLEY FASHION WEEK H'CAP 1m 1f 207y
2:00 (2:01) (Class 6) (0-65,65) 3-Y-O **£1,617** (£481; £240 ; £120) **Stalls** Low

Form RPR
004- **1** **Forster Street (IRE)**[342] 4898 3 -9-159...................... GrahamGibbons 8 69+
(Tim Easterby) *mde all: drvn 4 l clr 1f out: eased towards fin: cleverly* **8/1**
60-2 **2** *1/2* **Scarlet Prince**[25] 3355 3 -8-1155.. GrahamLee 5 62
(Tony Coyle) *in rr: effrt over 2f out: wnt 2nd 1f out: styd on towards fin: a hld* **9/2**[2]
021 **3** *2 3/4* **Miss Ella Jade**[15] 3694 3 -8-1155.. PaulQuinn 11 56
(Richard Whitaker) *swtchd rt s: in rr: effrt and nt clr run 2f out: kpt on fnl f* **7/2**[1]
0335 **4** *hd* **No Time To Cry**[8] 3907 3 -8-953...............................(v[1]) PaulMulrennan 7 54
(Ann Duffield) *rr-div: nt clr run and swtchd outside 2f out: kpt on fnl f* **12/1**
0040 **5** *nse* **Fine Kingdom**[8] 3914 3 -8-653 ow3.............................. PaulPickard(3) 3 54
(Brian Ellison) *chsd ldrs: one pce appr fnl f* **20/1**
0-60 **6** *3/4* **Firefly**[29] 3233 3 -8-852... JamesSullivan 1 51
(John Weymes) *in rr: hdwy on ins over 2f out: n.m.r: kpt on ins fnl f* **20/1**
426 **7** *1* **Gangsterbanksters (FR)**[29] 3212 3 -9-465.......(v[1]) MichaelMetcalfe(3) 9 62
(Mrs K Burke) *chsd ldrs: kpt on one pce fnl 2f* **17/2**
0040 **8** *5* **Capitol Gain (IRE)**[7] 3621 3 -9-664..................................(p) LukeMorris 4 51
(Brian Meehan) *s.i.s: t.k.h: hdwy to trck ldrs after 2f: hung lft bnd over 3f out: wknd jst ins fnl f* **11/2**
03-2 **9** *1/2* **Bada Bing**[34] 3025 3 -8-1256.. RobertWinston 6 42
(Scott Dixon) *sn trcking ldrs: chal over 2f out: wknd jst ins fnl f* **5/1**[3]
5000 **10** *2* **July Specialists**[19] 3547 3 -8-047 oh1 ow1.............. DeclanCannon(3) 2 29
(Richard Guest) *mid-div: hdwy 4f out: wknd over 1f out* **33/1**
0-56 **11** *22* **Pearl Catcher (IRE)**[25] 2771 3 -8-246 oh1.................. DuranFentiman 10
(Tim Easterby) *mid-div: lost pl over 2f out: bhd whn eased ins fnl f: t.o* **18/1**

2m 6.97s (-0.03)**Going Correction** 0.0s/f (Good) **11**Ran SP% **119.5**
Speed ratings (Par 98): **100,99,97,97,97 96,95,91,91,89 72**
toteswingers 1&2 £9.40, 1&3 £7.70, 2&3 £5.20 CSF £43.51 CT £152.44 TOTE £8.40 : £2.10 , £2.70, £1.30 ; EX 54.70 TRIFECTA Not won. .
Owner Liam Mulryan **Bred** L Mulryan **Trained** Great Habton, N Yorks

FOCUS
All distances as advertised. The ground was generally felt to be riding on the quick side of good by those who rode in the opener. The placed runners should have given the winner, who got first run, more to do. The winner made all in a modest time but was unexposed and still looked much the best.

Bada Bing Official explanation: trainer said filly failed to stay

4173 TYREGIANT.COM MAIDEN AUCTION STKS (DIV I) 5f
2:30 (2:35) (Class 5) 2-Y-O £2,264 (£673; £336; £168) Stalls Low

Form				RPR
	1		**Pure Excellence** 2-8-8 0 ... FrannyNorton 8 (Mark Johnston) *chsd ldrs: styd on wl to ld jst ins fnl f: kpt on wl* 6/1	72+
0	2	1	**Bogsnog (IRE)**[56] 2370 2-8-11 0 ... TomEaves 2 (Linda Stubbs) *led: hdd jst ins fnl f: kpt on same pce* 66/1	71
25	3	1 1/4	**Ayr Missile**[38] 2917 2-8-6 0 ... AmyRyan 5 (Kevin Ryan) *gave problems s: w ldr: wknd towards fin* 2/1[1]	62
55	4	hd	**Sleepy Haven (IRE)**[22] 3436 2-8-9 0 ... GrahamGibbons 4 (David Barron) *chsd ldrs: kpt on same pce fnl f* 10/1	64
3	5	1/2	**Red Gift (IRE)**[17] 3627 2-9-2 0 ... GrahamLee 6 (Brian Ellison) *mid-div: sn pushed along: kpt on fnl f* 9/2[3]	69
	6	1/2	**Dance Off (IRE)** 2-8-8 0 ... TonyHamilton 10 (Richard Fahey) *wnt lft s: mid-div: kpt on fnl f: nvr a threat* 12/1	59+
	7	2 3/4	**Hidden Asset** 2-8-13 0 ... LukeMorris 3 (Michael Appleby) *mid-div: sn pushed along: nvr a factor* 16/1	55
	8	2	**Cool Sea (IRE)** 2-8-4 0 ... AndrewMullen 1 (Nigel Tinkler) *s.s: sme hdwy on inner 2f out: nvr a factor* 50/1	38
6523	9	1/2	**Inchy Coo**[12] 3776 2-8-11 70 ...(p) DuranFentiman 7 (Tim Easterby) *sn wl outpcd and in rr: nvr on terms* 3/1[2]	44
0	10	7	**Chloe's Dream (IRE)**[23] 3415 2-8-4 0 ...(v[1]) JamesSullivan 9 (Ann Duffield) *t.k.h: sn trcking ldrs: lost pl over 1f out* 33/1	11

1m 5.72s (2.22) **Going Correction** +0.30s/f (Good) 10 Ran SP% **119.9**
Speed ratings (Par 94): **94,92,90,90,89 88,84,80,80,68**
toteswingers 1&2 £27.20, 1&3 £3.50, 2&3 £22.40 CSF £342.55 TOTE £8.40: £2.50, £14.40, £1.30; EX 325.00 Trifecta £470.00 Part won Pool: 635.24 - 0.39 winning units..
Owner Excellence Racing **Bred** Peter Harris **Trained** Middleham Moor, N Yorks

FOCUS
Few got into what was the first division of quite an ordinary juvenile maiden. The form fits with the race average. The winenr will be of interest in nurseries.

NOTEBOOK
Pure Excellence, half-sister to a 1m2f-1m3f winner, is entered in the Group 2 Lowther. She seemed to know her job well enough, got a nice tow into the race, and always looked likely to come out on top from over 1f out. The bare form is nothing special, but she should improve with a step up to 6f likely to suit. (op 5-1 tchd 9-2)
Bogsnog(IRE), 40-1 and tailed off on his debut at Kempton 56 days earlier, looked to have learnt plenty from that initial experience and stuck on really well once headed. He can win a small maiden on this evidence.
Ayr Missile, dropping a furlong and a half in trip, played up before the start and couldn't race on close home. She now has the option of nurseries. (op 9-4 tchd 7-4)
Sleepy Haven(IRE) got a bit wound up beforehand and proved one-paced under pressure. He should find opportunities over further in low-grade nurseries. (op 7-1)
Red Gift(IRE) should find opportunities over further in low-grade nurseries. (op 11-1)
Dance Off(IRE), whose dam is an unraced half-sister to numerous Flat winners from 1m up, made a satisfactory start and should improve. (op 10-1)
Cool Sea(IRE) Official explanation: jockey said filly was slowly away
Inchy Coo, the most experienced of these, was disappointing when considering the recent run of form her stable has been on. The drop to 5f on fast ground may have been against her. Official explanation: jockey said filly never travelled (tchd 7-2)

4174 TYREGIANT.COM SPRINT H'CAP 5f
3:00 (3:06) (Class 6) (0-60,60) 3-Y-O+ £1,617 (£481; £240; £120) Stalls Low

Form				RPR
50-5	1		**Holy Angel (IRE)**[38] 2928 3-9-2 56 ... DuranFentiman 16 (Tim Easterby) *dwlt: towards rr: hdwy on outer over 1f out: led wl ins fnl f: jst hld on* 12/1	63
05-0	2	hd	**Ypres**[22] 3442 3-9-0 57 ... GaryBartley(3) 12 (Jason Ward) *in rr: hdwy and nt clr run over 1f out: swtchd lft: styd on strly ins fnl f: jst failed* 22/1	64+
0400	3	hd	**Meandmyshadow**[10] 3845 4-9-10 60 ... RobertWinston 7 (Alan Brown) *w ldr: led 1f out: hdd and no ex last 50yds* 9/2[1]	67
2504	4	1 1/2	**Foreign Rhythm (IRE)**[9] 3893 7-9-5 60 ... GarryWhillans(5) 13 (Ron Barr) *in rr: hdwy over 1f out: hmpd ins fnl f: kpt on wl* 16/1	62
012	5	1 1/4	**Errigal Lad**[33] 3076 7-9-8 58 ... KellyHarrison 11 (Garry Woodward) *dwlt: in rr: hdwy and swtchd outside over 1f out: kpt on wl* 16/1	55+
0635	6	1/2	**Baybshambles (IRE)**[58] 2314 8-9-5 55 ... RoystonFfrench 6 (Ron Barr) *mid-div: effrt whn hmpd over 1f out: kpt on: nvr trbld ldrs* 8/1[3]	50+
404	7	3/4	**Mon Duchess**[24] 3406 4-9-2 52 ... DanielTudhope 4 (Lawrence Mullaney) *chsd ldrs: one pce appr fnl f* 14/1	45
2062	8	1 1/4	**Tom Sawyer**[43] 2749 4-9-10 60 ...(p) GrahamLee 8 (Julie Camacho) *in rr: hdwy 2f out: n.m.r over 1f out: fdd fnl 75yds* 17/2	48
0060	9	1/2	**Prince James**[36] 2982 5-9-1 58 ... DavidSimmonson(7) 1 (Michael Easterby) *chsd ldrs: one pce fnl 2f: b.b.v* 25/1	44
4400	10	1 3/4	**Ever Roses**[26] 3308 4-9-6 56 ...(v) RussKennemore 15 (Paul Midgley) *in rr: drvn over 2f out: nvr a factor* 33/1	36
-015	11	1 1/2	**Baltic Bomber (IRE)**[6] 3954 3-9-6 60 ... TomEaves 10 (John Quinn) *swtchd rt s: mid-div: hdwy and nt clr run over 2f out: nvr nr ldrs* 7/1[2]	34+
0265	12	1/2	**Chosen One (IRE)**[26] 3308 7-9-4 54 ... JamesSullivan 9 (Ruth Carr) *chsd ldrs: wknd over 1f out* 10/1	27
5246	13	3/4	**Imperial Legend (IRE)**[24] 3407 3-9-2 56 ... AdrianNicholls 5 (David Nicholls) *led tl hdd & wknd 1f out: heavily eased towards fin* 8/1[3]	25
6164	14	1/2	**Rio's Girl**[22] 3441 5-9-7 57 ... StephenCraine 17 (Tony Coyle) *in tch: drvn over 2f out: wknd over 1f out* 16/1	25
343-	15	2 1/4	**Headstight (IRE)**[267] 7058 3-9-4 58 ... MickyFenton 2 (Paul Midgley) *chsd ldrs on ins: wknd fnl f* 12/1	17
00-0	16	7	**Media Jury**[21] 3463 5-9-3 53 ...(b) DavidNolan 14 (John Wainwright) *mid-div on outer: rdn over 2f out: sn lost pl* 33/1	

1m 4.78s (1.28) **Going Correction** +0.30s/f (Good) 16 Ran SP% **126.3**
WFA 3 from 4yo+ 4lb
Speed ratings (Par 101): **101,100,100,97,95 95,93,91,91,88 85,85,83,83,79 68**
toteswingers 1&2 £52.00, 1&3 £21.60, 2&3 £32.80 CSF £266.48 CT £1437.34 TOTE £16.90: £3.70, £7.00, £1.10, £4.20; EX 425.30 TRIFECTA Not won..
Owner Three Jolly Farmers **Bred** Yeomanstown Stud **Trained** Great Habton, N Yorks
■ Arch Walker (6/1) was withdrawn after getting loose before the s. R4 applies, deduct 10p in the £. New market formed.
■ Stewards' Enquiry : Gary Bartley one-day ban: careless riding (Jul 31)

FOCUS
Plenty of pace on in this low-grade sprint and the race set up for the closers. A high draw was of no inconvenience the way the race played out and the winner rates a 7lb clear personal best. The second was possibly unlucky.
Errigal Lad Official explanation: jockey said gelding was denied a clear run
Baybshambles(IRE) Official explanation: jockey said gelding was denied a clear run
Prince James Official explanation: trainer's rep said gelding bled from the nose
Baltic Bomber(IRE) Official explanation: jockey said gelding was denied a clear run

4175 IRISHBIGRACETRENDS.COM H'CAP 1m 100y
3:30 (3:33) (Class 4) (0-80,80) 3-Y-O+ £4,204 (£1,251; £625; £312) Stalls Low

Form				RPR
5323	1		**Lockantanks**[17] 3615 5-9-12 78 ... LukeMorris 3 (Michael Appleby) *trckd ldrs: nt clr run over 2f out: led 1f out: all out* 7/2[2]	86
03-5	2	shd	**Christmas Light**[3] 4089 5-8-13 65 ... GrahamLee 4 (Brian Ellison) *trckd ldrs: nt clr run over 2f out: hdwy over 1f out: chal ins fnl f: jst failed* 12/1	73
2342	3	2 1/4	**Save The Bees**[10] 3859 4-9-7 73 ... DanielTudhope 2 (Declan Carroll) *t.k.h: sn trcking ldrs: led over 5f out: qcknd pce over 3f out: hdd 1f out: kpt on same pce last 100yds* 3/1[1]	70
5603	4	1/2	**Moheebb (IRE)**[20] 3492 8-9-5 71 ...(be) PJMcDonald 7 (Ruth Carr) *hld up in rr: drvn 3f out: kpt on ins fnl f* 6/1[3]	73
456	5	nk	**Fame Again**[59] 2262 4-9-4 70 ... JamesSullivan 9 (Michael Easterby) *led tl over 5f out: one pce fnl 2f* 16/1	71
3501	6	1/2	**Lady Chaparral**[20] 3492 5-10-0 80 ... TomEaves 8 (Michael Dods) *trckd ldrs: t.k.h: effrt over 2f out: hung rt: kpt on same pce* 3/1[1]	80
-053	7	1 1/2	**Change The Subject (USA)**[15] 3699 4-9-6 72 ...(t) AndrewMullen 6 (Peter Salmon) *hmpd s: hld up in rr: hdwy on ins over 2f out: n.m.r: one pce* 16/1	68
32-6	8	3 1/4	**Stylistickhill (IRE)**[17] 3616 4-8-9 61 oh1 ...(t) MircoDemuro 10 (Scott Dixon) *hld up in rr: hdwy on outside over 3f out: wknd over 1f out: eased clsng stages* 12/1	50

1m 46.99s (-0.61) **Going Correction** 0.0s/f (Good) 8 Ran SP% **113.7**
Speed ratings (Par 105): **103,102,100,100,99 97,97,94**
toteswingers 1&2 £8.70, 1&3 £3.00, 2&3 £5.30 CSF £43.45 CT £132.58 TOTE £5.20: £1.70, £4.50, £2.00; EX 49.90 Trifecta £224.90 Pool: 811.61 - 2.67 winning units..
Owner Dallas Racing **Bred** Jeremy Green And Sons **Trained** Danethorpe, Notts

FOCUS
Ordinary form for the grade, if straightforward enough, with the pace being fairly steady.

4176 127TH YEAR OF WATT MEMORIAL H'CAP 2m 35y
4:00 (4:00) (Class 4) (0-85,83) 3-Y-O+ £4,528 (£1,347; £673; £336) Stalls Low

Form				RPR
-525	1		**Moon Trip**[20] 3509 3-8-3 75 ... FrannyNorton 6 (Mark Johnston) *led after 1f: increased pce over 4f out: edgd rt over 1f out: styd on strly to forge clr* 7/2[2]	84
6-52	2	5	**Mojolika**[36] 2978 4-9-6 75 ... GrahamGibbons 1 (Tim Easterby) *t.k.h: trckd ldrs: chal on ins 2f out: kpt on same pce appr fnl f* 9/4[1]	78
0551	3	2	**Mohawk Ridge**[13] 3750 6-9-2 74 ...(p) LeeTopliss(3) 9 (Michael Dods) *t.k.h: trckd ldrs: chal 3f out: one pce over 1f out* 11/1	75
6-36	4	hd	**Stags Leap (IRE)**[19] 3519 5-8-10 65 ... DuranFentiman 3 (Dianne Sayer) *led 1f: chsd ldrs: drvn over 3f out: outpcd over 2f out: kpt on fnl f* 28/1	66
023	5	1/2	**Wild Desert (FR)**[16] 3661 7-9-11 83 ... MatthewCosham(3) 7 (Charlie Longsdon) *mid-div: drvn over 4f out: kpt on one pce fnl 2f* 8/1[3]	83
06-4	6	3/4	**Petella**[36] 2978 6-8-11 66 ... PJMcDonald 4 (George Moore) *hld up in rr: drvn over 4f out: kpt on fnl f* 8/1[3]	65
4113	7	1/2	**Blackstone Vegas**[23] 3419 6-8-12 67 ... TomEaves 5 (Derek Shaw) *t.k.h towards rr: hdwy on inner over 2f out: one pce* 10/1	66
1600	8	5	**Boss's Destination**[19] 3535 5-9-7 76 ... RobertWinston 2 (Alan Swinbank) *hld up in mid-div: t.k.h: effrt over 3f out: wknd over 1f out* 10/1	69
20-0	9	4	**Markington**[16] 3661 9-8-13 68 ...(t) PaulMulrennan 8 (Anthony Honeyball) *dwlt: hld up in rr: hdwy on outer to chse ldrs over 5f out: drvn over 3f out: lost pl over 1f out* 8/1[3]	56

3m 43.85s (4.05) **Going Correction** 0.0s/f (Good)
WFA 3 from 4yo+ 17lb 9 Ran SP% **116.3**
Speed ratings (Par 105): **89,86,85,85,85 84,84,82,80**
toteswingers 1&2 £2.40, 1&3 £7.30, 2&3 £5.40 CSF £11.89 CT £77.26 TOTE £5.60: £1.70, £1.20, £3.30; EX 13.70 Trifecta £77.90 Pool: 683.83 - 6.49 winning units..
Owner Sheikh Hamdan Bin Mohammed Al Maktoum **Bred** Darley **Trained** Middleham Moor, N Yorks

FOCUS
The early pace was a slow and front two more or less held their positions throughout. The winner improved 7lb, with the third and fourth helping with the standard.

4177 MR RAJARAMAN H'CAP 7f 100y
4:30 (4:30) (Class 5) (0-75,75) 3-Y-O+ £2,425 (£721; £360; £180) Stalls Low

Form				RPR
0-11	1		**Eeny Mac (IRE)**[21] 3460 5-8-10 60 ... JulieBurke(3) 3 (Neville Bycroft) *mde all: drvn over 2f out: kpt on wl* 11/8[1]	68
1216	2	1 1/4	**Violent Velocity (IRE)**[25] 3335 9-9-6 74 ... KevinLundie(7) 2 (John Quinn) *hld up in rr: hdwy over 3f out: swtchd to inner 2f out: styd on same pce fnl f* 10/1	79
0301	3	1 1/2	**First Class Favour (IRE)**[10] 3843 4-8-12 66 ... RachelRichardson(7) 5 (Tim Easterby) *wnt lft s: sn trcking ldrs: kpt on same pce over 1f out* 3/1[2]	67
0306	4	2 1/4	**Shadowtime**[27] 3274 7-9-8 69 ... FrannyNorton 8 (Tracy Waggott) *trckd ldrs: effrt over 2f out: one pce* 4/1[3]	64
30-0	5	1 1/2	**Sehnsucht (IRE)**[108] 1132 3-9-0 75 ... ThomasGarner(7) 7 (Alan McCabe) *bmpd s: hld up in rr: hdwy on outside over 2f out: one pce* 10/1	64
0-43	6	7	**Moorside Magic**[151] 604 3-8-7 61 ow1 ... TomEaves 4 (Richard Fahey) *trckd ldrs: lost pl over 2f out* 20/1	33
0050	7	1/2	**Wolf Spirit (IRE)**[32] 3111 3-8-6 60 ...(b) JamesSullivan 1 (Ruth Carr) *in rr: drvn over 3f out: edgd rt and wknd over 1f out* 20/1	31

1m 33.13s (-0.67) **Going Correction** 0.0s/f (Good)
WFA 3 from 4yo+ 7lb 7 Ran SP% **114.8**
Speed ratings (Par 103): **103,101,99,97,95 87,86**
toteswingers 1&2 £3.40, 1&3 £1.60, 2&3 £4.60 CSF £16.85 CT £35.40 TOTE £1.90: £1.20, £3.70; EX 16.20 Trifecta £36.80 Pool: 1,007.03 - 20.23 winning units..
Owner Mrs J Dickinson **Bred** Kenneth Heelan **Trained** Brandsby, N Yorks

FOCUS
Another race run at an ordinary gallop that suited those on the pace. The exposed runner-up sets the standard.

4178 TYREGIANT.COM MAIDEN AUCTION STKS (DIV II) 5f
5:00 (5:00) (Class 5) 2-Y-O £2,264 (£673; £336; £168) Stalls Low

Form				RPR
3	1		**Mitchell**[24] 3381 2-9-2 0 ... GrahamGibbons 8 (David Barron) *chsd ldrs: drvn 2f out: styd on to ld post* 9/4[1]	75

30 **2** *shd* **Balinka**[23] 3415 2-8-4 0 PJMcDonald 2 63
(Mel Brittain) *led: rdn over 1f out: edgd lft ins fnl f: hdd last stride* **14/1**

3 **3** *½* **Titus Titan (IRE)**[19] 3532 2-8-10 0 PaulPickard(3) 3 73+
(Brian Ellison) *sn outpcd and in rr: hdwy 2f out: kpt on ins fnl f* **12/1**

4 *1* **Fantasy Invader (IRE)** 2-8-13 0 TomEaves 1 66
(John Quinn) *rrd s: in rr: outpcd over 2f out: hdwy over 1f out: styd on wl towards fin* **7/1**

62 **5** *hd* **Red Cobra (IRE)**[13] 3748 2-8-11 0 DuranFentiman 6 64
(Tim Easterby) *chsd ldrs: kpt on same pce fnl f* **5/2**[2]

644 **6** *nse* **Art Mistress (IRE)**[23] 3415 2-8-11 65 JamesSullivan 5 63
(Tim Easterby) *chsd ldrs on inner: kpt on same pce fnl f* **5/1**[3]

7 *6* **Multisure** 2-8-9 0 PaulMulrennan 10 40
(Richard Fahey) *wnt lft s: sn trcking ldrs: wknd over 1f out* **9/1**

8 *3* **Cos I Can** 2-8-4 0 FrannyNorton 7 24
(Derek Shaw) *dwlt: outpcd in rr: lost pl over 2f out* **33/1**

1m 4.78s (1.28) **Going Correction** +0.30s/f (Good) 8 Ran SP% **115.8**
Speed ratings (Par 94): **101,100,100,98,98 98,88,83**
toteswingers 1&2 £6.50, 1&3 £5.90, 2&3 £7.90 CSF £34.99 TOTE £4.00: £1.50, £3.00, £3.90; EX 23.80 Trifecta £234.60 Pool: 948.09 - 2.99 winning units..

Owner A J Duffield **Bred** Conor J C Parsons & Brian M Parsons **Trained** Maunby, N Yorks

FOCUS
Fairly modest juvenile form, with division one looking stronger. The race averages and the winner's debut set the level.

NOTEBOOK
Mitchell stepped up on his debut effort, just about getting away with 5f on this faster surface. He will benefit from a step up to 6f and shouldn't be given too high a mark with nurseries in mind. (op 2-1 tchd 15-8)

Balinka returned to the level of her debut form, being cruelly denied in the final stride. Modest nurseries will be her thing. (op 11-1)

Titus Titan(IRE) is definitely the one to take from the race, and he may well have won had his rider been more vigorous/been able to get him organised sooner. Slowly away, it took him an age to be switched and once in the open his rider opted not to use the whip, presumably feeling it was too late. He'll benefit from an extra furlong and should be winning races this season. (op 8-1)

Fantasy Invader(IRE), a 14,000GBP 2yo, out of a 7f-1m1f winner, found this too sharp a test on debut, but should learn from the experience and will appreciate a stiffer test. (op 12-1)

Red Cobra(IRE) is likely to want further once contesting nurseries. (op 3-1)

Art Mistress(IRE) is likely to want further once contesting nurseries. (op 6-1 tchd 7-1)

4179 DOROTHY LAIRD MEMORIAL TROPHY H'CAP (LADIES RACES) 1m 1f 207y
5:30 (5:30) (Class 6) (0-65,65) 3-Y-O+ £1,617 (£481; £240; £120) Stalls Low

Form RPR

5-14 **1** **Tinseltown**[6] 3979 6-9-13 57 (p) AmyRyan 14 68
(Brian Rothwell) *mde all: edgd rt over 1f out: hld on nr fin* **5/1**[1]

0045 **2** *nk* **Gold Rules**[15] 3693 5-10-5 63 MissJCoward 8 73
(Michael Easterby) *trckd ldrs: effrt over 2f out: chsd wnr 1f out: styd on ins fnl f: no ex nr fin* **9/1**[2]

-202 **3** *¾* **Landesherr (GER)**[12] 3793 5-10-5 63 (t) LucyAlexander 12 72
(Steve Gollings) *mid-div: hdwy over 2f out: kpt on wl ins fnl f* **5/1**[1]

3204 **4** *2* **Shy**[15] 3693 7-9-12 61 (b) MissPhillipaTutty(5) 1 66
(Karen Tutty) *in rr-div: hdwy on inner over 2f out: n.m.r over 1f out: kpt on same pce ins fnl f* **10/1**[3]

2064 **5** *nk* **Edas**[29] 3213 10-9-12 56 MissHCuthbert 4 60
(Thomas Cuthbert) *s.i.s: hdwy 7f out: chsng ldrs over 3f out: one pce over 1f out* **20/1**

6340 **6** *4* **Tribal Myth (IRE)**[15] 3692 5-10-7 65 (p) JulieBurke 2 61
(Kevin Ryan) *in rr: hdwy on outer over 2f out: nvr trbld ldrs* **5/1**[1]

35-2 **7** *¾* **Honoured (IRE)**[15] 3699 5-9-12 56 (t) ShirleyTeasdale 7 50
(Michael Appleby) *mid-div: hdwy over 2f out: nt clr run and swtchd lft jst ins fnl f: kpt on* **11/1**

-055 **8** *nk* **Sharp Sovereign (USA)**[32] 2034 6-9-11 60 MissHBethell(5) 6 54
(Ian McInnes) *trckd ldrs: effrt over 2f out: one pce* **28/1**

4003 **9** *½* **Flag Of Glory**[15] 3692 5-10-0 63 MissMEdden(5) 5 56
(Peter Hiatt) *chsd ldrs: wknd fnl f* **18/1**

453 **10** *hd* **Nolecce**[3] 4088 5-9-11 60 (p) MrsAGuest(5) 13 52
(Richard Guest) *dwlt: swtchd rt after s: hdwy over 2f out: one pce* **20/1**

6200 **11** *¾* **Lakeman (IRE)**[32] 3129 6-9-10 59 MissJLambert(5) 16 50
(Brian Ellison) *in rr: kpt on fnl 2f: nvr a factor* **28/1**

45/3 **12** *nk* **Gulf Coast**[13] 3753 7-9-8 52 (p) GemmaTutty 9 42
(Tim Walford) *in rr-div: effrt on outer over 2f out: nvr a factor* **12/1**

6120 **13** *1* **Politbureau**[13] 3752 5-9-13 57 MissSBrotherton 10 45
(Michael Easterby) *mid-div: hdwy over 4f out: trcking ldrs 2f out: sn fdd* **14/1**

-040 **14** *4 ½* **Goodlukin Lucy**[22] 3440 5-9-6 50 MissECSayer 17 29
(Dianne Sayer) *mid-div: hdwy over 4f out: effrt on outside over 2f out: sn wknd* **25/1**

000/ **15** *1 ½* **Solis (GER)**[41] 6156 9-9-0 49 (e) MissRobynGray(5) 15 25
(Dianne Sayer) *dwlt: sn detachd in last: sme hdwy on wd outside over 2f out: sn wknd* **33/1**

3-06 **16** *26* **Rowan Lodge (IRE)**[50] 2536 10-9-11 55 (b) KellyHarrison 3
(Ollie Pears) *trckd ldrs: wknd 2f out: eased whn bhd: t.o* **33/1**

530/ **17** *¾* **Just Jimmy (IRE)**[606] 7502 7-9-1 50 MsDJones(5) 11
(Trevor Wall) *trckd wnr: lost pl over 2f out: bhd whn eased: t.o* **66/1**

2m 6.03s (-0.97) **Going Correction** 0.0s/f (Good) 17 Ran SP% **124.7**
Speed ratings (Par 101): **103,102,102,100,100 97,96,96,95,95 95,94,94,90,89 68,67**
toteswingers 1&2 £9.40, 1&3 £6.40, 2&3 £10.70 CSF £44.74 CT £244.93 TOTE £5.70: £2.40, £2.60, £1.10, £2.90; EX 30.40 Trifecta £139.80 Pool: 850.47 - 4.50 winning units..

Owner Tony Arnott **Bred** Biddestone Stud **Trained** Norton, N Yorks

■ Stewards' Enquiry : Miss H Cuthbert four-day ban: used whip above permitted level, down shoulder in the forehand (Jul 31,Aug,3,5,6)

FOCUS
An open lady riders' handicap. It was the pick of the round times, but was another race where few became involved. A 4lb personal best from the winner.

T/Jkpt: Part won. £162,058.70 to a £1 stake. T/Plt: £74.40 to a £1 stake. Pool: £106523.62 - 1044.69 winning tickets T/Qpdt: £19.80 to a £1 stake. Pool: £6241.32 - 233.21 winning tickets WG

FFOS LAS (L-H)
Tuesday, July 17

OFFICIAL GOING: Heavy (6.7)
Visibility poor and comments-in-running limited.
Wind: moderate against Weather: mist and drizzle

4180 32RED/BRITISH STALLION STUDS E B F MEDIAN AUCTION MAIDEN STKS 5f
2:15 (2:17) (Class 5) 2-Y-O £3,234 (£962; £481; £240) Stalls High

Form RPR

5 **1** **Blackdown Spirit**[22] 3444 2-9-3 0 JamesMillman 6 81
(Rod Millman) *racd koonly: cl up: let down to ld appr fnl f: rdn out* **4/1**[2]

2 **2** *2 ¼* **City Girl (IRE)**[20] 3504 2-8-12 0 RichardHughes 4 68
(Ralph Beckett) *led: rdn 2f out: hdd appr fnl f: no ex fnl 75yds* **1/3**[1]

3 *5* **Cashel's Missile (IRE)** 2-9-3 0 SamHitchcott 2 55
(John Spearing) *chsd ldrs: bustled along after 1f: wnt mod 3rd 2f out: r.o ins fnl f* **14/1**[3]

4 *6* **Scoobys Girl (IRE)** 2-8-7 0 MarkCoumbe(5) 3 28
(Daniel Mark Loughnane) *s.i.s: outpcd: rdn 1/2-way: passed wkng rival ins fnl f* **28/1**

5 *3 ¼* **Bounty Rock** 2-8-10 0 WilliamTwiston-Davies(7) 5 22
(Rebecca Curtis) *w ldr 2f: sn drvn: wknd wl over 1f out* **16/1**

1m 2.36s (4.06) **Going Correction** +0.675s/f (Yiel) 5 Ran SP% **111.0**
Speed ratings (Par 94): **94,90,82,72,67**
CSF £5.86 TOTE £3.90: £2.20, £1.02; EX 5.70.

Owner Rod Millman Racing Club **Bred** Brookridge Timber Ltd **Trained** Kentisbeare, Devon

FOCUS
An uncompetitive maiden run in bad ground, and long odds-on backers got their fingers burnt. The winner stepped up on his debut.

NOTEBOOK
Blackdown Spirit had finished an encouraging fifth of 14 on his Windsor debut last month and his sire's record with his progeny on testing ground gave every hope that he would handle these conditions. He was still on the bridle when collaring the favourite around 2f out and found plenty once off the bridle to keep the filly at bay. He should have a future in nurseries when able to get his toe in. (op 7-2)

City Girl(IRE) had been beaten a head in a six-runner fillies' maiden on her debut at Salisbury last month and was all the rage to go one better. She was soon taking them along, but her rider became animated passing the 2f pole, as the winner was brought to challenge, and the gelding saw his race out much better in the ground than she did. She is worth another chance back on a sound surface. (op 2-5)

Cashel's Missile(IRE), retained for 1,000GBP as a 2yo, is the first foal of the stable's 14-time winning sprinter Cashel Mead. He never got into this, but the yard are now just 2-69 with juvenile newcomers in the past ten seasons, so the best of him is likely to be well into the future. (op 12-1)

Scoobys Girl(IRE), a 6,000GBP 2yo, is closely related to a winner at up to 1m3f in Scandinavia and was always struggling after missing the break, but her stable is now 0-48 with juvenile debutants in the past ten seasons. (op 25-1)

Bounty Rock, retained for 14,000gns as a 2yo, is a half-brother to two winners in the US. He stayed with the two principals until feeling the pinch at halfway, but is another whose yard isn't renowned for 2yo winners. (tchd 20-1)

4181 £32 BONUS AT 32RED.COM H'CAP 1m 4f (R)
2:45 (2:45) (Class 6) (0-65,64) 3-Y-O+ £1,617 (£481; £240; £120) Stalls Low

Form RPR

-001 **1** **Astra Hall**[6] 3968 3-8-9 57 6ex RichardHughes 8 66+
(Ralph Beckett) *in tch: hdwy over 3f out: cl 2nd and stl on bridle 1f out: nudged into ld nr fin: cleverly* **1/3**[1]

0000 **2** *hd* **Femme Royale**[29] 3220 4-8-3 46 oh1 DanielMuscutt(7) 12 51
(Richard Price) *a.p: in narrow ld and rdn 1f out: hdd nr fin: no ch w wnr* **18/1**

-632 **3** *¾* **Barachiel**[33] 3081 4-9-8 61 CPGeoghegan(3) 11 65
(Ronald Harris) *hld up in tch: trcking ldrs over 3f out: 3rd and one pce fnl f* **11/2**[2]

306/ **4** *3 ½* **Bazart**[26] 3423 10-9-5 62 (tp) AliceHaynes(7) 6 60
(Bernard Llewellyn) *led: stl in ld over 2f out: 4th and btn 1f out* **28/1**

0-34 **5** *¾* **Taste The Wine (IRE)**[22] 3429 6-9-10 60 ChrisCatlin 9 57
(Bernard Llewellyn) *hld up in last pair: hdwy over 3f out: mod 5th 1f out* **10/1**[3]

-025 **6** *8* **Tijori (IRE)**[22] 3429 4-9-6 63 (p) RobertWilliams(7) 1 47
(Bernard Llewellyn) *cl up: rdn and wknd 4f out* **18/1**

0-00 **7** *nk* **Spinning Waters**[32] 3102 6-8-10 46 oh1 (p) SamHitchcott 5 30
(Dai Burchell) *s.i.s: hld up: a in last pair: wl btn 1f out* **25/1**

005 **8** *1* **David's Folly (IRE)**[32] 3100 3-8-6 59 (p) DarrenEgan(5) 3 41
(Bryn Palling) *cl up: in 2nd 5f out: rdn and wknd over 3f out* **11/1**

2m 58.76s (21.36) **Going Correction** +1.625s/f (Heav)
WFA 3 from 4yo+ 12lb 8 Ran SP% **125.6**
Speed ratings (Par 101): **93,92,92,90,89 84,84,83**
toteswingers 1&2 £5.00, 1&3 £1.70, 2&3 £10.40 CSF £11.65 CT £23.96 TOTE £1.40: £1.02, £5.30, £2.00; EX 16.00.

Owner G B Balding **Bred** Miss B Swire **Trained** Kimpton, Hants

FOCUS
The visibility was poor throughout this race and they appeared to go no pace in the early stages. This contest featured another long odds-on favourite, mainly due to the four non-runners. Astra Hall was a cosy winner of a weak race.

4182 32RED.COM MAIDEN FILLIES' STKS 1m 4f (R)
3:15 (3:15) (Class 5) 3-Y-O+ £2,264 (£673; £336) Stalls Low

Form RPR

6-52 **1** **Adeste**[25] 3352 3-9-0 78 ChrisCatlin 2 67+
(Noel Quinlan) *racd in 2nd: led over 3f out: sn rdn clr: wl in command 1f out: kpt up to work* **1/8**[1]

2 *9* **Maid Of Silk (IRE)**[26] 6-9-12 0 (t) RichardHughes 3 54
(Neil Mulholland) *led: shkn up over 4f out: hdd over 3f out: sn rdn: no ch w wnr 1f out: sn eased* **14/1**[3]

0- **3** *7* **End Of May (IRE)**[391] 3287 3-8-9 0 ow2 WilliamTwiston-Davies(7) 1 46
(Peter Bowen) *a in last: stl in tch 3f out: sn rdn and struggling* **7/1**[2]

3m 1.64s (24.24) **Going Correction** +1.625s/f (Heav)
WFA 3 from 6yo 12lb 3 Ran SP% **108.1**
Speed ratings (Par 100): **84,78,73**
CSF £2.88 TOTE £1.10; EX 2.00.

Owner Mrs Perle O'Rourke **Bred** Plantation Stud **Trained** Newmarket, Suffolk

■ Stewards' Enquiry : William Twiston-Davies three-day ban: weighed in 2lb heavy (Jul 31,Aug 2,3)

FOCUS
There won't be many weaker maidens run this year. It's doubtful the winner needed to match her debut form.

4183 32RED CASINO H'CAP 1m 2f (R)
3:45 (3:45) (Class 5) (0-70,70) 3-Y-0+ **£2,264** (£673; £336; £168) **Stalls** Low

Form RPR
5342 **1** **Pandorica**[9] 3891 4-9-3 **59**....(p) ChrisCatlin 7 67
(Bernard Llewellyn) *in tch on outer: clsd 5f out: led over 1f out: rdn out* **3/1**[2]
2500 **2** *1 ½* **Black Coffee**[12] 3782 7-0-12 **61**....(b) JackDuern(7) 2 66
(Mark Brisbourne) *s.i.s: in rr and sn chsd along: rdn 5f out: styd on fr 2f out: chsd wnr 1f out: kpt on same pce* **11/1**
00-6 **3** *2 ¼* **Spring Secret**[55] 2389 6-9-0 **61**.... DarrenEgan(5) 4 62
(Bryn Palling) *wnt to post early: prom: rdn 3f out: styd on same pce u.p* **7/2**[3]
0520 **4** *4 ½* **Lisselan Pleasure (USA)**[31] 3143 5-8-6 **55**....(t) DanielMuscutt(7) 3 47
(Bernard Llewellyn) *hld up in tch: clsd 5f out: rdn 3f out: one pce* **14/1**
0-00 **5** *hd* **Mr Udagawa**[20] 3485 6-9-2 **65** ow1....(p) RobertWilliams(7) 8 56
(Bernard Llewellyn) *prom: led 4f out: rdn over 2f out: hdd over 1f out: sn wknd* **25/1**
5336 **6** *nk* **Jalors (IRE)**[19] 3544 4-9-5 **64** ow1.... CPGeoghegan(3) 5 55
(Ronald Harris) *rdn along over 5f out: a towards rr* **9/2**
66B- **7** *8* **Misefi**[49] 5042 4-8-9 **51** oh3....[1] DavidProbert 6 26
(Martin Bosley) *wnt to post early: led tl hdd 4f out: sn rdn: wknd over 2f out* **50/1**
3-62 **8** *23* **Villa Royale**[22] 3430 3-9-4 **70**....(p) RichardHughes 1
(Harry Dunlop) *in tch: reminders 1/2-way: wknd over 3f out: sn eased: t.o* **5/2**[1]

2m 24.7s (15.30) **Going Correction** +1.625s/f (Heav)
WFA 3 from 4yo+ 10lb **8** Ran SP% **114.8**
Speed ratings (Par 103): **103,101,100,96,96 96,89,71**
toteswingers 1&2 £7.20, 1&3 £5.20, 2&3 £9.80 CSF £35.57 CT £119.85 TOTE £5.10: £1.40, £2.60, £1.30; EX 37.00.
Owner Alex James **Bred** Ambersham Stud **Trained** Fochriw, Caerphilly

FOCUS
An ordinary handicap. As in the second race, Bernard Llewellyn was responsible for three of the eight runners and managed to hit the target this time. Shaky form rated around the winner.
Villa Royale Official explanation: jockey said filly never travelled

4184 AT THE RACES H'CAP 1m 6f (R)
4:15 (4:15) (Class 4) (0-85,85) 4-Y-0+ **£4,204** (£1,251; £625; £312) **Stalls** Low

Form RPR
1 **1** **Asker (IRE)**[22] 3430 4-8-10 **81**....(b) KatiaScallan(7) 4 91
(Marcus Tregoning) *racd keenly: trckd ldrs: led over 4f out and qcknd the pce: rdn 3f out: jnd 1f out: jst did enough* **9/4**[2]
1111 **2** *shd* **Bilidn**[33] 3077 4-9-7 **85**.... ChrisCatlin 1 94
(Noel Quinlan) *hld up in last: hdwy over 4f out: rdn to chse wnr over 3f out: ev ch u.p thrght fnl f: jst hld* **15/8**[1]
3/56 **3** *15* **Mezzanisi (IRE)**[45] 2706 7-8-13 **77**.... RichardHughes 5 65
(Peter Bowen) *hld up in tch: rdn over 3f out: outpcd by ldrs 2f out: wnt mod 3rd 1f out* **5/2**[3]
6102 **4** *2* **Hamilton Hill**[22] 3429 5-8-4 **68**.... DavidProbert 3 53
(Dai Burchell) *s.i.s: hld up: hdwy into 3rd over 3f out: sn rdn and outpcd by ldrs: lost 3rd 1f out* **8/1**
00-5 **5** *7* **Praxiteles (IRE)**[32] 2423 8-8-9 **80**....(tp) WilliamTwiston-Davies(7) 2 55
(Rebecca Curtis) *cl up: rdn over 3f out: sn outpcd by ldrs: wknd 2f out* **14/1**
060- **6** *46* **Royal Reverie**[32] 5407 4-8-8 **72**.... JohnFahy 6
(Rebecca Curtis) *set stdy pce: hdd over 4f out: wknd qckly: t.o* **33/1**

3m 31.15s (27.35) **Going Correction** +1.625s/f (Heav) **6** Ran SP% **114.8**
Speed ratings (Par 105): **86,85,77,76,72 45**
toteswingers 1&2 £2.10, 1&3 £2.00, 2&3 £2.40 CSF £7.15 TOTE £3.70: £1.50, £2.90; EX 6.10.
Owner Nurlan Bizakov **Bred** Roncon Churchtown Bloodstock & Lane Ltd **Trained** Lambourn, Berks

FOCUS
A decent staying handicap and the in-form front pair pulled miles clear of the others. The winner is rated to the best view of his debut form.

4185 32REDPOKER.COM H'CAP 6f
4:45 (4:49) (Class 6) (0-55,55) 3-Y-0 **£1,617** (£481; £240; £120) **Stalls** High

Form RPR
4002 **1** **Purley Queen (IRE)**[35] 3005 3-8-13 **50**.... RichardHughes 6 58
(Sylvester Kirk) *trckd ldrs: wnt 2nd 2f out: led early ins fnl f: r.o wl: eased nr fin* **5/1**
0530 **2** *2 ¼* **Big Sylv (IRE)**[22] 3455 3-8-11 **48**.... DavidProbert 7 49
(James Unett) *led: rdn over 1f out: hdd early ins fnl f: sn outpcd by wnr* **4/1**[3]
04-0 **3** *4 ½* **Verus Delicia (IRE)**[55] 2388 3-8-4 **46** oh1.... MarkCoumbe(5) 5 34
(Daniel Mark Loughnane) *in tch: rdn and clsd 2f out: one pce and no imp on first pair fnl f* **11/1**
0000 **4** *1 ¼* **Compton Crofter**[15] 3706 3-8-11 **55**....(t) NicoleNordblad(7) 4 39
(Hans Adielsson) *hld up towards rr: rdn and hdwy 2f out: disp 3rd 1f out: sn no ex* **14/1**
02 **5** *6* **Bajan Hero**[22] 3433 3-9-1 **52**.... JohnFahy 8 18
(David Evans) *s.i.s and early reminder: sn chsng ldrs: rdn and wknd over 2f out* **3/1**[1]
2266 **6** *1* **First Rebellion**[20] 3489 3-8-4 **46** oh1.... DarrenEgan(5) 10 9
(Tony Carroll) *cl up: rdn 2f out: sn wknd* **7/2**[2]
600 **7** *3 ½* **Voodoo (IRE)**[46] 2665 3-8-9 **46** oh1....(t) ChrisCatlin 1
(Daniel Mark Loughnane) *unruly in paddock: chsd ldrs: rdn over 2f out: wknd over 1f out* **20/1**
0060 **8** *nk* **Lana (IRE)**[20] 3510 3-8-10 **54**.... WilliamTwiston-Davies(7) 2
(David Evans) *towards rr on outer: rdn over 2f out: sn wknd* **9/1**

1m 16.38s (6.38) **Going Correction** +1.025s/f (Soft) **8** Ran SP% **113.7**
Speed ratings (Par 98): **98,95,89,87,79 78,73,72**
CSF £24.96 CT £207.95 TOTE £7.40: £2.40, £1.10, £3.80; EX 19.00.
Owner D Boocock & P D Merritt **Bred** Mark & Pippa Hackett **Trained** Upper Lambourn, Berks

FOCUS
A moderate sprint handicap and they finished well spread out. Shaky form.

Voodoo(IRE) Official explanation: jockey said gelding hung right

4186 32REDBET.COM APPRENTICE TRAINING SERIES H'CAP 1m (R)
5:15 (5:16) (Class 6) (0-65,64) 3-Y-0 **£1,617** (£481; £240; £120) **Stalls** Far side

Form RPR
5-20 **1** **My Boy Ginger**[92] 1424 3-9-7 **64**.... ThomasBrown(3) 10 73
(Rod Millman) *in tch: chsd clr ldng pair 4f out: rdn to ld 2f out: clr ent fnl f: styd on wl* **11/4**[1]
4150 **2** *8* **Source Of Light (IRE)**[34] 3025 3-8-11 **58**.... LauraSimpson(7) 8 48
(Daniel Mark Loughnane) *racd keenly: w ldr tl tk narrow ld 4f out: rdn and hdd 2f out: no ex fnl f: jst hld 2nd* **14/1**
6044 **3** *hd* **Saint Irene**[16] 3665 3-9-1 **55**.... JakePayne 5 45
(Michael Blanshard) *towards rr: hdwy over 4f out: sn outpcd by ldrs: styd on u.p fnl f to cl on 2nd* **5/1**
012- **4** *9* **Compton Bird**[237] 7514 3-9-7 **61**....(t) NicoleNordblad 1 30
(Hans Adielsson) *hld up in rr: rdn 4f out: sn no ch w ldrs: plugged on fnl f* **11/2**
0002 **5** *hd* **Top Frock (IRE)**[22] 3454 3-9-5 **64**....(b) RyanTate(5) 9 33
(Clive Cox) *led to 4f out: rdn and wknd 2f out* **3/1**[2]
0060 **6** *2 ¼* **Rocquaine (IRE)**[22] 3443 3-8-11 **51**.... WilliamTwiston-Davies 7 15
(David Evans) *in rr: rdn over 3f out: wknd over 2f out* **9/2**[3]
0-05 **7** *20* **Idols Eye**[20] 3488 3-9-10 **64**....(t) DarrenEgan 2
(Martyn Meade) *t.k.h: chsd ldrs tl rdn and wknd 4f out: t.o* **22/1**

1m 52.6s (11.60) **Going Correction** +1.40s/f (Soft) **7** Ran SP% **112.9**
Speed ratings (Par 98): **98,90,89,80,80 78,58**
toteswingers 1&2 £7.80, 1&3 £4.10, 2&3 £11.60 CSF £38.96 CT £181.59 TOTE £3.90: £2.00, £3.20; EX 48.30.
Owner Coombeshead Racing **Bred** Percys (north Harrow) Ltd **Trained** Kentisbeare, Devon

FOCUS
Because of the heavy ground this race began with a 'flip' start. A moderate apprentice handicap, but the pick of the round times. Improvement from the winner, and the form could be rated higher.
T/Plt: £8.30 to a £1 stake. Pool: £51247.02 - 4461.35 winning tickets T/Qpdt: £10.30 to a £1 stake. Pool: £2933.12 - 209.40 winning tickets RL

4139 SOUTHWELL (L-H)
Tuesday, July 17

OFFICIAL GOING: Standard
Wind: Fresh half behind Weather: Cloudy with sunny periods

4187 BET TOTEPLACEPOT TEXT TOTE TO 89660 H'CAP 5f (F)
6:00 (6:01) (Class 5) (0-70,69) 3-Y-0+ **£2,264** (£673; £336; £168) **Stalls** High

Form RPR
0412 **1** **Just Like Heaven (IRE)**[34] 3028 3-9-0 **61**.... TedDurcan 14 74
(Tim Easterby) *mde virtually all: rdn over 1f out: edgd lft and clr ins fnl f: kpt on strly* **13/2**[2]
0031 **2** *4* **Spic 'n Span**[22] 3435 7-8-13 **56**....(b) LukeMorris 11 56
(Ronald Harris) *prom: rdn along wl over 1f out: kpt on same pce fnl f* **12/1**
3245 **3** *1* **Wreningham**[16] 3660 7-9-2 **64**....(p) DavidKenny(5) 9 60
(Pat Eddery) *trckd ldrs: rdn along 2f out: drvn and kpt on same pce fnl f* **16/1**
0004 **4** *nk* **Love You Louis**[5] 4003 6-9-12 **69**.... AdrianNicholls 8 64
(J R Jenkins) *cl up: rdn wl over 1f out: ev ch tl drvn and wknd ent fnl f* **13/2**[2]
4552 **5** *nk* **Soopacal (IRE)**[3] 4085 7-9-1 **58**.... SilvestreDeSousa 5 52+
(Brian Ellison) *dwlt: hmpd s: sn swtchd lft: outpcd and towards rr after 1f: swtchd rt and hdwy wl over 1f out: styd on fnl f: nrst fin* **2/1**[1]
4204 **6** *2* **Boucher Garcon (IRE)**[29] 3211 4-9-2 **64**.... NeilFarley(5) 3 51
(Declan Carroll) *wnt rt s: chsd ldrs: rdn along over 2f out: grad wknd* **14/1**
62-0 **7** *nk* **Irish Boy (IRE)**[53] 2439 4-9-8 **65**.... MickyFenton 1 51
(Paul Midgley) *prom on outer: rdn along bef 1/2-way: sn wknd* **12/1**
6000 **8** *shd* **Itum**[24] 3390 5-8-9 **52**....(v) BrettDoyle 2 37
(Christine Dunnett) *in tch: rdn along 2f out: no hdwy* **33/1**
223 **9** *nk* **The Magic Of Rio**[53] 2436 6-8-7 **50** oh5.... LiamKeniry 13 34
(John Balding) *in tch on wd outside: rdn along 2f out: sn btn* **25/1**
635 **10** *1 ½* **Strictly Pink (IRE)**[7] 3944 4-9-0 **64**.... RobertTart(7) 4 43
(Alan Bailey) *dwlt: hmpd s: a in rr* **9/1**[3]
0360 **11** *1 ¾* **Colourbearer (IRE)**[4] 4059 5-9-12 **69**....(t) RichardKingscote 7 41
(Milton Bradley) *dwlt: a in rr* **9/1**[3]
0-00 **12** *½* **Wake Up Sioux (IRE)**[14] 3730 3-8-7 **54**....(b[1]) KirstyMilczarek 6 24
(David C Griffiths) *dwlt: a in rr* **25/1**

58.2s (-1.50) **Going Correction** -0.225s/f (Stan)
WFA 3 from 4yo+ 4lb **12** Ran SP% **118.6**
Speed ratings (Par 103): **103,96,95,94,94 90,90,90,89,87 84,83**
toteswingers 1&2 £5.80, 1&3 £12.70, 2&3 £26.80 CSF £80.16 CT £829.17 TOTE £4.10: £1.90, £3.90, £2.50; EX 30.60 Trifecta £478.90 Part won. Pool: 647.29 - 0.39 winning units..
Owner D B Lamplough **Bred** Derek Veitch And Mark Tong **Trained** Great Habton, N Yorks

FOCUS
The stalls for the 5f races were on the outside while, for the remaining races, they were on the inside. A competitive sprint handicap run at a decent pace, with most of the field veering to the far side, and the impressive winner making all. He rates better than ever.
Soopacal(IRE) Official explanation: jockey said gelding suffered interference at start
Irish Boy(IRE) Official explanation: trainer said gelding finished distressed
Colourbearer(IRE) Official explanation: jockey said gelding never travelled
Wake Up Sioux(IRE) Official explanation: jockey said filly was outpaced throughout

4188 BET TOTEPOOL TEXT TOTE TO 89660 MEDIAN AUCTION MAIDEN STKS 1m 4f (F)
6:30 (6:30) (Class 5) 3-5-Y-0 **£2,385** (£704; £352) **Stalls** Low

Form RPR
4563 **1** **Adili (IRE)**[7] 3938 3-9-1 65.... PhillipMakin 3 74
(Brian Ellison) *towards rr: hdwy 5f out: rdn along to chse ldrs over 3f out: styng on whn n.m.r and swtchd lft over 1f out: sn drvn to chal: led ins fnl f: kpt on wl towards fin* **7/2**[3]
00- **2** *¾* **Echo Of Dream**[288] 6588 3-9-1 0....(p) RoystonFfrench 6 73
(Ismail Mohammed) *chsd ldng pair: hdwy over 3f out: chal over 2f out: rdn to ld wl over 1f out: drvn ent fnl f: sn hdd and no ex towards fin* **25/1**
044 **3** *4 ½* **Badea**[17] 3614 3-9-1 72....(v[1]) TonyHamilton 7 66
(Richard Fahey) *t.k.h: cl up: disp ld 1/2-way: led 4f out: rdn 3f out: drvn and hdd wl over 1f out: sn wknd* **15/8**[1]
0-34 **4** *18* **Muhamee (IRE)**[46] 2668 3-9-1 70....(b[1]) SilvestreDeSousa 4 37
(Saeed Bin Suroor) *t.k.h: led: jnd after 3f: rdn along and hdd 4f out: sn drvn and wknd 3f out* **2/1**[2]
00 **5** *29* **Omega Omega**[19] 3551 3-8-10 0.... BrettDoyle 5
(Julia Feilden) *in tch: rdn along bef 1/2-way: sn outpcd and bhd* **16/1**

6 34 **Primacy (IRE)** 3-8-10 0 .... RobertHavlin 1
(Hughie Morrison) *s.i.s and sn rdn along: a in rr: bhd fr 1/2-way* **10/1**

00 7 24 **Spanish Trail**[7] 3946 3-8-3 0 .... DannyBrock(7) 2
(Christopher Kellett) *prom early: sn outpcd and in rr: bhd fr 1/2-way* **100/1**

2m 38.6s (-2.40) **Going Correction** -0.15s/f (Stan) **7** Ran SP% **110.1**
Speed ratings (Par 103): **102,101,98,86,67 44,28**
toteswingers 1&2 £9.90, 1&3 £2.00, 2&3 £5.10 CSF £70.55 TOTE £8.90: £2.40, £13.40; EX 55.40 Trifecta £322.90 Pool: 838.02 - 1.92 winning units..
Owner Brian Ellison & Chris Lowther **Bred** His Highness The Aga Khan's Studs S C **Trained** Norton, N Yorks

FOCUS
This looked a very moderate maiden that was run at a sound pace, with the field well strung out crossing the line. The form is not easy to assess but hasn't been rated too positively

4189 BET TOTEQUADPOT TEXT TOTE TO 89660 H'CAP 1m 3f (F)
7:00 (7:00) (Class 6) (0-65,65) 3-Y-O+ **£1,940** (£577; £288; £144) **Stalls** Low

Form RPR

6201 1 **Kingaroo (IRE)**[11] 3814 6-9-5 **56** .... LukeMorris 10 65
(Garry Woodward) *chsd ldr: rdn along over 3f out: swtchd rt wl over 1f out: styd on to ld jst over 1f out: drvn and hdd ins fnl f: rallied and edgd rt nr fin: led again nr line* **7/1**

-430 2 *hd* **Bring Sweets (IRE)**[38] 2926 5-9-2 **53** .... SilvestreDeSousa 3 62
(Brian Ellison) *hld up: stdy hdwy 4f out: chsd ldng pair and swtchd rt wl over 1f out: sn rdn: styd on to chal ent fnl f: drvn and slt ld last 100yds: hmpd and hdd nr line* **8/1**

0602 3 *8* **Yas Marina (USA)**[7] 3942 4-8-9 **46** .... (b) GrahamGibbons 8 41
(David O'Meara) *led and set str pce: rdn along and hung bdly lft 2f out: sn drvn: hdd appr fnl f: sn wknd* **7/2**[1]

121/ 4 *5* **Tyrana (GER)**[56] 575 9-9-7 **58** .... StevieDonohoe 5 44
(Ian Williams) *hld up towards rr: stdy hdwy over 4f out: rdn to chse ldrs 2f out: kpt on same pce* **13/2**

0-00 5 *4 1/2* **Caledonian Lad**[38] 2941 3-8-7 **55** .... RobertHavlin 13 33
(Hughie Morrison) *in tch: rdn along 4f out: plugged on same pce fnl 3f* **9/2**[2]

56-0 6 *1 3/4* **Nha Trang (IRE)**[39] 105 5-8-9 **46** oh1 .... (be[1]) LiamKeniry 12 20
(Michael Appleby) *prom: chsd ldr 1/2-way: rdn along over 4f out: sn wknd* **28/1**

0105 7 *shd* **Run Of The Day**[33] 3072 3-8-4 **57** .... AmyScott(5) 1 31
(Eve Johnson Houghton) *in rr tl sme late hdwy* **12/1**

0400 8 *6* **Magnitude**[46] 2669 7-8-9 **46** .... (p) RoystonFfrench 11
(Brian Baugh) *a in rr* **33/1**

054/ 9 *6* **Moonstreaker**[58] 3314 9-8-13 **50** .... MichaelStainton 4
(Charles Pogson) *a in rr* **25/1**

00-0 10 *20* **Thoroughly Red (IRE)**[22] 3440 7-8-11 **55** .... JacobButterfield(7) 9
(Suzzanne France) *in tch: rdn along 4f out: sn wknd* **40/1**

-400 11 *7* **Sweet Grace**[33] 3066 3-8-0 **48** .... (t) NickyMackay 7
(David Brown) *trckd ldrs: hdwy 5f out: rdn along over 3f out: sn wknd* **20/1**

-153 12 *19* **The Blue Dog (IRE)**[89] 1485 5-10-0 **65** .... GrahamLee 2
(Michael Wigham) *a in rr: bhd fnl 4f* **6/1**[3]

2m 27.42s (-0.58) **Going Correction** -0.15s/f (Stan)
WFA 3 from 4yo+ 11lb **12** Ran SP% **116.8**
Speed ratings (Par 101): **96,95,90,86,83 81,81,77,73,58 53,39**
CSF £56.72 CT £230.62 TOTE £7.40: £2.10, £3.20, £2.10; EX 53.60 Trifecta £247.90 Pool: 425.61 - 1.27 winning units..
Owner J Pownall **Bred** Kevin Walsh **Trained** Bolham, Notts

FOCUS
An open looking middle-distance handicap that was run at a fierce pace, with the front two pulling a long way clear, and fighting out a thrilling finish. The winner is rated pretty much to his old best.
Tyrana(GER) Official explanation: jockey said mare hung left-handed throughout
Magnitude Official explanation: jockey said gelding never travelled
The Blue Dog(IRE) Official explanation: vet said mare was found to be in season

4190 RACING POST FORM WITH TOTEPOOL MOBILE H'CAP 7f (F)
7:30 (7:30) (Class 4) (0-85,85) 4-Y-O+ **£4,075** (£1,212; £606; £303) **Stalls** Low

Form RPR

-422 1 **Mingun Bell (USA)**[22] 3439 5-9-6 **84** .... LiamKeniry 7 96
(Ed de Giles) *dwlt and in rr: pushed along 1/2-way: rdn to chse ldrs 2f out: drvn to ld 1f out: styd on* **15/8**[1]

202 2 *3 1/4* **Alpha Tauri (USA)**[14] 3731 6-9-2 **80** .... (t) RobbieFitzpatrick 4 83
(David C Griffiths) *led: rdn wl over 1f out: drvn and hdd 1f out: kpt on u.p* **11/2**[3]

1120 3 *hd* **George Benjamin**[22] 3439 5-8-7 **78** .... RyanWhile(7) 2 80
(Christopher Kellett) *chsd ldrs: hdwy wl over 2f out: rdn and ev ch wl over 1f out: drvn and kpt on same pce fnl f* **16/1**

0020 4 *1 1/2* **Snow Bay**[32] 3128 6-9-7 **85** .... AdrianNicholls 5 83
(David Nicholls) *racd wd: prom: effrt and cl up 2f out: sn rdn and ev ch tl wknd ent fnl f* **3/1**[2]

3006 5 *1 1/4* **Eastern Hills**[12] 3779 7-8-10 **74** .... (p) GrahamLee 6 69
(Alan McCabe) *towards rr: rdn along wl over 2f out: kpt on appr fnl f: n.d* **13/2**

0010 6 *1 1/4* **St Oswald**[4] 4042 4-8-9 **80** .... (v) RobertTart(7) 3 72
(Alan Bailey) *cl up: rdn over 2f out and ev ch tl drvn and wknd over 1f out* **8/1**

0060 7 *29* **Point North (IRE)**[11] 3812 5-9-6 **84** .... (p) GrahamGibbons 1
(John Balding) *chsd ldrs on inner: rdn along 1/2-way: sn wknd* **18/1**

1m 28.18s (-2.12) **Going Correction** -0.15s/f (Stan) **7** Ran SP% **110.8**
Speed ratings (Par 105): **106,102,102,100,98 97,64**
toteswingers 1&2 £1.60, 1&3 £5.70, 2&3 £4.80 CSF £11.75 CT £115.25 TOTE £3.10: £2.10, £2.00; EX 5.90 Trifecta £36.50 Pool: 823.94 - 16.70 winning units..
Owner Blackham And Gould Partnership **Bred** Paula W Cline **Trained** Ledbury, H'fords

FOCUS
This decent handicap was run at a strong gallop and it suited those coming from off this pace, although few landed a blow. The winner is rated up 9lb on recent turf form, with another solid effort from the second.

4191 PLAY GOLF AT SOUTHWELL GOLF CLUB CLAIMING STKS 6f (F)
8:00 (8:00) (Class 6) 2-Y-O **£2,045** (£603; £302) **Stalls** Low

Form RPR

541 1 **Lord Avonbrook**[34] 3019 2-8-8 0 .... RyanWhile(7) 1 66+
(Bill Turner) *mde all: rdn wl over 1f out: clr appr fnl f: styd on strly* **15/2**

2403 2 *5* **Fly Fisher (IRE)**[6] 3951 2-8-12 79 .... TonyHamilton 3 48
(Richard Fahey) *cl up: effrt 2f out: sn rdn and ev ch tl drvn and one pce appr fnl f* **7/2**[3]

2 3 *5* **Vegas Belle**[19] 3533 2-9-0 0 .... TomEaves 5 35
(Ollie Pears) *cl up on outer: effrt over 2f out and ev ch rdn wl over 1f out and sn one pce* **11/4**[2]

64 4 *9* **Northern Harbour (IRE)**[29] 3224 2-8-12 0 .... (p) SilvestreDeSousa 4 6
(J S Moore) *cl up: rdn along wl over 2f out: sn wknd* **8/1**

301 P **Lexi The Princess (IRE)**[57] 2338 2-8-10 73 .... GrahamLee 2
(Kevin Ryan) *cl up: rdn along and lost action after 2f: sn bhd and p.u 1/2-way: lame* **13/8**[1]

1m 16.76s (0.26) **Going Correction** -0.15s/f (Stan) **5** Ran SP% **109.9**
Speed ratings (Par 92): **92,85,78,66,**
CSF £32.47 TOTE £8.20: £2.80, £1.10; EX 30.60.Lord Avonbrook was claimed by Mr A. Crook for £10,000.
Owner Mrs M S Teversham **Bred** Mrs Monica Teversham **Trained** Sigwells, Somerset

FOCUS
A weakish claimer run at a decent pace, with the field well strung out crossing the line. The form is rated negatively.

NOTEBOOK
Lord Avonbrook, an easy winner of a weak 5f Beverley claimer last time, looked to face a tough task in a better race here off top weight, but stepped up on that effort and ran out a convincing winner. The form of these juvenile claimers can often be misleading but the winner is clearly in good heart and is open to more improvement. He was claimed by Andy Crook for £10,000 (op 8-1 tchd 7-1)
Fly Fisher(IRE) raced up with the pace but found little for pressure on his first AW start and is becoming disappointing. (op 9-2)
Vegas Belle showed some promise when runner-up in a Newcastle maiden on her debut and again ran well enough for a yard which is yet to hit form this season. She may be more of a handicap project. (tchd 10-3)
Northern Harbour(IRE) ran better with cheekpieces applied at Windsor last time and again showed pace here, before weakening. He has now qualified for a mark. (op 7-1)
Lexi The Princess(IRE) was always struggling in behind the other runners and was pulled up some way out. Graham Lee reported that the filly lost her action, afterwards the veterinary officer reported she was lame. Official explanation: jockey said filly lost its action; vet said filly finished lame (tchd 11-8)

4192 ANCHOR INN WORKSOP H'CAP 7f (F)
8:30 (8:30) (Class 6) (0-60,60) 3-Y-O+ **£1,976** (£583; £292) **Stalls** Low

Form RPR

6000 1 **Monzino (USA)**[8] 3913 4-9-12 **60** .... RussKennemore 4 69
(Michael Chapman) *towards rr: hdwy over 2f out: rdn to chse ldrs whn swtchd rt over 1f out: str run ent fnl f: led last 50yds* **12/1**

43-0 2 *1 1/4* **Royal Holiday (IRE)**[33] 2239 5-9-8 **56** .... (p) PhillipMakin 10 62
(Marjorie Fife) *cl up: led after 2f: rdn over 2f out: drvn and hdd over 1f out: kpt on same pce fnl f* **33/1**

6433 3 *hd* **Rapid Water**[20] 3511 6-9-4 **52** .... (p) LukeMorris 6 57
(Pat Eddery) *in tch: hdwy to chse ldrs 3f out: effrt on inner to chal 2f out: rdn to ld appr fnl f: drvn: no ex and hdd last 50yds* **5/1**[3]

0-00 4 *1* **Boy The Bell**[21] 3460 5-9-5 **60** .... JacobButterfield(7) 13 63
(Ollie Pears) *cl up on outer: effrt 2f out: sn rdn and ev ch tl one pce ins fnl f* **9/1**

0000 5 *2* **Brailsford (IRE)**[19] 3548 3-9-3 **58** .... (v) RoystonFfrench 5 53
(Ismail Mohammed) *chsd ldrs: rdn along over 2f out: drvn and kpt on same pce appr fnl f* **22/1**

2205 6 *1* **Bonnie Prince Blue**[21] 3460 9-9-12 **60** .... (b) GrahamLee 8 55
(Ian McInnes) *bhd tl styd on fnl 2f: nrst fin* **15/2**

-003 7 *2* **This Ones For Eddy**[70] 1961 7-9-9 **57** .... GrahamGibbons 1 46
(John Balding) *nvr bttr than midfield* **7/1**

2132 8 *3 3/4* **Jonnie Skull (IRE)**[7] 3950 6-9-2 **57** .... (vt) DannyBrock(7) 9 36
(Phil McEntee) *led 2f: cl up: rdn along wl over 2f out: sn drvn and grad wknd* **10/3**[1]

0000 9 *3* **Ace Of Spies (IRE)**[7] 3941 7-9-12 **60** .... KirstyMilczarek 3 31
(Conor Dore) *nvr bttr than midfield* **20/1**

6050 10 *3* **Alabanda (IRE)**[18] 3555 3-9-3 **58** .... TedDurcan 12 19
(Tim Easterby) *in tch: rdn along wl over 2f out: n.d* **4/1**[2]

0/0- 11 *9* **Eye For The Girls**[402] 2920 6-8-11 **50** .... (t) DavidKenny(5) 11
(William Knight) *chsd ldrs on outer: rdn along wl over 2f out: sn wknd* **33/1**

0/00 12 *9* **King's Sabre**[6] 3964 6-9-5 **53** .... (p) KellyHarrison 7
(John Spearing) *s.i.s: a bhd* **40/1**

1m 29.48s (-0.82) **Going Correction** -0.15s/f (Stan)
WFA 3 from 4yo+ 7lb **12** Ran SP% **119.1**
Speed ratings (Par 101): **98,96,96,95,92 91,89,85,81,78 68,57**
toteswingers 1&2 £101.20, 1&3 £32.50, 2&3 £36.00 CSF £364.20 CT £2271.72 TOTE £17.90: £4.20, £14.00, £1.20; EX 872.70 TRIFECTA Not won..
Owner Mrs M Chapman **Bred** Pillar Property Services Inc **Trained** Market Rasen, Lincs

FOCUS
A competitive handicap run at a sound pace, with the winner the only one able to close from off the pace. The winner is likely to prove better on the AW than on turf.
Monzino(USA) Official explanation: trainer said, regarding apparent improvement in form, that the gelding appears better suited by the all-weather surface.
Jonnie Skull(IRE) Official explanation: jockey said gelding never travelled

4193 MEMBERSHIP AVAILABLE AT SOUTHWELL GOLF CLUB H'CAP 1m (F)
9:00 (9:00) (Class 6) (0-60,65) 3-Y-O+ **£1,908** (£563; £281) **Stalls** Low

Form RPR

0-01 1 **Kung Hei Fat Choy (USA)**[7] 3939 3-9-10 **65** 6ex .... (b) GrahamLee 9 79+
(James Given) *sn cl up: chal over 2f out: rdn to ld 1 1/2f out: clr ins fnl f: styd on* **8/11**[1]

5205 2 *3 1/4* **Putin (IRE)**[21] 3470 4-8-9 **47** .... (bt) LeonnaMayor(5) 10 56
(Phil McEntee) *cl up: led after 2f: rdn and jnd over 2f out: drvn and hdd 1 1/2f out: kpt on: no ch w wnr* **12/1**[3]

3002 3 *9* **Smart Affair**[7] 3938 3-8-7 **48** .... (v) LukeMorris 13 34
(Alan Bailey) *s.i.s and bhd: hdwy over 3f out: wd st and rdn wl over 2f out: drvn and styd on to take poor 3rd appr fnl f* **5/1**[2]

0 4 *2 3/4* **Praxios**[53] 2441 4-9-7 **57** .... GaryBartley(3) 2 39
(Noel Wilson) *chsd ldrs on inner: rdn along and swtchd wd st: drvn and styd on fnl 2f: nrst fin* **33/1**

1560 5 *shd* **Hilbre Court (USA)**[1] 4142 7-9-6 **53** .... (v) DuranFentiman 4 34
(Brian Baugh) *led 2f: cl up: rdn wl over 2f out and sn wknd* **33/1**

1026 6 *1* **Titan Diamond (IRE)**[15] 3713 4-8-9 **47** .... RachealKneller(5) 1 26
(Mark Usher) *cl up on inner: rdn along over 3f out: sn wknd* **25/1**

6003 7 *3/4* **Godwit**[15] 3713 4-8-5 45 **45** .... JoshBaudains(7) 5 22
(Eugene Stanford) *chsd ldrs: rdn wl over 2f out: sn wknd* **16/1**

4553 8 *1/2* **Gazboolou**[7] 3949 8-9-4 **51** .... (t) FergusSweeney 7 27
(Henry Candy) *chsd ldrs: rdn along 3f out: drvn and wknd over 2f out* **14/1**

0-63 **9** 2 ½ **Orpen Wide (IRE)**[84] 1583 10-9-1 **48**....................(b) RussKennemore 11 19
(Michael Chapman) *dwlt:a towards rr* **25/1**
4046 **10** 12 **Avalon Bay**[118] 988 4-8-12 **48**................................ MatthewCosham(3) 8
(Pat Eddery) *dwlt: a in rr* **16/1**
-340 **11** 11 **Bond Blade**[22] 3442 4-9-0 **54**................................ JacobButterfield(7) 3
(Suzzanne France) *trckd ldrs: hdwy 3f out: rdn over 2f out: wknd qckly* **33/1**

1m 41.91s (-1.79) **Going Correction** -0.15s/f (Stan)
WFA 3 from 4yo+ 8lb **11** Ran SP% **117.2**
Speed ratings (Par 101): **102,98,89,87,86 85,85,84,82,70 59**
toteswingers 1&2 £3.50, 1&3 £1.80, 2&3 £3.60 CSF £9.71 CT £26.97 TOTE £2.00: £1.20, £1.80, £1.10; EX 11.00 Trifecta £28.30 Pool: 1,161.88 - 30.36 winning units..
Owner Danethorpe Racing Partnership **Bred** Gilgai Farm **Trained** Willoughton, Lincs
FOCUS
An uncompetitive handicap run at a sound gallop, where again it paid to race up with the pace, with the front two pulling a long way clear. A weak race, but the winner confirmed last week's C&D romp.
T/Plt: £663.50 to a £1 stake. Pool: £67217.74 - 73.95 winning tickets T/Qpdt: £44.50 to a £1 stake. Pool: £7662.93 - 127.25 winning tickets JR

3973 YARMOUTH (L-H)
Tuesday, July 17

OFFICIAL GOING: Soft (6.4)
Wind: fairly light, across Weather: dry

4194 IRISH STALLION FARMS E B F / 4HEAD MAIDEN STKS 7f 3y
5:50 (5:51) (Class 5) 2-Y-O **£3,234** (£962; £481; £240) **Stalls** Centre

Form RPR
5 **1** **Makafeh**[24] 3397 2-9-3 0.. KierenFallon 6 76+
(Luca Cumani) *t.k.h: chsd ldrs: ev ch wl over 1f out: rdn and chsd ldr jst over 1f out: looked hld ins fnl f: styd on gamely fnl 100yds to ld cl home* **5/1**[3]
2 ½ **Huntsmans Close** 2-9-3 0.. JamieSpencer 4 76+
(Michael Bell) *t.k.h: hld up in tch in rr: hdwy to join ldrs on bit over 1f out: pushed into ld jst over 1f out: rdn ins fnl f: hdd cl home and eased last strides* **5/2**[1]
5 **3** ¾ **Disclaimer**[17] 3634 2-9-3 0.. TomQueally 9 73
(Sir Henry Cecil) *t.k.h: sn chsng ldr: led 2f out: sn rdn: hdd and sltly outpcd jst over 1f out: rallied and kpt on again fnl 75yds* **5/2**[1]
4 1 ¼ **Hazzaat (IRE)** 2-9-3 0.. NeilCallan 1 70+
(Roger Varian) *rn green: t.k.h: chsd ldrs: j. path over 5f out: rdn and unable qck ent fnl f: styd on same pce after* **3/1**[2]
0 **5** 3 **Jawinski (IRE)**[20] 3505 2-9-3 0.. AndreaAtzeni 5 62+
(David Evans) *in tch in rr: rdn over 2f out: outpcd 2f out: rallied and styd on again ins fnl f: no ch w ldrs* **66/1**
6 ½ **Lamusawama** 2-9-3 0.. PaulHanagan 7 61
(Ed Dunlop) *hld up in tch: rdn over 2f out: outpcd wl over 1f out: no threat to ldrs but plugged on fnl f* **25/1**
5 **7** 1 ¾ **Persian Wave**[11] 3824 2-9-3 0.. MartinDwyer 2 57
(James Tate) *led at stdy gallop tl rdn and hdd 2f out: sn outpcd u.p: wknd ent fnl f* **12/1**
8 1 ¾ **Topamichi** 2-8-12 0..(b¹) HarryPoulton(5) 8 52
(Mark H Tompkins) *s.i.s: in tch in rr: swtchd lft and hdwy to press ldr over 4f out: rdn and wandered u.p 2f out: sn wknd* **66/1**

1m 29.94s (3.34) **Going Correction** +0.15s/f (Good) **8** Ran SP% **113.3**
Speed ratings (Par 94): **86,85,84,83,79 79,77,75**
toteswingers 1&2 £2.50, 1&3 £2.10, 2&3 £2.40 CSF £17.57 TOTE £3.10: £1.10, £1.80, £1.10; EX 18.60.
Owner Sheikh Mohammed Obaid Al Maktoum **Bred** Highclere Stud And Floors Farming **Trained** Newmarket, Suffolk
FOCUS
Course at full width and distances as advertised. This looked a decent juvenile maiden and the first four all rate useful prospects. Kieren Fallon said afterwards it was good ground ground, while Neil Callan claimed it was dead and patchy.
NOTEBOOK
Makafeh advertised the clear benefit of his Newmarket debut last month and got off the mark in cosy fashion. He knew much more this time and was always up there, but had to dig deep from the furlong marker. Kieren Fallon got him up near the line as he found a second wind, though, and he looked to score with something left in the tank. There's a strong chance that he'll appreciate better ground and he looks a lovely prospect for races over 1m-1m2f at three, but there could well be a nice pot in him this year too. (op 11-2 tchd 6-1)
Huntsmans Close ◆, well backed, very nearly made a winning introduction. He cruised through the race and eased to the front 1f out. However, he probably got there a little too soon as the line came that bit too late in the day as the winner mugged him. Going better in something similar should prove a formality and perhaps a drop back to 6f would prove ideal in the short term, seeing as his dam won over that trip at two. (op 3-1 tchd 7-2)
Disclaimer again ran green and shaped as though this trip is on the sharp side, as he did on his debut at Newmarket 17 days earlier. He ought to be winning when faced with a stiffer test. (op 9-4)
Hazzaat(IRE)'s stable made it 7-10 juvenile winners for the year at Windsor the previous evening and this son of Ifraaj was unsurprisingly well backed to enhance that tally. He proved far too green to do himself full justice, though, and didn't appear to be liking the ground. Better can be expected next time out. Official explanation: trainer's rep said colt was struck into (op 7-2 tchd 4-1 and 11-4)
Jawinski(IRE) improved a good deal on his debut over 6f at Salisbury 20 days earlier and relished this extra furlong. Indeed he looks as though 1m will suit before long and he is one to keep an eye on. (op 50-1)

4195 DIOMED DEVELOPMENTS (S) NURSERY 7f 3y
6:20 (6:21) (Class 6) 2-Y-O **£1,617** (£481; £240; £120) **Stalls** Centre

Form RPR
405 **1** **Warrant Officer**[12] 3770 2-9-2 **62**.. MartinHarley 1 62
(Mick Channon) *chsd ldrs: rdn and ev ch 3f out: led ent fnl f: hrd drvn and hld on fnl 150yds: all out* **4/1**[3]
602 **2** nk **Blades Rose**[28] 3251 2-8-11 **57**.. PaulHanagan 5 56
(Richard Fahey) *led for over 1f: chsd ldrs after: rdn and edging lft fr 2f out: ev ch ins fnl f: hld hd high and nt qckn u.p fnl 100yds* **2/1**[1]
6203 **3** shd **Strawberry Duck (IRE)**[12] 3789 2-8-6 **52**........................ HayleyTurner 2 51
(Amy Weaver) *in tch: rdn 3f out: outpcd and looked btn wl over 1f out: rallied ent fnl f: ev ch fnl 100yds: kpt on* **7/1**
0503 **4** 4 ½ **Maypole Joe (IRE)**[33] 3084 2-8-5 **51**.. AndreaAtzeni 8 39
(David Evans) *in tch: rdn wl over 1f out: unable qck and sn struggling: plugged on but no threat to ldrs fnl f* **7/2**[2]
6200 **5** 1 ¼ **Alexandrakollontai (IRE)**[10] 3858 2-8-10 **56**............(p) JamieSpencer 3 41
(J S Moore) *early reminders and sn rdn to join ldr: led over 5f out: rdn over 3f out: edging lft u.p over 1f out: hdd ent fnl f: btn ins fnl f: eased fnl 100yds* **8/1**
005 **6** 27 **Myzamour**[29] 3224 2-8-10 **56**.. NeilCallan 7
(J S Moore) *dwlt: rdn along thrght and nvr gng wl: a bhd: lost tch 3f out: t.o* **8/1**

1m 30.8s (4.20) **Going Correction** +0.15s/f (Good) **6** Ran SP% **110.3**
Speed ratings (Par 92): **82,81,81,76,74 44**
toteswingers 1&2 £3.30, 1&3 £4.60, 2&3 £2.00 CSF £11.99 CT £48.42 TOTE £4.30: £2.50, £1.10; EX 8.90.There was no bid for the winner.
Owner Insignia Racing (Emblem) **Bred** Bambi Bloodstock **Trained** West Ilsley, Berks
FOCUS
This weak nursery threw up a tight three-way finish. The winner progressed a little.
NOTEBOOK
Warrant Officer ran out a gutsy winner. Mick Channon's colt had something to prove on this ground, but it was a significant drop in class on his handicap debut and that did the trick. He was there to be shot at throughout the final furlong, but was always just doing enough and evidently stays well. (tchd 9-2)
Blades Rose bumped into one in a 6f seller at Thirsk last time, but this was much easier for her and she ran a big race up in trip. No doubt she can be placed to strike soon enough. (op 5-2 tchd 7-4)
Strawberry Duck(IRE)'s two previous best efforts came over 6f on much quicker ground here. She looked to need every yard of this longer trip, however, and was only just held. (op 5-1)
Maypole Joe(IRE) finished third in a quick-ground C&D seller last month. He got badly outpaced before keeping on late. (tchd 10-3 and 4-1)
Alexandrakollontai(IRE) Official explanation: jockey said filly had no more to give
Myzamour Official explanation: trainer's rep said filly was in season

4196 AEROPAK H'CAP 6f 3y
6:50 (6:51) (Class 6) (0-60,60) 3-Y-O+ **£1,617** (£481; £240; £120) **Stalls** Centre

Form RPR
4441 **1** **Novalist**[22] 3442 4-9-5 **55**..(b) J-PGuillambert 14 66
(Robin Bastiman) *led: rdn 2f out: clr w runner-up ent fnl f: hdd ins fnl f: battled on u.p to ld again towards fin* **6/1**[2]
6363 **2** nk **Represent (IRE)**[20] 3489 3-9-5 **60**.. MartinHarley 15 69
(Mick Channon) *taken down early: hdwy to chse ldrs after 1f: chsd wnr over 3f out: rdn 2f out: ev ch and clr w wnr ent fnl f: hrd drvn to ld ins fnl f: hdd and no ex towards fin* **5/1**[1]
5030 **3** 4 **Anjomarba (IRE)**[7] 3943 5-9-6 **56**..............................(b) HayleyTurner 16 53
(Conor Dore) *dwlt: bhd: rdn and struggling 3f out: styd on wl fnl f: no ch w ldrs* **9/1**
35 **4** ¾ **Basle**[7] 3949 5-9-9 **59**..(t) NeilCallan 8 54
(Gay Kelleway) *in tch in midfield: rdn and effrt over 2f out: 3rd and no imp over 1f out: styd on same pce* **6/1**[2]
0206 **5** 4 **Jemimaville (IRE)**[14] 3718 5-8-10 **46** oh1........................ LiamJones 11 28
(Giles Bravery) *in tch in midfield: rdn and struggling over 2f out: wknd over 1f out* **40/1**
0251 **6** 1 **Mucky Molly**[14] 3718 4-9-2 **52**.. WilliamCarson 4 31
(Olivia Maylam) *in tch: rdn and struggling ent fnl 2f: wl btn over 1f out* **5/1**[1]
005 **7** ½ **Whiskey Junction**[34] 3052 8-9-4 **54**.. KierenFallon 5 31
(Michael Quinn) *chsd ldrs: rdn over 2f out: sn struggling and wl btn over 1f out* **11/1**
6035 **8** nse **Red Rhythm**[22] 3435 5-8-13 **49**.. TomQueally 1 26
(David Evans) *taken down early: t.k.h: hld up in midfield: rdn over 2f out: sn struggling and wl btn over 1f out* **15/2**[3]
0000 **9** shd **Shamakat**[29] 3218 3-8-13 **54**.. MartinLane 3 30
(Rae Guest) *bhd: struggling 3f out: n.d fnl 2f* **33/1**
0050 **10** 3 ¾ **Rasteau (IRE)**[19] 3546 4-8-3 **46** oh1........................ NoelGarbutt(7) 2
(Tom Keddy) *sn rdn along in rr: wl btn fnl 2f* **50/1**
0005 **11** ½ **Harry Lime**[6] 3974 4-8-10 **46**..(b¹) AndreaAtzeni 7
(Chris Dwyer) *in tch in midfield: rdn and struggling 3f out: wknd 2f out* **28/1**
30-0 **12** 8 **Tribouley**[14] 3735 4-9-7 **57**.. ShaneKelly 12
(Dean Ivory) *chsd ldr tl over 3f out: sn lost pl and hung lft wl bhd and eased fnl f* **16/1**
2346 **13** 5 **Fonterutoli (IRE)**[21] 3471 5-9-4 **54**..............................(v) PaulHanagan 10
(Roger Ingram) *bhd: hdwy to chse ldrs 4f out: wknd over 2f out: wl bhd and eased fnl f* **9/1**

1m 15.11s (0.71) **Going Correction** +0.15s/f (Good)
WFA 3 from 4yo+ 5lb **13** Ran SP% **118.7**
Speed ratings (Par 101): **101,100,95,94,88 87,86,86,86,81 81,70,63**
toteswingers 1&2 £6.40, 1&3 £10.70, 2&3 £10.00 CSF £34.79 CT £222.91 TOTE £6.20: £2.00, £2.00, £3.30; EX 27.20.
Owner Ms M Austerfield **Bred** Whitsbury Manor Stud **Trained** Cowthorpe, N Yorks
■ Stewards' Enquiry : J-P Guillambert two-day ban: used whip above permitted level (Jul 31, Aug 2)
FOCUS
A wide-open sprint handicap. Sound form for the class with the first two clear.

4197 IBULEVE H'CAP 5f 43y
7:20 (7:20) (Class 5) (0-70,65) 3-Y-O **£2,264** (£673; £336; £168) **Stalls** Centre

Form RPR
0622 **1** **One Kool Dude**[12] 3791 3-9-2 **60**..............................(v) JamieSpencer 1 70
(Michael Bell) *mde all: rdn over 1f out: pressed ins fnl f: fnd ex u.p and styd on wl* **13/8**[1]
3210 **2** ½ **Ooi Long**[12] 3791 3-8-10 **59**..............................(t) TobyAtkinson(5) 4 67
(Mark Rimmer) *t.k.h: hld up in tch: rdn and effrt to chse wnr jst over 1f out: swtchd lft and pressed wnr ins fnl f: kpt on but hld fnl 100yds* **7/1**
0201 **3** 5 **Seventeen Seventy**[20] 3489 3-9-6 **64**........................ FrankieMcDonald 2 54
(Alan Coogan) *chsd ldrs: rdn and hung lft 2f out: stl hanging and outpcd ent fnl f: hld on for 3rd but no ch w ldng pair fnl f* **7/2**[2]
-164 **4** nk **Pettochside**[20] 3488 3-9-7 **65**.. WilliamCarson 3 54
(Stuart Williams) *hld up in tch: effrt to chse ldrs ent fnl 2f: drvn and no ex over 1f out: outpcd by ldrs and btn 1f out: plugged on* **6/1**
-406 **5** 1 **Uncle Timmy**[28] 3245 3-9-0 **58**..............................(t) AndreaAtzeni 5 44
(David Evans) *chsd ldr tl unable qck over 1f out: outpcd by ldng pair and btn 1f out: plugged on* **5/1**[3]
-610 **6** 1 ¾ **Sarah Berry**[19] 3547 3-9-0 **58**.. LiamJones 6 37
(Chris Dwyer) *chsd ldrs: rdn and struggling over 2f out: wknd over 1f out* **10/1**

1m 4.01s (1.31) **Going Correction** +0.15s/f (Good) **6** Ran SP% **112.9**
Speed ratings (Par 100): **95,94,86,85,84 81**
toteswingers 1&2 £2.80, 1&3 £1.20, 2&3 £4.20 CSF £13.77 TOTE £1.80: £1.10, £4.20; EX 10.60.
Owner M L W Bell Racing Ltd **Bred** Catridge Farm Stud Ltd **Trained** Newmarket, Suffolk

FOCUS
A moderate 3-y-o sprint handicap where two came well clear. The winner is rated a length off his 2yo best. Again the action came down the centre of the track.

4198 FREEDERM H'CAP 1m 1f
7:50 (7:52) (Class 6) (0-55,58) 3-Y-O £1,617 (£481; £240; £120) Stalls Low

Form RPR
0-40 **1** **Norfolk Sky**34 3052 3-8-7 45 PaulHanagan 6 53
(Chris Wall) *chsd ldrs: wnt 2nd over 4f out: rdn over 2f out: pressed ldr 1f out: drvn and sustained chal fnl f to ld last strides* 8/1

6000 **2** *shd* **Goodie Goodie**6 3965 3-8-12 50 (t) MartinDwyer 8 57
(Sylvester Kirk) *sn led: rdn wl over 1f out: drvn and battled on wl fnl f tl hdd and no ex last strides* 18/1

236 **3** *1* **Thecornishcowboy**6 3966 3-9-1 53 (t) JimmyQuinn 1 58
(John Ryan) *hld up in tch towards rr: swtchd rt and hdwy 3f out: rdn to chse ldrs 2f out: pressed ldrs and hrd drvn jst ins fnl f: no ex fnl 50yds* 9/2²

0033 **4** *1 ¾* **Love Grows Wild (USA)**5 4006 3-9-0 52 (v) HayleyTurner 3 53
(Michael Bell) *t.k.h: chsd ldr tl 4f out: rdn and nt qckn over 1f out: styd on same pce ins fnl f* 7/1

60-0 **5** *6* **Siberian Belle (IRE)**71 1916 3-8-10 48 PatrickMathers 4 36
(Richard Fahey) *chsd ldrs: rdn and effrt over 2f out: 5th and no imp u.p over 1f out: wknd fnl f* 22/1

0040 **6** *1 ½* **Ossie's Dancer**34 3023 3-8-7 45 AndreaAtzeni 2 30
(Robert Cowell) *chsd ldrs: rdn and effrt over 2f out: 6th and btn over 1f out: wknd fnl f* 18/1

0-06 **7** *1 ½* **Connishka**22 3454 3-8-13 51 LiamJones 9 32
(Alan Bailey) *sn bustled along: in tch: outpcd u.p 3f out: no ch wl over 1f out* 17/2

000 **8** *2 ¾* **Roman Around**12 3786 3-8-8 46 (v¹) ShaneKelly 11 21
(William Knight) *hld up in last pair: rdn and fnd little over 2f out: sn btn* 33/1

3200 **9** *3* **Stag Hill (IRE)**16 3665 3-9-2 54 WilliamBuick 10 23
(Sylvester Kirk) *in tch in midfield: rdn and fnd little 3f out: wknd ent fnl 2f* 5/1³

0540 **10** *shd* **Majestic South**14 3717 3-9-1 53 MartinHarley 12 22
(Mick Channon) *hld up in tch in rr: effrt u.p 3f out: no prog ent fnl 2f: sn wknd* 14/1

-001 **11** *8* **Al Karlovyyh (IRE)**6 3978 3-9-3 58 6ex RyanPowell(3) 7
(Clive Brittain) *in tch: rdn and struggling over 3f out: sn btn: bhd fnl f* 4/1¹

-230 **12** *9* **Green Mountain (IRE)**26 3315 3-8-4 45 (t) AdamBeschizza(3) 5
(Philip McBride) *in tch in midfield: rdn and fnd little 3f out: sn lost pl: wl bhd fnl f: t.o* 20/1

1m 57.86s (2.06) **Going Correction** +0.075s/f (Good) 12 Ran SP% **118.2**
Speed ratings (Par 98): **93,92,92,90,85 83,82,80,77,77 70,62**
toteswingers 1&2 £11.90, 1&3 £7.00, 2&3 £25.10 CSF £138.12 CT £742.04 TOTE £6.00: £2.20, £8.70, £2.20; EX 191.50.
Owner FarandWide Partners **Bred** Farmers Hill Stud **Trained** Newmarket, Suffolk

FOCUS
This weak 3-y-o handicap was run at a fair pace, but still it proved hard work from off the pace and the first four dominated from 2f out. The first two oth ran their best races so far.
Al Karlovyyh(IRE) Official explanation: trainer's rep had no explanation for the poor form shown

4199 ADIOS H'CAP 1m 2f 21y
8:20 (8:20) (Class 4) (0-85,83) 3-Y-O+ £4,075 (£1,212; £606; £303) Stalls Low

Form RPR
1202 **1** **Spirit Of The Law (IRE)**31 3156 3-9-1 80 PaulHanagan 2 90
(Ed Dunlop) *racd keenly: mde all: rdn and qcknd 2f out: clr and styd on wl after: eased cl home* 7/4¹

1164 **2** *2 ¼* **Tilsworth Glenboy**40 2857 5-9-9 78 FrederikTylicki 8 83
(J R Jenkins) *hld up towards rr of main gp: hdwy on inner 4f out: swtchd rt and chsd clr wnr wl over 1f out: kpt on but no imp* 8/1

1-64 **3** *1 ½* **Miss Blink**47 2620 5-9-2 71 J-PGuillambert 9 73
(Robin Bastiman) *hld up towards rr: hdwy 3f out: rdn and chsd ldng pair wl over 1f out: kpt on but no imp after* 9/1

-104 **4** *½* **Twelve Strings (IRE)**38 2942 3-8-10 75 KierenFallon 10 76
(Luca Cumani) *in tch: rdn 5f out: swtchd rt and outpcd 3f out: rallied u.p over 1f out: kpt on fnl f* 7/2²

-103 **5** *½* **Miss Aix**35 3013 4-10-0 83 HayleyTurner 11 83
(Michael Bell) *v.s.a: bhd: clsd 4f out: swtchd rt and rdn 3f out: styd on fnl f: nvr trbld ldrs* 18/1

0165 **6** *4 ½* **Amoya (GER)**18 3594 5-9-9 78 MircoMimmocchi 1 69
(Philip McBride) *chsd ldrs tl wnt 2nd 6f out tl wl over 1f out: sn wknd* 28/1

5-04 **7** *7* **Antarctic (IRE)**18 3594 4-9-6 75 (b) WilliamBuick 5 52
(John Gosden) *in tch in midfield: rdn and fnd little ent fnl 2f: sn wknd* 7/1³

1066 **8** *6* **Blades Lad**23 3417 3-8-7 72 PatrickMathers 6 37
(Richard Fahey) *in tch: rdn and lost pl 3f out: wknd over 2f out* 22/1

0400 **9** *½* **Audacious**18 3574 4-8-11 71 TobyAtkinson(5) 4 35
(Michael Quinn) *chsd ldr tl 6f out: lost pl and bhd 3f out* 66/1

10 **10** *56* **Marine Girl**38 2942 3-8-10 75 TomQueally 7
(Sir Henry Cecil) *in tch tl 4f out: sn bhd: virtually p.u fnl 2f: t.o* 11/1

2m 9.96s (-0.54) **Going Correction** +0.075s/f (Good)
WFA 3 from 4yo+ 10lb 10 Ran SP% **115.1**
Speed ratings (Par 105): **105,103,102,101,101 97,92,87,86,42**
toteswingers 1&2 £2.80, 1&3 £4.70, 2&3 £6.70 CSF £15.99 CT £99.43 TOTE £3.70: £1.30, £2.50, £3.40; EX 16.80.
Owner R J Arculli **Bred** Georgestown Stud **Trained** Newmarket, Suffolk

FOCUS
A modest handicap where the winner dictated as he pleased. He's rated up 4lb.

4200 BAZUKA H'CAP 1m 6f 17y
8:50 (8:51) (Class 5) (0-70,67) 3-Y-O+ £2,264 (£673; £336; £168) Stalls Centre

Form RPR
0623 **1** **News Show**6 3968 3-8-12 65 MartinLane 7 82
(David Simcock) *stdd s: hld up in tch: hdwy to trck ldrs 4f out: rdn to ld ent fnl 2f: drvn and clr 1f out: styd on strly* 3/1¹

1255 **2** *9* **Quixote**33 3087 3-8-13 66 KierenFallon 6 70
(Clive Brittain) *in tch in last trio: pushed along and outpcd 5f out: styd on and hdwy over 2f out: chsd wnr u.p wl over 1f out: hung lft and btn 1f out: wknd ins fnl f* 11/2

5203 **3** *4 ½* **Lyric Poet (USA)**19 3552 5-9-12 65 (tp) WilliamCarson 1 63
(Anthony Carson) *chsd ldrs: nt clr run 4f out tl forced to switch arnd horses and drvn over 2f out: pressed ldrs 2f out: sn outpcd and wl btn 1f out* 3/1¹

545 **4** *4* **Authentication**14 3720 3-8-5 58 MircoDemuro 3 50
(Mark Johnston) *led: jnd and rdn 4f out: hdd 2f out: sn btn* 17/2

3203 **5** *17* **Chankillo**41 2818 3-8-8 61 PaulHanagan 5 29
(Mark H Tompkins) *t.k.h: chsd ldrs tl 4f out: sn struggling u.p: wl btn fnl 2f: eased ins fnl f: t.o* 4/1²

01/0 **6** *1* **Giant Sequoia (USA)**24 3400 8-9-9 62 DaraghO'Donohoe 2 29
(Barney Curley) *hld up in rr: struggling 5f out: wl bhd fnl 3f: eased ins fnl f: t.o* 66/1

03-0 **7** *4 ½* **Rishikesh**20 3484 4-10-0 67 JamieSpencer 4 28
(Michael Bell) *chsd ldr: rdn to chal 4f out tl ent fnl 2f: sn btn and bhd: eased fnl f: t.o* 5/1³

3m 9.89s (2.29) **Going Correction** +0.075s/f (Good)
WFA 3 from 4yo+ 14lb 7 Ran SP% **114.1**
Speed ratings (Par 103): **96,90,88,86,76 75,73**
toteswingers 1&2 £2.40, 1&3 £3.30, 2&3 £2.10 CSF £19.83 TOTE £5.70: £2.20, £1.90; EX 20.50.
Owner John Cook **Bred** Rabbah Bloodstock Limited **Trained** Newmarket, Suffolk
■ Stewards' Enquiry : William Carson one-day ban: careless riding (Jul 31)

FOCUS
An ordinary staying handicap. It proved a fair test and most were in trouble before 2f out. The winner produced a clear personal best.
T/Plt: £62.50 to a £1 stake. Pool: £69472.19 - 811.4 winning tickets T/Qpdt: £27.30 to a £1 stake. Pool: £6338.25 - 171.5 winning tickets SP

4201 - 4204a (Foreign Racing) - See Raceform Interactive

VICHY
Tuesday, July 17

OFFICIAL GOING: Turf: good to soft

4205a PRIX DES REVES D'OR - JACQUES BOUCHARA (LISTED RACE) (2YO) (TURF) 5f
1:20 (12:00) 2-Y-O £22,916 (£9,166; £6,875; £4,583; £2,291)

RPR
1 **Baileys Jubilee**17 3631 2-8-10 0 IoritzMendizabal 3 100
(Mark Johnston) *broke fast: settled in 2nd in slipstream of ldr: a gng wl: qcknd to ld 1f out: wnt clr: r.o wl fnl 100yds: comf* 23/10¹

2 *1 ½* **Faithfilly (IRE)**17 3604 2-8-10 0 MaximeGuyon 6 95
(Ed Walker) *broke wl: sn led travelling smoothly: hdd 1f out: rallied u.p ins fnl f to keep 2nd* 13/2³

3 *½* **Sorry Woman (FR)**9 2-8-10 0 FabriceVeron 8 93
(H-A Pantall, France) 73/10

4 *1* **Lasdramad (FR)**14 2-8-10 0 Jean-BaptisteHamel 1 89
(Y Durepaire, Spain) 10/1

5 *½* **Tipping Over (IRE)**17 3631 2-8-10 0 GeraldMosse 5 87
(Hugo Palmer) *outpcd fr s: styd on fnl f to go 5th but nvr a factor* 10/1

6 *½* **Tita Caty (FR)**4 2-8-10 0 StephanePasquier 2 86
(M Boutin, France) 10/1

7 *snk* **Style Boreale (FR)**19 2-8-10 0 RonanThomas 10 85
(J Heloury, France) 13/2³

8 *hd* **Thats Notall Folks (IRE)**8 3928 2-9-0 0 Christophe-PatriceLemaire 7 88
(F-H Graffard, France) 11/2²

9 *4* **Invincible Me (IRE)**9 2-8-10 0 Pierre-CharlesBoudot 9 70
(F-H Graffard, France) 47/1

10 *6* **Amicale (FR)** 2-8-10 0 (b) AnthonyTeissieux 4 48
(M Pimbonnet, France) 20/1

59.98s (59.98) 10 Ran SP% **118.5**
WIN (incl. 1 euro stake): 3.30. PLACES: 1.50, 2.10, 2.40. DF: 11.00. SF: 19.60.
Owner G R Bailey Ltd (Baileys Horse Feeds) **Bred** P And Mrs A G Venner **Trained** Middleham Moor, N Yorks

NOTEBOOK
Baileys Jubilee, third in the Empress Stakes last time out, travelled well in behind the leader and picked up well when asked to quicken. A speedy type, she could go for the Molecomb next, or perhaps the Prix de Cabourg at Deauville.
Faithfilly(IRE) made all at Sandown two starts back and tried to do the same again. She couldn't hold off the Mark Johnston-trained filly in the end but ran a sound race in defeat.
Tipping Over(IRE) found the trip too short and will appreciate returning to 6f.

3951 CATTERICK (L-H)
Wednesday, July 18

OFFICIAL GOING: Soft (6.7)
Wind: fairly strong half against Weather: mixture of sunshine and cloud

4206 ST TERESA'S HOSPICE NOVICE AUCTION STKS 7f
2:10 (2:10) (Class 5) 2-Y-O £2,264 (£673; £336) Stalls Centre

Form RPR
1 **1** **Lady Moonlight (IRE)**23 3436 2-8-8 71 GrahamLee 1 71
(Ann Duffield) *t.k.h early: trckd ldr: pushed along to chal over 1f out: rdn to ld ins fnl f: kpt on* 13/8²

21 **2** *¾* **Red Joker (IRE)**20 3520 2-9-3 0 PaulMulrennan 4 78
(Alan Swinbank) *led: rdn whn hdd ins fnl f: kpt on but a jst hld* 9/2³

1 **3** *7* **Silent Footsteps (IRE)**39 2923 2-9-3 0 TomEaves 3 63+
(Michael Dods) *trckd ldr on outer: pushed along and outpcd over 3f out: sn btn* 1/1¹

1m 30.48s (3.48) **Going Correction** +0.425s/f (Yiel) 3 Ran SP% **106.3**
Speed ratings (Par 94): **97,96,88**
CSF £7.04 TOTE £1.70; EX 7.40.
Owner M Wynne **Bred** Sean Madigan **Trained** Constable Burton, N Yorks

FOCUS
Top bend into home straight moved in 4yds to provide fresh ground. Only a handful of runners for this novice event but a fascinating race.

NOTEBOOK
Lady Moonlight(IRE) won in determined fashion to prove her 20-1 Thirsk success was no fluke. She had defied greenness when scoring on her debut last month, but she looked much wiser here and showed a good attitude. She travelled like the best horse, but did take a while to put the race to bed, rolling around under pressure in the testing conditions. She, like her two rivals, was tackling this trip for the first time and saw it out well. (op 15-8)
Red Joker(IRE) had been firmly put in his place by Silent Footsteps when they met at Newcastle, but he easily turned the tables on the disappointing favourite. Having won at Hamilton last time, he is improving and should continue to pay his way. (tchd 7-2)

Silent Footsteps(IRE) ran poorly. He was off the bridle from a very early stage and appeared ill-at-ease on the tight track. He had reportedly done well since making a winning introduction and it was worrying to see him beaten off before halfway. A return to a more galloping venue looks on the cards. Official explanation: trainer said gelding was unsuited by the track (op 10-11 tchd 11-10 in places)

4207 YORKSHIRE-OUTDOORS.CO.UK (S) STKS — 5f 212y
2:40 (2:42) (Class 6) 3-Y-O+ — **£1,704** (£503; £251) **Stalls** Low

Form — RPR

3301 **1** — **Red Cape (FR)**[28] 3276 9-9-6 70....(b) JamesSullivan 4 — 79
(Ruth Carr) *mde all: rdn 3 l clr over 1f out: drvn fnl f: hld on all out* **5/1**[3]

0U11 **2** ½ **Llewellyn**[37] 2972 4-8-13 72.... RyanWhile(7) 8 — 77
(Bill Turner) *dwlt: sn prom on outer: outpcd by wnr 2f out: kpt on fnl f* **6/4**[1]

0200 **3** ½ **Bay Of Fires (IRE)**[14] 3749 4-8-9 67....(p) TomEaves 6 — 65
(David O'Meara) *midfield: rdn and hdwy 2f out: kpt on* **10/1**

0 **4** 3¼ **China Excels**[19] 3561 5-9-0 0.... RussKennemore 7 — 59
(Sue Smith) *hld up in rr: pushed along and hdwy over 1f out: r.o wl fnl f: nrst fin* **150/1**

1510 **5** *nse* **Fol Hollow (IRE)**[6] 3993 7-9-6 73.... AdrianNicholls 12 — 65
(David Nicholls) *racd keenly: trckd ldr: rdn over 2f out: sn one pce: wknd ins fnl f: lost 4th post* **4/1**[2]

055 **6** 1½ **Northern Bolt**[15] 3730 7-9-0 65....(b) PatrickMathers 10 — 54
(Ian McInnes) *hld up in tch: rdn 1/2-way: bdly outpcd over 2f out: kpt on fnl f: nvr threatened* **12/1**

3042 **7** 3¼ **Middleton Flyer (IRE)**[20] 3540 3-8-4 62.... DuranFentiman 3 — 38
(Paul Midgley) *trckd ldrs: rdn over 2f out: wknd over 1f out* **6/1**

2616 **8** *shd* **Sophie's Beau (USA)**[22] 3463 5-9-6 53....(bt) GrahamLee 1 — 50
(Michael Chapman) *s.i.s: hld up: hdwy into midfield 1/2-way: wknd over 1f out* **50/1**

5 **9** 2 **Little Thief**[35] 3030 5-8-9 0.... LeeNewman 2 — 32
(Iain Jardine) *hld up in midfield: rdn over 2f out: sn wknd* **100/1**

10 11 **Keep Fighting** 4-8-10 0 ow1.... GrahamGibbons 5
(Tim Walford) *sn outpcd in rr: a bhd* **28/1**

1m 15.89s (2.29) **Going Correction** +0.425s/f (Yiel)
WFA 3 from 4yo+ 5lb — **10** Ran SP% **114.8**
Speed ratings (Par 101): **101,100,99,95,95 93,88,88,86,71**
toteswingers 1&2 £2.90, 2&3 £5.30, 1&3 £6.20 CSF £12.57 TOTE £4.20: £1.20, £1.50, £3.10; EX 16.30.There was no bid for the winner. Llewellyn was claimed by Mr D. Nicholls for £5,000.
Owner Middleham Park Racing LVI **Bred** Gilles And Mrs Forien **Trained** Huby, N Yorks

FOCUS
A fair seller, dominated by those that raced up with the pace.

4208 CATTERICKBRIDGE.CO.UK H'CAP — 5f
3:10 (3:10) (Class 4) (0-85,74) 3-Y-O — **£4,075** (£1,212; £606; £303) **Stalls** Low

Form — RPR

P-00 **1** — **Almond Branches**[18] 3613 3-9-1 **68**.... PJMcDonald 6 — 82
(George Moore) *hld up in tch: hdwy on outer 2f out: led appr fnl f: kpt on wl to go clr* **12/1**

5632 **2** 5 **Blue Shoes (IRE)**[7] 3954 3-8-9 **62**.... DavidAllan 5 — 58
(Tim Easterby) *chsd ldr: rdn over 2f out: kpt on: no ch w wnr* **11/4**[2]

6212 **3** 1¾ **Demora**[42] 2816 3-9-2 **69**.... TomEaves 4 — 59
(Michael Appleby) *chsd ldr: sltly short of room over 2f out: sn pushed along and outpcd: kpt on fnl f* **10/3**[3]

-231 **4** ¾ **Gowanharry (IRE)**[39] 2928 3-9-1 **68**....(t) PaulMulrennan 1 — 55
(Michael Dods) *briefly pushed along leaving stall: sn led: rdn whn hdd appr fnl f: wknd* **15/8**[1]

4-30 **5** 3¾ **Sunrise Dance**[18] 3623 3-9-7 **74**.... RobertWinston 2 — 48
(Robert Johnson) *chsd ldr: rdn over 2f out: wknd over 1f out* **14/1**

1130 **6** 8 **Laura's Bairn**[26] 3350 3-9-4 **71**....(v) FrederikTylicki 3 — 16
(J R Jenkins) *prom: rdn over 2f out: sn wknd: eased fnl f* **8/1**

1m 1.6s (1.80) **Going Correction** +0.425s/f (Yiel) — **6** Ran SP% **110.0**
Speed ratings (Par 102): **102,94,91,85,84 71**
toteswingers 1&2 £7.10, 1&3 £8.50, 2&3 £2.10 CSF £43.03 TOTE £12.20: £3.30, £1.20; EX 43.70.
Owner J A And M A Knox **Bred** J A And Mrs M A Knox **Trained** Middleham Moor, N Yorks

FOCUS
An interesting 3yo handicap, despite the small field, dominated by fillies.

4209 RACINGUK.COM CLAIMING STKS — 1m 3f 214y
3:40 (3:40) (Class 6) 3-Y-O+ — **£2,045** (£603; £302) **Stalls** Low

Form — RPR

2242 **1** — **Eijaaz (IRE)**[14] 3753 11-9-8 59....(p) PJMcDonald 2 — 62
(Geoffrey Harker) *hld up: rdn in 6th 3f out: gd hdwy 2f out: led 1f out: drvn 2 l clr bef idling towards fin* **11/2**

3630 **2** ½ **Zaplamation (IRE)**[27] 3307 7-9-3 62.... WilliamTwiston-Davies(7) 9 — 62
(John Quinn) *dwlt: sn midfield: pushed along over 3f out: trckd ldr whn briefly short of room over 2f out: led over 1f out: hdd 1f out: kpt on* **11/1**

2500 **3** 6 **Commander Veejay**[6] 3988 4-9-3 50....(p) JasonHart(7) 4 — 53
(Brian Rothwell) *trckd ldrs: rdn and outpcd over 2f out: plugged on fr over 1f out: no threat ldng pair* **50/1**

4351 **4** 1 **Elizabeth Coffee (IRE)**[26] 3355 4-9-9 73.... GrahamLee 8 — 50
(Ian Williams) *midfield: hdwy to trck ldrs 6f out: rdn to chal over 2f out: sn one pce* **15/8**[1]

2630 **5** 1½ **Tricksofthetrade (IRE)**[33] 3129 6-10-0 74....(p) RobertWinston 6 — 53
(Alan Swinbank) *trckd ldrs: led 3f out: rdn whn hdd over 1f out: grad wknd* **9/2**[3]

0-10 **6** 12 **Private Story (USA)**[29] 3241 5-9-12 80....(v[1]) DanielTudhope 1 — 31
(David O'Meara) *w ldr: led 9f out: rdn whn hdd 3f out: wknd fnl 2f* **9/4**[2]

4004 **7** 7 **Escape Artist**[28] 3277 5-9-8 45.... AndrewElliott 7 — 16
(David Thompson) *hld up: a bhd* **66/1**

050- **P** **Kathindi (IRE)**[218] 7743 5-9-2 30.... RobbieFitzpatrick 5
(Michael Chapman) *led: hdd over 9f out: remained prom tl lost pl qckly over 6f out: sn wl bhd: p.u over 2f out* **150/1**

2m 45.09s (6.19) **Going Correction** +0.425s/f (Yiel) — **8** Ran SP% **111.6**
Speed ratings (Par 101): **96,95,91,91,90 82,77,**
toteswingers 1&2 £4.00, 1&3 £17.90, 2&3 £18.10 CSF £58.19 TOTE £4.90: £1.90, £3.20, £10.70; EX 36.00.Elizabeth Coffee was claimed by Mr J. Weymes for £8,000.
Owner A S Ward **Bred** Shadwell Estate Company Limited **Trained** Thirkleby, N Yorks

FOCUS
Not many could be seriously fancied for this claimer and, with many of the market principals running below expectations, it was left to course-specialist Eijaaz to record a third win in this race.

Kathindi(IRE) Official explanation: trainer said gelding had a breathing problem

4210 AUGUST 17TH IS LADIES EVENING H'CAP — 1m 3f 214y
4:10 (4:12) (Class 5) (0-70,67) 3-Y-O — **£2,264** (£673; £336; £168) **Stalls** Low

Form — RPR

5352 **1** — **Red Tyke (IRE)**[35] 3023 3-8-4 **50**.... JimmyQuinn 13 — 60
(John Quinn) *trckd ldr: led over 2f out: sn drvn: strly pressed ins fnl f: hld on wl nr fin* **9/2**[2]

-065 **2** *nk* **Margo Channing**[16] 3697 3-8-4 **50**.... PJMcDonald 5 — 60
(Micky Hammond) *in tch: rdn over 3f out: hdwy to chal 2f out: upsides ins fnl f: kpt on: jst hld* **7/2**[1]

-001 **3** 3¼ **Fleeting Fashion**[35] 3023 3-8-4 **57**.... ShirleyTeasdale(7) 2 — 62
(Michael Appleby) *in tch: pushed along whn briefly short of room over 2f out: chsd ldng pair over 1f out: kpt on one pce* **7/2**[1]

-063 **4** 7 **Dr Irv**[30] 3212 3-8-6 **52**.... KellyHarrison 3 — 46
(Kate Walton) *hld up: pushed along 4f out: hdwy 3f out: short of room towards inner 2f out: no imp after* **8/1**[3]

060- **5** 1¾ **Sweet Fairnando**[326] 5464 3-8-13 **59**.... DavidAllan 7 — 50
(Tim Easterby) *hld up: pushed along over 3f out: nvr threatened* **8/1**[3]

3100 **6** 1½ **Fisher**[46] 2716 3-9-7 **67**.... AdrianNicholls 10 — 55
(David Nicholls) *trckd ldr: rdn over 2f out: wknd over 1f out* **8/1**[3]

0046 **7** 14 **Oops Caroline (IRE)**[15] 3729 3-8-3 **49**....(p) JamesSullivan 1 — 15
(David O'Meara) *trckd ldr: short of room and shuffled bk into midfield after 2f: rdn 4f out: sn wknd* **12/1**

0406 **8** 2 **Roughlyn**[21] 3483 3-8-7 **53** ow1....(v[1]) TomEaves 11 — 16
(Lisa Williamson) *sn led: rdn whn hdd over 2f out: wknd* **33/1**

000- **9** 2¾ **Willy McBay**[246] 7422 3-8-2 **48** oh3.... AndrewMullen 8
(George Moore) *hld up: a towards rr* **25/1**

2m 44.95s (6.05) **Going Correction** +0.425s/f (Yiel) — **9** Ran SP% **110.4**
Speed ratings (Par 100): **96,95,93,88,87 86,77,76,74**
toteswingers 1&2 £3.50, 1&3 £2.60, 2&3 £3.30 CSF £19.17 CT £56.56 TOTE £5.90: £1.90, £1.50, £1.20; EX 15.40.
Owner T G S Wood **Bred** Tally-Ho Stud **Trained** Settrington, N Yorks
■ Stewards' Enquiry : Jimmy Quinn two-day ban: used whip above permitted level (Aug 2-3)

FOCUS
Border Hill Jack was withdrawn after getting worked up in the stalls. This was a fair handicap, run at a steady pace.

4211 YORKSHIRE RACING SUMMER FESTIVAL MEDIAN AUCTION MAIDEN STKS — 7f
4:40 (4:40) (Class 6) 3-Y-O — **£2,045** (£603; £302) **Stalls** Centre

Form — RPR

-063 **1** — **Star City (IRE)**[41] 2865 3-9-3 63....(be[1]) PaulMulrennan 9 — 67
(Michael Dods) *led narrowly: rdn over 1f out 1f: hdd ins fnl f: rallied to ld again post* **5/1**

3-02 **2** *shd* **Eastlands Lad (IRE)**[14] 3751 3-9-3 63.... PJMcDonald 8 — 67
(Micky Hammond) *trckd ldr: rdn to ld narrowly ins fnl f: kpt on: hdd post* **7/2**[2]

340 **3** 3¾ **Admiralty**[23] 3447 3-9-3 72.... RoystonFfrench 10 — 57
(Ismail Mohammed) *trckd ldrs on outer: rdn 2f out: sn one pce* **9/2**[3]

6- **4** 1½ **Future Wonder (IRE)**[315] 5834 3-8-12 0.... ChrisCatlin 3 — 48+
(Rae Guest) *dwlt: hld up in rr: stl in last over 2f out: hdwy over 1f out: kpt on* **5/2**[1]

-555 **5** 1¾ **Landaho**[22] 3461 3-8-12 39.... JamesSullivan 6 — 44
(Hugh McWilliams) *hld up: pushed along over 2f out: kpt on: nvr threatened* **250/1**

-023 **6** ½ **Sabore**[35] 3024 3-8-12 72.... TonyHamilton 5 — 43
(Richard Fahey) *in tch: rdn over 2f out: sn one pce: wknd ins fnl f* **9/2**[3]

0 **7** 11 **Bandy Bob**[28] 3273 3-8-12 0.... GarryWhillans(5) 7 — 19
(Iain Jardine) *chsd ldrs: wknd over 2f out* **33/1**

00 **8** 13 **Connie Carlton**[9] 3913 3-8-12 0.... AndrewElliott 2
(David Thompson) *in tch: pushed along 1/2-way: sn wknd* **200/1**

0- **9** 4½ **Lollypop Lady**[387] 3452 3-8-12 0....(p) PhillipMakin 4
(Linda Perratt) *s.i.s: hld up in midfield: wknd over 2f out* **40/1**

-600 **10** 3 **Knight Vision**[19] 3567 3-9-3 62....(b[1]) AdrianNicholls 1
(David Nicholls) *t.k.h in midfield: wknd over 2f out: eased* **16/1**

1m 29.76s (2.76) **Going Correction** +0.425s/f (Yiel) — **10** Ran SP% **116.0**
Speed ratings (Par 98): **101,100,96,94,92 92,79,64,59,56**
toteswingers 1&2 £3.10, 1&3 £3.60, 2&3 £4.10 CSF £22.63 TOTE £5.70: £1.60, £1.10, £1.70; EX 28.00.
Owner Appleton Davison Dods **Bred** Michael Munnelly **Trained** Denton, Co Durham
■ Stewards' Enquiry : Paul Mulrennan two-day ban: used whip above permitted level (Aug 2-3)

FOCUS
Not a great deal of strength to this maiden, but it served up a thrilling finish with Star City just getting the verdict.
T/Plt: £106.20 to a £1 stake. Pool: £38938.16 - 267.58 winning tickets T/Qpdt: £16.10 to a £1 stake. Pool: £3237.32 -148.10 winning tickets AS

3965 LINGFIELD (L-H)
Wednesday, July 18

OFFICIAL GOING: Standard
Wind: medium, half behind Weather: overcast, dry

4212 LINGFIELD PARK LADIES EVENING 21ST JULY MAIDEN STKS (DIV I) — 1m (P)
2:00 (2:03) (Class 5) 3-4-Y-O — **£2,385** (£704; £352) **Stalls** High

Form — RPR

1 — **Royal Empire (IRE)** 3-9-3 0.... MickaelBarzalona 11 — 91+
(Saeed Bin Suroor) *hld up in midfield: rdn and hdwy over 2f out: chsd ldng pair over 1f out: str run to ld fnl 100yds: sn in command and gng away at fin* **5/4**[1]

6 **2** 2¼ **Gold Edition**[79] 1704 3-9-3 0....(v[1]) RyanMoore 9 — 82
(Jeremy Noseda) *led: increased gallop and clr 4f out: drvn and edgd rt over 1f out: hdd fnl 100yds: sn outpcd and btn: plugged on* **9/2**[2]

25 **3** 2 **Keyaadi**[60] 2273 3-9-3 0.... NeilCallan 10 — 77
(Roger Varian) *chsd ldr: drvn ent fnl 2f: hrd drvn and pressed ldr 1f out: outpcd by wnr and btn fnl 100yds: wknd towards fin* **5/1**[3]

3 **4** ½ **The Baronet**[12] 3809 3-9-3 0.... LukeMorris 12 — 76+
(Sir Mark Prescott Bt) *chsd ldrs: drvn and no imp 2f out: plugged on same pce fr over 1f out* **10/1**

4-0 **5** 7 **Mutasadder (USA)**[100] 1261 3-9-3 0....[1] PaulHanagan 1 — 59
(Roger Varian) *in tch: rdn and outpcd over 2f out: 5th and wknd over 1f out* **25/1**

0 **6** *nse* **Shahrazad (IRE)**[25] 3399 3-8-12 0 JamieMackay 8 54
(Patrick Gilligan) *hld up in last trio: pushed along over 3f out: sme hdwy and edging lft over 1f out: no imp and wl hld after* **150/1**

52 **7** *2 1/4* **Ukrainian Princess**[57] 2381 3-8-12 0 TomQueally 6 49
(Sir Henry Cecil) *t.k.h: in tch: rdn and struggling over 2f out: wknd wl over 1f out* **13/2**

0-0 **8** *1 1/4* **Simply**[19] 3565 3-8-12 0 WilliamCarson 4 46
(Eve Johnson Houghton) *dwlt: hld up in last trio: rdn and struggling 3f out: wknd wl over 1f out* **66/1**

9 *1 1/4* **Fly Haaf (IRE)** 3-9-3 0 JimCrowley 3 48
(William Knight) *dwlt: sn rcvrd and racd in midfield: rdn and struggling over 2f out: bhd over 1f out* **40/1**

0- **10** *7* **Pugnacious (IRE)**[396] 3182 3-9-3 0 SilvestreDeSousa 5 31
(Mark Johnston) *a towards rr: rdn and struggling in last over 3f out: lost tch 2f out* **25/1**

11 *12* **Cluaindubhloch (IRE)**[34] 4-9-11 0 KirstyMilczarek 7
(Tony Carroll) *t.k.h: hld up in tch in rr: rdn and struggling 3f out: sn lost tch: t.o* **100/1**

1m 38.1s (-0.10) **Going Correction** +0.075s/f (Slow)
WFA 3 from 4yo 8lb **11** Ran SP% **115.0**
Speed ratings (Par 103): **103,100,98,98,91 91,88,87,86,79 67**
toteswingers 1&2 £2.50, 1&3 £2.30, 2&3 £4.60 CSF £6.37 TOTE £2.50: £1.10, £1.50, £1.60; EX 9.00 Trifecta £40.70 Pool: 688.35 - 12.49 winning units..
Owner Godolphin **Bred** Twelve Oaks Stud **Trained** Newmarket, Suffolk

FOCUS
The market screamed that 200,000euros newcomer Royal Empire would make a winning introduction and he didn't disappoint, completing the task impressively.

4213 LINGFIELD PARK LADIES EVENING 21ST JULY MAIDEN STKS (DIV II) 1m (P)
2:30 (2:32) (Class 5) 3-4-Y-0 **£2,385** (£704; £352) **Stalls** High

Form RPR

62 **1** **Niger (IRE)**[41] 2865 3-9-3 0 WilliamBuick 11 78
(Jeremy Noseda) *sn chsng ldr: rdn and chal wl over 1f out: drvn to ld fnl 75yds: kpt on u.p* **6/4**[1]

50 **2** *nk* **Centrifugal (IRE)**[9] 3913 3-9-3 0 SilvestreDeSousa 10 77
(Mark Johnston) *led: rdn and hrd pressed wl over 1f out: hdd fnl 75yds: battled on gamely but a jst hld* **6/1**[3]

6 **3** *2 1/2* **Narcissist (IRE)**[15] 3735 3-9-3 0 GeorgeBaker 2 71
(Ed Dunlop) *broke wl: t.k.h: chsd ldng pair: rdn and effrt whn hung bdly lft over 1f out: no imp ins fnl f* **7/2**[2]

4 **4** *nk* **Iz She**[15] 3735 4-9-6 0 DarryllHolland 9 68
(William Knight) *taken down early: chsd ldng trio: rdn and sltly outpcd over 1f out: no threat to ldrs but kpt on again towards fin* **7/1**

5 *11* **Any Other Day** 3-8-12 0 JimCrowley 8 39
(William Knight) *in tch: lost pl and struggling u.p over 2f out: no ch over 1f out: plugged on to pass btn horses ins fnl f* **20/1**

6 *3/4* **Eamaadd** 3-9-3 0 NeilCallan 3 42+
(Roger Varian) *dwlt: in tch towards rr: rdn 5f out: hdwy into midfield over 2f out: outpcd and btn 2f out: wknd over 1f out* **15/2**

50 **7** *3/4* **Rowan Rhapsody**[17] 3666 3-8-12 0 PatCosgrave 1 36
(Jim Boyle) *in tch towards rr: rdn 4f out: struggling u.p over 2f out: wl btn fnl 2f* **100/1**

0-5 **8** *nk* **Clowance Keys**[100] 1256 3-9-3 0 JamesMillman 12 40
(Rod Millman) *in tch in midfield: rdn over 2f out: sn outpcd and btn 2f out: wknd over 1f out* **25/1**

0 **9** *1 3/4* **Suedehead**[58] 2344 3-8-12 0 MartinDwyer 5 31
(William Muir) *in tch in midfield: rdn and unable qck over 2f out: wknd wl over 1f out* **28/1**

5 **10** *12* **Friends Of Ama Gi**[194] 56 3-9-3 0 WilliamCarson 6
(Mark Hoad) *sn outpcd and pushed along in rr: lost tch 3f out* **66/1**

1m 38.42s (0.22) **Going Correction** +0.075s/f (Slow)
WFA 3 from 4yo 8lb **10** Ran SP% **115.3**
Speed ratings (Par 103): **101,100,98,97,86 86,85,85,83,71**
toteswingers 1&2 £3.40, 1&3 £2.20, 2&3 £5.10 CSF £10.19 TOTE £2.40: £1.10, £1.60, £1.70; EX 10.10 Trifecta £32.00 Pool: 776.88 - 17.94 winning units..
Owner Sir Robert Ogden **Bred** Tinnakill, F Craig & Cheveley Park Stud **Trained** Newmarket, Suffolk

FOCUS
This second division of the 1m maiden looked by some way weaker than the first. It paid to race handily and the first pair had it to themselves from the furlong marker.

4214 BREATHE SPA AT LINGFIELD MARRIOTT H'CAP 1m 4f (P)
3:00 (3:01) (Class 6) (0-60,60) 3-Y-O **£2,385** (£704; £352) **Stalls** Low

Form RPR

0404 **1** **Kaiser Wilhelm (IRE)**[21] 3483 3-8-13 52 (t) StevieDonohoe 8 64
(Paul Cole) *t.k.h: hld up in tch in midfield: rdn and hdwy to chse ldr 2f out: sn chalng and edging lft: led jst over 1f out: idling and racing awkwardly ins fnl f: drvn and a doing enough fnl 150yds* **5/1**[2]

00-2 **2** *1/2* **Silver Six**[53] 2495 3-8-11 50 ShaneKelly 14 61
(Sheena West) *stuck wd: in tch in midfield: pushed along and hdwy to ld over 5f out: clr 4f out: rdn 3f out: jnd and edgd rt wl over 1f out: hdd jst over 1f out: kpt on but a jst hld fnl f* **9/1**

3033 **3** *6* **Angel Cake (IRE)**[16] 3710 3-8-7 46 oh1 (p) SilvestreDeSousa 15 47
(Phil McEntee) *dropped in bhd after s: t.k.h: hld up in last trio: rdn and hdwy 3f out: 6th and styng on 2f out: swtchd rt over 1f out: wnt 3rd ins fnl f: no threat to ldrs* **20/1**

000 **4** *4* **Imperial Wave (IRE)**[15] 3735 3-9-4 57 (b[1]) TedDurcan 9 52
(David Lanigan) *in tch in midfield: hdwy to chse ldrs and gng wl 3f out: rdn and fnd little ent fnl 2f: 3rd and btn over 1f out: wknd fnl f* **6/1**[3]

000 **5** *hd* **Red Mystique (IRE)**[57] 2368 3-9-3 56 WilliamBuick 1 51
(Ed Dunlop) *hld up in last trio: stuck bhd horses and nt clr run wl over 3f out: swtchd rt over 2f out: stl plenty to do but hdwy 2f out: styd on ins fnl f: nvr trbld ldrs* **7/1**

05 **6** *4* **Flamborough Breeze**[18] 3622 3-9-7 60 (t) LukeMorris 12 48
(Ed Vaughan) *dropped in bhd after s: hld up in rr: rdn and effrt 4f out: no prog 3f out: wl btn and plugged on same pce after* **16/1**

00-0 **7** *2 1/2* **Zarosa (IRE)**[31] 3189 3-8-9 48 BrettDoyle 11 32
(John Berry) *stuck wd: in tch in midfield but pushed along thrght: struggling u.p over 4f out: wl btn over 2f out* **33/1**

-004 **8** *nk* **Polydamos**[54] 2445 3-9-6 59 KirstyMilczarek 2 43
(Tony Carroll) *restless in stalls: led tl over 5f out: chsd ldr after tl 2f out: wknd over 1f out: fdd fnl f* **16/1**

0-03 **9** *nk* **Dangerous To Know**[20] 3543 3-8-13 52 DarryllHolland 13 35
(Hughie Morrison) *chsd ldrs: drvn and no ex over 2f out: btn wl over 1f out: fdd fnl f* **13/2**

-636 **10** *8* **Blue Pencil**[68] 2049 3-8-4 46 oh1 RyanPowell(3) 10 17
(Roger Curtis) *chsd ldrs: rdn over 3f out: struggling u.p over 2f out: sn wknd* **25/1**

0-00 **11** *1/2* **Despatch**[62] 2204 3-9-3 56 [1] JimCrowley 6 26
(Ralph Beckett) *in tch: rdn along over 8f out: wknd u.p over 2f out: wl bhd fnl f* **3/1**[1]

2550 **12** *3 1/4* **Lady Romanza (IRE)**[21] 3483 3-9-2 60 DavidKenny(5) 4 25
(Brendan Powell) *restless in stalls: hld up in last trio: stuck bhd horses and nt clr run 4f out: rdn and stl plenty to do whn nt clr run again over 2f out: no ch* **16/1**

560- **13** *52* **Elammato (IRE)**[263] 7177 3-8-7 46 oh1 SamHitchcott 5
(Lisa Williamson) *in tch in midfield: rdn over 7f out: lost pl over 4f out: t.o fnl 3f* **125/1**

000 **14** *25* **Doyle's Dream**[26] 3340 3-8-4 46 oh1 SimonPearce(3) 7
(Michael Madgwick) *chsd ldr tl over 5f out: sn dropped out: t.o over 3f out* **125/1**

2m 33.27s (0.27) **Going Correction** +0.075s/f (Slow) **14** Ran SP% **122.6**
Speed ratings (Par 98): **102,101,97,95,94 92,90,90,90,84 84,82,47,30**
toteswingers 1&2 £11.60, 1&3 £11.40, 2&3 £7.40 CSF £48.54 CT £846.15 TOTE £6.80: £2.50, £1.90, £4.90; EX 70.00 Trifecta £467.20 Part won. Pool: 631.46 - 0.89 winning units..
Owner D S Lee **Bred** R N Auld **Trained** Whatcombe, Oxon

FOCUS
A weak 3yo handicap in which most failed to see out the trip and the first two came well clear.

4215 LINGFIELD PARK OWNERS GROUP H'CAP 2m (P)
3:30 (3:30) (Class 5) (0-75,80) 3-Y-0+ **£2,385** (£704; £352) **Stalls** Low

Form RPR

3112 **1** **Courtesy Call (IRE)**[18] 3605 3-8-9 72 NeilCallan 1 84
(Mark Johnston) *led for 2f: chsd ldr tl led again over 7f out: mde rest: rdn and qcknd clr over 2f out: in command and styd on wl fr over 1f out* **9/4**[2]

-001 **2** *5* **Trovare (USA)**[7] 3961 5-10-6 80 6ex JimCrowley 7 86
(Amanda Perrett) *hld up in tch in last pair: rdn and effrt to chse ldng pair 2f out: no imp on wnr but kpt on to go 2nd ins fnl f* **85/40**[1]

1121 **3** *1/2* **Alfraamsey**[19] 3572 4-9-13 73 JimmyFortune 6 78
(Sheena West) *in tch in last pair: rdn and effrt to chse wnr over 2f out: no imp and btn over 1f out: lost 2nd and kpt on same pce fnl f* **11/4**[3]

6103 **4** *14* **Frederick William**[7] 3961 4-9-10 70 (p) DaneO'Neill 3 59
(Chris Gordon) *dwlt: in tch: chsd wnr 4f out tl unable qck u.p over 2f out: 4th and wl btn over 1f out: eased wl ins fnl f* **12/1**

23-0 **5** *15* **Native Colony**[19] 3572 4-9-4 71 JeanVanOvermeire(7) 5 42
(Roger Varian) *led after 2f tl hdd over 7f out: chsd ldr tl 6f out: rdn and btn over 3f out: wl bhd 2f out* **25/1**

50/5 **6** *8* **Legend Erry (IRE)**[110] 1114 8-9-7 67 SilvestreDeSousa 4 28
(Venetia Williams) *t.k.h: chsd ldrs: wnt 2nd 6f out tl 4f out: sn wknd: wl bhd and eased fnl f: t.o* **8/1**

3m 25.97s (0.27) **Going Correction** +0.075s/f (Slow)
WFA 3 from 4yo+ 17lb **6** Ran SP% **112.1**
Speed ratings (Par 103): **102,99,99,92,84 80**
toteswingers 1&2 £1.70, 1&3 £2.20, 2&3 £1.80 CSF £7.44 TOTE £3.90: £2.50, £1.70; EX 8.30.
Owner A D Spence **Bred** Mrs James Wigan **Trained** Middleham Moor, N Yorks

FOCUS
A modest staying handicap. It was run at an uneven pace, but the form still looks reliable.

4216 PAUL KELLEWAY MEMORIAL H'CAP 1m 5f (P)
4:00 (4:00) (Class 3) (0-95,95) 3-Y-0+ **£6,663** (£1,982; £990; £495) **Stalls** Low

Form RPR

0-14 **1** **Viking Storm**[60] 2278 4-9-4 85 PaulHanagan 10 99
(Harry Dunlop) *hld up towards rr: stdy prog fr 8f out: rdn to ld ent fnl 2f: sn clr: r.o strly: eased towards fin* **14/1**

21 **2** *3* **Biographer**[31] 3181 3-8-5 85 TedDurcan 1 94+
(David Lanigan) *in tch: effrt u.p to chse ldng trio 2f out: outpcd by wnr over 1f out: styd on to go 2nd wl ins fnl f: no threat to wnr* **4/1**[2]

0-11 **3** *1 1/2* **The Holyman (IRE)**[144] 714 4-8-11 78 oh1 DaneO'Neill 11 85
(Jo Crowley) *chsd ldrs: chsd ldr 6f out tl led over 3f out: rdn and hdd 2f out: outpcd by wnr and btn ent fnl f: plugged on same pce and lost 2nd wl ins fnl f* **20/1**

-211 **4** *3/4* **Silent Moment (USA)**[7] 3962 3-8-6 86 6ex SilvestreDeSousa 3 92
(Saeed Bin Suroor) *led for 1f: chsd ldr tl 8f out: rdn and chsd ldng pair jst over 2f out: unable qck and btn 1f out: plugged on same pce and wl hld after* **11/10**[1]

0134 **5** *2 1/2* **Bute Hall**[11] 3859 3-7-13 79 (b[1]) MartinLane 7 81
(Mark Johnston) *dwlt: in tch towards rr: rdn and effrt over 2f out: nt clr run and hmpd bnd wl over 1f out: sme hdwy ent fnl f: styd on but no threat to ldrs* **25/1**

45- **6** *1 3/4* **Alsadaa (USA)**[329] 3794 9-9-3 84 AmirQuinn 8 83
(Laura Mongan) *hld up in midfield: sme hdwy u.p over 1f out: styd on same pce and no imp fnl f* **66/1**

2400 **7** *2 1/4* **Layline (IRE)**[19] 3594 5-9-13 94 NeilCallan 9 89
(Gay Kelleway) *stdd and dropped in bhd after s: t.k.h: hld up in last pair: rdn and effrt whn nt clr run and hmpd bnd 2f out: sme hdwy u.p over 1f out: nvr trbld ldrs* **25/1**

-104 **8** *2* **Old Hundred (IRE)**[14] 3766 5-10-0 95 (v) HayleyTurner 12 87
(James Fanshawe) *stdd and dropped in bhd after s: t.k.h: hld up in last trio: effrt on inner wl over 1f out: no imp: nvr trbld ldrs* **10/1**

2513 **9** *nse* **Sand Skier**[21] 3502 5-9-4 85 WilliamBuick 4 77
(Hans Adielsson) *chsd ldrs: wnt 2nd 8f out tl 6f out: rdn and unable qck over 2f out: edgd rt and wknd bnd 2f out* **16/1**

30-0 **10** *7* **Albaraka**[18] 3652 4-9-5 86 LukeMorris 2 67
(Sir Mark Prescott Bt) *dwlt: pushed along and rcvrd to ld after 1f: hdd and drvn jst over 3f out: wknd jst over 2f out: bhd and eased wl ins fnl f* **33/1**

0-13 **11** *1/2* **Kuda Huraa (IRE)**[72] 1940 4-8-13 80 JamieSpencer 6 60
(Roger Varian) *t.k.h: hld up in tch towards rr: rdn and effrt over 2f out: no imp and carried wd bnd 2f out: no ch after: eased wl ins fnl f* **11/2**[3]

250- **12** *1 3/4* **Aurorian (IRE)**[360] 4354 6-9-4 85 JimmyFortune 5 62
(Lawney Hill) *in tch: rdn and lost pl over 2f out: bhd and eased wl ins fnl f* **33/1**

2m 43.73s (-2.27) **Going Correction** +0.075s/f (Slow)
WFA 3 from 4yo+ 13lb **12** Ran SP% **124.5**
Speed ratings (Par 107): **109,107,106,105,104 103,101,100,100,96 95,94**
toteswingers 1&2 £8.50, 1&3 £12.20, 2&3 £11.70 CSF £68.00 CT £1164.95 TOTE £18.30: £3.20, £1.30, £6.80; EX 100.70 Trifecta £947.20 Part won. Pool: 1,280.01 - 0.20 winning units..
Owner Be Hopeful Partnership **Bred** Charlie Wyatt **Trained** Lambourn, Berks

FOCUS
This is a well-known event, but this was the first time it has been over the new, longer trip and as a handicap (formerly classified stakes). It was run at an uneven tempo until around 4f out and the injection of pace caught many out. The form still looks solid, though.

NOTEBOOK

Viking Storm took the race by the scruff of the neck under Paul Hanagan – a jockey back riding at the top of his game – and that proved a winning move as he had it in safe keeping from the furlong marker. He ran up to his mark in a very competitive race over a bit further on turf on his previous outing and his form figures at this venue now read 2211. There could be even more to come from him as a stayer. His trainer is hoping he makes the cut for the Ebor at York next month, but that does look unlikely even after a rise for this. (tchd 16-1)

Biographer won a 1m4f maiden on his second career start at Doncaster a month earlier. He got the inside trip from stall one, but was badly caught out when the winner kicked for home and was coming back at him all too late once getting organised in the home straight. He should build on this back on a stiffer track and is one to follow. (op 5-1)

The Holyman(IRE) arrived on this return from a 144-day break bidding for a hat-trick, and this was another sterling effort up in class from a 5lb higher mark (1lb out of the handicap). He's entitled to come on for it. (op 25-1)

Silent Moment(USA) was another searching for a hat-trick after her easy win from a decent benchmark at Kempton a week previously. She got the run of the race pretty much, but was another caught out by the winner's move and probably found this coming a little too soon. She's now due to race off a 6lb higher mark. (op Evens tchd 5-4)

Bute Hall, in first-time blinkers, was running on stoutly towards the finish having got well back when the winner kicked on for home.

4217 BRITISH STALLION STUDS SUPPORTING BRITISH RACING EBF MAIDEN FILLIES' STKS — 6f (P)

4:30 (4:32) (Class 5) 2-Y-O — **£3,169** (£943; £471; £235) **Stalls** Low

Form — RPR

20 **1** **Sugar House (USA)**[19] 3590 2-9-0 0 ... AhmedAjtebi 5 — 78
(Mahmood Al Zarooni) *led tl 1/2-way: chsd ldr after: rdn 2f out: drvn and rallied ins fnl f: r.o wl to ld again towards fin* **15/8**[1]

0 **2** 3/4 **Spicy (IRE)**[13] 3783 2-9-0 0 ... WilliamBuick 7 — 76
(Marco Botti) *chsd ldr tl led 1/2-way: rdn and clr 2f out: drvn over 1f out: kpt on tl hdd and no ex towards fin* **7/1**

3 5 **Ghostflower (IRE)** 2-9-0 0 ... MickaelBarzalona 6 — 61
(Mahmood Al Zarooni) *t.k.h: in tch: chsd ldrs 4f out: rn green and hung rt bnd 2f out: hung lft u.p and btn 1f out: wknd* **11/4**[2]

00 **4** 1 3/4 **Our Golden Girl**[21] 3487 2-9-0 0 ... DavidProbert 4 — 56
(Mark Usher) *chsd ldrs: rdn and outpcd 2f out: 4th and wl hld over 1f out: plugged on* **66/1**

0 **5** 1 3/4 **Starlight Symphony (IRE)**[26] 3339 2-9-0 0 ... TomQueally 9 — 50
(Eve Johnson Houghton) *in tch in midfield: outpcd over 2f out: no ch w ldrs but styd on again ins fnl f* **16/1**

6 2 1/2 **Flywheel (IRE)** 2-9-0 0 ... KierenFallon 11 — 43
(Brian Meehan) *in tch in midfield: rdn and outpcd over 2f out: 5th and wl btn over 1f out: wknd fnl f* **6/1**[3]

5 **7** 2 1/2 **Kunzea (IRE)**[21] 3487 2-9-0 0 ... MartinHarley 12 — 35
(Mick Channon) *hld up in last trio: rdn and struggling over 2f out: wknd 2f out: sn wl btn* **16/1**

8 3 **Misty Secret (IRE)** 2-9-0 0 ... BrettDoyle 3 — 26
(Jane Chapple-Hyam) *awkward leaving stalls: in tch in last trio: rdn and struggling over 2f out: wknd 2f out: bhd fnl f* **33/1**

9 shd **Choral Rhythm (IRE)** 2-9-0 0 ... JimmyFortune 2 — 26
(Richard Hannon) *v.s.a: rn green in rr: bhd fnl 2f* **8/1**

0 **10** 5 **Elounta**[21] 3506 2-9-0 0 ... LukeMorris 1 — 11
(John Best) *t.k.h: in tch in midfield: hmpd over 5f out: rdn and struggling over 2f out: fdd over 1f out* **25/1**

1m 13.33s (1.43) **Going Correction** +0.075s/f (Slow) — **10** Ran SP% **119.4**
Speed ratings (Par 91): **93,92,85,83,80 77,74,70,69,63**
toteswingers 1&2 £4.80, 1&3 £2.10, 2&3 £5.50 CSF £16.09 TOTE £3.10: £1.10, £1.70, £1.70; EX 18.40 Trifecta £56.10 Pool: 970.85 - 12.80 winning units..
Owner Godolphin **Bred** Darley **Trained** Newmarket, Suffolk

FOCUS

A modest juvenile fillies' maiden in which nothing got seriously involved from off the pace and it was another race where two came clear at the business end.

NOTEBOOK

Sugar House(USA) rallied gamely inside the final furlong and got on top near the line to shed her maiden tag at the third attempt. She flopped on turf last time, but was runner-up on her debut at Kempton the time before and this was a return to that sort of form. While not one of her stable's stars, she ought to enjoy another furlong and can find a nursery. (op 5-2)

Spicy(IRE), down the field on her Newbury debut 13 days earlier, shot into the lead leaving the back straight and looked to have nearly stolen the race. She was nabbed near the finish, but was a clear second-best and is obviously a fair filly. (tchd 13-2 and 15-2)

Ghostflower(IRE), stablemate of the runner-up, is the first foal of Ribblesdale winner Silkwood and there was every chance she'd find this sharp enough first time up. She displayed decent pace, though, and would have given the first two much more to think about had she not run so green under pressure. Another furlong ought to prove right up her street. (op 5-2 tchd 10-3)

Our Golden Girl showed up nicely through the early parts and, while ultimately well held, this was her most encouraging effort yet. She now qualifies for nurseries. (op 50-1)

Starlight Symphony(IRE) shaped as though she may benefit for a stiffer test. (op 14-1)

Flywheel(IRE) ran as though this initial outing was badly needed. (op 8-1)

Choral Rhythm(IRE), despite coming from leading quarters, proved easy to back ahead of this debut and lost any chance when falling out of the stalls. She ought to improve.

4218 RACING & MUSIC NIGHTS AT LINGFIELD PARK H'CAP — 6f (P)

5:00 (5:03) (Class 5) (0-75,75) 3-Y-O — **£2,385** (£704; £352) **Stalls** Low

Form — RPR

0-01 **1** **Take A Note**[15] 3732 3-9-0 **68** ... JimCrowley 8 — 76
(Patrick Chamings) *hld up in last quartet: rdn and effrt 2f out: str run ins fnl f to ld last strides* **7/2**[2]

5432 **2** hd **Ghost Train (IRE)**[14] 3762 3-9-1 **69** ... (p) NeilCallan 12 — 76
(Mark Johnston) *broke fast: led and crossed to inner rail: rdn and edgd rt over 1f out: wandered u.p 1f out: kpt on u.p tl edgd rt and hdd last strides* **11/2**

1060 **3** 1/2 **Boudoir (IRE)**[18] 3619 3-9-5 **73** ... SeanLevey 9 — 78
(Richard Hannon) *t.k.h: chsd ldrs: wnt 2nd over 4f out tl over 2f out: drvn and stl pressing ldrs 1f out: unable qck towards fin* **16/1**

4300 **4** 3/4 **Raffinn**[8] 3938 3-8-12 **66** ... LiamKeniry 1 — 69
(Sylvester Kirk) *in tch: rdn and effrt on inner 2f out: chsng ldrs and drvn jst ins fnl f: nt qckn and one pce after* **20/1**

2103 **5** shd **Sunley Pride**[16] 3698 3-9-5 **73** ... MartinHarley 5 — 76
(Mick Channon) *chsd ldrs: rdn and sltly outpcd over 1f out: rallied u.p 1f out and pressed ldrs ins fnl f: kpt on same pce fnl 75yds* **6/1**

014 **6** 1/2 **Bint Alzain (IRE)**[14] 3762 3-9-7 **75** ... LukeMorris 4 — 76
(Gerard Butler) *hld up in tch in midfield: effrt u.p over 1f out: one pce and no imp ins fnl f* **5/1**[3]

-313 **7** 1 1/2 **Sujet Bellagio**[9] 3912 3-9-7 **75** ... ShaneKelly 3 — 71
(Brian Meehan) *chsd ldrs: wnt 2nd and pressing ldr on inner 2f out: drvn and unable qck ent fnl f: wknd fnl 100yds* **3/1**[1]

-000 **8** 1 1/2 **Chalk And Cheese (USA)**[5] 4043 3-9-6 **74** ... (t) WilliamCarson 10 — 65
(Stuart Williams) *s.i.s: in tch in last pair: rdn over 2f out: styd on but no imp fr over 1f out* **25/1**

3-46 **9** shd **Topflight Princess**[21] 3488 3-9-4 **72** ... FergusSweeney 7 — 63
(Jeremy Gask) *stdd s: t.k.h: hld up in last pair: rdn and effrt over 1f out: kpt on but nvr gng pce to rch ldrs* **25/1**

46 **10** 1 3/4 **Sweet Ovation**[56] 2397 3-8-12 **66** ... HayleyTurner 2 — 52
(Mark Usher) *hld up in tch in last quartet: rdn and effrt ent fnl 2f: no imp: nvr trbld ldrs* **20/1**

3426 **11** hd **Mister Mackenzie**[7] 3972 3-8-12 **66** ... KierenFallon 6 — 51
(John Best) *sn pushed along to chse ldrs: sltly hmpd and dropped to midfield over 4f out: rdn and struggling over 2f out: wknd over 1f out* **16/1**

1m 12.41s (0.51) **Going Correction** +0.075s/f (Slow) — **11** Ran SP% **122.5**
Speed ratings (Par 100): **99,98,98,97,96 96,94,92,92,89 89**
toteswingers 1&2 £4.40, 1&3 £13.30, 2&3 £18.50 CSF £22.86 CT £233.92 TOTE £3.60: £1.30, £2.60, £6.90; EX 21.50 Trifecta £464.80 Pool: 1,042.79 - 1.66 winning units..
Owner The Foxford House Partnership **Bred** P J L Wright **Trained** Baughurst, Hants

FOCUS

This was a moderate sprint handicap, but it was competitive for the class and they went hard early on.

Sweet Ovation Official explanation: trainer's rep said filly finished distressed

4219 LADBROKES GAME ON! H'CAP — 1m 2f (P)

5:30 (5:32) (Class 6) (0-60,60) 3-Y-O+ — **£1,704** (£503; £251) **Stalls** Low

Form — RPR

2445 **1** **Jordaura**[86] 1562 6-9-12 **60** ... NeilCallan 14 — 67
(Gay Kelleway) *dwlt: hld up in tch: rdn and effrt whn nt much rooom jst over 2f out: gd hdwy over 1f out: led fnl 100yds: r.o wl* **16/1**

0004 **2** 1 1/4 **Secret Era**[30] 3236 5-9-8 **56** ... MartinDwyer 8 — 60
(William Muir) *chsd ldr tl rdn to ld ent fnl 2f: drvn and hrd pressed 1f out: hdd and one pce fnl 100yds* **9/1**

-050 **3** 1 1/4 **Formidable Guest**[16] 3704 8-9-6 **54** ... JimCrowley 6 — 56
(Jamie Poulton) *hld up in tch in midfield: nt clr run and swtchd rt wl over 1f out: hdwy u.p over 1f out: kpt on ins fnl f but nvr gng pce to chal* **10/1**

0-00 **4** 1/2 **Night Sky**[32] 3137 5-9-4 **52** ... KirstyMilczarek 4 — 53
(Tony Carroll) *in tch: rdn to chse ldrs over 2f out: drvn and chsd wnr over 1f out tl ent fnl f: one pce after* **40/1**

3506 **5** shd **Lytham (IRE)**[35] 3043 11-9-2 **50** ... FergusSweeney 12 — 50+
(Tony Carroll) *hld up in tch in last pair: stuck bhd horses over 3f out: sme hdwy and nt clr run over 1f out: swtchd rt and styd on strly fnl 100yds: nt rch ldrs* **16/1**

540 **6** 1/2 **Jumeirah Liberty**[32] 3153 4-9-7 **55** ... JamieGoldstein 7 — 54
(Zoe Davison) *in tch in midfield: rdn and unable qck over 2f out: outpcd and looked wl hld over 1f out: rallied and styd on wl fnl 100yds* **16/1**

0000 **7** 1/2 **Breakheart (IRE)**[23] 3454 5-9-12 **60** ... (p) KierenFallon 10 — 58
(Paul Howling) *t.k.h: chsd ldrs: rdn and unable qck jst over 1f out: drvn and btn 1f out: plugged on again ins fnl f* **18/1**

500- **8** 2 **Beat Up**[345] 4869 6-9-8 **56** ... GeorgeBaker 5 — 50
(Patrick Chamings) *hld up in tch in rr: effrt and nt clr run 2f out: swtchd ins and effrt over 1f out: no imp ins fnl f* **8/1**

2451 **9** hd **Lord Of The Storm**[25] 3392 4-9-12 **60** ... KierenFox 1 — 54
(Bill Turner) *chsd ldrs: rdn and unable qck whn n.m.r over 1f out: wknd ins fnl f* **4/1**[2]

5510 **10** 1/2 **Land Hawk (IRE)**[54] 2463 6-9-9 **60** ... SimonPearce(3) 11 — 53
(Lydia Pearce) *stuck wd: in tch in midfield: rdn and unable qck whn wd bnd 2f out: one pce and hld after* **6/1**[3]

0300 **11** 3 1/4 **Gallantry**[15] 3738 10-9-12 **60** ... TomMcLaughlin 3 — 46
(Paul Howling) *led tl rdn and hdd over 2f out: wknd 1f out: eased wl ins fnl f* **33/1**

00-3 **12** 13 **Mitch Rapp (USA)**[78] 1725 3-9-2 **60** ... JamieSpencer 9 — 20
(Harry Dunlop) *in tch in last quartet: rdn 4f out: hrd drvn and no rspnse over 3f out: lost tch 2f out: eased fnl f* **5/2**[1]

2m 7.59s (0.99) **Going Correction** +0.075s/f (Slow)
WFA 3 from 4yo+ 10lb — **12** Ran SP% **121.3**
Speed ratings (Par 101): **99,98,97,96,96 96,95,94,93,93 90,80**
toteswingers 1&2 £9.10, 1&3 £11.20, 2&3 £16.30 CSF £156.51 CT £1535.03 TOTE £23.40: £5.20, £2.90, £4.80; EX 91.60 Trifecta £878.20 Part won. Pool: 1,186.77 - 0.39 winning units..
Owner Miss Gay Kelleway **Bred** Pendley Farm **Trained** Exning, Suffolk

FOCUS

An ordinary handicap.

T/Jkpt: £8,914.30 to a £1 stake. Pool: £257385.84 - 20.50 winning tickets T/Plt: £51.50 to a £1 stake. Pool: £81184.79 - 1148.73 winning tickets T/Qpdt: £29.40 to a £1 stake. Pool: £4243.66 - 106.50 winning tickets SP

3876 SANDOWN (R-H)

Wednesday, July 18

OFFICIAL GOING: Soft (5.7)

Wind: Fresh, half against Weather: Overcast with showers

4220 DEVINE HOMES PLC MAIDEN — 5f 6y

5:55 (5:55) (Class 5) 2-Y-O — **£2,264** (£673; £336; £168) **Stalls** Low

Form — RPR

2 **1** **Dominate**[9] 3916 2-9-3 0 ... RichardHughes 6 — 84+
(Richard Hannon) *hld up in 4th: trckd ldr over 1f out: jst pushed along to ld ins fnl f: readily* **5/4**[1]

2 **2** 1/2 **Red Explorer (USA)**[25] 3381 2-9-3 0 ... MichaelHills 4 — 82
(Charles Hills) *trckd ldng pair: led against rail over 1f out: rdn and hdd ins fnl f: styd on but readily hld by wnr* **2/1**[2]

0 **3** 10 **Mullit (IRE)**[32] 3138 2-9-3 0 ... RichardKingscote 5 — 46
(Tom Dascombe) *taken v steadily to post: led: hung lft fr 2f out: hdd & wknd over 1f out* **25/1**

20 **4** hd **Starlight Angel (IRE)**[28] 3269 2-8-12 0 ... DaneO'Neill 7 — 41
(Ronald Harris) *t.k.h: pressed ldr: rdn whn carried lft and wknd over 1f out: carried further lft fnl f* **5/1**[3]

050 **5** 2 1/2 **Hats Off**[55] 2415 2-9-3 0 ... JohnFahy 1 — 36
(John Best) *in tch in 5th tl wknd fr 2f out* **66/1**

6 4 1/2 **Colourist** 2-9-3 0 ... RyanMoore 3 — 20
(Gary Moore) *s.v.s: rn green and a detached in last* **9/1**

1m 5.58s (3.98) **Going Correction** +0.775s/f (Yiel) — **6** Ran SP% **109.8**
Speed ratings (Par 94): **99,98,82,81,77 70**
toteswingers 1&2 £1.10, 1&3 £6.20, 2&3 £6.20 CSF £3.75 TOTE £2.00: £1.30, £1.60; EX 2.80.
Owner Godfrey Wilson **Bred** Mrs C R D Wilson **Trained** East Everleigh, Wilts

FOCUS
Far side rail on Sprint track moved 3yds inside. Round course dolled out up to 4yds from 7f to 2f adding about 5yds to distances on Round course.The course was dolled out from up to 4yds from the 7f to the 2f markers, adding approximately 5yds to the distances on the round course. After a dry day approximately 2mm of rain fell on the run up to the meeting and the time of the opener confirmed the ground was as the official. Not the most competitive of maidens but useful form from the two market leaders, who pulled clear late on. The second stepped up on his debut form. The gallop was a reasonable one.

NOTEBOOK
Dominate was down in trip but, after waiting to get a run, responded well to his rider's urgings to win a shade comfortably, in the process fully confirming debut promise. He'll be equally at home back over 6f and, although yet to tackle a sound surface, looks the type to win more races. (op Evens tchd 11-8)

Red Explorer(USA), just in front of a subsequent winner when showing fair form on his debut, got first run on the winner and ran at least as well. He has only tackled soft ground so far but a reproduction of either run should be more than good enough to win an ordinary maiden. (tchd 15-8)

Mullit(IRE) doesn't look straightforward as he was led to the start, took a good hold in front and hung left under pressure and, although he bettered his debut form, he's likely to remain vulnerable in this type of event. (op 33-1 tchd 22-1)

Starlight Angel(IRE), out of her depth in the Queen Mary, showed a tendency to race with the choke out and she was below the form she showed at Chester on her debut. (op 7-1 tchd 9-2)

Hats Off, back in trip and back in soft ground, again had his limitations firmly exposed on turf. His best effort came on Polytrack and a return to that surface and the switch to low-grade nurseries may be the way forward. (op 50-1)

Colourist, who cost 45,000GBP earlier this year and who is the second foal of a 7f Fibresand winner, was soundly beaten after a slow start and after running green but he's in good hands and he's entitled to come on for this experience. Official explanation: trainer said colt was slowly away (op 12-1 tchd 14-1)

4221 JAMCAP PROJECT FINANCE H'CAP 5f 6y
6:30 (6:31) (Class 4) (0-85,84) 3-Y-O **£4,075** (£1,212; £606; £303) **Stalls** Low

Form RPR

0503 **1** **Heartsong (IRE)**[11] 3861 3-9-1 **78**................................ StevieDonohoe 1 88
(John Gallagher) *mde virtually all against far side rail: clr over 3f out: rdn 2f out: kpt on wl: unchal* **12/1**

302 **2** *2 ¾* **Lupo D'Oro (IRE)**[25] 3396 3-8-12 **75**................................ JohnFahy 3 75
(John Best) *hld up in last: rdn whn looking for a gap over 1f out: styd on to take 2nd last strides* **13/2**

1411 **3** *shd* **Khubala (IRE)**[18] 3613 3-9-7 **84**................................(b) WilliamBuick 5 84
(Ed Dunlop) *trckd ldng pair: rdn over 2f out: chsd wnr over 1f out: no imp and lost 2nd last strides* **5/2**[2]

0446 **4** *2 ¾* **Mister Musicmaster**[23] 3445 3-8-13 **76**..................(b) JamesMillman 2 66
(Rod Millman) *best away but settled to trck wnr: rdn and fnd nil over 2f out: lost 2nd and btn over 1f out* **11/2**[3]

5312 **5** *¾* **Picture Dealer**[19] 3566 3-8-13 **76**................................ RyanMoore 6 63
(Gary Moore) *racd on outer: hld up in last pair: rdn and effrt over 2f out: no prog and btn over 1f out: fdd* **15/8**[1]

10 **6** *9* **Isola Verde**[40] 2893 3-8-10 **73** ow1................................ RichardHughes 4 28
(James Fanshawe) *hld up bhd ldrs and racd against rail: gng wl enough whn nt clr run over 1f out: sn wknd and eased* **9/1**

1m 5.13s (3.53) **Going Correction** +0.775s/f (Yiel) **6** Ran SP% **109.8**
Speed ratings (Par 102): **102,97,97,93,91 77**
CSF £79.41 TOTE £17.30: £5.20, £2.70; EX 106.20.
Owner Colin Rashbrook **Bred** Gerry And John Rowley **Trained** Chastleton, Oxon

FOCUS
A useful handicap and a decent gallop but a race in which only the enterprisingly ridden winner ever figured. The time was nearly half a second quicker than the opener. It's doubtful the form can be taken too literally with the first two in the betting below par.
Isola Verde Official explanation: jockey said filly stopped quickly

4222 CHILDREN'S TRUST MAIDEN AUCTION STKS 7f 16y
7:00 (7:01) (Class 5) 2-Y-O **£2,587** (£770; £384; £192) **Stalls** Low

Form RPR

53 **1** **Haatefina**[22] 3473 2-8-6 0................................ DavidProbert 8 70
(Mark Usher) *pressed ldr: c nr side st: overall ldr over 2f out: drvn and styd on wl* **2/1**[2]

2 *1* **Law Enforcement (IRE)** 2-8-13 0................................ RichardHughes 2 75+
(Richard Hannon) *sn trckd ldng pair: styd far side st: led gp wl over 1f out: drew clr after but a jst hld by wnr nr side* **13/8**[1]

4 **3** *5* **Dance With Dragons (IRE)**[9] 3916 2-9-1 0.............. StevieDonohoe 6 64
(Paul Cole) *hld up in tch: styd far side st: effrt and gng wl enough whn nt clr run wl over 1f out: swtchd rt and chsd ldr 1f out: no imp* **9/2**[3]

644 **4** *hd* **Northern Harbour (IRE)**[1] 4191 2-8-11 0....................(p) LiamKeniry 9 60
(J S Moore) *t.k.h: hld up in last pair: c nr side st w wnr in st: no imp fnl 2f* **25/1**

0 **5** *2 ½* **Sakhee's Ichigou**[36] 3009 2-8-4 0................................ HayleyTurner 1 46
(Michael Blanshard) *racd freely: led: hung lft bnd wl over 3f out: styd far side st: lost overall ld over 2f out but maintained gp ld tl wl over 1f out: wknd* **20/1**

00 **6** *nse* **Tomway**[56] 2384 2-8-13 0................................ RichardKingscote 3 55
(Tom Dascombe) *cl up: styd far side st: chal over 2f out: wknd over 1f out* **20/1**

7 *¾* **Benoni** 2-8-11 0................................ DaneO'Neill 4 51
(Henry Candy) *s.s and rousted along in last early: styd far side st: effrt and in tch over 2f out: wknd over 1f out* **8/1**

05 **8** *7* **Luckster**[45] 2729 2-8-9 0................................ LukeMorris 7 32
(David Evans) *pushed along in midfield bef 1/2-way: styd far side st: wknd over 2f out* **50/1**

1m 35.89s (6.39) **Going Correction** +0.60s/f (Yiel) **8** Ran SP% **116.1**
Speed ratings (Par 94): **87,85,80,79,77 77,76,68**
toteswingers 1&2 £1.80, 2&3 £2.80, 1&3 £2.40 CSF £5.44 TOTE £3.40: £1.20, £1.10, £1.80; EX 6.60 Trifecta £21.50 Pool: £1565.98 - 53.81 winning units..
Owner Ushers Court **Bred** D R Tucker **Trained** Upper Lambourn, Berks

FOCUS
Last year's winner Mister Music went on to show form bordering on smart but it'll be a surprise if this year's winner gets near that level. The gallop was an ordinary one and the winner and fourth tacked over to the stands rail early in the home straight. The winner probably stepped up on her debut form.

NOTEBOOK
Haatefina is a progressive sort who had the run of the race and showed a good attitude to get off the mark at the third attempt. It isn't easy to gauge how much tacking over to the stands rail aided her cause (if at all) but, although she lacks much in the way of physical scope, she should stay 1m and should continue to go well at a realistic level. (op 15-8 tchd 7-4)

Law Enforcement(IRE) ◆, who cost 18,000GBP and whose dam is a sister to Racing Post Trophy winner Armiger, is the one to take from the race. He showed a fair level of form to pull clear of those that raced on the far side. He'll stay 1m and should be able to pick up a similar event at the very least with this experience behind him. (op 9-4)

Dance With Dragons(IRE) had shown ability at a moderate level over 6f on his debut and bettered that upped to this trip. He has only raced in soft ground so far and he'll be of more interest when switched into run-of-the-mill nursery company. (tchd 6-1)

Northern Harbour(IRE), soundly beaten in a Fibresand claimer the previous evening, wasn't disgraced back on turf and on this first run over 7f but he's likely to remain vulnerable in this type of event. (op 20-1 tchd 18-1)

Benoni, a half-brother to several winners, including multiple 1m-1m5f winner Lennel, wasn't totally disgraced after a tardy start on this racecourse debut. He's entitled to improve for this experience. (tchd 10-1)

4223 JAMCAP PROPERTY DEVELOPMENT H'CAP 1m 14y
7:30 (7:31) (Class 4) (0-85,85) 3-Y-O+ **£4,075** (£1,212; £606; £303) **Stalls** Low

Form RPR

5352 **1** **My Lord**[16] 3705 4-8-12 **67** ow2................................ RichardHughes 1 78
(Luke Dace) *t.k.h: hld up in last pair: swtchd outside and prog wl over 1f out: decisive move to ld jst ins fnl f: wl in command after* **12/1**

0255 **2** *1 ½* **Shavansky**[21] 3508 8-9-13 **84**................................ JamesMillman 2 90
(Rod Millman) *c out of the stalls last: hld up: stl in last and pushed along over 1f out: swtchd to outer and styd on to take 2nd nr fin: no ch to chal* **9/2**[3]

2232 **3** *½* **Sir Mike**[9] 3917 3-9-2 **81**................................ JimCrowley 4 84
(Amanda Perrett) *hld up in 4th: waiting for gap bhd ldrs over 2f out tl rdn to chal 1f out: sn outpcd: kpt on* **3/1**[1]

605 **4** *nk* **Masters Blazing**[25] 3383 3-8-8 **73**................................(p) BrettDoyle 6 75
(John Ryan) *t.k.h: trckd ldr 3f: styd cl up: chal 2f out: led over 1f out tl jst ins fnl f: nt qckn* **10/1**

0-21 **5** *shd* **Hilali (IRE)**[22] 3475 3-8-13 **78**................................ RyanMoore 3 80
(Gary Brown) *sn hld up in 5th: rdn and prog on outer 2f out: chal and upsides jst over 1f out: nt qckn* **11/2**

-11U **6** *2 ¾* **Viscount Vert (IRE)**[9] 3917 3-9-3 **82**................................ DavidProbert 5 80
(Andrew Balding) *hld up towards rr: cl up bhd ldr over 2f out: rdn and nt qckn wl over 1f out: fdd* **7/1**

60-3 **7** *nk* **Star Surprise**[10] 3890 4-10-0 **85**................................ JamieSpencer 8 82
(Michael Bell) *sn led: brought field to nr side in st: hdd and fdd over 1f out* **4/1**[2]

0066 **8** *½* **Push Me (IRE)**[2] 4150 5-9-2 **73**................................ MartinLane 7 69
(Jamie Poulton) *prom: trckd ldr after 3f: rdn to chal 2f out: nt qckn over 1f out: fdd* **8/1**

1m 47.77s (4.47) **Going Correction** +0.60s/f (Yiel)
WFA 3 from 4yo+ 8lb **8** Ran SP% **119.0**
Speed ratings (Par 105): **101,99,99,98,98 95,95,95**
toteswingers 1&2 £11.40, 2&3 £3.80, 1&3 £4.30 CSF £67.68 CT £209.17 TOTE £13.30: £2.50, £2.20, £1.70; EX 120.50 Trifecta £1242.20 Part won. Pool: £1678.64 - 0.73 winning units..
Owner Mark Benton **Bred** Mrs Monica Teversham **Trained** Five Oaks, W Sussex
■ Stewards' Enquiry : Brett Doyle two-day ban: used whip above permitted level (Aug 2-3)

FOCUS
A useful handicap run at a reasonable gallop and, although the field tacked to the stands side early in the home straight, the group ended up racing in the centre of the track once the false rail dropped away. The first two came from the back and the winner more than confirmed his good reappearance.

4224 DEVINE HOMES PLC H'CAP 1m 2f 7y
8:05 (8:05) (Class 4) (0-80,77) 3-Y-O **£4,075** (£1,212; £606; £303) **Stalls** Low

Form RPR

2655 **1** **Sheila's Buddy**[23] 3448 3-9-1 **71**................................ LiamKeniry 6 79
(J S Moore) *hld up and sn in 5th: prog to chse ldr jst over 1f out: sustained chal fnl f: led last strides* **16/1**

02-2 **2** *hd* **Ace Of Valhalla**[93] 1414 3-9-6 **76**................................ TomQueally 2 84
(Sir Henry Cecil) *led at mod pce: brought field to nr side in st but styd away fr rail: rdn 2f out: styd on but hdd last strides* **7/2**[2]

-344 **3** *2* **Exning Halt**[18] 3622 3-9-1 **71**................................ HayleyTurner 1 75
(James Fanshawe) *trckd ldng pair: rdn to chse ldr briefly over 1f out: one pce after* **16/1**

4046 **4** *nse* **Whipcrackaway (IRE)**[9] 3920 3-9-3 **73**................................ DaneO'Neill 8 77
(Peter Hedger) *hld up in last pair: rdn over 2f out: taken wd and styd on fr over 1f out: nrly snatched 3rd* **8/1**

2663 **5** *1 ½* **Little Dutch Girl**[22] 3476 3-9-6 **76**................................(b) JohnFahy 5 77
(Clive Cox) *trckd ldr: chal 2f out: nt qckn and lost 2nd over 1f out: one pce* **4/1**[3]

-243 **6** *3 ¾* **Debating Society (IRE)**[15] 3737 3-9-7 **77**................................ RyanMoore 4 70
(Sir Michael Stoute) *hld up: n.m.r and dropped to last pair after 2f: rdn and no prog over 2f out: tried to cl over 1f out: no imp and eased* **2/1**[1]

40-0 **7** *3 ¾* **Maistro (IRE)**[72] 1922 3-9-1 **71**................................ KierenFallon 7 57
(Luca Cumani) *slowly away: pushed along to rcvr chsd ldrs after 2f: shkn up 3f out: dropped to last and wl btn over 1f out* **13/2**

2m 15.87s (5.37) **Going Correction** +0.60s/f (Yiel) **7** Ran SP% **111.8**
Speed ratings (Par 102): **102,101,100,100,99 96,93**
toteswingers 1&2 £5.80, 2&3 £8.00, 1&3 £13.50 CSF £67.79 CT £913.18 TOTE £12.10: £3.70, £2.30; EX 82.00 Trifecta £344.00 Pool: £1404.15 - 3.02 winning units..
Owner Ray Styles **Bred** Mrs Anita R Dodd **Trained** Upper Lambourn, Berks
■ Stewards' Enquiry : Liam Keniry two-day ban: used whip above permitted level (Aug 5-6)

FOCUS
A race that won by Group performers Presvis in 2008 and Aiken last year but no superstars on show in this field. The gallop was an ordinary one and the field all came stands' side early in the straight. The winner was the most exposed in the field and rates a 3lb personal best.

4225 XL GROUP H'CAP 1m 6f
8:35 (8:38) (Class 5) (0-75,75) 3-Y-O **£2,587** (£770; £384; £192) **Stalls** Low

Form RPR

6-46 **1** **Queen's Star**[33] 3100 3-8-2 **56** oh1................................ DavidProbert 1 64
(Andrew Balding) *dwlt: hld up in last trio: rdn 3f out: prog on outer 2f out: drvn to ld ins fnl f: hld on* **12/1**

2213 **2** *hd* **Bathwick Street**[19] 3592 3-8-13 **67**................................ StevieDonohoe 3 75
(David Evans) *trckd ldng pair: rdn 3f out: led 2f out: hdd ins fnl f: styd on: jst hld* **4/1**[2]

5661 **3** *4* **Byron Blue (IRE)**[13] 3781 3-9-4 **72**................................ JamieSpencer 2 74
(Jamie Osborne) *trckd ldrs: shkn up 3f out: nt qckn and no imp over 2f out: kpt on to take 3rd ins fnl f* **5/2**[1]

041 **4** *2 ¼* **Cellist**[16] 3710 3-9-7 **75**................................ RyanMoore 4 74
(William Haggas) *reluctant to enter stalls: mostly chsd ldr: pushed along 5f out: chal and upsides 4f out to 2f out: nt qckn* **5/1**

3100 **5** ¾ **Somemothersdohavem**[19] 3592 3 -9-371...........(p) DaraghO'Donohoe 6 69
(John Ryan) *stdd s: hld up in last: sme prog on outer over 2f out: no hdwy and btn over 1f out* **16/1**

4121 **6** *hd* **Dovils Date**[26] 3345 3 -9-472........................... JamesMillman 8 70
(Rod Millman) *hld up in last trio: rdn 3f out: no prog over 2f out: one pce and n.d after* **9/2**[3]

6611 **7** *6* **April Ciel**[20] 3543 3 -9-169.. LukeMorris 7 62
(Ronald Harris) *led at decent pce: jnd 4f out: hdd 2f out: wknd qckly jst over 1f out* **6/1**

0-30 **8** *6* **Stickleback**[42] 2818 3 -8-256 oh9.......................... MartinLane 5 37
(Harry Dunlop) *dwlt: trckd ldrs: shkn up 3f out: no prog and btn over 2f out: sn eased* **25/1**

3m 14.14s (9.64) **Going Correction** +0.60s/f (Yiel) **8**Ran SP% **115.1**
Speed ratings (Par 100): **96,95,93,92,91 91,88,84**
toteswingers 1&2 £13.40, 2&3 £2.40, 1&3 £4.10 CSF £59.87 CT £161.16 TOTE £10.60 : £3.00, £1.50, £1.50 ; EX 51.10 Trifecta £248.80 Pool: £1970.72 - 5.86 winning units.
Owner Sir Gordon Brunton **Bred** Sir Gordon Brunton **Trained** Kingsclere, Hants
■ Stewards' Enquiry : David Probert two-day ban: used whip above permitted level (Aug 2-3)

FOCUS
A fair handicap featuring a couple of unexposed types. The gallop was fair and, although the field tacked over to the stands rail early in the straight, the action played out in the centre of the track in the closing stages. Improvement from the winner.
April Ciel Official explanation: jockey said gelding had no more to give
T/Plt: £103.10 to a £1 stake. Pool of £79630.19 - 563.36 winning tickets. T/Qpdt: £13.30 to £1 stake. Pool £9576.86 - 531.79 w.tickets JN 4226a-4228a (Foreign Racing) See RI

4205 VICHY
Wednesday, July 18

OFFICIAL GOING: Turf: good to soft

4229a GRAND PRIX DE VICHY-AUVERGNE (GROUP 3) (3YO+) (TURF) 1m 2f
7:55 (12:00) 3-Y-0+ **£33,333** (£13,333; £10,000 ; £6,666 ; £3,333)

RPR

1 **No Risk At All (FR)**[37] 2989 5 -9-60........................... IoritzMendizabal 5 120+
(J-P Gallorini, France) *hld up towards rr: swtchd towards stands' side 2f out: qcknd wl to ld 1f out: sn wnt clr: eased towards fin: impressive* **3/5**[1]

2 2 ½ **Ok Coral (FR)**[18] 5 -9-20................................... NicolasPerret 7 109
(K Borgel, France) *hld up in last: shkn up ent fnl 1 1/2f: qcknd wl ins fnl f: fin strly to go 2nd fnl strides: no threat to wnr* **26/1**

3 ½ **Don Bosco (FR)**[22] 3482 5 -9-20.......................... GregoryBenoist 4 108
(D Smaga, France) *led fr s: set stdy pce: r.o wl u.p ent fnl f: hdd 1f out: styd on wl u.p fnl 100yds* **16/1**

4 *snk* **Pump Pump Boy (FR)**[22] 3178 4 -9-20.......................... MaximeGuyon 2 108
(M Pimbonnet, France) *racd midfield: u.p over 1 1/2f out: styd on wl fnl f* **30/1**

5 ½ **Aizavoski (IRE)**[53] 2518 6 -9-20.......................... ChristopheSoumillon 3 107
(E Lellouche, France) *racd in midfield: swtchd towards stands' side 2f out: u.p ent fnl f: no ex: styd on one pce: nt hrd rdn fnl 50yds* **5/2**[2]

6 *hd* **Pink Gin (FR)**[22] 3482 5 -9-20.......................... AntoineHamelin 6 107
(J-P Gauvin, France) *settled in 2nd: rdn to share ld 1 1/2f out: fnd no ex u.p: ins fnl f: wknd fnl 100yds* **9/1**[3]

7 3 ½ **Skallet (FR)**[18] 4 -8-130..(b) StephanePasquier 1 97
(S Wattel, France) *racd midfield: wnt 3rd ent st: rdn but fnd no ex 1 1/2f out: eased ins fnl f* **30/1**

2m 6.82s (-1.78) **7**Ran SP% **117.1**
WIN (incl. 1 euro stake): 1.60. PLACES: 1.20, 4.40, 2.60. DF: 88.20. SF: 191.50
Owner J-P Gallorini **Bred** Mme Sylvia Wildenstein **Trained** France

NOTEBOOK
No Risk At All (FR) who was given a waiting ride, picked up well to mow them down, and was eventually eased down to win. This was a good performance giving 4lb plus to the rest of the field, and he now has the Arc as his main objective, with an outing in the Prix Foy likely beforehand.

3483 BATH (L-H)
Thursday, July 19

OFFICIAL GOING: Good to soft (soft in places; 5.8)
Wind: Strong, against Weather: cloudy with sunny periods

4230 WINNING CONNECTIONS CLUB, BATH NURSERY 5f 11y
5:30 (5:30) (Class 5) (0-75,73) 2-Y-0 **£2,264** (£673; £336 ; £168) Stalls Centre

Form RPR

253 **1** **Barracuda Boy (IRE)**[45] 2763 2 -9-672.................... RichardKingscote 6 73
(Tom Dascombe) *trckd ldrs: rdn jst over 2f out: led over 1f out: hrd pressed thrght fnl f: kpt on and on top at fin* **10/3**[2]

4453 **2** ½ **Indian Affair**[33] 3138 2 -9-672.......................... RussKennemore 3 71
(Milton Bradley) *trckd ldrs: rdn 2f out: str chal ent fnl f: kpt on tl no ex towards fin* **8/1**

3431 **3** *2* **Windforpower (IRE)**[8] 3970 2 -9-273 6ex...................(p) DarrenEgan(5) 8 65
(Ronald Harris) *little slowly away: towards rr: rdn and hdwy over 3f out: chsd ldng pair over 1f out: kpt on same pce* **14/1**

4464 **4** *3* **Jimmy Elder**[19] 3617 2 -9-268.......................... RichardHughes 7 49
(Richard Hannon) *broke wl: sn stdd in rr: rdn 2f out: sme late prog: nvr a threat* **8/1**

050 **5** ½ **Kwanto**[41] 2868 2 -7-550 oh5.......................... KatiaScallan(7) 2 29
(Malcolm Saunders) *hld up: rdn over 2f out: sme late prog: nvr a danger* **33/1**

10 **6** *4* **Belle Intrigue**[29] 3269 2 -9-470.......................... EddieAhern 4 35
(Amanda Perrett) *in tch: rdn and hld whn squeezed up wl over 1f out: sn wknd* **13/2**[3]

4221 **7** ½ **Kicken Off (IRE)**[23] 3465 2 -9-073..........................(p) DannyBrock(7) 1 36
(Phil McEntee) *led for 2f: rdn 3f out: led briefly 2f out: edgd rt and wknd over 1f out* **10/1**

406 **8** ½ **Lawful**[20] 3569 2 -8-1365.......................... DaneO'Neill 9 26
(Paul Fitzsimons) *chsd ldrs: rdn over 2f out: wknd over 1f out* **20/1**

3322 **9** *8* **Opt Out**[10] 3902 2 -9-470.......................... MircoDemuro 5
(Mark Johnston) *prom: led 3f out: rdn and hdd 2f out: wknd tamely* **5/2**[1]

1m 5.35s (2.85) **Going Correction** +0.45s/f (Yiel) **9**Ran SP% **110.7**
Speed ratings (Par 94): **95,94,91,86,85 79,78,77,64**
Tote Swingers 1&2 £5.90, 2&3 £15.20, 1&3 £8.20 CSF £28.11 CT £311.43 TOTE £5.60 : £2.40, £3.30, £3.80 ; EX 40.60 .
Owner Laurence A Bellman **Bred** Mount Coote Partnership **Trained** Malpas, Cheshire

FOCUS
Races around bottom bend increased in distance by 12.5yds. The ground had dried a touch with Richard Kingscote describing it as being "just on the slow side of good". Quite a competitive sprint nursery and the form looks straightforward rated around the placed horses.

NOTEBOOK
Barracuda Boy (IRE) carried plenty of stable confidence ahead of this handicap debut and duly got it done, showing a really likeable attitude in the process. This looks his trip for now and he may win again. (tchd 3-1)
Indian Affair had run well here on a couple of occasions previously, and he put in a career-best on this nursery debut. He's now 0-5 but should find a small opening. (op 9-1)
Windforpower(IRE) ran well considering he was shouldering a 6lb penalty for his recent win in a less competitive race at Lingfield. (op 11-1)
Jimmy Elder was ridden with more restraint on this nursery debut, but didn't seem to improve.
Kwanto was 5lb wrong and will find easier opportunities. (op 50-1)
Belle Intrigue was already held when tightened up. (tchd 6-1)
Opt Out, who's twice had races taken off his hands late recently, looking a short runner, was disappointing. His stint in front lasted nowhere near as long this time, though, and he's left with plenty to prove having dropped right out. Official explanation: trainer's rep had no explanation for the poor form shown (op 11-4)

4231 RG KELLY WINDOWS H'CAP 5f 11y
6:00 (6:00) (Class 4) (0-85,83) 3-Y-0+ **£4,204** (£1,251; £625 ; £312) Stalls Centre

Form RPR

5-03 **1** **Rebecca Romero**[26] 3390 5 -8-1168.......................... RichardHughes 5 78
(Denis Coakley) *hld up: pushed along bhd ldrs whn nt clr run over 1f out: qcknd up wl whn gap appeared fnl 120yds: sn led: readily* **11/2**[2]

5-30 **2** 1 ¼ **Osiris Way**[18] 3660 10 -9-475.......................... GeorgeBaker 3 80
(Patrick Chamings) *led: rdn jst ins fnl f: hdd fnl 75yds: nt pce of wnr* **7/1**[3]

5004 **3** *nk* **Sulis Minerva (IRE)**[3] 3815 5 -9-175.......................... RaulDaSilva(3) 10 79
(Jeremy Gask) *in tch: nt clr run over 1f out: swtchd rt ent fnl f: sn rdn: r.o* **12/1**

0023 **4** ½ **Falasteen (IRE)**[17] 3707 5 -9-1283.......................... RichardKingscote 4 85
(Milton Bradley) *trckd ldrs: rdn over 2f out: kpt on same pce fnl f* **18/1**

0050 **5** ½ **Courageous (IRE)**[13] 3822 6 -9-778.......................... EddieAhern 7 78
(Milton Bradley) *hld up: hdwy 3f out: sn rdn to chse ldrs: kpt on same pce fnl f* **11/2**[2]

555 **6** ½ **Signifer (IRE)**[22] 3486 3 -9-080.......................... CharlesBishop(5) 8 79
(Mick Channon) *trckd ldrs: rdn to chse ldr over 1f out tl no ex fnl 120yds* **9/2**[1]

00-0 **7** 2 ¼ **Time Medicean**[33] 3139 6 -9-475.......................... StevieDonohoe 1 65
(Tony Carroll) *s.i.s: towards rr: rdn 2f out: nvr threatened* **11/1**

0021 **8** ½ **Wooden King (IRE)**[8] 3660 7 -9-677..........................(p) TomMcLaughlin 9 66
(Malcolm Saunders) *prom: rdn over 2f out: wknd ent fnl f* **9/2**[1]

6454 **9** *2* **Yurituni**[7] 4000 5 -9-778..........................(v) ShaneKelly 11 59
(Eve Johnson Houghton) *hld up: effrt 2f out: nvr gng pce to get involved: wknd fnl f* **7/1**[3]

1m 4.48s (1.98) **Going Correction** +0.45s/f (Yiel)
WFA 3 from 5yo+ 4lb **9**Ran SP% **113.4**
Speed ratings (Par 105): **102,100,99,98,97 97,93,92,89**
Tote Swingers 1&2 £6.10, 2&3 £19.20, 1&3 £11.50 CSF £42.76 CT £443.21 TOTE £4.70 : £1.40, £3.40, £5.00 ; EX 36.20 .
Owner Keepers Racing Ii **Bred** D W Armstrong **Trained** West Ilsley, Berks

FOCUS
An open sprint and any number held a chance over 1f out. Straightforward form.
Wooden King (IRE) Official explanation: jockey said gelding was unsuited by the good to soft (soft in places) ground

4232 VANS 2 GO H'CAP 1m 5y
6:30 (6:30) (Class 6) (0-60,60) 3-Y-0 **£1,617** (£481; £240 ; £120)

Form RPR

0152 **1** **Waspy**[23] 3470 3 -8-1049..........................(t) RichardHughes 6 57
(George Baker) *mid-div: rdn and stdy prog fr 2f out: led jst ins fnl f: styd on wl* **2/1**[1]

3000 **2** *2* **Macy Anne (IRE)**[10] 3920 3 -9-457.......................... StevieDonohoe 9 60
(Robert Mills) *trckd ldrs: rdn to ld over 2f out: hdd jst ins fnl f: styd on but sn hld by wnr* **7/1**[3]

0006 **3** *nk* **Essell**[30] 3248 3 -9-760.......................... PatCosgrave 5 62
(Mick Channon) *prom: rdn to chal over 2f out: styd on same pce fnl f* **5/1**[2]

020- **4** ¾ **Sovereign Waters**[331] 5342 3 -9-558.......................... JimmyFortune 11 58
(Eve Johnson Houghton) *t.k.h in tch: rdn 2f out: nt clr run and swtchd rt jst over 1f out: styd on* **18/1**

6-00 **5** *2* **Greatest Dancer (IRE)**[16] 3736 3 -9-760.......................... ShaneKelly 4 55
(Jamie Osborne) *hld up: pushed along over 3f out: rdn over 2f out: styd on steadily: nvr troubled ldrs* **9/1**

000 **6** 2 ¼ **Fight (IRE)**[16] 3719 3 -9-457..........................(b) GeorgeBaker 3 47
(Jeremy Gask) *sn pushed into ld: rdn and hdd over 2f out: kpt chsng ldrs tl wknd ent fnl f* **25/1**

0-00 **7** *shd* **Alnoomaas (IRE)**[35] 3079 3 -8-1357.......................... DarrenEgan(5) 1 47
(Ronald Harris) *hld up: hdwy on outer over 3f out: rdn to chal 2f out: fdd ent fnl f* **5/1**[2]

5050 **8** 2 ¼ **Petersboden**[64] 2162 3 -9-154.......................... DaneO'Neill 10 38
(Michael Blanshard) *mid-div tl dropped to last pair u.p 3f out: n.d after* **20/1**

0056 **9** *9* **Desert Red (IRE)**[8] 3965 3 -8-652..........................(t[1]) DannyBrock(7) 8 15
(Phil McEntee) *trckd ldrs: rdn to chal over 2f out: wknd over 1f out* **9/1**

1m 44.19s (3.39) **Going Correction** +0.375s/f (Good) **9**Ran SP% **113.0**
Speed ratings (Par 98): **98,96,95,94,92 90,90,88,79**
Tote Swingers 1&2 £3.10, 2&3 £5.80, 1&3 £3.30 CSF £15.96 TOTE £2.40 : £1.80, £2.10, £1.50 ; EX 11.60 .
Owner Patrick Milmo **Bred** Jeremy Gompertz **Trained** Whitsbury, Hants

FOCUS
A weak 3-y-o handicap but perhaps a little better than it looked. The form is sound at least.

4233 MB FRAMES H'CAP 1m 5y
7:05 (7:05) (Class 4) (0-80,80) 3-Y-0+ **£4,204** (£1,251; £625 ; £312)

Form RPR

-001 **1** **Philipstown**[52] 2557 3 -9-377.......................... RichardHughes 2 84
(Richard Hannon) *plld hrd in tch: tk clsr order 3f out: chal over 1f out: led ins fnl f: styd on: pushed out* **7/2**[2]

06-2 **2** *nk* **Miss Cap Estel**[19] 3619 3 -9-074.......................... JimmyFortune 10 80
(Andrew Balding) *led: rdn over 1f out: hdd ins fnl f: styd on but a being hld fnl 120yds* **5/2**[1]

054- **3** 1 ½ **Breaking The Bank**[273] 6970 3 -8-1070.......................... StevieDonohoe 9 73
(William Muir) *trckd ldrs tl lost pl on bnd over 3f out: hdwy over 2f out: sn rdn: styd on to snatch 3rd towards fin* **8/1**

1400 **4** *nk* **Alhaban (IRE)**[54] 2510 6-9-2 **73** DarrenEgan(5) 8 77
(Ronald Harris) *trckd ldr: rdn wl over 1f out: kpt on same pce: lost 3rd fnl strides* **10/1**

4111 **5** *1 ½* **Woolston Ferry (IRE)**[22] 3485 6-9-5 **71** DaneO'Neill 6 71
(Henry Candy) *cl up: rdn to chse ldrs 2f out: kpt on same pce tl no ex fnl 120yds* **7/2**[2]

-000 **6** *1 ¼* **Golden Tempest (IRE)**[38] 2975 4-10-0 **80** ShaneKelly 4 78
(Eve Johnson Houghton) *hld up: hdwy 3f out to trck ldrs: rdn over 1f out: nt pce to chal: fdd ins fnl f* **20/1**

3-43 **7** *4 ½* **Fabled City (USA)**[44] 2785 3-9-0 **74** (t) EddieAhern 5 59
(Clive Cox) *hld up: hdwy on outer over 3f out: effrt 2f out: hld whn squeezed up over 1f out* **5/1**[3]

1m 47.52s (6.72) **Going Correction** +0.375s/f (Good)
WFA 3 from 4yo+ 8lb 7 Ran SP% **114.6**
Speed ratings (Par 105): **81,80,79,78,77 76,71**
Tote Swingers 1&2 £2.90, 2&3 £6.30, 1&3 £7.10 CSF £12.78 CT £63.63 TOTE £4.70: £3.00, £1.70; EX 13.40.
Owner Dragon Gate **Bred** Whitsbury Manor Stud **Trained** East Everleigh, Wilts

FOCUS
Few got into this, with the 3-y-os dominating, and a progressive pair fought out the finish. The time was relatively slow.

4234 DAVE AND ROB'S BIG DAY OUT H'CAP 5f 161y
7:35 (7:35) (Class 3) (0-95,90) 3-Y-0 **£7,115** (£2,117; £1,058; £529) **Stalls** Centre

Form RPR

3111 **1** **Show Flower**[26] 3379 3-8-13 **82** PatCosgrave 6 94+
(Mick Channon) *nudged along in tch: hdwy to ld 2f out: rdn clr ent fnl f: r.o strly* **9/2**[2]

-601 **2** *1 ¾* **Alice's Dancer (IRE)**[27] 3343 3-8-11 **80** StevieDonohoe 5 85
(William Muir) *stirred up at s: awkward leaving stalls: last: rdn 2f out: hdwy over 1f out: r.o fnl f: wnt 2nd nring fin: no ch w wnr* **8/1**

-605 **3** *½* **Intransigent**[19] 3639 3-9-2 **85** JimmyFortune 9 88
(Andrew Balding) *hld up: hdwy 3f out: rdn 2f out: chsd wnr jst over 1f out: a being hld: lost 2nd nr fin* **5/1**[3]

5664 **4** *nk* **Fanrouge (IRE)**[19] 3639 3-9-4 **87** TomMcLaughlin 3 89
(Malcolm Saunders) *trckd ldrs: rdn 2f out: kpt on same pce fnl f* **8/1**

2131 **5** *hd* **Millibar (IRE)**[22] 3488 3-8-2 **74** (p) RaulDaSilva(3) 4 75+
(Nick Littmoden) *racd in cl 2nd tl short of room on rails bhd wkng ldr 2f out: swtchd rt: sn rdn: kpt on same pce fnl f* **12/1**

2-12 **6** *6* **Gabriel's Lad (IRE)**[33] 3165 3-9-3 **86** EddieAhern 7 67
(Denis Coakley) *trckd ldrs: ev ch 2f out: sn rdn and hld: wknd fnl f* **15/8**[1]

3115 **7** *3 ½* **Electric Qatar**[19] 3608 3-9-1 **84** RichardKingscote 8 53
(Tom Dascombe) *hld up: pushed along 3f out: nvr on terms: wknd over 1f out* **9/1**

6010 **8** *28* **Powerful Wind (IRE)**[40] 2914 3-9-2 **90** DarrenEgan(5) 2
(Ronald Harris) *led: rdn and hdd 2f out: sn wknd and eased* **33/1**

1m 13.26s (2.06) **Going Correction** +0.45s/f (Yiel) 8 Ran SP% **112.5**
Speed ratings (Par 104): **104,101,101,100,100 92,87,50**
Tote Swingers 1&2 £7.40, 2&3 £10.90, 1&3 £5.90 CSF £38.48 TOTE £5.60: £1.70, £3.00, £1.80; EX 37.00.
Owner Jaber Abdullah **Bred** Maywood Stud **Trained** West Ilsley, Berks

FOCUS
A decent 3yo sprint handicap that was always going to be run at a good clip with the trailblazing Powerful Wind in the field. Another personal best from the winner.

NOTEBOOK
Show Flower continued her progression with a fourth straight win, defying a 5lb rise in particularly gritty fashion. She'll reportedly be upped in grade now, with the aim presumably to gain black type at some stage. (op 4-1)
Alice's Dancer(IRE) needs her effort upgrading, getting worked up beforehand and losing ground at the start only to produce a sustained late run. She's much improved since wearing a hood (won off 8lb lower at Goodwood the time before) and remains capable of better. (tchd 7-1)
Intransigent moved strongly into contention from off the pace but not for the first time didn't see his race out. There's a race in him off this mark and a bare 5f may suit best. (op 11-2 tchd 13-2)
Fanrouge(IRE) ran right up to her best form at her favourite track. (op 13-2 tchd 17-2)
Millibar(IRE) was in the wrong place as Powerful Wind was weakening and looked unfortunate not to finish closer. (op 10-1)
Gabriel's Lad(IRE) looked the one to beat off only 2lb higher than when second in a valuable sprint at York but he found little for pressure and perhaps overdid it in the early stages, sitting close enough to the lead. Still, it was a disappointing run. Official explanation: jockey said gelding ran too free (op 9-4)

4235 PREMIER CONSERVATORY ROOFS FILLIES' H'CAP 5f 161y
8:10 (8:11) (Class 5) (0-75,75) 3-Y-0+ **£2,264** (£673; £336; £168) **Stalls** Centre

Form RPR

-332 **1** **School Fees**[27] 3343 3-9-1 **74** AmyScott(5) 7 85+
(Henry Candy) *s.i.s: towards rr: making hdwy whn stmbld bdly 3f out: hdwy over 2f out: nt clr run fr over 1f out tl swtchd lft whn gap appeared fnl 100yds: led nring fin: game* **5/1**[2]

6050 **2** *½* **Night Trade (IRE)**[8] 3960 5-9-7 **73** (p) RaulDaSilva(3) 8 81
(Ronald Harris) *trckd ldrs: swtchd rt over 1f out: sn rdn: r.o to ld jst ins fnl f: edgd lft: hdd nring fin* **8/1**

4113 **3** *¾* **Ginzan**[33] 3139 4-9-7 **70** TomMcLaughlin 4 75
(Malcolm Saunders) *led: rdn and narrowly hdd 2f out: styd pressing for ld: kpt on fnl f* **9/2**[1]

-401 **4** *½* **Sparking**[5] 4085 5-9-1 **67** 6ex RossAtkinson(3) 10 70+
(Tom Dascombe) *mid-div: rdn over 2f out: making hdwy whn swtchd rt ent fnl f: r.o* **11/2**[3]

3524 **5** *shd* **Ficelle (IRE)**[41] 2869 3-8-4 **63** DarrenEgan(5) 5 65
(Ronald Harris) *s.i.s: bhd: swtchd rt to centre over 2f out: sn rdn and hdwy: r.o wl fnl f* **14/1**

3-06 **6** *nk* **Iced Opal**[22] 3510 3-8-13 **67** DaneO'Neill 16 68
(Michael Blanshard) *mid-div: hdwy to trck ldrs 2f out: rdn over 1f out: kpt on same pce* **25/1**

2524 **7** *hd* **Whitecrest**[6] 4059 4-9-7 **70** PatCosgrave 3 71
(John Spearing) *trckd ldrs: rdn 2f out: kpt on same pce fnl f* **6/1**

5510 **8** *shd* **Dancing Welcome**[24] 3434 6-9-7 **70** (b) RichardKingscote 6 73+
(Milton Bradley) *prom: rdn to ld narrowly 2f out: strly pressed: hdd jst ins fnl f: disputing cl 3rd but hld whn badly squeezed out fnl 75yds* **10/1**

566- **9** *1 ¾* **Adventure Story**[264] 7172 5-9-0 **63** JimmyFortune 14 61+
(Tony Carroll) *s.i.s: bhd: hdwy on rails fr 2f out: nt clr run jst over 1f out: nt quick as wnr to use gap fnl 120yds and hmpd: no ch after* **28/1**

41-0 **10** *2 ¾* **Miriam's Song**[22] 3510 3-8-8 **62** ShaneKelly 12 47
(Stuart Kittow) *trckd ldrs: rdn over 2f out: fdd ins fnl f* **18/1**

050 **11** *11* **Jameela Girl**[19] 3618 4-9-7 **70** EddieAhern 9 18
(Robert Cowell) *prom: rdn over 2f out: wknd over 1f out* **16/1**

0006 **12** *3 ½* **Roodee Queen**[16] 3724 4-9-3 **66** (p) RussKennemore 15
(Milton Bradley) *in tch on outer: effrt over 2f out: wknd over 1f out* **25/1**

0000 **13** *6* **Marygold**[24] 3445 3-9-5 **73** (p) StevieDonohoe 1
(Lee Carter) *mid-div: rdn over 2f out: wknd over 1f out* **14/1**

1m 14.66s (3.46) **Going Correction** +0.45s/f (Yiel)
WFA 3 from 4yo+ 5lb 13 Ran SP% **120.3**
Speed ratings (Par 100): **94,93,92,91,91 91,90,90,88,84 70,65,57**
Tote Swingers 1&2 £12.20, 2&3 £7.30, 1&3 £4.70 CSF £44.13 CT £196.66 TOTE £7.00: £2.20, £2.10, £1.40; EX 53.70.
Owner Elias, Bennett, Mitchell & Newton **Bred** Benjamin Newton And Graycroft Farm **Trained** Kingston Warren, Oxon
■ Stewards' Enquiry : Raul Da Silva three-day ban: careless riding (Aug 2,3,5)
Amy Scott one-day ban: careless riding (Aug 2)

FOCUS
Plenty of pace on early and the race was set up nicely for the closers. This is sound form, and the winner rates better than the bare figures.

4236 K2 CONSERVATORIES H'CAP 5f 11y
8:40 (8:40) (Class 6) (0-65,64) 3-Y-0+ **£1,617** (£481; £240; £120) **Stalls** Centre

Form RPR

1654 **1** **Perlachy**[15] 3761 8-9-3 **60** (v) DarrenEgan(5) 9 72
(Ronald Harris) *hld up bhd: hdwy in centre fr over 2f out: rdn to chal jst over 1f out: led fnl 140yds: r.o* **8/1**

3501 **2** *1 ½* **Going French (IRE)**[34] 3098 5-9-12 **64** KellyHarrison 13 71
(Dai Burchell) *rn wout declared tongue tie: in tch on outer: hdwy to ld 2f out: sn rdn: hdd fnl 140yds: no ex* **9/2**[2]

5332 **3** *2 ¼* **One Last Dream**[22] 3489 3-8-4 **49** RaulDaSilva(3) 6 48
(Ron Hodges) *trckd ldrs: rdn over 2f out: nvr trbld ldrs: kpt on same pce* **5/2**[1]

030 **4** *¾* **Greyemkay**[34] 3098 4-8-1 **46** DanielMuscutt(7) 10 42
(Richard Price) *hld up towards rr: hdwy on outer over 2f out: sn rdn: kpt on same pce fnl f* **12/1**

6045 **5** *1 ½* **Bateleur**[7] 4003 8-9-3 **60** CharlesBishop(5) 4 50
(Mick Channon) *mid-div: rdn and hdwy over 2f out: kpt on same pce fnl f* **7/1**

611- **6** *2 ¼* **Steel Rain**[312] 5965 4-9-7 **59** RichardHughes 12 41
(Nikki Evans) *mid-div: rdn and hdwy whn nt clr run wl over 1f out: swtchd rt: no further imp fnl f* **5/1**[3]

0000 **7** *2 ¼* **Prize Point**[106] 1185 6-8-10 **48** ow1 (bt) StevieDonohoe 1 22
(Tom Gretton) *sn led: rdn and hdd 2f out: wknd* **33/1**

0-56 **8** *3* **Quadra Hop (IRE)**[45] 2760 4-8-8 **46** RussKennemore 2 9
(Bryn Palling) *trckd ldrs: rdn and ev ch 2f out: wknd ent fnl f* **12/1**

064 **9** *1* **Decider (USA)**[37] 3008 9-8-9 **50** (b) RossAtkinson(3) 7 10
(Ronald Harris) *drifted rt leaving stalls: chsd ldrs: rdn over 2f out: wknd over 1f out* **18/1**

50-0 **10** *1 ¼* **London Avenue (IRE)**[16] 3718 4-8-9 **47** (tp) EddieAhern 11
(Neil Mulholland) *v awkwardly away: struggling 1/2-way: a bhd* **28/1**

0040 **11** *7* **Atlantic Cycle (IRE)**[14] 3791 5-9-3 **55** (tp) RichardKingscote 3
(Milton Bradley) *mid-div: hdwy on inner over 3f out to trck ldrs: rdn over 2f out: wknd jst over 1f out* **16/1**

1m 4.84s (2.34) **Going Correction** +0.45s/f (Yiel)
WFA 3 from 4yo+ 4lb 11 Ran SP% **120.0**
Speed ratings (Par 101): **99,96,93,91,89 85,82,77,75,73 62**
Tote Swingers 1&2 £8.60, 2&3 £3.50, 1&3 £5.50 CSF £44.83 TOTE £11.80: £4.10, £1.60, £1.10; EX 75.60.
Owner Mrs N Macauley **Bred** J James **Trained** Earlswood, Monmouths

FOCUS
No hanging around here and the front pair had it to themselves from 1f out. The winner is rated close to his old turf best.
Going French(IRE) Official explanation: trainer said he was unable to fit tongue strap and gelding ran without it
T/Jkpt: £10,000.00 to a 1 stake. Pool £25,000. 2.50 winning tickets T/Plt: £64.70 to a 1 stake. Pool £60,549.03. 683.07 winning tickets T/Qpdt: £7.40 to a 1 stake. Pool £5,375.98. 532.55 winning tickets TM

3717 BRIGHTON (L-H)
Thursday, July 19

OFFICIAL GOING: Good to soft (5.9)
Wind: fresh, half against Weather: mainly dry, light showers

4237 SUPPORT ALBIONINTHECOMMUNITY.ORG.UK H'CAP 5f 59y
2:15 (2:15) (Class 6) (0-55,55) 3-Y-0+ **£1,617** (£481; £240; £120) **Stalls** Low

Form RPR

3011 **1** **Scommettitrice (IRE)**[16] 3717 4-8-11 **54** (p) WilliamTwiston-Davies(7) 5 67
(David Evans) *chsd ldrs: rdn and chsd ldr over 1f out: led jst ins fnl f: styd on strly and drew clr fnl 100yds* **8/1**[3]

5043 **2** *2 ¼* **Pharoh Jake**[6] 4059 4-8-10 **46** KieranO'Neill 13 51
(John Bridger) *chsd ldrs: rdn to chal 2f out: led over 1f out: drvn and hdd jst ins fnl f: outpcd by wnr and one pce fnl 100yds* **9/2**[1]

1-36 **3** *1 ½* **Dixie Gwalia**[73] 1934 4-8-10 **53** SiobhanMiller(7) 4 53
(David Simcock) *dwlt: towards rr: hdwy into midfield over 3f out: c centre and hdwy 1/2-way: styd on to chse ldng pair 1f out: no imp: eased cl home* **16/1**

5-00 **4** *2 ¼* **Depden (IRE)**[24] 3435 4-8-5 **46** oh1 MatthewLawson(5) 3 38
(Richard Price) *racd off the pce towards rr: rdn 1/2-way: hdwy u.p ent fnl f: styd on wl: no threat to ldrs* **33/1**

3044 **5** *¾* **Bitter Lemon**[22] 3489 3-8-12 **52** FergusSweeney 15 41
(Tony Newcombe) *in tch in midfield: c to r nr stands' rail 3f out: no imp and hung lft over 1f out: wl hld and plugged on same pce fnl f* **16/1**

0555 **6** *½* **Simple Rhythm**[14] 3791 6-8-10 **46** oh1 (v) DaraghO'Donohoe 9 34
(John Ryan) *hld up in tch: c towards centre and rdn over 2f out: no imp and no threat to ldrs fr over 1f out* **16/1**

4133 **7** *nk* **Tenancy (IRE)**[5] 4085 8-8-10 **53** (b) ShirleyTeasdale(7) 8 40
(Shaun Harris) *racd freely: chsd ldr tl led after 1f: hdd: edgd lft and hmpd rivals over 1f out: sn btn: wknd fnl f* **9/2**[1]

0-06 **8** *½* **King's Ciel**[16] 3719 3-9-0 **54** (v) LiamKeniry 11 39
(George Baker) *taken down early: hld up towards rr: effrt u.p over 2f out: no imp: nvr trbld ldrs* **16/1**

0132 **9** *¾* **Whiteoak Lady (IRE)**[16] 3718 7-9-5 **55** (p) AndreaAtzeni 14 37
(David Evans) *racd in midfield: rdn and swtchd rt towards stands' side over 2f out: no imp and wl hld over 1f out* **6/1**[2]

3000 **10** *nk* **White Shift (IRE)**[16] 3718 6-8-10 **46** oh1 JimmyQuinn 1 27+
(Paul Howling) *led for 1f: chsd ldr after: rdn whn pushed lft and squeezed over 1f out: lost all ch: and wknd ent fnl f* **22/1**

5-00 **11** *4* **Triple Salchow**[17] 3702 3-8-10 **55**.............................. LeonnaMayor(5) 7 22
(Alastair Lidderdale) *awkward leaving stalls and slowly away: a bhd* **28/1**

4423 **12** *35* **Perfect Honour (IRE)**[16] 3718 6-8-9 **48**..............(p) AdamBeschizza(3) 2 +
(Des Donovan) *taken down early: s.i.s: sn rcvrd and in midfield: hdwy and chsng ldrs whn squeezed for room and bdly hmpd over 1f out: lost all ch and eased after: t.o* **9/2**[1]

1m 5.23s (2.93) **Going Correction** +0.525s/f (Yiel)
WFA 3 from 4yo+ 4lb **12** Ran SP% **114.2**
Speed ratings (Par 101): **97,93,91,87,86 85,84,84,82,82 76,20**
toteswingers 1&2 £8.90, 2&3 £16.10, 1&3 £18.30 CSF £41.21 CT £571.53 TOTE £7.70: £2.60, £2.30, £5.00; EX 44.70 Trifecta £229.00 Pool: £473.56 - 1.53 winning units..
Owner Out Of Bounds Racing Club **Bred** L Mulryan **Trained** Pandy, Monmouths
■ Stewards' Enquiry : Shirley Teasdale eight-day ban: careless riding (Aug 2-9)

FOCUS
All races on Inner and distances as advertised. A moderate sprint handicap. They went an honest gallop on ground officially described as good to soft. The winning time was nearly five seconds slower than standard. The first two took the shortest route, sticking to the far side. The winner is rated back to her old best.
Tenancy(IRE) Official explanation: jockey said gelding hung left; vet said gelding sustained an overreach to right-fore

4238 EXTECH IT SOLUTIONS SUPPORTING AITC WANTTOWORK H'CAP 5f 213y
2:45 (2:45) (Class 5) (0-70,68) 3-Y-0+ **£2,264** (£673; £336; £168) **Stalls** Low

Form RPR

-522 **1** **Dear Maurice**[7] 4003 8-9-10 **66**..............................(t) MartinLane 1 76
(Tobias B P Coles) *s.i.s: in tch: rdn over 2f out: hdwy u.p over 1f out: nt clr run and swtchd rt ins fnl f: sustained effrt u.p to ld cl home* **9/2**[2]

4523 **2** *hd* **Bermondsey Bob (IRE)**[24] 3434 6-8-13 **62**. WilliamTwiston-Davies(7) 3 71
(John Spearing) *restless in stalls: broke wl: chsd ldrs: rdn to chse ldr 2f out: led jst ins fnl f: sn drvn: hdd and no ex cl home* **7/4**[1]

0160 **3** *2 1/4* **My Own Way Home**[14] 3790 4-9-6 **62**............................ AndreaAtzeni 2 64
(David Evans) *chsd ldr tl 2f out: stl pressing ldrs and drvn over 1f out: unable qck and pushed rt jst ins fnl f: plugged on same pce after: wnt 3rd on post* **9/2**[2]

3001 **4** *nse* **National Hope (IRE)**[17] 3701 4-9-4 **60**...........................(tp) PatCosgrave 8 62
(George Baker) *sn bustled along to ld: rdn and hrd pressed over 1f out: hdd jst ins fnl f: wknd fnl 50yds* **6/1**[3]

6506 **5** *3* **Muhandis (IRE)**[27] 3344 4-9-1 **64**..............................(b) JackDuern(7) 5 56
(Nick Littmoden) *s.i.s: in tch in rr: rdn and hdwy wl over 1f out: drvn and nt qckn ent fnl f: wknd fnl 150yds* **6/1**[3]

600- **6** *2 1/2* **Commandingpresence (USA)**[239] 7512 6-9-12 **68**....... KieranO'Neill 4 52
(John Bridger) *in tch: outpcd and dropped to rr whn squeezed for room and sltly hmpd over 1f out: swtchd lft and no prog 1f out: wknd ins fnl f* **20/1**

-000 **7** *1 1/4* **Stonecrabstomorrow (IRE)**[16] 3724 9-9-0 **61**.......(v) MarkCoumbe(5) 6 41
(Michael Attwater) *in tch: rdn and nt qckn over 1f out: wknd fnl f* **20/1**

1m 12.88s (2.68) **Going Correction** +0.525s/f (Yiel) **7** Ran SP% **110.8**
Speed ratings (Par 103): **103,102,99,99,95 92,90**
toteswingers 1&2 £1.40, 2&3 £3.20, 1&3 £3.70 CSF £11.99 CT £34.21 TOTE £3.20: £1.90, £2.30; EX 7.40 Trifecta £45.90 Pool: £830.00 - 13.38 winning units..
Owner Tobias B P Coles **Bred** Sheikh Abdulla Bin Isa Al-Khalifa **Trained** Newmarket, Suffolk

FOCUS
A modest sprint handicap. The winner is rated to his 2010 best.
Stonecrabstomorrow(IRE) Official explanation: trainer said gelding finished distressed

4239 SUSSEXSPORT MEDIAN AUCTION MAIDEN STKS 5f 213y
3:15 (3:15) (Class 6) 2-Y-0 **£1,617** (£481; £240; £120) **Stalls** Low

Form RPR

232 **1** **Super Simon (IRE)**[20] 3569 2-9-3 75..............................(v[1]) NeilCallan 3 77
(Paul D'Arcy) *t.k.h: upsides ldr: jinked rt after 1f: led over 2f out: rdn ent fnl 2f: forged clr jst over 1f out: styd on wl: rdn out* **8/11**[1]

6 **2** *5* **Man In The Arena**[19] 3617 2-9-3 0.................................. RobertHavlin 5 62
(Dr Jon Scargill) *t.k.h: chsd ldrs: rdn over 2f out: outpcd and dropped to rr 2f out: rallied to chse clr wnr ins fnl f: kpt on but no ch w wnr* **25/1**

43 **3** *2 3/4* **Petite Georgia (IRE)**[23] 3465 2-8-12 0............................ PatCosgrave 2 49
(George Baker) *awkward leaving stalls: chsd ldrs: rdn to chse wnr 2f out: no ex and btn ent fnl f: wknd fnl 100yds* **5/1**[3]

4 *shd* **Dream Cast (IRE)** 2-9-3 0.. MartinLane 4 54+
(David Simcock) *in tch in rr: clsd and gng wl 2f out: swtchd rt and effrt over 1f out: rn green: sn edgd lft and unable qck: wknd ins fnl f* **11/4**[2]

3 **5** *9* **Fruity Bun**[31] 3224 2-8-5 0.. IanBurns(7) 1 21
(Matthew Salaman) *led narrowly tl hdd over 2f out: rdn and unbalanced wl over 1f out: wknd over 1f out: bhd and eased ins fnl f* **16/1**

1m 13.65s (3.45) **Going Correction** +0.525s/f (Yiel) **5** Ran SP% **111.0**
Speed ratings (Par 92): **98,91,87,87,75**
CSF £19.62 TOTE £1.90: £1.10, £7.10; EX 25.80.
Owner Asiong Wong **Bred** Messrs A O'Callaghan & T Twomey **Trained** Newmarket, Suffolk

FOCUS
A fair juvenile maiden. The winner sets the level.

NOTEBOOK
Super Simon(IRE) was sporting a first-time visor for this fourth career start and had by far the best form, placing in all three previous starts, including posting a second consecutive RPR of 77 over 1f further at Folkestone last month. He was a bit keen early, but still found plenty, helped by his main market rival not picking up. He is reportedly likely to be sold to race in Hong Kong. (op Evens)
Man In The Arena finished a never-nearer last of six on debut over 1f shorter at Lingfield on good to firm the previous month. He showed he has gone the right way and looks likely to contest sprint nursery handicaps once qualified for a mark. (tchd 22-1 and 28-1)
Petite Georgia(IRE) finished third of five over C&D on her second start the previous month. She performed below that level this time, not helped by an awkward start. (op 9-2 tchd 4-1)
Dream Cast(IRE), who cost 90,000euros as a yearling, was hemmed in when travelling well around 2f out and ran green when seeing some daylight, not picking up as had looked likely. (op 3-1 tchd 10-3)

4240 1901 CLUB H'CAP (DIV I) 6f 209y
3:45 (3:45) (Class 6) (0-55,55) 3-Y-0+ **£1,617** (£481; £240; £120) **Stalls** Low

Form RPR

2604 **1** **Jackie Love (IRE)**[22] 3497 4-8-7 **46** oh1.......................(v) LauraPike(5) 6 58
(Olivia Maylam) *stdd s: hld up in rr of main gp: swtchd rt and effrt in centre 2f out: gd hdwy u.p over 1f out: led ins fnl f: edgd lft but sn clr: r.o strly* **6/1**[2]

3026 **2** *5* **Mark Anthony (IRE)**[5] 4087 5-8-12 **53**.................... ShirleyTeasdale(7) 4 52
(Shaun Harris) *led: rdn and edgd rt jst over 1f out: hdd ins fnl f: no ex and sn no ch w wnr: plugged on to hold 2nd* **7/4**[1]

00-0 **3** *2* **The Wonga Coup (IRE)**[23] 3470 5-8-12 **46**.................. KieranO'Neill 10 39
(Pat Phelan) *awkward and stmbld leaving stalls: bhd: hdwy u.p over 1f out: chsd ldrs 1f out: outpcd by wnr ins fnl f: plugged on* **14/1**

06-0 **4** *nk* **Crucis Abbey (IRE)**[20] 3559 4-9-3 **51**................................ LiamJones 1 43
(Mark Brisbourne) *in tch towards rr: swtchd rt and effrt 2f out: styd on u.p ins fnl f: no ch w wnr* **9/1**

0002 **5** *1 3/4* **Pose (IRE)**[17] 3701 5-9-4 **52**..(t) RobertHavlin 5 40
(Roger Ingram) *chsd ldrs: wnt 2nd jst over 2f out: rdn and unable qck ent fnl f: wknd ins fnl f* **6/1**[2]

00-6 **6** *hd* **Rafella (IRE)**[37] 3006 4-9-7 **55**......................................(p) HayleyTurner 7 42
(Michael Scudamore) *chsd ldrs: rdn over 2f out: unable qck over 1f out: wknd ins fnl f* **10/1**

0000 **7** *3 1/2* **Cuthbert (IRE)**[33] 3152 5-8-10 **49**............................ JemmaMarshall(5) 8 27
(Michael Attwater) *towards rr of main gp: rdn and hdwy to chse ldrs 2f out: no ex over 1f out: wknd fnl f* **33/1**

6002 **8** *5* **Bold Diva**[24] 3456 7-8-12 **46** oh1...(v) KierenFox 3 10
(Tony Carroll) *in tch in midfield: drvn and fnd little 2f out: wknd over 1f out: bhd ins fnl f* **8/1**[3]

0-00 **9** *5* **Lana Mae**[30] 3246 3-8-5 **46** oh1...................................... WilliamCarson 11
(Brendan Powell) *chsd ldr tl over 2f out: sn struggling: wknd wl over 1f out: bhd ins fnl f* **25/1**

-040 **10** *7* **Madame Feu**[22] 3489 3-8-13 **54**.................................... FergusSweeney 2
(Henry Candy) *in tch in midfield: rdn and unable qck over 2f out: wknd wl over 1f out: bhd and eased ins fnl f* **11/1**

1m 26.54s (3.44) **Going Correction** +0.525s/f (Yiel)
WFA 3 from 4yo+ 7lb **10** Ran SP% **116.9**
Speed ratings (Par 101): **101,95,93,92,90 90,86,80,75,67**
toteswingers 1&2 £4.00, 2&3 £16.30, 1&3 £26.70 CSF £16.89 CT £147.08 TOTE £6.20: £1.60, £1.50, £5.10; EX 29.40 Trifecta £350.70 Pool: £985.91 - 2.08 winning units..
Owner The Hookfield Racing Club **Bred** Bigwigs Bloodstock **Trained** Epsom, Surrey

FOCUS
The first division of a moderate 7f handicap, and slightly the quicker. The winner's first turf form, and there are doubts over the race.
Pose(IRE) Official explanation: trainer said tongue strap became adrift and couldn't be re-fitted which adversely affected mare's performance

4241 1901 CLUB H'CAP (DIV II) 6f 209y
4:15 (4:15) (Class 6) (0-55,54) 3-Y-0+ **£1,617** (£481; £240; £120) **Stalls** Low

Form RPR

0004 **1** **Whitstable Native**[9] 3949 4-9-3 **50**.................................... LiamKeniry 1 60
(Joseph Tuite) *broke wl and chsd ldrs early: stdd bk to rr after 2f: hdwy to chse ldrs and gng wl over 1f out: squeezed between horses to ld ins fnl f: sn in command and r.o strly* **11/1**

2533 **2** *2 3/4* **Baby Driver**[120] 988 4-9-6 **53**...............................(p) FergusSweeney 10 56
(Tony Newcombe) *chsd ldrs: wnt 2nd over 2f out: pushed along and hld hd high over 1f out: led ins fnl f: sn drvn and hdd: immediately btn and one pce after* **10/1**

00-4 **3** *1 1/4* **Trust Me Boy**[50] 2607 4-8-9 **45**................................ SimonPearce(3) 4 45
(John E Long) *chsd ldrs: rdn over 2f out: styng on same pce u.p whn n.m.r ent fnl f: hung lft and swtchd rt ins fnl f: styd on same pce fnl 100yds* **28/1**

2052 **4** *1/2* **Putin (IRE)**[2] 4193 4-8-9 **47**..................................(bt) LeonnaMayor(5) 6 45+
(Phil McEntee) *rrd as stalls opened and slowly away: rcvrd and hdwy to ld over 5f out: rdn and hrd pressed over 1f out: hdd ins fnl f: wknd fnl 75yds* **2/1**[1]

4000 **5** *2 1/4* **Rosy Dawn**[35] 3073 7-8-12 **45**...................................... KieranO'Neill 7 37
(John Bridger) *led tl over 5f out: chsd ldr tl rdn over 2f out: no ex u.p over 1f out: wknd ins fnl f* **20/1**

0002 **6** *nk* **Captainrisk (IRE)**[16] 3717 6-9-5 **52**...............................(v) IanMongan 3 43
(Christine Dunnett) *in tch: chsd ldrs and rdn over 1f out: fnd little u.p and btn 1f out: wknd ins fnl f* **5/1**[3]

2634 **7** *3 1/4* **Do More Business (IRE)**[8] 3964 5-9-0 **54**... WilliamTwiston-Davies(7) 8 37
(Alison Batchelor) *in tch in midfield on outer: effrt and rdn over 1f out: fnd little and sn btn: wknd fnl f* **11/4**[2]

1-63 **8** *3/4* **My Scat Daddy (USA)**[51] 2582 3-8-6 **51**...................... MarkCoumbe(5) 2 30
(Brett Johnson) *s.i.s: in tch: rdn wl over 1f out: switching rt and then lft jst over 1f out: sn struggling and wknd 1f out* **13/2**

1m 26.66s (3.56) **Going Correction** +0.525s/f (Yiel)
WFA 3 from 4yo+ 7lb **8** Ran SP% **115.6**
Speed ratings (Par 101): **100,96,95,94,92 91,88,87**
toteswingers 1&2 £5.40, 2&3 £13.00, 1&3 £14.50 CSF £114.20 CT £3000.68 TOTE £16.30: £3.60, £2.90, £7.10; EX 78.70 Trifecta £771.90 Part won. Pool: £1043.12 - 0.63 winning units..
Owner Bruce Woodward **Bred** D R Botterill **Trained** Great Shefford, Berks

FOCUS
The second leg of a moderate 7f handicap, and slightly the slower. A weak race, the winner rated to last year's best.
Baby Driver Official explanation: vet said gelding lost a left-hind shoe
My Scat Daddy(USA) Official explanation: trainer said gelding was unsuited by the track

4242 QSSD.COM VICENTE PLAZA H'CAP 7f 214y
4:45 (4:45) (Class 5) (0-70,70) 3-Y-0+ **£2,264** (£673; £336; £168) **Stalls** Low

Form RPR

5/05 **1** **Consider Yourself (USA)**[10] 3914 5-9-11 **67**............(p) WilliamCarson 6 76
(Anthony Carson) *in tch in midfield: rdn and effrt 2f out: hdwy u.p 1f out: wnt between horses and led fnl 50yds: r.o wl* **17/2**

0044 **2** *3/4* **Roedean (IRE)**[20] 3589 3-8-9 **64**...................................(tp) LauraPike(5) 7 69
(William Stone) *in tch: hdwy and chsd ldr 2f out: drvn and chal 1f out: led ins fnl f tl hdd and no ex fnl 50yds* **4/1**[2]

5 **3** *1* **Dundrum Dancer (IRE)**[32] 3207 5-9-2 **65**.. WilliamTwiston-Davies(7) 11 70
(Alex Hales) *stdd s: hld up in rr: hdwy 3f out: chsd ldrs 2f out: rdn and hung lft u.p ent fnl f: styd on same pce ins fnl f* **20/1**

5204 **4** *nk* **Satwa Laird**[10] 3914 6-10-0 **70**....................................... HayleyTurner 13 74
(Conor Dore) *chsd ldrs tl led ent fnl 2f: drvn and hrd pressed ent fnl f: hdd ins fnl f: no ex and wknd towards fin* **6/1**

2020 **5** *2* **Kelpie Blitz (IRE)**[30] 3246 3-9-1 **65**............................... FergusSweeney 1 62
(Seamus Durack) *dwlt: sn in tch in midfield: rdn and effrt to chse ldrs on inner ent fnl f: no ex fnl 150yds: wknd fnl 75yds* **5/1**[3]

3503 **6** *4 1/2* **Hereford Boy**[8] 3976 8-9-12 **68**.....................................(v) RobertHavlin 9 57
(Dean Ivory) *stdd after s: hld up in last trio: swtchd rt and effrt u.p over 1f out: no imp and btn 1f out: wl btn and eased towards fin* **6/1**

2-66 **7** *1 3/4* **Hint Of Mint**[41] 2866 3-9-6 **70**.. LiamKeniry 3 53
(Andrew Balding) *chsd ldr tl over 2f out: rdn and unable qck 2f out: drvn and btn over 1f out: wknd fnl f* **7/2**[1]

-000 **8** *3 3/4* **Ayaarah (IRE)**[28] 3318 4-8-6 **51** oh4.......................(v[1]) HarryBentley(3) 10 27
(William Knight) *t.k.h: chsd ldrs: wknd u.p over 1f out: fdd fnl f* **33/1**

2000 **9** 3 1/4 **Very Well Red**[118] 1009 9-8-6 **55** NoelGarbutt(7) 4 24
(Peter Hiatt) *led tl ent fnl 2f: sn u.p and struggling: wknd over 1f out* **25/1**
0640 **10** 19 **Tidy Affair (IRE)**[16] 3719 3-9-1 **65** JamieSpencer 12
(Murty McGrath) *stdd after s: styd wd: in tch in last trio: rdn 4f out: wknd 2f out: wl bhd and eased ins fnl f* **10/1**
1m 39.89s (3.89) **Going Correction** +0.525s/f (Yiel)
WFA 3 from 4yo+ 8lb 10 Ran SP% **118.6**
Speed ratings (Par 103): **101,100,99,98,96 92,90,86,83,64**
toteswingers 1&2 £2.60, 2&3 £14.30, 1&3 £24.20 CSF £42.29 CT £673.18 TOTE £11.90: £2.80, £1.60, £4.60; EX 47.60 Trifecta £568.60 Part won. Pool: £768.39 - 0.39 winning units..
Owner Christopher Wright & Minster Stud **Bred** Liberation Farm & Brandywine Farm **Trained** Newmarket, Suffolk
FOCUS
A fair handicap and pretty straightforward form.

4243 HARVEYS SUPPORTING ALBION IN THE COMMUNITY H'CAP 1m 1f 209y
5:15 (5:15) (Class 4) (0-80,79) 3-Y-0+ **£4,075** (£1,212; £606; £303) **Stalls** Centre

Form RPR
014 **1** **Sheikhzayedroad**[41] 2897 3-9-1 **76** JamieSpencer 1 91+
(David Simcock) *hld up in rr: clsd and travelling wl 2f out: pushed into ld and ducked rt ent fnl f: rn green and hung rt jst ins fnl f: in command but continued to r awkwardly after: pushed out* **4/7**[1]
3252 **2** 1 3/4 **Bayan (IRE)**[10] 3910 3-9-4 **79** (b) KierenFallon 5 88
(Brian Meehan) *led: rdn wl over 1f out: hdd ent fnl f: unable qck and pushed rt jst ins fnl f: one pce and wl hld after* **3/1**[2]
P453 **3** 4 1/2 **South Cape**[18] 3659 9-8-12 **66** HarryBentley(3) 3 66
(Gary Moore) *chsd ldng pair: rdn and effrt 2f out: one pce and struggling whn squeezed for room and hmpd jst over 1f out: wknd fnl f* **12/1**[3]
-062 **4** 2 1/4 **Hawaana (IRE)**[7] 3995 7-9-5 **73** AdamBeschizza(3) 4 69
(Gay Kelleway) *hld up in last pair: hdwy over 4f out: rdn and chsd ldrs over 2f out: wknd ent fnl f* **14/1**
30-6 **5** 10 **Brigadoon**[29] 3278 5-9-4 **76** WilliamTwiston-Davies(7) 6 52
(William Jarvis) *chsd ldr tl wl over 1f out: sn wknd* **14/1**
2m 8.62s (5.02) **Going Correction** +0.525s/f (Yiel)
WFA 3 from 5yo+ 10lb 5 Ran SP% **109.7**
Speed ratings (Par 105): **100,98,95,93,85**
CSF £2.49 TOTE £1.50: £1.10, £1.30; EX 2.50.
Owner Mohammed Jaber **Bred** Rabbah Bloodstock Limited **Trained** Newmarket, Suffolk
FOCUS
A fair handicap with the biggest prize-money purse on the card, but not strong form for the grade. The second sets the standard.

4244 AFINIS DIGITAL MARKETING SUPPORT AITC APPRENTICE H'CAP 1m 3f 196y
5:50 (5:50) (Class 6) (0-60,60) 4-Y-0+ **£1,617** (£481; £240; £120) **Stalls** Centre

Form RPR
005 **1** **Taroum (IRE)**[31] 3222 5-9-4 **57** KierenFox 10 68
(Tony Carroll) *hld up in tch: rdn and qcknd to ld 2f out: clr over 1f out: r.o wl: eased towards fin* **4/1**[2]
041 **2** 5 **Tawseef (IRE)**[16] 3721 4-8-13 **57** WilliamTwiston-Davies(5) 8 60
(Roy Brotherton) *hld up in last pair: rdn and effrt nrest stands' rail over 2f out: chsd clr wnr over 1f out: styd on but no imp* **6/5**[1]
4500 **3** 5 **Thundering Home**[18] 3659 5-9-0 **56** DavidKenny(3) 2 51
(Richard Mitchell) *in tch: chsd ldrs 1/2-way: rdn and effrt over 2f out: chsd wnr but outpcd wl over 1f out: 3rd and wl hld 1f out* **33/1**
5345 **4** 1 3/4 **Barbirolli**[20] 3573 10-8-7 **46** oh1 AdamBeschizza 4 38
(William Stone) *hld up in tch: effrt u.p over 2f out: 4th and no imp over 1f out: wl btn 1f out* **25/1**
0626 **5** 6 **Royal Defence (IRE)**[23] 3468 6-8-13 **55** TobyAtkinson(3) 3 38
(Michael Quinn) *led tl 2f out: sn struggling u.p and wknd over 1f out: wl btn and eased towards fin* **16/1**
3145 **6** 2 1/2 **King's Road**[23] 3468 7-9-7 **60** (t) HarryBentley 7 39
(Anabel K Murphy) *chsd ldr: upsides ldr over 2f out: rdn and unable qck 2f out: sn btn and wknd over 1f out: wl btn and eased wl ins fnl f* **10/1**
2543 **7** 13 **Crimson Monarch (USA)**[3] 4156 8-8-3 **47** NoelGarbutt(5) 1
(Peter Hiatt) *chsd ldrs: rdn over 2f out: sn struggling and wknd 2f out: wl bhd and eased ins fnl f* **5/1**[3]
0150 **8** 55 **Tallulah Mai**[8] 3969 5-8-10 **54** IanBurns(5) 9
(Matthew Salaman) *in tch tl rdn and dropped to rr over 6f out: lost tch 4f out: t.o and virtually p.u fnl 2f* **9/1**
2m 41.77s (9.07) **Going Correction** +0.525s/f (Yiel) 8 Ran SP% **113.9**
Speed ratings (Par 101): **90,86,83,82,78 76,67,31**
toteswingers 1&2 £2.30, 2&3 £6.90, 1&3 £10.70 CSF £9.09 CT £131.07 TOTE £3.10: £1.10, £1.80, £4.70; EX 6.10 Trifecta £191.70 Pool: £1147.66 - 4.43 winning units..
Owner Jason Tucker **Bred** His Highness The Aga Khan's Studs S C **Trained** Cropthorne, Worcs
FOCUS
A modest middle-distance handicap for older horses and restricted to apprentice riders. Not form to be too literal or positive about.
T/Plt: £253.90 to a £1 stake. Pool of £65659.78 - 188.75 winning tickets. T/Qpdt: £65.30 to a £1 stake. Pool of £4810.13 - 54.48 winning tickets. SP

3988 DONCASTER (L-H)
Thursday, July 19
OFFICIAL GOING: Good (good to soft in places; 7.6)
Wind: Moderate, half-behind Weather: Cloudy

4245 DULUX APPRENTICE H'CAP 5f
6:20 (6:20) (Class 6) (0-65,65) 3-Y-0+ **£1,617** (£481; £240; £120) **Stalls** High

Form RPR
-266 **1** **Fear Nothing**[168] 380 5-9-2 **58** DavidBergin(5) 2 69
(David O'Meara) *trckd ldrs: hdwy over 2f out: rdn to ld over 1f out: drvn and hung rt ins fnl f: kpt on* **11/1**
5055 **2** 1 **Spirit Of Coniston**[23] 3462 9-8-9 **53** DanielleMooney(7) 8 60
(Paul Midgley) *hld up: swtchd lft to outer and hdwy wl over 1f out: str run ent fnl f: nrst fin* **20/1**
3434 **3** 1 **Belinsky (IRE)**[47] 2690 5-9-9 **65** JacobButterfield(5) 15 68
(Julie Camacho) *towards rr: hdwy 2f out: sn rdn and styd on fnl f: nrst fin* **9/1**
5142 **4** shd **Another Citizen (IRE)**[9] 3944 4-9-7 **63** (b) RachelRichardson(5) 5 66
(Tim Easterby) *in tch: hdwy 2f out: sn rdn: kpt on fnl f* **7/2**[1]
-005 **5** 3/4 **Mecca's Team**[41] 2878 4-9-7 **61** (p) DavidSimmonson(3) 1 61
(Michael Dods) *sn led: rdn 2f out: edgd rt and hdd over 1f out: wknd ins fnl f* **14/1**
400- **6** 3/4 **Piste**[330] 5373 6-8-9 **46** oh1 (e[1]) RachealKneller 3 44
(Tina Jackson) *chsd ldrs: rdn along wl over 1f out: sn one pce* **100/1**
6040 **7** 1 1/4 **Lucky Art (USA)**[7] 3993 6-9-10 **61** NicoleNordblad 14 54
(Conor Dore) *chsd ldrs: rdn along over 2f out: sn wknd* **11/1**
2046 **8** nk **Boucher Garcon (IRE)**[2] 4187 4-9-6 **64** MichaelKenny(7) 6 56
(Declan Carroll) *chsd ldr: rdn 2f out: wknd wl over 1f out* **11/2**[3]
056 **9** nk **Majestic Angel (IRE)**[26] 3406 3-8-0 **46** oh1 EvaMoscrop(5) 4 37
(Brian Rothwell) *a towards rr* **50/1**
0125 **10** 1 3/4 **Errigal Lad**[2] 4174 7-9-4 **58** ThomasBrown(3) 11 43
(Garry Woodward) *s.i.s: a bhd* **9/2**[2]
0-02 **11** 1 1/4 **Myjestic Melody (IRE)**[30] 3256 4-9-0 **51** GeorgeChaloner 7 31
(Noel Wilson) *dwlt: a in rr* **8/1**
5000 **12** 61 **Liberty Ship**[7] 3993 7-9-11 **65** (t) LauraBarry(3) 13
(Mark Buckley) *v.s.a and lost many l s: a t.o* **9/1**
1m 0.42s (-0.08) **Going Correction** +0.025s/f (Good)
WFA 3 from 4yo+ 4lb 12 Ran SP% **117.9**
Speed ratings (Par 101): **101,99,97,97,96 95,93,92,92,89 87,**
Totc Swingcrs 1&2 £33.70, 2&3 £43.70, 1&3 £22.60 CSF £210.18 CT £2094.64 TOTE £17.60: £3.60, £2.90, £3.00; EX 173.80.
Owner C Maxsted & Miss S Iggulden **Bred** Houghton Bloodstock Uk Ltd **Trained** Nawton, N Yorks
FOCUS
A modest apprentice sprint handicap and the main action was towards the centre of the track. Straightforward form.
Liberty Ship Official explanation: jockey said gelding was slowly away

4246 EBF SAINT GOBAIN WEBER MAIDEN FILLIES' STKS 7f
6:50 (6:51) (Class 5) 2-Y-O **£3,169** (£943; £471; £235) **Stalls** High

Form RPR
0 **1** **Dusky Queen (IRE)**[20] 3560 2-9-0 0 TonyHamilton 5 73+
(Richard Fahey) *trckd ldrs: effrt 2f out: rdn over 1f out: styd on wl fnl f to ld nr line* **16/1**
36 **2** shd **Testamatta**[20] 3590 2-9-0 0 WilliamBuick 8 73
(Marco Botti) *trckd ldrs: hdwy on outer to ld 2f out: rdn: green and edgd rt ins fnl f: drvn and hdd towards fin* **9/2**[2]
2 **3** nk **Pompeia**[23] 3474 2-9-0 0 JimCrowley 2 72
(Ralph Beckett) *trckd ldrs: hdwy and cl up 3f out: chal 2f out: rdn and ev ch ent fnl f: no ex towards fin* **13/8**[1]
6 **4** 3/4 **Lady Marmelo (IRE)**[23] 3474 2-9-0 0 SamHitchcott 6 70
(Mick Channon) *trckd ldrs: hdwy 2f out: swtchd rt and rdn over 1f out: kpt on fnl f* **33/1**
5 1 1/4 **Deserted** 2-9-0 0 KirstyMilczarek 1 67+
(Luca Cumani) *dwlt and hld up towards rr: stdy hdwy on outer 1/2-way: effrt to chse ldrs over 2f out: rdn and ch over 1f out: one pce fnl f: improve* **9/2**[2]
5 **6** hd **Dixie Sky (USA)**[20] 3560 2-9-0 0 TomQueally 3 66
(Noel Quinlan) *dwlt: hld up towards rr: hdwy over 2f out: rdn to chse ldrs whn n.m.r and rn green over 1f out: no imp fnl f* **9/1**[3]
43 **7** 1 **Specialty (IRE)**[19] 3611 2-9-0 0 MickyFenton 7 64
(Pam Sly) *led: rdn along 3f out: hdd 2f out and grad wknd* **9/2**[2]
8 2 **Aeronwyn Bryn (IRE)** 2-9-0 0 PaulMulrennan 4 63+
(Michael Dods) *rn green and hld up in rr: sme hdwy fnl 2f* **33/1**
00 **9** 7 **Una Bella Cosa**[20] 3560 2-9-0 0 IPoullis 10 40
(Alan McCabe) *t.k.h: chsd ldr: rdn along over 2f out: sn wknd* **200/1**
00 **10** 39 **Diva Cavallina**[20] 3569 2-8-7 0 NoraLooby(7) 9
(Alan McCabe) *a in rr: rdn along and outpcd fr 1/2-way* **200/1**
1m 28.29s (1.99) **Going Correction** +0.025s/f (Good) 10 Ran SP% **115.4**
Speed ratings (Par 91): **89,88,88,87,86 86,84,82,74,30**
Tote Swingers 1&2 £11.60, 2&3 £1.80, 1&3 £6.80 CSF £85.01 TOTE £22.40: £4.30, £1.70, £1.20; EX 94.50.
Owner Mrs H Steel **Bred** Paul Hyland **Trained** Musley Bank, N Yorks
FOCUS
A fair maiden 2yo fillies' event with a tight three-way finish. The field finished quite compressed but there are some potential improvers.
NOTEBOOK
Dusky Queen(IRE) had clearly learnt plenty first time. She showed a good attitude to squeeze between horses and show ahead near the finish. She should improve again and looks a likely nursery type. A mile will suit her even better. (op 20-1)
Testamatta, who had run at a RPR of 76 on her two previous starts at Newmarket, just missed out. Her turn will surely come. (op 5-1 tchd 11-2)
Pompeia, who lacks a little substance, had clearly learnt from her first run and in the end came up only a fraction short. She has a round action and will appreciate give underfoot. (op 11-10 tchd Evens)
Lady Marmelo(IRE), about eight lengths behind Pompeia when both made their debut at Newbury, finished with quite a flourish. She will improve again and should have no difficulty finding a race. (op 50-1)
Deserted gave a problem or two in the paddock. Her dam was a winner over 1m6f and she will improve when stepped up to a mile. Official explanation: jockey said filly ran green (op 8-1 tchd 9-1)
Dixie Sky(USA) stayed on in her own time and looks more of a nursery type further down the road. (op 14-1)
Specialty(IRE) took them along but faded in rather disappointing fashion. Out of the stable's 1,000 Guineas winner Speciosa, she looks the type who might come into her own at three. (op 4-1 tchd 5-1)
Diva Cavallina Official explanation: jockey said filly never travelled

4247 STOBART NOVICE STKS 6f
7:25 (7:25) (Class 5) 2-Y-O **£2,264** (£673; £336; £168) **Stalls** High

Form RPR
1 **1** **Unsinkable (IRE)**[21] 3533 2-9-2 0 TonyHamilton 2 89
(Richard Fahey) *led: pushed along 2f out: sn jnd and rdn: hdd ins fnl f: drvn and rallied gamely to ld again on line* **7/2**[3]
1 **2** shd **Tickle Time (IRE)**[26] 3378 2-9-5 0 GrahamGibbons 1 92
(David Barron) *hld up: hdwy on outer and cl up 2f out: sn chal: rdn and slt ld ins fnl f: sn drvn: hdd and no ex on line* **15/8**[1]
1 **3** 2 **Elle Woods (IRE)**[49] 2631 2-9-0 0 PaulMulrennan 4 81
(Michael Dods) *t.k.h: stdd s and wnt lft after 100yds: trckd ldrs: effrt 2f out: sn rdn: chsd ldng pair ins fnl f: sn no imp* **3/1**[2]
4 1/2 **Veturia (USA)** 2-8-9 0 (t) PhillipMakin 5 75+
(Kevin Ryan) *t.k.h: chsd ldrs: rdn wl over 1f out: kpt on same pce* **13/2**
1 **5** 1 1/4 **Secret Look**[26] 3381 2-9-5 0 FrannyNorton 3 81
(Ed McMahon) *t.k.h: cl up: rdn along 2f out: grad wknd* **9/2**
1m 14.1s (0.50) **Going Correction** +0.025s/f (Good) 5 Ran SP% **113.5**
Speed ratings (Par 94): **97,96,94,93,91**
CSF £10.87 TOTE £2.30: £1.10, £1.40; EX 10.70.
Owner Penman Bond Partnership **Bred** Stephanie Hanly **Trained** Musley Bank, N Yorks
FOCUS
This novice event was won by subsequent Group 1 2yo winner Wootton Bassett in 2010. Four winners of their only previous race and a well regarded newcomer, and the form has been given a chance.

NOTEBOOK
Unsinkable(IRE), from the stable which won this with Wootton Bassett two years ago, had run out a wide-margin winner in bad ground at Newcastle. He set the pace and battled back in most willing fashion to get back up near the line. He will be even better suited by seven and looks a useful prospect. (op 10-3 tchd 3-1)
Tickle Time(IRE), a Gimcrack entry, was soon sitting upsides the winner seemingly to be travelling marginally better but in the end he just missed out. There will be other opportunities. (op 5-2 tchd 11-4 and 7-4)
Elle Woods(IRE), who accounted for two subsequent winners at Newcastle, is quite a big, rather ungainly filly. She will improve again and will be interesting in one of the sales races later on. (tchd 10-3)
Veturia(USA), a Lowther entry, took a keen hold on her debut. She showed a decent level of ability and a maiden would be a formality. (op 6-1 tchd 8-1)
Secret Look, who took an ordinary maiden at Hyadock, ran with the choke out and may be better back over five. (op 5-1 tchd 11-2)

4248 IRISH THOROUGHBRED MARKETING CONDITIONS STKS — 1m (S)
7:55 (7:55) (Class 3) 4-Y-O+ — **£6,792** (£2,021; £1,010; £505) **Stalls** High

Form				RPR
6023	**1**		**Dance And Dance (IRE)**[33] 3166 6-8-9 110 WilliamBuick 6 — (Ed Vaughan) *hld up in rr: smooth hdwy wl over 2f out: chal over 1f out: rdn to ld ins fnl f: styd on strly* **7/4**[1]	102+
2040	**2**	3	**Bridgefield (USA)**[29] 3268 4-8-9 99 MickaelBarzalona 4 — (Mahmood Al Zarooni) *trckd ldrs: hdwy over 2f out: led wl over 1f out: sn jnd and rdn: hdd ins fnl f: kpt on same pce* **9/4**[2]	97+
1031	**3**	3	**Madam Macie (IRE)**[21] 3522 5-8-4 96 JamesSullivan 5 — (David O'Meara) *led: rdn along over 2f out: hdd wl over 1f out: sn one pce* **7/2**[3]	83
3/2-	**4**	nk	**Self Employed**[423] 2361 5-8-9 73 MickyFenton 1 — (Garry Woodward) *dwlt and in rr: hdwy and in tch wl over 2f out: sn rdn and one pce* **66/1**	87?
6003	**5**	4 ½	**Sos Brillante (CHI)**[12] 3860 7-8-4 76 FrankieMcDonald 2 — (Terry Clement) *chsd ldrs: rdn along and wknd over 3f out* **40/1**	72
0265	**6**	5	**St Moritz (IRE)**[43] 2819 6-8-9 105 AdrianNicholls 3 — (David Nicholls) *trckd ldr: hdwy and cl up 3f out: sn rdn and wknd fnl 2f* **11/2**	66

1m 38.48s (-0.82) **Going Correction** +0.025s/f (Good) **6** Ran SP% **108.7**
Speed ratings (Par 107): **105,102,99,98,94 89**
Tote Swingers 1&2 £1.20, 2&3 £1.90, 1&3 £1.10 CSF £5.53 TOTE £3.30: £2.00, £1.10; EX 6.80.
Owner Mohammed Rashid **Bred** Darley **Trained** Newmarket, Suffolk

FOCUS
A typically muddling conditions race. Doubts over the form, and the first two are rated below their best.

NOTEBOOK
Dance And Dance(IRE), an infrequent winner, was clear on official ratings. Narrowly denied in a Group 3 at Epsom, he was never travelling when unsuited by the soft ground when a well-beaten third at York next time. Dropped in and ridden with bags of confidence, he won going away. He could well be soon on his travels. (op 2-1)
Bridgefield(USA), who finished last in the Royal Hunt Cup after becoming upset in the stalls, had 11lb to find with the winner. He looked likely to make a good race of it but was firmly put in his place. (tchd 5-2)
Madam Macie(IRE) raced with plenty of zest in front but proved no match for the two boys. She is happier on much easier ground. (op 4-1)
Self Employed, who had a mountain to climb, was having his first start for over a year. He ran way above his official mark of 73 and may well have been flattered but this 5yo can surely find a maiden.
Sos Brillante(CHI), rated just 76, is being set some stiff tasks at present. She was not disgraced but likewise may well have been flattered. (op 33-1)
St Moritz(IRE), absent for six weeks, is happier making the running. He challenged for the lead with three furlongs left to run but hung left and lookeds to throw in the towel completely. He is one to have reservations about now. (op 4-1)

4249 MIRROR PUNTERS CLUB H'CAP — 1m 2f 60y
8:30 (8:30) (Class 4) (0-85,85) 4-Y-O+ — **£4,204** (£1,251; £625; £312) **Stalls** Low

Form				RPR
1553	**1**		**Art Scholar (IRE)**[15] 3766 5-9-4 82 TomQueally 11 — (Michael Appleby) *hld up towards rr: hdwy on wd outside 3f out: rdn to chal and edgd lft 2f out: sn slt ld: drvn ins fnl f: edgd lft towards fin: jst hld on* **9/1**	89
0223	**2**	shd	**New Hampshire (USA)**[6] 4074 4-9-3 84 LeeTopliss(3) 12 — (Tony Coyle) *trckd ldr: hdwy to ld 3f out: sn rdn and jnd 2f out: drvn and hdd over 1f out: rallied ins fnl f and ev ch whn sltly hmpd and no ex nr line* **8/1**	91
3-52	**3**	½	**Kenyan Cat**[20] 3556 5-9-4 82 FrannyNorton 4 — (Ed McMahon) *hld up in midfield: hdwy over 2f out: rdn to chse ldrs over 1f out: styd on wl fnl f* **4/1**[2]	88
01-0	**4**	nk	**Novirak (IRE)**[62] 2248 4-8-9 73 TedDurcan 3 — (James Fanshawe) *midfield: hdwy on outer over 3f out: rdn to chse ldrs 2f out: drvn and kpt on fnl f* **7/1**[3]	78
0003	**5**	¾	**Kalk Bay (IRE)**[21] 3525 5-8-8 72 (t) PaulMulrennan 10 — (Michael Easterby) *hld up in rr: hdwy wl over 2f out: rdn over 1f out: styd on fnl f: nrst fin* **25/1**	76+
4133	**6**	3 ½	**Amazing Blue Sky**[10] 3906 6-9-1 79 (b) JamesSullivan 5 — (Ruth Carr) *led: rdn along 4f out: hdd 3f out: wknd over 2f out* **12/1**	76
0400	**7**	1	**Ailsa Craig (IRE)**[17] 3693 6-8-7 71 BarryMcHugh 8 — (Edwin Tuer) *chsd ldrs: rdn along 4f out: grad wknd* **25/1**	67
2001	**8**	hd	**Franco Is My Name**[20] 3574 6-9-2 80 JimCrowley 1 — (Peter Hedger) *chsd ldrs: hdwy 3f out: rdn over 2f out: sn wknd* **15/2**	75
	9	nk	**Nova Sam (FR)**[129] 4-9-4 82 LeeNewman 9 — (David Barron) *in tch on inner: hdwy wl over 2f out: rdn wl over 1f out: sn wknd* **33/1**	77
-110	**10**	13	**William Haigh (IRE)**[110] 1139 4-9-7 85 WilliamBuick 2 — (Alan Swinbank) *chsd ldng pair: rdn along 3f out: sn wknd* **9/1**	55
3455	**11**	7	**Tres Coronas (IRE)**[22] 3494 5-9-6 84 GrahamGibbons 7 — (David Barron) *rrd s and v.s.a: a t.o* **10/3**[1]	41

2m 11.88s (2.48) **Going Correction** +0.20s/f (Good) **11** Ran SP% **116.8**
Speed ratings (Par 105): **98,97,97,97,96 93,93,92,92,82 76**
Tote Swingers 1&2 £20.70, 2&3 £3.50, 1&3 £7.60 CSF £76.74 CT £336.65 TOTE £11.40: £3.80, £5.90, £1.60; EX 110.90.
Owner Mrs J Scrivens **Bred** John Ramsbottom **Trained** Danethorpe, Notts
■ Stewards' Enquiry : Lee Topliss two-day ban: used his whip above permitted level (Aug 2-3)

FOCUS
An open looking 71-85 handicap. The pace was just steady until turning in. Ordinary form, with the front three close to their recent marks.
Amazing Blue Sky Official explanation: jockey said gelding hung right-handed
William Haigh(IRE) Official explanation: trainer's rep said gelding was unsuited by the good (good to soft places) ground
Tres Coronas(IRE) Official explanation: jockey said he had been slow to remove blindfold and gelding was slowly away

4250 COOPERS MARQUEES H'CAP — 1m 2f 60y
9:00 (9:01) (Class 5) (0-70,70) 3-Y-O — **£2,264** (£673; £336; £168) **Stalls** Low

Form				RPR
0-06	**1**		**Calculated Risk**[31] 3228 3-8-10 59 WilliamBuick 5 — (Willie Musson) *hld up in rr: stdy hdwy on outer over 3f out: chsd ldrs and edgd lft 2f out: rdn to chal and hung lft ent fnl f: led and drvn clr last 100yds* **7/2**[1]	70
1233	**2**	3 ½	**Mistress Of Rome**[12] 3847 3-9-4 70 (p) LeeTopliss(3) 1 — (Michael Dods) *a.p: effrt to chal over 2f out: rdn to ld jst over 1f out: drvn and hdd ins fnl f: one pce* **11/2**[2]	74
3336	**3**	1 ½	**Feisty Champion (IRE)**[14] 3774 3-9-7 70 FrannyNorton 11 — (J W Hills) *in tch: pushed along 1/2-way: rdn along 3f out: hdwy 2f out: drvn and styd on fnl f: nrst fin* **7/2**[1]	71
1025	**4**	nk	**Dorry K (IRE)**[31] 3212 3-9-5 68 GrahamGibbons 6 — (David Barron) *trckd ldng pair: hdwy and cl up 4f out: led 2f out: sn jnd and rdn: hdd jst over 1f out sn drvn and wknd* **6/1**[3]	69
0-63	**5**	8	**Buster Brown (IRE)**[32] 3186 3-9-5 68 PaulMulrennan 10 — (James Given) *sn led: rdn along 4f out: hdd 2f out: sn wknd* **15/2**	53
-320	**6**	nse	**Island Melody (IRE)**[74] 1892 3-9-5 68 TedDurcan 4 — (J S Moore) *trckd ldrs: hdwy over 3f out: rdn to chse ldrs over 2f out: sn drvn and wknd* **16/1**	53
065	**7**	7	**In The Crowd (IRE)**[29] 3273 3-9-4 67 RobertWinston 8 — (Alan Swinbank) *chsd ldrs: rdn along over 3f out: wknd over 2f out* **14/1**	39
000	**8**	2 ¼	**Fuzzy Logic (IRE)**[35] 3079 3-8-13 62 JimCrowley 9 — (William Muir) *midfield: effrt and sme hdwy 4f out: sn rdn along and n.d* **10/1**	30
0056	**9**	1	**Icewan**[36] 3025 3-8-8 57 ow3 MickyFenton 2 — (Paul Midgley) *a in rr* **25/1**	23
5-65	**10**	½	**First Glance**[152] 620 3-7-13 51 oh2 DominicFox(3) 7 — (Michael Appleby) *dwlt: a in rr* **22/1**	16

2m 11.31s (1.91) **Going Correction** +0.20s/f (Good) **10** Ran SP% **115.7**
Speed ratings (Par 100): **100,97,96,95,89 89,83,81,81,80**
Tote Swingers 1&2 £5.80, 2&3 £5.90, 1&3 £4.10 CSF £22.33 CT £71.77 TOTE £3.40: £1.10, £1.50, £2.60; EX 25.10.
Owner A Duke & J Babbs **Bred** Newsells Park Stud **Trained** Newmarket, Suffolk

FOCUS
A modest but open-looking 3yo handicap run at a sound gallop and the winner came from off the pace under a well-judged ride. The time was relatively good and the winner is accorded an 8lb personal best.
Calculated Risk Official explanation: trainer said, regarding apparent improvement in form, that the gelding was suited by the strong pace and weaker race.
T/Plt: £63.90 to a 1 stake. Pool £63,183.68. 721.51 winning tickets. T/Qpdt: £7.80 to a 1 stake. Pool £6,057.43. 567.96 winning tickets. JR

3995 EPSOM (L-H)
Thursday, July 19
OFFICIAL GOING: Good to soft (last 5f good; 7.6)
Wind: Light, against Weather: Fine but cloudy, shower during Race 3

4251 MAY FAMILY LADIES' DERBY H'CAP (FOR LADY AMATEUR RIDERS) — 1m 4f 10y
6:10 (6:12) (Class 4) (0-80,80) 4-Y-O+ — **£4,367** (£1,354; £676; £338) **Stalls** Centre

Form				RPR
0000	**1**		**Epsom Salts**[29] 3278 7-10-2 72 MissSBrotherton 8 — (Pat Phelan) *hld up early: prog 1/2-way: wnt 3rd st: chsd ldr over 2f out: rdn to ld 1f out: styd on wl* **12/1**	79
3113	**2**	1 ½	**Rub Of The Relic (IRE)**[3] 4137 7-9-5 66 (v) MissHDukes(5) 9 — (Paul Midgley) *led: kpt on wl whn pressed over 3f out: hdd and one pce 1f out* **15/2**	71
0024	**3**	2 ¾	**Shesha Bear**[14] 3769 7-10-5 75 (p) MissEJJones 4 — (Jonathan Portman) *hld up in last pair: 8th and wl off the pce st: rdn and prog over 2f out: styd on fnl f to take 3rd post: hopeless task* **6/1**[3]	76
-656	**4**	hd	**Kings Troop**[14] 3769 6-9-13 69 (v[1]) MissJCoward 7 — (Alan King) *trckd ldrs: cl 4th st and clr of rest: rdn to chse ldng pair over 1f out: no imp: lost 3rd post* **8/1**	69
6462	**5**	2	**Brouhaha**[21] 3552 8-9-7 68 MissALMurphy(5) 5 — (Tom Dascombe) *hld up in last pair: rdn and prog over 4f out: 7th and off the pce st: kpt on after: nvr able to threaten* **12/1**	65
124	**6**	1 ¼	**O Ma Lad (IRE)**[27] 3341 4-10-5 80 MissCBoxall(5) 2 — (Sylvester Kirk) *hld up towards rr: prog into modest 5th st: sn rdn: one pce and nvr threatened* **5/2**[1]	75
4121	**7**	20	**The Ducking Stool**[14] 3794 5-9-1 62 MissSBirkett(5) 1 — (Julia Feilden) *trckd ldr: chal over 3f out: lost 2nd over 2f out: wknd qckly and eased over 1f out* **4/1**[2]	25
532-	**8**	23	**Carrowbeg (IRE)**[380] 3706 4-9-13 69 (t) MissGAndrews 6 — (Lawney Hill) *in tch in midfield early: lost pl bef 1/2-way: 9th and wkng st: t.o* **11/1**	
/41-	**9**	1	**Encircled**[533] 384 8-10-2 77 MissKMargarson(5) 3 — (J R Jenkins) *chsd ldng pair 4f: 6th and wkng st: t.o* **28/1**	

2m 46.95s (8.05) **Going Correction** +0.30s/f (Good) **9** Ran SP% **112.9**
Speed ratings (Par 105): **85,84,82,82,80 79,66,51,50**
Tote Swingers 1&2 £8.90, 2&3 £11.00, 1&3 £16.50 CSF £96.08 CT £595.17 TOTE £15.60: £3.30, £3.30, £2.60; EX 88.80 Trifecta £616.50 Part won. Pool 833.20 - 0.64 winning units..
Owner The Epsom Racegoers **Bred** Heatherwold Stud **Trained** Epsom, Surrey

FOCUS
Rail dolled out up to 7yds from 1m from there to Winning Post adding about 10yds to race distances. A fair lady amateurs' handicap, in which few could be confidently discounted. The winner matched last year's best.
Epsom Salts Official explanation: trainer said, regarding apparent improvement in form, that the gelding was better suited by a return to Epsom where it has previously been successful three times.
Carrowbeg(IRE) Official explanation: jockey said gelding never travelled

4252 DOWNLOAD EPSOM'S ANDROID OR IPHONE APP NOW CLAIMING STKS — 7f
6:40 (6:40) (Class 5) 3-Y-O+ — **£2,587** (£770; £384; £192) **Stalls** Low

Form				RPR
4605	**1**		**Fathsta (IRE)**[28] 3304 7-9-5 82 JamieSpencer 3 — (David Simcock) *hld up in rr: 7th and wl off the pce st: prog on outer over 2f out: rdn and styd on fr over 1f out to ld last 100yds: won gng away* **11/4**[1]	77

25 **2** *1* **Offbeat Safaris (IRE)**[19] 3609 4-9-1 0 SebSanders 1 70
(Brendan Powell) *pressed ldr: upsides ent st: hanging lft u.p fr over 2f out: hdd and outpcd last 100yds* **10/1**

530 **3** *nse* **Celtic Sultan (IRE)**[27] 3334 8-9-3 84 RoystonFfrench 8 72
(Paul Midgley) *fast away: led: jnd ent st: duelled after tl hdd and outpcd last 100yds* **7/2**[2]

1050 **4** *1 1/4* **Indian Art (IRE)**[17] 3703 6-8-12 76 SeanLevey 2 65
(Sylvester Kirk) *hld up: 6th and off the pce st: tried to cl on ldrs fr over 2f out: keeping on but hld whn nt clr run last 75yds* **8/1**

2050 **5** *1 1/2* **New Leyf (IRE)**[36] 3049 6-9-1 85 (v) NeilCallan 7 62
(Ed Walker) *chsd ldng pair: rdn over 2f out: one pce and no imp over 1f out: sn lost 3rd* **7/2**[2]

0005 **6** *shd* **Northern Spy (USA)**[22] 3511 8-8-9 55 SimonPearce(3) 5 59?
(Simon Dow) *hld up: detached last st: shkn up over 2f out: styd on steadily after: nrst fin* **40/1**

2044 **7** *6* **Standing Strong (IRE)**[12] 3843 4-8-8 72 (v[1]) DanielCremin(7) 4 46
(Robert Mills) *towards rr: 5th and nt on terms st: lost pl over 2f out: wknd* **16/1**

3-10 **8** *3/4* **Cool Rhythm**[22] 3503 4-9-1 77 MartinLane 6 44
(Ralph Beckett) *dwlt: chsd ldng trio: clr of rest st: wknd 2f out* **13/2**[3]

1m 26.49s (3.19) **Going Correction** +0.30s/f (Good) **8 Ran SP% 113.0**
Speed ratings (Par 103): **93,91,91,90,88 88,81,80**
Tote Swingers 1&2 £8.40, 2&3 £8.30, 1&3 £2.60 CSF £30.34 TOTE £3.20: £1.10, £3.20, £3.50; EX 32.00 Trifecta £240.80 Pool 771.39 - 2.37 winning units..Offbeat Safaris was claimed by Ron Harris for £10,000.
Owner Dr Marwan Koukash **Bred** Brian Miller **Trained** Newmarket, Suffolk

FOCUS
A competitive claimer, in which they finished in something of a heap. The modest time and the sixth limit the form.

4253 IRISH STALLION FARMS EBF MAIDEN STKS 7f
7:15 (7:15) (Class 5) 2-Y-O **£3,881** (£1,155; £577; £288) **Stalls Low**

Form RPR

0 **1** **Whipper's Boy (IRE)**[27] 3346 2-9-3 0 KierenFallon 8 88+
(Brian Meehan) *hld up in rr: sltly awkward downhill and 7th st: prog on outer over 2f out: led over 1f out: pushed along and sn clr: comf* **9/2**[3]

00 **2** *3 1/2* **Zanetto**[26] 3368 2-9-3 0 LiamKeniry 7 76
(Andrew Balding) *racd freely: mde most: pressed fr 1/2-way: hdd and outpcd over 1f out* **11/4**[2]

20 **3** *3 1/2* **Royal Skies (IRE)**[13] 3824 2-9-3 0 SilvestreDeSousa 1 67
(Mark Johnston) *pressed ldr: chal over 3f out: stl upsides as wnr wnt by over 1f out: fdd fnl f* **9/4**[1]

66 **4** *nk* **Aussie Reigns (IRE)**[27] 3346 2-9-3 0 NeilCallan 2 67
(William Knight) *chsd ldng pair: shkn up over 2f out: no imp after: one pce* **11/1**

0 **5** *3 3/4* **Nine Iron (IRE)**[35] 3067 2-9-3 0 MatthewDavies 4 57
(Mick Channon) *hld up in 5th: pushed along over 2f out: no imp wl over 1f out: fdd* **12/1**

5 **6** *3/4* **Stiff Upper Lip (IRE)**[18] 3658 2-9-3 0 SeanLevey 5 56
(Richard Hannon) *a in last trio: shkn up and no prog over 2f out: wl btn after* **11/2**

00 **7** *4 1/2* **Sekumkum (IRE)**[19] 3611 2-9-3 0 (b) MartinLane 3 44
(Marco Botti) *t.k.h early: trckd ldng trio tl wknd over 2f out* **20/1**

06 **8** *10* **Heliconia**[15] 3764 2-8-12 0 SebSanders 6 14
(Sir Mark Prescott Bt) *scrubbed along and outpcd in last: nvr a factor: t.o* **22/1**

1m 26.79s (3.49) **Going Correction** +0.30s/f (Good) **8 Ran SP% 116.1**
Speed ratings (Par 94): **92,88,84,83,79 78,73,61**
Tote Swingers 1&2 £4.30, 2&3 £2.00, 1&3 £3.60 CSF £17.62 TOTE £6.20: £1.50, £1.10, £1.30; EX 19.50 Trifecta £58.50 Pool 588.30 - 7.44 winning units..
Owner Trelawny II **Bred** D J Maher **Trained** Manton, Wilts

FOCUS
Just an average juvenile maiden, but a taking performance from the winner who produced a big step up.

NOTEBOOK
Whipper's Boy(IRE) was last of 11 on his Newmarket debut but, after being supported here, took a huge leap forward. Held up towards the rear in the early stages, he seemed not to be entirely happy on the bend. He was not that convincing on the camber early in the home straight, either, but once on an even keel made rapid progress 2f out and drew clear inside the last. Judged on this, he should make an impact in a higher grade. (op 7-2)
Zanetto, ninth of 14 in the Chesham Stakes, looks the most sensible marker for the form. Allowance has to be made, however, for the fact he raced keenly in the lead, which did not help when the winner swept past (op 7-2)
Royal Skies(IRE), second at Redcar on the first of his two previous outings but disappointing on his second start, probably ran to a level somewhere in between those two efforts. He led very briefly in the home straight, but faded late on. (op 3-1 tchd 10-3 in places)
Aussie Reigns(IRE) was stepping up in trip after two moderate 6f efforts, but it made little difference to his performance. He qualifies for nurseries now and may have better opportunities in those. (op 8-1)
Nine Iron(IRE) beat just one home on his Newbury debut five weeks earlier, so this has to go down as an improvement. He never seemed likely to make a major impact, though, and is another for whom handicaps beckon after he has run a third time. (op 16-1)
Stiff Upper Lip(IRE), who finished well when fifth of seven at Salisbury on his only previous start, was rather disappointing. Sixth was the best position he ever held. (op 5-1 tchd 13-2)

4254 WEATHERBYS BLOODSTOCK INSURANCE H'CAP 1m 2f 18y
7:45 (7:46) (Class 4) (0-80,76) 3-Y-O **£5,175** (£1,540; £769; £384) **Stalls Low**

Form RPR

0052 **1** **Mcvicar**[7] 3998 3-8-9 64 MartinDwyer 3 72
(Mick Channon) *trckd ldr: shkn up to take narrow ld over 2f out: asserted over 1f out: drvn out* **9/2**[3]

0431 **2** *3/4* **Jane Lachatte (IRE)**[7] 3998 3-9-4 73 6ex WilliamCarson 7 79
(Stuart Williams) *trckd ldng pair: shkn up 3f out: hanging lft and no inroads tl r.o to take 2nd last 150yds: clsng on wnr fin* **9/2**[3]

1-03 **3** *1 3/4* **Tamarrud**[25] 3417 3-9-7 76 SilvestreDeSousa 1 79
(Saeed Bin Suroor) *led: hdd and nt qckn over 2f out: hld over 1f out: lost 2nd last 150yds* **13/8**[1]

-400 **4** *3 1/2* **Instrumentalist (IRE)**[24] 3448 3-9-3 72 HayleyTurner 2 68
(John Best) *trckd ldng pair: rdn and nt qckn on inner over 2f out: fdd over 1f out* **14/1**

5204 **5** *1 1/2* **Daliance (IRE)**[16] 3736 3-9-4 73 KierenFallon 4 66
(Tom Dascombe) *hld up: cl 5th st: shkn up wl over 2f out: nt qckn and no prog: fdd over 1f out* **4/1**[2]

2423 **6** *2 1/2* **Cyrus Sod**[24] 3430 3-9-6 75 [1] JamieSpencer 6 63
(Ed Dunlop) *hld up: detached last and pushed along st: no prog* **17/2**

2m 15.05s (5.35) **Going Correction** +0.30s/f (Good) **6 Ran SP% 111.7**
Speed ratings (Par 102): **90,89,88,85,84 82**
Tote Swingers 1&2 £3.90, 2&3 £1.40, 1&3 £2.40 CSF £24.22 TOTE £4.90: £2.10, £2.70; EX 17.50.
Owner M Channon **Bred** J Breslin **Trained** West Ilsley, Berks

FOCUS
A competitive handicap, in which the top weight was rated 76. The winner, who reversed latest form with the second, is rated to his latest, with the second emerging with credit at the weights.

4255 TRY TOTEQUICKPICK IF YOU'RE FEELING LUCKY H'CAP 7f
8:20 (8:20) (Class 4) (0-85,82) 3-Y-O+ **£5,175** (£1,540; £769; £384) **Stalls Low**

Form RPR

6416 **1** **Dr Red Eye**[7] 3994 4-9-6 75 (p) SilvestreDeSousa 7 82
(Scott Dixon) *trckd ldr: rdn over 2f out: led over 1f out: drvn and in command fnl f* **5/2**[1]

0444 **2** *1 3/4* **Rigolleto (IRE)**[31] 3221 4-9-5 74 MatthewDavies 4 76
(Mick Channon) *led: rdn over 2f out: hdd over 1f out: one pce but hld on for 2nd* **5/1**[3]

1142 **3** *hd* **Abigails Angel**[38] 2988 5-8-12 72 MarkCoumbe(5) 1 74
(Brett Johnson) *trckd ldng pair: shkn up over 2f out: no imp tl styd on fnl f to press for 2nd nr fin* **4/1**[2]

6115 **4** *1 1/4* **Methayel (IRE)**[26] 3395 4-9-7 76 SebSanders 5 74
(Clive Brittain) *trckd ldng trio: shkn up over 2f out: nt qckn over 1f out: racd awkwardly fnl f* **13/2**

000 **5** *6* **Mr David (USA)**[26] 3394 5-9-13 82 HayleyTurner 6 64
(Jamie Osborne) *hld up: last but in tch st: pushed along and outpcd over 2f out: nvr on terms after* **4/1**[2]

6440 **6** *7* **Kylladdie**[54] 2487 5-9-7 76 (b) JamieSpencer 3 39
(Steve Gollings) *a in last pair: lost tch over 2f out: wl bhd after* **13/2**

1m 26.42s (3.12) **Going Correction** +0.30s/f (Good) **6 Ran SP% 111.9**
Speed ratings (Par 105): **94,92,91,90,83 75**
Tote Swingers 1&2 £2.10, 2&3 £7.30, 1&3 £1.30 CSF £15.10 TOTE £3.10: £1.90, £2.70; EX 17.10.
Owner The Red Eye Partnership **Bred** G E Amey **Trained** Babworth, Notts

FOCUS
An interesting handicap, with a top weight rated 82. The winner pretty much confirmed his penultimate Catterick win.

4256 EBBISHAM LANE H'CAP 1m 114y
8:50 (8:50) (Class 5) (0-75,75) 3-Y-O **£3,234** (£962; £481; £240) **Stalls Low**

Form RPR

-242 **1** **Benzanno (IRE)**[7] 3999 3-9-4 72 LiamKeniry 5 85+
(Andrew Balding) *trckd ldrs: 4th st: prog to go 2nd over 2f out: pushed into ld jst over 1f out: readily drew away* **11/4**[1]

14-6 **2** *2 1/4* **Fresa**[16] 3736 3-9-3 71 SebSanders 7 79
(Sir Mark Prescott Bt) *led: drvn over 2f out: hdd jst over 1f out: styd on but no ch w wnr* **11/2**[2]

2330 **3** *2 1/2* **Gold Show**[18] 3666 3-9-7 75 MatthewDavies 4 77
(Mick Channon) *trckd ldng pair: shkn up and outpcd in 4th wl over 1f out: kpt on to take 3rd again ins fnl f* **8/1**

06-1 **4** *1* **Malih**[21] 3539 3-9-4 72 FergusSweeney 8 72
(Jamie Osborne) *chsd ldr: rdn and nt qckn over 2f out: sn lost 2nd and outpcd: n.d after* **8/1**

6401 **5** *1/2* **Titus Bolt (IRE)**[18] 3671 3-8-6 60 (v) MartinDwyer 9 59
(Jim Boyle) *hld up in 6th: gng bttr than most 3f out: rdn and nt qckn over 2f out: outpcd wl over 1f out: no ch after* **10/1**

0646 **6** *3 1/4* **Alkadi (IRE)**[19] 3619 3-9-3 71 SilvestreDeSousa 3 63
(Mark Johnston) *hld up in 7th: rdn ent st: brief prog 2f out: sn no hdwy and btn* **7/1**

0330 **7** *1* **Attain**[27] 3338 3-8-11 68 AdamBeschizza(3) 6 57
(Julia Feilden) *hld up: 8th and rdn st: struggling after* **14/1**

1401 **8** *3/4* **Jumeirah Palm Star**[16] 3736 3-9-6 74 KieranO'Neill 2 62
(Richard Hannon) *chsd ldrs: 5th st: rdn over 2f out: sn wknd* **12/1**

-105 **9** *1/2* **Northern Territory (IRE)**[37] 3002 3-8-10 64 JamieSpencer 1 50
(Jim Boyle) *hld up in last: detached st: pushed along over 2f out: nvr in it* **6/1**[3]

1m 48.72s (2.62) **Going Correction** +0.30s/f (Good) **9 Ran SP% 114.5**
Speed ratings (Par 100): **100,98,95,94,94 91,90,90,89**
Tote Swingers 1&2 £2.70, 2&3 £13.60, 1&3 £3.30 CSF £17.40 CT £106.45 TOTE £3.60: £1.30, £1.10, £2.70; EX 11.10 Trifecta £293.50 Pool 628.14 - 1.58 winning units..
Owner Martin & Valerie Slade & Partner **Bred** Nanallac Stud **Trained** Kingsclere, Hants

FOCUS
A moderate finale but competitive on paper. The winner built on his latest C&D second, and the second rates a personal best.
Jumeirah Palm Star Official explanation: jockey said filly was unsuited by the good to soft (last 5f good) ground
T/Plt: £63.20 to a 1 stake. Pool £53,233.49. 614.47 winning tickets. T/Qpdt: £12.00 to a 1 stake. Pool £4,804.60. 295.90 winning tickets. JN

4083 HAMILTON (R-H)
Thursday, July 19

OFFICIAL GOING: Soft (7.1)
Wind: Almost nil Weather: Overcast

4257 IRISH STALLION FARMS EBF MAIDEN STKS 6f 5y
2:00 (2:02) (Class 5) 2-Y-O **£3,408** (£1,006; £503) **Stalls High**

Form RPR

2 **1** **Ginger Goose**[32] 3182 2-9-3 0 PaulHanagan 1 78
(Richard Fahey) *trckd ldrs: sn pushed along: hdwy 1/2-way: led over 1f out: hrd pressed ins fnl f: hld on wl u.p* **7/4**[1]

0 **2** *shd* **Dr Phibes (IRE)**[24] 3436 2-8-12 0 GarryWhillans(5) 4 77
(Alan Swinbank) *blkd s: chsd ldng gp: hdwy over 1f out: effrt and disp ld ins fnl f: kpt on wl: jst hld* **25/1**

3 *3 3/4* **Light Particle (IRE)**[27] 3358 2-9-3 0 LukeMorris 6 66
(John Patrick Shanahan, Ire) *prom: drvn and outpcd over 4f out: rallied over 1f out: kpt on fnl f: nt rch first two* **20/1**

5520 **4** *3/4* **Ouzinkie (IRE)**[5] 4093 2-9-3 75 (v[1]) MartinHarley 8 65
(Mick Channon) *trckd ldrs: effrt and rdn over 1f out: n.m.r briefly ent fnl f: kpt on same pce* **20/1**

3 **5** *1* **Nordikhab (IRE)**[26] 3378 2-9-3 0 PhillipMakin 7 61
(Kevin Ryan) *led: rdn and hdd over 1f out: one pce ins fnl f: no ex and lost two pls nr fin* **15/8**[2]

6 *17* **Funding Deficit (IRE)** 2-9-3 0.................................. GrahamGibbons 5 10
(David Barron) *t.k.h: w ldr tl rdn and wknd qckly over 1f out* **14/1[3]**
4 P **Elusive Heir (IRE)**[31] 3208 2-9-3 0.................................... TomEaves 2
(Bryan Smart) *appeared to be kicked in stalls: dwlt and blkd s: sn lost tch: t.o whn p.u 1/2-way* **18/1**
1m 16.22s (4.02) **Going Correction** +0.725s/f (Yiel) **7** Ran SP% **96.4**
Speed ratings (Par 94): **102,101,96,95,94 71,**
toteswingers 1&2 £6.40, 2&3 £25.20, 1&3 £4.80 CSF £32.61 TOTE £2.60: £1.60, £11.00; EX 31.80.
Owner City Vaults Racing 1 **Bred** Mrs C F Van Straubenzee And Partners **Trained** Musley Bank, N Yorks

FOCUS
Rail realignment around the loop bend added 25yds to races on Round course. Testing conditions. There was an incident at the start ahead of this fair-looking contest. Fraserburgh got upset in his stall, reared up and ended up on the floor. He was withdrawn (11/2, deduct 15p in the £ under R4). Elusive Heir was caught up in the incidident, but was allowed to run. The form makes sense and it's unlikely the winner had to improve.

NOTEBOOK
Ginger Goose put up a useful effort to divide Kimberella (just beaten in a Newmarket nursery off 86 the previous weekend) and Group 2 July Stakes runner-up Lewisham over this trip at Doncaster on his debut, and built on it to gain a narrow success under strong pressure. The ground may not have suited him but he was brave in victory. (op 6-4 tchd 15-8)
Dr Phibes(IRE) pushed the winner really hard in the final stages after still seeming green early. He should have little problem landing something similar if maintaining his progression. (op 22-1)
Light Particle(IRE) was one of the first under pressure, but did respond and finished off nicely. (op 25-1)
Ouzinkie(IRE), officially rated 75, was tried in first-time headgear after finishing last in the Super Sprint but didn't do a lot better for the visor even allowing for a bit of crowding about 1f out.
Nordikhab(IRE) proved to be one-paced inside the final 2f after having the stands' rail to run up. (op 9-4 tchd 7-4)
Elusive Heir(IRE) had to be backed out of the stalls and checked over after the horse in the next stall, which had reared over, had thrashed out into Elusive Heir's gate. Bryan Smart's runner was allowed his chance after being trotted up, but it quickly became evident that all was not right and he was soon pulled up. His backers can feel aggrieved, and interestingly the Stewards held an enquiry following a complaint by Bryan Smart as to why the colt was allowed to run. Having heard evidence from the trainer, Tom Eaves the rider, the Starter, the Veterinary Surgeon, the Veterinary Officer and the Clerk of the Course, and viewed recordings, the Stewards ordered a report to be forwarded to the BHA. (op 20-1 tchd 16-1)

4258 BRITISH STALLION STUDS SUPPORTING BRITISH RACING EBF CONDITIONS STKS 6f 5y
2:30 (2:30) (Class 2) 3-Y-O+ **£9,960** (£2,982; £1,491; £745; £372) **Stalls** High

Form RPR
1300 **1** **Colonel Mak**[5] 4086 5-8-13 104.................................... GrahamGibbons 5 95
(David Barron) *dwlt: trckd ldrs: nt clr run over 2f out and over 1f out: squeezed through to ld ins fnl f: kpt on strly* **10/11[1]**
0-00 **2** *3/4* **Victoire De Lyphar (IRE)**[74] 1885 5-8-13 92............... AdrianNicholls 4 93?
(David Nicholls) *led: rdn over 2f out: jnd over 1f out: hdd ins fnl f: kpt on towards fin* **7/1**
-605 **3** *1 1/2* **Oor Jock (IRE)**[19] 3648 4-8-13 87....................................(b) LukeMorris 2 88
(John Patrick Shanahan, Ire) *prom: rdn over 2f out: effrt over 1f out: ev ch ins fnl f: kpt on same pce towards fin* **9/2[3]**
0160 **4** *4* **Muaamara**[6] 4063 3-8-3 91.. PaulHanagan 3 70
(Mick Channon) *plld hrd: cl up: effrt and disp ld over 1f out to ent fnl f: wknd fnl 100yds* **3/1[2]**
0006 **5** *11* **Barbarella Blue (IRE)**[16] 3727 3-8-3 45.................... MatthewHopkins 1 35
(Alan Berry) *wnt rt s: in tch tl hung rt and wknd over 1f out* **100/1**
1m 15.5s (3.30) **Going Correction** +0.725s/f (Yiel)
WFA 3 from 4yo+ 5lb **5** Ran SP% **109.1**
Speed ratings (Par 109): **107,106,104,98,84**
CSF £7.80 TOTE £1.90: £1.60, £2.70; EX 6.60.
Owner Norton Common Farm Racing,O'Kane,Murphy **Bred** Peter Baldwin **Trained** Maunby, N Yorks

FOCUS
Not a result to go overboard about, as the runners were finding it really hard work in the going. The winner was clearly not at his best.

NOTEBOOK
Colonel Mak has been as good as ever this year and was far from disgraced over C&D in a fairly competitive handicap the previous weekend. Best in on BHA ratings, he was produced in the final stages after starting slowly and won a bit more comfortably than the winning margin suggests in ground that probably doesn't suit. David Barron said afterwards that the victory will rule the gelding out of the Stewards' Cup due to the penalty he has now picked up. (op 8-11 tchd Evens)
Victoire De Lyphar(IRE), who holds a Stewards' Cup entry, had been slightly disappointing since finishing second to Redford in 2010 Ayr Gold Cup but rallied quite well here after looking destined to be fourth at one point. Faster going also suits this gelding much better. (tchd 15-2)
Oor Jock(IRE) had blinkers on for only second time, but couldn't get on top while making his bid at least four horse widths from the stands' rail. (op 6-1)
Muaamara proved far too keen and unsurprisingly didn't pick up the moment she came off the bridle. The way she raced here strongly suggests she'll be of interest on a faster surface. (op 7-2 tchd 11-4)

4259 FOLLOW HAMILTONPARKRC ON TWITTER MAIDEN STKS 1m 3f 16y
3:00 (3:00) (Class 5) 3-Y-O+ **£3,234** (£962; £481; £240) **Stalls** Low

Form RPR
3-23 **1** **Mawaqeet (USA)**[22] 3484 3-9-3 82..............................(v[1]) PaulHanagan 5 86
(Sir Michael Stoute) *hld up: shkn up and stdy hdwy over 3f out: rdn to ld ins fnl f: edgd lft: sn clr: comf* **5/2[2]**
2 **2** *3* **Roc De Prince**[32] 3181 3-9-3 0...................................... FrederikTylicki 6 79
(Richard Fahey) *prom: n.m.r briefly over 2f out: sn rdn: chsd wnr wl ins fnl f: r.o* **4/1[3]**
22 **3** *1 1/4* **Sir Quintin (IRE)**[18] 3663 3-9-3 0...................................... DavidProbert 3 77
(Andrew Balding) *chsd ldrs: hdwy to ld 2f out: sn rdn and edgd rt: hdd ins fnl f: kpt on same pce* **11/8[1]**
53 **4** *5* **Echo Of Footsteps**[27] 3352 3-8-12 0.................................. TomEaves 2 63
(Michael Herrington) *hld up in midfield: effrt and pushed along over 3f out: kpt on same pce fr 2f out* **25/1**
2 **5** *9* **Madame Blavatsky (FR)**[21] 3521 4-9-9 0.................... PJMcDonald 4 47
(Karen McLintock) *led 3f: chsd clr ldr: led over 3f out to 2f out: wknd appr fnl f* **16/1**
04 **6** *5* **Laybach (IRE)**[20] 3580 8-10-0 0.. GrahamLee 7 43
(Jim Goldie) *hld up: drvn along over 3f out: wknd fr over 2f out* **100/1**
7 *6* **Cottesmore (USA)** 3-9-3 0... JoeFanning 9 32
(Mark Johnston) *unruly in preliminaries: cl up: rdn and ev ch over 3f out: wknd fr 2f out* **8/1**
8 *4* **Lillioftheballet (IRE)**[155] 5-9-4 0............................ LucyAlexander(5) 1 20
(Jim Goldie) *hld up: struggling over 4f out: sn btn* **100/1**
6 **9** *12* **Jim Tango (FR)**[32] 3181 8-10-0 0..............................(bt) PaddyAspell 11
(Brian Storey) *dwlt: hdwy to ld after 3f: sn clr: styd alone far side and hdd over 3f out: edgd lft and sn btn* **100/1**
10 *36* **Shatin Spirit (IRE)** 3-9-0 0... GaryBartley(3) 8
(Noel Wilson) *hld up: struggling over 4f out: sn wknd* **100/1**
2m 34.34s (8.74) **Going Correction** +0.725s/f (Yiel)
WFA 3 from 4yo+ 11lb **10** Ran SP% **115.5**
Speed ratings (Par 103): **97,94,93,90,83 80,75,72,64,37**
toteswingers 1&2 £2.80, 2&3 £2.30, 1&3 £1.90 CSF £12.70 TOTE £3.70: £1.30, £1.10, £1.90; EX 16.70.
Owner Hamdan Al Maktoum **Bred** London T'Bred Serv & Derry Meeting Farm **Trained** Newmarket, Suffolk

FOCUS
There was little depth to this maiden, but it was sound run and the form trio came to the form. Steps forward from the first two.

4260 TOTEPOOL.COM H'CAP 1m 1f 36y
3:30 (3:30) (Class 4) (0-80,77) 3-Y-O+ **£5,175** (£1,154; £1,154; £384) **Stalls** Low

Form RPR
3510 **1** **Double Cee**[20] 3555 3-8-8 66... PaulHanagan 7 74
(Richard Fahey) *chsd ldr: rdn over 2f out: led over 1f out: drvn out fnl f* **6/1**
0444 **2** *1 1/4* **High Resolution**[5] 4089 5-8-8 62.............................. ShaneBKelly(5) 5 67
(Linda Perratt) *s.i.s: hld up: hdwy and prom 2f out: sn rdn: swtchd rt and kpt on fnl f: dead-heated for 2nd on line* **8/1**
3034 **2** *dht* **I'm Super Too (IRE)**[29] 3274 5-9-9 77...................... GarryWhillans(5) 4 82
(Alan Swinbank) *led: rdn and hdd over 1f out: kpt on u.p ins fnl f: jnd for 2nd on line* **4/1[2]**
4 *1 1/4* **Lady Jock (IRE)**[20] 3597 3-8-11 69.................................... LukeMorris 2 70
(John Patrick Shanahan, Ire) *trckd ldrs: rdn over 2f out: edgd rt over 1f out: kpt on same pce fnl f* **5/1[3]**
4420 **5** *2* **Indian Giver**[17] 3694 4-8-8 60.................................... PaulPickard(3) 3 58
(Hugh McWilliams) *hld up: rdn and hdwy on outside 2f out: no imp fnl f* **16/1**
4062 **6** *2* **Botham (USA)**[21] 3525 8-9-4 67.. GrahamLee 8 60
(Jim Goldie) *in tch: rdn and outpcd over 2f out: no imp fnl f* **7/1**
0411 **7** *1/2* **King Of Paradise (IRE)**[16] 3727 3-8-5 70....................... JasonHart(7) 6 61
(Eric Alston) *plld hrd: prom: effrt and cl up over 3f out: wknd over 1f out* **9/4[1]**
1356 **8** *15* **Joshua The First**[16] 3728 3-9-0 72...................................... TomEaves 1 30
(Keith Dalgleish) *hld up: drvn and outpcd over 3f out: sn btn* **18/1**
2m 7.65s (7.95) **Going Correction** +0.725s/f (Yiel)
WFA 3 from 4yo+ 9lb **8** Ran SP% **116.5**
Speed ratings (Par 105): **93,91,91,90,89 87,86,73**PL: I'm Super Too £1.80, High Resolution £3.00 EX: Double Cee/IST: £16.00, DC/HR £27.10 CSF: DC/IST £15.40, DC/HR £26.77, TRI: DC/IST/HR £97.44 DC/HR/IST £107.97 toteswingers: 1&IST £5.60, 1&HR 6.50, IST&HR £3.90 CSF £26.77 CT £107.97 TOTE £6.00: £2.20; EX 27.10 27 Owner.

FOCUS
They didn't go a strong pace early and it developed into something of a sprint from the 4f marker. The winner is rated back to form but the favourite disappointed.
King Of Paradise(IRE) Official explanation: jockey said gelding ran too free

4261 GLASGOW STKS (LISTED RACE) 1m 3f 16y
4:00 (4:00) (Class 1) 3-Y-O **£20,720** (£7,836; £3,916; £1,956) **Stalls** Low

Form RPR
1160 **1** **Sparkling Portrait**[28] 3296 3-9-3 93.................................. PaulHanagan 1 107
(Richard Fahey) *hld up in tch: stdy hdwy 3f out: shkn up 2f out: led ins fnl f: edgd lft: rdn and r.o wl* **11/8[1]**
2166 **2** *3/4* **Goldoni (IRE)**[28] 3295 3-9-3 99...................................... DavidProbert 6 105
(Andrew Balding) *t.k.h early: cl up: led 4f out: rdn and edgd rt over 1f out: hdd ins fnl f: r.o* **4/1[3]**
10-3 **3** *2 1/4* **Albamara**[35] 3069 3-8-12 88... LukeMorris 3 96
(Sir Mark Prescott Bt) *trckd ldrs: drvn and outpcd over 2f out: rallied fnl f: nt gng pce of first two* **10/3[2]**
3412 **4** *6* **Naseem Alyasmeen (IRE)**[7] 4007 3-8-12 84................. MartinHarley 7 85
(Mick Channon) *hld up in tch: n.m.r and rdn 4f out: outpcd fr 2f out* **8/1**
5110 **5** *9* **Fennell Bay (IRE)**[7] 4009 3-9-3 91.................................. JoeFanning 9 74
(Mark Johnston) *in tch: stdy hdwy over 4f out: rdn and wknd fr 2f out* **9/1**
4411 **6** *22* **Act Your Shoe Size**[30] 3252 3-8-12 83................................ TomEaves 4 29
(Keith Dalgleish) *led at stdy pce to 4f out: rdn and wknd over 2f out: t.o* **25/1**
2m 32.01s (6.41) **Going Correction** +0.725s/f (Yiel) **6** Ran SP% **110.1**
Speed ratings (Par 108): **105,104,102,98,91 75**
toteswingers 1&2 £1.80, 2&3 £2.70, 1&3 £2.40 CSF £6.84 TOTE £2.10: £2.10, £1.70, £1.50; EX 7.70.
Owner Mike Browne **Bred** Dukes Stud & Overbury Stallions Ltd **Trained** Musley Bank, N Yorks

FOCUS
By some way, this was the best race of the day, although it was slightly weakened by the withdrawal of the promising Ed De Gas during the morning. The form is ordinary for the grade but well up to scratch for the race. Another personal best from Sparkling Portrait.

NOTEBOOK
Sparkling Portrait, who has a Great Voltigeur entry, was nearly brought down when making his effort at Royal Ascot behind Fennell Bay, and he met that rival on 8lb better terms here. He didn't look to be going as well as some rivals when heading into the home straight, but finished off strongly and ended up doing the job nicely. He shapes as though he'll get further. (op 6-4)
Goldoni(IRE), who also has a Great Voltigeur entry, finished a respectable sixth in Group 3 Tercentenary at Royal Ascot last month and gave the winner plenty to think about in the closing stages. He's an admirable type and could make someone a lovely hurdler should he ever be up for sale. (tchd 9-2)
Albamara finished third to subsequent Lancashire Oaks scorer Great Heavens in a muddling contest at Newbury on her latest start, and again looked in need of a sterner test after being caught for speed over 2f from home. (op 4-1)
Naseem Alyasmeen(IRE) chased home St Leger possible Shantaram in the Bahrain Trophy the previous week, but lost whatever chance she had when being squeezed up for room at a crucial stage. (op 11-2)
Fennell Bay(IRE) was easily seen off here and hasn't reproduced his Royal Ascot form in two subsequent starts. (op 8-1)

4262 FOLLOW @SCOTTISHRACINGGB ON TWITTER H'CAP 5f 4y
4:30 (4:31) (Class 6) (0-60,63) 3-Y-O+ **£1,940** (£577; £288; £144) **Stalls** High

Form RPR
2321 **1** **Economic Crisis (IRE)**[5] 4084 3-9-12 63 6ex.................. PaddyAspell 5 69
(Alan Berry) *cl up: rdn whn carried rt over 1f out: sn led: hrd pressed ins fnl f: hld on gamely* **3/1[2]**
6055 **2** *hd* **Weetentherty**[5] 4087 5-9-5 52......................................(p) FrederikTylicki 4 58
(Linda Perratt) *dwlt: bhd: rdn and hdwy over 1f out: kpt on wl fnl f: jst hld* **10/1**

2022	3	½	**Alpha Tauri (USA)**[2] 4190 6-9-3 **50**........................(t) RobbieFitzpatrick 6	54
			(David C Griffiths) *trckd ldrs: effrt and ev ch whn carried rt over 1f out: kpt on fnl f: hld nr fin* **2/1**[1]	
0-35	4	1	**Bridge Valley**[27] 3332 5-9-1 **48**.. MartinHarley 2	48
			(Jason Ward) *in tch: drvn and outpcd wl over 2f out: styd on fnl f: nrst fin* **11/2**	
2330	5	2¼	**Distant Sun (USA)**[10] 3905 8-9-4 **56**..........................(p) ShaneBKelly(5) 7	48
			(Linda Perratt) *racd alone towards stands' rail: prom: drvn along 1/2-way: sn no imp* **14/1**	
56	6	nk	**Pinball (IRE)**[36] 3020 6-9-5 **52**...(v) AmyRyan 8	43
			(Lisa Williamson) *dwlt: sn chsng ldrs: hdwy to ld over 2f out: hung rt and hdd over 1f out: no ex ins fnl f* **14/1**	
5403	7	3½	**Sharp Shoes**[21] 3523 5-9-10 **57**.....................................(p) GrahamLee 3	36
			(Ann Duffield) *led to over 2f out: rdn and carried rt over 1f out: sn wknd* **5/1**[3]	
/000	8	3¾	**Skiddaw View**[128] 887 4-8-12 **45**.................................(t) PJMcDonald 1	10
			(Maurice Barnes) *chsd ldrs to 1/2-way: sn rdn and wknd* **50/1**	

1m 3.46s (3.46) **Going Correction** +0.725s/f (Yiel)
WFA 3 from 4yo+ 4lb **8** Ran SP% **114.8**
Speed ratings (Par 101): **101,100,99,98,94 94,88,82**
toteswingers 1&2 £6.50, 2&3 £5.20, 1&3 £2.40 CSF £32.83 CT £72.57 TOTE £4.30: £2.60, £3.30, £1.60; EX 41.10.
Owner Mr & Mrs T Blane **Bred** Philip Hore Jnr **Trained** Cockerham, Lancs
■ Stewards' Enquiry : Amy Ryan three-day ban: careless riding (Aug 2,3,5)

FOCUS
A modest sprint that produced a close finish. The winner confirmed her recent improvement.

4263 BOOK NOW FOR LADIES NIGHT H'CAP 1m 65y
5:00 (5:00) (Class 6) (0-65,63) 3-Y-O **£1,940** (£577; £288; £144) **Stalls** Low

Form				RPR
0-02	1		**Lord Franklin**[10] 3908 3-8-4 **46**.. LukeMorris 9	58
			(Eric Alston) *t.k.h: cl up: led over 2f out: drvn and styd on wl fnl f* **2/1**[1]	
00-0	2	1	**Poontoon (IRE)**[61] 2262 3-8-11 **53**.............................. FrederikTylicki 6	63
			(Richard Fahey) *in tch: stdy hdwy over 3f out: effrt and chsd wnr over 1f out: kpt on ins fnl f* **13/2**[3]	
144	3	7	**Sweetnessandlight**[9] 3940 3-9-2 **63**........................... ShaneBKelly(5) 8	57
			(Jason Ward) *s.i.s: hld up: stdy hdwy and ev ch over 2f out: sn rdn: outpcd by first two fnl f* **3/1**[2]	
6000	4	4	**Tallula (IRE)**[20] 3567 3-8-5 **47** ow2.................................. PJMcDonald 7	31
			(Micky Hammond) *hld up: rdn and effrt over 3f out: no imp fr 2f out* **33/1**	
0-00	5	1½	**Sweet Liberta (IRE)**[18] 3666 3-9-3 **59**............................ DavidProbert 4	40
			(Andrew Balding) *cl up tl rdn and wknd fr 2f out* **17/2**	
504	6	2¼	**Well Bank (IRE)**[13] 3809 3-9-3 **59**...................................... TomEaves 2	35
			(Colin Teague) *hld up: n.m.r and outpcd over 4f out: sme late hdwy: nvr on terms* **15/2**	
0540	7	nk	**Alpha Arion (IRE)**[9] 3939 3-9-2 **58**................................... DavidAllan 3	33
			(Tim Easterby) *in tch: drvn and outpcd over 3f out: btn fnl 2f* **7/1**	
4050	8	1	**Hikma (USA)**[20] 3575 3-9-3 **59**... JoeFanning 5	32
			(Mark Johnston) *led tl rdn and hdd over 2f out: sn wknd* **12/1**	

1m 56.84s (8.44) **Going Correction** +0.725s/f (Yiel) **8** Ran SP% **117.1**
Speed ratings (Par 98): **86,85,78,74,72 70,69,68**
toteswingers 1&2 £3.90, 2&3 £6.00, 1&3 £2.40 CSF £16.16 CT £38.72 TOTE £3.80: £3.00, £2.70, £1.10; EX 20.10.
Owner Liam & Tony Ferguson **Bred** Tony Ferguson & Liam Ferguson **Trained** Longton, Lancs

FOCUS
A moderate handicap. The first two were clear and the winner rates a similar effort to Ayr.
Sweet Liberta(IRE) Official explanation: trainer's rep said filly was unsuited by the soft ground
T/Plt: £16.90 to a £1 stake. Pool of £59117.45 -2542.64 winning tickets. T/Qpdt: £12.40 to a £1 stake. Pool of £4276.25 - 255.06 winning tickets. RY

2783 LEICESTER (R-H)
Thursday, July 19

4264 Meeting Abandoned - waterlogged

4271 - 4275a (Foreign Racing) - See Raceform Interactive

4028 LEOPARDSTOWN (L-H)
Thursday, July 19

OFFICIAL GOING: Soft (soft to heavy in places) changing to soft after race 2 (6.15pm)

4276a SILVER FLASH STKS (GROUP 3) (FILLIES) 7f
6:45 (6:46) 2-Y-O **£25,729** (£7,520; £3,562; £1,187)

			RPR
1		**Harasiya (IRE)**[35] 3089 2-9-0 .... JohnnyMurtagh 7	104+
		(John M Oxx, Ire) *settled in 6th early: clsd home turn on outer: qcknd wl to ld appr fnl f: sn clr: comf* **11/8**[1]	
2	2½	**My Special J'S (USA)**[20] 3596 2-9-0 .... CO'Donoghue 3	98
		(John Patrick Shanahan, Ire) *attempted to make all: hdd appr fnl f: no ch w wnr but kpt on gamely* **8/1**	
3	1¼	**Roseraie (IRE)**[43] 2828 2-9-0 .... ChrisHayes 9	95
		(Kevin Prendergast, Ire) *hld up in rr: pushed along appr home turn: styd on wl ent fnl f to get up on post for 3rd* **14/1**	
4	nk	**Reglisse (IRE)**[14] 3797 2-9-0 .... FranBerry 4	94
		(Edward Lynam, Ire) *racd in 4th: pushed along to chse ldrs early in st: kpt on: ct cl home for 3rd* **12/1**	
5	1¾	**Snow Queen (IRE)**[14] 3797 2-9-0 .... JPO'Brien 8	90
		(A P O'Brien, Ire) *racd cl 3rd: briefly wnt 2nd over 1f out: wknd sn after* **9/1**	
6	¾	**Rawaaq**[19] 3644 2-9-0 .... PatSmullen 2	88
		(D K Weld, Ire) *hld up in rr: prog whn nt clr run early in st: nvr on terms* **11/2**[3]	
7	2¾	**Bronte**[20] 3596 2-9-0 .... WJLee 1	81
		(David Wachman, Ire) *trckd ldrs on inner tl outpcd over 1f out* **9/1**	
8	1	**True Verdict (IRE)**[18] 3674 2-9-0 102.............................. WayneLordan 6	79
		(David Wachman, Ire) *failed to settle: 2nd tl pushed along home turn: sn wknd* **10/3**[2]	

1m 31.31s (2.61) **Going Correction** +0.575s/f (Yiel) **8** Ran SP% **126.0**
Speed ratings: **108,105,103,103,101 100,97,96**
CSF £15.59 TOTE £2.00: £1.02, £2.30, £6.00; DF 11.40.
Owner H H Aga Khan **Bred** His Highness The Aga Khan's Studs S C **Trained** Currabeg, Co Kildare

FOCUS
A race won by many smart fillies in the past, most recently subsequent Group 1 winner Maybe a year ago. This looked a decent renewal but the form is hard to rate accurately.

NOTEBOOK
Harasiya(IRE), one of four winners in the line-up, had created a good impression when scoring over the C&D on her debut last month, and she confirmed that promise with a comfortably achieved success. She has now won on good and on soft and has the Group 1 Moyglare Stud Stakes as her target, with the Group 2 Debutante Stakes next month a possible prep. Stan James make her 12-1(from 25-1) second favourite behind Newfangled for the 1000 Guineas.
My Special J'S(USA), one of the maidens in the race, had lost out by a head over this trip on her debut at the Curragh. She had plenty more on her plate here and she acquitted herself well, making the running and sticking to her task when headed by the winner over 1f out.
Roseraie(IRE), successful over 6f on her debut at Fairyhouse last month, came from the back of the field and ran on for pressure from over 1f out to snatch third place close home.
Reglisse(IRE), third behind Harasiya on debut over the course and trip before winning well back here two weeks previously, raced a bit keenly and, after making headway to go third under 1f out, was unable to make much impression and was run out of third near the finish.
Snow Queen(IRE) had run quite green when fifth behind Reglisse on debut over the course and trip two weeks previously. She had every chance early in the straight but was beaten in third entering the final furlong.
True Verdict(IRE), runner-up on her two previous starts and tackling the trip for the first time having chased home subsequent Cherry Hinton winner, Sendmylovetorose, in a 6f Group 3 at the Curragh early this month, ran well below form and was a spent force early in the straight having raced prominently and quite keenly. Official explanation: jockey said filly ran flat

4277 - 4281a (Foreign Racing) - See Raceform Interactive

3368 ASCOT (R-H)
Friday, July 20

OFFICIAL GOING: Straight course - good to soft; round course - soft changing to straight course - good; round course good to soft after race 4 (3:55)
Wind: Light, half behind Weather: Fine but cloudy

4282 HELICAL BAR EBF MAIDEN FILLIES' STKS 6f
2:10 (2:11) (Class 3) 2-Y-O **£7,762** (£2,310; £1,154; £577) **Stalls** Centre

Form				RPR
2	1		**Diaminda (IRE)**[21] 3560 2-9-0 0.. JimCrowley 7	83+
			(Alan Jarvis) *hld up bhd ldrs: looking for room fr over 2f out: gap appeared over 1f out: rdn and prog to ld last 150yds: r.o wl* **7/2**[2]	
	2	2¼	**Serenity Spa** 2-9-0 0.. JamesDoyle 1	76+
			(Roger Charlton) *prog fr rr to press ldrs 1/2-way: rdn and sltly outpcd over 1f out: styd on fnl f to take 2nd last stride* **6/1**[3]	
2	3	nse	**Pearl Bell (IRE)**[21] 3590 2-9-0 0..................................... JamieSpencer 6	76
			(Brian Meehan) *w ldrs: chal and upsides over 2f out: hanging and nt qckn 1f out: sn outpcd* **5/6**[1]	
5	4	shd	**Woodlandsway**[16] 3764 2-9-0 0... RyanMoore 9	76
			(Richard Hannon) *led after 2f: jnd over 2f out: drvn over 1f out: hdd and outpcd last 150yds* **16/1**	
	5	1¾	**Uknowwhatushoulddo (IRE)** 2-9-0 0.............................. TedDurcan 5	71+
			(J S Moore) *dwlt: mostly in last pair: pushed along and outpcd 1/2-way: styd on wl fr over 1f out: nrst fin* **50/1**	
	6	¾	**Alhaarth Beauty (IRE)** 2-9-0 0.................................. RichardHughes 8	68
			(Richard Hannon) *sn trckd ldrs: rdn and one pce wl over 1f out: fdd ins fnl f* **8/1**	
40	7	3	**Shafaani**[28] 3326 2-9-0 0.. YasunariIwata 4	59
			(Clive Brittain) *racd freely: led 2f: styd w ldrs tl wknd over 1f out* **25/1**	
624	8	3½	**Hot Secret**[18] 3700 2-9-0 74.. JimmyFortune 2	49
			(Andrew Balding) *pressed ldrs: stl chalng wl over 1f out: wknd qckly sn after* **16/1**	
	9	7	**Dawn Rock** 2-9-0 0.. DarryllHolland 3	28
			(Simon Dow) *dwlt: a in last pair: bhd over 2f out* **100/1**	

1m 17.85s (3.35) **Going Correction** +0.425s/f (Yiel) **9** Ran SP% **120.7**
Speed ratings (Par 95): **94,91,90,90,88 87,83,78,69**
toteswingers 1&2 £4.50, 1&3 £1.50, 2&3 £2.50 CSF £25.84 TOTE £4.90: £1.60, £1.90, £1.10; EX 35.90 Trifecta £78.90 Pool £1,341.78 - 12.57 winning units..
Owner Market Avenue Racing Club Ltd **Bred** Canice Farrell Jnr **Trained** Twyford, Bucks

FOCUS
Round course rail between 9f to home straight moved out 2m and consequently 2yds added to Old Mile, 8yds to 10f race and 10yds to 12f &16f races. The round course rail was positioned approximately two metres out from 1m1f to the home straight, increasing distances by approximately the following: Old Mile: 2 yards, 1m2f: 8 yards, 1m4f and 2m: 10 yards. The time of this opening contest was the second slowest of 46 juvenile races run over C&D since 2006. This fillies' maiden has gone to a subsequent Group 1 winner three times in the last ten years, namely Carry On Katie (Cheveley Park), Silca's Sister (Prix Morny) and most recently White Moonstone (Fillies' Mile). This latest running looked a decent enough contest and they raced up the middle of the track.

NOTEBOOK
Diaminda(IRE) ◆ shaped well on her debut when a close second at 40-1 in a strong Doncaster maiden (6f, good) and proved herself to be quite useful. She was a bit keen early, but had plenty of cover and, once switched, picked up well to win convincingly. It wouldn't surprise if she was turned out quickly for the Group 3 Princess Margaret back over C&D on July 28 - a race her trainer has won a couple of times in recent years. (op 11-4 tchd 4-1)
Serenity Spa, a half-sister to useful 1m-1m4f winner and hurdles scorer Brunston, kept on nicely to grab second on the line. She can win a similar race granted normal improvement. (op 9-1)
Pearl Bell(IRE) failed to progress from her debut second at the Newmarket July course (6f, good), simply not picking up for pressure, although she still ran to a fair level in defeat. (op 10-11 tchd Evens)
Woodlandsway shaped just okay on her debut in a 7f Polytrack maiden, but this time she looked the winner for much the closing stages, trading at 1.44 in the win market on Betfair and 1.03 to place. She didn't see it out, but was up against some good fillies and can probably improve again. (op 14-1)
Uknowwhatushoulddo(IRE) ◆, who is out of a 6f Group 3 winner, made a really nice debut, staying on well after getting outpaced. This should have sharpened her up plenty.
Alhaarth Beauty(IRE), a 15,000GBP purchase out of an Italian 1m1f-1m3f winner, looked the Hannon first string but shaped as though the run was needed and wasn't given a hard time. (op 12-1)

4283 FOUNDATION DEVELOPMENTS NOVICE STKS 7f
2:45 (2:45) (Class 4) 2-Y-O **£6,469** (£1,925; £962; £481) **Stalls** Centre

Form				RPR
1	1		**Havana Gold (IRE)**[41] 2934 2-9-5 0............................. RichardHughes 5	91+
			(Richard Hannon) *hld up in 3rd: clsd over 2f out: rdn to ld jst ins fnl f: styd on wl* **6/5**[1]	
1	2	1¾	**Discernable**[30] 3282 2-9-0 0.. SilvestreDeSousa 1	81
			(Mark Johnston) *led: shkn up over 2f out: rdn and hdd jst ins fnl f: styd on same pce* **7/2**[3]	

31 **3** *1* **Glass Office**[17] 3733 2-9-2 0 .... JamieSpencer 4 81
(David Simcock) *hld up in last: effrt over 2f out: rdn over 1f out: hanging lft and nt qckn: wl hld fnl f* **3/1**[2]

4 **4** *3/4* **Millers Wharf (IRE)**[42] 2888 2-9-0 0 .... RyanMoore 3 77
(Richard Hannon) *trckd ldr: tried to chal over 2f out: lost 2nd over 1f out and sn outpcd* **11/2**

1m 31.24s (3.64) **Going Correction** +0.425s/f (Yiel) **4** Ran SP% **108.1**
Speed ratings (Par 96): **96,94,92,92**
CSF £5.57 TOTE £2.00; EX 4.00.
Owner Carmichael Humber **Bred** Sir Eric Parker **Trained** East Everleigh, Wilts

FOCUS
Like the opening race, the winning time was really slow, and again they raced up the middle. Hard to know the exact worth of this form, but the first three had all won their maidens last time, and there was much to like about Havana Gold, who did it easily.

NOTEBOOK
Havana Gold(IRE) ◆ was following up a surprise debut win on the Newmarket July course (6f, good to soft), when he defeated a useful-looking stablemate into second, and gave the impression there'll be more to come again when he gets a strong pace to chase. On this evidence he'll be well worth his place in Pattern company, but his trainer ruled out Goodwood. (tchd 11-10)
Discernable, who made all to justify favouritism on her debut over 7f on Polytrack, was allowed an uncontested lead but was simply beaten by a better one. She might want quicker ground. (op 3-1 tchd 11-4)
Glass Office probably didn't achieve much when winning a 6f Polytrack maiden on his second start and this was tougher. (op 7-2)
Millers Wharf(IRE) might have been a bit flattered to finish just over 4l behind his smart stablemate Olympic Glory on his debut at Goodwood (6f, good to soft), and he struggled this time. (op 6-1 tchd 13-2)

4284 CLOSE BROTHERS PROPERTY FINANCE H'CAP 2m
3:20 (3:20) (Class 3) (0-95,93) 3-Y-0+
£7,158 (£2,143; £1,071; £535; £267; £134) **Stalls** Low

Form RPR

2003 **1** **Romeo Montague**[27] 3373 4-9-11 **90** .... RyanMoore 1 99
(Ed Dunlop) *hld up wl in rr and off the pce early: stl in rr over 3f out: gd prog on inner over 2f out: led jst over 1f out: drvn and hld on wl* **4/1**[1]

2 *1/2* **Martial Law (IRE)**[29] 6-8-10 **82** ....(b) WilliamTwiston-Davies(7) 3 90
(David Pipe) *hld up: wl in tch fr 1/2-way: rdn over 2f out: styd on to chse wnr jst ins fnl f: chal last 100yds: a hld* **9/1**

0343 **3** *2 1/4* **Purification (IRE)**[21] 3564 4-9-6 **85** ....(b) WilliamBuick 5 90
(John Gosden) *hld up: prog to trck ldrs 1/2-way: wnt 3rd 6f out: rdn to ld 2f out: hdd and nt qckn jst over 1f out* **4/1**[1]

0-13 **4** *2 3/4* **Rockfella**[34] 3162 6-9-3 **82** .... JimmyFortune 4 84
(Denis Coakley) *trckd ldng pair and clr of rest early: wnt 2nd 11f out and led 1/2-way: drvn and hdd 2f out: one pce* **7/1**[3]

/0-0 **5** *9* **Liberate**[21] 3564 9-9-1 **80** .... JamesDoyle 10 71
(Anabel K Murphy) *hld up: wl in tch fr 1/2-way: drvn to chse ldng trio over 3f out: wknd qckly 2f out* **25/1**

-000 **6** *7* **Merchant Of Dubai**[20] 3625 7-9-9 **88** .... GrahamLee 9 71
(Jim Goldie) *hld up wl in rr: rdn and struggling 4f out: sn lost tch* **10/1**

00/0 **7** *1* **Call It On (IRE)**[31] 3241 6-9-4 **83** .... JamieSpencer 8 65
(Philip Kirby) *led at str pce but hdd over 11f out and stdd into 3rd: chsd ldr 6f out to wl over 2f out: wknd qckly* **12/1**

-206 **8** *4 1/2* **Spice Fair**[31] 3241 5-9-9 **88** .... RichardHughes 7 76
(Mark Usher) *hld up in last and wl off the pce: in tch fr 1/2-way: plld out wd and effrt over 2f out: sn hung bdly lft: ended against nr side rail and eased* **9/2**[2]

0240 **P** **Taikoo**[41] 2936 7-9-1 **80** .... DarryllHolland 2
(Hughie Morrison) *tried to ld but couldn't: pushed up to ld over 11f out: hdd 1/2-way: wknd rapidly 6f out: t.o whn p.u 5f out* **12/1**

5-00 **P** **Classic Vintage (USA)**[27] 3372 6-10-0 **93** .... JimCrowley 6
(Amanda Perrett) *chsd clr ldng trio 5f: sn wknd rapidly: t.o whn p.u 1/2-way: dismntd* **12/1**

3m 36.67s (7.67) **Going Correction** +0.525s/f (Yiel)
WFA 3 from 4yo+ 17lb **10** Ran SP% **116.7**
Speed ratings (Par 107): **101,100,99,98,93 90,89,87, ,**
toteswingers 1&2 £7.20, 1&3 £3.70, 2&3 £5.60 CSF £40.41 CT £153.82 TOTE £5.20: £2.00, £2.00, £1.70; EX 26.10 Trifecta £64.90 Pool £1,813.30 - 20.64 winning units..
Owner Mrs G A Rupert **Bred** Issa Syndicate **Trained** Newmarket, Suffolk

FOCUS
This unfolded in bizarre fashion. Call It On appeared to set off much too fast, and he was pursued by Taikoo and then Rockfella, with the others well strung out. The pace predictably slowed after a few furlongs and the chasing pair took turns in front, but the race still set up nicely for those ridden more sensibly. The final time was desperate. Another improved effort from the winner.

NOTEBOOK
Romeo Montague has a modest strike-rate for a horse of such ability - he's never convinced with his attitude - but he could hardly have had a kinder trip. The suicidal pace was in his favour and he enjoyed a ground-saving trip in the straight when getting an unlikely gap. He had shaped well when upped to just further than 2m5f in the Queen Alexandra at Royal Ascot, and clearly staying is his game. However, while this might have boosted his confidence, it's unlikely he'll enjoy such a favourable journey again anytime soon. (tchd 9-2)
Martial Law(IRE), formerly trained in France and Australia (won in both countries), had recently been successful over hurdles for this yard. This was an encouraging return to the Flat. (op 7-1)
Purification(IRE) again ran respectably without doing enough to suggest he's one to be following. (tchd 7-2)
Rockfella ◆ did well to finish so close considering his early exertions.
Spice Fair went badly left under pressure in the straight and may have had a problem. Official explanation: jockey said gelding hung badly left-handed in straight
Taikoo Official explanation: trainer said gelding had a breathing problem
Classic Vintage(USA) Official explanation: vet said gelding finished distressed

4285 CUSHMAN & WAKEFIELD H'CAP (FOR THE JOHN TRAVERS MEMORIAL TROPHY) 6f
3:55 (3:57) (Class 2) (0-105,100) 3-Y-0+
£9,960 (£2,982; £1,491; £745; £372; £187) **Stalls** Centre

Form RPR

2002 **1** **Shropshire (IRE)**[20] 3641 4-9-1 **94** .... MatthewLawson(5) 8 102
(Charles Hills) *sweating: trckd ldrs: pushed along over 2f out: prog to ld wl over 1f out: hrd pressed fnl f: hld on wl* **6/1**[3]

-330 **2** *nk* **Mac's Power (IRE)**[27] 3371 6-9-9 **97** ....(t) RyanMoore 12 104
(James Fanshawe) *w.w in tch: shkn up 2f out: prog to chse wnr 1f out: str chal fnl f: nt qckn last 75yds* **3/1**[1]

6-00 **3** *1* **Imperial Guest**[28] 3331 6-9-3 **94** .... AshleyHamblett(3) 4 98+
(George Margarson) *hld up in tch: trckd ldrs fr 1/2-way gng easily: no gap tl 1f out: r.o fnl f: no ch to chal* **7/1**

0-40 **4** *hd* **Lutine Bell**[20] 3641 5-9-1 **89** .... RichardHughes 10 92+
(Mike Murphy) *dwlt: t.k.h: hld up in last: stl there gng easily 2f out: prog jst over 1f out: r.o to press for 3rd nr fin: no ch to chal* **8/1**

-612 **5** *2* **Farlow (IRE)**[55] 2489 4-9-2 **90** .... JimCrowley 6 87
(Ralph Beckett) *w ldr: led over 2f out to wl over 1f out: fdd fnl f* **4/1**[2]

5005 **6** *1* **Thunderball**[6] 4086 6-9-0 **91** ....(p) RaulDaSilva(3) 1 85
(Scott Dixon) *racd freely: led at mod pce early: hdd over 2f out: wknd fnl f* **10/1**

-030 **7** *hd* **Top Cop**[34] 3165 3-9-0 **93** .... JimmyFortune 5 85
(Andrew Balding) *in tch towards rr: pushed along and no prog 2f out: fdd* **12/1**

5000 **8** *1 3/4* **Elna Bright**[14] 3822 7-8-9 **83** .... JimmyQuinn 3 70
(Peter Crate) *sltly short of room s: hld up in last pair: taken wd and shkn up briefly 2f out: nvr in it* **10/1**

-225 **9** *1 1/2* **Seeking Magic**[15] 3771 4-8-13 **87** ....(t) JohnFahy 2 70
(Clive Cox) *plld hrd: cl up bhd ldng pair to 2f out: wknd over 1f out* **11/1**

1m 16.76s (2.26) **Going Correction** +0.425s/f (Yiel)
WFA 3 from 4yo+ 5lb **9** Ran SP% **117.1**
Speed ratings (Par 109): **101,100,99,99,96 95,94,92,90**
toteswingers 1&2 £4.30, 1&3 £7.90, 2&3 £4.80 CSF £24.73 CT £131.40 TOTE £6.90: £2.20, £1.70, £2.60; EX 17.70 Trifecta £106.40 Pool £2,210.08 - 15.36 winning units..
Owner The Hon Mrs J M Corbett & C Wright **Bred** Tally-Ho Stud **Trained** Lambourn, Berks

FOCUS
A decent sprint handicap, although not a particularly big field and they didn't go that quick. They raced up the centre. Pretty ordinary form for the grade.

NOTEBOOK
Shropshire(IRE) was no match for the well-handicapped Rex Imperator at Windsor last time, but he was able to race from the same mark here and was reunited with 5lb claimer Matthew Lawson, who was aboard for the horse's most recent success and was replacing a fully fledged jockey. The winner got warm and was keen early, but he wanted it more than the runner-up when it mattered. He's in the Stewards' Cup, but now has a penalty and that will require more. (op 5-1 tchd 13-2)
Mac's Power(IRE) was produced with every chance, but looked happy to settle for second. He didn't carry his head high, but failed to convince he wanted to go past the winner and is on a 12-race losing streak dating back to 2010. (tchd 10-3)
Imperial Guest travelled well, but had to wait too long for a gap and couldn't get to the front two. (op 8-1)
Lutine Bell, who reportedly got upset in the stalls when below form last time, travelled well but the pace horses didn't come back to him, and the ground may have been a bit slower than ideal. It wasn't a bad run. (op 10-1 tchd 12-1)
Farlow(IRE) didn't see his race out and was well below form after 55 days off, perhaps just needing it on ground softer than he cares for. (op 6-1)

4286 CAPITAL & REGIONAL H'CAP 6f
4:30 (4:32) (Class 3) (0-90,89) 3-Y-0+ **£7,439** (£2,213; £1,106; £553) **Stalls** Centre

Form RPR

6265 **1** **Street Power (USA)**[9] 3960 7-8-11 **77** .... RaulDaSilva(3) 5 89
(Jeremy Gask) *hld up in last: prog on far side of gp fr 2f out to chse ldr jst over 1f out: narrow ld ins fnl f: hld on wl* **14/1**

2-31 **2** *nse* **Ladyship**[60] 2332 3-9-4 **86** .... RyanMoore 1 97
(Sir Michael Stoute) *hld up towards rr: prog on far side of gp to ld wl over 1f out: narrowly hdd ins fnl f: battled on wl: jst failed* **5/1**[2]

4000 **3** *4 1/2* **Tagula Night (IRE)**[15] 3771 6-9-5 **82** ....(b) TedDurcan 10 79
(Dean Ivory) *hld up towards rr: rdn 2f out: prog over 1f out: styd on to take 3rd ins fnl f: no ch* **25/1**

2500 **4** *1* **Baby Strange**[20] 3624 8-9-1 **85** .... MichaelJMMurphy(7) 9 79
(Derek Shaw) *wl in tch in midfield: gng strly jst over 2f out in centre of gp: rdn and nt qckn wl over 1f out: kpt on to take 4th nr fin* **9/1**

11 **5** *3/4* **Poole Harbour (IRE)**[21] 3571 3-9-7 **89** .... RichardHughes 11 80
(Richard Hannon) *trckd ldrs towards far side of gp: clsd and wl on terms 2f out: sn outpcd: one pce fnl f* **8/1**[3]

2041 **6** *hd* **Beckermet (IRE)**[14] 3812 10-9-11 **88** .... PJMcDonald 19 79
(Ruth Carr) *led and clr towards nr side of gp: hdd wl over 1f out: fdd* **12/1**

1-25 **7** *shd* **Magic Secret**[15] 3778 4-9-3 **80** .... JimmyFortune 13 71
(Jeremy Gask) *wl in tch in chsng gp: cl enough 2f out: sn outpcd* **4/1**[1]

-032 **8** *nk* **Apollo D'Negro (IRE)**[42] 2870 4-9-2 **79** ....(v) JohnFahy 2 69
(Clive Cox) *towards rr: rdn and prog towards far side and cl up 2f out: sn outpcd and btn* **14/1**

000 **9** *1* **Masked Dance (IRE)**[6] 4086 5-9-7 **84** ....(p) MircoDemuro 4 71
(Scott Dixon) *wl in tch: clsd and on terms 2f out: sn outpcd: fdd fnl f* **50/1**

4030 **10** *nk* **We Have A Dream**[21] 3571 7-9-4 **81** .... MartinDwyer 12 67
(William Muir) *chsd clr ldr to 2f out: steadily wknd over 1f out* **33/1**

2500 **11** *1/2* **Bravo Echo**[38] 3004 6-9-3 **80** .... JimmyQuinn 3 64
(Michael Attwater) *t.k.h: hld up in rr: effrt towards far side 2f out: nvr gng pce to threaten: kpt on* **33/1**

1656 **12** *3* **Caldercruix (USA)**[27] 3394 5-9-5 **82** .... DarryllHolland 17 57
(James Evans) *prom in chsng gp towards nr side: wknd fr 2f out* **33/1**

1223 **13** *3/4* **Moretta Blanche**[21] 3593 5-9-8 **85** ....(t) JimCrowley 7 57
(Ralph Beckett) *stdd s: hld up wl in rr: shkn up and no prog 2f out: wl btn after* **8/1**[3]

-023 **14** *1/2* **Novellen Lad (IRE)**[53] 2558 7-9-12 **89** .... WilliamBuick 18 60
(Willie Musson) *slowest away: hld up in rr: shkn up and no prog 2f out: sn btn* **14/1**

0340 **15** *3/4* **Rothesay Chancer**[11] 3903 4-8-13 **76** .... GrahamLee 6 44
(Jim Goldie) *hld up in rr: rdn and no prog 2f out: sn btn* **16/1**

0045 **16** *1* **Quasi Congaree (GER)**[27] 3394 6-9-5 **82** ....(tp) SilvestreDeSousa 16 47
(Ian Wood) *wl in tch in chsng gp towards nr side: wknd 2f out* **25/1**

1410 **17** *3* **Italian Tom (IRE)**[15] 3771 5-9-5 **87** .... DarrenEgan(5) 15 42
(Ronald Harris) *wl in tch on nr side of gp: wknd 2f out: eased whn no ch* **14/1**

-031 **18** *1 1/2* **Barons Spy (IRE)**[32] 3221 11-9-8 **85** .... JamesDoyle 14 36
(Richard Price) *awkward s: in tch on nr side of gp but nvr gng wl: btn 2f out: eased: sddle slipped* **25/1**

1m 15.2s (0.70) **Going Correction** +0.425s/f (Yiel)
WFA 3 from 4yo+ 5lb **18** Ran SP% **131.5**
Speed ratings (Par 107): **112,111,105,104,103 103,103,102,101,101 100,96,95,94,93 92,88,86**
toteswingers 1&2 £21.70, 1&3 £66.70, 2&3 £45.30 CSF £82.13 CT £1861.98 TOTE £19.30: £4.20, £1.90, £5.90, £2.60; EX 122.60 TRIFECTA Not won..
Owner Horses First Racing Limited **Bred** John Hawkins **Trained** Sutton Veny, Wilts

FOCUS
The ground on the straight course was changed to 'good' all over ahead of this contest. Earlier race times did not support that view, but conditions were drying out all the time and this looked to be the first race on the straight track to be run at a true gallop. Consequently, the time was much the quickest of three races at the distance. This was a competitive sprint handicap, yet two horses finished well clear. The field raced up the centre before gradually edging towards the far side, and the first two raced closest to the far rail for much of the way. A low draw was helpful. The first two were clear and the winner rates a turf personal best.

NOTEBOOK

Street Power(USA) gained his second course win from four starts here, defying a mark 4lb higher than when a close second to Italian Tom at Ascot on his last turf start in May. He's well suited by a strongly run race, and the draw helped, so it's fair to say this set up nicely for him. (op 16-1)

Ladyship ◆ had been absent since winning a Leicester maiden (6f, good to soft) in May, but she improved again on this handicap debut. She was bumped ever so slightly by the winner late on, but it didn't look to cost her and she was nicely clear of the others. There should be plenty more to come. (tchd 13-2)

Tagula Night(IRE) was back on his last winning mark and shaped nicely, suggesting he may soon go in again.

Baby Strange found the main action unfolding away from him. He's not easy to win with these days, however. (tchd 10-1)

Poole Harbour(IRE) was on a hat-trick, but appeared to be found out by his latest 4lb rise. (tchd 15-2, 17-2 in a place)

Beckermet(IRE) may not have been helped by his draw. (op 14-1)

Magic Secret should have finished closer at Haydock on her previous start and was made favourite this time, but she lacked the required pace. This trip on drying ground didn't suit her and she should appreciate a return to soft going and/or a step up in trip. (op 11-2 tchd 6-1)

Barons Spy(IRE) Official explanation: jockey said saddle slipped

4287 DELANCEY H'CAP — 1m (R)

5:05 (5:07) (Class 3) (0-90,94) 3-Y-O+ **£7,439** (£2,213; £1,106; £553) **Stalls** Low

Form — RPR

0131 **1** **Hefner (IRE)**[16] 3767 3-9-3 **87** .... RichardHughes 8 — 92
(Richard Hannon) *trckd ldr: hld together tl sent into ld over 1f out: immediately pressed and drvn: hld on wl fnl f* — **9/2**[3]

5021 **2** *hd* **Dubai Dynamo**[4] 4136 7-10-4 **94** 6ex .... PJMcDonald 1 — 100
(Ruth Carr) *hld up in 5th: clsd on ldrs 2f out: swtchd lft over 1f out: r.o to take 2nd last 100yds: pressed wnr after: jst hld* — **4/1**[2]

0610 **3** *1/2* **Starwatch**[19] 3667 5-9-6 **89** .... WilliamTwiston-Davies(7) 7 — 94
(John Bridger) *chsd ldng trio: rdn over 2f out: styd on fr over 1f out on outer: chal last 100yds: nt qckn nr fin* — **20/1**

060 **4** *1 3/4* **Fantasy Gladiator**[23] 3508 6-9-2 **78** .... (p) JimmyQuinn 2 — 79
(Robert Cowell) *chsd ldng pair: clsd 2f out: rdn to press wnr jst over 1f out: no ex and lost 2nd last 100yds* — **25/1**

31 **5** *nk* **Fluctuate (USA)**[81] 1716 3-9-6 **90** .... WilliamBuick 3 — 88+
(John Gosden) *hld up off the pce disputing 6th: rdn wl over 2f out: nvr on terms but styd on fr over 1f out: nrst fin* — **11/10**[1]

0 **6** *3 1/4* **Silver Sycamore (USA)**[19] 3667 3-9-3 **87** .... TedDurcan 9 — 78
(David Lanigan) *hld up off the pce disputing 6th: pushed along briefly bef 1/2-way: no prog whn sltly impeded 2f out: no ch but kpt on steadily fnl f* — **10/1**

1455 **7** *nse* **Bloodsweatandtears**[15] 3774 4-8-6 **73** .... (b) DavidKenny(5) 5 — 66
(William Knight) *led at gd pce and stretched field: hdd over 1f out: sn wknd* — **25/1**

-050 **8** *6* **Ellie In The Pink (IRE)**[15] 3772 4-9-0 **76** .... JimCrowley 4 — 55
(Alan Jarvis) *s.s: hld up in last pair and wl off the pce: rdn and no prog over 2f out* — **16/1**

-000 **9** *9* **Golden Desert (IRE)**[15] 3771 8-9-6 **82** .... JimmyFortune 6 — 40
(Simon Dow) *hld up in last pair and wl off the pce: rdn over 2f out: sn wknd* — **66/1**

1m 43.32s (2.62) **Going Correction** +0.525s/f (Yiel)
WFA 3 from 4yo+ 8lb — **9** Ran SP% **114.7**
Speed ratings (Par 107): **107,106,106,104,104 101,100,94,85**
toteswingers 1&2 £2.80, 1&3 £12.70, 2&3 £9.60 CSF £21.62 CT £325.08 TOTE £4.30: £1.40, £1.70, £5.90; EX 26.30 Trifecta £269.40 Pool £2,625.30 - 7.21 winning units..
Owner Mrs J Wood **Bred** Denis A McCarthy **Trained** East Everleigh, Wilts

FOCUS

A decent handicap run at a reasonable pace. Another step forward from the winner.

NOTEBOOK

Hefner(IRE) looked a fortunate winner at Kempton last time (runner-up had a tough trip), but he defied a 6lb higher mark on this return to turf, sticking on gamely after managing to get a decent position from his wide draw. He's now won three of his last four starts and there might be more to come. (op 13-2)

Dubai Dynamo, carrying a penalty for a 5l win at Ayr (1m, good) four days earlier, travelled well as is often the case, but his rider took a while to get after him and the gelding had to be switched to get a run. It's possible to argue he should have won, but the winner was finding plenty for pressure. (op 3-1)

Starwatch was helped by having a decent 7lb claimer taking over from a fully fledged rider and ran well. (op 16-1)

Fantasy Gladiator couldn't take advantage of a mark 1lb lower than when runner-up in this race 12 months earlier. (op 33-1)

Fluctuate(USA) made all when an impressive winner of an uncompetitive Wolverhampton maiden on his second start, confirming his debut promise, but he has looked immature and that was his undoing here after 81 days off. Under contrasting tactics, he took an age to pick up and didn't look to be helping his rider. If he gets his act together then he could be quite decent, but it's possible he's the type who will never really grow up. (op 5-4 tchd Evens, 11-8 in a place)

4288 TRIBECA HOLDINGS APPRENTICE H'CAP — 1m (S)

5:35 (5:37) (Class 4) (0-85,85) 3-Y-O **£6,145** (£1,828; £913; £456) **Stalls** Centre

Form — RPR

4035 **1** **Halling Dancer**[17] 3736 3-8-11 **72** .... KierenFox 7 — 80
(Lee Carter) *mde all: drvn 2f out and 3 l clr: hrd pressed fnl f: hld on wl* — **10/1**

-503 **2** *nk* **Jungle Beat (IRE)**[19] 3668 3-9-7 **85** .... (b) TobyAtkinson(3) 2 — 92
(John Gosden) *hld up in last pair: pushed along and stdy prog over 3f out: chsd wnr wl over 1f out: str chal fnl f: r.o but a jst hld* — **6/1**

0-06 **3** *1 1/2* **Feelthedifference**[20] 3643 3-8-1 **69** .... AmeliaGreen(7) 5 — 73
(Sir Henry Cecil) *hld up in last pair: stdy prog fr 3f out: disp 2nd wl over 1f out: cl enough sn after: pushed along and nt qckn* — **14/1**

-221 **4** *9* **Sir Fredlot (IRE)**[28] 3333 3-9-0 **78** .... MatthewLawson(3) 1 — 61
(Charles Hills) *t.k.h: chsd wnr to wl over 1f out: wknd* — **5/1**[3]

1200 **5** *1 3/4* **Oratorian (IRE)**[25] 3446 3-8-9 **75** .... WilliamTwiston-Davies(5) 10 — 54
(Sylvester Kirk) *hld up in rr: rdn over 2f out: sme prog over 1f out but nvr on terms: no hdwy fnl f* — **40/1**

0-00 **6** *1/2* **Cape Rainbow**[57] 2428 3-8-1 **67** .... RachealKneller(5) 8 — 45
(Mark Usher) *hld up towards rr: rdn wl over 2f out: no real prog* — **25/1**

105 **7** *4* **Dutch Old Master**[27] 3393 3-9-3 **78** .... HarryBentley 9 — 46
(Gary Moore) *t.k.h early: trckd ldng trio: rdn wl over 2f out: nt qckn and sn btn* — **11/4**[2]

21-3 **8** *3 3/4* **Restaurateur (IRE)**[25] 3446 3-8-10 **76** .... ThomasBrown(5) 4 — 36
(Andrew Balding) *chsd wnr to 2f out: wknd qckly* — **5/2**[1]

42-0 **9** *5* **Opera Buff**[44] 2813 3-9-0 **75** .... RaulDaSilva 6 — 23
(Sylvester Kirk) *sn pushed along in midfield: dropped to rr bef 1/2-way: wl bhd fnl 2f* — **14/1**

450- **10** *3/4* **Farleaze**[275] 6950 3-8-6 **70** .... DarrenEgan(3) 3 — 17
(Martyn Meade) *t.k.h: chsd ldrs to 1/2-way: sn lost pl and btn* — **40/1**

1m 43.62s (2.82) **Going Correction** +0.425s/f (Yiel) — **10** Ran SP% **117.3**
Speed ratings (Par 102): **102,101,100,91,89 88,84,81,76,75**
toteswingers 1&2 £7.60, 1&3 £7.90, 2&3 £10.50 CSF £68.16 CT £860.14 TOTE £12.80: £3.10, £2.60, £3.20; EX 84.30 Trifecta £1395.90 Part won. Pool £1,886.38 - 0.40 winning units..
Owner Tattenham Corner Racing IV **Bred** Meon Valley Stud **Trained** Epsom, Surrey
■ Stewards' Enquiry : Kieren Fox seven-day ban: used whip above permitted level (Aug 3-9)

FOCUS

A fair handicap in which Halling Dancer set a good pace in an uncontested lead and just kept rolling, proving more resolute than the next two finishers, with the trio well clear. There were a few disappointments and the form has not been rated too positively.

T/Plt: £55.10 to a £1 stake. Pool: £129196.07 - 1710.39 winning tickets T/Qpdt: £18.10 to a £1 stake. Pool: £8981.76 - 366.92 winning tickets JN

3855 HAYDOCK (L-H)

Friday, July 20

OFFICIAL GOING: Home straight - good (good to soft in places); back straight - good to soft (soft in places) changing to home straight - good to soft ; back straight - soft after race 1 (2:00)

Wind: Light, half behind Weather: Cloudy

4289 STEPS IN CONCERT HERE 21ST JULY H'CAP — 1m 2f 95y

2:00 (2:01) (Class 5) (0-75,80) 3-Y-O **£2,264** (£673; £336; £168) **Stalls** High

Form — RPR

5040 **1** **Now My Sun**[15] 3775 3-9-0 67 .... PhillipMakin 9 — 80
(Mrs K Burke) *hld up in last pl: hdwy over 2f out: rdn to ld over 1f out: styd on wl to draw clr fnl 100yds* — **9/2**[3]

-033 **2** *4 1/2* **Highland Duke (IRE)**[19] 3671 3-8-10 70 .... RyanTate(7) 6 — 74
(Clive Cox) *trckd ldrs: effrt 2f out: chalng over 1f out: sn sed to hang lft: unable to go w wnr fnl 100yds* — **9/2**[3]

0631 **3** *1 1/4* **Paddyfrommenlo (IRE)**[7] 4046 3-9-13 80 6ex .... SebSanders 1 — 83
(J W Hills) *racd keenly: chsd ldr tl rdn over 2f out: nt qckning whn sltly short of room and checked over 1f out: sn swtchd rt and outpcd: styd on towards fin* — **9/4**[1]

0035 **4** *nk* **Elkhart (IRE)**[30] 3280 3-9-7 74 .... JoeFanning 8 — 76
(Mark Johnston) *led: rdn over 2f out: hdd over 1f out: no ex ins fnl f* — **11/1**

22-1 **5** *2* **Bold Cuffs**[20] 3622 3-9-5 72 .... ChrisCatlin 4 — 70
(Sir Mark Prescott Bt) *trckd ldrs: pushed along over 3f out: sn lost pl and outpcd: no imp after* — **3/1**[2]

U034 **6** *4 1/2* **Tweet Lady**[25] 3443 3-8-13 66 .... JamesMillman 5 — 55
(Rod Millman) *hld up: pushed along 3f out: nvr able to chal: lft bhd ins fnl f* — **10/1**

2m 15.77s (0.27) **Going Correction** +0.10s/f (Good) — **6** Ran SP% **109.6**
Speed ratings (Par 100): **102,98,97,97,95 91**
toteswingers 1&2 £4.70, 1&3 £5.60, 2&3 £2.80 CSF £23.28 CT £51.27 TOTE £4.50: £1.50, £2.70; EX 23.30.
Owner Ray Bailey **Bred** Ray Bailey **Trained** Middleham Moor, N Yorks

FOCUS

All races on Outer home straight and races on Round course run over approximately 6yds further than advertised except 1m 6f race which increased by 56yds. All races were run on the outer home straight. Jockeys involved in the first reported that the ground was basically riding soft. They went a fairly steady pace in this ordinary handicap. A step up from the winner, with the next two helping set the level.

4290 BRITISH STALLION STUDS SUPPORTING BRITISH RACING EBF MAIDEN STKS — 6f

2:30 (2:30) (Class 5) 2-Y-O **£3,234** (£962; £481; £240) **Stalls** High

Form — RPR

1 **Professor** 2-9-3 0 .... SeanLevey 4 — 84+
(Richard Hannon) *a.p: led over 2f out: r.o wl to draw clr ins fnl 100yds: eased cl home* — **11/8**[1]

6 **2** *3 1/4* **Great Run**[33] 3191 2-9-3 0 .... KieranO'Neill 1 — 72+
(Richard Hannon) *wnt lft and awkward s: hld up in tch: chsd wnr over 2f out: carried hd high u.p: no ch ins fnl f* — **20/1**

0 **3** *1 1/2* **Madame Elizabeth**[37] 3034 2-8-12 0 .... RussKennemore 7 — 63
(Reg Hollinshead) *hld up: swtchd lft and hdwy over 2f out: chsd ldrs u.p over 1f out: kpt on same pce ins fnl f* — **20/1**

05 **4** *6* **Smooth Handle**[25] 3452 2-9-3 0 .... RichardKingscote 2 — 50
(Tom Dascombe) *midfield: outpcd 1/2-way: plugged on at one pce and no imp fr over 1f out* — **33/1**

0 **5** *4* **Unassailable**[76] 1842 2-9-3 0 .... PhillipMakin 8 — 38
(Kevin Ryan) *hld up: outpcd over 2f out: kpt on to chse ldrs but no ch whn hung lft over 1f out: wl btn fnl f* — **9/2**[3]

0 **6** *2 1/2* **Tussy Marx**[16] 3747 2-8-12 0 .... GrahamGibbons 5 — 25
(David Barron) *midfield: pushed along and outpcd over 2f out: n.d after* — **8/1**

5 **7** *11* **Mushaakis (IRE)**[44] 2822 2-9-3 0 .... TadhgO'Shea 6
(Mark Johnston) *prom tl rdn and wknd 2f out* — **11/4**[2]

0 **8** *hd* **Lady Of Seville (IRE)**[83] 1671 2-8-12 0 .... MickyFenton 3
(Tom Tate) *led: hung lft and hdd over 2f out: wknd over 1f out* — **33/1**

1m 14.63s (0.83) **Going Correction** +0.10s/f (Good) — **8** Ran SP% **113.5**
Speed ratings (Par 94): **98,93,91,83,78 75,60,60**
toteswingers 1&2 £5.50, 1&3 £11.20, 2&3 £18.50 CSF £34.27 TOTE £2.80: £1.50, £3.90, £6.50; EX 14.90.
Owner Mrs P Good **Bred** Exors Of The Late J R Good **Trained** East Everleigh, Wilts

FOCUS

The going was officially changed before this race, to soft in the back straight and good to soft in the home straight. An ordinary maiden, the best recent winner of which was 2003 scorer Peak To Creek who won the Horris Hill later in the season. With the second favourite failing to run his race the form is limited, but the winner did it nicely.

NOTEBOOK

Professor is out of a half-sister to Tadeo, a one-time smart sprinter in these colours. Reportedly fractious in the preliminaries, he did nothing wrong once in action, running on for a comfortable victory. Things will be tougher for him up in grade but this was a pleasing start. (op 13-8, tchd 7-4 in places)

Great Run, whose debut was over almost as soon as it had begun, was no match for his stablemate and held his head high under pressure, probably through greenness. (op 12-1 tchd 11-1)

Madame Elizabeth picked up well from the rear once switched to the outer, without threatening the winner. This was a marked improvement on her debut effort over C&D. (op 33-1)

Smooth Handle was well held, but is now eligible for nurseries. (op 28-1)

Unassailable never really figured and appeared ill-at-ease on the ground in the latter stages. (op 4-1 tchd 5-1)

Mushaakis(IRE), fifth to Chesham winner Tha'Ir on his Ripon debut, ran no sort of race, his rider first appearing concerned after just a couple of furlongs. This was clearly not his running. (op 7-2 tchd 5-2)

4291 PARRY & CO SOLICITORS ANNUAL H'CAP 6f
3:05 (3:05) (Class 4) (0-85,83) 3-Y-O **£4,204** (£1,251; £625; £312) **Stalls** High

Form RPR

0321 **1** **Henry Bee**[13] 3848 3-8-10 **72**.......... FrederikTylicki 6 81
(Richard Fahey) *in rr: pushed along whn struggling to go pce over 4f out: swtchd lft and hdwy over 1f out: styd on to ld wl ins fnl f: in command towards fin* **9/2**[2]

2052 **2** 1 1/4 **Tip Top Gorgeous (IRE)**[11] 3912 3-8-9 **78**.......... DavidBergin(7) 1 83
(David O'Meara) *hld up: swtchd lft and hdwy over 1f out: sn led: hdd wl ins fnl f: hld towards fin* **8/1**

0312 **3** 2 1/2 **Goldream**[20] 3613 3-9-7 **83**.......... J-PGuillambert 7 80
(Luca Cumani) *chsd ldrs: pushed along over 2f out: rdn and chalng 1f out: no ex fnl 110yds* **6/4**[1]

-060 **4** 4 1/2 **Pea Shooter**[34] 3165 3-9-7 **83**.......... PhillipMakin 4 66
(Kevin Ryan) *led: rdn and hdd over 1f out: wknd ins fnl f* **6/1**[3]

-001 **5** 3 **Indego Blues**[18] 3698 3-8-9 **78**.......... ShirleyTeasdale(7) 2 51
(David Nicholls) *w ldr: rdn over 1f out: sn wknd* **13/2**

6030 **6** 3/4 **Dubai Sunshine (IRE)**[27] 3379 3-9-4 **80**..........(v[1]) HayleyTurner 5 51
(Michael Bell) *s.i.s: sn prom: rdn over 2f out: wknd over 1f out* **13/2**

1m 14.03s (0.23) **Going Correction** +0.10s/f (Good) 6 Ran SP% **110.2**
Speed ratings (Par 102): **102,100,97,91,87 86**
toteswingers 1&2 £1.60, 1&3 £1.30, 2&3 £2.70 CSF £36.45 TOTE £4.20: £2.30, £2.30; EX 26.90.
Owner Wildcard Racing Syndicate X2 **Bred** T M M Partnership **Trained** Musley Bank, N Yorks

FOCUS
They went a solid pace in this fair sprint handicap and the first three came from the rear half of the field. Some of the winner's earlier form could rate this high.

4292 BLUE PRISM H'CAP 5f
3:40 (3:42) (Class 4) (0-80,80) 3-Y-O+ **£4,075** (£1,212; £606; £303) **Stalls** High

Form RPR

2512 **1** **Cruise Tothelimit (IRE)**[4] 4146 4-8-11 **68**.......... RyanPowell(3) 4 80
(Ian Williams) *a.p: led jst over 2f out: rdn and edgd lft over 1f out: r.o wl fnl f* **9/4**[1]

0002 **2** 2 **Macdillon**[11] 3919 6-9-3 **71**.......... LiamKeniry 2 76
(Stuart Kittow) *chsd ldrs: rdn over 1f out: hung lft and wnt 2nd ins fnl f: no imp on wnr* **7/1**[3]

0000 **3** 1 1/4 **Cocktail Charlie**[35] 3127 4-9-10 **78**..........(p) DavidAllan 5 79
(Tim Easterby) *chsd ldrs: swtchd lft wl over 1f out: kpt on ins fnl f: nt quite gng pce to chal ldrs* **7/2**[2]

6242 **4** 3/4 **Haajes**[11] 3903 8-9-9 **77**.......... MickyFenton 3 75
(Paul Midgley) *in tch: pushed along and outpcd over 2f out: kpt on ins fnl f: nvr able to chal* **7/2**[2]

0206 **5** shd **Bronze Beau**[13] 3845 5-9-12 **80**..........(t) KirstyMilczarek 6 77
(Linda Stubbs) *led: rdn and hdd jst over 2f out: stl cl up over 1f out: no ex fnl 75yds* **10/1**

0531 **6** 1 3/4 **Captain Scooby**[13] 3845 6-9-6 **77**.......... DeclanCannon(3) 7 68
(Richard Guest) *dwlt: in rr: sn pushed along: nvr gng pce to chal* **9/1**

02-0 **7** 2 1/2 **Ishetoo**[44] 2809 8-9-1 **69**.......... RobbieFitzpatrick 8 51
(Peter Grayson) *in rr: pushed along over 2f out: nvr on terms w ldrs* **66/1**

0042 **8** 2 1/2 **Wicked Wilma (IRE)**[17] 3730 8-8-6 **67**.......... MatthewHopkins(7) 1 40
(Alan Berry) *prom: rdn 2f out: wknd over 1f out* **25/1**

1m 0.66s (-0.14) **Going Correction** +0.10s/f (Good) 8 Ran SP% **112.1**
Speed ratings (Par 105): **105,101,99,98,98 95,91,87**
toteswingers 1&2 £3.00, 1&3 £2.40, 2&3 £8.80 CSF £18.00 TOTE £3.10: £1.30, £2.80, £1.40; EX 22.10.
Owner Odysian Ltd T/A Cruise Nightspot **Bred** D And Mrs D Veitch **Trained** Portway, Worcs

FOCUS
A run-of-the-mill sprint handicap. The first two ended up racing towards the centre of the track. The winner is rated back to his old best.

4293 LANCASHIRE LIFE MAIDEN STKS 1m
4:15 (4:16) (Class 5) 3-Y-O+ **£2,264** (£673; £336; £168) **Stalls** Low

Form RPR

2 **1** **Mean It (IRE)**[27] 3384 3-9-3 0.......... MickyFenton 11 79+
(Tom Tate) *midfield: hdwy 3f out: led wl over 1f out: sn rdn: r.o wl to draw clr fnl 150yds* **8/13**[1]

2- **2** 3 1/2 **Sunnybridge Boy (IRE)**[391] 3382 3-9-0 0.......... MichaelMetcalfe(3) 12 71+
(Mrs K Burke) *a.p: led over 3f out: rdn and hdd wl over 1f out: no imp on wnr ins fnl f: no ch fnl 150yds* **9/4**[2]

0/0 **3** 3 3/4 **Gavi**[19] 3663 6-9-6 0.......... DeanHeslop(5) 1 60
(Karen George) *dwlt: racd keenly: midfield: n.m.r and checked on bnd 6f out: swtchd rt over 2f out: hdwy to chse ldrs and hung lft over 1f out: styd on same pce and no imp fnl f* **80/1**

4 1 1/2 **Maska Pony (IRE)**[397] 8-9-11 0.......... TomEaves 9 56+
(George Moore) *stdd s: hld up in rr: pushed along to go pce over 3f out: swtchd rt over 1f out: styd on ins fnl f: nt pce to rch ldrs* **14/1**[3]

5 nk **Tenacity** 3-9-3 0.......... PaddyAspell 14 58
(Kate Walton) *hld up: pushed along over 2f out: rdn and hung lft over 1f out: hung markedly lft and styd on fnl 110yds: nt rch ldrs* **33/1**

00 **6** 2 1/2 **Scarborough Rock**[53] 2553 3-9-3 0.......... ChrisCatlin 7 52
(Tom Symonds) *racd keenly: disp ld tl def advantage over 4f out: hdd over 3f out: sn rdn: one pce u.p over 1f out: wl btn fnl 100yds* **100/1**

6-0 **7** 1/2 **Daffyd**[55] 2501 3-9-3 0.......... PhillipMakin 5 50
(Kevin Ryan) *racd keenly: trckd ldrs: rdn over 2f out: one pce u.p over 1f out: wl btn fnl 100yds* **20/1**

8 1 1/4 **My Stroppy Poppy** 3-8-12 0..........(t) SebSanders 3 44
(Frank Sheridan) *s.i.s: in rr: pushed along over 2f out: sme hdwy over 1f out: nvr able to get on terms w ldrs: wl btn ins fnl f* **33/1**

40 **9** 2 1/4 **Thats Molly (IRE)**[8] 3990 3-8-12 0.......... FrederikTylicki 8 37
(Eric Alston) *racd keenly: trckd ldrs: rdn over 2f out: wknd over 1f out* **16/1**

0/ **10** 2 **Smirfys Emerald (IRE)**[650] 6743 4-9-11 0.......... SeanQuinlan 10 35
(Michael Mullineaux) *hld up: pushed along 4f out: rdn over 2f out and sn hung lft: no imp* **100/1**

30 **11** 2 1/4 **Native Eight (USA)**[15] 3786 3-9-0 0.......... RyanPowell(3) 6 32
(Ian Williams) *disp ld tl hdd over 4f out: wknd 3f out* **16/1**

63 **12** 1 **One For The Girls**[27] 3384 3-9-3 0.......... RussKennemore 13 29
(Nicky Vaughan) *midfield: hdwy 4f out: effrt and prom 3f out: wknd 2f out* **40/1**

1m 45.67s (1.97) **Going Correction** +0.10s/f (Good)
WFA 3 from 4yo+ 8lb 12 Ran SP% **127.4**
Speed ratings (Par 103): **94,90,86,85,84 82,81,80,78,76 74,73**
toteswingers 1&2 £1.20, 1&3 £16.60, 2&3 £19.00 CSF £2.20 TOTE £1.80: £1.10, £1.10, £12.90; EX 3.10.
Owner Mrs Fitri Hay **Bred** Lynch Bages Ltd & Samac Ltd **Trained** Tadcaster, N Yorks

FOCUS
There was a decided lack of depth to this maiden, where they bet 14-1 bar two, and that pair duly dominated. However, they didn't show their best off a muddling pace.

4294 BROWN SHIPLEY WEALTH WELL MANAGED H'CAP 1m 6f
4:50 (4:50) (Class 4) (0-85,84) 3-Y-O **£4,204** (£1,251; £625; £312) **Stalls** Low

Form RPR

5513 **1** **Flashman**[18] 3697 3-8-3 **66**.......... PatrickMathers 2 83
(Richard Fahey) *prom: wnt 2nd 5f out: led over 2f out: rdn clr over 1f out: styd on wl and in command fnl f: eased cl home* **7/2**[3]

2110 **2** 10 **Rocktherunway (IRE)**[29] 3296 3-9-4 **84**.......... LeeTopliss(3) 3 86
(Michael Dods) *s.i.s: hld up: hdwy over 3f out: rdn to chse wnr over 2f out: one pce over 1f out: no ch fnl f* **2/1**[1]

2230 **3** 1 **Pistol (IRE)**[21] 3592 3-9-1 **78**..........(v[1]) TomEaves 6 79
(Sir Michael Stoute) *s.s: hld up: rdn and hdwy to chse ldrs over 3f out: one pce over 1f out: hung lft ent fnl f: plugged on at same pce* **9/2**

315 **4** 9 **Fleeting Image**[13] 3859 3-8-6 **76**..........(p) NatashaEaton(7) 4 64
(Alan Bailey) *racd keenly: led: pushed along 3f out: rdn and hdd over 2f out: no ex over 1f out: wl btn fnl f* **12/1**

346 **5** 18 **Aliante**[42] 2885 3-8-4 **67**.......... JoeFanning 5 30
(Mark Johnston) *chsd ldr to 5f out: pushed along and lost pl over 4f out: sn bhd: lost tch 2f out: t.o* **25/1**

5452 **R** **Juno The Muffinman (IRE)**[15] 3781 3-8-7 **70**.....(v) RichardKingscote 1
(Tom Dascombe) *ref to r: tk no part* **3/1**[2]

3m 2.29s (0.29) **Going Correction** +0.10s/f (Good) 6 Ran SP% **110.3**
Speed ratings (Par 102): **103,97,96,91,81**
toteswingers 1&2 £1.90, 1&3 £1.80, 2&3 £2.30 CSF £10.53 TOTE £3.80: £2.50, £1.20; EX 14.00.
Owner The G-Guck Group **Bred** Avenue Farm Stud **Trained** Musley Bank, N Yorks

FOCUS
This race, a reasonable staying handicap run at a fair pace, was run over 56 yards further than advertised. It was won 12 months ago by Colour Vision, who took this year's Gold Cup at Ascot. Flashman rates a 7lb best, but the next pair were not at their best.

4295 BETDAQ HAYDOCK PARK APPRENTICE TRAINING SERIES H'CAP (PART OF THE RACING EXCELLENCE INITIATIVE) 1m
5:25 (5:25) (Class 5) (0-75,71) 4-Y-O+ **£2,264** (£673; £336; £168) **Stalls** Low

Form RPR

3063 **1** **Chosen Character (IRE)**[21] 3559 4-9-6 **70**..........(vt) NatashaEaton(3) 2 79
(Tom Dascombe) *plld hrd: sn led: rdn over 1f out: kpt on wl towards fin* **5/2**[2]

5213 **2** 1 3/4 **Hayek**[7] 4042 5-9-5 **66**..........(b) AdamCarter 4 71+
(Tim Easterby) *hld up: hdwy over 2f out: wnt 2nd over 1f out: nvr able to chal wnr* **9/4**[1]

0303 **3** 2 **Rasselas (IRE)**[27] 3405 5-8-9 **59**..........(v) ShirleyTeasdale(3) 1 59
(David Nicholls) *plld hrd: prom: trckd ldr after 2f: lost 2nd 3f out: remained handy: pushed along and nt qckn over 1f out: no ex fnl 100yds* **16/1**

06-0 **4** 3 3/4 **Buzz Law (IRE)**[45] 2792 4-9-5 **71**.......... RyanTate(5) 5 63
(Mrs K Burke) *midfield: rdn over 2f out: one pce and no imp over 1f out* **4/1**[3]

0413 **5** 3/4 **Jupiter Fidius**[21] 3581 5-8-8 **60**..........(p) GemmaTutty(5) 7 50
(Karen Tutty) *hld up in rr: rdn over 2f out: no imp* **9/1**

0050 **6** 1/2 **Flipping**[21] 3559 5-9-0 **64**.......... DarylByrne(3) 3 53
(Eric Alston) *prom: wnt 2nd 3f out: lost 2nd over 1f out: wknd ins fnl f* **9/1**

/1-0 **7** 3 **Cyril The Squirrel**[19] 3659 8-9-4 **65**.......... DeanHeslop 8 47
(Karen George) *s.i.s: hld up: pushed along 3f out: no imp: wl btn ins fnl f* **16/1**

0 **8** 24 **De Lesseps (USA)**[32] 3215 4-8-3 **55**.......... MatthewHopkins(5) 6
(Alan Berry) *in tch: lost pl over 4f out: struggling over 3f out: lft bhd over 2f out: t.o* **100/1**

1m 45.3s (1.60) **Going Correction** +0.10s/f (Good) 8 Ran SP% **112.1**
Speed ratings (Par 103): **96,94,92,88,87 87,84,60**
toteswingers 1&2 £1.90, 1&3 £4.40, 2&3 £3.50 CSF £8.17 CT £67.80 TOTE £3.50: £1.60, £1.20, £3.70; EX 8.60.
Owner Aykroyd And Sons Ltd **Bred** Moyglare Stud Farm Ltd **Trained** Malpas, Cheshire
■ Stewards' Enquiry : Ryan Tate seven-day ban: used whip contrary to race rules (tbn)

FOCUS
This was a modest apprentice handicap in which the winner had his own way in front. The third looks the best guide.
T/Plt: £70.90 to a £1 stake. Pool: £54838.68 - 564.38 winning tickets T/Qpdt: £16.30 to a £1 stake. Pool: £5086.60 - 230.42 winning tickets DO

4097 NEWMARKET (R-H)
Friday, July 20

OFFICIAL GOING: Soft
Wind: Light across Weather: Showers

4296 0843 FREE DIVERT TO MOBILE @ OPTELECOM.CO.UK H'CAP (BETFAIR 10 FURLONG FLAT SERIES QUALIFIER) 1m 2f
5:40 (5:42) (Class 5) (0-70,73) 3-Y-O+ **£3,234** (£962; £481; £240) **Stalls** Centre

Form RPR

5450 **1** **Minstrel Lad**[37] 3043 4-8-6 **50** oh1.......... SimonPearce(3) 4 62
(Lydia Pearce) *hld up: hdwy over 3f out: led over 1f out: sn rdn: jst hld on* **25/1**

236 **2** hd **Laconicos (IRE)**[17] 3721 10-8-7 **53**..........(t) LauraPike(5) 5 65
(William Stone) *hld up: hdwy over 3f out: rdn to chse wnr over 1f out: edgd lft ins fnl f: styd on* **33/1**

6-00 **3** 5 **Royal Dutch**[70] 2042 3-8-10 **61**.......... EddieAhern 3 63
(Denis Coakley) *chsd ldrs: rdn over 2f out: no ex fnl f* **15/2**[3]

2000 **4** 2 **Hurricane Hymnbook (USA)**[21] 3594 7-9-10 **65**.......... StevieDonohoe 9 63
(Willie Musson) *hld up: hdwy over 2f out: sn rdn: styd on: nt rch ldrs* **6/1**[2]

-150 **5** 3 1/2 **Rockweiller**[15] 3775 5-9-9 **64**..........(v) PaulHanagan 13 55
(Steve Gollings) *chsd ldrs: rdn over 3f out: wknd fnl f* **11/1**

4-20 **6** *2 ¾* **Enriching (USA)**[21] 3589 4-8-12 **53**.................................... MartinLane 2 39
(Lydia Pearce) *chsd ldr tl led over 4f out: sn clr: rdn and hdd over 1f out: wknd fnl f* **28/1**

1065 **7** *1* **Darsan (IRE)**[41] 2937 4-9-6 **61**..................................[1] TomMcLaughlin 12 45
(Phil McEntee) *hld up: rdn over 2f out: nt trble ldrs* **40/1**

3521 **8** *3 ¾* **Cantor**[8] 3995 4-8-12 **56**... AdamBeschizza(3) 15 32
(Giles Bravery) *mid-div: hdwy over 5f out: rdn over 3f out: wknd over 1f out* **7/4**[1]

30-0 **9** *6* **No Larking (IRE)**[17] 3723 4-9-8 **63**.................................... DaneO'Neill 16 27
(Henry Candy) *hld up: rdn over 2f out: n.d* **16/1**

2650 **10** *6* **Cairanne**[11] 3920 4-9-2 **57**.. RobertHavlin 11
(Tom Keddy) *hld up: rdn over 2f out: n.d* **20/1**

/514 **11** *6* **Pindar (GER)**[21] 3573 8-8-11 **52**.............................. DaraghO'Donohoe 10
(Barney Curley) *prom: lost pl 1/2-way: wknd 3f out: t.o* **25/1**

6263 **12** *2 ¾* **Graylyn Valentino**[11] 3920 3-8-12 **63**................................ BrettDoyle 8
(Robin Dickin) *mid-div: wknd over 3f out: t.o* **10/1**

-530 **13** *12* **Porcini**[15] 3793 3-9-4 **69**.. MickaelBarzalona 6
(Philip McBride) *hld up and a in rr: t.o* **8/1**

1621 **14** *3* **Hail Promenader (IRE)**[9] 3976 6-10-4 **73** 6ex...........(p) WilliamCarson 7
(Anthony Carson) *hld up: hdwy 1/2-way: wknd 3f out: t.o* **9/1**

0000 **15** *21* **Bonbon Bonnie**[10] 3946 4-8-2 **50** oh5.......................... DannyBrock(7) 14
(Phil McEntee) *set str pce tl wknd and hdd over 4f out: t.o* **100/1**

2m 12.18s (6.68) **Going Correction** +0.75s/f (Yiel)
WFA 3 from 4yo+ 10lb **15** Ran SP% **129.1**
Speed ratings (Par 103): **103,102,98,97,94 92,91,88,83,78 74,71,62,59,43**
toteswingers 1&2 £117.50, 1&3 £29.70, 2&3 £44.20. CSF £689.82 CT £6652.89 TOTE £31.90: £9.80, £10.10, £2.50; EX 655.10 TRIFECTA Not won..
Owner Dick Devereux **Bred** Theresa Fitsall **Trained** Newmarket, Suffolk
■ Stewards' Enquiry : Laura Pike four-day ban: used whip above permitted level (Aug 3,5-7)
Simon Pearce four-day ban: used whip above permitted level (Aug 3,5-7)

FOCUS
Stands Side track used with Stalls on Far Side except 10f: Centre. The going was soft after 6mm of rain the previous night and 21 horses had been withdrawn prior to racing. A modest handicap run at a good early gallop, but the fact that the overall time was slow indicates the ground was pretty testing. There was a surprise result with two outsiders dominating and the form looks dubious. It has been rated around the runner-up.
Cantor Official explanation: trainer said gelding finished distressed

4297 POPTELECOM.CO.UK HUGE DISCOUNTS ON 0800 MAIDEN FILLIES' STKS 7f
6:10 (6:10) (Class 5) 2-Y-O **£3,234** (£962; £481; £240) **Stalls** High

Form RPR

45 **1** **Mystical Moment**[28] 3339 2-9-0 0.. DaneO'Neill 2 81+
(Richard Hannon) *mde all: rdn and hung lft fr over 1f out: styd on* **15/2**[3]

3 **2** *2 ½* **Nargys (IRE)**[21] 3590 2-9-0 0.. KierenFallon 3 75
(Luca Cumani) *trckd wnr: racd keenly: shkn up over 1f out: no ex ins fnl f* **10/11**[1]

3 *1* **Heading North** 2-9-0 0... RichardMullen 12 74+
(Richard Hannon) *hld up: hdwy over 1f out: sn rdn and edgd lft: styd on: nt rch ldrs* **16/1**

4 *nk* **Of Course Darling** 2-9-0 0... PaulHanagan 10 74+
(Ed Dunlop) *hld up: hdwy over 1f out: styd on: nrst fin* **20/1**

5 *nk* **My Flaming Cat (USA)** 2-9-0 0.. NeilCallan 5 71+
(Roger Varian) *chsd ldrs: shkn up over 2f out: styd on same pce fr over 1f out* **20/1**

6 *¾* **Vanity Rules** 2-9-0 0.. RobertHavlin 11 69
(John Gosden) *a.p: shkn up over 2f out: no ex fnl f* **7/2**[2]

7 *6* **Willowing (USA)** 2-9-0 0... MickaelBarzalona 4 54
(Mahmood Al Zarooni) *prom: pushed along 4f out: rdn and wknd over 1f out* **17/2**

8 *hd* **Duchess Of Gazeley (IRE)** 2-9-0 0.......................... StevieDonohoe 9 54
(Lydia Pearce) *hld up: pushed along over 2f out: a in rr* **100/1**

9 *nk* **Silk Fairy (IRE)** 2-9-0 0... EddieAhern 7 53
(Noel Quinlan) *s.i.s: hld up: pushed along and wknd over 2f out* **40/1**

10 *1 ¼* **Super Cookie** 2-9-0 0.. MircoMimmocchi 8 50
(Philip McBride) *mid-div: hdwy 3f out: rdn and wknd over 1f out* **66/1**

1m 31.22s (5.52) **Going Correction** +0.75s/f (Yiel) **10** Ran SP% **117.2**
Speed ratings (Par 91): **98,95,94,93,93 92,85,85,85,83**
toteswingers 1&2 £3.00, 1&3 £14.10, 2&3 £4.50. CSF £14.30 TOTE £9.00: £2.50, £1.10, £3.60; EX 18.00 Trifecta £175.70 Pool: £766.96 - 3.23 winning units..
Owner Mrs Amanda Turner **Bred** Denis Barry **Trained** East Everleigh, Wilts

FOCUS
Debutantes had dominated this fillies' maiden in recent seasons and it has thrown up several useful sorts, the best of them being the dual Group 1 winner Rainbow View. However, that was not the case this year as the race was dominated by the two fillies with previous racecourse experience.

NOTEBOOK
Mystical Moment had shown promise on her second start when she did not get the best of runs at Goodwood in June, but was stepping up in trip on this third start and the ground was an unknown. However, she set off in front and produced extra up the hill to pull away from the favourite and score quite nicely. Nurseries look likely to be the next port of call. (op 8-1)
Nargys(IRE), a 125,000euros daughter of a 7f winner who is related to Listed performers, had run a promising race when third on her debut over 6f of this track at the end of June. She had every chance if a little free early, but did not appear to get home. That said the runner-up in that race was also a beaten odds-on favourite earlier in the afternoon and perhaps the form might not prove as good as it originally looked. (op Evens tchd 11-10)
Heading North, a stable companion of the winner and the first foal of a lightly raced 1m winner from the family of Rock City and Kerrera, was slowly into her stride on this debut but got the idea from halfway and stayed on to finish on the heels of the first two. She should benefit greatly from the experience. (tchd 14-1)
Of Course Darling, a half-sister to the very useful Valiant out of a Group 3 winner, was settled early before keeping on late and should come on for the outing. (op 16-1)
My Flaming Cat(USA), a $120,000 first foal of a half-sister to a couple of winners at around 1m in the US, chased the pace but could not pick up under pressure. Faster ground might suit her in future (op 14-1)
Vanity Rules, the fifth foal of a couple of multiple winners at 1m plus (General Tufto and Smart Step) out of a Listed winner, ran as if the outing would bring her on and she should be sharper next time. (tchd 4-1)
Willowing(USA)'s trainer was bidding to win this for the third successive year, but was very green and was struggling before halfway. (op 10-1)

4298 INVESCO PERPETUAL H'CAP 7f
6:45 (6:46) (Class 4) (0-85,85) 3-Y-O **£4,528** (£1,347; £673; £336) **Stalls** High

Form RPR

012 **1** **Serene Oasis (IRE)**[9] 3952 3-8-6 **70**..........................(v) SamHitchcott 10 79
(Mick Channon) *led: rdn and hdd over 1f out: rallied u.str.p to ld wl ins fnl f: all out* **9/1**

600 **2** *hd* **Swing Alone (IRE)**[29] 3294 3-9-7 **85**.................................. EddieAhern 2 93
(Gay Kelleway) *hld up: hdwy over 2f out: rdn to ld over 1f out: hdd wl ins fnl f: r.o* **16/1**

-006 **3** *¾* **Elusive Flame**[27] 3393 3-9-2 **80**.. DaneO'Neill 3 86
(David Elsworth) *s.i.s: swtchd to r alone towards stands' side and sn prom: rdn over 1f out: hung lft ins fnl f: r.o* **12/1**

-442 **4** *½* **Amadeus Wolfe Tone (IRE)**[27] 3393 3-9-4 **82**..........(p) KierenFallon 12 87
(Jamie Osborne) *hld up: hdwy over 2f out: rdn and ev ch ins fnl f: unable qck towards fin* **11/4**[1]

5212 **5** *2* **Rocky Reef**[13] 3876 3-8-11 **75**..(v) DavidProbert 5 75
(Andrew Balding) *chsd ldrs: shkn up over 2f out: rdn over 1f out: no ex ins fnl f* **9/1**

15-2 **6** *3* **Ruby Night (IRE)**[45] 2785 3-9-7 **85**................................ JamieSpencer 6 77
(Michael Bell) *hld up: hdwy over 1f out: sn rdn: wknd and eased wl ins fnl f* **3/1**[2]

4-21 **7** *5* **Al Wajba (USA)**[49] 2672 3-8-13 **80**.......................... AdamBeschizza(3) 1 58
(William Haggas) *chsd ldrs tl rdn and wknd over 1f out* **8/1**

-160 **8** *14* **Muarrab**[76] 1858 3-9-3 **81**... PaulHanagan 13 21
(Ed Dunlop) *hld up: wknd wl over 1f out* **13/2**[3]

32-1 **9** *2 ¾* **Don Libre**[34] 3155 3-8-11 **75**... NeilCallan 4
(Paul Cole) *prom: racd keenly: rdn over 2f out: wknd over 1f out* **20/1**

1m 30.37s (4.67) **Going Correction** +0.75s/f (Yiel) **9** Ran SP% **114.4**
Speed ratings (Par 102): **103,102,101,101,99 95,89,73,70**
toteswingers 1&2 £24.50, 1&3 £20.90, 2&3 £36.20. CSF £138.61 CT £1733.98 TOTE £10.30: £2.90, £4.30, £3.40; EX 140.00 TRIFECTA Not won..
Owner Doric Racing **Bred** Round Hill Stud **Trained** West Ilsley, Berks

FOCUS
A competitive handicap despite the withdrawals and the time compared unfavourably with the preceding juvenile maiden. The winner is rated similar to her Catterick form.

4299 POPTELECOM.CO.UK ESSENTIAL BUSINESS TARIFF CONDITIONS STKS 5f
7:15 (7:15) (Class 3) 3-Y-O+ **£7,470** (£2,236; £1,118; £559; £279) **Stalls** High

Form RPR

3600 **1** **Elusivity (IRE)**[13] 3877 4-8-9 106......................................(b) EddieAhern 2 101
(Brian Meehan) *trckd ldr: racd keenly: led 2f out: rdn over 1f out: r.o* **9/4**[2]

0265 **2** *1* **Elnawin**[6] 4092 6-8-9 109.. RichardHughes 4 98
(Richard Hannon) *racd keenly: set stdy pce tl qcknd 1/2-way: hdd 2f out: shkn up over 1f out: unable qck towards fin* **11/10**[1]

-605 **3** *1 ½* **Dinkum Diamond (IRE)**[13] 3877 4-8-9 103.......................... DaneO'Neill 3 92
(Henry Candy) *trckd ldrs: plld hrd: rdn over 1f out: styd on same pce* **9/2**[3]

1-00 **4** *2 ¼* **Beach Candy (IRE)**[74] 1921 3-8-0 75................................ JimmyQuinn 1 78?
(Phil McEntee) *s.i.s: hld up: pushed along 1/2-way: styd on to go 4th nr fin: nvr trbld ldrs* **100/1**

-643 **5** *½* **Noble Storm (USA)**[49] 2664 6-8-9 105.......................... RichardMullen 5 82
(Ed McMahon) *s.i.s: plld hrd and sn prom: rdn over 1f out: wknd ins fnl f* **8/1**

1m 2.2s (3.10) **Going Correction** +0.75s/f (Yiel)
WFA 3 from 4yo+ 4lb **5** Ran SP% **108.7**
Speed ratings (Par 107): **105,103,101,97,96**
toteswinger 1&2 £1.70. CSF £4.97 TOTE £3.50: £1.60, £1.40; EX 4.60.
Owner Mrs P Good **Bred** J Costello **Trained** Manton, Wilts

FOCUS
This looked a strong, competitive conditions sprint before the withdrawals but the previous two winners of the race stood their ground. The rain had returned before this contest and the field stuck to the fair rail, where the stalls were placed. The race was rather confused when the expected pacesetter missed the break and the gallop was steady until past halfway. Muddling conditions form, with the fourth limiting.

NOTEBOOK
Elusivity(IRE) is consistent at 5-7f but does not win that often and looked to have a little to find with his rivals over this trip. However, he was able to sit close to the leader and make his move when he wanted, then proved the strongest up the hill. The blinkers looked to have had a positive effect. (op 2-1 tchd 5-2)
Elnawin, the 2010 winner, handles cut but is best on fast and, although he likes to race prominently, was not suited by making the running. His rider tried to dictate a steady pace and then kick but the winner gave him no leeway and the tactics did not work. (op 6-4)
Dinkum Diamond(IRE), last year's winner, handles cut but is probably best on fast and would have preferred a stronger gallop. He was also keen after being restrained having jumped best of all from the stalls. (op 7-2)
Beach Candy(IRE) had upwards of two stone to find with her rivals and the fact she finished so close casts doubts over the form. Her handicap mark will be blown apart if the handicapper takes this form at face value.
Noble Storm(USA) is best on fast although he seems to handle softer ground, but he likes to lead and could not do so after blowing the start and being trapped on the rail. He was too keen under restraint and this run can be ignored. Official explanation: jockey said horse was slowly away (op 7-1 tchd 9-1)

4300 POPTELECOM.CO.UK UNLIMITED BROADBAND H'CAP (BETFAIR SPRINT FLAT SERIES QUALIFIER) 6f
7:50 (7:51) (Class 4) (0-80,78) 3-Y-O+ **£5,175** (£1,540; £577; £577) **Stalls** High

Form RPR

1121 **1** **Trojan Rocket (IRE)**[27] 3394 4-9-11 **77**................. MickaelBarzalona 12 84
(Michael Wigham) *dwlt: hdwy over 4f out: rdn over 1f out: r.o to ld nr fin* **4/1**[2]

-222 **2** *nse* **Rivas Rhapsody (IRE)**[23] 3500 4-9-11 **77**................... RichardHughes 5 84
(Ian Wood) *hld up: rdn over 1f out: r.o wl ins fnl f: nt quite get up* **2/1**[1]

413 **3** *shd* **Crew Cut (IRE)**[27] 3394 4-9-12 **78**.................................(p) JamieSpencer 7 85
(Jeremy Gask) *hld up: pushed along 1/2-way: hdwy and nt clr run over 1f out: r.o wl u.p: jst failed* **7/1**

2-15 **3** *dht* **Delft**[28] 3342 3-9-7 **78**.. RyanMoore 13 84
(Jeremy Noseda) *chsd ldr: rdn to ld over 1f out: hdd nr fin* **11/2**[3]

3020 **5** *1 ¾* **Amazon Twilight**[86] 1614 4-9-4 **70**.................................... DavidProbert 11 71
(Brett Johnson) *led: rdn and hdd over 1f out: no ex towards fin* **50/1**

-663 **6** *2 ¾* **Rash Judgement**[15] 3778 7-9-7 **73**.................................. FergusSweeney 9 66
(Stuart Kittow) *hld up: hdwy over 1f out: sn rdn: no ex ins fnl f* **9/1**

0040 **7** *1 ½* **Rafaaf (IRE)**[14] 3822 4-9-12 **78**.. AndreaAtzeni 2 66
(Robert Eddery) *prom: rdn: edgd lft and ev ch over 1f out: wknd ins fnl f* **10/1**

1505 **8** *1* **Aqua Ardens (GER)**[46] 2758 4-9-5 **71**................................ DaneO'Neill 1 56
(George Baker) *hld up: shkn up and edgd lft over 1f out: nvr nr to chal* **33/1**

210 **9** *½* **Caramelita**[25] 3434 5-9-3 **69**..(v) PaulHanagan 10 52
(J R Jenkins) *prom: rdn over 1f out: wknd ins fnl f* **16/1**

00 **10** *3 ¼* **Celtic Sixpence (IRE)**[23] 3500 4-9-9 **75**............................ TomQueally 4 48
(Noel Quinlan) *chsd ldrs: rdn over 1f out: wknd fnl f* **20/1**

2561 **11** *7* **The Strig**[17] 3724 5-9-1 **67**.............. WilliamCarson 3 17
(Stuart Williams) *racd alone towards centre: nvr really up w the pce: hung lft and wknd over 1f out* **25/1**

1m 17.22s (4.72) **Going Correction** +0.75s/f (Yiel)
WFA 3 from 4yo+ 5lb **11 Ran SP% 119.7**
Speed ratings (Par 105): **98,97,97,97,95 91,89,88,87,83 74**Places: Trojan Rocket £1.90, Rivas Rhapsody £1.20, Crew Cut £1.00, Delft £1.30. Tricast: TR, RR & CC £28.32, TR, RR & D £23.01. toteswingers 1&2 £3.90, 1&CC £1.40, 1&D £3.20, 2&CC £1.60, 2&D £1.60. CSF £12.12 TOTE £4.10; EX 11.30 TRIFECTA27 Owner.

FOCUS
A fair contest and not strong run, but another competitive handicap and a blanket finish. The winner and Crew Cut are rated pretty much to their C&D latest.

4301 POPTELECOM.CO.UK 0845 & 0870 FREE CALLS MAIDEN STKS 1m
8:25 (8:30) (Class 5) 3-Y-O **£3,234** (£962; £481; £240) **Stalls High**

Form RPR

3 **1** **Zamdy Man**[34] 3161 3-9-3 0.............. EddieAhern 8 86+
(Venetia Williams) *racd far side: mde all: shkn up over 1f out: styd on wl: eased towards fin* **6/4**[2]

6-3 **2** *4* **Alraased (USA)**[27] 3399 3-9-3 0.............. PaulHanagan 3 74
(John Dunlop) *racd centre: chsd ldr tl led that gp over 3f out: hung lft fr over 2f out: rdn over 1f out: wknd fnl f* **5/4**[1]

06 **3** *3 ¾* **Made Of More**[8] 4001 3-9-3 0.............. RobertHavlin 10 65
(Roger Ingram) *racd far side: hld up: hdwy to chse ldr 1/2-way: sn pushed along: outpcd over 2f out: hung rt over 1f out: styd on to go 3rd post* **50/1**

4 *shd* **Spring Tonic** 3-9-3 0.............. KierenFallon 5 65
(Luca Cumani) *racd centre: chsd ldrs: rdn to go 3rd over 1f out: styd on same pce: lost 3rd post* **10/1**

0 **5** *11* **Cool As Cash**[17] 3735 3-9-3 0.............. NeilCallan 4 40
(Paul D'Arcy) *led centre over 4f: edgd lft and wknd over 2f out* **7/1**[3]

6 *¾* **Summer Sun** 3-8-12 0.............. TomMcLaughlin 1 33
(Phil McEntee) *racd centre: s.i.s: hdwy over 6f out: chsd ldr centre over 2f out: rdn and wknd over 1f out* **40/1**

0 **7** *2 ¾* **Magma**[88] 1567 3-8-12 0.............. DavidProbert 6 27
(Andrew Balding) *racd far side: chsd wnr to 1/2-way: sn hung rt: wknd over 2f out* **16/1**

8 *23* **Peace In Our Time** 3-9-3 0.............. WilliamCarson 7
(Anthony Carson) *racd centre: s.i.s: sn pushed along in rr: wknd over 2f out: t.o* **20/1**

1m 45.74s (5.74) **Going Correction** +0.75s/f (Yiel) **8 Ran SP% 121.1**
Speed ratings (Par 100): **101,97,93,93,82 81,78,55**
toteswingers 1&2 £1.10, 1&3 £27.80, 2&3 £8.20. CSF £3.95 TOTE £2.40: £1.10, £1.10, £10.60; EX 3.90 Trifecta £77.60 Pool: £680.74 - 77.60 winning units..
Owner Muhammad Nadeem Khan **Bred** The Kathryn Stud **Trained** Kings Caple, H'fords

FOCUS
Not much form to go on in this 3yo maiden and it was dominated by the market leaders. It was a weak maiden for the track, lacking depth, and the form pair were 1-2.

4302 POPTELECOM.CO.UK GET CONNECTED H'CAP 7f
8:55 (8:57) (Class 5) (0-75,75) 4-Y-0+ **£2,587** (£770; £384; £192) **Stalls High**

Form RPR

13-3 **1** **Forks**[22] 3549 5-9-1 **69**.............. MickaelBarzalona 19 77
(Jane Chapple-Hyam) *trckd ldrs: plld hrd: rdn to ld ins fnl f: hung rt towards fin: jst hld on* **12/1**

-050 **2** *shd* **Frozen Over**[23] 3485 4-8-7 **61**.............. SilvestreDeSousa 14 69
(Stuart Kittow) *hld up: hdwy over 2f out: rdn over 1f out: r.o* **7/1**

0542 **3** *½* **My Single Malt (IRE)**[7] 4042 4-9-4 **72**.............. PaulHanagan 5 78
(Julie Camacho) *chsd ldrs: rdn over 2f out: r.o* **11/4**[1]

-504 **4** *nk* **Two Sugars**[8] 3994 4-8-2 **56** oh1.............. MartinLane 8 62
(Louise Best) *chsd ldr tl led 2f out: rdn over 1f out: hdd ins fnl f: r.o* **16/1**

5-44 **5** *2* **Schoolmaster**[17] 3720 4-9-6 **74**.............. WilliamCarson 9 74
(Giles Bravery) *plld hrd: led: rdn and hdd 2f out: no ex ins fnl f* **6/1**[3]

323 **6** *3 ¼* **First Class**[15] 3790 4-8-4 **58**.............. DavidProbert 12 49
(Rae Guest) *hld up: rdn over 2f out: edgd lft and styd on ins fnl f: nvr nrr* **4/1**[2]

1004 **7** *½* **Spin Again (IRE)**[4] 4155 7-8-10 **64**.............. BrettDoyle 18 54
(John Ryan) *hld up: rdn over 1f out: styd on ins fnl f: nrst fin* **14/1**

0-00 **8** *2 ¾* **Bassett Road (IRE)**[21] 3589 4-8-7 **61**.............. JamieMackay 17 44
(Willie Musson) *hld up: hdwy over 1f out: wknd ins fnl f* **33/1**

140- **9** *6* **Dashwood**[212] 7847 5-9-0 **75**.............. SiobhanMiller(7) 6 41
(Anthony Carson) *hld up: pushed along over 2f out: a in rr* **14/1**

0-50 **10** *3 ¼* **Saskia's Dream**[27] 3395 4-9-4 **72**.............. JimmyQuinn 16 30
(Jane Chapple-Hyam) *hld up in tch: rdn over 2f out: wknd over 1f out* **6/1**[3]

-000 **11** *3* **Darcey**[28] 3344 6-8-8 **62**.............. DaraghO'Donohoe 15 12
(Amy Weaver) *prom tl rdn and wknd over 2f out* **50/1**

1m 31.45s (5.75) **Going Correction** +0.75s/f (Yiel) **11 Ran SP% 119.5**
Speed ratings (Par 103): **97,96,96,95,93 89,89,86,79,75 72**
toteswingers 1&2 £12.70, 1&3 £4.10, 2&3 £6.70. CSF £95.13 CT £308.20 TOTE £10.40: £2.30, £2.20, £1.80; EX 68.20 Trifecta £94.90 Pool: £944.79 - 7.36 winning units..
Owner Mrs Julie Martin **Bred** Julie Routledge-Martin **Trained** Dalham, Suffolk

FOCUS
The big field for this ordinary handicap was reduced by nearly half owing to withdrawals. The rain had got into the ground and the time was the slowest of the three races over the trip on the night. It looked hard work for the horses but resulted in another close finish. The winner is rated to his best.
Bassett Road(IRE) Official explanation: jockey said he was slow to remove blindfold and gelding was slowly away
T/Plt: £163.60 to a £1 stake. Pool: £73,273.17 - 326.83 winning tickets. T/Qpdt: £17.20 to a £1 stake. Pool: £6,912.13 - 297.30 winning tickets. CR

3074 NOTTINGHAM (L-H)
Friday, July 20

4303 Meeting Abandoned - waterlogged

3692 PONTEFRACT (L-H)
Friday, July 20

OFFICIAL GOING: Good to soft (soft in places) changing to soft (heavy in places) after race 1 (6.25).
Wind: Almost nil Weather: Overcast, light showers

4310 COUNTRYWIDE FREIGHT MAIDEN AUCTION STKS 6f
6:25 (6:26) (Class 4) 2-Y-O **£3,428** (£1,020; £509; £254) **Stalls Low**

Form RPR

56 **1** **Mystical Man**[9] 3973 2-9-2 0.............. IanMongan 5 82
(James Tate) *mde all: drvn 2 l clr over 1f out: hung lft: wandered ins fnl f: hld on towards fin* **16/1**

2 *1* **Laudate Dominum (IRE)** 2-8-4 0.............. BarryMcHugh 16 67+
(Richard Fahey) *in rr: hdwy over 1f out: 6th 100yds out: styd on strly: tk 2nd clsng stages: nt rch wnr* **11/2**[3]

3 *1* **Scentpastparadise** 2-8-6 0.............. RoystonFfrench 2 66
(Ann Duffield) *carried lft s: sn chsng ldrs: wnt 2nd over 2f out: kpt on same pce fnl f* **25/1**

4 *¾* **Spirit Of Rio (IRE)** 2-8-11 0.............. PaulMulrennan 7 68
(Ann Duffield) *dwlt: in rr: hdwy over 2f out: kpt on fnl f: will improve* **11/1**

352 **5** *1 ¾* **Twilight Pearl**[6] 4083 2-8-4 0.............. DuranFentiman 13 56
(Tim Easterby) *chsd ldrs: fdd appr fnl f* **5/1**[2]

40 **6** *3 ¼* **Marabout (IRE)**[25] 3436 2-8-9 0.............. RobertWinston 9 51
(Mel Brittain) *chsd ldrs: drvn over 2f out: wknd over 1f out* **8/1**

7 *1 ½* **Precision Strike** 2-8-11 0.............. RobbieFitzpatrick 10 49
(Richard Guest) *s.i.s: in rr: hdwy over 1f out: nvr nr ldrs* **50/1**

0 **8** *11* **Vision Of Judgment**[32] 3208 2-8-9 0.............. TonyHamilton 6 14
(Ollie Pears) *s.i.s: sn drvn along: nvr a factor* **33/1**

00 **9** *2 ¾* **Likelikelikelikeit**[15] 3788 2-8-4 0.............. AndrewMullen 3
(Mark H Tompkins) *wnt lft s: in rr: nvr on terms* **33/1**

00 **10** *1* **Twinwood Star (IRE)**[46] 2770 2-7-13 0.............. NeilFarley(5) 12
(John Weymes) *t.k.h: trckd ldrs: lost pl over 2f out* **50/1**

6 **11** *hd* **Garmelow Girl**[25] 3436 2-8-6 0.............. AmyRyan 17
(Kevin Ryan) *wnt rt s: swtchd lft after s: a in rr* **11/2**[3]

12 *shd* **Millkwood** 2-8-9 0.............. JamesSullivan 8 2
(John Davies) *mid-div: lost pl over 1f out* **18/1**

02 **13** *8* **Secret Symphony**[17] 3733 2-8-13 0.............. LiamKeniry 11
(Sylvester Kirk) *chsd ldrs: drvn over 2f out: lost pl wl over 1f out* **9/4**[1]

05 **14** *2 ¾* **Tyson The Byson**[55] 2469 2-8-9 0.............. KirstyMilczarek 15
(David C Griffiths) *s.i.s: mid-div: lost pl over 2f out: sn bhd* **66/1**

1m 21.07s (4.17) **Going Correction** +0.425s/f (Yiel) **14 Ran SP% 123.9**
Speed ratings (Par 96): **89,87,86,85,83 78,76,62,58,57 56,56,45,42**
toteswingers 1&2 £12.90, 1&3 £18.00, 2&3 £64.10. CSF £100.42 TOTE £19.90: £3.80, £2.70, £6.70; EX 192.90.
Owner Saeed Manana **Bred** Lady Hardy **Trained** Newmarket, Suffolk

FOCUS
False rail removed and distances as advertised. Following 2mm of overnight rain and a further 8mm in the morning, the ground was eased to good to soft and was changed to soft, heavy in places after the first. Ian Mongan reported the ground was "soft" and Robert Winston stated it was "very soft". No more than a modest maiden but a couple of these showed promise, not least the runner-up. The gallop was an ordinary one and the field stayed far side in the straight.

NOTEBOOK
Mystical Man, who had shown only moderate form over 5f, appreciated the step up to this trip and showed improved form, despite veering both ways under pressure. He may do better still but wouldn't be certain to confirm placings with the runner-up should the pair meet again. (op 14-1)
Laudate Dominum(IRE) ◆, who cost 6,000gns and is a half-sister to the yard's modest dual 6f winner Sunny Side Up, created a favourable impression, despite her greenness, on this racecourse debut and is the one to take from the race. She should appreciate the step up to 7f and is sure to win an ordinary event. (tchd 5-1 and 6-1)
Scentpastparadise, the first foal of a useful (at best) but inconsistent 7f winner, herself a half-sister to the smart 7f-1m2f performer Barefoot Lady, posted a pleasing debut effort and is sure to improve for the experience. She should win a race. (op 28-1)
Spirit Of Rio(IRE), an 18,000gns half-brother to 5f-1m (Group 3) winner Stay Young and to multiple 7f-1m winner Dakota Sioux, was fairly easy in the market but shaped pleasingly on this racecourse debut. He should stay 7f and can improve. (op 16-1 tchd 20-1)
Twilight Pearl had shown moderate form in three previous starts but didn't get home in the anticipated manner over a trip that had looked likely to suit. Run-of-the-mill nurseries will be the way forward with her. (op 7-2)
Precision Strike, a 12,000GBP half-brother to dual 1m Polytrack winner Complex, is entered in a couple of sales races and showed ability after a tardy start. He'll be suited by a stiffer test of stamina and should improve. (op 40-1)
Secret Symphony, who had shown form bordering on fair on Polytrack on her previous start, was the disappointment. Conditions here may have been against him, though and he'll be worth another chance returned to artificial surfaces. Official explanation: trainer's rep said colt was unsuited by the soft (heavy in places) ground (op 10-3)

4311 TOTEPOOL FILLIES' H'CAP 1m 4f 8y
7:00 (7:02) (Class 5) (0-75,75) 3-Y-0+ **£2,264** (£673; £336; £168) **Stalls Low**

Form RPR

5303 **1** **Maybeagrey**[11] 3910 3-8-3 **62**.............. DuranFentiman 4 76
(Tim Easterby) *hld up in mid-div: hdwy over 2f out: styd on wl to ld appr fnl f: drvn out* **7/2**[3]

443 **2** *2 ¾* **Kunegunda**[32] 3227 3-9-2 **75**.............. HayleyTurner 6 85+
(James Fanshawe) *trckd ldrs: wnt 2nd over 2f out: led over 1f out: sn hdd: styd on same pce* **5/2**[1]

0000 **3** *2 ¾* **Song Of The Siren**[4] 4141 4-9-5 **66**.............. DanielTudhope 9 71
(David O'Meara) *led: t.k.h: hdd over 1f out: one pce* **33/1**

5013 **4** *6* **Zowaina**[18] 3704 3-8-8 **70**.............. DominicFox(3) 7 66
(Roger Varian) *rn in snatches: lost pl after 4f: hdwy 4f out: outpcd over 2f out: kpt on fnl f to take modest 4th nr fin* **11/4**[2]

3000 **5** *nk* **So Cheeky**[15] 3781 3-7-12 **57** oh7.............. (p) AndrewMullen 2 52
(Peter Salmon) *sn trcking ldrs: drvn over 2f out: wknd over 1f out* **16/1**

0-00 **6** *13* **Zennor**[22] 3550 5-9-11 **72**.............. RobertWinston 1 46
(George Margarson) *chsd ldr: effrt over 2f out: lost pl over 1f out* **14/1**

445 **7** *4* **Jorum**[15] 3773 3-9-1 **74**.............. IanMongan 3 42
(Sir Henry Cecil) *s.i.s: in rr: hdwy on outside over 5f out: sn drvn: lost pl over 3f out: sn bhd* **9/2**

100- **8** *3 ¼* **Cat O' Nine Tails**[277] 6916 5-9-3 **64**.............. BarryMcHugh 8 27
(Brian Rothwell) *hld up in rr: drvn over 3f out: sn lost pl and bhd* **33/1**

2m 45.87s (5.07) **Going Correction** +0.425s/f (Yiel)
WFA 3 from 4yo+ 12lb **8 Ran SP% 114.1**
Speed ratings (Par 100): **100,98,96,92,92 83,80,78**
toteswingers 1&2 £2.50, 1&3 £11.40, 2&3 £14.30. CSF £12.62 CT £234.42 TOTE £3.10: £1.10, £1.80, £14.70; EX 16.40.

Owner Habton Farms **Bred** J K Beckitt And Son **Trained** Great Habton, N Yorks
FOCUS
No more than a fair fillies' handicap and one in which the gallop was only ordinary. They finished well strung out and the winner is rated back to her 2yo best.

4312 BETFRED H'CAP 5f
7:35 (7:35) (Class 3) (0-95,94) 3-Y-O+
£6,411 (£1,919; £959; £479; £239; £120) **Stalls** Low

Form RPR
2121 **1** **Silvanus (IRE)**[20] 3608 7-9-3 **85** RussKennemore 2 94
(Paul Midgley) *trckd ldrs: t.k.h: wnt 2nd appr fnl f: r.o to ld last 75yds* **7/1**
6242 **2** ¾ **Noodles Blue Boy**[13] 3845 6-9-1 **83** TonyHamilton 1 89
(Ollie Pears) *w ldr: led over 2f out: hdd and no ex wl ins fnl f* **6/1**[3]
5104 **3** 2 **Caranbola**[13] 3845 6-8-12 **80** RobertWinston 8 79
(Mel Brittain) *led: hdd over 2f out: one pce fnl f* **12/1**
3652 **4** ½ **Green Park (IRE)**[20] 3608 9-8-5 **80** (b) JasonHart[(7)] 9 77
(Declan Carroll) *sn chsng ldrs: drvn and outpcd over 2f out: kpt on fnl f* **8/1**
-120 **5** 1 ½ **Oldjoesaid**[14] 3822 8-8-11 **79** MickyFenton 13 71
(Paul Midgley) *in tch on outer: outpcd over 2f out: kpt on fnl f* **25/1**
030- **6** shd **Singeur (IRE)**[272] 7018 5-9-12 **94** DanielTudhope 5 85
(Robin Bastiman) *trckd ldrs: t.k.h: effrt over 1f out: kpt on same pce* **5/1**[2]
1313 **7** ¾ **Head Space (IRE)**[11] 3903 4-9-9 **91** JamesSullivan 10 80+
(Ruth Carr) *in rr: drvn and outpcd over 2f out: nt clr run 1f out: kpt on towards fin* **5/2**[1]
200 **8** ¾ **Blue Jack**[35] 3127 7-9-11 **93** (b) RichardKingscote 4 79
(Tom Dascombe) *in rr: effrt on inner over 2f out: nvr a factor* **7/1**
0404 **9** 2 **Lost In Paris (IRE)**[22] 3541 6-8-9 **77** (p) DavidAllan 11 56
(Tim Easterby) *chsd ldrs: wknd appr fnl f* **14/1**
1m 5.42s (2.12) **Going Correction** +0.60s/f (Yiel) **9** Ran SP% **113.8**
Speed ratings (Par 107): **107,105,102,101,99 99,98,96,93**
toteswingers 1&2 £4.00, 1&3 £18.00, 2&3 £16.90. CSF £47.78 CT £497.39 TOTE £10.40: £2.60, £2.60, £4.30; EX 38.80.
Owner Colin Alton **Bred** Barronstown Stud And Mrs T Stack **Trained** Westow, N Yorks
FOCUS
A very useful handicap but, although the gallop seemed reasonable, those held up were at a disadvantage. The level is set around the runner-up.
NOTEBOOK
Silvanus(IRE) has improved significantly this year and turned in a career-best effort, despite once again failing to settle, in the process confirming his ability to handle very testing ground. He won't be going up too much for this and may be able to step up again back on a sounder surface. (op 13-2 tchd 6-1)
Noodles Blue Boy had the run of the race and, although his trainer has struggled for winners this season, he extended his run of creditable efforts. Things were in his favour and he'll be up again in the weights for this but he should continue to give it his best shot. (tchd 7-1)
Caranbola, whose best efforts have come at the stiff Beverley track, was well placed given the way things panned out and seemed to give it her best shot. The return to the East Yorkshire venue should suit but she has little margin for error from her current mark. (op 16-1 tchd 18-1)
Green Park(IRE), another fairly reliable yardstick, finished a bit further behind the winner than at Chester on his previous start but he's going to have to raise his game to win a competitive handicap from his current mark. (op 11-1)
Oldjoesaid hadn't been at his best on his previous start but he looks a bit better than he was able to show here in a race that suited the prominent-racers. He's not a regular winner, though, and is the type that needs things to drop right. (op 20-1)
Singeur(IRE), with the headgear left off this time, wasn't at his very best and, although he'd almost certainly prefer better underfoot conditions than the ones he encountered here, he is vulnerable to the better handicapped or more progressive types from this mark. (op 6-1 tchd 9-2)
Head Space(IRE) wasn't seen to best effect in a race where those held up never got involved but, even though he has his quirks, the way he quickened on good ground when successful at Ayr last month remains fresh in the mind and he'll be worth a chance back on a sounder surface when a good gallop looks likely. Official explanation: trainer said gelding was unsuited by the soft (heavy in places) ground (op 2-1 tchd 11-4)

4313 COLSTROPE CUP H'CAP 1m 4y
8:10 (8:10) (Class 5) (0-70,70) 3-Y-O+ **£2,264** (£673; £336; £168) **Stalls** Low

Form RPR
4-03 **1** **Rex Romanorum (IRE)**[56] 2441 4-9-7 **63** DanielTudhope 2 72
(Patrick Holmes) *led: qcknd pce 3f out: drvn and styd on strly over 1f out* **11/8**[1]
0402 **2** 3 ¼ **Elijah Pepper (USA)**[28] 3335 7-10-0 **70** GrahamGibbons 4 73
(David Barron) *trckd ldrs: effrt over 2f out: chsd wnr over 1f out: no imp* **2/1**[2]
-140 **3** 6 **Kian's Joy**[15] 3775 3-8-1 **51** (p) AndrewMullen 5 37
(Jedd O'Keeffe) *s.i.s: sn trcking ldrs: t.k.h: effrt 3f out: sn outpcd: kpt on to take 3rd last 50yds* **4/1**[3]
-606 **4** 2 **Only A Round (IRE)**[26] 3421 3-7-10 **51** oh6 NeilFarley[(5)] 3 33
(Micky Hammond) *sn trcking wnr: t.k.h: drvn over 2f out: wknd appr fnl f* **20/1**
0650 **5** ½ **Strong Man**[24] 3460 4-9-4 **60** JamesSullivan 7 42
(Michael Easterby) *t.k.h in last: drvn over 3f out: sn lost pl* **15/2**
1m 50.5s (4.60) **Going Correction** +0.60s/f (Yiel)
WFA 3 from 4yo+ 8lb **5** Ran SP% **112.0**
Speed ratings (Par 103): **101,97,91,89,89**
toteswinger 1&2 £4.90. CSF £4.51 TOTE £2.60: £2.20, £1.10; EX 4.90.
Owner Foulrice Park Racing Limited **Bred** Swettenham, Carradale, S Cosgrove & T Stack **Trained** Brandsby, N. Yorks
FOCUS
A depleted field due to the testing conditions and modest handicap in which the gallop was an ordinary one. The two market leaders pulled clear in the straight and the winner is rated up 3lb.

4314 THE HOUSE THAT JACK BUILT MAIDEN H'CAP 1m 2f 6y
8:40 (8:40) (Class 5) (0-70,70) 3-Y-O+ **£2,264** (£673; £336; £168) **Stalls** Low

Form RPR
6-3 **1** **Xclaim**[28] 3353 4-9-11 **67** MichaelO'Connell 1 74+
(Micky Hammond) *t.k.h in rr: drvn and outpcd over 2f out: plld wd over 1f out: styd on wl to ld towards fin* **9/4**[1]
0642 **2** ¾ **Tobrata**[7] 4048 6-8-9 **58** RobertDodsworth[(7)] 9 62
(Mel Brittain) *s.i.s: sn trcking ldrs: led wl over 1f out: hdd and no ex last 50yds* **4/1**[2]
32-0 **3** 1 ¼ **Oliver's Gold**[12] 1299 4-8-6 **55** ShirleyTeasdale[(7)] 11 56
(Shaun Harris) *hld up in rr: hdwy 5f out: chsng ldrs over 2f out: edgd lft over 1f out: kpt on same pce fnl f* **22/1**
06-0 **4** ½ **Zaahya (IRE)**[23] 3507 3-8-12 **64** TadhgO'Shea 8 64
(John Dunlop) *hld up in rr: hdwy and upsides 2f out: kpt on same pce fnl f* **11/2**
402 **5** 14 **The Lodge Road (IRE)**[41] 2926 4-9-12 **68** PaulMulrennan 7 40
(Martin Todhunter) *t.k.h in mid-div: effrt over 2f out: sn chsng ldrs: wknd fnl f* **5/1**[3]
0/4 **6** 3 ¼ **Glendaragh (IRE)**[10] 3939 4-9-1 **57** DanielTudhope 4 23
(David O'Meara) *set stdy gallop: increased pce over 3f out: hdd wl over 1f out: wknd fnl f* **8/1**
4000 **7** 1 **Kata Rock (USA)**[53] 2555 5-8-11 **53** BarryMcHugh 5 17
(Brian Rothwell) *w ldr: wkng whn n.m.r over 1f out* **33/1**
625- **8** 44 **Lady Bellatrix**[321] 5698 3-9-1 **67** RobertWinston 2
(Mark H Tompkins) *dwlt: t.k.h: sn trcking ldrs: sddle appeared to slip forward bnd after 2f: drvn and lost pl 2f out: sn bhd and heavily eased: t.o* **15/2**
2m 22.47s (8.77) **Going Correction** +0.775s/f (Yiel)
WFA 3 from 4yo+ 10lb **8** Ran SP% **113.0**
Speed ratings (Par 103): **95,94,93,93,81 79,78,43**
toteswingers 1&2 £1.90, 1&3 £14.90, 2&3 £19.00. CSF £10.94 CT £149.70 TOTE £2.70: £1.10, £1.90, £4.10; EX 9.70.
Owner Mike And Eileen Newbould **Bred** Whitsbury Manor Stud **Trained** Middleham Moor, N Yorks
■ Stewards' Enquiry : Shirley Teasdale one-day ban: careless riding (Aug 10)
FOCUS
A modest handicap run at a fairly steady gallop. The first four pulled clear in the straight and the form seems sound enough.
Lady Bellatrix Official explanation: trainer said gelding was unsuited by the soft (heavy in places) ground

4315 YORKSHIRE RACING SUMMER FESTIVAL H'CAP 6f
9:10 (9:11) (Class 5) (0-75,75) 3-Y-O+ **£2,264** (£673; £336; £168) **Stalls** Low

Form RPR
-561 **1** **Dream Catcher (FR)**[11] 3915 4-8-11 **65** AmyScott[(5)] 11 78
(Henry Candy) *mde all: qcknd clr over 2f out: styd on strly: eased nr fin* **9/4**[1]
1-25 **2** 2 ¾ **Bid For Gold**[17] 3731 8-9-0 **63** TonyHamilton 3 65
(Jedd O'Keeffe) *chsd ldrs: styd on to take 2nd last 100yds: no imp* **9/1**
0104 **3** 1 ¼ **Steel Stockholder**[7] 4043 6-9-4 **67** RobertWinston 5 63
(Mel Brittain) *w wnr: kpt on same pce fnl 2f* **8/1**[3]
0650 **4** nk **Reason To Believe (IRE)**[17] 3731 4-8-11 **60** (p) JamesSullivan 2 55
(Ben Haslam) *chsd ldrs: kpt on one pce fnl 2f* **8/1**[3]
00 **5** ¾ **Handheld**[37] 3045 5-9-9 **72** LiamKeniry 9 65
(Ed de Giles) *sn bhd: hdwy 2f out: kpt on fnl f* **25/1**
5-00 **6** 5 **Mount Hollow**[42] 2870 7-9-5 **75** (p) JackDuern[(7)] 8 52
(Reg Hollinshead) *mid-div: sn drvn along: outpcd over 2f out: wknd fnl 150yds* **9/2**[2]
0-15 **7** 2 ½ **Half A Crown (IRE)**[69] 2096 7-9-4 **67** AndrewMullen 17 36
(Peter Salmon) *stmbld s: sn chsng ldrs: wknd fnl f* **10/1**
-613 **8** 16 **Secret City (IRE)**[46] 2750 6-9-7 **70** (b) DanielTudhope 1
(Robin Bastiman) *in rr: bhd and drvn 3f out: heavily eased over 1f out: t.o* **9/2**[2]
4540 **9** 10 **Dickie Le Davoir**[83] 1650 8-9-11 **74** (b) J-PGuillambert 16
(Richard Guest) *drvn to chse ldrs: lost pl over 2f out: sn bhd: heavily eased 1f out: t.o* **14/1**
1m 21.0s (4.10) **Going Correction** +0.775s/f (Yiel) **9** Ran SP% **119.0**
Speed ratings (Par 103): **103,99,97,96,95 88,85,64,50**
toteswingers 1&2 £6.30, 1&3 £5.60, 2&3 £2.70. CSF £24.70 CT £143.12 TOTE £4.20: £1.90, £2.40, £1.80; EX 17.40.
Owner Miss N M Haine **Bred** Daniel Cherdo **Trained** Kingston Warren, Oxon
FOCUS
Exposed performers and several ground-related non-runners in an ordinary handicap. The gallop was a reasonable one but, once again in sprints on this card, those held up never figured. The winner is rated back to his 3yo best.
Secret City(IRE) Official explanation: trainer had no explanation for the poor form shown
T/Jkpt: Not won. T/Plt: £87.90 to a £1 stake. Pool: £72,455.14 - 601.60 winning tickets. T/Qpdt: £5.60 to a £1 stake. Pool: £6,711.47 - 882.72 winning tickets. WG

4229 VICHY
Friday, July 20
OFFICIAL GOING: Turf: good to soft

4316a PRIX JACQUES DE BREMOND (LISTED RACE) (4YO+) (TURF) 1m
2:20 (12:00) 4-Y-O+ **£21,666** (£8,666; £6,500; £4,333; £2,166)

RPR
1 **Making Eyes (IRE)**[42] 2882 4-8-8 0 IoritzMendizabal 14 100
(Hugo Palmer) *broke wl fr outside draw: racd freely in 3rd: wnt 2nd bef st: chal for ld over 350yds out: tk ld u.p 250yds out: wnt clr: r.o wl fnl 100yds: hld on wl* **27/1**
2 ½ **Ball Prince (IRE)**[34] 5-8-11 0 FlavienPrat 3 102
(T Clout, France) **18/1**
3 snk **Abdel (FR)**[18] 3716 4-9-2 0 AnthonyCrastus 1 107
(C Laffon-Parias, France) **6/1**[2]
4 hd **Pareo (FR)**[18] 3716 4-8-11 0 (p) AntoineHamelin 5 102
(A De Royer-Dupre, France) **18/1**
5 ¾ **Sulle Orme (FR)**[20] 3657 4-9-2 0 JulienAuge 4 105
(C Ferland, France) **78/10**[3]
6 ½ **Red Dubawi (IRE)**[18] 3716 4-8-11 0 AlexandreRoussel 12 99
(A De Royer-Dupre, France) **18/1**
7 ¾ **Ch'Tio Bilote (FR)**[20] 3657 4-8-11 0 GaetanMasure 11 97
(J-P Gallorini, France) **27/1**
8 1 ¼ **Stand My Ground (IRE)**[12] 3900 5-8-11 0 Christophe-PatriceLemaire 6 94
(Mme Pia Brandt, France) **12/1**
9 2 ½ **Toss The Dice (IRE)**[47] 4-8-11 0 GeraldMosse 9 88
(A De Royer-Dupre, France) **30/1**
10 3 **Rayeni (IRE)**[362] 6-8-11 0 UmbertoRispoli 2 81
(C Scandella, France) **42/1**
0 **Royal Bench (IRE)**[34] 5-8-11 0 SebastienMaillot 10
(Robert Collet, France) **2/1**[1]
0 **Iokastos**[47] 5-8-11 0 ThomasMessina 8
(Mlle C Cardenne, France) **23/1**
0 **Roches Cross (IRE)**[61] 2322 4-8-11 0 GregoryBenoist 7
(Josef Vana II, Czech Republic) **26/1**
0 **Nova Valorem (IRE)**[47] 4-8-11 0 MaximeGuyon 13
(F Rohaut, France) **6/1**[2]
1m 39.61s (99.61) **14** Ran SP% **117.3**
WIN (incl. 1 euro stake): 28.10. PLACES: 9.00, 6.50, 2.90. DF: 258.00. SF: 545.90.
Owner Starter For Ten Partnership **Bred** F Dunne **Trained** Newmarket, Suffolk

NOTEBOOK
Making Eyes(IRE), the only filly in the line-up, stepped up on her previous efforts in handicap company to take this Listed event. Her trainer now has the Group 3 Landwades Stud Fillies Stakes at the Curragh at the end of August in mind for her.

4282 ASCOT (R-H)
Saturday, July 21

OFFICIAL GOING: Straight course - good; round course - good to soft (stands' side 8.2, centre 8.5, far side 8.3, round 6.6
Wind: gentle breeze Weather: cloudy with sunny periods

4317 LONGINES H'CAP (LADIES' RACE) 7f
1:35 (1:35) (Class 3) (0-90,90) 3-Y-O+ **£8,110** (£2,515; £1,257; £629) **Stalls** Centre

Form RPR
0534 **1** **Redvers (IRE)**[28] 3403 4-10-1 **84**.....................(b) MissHayleyMoore(3) 22 94
(Ed Vaughan) *hld up in rr on stands' side: hdwy over 2f out: sn rdn: led narrowly over 1f out: strly chal thrght fnl f: jst hld on: all out* **12/1**
1000 **2** *nse* **Apostle (IRE)**[30] 3294 3-9-11 **87**............................ MissLMasterton(3) 18 95
(Michael Bell) *chsd ldrs on stands' side: rdn upsides wnr over 1f out: ev ch thrght fnl f: jst denied* **14/1**
0041 **3** *2* **Day Of The Eagle (IRE)**[8] 4043 6-9-0 **71**......... MissJoannaMason(5) 16 76
(Michael Easterby) *chsd ldrs on stands' side: led and overall ldr narrowly over 2f out: hdd over 1f out: kpt on same pce fnl f* **9/1**[3]
1442 **4** *¾* **Great Shot**[10] 3963 4-9-4 **75**.. MissCBoxall(5) 7 78
(Sylvester Kirk) *chsd ldrs on far side: rdn over 2f out: led gp and ev ch w stands' side over 1f out: kpt on* **12/1**
1340 **5** *nk* **Orpsie Boy (IRE)**[42] 2910 9-10-6 **86**......................... MissSBrotherton 20 88
(Ruth Carr) *s.i.s: mid-div on stands' side: hdwy 2f out: pressed ldrs ent fnl f: kpt on same pce* **14/1**
0250 **6** *2* **Majestic Dream (IRE)**[7] 4110 4-9-11 **77**...................(b[1]) MissJCoward 4 73
(Michael Easterby) *led far side gp and overall advantage tl hdd over 1f out: kpt on same pce* **10/1**
1606 **7** *½* **Viva Ronaldo (IRE)**[23] 3534 6-10-2 **87**................. MissPhillipaTutty(5) 21 82
(Richard Fahey) *hld up in rr on stands' side: struggling 3f out: edgd rt over 2f out: r.o ins fnl f: nvr a threat* **25/1**
1231 **8** *½* **Our Boy Jack (IRE)**[7] 4082 3-9-10 **83**............................ MissADeniel 13 75+
(Richard Fahey) *mid-div on farside: hdwy to chse ldrs u.p over 1f out: kpt on same pce fnl f* **15/2**[1]
0050 **9** *nk* **Perfect Cracker**[24] 3503 4-9-10 **79**....................... MissRachelKing(3) 17 72
(Clive Cox) *a in mid-div on stands' side* **20/1**
0000 **10** *¾* **Cool Marble (IRE)**[24] 3492 5-9-3 **74**.........................(b) MissRSmith(5) 12 65
(Jeremy Gask) *chsd ldrs on farside: rdn over 2f out: one pce fnl f* **20/1**
-225 **11** *shd* **Angelic Upstart (IRE)**[63] 2274 4-9-3 **72**................. MissAZetterholm(3) 3 63
(Andrew Balding) *chsd ldrs on far side: rdn over 2f out: one pce fnl f* **14/1**
4-64 **12** *¾* **Magical Speedfit (IRE)**[39] 2994 7-9-0 **71** oh2.... MissKMargarson(5) 24 60
(George Margarson) *led stands' side gp tl 2f out: grad fdd* **66/1**
0-00 **13** *nk* **White Frost (IRE)**[36] 3128 4-10-8 **88**............................ MsNCarberry 15 76
(Charles Hills) *mid-div on stands' side: hdwy over 2f out: sn rdn: one pce fnl f* **8/1**[2]
6223 **14** *½* **Lindoro**[30] 3314 7-9-5 **71** oh2.. MsKWalsh 5 57
(Brian Ellison) *mid-div on far side: effrt 2f out: fdd fnl f* **9/1**[3]
0100 **15** *4* **Shifting Star (IRE)**[24] 3508 7-10-8 **88**.......................... MissEJJones 8 64
(John Bridger) *chsd ldrs on far side tl wknd ent fnl f* **33/1**
0113 **16** *nk* **Benandonner (USA)**[44] 2845 9-9-7 **78**........................... MissMBryant(5) 23 53
(Paddy Butler) *racd stands' side: wnt rt s: nvr bttr than mid-div* **50/1**
0-54 **17** *shd* **Moynahan (USA)**[96] 1416 7-9-8 **77**........................(p) MissHCuthbert(3) 6 51
(Thomas Cuthbert) *racd far side: sme late prog but mainly towards rr* **20/1**
061 **18** *nk* **Kingswinford (IRE)**[39] 3011 6-10-2 **82**.............................. MrsEEvans 10 56
(David Evans) *mid-div on far side: rdn over 2f out: wknd ent fnl f* **33/1**
0100 **19** *nk* **Northern Fling**[13] 3890 8-9-6 **72**.. MrsCBartley 14 45
(Jim Goldie) *a towards rr on far side* **33/1**
6130 **20** *nk* **Avonrose**[9] 3696 5-9-2 **71** oh1..................................(v) MissWGibson(3) 19 43
(Derek Shaw) *a towards rr on stands' side* **50/1**
2513 **21** *2 ¼* **Moody Tunes**[19] 3693 9-9-2 **73**................................ MissALMurphy(5) 11 39
(Tom Dascombe) *a towards rr on far side* **33/1**
005 **22** *3* **Star Rover (IRE)**[12] 3919 5-9-4 **75**.............................. MissJoeyEllis(5) 9 33
(David Evans) *racd freely trcking ldrs on farside tl 2f out* **50/1**
0034 **23** *1 ¾* **Sohraab**[16] 3771 8-10-5 **90**.. MissNDumelow(5) 2 43
(Hughie Morrison) *prom on far side: rdn over 2f out: sn wknd: eased* **20/1**
6444 **24** *1 ¾* **Haadeeth**[12] 3919 5-9-9 **75**.. MissZoeLilly 1 23
(David Evans) *mid-div on far side tl wknd over 2f out* **50/1**

1m 28.3s (0.70) **Going Correction** +0.275s/f (Good)
WFA 3 from 4yo+ 7lb **24 Ran SP% 131.3**
Speed ratings (Par 107): **107,106,104,103,103 101,100,100,99,98 98,97,97,96,92 92,91,91,91,90 88,84,82,80**
toteswingers 1&2 £49.70, 2&3 £45.40, 1&3 £54.80 CSF £147.97 CT £1620.93 TOTE £15.20: £4.00, £4.20, £2.80, £2.90; EX 348.90 TRIFECTA Not won..
Owner M J C Hawkes and E J C Hawkes **Bred** Peter Jones And G G Jones **Trained** Newmarket, Suffolk
■ Stewards' Enquiry : Miss Hayley Moore four-day ban: used whip above permitted level (tbn)

FOCUS
Round course rail between 9f to home straight moved out 2m and consequently 2yds added to Old Mile, 8yds to 10f race and 10yds to 12f &16f races. The traditional start to King George day and a typically competitive race for lady amateur riders. Predictably the field soon split into two with the larger group of 14 going far side and ten coming stands' side, but the smaller group provided four of the first five home. A decent time, and the first two rate small personal bests.

NOTEBOOK
Redvers(IRE) was 4lb higher than for his last win over a year ago and had yet to win over this far, but his recent efforts over this trip on soft ground suggested that stamina wasn't going to be an issue. Making his move from off the pace in the nearside group over a furlong out, he may have hit the front soon enough and he only just managed to hold on by the skin of his teeth, but it was enough to give his rider her second consecutive win in this race.
Apostle(IRE), well beaten in three tries over 1m since winning over this trip on his Salisbury reappearance, appreciated the return to 7f. Never far off the pace in the stands' side group, he was passed by the winner a furlong out as both made their efforts, but rallied gamely and very nearly got up. (op 22-1 tchd 25-1)
Day Of The Eagle(IRE) was put up 5lb after bouncing back to winning form at Chester eight days earlier, but was winning off a 13lb higher mark just over two years ago so it was little surprise that he put in a big run. He looked the one to beat when taking over in the nearside group over 2f out, but couldn't respond when the front pair tackled him a furlong later. (op 8-1)
Great Shot ◆ was racing over a trip shorter than 1m for the first time in his 15th outing and can be considered unlucky, as all he did was find himself in the wrong group rather than the trip proving inadequate. He came through to win the race on his flank inside the last furlong clearly and can be considered a winner without a penalty, provided the handicapper doesn't hit him. (op 14-1)
Orpsie Boy(IRE) had every chance in the nearside group until getting outpaced inside the last furlong, but was racing in the right group. He is still 5lb higher than when winning at Thirsk in May.
Majestic Dream(IRE) ◆, without a win since October 2010, continues to slip down the weights and had blinkers on for the first time. He made much of the running in the far-side group and only the eventual fourth was able to get past him on his side. He is worth keeping an eye on.
Viva Ronaldo(IRE) gave himself plenty to do in the nearside group and, although staying on late, was never going to get there. This was still a fair effort as he probably needs a turning left-handed track, with his best turf form coming at Chester. (op 33-1)
Our Boy Jack(IRE) has been running consistently well this year, but was put up another 4lb for his recent Chester win and was only getting there slowly in the far-side group. (op 8-1)
Perfect Cracker had been disappointing in his previous four starts, all over 1m, and this was only marginally better back at 7f.
Cool Marble(IRE), formerly trained in Ireland and France, ran creditably in the Victoria Cup over C&D on his debut for this yard, but had shown little in three starts over further since. Although only 10th here overall having raced in the far-side group, he did again suggest that he retains some ability. (op 25-1)
Angelic Upstart(IRE) ran a fair race in the far-side group, but has shown his best form up to now on Polytrack. (op 12-1)
White Frost(IRE)'s rider took a little while to decide which group to join, eventually tagging on to the nearside flank, but he faded tamely inside the last 2f and continues to under-perform this season. (tchd 9-1)

4318 CARRAIG INSURANCE WINKFIELD STKS (LISTED RACE) 7f
2:10 (2:12) (Class 1) 2-Y-O
£13,043 (£4,945; £2,474; £1,232; £618; £310) **Stalls** Centre

Form RPR
1 **1** **Toronado (IRE)**[37] 3067 2-9-2 0..................................... RichardHughes 6 99+
(Richard Hannon) *stdd s: racd in cl 6th: crept clsr over 1f out: led ent fnl f: r.o wl: pushed out* **1/3**[1]
24 **2** *2* **Strictly Silca**[25] 3474 2-8-11 0.. MartinHarley 3 87
(Mick Channon) *racd in cl 5th: swtchd rt and hdwy over 2f out: rdn and ev ch ent fnl f: kpt on but nt gng pce of wnr* **25/1**
1 **3** *2 ½* **Verdane**[24] 3506 2-9-2 77... RyanMoore 4 85
(David Evans) *trckd ldr tl sltly outpcd 3f out: styd on ins fnl f: snatched 3rd fnl stride* **11/1**[3]
52 **4** *shd* **Letstalkaboutmoney (IRE)**[37] 3062 2-9-2 0.................(v) JimCrowley 5 85
(Mrs K Burke) *trckd ldr: led narrowly wl over 1f out: sn rdn: hdd ent fnl f: nt gng pce of ldng pair: lost 3rd fnl stride* **12/1**
1 **5** *2 ½* **Arthurs Secret**[25] 3457 2-9-2 0.................................... MichaelO'Connell 2 78
(John Quinn) *trckd ldr: rdn wl over 1f out: fdd ins fnl f* **6/1**[2]
01 **6** *1 ½* **Claude Greenwood**[26] 3452 2-9-2 81............................ JimmyFortune 1 74
(Sylvester Kirk) *led: rdn and narrowly hdd wl over 1f out: fdd ins fnl f* **40/1**

1m 30.47s (2.87) **Going Correction** +0.275s/f (Good) **6 Ran SP% 111.6**
Speed ratings (Par 102): **94,91,88,88,85 84**
toteswingers 1&2 £4.10, 2&3 £10.10, 1&3 £1.60 CSF £11.63 TOTE £1.30: £1.10, £6.10; EX 11.80.
Owner Carmichael Humber **Bred** Paul Nataf **Trained** East Everleigh, Wilts

FOCUS
A race that went to subsequent Breeders' Cup Classic winner Raven's Pass back in 2007. They seemed to go just a steady pace in this latest running, and the form is probably nothing special, but the winner was much the best.

NOTEBOOK
Toronado(IRE) had reportedly been considered for the Chesham Stakes following an impressive debut success at Newbury (7f, good to soft), but his connections opted to give him time. He was still a touch green when first coming under pressure, but nevertheless he picked up in pretty decent style, and that's despite the lack of pace in the race. It's likely we'll see better from him when he gets a stronger gallop and he'll surely stay further. He looks a Group horse in the making and his trainer already has one eye on next year's 2000 Guineas. Boylesports offered 33s, but William Hill were ducking him at 16-1. (op 4-9 tchd 1-2 in places)
Strictly Silca, the only filly in the line-up, had run to just a fair level when beaten in maidens on her first two starts, but there was plenty to like about this performance, travelling well and pulling away from all bar the smart winner. She's from a family her owner and trainer have enjoyed plenty of success with, and she looks pretty decent. (tchd 22-1)
Verdane managed to win over 6f on his debut at Salisbury (jumped the winning line), but he didn't have the speed for this steadily run 7f in better company. He looked set to finish well beaten when first coming under pressure, but there was much to like about how well he kept on, albeit the horse he nabbed for third had been keen. There's plenty of stamina in his pedigree and it's not out of the question he could reach a smart level over longer trips in time. (op 17-2)
Letstalkaboutmoney(IRE) was too keen without cover and did well to last so long. He's useful. (tchd 14-1)
Arthurs Secret won a Beverley maiden (7.5, good to soft) by 8l on his debut, but it was difficult to know exactly what he achieved. This proved more of a speed test and he wasn't up to it. (op 11-2 tchd 13-2)
Claude Greenwood, successful in a 6f Polytrack maiden on his second start, didn't see his race out despite being allowed an easy enough lead. (op 25-1)

4319 DELOITTE H'CAP 1m (S)
2:45 (2:47) (Class 2) 3-Y-O
£28,012 (£8,388; £4,194; £2,097; £1,048; £526) **Stalls** Centre

Form RPR
2-61 **1** **Chil The Kite**[22] 3563 3-9-1 **91**.. RyanMoore 10 103+
(Hughie Morrison) *hld up: hung rt but hdwy 2f out: led over 1f out: sn rdn and drifted bdly rt but clr: a enough in hand: rdn out: readily* **5/2**[1]
4251 **2** *1 ½* **Takeitfromalady (IRE)**[12] 3917 3-8-10 **86**.....................(b) JimCrowley 9 94+
(Ralph Beckett) *mid-div: pushed along but nt clrest of runs bhd wall of horses fr 2f out tl 1f out: rdn and r.o wl ins fnl f: rdr lost whip fnl 75yds: wnt 2nd nr fin* **6/1**[3]
-010 **3** *nk* **Flaxen Flare (IRE)**[58] 2428 3-8-4 **80**..............................(v[1]) DavidProbert 3 86
(Andrew Balding) *led: rdn whn hdd jst over 1f out: kpt on gamely but sn nt gng pce of wnr* **25/1**
2513 **4** *nse* **Lady Loch**[28] 3383 3-8-2 **78**..(b) PaulHanagan 4 84
(Richard Fahey) *hld up: nudged along 1/2-way: rdn over 2f out: hdwy ent fnl f: r.o: snatched 4th fnl stride* **9/1**
0122 **5** *nse* **Fire Ship**[7] 4097 3-8-8 **84**.. WilliamBuick 12 90
(William Knight) *trckd ldr: rdn and ev ch jst over 1f out: kpt on but nt gng pce of wnr* **11/2**[2]
1003 **6** *½* **Arnold Lane (IRE)**[7] 4095 3-9-7 **97**.................................. MartinHarley 2 102
(Mick Channon) *mid-div: nt best of runs fr 2f out: rdn and r.o whn gap appeared to press ldrs ent fnl f: kpt on but no ex nring fin* **16/1**
2003 **7** *½* **Miblish**[21] 3630 3-9-7 **97**..(t) YasunariIwata 1 100
(Clive Brittain) *mid-div: hdwy 2f out: sn rdn: ev ch whn hung lft jst over 1f out: kpt on but no ex towards fin* **28/1**
530 **8** *3 ½* **Prince Alzain (USA)**[30] 3294 3-9-0 **90**............................ FrankieDettori 8 85
(Gerard Butler) *mid-div: effrt wl over 1f out: wknd ins fnl f* **9/1**

2620 **9** *3* **Lucky Henry**[30] 3294 3-8-11 **87** JohnFahy 7 75
(Clive Cox) *racd keenly trcking ldrs: rdn and ev ch jst over 1f out: fdd ins fnl f* **14/1**

0-32 **10** *2 ¼* **My Queenie (IRE)**[70] 2067 3-8-12 **88** RichardHughes 6 70
(Richard Hannon) *hld up: nt clrest of runs whn rdn 2f out but nvr finding pce to get on terms* **7/1**

55-4 **11** *4 ½* **Red Art (IRE)**[21] 3607 3-9-6 **96** MichaelHills 5 68
(Charles Hills) *trckd ldrs: rdn 2f out: wknd ent fnl f* **14/1**

1m 42.54s (1.74) **Going Correction** +0.275s/f (Good) **11** Ran SP% **117.3**
Speed ratings (Par 106): **102,100,100,100,100 99,99,95,92,90 85**
toteswingers 1&2 £3.50, 2&3 £25.50, 1&3 £15.90 CSF £16.87 CT £310.21 TOTE £3.50: £1.60, £2.00, £7.40; EX 16.60 Trifecta £169.40 Pool: £2657.15 - 11.60 winning units..
Owner Hazel Lawrence & Graham Doyle **Bred** Whitsbury Manor Stud & Pigeon House Stud **Trained** East Ilsley, Berks

FOCUS
The ten runners in this decent handicap all came up the centre of the track. This race has been won by some decent sorts in recent years, with the likes of Dunelight, Perfect Stride and Sri Putra all going on to success at Pattern level. This year's winner looks as though he will be going places too. However the pace was not strong and the form is a little muddling. The winner is value for extra than the bare form.

NOTEBOOK
Chil The Kite ◆ was raised 6lb for last month's Doncaster success and followed up here under a cool ride from Ryan Moore, who settled him in last early before delivering him with an impressive turn of foot on the nearside to lead over a furlong out. However, just as at Doncaster he hung violently away to his right and it was fortunate that he was well clear of his rivals at the time with the race won. As this was only his sixth start, it's worth giving him the benefit of the doubt and once the greenness is finally out of him, he could develop into a really smart performer. (op 11-4 tchd 3-1 in places)
Takeitfromalady(IRE), 4lb higher than when winning at Windsor last time, has gained all three of his wins in testing ground, but he has plenty of form on a quicker surface as well. Held up early, he had a wall of horses in front of him as he tried to get closer over a furlong out and finished well when seeing daylight, but he was very much second-best on the day. He remains at the top of his game. (op 7-1)
Flaxen Flare(IRE) would have appreciated the return to an easier surface following a moderate effort on his handicap debut at Sandown and had a visor on for the first time. Having made much of the running, he looked sure to drop away once headed passing the 2f pole, but he rallied gamely and was coming back for more at the line. Like the winner, this was only his sixth start so he may still have improvement left.
Lady Loch was the first off the bridle, but kept plugging away. She was shoved up 8lb for her success in first-time blinkers two starts back and seems unlikely to be given much respite after this. (op 17-2 tchd 8-1)
Fire Ship, up another 2lb after his narrow defeat at Newmarket, was never far away and there seemed no obvious excuses. (op 7-1)
Arnold Lane(IRE) was staying on when getting a bump from Miblish inside the last furlong, but it didn't make that much of a difference. (op 11-1 tchd 10-1)
Miblish was back down to 1m for this handicap debut after finishing third behind St Leger hope Michelangelo over 2f further at Newmarket last time. He had every chance over a furlong from home, but then started to hang about under pressure and had no more to give.
Prince Alzain(USA), minus the hood this time after finishing out with the washing in the Britannia, faded out of it late on and probably needs a faster surface or Polytrack. (tchd 10-1)
Lucky Henry, another well beaten in the Britannia, eventually paid for taking a keen hold through the early stages. (op 16-1)
My Queenie(IRE) was only narrowly beaten on her handicap debut in an all-age fillies' event over C&D last time, but she was making hard work of it from some way out here and proved disappointing. (tchd 15-2)

4320 TRANSFORMERS & RECTIFIERS SUMMER MILE STKS (GROUP 2) 1m (R)

3:20 (3:22) (Class 1) 4-Y-0+

£56,710 (£21,500; £10,760; £4,025; £4,025; £1,350) **Stalls** Low

Form RPR

-000 **1** **Fanunalter**[142] 758 6-9-1 113 OlivierPeslier 1 117
(Michael Wigham) *travelled wl in tch: hdwy 2f out: sn nt clr run: swtchd lft to get out ent fnl f: qcknd up wl to ld fnl 120yds: hld on wl: rdn out* **33/1**

-610 **2** *nk* **Pastoral Player**[28] 3370 5-9-1 112 DarryllHolland 4 116
(Hughie Morrison) *v awkward leaving stalls: bhd: shkn up and hdwy on rails whn swtchd rt wl over 1f out: str run whn gap appeared fnl 120yds: sn pressing wnr: hld nr fin* **18/1**

-111 **3** *¾* **Tullius (IRE)**[35] 3166 4-9-1 112 JimmyFortune 2 115
(Andrew Balding) *trckd ldrs: rdn 2f out: slt bump ent fnl f: styd on fnl 120yds* **6/1**[3]

2363 **4** *1* **Cai Shen (IRE)**[15] 3825 4-9-1 105 RichardHughes 3 112
(Richard Hannon) *led: rdn and narrowly hdd 2f out: styd pressing ldr: ev ch tl drifted lft and no ex fnl 120yds* **16/1**

4-12 **4** *dht* **Carlton House (USA)**[31] 3267 4-9-1 119 RyanMoore 8 112
(Sir Michael Stoute) *racd freely: sn w ldr: rdn to ld narrowly 2f out: no ex whn hdd fnl 120yds* **4/7**[1]

320- **6** *1 ¼* **Set The Trend**[294] 6556 6-9-1 113 DanielTudhope 6 109
(David O'Meara) *trckd ldrs: rdn over 2f out: swtchd lft over 1f out: kpt on same pce* **20/1**

3124 **7** *1 ¼* **Questioning (IRE)**[72] 1994 4-9-1 114 (p) WilliamBuick 7 107
(John Gosden) *trckd ldrs: rdn over 2f out: kpt on same pce fnl f* **11/2**[2]

3140 **8** *¾* **Red Jazz (USA)**[32] 3237 5-9-1 112 MichaelHills 5 105
(Charles Hills) *hld up: swtchd lft and rdn over 2f out: nt gng pce to get involved* **16/1**

1m 41.36s (0.66) **Going Correction** +0.375s/f (Good) **8** Ran SP% **118.1**
Speed ratings (Par 115): **111,110,109,108,108 107,106,105**
toteswingers 1&2 £41.20, 2&3 £9.40, 1&3 £17.70 CSF £511.22 TOTE £54.30: £7.30, £4.40, £1.80; EX 605.50 TRIFECTA Not won..
Owner A Al Kathiri **Bred** Azienda Agricola Francesca **Trained** Newmarket, Suffolk
■ Michael Wigham's first Group winner and runner.
■ Stewards' Enquiry : Olivier Peslier one-day ban: careless riding (Aug 5)

FOCUS
Not a strong running of this Group 2, but it could barely have panned out any better for a tricky customer like the winner. The pace wasn't strong and the favourite disappointed, but the winner is rated close to his form when runner-up in this last year.

NOTEBOOK
Fanunalter is a horse who likes to find trouble and has a fine change of pace, so the steady pace was in his favour as it meant the field were still well bunched early in the relatively short home straight. He had to wait for a clear run before being switched, but that ensured he wasn't in front too soon and he did just enough. He was below form in three starts in Dubai earlier in the year and had since been sold out of Marco Botti's yard for 67,000gns, but he's always had a ton of talent, as he had shown when runner-up to Dick Turpin in this race last season. Clearly he retains all of his ability and he might win again when things drop right.
Pastoral Player has long had an issue with the stalls and an awkward start didn't help. However, the steady pace suited considering he's a speedy horse who was up to this trip for the first time, and he got a good run against the inside rail, so it would be dangerous to suggest he was unlucky. He'll be worth another try at 1m, but might not want a proper test at the distance. (op 14-1)
Tullius(IRE) was keen early and then, as usual, looked a bit awkward under pressure, not really helping his rider, but it didn't stop him running another sound race. He had won his first three starts for this yard, including two Listed events, and showed he's not out of place at Group level. Jimmy Fortune reported the gelding hung right. Official explanation: jockey said gelding hung right
Cai Shen(IRE) was responsible for the modest gallop and ran better than he was entitled to at the weights. (op 20-1)
Carlton House(USA) is a free-going sort, but it was still a surprise to see him pull so hard considering he was back down to 1m for the first time since winning his maiden, and he ran nowhere near the level he reached when runner-up to So You Think in the Prince Of Wales's Stakes. The trip wasn't to blame - he was just unsuited by the steady pace and his wide draw, meaning he couldn't get any cover. He's not one to give up on. (op 20-1)
Set The Trend, having his first start since leaving Andrew Balding and returning from a 294-day break, raced a touch keenly and was going nowhere for much of the straight, but he made some pleasing late progress. He should improve plenty for this. (op 16-1)
Questioning(IRE), returning from a 72-day break, had a wide trip and was eased once beaten. (op 6-1)
Red Jazz(USA), last year's fourth, was also stuck out wide but that was no excuse for such a poor performance.

4321 BETFAIR SUMMER DOUBLE INTERNATIONAL STKS (HERITAGE H'CAP) 7f

3:55 (3:55) (Class 2) 3-Y-0+

£62,250 (£18,640; £9,320; £4,660; £2,330; £1,170) **Stalls** Centre

Form RPR

0040 **1** **Field Of Dream**[14] 3878 5-8-11 **99** (b) RichardHughes 22 109
(Jamie Osborne) *hld up bhd: hdwy 2f out: sn rdn: str run ent fnl f: led nring fin* **25/1**

-402 **2** *½* **Edinburgh Knight (IRE)**[21] 3633 5-9-2 **104** WilliamBuick 18 113
(Paul D'Arcy) *hmpd s: towards rr: stdy prog fr over 2f out: swtchd rt and rdn wl over 1f out: qcknd up wl: led wl ins fnl f: ct nring fin* **12/1**[3]

0040 **3** *hd* **Bertiewhittle**[21] 3648 4-7-13 **90** HarryBentley(3) 23 98
(David Barron) *hld up towards rr: hdwy 2f out: sn swtchd rt and rdn: led briefly ins fnl f: kpt on* **20/1**

1314 **4** *¾* **Global Village (IRE)**[29] 3331 7-8-3 **94** RyanClark(3) 5 100
(Brian Ellison) *mid-div: rdn and hdwy fr 2f out: ch ent fnl f: kpt on* **14/1**

2111 **5** *1* **Highland Colori (IRE)**[51] 2642 4-8-0 **88** DavidProbert 1 91+
(Andrew Balding) *racd w one other on far side: chsd ldr: overall ldr 2f out: sn rdn: hdd ins fnl f: kpt on but no ex* **14/1**

62 **6** *1* **Noble Citizen (USA)**[58] 2409 7-8-4 **92** (b) MartinLane 7 93
(David Simcock) *mid-div: rdn over 2f out: styd on fnl f* **16/1**

-035 **7** *1 ¼* **Hawkeyethenoo (IRE)**[7] 4100 6-9-1 **103** GrahamLee 12 100+
(Jim Goldie) *mid-div: rdn over 2f out: no imp tl r.o wl ins fnl f* **12/1**[3]

2601 **8** *hd* **Bonnie Brae**[7] 4099 5-9-0 **102** 3ex RyanMoore 25 99
(David Elsworth) *hld up towards rr: rdn 2f out: hdwy over 1f out: r.o fnl f: nvr trbld ldrs* **8/1**[1]

-004 **9** *nk* **Joe Packet**[21] 3641 5-8-7 **95** MartinHarley 4 91
(Jonathan Portman) *sn swtchd lft: mid-div: effrt 2f out: kpt on same pce fnl f* **33/1**

1036 **10** *½* **Imperial Djay (IRE)**[7] 4078 7-8-9 **97** PJMcDonald 29 92
(Ruth Carr) *mid-div: rdn over 2f out: styd on ins fnl f: nvr threatened ldrs* **40/1**

2004 **11** *¾* **Bannock (IRE)**[21] 3633 3-8-12 **107** KierenFallon 27 98
(Mark Johnston) *chsd ldrs: rdn 2f out: fdd ins fnl f* **33/1**

4150 **12** *nk* **Bronze Prince**[29] 3331 5-8-7 **95** JimCrowley 20 87
(Michael Attwater) *wnt bdly rt s: a in mid-div* **33/1**

0623 **13** *½* **Al Muheer (IRE)**[12] 3911 7-8-2 **90** (b) JamesSullivan 28 80
(Ruth Carr) *hld up in last: rdn over 2f out: no imp tl styd on ins fnl f* **14/1**

3-00 **14** *½* **Castles In The Air**[29] 3331 7-8-2 **93** RaulDaSilva(3) 14 82
(Richard Fahey) *chsd ldrs: rdn 2f out: fdd ins fnl f* **22/1**

4402 **15** *1 ¼* **Brae Hill (IRE)**[21] 3626 6-8-10 **98** PaulHanagan 15 84
(Richard Fahey) *sn prom: (led main gp): rdn 2f out: wknd ent fnl f* **20/1**

-501 **16** *1 ¼* **Eton Forever (IRE)**[29] 3331 5-9-7 **109** NeilCallan 21 91
(Roger Varian) *rdn 3f out: nvr bttr than mid-div* **8/1**[1]

3100 **17** *¾* **Capaill Liath (IRE)**[31] 3268 4-8-1 **92** (p) JulieBurke(3) 9 72
(Kevin Ryan) *prom: rdn over 2f out: wknd ent fnl f* **33/1**

0-02 **18** *2 ½* **Excellent Guest**[31] 3268 5-8-10 **98** FrankieDettori 6 72+
(George Margarson) *hld up towards rr: travelling wl enough but nvr a clr passage fr 2f out: sme prog ent fnl f: sn stopped again: eased whn no ch ins fnl f* **10/1**[2]

1421 **19** *¾* **Ducal**[39] 3004 4-8-2 **90** JohnFahy 8 62
(Mike Murphy) *chsd ldrs tl wknd over 1f out* **33/1**

3410 **20** *1 ¼* **Dubai Hills**[21] 3626 6-8-4 **92** ow1 RoystonFfrench 17 60
(Bryan Smart) *hmpd s: sn chsng ldrs: wknd over 1f out* **66/1**

1-50 **21** *1 ¼* **Lightning Cloud (IRE)**[28] 3371 4-8-6 **94** AmyRyan 10 59
(Kevin Ryan) *chsd ldrs tl wknd over 1f out* **8/1**[1]

0324 **22** *1* **Esprit De Midas**[14] 3855 6-8-6 **94** JimmyQuinn 16 56
(Dean Ivory) *mid-div: losing pl whn short of room 2f out: wknd sn after* **50/1**

-040 **23** *shd* **Deire Na Sli (IRE)**[14] 3878 4-7-7 **88** (b) JoeyHaynes(7) 19 50
(Martyn Meade) *bdly hmpd s: sn chsng ldrs: wknd 2f out* **66/1**

601 **24** *¾* **Van Ellis**[21] 3607 3-8-4 **99** 3ex JoeFanning 3 57
(Mark Johnston) *racd w one other on far side: overall ldr tl rdn 2f out: sn wknd* **16/1**

0016 **25** *1* **Escape To Glory (USA)**[43] 2896 4-7-13 **87** FrankieMcDonald 26 44
(Mikael Magnusson) *a towards rr* **50/1**

1160 **26** *4* **Justonefortheroad**[31] 3268 6-8-10 **98** FrederikTylicki 13 44
(Richard Fahey) *chsd ldrs: rdn 3f out: wknd 2f out* **33/1**

324 **27** *9* **Van Der Art**[22] 3563 3-7-9 **93** oh1 SimonPearce(3) 2
(Alan Jarvis) *dwlt v bdly: nvr recoevered: a wl bhd* **16/1**

1m 27.47s (-0.13) **Going Correction** +0.275s/f (Good)
WFA 3 from 4yo+ 7lb **27** Ran SP% **140.2**
Speed ratings (Par 109): **111,110,110,109,108 107,105,105,105,104 103,103,102,102,100 99,98,95,94,93 91,90,90,89,88 84,**
toteswingers 1&2 £60.70, 2&3 £77.40, 1&3 £116.10 CSF £286.04 CT £6091.12 TOTE £25.60: £5.40, £3.50, £6.00, £4.70; EX 385.10 Trifecta £19871.80 Part won. Pool: £59078.44 - 2.20 winning units..
Owner K J P Gundlach **Bred** Grundy Bloodstock S R L **Trained** Upper Lambourn, Berks

FOCUS

A fiercely competitive handicap as it should be for the money. Winners during the previous ten years include the subsequent Sussex Stakes winner Court Masterpiece, the Group winners Crystal Castle and Laa Rayb, plus the Listed winners Third Set and New Seeker (who won this twice). They went a decent pace and apart from two who raced close to the far rail plus one horse who was tailed off from the start, the other 24 raced as one bunch down the centre of the track. It was strong run, perhaps overly as the time was disappointing compared with the earlier handicap. Solid form.

NOTEBOOK

Field Of Dream never got into the race in a visor at Sandown last time, but had the blinkers back on in which he finished a luckless fourth in the Royal Hunt Cup the time before. Given a very confident ride over this shorter trip, his run was timed to perfection on this occasion and he was delivered from well back to hit the front close to the line. For a horse of his ability, it's surprising that this was only his second win in 19 starts since arriving from Italy. This was also vintage Hughes. He is a leading fancy for the Betfred Mile at Goodwood, but is not a certain runner.

Edinburgh Knight(IRE) would have had another 5lb to carry had his narrow defeat by Libranno in the Group 3 Criterion Stakes been taken into account. Another to travel comfortably off the pace, he picked up well after being switched right over a furlong from home and may have hit the front briefly before the winner mugged him close to the line. His imminent rise may mean he has to return to conditions events. (op 10-1)

Bertiewhittle has been running over 6f for most of the past year and his two wins over this trip last summer came on easier tracks than this, but he was delivered from off the pace to hit the front inside the last, only to just get run out of it. It would be harsh to blame stamina for this defeat and this was a decent effort. (op 22-1)

Global Village(IRE), winner of the Victoria Cup off 6lb lower over C&D in May, was another to finish well after being switched right for his effort over a furlong out. Although he raced in the main group, unlike the three who beat him he started from a low draw, so deserves plenty of credit for finishing so close. He was winning off a mark of just 63 on Polytrack last October, so is a credit to current connections. (op 16-1 tchd 20-1 in a place)

Highland Colori(IRE) ◆ has been in rude health this season and was bidding for a four-timer off a 3lb higher mark. Considering he only had Van Ellis keeping him company towards the far rail for most of the journey, he did incredibly well to stay in the thick of the action for so long and this effort can be marked up plenty. (op 16-1)

Noble Citizen(USA), second in this race in 2010 and third last year, would have appreciated the ground drying out and finished well to record another decent effort at Ascot.

Hawkeyethenoo(IRE) ◆ had run blinders in his previous two starts, finishing third in the Wokingham and fifth in the July Cup, but he enjoyed no luck at all this time. He was all dressed up with nowhere to go coming to the last 2f and by the time he saw daylight his task was hopeless. There is still a big race in him, with the Ayr Gold Cup an obvious option. (op 10-1)

Bonnie Brae, carrying a 3lb penalty for her win in the Bunbury Cup seven days earlier, finished well towards the nearside of the track but could probably have done without the ground drying out. She is already set for another 3lb rise. (op 10-1)

Joe Packet looked like playing a part when moving into contention over 2f out, but he does most of his racing over 6f these days and his stamina then appeared to desert him.

Imperial Djay(IRE) was far from disgraced considering he seems to reserve his very best form for turning left-handed tracks.

Bannock(IRE), bidding to become the first 3yo since New Seeker in 2003 to win this and held by Edinburgh Knight on Criterion Stakes running, was always likely to find this quite a test of stamina. He was being niggled along from some away out and it was down to his rider's persistence that his challenge lasted for as long as it did. He will remain tricky to place.

Al Muheer(IRE) ◆, 9lb lower than when taking this race for Clive Brittain in 2009, can be given some credit as he only had the tailed-off Van Der Art behind him passing the 2f pole, yet made up plenty of late ground to finish where he did.

Eton Forever(IRE) was put up 6lb for his success in the Buckingham Palace over C&D at the Royal meeting, but was still disappointing, finding little once coming under pressure over 2f out. (op 9-1 tchd 10-1)

Excellent Guest has run several good races here and was put up 4lb following his narrow defeat in the Royal Hunt Cup, but having travelled well off the pace he met plenty of trouble when trying to get closer and his jockey eventually gave up. His rider also reported that the gelding hit the stalls and missed the break, so a line can be put through this. Official explanation: jockey said gelding hit the stalls and missed the break (op 14-1)

Lightning Cloud(IRE), a most progressive 7f handicapper last season, had excuses for his two unplaced efforts this year, being drawn on the wrong side in the Victoria Cup and lacking the necessary speed dropped to 6f in the Wokingham having been sent off favourite. He was well supported again, but this time he seemed to have every chance having raced handily, yet dropped tamely away. (tchd 15-2)

Esprit De Midas Official explanation: jockey said gelding suffered interference in running

Escape To Glory(USA) Official explanation: jockey said colt got upset in stalls

Van Der Art Official explanation: jockey said filly was reluctant to race

4322 KING GEORGE VI AND QUEEN ELIZABETH STKS SPONSORED BY BETFAIR (BRITISH CHAMPIONS SERIES) (GROUP 1) 1m 4f

4:35 (4:35) (Class 1) 3-Y-O+

£567,100 (£215,000; £107,600; £53,600; £26,900; £13,500) **Stalls** Low

Form RPR

6-14 **1** **Danedream (GER)**[27] 3424 4-9-4 **128**........ AStarke 4 124
(P Schiergen, Germany) *trckd ldrs: rdn over 2f out: steadily clsd on ldr to chal ins fnl f: upsides fnl 75yds: won on nod* **9/1**

15-1 **2** *nse* **Nathaniel (IRE)**[14] 3880 4-9-7 **126**........ WilliamBuick 3 127
(John Gosden) *trckd ldrs in 4th: tk clsr order 3f out: sn rdn: led over 1f out: fnd more whn chal ins fnl f: lost on nod* **5/2**[2]

-221 **3** *1 ½* **St Nicholas Abbey (IRE)**[49] 2703 5-9-7 **124**........ JPO'Brien 8 124+
(A P O'Brien, Ire) *hld up wl off pce: swtchd out and rdn over 2f out: hdwy fr wl over 1f out: styd on fnl f: wnt 3rd nring fin but nvr threatening ldng pair* **5/1**[3]

-304 **4** *hd* **Reliable Man**[31] 3267 4-9-7 **118**........(t) OlivierPeslier 9 124
(A De Royer-Dupre, France) *hld up: rdn and hdwy over 2f out: styd on: wnt 3rd ins fnl f: lost 3rd fnl stride* **20/1**

2-11 **5** *½* **Sea Moon**[28] 3369 4-9-7 **124**........ RyanMoore 6 123
(Sir Michael Stoute) *hld up in last pair: rdn over 2f out: hdwy fr wl over 1f out: styd on fnl f: nvr threatened* **2/1**[1]

-332 **6** *1 ¼* **Dunaden (FR)**[28] 3369 6-9-7 **118**........ CraigAWilliams 2 121
(M Delzangles, France) *led for over 3f: trckd ldr: led over 3f out: rdn and hdd 2f out: styd on same pce tl no ex fnl 120yds* **8/1**

2-41 **7** *½* **Brown Panther**[27] 3418 4-9-7 **117**........ KierenFallon 10 120
(Tom Dascombe) *trckd ldrs: chal 3f out: sn rdn: led 2f out tl over 1f out: styd on same pce fnl f* **20/1**

8 *10* **Deep Brillante (JPN)**[55] 3-8-9 **118**........ Yasunarilwata 7 104
(Yoshito Yahagi, Japan) *mid-div: effrt over 2f out: wknd over 1f out* **20/1**

0-03 **9** *½* **Masked Marvel**[49] 2703 4-9-7 **119**........ FrankieDettori 5 108
(John Gosden) *mid-div: effrt over 2f out: wknd over 1f out* **25/1**

4360 **10** *40* **Robin Hood (IRE)**[31] 3267 4-9-7 **99**........(v) SeamieHeffernan 1 40
(A P O'Brien, Ire) *chsd ldr: led after 3f: hdd over 3f out: sn btn and eased* **100/1**

2m 31.62s (-0.88) **Going Correction** +0.375s/f (Good)
WFA 3 from 4yo+ 12lb **10** Ran SP% **118.8**
Speed ratings (Par 117): **117,116,115,115,115 114,114,107,107,80**
toteswingers 1&2 £6.80, 2&3 £3.10, 1&3 £11.20 CSF £30.37 CT £129.83 TOTE £11.20: £3.20, £1.40, £1.70; EX 40.60 Trifecta £148.90 Pool: £20780.24 - 103.23 winning units..
Owner Gestut Burg Eberstein & Teruya Yoshida **Bred** Gestut Brummerhof **Trained** Germany

■ Danedream is the first German-trained winner of the King George, and the first filly or mare to do the Arc-King George double.

■ Stewards' Enquiry : J P O'Brien seven-day ban & £900 fine: used whip above permitted level (Aug 4-10)
William Buick two-day ban: used whip above permitted level (Aug 5-6)
A Starke six-day ban: used whip above permitted level and incorrect place (Aug 4-9)

FOCUS

Seven of the ten-strong field had won 14 top-level contests between them, including some of the most prestigious races in the world. Last year's winner also lined up, and the only slight disappointment was the shortage of three-year-olds. After starting slowly, the pacemaker took a while to get to the front, meaning the early gallop wasn't as strong as expected. The tempo lifted soon enough, but the hold-up horses didn't have much hope, and in contrast the winner and runner-up had just about the ideal trips. This looked a good renewal on paper, albeit lacking 3yos, but the bare form is only just up to scratch off an ordinary pace. Danedream was a length off her Arc form, and Nathaniel a length off his Eclipse figure. The fourth and seventh may be the best guides to the form.

NOTEBOOK

Danedream(GER) hadn't been at her best in three starts since breaking the course record in last year's Arc, and there had to be doubts that she'd ever recapture such form, particularly after trailing in last of four in the Grand Prix de Saint-Cloud on her most recent outing. However, she was able to return to peak form and proved once and for all that she's a genuinely top-class filly, even if it was her generous 3lb sex allowance that made the difference. This was her fourth Group 1 win in total (other two gained in her native Germany) and it's all systems go for a repeat Arc bid, although she's likely to face a stronger challenge from the three-year-olds back at Longchamp. She's likely to take the same route to the Arc, bidding for a repeat win in the Grosser Preis von Baden.

Nathaniel(IRE), last year's winner, ran a mighty race just 14 days after making a successful reappearance in the Eclipse. He got warm beforehand, but that's often the case and he did absolutely nothing wrong in the race. John Gosden's colt emerges as the best horse at the weights and he has plenty of options. (op 11-4 tchd 3-1 in places)

St Nicholas Abbey(IRE) looked to be given a poor ride, but his connections were quick to blame the ground, saying it wasn't quick enough. It also didn't help that the pacemaker failed to carry out his job particularly well, but Joseph O'Brien's mount was set an awful lot to do, racing in an almost detached last for some of the way, and then receiving a hard ride when trying to make up the lost ground. The dual Coronation Cup winner, who had filled the same position in this race last year, did well to get so close and there are more 1m4f Group 1 races to be won with him. (op 7-2)

Reliable Man's camp had no complaints. The horse ran well but simply wasn't good enough and he'll be best off avoiding top-level European competition.

Sea Moon was hopelessly placed and found a bit of trouble early in the straight, although his connections suggested afterwards the horse didn't travel as well as in the Hardwicke. He's yet to prove he has what it takes to win a top-notch Group 1. (op 11-4)

Dunaden(FR) found himself in front early on and was too free. His trainer was quoted as saying "the race went the worst possible way" as the horse needs to be covered up. While it's questionable whether he would have been good enough anyway, he can be excused this performance. There is no decision yet on the Arc or whether he'll bid to follow-up last year's Melbourne Cup success. (op 15-2)

Brown Panther raced bang on the pace and was keen enough. He went well for a long way and might have fared even better had he been able to save something for the finish. The Irish St Leger could be his target. (op 25-1)

Deep Brillante(JPN) was the sole runner from the Classic generation and while he was potentially exciting, having won the Japanese Derby on his most recent start, he raced too keenly and failed to give his true running. (op 25-1)

Masked Marvel couldn't match the form he showed when third to St Nicholas Abbey in the Coronation Cup, being eased once beaten. (op 40-1)

4323 CANISBAY BLOODSTOCK H'CAP 1m 4f

5:10 (5:11) (Class 4) (0-85,84) 3-Y-O **£6,469** (£1,925; £962; £481) **Stalls** Low

Form RPR

3-1 **1** **Gospel Choir**[20] 3664 3-9-7 **84**........ RyanMoore 1 101
(Sir Michael Stoute) *in tch: rdn over 3f out: str run over 1f out: led ins fnl f: styd on: drvn out* **4/1**[2]

0-31 **2** *1 ¼* **Sun Central (IRE)**[21] 3606 3-9-5 **82**........ JPO'Brien 7 97
(William Haggas) *trckd ldrs: rdn over 2f out: led jst over 1f out: hdd ins fnl f: styd on but no ex* **11/4**[1]

2014 **3** *1 ¾* **Burnham**[26] 3448 3-8-8 **71**........ DarryllHolland 10 83
(Hughie Morrison) *mid-div: nudged along fr over 7f out: rdn over 3f out: stdy prog fr 2f out: wnt 3rd ins fnl f: styd on* **9/1**

4033 **4** *¾* **Ex Oriente (IRE)**[38] 3042 3-9-5 **82**........ WilliamBuick 5 93
(John Gosden) *hmpd s: towards rr: rdn and hdwy over 2f out: styd on fnl f* **10/1**

-223 **5** *3 ½* **Bank Bonus**[16] 3786 3-9-3 **80**........ JimmyFortune 6 85
(Andrew Balding) *wnt lft s: towards rr: rdn and hdwy fr 2f out: styd on tl no ex fnl 120yds* **14/1**

5031 **6** *½* **The Quarterjack**[24] 3483 3-8-0 **66** oh1 ow1........ RaulDaSilva(3) 4 71+
(Ron Hodges) *mid-div tl dropped to rr over 3f out: swtchd wd ent st: sn rdn: drifted to stands' side fnl f: styd on same pce* **16/1**

-061 **7** *1 ¼* **Moidore**[16] 3787 3-9-4 **81**........ GeorgeBaker 3 84
(Roger Charlton) *led: rdn over 2f out: hdd jst over 1f out: fdd ins fnl f* **4/1**[2]

0316 **8** *5* **Take Two**[16] 3792 3-9-0 **77**........ FergusSweeney 8 72
(John O'Shea) *hld up: rdn over 3f out: nvr any real imp on ldrs* **25/1**

0103 **9** *4* **Hyperlink (IRE)**[9] 3998 3-8-10 **73**........ JoeFanning 2 61
(Mark Johnston) *trckd ldr: rdn to chal over 2f out: wknd ent fnl f* **33/1**

0634 **10** *5* **Black Mascara (IRE)**[16] 3786 3-9-1 **78**........ JimCrowley 9 58
(Richard Hannon) *in tch: rdn 3f out: wknd 2f out* **25/1**

1624 **11** *5* **Hurricane In Dubai (IRE)**[18] 3737 3-8-13 **76**........ KierenFallon 11 48+
(Denis Coakley) *hld up: pushed along over 4f out: rdn over 3f out: looked to be styng on whn bdly squeezed up 2f out: no ch after* **15/2**[3]

2m 35.13s (2.63) **Going Correction** +0.375s/f (Good) **11** Ran SP% **120.7**
Speed ratings (Par 102): **106,105,104,103,101 100,100,96,94,90 87**
toteswingers 1&2 £2.40, 2&3 £6.40, 1&3 £3.80 CSF £15.52 CT £95.92 TOTE £4.60: £2.30, £1.50, £2.80; EX 9.00 Trifecta £43.00 Pool: £3,644.65 - 62.57 winning units..
Owner Cheveley Park Stud **Bred** Cheveley Park Stud Ltd **Trained** Newmarket, Suffolk

FOCUS

Last year this race was won by recent Group 2 winner Aiken, so it can produce a good one and it was encouraging that the finish was fought out by the two least-exposed runners in the field. The pace seemed generous enough, despite the time being 3.51 seconds slower than the King George, but the pair who forced it may have done too much as both eventually faded out of it. The form is rated around the fourth, with the first two stepping up on their maiden form.

The Quarterjack Official explanation: jockey said gelding hung left

T/Jkpt: Not won. T/Plt: £883.90 to a £1 stake. Pool of £225245.15 - 186.02 winning tickets. T/Qpdt: £116.90 to a £1 stake. Pool of £12724.83 - 80.55 winning tickets. TM

4289 HAYDOCK (L-H)

Saturday, July 21

OFFICIAL GOING: Home straight - good to soft; back straight - soft (7.2)

Wind: Light, against Weather: Fine and dry

4324 32RED CASINO NURSERY — 5f

6:30 (6:30) (Class 5) 2-Y-O — £2,911 (£866; £432; £216) Stalls High

Form — RPR

140 **1** **Tharawal Lady (IRE)**[52] 2603 2-9-2 **74** .... SeanLevey 3 — 75
(John Quinn) *cl up: effrt to chal over 1f out: rdn to ld jst ins fnl f: styd on wl* **8/1**

0543 **2** 1 1/4 **Millie N Aire**[7] 4076 2-8-7 **65** .... ChrisCatlin 2 — 62
(Danielle McCormick) *in tch: hdwy on outer to chse ldrs over 2f out: rdn wl over 1f out: kpt on u.p fnl f* **5/1**

603 **3** hd **Bentleysoysterboy (IRE)**[45] 2817 2-8-9 **70** ......(p) DeclanCannon(3) 4 — 67
(David Elsworth) *cl up: led after 1 1/2f: jnd and rdn over 1f out: hdd and edgd lft ins fnl f: drvn and hung lft and hmpd nr fin: lost 2nd on line* **10/3**[2]

1353 **4** 3/4 **Ishi Honest**[20] 3662 2-9-7 **79** .... RobertWinston 5 — 72
(Mark Usher) *trckd ldrs: effrt 2f out: sn swtchd rt to rails and rdn: drvn and one pce ent fnl f* **9/2**[3]

650 **5** 3 1/4 **Mace The Ace**[57] 2437 2-7-10 **61** .... IanBurns(7) 1 — 43
(David C Griffiths) *sn rdn along and outpcd in rr: sme late hdwy* **25/1**

4501 **6** 1 3/4 **Lucy Bee**[7] 4083 2-8-5 **63** .... AndrewMullen 7 — 38
(Keith Dalgleish) *in tch: effrt 1/2-way: sn rdn along and n.d* **13/2**

4342 **7** 3 **Mandy Lexi (IRE)**[7] 4076 2-9-5 **77** .... FrannyNorton 6 — 42
(Patrick Morris) *led 1 1/2f: sn rdn along: lost pl 1/2-way: sn bhd* **3/1**[1]

1m 1.86s (1.06) **Going Correction** +0.125s/f (Good) **7** Ran SP% **111.2**

Speed ratings (Par 94): **96,94,93,92,87 84,79**

toteswingers: 1&2 £5.70, 1&3 £5.10, 2&3 £3.00 CSF £44.45 CT £154.65 TOTE £9.70: £4.00, £2.20; EX 68.00 Trifecta £171.10 Pool: £328.37 - 1.42 winning units..

Owner Highfield Racing **Bred** Rathbarry Stud **Trained** Settrington, N Yorks

FOCUS

All races on Outer home straight and races on Round course run over approximately 6yds further than advertised except 1m 6f race which increased by 56yds. All races took place on the outer straight with exact distances apparently 7f 6y, 1m2f 101y and 1m6f 56y. An uncompetitive run-of-the-mill nursery with two at the bottom looking to have a lot on at the weights and the favourite running poorly.

NOTEBOOK

Tharawal Lady(IRE) was taking a drop in class after making limited impact at best in decent fillies' races on her last two starts and prevailed after a good tussle with the eventual third. She's closely related to the smart sprinter Knot In Wood and might yet progress a bit more now she's back at a more realistic level. (op 13-2)

Millie N Aire was never a threat, rather getting second by default late on, but this run showed that she's likely to be at least as effective at 6f. (op 13-2 tchd 7-1)

Bentleysoysterboy(IRE), with cheekpieces replacing blinkers, was having his first run since being gelded but still ruined his chance by racing too keenly after looking as capable as the winner for much of the way, just held when veering left late on as he tired and lost second. He's speedy and will be more effective on faster ground. (op 9-2)

Ishi Honest got the perfect tow into the race tracking the early pace but couldn't muster the pace to take advantage. She looks in need of a step up to 6f. (op 7-2)

Mace The Ace showed more than last time but still not enough to think she will be competitive outside of selling company or at distances shorter than 6f.

Lucy Beedidn't get anything like the same stamina test as at Hamilton last week, though that poor race rather fell apart in front of her and her current mark looks stiff. (op 6-1 tchd 5-1)

Mandy Lexi(IRE) dropped away very tamely after racing up with the pace on the rail for 2f and can't have been right. Official explanation: trainer said, regarding running, that filly was in season (op 7-2)

4325 32REDPOKER.COM H'CAP — 1m 2f 95y

7:00 (7:00) (Class 5) (0-75,75) 3-Y-O+ — £2,911 (£866; £432; £216) Stalls High

Form — RPR

4256 **1** **Third Half**[22] 3558 3-8-12 **69** .... RichardKingscote 10 — 77
(Tom Dascombe) *in tch: hdwy on outer wl over 2f out: chal over 1f out: rdn ins fnl f: styd on to ld last 75yds* **9/2**[2]

2366 **2** hd **Dazzling Valentine**[16] 3775 4-8-10 **64** .... NatashaEaton(7) 9 — 72
(Alan Bailey) *trckd ldng pair: hdwy to chal over 2f out: rdn to ld over 1f out: edgd lft ins fnl f: hdd and no ex last 75yds* **20/1**

5532 **3** 1 1/4 **Skyfire**[16] 3775 5-9-6 **67** .... MichaelStainton 8 — 72
(Nick Kent) *led: rdn along wl over 2f out: drvn and hdd over 1f out: edgd lft and kpt on fnl f* **4/1**[1]

0614 **4** 1 1/4 **Cosmic Moon**[19] 3692 4-8-10 **60** .... LeeTopliss(3) 6 — 64
(Richard Fahey) *in tch: hdwy over 2f out: effrt on inner and n.m.r over 1f out: nt clr run and swtchd rt ins fnl f: kpt on same pce* **6/1**[3]

-031 **5** 1 **Rosselli (IRE)**[31] 3273 3-9-0 **74** .... MichaelMetcalfe(3) 5 — 75
(Mrs K Burke) *trckd ldng pair on inner: pushed along over 2f out: rdn wl over 1f out and grad wknd* **7/1**

5233 **6** 2 1/2 **Regal Swain (IRE)**[56] 2510 4-9-12 **73** .... RobertWinston 7 — 69
(Alan Swinbank) *hld up in rr: hdwy on outer 3f out: rdn along 2f out: sn no imp* **9/2**[2]

0433 **7** nk **Climaxfortackle (IRE)**[22] 3589 4-9-0 **61** ......(v) FrannyNorton 3 — 57
(Derek Shaw) *s.i.s: a in rr* **16/1**

50-1 **8** 1 **Livia's Dream (IRE)**[26] 3443 3-9-3 **74** .... ChrisCatlin 2 — 68
(Ed Walker) *hld up towards rr: effrt and sme hdwy 3f out: rdn along over 2f out and n.d* **9/2**[2]

0-00 **9** 16 **Desert Vision**[56] 2510 8-9-9 **70** ......(vt) PhillipMakin 11 — 33
(Michael Easterby) *cl up: rdn along wl over 2f out: wknd qckly* **20/1**

2m 13.51s (-1.99) **Going Correction** -0.10s/f (Good)

WFA 3 from 4yo+ 10lb **9** Ran SP% **116.7**

Speed ratings (Par 103): **103,102,101,100,100 98,97,97,84**

toteswingers: 1&2 £26.40, 1&3 £5.80, 2&3 £11.80 CSF £88.59 CT £384.14 TOTE £4.40: £1.40, £5.10, £1.90; EX 118.50 TRIFECTA Not won..

Owner Owen Promotions Limited **Bred** Owen Promotions Ltd **Trained** Malpas, Cheshire

FOCUS

An ordinary handicap which was run at no more than a fair pace and went the way of one of the less exposed runners. Sound form.

4326 32RED.COM H'CAP — 1m 6f

7:30 (7:30) (Class 4) (0-80,80) 4-Y-O+ — £5,175 (£1,540; £769; £384) Stalls Low

Form — RPR

0232 **1** **Cape Rising (IRE)**[28] 3377 5-9-4 **77** .... RobertWinston 13 — 84
(Alan Swinbank) *a.p: effrt to ld wl over 2f out: rdn over 1f out: hdd ent fnl f: sn drvn and rallied gamely on inner to ld again nr fin* **7/2**[1]

-010 **2** hd **Dark Dune (IRE)**[24] 3494 4-9-5 **78** .... DavidAllan 5 — 85
(Tim Easterby) *hld up and bhd: smooth hdwy wl over 2f out: chal over 1f out: rdn to ld ent fnl f and sn edgd lft: drvn and wandered last 100yds: hdd and no ex towards fin* **8/1**

24-0 **3** 3/4 **Gordonsville**[28] 3377 9-9-7 **80** .... ChrisCatlin 12 — 86
(Jim Goldie) *hld up in rr: hdwy 6f out: trckd ldrs on outer over 3f out: chsd wnr 2f out: sn rdn: drvn and ev ch ent fnl f: sn n.m.r and swtchd rt: kpt on same pce* **25/1**

-230 **4** hd **Sugar Hiccup (IRE)**[28] 3400 4-8-13 **72** .... RichardMullen 2 — 78
(David Simcock) *hld up: hdwy on inner and in tch whn n.m.r and hmpd bnd over 5f out: sn towards rr: swtchd rt and hdwy 3f out: rdn to chse ldrs over 1f out: kpt on fnl f: nrst fin* **7/1**[3]

0005 **5** 1 **Bowdler's Magic**[17] 3766 5-9-3 **76** .... FrannyNorton 6 — 81
(Mark Johnston) *chsd ldrs: rdn along 3f out: drvn wl over 1f out: kpt on u.p fnl f* **9/1**

51 **6** 1 **Jamarjo (IRE)**[9] 3988 5-9-2 **75** .... SeanLevey 11 — 78
(Steve Gollings) *hld up towards rr: stdy hdwy over 5f out: trckd ldrs 4f out: rdn to chse ldrs 2f out: drvn and one pce appr fnl f* **10/1**

0-42 **7** 1 **Dawn Gale (IRE)**[28] 3400 4-9-0 **80** ......(t) WilliamTwiston-Davies(7) 3 — 82
(Hughie Morrison) *hld up in midfield: swtchd rt and hdwy 3f out: rdn to chse ldrs 2f out: drvn and no imp appr fnl f* **4/1**[2]

6600 **8** 2 1/4 **English Summer**[32] 3253 5-8-9 **71** .... RyanPowell(3) 8 — 69
(Patrick Morris) *cl up: rdn to ld briefly over 3f out: hdd wl over 2f out and grad wknd* **33/1**

00-0 **9** 1 **Sea Change (IRE)**[28] 3377 5-8-9 **68** .... WilliamCarson 9 — 65
(Jim Goldie) *hld up: a towards rr* **40/1**

5066 **10** 1/2 **Sherman McCoy**[20] 3661 6-9-3 **76** .... JamesMillman 7 — 72
(Rod Millman) *led: rdn along and hdd over 3f out: sn wknd* **20/1**

3043 **11** nk **Sohcahtoa (IRE)**[29] 3337 6-8-11 **70** .... GrahamGibbons 4 — 66
(David Barron) *hld up towards rr: gd hdwy on inner 1/2-way and sn trcking ldrs: pushed along over 3f out: sn rdn and wknd* **8/1**

135- **12** nk **Body Language (IRE)**[222] 7738 4-9-1 **74** .... StevieDonohoe 1 — 69
(Ian Williams) *cl up: rdn along 4f out: sn wknd* **14/1**

0020 **13** 1 1/4 **King Kurt (IRE)**[24] 3494 4-9-7 **80** .... PhillipMakin 10 — 74
(Kevin Ryan) *t.k.h: chsd ldrs 3f: sn dropped to rr: hdwy on wd outside 3f out: rdn to chse ldrs over 2f out: sn wknd* **14/1**

3m 0.43s (-1.57) **Going Correction** -0.10s/f (Good) **13** Ran SP% **123.4**

Speed ratings (Par 105): **100,99,99,99,98 98,97,96,95,95 95,95,94**

toteswingers: 1&2 £6.40, 1&3 £18.90, 2&3 £43.20 CSF £31.48 CT £628.32 TOTE £3.50: £1.50, £2.80, £7.30; EX 37.10 Trifecta £210.90 Pool: £285.06 - 1.00 winning units..

Owner John Wills **Bred** J R Wills **Trained** Melsonby, N Yorks

FOCUS

A fair handicap and an open one too with nothing either very progressive or standing out at the weights. The pace was a decent one overall if slightly uneven and there didn't appear to be an advantage ridden one way or another. There was a bunch finish and it's hard to rate the form too highly.

4327 £32 BONUS AT 32RED.COM MAIDEN STKS — 7f

8:00 (8:02) (Class 5) 2-Y-O — £2,911 (£866; £432; £216) Stalls Low

Form — RPR

02 **1** **Deauville Prince (FR)**[50] 2662 2-9-3 0 .... RichardKingscote 6 — 87+
(Tom Dascombe) *mde all: rdn and qcknd clr wl over 1f out: heavily eased last 100yds* **3/1**[2]

2 hd **Steeler (IRE)** 2-9-3 0 .... FrannyNorton 7 — 85+
(Mark Johnston) *s.i.s and green in rr: hdwy 4f out: pushed along on inner 3f out: rdn to chse ldrs over 2f out: swtchd to outer over 1f out and styd on strly fnl f* **5/2**[1]

3 2 1/4 **Arlecchino (IRE)** 2-9-3 0 .... SeanLevey 2 — 78
(Ed McMahon) *prom: pushed along to chse wnr 2f out: rdn: edgd lft and rn green appr fnl f: sn one pce* **7/1**

02 **4** 6 **Noble Bull (IRE)**[21] 3634 2-9-3 0 .... RobertWinston 1 — 63
(Charles Hills) *cl up: rdn along 3f out: wknd 2f out* **11/2**

2 **5** 1 **French Press (IRE)**[21] 3611 2-9-3 0 .... RichardMullen 5 — 60
(David Brown) *in tch: pushed along bef 1/2-way: rdn wl over 2f out and n.d* **10/3**[3]

0 **6** 2 **Gabrial The Boss (USA)**[24] 3499 2-9-3 0 .... ChrisCatlin 3 — 55
(David Simcock) *green and outpcd in rr: sme hdwy 3f out: nvr a factor* **25/1**

05 **7** 31 **Cielo Rojo (IRE)**[25] 3457 2-9-0 0 .... LeeTopliss(3) 8
(Richard Fahey) *a in rr: outpcd and bhd fr 1/2-way* **33/1**

1m 30.21s (-0.49) **Going Correction** -0.10s/f (Good) **7** Ran SP% **111.3**

Speed ratings (Par 94): **98,97,95,88,87 84,49**

toteswingers: 1&2 £3.30, 1&3 £4.30, 2&3 £6.30 CSF £10.32 TOTE £4.90: £2.70, £1.30; EX 13.60 Trifecta £87.00 Pool: £308.04 - 2.62 winning units..

Owner N & S Mather, C Ledigo, L Basran **Bred** Ecurie Haras Du Cadran Et Al **Trained** Malpas, Cheshire

FOCUS

An above-average maiden in which the field soon got strung out behind an honest gallop and the winner put his experience to good use.

NOTEBOOK

Deauville Prince(FR) had shaped well here last time despite things not going his way and he shed his maiden tag with more in hand than the margin suggests, eased prematurely and nearly caught after being around three lengths up and still going strongly inside the last. He looked much happier at this trip than 6f last time and might well be good enough to win a minor event. (op 7-2 tchd 4-1 in a place)

Steeler(IRE), a half-brother to a couple of useful winners over 1m2f and more, shouldn't be long in winning a race. He got behind early having run green and then took all of the straight to find his stride but he stayed on very well and already looks as if he will appreciate 1m. (op 2-1)

Arlecchino(IRE), by Hernando and the third foal of a 1m3f winner, shaped promisingly if looking to lack the scope of the runner-up, and he is another that should improve as he tackles longer distances. (op 17-2 tchd 10-1)

Noble Bull(IRE) had finished second in a Newmarket maiden last time and was given every chance to run his race here, upsides the winner for a long way. (tchd 5-1)

French Press(IRE) had shaped well at Doncaster on his debut but the form of that race has already taken a few knocks and he never got competitive after looking awkward around the home bend. (op 4-1)

Gabrial The Boss(USA) still looks something of a big baby and is unlikely to grow up enough to show what he is properly capable of before he goes into nurseries. (tchd 28-1)
Cielo Rojo(IRE) needs his sights lowering as he once again showed little, quickly left behind once the race began in earnest. (op 20-1)

4328 32RED CONDITIONS STKS 7f
8:30 (8:31) (Class 3) 3-Y-O+ **£8,409** (£2,502; £1,250; £625) **Stalls** Low

Form RPR
-050 **1** **Rhythm Of Light**[31] 3266 4-8-10 **103**........................ RichardKingscote 2 106
(Tom Dascombe) *hld up in rr: swtchd to outer and smooth hdwy to ld 2f out: rdn and qcknd over 1f out: styd on wl* **11/4**[2]

1234 **2** *2* **Lethal Force (IRE)**[31] 3265 3-8-8 **107**..............................(p) JohnFahy 3 104
(Clive Cox) *trckd ldng pair: tk clsr order over 2f out: rdn to chse wnr whn rdr dropped whip over 1f out: no imp fnl f* **4/6**[1]

2636 **3** *2 ½* **Regal Parade**[7] 4092 8-9-1 **105**........................ WilliamCarson 4 99
(Milton Bradley) *cl up: led 3f out: rdn and hdd 2f out: sn one pce* **7/2**[3]

00 **4** *23* **De Lesseps (USA)**[1] 4295 4-8-8 **55**........................ MatthewHopkins(7) 1 37?
(Alan Berry) *set stdy pce: rdn along 4f out: hdd 3f out and sn outpcd* **66/1**

1m 28.85s (-1.85) **Going Correction** -0.10s/f (Good)
WFA 3 from 4yo+ 7lb **4 Ran SP% 110.4**
Speed ratings (Par 107): **106,103,100,74**
CSF £5.19 TOTE £2.90; EX 5.40.
Owner Lowe Silver Deal **Bred** Hermes Services Ltd **Trained** Malpas, Cheshire

FOCUS
A useful minor event but a tactical one with the pace set by the rank outsider De Lesseps only modest. Muddling conditions form with the winner rated to his best.

NOTEBOOK
Rhythm Of Light hadn't won since landing the Sandringham Handicap at Royal Ascot last year but she hadn't fared too badly in three Group 2 events at Meydan earlier this year and proved much too good on this drop in grade, quickening to the front readily despite being held up in last place and then always looking likely to hold on readily. It wouldn't be a surprise to see her come back for the Listed Dick Hern Stakes here next month as she's more than good enough to win that race if previous renewals are anything to go by. (op 9-4)
Lethal Force(IRE) had the highest official rating of the quartet by dint of his fourth last time out in the Jersey Stakes but that contest looks a bit substandard this year and he was beaten fair and square for all the winner might have got first run on him under a superior tactical ride. (op 4-5 tchd 8-13)
Regal Parade was too keen on the heels of the pacesetter and would have fared better given a stronger gallop but his current BHA mark of 105 is starting to look to flatter him. (op 4-1 tchd 9-2)

4329 TEXT 32RED TO 89932 H'CAP 1m
9:00 (9:02) (Class 5) (0-75,75) 3-Y-O **£2,911** (£866; £432; £216) **Stalls** Low

Form RPR
034 **1** **Ascription (IRE)**[37] 3079 3-9-2 **70**........................ PaulMulrennan 1 85+
(Ed Dunlop) *stdd s and hld up in rr: tk clsr order 3f out: nt clr run 2f out: swtchd rt and smooth hdwy to chse ldr ent fnl f: sn rdn and edgd lft: drvn and styd on wl to ld nr line* **4/1**[1]

4514 **2** *hd* **Hi There (IRE)**[21] 3629 3-8-10 **67**........................ LeeTopliss(3) 10 78+
(Richard Fahey) *hld up towards rr: smooth hdwy 3f out: led wl over 1f out: sn rdn clr: drvn ins fnl f: hdd and no ex nr line* **9/2**[2]

150 **3** *6* **Exclusive Dancer**[21] 3616 3-9-0 **68**........................ PJMcDonald 13 65
(George Moore) *hld up and bhd: hdwy on outer 3f out: rdn to chse ldr 1 1/2f out: drvn and one pce ent fnl f* **11/2**[3]

3210 **4** *6* **Silvas Romana (IRE)**[22] 3558 3-9-4 **75**........................ RyanClark(3) 14 59
(Mark Brisbourne) *trckd ldrs: smooth hdwy on outer 3f out: led wl over 2f out: rdn and hdd wl over 1f out: kpt on same pce* **15/2**

40-4 **5** *½* **Elbow Beach**[16] 3780 3-9-1 **69**........................ JamesMillman 4 51
(Rod Millman) *trckd ldrs on inner: rdn along and outpcd wl over 2f out: kpt on u.p fnl f* **22/1**

00 **6** *½* **Gabrial's Gift (IRE)**[16] 3790 3-9-2 **70**........................ ChrisCatlin 7 51
(David Simcock) *set gd pce: rdn along 3f out: sn hdd and grad wknd* **11/1**

4130 **7** *1 ¾* **On The Hoof**[28] 3383 3-9-5 **73**........................ DavidNolan 8 50
(Michael Easterby) *chsd ldrs: rdn along 1/2-way: sn wknd* **10/1**

534P **8** *1 ¼* **Chester Aristocrat**[7] 4082 3-9-0 **68**........................ GrahamGibbons 9 42
(Eric Alston) *cl up: rdn along over 3f out: sn wknd* **6/1**

10-0 **9** *8* **Passionada**[58] 2416 3-9-2 **70**........................ LeeNewman 6 26
(David Barron) *in tch: rdn along 3f out: sn wknd* **14/1**

541- **10** *2 ¾* **Medieval Bishop (IRE)**[285] 6743 3-9-7 **75**........................ DuranFentiman 2 25
(Tim Walford) *a towards rr* **20/1**

-515 **11** *1* **Bitaphon (IRE)**[43] 2883 3-8-11 **70**........................ JustinNewman(5) 11 17
(John Balding) *prom: chsd ldr 1/2-way: rdn wl over 2f out and sn wknd* **16/1**

4050 **12** *8* **Moataz (USA)**[37] 3066 3-8-6 **60**........................ FrannyNorton 5
(Patrick Morris) *midfield: rdn along over 3f out: sn wknd* **25/1**

1m 41.98s (-1.72) **Going Correction** -0.10s/f (Good) **12 Ran SP% 122.5**
Speed ratings (Par 100): **104,103,97,91,91 90,89,87,79,77 76,68**
toteswingers: 1&2 £5.20, 1&3 £8.50, 2&3 £9.60 CSF £21.79 CT £104.25 TOTE £3.80: £1.10, £2.70, £2.90; EX 15.00 Trifecta £78.50 Pool: £262.03 - 2.47 winning units..
Owner V I Araci **Bred** Haras De Manneville **Trained** Newmarket, Suffolk

FOCUS
A strongly-run finale in which the leaders set it up for the first two who were ridden with plenty of restraint. All the same they looked easily the best handicapped horses and the winner would have been unlucky had he not prevailed. The winner looked better than the bare form.
T/Plt: £398.40 to a £1 stake. Pool: £65,556.11. 120.12 winning tickets. T/Qpdt: £29.80 to a £1 stake. Pool: £5,713.78. 141.50 winning tickets. JR

4212 LINGFIELD (L-H)
Saturday, July 21
OFFICIAL GOING: Turf course - good (7.0); all-weather - standard
Wind: Virtually nil Weather: Dry, bright spells

4330 IRISH STALLION FARMS E B F MAIDEN STKS (TURF) 7f
6:15 (6:16) (Class 5) 2-Y-O **£4,022** (£1,187; £594) **Stalls** High

Form RPR
2 **1** **Tobacco Road (IRE)**[24] 3499 2-9-3 0........................ RichardHughes 5 78+
(Richard Hannon) *trckd ldrs: rdn and qcknd to ld over 1f out: hrd pressed ins fnl f: edgd lft but r.o wl to assert fnl 75yds* **13/8**[1]

0 **2** *1* **Swift Cedar (IRE)**[26] 3444 2-8-10 0........................ MichaelJMMurphy(7) 3 76+
(Alan Jarvis) *in tch: rdn and effrt to chse wnr over 1f out: ev ch jst ins fnl f: edgd lft u.p and no ex fnl 75yds* **14/1**

0 **3** *4 ½* **Digress**[24] 3505 2-9-3 0........................ RyanMoore 7 64+
(Sir Michael Stoute) *in tch in last pair: swtchd lft and effrt ent fnl 2f: pressed ldrs u.p but unable qck 1f out: wknd ins fnl f* **9/2**[3]

4 *1 ½* **Fehaydi** 2-9-0 0........................ AdamBeschizza(3) 4 61+
(William Haggas) *rn green and sn pushed along: in tch in rr: rdn and hdwy wl over 1f out: outpcd and btn ent fnl f: no ch but plugged on fnl f* **15/2**

50 **5** *3* **Persian Marvel (IRE)**[21] 3637 2-9-3 0........................ MatthewDavies 2 53
(Jim Boyle) *sltly hmpd sn after s: sn pressing ldr: rdn ent fnl 2f: led wl over 1f out: sn hdd & wknd ent fnl f* **66/1**

6 *4* **Yul Finegold (IRE)** 2-9-3 0........................ PatCosgrave 6 45+
(George Baker) *in tch: rdn and effrt over 2f out: wknd over 1f out: fdd fnl f* **16/1**

3 **7** *2 ¾* **Yellow Mountain (IRE)**[28] 3397 2-9-3 0........................ MartinHarley 1 36
(Marco Botti) *sn pushed along to ld and crossed to r against stands' rail: rdn and hdd wl over 1f out: sn struggling and wknd over 1f out* **2/1**[2]

1m 23.67s (0.37) **Going Correction** -0.05s/f (Good) **7 Ran SP% 115.4**
Speed ratings (Par 94): **95,93,88,87,83 79,75**
toteswingers: 1&2 £5.20, 1&3 £2.50, 2&3 £9.40 CSF £25.99 TOTE £3.00: £1.80, £2.90; EX 28.40.
Owner Noodles Racing **Bred** Minch Bloodstock **Trained** East Everleigh, Wilts

FOCUS
Not many could be seriously considered for this juvenile event.

NOTEBOOK
Tobacco Road(IRE), who had shown potential when finishing runner-up over this trip on the AW on debut at Kempton, put that experience to full use and, despite needing plenty of driving, came clear to record a first victory. Having cost 38,000gns as a yearling, he's expected to come into his own once tackling longer trips and appears to have a bright future ahead of him. He holds no big-race entries at present but ought to make an impression in nurseries over a mile. (tchd 6-4 and 7-4)
Swift Cedar(IRE) had only shown limited promise on his introduction, but he looked to step up considerably on that effort. He was certainly wiser for his experience at Wolverhampton and got this trip well, despite being overhauled late on. Connections should have no problem finding him a race. (op 9-1)
Digress made a significant forward move with 2f remaining, but weakened out of it having raced on the unfavourable part of the track. (op 6-1)
Fehaydi made a pleasing debut, but was never able to get involved. (op 8-1 tchd 6-1)
Persian Marvel(IRE) showed good early speed and is an interesting prospect at a lower grade for the remainder of the season.
Yellow Mountain(IRE) was a real disappointment. He had looked nailed on for a place beforehand and, despite racing against the favoured rail, dropped out quickly and now has questions to answer. (op 5-2 tchd 11-4)

4331 CROWHURST NURSERY (TURF) 6f
6:45 (6:46) (Class 5) (0-75,71) 2-Y-O **£3,067** (£905; £453) **Stalls** High

Form RPR
204 **1** **Equitania**[16] 3783 2-9-7 **71**........................ RichardHughes 1 82+
(Richard Hannon) *chsd ldr: clsd and jnd ldr on bit over 1f out: rdn to ld jst ins fnl f: sn wnt clr and r.o wl: comf* **13/8**[1]

406 **2** *4 ½* **Frosted Off**[28] 3387 2-8-12 **62**........................ CathyGannon 6 58
(John Spearing) *taken down early: led and sn clr: rdn wl over 1f out: hdd jst ins fnl f and sn outpcd by wnr: plugged on to hold 2nd* **10/1**

605 **3** *1* **Little Miss Zuri (IRE)**[19] 3700 2-8-1 **51**........................ KieranO'Neill 3 44
(Sylvester Kirk) *stdd after s: hld up off the pce in midfield: rdn and sme hdwy over 1f out: swtchd lft jst ins fnl f: styd on but no ch w wnr* **8/1**[3]

0520 **4** *1 ¼* **Baltic Gin (IRE)**[39] 3009 2-8-13 **63**........................ TomMcLaughlin 7 52
(Malcolm Saunders) *chsd ldng pair: rdn and edgd lft 2f out: no ch w wnr and plugged on same pce fr over 1f out* **9/1**

1 **5** *3* **Risky Rizkova**[35] 3140 2-9-6 **70**........................ MatthewDavies 4 50
(Jonathan Portman) *a off the pce in last trio: rdn and hung lft over 3f out: n.d* **4/1**[2]

404 **6** *12* **Tough Lady (IRE)**[22] 3554 2-9-4 **68**........................ JoeFanning 5 15
(Mark Johnston) *short of room sn after s: nvr gng wl and a struggling in last pair: hung lft 4f out: no hdwy and edgd bk rt 2f out: nvr on terms* **4/1**[2]

6310 **7** *½* **Captain Blue**[46] 2797 2-8-9 **66**........................ RyanWhile(7) 2 9
(Bill Turner) *sn outpcd in rr: detached last 4f out: n.d* **25/1**

1m 11.13s (-0.07) **Going Correction** -0.05s/f (Good) **7 Ran SP% 112.1**
Speed ratings (Par 94): **98,92,90,89,85 69,68**
toteswingers: 1&2 £4.90, 1&3 £4.30, 2&3 £12.20 CSF £18.49 TOTE £2.60: £1.80, £6.60; EX 19.70.
Owner Carmichael Humber **Bred** Longdon Stud **Trained** East Everleigh, Wilts

FOCUS
An interesting nursery, run at a strong pace.

NOTEBOOK
Equitania showed her rivals a clean pair of heels en-route to a first success. The filly had shown definite signs of ability in three run maiden outings and she duly enhanced her paddock value with a smooth victory. Always travelling well under her in-form pilot, she barely needed to be shaken up to score and looks more than capable of following up once reassessed. (op 15-8 tchd 2-1)
Frosted Off showed good early pace but was ultimately no match for the easy winner. He proved reluctant to load but broke alertly and deserves plenty of credit as he finished well clear of the remainder. He was arguably unlucky to bump into such a well handicapped rival and compensation surely awaits. (tchd 14-1)
Little Miss Zuri(IRE) performed creditably, though not well enough to reward those that got involved in the gamble. It's hard to know what she achieved here but she was doing some good late work and ought to remain competitive. (op 10-1 tchd 12-1)
Tough Lady(IRE) was slow to go and and never threatened to get involved. He's clearly got his limitations. (op 7-2)

4332 LINGFIELD PARK OWNERS GROUP H'CAP (TURF) 6f
7:15 (7:16) (Class 6) (0-65,65) 3-Y-O+ **£2,181** (£644; £322) **Stalls** High

Form RPR
3-20 **1** **Golden Compass**[45] 2811 4-9-8 **64**........................ AdamBeschizza(3) 16 77
(Giles Bravery) *mde all and crossed to r against stands' rail over 4f out: kpt on wl u.p fr over 1f out: rdn out* **13/2**

/105 **2** *¾* **Ansells Pride (IRE)**[19] 3709 9-9-0 **60**........................(p) JakePayne(7) 10 71
(Bill Turner) *taken down early: chsd ldrs tl pressed wnr fr over 4f out: rdn over 1f out: kpt on but a hld fnl f* **33/1**

552 **3** *nk* **Links Drive Lady**[39] 3007 4-9-9 **62**........................ RichardHughes 8 72+
(Dean Ivory) *stdd and dropped in bhd after s: bhd: rdn and stl plenty to do 2f out: swtchd lft and hdwy over 1f out: r.o wl ins fnl f: nt quite rch ldrs* **11/1**

5232 **4** *½* **Bermondsey Bob (IRE)**[2] 4238 6-9-2 **62**........................ RyanWhile(7) 17 70
(John Spearing) *chsd wnr tl sltly hmpd over 4f out: chsd ldng pair after: rdn and no imp over 1f out: swtchd lft and kpt on wl fnl 50yds* **10/3**[1]

2201 **5** *¾* **Sarangoo**[5] 4146 4-9-3 **61**........................(p) MatthewLawson(5) 6 67+
(Malcolm Saunders) *bhd: rdn 3f out: hdwy towards centre of crse over 1f out: kpt on u.p fnl f: nvr looked like rching ldrs* **7/2**[2]

0464 **6** *1* **Memphis Man**[19] 3701 9-8-11 **53**.......................... MatthewCosham(3) 18 55
(David Evans) *taken down early: racd in midfield: rdn and no imp 2f out: styd on ins fnl f: nvr gng pce to rch ldrs* **25/1**

6101 **7** *2* **Silvee**[9] 4000 5-9-11 **64**.. KieranO'Neill 11 60
(John Bridger) *racd off the pce in midfield: u.p and no imp 1/2-way: kpt on ins fnl f: nvr trbld ldrs* **12/1**

0030 **8** *¾* **Huzzah (IRE)**[11] 3950 7-9-7 **60**... KierenFallon 7 54
(Paul Howling) *bhd and sn niggled along: swtchd lft and sme hdwy over 1f out: kpt on but no threat to ldrs fnl f* **6/1**[3]

0025 **9** *1 ½* **Pose (IRE)**[2] 4240 5-8-13 **52**.....................................(t) CathyGannon 4 41
(Roger Ingram) *hld up off the pce towards rr: hdwy and n.m.r jst over 1f out: rdn and kpt on ins fnl f: nvr trbld ldrs* **20/1**

4100 **10** *2 ½* **Proper Charlie**[23] 3549 4-9-12 **65**.................................... JimCrowley 15 46
(William Knight) *chsd ldrs: rdn and unable qck over 2f out: btn over 1f out: wknd fnl f* **14/1**

5102 **11** *½* **Danzoe (IRE)**[9] 4000 5-9-9 **62**...................................... TomMcLaughlin 1 41
(Christine Dunnett) *bhd: u.p after 2f: modest hdwy fnl f: n.d* **20/1**

1320 **12** *3* **Whiteoak Lady (IRE)**[2] 4237 7-9-2 **55**...........................(p) AndreaAtzeni 3 25
(David Evans) *a in rr: rdn 1/2-way: n.d* **25/1**

30-0 **13** *nk* **Royale Ransom**[25] 3475 3-9-4 **62**.. LiamKeniry 2 31
(Sylvester Kirk) *stdd and dropped in bhd after s: a bhd: lost tch 2f out* **25/1**

4400 **14** *1* **Smoky Cloud (IRE)**[11] 3950 5-9-6 **59**................................... NeilCallan 9 24
(Tony Newcombe) *chsd ldrs and crossed to r against stands' rail: rdn and no prog ent fnl 2f: btn 1f out: eased ins fnl f* **33/1**

1220 **15** *1 ½* **Mary's Pet**[21] 3618 5-9-9 **62**.. AmirQuinn 14 23
(Lee Carter) *racd off the pce towards rr: rdn and lost pl ent fnl 2f: wknd wl over 1f out: bhd fnl f* **20/1**

1m 10.65s (-0.55) **Going Correction** -0.05s/f (Good)
WFA 3 from 4yo+ 5lb **15** Ran SP% **127.3**
Speed ratings (Par 101): **101,100,99,98,97 96,93,92,90,87 86,82,82,81,79**
toteswingers: 1&2 £97.00, 1&3 £7.40, 2&3 £69.70 CSF £217.24 CT £2391.12 TOTE £5.40: £1.80, £14.20, £3.70; EX 474.70.
Owner J P Carrington **Bred** Mrs F Bravery **Trained** Newmarket, Suffolk

FOCUS
It paid to be up with the pace in this 6f handicap. Straightforward form amongst the principals.
Silvee Official explanation: trainer said mare was unsuited by going.
Huzzah(IRE) Official explanation: jockey said gelding was denied a clear run

4333 GREASE NIGHT! SAT 11TH AUGUST CLASSIFIED (S) STKS 1m 2f (P)
7:45 (7:45) (Class 6) 3-Y-O+ **£2,181** (£644; £322) **Stalls** Low

Form RPR

-320 **1** **Officer In Command (USA)**[10] 3962 6-9-5 70.............(p) JamesDoyle 4 65
(Paul Rich) *in tch: rdn and effrt to press ldrs 2f out: ev ch ent fnl f: drvn to ld ins fnl f: kpt on and a doing enough towards fin: rdn out* **2/1**[1]

665 **2** *nk* **Conducting**[72] 2011 4-9-5 65.. JimmyFortune 5 64
(Gay Kelleway) *chsd ldr: ev ch 2f out: drvn ent fnl f: hrd drvn and kpt on same pce fnl 100yds* **3/1**[3]

2326 **3** *nk* **Potentiale (IRE)**[18] 3723 8-9-5 62....................................(v) SebSanders 3 63
(J W Hills) *led: jnd 2f out: rdn jst over 1f out: hdd ins fnl f: unable qck u.p fnl 100yds* **9/2**

3306 **4** *5* **Catchanova (IRE)**[24] 3485 5-9-5 66...................................... NeilCallan 7 53
(Eve Johnson Houghton) *t.k.h: hld up in tch: rdn and effrt on inner to chse ldrs 2f out: drvn pressed ldrs over 1f out: btn ins fnl f: wknd fnl 100yds* **9/4**[2]

0000 **5** *¾* **Castalian Spring (IRE)**[10] 3968 3-8-9 35.......................... JimmyQuinn 6 52?
(Terry Clement) *t.k.h: hld up in tch in rr: pushed along and effrt 2f out: no ex ent fnl f: drvn and wknd ins fnl f* **66/1**

000- **6** *17* **The Boomingbittern**[339] 5170 3-8-4 25.....................[1] MarkCoumbe(5) 2 18
(Roger Teal) *chsd ldrs tl rdn and lost pl over 3f out: bhd 2f out: sn lost tch* **33/1**

0006 **R** **Littlemissperfect**[50] 2651 4-9-5 32....................................... AmirQuinn 1
(Richard Rowe) *rrd as stalls opened and ref to r: tk no part* **50/1**

2m 8.71s (2.11) **Going Correction** +0.225s/f (Slow)
WFA 3 from 4yo+ 10lb **7** Ran SP% **113.7**
Speed ratings (Par 101): **100,99,99,95,94 81,**
toteswingers: 1&2 £1.90, 1&3 £1.90, 2&3 £1.90 CSF £8.29 TOTE £2.80: £1.60, £2.50; EX 9.60.There was no bid for the winner.
Owner P M Rich **Bred** Blooming Hills Inc **Trained** Newport, Gwent

FOCUS
Only a classified selling stakes, but it served up a good finish. The form is rated negatively.

4334 PORTO RACING CLAIMING STKS 1m (P)
8:15 (8:15) (Class 6) 3-5-Y-O **£2,181** (£644; £322) **Stalls** High

Form RPR

5100 **1** **Munsarim (IRE)**[49] 2720 5-9-6 84................................(b) FrederikTylicki 6 88
(Richard Fahey) *hld up in tch in last trio: hdwy on inner to join ldrs on bit over 1f out: shkn up to ld 1f out and sn clr: easily* **11/10**[1]

3501 **2** *6* **Aciano (IRE)**[11] 3947 4-9-1 70.. SebSanders 1 69
(Brendan Powell) *led: rdn ent fnl 2f: hdd 1f out and immediately outpcd by wnr and wl btn: kpt on for clr 2nd* **15/2**

-200 **3** *3 ½* **Titus Star (IRE)**[58] 2408 3-9-0 68.. LiamKeniry 4 66
(J S Moore) *chsd ldr tl 3f out: drvn to chse ldr again 2f out tl over 1f out: 3rd and btn 1f out: wknd fnl f* **7/2**

0000 **4** *3 ½* **Tiradito (USA)**[28] 3388 5-8-10 67...........................(p) MarkCoumbe(5) 10 53
(Michael Attwater) *in tch in midfield: rdn and effrt over 1f out: hrd drvn and btn over 1f out: sn wknd* **28/1**

40-0 **5** *1 ¼* **Fremont (IRE)**[22] 3594 5-9-3 73....................................(b[1]) JamesDoyle 3 52
(Hugo Palmer) *t.k.h: chsd ldrs: wnt 2nd 3f out tl nt qckn u.p 2f out: wknd over 1f out* **7/1**[3]

2410 **6** *½* **Sandbetweenourtoes (IRE)**[5] 4155 3-9-0 75....(p) MatthewLawson(5) 9 59
(Roger Curtis) *in tch in midfield on outer: effrt u.p and stl wd bnd 2f out: wknd over 1f out* **8/1**

0-00 **7** *8* **Fireback**[22] 3557 5-9-9 82...(bt[1]) MickaelBarzalona 5 39
(Daniel Kubler) *taken down early and led to post: fly-jmpd as stalls opened and slowly away: sn rcvrd and in tch in last trio: rdn 4f out: struggling ent fnl 2f: sn wknd* **11/2**[2]

3000 **8** *2* **Darrow (IRE)**[10] 3952 3-8-3 68.. JimmyQuinn 8 20
(Noel Quinlan) *t.k.h: chsd ldrs: rdn and unable qck over 2f out: drvn wl over 1f out: sn wknd* **12/1**

0 **9** *3 ¾* **Medeeba**[18] 3735 3-9-0 0.. JamieGoldstein 2 22
(Zoe Davison) *in tch in last trio: rdn and struggling over 3f out: wll bhd fnl 2f* **100/1**

1m 38.16s (-0.04) **Going Correction** +0.225s/f (Slow)
WFA 3 from 4yo+ 8lb **9** Ran SP% **118.8**
Speed ratings (Par 101): **109,103,99,96,94 94,86,84,80**
toteswingers: 1&2 £1.40, 1&3 £3.10, 2&3 £10.10 CSF £10.59 TOTE £2.30: £1.10, £2.50, £2.00; EX 9.60.The winner was claimed by Mr Richard Rowe for £13,000.
Owner M A Leatham & G H Leatham **Bred** Shadwell Estate Company Limited **Trained** Musley Bank, N Yorks

FOCUS
A fair claimer which was well run. The form is rated around the winner.
Munsarim(IRE) Official explanation: trainer's rep said, regarding apparent improvement in form, that the gelding was better suited by a return to claiming company.

4335 LADBROKES GAME ON! FILLIES' H'CAP 1m 2f (P)
8:45 (8:45) (Class 5) (0-75,75) 3-Y-O+ **£3,067** (£905; £453) **Stalls** Low

Form RPR

1-04 **1** **Hayaku (USA)**[57] 2465 4-10-0 **75**...................................(t) JimCrowley 12 81
(Ralph Beckett) *chsd ldr tl rdn to ld 2f out: kpt on wl fnl f: fnd ex whn hrd pressed wl ins fnl f and hld on cl home* **22/1**

30-0 **2** *½* **Jewelled**[103] 1266 6-9-9 **70**.. SebSanders 8 75+
(Lady Herries) *stdd s: hld up in rr: hdwy on outer over 2f out: forced to go v wd and no hdwy bnd 2f out: str run fnl f to chal wl ins fnl f: hld cl home* **33/1**

2-05 **3** *¾* **Srinagar Girl**[61] 2335 3-9-4 **75**.. IanMongan 3 78
(Sir Henry Cecil) *in tch in midfield: nt clr run on inner bnd 2f out: rdn and gd hdwy over 1f out: chsd wnr 1f out: no ex and btn fnl 75yds* **12/1**

50-5 **4** *1 ¾* **Buzkashi (IRE)**[58] 2431 3-9-3 **74**... TedDurcan 5 74
(David Lanigan) *in tch in midfield: rdn and unable qck whn short of room wl over 1f out: swtchd rt 1f out: styd on fnl 150yds* **10/1**

-410 **5** *hd* **Talk Of The North**[35] 3142 3-9-0 **71**................................ JamesDoyle 11 70
(Hugo Palmer) *t.k.h: in tch: rdn and effrt to chse ldrs 2f out outpcd ent fnl f: kpt on again but no threat to ldrs fnl 100yds* **6/1**[3]

0235 **6** *nk* **Song Of Joy (IRE)**[44] 2850 3-8-2 **59**.............................. KieranO'Neill 7 58
(Paul D'Arcy) *dwlt and pushed along early: racd in tch in last quartet: rdn over 2f out: no imp and n.m.r over 1f out: hdwy u.p and styd on ins fnl f* **25/1**

4055 **7** *¾* **Bramshill Lass**[39] 3003 3-8-10 **67**................................(v[1]) JimmyQuinn 2 64
(Amanda Perrett) *t.k.h: hld up in tch in last quartet: stuck bhd horses over 2f out: hdwy u.p on inner jst over 1f out: styd on same pce ins fnl f* **50/1**

6363 **8** *1 ¼* **Sail Home**[23] 3550 5-9-7 **71**..................................... AdamBeschizza(3) 4 66
(Julia Feilden) *led and set stdy gallop: rdn and hdd 2f out: lost 2nd 1f out: wknd ins fnl f* **20/1**

212 **9** *hd* **Roxelana (IRE)**[57] 2448 3-9-4 **75**...................................... JimmyFortune 1 69
(Jeremy Noseda) *chsd ldrs: rdn and unable qck ent fnl 2f: btn 1f out: wknd ins fnl f* **5/2**[2]

01 **10** *¾* **Lashyn (USA)**[53] 2585 3-9-3 **74**.. RyanMoore 13 67
(Sir Michael Stoute) *t.k.h: chsd ldrs: rdn and unable qck 2f out: btn ent fnl f: wknd fnl 150yds* **6/4**[1]

3020 **11** *nk* **Midas Moment**[20] 3659 4-9-12 **73**.................................. GeorgeBaker 10 65
(William Muir) *hld up in tch in last quartet: hdwy to chse ldrs ent fnl 2f: rdn and fnd little over 1f out: wknd fnl f* **25/1**

2m 7.92s (1.32) **Going Correction** +0.225s/f (Slow)
WFA 3 from 4yo+ 10lb **11** Ran SP% **121.3**
Speed ratings (Par 100): **103,102,102,100,100 100,99,98,98,97 97**
toteswingers: 1&2 £26.50, 1&3 £16.10, 2&3 £29.70 CSF £574.03 CT £8782.65 TOTE £39.40: £10.00, £4.90, £5.50; EX 307.50.
Owner G B Partnership **Bred** George Strawbridge & London Thoroughbred Services **Trained** Kimpton, Hants

FOCUS
A fair fillies' handicap. There was a compressed finish and the form is ordinary.
T/Plt: £446.20 to a £1 stake. Pool: £75,276.03. 123.14 winning tickets. T/Qpdt: £128.20 to a £1 stake. Pool: £6,185.98. 35.70 winning tickets. SP

4296 NEWMARKET (R-H)
Saturday, July 21

OFFICIAL GOING: Soft (7.1)
Wind: Light across Weather: Cloudy with sunny spells

4336 BET AT BLUESQUARE ON YOUR MOBILE EBF FILLIES' H'CAP 6f
2:00 (2:00) (Class 3) (0-95,93) 3-Y-O+
£8,715 (£2,609; £1,304; £652; £326; £163) **Stalls** Low

Form RPR

-034 **1** **Ultrasonic (USA)**[22] 3593 3-9-7 **93**.......................................[1] PatDobbs 2 105
(Sir Michael Stoute) *racd stands' side: s.i.s: hld up: hdwy over 1f out: led ins fnl f: sn rdn and hung rt: r.o wl* **15/2**[3]

1366 **2** *2 ½* **Sugar Beet**[63] 2286 4-9-10 **91**.. LukeMorris 3 96
(Ronald Harris) *racd stands' side: hld up: rdn over 1f out: nt clr run and swtchd lft ins fnl f: r.o wl to go 2nd nr fin: no ch w wnr* **20/1**

1315 **3** *nk* **Charlotte Rosina**[23] 3542 3-9-2 **88**................................. SebSanders 8 91
(Roger Teal) *racd stands' side: led: rdn over 1f out: hdd and unable qck ins fnl f: lost 2nd nr fin* **7/2**[1]

6004 **4** *½* **Coolminx (IRE)**[19] 3696 5-9-2 **83**................................... BarryMcHugh 9 85
(Richard Fahey) *led centre pair tl jnd stands' side over 2f out: rdn over 1f out: styd on same pce ins fnl f* **9/2**[2]

0020 **5** *1 ¼* **Button Moon (IRE)**[10] 3960 4-8-11 **78**......................(p) CathyGannon 10 76
(Ian Wood) *chsd ldr stands' side: rdn and ev ch over 1f out: no ex ins fnl f* **16/1**

1022 **6** *½* **Choral**[38] 3045 4-9-0 **81**.. DaneO'Neill 7 78
(Richard Hannon) *prom: shkn up over 2f out: rdn over 1f out: no ex ins fnl f* **15/2**[3]

0342 **7** *2 ¼* **Bouncy Bouncy (IRE)**[19] 3696 5-8-12 **79**.....................(t) HayleyTurner 5 69
(Michael Bell) *racd stands' side: prom: rdn over 1f out: wknd ins fnl f* **8/1**

150- **8** *2 ½* **Elbe**[324] 5656 3-8-12 **84**... TomQueally 12 65
(Sir Henry Cecil) *s.i.s: trckd ldr in centre: plld hrd: jnd stands' side over 2f out: effrt and nt clr run over 1f out: sn wknd* **12/1**

20-0 **9** *1 ¼* **Al Mayasah (IRE)**[37] 3085 4-9-1 **82**..........................(p) JamieSpencer 1 60
(David Simcock) *racd stands' side: chsd ldrs: effrt over 1f out: sn wknd* **10/1**

1m 14.03s (1.53) **Going Correction** +0.325s/f (Good)
WFA 3 from 4yo+ 5lb **9** Ran SP% **102.5**
Speed ratings (Par 104): **102,98,98,97,95 95,92,88,87**
toteswingers 1&2 £17.00, 2&3 £7.00, 1&3 £2.00 CSF £108.07 CT £393.33 TOTE £7.70: £2.20, £5.20, £1.70; EX 81.70 Trifecta £249.20 Part won. Pool: £336.77 - 0.64 winning units..

Owner K Abdulla **Bred** Juddmonte Farms Inc **Trained** Newmarket, Suffolk
■ Lollina Paulina was withdrawn (5/1, broke out of stalls). Deduct 15p in the £ under R4.

FOCUS
Stands Side track used with Stalls on Stands Side except 10f & 12f: Centre. A pretty smart performance from the progressive winner, who readily took care of some pretty useful opposition and posted a clear personal best.

NOTEBOOK
Ultrasonic(USA) had been a shade disappointing here last time but that was a muddling affair and she was firmly back on the up in a first-time hood, travelling strongly under restraint and not subjected to strong pressure to come clear inside the last. From a yard enjoying an excellent run at present, she could easily have more to give after just six starts and is up to winning at Listed level among her own sex before long on this evidence. (op 13-2)
Sugar Beet put a couple of slightly below-par efforts behind her, proving herself on soft going in the process. No threat to the winner, she'll always be vulnerable to anything remotely progressive off this sort of mark.
Charlotte Rosina was suited by the return to 6f and matched the form she showed when winning over C&D last month, just leaving the impression the handicapper probably has her about right after an 8lb rise for that success. (tchd 4-1)
Coolminx(IRE) is back down to her last winning mark now but there was no obvious indication she's in good enough form to take advantage, for all this is clearly a respectable effort. (op 11-2)
Button Moon(IRE) wasn't discredited back on turf, but the fact she has just a maiden success to her name pretty much sums her up and she'll remain opposable for win purposes. (op 18-1)
Choral came here on the back of a couple of good runs over 7f, but wasn't at her best down in trip. Her overall record suggests she's likely to bounce back before long. (op 6-1)
Bouncy Bouncy(IRE) is normally reliable, so is likely to leave this effort behind. (tchd 15-2 and 9-1)
Elbe was a bit disappointing after her maiden win last year and is in danger of going the wrong way, though there is a chance the soft ground may have been against her on her return. (op 14-1)
Al Mayasah(IRE) had the speed to cope with the drop to 6f, but found disappointingly little in first-time cheekpieces. (op 11-1 tchd 12-1)

4337 NOVAE BLOODSTOCK INSURANCE H'CAP 5f
2:35 (2:35) (Class 3) (0-95,92) 3-Y-0+ **£8,409** (£2,502; £1,250; £625) **Stalls** Low

Form RPR
3053 **1** **Steps (IRE)**[8] 4073 4-9-10 **90**.........(b) AndreaAtzeni 4 101
(Roger Varian) *hld up: hdwy and nt clr run over 1f out: rdn and edgd lft ins fnl f: qcknd to ld towards fin: readily* **3/1**[1]
3001 **2** 1 1/4 **Noverre To Go (IRE)**[10] 3960 6-9-4 **84**......... LukeMorris 3 91
(Ronald Harris) *awkward leaving stalls: hdwy 1/2-way: rdn over 1f out: led wl ins fnl f: sn hdd and unable qck* **7/1**
0210 **3** *hd* **Kyleakin Lass**[12] 3912 3-9-3 **87**......... PatDobbs 6 92
(Ian Wood) *stdd s: hld up: hdwy over 1f out: rdn and ev ch wl ins fnl f: styd on same pce* **6/1**
-125 **4** 3/4 **Kingsgate Choice (IRE)**[28] 3374 5-9-8 **88**......... LiamKeniry 5 91
(Ed de Giles) *a.p: chsd ldr 3f out: rdn to ld 1f out: sn edgd lft: hdd and no ex wl ins fnl f* **7/1**
0160 **5** 1/2 **Damika (IRE)**[7] 4086 9-9-7 **87**.........(b1) MichaelStainton 2 89
(David Brown) *prom: rdn over 1f out: styng on same pce whn nt clr run wl ins fnl f* **12/1**
500- **6** 3 **R Woody**[268] 7127 5-9-7 **87**......... ShaneKelly 8 78
(Robert Cowell) *chsd ldrs: rdn over 1f out: wknd ins fnl f* **10/1**
0451 **7** *hd* **West Coast Dream**[12] 3919 5-9-12 **92**......... IanMongan 7 82
(Roy Brotherton) *led 4f out: rdn and hdd 1f out: sn wknd* **5/1**[2]
5230 **8** 2 **Whozthecat (IRE)**[14] 3845 5-8-9 **80**.........(v) NeilFarley(5) 1 63
(Declan Carroll) *led 1f: chsd ldr tl drvn along 3f out: wknd fnl f* **11/2**[3]
554 **9** 7 **Estonia**[22] 3595 5-8-7 **73** oh6......... CathyGannon 9 31
(Michael Squance) *dwlt: hld up: rdn and wknd over 1f out* **33/1**

59.84s (0.74) **Going Correction** +0.325s/f (Good)
WFA 3 from 4yo+ 4lb **9** Ran SP% **116.1**
Speed ratings (Par 107): **107,105,104,103,102 97,97,94,83**
toteswingers 1&2 £5.90, 2&3 £6.60, 1&3 £3.80 CSF £24.56 CT £118.92 TOTE £3.40: £1.60, £2.10, £1.90; EX 13.50 Trifecta £35.50 Pool: £933.09 - 19.45 winning units..
Owner Michael Hill **Bred** Eamon Beston **Trained** Newmarket, Suffolk

FOCUS
Some in-form horses fought out the finish of this sprint and the form should prove solid for this level. The time was reasonable.

NOTEBOOK
Steps(IRE) had a hood added to the blinkers he wore last time and clearly reacted well to it, quickening up nicely once a gap opened up for him towards the rail. There's no reason he won't continue to give a good account. (tchd 7-2)
Noverre To Go(IRE) hasn't always been the most consistent, but backed up his Kempton win here, getting to the front briefly before the winner. All ground seems to come alike to him. (tchd 13-2 and 15-2)
Kyleakin Lass was suited by the return to 5f and showed she's still at the top of her game, typically impressing with the way she travelled. She's going to have to pull out a bit more to defy this mark, though. (op 5-1 tchd 13-2)
Kingsgate Choice(IRE) is another sprinter in form, but the handicapper perhaps has about right for now. (tchd 13-2 and 15-2)
Damika(IRE) wasn't disgraced with blinkers replacing the visor he's worn of late. (tchd 14-1)
R Woody, who was making his debut for Robert Cowell, left the impression his first run since October was probably just needed. He'll come down a little in the weights for this and is potentially well treated. (op 14-1)
West Coast Dream had won a weak race at Windsor and a 10lb rise was more than enough to stop him. (tchd 11-2)
Whozthecat(IRE) has yet to show his form on soft ground and was in trouble a long way out. (op 7-1)

4338 NEWSELLS PARK STUD STKS (REGISTERED AS THE APHRODITE STAKES) (LISTED RACE) 1m 4f
3:10 (3:11) (Class 1) 3-Y-0+
£22,684 (£8,600; £4,304; £2,144; £1,076; £540) **Stalls** Centre

Form RPR
2-20 **1** **Hazel Lavery (IRE)**[30] 3292 3-8-4 92......... WilliamCarson 3 103
(Charles Hills) *hld up: hdwy over 2f out: rdn to ld and hung rt ins fnl f: drvn clr* **5/1**[3]
30-6 **2** 3 3/4 **Dorcas Lane**[49] 2711 4-9-2 107......... TedDurcan 10 97
(David Lanigan) *hld up: hdwy over 3f out: led 2f out: sn rdn and hung rt: hdd ins fnl f: hmpd and no ex sn after* **9/2**[2]
10-1 **3** *nk* **Ambivalent (IRE)**[37] 3080 3-8-4 85......... AndreaAtzeni 8 96
(Roger Varian) *chsd ldr tl led over 2f out: sn rdn and hdd: styd on same pce fnl f* **11/4**[1]
551 **4** 2 3/4 **Bolivia (GER)**[35] 3162 6-9-2 91.........(t1) EddieAhern 4 92
(Lucy Wadham) *led: shkn up and hdd over 2f out: wknd fnl f* **6/1**
0501 **5** 2 **Bollin Greta**[8] 4072 7-9-2 87......... LukeMorris 9 89
(Tim Easterby) *hld up: rdn and swtchd lft over 2f out: hung rt and wknd over 1f out* **8/1**
-004 **6** 1 **Qushchi**[21] 3635 4-9-2 92......... TomQueally 6 87
(William Jarvis) *hld up in tch: rdn over 2f out: wknd over 1f out* **10/1**
0-51 **7** 15 **Saint Hilary**[47] 2768 3-8-4 87......... SilvestreDeSousa 11 63
(William Muir) *prom: pushed along over 4f out: rdn over 2f out: wknd and eased over 1f out* **8/1**
-100 **8** 43 **Inchina**[30] 3292 3-8-4 85......... MickaelBarzalona 5
(Roger Charlton) *chsd ldrs: rdn over 2f out: sn wknd and eased: t.o* **12/1**

2m 33.48s (0.58) **Going Correction** +0.325s/f (Good)
WFA 3 from 4yo+ 12lb **8** Ran SP% **114.8**
Speed ratings (Par 111): **111,108,108,106,105 104,94,65**
toteswingers 1&2 £4.30, 2&3 £3.40, 1&3 £2.90 CSF £27.84 TOTE £5.20: £1.60, £1.60, £1.80; EX 35.40 Trifecta £132.30 Pool: £1,089.29 - 6.09 winning units..
Owner R Morecombe, E O'Leary, R Scarborough **Bred** Longueville Bloodstock **Trained** Lambourn, Berks

FOCUS
The trio at the the head of the market in the morning were all taken out and this doesn't look the strongest of Listed races. A fairly negative view of the form has been taken, but this was still a clear personal best from the winner. The first two home came from off the pace, although the gallop did not look overly strong.

NOTEBOOK
Hazel Lavery(IRE), runner-up in the Pretty Polly here on her return, didn't see her race out in the Ribblesdale but proved herself at 1m4f in no uncertain terms this time, looking better the further she went. She's only had half a dozen starts so may not have reached her limit yet. Official explanation: trainer's rep said, regarding apparent improvement in form, that the yard is now in better form than it was in June. (op 11-2 tchd 13-2)
Dorcas Lane bettered her reappearance, showing herself as good as ever on her second start for the yard, though no match for the winner in the end after moving up smoothly. (op 4-1 tchd 7-2)
Ambivalent(IRE) was sent off favourite but had a fair bit to find in form terms pitched straight into Listed company after her Nottingham handicap success and this is another improved effort. It's not out of the question she could have more to give the way her career's gone to date. (tchd 3-1)
Bolivia(GER) faced a stiffish task back up in class and fared as well as could be expected. (tchd 7-1)
Bollin Greta was always likely to find it tough up at this level and never threatened a serious blow.
Qushchi had shaped as if she'd benefit from the return to 1m4f, but it didn't prove to be the case, weakening in the end. (op 8-1)
Saint Hilary's maiden form had been boosted since and she might have been expected to fare a lot better, beaten a long way out. (op 13-2)
Inchina hasn't progressed as might have been expected, but there's a chance she wasn't right here. (op 14-1)

4339 GET YOUR BET ON AT BLUE SQUARE H'CAP 1m
3:45 (3:45) (Class 2) (0-105,97) 3-Y-0+
£18,675 (£5,592; £2,796; £1,398; £699; £351) **Stalls** Low

Form RPR
1200 **1** **Mull Of Killough (IRE)**[31] 3268 6-9-10 **97**......... JamieSpencer 2 103
(Jane Chapple-Hyam) *led over 4f: led again 2f out: sn rdn and hung rt: styd on u.p* **6/1**
4532 **2** 1 **Vainglory (USA)**[14] 3878 8-9-0 **92**......... LauraPike(5) 7 96
(David Simcock) *s.i.s: hld up: hdwy over 2f out: rdn and ev ch over 1f out: styd on same pce ins fnl f* **11/2**[3]
2450 **3** 1 **Kyllachy Star**[14] 3878 6-9-2 **89**......... DavidNolan 3 91
(Richard Fahey) *hld up: hdwy over 2f out: rdn over 1f out: styd on same pce fnl f* **7/1**
5010 **4** 3/4 **Emilio Largo**[29] 3331 4-9-5 **92**......... TomQueally 1 92
(Sir Henry Cecil) *trckd ldrs: racd keenly: rdn over 1f out: styd on same pce* **10/3**[1]
4020 **5** 2 1/4 **Mon Brav**[21] 3624 5-8-9 **82**......... BarryMcHugh 8 77
(Brian Ellison) *prom: rdn over 1f out: wknd ins fnl f* **25/1**
6112 **6** *nse* **Levitate**[7] 4110 4-9-4 **91**.........(v) ShaneKelly 9 86
(Alan McCabe) *s.i.s: hld up: rdn over 1f out: hung lft and wknd ins fnl f* **5/1**[2]
006 **7** 1/2 **Pravda Street**[30] 3306 7-8-7 **80**.........(p) MircoDemuro 6 74
(Brian Ellison) *chsd ldr tl led over 3f out: rdn and hdd 2f out: wknd ins fnl f* **20/1**
030 **8** *shd* **Mabait**[31] 3268 6-9-1 **95**.........(p) AliceHaynes(7) 10 88
(David Simcock) *hld up: racd keenly: rdn over 1f out: wkng whn rdr dropped reins ins fnl f* **12/1**
3040 **9** 7 **Switzerland (IRE)**[14] 3878 3-8-9 **90**......... SilvestreDeSousa 4 65
(Mark Johnston) *swtchd to r alone towards stands' side over 6f out: up w the pce: rdn over 2f out: sn edgd lft: wknd over 1f out* **6/1**

1m 44.01s (4.01) **Going Correction** +0.325s/f (Good)
WFA 3 from 4yo+ 8lb **9** Ran SP% **112.5**
Speed ratings (Par 109): **92,91,90,89,87 86,86,86,79**
toteswingers 1&2 £5.10, 2&3 £7.40, 1&3 £4.10 CSF £37.67 CT £235.10 TOTE £7.40: £2.20, £1.80, £2.40; EX 47.20 Trifecta £165.90 Pool: £589.89 - 2.63 winning units..
Owner Invictus **Bred** Owenstown Stud **Trained** Dalham, Suffolk

FOCUS
A useful handicap, although the gallop was no better than modest, and the form perhaps has the potential to prove a little muddling. The winner always well placed the way things developed and rates a narrow personal best.

NOTEBOOK
Mull Of Killough(IRE) put a couple of blips behind him, bouncing back to his Lincoln form here. He was always to the fore and pulled out more when the runner-up got upsides. He's not sure to have things go quite so much his way next time. (op 15-2)
Vainglory(USA) continued his good run of form and was arguably better than the bare result as he came from further back than ideal. He's not a frequent winner, but there's no reason he won't continue to give a good account. (op 9-2)
Kyllachy Star is reliable, but doesn't have anything in hand of his mark at present. (op 11-2)
Emilio Largo has perhaps found his level for now, though there's just a chance a stronger gallop would have seen him in a better light. He was a bit keen for his own good if anything and one-paced when it mattered. (op 4-1)
Mon Brav has raced over shorter trips than this previously and he didn't appear to see this out despite the steady gallop.
Levitate wasn't suited by the way things developed and chances are he remains in good form. (op 11-2)
Switzerland(IRE) did race isolated for a long way, but that doesn't really excuse this and he's in danger of becoming disappointing. (op 7-1 tchd 15-2)

4340 BET AT BLUESQUARE.COM MAIDEN STKS 7f
4:25 (4:25) (Class 5) 2-Y-0 **£3,234** (£962; £481; £240) **Stalls** Low

Form RPR
1 **Al Waab (IRE)** 2-9-3 0......... TomQueally 8 79+
(Sir Henry Cecil) *s.i.s: hld up: hdwy over 2f out: rdn to ld ins fnl f: edgd rt: r.o: readily* **7/1**
4 **2** 1/2 **Glory City (IRE)**[21] 3634 2-9-3 0......... SebSanders 4 78
(Marco Botti) *led: rdn and hdd ins fnl f: r.o* **2/1**[1]

3 nk **Country Western** 2-9-3 0 ... JamesDoyle 1 77+
(Charles Hills) *a.p: racd keenly: chsd ldr over 2f out: rdn over 1f out: r.o* **7/1**

6 **4** 2 1/4 **Hands Of Time**[37] 3067 2-9-3 0 ... PatDobbs 6 72
(Richard Hannon) *chsd ldrs: rdn over 1f out: no ex ins fnl f* **4/1**[2]

0 **5** 1 **Abraq**[8] 4066 2-9-3 0 ... TomMcLaughlin 7 69
(Ed Dunlop) *hld up: pushed along and nt clr run over 2f out: hung lft and styd on ins fnl f: nvr trbld ldrs* **40/1**

40 **6** 14 **Quintilian (IRE)**[21] 3634 2-9-3 0 ... AhmedAjtebi 11 39+
(Mahmood Al Zarooni) *s.i.s: hld up: hdwy over 2f out: rdn: hung lft and wknd over 1f out: eased* **10/1**

0 **7** 7 **Shooting Jacket (USA)**[54] 2550 2-9-3 0 ... MickaelBarzalona 2 32
(Mahmood Al Zarooni) *prom tl wknd and eased over 1f out* **6/1**[3]

8 3 1/2 **Karr Wa Farr (IRE)** 2-9-3 0 ... LukeMorris 9
(Ed Vaughan) *chsd ldr tl rdn over 2f out: wknd over 1f out* **25/1**

9 3/4 **Winslow Arizona (IRE)** 2-9-3 0 ... JamieSpencer 3
(Michael Bell) *s.i.s: hld up: a in rr: wknd 2f out* **16/1**

1m 29.83s (4.13) **Going Correction** +0.325s/f (Good) **9** Ran SP% **113.9**
Speed ratings (Par 94): **89,88,88,85,84 68,60,56,55**
toteswingers 1&2 £4.90, 2&3 £4.80, 1&3 £5.50 CSF £21.06 TOTE £9.90: £2.50, £1.40, £1.90; EX 25.60 Trifecta £170.10 Pool: £441.38 - 1.92 winning units..
Owner Mubarak Al Naemi **Bred** Aunt Julia Syndicate **Trained** Newmarket, Suffolk

FOCUS
This maiden wasn't as strong in depth as quite a few run here, but the first three home all look to have bright futures.

NOTEBOOK
Al Waab(IRE), a Danehill Dancer colt out of a useful 1m2f winner, made a promising start and looks sure to build on this, coming from further back than the second and third and requiring just one smack to get on top inside the last. He was the yard's first juvenile winner of the season from just its third individual runner. (tchd 6-1 and 15-2)
Glory City(IRE) duly built on last month's promising C&D debut and should have little difficulty winning a maiden, particularly at one of the smaller tracks. (op 3-1 tchd 7-2 in a place)
Country Western, an Oasis Dream colt, holds a Gimcrack entry and is unlikely to remain a maiden for much longer, travelling strongly for a long way and sticking to his task under pressure. A drop to 6f wouldn't inconvenience him at this stage of his career. (op 5-1)
Hands Of Time clearly isn't one of his yard's leading lights, but he built on his debut and is the type to keep on improving with racing, with nurseries an option after his next run. (op 7-2 tchd 9-2)
Abraq offered more than last week's debut, but chances are he won't be of any real interest until he's got a handicap mark. (op 33-1)

4341 ATKINSON BOLTON MAIDEN STKS 7f
5:00 (5:01) (Class 5) 3-Y-O **£3,234** (£962; £481; £240) **Stalls** Low

Form RPR

1 **Selkie's Friend** 3-9-3 0 ... DaneO'Neill 14 81
(Henry Candy) *s.s: hld up: hdwy over 2f out: rdn to ld over 1f out: edgd rt: r.o: comf* **40/1**

6622 **2** 1 1/4 **Pashan Garh**[15] 3809 3-9-3 74 ... LukeMorris 8 77
(Pat Eddery) *chsd ldr tl led wl over 1f out: sn rdn and hdd: styd on same pce ins fnl f* **5/1**[2]

-362 **3** 1/2 **Cathedral**[12] 3913 3-9-3 79 ... JamieSpencer 1 76
(Brian Meehan) *hld up: hdwy over 2f out: rdn and edgd lft over 1f out: no ex towards fin* **11/10**[1]

00- **4** 4 1/2 **Storm King**[270] 7082 3-9-3 0 ... BrettDoyle 11 64
(Jane Chapple-Hyam) *chsd ldrs: rdn over 2f out: styd on same pce appr fnl f* **40/1**

0- **5** nk **Dawn Glory**[335] 5299 3-8-12 0 ... JamesDoyle 5 58+
(Roger Charlton) *prom: racd keenly: rdn over 2f out: wknd ins fnl f* **12/1**

0-0 **6** 4 1/2 **Princess Of Rock**[28] 3398 3-8-12 0 ... SamHitchcott 6 47
(Mick Channon) *hld up: rdn over 2f out: nvr nrr* **66/1**

500 **7** 1 3/4 **Monymusk**[12] 3917 3-9-3 68 ... LiamKeniry 7 47
(David Elsworth) *led: rdn and hdd wl over 1f out: sn edgd rt and wknd* **25/1**

8 shd **Garrisson (IRE)** 3-9-3 0 ... HayleyTurner 13 47+
(Charles Hills) *s.s: rdn over 2f out: nvr nrr* **16/1**

9 1 1/2 **Blue Dune** 3-8-12 0 ... SilvestreDeSousa 10 38+
(Mark Johnston) *mid-div: rdn and wknd over 2f out* **17/2**

0 **10** 1/2 **Moss Hill**[94] 1450 3-9-0 0 ... SophieDoyle(3) 12 42
(Charles Hills) *plld hrd and prom: wknd wl over 1f out* **66/1**

0-0 **11** nk **Galletto (IRE)**[63] 2279 3-8-12 0 ... HarryPoulton(5) 9 41
(Terry Clement) *sn pushed along and a in rr* **150/1**

5 **12** nk **Sir Palomides (USA)**[18] 3735 3-9-3 0 ... LiamJones 2 40
(William Haggas) *mid-div: pushed along over 4f out: wknd over 2f out* **11/2**[3]

0-5 **13** 3 1/4 **Salutary**[23] 3539 3-9-3 0 ... SebSanders 4 32
(Jane Chapple-Hyam) *chsd ldrs: rdn over 2f out: wknd over 1f out* **50/1**

5 **14** 1 **Chuckle**[135] 838 3-8-12 0 ... TedDurcan 3 24
(Rae Guest) *s.i.s: a in rr: lost tch fr over 2f out* **20/1**

1m 28.45s (2.75) **Going Correction** +0.325s/f (Good) **14** Ran SP% **122.9**
Speed ratings (Par 100): **97,95,95,89,89 84,82,82,80,79 79,79,75,74**
toteswingers 1&2 £25.40, 2&3 £2.20, 1&3 £15.90 CSF £228.39 TOTE £55.30: £9.30, £1.50, £1.10; EX 323.70 TRIFECTA Not won..
Owner Henry Candy **Bred** J W P Clark **Trained** Kingston Warren, Oxon

FOCUS
Three-year-old maidens at this stage of the season are seldom strong and this was no exception. The level is set around the second and third.

4342 ATKINSON BOLTON H'CAP (IN MEMORY OF REG DAY) 1m 2f
5:35 (5:35) (Class 3) (0-95,87) 3-Y-O
£8,092 (£2,423; £1,211; £605; £302; £152) **Stalls** Centre

Form RPR

5100 **1** **Prussian**[9] 4009 3-9-6 **86** ... SilvestreDeSousa 4 94
(Mark Johnston) *mde all: rdn and hung lft fr over 1f out: styd on* **8/1**

6-14 **2** 1/2 **Dark Stranger (USA)**[35] 3156 3-9-6 **86** ... RobertHavlin 7 93
(John Gosden) *trckd ldrs: rdn to chse wnr over 1f out: carried lft ins fnl f: styd on* **7/4**[1]

0300 **3** nse **Ghost Protocol (IRE)**[9] 4009 3-9-5 **85** ... (p) JamieSpencer 1 92
(David Simcock) *hld up: hdwy over 2f out: rdn over 1f out: carried lft ins fnl f: styd on* **7/2**[2]

122 **4** 2 3/4 **Prophesy (IRE)**[13] 3890 3-8-9 **80** ... NeilFarley(5) 5 81
(Declan Carroll) *prom: rdn over 1f out: styd on same pce* **13/2**

015 **5** 3/4 **Educate**[7] 4103 3-9-2 **82** ... (v[1]) JamesDoyle 2 82
(Ismail Mohammed) *hld up: rdn and hung lft over 1f out: nt run on* **9/2**[3]

216 **6** 1/2 **Perfect Delight**[21] 3630 3-9-3 **83** ... EddieAhern 8 82
(Clive Cox) *chsd wnr tl rdn over 1f out: no ex fnl f* **13/2**

2m 11.51s (6.01) **Going Correction** +0.325s/f (Good) **6** Ran SP% **114.5**
Speed ratings (Par 104): **88,87,87,85,84 84**
toteswingers 1&2 £5.30, 2&3 £2.00, 1&3 £5.00 CSF £23.18 CT £58.88 TOTE £10.20: £3.80, £1.70; EX 25.60 Trifecta £155.70 Pool: £918.11 - 4.36 winning units..
Owner Sheikh Hamdan Bin Mohammed Al Maktoum **Bred** Darley **Trained** Middleham Moor, N Yorks

FOCUS
Not that competitive as three-year-old handicaps go. It was steadily run to boot. The winner is rated back to her best.

NOTEBOOK
Prussian had been below par the last twice but those had been strong handicaps and she appreciated the return to calmer waters, being able dictate another thing in her favour, always pulling out just enough. She may not be able to dominate to this extent next time. (op 10-1 tchd 12-1)
Dark Stranger(USA)'s Sandown form has worked out well and he performed with credit, although it's hardly an effort which marks him down as one of the yard's real progressive types, having every chance, though the winner carrying him left in the final furlong probably didn't help. (tchd 2-1)
Ghost Protocol(IRE) ran up to his best, but there's no obvious sign he has a great deal in hand of his mark. (op 9-2 tchd 5-1 in a place)
Prophesy(IRE) wasn't at his very best, though it would be hard to argue he didn't stay the trip, albeit the way the race unfolded hardly placed massive emphasis on stamina. (op 6-1 tchd 7-1)
Educate hadn't looked entirely straightforward here last time and looked very wayward on this occasion, hanging badly left under pressure in a first-time visor. Official explanation: jockey said colt hung badly right (tchd 5-1)
Perfect Delight is usually consistent, but had an off-day here. (op 7-1 tchd 11-2)
T/Plt: £12.10 to a £1 stake. Pool of £112683.82 -6796.45 winning tickets. T/Qpdt: £3.80 to a £1 stake. Pool of £5006.73 - 968.84 winning tickets. CR

3909 RIPON (R-H)
Saturday, July 21
OFFICIAL GOING: Good (good to soft in places; 7.8)
Wind: Breezy, across Weather: Cloudy

4343 DOBSONS GASKETS (S) STKS 6f
1:55 (1:57) (Class 6) 2-Y-O **£2,587** (£770; £384; £192) **Stalls** High

Form RPR

4045 **1** **Windsor Rose (IRE)**[22] 3554 2-8-6 52 ... FrannyNorton 5 57
(Mark Brisbourne) *mde all: rdn and edgd rt over 1f out: drifted rt ins fnl f: kpt on wl* **8/1**

3 **2** 2 3/4 **Tricky Madam**[29] 3351 2-8-6 0 ... DavidAllan 2 49
(Tim Easterby) *pressed wnr: drvn and outpcd over 1f out: rallied to regain 2nd ins fnl f: r.o* **2/1**[2]

6630 **3** 1/2 **Moss Quito (IRE)**[26] 3436 2-8-4 67 ... DavidBergin(7) 4 52
(David O'Meara) *trckd ldrs: rdn and chsd wnr over 1f out to ins fnl f: one pce* **11/8**[1]

3544 **4** 1 3/4 **Wordsaplenty (IRE)**[10] 3970 2-8-3 60 ... RyanPowell(3) 3 42
(J S Moore) *unruly in preliminaries and reluctant to go to post: s.i.s and blkd s: sn outpcd: effrt and hung rt over 2f out: kpt on fnl f: no imp* **10/3**[3]

1m 15.14s (2.14) **Going Correction** -0.175s/f (Firm) **4** Ran SP% **109.6**
Speed ratings (Par 92): **78,74,73,71**
CSF £23.77 TOTE £10.60; EX 17.90.The winner was bought in for 4,200gns.
Owner Peter Mort **Bred** Rossenarra Bloodstock Limited **Trained** Great Ness, Shropshire

FOCUS
Rail on bend from back straight to home straight moved out 2m adding about 6yds to distances on Round course. A fair juvenile seller. They went an honest gallop on ground officially described as Good (Good to soft in places). The jockeys reported the ground to be riding on the slower side of good.

NOTEBOOK
Windsor Rose(IRE) ran poorly in first-time cheekpieces over 7f at Chester the previous month and she raced without headgear over this 1f shorter trip. On the book, she had a few lengths to find with two of her three rivals on these unfavourable terms, the pick of her form being her fourth over 5f at Wolverhampton in April when gaining an RPR of 53. She was quick to grab the rail from a handy stands' side draw and asserted when challenged inside the 2f marker to make all the running, despite drifting right off the rail inside the final furlong. She is progressing and is certainly capable of winning again under these conditions, possibly a low-grade nursery handicap. She was retained by trainer Mark Brisbourne for £4,200 in the subsequent auction. (op 9-1 tchd 15-2)
Tricky Madam got just about upsides the winner at the 2f pole but became outpaced before running on again. She ran encouragingly over 7f on good to soft ground in another seller at Redcar on debut the previous month, and performed to a similar level this time. (tchd 15-8 and 9-4)
Moss Quito(IRE) looked a potential threat over 1f out but failed to pick up as had seemed likely. (op 15-8 tchd 2-1 and 5-4)
Wordsaplenty(IRE) was unruly in the preliminaries, before missing the break in the race itself, and did reasonably well to finish as close as she did. (op 5-2)

4344 EBF YORKSHIRE.COM BACK LE BID MAIDEN STKS 5f
2:30 (2:31) (Class 4) 2-Y-O **£5,175** (£1,540; £769; £384) **Stalls** High

Form RPR

1 **Rosdhu Queen (IRE)** 2-8-12 0 ... PhillipMakin 10 88+
(William Haggas) *mde all stands' side: clr over 2f out: kpt on wl fnl f: readily: 1st of 9 in gp* **7/2**[2]

42 **2** 2 1/4 **Bachotheque (IRE)**[7] 4114 2-9-3 0 ... DavidAllan 4 82
(Tim Easterby) *chsd far side ldrs: effrt and led that gp over 1f out: kpt on wl fnl f: nt gng pce of stands' side wnr: 1st of 5 in gp* **9/4**[1]

52 **3** 2 1/4 **Dusty Storm (IRE)**[19] 3700 2-8-12 0 ... FrannyNorton 1 69
(Ed McMahon) *cl up far side: effrt and rdn over 1f out: kpt on same pce ins fnl f: 2nd of 5 in gp* **5/1**[3]

302 **4** nk **Balinka**[4] 4178 2-8-5 0 ... RobertDodsworth(7) 2 68
(Mel Brittain) *plld hrd: led far side gp tl edgd lft and hdd over 1f out: one pce ins fnl f: 3rd of 5 in gp* **12/1**

5 1 3/4 **Melody Of Love** 2-8-12 0 ... PaulMulrennan 8 62
(Ann Duffield) *midfield stands' side: rdn over 2f out: hdwy over 1f out: chsd (clr) wnr and edgd rt ins fnl f: kpt on: 2nd of 9 in gp* **40/1**

6 shd **First Serve (IRE)** 2-8-12 0 ... GrahamGibbons 3 61
(David Barron) *unruly bef s: cl up far side tl rdn and no ex over 1f out: 4th of 5 in gp* **25/1**

05 **7** 3/4 **Ena Sharples**[17] 3747 2-8-12 0 ... AdrianNicholls 7 58
(David Nicholls) *chsd wnr stands' side: rdn over 2f out: no ex and lost 2nd ins fnl f: 3rd of 9 in gp* **25/1**

0 **8** 1 3/4 **On The Bias (USA)**[22] 3590 2-8-12 0 ... (b[1]) RobertWinston 13 52
(Brian Meehan) *hld up stands' side: effrt and rdn over 2f out: hung rt: no imp fnl f: 4th of 9 in gp* **10/1**

9 3/4 **Done Dreaming (IRE)** 2-9-3 0 TonyHamilton 9 54+
(Richard Fahey) *in tch stands' side: drvn over 2f out: no imp over 1f out: 5th of 9 in gp* **8/1**

0 10 1/2 **Monsieur Royale**[49] 2686 2-9-0 0 DaleSwift(3) 14 53
(Geoffrey Oldroyd) *bhd and sn pushed along stands' side: drvn over 3f out: nvr able to chal: 6th of 9 in gp* **10/1**

11 1 1/2 **Pipers Note** 2-9-3 0 RussKennemore 11 47
(Richard Whitaker) *missed break: bhd stands' side: drvn 1/2-way: nvr on terms: 7th of 9 in gp* **50/1**

12 1/2 **Megaleka** 2-8-12 0 DuranFentiman 6 40
(Chris Fairhurst) *dwlt: bhd stands' side: sn pushed along: nvr on terms: 8th of 9 in gp* **66/1**

00 13 10 **Cromwell Rose (IRE)**[24] 3490 2-8-12 0 TomEaves 12 4
(John Weymes) *cl up stands' side tl rdn and wknd fr 2f out: last of 9 in gp* **80/1**

14 3 **Hazard Warning (IRE)** 2-8-12 0 DarylByrne(5) 5
(Tim Easterby) *missed break: sn t.o far side: nvr on terms: last of 5 in gp* **25/1**

59.93s (-0.77) **Going Correction** -0.175s/f (Firm) **14** Ran SP% **125.3**
Speed ratings (Par 96): **99,95,91,91,88 88,87,84,83,82 79,79,63,58**
toteswingers 1&2 £1.40, 2&3 £2.90, 1&3 £4.80 CSF £11.62 TOTE £5.10: £1.90, £1.20, £2.30; EX 15.10.
Owner Clipper Logistics **Bred** Old Carhue & Graeng Bloodstock **Trained** Newmarket, Suffolk

FOCUS
A decent juvenile maiden. They split into two groups with five racing far side from their low draws and the remaining nine competing up the stands' side.

NOTEBOOK
Rosdhu Queen(IRE) was a 65,000 guineas purchase from the juvenile breeze-up sales in April. She is a half-sister to two fair winners at up to 6f out of a 1m French Group 3 juvenile winner. She made all the running here up the stands' rail in splendid isolation. She holds an entry in the Group 2 Lowther Stakes over this trip at York in August and did nothing to discourage such aspirations. (op 4-1)
Bachotheque(IRE) set the form standard after improving to finish a close second of 13 on good ground at York on his second start this month, gaining an RPR of 89. He won his race over this 1f shorter trip on the far side but proved no match for the useful looking debutante on the opposite rail. He gives this form real substance and looks very likely to win a similar contest at up to 6f. He will make up into a decent sprinter in any case. (op 2-1)
Dusty Storm(IRE) gives further substance to this form in third, after finishing second of those to race in the far side group. She improved to finish about 1l second of eight at Windsor on good ground on her second start this month and posted slightly better form in this company. (op 9-2 tchd 11-2)
Balinka produced a slightly improved effort in fourth and may be one to note in a 5f fillies' nursery handicap.
Melody Of Love finished second on the stands' side but fifth overall and will benefit from this debut experience. (op 50-1)
Done Dreaming(IRE) is another debutant who will improve for the run. (op 11-1)
Cromwell Rose(IRE) Official explanation: trainer said filly was unsuited by the track

4345 RIPON-RACES.CO.UK H'CAP 1m
3:05 (3:05) (Class 4) (0-85,84) 3-Y-O+ **£6,301** (£1,886; £943; £472; £235) **Stalls** Low

Form RPR

3231 1 **Lockantanks**[4] 4175 5-9-9 84 6ex CharlesBishop(5) 4 95
(Michael Appleby) *t.k.h early: prom: smooth hdwy 2f out: rdn to ld ins fnl f: edgd rt: kpt on* **5/1**[2]

0-61 2 1/2 **Venutius**[28] 3385 5-9-13 83 FrannyNorton 1 93
(Ed McMahon) *mde most tl rdn and hdd ins fnl f: rallied: hld towards fin* **17/2**

211 3 2 1/4 **Eastward Ho**[21] 3615 4-9-0 70 RobertWinston 3 75
(Jason Ward) *prom: effrt and rdn over 2f out: cl up over 1f out: kpt on same pce ins fnl f* **7/2**[1]

25 4 6 **Just Bond (IRE)**[103] 1249 10-9-9 82 DaleSwift(3) 6 73
(Geoffrey Oldroyd) *t.k.h: hld up: rdn over 3f out: hdwy wl over 1f out: kpt on fnl f: nvr able to chal* **20/1**

-021 5 1 1/2 **Ingleby Exceed (IRE)**[26] 3439 4-9-10 80 TomEaves 8 68
(David O'Meara) *t.k.h: cl up tl rdn and wknd wl over 1f out* **8/1**

10-0 6 3/4 **So Wise (USA)**[30] 3306 4-9-1 78 DavidBergin(7) 7 64
(David O'Meara) *hld up: rdn over 3f out: hdwy on outside and edgd rt wl over 1f out: nvr able to chal* **25/1**

6034 7 1 **Dolphin Rock**[28] 3385 5-9-5 75 LeeNewman 9 59
(David Barron) *midfield: drvn over 3f out: edgd rt and wknd wl over 1f out* **9/1**

4503 8 1/2 **Icy Blue**[12] 3914 4-8-11 67 TonyHamilton 5 50+
(Richard Whitaker) *s.i.s: hld up ins: hmpd and snatched up over 3f out: sme late hdwy: nvr rchd ldrs* **15/2**[3]

0213 9 1 **No Poppy (IRE)**[9] 3991 4-9-9 84 [1] AdamCarter(5) 11 64
(Tim Easterby) *sn pushed along towards rr: drvn 3f out: nvr able to chal* **10/1**

21 10 nk **Daruband**[22] 3589 4-9-1 78 (v) WilliamTwiston-Davies(7) 2 58
(Alan McCabe) *s.i.s: sn midfield on ins: outpcd over 2f out: sn struggling* **9/1**

0000 11 6 **Mujaadel (USA)**[28] 3403 7-9-4 74 (p) AndrewMullen 10 40
(David Nicholls) *prom tl rdn and wknd over 2f out* **66/1**

21-0 12 2 1/2 **Imperator Augustus (IRE)**[63] 2285 4-9-12 82 DuranFentiman 15 42
(Patrick Holmes) *midfield on outside: struggling over 2f out: edgd rt and btn over 1f out* **25/1**

-256 13 hd **Sunnyside Tom (IRE)**[178] 299 8-9-1 78 EireannCagney(7) 13 38
(Richard Fahey) *w ldr: rdn over 3f out: wknd 2f out* **33/1**

4026 14 31 **Amazing Star (IRE)**[21] 3609 7-9-3 73 GrahamGibbons 12
(Declan Carroll) *s.i.s: bhd: lost tch 1/2-way: t.o* **33/1**

1m 39.2s (-2.20) **Going Correction** -0.175s/f (Firm) **14** Ran SP% **121.2**
Speed ratings (Par 105): **104,103,101,95,93 93,92,91,90,90 84,81,81,50**
toteswingers 1&2 £12.70, 2&3 £7.30, 1&3 £7.30 CSF £43.56 CT £153.70 TOTE £5.60: £1.80, £3.00, £1.50; EX 69.00.
Owner Dallas Racing **Bred** Jeremy Green And Sons **Trained** Danethorpe, Notts

FOCUS
A decent handicap. They went a strongly contested pace and the winning time looks very respectable. The first three home all won their previous starts. The winner is rated back to his best.
Amazing Star(IRE) Official explanation: jockey said gelding never travelled

4346 RIPON BELL-RINGER H'CAP 1m 4f 10y
3:40 (3:41) (Class 2) (0-100,88) 3-Y-**£12,450** (£3,728; £1,864; £932; £466) **Stalls** Centre

Form RPR

21 1 **Guarantee**[16] 3786 3-9-6 87 PhillipMakin 5 96+
(William Haggas) *prom: niggled along 4f out: pushed along and hdwy over 1f out: edgd rt: led 1f out: rdn out fnl f* **5/4**[1]

6413 2 3 3/4 **Choisan (IRE)**[14] 3859 3-8-12 79 DavidAllan 6 82
(Tim Easterby) *led at stdy gallop: rdn over 3f out: hdd 1f out: kpt on fnl f: nt gng pce of wnr* **4/1**[3]

-205 3 1 1/4 **Maastricht (IRE)**[7] 4079 3-8-12 79 FrannyNorton 2 80
(Mark Johnston) *trckd ldr 2f: cl up: rdn and outpcd over 2f out: rallied appr fnl f: nt gng pce of first two* **6/1**

54-3 4 3/4 **Toptempo**[64] 2249 3-9-4 85 PaulMulrennan 3 85
(Mark H Tompkins) *stdd in last pl but in tch: rdn and outpcd 4f out: rallied over 1f out: no imp fnl f* **8/1**

3106 5 7 **Yazdi (IRE)**[9] 4007 3-9-7 88 (b1) RobertWinston 4 85
(Brian Meehan) *dwlt: t.k.h and chsd ldr after 2f: drvn over 2f out: hung bdly lft fr over 1f out: kpt hanging and eased ins fnl f* **7/2**[2]

2m 38.27s (1.57) **Going Correction** -0.175s/f (Firm) **5** Ran SP% **112.1**
Speed ratings (Par 106): **87,84,83,83,78**
CSF £6.72 TOTE £2.00: £1.40, £2.00; EX 6.80.
Owner Highclere Thoroughbred Racing-Authorized **Bred** Highbury Stud Ltd **Trained** Newmarket, Suffolk

FOCUS
An above average middle-distance 3yo handicap and the feature race on the card. They went an even pace at best and the winning time was nothing to write home about. The race did not take as much winning as might have been expected from the grade, but Guarantee can step up again.

NOTEBOOK
Guarantee looked a good-class handicapper in the making when winning his Newbury maiden in fine style over this 1m4f trip on good to soft ground, just over a fortnight previous to this contest. He took over with a furlong to go here and powered away for an authoritative success off an initial BHB rating of 87. He looks progressive in this sort of company under these conditions. Trainer William Haggas now has a very healthy 57% strike-rate in 3yo handicaps here since 2008. (op 6-4)
Choisan(IRE) didn't go down without a fight after setting his own even pace but had no answer to the winner inside the final furlong. He won a soft-ground C&D handicap off 4lb lower the previous month and may prove hard to win with on drying ground in the coming weeks. (op 9-2 tchd 7-2)
Maastricht(IRE) ran poorly the last twice after a good second at Newmarket in May. He should be able to build on this much better display in third. (tchd 5-1)
Toptempo was returning from a two-month break and remains a maiden after four starts. She looks a shade high in the weights currently. (op 11-2)
Yazdi(IRE) started slowly and raced far too keenly in first-time blinkers, before hanging badly to his left from over 1f out. Official explanation: jockey said colt hung left and did not face the first-time blinkers (op 4-1)

4347 SKY BET SUPPORTING THE YORKSHIRE RACING SUMMER FESTIVAL H'CAP 1m 1f 170y
4:20 (4:21) (Class 4) (0-85,84) 3-Y-O+ **£6,301** (£1,886; £943; £472; £235) **Stalls** Low

Form RPR

3024 1 **Muffin McLeay (IRE)**[24] 3494 4-10-0 84 GrahamGibbons 4 96
(David Barron) *t.k.h early: prom: smooth hdwy to ld over 2f out: rdn and edgd rt over 1f out: hld on gamely fnl f* **15/8**[1]

0530 2 3/4 **Assizes**[7] 4110 3-9-0 80 FrannyNorton 9 90
(Mark Johnston) *towards rr: pushed along 1/2-way: hdwy to chse wnr 2f out: edgd rt over 1f out: kpt on wl u.p ins fnl f: hld nr fin* **13/2**[3]

1345 3 7 **Carragold**[25] 3459 6-9-7 77 PaulMulrennan 5 72
(Mel Brittain) *hld up: smooth hdwy whn nt clr run over 2f out: sn chsng clr ldng pair: no imp fnl f* **10/1**

-654 4 3 1/4 **Robert The Painter (IRE)**[7] 4080 4-9-6 76 TomEaves 1 64
(David O'Meara) *prom: rdn whn n.m.r briefly over 2f out: sn n.d* **15/2**

4303 5 4 **Jonny Lesters Hair (IRE)**[30] 3306 7-9-9 79 DavidAllan 6 59
(Tim Easterby) *w ldr: rdn over 3f out: wknd 2f out* **10/3**[2]

0030 6 2 **Kinyras (IRE)**[8] 4072 4-8-12 75 DavidSimmonson(7) 10 51
(Michael Easterby) *s.i.s: hld up: hdwy on outside over 2f out: edgd rt and wknd wl over 1f out* **25/1**

-200 7 6 **Lucky Windmill**[24] 3494 5-9-6 76 RobertWinston 8 39
(Alan Swinbank) *s.i.s: hld up: rdn and hdwy over 3f out: wknd over 2f out* **13/2**[3]

3-00 8 3/4 **Brocklebank (IRE)**[27] 3417 3-9-1 81 PhillipMakin 2 43
(Kevin Ryan) *t.k.h: led to over 2f out: sn n.m.r and wknd* **33/1**

01-0 9 5 **Ultimate**[56] 2504 6-9-9 82 PaulPickard(3) 7 33
(Brian Ellison) *trckd ldrs on outside tl rdn and wknd fr 3f out* **20/1**

2m 2.29s (-3.11) **Going Correction** -0.175s/f (Firm)
WFA 3 from 4yo+ 10lb **9** Ran SP% **116.9**
Speed ratings (Par 105): **105,104,98,96,93 91,86,86,82**
toteswingers 1&2 £3.50, 2&3 £7.30, 1&3 £5.40 CSF £14.48 CT £98.04 TOTE £2.50: £1.20, £2.40, £1.70; EX 17.20.
Owner Harrowgate Bloodstock Ltd **Bred** Mrs Josephine Hughes **Trained** Maunby, N Yorks

FOCUS
A decent handicap for 3yos and up. They went a very honest gallop and the winning time was reasonable. The first two were clear and it's worth being slightly positive about the form.

4348 GO RACING IN YORKSHIRE MAIDEN H'CAP 6f
4:55 (4:56) (Class 5) (0-70,70) 3-Y-O+ **£3,234** (£962; £481; £240) **Stalls** High

Form RPR

05-6 1 **Trust Fund Babe (IRE)**[29] 3357 3-8-7 56 DavidAllan 4 63
(Tim Easterby) *mde all far side: rdn 2f out: hld on gamely fnl f: 1st of 4 in gp* **20/1**

2025 2 1/2 **Ambitious Icarus**[22] 3566 3-8-11 60 (e) RobbieFitzpatrick 1 65
(Richard Guest) *bhd far side: gd hdwy over 1f out: chsd wnr ins fnl f: kpt on: hld nr fin: 2nd of 4 in gp* **16/1**

5-02 3 nk **Ypres**[4] 4174 3-8-8 57 TonyHamilton 2 61
(Jason Ward) *cl up far side: effrt and chsd wnr over 1f out to ins fnl f: kpt on same pce towards fin: 3rd of 4 in gp* **4/1**[1]

4342 4 3/4 **Art Form**[22] 3561 3-9-0 70 (t) WilliamTwiston-Davies(7) 15 72+
(Alan McCabe) *prom stands' side: gng wl over 2f out: led that gp appr fnl f: kpt on fnl f: nt rch far side wnr: 1st of 11 in gp* **4/1**[1]

-525 5 3 **Slenningford**[17] 3751 3-8-12 61 PaulMulrennan 13 53
(Ollie Pears) *led stands' side tl edgd rt and hdd appr fnl f: sn outpcd: 2nd of 11 in gp* **18/1**

2220 6 nk **Fama Mac**[26] 3442 5-8-9 56 (b1) DaleSwift(3) 10 48
(Neville Bycroft) *prom stands' side: effrt and rdn over 2f out: outpcd appr fnl f: 3rd of 11 in gp* **4/1**[1]

0-02 7 3 3/4 **Ingleby Angel (IRE)**[26] 3442 3-8-3 52 DuranFentiman 9 31
(David O'Meara) *towards rr stands' side: rdn over 2f out: styd on fnl f: nvr able to chal: 4th of 11 in gp* **6/1**[2]

-060 8 nse **Cottam Stella**[40] 2981 4-8-0 51 oh6 (t) RobertDodsworth(7) 5 31
(Mel Brittain) *sn bhd on outside of stands' side gp: drvn 1/2-way: sme late hdwy: nvr rchd ldrs: 5th of 11 in gp* **50/1**

3044 9 hd **Dartrix**[13] 3892 3-8-7 56 (v1) TomEaves 3 35
(Michael Dods) *taken early to post: chsd wnr far side tl edgd rt and wknd over 1f out: last of 4 in gp* **10/1**

0056 **10** *nk* **Queen's Princess**[25] 3462 4-8-3 **54** oh6 ow3............(p) DavidBergin(7) 7 33
(John Wainwright) *towards rr stands' side: rdn and effrt over 2f out: nvr able to chal: 6th of 11 in gp* **66/1**

3-50 **11** *1 1/4* **Endless Applause**[34] 3184 3-8-6 **55**............................(v1) PaulQuinn 11 29
(Richard Whitaker) *dwlt: bhd stands' side: rdn 1/2-way: sme late hdwy: nvr on terms: 7th of 11 in gp* **12/1**

3025 **12** *6* **Brunswick Vale (IRE)**[14] 3848 3-8-4 **53**......................(b) KellyHarrison 6
(Paul Midgley) *towards rr stands' side: drvn along 1/2-way: btn fnl 2f: 8th of 11 in gp* **28/1**

0-36 **13** *1* **Toffee Nose**[13] 3893 5-8-7 **51** oh4............................... PatrickMathers 12
(Ron Barr) *cl up stands' side tl wknd over 2f out: 9th of 11 in gp* **20/1**

000 **14** *nk* **Busy Bimbo (IRE)**[25] 3462 3-7-12 **54** oh2 ow3..(p) MatthewHopkins(7) 8
(Alan Berry) *in tch on outside of stands' side gp tl rdn and wknd wl over 1f out: 10th of 11in gp* **66/1**

565 **15** *6* **John Coffey (IRE)**[26] 3438 3-8-6 **55**............................ AdrianNicholls 14
(David Nicholls) *chsd ldrs: drvn over 2f out: wknd wl over 1f out: last of 11 in gp* **8/1**[3]

1m 12.76s (-0.24) **Going Correction** -0.175s/f (Firm)
WFA 3 from 4yo+ 5lb **15** Ran SP% **131.2**
Speed ratings (Par 103): **94,93,92,91,87 87,82,82,82,81 80,72,70,70,62**
toteswingers 1&2 £37.00, 2&3 £18.80, 1&3 £24.60 CSF £316.27 CT £1106.42 TOTE £21.20: £4.50, £5.50, £2.20; EX 252.70.
Owner The Mutineers & Habton Farms **Bred** John Hutchinson **Trained** Great Habton, N Yorks

FOCUS
A fair maiden sprint handicap for 3yos and up. They split into two groups eventually, once those in the centre of the course realised they were in no-man's land and came over to the larger stands' side cluster. The first three horses home raced far side from stalls 4, 1 and 2 in a group of only four. The runner-up sets the standard.
John Coffey(IRE) Official explanation: jockey said gelding lost its action

4349 TYREGIANT.COM H'CAP (DIV I) 1m 1f 170y
5:30 (5:30) (Class 6) (0-60,60) 3-Y-0+ **£2,587** (£770; £384; £192) **Stalls** Low

Form RPR

5-20 **1** **Honoured (IRE)**[4] 4179 5-9-10 **56**..................................(t) TomEaves 8 68
(Michael Appleby) *prom: hdwy to ld over 1f out: rdn clr ins fnl f: eased cl home* **7/2**[1]

4400 **2** *2 1/2* **Border Bandit (USA)**[29] 3353 4-9-9 **60**..................... GarryWhillans(5) 5 66
(Tracy Waggott) *prom: effrt whn nt clr run over 2f out: hdwy over 1f out: chsd (clr) wnr wl ins fnl f: r.o* **12/1**

3063 **3** *1* **Market Puzzle (IRE)**[18] 3721 5-8-11 **48**..............(p) RachealKneller(5) 11 52
(Mark Brisbourne) *hld up in midfield on outside: hdwy on outside to ld over 2f out: hdd over 1f out: one pce ins fnl f* **13/2**[2]

56-0 **4** *3/4* **Think**[71] 2048 5-9-2 **48**...(t) PaddyAspell 9 51
(Clive Mulhall) *hld up: rdn along and hdwy 2f out: kpt on fnl f: nvr able to chal* **16/1**

00-0 **5** *hd* **Valentine's Gift**[46] 2791 4-9-0 **46** oh1............................ DuranFentiman 3 48
(Neville Bycroft) *hld up: hdwy and in tch wl over 1f out: kpt on fnl f: no imp* **33/1**

0362 **6** *1 1/4* **Mangham (IRE)**[13] 3889 7-9-10 **56**..............................(p) LeeNewman 14 55
(George Foster) *s.i.s: hld up towards rr: hdwy to chal over 2f out to over 1f out: outpcd ins fnl f* **13/2**[2]

30-0 **7** *nk* **Dandarrell**[12] 3914 5-9-3 **49**.. TonyHamilton 4 47
(Julie Camacho) *s.i.s: t.k.h: hld up: rdn over 2f out: styd on fnl f: nvr able to chal* **13/2**[2]

5043 **8** *1 1/2* **Sposalizio (IRE)**[31] 3277 5-8-9 **46** oh1...........................(p) LMcNiff(5) 12 41
(Colin Teague) *anticipated s: led to over 2f out sn rdn and outpcd* **11/1**

-104 **9** *1/2* **Ptolomeos**[37] 3081 9-9-2 **55**......................................(p) GemmaTutty(7) 2 49
(Sean Regan) *hld up: hdwy on outside over 2f out: wknd appr fnl f* **12/1**

00-3 **10** *3/4* **Red Mercury (IRE)**[52] 1673 4-9-6 **52**......................(b1) PaulMulrennan 6 45
(Ollie Pears) *t.k.h: hld up in tch: smooth hdwy to chal over 2f out: rdn and wknd appr fnl f* **12/1**

5-05 **11** *3/4* **Catramis**[18] 3727 3-8-8 **53**... DaleSwift(3) 1 44
(Geoffrey Oldroyd) *chsd ldrs: rdn whn nt clr run over 2f out: sn rdn and wknd* **8/1**[3]

0200 **12** *7* **Srimenanti**[26] 3440 4-9-0 **46** oh1....................................(p) MickyFenton 7 22
(Brian Rothwell) *prom tl rdn and wknd over 3f out* **50/1**

-020 **13** *1/2* **Penderyn**[37] 3081 5-9-0 **46** oh1................................ RobbieFitzpatrick 13 21
(Charles Smith) *cl up tl rdn and wknd fr 3f out* **25/1**

036 **14** *24* **Airmyles**[29] 3352 4-9-9 **58**... PaulPickard(3) 10
(Tracy Waggott) *in tch tl rdn and wknd over 3f out: sn lost tch: t.o* **22/1**

2m 5.54s (0.14) **Going Correction** -0.175s/f (Firm)
WFA 3 from 4yo+ 10lb **14** Ran SP% **123.7**
Speed ratings (Par 101): **92,90,89,88,88 87,87,86,85,85 84,78,78,59**
toteswingers 1&2 £16.30, 2&3 £19.00, 1&3 £5.30 CSF £47.11 CT £272.61 TOTE £4.60: £1.60, £7.00, £2.80; EX 77.90.
Owner Dallas Racing **Bred** Kilfrush Stud **Trained** Danethorpe, Notts

FOCUS
The first and slower division of a moderate handicap for 3yos and up. They appeared to go a steady gallop and the winning time reflects that observation. The second and third set the standard.

4350 TYREGIANT.COM H'CAP (DIV II) 1m 1f 170y
6:05 (6:05) (Class 6) (0-60,59) 3-Y-0+ **£2,587** (£770; £384; £192) **Stalls** Low

Form RPR

5-52 **1** **Celtic Step**[33] 3236 8-9-0 **48**... DaleSwift(3) 2 59
(Peter Niven) *in tch: effrt 2f out: shkn up to ld ins fnl f: kpt on wl: comf* **3/1**[1]

20-6 **2** *2* **Haka Dancer (USA)**[47] 2775 9-9-0 **45**..................(p) RussKennemore 14 52
(Philip Kirby) *chsd ldrs: rdn 4f out: rallied and led over 2f out: hdd ins fnl f: kpt on: nt pce of wnr* **25/1**

3004 **3** *5* **General Tufto**[38] 3022 7-9-3 **48**..............................(b) RobbieFitzpatrick 3 45
(Charles Smith) *hld up: rdn and outpcd over 3f out: styd on fr 2f out: nt pce to rch first two* **20/1**

006- **4** *1 1/2* **Carlitos Spirit (IRE)**[62] 7119 8-9-0 **50**............................(v) LMcNiff(5) 11 43
(Ian McInnes) *w ldr: led 1/2-way: edgd rt and hdd over 2f out: no ex over 1f out* **8/1**[3]

0-20 **5** *hd* **Petrocelli**[13] 3889 5-9-6 **54**... DominicFox(3) 1 47
(Wilf Storey) *hld up in tch: effrt and rdn 3f out: no imp fr 2f out* **12/1**

4000 **6** *hd* **Petsas Pleasure**[22] 3589 6-9-4 **56**.............................. JacobButterfield(7) 10 49
(Ollie Pears) *s.s: bhd: stdy hdwy on outside over 2f out: rdn and no imp fnl f* **14/1**

6612 **7** *2* **Izzet**[12] 3914 4-9-13 **58**.. PatrickMathers 9 46+
(Ron Barr) *s.i.s: bhd: rdn and hdwy on outside over 2f out: btn fnl f* **3/1**[1]

0050 **8** *8* **Decadence**[22] 3577 4-9-0 **45**.. MickyFenton 5 17
(Nigel Tinkler) *led to 1/2-way: cl up tl rdn and wknd 2f out* **40/1**

0-66 **9** *1 3/4* **Catcher Of Dreams (IRE)**[13] 3889 6-8-7 **45**.....(p) MatthewHopkins(7) 6 13
(George Foster) *in tch tl rdn: edgd rt and wknd over 2f out* **12/1**

-536 **10** *1* **Sinatramania**[29] 3355 5-9-10 **55**... TomEaves 12 21
(Tracy Waggott) *t.k.h: hld up: stdy hdwy over 3f out: edgd rt and wknd 2f out* **6/1**[2]

530 **11** *7* **Nolecce**[4] 4179 5-10-0 **59**...(p) J-PGuillambert 13 10
(Richard Guest) *hld up: rdn over 3f out: btn fnl 2f* **9/1**

6300 **12** *1 3/4* **Norton Girl**[29] 3355 4-9-0 **45**.. PaulMulrennan 4
(Tracy Waggott) *chsd ldrs tl edgd rt and wknd fr 2f out* **25/1**

-500 **13** *6* **Bells Of Berlin**[16] 3781 3-8-6 **47**...............................(vt) DuranFentiman 7
(Alan McCabe) *s.i.s: bhd and sn pushed along: struggling fr over 4f out* **25/1**

50-0 **14** *4 1/2* **Northgate Lodge (USA)**[29] 3356 7-8-9 **47**.......... RobertDodsworth(7) 8
(Mel Brittain) *plld hrd towards rr: struggling over 4f out: sn btn: t.o* **50/1**

2m 4.42s (-0.98) **Going Correction** -0.175s/f (Firm)
WFA 3 from 4yo+ 10lb **14** Ran SP% **128.1**
Speed ratings (Par 101): **96,94,90,89,89 88,87,80,79,78 73,71,66,63**
toteswingers 1&2 £25.00, 2&3 £22.20, 1&3 £8.60 CSF £97.65 CT £1353.51 TOTE £4.60: £2.10, £6.30, £6.50; EX 86.70.
Owner Mrs Muriel Ward **Bred** Woodcote Stud Ltd **Trained** Barton-le-Street, N Yorks

FOCUS
The second instalment of a moderate handicap for 3yos and up. The winning time was significantly better than the first division, and the form is similar but perhaps that bit more solid. The first pair came clear and the winner is weighted to win again.
Izzet Official explanation: jockey said gelding never travelled
Norton Girl Official explanation: jockey said filly hung right in straight
T/Plt: £534.70 to a £1 stake. Pool of £57169.79 - 78.05 winning tickets. T/Qpdt: £42.10 to a £1 stake. Pool of £4280.44, 75.11 winning tickets. RY

4351 - 4353a (Foreign Racing) - See Raceform Interactive

3672 CURRAGH (R-H)
Saturday, July 21

OFFICIAL GOING: Heavy (soft in places)

4354a KARE RACE DAY MINSTREL STKS (GROUP 3) 7f
3:45 (3:45) 3-Y-0+ **£31,145** (£9,104; £4,312)

RPR

1 **Takar (IRE)**[30] 3322 3-9-2 108....................................(t) JohnnyMurtagh 1 102+
(John M Oxx, Ire) *racd in 2nd tl sent on over 2f out: sn clr: easily* **1/7**[1]

2 *3* **Singing Bird (IRE)**[10] 3983 3-8-13 93............................ WayneLordan 2 91
(David Wachman, Ire) *hld up in 3rd: chsd wnr fnl 2f but nvr on terms* **10/1**[3]

3 *11* **Among Equals**[38] 3055 3-9-2 95...................................... CO'Donoghue 3 64+
(A P O'Brien, Ire) *led tl hdd appr 2f out: lost action and sn dropped away* **7/1**[2]

1m 33.08s (2.28) **Going Correction** +0.50s/f (Yiel) **3** Ran SP% **109.1**
Speed ratings: **106,102,90**
CSF £2.43 TOTE £1.10; DF 2.10.
Owner H H Aga Khan **Bred** His Highness The Aga Khan's Studs S C **Trained** Currabeg, Co Kildare

FOCUS
A truly awful Group 3. The winner is a genuine Group-performer but his two rivals were massively inferior and the race itself was as straightforward as it looked beforehand. The runner-up has been rated to her best.

NOTEBOOK
Takar(IRE) has always looked classy and, had he not produced a pretty tame effort in the Irish 2,000 Guineas here in May, he would be very high in the pecking order in the 3yo division over 1m. He had his confidence restored at Leopardstown on deep ground and handled the testing conditions here too. He tracked Among Equals but cruised past 3f out and was always holding the runner-up. It wasn't hugely impressive, but it didn't have to be, and he was probably dossing a bit in front. He'll head for the Desmond Stakes now and is likely to take some beating in that, especially if the ground continues like this.
Singing Bird(IRE) showed her liking for this type of ground when winning well on debut over this C&D. She was given a nice ride here, allowed to settle at the rear of the three runners and she was second best by quite some considerable margin. She could turn out to be useful when things fall her way.
Among Equals didn't go off fast and perhaps tried to catch the long odds-on favourite out for speed. That didn't happen and the result was a foregone conclusion from 3f out.

4355 - 4358a (Foreign Racing) - See Raceform Interactive

3654 JAGERSRO (R-H)
Saturday, July 21

OFFICIAL GOING: Dirt: standard

4359a SVENSKT OAKS (CONDITIONS) (3YO FILLIES) (DIRT) 1m 4f
6:11 (12:00) 3-Y-0
£36,073 (£16,593; £7,214; £5,050; £3,607; £2,164)

RPR

1 **Summertime (DEN)**[27] 3-9-4 0.................................. ManuelMartinez 3
(Francisco Castro, Sweden) **5/1**[2]

2 *2* **Blue Saphire (DEN)**[27] 3-9-4 0................................. MartinRodriguez 1
(Bettina Wilson, Denmark) **38/1**

3 *1 1/4* **Beauchamp Castle**[10] 3968 3-9-4 0..........................(b) ElioneChaves 6
(Hans Adielsson) *trckd ldrs: 5th towards outside 1/2-way: pushed along to hold pl 2 1/2f out: c wdst of all bnd into st: kpt on u.p fnl 1 1/2f: nt pce to chal first two* **145/10**

4 *1 1/2* **Zegna (GER)** 3-9-4 0.. EspenSki 9
(Fredrik Reuterskiold, Sweden) **163/10**

5 *1 1/2* **Magica Von Tryll (GER)**[30] 3-9-4 0.............................. FJohansson 7
(Wido Neuroth, Norway) **183/10**

6 *1/2* **Novagem (SWE)** 3-9-4 0... JacobJohansen 10
(Mikael Tjernstrom, Sweden) **18/1**

7 *nse* **Hanna (SWE)**[27] 3-9-4 0.. CarlosLopez 5
(Bent Olsen, Denmark) **35/1**

8 *1/2* **Truly Charming (GER)** 3-9-4 0.......................... Per-AndersGraberg 12
(Fredrik Reuterskiold, Sweden) **83/10**[3]

9 *hd* **Madame Jane (IRE)**[349] 4841 3-9-4 0.......................... ShaneKarlsson 8
(Ole Larsen, Sweden) **29/1**

10 *2 1/2* **Mrs Perry (SWE)** 3-9-4 0.. DannyPatil 2
(Hans-Inge Larsen, Sweden) **44/1**

11 *nse* **Matauri Pearl (IRE)**[30] 3-9-4 0.................................. ValmirDeAzeredo 11
(Fredrik Reuterskiold, Sweden) **4/5**[1]

12 1 1/4 **Imagine (DEN)** 3-9-4 0 OliverWilson 13
(Soren Jensen, Denmark) 92/10
2m 35.4s (155.40) 12 Ran SP% 126.4
PARI-MUTUEL (all including 1sek stake): WIN 5.95; PLACE 2.24, 9.06, 4.77; SF 157.23.
Owner Kentaur A/S **Bred** Light Valley Stud **Trained** Sweden

4360 - 4361a (Foreign Racing) - See Raceform Interactive

4317 ASCOT (R-H)
Sunday, July 22

OFFICIAL GOING: Straight course - good; round course - good to soft (stands' side 8.5, centre 8.7, far side 8.4, round 7.0)
Wind: Moderate, half-against Weather: dry, bright spells

4362 ANDERS FOUNDATION EBF CROCKER BULTEEL MAIDEN STKS (C&G) 6f
2:15 (2:16) (Class 2) 2-Y-O £12,938 (£3,850; £1,924; £962) Stalls Centre

Form				RPR
	1		**Moohaajim (IRE)** 2-9-0 0 AndreaAtzeni 9 (Marco Botti) *trckd ldrs and travelled wl: rdn and qcknd to ld over 1f out: clr and r.o wl ins fnl f* 13/2	84+
	2	1 3/4	**Sea Shanty (USA)** 2-9-0 0 RichardHughes 3 (Richard Hannon) *hld up in tch: rdn and sltly outpcd over 1f out: swtchd lft and rallied ins fnl f: r.o strly fnl 100yds: wnt 2nd cl home* 9/2[3]	79+
	3	hd	**Rivellino** 2-9-0 0 JimCrowley 10 (Mrs K Burke) *restless in stalls: in tch: effrt and rdn over 1f out: chsd wnr jst ins fnl f: r.o but a hld: lost 2nd last strides* 7/2[1]	78+
	4	nse	**Exotic Guest** 2-9-0 0 IanMongan 1 (George Margarson) *hld up in tch in midfield: rdn and effrt u.p to chse ldrs 1f out: styd on same pce ins fnl f* 40/1	78
	5	1/2	**Amralah (IRE)** 2-9-0 0 JamesDoyle 11 (Mick Channon) *s.i.s: hld up in tch in rr: effrt and n.m.r over 1f out: swtchd lft and hdwy 1f out: styd on wl fnl 100yds* 11/2	77+
	6	hd	**Saint Jerome (IRE)** 2-9-0 0 HayleyTurner 8 (Marcus Tregoning) *in tch in midfield: rdn and sltly outpcd over 1f out: n.m.r ent fnl f: rallied and styd on fnl 100yds* 22/1	76+
	7	1 1/2	**Excuse To Linger** 2-9-0 0 FrankieDettori 5 (Jeremy Noseda) *led: rdn and hdd over 1f out: stl pressing ldrs but unable qck 1f out: wknd fnl 100yds* 11/1	71
	8	hd	**Purcell (IRE)** 2-9-0 0 JimmyFortune 2 (Andrew Balding) *restless in stalls: chsd ldrs: rdn and pressed ldrs over 1f out: no ex 1f out: wknd ins fnl f* 14/1	71
	9	1 1/4	**Shaishee (USA)** 2-9-0 0 PaulHanagan 12 (Charles Hills) *hld up in tch: rdn and effrt over 1f out: unable qck ent fnl f: wknd fnl 100yds* 4/1[2]	67
	10	1	**Izzy Boy (USA)** 2-9-0 0 JoeFanning 4 (Mark Johnston) *racd keenly: w ldr: rdn and unable qck over 1f out: wknd ins fnl f* 16/1	64
	11	1	**Shiatsu** 2-9-0 0 SeanLevey 7 (Richard Hannon) *wnt bdly rt s: hld up in tch: swtchd rt and effrt 2f out: no imp over 1f out: wknd fnl f* 20/1	61+
	P		**Sabre Tiger** 2-9-0 0 NeilCallan 13 (Alan Jarvis) *wnt bdly lft s: a bhd: rdn 1/2-way: lost action over 2f out: p.u and dismntd 2f out: fatally injured* 50/1	

1m 16.18s (1.68) **Going Correction** +0.125s/f (Good) 12 Ran SP% 123.5
Speed ratings (Par 100): **93,90,90,90,89 89,87,87,85,84 82,**
Tote Swingers 1&2 £9.00, 2&3 £6.60, 1&3 £7.90 CSF £36.06 TOTE £9.30: £2.70, £2.10, £2.20; EX 47.50 Trifecta £541.40 Part won. Pool £731.74 - 0.40 winning units..
Owner Sheikh Mohammed Bin Khalifa Al Maktoum **Bred** Castlemartin Sky & Skymarc Farm **Trained** Newmarket, Suffolk

FOCUS
Round course rail between 9f to home straight moved out 2m and consequently 2yds added to Old Mile, 8yds to 10f race and 10yds to 12f &16f races. The official going was unchanged despite warm and sunny conditions and the jockeys reported it was riding pretty much as described. This newcomers' race has been a source of handicappers rather than Pattern performers in recent years. The prize was big for this Racing Post Yearling Bonus race and the form is rated a shade positively.

NOTEBOOK
Moohaajim(IRE) ◆, a 200,000gns first foal of a mare who won her only race as a juvenile, is related to Group and Graded winners and gave the impression he might be able to join that list and justify his purchase price with a taking debut. He tracked the pace and found plenty when asked, eventually running out a cosy winner. He looks one to keep on-side on this evidence. (op 7-1 tchd 6-1)
Sea Shanty(USA) was held up and did not get the clearest of runs before finishing best of all. The first foal of a 6f-1m winner, including at Listed level, he can be expected to come on considerably for the outing. (op 5-1 tchd 11-2)
Rivellino, a speedily bred 57,000gns breeze-up purchase, made an encouraging debut, coming through to chase the winner before his effort flattened out late on. (op 5-1)
Exotic Guest was held up on the far side of the back and showed a good attitude to keep on under pressure, just missing out on a place. A 67,000gns half-brother to six winners from a middle-distance family, he looks likely to appreciate further, despite being by a sprinter. (op 33-1 tchd 50-1 in a place)
Amralah(IRE) was held up out the back before staying on in the latter stages. A 50,000gns colt from the family of Reams Of Verse and Elmaamul, he is another likely to be seen to better effect over longer trips. (op 5-1 tchd 9-2)
Saint Jerome(IRE), the £55,000 first foal of a dual 1m2f winner, stayed on quite nicely in the closing stages and should be better for the experience and a slightly longer trip. (op 25-1)
Shaishee(USA), a $325,000 first foal of a multiple winner in North America, was sent off second favourite and tracked the pace, but did not pick up when asked to make his effort. (op 7-2)

4363 GL EVENTS OWEN BROWN STKS (H'CAP) 1m 4f
2:50 (2:52) (Class 2) (0-105,104) 3-Y-O+
£12,450 (£3,728; £1,864; £932; £466; £234) Stalls Low

Form				RPR
0424	1		**Fattsota**[16] 3826 4-9-1 **91** MircoDemuro 4 (Marco Botti) *sn led and mde rest: rdn and kpt finding ex fr 2f out: styd on wl and in command fnl 100yds: eased nr fin* 7/1	100
-454	2	1 1/2	**Cill Rialaig**[16] 3825 7-9-6 **96** JimmyFortune 10 (Hughie Morrison) *hld up in last trio: clsd and gng wl over 2f out: rdn and effrt 2f out: chsd wnr 1f out: styd on but no imp fnl 100yds* 9/2[2]	103
/42-	3	1 1/2	**Willing Foe (USA)**[260] 7297 5-9-11 **101** FrankieDettori 7 (Saeed Bin Suroor) *hld up in midfield: rdn and hdwy over 2f out: chsd ldrs and edgd rt ent fnl f: continued edging lft styd on same pce after* 7/2[1]	105
4043	4	nk	**Barbican**[22] 3632 4-10-0 **104** RichardHughes 9 (Alan Bailey) *chsd ldng pair: wnt 2nd ent fnl 3f: rdn and tried to chal wnr 2f out: no ex and btn 1f out: styd on same pce after* 15/2	108
1-02	5	1/2	**Rawaki (IRE)**[22] 3642 4-8-9 **85** DavidProbert 8 (Andrew Balding) *in tch in midfield: rdn and effrt over 2f out: styng on same pce whn n.m.r 1f out: no imp fnl f: swtchd lft cl home* 5/1[3]	88
-013	6	2 3/4	**Tropical Beat**[16] 3826 4-9-2 **92** EddieAhern 6 (John Gosden) *hld up in last trio: swtchd rt and effrt over 2f out: nt clr run 2f out: swtchd lft and rdn over 1f out: no imp* 11/2	91
-001	7	8	**Rock A Doodle Doo (IRE)**[18] 3766 5-9-7 **97** PaulHanagan 11 (William Jarvis) *hld up in last trio: effrt on outer bnd over 2f out: rdn and edgd rt over 1f out: sn wknd: eased towards fin* 8/1	83
3030	8	7	**Oceanway (USA)**[20] 3417 4-8-12 **88** JoeFanning 3 (Mark Johnston) *chsd ldr tl ent fnl 3f: struggling u.p 2f out: wknd over 1f out: bhd ins fnl f* 25/1	63
1/6	9	9	**Starluck (IRE)**[113] 1139 7-9-5 **95** LiamKeniry 1 (David Arbuthnot) *t.k.h: hld up in tch towards rr: rdn and no rspnse over 2f out: wknd 2f out: bhd and eased ins fnl f* 20/1	55
260/	10	12	**Adelar (GER)**[840] 6506 7-9-13 **103** JamesDoyle 5 (Venetia Williams) *hld up in midfield: rdn 3f out: struggling u.p over 2f out: sn wknd: wl bhd and eased ins fnl f: t.o* 66/1	44

2m 31.17s (-1.33) **Going Correction** +0.125s/f (Good) 10 Ran SP% 117.9
Speed ratings (Par 109): **109,108,107,106,106 104,99,94,88,80**
Tote Swingers 1&2 £7.00, 2&3 £4.30, 1&3 £6.30 CSF £38.27 CT £130.90 TOTE £8.90: £3.10, £1.90, £1.70; EX 45.50 Trifecta £277.10 Pool £1,576.47 - 4.21 winning units..
Owner Scuderia Rencati Srl **Bred** Azienda Agricola Francesca **Trained** Newmarket, Suffolk

FOCUS
A high-class handicap run at a fair gallop and in a decent time. Solid form but the race lacked improvers.

NOTEBOOK
Fattsota made all under a fine ride from Mirco Demuro. Back on better ground and trying his longest trip to-date, he reverted to positive tactics and they seemed to suit, as he found plenty for pressure to beat off several challengers in the last 2f. His half-brother Falbrav progressed as he got older and, although obviously not in that class, he could follow suit. (op 15-2 tchd 8-1)
Cill Rialaig, who is in-foal to Pastoral Pursuits and was probably having her final race, came from the back of the field with what looked a winning run but the leader found extra and she was held in the last half-furlong. A winner at Royal Ascot and Listed placed, she has won in excess of £97,000 in her career and is a credit to connections. (tchd 5-1)
Willing Foe(USA) is lightly raced but goes well fresh and was sent off favourite. He came to have his chance in the straight but drifted right under pressure and had no more to offer in the last furlong. (op 4-1)
Barbican was 2-2 on this track before this and, although proving difficult to load and drifting in the betting, ran his race and looked to be running back into form. He really hit his stride from August onwards last season and that may prove to be the case again this year. (op 6-1)
Rawaki(IRE), raised 2lb for his good effort at Windsor, tracked the pace and was held but staying on when short of room inside the last furlong. He is inexperienced for his age and might be worth trying over a little further. (op 13-2)
Tropical Beat, stepping up in distance, was held up but failed to land a blow. (op 7-1)
Rock A Doodle Doo(IRE) was forced to race wide from his outside draw and his effort turning for home proved short-lived. (op 7-1)

4364 BETFAIR. DON'T SETTLE FOR LESS H'CAP 6f
3:25 (3:25) (Class 4) (0-85,85) 3-Y-O £6,469 (£1,925; £962; £481) Stalls Centre

Form				RPR
122	1		**Nassau Storm**[22] 3639 3-9-6 **84** JimCrowley 11 (William Knight) *hld up in tch in rr: rdn and effrt over 1f out: chal 1f out: led fnl 100yds: r.o strly and gng away at fin* 3/1[1]	94+
041	2	1 1/2	**Nocturn**[20] 3702 3-9-0 **78** JimmyFortune 8 (Jeremy Noseda) *chsd ldrs: rdn and effrt over 1f out: ev ch jst ins fnl f: battling for 2nd and styd on same pce fnl 100yds* 4/1[2]	83
-053	3	shd	**Generalyse**[18] 3762 3-8-7 **71** (p) JohnFahy 7 (Ben De Haan) *chsd ldrs: rdn and chal over 1f out: led jst ins fnl f: hdd and styd on same pce fnl 100yds* 25/1	76
341	4	3 1/4	**Lady Gibraltar**[22] 3618 3-8-6 **77** (v) MichaelJMMurphy(7) 5 (Alan Jarvis) *sddle slipped sn after s: sn led: rdn over 1f out: hdd jst ins fnl f: wknd fnl 100yds* 10/1	72
-402	5	1/2	**Jack Who's He (IRE)**[27] 3445 3-9-7 **85** RichardHughes 3 (David Evans) *hld up in tch in rr: rdn and effrt whn hung rt over 1f out: no prog and wl hld ins fnl f* 4/1[2]	78
2264	6	1 1/4	**Royal Reyah**[27] 3445 3-8-11 **75** FergusSweeney 4 (Stuart Kittow) *chsd ldr: rdn and pressed ldr over 1f out: sn drvn and unable qck: wknd ins fnl f* 8/1	64
0242	7	3/4	**Church Music (IRE)**[15] 3861 3-9-5 **83** (p) MircoDemuro 1 (Michael Scudamore) *in tch in rr: hdwy 1/2-way: rdn and effrt to chse ldrs over 1f out: no ex 1f out: wknd ins fnl f* 12/1	70
3-13	8	1 3/4	**Fast Finian (IRE)**[27] 3445 3-8-9 **73** PaulHanagan 6 (Paul D'Arcy) *t.k.h: hld up in tch: rdn and unable qck over 1f out: wknd 1f out* 13/2[3]	54
200	9	2	**Sans Loi (IRE)**[50] 2714 3-8-13 **84** (p) WilliamTwiston-Davies(7) 2 (Alan McCabe) *awkward leaving stalls and slowly away: t.k.h: hld up in rr: hdwy into midfield 1/2-way: rdn over 1f out: wknd 1f out* 12/1	59

1m 15.17s (0.67) **Going Correction** +0.125s/f (Good) 9 Ran SP% 117.8
Speed ratings (Par 102): **100,98,97,93,92 91,90,87,85**
Tote Swingers 1&2 £3.20, 2&3 £21.10, 1&3 £14.40 CSF £15.28 CT £228.05 TOTE £4.30: £1.90, £1.50, £6.70; EX 12.50 Trifecta £93.00 Pool £866.05 - 6.89 winning units..
Owner The Oil Men Partnership **Bred** Glebe Stud & J F Dean **Trained** Patching, W Sussex

FOCUS
A good, competitive 3yo sprint that has thrown up a couple of subsequent Listed winners in recent seasons. The early pace was not strong. The form is rated around the third.
Lady Gibraltar Official explanation: jockey said saddle slipped

4365 KELTBRAY H'CAP 1m 2f
4:00 (4:02) (Class 3) (0-95,95) 3-Y-O+
£8,092 (£2,423; £1,211; £605; £302; £152) Stalls Low

Form				RPR
-243	1		**Ahzeemah (IRE)**[37] 3124 3-8-9 **86** (p) SilvestreDeSousa 6 (Saeed Bin Suroor) *in tch: chsd ldrs and swtchd lft over 1f out: rdn to ld 1f out: styd on wl fnl f: rdn out* 10/3[1]	94
0002	2	3/4	**Las Verglas Star (IRE)**[31] 3306 4-9-2 **86** LeeTopliss(3) 1 (Richard Fahey) *pushed along leaving stalls: in tch in midfield: nt clr run and shuffled bk towards rr 2f out: swtchd lft and hdwy over 1f out: r.o wl u.p to go 2nd towards fin* 10/1	94+
2406	3	1/2	**Tinshu (IRE)**[16] 3826 6-9-3 **84** (p) DaneO'Neill 2 (Derek Haydn Jones) *hld up in tch towards rr: effrt on inner and travelling strly whn nt clr run wl over 1f out: swtchd lft and hdwy jst ins fnl f: running on whn nt clr run again and swtchd rt fnl 75yds: r.o strly after* 20/1	91+

0010 **4** *hd* **Cool Macavity (IRE)**[16] 3826 4-9-4 **85**........................ RobertWinston 10 90
(Charles Hills) *hld up in tch in last quartet: hdwy on outer 2f out: rdn and chsd wnr 1f out: styd on same pce fnl 100yds and lost 2 pls towards fin* **12/1**

2211 **5** *½* **Lieutenant Kojak**[10] 3997 4-8-13 **80**.................................. EddieAhern 8 84+
(Peter Charalambous) *in tch towards rr: nt clr run 2f out: swtchd lft and hdwy over 1f out: chsd ldrs and drvn jst ins fnl f: kpt on* **10/1**

1642 **6** *1* **Tilsworth Glenboy**[5] 4199 5-8-11 **78**........................... FrederikTylicki 4 80
(J R Jenkins) *hld up in tch in midfield: nt clr run briefly 2f out: rdn and hdwy to chse ldrs over 1f out: no ex and one pce ins fnl f* **12/1**

3000 **7** *hd* **Sirvino**[22] 3642 7-10-0 **95**... PhillipMakin 14 97
(David Barron) *slowly away and pushed along leaving stalls: hld up in tch in rr: rdn and hdwy on outer over 1f out: kpt on ins fnl f but nvr gng pce to rch ldrs* **11/1**

5031 **8** *¾* **Union Island (IRE)**[22] 3628 6-8-13 **83**............................. DaleSwift(3) 11 83
(Brian Ellison) *in tch: effrt to chse ldrs 3f out: rdn and unable qck 2f out: drvn and no ex 1f out: wknd fnl 100yds* **8/1**

1-10 **9** *¾* **Eshtibaak (IRE)**[113] 1139 4-9-13 **94**................................ PaulHanagan 3 93+
(John Gosden) *in tch: nt clr run 2f out: rdn and effrt over 1f out: nt clr run again ent fnl f: unable to make hdwy and nt pushed along ins fnl f* **9/2**[2]

0130 **10** *½* **Weapon Of Choice (IRE)**[36] 3157 4-9-10 **91**................. IanMongan 12 89
(Stuart Kittow) *chsd ldrs: wnt 2nd 5f out: drvn to ld over 1f out: hdd 1f out: wknd ins fnl f* **14/1**

2010 **11** *6* **Megalala (IRE)**[18] 3767 11-9-2 **83**..................................... KieranO'Neill 9 69
(John Bridger) *led: rdn 3f out: hdd over 1f out: fdd fnl f* **40/1**

140- **12** *4 ½* **You've Been Mowed**[267] 7178 6-8-8 **80**................ MatthewLawson(5) 5 57
(Richard Price) *chsd ldr tl 5f out: wknd u.p over 1f out: fdd fnl f* **40/1**

122 **13** *4* **Prince Of Sorrento**[24] 3534 5-9-11 **92**........................ StevieDonohoe 13 61
(Lee Carter) *in tch in midfield on outer: rdn and no imp 2f out: wknd and dropped to rr over 1f out: fdd fnl f* **15/2**[3]

2m 7.57s (0.17) **Going Correction** +0.125s/f (Good)
WFA 3 from 4yo+ 10lb **13** Ran SP% **122.3**
Speed ratings (Par 107): **104,103,103,102,102 101,101,100,100,99 95,91,88**
Tote Swingers 1&2 £10.10, 2&3 £52.90, 1&3 £19.50 CSF £37.64 CT £590.03 TOTE £3.70: £1.30, £4.00, £6.40; EX 40.00 Trifecta £367.30 Pool £2,184.23 - 4.40 winning units..
Owner Godolphin **Bred** G O'Brien **Trained** Newmarket, Suffolk

FOCUS

This decent handicap has been won by some useful performers and 3yos have a particularly good record, which was improved when the only runner of that age prevailed. However, there were several hard-luck stories in behind, notably the second and third. The pace was strong.

NOTEBOOK

Ahzeemah(IRE), who ran the subsequent Derby second to half a length at Newmarket in April, had been beaten twice on softer going since but the drying ground here came in his favour. He got the gaps at the right time when others didn't and did enough to justify favouritism. He might find it difficult to follow up of a higher mark, although better ground may help in that respect. (op 9-2 tchd 3-1)

Las Verglas Star(IRE) ◆, 7lb better off with the fifth compared with their Ripon running, reversed that form despite looking unlucky. He was short of room 2f out before getting a gap towards the outside and finishing well, but not quite in time to catch the winner. His turn does not look far away. (op 7-1)

Tinshu(IRE) ◆ was another who was unlucky, as she was held up and failed to get a run when required over a furlong out. Once in the clear she finished really well and would have probably won with a clear passage. She is likely to come back here next week and might be able to gain quick compensation with better luck in running. (op 16-1 tchd 14-1)

Cool Macavity(IRE) was held up at the back but made smooth progress around the outside of his field, avoiding any trouble. He had every chance but his effort petered out inside the last and he was run out of the places.

Lieutenant Kojak has been running really well on soft going but did not perform badly on this faster surface, finishing on the heels of the placed horses in a messy contest. He looks to be holding his form, but much depends on whether the ground gets really fast in the short term.

Tilsworth Glenboy, another who ideally prefers softer ground than he got here, ran a decent race and helps set the level of the form.

Eshtibaak(IRE), having his first start since March, tracked the pace but was locked in with nowhere to go for most of the straight, which was confirmed by his jockey. This effort can be discounted. Official explanation: jockey said colt was denied a clear run (op 5-1)

4366 BETTER PRICES ON BETFAIR MOBILE MAIDEN FILLIES' STKS 1m (S)

4:35 (4:40) (Class 4) 3-Y-O **£5,175** (£1,540; £769; £384) **Stalls** Centre

Form RPR

6-42 **1** **Dalkova**[25] 3507 3-9-0 81..(t) RichardHughes 14 84
(Richard Hannon) *in tch: rdn over 2f out: drvn to chse ldrs over 1f out: chal ins fnl f: led fnl 50yds: r.o wl and forged ahd cl home* **11/4**[2]

6 **2** *¾* **Light Shine**[32] 3279 3-9-0 0.. RobertHavlin 12 81
(John Gosden) *pressed ldrs: chsd ldr 1/2-way: rdn and ev ch whn edgd rt jst over 1f out: unable qck fnl 100yds* **2/1**[1]

553 **3** *hd* **Khazeena**[45] 2848 3-9-0 79... PaulHanagan 5 81
(William Haggas) *w ldr tl led 1/2-way: rdn 2f out: hrd pressed over 1f out: battled on u.p tl hdd and no ex fnl 50yds* **7/2**[3]

4 **4** *4* **Eponastone (IRE)**[21] 3666 3-9-0 0................................ FrankieDettori 13 71
(Gerard Butler) *in tch in midfield: rdn 3f out: hdwy u.p over 1f out: kpt on but no imp on ldrs fnl f* **12/1**

4 **4** *dht* **Urban Daydream (IRE)**[16] 3811 3-9-0 0.......................... NeilCallan 10 71
(Roger Varian) *led tl 1/2-way: pressed ldrs after: rdn over 2f out: no ex over 1f out and btn ent fnl f: wknd ins fnl f* **12/1**

6 **6** *1 ½* **Mama Quilla (USA)**[21] 3666 3-9-0 0................................... LiamJones 1 68
(William Haggas) *t.k.h: in tch: hdwy to chse ldrs and rdn 3f out: no ex and btn over 1f out: wknd fnl f* **18/1**

0 **7** *¾* **Divea**[13] 3918 3-9-0 0.. RobertWinston 7 66+
(Charles Hills) *s.i.s: hld up in rr: hdwy into midfield: rdn and m green 2f out: wknd over 1f out* **33/1**

8 *9* **Elsie Bay** 3-9-0 0.. DaneO'Neill 8 44
(Mark Usher) *hld up towards rr: rdn and struggling 1/2-way: no ch w ldrs fnl 2f* **100/1**

00 **9** *¾* **Regalo Rosado**[29] 3398 3-9-0 0.. KieranO'Neill 6 43
(Mike Murphy) *wnt lft s: t.k.h: hld up in rr: lost tch over 3f out: plugged on past btn horses fnl f: n.d* **100/1**

10 *1 ½* **Rokcella** 3-9-0 0.. JohnFahy 11 39
(Clive Cox) *in tch tl lost pl 1/2-way: bhd fnl 2f* **40/1**

6 **11** *4* **Treasured Dream**[35] 3189 3-9-0 0.................................... EddieAhern 2 29+
(Amanda Perrett) *chsd ldrs: rdn over 2f out: struggling and btn whn short of room over 1f out: sn wknd and eased ins fnl f* **20/1**

12 *¾* **Vivacious Way** 3-9-0 0.. JimmyFortune 3 28
(Andrew Balding) *t.k.h: hld up towards rr: rdn and struggling 3f out: edgd rt and bhd wl over 1f out* **25/1**

13 *nk* **Fever Few** 3-9-0 0.. BrettDoyle 9 27
(Jane Chapple-Hyam) *chsd ldrs tl 1/2-way: sn rdn and lost pl: bhd fnl 2f* **50/1**

06 **14** *1 ½* **Not Now Katie**[17] 3786 3-9-0 0.. LiamKeniry 4 23
(Chris Gordon) *in tch in midfield: rdn and struggling over 2f out: sn wknd: bhd fnl f* **33/1**

1m 42.22s (1.42) **Going Correction** +0.125s/f (Good) **14** Ran SP% **123.7**
Speed ratings (Par 99): **97,96,96,92,92 90,89,80,80,78 74,73,73,72**
Tote Swingers 1&2 £2.30, 2&3 £2.50, 1&3 £3.00 CSF £8.27 TOTE £3.80: £1.40, £1.40, £1.60; EX 10.90 Trifecta £27.10 Pool £1,985.23 - 54.10 winning units..
Owner Andrew Tinkler **Bred** Balmerino Bloodstock & Plantation Stud **Trained** East Everleigh, Wilts

FOCUS

Not much form on offer in this 3yo fillies' maiden but a couple with official ratings around 80 set a reasonable standard and they fought out the finish with the favourite. The race was sound run and the form makes a fair bit of sense.

4367 SIS SPRINT (H'CAP) 5f

5:05 (5:12) (Class 2) 3-Y-O+

£28,012 (£8,388; £4,194; £2,097; £1,048; £526) **Stalls** Centre

Form RPR

0243 **1** **Taajub (IRE)**[17] 3771 5-8-10 **92**.. EddieAhern 12 102
(Peter Crate) *racd far side: in tch: rdn and effrt to chse ldrs over 1f out: led fnl 100yds: kpt on u.p* **14/1**

5253 **2** *hd* **Mass Rally (IRE)**[8] 4086 5-8-8 **90**.......................(b) PaulMulrennan 11 99
(Michael Dods) *racd far side: hld up in midfield: smooth hdwy over 1f out: cruised upsides wnr ins fnl f: shkn up and nt qckn nr fin: 2nd of 15 in gp* **9/1**[2]

406 **3** *½* **Fratellino**[51] 2664 5-8-8 **90**..(t) RobertWinston 1 97
(Alan McCabe) *racd far side: in tch in midfield: rdn and effrt to chse ldrs over 1f out: kpt on wl u.p ins fnl f: 3rd of 15 in gp* **33/1**

0361 **4** *nk* **Jedward (IRE)**[10] 4013 5-8-5 **87**...................................... PaulHanagan 4 93
(Richard Fahey) *racd far side: chsd ldr: rdn and ev ch over 1f out: led ins fnl f: hdd and no ex fnl 100yds: 4th of 15 in gp* **10/1**[3]

0-05 **5** *hd* **Dungannon**[29] 3371 5-9-1 **97**.. JimmyFortune 22 105+
(Andrew Balding) *racd nr side: hld up towards rr: rdn and hdwy over 1f out: led gp and chsd overall ldrs fnl 100yds: kpt on wl: 1st of 6 in gp* **7/2**[1]

-000 **6** *hd* **Barnet Fair**[22] 3641 4-8-6 **88**.. KierenFox 18 93
(Richard Guest) *uns rdr and galloped loose to s: racd far side: hld up in rr: rdn and hdwy over 1f out: kpt on wl ins fnl f: 5th of 15 in gp* **12/1**

1153 **7** *nse* **Jack Dexter**[29] 3374 3-7-7 **84**.. NeilFarley(5) 8 89+
(Jim Goldie) *racd far side: towards rr and rdn along after 2f: hdwy over 1f out: styd on wl ins fnl f: nt rch ldrs: 6th of 15 in gp* **12/1**

0120 **8** *½* **Judge 'n Jury**[15] 3877 8-9-4 **105**................................(t) DarrenEgan(5) 10 108
(Ronald Harris) *racd far side: overall ldr: rdn over 1f out: hdd ins fnl f: no ex fnl 100yds: 7th of 15 in gp* **16/1**

0505 **9** *½* **Courageous (IRE)**[3] 4231 6-7-12 **80** oh2......................... KellyHarrison 5 81+
(Milton Bradley) *racd far side: bhd: hdwy over 1f out: styng on wl whn nt clr run fnl 75yds: unable to chal: 8th of 15 in gp* **25/1**

10-0 **10** *½* **Ajjaadd (USA)**[22] 3641 6-8-8 **90**...................................... KieranO'Neill 7 89+
(Ted Powell) *racd far side: in tch: rdn and effrt over 1f out: n.m.r 1f out: keeping on same pce whn nt clr run wl ins fnl f: 9th of 15 in gp* **33/1**

0042 **11** *nse* **Secret Witness**[9] 4073 6-9-10 **106**..............................(b) JamesDoyle 13 105
(Ronald Harris) *racd far side: hld up in midfield: effrt u.p over 1f out: kpt on same pce and no imp fnl 100yds: 10th of 15 in gp* **9/1**[2]

0-05 **12** *nk* **B Fifty Two (IRE)**[81] 1751 3-9-3 **103**................................. SebSanders 19 101
(J W Hills) *racd nr side: midfield overall: rdn and effrt 2f out: led gp and chsd ldrs 1f out: styd on same pce ins fnl f: 2nd of 6 in gp* **25/1**

2015 **13** *hd* **Magical Macey (USA)**[8] 4113 5-9-5 **101**.....................(b) PhillipMakin 14 98
(David Barron) *racd far side: in tch in midfield: rdn over 1f out: styd on same pce and no imp ins fnl f: 11th of 15 in gp* **20/1**

00-3 **14** *¾* **Burning Thread (IRE)**[50] 2717 5-8-10 **92**..................... StevieDonohoe 20 86
(Tim Etherington) *racd nr side: midfield overall: rdn 2f out: drvn and one pce fr over 1f out: 3rd of 6 in gp* **33/1**

1004 **15** *hd* **Dancing Freddy (IRE)**[10] 4013 5-8-7 **89**.................(tp) WilliamCarson 16 83
(Richard Guest) *racd nr side: led gp and chsd ldrs overall tl over 1f out: wknd ins fnl f: 4th of 6 in gp* **33/1**

320 **16** *hd* **Bathwick Bear (IRE)**[37] 3127 4-8-5 **87**.......................... CathyGannon 23 80
(David Evans) *racd nr side: midfield overall: rdn ent fnl 2f: styd on same pce and no imp fr over 1f out: 5th of 6 in gp* **16/1**

1110 **17** *1 ¼* **Best Trip (IRE)**[17] 3778 5-7-12 **80** oh1.................... SilvestreDeSousa 17 68
(Brian Ellison) *swtchd to r in far side gp after 1f: a towards rr: no hdwy u.p fr over 1f out: 12th of 15 in gp* **10/1**[3]

5216 **18** *¾* **Rasaman (IRE)**[6] 4133 8-8-0 **82** ow2.............................. AndreaAtzeni 6 68
(Jim Goldie) *racd far side: bhd: rdn wl over 1f out: swtchd rt 1f out: kpt on but nvr trbld ldrs: 13th of 15 in gp* **14/1**

1-05 **19** *¾* **Verinco**[9] 4073 6-8-13 **95**..(v) TomEaves 2 78
(Bryan Smart) *racd far side: chsd ldr tl over 1f out: btn 1f out: fdd ins fnl f: 14th of 15 in gp* **33/1**

0150 **20** *2* **Taurus Twins**[10] 4013 6-8-5 **87**....................................(b) DavidProbert 15 63
(Richard Price) *racd far side: in tch: rdn and struggling 2f: wknd over 1f out: 15th of 15 in gp* **33/1**

1-00 **21** *5* **Expose**[29] 3394 4-7-13 **81**.. NickyMackay 21 39
(William Haggas) *racd nr side: a bhd: 6th of 6 in gp* **14/1**

1m 0.03s (-0.47) **Going Correction** +0.125s/f (Good)
WFA 3 from 4yo+ 4lb **21** Ran SP% **137.7**
Speed ratings (Par 109): **108,107,106,106,106 105,105,104,104,103 103,102,102,101,100 100,98,97,96,92 84**
Tote Swingers 1&2 £45.60, 2&3 £42.90, 1&3 £8.30 CSF £132.48 CT £4146.39 TOTE £19.30: £3.80, £2.90, £9.80, £3.10; EX 127.10 Trifecta £1867.50 Pool £3,482.64 - 1.38 winning units..
Owner Peter Crate **Bred** Rabbah Bloodstock Limited **Trained** Newdigate, Surrey

FOCUS

This hot handicap usually falls to an experienced, if improving, older sprinter and that could be said to have been the same case again. With a big field they split into two groups, and those in the bigger section towards the far side prevailed. Solid form.

NOTEBOOK

Taajub(IRE) has re-discovered his form this year aided by a drop in the weights and ran a game race to score, having been in the firing line throughout, although he was helped by the reluctance of the runner-up. This was only his second win on turf but he is versatile regarding ground and could have more good handicaps in him. (op 12-1 tchd 16-1)

Mass Rally(IRE) has plenty of ability but finds nothing once let down and must be very frustrating for connections. He cruised into contention with his rider motionless but would not go by the winner. He needs everything to fall just right and is one punters should avoid for win-only purposes, but connections deserve a bit of luck after several near-misses. Official explanation: jockey said, regarding riding, that the gelding has to be held up and as soon as pressure is applied it does not respond and goes backwards. (tchd 8-1 and 10-1)

Fratellino ◆, without the visor he wore last time but with the tongue tie back on, got a good tow into the race and was right there at the finish. A stiff 5f suits him well and drying ground is in his favour, so he is one to keep an eye on.
Jedward(IRE) has been pretty consistent on softer ground of late but, racing off 7lb higher than her last winning mark, ran her race on this faster surface, having been in the firing line throughout. (op 14-1)
Dungannon was sent off favourite and ran a fine race, doing best of those racing in the group towards the stands' side and just missing out on a place. He won at the Shergar Cup meeting here last August and presumably that will be on the agenda again. (op 9-2)
Barnet Fair ◆, who got loose before the start, ran on well late and looks one to bear in mind with the drying ground likely to be in his favour. (op 16-1)
Jack Dexter ◆, a lightly raced 3-y-o, put up a decent effort and, already a winner over 6f, could be the sort for one of the Ayr Gold Cup consolation races in September, providing the ground is good or softer.
Judge 'n Jury made the running on the far side but was challenged on all sides entering the last furlong and was run out of it, although not beaten far. (op 14-1)
Courageous(IRE) has yet to hit form for his new trainer but looked unlucky here, finishing on the heels of the principals but not getting a clear run. If this was a sign of a revival he is very well handicapped on his best form.
Secret Witness, who has been in good form but as a result is off a career-high mark, ran reasonably but is not as effective at this track as he is at, for instance, York. He is one to bear in mind for the Ebor meeting. (tchd 8-1 and 10-1)
T/Jkpt: Not won. T/Plt: £44.20 to a £1 stake. Pool £187,053.46 - 3,083.83 winning tickets.
T/Qpdt: £11.80 to a £1 stake. Pool £10,542.51 - 660.97 winning tickets. SP

3401 REDCAR (L-H)
Sunday, July 22
4368 Meeting Abandoned - waterlogged

4351 CURRAGH (R-H)
Sunday, July 22
OFFICIAL GOING: Soft (heavy in places)

4376a KILBOY ESTATE STKS (GROUP 3) (F&M) — 1m 1f
2:10 (2:10) 3-Y-0+ — **£32,500** (£9,500; £4,500; £1,500)

RPR
1 **Tannery (IRE)**[30] 3361 3-9-0 109 ... WayneLordan 4 — 109+
(David Wachman, Ire) *plld hrd in 3rd early: rdn over 2f out and wnt 2nd ins fnl f: kpt on wl to ld fnl 50yds: all out* — **5/1**[3]
2 ½ **Caponata (USA)**[25] 3516 3-9-0 110 ... PatSmullen 6 — 108
(D K Weld, Ire) *chsd ldr in 2nd: travelled wl to ld 2f out and sn edgd rt: rdn and strly pressed ins fnl f: hdd fnl 50yds* — **11/10**[1]
3 nk **Up (IRE)**[21] 3676 3-9-0 111 ... JPO'Brien 3 — 107+
(A P O'Brien, Ire) *hld up in tch: pushed along over 2f out and clsd on outer into 3rd fnl 150yds: kpt on wl: jst hld for 2nd* — **11/4**[2]
4 2 **Spirit Of Cuba (IRE)**[57] 2515 4-9-9 94 ... DeclanMcDonogh 2 — 104?
(Kevin Prendergast, Ire) *hld up towards rr: rdn in 5th appr fnl f: kpt on wout ever threatening principals to take 4th on line* — **50/1**
5 hd **Shebella (IRE)**[25] 3516 3-9-0 105 ... JohnnyMurtagh 5 — 103
(John M Oxx, Ire) *led: pushed along and hdd 2f out: sn n.m.r on inner and one pce ins fnl f* — **9/1**
6 4 ¼ **Soon (IRE)**[25] 3516 3-9-0 99 ... SeamieHeffernan 1 — 94
(A P O'Brien, Ire) *chsd ldrs: in 4th: rdn under 2f out and sn no imp* — **14/1**
7 4 ¾ **Princess Sinead (IRE)**[56] 2527 3-9-0 103 ... FranBerry 7 — 84
(Mrs John Harrington, Ire) *hld up in rr: rdn over 3f out and sn no imp: eased* — **10/1**
2m 1.18s (6.28) **Going Correction** +0.35s/f (Good) — 7 Ran SP% **118.7**
WFA 3 from 4yo 9lb
Speed ratings: **86,85,85,83,83 79,75**
CSF £11.56 TOTE £5.30: £2.80, £1.40; DF 15.70.
Owner Mrs D P Magnier **Bred** Grange Stud **Trained** Goolds Cross, Co Tipperary
■ Stewards' Enquiry : J P O'Brien two-day ban: used whip without giving filly time to respond (Aug 13,15)

FOCUS
David Wachman won this Group 3 event for the third time in five years, courtesy of Tannery, who has made sustained progress since starting the campaign as a 75-rated maiden. The form is rated around the fifth.

NOTEBOOK
Tannery(IRE) has really come into her own on soft ground on turf, winning Listed events at Gowran and Limerick this. The Limerick race was over a bit further than 1m3f, so it was not surprising that she showed reserves of stamina to wear down the favourite. Quote David Wachman, trainer of Tannery: "She's a very tough filly who seems to handle any ground. There's a good programme of races for her and she may go for the Blandford Stakes."
Caponata(USA) was ridden prominently before taking the lead two furlongs down. The second is a relatively inexperienced filly, and her showing relative to the pace-setting Shebella, who dropped away to finish fifth, was consistent with her win at Naas on her second start.
Up(IRE) has only one win to her name, in a maiden at Dundalk last September. She was not beaten far in third, but such is her profile one could not be confident about predicting further success for the daughter of Galileo.
Spirit Of Cuba(IRE) achieved the second of two handicap wins last season off a modest 76 at Down Royal, is being ambitiously campaigned this season. With a few of her rivals performing below optimum she managed a creditable fourth.
Shebella(IRE) dropped away to finish fifth.
Soon(IRE) has now had 11 more races since winning a Galway maiden almost a year ago.
Princess Sinead(IRE) was never in the hunt and was eased after it had become clear she was making no impact. Official explanation: jockey said filly lost its action

4377a JEBEL ALI STABLES & RACECOURSE ANGLESEY STKS (GROUP 3) — 6f 63y
2:45 (2:45) 2-Y-0 — **£28,166** (£8,233; £3,900; £1,300)

RPR
1 **Grafelli (IRE)**[11] 3980 2-9-3 ... KevinManning 6 — 108+
(J S Bolger, Ire) *missed kick: pushed along to take clsr order in 3rd: chal on outer 2f out and led under 1 1/2f out: sn edgd lft to nrside rail and drew clr: easily* — **9/4**[2]
2 6 ½ **Hard Yards (IRE)**[13] 3922 2-9-3 86 ... ChrisHayes 4 — 88
(A Oliver, Ire) *broke wl to ld narrowly: chal after 1/2-way and sn rdn: hdd 1 1/2f out and no ch w wnr ent fnl f: kpt on* — **8/1**
3 1 ¾ **Count Of Limonade (IRE)**[13] 3921 2-9-3 90 ... JPO'Brien 3 — 83
(A P O'Brien, Ire) *broke wl to r a cl 2nd: almost on terms after 1/2-way: sn hrd rdn and no ex appr fnl f* — **7/4**[1]
4 4 ½ **Hard Core Debt**[17] 3796 2-9-3 86 ... ShaneFoley 5 — 69
(A Oliver, Ire) *hld up in rr: wnt 4th after 1/2-way and sn rdn to keep in tch: one pce fnl 2f* — **12/1**
5 19 **Smoker**[29] 3409 2-9-3 ... CO'Donoghue 2 — 12
(P J Prendergast, Ire) *chsd ldrs in 4th on outer: niggled after 1/2-way and relegated to rr: no imp fnl 2f: eased fnl f* — **11/4**[3]
1m 21.74s (2.64) **Going Correction** +0.65s/f (Yiel) — 5 Ran SP% **112.6**
Speed ratings: **105,96,94,88,62**
CSF £19.18 TOTE £3.50: £1.60, £2.10; DF 17.80.
Owner Sylvain Benillouche **Bred** F Benillouche **Trained** Coolcullon, Co Carlow

FOCUS
Possibly not much strength-in-depth, but Jim Bolger, who handles leading juvenile Dawn Approach, has another smart two-year-old prospect in Grafelli who won with authority on the third outing of his career. He could easily be worth another 4lb.

NOTEBOOK
Grafelli(IRE) showed he had made good progress since a Naas maiden win less than a fortnight ago, going clear inside the last in the style of a colt who should be able to stay one mile in due course. After his maiden win Bolger was talking in terms of a possible nursery mark. This win means that he will remain part of the Pattern scene instead.Quote Jim Bolger, trainer of Grafelli: "He handled the ground well, but I think he will be even better on better ground,and I expect him to get a mile. We will step him up to a Group 2 next."
Hard Yards(IRE) was no match for the winner, but emerged with credit in taking second place.
Count Of Limonade(IRE) became Aidan O'Brien's sole runner after the defection of Coventry Stakes third Cristoforo Colombo because of the ground. He did most of the donkey work before Grafelli asserted and drew clear.
Hard Core Debt posed no threat.
Smoker laboured before being eased down.

4378a DARLEY IRISH OAKS (GROUP 1) (FILLIES) — 1m 4f
3:20 (3:21) 3-Y-0 — **£193,333** (£63,333; £30,000; £10,000; £6,666; £3,333)

RPR
1 **Great Heavens**[15] 3856 3-9-0 ... WilliamBuick 1 — 118+
(John Gosden) *broke wl and settled in 3rd: niggled in 5th into st: pushed along over 2f out and swtchd lft over 1 1/2f out: r.o strly to ld 100yds out and drew clr in clsng stages: comf* — **5/4**[1]
2 3 **Shirocco Star**[31] 3292 3-9-0 ... JohnnyMurtagh 4 — 113
(Hughie Morrison) *hld up in tch: 4th 6f out and clsd on outer to ld under 3f out: edgd rt u.p 1 1/2f out and again ins fnl f: hdd 100yds out and sn no ch w wnr: kpt on* — **7/1**
3 1 ¾ **Princess Highway (USA)**[31] 3292 3-9-0 117 ... PatSmullen 5 — 110
(D K Weld, Ire) *hld up towards rr: clsr on outer in 4th 3f out: unable qck in 3rd ent fnl f: kpt on* — **9/4**[2]
4 ½ **Was (IRE)**[51] 2658 3-9-0 113 ... JPO'Brien 6 — 109
(A P O'Brien, Ire) *chsd ldr in 2nd: travelled wl into st and sn pushed along: cl 2nd under 2f out and rdr forced to snatch up ins fnl f: sn n.d: kpt on* — **5/1**[3]
5 1 ¾ **Devotion (IRE)**[32] 3270 3-9-0 105 ... CO'Donoghue 2 — 107
(A P O'Brien, Ire) *hld up in 5th: relegated to last 3f out: kpt on fnl 2f: n.d* — **50/1**
6 ¾ **Colliding Worlds (IRE)**[10] 4030 3-9-0 ... FranBerry 3 — 105
(Edward Lynam, Ire) *in rr: wnt 6th 3f out: kpt on wout ever threatening fnl 2f* — **25/1**
7 4 ¼ **Twirl (IRE)**[31] 3292 3-9-0 103 ... (b[1]) SeamieHeffernan 7 — 99
(A P O'Brien, Ire) *sn led: hdd 3f out and wknd fnl 2f: allowed edge lft and eased fnl 150yds* — **14/1**
2m 42.92s (4.42) **Going Correction** +0.35s/f (Good) — 7 Ran SP% **116.9**
Speed ratings: **99,97,95,95,94 93,91**
CSF £11.58 TOTE £2.00: £1.30, £2.00; DF 9.30.
Owner Lady Rothschild **Bred** Kincorth Investments Inc **Trained** Newmarket, Suffolk
■ Stewards' Enquiry : Johnny Murtagh two-day ban: careless riding (Aug 5-6)

FOCUS
Another Group 1 triumph in a terrific season for John Gosden who sent out Great Heavens to become the fourth successive British-trained winner of the event. The winner is progressive, and has been rated at the mid-point of the race averages. The fifth and sixth, plus the time, help limit the form.

NOTEBOOK
Great Heavens was proven on soft ground by virtue of an impressive victory at Group 2 level in the Lancashire Oaks, and ran out comprehensive winner after it had appeared she might struggle to extract herself from potential trouble on the inner. She came home strongly when switched, showing a strong element of stamina that could ultimately make her a credible opponent for Camelot in the St Leger. The Yorkshire Oaks is the logical target in the more immediate term. John Gosden, trainer of Great Heavens: "I had nearly given up hope two furlongs out, but she is classy and she answered a big question in the final furlong".
Shirocco Star has only a Newbury maiden win to her name, but she is proving a very smart filly and deserves to pick up a big prize. On much softer ground she managed to reverse form with the Ribblesdale winner Princess Highway.
Princess Highway(USA)'s trainer and rider thought that the going would not be ideal and while this was a satisfactory effort, those reservations proved well-founded.
Was(IRE) suffered interference as the runner-up drifted right from over a furlong out. The ensuing stewards' enquiry produced no alteration. This was well below the form she showed at Epsom, however.
Colliding Worlds(IRE) will find easier opportunities in the future.

4380a BETTOR.COM ROCKINGHAM H'CAP — 5f
4:30 (4:30) 3-Y-0+ — **£42,000** (£13,300; £6,300; £2,100; £1,400; £700)

RPR
1 **Bubbly Bellini (IRE)**[7] 4124 5-9-4 81 ... (p) IJBrennan(3) 5 — 91
(Adrian McGuinness, Ire) *mid-div: pushed along bef 1/2-way: clsd to ld narrowly 1f out and kpt on wl u.p in clsng stages* — **11/2**[3]
2 ¾ **First In Command (IRE)**[29] 3382 7-9-4 78 ... (t) ShaneKelly 10 — 85
(Daniel Mark Loughnane) *cl up: almost on terms on nr side ent fnl f: kpt on wl: hld* — **7/1**
3 nk **An Saighdiur (IRE)**[22] 3648 5-9-7 86 ... MACleere(5) 6 — 92
(Andrew Slattery, Ire) *in tch: 3rd on outer at 1/2-way: no ex ins fnl f* — **9/2**[1]
4 shd **Bogini (IRE)**[16] 3837 3-9-10 88 ... (b) WilliamBuick 8 — 93
(M D O'Callaghan, Ire) *hld up towards rr: travelling wl in bhd ldrs whn swtchd rt to mount chal on outer: kpt on* — **10/1**
5 ½ **Possible**[21] 3677 3-9-5 83 ... FranBerry 2 — 86+
(Charles O'Brien, Ire) *bhd: 7th bef 1/2-way: clsd under 2f out and short of room ins fnl f: kpt on again cl home* — **9/2**[1]

6 hd **Statue Of Dreams (IRE)**[6] 3836 6 -8-767....................(tp) ChrisHayes 7 70
(James Bernard McCabe, Ire) *cl up 2nd in centre: rdn and lost pl appr fnl f: one pce in clsng stages* **8/1**

7 1/2 **Nini Ok (IRE)**[6] 3837 3 -9-280...(b) ShaneFoley 4 80
(John Joseph Murphy, Ire) *bhd: in rr 1/2-way: swtchd rt and kpt on u.p ins fnl f wout ever threatening* **9/1**

8 hd **Allegra Tak (ITY)**[21] 3677 6 -9-579..................................(t) PatSmullen 9 80
(H Rogers, Ire) *broke wl to ld on nrside: hdd 1f out and no ex in clsng stages* **16/1**

9 3 3/4 **Little Village (IRE)**[11] 3982 6 -8-065 oh4 ow1............ LeighRoche(5) 11 51
(Kieran P Cotter, Ire) *cl up on inner early: wknd fr 1/2-way* **11/1**

10 2 **Empirico (FR)**[21] 3677 6 -9-680... FergalLynch 1 60
(David Marnane, Ire) *bhd: rdn over 2f out and sn no imp: eased* **5/1**[2]

1m 3.0s (0.10)**Going Correction** +0.65s/f (Yiel)
WFA 3 from 4yo+ 4lb 10Ran SP%125.3
Speed ratings: **107,105,105,105,104 104,103,102,96,93**
CSF £47.37 CT £199.13 TOTE £5.60 : £1.90 , £2.50 , £2.00 ; DF 67.50 .
Owner Gary Devlin **Bred** J P Hand **Trained** Lusk, Co Dublin

FOCUS
Win number four of the season, and the ninth success overall, for the admirably consistent Bubbly Bellini.

NOTEBOOK
Bubbly Bellini (IRE)has done most of his winning over 7f or 6f but the testing ground made it more of a stamina test than usual and played to his strengths. He tracked the leaders and was already under pressure when going to the front well over 1f out, but he battled on well to win all out.
First In Command (IRE)a seven-time winner who scored over the trip at Haydock on his previous start, has shown himself to be adaptable in terms of ground and he ran a good race, raised 5lb for his recent win. He tracked the leaders and responded for pressure to press the winner over the final furlong, keeping on without quite getting on terms.
An Saighdiur (IRE)ran a fine race and made his bid over 2f out. He soon had every chance and kept on for pressure.
Bogini(IRE) had completed a hat-trick before running below form at Bellewstown only 24 hours after winning at Leopardstown. This was a better effort and after being switched to begin her run well over 1f out she kept on without posing a serious threat.
Possible, winner of a handicap over the trip at Naas and placed on her two subsequent starts, has been creeping up the ratings. Held up, she made headway 2f out and kept on without looking as if she get into serious contention. 4379a, 4381a-4382a (Foreign Racing) See RI

2530 HOPPEGARTEN (R-H)
Sunday, July 22

OFFICIAL GOING: Turf: good

4383a GROSSER PREIS VON BERLIN (GROUP 1) (3YO+) (TURF) 1m 4f
4:00 (12:00) 3-Y-0+
£83,333 (£33,333; £16,666 ; £6,666 ; £3,750 ; £2,083)

RPR

1 **Meandre (FR)**[28] 3424 4 -9-60.. MaximeGuyon 3 119+
(A Fabre, France) *t.k.h early: midfield on outer: prom in 3rd over 4f out: rdn 2 1/2f out: edgd rt: r.o to ld over 1f out: wnt clr ins fnl f: drvn out* **4/5**[1]

2 1 1/4 **Earl Of Tinsdal (GER)**[42] 2968 4 -9-60.................................... AStarke 1 116
(A Wohler, Germany) *broke wl to ld: set stdy pce: rdn to increase tempo 2 1/2f out: hdd over 1f out: kpt on gamely u.p to hold 2nd cl home* **12/5**[2]

3 1/2 **Baschar**[19] 3746 5 -9-60.. APietsch 2 115
(M G Mintchev, Germany) *trckd ldr in 2nd: rdn 2f out: brief effrt to chal 1 1/2f out: sn outpcd by wnr: kpt on u.p ins fnl f: jst hld on for 3rd* **116/10**

4 shd **Ovambo Queen (GER)**[19] 3746 5 -9-30.............................. ADeVries 6 112
(Dr A Bolte, Germany) *hld up in last pair: rdn to improve 2 1/2f out: plugged on to go 4th last strides: nt pce to chal* **18/5**[3]

5 shd **Sir Lando**[15] 3886 5 -9-60... FJohansson 4 115
(Wido Neuroth, Norway) *midfield on inner: rdn and outpcd over 3f out: plugged on u.p ins fnl 2f: ct for 4th last strides* **118/10**

6 1 3/4 **Silvaner (GER)**[19] 3746 4 -9-60.. FilipMinarik 5 112
(P Schiergen, Germany) *slow to stride and hld up in last: rdn to try and improve over 2f out: outpcd and btn over 1f out: plugged on* **138/10**

2m 31.5s (2.20) 6Ran SP%129.2
WIN (incl. 10 euro stake): 18. PLACES: 14, 17. SF: 40
Owner Rothschild Family **Bred** Famille Rothschild **Trained** Chantilly, France

FOCUS
They went a steady early pace, but the form has been rated at face value.

NOTEBOOK
Meandre(FR), who got his favoured going, followed up his Grand Prix de Saint-Cloud win, in which Danedream was last of four. His supporters had a few anxious moments early in the straight as Guyon had to scrub his mount along, but the grey responded well and suddenly found another gear, quickly passing the long-time leader Earl of Tinsdal to go two lengths clear, and soon out of danger. The official winning distance understates his superiority by some margin. The Grosser Preis von Baden is a possible target, followed by the Arc, in which he was sixth last year.
Earl Of Tinsdal (GER)appeared beaten at the distance after setting the fractions in front, but rallied strongly to take second place. He wants much easier ground than this and should be given another chance when getting ideal conditions.

3987 MAISONS-LAFFITTE (R-H)
Sunday, July 22

OFFICIAL GOING: Turf: good

4384a PRIX ROBERT PAPIN (GROUP 2) (2YO COLTS & FILLIES) (TURF) 5f 110y
1:30 (12:00) 2-Y-0 **£61,750** (£23,833; £11,375 ; £7,583 ; £3,791)

RPR

1 **Reckless Abandon**[31] 3291 2 -9-20.............................. GeraldMosse 3 115+
(Clive Cox) *broke smartly: sn led: clr ld 1f out: jinked lft ins fnl f: r.o wl: eased fnl 50yds: comf* **9/4**[1]

2 1 1/2 **Sir Prancealot (IRE)**[33] 3240 2 -9-20.............................. RyanMoore 1 110
(Richard Hannon) *towards rr: swtchd away fr stands' rail 1 1/2f out: fnd opening: r.o wl fnl f: no threat to wnr* **10/3**[3]

3 2 1/2 **Snowday (FR)**[21] 3680 2 -9-20.............................. OlivierPeslier 5 102
(C Laffon-Parias, France) *racd 4th on outside of field: u.p 1f out: styd on wl fnl 100yds: wnt 3rd cl home* **6/1**

4 shd **Penny's Picnic (IRE)**[44] 2907 2 -9-20.............................. ThierryJarnet 2 101
(D Guillemin, France) *broke wl: racd cl 2nd on stands' rail: rdn 1f out: nt pce to cl on ldr: styd on fnl 100yds: lost 3rd cl home* **5/2**[2]

5 hd **To My Valentine (FR)**[31] 3680 2 -8-130............. ChristopheSoumillon 8 98
(F-H Graffard, France) *settled towards rr: swtchd away fr stands' rail 1f out: r.o u.p* **14/1**

6 shd **Sara Lucille**[24] 2 -8-130.. AurelienLemaitre 7 97
(F Head, France) *bkmarker fr s: swtchd to wd outside 1 1/2f out: r.o u.p fnl f* **18/1**

7 hd **Sage Melody (FR)**[21] 3680 2 -8-130........... Christophe-PatriceLemaire 4 97
(P Demercastel, France) *racd towards rr: rdn 1 1/2f out: r.o u.p fnl 100yds* **20/1**

8 3 **Via Chope (FR)**[24] 2 -8-130... IoritzMendizabal 6 87
(Y Barberot, France) *broke wl to r 3rd bhd ldrs: rdn 1 1/2f out: no ex: fdd* **33/1**

1m 4.0s (-3.30) 8Ran SP%116.3
WIN (incl. 1 euro stake): 3.40. PLACES: 1.70, 1.50, 1.80. DF: 5.20. SF: 9.70
Owner Miss J Deadman & S Barrow **Bred** Car Colston Hall Stud **Trained** Lambourn, Berks

FOCUS
The form has a solid look to it.

NOTEBOOK
Reckless Abandon, winner of the Norfolk, made every yard to win easily enough. He did jink left when asked to quicken (had gone left in his previous two starts as well), but as he had the rail to help it wasn't a problem on this occasion, but it might be something to worry about longer term. The Group 1 Prix Morny on August 19 will apparently be his next race.
Sir Prancealot (IRE) fourth in the Coventry, finished fast to make it a one-two for British-trained runners, but never really threatened to get to the winner. He could well take on the winner again in the Morny.

4385a PRIX EUGENE ADAM (GRAND PRIX DE MAISONS-LAFFITTE) (GROUP 2) (3YO) (TURF) 1m 2f (S)
2:40 (12:00) 3-Y-0 **£61,750** (£23,833; £11,375 ; £7,583 ; £3,791)

RPR

1 **Bayrir (FR)**[28] 3422 3 -8-110......................... Christophe-PatriceLemaire 2 114
(A De Royer-Dupre, France) *settled towards rr on stands' rail: patiently rdn while waiting for opening 1f out: qckند wl 150yds out whn gap opened: led 100yds out: r.o wl: comf* **4/1**[2]

2 1 1/2 **Cogito (USA)**[33] 3239 3 -8-110.. KierenFallon 4 111
(Brian Meehan) *hld up at rr: racing freely: swtchd to outside 2f out to go cl 3rd: r.o wl fnl f to go 2nd 100yds out: styd on wl: jst hld 2nd* **4/1**[2]

3 shd **Fractional (IRE)**[25] 3 -8-110................................ Pierre-CharlesBoudot 5 111
(A Fabre, France) *racd cl 3rd bhd ldrs: relegated to last 2f out: swtchd to outside 1 1/2f out: r.o wl u.p fnl 150yds: narrowly missed 2nd* **6/4**[1]

4 3/4 **Starboard**[43] 2920 3 -8-110.. RyanMoore 1 109
(John Gosden) *broke wl to ld on stands' rail: u.p over 250yds out: hdd 100yds out: styd on* **4/1**[2]

5 8 **Loi (IRE)**[32] 3 -8-110.. OlivierPeslier 3 93
(J-M Beguigne, France) *broke smartly to be cl 2nd on outside of ldr: shared ld 1 1/2f out: rdn but fnd no ex fr 1f out: wknd and eased fnl 100yds* **7/1**[3]

2m 2.4s 5Ran SP%112.5
WIN (incl. 1 euro stake): 4.20. PLACES: 2.00, 2.40. SF: 19.30
Owner H H Aga Khan **Bred** S A Aga Khan **Trained** Chantilly, France

FOCUS
The race has been rated around the averages for this race.

NOTEBOOK
Bayrir(FR), with the rail to help, picked up well from off the pace and won in the style of a smart horse. He holds an entry in the Group 1 Preis Von Europa at Cologne over 1m4f in September, and it doesn't look like he'd have a problem with the longer trip.
Cogito(USA), who was one of those hampered at Ascot last time, handled the step up in trip well. He couldn't quite live with the winner at the end but he's lightly raced and open to further improvement.
Fractional(IRE), winner of his first two starts, was taking a big step up in class. He got shuffled back to last 2f out before finishing well after being switched, and is another who is open to further improvement.
Starboard, who tried to make all, was there to be shot at from a furlong out.

4386a PRIX DE LA PEPINIERE (LISTED RACE) (4YO+ FILLIES & MARES) (TURF) 1m 2f (S)
3:10 (12:00) 4-Y-0+ **£21,666** (£8,666; £6,500 ; £4,333 ; £2,166)

RPR

1 **Pirika (IRE)**[271] 7090 4 -8-110............................. Pierre-CharlesBoudot 3 109
(A Fabre, France) **181/10**

2 1/2 **La Pomme D'Amour**[22] 4 -8-110.............................. MlleAmelieFoulon 1 108
(A Fabre, France) **16/5**[2]

3 1/2 **Mid Mon Lady (IRE)**[8] 4112 7 -8-110................................. LukeMorris 6 107
(Sir Mark Prescott Bt) *racd cl 5th bhd ldrs: wnt 2nd on outside at 1/2-way: rdn over 1 1/2f out: r.o u.str.p to ld 100yds out: hdd 50yds out: r.o wl* **9/1**[3]

4 1 1/2 **Navarra Queen**[26] 3482 4 -8-110.................................... GeraldMosse 9 104
(P Schiergen, Germany) **14/5**[1]

5 2 **Divine Music (IRE)**[65] 2570 5 -8-110.......................(p) RonanThomas 11 100
(P Van De Poele, France) **10/1**

6 1 **Amare**[47] 2805 5 -8-110...(b) StephanePasquier 12 98
(P Harley, Germany) **11/1**

7 hd **Global Magic (GER)**[28] 4 -8-110.............................(p) UmbertoRispoli 4 98
(A Wohler, Germany) **12/1**

8 1 1/4 **Siete Vidas (IRE)**[22] 4 -8-110.. GregoryBenoist 2 95
(M Delzangles, France) **17/1**

9 3 **Pagera (FR)**[36] 3178 4 -8-110............................. ChristopheSoumillon 10 89
(H-A Pantall, France) **19/1**

10 18 **Acacalia (GER)**[43] 4 -8-110.. JohanVictoire 5 53
(C Sprengel, Germany) **49/1**

0 **Aspasia De Mileto**[291] 6642 4 -8-110............................... OlivierPeslier 7
(C Laffon-Parias, France) **10/1**

0 **Yukatana (FR)**[22] 4 -8-110... AlexandreRoussel 8
(C Lotoux, France) **16/1**

2m 4.43s (2.03) 12Ran SP%118.0
WIN (incl. 1 euro stake): 19.10. PLACES: 5.70, 1.80, 3.40. DF: 30.60. SF: 57.20
Owner Teruya Yoshida **Bred** Shadai Farm **Trained** Chantilly, France

NOTEBOOK
Mid Mon Lady (IRE)runner-up in the John Smith's Cup last time out, backed that up with a solid effort in Listed company. She has never been in better heart.

[4132]AYR (L-H)

Monday, July 23

OFFICIAL GOING: Soft changing to soft (heavy in places) after race 6 (4.45)

Home bend out 6m from inner line and straight out 4m from inner line. 18yds added to races between 7f and 10f and 30yds to others race on Round course.
Wind: Almost nil Weather: Overcast, persistent rain

4387 BET TOTEPLACEPOT TEXT TOTE TO 89660 EBF MAIDEN STKS 7f 50y
2:00 (2:01) (Class 4) 2-Y-O **£4,398** (£1,309; £654; £327) **Stalls** High

Form RPR

22 **1** **One Word More (IRE)**[10] 4056 2-9-3 0 .... WilliamCarson 1 83+
(Charles Hills) *dwlt: t.k.h and sn trcking ldrs: smooth hdwy to ld over 2f out: shkn up and edgd lft appr fnl f: kpt on wl: comf* **1/5**[1]

5 **2** *2* **Dark Ocean (IRE)**[30] 3401 2-9-3 0 .... PJMcDonald 6 74
(Jedd O'Keeffe) *prom: effrt and rdn over 2f out: chsd wnr ent fnl f: kpt on* **16/1**[3]

3 *2 ½* **Greeleys Love (USA)** 2-9-3 0 .... PhillipMakin 2 67+
(Kevin Ryan) *s.i.s: hld up: in tch: rdn and rn green over 2f out: kpt on fnl f: bttr for r* **14/1**[2]

0 **4** *1 ¼* **Foolbythepool**[7] 4132 2-9-3 0 .... TomEaves 5 63+
(Keith Dalgleish) *pressed ldr: effrt and ev ch over 2f out: sn rdn: outpcd ins fnl f* **100/1**

5 *1 ¾* **Causeway Foot (USA)** 2-9-3 0 .... DanielTudhope 7 59
(Jedd O'Keeffe) *s.i.s: hld up: hdwy over 2f out: sn rdn: wknd ins fnl f* **28/1**

0 **6** *2 ¼* **Sennockian Star**[44] 2934 2-9-3 0 .... JoeFanning 4 64
(Mark Johnston) *led: rdn and hdd over 2f out: rallied: wknd ins fnl f* **14/1**[2]

4555 **7** *4* **Someone's Darling**[46] 2837 2-8-12 62 .... GrahamLee 8 35
(Jim Goldie) *hld up on outside: struggling over 2f out: sn btn* **40/1**

5 **8** *6* **Salvatore Fury (IRE)**[20] 3725 2-9-3 0 .... RoystonFfrench 3 22
(Keith Dalgleish) *s.i.s: t.k.h: hld up towards rr: struggling over 2f out: sn btn* **100/1**

1m 36.93s (3.53) **Going Correction** +0.475s/f (Yiel) **8** Ran SP% **110.4**
Speed ratings (Par 96): **98,95,92,90,88 84,79,71**
Tote Swingers: 1&2 £2.10, 1&3 £2.30, 2&3 £3.40 CSF £4.00 TOTE £1.20: £1.02, £2.40, £2.10; EX 5.50 Trifecta £27.90 Pool: £312.93 - 27.90 winning units..
Owner Tony Wechsler & Ann Plummer **Bred** John Fielding **Trained** Lambourn, Berks

FOCUS
Despite the rain during the morning the ground was still officially described as Good going into the opener (GoingStick 9.2). However, it was plainly far softer than that and the going was changed to Soft before the next. This was an uncompetitive maiden, dominated by the long odds-on favourite. The winner did not need to match his best to score.

NOTEBOOK
One Word More(IRE) had the misfortune to come up against two smart Richard Hannon-trained juveniles in his first two starts at Newbury, including Saturday's Ascot winner Toronado, but was up against nothing off that calibre here. Always travelling well behind the leaders, he had to be nudged out after leading 2f from home to make sure of it, but never looked in any danger. He seems bound for something better now. (op 2-9)
Dark Ocean(IRE) showed plenty of promise when fifth of eight behind a decent sort on last month's Redcar debut and stepped up from that, staying on late to keep the winner honest. Whether finishing so close to such a talented rival will affect his potential nursery mark remains to be seen, but he can certainly win races. (op 12-1)
Greeleys Love(USA) ◆, a $105,000 colt out of a half-sister to the Group 1 winning juvenile Pearl Of Love and a Grade 3 winner in the US, betrayed his inexperience with a slow start and, although soon back in touch, came off the bridle sooner than most, but he stayed on in pleasing fashion and can only come on from this. (op 10-1)
Foolbythepool was always handy and ran much better than when last of eight on his debut over 6f here seven days earlier. (op 66-1)
Causeway Foot(USA), a 55,000GBP 2yo and stablemate of the runner-up, is closely related to a 7f winning juvenile in Ireland and a half-brother to a 1m Listed winner in the US. Despite racing in last for much of the way, he showed ability as the race progressed and will improve. (op 25-1)
Sennockian Star made the early running, but again didn't see his race out. (op 12-1)

4388 TOTEPOOL MOBILE TEXT TOTE TO 89660 H'CAP 7f 50y
2:30 (2:32) (Class 5) (0-75,75) 3-Y-O+ **£2,458** (£731; £365; £182) **Stalls** High

Form RPR

0631 **1** **Chosen Character (IRE)**[3] 4295 4-9-2 70 ....(vt) NatashaEaton(7) 7 81
(Tom Dascombe) *t.k.h: prom: rdn over 2f out: led appr fnl f: kpt on wl* **7/4**[1]

6600 **2** *1 ¾* **Chookie Avon**[7] 4134 5-8-12 64 ....(p) LMcNiff(5) 10 69
(Keith Dalgleish) *t.k.h: prom: smooth hdwy to chal over 2f out: rdn over 1f out: kpt on fnl f: nt rch wnr* **22/1**

0040 **3** *1 ¼* **Dhhamaan (IRE)**[28] 3455 7-8-9 56 ....(b) PJMcDonald 1 58
(Ruth Carr) *led: rdn and hdd appr fnl f: kpt on same pce* **14/1**

5452 **4** *1 ¾* **Silver Rime (FR)**[7] 4135 7-9-11 72 .... PhillipMakin 8 69
(Linda Perratt) *s.i.s: hld up: stdy hdwy over 2f out: sn rdn and edgd lft over 1f out: no imp fnl f* **6/1**[3]

-003 **5** *2* **Namwahjobo (IRE)**[14] 3905 4-9-10 71 ....(v) DanielTudhope 6 63
(Jim Goldie) *cl up: rdn over 2f out: no ex wl over 1f out* **16/1**

36-1 **6** *4 ½* **Burnwynd Boy**[53] 2621 7-8-9 56 oh3 .... RoystonFfrench 3 36
(Ian Semple) *t.k.h: in tch on ins: rdn over 2f out: btn fnl f* **14/1**

20-5 **7** *1* **Opus Dei**[7] 4142 5-9-5 69 .... GaryBartley(3) 4 47
(Noel Wilson) *hld up towards rr: drvn along over 2f out: nvr on terms* **33/1**

0-21 **8** *¾* **Iffraam (IRE)**[46] 2864 3-9-7 75 .... TomEaves 9 49
(Michael Dods) *in tch on outside: pushed along after 3f: struggling fr wl over 2f out: sn n.d* **4/1**[2]

5-10 **9** *6* **Safe House (IRE)**[13] 3940 3-9-7 75 .... JoeFanning 5 33
(Mark Johnston) *dwlt: sn cl up: rdn and wknd wl over 2f out* **8/1**

050- **10** *½* **Music Festival (USA)**[226] 7716 5-9-3 64 .... GrahamLee 2 23
(Jim Goldie) *hld up on ins: drvn along over 2f out: sn struggling* **12/1**

1m 36.12s (2.72) **Going Correction** +0.475s/f (Yiel)
WFA 3 from 4yo+ 7lb **10** Ran SP% **116.0**
Speed ratings (Par 103): **103,101,99,97,95 90,89,88,81,80**
Tote Swingers: 1&2 £11.00, 1&3 £8.00, 2&3 £30.80 CSF £46.90 CT £431.21 TOTE £3.10: £1.90, £5.10, £6.00; EX 39.40 Trifecta £326.90 Part won. Pool: £411.81 - 0.63 winning units..
Owner Aykroyd And Sons Ltd **Bred** Moyglare Stud Farm Ltd **Trained** Malpas, Cheshire

FOCUS
A modest handicap, though the pace was sound. The winner got closer to his 2yo form.

Iffraam(IRE) Official explanation: trainer's rep said colt was unsuited by the soft ground

4389 RACING POST FORM WITH TOTEPOOL MOBILE H'CAP (DIV I) 1m
3:05 (3:05) (Class 6) (0-65,70) 3-Y-O+ **£1,704** (£503; £251) **Stalls** Low

Form RPR

0342 **1** **Uncle Brit**[7] 4142 6-9-0 50 .... PJMcDonald 1 59
(Malcolm Jefferson) *trckd ldrs: smooth hdwy to ld 2f out: sn rdn: hld on wl fnl f* **7/2**[2]

03-4 **2** *1 ¼* **Military Call**[38] 3115 5-9-8 58 .... DanielTudhope 2 64
(Alistair Whillans) *hld up: stdy hdwy over 2f out: edgd lft: chsd ldrs over 1f out: kpt on to take 2nd cl home: nt rch wnr* **6/1**

0621 **3** *shd* **Master Of Dance (IRE)**[7] 4134 5-10-1 70 6ex ....(p) LMcNiff(5) 9 76
(Keith Dalgleish) *trckd ldrs: effrt over 2f out: chsd wnr and hung lft over 1f out: kpt on fnl f: lost 2nd cl home* **4/1**[3]

3311 **4** *3 ½* **Cheeky Wee Red**[24] 3581 4-8-13 54 .... ShaneBKelly(5) 7 52
(Richard Fahey) *prom: rdn and outpcd over 2f out: kpt on fnl f: nvr able to chal* **11/4**[1]

4660 **5** *1 ½* **Deep Applause**[14] 3907 4-8-12 48 ....(b) TomEaves 8 42
(Michael Dods) *s.i.s: hld up: effrt and rdn over 2f out: no imp fnl f* **22/1**

3006 **6** *shd* **Monsieur Pontaven**[14] 3907 5-8-11 47 ....(b) PhillipMakin 11 41
(Robin Bastiman) *hld up: rdn and edgd lft over 2f out: kpt on fnl f: nvr able to chal* **16/1**

0-43 **7** *1* **Let's Face Facts**[7] 4134 5-9-3 53 ....(v) GrahamLee 3 45
(Jim Goldie) *t.k.h: hld up in tch: drvn over 2f out: btn over 1f out* **7/1**

5246 **8** *2 ½* **Hellbender (IRE)**[35] 3209 6-9-3 60 .... JasonHart(7) 4 46
(George Foster) *t.k.h: w ldr: rdn and hdd 2f out: sn outpcd* **20/1**

4000 **9** *7* **Shunkawakhan (IRE)**[15] 3889 9-8-9 45 ....(p) JoeFanning 5 15
(Linda Perratt) *t.k.h: slt ld to 1/2-way: rdn and wknd fr 2f out* **33/1**

644 **10** *5* **Cheers Buddy (IRE)**[50] 2735 4-9-8 58 ....(e[1]) RoystonFfrench 12 17
(Ian Semple) *t.k.h: in tch on outside tl rdn and wknd over 2f out* **14/1**

1m 47.92s (4.12) **Going Correction** +0.55s/f (Yiel)
WFA 3 from 4yo+ 8lb **10** Ran SP% **120.3**
Speed ratings (Par 101): **101,99,99,96,94 94,93,91,84,79**
Tote Swingers: 1&2 £4.90, 1&3 £4.50, 2&3 £5.20 CSF £25.11 CT £91.49 TOTE £4.20: £1.80, £1.10, £2.20; EX 32.20 Trifecta £254.90 Part won. Pool: £344.53 - 0.89 winning units..
Owner J M Jefferson **Bred** Heather Raw **Trained** Norton, N Yorks

FOCUS
A poor handicap in which the runners spurned the inside rail in the home straight, which set the trend for the following races on the round course. It was 9lb quicker than division II and looks the sounder form. The third sets the standard.

4390 RACING POST FORM WITH TOTEPOOL MOBILE H'CAP (DIV II) 1m
3:35 (3:38) (Class 6) (0-65,60) 3-Y-O+ **£1,704** (£503; £251) **Stalls** Low

Form RPR

6015 **1** **Mr Chocolate Drop (IRE)**[28] 3454 8-9-9 55 ....(t) PhillipMakin 12 65
(Mandy Rowland) *s.i.s: hld up: rdn and gd hdwy wl over 1f out: led ins fnl f: r.o wl* **14/1**

0262 **2** *1 ¾* **Mark Anthony (IRE)**[4] 4240 5-9-0 53 .... ShirleyTeasdale(7) 2 59
(Shaun Harris) *led and sn wl clr: rdn over 2f out: hdd ins fnl f: kpt on same pce* **10/3**[1]

2343 **3** *3 ½* **Kyllachykov (IRE)**[15] 3889 4-9-2 48 ....(p) DanielTudhope 3 46
(Robin Bastiman) *prom: drvn and outpcd wl over 1f out: r.o ins fnl f: nt pce to chal* **10/3**[1]

4413 **4** *nk* **Social Rhythm**[40] 3032 8-10-0 60 .... PaddyAspell 9 57
(Alistair Whillans) *hld up: hdwy on outside over 2f out: rdn and styd on fnl f: nvr able to chal* **8/1**[3]

0343 **5** *¾* **Georgebernardshaw (IRE)**[9] 4089 7-9-11 60 .... DeclanCannon(3) 10 56
(Richard Guest) *prom: chsd clr ldr 1/2-way: effrt over 2f out: wandered and lost 2nd over 1f out: sn no ex* **7/2**[2]

0540 **6** *1 ¼* **Glenluji**[15] 3889 7-9-7 53 .... GrahamLee 4 46
(Jim Goldie) *hld up: rdn along over 2f out: hdwy over 1f out: nvr able to chal* **14/1**

0560 **7** *5* **Viking Dancer**[7] 4134 5-8-13 45 ....(b) PJMcDonald 8 26
(Ruth Carr) *s.i.s: rdn in rr over 2f out: nvr able to chal* **25/1**

0503 **8** *shd* **Poppy Golightly**[21] 3712 5-8-8 47 .... JasonHart(7) 7 28
(Declan Carroll) *prom: drvn over 2f out: wknd wl over 1f out* **8/1**[3]

04 **9** *1 ½* **Praxios**[6] 4193 4-9-8 57 .... GaryBartley(3) 1 34
(Noel Wilson) *prom tl rdn and wknd over 2f out* **16/1**

-000 **10** *10* **Champagne Valley**[28] 3456 3-8-5 45 .... JoeFanning 11
(Sharon Watt) *in tch: rdn along over 3f out: wknd fr 2f out* **33/1**

0-00 **11** *24* **Sheedal (IRE)**[46] 2840 4-8-13 45 ....(e[1]) LeeNewman 5
(Ian Semple) *chsd clr ldr to 1/2-way: rdn and wknd over 3f out: lost tch fnl 2f* **80/1**

1m 48.88s (5.08) **Going Correction** +0.55s/f (Yiel)
WFA 3 from 4yo+ 8lb **11** Ran SP% **117.8**
Speed ratings (Par 101): **96,94,90,90,89 88,83,83,81,71 47**
Tote Swingers: 1&2 £8.70, 1&3 £11.60, 2&3 £3.30 CSF £59.84 CT £201.22 TOTE £13.30: £3.40, £1.30, £1.50; EX 73.10 Trifecta £242.00 Pool: £467.75 - 1.43 winning units..
Owner Miss M E Rowland **Bred** P J Munnelly **Trained** Lower Blidworth, Notts

FOCUS
Thanks to the runner-up this was run at a searching early gallop, but the pace eventually collapsed and the winning time was nearly a second slower than the first division. The winner's first turf form since last summer, but the form is a bit shaky.

4391 TOTEPOOL.COM SPORTS, GAMES, BINGO & MORE H'CAP 1m 2f
4:10 (4:10) (Class 5) (0-70,70) 3-Y-O+ **£2,458** (£731; £365; £182) **Stalls** Low

Form RPR

0421 **1** **Luctor Emergo (IRE)**[14] 3907 3-8-9 58 ....(p) TomEaves 9 68+
(Keith Dalgleish) *cl up: led gng wl over 2f out: sn rdn: kpt on strly fnl f* **6/4**[1]

5333 **2** *1 ½* **Cadgers Brig**[7] 4138 4-9-8 61 ....(p) RoystonFfrench 5 68
(Keith Dalgleish) *led 1f: cl up: rdn and ev ch over 2f out: kpt on fnl f: nt pce of wnr* **8/1**

6605 **3** *2 ¼* **Chatterati (USA)**[16] 3847 3-8-8 57 .... JoeFanning 1 60
(Mark Johnston) *hld up in tch: stdy hdwy over 2f out: rdn over 1f out: kpt on same pce ins fnl f* **5/1**[3]

1006 **4** *½* **Sedgwick**[12] 3962 10-9-4 64 .... ShirleyTeasdale(7) 2 66
(Shaun Harris) *hld up in tch: effrt and rdn over 2f out: one pce fnl f* **11/1**

5 *7* **Shisha Threesixty (IRE)**[47] 855 4-9-2 60 ....(p) LMcNiff(5) 4 48
(Lucinda Russell) *s.i.s: hld up: rdn and effrt over 2f out: wknd over 1f out* **12/1**

2436 **6** *½* **Free Art**[31] 3353 4-10-0 67 .... PJMcDonald 11 54
(Geoffrey Harker) *hld up in tch: effrt and rdn over 2f out: wknd wl over 1f out* **11/4**[2]

The Form Book Flat, Raceform Ltd, Compton, RG20 6NL

0/-0 7 3 ½ **Toledo Gold (IRE)**[12] 3953 6-9-4 57................................(t) PaddyAspell 7 37
(Maurice Barnes) *led after 1f to over 2f out: sn struggling* **16/1**

2m 20.16s (8.16) **Going Correction** +0.55s/f (Yiel)
WFA 3 from 4yo+ 10lb 7 Ran SP% **116.4**
Speed ratings (Par 103): **89,87,86,85,80 79,76**
Tote Swingers: 1&2 £2.00, 1&3 £3.50, 2&3 £5.70 CSF £15.10 CT £49.67 TOTE £1.80: £1.10, £3.10; EX 9.00 Trifecta £50.10 Pool: £555.91 - 8.20 winning units..
Owner Gordon McDowall **Bred** Kilnamoragh Stud **Trained** Carluke, S Lanarks

FOCUS
A modest handicap and the first race on the card to be significantly hit by non-runners. It resulted in a 1-2 for trainer Keith Dalgleish. The winner posted a length personal best but the second favourite disappointed.

4392 YOUR FAVOURITE POOL BETS AT TOTEPOOL.COM H'CAP 5f
4:45 (4:45) (Class 6) (0-65,64) 3-Y-O+ **£1,704** (£503; £251) **Stalls** Centre

Form RPR
6006 1 **Blown It (USA)**[24] 3578 6-9-12 64... JoeFanning 2 72
(Keith Dalgleish) *stdd in tch: hdwy over 1f out: swtchd lft and led ins fnl f: pushed out* **7/2**[3]
5360 2 ¾ **Amno Dancer (IRE)**[15] 3893 5-8-9 47................................ LeeNewman 3 52
(Ian Semple) *t.k.h early: cl up: rdn to ld briefly ins fnl f: kpt on towards fin* **6/1**
3305 3 4 **Distant Sun (USA)**[4] 4262 8-9-5 57................................(p) PhillipMakin 6 48
(Linda Perratt) *led: rdn over 1f out: hdd ins fnl f: sn outpcd* **4/1**
6234 4 ¾ **Here Now And Why (IRE)**[46] 2839 5-9-8 60...................(p) TomEaves 5 48
(Ian Semple) *t.k.h early: cl up: effrt and rdn over 1f out: wknd ins fnl f* **2/1**[1]
0550 5 3 ¾ **Glenlini**[15] 3893 6-9-0 52... GrahamLee 9 26
(Jim Goldie) *trckd ldrs tl rdn and wknd 2f out* **10/3**[2]

1m 3.94s (4.54) **Going Correction** +0.825s/f (Soft)
WFA 3 from 4yo+ 4lb 5 Ran SP% **112.9**
Speed ratings (Par 101): **96,94,88,87,81**
CSF £23.45 TOTE £6.30: £2.70, £2.90; EX 28.50 Trifecta £76.90 Pool: £237.10 - 2.28 winning units..
Owner D G Savala **Bred** H & W Thoroughbreds & Adrian Regan **Trained** Carluke, S Lanarks

FOCUS
An already moderate spring handicap was weakened further by the absence of half the intended runners. Modest form.

4393 BET ON LIVE DARTS AT TOTEPOOL.COM H'CAP 6f
5:15 (5:16) (Class 5) (0-70,70) 3-Y-O+ **£2,458** (£731; £365; £182) **Stalls** Centre

Form RPR
-221 1 **Sovereign Street**[20] 3731 4-9-12 70.................................. GrahamLee 1 87
(Ann Duffield) *t.k.h: in tch: shkn up and hdwy to ld 1f out: pushed out: comf* **2/1**[1]
-414 2 1 ¾ **Colbyor**[53] 2616 3-9-0 68.. ShaneBKelly(5) 13 77
(Richard Fahey) *trckd ldrs: effrt and rdn 2f out: chsd wnr ins fnl f: kpt on* **9/2**[3]
5406 3 3 ¾ **Chookie Royale**[14] 3905 4-9-12 70.................................... JoeFanning 4 68
(Keith Dalgleish) *dwlt: t.k.h: in tch: rdn and outpcd 2f out: styd on fnl f: nvr able to chal* **8/1**
1424 4 nk **Another Citizen (IRE)**[4] 4245 4-9-8 66..........................(b) PhillipMakin 7 63
(Tim Easterby) *led tl rdn and hdd 1f out: sn wknd* **11/4**[2]
2002 5 13 **Saxonette**[14] 3905 4-8-8 57...(p) LMcNiff(5) 3 12
(Linda Perratt) *trckd ldr tl rdn and wknd qckly over 1f out* **16/1**
6155 6 3 ¼ **Argentine (IRE)**[33] 3276 8-9-2 63.................................(b) LeeTopliss(3) 8 8
(Ian Semple) *rrd s: in tch tl rdn and wknd over 2f out* **25/1**
0552 7 4 ½ **Weetentherty**[4] 4262 5-8-7 51 oh1...............................(p) WilliamCarson 11
(Linda Perratt) *hld up in tch: rdn and struggling over 2f out: sn btn* **7/1**

1m 17.83s (5.43) **Going Correction** +0.825s/f (Soft)
WFA 3 from 4yo+ 5lb 7 Ran SP% **111.5**
Speed ratings (Par 103): **96,93,88,88,70 66,60**
Tote Swingers: 1&2 £2.70, 1&3 £3.50, 2&3 £6.40 CSF £10.75 CT £55.30 TOTE £4.00: £2.00, £2.30; EX 12.40 Trifecta £101.20 Pool: £298.28 - 2.18 winning units..
Owner Evelyn Duchess Of Sutherland **Bred** Evelyn Duchess Of Sutherland **Trained** Constable Burton, N Yorks

FOCUS
The ground was changed to soft, heavy in places before this race. Only seven of the 13 intended runners stood their ground for this modest handicap. The winner continues to improve.
Weetentherty Official explanation: trainer said, regarding running, having run four days earlier, the race came too soon for the gelding

4394 DEAL OR NO DEAL AT TOTEPOOL.COM H'CAP 6f
5:45 (5:46) (Class 6) (0-60,60) 3-Y-O **£1,704** (£503; £251) **Stalls** Centre

Form RPR
0404 1 **Orwellian**[7] 4134 3-9-2 55... TomEaves 2 65
(Bryan Smart) *hld up: smooth hdwy wl over 1f out: rdn to ld ins fnl f: kpt on strly* **2/1**[1]
4U 2 1 ½ **Oakbrook**[14] 3908 3-8-13 52.. GrahamLee 1 57
(Ann Duffield) *trckd ldrs: effrt and disp ld over 1f out to ins fnl f: kpt on: nt pce of wnr* **5/1**[3]
0000 3 ¾ **Great Nicanor (IRE)**[28] 3456 3-8-7 46 oh1..............(p) RoystonFfrench 4 49
(Ian Semple) *led: rdn 2f out: hdd ins fnl f: kpt on same pce* **16/1**
06-0 4 5 **Findhornbay**[20] 3731 3-9-4 57.. JoeFanning 5 44
(Keith Dalgleish) *t.k.h: trckd ldrs tl rdn and wknd over 1f out* **7/1**
5050 5 1 **Chapellerie (IRE)**[106] 1241 3-9-6 59...........................(b) WilliamCarson 9 43
(Richard Guest) *t.k.h: in tch tl rdn and wknd over 1f out* **7/2**[2]
0050 6 2 ½ **First Fast Now (IRE)**[30] 3407 3-9-2 55...................(p) PhillipMakin 10 31
(Nigel Tinkler) *hld up in tch: rdn over 2f out: wknd wl over 1f out* **6/1**
154- 7 13 **Make Up**[224] 7735 3-9-4 60.. GaryBartley(3) 6
(Noel Wilson) *t.k.h: trckd ldrs tl rdn and wknd fr 2f out* **11/1**

1m 17.65s (5.25) **Going Correction** +0.825s/f (Soft) 7 Ran SP% **113.2**
Speed ratings (Par 98): **98,96,95,88,87 83,66**
Tote Swingers: 1&2 £2.60, 1&3 £7.80, 2&3 £7.00 CSF £12.07 CT £120.52 TOTE £2.00: £1.10, £3.30; EX 12.00 Trifecta £101.70 Pool: £402.86 - 2.93 winning units..
Owner Just For Girls Partnership **Bred** Mrs Fiona Denniff **Trained** Hambleton, N Yorks

FOCUS
Another modest sprint handicap, this time restricted to 3yos, and it was probably no coincidence that the front three had all shown form over further. There's a bit of doubt over the form.
Chapellerie(IRE) Official explanation: jockey said filly ran too free
T/Plt: £61.80 to a £1 stake. Pool: £55,867.00 - 659.88 winning tickets. T/Qpdt: £21.60 to a £1 stake. Pool: £4,290.00 - 146.70 winning tickets. RY

4172 BEVERLEY (R-H)
Monday, July 23

OFFICIAL GOING: Good to firm (8.4)
Wind: Fresh across Weather: sunny

4395 YORKSHIRE.COM BACK LE BID CLAIMING STKS 5f
6:30 (6:33) (Class 5) 2-Y-O **£2,385** (£704; £352) **Stalls** Low

Form RPR
3 1 **Findog**[33] 3286 2-9-0 0... PaulMulrennan 1 71+
(Ollie Pears) *trckd ldrs on inner: swtchd lft and hdwy to chal jst over 1f out: sn rdn: led last 100yds: styd on strly* **6/4**[1]
05 2 2 ¼ **Autumn Shadow (IRE)**[18] 3776 2-8-9 0......................... TonyHamilton 4 58
(Richard Fahey) *cl up: led after 2f: rdn over 1f out: drvn ent fnl f: hdd and one pce last 100yds* **5/1**[3]
03 3 2 ½ **Edith Anne**[16] 3844 2-9-0 0.. MickyFenton 3 54
(Paul Midgley) *s.i.s and in rr: hdwy on inner over 1f out: sn rdn and kpt on fnl f* **8/1**
065 4 2 ½ **Madam Moreton**[18] 3789 2-7-13 44....................................... RyanPowell(3) 7 33
(George Margarson) *chsd ldrs on outer: rdn along wl over 1f out: kpt on same pce* **66/1**
0023 5 ¾ **Red Highlites (IRE)**[9] 4083 2-8-9 67.....................(p) SilvestreDeSousa 6 37
(Ann Duffield) *dwlt and awkward s: keen and sn chsng ldrs: rdn 2f out: sn btn* **5/2**[2]
0024 6 1 ½ **Sulky Sheila (IRE)**[12] 3951 2-8-4 47.........................(b[1]) DuranFentiman 2 27
(Tim Easterby) *plld hrd: a towards rr* **11/1**
00 7 1 ¼ **Vida Eterna (IRE)**[14] 3909 2-8-9 0................................... JamesSullivan 5 27
(Ollie Pears) *led 2f: cl up: rdn along over 2f out and sn wknd* **20/1**
0 8 nse **Elusive Shadow**[79] 1861 2-8-4 0.. JimmyQuinn 9 22
(Alan Brown) *a towards rr* **66/1**

1m 4.51s (1.01) **Going Correction** -0.075s/f (Good) 8 Ran SP% **112.4**
Speed ratings (Par 94): **88,84,80,76,75 72,70,70**
Tote Swingers: 1&2 £3.60, 1&3 £3.10, 2&3 £4.60 CSF £9.09 TOTE £3.10: £1.50, £1.10, £1.60; EX 12.30.Winner claimed by Mr Ken McGarrity for £10,000.
Owner John J Maguire **Bred** D R Tucker **Trained** Norton, N Yorks

FOCUS
After a hot sunny day the going was changed to good to firm. They went a decent pace in this 2yo claimer and the favourite scored in good style. The winner looks a fair prospect and the second also produced a step up.

NOTEBOOK
Findog had solid claims on his promising 12-1 third in a 5f Ripon maiden on debut. He travelled well tucked away against the far rail and got a split when he needed one before finding a surging run to win with plenty in hand. A gelded half-brother to four winners in Italy, he looks a fair type and could stay an extra furlong or two this season. (op 13-8 tchd 15-8)
Autumn Shadow(IRE) couldn't repel the fast-finishing winner by she showed a decent attitude to finish clear of the rest. She looks a speedy sort who has improved with each of three starts and is a 25,000euros half-sister to a French 6.7f-1m winner. (tchd 11-2)
Edith Anne got tapped for pace before staying on late dropped into a claimer on her third run. A 5,000euros half-sister to German Listed-placed 1m 2yo winner Enjoy The Life, she is progressing and is bred to be suited by longer trips. (tchd 17-2)
Madam Moreton showed a first glimmer of ability when a 50-1 fifth of six in a seller last time and confirmed that with a respectable effort at another big price. (op 50-1)
Red Highlites(IRE) had a decent chance on her best form and was solid in the market, but she put a dent in her chance by starting slowly and found a limited response. Official explanation: jockey said filly hung right-handed (op 11-4 tchd 9-4)

4396 SWAN INDUSTRIAL DRIVES H'CAP 1m 1f 207y
7:00 (7:01) (Class 5) (0-75,75) 3-Y-O+ **£2,264** (£673; £336; £168) **Stalls** Low

Form RPR
-032 1 **King Of The Celts (IRE)**[27] 3459 4-9-10 71....................... EddieAhern 3 81
(Tim Easterby) *mde virtually all: jnd and rdn over 1f out: kpt on wl fnl f* **11/4**[1]
-005 2 ½ **Arashi**[49] 2767 6-8-9 56 oh2.. JimmyQuinn 10 65
(Derek Shaw) *trckd ldrs: gd hdwy wl over 2f out: rdn to chal over 1f out: ev ch tl drvn and no ex last 50yds* **25/1**
-155 3 2 ¼ **Saint Thomas (IRE)**[60] 2414 5-9-2 63.............................. FrannyNorton 2 68
(John Mackie) *trckd ldng pair on inner: effrt and n.m.r 2f out: rdn and nt clr run over 1f out: sn swtchd lft and kpt on fnl f* **9/2**[3]
6621 4 1 ½ **Enery (IRE)**[13] 3945 3-9-4 75.................................. SilvestreDeSousa 6 77+
(Mark Johnston) *hld up: pushed along and sltly outpcd over 3f out: rdn over 2f out: swtchd lft to outer over 1f out: kpt on: nrst fin* **7/2**[2]
0-05 5 ½ **Dean Iarracht (IRE)**[52] 2670 6-8-9 56 oh1..................(p) BarryMcHugh 7 57
(Tracy Waggott) *s.i.s and bhd: hdwy on wd outside 2f out: sn rdn and styd on fnl f: nrst fin* **14/1**
400- 6 2 ¾ **Major Domo (FR)**[130] 5639 4-9-3 64.............................. FrederikTylicki 12 59
(Micky Hammond) *hld up: hdwy 4f out: rdn along wl over 2f out: sn no imp* **50/1**
0065 7 2 **Goldenveil (IRE)**[15] 3889 4-8-9 56.................................. TonyHamilton 9 47
(Richard Fahey) *towards rr: pushed along 4f out: rdn 3f out: n.d* **9/1**
0005 8 ¾ **Tiger Webb**[23] 3628 4-9-5 66... PaulMulrennan 4 56
(Michael Easterby) *in tch: rdn along wl over 2f out: sn wknd* **7/1**
2416 9 1 ¾ **Brockfield**[9] 4080 6-10-0 75... RobertWinston 13 61
(Mel Brittain) *in tch: hdwy to chse ldrs 3f out: rdn along over 2f out: sn btn* **7/1**
0350 10 2 ¼ **Triple Eight (IRE)**[14] 3914 4-9-3 64.........................(b) MichaelO'Connell 11 46
(Philip Kirby) *cl up: rdn along wl over 2f out: wknd wl over 1f out* **22/1**

2m 2.93s (-4.07) **Going Correction** -0.325s/f (Firm)
WFA 3 from 4yo+ 10lb 10 Ran SP% **118.9**
Speed ratings (Par 103): **103,102,100,99,99 97,95,94,93,91**
Tote Swingers: 1&2 £10.70, 1&3 £2.20, 2&3 £29.30 CSF £79.16 CT £308.88 TOTE £3.10: £1.10, £9.60, £2.00; EX 65.40.
Owner Mrs B Oughtred **Bred** Gerrardstown House Stud **Trained** Great Habton, N Yorks

FOCUS
This handicap was weakened by four withdrawals. The pace was not very strong but the favourite put in a gritty effort to deliver under a prominent ride. He's rated back to his best.
Goldenveil(IRE) Official explanation: jockey said filly was denied a clear run

4397 SKYBET SUPPORTING YORKSHIRE RACING SUMMER FESTIVAL H'CAP 7f 100y
7:30 (7:32) (Class 6) (0-65,65) 3-Y-O **£1,811** (£539; £269; £134) **Stalls** Low

Form RPR
0621 1 **Daddy Warbucks (IRE)**[13] 3938 3-9-7 65........................ AdrianNicholls 7 71
(David Nicholls) *mde all: rdn wl over 1f out: drvn ins fnl f: hld on gamely* **9/2**[1]

1322 **2** *nk* **Dream Walker (FR)**^{24} 3567 3-9-6 **64**.......................... PatrickMathers 6 69
(Ian McInnes) *trckd ldrs: hdwy 2f out: rdn over 1f out: drvn to chal ins fnl f: ev ch tl no ex nr fin* **8/1**^{3}

5-00 **3** *¾* **Kathleensluckylad (IRE)**^{77} 1916 3-8-12 **56**.............. PaulMulrennan 3 59
(Kevin Ryan) *prom on inner: effrt over 2f out: rdn to chal over 1f out: ev ch tl drvn and one pce wl ins fnl f* **14/1**

66-5 **4** *½* **Gibraltar Road**^{76} 1953 3-8-12 **56**.......................... MichaelO'Connell 14 58
(John Quinn) *hld up: hdwy on outer 2f out: rdn over 1f out: styd on fnl f: nrst fin* **9/1**

0-00 **5** *½* **Blue Top**^{52} 2673 3-8-10 **54**......................................(b^{1}) TonyHamilton 12 55
(Tim Walford) *hld up: hdwy 3f out: rdn wl over 1f out: kpt on fnl f: nrst fin* **20/1**

01 **6** *½* **Military Green (FR)**^{30} 3406 3-8-9 **53**...................... DuranFentiman 16 53+
(Tim Easterby) *trckd ldng pair on outer: hdwy and cl up wl over 2f out: sn rdn to chal and ch tl drvn and one pce ent fnl f* **16/1**

-000 **7** *1* **Minty Jones**^{24} 3555 3-8-9 **53**.......................................(b) JimmyQuinn 8 50
(Michael Mullineaux) *midfield: rdn along wl over 2f out: drvn and kpt on appr fnl f* **20/1**

0500 **8** *hd* **Alabanda (IRE)**^{6} 4192 3-9-0 **58**.. DavidAllan 11 55+
(Tim Easterby) *hld up towards rr: hdwy over 2f out: rdn over 1f out: chsd ldrs and styng on whn n.m.r ent fnl f: one pce after* **8/1**^{3}

-003 **9** *¾* **Jay Kay**^{24} 3555 3-8-10 **54**... JamesSullivan 1 49
(Danielle McCormick) *in tch: hdwy 2f out: rdn to chse ldrs over 1f out: n.m.r and one pce ins fnl f* **7/1**^{2}

5243 **10** *½* **Red Shadow**^{30} 3407 3-8-10 **54**.............................. SilvestreDeSousa 15 48+
(Alan Brown) *prom: effrt and cl up over 2f out: sn rdn and ev ch tl drvn and wknd appr fnl f* **16/1**

005 **11** *hd* **Hurricane Max (IRE)**^{52} 2680 3-8-11 **58**.......................... DaleSwift$^{(3)}$ 2 55+
(Chris Fairhurst) *dwlt and hld up in rr: hdwy and nt clr run on inner over 1f out: swtchd lft ent fnl f: sn nt clr run and hmpd: nt rcvr* **14/1**

4503 **12** *nk* **Divine Success (IRE)**^{24} 3575 3-8-6 **50**.....................(b) BarryMcHugh 4 42
(Richard Fahey) *dwlt and reminders s: a bhd* **20/1**

5-32 **13** *3½* **Mad For Fun (IRE)**^{56} 2540 3-8-8 **52**............................... MickyFenton 5 36
(Paul Midgley) *a towards rr* **9/1**

6450 **14** *3½* **Ma Kellys (IRE)**^{21} 3713 3-8-11 **55**............................. FrederikTylicki 9 30
(Micky Hammond) *midfield: rdn along on outer 1/2-way: sn lost pl and bhd* **8/1**^{3}

1m 32.32s (-1.48) **Going Correction** -0.325s/f (Firm) 14 Ran SP% **123.4**
Speed ratings (Par 98): **95,94,93,93,92 92,90,90,89,89 89,88,84,80**
Tote Swingers: 1&2 £4.70, 1&3 £8.30, 2&3 £16.00 CSF £38.86 CT £462.61 TOTE £3.40: £1.10, £4.00, £5.60; EX 27.50.
Owner Martin Love **Bred** Edmond Kent **Trained** Sessay, N Yorks

FOCUS
A minor handicap. It was run at a stop-start gallop and they finished in a bunch. The form is sound enough, with a turf personal best from the winner.
Hurricane Max(IRE) Official explanation: jockey said colt was denied a clear run

4398 TYREGIANT.COM H'CAP 1m 100y
8:00 (8:01) (Class 5) (0-75,75) 3-Y-O+ **£2,587** (£770; £384; £192) **Stalls** Low

Form RPR

0020 **1** **Last Destination (IRE)**^{21} 3705 4-8-9 **56**.............. SilvestreDeSousa 10 64
(Nigel Tinkler) *midfield: hdwy and in tch on inner over 3f out: chsd ldrs over 1f out: sn rdn and styd on wl to ld nr line* **16/1**

0 **2** *nk* **Sir Trevor (IRE)**^{75} 1978 3-9-3 **72**.................................. StephenCraine 9 77
(Tom Dascombe) *slt ld: rdn along 2f out: drvn over 1f out: kpt on gamely ins fnl f tl edgd lft and hdd nr line* **9/2**^{1}

0006 **3** *hd* **Switchback**^{19} 3749 4-9-9 **70**...................................... PaulMulrennan 11 77
(Michael Easterby) *trckd ldng pair: pushed along wl over 1f out: rdn ent fnl f: styd on wl towards fin* **14/1**

3064 **4** *½* **Shadowtime**^{6} 4177 7-9-8 **69**... FrannyNorton 7 74
(Tracy Waggott) *hld up towards rr: hdwy on outer 2f out: sn rdn and styd on fnl f: nrst fin* **7/1**^{3}

453 **5** *hd* **Sir George (IRE)**^{7} 4142 7-9-8 **69**.................................. BarryMcHugh 3 74
(Ollie Pears) *hld up towards rr: hdwy 2f out: effrt and nt clr run ent fnl f: sn swtchd lft and rdn: ch whn swtchd rt and no ex towards fin* **15/2**

3330 **6** *1* **Striker Torres (IRE)**^{18} 3775 6-9-7 **68**..........................(v) LukeMorris 12 71
(Ian McInnes) *stdd and swtchd rt s: hld up in rr: hdwy on outer wl over 1f out: sn rdn and styd on fnl f* **16/1**

40-4 **7** *1¼* **Tukitinyasok (IRE)**^{21} 3699 5-8-10 **57**......................(p) TonyHamilton 2 57
(Clive Mulhall) *chsd ldrs on inner: rdn along 2f out: drvn appr fnl f and grad wknd* **20/1**

0113 **8** *nse* **Cono Zur (FR)**^{31} 3335 5-10-0 **75**..................................... JamesSullivan 4 75
(Ruth Carr) *cl up: rdn along 2f out: drvn and ev ch ent fnl f: sn wknd* **9/2**^{1}

0001 **9** *2¼* **Collateral Damage (IRE)**^{9} 4089 9-9-7 **68**......................(t) DavidAllan 1 62
(Tim Easterby) *in tch: hdwy to chse ldrs over 3f out: rdn 2f out: wknd appr fnl f* **11/2**^{2}

304- **10** *¾* **Auto Mac**^{265} 7214 4-9-2 **66**... JulieBurke$^{(3)}$ 5 59
(Neville Bycroft) *dwlt: a in rr* **14/1**

3620 **11** *3½* **Seldom (IRE)**^{44} 2922 6-9-4 **65**..................................... RobertWinston 13 50
(Mel Brittain) *chsd ldrs: rdn along over 2f out: grad wknd* **12/1**

0-00 **12** *5* **Stilettoesinthemud (IRE)**^{28} 3456 4-8-10 **60**.................. DaleSwift$^{(3)}$ 6 33
(James Given) *a towards rr* **66/1**

5501 **13** *20* **Foursquare Funtime**^{16} 3846 3-9-1 **70**..................... RussKennemore 8
(Reg Hollinshead) *midfield: rdn along over 3f out: sn wknd* **25/1**

1m 44.23s (-3.37) **Going Correction** -0.325s/f (Firm)
WFA 3 from 4yo+ 8lb 13 Ran SP% **118.9**
Speed ratings (Par 103): **103,102,102,102,101 100,99,99,97,96 93,88,68**
Tote Swingers: 1&2 £15.00, 1&3 £29.70, 2&3 £8.30 CSF £84.65 CT £760.97 TOTE £23.90: £6.60, £1.10, £2.10; EX 100.10.
Owner A Killoran **Bred** Pier House Stud **Trained** Langton, N Yorks

FOCUS
A competitive handicap. The pace was just fair and the winner can be marked up a bit for scoring from some way back. Sound form.

4399 KINGSTON BYPASS MAIDEN H'CAP 2m 35y
8:30 (8:30) (Class 6) (0-65,63) 3-Y-O **£1,617** (£481; £240; £120) **Stalls** Low

Form RPR

-032 **1** **Solar View (IRE)**^{7} 4153 3-8-6 **48**.. LukeMorris 6 61
(Sir Mark Prescott Bt) *in tch: hdwy 6f out: led 2f out: sn rdn: drvn ins fnl f: hung bdly lft towards fin: kpt on* **11/10**^{1}

0230 **2** *¾* **Looks Like Rain**^{26} 3483 3-8-10 **55**................................. DaleSwift$^{(3)}$ 11 67
(Brian Ellison) *hld up: hdwy on outer over 2f out: rdn to chse ldrs over 1f out: styng on strly whn sltly hmpd nr fin* **14/1**

0634 **3** *2½* **Dr Irv**^{5} 4210 3-8-10 **52**.. MichaelO'Connell 10 61
(Kate Walton) *in tch: hdwy over 3f out: swtchd lft and rdn to chse ldrs over 1f out: drvn to chal jst ins fnl f: sn one pce* **18/1**

0302 **4** *1¼* **Vexillum (IRE)**^{12} 3965 3-9-0 **56**.................................... SamHitchcott 7 64
(Mick Channon) *hld up: hdwy over 4f out: rdn 2f out: drvn and styd on appr fnl f: nrst fin* **12/1**

0-60 **5** *2¾* **Astonished Harry (GER)**^{21} 3697 3-8-9 **51**............. RussKennemore 15 55
(Reg Hollinshead) *hld up and bhd: hdwy wl over 2f out: styd on appr fnl f: nrst fin* **33/1**

0404 **6** *2¾* **Eanans Bay (IRE)**^{18} 3781 3-8-13 **55**............................ RobertWinston 9 56
(Mark H Tompkins) *in tch: hdwy wl over 2f out: rdn wl over 1f out: kpt on same pce appr fnl f* **8/1**^{2}

-050 **7** *hd* **Single Girl (IRE)**^{39} 3087 3-8-7 **49**..........................(p) DuranFentiman 13 50
(Jonathan Portman) *trckd ldrs: hdwy and cl up 5f out: rdn along over 2f out: sn drvn and grad wknd* **16/1**

60-5 **8** *3¼* **Sweet Fairnando**^{5} 4210 3-9-3 **59**... DavidAllan 12 56
(Tim Easterby) *hld up: a towards rr* **20/1**

0004 **9** *¾* **Brasingaman Espee**^{21} 3697 3-8-4 **46**.......................... AndrewElliott 14 42
(George Moore) *hld up in rr: sme hdwy 3f out: rdn along and styng on whn n.m.r wl over 1f out: n.d* **20/1**

5454 **10** *2* **Authentication**^{6} 4200 3-9-2 **58**................................ SilvestreDeSousa 3 51
(Mark Johnston) *in tch: hdwy to chse ldr after 5f: led over 5f out: rdn and hdd 2f out: sn drvn and wknd* **10/1**^{3}

0044 **11** *1¾* **Hulwa (USA)**^{49} 2771 3-8-3 **45**.. FrannyNorton 8 36
(Tracy Waggott) *prom: effrt over 2f out: sn rdn and wknd* **14/1**

5202 **12** *6* **Minnie Diva (IRE)**^{47} 2818 3-9-7 **63**.............................. PaulMulrennan 1 47+
(Kevin Ryan) *trckd ldrs: rdn along over 3f out: sn wknd* **10/1**^{3}

06-0 **13** *7* **Hawkino (IRE)**^{30} 3399 3-8-3 **45**.....................................(v) JimmyQuinn 16 21
(Derek Shaw) *a bhd* **100/1**

00-0 **14** *12* **Willy McBay**^{5} 4210 3-8-3 **45**.. AndrewMullen 2
(George Moore) *chsd ldrs: rdn along 6f out: sn wknd* **100/1**

0-04 **15** *99* **Letham Cottage**^{11} 4005 3-8-3 **45**...................................(b) MartinLane 5
(Brian Meehan) *led: hdd over 5f out: sn wknd and bhd fnl 3f* **40/1**

3m 37.91s (-1.89) **Going Correction** -0.325s/f (Firm) 15 Ran SP% **126.0**
Speed ratings (Par 98): **91,90,89,88,87 86,85,84,83,82 82,79,75,69,20**
Tote Swingers: 1&2 £7.90, 1&3 £5.00, 2&3 £9.50 CSF £17.99 CT £209.40 TOTE £2.30: £1.40, £4.60, £5.60; EX 21.90.
Owner Neil Greig - Osborne House **Bred** Lady Richard Wellesley **Trained** Newmarket, Suffolk
■ Stewards' Enquiry : Michael O'Connell one-day ban: careless riding (Aug 6)

FOCUS
A minor staying handicap but the unexposed Sir Mark Prescott-trained winner landed a gamble with a bit in hand and the form has been rated slightly positively. The winner did not need to match his latest effort.

4400 BEVERLEY FASHION WEEK 23 - 28 JULY H'CAP 5f
9:00 (9:01) (Class 5) (0-75,75) 3-Y-O+ **£2,264** (£673; £336; £168) **Stalls** Low

Form RPR

3060 **1** **Last Sovereign**^{37} 3169 8-9-5 **75**.........................(b) JacobButterfield$^{(7)}$ 8 84
(Ollie Pears) *in rr and pushed along 1/2-way: rdn 2f out: swtchd lft and hdwy over 1f out: squeezed through ent fnl f: styd on strly to ld nr line* **20/1**

045 **2** *hd* **Select Committee**^{42} 2982 7-9-10 **73**....................(b) MichaelO'Connell 7 81
(John Quinn) *trckd ldrs: hdwy wl over 1f out: rdn to chse ldr ent fnl f: sn drvn and led last 50yds: hdd nr line* **10/1**

4203 **3** *hd* **Tabaret**^{13} 3944 9-9-5 **68**...(p) AmyRyan 3 75
(Richard Whitaker) *prom: hdwy to ld 1 1/2f out: rdn and edgd lft ins fnl f: sn drvn: hdd and no ex last 50yds* **9/2**^{2}

2510 **4** *2¼* **Steelcut**^{18} 3778 8-9-9 **72**..(p) FrederikTylicki 13 71
(Mark Buckley) *in tch: hdwy and nt clr run 1f out: sn rdn and styd on wl: nrst fin* **10/1**

2110 **5** *shd* **Mercers Row**^{48} 2793 5-9-12 **75**.............................. SilvestreDeSousa 12 74
(Noel Wilson) *in tch: hdwy wl over 1f out: rdn to chse ldng trio ins fnl f: kpt on same pce* **15/2**^{3}

-000 **6** *1½* **Indian Trail**^{51} 2719 12-9-7 **70**..(b) PaulQuinn 1 63
(David Nicholls) *chsd ldrs on inner: rdn along over 1f out: kpt on same pce* **10/1**

-004 **7** *½* **Lady Kildare (IRE)**^{42} 2982 4-8-13 **62**............................ AndrewElliott 17 54
(Jedd O'Keeffe) *in tch on wd outside: hdwy to chse ldrs 2f out: sn rdn and kpt on same pce fnl f* **25/1**

150 **8** *¾* **Gorgeous Goblin (IRE)**^{11} 4013 5-9-4 **74**(t) WilliamTwiston-Davies$^{(7)}$ 14 63
(David C Griffiths) *hld up towards rr: hdwy over 1f out: sn rdn and kpt on fnl f: nt rch ldrs* **20/1**

0311 **9** *1½* **Choc'A'Moca (IRE)**^{45} 2878 5-9-4 **67**.........................(v) MickyFenton 5 51
(Paul Midgley) *stmbld s: sn cl up: rdn along wl over 1f out: hld whn hmpd and wknd 1f out* **4/1**^{1}

0530 **10** *½* **Master Of Disguise**^{18} 3778 6-9-12 **75**.....................(t) DuranFentiman 15 57
(Brian Baugh) *chsd ldrs: rdn along wl over 1f out: sn wknd* **10/1**

0000 **11** *hd* **Ingleby Star (IRE)**^{42} 2982 7-9-6 **69**.........................(p) PatrickMathers 4 50
(Ian McInnes) *cl up: rdn and led briefly 2f out: sn hdd and wkng whn hmpd 1f out* **20/1**

-006 **12** *2* **Nickel Silver**^{48} 2793 7-9-2 **70**................................(v) JustinNewman$^{(5)}$ 11 44
(Bryan Smart) *hld up: effrt whn nt clr run and hmpd 1f out: sn swtchd rt and nt rcvr* **25/1**

000- **13** *1¼* **Major Muscari (IRE)**^{277} 6979 4-9-4 **70**............................ DaleSwift$^{(3)}$ 6 39
(Geoffrey Oldroyd) *cl up: led 1/2-way: hdd and rdn 2f out: sn wknd* **20/1**

0030 **14** *½* **Black Annis Bower**^{11} 3993 4-9-3 **66**.............................. JamesSullivan 16 34
(Michael Easterby) *a in rr* **28/1**

40-3 **15** *1* **Secret Venue**^{48} 2793 6-9-3 **66**....................................... TonyHamilton 10 30
(Jedd O'Keeffe) *led: hdd 1/2-way: sn rdn along and wknd wl over 1f out* **12/1**

1m 2.64s (-0.86) **Going Correction** -0.075s/f (Good)
WFA 3 from 4yo+ 4lb 15 Ran SP% **124.2**
Speed ratings (Par 103): **103,102,102,98,98 96,95,94,91,91 90,87,85,84,83**
Tote Swingers: 1&2 £16.50, 1&3 £33.60, 2&3 £5.20 CSF £195.50 CT £1080.10 TOTE £37.50: £11.90, £2.80, £2.10; EX 148.80.
Owner Richard Walker **Bred** Gestut Hof Ittlingen & Cheveley Park Stud Ltd **Trained** Norton, N Yorks

FOCUS
A big-priced runner prevailed in a tight three-way finish in this sprint handicap. The first three raced towards the far rail and the second and third are the best guides.
Ingleby Star(IRE) Official explanation: jockey said gelding hung left-handed
T/Jkpt: Not won. T/Plt: £137.80 to a £1 stake. Pool: £71,209.77 - 377.04 winning tickets. T/Qpdt: £19.50 to a £1 stake. Pool: £7,815.25 - 295.66 winning tickets. JR

[4187] SOUTHWELL (L-H)

Monday, July 23

OFFICIAL GOING: Standard

Wind: Light across Weather: Fine and sunny

4401 32RED.COM H'CAP 7f (F)
2:10 (2:11) (Class 4) (0-80,80) 3-Y-0+ **£4,851** (£1,443; £721; £360) **Stalls** Low

Form RPR

1116 **1** **Only Ten Per Cent (IRE)**[76] 1958 4-9-6 72 .... DarryllHolland 6 82+
(J R Jenkins) *a.p: chsd ldr 1/2-way: led over 2f out: drvn out* **15/2**

0361 **2** ½ **Anton Chigurh**[11] 3994 3-9-7 80 .... RichardKingscote 2 87
(Tom Dascombe) *s.i.s: hld up: hdwy over 1f out: r.o to go 2nd nr fin: nt quite rch wnr* **6/4**[1]

0040 **3** *nk* **Follow The Flag (IRE)**[73] 2051 8-9-11 77 ....(v) LukeMorris 7 85
(Alan McCabe) *sn outpcd: hdwy over 2f out: rdn to chse wnr over 1f out: r.o* **25/1**

0601 **4** 4½ **Flying Pickets (IRE)**[7] 4141 3-8-9 75 6ex(be) WilliamTwiston-Davies[(7)] 3 69
(Alan McCabe) *sn outpcd: rdn and hung lft over 2f out: styd on fr over 1f out: nt trble ldrs* **16/1**

3402 **5** 2¾ **Tahnee Mara (IRE)**[13] 3940 3-8-7 66 .... AmyRyan 5 52
(Kevin Ryan) *chsd ldrs: rdn over 2f out: wknd over 1f out* **6/1**[3]

0223 **6** 4½ **Alpha Tauri (USA)**[4] 4262 6-9-7 80 ....(t) ThomasBrown[(7)] 4 56
(David C Griffiths) *led: rdn and hdd over 2f out: wknd wl over 1f out* **6/1**[3]

6001 **7** 4½ **Mazovian (USA)**[7] 4143 4-9-0 73 6ex .... DannyBrock[(7)] 1 37
(Michael Chapman) *chsd ldrs: sn drvn along: lost pl 5f out: sn bhd: eased fr over 1f out* **14/1**

-440 **8** 2 **Dark Falcon (IRE)**[48] 2785 3-8-13 72 ....(p) MartinLane 8 29
(James Tate) *chsd ldr to 1/2-way: rdn and wknd over 2f out* **9/2**[2]

1m 28.23s (-2.07) **Going Correction** -0.125s/f (Stan)
WFA 3 from 4yo+ 7lb **8** Ran SP% **114.9**
Speed ratings (Par 105): **106,105,105,99,96 91,86,84**
Tote Swingers: 1&2 £3.10, 1&3 £6.80, 2&3 £9.30 CSF £19.32 CT £274.28 TOTE £5.80: £1.50, £2.90, £7.20; EX 22.90.
Owner B Silkman **Bred** Sandro Garavelli **Trained** Royston, Herts

FOCUS
A competitive handicap on paper but the pace, set by Alpha Tauri, looked suicidal and only served to set things up for those in behind. The first three home all came from well off the gallop. The winner resumed his progress on this surface.

4402 32REDPOKER.COM H'CAP 1m 4f (F)
2:40 (2:40) (Class 6) (0-65,65) 4-Y-0+ **£1,681** (£500; £250; £125) **Stalls** Low

Form RPR

06-5 **1** **Layla's Boy**[7] 4156 5-8-9 53 ....(bt) FrannyNorton 9 69
(John Mackie) *chsd ldrs tl led over 3f out: rdn clr fr over 2f out: easily* **16/1**

2000 **2** 12 **Lakeman (IRE)**[6] 4179 6-8-12 59 ....(v) PaulPickard[(3)] 3 56
(Brian Ellison) *prom: chsd ldr 8f out tl led over 4f out: hdd over 3f out: sn rdn: wknd over 1f out* **12/1**

503 **3** 2¾ **Naburn**[14] 3913 4-9-2 65 .... GarryWhillans[(5)] 7 57
(Alan Swinbank) *hld up: pushed along over 9f out: hdwy over 5f out: rdn over 3f out: wknd over 2f out* **3/1**[2]

4302 **4** 1¾ **Bring Sweets (IRE)**[6] 4189 5-8-7 54 ow1 .... DaleSwift[(3)] 5 44
(Brian Ellison) *prom: rdn over 3f out: wknd over 2f out* **7/4**[1]

06-0 **5** ¾ **Mahayogin (USA)**[18] 3786 4-8-9 60 ....(tp) WilliamTwiston-Davies[(7)] 6 48
(Charlie Mann) *prom: rdn over 4f out: wknd over 2f out* **7/1**[3]

-040 **6** *hd* **Runaway Tiger (IRE)**[11] 3988 4-8-8 52 ....(v) LiamJones 10 40
(Paul D'Arcy) *hld up: rdn over 3f out: n.d* **9/1**

3005 **7** 7 **Swords**[59] 2454 10-8-2 46 oh1 .... JimmyQuinn 1 23
(Ray Peacock) *led: rdn and hdd over 4f out: wknd over 3f out* **40/1**

4160 **8** 3¼ **Sky Diamond (IRE)**[32] 3317 4-8-2 53 .... DannyBrock[(7)] 8 25
(John Mackie) *hld up: rdn over 3f out: a in rr* **12/1**

0650 **9** 58 **Darsan (IRE)**[3] 4296 4-9-3 61 .... SilvestreDeSousa 2
(Phil McEntee) *chsd ldr 4f: sn pushed along and lost pl: bhd fnl 6f: eased: t.o* **11/1**

2m 37.72s (-3.28) **Going Correction** -0.125s/f (Stan) **9** Ran SP% **115.9**
Speed ratings (Par 101): **105,97,95,94,93 93,88,86,47**
Tote Swingers: 1&2 £7.50, 1&3 £9.50, 2&3 £6.60 CSF £191.42 CT £738.74 TOTE £15.80: £3.40, £1.70, £1.40; EX 127.60.
Owner RJM Racing **Bred** Wickfield Stud And Hartshill Stud **Trained** Church Broughton , Derbys

FOCUS
A poor race in truth, with the favourite disappointing. A surprise winner, rated back to something like his 2yo form.
Layla's Boy Official explanation: trainer had no explanation for the apparent improvement in form
Bring Sweets(IRE) Official explanation: jockey said gelding never travelled
Darsan(IRE) Official explanation: trainer's rep said filly lost a front shoe

4403 32RED CASINO H'CAP 1m 4f (F)
3:15 (3:15) (Class 5) (0-75,71) 3-Y-0 **£2,328** (£693; £346; £173) **Stalls** Low

Form RPR

0000 **1** **Three Bards (IRE)**[27] 3475 3-9-7 71 .... SilvestreDeSousa 4 84+
(Mark Johnston) *a.p: chsd ldr over 10f out: led over 7f out: rdn: hung rt and lft fr over 2f out: styd on* **11/4**[2]

6231 **2** 2½ **News Show**[6] 4200 3-9-0 71 6ex .... AliceHaynes[(7)] 5 80
(David Simcock) *s.i.s: hld up: hdwy over 5f out: chsd wnr over 2f out: sn rdn: styd on same pce fnl f* **11/10**[1]

5045 **3** 5 **Rano Pano (USA)**[23] 3621 3-8-2 52 oh2 .... JamesSullivan 3 53
(Brian Ellison) *plld hrd: trckd ldr over 1f: remained handy: chsd wnr over 6f out tl rdn over 2f out: styd on same pce appr fnl f* **15/2**

055 **4** 21 **Zain Glory**[23] 3606 3-9-5 69 .... LukeMorris 2 36
(Gerard Butler) *s.i.s: sn prom: rdn over 4f out: wknd wl over 2f out* **4/1**[3]

0500 **5** 60 **Tooley Woods (IRE)**[13] 3939 3-8-0 57 .... DannyBrock[(7)] 1
(Alan McCabe) *led over 4f: sn drvn along: wknd over 5f out: t.o* **40/1**

2m 38.62s (-2.38) **Going Correction** -0.125s/f (Stan) **5** Ran SP% **108.5**
Speed ratings (Par 100): **102,100,97,83,43**
CSF £6.01 TOTE £9.90: £3.10, £1.10; EX 8.90.
Owner Sheikh Hamdan Bin Mohammed Al Maktoum **Bred** Thomas G Cooke **Trained** Middleham Moor, N Yorks

FOCUS
A small field with little depth. The winner's previous best was on his only other run here.

4404 £32 BONUS AT 32RED.COM MAIDEN STKS 7f (F)
3:45 (3:46) (Class 5) 2-Y-0 **£2,328** (£693; £346; £173) **Stalls** Low

Form RPR

4 **1** **Hunting Rights (USA)**[15] 3887 2-9-3 0 .... SilvestreDeSousa 3 73+
(Mark Johnston) *led: rdn and hdd over 2f out: hung lft over 1f out: rallied to ld ins fnl f: edgd rt: styd on* **8/13**[1]

6 **2** 1¾ **Zain Spirit (USA)**[26] 3499 2-9-3 0 .... LukeMorris 1 68
(Gerard Butler) *trckd wnr tl led over 2f out: rdn and hung lft over 1f out: edgd rt and hdd ins fnl f: styd on same pce* **5/2**[2]

00 **3** 12 **Holding Fast (IRE)**[12] 3973 2-9-3 0 .... MartinLane 4 37
(Tobias B P Coles) *s.i.s: sn chsng ldrs: rdn and hung lft over 2f out: wknd over 1f out* **20/1**

50 **4** 12 **Buxted's Choice (IRE)**[10] 4056 2-9-3 0 .... StevieDonohoe 2 6
(Robert Mills) *hld up in tch: racd keenly: rdn 1/2-way: sn wknd* **13/2**[3]

1m 31.19s (0.89) **Going Correction** -0.125s/f (Stan) **4** Ran SP% **108.6**
Speed ratings (Par 94): **89,87,73,59**
CSF £2.42 TOTE £1.60; EX 2.00.
Owner Sheikh Hamdan Bin Mohammed Al Maktoum **Bred** Darley **Trained** Middleham Moor, N Yorks

FOCUS
The betting suggested this was effectively a match, and the big two came a long way clear of the two outsiders. Tricky to pin down the level of the form.

NOTEBOOK
Hunting Rights(USA) is a big, scopey colt from a smart US family and he showed all the right qualities to dig deep and see off what looked a very strong challenge from Zain Glory early in the straight. Although the winning time was quite modest (much slower than opening handicap over this trip) he could have a bright future, especially on AW surfaces which he is bred to excel on. (op 4-6 tchd 8-11)
Zain Spirit(USA) posted a cracking effort in defeat and has clearly come on a good deal from his Kempton debut. He'll not be long in going one better, perhaps on the AW. (op 3-1 tchd 9-4)
Holding Fast(IRE) appears to be regressing with racing. (op 18-1 tchd 25-1)
Buxted's Choice(IRE) appears to be regressing with racing. (op 5-1 tchd 7-1)

4405 32REDBET.COM H'CAP 1m (F)
4:20 (4:21) (Class 6) (0-60,63) 3-Y-0+ **£1,772** (£523; £261) **Stalls** Low

Form RPR

0-00 **1** **Applaude**[63] 2348 7-8-12 46 oh1 ....(b) MichaelStainton 8 55
(Chris Bealby) *a.p: chsd ldr over 5f out tl led over 3f out: rdn over 1f out: styd on* **40/1**

5062 **2** 1½ **Symphony Star (IRE)**[13] 3939 3-8-12 54 .... LukeMorris 9 58
(Paul D'Arcy) *sn pushed along in rr: hdwy u.p 1/2-way: styd on to go 2nd wl ins fnl f: nt rch wnr* **4/1**[2]

0001 **3** 1¼ **Monzino (USA)**[6] 4192 4-10-1 63 6ex .... RussKennemore 10 66
(Michael Chapman) *s.i.s: hdwy over 4f out: rdn to chse wnr 2f out: styd on: lost 2nd wl ins fnl f* **4/1**[2]

2056 **4** 4½ **Bonnie Prince Blue**[6] 4192 9-9-9 60 ....(b) DaleSwift[(3)] 7 53
(Ian McInnes) *sn outpcd: hdwy u.p fnl 2f: nvr trbld ldrs* **10/1**

0030 **5** 3¼ **This Ones For Eddy**[6] 4192 7-9-9 57 .... MartinLane 6 42
(John Balding) *sn pushed along in rr: drvn along 1/2-way: styd on u.p: nvr on terms* **16/1**

/000 **6** ½ **Gifted Heir (IRE)**[136] 848 8-8-9 46 oh1 .... MichaelMetcalfe[(3)] 11 30
(Ray Peacock) *chsd ldrs: rdn over 3f out: wknd over 1f out* **100/1**

000 **7** 2 **One Bid Too Many (USA)**[24] 3561 3-8-4 46 oh1 ....(v[1]) JimmyQuinn 2 23
(Derek Shaw) *sn led: hdd over 3f out: wknd over 2f out* **33/1**

-305 **8** 1½ **Allanit (GER)**[12] 3976 8-9-10 58 .... DaraghO'Donohoe 3 34
(Barney Curley) *stdd s: hld up and bhd: shkn up over 2f out: eased fr over 1f out: nvr nr to chal* **33/1**

5346 **9** ½ **Brown Pete (IRE)**[9] 4089 4-9-12 60 ....(e) CathyGannon 5 35
(Richard Guest) *mid-div: hdwy u.p over 3f out: wknd over 2f out* **6/1**[3]

5605 **10** 13 **Hilbre Court (USA)**[6] 4193 7-9-5 53 ....(v) J-PGuillambert 1
(Brian Baugh) *led early: sn drvn along and lost pl: wknd over 4f out* **25/1**

6023 **11** 7 **Yas Marina (USA)**[6] 4189 4-8-13 47 ....(b) SilvestreDeSousa 13
(David O'Meara) *sn pushed along in rr: hdwy 5f out: rdn and hung rt over 4f out: wknd and eased over 3f out: t.o* **7/2**[1]

000- **12** 51 **Irish Law**[209] 7886 4-8-12 46 oh1 .... FrannyNorton 4
(John Balding) *chsd ldr over 2f: wknd 1/2-way: t.o* **50/1**

1m 42.69s (-1.01) **Going Correction** -0.125s/f (Stan)
WFA 3 from 4yo+ 8lb **12** Ran SP% **106.6**
Speed ratings (Par 101): **100,98,97,92,89 89,87,85,85,72 65,14**
Tote Swingers: 1&2 £22.60, 1&3 £33.30, 2&3 £3.00 CSF £153.84 CT £602.94 TOTE £45.40: £10.50, £1.10, £1.10; EX 253.70.
Owner Miss F E Harper **Bred** G Reed **Trained** Barrowby, Lincs
■ Scarborough Lily (8/1) was withdrawn on vet's advice. Deduct 10p in the £ under R4.

FOCUS
Low-grade stuff and a shock result. The winner's best form for two years.
Yas Marina(USA) Official explanation: jockey said gelding had no more to give

4406 32REDBINGO.COM H'CAP 7f (F)
4:55 (4:59) (Class 6) (0-65,63) 3-Y-0+ **£1,772** (£523; £261) **Stalls** Low

Form RPR

5525 **1** **Soopacal (IRE)**[6] 4187 7-9-6 58 .... DaleSwift[(3)] 12 72
(Brian Ellison) *mde all: rdn and hung lft ins fnl f: styd on* **7/2**[1]

2006 **2** 3 **Beachwood Bay**[13] 3941 4-10-0 63 .... J-PGuillambert 2 69
(Jo Hughes) *a.p: rdn to chse wnr and hung lft over 2f out: styd on same pce fnl f* **15/2**

0524 **3** *shd* **Putin (IRE)**[4] 4241 4-8-12 47 ....(bt) LukeMorris 7 53
(Phil McEntee) *chsd ldrs: rdn over 2f out: styd on same pce fnl f* **7/2**[1]

56-2 **4** 4 **Elusive Warrior (USA)**[7] 4141 9-9-0 56 .... NoraLooby[(7)] 8 51
(Alan McCabe) *prom: rdn over 2f out: hung lft and wknd over 1f out* **11/2**[3]

4-05 **4** *dht* **Spitfire**[38] 3103 7-10-0 63 .... FrederikTylicki 9 58
(J R Jenkins) *n.m.r sn after s: hld up: hdwy 2f out: sn rdn: wknd fnl f* **5/1**[2]

0606 **6** 8 **Amber Moon**[7] 4142 7-8-5 45 ....(b) AnnStokell[(5)] 10 18
(Ann Stokell) *sn pushed along and prom: lost pl over 4f out: n.d after* **66/1**

0000 **7** ¾ **Abdul Malik**[21] 3713 3-8-3 45 ....(e) CathyGannon 6 14
(Kate Walton) *chsd ldrs: rdn 1/2-way: wknd over 1f out* **16/1**

6000 **8** 1¼ **Bridal Medic**[25] 3543 3-8-3 45 .... MartinLane 1 11
(John Mackie) *sn outpcd: hdwy and nt clr run over 4f out: rdn and wknd over 2f out* **22/1**

5564 **9** ½ **Crocodile Bay (IRE)**[28] 3455 9-8-10 45 ....(p) RobbieFitzpatrick 11 12
(Richard Guest) *chsd ldrs: rdn 1/2-way: wknd over 2f out* **16/1**

5-60 **10** *nk* **Norcroft**[40] 3053 10-8-11 46 ....(p) TomMcLaughlin 3 12
(Christine Dunnett) *sn outpcd* **25/1**

0000 **11** *1 ¼* **Avec Moi**[20] 3721 5-8-7 45 .... AdamBeschizza(3) 5
(Christine Dunnett) *sn outpcd* **50/1**
0066 **12** *1* **Kieron's Rock (IRE)**[31] 3356 3-8-6 48 .... AndrewElliott 4
(Jedd O'Keeffe) *prom: rdn 1/2-way: wknd over 2f out* **12/1**
1m 28.9s (-1.40) **Going Correction** -0.125s/f (Stan)
WFA 3 from 4yo+ 7lb **12** Ran SP% **119.4**
Speed ratings (Par 101): **103,99,99,94,94 85,84,83,82,82 81,79**
Tote Swingers: 1&2 £8.50, 1&3 £4.20, 2&3 £6.50 CSF £29.55 CT £101.61 TOTE £4.80: £2.00, £3.80, £2.10; EX 39.20.
Owner Mrs Claire Ellison **Bred** Paul Trainor **Trained** Norton, N Yorks

FOCUS
It paid to race prominently here as the first three home were always on or close to the speed. Sound form.

4407 32RED FILLIES' H'CAP — 1m (F)
5:25 (5:25) (Class 4) (0-85,80) 3-Y-0+ **£4,851** (£1,443; £721; £360) **Stalls** Low

Form RPR
-042 **1** **Saaboog**[12] 3978 3-8-4 64 .... MartinLane 2 72+
(James Tate) *broke wl and led early: sn stdd and lost pl: hld up: hmpd over 3f out: swtchd rt sn after: hdwy to ld 2f out: clr over 1f out: edgd lft: easily* **4/1**[2]
264 **2** *3 ½* **Certral**[58] 2504 4-9-11 80 .... PaulPickard(3) 3 82+
(Brian Ellison) *chsd ldrs: hmpd and lost pl over 3f out: rallied over 1f out: styd on: no ch w wnr* **2/1**[1]
0606 **3** *½* **Imaginary World (IRE)**[59] 2465 4-9-0 73(be) WilliamTwiston-Davies(7) 4 74
(Alan McCabe) *hld up in tch: rdn over 1f out: styd on same pce fnl f* **6/1**[3]
656U **4** *3 ½* **Inpursuitoffreedom**[31] 3344 5-8-12 64 .... (v) LukeMorris 6 57
(Philip McBride) *chsd ldrs: led over 2f out: sn hdd: rdn and wknd fnl f* **6/1**[3]
30- **5** *5* **Shayla**[282] 6867 5-8-11 68 .... GarryWhillans(5) 8 50
(Alan Swinbank) *chsd ldrs: rdn over 4f out: wknd over 1f out* **8/1**
00-2 **6** *1 ¾* **Kampai**[20] 3720 4-9-3 72 .... AdamBeschizza(3) 5 50
(Julia Feilden) *s.i.s: hdwy over 6f out: led over 3f out: rdn and hdd over 2f out: wknd over 1f out* **16/1**
1005 **7** *9* **Hold The Star**[13] 3940 6-8-4 61 oh6 .... AnnStokell(5) 1 18
(Ann Stokell) *sn pushed along in rr: bhd fr 1/2-way* **40/1**
1205 **8** *1 ¾* **Cut The Cackle (IRE)**[9] 4085 6-8-12 64 .... (bt) CathyGannon 7 17
(Richard Guest) *sn led: rdn and hdd over 3f out: wknd 2f out* **8/1**
1m 43.57s (-0.13) **Going Correction** -0.125s/f (Stan)
WFA 3 from 4yo+ 8lb **8** Ran SP% **112.4**
Speed ratings (Par 102): **95,91,91,87,82 80,71,70**
CSF £11.98 CT £45.38 TOTE £4.60: £1.10, £3.60, £1.30; EX 10.50.
Owner Saif Ali **Bred** Rabbah Bloodstock Limited **Trained** Newmarket, Suffolk

FOCUS
Mostly exposed performers in this ordinary fillies' handicap. The time was slow but the winner is gradually getting her act together.
Cut The Cackle(IRE) Official explanation: jockey said mare hung left
T/Plt: £49.50 to a £1 stake. Pool: £46,996.00 - 692.85 winning units. T/Qpdt: £7.20 to a £1 stake. Pool: £4,029.00 - 410.02 winning units. CR

4146 WINDSOR (R-H)
Monday, July 23

OFFICIAL GOING: Good (7.7)
Straight dolled out 3yds at 6f to intersection, reducing to full course width at winning post. Top bend out 1yd from normal, adding 5yds to races of 1m plus.
Wind: Nil Weather: Sunny early, getting darker

4408 EBF TATTERSALLS IRELAND SEPTEMBER YEARLING SALE MAIDEN FILLIES' STKS — 6f
6:10 (6:11) (Class 5) 2-Y-0 **£3,557** (£1,058; £529; £264) **Stalls** Low

Form RPR
43 **1** **Califante**[27] 3474 2-9-0 0 .... RichardHughes 8 81+
(Richard Hannon) *trckd ldrs: led appr fnl f: sn qcknd to assert: comf* **13/8**[1]
55 **2** *2* **Annie's Fortune (IRE)**[45] 2892 2-8-7 0 .... MichaelJMMurphy(7) 12 75
(Alan Jarvis) *chsd ldrs: drvn to go 2nd 1f out but no ch w wnr: edgd rt u.p clsng stages* **17/2**
505 **3** *1 ¼* **This Is Nice (IRE)**[12] 3959 2-9-0 72 .... KierenFallon 4 71
(Tom Dascombe) *pressed ldrs: chal fr over 2f out tl over 1f out: no ex and dropped to 3rd fnl f* **5/1**[3]
0 **4** *2 ½* **Take The Lead**[24] 3560 2-9-0 0 .... DaneO'Neill 3 64
(Richard Hannon) *led: rdn and jnd over 2f out: hdd appr fnl f and sn wknd* **20/1**
5 **5** *1 ¾* **Invincible Cara (IRE)**[24] 3590 2-9-0 0 .... RyanMoore 7 59
(John Dunlop) *s.i.s: rcvrd and in tch over 3f out: drvn over 2f out and no imp on ldrs: kpt on same pce* **5/2**[2]
65 **6** *hd* **Meet Me Halfway**[18] 3788 2-9-0 0 .... TedDurcan 9 58
(Chris Wall) *mid-div: pushed along over 2f out: kpt on same pce* **66/1**
7 *nse* **Koharu** 2-9-0 0 .... SebSanders 2 58+
(Peter Makin) *chsd ldrs: pushed along over 2f out: styd on same pce* **28/1**
4 **8** *2 ¼* **Silver Arny**[26] 3487 2-9-0 0 .... KirstyMilczarek 1 51
(Brendan Powell) *in tch: pushed along 1/2-way and styd on same pce* **50/1**
9 *nse* **Fair Comment** 2-9-0 0 .... FergusSweeney 10 51+
(Michael Blanshard) *in rr: pushed along after 2f: styd on fnl f* **100/1**
10 *4* **Entwined (IRE)** 2-9-0 0 .... JohnFahy 11 39
(Clive Cox) *a outpcd* **33/1**
5 **11** *5* **Linda's Icon**[10] 4055 2-9-0 0 .... ChrisCatlin 5 24
(Mick Channon) *s.i.s: a outpcd* **18/1**
000 **12** *nse* **I'm Watching**[46] 2844 2-9-0 0 .... MickaelBarzalona 13 24
(George Baker) *chsd ldrs over 3f* **100/1**
13 *3 ½* **Be Very Careful** 2-9-0 0 .... SeanLevey 6 13
(Richard Hannon) *outpcd* **40/1**
1m 11.56s (-1.44) **Going Correction** -0.325s/f (Firm) **13** Ran SP% **118.1**
Speed ratings (Par 91): **96,93,91,88,86 85,85,82,82,77 70,70,65**
Tote Swingers: 1&2 £4.80, 1&3 £2.70, 2&3 £9.10 CSF £15.41 TOTE £2.50: £1.10, £2.60, £2.10; EX 17.60 Trifecta £181.80 Pool: £535.33 - 2.17 winning units..
Owner Rockcliffe Stud **Bred** J Hicks, K Nikkel & S Robertson **Trained** East Everleigh, Wilts

FOCUS
The inner of the straight was dolled out three yards at 6f down to the intersection, then reducing to full racecourse width at the winning post. The top bend was dolled out one yard from normal inner configuration, adding five yards to race distances at 1m-plus. On a warm day, the ground was drying out all the time. This looked just a fair fillies' maiden. The winner did this in the style of a filly who can rate a bit higher.

NOTEBOOK
Califante, who had recorded RPRs in the 70s on her first two starts, found this straightforward. She was dropping back in trip and racing on quickish ground for the first time, but she had more than enough speed to cope. (op 11-10)
Annie's Fortune(IRE) had shown ability on her first two starts, albeit her level of form was a notch or two below Califante's, and she again ran well. She might win an ordinary maiden and nurseries are now an option. (op 14-1)
This Is Nice(IRE) showed speed but just wasn't good enough. She might be better off in nurseries. (tchd 6-1)
Invincible Cara(IRE) was fifth on her debut in a July course maiden in which could be working out better, and became another to let the form down. She never threatened after missing the break and, considering she's out of a 1m4f winner, this sharper track probably didn't suit. (op 4-1)
Meet Me Halfway can now contest nurseries and there should be more to come from her.

4409 GO RACING IN IRELAND CLASSIFIED (S) STKS — 1m 3f 135y
6:40 (6:40) (Class 5) 3-Y-0+ **£2,264** (£673; £336; £168) **Stalls** Centre

Form RPR
-006 **1** **Into The Wind**[37] 3137 5-9-6 46 .... IanMongan 4 67
(Rod Millman) *racd in 4th tl hdwy 4f out: chal over 2f out and sn narrow ld: sn drvn and hrd pressed tl styd on wl fnl 150yds* **10/1**
3/61 **2** *1 ½* **King's Masque**[12] 3967 6-9-4 72 .... RobertWilliams(7) 1 69
(Bernard Llewellyn) *racd in cl 3rd: hdwy 4f out: sn chalng: pressed wnr fr over 2f out tl no ex and btn fnl 150yds* **5/2**[2]
5641 **3** *8* **Kiss A Prince**[23] 3620 6-9-11 63 .... (p) RichardHughes 5 55
(Dean Ivory) *stdd s and hld up in last pl taking t.k.h: shkn up 4f out: tk mod 3rd but no ch whn hung lft to centre of crse fnl 2f* **9/4**[1]
/0-4 **4** *1 ¼* **Goodwood Starlight (IRE)**[12] 3967 7-9-6 70 .... (t) GeorgeBaker 3 48
(Jim Best) *plld hrd: chsd ldr tl led over 6f out: jnd over 4f out: sn rdn: wknd over 2f out* **9/2**
0/13 **5** *1 ¼* **Reaction**[12] 3967 6-9-6 65 .... (p) HarryPoulton(5) 2 51
(Sheena West) *led tl over 6f out: drvn to chal 4f out: wkng whn hmpd appr fnl 2f* **7/2**[3]
2m 29.1s (-0.40) **Going Correction** -0.325s/f (Firm) **5** Ran SP% **108.8**
Speed ratings (Par 103): **88,87,81,80,80**
CSF £33.92 TOTE £9.40: £3.20, £1.90; EX 43.60.Kiss A Prince was bought by Mrs J. Holder for £6,000. The winner was bought in for £3,600.
Owner Eric Gadsden **Bred** Mrs M Fairbairn And E Gadsden **Trained** Kentisbeare, Devon

FOCUS
A weak, slowly run seller. Shaky form, which could rate higher at face value.
Goodwood Starlight(IRE) Official explanation: jockey said gelding ran too freely

4410 ITM PROMOTING IRISH BLOODSTOCK MAIDEN STKS — 1m 2f 7y
7:10 (7:12) (Class 5) 3-4-Y-0 **£2,264** (£673; £336; £168) **Stalls** Centre

Form RPR
1 **Surprise Moment (IRE)** 3-8-12 0 .... MickaelBarzalona 7 84+
(Saeed Bin Suroor) *in rr: hdwy on outside and rdn over 3f out: stl wd and plenty to do w ldng duo whn tk 3rd 2f out: str run ins fnl f to ld clsng stages: won gng away* **4/1**[2]
62 **2** *½* **Courage (IRE)**[69] 2143 3-9-3 0 .... RyanMoore 14 88
(Sir Michael Stoute) *trckd ldrs: wnt 2nd 2 l off wnr and 5 l clr of main gp wl over 3f out: drvn to chal wl over 1f out: led ins fnl f: hdd and outpcd clsng stages* **11/8**[1]
0 **3** *1* **Zanotti**[67] 2196 3-9-3 0 .... (t[1]) NeilCallan 16 86
(Roger Varian) *sn led: 2 l clr of 2nd and 5 l clr of main gp wl over 3f out: jnd wl over 1f out: hdd ins fnl f: one pce and dropped to 3rd clsng stages* **20/1**
5 **4** *14* **Castilo Del Diablo (IRE)**[55] 2584 3-9-3 0 .... RichardHughes 3 58+
(David Simcock) *in tch 1/2-way: pushed along over 3f out: no ch w ldng trio and wl btn fnl 2f* **9/2**[3]
0 **5** *1 ¼* **Comedy House**[23] 3622 4-9-13 0 .... JamieGoldstein 11 56
(Michael Madgwick) *chsd ldrs: rdn over 3f out: nvr any ch w ldng duo and btn over 2f out* **125/1**
00 **6** *2* **Semeen**[44] 2941 3-9-3 0 .... KierenFallon 13 52+
(Luca Cumani) *chsd ldrs: rdn over 3f out: sn btn* **14/1**
00 **7** *shd* **Albonny (IRE)**[44] 2941 3-8-10 0 .... MichaelJMMurphy(7) 8 51
(Alan Jarvis) *in tch 1/2-way: rdn and no ch w ldrs fnl 3f: hung lft u.p 1f out* **150/1**
6 **8** *shd* **On Stage**[77] 1937 3-8-12 0 .... IanMongan 2 46+
(Stuart Kittow) *in rr: mod hdwy over 2f out: no ch whn pushed lft 1f out* **33/1**
9 *1* **El Camino Real (IRE)**[335] 5358 4-9-13 0 .... (t) LiamKeniry 6 49
(Charlie Longsdon) *chsd ldrs over 6f* **33/1**
0-5 **10** *½* **Mabel's Song**[22] 3664 3-8-12 0 .... DaneO'Neill 12 43
(Henry Candy) *a towards rr* **40/1**
11 *¾* **Addazero** 3-9-3 0 .... JohnFahy 15 47
(Alastair Lidderdale) *chsd ldrs: rdn over 4f out: sn btn* **100/1**
0- **12** *2* **Maria Letizia**[352] 4804 3-8-12 0 .... WilliamBuick 1 38+
(John Gosden) *in rr: in tch 1/2-way: pushed along and btn 4f out* **7/1**
13 *3 ¼* **Broughtons Maxim** 3-9-3 0 .... JamieMackay 4 36
(Willie Musson) *s.i.s: a in rr* **100/1**
0 **14** *6* **Douro**[33] 3279 3-8-12 0 .... JamesDoyle 9 19
(Roger Charlton) *a in rr* **25/1**
0 **15** *12* **Oh So Charming**[35] 3227 3-8-12 0 .... MatthewLawson(5) 10
(Andy Turnell) *a in rr* **100/1**
0-0 **16** *5* **Time For A Tiger**[23] 3622 3-8-12 0 .... FergusSweeney 5
(Henry Candy) *a in rr* **100/1**
2m 4.68s (-4.02) **Going Correction** -0.325s/f (Firm)
WFA 3 from 4yo 10lb **16** Ran SP% **121.8**
Speed ratings (Par 103): **103,102,101,90,89 88,87,87,87,86 86,84,81,77,67 63**
Tote Swingers: 1&2 £1.60, 1&3 £21.70, 2&3 £10.70 CSF £9.19 TOTE £5.30: £1.80, £1.20, £4.50; EX 12.70 Trifecta £321.50 Part won. Pool: £434.54 - 0.74 winning units..
Owner Godolphin **Bred** Darley **Trained** Newmarket, Suffolk

FOCUS
An interesting maiden in which three runners finished a long way clear of the remainder. The time was only fractionally slower than the following Class 5 handicap. The winner may improve considerably on this.
Castilo Del Diablo(IRE) Official explanation: jockey said colt hung left
Semeen Official explanation: jockey said colt lost its action

Maria Letizia Official explanation: jockey said he lost a stirrup coming out of stalls

4411 IRELANDS BEST AT GOFFS ORBY SALE H'CAP 1m 2f 7y
7:40 (7:43) (Class 5) (0-70,70) 3-Y-0+ £2,264 (£673; £336; £168) Stalls Centre

Form				RPR
5-44	1		**Ambala**[44] 2915 4-9-9 65 GeorgeBaker 9	75
			(Chris Wall) *stdd in tch: drvn and hdwy over 2f out: led over 1f out: drvn out* 4/1[1]	
-125	2	1 1/4	**Spartan Spirit (IRE)**[39] 3073 4-9-7 63 RyanMoore 7	71
			(Hughie Morrison) *in rr: hdwy over 2f out: drvn to chse wnr 1f out: no imp and one pce ins fnl f* 7/1	
02-0	3	2 3/4	**Wordiness**[10] 4061 4-9-8 64 JamesDoyle 4	66
			(Seamus Durack) *in rr: hdwy 2f out: rdn and swtchd lft over 1f out: styd on fnl f to take 3rd ins fnl f but no ch w ldng duo* 25/1	
1-03	4	shd	**Librettela**[27] 3472 4-9-4 67 MichaelJMMurphy(7) 10	69
			(Alan Jarvis) *sn led: rdn and jnd 3f out: kpt narrow ld u.p fr over 2f out: hdd over 1f out: wknd ins fnl f* 16/1	
0664	5	1/2	**Larkrise Star**[14] 3920 5-9-8 64 TedDurcan 16	65
			(Dean Ivory) *in rr: hdwy over 2f out: sn rdn: styd on fnl f but nvr gng pce to get into contention* 12/1	
0123	6	hd	**Ryedale Lass**[27] 3468 4-9-7 63 LiamKeniry 8	63
			(Joseph Tuite) *chsd ldrs pushed along and one pce 2f out: kpt on again clsng stages* 16/1	
-000	7	3/4	**Mahadee (IRE)**[21] 3703 7-9-12 68 (p) JohnFahy 6	67
			(Ed de Giles) *chsd ldrs: rdn 3f out: wknd fnl f* 40/1	
4-05	8	hd	**Hawridge Song**[22] 3659 4-9-9 65 (b[1]) IanMongan 15	64
			(Rod Millman) *chsd ldrs: chal 3f out to 2f out: wknd fnl f* 25/1	
6-30	9	6	**Cool Hand Jake**[26] 3485 6-9-6 62 DavidProbert 13	49
			(Jamie Osborne) *in rr: rdn along on outside over 3f out: clsd on ldrs 2f out: wknd sn after* 16/1	
-021	10	3 1/2	**Bernisdale**[21] 3704 4-10-0 70 RichardHughes 1	50
			(John Flint) *chsd ldrs: pushed along and fdd fr 2f out* 9/2[2]	
4400	11	2	**Highlife Dancer**[48] 2792 4-9-6 62 MatthewDavies 11	38
			(Mick Channon) *chsd ldrs: rdn 3f out: sn wknd* 20/1	
4000	12	2 1/2	**Orpen'Arry (IRE)**[20] 3738 4-9-11 67 KieranO'Neill 14	38
			(Jimmy Fox) *t.k.h: a in rr* 33/1	
6054	13	15	**Rogue Reporter (IRE)**[18] 3793 3-8-11 63 WilliamBuick 12	
			(Stuart Williams) *pressed ldrs: pushed along and hung lft fr 4f out: wknd fr 3f out* 11/2[3]	
-300	14	75	**Acer Diamonds (IRE)**[22] 3671 3-9-1 67 BrettDoyle 3	
			(Julia Feilden) *sn t.o* 14/1	
2014	U		**Royal Etiquette (IRE)**[21] 3703 5-9-5 66 LeonnaMayor(5) 2	
			(Lawney Hill) *uns rdr s* 9/1	

2m 4.61s (-4.09) **Going Correction** -0.325s/f (Firm)
WFA 3 from 4yo+ 10lb 15 Ran SP% 125.9
Speed ratings (Par 103): **103,102,99,99,99 99,98,98,93,90 89,87,75,15,**
Tote Swingers: 1&2 £7.60, 1&3 £33.10, 2&3 £68.50 CSF £30.87 CT £647.11 TOTE £5.40: £1.90, £2.80, £9.80; EX 34.30 TRIFECTA Not won..
Owner Mrs Claude Lilley **Bred** Mrs David Low **Trained** Newmarket, Suffolk

FOCUS
A fair handicap, weakened somewhat with Royal Etiquette unseating his rider soon after the start. The form is fairly sound.
Bernisdale Official explanation: trainer said filly would prefer softer ground; vet said filly was in season

4412 GORESBRIDGE BREEZE UP SALE H'CAP 6f
8:10 (8:13) (Class 4) (0-85,82) 3-Y-0 £4,204 (£1,251; £625; £312) Stalls Low

Form				RPR
412	1		**Jocasta Dawn**[38] 3118 3-8-12 73 FergusSweeney 2	81
			(Henry Candy) *mde virtually all: shkn up 2f out: sn rdn: jnd and strly chal thrght fnl f: jst hld on* 4/1[2]	
-010	2	hd	**Orders From Rome (IRE)**[42] 2979 3-8-9 75 AmyScott(5) 7	82
			(Eve Johnson Houghton) *in rr: gd hdwy over 2f out: chsd wnr over 1f out: sn upsides and str chal thrght fnl f: no ex last stride* 12/1	
4021	3	1 1/4	**Uprise**[24] 3561 3-9-1 76 WilliamBuick 8	79
			(George Margarson) *in rr but in tch: hdwy 2f out: rdn to chse ldng duo ins fnl f but no imp* 10/1	
1113	4	hd	**Dark Ages (IRE)**[9] 4081 3-8-9 75 (t) DavidKenny(5) 1	77
			(Paul Burgoyne) *chsd ldrs: rdn 2f out: styd on fnl f: nvr quite gng pce of ldng duo* 5/1	
0-00	5	hd	**Gung Ho Jack**[28] 3445 3-9-2 77 AndreaAtzeni 6	79
			(John Best) *chsd wnr: rdn and ev ch fr over 2f out: kpt on same pce fnl f* 16/1	
5564	6	1 3/4	**Red Senor (IRE)**[26] 3486 3-8-13 74 MatthewChadwick 4	70
			(Charles Hills) *in tch: pushed along 2f out: kpt on fnl f but nvr gng pce to get into contention* 8/1	
01-4	7	1 3/4	**Solfilia**[33] 3284 3-9-3 78 DarryllHolland 3	69
			(Hughie Morrison) *in tch: rdn 2f out: sn outpcd* 7/2[1]	
51	8	nk	**Impel (IRE)**[19] 3762 3-9-6 81 RichardHughes 9	71
			(Richard Hannon) *chsd ldrs: pushed along 2f out: wknd over 1f out* 9/2[3]	
0-00	9	2	**Charitable Act (FR)**[65] 2265 3-9-4 79 GeorgeBaker 10	62
			(William Muir) *outpcd* 14/1	

1m 11.91s (-1.09) **Going Correction** -0.325s/f (Firm) 9 Ran SP% 117.5
Speed ratings (Par 102): **94,93,92,91,91 89,86,86,83**
Tote Swingers: 1&2 £9.40, 1&3 £4.30, 2&3 £20.40 CSF £51.73 CT £454.33 TOTE £4.20: £1.90, £4.90, £3.00; EX 79.30 TRIFECTA Not won..
Owner Mrs David Blackburn & M Blackburn **Bred** Mrs M J Blackburn **Trained** Kingston Warren, Oxon

FOCUS
A competitive sprint handicap run in a relatively modest time. An improved effort from the winner.

4413 THINK THOROUGHBRED...THINK IRELAND H'CAP 1m 67y
8:40 (8:40) (Class 5) (0-75,74) 3-Y-0+ £2,264 (£673; £336; £168) Stalls Low

Form				RPR
-225	1		**Juvenal (IRE)**[22] 3667 3-9-6 74 (p) RichardHughes 13	80+
			(Richard Hannon) *hmpd and dropped to rr after 2f: gd hdwy over 2f out: drvn and qcknd fnl f to ld fnl 50yds: readily* 5/1[2]	
2114	2	1/2	**Know No Fear**[10] 4061 7-8-13 64 (p) AmyScott(5) 11	71
			(Alastair Lidderdale) *in rr: hdwy 5f out: led over 2f out: hrd pressed but kpt advantage fr over 1f out tl hdd and outpcd fnl 50yds* 10/1	
2044	3	3/4	**Satwa Laird**[4] 4242 6-9-9 69 HayleyTurner 14	74
			(Conor Dore) *chsd ldrs: rdn and ev ch fr 2f out: styd on same pce ins fnl f* 9/1	
-320	4	hd	**The Noble Ord**[20] 3736 3-9-4 72 JamesDoyle 7	75+
			(Sylvester Kirk) *hmpd and towards rr after 2f: hdwy over 2f out: chsd ldr over 1f out: no ex and one pce u.p ins fnl f* 11/1	
-004	5	1/2	**Blue Maisey**[26] 3485 4-9-5 65 SebSanders 2	69
			(Peter Makin) *chsd ldrs and hmpd after 2f: sn rcvrd and chsd ldrs again: rdn over 2f out: one pce ins fnl f* 16/1	
0-32	6	2	**Patavium Prince (IRE)**[27] 3471 9-9-11 71 DaneO'Neill 10	70
			(Jo Crowley) *hmpd and lost pl after 2f: hdwy 3f out: chsd ldrs fr 2f out: wknd fnl f* 16/1	
5415	7	2 1/4	**Tenbridge**[23] 3619 3-9-4 72 (p) AndreaAtzeni 5	64
			(Derek Haydn Jones) *chsd ldr after 2f: rdn and ev ch fr 3f out: wknd fnl f* 16/1	
2522	8	nk	**Good Luck Charm**[34] 3248 3-9-1 69 RyanMoore 4	60+
			(Gary Moore) *bdly hmpd and dropped to rr after 2f: rdn and sme hdwy 2f out: nvr in contention* 9/4[1]	
-056	9	5	**Whitechapel**[115] 1108 5-9-8 68 MickaelBarzalona 8	50
			(Daniel Kubler) *chsd ldrs: led over 3f out: hdd over 2f out: sn btn* 25/1	
1046	10	1	**Katmai River (IRE)**[35] 3226 5-9-8 68 DavidProbert 6	47
			(Mark Usher) *chsd ldrs: rdn 3f out: wknd fr 2f out* 33/1	
003	11	1	**Calypso Magic (IRE)**[21] 3705 4-9-4 64 (t) KirstyMilczarek 3	41
			(Olivia Maylam) *lft in ld after 2f: hdd over 3f out: wknd 2f out* 20/1	
0323	12	2	**Blue Deer (IRE)**[11] 3995 4-9-0 67 AaronChave(7) 9	40+
			(Lee Carter) *hmpd after 2f: a in rr* 33/1	
-000	13	29	**Uncle Fred**[26] 3503 7-10-0 74 GeorgeBaker 1	+
			(Patrick Chamings) *hmpd after 2f: a in rr* 11/2[3]	
6515	P		**Ken's Girl**[18] 3780 8-9-12 72 IanMongan 12	
			(Stuart Kittow) *led tl wnt lame and p.u after 2f* 16/1	

1m 42.75s (-1.95) **Going Correction** -0.325s/f (Firm)
WFA 3 from 4yo+ 8lb 14 Ran SP% 128.3
Speed ratings (Par 103): **96,95,94,94,94 92,89,89,84,83 82,80,51,**
Tote Swingers: 1&2 £11.90, 1&3 £7.70, 2&3 £14.40 CSF £55.91 CT £345.91 TOTE £5.80: £2.00, £2.60, £3.40; EX 61.80 Trifecta £126.60 Pool: £376.59 - 2.20 winning units..
Owner Noodles Racing **Bred** Gerard Callanan **Trained** East Everleigh, Wilts

FOCUS
Form to treat with caution as, shortly after the start, something went wrong with early leader Ken's Girl and several of the runners were hampered as she dropped through the field. A length personal best from the winner.
The Noble Ord Official explanation: jockey said gelding suffered interference on first bend
Good Luck Charm Official explanation: jockey said gelding suffered interference on first bend
Blue Deer(IRE) Official explanation: jockey said gelding suffered interference on first bend
Uncle Fred Official explanation: jockey said gelding suffered interference on first bend
T/Plt: £84.60 to a £1 stake. Pool: £92,181.00 - 795.27 winning tickets. T/Qpdt: £19.50 to a £1 stake. Pool: £7,815.00 - 295.66 winning tickets. ST

4414 - 4418a (Foreign Racing) - See Raceform Interactive

4180 FFOS LAS (L-H)
Tuesday, July 24

OFFICIAL GOING: Good (good to soft in places) changing to good after race 2 (6.35)
Wind: Almost nil Weather: Fine

4419 32RED.COM MAIDEN STKS 5f
6:05 (6:07) (Class 5) 2-Y-0 £2,264 (£673; £336; £168) Stalls Centre

Form				RPR
22	1		**Red Explorer (USA)**[6] 4220 2-9-3 0 MatthewChadwick 2	70+
			(Charles Hills) *mde virtually all: shkn up ins fnl f: r.o* 4/5[1]	
	2	1/2	**Vincentti (IRE)** 2-9-3 0 JamesDoyle 4	66
			(Ronald Harris) *chsd wnr: pushed along 1/2-way: outpcd over 1f out: rdn: edgd lft and r.o ins fnl f* 25/1	
	3	3/4	**Stand Of Glory (USA)** 2-9-3 0 MartinLane 7	64
			(David Simcock) *a.p: rdn over 1f out: edgd lft: r.o* 11/4[2]	
	4	1 1/2	**Reinvigorate (IRE)** 2-8-12 0 SeanLevey 6	53
			(Richard Hannon) *hld up in tch: rdn over 1f out: styd on same pce ins fnl f* 8/1[3]	
0	5	3/4	**Katy Spirit (IRE)**[27] 3487 2-8-12 0 LiamKeniry 1	50
			(Michael Blanshard) *wnt lft s: sn chsng ldrs: rdn and ev ch over 1f out: edgd lft and no ex ins fnl f* 100/1	
023	6	1 1/2	**Hardy Red (IRE)**[43] 2970 2-9-3 0 FergusSweeney 3	50
			(Jamie Osborne) *chsd ldrs: rdn over 1f out: no ex fnl f* 10/1	
	7	9	**Sand Boy (IRE)** 2-8-12 0 MatthewLawson(5) 8	18
			(Charles Hills) *dwlt: outpcd* 20/1	

58.98s (0.68) **Going Correction** -0.025s/f (Good) 7 Ran SP% 112.0
Speed ratings (Par 94): **93,92,91,88,87 85,70**
toteswingers: 1&2 £5.10, 2&3 £12.40, 1&3 £1.60 CSF £26.39 TOTE £1.90: £1.10, £21.00; EX 24.90 Trifecta £88.20 Pool £627.29 - 5.26 winning units..
Owner R J Arculi & Robert Ng **Bred** E Hernandez, K Hernandez & J Duvieilh **Trained** Lambourn, Berks

FOCUS
A modest maiden. The second and fifth are perhaps the long-term keys.

NOTEBOOK
Red Explorer(USA) set a fair standard on his runner-up efforts in 5f maidens at Haydock and Sandown. Kept to the minimum, the son of Henrythenavigator showed the benefit of experience to record a professional success. A fluent mover, this was the quickest surface he had encountered and he's likely to be competitive in nurseries. (op 4-7)
Vincentti(IRE), an expensive purchase for this stable, is related to winners over a variety of trips. He put in a promising effort and will have chances of winning a similar maiden with 6f within his compass. (op 28-1 tchd 33-1)
Stand Of Glory(USA), ran with credit without ever looking like rewarding his supporters. He was a costly breeze-up purchase and his yard have run some of their better juveniles here in the past, so he is expected to progress. (op 5-1)
Reinvigorate(IRE) is from a fast family and wasn't disgraced on debut. (op 11-1 tchd 7-1)
Sand Boy(IRE) Official explanation: jockey said colt was slowly away

4420 32RED CASINO FILLIES' H'CAP 6f
6:35 (6:35) (Class 5) (0-75,75) 3-Y-0+ £2,264 (£673; £336; £168) Stalls Centre

Form				RPR
0502	1		**Night Trade (IRE)**[5] 4235 5-9-5 71 (p) RaulDaSilva(3) 4	82
			(Ronald Harris) *a.p: rdn to chse ldr over 1f out: sn hung lft: r.o to ld wl ins fnl f* 11/4[2]	
0404	2	3/4	**Selfara**[41] 3044 3-8-12 66 (b[1]) JamesDoyle 3	74
			(Roger Charlton) *led: clr 4f out: rdn over 1f out: sn hung lft: hdd wl ins fnl f* 5/1[3]	
-233	3	2 1/2	**Shaleek**[47] 2846 3-9-4 75 (b) DominicFox(3) 8	75
			(Roger Varian) *chsd ldrs: rdn to go 2nd and hung lft fr over 2f out: styd on same pce fnl f* 6/1	
4014	4	1	**Sparking**[5] 4235 5-8-13 65 RossAtkinson(3) 9	62
			(Tom Dascombe) *hld up: rdn over 2f out: hdwy u.p and edgd lft fr over 1f out: nt rch ldrs* 6/1	

5040 **5** *1* **Cockney Fire**[24] 3613 3-9-2 **70** .... SeanLevey 1 63
(David Evans) *chsd ldr over 3f: sn rdn: hung lft over 1f out: wknd ins fnl f* **16/1**

0121 **6** *2 ¾* **Full Shilling (IRE)**[29] 3434 4-8-13 **69** .... WilliamTwiston-Davies(7) 6 54
(John Spearing) *s.i.s: rdn and hung lft over 2f out: nvr on terms* **5/2**[1]

3033 **7** *3 ¼* **Hey Fiddle Fiddle (IRE)**[27] 3510 3-8-3 **62** ....(b) MatthewLawson(5) 7 37
(Charles Hills) *hld up: pushed along 4f out: wknd over 2f out* **16/1**

1m 10.12s (0.12) **Going Correction** -0.025s/f (Good)
WFA 3 from 4yo+ 5lb **7** Ran SP% **112.2**
Speed ratings (Par 100): **98,97,93,92,91 87,83**
toteswingers:1&2 £4.90, 2&3 £1.40, 1&3 £2.90 CSF £16.19 CT £73.71 TOTE £2.60: £1.50, £3.10; EX 15.70 Trifecta £93.60 Pool £445.70 - 3.52 winning units..
Owner Alan & Adam Darlow, A Darlow Productions **Bred** John Foley **Trained** Earlswood, Monmouths

FOCUS
A weak fillies' handicap.

4421 32REDBET.COM NURSERY 6f
7:05 (7:06) (Class 6) (0-65,63) 2-Y-O **£1,746** (£519; £259; £129) **Stalls** Centre

Form RPR

050 **1** **Khefyn (IRE)**[38] 3138 2-9-2 58 .... JamesDoyle 4 61+
(Ronald Harris) *s.i.s: sn prom: led and hung bdly lft ins fnl f: drvn out* **5/2**[2]

5444 **2** *2* **Wordsaplenty (IRE)**[3] 4343 2-9-4 60 ....[1] LiamKeniry 5 57
(J S Moore) *chsd ldr: rdn to ld over 1f out: hdd and hmpd ins fnl f: styd on same pce* **15/2**

6401 **3** *2 ½* **Lucky Suit (IRE)**[36] 3224 2-9-2 63 .... DarrenEgan(5) 2 53
(Ronald Harris) *hld up in tch: rdn over 2f out: styd on same pce fr over 1f out: wnt 3rd post* **9/4**[1]

01 **4** *nse* **Senora Lobo (IRE)**[19] 3789 2-9-1 57 .... RoystonFfrench 6 52
(Lisa Williamson) *sn led: rdn and hdd over 1f out: ev ch whn bdly hmpd ins fnl f: nt rcvr: lost 3rd post* **3/1**[3]

601 **5** *5* **Missing Agent**[40] 3084 2-9-1 60 .... MatthewCosham(3) 1 34
(David Evans) *s.i.s: sn chsng ldrs: drvn along 1/2-way: wknd over 1f out* **6/1**

1m 11.42s (1.42) **Going Correction** -0.025s/f (Good) **5** Ran SP% **110.4**
Speed ratings (Par 92): **89,86,83,82,76**
CSF £19.70 TOTE £5.50: £2.20, £2.80; EX 26.10.
Owner Robert & Nina Bailey **Bred** Ms Kate Wilson **Trained** Earlswood, Monmouths

FOCUS
After the second race jockeys reported the ground was on the fast side of good, a significant change from ground conditions at declaration time. Despite the lowly grade, three of them came into this on the back of a victory. The form is weak.

NOTEBOOK
Khefyn(IRE) came into this with form figures of 858 with all of those runs coming at Bath. Strong in the market, he was spotted travelling sweetly with 2f to run. Once sent to the front he veered violently left, hampering Senora Lobo in the process. He continued to go forward however, and won comfortably in the end, despite having to survive a stewards' enquiry. This was the quickest ground he'd encountered and he clearly relished it. The handicapper will have to take action but this was the first time he'd been involved at the business end and he should continue to improve.
Official explanation: trainer said, regarding apparent improvement in form, that the colt may have been suited by the good ground, having previously run on much softer. (op 5-1)
Wordsaplenty(IRE) had been beaten in a seller at Ripon just three days ago when she was slowly away. Equipped with a hood, she was much more alertly out the stalls and ran a fair race without looking like winning. (op 8-1 tchd 17-2 and 7-1)
Lucky Suit(IRE), making her debut for Ron Harris, finished strongly having been initially outpaced. She was fortunate to finish third. (op 7-4)
Senora Lobo(IRE), a winner of a Yarmouth seller on her last start, still had running to give when being hampered and can have this effort upgraded. She raced enthusiastically and a drop back to 5f shouldn't be ruled out. (op 11-4 tchd 7-2)

4422 32REDPOKER.COM H'CAP 5f
7:35 (7:36) (Class 6) (0-55,53) 3-Y-O+ **£1,746** (£519; £259; £129) **Stalls** Centre

Form RPR

0350 **1** **Red Rhythm**[7] 4196 5-9-1 49 ....(v[1]) JamesDoyle 7 62
(David Evans) *trckd ldrs: led over 3f out: edgd lft ins fnl f: drvn out* **9/2**[3]

0002 **2** *2* **Griffin Point (IRE)**[11] 4059 5-9-5 53 ....(b) DavidProbert 5 60
(William Muir) *a.p: rdn to chse wnr over 1f out: hung lft ins fnl f: styd on same pce* **4/1**[2]

-363 **3** *nk* **Dixie Gwalia**[5] 4237 4-9-5 53 .... MartinLane 6 59
(David Simcock) *hld up: hdwy 1/2-way: rdn over 1f out: styd on same pce ins fnl f* **9/4**[1]

4500 **4** *2 ¾* **Forty Proof (IRE)**[19] 3791 4-8-12 49 ....(vt) MatthewCosham(3) 3 46
(David Evans) *drvn along thrght: prom: lost pl over 3f out: sme hdwy over 1f out: no imp fnl f* **12/1**

-434 **5** *½* **The Jailer**[19] 3791 9-8-12 53 ....(p) WilliamTwiston-Davies(7) 4 48
(John O'Shea) *led: hdd over 3f out: chsd wnr tl rdn over 1f out: wknd fnl f* **5/1**

640 **6** *2 ¾* **Decider (USA)**[5] 4236 9-8-11 50 ....(b) DarrenEgan(5) 8 36
(Ronald Harris) *mid-div: rdn 1/2-way: wknd fnl f* **8/1**

7 *1* **Boudicca (IRE)**[337] 5330 3-8-7 45 .... FrankieMcDonald 2 27
(Daniel Mark Loughnane) *chsd ldrs: rdn 1/2-way: wknd over 1f out* **7/1**

00-0 **8** *8* **Glitter (IRE)**[9] 2387 3-8-5 48 ow3 .... JamesRogers(5) 1
(Laura Young) *sn pushed along in rr: bhd fnl 2f* **100/1**

58.03s (-0.27) **Going Correction** -0.025s/f (Good)
WFA 3 from 4yo+ 4lb **8** Ran SP% **117.9**
Speed ratings (Par 101): **101,97,97,92,92 87,86,73**
toteswingers:1&2 £5.30, 2&3 £4.20, 1&3 £7.90 CSF £23.66 CT £51.11 TOTE £4.40: £1.90, £1.90, £1.10; EX 30.80 Trifecta £88.20 Pool £362.45 - 3.04 winning units..
Owner J Babb **Bred** W Jenks, H Fowler & Mrs J Minton **Trained** Pandy, Monmouths

FOCUS
Another modest contest.

4423 32RED FILLIES' H'CAP 5f
8:05 (8:06) (Class 4) (0-80,83) 3-Y-O+ **£4,204** (£1,251; £625; £312) **Stalls** Centre

Form RPR

5404 **1** **Pale Orchid (IRE)**[11] 4044 3-9-7 83 .... JamesDoyle 3 88
(David Evans) *chsd ldrs: rdn to ld and edgd lft ins fnl f: drvn out* **5/4**[1]

1141 **2** *1* **Redair (IRE)**[47] 2861 3-8-13 78 .... MatthewCosham(3) 4 79
(David Evans) *led: rdn over 1f out: hdd and carried lft ins fnl f: unable qck towards fin* **5/1**[3]

5351 **3** *1 ¾* **Charming (IRE)**[12] 4003 3-8-7 69 .... DavidProbert 1 64
(Olivia Maylam) *chsd ldrs: rdn to go 2nd wl over 1f out: styd on same pce ins fnl f* **6/4**[2]

0-00 **4** *2* **Berberana (IRE)**[27] 3496 4-9-3 78 ....(t) RaulDaSilva(3) 2 66
(Jeremy Gask) *w ldr tl pushed along 1/2-way: no ex fnl f* **9/1**

58.81s (0.51) **Going Correction** -0.025s/f (Good)
WFA 3 from 4yo 4lb **4** Ran SP% **111.1**
Speed ratings (Par 102): **94,92,89,86**
CSF £7.72 TOTE £2.10; EX 4.90.
Owner A F O'Callaghan **Bred** Mrs A J Donnelly **Trained** Pandy, Monmouths

FOCUS
The feature fillies' handicap attracted just four runners. The finish was fought out by the David Evans-trained pair.

4424 £10 FREE AT 32REDBINGO.COM H'CAP 6f
8:35 (8:36) (Class 6) (0-55,56) 3-Y-O **£1,746** (£519; £259; £129) **Stalls** Centre

Form RPR

4-03 **1** **Verus Delicia (IRE)**[7] 4185 3-8-6 45 .... MarkCoumbe(5) 3 63
(Daniel Mark Loughnane) *led 1f: led again 1/2-way: rdn clr fr over 1f out: hung lft fnl f* **7/1**[3]

0021 **2** *4* **Purley Queen (IRE)**[7] 4185 3-9-1 56 6ex .... ThomasBrown(7) 4 61
(Sylvester Kirk) *chsd ldrs: rdn whn nt clr run over 1f out: styd on to go 2nd wl ins fnl f: no ch w wnr* **11/10**[1]

5-00 **3** *2 ½* **Spellmaker**[31] 3389 3-9-1 49 .... FergusSweeney 7 46
(Tony Newcombe) *chsd ldrs: rdn 1/2-way: hung lft fr over 1f out: wknd ins fnl f* **10/3**[2]

0-00 **4** *1 ½* **La Sonadora**[27] 3489 3-8-11 45 ....(b) JamesDoyle 5 37
(John Spearing) *chsd ldrs: rdn over 1f out: sn edgd lft and wknd* **9/1**

0400 **5** *9* **Tenderly Place**[27] 3510 3-8-13 52 .... DavidKenny(5) 6
(William Knight) *s.s: hld up: plld hrd: rdn: hung lft and wknd over 1f out* **10/1**

000 **6** *7* **Starlight Secret**[63] 2361 3-9-1 49 .... DavidProbert 2
(Simon Earle) *sn outpcd* **22/1**

000 **7** *14* **Boragh Waters (IRE)**[45] 2935 3-8-11 45 ....(bt[1]) MartinLane 1
(Brian Meehan) *s.s: hdwy to ld 5f out: hdd 1/2-way: rdn and wknd over 1f out: t.o* **14/1**

1m 10.25s (0.25) **Going Correction** -0.025s/f (Good) **7** Ran SP% **113.3**
Speed ratings (Par 98): **97,91,88,86,74 65,46**
toteswingers:1&2 £1.02, 2&3 £4.20, 1&3 £3.90 CSF £14.92 TOTE £10.30: £3.40, £1.10; EX 18.10.
Owner G J McGuinness & J Corcoran **Bred** R Fagan **Trained** Baldwin's Gate, Staffs

FOCUS
A desperate three-year-old handicap.
Tenderly Place Official explanation: jockey said filly was slowly away

4425 £32 BONUS AT 32RED.COM H'CAP 5f
9:05 (9:09) (Class 5) (0-70,66) 3-Y-O+ **£2,264** (£673; £336; £168) **Stalls** Centre

Form RPR

111 **1** **Scommettitrice (IRE)**[5] 4237 4-8-13 60 6ex(p) WilliamTwiston-Davies(7) 1 69
(David Evans) *chsd ldrs: rdn 1/2-way: r.o to ld post* **10/3**[2]

0-03 **2** *nk* **My Meteor**[78] 1910 5-9-7 61 .... FergusSweeney 3 69
(Tony Newcombe) *hld up: hdwy 1/2-way: shkn up to ld over 1f out: rdn ins fnl f: hdd post* **8/1**

0312 **3** *½* **Spic 'n Span**[7] 4187 7-8-10 50 ....(b) JamesDoyle 6 56
(Ronald Harris) *led: rdn: hdd and hung lft fr over 1f out: r.o* **11/4**[1]

053- **4** *1 ½* **Crazy Too (IRE)**[267] 7194 3-9-7 65 .... MartinLane 5 65
(David Simcock) *chsd ldrs: rdn over 1f out: r.o* **9/2**[3]

11-6 **5** *nk* **Steel Rain**[5] 4236 4-9-5 59 .... DavidProbert 4 59
(Nikki Evans) *chsd ldrs: rdn 1/2-way: styd on same pce ins fnl f* **5/1**

4403 **6** *6* **Just For Mary**[12] 3993 8-9-12 66 ....(bt) StephenCraine 2 44
(Daniel Mark Loughnane) *dwlt: outpcd* **9/2**[3]

57.93s (-0.37) **Going Correction** -0.025s/f (Good)
WFA 3 from 4yo+ 4lb **6** Ran SP% **113.9**
Speed ratings (Par 103): **101,100,99,97,96 87**
toteswingers:1&2 £5.80, 2&3 £4.40, 1&3 £2.80 CSF £29.17 TOTE £3.50: £2.60, £3.00; EX 29.50.
Owner Out Of Bounds Racing Club **Bred** L Mulryan **Trained** Pandy, Monmouths

FOCUS
A competitive closer despite the small field.
T/Plt: £180.90 to a £1 stake. Pool £52,872.83 -213.31 winning units. T/Qpdt: £30.60 to a £1 stake. Pool £4,641.56 - 111.90 winning units. CR

3575 MUSSELBURGH (R-H)
Tuesday, July 24

OFFICIAL GOING: Soft (good to soft in places; 6.8)
Back straight out 3m from stands bend to road crossing, bottom bend out 2m and all distances as advertised.
Wind: Virtually nil Weather: Cloudy and humid

4426 TURFTV H'CAP 1m 1f
2:00 (2:00) (Class 5) (0-70,69) 3-Y-O+ **£2,587** (£770; £384; £192) **Stalls** Low

Form RPR

326 **1** **Raheeba**[18] 3811 3-9-5 69 .... JoeFanning 6 74
(Mark Johnston) *slt ld: pushed along over 2f out: rdn wl over 1f out: drvn and wandered wl ins fnl f: jst hld on* **15/8**[2]

0400 **2** *nse* **Sangar**[24] 3616 4-9-8 63 .... PaulMulrennan 9 69
(Ollie Pears) *cl up: rdn over 2f out: drvn and ev ch ins fnl f: jst failed* **10/3**[3]

3-52 **3** *2 ¼* **Christmas Light**[7] 4175 5-9-5 63 .... DaleSwift(3) 4 64
(Brian Ellison) *trckd ldng pair: effrt wl over 2f out: sn rdn along and no imp fnl f* **6/5**[1]

-500 **4** *33* **Naafetha (IRE)**[32] 3332 4-8-10 51 ....(p) LeeNewman 8
(George Foster) *trckd ldng pair: rdn along 3f out: sn outpcd and bhd* **25/1**

1m 59.44s (5.54) **Going Correction** +0.70s/f (Yiel)
WFA 3 from 4yo+ 9lb **4** Ran SP% **107.2**
Speed ratings (Par 103): **103,102,100,71**
CSF £7.99 TOTE £3.50; EX 7.80.
Owner Sheikh Hamdan Bin Mohammed Al Maktoum **Bred** Mrs C R Philipson & Lofts Hall Stud **Trained** Middleham Moor, N Yorks

FOCUS
This modest handicap was reduced to a field of four females and it proved a tactical affair with the first two dominating throughout. The time was reasonable and the winner is accorded a length personal best.

4427 BRITISH STALLION STUDS EBF MAIDEN STKS — 7f 30y
2:30 (2:34) (Class 5) 2-Y-O — **£3,234** (£962; £481; £240) **Stalls** Low

Form — RPR

1 — **Polar Chief** 2-9-3 0 .... JamesSullivan 3 — 70+
(Linda Stubbs) *dwlt: sn in tch: hdwy on outer 3f out: chal and hung rt 2f out: sn rdn: rn green and wandered ent fnl f: styd on to ld last 50yds* **20/1**

05 2 *hd* **Marhaba Malayeen (IRE)**[27] 3491 2-9-3 0 .... PhillipMakin 7 — 70
(Kevin Ryan) *led: rdn along over 2f out: drvn ent fnl f: hdd and no ex last 50yds* **13/2**

3 *2 ½* **Excellent Mariner (IRE)** 2-8-12 0 .... JoeFanning 1 — 60+
(Mark Johnston) *in tch: green and pushed along 1/2-way: hdwy on inner over 2f out: rdn and kpt on same pce fnl f* **9/4**[2]

63 4 *2 ¾* **Chant (IRE)**[14] 3948 2-9-3 0 .... GrahamLee 5 — 57
(Ann Duffield) *chsd ldr: cl up 1/2-way: rdn along whn hmpd 2f out: sn wknd* **6/1**[3]

322 5 *1 ½* **Lady Margaeux (IRE)**[25] 3554 2-8-12 0 .... DanielTudhope 4 — 50
(David O'Meara) *trckd ldrs: hdwy 3f out: pushed along and cl up whn hmpd 2f out: sn btn* **6/5**[1]

6 *20* **Ragnarr** 2-9-3 0 .... LeeNewman 2
(Ian Semple) *s.i.s: a bhd* **33/1**

1m 36.24s (7.24) **Going Correction** +0.775s/f (Yiel) — **6** Ran SP% **111.5**
Speed ratings (Par 94): **89,88,85,82,81 58**
toteswingers 1&2 £6.50, 2&3 £2.00, 1&3 £3.60 CSF £134.20 TOTE £17.30: £7.50, £3.00; EX 118.00.
Owner P & L Partners **Bred** J W Mitchell **Trained** Norton, N Yorks

FOCUS
An ordinary juvenile maiden, and surely modest form.

NOTEBOOK
Polar Chief, an already gelded half-brother to five previous winners over a variety of distances, showed a professional attitude and ran out a game debut winner. He was well placed off the home turn and knew his job when asked for his effort. His sire's progeny like cut in the ground and he clearly stays well so the future looks bright, for all that he may be tricky to place in the short term. (op 18-1 tchd 14-1)
Marhaba Malayeen(IRE) was having his third outing and his previous experience told as he took them along early. He had something to prove on this debut over the extra furlong, but saw it out really well and was only just denied. He now qualifies for nurseries and is improving. (op 14-1 tchd 6-1)
Excellent Mariner(IRE) is a half-sister to Pure Champion, a dual Group 3 winner formerly known as Steinbeck when with Aidan O'Brien in Ireland. She ran green from the start, but would have gone a little closer with more room on the far rail around 1f out and this was an encouraging introduction. (op 3-1 tchd 10-3)
Chant(IRE) got a positive ride, but paid for his early exertions before the final furlong. He was outclassed, but probably wants a sounder surface and should nick a small race this year. (op 11-1 tchd 12-1)
Lady Margaeux(IRE) set the standard having finished runner-up the last twice. She was in trouble 2f out and looked awkward under pressure. (op 4-6 tchd 5-4)

4428 SCOTTISH RACING H'CAP — 5f
3:00 (3:01) (Class 6) (0-65,65) 3-Y-O — **£1,940** (£577; £288; £144) **Stalls** High

Form — RPR

02-0 1 — **Alnair (IRE)**[131] 905 3-9-2 60 .... DanielTudhope 3 — 65
(Declan Carroll) *promilnent: rdn to chal 2f out: ev ch whn hmpd jst over 1f out: drvn to ld ins fnl f: kpt on wl* **5/1**

5324 2 *nk* **Elegant Girl (IRE)**[17] 3848 3-9-7 65 ....(p) DavidAllan 10 — 69+
(Tim Easterby) *hld up: swtchd rt and hdwy over 1f out: rdn and styd on to chal ins fnl f: ev ch tl nt qckn towards fin* **4/1**[3]

0-23 3 *¾* **Majestic Manannan (IRE)**[8] 4144 3-9-2 60 .... AdrianNicholls 6 — 61+
(David Nicholls) *hld up: hdwy on outer 2f out: rdn to chal over 1f out: ev ch tl drvn ins fnl f and no ex last 75yds* **7/2**[2]

2460 4 *3* **Imperial Legend (IRE)**[7] 4174 3-8-12 56 .... AndrewMullen 2 — 48
(David Nicholls) *wnt rt s: chsd ldrs: hdwy to ld wl over 1f out: sn rdn and hung lft: drvn and hdd jst ins fnl f: sn wknd* **11/1**

6411 5 *1 ¼* **Tuibama (IRE)**[35] 3256 3-9-6 64 ....(p) FrannyNorton 13 — 50
(Tracy Waggott) *led: rdn along 2f out: sn hdd & wknd* **5/2**[1]

-505 6 *hd* **Roy's Legacy**[10] 4084 3-8-4 55 .... ShirleyTeasdale(7) 9 — 40
(Shaun Harris) *chsd ldng pair: rdn along 2f out: wknd over 1f out* **10/1**

0560 7 *3 ½* **Majestic Angel (IRE)**[5] 4245 3-8-2 46 oh1 .... JoeFanning 11 — 18
(Brian Rothwell) *a in rr* **10/1**

1m 2.87s (2.47) **Going Correction** +0.325s/f (Good) — **7** Ran SP% **114.0**
Speed ratings (Par 98): **93,92,91,86,84 84,78**
toteswingers 1&2 £4.40, 2&3 £2.80, 1&3 £6.00 CSF £24.99 CT £78.16 TOTE £5.80: £4.30, £2.50; EX 32.40 Trifecta £176.60 Pool: £529.84 - 2.22 winning units..
Owner K McConnell **Bred** James Burns And A Moynan **Trained** Sledmere, E Yorks
■ Stewards' Enquiry : Andrew Mullen one-day ban: careless riding (Aug 7)

FOCUS
A moderate 3yo sprint handicap, decimated by withdrawals.
Roy's Legacy Official explanation: trainer's rep said colt lost off-fore shoe

4429 BROWN SHIPLEY WEALTH WELL MANAGED H'CAP — 1m 4f 100y
3:30 (3:30) (Class 5) (0-70,70) 4-Y-O+ — **£2,587** (£770; £384; £192) **Stalls** Low

Form — RPR

50-3 1 — **Houston Dynimo (IRE)**[60] 2454 7-9-5 68 .... PaulMulrennan 6 — 76
(Nicky Richards) *mde all: rdn along over 2f out: styd on strly appr fnl f* **6/5**[1]

44-5 2 *6* **Ravi River (IRE)**[27] 3492 8-9-7 70 .... PaddyAspell 5 — 69
(Alistair Whillans) *hld up in rr: hdwy 3f out: rdn to chse wnr wl over 1f out: sn edgd rt: drvn and one pce fnl f* **2/1**[2]

46-4 3 *1 ¾* **A Southside Boy (GER)**[16] 3891 4-7-11 51 oh6 .... NeilFarley(5) 1 — 47
(Jim Goldie) *in tch: pushed along 3f out: rdn 2f out and sn one pce* **8/1**

0-60 4 *12* **Cadore (IRE)**[41] 3031 4-9-0 63 ....(p) TomEaves 9 — 40
(Lucinda Russell) *chsd wnr: rdn along 3f out: wknd 2f out* **9/2**[3]

2m 51.34s (9.34) **Going Correction** +0.775s/f (Yiel) — **4** Ran SP% **108.1**
Speed ratings (Par 103): **99,95,93,85**
CSF £3.85 TOTE £2.30; EX 3.50.
Owner Miss J R Richards **Bred** Sweetmans Bloodstock **Trained** Greystoke, Cumbria

FOCUS
This ordinary handicap was another event badly hit by non-runners. The winner is rated to his British best.

4430 MUSSELBURGH FESTIVAL H'CAP — 5f
4:00 (4:03) (Class 4) (0-80,80) 3-Y-O+ — **£4,528** (£1,347; £673; £336) **Stalls** High

Form — RPR

2533 1 — **Crimson Knot (IRE)**[8] 4133 4-9-10 78 .... TomEaves 9 — 86
(Alan Berry) *in rr and sn pushed along: rdn 1/2-way: sn swtchd rt to outer and hdwy over 1f out: rdn to chal ins fnl f: drvn and styd on wl to ld last 50yds* **5/2**[2]

0112 2 *nk* **The Nifty Fox**[8] 4133 8-9-11 79 ....(p) DavidAllan 5 — 86
(Tim Easterby) *trckd ldrs: hdwy wl over 1f out: rdn to ld jst ins fnl f: hdd and no ex last 50yds* **5/4**[1]

0-4 3 *2* **Quaroma**[40] 3065 7-9-8 76 .... MickyFenton 6 — 78
(Paul Midgley) *trckd ldng pair: effrt 2f out: sn rdn and kpt on same pce fnl f* **7/2**[3]

1134 4 *½* **Sandwith**[25] 3578 9-8-8 67 ....(p) LMcNiff(5) 1 — 65
(George Foster) *cl up: rdn to ld 2f out: drvn and hdd jst ins fnl f: sn wknd* **14/1**

2065 5 *6* **Bronze Beau**[4] 4292 5-9-12 80 ....(t) JamesSullivan 4 — 56
(Linda Stubbs) *led: rdn along and hdd 2f out: sn wknd* **13/2**

0544 6 *¾* **Angelo Poliziano**[26] 3523 6-8-12 66 ....(t) LeeNewman 3 — 40
(George Foster) *dwlt: effrt and sme hdwy on outer 1/2-way: sn rdn and wknd* **25/1**

1m 1.3s (0.90) **Going Correction** +0.325s/f (Good) — **6** Ran SP% **119.1**
Speed ratings (Par 105): **105,104,101,100,90 89**
toteswingers 1&2 £2.10, 2&3 £2.10, 1&3 £3.00 CSF £6.54 CT £10.42 TOTE £4.20: £2.30, £1.70; EX 7.50 Trifecta £11.20 Pool: £301.22 - 19.77 winning units..
Owner William Burns **Bred** Iona Equine **Trained** Cockerham, Lancs

FOCUS
A modest sprint handicap, run at a decent pace.
Angelo Poliziano Official explanation: jockey said blindfold became stuck on bridle and gelding was slowly away

4431 RACING UK THE UK'S BEST RACECOURSES LIVE H'CAP — 2m
4:30 (4:30) (Class 6) (0-65,63) 4-Y-O+ — **£1,940** (£577; £288; £144) **Stalls** High

Form — RPR

-602 1 — **Jan Smuts (IRE)**[20] 3752 4-8-9 51 ow3 ....(tp) GrahamLee 2 — 62
(Wilf Storey) *hld up in tch: hdwy 4f out: chsd ldr wl over 1f out: rdn to ld ent fnl f: drvn out* **6/1**

0010 2 *4* **Vittachi**[25] 3579 5-9-2 63 .... GarryWhillans(5) 8 — 69
(Alistair Whillans) *trckd ldng pair: hdwy 3f out: led over 2f out: rdn and hdd ent fnl f: kpt on same pce* **5/1**[3]

-000 3 *6* **Purkab**[8] 4137 4-8-5 47 .... JoeFanning 13 — 46
(Jim Goldie) *hld up in rr: hdwy over 4f out: rdn along over 2f out: chsd ldng pair appr fnl f: no imp* **12/1**

/604 4 *½* **Sydney Cove (IRE)**[3] 3519 6-8-3 45 ....(p) FrannyNorton 1 — 43
(Iain Jardine) *hld up in rr: hdwy over 3f out: rdn along over 2f out: n.d* **4/1**[2]

00-5 5 *4* **Word Of Warning**[9] 3402 8-8-11 53 .... PaulMulrennan 5 — 46
(Martin Todhunter) *trckd ldrs: hdwy 7f out: led over 3f out: sn rdn and hdd over 2f out: sn wknd* **7/1**

0/0- 6 *14* **Almutaham (USA)**[38] 2733 5-8-6 48 ....(p) JamesSullivan 12 — 24
(Martin Todhunter) *led: rdn along 1/2-way: sn hdd & wknd* **11/2**

32-0 7 *35* **Rhyton (IRE)**[8] 4138 5-9-6 62 ....(b) PJMcDonald 7
(Brian Storey) *cl up: led 7f out: rdn along and hdd over 3f out: sn wknd* **28/1**

0 R — **Sinnamara (IRE)**[37] 3180 4-9-4 60 .... DanielTudhope 10
(John Wainwright) *ref to r: tk no part* **2/1**[1]

3m 45.68s (12.18) **Going Correction** +0.775s/f (Yiel) — **8** Ran SP% **123.3**
Speed ratings (Par 101): **100,98,95,94,92 85,68,**
toteswingers 1&2 £3.80, 2&3 £9.20, 1&3 £7.70 CSF £38.94 CT £361.02 TOTE £8.20: £2.30, £1.90, £4.70; EX 27.10 Trifecta £147.50 Pool: £672.02 - 3.37 winning units..
Owner H S Hutchinson **Bred** Tipper House Stud **Trained** Muggleswick, Co Durham

FOCUS
A weak staying handicap, rated around the runner-up.

4432 WATCH RACING UK ON SKY 432 H'CAP — 7f 30y
5:00 (5:00) (Class 5) (0-70,67) 3-Y-O+ — **£2,587** (£770; £384; £192) **Stalls** Low

Form — RPR

6501 1 — **Florio Vincitore (IRE)**[36] 3231 5-9-1 58 ....(v) DaleSwift(3) 3 — 79+
(Brian Ellison) *trckd ldr: smooth hdwy to ld over 2f out: sn clr: comf* **3/1**[1]

0420 2 *6* **Sabratha (IRE)**[8] 4134 4-9-10 64 .... PhillipMakin 6 — 66
(Linda Perratt) *trckd ldrs: hdwy 3f out: rdn to chse wnr 2f out: drvn and no imp fnl f* **14/1**

000 3 *nk* **Berbice (IRE)**[8] 4134 7-9-3 60 .... JulieBurke(3) 1 — 61
(Linda Perratt) *dwlt and in rr: stdy hdwy on inner wl over 2f out: rdn wl over 1f out: kpt on fnl f: nrst fin* **22/1**

0006 4 *½* **Keys Of Cyprus**[11] 4042 10-9-8 62 .... AdrianNicholls 11 — 62
(David Nicholls) *in tch: hdwy over 3f out: rdn along over 2f out: drvn and one pce fr wl over 1f out* **8/1**

-10R 5 *2* **Nadeen (IRE)**[52] 2696 5-9-13 67 .... AndrewMullen 12 — 62
(Michael Smith) *s.i.s and bhd: hdwy 3f out: rdn to chse ldrs 2f out: sn drvn and no imp* **14/1**

-106 6 *¾* **Cannon Bolt (IRE)**[39] 3115 4-9-4 58 ....(b) DanielTudhope 2 — 51
(Robin Bastiman) *led: rdn along and hdd over 2f out: grad wknd* **7/1**[3]

2131 7 *1 ¾* **Mick Slates (IRE)**[13] 3952 3-8-11 63 .... NeilFarley(5) 9 — 49
(Declan Carroll) *in rr and rdn along sn after s: sme hdwy 3f out: sn drvn and nvr a factor* **3/1**[1]

22U1 8 *4* **Goninodaethat**[16] 3888 4-9-4 58 .... GrahamLee 4 — 36
(Jim Goldie) *prom: rdn along over 2f out: sn drvn and wknd* **4/1**[2]

0-00 9 *9* **Nufoudh (IRE)**[20] 3749 8-9-6 60 .... FrannyNorton 5
(Tracy Waggott) *prom: pushed along 3f out: rdn over 2f out and sn wknd* **20/1**

1m 33.78s (4.78) **Going Correction** +0.775s/f (Yiel)
WFA 3 from 4yo+ 7lb — **9** Ran SP% **116.1**
Speed ratings (Par 103): **103,96,95,95,92 92,90,85,75**
toteswingers 1&2 £6.80, 2&3 £18.30, 1&3 £11.90 CSF £47.31 CT £788.58 TOTE £3.50: £1.10, £2.90, £8.00; EX 51.70 Trifecta £282.50 Pool: £473.48 - 1.24 winning units..
Owner L S Keys & Kristian Strangeway **Bred** Newsells Park Stud **Trained** Norton, N Yorks

FOCUS
This looked competitive, but the well-treated winner hosed up.
Mick Slates(IRE) Official explanation: jockey said gelding never travelled
T/Jkpt: £106,047.20 to a £1 stake. Pool of £149362.39 - 1 winning ticket. T/Plt: £1,747.00 to a £1 stake. Pool of £53632.60 - 22.41 winning tickets. T/Qpdt: £15.10 to a £1 stake. Pool of £4171.70 - 204.15 winning tickets. JR

[4194]YARMOUTH (L-H)

Tuesday, July 24

OFFICIAL GOING: Good to firm (7.2)

Wind: light, against Weather: hot and sunny

4433 JOHN WILLIAMS CELEBRATING A LIFETIME IN RACING MAIDEN AUCTION STKS 6f 3y

2:20 (2:26) (Class 5) 2-Y-O **£2,264** (£673; £336; £168) **Stalls** Centre

Form				RPR
6	1		**Sound Of Guns**[32] 3339 2-8-11 0 WilliamBuick 8 (Ed Walker) *stdd s: t.k.h: hld up in rr: swtchd rt and hdwy 2f out: rdn to ld ent fnl f: r.o wl* **15/8**[1]	85+
3250	2	1 ¼	**Vestibule**[10] 4093 2-8-4 74 CathyGannon 12 (Eve Johnson Houghton) *sn led: rdn and drew clr w wnr over 1f out: hdd ent fnl f: kpt on but a hld fnl f* **2/1**[2]	74
	3	6	**American Impact (USA)** 2-8-12 0 BarryMcHugh 2 (Tony Coyle) *in tch: drvn 2f out: outpcd by ldng pair and btn over 1f out: kpt on ins fnl f* **12/1**	64
20	4	1 ¼	**Not Now Blondie**[12] 4011 2-8-7 0 AndreaAtzeni 4 (Chris Dwyer) *t.k.h: sn chsng ldrs: chsd ldr and rdn over 2f out: outpcd and btn over 1f out: wknd fnl f* **12/1**	55
	5	3	**Little Indian** 2-8-12 0 FrederikTylicki 13 (J R Jenkins) *in tch: rdn 2f out: sn outpcd and struggling over 1f out: 5th and wl hld fnl f* **40/1**	51
	6	1 ¾	**Daisie Cutter** 2-8-1 0 SimonPearce(3) 15 (Lydia Pearce) *in tch in midfield: rdn ent fnl 2f: outpcd by ldng pair and btn over 1f out: wknd fnl f* **50/1**	38
60	7	nse	**Fit For A King (IRE)**[12] 3996 2-9-2 0 GeorgeBaker 10 (John Best) *led most of way to s: t.k.h: hld up in tch: rdn and effrt 2f out: sn no imp and wl hld: wknd fnl f* **16/1**	50
00	8	nse	**Perseverent Pete (USA)**[12] 3996 2-8-13 0 RyanClark(3) 11 (Christine Dunnett) *in tch: rdn and unable qck 2f out: sn outpcd and btn over 1f out: wknd fnl f* **33/1**	50
64	9	6	**Annie Besant**[11] 4045 2-8-1 0 HarryBentley(3) 9 (David C Griffiths) *in tch: hmpd and lost pl over 2f out: sn struggling and no ch over 1f out* **33/1**	20
425	10	1 ½	**Gold Beau (FR)**[26] 3520 2-8-12 73 DarryllHolland 5 (Linda Stubbs) *t.k.h early: in tch in midfield: pushed along over 3f out: lost pl and bhd 2f out* **9/1**[3]	23
300	11	½	**Simply Dreaming**[8] 4152 2-8-4 0 JamieMackay 6 (Michael Squance) *t.k.h: chsd ldr tl over 2f out: sn edging lft and wkng: fdd and bhd over 1f out* **100/1**	14
	12	5	**Star Sequence (IRE)** 2-8-7 0 MartinDwyer 7 (Hugo Palmer) *a towards rr: lost tch 2f out* **33/1**	
	13	3 ¼	**Divine Angel (IRE)** 2-8-11 0 ChrisCatlin 14 (Rae Guest) *a in rr: struggling and rdn 1/2-way: bhd fnl 2f* **12/1**	

1m 14.03s (-0.37) **Going Correction** -0.175s/f (Firm) **13** Ran SP% **121.3**

Speed ratings (Par 94): **95,93,85,83,79 77,77,77,69,67 66,59,55**

toteswingers 1&2 £2.00, 2&3 £7.30, 1&3 £6.60 CSF £5.55 TOTE £3.30: £1.20, £1.10, £3.90; EX 7.50.

Owner Howard J A Russell **Bred** Helier Stud **Trained** Newmarket, Suffolk

FOCUS

A fair juvenile maiden. They went a respectable gallop at best on drying ground officially described as Good to Firm on a hot and sunny afternoon. The first pair came clear but there was an obvious lack of depth behind them.

NOTEBOOK

Sound Of Guns finished about 5l sixth of 13 in a decent Goodwood maiden over this trip on debut the previous month, recording an RPR of 64. She reportedly looked scopey in the paddock and duly built on that promise here. She didn't make the best of starts and raced slightly keenly, but as soon as she was switched to her right, in behind the leader with 2f to go, she settled. The outcome was in little doubt when asked to go on just over 1f out and she did this nicely in the end. She is the third foal out a stakes-placed dam in the USA, who is out of a half-sister to Irish 2,000 Guineas winner Shaadi, She looks a nice sprinter in the making. (op 2-1)

Vestibule looked well beforehand and travelled well on the lead in the race itself. She had no answer to the winner once passed just over 1f out but there was a significant break back to the third. She would be of interest in sprint nurseries going forward. (op 10-3)

American Impact(USA) has an American pedigree and seemed to appreciate the ground. He is well related on the damside of his pedigree and should appreciate a step up to 7f. This was a fair debut and he will know more next time. (tchd 10-1)

Not Now Blondie will be qualified for lowly nurseries after this. (tchd 14-1)

Little Indian has something to build on at least after this modest debut fifth. (tchd 33-1)

Annie Besant Official explanation: jockey said filly suffered interference approaching 1f out

Simply Dreaming Official explanation: jockey said filly was struck into

4434 STANLEY THREADWELL MEMORIAL MAIDEN FILLIES' STKS 6f 3y

2:50 (2:53) (Class 5) 3-4-Y-O **£2,264** (£673; £336; £168) **Stalls** Centre

Form				RPR
-233	1		**Ihtifal**[45] 2935 3-8-12 87 (t) SilvestreDeSousa 6 (Saeed Bin Suroor) *taken down early and ponied to s: mde all: pushed clr over 1f out: in n.d fnl f: comf* **10/11**[1]	89+
	2	5	**Tahlia Ree (IRE)** 3-8-12 0 HayleyTurner 3 (Michael Bell) *s.i.s: hld up towards rr: rdn and hdwy over 1f out: chsd clr wnr ins fnl f: r.o for clr 2nd but no ch w wnr* **16/1**	73+
24	3	2 ¼	**Palmette**[25] 3568 3-8-12 0 WilliamBuick 2 (John Gosden) *chsd ldrs: rdn 1/2-way: drvn 2f out: sn nt qckn and no ch w wnr 1f out: 3rd and one pce ins fnl f* **2/1**[2]	66
4-0	4	1 ½	**It's My Time**[96] 1472 3-8-12 0 DaneO'Neill 1 (David Simcock) *s.i.s: towards rr: rdn and struggling 1/2-way: rallied over 1f out: no ch w wnr but kpt on ins fnl f* **25/1**	61
34	5	1 ½	**If So**[33] 3312 3-8-12 0 MickaelBarzalona 7 (James Fanshawe) *t.k.h: chsd wnr after 2f: rdn and outpcd over 1f out: wl hld 1f out: lost 2nd ins fnl f: wknd fnl 100yds* **7/1**[3]	57
0446	6	½	**Miakora**[25] 3568 4-8-12 46 TobyAtkinson(5) 9 (Michael Quinn) *chsd ldr for 2f: drvn and outpcd over 1f out: pressing for placings but no ch w wnr 1f out: wknd ins fnl f* **200/1**	56
0	7	2	**I Stand Corrected**[26] 3539 3-8-12 0 JamieSpencer 10 (Ed Walker) *in rr of main gp: rdn 1/2-way: modest hdwy fnl f: n.d* **33/1**	49
6	8	nk	**Summer Sun**[4] 4301 3-8-12 0 JimmyQuinn 4 (Phil McEntee) *t.k.h: hld up in midfield: rdn over 2f out: no prog and btn over 1f out: wknd* **66/1**	48
0-0	9	nse	**Toothache**[18] 3811 4-9-3 0 KirstyMilczarek 11 (Garry Woodward) *plld hrd: hld up in rr of main gp: swtchd rt and effrt ent fnl 2f: pressing for placings but outpcd by wnr over 1f out: wknd 1f out: fdd ins fnl f* **40/1**	48
0	10	11	**Choice Pearl (USA)**[12] 3990 3-8-9 0 HarryBentley(3) 5 (Tobias B P Coles) *chsd ldrs tl 1/2-way: sn lost pl and struggling: wl bhd fnl f* **33/1**	
0	11	3 ¾	**Venetias Dream (IRE)**[13] 3972 3-8-12 0 (t) SaleemGolam 12 (Stuart Williams) *v.s.a: a wl detached in last* **100/1**	

1m 12.28s (-2.12) **Going Correction** -0.175s/f (Firm)

WFA 3 from 4yo 5lb **11** Ran SP% **119.2**

Speed ratings (Par 100): **107,100,97,95,93 92,90,89,89,74 69**

toteswingers 1&2 £5.70, 2&3 £5.00, 1&3 £1.40 CSF £18.67 TOTE £1.90: £1.10, £1.90, £1.20; EX 26.90.

Owner Godolphin **Bred** Darley **Trained** Newmarket, Suffolk

FOCUS

A fair fillies' maiden for 3-4yos.

Summer Sun Official explanation: trainer saidn filly was unsuited by the good to firm ground

4435 EASTANGLIANAIRAMBULANCE.ORG.UK FILLIES' H'CAP (DIV I) 1m 3y

3:20 (3:20) (Class 5) (0-70,71) 3-Y-O+ **£2,264** (£673; £336; £168) **Stalls** Centre

Form				RPR
/051	1		**Consider Yourself (USA)**[5] 4242 5-10-1 71 6ex (p) WilliamCarson 6 (Anthony Carson) *hld up wl in tch: rdn and chsd ldr 2f out: ev ch and drvn ins fnl f: r.o gamely to ld last stride* **7/2**[2]	77
-430	2	shd	**Travelling**[24] 3643 3-9-3 67 MartinHarley 2 (Marco Botti) *hld up in tch in last trio: effrt ent fnl 2f: chsd ldrs and drvn 1f out: str chal ins fnl f: led towards fin tl hdd last stride* **9/2**[3]	71
-066	3	nk	**Exopuntia**[13] 3978 6-8-6 51 oh2 AdamBeschizza(3) 5 (Julia Feilden) *chsd ldr tl led ent fnl 2f: sn hrd pressed and rdn: battled on wl u.p tl hdd and no ex towards fin* **20/1**	56
50-6	4	2	**Twin Shadow (IRE)**[31] 3398 3-8-13 63 JamieSpencer 1 (James Fanshawe) *hld up in tch in rr: hdwy and n.m.r ent fnl 2f: rdn to chse ldrs over 1f out: drvn and one pce ins fnl f* **3/1**[1]	62+
660	5	1 ¼	**Divine Pamina (IRE)**[24] 3630 3-9-2 65 TomQueally 8 (Jim Boyle) *hld up in tch in last trio: hdwy over 2f out: rdn and chsd ldrs over 1f out: no ex 1f out: wknd ins fnl f* **8/1**	62
0400	6	2 ½	**Gay Gallivanter**[21] 3721 4-8-9 51 oh6 AndreaAtzeni 9 (Michael Quinn) *chsd ldrs: rdn 3f out: outpcd and drvn wl over 1f out: styd on same pce after* **66/1**	43
5034	7	nk	**Director's Dream (IRE)**[13] 3978 4-8-4 51 oh1 (tp) TobyAtkinson(5) 7 (Mark Rimmer) *hld up in tch in midfield: rdn and unable qck whn hung lft wl over 1f out: plugged on same pce but no threat to ldrs fnl f* **10/1**	42
002	8	11	**Virginia Galilei (IRE)**[15] 3918 3-9-6 70 TedDurcan 4 (David Lanigan) *hld up in tch in last trio: rdn and no rspnse over 2f out: btn over 1f out: eased ins fnl f* **7/2**[2]	34
20-0	9	10	**Yanbu (USA)**[160] 561 7-8-12 54 (t) DarryllHolland 3 (Michael Murphy) *led tl hdd ent fnl 2f: sn hld hd high u.p and lost pl: wl bhd and eased ins fnl f* **25/1**	

1m 39.77s (-0.83) **Going Correction** -0.175s/f (Firm)

WFA 3 from 4yo+ 8lb **9** Ran SP% **117.9**

Speed ratings (Par 100): **97,96,96,94,93 90,90,79,69**

toteswingers 1&2 £4.30, 2&3 £17.40, 1&3 £12.60 CSF £19.74 CT £278.94 TOTE £4.30: £1.10, £1.90, £7.60; EX 20.80.

Owner Christopher Wright & Minster Stud **Bred** Liberation Farm & Brandywine Farm **Trained** Newmarket, Suffolk

FOCUS

The first instalment of a fair fillies' handicap for 3yos and up. The gallop was respectable at best.

Virginia Galilei(IRE) Official explanation: jockey said filly never travelled

Yanbu(USA) Official explanation: trainer said mare was unsuited by the good to firm ground

4436 EASTANGLIANAIRAMBULANCE.ORG.UK FILLIES' H'CAP (DIV II) 1m 3y

3:50 (3:50) (Class 5) (0-70,69) 3-Y-O+ **£2,264** (£673; £336; £168) **Stalls** Centre

Form				RPR
-035	1		**Darling Grace**[13] 3978 3-8-10 62 AdamBeschizza(3) 6 (William Haggas) *awkward leaving stalls and s.i.s: sn niggled along in last pair: swtchd lft and effrt 3f out: chsd ldrs and hrd drvn over 1f out: chal ins fnl f: led fnl 50yds: kpt on* **6/1**	67
1255	2	nk	**Viking Rose (IRE)**[26] 3550 4-9-13 68 CathyGannon 1 (James Eustace) *w ldr: rdn 2f out: drvn to ld ld fnl 150yds: sn hrd pressed: hdd and no ex fnl 50yds* **5/2**[1]	74
000-	3	1	**Soho Rocks**[297] 6526 3-9-6 69 RobertHavlin 9 (James Toller) *t.k.h: hld up in tch in rr: hdwy and gng best over 2f out: rdn ent fnl f: edgd lft and styd on same pce ins fnl f* **5/1**[3]	71
003	4	nk	**Zuzu Angel (IRE)**[35] 3248 3-8-5 57 HarryBentley(3) 2 (William Knight) *led tl over 4f out: chsd ldr after: rdn over 2f out: stl chsng ldrs whn edgd lft u.p 1f out: styd on same pce ins fnl f* **8/1**	58
34-3	5	2 ½	**Alice Rose (IRE)**[21] 3719 3-9-4 67 NickyMackay 3 (Rae Guest) *w ldr tl led over 4f out: pushed along ent fnl 2f: rdn and flashed tail ent fnl f: hdd fnl 150yds: btn fnl 100yds and wknd towards fin* **11/4**[2]	62
0560	6	4	**Desert Red (IRE)**[5] 4232 3-8-1 50 oh1 (t) JimmyQuinn 5 (Phil McEntee) *hld up in tch: rdn and unable qck over 2f out: wknd ent fnl f* **28/1**	36
0303	7	3 ¼	**Anjomarba (IRE)**[7] 4196 5-9-1 56 HayleyTurner 4 (Conor Dore) *t.k.h: hld up wl in tch: rdn and effrt 3f out: wknd u.p over 1f out* **12/1**	37
0-10	8	14	**Carpentras**[27] 3497 4-8-12 53 DarryllHolland 8 (Dr Jon Scargill) *in tch in rr: rdn 1/2-way: wknd and lost tch 2f out: eased ins fnl f* **11/1**	

1m 39.92s (-0.68) **Going Correction** -0.175s/f (Firm)

WFA 3 from 4yo+ 8lb **8** Ran SP% **116.8**

Speed ratings (Par 100): **96,95,94,94,91 87,84,70**

toteswingers 1&2 £3.70, 2&3 £4.40, 1&3 £7.70 CSF £21.92 CT £82.01 TOTE £10.00: £2.50, £1.40, £3.60; EX 25.20.

Owner Mrs Deborah June James **Bred** Exors Of The Late F C T Wilson **Trained** Newmarket, Suffolk

FOCUS

This looked the weaker division of a fair fillies' handicap for 3yos and up.

Carpentras Official explanation: jockey said filly never travelled

4437 WELL BALANCED LEDGER AT J&H SIMPSON H'CAP 6f 3y

4:20 (4:20) (Class 4) (0-85,85) 3-Y-O+ **£4,075** (£1,212; £606; £303) **Stalls** Centre

Form				RPR
-552	1		**Picabo (IRE)**[18] 3822 4-9-2 75 DaneO'Neill 2 (Henry Candy) *hld up in tch: swtchd lft and effrt to chse ldr ent fnl f: rdn and qcknd to ld ins fnl f: sn clr: eased cl home* **4/1**[3]	88

02- **2** 3 1/4 **Soap Wars**[288] 6761 7 -9-12**85**........ WilliamBuick 3 88
(Hugo Palmer) *led: rdn over 1f out: hdd ins fnl f: no ex and immediately outpcd by wnr: kpt on for clr 2nd* **10/3**[2]
3000 **3** 2 1/2 **Five Star Junior (USA)**[32] 3336 6 -9-11**84**........ DarryllHolland 7 79
(Linda Stubbs) *bhd: rdn and hdwy jst over 1f out: edging lft and styd on u.p to go 3rd wl ins fnl f: nvr trbld ldrs* **10/1**
-003 **4** 1/2 **Kuanyao (IRE)**[41] 3049 6 -9-9**82**........ SebSanders 4 75
(Peter Makin) *chsd ldr: rdn over 2f out: drvn and unable qck over 1f out: lost 2nd and wl hld fnl f* **11/4**[1]
-004 **5** 2 1/4 **Beach Candy (IRE)**[1] 4299 3 -8-11**75**........ JimmyQuinn 8 61
(Phil McEntee) *t.k.h: chsd ldrs: rdn and unable qck 2f out: wknd u.p jst over 1f out: fdd fnl f* **16/1**
0003 **6** 1 **The Guru Of Gloom (IRE)**[8] 3772 4 -9-7**80**........ MartinDwyer 1 63
(William Muir) *t.k.h: chsd ldrs: rdn and unable qck 2f out: wknd over 1f out: fdd fnl f* **9/1**
0305 **7** 4 **Prime Exhibit**[24] 3626 7 -9-12**85**........(p) WilliamCarson 9 55
(Milton Bradley) *hld up in rr: rdn and no rspnse wl over 1f out: n.d* **13/2**
2660 **8** 3/4 **Piscean (USA)**[25] 3571 7 -9-11**84**........ JamieSpencer 5 51
(Tom Keddy) *racd in last trio: rdn and no hdwy 2f out: wknd over 1f out* **14/1**

1m 12.46s (-1.94)**Going Correction** -0.175s/f (Firm)
WFA 3 from 4yo+ 5lb 8Ran SP%114.7
Speed ratings (Par 105): **105,100,97,96,93 92,87,86**
toteswingers 1&2 £3.80, 2&3 £8.80, 1&3 £9.50 CSF £17.83 CT £123.86 TOTE £4.60 : £2.00, £2.20, £4.40 ; EX 13.40 .
Owner Tom Ford **Bred** A B Mulholland **Trained** Kingston Warren, Oxon

FOCUS
A decent sprint handicap for 3yos and upwards and the feature race on the card. The early gallop didn't appear strong with a few horses pulling hard, but they came home quickly enough in a fair time for the grade.

4438 VIKING FAMILY SUPPORT GROUP H'CAP 6f 3y
4:50 (4:51) (Class 6) (0-60,60) 3-Y-O+ £1,617 (£481; £240 ; £120) Stalls Centre

Form RPR
3-00 **1** **Elusive Hawk (IRE)**[12] 3994 8 -9-10**60**........ TomQueally 2 73
(Barney Curley) *chsd ldng pair: trckd ldr over 2f out: pushed into ld over 1f out: in command and pushed out hands and heels fnl f* **4/1**[2]
600 **2** 1 **Arch Walker (IRE)**[9] 3791 5 -9-8**58**........(b) DarryllHolland 5 67
(John Weymes) *led: rdn 2f out: hdd over 1f out: styd on same pce and a hld fnl f: swtchd lft fnl 50yds* **15/2**
224 **3** 1 1/4 **Yankee Storm**[26] 3546 7 -9-8**58**........(p) JimmyQuinn 10 63
(Michael Wigham) *hld up towards rr: swtchd lft and effrt u.p wl over 1f out: chsd ldng pair fnl f: no imp* **3/1**[1]
32-0 **4** 1/2 **Excellent Aim**[26] 3546 5 -9-7**57**........(t) JamieSpencer 6 60
(George Margarson) *chsd ldrs: rdn and racd awkwardly 2f out: styd on same pce u.p fnl f* **16/1**
2530 **5** 4 1/2 **Illustrious Lad (IRE)**[38] 3151 3 -9-0**55**........ WilliamBuick 8 44
(Jim Boyle) *in tch in midfield: rdn and unable qck wl over 2f out: no imp over 1f out: 5th and wl hld fnl f* **16/1**
0033 **6** 1/2 **Red Scintilla**[10] 4087 5 -8-11**47**........(p) SilvestreDeSousa 16 34+
(Nigel Tinkler) *towards rr: effrt u.p and edgd rt wl over 1f out: plugged on fnl f: nvr trbld ldrs* **6/1**[3]
1250 **7** 2 1/4 **Errigal Lad**[5] 4245 7 -9-8**58**........ KellyHarrison 4 38
(Garry Woodward) *s.i.s: bhd: rdn over 2f out: sme hdwy but stl plenty to do whn nt clr run and swtchd lft over 1f out: nvr trbld ldrs* **8/1**
0-04 **8** hd **Bahri Sheen (IRE)**[13] 3972 4 -9-10**60**........ GeorgeBaker 3 40
(John Best) *stdd s: hld up in rr: swtchd lft and effrt over 2f out: no imp and wknd over 1f out* **16/1**
5105 **9** hd **Compton Target (IRE)**[14] 3950 3 -9-1**56**........(t) CathyGannon 11 35
(Milton Bradley) *in tch in midfield: rdn and unable qck over 2f out: no threat to ldrs fr over 1f out* **14/1**
4604 **10** 1/2 **Microlight**[21] 3718 4 -8-11**47**........ RichardThomas 14 24
(John E Long) *in tch: rdn and unable qck over 2f out: edgd rt and wknd over 1f out* **12/1**
0200 **11** 3/4 **Flaxen Lake**[28] 3466 5 -9-0**50**........(p) DaneO'Neill 13 25
(Milton Bradley) *a towards rr: effrt u.p 2f out: stl plenty to do whn nt clr run wl over 1f out: nvr trbld ldrs* **18/1**
6-30 **12** 3 1/2 **Abadejo**[38] 3151 4 -9-8**58**........[1] FrederikTylicki 1 22
(J R Jenkins) *chsd ldr tl over 2f out: sn struggling u.p: wknd wl over 1f out* **33/1**
-000 **13** 3 1/2 **Baltic Flyer (IRE)**[22] 3701 3 -9-0**55**........(p) AndreaAtzeni 12
(Robert Eddery) *a towards rr: rdn 1/2-way: no rspnse and bhd wl over 1f out: eased wl ins fnl f* **40/1**
-006 **14** 2 **Sapphire Seeker**[49] 2803 3 -9-1**56**........ MartinHarley 15
(Des Donovan) *chsd ldrs: struggling and rdn 1/2-way: wknd 2f out: bhd fnl f* **14/1**

1m 13.25s (-1.15)**Going Correction** -0.175s/f (Firm)
WFA 3 from 4yo+ 5lb 14Ran SP%131.5
Speed ratings (Par 101): **100,98,97,96,90 89,86,86,86,85 84,79,75,72**
toteswingers 1&2 £9.40, 2&3 £6.60, 1&3 £8.70 CSF £37.91 CT £112.00 TOTE £8.80 : £3.10, £2.40, £1.10 ; EX 52.50 .
Owner Curley Leisure **Bred** J Fike **Trained** Newmarket, Suffolk

FOCUS
A moderate sprint handicap for 3yos and up. They went a respectable gallop.
Elusive Hawk (IRE) Official explanation: trainer said, regarding apparent improvement in form, that the gelding had been suited by the good to firm ground, drop in trip and benefited from the application of stick-on-shoes .
Errigal Lad Official explanation: jockey said gelding hung right

4439 SHAMROCK MOTOR COMPANY H'CAP 5f 43y
5:20 (5:21) (Class 6) (0-60,59) 4-Y-O+ £1,617 (£481; £240 ; £120) Stalls Centre

Form RPR
0060 **1** **Speedyfix**[22] 3707 5 -9-0**52**........(t) JimmyQuinn 4 62
(Christine Dunnett) *chsd ldrs and travelled wl: rdn to chal ent fnl f: led ins fnl f: r.o wl* **25/1**
5123 **2** 1 1/2 **Autocracy**[19] 3791 5 -9-7**59**........(bt) MickaelBarzalona 6 64
(Daniel Kubler) *in tch in midfield: swtchd rt and effrt 2f out: chsd ldrs and drvn 1f out: styd on same pce ins fnl f: wnt 2nd last strides* **9/4**[1]
0400 **3** hd **Miss Polly Plum**[19] 3791 5 -9-1**53**........(p) AndreaAtzeni 3 57
(Chris Dwyer) *taken down early: led: rdn and hrd pressed ent fnl f: no ex and styd on same pce after: lost 2nd last strides* **10/1**
0056 **4** 1 **See The Storm**[12] 4003 4 -8-9**47** ow1........(v) FrederikTylicki 2 47
(Lisa Williamson) *in tch: rdn over 2f out: kpt on same pce u.p fnl f* **7/2**[2]
0000 **5** 1/2 **Silver Linnet (IRE)**[14] 3943 5 -9-3**55**........(v) TomQueally 8 54
(John Butler) *pressed ldr tl rdn and unable qck over 1f out: wknd ins fnl f* **4/1**[3]

4546 **6** 2 3/4 **Imaginary Diva**[28] 3464 6 -9-6**58**........ JamieSpencer 7 47
(George Margarson) *hld up in last pair: rdn and effrt 2f out: styd on same pce and no imp after* **4/1**[3]
4500 **7** 2 1/4 **Court Applause (IRE)**[12] 4003 4 -9-7**59**........(p) MartinDwyer 5 40
(William Muir) *hld up in rr: effrt ent fnl 2f: racd awkwardly and edgd lft wl over 1f out: no prog* **11/1**

1m 2.71s (0.01)**Going Correction** -0.175s/f (Firm) 7Ran SP%114.3
Speed ratings (Par 101): **92,89,89,87,86 82,78**
toteswingers 1&2 £6.30, 2&3 £3.30, 1&3 £10.70 CSF £81.07 CT £624.72 TOTE £36.40 : £7.40 , £1.60; EX 103.30 .
Owner Mrs Christine Dunnett **Bred** Mrs Christine Dunnett **Trained** Hingham, Norfolk

FOCUS
A moderate sprint handicap for older horses. They went an even pace.
Speedyfix Official explanation: trainer said, regarding apparent improvement in form, that the gelding had benefited from the weaker race.
See The Storm Official explanation: jockey said gelding hung right
Imaginary Diva Official explanation: trainer said mare was unsuited by the good to firm ground

4440 GRANGE HOTEL ORMESBY ST MARGARET H'CAP 1m 3f 101y
5:50 (5:51) (Class 6) (0-65,64) 3-Y-O £1,617 (£481; £240 ; £120) Stalls Low

Form RPR
-224 **1** **Seven Veils (IRE)**[24] 3621 3 -9-7**64**........ ChrisCatlin 10 81
(Sir Mark Prescott Bt) *mde all: pushed along and increased gallop 4f out: rdn clr over 2f out: in n.d over 1f out: styd on wl: eased nr fin* **3/1**[1]
-4-06 **2** 6 **Attraction Ticket**[39] 3122 3 -8-12**58**........ AdamBeschizza(3) 11 64
(David Simcock) *in tch: rdn and effrt 3f out: outpcd by wnr over 2f out: wl hld but battling for 2nd fr wl over 1f out: wnt 2nd ins fnl f* **6/1**
3401 **3** 1 1/4 **Eightfold**[13] 3966 3 -9-4**61**........(t) GeorgeBaker 9 65
(Seamus Durack) *t.k.h: hld up in midfield: hdwy 4f out: drvn and chsd clr ldr 2f out: no imp and wl btn over 1f out: lost 2nd ins fnl f* **4/1**[3]
0-22 **4** 4 1/2 **Scarlet Prince**[7] 4172 3 -8-12**55**........ BarryMcHugh 2 52
(Tony Coyle) *in tch in midfield: rdn and outpcd over 2f out: no ch w wnr fnl 2f: plugged on ins fnl f* **7/2**[2]
-000 **5** 2 **Denton Dancer**[49] 2803 3 -9-0**57**........ CathyGannon 5 50
(James Eustace) *t.k.h: chsd ldrs: rdn and outpcd by wnr over 2f out: wknd over 1f out* **40/1**
4340 **6** shd **Dropzone (USA)**[19] 3781 3 -9-7**64**........ MartinHarley 3 57
(Marco Botti) *hld up in last trio: n.m.r jst over 4f out: drvn and no prog 3f out: edgd rt and wl btn 2f out: plugged on ins fnl f* **7/1**
0406 **7** 1 1/2 **Ossie's Dancer**[7] 4198 3 -8-2**45**........ JimmyQuinn 7 35
(Robert Cowell) *t.k.h: chsd ldr: rdn and outpcd over 2f out: lost 2nd and btn 2f out: wknd over 1f out* **28/1**
60-3 **8** 6 **Skyblue**[202] 30 3 -8-2**45**........ NickyMackay 6 25
(Tobias B P Coles) *rel to r and v.s.a: grad clsd and latched on to bk of field over 6f out: rdn and no rspnse over 2f out: sn wknd* **40/1**
0-00 **9** 1/2 **Karistar (IRE)**[31] 3399 3 -8-6**52**........ RyanClark(3) 1 31
(Tom Keddy) *hld up in last trio: rdn and effrt over 3f out: sn toiling: wl bhd fnl 2f* **33/1**
-024 **10** 21 **Hollywood All Star (IRE)**[13] 3966 3 -8-8**51**........ MartinDwyer 4
(William Muir) *in tch in midfield: rdn 3f out: rdr immediately looking down and nt moving wl: bhd and eased off fnl 2f* **13/2**

2m 27.68s (-1.02)**Going Correction** -0.175s/f (Firm) 10Ran SP%118.6
Speed ratings (Par 98): **96,91,90,87,86 85,84,80,80,64**
toteswingers 1&2 £5.10, 2&3 £7.60, 1&3 £4.50 CSF £21.23 CT £72.70 TOTE £4.30 : £1.70 , £3.10, £1.80 ; EX 27.50 .
Owner Mrs Olivia Hoare **Bred** Lynch Bages Ltd & Samac Ltd **Trained** Newmarket, Suffolk

FOCUS
A modest middle-distance 3yo handicap. They went a steady enough gallop, allowing Skyblue, who missed the break by 20l, to catch up before turning in.
Skyblue Official explanation: jockey said filly was slowly away
Hollywood All Star (IRE) Official explanation: vet said gelding finished lame behind
T/Plt: £14.60 to a £1 stake. Pool of £70367.58 - 3511.13 winning tickets. T/Qpdt: £15.80 to a £1 stake. Pool £3753.50 - 75.59 w. tickets SP 4441a-4447a (Foreign Racing) See RI

4206 CATTERICK (L-H)
Wednesday, July 25

OFFICIAL GOING: Good to firm (good in places; 8.8)
Wind: Moderate, half against Weather: overcast, light showers after race 3

4448 BRITISH STALLION STUDS SUPPORTING BRITISH RACING EBF MAIDEN STKS 5f 212y
2:00 (2:03) (Class 5) 2-Y-O £3,169 (£943; £471 ; £235) Stalls Low

Form RPR
64 **1** **Flighty Clarets (IRE)**[22] 3725 2 -8-12**0**........ TonyHamilton 9 66+
(Richard Fahey) *t.k.h: trckd ldrs: led over 1f out: edgd lft: drvn out* **10/1**
555 **2** hd **Grievous Angel (IRE)**[16] 3909 2 -8-12**67**........ GrahamLee 8 67
(Ann Duffield) *hld up towards rr: hdwy over 2f out: str run last 100yds: hung lft: jst failed* **10/3**[2]
00 **3** 1 1/4 **Salutation (IRE)**[11] 4114 2 -9-3**0**........ JoeFanning 3 66
(Mark Johnston) *w ldr: led over 4f out: hdd over 1f out: n.m.r and swtchd rt: styd on same pce* **11/2**
4 1 **Hit The Lights (IRE)** 2 -9-3**0**........ TomEaves 6 63+
(Ollie Pears) *t.k.h: sn trcking ldrs: effrt on outer over 2f out: sltly hmpd ins fnl f: kpt on same pce* **11/4**[1]
U30 **5** 2 **Panama Cat (USA)**[26] 3560 2 -8-12**0**........ PhillipMakin 4 52
(Kevin Ryan) *led tl over 4f out: one pce fnl 2f* **5/1**[3]
0 **6** 4 **Joeluke**[18] 3844 2 -9-3**0**........ MickyFenton 5 44+
(Paul Midgley) *s.i.s: bhd: sme hdwy over 2f out: hung lft over 1f out: kpt on* **28/1**
00 **7** 3/4 **Jomari (IRE)**[46] 2923 2 -9-3**0**........ GrahamGibbons 1 42
(Declan Carroll) *chsd ldrs: wknd 2f out* **50/1**
50 **8** 1 1/4 **Pacquiao (IRE)**[32] 3381 2 -9-3**0**........ MichaelO'Connell 10 38
(John Quinn) *wnt rt s: mid-div: effrt outer over 2f out: hung lft and sn wknd* **12/1**
050 **9** 4 **El Molino Blanco**[40] 3123 2 -8-12**0**........ JamesSullivan 2 21
(Michael Easterby) *sn wl outpcd and bhd* **40/1**
0 **10** 2 1/4 **Dinkie**[61] 2437 2 -8-12**0**........ PaulMulrennan 7 14
(Ollie Pears) *s.i.s: sn mid-div: effrt over 2f out: sn wknd* **12/1**

1m 13.84s (0.24)**Going Correction** -0.125s/f (Firm) 10Ran SP%114.1
Speed ratings (Par 94): **93,92,91,89,87 81,80,79,73,70**
toteswingers: 1&2 £4.60, 1&3 £7.10, 2&3 £3.60 CSF £41.95 TOTE £8.10 : £2.90 , £1.10 , £2.80 ; EX 48.60 .
Owner The Matthewman One Partnership **Bred** R A Fahey **Trained** Musley Bank, N Yorks

FOCUS

A modest juvenile maiden. They went an honest gallop and, with the winning time was just over 2secs slower than standard, it suggests the ground description was accurate. The winner improved for the better ground while the runner-up sets the level.

NOTEBOOK

Flighty Clarets(IRE) progressed markedly from her first two 6f starts on the quickest ground she has encountered. The first foal of John Smith's Cup winner Flying Clarets, who is a half-sister to fairly useful 6f-7f winner Celtic Lynn, she handled the turning track and good to firm ground well. She came around the leaders to challenge at the 2f pole, and just held off the fast-finishing runner-up after getting on top with a furlong to go. She will probably remain at this trip for a modest nursery handicap campaign in the coming weeks. (op 12-1)

Grievous Angel(IRE) set the form standard having achieved a BHB rating of 67 for finishing fifth in all three starts at up to 6f on softer ground. She is a good hook for the level of form on offer. Given plenty to do, she came home with a wet sail inside the final furlong but hung to her left under pressure. She appears versatile in terms of ground and looks likely to get 7f in modest nursery handicaps. (tchd 3-1)

Salutation(IRE) showed improved form on this third start. A drop to 5f in a modest nursery handicap may bear fruit. (op 5-1 tchd 7-1)

Hit The Lights(IRE) reportedly stood out in terms of looks in the preliminaries. He raced too freely here on debut but will know more next time. (op 4-1)

Panama Cat(USA) may appreciate a drop back to 5f on good ground. (op 9-2 tchd 4-1)

Joeluke was given a kind introduction after a slow start. (op 50-1 tchd 25-1)

Pacquiao(IRE)'s rider reported that the colt hung left in the straight. Official explanation: jockey said colt hung left in straight (op 11-1)

4449 STEVEN AND SHIREE WYLIE SILVER WEDDING (S) STKS — 7f

2:30 (2:31) (Class 6) 2-Y-O — **£2,045** (£603; £302) **Stalls** Centre

Form			Horse	Jockey	RPR
0	1		**Bear Totem (IRE)**[9] 4152 2-8-11 0	J-PGuillambert 4	59
			(Jo Hughes) *w ldrs: t.k.h: styd on to ld last 75yds: hld on towards fin*	**7/2**[2]	
	2	*nk*	**Juana Belen** 2-8-7 0 ow1	GrahamGibbons 2	54+
			(David Barron) *chsd ldrs: drvn over 4f out: swtchd lft 100yds out: styd on: jst hld*	**6/4**[1]	
000	3	*3/4*	**Special Report (IRE)**[40] 3126 2-8-11 32	PaulMulrennan 3	56
			(Nigel Tinkler) *led: hdd ins fnl f: kpt on same pce*	**25/1**[3]	
32	4	*8*	**Tricky Madam**[4] 4343 2-8-6 0	DavidAllan 1	30
			(Tim Easterby) *sn drvn along in rr: hdwy and swtchd outside over 2f out: chsng ldrs over 1f out: wknd fnl f*	**6/4**[1]	
00	5	*14*	**Poppy's Purse**[21] 3747 2-8-6 0	JamesSullivan 6	
			(Ollie Pears) *trckd ldrs: t.k.h: lost pl over 1f out: eased towards fin*	**33/1**	

1m 28.21s (1.21) **Going Correction** -0.125s/f (Firm) **5** Ran SP% **109.0**

Speed ratings (Par 92): **88,87,86,77,61**

CSF £9.03 TOTE £2.40: £1.40, £1.50; EX 9.90.There was no bid for the winner. Juana Belen was subject to a friendly claim.

Owner Mrs Joanna Hughes **Bred** Henry O'Callaghan **Trained** Lambourn, Berks

FOCUS

A moderate juvenile seller in which the form is taken at face value.

NOTEBOOK

Bear Totem(IRE) achieved little on his debut over 6f at Wolverhampton, but had clearly benefited greatly from that experience and won this well. He raced handily but keenly, and asserted inside the final furlong. He appears suited by this 7f trip on good to firm ground and may be able to win again in a similar grade, if continuing to improve. There was no bid for him at the subsequent auction. (op 9-2)

Juana Belen is the one to take out of this contest. Carrying 1lb overweight, she showed promise on her debut, and will know more next time, probably when racing over further. (op 5-2)

Special Report(IRE) stuck to his task in game fashion, showing improved form on his return from a six-week break. He may be able to win a similar contest back over 6f. (op 18-1)

Tricky Madam was never travelling on the quickest ground she has encountered. (op Evens tchd 13-8)

4450 PIN POINT RECRUITMENT NURSERY — 7f

3:00 (3:02) (Class 5) (0-75,70) 2-Y-O — **£2,264** (£673; £336; £168) **Stalls** Centre

Form			Horse	Jockey	RPR
064	1		**Charlie Em**[16] 3909 2-9-0 66	LeeTopliss(3) 2	68
			(Richard Fahey) *chsd ldrs: wnt 2nd over 2f out: hung lft and kpt on to ld last 100yds: hld on towards fin*	**9/2**[3]	
4046	2	*nk*	**Out Of The Blocks**[18] 3858 2-9-1 64	PJMcDonald 3	64
			(Ruth Carr) *mid-div: hdwy over 2f out: swtchd rt over 1f out: styd on towards fin*	**8/1**	
052	3	*nk*	**Sandy's Row (USA)**[22] 3725 2-9-1 64	JoeFanning 4	63
			(Mark Johnston) *led: hdd ins fnl f: no ex*	**3/1**[1]	
0000	4	*2 3/4*	**Delores Rocket**[18] 3858 2-9-1 64	PhillipMakin 7	56
			(Kevin Ryan) *chsd ldrs on outer: one pce fnl 2f*	**20/1**	
000	5	*nk*	**Clock On Tom**[47] 2880 2-8-8 57	JamesSullivan 6	48
			(Michael Easterby) *in rr: hdwy over 2f out: nvr rchd ldrs*	**66/1**	
3321	6	*shd*	**Yorkshire Icon**[18] 3842 2-9-7 70	(p) PaulMulrennan 1	61
			(Ann Duffield) *trckd ldrs: plunged and lost pl after 150yds: tk fierce hold after in rr: hdwy on ins 3f out: sn chsng ldrs: one pce over 1f out*	**15/2**	
660	7	*1 1/4*	**Lea Valley Black**[64] 2370 2-9-4 67 [1]	RichardKingscote 11	55
			(Tom Dascombe) *chsd ldrs on outer: outpcd and lost pl over 2f out: kpt on fnl f*	**11/1**	
0402	8	*4 1/2*	**Relight My Fire**[9] 4139 2-8-11 60	DavidAllan 5	36
			(Tim Easterby) *chsd ldrs: sn drvn along wknd appr fnl f*	**7/2**[2]	
005	9	*3*	**Another Ponty**[50] 2790 2-8-6 55	DuranFentiman 8	23
			(Tim Easterby) *chsd ldrs: drvn over 4f out: sltly hmpd over 1f out: sn wknd*	**16/1**	
4640	10	*2 1/4*	**Until It Sleeps**[63] 2402 2-7-13 55	DannyBrock(7) 9	17
			(Alan McCabe) *s.s: nvr on terms*	**50/1**	
600	11	*5*	**Strasbourg Place**[31] 3415 2-7-13 51	(p) DeclanCannon(3) 10	
			(Nigel Tinkler) *s.i.s: in rr: bhd fnl 3f*	**25/1**	
3100	12	*6*	**Vanessa**[11] 4116 2-9-2 65	GrahamLee 12	
			(Jim Goldie) *gave problems s: rrd and s.v.s: a detached in last*	**28/1**	

1m 28.03s (1.03) **Going Correction** -0.125s/f (Firm) **12** Ran SP% **118.0**

Speed ratings (Par 94): **89,88,88,85,84 84,83,78,74,72 66,59**

toteswingers: 1&2 £9.20, 1&3 £4.40, 2&3 £8.50 CSF £37.77 TOTE £5.10: £1.70, £2.60, £2.60; EX 48.00.

Owner Mrs E Armstrong & R Marshall **Bred** Highfield Farm Llp **Trained** Musley Bank, N Yorks

FOCUS

A modest nursery handicap in which the form is straightforward and solid.

NOTEBOOK

Charlie Em ◆ had shown quietly progressive form in her three previous starts, managing to qualify for a race of this nature with a peak fourth over 6f at Ripon on soft ground this month. She looked potentially well treated off an initial mark of 66, stepping up to 7f on better ground, and so it proved. She had the benefit of a low draw and was able to race handily, came with a good sustained challenge from 2f out and convinced herself she had done more than enough when eventually getting on top well inside the final furlong, pricking her ears passing the post in front. There is probably more to come from her. (tchd 11-2)

Out Of The Blocks had the most experience in the field after seven starts. He came home strongly into second from midfield and looks capable of picking up a similar contest over this 7f trip on decent ground. (op 15-2)

Sandy's Row(USA) attempted to make all the running and looked like achieving the feat about 1f out. She stuck to her task in game fashion but had to give best well inside the final furlong. She may appreciate a drop back to 6f on a similarly turning track. (op 4-1)

Delores Rocket didn't appreciate racing downhill around the home turn and could never get to the principals. (tchd 16-1)

Clock On Tom showed his first real promise on this fourth start.

Yorkshire Icon raced very freely after taking a false step early in the race. This was a fair effort in the circumstances. (op 5-1 tchd 8-1)

Lea Valley Black appeared to show the benefit of a first-time hood on his return from a two-month break. (op 16-1)

Relight My Fire appeared not to handle the downhill turn for home. (tchd 4-1)

Vanessa's rider reported that the filly reared as the stalls opened. Official explanation: jockey said filly reared as stalls opened (op 25-1 tchd 33-1)

4451 SKYBET SUPPORTING THE YORKSHIRE RACING SUMMER FESTIVAL H'CAP — 5f

3:30 (3:30) (Class 4) (0-85,84) 3-Y-0+ — **£4,075** (£1,212; £606; £303) **Stalls** Low

Form			Horse	Jockey	RPR
4040	1		**Lost In Paris (IRE)**[5] 4312 6-9-5 77	(p) DavidAllan 3	85
			(Tim Easterby) *mde virtually all: kpt on fnl f: all out*	**5/2**[2]	
0-00	2	*nse*	**Master Rooney (IRE)**[65] 2337 6-9-7 84	JustinNewman(5) 6	92
			(Bryan Smart) *tubed: chsd ldrs on outer: upsides jst ins fnl f: jst failed*	**11/1**	
001	3	*nk*	**Almond Branches**[7] 4208 3-8-12 74 6ex	PJMcDonald 1	80
			(George Moore) *chsd ldrs: outpcd 3f out: hdwy over 1f out: nt clr run ins fnl f: swtchd lft: styd on wl towards fin*	**7/4**[1]	
4603	4	*2 1/2*	**Jamesway (IRE)**[30] 3441 4-9-10 82	JamesSullivan 4	80
			(Ruth Carr) *trckd ldrs: effrt over 1f out: kpt on same pce*	**5/1**[3]	
011	5	*1 1/2*	**Nomoreblondes**[61] 2439 8-9-0 77	(v) LMcNiff(5) 2	69
			(Paul Midgley) *w wnr: wkng on ins whn hmpd last 50yds*	**10/1**	
0420	6	*1 3/4*	**Wicked Wilma (IRE)**[5] 4292 8-8-6 67	JulieBurke(3) 7	53
			(Alan Berry) *swvd rt s: in rr: kpt on fnl f: nvr a factor*	**22/1**	
625-	7	*3 3/4*	**Mey Blossom**[264] 7265 7-8-7 65	TomEaves 5	38
			(Richard Whitaker) *chsd ldrs: outpcd and lost pl 3f out*	**18/1**	

59.05s (-0.75) **Going Correction** -0.025s/f (Good)

WFA 3 from 4yo+ 4lb **7** Ran SP% **108.6**

Speed ratings (Par 105): **105,104,104,100,98 95,89**

toteswingers: 1&2 £8.20, 1&3 £1.20, 2&3 £2.70 CSF £26.09 TOTE £3.40: £2.30, £4.30; EX 32.90.

Owner W H Ponsonby **Bred** Yeomanstown Stud **Trained** Great Habton, N Yorks

■ Stewards' Enquiry : P J McDonald two-day ban: careless riding (Aug 8-9)

FOCUS

A decent sprint handicap.

4452 TYREGIANT.COM H'CAP (DIV I) — 5f 212y

4:00 (4:03) (Class 6) (0-60,60) 3-Y-0+ — **£1,940** (£577; £288; £144) **Stalls** Low

Form			Horse	Jockey	RPR
0325	1		**Ferdy (IRE)**[12] 4043 3-8-11 52	FrannyNorton 11	64
			(Paul Green) *chsd ldr: wnt 2nd over 3f out: led last 150yds: kpt on wl*	**4/1**[1]	
2650	2	*1 1/2*	**Chosen One (IRE)**[8] 4174 7-9-4 54	JamesSullivan 8	61
			(Ruth Carr) *led: t.k.h: drvn over 2f out: hdd jst ins fnl f: no ex*	**12/1**	
6356	3	*1 1/2*	**Baybshambles (IRE)**[8] 4174 8-9-5 55	TomEaves 12	57
			(Ron Barr) *chsd ldrs: wnt 3rd over 1f out: kpt on same pce*	**9/1**	
0063	4	*3/4*	**Green Warrior**[27] 3546 4-8-11 50	(e) DeclanCannon(3) 1	50
			(Richard Guest) *chsd ldrs: drvn over 2f out: kpt on fnl f*	**14/1**	
-004	5	*nk*	**Boy The Bell**[8] 4192 5-9-3 60	JacobButterfield(7) 2	59
			(Ollie Pears) *mid-div: hdwy over 2f out: kpt on fnl f*	**5/1**[3]	
-003	6	*1 1/2*	**Sir Windsorlot (IRE)**[26] 3566 3-9-5 60	(t) MichaelO'Connell 9	54
			(John Quinn) *mid-div: hdwy over 2f out: kpt on fnl f*	**9/2**[2]	
00-6	7	*1*	**Piste**[6] 4245 6-8-7 46 oh1	(e) JulieBurke(3) 4	37
			(Tina Jackson) *s.i.s: in rr: hdwy on outer 2f out: kpt on towards fin*	**14/1**	
0640	8	*shd*	**Elusive Island (USA)**[11] 4087 3-8-9 50	(p) PaulMulrennan 10	41+
			(Ann Duffield) *rrd s: in rr: last 3f out: hdwy 2f out: kpt on ins fnl f*	**12/1**	
0-60	9	*1 1/2*	**Peteron**[18] 3848 4-8-11 47	PaddyAspell 6	33
			(Colin Teague) *chsd ldrs: wknd over 1f out*	**66/1**	
0000	10	*1 3/4*	**Sleights Boy (IRE)**[22] 3731 4-8-12 48	(v) PatrickMathers 7	28
			(Ian McInnes) *hmpd s: in rr: wd bnd 3f out: nvr on terms*	**25/1**	
2336	11	*5*	**Besty**[22] 3730 5-9-9 59	MickyFenton 5	23
			(Paul Midgley) *mid-div: lost pl over 4f out: sme hdwy over 2f out: lost pl over 1f out: eased clsng stages*	**5/1**[3]	
-000	12	*nk*	**Chambers (IRE)**[55] 2618 6-8-10 46 oh1	(b[1]) GrahamLee 3	
			(Richard Ford) *in rr: sme hdwy on inner over 2f out: wknd over 1f out*	**40/1**	

1m 12.77s (-0.83) **Going Correction** -0.125s/f (Firm)

WFA 3 from 4yo+ 5lb **12** Ran SP% **118.0**

Speed ratings (Par 101): **100,98,96,95,94 92,91,91,89,86 80,79**

toteswingers 1&2 £11.30, 1&3 £8.10, 2&3 £14.80 CSF £51.93 CT £412.48 TOTE £3.90: £1.20, £5.00, £2.70; EX 65.30.

Owner E Sciarrillo **Bred** David And Elizabeth Kennedy **Trained** Lydiate, Merseyside

FOCUS

The first instalment of a modest sprint handicap. The winning time was very respectable for the grade.

Besty Official explanation: trainer said gelding was unsuited by the track

4453 TYREGIANT.COM H'CAP (DIV II) — 5f 212y

4:30 (4:31) (Class 6) (0-60,60) 3-Y-0+ — **£1,940** (£577; £288; £144) **Stalls** Low

Form			Horse	Jockey	RPR
4U2	1		**Oakbrook**[2] 4394 3-8-11 52	PaulMulrennan 2	60
			(Ann Duffield) *mid-div: effrt and swtchd ins over 2f out: styd on to ld last 100yds: kpt on wl*	**7/2**[1]	
0-35	2	*3/4*	**Ursus**[37] 3210 7-8-11 47	(p) PaddyAspell 7	53
			(Christopher Wilson) *chsd ldrs: led over 2f out: hdd ins fnl f: no ex*	**14/1**	
0-36	3	*3/4*	**Lady Del Sol**[34] 3308 4-9-10 60	PhillipMakin 12	63
			(Marjorie Fife) *dwlt: swtchd lft s: in rr: hdwy over 2f out: kpt on wl ins fnl f*	**7/1**	
0-60	4	*nk*	**Irrational**[26] 3566 3-9-3 58	TomEaves 5	60
			(Bryan Smart) *in rr: hdwy ins 2f out: kpt on wl fnl f*	**14/1**	
2-30	5	*shd*	**Karate Queen**[42] 3026 7-8-5 46 oh1	ShaneBKelly(5) 11	48
			(Ron Barr) *dwlt: in rr: hdwy over 2f out: kpt on fnl f*	**9/1**	
0002	6	*1*	**Dunmore Boy (IRE)**[9] 4143 4-9-8 58	(p) TonyHamilton 10	57
			(Richard Fahey) *chsd ldrs: drvn over 2f out: hung lft and wknd ins fnl f*	**5/1**[2]	

4202 **7** *hd* **Drumpellier (IRE)**[29] 3462 5-9-0 **50** AmyRyan 8 48
(Simon West) *chsd ldrs: effrt on outer over 2f out: kpt on one pce over 1f out* **8/1**

1023 **8** *½* **Dotty Darroch**[29] 3462 4-9-5 **55** DanielTudhope 1 57+
(Robin Bastiman) *hld up towards rr: effrt and nt clr run 2f out: styng on whn nt clr run wl ins fnl f* **11/2**[3]

0500 **9** *2* **Downtown Boy (IRE)**[33] 3353 4-8-10 **46** oh1 (p) MickyFenton 6 36
(Ray Craggs) *led tl over 2f out: wknd and eased fnl 75yds* **18/1**

2050 **10** *7* **Meydan Style (USA)**[83] 1799 6-8-10 **46** oh1 (p) GrahamLee 3 14
(Richard Ford) *chsd ldrs: lost pl over 2f out: eased whn bhd* **28/1**

0004 **11** *6* **Grand Stitch (USA)**[29] 3462 6-8-7 **48** NeilFarley(5) 4
(Declan Carroll) *chsd ldrs: wknd 2f out: eased clsng stages* **12/1**

1m 13.32s (-0.28) **Going Correction** -0.125s/f (Firm)
WFA 3 from 4yo+ 5lb **11** Ran SP% **117.6**
Speed ratings (Par 101): **98,95,94,93,93 92,91,91,88,79 71**
toteswingers 1&2 £10.40, 1&3 £7.90, 2&3 £24.20 CSF £54.96 CT £334.66 TOTE £3.10: £1.20, £4.00, £2.20; EX 43.00.
Owner James Warrender & Mrs Elaine Culf **Bred** W H R John And Partners **Trained** Constable Burton, N Yorks

FOCUS
The second division of a modest sprint handicap for 3yos and up. The winning time was slower than the first leg.
Karate Queen Official explanation: jockey said mare missed the break
Dunmore Boy(IRE) Official explanation: jockey said gelding hung left
Dotty Darroch Official explanation: jockey said filly was denied a clear run

4454 YORKSHIRE.COM BACK LE BID CLAIMING STKS 5f
5:00 (5:00) (Class 6) 3-Y-O+ **£2,045** (£603; £302) **Stalls** Low

Form RPR

06 **1** **Kyzer Chief**[61] 2436 7-8-7 57 [1] ShaneBKelly(5) 5 69
(Ron Barr) *led: narrowly hdd last 75yds: rallied to ld cl home* **50/1**

1000 **2** *nk* **Partner (IRE)**[32] 3374 6-9-7 90 (b) GrahamLee 1 77
(Kevin Ryan) *towards rr: hdwy on inner whn nt clr run over 2f out: swtchd rt: styd on to take narrow ld ins fnl f: hdd fnl strides* **9/2**[3]

0610 **3** *¾* **No Hubris (USA)**[9] 4133 5-9-3 79 (b) JamesSullivan 2 70
(Ruth Carr) *towards rr: hdwy and edgd lft 2f out: sn chsng ldrs: no ex last 50yds* **8/1**

0020 **4** *2* **What About You (IRE)**[16] 3903 4-9-0 75 (b) FrederikTylicki 8 60
(Richard Fahey) *outpcd and towards rr: hdwy 2f out: edgd lft: kpt on fnl f* **4/1**[2]

5105 **5** *nk* **Fol Hollow (IRE)**[7] 4207 7-8-9 73 ShirleyTeasdale(7) 7 61
(David Nicholls) *chsd ldrs: drvn and outpcd over 2f out: fdd appr fnl f* **9/1**

4400 **6** *1½* **Mango Music**[13] 3993 9-8-6 65 (p) KellyHarrison 4 46
(David Thompson) *s.s: detached in last: styd on over 1f out: nvr a factor* **50/1**

4505 **7** *nk* **Foxy Music**[16] 3903 8-9-2 90 GrahamGibbons 6 54
(Eric Alston) *w ldrs: rdn 2f out: eased whn btn last 100yds* **7/4**[1]

0302 **8** *1¼* **Crimea (IRE)**[23] 3707 6-9-2 75 AdrianNicholls 3 50
(David Nicholls) *sn trcking ldrs: rdn 2f out: wknd appr fnl f* **8/1**

050 **9** *5* **Lady By Red (IRE)**[37] 3210 4-8-6 44 DuranFentiman 9 22
(David Thompson) *chsd ldrs on outer: wknd over 1f out* **200/1**

59.05s (-0.75) **Going Correction** -0.025s/f (Good) **9** Ran SP% **111.2**
Speed ratings (Par 101): **105,104,103,100,99 97,96,94,86**
toteswingers 1&2 £10.10, 2&3 £4.70, 1&3 £18.40 CSF £250.26 TOTE £33.00: £5.90, £1.10, £3.90; EX 174.30.
Owner R E Barr **Bred** Mrs H F Mahr **Trained** Seamer, N Yorks

FOCUS
A good claiming sprint.
Foxy Music Official explanation: trainer's rep said, regarding running, that the gelding was unable to dominate.

4455 YORKSHIRE RADIO APPRENTICE H'CAP 1m 3f 214y
5:30 (5:31) (Class 6) (0-65,65) 4-Y-O+ **£2,045** (£603; £302) **Stalls** Low

Form RPR

-141 **1** **Tinseltown**[8] 4179 6-9-8 **63** 6ex (p) JasonHart 8 73
(Brian Rothwell) *mde all: increased pce over 4f out: styd on wl: hld on towards fin* **7/2**[2]

/30- **2** *¾* **Sheila's Castle**[295] 6600 8-9-0 **55** JackDuern 1 64
(Sean Regan) *chsd ldrs: wnt 2nd over 4f out: kpt on fnl f: a jst hld* **25/1**

024 **3** *2* **Snooker (GER)**[20] 3775 6-9-5 **60** HarryChalloner 10 66
(Rose Dobbin) *mid-div: hdwy to chse wnr over 3f out: kpt on same pce over 1f out* **14/1**

-406 **4** *6* **King's Counsel (IRE)**[4] 4048 6-9-5 **65** (v) DavidBergin(5) 2 61
(David O'Meara) *sn outpcd: chsd ldrs: drvn 4f out: kpt on one pce to take 4th over 1f out* **9/2**[3]

0335 **5** *5* **Dubara Reef (IRE)**[41] 3061 5-8-8 **49** (v) JoshBaudains 11 37
(Paul Green) *chsd ldrs: hrd drvn over 4f out: wknd over 1f out* **9/1**

560- **6** *½* **Muwalla**[56] 7215 5-9-7 **62** (p) GeorgeChaloner 14 50
(Chris Grant) *mid-div: effrt over 3f out: nvr nr ldrs* **18/1**

32-0 **7** *1½* **Phase Shift**[20] 3775 4-8-12 **56** LauraBarry(3) 9 41+
(Brian Ellison) *hld up in mid-div: effrt over 3f out: hung rt over 1f out: nvr a factor* **11/4**[1]

0643 **8** *4* **Amir Pasha (UAE)**[21] 3752 7-8-6 **54** (p) KatieDowson(7) 6 33
(Micky Hammond) *in rr: hmpd and lost pl bnd after 3f: sn drvn along: sme hdwy over 2f out: nvr on terms* **9/1**

00-3 **9** *hd* **Into The Light**[101] 632 7-8-2 **48** (p) EvaMoscrop(5) 7 26
(Philip Kirby) *trckd ldrs: lost pl over 6f out* **40/1**

5/30 **10** *1¼* **Gulf Coast**[8] 4179 7-8-8 **52** (p) GemmaTutty(3) 12 28
(Tim Walford) *chsd ldrs: outpcd over 3f out: hung lft and wknd over 1f out* **12/1**

60-0 **11** *11* **Gumnd (IRE)**[21] 3752 5-8-1 **47** KevinLundie(5) 4
(Chris Grant) *dwlt: in rr: bhd fnl2f* **50/1**

2004 **12** *1¾* **Arizona High**[21] 3752 4-8-5 **46** (v) NatashaEaton 3
(Andrew Crook) *in rr: hdwy on outer 6f out: lost pl over 3f out* **28/1**

600- **13** *32* **Friday Night Lad (IRE)**[241] 6870 5-8-5 **46** DannyBrock 15
(Dianne Sayer) *swvd rt s: in rr: sme hdwy on outer over 5f out: lost pl over 3f out: sn bhd: t.o* **66/1**

2m 36.83s (-2.07) **Going Correction** -0.125s/f (Firm) **13** Ran SP% **119.9**
Speed ratings (Par 101): **101,100,99,95,91 91,90,87,87,86 79,78,57**
toteswingers 1&2 £13.20, 1&3 £8.20, 2&3 £25.40 CSF £97.83 CT £1113.36 TOTE £5.40: £2.60, £7.50, £5.50; EX 94.60.
Owner Tony Arnott **Bred** Biddestone Stud **Trained** Norton, N Yorks

FOCUS
A modest middle-distance handicap restricted to apprentice riders.
T/Plt: £207.10 to a £1 stake. Pool: £48,362.17. 170.45 winning tickets. T/Qpdt: £47.10 to a £1 stake. Pool: £3,943.80. 61.86 winning tickets. WG

[2783]LEICESTER (R-H)
Wednesday, July 25

OFFICIAL GOING: Good to soft (good in places) changing to good (good to soft in places) after race 1 (6.10)
Far side rail on Sprint track moved 3yds inside. Inner configuration on Round course and all distances as advertised.
Wind: Nil Weather: Fine

4456 ATTHERACES.COM FREE REPLAYS MAIDEN STKS 5f 2y
6:10 (6:12) (Class 5) 3-Y-O+ **£2,264** (£673; £336; £168) **Stalls** Low

Form RPR

424 **1** **Supreme Quest**[37] 3235 3-8-12 78 JamesDoyle 6 73+
(Roger Charlton) *mde virtually all: racd keenly: shkn up ins fnl f: styd on* **5/4**[1]

3 **2** *1½* **Angelito**[23] 3702 3-9-3 0 RichardMullen 3 71
(Ed McMahon) *a.p: pushed along 1/2-way: rdn to chse wnr fnl f: r.o* **5/2**[2]

0 **3** *2¼* **Red Baron (IRE)**[13] 3990 3-9-3 0 JimmyQuinn 2 63
(Eric Alston) *a.p: rdn to chse wnr over 1f out: styd on same pce fnl f* **33/1**

4 *¾* **Bull Bay** 3-9-3 0 RobertHavlin 9 60+
(Jane Chapple-Hyam) *s.i.s: rn green in rr: rdn 1/2-way: r.o ins fnl f: nrst fin* **14/1**

0-6 **5** *8* **Black Douglas**[13] 3990 3-9-3 0 JoeFanning 8 31
(William Jarvis) *chsd ldrs: rdn 1/2-way: wknd over 1f out* **9/2**[3]

00 **6** *½* **Barnacle**[23] 3702 3-9-3 0 JohnFahy 1 30
(Pat Eddery) *s.i.s: sn outpcd* **66/1**

-202 **7** *2* **Miss Noble**[56] 2611 3-8-12 60 NeilCallan 7 17
(Stuart Williams) *trckd wnr: racd keenly: rdn 1/2-way: wknd over 1f out* **12/1**

8 *9* **Euroquip Rose** 3-8-7 0 RachealKneller(5) 4
(Michael Scudamore) *s.s: outpcd* **28/1**

59.57s (-0.43) **Going Correction** +0.025s/f (Good)
WFA 3 from 4yo 4lb **8** Ran SP% **113.4**
Speed ratings (Par 103): **104,101,98,96,84 83,80,65**
toteswingers: 1&2 £1.20, 1&3 £6.30, 2&3 £17.80 CSF £4.35 TOTE £1.80: £1.10, £1.40, £7.60; EX 4.60.
Owner Inglett, Allen, Carter and Kennedy **Bred** A Parker & Bullard Bloodstock Ltd **Trained** Beckhampton, Wilts

FOCUS
There was an area dolled off between the 2f and 3f poles on the stands' side for approximately 100 yards. The course had seen an unwelcome amount of rain recently, 317mm in the past six weeks to be precise, and had lost its last five meetings. The ground was finally drying out, and this was a particularly warm day. Following this opening race the going was changed to good, good to soft in places, and the winning time suggests conditions were not at all bad. The time was marginally quicker than the closing Class 5 handicap.

4457 ATTHERACES.COM EXCLUSIVE WILLIAM BUICK BLOG (S) STKS 1m 60y
6:40 (6:40) (Class 6) 3-Y-O **£1,617** (£481; £240; £120) **Stalls** Low

Form RPR

6-4 **1** **Future Wonder (IRE)**[7] 4211 3-8-6 0 ChrisCatlin 2 59+
(Rae Guest) *a.p: swtchd lft and chsd ldr 2f out: rdn to ld ins fnl f: sn hung rt: styd on wl* **2/1**[2]

450U **2** *3½* **Mitie Mouse**[24] 3671 3-8-11 67 NeilCallan 6 56
(Mike Murphy) *led: racd keenly and hung lft tl over 4f out: rdn over 1f out: hdd and unable qck ins fnl f* **9/1**

5145 **3** *1¾* **Final Delivery**[15] 3938 3-8-11 66 (p) FrankieDettori 4 54
(George Baker) *hld up: rdn over 2f out: hdwy u.p over 1f out: no ex ins fnl f: eased nr fin* **13/8**[1]

6460 **4** *nk* **High Five Prince (IRE)**[15] 3938 3-8-6 42 RachealKneller(5) 1 51?
(Mark Usher) *hld up: plld hrd: hdwy 2f out: rdn over 1f out: styd on same pce fnl f* **25/1**

6045 **5** *8* **Armiger**[32] 3391 3-8-8 46 RaulDaSilva(3) 5 33
(William Muir) *prom: rdn over 3f out: wknd over 2f out* **25/1**

0-50 **6** *hd* **Clowance Keys**[7] 4213 3-8-11 0 JamesDoyle 8 38
(Rod Millman) *hld up: hung lft 6f out: hdwy over 3f out: rdn and wknd over 1f out* **4/1**[3]

0500 **7** *1¾* **Gadreel (IRE)**[38] 3193 3-8-11 41 JohnFahy 9 28
(Anthony Middleton) *chsd ldrs: rdn over 2f out: sn wknd* **50/1**

-000 **8** *8* **Mae Rose Cottage (IRE)**[30] 3451 3-8-6 53 JimmyQuinn 7
(Barney Curley) *trckd ldr: plld hrd: rdn over 2f out: sn wknd* **20/1**

-000 **9** *nk* **Peg Peg**[28] 3489 3-7-13 41 NoelGarbutt(7) 3
(Nerys Dutfield) *s.s: a in rr: wknd over 2f out* **80/1**

1m 44.97s (-0.13) **Going Correction** -0.125s/f (Firm) **9** Ran SP% **117.1**
Speed ratings (Par 98): **95,91,89,89,81 81,79,71,71**
toteswingers: 1&2 £3.20, 1&3 £1.10, 2&3 £2.10 CSF £18.75 TOTE £3.00: £1.10, £1.90, £1.10; EX 20.20.The winner was bought in for 6,500gns.
Owner Barry Stewart **Bred** Peter Thome **Trained** Newmarket, Suffolk

FOCUS
A moderate race.
Clowance Keys Official explanation: jockey said gelding lost its action

4458 JOIN AT THE RACES ON FACEBOOK MEDIAN AUCTION MAIDEN STKS 1m 1f 218y
7:15 (7:15) (Class 6) 3-4-Y-O **£1,940** (£577; £288; £144) **Stalls** Low

Form RPR

4- **1** **Pallasator**[233] 7634 3-9-3 0 ChrisCatlin 2 90+
(Sir Mark Prescott Bt) *hld up: hdwy to chse ldr over 2f out: rdn over 1f out: styd on u.p to ld nr fin* **9/4**[2]

4035 **2** *nk* **Sound Hearts (USA)**[22] 3737 3-8-12 77 NeilCallan 5 84
(Roger Varian) *led: rdn over 1f out: hdd nr fin* **11/8**[1]

6 **3** *7* **Caption**[32] 3399 3-8-12 0 RichardMullen 1 70
(Sir Michael Stoute) *chsd ldrs tl rdn and wknd over 1f out* **3/1**[3]

-630 **4** *5* **Choral Bee**[28] 3483 3-8-12 57 (v[1]) DaneO'Neill 3 60
(Henry Candy) *chsd ldr tl rdn and wknd over 2f out* **12/1**

2m 5.58s (-2.32) **Going Correction** -0.125s/f (Firm) **4** Ran SP% **105.6**
Speed ratings (Par 101): **104,103,98,94**
CSF £5.49 TOTE £3.40; EX 5.90.
Owner Baxter, Gregson, Jenkins & Warman **Bred** Newsells Park Stud **Trained** Newmarket, Suffolk

FOCUS
Only four runners, but a fair standard of form and a winner who is open to plenty of improvement. The time was only 0.19 seconds slower than the following Class 4 handicap.

4459 AT THE RACES SKY 415 EBF H'CAP 1m 1f 218y
7:45 (7:45) (Class 4) (0-85,86) 3-Y-O £5,175 (£1,540; £769; £384) **Stalls** Low

Form				RPR
-204	1		**Deia Sunrise (IRE)**46 2930 3-9-7 84 RobertHavlin 4 (John Gosden) *led 9f out: rdn over 1f out: styd on wl* 5/2[2]	96
0201	2	2 ¾	**Queen's Estate (GER)**11 4088 3-8-13 76 JoeFanning 1 (Mark Johnston) *hld up: hdwy over 2f out: rdn to chse wnr over 1f out: styd on same pce ins fnl f* 10/1	82
41-0	3	1 ¼	**Saytara (IRE)**22 3737 3-9-2 79 FrankieDettori 7 (Saeed Bin Suroor) *s.i.s: hld up: hdwy over 2f out: rdn over 1f out: edgd rt and styd on same pce ins fnl f* 6/5[1]	83
2021	4	4 ½	**Spirit Of The Law (IRE)**8 4199 3-9-4 86 6ex AshleyMorgan(5) 2 (Ed Dunlop) *plld hrd: led 1f: trckd ldr tl rdn over 2f out: wknd over 1f out* 3/1[3]	81
3236	5	10	**Tidal Way (IRE)**12 4046 3-8-11 74 (v1) SamHitchcott 6 (Mick Channon) *stmbld s: chsd ldrs: rdn over 3f out: wknd over 2f out* 14/1	49

2m 5.39s (-2.51) **Going Correction** -0.125s/f (Firm) 5 Ran SP% **111.6**
Speed ratings (Par 102): **105,102,101,98,90**
CSF £33.36 TOTE £5.80: £2.90, £4.40; EX 22.70.
Owner M Kerr-Dineen M Hughes Ms R Hood **Bred** John O'Connor **Trained** Newmarket, Suffolk

FOCUS
A small field, but fair enough form.

4460 AT THE RACES VIRGIN 534 H'CAP 1m 3f 183y
8:20 (8:20) (Class 4) (0-85,84) 4-Y-O+ £4,075 (£1,212; £606; £303) **Stalls** Low

Form				RPR
-015	1		**Lily In Pink**24 3661 4-9-7 84 JamesDoyle 3 (Jonathan Portman) *hld up: hdwy over 3f out: rdn to join ldr over 1f out: led ins fnl f: drvn out* 9/2[2]	94
0022	2	hd	**Daring Indian**11 4088 4-8-8 71 RichardKingscote 4 (Tom Dascombe) *a.p: led wl over 1f out: sn rdn: hdd ins fnl f: r.o* 4/1[1]	80
5130	3	1 ¾	**Sand Skier**7 4216 5-8-7 77 NicoleNordblad(7) 5 (Hans Adielsson) *chsd ldrs: lost pl 7f out: hdwy over 2f out: rdn over 1f out: styd on* 9/2[2]	83
2241	4	2 ¾	**The Lock Master (IRE)**13 3992 5-8-6 69 LukeMorris 10 (Michael Appleby) *hld up: hdwy over 1f out: rdn and no imp ins fnl f* 7/1[3]	71
-450	5	6	**Jeu De Vivre (IRE)**80 1880 4-9-0 77 JoeFanning 8 (Mark Johnston) *prom: rdn over 2f out: wknd fnl f* 10/1	69
-002	6	2	**Reflect (IRE)**25 3609 4-9-7 84 (t) DaneO'Neill 6 (Tim Vaughan) *hld up: hdwy over 3f out: rdn and hung lft over 2f out: sn wknd* 12/1	73
0456	7	1	**Royal Trooper (IRE)**13 3992 6-8-11 74 GrahamLee 9 (James Given) *chsd ldr tl led over 3f out: rdn: hdd and n.m.r wl over 1f out: wknd fnl f* 9/2[2]	62
6515	8	5	**Achalas (IRE)**34 3316 4-8-13 76 TadhgO'Shea 2 (Heather Main) *s.s: a bhd* 12/1	56
4440	9	1 ¼	**Steuben (GER)**12 4072 6-9-5 82 MickyFenton 1 (Barney Curley) *plld hrd: sn led: hdd over 3f out: wknd over 2f out* 20/1	60

2m 30.66s (-3.24) **Going Correction** -0.125s/f (Firm) 9 Ran SP% **116.3**
Speed ratings (Par 105): **105,104,103,101,97 96,95,92,91**
toteswingers: 1&2 £3.40, 1&3 £5.80, 2&3 £3.10 CSF £23.06 CT £85.68 TOTE £7.00: £1.80, £1.90, £1.40; EX 22.70.
Owner Mrs S L Morley **Bred** J Ford & Peter J Skinner **Trained** Compton, Berks

FOCUS
A fair handicap.
Achalas(IRE) Official explanation: jockey said gelding became upset in the stalls and missed the break

4461 FOLLOW AT THE RACES ON TWITTER H'CAP 5f 2y
8:50 (8:50) (Class 5) (0-75,74) 3-Y-O+ £2,587 (£770; £384; £192) **Stalls** Low

Form				RPR
4424	1		**Rylee Mooch**13 3993 4-9-5 74 (e) JasonHart(7) 5 (Richard Guest) *trckd ldr: plld hrd: rdn to ld over 1f out: r.o* 7/2[3]	81
0263	2	¾	**Rambo Will**16 3915 4-9-9 71 DaneO'Neill 1 (J R Jenkins) *sn led: rdn and hdd over 1f out: r.o* 3/1[2]	75
0060	3	nk	**Swendab (IRE)**16 3915 4-9-10 72 (b1) LukeMorris 8 (John O'Shea) *chsd ldrs: pushed along 1/2-way: rdn over 1f out: hung lft wl ins fnl f: r.o* 12/1	75
4305	4	¾	**Sally's Swansong**32 3382 6-8-7 55 oh5 (b) JimmyQuinn 3 (Eric Alston) *s.i.s: sn chsng ldrs: rdn over 1f out: styd on* 16/1	56
1000	5	¾	**Red Roar (IRE)**11 4085 5-9-6 68 GrahamLee 2 (Alan Berry) *chsd ldrs: rdn over 1f out: styd on* 9/1	66
2134	6	1 ½	**Celestial Dawn**14 3954 3-8-10 62 ChrisCatlin 7 (John Weymes) *s.i.s: outpcd: r.o ins fnl f: nvr nrr* 8/1	53
5021	7	1 ½	**Sir Geoffrey (IRE)**13 3993 6-9-12 74 (p) RobertWinston 9 (Scott Dixon) *sn pushed along in rr: edgd rt 1/2-way: nvr trbld ldrs* 5/2[1]	61
00-5	8	½	**Dubai Rythm**43 3005 3-8-0 55 oh10 (b) RaulDaSilva(3) 4 (Michael Appleby) *sn pushed along in rr: bhd fr 1/2-way* 16/1	39

59.74s (-0.26) **Going Correction** +0.025s/f (Good)
WFA 3 from 4yo+ 4lb 8 Ran SP% **116.4**
Speed ratings (Par 103): **103,101,101,100,98 96,94,93**
toteswingers: 1&2 £2.00, 1&3 £6.10, 2&3 £19.40 CSF £14.76 CT £113.21 TOTE £3.80: £1.20, £1.10, £4.50; EX 16.60.
Owner Katie Hughes,Julie McCarlie,Sheila White **Bred** Mrs Sheila White **Trained** Stainforth, S Yorks

FOCUS
A modest sprint handicap.
Swendab(IRE) Official explanation: jockey said gelding hung left
Sir Geoffrey(IRE) Official explanation: jockey said gelding was unsuited by being held up
T/Plt: £41.30 to a £1 stake. Pool: £51,418.80. 908.48 winning tickets. T/Qpdt: £36.90 to a £1 stake. Pool: £4,426.70. 88.60 winning tickets. CR

4330 LINGFIELD (L-H)
Wednesday, July 25

OFFICIAL GOING: Standard
Wind: Virtually nil Weather: Hot and sunny

4462 TOTEPLACEPOT WIN WITHOUT BACKING A WINNER CLAIMING STKS 6f (P)
2:10 (2:13) (Class 6) 2-Y-O £1,704 (£503; £251) **Stalls** Low

Form				RPR
000	1		**Grace Of Hearts**14 3971 2-8-2 58 ow1 (p) AndreaAtzeni 3 (Robert Eddery) *chsd ldr: rdn to ld and racd awkwardly bnd wl over 1f out: sn hrd pressed: drvn and a jst holding runner-up fnl f* 20/1	58
46	2	nse	**Augustinian**49 2808 2-8-8 0 RyanMoore 8 (Richard Hannon) *t.k.h: hld up in tch: rdn and effrt to chal between horses wl over 1f out: ev ch after: drvn fnl f: a jst hld* 15/8[1]	64
0	3	1 ¾	**Age Of Bronze**26 3569 2-8-8 0 SeanLevey 7 (Richard Hannon) *chsd ldrs: rdn and effrt wl over 1f out: kpt on same pce fnl f* 8/1[3]	59
2005	4	1 ¾	**Alexandrakollontai (IRE)**8 4195 2-8-0 56 (b1) SilvestreDeSousa 9 (J S Moore) *wnt bdly rt s and slowly away: racd in last trio and sn rdn along: hdwy over 1f out: kpt on same pce ins fnl f* 8/1[3]	45
	5	1 ¼	**Hardy Blue (IRE)** 2-8-4 0 LukeMorris 4 (Jamie Osborne) *sn rdn along in last trio: sme hdwy over 2f out: styd on same pce and no imp fr over 1f out* 8/1[3]	46
1235	6	8	**Just Past Andover (IRE)**25 3604 2-8-11 79 JakePayne(7) 2 (Bill Turner) *led and racd freely: rdn and hdd wl over 1f out: sn struggling and wknd over 1f out* 11/4[2]	36
3613	7	1	**Suivez L'Argent**50 2798 2-7-11 58 DarrenEgan(5) 6 (Joseph Tuite) *slowly away: sn rdn along in rr: drvn and no prog over 2f out: sn wknd* 8/1[3]	17
5	8	7	**My Lagan Love (IRE)**61 2462 2-7-12 0 ow1 RyanPowell(3) 1 (J S Moore) *hld up in midfield: rdn 4f out: wknd over 2f out: wl bhd over 1f out* 40/1	

1m 14.2s (2.30) **Going Correction** +0.175s/f (Slow) 8 Ran SP% **113.1**
Speed ratings (Par 92): **91,90,88,86,84 73,72,63**
toteswingers: 1&2 £9.10, 1&3 £16.20, 2&3 £6.00 CSF £56.75 TOTE £16.90: £3.70, £1.40, £2.90; EX 80.20 Trifecta £369.20 Pool: £638.70 - 1.28 winning units..Augustinian was claimed by Mr Claes Bjorling £6000.
Owner Phillips, Donaldson, Anderson & Mathews **Bred** Kirtlington Stud Ltd **Trained** Newmarket, Suffolk

FOCUS
A modest juvenile claimer, but a thrilling finish. The first two set the level.

NOTEBOOK
Grace Of Hearts had finished well beaten in three maidens, but was tried in cheekpieces on this drop in class and the difference was dramatic. Always handy, she took over in front coming to the last furlong and, despite appearing to be headed for a few strides well inside the last, forced her nose in front on the line, which may have been a relief to her rider who put up 1lb overweight. Whether she will reproduce this next time is anyone's guess. Official explanation: trainer said, regarding apparent improvement in form, that the filly benefited from first-time cheek pieces and the drop in class. (op 14-1 tchd 12-1)
Augustinian, very disappointing at Kempton last time having shown a hint of ability on his debut here, looked to have been delivered with his effort at just the right time and seemed to be in front for a few strides approaching the finish, but not only did he lose out in the photo he also rubbed salt into the wound by dumping his rider on the deck after the line. He looks very limited. (op 2-1 tchd 9-4)
Age Of Bronze was always in about the same place and, although he may not have achieved that much here, this was better than when a tailed-off last of eight on last month's Folkestone debut. (op 11-1 tchd 12-1)
Alexandrakollontai(IRE), dropping back in trip and tried in blinkers for this AW debut, veered out to her right exiting the stalls and ran wide off the final bend, so did well to finish where she did, but she doesn't look straightforward. (tchd 9-1)
Hardy Blue(IRE), a 35,000euros filly out of a half-sister to six winners including the dual Group 3 winning sprinter Triple Aspect, didn't set the world alight on this debut. (op 9-1)
Just Past Andover(IRE) was attempting 6f for the first time on this AW debut and didn't get home after making the running to over a furlong out. (op 7-2 tchd 5-2)

4463 TOTEEXACTA YOUR BETTER VALUE FORECAST MEDIAN AUCTION MAIDEN STKS 7f (P)
2:40 (2:42) (Class 6) 2-Y-O £1,704 (£503; £251) **Stalls** Low

Form				RPR
62	1		**Great Run**5 4290 2-9-3 0 RyanMoore 13 (Richard Hannon) *chsd ldr and grad crossed over towards inner: rdn and effrt to chal over 1f out: drvn to ld 1f out: styd on wl and drew clr fnl 100yds* 5/2[1]	81
6	2	3	**Labienus**19 3824 2-9-3 0 TedDurcan 5 (David Lanigan) *led: rdn and jnd over 1f out: hdd 1f out: no ex and btn fnl 100yds* 5/2[1]	73
	3	1	**Lord Of Leitrim (IRE)** 2-9-3 0 ShaneKelly 1 (Brian Meehan) *hld up in tch in midfield: effrt towards inner over 1f out: kpt on steadily under hands and heels riding and edgd rt ins fnl f: wnt 3rd cl home* 25/1	71+
	4	nse	**Canadian Run (IRE)** 2-9-3 0 StevieDonohoe 4 (Robert Mills) *chsd ldrs: rdn and effrt 2f out: unable qck over 1f out: styd on same pce fnl f* 20/1[2]	70+
35	5	5	**Bay Laurel (IRE)**14 3971 2-8-12 0 MickaelBarzalona 6 (Harry Dunlop) *in tch: hdwy to chas ldrs 3f out: rdn and unable qck ent fnl 2f: wknd over 1f out* 5/2[1]	52
00	6	2 ¾	**Alpine Mysteries (IRE)**21 3764 2-8-12 0 DaneO'Neill 10 (John Dunlop) *s.i.s: bhd: pushed along ent fnl 2f: sme hdwy over 1f out: kpt on but nvr trbld ldrs* 40/1	45
	7	1	**Hadeeya** 2-8-12 0 SilvestreDeSousa 3 (Clive Brittain) *racd in last trio: rdn over 3f out: struggling and btn 2f out: nvr trbld ldrs* 22/1[3]	43
0	8	½	**Elvin**28 3506 2-9-3 0 JimCrowley 9 (Amanda Perrett) *t.k.h: chsd ldrs: rdn and struggling jst over 2f out: wknd wl over 1f out* 20/1[2]	46
0	9	1 ½	**Progenitor (IRE)**12 4066 2-9-3 0 FrankieMcDonald 2 (David Lanigan) *bhd: struggling over 2f out: no ch wl over 1f out* 20/1[2]	43
	10	7	**Pink Mischief** 2-8-12 0 LukeMorris 11 (Harry Dunlop) *in tch in midfield on outer: rdn and struggling over 2f out: wknd 2f out and sn bhd* 20/1[2]	19

005 **11** *3 ¼* **Tough Question**[36] 3244 2-9-3 0 .... JamieGoldstein 8 16
(Michael Madgwick) *in tch in midfield: rdn and lost pl over 2f out: bhd wl over 1f out* **200/1**

1m 26.44s (1.64) **Going Correction** +0.175s/f (Slow) **11** Ran SP% **115.9**
Speed ratings (Par 92): **97,93,92,92,86 83,82,81,80,72 68**
toteswingers: 1&2 £1.90, 1&3 £10.60, 2&3 £13.80 CSF £7.29 TOTE £4.00: £2.00, £1.10, £5.90; EX 10.50 Trifecta £88.50 Pool: £617.79 - 5.16 winning units..
Owner Senta Wong **Bred** N Poole And A Franklin **Trained** East Everleigh, Wilts

FOCUS
An ordinary maiden for the track, but a few did show promise. The first four pulled clear and there was improvement from the first two.

NOTEBOOK
Great Run improved from his debut effort when runner-up to a stablemate at Haydock five days earlier and took another step forward here. Soon handy from the widest draw, he was off the bridle on the home bend but responded to pressure and was in front over a furlong from home. The only negative was that he again did a fair amount of stargazing and it might be interesting to see how he would respond to some form of headgear. (op 7-2)
Labienus caught the eye when a staying-on sixth of ten on his Sandown debut earlier this month, but was ridden much more positively this time and made the running to over a furlong out. He ought to improve again. (op 3-1)
Lord Of Leitrim(IRE), a 57,000gns 2yo and a half-brother to two winners at up to 1m4f (one of whom also scored over hurdles), stayed on to fare best of the newcomers. He seems sure to come on from this debut and should appreciate further in due course. (tchd 22-1)
Canadian Run(IRE) was always close to the pace and this 47,000euros half-brother to the multiple winning juvenile Bilko Pak seems sure to find an opportunity. (op 16-1)
Bay Laurel(IRE) was probably unlucky not to win over 6f here a fortnight earlier, but got a clear run this time and it was disappointing to see her finish tamely after holding every chance. Perhaps the extra furlong was against her and she now gets a nursery mark. (op 9-4 tchd 11-4)
Alpine Mysteries(IRE) made limited late progress, but also now gets a mark and may yet be capable of better. (op 33-1)

4464 THAKEHAM HOMES FRANKLINS GARDENS MAIDEN STKS (DIV I) 1m 4f (P)
3:10 (3:11) (Class 5) 3-Y-0+ **£2,385** (£704; £352) **Stalls** Low

Form RPR
-056 **1** **Zenaat**[25] 3605 3-8-10 77 .... (v¹) RyanMoore 6 80
(Sir Michael Stoute) *t.k.h: hld up in tch: rdn and effrt 2f out: drvn to ld ins fnl f: forged ahd fnl 100yds* **7/1³**
0 **2** *1 ¼* **Cottesmore (USA)**[6] 4259 3-9-1 0 .... SilvestreDeSousa 4 83
(Mark Johnston) *chsd ldr: upsides ldr 3f out: rdn to ld 2f out: hrd pressed ent fnl f: hdd ins fnl f: one pce after* **8/1**
022 **3** *3* **Mashaari (IRE)**[31] 3420 3-9-1 86 .... PaulHanagan 2 78
(John Gosden) *led: jnd 3f out: sn rdn: hdd 2f out: 3rd and one pce fnl f* **2/5¹**
0-2 **4** *1 ½* **Al Mamzar (IRE)**[62] 2418 3-9-1 0 .... JamieSpencer 1 76
(David Simcock) *trckd ldrs: rdn and effrt whn swtchd rt over 1f out: fnd little and btn 1f out* **11/2²**
5 *9* **Ahuqd (IRE)** 3-8-10 0 .... SebSanders 10 56
(Clive Brittain) *towards rr and rdn along 8f out: sme hdwy u.p over 4f out: no ch w ldrs fnl 3f* **20/1**
5 **6** *9* **Benartic (IRE)**[28] 3484 8-9-13 0 .... DaneO'Neill 8 47
(Harry Dunlop) *towards rr: pushed along and hdwy to chse ldrs 7f out: rdn and wknd over 3f out: sn wl btn* **33/1**
06 **7** *2* **Dee Ee Williams (IRE)**[21] 3763 9-9-13 0 .... JimCrowley 7 44
(Nick Gifford) *a towards rr: rdn 7f out: lost tch over 3f out* **20/1**
0 **8** *½* **Cometography (IRE)**[33] 3349 3-9-1 0 .... RoystonFfrench 9 43
(Ismail Mohammed) *s.i.s: sn rdn along: rn in snatches and a towards rr: lost tch u.p over 3f out* **50/1**
5-0 **9** *1 ¾* **Scotsbrook Cloud**[4] 3373 7-9-10 0 .... RichardEvans(3) 3 40
(David Evans) *a in rr: rdn over 4f out: lost tch over 3f out* **33/1**
6 **10** *shd* **Ice Apple**[22] 3720 4-9-8 0 .... RichardThomas 5 35
(John E Long) *s.i.s and rdn along early: in tch in midfield after: rdn and struggling over 4f out: lost tch over 3f out* **100/1**

2m 33.78s (0.78) **Going Correction** +0.175s/f (Slow)
WFA 3 from 4yo+ 12lb **10** Ran SP% **128.8**
Speed ratings (Par 103): **104,103,101,100,94 88,86,86,85,85**
toteswingers: 1&2 £7.30, 1&3 £1.90, 2&3 £2.70 CSF £60.48 TOTE £7.70: £1.50, £2.10, £1.10; EX 76.80 Trifecta £126.80 Pool: £1,035.46 - 6.04 winning units..
Owner H H Sheikh Mohammed Bin Khalifa Al Thani **Bred** Balmerino Bldstock & Newsells Park Stud **Trained** Newmarket, Suffolk

FOCUS
This modest middle-distance maiden only concerned the 3yos.
Mashaari(IRE) Official explanation: jockey said gelding hung both ways

4465 THAKEHAM HOMES FRANKLINS GARDENS MAIDEN STKS (DIV II) 1m 4f (P)
3:40 (3:40) (Class 5) 3-Y-0+ **£2,385** (£704; £352) **Stalls** Low

Form RPR
323 **1** **Scottish Vespers (IRE)**[22] 3720 3-9-1 80 .... (v¹) RyanMoore 6 83
(Sir Michael Stoute) *mde all: rdn and forged clr 2f out: drvn and kpt on fnl f* **13/8¹**
0 **2** *4 ½* **City Of Canton (IRE)**[33] 3349 3-9-1 0 .... KierenFallon 8 76
(Luca Cumani) *in tch in midfield: rdn and effrt to chse ldng pair 3f out: chsd clr wnr and edgd lft 1f out: no imp fnl f* **15/8²**
00 **3** *2* **Stunning View (USA)**[35] 3279 3-8-10 0 .... NickyMackay 3 68
(John Gosden) *chsd ldrs tl wnt 2nd 5f out: rdn and unable qck over 2f out: 3rd and one pce fr over 1f out* **13/2³**
00 **4** *3* **Chella Thriller (SPA)**[34] 3292 3-8-10 0 .... MartinHarley 1 63
(Alastair Lidderdale) *chsd wnr tl over 5f out: 4th and rdn 3f out: styd on same pce fr over 2f out* **10/1**
5 **5** *8* **Murphy (IRE)**[21] 3763 10-9-13 0 .... (t) GeorgeBaker 2 55
(Nick Gifford) *in tch: rdn and struggling in 5th 4f out: wl btn fnl 3f* **33/1**
0-0 **6** *17* **Pugnacious (IRE)**[7] 4212 3-9-1 0 .... SilvestreDeSousa 7 28
(Mark Johnston) *in tch in midfield: pushed along 8f out: rdn 6f out: 6th and wl btn over 3f out: t.o* **25/1**
40 **7** *1 ½* **Crystal Monarch (IRE)**[20] 3786 3-9-1 0 .... TomQueally 9 25
(Sir Henry Cecil) *s.i.s: sn pushed along and a towards rr: lost tch 4f out: t.o* **9/1**
8 *3 ¾* **Mummyow (IRE)**[14] 4-9-8 0 .... FrankieMcDonald 5 14
(Terry Clement) *taken down early: s.i.s: hld up in rr of main gp: lost tch 4f out: t.o* **100/1**
9 *62* **Lets Go Boogie** 4-9-8 0 .... JamieJones(5) 4
(Mark Hoad) *dropped to last and rdn after 2f: lost tch 6f out: t.o fnl 5f* **80/1**

2m 33.98s (0.98) **Going Correction** +0.175s/f (Slow)
WFA 3 from 4yo+ 12lb **9** Ran SP% **114.3**
Speed ratings (Par 103): **103,100,98,96,91 80,79,76,35**
toteswingers: 1&2 £3.10, 1&3 £2.60, 2&3 £1.30 CSF £4.69 TOTE £2.60: £1.10, £1.20, £1.30; EX 4.80 Trifecta £13.40 Pool: £907.57 - 49.96 winning units..
Owner Ballymacoll Stud **Bred** Ballymacoll Stud Farm Ltd **Trained** Newmarket, Suffolk

FOCUS
Again this only concerned the 3yos and yet another winner sporting first-time headgear. The winning time was 1/5 of a second slower than division one.

4466 M & P MANAGING TO WIN H'CAP 1m 4f (P)
4:10 (4:10) (Class 5) (0-75,75) 3-Y-0 **£2,385** (£704; £352) **Stalls** Low

Form RPR
400- **1** **Kiwayu**[288] 6768 3-9-1 69 .... (t) KierenFallon 5 89
(Luca Cumani) *hld up in last pair early: pushed along and stdy hdwy 8f out: chsd ldrs 6f out: rdn to ld jst over 2f out: drvn and clr 1f out: styd on wl* **10/1**
-131 **2** *6* **Tis Rock 'N' Roll (USA)**[20] 3793 3-9-6 74 .... TedDurcan 8 84
(David Lanigan) *stdd and dropped in after s: hld up in midfield: rdn and effrt to press wnr wl over 1f out: no ex and btn whn edgd lft 1f out: wknd ins fnl f* **5/2¹**
-544 **3** *10* **District Attorney (IRE)**[26] 3558 3-8-12 66 .... (b¹) RyanMoore 2 60
(William Haggas) *t.k.h: chsd ldrs: rdn over 2f out: no ex and btn 2f out: 4th and wl btn over 1f out: plugged on to go modest 3rd nr fin* **4/1²**
5422 **4** *¾* **Holly Martins**[25] 3655 3-9-0 75 .... (t) NicoleNordblad(7) 4 68
(Hans Adielsson) *led: hdd and rdn jst over 2f out: sn struggling and wl btn over 1f out: wknd* **7/1**
1604 **5** *1 ¾* **Ukrainian (IRE)**[23] 3711 3-9-7 75 .... SilvestreDeSousa 6 65
(Mark Johnston) *in tch: rdn 5f out: struggling and outpcd in last trio over 3f out: lost tch over 2f out* **9/2³**
433 **6** *11* **Regal Aura**[21] 3763 3-9-3 71 .... MickaelBarzalona 7 43
(John Gosden) *chsd ldr: jnd ldr 6f out tl jst over 2f out: sn u.p and btn: fdd wl over 1f out: eased ins fnl f* **8/1**
3-50 **7** *1 ¾* **Between Us**[47] 2877 3-9-1 69 .... LukeMorris 1 39
(Sir Mark Prescott Bt) *in tch towards rr: rdn 7f out: reminders over 6f out and nvr gng wl after: lost tch wl over 2f out* **14/1**
1210 **8** *7* **Hector's Chance**[42] 3042 3-9-6 74 .... TomQueally 3 32
(Heather Main) *a in rr and nvr gng wl: rdn and struggling over 4f out: lost tch 3f out: t.o* **8/1**

2m 33.07s (0.07) **Going Correction** +0.175s/f (Slow) **8** Ran SP% **117.2**
Speed ratings (Par 100): **106,102,95,94,93 86,85,80**
toteswingers: 1&2 £6.60, 1&3 £6.80, 2&3 £2.50 CSF £36.28 CT £120.48 TOTE £10.30: £2.60, £1.80, £2.00; EX 61.70 Trifecta £79.60 Pool: £568.31 - 5.28 winning units..
Owner Fittocks Stud **Bred** Fittocks Stud Ltd **Trained** Newmarket, Suffolk

FOCUS
They went a decent pace in this 3yo handicap and staying was the name of the game. The winning time was comfortably faster than both divisions of the maiden and yet again the winner benefited from the application of an aid.

4467 HENRY STREETER LTD H'CAP 5f (P)
4:40 (4:41) (Class 6) (0-65,63) 3-Y-0+ **£1,704** (£503; £251) **Stalls** High

Form RPR
0545 **1** **Hannibal Hayes (USA)**[24] 3670 3-9-3 59 .... RyanMoore 6 65
(Jeremy Noseda) *pressed ldr: rdn and ev ch wl over 1f out: drvn ent fnl f: led ins fnl f: kpt on wl: drvn out* **4/1¹**
0000 **2** *hd* **Brandywell Boy (IRE)**[29] 3477 9-8-11 49 .... (t) SilvestreDeSousa 8 55
(Dominic Ffrench Davis) *led: rdn ent fnl 2f: hdd ins fnl f: kpt on gamely but a jst hld* **9/1**
1640 **3** *2 ¼* **Russian Bullet**[28] 3489 3-9-7 63 .... FergusSweeney 4 60+
(Jamie Osborne) *dwlt: t.k.h and hld up in midfield: rdn and effrt over 1f out: chsd ldng pair ins fnl f: no imp fnl 100yds* **6/1**
550- **4** *½* **Cincinnati Kit**[218] 7830 3-9-2 58 .... (t) WilliamCarson 9 53
(Stuart Williams) *in tch on outer: hdwy to chse ldrs and rdn 2f out: unable qck over 1f out: one pce fnl f* **9/2²**
0632 **5** *hd* **Blueberry Fizz (IRE)**[15] 3943 4-9-4 56 .... (v) BrettDoyle 2 52
(John Ryan) *s.i.s: bhd and sn pushed along: stl bhd and swtchd rt 1f out: styd on u.p fnl f: nvr able to chal* **11/2³**
0432 **6** *½* **Pharoh Jake**[6] 4237 4-8-11 49 .... KieranO'Neill 5 43
(John Bridger) *in tch: swtchd lft and effrt to chse ldrs ent fnl f: no imp and one pce ins fnl f* **13/2**
5006 **7** *hd* **Christopher Chua (IRE)**[22] 3732 3-9-3 59 .... SebSanders 1 50
(Simon Dow) *taken down early: in tch in midfield: rdn and effrt 2f out: swtchd rt and hdwy over 1f out: styng on same pce and hld whn n.m.r ins fnl f* **13/2**
0054 **8** *1 ½* **Sherjawy (IRE)**[29] 3467 8-9-3 55 .... KirstyMilczarek 3 43
(Zoe Davison) *chsd ldrs tl jst over 2f out: no ex u.p over 1f out: wknd ins fnl f* **16/1**
0005 **9** *½* **Replicator**[29] 3467 7-8-8 46 .... (e) JamieMackay 10 32
(Patrick Gilligan) *stdd and dropped in bhd after s: hld up in last pair: rdn and effrt over 1f out: no hdwy: n.d* **25/1**

1m 0.51s (1.71) **Going Correction** +0.175s/f (Slow)
WFA 3 from 4yo+ 4lb **9** Ran SP% **114.2**
Speed ratings (Par 101): **93,92,89,88,87 87,86,84,83**
toteswingers: 1&2 £7.50, 1&3 £5.20, 2&3 £12.40 CSF £39.75 CT £212.75 TOTE £4.10: £1.30, £4.20, £3.30; EX 39.30 Trifecta £245.50 Pool: £793.15 - 2.39 winning units..
Owner G C Stevens **Bred** John T Crane & Margaret M Crane **Trained** Newmarket, Suffolk

FOCUS
A moderate sprint handicap in which it was crucial to be handy. The front pair were on the pace throughout and there never appeared to be more than a head between them.

4468 ADRIAN HALL MEMORIAL H'CAP 6f (P)
5:10 (5:12) (Class 5) (0-70,70) 3-Y-0+ **£2,385** (£704; £352) **Stalls** Low

Form RPR
1000 **1** **Proper Charlie**[4] 4332 4-9-10 68 .... JimCrowley 3 78
(William Knight) *t.k.h: chsd ldrs: wnt 2nd 2f out: rdn to ld 1f out: drvn and r.o wl to assert fnl 75yds* **5/1²**
4322 **2** *¾* **Ghost Train (IRE)**[7] 4218 3-9-6 69 .... (v¹) RyanMoore 4 76
(Mark Johnston) *led: rdn wl over 1f out: drvn and hdd 1f out: no ex and one pce fnl 100yds* **6/5¹**
0400 **3** *1 ½* **Hoover**[102] 1378 4-9-8 66 .... (t) TomQueally 8 69
(Jim Boyle) *in tch in midfield: effrt u.p to chse ldrs over 1f out: kpt on towards fin but nvr gng pce to rch ldrs* **9/1**
240 **4** *nk* **Cheers**[28] 3485 4-9-7 65 .... (tp) FrankieMcDonald 5 67
(Oliver Sherwood) *awkward leaving stalls: hld up in tch in midfield: rdn and effrt to chse ldrs over 1f out: kpt on towards fin bt nt gng pce to rch ldrs* **6/1³**
0626 **5** *nk* **Amba**[22] 3738 6-8-13 60 .... AdamBeschizza(3) 9 61+
(Des Donovan) *taken down early: in tch on outer: wd and lost pl bnd 2f out: rallied and kpt on wl ins fnl f* **12/1**

3520 **6** 2 **Chjimes (IRE)**[15] 3944 8-9-8 **66**....................................(b) HayleyTurner 6 61
(Conor Dore) *hld up in tch: effrt whn n.m.r wl over 1f out: styd on u.p fnl f but nvr gng pce to threaten ldrs* **18/1**

4100 **7** 4 ½ **Stevie Gee (IRE)**[9] 4155 8-9-9 **70**....................................(v) RyanClark[(3)] 7 50
(Mark Buckley) *chsd ldrs: rdn and struggling whn edgd rt bnd 2f out: wknd over 1f out* **16/1**

6000 **8** 1 **Elhamri**[15] 3941 8-9-2 **60**.. KirstyMilczarek 1 37
(Conor Dore) *chsd ldr tl 2f out: sn struggling u.p: wknd over 1f out* **50/1**

6000 **9** ¾ **Alfresco**[24] 3660 8-9-4 **62**..(b) GeorgeBaker 2 37
(John Best) *hld up in rr: hung lft jst over 2f out: no hdwy and wl hld over 1f out* **25/1**

260 **10** 1 ¼ **Cliffords Reprieve**[49] 2809 4-9-2 **60**............................(b) SebSanders 10 31
(Eric Wheeler) *taken down early: hld up towards rr: rdn and effrt wl over 1f out: no prog and wl hld fnl f* **18/1**

3420 **11** 26 **Waterloo Dock**[105] 1307 7-9-8 **66**.................................. AndreaAtzeni 11
(Michael Quinn) *dropped to rr after 1f: sn rdn and struggling: lost tch 2f out: eased ins fnl f: t.o* **33/1**

1m 13.13s (1.23) **Going Correction** +0.175s/f (Slow)
WFA 3 from 4yo+ 5lb **11 Ran SP% 119.3**
Speed ratings (Par 103): **98,97,95,94,94 91,85,84,83,81 46**
toteswingers 1&2 £2.30, 1&3 £8.00, 2&3 £3.80 CSF £11.30 CT £55.27 TOTE £6.10: £2.00, £1.30, £1.90; EX 14.80 Trifecta £116.10 Pool: £1,263.48 - 8.05 winning units..
Owner Peter Oakley & Charles Whittaker **Bred** P And Mrs A G Venner **Trained** Patching, W Sussex

FOCUS
A modest sprint handicap and again it paid to race handily.
Proper Charlie Official explanation: trainer's said, regarding apparent improvement in form, that the gelding appreciated the return to the all-weather surface.
Alfresco Official explanation: jockey said gelding hung left
Waterloo Dock Official explanation: jockey said gelding never travelled

4469 FOLLOW TOTEPOOL ON FACEBOOK AND TWITTER H'CAP 7f (P)
5:40 (5:41) (Class 5) (0-70,69) 3-Y-0+ **£2,385** (£704; £352) **Stalls** Low

Form RPR

-633 **1** **Paphos**[14] 3958 5-9-6 **65**..(v) RyanClark[(3)] 13 74
(Stuart Williams) *dwlt and rdn along leaving stalls: sn in tch in midfield: reminder 4f out: hdwy and rdn to chse ldr wl over 1f out: led ins fnl f: in command and idling fnl 50yds: rdn out* **6/1[3]**

2241 **2** 1 **Cyflymder (IRE)**[12] 4042 6-9-12 **68**.................................. GeorgeBaker 8 74+
(David C Griffiths) *hld up in tch in midfield: chsd ldrs 2f out: kpt on wl u.p ins fnl f to go 2nd towards fin* **5/2[1]**

3322 **3** 1 **Homeboy (IRE)**[12] 4043 4-9-9 **65**.................................... HayleyTurner 11 69
(Marcus Tregoning) *racd freely: pressed ldr tl led over 2f out: rdn 2f out: hdd ins fnl f: no ex and wknd towards fin* **9/2[2]**

1240 **4** nk **Dvinsky (USA)**[14] 3958 11-9-8 **64**...............................(b) TomMcLaughlin 1 67
(Paul Howling) *sn rdn along to chse ldrs: rdn and chsd ldr briefly 2f out: styng on same pce and swtchd rt ins fnl f: wknd towards fin* **20/1**

-032 **5** 1 ¼ **Mudhish (IRE)**[30] 3455 7-9-5 **61**....................................(b) BrettDoyle 6 60
(Clive Brittain) *towards rr on outer: hdwy over 1f out: kpt on fnl f but nvr gng pce to threaten ldrs* **10/1**

044 **6** hd **Bold Ring**[16] 3915 6-8-13 **58**... SophieDoyle[(3)] 7 57
(Eric Wheeler) *hld up in tch towards rr: n.m.r over 2f out: rdn and hdwy over 1f out: kpt on fnl f: nvr trbld ldrs* **12/1**

0-64 **7** 1 **Reginald Claude**[41] 3076 4-9-0 **61**................................ LeeNewnes[(5)] 9 57
(Mark Usher) *hld up wl in tch: swtchd rt and effrt wl over 1f out: styd on same pce fnl f* **20/1**

2100 **8** 2 ¼ **Diplomatic (IRE)**[12] 4068 7-9-11 **67**................................. CathyGannon 5 57
(Michael Squance) *dropped to rr and rdn after 1f out: styd on past btn horses fnl f: nvr trbld ldrs* **14/1**

610 **9** nk **Zing Wing**[25] 3643 4-9-8 **69**.. DuilioDaSilva[(5)] 2 58
(Paul Cole) *hld up in tch in midfield: nt clr run and shuffled bk over 2f out: swtchd rt and rallied over 1f out: no imp fnl f* **14/1**

6526 **10** ½ **Highland Harvest**[36] 3249 8-9-9 **65**.................................... IanMongan 4 53
(Jamie Poulton) *hld up towards rr: rdn and hdwy wl over 1f out: no imp 1f out and wl hld fnl f* **33/1**

0-06 **11** nk **Primo Lady**[27] 3549 4-9-12 **68**...................................(v) StevieDonohoe 14 55
(Gay Kelleway) *chsd ldrs: rdn and struggling whn short of room over 1f out: wknd ent fnl f* **16/1**

2500 **12** hd **Perfect Ch'I (IRE)**[14] 3958 5-9-9 **65**.................................. JimCrowley 3 52
(Ian Wood) *hld up in rr: c wd and effrt wl over 1f out: no prog: n.d* **20/1**

4-00 **13** 22 **Greek Islands (IRE)**[63] 2399 4-9-11 **67**............................ LiamKeniry 10
(Ed de Giles) *led tl rdn and hdd over 2f out: fdd rapidly wl over 1f out: wl bhd and eased ins fnl f* **12/1**

1m 26.37s (1.57) **Going Correction** +0.175s/f (Slow) **13 Ran SP% 122.0**
Speed ratings (Par 103): **98,96,95,95,93 93,92,90,89,89 88,88,63**
toteswingers 1&2 £4.40, 1&3 £4.80, 2&3 £3.30 CSF £20.51 CT £77.14 TOTE £8.70: £3.10, £1.20, £1.50; EX 29.30 Trifecta £48.50 Pool: £614.39 - 9.36 winning units..
Owner Stuart C Williams **Bred** L Ellinas And Old Mill Stud Ltd **Trained** Newmarket, Suffolk
■ Stewards' Enquiry : George Baker one-day ban: careless riding (Aug 8)

FOCUS
Another modest handicap.
T/Plt: £11.50 to a £1 stake. Pool: £58,710.65. 3,702.09 winning tickets. T/Qpdt: £4.50 to a £1 stake. Pool: £4,182.36. 672.88 winning tickets. SP

4220 SANDOWN (R-H)
Wednesday, July 25

OFFICIAL GOING: Sprint course - good (good to firm in places; 8.4); round course - good to firm (good in places; 8.6)
Far side rail on Sprint track moved 3yds inside. Inner configuration on Round course and all distances as advertised.
Wind: Almost nil Weather: Sunny, hot

4470 HAAGEN-DAZS APPRENTICE H'CAP 1m 2f 7y
5:50 (5:50) (Class 5) (0-75,75) 4-Y-0+ **£2,264** (£673; £336; £168) **Stalls** Low

Form RPR

3032 **1** **Hurakan (IRE)**[24] 3659 6-8-11 **67**.............................(p) DanielMuscutt[(5)] 4 77
(Richard Price) *trckd ldng pair: led jst over 3f out and kicked on: drew clr over 1f out: styd on wl* **7/2[1]**

02-0 **2** 4 ½ **Looking On**[79] 1939 4-9-10 **75**.. AmyScott 10 77+
(Henry Candy) *hld up and last early: effrt on outer and rdn over 2f out: prog to take 2nd last 150yds: no imp on wnr* **11/2[3]**

4533 **3** ¾ **South Cape**[6] 4243 9-9-1 **66**.. HarryBentley 3 67
(Gary Moore) *hld up in rr: rdn and nt qckn over 2f out: styd on fr over 1f out to take 3rd nr fin* **6/1**

3216 **4** 1 ½ **Strawberrymystique**[27] 3550 4-9-8 **73**................................ KierenFox 7 71
(Marco Botti) *trckd ldng trio: prog to chse wnr over 2f out and cl enough: no imp over 1f out: wknd fnl f* **7/2[1]**

1030 **5** 1 ¼ **Ssafa**[27] 3550 4-9-5 **70**... PatrickHills 8 65
(J W Hills) *chsd ldr to 4f out: chsd wnr briefly wl over 2f out: sn rdn and nt qckn: steadily fdd* **18/1**

5 **6** hd **Amistress**[20] 3793 4-9-0 **65**.. DarrenEgan 5 60
(Eve Johnson Houghton) *sn hld up in rr: rdn and no prog wl over 2f out: wl btn after: plugged on fnl f* **4/1[2]**

-021 **7** 6 **James Pollard (IRE)**[22] 3429 7-9-6 **71**..........................(t) RobertWilliams 1 54
(Bernard Llewellyn) *hld up in midfield: rdn and no prog over 2f out: wl btn after* **14/1**

111- **8** 4 ½ **Eseej (USA)**[347] 671 7-9-10 **75**.................................... MatthewLawson 9 49
(Geoffrey Deacon) *led at gd pce: hdd jst over 3f out: sn wknd* **16/1**

4-00 **9** 20 **Songburst**[16] 3920 4-9-4 **69**.. SeanLevey 6
(Richard Hannon) *t.k.h: hld up in rr: wknd 3f out: t.o* **25/1**

2m 7.57s (-2.93) **Going Correction** -0.20s/f (Firm) **9 Ran SP% 115.8**
Speed ratings (Par 103): **103,99,98,97,96 96,91,88,72**
toteswingers: 1&2 £4.40, 1&3 £3.10, 2&3 £6.40 CSF £23.09 CT £111.67 TOTE £5.00: £1.80, £2.20, £1.60; EX 27.50 Trifecta £153.30 Pool: £261.18 - 1.26 winning units..
Owner Derek & Cheryl Holder **Bred** Newberry Stud Company **Trained** Ullingswick, H'fords

FOCUS
it paid to race handily in this moderate handicap for apprentices and the form is straightforward.

4471 MOLESEY NURSERY 5f 6y
6:20 (6:23) (Class 5) (0-75,75) 2-Y-0 **£2,587** (£770; £384; £192) **Stalls** Low

Form RPR

040 **1** **Danz Choice (IRE)**[39] 3138 2-8-11 **65**.................................. RyanMoore 1 70
(Richard Hannon) *pushed along in last pair 1/2-way: prog against far rail over 1f out: drvn and r.o to ld last 75yds: hung lft but styd on wl* **7/2[2]**

333 **2** ¾ **Dream Maker (IRE)**[21] 3747 2-8-9 **66**.......................... RossAtkinson[(3)] 2 68
(Tom Dascombe) *led and grabbed far rail: edgd lft fr 1/2-way: hdd and one pce last 75yds* **7/2[2]**

2231 **3** nk **Uncomplicated**[14] 3973 2-9-7 **75**...................................... PatCosgrave 5 76
(Jim Boyle) *racd on outer: pressed ldng pair: rdn to chal over 1f out: upsides ent fnl f: carried lft and nt qckn* **7/2[2]**

21 **4** ½ **Megamunch (IRE)**[16] 3902 2-9-7 **75**................................ DarryllHolland 3 74
(Linda Stubbs) *in tch in last pair: swtchd out wdst of all 2f out: drvn and nt qckn over 1f out: carried lft and styd on fnl f* **11/4[1]**

500 **5** 1 ½ **Why So Fast (IRE)**[14] 3971 2-8-9 **66**............................ HarryBentley[(3)] 4 60
(Stuart Williams) *reluctant to enter stalls: pressed ldr: rdn to chal 2f out: nt qckn over 1f out: racd awkwardly and j. path jst ins fnl f: wknd* **5/1[3]**

1m 2.01s (0.41) **Going Correction** -0.05s/f (Good) **5 Ran SP% 110.0**
Speed ratings (Par 94): **94,92,92,91,89**
CSF £15.67 TOTE £3.40: £2.40, £2.70; EX 11.10.
Owner Dragon Gate **Bred** J & J Waldron **Trained** East Everleigh, Wilts
■ Stewards' Enquiry : Ross Atkinson four-day ban: used whip above permitted level (Aug 8-11)

FOCUS
This modest nursery was a tight-looking affair and it saw a close finish. The form fits well.

NOTEBOOK
Danz Choice(IRE) forged to the front inside the final furlong under his bang in-form rider and opened his account at the fourth attempt. He came from last to first from the furlong marker and it was probably down to inexperience that he drifted left near the line. (op 4-1)
Dream Maker(IRE) was intent on getting over to the far rail and thus set the pace. She made a bold bid and has developed a very consistent profile, so certainly deserves to go one better. (op 3-1)
Uncomplicated was always up there and posted a game effort, but was held prior to being slightly hampered late on. It was her first outing away from soft ground. Reverting to slightly easier ground will probably be up her street. (tchd 3-1 and 4-1)
Megamunch(IRE) looked in need of all of this trip when winning at Ayr last time out. On much quicker ground, it wasn't surprising to see him feeling the pinch in the final 2f. He did well to finish so close as the surface looked against him. (op 7-2)
Why So Fast(IRE), much better than the bare form on Polytrack last time, was back down in trip for this nursery debut. She was up there early, but did too much too soon and paid entering the last furlong. She looks to need more time. (op 4-1)

4472 BCL BURTON COPELAND / BRITISH STALLION STUDS SUPPORTING BRITISH RACING EBF MAIDEN STKS 7f 16y
6:55 (6:57) (Class 5) 2-Y-0 **£3,881** (£1,155; £577; £288) **Stalls** Low

Form RPR

1 **Kerbaaj (USA)** 2-9-3 0... PaulHanagan 6 83+
(Charles Hills) *wl in rr: taken to outer 3f out: prog 2f out: rdn and sustained effrt fr over 1f out to ld last 50yds* **25/1**

62 **2** ½ **Tropical Song**[19] 3824 2-9-3 0.. EddieAhern 5 82
(John Gosden) *trckd ldng pair: rdn to ld over 1f out: r.o fnl f: hdd last 50yds* **5/2[1]**

4 **3** 1 ¼ **Monsieur Rieussec**[41] 3067 2-9-3 0.................................. JimmyFortune 2 79
(Jonathan Portman) *t.k.h: trckd ldng trio: effrt 2f out: chal 1f out: styd on same pce* **13/2[3]**

4 2 ½ **Lightning Launch (IRE)** 2-9-3 0.. MartinHarley 4 72+
(Mick Channon) *wl in tch in midfield: trckd ldrs and looking for room 2f out: tried to cl over 1f out: shkn up and one pce after* **12/1**

6 **5** ¾ **Colmar Kid (IRE)**[12] 4056 2-9-3 0................................... JamieSpencer 9 70
(Richard Hannon) *racd wd early: mostly chsd ldr to 2f out: stl cl enough 1f out: fdd* **7/2[2]**

5045 **6** 1 ¼ **Walter White (IRE)**[18] 3858 2-9-3 71.................................. DavidProbert 8 67
(Andrew Balding) *trckd ldrs: rdn and cl enough on outer 2f out: fdd over 1f out* **20/1**

7 nk **Erodium** 2-9-3 0... PatDobbs 1 66+
(Richard Hannon) *trckd ldrs on inner: pushed along 2f out: no imp over 1f out: steadily fdd: nt disgracd* **22/1**

8 nk **Roman Order (IRE)** 2-9-3 0.. KierenFallon 7 65+
(Brian Meehan) *towards rr: pushed along over 2f out: no prog tl styd on fnl f* **16/1**

0 **9** hd **Eton Rambler (USA)**[28] 3506 2-9-3 0................................ PatCosgrave 10 65
(George Baker) *a in midfield: pushed along 1/2-way: rdn and outpcd over 2f out: kpt on fnl f* **40/1**

10 ¾ **Felix Fabulla** 2-9-3 0.. DarryllHolland 3 63+
(Hughie Morrison) *dwlt: mostly in last pair: sme prog 2f out: pushed along and rn green over 1f out: no hdwy after* **50/1**

03 **11** ½ **Wellingrove (IRE)**[40] 3112 2-9-3 0.............................. SilvestreDeSousa 15 62
(Mark Johnston) *racd freely: sn led and crossed to inner: rdn and hdd over 1f out: wknd and eased* **14/1**

12 ½ **Master Ming (IRE)** 2-9-3 0.. MartinDwyer 11 60
(Brian Meehan) *dwlt: mostly in last pair: pushed along fr 3f out: sme prog on inner 2f out: no hdwy fnl f* **66/1**

13 *1 ¼* **Altruism (IRE)** 2-9-3 0.. MickaelBarzalona 12 57
(Mahmood Al Zarooni) *slowest away: racd wd in rr: prog on outer 3f out: no hdwy 2f out: wknd over 1f out* **7/1**

14 *3 ¼* **Shades Of Silver** 2-9-3 0.. RyanMoore 14 49+
(Sir Michael Stoute) *chsd ldrs early: dropped to rr by 1/2-way: rn green and n.d after* **8/1**

15 *shd* **Ivanhoe** 2-9-3 0.. FergusSweeney 13 48
(Michael Blanshard) *a in rr: shkn up 3f out: sn btn* **100/1**

1m 28.18s (-1.32) **Going Correction** -0.20s/f (Firm) **15** Ran SP% **127.8**
Speed ratings (Par 94): **99,98,97,94,93 91,91,91,90,90 89,88,87,83,83**
toteswingers: 1&2 £9.50, 1&3 £43.40, 2&3 £6.60 CSF £88.01 TOTE £25.00: £7.40, £1.10, £2.20; EX 66.30 Trifecta £414.20 Part won. Pool: £559.73 - 0.39 winning units..
Owner Hamdan Al Maktoum **Bred** Shadwell Farm LLC **Trained** Lambourn, Berks

FOCUS
A fair juvenile maiden. There were conflicting opinions about the ground as plenty kept wide into the first bend, but there appeared to be no real advantage in doing so. They finished compressed and the form fits with the race averages.

NOTEBOOK
Kerbaaj(USA) ◆, easy to back for this debut, was nearer last than first straightening for home, but he picked up strongly out wide once asked for his effort and was always just going to get up near the business end. He was well on top shortly after the line and this was a promising initial effort. He holds a Gimcrack entry, but clearly stays well and dropping back to 6f doesn't appear the way to go with him. Either way he's one to follow and a step up in class will tell us more about him. (op 20-1 tchd 16-1)
Tropical Song set the standard on his staying-on second over C&D on easier ground last time out. He was angled out to lead from 2f out, but still looked somewhat green under pressure and was mugged late on. He evidently has an engine and can soon be placed to strike, but his brother Tropical Beat is a tricky sort and he now has a little to prove with his attitude. (op 3-1 tchd 10-3)
Monsieur Rieussec posted an encouraging debut effort behind subsequent Listed winner Toronado on his Newbury debut last month. He ran another pleasing race up in trip on the quicker ground and looks a winner waiting to happen. (op 11-2)
Lightning Launch(IRE) ◆ travelled nicely into contention and clearly has a future. The market suggested this half-brother to former stable star Halicarnassus would need this initial outing and, well entered up, he ought to go very close next time. (op 11-1)
Colmar Kid(IRE), one of the first to go wide early, was always up there and held every chance but ran out of steam from half a furlong out. This was an improved effort, but he's now looking more of one for nurseries after his next assignment. (op 11-2)
Roman Order(IRE) ◆ kept on steadily without being given a hard time and he seems sure to improve a deal for this debut outing. (tchd 14-1 and 20-1)

4473 TOTEPOOL MOBILE TEXT "TOTE" TO 89660 H'CAP — 7f 16y
7:30 (7:31) (Class 3) (0-90,89) 3-Y-O **£6,663** (£1,982; £990; £495) **Stalls** Low

Form RPR

4341 **1** **Stirring Ballad**[13] 4001 3-8-8 **76**.. DavidProbert 6 83+
(Andrew Balding) *hld up in 6th: clsd on ldrs fr 2f out: rdn and gd burst between rivals ins fnl f to ld last 50yds* **9/1**

4123 **2** *½* **Dutch Supreme**[18] 3876 3-9-7 **89**.. TedDurcan 1 95
(David Lanigan) *led: narrowly hdd over 2f out: hrd rdn and rallied over 1f out: forced way bk into ld last 75yds: sn hdd and outpcd* **10/3**[1]

606 **3** *hd* **Sheikh The Reins (IRE)**[54] 2660 3-8-3 **76**.................... DarrenEgan(5) 8 81
(John Best) *pressed ldr: narrow ld over 2f out: sn rdn: hdd jst ins fnl f: styd on* **16/1**

-104 **4** *½* **Obliteright (IRE)**[32] 3393 3-8-12 **80**................................ JimCrowley 5 84
(William Knight) *trckd ldrs in 5th: prog on inner fr 2f out: drvn to ld narrowly jst ins fnl f: hdd and outpcd last 75yds* **13/2**

61-0 **5** *¾* **Usain Colt**[96] 1500 3-9-5 **87**.. RyanMoore 4 89+
(Richard Hannon) *awkward s: hld up in last: pushed along over 2f out: taken to outer and rdn over 1f out w plenty to do: r.o fnl f: clsng at fin* **5/1**[3]

4450 **6** *½* **Solar Deity (IRE)**[14] 3977 3-9-2 **84**..............................(b) MartinHarley 10 84
(Marco Botti) *trckd ldng trio: hrd rdn fr 2f out: no imp on ldrs over 1f out: kpt on* **8/1**

5531 **7** *3 ¼* **Johnno**[18] 3876 3-9-2 **84**.. SebSanders 9 76+
(J W Hills) *stmbld s: a towards rr: rdn wl over 2f out: no prog over 1f out: wknd* **9/2**[2]

4004 **8** *1* **Kinloch Castle**[20] 3779 3-8-11 **79**............................. SilvestreDeSousa 2 68
(Mark Johnston) *trckd ldng pair: rdn over 2f out: wknd wl over 1f out* **8/1**

-040 **9** *7* **Sir Glanton (IRE)**[32] 3393 3-8-12 **80**...................................[1] PatDobbs 3 50
(Amanda Perrett) *in tch tl wknd 3f out: sn last and bhd* **20/1**

1m 28.88s (-0.62) **Going Correction** -0.20s/f (Firm) **9** Ran SP% **114.1**
Speed ratings (Par 104): **95,94,94,93,92 92,88,87,79**
toteswingers: 1&2 £4.80, 1&3 £44.10, 2&3 £12.60 CSF £38.65 CT £479.42 TOTE £9.60: £3.20, £1.50, £4.70; EX 25.50 Trifecta £437.00 Part won. Pool: £590.63 - 0.83 winning units..
Owner George Strawbridge **Bred** George Strawbridge **Trained** Kingsclere, Hants

FOCUS
A fair 3-y-o handicap with a wide-open look about it. This time the entire field shunned the inside rail before turning into the bend and the dash for home developed 3f out.

NOTEBOOK
Stirring Ballad ◆ mowed down rivals late on to follow up her Folkestone maiden success 13 days earlier. This was tougher, but running between horses the last day proved a lot more to her liking and, doing the same late on here, connections have obviously now found the key to her. The handicapper will now react, but she's well bred and could very well have a lot more to offer. (tchd 8-1)
Dutch Supreme was ridden a lot more positively than had been the case when fourth here on easier ground last time. He kept on at the same pace from 2f out, but was only just held and still looks to be learning his trade somewhat. (op 4-1 tchd 3-1)
Sheikh The Reins(IRE) was always well placed and this was a solid effort from him back off a 54-day break. He's on a workable mark. (tchd 12-1)
Obliteright(IRE) found a nice run on the inside from 2f out and threw down a strong challenge, posting a sound effort in defeat. He can find a race on turf before long. (op 6-1 tchd 7-1)
Usain Colt ◆, who reportedly had a lung infection after his comeback run in April, was expected to relish this quicker ground. After taking a keen hold he found himself too far back when the pace increased 3f out, however, and is a good deal better than he could show. Indeed there was much to like about his finishing kick and, unexposed, he strongly appeals as one to be with next time out. Official explanation: jockey said colt left the stalls awkwardly (op 4-1 tchd 7-2)
Johnno was up 5lb for beating the runner-up on soft ground over C&D last time. He forfeited any chance of sitting handy here by messing up the start, however, and this is best forgiven (op 5-1 tchd 11-2)

4474 RACING POST FORM WITH TOTEPOOL MOBILE H'CAP — 1m 14y
8:05 (8:05) (Class 4) (0-85,85) 3-Y-O+ **£4,075** (£1,212; £606; £303) **Stalls** Low

Form RPR

0-01 **1** **Jacob Cats**[62] 2428 3-9-6 **85**.. RyanMoore 2 98+
(Richard Hannon) *patiently rdn in last trio: taken to outer over 2f out: gd prog after: led last 150yds: drvn and asserted after* **15/8**[1]

4116 **2** *1 ¼* **Burke's Rock**[51] 2772 3-9-0 **79**.. JimmyFortune 1 89
(Jeremy Noseda) *pressed ldrs: wnt 2nd over 3f out: rdn to ld jst over 2f out: hdd last 150yds: styd on wl but no match for wnr after* **17/2**[3]

113 **3** *1 ¾* **Postscript (IRE)**[32] 3385 4-9-8 **79**.................................... JamieSpencer 5 87
(Ian Williams) *trckd ldrs: cl up and looking for room 2f out: drvn and styng on whn bmpd jst ins fnl f: kpt on* **15/2**[2]

-001 **4** *1 ¼* **Pendragon (USA)**[42] 3030 9-9-6 **80**................................... DaleSwift(3) 8 85
(Brian Ellison) *settled in midfield: pushed along on outer 3f out: prog u.p fr 2f out: trying to cl whn wnr wnt by jst over 1f out: one pce* **9/1**

6430 **5** *¾* **First Post (IRE)**[28] 3508 5-9-10 **81**.................................. AndreaAtzeni 11 86
(Derek Haydn Jones) *prom: rdn to chse ldr wl over 1f out: hld and sing to lose pl whn bmpd jst ins fnl f: nt rcvr* **9/1**

4504 **6** *½* **Rock Anthem (IRE)**[23] 3705 8-8-9 **66**............................. KieranO'Neill 14 68
(Mike Murphy) *dwlt: hld up in last: prog 2f out: hanging it over 1f out: styd on wl fnl f: nrst fin* **33/1**

-366 **7** *shd* **Dynamic Duo (IRE)**[46] 2941 3-8-9 **74**................................. PatDobbs 3 75
(Richard Hannon) *trckd ldrs on inner: nowhere to go over 2f out: plld out over 1f out: kpt on but no ch to be involved* **14/1**

0303 **8** *nk* **Yojimbo (IRE)**[13] 3999 4-9-8 **79**.................................... MatthewDavies 6 80
(Mick Channon) *hld up towards rr: gng wl enough over 2f out: rdn and nt qckn wl over 1f out: kpt on fnl f: n.d* **14/1**

-214 **9** *3 ¾* **Henry Clay**[13] 3999 3-8-12 **77**................................. SilvestreDeSousa 12 71
(Mark Johnston) *mde most to jst over 2f out: drvn and wknd over 1f out: sn eased* **9/1**

0-00 **10** *4 ½* **Obligada (IRE)**[27] 3550 4-9-7 **78**..............................(b[1]) StevieDonohoe 7 60
(Tobias B P Coles) *n.m.r s: hld up in rr: effrt on inner 3f out: sn no prog and wknd* **20/1**

2332 **11** *3 ¼* **Choral Festival**[9] 4150 6-9-5 **76**.. SeanLevey 4 51
(John Bridger) *prom: lost pl fr 3f out: struggling in rr 2f out* **12/1**

001 **12** *4* **Silverware (USA)**[55] 2619 4-9-7 **78**................................ DarryllHolland 13 44
(Linda Stubbs) *pressed ldr to over 3f out: wknd over 2f out* **20/1**

14-0 **13** *12* **Sugarformyhoney (IRE)**[16] 3917 3-9-2 **81**....................... GeorgeBaker 9 17
(Seamus Durack) *stdd s: hld up wl in rr: nudged along and no prog over 2f out: wknd and t.o* **33/1**

1m 40.52s (-2.78) **Going Correction** -0.20s/f (Firm)
WFA 3 from 4yo+ 8lb **13** Ran SP% **123.5**
Speed ratings (Par 105): **105,103,102,100,100 99,99,99,95,90 87,83,71**
toteswingers: 1&2 £3.70, 1&3 £1.70, 2&3 £10.80 CSF £17.57 CT £100.17 TOTE £2.10: £1.10, £3.30, £3.20; EX 15.70 Trifecta £70.00 Pool: £474.91 - 5.02 winning units..
Owner Michael Pescod & Justin Dowley **Bred** Highclere Stud **Trained** East Everleigh, Wilts

FOCUS
Not a bad handicap and the form looks solid.
Henry Clay Official explanation: jockey said colt had no more to give
Silverware(USA) Official explanation: jockey said gelding ran too free

4475 HAAGEN-DAZS SECRET SENSATIONS H'CAP — 1m 6f
8:40 (8:40) (Class 4) (0-80,80) 4-Y-O+ **£4,075** (£1,212; £606; £303) **Stalls** Low

Form RPR

011 **1** **Callisto Moon**[33] 3337 8-8-10 **69**................................(p) DarryllHolland 7 80
(Jo Hughes) *sn t.k.h and trckd ldng pair: decisive move to ld over 2f out and stormed clr: maintained gallop to the fin: impressive* **9/2**

0335 **2** *4 ½* **Ampleforth**[13] 3997 4-8-11 **70**......................................(v[1]) JamieSpencer 6 76
(Ian Williams) *hld up in last pair: urged along fr 5f out and nt look keen: responded fnlly and prog to chse wnr over 1f out: styd on but no ch* **9/2**

113 **3** *5* **The Holyman (IRE)**[7] 4216 4-9-4 **77**.................................. IanMongan 5 75
(Jo Crowley) *pressed ldr: chalng whn wnr shot past over 2f out: chsd him to over 1f out: fdd* **11/4**[1]

03-0 **4** *2 ½* **Sirius Superstar**[21] 3765 4-9-4 **77**.................................. DavidProbert 2 72
(Andrew Balding) *trckd ldrs: rdn and nt qckn over 2f out: sn lft bhd and wl btn* **3/1**[2]

0602 **5** *10* **Lady of Burgundy**[14] 3961 6-8-2 **66**............................. DarrenEgan(5) 3 47
(Mark Usher) *dwlt: t.k.h in last pair: rdn 3f out: no rspnse and sn wl btn* **7/2**[3]

04/0 **6** *½* **Moose Moran (USA)**[21] 3765 5-9-7 **80**.......................(v[1]) GeorgeBaker 9 60
(Olivia Maylam) *mde most to over 2f out: wknd qckly* **25/1**

3m 2.5s (-2.00) **Going Correction** -0.20s/f (Firm) **6** Ran SP% **114.1**
Speed ratings (Par 105): **97,94,91,90,84 84**
toteswingers: 1&2 £2.40, 1&3 £3.40, 2&3 £2.30 CSF £25.10 CT £64.96 TOTE £3.80: £2.40, £4.20; EX 28.50 Trifecta £44.80 Pool: £364.35 - 6.01 winning units..
Owner B Bedford & Mrs Gill White **Bred** Barton Stud **Trained** Lambourn, Berks
■ Stewards' Enquiry : Jamie Spencer two-day ban: careless riding (Aug 8-9)

FOCUS
A modest staying handicap.
T/Jkpt: Not won. T/Plt: £82.10 to a £1 stake. Pool: £83,719.76. 743.71 winning tickets. T/Qpdt: £11.50 to a £1 stake. Pool: £6,571.23. 419.45 winning tickets. JN

DIEPPE (R-H)
Wednesday, July 25

OFFICIAL GOING: Turf: good to soft

4476a PRIX CAMILLE SAINT-SAENS (MAIDEN) (2YO) (TURF) — 5f 110y
11:30 (12:00) 2-Y-O **£8,333** (£3,333; £2,500; £1,666; £833)

RPR

1 **Style Vendome (FR)**[27] 3553 2-9-2 0................................ ThierryThulliez 3 91
(N Clement, France) **1/2**[1]

2 *4* **Lykea (IRE)** 2-8-8 0.. AnthonyCrastus 7 70
(C Laffon-Parias, France) **43/10**[2]

3 *6* **Starlette (FR)**[16] 2-8-9 0.. AntoineCoutier(4) 4 55
(P Bary, France) **12/1**

4 *½* **Adira (GER)** 2-8-13 0... UmbertoRispoli 6 53
(J-P Carvalho, Germany) **30/1**

5 *6* **Lewamy (IRE)**[16] 3928 2-9-2 0.................................. StephanePasquier 1 37
(John Best) *broke wl on ins rail: led after 1f: hdd at 1/2-way: no rspnse u.p: wknd qckly* **5/1**[3]

6 *8* **Telmo (FR)** 2-9-2 0.. FabienLefebvre 2 10
(A Lamotte D'Argy, France) **37/1**

1m 7.7s (67.70) **6** Ran SP% **115.8**
WIN (incl. 1 euro stake): 1.50. PLACES: 1.10, 1.50. SF: 5.20.
Owner Comte Andre de Ganay **Bred** Guy Pariente **Trained** Chantilly, France

4477a PRIX PICHEGRU (MAIDEN) (3YO) (TURF) 5f 110y

12:30 (12:00) 3-Y-O **£8,333** (£3,333; £2,500; £1,666; £833)

RPR

1 **Derivatives (IRE)**[105] 1313 3-8-13 0 .... FabriceVeron 9 75
(H-A Pantall, France) **26/5**[3]

2 2 **Contender (FR)**[40] 3-9-2 0 .... (p) SylvainRuis 3 71
(X Nakkachdji, France) **6/1**

3 1 ½ **Poppet's Passion**[40] 3-8-13 0 .... RonanThomas 6 63
(R Pritchard-Gordon, France) **53/10**

4 nk **American Saga (FR)**[16] 3-8-13 0 .... DavyBonilla 5 62
(M Delzangles, France) **9/2**[2]

5 1 ½ **Lupo D'Oro (IRE)**[7] 4221 3-9-2 0 .... StephanePasquier 8 60
(John Best) *broke awkwardly: sn racd midfield: gd prog to go 3rd at 1/2-way: u.p 1 1/2f out: no ex: styd on one pce fnl f* **14/5**[1]

6 2 **Mossa (IRE)**[205] 17 3-8-3 0 .... StephaneLaurent(5) 10 45
(Mme J Bidgood, France) **50/1**

7 1 **Manisa (FR)** 3-8-8 0 .... (b) UmbertoRispoli 4 42
(E Kurdu, Germany) **23/1**

8 ¾ **Begonia (FR)**[21] 3-8-8 0 .... FlavienPrat 7 40
(M Nigge, France) **35/1**

9 2 **Chief Hawkeye (IRE)**[21] 3-9-2 0 .... (b1) AlexisBadel 1 41
(J-V Toux, France) **13/1**

10 5 **Queenoftheprairie**[36] 3-8-5 0 .... MatthieuAutier(3) 2 17
(J E Pease, France) **19/1**

0 **Macicka (FR)**[16] 3-8-8 0 .... (b) WilliamsSaraiva 11
(Mme J Bidgood, France) **35/1**

0 **So Grateful (FR)**[44] 3-8-3 0 .... MarcLerner(5) 12
(F Pedrono, France) **71/1**

1m 4.71s (64.71) **12** Ran SP% **116.0**
WIN (incl. 1 euro stake): 6.20. PLACES: 2.30, 2.20, 1.90. DF: 24.40. SF: 47.00.
Owner Sheikh Mohammed **Bred** Darley **Trained** France

4360 SARATOGA (R-H)

Wednesday, July 25

OFFICIAL GOING: Turf: firm

4478a LAKE GEORGE STKS (GRADE 2) (3YO FILLIES) (TURF) 1m 110y

10:30 (12:00) 3-Y-O

£77,419 (£25,806; £12,903; £6,451; £3,870; £860)

RPR

1 **Centre Court (USA)**[38] 3-8-10 0 .... JRLeparoux 3 107
(George R Arnold II, U.S.A) **11/4**[2]

2 nk **Better Lucky (USA)**[58] 3-8-10 0 .... ECastro 4 106
(Thomas Albertrani, U.S.A) **158/10**

3 hd **Samitar**[33] 3328 3-8-10 0 .... RADominguez 6 106
(Mick Channon) **14/5**[3]

4 hd **Stephanie's Kitten (USA)**[82] 3-8-8 0 .... JRVelazquez 2 103
(Wayne Catalano, U.S.A) **23/10**[1]

5 ¾ **Medolina (USA)** 3-8-8 0 .... JJCastellano 8 101
(Todd Pletcher, U.S.A) **49/10**

6 hd **Somali Lemonade (USA)**[32] 3-8-8 0 .... JRosario 7 101
(Michael Matz, U.S.A) **154/10**

7 2 ¼ **Dancing Solo (USA)**[32] 3-8-10 0 .... JBravo 5 98
(Todd Pletcher, U.S.A) **16/1**

8 hd **Elusive Rumour (USA)** 3-8-4 0 .... (b) JAlvarado 1 92
(Thomas Albertrani, U.S.A) **56/1**

1m 41.71s (101.71) **8** Ran SP% **119.9**
PARI-MUTUEL (all including $2 stakes): WIN 7.50; PLACE (1-2) 3.80, 12.00; SHOW (1-2-3) 2.80, 6.10, 4.20; SF 77.00.
Owner G Watts Humphrey Jr **Bred** G Watts Humphrey Jr & Louise Ireland Humphrey Revo **Trained** USA

NOTEBOOK
Samitar, the Irish Guineas winner, will now stay in the US to be trained by Chad Brown.

4479 - 4481a (Foreign Racing) - See Raceform Interactive

3980 NAAS (L-H)

Wednesday, July 25

OFFICIAL GOING: Soft to heavy

4482a DARK ANGEL EUROPEAN BREEDERS FUND SWEET MIMOSA STKS (LISTED RACE) (FILLIES) 6f

7:25 (7:25) 3-Y-0+ **£34,666** (£10,133; £4,800; £1,600)

RPR

1 **Empowering (IRE)**[25] 3650 4-9-5 95 .... JPO'Brien 10 104
(A P O'Brien, Ire) *racd in 2nd: pushed along to go w ldr appr fnl f: styd on wl to get up ins fnl 50yds* **12/1**

2 ½ **Caprella**[14] 3983 3-9-0 94 .... JohnnyMurtagh 6 101
(P D Deegan, Ire) *sn led: qcknd 2f out: kpt on gamely: only ct ins fnl 50yds* **7/1**[3]

3 nse **After (IRE)**[10] 4123 3-9-0 105 .... SeamieHeffernan 7 101+
(A P O'Brien, Ire) *hld up towards rr: swtchd out over 1f out: styd on strly clsng stages* **5/2**[2]

4 1 ½ **Colour Of Love (IRE)**[10] 4124 4-9-5 86 .... (b) DeclanMcDonogh 5 97+
(W McCreery, Ire) *hld up on inner far side: unable to go pce 1/2-way: last ins fnl 2f: styd on wl for press to go 4th fnl 100yds* **8/1**

5 2 ½ **Lady Wingshot (IRE)**[304] 6389 3-9-0 101 .... KevinManning 2 88
(J S Bolger, Ire) *hld up against far rails: short of room 2f out and swtchd then snatched up: styd on wl ins fnl f* **8/1**

6 ½ **Rock On Ciara (IRE)**[16] 3923 6-9-5 83 .... ShaneFoley 8 87
(Joseph G Murphy, Ire) *trckd ldrs in 5th tl pushed along 2f out: no ex appr fnl f* **9/1**

7 1 ½ **Redoutable (IRE)**[25] 3645 3-9-0 80 .... ChrisHayes 1 82
(Kevin Prendergast, Ire) *broke wl and racd in 3rd against far rails: pushed along 2f out: wknd ent fnl f* **14/1**

8 7 ½ **Miss Complex**[30] 3438 3-9-0 .... PatSmullen 11 58
(Brian Meehan) *jinked rt leaving stalls: racd on outer tl wkng over 1f out* **20/1**

9 12 **Katla (IRE)**[25] 3650 4-9-8 99 .... WJLee 4 23
(J F Grogan, Ire) *trckd ldrs in 4th tl qckly losing position appr fnl f: eased down* **9/4**[1]

1m 14.1s (0.90)
WFA 3 from 4yo+ 5lb **9** Ran SP% **123.2**
CSF £99.05 TOTE £8.90: £3.20, £2.20, £1.40; DF 69.30.
Owner Mrs A M O'Brien & Mrs John Magnier **Bred** Whisperview Trading Ltd **Trained** Ballydoyle, Co Tipperary

FOCUS
The withdrawal of the morning-line favourite thieved this race of much of its lustre. Even so, it was quite a fascinating race to watch. The second and fourth have been rated as running personal bests.

NOTEBOOK
Empowering(IRE) showed great resolution to get up close home. A tough sort who stays further, she has been disappointing this year but bounced back and needed to be up with the pace, as she would struggle to do them for toe over 6f. Around a furlong out she started to reel in the pacemaker and the run was perfectly timed. She is now a Group 3 and Listed winner and is really game. The stiff finish here is right up her street.
Caprella ♦, who is in foal to the stallion honoured in the race title, ran a startling race. She showed buckets of pace and only started to falter in the final furlong. On this evidence she is well worth a try at 5f as her rider's main problem seemed to be to restrain her.
After(IRE) had a fair bit of ground to make up on her stablemate as the race developed and she was gaining quite fast in the last furlong. This was a decent effort from one who has been kept busy.
Colour Of Love(IRE) ran bravely as she was one of the first under duress. A game sort, she will surely have a few more tries at black-type placing.
Lady Wingshot(IRE) was the eyecatcher, having a nightmare passage on the inner and losing a great deal of ground at critical stages. It is to her credit that she managed to come fifth and she is one to note next time. Official explanation: jockey said filly got no clear run final stages
Katla(IRE), who edged Empowering last year, travelled to the 2f pole but faded quickly thereafter. The suspicion lingers that 6f on deep ground is not ideal for her and she was also giving weight away. Official explanation: vet said filly returned clinically abnormal

4483 - 4485a (Foreign Racing) - See Raceform Interactive

4230 BATH (L-H)

Thursday, July 26

OFFICIAL GOING: Firm (good to firm in places; 10.6)
Races around bottom bend increased in distance by 12.5yds.
Wind: virtually nil Weather: sunny, very warm

4486 TONY FOXWELL MEMORIAL FILLIES' H'CAP 1m 2f 46y

2:10 (2:10) (Class 5) (0-70,70) 3-Y-O **£2,264** (£673; £336; £168) **Stalls** Low

Form RPR

2341 1 **Play Street**[13] 4057 3-9-4 **70** .... HarryBentley(3) 13 83+
(Jonathan Portman) *trckd ldrs: jnd ldr over 3f out: led 2f out: pushed clr: readily* **15/8**[1]

30-0 2 1 ¼ **Hesperides**[61] 2497 3-8-11 **60** .... DavidProbert 4 67
(Harry Dunlop) *mid-div: pushed along 5f out: rdn 3f out: hdwy over 1f out: styd on ins fnl f: wnt 2nd towards fin: no ch w wnr* **40/1**

0-02 3 ¾ **Kittens**[14] 4006 3-8-9 **58** .... WilliamCarson 3 63
(William Muir) *prom tl rdn to chse ldrs over 3f out: styd on ins fnl f: wnt 3rd towards fin* **12/1**

0-04 4 ¾ **Cape Joy (IRE)**[25] 3663 3-9-0 **63** .... PatCosgrave 5 67
(Richard Hannon) *led: rdn and hdd 2f out: sn hld by wnr: no ex and lost pls ins fnl f* **11/1**

-243 5 2 **Idyllic Star (IRE)**[31] 3443 3-9-4 **67** .... LiamKeniry 9 67
(J S Moore) *mid-div: rdn 3f out: styd on fnl f: nvr a danger* **3/1**[2]

050 6 2 **Poly Pomona**[25] 3666 3-9-5 **68** .... (t) SeanLevey 6 64
(Richard Hannon) *mid-div: rdn over 3f out: sme late prog: nvr a danger* **16/1**

0250 7 ½ **Musically**[15] 3966 3-8-8 **57** .... ChrisCatlin 11 52
(Mick Channon) *towards rr: rdn 3f out: sme imp into midfield: nvr threatened ldrs* **9/1**[3]

000 8 3 **Riviera Romance**[23] 3720 3-8-5 **54** .... MircoDemuro 10 46
(J W Hills) *mid-div: rdn over 2f out: no imp* **20/1**

-335 9 3 ¼ **Trusting (IRE)**[16] 3939 3-8-9 **58** .... NeilCallan 2 47
(Eve Johnson Houghton) *trckd ldrs: rdn over 3f out: fdd ent fnl f* **9/1**[3]

050- 10 17 **Lady Lyricist**[223] 7783 3-8-10 **59** .... RussKennemore 8
(Reg Hollinshead) *a towards rr: eased whn btn over 1f out* **40/1**

0-00 11 6 **Glaze**[25] 3665 3-8-4 **53** .... (t) NickyMackay 7
(Hughie Morrison) *mid-div tl bdly hmpd and dropped in rr on bnd over 5f out: nvr rcvrd: eased whn btn fr over 1f out* **25/1**

4020 12 10 **Swift Act**[39] 3192 3-9-2 **68** .... SophieDoyle(3) 1
(Ronald Harris) *prom tl rdn 3f out: sn wknd: eased whn btn over 1f out* **18/1**

2m 8.4s (-2.60) **Going Correction** -0.275s/f (Firm) **12** Ran SP% **120.4**
Speed ratings (Par 97): **99,98,97,96,95 93,93,90,88,74 69,61**
toteswingers 1&2 £22.00, 2&3 £46.60, 1&3 £4.70 CSF £102.98 CT £737.80 TOTE £2.80: £1.50, £10.60, £2.50; EX 120.50.
Owner Anthony Boswood **Bred** The Hon Mrs R Pease **Trained** Compton, Berks

FOCUS
The going was firm, good to firm in places on a hot sunny day. A progressive type landed a gamble eased down in this strongly-run fillies' handicap. Sound form, if a bit limited. The winner is value for a bit extra.
Trusting(IRE) Official explanation: jockey said filly had no more to give

4487 THERMOLAST ROOFING MEDIAN AUCTION MAIDEN STKS 5f 161y

2:40 (2:41) (Class 6) 2-Y-O **£1,617** (£481; £240; £120) **Stalls** Centre

Form RPR

0 1 **Rafale**[49] 2844 2-9-3 0 .... FrankieMcDonald 7 73+
(Richard Hannon) *outpcd in rr early: hdwy fr over 2f out: str run ent fnl f: led nring finsh* **20/1**[3]

23 2 1 **Whistling Buddy**[44] 2995 2-9-3 0 .... SebSanders 8 70
(Peter Makin) *chsd ldrs: rdn to ld jst ins fnl f: hdd nring fin* **9/2**[2]

3 1 **Dawn Catcher** 2-8-12 0 .... KirstyMilczarek 17 62+
(Tony Carroll) *led at gd pce: rdn over 1f out: hdd jst ins fnl f: kpt on gamely* **40/1**

6323 4 ½ **The Sixties**[13] 4071 2-9-3 79 .... PatCosgrave 1 65
(Mick Channon) *prom: rdn over 2f out: kpt on tl no ex ins fnl f* **13/8**[1]

0 5 nk **Girl Of Cadiz**[13] 4055 2-8-12 0 .... SeanLevey 11 59
(Richard Hannon) *in tch: rdn wl over 2f out: kpt on same pce fnl f* **20/1**[3]

0 6 2 **Imperial Spirit**[13] 4056 2-9-3 0 .... ChrisCatlin 15 57
(Mick Channon) *mid-div on outer: rdn over 2f out: kpt on same pce fr over 1f out* **9/2**[2]

00 **7** *nk* **Michael's Song (IRE)**[13] 4055 2-8-12 0 CathyGannon 4 51
(Mick Channon) *mid-div: rdn over 2f out: kpt on same pce fnl f* **33/1**

0 **8** *5* **Keene's Pointe**[45] 2983 2-9-3 0 MircoDemuro 6 40
(J W Hills) *a towards rr* **20/1**[3]

9 *1* **Stormy Times (IRE)** 2-8-12 0 DavidProbert 5 32
(Mark Usher) *s.i.s: a towards rr* **28/1**

10 *nk* **Complexity** 2-9-3 0 NeilCallan 10 36
(Charles Hills) *a towards rr* **9/2**[2]

00 **11** *1* **Kalahari Breeze (IRE)**[15] 3971 2-8-12 0 WilliamCarson 12 27
(William Muir) *chsd ldrs tl wknd over 2f out* **25/1**

060 **12** *3 ¼* **Icanboogie**[63] 2420 2-9-3 53 (p) TomMcLaughlin 9 22
(Karen George) *mid-div tl wknd over 2f out* **66/1**

0 **13** *63* **Cerys**[10] 4152 2-8-12 0 (p) NickyMackay 2
(Derek Haydn Jones) *sn outpcd in rr: t.o* **100/1**

1m 9.92s (-1.28) **Going Correction** -0.275s/f (Firm) **13** Ran SP% **122.1**
Speed ratings (Par 92): **97,95,94,93,93 90,90,83,82,81 80,76,**
toteswingers 1&2 £13.40, 2&3 £28.80, 1&3 £79.10 CSF £101.59 TOTE £27.40: £6.00, £1.60, £11.40; EX 133.50.
Owner M S Al Shahi **Bred** S A Douch **Trained** East Everleigh, Wilts

FOCUS
It was fast and furious in this fair maiden auction. The favourite was a bit disappointing and a big-priced Richard Hannon-trained runner swooped late.

NOTEBOOK
Rafale didn't show much when 10-1 in a Lingfield maiden on debut and he was sent off at a biggish price here. He was slowly away and looked unlikely to get involved when still out the back turning in but he produced a power-packed finish to lead close home. The pace probably collapsed in a race where the leaders did too much too soon but there was still a lot to like about this much-improved performance from a £22,000 Sleeping Indian half-brother to three winners at 8.6f-2m1f. (op 12-1)
Whistling Buddy finished last of three at odds-on in a Brighton maiden last time but the soft ground may have been against him and he had claims on his promising debut second at Goodwood. Solid in the market, he travelled smoothly just behind the leaders and looked likely to collect when hitting the front inside the final furlong but he was reeled in by a fast finisher. (op 4-1 tchd 5-1)
Dawn Catcher, a half-sister to 1m2f Ryedale Lass and 5f 2yo winner First Rebellion, did well to hang on for a 40-1 third after setting a brutal pace on her debut. This Bertolini filly has a lot of natural speed and could take some catching in a similar race next time. (op 33-1)
The Sixties set the standard on his nose defeat in a Yarmouth maiden two runs back and his close third off 79 in a York nursery last time. He grabbed a prominent early position from stall one but there were warning signs some way out and he could only plug on for fourth. (op 7-4)
Girl Of Cadiz, a stablemate of the winner, finished last of nine in a soft-ground Newbury maiden on debut but she stayed on steadily in this improved run switched to fast ground. (op 14-1)
Imperial Spirit was a big market springer on his second run but he couldn't land a blow from off the pace. (op 12-1)
Keene's Pointe Official explanation: jockey said, regarding running and riding, that his orders were settle the colt in early and be handy in latter stages before making a challenge, he was unable to carry these out as it is very green and was frightened to go between other horses; trainer confirmed saying that it was only the colt's second run and it probably needs further.
Complexity was also well backed but this Gimcrack-entered colt ran green and was never involved on his debut. (op 7-1)

4488 BRITISH STALLION STUDS SUPPORTING BRITISH RACING E B F NOVICE STKS 5f 11y
3:15 (3:15) (Class 4) 2-Y-O **£4,463** (£1,328; £663; £331) **Stalls** Centre

Form RPR

1300 **1** **Liber**[12] 4093 2-9-2 98 ChrisCatlin 8 94
(Sir Mark Prescott Bt) *hld up: pushed along and hdwy fr 3f out: led jst ins fnl f: r.o wl* **5/2**[2]

2251 **2** *1 ¾* **Lucky Beggar (IRE)**[10] 4148 2-9-0 79 MatthewLawson(5) 5 91
(Charles Hills) *hld up: pushed along wl over 2f out: rdn and hdwy over 1f out: r.o strly ins fnl f: wnt 2nd nring fin* **16/1**

51 **3** *hd* **Blackdown Spirit**[9] 4180 2-9-2 0 JamesMillman 3 87
(Rod Millman) *prom: led jst over 2f out: sn jnd and rdn: hdd jst ins fnl f: kpt on same pce* **16/1**

0 **4** *¾* **New Fforest**[14] 4011 2-8-9 0 LiamKeniry 4 78
(Andrew Balding) *trckd ldrs: rdn to dispute ld wl over 1f out tl ent fnl f: no ex* **12/1**[3]

1 **5** *1 ½* **Normal Equilibrium**[26] 3617 2-9-5 0 NeilCallan 6 82
(Roger Varian) *trckd ldrs: effrt over 2f out: ev ch over 1f out: no ex fnl f* **2/1**[1]

10 **6** *nk* **The Taj (USA)**[37] 3240 2-9-5 0 TadhgO'Shea 1 84
(Richard Hannon) *trckd ldrs: nt clrest of runs 2f out: swtchd lft and rdn over 1f out: edgd lft: nt gng pce to get on terms* **5/2**[2]

615 **7** *4* **Majestic Red (IRE)**[40] 3138 2-8-11 75 TomMcLaughlin 2 59
(Malcolm Saunders) *sn pushed along in last trio: nvr gng pce to get involved* **66/1**

531 **8** *1* **Snow Angel (IRE)**[14] 4002 2-9-0 0 SebSanders 7 58
(J W Hills) *led tl jst over 2f out: sn rdn: wknd ent fnl f* **25/1**

1m 0.39s (-2.11) **Going Correction** -0.275s/f (Firm) **8** Ran SP% **115.3**
Speed ratings (Par 96): **105,102,101,100,98 97,91,89**
toteswingers 1&2 £7.00, 2&3 £10.30, 1&3 £7.20 CSF £41.44 TOTE £3.30: £1.20, £4.30, £4.80; EX 44.90.
Owner William Charnley & Richard Pegum **Bred** Redmyre Bloodstock Ltd **Trained** Newmarket, Suffolk

FOCUS
A useful novice event. The winner scored with authority but the sixth looked unlucky. The time was 0.61 seconds faster than standard.

NOTEBOOK
Liber had been beaten less than 3l in the Windsor Castle at Royal Ascot and the Super Sprint at Newbury on his last two runs. He had a clear form chance at the weights and found a surging run out wide to score in good style. His limitations have been exposed in stronger company but he is a very likeable, strong-galloping type with a good attitude and he is bred to stay further than this next season. (op 11-4 tchd 7-2)
Lucky Beggar(IRE) hammered his rivals under a forcing ride in a heavy-ground Windsor maiden on his fourth start. This 79-rated colt had plenty to find in this stronger race on much faster ground and was outpaced and a bit detached around the final turn but he finished well to snatch second. (tchd 20-1)
Blackdown Spirit gave it a decent try in his bid to add to his heavy-ground Ffos Las maiden win but his effort flattened out in the closing stages. (op 12-1)
New Fforest had been beaten 14l in a Newmarket maiden on her debut but it was interesting that she was sent here instead of sticking to maiden company and she ran a big race. This was a good leap forward from a half-sister to six winners, notably 6f-1m (Group 3) scorer Border Patrol and prolific 5f-7f (including Group 3) winner Eisteddfod. (tchd 11-1 and 14-1)
Normal Equilibrium overcame inexperience when winning a 5f Lingfield maiden on debut last month. This £85,000 brother to Group 3 2yo AW winner Elnawin was heavily-backed switched to novice company but he raced too freely early on and couldn't pick up. (op 11-4 tchd 15-8)
The Taj(USA) travelled well behind the leaders but he ran into repetitive traffic problems before coasting home for a close sixth. Official explanation: jockey said colt was denied a clear run (tchd 9-4 and 11-4)

4489 EWART ADAMS H'CAP 5f 11y
3:50 (3:50) (Class 5) (0-70,68) 3-Y-O **£2,264** (£673; £336; £168) **Stalls** Centre

Form RPR

4130 **1** **Trending (IRE)**[31] 3442 3-8-6 56 (b) RaulDaSilva(3) 3 66
(Jeremy Gask) *chsd ldrs: r.o to ld fnl 140yds: sn in command: rdn out* **8/1**[3]

436 **2** *2 ¼* **Funcheon Vale (IRE)**[24] 3702 3-8-11 58 MircoDemuro 2 60+
(Hughie Morrison) *wnt to s early: set decent pce: rdn over 1f out: no ex whn hdd fnl 140yds* **6/1**[2]

0043 **3** *¾* **West Leake Hare (IRE)**[26] 3613 3-9-7 68 (p) NeilCallan 8 67
(Charles Hills) *awkward leaving stalls: sn pushed along towards rr: rdn and hdwy 2f out: kpt on ins fnl f* **1/1**[1]

5365 **4** *nk* **Le King Beau (USA)**[22] 3762 3-9-5 66 (v) SeanLevey 7 64
(John Bridger) *chsd ldrs: rdn over 2f out: kpt on ins fnl f* **12/1**

0252 **5** *2 ¼* **Ocean Myth**[29] 3510 3-9-4 65 NickyMackay 1 55
(Jonathan Portman) *prom: rdn over 2f out: fdd ins fnl f* **6/1**[2]

-066 **6** *nse* **Too Ambitious**[19] 3848 3-8-4 51 oh3 ow2 ChrisCatlin 9 41
(Reg Hollinshead) *prom: rdn over 2f out: fdd ins fnl f* **16/1**

4-40 **7** *8* **Selinda**[29] 3489 3-8-2 49 CathyGannon 4
(Mick Channon) *s.i.s: sn struggling: a in rr* **28/1**

6200 **8** *6* **Monty Fay (IRE)**[25] 3670 3-8-8 55 (t) DavidProbert 6
(Derek Haydn Jones) *rrd bdly and lft in stalls: a bhd and nvr any ch* **12/1**

1m 1.08s (-1.42) **Going Correction** -0.275s/f (Firm) **8** Ran SP% **114.4**
Speed ratings (Par 100): **100,96,95,94,91 91,78,68**
toteswingers 1&2 £7.60, 2&3 £2.50, 1&3 £3.20 CSF £54.94 CT £88.88 TOTE £7.80: £1.70, £2.30, £1.10; EX 50.20.
Owner The Twitterati **Bred** Thomas Hassett **Trained** Sutton Veny, Wilts

FOCUS
They went a strong pace in this sprint handicap. The winner posted a 6lb personal best.

4490 TRENT SERVICES H'CAP 1m 5y
4:25 (4:25) (Class 6) (0-60,60) 3-Y-O **£1,617** (£481; £240; £120) **Stalls** Low

Form RPR

-000 **1** **Cha Ching (IRE)**[16] 3950 3-9-2 55 MircoDemuro 11 64
(J W Hills) *hld up bhd: rdn and hdwy on outer fr over 2f out: led ins fnl f: r.o: readily* **16/1**

3062 **2** *1 ½* **Authoritarian**[15] 3966 3-9-5 58 SeanLevey 16 63
(Richard Hannon) *in tch: rdn and hdwy to ld 2f out: hdd ins fnl f: kpt on but sn hld* **5/1**

-000 **3** *1 ¾* **Poetry Writer**[22] 3762 3-9-7 60 FergusSweeney 12 61
(Michael Blanshard) *mid-div: rdn and hdwy to chse ldrs 2f out: wnt 2nd briefly jst over 1f out: kpt on same pce fnl f* **25/1**

0-65 **4** *2 ½* **Dana's Present**[65] 2374 3-9-1 54 LiamKeniry 4 49
(George Baker) *trckd ldrs: ev ch 2f out: sn rdn: one pce fnl f* **7/2**[1]

0063 **5** *½* **Essell**[7] 4232 3-9-7 60 PatCosgrave 10 54
(Mick Channon) *chsd ldrs tl outpcd over 3f out: kpt on fnl f* **9/2**[3]

6060 **6** *½* **Scarlett Fever**[26] 3621 3-8-13 52 (p) DavidProbert 13 45
(Marcus Tregoning) *hld up towards rr: rdn 3f out: no imp tl styd on fnl f* **14/1**

0604 **7** *¾* **Winter Dress**[15] 3965 3-9-2 58 (v) HarryBentley(3) 7 49
(Roger Teal) *prom: led over 5f out tl rdn 2f out: wknd fnl f* **4/1**[2]

0600 **8** *hd* **Opus (IRE)**[28] 3543 3-9-2 55 (t) FrankieMcDonald 5 46
(Amanda Perrett) *s.i.s: a towards rr* **18/1**

0044 **9** *2 ¼* **Athletic**[27] 3575 3-9-2 55 (p) WilliamCarson 15 41
(Andrew Reid) *trckd ldrs: led 4f out tl rdn 2f out: wknd ins fnl f* **9/1**

0000 **10** *2* **Findeln**[15] 3966 3-9-2 55 (t) CathyGannon 3 36
(Eve Johnson Houghton) *racd keenly: hld up towards rr: midfield 5f out: rdn 3f out: no further imp* **33/1**

0300 **11** *22* **Sangrail**[26] 3619 3-9-3 59 RaulDaSilva(3) 14
(William Muir) *led tl over 5f out: wknd 2f out* **12/1**

1m 40.23s (-0.57) **Going Correction** -0.275s/f (Firm) **11** Ran SP% **119.4**
Speed ratings (Par 98): **91,89,87,85,84 84,83,83,81,79 57**
toteswingers 1&2 £18.80, 2&3 £12.60, 1&3 £37.20 CSF £95.63 CT £2057.95 TOTE £30.10: £8.80, £2.00, £9.40; EX 183.20.
Owner Mrs John Fenton **Bred** J F Tuthill **Trained** Upper Lambourn, Berks

FOCUS
A minor handicap. It was run at just a fair pace and the surprise winner deserves extra credit for scoring from some way back.
Cha Ching(IRE) Official explanation: trainer said, regarding apparent improvement in form, that the filly had been disappointing this season and had a rough race at Wolverhampton over 7f last time.
Sangrail Official explanation: jockey said filly had a breathing problem

4491 VISIT BATH H'CAP 1m 5f 22y
5:00 (5:00) (Class 6) (0-65,64) 4-Y-0+ **£1,617** (£481; £240; £120) **Stalls** High

Form RPR

224 **1** **Laser Blazer**[36] 3283 4-8-13 56 (p) MircoDemuro 9 66
(Jeremy Gask) *hld up towards rr: rdn and hdwy fr over 2f out: led ent fnl f: styd on strly* **8/1**

2203 **2** *1 ½* **Holden Eagle**[53] 2732 7-9-0 64 IanBurns(7) 6 72
(Tony Newcombe) *in tch: hdwy 3f out: rdn and ev ch 2f out tl jst ins fnl f: styd on* **16/1**

0051 **3** *nk* **Taroum (IRE)**[7] 4244 5-9-0 57 KierenFox 8 65
(Tony Carroll) *mid-div: rdn and hdwy fr wl over 2f out: led wl over 1f out: hdd ent fnl f: styd on but no ex* **13/8**[1]

4062 **4** *3 ½* **Beneath**[50] 2137 5-9-1 58 (bt) LiamKeniry 11 60
(Neil Mulholland) *hld up towards rr: hdwy 3f out: sn rdn: styd on same pce fnl 2f* **33/1**

-303 **5** *2 ¾* **The Calling Curlew**[23] 3722 4-9-1 63 AmyScott(5) 14 61
(Henry Candy) *mid-div: hdwy 3f out: sn rdn: styd on same pce fnl 2f* **7/1**[3]

50 **6** *1 ½* **Belleau (IRE)**[13] 4061 4-8-9 57 (b) CharlesBishop(5) 2 53
(Matt Sheppard) *mid-div: rdn whn lost pl and squeezed up over 1f out: nt a threat after* **20/1**

44-5 **7** *shd* **Eastern Magic**[69] 2237 5-8-8 58 JackDuern(7) 10 54
(Reg Hollinshead) *in tch: hdwy to dispute ld over 3f out: sn rdn: hdd wl over 1f out: fdd ent fnl f* **9/1**

5-50 **8** *1 ¼* **Pelham Crescent (IRE)**[65] 2363 9-9-2 62 RaulDaSilva(3) 4 56
(Bryn Palling) *hld up towards rr: hdwy into midfield u.p over 2f out: no further imp fr wl over 1f out* **20/1**

064/ **9** *10* **Rio Gael (IRE)**[69] 7011 6-8-13 56 TomMcLaughlin 1 35
(Peter Bowen) *chsd clr ldr tl rdn 3f out: sn btn: wknd over 1f out* **4/1**[2]

532- **10** 3/4 **Astroleo**[380] 3946 6-8-8 **51** ChrisCatlin 7 29
(Mark H Tompkins) *chsd clr ldr: led 4f out: sn rdn and jnd: hdd wl over 1f out: sn wknd* **22/1**

0-15 **11** 87 **Dove Cottage (IRE)**[53] 2732 10-9-6 **63** (v) FergusSweeney 13
(Stuart Kittow) *led: sn clr: hdd 4f out: wknd qckly: virtually p.u* **12/1**

3/0- **S** **Colonel Flay**[301] 6476 8-8-12 **56** ow1 AmirQuinn 12
(Nerys Dutfield) *hld up: stmbld bdly and slipped up after 1f: fatally injured* **50/1**

2m 49.21s (-2.79) **Going Correction** -0.275s/f (Firm) **12** Ran SP% **124.1**
Speed ratings (Par 101): **97,96,95,93,92 91,91,90,84,83 30,**
toteswingers 1&2 £18.60, 2&3 £8.10, 1&3 £3.80 CSF £122.92 CT £315.22 TOTE £7.00: £2.40, £3.90, £1.40; EX 139.30.
Owner Calne Engineering Ltd **Bred** Edward J G Young **Trained** Sutton Veny, Wilts

FOCUS
A staying handicap. Veteran Dove Cottage set a strong pace before fading and the winner came from a long way back. There was a horrible incident when Colonel Flay stumbled and took a nasty fall early on. The winner was entitled to take this on a best view of his penultimate run. The third was 4lb off his Brighton run.

4492 BATH TOURISM PLUS H'CAP (DIV I) 5f 161y
5:30 (5:31) (Class 6) (0-65,66) 3-Y-0+ **£1,617** (£481; £240; £120) **Stalls** Centre

Form RPR

2324 **1** **Bermondsey Bob (IRE)**[5] 4332 6-9-12 **62** ChrisCatlin 5 69
(John Spearing) *led for 1f: prom: rdn wl over 2f out: kpt on v gamely to ld ins fnl f: drvn out* **7/4**[1]

0000 **2** nk **Sermons Mount (USA)**[16] 3949 6-9-7 **57** (p) TomMcLaughlin 9 63
(Paul Howling) *s.i.s: sn pushed along towards rr: rdn over 2f out: hdwy over 1f out: r.o wl fnl 140yds: wnt 2nd fnl strides* **11/1**

/000 **3** nk **Red Avalanche (IRE)**[59] 2555 5-9-7 **57** KirstyMilczarek 3 62
(Tony Newcombe) *s.i.s: in rr: rdn and hdwy over 1f out: swtchd rt ent fnl f: r.o: wnt 3rd fnl strides* **8/1**[3]

-55 **4** hd **Ridgeway Sapphire**[30] 3466 5-8-11 **47** (v) DavidProbert 14 51
(Mark Usher) *w ldrs: rdn to ld 2f out: sn 1 1/2 l clr: hdd ins fnl f: no ex and lost 2 pls fnl strides* **12/1**

0002 **5** 2 1/4 **Brandywell Boy (IRE)**[1] 4467 9-8-13 **49** (t) RichardThomas 2 45
(Dominic Ffrench Davis) *chsd ldrs: rdn over 2f out: one pce fnl f* **9/1**

0455 **6** 2 1/4 **Bateleur**[7] 4236 8-9-10 **60** CathyGannon 1 49
(Mick Channon) *chsd ldrs: rdn wl over 2f out: one pce fnl f* **10/1**

60-0 **7** 3/4 **One Cool Chick**[10] 4146 4-9-8 **58** SeanLevey 15 44
(John Bridger) *s.i.s: sn in tch: rdn over 2f out: fdd fnl f* **40/1**

4345 **8** 2 1/2 **The Jailer**[2] 4422 9-9-0 **53** (p) RaulDaSilva(3) 10 31
(John O'Shea) *led after 1f: rdn and hdd 2f out: sn btn* **9/1**

6541 **9** 1/2 **Perlachy**[7] 4236 8-9-13 **66** 6ex (v) CPGeoghegan(3) 13 42+
(Ronald Harris) *chsd ldrs: rdn over 2f out: squeezed up over 1f out: hld after* **7/1**[2]

200 **10** 3 1/2 **Secret Queen**[70] 2207 5-9-4 **61** (b) RyanTate(7) 12 25
(Martin Hill) *in tch on outer tl dropped to last pair 3f out: sn rdn: nvr a threat after* **8/1**[3]

1m 10.08s (-1.12) **Going Correction** -0.275s/f (Firm)
WFA 3 from 4yo+ 5lb **10** Ran SP% **118.6**
Speed ratings (Par 101): **96,95,95,94,91 88,87,84,83,79**
toteswingers 1&2 £5.80, 2&3 £14.90, 1&3 £5.00 CSF £23.18 CT £128.32 TOTE £2.70: £1.10, £3.40, £4.20; EX 26.40.
Owner A A Campbell **Bred** Pier House Stud **Trained** Kinnersley, Worcs

FOCUS
There was a tight-four-way finish in this minor sprint handicap which was a race of changing fortunes. Ordinary form.

4493 BATH TOURISM PLUS H'CAP (DIV II) 5f 161y
5:55 (6:04) (Class 6) (0-65,63) 3-Y-0+ **£1,617** (£481; £240; £120) **Stalls** Centre

Form RPR

6-64 **1** **Crimson Queen**[31] 3435 5-9-6 **57** (b) ChrisCatlin 9 80
(Roy Brotherton) *mde all: pushed clr over 1f out: easily* **7/1**[3]

5015 **2** 7 **Catalinas Diamond (IRE)**[13] 4059 4-9-12 **63** (t) FergusSweeney 14 62
(Pat Murphy) *hld up in tch: pushed along and hdwy fr 3f out: rdn to chse wnr over 1f out but nvr any ch* **8/1**

-345 **3** 2 1/2 **Trade Centre**[23] 3718 7-8-12 **49** CathyGannon 5 40
(Milton Bradley) *chsd ldrs: rdn over 2f out: kpt on same pce fr over 1f out* **8/1**

2015 **4** 3/4 **Sarangoo**[5] 4332 4-9-10 **61** (p) KirstyMilczarek 6 49
(Malcolm Saunders) *s.i.s: in last: swtchd wd 3f out: sn rdn: kpt on ins fnl f: nvr trbld ldrs* **13/8**[1]

5522 **5** 1/2 **Auntie Mabel**[99] 1445 3-9-2 **58** LiamKeniry 8 44
(Andrew Balding) *chsd wnr tl over 1f out: no ex fnl f* **4/1**[2]

6000 **6** 1 **Not My Choice (IRE)**[16] 3949 7-9-6 **57** (t) TomMcLaughlin 12 40
(Paul Howling) *chsd ldrs: rdn over 2f out: sn one pce* **22/1**

-005 **7** nk **Pindrop**[29] 3510 3-8-6 **55** RyanTate(7) 7 37
(Clive Cox) *hld up in last pair: rdn 3f out: nvr gng pce to get involved* **12/1**

-006 **8** 1 1/2 **Crabbies Ginger**[21] 3791 4-8-9 **46** DavidProbert 10 23
(Lisa Williamson) *chsd ldrs: rdn over 2f out: wknd over 1f out* **20/1**

1m 9.58s (-1.62) **Going Correction** -0.275s/f (Firm)
WFA 3 from 4yo+ 5lb **8** Ran SP% **109.6**
Speed ratings (Par 101): **99,89,86,85,84 83,82,80**
toteswingers 1&2 £7.50, 2&3 £8.70, 1&3 £7.80 CSF £55.90 CT £425.55 TOTE £5.30: £1.50, £2.30, £2.30; EX 48.90.
Owner Arthur Clayton **Bred** Cheveley Park Stud Ltd **Trained** Elmley Castle, Worcs

FOCUS
The second division of a sprint handicap. Maltease Ah got loose at the start and was withdrawn. Molly Jones got unruly in the stalls and was also taken out of the race along with London Avenue. It was the quicker division and the winner looks better than ever.

T/Plt: £238.00 to a £1 stake. Pool of £60507.27 - 185.52 winning tickets. T/Qpdt: £17.30 to a £1 stake. Pool of £4284.56 - 182.35 winning tickets. TM

4245 DONCASTER (L-H)
Thursday, July 26

OFFICIAL GOING: Good to firm (firm in places; 9.1)
Wind: Moderate across Weather: Sunny periods

4494 OLIVIA ADAMS IS A TEENAGER TODAY MAIDEN AUCTION FILLIES' STKS 7f
6:10 (6:11) (Class 5) 2-Y-O **£2,264** (£673; £336; £168) **Stalls** High

Form RPR

05 **1** **Starlight Symphony (IRE)**[8] 4217 2-8-8 0 ow2 TedDurcan 14 77
(Eve Johnson Houghton) *towards rr: hdwy over 2f out: rdn over 1f out: styd on to chal ins fnl f: drvn to ld last 40yds* **33/1**

4 **2** 1/2 **Sorella Bella (IRE)**[13] 4055 2-8-6 0 SamHitchcott 4 74
(Mick Channon) *trckd ldrs: hdwy to ld and edgd rt 1 1/2f out: sn jnd and rdn: drvn ins fnl f: hdd and no ex last 40yds* **10/1**[3]

56 **3** 1 **Becky Lou (USA)**[34] 3326 2-8-9 0 KierenFallon 15 75+
(Jeremy Noseda) *in tch: pushed along bef 1/2-way: hdwy over 2f out: rdn to chse ldrs and hung bdly lft over 1f out: drvn and styng on whn n.m.r ins fnl f: kpt on u.p towards fin* **8/11**[1]

4 shd **Society Pearl (IRE)** 2-8-10 0 MichaelHills 1 75+
(Charles Hills) *dwlt and towards rr: gd hdwy wl over 2f out: chal over 1f out: rdn ins fnl f and ev ch tl wknd last 100yds* **9/1**[2]

5 3 **Indigo Lady** 2-8-6 0 AndreaAtzeni 13 63
(Peter Chapple-Hyam) *dwlt: sn in tch: hdwy over 2f out: rdn wl over 1f out: kpt on same pce fnl f* **12/1**

6 3/4 **Amirah (IRE)** 2-8-8 0 GrahamGibbons 6 64
(Alan McCabe) *led: rdn along over 2f out: hdd and sltly hmpd 1 1/2f out: sn wknd* **20/1**

0 **7** 1 1/4 **Good Speech (IRE)**[26] 3611 2-8-6 0 AndrewMullen 10 58
(Tom Tate) *chsd ldrs: rdn along wl over 2f out: grad wknd* **150/1**

0 **8** 3/4 **Aeronwyn Bryn (IRE)**[7] 4246 2-8-8 0 PaulMulrennan 8 58
(Michael Dods) *chsd ldrs: pushed along wl over 2f out: grad wknd* **20/1**

43 **9** 1 **Aseela (IRE)**[24] 3708 2-8-10 0 RobertWinston 9 58
(Clive Brittain) *in rr: pushed along 1/2-way: rdn over 2f out: styd on appr fnl f* **16/1**

65 **10** 1 1/4 **Trymyluck**[19] 3842 2-8-5 0 DuranFentiman 12 49
(Pam Sly) *prom: rdn along over 2f out: sn wknd* **33/1**

0 **11** 3/4 **Ceekay's Girl**[21] 3776 2-8-6 0 PJMcDonald 2 48
(Mrs K Burke) *nvr bttr than midfield* **25/1**

03 **12** 8 **Our Sweet Art**[15] 3971 2-8-7 0 LiamJones 7 29
(John Best) *prom: rdn along wl over 2f out: sn wknd* **12/1**

5 **13** 1 3/4 **Alex Zara**[10] 4132 2-8-0 0 NeilFarley(5) 5 22
(Jim Goldie) *dwlt: a towards rr* **50/1**

14 1 1/4 **Chloe's Image** 2-8-4 0 JamesSullivan 11 18
(Philip Kirby) *a in rr* **100/1**

40 **15** 1 **Rio Cato**[16] 3948 2-8-6 0 JimmyQuinn 3 17
(Ed Dunlop) *midfield: effrt wl over 2f out: sn rdn and wknd* **50/1**

1m 24.5s (-1.80) **Going Correction** -0.475s/f (Firm) **15** Ran SP% **123.1**
Speed ratings (Par 91): **91,90,89,89,85 84,83,82,81,80 79,70,68,66,65**
toteswingers: 1&2 £42.20, 1&3 £12.60, 2&3 £2.80. CSF £318.41 TOTE £43.40: £8.40, £2.10, £1.02; EX 342.60.
Owner Brian & Liam McNamee, Les & Ian Dawson **Bred** Patrick Byrnes **Trained** Blewbury, Oxon
■ Stewards' Enquiry : Sam Hitchcott caution: careless riding.

FOCUS
Following a dry run up to the meeting the ground was altered to 'good to firm, firm in places'. Jimmy Quinn reported the ground to be "on the fast side but with no jar". Not much in the way of strength in this ordinary maiden and a race that didn't take as much winning as had seemed likely with the market leader disappointing. The gallop was reasonable and the first four pulled clear in the closing stages.

NOTEBOOK
Starlight Symphony(IRE) had shown only moderate form at best in two outings over 6f but turned in a much-improved display over this longer trip back on grass, despite her rider posting 2lb overweight. She'll be equally effective over 1m and may do better granted a suitable test.
Sorella Bella(IRE) had shaped well over 6f in soft ground on her debut but she ran to a similar level over this longer trip on this much quicker ground. While she's likely to remain vulnerable to the better sorts in this grade, she's more than capable of picking up a small event. (op 8-1)
Becky Lou(USA) was upped to a trip that looked sure to suit but she didn't fill the eye in the preliminaries and failed to reproduce the useful form she showed when sixth in the much stronger Albany at Royal Ascot and proved disappointing. She's capable of winning a race and easier ground may suit given the way she hung but she doesn't look one to take too short a price about in this grade. (op 4-5)
Society Pearl(IRE) ◆, a 37,000euro yearling out of a dam who stayed 2m, shaped with a fair degree of promise after attracting a bit of support on this racecourse debut and after travelling strongly for a long way. She'll be all the better for this and should be able to win a similar event. (op 14-1)
Indigo Lady, an 11,000gns yearling with a stack of winners over a variety of distances in her pedigree, wasn't disgraced on this racecourse debut and is open to improvement. Official explanation: jockey said filly was slowly away (tchd 11-1 and 14-1)
Amirah(IRE), closely related to fair 6f Polytrack winner Golden Taurus and is also a half-sister to very useful 6f-1m winner Estidihaaf, showed ability on this racecourse debut and should improve for the run. (op 16-1)

4495 YORKSHIRE.COM JACKSONS CHAMPION BREAD H'CAP 6f
6:45 (6:46) (Class 5) (0-70,70) 4-Y-O+ **£2,385** (£704; £352) **Stalls** High

Form RPR

5000 **1** **Sleepy Blue Ocean**[55] 2674 6-9-2 **65** (p) RobertWinston 13 76
(John Balding) *prom: led 2f out: rdn ent fnl f: drvn towards fin and hld on gamely* **16/1**

6025 **2** nk **Song Of Parkes**[24] 3696 5-9-6 **69** DavidAllan 4 79
(Eric Alston) *cl up: led after 2f: hdd 2f out: rdn over 1f out and ev ch tl drvn ins fnl f and no ex towards fin* **5/1**[1]

2033 **3** 1 3/4 **Tabaret**[3] 4400 9-9-5 **68** (p) AmyRyan 5 72
(Richard Whitaker) *in tch: hdwy to chse ldng pair over 1f out: sn rdn and kpt on fnl f* **11/2**[2]

-066 **4** 3/4 **Drift And Dream**[29] 3500 5-9-7 **70** TedDurcan 10 72
(Chris Wall) *in tch: hdwy to chse ldrs 2f out: sn rdn: drvn and one pce fnl f* **15/2**[3]

00-0 **5** 1 1/4 **Dubai Celebration**[52] 2750 4-8-9 **58** GrahamLee 6 56
(Julie Camacho) *hld up: hdwy 2f out: rdn over 1f out: styd on fnl f: nrst fin* **25/1**

1-00 **6** 1 1/4 **Henry Morgan**[59] 2538 5-9-1 **64** (p) TomEaves 18 58
(Bryan Smart) *towards rr: hdwy 2f out: sn rdn and styd on wl fnl f: nrst fin* **14/1**

532 **7** ½ **Consistant**[45] 2981 4-9-0 **63** DuranFentiman 14 55
(Brian Baugh) *prom: rdn along over 2f out: grad wknd appr fnl f* **9/1**

05 **8** *nk* **Powerful Pierre**[45] 2981 5-9-0 **66** (b) DaleSwift(3) 19 57
(Ian McInnes) *towards rr: hdwy 2f out: sn rdn and styd on fnl f: nrst fin* **20/1**

000 **9** *nse* **Ryedale Dancer (IRE)**[157] 633 4-8-10 **59** GrahamGibbons 8 50
(Richard Guest) *hld up towards rr: hdwy 2f out: rdn over 1f out: kpt on fnl f: nrst fin* **40/1**

3314 **10** *nk* **Avonvalley**[33] 3382 5-8-11 **60** RobbieFitzpatrick 9 50
(Peter Grayson) *in rr: hdwy wl over 1f out: rdn and styd on fnl f: nrst fin* **16/1**

/004 **11** *1* **Loukoumi**[21] 3778 4-8-13 **62** (b) DanielTudhope 2 49
(Tim Easterby) *towards rr: hdwy 1/2-way: rdn to chse ldrs 2f out: wknd over 1f out* **8/1**

3550 **12** *4* **Brave Battle**[13] 4042 4-8-5 **59** ow2 ShaneBKelly(5) 17 33
(Ron Barr) *sn rdn along: a in rr* **16/1**

5666 **13** *1* **Mawjoodah**[16] 3943 4-8-4 **53** JamesSullivan 3 24
(Brian Ellison) *s.i.s: a in rr* **11/1**

3110 **14** ¾ **Choc'A'Moca (IRE)**[3] 4400 5-9-4 **67** (v) MickyFenton 7 36
(Paul Midgley) *broke wl and prom for 2f: sn lost pl and bhd* **12/1**

-000 **15** *1¼* **Deliberation (IRE)**[61] 2475 4-8-13 **65** JulieBurke(3) 11 30
(Mark Buckley) *sn led: hdd after 2f: cl up tl rdn along wl over 2f out and sn wknd* **50/1**

0030 **16** *1½* **Kapunda**[23] 3731 4-8-2 **51** oh4 FrannyNorton 12 11
(Jedd O'Keeffe) *in tch: rdn along over 2f out: sn wknd* **33/1**

-150 **17** *8* **Half A Crown (IRE)**[6] 4315 7-9-4 **67** AndrewMullen 1
(Peter Salmon) *prom on outer: rdn along bef 1/2-way: sn lost pl and bhd* **20/1**

1m 10.64s (-2.96) **Going Correction** -0.475s/f (Firm) **17** Ran SP% **126.0**
Speed ratings (Par 103): **100,99,97,96,94 92,92,91,91,91 90,84,83,82,80 78,68**
toteswingers: 1&2 £28.80, 1&3 £36.10, 2&3 £7.80. CSF £89.28 CT £533.37 TOTE £21.50: £5.10, £1.90, £2.20, £2.30; EX 152.40.

Owner Tykes And Terriers Racing Club **Bred** Exors Of The Late N Ahamad & P C Scott **Trained** Scrooby, Notts

FOCUS
Exposed performers in a modest handicap. The gallop was sound throughout but those held up could never get involved. Straightforward form.

Ryedale Dancer(IRE) Official explanation: trainer said filly was unsuited by the good to firm (firm in places) ground

Half A Crown(IRE) Official explanation: jockey said gelding never travelled

4496 SKYBET SUPPORTING YORKSHIRE RACING SUMMER FESTIVAL H'CAP 6f

7:15 (7:18) (Class 4) (0-80,80) 3-Y-O **£4,204** (£1,251; £625; £312) **Stalls** High

Form RPR

522 **1** **Pearl Nation (USA)**[14] 3990 3-9-0 **73** FrederikTylicki 15 84
(Brian Baugh) *hld up: hdwy and in tch 1/2-way: chsd ldrs 2f out: rdn to chal 1f out: led last 100yds: kpt on strly* **14/1**

-010 **2** ¾ **Decision By One**[26] 3607 3-9-7 **80** (t) RichardKingscote 13 88
(Tom Dascombe) *a.p: rdn to ld over 1f out: drvn ins fnl f: hdd and no ex last 100yds* **8/1**

462 **3** *2* **Discression**[33] 3379 3-9-1 **74** GrahamLee 6 76
(Kevin Ryan) *towards rr: hdwy 1/2-way: rdn to chse ldrs whn edgd rt ent fnl f: kpt on to take 3rd nr line* **8/1**

-423 **4** *shd* **Love Island**[50] 2824 3-8-4 **63** oh1 ow2 AmyRyan 11 65
(Richard Whitaker) *prom: led 2f out: sn rdn and hdd over 1f out: sn edgd lft and kpt on same pce: lost 3rd nr line* **7/1**[3]

-316 **5** *2¾* **Duke Of Aricabeau (IRE)**[17] 3912 3-8-11 **70** RobertWinston 16 63
(Mrs K Burke) *in tch: hdwy to chse ldrs 2f out: rdn and edgd lft appr fnl f: kpt on same pce* **9/1**

3230 **6** ¾ **Wahylah (IRE)**[13] 4062 3-9-7 **80** KierenFallon 17 80
(Clive Brittain) *dwlt and bhd: rdn along bef 1/2-way: hdwy wl over 1f out: styng on to chse ldrs whn n.m.r and hmpd ent fnl f: one pce after* **6/1**[2]

2100 **7** *2¼* **Available (IRE)**[26] 3613 3-9-0 **73** FrannyNorton 10 56
(John Mackie) *chsd ldrs: edgd lft after 2f: rdn along over 2f out: wknd over 1f out* **28/1**

1011 **8** *2¼* **Johnny Cavagin**[27] 3567 3-8-5 **71** (t) JasonHart(7) 9 47
(Richard Guest) *chsd ldrs whn n.m.r and hmpd after 2f: effrt over 2f out: sn rdn and no imp* **3/1**[1]

0-06 **9** ¾ **Airborne Again (IRE)**[80] 1921 3-9-4 **77** DanielTudhope 14 51
(Harry Dunlop) *chsd ldrs: rdn along over 2f out: grad wknd* **33/1**

4153 **10** ½ **Willies Wonder (IRE)**[36] 3284 3-9-4 **77** MichaelHills 5 49
(Charles Hills) *sltly hmpd s: towards rr: hdwy wl over 2f out: sn rdn and n.d* **10/1**

34R **11** *1¾* **Scrooby Doo**[15] 3954 3-8-8 **67** MickyFenton 4 33
(Scott Dixon) *prom: rdn along over 2f out: drvn and wknd over 1f out* **40/1**

-000 **12** *1* **Hot Sugar (USA)**[52] 2764 3-8-12 **71** (b[1]) PhillipMakin 2 34
(Kevin Ryan) *chsd ldrs on outer: rdn along wl over 2f out: sn wknd* **25/1**

264 **13** *nk* **Reve Du Jour (IRE)**[10] 4143 3-8-8 **67** IPoullis 7 29
(Alan McCabe) *led: rdn along over 2f out: sn hdd & wknd* **33/1**

3115 **14** *12* **Art Dzeko**[62] 2459 3-8-10 **69** DavidAllan 12
(Tim Easterby) *a towards rr* **16/1**

2-10 **15** *19* **By Invitation (USA)**[61] 2503 3-8-12 **71** NeilCallan 1
(Ralph Beckett) *towards rr: rdn along 1/2-way: sn outpcd and bhd* **25/1**

1m 10.37s (-3.23) **Going Correction** -0.475s/f (Firm) **15** Ran SP% **125.1**
Speed ratings (Par 102): **102,101,98,98,94 93,90,87,86,85 83,82,81,65,40**
toteswingers: 1&2 £19.70, 1&3 £24.00, 2&3 £9.50. CSF £117.14 CT £1003.44 TOTE £15.00: £4.00, £3.90, £3.30; EX 160.50.

Owner Chris Iddon **Bred** William A Carl Estate **Trained** Audley, Staffs

FOCUS
A fair handicap run at a decent gallop and this form should prove reliable. The winner is rated up 6lb.

Johnny Cavagin Official explanation: trainer said gelding was unsuited by the good to firm (firm in places) ground

Willies Wonder(IRE) Official explanation: jockey said colt lost its action

4497 ESQUIRES COFFEE WHEATLEY RETAIL PARK FILLIES' H'CAP 7f

7:50 (7:51) (Class 3) (0-90,90) 3-Y-O+ **£6,792** (£2,021; £1,010; £505) **Stalls** High

Form RPR

-003 **1** **Shesastar**[20] 3812 4-9-8 **84** GrahamGibbons 3 93
(David Barron) *hld up towards rr: hdwy 1/2-way: chsd ldrs wl over 1f out: rdn ent fnl f: led last 50yds: edgd lft towards fin and jst hld on* **9/2**[2]

2210 **2** *shd* **Dancheur (IRE)**[22] 3762 3-8-6 **75** PJMcDonald 8 82
(Mrs K Burke) *set str pce: clr after 2f: rdn wl over 1f out: edgd rt ent fnl f: hdd and no ex last 50yds* **13/2**[3]

5-12 **3** *nk* **Perfect Step (IRE)**[76] 2022 3-9-5 **88** NeilCallan 6 94
(Roger Varian) *trckd ldrs: hdwy over 2f out: rdn to chse ldng pair whn swtchd lft ent fnl f: sn drvn to chal and ev ch tl no ex towards fin* **13/8**[1]

563 **4** *3¾* **Colorful Notion (IRE)**[147] 754 3-9-6 **89** AndreaAtzeni 9 85
(Marco Botti) *chsd ldr: tk clsr order 2f out: rdn and ch over 1f out: sn drvn: edgd lft one pce fnl f* **12/1**

-200 **5** *5* **Lady Layla**[33] 3376 3-8-8 **77** TomEaves 5 60
(Bryan Smart) *towards rr: effrt and sme hdwy wl over 2f out: sn rdn and no imp* **16/1**

-004 **6** *1¼* **Nemushka**[52] 2752 3-8-10 **79** (p) FrederikTylicki 1 58
(Richard Fahey) *chsd ldrs: rdn along over 2f out: sn btn* **13/2**[3]

0005 **7** *1½* **Fillionaire**[19] 3879 3-9-7 **90** SamHitchcott 7 65
(Mick Channon) *a towards rr* **14/1**

0 **8** *11* **Mortitia**[34] 3336 4-9-9 **85** (bt[1]) RobertWinston 2 32
(Brian Meehan) *dwlt: a in rr* **20/1**

60-6 **9** *1¾* **Besito (IRE)**[48] 2893 3-8-9 **78** KierenFallon 4 19
(William Jarvis) *chsd ldrs: rdn along 3f out: sn wknd* **16/1**

1m 23.09s (-3.21) **Going Correction** -0.475s/f (Firm)
WFA 3 from 4yo 7lb **9** Ran SP% **113.8**
Speed ratings (Par 104): **99,98,98,94,88 87,85,72,70**
toteswingers: 1&2 £2.80, 1&3 £1.80, 2&3 £3.70. CSF £33.25 CT £66.28 TOTE £5.50: £1.50, £2.10, £1.20; EX 42.00.

Owner Star Alliance 4 - Lancs 2 Lincs **Bred** The Welcome Alliance **Trained** Maunby, N Yorks

FOCUS
A useful fillies' handicap in which the gallop was sound and the first three pulled clear. Sound looking form if hard to rate too positively.

NOTEBOOK
Shesastar, a dual 6f winner at this course, appreciated the decent gallop and showed a good attitude to confirm the promise shown on her previous start. It is unlikely she'll be going up too much for this and she's likely to remain competitive in similar events after reassessment. (op 5-1 tchd 11-2)

Dancheur(IRE) emerges with plenty of credit on her first start over 7f after setting and almost sustaining a decent gallop. She is by no means fully exposed and she's more than capable of adding to her tally. (op 15-2 tchd 8-1)

Perfect Step(IRE), the least experienced member of this field, ran creditably, despite looking less than happy on this first run on very quick ground since her debut. She's in very good hands and is capable of winning a reasonable handicap, especially when there is a bit more give in the ground. (op 6-4 tchd 7-4)

Colorful Notion(IRE) is a reliable sort who didn't help her cause by hanging but she was far from disgraced back in handicap on this first start since running well in the face of a stiff task in the UAE in March. She'll have to improve to win a competitive handicap on turf from this mark, though. (op 11-1)

Lady Layla continues below the pick of her form last year and on her reappearance and may be suited by easier ground. (tchd 14-1)

Nemushka was again a long way below the form she showed in three runs last year and, although her stable continues in good form, she's one to tread carefully with. (op 7-1 tchd 6-1)

4498 NAPOLEONS CASINOS SHEFFIELD H'CAP 1m 2f 60y

8:25 (8:26) (Class 5) (0-75,75) 3-Y-O **£2,264** (£673; £336; £168) **Stalls** Low

Form RPR

-030 **1** **Keepax**[24] 3703 3-9-7 **75** GeorgeBaker 8 83
(Chris Wall) *hld up in midfield: stdy hdwy on inner 3f out: chsd ldrs over 1f out: rdn to chal ins fnl f: styd on to ld nr fin* **9/1**

4004 **2** ½ **Instrumentalist (IRE)**[7] 4254 3-9-4 **72** FrederikTylicki 13 79
(John Best) *in tch: hdwy over 3f out: chal 2f out: rdn to ld jst over 1f out: drvn ins fnl f: hdd and ex nr fin* **40/1**

4-12 **3** *1¼* **Watheeq (USA)**[27] 3574 3-9-5 **73** TadhgO'Shea 15 78
(Roger Varian) *hld up in rr: gd hdwy on wd outside over 3f out: chsd ldrs 2f out: rdn to chal jst over 1f out and ev ch tl drvn and one pce last 75yds* **9/2**[2]

06 **4** *3* **Romantic (IRE)**[62] 2449 3-8-13 **67** (b) IanMongan 4 66
(Sir Henry Cecil) *trckd ldrs: hdwy over 3f out: rdn 2f out: drvn and kpt on same pce appr fnl f* **20/1**

0434 **5** *1½* **Scrupul (IRE)**[19] 3882 3-9-7 **75** KierenFallon 9 71
(Luca Cumani) *t.k.h: chsd ldrs: cl up 5f out: led over 2f out: sn rdn and hdd over 1f out: wknd ent fnl f* **7/2**[1]

056 **6** *hd* **Sky Khan**[58] 2584 3-9-0 **68** PaulMulrennan 16 64
(Ed Dunlop) *hld up in midfield: hdwy 3f out: rdn wl over 1f out: styd on in fnl f: nrst fin* **11/2**[3]

1005 **7** ¾ **Good Of Luck**[37] 3248 3-9-4 **72** SamHitchcott 10 66
(Mick Channon) *hld up in rr: hdwy 3f out: effrt 2f out and n.m.r: swtchd lft to inner over 1f out: sn rdn and no imp* **22/1**

-500 **8** *hd* **Finbar**[50] 2813 3-9-6 **74** GrahamLee 14 68
(James Given) *hld up in midfield: hdwy 3f out: rdn 2f out: styd on appr fnl f: nt rch ldrs* **20/1**

2560 **9** ¾ **Sardanapalus**[13] 4046 3-9-5 **73** PhillipMakin 12 65
(Kevin Ryan) *hld up in rr: hdwy over 3f out: rdn over 2f out: n.d* **25/1**

504U **10** *3¼* **No Dominion (IRE)**[26] 3630 3-8-8 **62** JamesSullivan 2 48
(James Given) *a towards rr* **28/1**

00-1 **11** ¾ **Up Ten Down Two (IRE)**[10] 4153 3-8-2 **56** 6ex (t) AndreaAtzeni 1 41
(Michael Easterby) *cl up: rdn along over 3f out: sn wknd* **7/1**

0355 **12** *nk* **Chelsea Mick**[27] 3558 3-8-7 **68** JoshBaudains(7) 5 52
(John Mackie) *led: rdn along over 3f out: hdd 2f out and sn wknd* **16/1**

06-5 **13** ¾ **Holy Roman Warrior (IRE)**[99] 1442 3-9-4 **72** TonyHamilton 6 55
(Richard Fahey) *a towards rr* **40/1**

-300 **14** *1½* **Virginia Gallica (IRE)**[40] 3161 3-9-4 **72** MichaelHills 11 52
(J W Hills) *a towards rr* **50/1**

42 **15** *1* **Sarmatian Knight (IRE)**[21] 3792 3-9-2 **70** NeilCallan 7 48
(Ian Williams) *chsd ldrs: rdn along 3f out: sn wknd* **8/1**

166 **16** *nk* **Falcon's Reign (FR)**[12] 4094 3-9-3 **71** TomEaves 3 49
(Michael Appleby) *t.k.h: in tch on inner: effrt to chse ldrs over 3f out: sn rdn and wknd over 2f out* **33/1**

2m 6.52s (-2.88) **Going Correction** -0.475s/f (Firm) **16** Ran SP% **126.2**
Speed ratings (Par 100): **92,91,90,88,87 86,86,86,85,82 82,82,81,80,79 79**
toteswingers 1&2 £27.20, 1&3 £8.50, 2&3 £25.80 CSF £343.49 CT £1855.14 TOTE £14.20: £2.10, £8.30, £1.90, £4.10; EX 555.40.

Owner Follow The Flag Partnership **Bred** Follow The Flag Partnership **Trained** Newmarket, Suffolk

FOCUS
A fair handicap run at a reasonable gallop. The winner built on his reappearance promise.

Sky Khan Official explanation: trainer said gelding was unsuited by the good to firm (firm in places) ground

Sarmatian Knight(IRE) Official explanation: jockey said gelding ran too free and had no more to give

4499 TYREGIANT.COM H'CAP — 1m 4f

8:55 (8:56) (Class 5) (0-75,75) 3-Y-0+ **£2,264** (£673; £336; £168) **Stalls** Low

Form				RPR
61	**1**		**The High Man**[40] 3154 4-9-13 **74** ... GeorgeBaker 8 (Ed Walker) *prom: chsd clr ldr after 4f: tk clsr order on bit 4f out: led 3f out: pushed clr wl over 1f out: comf* **4/1**[1]	90+
1233	**2**	3 ¾	**Arizona John (IRE)**[55] 2676 7-10-0 **75** ... FrannyNorton 3 (John Mackie) *hld up in midfield: stdy hdwy 3f out: rdn to chse ldrs 2f out: styd on fnl f: no ch w wnr* **11/2**[2]	81
0005	**3**	*nk*	**Meetings Man (IRE)**[41] 3129 5-9-1 **67** ... GarryWhillans(5) 6 (Micky Hammond) *trckd ldrs: chsd ldng pair after 4f: effrt over 3f out: sn chsng wnr and rdn: drvn wl over 1f out and kpt on same pce* **15/2**	73
0134	**4**	*2*	**Scottish Star**[36] 3278 4-10-0 **75** ... MickyFenton 2 (James Eustace) *hld up in midfield: hdwy on outer 3f out: rdn wl over 1f out: sn no imp* **13/2**[3]	77
-10	**5**	*4*	**Artisan**[41] 3129 4-9-3 **67** ... DaleSwift(3) 4 (Brian Ellison) *towards rr: hdwy 4f out: rdn 3f out: plugged on: nvr nr ldrs* **8/1**	63
0530	**6**	3 ¾	**Change The Subject (USA)**[9] 4175 4-9-11 **72** ...(t) AndrewMullen 12 (Peter Salmon) *in tch: pushed along 1/2-way: hdwy to chse ldng pair 3f out: rdn over 2f out: sn wknd* **33/1**	62
415	**7**	*3*	**Al Furat (USA)**[34] 3353 4-9-1 **67** ... ShaneBKelly(5) 11 (Ron Barr) *s.i.s and rdn sn after s: bhd: sme hdwy u.p over 3f out: drvn over 2f out and nvr a factor* **7/1**	52
61/5	**8**	*13*	**Jolly Roger (IRE)**[13] 4061 5-9-12 **73** ... FrederikTylicki 9 (Tony Carroll) *bhd: pushed along 1/2-way: rdn and detached 5f out: nvr a factor* **8/1**	37
-006	**9**	2 ¼	**Tartan Gunna**[33] 3386 6-9-8 **69** ...(b) GrahamLee 10 (James Given) *midfield: rdn along 4f out: sn outpcd and bhd* **16/1**	30
030	**10**	*hd*	**Azerodegree (IRE)**[42] 3079 3-8-11 **70** ... AndreaAtzeni 5 (Marco Botti) *chsd ldrs: rdn along over 3f out: sn wknd* **12/1**	30
-246	**11**	*8*	**Woop Woop (IRE)**[26] 3610 4-9-7 **71** ... RyanPowell(3) 1 (Ian Williams) *chsd ldr 4f: prom tl rdn along over 4f out and sn wknd* **14/1**	19
60-0	**12**	¾	**Oriental Cavalier**[63] 2414 6-9-11 **72** ...(v) GrahamGibbons 7 (Mark Buckley) *led and sn wl clr: pushed along 4f out: hdd & wknd 3f out* **25/1**	18

2m 29.31s (-5.59) **Going Correction** -0.475s/f (Firm) 12 Ran SP% **122.2**
WFA 3 from 4yo+ 12lb
Speed ratings (Par 103): **99,96,96,94,92 89,87,79,77,77 72,71**
toteswingers 1&2 £1.50, 1&3 £7.80, 2&3 £3.10 CSF £26.01 CT £164.06 TOTE £5.90: £3.20, £1.10, £4.20; EX 27.20.
Owner Dubai Thoroughbred Racing **Bred** Cheveley Park Stud Ltd **Trained** Newmarket, Suffolk

FOCUS
A fair handicap run at a reasonable gallop but a race in which very few got involved. The winner was value for 6l and the runner-up sets the standard.
Change The Subject(USA) Official explanation: jockey said colt never travelled
Jolly Roger(IRE) Official explanation: jockey said gelding never travelled
Azerodegree(IRE) Official explanation: jockey said gelding hung left-handed
T/Jkpt: Not won. T/Plt: £45.00 to a £1 stake. Pool: £75,559.22 - 1223.26 winning tickets T/Qpdt: £21.10 to a £1 stake. Pool: £4729.10 - 165.6 winning tickets JR

4251 EPSOM (L-H)

Thursday, July 26

OFFICIAL GOING: Good to firm (good in places; sprint 8.7, derby 8.5)
Rail dolled out up to 4yds from 1m from there to Winning Post adding about 8yds to race distances.
Wind: Almost nil Weather: Sunny, hot

4500 DOWNLOAD EPSOM'S ANDROID OR IPHONE APP NOW H'CAP — 5f

6:00 (6:00) (Class 4) (0-80,80) 3-Y-0 **£4,528** (£1,347; £673; £336) **Stalls** High

Form				RPR
414	**1**		**Lady Gibraltar**[4] 4364 3-8-11 **77** ...(v) MichaelJMMurphy(7) 2 (Alan Jarvis) *racd three off the rail: pressed ldrs: shkn up to chal fr 2f out: narrow ld ins fnl f: jst hld on* **11/4**[2]	84
222	**2**	*shd*	**Wild Sauce**[33] 3404 3-9-0 **73** ...(b) PaulHanagan 6 (Bryan Smart) *racd against rail: disp ld: narrowly hdd ins fnl f: kpt on wl: jst hld* **15/8**[1]	80
10-0	**3**	*1*	**Sandfrankskipsgo**[66] 2347 3-9-3 **76** ... JoeFanning 1 (Peter Crate) *racd wdst of all: disp ld: rdn over 1f out: nt qckn fnl f* **16/1**	79
0604	**4**	2 ¼	**Jinker Noble**[38] 3234 3-9-2 **75** ...(p) JohnFahy 3 (Clive Cox) *mostly in last pair: rdn and racd awkwardly 2f out: n.d after: styd on ins fnl f* **8/1**	70
556	**5**	*nk*	**Signifer (IRE)**[7] 4231 3-9-7 **80** ...(v) MatthewDavies 5 (Mick Channon) *racd one off of the rail: disp ld tl wknd jst over 1f out* **13/2**	74
1-16	**6**	2 ½	**Blanc De Chine (IRE)**[29] 3486 3-9-4 **77** ... JimmyFortune 4 (Peter Makin) *hld up in last pair: effrt 2f out: no imp over 1f out: eased whn btn* **4/1**[3]	62

54.53s (-1.17) **Going Correction** -0.175s/f (Firm) 6 Ran SP% **111.8**
Speed ratings (Par 102): **102,101,100,96,96 92**
toteswingers: 1&2 £1.30, 1&3 £12.40, 2&3 £7.70. CSF £8.26 TOTE £3.40: £1.50, £2.40; EX 6.10.
Owner Buckingham Flooring **Bred** Netherfield House Stud **Trained** Twyford, Bucks

FOCUS
A competitive small-field handicap to open the card. The finish was fought out by two of the three fillies in the race. There are one or two doubts over the form.

4501 TRY TOTEQUICKPICK IF YOU'RE FEELING LUCKY H'CAP — 5f

6:35 (6:36) (Class 4) (0-85,85) 4-Y-0+ **£5,175** (£1,540; £769; £384) **Stalls** High

Form				RPR
020	**1**		**Fair Value (IRE)**[20] 3822 4-9-6 **84** ... SebSanders 8 (Simon Dow) *hanging lft much of way: chsd ldr: led 2f out: sn clr: unchal* **9/2**[2]	95
-004	**2**	1 ¾	**Ryan Style (IRE)**[17] 3905 6-8-6 **72** ...(v) SilvestreDeSousa 10 (Lisa Williamson) *disp 3rd and in tch: rdn over 2f out: styd on fnl f to take 2nd last stride* **5/1**[3]	75
3024	**3**	*shd*	**Flash City (ITY)**[41] 3127 4-9-7 **85** ...(v) PaulHanagan 3 (Bryan Smart) *disp 3rd and in tch: rdn to chse wnr jst ins fnl f: no imp: pushed along and lost 2nd post* **15/8**[1]	88
0234	**4**	2 ¾	**Falasteen (IRE)**[7] 4231 5-9-5 **83** ... LukeMorris 7 (Milton Bradley) *sn rdn and outpcd in rr: no hdwy tl styd on ins fnl f* **9/1**	76
0605	**5**	*hd*	**Volcanic Dust (IRE)**[53] 2731 4-8-13 **77** ... TomQueally 5 (Milton Bradley) *dwlt and n.m.r s: outpcd in last: no prog tl styd on wl fnl f: nrst fin* **25/1**	69
050	**6**	¾	**Bertoliver**[14] 4013 8-8-11 **75** ...(b) DaneO'Neill 2 (Stuart Williams) *gd spd to ld and crossed to nr side rail: hdd 2f out: lost 2nd and wknd qckly jst ins fnl f* **12/1**	65
0300	**7**	½	**Diamond Charlie (IRE)**[21] 3771 4-9-3 **84** ... SimonPearce(3) 4 (Simon Dow) *n.m.r s: hld up in rr: pushed along on outer 1/2-way: no prog* **10/1**	72
-302	**8**	1 ¾	**Osiris Way**[7] 4231 10-8-11 **75** ... JimCrowley 9 (Patrick Chamings) *sn outpcd in rr: pushed along 2f out: no prog: eased whn no ch ins fnl f* **15/2**	57

54.19s (-1.51) **Going Correction** -0.175s/f (Firm) 8 Ran SP% **112.0**
Speed ratings (Par 105): **105,102,102,97,97 96,95,92**
toteswingers: 1&2 £4.70, 1&3 £2.60, 2&3 3.20. CSF £26.02 CT £55.00 TOTE £5.10: £1.80, £1.40, £1.10; EX 30.50 Trifecta £85.40 Pool: £511.51 - 4.43 winning units..
Owner Edward Hyde **Bred** Edward Hyde **Trained** Epsom, Surrey

FOCUS
The turn of the older horses to strut their stuff down the world's fastest 5f. Not the strongest form for the grade.
Flash City(ITY) Official explanation: jockey said gelding became unbalanced final furlong, attempted to hang left and had nothing more to give at the finish.
Diamond Charlie(IRE) Official explanation: jockey said gelding lost its action

4502 BRITISH STALLION STUDS SUPPORTING BRITISH RACING E B F MAIDEN STKS — 6f

7:05 (7:06) (Class 5) 2-Y-0 **£3,881** (£1,155; £577; £288) **Stalls** High

Form				RPR
0	**1**		**Meringue Pie**[101] 1411 2-9-3 0 ... DaneO'Neill 1 (Richard Hannon) *trckd ldng pair: wnt 2nd over 2f out: shkn up and r.o to ld last 100yds: readily* **11/1**	81+
24	**2**	1 ¼	**Black Monk (IRE)**[63] 2420 2-9-3 0 ... PatDobbs 7 (Richard Hannon) *led after 1f: rdn 2f out: styd on wl but hdd and outpcd last 100yds* **11/4**[1]	77
03	**3**	*7*	**Blazing Knight (IRE)**[26] 3638 2-9-3 0 ... JimCrowley 5 (Ralph Beckett) *chsd ldrs in 4th: awkward whn rdn over 2f out: wnt 3rd wl over 1f out but ldng pair already clr* **3/1**[2]	56
6	**4**	2 ¼	**Pearl Bounty (IRE)**[63] 2420 2-9-3 0 ... JimmyFortune 6 (Andrew Balding) *hld up in 6th: outpcd whn rdn 2f out: n.d after* **4/1**[3]	49
3	**5**	½	**Clement (IRE)**[39] 3191 2-9-3 0 ... SebSanders 4 (Eve Johnson Houghton) *hld up in 5th: effrt to dispute 3rd 2f out: wknd over 1f out* **6/1**	48
00	**6**	*5*	**Birdy Boy (USA)**[29] 3491 2-9-3 0 ... JoeFanning 9 (Mark Johnston) *led 1f: chsd ldr to over 2f out: wknd* **20/1**	33
0264	**P**		**Cappadocia (IRE)**[14] 3996 2-9-3 69 ... MatthewDavies 3 (Mick Channon) *awkward s: detached in last whn appeared to lose action over 4f out: t.o whn p.u 3f out: dismntd* **11/2**	

1m 9.09s (-0.31) **Going Correction** -0.175s/f (Firm) 7 Ran SP% **114.4**
Speed ratings (Par 94): **95,93,84,81,80 73,**
toteswingers 1&2 £6.90, 1&3 £5.50, 2&3 £1.50 CSF £41.43 TOTE £11.90: £4.00, £2.20; EX 32.50 Trifecta £333.00 Pool: £561.15 - 1.24 winning units..
Owner R Morecombe, D Anderson, M Hughes **Bred** Mrs T Brudenell **Trained** East Everleigh, Wilts

FOCUS
This didn't look a strong maiden on paper, however the front pair pulled clear and both could be nice prospects.

NOTEBOOK
Meringue Pie disappointed when sent off favourite for the opening two-year-old race of Windsor's season but there was no disappointment here as he showed a fair level of ability to master a professional stablemate. A 60,000euros yearling from the first crop of Sakhee's Secret, he'll stay further and should make up into a nice prospect. (op 14-1 tchd 10-1)
Black Monk(IRE) stepped up on his first two starts (sent off favourite both times), attempting to make all. He had all bar his stablemate beat 2f out but couldn't muster a renewed effort when headed. This looks his trip and he should pay his way in nurseries. (op 5-2 tchd 10-3)
Blazing Knight(IRE) attracted support but looked limited being readily left behind. (op 11-4 tchd 9-4)
Pearl Bounty(IRE) was also left behind but might benefit from a step up in trip. (op 13-2)
Cappadocia(IRE) had run creditably here two weeks previously but took a false step early and was quickly eased off. Official explanation: jockey said colt stumbled leaving stalls and pulled up fearing injury (tchd 13-2)

4503 TOTAL DATA MANAGEMENT H'CAP — 7f

7:40 (7:41) (Class 4) (0-85,83) 3-Y-0+ **£5,175** (£1,540; £769; £384) **Stalls** Low

Form				RPR
1-40	**1**		**Go Dutch (IRE)**[47] 2930 3-9-5 **81** ... JimmyFortune 3 (Roger Varian) *trckd ldrs: 3rd st: pressed ldr jst over 2f out: rdn to ld jst over 1f out: drvn clr* **3/1**[1]	92+
22	**2**	1 ¾	**My Kingdom (IRE)**[27] 3557 6-10-0 **83** ...(t) StephenCraine 2 (Ian Williams) *trckd ldrs: 5th st: effrt on inner 2f out: drvn and r.o fnl f to take 2nd nr fin* **9/2**[2]	91
4161	**3**	½	**Dr Red Eye**[7] 4255 4-9-12 **81** 6ex ...(p) SilvestreDeSousa 1 (Scott Dixon) *led: rdn 2f out: hdd and one pce jst over 1f out: lost 2nd nr fin* **6/1**[3]	88
1030	**4**	*5*	**Aldermoor (USA)**[59] 2545 6-9-8 **77** ... WilliamCarson 6 (Stuart Williams) *wl in rr: 9th st: effrt and looking for room over 2f out: kpt on to take modest 4th fnl f: no ch* **18/1**	70
1620	**5**	*4*	**Tea Cup**[10] 4150 3-9-2 **78** ... PatDobbs 7 (Richard Hannon) *taken down early: pressed ldr to jst over 2f out: wknd qckly over 1f out* **10/1**	58
0552	**6**	2 ½	**Emiratesdotcom**[21] 3778 6-9-6 **75** ... LukeMorris 11 (Milton Bradley) *in tch: 7th and rdn st: outpcd over 2f out: n.d after* **16/1**	51
4-06	**7**	½	**Rondeau (GR)**[21] 3772 7-9-13 **82** ... JimCrowley 9 (Patrick Chamings) *taken down early: jockey removed blindfold after stalls opened: slowly away: wl bhd: 11th st: pushed along on wd outside over 2f out: passed btn rivals fr over 1f out: nvr involved* **14/1**	56+
642	**8**	2 ½	**Perfect Mission**[15] 3958 4-8-10 **72** ...(v) DanielMuscutt(7) 14 (Andrew Balding) *hld up fr wd draw: 8th st: rdn and no prog whn sltly hmpd 2f out: no ch after* **12/1**	40
-046	**9**	*shd*	**Batchelors Star (IRE)**[41] 3105 4-9-10 **79** ...(t[1]) JoeFanning 5 (Jim Boyle) *chsd ldrs: 6th st: sn rdn: outpcd over 2f out: wknd* **20/1**	46
-000	**10**	1 ¼	**Rulesn'regulations**[27] 3557 6-9-11 **80** ...(be) TomQueally 15 (Matthew Salaman) *c out of stalls slowly: wl in rr: 10th st: pushed along on outer over 2f out: no prog: hmpd and eased last 100yds* **20/1**	44
2-31	**11**	*1*	**Moodhill**[20] 3809 3-9-1 **77** ... PaulHanagan 4 (Charles Hills) *chsd ldrs: 4th and rdn st: sn lost pl and btn* **9/2**[2]	36

2-00 **12** *29* **Regal Approval**[45] 2975 4-9-6 **75** DaneO'Neill 13
(Jim Boyle) *jockey removed blindfold sme time after stalls opened: immediately t.o* **50/1**
1m 21.43s (-1.87) **Going Correction** -0.175s/f (Firm)
WFA 3 from 4yo+ 7lb **12** Ran SP% **121.7**
Speed ratings (Par 105): **103,101,100,94,90 87,86,83,83,82 81,48**
toteswingers: 1&2 £3.50, 1&3 £3.50, 2&3 £2.80. CSF £15.97 CT £77.06 TOTE £4.20: £1.90, £1.70, £3.80; EX 22.10 Trifecta £76.80 Pool: £542.30 - 5.22 winning units..
Owner K Allen, R Marchant, G Moss & G Jarvis **Bred** Wiji Bloodstock & Gerry Mullins **Trained** Newmarket, Suffolk
■ Stewards' Enquiry : William Carson two-day ban: careless riding (Aug 9-10)

FOCUS
A strong handicap featuring a smart performance from the well-backed three-year-old to beat two in-form older horses. The runner-up sets the standard.
Go Dutch(IRE) Official explanation: trainer's rep said, regarding apparent improvement in form, that the colt was suited by the better ground, drop in trip and class.
Regal Approval Official explanation: jockey said gelding was slowly away

4504 AGENTCITE H'CAP 1m 4f 10y
8:15 (8:20) (Class 5) (0-70,70) 3-Y-O+ **£3,234** (£962; £481; £240) **Stalls** Centre

Form RPR
0052 **1** **Arashi**[3] 4396 6-8-12 **54** (v) SilvestreDeSousa 3 68
(Derek Shaw) *a gng wl: trckd ldrs: 5th st: prog to go 2nd 2f out and led over 1f out: sn rdn clr* **4/1**[1]
2250 **2** *4* **Reset City**[52] 2751 6-9-8 **64** TomQueally 4 71
(Ian Williams) *hld up in midfield gng wl: 9th st: stdy prog on outer fr 3f out: rdn over 1f out: styd on to take 2nd last 50yds: no ch w wnr* **9/2**[2]
4-61 **3** *½* **Bouggatti**[30] 3468 4-10-0 **70** SebSanders 6 76
(Lady Herries) *sn prom: 3rd st: chsd ldr over 3f out to 2f out: styd on to chse wnr 1f out: no imp: lost 2nd last 50yds* **5/1**[3]
0360 **4** *1* **Iguacu**[33] 3392 8-8-9 **51** oh2 (p) LukeMorris 14 56
(Richard Price) *chsd ldrs: 6th st: sn rdn: styd on fr 2f out: tk 4th ins fnl f* **22/1**
0136 **5** *3* **Spiritual Art**[84] 1770 6-8-13 **55** (v[1]) StephenCraine 2 55
(Luke Dace) *pressed ldr: led 5f out: kicked clr ent st: hdd & wknd over 1f out* **20/1**
3606 **6** *5* **Rather Cool**[15] 3969 4-8-9 **51** oh4 (t) WilliamCarson 13 43
(John Bridger) *a in midfield on outer: pushed along in 7th st: plugged on fr over 2f out: no ch* **40/1**
002 **7** *1 ½* **El Libertador (USA)**[27] 3573 6-8-12 **54** (b) JimmyFortune 9 44
(Eric Wheeler) *towards rr: 11th st: rdn 3f out: kpt on but nvr gng pce to threaten* **20/1**
5025 **8** *½* **Coup De Grace (IRE)**[15] 3966 3-8-0 **59** JemmaMarshall(5) 12 48
(Pat Phelan) *hld up wl in rr: 13th st: nudged along and passed sme stragglers fr 2f out: nvr remotely involved* **16/1**
3-65 **9** *1 ½* **Squad**[174] 400 6-9-4 **63** (v) SimonPearce(3) 5 49
(Simon Dow) *v.s.a: hld up in last trio: 12th st: rdn 3f out: no great prog* **33/1**
0400 **10** *1 ¼* **Yes Chef**[21] 3782 5-9-8 **64** DaneO'Neill 7 48
(Chris Gordon) *sn restrained into midfield: 8th st: rdn 3f out: no prog and sn btn* **20/1**
3201 **11** *1 ¾* **Rodrigo De Freitas (IRE)**[27] 3573 5-9-3 **59** (v) PatCosgrave 16 44
(Jim Boyle) *trckd ldrs: 4th st: sn rdn and lost pl: eased fnl 2f* **20/1**
6- **12** *13* **Amen (IRE)**[23] 3990 4-9-11 **67** PatDobbs 8 28
(Gary Moore) *taken down early: hld up in last: shkn up 3f out: no prog and sn wknd* **20/1**
00-0 **13** *4 ½* **Comical**[62] 2440 3-9-2 **70** JoeFanning 15 24
(Mark Johnston) *led to 5f out: 2nd and rdn st: sn wknd qckly* **10/1**
010 **14** *29* **Autarch (USA)**[26] 3621 3-8-11 **65** JimCrowley 11
(Amanda Perrett) *prom to 5f out: 10th and wkng rapidly st: t.o* **14/1**
3342 **U** **Viola Da Gamba (IRE)**[31] 3448 3-8-5 **64** DavidKenny(5) 1
(William Knight) *rrd over and uns rdr as stalls opened* **11/2**
2m 37.83s (-1.07) **Going Correction** -0.175s/f (Firm)
WFA 3 from 4yo+ 12lb **15** Ran SP% **125.4**
Speed ratings (Par 103): **96,93,93,92,90 87,86,85,84,83 82,74,71,51,**
toteswingers: 1&2 £4.60, 1&3 £3.90, 2&3 £5.00. CSF £19.11 CT £96.43 TOTE £4.20: £1.30, £2.40, £2.30; EX 23.60 Trifecta £177.80 Pool: £569.59 - 2.37 winning units..
Owner Stuart Barnett **Bred** Wyck Hall Stud Ltd **Trained** Sproxton, Leics

FOCUS
An eventful start to the 1m4f handicap with Viola De Gamba rearing over as the stalls opened unseating David Kenny. Sound form for the grade and track.
Viola Da Gamba(IRE) Official explanation: jockey said filly reared as stalls opened and unseated

4505 PADDOCKS FILLIES' H'CAP 1m 2f 18y
8:45 (8:48) (Class 5) (0-75,75) 3-Y-O+ **£3,234** (£962; £481; £240) **Stalls** Low

Form RPR
4-62 **1** **Fresa**[7] 4256 3-9-0 **71** LukeMorris 6 77+
(Sir Mark Prescott Bt) *taken down early: sn trckd ldr: led over 2f out and sn drvn 2 l clr: all out to hold on nr fin* **2/1**[1]
03-0 **2** *hd* **Monopoli**[23] 3735 3-8-8 **65** JimCrowley 3 70+
(Ralph Beckett) *hld up in rr: disp 8th st: prog on wd outside over 2f out: chsd wnr 1f out: styd on: jst failed* **12/1**
20-3 **3** *shd* **Ice Nelly (IRE)**[52] 2767 4-9-5 **66** JimmyFortune 5 73+
(Hughie Morrison) *dwlt: hld up in last: effrt and 7th st: nt clr run 3f out to over 2f out: plenty to do after: prog on outer over 1f out: hrd rdn and hung lft ent fnl f: r.o after: jst too much to do* **6/1**[3]
1324 **4** *¾* **Dutch Diamond**[30] 3476 3-9-4 **75** NickyMackay 2 79
(John Gosden) *trckd ldrs: pushed along after 3f: lost pl downhill and disp 8th st: renewed effrt over 2f out: pressed for a pl fr over 1f out: styd on* **7/2**[2]
3303 **5** *1 ½* **Gold Show**[7] 4256 3-9-4 **75** MatthewDavies 10 76
(Mick Channon) *taken down early: rdn to ld: hdd over 2f out: chsd wnr to 1f out: one pce after* **10/1**
-044 **6** *1 ¾* **Emmuska**[12] 4091 3-9-2 **73** PatDobbs 1 70
(Richard Hannon) *hld up in tch: 5th st: rdn over 2f out: one pce and no real imp on ldrs* **13/2**
402 **7** *1* **Mount Abora (IRE)**[15] 3967 5-9-0 **61** AmirQuinn 7 56
(Laura Mongan) *cl up: 3rd st: rdn 3f out: one pce after: fdd over 1f out* **33/1**
0050 **8** *6* **Abishena (IRE)**[12] 4091 3-9-4 **75** JoeFanning 4 58
(Mark Johnston) *taken down early: prom: 4th st: sn rdn: one pce after tl wknd over 1f out: eased* **20/1**
662 **9** *2 ½* **Ermyntrude**[43] 3043 5-8-4 **56** oh1 JemmaMarshall(5) 9 34
(Pat Phelan) *hld up: 6th st: rdn over 2f out: no prog and wknd over 1f out* **16/1**
2m 9.9s (0.20) **Going Correction** -0.175s/f (Firm)
WFA 3 from 4yo+ 10lb **9** Ran SP% **113.5**
Speed ratings (Par 100): **92,91,91,91,89 88,87,82,80**
toteswingers 1&2 £7.00, 1&3 £1.60, 2&3 £8.30 CSF £27.45 CT £123.13 TOTE £2.90: £1.50, £4.30, £1.10; EX 28.90 Trifecta £183.00 Pool: £581.79 - 2.35 winning units..
Owner Miss K Rausing **Bred** Miss K Rausing **Trained** Newmarket, Suffolk

FOCUS
Another competitive affair to close the card. Ordianry form and the second and third were both perhaps unfortunate not to win.
T/Plt: £17.40 to a £1 stake. Pool: £62448.24 - 2618.97 winning tickets T/Qpdt: £6.40 to £1 stake. Pool: £4140.85 - 477.85 winning tickets JN

4001 FOLKESTONE (R-H)
Thursday, July 26

OFFICIAL GOING: Good to firm (watered; round course 8.5; straight course: stands' side 9.2; far side 8.5)
Wind: virtually nil Weather: hot and sunny

4506 KMFM KENT'S BIGGEST HITS H'CAP 7f (S)
5:50 (5:52) (Class 6) (0-60,60) 3-Y-O **£1,704** (£503; £251) **Stalls** High

Form RPR
3632 **1** **Represent (IRE)**[9] 4196 3-9-7 **60** SaleemGolam 5 70
(Mick Channon) *stdd s: hld up towards rr: effrt and nt clr run briefly 2f out: rdn and gd hdwy over 1f out: led ins fnl f: sn clr and r.o strly: readily* **9/2**[3]
4221 **2** *3 ¼* **Marinus (IRE)**[16] 3943 3-8-12 **58** ThomasBrown(7) 9 59
(Sylvester Kirk) *in tch: swtchd rt and effrt 2f out: rdn to ld over 1f out: hdd ins fnl f: sn outpcd by wnr and kpt on same pce* **4/1**[2]
-550 **3** *½* **Arrow Lake (FR)**[24] 3694 3-9-4 **57** JamesDoyle 7 57
(Noel Quinlan) *hld up towards rr: swtchd rt and gd hdwy to chse ldrs and drvn jst over 1f out: styd on same pce fnl f* **20/1**
44-0 **4** *shd* **Classic Falcon (IRE)**[96] 1529 3-9-4 **60** [1] AdamBeschizza(3) 8 60
(William Haggas) *hld up in midfield: rdn and effrt 2f out: chsd ldrs and drvn over 1f out: styd on same pce fnl f* **10/1**
00-2 **5** *3* **Scouting For Girls**[132] 917 3-9-5 **58** ShaneKelly 12 50+
(Jim Boyle) *trckd ldrs on stands' rail: wnt 2nd over 2f out: gng wl but nt clr run 2f out: lost pl and eventually managed to switch rt 1f out and kpt on: no ch w ldrs* **14/1**
5463 **6** *hd* **Joyful Spirit (IRE)**[15] 3966 3-9-4 **57** (b) EddieAhern 14 48
(John Dunlop) *led and racd against stands' rail: rdn and hdd over 1f out: sn btn: wknd fnl f* **7/2**[1]
150 **7** *3 ¼* **Atlantis Crossing (IRE)**[28] 3547 3-9-0 **58** NathanAlison(5) 13 40
(Jim Boyle) *t.k.h: hld up in rr and racd against stands' rail: effrt and nt clr run 2f out: lost all ch and fnlly swtchd rt 1f out: kpt on but no ch* **9/1**
0005 **8** *1 ¾* **Brailsford (IRE)**[9] 4192 3-9-5 **58** (v) RoystonFfrench 10 35
(Ismail Mohammed) *chsd ldr tl over 2f out: sn struggling u.p: wkng whn hmpd 2f out: no ch after* **40/1**
0-00 **9** *hd* **Whinging Willie (IRE)**[56] 2628 3-9-7 **60** (p) RichardMullen 6 37
(Gary Moore) *hld up towards rr: effrt u.p over 2f out: no imp over 1f out: wknd fnl f* **33/1**
6-40 **10** *7* **Allegra Byron**[87] 1705 3-9-6 **59** LeeNewman 1 17
(Jonathan Portman) *s.i.s: a towards rr and racd towards centre: wknd 2f out: bhd fnl f* **50/1**
305 **11** *3 ¼* **Exceedexpectations (IRE)**[15] 3972 3-9-7 **60** HayleyTurner 2
(Michael Bell) *chsd ldrs: rdn and struggling over 2f out: wknd wl over 1f out: bhd fnl f* **8/1**
5462 **12** *2 ½* **Moody Dancer**[16] 3949 3-9-2 **58** MatthewCosham(3) 4
(William Muir) *in tch towards centre: rdn and fnd nil ent fnl 2f: sn wknd and bhd fnl f* **11/1**
-005 **13** *4 ½* **Strategic Action (IRE)**[14] 4001 3-8-13 **52** (p) MartinLane 11
(Linda Jewell) *chsd ldrs tl 1/2-way: sn lost pl: bhd over 1f out* **28/1**
1m 26.29s (-1.01) **Going Correction** -0.225s/f (Firm) **13** Ran SP% **121.2**
Speed ratings (Par 98): **96,92,91,91,88 87,84,82,82,74 70,67,62**
toteswingers: 1&2 £4.90, 1&3 £24.00, 2&3 £33.50. CSF £21.93 CT £335.71 TOTE £5.50: £1.90, £2.00, £7.30; EX 26.40.
Owner Insignia Racing (Ensign) **Bred** Whatton Manor Stud **Trained** West Ilsley, Berks

FOCUS
Low-grade stuff and, barring a couple of exceptions, these were a fairly exposed bunch. The principals all came from off the pace suggesting the gallop was sound. The winner ran to a similar level as her Yarmouth run but this form is not the most solid.
Arrow Lake(FR) Official explanation: jockey said filly suffered interference in running
Moody Dancer Official explanation: jockey said filly suffered interference in running

4507 IRISH STALLION STUD FARMS E B F MAIDEN STKS 7f (S)
6:20 (6:21) (Class 5) 2-Y-O **£3,234** (£962; £481; £240) **Stalls** High

Form RPR
4344 **1** **Ayaar (IRE)**[13] 4056 2-9-3 93 MartinHarley 9 86
(Mick Channon) *hld up towards rr: hdwy over 2f out: rdn to chal ent fnl f: led ins fnl f: r.o wl* **11/4**[1]
2 *1 ¾* **Brave Command (USA)** 2-9-3 0 ShaneKelly 13 83+
(Mahmood Al Zarooni) *t.k.h: hld up in midfield: nt clr run and shuffled bk ent fnl 2f: swtchd rt and hdwy towards centre jst over 1f out: r.o wl to go 2nd wl ins fnl f* **3/1**[2]
30 **3** *1 ¾* **Requested**[13] 4066 2-9-3 0 AhmedAjtebi 12 77
(Mahmood Al Zarooni) *in tch in midfield: hdwy to chse ldrs 3f out: chsd ldr 2f out: sn rdn and ld jst over 1f out: hdd and no ex ins fnl f* **10/3**[3]
42 **4** *hd* **Mayaasem**[21] 3777 2-9-3 0 JamesDoyle 3 76
(Charles Hills) *led and crossed to r against stands' rail: rdn and hrd pressed wl over 1f out: hdd jst over 1f out: no ex and outpcd fnl 150yds* **9/2**
43 **5** *1 ¾* **Pira Palace (IRE)**[27] 3554 2-8-12 0 RichardMullen 6 67
(Sir Michael Stoute) *chsd ldng pair: rdn and unable qck wl over 1f out: outpcd fnl f* **17/2**
6 *nse* **Captain McCaw** 2-9-3 0 MartinDwyer 5 72
(Brian Meehan) *dwlt: t.k.h and sn rcvrd to chse ldrs: rdn wl over 1f out: unable qck and btn 1f out: kpt on same pce* **28/1**
40 **7** *6* **Ana Shababiya (IRE)**[47] 2929 2-8-12 0 RoystonFfrench 7 51
(Ismail Mohammed) *stdd s: hld up towards rr: rdn 3f out: wknd wl over 1f out* **66/1**
8 *nk* **Knight's Parade (IRE)** 2-9-3 0 HayleyTurner 8 55
(Amanda Perrett) *rn green and sn rdn along in rr: sme hdwy over 2f out: wknd wl over 1f out* **16/1**

9 4 **Thomasina** 2-8-12 0 ..... EddieAhern 2 40
(Denis Coakley) *s.i.s: hld up in tch in midfield: rdn over 2f out: sn struggling and wknd wl over 1f out* **22/1**

0 10 ½ **Rosia Bay**[22] 3764 2-8-12 0 ..... MatthewChadwick 1 39
(Charles Hills) *chsd ldr tl 2f out: sn lost pl and bhd 1f out* **50/1**

1m 26.76s (-0.54) **Going Correction** -0.225s/f (Firm) **10** Ran SP% **120.6**
Speed ratings (Par 94): **94,92,90,89,87 87,80,80,75,75**
toteswingers: 1&2 £3.80, 1&3 £1.10, 2&3 £4.70. CSF £11.36 TOTE £3.40: £1.10, £1.50, £1.90; EX 9.20.
Owner Sheikh Mohammed Bin Khalifa Al Maktoum **Bred** Blue Bloodstock Ltd **Trained** West Ilsley, Berks

FOCUS
Not a bad maiden by the looks of things and a few of these could be useful.

NOTEBOOK
Ayaar(IRE) has already proved himself to be quite smart having only been beaten four lengths in a Group 2 in Ireland this season and although disappointing back in maiden company at Newbury last time, he bounced back in good style to sweep down the outside of the field and win this decisively. This was Ayaar's first try on ground faster than good and he clearly handles it well, indeed it might even be the making of him. He's in the Gimcrack and we might not have seen the best of this colt just yet. (op 5-2)
Brave Command(USA) cost a packet as a 2yo and shaped with a deal of promise in second. Given the way he finished, he might well have won had he not been shuffled back when the race was beginning to unwind entering the final two furlongs. He already looks good enough to win in ordinary maiden company and could be a decent prospect. (op 11-4 tchd 5-2)
Requested, a stablemate of the second, bounced back from his disappointing run at Newmarket last time and looks the type to do better in handicaps down the line, especially when stepped up in trip (quite stoutly bred on dam's side). (op 11-2)
Mayaasem, who made the running, clearly has ability and is qualified for a handicap mark now, although this step up to 7f didn't bring about any significant improvement. (op 11-2 tchd 6-1)
Ana Shababiya(IRE) Official explanation: jockey said filly ran too freely

4508 KMFM RADIO MADE IN KENT (S) STKS 6f
6:55 (6:55) (Class 6) 3-Y-O+ **£1,704** (£503; £251) **Stalls** High

Form RPR

03 1 **Desert Strike**[55] 2647 6-9-6 68 ..... (p) MatthewChadwick 1 79
(Charles Hills) *taken down early: mde all and sn crossed to r against stands' rail: pushed along over 1f out: in command and kpt on wl fnl f* **15/2**

0660 2 1¾ **Efistorm**[16] 3944 11-9-6 72 ..... HayleyTurner 5 73
(Joseph Tuite) *chsd ldrs: chsd wnr over 2f out: rdn and styd on same pce fr over 1f out* **5/1**[3]

610 3 1¼ **Kingswinford (IRE)**[5] 4317 6-9-3 82 ..... MatthewCosham(3) 3 69
(David Evans) *in tch: niggled along 1/2-way: rdn and chsd ldng pair wl over 1f out: styd on same pce and no imp after* **10/11**[1]

4-04 4 hd **Silver Wind**[181] 328 7-9-0 74 ..... (v) ShaneKelly 6 63
(Alan McCabe) *stdd s: hld up in rr: nt clr run over 2f out: rdn and hdwy wl over 1f out: kpt on fnl f: no ch w wnr* **7/2**[2]

-046 5 7 **Louphole**[23] 3717 10-9-0 53 ..... EddieAhern 2 40
(J R Jenkins) *chsd ldrs: rdn and unable qck 2f out: wknd u.p over 1f out* **14/1**

-550 6 1½ **Norwood Lane**[35] 3314 3-8-9 54 ..... (b[1]) RoystonFfrench 4 35
(Peter Hedger) *stdd s: hld up in rr: effrt whn sltly hmpd and swtchd rt 2f out: sn rdn and no prog: wknd over 1f out* **33/1**

4 7 1¾ **Toms River Tess (IRE)**[30] 3466 4-8-9 41 ..... KellyHarrison 8 25
(Zoe Davison) *chsd ldrs: rdn wl over 2f out: edgd rt and wknd over 1f out* **33/1**

4-60 8 6 **Thalia Grace**[28] 3546 5-8-9 45 ..... MartinDwyer 7
(William Knight) *taken down early: chsd wnr tl over 2f out: sn lost pl and towards rr whn edgd rt 2f out: bhd fnl f* **22/1**

1m 11.61s (-1.09) **Going Correction** -0.225s/f (Firm)
WFA 3 from 4yo+ 5lb **8** Ran SP% **119.9**
Speed ratings (Par 101): **98,95,94,93,84 82,80,72**
toteswingers: 1&2 £5.30, 1&3 £2.90, 2&3 £1.70. CSF £45.71 TOTE £10.20: £3.50, £1.10, £1.02; EX 42.00.The winner was bought in for 8,000gns.
Owner S E Sangster & Richard Morecombe **Bred** Mrs Mary Rowlands **Trained** Lambourn, Berks

FOCUS
The first pair in the market disappointed in this ordinary handicap. The winner is rated back to his old turf best.
Toms River Tess(IRE) Official explanation: jockey said filly hung right
Thalia Grace Official explanation: jockey said mare hung right

4509 LADBROKES.COM H'CAP 6f
7:25 (7:25) (Class 5) (0-70,70) 3-Y-O **£2,385** (£704; £352) **Stalls** High

Form RPR

053 1 **Tinzapeas**[15] 3954 3-9-2 65 ..... (v) MartinHarley 6 69
(Mick Channon) *hld up in tch: gng wl but nt clr run 2f out: rdn and effrt to chal ent fnl f: drvn to ld jst ins fnl f: hld on cl home* **9/2**[3]

001 2 hd **Rum Punch**[57] 2611 3-9-2 65 ..... EddieAhern 4 68
(Eve Johnson Houghton) *travelled wl: chsd ldr tl led 2f out: rdn over 1f out: hdd jst ins fnl f: rallied gamely u.p fnl 75yds: jst hld* **7/2**[2]

0650 3 2½ **Judas Jo (FR)**[22] 3762 3-9-7 70 ..... (p) StevieDonohoe 7 65
(Gay Kelleway) *s.i.s: in tch in rr: switching out rt over 3f out: hdwy ent fnl 2f: drvn and pressed ldr over 1f out: no ex 1f out: wknd towards fin* **6/1**

6516 4 8 **Maria Montez**[34] 3343 3-8-11 60 ..... MartinLane 1 30
(J W Hills) *chsd ldrs: pressing ldrs and rdn over 1f out: fnd little and btn 1f out: wknd fnl f* **11/1**

-336 5 ½ **Conowen**[27] 3567 3-9-4 67 ..... HayleyTurner 3 35
(William Jarvis) *led tl rdn and hdd 2f out: sn drvn and btn over 1f out: wknd fnl f* **6/1**

0-06 6 2½ **Willow Beauty**[57] 2610 3-8-2 51 oh2 ..... KieranO'Neill 5 11
(J R Jenkins) *pushed along leaving stalls: sn in tch in midfield: rdn and lost pl jst over 2f out: wknd over 1f out* **25/1**

2-50 7 3½ **Dark Don (IRE)**[24] 3702 3-9-6 69 ..... JamesDoyle 2 18
(Charles Hills) *sn pushed along in last trio: drvn and no prog ent fnl 2f: wknd over 1f out: wl btn and eased ins fnl f* **2/1**[1]

1m 12.27s (-0.43) **Going Correction** -0.225s/f (Firm) **7** Ran SP% **114.5**
Speed ratings (Par 100): **93,92,89,78,78 74,70**
toteswingers: 1&2 £2.10, 1&3 £5.20, 2&3 £4.80. CSF £20.63 TOTE £5.70: £4.60, £3.80; EX 21.20.
Owner M Channon **Bred** Mike Channon Bloodstock Ltd **Trained** West Ilsley, Berks

FOCUS
Not the most competitive of handicaps and very few got into it. The front two, who were always close the pace, came nicely clear. The winner is rated back to last October's winning form with a step up from the runner-up.

Dark Don(IRE) Official explanation: trainer's rep said colt did not handle the track

4510 HAYNES TRUCKS H'CAP 1m 4f
8:00 (8:00) (Class 6) (0-60,60) 3-Y-O **£1,704** (£503; £251) **Stalls** High

Form RPR

4041 1 **Kaiser Wilhelm (IRE)**[8] 4214 3-9-5 58 6ex ..... (t) StevieDonohoe 1 69+
(Paul Cole) *chsd ldrs: rdn to chse ldr and swtchd lft over 1f out: qcknd to ld 1f out: r.o wl and a readily holding runner-up ins fnl f* **4/1**[2]

6-46 2 1 **Geanie Mac (IRE)**[145] 784 3-9-6 59 ..... (b[1]) ShaneKelly 3 66
(Tim Pitt) *led: rdn 2f out: hdd 1f out: kpt on wl for clr 2nd but readily hld by wnr fnl f* **25/1**

006 3 7 **Runway Girl (IRE)**[25] 3664 3-9-6 59 ..... JamesDoyle 10 55+
(Roger Charlton) *s.i.s: racd off the pce in last quartet: stl plenty to do and effrt 2f out: hdwy jst over 1f out: no ch w ldng pair but kpt on to go 3rd ins fnl f* **15/2**

0-22 4 hd **Silver Six**[8] 4214 3-8-11 50 ..... EddieAhern 4 46+
(Sheena West) *in tch in midfield: rdn and effrt to chse ldrs over 1f out: keeping on same pce whn hmpd 1f out: no ch w ldrs but pressing for 3rd and kpt on ins fnl f* **7/2**[1]

4300 5 2 **Bondi Mist (IRE)**[25] 3671 3-9-5 58 ..... LeeNewman 11 50
(Jonathan Portman) *t.k.h: chsd ldrs: rdn and effrt jst over 2f out: 4th and outpcd whn sltly hmpd ent fnl f: no threat to ldrs and one pce after* **22/1**

-064 6 hd **Camrock Star (IRE)**[34] 2787 3-9-0 56 ..... MatthewCosham(3) 12 48
(David Evans) *stdd s: hld up in last quartet: rdn and hdwy on outer over 2f out: no imp on ldng pair and one pce fr over 1f out* **12/1**

-405 7 1¼ **Onertother**[10] 4153 3-9-7 60 ..... MartinHarley 6 50
(Joseph Tuite) *t.k.h: chsd ldr for 2f: wnt 2nd again over 7f out tl over 1f out: 3rd and wkng whn hung rt 1f out: fdd ins fnl f* **6/1**[3]

0000 8 3¼ **Fleeting Indian (IRE)**[15] 3966 3-8-7 46 oh1 ..... SaleemGolam 2 31
(Linda Jewell) *hld up in midfield: effrt on inner 2f out: sme hdwy but stl plenty to do whn n.m.r over 1f out: wl btn fnl f* **80/1**

0-43 9 1 **Isobella**[29] 3483 3-9-1 54 ..... RichardMullen 5 37
(Hughie Morrison) *hld up in last quartet: rdn and effrt ent fnl 2f: no prog and wl btn over 1f out* **4/1**[2]

1466 10 nk **Excellent News (IRE)**[58] 2578 3-9-4 57 ..... MartinLane 7 40
(J W Hills) *stdd s: t.k.h: hld up in midfield: rdn and no hdwy jst over 2f out: wl btn over 1f out* **20/1**

0-00 11 1½ **Feb Thirtyfirst**[15] 3965 3-9-1 54 ..... KieranO'Neill 13 34
(Sheena West) *t.k.h: chsd ldr after 2f tl over 7f out: steadily lost pl: bhd and rdn jst over 2f out: wknd 2f out* **16/1**

0004 12 3 **Imperial Elegance**[14] 4006 3-8-7 46 oh1 ..... RoystonFfrench 8 22
(Mick Channon) *hld up in midfield: lost pl and dropped to last pair 3f out: wl btn fnl 3f* **33/1**

0500 13 8 **Scripturist**[66] 2353 3-8-7 46 oh1 ..... HayleyTurner 9 9
(William Jarvis) *a in rr: toiling 3f out: wl bhd fnl 2f* **25/1**

2m 38.73s (-2.17) **Going Correction** -0.225s/f (Firm) **13** Ran SP% **122.8**
Speed ratings (Par 98): **98,97,92,92,91 91,90,88,87,87 86,84,78**
toteswingers: 1&2 £19.60, 1&3 £15.00, 2&3 £96.70. CSF £111.37 CT £743.05 TOTE £5.50: £1.70, £11.40, £3.00; EX 197.00.
Owner D S Lee **Bred** R N Auld **Trained** Whatcombe, Oxon
■ Stewards' Enquiry : Stevie Donohoe caution: careless riding.

FOCUS
Not much depth to this handicap and the pace looked steady until things quickened up sharply on the turn for home. Those to the fore were clear best placed to take advantage and the front two had it between them in the straight.

4511 LADBROKESBINGO.COM H'CAP 1m 1f 149y
8:35 (8:38) (Class 5) (0-70,70) 3-Y-O+ **£2,385** (£704; £352) **Stalls** Centre

Form RPR

0-00 1 **Croquembouche (IRE)**[34] 3347 3-9-4 70 ..... EddieAhern 1 81+
(Ed de Giles) *pushed along to ld after 1f: mde rest and set gd gallop: rdn and fnd ex 2f out: 2 l clr and in command fnl 100yds: eased towards fin: pressed and pushed along again last strides* **5/1**[3]

0030 2 nk **Standpoint**[29] 3503 6-10-0 70 ..... HayleyTurner 7 78
(Conor Dore) *in tch in midfield: rdn and effrt ent fnl 2f: hdwy to chse clr wnr over 1f out: styd on but no imp tl clsd qckly on eased wnr towards fin* **7/1**

0/00 3 hd **Seeking The Buck (USA)**[36] 3278 8-9-12 68 ..... MartinDwyer 6 76+
(Amy Weaver) *racd off the pce in last trio: rdn and stl plenty to do and rdn wl over 1f out: hdwy and swtchd lft ent fnl f: r.o v strly fnl 100yds: nt quite get up* **12/1**

4410 4 2 **Foster's Road**[11] 1982 3-8-9 61 ..... MartinHarley 5 65
(Mick Channon) *in tch in midfield: effrt u.p jst over 2f out: styd on ins fnl f but nvr quite gng pce to chal* **12/1**

540 5 1 **Tallevu (IRE)**[24] 3697 3-8-11 63 ..... JamesDoyle 4 65
(Tom Dascombe) *chsd ldrs: rdn over 2f out: edgd rt u.p and unable qck 2f out: kpt on but no threat to wnr fnl f* **2/1**[1]

6-35 6 nk **Gold Sceptre (FR)**[34] 3347 3-9-4 70 ..... (b[1]) KieranO'Neill 11 71
(Richard Hannon) *racd off the pce in last quartet: rdn and effrt over 2f out: styng on but no threat to wnr whn short of room 1f out: one pce after* **4/1**[2]

0340 7 ½ **Regal Rave (USA)**[49] 2851 5-8-9 51 oh3 ..... (v) RoystonFfrench 8 51
(Peter Hedger) *hld up off the pce in last trio: rdn and effrt 2f out: drvn and hdwy 1f out: styd on wl ins fnl f: nvr trbld ldrs* **20/1**

504 8 4½ **Saucy Buck (IRE)**[40] 3153 4-9-5 61 ..... (t) ShaneKelly 2 52
(Jamie Poulton) *chsd ldrs: rdn and effrt on inner whn hung rt u.p over 1f out: wknd ins fnl f* **14/1**

0533 9 4 **Taqaat (USA)**[27] 3573 4-9-2 58 ..... RichardMullen 3 40
(Tim McCarthy) *sn pushed along to ld: hdd after 1f: chsd ldr after tl unable qck u.p wl over 1f out: wknd 1f out* **10/1**

26/0 10 ¾ **King Of The Moors (USA)**[56] 2621 9-9-2 58 ..... (p) KellyHarrison 10 39
(John Spearing) *hld up wl off the pce in last trio: n.d* **25/1**

2m 3.17s (-1.73) **Going Correction** -0.225s/f (Firm)
WFA 3 from 4yo+ 10lb **10** Ran SP% **122.3**
Speed ratings (Par 103): **97,96,96,95,94 93,93,89,86,86**
toteswingers 1&2 £8.10, 1&3 £10.80, 2&3 £10.60 CSF £42.09 CT £409.63 TOTE £12.90: £4.10, £4.40, £5.90; EX 57.40.
Owner John Manser **Bred** Ballymacoll Stud Farm Ltd **Trained** Ledbury, H'fords

FOCUS
Most of these had something to prove and the form probably isn't that strong, even for this level. The winner is rated back to his 2yo best.
T/Plt: £129.60 to a £1 stake. Pool: £45817.29 - 258.0 winning tickets T/Qpdt: £85.80 to a £1 stake. Pool: £3479.02 - 30.0 winning tickets SP

4470 **SANDOWN** (R-H)

Thursday, July 26

OFFICIAL GOING: Good to firm (firm in places on round course)

Far side rail on Sprint track moved 3yds inside. Inner configuration on Round course and all distances as advertised.

Wind: Nil Weather: Sunny

4512 BRITISH STALLION STUDS SUPPORTING BRITISH RACING EBF MAIDEN STKS 5f 6y

2:00 (2:00) (Class 5) 2-Y-O **£3,881** (£1,155; £577; £288) **Stalls** Low

Form					RPR
2	**1**		**Pearl Acclaim (IRE)**[47] 2934 2-9-3 0 ... PatDobbs 8 (Richard Hannon) *trckd ldrs: chal 2f out: sn ld: qcknd fnl f: easily* **2/11**[1]		86+
	2	*3*	**Baron Run** 2-9-0 0 ... MichaelMetcalfe(3) 2 (Mrs K Burke) *trckd ldrs: drvn over 1f out: styd on to take 2nd fnl 120yds but nvr any ch w easy wnr* **14/1**		72+
04	**3**	*3/4*	**Pal Of The Cat**[10] 4148 2-9-0 0 ... AdamBeschizza(3) 6 (Brian Gubby) *led: rdn and jnd 2f out: hdd sn after: one pce and lost 2nd fnl 120yds* **66/1**		69
40	**4**	*2*	**Red Star Lady (IRE)**[68] 2261 2-8-12 0 ... MartinHarley 3 (Mrs K Burke) *chsd ldrs: rdn over 2f out: wknd ins fnl f* **20/1**		57
6	**5**	*hd*	**Red Dragon (IRE)**[75] 2073 2-9-3 0 ... MatthewChadwick 1 (Charles Hills) *in rr but in tch: pushed along fr 2f out and styd on same pce* **12/1**[3]		61
	6	*hd*	**Betzyoucan** 2-8-12 0 ... SilvestreDeSousa 7 (Mark Johnston) *in tch: drvn along 1/2-way: styd on fnl f but nvr gng pce to get into contention* **10/1**[2]		56

1m 1.09s (-0.51) **Going Correction** -0.25s/f (Firm) **6** Ran SP% **114.3**

Speed ratings (Par 94): **94,89,88,84,84 84**

toteswingers 1&2 £2.10, 2&3 £10.40, 1&3 £3.9 CSF £4.62 TOTE £1.30: £1.02, £7.30; EX 5.40 Trifecta £85.30 Pool: £792.29 - 6.87 winning units..

Owner Pearl Bloodstock Ltd **Bred** Awbeg Stud **Trained** East Everleigh, Wilts

FOCUS

The ground had firmed up from the previous evening with the sprint course Good to Firm (GoingStick 8.6) and the round course Good to Firm, Firm in places (GoingStick 9.0). An uncompetitive maiden and long odds-on backers had few worries. The bare form can't be rated any better and the winner may get a good nursery mark.

NOTEBOOK

Pearl Acclaim(IRE) ♦'s second to his stablemate Havana Gold on his Newmarket debut over 6f last month has since been boosted, with the winner going in again, and he had little difficulty in going one better, travelling well on the outside of the field and finding plenty once asked. He appeared to take to the quicker surface well and, with a return to further unlikely to bother him, he looks set for better things.

Baron Run, an already gelded 13,000GBP yearling out of a dual winner at up to 1m in Italy, made a taking debut, especially as he was keen early and looked uncomfortable on the ground in the second half of the contest. Despite that he came home well and it shouldn't be long before he gets off the mark. (tchd 12-1)

Pal Of The Cat hadn't looked an easy ride in his first two starts, but didn't seem to do much wrong this time under positive tactics. He was just outclassed by the front pair from over a furlong out and now gets a nursery mark.

Red Star Lady(IRE), well beaten in her previous start having shown ability on her Kempton debut, was another to show good pace for much of the journey and also now gets a mark. (op 25-1)

Red Dragon(IRE) never got into it following a slow break on his Haydock debut back in May and didn't make much impression from the back of the field this time either. (op 14-1)

Betzyoucan, who cost 20,000gns as a 2-y-o, is a sister to a winner at up to 1m1f and a half-sister to three other winners, but she proved far too green to do herself justice on this debut. (op 12-1)

4513 YOUNG STAYERS H'CAP 1m 6f

2:30 (2:30) (Class 3) (0-90,88) 3-Y-O **£6,663** (£1,982; £990; £495) **Stalls** Low

Form					RPR
4112	**1**		**Bridgehampton**[26] 3621 3-8-2 **69** ... HayleyTurner 5 (Michael Bell) *trckd ldr: chal 3f out: sn led and drvn: rdn fnl f: styd strly* **9/2**[2]		77
3221	**2**	*1*	**Muntasir (IRE)**[22] 3763 3-9-6 **87** ... FrankieDettori 2 (Saeed Bin Suroor) *hld up in rr: gd hdwy over 2f out: chsd wnr 1f out and sn drvn: no imp and hld fnl 120yds* **11/4**[1]		93
3-32	**3**	*1 1/2*	**Daneking**[69] 2258 3-8-13 **80** ... RobertHavlin 9 (John Gosden) *sn led: jnd 3f out: sn hdd: one pce 2f out: rallied on ins but nt much daylight fnl 120yds: tk 3rd last strides* **6/1**[3]		84
-413	**4**	*shd*	**Winner's Wish**[43] 3033 3-9-1 **82** ... ShaneKelly 6 (Jeremy Noseda) *chsd ldrs: rdn and flashed tail 2f out whn chsng wnr: no imp and one pce fnl f: lost 3rd last strides* **7/1**		86
-401	**5**	*2*	**Mubaraza (IRE)**[27] 3592 3-9-4 **85** ... PaulHanagan 1 (John Dunlop) *in rr: rdn and hdwy over 2f out: nvr gng pce to rch wnr: wknd fnl f* **11/4**[1]		86
0013	**6**	*1 3/4*	**Tingo In The Tale (IRE)**[24] 3711 3-8-8 **75** ... SilvestreDeSousa 3 (David Arbuthnot) *chsd ldrs: rdn and hung rt 2f out: sn btn* **25/1**		74
31	**7**	*7*	**New Youmzain (FR)**[68] 2288 3-8-13 **80** ... SamHitchcott 8 (Mick Channon) *in rr: rdn and no ch fr 3f out* **10/1**		69

3m 6.22s (1.72) **Going Correction** -0.15s/f (Firm) **7** Ran SP% **111.2**

Speed ratings (Par 104): **89,88,87,87,86 85,81**

toteswingers 1&2 £1.10, 2&3 £2.90, 1&3 £4.30 CSF £16.30 CT £70.61 TOTE £7.10: £2.70, £1.10; EX 16.00 Trifecta £47.90 Pool: £765.60 - 11.80 winning units..

Owner M B Hawtin **Bred** The Kingwood Partnership **Trained** Newmarket, Suffolk

FOCUS

This trip was a new experience for the majority of these and the pace looked solid enough, but the time was quite slow. The form should work out and the winner looks capable of better.

NOTEBOOK

Bridgehampton had been narrowly thwarted in his bid for a hat-trick on the Lingfield Polytrack last time and was up another 4lb over an extra 2f, but he put matters right here having been ridden much more prominently than last time. Sent to the front over 2f out, he showed a good attitude to keep his rivals at bay and had no problem with this much quicker ground. He has more to offer as a stayer. (op 4-1)

Muntasir(IRE) was also up another 2f in trip after comfortably winning a Kempton Polytrack maiden and was 5lb higher. He looked a danger when making up ground on the wide outside coming to the last quarter-mile, but he tended to hang about inside the last furlong and could never quite get to the winner. He may not want the ground quite this quick. (op 3-1 tchd 5-2)

Daneking, taking another step up in trip off a 3lb higher mark, was soon sent to the front and set a reasonable pace, but despite being headed by the winner over 2f from home he rallied well and managed to get back up for third close home. He stayed the trip alright, but may need an easier surface to show his best. (op 4-1)

Winner's Wish proved her stamina when winning over this C&D in May and moved up to hold every chance halfway up the straight, but her effort eventually flattened out. She was 9lb higher than for her win here, so may need to drop a bit. (op 13-2 tchd 8-1)

Mubaraza(IRE) appreciated the step up to 1m5f when winning at Newmarket last time and was put up 6lb for that, but he never made much impression from off the pace here. (op 9-2)

Tingo In The Tale(IRE), another up 2f in trip, didn't have much room to play with from over 2f out but it didn't make that much difference. He lacks the scope of a few of these, but really needs softer ground.

New Youmzain(FR), making his handicap debut on his third outing, was never out of last place and was beaten a long way out. (op 8-1)

4514 WEATHERBYS VAT SERVICES STAR STKS (LISTED RACE) (FILLIES) 7f 16y

3:05 (3:05) (Class 1) 2-Y-O

£13,043 (£4,945; £2,474; £1,232; £618; £310) **Stalls** Low

Form					RPR
01	**1**		**Roz**[22] 3764 2-8-12 0 ... JimCrowley 7 (Harry Dunlop) *mde all: rdn over 2f out: styd on gamely thrght fnl f* **28/1**		100
21	**2**	*1 3/4*	**Savanna La Mar (USA)**[27] 3554 2-8-12 0 ... LukeMorris 8 (Sir Mark Prescott Bt) *sn chsng ldr: rdn over 3f out: styd on fnl f but a being hld by wnr* **13/2**		95
1	**3**	*3/4*	**Purr Along**[16] 3948 2-8-12 0 ... MartinDwyer 2 (William Muir) *t.k.h early: chsd ldrs: rdn over 2f out: kpt on same pce u.p fnl f* **12/1**		94
1	**4**	*shd*	**Go Angellica (IRE)**[47] 2917 2-8-12 0 ... MartinLane 1 (David Simcock) *t.k.h in rr: hdwy and rdn 2f out: styd on fnl f to cl on 3rd but nvr any ch of rching wnr* **10/1**		93
14	**5**	*6*	**Amazonas (IRE)**[34] 3326 2-8-12 0 ... FrankieDettori 10 (Ed Dunlop) *chsd ldrs: pushed along 2f out: wknd over 1f out* **10/3**[2]		78
21	**6**	*4 1/2*	**Mollyvator (IRE)**[21] 3776 2-8-12 78 ... MartinHarley 4 (Mrs K Burke) *in rr: rdn and sme hdwy 3f out: faltered sn after and then hung lft and btn* **5/1**[3]		66
21	**7**	*15*	**Miss You Too**[13] 4069 2-8-12 0 ... MatthewDavies 9 (Mick Channon) *s.i.s racd on outside: hung bdly lft to stands' side fr 3f out and no ch 2f out: eased fnl f* **12/1**		27+
1	**8**	*6*	**Rayaheen**[42] 3074 2-8-12 0 ... PaulHanagan 5 (Richard Hannon) *in tch: rdn and btn 2f out: eased fnl f* **2/1**[1]		37+

1m 28.22s (-1.28) **Going Correction** -0.15s/f (Firm) **8** Ran SP% **114.3**

Speed ratings (Par 99): **101,99,98,98,91 86,68,62**

toteswingers 1&2 £11.10, 2&3 £6.30, 1&3 £20.50 CSF £197.40 TOTE £35.80: £5.40, £1.90, £2.70; EX 100.00 Trifecta £671.30 Pool: £1261.10 - 1.39 winning units..

Owner Mrs Mary-Anne Parker **Bred** Darley **Trained** Lambourn, Berks

■ Stewards' Enquiry : Jim Crowley two-day ban: careless riding (Aug 9-10)

FOCUS

This race was taken by the subsequent Prix de Diane winner Confidential Lady in 2005, but none of the last four winners managed to win again and the feeling is that this form should be taken with a pinch of salt. The fillies in first, second and third places after 2f were also in those positions crossing the line and many of those in behind pulled their chances away and/or hated the fast ground. This is likely to prove a lesser renewal of this event.

NOTEBOOK

Roz caused a 40-1 surprise in a Kempton maiden over this trip on her second start and this was just as big a shock, but to be fair her rider got the tactics spot on. Left alone to do her own thing out in front, she kept enough in reserve to see her race out and coped fine with the quick ground, whilst several of her rivals couldn't handle it at all. It's hard to believe that she can better this, but that may not matter now that she has earned some black type. (op 25-1)

Savanna La Mar(USA), whose stable had won this race twice in the previous seven years, was always in the same place but was off the bridle as soon as the field reached the home straight. To her credit, she kept staying on and would surely reverse form with the winner were they to meet again in a race run at a more routine tempo. (op 15-2 tchd 6-1)

Purr Along stayed this trip well when bolting up on her debut in a Wolverhampton Polytrack maiden earlier this month and ran well, but was another who benefited from racing close to the pace. (op 14-1)

Go Angellica(IRE) was up half a furlong after her successful debut in a Doncaster fillies' maiden last month which is working out well and she earns credit for this effort, as she was one of those to pull hard early and did best of those trying to come from well off this pace. She still has a bright future. (op 8-1)

Amazonas(IRE), up a furlong after finishing a fine fourth in the Albany at Royal Ascot, made a brief effort coming to the last 2f, but never looked that happy and soon folded. It's worth giving her another chance. Official explanation: jockey said filly hung left (op 4-1)

Mollyvator(IRE) shaped as though this extra furlong would suit when bolting up in a Haydock maiden on her second start, but she was another to pull hard off the pace early and looked to be hating the ground when let down. (op 13-2)

Miss You Too didn't look straightforward when easily winning a five-runner York maiden over this trip a fortnight earlier and hung over to the stands' rail after turning in here. She looks one to avoid. Official explanation: jockey said filly hung badly left (tchd 14-1)

Rayaheen landed a 6f Nottingham maiden in decent style on her debut last month and that form has been boosted, but having pulled hard early she found nothing off the bridle and was eased right off. Richard Hannon jnr said that the filly had been struck into rounding the home bend and the vet reported that she was lame on her near hind. Official explanation: vet said filly was lame near-hind leg (op 7-4)

4515 ODGERS BERNDTSON H'CAP 1m 2f 7y

3:40 (3:40) (Class 4) (0-85,85) 3-Y-O+ **£4,075** (£1,212; £606; £303) **Stalls** Low

Form					RPR
42	**1**		**Angel Gabrial (IRE)**[27] 3558 3-8-11 **78** ... JamieSpencer 1 (Ian Williams) *hld up in rr: hdwy on outside over 1f out: str run whn u.p ins fnl f: led last stride* **4/1**[2]		86+
1-14	**2**	*shd*	**Night And Dance (IRE)**[89] 1656 4-9-11 **82** ... FrankieDettori 9 (Clive Cox) *in rr: hdwy over 2f out: str run fnl f to chal fnl 120yds: slt advantage whn faltered: wnt lft: and hdd last stride* **10/1**		90
2-00	**3**	*shd*	**Fadhaa (IRE)**[26] 3635 4-9-10 **81** ... PaulHanagan 6 (Charles Hills) *trckd ldrs: chal 3f out: sn led: drvn fr 2f out and sn jnd: kpt on gamely thrght fnl f whn hrd pressed: hdd last strides* **9/2**[3]		89
456	**4**	*2*	**Sash Of Honour (IRE)**[38] 3227 3-9-1 **82** ... (v[1]) JimmyFortune 4 (Sir Michael Stoute) *chsd ldr: jnd over 3f out: sn hdd: one pce 2f out: drvn over 1f out: styd on again in clsng stages* **6/1**		86
0441	**5**	*nk*	**Odin (IRE)**[25] 3659 4-9-5 **76** ... SilvestreDeSousa 7 (David Elsworth) *in rr: hung rt and looked in trble 3f out: styd on over 1f out: stl hanging and: n.m.r ins fnl f but styd on wl: gng on cl home* **7/1**		79+
1-6	**6**	*1/2*	**Kiz Kulesi**[33] 3383 3-9-1 **82** ... MickaelBarzalona 3 (Mahmood Al Zarooni) *chsd ldrs: wnt 2nd 2f out: chal over 1f out tl wknd fnl 120yds* **7/2**[1]		84
0-42	**7**	*3/4*	**Destiny Of Dreams**[24] 3703 4-9-10 **81** ... DaneO'Neill 8 (Jo Crowley) *chsd ldrs: rdn over 2f out: no imp on ldrs and one pce ins fnl f* **14/1**		82

-150 8 ½ **Freddy Q (IRE)**[25] [3668] 3-9-4 **85**............ PatDobbs 5 85
(Richard Hannon) *towards rr: rdn and sme hdwy fr 2f out: nvr rchd ldrs and styd on same pce fr over 1f out* **10/1**

-114 9 9 **Sula Two**[20] [3813] 5-8-13 **77**............ PhilipPrince(7) 2 59
(Ron Hodges) *led tl hdd 3f out: wknd over 2f out* **16/1**

2m 7.68s (-2.82) **Going Correction** -0.15s/f (Firm)
WFA 3 from 4yo+ 10lb **9** Ran SP% **117.9**
Speed ratings (Par 105): **105,104,104,103,103 102,102,101,94**
toteswingers 1&2 £2.90, 2&3 £10.80, 1&3 £5.10 CSF £44.44 CT £189.10 TOTE £3.60: £1.10, £3.50, £2.10; EX 20.10 Trifecta £146.00 Pool: £1302.44 - 6.60 winning units..
Owner Dr Marwan Koukash **Bred** K And Mrs Cullen **Trained** Portway, Worcs

FOCUS
A fair handicap and it was noticeable the runners spurned the inside rail down the back straight. It produced a bunch finish and the third sets the standard.
Sula Two Official explanation: jockey said pin came out of stirrup leather

4516 TWICKENHAM MAIDEN STKS 1m 14y
4:15 (4:16) (Class 5) 3-4-Y-0 **£2,264** (£673; £336; £168) **Stalls** Low

Form RPR

5- 1 **Invisible Hunter (USA)**[275] [7080] 3-9-2 0............(t) FrankieDettori 3 93+
(Saeed Bin Suroor) *mde all: drvn over 2f out: styd on strly appr fnl f: unchal* **3/1**[2]

-240 2 3 ¼ **Dream Tune**[49] [2856] 3-9-2 88............ PatDobbs 6 86
(Clive Cox) *chsd wnr: drvn 2f out: no imp over 1f out and styd on same pce* **5/2**[1]

4 3 1 ¾ **Afraah (USA)**[33] [3399] 3-8-11 0............ TomQueally 4 77+
(Roger Varian) *chsd ldrs: rdn to take 3rd ins fnl 2f: no imp on ldng trio and one pce fnl f* **12/1**

2 4 3 ¾ **Estebsaal (IRE)**[33] [3398] 3-9-2 0............ PaulHanagan 10 73
(John Dunlop) *chsd ldrs and t.k.h: rdn 2f out: hung rt and wknd appr fnl f* **5/1**[3]

0 5 1 **Taglietelle**[202] [56] 3-8-9 0............ JoeyHaynes(7) 13 71+
(Andrew Balding) *in rr: hdwy towards outside fr 2f out: styd on ins fnl f but nvr a threat* **40/1**

4-4 6 1 ½ **Abbraccio**[61] [2496] 4-9-10 0............ MickaelBarzalona 1 70
(James Fanshawe) *chsd ldrs: drvn 3f out: wknd 2f out* **8/1**

602 7 1 ¼ **Cool Sky**[31] [3447] 3-9-2 78............ JimCrowley 14 65
(William Knight) *chsd ldrs: drvn 3f out: wknd 2f out* **16/1**

00 8 nk **Flashy Star**[38] [3227] 3-8-11 0............(v[1]) MatthewDavies 7 59
(Mick Channon) *in rr: pushed along 3f out: mod prog ins fnl f* **50/1**

9 2 ¼ **Who's That Chick (IRE)** 3-8-5[0] ow1............ DanielCremin(7) 2 55
(Ralph Smith) *s.i.s: in rr tl mod late prog* **66/1**

0 10 3 ½ **Tenure**[98] [1467] 3-9-2 0............ JimmyFortune 8 51
(Sir Michael Stoute) *got loose in paddock: a towards rr* **5/1**[3]

3-0 11 2 ¾ **Sweet Ophelia**[92] [1610] 3-8-6 0............ DavidKenny(5) 9 39
(George Baker) *bhd most of way* **40/1**

05 12 nk **Iron Butterfly**[59] [2560] 3-8-11 0............ LukeMorris 12 39
(James Eustace) *bhd most of way* **33/1**

0 13 2 **Red Protector (IRE)**[13] [4067] 3-9-2 0............ DaneO'Neill 5 39
(Amy Weaver) *chsd ldrs: rdn over 3f out: sn wknd* **100/1**

1m 40.76s (-2.54) **Going Correction** -0.15s/f (Firm)
WFA 3 from 4yo 8lb **13** Ran SP% **123.9**
Speed ratings (Par 103): **106,102,101,97,96 94,93,93,90,87 84,84,82**
toteswingers 1&2 £3.30, 2&3 £8.90, 1&3 £7.80 CSF £11.04 TOTE £3.50: £1.20, £1.60, £3.30; EX 17.90 Trifecta £239.70 Pool: £1924.62 - 5.94 winning units..
Owner Godolphin **Bred** Charles H Deters Et Al **Trained** Newmarket, Suffolk

FOCUS
The last two winners of this maiden, Nationalism and Dare To Dance, both went on to prove smart and this may have been won by a nice type too, even though plenty went his way. The form looks sound enough among the principals.

4517 LUBRICATORS H'CAP 7f 16y
4:50 (4:51) (Class 5) (0-75,75) 3-Y-0+ **£2,587** (£770; £384; £192) **Stalls** Low

Form RPR

-430 1 **Annes Rocket (IRE)**[29] [3511] 7-8-8 **62**............(p) KatiaScallan(7) 5 73
(Jimmy Fox) *in rr: gd hdwy wl over 1f out: edging rt and led ins fnl f: pushed out* **33/1**

6-02 2 2 ¼ **Buckland (IRE)**[10] [4155] 4-9-2 **70**............ NicoleNordblad(7) 12 75
(Hans Adielsson) *chsd ldrs: led over 2f out: pushed along and hdd ins fnl f: nt pce of wnr but hld on wl for 2nd* **8/1**

04-5 3 ¾ **Bajan Bear**[33] [3388] 4-9-9 **70**............ DaneO'Neill 1 76+
(Michael Blanshard) *towards rr: swtchd lft and hdwy appr fnl f: styd on to take 3rd last strides but no imp on ldng duo* **8/1**

0400 4 shd **Cravat**[15] [3977] 3-9-6 **74**............ SilvestreDeSousa 11 75+
(Mark Johnston) *in rr: drvn 3f out: styd on fnl f to take 3rd briefly nr fin but no imp on ldng duo* **7/1**[3]

-006 5 ¾ **Poetic Lord**[31] [3446] 3-9-7 **75**............(b[1]) PatDobbs 3 74
(Richard Hannon) *led 1f: styd chsng ldrs: rdn over 2f out: styd on fnl f: sn pushed rt: kpt on same pce* **9/2**[1]

0106 6 shd **Shamrocked (IRE)**[12] [4082] 3-9-7 **75**............ MatthewDavies 8 73
(Mick Channon) *led after 1f: hdd over 2f out: no ex fnl f* **8/1**

-053 7 2 ¼ **Flavius Victor (IRE)**[25] [3671] 3-8-11 **65**............(t) LukeMorris 2 57
(Richard Hannon) *s.i.s: in rr: rdn over 2f out: sme prog u.p fnl f* **6/1**[2]

216 8 ¾ **Loyal N Trusted**[65] [2373] 4-8-5 **59**............(p) PhilipPrince(7) 13 51
(Richard Price) *chsd ldrs: pushed along 2f out: hung rt and wknd ins fnl f* **12/1**

0440 9 1 **Standing Strong (IRE)**[7] [4252] 4-9-4 **72**............[1] DanielCremin(7) 10 62
(Robert Mills) *in rr: pushed along over 2f out: sme late prog* **20/1**

3535 10 2 ¾ **Batgirl**[26] [3615] 5-9-7 **68**............ FrankieDettori 6 50
(John Berry) *in tch: rdn 3f out: sn btn* **9/2**[1]

000 11 2 **Local Singer (IRE)**[15] [3958] 4-9-2 **63**............ J-PGuillambert 4 45
(Paul Howling) *led 1f: chsd ldr to 3f out: wknd 2f out* **16/1**

-062 12 4 ½ **Khazium (IRE)**[41] [3098] 3-8-10 **69**............(v) DavidKenny(5) 7 32
(Pat Eddery) *s.i.s: t.k.h: sn in tch: rdn and btn 3f out* **16/1**

1m 27.67s (-1.83) **Going Correction** -0.15s/f (Firm)
WFA 3 from 4yo+ 7lb **12** Ran SP% **123.6**
Speed ratings (Par 103): **104,101,100,100,99 99,96,96,94,91 89,84**
toteswingers 1&2 £33.60, 2&3 £13.30, 1&3 £50.10 CSF £289.97 CT £2384.74 TOTE £42.60: £9.00, £3.20, £3.30; EX 379.50 Trifecta £662.30 Part won. Pool: £895.06 - 0.64 winning units..
Owner Claire Underwood, Fay Thomas & S-J Fox **Bred** S Coughlan **Trained** Collingbourne Ducis, Wilts

FOCUS
Not the best handicap Sandown will ever stage, but competitive nonetheless and the pace was good. A personal best from the winner.
T/Plt: £238.90 to a £1 stake. Pool of £70780.32 - 216.24 winning tickets. T/Qpdt: £158.60 to a £1 stake. Pool of £4458.28 - 20.79 winning tickets. ST

4518 - (Foreign Racing) - See Raceform Interactive

4274 LEOPARDSTOWN (L-H)
Thursday, July 26

OFFICIAL GOING: Good (good to soft in places)

4519a KOREAN RACING AUTHORITY TYROS STKS (GROUP 3) 7f
6:15 (6:15) 2-Y-0 **£25,729** (£7,520; £3,562; £1,187)

RPR

1 **Grafelli (IRE)**[4] [4077] 2-9-0 107............ KevinManning 1 107
(J S Bolger, Ire) *racd in 2nd: drvn to ld fnl f: kpt on wl whn chal ins fnl f: all out* **13/8**[2]

2 nk **Lines Of Battle (USA)**[37] [3240] 2-9-3............ JPO'Brien 5 103
(A P O'Brien, Ire) *racd in 3rd: upsides wnr and ev ch fnl f: kpt on wl but no ex cl home* **5/6**[1]

3 hd **Kingston Jamaica (IRE)**[34] [3358] 2-9-3............ SeamieHeffernan 2 103
(A P O'Brien, Ire) *led: drvn and hdd fnl f: cl 3rd and no ex cl home* **9/1**

4 1 **Reglisse (IRE)**[7] [4276] 2-9-0 97............ ShaneFoley 4 97
(Edward Lynam, Ire) *racd in 4th: kpt on wl st but nt rch ldrs* **8/1**[3]

5 10 **Ella's Kitten (USA)**[21] [3796] 2-9-3............ PatSmullen 3 74
(D K Weld, Ire) *racd in 5th: no imp fr over 2 out* **25/1**

1m 30.31s (1.61) **Going Correction** +0.15s/f (Good) **5** Ran SP% **117.6**
Speed ratings: **96,95,95,94,82**
CSF £3.64 TOTE £2.90: £1.10, £1.30; DF 5.10.
Owner Sylvain Benillouche **Bred** F Benillouche **Trained** Coolcullen, Co Carlow

FOCUS
An illustrious list of previous winners, especially in the last decade with the likes of Teofilo, New Approach and Cape Blanco winning this on the way to becoming outstanding Group 1 performers. There was a compressed finish and there's a suspicion that the winner was perhaps a fraction below best/potential best given he'd won a Group 3 race four days earlier.

NOTEBOOK
Grafelli(IRE) ◆ followed up his landslide victory in last Sunday's Anglesey Stakes with a more hard-earned one. After tracking the pace throughout, he was shoved into a narrow lead 1f out and, while the winning margin was narrow, he showed a likeable attitude when challenged by the runner-up and gave the impression he'd relish another furlong or two. He might not ooze the same class as his more esteemed stable companion Dawn Approach, but he races in a similar fashion and appears very straightforward. The Prix Jean-Luc Lagardere on Arc Day at Longchamp was nominated as his end of season target but we will probably see him again before then.
Lines Of Battle(USA) gives the form a solid look. He was sixth to Dawn Approach in the Coventry Stakes and might have finished closer had he not been forced to switch at a vital stage. Here, he was last to come off the bridle and looked the likeliest winner on the outside 2f out. He was just outfought by the winner in the closing stages but there's no shame in that and a Group race should come his way before too long, perhaps back over 6f.
Kingston Jamaica(IRE) looked a real grinder when winning at Limerick and tried to make this into a true test of stamina. His rider made the clever move of trying to kick for home rounding the final bend and, at one stage, it looked as though it would reap handsome dividends. But the main two in the market challenged inside the final furlong and he couldn't retain his lead. He will surely improve over further and isn't one to write off.
Reglisse(IRE) possibly turned in her best performance to date. She may have finished second last but she was beaten less than two lengths and moved through the race like a decent animal. She keeps progressing and will be a big player when she faces her own sex over this trip.
Ella's Kitten(USA) was not surprisingly outclassed but, even so, one would have expected him to be more competitive than he was.

4521a JOCKEY CLUB OF TURKEY MELD STKS (GROUP 3) 1m 1f
7:20 (7:24) 3-Y-0+ **£31,145** (£9,104; £4,312; £1,437)

RPR

1 **Famous Name**[25] [3675] 7-9-12 115............ PatSmullen 3 118+
(D K Weld, Ire) *trckd ldrs: 3rd 1/2-way: prog to ld over 1f out: r.o wl: easily* **30/100**[1]

2 5 ½ **Ballybacka Lady (IRE)**[327] [5745] 4-9-6 102............ FranBerry 2 100
(Mrs John Harrington, Ire) *trckd ldrs: 5th 1/2-way: 4th and kpt on best of the remainder fnl f: no ch w easy wnr* **33/1**

3 ¾ **Native Khan (FR)**[25] [3675] 4-9-9 113............ JohnnyMurtagh 1 101
(John M Oxx, Ire) *trckd ldrs: 4th 1/2-way: drvn over 2 out: kpt on one pce fnl f* **4/1**[2]

4 ¾ **Defining Year (IRE)**[17] [3926] 4-9-9 105............ ShaneFoley 6 100
(M Halford, Ire) *led: chal and hdd over 1f out: 3rd and no ex fnl f* **12/1**[3]

5 1 ¼ **Windsor Palace (IRE)**[25] [3675] 7-9-12 106............(b) JPO'Brien 5 100
(A P O'Brien, Ire) *trckd ldrs: racd wd: 2nd 1/2-way: ev ch over 2 out: 5th and no imp fnl f* **14/1**

6 6 ½ **Barack (IRE)**[7] [4279] 6-9-9 97............(bt) BenCurtis 4 84
(W McCreery, Ire) *racd in 6th thrght: nvr a factor* **25/1**

1m 54.6s (0.50) **Going Correction** +0.15s/f (Good) **6** Ran SP% **118.1**
Speed ratings: **103,98,97,96,95 89**
CSF £17.11 TOTE £1.30: £1.02, £9.50; DF 22.60.
Owner K Abdulla **Bred** Juddmonte Farms Ltd **Trained** The Curragh, Co Kildare

FOCUS
The winning time wasn't great but Famous Name took this with some ease. He sets the standard, along with the third to his previous outing.

NOTEBOOK
Famous Name is a standing dish at this track and a formidable performer at this level of competition. He showed that here, recording the 18th win of his 35-race career, his 11th victory at Group 3 level and his 12th success over the course. He proved much too good for his rivals, closing in third before the straight, swinging wide and hitting the front one and a half furlongs out before settling the issue in a matter of strides, He is likely to seek a first Group 2 win in the Royal Whip Stakes at the Curragh on August 12.
Ballybacka Lady(IRE), a Group 3 winner here early last season, was having her first run since finishing sixth in the Group 1 Matron Stakes at the same course in September. Covered by Dream Ahead, this was her first start for Jessica Harrington and although she never posed a theat to the winner, she ran a good race, making headway from 2f out and staying on for second in the closing stages.
Native Khan(FR) had finished third behind Famous Name at the Curragh when making his debut for John Oxx early this month. He was beaten by only a slightly shorter margin on this occasion and while he would probably prefer quicker ground he proved disappointing. He failed to pick up when asked for his effort and could only keep on at the same pace.
Defining Year(IRE) had split Famous Name and Native Khan at the Curragh on his previous start and after disappointing when upped in trip in a 1m4f Listed event at Roscommon he was back to a more suitable distance here. As at the Curragh he made the running but after being ridden along into the straight he had no more to offfer when tackled by the winner.
Windsor Palace(IRE), fourth in the Curragh event in which Famous Name beat Defining Year and Native Khan, raced wide of his rivals for most of the journey. He disputed the lead from halfway but began to struggle turning for home and was soon beaten.
Barack(IRE) Official explanation: jockey said gelding sat back as stalls opened and missed break

The Form Book Flat, Raceform Ltd, Compton, RG20 6NL

4520a, 4522a - 4524a (Foreign Racing) - See Raceform Interactive

4362 **ASCOT** (R-H)

Friday, July 27

OFFICIAL GOING: Firm (good to firm in places)

Wind: Light, against Weather: Grey

4525 JOHN GUEST IRISH EBF MAIDEN FILLIES' STKS 7f

2:20 (2:21) (Class 4) 2-Y-O **£6,469** (£1,925; £962 ; £481) **Stalls** High

Form RPR

2 **1** **Fleeting Smile (USA)**[49] 2892 2 -9-0 0 .... TadhgO'Shea 4 85
(Richard Hannon) *mde virtually all: shkn up over 2f out: hrd pressed and drvn over 1f out: styd on wl and asserted ins fnl f* **11/8**[1]

2 *1* **Flawless Beauty** 2 -9-0 0 .... MichaelHills 2 82+
(Hugo Palmer) *hld up: prog on outer to chse wnr 3f out: str chal fr 2f out tl no ex ins fnl f* **14/1**

30 **3** *1* **Summer Dream (IRE)**[28] 3590 2 -9-0 0 .... TedDurcan 6 79+
(Marco Botti) *trckd wnr 2f: styd cl up: rdn to chse ldng pair 2f out: hanging and nt qckn over 1f out: styd on ins fnl f* **4/1**[3]

4 *4 ½* **Close At Hand** 2 -9-0 0 .... WilliamBuick 10 68+
(John Gosden) *rn green and sn last: taken to wd outside and prog over 2f out: tk 4th over 1f out: no hdwy after* **3/1**[2]

56 **5** *1* **Jathabah (IRE)**[14] 4055 2 -9-0 0 .... MartinDwyer 8 64
(Clive Brittain) *prog to press wnr after 2f to 3f out: steadily wknd fnl 2f* **16/1**

6 *1 ¾* **Dark Justice (IRE)** 2 -9-0 0 .... RobertHavlin 3 60
(Tim Pitt) *s.s and tail swishing: sn in tch: effrt on outer over 2f out: no hdwy over 1f out: fdd* **40/1**

2 **7** *5* **Solvanna**[16] 3971 2 -9-0 0 .... EddieAhern 1 46
(Heather Main) *trckd ldrs tl wknd over 2f out* **16/1**

4 **8** *6* **Poetic Belle**[23] 3764 2 -9-0 0 .... JamesDoyle 5 30
(Alan Jarvis) *cl up tl wknd qckly over 2f out* **14/1**

9 *9* **Sol Diva** 2 -9-0 0 .... MartinHarley 9
(Mick Channon) *t.k.h: hld up in tch: wknd 3f out: t.o* **12/1**

1m 28.58s (0.98) **Going Correction** -0.05s/f (Good) **9** Ran SP% **122.3**

Speed ratings (Par 93): **92,90,89,84,83 81,75,68,58**

toteswingers 1&2 £7.50, 2&3 £10.00, 1&3 £1.50 CSF £26.01 TOTE £2.30 : £1.10 , £3.90 , £1.60 ; EX 27.20 Trifecta £108.40 Pool: £1677.18 - 11.44 winning units.

Owner Hamdan Al Maktoum **Bred** Summer Wind Farm **Trained** East Everleigh, Wilts

FOCUS

This juvenile fillies' maiden was run at a sluggish early pace and no doubt it proved an advantage to race handily. The principals dominated from the furlong marker. The winner and third were the best guide and close to their debut form with Newfangled.

NOTEBOOK

Fleeting Smile (USA)made most and opened her account at the second attempt. She was a beaten favourite on her Newmarket debut last month, but did finish a clear second-best to impressive subsequent Albany winner Newfangled that day, the form of which entitled her to win this. She has been waiting for quicker ground since and reportedly worked well earlier in the week, but one couldn't give her away in the betting as she moved to post. This was only workmanlike yet she did it the hard way and saw out the extra furlong well. She's highly regarded and entered in the Group 1 Fillies' Mile at Newmarket later on, although this will need improving on if she's to score in Pattern company at two. Trainer Richard Hannon later said he wouldn't overdo her this year. Evens tchd 10-11)

Flawless Beauty ◆ looked beforehand as though the run would bring her on somewhat, but she ran a blinder. A half-sister to Breeders' Cup Juvenile winner Wrote, she travelled kindly on the outside and was sensibly sent closer to the ordinary pace from halfway. Ultimately she made the winner work hard and surely will be going one better soon.

Summer Dream (IRE)was better than her previous eighth at Newmarket and had finished one place behind Fleeting Smile on her debut there the time before. She bagged the near rail early and tracked her old rival, but despite having her chance she never seriously threatened to reverse form. This ground looked quick enough for her and she can soon find a maiden if sent to one of the smaller tracks. (op 6-1)

Close At Hand, whose dam was a useful 1m2f performer, attracted support and was drawn nearest the stands' rail. Due to being held up she ended up coming widest of all with her challenge and really proved too green to do herself full justice. She can get a lot closer with the initial experience now behind her. (op 11-2)

Jathabah(IRE) was in the firing line 3f out, but failed to quicken when the tempo became serious. Her best trip is still unknown, but she may be better off now she can enter nurseries. (op 14-1)

Dark Justice (IRE)is bred to come into her own over longer trips, being a half-sister to her stable's winning stayers Dark Ranger and Dark Spirit. She ran with some encouragement after missing the break. (op 33-1)

Sol Diva Official explanation: jockey said saddle slipped after 1/2f

4526 HOUGHTON STONE NURSERY 6f

2:55 (2:55) (Class 4) (0-85,83) 2-Y-O **£6,469** (£1,925; £962 ; £481) **Stalls** High

Form RPR

024 **1** **Carlton Blue (IRE)**[27] 3638 2 -8-7 74 .... AshleyMorgan(5) 10 81+
(Paul Cole) *w ldr gng strly: led wl over 1f out: shifted rt after and hrd pressed fnl f: r.o wl last 100yds* **8/1**

4520 **2** *1 ¼* **Star Of Rohm**[34] 3378 2 -9-2 78 .... WilliamBuick 8 81
(Michael Bell) *hld up in last trio: stl there over 1f out: gd prog after: hrd rdn and r.o to take 2nd nr fin: no imp on wnr* **7/1**[3]

321 **3** *¾* **Dansili Dual (IRE)**[39] 3223 2 -9-1 77 .... RichardHughes 1 78
(Richard Hannon) *hld up in rr: smooth prog on outer over 2f out: chal and w wnr 1f out: nt qckn fnl f: lost 2nd nr fin* **3/1**[1]

4104 **4** *¾* **Party Royal**[14] 4047 2 -9-2 78 .... JoeFanning 2 77
(Mark Johnston) *cl up: wl on terms w ldrs over 1f out: nt qckn and hld sn after: styd on nr fin* **9/1**

250 **5** *nk* **Newstead Abbey**[40] 3182 2 -9-4 80 .... RichardMullen 7 78
(David Brown) *hld up in tch against rail: rdn 2f out: hanging and nt qckn over 1f out: styd on ins fnl f* **10/1**

61 **6** *2 ¾* **Front Page News**[32] 3444 2 -9-0 76 .... AndreaAtzeni 4 68+
(Robert Eddery) *trckd ldrs: pushed along over 2f out: nt clr run briefly over 1f out: stl pushed along and one pce* **9/2**[2]

5512 **7** *½* **Bheleyf (IRE)**[16] 3970 2 -9-0 76 .... LiamKeniry 5 63
(Joseph Tuite) *hld up in rr: effrt and cl up bhd ldrs over 1f out: sn fdd* **33/1**

3224 **8** *hd* **Echion (IRE)**[13] 4102 2 -8-13 75 .... JimmyFortune 3 62
(Richard Hannon) *chsd ldng pair to over 1f out: wknd fnl f* **8/1**

210 **9** *nse* **Sharaarah (IRE)**[37] 3269 2 -9-6 82 .... TadhgO'Shea 6 68
(Ed Dunlop) *hld up in last pair: effrt on outer over 2f out: sn no hdwy and btn* **8/1**

2102 **10** *½* **Hillbilly Boy (IRE)**[4] 4047 2 -9-0 83 .... RyanWhile(7) 9 69
(Bill Turner) *mde most tl wl over 1f out: bmpd along and wknd qckly* **11/1**

1m 13.38s (-1.12) **Going Correction** -0.05s/f (Good) **10** Ran SP% **119.4**

Speed ratings (Par 96): **105,103,102,101,100 97,96,96,96,95**

toteswingers 1&2 £11.00, 2&3 £3.60, 1&3 £4.80 CSF £64.51 CT £213.24 TOTE £9.50 : £2.80 , £2.50, £1.50 ; EX 64.90 Trifecta £845.10 Pool: £1313.41 - 1.15 winning units.

Owner Meyrick, Dunnington-Jefferson & Wright **Bred** Eoghan Grogan **Trained** Whatcombe, Oxon

■ Stewards' Enquiry : Ryan While five-day ban: used whip when out of contention (Aug 10-14)

FOCUS

Six of the runners in this decent nursery had previously won a race and it looked an open race. There was an average pace on those racing nearer the stands' rail seemed at an advantage. Sound form.

NOTEBOOK

Carlton Blue (IRE) reportedly struck into when a beaten favourite last time, was drawn nearest the rail and dug deep late on to open his account on this nursery debut. He was always up there and kept finding for pressure from the furlong marker, despite still looking green. He has plenty of scope, evidently enjoyed the quick ground and should go on from this. A stiffer test may also suit him ideally and a quick turnout at Goodwood next week over an extra furlong is now on the cards.

Star Of Rohm came from out the back with a strong burst, but the winner was gone beyond recall. This ground suited better and a more prominent ride can see him off the mark in something similar. (op 8-1)

Dansili Dual (IRE) off the mark at Windsor last month, was making his nursery debut and is bred to enjoy quick ground. He took time to settle and got buried away, with Richard Hughes producing him to close up quickly widest of all 2f out. He was done with with half a furlong to run, but covered more ground than the first pair and is well up to landing one of these. (op 7-2 tchd 4-1 in places)

Party Royal shaped better again for the return to a quicker surface and reversed last-time-out Chester form with Hillbilly Boy. He looks ready for another furlong. (op 8-1)

Newstead Abbey, another making his debut in this sphere, raced against the stands' rail and did his best work late in the day. He may now appreciate another furlong, but it was his first run on quick ground. (op 14-1)

Front Page News was a clear-cut winner at Windsor last month and she got very well backed for this nursery debut. Her response under pressure was most limited 2f out and she now has something to prove. (op 4-1)

4527 WOODCOTE STUD EBF VALIANT STKS (LISTED RACE) (F&M) 1m (R)

3:30 (3:30) (Class 1) 3-Y-O+

£18,714 (£7,095; £3,550 ; £1,768 ; £887 ; £445) **Stalls** Low

Form RPR

35-1 **1** **Thistle Bird**[27] 3640 4 -9-5 108 .... JamesDoyle 5 107
(Roger Charlton) *trckd ldr: led jst over 2f out gng strly: shkn up and 2 l clr over 1f out: drvn and styd on wl fnl f* **4/1**

5646 **2** *2 ¾* **Villeneuve**[16] 3987 3 -8-7 93 .... MartinDwyer 6 94
(William Muir) *trckd ldng pair: rdn over 2f out: styd on to take 2nd over 1f out: no imp on wnr* **20/1**

1401 **3** *hd* **Moone's My Name**[27] 3636 4 -9-1 94 .... RichardHughes 2 96+
(Ralph Beckett) *rrd s and lost several l: t.k.h and in tch in last pair: rdn and outpcd over 2f out: styd on fr over 1f out: nrly snatched 2nd* **10/3**[2]

5301 **4** *¾* **Free Verse**[14] 4062 3 -8-7 94 .... KieranO'Neill 9 92
(Richard Hannon) *awkward s: hld up in last trio: rdn over 3f out and sn struggling: brought wd in st and styd on fr over 1f out: nrst fin* **11/2**

4526 **5** *2 ¼* **Night Lily (IRE)**[56] 2654 6 -9-1 85 .... NeilCallan 1 88
(Paul D'Arcy) *led to jst over 2f out: steadily fdd over 1f out* **16/1**

3355 **6** *1 ¾* **Beatrice Aurore (IRE)**[37] 3266 4 -9-1 109 .... WilliamBuick 3 84
(John Dunlop) *uns rdr coming out on to the trck and galloped flat out to post: dwlt: in tch in rr: hanging lft bnd 3f out: effrt over 2f out: wknd over 1f out* **11/4**[1]

4-05 **7** *6* **I Love Me**[13] 4078 4 -9-1 105 .... JimmyFortune 7 70
(Andrew Balding) *trckd ldng pair: rdn over 2f out: sn wknd* **7/2**[3]

1m 38.65s (-2.05) **Going Correction** -0.05s/f (Good)

WFA 3 from 4yo+ 8lb **7** Ran SP% **118.0**

Speed ratings (Par 111): **108,105,105,104,102 100,94**

toteswingers 1&2 £16.30, 2&3 £17.10, 1&3 £3.00 CSF £75.58 TOTE £5.00 : £3.30 , £6.20 ; EX 94.50 Trifecta £1293.80 Part won. Pool of £1748.42 - 0.72 winning units.

Owner Lady Rothschild **Bred** The Rt Hon Lord Rothschild **Trained** Beckhampton, Wilts

FOCUS

The classic generation have dominated this fillies' and mares' Listed event in the past, but older horses held a stronger hand this year. The pair of 3-y-os still both made the frame, though. They didn't go a great pace early and this wasn't a strong race for the grade.

NOTEBOOK

Thistle Bird was always in the right place. She looked vulnerable under her penalty and isn't straightforward (mounted on the track). However, the race fell into her lap from 2f out and her main rivals in behind had excuses. She's now 2-2 in Listed company since resuming this term, though, and is lightly raced enough to think she can make an impact in Group races on suitably quick ground this year. Her entry in a Group 3 at the Curragh later next month looks a most viable target, but after this her trainer didn't rule out a quick reappearance in the Group 1 Nassau Stakes at Goodwood next week. (tchd 7-2)

Villeneuve, fourth in the Listed Sandringham Handicap at the Royal Meeting last month, has been highly tried since her maiden success last year. She never threatened the winner, but stayed on well late and probably ran a personal-best in defeat. (op 22-1 tchd 25-1)

Moone's My Name ◆ would have probably taken all the beating but for rearing as the stalls opened. She forfeited around six lengths in doing so and thus was unable to race handily, which she seems to like. There was a lot to like about her finishing effort in the circumstances and it confirms she's well up to success at this sort of level. (op 4-1)

Free Verse won comfortably on soft ground at Newmarket last time. Ridden to get the extra furlong, she was in trouble turning for home. She deserves credit for rallying as she did late on, on ground surely against her, considering this was not a race where being held up suited (op 8-1)

Night Lily (IRE)proved keen out in front and was a sitting duck for the winner. She's tricky to place these days, but is more effective on the AW. (op 20-1)

Beatrice Aurore (IRE)ran a solid race when fifth in the Group 2 Windsor Forest here last month. She petered out late on and wasn't helped by the lack of pace on, but getting loose and sprinting away beforehand surely did for her chances. She deserves a change of luck. Official explanation: jockey said filly got loose on way to start (op 9-4 tchd 85-40 in a place)

I Love Me, back on quicker ground, again failed to settle and now has questions to answer, but her rider later reported she banged herself entering the stalls. Official explanation: trainer said filly banged itself entering stalls (op 9-2)

4528 JOHN GUEST BROWN JACK STKS (H'CAP) 2m

4:05 (4:05) (Class 2) (0-100,95) 3-Y-O+ **£14,231** (£4,235; £2,116 ; £1,058) **Stalls** Low

Form RPR

541 **1** **Montaser (IRE)**[62] 2484 3 -8-3 87 .... FrannyNorton 9 97+
(David Simcock) *dwlt and swvd lft s: hld up in 5th: prog over 3f out: led over 2f out: shkn up and drew clr over 1f out: pushed out: decisively* **7/4**[1]

0-61 **2** *3 ¾* **Western Prize**[26] 3661 4 -9-5 86 .... RichardHughes 1 92+
(Ralph Beckett) *trckd ldr 4f: styd cl up: gng wl but lost pl on inner over 2f out: renewed effrt to chse wnr over 1f out: styd on but no ch* **5/2**[2]

3005 **3** *2 1/4* **Montaff**[27] 3625 6-9-9 **90** .... MartinHarley 4 93
(Mick Channon) *hld up in last pair: prog fr 3f out to chse wnr 2f out: no imp and lost 2nd over 1f out: one pce* **8/1**

0-05 **4** *nse* **Mystery Star (IRE)**[62] 2506 7-9-10 **91** .... NeilCallan 5 94
(Mark H Tompkins) *hld up in 4th: lost pl over 3f out: effrt again 2f out: kpt on one pce after and no threat* **33/1**

1112 **5** *3* **Bilidn**[10] 4184 4-9-4 **85** .... ChrisCatlin 3 84
(Noel Quinlan) *stdd s: hld up in last pair: rdn and effrt on outer over 2f out: no prog over 1f out* **6/1**[3]

2220 **6** *0* **Dark Ranger**[38] 2241 6-9-6 **86** .... EddieAhern 0 75
(Tim Pitt) *trckd ldr after 4f: rdn over 3f out: wknd over 2f out* **9/1**

1010 **7** *13* **Kangaroo Court (IRE)**[34] 3373 8-8-13 **80** .... WilliamBuick 6 53
(Emma Lavelle) *led: stretched field fr 6f out: hdd & wknd rapidly over 2f out: eased and t.o* **9/1**

3m 29.6s (0.60) **Going Correction** -0.05s/f (Good)
WFA 3 from 4yo+ 17lb **7** Ran SP% **113.3**
Speed ratings (Par 109): **96,94,93,92,91 86,80**
toteswingers 1&2 £2.30, 2&3 £4.10, 1&3 £4.10 CSF £6.14 CT £25.10 TOTE £2.60: £1.30, £2.40; EX 6.60 Trifecta £38.10 Pool: £ 1862.45 - 36.11 winning units..

Owner Dr Marwan Koukash **Bred** Airlie Stud **Trained** Newmarket, Suffolk

FOCUS

A good staying handicap but the bare form is muddling and rather ordinary for the grade. The winner is rated up 4lb, and he and the second are progressive.

NOTEBOOK

Montaser(IRE) ◆ followed up his Haydock success over 1m4f when last seen 62 days earlier, off an 8lb higher mark, and looks a stayer going places. He hampered his cause with a messy start, but the lack of early pace helped on that front. Just as his main rival found trouble on the inside as things quickened up in the home straight he found first run, but this ground would have been plenty quick enough for him and he saw it out really well. Indeed he reminds one of his stable's former winner of this event in Darley Sun 2009, who went on to land the Cesarewitch later that year before joining Godolphin, and bigger prizes surely now await this progressive colt. Looking further ahead and bearing in mind his owner, the Chester Cup next year must be a target. (op 2-1 tchd 9-4)

Western Prize ◆ was 5lb higher than when scoring at Salisbury 26 days previously. He was confidently ridden on the inside, but had to wait for the gap to appear 2f out and thus gifted first run to the winner, to whom he was conceding over a stone. He's better than the bare form and remains unexposed as a stayer. (op 3-1)

Montaff did best of those held up off the uneven pace and this was a step back in the right direction, but his losing run goes on. (op 10-1)

Mystery Star(IRE), back from a 62-day break, would have no doubt enjoyed more of a test and so he wasn't disgraced. (op 28-1)

Bilidn came here in the form of her life. It was her toughest assignment to date and she faced contrasting ground, but the tactical nature of the race found her out. She's now due a 5lb rise. (op 5-1)

Dark Ranger failed to respond sufficiently when the tempo increased around 3f out and was well beaten off, but this wasn't run to suit. (op 8-1 tchd 15-2)

4529 NEWSMITH OCTOBER CLUB CHARITY H'CAP — 1m 2f

4:40 (4:40) (Class 2) (0-100,90) 3-Y-O+

£12,450 (£3,728; £1,864; £932; £466; £234) **Stalls** Low

Form RPR

1126 **1** **Hajras (IRE)**[15] 4009 3-9-4 **90** .... TadhgO'Shea 5 100+
(Mark Johnston) *hld up in 6th: shkn up and prog on outer wl over 2f out: wnt 2nd and edgd rt 1f out: r.o to ld last 75yds* **5/2**[1]

1122 **2** *1* **Love Your Looks**[27] 3636 4-9-11 **87** .... MartinDwyer 8 95
(Mike Murphy) *t.k.h: trckd ldr: led after 4f and increased already fair pce: drvn 2 l clr over 1f out: collared last 75yds* **9/2**[3]

03-5 **3** *2 1/4* **Haylaman (IRE)**[56] 2655 4-9-11 **87** .... NeilCallan 2 91
(David Simcock) *trckd ldng pair: rdn wl over 2f out: prog to chse ldr briefly over 1f out: styd on same pce after* **10/3**[2]

3401 **4** *3 1/4* **Clare Island Boy (IRE)**[42] 3106 3-9-2 **88** .... JimmyFortune 6 85
(Richard Hannon) *led 4f: chsd ldr: rdn to try to chal 2f out: lost 2nd over 1f out: wl hld whn sltly impeded jst ins fnl f* **9/1**

6103 **5** *shd* **Starwatch**[7] 4287 5-9-8 **89** .... DavidKenny(5) 3 86
(John Bridger) *hld up in 5th: rdn over 2f out and no prog: kpt on fr over 1f out* **16/1**

-600 **6** *6* **Roayh (USA)**[21] 3826 4-10-0 **90** .... MickaelBarzalona 1 77
(Saeed Bin Suroor) *hld up in last: pushed along after 4f: a struggling after: rdn and no prog over 2f out* **13/2**

01-6 **7** *hd* **Dandy (GER)**[20] 3882 3-8-11 **83** .... (v1) EddieAhern 7 67
(Andrew Balding) *trckd ldng trio to 3f out: wknd* **6/1**

2m 5.73s (-1.67) **Going Correction** -0.05s/f (Good)
WFA 3 from 4yo+ 10lb **7** Ran SP% **113.3**
Speed ratings (Par 109): **104,103,101,98,98 93,93**
toteswingers 1&2 £2.30, 2&3 £3.50, 1&3 £2.50 CSF £13.76 CT £36.65 TOTE £3.00: £1.50, £2.40; EX 10.10 Trifecta £29.40 Pool: £1494.64 - 37.59 winning units..

Owner Hamdan Al Maktoum **Bred** Shadwell Estate Company Limited **Trained** Middleham Moor, N Yorks

■ Stewards' Enquiry : Tadhg O'Shea one-day ban: careless riding (Aug 10)

FOCUS

A fair handicap, run at a sound pace. The first two continue to progress.

NOTEBOOK

Hajras(IRE) struck another blow for the classic generation with a gutsy success to make it 3-6 for the year. The lightly raced colt ran a solid race on his return from a break at Newmarket last tie, when better than the bare form, and won this despite having been set plenty to do off the pace. He also looked to be hanging under pressure from 2f out, possibly on account of the ground, and so really did well to master the in-form runner-up late on. There's little doubt he's capable of rating higher yet this year. (op 11-4)

Love Your Looks, 5lb higher up in trip, is a really consistent filly and this brave effort rates another career-best in defeat. She'll go up again for this, but her attitude means that further success cannot be ruled out yet. (tchd 4-1)

Haylaman(IRE) posted a promising effort on Derby day at Epsom on his seasonal reappearance when making his debut for the yard. He was well placed turning for home, but couldnt quicken sufficiently when asked for his effort and may just have needed it. (op 11-4 tchd 7-2)

Clare Island Boy(IRE) was 2lb higher than when just making all at Goodwood 42 six weeks earlier. He wasn't helped by being taken on and passed by the runner-up 3lf out, so this was a fair effort in defeat. (op 14-1)

Starwatch travelled enthusiastically, but didnt convince he wants to go this far and is weighted right up to his best at present. (op 14-1)

Roayh(USA) got markedly outpaced on the far side and is struggling for form. (op 9-1)

Dandy(GER), in a first-time visor, posted a tame effort and now has plenty to prove.

4530 JOHN GUEST H'CAP — 5f

5:15 (5:15) (Class 4) (0-85,85) 3-Y-O+

£5,175 (£1,540; £769; £384) **Stalls** High

Form RPR

0-53 **1** **Best Be Careful (IRE)**[62] 2494 4-8-5 **71** .... RachealKneller(5) 14 81
(Mark Usher) *trckd ldrs: prog to ld 2f out gng easily: pressed and urged along fnl f: a holding on* **8/1**

0-10 **2** *nk* **Larwood (IRE)**[79] 1983 3-9-0 **79** .... FergusSweeney 12 87
(Henry Candy) *trckd ldrs: prog 2f out: rdn to chse wnr jst ins fnl f: sn chalng: r.o but a hld* **6/1**[0]

0 **3** *1 1/4* **Rowe Park**[21] 3822 9-9-6 **81** .... (p) SaleemGolam 2 85
(Linda Jewell) *hld up in rr: prog on outer fr 2f out: rdn to take 3rd fnl f: styd on same pce* **33/1**

3226 **4** *1/2* **Arctic Lynx (IRE)**[28] 3571 5-9-9 **84** .... StephenCraine 11 87
(John Best) *hld up in rr: prog 2f out: hrd rdn over 1f out: styd on same pce ins fnl f* **15/2**

0303 **5** *1/2* **Sutton Veny (IRE)**[27] 3612 6-9-10 **85** .... MartinDwyer 9 86
(Jeremy Gask) *hld up: effrt 2f out: hrd rdn jst over 1f out: styd on but nt gng pce to threaten* **5/1**[2]

12 **6** *nk* **Cut Across (IRE)**[66] 2360 4-8-11 **72** .... NeilCallan 4 72
(Nick Littmoden) *trckd ldrs: drvn 2f out: nt qckn and outpcd over 1f out: styd on again fnl f* **4/1**[1]

20-0 **7** *nk* **Invincible Lad (IRE)**[26] 3660 8-9-0 **75** .... MarcHalford 8 74
(Milton Bradley) *taken down early and free to post: dwlt: hld up last: pushed along and sme prog over 1f out: styd on fnl f: nvr in it* **28/1**

-012 **8** *1* **Avonmore Star**[16] 3960 4-9-5 **80** .... JimmyFortune 6 77
(Richard Hannon) *pressed ldrs: drvn to chse wnr over 1f out tl jst ins fnl f: fdd* **6/1**[3]

1262 **9** *shd* **Clear Praise (USA)**[27] 3618 5-8-13 **74** .... EddieAhern 7 69
(Simon Dow) *led to 2f out: wknd fnl f* **9/1**

0210 **10** *8* **Wooden King (IRE)**[8] 4231 7-9-1 **76** .... (p) TomMcLaughlin 13 42
(Malcolm Saunders) *pressed ldr to 1/2-way: wknd rapidly 2f out* **8/1**

63-0 **11** *1 1/4* **Foxtrot India (IRE)**[21] 3822 3-9-2 **81** .... RenatoSouza 1 41
(Jeremy Gask) *swvd rt s and lost grnd: spd to chse ldrs 3f: wknd rapidly* **25/1**

1m 0.57s (0.07) **Going Correction** -0.05s/f (Good)
WFA 3 from 4yo+ 4lb **11** Ran SP% **119.5**
Speed ratings (Par 105): **97,96,94,93,92 92,91,90,90,77 75**
toteswingers 1&2 £10.80, 2&3 £24.80, 1&3 £55.20 CSF £55.24 CT £1544.05 TOTE £10.80: £3.10, £2.20, £9.50; EX 70.80 Trifecta £1525.60 Part won. Pool of £2061.67 - 0.60 winning units..

Owner Mrs Jill Pellett **Bred** M Phelan **Trained** Upper Lambourn, Berks

FOCUS

A typically open and competitive sprint handicap for the class. The main action developed off the stands' rail late on. The winner picked up her 3yo progress for a 7lb personal best.

T/Plt: £147.20 to a £1 stake. Pool of £120018.73 - 594.82 winning tickets. T/Qpdt: £56.40 to a £1 stake. Pool of £7045.62 - 92.40 winning tickets. JN

3429 CHEPSTOW (L-H)

Friday, July 27

OFFICIAL GOING: Firm (good to firm in places; 8.7)

Wind: Moderate behind Weather: Sunny early, getting darker

4531 BREWIN DOLPHIN CARDIFF OFFICE H'CAP — 1m 14y

5:45 (5:46) (Class 5) (0-70,76) 3-Y-O+

£2,264 (£673; £336; £168) **Stalls** Centre

Form RPR

6311 **1** **Chosen Character (IRE)**[4] 4388 4-9-13 **76** 6ex .... (vt) RyanTate(7) 10 86
(Tom Dascombe) *trckd ldrs: wnt 2nd over 2f out: led ins fnl f and sn 1 l up: rdn and one pce clsng stages: jst hld on* **5/2**[1]

-310 **2** *nse* **Supaheart**[60] 2557 3-9-6 **70** .... DarryllHolland 16 78
(Hughie Morrison) *sn led: rdn 2f out: c to stands' side sn after: hdd ins fnl f and sn 1 l down: rallied strly in clsng stages: fin wl: jst failed* **11/2**[3]

1260 **3** *1 1/2* **Temuco (IRE)**[18] 3920 3-9-0 **67** .... MatthewCosham(3) 6 71
(David Evans) *in rr: hdwy 3f out: drvn and styd on to take 3rd jst ins fnl f but nvr gng pce of ldng duo* **16/1**

-314 **4** *3/4* **Derfenna Art (IRE)**[43] 3068 3-9-6 **70** .... (t) LukeMorris 13 73
(Seamus Durack) *chsd ldrs: rdn fr over 3f out: styd on for one pce 4th ins fnl f* **8/1**

3016 **5** *2 3/4* **Polar Auroras**[17] 3950 4-9-2 **58** .... (t) DavidProbert 5 56
(Tony Carroll) *in rr: hdwy 3f out: styd on to chse ldrs fr 2f out: wknd ins fnl f* **20/1**

-003 **6** *2 1/4* **Caterina**[24] 3732 3-8-9 **64** .... (b) AmyScott(5) 3 55
(Richard Hannon) *in rr: pushed along over 2f out: styd on fnl f: nvr a threat* **12/1**

-201 **7** *shd* **My Boy Ginger**[10] 4186 3-9-0 **64** .... JamesMillman 14 55
(Rod Millman) *chsd ldr 3f: stl front rnk tl wknd fnl f* **9/2**[2]

2404 **8** *1 1/2* **Signora Frasi (IRE)**[29] 3544 7-9-3 **59** .... WilliamCarson 15 49
(Tony Newcombe) *s.i.s: in rr: rdn and sme prog fr 3f out: wknd over 1f out* **14/1**

0445 **9** *3/4* **Sir Bruno (FR)**[39] 3230 5-9-13 **69** .... (p) CathyGannon 12 57
(Bryn Palling) *s.i.s: sn pushed along and in tch: rdn over 2f out: wknd over 1f out* **20/1**

-005 **10** *3/4* **Mr Udagawa**[10] 4183 6-9-1 **64** .... (p) AliceHaynes(7) 1 50
(Bernard Llewellyn) *in tch: rdn 3f out: wknd fr 2f out* **33/1**

-032 **11** *1* **Princess Maya**[29] 3547 3-8-7 **62** .... NathanSweeney(5) 11 44
(Jo Crowley) *chsd ldrs over 5f* **14/1**

1024 **12** *4* **Hamilton Hill**[10] 4184 5-9-5 **68** .... (t) DanielMuscutt(7) 17 43
(Dai Burchell) *s.i.s: bhd most of way* **18/1**

650 **13** *9* **One Way Or Another (AUS)**[17] 3944 9-9-6 **62** .... (bt) RichardThomas 7 16
(David Evans) *chsd ldrs tl rdn and wknd 3f out* **16/1**

1m 32.23s (-3.97) **Going Correction** -0.45s/f (Firm)
WFA 3 from 4yo+ 8lb **13** Ran SP% **123.8**
Speed ratings (Par 103): **101,100,99,98,95 93,93,92,91,90 89,85,76**
toteswingers: 1&2 £7.40, 1&3 £32.00, 2&3 £89.00 CSF £15.70 CT £198.24 TOTE £4.00: £1.20, £2.20, £11.70; EX 23.10.

Owner Aykroyd And Sons Ltd **Bred** Moyglare Stud Farm Ltd **Trained** Malpas, Cheshire

FOCUS

Low grade handicap form, but a few of these were in decent heart and the winning time was inside standard, which suggests the ground was definitely on the quick side. Thwe winner was back to his 3yo best.

My Boy Ginger Official explanation: jockey said gelding hung left

One Way Or Another(AUS) Official explanation: vet said gelding bled from the nose

4532 BREWIN DOLPHIN SWANSEA OFFICE MAIDEN AUCTION STKS 6f 16y
6:20 (6:20) (Class 5) 2-Y-O £2,264 (£673; £336; £168) Stalls Centre

Form RPR

1 **Ninjago** 2-9-2 0 RichardHughes 1 88+
(Richard Hannon) *trckd ldrs: upsides fr 2f out: qckngd to ld 1f out: shkn up fnl 120yds: cosily* **11/10**[1]

2 *nk* **Almalekiah (IRE)** 2-8-4 0 DavidProbert 6 73+
(J S Moore) *s.i.s: in rr tl gd hdwy to trck ldrs 3f out: chsd wnr jst ins fnl f and styd on strly but a comf hld* **20/1**

04 3 *3 ¾* **Secret Beau**[26] 3658 2-8-13 0 PatCosgrave 4 70
(George Baker) *trckd ldrs: chal 3f out tl slt ld jst ins fnl 2f: hdd 1f out: wknd fnl f* **9/2**[3]

04 4 *2 ¾* **Al Muntazah (IRE)**[21] 3824 2-9-2 0 LukeMorris 5 64
(Ronald Harris) *pressed ldrs: slt ld 3f out: sn rdn: hdd ins fnl 2f: wknd fnl f* **3/1**[2]

46 5 *4 ½* **Kryena's Rose**[100] 1435 2-8-4 0 CathyGannon 2 38
(Mick Channon) *chsd ldrs: wknd over 2f out* **11/1**

05 6 *2 ¼* **Frans Hals**[15] 3996 2-8-11 0 DarryllHolland 9 37
(Dominic Ffrench Davis) *led 3f: wknd over 2f out* **10/1**

0 7 *10* **Stockholm**[26] 3658 2-8-11 0 ow2 JamesMillman 3
(Rod Millman) *chsd ldrs: upsides 3f out: wknd over 2f out* **50/1**

8 *17* **Just Duchess** 2-8-4 0 WilliamCarson 8
(Michael Blanshard) *sn t.o* **33/1**

1m 8.5s (-3.50) **Going Correction** -0.45s/f (Firm) 2y crse rec **8** Ran SP% **117.9**
Speed ratings (Par 94): **105,104,99,95,89 86,73,50**
toteswingers: 1&2 £5.70, 1&3 £2.10, 2&3 £16.20 CSF £29.61 TOTE £2.30: £1.50, £9.80, £1.40; EX 36.50.
Owner J Palmer-Brown & Potensis Ltd **Bred** Newsells Park Stud **Trained** East Everleigh, Wilts

FOCUS
Not much depth to this maiden but the third and fourth had shown a reasonable level of form in two previous starts, so the two newcomers that beat them might be pretty useful, especially the winner. He is rated value a length.

NOTEBOOK
Ninjago ◆, whom the market strongly favoured, didn't disappoint, despite racing widest of all down the middle of the track. He only needed nudging along to move into a challenging position and, although the winning margin was only slight, his rider never once had to get serious and there looked to be a lot still left in the tank. He doesn't have any entries at this stage but looks yet another potentially decent juvenile from this yard. (tchd 11-8)
Almalekiah(IRE) ◆ is clearly no slouch, having seen off more experienced rivals, and she impressed with the way she travelled before just finding the winner having a class edge in the closing stages. She looks a certainty to win her maiden on this evidence. (op 16-1)
Secret Beau travelled well and had every chance but had his limitations exposed in the closing stages. He certainly looks to have enough ability to win races though and is qualified for a mark now. (tchd 4-1 and 5-1)
Al Muntazah(IRE), whom the drop back in trip didn't help, didn't build on his first two starts. Nurseries beckon for him. (op 9-2)

4533 IDEAL CARIBBEAN INVESTMENT PROPERTIES FILLIES' H'CAP 7f 16y
6:50 (6:51) (Class 5) (0-70,70) 3-Y-O+ £2,264 (£673; £336; £168) Stalls Centre

Form RPR

4045 1 **Shes Rosie**[22] 3785 4-9-5 66 MarkCoumbe(5) 7 76+
(John O'Shea) *mde virtually all: pushed 3 l clr fnl f: eased considerably fnl 25yds: unchal* **6/1**[3]

64-1 2 *1* **Pawprints (IRE)**[63] 2461 3-9-4 70 AdamBeschizza(3) 3 72+
(William Haggas) *in rr and sn pushed along: hdwy over 2f out: styd on to go 3rd ins fnl f: clsd on eased down wnr clsng stages* **7/1**

21-0 3 *nk* **Royal Selection (IRE)**[107] 1306 4-9-2 58 KirstyMilczarek 10 61
(Karen George) *chsd wnr: rdn 2f out: no imp: one pce fnl f: kpt on as wnr eased: lost 2nd clsng stages* **33/1**

0420 4 *1 ¾* **Collectable**[52] 2802 3-8-3 52 ow1 (t) WilliamCarson 11 48+
(Jonathan Portman) *chsd ldrs: n.m.r 2f out: rdn and rallied fnl f: styd on but nvr a threat* **16/1**

1411 5 *1* **Lady Mango (IRE)**[16] 3958 4-9-7 63 LukeMorris 6 59
(Ronald Harris) *chsd ldrs: rdn 2f out: styd on same pce* **11/2**[2]

24-4 6 *nk* **Gifted Dancer**[27] 3619 3-9-2 70 AmyScott(5) 9 63
(Henry Candy) *in tch: pushed along and hdwy over 2f out: styd on same pce fnl f* **3/1**[1]

1-52 7 *2 ¼* **Daffydowndilly**[38] 3247 4-9-4 60 (t) DarryllHolland 14 49
(Hughie Morrison) *chsd ldrs: rdn and outpcd over 2f out: styd on again clsng stages* **3/1**[1]

0-00 8 *hd* **Bidable**[30] 3485 8-9-4 63 MatthewCosham(3) 15 51
(Bryn Palling) *in rr: pushed along 1/2-way: styd on fnl f: nvr in contention* **25/1**

35-0 9 *1 ¾* **Sea Anemone**[156] 660 3-8-3 52 DavidProbert 2 33
(Andrew Balding) *in rr: drvn along over 3f out: mod prog fnl f* **33/1**

5100 10 *hd* **Dancing Welcome**[8] 4235 6-10-0 70 (b) CathyGannon 16 53
(Milton Bradley) *outpcd most of way* **14/1**

0500 11 *2 ½* **Sienna Blue**[144] 804 4-8-5 54 JakePayne(7) 13 30
(Simon Hodgson) *chsd ldrs: rdn over 3f out: wknd sn after* **40/1**

-004 12 *5* **Red Mischief (IRE)**[30] 3510 3-9-4 67 JohnFahy 12 28
(Harry Dunlop) *pressed ldrs: rdn 3f out: wknd sn after* **16/1**

0060 13 *4* **Roodee Queen**[8] 4235 4-9-10 66 (be) LiamKeniry 5 18
(Milton Bradley) *in tch 4f* **33/1**

1m 20.7s (-2.50) **Going Correction** -0.45s/f (Firm)
WFA 3 from 4yo+ 7lb **13** Ran SP% **125.7**
Speed ratings (Par 100): **96,94,94,92,91 91,88,88,86,86 83,77,72**
toteswingers: 1&2 £11.00, 1&3 £60.20, 2&3 £39.60 CSF £47.94 CT £1319.63 TOTE £8.20: £2.60, £2.70, £9.50; EX 76.90.
Owner S G Martin **Bred** Stewart Martin And Alan Purvis **Trained** Elton, Gloucs

FOCUS
Run-of-the-mill handicap form, in which it proved very difficult to land a blow from off the pace. The winner was value for an extra length or so.

4534 FREEBETS.CO.UK H'CAP 7f 16y
7:20 (7:21) (Class 5) (0-75,75) 3-Y-O £2,264 (£673; £336; £168) Stalls Centre

Form RPR

6360 1 **Verse Of Love**[26] 3667 3-9-6 74 CathyGannon 2 81
(David Evans) *chsd ldrs: rdn fr 3f out: led wl over 1f out: styd on strly clsng stages* **4/1**[3]

2125 2 *1 ¼* **Rocky Reef**[7] 4298 3-9-0 75 (v) DanielMuscutt(7) 7 79
(Andrew Balding) *towards rr but in tch: hdwy and rdn wl over 1f out: styd on to take 2nd fnl 120yds but no imp on wnr* **11/4**[1]

5-00 3 *1* **Tidal's Baby**[60] 2557 3-9-0 68 DavidProbert 9 69
(Tony Carroll) *towards rr but in tch: hdwy and drvn 2f out: styd on u.p fnl f to cl on 2nd nr fin but no imp on wnr* **16/1**

0-04 4 *1* **Parisian Princess (IRE)**[39] 3214 3-8-11 65 DarryllHolland 3 63
(Hughie Morrison) *sn led: hdd wl over 3f out: rdn and styd chsng ldrs tl no ex fnl f* **7/1**

1035 5 *½* **Sunley Pride**[9] 4218 3-9-5 73 SamHitchcott 10 70
(Mick Channon) *in tch: rdn and outpcd 2f out: styd on again clsng stages* **7/2**[2]

-206 6 *¾* **Uncle Roger (IRE)**[53] 2756 3-8-12 66 (b[1]) WilliamCarson 5 61
(Eve Johnson Houghton) *s.i.s sn drvn and rcvrd to ld wl over 3f out: hdd u.p wl over 1f out: wknd fnl f* **16/1**

-050 7 *11* **Silkee Supreme**[41] 3161 3-9-3 71 RichardHughes 6 36
(Richard Hannon) *s.i.s: sn in tch: rdn over 3f out: sn btn* **12/1**

0030 8 *14* **Sir Dylan**[24] 3719 3-8-2 56 KierenFox 1
(Ronald Harris) *sn bhd* **33/1**

6514 9 *5* **New Decade**[28] 3566 3-8-11 65 LukeMorris 11
(Milton Bradley) *in tch 4f* **13/2**

1m 20.03s (-3.17) **Going Correction** -0.45s/f (Firm) **9** Ran SP% **117.1**
Speed ratings (Par 100): **100,98,97,96,95 94,82,66,60**
toteswingers 1&2 £3.30, 1&3 £19.50, 2&3 £9.00 CSF £15.68 CT £159.85 TOTE £4.70: £1.90, £1.10, £6.50; EX 15.00.
Owner Wayne Clifford **Bred** Mrs S Clifford **Trained** Pandy, Monmouths

FOCUS
A soundly run 7f in which the outcome was settled just inside the 2f pole. The first two were pretty much to form.
New Decade Official explanation: jockey said gelding was unsuited by the firm (good to firm places) ground

4535 FREEBETS.CO.UK FREE BETS H'CAP 5f 16y
7:50 (7:50) (Class 5) (0-70,69) 3-Y-O+ £2,264 (£673; £336; £168) Stalls Centre

Form RPR

5560 1 **Two Turtle Doves (IRE)**[19] 3893 6-8-12 55 SeanQuinlan 12 64
(Michael Mullineaux) *chsd ldrs: wnt 2nd over 1f out: str run clsng stages to ld last stride* **20/1**

3501 2 *nse* **Red Rhythm**[3] 4422 5-8-12 55 6ex (v) DavidProbert 5 64
(David Evans) *led: rdn and kpt on wl fnl f: hdd last stride* **4/1**[1]

354 3 *nk* **Sole Danser (IRE)**[16] 3960 4-9-10 67 LiamKeniry 9 75
(Milton Bradley) *in tch: rdn and hdwy over 1f out: str run fnl f to take 3rd fnl 75yds: clsng on ldng duo cl home* **11/2**[2]

5240 4 *1 ¼* **Whitecrest**[8] 4235 4-9-12 69 PatCosgrave 1 72
(John Spearing) *racd wd towards far side and outpcd: drvn and styd on to chse ldrs ins fnl f one pce in clsng stages* **7/1**

3663 5 *½* **Mother Jones**[11] 4154 4-9-6 66 MatthewCosham(3) 4 68
(David Evans) *in tch: drvn and hdwy to chse ldrs over 1f out: one pce ins fnl f* **16/1**

0-63 6 *hd* **Belle Bayardo (IRE)**[11] 4146 4-9-10 67 LukeMorris 11 68
(Ronald Harris) *in tch: rdn 3f out: one pce 2f out: kpt on again fnl 120yds* **11/2**[2]

0336 7 *2 ¾* **Cape Royal**[14] 4059 12-9-7 64 (tp) CathyGannon 7 55
(Milton Bradley) *chsd ldrs: rdn 2f out: wknd fnl f* **20/1**

5-02 8 *nk* **Valdaw**[65] 2385 4-8-12 55 StevieDonohoe 2 45
(Tony Carroll) *in rr: wl adrift 1/2-way and stl plenty to do in last pl appr fnl f: styd on wl fnl 150yds but nvr a threat* **14/1**

1-65 9 *4 ½* **Steel Rain**[3] 4425 4-9-2 59 RichardHughes 6 33
(Nikki Evans) *s.i.s: outpcd most of way* **15/2**

2013 10 *2* **Seventeen Seventy**[10] 4197 3-9-3 64 FrankieMcDonald 10 31
(Alan Coogan) *outpcd fr 1/2-way* **14/1**

0311 11 *16* **Festival Dance**[14] 4059 4-9-8 65 WilliamCarson 3
(Ron Hodges) *chsd ldr tl over 1f out: wknd appr fnl f: eased whn no ch* **6/1**[3]

57.84s (-1.46) **Going Correction** -0.45s/f (Firm)
WFA 3 from 4yo+ 4lb **11** Ran SP% **118.1**
Speed ratings (Par 103): **93,92,92,90,89 89,84,84,77,74 48**
toteswingers: 1&2 £23.40, 1&3 £24.80, 2&3 £3.50 CSF £98.93 CT £519.25 TOTE £19.90: £4.80, £1.20, £3.10; EX 102.40.
Owner George Cornes **Bred** M Sharkey **Trained** Alpraham, Cheshire
■ Sean Quinlan's first Flat winner.

FOCUS
Again the speed held up and Red Rhythm went agonisingly close to following up Tuesday's Ffos Las win but he was chinned on the line. The winner is rated up a length on this year's form.
Festival Dance Official explanation: vet said filly bled from the nose

4536 FREEBETS.CO.UK FREE BETTING H'CAP 1m 4f 23y
8:20 (8:21) (Class 6) (0-65,66) 3-Y-O+ £1,617 (£481; £240; £120) Stalls Low

Form RPR

-420 1 **Before Bruce**[16] 3969 5-8-13 57 (vt) ThomasGarner(7) 14 66
(Brendan Powell) *w ldrs tl led 5f out: shkn up whn jnd 3f out: drvn clr ins fnl 2f: comf* **40/1**

5-14 2 *2 ¼* **Abundantly**[39] 3212 3-8-13 62 DarryllHolland 15 67+
(Hughie Morrison) *in rr: rdn and hdwy fr 3f out: swtchd rt to outer fr 2f out: styd on wl fnl f to take 2nd last strides but no ch w wnr* **5/2**[2]

0513 3 *shd* **Taroum (IRE)**[1] 4491 5-9-6 57 KierenFox 2 62
(Tony Carroll) *in tch: hdwy 4f out: chal 3f out: styd chsng wnr but outpcd ins fnl 2f: one pce fnl f and ct for 2nd last strides* **2/1**[1]

3366 4 *1 ½* **Jalors (IRE)**[10] 4183 4-9-12 63 LukeMorris 10 66
(Ronald Harris) *chsd ldrs: rdn and one pce 3f out: styd on again fnl f* **10/1**

-345 5 *shd* **Taste The Wine (IRE)**[10] 4181 6-9-2 60 DanielMuscutt(7) 13 62
(Bernard Llewellyn) *chsd ldrs: chal 3f out: wknd fnl f* **16/1**

06/4 6 *5* **Bazart**[10] 4181 10-9-4 62 (tp) AliceHaynes(7) 5 56
(Bernard Llewellyn) *in rr: drvn along over 3f out: sme hdwy fnl f* **25/1**

-000 7 *hd* **Belle Park**[41] 3137 5-8-12 49 KirstyMilczarek 4 43
(Karen George) *s.i.s: in rr: drvn and styd on fnl 2f but nvr gng pce to get into contention* **28/1**

6426 8 *1 ½* **Pahente**[41] 3143 4-8-9 46 StevieDonohoe 11 41
(Tony Carroll) *led after 2f: hdd 5f out: stl upsides fr 3f out to 2f out: wknd and eased fnl f* **20/1**

000 9 *7* **Scribe (IRE)**[39] 3236 4-9-1 55 (v) MatthewCosham(3) 7 36
(David Evans) *nvr bttr than mid-div* **16/1**

0-30 10 *1 ¼* **Grande Illusion**[16] 3966 3-8-1 50 FrankieMcDonald 1 29
(J W Hills) *towards rr most of way* **40/1**

0-03 11 *8* **Sweet World**[32] 3429 8-9-8 62 AdamBeschizza(3) 9 28
(Bernard Llewellyn) *led 2f: chsd ldrs to 3f out* **14/1**

0060 12 *2 ¼* **Crazy Chris**[41] 3137 7-8-9 46 (b) CathyGannon 16
(Milton Bradley) *chsd ldrs to 3f out* **25/1**

004 **13** *10* **Carmen's Concerto**[26] 3664 3-9-0 **63**............................ DavidProbert 6
(Andrew Balding) *a in rr* **7/1**[3]
005 **14** *23* **Moonshine Ruby**[26] 3663 6-9-5 **56**............................ WilliamCarson 12
(Peter Hiatt) *chsd ldrs 5f out: wknd over 3f out* **20/1**
2m 38.01s (-0.99) **Going Correction** -0.05s/f (Good)
WFA 3 from 4yo+ 12lb **14** Ran SP% **127.5**
Speed ratings (Par 101): **101,99,99,98,98 95,94,93,89,88 83,81,74,59**
toteswingers 1&2 £111.70, 2&3 £3.00, 1&3 £11.50 CSF £137.94 CT £317.11 TOTE £91.00: £16.50, £1.30, £1.30; EX 761.80.
Owner McNamee,Peachey,Chapman,Guest,Smith **Bred** Miss S J Turner **Trained** Upper Lambourn, Berks
FOCUS
Low-grade stuff with a couple of potential improvers on show but there was a surprising winner. It was steadily run and the form is muddling.

4537 BREWIN DOLPHIN SUPPORTS TENOVUS H'CAP 2m 49y
8:55 (8:55) (Class 6) (0-60,61) 3-Y-O+ £1,617 (£481; £240; £120) Stalls Low

Form RPR
0321 **1** **Solar View (IRE)**[4] 4399 3-8-6 **54** 6ex................................ LukeMorris 6 63+
(Sir Mark Prescott Bt) *sn chsng ldr: drvn over 5f out: led over 4f out: sn drvn again and idling fr over 2f out and thrght fnl f but a doing enough* **1/2**[1]
5500 **2** *1 ½* **Lucky Diva**[147] 772 5-8-13 **51**......................................(p) JakePayne(7) 2 56
(Bill Turner) *in rr: hdwy to chse ldrs 5f out: chsd wnr fr 4f out: kpt on u.p but a hld* **16/1**[3]
-000 **3** *2* **Spinning Waters**[10] 4181 6-9-0 **45**................................ KellyHarrison 1 48
(Dai Burchell) *in tch: styd on to chse ldng duo over 3f out: one pce fnl 2f* **20/1**
5030 **4** *1 ¼* **Sacco D'Oro**[39] 3216 6-9-3 **48**......................................(v[1]) SeanQuinlan 5 49
(Michael Mullineaux) *in rr: hdwy fr 4f out: styd on fnl 2f but nvr gng pce to rch ldrs* **33/1**
-461 **5** *4* **Queen's Star**[9] 4225 3-8-13 **61** 6ex.................................. DavidProbert 8 57
(Andrew Balding) *led at modest pce tl hdd over 4f out: wknd fr 3f out* **11/4**[2]
6360 **6** *8* **Blue Pencil**[9] 4214 3-7-12 **49** oh1 ow3........................... RyanPowell(3) 4 36
(Roger Curtis) *chsd ldrs to 4f out: sn btn* **50/1**
-054 **7** *26* **Ladram Bay (IRE)**[11] 4147 3-7-5 **46** oh1........................ KatiaScallan(7) 7
(Jonathan Portman) *in rr: lost tch fnl 5f* **33/1**
0-60 **8** *¾* **Kings Apollo**[12] 1867 3-8-6 **57**...................................(p) SimonPearce(3) 9
(Tom Symonds) *stdd s t.k.h in rr tl lost tch fnl 7f* **33/1**
0050 **9** *1 ¾* **David's Folly (IRE)**[10] 4181 3-8-11 **59**........................ CathyGannon 3
(Bryn Palling) *in tch 9f* **25/1**
3m 45.86s (6.96) **Going Correction** -0.05s/f (Good)
WFA 3 from 5yo+ 17lb **9** Ran SP% **118.6**
Speed ratings (Par 101): **80,79,78,77,75 71,58,58,57**
toteswingers 1&2 £2.40, 2&3 £12.90, 1&3 £4.90 CSF £9.80 CT £91.05 TOTE £1.40: £1.10, £3.80, £3.30; EX 14.10.
Owner Neil Greig - Osborne House **Bred** Lady Richard Wellesley **Trained** Newmarket, Suffolk
FOCUS
Two penalised/progressive runners in an otherwise poor staying handicap. It was slowly run and the winner did not need to improve.
Kings Apollo Official explanation: jockey said gelding lost its action
T/Plt: £47.30 to a £1 stake. Pool of £53745.89 - 829.42 winning tickets. T/Qpdt: £20.90 to a £1 stake. Pool of £5150.33 - 182.15 winning tickets. ST

4336 NEWMARKET (R-H)
Friday, July 27

OFFICIAL GOING: Good to firm (8.7)
Far Side track used with Stalls on Stands Side except 10f &12f: Centre.
Wind: virtually nil Weather: warm, light cloud

4538 VINDIS GROUP FILLIES' H'CAP 1m 2f
5:35 (5:39) (Class 5) (0-70,70) 3-Y-O+ £2,587 (£770; £384; £192) Stalls Centre

Form RPR
0503 **1** **Candycakes (IRE)**[16] 3978 3-9-4 **70**................................ JamieSpencer 4 82
(Michael Bell) *mde all: 5 l clr 3f out: rdn over 1f out: drvn ent fnl f: kpt on wl u.p* **7/1**[2]
054 **2** *2 ½* **Spey Song (IRE)**[64] 2414 4-9-7 **63**..............................(b) FrankieDettori 9 70
(James Bethell) *stdd s: t.k.h: hld up towards rr: nt clr run 3f out: hdwy to chse clr wnr over 1f out: kpt on u.p fnl f but nvr able to chal* **8/1**[3]
3662 **3** *6* **Dazzling Valentine**[6] 4325 4-9-1 **64**............................ NatashaEaton(7) 8 59
(Alan Bailey) *chsd ldrs: chsd wnr over 3f out and sn rdn: no imp and lost 2nd over 1f out: no ch w ldng pair but battled on to hold 3rd fnl f* **7/1**[2]
06-0 **4** *1 ¾* **Peachez**[41] 3154 4-9-7 **68**.......................................(p) LeonnaMayor(5) 14 60
(Alastair Lidderdale) *stdd and dropped in bhd after s: t.k.h: hld up in rr tl hdwy 1/2-way: chsd ldrs and rdn over 2f out: no ex and btn over 1f out: no ch w wnr but plugged on fnl f* **9/1**
2-60 **5** *hd* **Stylistickhill (IRE)**[10] 4175 4-9-4 **60**..........................(t) MircoDemuro 13 51
(Scott Dixon) *stdd s: hld up off the pce in towards rr: swtchd lft and effrt over 3f out: chsng ldrs and drvn over 2f out: no ex over 1f out and wl hld 1f out: plugged on* **14/1**
0333 **6** *½* **Angel Cake (IRE)**[9] 4214 3-7-13 **51** oh6.....................(p) JamieMackay 6 41
(Phil McEntee) *racd in midfield: rdn over 3f out: no prog tl hdwy ent fnl f: styd on u.p: nvr trbld ldrs* **40/1**
00-0 **7** *nse* **Kaylena**[69] 2279 3-8-11 **63**.. RoystonFfrench 7 53
(Jeremy Noseda) *in tch in midfield: rdn effrt over 2f out: unable qck 2f out and no ch w wnr over 1f out: plugging on same pce whn nt clr run and swtchd rt ins fnl f* **12/1**
5253 **8** *2 ½* **So Is She (IRE)**[36] 3317 4-8-2 **51** oh1.......................(be) IanBurns(7) 11 36
(Alan Bailey) *hld up in rr: rdn and effrt 4f out: styd on past btn horses ins fnl f: nvr trbld ldrs* **22/1**
-514 **9** *¾* **Chignon (IRE)**[45] 2999 3-8-11 **63**.................................. TomQueally 3 47
(Sir Henry Cecil) *in tch: rdn and struggling over 2f out: wknd over 1f out* **4/1**[1]
0340 **10** *4* **Director's Dream (IRE)**[3] 4435 4-8-4 **51** oh1..........(b) TobyAtkinson(5) 1 27
(Mark Rimmer) *chsd wnr tl over 3f out: sn struggling u.p: wkng whn hung lft wl over 1f out: bhd and edgd rt fnl f* **33/1**
0-00 **11** *1 ¾* **Height Of Summer (IRE)**[57] 2637 4-9-11 **67**................ TedDurcan 12 39
(Chris Wall) *racd in midfield: rdn and no prog whn sltly hmpd and wnt lft jst over 2f out: bhd fnl f: eased towards fin* **7/1**[2]
6-54 **12** *3* **Valley Queen**[40] 3189 3-9-3 **69**...................................... PatDobbs 10 35
(Mark Usher) *chsd ldrs: lost pl and rdn over 3f out: towards rr and hmpd 2f out: wl bhd whn hmpd and eased wl ins fnl f* **20/1**

460 **13** *5* **Moonglow**[22] 3786 3-9-3 **69**...................................... RobertHavlin 2 25
(John Gosden) *chsd ldrs: rdn and losing pl whn edgd lft and hmpd jst over 2f out: sn wknd: wl bhd and eased ins fnl f* **9/1**
2m 4.53s (-0.97) **Going Correction** -0.15s/f (Firm)
WFA 3 from 4yo 10lb **13** Ran SP% **117.5**
Speed ratings (Par 100): **97,95,90,88,88 88,88,86,85,82 81,78,74**
toteswingers 1&2 £10.30, 2&3 £9.10, 1&3 £6.00 CSF £58.10 CT £410.55 TOTE £7.70: £2.30, £3.30, £2.30; EX 36.90 Trifecta £379.00 Pool: £563.48 - 1.10 winning units..
Owner J Acheson **Bred** Roland H Alder **Trained** Newmarket, Suffolk
■ Stewards' Enquiry : Toby Atkinson 1st incident, two-day ban: careless riding (Aug 10-11); 2nd, one-day ban: (careless riding) Aug 12
FOCUS
They went a decent pace in this handicap and raced towards the near rail. The winner put in a dominant display from the slightly unlucky runner-up, and the pair pulled clear. The form is taken at face value.

4539 AUDI CAMBRIDGE MEDIAN AUCTION MAIDEN STKS 6f
6:10 (6:10) (Class 5) 2-Y-O £3,234 (£962; £481; £240) Stalls Low

Form RPR
35 **1** **The Gold Cheongsam (IRE)**[35] 3326 2-8-12 0........... FrankieDettori 7 82+
(Jeremy Noseda) *wnt lft s: trckd ldrs: swtchd rt and effrt over 1f out: rdn to ld ins fnl f: r.o strly: gng away at fin* **5/4**[1]
4620 **2** *2 ¾* **Kalicamix**[14] 4056 2-8-12 74... DuilioDaSilva(5) 13 78
(Paul Cole) *led and set stdy gallop: qcknd 2f out: rdn and fnd ex over 1f out: hdd ins fnl f and outpcd by wnr: hld on for 2nd cl home* **20/1**
3 *shd* **Lord Of The Garter (IRE)** 2-9-3 0.............................. MartinLane 2 78+
(Brian Meehan) *t.k.h: hld up wl in tch: rdn and effrt over 1f out: sltly outpcd 1f out: rallied and styd on strly fnl 100yds: no threat to wnr* **40/1**
4 *nk* **Theodore Gericault (IRE)** 2-9-3 0................................ PatDobbs 11 77+
(Sir Michael Stoute) *hld up in tch: effrt and swtchd lft over 1f out: hdwy to chse ldrs ins fnl f: kpt on but nt gng pce of wnr fnl 100yds* **12/1**[3]
36 **5** *½* **Sejalaat (IRE)**[26] 3658 2-9-3 0.................................... TedDurcan 4 76
(John Dunlop) *hld up wl in tch in midfield: rdn and effrt over 1f out: kpt on fnl 100yds: no threat to wnr* **12/1**[3]
4 **6** *1 ¼* **Oscars Journey**[16] 3973 2-9-3 0.............................. FrederikTylicki 12 72
(J R Jenkins) *t.k.h: sn chsng ldrs: pressed ldr 1/2-way: ev ch and rdn 2f out: unable qck ent fnl f: wknd fnl 100yds* **25/1**
7 *1 ¾* **Seven Of Clubs (IRE)** 2-9-3 0..................................... JamesDoyle 10 66+
(Noel Quinlan) *hld up in tch in last quartet: hdwy and switching lft over 1f out: rdn: rn green and hung lft 1f out: styd on same pce ins fnl f* **16/1**
5 **8** *2* **Hot Mustard**[11] 4149 2-9-3 0.. TomQueally 8 60+
(Michael Bell) *hld up in last quartet: rdn and effrt but stl plenty to do whn nt clr run and swtchd rt 1f out: kpt on but no threat to wnr fnl f* **25/1**
3 **9** *½* **Echo Of Silence (FR)**[29] 3545 2-9-3 0........................ JamieSpencer 5 61
(Marco Botti) *in tch in midfield: swtchd lft 2f out and sn rdn: no imp ent fnl f: wl hld and eased towards fin* **9/4**[2]
00 **10** *hd* **Romanoff (IRE)**[13] 4114 2-9-3 0................................. J-PGuillambert 3 57
(Luca Cumani) *t.k.h: chsd ldr tl 1/2-way: rdn and unable qck jst over 2f out: lost pl over 1f out: wknd ins fnl f* **40/1**
62 **11** *3 ¾* **Man In The Arena**[8] 4239 2-9-3 0............................... RobertHavlin 14 45
(Dr Jon Scargill) *hld up in last quarter: rdn and effrt 2f out: sn struggling and edging lft: wknd 1f out* **80/1**
12 *¾* **Seemenomore** 2-9-3 0.. MartinHarley 9 43
(Michael Bell) *squeezed for room leaving stalls: in tch in rr: rdn and no hdwy 2f out: wknd over 1f out* **50/1**
4 **13** *hd* **Rosie Future (IRE)**[54] 2729 2-8-12 0............................... ChrisCatlin 1 37
(Rae Guest) *hld up in tch in last quartet: rdn and struggling 2f out: wknd over 1f out* **50/1**
1m 13.72s (1.22) **Going Correction** -0.15s/f (Firm) **13** Ran SP% **119.0**
Speed ratings (Par 94): **85,81,81,80,80 78,76,73,72,72 67,66,66**
toteswingers 1&2 £9.80, 2&3 £103.10, 1&3 £16.70 CSF £35.00 TOTE £1.80: £1.10, £5.00, £6.90; EX 29.40 TRIFECTA Not won..
Owner Arashan Ali **Bred** Tally-Ho Stud **Trained** Newmarket, Suffolk
FOCUS
A useful maiden. The pace was not very strong and they raced down the centre to near side. The winner did not need to match her Albany form.
NOTEBOOK
The Gold Cheongsam(IRE) set a clear standard on her fifth in the Albany Stakes. Unfazed by a return to fast ground, she travelled well just behind the pace before finding a sustained burst to get off the mark on her third start. She looks a speedy and professional type at this early stage of her career and is out of a 1m-9.4f winning half-sister to 6f Listed winner Sir Xaar, and also Chester Cup/smart jumps winner Mamlook. (op 11-8 tchd 6-5)
Kalicamix got an easy lead but he ran a big race and did well to hold off everything except for the favourite. This fairly exposed 74-rated colt holds the form down a bit but he is a willing type and he could have improved for this switch to fast ground. (op 16-1)
Lord Of The Garter(IRE), a 55,000euros Royal Applause colt who holds an entry in the Royal Lodge and Champagne Stakes, showed plenty to promise staying on strongly against the near rail on his debut.
Theodore Gericault(IRE) showed signs of inexperience but he did well to work his way into a dangerous position out wide and kept battling. This was an encouraging start by a Sir Percy colt who is out of the same connections' fair 7f 3yo winner Tableau Vivant. (op 11-1)
Sejalaat(IRE) was low-key at Salisbury last time but he was backed at biggish prices here and stayed on steadily to confirm the promise on his debut third at this track last month. (op 20-1)
Oscars Journey raced a bit keenly but he shaped with promise on his second start. He needs to learn to settle better but he is gelded second foal of useful prolific 5f-1m winner Fruit Of Glory who has quite a bit of potential for progress. (op 18-1)
Echo Of Silence(FR) raced a bit keenly but he shaped with promise on his second start. He needs to learn to settle better but he is gelded second foal of useful prolific 5f-1m winner Fruit Of Glory who has quite a bit of potential for progress. (op 5-2)

4540 VINDIS FAMILY NURSERY 7f
6:40 (6:40) (Class 4) (0-85,80) 2-Y-O £3,881 (£1,155; £577; £288) Stalls Low

Form RPR
500 **1** **Magic Channel (USA)**[24] 3733 2-8-0 **62**....................... RaulDaSilva(3) 7 66
(Richard Hannon) *chsd ldr: rdn over 2f out: kpt on u.p and ev ch ins fnl f: led fnl 75yds: styd on wl* **14/1**
0212 **2** *¾* **Oasis Cannes**[13] 4102 2-9-7 **80**.................................... ChrisCatlin 6 83
(Sir Mark Prescott Bt) *sn pushed along to ld: rdn 2f out: drvn and pressed ins fnl f: hdd and one pce fnl 75yds* **6/4**[1]
133 **3** *1* **Beedee**[42] 3097 2-9-7 **80**... PatDobbs 8 79
(Richard Hannon) *hld up in tch in last pair: effrt over 1f out: chsd ldrs and kpt on u.p ins fnl f* **5/1**[3]
055 **4** *nk* **Santo Prince (USA)**[29] 3545 2-8-13 **72**........................ JamieSpencer 2 70
(Michael Bell) *hld up in tch: swtchd lft and drvn over 1f out: kpt on same pce u.p ins fnl f* **10/3**[2]

5052 **5** *6* **Royal Mizar (SPA)**[13] [4090] 2-8-12 **71**.............................. TomQueally 4 53
(Alastair Lidderdale) *in tch: swtchd lft and effrt 2f out: no ex ent fnl f: wknd ins fnl f* **14/1**

440 **6** *3 ½* **Composed**[46] [2983] 2-8-5 **69**.. AshleyMorgan(5) 5 41
(Paul Cole) *chsd ldrs: rdn over 2f out: drvn and struggling over 1f out: wknd fnl f: wl hld and eased towards fin* **9/1**

540 **7** *4* **Standing Bear (IRE)**[24] [3733] 2-8-7 **71** ow1................ DuilioDaSilva(5) 1 33
(Paul Cole) *a in rr: rdn 3f out: wknd over 1f out: bhd ins fnl f* **16/1**

1210 **U** **Rated**[13] [4102] 2-9-5 **78**.. MartinHarley 3
(Mick Channon) *ducked rt and uns rdr sn after s* **20/1**

1m 25.78s (0.08) **Going Correction** -0.15s/f (Firm) **8** Ran SP% **113.7**
Speed ratings (Par 96): **93,92,91,90,83 79,75,**
toteswingers 1&2 £6.50, 2&3 £1.30, 1&3 £10.50 CSF £35.19 CT £124.05 TOTE £20.20: £6.10, £1.10, £1.40; EX 71.60 Trifecta £402.00 Pool: £776.86 - 1.43 winning units..
Owner Abdulla Al Mansoori **Bred** Bluegrass Hall Llc **Trained** East Everleigh, Wilts

FOCUS
A fair nursery. It was run at a solid pace and the first four pulled clear. Sound form judged around the second.

NOTEBOOK
Magic Channel(USA) was a bit disappointing as favourite in his first two maiden runs and finished tailed off at Kempton last time, but a step up to 7f on fast ground worked for him and he found a sustained run out wide to reel in the long-time leader on his nursery debut. He is a half-brother to two winners in the US and should be capable of more improvement at this trip and a bit further. Official explanation: trainer's rep said, regarding apparent improvement in form, that the colt benefited from the good to firm ground. (op 16-1)
Oasis Cannes landed the odds in a 7f Wolverhampton maiden before going very close on heavy ground in a 7f nursery here last time. Heavily backed, he looked in control for a long way against the near rail but he was worn down close home. (tchd 11-8)
Beedee got a bit tapped for speed before staying on well in a close third behind his bigger-priced stablemate. This was a solid first nursery run and he is by Beat Hollow out of a useful and progressive 1m-1m2f winner, so should appreciate a step up to 1m. (op 9-2)
Santo Prince(USA), a market mover in the morning, couldn't land a serious blow but he rallied well to finish at the back on the leading bunch on his nursery debut. (op 4-1)
Royal Mizar(SPA) raced a bit freely early on and couldn't find a finishing effort. (op 12-1)
Rated swerved and unseated his rider exiting the stalls. (op 16-1 tchd 22-1)

4541 BENTLEY CAMBRIDGE H'CAP 1m
7:10 (7:10) (Class 5) (0-75,74) 4-Y-O+ **£2,587** (£770; £384; £192) **Stalls** Low

Form RPR

4510 **1** **Copperwood**[25] [3699] 7-9-4 **71**.. FrannyNorton 10 79
(Mark Johnston) *racd in centre tl over 3f out: pressed overall ldr tl rdn to ld 2f out: sustained duel w rival ins fnl f: forged ahd cl home: all out: gamely* **16/1**

1600 **2** *nk* **McCool Bannanas**[28] [3559] 4-8-9 **62**.................................. LiamJones 8 69
(James Unett) *racd in centre tl 3f out: chsd ldrs overall: rdn and effrt 2f out: ev ch 1f out: sustained chal tl no ex and btn cl home* **20/1**

3533 **3** *¾* **Red Shuttle**[28] [3594] 5-9-4 **71**....................................(t) JamieSpencer 11 77
(Noel Quinlan) *racd in centre tl 3f out: hld up in rr: effrt over 1f out: chsd ldng pair and drvn ins fnl f: racd awkwardly but kpt on towards fin* **4/1**[3]

223 **4** *3* **Whitby Jet (IRE)**[28] [3574] 4-9-7 **74**.................................... WilliamBuick 3 73
(Ed Vaughan) *racd nrside thrght: hld up towards rr: drvn and effrt 2f out: styd on same pce u.p fnl f* **7/2**[2]

-111 **5** *nk* **Toga Tiger (IRE)**[31] [3470] 5-8-12 **68**.............................. RaulDaSilva(3) 5 66
(Jeremy Gask) *racd nrside thrght: in tch: effrt over 2f out: ev ch and rdn wl over 1f out: no ex 1f out: outpcd and btn ins fnl f* **11/10**[1]

0000 **6** *1* **Pat's Legacy (USA)**[15] [3999] 6-9-5 **72**........................... J-PGuillambert 1 68
(Jo Hughes) *racd nr side thrght: sn rdn along to ld overall: hdd and rdn 2f out: outpcd and btn 1f out: plugged on* **10/1**

4003 **7** *4* **Prince Namid**[30] [3485] 10-7-9 **55** oh4................................. IanBurns(7) 4 41
(Jonathen de Giles) *racd nr side thrght: in tch in last trio: rdn and struggling 3f out: outpcd and no threat to ldrs fr over 1f out* **66/1**

0050 **8** *16* **Rufus Stone (USA)**[22] [3793] 4-8-5 **58**............................ MircoDemuro 2 8
(Jane Chapple-Hyam) *racd nr side thrght: in tch: rdn and effrt 3f out: btn 2f out: sn wknd and wl bhd fnl f:* **20/1**

560- **9** *½* **Roy The Boy (USA)**[314] [6167] 4-9-7 **74**......................(v[1]) PadraigBeggy 7 23
(Alan Bailey) *t.k.h: swtchd to r nr side sn after s: hld up in tch: rdn and fnd nil 2f out: sn fdd and wl bhd fnl f* **25/1**

4-00 **10** *7* **Clearing House**[11] [4158] 7-7-13 **59**.............................. BradleyBosley(7) 9
(John Ryan) *awkward leaving stalls and rdr lost iron: racd in centre tl 3f out: t.k.h: in tch tl lost pl 3f out: sn bhd: no ch whn rdr lost iron again 1f out* **100/1**

1m 38.19s (-1.81) **Going Correction** -0.15s/f (Firm) **10** Ran SP% **120.7**
Speed ratings (Par 103): **103,102,101,98,98 97,93,77,77,70**
toteswingers 1&2 £4.30, 2&3 £6.00, 1&3 £1.20 CSF £287.88 CT £1131.28 TOTE £18.20: £4.40, £7.30, £1.20; EX 329.80 Trifecta £428.40 Pool: £1018.97 - 1.76 winning units..
Owner Always Trying Partnership VIII (E) **Bred** Hertford Offset Press **Trained** Middleham Moor, N Yorks
■ Stewards' Enquiry : Liam Jones two-day ban: used whip above permitted level (Aug 10-11)

FOCUS
There was a tight finish in this steadily run handicap and the hot favourite ran flat. Ordinary form.
Toga Tiger(IRE) Official explanation: trainer's rep said gelding was unsuited by the good to firm ground
Clearing House Official explanation: jockey said he lost an iron on leaving stalls

4542 FRANK VINDIS MAIDEN STKS 1m 4f
7:40 (7:40) (Class 5) 3-Y-O **£3,234** (£962; £481; £240) **Stalls** Centre

Form RPR

3-42 **1** **Stencive**[51] [2826] 3-9-3 85.. FrankieDettori 6 95
(William Haggas) *stdd s: t.k.h: hld up in midfield: clsd to chse ldr 3f out: rdn to ld wl over 1f out: styd on wl ins fnl f* **5/2**[1]

45 **2** *2* **Dr Yes (FR)**[35] [3349] 3-9-3 0... TomQueally 5 92
(Sir Henry Cecil) *chsd ldr for 2f: chsd clr ldng pair after: clsd and pressed ldr 3f out: rdn and chsd wnr over 1f out: edgd lft and styd on same pce ins fnl f* **7/2**[2]

23 **3** *2 ½* **Suegioo (FR)**[35] [3349] 3-9-3 0...................................... MircoDemuro 11 88
(Marco Botti) *stdd s: hld up towards rr: clsd on ldrs 3f out: rdn to chse ldng pair over 1f out: edgd lft and btn ins fnl f: eased towards fin* **13/2**

-020 **4** *2 ½* **Coplow**[28] [3565] 3-8-12 80... PatDobbs 2 79
(Richard Hannon) *stdd: wnt lft and bmpd rival s: t.k.h: chsd ldr after 2f tl led and clr w rival 8f out: rdn over 2f out: hdd wl over 1f out: no ex and btn 1f out: plugged on same pce* **9/1**

24 **5** *½* **Infinitum**[22] [3773] 3-8-12 0... WilliamBuick 3 78
(John Gosden) *bmpd s: hld up towards rr: hdwy into midfield 6f out: clsd on ldrs 3f out: drvn and chsd ldrs 2f out: unable qck and btn 1f out: plugged on same pce after* **4/1**[3]

0 **6** *1 ¾* **Leo Luna**[14] [4067] 3-9-3 0.. RichardMullen 8 80
(Sir Michael Stoute) *prom in main gp: rdn along and clsd on ldrs 4f out: struggling u.p 2f out: 6th and wl hld 1f out* **11/2**

0 **7** *10* **Sanctioned**[22] [3786] 3-9-3 0.. JamesDoyle 12 64
(Roger Charlton) *bhd: pushed along 8f out: rdn and struggling 4f out: lost tch and bhd fnl 2f* **20/1**

50 **8** *6* **Bobs Her Uncle**[28] [3565] 3-8-12 0..................................... TedDurcan 7 50
(James Bethell) *wnt lft s: t.k.h: hld up off the pce in midfield: clsd on ldrs 4f out: rdn over 2f out and sn btn: wknd 2f out* **66/1**

0 **9** *4 ½* **Autumnus (IRE)**[23] [3763] 3-9-3 0..............................(p) RoystonFfrench 9 48
(Ismail Mohammed) *led tl 10f out: chsd ldr and clr of field 8f out: lost 2nd 3f out: sn lost pl and racd awkwardly wl over 1f out: bhd fnl f* **150/1**

0-3 **10** *18* **End Of May (IRE)**[10] [4182] 3-8-12 0.................................... ChrisCatlin 1 14
(Peter Bowen) *hld up off the pce towards rr: clsd on ldrs 4f out: rdn and struggling 3f out: sn wknd: wl bhd and eased ins fnl f* **100/1**

2m 30.92s (-1.98) **Going Correction** -0.15s/f (Firm) **10** Ran SP% **117.4**
Speed ratings (Par 100): **100,98,97,95,95 93,87,83,80,68**
toteswingers 1&2 £4.30, 2&3 £6.00, 1&3 £1.20 CSF £11.26 TOTE £4.30: £1.60, £1.10, £2.80; EX 15.10 Trifecta £53.10 Pool: £599.48 - 8.34 winning units..
Owner B Kantor & M Jooste **Bred** Castlemartin Stud And Skymarc Farm **Trained** Newmarket, Suffolk

FOCUS
A hot maiden. The early pace was steady but it quickened before the halfway point and the favourite scored in good style. The form makes sense.

4543 DEYTON BELL ECONOMIC AND COMMERCIAL DEVELOPMENT H'CAP 1m 4f
8:10 (8:12) (Class 3) (0-90,86) 3-Y-O+ **£7,115** (£2,117; £1,058; £529) **Stalls** Centre

Form RPR

1-02 **1** **Expert Fighter (USA)**[37] [3280] 3-8-13 **83**........................ FrankieDettori 6 92+
(Saeed Bin Suroor) *mde all: rdn 2f out: fnd ex and clr ent fnl f: r.o wl: readily* **15/8**[1]

-421 **2** *3* **Cresta Star**[48] [2942] 3-8-11 **81**.. PatDobbs 1 84
(Richard Hannon) *chsd ldrs: wnt 2nd over 3f out: rdn and unable qck w wnr over 1f out: styd on same pce fnl f* **3/1**[2]

5620 **3** *2* **Hong Kong Island (IRE)**[30] [3494] 5-9-12 **84**................ FrederikTylicki 3 84
(Micky Hammond) *hld up in last pair: rdn and effrt 2f out: styd on same pce fnl f* **3/1**[2]

0616 **4** *1 ½* **Tartan Gigha (IRE)**[42] [3114] 7-10-0 **86**........................ RoystonFfrench 5 83
(Geoffrey Harker) *hld up in last pair: effrt and rdn ent fnl 2f: drvn and styd on same pce fr over 1f out* **12/1**

0-00 **5** *1 ¾* **Granston (IRE)**[62] [2504] 11-9-6 **78**.................................... TomQueally 2 73
(James Bethell) *t.k.h: hld up in tch: chsd ldrs 3f out: rdn and unable qck ent fnl 2f: wknd ins fnl f* **11/1**

/563 **6** *dist* **Mezzanisi (IRE)**[10] [4184] 7-9-5 **77**.................................. JamieSpencer 8
(Peter Bowen) *chsd ldr tl over 3f out: sn dropped out and eased: virtually p.u fnl 2f* **8/1**[3]

-00L **R** **Gunslinger (FR)**[15] [3997] 7-9-2 **79**.............................. MircoDemuro(5) 7
(Michael Scudamore) *ref to r: tk no part* **33/1**

2m 32.11s (-0.79) **Going Correction** -0.15s/f (Firm)
WFA 3 from 5yo+ 12lb **7** Ran SP% **114.9**
Speed ratings (Par 107): **96,94,92,91,90 ,**
toteswingers 1&2 £1.70, 2&3 £2.30, 1&3 £2.20 CSF £7.79 CT £15.38 TOTE £1.80: £1.10, £2.10; EX 7.20 Trifecta £16.90 Pool: £745.30 - 32.52 winning units..
Owner Godolphin **Bred** Darley **Trained** Newmarket, Suffolk

FOCUS
A decent handicap. The pace was steady but the unexposed favourite powered clear under a front-running ride. He could be capable of better still.

NOTEBOOK
Expert Fighter(USA) coped well with a step up to 1m4f, running his rivals into submission to add to his 1m Brighton maiden win in October. He did have the run of things in a race where several of his rivals took a strong hold but there was a lot to like about the style of the win. A lightly raced and progressive half-brother to Dubai World Cup winner Monterosso, he has scope for further improvement in middle-distance handicaps and it is worth noting that his one blip was on slow ground. (op 13-8 tchd 2-1)
Cresta Star was a bit keen on her first run at 1m4f but she battled on well in a respectable run off 5lb higher than for her 1m2f win on slow ground at Windsor last month. She could resume her progress in a more strongly run race next time. (op 7-2 tchd 4-1)
Hong Kong Island(IRE) was market springer in his bid to bounce back from a rare below-par effort last time but he couldn't land a blow in a race that didn't set up for his closing style. (op 5-1 tchd 11-2)
Tartan Gigha(IRE) stayed on late when it was all over in a race that wasn't run to suit. An inconsistent profile casts a cloud over his prospects but he scored in good style at Carlisle last month and remains well treated on his old form for Mark Johnston. (op 8-1)
Granston(IRE) shaped with a bit of promise before his effort petered out on his third run back from a layoff. He still seems to have ability but he is well into the veteran stage and has managed just one win since May 2010. (op 14-1 tchd 9-1)
Mezzanisi(IRE) Official explanation: jockey said gelding lost its action

4544 DEYTON BELL TRANSATLANTIC BUSINESS DEVELOPMENT H'CAP 1m
8:45 (8:45) (Class 5) (0-75,74) 3-Y-O **£2,587** (£770; £288; £288) **Stalls** Low

Form RPR

0-03 **1** **Siouxperhero (IRE)**[32] [3432] 3-8-11 **64**................................ NeilCallan 7 71
(William Muir) *mde all: rdn 2f out: drvn and kpt on gamely fnl f: jst hld on: all out* **12/1**

0442 **2** *shd* **Roedean (IRE)**[8] [4242] 3-8-11 **64**................................(tp) FrankieDettori 2 71
(William Stone) *in tch: effrt u.p over 1f out: chsd wnr jst ins fnl f: styd on strly fnl 100yds: jst failed* **4/1**[2]

1-03 **3** *1 ¾* **Afnoon (USA)**[35] [3347] 3-9-4 **71**.. TadhgO'Shea 3 74
(John Dunlop) *in tch: gng wl but nt clr run 2f out: switching rt and lft over 1f out: in the clr and drvn to chse ldrs jst ins fnl f: one pce fnl 100yds* **4/1**[2]

433 **3** *dht* **Engrossing**[15] [4001] 3-9-6 **73**.. PatDobbs 4 76+
(Richard Hannon) *s.i.s: hld up in rr: rdn and effrt over 1f out: r.o wl ins fnl f: unable to chal* **5/2**[1]

405 **5** *1 ¼* **Thereabouts (USA)**[21] [3809] 3-9-5 **72**.............................. MartinHarley 10 72
(Marco Botti) *t.k.h: chsd ldrs: rdn and effrt 2f out: drvn and unable qck over 1f out: wknd ins fnl f* **9/1**

2426 **6** *1 ¾* **Santadelacruze**[35] [3338] 3-9-0 **67**..............................(p) TomQueally 8 64
(Gary Moore) *chsd ldr: rdn 2f out: lost 2nd jst ins fnl f and struggling whn short of room and hmpd sn after: wknd* **20/1**

-030 **7** *11* **Amoralist**[24] [3736] 3-9-7 **74**.. WilliamBuick 9 43
(Ed Dunlop) *t.k.h: chsd ldrs: rdn and unable qck 2f out: sn short of room and hmpd: wknd over 1f out: eased wl ins fnl f* **7/1**[3]

140- **8** 4 ½ **Broxbourne (IRE)**[351] 4943 3-9-3 **70**.............................. FrannyNorton 6 28
(Mark Johnston) *in tch in last pair: rdn 3f out: struggling u.p 2f out: wknd over 1f out* **8/1**

1m 42.71s (2.71) **Going Correction** -0.15s/f (Firm) **8** Ran SP% **114.6**
Speed ratings (Par 100): **80,79,78,78,76 75,64,59**PL: Engrossing £0.50 Afnoon £1.00 TRICAST: Siouxperhero/Rodean/E £81.01 S/R/A £115.70.t oteswingers: 1&2 £7.40, 1&A £4.60, 1&E £5.90, 2&E £1.20, 2&A £1.10 CSF £59.62 TOTE £20.10: £3.40, £1.20; EX 63.00 TRIFECTA £132.10. Pool: £439.37 - 1.23 winning unit27 Owner.

FOCUS
A competitive handicap run at a steady pace. There was a surprise result and John Dunlop's runner didn't get any luck. The form looks sound enough.
Amoralist Official explanation: trainer's rep said colt was unsuited by the good to firm ground
T/Plt: £40.30 to a £1 stake. Pool of £51903.19 - 938.52 winning tickets. T/Qpdt: £10.90 to a £1 stake. Pool of £4107.84, 276.55 winning tickets. SP

3436 THIRSK (L-H)
Friday, July 27

OFFICIAL GOING: Good to firm (good in places; 9.5)
Wind: Fresh, half behind Weather: Cloudy, bright

4545 BRITISH STALLION STUDS SUPPORTING BRITISH RACING EBF MAIDEN STKS 5f
2:10 (2:11) (Class 5) 2-Y-O **£3,234** (£962; £481; £240) **Stalls** High

Form RPR

1 **Fire Eyes** 2-9-0 0.. HarryBentley(3) 4 85+
(David Brown) *trckd ldr far side: led gp over 2f out: sn in overall command: kpt on wl* **14/1**

3 **2** 2 ¼ **Avec Rose**[39] 3217 2-8-12 0.. PaulHanagan 17 71+
(Richard Fahey) *racd stands' side: chsd ldr: rdn 2f out: kpt on: led gp ins fnl f but no ch w wnr* **9/4**[1]

5 **3** 1 ½ **Queen Flush (IRE)**[17] 3937 2-8-12 0.......................... AdrianNicholls 14 66+
(David Nicholls) *led stands' side: rdn and hung lft over 1f out: sn no ch w wnr on far side: lost overall 2nd ins fnl f: 2nd of 12 in gp* **13/2**[3]

4 ½ **Kamchatka** 2-9-3 0... RobertWinston 3 69+
(Alan Swinbank) *chsd ldng pair far side: rdn 2f out: kpt on: no threat wnr: 2nd of 6 in gp* **9/2**[2]

5 ¾ **Bapak Pesta (IRE)** 2-9-3 0.. PhillipMakin 19 66+
(Kevin Ryan) *racd stands' side: in tch: pushed along whn swtchd lft over 1f out: kpt on fnl f: 3rd of 12 in gp* **8/1**

6 ½ **Different** 2-8-12 0.. TomEaves 16 60
(Bryan Smart) *racd stands' side: in tch: rdn over 1f out: kpt on: 4th of 12 in gp* **9/1**

00 **7** 1 ¼ **Modern Lady**[37] 3269 2-8-12 0.................................. RobbieFitzpatrick 7 55
(Richard Guest) *racd far side: hld up: pushed along 1/2-way: kpt on: 3rd of 6 in gp* **66/1**

7 dht **Star Spun (USA)** 2-9-3 0... GrahamGibbons 12 60
(David Barron) *racd stands' side: s.i.s: sn midfield: pushed along 1/2-way: kpt on fnl f: 5th of 12 in gp* **11/1**

3 **9** 2 ¾ **Municipal (IRE)**[18] 3902 2-9-3 0.. PaulMulrennan 2 50
(Michael Dods) *led far side: hdd over 2f out: wknd over 1f out: 4th of 6 in gp* **20/1**

40 **10** ½ **Confidential Creek**[42] 3110 2-9-3 0................................ GrahamLee 11 48
(Ollie Pears) *racd stands' side: midfield: pushed along 1/2-way: nvr threatened: 6th of 12 in gp* **14/1**

0 **11** hd **Portside Blue**[13] 4114 2-9-3 0.. BarryMcHugh 5 48
(Tony Coyle) *hld up far side: pushed along bef 1/2-way: nvr threatened: 5th of 6 in gp* **100/1**

06 **12** hd **Grand Jipeck (IRE)**[20] 3844 2-9-3 0..........................(t) PatrickMathers 6 47
(Ian McInnes) *s.i.s: a bhd far side: last of 6 in gp* **100/1**

250 **13** 1 **Ryedale Valley**[43] 3062 2-9-3 53...................................... DuranFentiman 18 43
(Tim Easterby) *chsd ldrs stands' side: wknd over 1f out: 7th of 12 in gp* **28/1**

14 1 **Abraham Monro** 2-9-3 0.. MichaelO'Connell 8 40
(Kate Walton) *racd stands' side: midfield: pushed along 1/2-way: sn btn: 8th of 12 in gp* **40/1**

260 **15** 2 ¼ **Cymeriad**[23] 3747 2-8-12 59.. JamesSullivan 13 27
(Michael Easterby) *chsd ldrs stands' side: wknd over 1f out: 9th of 12 in gp* **40/1**

400 **16** shd **Betty Boo (IRE)**[37] 3286 2-8-5 56........................(e[1]) ShirleyTeasdale(7) 15 26
(Shaun Harris) *chsd ldrs stands' side: wknd fnl 2f: 10th of 12 in gp* **66/1**

40 **17** hd **Oh Boy Oh Boy**[34] 3381 2-9-3 0.. PaddyAspell 9 30
(James Moffatt) *hld up stands' side: a bhd: 11th of 12 in gp* **150/1**

18 1 ½ **Itsallinthemind** 2-8-12 0.. DavidAllan 10 20
(Tim Easterby) *dwlt: a towards rr stands' side: last of 12 in gp* **40/1**

57.84s (-1.76) **Going Correction** -0.375s/f (Firm) **18** Ran SP% **126.2**
Speed ratings (Par 94): **99,95,93,92,91 90,88,88,83,83 82,82,80,79,75 75,75,72**
toteswingers 1&2 £8.80, 2&3 £4.80, 1&3 £16.80 CSF £44.33 TOTE £16.30: £4.00, £1.50, £2.50; EX 71.10.
Owner Qatar Racing Limited **Bred** J Ellis **Trained** Averham Park, Notts

FOCUS
A decent looking maiden on paper, with some interesting types making their debuts up against some 2yos who were expected to build upon the favourable impressions they'd made on their first starts. The field split into two groups off a strong pace with the winner coming from the smaller group on the unfavourable far side. The form looks solid, rated towards the top end of the race averages, and should produce plenty of winners, as the time was just under standard and only a touch over the course record.

NOTEBOOK
Fire Eyes is out of Flying Childers and Molecomb winner Wunders Dream and was a £300,000 purchase earlier this term. He was an eye-catching colt beforehand and showed good speed, sitting prominently throughout before quickening clear in the final furlong. There was a lot to like about this performance and he looks a very exciting 2yo and, with some improvement guaranteed, he can be certain to make his presence felt in the better juvenile races this season. (tchd 12-1)
Avec Rose had been well supported on her debut but probably got bogged down in the conditions. Highly regarded at home, this went some way to confirming that belief as she was a little unlucky to bump into a potentially very useful juvenile ands she ran out a clear second. She looks sure to go one better. (op 2-1 tchd 15-8)
Queen Flush(IRE) had clearly benefited from her experience when only producing a fair effort on debut (beaten favourite), but is clearly held in some regard as she was again well-backed. She cut out a furious pace and, apart from drifting left in the final furlong, did little wrong in defeat, and is one to keep on-side. (op 9-1 tchd 10-1)
Kamchatka cost 150,000gns earlier this year and hails from a stable whose 2yos are performing well. The son of Sakhee's Secret was very well-supported and ran with plenty of credit, but things appeared to be happening all too quick for him on this debut and he will have benefited from the experience. He is another to keep on-side. (op 9-1)
Bapak Pesta(IRE), a 100,000euros purchase, is a half-brother to three winners, including 7f winner Diamond Penny, and is another to take of note as he was doing all his best work in the latter stages. (tchd 17-2)
Different, a well-related sister to two winners, notably the stable's 5f 100-rated juvenile Mary Read, and a half-sister to another three. She chased the leaders from the off but could not quite find the pace to lay down a challenge before drifting to her left in the final furlong. (op 10-1 tchd 17-2)
Modern Lady Official explanation: jockey said filly hung right throughout (op 10-1)
Star Spun(USA) hails from a stable having a fine time with juveniles this season. He came here with a big reputation but ran into some useful sorts although he showed plenty of promise. (op 10-1)
Municipal(IRE) showed good early pace to press the winner on the far side but probably paid the price for doing so. (op 18-1)
Grand Jipeck(IRE) Official explanation: trainer said gelding was unsuited by the good to firm (good in places) ground

4546 BRITISH STALLION STUDS SUPPORTING BRITISH RACING EBF MAIDEN FILLIES' STKS 7f
2:45 (2:46) (Class 4) 2-Y-O **£4,528** (£1,347; £673; £336) **Stalls** Low

Form RPR

2 **1** **Simply Shining (IRE)**[19] 3887 2-9-0 0.............................. PaulHanagan 6 80+
(Richard Fahey) *trckd ldrs: rdn to ld over 1f out: kpt on strly fnl f* **2/1**[1]

52 **2** 2 **New Falcon (IRE)**[60] 2541 2-9-0 0................................ PaulMulrennan 9 72
(James Tate) *t.k.h early: prom: effrt and rdn over 2f out: chsd wnr ins fnl f: r.o* **6/1**[3]

3 1 **Iberis** 2-9-0 0... IanMongan 11 70+
(Sir Henry Cecil) *dwlt: sn in tch on outside: effrt and pushed along over 2f out: kpt on same pce ins fnl f* **5/2**[2]

4 hd **Ella Motiva (IRE)** 2-9-0 0.. RobbieFitzpatrick 8 69+
(Mark Brisbourne) *dwlt: hld up: pushed along over 2f out: hdwy and swtchd rt over 1f out: kpt on fnl f: no imp* **40/1**

0 **5** shd **Noosa Sound**[22] 3776 2-9-0 0.. PJMcDonald 10 69
(John Davies) *cl up: led over 2f out to over 1f out: no ex ins fnl f* **150/1**

6 hd **Spirit Of Success** 2-9-0 0... AhmedAjtebi 2 68+
(Mahmood Al Zarooni) *t.k.h: hld up: rdn and m green 2f out: kpt on fnl f: nvr able to chal* **13/2**

7 2 ½ **Kat Moon** 2-9-0 0.. DavidAllan 3 61+
(Tim Easterby) *dwlt: bhd: pushed along and m green 2f out: kpt on ins fnl f: nvr on terms* **20/1**

5025 **8** 2 ½ **Blue Clumber**[20] 3844 2-9-0 83.................................... GrahamGibbons 7 55
(Shaun Harris) *led at ordinary gallop to over 2f out: sn rdn: wknd fnl f* **12/1**

9 2 **Trinket Box (USA)** 2-8-9 0.. AntiocoMurgia(5) 1 49
(Mahmood Al Zarooni) *hld up: rdn along and drifted lft 2f out: sn n.d* **12/1**

0 **10** 9 **Juhaina (IRE)**[18] 3909 2-9-0 0... GrahamLee 5 25
(Ann Duffield) *midfield on ins: struggling over 3f out: sn btn* **50/1**

11 ½ **Rosie Hall (IRE)** 2-9-0 0.. TomEaves 4 24
(Bryan Smart) *s.i.s: bhd on outside: struggling 3f out: sn btn* **28/1**

1m 27.2s **Going Correction** -0.325s/f (Firm) **11** Ran SP% **118.2**
Speed ratings (Par 93): **87,84,83,83,83 83,80,77,75,64 64**
toteswingers 1&2 £2.40, 2&3 £4.30, 1&3 £3.00 CSF £14.00 TOTE £2.90: £1.40, £1.10, £1.10; EX 11.50.
Owner Mrs H Steel **Bred** Ennistown Stud **Trained** Musley Bank, N Yorks

FOCUS
A reasonable pace for this fair 7f fillies' maiden which featured some interesting newcomers. The form is rated around the race averages.

NOTEBOOK
Simply Shining(IRE) had shown some promise when runner-up in a 7f maiden at Ayr on soft ground earlier this month. She handled the quicker ground well enough although changing her legs a couple of times when asked to quicken, and she won with something in hand. Shaped as though she will get at least a mile and depending on what the handicapper makes of this she should have plenty of options in the future. (tchd 9-4)
New Falcon(IRE) had improved with each run over 6f and appeared to appreciate this slight step up in trip. She looks a little one-paced but should find an opening when switching to nurseries. (op 13-2 tchd 7-1)
Iberis was making her debut and had attracted some support beforehand. She ran well enough in defeat but could only stay on at the same pace when the tempo increased in the straight. She is entitled to come on for this. (op 7-2)
Ella Motiva(IRE) ran with credit on her debut doing all her best work late on and, being by Motivator, should be a better proposition when stepped up in trip further down the line.
Noosa Sound finished a well-beaten eighth on her debut, but this was a much improved effort having travelled well for a long way before flattening out in the latter stages.
Spirit Of Success, a 65,000gns purchase, has some decent entries but could never get involved and she will have to come on for this considerably if he is to take them up. (op 7-1 tchd 15-2)

4547 STANLAND GROUP FILLIES' H'CAP 6f
3:20 (3:21) (Class 5) (0-70,70) 3-Y-O+ **£2,328** (£693; £346; £173) **Stalls** High

Form RPR

4003 **1** **Meandmyshadow**[10] 4174 4-9-2 **60**.............................. RobertWinston 9 71
(Alan Brown) *chsd far side ldrs: effrt and edgd lft over 1f out: led wl ins fnl f: r.o: 1st of 10 in gp* **5/1**[1]

0001 **2** nk **Sunny Side Up (IRE)**[58] 2595 3-9-0 **63**.......................... PaulHanagan 8 73
(Richard Fahey) *t.k.h: cl up far side: led that gp over 2f out: sn rdn: hdd wl ins fnl f: r.o: 2nd of 10 in gp* **6/1**[3]

0/1- **3** ¾ **Willbeme**[416] 2781 4-9-2 **60**.. MichaelO'Connell 12 68+
(Neville Bycroft) *dwlt: sn trcking stands' side ldrs: led that gp and effrt over 1f out: kpt on fnl f: nt rch first two far side: 1st of 7 in gp* **14/1**

2003 **4** ¾ **Bay Of Fires (IRE)**[9] 4207 4-9-9 **67**.........................(p) DanielTudhope 4 72
(David O'Meara) *cl up far side gp: effrt on outside over 1f out: nt qckn wl ins fnl f: 3rd of 10 in gp* **20/1**

4601 **5** 1 ½ **Majestic Breeze (IRE)**[25] 3706 3-8-4 **53**.............................. AmyRyan 3 53
(Brian Ellison) *trckd far side ldrs: effrt and rdn over 2f out: one pce fnl f: 4th of 10 in gp* **16/1**

0040 **6** hd **Lady Kildare (IRE)**[4] 4400 4-9-4 **62**............................... AndrewElliott 20 62
(Jedd O'Keeffe) *in tch stands' side: effrt over 1f out: wnt 2nd that gp ins fnl f: kpt on: 2nd of 7 in gp* **6/1**[3]

-406 **7** shd **Fair Bunny**[44] 3018 5-8-7 **51** oh3..................................(b) JimmyQuinn 14 50
(Alan Brown) *slt ld stands' side gp to over 1f out: kpt on same pce ins fnl f: 3rd of 7 in gp* **50/1**

0640 **8** ¾ **Lizzie (IRE)**[15] 3994 4-9-2 **60**..................................(b) GrahamGibbons 18 57
(Tim Easterby) *bhd and sn pushed along stands' side gp: sme hdwy fnl f: nvr on terms: 4th of 7 in gp* **5/1**[2]

5044 **9** 1 ¼ **Foreign Rhythm (IRE)**[10] 4174 7-8-11 **60**............... GarryWhillans(5) 11 53
(Ron Barr) *cl up on outside of stands' side gp: drvn over 2f out: no ex over 1f out: 5th of 7 in gp* **14/1**

-330 **10** *nk* **Code Six (IRE)**[134] 905 3-9-3 **66** TomEaves 19 58
(Bryan Smart) *taken early to post: w stands' side ldr to over 2f out: no ex over 1f out: 6th of 7 in gp* **20/1**

1236 **11** *shd* **Untold Melody**[16] 3954 3-9-3 **66** (t) PhillipMakin 10 58
(Kevin Ryan) *swtchd lft and hld up far side: effrt over 2f out: no imp over 1f out: 5th of 10 in gp* **14/1**

-060 **12** *2¾* **Taro Tywod (IRE)**[16] 3954 3-9-0 **63** (p) GrahamLee 5 46
(Ann Duffield) *towards rr far side: drvn 1/2-way: nvr able to chal: 6th of 10 in gp* **12/1**

-000 **13** *¾* **Spoken Words**[39] 3209 3-8-2 **51** oh2 (p) JamesSullivan 13 32
(Hugh McWilliams) *prom stands' side: drvn over 2f out: wknd over 1f out: last of 7 in gp* **50/1**

5206 **14** *1¼* **Scarlet Rocks (IRE)**[25] 3701 4-9-2 **60** (t) RobbieFitzpatrick 2 37
(Ron Barr) *dwlt: sn midfield far side: drvn over 2f out: wknd wl over 1f out: 7th of 10 in gp* **25/1**

6322 **15** *2* **Blue Shoes (IRE)**[9] 4208 3-9-1 **64** DavidAllan 7 34
(Tim Easterby) *led far side gp to over 2f out: wknd over 1f out: 8th of 10 in gp* **9/1**

0000 **16** *2¼* **Busy Bimbo (IRE)**[6] 4348 3-8-2 **51** oh2 (p) PatrickMathers 1 14
(Alan Berry) *towards rr and drvn along far side: struggling over 2f out: sn btn: 9th of 10 in gp* **100/1**

6-00 **17** *nk* **Sinai (IRE)**[55] 2689 3-9-6 **69** PJMcDonald 6 31
(Geoffrey Harker) *missed break: a bhd far side: last of 10 in gp* **12/1**

1m 10.45s (-2.25) **Going Correction** -0.375s/f (Firm)
WFA 3 from 4yo+ 5lb **17** Ran SP% **131.5**
Speed ratings (Par 100): **100,99,98,97,95 95,95,94,92,92 92,88,87,85,83 80,79**
toteswingers 1&2 £6.00, 2&3 £9.50, 1&3 £32.00 CSF £34.02 CT £419.76 TOTE £7.70: £1.90, £1.80, £4.40, £6.10; EX 25.80.
Owner G Morrill **Bred** M J Dawson **Trained** Yedingham, N Yorks

FOCUS
A competitive 51-75 sprint handicap where the field split into two groups and, as in the first race, the far side came out on top off a strong gallop. The winner is rated back to her best.
Untold Melody Official explanation: jockey said filly hung right throughout
Sinai(IRE) Official explanation: jockey said filly reared as gates opened

4548 TYREGIANT.COM H'CAP 1m 4f
3:55 (3:56) (Class 4) (0-80,80) 3-Y-O **£4,140** (£1,232; £615; £307) **Stalls** Low

Form RPR

0-62 **1** **Sequence (IRE)**[57] 2633 3-9-5 **78** RobertWinston 4 95+
(Sir Michael Stoute) *prom: effrt and pushed along over 2f out: led and edgd lft over 1f out: styd on strly fnl f* **9/2**[2]

1-50 **2** *3* **Gabrial's Star**[46] 2980 3-9-3 **76** TomEaves 3 88
(Bryan Smart) *dwlt: sn trcking ldrs: drvn and outpcd over 3f out: rallied over 1f out: chsd (clr) wnr ins fnl f: rn no* **11/2**

454 **3** *1* **Cactus Valley (IRE)**[39] 3227 3-9-5 **78** GeorgeBaker 1 88+
(Roger Charlton) *t.k.h: hld up in tch: swtchd rt and effrt over 2f out: chsd wnr over 1f out to ins fnl f: no ex* **11/8**[1]

0036 **4** *4½* **Saffa Hill (IRE)**[25] 3697 3-8-9 **68** DavidAllan 2 71
(Tim Easterby) *led: hung bdly rt bnd ent bk st after 3f: sn hdd: cl up: drvn and ev ch wl over 1f out: wknd fnl f* **6/1**

40-0 **5** *12* **Northern Jewel (IRE)**[63] 2449 3-8-2 **61** oh2 PatrickMathers 6 45
(Richard Fahey) *hld up in tch: rdn along 1/2-way: short lived effrt on outside over 2f out: sn struggling* **33/1**

2-04 **6** *10* **Almaas (USA)**[27] 3606 3-9-7 **80** PaulHanagan 5 48
(Saeed Bin Suroor) *t.k.h: pressed ldr: carried wd bnd ent bk st after 3f: sn led: rdn and hdd over 1f out: sn btn and eased* **5/1**[3]

2m 33.04s (-3.16) **Going Correction** -0.325s/f (Firm) **6** Ran SP% **109.6**
Speed ratings (Par 102): **97,95,94,91,83 76**
toteswingers 1&2 £3.00, 2&3 £2.70, 1&3 £2.10 CSF £27.07 TOTE £4.80: £2.50, £2.20; EX 27.40.
Owner The Queen **Bred** His Highness The Aga Khan's Studs S C **Trained** Newmarket, Suffolk

FOCUS
A fair staying handicap in principal but with some questions marks hanging over some of the runners it might be worthwhile to treat the race with caution. The winner was on a good mark on a literal reading of her Newcastle form.

4549 YORKSHIRE.COM BACK LE BID (S) H'CAP 1m
4:30 (4:32) (Class 6) (0-65,63) 3-Y-O **£1,940** (£577; £288; £144) **Stalls** Low

Form RPR

443 **1** **Sweetnessandlight**[8] 4263 3-9-7 **63** KierenFallon 10 74+
(Jason Ward) *hld up in midfield: gd hdwy on outside to ld over 2f out: pushed clr fnl f: comf* **7/2**[1]

0360 **2** *2¾* **Remember Rocky**[52] 2788 3-8-11 **53** (p) RobertWinston 4 55
(Steve Gollings) *hld up: rdn and hdwy over 2f out: edgd lft over 1f out: styd on to take 2nd cl home: no ch w wnr* **7/1**[2]

500 **3** *½* **Outlaw Torn (IRE)**[29] 3548 3-9-1 **57** (e) RobbieFitzpatrick 9 58
(Richard Guest) *trckd ldrs: effrt and ev ch over 2f out: sn chsng wnr: one pce fnl f: lost 2nd nr fin* **12/1**

0505 **4** *5* **Magic Bounty**[28] 3567 3-8-10 **52** DavidAllan 8 41
(Tim Easterby) *trckd ldrs: rdn and ev ch over 2f out: outpcd fnl f* **7/1**[2]

0-00 **5** *1* **Bedlam**[22] 3781 3-9-1 **57** (b) DanielTudhope 5 44
(Tim Easterby) *midfield on ins: effrt and rdn over 2f out: no imp wl over 1f out* **17/2**[3]

5555 **6** *1½* **Landaho**[9] 4211 3-8-3 **45** JamesSullivan 3 29
(Hugh McWilliams) *hld up: pushed along over 2f out: kpt on fnl f: nvr able to chal* **33/1**

06-0 **7** *¾* **Justine Time (IRE)**[36] 3315 3-8-8 **50** BarryMcHugh 6 32
(Julie Camacho) *s.i.s: hld up: stdy hdwy on ins over 3f out: rdn and no imp fnl 2f* **25/1**

0000 **8** *3* **July Specialists**[10] 4172 3-8-3 **45** JimmyQuinn 2 20
(Richard Guest) *trckd ldrs tl rdn and wknd over 1f out* **20/1**

0-04 **9** *¾* **Baileys Over Ice**[20] 3847 3-8-13 **55** GrahamLee 14 28
(James Given) *hld up towards rr: drvn and edgd lft over 2f out: nvr on terms* **7/2**[1]

-056 **10** *1¾* **Time To Excel**[35] 3333 3-8-8 **50** PaulMulrennan 15 19
(Michael Dods) *t.k.h: in tch on outside: rdn and hung lft over 2f out: btn over 1f out* **14/1**

006 **11** *¾* **Medecis Mountain**[37] 3273 3-8-3 **45** (p) PatrickMathers 16 13
(John Wainwright) *bhd: drvn along over 3f out: nvr on terms* **50/1**

0030 **12** *5* **Hopes Rebellion**[52] 2787 3-7-12 **45** NeilFarley(5) 13
(Declan Carroll) *towards rr: drvn over 3f out: nvr able to chal* **25/1**

00 **13** *6* **Nakuru Breeze (IRE)**[27] 3616 3-9-3 **59** (t[1]) MichaelO'Connell 7
(David Thompson) *taken early to post: cl up tl rdn and wknd over 2f out* **33/1**

0660 **14** *1¼* **Kieron's Rock (IRE)**[4] 4406 3-8-6 **48** (b[1]) AndrewElliott 1
(Jedd O'Keeffe) *led at decent gallop to over 2f out: sn rdn and wknd* **16/1**

05-0 **15** *31* **Come To Mind**[13] 4087 3-8-3 **45** DuranFentiman 12
(Alan Berry) *bhd: drvn along 1/2-way: btn and eased fnl 2f* **100/1**

1m 37.89s (-2.21) **Going Correction** -0.325s/f (Firm) **15** Ran SP% **121.5**
Speed ratings (Par 98): **98,95,94,89,88 87,86,83,82,81 80,75,69,68,37**
toteswingers 1&2 £6.10, 2&3 £18.20, 1&3 £10.40 CSF £25.59 CT £278.88 TOTE £3.90: £1.90, £1.50, £3.80; EX 31.60.The winner was bought in for 8,500ngs.
Owner Mrs Jill Ward **Bred** Dxb Bloodstock Ltd **Trained** Middleham, N Yorks

FOCUS
Not the strongest of sellers, but it was sound run and the winner is still improving.

4550 SKYBET SUPPORTING YORKSHIRE RACING SUMMER FESTIVAL MAIDEN STKS (DIV I) 7f
5:00 (5:03) (Class 5) 3-Y-O+ **£2,328** (£693; £346; £173) **Stalls** Low

Form RPR

44 **1** **Evanescent (IRE)**[15] 3990 3-9-3 0 KierenFallon 10 68+
(Alan McCabe) *mde all: rdn over 2f out: edgd rt ins fnl f: jst hld on* **4/1**[2]

42-0 **2** *nse* **Qannaas (USA)**[100] 1450 3-9-3 80 PaulHanagan 9 68+
(Charles Hills) *sn pressing wnr: rdn and hung lft over 1f out: brushed by wnr ins fnl f: kpt on wl: jst hld* **4/11**[1]

0-6 **3** *2½* **Morna's Glory**[18] 3913 3-8-12 0 MichaelStainton 4 56
(Jason Ward) *trckd ldrs: rdn over 2f out: kpt on same pce fnl f* **11/1**[3]

03 **4** *2¼* **Stormont Bridge**[28] 3580 4-9-10 0 (t) PaulMulrennan 6 57?
(Maurice Barnes) *hld up: pushed along and hdwy over 1f out: kpt on fnl f: nvr able to chal* **50/1**

5 *nse* **Symphony Of Stars** 3-8-9 0 DominicFox(3) 1 50
(Michael Appleby) *in tch: pushed along over 2f out: no imp fr over 1f out* **25/1**

04 **6** *1½* **China Excels**[9] 4207 5-9-10 0 RussKennemore 2 53+
(Sue Smith) *s.i.s: t.k.h in rr: pushed along over 2f out: sme late hdwy: n.d* **16/1**

40 **7** *5* **Charmel's Delight**[20] 3848 3-8-9 0 DaleSwift(3) 7 32
(Geoffrey Oldroyd) *trckd ldrs tl rdn and wknd over 2f out* **25/1**

0 **8** *2* **Icing Sugar**[18] 3913 4-9-5 0 PatrickMathers 12 29
(Mike Sowersby) *cl up: rdn over 2f out: sn wknd* **100/1**

0-00 **9** *4* **Red All Over (IRE)**[20] 3848 3-8-12 30 PaddyAspell 8 16
(Alan Berry) *hld up towards rr: drvn and hung lft 2f out: sn btn* **100/1**

0 **10** *13* **Miss Matiz**[21] 3811 5-9-2 0 PaulPickard(3) 5
(Alan Kirtley) *bhd: rdn and c alone towards stands' side ent st: sn struggling: t.o* **100/1**

0 **11** *13* **Bez**[53] 2765 4-9-10 0 (b) JimmyQuinn 3
(Nicky Vaughan) *hld up: rdn and struggling over 2f out: sn btn: t.o* **66/1**

1m 27.08s (-0.12) **Going Correction** -0.325s/f (Firm)
WFA 3 from 4yo+ 7lb **11** Ran SP% **121.6**
Speed ratings (Par 103): **87,86,84,81,81 79,74,71,67,52 37**
toteswingers 1&2 £1.40, 2&3 £1.80, 1&3 £2.60 CSF £5.85 TOTE £5.20: £1.30, £1.10, £2.10; EX 8.60.
Owner Charles Wentworth **Bred** Oliver Donlon **Trained** Averham Park, Notts

FOCUS
A weak maiden and a match on paper which it proved to be, but not in the way supporters of the odds-on favourite would have hoped for, especially after a stewards' enquiry which looked tight enough considering the winner only held on by the narrowest of margins. It was the slower division and the time was poor.
China Excels Official explanation: jockey said gelding hung right in straight

4551 SKYBET SUPPORTING YORKSHIRE RACING SUMMER FESTIVAL MAIDEN STKS (DIV II) 7f
5:30 (5:31) (Class 5) 3-Y-O+ **£2,328** (£693; £346; £173) **Stalls** Low

Form RPR

3-5 **1** **Epoque (USA)**[97] 1532 3-8-12 0 IanMongan 4 67+
(Sir Henry Cecil) *t.k.h: prom: gd hdwy to ld over 2f out: pushed out fnl f* **8/15**[1]

0236 **2** *2¾* **Sabore**[9] 4211 3-8-12 72 TonyHamilton 5 59+
(Richard Fahey) *trckd ldrs: effrt and wnt 2nd wl over 1f out: kpt on same pce last 100yds* **6/1**[3]

3 *3¼* **Lieutenant Dan (IRE)**[280] 5-9-7 0 DominicFox(3) 1 57
(Michael Appleby) *hld up: rdn and hdwy over 2f out: kpt on fnl f: nvr able to chal* **20/1**

0000 **4** *½* **Benidorm**[35] 3356 4-9-5 48 (v[1]) AdamCarter(5) 10 56
(John Wainwright) *cl up: rdn and ev ch over 2f out: no ex over 1f out* **40/1**

0 **5** *5* **Double Proposition**[67] 2335 3-8-12 0 PaulMulrennan 8 36+
(Bryan Smart) *s.i.s: bhd tl styd on fr 2f out: nvr nr ldrs* **33/1**

0-0 **6** *¾* **Misty Eyes**[35] 3352 3-8-12 0 PJMcDonald 6 33
(Geoffrey Harker) *cl up tl rdn and outpcd fr 2f out* **50/1**

3-0 **7** *4* **Three Darlings (IRE)**[110] 1238 3-8-12 0 AdrianNicholls 11 23
(David Nicholls) *t.k.h: led to over 2f out: sn rdn and outpcd* **5/1**[2]

8 *2¾* **Lady Bentinck (IRE)** 3-8-12 0 PaddyAspell 3 15
(Alan Berry) *s.i.s: bhd and outpcd: nvr on terms* **100/1**

9 *2¼* **Roc Fort** 3-9-3 0 JamesSullivan 9 14
(Ruth Carr) *bhd and outpcd: nvr on terms* **10/1**

0 **10** *5* **Keep Fighting**[9] 4207 4-9-5 0 DuranFentiman 7
(Tim Walford) *plld hrd: in tch tl rdn and wknd over 2f out* **66/1**

11 *1¾* **Urbonite (IRE)** 3-9-3 0 AndrewElliott 2
(Alan Swinbank) *towards rr and sn struggling: no ch fr 1/2-way* **20/1**

1m 25.49s (-1.71) **Going Correction** -0.325s/f (Firm)
WFA 3 from 4yo+ 7lb **11** Ran SP% **124.6**
Speed ratings (Par 103): **96,92,89,88,82 82,77,74,71,66 64**
toteswingers 1&2 £2.50, 2&3 £8.60, 1&3 £6.00 CSF £4.35 TOTE £1.70: £1.02, £1.80, £5.90; EX 5.60.
Owner K Abdulla **Bred** Juddmonte Farms Inc **Trained** Newmarket, Suffolk

FOCUS
Another weak maiden with a workmanlike performance from the odds-on favourite. The faster division but still modest and shaky form.

4552 YORKSHIRE RADIO "HANDS AND HEELS" APPRENTICE SERIES H'CAP (RACING EXCELLENCE INITIATIVE) 5f
5:55 (5:59) (Class 5) (0-75,73) 3-Y-O+ **£2,328** (£693; £346; £173) **Stalls** High

Form RPR

0055 **1** **Mecca's Team**[8] 4245 4-9-0 **61** (p) DavidSimmonson 11 70
(Michael Dods) *cl up stands' rail: led 2f out: rdn and hld on wl fnl f* **9/2**[2]

6062 **2** *1¼* **Waking Warrior**[15] 3993 4-9-5 **71** (tp) KevinStott(5) 1 76
(Kevin Ryan) *cl up: effrt over 2f out: chsd wnr over 1f out: kpt on ins fnl f* **7/1**

3424 **3** *nk* **Art Form**[6] 4348 3-9-5 **70** GemmaTutty 7 73+
(Alan McCabe) *hld up: rdn and hdwy over 1f out: kpt on fnl f: nrst fin* **3/1**[1]

5631 **4** *¾* **Ice Trooper**[11] 4154 4-9-5 **71** 6ex (p) GerJohnson(5) 4 72
(Linda Stubbs) *cl up: drvn along 1/2-way: nt qckn fnl f* **18/1**

2600 **5** 1 3/4 **Illustrious Prince (IRE)**[14] 4042 5-9-7 **73**................ LukeLeadbitter(5) 8 67
(Declan Carroll) *sn drvn along towards rr: hdwy over 1f out: kpt on fnl f: nvr able to chal* **5/1**[3]

420- **6** shd **Feel The Heat**[364] 4516 5-9-8 **72**................................(p) PeterSword(3) 9 66
(Bryan Smart) *midfield centre: drvn along 1/2-way: no imp fr over 1f out* **9/1**

0-30 **7** 1 3/4 **Secret Venue**[4] 4400 6-9-0 **66**.................................. KatieDowson(5) 10 54
(Jedd O'Keeffe) *cl up tl rdn and wknd over 1f out* **12/1**

-500 **8** 1/2 **On The High Tops (IRE)**[55] 2690 4-8-12 **59**..........(b) ShirleyTeasdale 2 45
(Ruth Carr) *led at decent gallop: swtchd to stands' rail 1/2-way: hdd 2f out: sn rdn: wknd fnl f* **11/1**

4601 **9** 1 **Ryedane (IRE)**[19] 3893 10-8-11 **61**...................(b) RachelRichardson(3) 5 43
(Tim Easterby) *bhd and sn drvn along: nvr on terms* **12/1**

026 **10** 7 **Compton Time**[37] 3289 3-8-9 **65**................................ ConnorNichol(5) 3 22
(Michael Dods) *bhd and sn drvn along: struggling 1/2-way: sn btn* **14/1**

58.46s (-1.14) **Going Correction** -0.375s/f (Firm)
WFA 3 from 4yo+ 4lb **10** Ran SP% **118.0**
Speed ratings (Par 103): **94,92,91,90,87 87,84,83,82,70**
toteswingers 1&2 £6.00, 2&3 £3.90, 1&3 £4.60 CSF £35.05 CT £99.59 TOTE £6.80: £2.40, £2.60, £1.20; EX 36.90.
Owner David T J Metcalfe **Bred** Redmyre Bloodstock Ltd **Trained** Denton, Co Durham

FOCUS
A modest apprentice sprint. The winner got the rail and is rated back to her best.
T/Plt: £18.20 to a £1 stake. Pool of £50791.26 - 2032.28 winning tickets. T/Qpdt: £10.80 to a £1 stake. Pool of £2848.55 - 193.75 winning tickets. RY

4110 YORK (L-H)
Friday, July 27

OFFICIAL GOING: Good to firm (8.0)
Rail out 4m from inside line to give fresh ground from 9f to entrance to home straight; races of 1m and over reduced by 16yds from advertised distance.
Wind: Fresh half against Weather: Fine and dry

4553 FUTURE CLEANING SERVICES APPRENTICE STKS (H'CAP) 1m
6:00 (6:01) (Class 4) (0-80,80) 3-Y-0 **£5,175** (£1,540; £769; £384) **Stalls** Low

Form RPR

1-03 **1** **Elegant Flight**[31] 3475 3-8-5 **66**.........................(v) MichaelJMMurphy(5) 9 74
(Alan Jarvis) *t.k.h: trckd ldrs: hdwy and cl up 1/2-way: slt ld 3f out: rdn and edgd lft appr fnl f: kpt on wl* **16/1**

-212 **2** 1 **Henry Allingham**[22] 3772 3-9-7 **77**................................... DarrenEgan 11 82
(Roger Varian) *awkward s: hld up in rr: hdwy over 3f out: rdn to chse ldrs 2f out: drvn and kpt on same pce fnl f* **7/2**[1]

-12 **3** 1/2 **Miss Ellany (IRE)**[23] 3749 3-9-2 **77**............................... DavidBergin(5) 2 81
(David O'Meara) *t.k.h: trckd ldrs on inner: effrt wl over 2f out: rdn over 1f out: drvn and kpt on same pce fnl f* **7/2**[1]

2024 **4** 3 3/4 **Vital Calling**[35] 3333 3-9-5 **75**.. LMcNiff 6 69
(David Barron) *trckd ldrs: effrt on wd outside 3f out: rdn along 2f out: drvn over 1f out and sn no imp* **8/1**[3]

-022 **5** hd **Eastlands Lad (IRE)**[9] 4211 3-8-7 **63**........................... GarryWhillans 3 56
(Micky Hammond) *towards rr: hdwy 3f out: rdn over 2f out: sn one pce* **9/1**

050- **6** 3/4 **Giorgio's Dragon (IRE)**[331] 5618 3-8-5 **61** oh2............ ShaneBKelly 10 52
(Richard Fahey) *t.k.h: cl up: slt ld 4f out: rdn and hdd 3f out: drvn and hld whn n.m.r appr fnl f: wknd after* **20/1**

304 **7** nk **Running Reef (IRE)**[13] 4082 3-8-8 **67**.......................... DarylByrne(3) 7 57
(Tracy Waggott) *dwlt: hld up in rr: effrt and sme hdwy 3f out: sn rdn and n.d* **22/1**

4640 **8** nk **Just Fabulous**[20] 3882 3-9-7 **80**...................................... JasonHart(3) 4 69
(George Moore) *t.k.h early: trckd ldrs: effrt 3f out: sn rdn: n.m.r and swtchd lft wl over 1f out: sn wknd* **6/1**[2]

-003 **9** 10 **Sound Advice**[37] 3274 3-9-9 **79**....................................... DeanHeslop 8 41
(Keith Dalgleish) *led: pushed along 1/2-way: hdd 4f out: wknd wl over 2f out* **9/1**

4012 **10** 13 **Dansili Dutch (IRE)**[27] 3616 3-8-12 **68** ow1................ JustinNewman 1
(Andrew Crook) *towards rr: rdn along 1/2-way: sn outpcd and bhd* **8/1**[3]

1m 36.98s (-2.02) **Going Correction** -0.20s/f (Firm) **10** Ran SP% **115.9**
Speed ratings (Par 102): **102,101,100,96,96 95,95,95,85,72**
toteswingers: 1&2 £9.40, 1&3 £24.30, 2&3 £5.00 CSF £71.10 CT £252.34 TOTE £22.50: £5.10, £1.50, £1.90; EX 104.70.
Owner Grant & Bowman Limited **Bred** Mrs Ann Jarvis **Trained** Twyford, Bucks

FOCUS
The rail had been moved to give fresh ground, meaning all races beyond 1m were reportedly 16 yards shorter than the published distances. A fair apprentice handicap, but it was something of a muddling affair with several runners pulling hard early on. A prominent position was an advantage and the effort of the second needs marking up. The form is rated around the second and third.
Giorgio's Dragon(IRE) Official explanation: jockey said colt ran too free
Just Fabulous Official explanation: trainer said filly was unsuited by the good to firm ground

4554 SEDDON PROPERTY SERVICES STKS (H'CAP) 6f
6:30 (6:31) (Class 4) (0-80,80) 4-Y-0+ **£5,175** (£1,540; £769; £384) **Stalls** Low

Form RPR

5114 **1** **Julius Geezer (IRE)**[37] 3272 4-9-7 **80**.................... RichardKingscote 3 89
(Tom Dascombe) *a.p: cl up 2f out: sn led and rdn over 1f out: drvn ins fnl f: jst hld on* **12/1**

14-2 **2** nse **Prodigality**[51] 2815 4-8-11 **75**.. DarrenEgan(5) 20 84
(Ronald Harris) *towards rr: hdwy and in tch 1/2-way: rdn to chse ldrs over 1f out: styd on strly ins fnl f: jst failed* **11/2**[1]

326 **3** shd **Showboating (IRE)**[15] 4013 4-9-3 **76**...........................(tp) SeanLevey 11 85
(Alan McCabe) *in rr: hdwy 2f out: sn rdn: styd on strly ins fnl f: jst failed* **12/1**

6646 **4** 1/2 **Barney McGrew (IRE)**[16] 3960 9-9-5 **78**........................... TomEaves 2 85
(Michael Dods) *in tch: hdwy to chse ldrs 2f out: drvn and ch ent fnl f: kpt on towards fin* **16/1**

00-0 **5** 2 1/2 **Kellys Eye (IRE)**[99] 1478 5-9-4 **77**.............................. PhillipMakin 16 76
(David Brown) *chsd ldrs: rdn wl over 1f out: one pce fnl f* **18/1**

5460 **6** shd **Lucky Numbers (IRE)**[28] 3557 6-9-5 **78**..................[1] DanielTudhope 15 77
(David O'Meara) *hmpd by blind removed fr next stall and slowly away: hdwy 2f out: sn rdn and styd on wl fnl f: nrst fin* **14/1**

0003 **6** dht **Cocktail Charlie**[7] 4292 4-9-5 **78**..................................(p) DavidAllan 10 77
(Tim Easterby) *cl up: led 1/2-way: rdn 2f out: hdd wl over 1f out: ev ch tl drvn ent fnl f and sn wknd* **11/1**[3]

6524 **8** 3/4 **Green Park (IRE)**[7] 4312 9-9-0 **80**...............................(b) JasonHart(7) 6 77
(Declan Carroll) *chsd ldrs: rdn along wl over 1f out: wknd appr fnl f* **12/1**

2310 **9** 1 **Barkston Ash**[22] 3778 4-9-2 **75**... ShaneKelly 18 68
(Eric Alston) *towards rr: hdwy wl over 1f out: sn rdn and kpt on fnl f: nt rch ldrs* **11/1**[3]

4060 **10** 2 **Another Try (IRE)**[42] 3128 7-9-0 **80**................. MichaelJMMurphy(7) 13 67
(Alan Jarvis) *nvr bttr than midfield* **16/1**

6300 **11** 1/2 **Baldemar**[13] 4077 7-9-7 **80**... PaulHanagan 19 65
(Richard Fahey) *chsd ldrs: rdn along over 2f out: grad wknd* **14/1**

03P4 **12** 1 3/4 **Toby Tyler**[11] 4133 6-9-5 **78**...................................(v) MickyFenton 12 58
(Paul Midgley) *chsd ldrs: rdn along over 2f out: grad wknd* **20/1**

053- **13** 3/4 **Dominium (USA)**[254] 7439 5-9-0 **76**.............................. HarryBentley(3) 7 53
(Jeremy Gask) *a towards rr* **25/1**

0005 **14** 1 1/4 **Mandalay King (IRE)**[30] 3496 7-8-13 **75**.....................(p) JulieBurke(3) 8 48
(Marjorie Fife) *a in rr* **40/1**

0005 **15** hd **Medici Time**[15] 4013 7-9-7 **80**..(p) KierenFallon 14 53
(Tim Easterby) *a in rr* **7/1**[2]

20-0 **16** 1 1/4 **Eland Ally**[52] 2793 4-9-6 **79**... GrahamLee 4 48
(Tom Tate) *a towards rr* **25/1**

6205 **17** nse **Defence Council (IRE)**[13] 4077 4-9-7 **80**...................... RobertWinston 5 49
(Mel Brittain) *chsd ldrs: rdn along wl over 2f out: sn wknd* **14/1**

2300 **18** 2 **Whozthecat (IRE)**[6] 4337 5-9-2 **80**..............................(v) NeilFarley(5) 9 42
(Declan Carroll) *led to 1/2-way: sn rdn along and wknd* **14/1**

-000 **19** 6 **Wildcat Wizard (USA)**[35] 3336 6-9-7 **80**..................... RussKennemore 1 23+
(Paul Midgley) *dwlt: a in rr* **40/1**

1m 11.59s (-0.31) **Going Correction** +0.075s/f (Good) **19** Ran SP% **128.7**
Speed ratings (Par 105): **105,104,104,104,100 100,100,99,98,95 95,92,91,90,89 88,88,85,77**
toteswingers: 1&2 £10.00, 1&3 £22.20, 2&3 £20.40 CSF £74.48 CT £857.39 TOTE £14.30: £3.10, £1.90, £3.30, £3.80; EX 57.10.
Owner Basing Bellman Stroud **Bred** Ballyhane Stud **Trained** Malpas, Cheshire

FOCUS
A wide-open sprint handicap in which the runners came down the centre of the course. There seemed no advantage in the draw, but it wasn't easy to come from off the pace. Sound form.
Whozthecat(IRE) Official explanation: jockey said he lost an iron

4555 BATLEYS CASH AND CARRY MEDIAN AUCTION MAIDEN STKS 7f
7:00 (7:01) (Class 4) 2-Y-0 **£5,175** (£1,540; £769; £192; £192) **Stalls** Low

Form RPR

1 **Ebn Arab (USA)** 2-9-3 0... PaulHanagan 2 94+
(Charles Hills) *hld up in tch: smooth hdwy to trck ldrs over 2f out: sn swtchd rt and cl up: led appr fnl f and sn pushed clr* **5/2**[1]

4 **2** 5 **Related**[30] 3506 2-9-3 0... GrahamLee 10 81
(Clive Cox) *led: rdn along and jnd 2f out: drvn and hdd over 1f out: kpt on: no ch w wnr* **3/1**[2]

0 **3** 2 3/4 **Cash Is King**[41] 3168 2-9-3 0.. TonyHamilton 7 74
(Richard Fahey) *trckd ldrs: hdwy on outer to chal wl over 2f out: ev ch tl rdn and one pce fr over 1f out* **11/1**

32 **4** 2 3/4 **Red Refraction (IRE)**[26] 3658 2-9-3 0................................ DavidAllan 3 67
(Richard Hannon) *trckd ldrs: hdwy and cl up 2f out: sn rdn and wknd appr fnl f* **9/2**[3]

0 **4** dht **Mandeville (IRE)**[15] 4011 2-8-12 0.................................... SeanLevey 5 62+
(Richard Hannon) *chsd ldrs: rdn along over 2f out: kpt on same pce* **7/1**

6 2 3/4 **Red Runaway** 2-9-3 0... PaulMulrennan 11 60+
(Ed Dunlop) *green and wnt bdly rt s: in rr: hdwy over 2f out: n.d* **25/1**

7 2 **Red Eight (USA)** 2-9-3 0... MichaelO'Connell 4 55
(John Quinn) *a towards rr* **14/1**

8 8 **Silvio Dante (USA)** 2-9-3 0.. PhillipMakin 8 34
(Kevin Ryan) *cl up: rdn along 3f out: sn wknd* **16/1**

9 3 **Mirlo Blanco (IRE)** 2-9-0 0.. LeeTopliss(3) 9 26
(Richard Fahey) *wnt lft s: rn green and a in rr* **16/1**

10 14 **Khelac** 2-9-3 0.. RobertWinston 1
(Alan Swinbank) *sn outpcd and green in rr: a bhd* **33/1**

1m 25.11s (-0.19) **Going Correction** -0.125s/f (Firm) **10** Ran SP% **117.8**
Speed ratings (Par 96): **96,90,87,84,84 80,78,69,66,50**
toteswingers: 1&2 £2.50, 1&3 £11.80, 2&3 £4.30 CSF £10.08 TOTE £3.20: £1.50, £1.60, £2.30; EX 10.90.
Owner Hamdan Al Maktoum **Bred** Shadwell Farm LLC **Trained** Lambourn, Berks
■ Stewards' Enquiry : Sean Levey three-day ban: failed to ride out for 4th (Aug 10-12)

FOCUS
Mostly newcomers in what will probably turn out to be quite a useful median auction maiden. The pace looked decent and the winner created a good impression. He is an above average winner of this event.

NOTEBOOK
Ebn Arab(USA), a colt by Dixie Union and half-brother to a winner in USA out of a half-sister to a Grade 1 1m3f winner, holds entries in the Gimcrack and Royal Lodge and as those suggest looks destined for better things. He doesn't appeal as having the pace to drop back to 6f in good company, as it was only inside the last furlong he began to draw clear, but the distance he put between himself and the rest in a short space of time was impressive and he looks ready for an immediate step up to Listed company. (op 7-2)
Related disputed the lead and beat the rest comfortably enough without being any match for the winner once he hit top gear. For a race of this type he was unlucky to come up against an above-average rival and should win a similar event without much trouble. (tchd 10-3)
Cash Is King showed much more than he did on his debut in very testing conditions, but still looked green off the bridle and will improve again. (op 14-1)
Red Refraction(IRE) looked to have just about the best form on offer but came up short. This might be as good as he is, but he looked to be floundering in the last furlong and might be better dropped back to 6f for now. (op 11-1)
Mandeville(IRE) just got up for a share of fourth without either being given a hard time or looking the finished article. He should improve again, not least when stepped up to 1m. (op 11-1)
Red Runaway, a colt by Medicean out of a dam who is a half-sister to the Irish St Leger winner Sans Frontiers, was very green, swerving badly to his right leaving the stalls, and never got involved. There were signs the penny was dropping late on, however, and he's a sure improver, given time and more distance. (op 18-1)

4556 EBF STOBART PJA TESTIMONIAL LYRIC FILLIES' STKS (LISTED RACE) 1m 2f 88y
7:30 (7:31) (Class 1) 3-Y-0+
£19,848 (£7,525; £3,766; £1,876; £941; £472) **Stalls** Low

Form RPR

4346 **1** **Barefoot Lady (IRE)**[14] 4065 4-9-4 **106**......................... TonyHamilton 7 110
(Richard Fahey) *hld up towards rr: hdwy on outer 3f out: led 2f out: rdn over 1f out: edgd lft and hdd ins fnl f: drvn and rallied gamely to ld again nr fin* **10/3**[1]

61 **2** nk **Emirates Queen**[28] 3565 3-8-8 **89**................................... KierenFallon 5 109+
(Luca Cumani) *hld up towards rr: niggled along 1/2-way: hdwy 3f out: nt clr run and swtchd lft wl over 1f out: rdn and styd on to ld ins fnl f: sn drvn: hdd and no ex nr fin* **7/2**[2]

1-30 **3** *6* **Gathering (USA)**[26] 3682 3-8-8 99.............................(b[1]) NickyMackay 3 98
(John Gosden) *set stdy pce: qcknd 4f out: rdn along 3f out: hdd 2f out: sn drvn and edgd rt: one pce ent fnl f* **9/1**

410 **4** *1* **Momentary**[36] 3292 3-8-11 105.. HayleyTurner 1 99
(Michael Bell) *trckd ldrs: hdwy over 3f out: chal 2f out: sn rdn and ev ch tl drvn and wknd appr fnl f* **8/1**

13-0 **5** *nk* **Firdaws (USA)**[70] 2232 3-8-8 97...................................... PaulHanagan 8 96
(Roger Varian) *t.k.h: cl up: rdn along 3f out: wknd 2f out* **9/1**

212/ **6** *1 1/4* **Elas Diamond**[636] 7235 4-9-4 97.. ShaneKelly 6 93
(Jeremy Noseda) *trckd ldrs: hdwy 3f out: rdn 2f out: sn drvn and wknd* **12/1**

2323 **7** *1 3/4* **Mid Mon Lady (IRE)**[5] 4386 7-9-4 102............................(b) TomEaves 4 90
(Sir Mark Prescott Bt) *dwlt: t.k.h in rr: hdwy on inner 4f out: rdn along over 3f out and sn btn* **4/1**[3]

1322 **8** *25* **Dragonera**[39] 3219 4-9-4 98... PaulMulrennan 2 42
(Ed Dunlop) *trckd ldrs: effrt over 3f out: sn rdn and wknd* **10/1**

2m 7.86s (-4.64) **Going Correction** -0.20s/f (Firm)
WFA 3 from 4yo+ 10lb **8** Ran SP% **113.2**
Speed ratings (Par 108): **110,109,104,104,103 102,101,81**
toteswingers 1&2 £2.60, 1&3 £6.70, 2&3 £9.70 CSF £14.89 TOTE £3.90: £1.70, £1.70, £2.70; EX 11.50.
Owner Mrs H Steel **Bred** Arbawny Ventures 2000uc **Trained** Musley Bank, N Yorks
■ Stewards' Enquiry : Nicky Mackay two-day ban: careless riding (Aug 10-11)

FOCUS
An above-average Listed fillies' event and an open one too, with the outsider only 12-1. The pace was uneven and largely modest, so it's to the credit of the first two that they were able to pull so far clear, having been held up in rear. The winner sets the standard.

NOTEBOOK
Barefoot Lady(IRE) is a cut above this grade at her best, having won a Group 3 event and twice made the frame in Group 1 contests, but she was made to work hard for success by a lightly raced improver, needing to show all her battling qualities to rally after the runner-up had got her head in front. She's consistent and must have good prospects of winning another Listed race before the season is out, as she takes her racing well and ground conditions come alike to her. (op 4-1)
Emirates Queen looked an unlucky loser as she was never travelling particularly well yet still managed to work her way into contention and led for much of the last furlong (having wandered around when hitting the front) before being mugged close home by one still effective at 1m. Open to plenty more improvement, she'd have beaten the winner had this race been run at a stronger gallop and she won't be long in winning a similar event with the Upavon Stakes at Salisbury in the middle of August an obvious target. (tchd 4-1)
Gathering(USA) probably didn't show any improvement in first-time blinkers after dictating the pace but began to stay on again towards the finish and might fare a bit better another time if her stamina is tested more. (op 10-1)
Momentary's Newbury defeat of Shirocco Star looks good form, given that one's subsequent efforts, but she looked very one paced after travelling well into the race. This was the fastest ground she has encountered and she looked as though she found the emphasis too much on speed. (op 7-1 tchd 17-2)
Firdaws(USA) is worth another chance as she was squeezed out with 2f to run and then took an age to get going again before finishing well. She looked third best on the day and, like her dam, might well show even better form at 1m4f. (op 8-1 tchd 10-1)
Elas Diamond was another quickly put in her place when the race developed in earnest. (op 11-1 tchd 14-1)
Mid Mon Lady(IRE) pulled hard in rear after a slow start and never looked happy turned out quickly after running in France last weekend. Official explanation: jockey said mare ran too free (op 9-2 tchd 7-2)
Dragonera Official explanation: trainer's rep said filly was unsuited by the good to firm ground

4557 SKYBET SUPPORTING THE YORKSHIRE RACING FESTIVAL STKS (H'CAP) 1m
8:00 (8:00) (Class 2) (0-100,98) 3-Y-0+ **£11,450** (£3,407; £1,702; £851) **Stalls** Low

Form RPR

2521 **1** **Anderiego (IRE)**[13] 4110 4-9-4 87............................... DanielTudhope 11 95
(David O'Meara) *trckd ldrs: smooth hdwy 3f out: led wl over 1f out: rdn and kpt on wl fnl f* **9/2**[1]

0040 **2** *1* **Askaud (IRE)**[14] 4072 4-9-0 83.................................(b[1]) RobertWinston 3 88
(Scott Dixon) *set stdy pce: qcknd 3f out: rdn over 2f out: hdd wl over 1f out: kpt on u.p fnl f* **14/1**

0000 **3** *1 1/2* **Take It To The Max**[13] 4112 5-9-6 89................................ DavidNolan 6 91+
(Richard Fahey) *hld up in tch: hdwy 3f out: rdn to chse ldrs wl over 1f out: drvn and one pce fnl f* **14/1**

1-20 **4** *nk* **Terdaad (IRE)**[57] 2642 4-9-8 91.....................................(tp) PhillipMakin 7 92
(Saeed Bin Suroor) *hld up: hdwy 3f out: rdn to chse ldrs wl over 1f out: edgd lft and one pce fnl f* **7/1**

0212 **5** *1 3/4* **Dubai Dynamo**[7] 4287 7-10-1 98 6ex.............................. PJMcDonald 5 95
(Ruth Carr) *chsd ldrs: rdn along wl over 2f out: kpt on same pce* **5/1**[2]

4302 **6** *1* **Lord Aeryn (IRE)**[22] 3779 5-9-5 88.................................. PaulHanagan 9 83
(Richard Fahey) *hld up towards rr: hdwy wl over 2f out: rdn wl over 1f out: kpt on fnl f: nrst fin* **13/2**

-000 **7** *1 1/2* **Fighter Boy (IRE)**[13] 4110 5-8-9 78.............................. PaulMulrennan 1 69+
(Michael Easterby) *plld hrd: hld up in rr: hdwy 2f out: kpt on fnl f: nt rch ldrs* **14/1**

5053 **8** *1/2* **Crown Counsel (IRE)**[26] 3667 4-9-2 85........................... KierenFallon 2 75
(Mark Johnston) *trckd ldr: effrt and cl up 3f out: sn rdn and wknd fnl 2f* **11/2**[3]

54 **9** *1 1/2* **Just Bond (IRE)**[6] 4345 10-8-10 82................................ DaleSwift[(3)] 12 68
(Geoffrey Oldroyd) *plld hrd: hld up: a in rr* **20/1**

0-00 **10** *1 1/4* **Moon Pearl (USA)**[36] 3294 3-8-10 90.......................... HarryBentley[(3)] 4 74
(Ralph Beckett) *trckd ldng pair: rdn along 3f out: wknd over 2f out* **9/1**

0530 **11** *3 1/2* **Roger Sez (IRE)**[14] 4062 3-9-6 97...................................(p) DavidAllan 8 73
(Tim Easterby) *hld up: a in rr* **20/1**

1m 38.1s (-0.90) **Going Correction** -0.20s/f (Firm)
WFA 3 from 4yo+ 8lb **11** Ran SP% **115.6**
Speed ratings (Par 109): **96,95,93,93,91 90,88,88,86,85 82**
toteswingers 1&2 £9.60, 2&3 £94.50, 1&3 £24.90 CSF £66.65 CT £818.98 TOTE £5.10: £1.90, £4.20, £4.00; EX 75.20.
Owner Ebor Racing Club **Bred** Gerrardstown House Stud **Trained** Nawton, N Yorks
■ Stewards' Enquiry : Phillip Makin two-day ban: careless riding (Aug 10-11)

FOCUS
Quite a useful handicap but a race near-worthless as a form guide, given it was run at a slow pace with the unfancied runner-up dictating, and it was almost impossible for those held up to make much impact. The winner continued his improvement.

NOTEBOOK
Anderiego(IRE) finally looks to be back on the up now his stable have had time to get to know him and he followed up his C&D win earlier this month readily, for all he was favoured by being ridden close to the pace. He's probably got more progress in him and won't be one to dismiss lightly in his bid for a three-timer.
Askaud(IRE) hasn't been firing of late and has received a deal of respite from the handicapper as a result, but it was more the slow pace she was allowed to set that saw her finishing as close as she did here. Whether she achieved what it seems she did on paper is open to doubt. (op 12-1)
Take It To The Max has dropped to a mark just 1lb above that from which he won a valuable handicap in Ireland last season. He showed his first encouragement since, not least as he was set more to do than the pair that beat him, but this isn't form to be relying on greatly. (op 16-1)
Terdaad(IRE) looked a difficult ride, pulling hard, carrying his head awkwardly and then hanging left without looking as if he was putting it all in. It's easy to see why he wears cheekpieces. (op 6-1)
Dubai Dynamo never threatened from midfield and found the slow gallop no use to him. (op 6-1)
Lord Aeryn(IRE)'s effort is also best overlooked, seeing as he was settled too far back. (tchd 7-1)
Fighter Boy(IRE) ◆ flew home from an unpromising position and certainly isn't the back number he has looked for his current yard so far this season. Officially rated 99 just three runs ago, he's worth a second look next time. (op 20-1)
Crown Counsel(IRE) isn't the most consistent but was very disappointing even so, given he stalked the slow gallop. (op 9-2)

4558 YORKSHIRE.COM BACK LE BID STKS (H'CAP) 5f 89y
8:30 (8:31) (Class 4) (0-85,85) 3-Y-0 **£5,175** (£1,540; £769; £384) **Stalls** Low

Form RPR

3553 **1** **Waseem Faris (IRE)**[14] 4044 3-9-0 78....................... PaulMulrennan 13 87
(Mick Channon) *hld up in tch: smooth hdwy 2f out: rdn to ld ins fnl f: hld on wl towards fin* **12/1**

0-45 **2** *nk* **Kool Henry (IRE)**[14] 4044 3-9-7 85................................ DanielTudhope 4 93
(David O'Meara) *in rr: swtchd to outer and gd hdwy wl over 1f out: sn rdn and styd on strly ins fnl f: jst failed* **12/1**

0013 **3** *1 1/4* **Almond Branches**[2] 4451 3-8-10 74 6ex........................ PJMcDonald 9 78
(George Moore) *towards rr: gd hdwy on outer 2f out: rdn to chse ldrs over 1f out: drvn to chal ent fnl f: ev ch tl no ex last 75yds* **8/1**[3]

4121 **4** *3/4* **Just Like Heaven (IRE)**[10] 4187 3-8-3 67 6ex............ DuranFentiman 5 68
(Tim Easterby) *cl up: rdn to ld over 1f out: drvn and hdd ins fnl f: kpt on same pce* **10/1**

4116 **5** *1* **El McGlynn (IRE)**[14] 4044 3-7-11 68............................ HannahNunn[(7)] 6 65
(Peter Salmon) *chsd ldrs: rdn to chal over 1f out and ev ch tl wknd ins fnl f* **33/1**

0604 **6** *1/2* **Pea Shooter**[7] 4291 3-9-5 83... PhillipMakin 7 79+
(Kevin Ryan) *in tch: hdwy whn nt clr run wl over 1f out: sn rdn and kpt on towards fin* **6/1**[2]

2361 **7** *1* **Phoenix Clubs (IRE)**[34] 3404 3-8-6 70........................ BarryMcHugh 10 62+
(Paul Midgley) *hld up: hdwy whn nt clr run over 1f out: no imp after* **14/1**

5116 **8** *1* **Cats Eyes**[35] 3350 3-8-10 74.. ShaneKelly 2 63
(Robert Cowell) *chsd ldrs: rdn along 2f out: grad wknd* **14/1**

0043 **9** *shd* **Come On Dave (IRE)**[28] 3578 3-8-2 66........................... AndrewMullen 12 54
(David Nicholls) *sn led: rdn 2f out: drvn: edgd lft and hdd over 1f out: sn wknd* **14/1**

-411 **10** *2 1/4* **Lupin Pooter**[35] 3350 3-9-1 79................................... GrahamGibbons 14 59
(David Barron) *swtchd lft s: hld up in tch: effrt over 2f out: sn rdn and wknd* **2/1**[1]

500 **11** *hd* **Monnoyer**[59] 2591 3-8-10 74 ow1................................... RobertWinston 8 54
(Scott Dixon) *chsd ldng pair: rdn along 2f out: wknd over 1f out* **50/1**

1-60 **12** *3* **Taffe**[27] 3613 3-9-1 79..(b[1]) GrahamLee 11 48
(James Given) *dwlt: a in rr* **33/1**

0101 **13** *3* **Towbee**[13] 4081 3-9-5 83.. JamesSullivan 3 42
(Michael Easterby) *dwlt: a in rr* **16/1**

1m 4.06s (-0.04) **Going Correction** +0.075s/f (Good) **13** Ran SP% **116.9**
Speed ratings (Par 102): **103,102,100,99,97 96,95,93,93,89 89,84,80**
toteswingers 1&2 £19.00, 2&3 £13.90, 1&3 £15.00 CSF £143.30 CT £1266.96 TOTE £12.80: £4.00, £4.90, £2.30; EX 212.90.
Owner The Living Legend Racing Partnership II **Bred** Rabbah Bloodstock Limited **Trained** West Ilsley, Berks

FOCUS
A fair sprint handicap to end proceedings and one run at a decent gallop that soon had the field strung out with the first three coming from off the pace. The winner is rated in line with a best view of his winter form. Profile Star was withdrawn after trying to escape under the stalls.
Lupin Pooter Official explanation: trainer had no explanation for the poor form shown
Monnoyer Official explanation: jockey said gelding hung left-handed
T/Jkpt: Not won. T/Plt: £130.60 to a £1 stake. Pool of £84930.28 - 474.45 winning tickets. T/Qpdt: £40.10 to a £1 stake. Pool of £5151.41 - 94.90 winning tickets. JR

4559 - 4573a (Foreign Racing) - See Raceform Interactive

[4525] ASCOT (R-H)
Saturday, July 28

OFFICIAL GOING: Firm (good to firm in places; stands' side 10.7; centre 10.9; far side 11.2; round 10.1)
Wind: Almost nil Weather: Fine but cloudy

4574 KELLY GROUP FILLIES' NURSERY 7f
1:45 (1:46) (Class 4) (0-85,85) 2-Y-0 **£6,469** (£1,925; £962; £481) **Stalls** High

Form RPR

1 **1** **Redressthebalance (IRE)**[31] 3487 2-8-11 75................. JamesDoyle 7 86+
(Ralph Beckett) *hld up in midfield: smooth prog to ld wl over 1f out: stl gng easily ent fnl f: shkn up and qckly drew clr* **7/2**[2]

12 **2** *2 1/4* **Rebel Magic**[42] 3138 2-9-7 85.................................... RichardHughes 6 88
(Richard Hannon) *hld up in rr: prog jst over 2f out: drvn to chse wnr 1f out: styd on but no ch* **11/4**[1]

0364 **3** *1 1/4* **Bayan Kasirga (IRE)**[21] 3858 2-8-5 69....................... RoystonFfrench 11 69
(Richard Fahey) *hld up towards rr: rdn over 2f out: prog over 1f out: styd on fnl f to take 3rd last strides* **20/1**

006 **4** *1/2* **We Are City**[16] 3996 2-7-10 63..................................... RyanPowell[(3)] 4 62
(Michael Bell) *hld up in rr: stdy prog on outer of gp 3f out: chal 2f out: no ch w wnr and lost 2nd 1f out: one pce* **20/1**

500 **5** *1 1/2* **Masarah (IRE)**[15] 4064 2-8-6 70...................................... MartinDwyer 9 65
(Clive Brittain) *pressed ldr: upsides 2f out: outpcd over 1f out* **12/1**

623 **6** *1 1/2* **Mrs Warren**[18] 3937 2-8-3 67... WilliamCarson 5 58
(Charles Hills) *hld up in midfield: prog to trck ldrs 2f out gng wl: rdn over 1f out: no rspnse* **11/1**

402 **7** *nse* **Must Be Me**[32] 3465 2-8-1 65....................................... CathyGannon 10 55
(Eve Johnson Houghton) *t.k.h: trckd ldrs: gng wl whn nt clr run 2f out: rdn over 1f out: fdd tamely* **28/1**

303 **8** *1/2* **Cio Cio San (IRE)**[31] 3487 2-8-3 67............................... KieranO'Neill 8 56
(Richard Hannon) *mde most to wl over 1f out: wknd fnl f* **6/1**[3]

402 **9** *3 3/4* **Sojoum**[40] 3224 2-7-8 63... DarrenEgan[(5)] 3 42
(Mick Channon) *hld up in last pair: rdn and no prog over 2f out: no ch after* **20/1**

1063 **10** *nk* **Sylvia Pankhurst (IRE)**[15] 4047 2-8-5 **69**........................ DavidProbert 2 47
(David C Griffiths) *trckd ldrs to 2f out: wknd over 1f out* **25/1**

3561 **11** *2 ½* **Poetic Princess**[12] 4140 2-8-3 **67**.................................. HayleyTurner 12 38
(Jo Hughes) *pressed ldng pair to over 2f out: steadily wknd* **12/1**

042 **12** *20* **Bountybeamadam**[23] 3783 2-9-1 **79**.............................. PatCosgrave 13
(George Baker) *awkward s and slowly away: in tch in midfield tl wknd rapidly 2f out: t.o* **12/1**

1m 29.27s (1.67) **Going Correction** +0.075s/f (Good) 12 Ran SP% **116.2**
Speed ratings (Par 93): **93,90,89,88,86 85,84,84,80,79 76,54**
toteswingers 1&2 £2.20, 1&3 £14.40, 2&3 £12.10 CSF £11.88 CT £169.08 TOTE £4.20: £2.10, £1.50, £4.20; EX 10.40 Trifecta £104.70 Pool: £704.74 - 4.98 winning units.
Owner R A Pegum **Bred** Kevin Walsh **Trained** Kimpton, Hants
■ Stewards' Enquiry : James Doyle one-day ban: careless riding (Aug 11)

FOCUS
The winning jockey in the first confirmed that the ground was very fast. They came down the centre of the track in this fair fillies' nursery, but the principals raced on the far side of the group. The initial pace was modest and the time was around three seconds outside the standard, not especially quick given the conditions. The form makes sense.

NOTEBOOK
Redressthebalance(IRE), a gritty winner on her debut at Bath, retained her unbeaten status in very different fashion. She hit the front still on the bridle and found plenty once her rider finally let her down. The extra yardage suited and she had no problem with the very different ground. (op 3-1 tchd 11-4)
Rebel Magic, like the winner, had done her previous racing at Bath, and was taking a sizeable step up in trip. The topweight, conceding 6lb and more to her rivals, ran on well for pressure once switched to the far side of the bunch but the winner had her covered. She should remain competitive, and may come back here for a sales race later in the summer. (tchd 3-1 in a place)
Bayan Kasirga(IRE), in contrast to the first two, came down the stands' flank, finishing well to snatch third. She may get another furlong. (op 22-1 tchd 25-1)
We Are City was unplaced in three auction maidens but showed more on this nursery debut. However, she could have been flattered by delivering her challenge towards the far side.
Masarah(IRE) found this company more suitable after Group 2 assignments on her last couple of starts, but was still comfortably held. (op 14-1)
Mrs Warren didn't find anything when push came to shove. (tchd 10-1)
Cio Cio San(IRE), the long-time leader, finished further behind today's winner than she had at Bath last time. (op 7-1 tchd 15-2)

4575 BATTERSEA DOGS & CATS HOME H'CAP 1m 4f
2:20 (2:20) (Class 2) (0-105,102) 3-Y-0+

£18,675 (£5,592; £2,796; £1,398; £699; £351) **Stalls** Low

Form RPR

1121 **1** **Scatter Dice (IRE)**[56] 2718 3-7-10 **87**............................ DarrenEgan(5) 8 95
(Mark Johnston) *hld up in 4th: prog over 2f out: rdn to ld over 1f out: hrd pressed after but a holding on* **2/1**[1]

400 **2** *nk* **Address Unknown**[43] 3125 5-9-2 **90**.................................(vt) FranBerry 6 97
(Ian Williams) *trckd ldr: rdn to ld briefly wl over 1f out: pressed wnr after: styd on wl but a jst hld* **15/2**

2-06 **3** *2 ½* **Warlu Way**[28] 3642 5-9-2 **90**.. TedDurcan 9 93
(John Dunlop) *hld up in last pair: effrt over 2f out and hanging: styd on to take 3rd fnl f: no ch w front pair* **8/1**

0501 **4** *1* **Fiery Lad (IRE)**[56] 2706 7-10-0 **102**................................ JamieSpencer 4 104
(Luca Cumani) *hld up in 5th: shkn up 2f out: chsd ldng pair jst over 1f out but already outpcd by them: one pce after* **3/1**[2]

-236 **5** *1 ¾* **High Office**[28] 3625 6-9-1 **89**.. GrahamGibbons 5 88
(Richard Fahey) *trckd ldng pair: rdn over 2f out: lost pl sn after: fdd over 1f out* **5/1**[3]

-000 **6** *3* **Becausewecan (USA)**[21] 3857 6-8-12 **86**........................ JoeFanning 1 80
(Mark Johnston) *led to wl over 1f out: wknd and eased* **16/1**

042- **7** *2 ¾* **Downhiller (IRE)**[337] 5448 7-9-1 **89**.................................. EddieAhern 7 79
(John Dunlop) *hld up in last: pushed along on inner over 2f out: no prog* **12/1**

2m 32.14s (-0.36) **Going Correction** +0.075s/f (Good)
WFA 3 from 4yo+ 12lb 7 Ran SP% **111.5**
Speed ratings (Par 109): **104,103,102,101,100 98,96**
toteswingers 1&2 £4.00, 1&3 £3.80, 2&3 £8.30 CSF £16.68 CT £94.34 TOTE £2.60: £1.80, £3.30; EX 20.40 Trifecta £126.90 Pool: £740.48 - 4.31 winning units..
Owner Sheikh Hamdan Bin Mohammed Al Maktoum **Bred** Darley **Trained** Middleham Moor, N Yorks
■ Stewards' Enquiry : Fran Berry four-day ban: used whip above permitted level (Aug 11-14)

FOCUS
A good-quality handicap, but not as competitive as this race usually is. The pace was ordinary and the order remained unchanged until they turned for home. The winner gave connections their second victory in three years after Bay Willow in 2010. The winner continues to progress but this is not form to take too literally.

NOTEBOOK
Scatter Dice(IRE) has been in fine form this summer and she made it four wins from her last five, following up her victory in the Edinburgh Gold Cup at Musselburgh to score off 23lb higher than when winning at Redcar in April. She was the only 3-y-o in the field and, with her rider's claim, was receiving upwards of 16lb from her rivals. Sticking her neck out gamely to hold off the runner-up, she is remarkably tough and would have prospects if turning out under a penalty at Goodwood on Wednesday. (op 13-8 tchd 6-4)
Address Unknown ran his best race of the campaign, finding only a very tough filly too strong. The faster ground and reuse of the tongue-tie were surely positive factors, as was his falling handicap mark.
Warlu Way did the better of the Dunlop pair, running on down the outside for third. He is reasonably treated at present.
Fiery Lad(IRE) was never quite able to deliver a meaningful challenge, with the way the race was not run not really suiting him. This mark should not be beyond him on his best efforts. (op 7-2 tchd 4-1)
High Office, back down in trip, appeared to have no real excuse. (tchd 6-1)
Becausewecan(USA), the winner's stablemate, was able to dictate, but couldn't hold on once pressed. This trip is a bare minimum for him. (tchd 14-1)

4576 BETFRED MOBILE SPORTS H'CAP 5f
2:55 (2:57) (Class 2) 3-Y-0+

£62,250 (£18,640; £9,320; £4,660; £2,330; £1,170) **Stalls** High

Form RPR

0006 **1** **Barnet Fair**[6] 4367 4-8-3 **88**... KierenFox 18 97
(Richard Guest) *taken down early: wl in rr: str reminders jst over 2f out: prog over 1f out: r.o fnl f on nr side to ld last strides* **7/1**[3]

2431 **2** *nk* **Taajub (IRE)**[6] 4367 5-8-13 **98** 6ex................................... SebSanders 13 106
(Peter Crate) *trckd ldrs: swtchd rt over 1f out: drvn and r.o to take narrow ld wl ins fnl f: hdd last strides* **17/2**

5-03 **3** *shd* **Zero Money (IRE)**[28] 3641 6-8-13 **98**..............................(b) JamesDoyle 9 106
(Roger Charlton) *pressed ldr: led over 2f out: drvn and hdd wl ins fnl f: styd on* **5/1**[1]

120 **4** *nk* **Whaileyy (IRE)**[70] 2268 4-8-9 **94**....................................(b) MartinHarley 15 100
(Marco Botti) *dwlt: sn trckd ldrs: rdn to cl over 1f out on nr side: tried to chal fnl f: a jst hld* **20/1**

4063 **5** *nk* **Fratellino**[6] 4367 5-8-0 **90**..(t) DarrenEgan(5) 6 95+
(Alan McCabe) *sn pushed along and wl in rr: styd on fr over 1f out: gaining at fin* **11/1**

000 **6** *½* **Fitz Flyer (IRE)**[56] 2704 6-8-5 **90**..................................... MartinDwyer 16 94
(David Nicholls) *towards rr: effrt fr 1/2-way: styd on fr over 1f out: nvr quite able to threaten* **33/1**

0-30 **7** *nk* **Burning Thread (IRE)**[6] 4367 5-8-7 **92**.............................. TedDurcan 3 95
(Tim Etherington) *wl in tch: rdn over 1f out: kpt on but nvr gng pce to chal* **25/1**

-020 **8** *½* **Desert Law (IRE)**[35] 3371 4-9-3 **102**.......................... RichardHughes 11 103
(Andrew Balding) *dwlt: wl in rr: rdn and styd on fr 2f out: nrst fin but n.d* **13/2**[2]

300 **9** *shd* **Excel Bolt**[56] 2717 4-8-5 **90**.. RoystonFfrench 14 90
(Bryan Smart) *v prom: pressed ldr 2f out to jst over 1f out: fdd* **25/1**

0-00 **10** *½* **Ajjaadd (USA)**[6] 4367 6-8-5 **90**.. KieranO'Neill 20 89
(Ted Powell) *hld up towards rr: effrt 2f out: tried to cl on ldrs on nr side 1f out: kpt on one pce* **25/1**

-236 **11** *shd* **Catfish (IRE)**[29] 3593 4-8-6 **91**.. HayleyTurner 19 89
(Brian Meehan) *taken down early: dwlt: wl in rr: rdn wl over 1f out: styd on fnl f: nrst fin* **11/1**

0340 **12** *3 ¾* **Sohraab**[7] 4317 8-8-4 **89**.. NickyMackay 1 74
(Hughie Morrison) *racd towards far side: wl in rr: rdn 2f out: no real prog* **20/1**

2111 **13** *nk* **Bosun Breese**[35] 3374 7-8-8 **93**................................ GrahamGibbons 10 77
(David Barron) *chsd ldrs to 2f out: steadily wknd* **12/1**

4220 **14** *hd* **Es Que Love (IRE)**[35] 3370 3-9-4 **107**............................... JoeFanning 2 90
(Mark Johnston) *w ldrs to 2f out: wknd* **12/1**

0040 **15** *nse* **Dancing Freddy (IRE)**[6] 4367 5-8-4 **89**...................(tp) WilliamCarson 7 72
(Richard Guest) *racd on outer of gp in midfield: rdn 2f out: edgd rt and wknd over 1f out* **33/1**

0-01 **16** *1 ¾* **La Fortunata**[29] 3593 5-8-0 **90**.. AmyScott(5) 8 66
(Eve Johnson Houghton) *taken down early: led to over 2f out: lost pl qckly* **33/1**

310 **17** *3* **Bajan Tryst (USA)**[28] 3648 6-9-2 **101**.......................... JamieSpencer 12 67
(Kevin Ryan) *dwlt: a in last of main gp: struggling fr 1/2-way* **25/1**

2261 **18** *11* **Hazelrigg (IRE)**[15] 4073 7-8-7 **92**.. EddieAhern 5 18
(Tim Easterby) *awkward as stalls opened: walked out of them w blindfold stl on and then turned lft: allowed to come home in own time* **20/1**

59.66s (-0.84) **Going Correction** +0.075s/f (Good)
WFA 3 from 4yo+ 4lb 18 Ran SP% **123.6**
Speed ratings (Par 109): **109,108,108,107,107 106,106,105,105,104 104,98,97,97,97 94,89,72**
toteswingers 1&2 £17.10, 1&3 £15.50, 2&3 £9.00 CSF £55.35 CT £337.07 TOTE £7.60: £2.50, £2.60, £1.70, £4.90; EX 88.30 Trifecta £1135.60 Pool: £2,654.88 - 1.73 winning units..
Owner Donald Wheatley **Bred** Mrs J M Russell **Trained** Stainforth, S Yorks
■ Stewards' Enquiry : Seb Sanders two-day ban: used whip above permitted level (Aug 13-14)
Kieren Fox seven-day ban: used whip above permitted level (Aug 11-17)

FOCUS
A hotly contested contest for a very valuable prize, and pretty solid handicap form. They raced down the centre and this time the main players were on the stands' side of the pack. The winner is rated back to his best.

NOTEBOOK
Barnet Fair delivered his challenge nearest to the stands' side, running on from the back to get up close home. The bottomweight had caught the eye when sixth to Taajub here last Sunday, after running loose before the off, and had his favoured quick ground here. He was also well handicapped on his form from this time last year. Richard Guest is now eyeing valuable sprints at Deauville in the next month or so. (op 15-2 tchd 13-2)
Taajub(IRE), a recent C&D winner, came close to bagging a lucrative double, but was just denied under his penalty. He was Group-placed at two and remains well treated on his best form. (op 12-1 tchd 8-1)
Zero Money(IRE) had his ideal conditions back at 5f and ran a big race, always up with the speed and missing out narrowly. (op 6-1 tchd 13-2)
Whaileyy(IRE), another drawn high, ran well on this first try at 5f. He's relatively lightly raced and may have more to offer in the blinkers. (op 25-1)
Fratellino, third in Taajub's recent race over C&D, was first home here among those who raced towards the far side. He is in fine heart at present. (op 10-1)
Fitz Flyer(IRE) ◆ didn't get the best of breaks then raced away from the pace, so deserves marking up for this effort. He's well treated on his best form and could be interesting at Goodwood, where he holds a couple of entries.
Burning Thread(IRE) showed more than he had in Taajub's race here last week, despite an unhelpful draw.
Desert Law(IRE), 5lb higher than when well beaten in the Wokingham, was one of the few running on from the back. Richard Hughes reported that the gelding slipped leaving the stalls. Official explanation: jockey said gelding slipped on leaving stalls (tchd 6-1 and 7-1)
Excel Bolt was up with the pace from the start until fading under pressure. He had ground and draw in his favour.
Ajjaadd(USA) Official explanation: jockey said gelding jumped right leaving stalls
Catfish(IRE), reportedly in season last time, wasn't the best away here but put in some decent late work. (op 12-1 tchd 14-1)
Bosun Breese was well held on this bid for a four-timer, but his rider did not persevere once his chance had gone. Graham Gibbons reported that his mount slipped leaving the stalls. Official explanation: jockey said gelding slipped on leaving stalls (op 10-1)
Hazelrigg(IRE) lost his race at the start, appearing to burst his stall open and emerging with the blindfold still on. Eddie Ahern reported that his mount charged the gate. Official explanation: jockey said as he went to remove blindfold gelding jumped forward and hit gate and was slowly away.

4577 PRINCESS MARGARET JUDDMONTE STKS (GROUP 3) (FILLIES) 6f
3:25 (3:25) (Class 1) 2-Y-0

£28,355 (£10,750; £5,380; £2,680; £1,345; £675) **Stalls** High

Form RPR

12 **1** **Maureen (IRE)**[15] 4064 2-8-12 0.................................... RichardHughes 1 107+
(Richard Hannon) *sn hld up bhd ldrs: prog to ld over 1f out: shkn up and wl in command fnl f: readily* **5/6**[1]

12 **2** *2 ¼* **Sandreamer (IRE)**[28] 3631 2-8-12 0................................ MartinHarley 3 99
(Mick Channon) *hld up last: prog fr 2f out to chse wnr 1f out: styd on but no ch* **11/1**

221 **3** *1 ¼* **Hoyam**[26] 3700 2-8-12 99.. JamieSpencer 2 95
(Michael Bell) *restrained early but moved up to ld over 4f out: rdn and hdd over 1f out: one pce* **5/2**[2]

61 **4** 1 1/4 **Jollification (IRE)**[31] 3504 2-8-12 0 PatCosgrave 5 91
(George Baker) *hld up in tch: effrt 2f out: cl enough over 1f out: fdd fnl f* **40/1**

0 **5** 3/4 **Mironica (IRE)**[38] 3269 2-8-12 0 WayneLordan 6 89
(David Wachman, Ire) *t.k.h: hld up: effrt 2f out: no prog and btn over 1f out* **8/1**[3]

1 **6** 5 **Strange Magic (IRE)**[24] 3748 2-8-12 0 GrahamGibbons 8 73
(Richard Fahey) *led to over 4f out: w ldr to over 2f out: wknd* **20/1**

1m 14.4s (-0.10) **Going Correction** +0.075s/f (Good) **6** Ran SP% **109.8**
Speed ratings (Par 101): **103,100,98,96,95 89**
toteswingers 1&2 £2.10, 1&3 £1.10, 2&3 £2.90 CSF £10.85 TOTE £1.60: £1.20, £3.00; EX 7.60 Trifecta £17.80 Pool: £1,983.78 - 82.13 winning units..

Owner Ahmad Alkhallafi **Bred** C McEvoy **Trained** East Everleigh, Wilts

FOCUS
Russian Rhythm, successful in 2002 and winner of the following year's 1000 Guineas, was the last real star to take this event, which has held Group 3 status since 1986. This was the smallest field since 2004. The runners raced alongside the stands' rail and the early pace was by no means strong. This weas a slightly below standard edition and Maureen didn't need to match her Cherry Hinton form.

NOTEBOOK
Maureen(IRE) ◆ was very much the form pick after her luckless second to Sendmylovetorose in the Cherry Hinton at Newmarket, and followed up fellow runners-up in that race, Enthused and Soraaya, in winning this. She was only Richard Hannon's second Princess Margaret winner, the first having been A Smooth One back in 1993. Connections had been worried about the prospect of a muddling pace, which duly materialised, but the filly soon settled behind the leading pair and did her work fluently once produced to lead. She must hold strong claims in the Lowther Stakes at York next month, while longer term she could well make a Cheveley Park filly. She appears to handle most types of ground. (op 10-11)

Sandreamer(IRE), from the yard successful with Soraaya two years ago, had her favoured quick ground. Runner-up to Maureen's stablemate City Image in Listed company last time, she ran on well from the rear of the field but the winner was too classy for her. This was a step up. (op 10-1 tchd 12-1)

Hoyam, the Queen Mary runner-up, looked the principal danger to the winner on form. She could have done with some cover, but with the pace so steady her rider let her stride along after a couple of furlongs. Once tackled she was unable to quicken up, but there was something to like about the way she stuck to her task and she merits another chance over this trip. (tchd 11-4)

Jollification(IRE), a Salisbury maiden winner, handled the ground well and ran respectably to reach the frame. (tchd 33-1)

Mironica(IRE) has disappointed in two trips over to Ascot now. The return to 6f should not have posed her a problem but the firm ground is a plausible excuse. (op 9-1 tchd 10-1)

Strange Magic(IRE), a Catterick maiden scorer, was not up to this big leap in grade, fading after helping to set the pace. (op 16-1)

4578 ROYAL ASCOT BEST EVENT FOR GROUPS H'CAP 1m 2f
3:55 (3:56) (Class 3) (0-90,88) 3-Y-O+ **£8,409** (£2,502; £1,250; £625) **Stalls** Low

Form RPR

1656 **1** **Amoya (GER)**[11] 4199 5-8-13 76 RaulDaSilva(3) 10 84
(Philip McBride) *qckly away fr wd draw and crossed to inner: mde all: rdn 2f out: edgd lft over 1f out: hld on nr fin* **20/1**

0421 **2** hd **John Biscuit (IRE)**[23] 3774 4-9-8 82 DavidProbert 2 90
(Andrew Balding) *hld up in 4th: brought wd and effrt 2f out: drvn to chse wnr 1f out: clsd nr fin: jst failed* **6/1**[3]

5400 **3** 1 **Colour Guard**[12] 4136 4-9-10 84 JoeFanning 4 90
(Mark Johnston) *trckd wnr: rdn 2f out: tried to cl over 1f out: lost 2nd fnl f: styd on* **14/1**

-350 **4** 1 **Indian Jack (IRE)**[50] 2882 4-10-0 88 JamieSpencer 5 92+
(Luca Cumani) *restless stalls: stdd s: hld up in last pair: plenty to do 3f out: taken out wd and prog 2f out: clsd on ldrs 1f out: one pce after* **10/3**[2]

521 **5** 1 1/2 **Mcvicar**[9] 4254 3-7-13 69 oh2 CathyGannon 7 70
(Mick Channon) *trckd wnr: rdn over 2f out: tried to cl over 1f out: fdd ins fnl f* **7/1**

6-05 **6** 8 **Greylami (IRE)**[43] 3121 7-9-8 82 StevieDonohoe 1 67
(Robert Mills) *hld up in 5th: plenty to do 3f out: rdn and no prog on inner over 2f out: wl btn after* **15/2**

/000 **7** 3/4 **Toughness Danon**[31] 3502 6-9-3 77 FranBerry 9 61
(Brendan Powell) *stmbld s: hld up in last pair: rdn and no prog over 2f out: wl btn after* **40/1**

2-34 **8** 11 **Robin Hoods Bay**[28] 3642 4-9-13 87 RichardHughes 3 74
(Ed Vaughan) *dwlt: hld up in 6th: plenty to do 3f out: rdn and effrt over 2f out: no imp over 1f out: virtually p.u ins fnl f: dismntd after line* **13/8**[1]

2m 6.1s (-1.30) **Going Correction** +0.075s/f (Good)
WFA 3 from 4yo+ 10lb **8** Ran SP% **113.6**
Speed ratings (Par 107): **108,107,107,106,105 98,98,89**
toteswingers 1&2 £17.20, 1&3 £13.10, 2&3 £9.30 CSF £132.21 CT £1744.83 TOTE £29.80: £5.30, £1.60, £3.30; EX 186.00 Trifecta £1354.30 Part won. Pool: £1,830.21 - 0.10 winning units..

Owner Black Star Racing **Bred** Gestut Ebbesloh **Trained** Newmarket, Suffolk

■ Stewards' Enquiry : Raul Da Silva one-day ban: careless riding (Aug 11)

FOCUS
The winner set a reasonable pace in this ordinary handicap for the track and grade. A British best from the winner.

NOTEBOOK
Amoya(GER) got over from the outside stall to make all the running. The challengers were coming in up the straight, but she held on well despite wandering a bit in front. She was just 1lb higher than when winning at Yarmouth in May, which also came on firm ground. Official explanation: trainer said, regarding apparent improvement in form, that the mare was better suited by being allowed to dominate. (op 16-1)

John Biscuit(IRE) took time to settle but was running on well down the outside at the death, needing another stride or two. Still reasonably handicapped despite the 4lb rise for his Epsom win, he will probably stay 1m4f. (op 11-2 tchd 13-2)

Colour Guard has limited experience on turf and ran a decent race in an event in which his trainer has a good record. He got the trip well enough. (op 11-1)

Indian Jack(IRE) could never reach a challenging position after a tardy start, and his effectiveness at this distance remains unproven. (op 4-1)

Mcvicar, effectively 5lb higher than when winning at Epsom, may not have found these underfoot conditions so suitable. (op 8-1)

Robin Hoods Bay's Newmarket third in May looked strong form, but he was never able to get into this. He was eased right down inside the last and Richard Hughes quickly dismounted after the finish. Hughes reported that the gelding felt wrong. Official explanation: jockey said gelding felt wrong (op 9-4)

4579 NORMAN COURT STUD FILLIES' H'CAP 1m (S)
4:30 (4:30) (Class 3) (0-90,90) 3-Y-O+ **£8,409** (£2,502; £1,250; £625) **Stalls** High

Form RPR

2-10 **1** **Dank**[70] 2263 3-9-4 88 RichardHughes 10 99+
(Sir Michael Stoute) *hld up towards rr: shkn up and prog jst over 2f out to ld over 1f out: r.o wl: comf* **3/1**[2]

6-10 **2** 1 3/4 **Rugosa**[28] 3643 3-8-3 73 WilliamCarson 1 80
(Charles Hills) *dwlt: hld up in last pair: prog 2f out: chsd wnr jst over 1f out: shkn up and r.o but no imp* **16/1**

601 **3** 2 3/4 **Forgive**[28] 3643 3-8-7 77 SeanLevey 13 78
(Richard Hannon) *trckd ldrs: rdn and nt qckn 2f out: styd on again fnl f to take 3rd last strides* **9/1**

1-06 **4** nk **Diala (IRE)**[30] 3542 3-9-6 90 EddieAhern 12 92+
(William Haggas) *t.k.h: hld up on inner: dropped to last pair 1/2-way: prog 2f out: rn into trble briefly over 1f out: pushed along and styd on fnl f: nvr any threat* **9/4**[1]

5-10 **5** nse **Lady Macduff (IRE)**[73] 2182 3-8-12 82 JoeFanning 6 82
(Mark Johnston) *mde most to over 1f out: outpcd* **25/1**

1-36 **6** 2 **Estrela**[65] 2410 3-9-6 90 JamesDoyle 11 85
(Roger Charlton) *mostly chsd ldr to wl over 1f out: wknd* **11/2**[3]

1132 **7** 2 3/4 **Russian Rave**[14] 4091 6-9-13 89 StephenCraine 4 80
(Jonathan Portman) *dwlt: hld up in last pair: rdn over 2f out: no prog* **10/1**

-050 **8** 10 **Diverting**[28] 3636 4-9-5 84 RaulDaSilva(3) 2 52
(William Jarvis) *racd wd of rest: wl in tch: rdn 3f out: wknd rapidly over 1f out: t.o* **16/1**

-211 **9** 6 **Laverre (IRE)**[30] 3550 5-9-1 77 HayleyTurner 7 31
(Lucy Wadham) *prom tl wknd 2f out: eased and t.o* **8/1**

1m 40.58s (-0.22) **Going Correction** +0.075s/f (Good)
WFA 3 from 4yo+ 8lb **9** Ran SP% **117.0**
Speed ratings (Par 104): **104,102,99,99,99 97,94,84,78**
toteswingers 1&2 £12.50, 1&3 £7.10, 2&3 £9.70 CSF £50.34 CT £395.19 TOTE £4.10: £1.50, £3.90, £2.40; EX 55.60 Trifecta £541.50 Pool: £1,631.98 - 2.23 winning units..

Owner James Wigan **Bred** London Thoroughbred Services Ltd **Trained** Newmarket, Suffolk

FOCUS
A decent fillies' handicap in which the field raced against the stands' rail. The pace was fairly steady and there were one or two traffic problems. The first two were unexposed and there's more to come from them.

NOTEBOOK
Dank quickened nicely to assume control and ran out a ready winner. Off since disappointing when favourite for a Doncaster handicap in May, she looked a smart filly here, one well capable of earning some black type. In fact, she had been declared for a Listed race at Sandown earlier in the month, but the easy ground was thought unsuitable. (op 7-2)
Rugosa ◆ was carried to her right leaving the stalls. Travelling well, she tracked the winner through, but lacked the pace of her rival. She lost a shoe when disappointing at Windsor last time and turned round the form with the winner that day. A handicap should come her way. (op 12-1)
Forgive, raised 4lb for her Windsor success, plugged on against the rail and, on this evidence, would be worth another crack at 1m2f. She deserves some credit for being the only one of the first four to race up with the pace. (op 10-1)
Diala(IRE)was an interesting runner, quietly fancied when down the field for the 1,000 Guineas on her reappearance before a below-par effort in a Listed race. This quick ground was expected to suit and she ran a better race, but things did not go her way as she found herself having to wait for a run, then lost more momentum when out in the clear. She can't be classed as unlucky, but would have finished closer and remains capable of better. (op 7-2)
Lady Macduff(IRE), ran a fair race from the front on this first start since mid-May, losing two places in the latter stages. (op 16-1)
Estrela faded after tracking the pace, the drop in trip failed to do the trick. (op 9-2)
Laverre(IRE), on a hat-trick but down in trip, dropped right away.

4580 MITIE TOTAL SECURITY MANAGEMENT H'CAP 7f
5:00 (5:01) (Class 4) (0-85,85) 3-Y-O+ **£6,469** (£1,925; £962; £481) **Stalls** High

Form RPR

4442 **1** **Corporal Maddox**[14] 4077 5-10-0 85 JamieSpencer 3 95
(Patrick Morris) *dwlt: hld up in last pair: stl covered up there 2f out: gd prog over 1f out: rdn and r.o to ld ins fnl f: sn clr* **5/1**[3]

12 **2** 1 1/2 **Gaul Wood (IRE)**[14] 4082 3-9-4 82 RichardKingscote 4 86+
(Tom Dascombe) *prom on outer: shkn up to ld wl over 1f out: hdd and outpcd ins fnl f* **11/4**[1]

-241 **3** 1 1/4 **Good Authority (IRE)**[45] 3045 5-9-7 78 TomMcLaughlin 7 81
(Karen George) *hld up in last pair: stdy prog jst over 2f out: wnt 2nd briefly 1f out: rdn and styd on same pce after* **10/1**

0-10 **4** 3 **Ongoodform (IRE)**[70] 2274 5-9-8 79 (v) EddieAhern 13 73
(Paul D'Arcy) *cl up gng wl: asked for effrt over 1f out: one pce and easily lft bhd fnl f* **16/1**

-000 **5** 1 1/4 **George Baker (IRE)**[64] 2444 5-9-6 77 PatCosgrave 6 68
(George Baker) *hld up towards rr: effrt over 2f out: rdn and sme prog over 1f out: nvr gng pce to threaten* **14/1**

0000 **6** 3/4 **The Tichborne (IRE)**[23] 3772 4-8-7 67 (v) RaulDaSilva(3) 14 56
(Roger Teal) *led to wl over 1f out: steadily wknd fnl f* **16/1**

1550 **7** 4 **Masai Moon**[36] 3348 8-9-4 75 JamesMillman 17 53
(Rod Millman) *cl up 3f: lost pl sn after: wknd 2f out* **16/1**

000 **8** 1/2 **Azrael**[36] 3348 4-9-10 81 MartinHarley 12 58
(Alan McCabe) *prom: rdn over 2f out: wknd wl over 1f out* **33/1**

0000 **9** 1 **Lowther**[16] 3999 7-9-9 80 KierenFox 15 54
(Brett Johnson) *wl in tch in midfield: rdn over 2f out: wknd wl over 1f out* **20/1**

0604 **10** nk **Fantasy Gladiator**[8] 4287 6-9-5 76 [1] JamesDoyle 2 49
(Robert Cowell) *nvr really gng: in tch to over 2f out: wknd* **8/1**

6564 **11** 3/4 **Kakapuka**[17] 3963 5-9-6 77 HayleyTurner 8 48
(Anabel K Murphy) *awkward s: in tch in midfield: shkn up wl over 2f out: sn wknd* **16/1**

4221 **12** 1 **Mingun Bell (USA)**[11] 4190 5-9-11 82 LiamKeniry 16 51
(Ed de Giles) *mostly chsd ldr to 2f out: wknd qckly* **4/1**[2]

1m 26.97s (-0.63) **Going Correction** +0.075s/f (Good)
WFA 3 from 4yo+ 7lb **12** Ran SP% **121.4**
Speed ratings (Par 105): **106,104,102,99,98 97,92,92,90,90 89,88**
toteswingers 1&2 £4.00, 1&3 £8.80, 2&3 £6.20 CSF £19.56 CT £137.27 TOTE £5.20: £2.10, £1.50, £2.80; EX 17.50 Trifecta £57.10 Pool: £1,461.82 - 18.92 winning units..

Owner Dr Marwan Koukash **Bred** Theobalds Stud **Trained** Tarporley, Cheshire

FOCUS
A reasonable handicap where those drawn low were seen to best effect. The pace was strong and the winner is rated to last year's best.

T/Plt: £92.70 to a £1 stake. Pool: £13,8580.60 - 1,091.14 winning tickets T/Qpdt: £47.60 to a £1 stake. Pool: £7,305.57 - 113.52 winning tickets JN

4462 LINGFIELD (L-H)

Saturday, July 28

OFFICIAL GOING: Turf course - good to firm (watered; 9.1); all-weather - standard

Wind: Light, across Weather: Dry, bright spells

4581 CYPRIUM BAR AT MARRIOTT LINGFIELD MAIDEN AUCTION STKS — 5f

5:55 (5:58) (Class 6) 2-Y-O — **£2,181** (£644; £322) **Stalls** High

Form — RPR

6 **1** **Ovett**[17] 3971 2-8-7 0 ow1 .... AdamBeschizza(3) 1 — 74+
(Gary Moore) *dwlt: sn rcvrd and in tch: chsd ldr over 3f out: rdn to ld 1f out: rdn out hands and heels and r.o wl fnl f* **15/8**[1]

06 **2** *nk* **Silverrica (IRE)**[31] 3506 2-8-2 0 .... DarrenEgan(5) 4 — 70+
(Malcolm Saunders) *racd keenly: chsd ldr tl over 3f out: hmpd and stmbld 3f out: rdn wl over 1f out: squeezed through on rail and chsd wnr ins fnl f: styd on wl u.p fnl 100yds* **11/4**[2]

204 **3** *2* **Jet Acclaim (IRE)**[17] 3971 2-8-5 66 .... NickyMackay 2 — 60
(Marco Botti) *led: rdn over 1f out: hdd 1f out: no ex and lost 2nd ins fnl f: wknd towards fin* **3/1**[3]

40 **4** *2 3/4* **Moonlit Dancer (IRE)**[32] 3473 2-8-9 0 ....(t) WilliamCarson 6 — 54
(J W Hills) *dwlt: in tch in last pair: edging out lft and effrt over 2f out: kpt on same pce fnl f* **15/2**

0 **5** *3 1/2* **Southern Sapphire**[17] 3973 2-8-11 0 .... ShaneKelly 5 — 44
(Linda Stubbs) *awkward leaving stalls: sn in tch: rdn: rn green and edgd lft over 2f out: wknd over 1f out* **12/1**

00 **6** *9* **Casta Diamante**[12] 4149 2-8-4 0 .... RichardThomas 3
(Ralph Beckett) *a in rr: rdn and struggling over 2f out: wknd wl over 1f out* **16/1**

58.34s (0.14) **Going Correction** -0.325s/f (Firm) — **6** Ran SP% **111.8**
Speed ratings (Par 92): **85,84,81,76,71 56**
toteswingers: 1&2 £2.00, 1&3 £2.00, 2&3 £1.70. CSF £7.21 TOTE £2.90: £2.10, £1.70; EX 10.20.
Owner G L Moore **Bred** Whatton Manor Stud **Trained** Lower Beeding, W Sussex
■ Stewards' Enquiry : Nicky Mackay two-day ban: careless riding (Aug 12-13)

FOCUS
The going was good to firm and the clerk of the course reported that there was a quicker strip of ground against the stands' rail. The three market leaders dominated this minor maiden and the winner was value for a bit more than the winning margin.\n

NOTEBOOK
Ovett finished two places behind Jet Acclaim in a bunch finish in a 6f AW maiden here on debut. A solid favourite in his bid to turn that form around, he coped well with a drop back to 5f and found A sustained run to score with a bit in hand. He is a scopey half-brother to a decent 1m winner and a minor 3m hurdles winner, but he also has quite a bit of speed on both sides of his pedigree and should continue to progress. (op 5-2 tchd 7-4)
Silverrica(IRE) showed good speed but paid the price for pulling hard when 66-1 in a Salisbury maiden last time. She was a bit keen again dropped in grade and trip but did well to rally for a close second. A half-sister to smart prolific 5f-7f winner Miss Gorica and three other winners, she is getting better with practice and could raise her form several notches when she learns to settle better. Official explanation: jockey said filly suffered interference in running (op 3-1 tchd 7-2)
Jet Acclaim(IRE), a 66-rated filly, set the pace against the favoured stands' rail but couldn't hold off the less exposed winner and more progressive second. (op 11-4 tchd 10-3)
Moonlit Dancer(IRE) was never dangerous and a tongue-tie and switch to 5f on fast ground didn't work for him. (op 7-1 tchd 11-2)
Casta Diamante Official explanation: trainer's rep said filly was unsuited by the good to firm ground

4582 BREATHE SPA AT MARRIOTT LINGFIELD MEDIAN AUCTION MAIDEN STKS — 7f

6:25 (6:28) (Class 6) 3-5-Y-O — **£2,181** (£644; £322) **Stalls** High

Form — RPR

0-5 **1** **Catherine Laboure (IRE)**[31] 3507 3-8-12 0 .... WilliamCarson 15 — 75+
(Eve Johnson Houghton) *chsd ldr tl led 2f out: sn rdn clr: in command but hung lft fr over 1f out: comf* **5/4**[1]

2453 **2** *2 1/2* **Gunner Will (IRE)**[25] 3736 3-9-3 72 .... TedDurcan 4 — 70
(Jamie Osborne) *racd off the pce in midfield: rdn and chsd ldng trio 4f out: styd on to chse wnr jst ins fnl f: kpt on* **9/2**[2]

6 **3** *2 1/2* **Ifan (IRE)**[66] 2387 4-9-5 0 .... DarrenEgan(5) 5 — 65+
(Bryn Palling) *wl off the pce towards rr: sme hdwy 4f out: modest 6th 2f out: styd on wl u.p fnl f to go 3rd wl ins fnl f: no threat to wnr* **40/1**

0-4 **4** *3* **Mulberry Brite**[156] 663 4-9-0 0 .... AmyScott(5) 8 — 52
(Alastair Lidderdale) *led tl hdd and rdn 2f out: btn over 1f out: wknd and lost 2 pls ins fnl f* **80/1**

63 **5** *3 1/2* **Shore Performer (IRE)**[22] 3811 3-8-12 0 .... ShaneKelly 2 — 41
(William Haggas) *chsd ldng piar: rdn and unable qck 2f out: 4th and btn over 1f out: wknd fnl f* **6/1**[3]

60-3 **6** *1 1/2* **Pastures New**[42] 3155 4-9-7 60 .... AdamBeschizza(3) 7 — 44
(Des Donovan) *chsd ldrs: rdn after 2f and sn struggling: 5th and btn 2f out: wknd* **33/1**

6 *dht* **Ever Fortune (USA)** 3-9-3 0 .... MartinDwyer 14 — 42
(Rae Guest) *bhd: sme hdwy past btn horses whn nt clr run and swtchd rt over 1f out: kpt on but n.d* **12/1**

6 **8** *4 1/2* **Yogic Flyer**[42] 3155 3-8-12 0 .... StevieDonohoe 1 — 24
(Gay Kelleway) *racd off the pce in midfield: rdn and struggling 1/2-way: wknd over 2f out* **66/1**

0 **9** *1/2* **Neat Little Rows (IRE)**[16] 4001 3-8-12 0 .... NickyMackay 12 — 23
(Marco Botti) *sn struggling to go pce and pushed along towards rr: sme hdwy 2f out: no imp after: n.d* **16/1**

10 *2 1/4* **Siena Street** 3-8-12 0 .... FergusSweeney 9 — 17
(Henry Candy) *sn pushed along and rn green towards rr: n.d* **20/1**

0-0 **11** *nk* **Saffron Park**[42] 3155 3-9-3 0 .... RichardThomas 10 — 21
(John Best) *stdd s: t.k.h: hld up in midfield: rdn over 2f out: sn wknd* **33/1**

12 *2 1/4* **Captain Hero (IRE)**[52] 5-9-3 0 .... CharlotteJenner(7) 13 — 17
(Laura Mongan) *a outpcd towards rr: n.d* **150/1**

13 *2* **Maligned (USA)** 3-8-12 0 .... SeanLevey 11
(Richard Hannon) *racd in midfield but nvr on terms: struggling 4f out: bhd fnl 2f* **12/1**

UR05 **14** *35* **Aurens (IRE)**[35] 3389 3-9-3 70 ....(v) AmirQuinn 3
(Gary Moore) *v awkward leaving stalls and virtually ref to r: a t.o* **22/1**

1m 21.88s (-1.42) **Going Correction** -0.325s/f (Firm)
WFA 3 from 4yo+ 7lb — **14** Ran SP% **119.0**
Speed ratings (Par 101): **95,92,89,85,81 80,80,75,74,71 71,68,66,26**
toteswingers: 1&2 £2.20, 1&3 £13.60, 2&3 £48.10. CSF £5.76 TOTE £2.20: £1.10, £1.60, £8.00; EX 7.80.
Owner Exors of the Late George Ward **Bred** Declan Johnson **Trained** Blewbury, Oxon

FOCUS
There was little strength in depth in this maiden auction. The well-backed favourite was a comfortable winner and only a few runners got involved. The winner is rated in line with her reappearance

4583 FOLLOW US ON TWITTER @LINGFIELDPARK H'CAP — 7f

7:00 (7:02) (Class 5) (0-70,70) 3-Y-O — **£3,067** (£905; £453) **Stalls** High

Form — RPR

14 **1** **Shena's Dream (IRE)**[32] 3475 3-9-4 67 .... LiamJones 6 — 79+
(William Haggas) *rring in stalls: broke fast: mde all and crossed to r against stands' rail: rdn ent fnl 2f: clr and in command over 1f out: eased towards fin* **11/10**[1]

4550 **2** *2* **Al's Memory (IRE)**[29] 3555 3-9-4 67 .... ShaneKelly 12 — 71
(David Evans) *in tch: rdn to chse clr wnr over 1f out: kpt on same pce fnl f* **4/1**[2]

36-0 **3** *3/4* **I'm Harry**[26] 3705 3-9-3 66 .... MartinDwyer 10 — 68
(George Baker) *hld up in last pair: rdn and hdwy to go 3rd over 1f out: swtchd lft and styd on same pce ins fnl f* **12/1**

00-0 **4** *7* **Clapped**[74] 2147 3-8-9 58 .... TedDurcan 9 — 41
(Ed Vaughan) *stdd s: hld up in tch in midfield: swtchd lft and effrt 2f out: sn rdn and outpcd: 4th and wl btn fnl f* **33/1**

5-05 **5** *1* **Operation Tracer**[23] 3792 3-8-12 61 .... FergusSweeney 11 — 41
(Michael Bell) *chsd ldrs: rdn and edgd lft over 2f out: outpcd and btn over 1f out: wknd fnl f* **4/1**[2]

0136 **6** *3/4* **The New Black (IRE)**[27] 3671 3-9-3 66 .... StevieDonohoe 5 — 44
(Gay Kelleway) *hld up in rr: rdn 3f out: no prog 2f out: wknd over 1f out* **10/1**[3]

06-0 **7** *2* **Silver Marizah (IRE)**[75] 2136 3-8-13 62 ....(p) RichardMullen 1 — 35
(Gary Moore) *in tch in midfield: rdn and effrt 2f out: no hdwy and sn btn: wknd over 1f out* **25/1**

0-04 **8** *3 1/4* **Arctic Stryker**[78] 2045 3-9-2 70 .... DarrenEgan(5) 4 — 34
(John Best) *chsd ldr tl wl over 1f out: sn btn: wknd over 1f out: fdd ins fnl f* **16/1**

1m 21.86s (-1.44) **Going Correction** -0.325s/f (Firm) — **8** Ran SP% **117.1**
Speed ratings (Par 100): **95,92,91,83,82 81,79,75**
toteswingers: 1&2 £2.40, 1&3 £4.90, 2&3 £5.90. CSF £5.88 CT £34.60 TOTE £1.90: £1.30, £1.30, £3.90; EX 7.00.
Owner Miss Pat O'Kelly **Bred** Kilcarn Stud **Trained** Newmarket, Suffolk

FOCUS
The unexposed hot favourite put in a dominant display and the placed horses finished a long way clear of the rest in this handicap. The first three raced on the rail and the form among them makes sense.

4584 LINGFIELD PARK GOLF CLUB H'CAP — 7f 140y

7:30 (7:32) (Class 6) (0-65,65) 3-Y-O+ — **£2,181** (£644; £322) **Stalls** Centre

Form — RPR

6265 **1** **Amba**[3] 4468 6-9-6 60 .... AdamBeschizza(3) 4 — 72+
(Des Donovan) *sn pushed along to chse ldr: rdn 3f out: drvn 2f out: led 1f out: kpt on wl u.p fnl f* **12/1**

0-31 **2** *1 3/4* **For What (USA)**[12] 4142 4-9-12 63 .... TedDurcan 14 — 71+
(David Lanigan) *hld up in midfield: switching lft and effrt over 1f out: kpt on u.p ins fnl f to go 2nd towards fin: no threat to wnr* **2/1**[1]

1142 **3** *1/2* **Know No Fear**[5] 4413 7-9-6 64 ....(p) SemiraPashai(7) 9 — 70
(Alastair Lidderdale) *in tch: pushed along to chse ldrs ent fnl 2f: styd on same pce ins fnl f: wnt 3rd cl home* **9/2**[3]

0001 **4** *hd* **Comadoir (IRE)**[39] 3249 6-9-6 62 ....(p) NathanSweeney(5) 12 — 68
(Jo Crowley) *led: rdn over 1f out: hdd 1f out: no ex and one pce after: lost 2 pls towards fin* **16/1**

42-4 **5** *3 1/2* **Beauchamp Zorro**[36] 3344 4-9-12 63 .... FergusSweeney 13 — 60
(Henry Candy) *hld up in tch: shkn up and effrt 2f out: fnd little u.p over 1f out: wknd ins fnl f* **4/1**[2]

4434 **6** *1 1/2* **Unlimited**[26] 3709 10-9-9 60 .... J-PGuillambert 15 — 53
(Tony Carroll) *hld up in tch in midfield: rdn and effrt over 1f out: no imp 1f out: wknd ins fnl f* **16/1**

0-00 **7** *2 1/2* **No Larking (IRE)**[8] 4296 4-9-5 61 ....(p) AmyScott(5) 3 — 48
(Henry Candy) *chsd ldrs: rdn and unable qck 2f out: wknd ent fnl f* **16/1**

6400 **8** *3 1/4* **Tidy Affair (IRE)**[9] 4242 3-9-1 60 .... ShaneKelly 6 — 37
(Murty McGrath) *stdd and dropped in bhd after s: rdn and effrt over 2f out: stl plenty to do and nt clr run 2f out: swtchd lft and drvn over 1f out: no ch* **40/1**

/0-0 **9** *7* **Eye For The Girls**[11] 4192 6-8-8 50 ....(t) DavidKenny(5) 1
(William Knight) *towards rr: rdn over 3f out: sme hdwy u.p 3f out: wknd wl over 1f out* **50/1**

0000 **10** *1* **Luna Rosa (IRE)**[16] 4006 3-8-6 51 .... NickyMackay 8
(Clive Cox) *taken down early: hld up in midfield: rdn and struggling 1/2-way: wknd 2f out* **40/1**

000- **11** *3 3/4* **Navajo Charm**[281] 6991 3-8-7 59 .... MichaelJMMurphy(7) 5
(Alan Jarvis) *sn pushed along towards rr and nvr gng wl: wknd 2f out* **33/1**

440 **12** *1 1/4* **Zaheeb**[51] 2847 4-9-11 62 .... WilliamCarson 17
(Dave Morris) *in tch in midfield: rdn over 2f out: sn struggling: bhd fnl f* **7/1**

0060 **13** *4 1/2* **Holyfield Warrior (IRE)**[31] 3497 8-8-5 47 oh1 ow1.. MarkCoumbe(5) 11
(Michael Attwater) *a in rr: lost tch 2f out* **50/1**

1m 29.34s (-2.96) **Going Correction** -0.325s/f (Firm)
WFA 3 from 4yo+ 8lb — **13** Ran SP% **121.1**
Speed ratings (Par 101): **101,99,98,98,95 93,91,87,80,79 76,74,70**
toteswingers: 1&2 £9.00, 1&3 £14.80, 2&3 £2.20. CSF £35.76 CT £135.46 TOTE £16.80: £4.50, £1.40, £2.10; EX 43.50.
Owner Mrs Jackie Cornwell **Bred** Mrs J A Cornwell **Trained** Exning, Suffolk

FOCUS
A competitive handicap. It was run at a fair pace and the favourite didn't get any luck. The form seems sound overall.

4585 FAMILY FUN DAY 10TH AUGUST H'CAP — 2m (P)
8:00 (8:01) (Class 5) (0-70,70) 3-Y-O+ — **£3,067** (£905; £453) **Stalls** Low

Form				RPR
35-6	**1**		**No Time To Lose**[61] 2544 3-8-11 **70** FergusSweeney 7 (Jamie Osborne) *chsd ldrs: rdn over 4f out: drvn over 2f out: hdwy to press ldrs ent fnl f: led fnl 100yds: styd on wl* **6/1**[3]	80
-245	**2**	1 ¾	**Wayne Manor (IRE)**[52] 2818 3-8-4 **63** RichardThomas 4 (Ralph Beckett) *hld up in midfield: hdwy to chse ldrs 7f out: rdn and chsd ldr over 2f out: drvn over 1f out: styd on same pce ins fnl f* **14/1**	71
2241	**3**	2 ¼	**Seven Veils (IRE)**[4] 4440 3-8-11 **70** 6ex ChrisCatlin 3 (Sir Mark Prescott Bt) *chsd ldr tl rdn to ld wl over 2f out: hrd pressed and drvn over 1f out: hdd and one pce fnl 100yds* **5/6**[1]	75+
-243	**4**	3 ¼	**Suzi's A Class Act**[17] 3979 4-9-11 **67** (p) AndreaAtzeni 5 (James Eustace) *chsd ldrs: rdn 3f out: unable qck u.p 2f out: 4th and btn 1f out: plugged on* **11/2**[2]	68
3100	**5**	1 ¾	**Quiet Appeal (IRE)**[20] 3891 3-8-3 **62** JoeFanning 9 (Mark Johnston) *hld up in tch: nt clr run on inner jst over 2f out: effrt on inner over 1f out: no prog and btn 1f out* **12/1**	61
-130	**6**	2	**Passion Play**[47] 2978 4-9-5 **66** DavidKenny[(5)] 1 (William Knight) *led and set stdy gallop: rdn and hdd wl over 2f out: wknd u.p over 1f out* **16/1**	63
64-5	**7**	3 ¼	**Stentorian (IRE)**[37] 2447 4-9-13 **69** (be) RichardMullen 11 (Gary Moore) *s.i.s and rdn along early: sn rcvrd and in tch in midfield: rdn and fnd little over 2f out: wknd wl over 1f out* **20/1**	62
60/	**8**	15	**Pepito Collonges (FR)**[48] 3137 9-8-2 **51** oh4 CharlotteJenner[(7)] 6 (Laura Mongan) *s.i.s: a bhd: lost tch over 3f out* **100/1**	26
4314	**9**	1 ¾	**Bennelong**[27] 3659 6-9-13 **69** AmirQuinn 8 (Richard Rowe) *hld up in last trio: sme hdwy over 5f out: rdn and btn 3f out: bhd and eased ins fnl f* **20/1**	42
425/	**10**	4	**Leopard Hills (IRE)**[54] 5243 5-9-4 **60** KierenFox 2 (Tony Carroll) *a towards rr: rdn and struggling 5f out: lost tch over 3f out: t.o* **50/1**	28
12-0	**11**	4 ½	**Tanjung Agas (IRE)**[16] 3997 4-8-12 **59** (p) MarkCoumbe[(5)] 10 (Christopher Kellett) *in tch in midfield: pushed along and nt gng wl 8f out: steadily lost pl: lost tch over 3f out: t.o* **100/1**	21

3m 27.14s (1.44) **Going Correction** +0.20s/f (Slow)
WFA 3 from 4yo+ 17lb — 11 Ran SP% 117.9
Speed ratings (Par 103): **104,103,102,100,99 98,96,89,88,86 84**
toteswingers: 1&2 £7.20, 1&3 £2.80, 2&3 £5.50. CSF £80.49 CT £138.66 TOTE £5.50: £2.20, £4.90, £1.02; EX 82.80.
Owner Michael Buckley **Bred** Carmel Stud **Trained** Upper Lambourn, Berks

FOCUS
The hot favourite was overhauled by two rivals in this staying handicap which was run at a reasonable pace. The form has been given a bit of a chance.
Passion Play Official explanation: jockey said filly hung right

4586 LADBROKES GAME ON! H'CAP — 1m 2f (P)
8:30 (8:32) (Class 6) (0-65,65) 3-Y-O+ — **£2,181** (£644; £322) **Stalls** Low

Form				RPR
4420	**1**		**Ostentation**[23] 3794 5-9-7 **63** (b) LeonnaMayor[(5)] 10 (Alastair Lidderdale) *stdd and dropped out in detached last early: gd hdwy on outer over 5f out: led 4f out: rdn and qcknd clr 2f out: tiring ins fnl f but a gng to hold on* **10/1**	71
-153	**2**	¾	**Ishikawa (IRE)**[33] 3454 4-10-0 **65** FergusSweeney 4 (Alan King) *in tch in midfield: rdn and effrt to chse ldrs 2f out: no imp on wnr tl wnt 2nd and styd on ins fnl f: nvr quite getting to wnr* **3/1**[1]	71+
0025	**3**	nk	**Top Frock (IRE)**[11] 4186 3-9-3 **64** (b) WilliamCarson 2 (Clive Cox) *chsd ldr tl over 4f out: drvn to chse wnr 2f out: no imp tl styd on u.p fnl 100yds: nvr looked like getting to wnr* **14/1**	69
5065	**4**	1 ¾	**Lytham (IRE)**[10] 4219 11-8-8 **50** DarrenEgan[(5)] 6 (Tony Carroll) *t.k.h: hld up in midfield: stl gng strly and n.m.r ent fnl 2f: hdwy u.p jst over 1f out: swtchd lft and styd on ins fnl f* **12/1**	51
0000	**5**	1 ½	**Fuzzy Logic (IRE)**[9] 4250 3-8-13 **60** MartinDwyer 3 (William Muir) *in tch: rdn 3f out: unable qck u.p ent fnl 2f: drvn and styd on same pce fnl f* **33/1**	58
4451	**6**	2	**Jordaura**[10] 4219 6-10-0 **65** StevieDonohoe 11 (Gay Kelleway) *in tch in midfield: rdn and sme hdwy over 2f out: drvn and no imp 2f out: styd on same pce and wl hld after* **13/2**[3]	59
0-05	**7**	2 ¼	**Garzoni**[19] 3918 3-9-0 **61** ChrisCatlin 7 (Sir Mark Prescott Bt) *chsd ldrs: rdn along briefly 5f out: unable qck over 2f out: rn green and wknd over 1f out* **4/1**[2]	51
4410	**8**	2 ¼	**Always Eager**[25] 3727 3-9-3 **64** JoeFanning 5 (Mark Johnston) *sn led: hdd 4f out: rdn over 3f out: lost 2nd 2f out and sn struggling: wl btn and eased ins fnl f* **7/1**	49
000	**9**	shd	**Opus Maximus (IRE)**[42] 3154 7-9-10 **61** KirstyMilczarek 8 (Conor Dore) *stdd after s: t.k.h: hld up in rr: rdn and effrt wl over 1f out: no prog and nvr trbld ldrs* **20/1**	46
1550	**10**	8	**Lightning Spirit**[17] 3964 4-9-5 **56** (p) RichardMullen 9 (Gary Moore) *s.i.s: hld up towards rr: rdn over 3f out: bhd fnl 2f* **14/1**	25
260-	**11**	8	**Ebony Song (USA)**[285] 6924 4-10-0 **65** IanMongan 12 (Jo Crowley) *awkward leaving stalls: hld up towards rr: effrt and sme hdwy on outer over 2f out: no hdwy 2f out and sn wknd: bhd and eased ins fnl f* **20/1**	18
4350	**12**	15	**Lisahane Bog**[50] 2886 5-9-12 **63** (b) TomMcLaughlin 1 (Peter Hedger) *rdn along leaving stalls: in tch in midfield: u.p and dropped to rr over 3f out: lost tch 2f out: eased fnl f: t.o* **10/1**	

2m 8.64s (2.04) **Going Correction** +0.20s/f (Slow)
WFA 3 from 4yo+ 10lb — 12 Ran SP% 122.5
Speed ratings (Par 101): **99,98,98,96,95 93,92,90,90,83 77,65**
toteswingers: 1&2 £6.20, 1&3 £43.10, 2&3 £20.80. CSF £40.41 CT £440.19 TOTE £14.70: £4.10, £1.50, £4.60; EX 61.30.
Owner Chris Beek Racing **Bred** Wellsummers Stud **Trained** Lambourn, Berks

FOCUS
A low-grade handicap, but it was run at a decent pace and the winner was quite impressive in adverse circumstances. Ordinary form.
T/Plt: £14.20 to a £1 stake. Pool: £65,792.33 - 3,377.64 winning tickets. T/Qpdt: £7.20 to a £1 stake. Pool: £5,786.28 - 590.61 winning tickets. SP

3623 NEWCASTLE (L-H)
Saturday, July 28
OFFICIAL GOING: Good to firm (firm in places; 8.4)
Wind: Fresh, half against Weather: Cloudy

4587 NEW COUNTY GROUP MAIDEN AUCTION STKS — 7f
1:55 (1:55) (Class 4) 2-Y-O — **£4,398** (£1,309; £654; £327) **Stalls** Centre

Form				RPR
3	**1**		**Beat The Tide**[35] 3401 2-8-11 0 PaulMulrennan 9 (Michael Dods) *hld up: shkn up over 2f out: rdn and hdwy over 1f out: led wl ins fnl f: styd on wl* **9/4**[1]	70+
03	**2**	¾	**Surround Sound**[21] 3842 2-8-9 0 DuranFentiman 4 (Tim Easterby) *cl up: led over 2f out: rdn and qcknd over 1f out: hdd wl ins fnl f: kpt on* **16/1**	66
5204	**3**	2 ½	**Ouzinkie (IRE)**[9] 4257 2-8-11 74 SamHitchcott 1 (Mick Channon) *t.k.h: prom: effrt and rdn over 2f out: kpt on same pce fnl f* **9/2**[2]	61
0	**4**	¾	**Captain's Dream (IRE)**[28] 3611 2-8-12 0 MickyFenton 5 (Jedd O'Keeffe) *led to over 2f out: sn rdn: kpt on same pce over 1f out* **33/1**	60
	5	½	**Alkcama (IRE)** 2-8-9 0 JimmyQuinn 11 (John Weymes) *dwlt: hld up: pushed along over 2f out: styd on fnl f: nvr able to chal* **40/1**	56+
5	**6**	¾	**Inovate (IRE)**[15] 4069 2-8-5 0 DarylByrne[(5)] 2 (Tim Easterby) *t.k.h: prom: outpcd over 2f out: no imp fnl f* **8/1**[3]	55+
0	**7**	1	**Precision Strike**[8] 4310 2-8-10 0 RobbieFitzpatrick 7 (Richard Guest) *trckd ldrs: drvn over 2f out: btn fnl f* **12/1**	52
	8	2	**Just Paul (IRE)** 2-8-11 0 MichaelO'Connell 8 (Kate Walton) *t.k.h: trckd ldrs: rdn over 2f out: wknd fnl f* **17/2**	48+
0	**9**	1 ¼	**French Revolution**[21] 3842 2-8-10 0 AndrewMullen 6 (Jedd O'Keeffe) *slowly away: hld up bhd ldng gp: struggling wl over 2f out: sn btn* **80/1**	43
0	**10**	½	**Bain's Pass (IRE)**[41] 3182 2-8-12 0 AmyRyan 3 (Kevin Ryan) *t.k.h: trckd ldrs tl wknd over 2f out* **9/2**[2]	44
	11	14	**Denton Skyline (IRE)** 2-8-9 0 TomEaves 10 (Michael Dods) *dwlt: bhd: rdn and struggling after 3f: sn lost tch* **14/1**	

1m 29.73s (1.93) **Going Correction** -0.125s/f (Firm) — 11 Ran SP% 115.6
Speed ratings (Par 96): **83,82,79,78,77 77,75,73,72,71 55**
Tote Swingers: 1&2 £10.10, 1&3 £1.30, 2&3 £12.80 CSF £41.69 TOTE £3.40: £1.30, £3.70, £2.20; EX 51.70.
Owner J A Wynn-Williams & D Neale **Bred** C E Stedman **Trained** Denton, Co Durham
■ Stewards' Enquiry : Paul Mulrennan caution: careless riding.

FOCUS
An ordinary maiden to kick off proceedings, run on ground described as being fast by jockeys. The gallop was very steady until halfway. The form is rated around the race standard.

NOTEBOOK
Beat The Tide, who'd been third behind a useful sort on his debut, probably wasn't ideally suited by the sedate gallop (off bridle before most) but responded well to get on top near the finish. There'll be more to come from him as his stamina is drawn out, with nurseries presumably the next port of call. (tchd 2-1 and 5-2)
Surround Sound hadn't achieved a great deal when a well-held third at Beverley and this undoubtedly represents an improvement, the quicker ground presumably in his favour. He also now has nuseries as an option. (op 14-1)
Ouzinkie(IRE) wasn't disgraced but already looks thoroughly exposed and it'll be a very weak maiden he wins. (op 4-1 tchd 7-2)
Captain's Dream(IRE) stepped up on his debut, though well placed the way things unfolded, not offering enough to suggest he's one to be interested in at a similar level next time. (op 40-1)
Alkcama(IRE), a gelded son of Camacho out of a winner in Norway, was just about the last off the bridle and did stick to his task under pressure. He's entitled to build on this, though it's worth bearing in mind the bare form almost certainly isn't anything special. (op 33-1)
Inovate(IRE) is probably more of a nursery type but leaves the impression he's capable of better at some stage, keen in the first half of the race and not unduly knocked about in the final 2f. (op 9-1 tchd 15-2)
Precision Strike is another who looks to have a bit of ability but won't be of interest until contesting handicaps. (op 14-1)
Just Paul(IRE), a son of Clodovil, travelled comfortably enough for a long way and possibly just needed the run. He's likely to improve. (op 10-1)
Bain's Pass(IRE) was prominent in the betting but failed to step up on his debut effort and was in trouble the moment the pace increased. (op 5-1 tchd 11-2)

4588 NEW COUNTY ROAD SURFACING H'CAP — 6f
2:30 (2:30) (Class 3) (0-90,89) 3-Y-O — **£8,409** (£2,502; £1,250; £625) **Stalls** Centre

Form				RPR
-302	**1**		**Springinmystep (IRE)**[47] 2979 3-9-3 **85** PaulMulrennan 9 (Michael Dods) *hld up: rdn and hdwy over 1f out: styd on wl to ld towards fin* **5/1**[2]	94
1111	**2**	hd	**Show Flower**[9] 4234 3-9-7 **89** SamHitchcott 10 (Mick Channon) *hld up: stdy hdwy over 2f out: rdn to ld ent fnl f: kpt on: hdd towards fin* **4/1**[1]	97
4346	**3**	2 ½	**Personal Touch**[15] 4075 3-8-5 **78** ShaneBKelly[(5)] 5 (Richard Fahey) *prom: effrt and rdn over 2f out: kpt on same pce ins fnl f* **8/1**	78
1400	**4**	½	**Nameitwhatyoulike**[29] 3563 3-8-6 **81** DavidSimmonson[(7)] 1 (Michael Easterby) *led: rdn over 2f out: hdd ent fnl f: kpt on same pce* **18/1**	79
0304	**5**	1	**Whisky Bravo**[28] 3613 3-8-6 **74** MichaelStainton 3 (David Brown) *hld up: hdwy on outside over 2f out: sn rdn: kpt on same pce fnl f* **16/1**	69
3113	**6**	¾	**All Or Nothin (IRE)**[28] 3607 3-9-1 **83** MichaelO'Connell 8 (John Quinn) *t.k.h: in tch: effrt over 2f out: btn ins fnl f* **4/1**[1]	76
-000	**7**	3 ½	**Ralphy Boy (IRE)**[63] 2490 3-9-3 **85** AmyRyan 11 (Kevin Ryan) *prom: rdn and outpcd over 2f out: n.d after* **7/1**[3]	67
0522	**8**	6	**Tip Top Gorgeous (IRE)**[8] 4291 3-8-5 **80** DavidBergin[(7)] 2 (David O'Meara) *trckd ldrs tl rdn and wknd wl over 1f out* **8/1**	42
-640	**9**	½	**Rafeej**[47] 2979 3-9-5 **87** FrannyNorton 4 (Mark Johnston) *prom tl rdn and hung lft wl over 1f out: sn wknd* **8/1**	48
-010	**10**	2	**Daunt (IRE)**[39] 3248 3-8-4 **72** DuranFentiman 7 (John Quinn) *hld: bhd: drvn along 1/2-way: nvr on terms* **33/1**	26
-305	**11**	2 ¾	**Sunrise Dance**[10] 4208 3-8-2 **70** JimmyQuinn 6 (Robert Johnson) *cl up tl rdn and wknd wl over 1f out* **50/1**	16

1m 13.12s (-1.48) **Going Correction** -0.125s/f (Firm) — 11 Ran SP% 118.5
Speed ratings (Par 104): **104,103,100,99,98 97,92,84,84,81 77**
Tote Swingers: 1&2 £4.10, 1&3 £16.70, 2&3 £10.70 CSF £25.54 CT £162.31 TOTE £5.60: £1.90, £2.10, £2.50; EX 30.90.

Owner Andrew Tinkler **Bred** Dr D Harron **Trained** Denton, Co Durham

FOCUS

A fairly useful handicap. The gallop appeared sound enough, the first two home both coming from off the pace, and the time was good. The winner reversed Pontefract form with the sixth.

NOTEBOOK

Springinmystep(IRE) had run well when second at Pontefract last time but has almost certainly found a bit more improvement to go one better here, travelling well under restraint and finding plenty to nail a bang-in-form rival near the finish. He's a strong-travelling type and should be up to holding his own in better-class handicaps. (op 13-2)

Show Flower's winning run came to an end but she lost little in defeat, running at least as well as previously. She'll go up a little more in the weights but it won't prevent her being of interest again next time. (op 9-2)

Personal Touch hails from a yard in top form and bounced back from a lesser run at York, though there's nothing in his record to suggest he has much in hand off his current mark. (op 15-2)

Nameitwhatyoulike ran well enough but look in the handicapper's grip. (op 16-1 tchd 20-1)

Whisky Bravo was another who ran well enough but both look in the handicapper's grip. (op 11-1)

All Or Nothin(IRE) had beaten Springinmystep at Pontefract a couple of starts back but wasn't at his best this time, carrying his head a shade awkwardly under pressure. Official explanation: trainer's rep said gelding was unsuited by the good to firm (firm in places) ground (tchd 9-2)

Ralphy Boy(IRE) had switched yards since last seen a couple of months previously but it didn't bear any immediate dividends. (op 17-2 tchd 13-2)

Tip Top Gorgeous(IRE) came into the race in form but backed out of things pretty tamely. (tchd 7-1)

Rafeej's Newmarket fourth is beginning to look a bit of a stand-out effort. (op 9-1)

Sunrise Dance Official explanation: jockey said filly lost its action

4589 NEW COUNTY PLANING "BEESWING" H'CAP 7f

3:05 (3:05) (Class 3) (0-95,91) 3-Y-O+ **£8,409** (£2,502; £1,250; £625) **Stalls** Centre

Form RPR

40-0 **1** **Dubawi Sound**[98] 1510 4-9-9 **86**.....(t) FrannyNorton 12 105
(David Brown) *t.k.h: cl up: led gng wl over 2f out: pushed clr fnl f: readily* **11/4**[1]

0000 **2** 6 **Stevie Thunder**[14] 4099 7-9-11 **91**..... RyanClark(3) 4 94
(Ian Williams) *trckd ldrs: effrt and rdn over 2f out: chsd (clr) wnr ins fnl f: kpt on* **13/2**

3011 **3** 1 **King Of Eden (IRE)**[12] 4135 6-9-13 **90**..... JimmyQuinn 5 90
(Eric Alston) *hld up: rdn and hdwy to chse wnr over 1f out to ins fnl f: no imp* **6/1**

6532 **4** 3/4 **Roker Park (IRE)**[14] 4086 7-9-2 **86**..... DavidBergin(7) 1 84
(David O'Meara) *trckd ldrs: effrt and rdn over 2f out: kpt on same pce fnl f* **5/1**[3]

2130 **5** 1/2 **No Poppy (IRE)**[7] 4345 4-9-2 **84**..... AdamCarter(5) 7 81
(Tim Easterby) *blindfold slow to remove and s.s: bhd: rdn and hdwy over 2f out: nvr able to chal* **14/1**

6051 **6** 1 1/4 **Fathsta (IRE)**[9] 4252 7-9-8 **85**..... SamHitchcott 6 79
(David Simcock) *t.k.h: in tch: rdn and outpcd over 2f out: rallied over 1f out: no imp* **12/1**

6230 **7** 1 1/2 **Al Muheer (IRE)**[7] 4321 7-9-8 **90**.....(b) ShaneBKelly(5) 11 80
(Ruth Carr) *hld up: shkn up whn nt clr run over 1f out: nvr able to chal* **9/2**[2]

1025 **8** 2 1/4 **Polish World (USA)**[22] 3812 8-9-9 **86**..... MickyFenton 3 69
(Paul Midgley) *led to over 2f out: rdn and wknd over 1f out* **7/1**

1m 26.59s (-1.21) **Going Correction** -0.125s/f (Firm) **8** Ran SP% **116.0**

Speed ratings (Par 107): **101,94,93,92,91 90,88,85**

Tote Swingers: 1&2 £3.30, 1&3 £2.90, 2&3 £5.90 CSF £21.42 CT £99.85 TOTE £4.40: £1.60, £2.80, £1.80; EX 31.70.

Owner Pearl Bloodstock Ltd **Bred** Derek R Price **Trained** Averham Park, Notts

FOCUS

A very one-sided handicap, the winner impressing in a good time. The winner is obviously smart.

NOTEBOOK

Dubawi Sound ◆ showed himself well ahead of his mark on his first outing for David Brown, soon tanking in behind the leader and pushed clear in the final 2f. Gelded since joining the yard and fitted with a tongue-strap here, he's entered in the final race at Goodwood on Wednesday and will take a lot of stopping under a penalty if turning up in similar form. (op 5-1)

Stevie Thunder had got stuck in the mud at Newmarket last time but showed himself in good form here, just no match for a very well-treated rival. (tchd 7-1)

King Of Eden(IRE) had gone up 8lb for Ayr and ran creditably while leaving the impression the handicapper probably has him right for now. (op 4-1)

Roker Park(IRE) made the frame again but probably wasn't quite at his best, one paced after having every chance. (op 9-2 tchd 4-1)

No Poppy(IRE), with the hood on again, missed the break after the blindfold was not removed quickly enough. She did well to finish as close as she did to the placed horses. Official explanation: jockey said filly was slow to start as it had turned its head to the left making it difficult to remove blindfold; jockey said filly was denied a clear run

Fathsta(IRE) had won in claiming company last time but didn't cut much ice back in a handicap. (op 9-1)

Al Muheer(IRE) has been hard to predict all season, this clearly one of his lesser efforts. (op 11-2)

Polish World(USA) had an uncontested lead but faded pretty tamely in the end, well below par for the third start running. (tchd 6-1 and 15-2)

4590 NEW COUNTY TRAFFIC MANAGEMENT H'CAP 2m 19y

3:35 (3:35) (Class 5) (0-70,69) 4-Y-O+ **£2,911** (£866; £432; £216) **Stalls** Low

Form RPR

-265 **1** **Come Here Yew (IRE)**[38] 3290 4-9-0 **67**..... NeilFarley(5) 1 75
(Declan Carroll) *led: rdn 3f out: hld on wl fnl f* **8/1**

55-5 **2** 1/2 **Dr Finley (IRE)**[29] 3572 5-8-11 **62**..... SimonPearce(3) 4 70
(Lydia Pearce) *midfield on ins: hdwy over 2f out: chsd wnr fnl f: r.o* **14/1**

1460 **3** 1 1/4 **Bradbury (IRE)**[29] 3564 4-9-6 **68**.....(p) JimmyQuinn 7 74
(James Bethell) *hld up: rdn and hdwy over 2f out: rdn and kpt on ins fnl f* **12/1**

6021 **4** nk **Jan Smuts (IRE)**[4] 4431 4-8-3 **54** 6ex.....(tp) DominicFox(3) 11 62+
(Wilf Storey) *hld up: effrt whn nt clr run over 2f out: styd on wl fnl f: nrst fin* **10/1**

-364 **5** 2 3/4 **Stags Leap (IRE)**[5] 4176 5-9-2 **64**..... DuranFentiman 9 66
(Dianne Sayer) *prom: drvn over 3f out: kpt on same pce fnl f* **14/1**

2-41 **6** nk **Madrasa (IRE)**[54] 2775 4-9-6 **68**.....(bt) TomEaves 2 70
(Keith Reveley) *hld up: rdn along 3f out: kpt on fnl f: nvr able to chal* **4/1**[1]

6-30 **7** hd **Strikemaster (IRE)**[33] 3437 6-8-4 **59**.....(t) JacobButterfield(7) 12 61
(Lee James) *hld up: pushed along over 2f out: hdwy over 1f out: nvr able to chal* **20/1**

0655 **8** hd **Descaro (USA)**[24] 3750 6-8-9 **64**.....(v) DavidBergin(7) 3 66
(David O'Meara) *hld up: stdy hdwy over 3f out: rdn over 1f out: carried hd high: sn no ex* **7/1**

/6-2 **9** 7 **Rock Relief (IRE)**[30] 3535 6-9-3 **65**..... FrannyNorton 6 58
(Chris Grant) *trckd ldrs: drvn over 3f out: wknd over 1f out* **9/2**[2]

3-00 **10** 3 1/2 **Jeu De Roseau (IRE)**[17] 3953 8-9-3 **65**..... AmyRyan 10 54
(Chris Grant) *chsd ldng gp: stdy hdwy 1/2-way: rdn 3f out: wknd over 1f out* **17/2**

4006 **11** 1 1/2 **Zefooha (FR)**[24] 3750 8-8-10 **65**..... GemmaTutty(7) 5 52
(Tim Walford) *hld up towards rr: rdn and lost pl over 5f out: n.d after* **33/1**

1432 **12** 1/2 **Golden Future**[13] 3114 9-9-7 **69**..... PaulMulrennan 13 56
(Peter Niven) *hld up on outside: hdwy to press wnr after 4f: rdn over 2f out: sn wknd: eased whn btn fnl f* **13/2**[3]

30/0 **13** nk **Prairie Hawk (USA)**[33] 3440 7-8-2 **50**..... PatrickMathers 8 36
(Brian Rothwell) *prom: drvn along over 5f out: rallied: wknd over 2f out* **33/1**

3m 34.99s (-4.41) **Going Correction** -0.20s/f (Firm) **13** Ran SP% **126.4**

Speed ratings (Par 103): **103,102,102,101,100 100,100,100,96,95 94,94,93**

Tote Swingers: 1&2 £44.30, 1&3 £17.80, 2&3 £51.80 CSF £110.26 CT £1358.02 TOTE £9.50: £2.60, £6.70, £4.40; EX 196.00.

Owner K MacKay & L Ibbotson **Bred** Norelands Bloodstock **Trained** Sledmere, E Yorks

FOCUS

A modest staying event. The winner was able to dictate what was just a pretty ordinary gallop, and it wasn't easy to get into it from behind. The fotrm is rated around the second.

Golden Future Official explanation: jockey said gelding ran too free

4591 NEW COUNTY UTILITIES H'CAP 5f

4:10 (4:14) (Class 4) (0-85,85) 3-Y-O+ **£5,175** (£1,540; £769; £384) **Stalls** Centre

Form RPR

2422 **1** **Noodles Blue Boy**[8] 4312 6-9-5 **85**..... JacobButterfield(7) 13 91
(Ollie Pears) *cl up: rdn over 2f out: led ins fnl f: hld on wl* **13/8**[1]

-415 **2** 1/2 **Liberty Island (IRE)**[29] 3578 7-8-13 **75**.....(p) LeeTopliss(3) 8 79
(Ian Semple) *slt ld to ins fnl f: kpt on: hld nr fin* **5/1**[2]

0200 **3** 1 **Even Stevens**[44] 3065 4-9-5 **78**.....(p) MichaelO'Connell 6 78
(Scott Dixon) *disp ld: rdn over 1f out: kpt on same pce wl ins fnl f* **7/1**

5400 **4** 1 1/4 **Dickie Le Davoir**[8] 4315 8-8-10 **72**.....(v) DeclanCannon(3) 5 68
(Richard Guest) *s.i.s: outpcd and sn wl bhd: gd hdwy over 1f out: nvr rchd ldrs* **14/1**

030 **5** 1 **Tyfos**[28] 3608 7-9-10 **83**..... DuranFentiman 7 75
(Brian Baugh) *trckd ldrs: rdn along over 2f out: kpt on same pce fnl f* **17/2**

6004 **6** 2 **I'll Be Good**[21] 3861 3-8-13 **76**..... AmyRyan 1 61
(Robert Johnson) *sn outpcd bhd ldng gp: sme hdwy and edgd lft over 1f out: nvr able to chal* **8/1**

01-6 **7** 1 3/4 **We'll Deal Again**[74] 2140 5-8-13 **72**.....(b) PaddyAspell 10 51
(Michael Easterby) *trckd ldrs tl rdn and wknd over 1f out* **11/2**[3]

000- **8** 54 **Archers Road (IRE)**[115] 1194 5-9-4 **82**.....(t) LMcNiff(5) 3
(Mark Michael McNiff, Ire) *reluctant to enter stalls: virtually ref to r: t.o* **16/1**

1m 1.22s (0.12) **Going Correction** -0.125s/f (Firm)

WFA 3 from 4yo+ 4lb **8** Ran SP% **116.8**

Speed ratings (Par 105): **94,93,91,89,88 84,82,**

Tote Swingers: 1&2 £2.80, 1&3 £2.50, 2&3 £3.60 CSF £10.15 CT £45.46 TOTE £2.60: £1.20, £1.80, £2.50; EX 11.90.

Owner Keith Taylor & Keith West **Bred** Fifehead Farms M C Denning **Trained** Norton, N Yorks

■ Pivotal Prospect was withdrawn (rider injured, 12/1.) Deduct 5p in the £ under R4. New market formed.

FOCUS

Not the most competitive of sprint handicaps, and the time was modest. The winner is rated to his old best.

Archers Road(IRE) Official explanation: jockey said gelding froze when gates opened

4592 NEWCOUNTY.CO.UK H'CAP (DIV I) 5f

4:45 (4:45) (Class 6) (0-60,63) 3-Y-O+ **£2,070** (£616; £307; £153) **Stalls** Centre

Form RPR

2661 **1** **Fear Nothing**[9] 4245 5-9-6 **63**..... DavidBergin(7) 1 81
(David O'Meara) *prom centre: hdwy: edgd to stands' side and led 1f out: rdn clr: readily* **5/2**[1]

0346 **2** 3 3/4 **Ballarina**[35] 3382 6-9-6 **56**..... JimmyQuinn 11 61
(Eric Alston) *overall ldr on stands' rail: hdd 1f out: kpt on: nt pce of wnr* **13/2**[3]

020 **3** 1 1/2 **Myjestic Melody (IRE)**[9] 4245 4-9-1 **51**..... DuranFentiman 12 50
(Noel Wilson) *chsd ldr stands' rail: rdn over 2f out: kpt on same pce ins fnl f* **16/1**

5004 **4** 4 1/2 **Star Kingdom (IRE)**[25] 3719 3-9-2 **56**..... AmyRyan 3 39
(Brian Ellison) *s.i.s: bhd and outpcd centre: hdwy over 1f out: r.o fnl f: nvr able to chal* **3/1**[2]

-004 **5** nk **Duke Of Rainford**[39] 3256 5-8-12 **48**..... TomEaves 5 30
(Michael Herrington) *t.k.h: in tch centre: drvn along over 2f out: no imp over 1f out* **16/1**

14-4 **6** 1 **Cri Na Mara (IRE)**[166] 544 4-8-9 **50**.....(t) LMcNiff(5) 9 28
(Mark Michael McNiff, Ire) *prom: swtchd to stands' side over 3f out: outpcd 2f out: n.d after* **12/1**

036 **7** 1/2 **Greenhead High**[50] 2878 4-9-3 **60**..... ShirleyTeasdale(7) 10 36
(David Nicholls) *cl up centre tl rdn and wknd over 1f out* **10/1**

0000 **8** 1 3/4 **Not Bad For A Boy (IRE)**[14] 4082 3-8-13 **58**..... DeanHeslop(5) 7 28
(Barry Leavy) *prom centre: lost pl 1/2-way: n.d after* **25/1**

00-0 **9** 1/2 **Carrie's Magic**[25] 3731 5-8-11 **52**.....(p) GarryWhillans(5) 6 20
(Alistair Whillans) *s.i.s: hld up in tch centre: drvn and outpcd 2f out: sn n.d* **9/1**

4344 **10** 1/2 **Miserere Mei (IRE)**[14] 4087 3-8-3 **46**.....(e) DeclanCannon(3) 4 13
(Richard Guest) *prom centre tl rdn and wknd over 1f out* **20/1**

4030 **11** 4 **Sharp Shoes**[9] 4262 5-9-6 **56**.....(v[1]) PaulMulrennan 2
(Ann Duffield) *dwlt: sn in tch on outside of centre gp: effrt over 2f out: wknd over 1f out* **11/1**

1m 0.94s (-0.16) **Going Correction** -0.125s/f (Firm)

WFA 3 from 4yo+ 4lb **11** Ran SP% **122.4**

Speed ratings (Par 101): **96,90,87,80,79 78,77,74,73,73 66**

Tote Swingers: 1&2 £5.90, 1&3 £19.50, 2&3 £11.10 CSF £20.14 CT £227.79 TOTE £4.10: £1.80, £2.60, £5.60; EX 31.40.

Owner C Maxsted & Miss S Iggulden **Bred** Houghton Bloodstock Uk Ltd **Trained** Nawton, N Yorks

FOCUS

Run-of-the-mill fare. Not many got competitive, the winner edging across to the stands' rail late on, the second and third having raced there throughout. The time was fast and the winner is rated back to his old best.

4593 NEWCOUNTY.CO.UK H'CAP (DIV II) 5f

5:15 (5:18) (Class 6) (0-60,60) 3-Y-O+ **£2,070** (£616; £307; £153) **Stalls** Centre

Form RPR

0150 **1** **Baltic Bomber (IRE)**[11] 4174 3-9-6 **60**..... MichaelO'Connell 6 65
(John Quinn) *t.k.h: trckd ldrs: effrt over 1f out: edgd lft and bmpd rival cl home: led post* **4/1**[2]

0406 **2** nse **Cross Of Lorraine (IRE)**[14] 4085 9-9-6 **56**....................(b) AmyRyan 10 62
(Chris Grant) *led: rdn 2f out: edgd both ways ins fnl f: bmpd cl home: hdd post* **9/2**[3]
3602 **3** 3/4 **Amno Dancer (IRE)**[5] 4392 5-8-11 **47**............................(b) TomEaves 14 50
(Ian Semple) *t.k.h: trckd ldrs: effrt over 1f out: kpt on ins fnl f* **11/2**
0-03 **4** 5 **Cataract**[55] 2730 3-8-6 **46**..(b) JimmyQuinn 1 30
(John Weymes) *hld up: pushed along 1/2-way: plugged on fnl f: nvr able to chal* **14/1**
0000 **5** 1/2 **Skiddaw View**[9] 4262 4-8-10 **46** oh1...........................(t) AndrewMullen 13 29
(Maurice Barnes) *disp ld to wl over 1f out: wknd ins fnl f* **25/1**
212 **6** 33 **Lord Buffhead**[14] 4084 3-8-10 **57**...................................... JasonHart(7) 5
(Richard Guest) *trckd ldrs tl rdn and wknd over 1f out: eased whn btn ins fnl f* **3/1**[1]

1m 2.82s (1.72) **Going Correction** -0.125s/f (Firm)
WFA 3 from 4yo+ 4lb **6** Ran SP% **89.1**
Speed ratings (Par 101): **81,80,79,71,70 18**
Tote Swingers: 1&2 £3.00, 1&3 £3.80, 2&3 £1.90 CSF £13.38 CT £39.75 TOTE £3.80: £1.80, £2.20; EX 11.80.
Owner The New Century Partnership **Bred** D And Mrs D Veitch **Trained** Settrington, N Yorks
■ Lees Anthem (17/2, broke out of stall) and Ingenti (9/2, refused to enter stalls) were withdrawn. Deduct 15p in the £ under R4.

FOCUS
A race which was decimated by non-runners and without question the weaker of the two divisions.
Lord Buffhead Official explanation: trainer's rep said gelding lost its action

4594 NEW COUNTY 0191 410 9061 APPRENTICE H'CAP 1m 2f 32y
5:45 (5:45) (Class 6) (0-60,60) 3-Y-0+ **£2,070** (£616; £307; £153) **Stalls** Low

Form RPR
1350 **1** **Call Of Duty (IRE)**[31] 3492 7-9-10 **60**.............................. JoshCrane(4) 6 72
(Dianne Sayer) *hld up: gd hdwy over 2f out: led over 1f out: sn clr* **9/2**[1]
010/ **2** 4 **Dream Risk (FR)**[305] 6921 6-9-0 **52**...................... RobertDodsworth(6) 9 56
(Brian Ellison) *t.k.h: prom: pushed along over 2f out: chsd (clr) wnr ins fnl f: r.o* **5/1**[2]
0000 **3** 1 1/4 **Sally Friday (IRE)**[38] 3290 4-9-8 **54**..............................(p) LauraBarry 11 55
(Edwin Tuer) *chsd ldrs: effrt over 2f out: ev ch over 1f out: one pce ins fnl f* **14/1**
324 **4** 1 **Barton Bounty**[56] 2692 5-9-0 **50**......................... FrancescaWolter(4) 15 49
(Peter Niven) *hld up: shkn up 2f out: styd on wl fnl f: nvr able to chal* **9/2**[1]
4 **5** nse **Asteroid Belt (IRE)**[44] 3093 3-9-0 **58**.......................... DavidBergin(2) 16 57
(Chris Grant) *midfield: rdn and outpcd over 2f out: styd on fnl f: nrst fin* **13/2**
-205 **6** nk **Petrocelli**[7] 4350 5-9-2 **52**...(t) EvaMoscrop(4) 13 50
(Wilf Storey) *in tch: drvn along over 2f out: effrt over 1f out: sn one pce* **9/1**
-055 **7** 3/4 **Dean Iarracht (IRE)**[5] 4396 6-9-9 **55**.........................(p) GemmaTutty 12 52
(Tracy Waggott) *missed break: bhd: rdn over 2f out: styd on fnl f: nvr able to chal* **6/1**[3]
3230 **8** 1/2 **Kames Park (IRE)**[33] 3449 10-9-7 **53**......................... ThomasGarner 17 49
(Richard Guest) *s.i.s: hld up: rdn and hdwy on outside over 2f out: kpt on fnl f: nrst fin* **12/1**
0336 **9** 1/2 **Bygones For Coins (IRE)**[49] 2925 4-8-12 **50**................ KevinStott(6) 5 45
(Robert Johnson) *led and sn clr: rdn and hdd over 1f out: sn btn* **16/1**
5200 **10** 8 **Diamond Twister (USA)**[19] 3907 6-8-8 **46** oh1..(t) MatthewMcGhee(6) 4 25
(Lisa Williamson) *hld up: shkn up over 3f out: btn fnl 2f* **28/1**
3000 **11** 1 **Norton Girl**[7] 4350 4-8-8 **46** oh1............................ DanielleMooney(6) 10 23
(Tracy Waggott) *t.k.h: chsd clr ldr to over 2f out: sn wknd* **40/1**
/0-4 **12** 2 3/4 **Hoar Frost**[29] 3579 7-9-1 **47**..(tp) NoelGarbutt 8 18
(Karen Tutty) *hld up: pushed along over 4f out: nvr on terms* **33/1**
020 **13** 41 **Media Stars**[36] 3353 7-9-2 **52**......................................(p) PeterSword(4) 1
(Robert Johnson) *hld up in tch: rdn over 2f out: wknd wl over 1f out* **20/1**

2m 9.39s (-2.51) **Going Correction** -0.20s/f (Firm)
WFA 3 from 4yo+ 10lb **13** Ran SP% **124.5**
Speed ratings (Par 101): **102,98,97,97,96 96,96,95,95,88 88,85,53**
Tote Swingers 1&2 £9.90, 2&3 £13.60, 1&3 £25.10 CSF £26.73 CT £303.98 TOTE £3.30: £1.50, £2.80, £4.50; EX 85.50.
Owner T W Rebanks **Bred** Gainsborough Stud Management Ltd **Trained** Hackthorpe, Cumbria

FOCUS
A modest apprentice event. Confirmed front-runner Bygones For Coins ensured a sound pace.
Call Of Duty(IRE) ◆ Official explanation: trainer said, regarding apparent improvement in form, that the gelding was better suited by the faster ground
T/Plt: £126.40 to a £1 stake. Pool: £69,913.47 - 403.70 winning tickets T/Qpdt: £63.30 to a £1 stake. Pool: £3,927.40 - 45.90 winning tickets RY

4538 NEWMARKET (R-H)
Saturday, July 28

OFFICIAL GOING: Good to firm (8.6)
Far Side track used with Stalls on Far Side except 10f & 13f: Centre. Repositioning of the rail into home straight added 18m to 10f &13f races.
Wind: Light across Weather: Cloudy with sunny spells

4595 NSPCC BALLYGALLON STUD IRELAND EBF MAIDEN STKS 7f
2:15 (2:18) (Class 4) 2-Y-0 **£4,528** (£1,347; £673; £336) **Stalls** High

Form RPR
1 **Timoneer (USA)** 2-9-3 0.. MickaelBarzalona 12 82+
(Mahmood Al Zarooni) *dwlt and hmpd s: racd keenly: hdwy over 4f out: rdn to ld ins fnl f: r.o* **11/4**[1]
0 **2** nk **Blue Wave (IRE)**[28] 3634 2-8-12 0........................... AntiocoMurgia(5) 13 81
(Mahmood Al Zarooni) *hmpd s: sn prom: rdn and ev ch ins fnl f: edgd rt: r.o* **12/1**
3 3/4 **Bright Strike (USA)** 2-9-3 0... WilliamBuick 8 79+
(John Gosden) *hld up: racd keenly: hdwy over 1f out: rdn and edgd lft ins fnl f: r.o* **7/2**[2]
4 1 1/2 **Al Mukhdam** 2-9-3 0.. RobertHavlin 14 75+
(Peter Chapple-Hyam) *wnt rt s: sn chsng ldr: led and hung rt over 1f out: sn rdn: hdd and unable qck ins fnl f* **12/1**
5 2 1/2 **Emulating (IRE)** 2-9-3 0.. PatDobbs 10 68+
(Richard Hannon) *chsd ldrs: rdn over 1f out: edgd rt: styd on same pce* **12/1**
6 1/2 **Claim (IRE)** 2-9-3 0.. RyanMoore 15 67
(Sir Michael Stoute) *prom: pushed along over 2f out: styd on same pce fnl f* **8/1**[3]
63 **7** shd **Tuffan (USA)**[43] 3119 2-9-3 0... BrettDoyle 7 67
(Clive Brittain) *led: rdn and hdd over 1f out: no ex ins fnl f* **100/1**
8 nk **Ersaal** 2-9-3 0... PaulHanagan 2 66+
(Roger Varian) *s.i.s and wnt rt s: racd keenly: hdwy over 4f out: shkn up and edgd rt over 1f out: styd on same pce* **7/2**[2]
9 3 **Rhombus (IRE)** 2-9-3 0.. LiamJones 3 58+
(William Haggas) *s.s: sn pushed along in rr: styd on ins fnl f: nvr nrr* **22/1**
06 **10** nk **Gabrial The Boss (USA)**[7] 4327 2-9-3 0.................... RichardMullen 11 57+
(David Simcock) *hld up: shkn up over 1f out: nvr on terms* **66/1**
11 1 1/4 **Sioux Chieftain (IRE)** 2-9-3 0... ShaneKelly 9 53
(Tim Pitt) *sn pushed along in rr: rdn over 2f out: n.d* **66/1**
12 1 1/2 **Dark Templar** 2-9-3 0.. ChrisCatlin 4 49
(Ed Vaughan) *hld up: pushed along 1/2-way: a in rr* **50/1**
13 2 **Go Far** 2-9-3 0... PadraigBeggy 5 44
(Alan Bailey) *hld up: rdn over 2f out: sn wknd* **50/1**
14 1 **Queen Of Sacrmento** 2-8-12 0.. JohnFahy 6 36
(Dr Jon Scargill) *s.i.s: sn pushed along in rr: rdn over 2f out: sn wknd* **150/1**

1m 26.63s (0.93) **Going Correction** -0.15s/f (Firm) **14** Ran SP% **118.2**
Speed ratings (Par 96): **88,87,86,85,82 81,81,81,77,77 76,74,72,70**
Tote Swingers: 1&2 £9.70, 1&3 £2.60, 2&3 £12.00 CSF £36.15 TOTE £3.50: £1.70, £3.60, £1.80; EX 41.50.
Owner Godolphin **Bred** Darley **Trained** Newmarket, Suffolk

FOCUS
Racing took place on the far-side track. The ground had dried up overnight, with 'firm in places' added to the description, despite watering. A decent maiden in which the last two renewals had been won by subsequent Group-race performers Farhh and Entifaadha. Very few of the runners had previous experience and the market was dominated by newcomers. The race provided a 1-2 for Godolphin horses.

NOTEBOOK
Timoneer(USA), the first foal of a half-sister to Raven's Pass and by the same sire as that colt, Timoneer made a good start to his career, running on gamely to hold off the challenge of his stablemate. He had quite a hard race here though and much depends on how he goes on from this. (op 3-1 tchd 7-2)
Blue Wave(IRE), unfancied when well beaten in an ordinary maiden here on his debut, was the stable second string but not such a long-shot this time and improved significantly, pushing his stablemate all the way. He should win races based on this evidence. (op 14-1 tchd 16-1)
Bright Strike(USA) ◆, a half-brother to a couple of 1m-1m2f performers from the family of Selkirk, was held up before making good headway to challenge entering the final furlong but could not quite get there. He did best of those held up and, entered in the Champagne and Royal Lodge, he can be expected to win his maiden before going on to better things. (op 4-1)
Al Mukhdam, a half-brother to a couple of 1m winners by a speedy sire, was a market drifter but showed plenty of ability, having his chance in the Dip before being run out of it up the hill. (op 9-1)
Emulating(IRE) ◆, a 50,000gns half-brother to three middle-distance winners, was never far away on this debut and this was an encouraging effort given his pedigree. (op 11-1 tchd 14-1)
Claim(IRE), a half-brother to five winners whose price steadily increased to 77,000gns at the breeze-ups, showed up early on this debut before fading.
Tuffan(USA), a well-beaten third of four on his second start, made the running and is probably the best guide to the level.
Ersaal, the first foal of a Listed-placed mile winner, was relatively easy to back but travelled well until let down. Being by Dubawi he might prefer easier ground and Group-race entries suggest he is well regarded, so he can be given another chance. (op 4-1 tchd 10-3)

4596 RAY & JOYCE DIAMOND WEDDING ANNIVERSARY H'CAP 1m 2f
2:45 (2:47) (Class 3) (0-95,95) 3-Y-0+
£8,715 (£2,609; £1,304; £652; £326; £163) **Stalls** Centre

Form RPR
0432 **1** **Unex El Greco**[28] 3635 4-9-8 **89**....................................... WilliamBuick 1 98
(John Gosden) *plld hrd and a.p: rdn to ld over 1f out: edgd rt ins fnl f: styd on u.p* **2/1**[1]
1001 **2** 3/4 **Prussian**[7] 4342 3-8-12 **89**.. RyanMoore 8 96
(Mark Johnston) *w ldr tl led wl over 1f out: sn rdn and hdd: nt clr run ins fnl f: styd on* **11/4**[2]
5-40 **3** 3/4 **Ellemujie**[31] 3502 7-8-13 **83**...(p) PatrickHills(3) 6 88
(Dean Ivory) *chsd ldrs: rdn over 3f out: unable qck towards fin* **14/1**
0226 **4** 2 1/2 **Proud Chieftain**[28] 3632 4-9-7 **88**... PatDobbs 2 88
(Clifford Lines) *hld up: rdn over 3f out: hdwy over 1f out: no imp ins fnl f* **11/2**[3]
3-00 **5** 1 1/4 **Classic Punch (IRE)**[28] 3635 9-10-0 **95**............................ IanMongan 3 93
(David Elsworth) *led: rdn over 2f out: hdd wl over 1f out: no ex fnl f* **8/1**
-000 **6** hd **Demolition**[15] 4072 8-9-3 **87**.. GaryBartley(3) 5 84
(Noel Wilson) *hld up: pushed along over 4f out: rdn over 2f out: nvr trbld ldrs* **11/1**
2120 **7** nse **Focail Maith**[17] 3953 4-8-13 **80**... ShaneKelly 7 77
(Tim Pitt) *hld up: rdn over 2f out: nvr on terms* **40/1**
1-22 **8** 57 **Tornado Force (IRE)**[168] 529 4-9-7 **88**........................ PaulHanagan 4
(Jeremy Noseda) *chsd ldrs: rdn over 3f out: hung lft and wknd over 2f out: eased: t.o* **10/1**

2m 3.73s (-1.77) **Going Correction** -0.15s/f (Firm)
WFA 3 from 4yo+ 10lb **8** Ran SP% **113.0**
Speed ratings (Par 107): **101,100,99,97,96 96,96,51**
Tote Swingers: 1&2 £1.50, 1&3 £3.90, 2&3 £13.60 CSF £7.35 CT £55.81 TOTE £3.00: £1.10, £1.30, £3.50; EX 8.90.
Owner W J Gredley **Bred** Middle Park Stud Ltd **Trained** Newmarket, Suffolk
■ Stewards' Enquiry : Patrick Hills four-day ban: used whip above permitted level (Aug 11-14)

FOCUS
A good quality handicap.

NOTEBOOK
Unex El Greco benefited from the gallop as his rider was able to settle him after the gelding was keen early on. He cruised into contention inside the last 2f but his rider had to work pretty hard to get him home. (op 9-4)
Prussian, the only 3-y-o and sole filly in the line-up, helped force the pace, but as soon as she won the battle for the lead she was challenged by the winner and the third. She showed commendable gameness to rally and looks still on the upgrade. (op 7-2)
Ellemujie has gone well here in the past and ran his best race of the season with the cheekpieces back on, just losing out up the hill. (op 9-1)
Proud Chieftain goes well on this track but never got into contention having been held up. (op 8-1)
Classic Punch(IRE) was bidding to repeat his 2010 success. He had a good battle for the lead with the runner-up, but paid for his efforts in the latter stages. (op 10-1 tchd 11-1)

Tornado Force(IRE) was eased and finished tailed off on this return from a break and has yet to prove he handles turf anywhere near as well as he does the all-weather. Paul Hanagan reported his mount lost his action and the stewards ordered the gelding to be routine tested. Official explanation: jockey said gelding lost its action (op 6-1)

4597 BOYLESPORTS.COM FREE PHONE BETTING 0800 440000 FILLIES' STKS (H'CAP) 7f

3:20 (3:20) (Class 2) (0-100,102) 3-Y-0+ **£12,938** (£3,850; £1,924; £962) **Stalls** High

Form	Pos	Dist	Horse	Jockey / Draw	RPR
3110	**1**		**I'm So Glad**[26] 3696 3-8-6 **90** (Mick Channon) *mde all: rdn over 1f out: styd on u.p* **16/1**	CharlesBishop(5) 6	100
2212	**2**	3/4	**Riot Of Colour**[15] 4062 3-8-2 **84** (Ralph Beckett) *hld up in tch: chsd wnr over 2f out: hrd rdn fr over 1f out: styd on* **11/4**[1]	(p) HarryBentley[illegible] 2	[illegible]
0063	**3**	3/4	**Elusive Flame**[8] 4298 3-8-4 **83** ow2 (David Elsworth) *chsd ldrs: rdn and hung lft fr over 1f out: styd on* **11/2**[3]	ChrisCatlin 3	89
10-0	**4**	2	**Instance**[73] 2177 4-9-4 **90** (Jeremy Noseda) *hld up: rdn over 1f out: r.o ins fnl f: nrst fin* **8/1**	WilliamBuick 4	93
0-02	**5**	shd	**Miss Azeza**[15] 4075 3-8-11 **90** (David Simcock) *hld up: hdwy over 2f out: rdn over 1f out: styd on* **10/1**	RichardMullen 11	90
1-10	**6**	nk	**Priceless Jewel**[42] 3165 3-8-11 **90** (Roger Charlton) *chsd ldrs: rdn over 1f out: no ex ins fnl f* **10/3**[2]	PatDobbs 9	90
2226	**7**	3 3/4	**Gouray Girl (IRE)**[22] 3812 5-9-2 **88** (Henry Candy) *s.i.s: hld up: plld hrd: rdn over 1f out: nvr trbld ldrs* **9/1**	FergusSweeney 8	79
-306	**8**	3	**Hello Glory**[15] 4062 3-8-11 **90** (David Simcock) *prom: rdn over 2f out: wknd fnl f* **10/1**	MickaelBarzalona 7	71
10-0	**9**	12	**Self Centred**[99] 1500 3-8-5 **84** (Charles Hills) *chsd wnr tl rdn over 2f out: wknd over 1f out* **14/1**	PaulHanagan 12	33

1m 24.41s (-1.29) **Going Correction** -0.15s/f (Firm)
WFA 3 from 4yo+ 7lb **9** Ran SP% **117.0**
Speed ratings (Par 96): **101,100,99,97,96 96,92,88,75**
Tote Swingers: 1&2 £34.70, 1&3 £11.80, 2&3 £2.50 CSF £60.79 CT £283.75 TOTE £4.10: £1.50, £1.50, £2.10; EX 21.80.
Owner Chris Wright & The Hon Mrs J M Corbett **Bred** Stratford Place Stud **Trained** West Ilsley, Berks

FOCUS

A good quality fillies' handicap in which the pace was reasonable and the time was 2.22sec faster than the opening juvenile event.

NOTEBOOK

I'm So Glad has progressed really well this summer and the faster ground was no problem to her, as she won her maiden on it. She made all and, despite flashing her tail under pressure, found more than enough to hold off the favourite and proved her stamina for the trip at the same time. She was rated 90 here, so connections may be tempted to try to pick up some black type with her now. (tchd 18-1)

Riot Of Colour, wearing first-time cheekpieces, appeared to have every chance but never looked like going past the winner. This was her first try on fast ground, but her record of one win and six seconds in seven starts indicates she is consistent but maybe not the toughest in a battle. (op 9-2)

Elusive Flame made the running up the centre before the groups merged and then rallied under pressure. This was her best effort on ground this fast but she does run well at this track. (op 13-2 tchd 7-1)

Instance struggled for the third successive time having been a beaten odds-on favourite in this race last season, after which she missed the remainder of the campaign. However, there were signs, with her staying on late, that much of her ability remains.

Miss Azeza, the least experienced in the line-up, ran well on this return to fast ground but her 4lb rise following her last effort seemed enough to hold her back. It might be that flatter tracks suit her best. (op 7-1)

Priceless Jewel won her maiden on fast going but was disappointing on soft ground last time. She was keen early on here but had her chance and could not pick up. This was her first run on an undulating track but there was no other obvious excuse. (op 5-2)

4598 BOYLESPORTS.COM MOBILE BETTING H'CAP 6f

4:00 (4:03) (Class 2) (0-105,104) 3-Y-0 **£29,110** (£8,662; £4,329; £2,164) **Stalls** High

Form	Pos	Dist	Horse	Jockey / Draw	RPR
1061	**1**		**Fulbright**[15] 4063 3-9-6 **103** (Mark Johnston) *chsd ldrs tl led 1/2-way: rdn ins fnl f: jst hld on* **8/1**	RobertHavlin 4	114
1-01	**2**	nse	**Duke Of Firenze**[33] 3445 3-8-6 **89** ow1 (Sir Michael Stoute) *hld up: hdwy over 2f out: rdn to chse wnr over 1f out: ev ch ins fnl f: r.o* **3/1**[2]	RyanMoore 5	100
-363	**3**	1 1/2	**Heeraat (IRE)**[35] 3396 3-8-5 **88** (William Haggas) *s.i.s: hld up: hdwy over 1f out: r.o: nt rch ldrs* **9/1**	PaulHanagan 1	94
5-51	**4**	nk	**Rex Imperator**[28] 3641 3-9-7 **104** (Roger Charlton) *trckd ldrs: plld hrd: shkn up over 1f out: rdn and edgd lft ins fnl f: no ex* **11/4**[1]	PatDobbs 10	109+
-503	**5**	1 1/2	**Gatepost (IRE)**[15] 4063 3-8-13 **96** (Richard Fahey) *chsd ldrs: rdn over 1f out: styd on same pce fnl f* **10/1**	DavidNolan 2	96
0360	**6**	1/2	**Lady Gorgeous**[15] 4070 3-9-3 **100** (Mick Channon) *hld up: rdn over 1f out: edgd lft ins fnl f: r.o: nt trble ldrs* **25/1**	ShaneKelly 3	99
-035	**7**	3/4	**Balty Boys (IRE)**[57] 2659 3-9-4 **101** (Charles Hills) *chsd ldr to 1/2-way: sn rdn: no ex fnl f* **15/2**[3]	IanMongan 14	97
1060	**8**	1	**Accession (IRE)**[15] 4063 3-8-11 **94** (Clive Cox) *hld up: hdwy u.p over 2f out: styd on same pce fnl f* **28/1**	(p) JohnFahy 8	87
1-40	**9**	shd	**Solfilia**[5] 4412 3-7-5 **81** oh3 (Hughie Morrison) *edgd rt s: led to 1/2-way: sn rdn: styd on same pce fr over 1f out* **40/1**	KatiaScallan(7) 7	74
-035	**10**	1 1/2	**Samminder (IRE)**[56] 2712 3-9-5 **102** (Peter Chapple-Hyam) *hld up: hdwy over 1f out: wknd wl ins fnl f* **16/1**	WilliamBuick 9	90
1315	**11**	1 1/4	**Millibar (IRE)**[9] 4234 3-7-12 **81** oh7 (Nick Littmoden) *prom: rdn over 2f out: wknd over 1f out* **66/1**	(p) JamieMackay 11	65
1125	**12**	nk	**Bartolomeu**[35] 3396 3-8-8 **91** (Marco Botti) *hld up: hdwy 1/2-way: rdn over 1f out: wknd fnl f* **16/1**	LiamJones 13	74
0300	**13**	3/4	**Top Cop**[8] 4285 3-8-1 **91** (Andrew Balding) *hmpd s: sn prom: shkn up over 2f out: wknd over 1f out* **16/1**	DanielMuscutt(7) 6	72

1m 10.63s (-1.87) **Going Correction** -0.15s/f (Firm) **13** Ran SP% **122.5**
Speed ratings (Par 106): **106,105,103,103,101 100,99,98,98,96 94,94,93**
Tote Swingers: 1&2 £6.40, 1&3 £18.80, 2&3 £8.30 CSF £32.11 CT £199.90 TOTE £10.70: £3.60, £1.90, £3.30; EX 38.80 TRIFECTA Pool: £1,195.89 - 3.29 winning units..
Owner Sheikh Hamdan Bin Mohammed Al Maktoum **Bred** R F And S D Knipe **Trained** Middleham Moor, N Yorks

FOCUS

Decent prize-money resulted in a strong line-up for this sprint, the time was good and the form looks sound. The first four all raced centre to stands' side.

NOTEBOOK

Fulbright, from a yard in good form, put up a game performance to record his third win of the season and retain his unbeaten record at the track. He was in the firing line throughout and answered every question, despite having been raised 8lb for his success in an even more valuable contest at the July festival, with his stamina for 7f proving an asset. He looks sure to win again and no doubt connections will be looking for an opportunity to return here. (op 9-1)

Duke Of Firenze ◆, the least experienced in the field, came through to challenge in the Dip and stuck on under pressure all the way to the line. He lost little in defeat and this well-bred colt looks sure to gain compensation before long. (op 9-2)

Heeraat(IRE) was ridden more patiently than he had been when third over 5f here earlier in the month and finished nicely. Evidence suggests a stiff 6f suits him ideally and he could well build on this. (op 12-1)

Rex Imperator was impressive when scoring at Windsor from a subsequent winner, and a 6lb rise for that looked fair. He was keen early but travelled well into contention only to find very little up the hill. His previous record suggests he might be best suited by a flat track, so he could be the sort to bounce back at York's Ebor meeting. (op 3-1 tchd 7-2)

Gatepost(IRE) was 6lb better off with today's winner compared with their meeting over C&D earlier in the month. He nevertheless ran well on his second start for his new trainer and should win a handicap before too long. (tchd 11-1)

Lady Gorgeous has generally been running reasonably and did much better back on this faster ground after being well beaten on soft on her previous start. She stayed on from the rear late but might need to drop a few more pounds to win at this level. (op 22-1)

Balty Boys(IRE), dropping back in trip after a couple of months off, made the running but could not sustain his effort. Nevertheless, he looks likely to be more effective at this distance. (op 7-1)

4599 NSPCC IRISH STALLION FARMS EBF CONDITIONS STKS 6f

4:35 (4:35) (Class 3) 2-Y-0 **£7,762** (£2,310; £1,154; £577) **Stalls** High

Form	Pos	Dist	Horse	Jockey / Draw	RPR
1	**1**		**Ollie Olga (USA)**[23] 3783 2-9-0 79 (Mick Channon) *s.i.s: hld up: hdwy over 1f out: r.o to ld nr fin* **12/1**	MatthewDavies 2	91
1	**2**	hd	**Rocky Ground (IRE)**[30] 3545 2-9-5 0 (Roger Varian) *trckd ldrs: plld hrd: rdn to ld ins fnl f: hung rt: hdd nr fin* **8/11**[1]	WilliamBuick 6	95
2102	**3**	2 1/2	**Miss Diva**[27] 3669 2-9-0 88 (Richard Hannon) *led: shkn up over 1f out: rdn and hdd ins fnl f: hld whn hmpd towards fin* **9/1**[3]	RyanMoore 4	82
5213	**4**	2	**Kimberella**[14] 4102 2-8-10 88 (Michael Bell) *prom: jnd ldr 1/2-way: shkn up over 2f out: rdn: hung lft and no ex fnl f* **9/2**[2]	IanBurns(7) 3	79
1	**5**	3 1/4	**I'm Back (IRE)**[28] 3637 2-9-5 0 (Saeed Bin Suroor) *chsd ldr: rdn over 1f out: wknd fnl f* **9/2**[2]	MickaelBarzalona 5	70

1m 12.83s (0.33) **Going Correction** -0.15s/f (Firm) **5** Ran SP% **112.0**
Speed ratings (Par 98): **91,90,87,84,80**
CSF £22.21 TOTE £12.70: £2.90, £1.50; EX 27.60.
Owner Nick & Olga Dhandsa & John & Zoe Webster **Bred** Greenwood Lodge Farm Inc **Trained** West Ilsley, Berks
■ Stewards' Enquiry : William Buick two-day ban: careless riding (Aug 11-12)

FOCUS

Subsequent Group 1 winner Excelebration is the best past winner of this conditions stakes and there was plenty of interest with four of the six runners previously unbeaten, and two of those fought out the finish.

NOTEBOOK

Ollie Olga(USA) ◆ won nicely on easy ground on her debut at Newbury and the fourth had scored since. She was bumped at the start but settled at the back before pulling out and running on strongly down the outside to get to the front near the line. She has a number of good entries, including all the top fillies' races, and could well prove to be Group class on this evidence, with the Lowther a possible target. (op 10-1)

Rocky Ground(IRE) impressed when beating a subsequent winner by 4l on his debut at Yarmouth and was sent off favourite. Keen early, he came through to have every chance but wandered under pressure up the hill and was just caught. He remains a colt of some potential. (op 11-10)

Miss Diva ran a decent race in a similar contest over 5f last time and handled this step up in trip well enough. She made the running and rallied well under pressure, but was done no favours by the runner-up on the climb to the line and was eased a little, otherwise she would have finished closer. She has no big entries but something like the Firth of Clyde at Ayr might suit her later on. (op 15-2)

Kimberella had shown his form on softer ground that this and he did not pick up after appearing to have every chance. (op 7-2)

I'm Back(IRE) was edgy at the start and a little keen in the race. He did not find much when ridden and this was disappointing. (op 4-1)

4600 NSPCC H'CAP 1m

5:05 (5:06) (Class 3) (0-90,89) 3-Y-0

£8,715 (£2,609; £1,304; £652; £326; £163) **Stalls** High

Form	Pos	Dist	Horse	Jockey / Draw	RPR
0354	**1**		**Elkhart (IRE)**[8] 4289 3-8-4 **72** (Mark Johnston) *led over 5f: rdn and edgd lft over 1f out: r.o to ld post* **8/1**	JamieMackay 5	77
10-0	**2**	hd	**Nawwaar (USA)**[37] 3294 3-9-5 **87** (John Dunlop) *trckd ldrs: racd keenly: rdn over 1f out: r.o to ld wl ins fnl f: hdd post* **11/2**[3]	PaulHanagan 10	91
-030	**3**	hd	**Nelson's Bay**[49] 2930 3-8-11 **79** (Brian Meehan) *wnt lft s: sn chsng wnr: rdn and ev ch fr over 2f out: r.o* **10/1**	(t) MickaelBarzalona 6	83
3-02	**4**	nse	**Devdas (IRE)**[64] 2452 3-8-12 **80** (Clive Cox) *chsd ldrs: pushed along to ld over 2f out: rdn over 1f out: hdd wl ins fnl f: r.o* **3/1**[1]	WilliamBuick 12	84
-210	**5**	shd	**Come On Blue Chip (IRE)**[37] 3294 3-9-3 **85** (Paul D'Arcy) *hld up: hdwyy u.p over 1f out: r.o* **20/1**	(b) PatDobbs 1	89
-620	**6**	3/4	**Strada Facendo (USA)**[23] 3792 3-8-11 **79** (Luca Cumani) *hld up: hdwy over 2f out: rdn and ev ch whn hung lft ins fnl f: unable qck nr fin* **9/1**	KirstyMilczarek 11	81+
4303	**7**	1/2	**Mr Spiggott (IRE)**[28] 3629 3-9-0 **82** (Mick Channon) *hmpd s: sn prom: rdn and nt clr run over 1f out: r.o* **14/1**	MatthewDavies 7	83
215	**8**	2 1/4	**Legendary**[49] 2930 3-9-0 **82** (Ed Vaughan) *hld up: hdwy u.p and hung lft over 1f out: styd on same pce ins fnl f* **9/2**[2]	ChrisCatlin 9	77
0115	**9**	1 3/4	**Ardmay (IRE)**[14] 4097 3-9-6 **88** (Kevin Ryan) *prom: racd keenly: shkn up over 2f out: rdn over 1f out: no ex fnl f* **7/1**	DavidNolan 3	79
0-	**10**	2 1/2	**Aquilonius (IRE)**[63] 2517 3-9-3 **85** (Stuart Williams) *hld up: rdn over 2f out: wknd over 1f out* **14/1**	BrettDoyle 4	70

1m 41.16s (1.16) **Going Correction** -0.15s/f (Firm) **10** Ran SP% **119.4**
Speed ratings (Par 104): **88,87,87,87,87 86,86,83,82,79**
Tote Swingers: 1&2 £12.70, 1&3 £10.70, 2&3 £17.00 CSF £52.88 CT £453.19 TOTE £9.80: £3.20, £2.60, £3.40; EX 87.10.
Owner Sheikh Hamdan Bin Mohammed Al Maktoum **Bred** Darley **Trained** Middleham Moor, N Yorks

FOCUS
Another good, competitive 3yo handicap and a tremendous blanket finish resulting in another success for the Mark Johnston-Sheikh Hamdan bin Mohammed combination.
NOTEBOOK
Elkhart(IRE) saves his best efforts for when there is fast ground and put up a terrific show. He led early up the centre but looked set to drop away when the winner struck for home. However, in a fashion typical of runners from the stable, he dug in up the hill and refused to be beaten. He had dropped quite a way in the handicap and could prove well treated, even after reassessment. (op 15-2 tchd 10-1)
Nawwaar(USA) had not really built on his maiden win of nearly a year ago, but he was backed here and ran really well, only losing out to a determined rival from an in-form stable. Perhaps he can build on this and fulfil the potential that was evident last season. (op 10-1 tchd 11-1)
Nelson's Bay was closely matched with Devdas on Haydock running, and the fact they finished upsides helps suggest this form is sound. He should be up to winning a decent fast-ground handicap.
Devdas(IRE), who looked unlucky when last seen at Haydock in May, was never far away here and came through to lead over 2f out. However, he was then faced with a number of challenges and, despite battling on, could not hold them off. Perhaps he would have been helped by getting more cover. (op 10-3 tchd 7-2)
Come On Blue Chip(IRE), all of whose wins have been on Polytrack, was held up before coming through late and only just missing out on a place. He looks capable of winning on turf judged on this effort. (op 14-1)
Strada Facendo(USA) was held up before making his effort more towards the far side and, as in earlier races, the principals raced more towards the centre, so this effort can be marked up a little. (op 8-1)
Mr Spiggott(IRE) did not run badly, having tracked the pace throughout, but all his best efforts have been with more cut in the ground. (tchd 11-1)
Legendary, having just his second start on turf and running on the fastest ground he has encountered, was held up and never got competitive, finding little when put under pressure. (op 5-1)

4601 NSPCC FAMILY DAY H'CAP 1m 5f
5:35 (5:36) (Class 4) (0-80,80) 3-Y-O £5,175 (£1,540; £769; £384) Stalls Centre

Form RPR
002 1 **Bite Of The Cherry**[23] 3773 3-9-6 **79** RyanMoore 2 95
(Michael Bell) *led after 1f: sn clr: rdn over 1f out: styd on wl: unchal* 5/1[2]
1-45 2 5 **Aazif (IRE)**[70] 2281 3-9-6 **79** PaulHanagan 9 87
(John Dunlop) *hld up: hdwy over 3f out: rdn to go 2nd over 1f out: nvr any ch* 3/1[1]
5251 3 4 **Moon Trip**[11] 4176 3-9-7 **80** MickaelBarzalona 4 82
(Mark Johnston) *led 1f: chsd wnr who sn wnt clr: rdn and lost 2nd over 1f out: styd on same pce* 3/1[1]
0213 4 1 1/2 **Venegazzu (IRE)**[18] 3945 3-9-4 **77** (v) RobertHavlin 1 77
(Peter Chapple-Hyam) *hld up: hdwy to go 4th 2f out: sn rdn and hung lft: no imp* 6/1[3]
-104 5 7 **Almuftarris (USA)**[63] 2484 3-9-3 **76** ChrisCatlin 3 65
(Ed Dunlop) *stdd s: hld up: rdn over 2f out: nvr on terms* 8/1
4-00 6 1 1/2 **Paramythi (IRE)**[60] 2584 3-8-7 **66** (v[1]) KirstyMilczarek 5 53
(Luca Cumani) *mid-div: pushed along over 4f out: wknd 2f out* 12/1
0000 7 9 **Cape Safari (IRE)**[28] 3630 3-8-12 **78** (p) NatashaEaton(7) 6 52
(Alan Bailey) *mid-div: hdwy over 3f out: sn rdn: wknd over 2f out* 40/1
030 8 33 **Rayvin Black**[28] 3605 3-9-7 **80** WilliamBuick 8
(Mark H Tompkins) *trckd ldrs: racd keenly: rdn: hung lft and wknd over 2f out: t.o* 7/1
2m 44.26s (0.26) **Going Correction** -0.15s/f (Firm) 8 Ran SP% **114.7**
Speed ratings (Par 102): **93,89,87,86,82 81,75,55**
Tote Swingers: 1&2 £5.80, 1&3 £2.40, 2&3 £3.70 CSF £20.48 CT £52.24 TOTE £6.10: £2.30, £1.40, £1.40; EX 18.10.
Owner R L W Frisby **Bred** Palm Tree Thoroughbreds **Trained** Newmarket, Suffolk
FOCUS
This fair but tightly knit staying handicap was won in enterprising fashion.
T/Plt: £80.50 to a £1 stake. Pool: £84,024.34 - 761.55 winning tickets T/Qpdt: £54.50 to a £1 stake. Pool: £3,499.76 - 47.50 winning tickets CR

3658 SALISBURY (R-H)
Saturday, July 28
OFFICIAL GOING: Firm (good to firm in places; 9.4)
Wind: Mild breeze Weather: Sunny

4602 PICADOR CHEVROLET "CARNARVON" H'CAP (FOR GENTLEMAN AMATEUR RIDERS) 1m
6:10 (6:11) (Class 5) (0-75,74) 3-Y-O+ £2,807 (£870; £435; £217) Stalls High

Form RPR
2-0 1 **Fire King**[31] 3485 6-10-7 **65** (p) MrFMitchell(5) 10 72
(Natalie Lloyd-Beavis) *s.i.s: towards rr: hdwy over 2f out: led over 1f out: strly pressed ins fnl f: jst hld on* 20/1
3263 2 nse **Potentiale (IRE)**[7] 4333 8-10-2 **62** (v) MrEdwardSibbick(7) 1 69
(J W Hills) *hld up towards rr: smooth hdwy over 2f out: nt clr run and swtchd lft over 1f out: sn rdn: r.o to chal ins fnl f: jst failed on nod* 9/1
5-06 3 2 **Gallego**[31] 3511 10-10-1 **57** ow1 MrMPrice(3) 14 59
(Richard Price) *wnt to s early: hld up bhd: swtchd to centre 2f out: sn rdn and hdwy: styd on: nvr rchd ldrs* 4/1[1]
6002 4 1 3/4 **George Thisby**[31] 3511 6-10-6 **64** (p) MrPMillman(5) 4 62
(Rod Millman) *s.i.s: towards rr: rdn and hdwy 2f out: styd on same pce fnl f* 7/1
6000 5 shd **Smarty Time**[12] 4150 5-9-5 **55** oh5 MrAJones(7) 6 53
(John Bridger) *chsd ldrs: rdn 2f out: one pce fnl f* 66/1
3632 6 1 3/4 **Lady Sylvia**[27] 3671 3-10-3 **67** MrNdeBoinville(3) 3 59
(Joseph Tuite) *mid-div: chsd ldrs 2f out: sn rdn: fdd ins fnl f* 6/1[3]
2352 7 1/2 **The Name Is Frank**[42] 3153 7-10-6 **64** MrKevinJones(5) 13 57
(Mark Gillard) *wnt to s early: chsd ldrs: rdn over 2f out: one pce fnl f* 9/1
-054 8 1 1/4 **Frederickthegreat**[18] 3938 3-9-10 **62** (t) MrJSherwood(5) 7 50
(Hughie Morrison) *chsd ldr: led over 2f out: sn rdn: hdd over 1f out: fdd ins fnl f* 14/1
1202 9 2 1/2 **Frosty Berry**[26] 3694 3-10-2 **70** MrAFrench(7) 8 52
(John Wainwright) *mid-div: rdn 2f out: wknd fnl f* 11/2[2]
0-52 10 2 1/4 **Sasheen**[67] 2362 5-10-2 **62** MrLKilgarriff(7) 9 41
(Jeremy Gask) *chsd ldrs tl 2f out* 9/1
-000 11 2 1/4 **Green Pearl (IRE)**[66] 2385 4-9-11 **55** oh10..(t) MrCharlieDuckworth(5) 12 29
(Ralph Beckett) *unsettled in stalls: s.i.s: racd in centre: a towards rr* 33/1
-260 12 1 3/4 **Glass Mountain (IRE)**[68] 2328 4-11-2 **74** MrJHodson(5) 2 44
(Ian Williams) *mid-div: effrt over 2f out: wknd over 1f out* 16/1
4440 13 3 **Haadeeth**[7] 4317 5-11-6 **73** MrFWindsorClive 11 36
(David Evans) *wnt to s early: led tl over 2f out: wknd over 1f out* 25/1
1m 44.37s (0.87) **Going Correction** -0.15s/f (Firm)
WFA 3 from 4yo+ 8lb 13 Ran SP% **117.8**
Speed ratings (Par 103): **89,88,86,85,85 83,82,81,79,76 74,72,69**
toteswingers: 1&2 £47.80, 1&3 £22.80, 2&3 £15.10. CSF £182.24 CT £907.52 TOTE £32.30: £7.20, £3.20, £1.90; EX 374.80 TRIFECTA Not won..
Owner Miss S Wicks & J McCarthy **Bred** Dr J M Leigh **Trained** East Garston, Berks
FOCUS
A wide-open handicap, confined to gentleman amateur riders.

4603 DEREK BURRIDGE GOLF & RACING TROPHIES CLASSIFIED CLAIMING STKS 1m
6:40 (6:40) (Class 5) 3-4-Y-O £2,911 (£866; £432; £216) Stalls High

Form RPR
-060 1 **Rossetti**[24] 3767 4-9-1 71 JamesDoyle 7 81
(Ian Williams) *hld up: hdwy over 2f out: led fnl 140yds: r.o wl: pushed out* 10/1
2233 2 1 3/4 **Mayo Lad (IRE)**[35] 3388 3-8-12 74 RichardHughes 1 80
(Richard Hannon) *v.s.a: bhd: swtchd lft over 2f out: gd hdwy to ld over 1f out: sn rdn: no ex whn hdd fnl 140yds* 5/2[2]
5012 3 10 **Aciano (IRE)**[7] 4334 4-8-13 70 (t) SebSanders 4 52
(Brendan Powell) *wnt lft s: trckd ldr: rdn 3f out: wknd fnl f* 11/1
-043 4 1 1/4 **Tony Hollis**[18] 3939 4-8-12 50 DavidProbert 2 48
(Rod Millman) *led: rdn over 2f out: hdd over 1f out: wknd fnl f* 40/1
0046 5 3 3/4 **Netley Marsh**[32] 3475 3-8-5 62 KieranO'Neill 8 38
(Richard Hannon) *in tch: sltly outpcd over 3f out: n.d after* 12/1
14 6 nk **Purple 'n Gold (IRE)**[29] 3591 3-8-6 74 (v) MatthewChadwick 9 39
(George Baker) *in tch: jnd ldrs 4f out: rdn over 2f out: hld fr over 1f out: wknd fnl f* 9/2[3]
2003 7 1 1/4 **Titus Star (IRE)**[7] 4334 3-8-8 68 FrankieMcDonald 3 38
(J S Moore) *trckd ldrs: rdn wl over 2f out: wknd over 1f out* 20/1
5300 8 3 1/4 **Four Richer**[18] 3938 3-8-4 68 (b) CathyGannon 5 26
(Jamie Osborne) *bmpd leaving stalls: pushed along in midfield fr over 5f out: rdn and no imp whn bmpd over 2f out: wknd fnl f* 33/1
2421 9 4 **Benzanno (IRE)**[9] 4256 3-9-6 79 LiamKeniry 10 33
(Andrew Balding) *trckd ldrs: ev ch over 2f out: sn rdn: qckly btn* 2/1[1]
1m 41.72s (-1.78) **Going Correction** -0.15s/f (Firm)
WFA 3 from 4yo 8lb 9 Ran SP% **115.3**
Speed ratings (Par 103): **102,100,90,89,85 84,83,80,76**
toteswingers: 1&2 £9.20, 1&3 £39.30, 2&3 £6.60. CSF £34.66 TOTE £11.40: £2.10, £1.90, £3.20; EX 43.40 Trifecta £432.20 Pool: £646.24 - 1.13 winning units..Rosetti was the subject of a friendly claim.
Owner Paul Wildes **Bred** Bricklow Ltd **Trained** Portway, Worcs
FOCUS
Not a bad claimer.
Tony Hollis Official explanation: jockey said gelding hung right

4604 K J PIKE & SONS LTD MAIDEN STKS 6f
7:15 (7:15) (Class 5) 2-Y-O £2,911 (£866; £432; £216) Stalls Low

Form RPR
1 **Waterway Run (USA)** 2-8-12 0 RichardKingscote 2 80+
(Ralph Beckett) *trckd ldrs: swtchd lft whn nt clr run on rails ent fnl f: rdn and str run to ld fnl strides* 14/1
32 2 hd **Bold Prediction (IRE)**[28] 3637 2-9-3 0 RichardHughes 1 82
(Richard Hannon) *wnt lft s: led: rdn whn briefly hdd 2f out: kpt on: hdd fnl strides* 7/4[2]
3 3 4 **Bravo Youmzain (IRE)**[36] 3346 2-9-3 0 MartinHarley 4 69+
(Marco Botti) *w ldr: rdn to ld briefly 2f out: kpt on same pce fnl f* 13/8[1]
4 2 1/4 **Vectis** 2-9-3 0 HayleyTurner 8 62
(Harry Dunlop) *racd keenly: trckd ldrs: rdn over 2f out: kpt on same pce* 14/1
5 1 **Newtown Cross (IRE)** 2-9-3 0 LiamKeniry 10 59+
(Jimmy Fox) *s.i.s: towards rr: nt clr run on rails over 2f out: swtchd lft wl over 1f out: r.o fnl f: wnt 5th nring fin* 66/1
6 6 1/2 **Colourist**[10] 4220 2-9-0 0 HarryBentley(3) 9 57
(Gary Moore) *trckd ldrs: rdn over 2f out: nt pce to chal: no ex fnl f* 25/1
7 1 1/2 **Storming (IRE)** 2-9-3 0 DavidProbert 12 52
(Andrew Balding) *mid-div: rdn over 2f out: nvr any imp* 10/1[3]
8 2 1/4 **Rutherglen** 2-9-3 0 PatCosgrave 5 45
(George Baker) *trckd ldrs tl outpcd 3f out* 33/1
9 2 **Shades Of Light** 2-8-12 0 SebSanders 11 34
(Peter Makin) *s.i.s: a towards rr* 40/1
10 2 **Madame Scarlett (IRE)** 2-8-12 0 FrankieMcDonald 14 27
(Jo Crowley) *s.i.s fr poor draw: sn mid-div: pushed along over 3f out: wknd over 1f out* 50/1
11 1 1/2 **Lyrical Vibe** 2-8-12 0 CathyGannon 3 23
(David Evans) *hmpd s: a towards rr* 50/1
12 1/2 **Intrigo** 2-9-3 0 KieranO'Neill 6 26
(Richard Hannon) *s.i.s: sn struggling: a bhd* 16/1
13 13 **Admirals Walk (IRE)** 2-9-3 0 JamesDoyle 13
(Sylvester Kirk) *mid-div: effrt over 2f out: wknd qckly wl over 1f out* 25/1
1m 14.8s **Going Correction** -0.15s/f (Firm) 13 Ran SP% **121.3**
Speed ratings (Par 94): **94,93,88,85,84 83,81,78,75,73 71,70,53**
toteswingers: 1&2 £9.30, 1&3 £6.30, 2&3 £1.10. CSF £37.69 TOTE £18.80: £3.80, £1.10, £1.10; EX 52.90 Trifecta £72.60 Pool: £582.16 - 5.93 winning units..
Owner Thurloe Thoroughbreds XX **Bred** Dorothy Alexander Matz **Trained** Kimpton, Hants
FOCUS
The principals dominated this juvenile maiden and the first pair were nicely clear.
NOTEBOOK
Waterway Run(USA) ◆, who has a US pedigree, got on top nearing the finish and ran out a taking debut winner. She knew her job and took advantage of her decent draw on the inside. Indeed she got a lovely trip through the race and there was plenty to like about her effort when the penny dropped. Her trainer advertises each season what he can do with a decent filly and, while she has no fancy entries, she looks potentially very useful as she ought to improve plenty for the outing. (tchd 12-1 and 16-1)
Bold Prediction(IRE) did his very best and nearly made most of the running, but again just failed near the finish. Taking time to settle probably just cost him, but he was a clear second-best and should be winning before long. Nurseries are now an option. (op 2-1)
Bravo Youmzain(IRE) was a promising third on his Newmarket debut last month and got very well backed to score here. He was always up there, but couldnt respond half a furlong out and was ultimately well held. This was very different ground for him, however, and he's worth another chance on an easier surface. (op 9-4)
Vectis, whose yard is doing well with juveniles so far this year, ran with promise considering he refused to settle. He should improve a deal and may appreciate a stiffer test before long. (op 12-1)
Newtown Cross(IRE) ◆ found a troubled passage when trying to improve from off the pace and stayed on nicely when in the clear. He's one to keep an eye on. (op 50-1)

Colourist showed a lot more on this quicker ground and will be eligible for nurseries after his next outing. (op 20-1)
Intrigo Official explanation: jockey said colt was slowly away

4605 ELLIE GRIMES BIRTHDAY CELEBRATION MAIDEN STKS 6f
7:45 (7:45) (Class 5) 3-Y-O+ **£2,911** (£866; £432; £216) **Stalls** Low

Form | | | | RPR

0-63 **1** **Saloomy**[50] 2881 3-9-3 72 RichardHughes 4 84
(David Simcock) *wnt lft s: led tl 4f out: prom: led over 1f out: qckd clr: readily* **8/11**[1]

[illegible] **2** *1 ¾* **Stir Trader (IRE)**[96] 1560 3-9-3 0 JamesDoyle 2 77
(Roger Charlton) *trckd ldrs: swtchd lft to chse wnr over 1f out: kpt on but nvr gng pce to threaten* **9/4**[2]

44 **3** *5* **Bajan Story**[46] 3012 3-9-3 0 LiamKeniry 1 61
(Michael Blanshard) *hld up bhd ldrs: swtchd lft 2f out: sn rdn to chse ldng pair: kpt on same pce fnl f* **9/1**[3]

0-0 **4** *9* **Your Word**[31] 3507 3-8-12 0 JohnFahy 8 28
(Clive Cox) *racd keenly: trckd ldrs: led over 2f out: rdn and hdd over 1f out: wknd fnl f* **14/1**

00 **5** *2* **Rupeetoups**[26] 3702 4-9-8 0 CathyGannon 7 26
(Henry Candy) *carried lft leaving stalls: cl up: led 4f out tl rdn over 2f out: wknd jst over 1f out* **50/1**

6 *13* **Multiply** 3-9-3 0 SebSanders 5
(Peter Makin) *sltly hmpd s: cl up: rdn wl over 2f out: wknd over 1f out* **20/1**

1m 14.72s (-0.08) **Going Correction** -0.15s/f (Firm)
WFA 3 from 4yo 5lb **6** Ran SP% **112.1**
Speed ratings (Par 103): **94,91,85,73,70 53**
toteswingers: 1&2 £1.02, 1&3 £2.80, 2&3 £2.40. CSF £2.53 TOTE £1.80: £1.10, £1.60; EX 3.00 Trifecta £9.40 Pool: £464.84 - 36.55 winning units..
Owner Saleh Al Homaizi & Imad Al Sagar **Bred** D J And Mrs Deer **Trained** Newmarket, Suffolk

FOCUS
A modest sprint maiden and straightforward form.

4606 FAMOUS GROUSE H'CAP 1m 6f 21y
8:15 (8:15) (Class 5) (0-75,73) 3-Y-O+ **£2,911** (£866; £432; £216)

Form | | | | RPR

122 **1** **Teak (IRE)**[44] 3061 5-9-12 71 JamesDoyle 4 80
(Ian Williams) *mid-div: hdwy on rails to chal 3f out: rdn to ld 2f out: styd on wl fnl f* **6/1**[3]

452R **2** *1 ¼* **Juno The Muffinman (IRE)**[8] 4294 3-8-11 70 RichardKingscote 1 77
(Tom Dascombe) *hld up: hdwy over 3f out: styd on steadily but nvr clrest of runs: wnt 2nd ins fnl f* **11/2**[2]

1103 **3** *1 ¾* **Steely**[23] 3769 4-9-11 70 [1] MartinHarley 5 75
(Gary Moore) *wnt to s early: trckd clr ldr in clr 2nd: rdn and ev ch 3f out tl over 1f out: kpt on but no ex whn lost 2nd wl ins fnl f* **20/1**

-110 **4** *1 ¼* **Maydream**[41] 3187 5-9-11 70 KieranO'Neill 13 73+
(Jimmy Fox) *wnt to s early: hld up: rdn and stdy prog fr 3f out: styd on fnl f* **14/1**

2132 **5** *1* **Bathwick Street**[10] 4225 3-8-12 71 (v[1]) CathyGannon 6 73
(David Evans) *mid-div: hdwy to ld over 3f out: rdn and hdd 2f out: kpt on tl no ex fnl f* **6/1**[3]

1213 **6** *9* **Alfraamsey**[10] 4215 4-9-13 72 RichardHughes 10 61
(Sheena West) *trckd ldrs: rdn and ch fr over 2f out tl fdd ent fnl f* **15/2**

36-2 **7** *1 ½* **Dora's Gift**[42] 3142 3-8-6 68 HarryBentley[(3)] 8 55
(Hughie Morrison) *hld up: struggling 5f out: nvr any imp* **3/1**[1]

64-4 **8** *7* **Spensley (IRE)**[24] 3765 6-10-0 73 HayleyTurner 12 50
(James Fanshawe) *trckd ldrs: rdn over 3f out: wknd 2f out: eased fnl f* **8/1**

15-0 **9** *11* **Hawridge King**[65] 2423 10-9-11 70 (v) LiamKeniry 3 32
(Stuart Kittow) *hld up: pushed along over 4f out: sme prog over 3f out: wknd over 1f out* **18/1**

06/0 **10** *2 ¼* **Curacao**[17] 3962 6-10-0 73 SebSanders 11 32
(Amanda Perrett) *pushed along over 5f out: a towards rr* **25/1**

-664 **11** *½* **Poetic Power (IRE)**[44] 3072 3-8-13 72 DavidProbert 9 30
(David Elsworth) *wnt to s early: led: clr 7f out: rdn and hdd over 3f out: sn btn* **12/1**

3m 1.13s (-6.27) **Going Correction** -0.35s/f (Firm)
WFA 3 from 4yo+ 14lb **11** Ran SP% **120.1**
Speed ratings (Par 103): **103,102,101,100,100 94,94,90,83,82 82**
toteswingers: 1&2 £5.40, 1&3 £21.60, 2&3 £44.40. CSF £39.91 CT £632.06 TOTE £6.90: £1.90, £2.30, £6.00; EX 39.60 Trifecta £380.30 Part won. Pool: £513.91 - 0.73 winning units..
Owner Farranamanagh **Bred** Michael Morrissey **Trained** Portway, Worcs

FOCUS
This modest staying handicap was a very competitive race for the class. It was run at a good gallop and the first five pulled clear.

4607 CATHEDRAL HOTEL SALISBURY H'CAP 6f 212y
8:45 (8:45) (Class 4) (0-85,85) 3-Y-O **£5,175** (£1,540; £769; £384) **Stalls** High

Form | | | | RPR

4424 **1** **Amadeus Wolfe Tone (IRE)**[8] 4298 3-9-4 82 (p) JamesDoyle 5 93+
(Jamie Osborne) *trckd ldr: rdn to ld wl over 1f out: strly pressed fnl 140yds: jst hld on* **6/4**[1]

0-04 **2** *nse* **Whimsical (IRE)**[28] 3636 3-9-1 79 RichardHughes 1 90+
(Richard Hannon) *hld up: smooth hdwy on rails over 2f out: swtchd lft over 1f out: sn pushed upsides wnr: unlucky to lose on nod* **5/1**[3]

4025 **3** *3 ¾* **Jack Who's He (IRE)**[6] 4364 3-9-7 85 PatCosgrave 2 86
(David Evans) *hld up in tch: rdn over 2f out: swtchd lft over 1f out: r.o to go 3rd fnl 100yds* **10/1**

0121 **4** *2 ¼* **Serene Oasis (IRE)**[8] 4298 3-8-11 75 (v) MartinHarley 6 70
(Mick Channon) *led: rdn and hdd wl over 1f out: kpt on same pce fnl f* **9/2**[2]

6116 **5** *1* **Xinbama (IRE)**[35] 3376 3-9-0 78 SebSanders 3 70
(J W Hills) *squeezed out after 1f: in tch but last: rdn over 2f out: nt gng pce to get on terms* **9/1**

2-10 **6** *1* **Don Libre**[8] 4298 3-8-8 72 HayleyTurner 8 61
(Paul Cole) *wnt lft s: sn trcking ldrs: jnd ldr after 2f: rdn 2f out: wknd fnl 120yds* **16/1**

2300 **7** *hd* **Beau Duke (IRE)**[61] 2557 3-8-3 67 DavidProbert 7 56
(Andrew Balding) *trckd ldr: rdn over 2f out: wknd over 1f out* **16/1**

15 **8** *18* **Ivor's Princess**[21] 3876 3-9-1 82 (b) HarryBentley[(3)] 4 22
(Rod Millman) *in tch: rdn over 3f out: nvr gng pce to get on terms: wknd over 1f out* **17/2**

1m 27.13s (-1.47) **Going Correction** -0.15s/f (Firm) **8** Ran SP% **116.2**
Speed ratings (Par 102): **102,101,97,95,93 92,92,72**
toteswingers: 1&2 £4.80, 1&3 £4.00, 2&3 £8.00. CSF £9.36 CT £56.10 TOTE £2.30: £1.10, £2.30, £2.10; EX 12.60 Trifecta £64.30 Pool: £492.86 - 5.67 winning units..
Owner B T McDonald **Bred** Brian Williamson **Trained** Upper Lambourn, Berks

FOCUS
The first pair drew right away late on in this 3yo handicap, which was run at just an ordinary pace.
T/Plt: £38.00 to a £1 stake. Pool: £65,453.06 - 1,256,27 winning tickets. T/Qpdt: £6.40 to a £1 stake. Pool: £5,238.46 - 596.82 winning tickets. TM

4553 YORK (L-H)
Saturday, July 28

OFFICIAL GOING: Good to firm (overall 8.0; home straight: far side 7.9, centre 7.9, stands' side 8.0)
Rail out 4m from inside line to give fresh ground from 9f to entrance to home straight; races of 1m and over reduced by 16yds from advertised distance.
Wind: moderate 1/2 against Weather: overcast, shower race 6

4608 SKY BET MOBILE EBF FILLIES' STKS (H'CAP) 1m 2f 88y
2:05 (2:05) (Class 3) (0-90,90) 3-Y-O+ **£9,703** (£2,887; £1,443; £721) **Stalls** Low

Form | | | | RPR

1332 **1** **Maven**[22] 3813 4-9-1 77 DavidAllan 2 88
(Tim Easterby) *hld up in rr: hdwy over 3f out: r.o to ld last 150yds: edgd rt and styd on wl* **10/1**

21 **2** *2 ½* **Hippy Hippy Shake**[27] 3663 3-9-0 86 KierenFallon 10 92+
(Luca Cumani) *hdwy to trck ldrs 7f out: led over 2f out: hdd and no ex ins fnl f* **11/4**[1]

0052 **3** *1 ¼* **Napoleon's Muse (IRE)**[21] 3847 3-7-13 71 MartinLane 9 75
(Ralph Beckett) *led: qcknd pce over 4f out: hdd over 2f out: kpt on same pce* **25/1**

-001 **4** *¾* **Popular**[51] 2848 3-8-10 82 TomQueally 1 85
(Sir Henry Cecil) *t.k.h towards rr: hdwy 4f out: upsides over 2f out: one pce* **13/2**[2]

0620 **5** *2 ¾* **Bridle Belle**[15] 4072 4-9-3 86 GeorgeChaloner[(7)] 6 83
(Richard Fahey) *chsd ldrs: kpt on same pce fnl 2f* **20/1**

11- **6** *3* **Anjaz (USA)**[322] 5931 3-9-4 90 FrankieDettori 5 82
(Saeed Bin Suroor) *trckd ldrs: drvn 4f out: fdd fnl f* **11/4**[1]

100 **7** *1 ½* **Zaina (IRE)**[16] 4009 3-8-12 84 LukeMorris 3 73
(Gerard Butler) *hld up in mid-div: drvn 4f out: wknd over 1f out* **16/1**

642 **8** *1 ½* **Certral**[5] 4407 4-9-1 80 PaulPickard[(3)] 7 66
(Brian Ellison) *s.v.s: hdwy wd outside over 3f out: wknd 2f out* **9/1**[3]

12-0 **9** *9* **Kunooz (IRE)**[21] 3879 3-9-4 90 AhmedAjtebi 8 59
(Mahmood Al Zarooni) *hld up in rr: hdwy over 3f out: sn chsng ldrs: wknd over 1f out: eased* **16/1**

0041 **10** *12* **Fork Handles**[14] 4080 4-9-9 85 (v) NeilCallan 11 31
(Mick Channon) *t.k.h: w ldr: lost pl wl over 1f out: eased clsng stages* **11/1**

100- **11** *3 ¾* **Apache Glory (USA)**[353] 4914 4-9-4 80 AdamKirby 4 19
(John Stimpson) *trckd ldrs: upsides over 3f out: lost pl 2f out: bhd whn eased* **50/1**

1-55 **12** *1 ¾* **Zimira (IRE)**[65] 2410 3-9-1 87 GeorgeBaker 12 23
(Ed Dunlop) *chsd ldrs: lost pl 2f out: bhd whn eased* **20/1**

2m 7.55s (-4.95) **Going Correction** -0.30s/f (Firm)
WFA 3 from 4yo 10lb **12** Ran SP% **121.2**
Speed ratings (Par 104): **107,105,104,103,101 98,97,96,89,79 76,75**
toteswingers 1&2 £6.80, 1&3 £37.70, 2&3 £18.80 CT £697.34 TOTE £11.80: £3.80, £1.50, £6.50; EX 53.50 Trifecta £551.60 Part won. Pool: £745.50 - 0.78 winning units..
Owner Habton Farms **Bred** Habton Farms **Trained** Great Habton, N Yorks

FOCUS
The early fractions for the opener weren't that quick, but the winner won nicely despite taking a keen hold in rear. A decent fillies' handicap, and sound form.

NOTEBOOK
Maven travelled really strongly out the back before coming with a powerful effort over 2f from home. She was more than good enough once in front to hang on for an in-form stable. Runner-up in heavy going last time, she appears to handle most ground and is a likeable sort. (tchd 9-1)
Hippy Hippy Shake ◆ looked promising when landing a Salisbury maiden on her previous outing, this after chasing home Popular on debut, and improved on that effort here. One would suspect she'll progress again after being in amongst useful sorts for the first time. A step up in distance doesn't look like it would be a problem. (op 3-1)
Napoleon's Muse(IRE) was well ridden to make use of bottom weight and battled on to claim third. (op 28-1 tchd 33-1)
Popular, off since beating Hippy Hippy Shake in a Lingfield maiden during June, hit a flat spot when the tempo increased and shapes like a filly that is a galloper rather than one with a turn-of-foot. (op 7-1)
Bridle Belle, taking another drop in distance, plugged on for pressure. (op 16-1)
Anjaz(USA), not seen out since September 2011, needed plenty of pushing to get into a prominent position from the home bend but wasn't given an unduly hard time when it was obvious she was beaten. Something may have been amiss. (op 10-3)
Apache Glory(USA) Official explanation: jockey said filly hung left

4609 SPORTINGLIFE.COM STKS (H'CAP) 7f
2:35 (2:41) (Class 2) (0-105,104) 3-Y-O+ **£12,938** (£3,850; £1,924; £962) **Stalls** Low

Form | | | | RPR

1-20 **1** **Dimension**[38] 3268 4-9-8 98 TomQueally 15 111
(James Fanshawe) *stdd s: hld up in rr: gd hdwy on outer over 1f out: r.o to ld fnl 30yds* **4/1**[1]

-000 **2** *½* **White Frost (IRE)**[7] 4317 4-8-10 86 MichaelHills 7 97
(Charles Hills) *w ldr: led after 1f: no ex and hdd nr fin* **9/1**[3]

0360 **3** *4* **Imperial Djay (IRE)**[7] 4321 7-9-6 96 PJMcDonald 11 97
(Ruth Carr) *in rr-div: hdwy over 2f out: styd on fnl f: tk 3rd post* **16/1**

0300 **4** *nse* **Advanced**[14] 4086 9-9-2 92 PhillipMakin 14 93
(Kevin Ryan) *chsd ldrs: kpt on same pce appr fnl f* **33/1**

-030 **5** *nk* **Citrus Star (USA)**[14] 4099 5-9-3 93 GeorgeBaker 6 93+
(Chris Wall) *hld up in rr: hdwy over 2f out: repeatedly denied clr run: styd on wl ins fnl f* **10/1**

003 **6** *1 ¾* **Greensward**[63] 2489 6-8-12 88 RobertWinston 5 83
(Mike Murphy) *s.i.s: sn chsng ldrs: drvn 3f out: one pce* **20/1**

0310 **7** *½* **Atlantic Sport (USA)**[14] 4099 7-9-7 97 LukeMorris 8 91
(Mick Channon) *in rr-div: kpt on fnl 2f: nvr a threat* **20/1**

3405 **8** *hd* **Orpsie Boy (IRE)**[7] 4317 9-8-7 86 DaleSwift[(3)] 10 79
(Ruth Carr) *in rr-div: kpt on fnl 2f: nvr a threat* **16/1**

0104 **9** *shd* **Quick Wit**[147] 792 5-10-0 104 FrankieDettori 4 97
(Saeed Bin Suroor) *trckd ldrs: effrt 2f out: kpt on same pce* **8/1**[2]

5413 **10** *1 ¾* **Able Master (IRE)**[30] 3524 6-8-9 85 KierenFallon 9 73
(David O'Meara) *s.i.s: bhd and drvn along: hdwy wd outside over 1f out: nvr nr ldrs* **11/1**

1314 **11** *hd* **Haamaat (IRE)**[56] 2713 4-9-4 **94** .... TadhgO'Shea 12 82
(William Haggas) *mid-div: hdwy over 2f out: rdn and one pce whn n.m.r over 1f out* **8/1**[2]

1-44 **12** *¾* **Yair Hill (IRE)**[36] 3348 4-8-11 **87** .... JimmyFortune 3 73
(John Dunlop) *in rr-div: effrt over 2f out: nvr rchd ldrs* **9/1**[3]

26 **13** *shd* **Noble Citizen (USA)**[7] 4321 7-9-2 **92** .... (b) MartinLane 2 77
(David Simcock) *s.i.s: in rr: sme hdwy 3f out: lost pl over 1f out* **12/1**

1600 **14** *hd* **Justonefortheroad**[7] 4321 6-8-13 **96** .... GeorgeChaloner(7) 13 81
(Richard Fahey) *in tch on outer: drvn 3f out: wknd fnl f* **14/1**

5406 **15** *15* **Parisian Pyramid (IRE)**[14] 4077 6-8-12 **88** .... NeilCallan 1 32
(Patrick Morris) *led 1f: w ldr: lost pl 2f out: heavily eased: t.o* **20/1**

1m 21.83s (-3.47) **Going Correction** -0.25s/f (Firm) course record **15** Ran SP% **123.0**
Speed ratings (Par 109): **109,108,103,103,103 101,100,100,100,98 98,97,97,97,79**
toteswingers 1&2 £4.00, 1&3 £3.80, 2&3 £8.30 CSF £36.80 CT £547.66 TOTE £2.60: £1.80, £3.30; EX 20.40 TRIFECTA Not won..
Owner Cheveley Park Stud **Bred** Cheveley Park Stud Ltd **Trained** Newmarket, Suffolk

FOCUS
A strong race in which it was easy to make a solid case for then majority of the runners. It wasn't a surprise to see a new course record set. A personal best from the winner with the first pair clear.

NOTEBOOK
Dimension ◆, dropping back to 7f, had been well fancied this season for a couple of decent races but hadn't been able to get his head to the front. For a large portion of the home straight success looked unlikely again, but he showed a good attitude under Tom Queally towards the stands' rail and was nicely on top at the end. He's just the sort of horse his trainer has often done well with, but he'll be faced with carrying big weights in handicaps for quite a while or trying to bridge the gap to Pattern level. The Group 2 Park Stakes is an entry he already holds. (op 5-1)
White Frost(IRE) bounced back to something resembling his 3yo promise under a prominent ride. If his official mark doesn't go up much for this, he can continue to hold his own in decent contests. (op 12-1 tchd 14-1)
Imperial Djay(IRE) travelled kindly for quite a while, as he can do, and kept on well once hitting top gear. He is enjoying a fine season. (tchd 20-1)
Advanced prefers a decent surface and it wasn't surprising to see a better effort from him as a result.
Citrus Star(USA) ◆ looked really unlucky, as he met traffic problems when trying to make ground through runners and didn't get in the clear until too late. (op 9-1 tchd 8-1)
Quick Wit, off the track since running at Meydan in March, has gone well fresh previously so this was a little disappointing. (op 9-1)
Haamaat(IRE), the only filly in the contest, was stuck in midfield throughout and didn't see lots of room. She may not have been good enough anyway, but can be allowed another chance. (op 7-1)
Yair Hill(IRE) has only ever won Class 4 and 5 races, so probably finds this level a bit too tough to win in. (op 8-1)

4610 SKY BET YORK STKS (GROUP 2) 1m 2f 88y
3:10 (3:12) (Class 1) 3-Y-O+
£56,710 (£21,500; £10,760; £5,360; £2,690; £1,350) **Stalls** Low

Form RPR

1650 **1** **Sri Putra**[21] 3880 6-9-2 116 .... (b) NeilCallan 4 118
(Roger Varian) *hld up: hdwy 3f out: swtchd lft and effrt 2f out: rdn to chse ldr ent fnl f: sn drvn and hung lft: styd on to ld nr fin* **12/1**

-421 **2** *nk* **Afsare**[22] 3825 5-9-2 113 .... KierenFallon 1 117
(Luca Cumani) *hld up in tch on inner: hdwy 4f out: chal 2f out: sn rdn to ld and hung bdly rt wl over 1f out: drvn and hung bdly lft ins fnl f: hdd and no ex nr fin* **9/4**[1]

5313 **3** *3¾* **Side Glance**[39] 3237 5-9-2 114 .... JimmyFortune 7 110
(Andrew Balding) *trckd ldrs: hdwy over 3f out: chal over 2f out: rdn and ev ch whn sltly hmpd wl over 1f out: kpt on same pce* **6/1**

-113 **4** *2¾* **Jet Away**[34] 3418 5-9-2 114 .... TomQueally 11 105+
(Sir Henry Cecil) *s.i.s and in rr: hdwy on wd outside 3f out: chsd ldrs 2f out: rdn and ch whn n.m.r wl over 1f out: sn hmpd and one pce after* **7/2**[2]

0-05 **5** *1* **Ransom Note**[70] 2270 5-9-2 113 .... MichaelHills 6 103
(Charles Hills) *trckd ldrs: hdwy over 3f out: led over 2f out: sn rdn: hdd: n.m.r and hmpd over 1f out: one pce after* **8/1**

4430 **6** *1¾* **Wigmore Hall (IRE)**[38] 3267 5-9-2 115 .... GrahamLee 8 100+
(Michael Bell) *hld up in tch: hdwy 3f out: trckd ldrs and ch whn bdly hmpd wl over 1f out: nt rcvr* **5/1**[3]

6515 **7** *3¼* **Marcret (ITY)**[57] 2656 5-9-2 111 .... AdamKirby 3 94
(Marco Botti) *t.k.h: trckd ldr on inner: effrt over 3f out: sn rdn along and wknd 2f out* **25/1**

60-0 **8** *10* **Pekan Star**[57] 2655 5-9-2 90 .... [1] MartinLane 10 75
(Roger Varian) *led: rdn along over 3f out: hdd over 2f out: sn wknd* **50/1**

-110 **9** *¾* **Premio Loco (USA)**[39] 3237 8-9-2 113 .... GeorgeBaker 9 73
(Chris Wall) *t.k.h: trckd ldrs on outer: effrt 3f out: rdn and wkng whn n.m.r wl over 1f out: sn eased* **11/1**

2m 5.74s (-6.76) **Going Correction** -0.30s/f (Firm) **9** Ran SP% **116.9**
Speed ratings (Par 115): **115,114,111,109,108 107,104,96,96**
toteswingers 1&2 £7.90, 1&3 £13.20, 2&3 £4.30 CSF £39.81 TOTE £14.30: £3.70, £1.20, £2.20; EX 45.50 Trifecta £484.40 Pool: £2,108.05 - 3.22 winning units..
Owner H R H Sultan Ahmad Shah **Bred** Glebe Stud And Partners **Trained** Newmarket, Suffolk
■ Stewards' Enquiry : Michael Hills three-day ban: careless riding (Aug 11-13)

FOCUS
Sadly no 3yos took their chance, but this was a good field, full of horses up to the required level. It produced a slightly messy finish when a few horses came rather close to each other. The pace was only reasonable but the form is up to scratch for the race and grade.

NOTEBOOK
Sri Putra, wearing a hood for the first time, and having blinkers reintroduced after ten runs without them, burst through to challenge. Neil Callan's mount is a likeable old character and was the highest-rated of these after the late defection of Planteur. However, it remains to be seen if the headgear combination works in the future. (op 17-2)
Afsare loves really quick ground, he had form figures of 111 on officially good to firm going prior to this, but didn't help his chances of gaining a first Group success here by hanging both ways under pressure. Had he kept dead straight, he may well have won considering the margin of defeat. (op 3-1)
Side Glance was being tried over this distance for the first time after a great effort in the Queen Anne but didn't have the pace when needed to go with the first two. He was carried right as Afsare made his bid, which obviously didn't help.
Jet Away, whose connections took this race last year with Twice Over, was back down to what seemed a more suitable distance but didn't aid his cause here after being slowly away. He made his challenge up the rail once in the home straight and was undoubtedly hampered, but didn't appear to be going forward quickly at the time. (op 9-2 tchd 3-1)
Ransom Note, second in this last year, had been off since the Lockinge Stakes and ran respectably until tightened for room. (tchd 10-1)
Wigmore Hall(IRE), who won the John Smith's Cup on his only other try here, was just starting to come under strong pressure when forced to snatch up - Michael Hills was given a ban for careless riding on Ransom Note, the horse that came across him. He had looked a shade outpaced at that stage. (tchd 9-2)
Pekan Star, running for the first time in Group company and in a hood, went off in front and set what looked only a reasonable gallop. He was readily beaten off. (tchd 66-1)

4611 SKY BET DASH STKS (H'CAP) 6f
3:45 (3:48) (Class 2) (0-105,102) 3-Y-O+**£32,345** (£9,625; £4,810; £2,405) **Stalls** Low

Form RPR

010 **1** **Van Ellis**[7] 4321 3-9-3 **100** .... KierenFallon 1 111
(Mark Johnston) *chsd ldrs on outer: led over 1f out: edgd rt: kpt on wl* **8/1**[2]

0000 **2** *1¼* **Gramercy (IRE)**[14] 4099 5-9-0 **92** .... NeilCallan 14 102+
(David Simcock) *mid-div: hdwy and nt clr run over 1f out: styd on ins fnl f: tk 2nd nr fin* **20/1**

6664 **3** *½* **Tax Free (IRE)**[35] 3374 10-9-0 **92** .... AdrianNicholls 8 97
(David Nicholls) *w ldrs: led after 2f: hdd over 1f out: styd on same pce* **14/1**

000 **4** *1* **Nasri**[28] 3641 6-8-10 **88** .... LukeMorris 7 90
(Milton Bradley) *reminders after s: hdwy to chse ldrs over 4f out: kpt on same pce fnl f* **14/1**

3001 **5** *½* **Colonel Mak**[9] 4258 5-9-10 **102** .... GeorgeBaker 15 102
(David Barron) *hld up: hdwy over 2f out: kpt on same pce fnl f* **14/1**

3130 **6** *hd* **Head Space (IRE)**[8] 4312 4-9-2 **94** .... PJMcDonald 2 94
(Ruth Carr) *chsd ldrs: styd on same pce fnl f* **6/1**[1]

0-06 **7** *shd* **Kaldoun Kingdom (IRE)**[15] 4073 7-9-2 **94** .... BarryMcHugh 16 96+
(Richard Fahey) *s.i.s: hdwy and nt clr run over 1f out: kpt on towards fin* **14/1**

0016 **8** *¾* **Fast Shot**[14] 4086 4-9-0 **92** .... DavidAllan 17 89
(Tim Easterby) *in rr-div: styd on fnl 2f: nt rch ldrs* **14/1**

1000 **9** *½* **Capaill Liath (IRE)**[7] 4321 4-8-10 **91** .... (p) JulieBurke(3) 13 86
(Kevin Ryan) *s.i.s: detached in last: hdwy and swtchd far side over 1f out: styd on ins fnl f* **25/1**

1113 **10** *nk* **Powerful Presence (IRE)**[28] 3624 6-9-1 **93** .... DanielTudhope 4 87
(David O'Meara) *w ldrs: fdd fnl f* **8/1**[2]

0-00 **11** *1¾* **Breathless Kiss (USA)**[14] 4113 5-9-1 **93** .... (b) PhillipMakin 5 82
(Kevin Ryan) *s.i.s: hdwy and n.m.r over 1f out: nvr trbld ldrs* **40/1**

1114 **12** *nse* **Klynch**[14] 4086 6-8-13 **94** .... (b) DaleSwift(3) 6 83
(Ruth Carr) *chsd ldrs: one pce over 1f out* **12/1**[3]

0241 **13** *¾* **Sacrosanctus**[23] 3771 4-8-10 **88** .... TomQueally 12 74
(Scott Dixon) *in tch: effrt over 2f out: one pce* **16/1**

002 **14** *nk* **Swiss Cross**[23] 3771 5-9-2 **94** .... (t) FrankieDettori 3 79
(Phil McEntee) *led 2f: w ldrs: wknd appr fnl f* **16/1**

2-06 **15** *½* **Chunky Diamond (IRE)**[42] 3158 3-9-3 **100** .... JimmyFortune 18 84
(Peter Chapple-Hyam) *in rr: sme hdwy over 2f out: nvr a factor* **20/1**

-605 **16** *½* **El Viento (FR)**[49] 2931 4-8-10 **88** .... TonyHamilton 9 70
(Richard Fahey) *chsd ldrs: drvn over 2f out: fdd over 1f out* **14/1**

0132 **17** *½* **Misplaced Fortune**[28] 3624 7-9-0 **92** .... GrahamLee 11 72+
(Nigel Tinkler) *in rr-div: effrt and nt clr run over 1f out: nvr a factor* **16/1**

0260 **18** *1* **Last Bid**[15] 4063 3-8-9 **92** .... FrederikTylicki 10 69
(Tim Easterby) *chsd ldrs: lost pl over 1f out* **25/1**

5501 **19** *1¾* **Grissom (IRE)**[14] 4086 6-9-2 **94** .... AndrewElliott 20 66
(Tim Easterby) *a towards rr* **16/1**

6125 **20** *1* **Farlow (IRE)**[8] 4285 4-8-12 **90** .... MartinLane 19 58
(Ralph Beckett) *a in rr* **14/1**

1m 10.78s (-1.12) **Going Correction** -0.25s/f (Firm)
WFA 3 from 4yo+ 5lb **20** Ran SP% **134.1**
Speed ratings (Par 109): **97,95,94,93,92 92,92,91,90,90 87,87,86,86,85 85,84,83,80,79**
toteswingers 1&2 £83.00, 1&3 £60.90, 2&3 £139.50 CSF £174.49 CT £2302.81 TOTE £8.90: £2.60, £5.80, £2.70, £4.80; EX 221.10 Trifecta £5945.20 Pool: £47,023.83 - 5.85 winning units..
Owner Sheikh Hamdan Bin Mohammed Al Maktoum **Bred** D A Yardy **Trained** Middleham Moor, N Yorks

FOCUS
This was won by smart sprinters Hoof It (who won the Stewards' Cup a week later) in 2011 and Hawkeyethenoo the year previously, so potentially the winner could be up to holding his own at a higher level. A competitive handicap and the form is taken at face value.

NOTEBOOK
Van Ellis ◆, who is felt to be at his best on decent ground, came in for plenty of market support but things didn't look good for his supporters as he was being pushed along quite early to keep tabs on the leaders. However, Kieren Fallon slowly gathered them in and the pair won going away despite hanging right across the course towards the stands' side from over a furlong out. Connections have the colt in three races at Goodwood next week, including two Group contests, and a return to 7f clearly won't be an issue. The last 3yo to win this ended up being Group 1-placed. (op 10-1)
Gramercy(IRE) had run badly on the other occasions he'd been to York, so made a positive step in the right direction here. He's down to a fair mark and should be of interest next time.
Tax Free(IRE) ◆ gets little respite from the handicapper due to his consistency and he ran another cracker from a prominent position. He will run well if having another go at the Stewards' Cup next weekend, granted a good draw.
Nasri ◆ has dropped to a really good mark. Having only his second start for Milton Bradley, he was two places behind Tax Free in 2011 at Goodwood, but was running off a mark of 97 then, so his chances of reversing placing appear obvious. Odds of 33-1 for that contest look tempting. (op 16-1 tchd 20-1)
Colonel Mak was another who hadn't run well here in the past, so this was a big performance giving weight away. (op 12-1)
Head Space(IRE) made his challenge quite late but seemed comfortably held by those in front of him. This was his first venture to Class 2 company and he was far from disgraced. (op 13-2 tchd 7-1)
Kaldoun Kingdom(IRE), second in this in 2010 off a BHA mark of 101, got squeezed for room at a crucial stage before staying on. (op 12-1)
Capaill Liath(IRE) was slightly detached after a furlong but made good headway inside the final stages. (op 40-1)
Powerful Presence(IRE) goes really well on officially fast ground but didn't look to have too many excuses here. (op 12-1)
Sacrosanctus seemed to find a little bit of trouble in running.
Chunky Diamond(IRE) needed switching while travelling strongly and is better than his final position. (op 25-1)
Misplaced Fortune was denied a clear run. Official explanation: jockey said mare was denied a clear run (tchd 20-1)

4612 SKY SPORTS MEDIAN AUCTION MAIDEN STKS 6f
4:20 (4:20) (Class 4) 2-Y-O **£6,469** (£1,925; £962; £481) **Stalls** Low

Form RPR

3 **1** **Burning Blaze**[20] 3887 2-9-3 0 .... PhillipMakin 5 87+
(Kevin Ryan) *mde most: rdn wl over 1f out: drvn ins fnl f: styd on wl towards fin* **11/4**[1]

2 *1* **Cour Valant** 2-9-3 0 .... NeilCallan 8 83
(Noel Quinlan) *in tch: hdwy over 2f out: rdn to chal over 1f out: ev ch tl drvn: rn green and no ex wl ins fnl f* **33/1**

03 **3** 1 ¾ **Medicoe**[17] 3973 2-9-3 0 LukeMorris 2 77
(Sir Mark Prescott Bt) *cl up: rdn along over 2f out: drvn appr fnl f: kpt on same pce* **8/1**[2]

02 **4** 1 ½ **Ajmany (IRE)**[23] 3788 2-9-3 0 KierenFallon 3 72
(Luca Cumani) *trckd ldrs: rdn along and sltly outpcd wl over 1f out: kpt on fnl f* **11/4**[1]

422 **5** ¾ **Bachotheque (IRE)**[7] 4344 2-9-3 82 DavidAllan 7 70
(Tim Easterby) *chsd ldrs: rdn along over 2f out: grad wknd* **11/4**[1]

64 **6** 11 **Monkey Bar Flies (IRE)**[58] 2614 2-9-3 0 BarryMcHugh 9 35
(Richard Fahey) *prom: cl up 1/2-way: rdn along over 2f out: sn wknd* **12/1**[3]

7 hd **Khelman (IRE)** 2-9-3 0 TonyHamilton 13 34
(Richard Fahey) *trckd ldrs: cl up 1/2-way: rdn along over 2f out and sn wknd* **18/1**

33 **8** 2 **Dark Opal (IRE)**[31] 3491 2-8-12 0 JimmyFortune 10 23
(John Weymes) *a towards rr* **14/1**

00 **9** 16 **Grey Destiny**[21] 3844 2-9-3 0 RobertWinston 11
(Mel Brittain) *rrd s and s.i.s and a bhd* **33/1**

1m 11.13s (-0.77) **Going Correction** -0.25s/f (Firm) **9** Ran SP% **116.6**
Speed ratings (Par 96): **95,93,91,89,88 73,73,70,49**
toteswingers 1&2 £86.30, 1&3 £10.10, 2&3 £59.90 CSF £110.97 TOTE £3.90: £1.30, £11.40, £2.80; EX 166.30.
Owner Qatar Racing Limited **Bred** Redland Bs, Baroness Bs & D Redvers **Trained** Hambleton, N Yorks

FOCUS
Good maiden form, in a decent time. The winner built on his debut promise.

NOTEBOOK
Burning Blaze, who travelled best of all on his debut at Ayr over 7f but failed to see his race out on soft ground, looks sure to make progression. His attitude is hard to fault and he has the scope to do well as a juvenile. (op 3-1 tchd 5-2)
Cour Valant, whose dam was smart as a 2yo, made an excellent start to his career and split some pretty decent types. If he makes normal progress, it'll take a good horse to beat him on his next start if kept to a realistic level.
Medicoe was racing on fast ground for the first time, and shaped as though further might help him in the future. (tchd 17-2)
Ajmany(IRE) hit a flat spot some way out but kept on under pressure to finish fourth. His dam was a middle-distance winner in soft ground, so he'll be one to watch out for in handicaps up in distance. (op 9-4)
Bachotheque(IRE) had run well over C&D previously but was disappointing here. There is no way he ran up to his official mark and he may want a bit more ease in the going. He has plenty of size and is probably one for the long-term. (op 7-2)

4613 SKY BET MOBILE FOR IPAD STKS (H'CAP) 2m 88y
4:50 (4:50) (Class 3) (0-90,90) 4-Y-0+ **£8,409** (£2,502; £1,250; £625) **Stalls** Low

Form RPR

1320 **1** **Herostatus**[14] 4115 5-9-0 83 (p) DanielTudhope 9 91
(David O'Meara) *hmpd after 1f: chsd ldrs: styd on fnl f: led nr fin* **16/1**

5-34 **2** nk **Eagle Rock (IRE)**[42] 3163 4-8-10 79 MartinLane 4 87
(Tom Tate) *led 1f: sn hmpd bnd: chsd ldrs: chal over 2f out: led over 1f out: hdd and no ex nr fin* **8/1**

0-50 **3** 1 ½ **Itlaaq**[42] 3163 6-9-7 90 (t) FrankieDettori 13 96
(Michael Easterby) *hld up in last: effrt over 3f out: swtchd rt 2f out: sn chsng ldrs: kpt on same pce ins fnl f* **15/2**[3]

522 **4** ½ **Mojolika**[11] 4176 4-8-6 75 BarryMcHugh 6 81
(Tim Easterby) *hmpd after 1f: t.k.h in midfield: effrt over 3f out: chsng ldrs over 1f out: kpt on same pce last 75yds* **16/1**

1060 **5** nk **Deauville Flyer**[21] 3857 6-9-6 89 (p) DavidAllan 10 94
(Tim Easterby) *hld up in rr: hdwy 9f out: swtchd towards stands' side 4f out: chsng ldrs over 1f out: kpt on same pce last 150yds* **12/1**

0346 **6** nk **The Bells O Peover**[24] 3765 4-8-8 77 (b) KierenFallon 15 82
(Mark Johnston) *swtchd lft after s: t.k.h: sn trcking ldr: led after 5f: qcknd pce 4f out: hdd over 1f out: wknd towards fin* **12/1**

0-02 **7** 1 ¼ **Dazinski**[56] 2709 6-9-6 89 TomQueally 11 92
(Mark H Tompkins) *sn trcking ldrs: effrt over 3f out: one pce fnl 2f* **6/1**[1]

-660 **8** 5 **Hawk Mountain (UAE)**[73] 2180 7-9-0 83 JimmyFortune 8 80
(John Quinn) *hmpd on bnd after 1f: mid-div: effrt in centre over 3f out: nvr a threat* **9/1**

5353 **9** 1 ½ **Noble Alan (GER)**[28] 3610 9-9-2 85 GrahamLee 1 81
(Nicky Richards) *in rr whn hmpd after 1f: hld up: sme hdwy over 2f out: nvr a factor* **7/1**[2]

-312 **10** 2 ¾ **Reem Star**[14] 4115 4-9-2 88 JulieBurke(3) 7 80
(Kevin Ryan) *led after 1f: hdd after 5f: lost pl over 1f out* **15/2**[3]

0141 **11** 1 ¾ **La Bacouetteuse (FR)**[51] 2842 7-8-2 71 (p) LukeMorris 2 61
(Iain Jardine) *in rr whn hmpd after 1f: hdwy 9f out: drvn 6f out: lost pl over 2f out* **25/1**

3211 **12** 1 **Rosairlie (IRE)**[22] 3827 4-8-7 76 PJMcDonald 14 65
(Micky Hammond) *sn chsng ldrs: drvn over 3f out: wknd over 1f out* **11/1**

3-24 **13** 18 **French Hollow**[28] 3625 7-8-13 82 FrederikTylicki 12 49
(Tim Fitzgerald) *hld up in rr: hdwy to trck ldrs after 5f: lost pl over 2f out: sn eased: t.o* **8/1**

0-P6 **14** 19 **Kazbow (IRE)**[56] 2709 6-9-7 90 TonyHamilton 3 35
(Chris Grant) *hmpd and lost pl after 1f: in rr-div: bhd fnl 3f: t.o* **22/1**

3m 30.55s (-3.95) **Going Correction** -0.30s/f (Firm) course record **14** Ran SP% **126.2**
Speed ratings (Par 107): **97,96,96,95,95 95,94,92,91,90 89,88,79,70**
toteswingers 1&2 £15.90, 1&3 £31.40, 2&3 £16.00 CSF £145.34 CT £1067.37 TOTE £21.70: £7.00, £3.10, £2.50; EX 241.10.
Owner R Naylor **Bred** Darley **Trained** Nawton, N Yorks

FOCUS
A fair range of ability took their chance in this staying contest. The early gallop was sensible for the distance. The winner is rated back to his old best.

NOTEBOOK
Herostatus, seventh over C&D last time, was tried in cheekpieces and that aid may have given him the sufficient boost he needed to get his head back in front. The gelding has maintained a useful level of ability this season, and kept on gamely enough here despite wandering under pressure. (tchd 20-1)
Eagle Rock(IRE) had never raced over 2m on the Flat, but looked to appreciate the step up in trip after being narrowly beaten in a driving finish. (tchd 15-2)
Itlaaq, with a tongue-tie back on, won this last year off a 2lb lower mark and was produced to have every chance after being out the back early. He couldn't force his way to the front and was comfortably held. (op 10-1 tchd 7-1)
Mojolika, like many, got outpaced but showed plenty of resolution to keep on. Both of his victories have come off official marks in the 60s.
Deauville Flyer was deliberately moved towards the centre of the course on turning in but it didn't prove to be a hugely advantageous tactic. (tchd 10-1)
The Bells O Peover, back in blinkers, kept on well after leading for a large part of the race. (op 11-1 tchd 14-1)
Dazinski, given a break since a useful effort at Haydock in early June, didn't look to have any obvious excuses. (op 15-2)
Noble Alan(GER), up over 4f in trip for his second start in a handicap, moved powerfully approaching the 2f pole after being in rear but couldn't quicken. Nicky Richards reported that the gelding was unsuited by the good to firm ground. Official explanation: trainer said gelding was unsuited by the good to firm ground (tchd 6-1)

4614 SKY BET MOBILE FOR IPHONE STKS (NURSERY H'CAP) 5f
5:20 (5:20) (Class 3) (0-95,85) 2-Y-0 **£7,439** (£2,213; £1,106; £553) **Stalls** Low

Form RPR

5215 **1** **Lady Poppy**[39] 3250 2-8-11 75 PJMcDonald 2 80
(George Moore) *mde all: shkn up over 1f out: kpt on wl last 75yds* **5/1**[2]

6654 **2** 1 ½ **Bispham Green**[15] 4071 2-8-7 71 BarryMcHugh 3 71
(Richard Fahey) *chsd ldrs: wnt 2nd over 1f out: kpt on same pce last 100yds* **17/2**

1540 **3** 1 ½ **Tatlisu (IRE)**[14] 4093 2-9-4 82 TonyHamilton 7 77
(Richard Fahey) *rrd s: hdwy over 2f out: styd on fnl f to take 3rd nr fin* **5/1**[2]

2541 **4** hd **Mayfield Girl (IRE)**[15] 4071 2-9-4 82 RobertWinston 6 76+
(Mel Brittain) *rrd s: sn outpcd and bhd: hdwy to chse ldrs over 1f out: kpt on same pce last 150yds* **13/2**[3]

421 **5** 4 ½ **Three Crowns**[27] 3669 2-9-7 85 NeilCallan 8 63
(Ian Wood) *sn outpcd and in rr: hdwy over 2f out: chsng ldrs over 1f out: sn wknd* **7/1**

051 **6** 7 **Our Diane (IRE)**[24] 3747 2-8-10 74 DanielTudhope 4 26
(David O'Meara) *trckd ldrs: wknd over 1f out* **9/4**[1]

4012 **7** 6 **Blue Lotus (IRE)**[15] 4071 2-9-1 79 DavidAllan 5
(Tim Easterby) *sn outpcd in rr: hdwy to chse ldrs over 1f out: wknd fnl f: eased* **5/1**[2]

58.21s (-1.09) **Going Correction** -0.25s/f (Firm) **7** Ran SP% **117.1**
Speed ratings (Par 98): **98,95,93,92,85 74,64**
toteswingers 1&2 £16.80, 1&3 £3.60, 2&3 £22.50 CSF £47.16 CT £225.05 TOTE £6.90: £2.20, £5.70; EX 69.80.
Owner Ingham Racing Syndicate **Bred** Whatton Manor Stud **Trained** Middleham Moor, N Yorks

FOCUS
It's still a bit early to be working out how good juvenile handicap form is but the winner did it nicely. The figures make sense.

NOTEBOOK
Lady Poppy, having her first try in that handicaps, blasted out of the stalls and made every yard of the running. She'll always be of some interest on speed-favouring courses. (op 6-1 tchd 13-2)
Bispham Green reversed form with Mayfield Girl and Blue Lotus on their recent meeting after showing pace. He can collect a small race to shed his maiden tag. (op 12-1)
Tatlisu(IRE), not beaten far in the Super Sprint two weeks previously, didn't have a visor on this time but flashed his tail under pressure when staying on, suggesting he isn't completely straightforward. (op 6-1 tchd 7-1)
Mayfield Girl(IRE) got herself detached at one point before staying on well towards the inside rail, and emerges with plenty of credit. (op 6-1)
Three Crowns appeared anchored under her big weight. (op 15-2 tchd 13-2)
Our Diane(IRE) dropped out after racing up with the leader early. (op 2-1 tchd 7-4)
Blue Lotus(IRE) Official explanation: trainer's rep said gelding was unsuited by the good to firm ground
T/Jkpt: Not won. T/Plt: £1,819.80 to a £1 stake. Pool: £177,304.84 - 71.12 winning tickets
T/Qpdt: £330.10 to a £1 stake. Pool: £8632.49 -19.35 winning tickets WG

3884 DEAUVILLE (R-H)
Saturday, July 28

OFFICIAL GOING: Turf: good; fibresand: standard

4615a PRIX SIX PERFECTIONS (LISTED RACE) (2YO FILLIES) (TURF) 7f
4:45 (12:00) 2-Y-0 **£22,916** (£9,166; £6,875; £4,583; £2,291)

RPR

1 **Discernable**[8] 4283 2-9-0 0 IoritzMendizabal 2 99
(Mark Johnston) *broke wl: settled in ld after 1f: shkn up early in st: wnt clr 1f out: r.o wl* **22/5**[3]

2 ¾ **Khadima (FR)**[24] 2-9-0 0 Christophe-PatriceLemaire 1 97
(J-C Rouget, France) **6/4**[1]

3 ½ **Sheistheboss (FR)**[66] 2-9-0 0 ChristopheSoumillon 4 96
(C Lerner, France) **43/10**[2]

4 snk **Grey Perle (FR)**[9] 2-9-0 0 RonanThomas 5 96
(J Heloury, France) **9/1**

5 3 ½ **Zazera (FR)**[17] 2-9-0 0 OlivierPeslier 7 86
(Mario Hofer, Germany) **9/1**

6 nk **Her Star (USA)**[45] 2-9-0 0 StephanePasquier 3 85
(P Bary, France) **5/1**

7 1 ¾ **Riskhana (FR)**[20] 2-9-0 0 AllanBonnefoy 6 81
(F Sanchez, France) **33/1**

1m 27.61s (-0.69) **7** Ran SP% **117.0**
WIN (incl. 1 euro stake): 5.40. PLACES: 2.10, 1.40. SF: 14.60.
Owner Sheikh Hamdan Bin Mohammed Al Maktoum **Bred** Newsells Park Stud **Trained** Middleham Moor, N Yorks

NOTEBOOK
Discernable was up in class but was allowed to dominate and, when asked to quicken, comfortably held off the pack.

4616a PRIX DE PSYCHE (GROUP 3) (3YO FILLIES) (TURF) 1m 2f
5:45 (12:00) 3-Y-0 **£33,333** (£13,333; £10,000; £6,666; £3,333)

RPR

1 **Leaupartie (IRE)**[41] 3203 3-8-11 0 GregoryBenoist 8 107
(F Chappet, France) *settled in 2nd trcking ldr: rdn over 1 1/2f out: qcknd to ld 1f out: r.o wl u.p fnl f: hld on wl* **57/10**[3]

2 ½ **Romantica**[27] 3682 3-8-11 0 MaximeGuyon 5 106
(A Fabre, France) *settled in 3rd: shaklen up early in st: nt qckn immediately: r.o wl u.p ent fnl f: clst at fin* **13/10**[1]

3 snk **Bugie D'Amore**[36] 3328 3-8-11 0 ChristopheSoumillon 3 106
(A De Royer-Dupre, France) *racd in 6th on ins rail: mde gd prog over 1 1/2f out: r.o wl u.p ins fnl f: narrowly missed 2nd* **7/2**[2]

4 4 **Magic Motif (USA)**[31] 3682 3-8-11 0 (b[1]) FlavienPrat 6 98
(A Fabre, France) *led fr s: set gd pce: u.p 1 1/2f out: hdd 1f out: styd on fnl f* **14/1**

5 1 ¾ **Dark Orchid (USA)**[27] 3682 3-8-11 0 Pierre-CharlesBoudot 1 94
(A Fabre, France) *hld up towards rr: rdn 1 1/2f out: no ex: styd on fnl f: nvr a factor* **9/1**

6 *hd* **Falls Of Lora (IRE)**[21] 3879 3-9-2 0........... Christophe-PatriceLemaire 4 99
(Mahmood Al Zarooni) *racd in midfield towards outside: shkn up 2f out: rdn but no ex fr 1 1/2f out: styd on at one pce fnl 150yds* **11/1**
7 *1* **Lady Of Budysin (GER)**[23] 3802 3-8-11 0.................. DavyBonilla 2 92
(Andreas Lowe, Germany) *hld up at rr: swtchd to outside in st: styd on fnl 2f: nvr a factor* **24/1**
8 *6* **Aghareed (USA)**[27] 3-8-11 0.. GeraldMosse 7 80
(J E Hammond, France) *settled in 4th towards outside: rdn 2f out: nt qckn: grad fdd ins fnl f tl eased fnl 100yds* **9/1**

2m 4.3s (-5.90) **8** Ran SP% **119.6**
WIN (incl. 1 euro stake): 6.70. PLACES: 1.40, 1.10, 1.30. DF: 6.40. SF: 13.80.
Owner Gerard Augustin-Normand **Bred** M Henochsberg, Pontchartrain Stud, Haras d'Etreham **Trained** France

NOTEBOOK
Leaupartie(IRE), who was supplemented into the Prix de Diane last month but could only finish sixth, appreciated the drop in grade and quickened up well to score. She has plenty of options but the Opera looks the logical autumn target.
Falls Of Lora(IRE) lacked the required change of gear, but she's possibly more at home over a mile.

4478 SARATOGA (R-H)
Saturday, July 28
OFFICIAL GOING: Turf: good; dirt: sloppy

4617a DIANA STKS (GRADE 1) (3YO+ FILLIES & MARES) (TURF) 1m 1f
10:12 (10:12) 3-Y-0+
£232,258 (£77,419; £38,709; £19,354; £11,612; £7,741)

RPR
1 **Winter Memories (USA)**[49] 2952 4-8-8 0........................ JJCastellano 5 117
(James J Toner, U.S.A) **7/4**[1]
2 *1 ½* **Dream Peace (IRE)**[69] 2327 4-8-6 0................................ JRLeparoux 4 112
(Robert Collet, France) **15/2**
3 *3 ¼* **Zagora (FR)**[70] 5-8-8 0.. RADominguez 3 107
(Chad C Brown, U.S.A) **41/10**
4 *nk* **Tapitsfly (USA)**[49] 2952 5-8-8 0... JRosario 1 106
(Dale Romans, U.S.A) **51/20**[2]
5 *½* **Hungry Island (USA)**[49] 2952 4-8-8 0............................ JRVelazquez 6 105
(Claude McGaughey III, U.S.A) **77/20**[3]
6 *27* **Law Of The Range**[38] 3266 5-8-6 0....................................... RMaragh 2 47
(Marco Botti) **269/10**

1m 48.5s (108.50) **6** Ran SP% **120.1**
PARI-MUTUEL (all including $2 stakes): WIN 5.50; PLACE (1-2) 3.40, 6.40; SHOW (1-2-3) 2.60, 3.70, 3.00; SF 42.20.
Owner Phillips Racing Partnership **Bred** Phillips Racing Partnership **Trained** USA

3490 CARLISLE (R-H)
Sunday, July 29
OFFICIAL GOING: Good (good to soft in places; 7.5)
Wind: Fresh, half against Weather: Cloudy, showers

4618 READ HAYLEY AT RACINGUK.COM EVERY FRIDAY MAIDEN AUCTION STKS 5f 193y
2:10 (2:12) (Class 5) 2-Y-0 **£2,911** (£866; £432; £216) **Stalls** Low

Form RPR
0 1 **Ishigunnaeatit**[79] 2047 2-8-7 0.. LukeMorris 9 72
(Mrs K Burke) *t.k.h: trckd ldrs: hdwy to ld over 1f out: edgd rt ins fnl f: rdn out* **22/1**
02 2 *1 ¼* **Dr Phibes (IRE)**[10] 4257 2-8-9 0...................................... AndrewElliott 8 70
(Alan Swinbank) *hld up: effrt and rdn on outside over 2f out: styd on fnl f to go 2nd towards fin: nt rch wnr* **7/2**[3]
2 3 *nk* **Rocky Two (IRE)**[32] 3491 2-9-1 0................................ PaulMulrennan 1 75
(Michael Dods) *led: rdn and hdd over 1f out: rallied: no ex and lost 2nd towards fin* **2/1**[1]
0 4 *2 ¾* **Byron's Dream**[20] 3611 2-8-9 0...................................... FrederikTylicki 7 60
(Jedd O'Keeffe) *bhd and sn pushed along: hdwy on outside over 2f out: kpt on fnl f: nvr able to chal* **50/1**
50 5 *1 ½* **Unidexter (IRE)**[73] 2213 2-8-12 0.................................... SamHitchcott 6 58
(Mick Channon) *bhd and sn pushed along: hdwy on ins rail over 1f out: kpt on fnl f: nrst fin* **40/1**
32 6 *2 ¼* **Bondesire**[20] 3909 2-8-4 0.. JoeFanning 12 43
(David O'Meara) *in tch on outside: effrt and rdn over 2f out: hung rt and wknd over 1f out* **3/1**[2]
7 *½* **Welliesinthewater (IRE)** 2-8-10 0 ow1.................. GrahamGibbons 5 48
(Derek Shaw) *s.i.s: bhd and outpcd: hung lft and hdwy on wd outside over 2f out: rdn and no imp fnl f* **100/1**
625 8 *2 ¼* **Red Cobra (IRE)**[12] 4178 2-8-9 77..................................... DavidAllan 10 39
(Tim Easterby) *cl up: ev ch over 2f out to over 1f out: wknd ins fnl f* **15/2**
6 9 *4 ½* **By A Wiska**[22] 3842 2-8-12 0.. PhillipMakin 2 28
(Ann Duffield) *trckd ldrs tl rdn and wknd fr 2f out* **25/1**
10 *1 ½* **Don't Tell** 2-8-4 0.. AndrewMullen 11 15
(George Moore) *mounted on crse and keen to post: t.k.h: hld up: rdn over 3f out: wknd fnl 2f* **33/1**
0 11 *¾* **Armada Bay (IRE)**[22] 3844 2-9-1 0............................. RoystonFfrench 3 24
(Bryan Smart) *midfield on ins: rdn and struggling 2f out: sn wknd* **33/1**
U P **Fenwick Gale (IRE)**[48] 2977 2-8-7 0.................................... AmyRyan 4
(Kevin Ryan) *sn lost pl and virtually unrideable: p.u after 1f* **14/1**

1m 14.83s (1.13) **Going Correction** +0.05s/f (Good) **12** Ran SP% **118.5**
Speed ratings (Par 94): **94,92,91,88,86 83,82,79,73,71 70,**
Tote Swingers: 1&2 £13.40, 1&3 £8.00, 2&3 £2.20 CSF £94.12 TOTE £24.20: £5.00, £1.40, £1.10; EX 129.20.
Owner D Redvers & Mrs E Burke **Bred** Redmyre Bloodstock & Sunday Club **Trained** Middleham Moor, N Yorks

FOCUS
A modest juvenile maiden.

NOTEBOOK
Ishigunnaeatit showed the clear benefit of her debut run at Nottingham and relished this better ground. She did well to see it out despite refusing to settle and her future now lies with the handicapper. (op 20-1)
Dr Phibes(IRE) again found one too good, but turned in another solid display and rates the benchmark. Nurseries are now an option. (tchd 4-1)
Rocky Two(IRE) finished second on his debut here last month and he too helps to set the standard of this form. He's now looking more of one for nurseries after his next assignment. (op 5-2)
Byron's Dream wasn't so suited by this drop in trip, but it was still an improved effort in defeat and he needs one more outing before qualifying for nurseries. (op 80-1)
Bondesire got little cover and hung-fire when asked for maximum effort. She now has something to prove. (op 11-4)

4619 GOOD LUCK TEAM GB H'CAP 5f
2:40 (2:41) (Class 5) (0-70,70) 3-Y-0 **£2,911** (£866; £432; £216) **Stalls** Low

Form RPR
-233 1 **Majestic Manannan (IRE)**[5] 4428 3-8-13 60................ AndrewMullen 6 74
(David Nicholls) *t.k.h: mde all: rdn over 1f out: kpt on strly fnl f* **7/2**[2]
2641 2 *3* **Ghazeer (IRE)**[31] 3540 3-8-13 60.......................................(v) JoeFanning 2 63
(Derek Shaw) *trckd ldrs: effrt and wnt 2nd over 1f out: kpt on fnl f: nt pce of wnr* **6/1**
531 3 *2 ¼* **Tinzapeas**[3] 4509 3-9-9 70 6ex.......................................(v) SamHitchcott 4 65
(Mick Channon) *in tch: pushed along over 3f out: effrt on outside over 1f out: kpt on fnl f: nvr able to chal* **9/2**
2314 4 *shd* **Gowanharry (IRE)**[11] 4208 3-9-7 68.............................. PaulMulrennan 9 63
(Michael Dods) *chsd wnr to over 1f out: sn rdn and one pce* **4/1**[3]
0542 5 *2 ½* **Script**[21] 3892 3-8-2 49 oh3.. LukeMorris 7 35
(Alan Berry) *hld up bhd ldng gp: rdn 1/2-way: effrt over 1f out: no imp fnl f* **20/1**
0-51 6 *1 ¾* **Holy Angel (IRE)**[12] 4174 3-8-13 60.................................... DavidAllan 5 39
(Tim Easterby) *dwlt and pckd sn after s: bhd and pushed along: hdwy 1/2-way: no further imp over 1f out* **11/4**[1]
146- 7 *7* **Twilight Allure**[213] 7905 3-9-2 66.....................................(t) JulieBurke[(3)] 8 20
(Kevin Ryan) *hld up on outside: drvn and effrt over 2f out: wknd over 1f out* **20/1**
4-60 8 *2 ¼* **Lowtherwood**[65] 2460 3-8-5 52..................................(p) RoystonFfrench 1
(Bryan Smart) *prom tl rdn and wknd 1/2-way* **33/1**

1m 1.3s (0.50) **Going Correction** +0.05s/f (Good) **8** Ran SP% **113.8**
Speed ratings (Par 100): **98,93,89,89,85 82,71,67**
Tote Swingers: 1&2 £4.70, 1&3 £4.10, 2&3 £6.20 CSF £23.68 CT £94.68 TOTE £4.40: £1.40, £2.60, £2.10; EX 27.90.
Owner Mark & Maureen Schofield **Bred** Curlew Partnership **Trained** Sessay, N Yorks

FOCUS
A moderate sprint handicap.

4620 GRAFIX SIGNS CLAIMING STKS 7f 200y
3:10 (3:10) (Class 6) 3-Y-0+ **£2,070** (£616; £307; £153) **Stalls** Low

Form RPR
0503 1 **Mirrored**[29] 3609 6-9-12 86.. DuranFentiman 3 81
(Tim Easterby) *hld up in midfield: hdwy on outside over 2f out: led over 1f out: edgd rt: kpt on wl* **7/2**[2]
0523 2 *3 ¼* **Abidhabidubai**[23] 3810 4-8-9 74.................................... KevinLundie[(7)] 5 64
(John Quinn) *hld up in tch: effrt and rdn over 2f out: chsd wnr ent fnl f: kpt on: no imp* **10/1**
-000 3 *¾* **City Of The Kings (IRE)**[39] 3287 7-9-12 83...........(p) PaulMulrennan 10 72
(Ollie Pears) *trckd ldrs on outside: rdn to ld 2f out: hdd over 1f out: kpt on same pce ins fnl f* **14/1**
2401 4 *shd* **Kay Gee Be (IRE)**[23] 3810 8-9-5 85.............................. ShaneBKelly[(5)] 6 70
(Richard Fahey) *midfield: drvn and outpcd over 3f out: rallied over 1f out: kpt on fnl f: nvr able to chal* **85/40**[1]
3033 5 *nk* **Rasselas (IRE)**[9] 4295 5-9-0 57............................(v) ShirleyTeasdale[(7)] 9 66
(David Nicholls) *in tch: rdn and hung lft over 2f out: kpt on same pce fnl f* **40/1**
6034 6 *nk* **Moheebb (IRE)**[12] 4175 8-9-2 70................................(be) PhillipMakin 12 60
(Ruth Carr) *hld up: rdn over 3f out: hdwy wl over 1f out: nvr able to chal* **9/2**[3]
0-5 7 *4 ½* **Shayla**[6] 4407 5-8-10 68.. AndrewElliott 11 44
(Alan Swinbank) *s.i.s: bhd: rdn over 3f out: hdwy over 1f out: nrst fin* **28/1**
4024 8 *6* **River Ardeche**[36] 3405 7-9-0 63.................................... PaulPickard[(3)] 4 37
(Tracy Waggott) *trckd ldrs tl rdn and wknd wl over 1f out* **40/1**
-405 9 *7* **Monthly Medal**[21] 3888 9-8-12 56..................................(t) DominicFox[(3)] 1 19
(Wilf Storey) *slt ld to 2f out: sn rdn and wknd* **50/1**
0105 10 *2 ¾* **Miami Gator (IRE)**[20] 3911 5-9-8 80....................(v) MichaelMetcalfe[(3)] 7 23
(Mrs K Burke) *disp ld to 2f out: sn rdn and wknd* **7/1**
50 11 *shd* **Little Thief**[11] 4207 5-8-10 0.. DavidAllan 8 8
(Iain Jardine) *hld up: struggling over 3f out: sn btn* **200/1**
100- 12 *2* **Shotley Mac**[288] 6868 8-9-2 75....................................... JulieBurke[(3)] 2 12
(Neville Bycroft) *bhd: drvn over 4f out: nvr on terms* **25/1**

1m 39.49s (-0.51) **Going Correction** +0.05s/f (Good) **12** Ran SP% **115.3**
Speed ratings (Par 101): **104,100,100,99,99 99,94,88,81,79 78,76**
Tote Swingers: 1&2 £25.40, 1&3 £7.20, 2&3 £15.10 CSF £34.72 TOTE £6.20: £1.80, £2.90, £5.90; EX 44.90.
Owner Middleham Park Racing XXX **Bred** Millsec Limited **Trained** Great Habton, N Yorks

FOCUS
A fair claimer.
Shotley Mac Official explanation: trainer's rep said gelding bled from the nose

4621 CARLISLE BOWL H'CAP 1m 3f 107y
3:40 (3:40) (Class 4) (0-85,85) 3-Y-0+ **£5,175** (£1,540; £769; £384) **Stalls** High

Form RPR
2232 1 **New Hampshire (USA)**[10] 4249 4-9-10 84.................... LeeTopliss[(3)] 8 93
(Tony Coyle) *trckd ldrs: rdn to ld over 2f out: hld on wl fnl f* **13/2**
0660 2 *¾* **Northside Prince (IRE)**[32] 3494 6-9-9 85.............. GarryWhillans[(5)] 12 93
(Alan Swinbank) *hld up: rdn and hdwy on outside over 2f out: edgd rt over 1f out: styd on to take 2nd towards fin* **20/1**
3206 3 *¾* **Eltheeb**[32] 3494 5-9-11 82.. GrahamGibbons 7 88
(David O'Meara) *in tch: effrt and rdn over 2f out: chsd wnr and hung rt over 1f out: kpt on ins fnl f: lost 2nd towards fin* **9/2**[2]
1-00 4 *2 ¾* **Ultimate**[8] 4347 6-9-5 79.. PaulPickard[(3)] 11 81
(Brian Ellison) *cl up: led after 2f tl over 2f out: sn drvn: kpt on same pce fr over 1f out* **33/1**
-411 5 *1* **Just Lille (IRE)**[29] 3609 9-10-0 85......................................(p) AmyRyan 3 85
(Ann Duffield) *prom: rdn and outpcd wl over 2f out: rallied appr fnl f: no imp* **10/1**
1F44 6 *¾* **Star Date (IRE)**[15] 4103 3-9-0 82.. LukeMorris 1 81
(Gerard Butler) *hld up: drvn along on ins over 2f out: no imp over 1f out* **11/4**[1]
112 7 *1 ¼* **Bright Applause**[15] 4080 4-9-1 72................................ FrederikTylicki 9 69
(Tracy Waggott) *trckd ldrs: effrt and rdn over 2f out: outpcd appr fnl f* **10/1**

2210 **8** *5* **Entihaa**[32] 3494 4-9-8 **79** AndrewElliott 5 67
(Alan Swinbank) *hld up: rdn along over 3f out: nvr able to chal* **22/1**

0534 **9** *7* **Snow Dancer (IRE)**[55] 2751 8-9-6 **77** PaulMulrennan 4 53
(Hugh McWilliams) *bhd: drvn along over 4f out: nvr on terms* **14/1**

4-52 **10** *3 1/4* **Ravi River (IRE)**[5] 4429 8-8-13 **70** PhillipMakin 13 41
(Alistair Whillans) *cl up on outside tl rdn: edgd rt and wknd 2f out* **28/1**

0102 **11** *19* **Dark Dune (IRE)**[8] 4326 4-9-8 **79** DavidAllan 6 17
(Tim Easterby) *hld up: drvn along over 3f out: sn struggling: t.o* **11/2**[3]

6 **12** *5* **Pirate Chest (IRE)**[46] 3038 4-9-6 **77** DuranFentiman 10
(Patrick Holmes) *t.k.h: midfield on outside: struggling over 4f out: sn btn: t.o* **40/1**

2m 24.37s (1.27) **Going Correction** +0.05s/f (Good)
WFA 3 from 4yo+ 11lb 12 Ran SP% **116.4**
Speed ratings (Par 105): **97,96,95,93,93 92,91,88,83,80 66,63**
Tote Swingers: 1&2 £25.40, 1&3 £7.20, 2&3 £15.10 CSF £133.13 CT £646.03 TOTE £6.70: £2.40, £5.20, £2.10; EX 130.70.
Owner B Dunn **Bred** Everest Stables Inc **Trained** Norton, N Yorks

FOCUS
A fair handicap, run at a sound pace.
Dark Dune(IRE) Official explanation: jockey said gelding ran flat

4622 GET FREE BETS AT FREEBETTING.CO.UK MAIDEN STKS 1m 1f 61y
4:10 (4:11) (Class 5) 3-Y-0+ **£2,911** (£866; £432; £216) **Stalls** Low

Form RPR
4-22 **1** **Commend**[70] 2313 3-9-3 82 RyanMoore 6 88+
(Sir Michael Stoute) *trckd ldrs: smooth hdwy to ld over 2f out: shkn up and edgd rt over 1f out: pushed clr: comf* **2/5**[1]

44 **2** *5* **Urban Daydream (IRE)**[7] 4366 3-8-12 0 NeilCallan 11 72+
(Roger Varian) *t.k.h: prom: effrt and rdn over 2f out: rallied and edgd rt over 1f out: chsd (clr) wnr ins fnl f: r.o* **9/2**[2]

2336 **3** *3/4* **Regal Swain (IRE)**[8] 4325 4-9-12 73 JoeFanning 7 76
(Alan Swinbank) *led: rdn and hdd over 2f out: sn one pce: lost 2nd ins fnl f* **5/1**[3]

60 **4** *6* **Jim Tango (FR)**[10] 4259 8-9-12 0 (bt) PaulMulrennan 1 63
(Brian Storey) *dwlt: hld up: rdn and hdwy 2f out: kpt on fnl f: no imp* **100/1**

044 **5** *4 1/2* **Artistic Dawn (IRE)**[31] 3521 3-8-12 69 LukeMorris 9 47
(John Weymes) *plld hrd early: in tch: drvn over 4f out: outpcd over 2f out: n.d after* **25/1**

60 **6** *hd* **Seagoing**[46] 3035 3-8-12 0 DavidAllan 4 46
(Tim Easterby) *plld hrd: hld up: rdn and outpcd over 3f out: n.d after* **25/1**

4 **7** *1 3/4* **Maska Pony (IRE)**[9] 4293 8-9-12 0 PhillipMakin 8 49
(George Moore) *hld up: drvn along and shortlived effrt on outside wl over 2f out: sn btn* **12/1**

- **8** *4 1/2* **Dancing Paddy (IRE)** 4-9-7 0 GarryWhillans(5) 10 39
(Alan Swinbank) *sn pressing ldr: drvn and edgd lft over 2f out: sn btn* **25/1**

06 **9** *2 1/2* **Tomasini**[55] 2774 3-9-3 0 DuranFentiman 2 32
(John Weymes) *hld up on ins: struggling over 3f out: sn btn* **125/1**

6 **10** *4* **Mountain Summit**[36] 3384 3-8-9 0 LeeTopliss(3) 3 18
(Richard Fahey) *midfield on ins: rdn after 3f: struggling over 3f out: sn btn* **40/1**

1m 57.64s (0.04) **Going Correction** +0.05s/f (Good)
WFA 3 from 4yo+ 9lb 10 Ran SP% **129.7**
Speed ratings (Par 103): **101,96,95,90,86 86,84,80,78,75**
Tote Swingers: 1&2 £1.50, 1&3 £1.80, 2&3 £3.30 CSF £3.11 TOTE £1.50: £1.10, £1.60, £1.10; EX 3.00.
Owner Highclere Thoroughbred Racing-Rock Sand **Bred** Cheveley Park Stud Ltd **Trained** Newmarket, Suffolk

FOCUS
A modest maiden and the winner won as he was entitled to.

4623 ULTIMATE LADIES NIGHT ON AUGUST 6TH H'CAP 1m 1f 61y
4:40 (4:40) (Class 5) (0-70,69) 3-Y-0 **£2,911** (£866; £432; £216) **Stalls** Low

Form RPR
5005 **1** **Bountiful Girl**[20] 3906 3-9-4 **66** FrederikTylicki 2 78
(Richard Fahey) *trckd ldrs: effrt and swtchd lft over 1f out: sn led: rdn and edgd lft ins fnl f: kpt on wl* **3/1**[2]

011- **2** *3/4* **Docs Legacy (IRE)**[274] 7157 3-9-2 **69** ShaneBKelly(5) 1 79
(Richard Fahey) *hld up in tch: effrt on outside over 2f out: rdn and ev ch whn rdr dropped whip appr fnl f: struck over face by rivals whip ins fnl f: kpt on* **9/2**[3]

-645 **3** *7* **Baltic Fizz (IRE)**[58] 2672 3-9-1 **66** MichaelMetcalfe(3) 7 61
(Mrs K Burke) *hld up: drvn along over 3f out: kpt on fnl f: no ch w first two* **10/1**

1413 **4** *3/4* **Fine Altomis**[26] 3727 3-9-4 **69** LeeTopliss(3) 8 62
(Michael Dods) *t.k.h: pressed ldr: led over 2f out to over 1f out: sn outpcd* **9/4**[1]

06-0 **5** *9* **Last Zak**[39] 3275 3-7-13 **50** oh3 JulieBurke(3) 4 24
(Michael Easterby) *in tch: drvn and outpcd over 3f out: sn n.d* **25/1**

04-1 **6** *1 1/2* **Forster Street (IRE)**[12] 4172 3-9-3 **65** GrahamGibbons 6 35
(Tim Easterby) *t.k.h: led to over 2f out: wknd over 1f out* **3/1**[2]

160- **7** *10* **Artlana**[244] 7568 3-8-8 **56** AmyRyan 5
(Julie Camacho) *plld hrd: cl up: rn wd first bnd over 8f out: rdn and wknd fr 2f out* **25/1**

1m 57.48s (-0.12) **Going Correction** +0.05s/f (Good) 7 Ran SP% **115.7**
Speed ratings (Par 100): **102,101,95,94,86 85,76**
Tote Swingers: 1&2 £3.60, 1&3 £4.70, 2&3 £3.20 CSF £17.33 CT £115.47 TOTE £4.70: £2.90, £2.00; EX 20.90.
Owner D W Barker **Bred** E J Harper & Whitsbury Manor Stud **Trained** Musley Bank, N Yorks

FOCUS
A moderate handicap in which the first pair, both stablemates, came well clear.
Forster Street(IRE) Official explanation: trainer had no explanation for the poor form shown

4624 EDINBURGH WOOLLEN MILL H'CAP 6f 192y
5:10 (5:20) (Class 5) (0-75,75) 3-Y-0+ **£2,911** (£866; £432; £216) **Stalls** Low

Form RPR
2132 **1** **Hayek**[9] 4295 5-9-0 **66** (b) AdamCarter(5) 4 74
(Tim Easterby) *hld up: rdn and hdwy on outside over 2f out: led ins fnl f: idled: hld on* **3/1**[2]

3-05 **2** *hd* **Amoure Medici**[39] 3284 3-9-2 **70** RoystonFfrench 7 75
(Ann Duffield) *plld hrd: hld up in tch: hdwy to ld over 1f out: hdd ins fnl f: rallied: kpt on* **18/1**

4221 **3** *nse* **Horatio Carter**[20] 3914 7-9-11 **72** GrahamGibbons 11 79
(David O'Meara) *t.k.h: cl up on outside: effrt and disp ld over 1f out to ins fnl f: kpt on: hld cl home* **15/8**[1]

0455 **4** *6* **Clumber Place**[25] 3749 6-9-0 **61** JoeFanning 9 52
(James Given) *led: rdn and hdd over 1f out: wknd ins fnl f* **8/1**

2645 **5** *1 1/2* **Dubious Escapade (IRE)**[18] 3952 3-9-1 **69** PaulMulrennan 6 54
(Ann Duffield) *prom tl rdn and wknd over 1f out* **7/1**

42 **6** *4 1/2* **Rigolleto (IRE)**[10] 4255 4-9-13 **74** SamHitchcott 10 49
(Mick Channon) *cl up: drvn over 2f out: wknd over 1f out* **7/2**[3]

6-50 **7** *nk* **Nasharra (IRE)**[13] 4135 4-9-8 **69** PhillipMakin 1 43
(Kevin Ryan) *trckd ldrs tl rdn and wknd fr 2f out* **25/1**

1m 26.87s (-0.23) **Going Correction** +0.05s/f (Good)
WFA 3 from 4yo+ 7lb 7 Ran SP% **114.7**
Speed ratings (Par 103): **103,102,102,95,94 89,88**
Tote Swingers: 1&2 £9.10, 1&3 £2.20, 2&3 £6.70 CSF £51.66 CT £125.77 TOTE £3.70: £2.30, £5.20; EX 23.30.
Owner Numac Engineering Ltd **Bred** Cranford Stud **Trained** Great Habton, N Yorks

FOCUS
This looked competitive enough and the form should work out.
T/Plt: £80.30 to a £1 stake. Pool: £69,968.98 - 635.38 winning tickets. T/Qpdt: £23.60 to a £1 stake. Pool: £4,175.67 - 130.70 winning tickets. RY

4310 PONTEFRACT (L-H)
Sunday, July 29

OFFICIAL GOING: Good to firm (8.5)
Wind: moderate 1/2 behind Weather: fine, showers

4625 YORKSHIRE.COM BACK LE BID MAIDEN STKS 5f
2:20 (2:21) (Class 4) 2-Y-0 **£4,398** (£1,309; £654; £327) **Stalls** Low

Form RPR
40 **1** **Ziggy's Secret**[17] 4011 2-8-12 0 EddieAhern 10 74
(Lucy Wadham) *trckd ldrs: t.k.h: led jst ins fnl f: pushed out* **11/4**[2]

03 **2** *1* **Shillito**[17] 3989 2-9-3 0 BarryMcHugh 7 75
(Tony Coyle) *w ldr: led over 1f out: hdd and no ex ins fnl f* **7/1**[3]

3 *1* **Moviesta (USA)** 2-9-3 0 TomEaves 9 71+
(Bryan Smart) *trckd ldrs on outer: drvn over 2f out: sn outpcd: styd on fnl f: will improve* **9/4**[1]

002 **4** *2 1/4* **Pippy**[48] 2970 2-9-3 0 RichardKingscote 3 63
(Tom Dascombe) *chsd ldrs: one pce appr fnl f* **7/1**[3]

0 **5** *1/2* **Multisure**[12] 4178 2-9-3 0 PatrickMathers 2 62
(Richard Fahey) *mid-div: kpt on fnl 2f* **22/1**

040 **6** *1 1/4* **Colours Of Nature**[39] 3286 2-9-3 62 ShaneKelly 6 57
(Eric Alston) *led tl over 1f out: wknd fnl 150yds* **25/1**

7 *8* **Annalova** 2-8-12 0 TonyHamilton 1 23+
(Richard Fahey) *s.s: nvr on terms* **9/1**

04 **8** *hd* **Purple Day**[22] 3844 2-9-3 0 MickyFenton 4 27
(Pam Sly) *mid-div: outpcd over 2f out: wknd over 1f out* **22/1**

9 *2 3/4* **Knockamany Bends (IRE)** 2-9-3 0 PaddyAspell 5 18
(John Wainwright) *prom: lost pl over 2f out* **100/1**

10 *6* **Black Truffle (FR)** 2-9-3 0 HayleyTurner 8
(Michael Bell) *dwlt: sn chsng ldrs: lost pl over 2f out: sn bhd* **10/1**

1m 3.46s (0.16) **Going Correction** -0.05s/f (Good) 10 Ran SP% **115.1**
Speed ratings (Par 96): **96,94,92,89,88 86,73,73,68,59**
Tote Swingers: 1&2 £5.90, 1&3 £2.90, 2&3 £6.60 CSF £20.95 TOTE £3.50: £1.30, £2.30, £1.70; EX 23.30 Trifecta £83.30 Pool: £336.91 - 2.99 winning units..
Owner Mr And Mrs A E Pakenham **Bred** Honeypuddle Stud **Trained** Newmarket, Suffolk

FOCUS
Probably only a fair maiden to start the meeting off with, on ground that had dried out to good to firm.

NOTEBOOK
Ziggy's Secret, the best of these on RPRs, took this nicely after being well positioned throughout. One would imagine handicaps are next for her. A return to 6f won't be a problem. (op 10-3 tchd 7-2)
Shillito, taking another step down in distance, unsurprisingly raced prominently and was always going to see out the trip. He's another who will presumably head to nurseries now. (op 9-2)
Moviesta(USA) ◆, who cost 44,000gns in April, attracted market support and ran okay but ultimately looked too green on debut. He should come on mentally and will be better assessed after his next start. (op 7-2)
Pippy stayed on from midfield but never threatened to get to the front. (op 5-1)
Colours Of Nature showed good pace until about 1f out. He might be of interest in a low-grade contest at a sharp track.
Annalova, whose dam's only victory came in 1m2f seller, lost all chance with a slow start. (op 12-1)
Black Truffle(FR), who is out of 1m1f AW winning half-sister to top-class Primo Valentino, didn't show much after emerging from a wide draw but should derive plenty of improvement for the outing. (op 8-1 tchd 15-2)

4626 MOOR TOP FARM SHOP HEMSWORTH H'CAP 1m 4f 8y
2:50 (2:53) (Class 5) (0-70,70) 3-Y-0+ **£2,911** (£866; £432; £216) **Stalls** Low

Form RPR
0003 **1** **Song Of The Siren**[9] 4311 4-9-9 **65** DanielTudhope 4 78
(David O'Meara) *mde all: qcknd over 2f out: drvn out: unchal* **14/1**

6231 **2** *3 1/4* **Mr Snoozy**[27] 3697 3-8-6 **60** PJMcDonald 12 68
(Tim Walford) *trckd ldrs: wnt 2nd over 2f out: kpt on: no imp* **4/1**[1]

3-04 **3** *3 1/2* **Pinotage**[37] 3353 4-9-7 **63** GrahamLee 1 65
(Peter Niven) *s.i.s: hld up in rr: hdwy 4f out: struck over hd by rival rdr's whip appr fnl f: styd on to take 3rd last 100yds* **9/1**[3]

6253 **4** *1/2* **Anna's Arch (IRE)**[25] 3750 5-10-0 **70** RobertWinston 5 71
(Alan Swinbank) *trckd ldrs: wnt 3rd over 1f out: one pce* **14/1**

-254 **5** *4 1/2* **Mafeteng**[53] 2814 4-9-7 **63** TomQueally 6 57
(John Dunlop) *in rr: effrt over 2f out: nvr nr ldrs* **14/1**

105 **6** *3 1/2* **Artisan**[3] 4499 4-9-11 **67** BarryMcHugh 2 56
(Brian Ellison) *hld up in rr: effrt on ins 3f out: nvr nr ldrs* **13/2**[2]

0040 **7** *1* **Mazij**[27] 3704 4-9-11 **67** ShaneKelly 8 54
(Peter Hiatt) *chsd ldrs: drvn over 2f out: wknd over 1f out* **28/1**

3204 **8** *3/4* **Coax**[25] 3753 4-8-13 **60** NeilFarley(5) 9 46
(Patrick Holmes) *hld up in mid-div: effrt over 2f out: nvr a factor* **16/1**

6613 **9** *1 1/2* **Fleeting Fashion**[11] 4210 3-8-3 **57** DavidProbert 11 40
(Michael Appleby) *chsd ldrs: lost pl 2f out: eased over 1f out* **13/2**[2]

562 **10** *2 1/2* **Maid Of Meft**[34] 3449 5-9-6 **62** MickyFenton 13 41
(Paul Midgley) *s.i.s: nvr on terms* **20/1**

2-22 **11** *shd* **Falcun**[36] 3402 5-9-2 **58** (p) TomEaves 7 37
(Micky Hammond) *s.i.s: bhd and sn drvn along: nvr on terms* **10/1**

6422 **12** *3* **Tobrata**[9] 4314 6-8-12 **61** RobertDodsworth(7) 10 35
(Mel Brittain) *in rr: hdwy on outer 5f out: lost pl over 2f out* **16/1**

2-00 **13** *2 1/2* **Singzak**[30] 3564 4-9-12 **68** PaddyAspell 15 38
(Michael Easterby) *chsd ldrs: lost pl over 2f out* **12/1**

0004 **14** *10* **Hyson**^{31} [3543] 3-8-13 **67**.. RussKennemore 14 21
(Reg Hollinshead) *mid-div: sn drvn along: lost pl over 3f out: sn bhd* **16/1**

2m 36.99s (-3.81) **Going Correction** -0.30s/f (Firm)
WFA 3 from 4yo+ 12lb **14** Ran SP% **119.3**
Speed ratings (Par 103): **100,97,95,95,92 89,89,88,87,86 85,83,82,75**
Tote Swingers: 1&2 £11.20, 1&3 £42.70, 2&3 £11.60 CSF £68.46 CT £548.58 TOTE £19.70: £6.60, £1.60, £3.90; EX 51.40 Trifecta £312.50 Part won. Pool: £422.38 - 0.73 winning units..
Owner George Leggott & John Haydock **Bred** Miss K Rausing **Trained** Nawton, N Yorks

FOCUS
Nothing more than a modest event, in which the winner led from start to finish.
Fleeting Fashion Official explanation: trainer sasid filly was unsuited by the good to firm ground

4627 GRAHAM ROCK MEMORIAL H'CAP — 1m 2f 6y
3:20 (3:23) (Class 5) (0-70,68) 3-Y-O+ **£2,911** (£866; £432; £216) **Stalls** Low

Form RPR
0025 **1** **Painted Tail (IRE)**^{27} [3704] 5-9-11 **66**.......................... RobertWinston 2 75
(Alan Swinbank) *hld up in mid-div on inner: nt clr run over 3f out tl over 2f out: styd on to ld ins fnl f: drvn out* **13/2**^{3}
-201 **2** *1 ¼* **Honoured (IRE)**^{8} [4349] 5-9-6 **61**....................................(t) TomQueally 9 68
(Michael Appleby) *trckd ldrs: led 1f out: hdd and no ex last 100yds* **11/2**^{2}
-321 **3** *1 ¼* **Circle Of Angels**^{29} [3616] 4-9-9 **64**........................... JamieSpencer 5 69
(Ian Williams) *dwlt: hld up in rr: hdwy and swtchd wd outside over 1f out: styd on to take 3rd last 100yds: nt rch 1st 2* **3/1**^{1}
0525 **4** *1 ¾* **Tenhoo**^{16} [4048] 6-9-6 **68**.. JasonHart$^{(7)}$ 8 69
(Eric Alston) *stdd s: hld up: hdwy 6f out: swtchd outside over 2f out: kpt on fnl f: tk 4th last 50yds* **7/1**
-500 **5** *1 ½* **Dream Win**^{13} [4142] 6-9-7 **65**.. DaleSwift$^{(3)}$ 1 63
(Brian Ellison) *led: hdd 1f out: fdd last 100yds* **11/2**^{2}
4002 **6** *3* **Border Bandit (USA)**^{8} [4349] 4-9-5 **60**.......................... PaddyAspell 10 52
(Tracy Waggott) *trckd ldrs: drvn 3f out: wknd fnl f* **16/1**
-000 **7** *¾* **Mr Perceptive (IRE)**^{27} [3693] 4-9-10 **65**....................(p) PJMcDonald 4 55
(Micky Hammond) *mid-div: effrt over 2f out: nvr trbld ldrs* **16/1**
-001 **8** *3 ½* **Master Of Song**^{62} [2555] 5-9-3 **63**............................(p) MarkCoumbe$^{(5)}$ 6 46
(Roy Bowring) *mid-div: effrt over 2f out: sn chsng ldrs: wknd over 1f out* **10/1**
-500 **9** *1 ½* **Betteras Bertie**^{61} [2593] 9-9-8 **63**................................(p) BarryMcHugh 12 43
(Tony Coyle) *s.i.s: swtchd lft after s: kpt on fnl 2f: nvr on terms* **25/1**
6045 **10** *1 ½* **My Mate Jake (IRE)**^{38} [3309] 4-9-5 **60**.........................(b) GrahamLee 3 37
(James Given) *chsd ldrs: effrt over 2f out: lost pl over 1f out* **16/1**
0600 **11** *22* **Wiseman's Diamond (USA)**^{20} [3914] 7-9-9 **64**..........(p) MickyFenton 11
(Paul Midgley) *chsd ldrs: drvn over 3f out: lost pl over 2f out: sn eased and bhd: t.o* **25/1**

2m 12.52s (-1.18) **Going Correction** -0.30s/f (Firm) **11** Ran SP% **116.0**
Speed ratings (Par 103): **92,91,90,88,87 85,84,81,80,79 61**
Tote Swingers: 1&2 £6.70, 1&3 £3.80, 2&3 £2.30 CSF £41.56 CT £127.79 TOTE £7.60: £2.60, £1.90, £1.50; EX 54.20 Trifecta £183.00 Pool: £798.80 - 3.23 winning units..
Owner Matthew Green **Bred** Rabbah Bloodstock Limited **Trained** Melsonby, N Yorks

FOCUS
The leaders didn't seem to go a great pace but plenty of these look tired once in the home straight.
Circle Of Angels ◆ Official explanation: jockey said filly was slowly away

4628 SKYBET SUPPORTING YORKSHIRE RACING SUMMER FESTIVAL POMFRET STKS (LISTED RACE) — 1m 4y
3:50 (3:51) (Class 1) 3-Y-O+
£18,714 (£7,095; £3,550; £1,768; £887; £445) **Stalls** Low

Form RPR
3013 **1** **Highland Knight (IRE)**^{29} [3640] 5-9-1 **104**....................(t) DavidProbert 9 113
(Andrew Balding) *trckd ldr: effrt on ins 2f out: r.o to ld last 100yds* **10/1**
1-30 **2** *1 ½* **Rugged Cross**^{57} [2705] 3-8-7 **104**................................. FergusSweeney 6 108+
(Henry Candy) *hld up in mid-div: effrt over 2f out: checked 100yds out: styd on to take 2nd nr fin* **10/3**^{2}
20-6 **3** *nk* **Set The Trend**^{8} [4320] 6-9-1 **110**................................... DanielTudhope 1 109
(David O'Meara) *set str pce: hdd and no ex ins fnl f* **5/2**^{1}
0040 **4** *nse* **Bannock (IRE)**^{8} [4321] 3-8-7 **107**...................................... FrannyNorton 4 108
(Mark Johnston) *trckd ldrs: wnt 3rd over 2f out: almost upsides whn swvd rt 100yds out: kpt on nr fin* **15/2**
1-21 **5** *2 ¾* **Prince Of Johanne (IRE)**^{39} [3268] 6-9-1 **106**....................(p) JohnFahy 5 102
(Tom Tate) *towards rr: hdwy on outer over 4f out: outpcd over 2f out: hdwy over 1f out: keeping on same pce whn checked and rdr dropped whip 100yds out: eased nr fin* **10/3**^{2}
-232 **6** *½* **Ladys First**^{22} [3879] 3-8-2 **100**.. PatrickMathers 8 94
(Richard Fahey) *chsd ldrs: drvn 3f out: one pce over 1f out* **7/1**^{3}
2656 **7** *14* **St Moritz (IRE)**^{10} [4248] 6-9-1 **102**...............................(p) AdrianNicholls 2 76
(David Nicholls) *strated slowly: a last: drvn 3f out: nvr on terms: heavily eased last 75yds* **28/1**

1m 41.24s (-4.66) **Going Correction** -0.30s/f (Firm)
WFA 3 from 4yo+ 8lb **7** Ran SP% **111.5**
Speed ratings (Par 111): **111,109,109,109,106 105,91**
Tote Swingers: 1&2 £3.90, 1&3 £12.40, 2&3 £2.80 CSF £41.05 TOTE £11.60: £6.20, £3.80; EX 51.40 Trifecta £278.30 Pool: £850.23 - 2.26 winning units..
Owner J C Smith **Bred** Littleton Stud **Trained** Kingsclere, Hants

FOCUS
With plenty of runners who like to force the pace, this was always going to be a well-run affair.

NOTEBOOK
Highland Knight(IRE) can make the running but David Probert was happy to take a lead on his mount before staying on really strongly up the inside rail. The Group 2 Darley Oettingen-Rennen in late August is a possible target for the gelding. (tchd 12-1)
Rugged Cross ◆, absent since finishing down the field in the Epsom Derby, looked the most interesting runner but didn't really get going until it was all too late. That said, it was still a good performance and he should have more to come. (op 5-2 tchd 7-2)
Set The Trend shaped respectably on his first start for David O'Meara at Ascot recently and got a fairly easy lead here before being swallowed up. It's entirely possible that this came too soon after his seasonal return, as he should have been good enough at these weights to hold on considering the position he held turning in. (op 4-1 tchd 9-2)
Bannock(IRE) has been running quite well as a 3yo without getting his head to the front, and looked poised to go really close again until jinking right about half a furlong out. The fact he finished fourth suggests he wouldn't have won even had he remained straight. (op 7-1 tchd 8-1)
Prince Of Johanne(IRE), the Royal Hunt Cup winner, was being ridden along over 3f out and then got hampered by the errant Bannock, causing John Fahy to lose his whip. He was just in front of the runner-up at that point, keeping on. (op 3-1 tchd 11-4)

4629 TYREGIANT.COM H'CAP — 6f
4:20 (4:20) (Class 3) (0-90,90) 3-Y-O+
£8,092 (£2,423; £1,211; £605; £302; £152) **Stalls** Low

Form RPR
0430 **1** **Orbit The Moon (IRE)**^{13} [4135] 4-9-0 **78**.........................(tp) TomEaves 11 85
(Michael Dods) *chsd ldrs on outer: led 100yds out: all out* **20/1**
1040 **2** *shd* **Solar Spirit (IRE)**^{15} [4078] 7-9-5 **83**................................... FrannyNorton 4 90
(Tracy Waggott) *trckd ldrs: upsides fnl 100yds: jst denied* **20/1**
22 **3** *1 ¼* **My Kingdom (IRE)**^{3} [4503] 6-9-7 **85**..............................(t) JamieSpencer 1 88+
(Ian Williams) *s.o: on mid-div: chsng ldrs over 1f out: nt clr run jst ins fnl f: swtchd lft and kpt on wl to snatch 3rd post* **7/4**^{1}
1605 **4** *nse* **Damika (IRE)**^{8} [4337] 9-9-8 **86**....................................(v) MichaelStainton 9 89
(David Brown) *w ldrs: led over 1f out: hdd last 100yds: no ex* **12/1**^{3}
0416 **5** *½* **Beckermet (IRE)**^{9} [4286] 10-9-10 **88**................................. PJMcDonald 2 89
(Ruth Carr) *chsd ldrs on inner: kpt on same pce fnl f* **10/1**^{2}
0041 **6** *¾* **Johannes (IRE)**^{29} [3612] 9-9-4 **89**.......................... GeorgeChaloner$^{(7)}$ 13 88
(Richard Fahey) *chsd ldrs: kpt on same pce appr fnl f* **12/1**^{3}
0020 **7** *1* **Fred Willetts (IRE)**^{15} [4077] 4-9-0 **85**................(v) DavidSimmonson$^{(7)}$ 7 80
(Tony Coyle) *w ldrs: wknd fnl 50yds* **18/1**
140 **8** *1 ½* **Close To The Edge (IRE)**^{18} [3960] 4-9-1 **79**........................ ShaneKelly 6 70+
(Alan McCabe) *rrd s: hdwy to chse ldrs after 2f: one pce over 1f out* **14/1**
4102 **9** *shd* **Bond Fastrac**^{22} [3845] 5-9-0 **81**... DaleSwift$^{(3)}$ 14 71
(Geoffrey Oldroyd) *in rr: hdwy wd outside 2f out: kpt on fnl f* **25/1**
2201 **10** *shd* **Trade Secret**^{40} [3255] 5-9-3 **81**.. RobertWinston 12 71
(Mel Brittain) *rrd s: hdwy over 2f out: chsng ldrs over 1f out: kpt on same pce: eased nr fin* **12/1**^{3}
0205 **11** *½* **Mon Brav**^{8} [4339] 5-9-2 **80**..(b) BarryMcHugh 5 68
(Brian Ellison) *in rr: reminders after s: styd on ins fnl f: nvr a factor* **12/1**^{3}
4400 **12** *¾* **Global City (IRE)**^{53} [2825] 6-9-12 **90**....................(t) MickaelBarzalona 10 76
(Saeed Bin Suroor) *dwlt: sn mid-div: effrt over 2f out: wknd last 150yds* **10/1**^{2}
0204 **13** *¾* **Arganil (USA)**^{15} [4077] 7-9-9 **87**....................................(p) GrahamLee 16 70
(Kevin Ryan) *in rr: edgd lft and kpt on fnl f: nvr a factor* **25/1**
-035 **14** *¾* **Another Wise Kid (IRE)**^{22} [3845] 4-9-4 **82**...................... MickyFenton 3 63
(Paul Midgley) *led: hdd over 1f out: wknd fnl 150yds* **16/1**
1-00 **15** *3 ¾* **Imperator Augustus (IRE)**^{8} [4345] 4-9-2 **80**............. DanielTudhope 15 49
(Patrick Holmes) *swtchd lft after s: chsd ldrs on outer: lost pl over 1f out: eased towards fin* **20/1**
0010 **16** *1 ¾* **Byronic Hero**^{24} [3778] 3-8-11 **80**..................................(p) TonyHamilton 8 43
(Jedd O'Keeffe) *dwlt: swtchd lft and reminders after s: a in rr: bhd fnl 2f* **22/1**

1m 15.46s (-1.44) **Going Correction** -0.05s/f (Good)
WFA 3 from 4yo+ 5lb **16** Ran SP% **129.5**
Speed ratings (Par 107): **107,106,105,105,104 103,102,100,100,99 99,98,97,96,91 88**
Tote Swingers: 1&2 £124.10, 2&3 £14.40 CSF £365.06 CT £1112.15 TOTE £29.60: £5.50, £4.70, £1.20, £3.10; EX 521.30 Trifecta £643.70 Part won. Pool: £869.97 - 0.78 winning units..
Owner Andrew Tinkler **Bred** Michael Collins **Trained** Denton, Co Durham

FOCUS
Competitive stuff.

NOTEBOOK
Orbit The Moon(IRE), never far away after breaking from a moderate stalls position, fought on well towards the centre of the track in headgear for the first time. The drop back to sprinting possibly helped (his half-brother Song Of My Heart was a smart sprinter in Ireland as a 2yo) and this gelding still has the scope for more improvement. (op 14-1)
Solar Spirit(IRE) looked a touch high in the weights on his winning form, so this was a fine effort. He has a reasonable record at Pontefract. (op 25-1)
My Kingdom(IRE)was ridden to get there right on the line but wasn't able to reel in the leaders after being stopped in his run. He seemed unlucky but his form figures are a concern for win purposes. Jamie Spencer reported that the gelding was denied a clear run. Official explanation: jockey said gelding was denied a clear run (op 3-1)
Damika(IRE), back in a visor, has been running creditably since headgear was introduced and ran another cracker after racing up with the speed. (tchd 11-1)
Beckermet(IRE) had a favourable draw to emerge from and stayed on nicely up the inside rail once he found a clear route. (op 12-1)
Johannes(IRE), up 6lb for his Doncaster victory, was drawn pretty wide, so can be given another chance. (op 9-1)

4630 LADIES DAY ON WEDNESDAY 8TH AUGUST MAIDEN STKS — 1m 4y
4:50 (4:55) (Class 5) 3-4-Y-O **£2,911** (£866; £432; £216) **Stalls** Low

Form RPR
6-23 **1** **Warcrown (IRE)**^{75} [2143] 3-9-3 **75**................................. TonyHamilton 11 79+
(Richard Fahey) *mde all: drvn 3 l clr over 1f out: jst lasted* **3/1**^{2}
2-50 **2** *nk* **Isatis**^{70} [2313] 3-8-12 **72**.. TomQueally 7 73
(Sir Henry Cecil) *trckd ldrs: wnt 2nd over 1f out: styd on: no ex nr fin* **11/2**^{3}
5- **3** *1 ¼* **Noble Silk**^{386} [3878] 3-9-3 0... EddieAhern 10 75
(Lucy Wadham) *trckd ldrs: drvn 3f out: kpt on one pce to take 3rd 1f out* **7/1**
4 *4 ½* **Intent (IRE)** 3-8-12 0... HayleyTurner 9 60+
(Michael Bell) *in rr: hdwy over 2f out: kpt on to take 4th last 100yds* **25/1**
50 **5** *6* **Hummingbird**^{20} [3918] 3-8-12 0... LiamJones 1 46
(William Haggas) *chsd ldrs: drvn over 2f out: wknd over 1f out* **9/1**
2 **6** *½* **Eltifaat (IRE)**^{26} [3735] 3-9-3 0.. TadhgO'Shea 14 50
(Sir Michael Stoute) *s.s and wnt rt s: sn trcking ldrs: wnt 2nd over 4f out: rdn 2f out: wknd over 1f out: fin lame* **13/8**^{1}
0 **7** *2* **Blue Dune**^{8} [4341] 3-8-12 0... FrannyNorton 13 41
(Mark Johnston) *s.i.s: sn prom: outpcd over 2f out: kpt on fnl f* **16/1**
0 **8** *7* **Shavalley (USA)**^{20} [3913] 3-8-12 0................................... AdrianNicholls 12 24
(David Nicholls) *chsd ldrs: lost pl over 2f out* **80/1**
0 **9** *1* **Tysoe Lad**^{54} [2800] 4-9-11 0.. DavidProbert 8 29
(Michael Appleby) *reluctant and led rdrless to post: s.i.s: sn drvn and a in rr* **150/1**
36 **10** *3 ½* **Plus Fours (USA)**^{81} [1981] 3-9-3 0...................................... MickyFenton 6 19
(Charles Smith) *mid-div: drvn and lost pl over 2f out* **25/1**
00 **11** *hd* **Destiny Awaits (IRE)**^{13} [4157] 3-9-3 0.................................. TomEaves 2 19
(Ian Semple) *mid-div: drvn and lost pl 3f out: sn bhd* **66/1**
0 **12** *4 ½* **Nowdoro**^{20} [3913] 3-9-0 0.. DaleSwift$^{(3)}$ 4
(Julie Camacho) *in rr: drvn 4f out: sn bhd* **66/1**

1m 44.46s (-1.44) **Going Correction** -0.30s/f (Firm)
WFA 3 from 4yo 8lb **12** Ran SP% **119.4**
Speed ratings (Par 103): **95,94,93,88,82 82,80,73,72,68 68,64**
Tote Swingers: 1&2 £3.80, 1&3 £4.90, 2&3 £6.90 CSF £19.37 TOTE £4.30: £1.90, £2.10, £2.20; EX 24.40 Trifecta £161.80 Pool: £1,187.89 - 5.43 winning units..

Owner Mrs H Steel **Bred** Abbeville And Meadow Court Partners **Trained** Musley Bank, N Yorks

FOCUS

The first two home were rated in the 70s, suggesting this was a fair race.

Eltifaat(IRE) Official explanation: trainer's rep said colt finished lame

4631 YORKSHIRE RADIO H'CAP 5f

5:20 (5:25) (Class 5) (0-70,70) 3-Y-O+ **£2,911** (£866; £432; £216) **Stalls** Low

Form RPR

6502 **1** **Chosen One (IRE)**[4] 4452 7-8-9 **53** PJMcDonald 3 64
(Ruth Carr) *chsd ldrs on inner: styd on to ld ins fnl 100yds: kpt on wl* **5/2**[1]

0002 **2** 1 1/2 **Arch Walker (IRE)**[5] 4438 5-9-0 **58** (b) DavidProbert 15 64+
(John Weymes) *w ldrs: led over 1f out: hdd and no ex last 100yds* **11/2**[2]

4343 **3** 1 3/4 **Belinsky (IRE)**[10] 4245 5-9-4 **65** (v[1]) DaleSwift(3) 14 64+
(Julie Camacho) *chsd ldrs on outer: kpt on wl to take 3rd last 50yds* **9/1**

1640 **4** 1 1/4 **Rio's Girl**[12] 4174 5-8-12 **56** BarryMcHugh 5 51
(Tony Coyle) *chsd ldrs: kpt on same pce fnl f* **16/1**

0-00 **5** 1 **Media Jury**[12] 4174 5-8-7 **51** oh1 (v) PatrickMathers 4 42
(John Wainwright) *in rr: hdwy 2f out: styng on at fin* **50/1**

454- **6** *hd* **Above The Stars**[222] 7834 4-9-3 **68** LauraBarry(7) 9 58+
(Richard Fahey) *dwlt: in rr: hdwy on outer 2f out: kpt on fnl f* **12/1**

1556 **7** 1 1/4 **Argentine (IRE)**[6] 4393 8-9-5 **63** (b) TomEaves 8 49
(Ian Semple) *in rr: swtchd lft after s: effrt and nt clr run bnd over 2f out: kpt on fnl f* **25/1**

50-0 **8** 1/2 **Mr Wolf**[48] 2982 11-9-4 **62** (p) TonyHamilton 2 46
(Paul Midgley) *led: hdd over 1f out: edgd rt and fdd last 100yds* **16/1**

2060 **9** 1 **Divertimenti (IRE)**[46] 3018 8-9-0 **63** (b) MarkCoumbe(5) 6 44
(Roy Bowring) *mid-div: effrt over 2f out: one pce* **14/1**

0006 **10** 1 **Indian Trail**[6] 4400 12-9-12 **70** (b) PaulQuinn 16 47
(David Nicholls) *in rr: effrt over 2f out: kpt on fnl f* **20/1**

-001 **11** 7 **Jack Smudge**[27] 3707 4-9-4 **62** (b) GrahamLee 12 14
(James Given) *chsd ldrs: lost pl over 1f out: eased towards fin* **14/1**

052 **12** 2 3/4 **Kyllachy Dancer**[27] 3706 3-8-13 **61** (v) MichaelO'Connell 7
(John Quinn) *mid-div: lost pl over 2f out: bhd whn eased nr fin* **17/2**

25-0 **13** 4 **Mey Blossom**[4] 4451 7-9-7 **65** RobertWinston 11
(Richard Whitaker) *outpcd in rr: eased whn bhd ins fnl f* **20/1**

00-0 **14** 16 **Gottcher**[53] 2809 4-9-7 **65** JamieSpencer 10
(David Barron) *chsd ldrs: wknd rapidly over 2f out: sn bhd: eased whn t.o ins fnl f* **15/2**[3]

1m 2.46s (-0.84) **Going Correction** -0.05s/f (Good)
WFA 3 from 4yo+ 4lb **14** Ran SP% **124.4**
Speed ratings (Par 103): **104,101,98,96,95 94,92,92,90,88 77,73,66,41**
Tote Swingers: 1&2 £5.40, 1&3 £6.50, 2&3 £13.50 CSF £14.66 CT £116.02 TOTE £3.60: £1.90, £2.60, £4.10; EX 19.60 Trifecta £202.50 Pool: £611.29 - 2.23 winning units..
Owner Bridget Houlston, Chris Jeffery & Co **Bred** Carl Holt **Trained** Huby, N Yorks

FOCUS

Fast and furious stuff from the outset, which was always likely to favour a closer.

Gottcher Official explanation: jockey said gelding lost its action

T/Jkpt: Not won. T/Plt: £127.20 to a £1 stake. Pool: £92,450.02 - 530.29 winning tickets. T/Qpdt: £37.80 to a £1 stake. Pool: £4,175.67 - 105.12 winning tickets. WG

4615 DEAUVILLE (R-H)

Sunday, July 29

OFFICIAL GOING: Turf: good; fibresand: standard

4632a PRIX DE CABOURG - JOCKEY CLUB DE TURQUIE (GROUP 3) (2YO) (TURF) 6f

1:00 (12:00) 2-Y-O **£33,333** (£13,333; £10,000; £6,666; £3,333)

RPR

1 **Mazameer (IRE)**[23] 2-8-11 0 ThierryJarnet 1 108
(F Head, France) *broke fast to ld: clr ld over 1f out: chal ins fnl f: r.o wl under hands and heels ride: hld on wl* **5/1**[3]

2 *snk* **Baileys Jubilee**[12] 4205 2-8-8 0 IoritzMendizabal 5 105
(Mark Johnston) *racd in 4th on outside: qcknd wl 1 1/2f out to go 2nd: chal ldr fnl 100yds: fin wl: jst hld* **6/1**

3 2 1/2 **Pearl Flute (IRE)**[31] 3553 2-8-11 0 Christophe-PatriceLemaire 2 100
(F-H Graffard, France) *racd in cl 2nd: rdn ent fnl f: no ex: styd on at one pce* **13/8**[1]

4 1 1/2 **Wild Horse (IRE)**[23] 2-8-11 0 ChristopheSoumillon 4 95
(J-C Rouget, France) *settled in 3rd on ins rail: swtchd away fr rail 2f out: rdn 1 1/2f out: no ex: styd on fnl f* **2/1**[2]

5 1 **Cucuma (FR)**[15] 4118 2-8-8 0 StephanePasquier 6 89
(P Bary, France) *a towards rr: rdn but no ex fr 1 1/2f out: nvr a factor* **16/1**

6 1/2 **You're Golden (IRE)**[26] 2-8-11 0 JulienAuge 3 90
(C Ferland, France) *a in rr: rdn but fnd no ex fnl 2f: nvr figured* **14/1**

1m 9.3s (-1.70) **Going Correction** -0.075s/f (Good) **6** Ran SP% **114.9**
Speed ratings: **108,107,104,102,101 100**
WIN (incl. 1 euro stake): 5.50. PLACES: 3.00, 4.00. SF: 31.40.
Owner Hamdan Al Maktoum **Bred** S Kennedy & P Carmody **Trained** France

NOTEBOOK

Mazameer(IRE), beaten at odds-on last time, bounced back with an all-the-way win on the favoured stands' rail. A speedy type, a further rise in class now beckons for him, with the Prix Morny his target.

Baileys Jubilee, a winner of a Listed race at Vichy last time out, pushed the winner all the way to the line but couldn't quite get by. She might reoppose the winner in the Morny, but returning to fillies' only company in the Lowther at York is also an option short-term.

4633a PRIX ROTHSCHILD (GROUP 1) (3YO+ FILLIES & MARES) (TURF) 1m (R)

1:30 (12:00) 3-Y-O+ **£142,850** (£57,150; £28,575; £14,275; £7,150)

RPR

1 **Elusive Kate (USA)**[16] 4065 3-8-9 0 ow1 WilliamBuick 3 118
(John Gosden) *led fr s: qcknd wl 3f out: established clr ld 1 1/2f out: r.o wl fnl f: nvr threatened: comf* **9/4**[2]

2 1 1/4 **Golden Lilac (IRE)**[16] 4065 4-9-2 0 MaximeGuyon 1 116+
(A Fabre, France) *settled in 3rd on stands' rail: rdn 2f out: chsd ldr fnl f: clst at fin* **5/4**[1]

3 2 1/2 **Mashoora (IRE)**[29] 3657 3-8-8 0 ChristopheSoumillon 4 108
(J-C Rouget, France) *racd 2nd on outside: relegated to 3rd 2f out: nt qckn u.p 1 1/2f out: styd on* **8/1**

4 1/2 **Sagawara**[42] 3203 3-8-8 0 Christophe-PatriceLemaire 5 107
(A De Royer-Dupre, France) *racd in 4th on outside: rdn 2f out: no ex: styd on fnl f* **14/1**

5 3 1/2 **Immortal Verse (IRE)**[252] 4-9-2 0 GeraldMosse 2 101
(Robert Collet, France) *a at rr: rdn but no ex fr 2f out: nvr figured* **6/1**[3]

1m 37.4s (-3.40) **Going Correction** -0.075s/f (Good)
WFA 3 from 4yo 8lb **5** Ran SP% **107.3**
Speed ratings: **114,112,110,109,106**
WIN (incl. 1 euro stake): 3.70. PLACES: 1.60, 1.40. SF: 8.30.
Owner Teruya Yoshida **Bred** Clovelly Farms **Trained** Newmarket, Suffolk

FOCUS

Even without Goldikova (winner of the last four renewals), this was a high class contest.

NOTEBOOK

Elusive Kate(USA) closed her European 2yo career with success in the Prix Marcel Boussac (crowned French champion 2yo filly). With ground conditions soft all over Europe she didn't mount a challenge on any of the classics and hadn't been seen as a 3yo until reappearing in Newmarket's Falmouth Stakes 16 days previously. She ran a stormer that day on ground still far softer than suitable, finishing runner-up behind Giofra. Quickly away here, she settled in front with her jockey dictating only a modest pace. She had all the field in trouble when making her move and, despite the runner-up getting to her girths well inside the final furlong, she ran out a comfortable winner. The quicker ground conditions suited this fluent mover and she can go on to confirm herself as European champion filly with victory in the Sun Chariot or Prix Jacques Le Marois, and considering her Japanese ownership a tilt at the Mile Championship at Kyoto in November may be where she closes her season.

Golden Lilac(IRE), who had the excuse of soft ground when below par in the Falmouth Stakes, had no such excuses here. Settled on the rail, she was brought with her challenge in plenty of time but wasn't good enough. Her free nature means she has to be settled and often gives away first run to her rivals. She has won over as far as 1m3f and a step up in trip is in the offing.

Mashoora(IRE) was a touch keen on the outside and, despite threatening to challenge the winner, wasn't good enough. She isn't quite up to winning a Group 1 yet.

Immortal Verse(IRE) had been given a lengthy break after finishing last season late. Settled in rear, she never looked like getting competitive and is expected to come on significantly for the run.

4634a PRIX DU CARROUSEL (LISTED RACE) (4YO+) (TURF) 1m 7f

3:10 (12:00) 4-Y-O+ **£21,666** (£8,666; £6,500; £4,333; £2,166)

RPR

1 **Lone Ranger (FR)**[37] 3367 4-8-11 0 (p) ChristopheSoumillon 11 105
(A De Royer-Dupre, France) **53/10**[3]

2 *snk* **Flamingo Fantasy (GER)**[25] 3768 7-8-11 0 (p) StephanePasquier 10 105
(S Smrczek, Germany) **26/1**

3 1 **Inside Man (IRE)**[37] 3367 6-9-1 0 (b) AnthonyCrastus 3 108
(E Lellouche, France) **11/2**

4 *shd* **Tres Rock Danon (FR)**[25] 3768 6-9-4 0 (p) GeraldMosse 4 111
(W Hickst, Germany) **48/10**[2]

5 *snk* **Thimaar (USA)**[22] 3881 4-9-1 0 PaulHanagan 8 108
(John Gosden) *led fr s: set modest pce: qcknd tempo 6f out: led into st: r.o wl: clr but u.p 1f out: hdd 75yds out: styd on wl* **9/1**

6 3/4 **Silver Valny (FR)**[231] 7733 6-8-11 0 ThomasMessina 6 103
(Mlle M-L Mortier, France) **32/1**

7 1 1/4 **Gulf Of Naples (IRE)**[29] 3625 4-8-11 0 SilvestreDeSousa 9 101
(Mark Johnston) *settled in 2nd: rdn early in st: r.o wl u.p: no ex fr 1f out: styd on one pce* **7/1**

8 *nk* **Marceti (IRE)**[120] 5-8-11 0 ThierryJarnet 2 101
(E Leenders, France) **20/1**

9 2 **Tidespring (IRE)**[25] 3768 4-8-8 0 MaximeGuyon 7 95
(H-A Pantall, France) **19/5**[1]

10 *snk* **Caudillo (GER)**[64] 9-9-4 0 IoritzMendizabal 5 105
(Dr A Bolte, Germany) **19/1**

0 **Lacateno**[37] 3367 5-8-11 0 OlivierPeslier 1
(W Hickst, Germany) **11/1**

3m 9.5s (-9.60) **11** Ran SP% **116.7**
WIN (incl. 1 euro stake): 6.30. PLACES: 2.40, 5.40, 2.10. DF: 66.30. SF: 114.50.
Owner Ecurie Wildenstein **Bred** Dayton Investments Ltd **Trained** Chantilly, France

4635 - (Foreign Racing) - See Raceform Interactive

2569 MUNICH (L-H)

Sunday, July 29

OFFICIAL GOING: Turf: soft

4636a GROSSER DALLMAYR-PREIS - BAYERISCHES ZUCHTRENNEN (GROUP 1) (3YO+) (TURF) 1m 2f

4:20 (4:21) 3-Y-O+ **£75,833** (£30,000; £15,000; £8,333)

RPR

1 **Pastorius (GER)**[28] 3683 3-8-10 0 AStarke 7 122
(Mario Hofer, Germany) *prom thrght: rdn to ld over 2f out: qcknd smartly and sn clr: styd on strly to extend advantage ins fnl f: impressive* **3/1**[2]

2 8 **Durban Thunder (GER)**[231] 7732 6-9-6 0 MartinHarley 6 106
(P Harley, Germany) *led: rdn and hdd over 2f out: qckly outpcd by wnr: plugged on ins fnl 1 1/2f: got bk up for 2nd cl home* **121/10**

3 1/2 **Zazou (GER)**[70] 2327 5-9-6 0 ASuborics 8 105
(W Hickst, Germany) *hld up in last: rdn to improve over 2 1/2f out: outpcd by wnr over 1 1/2f out: kpt on to go 2nd over 1f out: no ex and dropped to* **7/5**[1]

4 1/2 **Waldpark (GER)**[26] 3746 4-9-6 0 EPedroza 1 104
(A Wohler, Germany) *midfield on inner: dropped to rr and rdn over 3f out: outpcd over 2 1/2f out: plugged on to go 4th ins fnl f* **4/1**[3]

5 1/2 **Feuerblitz (GER)**[28] 3683 3-8-10 0 RobertHavlin 2 103
(M Figge, Germany) *midfield: rdn and brief effrt over 2f out: sn outpcd: plugged on* **58/10**

6 1/2 **Pakal (GER)**[14] 4171 3-8-10 0 KKerekes 3 102
(W Figge, Germany) *restrained early stages and trckd ldr in 2nd: rdn and lost pl over 2 1/2f out: sn btn: plugged on* **78/10**

7 3 **King's Hall**[50] 4-9-6 0 (p) LennartHammer-Hansen 4 96
(A Wohler, Germany) *hld up in last pair on outer: rdn and outpcd 3f out: plugged on: nvr a factor* **174/10**

2m 12.04s (3.07)
WFA 3 from 4yo+ 10lb **7** Ran SP% **125.8**
WIN (incl. 10 euro stake): 40. PLACES: 14, 19, 12. SF: 576.
Owner Stall Antanando **Bred** Franz Prinz Von Auersperg & Florian Haffa **Trained** Germany

NOTEBOOK
Pastorius(GER), who overturned odds-on favourite Novellist in the German Derby, ran out a most impressive winner against these older rivals. There are question marks over whether those in behind ran close to their best in the soft ground, but this was still a very taking display by this improving 3yo, and he'll now be pointed towards the Grosser Preis von Baden, where the opposition will likely include Danedream. A victory there would put him firmly in the Arc picture.

4387 AYR (L-H)
Monday, July 30

OFFICIAL GOING: Good (good to soft in places; 8.9)
Wind: Fresh, half against Weather: Cloudy

4637 BETTOR.COM STARTING COMMISSION OF 1.5% MEDIAN AUCTION MAIDEN 6f
2:05 (2:06) (Class 5) 2-Y-O £2,458 (£731; £365; £182) Stalls High

Form RPR
2 **1** **Majestic Moon (IRE)**[14] 4132 2-9-3 0 TonyHamilton 6 87+
(Richard Fahey) *trckd ldrs: smooth hdwy to ld over 1f out: shkn up and qcknd clr fnl f: readily* **10/11**[1]
2 5 **Kolonel Kirkup** 2-9-3 0 PaulMulrennan 1 68+
(Michael Dods) *hld up in tch: hdwy to chse wnr 1f out: kpt on fnl f: no imp* **14/1**
3 1 1/4 **Hello Gorgeous** 2-8-12 0 TomEaves 3 59
(Keith Dalgleish) *t.k.h: trckd ldrs: effrt and edgd lft over 1f out: kpt on same pce* **50/1**
4 **4** nk **Fife Jo**[45] 3112 2-9-3 0 GrahamLee 5 63+
(Jim Goldie) *dwlt: sn pushed along in rr: hdwy over 1f out: nvr able to chal* **18/1**
2363 **5** hd **Red Style (IRE)**[14] 4132 2-9-3 70 MickyFenton 2 62
(Paul Midgley) *hld up in tch: hung lft and nt clr run wl over 1f out: sn n.d* **12/1**[3]
040 **6** 3 3/4 **Ana Emaratiya**[38] 3326 2-8-12 85 PhillipMakin 8 45
(Kevin Ryan) *disp ld: rdn over 2f out: wknd appr fnl f* **7/4**[2]
0020 **7** nse **Amelia Jay**[25] 3776 2-8-5 62 JasonHart(7) 4 45
(Danielle McCormick) *t.k.h: led to over 1f out: sn wknd* **100/1**

1m 14.3s (1.90) **Going Correction** +0.375s/f (Good) 7 Ran SP% 111.3
Speed ratings (Par 94): **102,95,93,93,93 88,87**
toteswingers: 1&2 £3.10, 1&3 £6.60, 2&3 £20.40 CSF £15.00 TOTE £2.40: £1.40, £4.20; EX 18.60 Trifecta £275.80 Pool: £764.26 - 2.05 winning units..
Owner James Gaffney **Bred** Tony Cosgrave **Trained** Musley Bank, N Yorks

FOCUS
Home bend out 8m from inner line and straight out 6m from inner line and Stands bend moved out 6m. 24yds added to races between 7f and 10f and 60yds to other races on Round course. Ordinary maiden form rated around the fourth.

NOTEBOOK
Majestic Moon(IRE) won with tons in hand having travelled well, and can yet rate higher. He had finished second over C&D on debut and, being a brother to the yard's useful Listed winner Majestic Myles, should progress, with 7f unlikely be an issue. (op Evens)
Kolonel Kirkup, whose dam won up to 1m2f, is from a yard going well and he made a promising start. Normal progress may seem him winning a minor 7f maiden. (op 12-1)
Hello Gorgeous, whose dam was a modest maiden, showed a bit of ability but improvement will be required if she's to win a maiden.
Fife Jo ran well considering he was squeezed out at the start and soon on the back foot. He was dropping from 7f and will be helped by a return to a longer distance. (op 16-1 tchd 20-1)
Red Style(IRE) will stand more of a chance in modest nurseries. Official explanation: jockey said gelding hung left (tchd 14-1)
Ana Emaratiya, seventh in the Albany, was unable to build on that back down in grade and clearly failed to give her running, having cut out the early running. Official explanation: trainer's rep had no explanation for the poor form shown (op 2-1)
Amelia Jay was disputing the running early, but stopped quickly. (op 66-1)

4638 BETTOR.COM SOCIAL BETTING H'CAP 6f
2:35 (2:38) (Class 5) (0-75,75) 3-Y-0+ £2,458 (£731; £365; £182) Stalls High

Form RPR
0-30 **1** **Dutch Heritage**[21] 3912 3-9-1 69 (b[1]) TonyHamilton 7 78
(Richard Fahey) *s.s: bhd and drvn along: gd hdwy on outside over 1f out: led last 50yds: kpt on wl* **11/4**[1]
0035 **2** 3/4 **Namwahjobo (IRE)**[7] 4388 4-9-8 71 (v) DanielTudhope 9 78
(Jim Goldie) *hld up: hdwy and weaved through over 1f out: led ins fnl f: hdd last 50yds: kpt on* **11/2**[3]
-505 **3** 1 1/2 **Midnight Dynamo**[21] 3905 5-9-0 63 GrahamLee 4 65
(Jim Goldie) *rrd s: bhd: rdn and hdwy over 1f out: kpt on ins fnl f* **14/1**
0042 **4** 3 1/2 **Ryan Style (IRE)**[4] 4501 6-9-6 72 (v) LeeTopliss(3) 6 63
(Lisa Williamson) *chsd clr ldr: rdn over 2f out: effrt over 1f out: no ex ins fnl f* **4/1**[2]
5/00 **5** 2 3/4 **Jebel Tara**[14] 4134 7-8-7 56 oh5 (bt) DuranFentiman 3 38
(Ian Semple) *led and sn clr: rdn over 2f out: hdd ins fnl f: sn btn* **100/1**
5520 **6** shd **Weetentherty**[7] 4393 5-8-7 56 oh1 (p) LukeMorris 2 38
(Linda Perratt) *hld up in tch: rdn over 2f out: effrt over 1f out: sn no imp* **33/1**
21/0 **7** nk **Jinky**[14] 4133 4-9-12 75 PhillipMakin 5 56
(Linda Perratt) *hld up on outside: rdn over 2f out: outpcd over 1f out: sn n.d* **12/1**
0025 **8** nse **Saxonette**[7] 4393 4-8-8 57 (p) PJMcDonald 10 38
(Linda Perratt) *t.k.h: hld up in tch: drvn over 2f out: no imp over 1f out* **25/1**
0061 **9** 1 1/2 **Blown It (USA)**[7] 4392 6-9-7 70 6ex TomEaves 1 46
(Keith Dalgleish) *hld up: rdn and hdwy over 1f out: wknd ins fnl f* **18/1**
0036 **10** 1/2 **Ballinargh Girl (IRE)**[32] 3524 4-8-11 67 JasonHart(7) 8 41
(Danielle McCormick) *midfield: rdn over 2f out: wknd over 1f out* **7/1**
021 **11** 1/2 **Commanche Raider (IRE)**[49] 2982 5-9-10 73 (b) PaulMulrennan 11 46+
(Michael Dods) *hld up on ins: nt clr run over 2f out to ins fnl f: no imp* **8/1**

1m 14.09s (1.69) **Going Correction** +0.375s/f (Good)
WFA 3 from 4yo+ 5lb 11 Ran SP% 113.1
Speed ratings (Par 103): **103,102,100,95,91 91,91,91,89,88 87**
toteswingers: 1&2 £4.40, 1&3 £11.40, 2&3 £16.90 CSF £16.66 CT £179.50 TOTE £3.90: £1.70, £2.10, £4.60; EX 17.90 Trifecta £372.00 Part won. Pool: £502.76 - 0.63 winning units..
Owner P Timmins & A Rhodes Haulage **Bred** Red House Stud **Trained** Musley Bank, N Yorks

FOCUS
Outsider Jebel Tara was responsible for setting a fast pace and it paid to be held up.
Ryan Style(IRE) Official explanation: jockey said gelding hung right throughout
Ballinargh Girl(IRE) Official explanation: jockey said filly never travelled
Commanche Raider(IRE) Official explanation: jockey said gelding was denied a clear run

4639 BETTOR.COM BET AGAINST OTHER SPORTS FANS H'CAP 1m 5f 13y
3:05 (3:05) (Class 5) (0-75,75) 3-Y-0+ £2,458 (£731; £365; £182) Stalls Low

Form RPR
4421 **1** **Lady Bluesky**[14] 4138 9-9-6 67 PaulMulrennan 4 77
(Alistair Whillans) *trckd ldrs: led over 2f out: sn hrd pressed: hld on gamely fnl f* **11/4**[2]
5-25 **2** 1/2 **Yours Ever**[20] 3945 3-8-13 73 LukeMorris 2 82
(Sir Mark Prescott Bt) *led: rdn and hdd over 2f out: rallied and ev ch fnl f: kpt on: hld nr fin* **2/1**[1]
-031 **3** 2 1/2 **The Oil Magnate**[22] 3891 7-10-0 75 TomEaves 3 80
(Michael Dods) *hld up: hdwy to chse ldrs over 3f out: rdn and kpt on fnl f: nt pce of first two* **5/1**[3]
-646 **4** 7 **Forrest Flyer (IRE)**[21] 3904 8-9-3 64 GrahamLee 5 59
(Jim Goldie) *chsd ldr: drvn and outpcd over 3f out: no imp fr 2f out* **17/2**
4625 **5** 12 **Brouhaha**[11] 4251 8-9-6 67 RichardKingscote 8 44
(Tom Dascombe) *prom: rdn and outpcd wl over 3f out: sn btn* **8/1**
0406 **6** 7 **Chookie Hamilton**[38] 3337 8-9-6 72 GarryWhillans(5) 7 38
(Ian Semple) *hld up in tch: drvn and struggling over 3f out: sn btn* **16/1**
/-31 **7** 3 1/2 **Dispol Diva**[31] 3577 6-9-4 65 (v) MickyFenton 9 26
(Paul Midgley) *hld up on outside: outpcd after 4f: struggling 4f out: sn btn* **11/1**

2m 55.71s (1.71) **Going Correction** +0.075s/f (Good)
WFA 3 from 5yo+ 13lb 7 Ran SP% 112.5
Speed ratings (Par 103): **97,96,95,90,83 79,77**
toteswingers: 1&2 £1.80, 1&3 £2.40, 2&3 £2.80 CSF £8.38 CT £24.04 TOTE £6.40: £2.40, £1.10; EX 11.70 Trifecta £31.70 Pool: £506.80 - 11.80 winning units..
Owner Mrs S Harrow Mrs L M Whillans **Bred** C E Whiteley **Trained** Newmill-On-Slitrig, Borders

FOCUS
The front pair had this to themselves from the home bend. Fair form for the grade rated around the third.

4640 BETTOR.COM BETTING EXCHANGE H'CAP 7f 50y
3:40 (3:41) (Class 4) (0-85,84) 3-Y-0+ £4,204 (£1,251; £625; £312) Stalls High

Form RPR
1633 **1** **Ballista (IRE)**[31] 3557 4-10-0 84 RichardKingscote 6 93
(Tom Dascombe) *mde all: qcknd clr over 1f out: kpt on wl: unchal* **1/1**[1]
103 **2** 5 **Frequency**[27] 3726 5-9-6 76 (b) TomEaves 1 72
(Keith Dalgleish) *hld up in last pl: stdy hdwy to chse wnr over 2f out: rdn over 1f out: no imp* **16/1**
4153 **3** 4 1/2 **Emeralds Spirit (IRE)**[22] 3888 5-8-10 66 LukeMorris 2 50
(John Weymes) *cl up: wnt 2nd over 3f out to over 2f out: edgd lft and sn outpcd* **10/3**[2]
04-0 **4** 1 3/4 **Roninski (IRE)**[120] 1161 4-9-7 82 JustinNewman(5) 7 62
(Bryan Smart) *prom on outside: rdn over 2f out: btn fnl f* **4/1**[3]
4202 **5** 10 **Sabratha (IRE)**[6] 4432 4-8-9 65 oh1 PJMcDonald 5 19
(Linda Perratt) *chsd wnr to over 3f out: sn rdn and wknd* **7/1**
266- **6** 19 **Eilean Mor**[7] 1543 4-8-9 65 oh1 DuranFentiman 4
(R Mike Smith) *unruly bef s: cl up tl rdn and wknd over 3f out* **40/1**

1m 32.93s (-0.47) **Going Correction** +0.075s/f (Good) 6 Ran SP% 113.9
Speed ratings (Par 105): **105,99,94,92,80 59**
toteswingers: 1&2 £3.70, 1&3 £1.70, 2&3 £3.60 CSF £19.67 TOTE £2.10: £1.10, £3.20; EX 12.30.
Owner Well Done Top Man Partnership **Bred** Sj Partnership **Trained** Malpas, Cheshire

FOCUS
The runners finished quite well strung out and the winner has been rated to last year's best.

4641 BETTOR.COM LATEST SPORTS NEWS H'CAP 1m 1f 20y
4:15 (4:17) (Class 5) (0-75,75) 3-Y-0+ £2,458 (£731; £365; £182) Stalls Low

Form RPR
3421 **1** **Uncle Brit**[7] 4389 6-8-9 56 6ex PJMcDonald 4 64
(Malcolm Jefferson) *trckd ldrs: rdn over 2f out: led 1f out: drvn out* **11/2**[3]
000U **2** 1/2 **King Of Windsor (IRE)**[37] 3380 5-10-0 75 (p) PaulMulrennan 1 84+
(Keith Dalgleish) *hld up in tch: repeatedly denied room fr 3f out to ins fnl f: styd on wl towards fin: nt rch wnr* **7/2**[1]
3423 **3** nse **Save The Bees**[13] 4175 4-9-4 72 JasonHart(7) 3 79
(Declan Carroll) *t.k.h: trckd ldrs: drvn whn n.m.r briefly over 2f out: rallied over 1f out: kpt on fnl f* **9/2**[2]
3014 **4** 1/2 **Le Chat D'Or**[22] 3890 4-9-11 72 TomEaves 5 79+
(Michael Dods) *rn wout declared tongue-tie: hld up: rdn whn nt clr run over 2f out: nt clr run and swtchd rt ent fnl f: styd on wl nr fin* **7/1**
0100 **5** 1/2 **Spavento (IRE)**[25] 3775 6-9-3 64 LukeMorris 10 69
(Eric Alston) *hld up: stdy hdwy to chal over 1f out: kpt on same pce ins fnl f* **14/1**
6623 **6** 1 **Dazzling Valentine**[3] 4538 4-8-12 66 NatashaEaton(7) 8 69
(Alan Bailey) *cl up: rdn to ld briefly over 1f out: no ex ins fnl f* **9/1**
5025 **7** 3 1/4 **Hawdyerwheesht**[14] 4137 4-8-13 60 (v) DanielTudhope 7 56
(Jim Goldie) *t.k.h: trckd ldrs: led over 2f out: rdn: edgd lft and hdd over 1f out: wknd fnl f* **11/1**
1-36 **8** 3/4 **All For You (IRE)**[53] 2840 6-9-5 66 GrahamLee 6 60
(Jim Goldie) *hld up in tch: stdy hdwy over 2f out: rdn over 1f out: sn wknd* **20/1**
4442 **9** 1/2 **High Resolution**[11] 4260 5-8-10 62 ShaneBKelly(5) 2 55
(Linda Perratt) *s.i.s: hld up: effrt on ins whn nt clr run over 2f out: swtchd rt and no imp over 1f out* **12/1**
6144 **10** 14 **Cosmic Moon**[9] 4325 4-8-13 60 TonyHamilton 9 22
(Richard Fahey) *led to over 2f out: wknd over 1f out: eased whn btn* **13/2**

1m 59.84s (2.34) **Going Correction** +0.075s/f (Good) 10 Ran SP% 119.1
Speed ratings (Par 103): **92,91,91,91,90 89,86,86,85,73**
toteswingers 1&2 £4.90, 1&3 £5.20, 2&3 £4.90 CSF £25.67 CT £95.82 TOTE £5.20: £1.70, £1.30, £2.10; EX 27.50 Trifecta £454.40 Pool: £632.48 - 1.03 winning units..
Owner J M Jefferson **Bred** Heather Raw **Trained** Norton, N Yorks

FOCUS
Any number held a chance in what was a low-grade handicap. Messy form which isn't sure to work out.
King Of Windsor(IRE) Official explanation: jockey said gelding was denied a clear run

4642 BETTOR.COM BACK AND LAY H'CAP 1m 2f
4:45 (4:45) (Class 6) (0-65,65) 3-Y-O £1,704 (£503; £251) Stalls Low

Form RPR
4211 **1** **Luctor Emergo (IRE)**[7] 4391 3-9-6 64 6ex (p) TomEaves 6 73+
(Keith Dalgleish) *trckd ldr: drvn over 2f out: led over 1f out: hrd rdn: hld on wl fnl f* **2/1**[1]

4534 **2** *hd* **Arley Hall**[21] 3910 3-9-4 **65**.. LeeTopliss(3) 5 73+
(Richard Fahey) *led: rdn over 2f out: hdd over 1f out: rallied and ev ch fnl f: kpt on: jst hld* **5/2**[2]

3232 **3** *hd* **Schmooze (IRE)**[14] 4137 3-8-10 **54**.................................... GrahamLee 1 62
(Linda Perratt) *trckd ldrs: drvn along over 2f out: edgd rt: kpt on wl fnl f: jst hld* **5/1**

-021 **4** *9* **Lord Franklin**[11] 4263 3-8-11 **55**.. LukeMorris 2 45
(Eric Alston) *prom: rdn over 3f out: wknd over 2f out* **11/4**[3]

-606 **5** *9* **Firefly**[13] 4172 3-8-6 **50**.. DuranFentiman 3 22
(John Weymes) *hld up in tch: struggling over 2f out: sn btn* **22/1**

2m 13.71s (1.71) **Going Correction** +0.075s/f (Good) **5** Ran SP% **109.6**
Speed ratings (Par 98): **96,95,95,88,81**
CSF £7.23 TOTE £2.50: £2.30, £1.90; EX 8.70.
Owner Gordon McDowall **Bred** Kilnamoragh Stud **Trained** Carluke, S Lanarks
■ Stewards' Enquiry : Tom Eaves four-day ban: used whip above permitted level (Aug 13-16)

FOCUS
The front three pulled clear, with little separating them at the line, and the form looks reasonable for the grade rated around the third.

4643 BETTOR.COM FINALE LAST CHANCE TO BET APPRENTICE H'CAP 1m
5:20 (5:21) (Class 6) (0-60,60) 3-Y-0+ **£1,704** (£503; £251) **Stalls** Low

Form RPR

3114 **1** **Cheeky Wee Red**[7] 4389 4-9-5 **54**................................(p) LauraBarry(3) 8 62
(Richard Fahey) *hld up in tch: hdwy over 2f out: led over 1f out: rdn out fnl f* **5/2**[2]

3626 **2** *¾* **Mangham (IRE)**[9] 4349 7-9-10 **56**............................(p) GeorgeChaloner 9 62
(George Foster) *s.i.s: hld up: hdwy on outside and ev ch over 1f out: kpt on ins fnl f* **6/1**[3]

3-42 **3** *1* **Military Call**[7] 4389 5-9-12 **58**...(p) JasonHart 1 62
(Alistair Whillans) *hld up in tch: drvn along over 3f out: rallied over 1f out: kpt on fnl f: nrst fin* **6/4**[1]

2530 **4** *1 ¾* **So Is She (IRE)**[3] 4538 4-9-4 **50**.................................(be) NatashaEaton 3 50
(Alan Bailey) *hld up in tch: rdn and outpcd over 2f out: rallied fnl f: no imp* **7/1**

0-05 **5** *½* **Siberian Belle (IRE)**[13] 4198 3-8-6 **46**.................................. DarylByrne 5 43
(Richard Fahey) *w ldr to over 2f out: rdn and one pce over 1f out* **14/1**

0000 **6** *2* **Shunkawakhan (IRE)**[7] 4389 9-8-9 **46** oh1................(tp) RossSmith(5) 4 40
(Linda Perratt) *trckd ldrs: led over 2f out to over 1f out: sn no ex* **50/1**

5406 **7** *4 ½* **Glenluji**[7] 4390 7-9-7 **53**.. NoraLooby 7 37
(Jim Goldie) *s.i.s: bhd: struggling 1/2-way: nvr rchd ldrs* **16/1**

6500 **8** *3 ½* **Just Five (IRE)**[14] 4142 6-9-11 **60**........................(v) DavidSimmonson(3) 2 36
(John Weymes) *prom tl rdn: edgd rt and wknd over 2f out* **25/1**

-660 **9** *2 ¼* **Catcher Of Dreams (IRE)**[9] 4350 6-8-9 **46** oh1........(p) DavidBergin(5) 6 17
(George Foster) *led to over 2f out: sn rdn and wknd* **28/1**

1m 44.41s (0.61) **Going Correction** +0.075s/f (Good)
WFA 3 from 4yo+ 8lb **9** Ran SP% **117.2**
Speed ratings (Par 101): **99,98,97,95,95 93,88,85,82**
toteswingers: 1&2 £3.70, 1&3 £2.00, 2&3 £3.20 CSF £17.97 CT £29.43 TOTE £3.10: £1.50, £1.90, £1.60; EX 17.97 Trifecta £17.10 Pool: £384.36 - 16.57 winning units..
Owner Eildon Hill Racing **Bred** Thoroughbred Farms Ltd **Trained** Musley Bank, N Yorks
■ Stewards' Enquiry : Jason Hart two-day ban: used whip above permitted level (Aug 13-14)

FOCUS
The pace seemed fair enough and those coming from off the speed were at an advantage. The runner-up has been rated to the best of this year's form.
Glenluji Official explanation: jockey said saddle slipped
T/Plt: £20.90 to a £1 stake. Pool: £50577.27 - 1764.37 winning tickets T/Qpdt: £7.20 to a £1 stake. Pool: £3361.96 - 345.16 winning tickets RY

4581 LINGFIELD (L-H)
Monday, July 30

OFFICIAL GOING: Standard
Wind: moderate breeze, half behind Weather: sunny with cloudy periods

4644 32REDBET.COM CLAIMING STKS 6f (P)
2:25 (2:25) (Class 6) 3-Y-0 **£1,704** (£503; £251) **Stalls** Low

Form RPR

40 **1** **Ziefhd**[25] 3785 3-8-6 **78**..(p) ChrisCatlin 2 68
(Paul Cole) *led after 1f: rdn and hrd pressed fr over 1f out: hld on gamely: on top at fin* **11/4**[3]

5500 **2** *nk* **Adranian (IRE)**[16] 4081 3-9-1 **73**.......................................(b[1]) WilliamBuick 4 76
(David C Griffiths) *led for 1f: w wnr: rdn and ev ch fr wl over 1f out tl no ex fnl 50yds* **9/1**

1412 **3** *1 ¼* **Redair (IRE)**[6] 4423 3-8-9 **78**.. PaulHanagan 6 66+
(David Evans) *in last pair but wl in tch: rdn 2f out: no imp tl r.o ins fnl f: wnt 3rd nr fin: nt rch ldrs* **9/5**[1]

306 **4** *¾* **Asian Trader**[24] 3809 3-8-12 **70**.......................................(t) RyanMoore 7 67
(William Haggas) *s.i.s: in last pair but wl in tch: rdn and hdwy 2f out: kpt on same pce fnl f: lost 3rd nr fin* **5/2**[2]

0000 **5** *½* **Chalk And Cheese (USA)**[12] 4218 3-8-12 **72**..........(t) WilliamCarson 8 65
(Stuart Williams) *hld up in tch on outer: rdn to chse ldrs 2f out: kpt on same pce* **16/1**

5340 **6** *4* **Saint Boniface**[35] 3450 3-9-0 **64**.. SebSanders 3 54
(Peter Makin) *racd keenly trcking ldrs: rdn over 2f out: wknd ins fnl f* **50/1**

0000 **7** *nk* **Johnny Splash (IRE)**[27] 3724 3-8-13 **48**.........................(p) DaneO'Neill 1 52?
(Roger Teal) *trckd ldrs: pushed along over 3f out: rdn over 2f out: wknd fnl f* **100/1**

1m 11.99s (0.09) **Going Correction** +0.10s/f (Slow) **7** Ran SP% **109.8**
Speed ratings (Par 98): **83,82,80,79,79 73,73**
toteswingers: 1&2 £7.40, 1&3 £1.10, 2&3 £6.50 CSF £24.76 TOTE £2.90: £1.90, £3.50; EX 26.50.Ziefhd was claimed by Mr P. D. Evans for £7,000.
Owner The Fairy Story Partnership **Bred** Deepwood Farm Stud **Trained** Whatcombe, Oxon

FOCUS
A fair claimer. They were tightly bunched for a long way in a steadily run race and the 78-rated winner put in a determined front-running effort. It's been rated through the runner-up and fourth.
Redair(IRE) Official explanation: jockey said filly hung right

4645 £32 BONUS AT 32RED.COM MAIDEN FILLIES' STKS 6f (P)
2:55 (2:55) (Class 5) 2-Y-0 **£2,726** (£805; £402) **Stalls** Low

Form RPR

22 **1** **City Girl (IRE)**[13] 4180 2-9-0 **0**... JimCrowley 7 81
(Ralph Beckett) *trckd ldr: rdn 2f out: led ent fnl f: drifted rt: kpt on wl to assert fnl 100yds* **8/11**[1]

02 **2** *1 ½* **Spicy (IRE)**[12] 4217 2-9-0 **0**.. AdamKirby 1 76
(Marco Botti) *led: rdn 2f out: hdd ent fnl f: kpt on: hld fnl 100yds* **15/8**[2]

6 **3** *3 ½* **Our Three Graces (IRE)**[28] 3700 2-9-0 **0**.......................... RyanMoore 4 65
(Gary Moore) *trckd ldrs: rdn over 2f out: sn outpcd by ldng pair: kpt on ins fnl f* **16/1**

00 **4** *1 ¾* **Iris Blue**[19] 3959 2-9-0 **0**.. WilliamBuick 3 59
(John Gosden) *trckd ldrs: rdn jst over 2f out: sn outpcd by front pair* **14/1**[3]

0 **5** *3 ¾* **Idle Curiosity (IRE)**[18] 4002 2-9-0 **0**.................................. JamesDoyle 5 47
(Jim Boyle) *racd keenly: trckd ldrs: rdn over 2f out: outpcd by ldng pair sn after: wknd fnl f* **33/1**

6 *7* **Jubilini** 2-9-0 **0**.. KierenFox 6 25
(Brett Johnson) *wnt rt and slowly away: sn pushed along in last: nvr a threat* **66/1**

1m 12.86s (0.96) **Going Correction** +0.10s/f (Slow) **6** Ran SP% **109.7**
Speed ratings (Par 91): **97,95,90,88,83 73**
toteswingers: 1&2 £1.02, 1&3 £3.10, 2&3 £3.20 CSF £2.13 TOTE £1.40: £1.10, £1.10; EX 2.60.
Owner J C Smith **Bred** Littleton Stud **Trained** Kimpton, Hants

FOCUS
The two market leaders dominated this decent fillies' maiden and the winner was value for a bit more than the winning margin. The first two have been rated pretty much to form, but the time was modest.

NOTEBOOK
City Girl(IRE) was heavily backed and produced a sustained run out wide to get off the mark and bounce back from a disappointment on heavy ground last time. A useful and professional type, she is out of a smart 6f/7f winning half-sister to a 5f Listed winner and has plenty of scope for further improvement. (op 4-5 tchd 5-6)
Spicy(IRE) showed much-improved form when just caught in a similar C&D race last time and she made another bold bid but was run down again. A speedy half-sister to 2yo Listed winner Geesala, she has been a bit unlucky to run into a couple of useful rivals on her last two starts and should be able to find a good opportunity to get off the mark. (op 2-1)
Our Three Graces(IRE) was left behind when the front two kicked on but she deserves credit for rallying and was not beaten far on her second start. A half-sister to five winners at 5f-1m2f, she should continue to progress with time and distance.
Iris Blue got tapped for speed when the pace increased before staying on late. (op 10-1)
Jubilini Official explanation: jockey said filly never travelled

4646 32REDPOKER.COM MEDIAN AUCTION MAIDEN STKS 7f (P)
3:30 (3:31) (Class 6) 2-Y-0 **£2,045** (£603; £302) **Stalls** Low

Form RPR

0 **1** **No Jet Lag (USA)**[17] 4066 2-9-3 **0**.. TedDurcan 6 83+
(David Lanigan) *s.i.s: racd keenly: trckd ldrs: drvn upsides ins fnl f: edgd lft fnl 100yds: led fnl strides* **6/5**[1]

2 *shd* **Mocenigo (IRE)** 2-9-3 **0**.. RobertHavlin 3 82+
(Peter Chapple-Hyam) *trckd ldrs: rdn to ld ent fnl f: edgd rt fnl 100yds: hdd fnl strides* **6/4**[2]

40 **3** *2 ¼* **Frege (USA)**[37] 3368 2-8-12 **0**.. KierenFallon 5 74
(Brian Meehan) *led: rdn and hdd over 1f out: disputing v cl 3rd whn bdly hmpd fnl 100yds: hld after* **9/2**[3]

4 *hd* **Piper's Lass (IRE)** 2-8-12 **0**... JoeFanning 7 73+
(Mark Johnston) *prom: rdn to ld briefly over 1f out: disputing v cl 3rd whn squeezed out fnl 100yds: hld after* **14/1**

0 **5** *6* **Day In Day Out**[17] 4066 2-9-3 **0**... JimCrowley 1 59
(Ralph Beckett) *mid-div: rdn over 2f out: sn outpcd* **16/1**

05 **6** *1 ¼* **Sakhee's Ichigou**[12] 4222 2-8-12 **0**.................................... DaneO'Neill 8 51
(Michael Blanshard) *mid-div: rdn over 2f out: sn outpcd* **66/1**

0 **7** *1 ¾* **Ropehanger**[35] 3444 2-8-12 **0**.. KierenFox 2 46
(Lee Carter) *poined to s: hld up: hdwy on outside fr 3f out: rdn to chse ldrs 2f out: wknd fnl f* **50/1**

0 **8** *19* **Kimvara**[38] 3339 2-8-12 **0**... ChrisCatlin 4
(Joseph Tuite) *mid-div tl 3f out: sn rdn: wknd 2f out* **66/1**

1m 27.47s (2.67) **Going Correction** +0.10s/f (Slow) **8** Ran SP% **121.1**
Speed ratings (Par 92): **88,87,85,85,78 76,74,53**
toteswingers: 1&2 £1.10, 1&3 £1.70, 2&3 £1.90 CSF £3.52 TOTE £2.10: £1.10, £1.70, £1.10; EX 4.50.
Owner William McAlpin **Bred** Greenwood Lodge Farm Inc **Trained** Upper Lambourn, Berks
■ Stewards' Enquiry : Robert Havlin three-day ban: careless riding (Aug 13-15)

FOCUS
They went a steady pace in this maiden. There was an exciting finish between the two market leaders and the first four pulled clear. The hampered third is probably the best guide to the level.

NOTEBOOK
No Jet Lag(USA) had fair claims on his promising 40-1 seventh in a 7f soft-ground Newmarket maiden on debut and was heavily backed. Things didn't look very promising when he took a fierce hold early on, and he was forced to switch widest of all in the straight, but he managed to find a strong burst and just prevailed. This was a highly creditable effort in adverse circumstances from this half-brother to French Group-placed 6f 2yo winner Optari and he has plenty of potential for further improvement. (op 2-1)
Mocenigo(IRE), a big market mover in the morning but a drifter on course, tracked the pace before quickening into the lead 1f out but he was just worn down by an experienced rival. This was a big debut run from a well-regarded Refuse To Bend colt who holds entries in The Champagne Stakes and Royal Lodge. (tchd 11-8 and 2-1)
Frege(USA) set the standard on her respectable seventh in the Chesham and had an easy lead for most of the way, but she had no answer when the front two attacked on both sides. (op 3-1)
Piper's Lass(IRE), a Singspiel filly who is a sister to useful 1m2f/1m3f winner Cairnsmore out of a dam who finished third in the Lowther, ran a big race at 14-1 on her debut and would have finished closer if she hadn't been squeezed out by the front two in the closing stages.
Day In Day Out finished around 4l closer to No Jet Lag than he did on his debut. (op 25-1)

4647 32RED.COM FILLIES' H'CAP 7f (P)
4:05 (4:05) (Class 4) (0-85,78) 3-Y-0 **£4,528** (£1,347; £673; £336) **Stalls** Low

Form RPR

-104 **1** **Dance Company**[46] 3085 3-9-5 **76**.. JimCrowley 8 87+
(William Knight) *in tch: rdn and hdwy 2f out: led ent fnl f: hld on* **2/1**[1]

4121 **2** *hd* **Subtle Knife**[27] 3719 3-8-13 **70**....................................... WilliamCarson 2 80+
(Giles Bravery) *in tch: rdn 2f out: str run ent fnl f: clsng on wnr at fin: jst failed* **9/2**[2]

0146 **3** *3 ¾* **Bint Alzain (IRE)**[12] 4218 3-9-4 **75**.. RyanMoore 1 75
(Gerard Butler) *hld up: rdn and gd hdwy on inner wl over 1f out: wnt 3rd ent fnl f: kpt on same pce* **6/1**[3]

0215 **4** *½* **Negin**[18] 3991 3-9-7 **78**..[1] WilliamBuick 4 77
(Ed Dunlop) *hld up: rdn whn coming wdst ent st: r.o ins fnl f: wnt 4th nring fin* **8/1**

4-16 **5** *¾* **Balady (IRE)**[54] 2820 3-9-7 **78**... PaulHanagan 5 75
(John Dunlop) *trckd ldr: rdn over 2f out: one pce fnl f* **9/1**

-234 **6** *nk* **Saratoga Slew (IRE)**[43] 3192 3-9-2 **73**.................................. AdamKirby 7 69
(Marco Botti) *led: rdn and hdd over 2f out: kpt on tl no ex fnl 120yds* **7/1**

5333 **7** *½* **Red Larkspur (IRE)**[33] 3500 3-9-7 **78**.................................. JamesDoyle 6 72
(Roger Teal) *trckd ldrs after 1f: rdn to ld over 2f out: hdd ent fnl f: no ex fnl 120yds* **7/1**

-435 **8** *1 ¼* **Cynthia Calhoun**47 3044 3-8-10 67 .... JohnFahy 3 58
(Clive Cox) *trckd ldrs: rdn over 2f out: sn one pce* **16/1**

1m 24.48s (-0.32) **Going Correction** +0.10s/f (Slow) **8** Ran SP% **117.8**
Speed ratings (Par 99): **105,104,100,99,99 98,98,96**
toteswingers 1&2 £2.90, 1&3 £3.70, 2&3 £4.60 CSF £11.42 CT £46.83 TOTE £3.80: £1.80, £1.10, £1.90; EX 15.00.
Owner Mrs P G M Jamison **Bred** David Jamison Bloodstock **Trained** Patching, W Sussex

FOCUS
The top weight was 7lb below the ceiling in this handicap and the pace was not very strong, but there was a tight finish between the two market leaders who pulled clear. The third has been used to rate the race.
Cynthia Calhoun Official explanation: jockey said filly hung right

4648 32RED CASINO MAIDEN STKS 1m 4f (P)
4:35 (4:36) (Class 5) 3-Y-O+ **£2,726** (£805; £402) **Stalls** Low

Form RPR
4-35 **1** **Aniseed (IRE)**75 2178 3-8-10 88 .... RyanMoore 6 86
(William Haggas) *trckd ldrs: wnt 2nd over 6f out: pushed along over 3f out: drvn upsides 2f out: led jst over 1f out: styd on strly: rdn out* **4/5**[1]

40 **2** *1 ¼* **Caphira**40 3279 3-8-10 0 .... JimCrowley 7 84
(William Knight) *led after 1f: rdn whn chal over 2f out: hdd jst over 1f out: kpt on but no ex fnl 120yds* **8/1**[3]

3463 **3** *3 ¼* **Disposition**25 3792 3-8-10 77 .... WilliamBuick 1 79
(John Gosden) *led for 1f: trckd ldr tl over 6f out: rdn over 3f out: styd on same pce fnl 2f* **5/2**[2]

4 *nk* **Maun Vrat (IRE)** 3-8-10 0 .... PaulHanagan 2 78
(Ed Dunlop) *s.i.s: bhd: hdwy fr 3f out: rdn over 2f out: chal for 3rd ins fnl f: styd on same pce* **14/1**

0556 **5** *9* **Bohemian Rhapsody (IRE)**20 3945 3-9-1 72 ....(p) SebSanders 4 69
(J W Hills) *racd keenly early: trckd ldrs: rdn wl over 2f out: sn btn* **10/1**

56 **6** *7* **Benartic (IRE)**5 4464 8-9-13 0 .... DaneO'Neill 5 58
(Harry Dunlop) *s.i.s: towards rr: rdn 4f out: nvr any imp: wknd over 1f out* **50/1**

P **Totally Addicted**19 6-9-13 0 .... WilliamCarson 3
(Mark Hoad) *trckd ldrs tl lost pl qckly over 4f out: sn bhd: p.u over 1f out* **200/1**

2m 34.19s (1.19) **Going Correction** +0.10s/f (Slow)
WFA 3 from 6yo+ 12lb **7** Ran SP% **113.5**
Speed ratings (Par 103): **100,99,97,96,90 86,**
toteswingers 1&2 £1.70, 1&3 £1.60, 2&3 £2.50 CSF £8.35 TOTE £2.20: £1.10, £2.80; EX 6.50.
Owner M J & L A Taylor **Bred** Grangecon Stud **Trained** Newmarket, Suffolk

FOCUS
The favourite had to work hard before scoring with something in hand in this decent maiden, and she's been rated as running below her best.
Totally Addicted Official explanation: vet said gelding pulled up lame

4649 32RED H'CAP 1m 4f (P)
5:10 (5:11) (Class 4) (0-80,78) 3-Y-O **£4,528** (£1,347; £673; £336) **Stalls** Low

Form RPR
5-13 **1** **Arch Villain (IRE)**45 3104 3-9-1 72 .... JimCrowley 4 81+
(Amanda Perrett) *trckd ldrs: jnd ldr over 5f out: rdn to ld over 2f out: styd on strly to assert fnl 120yds* **4/1**[3]

0001 **2** *1 ¾* **Three Bards (IRE)**7 4403 3-9-6 77 6ex .... JoeFanning 2 84+
(Mark Johnston) *led for 1f: rdn whn nt clr run over 1f out: styd on whn clr run jst ins fnl f: sn chsng wnr but a being hld* **11/2**

5402 **3** *shd* **Mizbah**20 3945 3-9-5 76 .... FrankieDettori 3 82
(Saeed Bin Suroor) *stdd s: in last but in tch: pushed along over 2f out: swtchd rt and rdn over 1f out: sn hung lft: styd on ins fnl f: wnt 3rd fnl stride* **13/8**[1]

-001 **4** *½* **Dont Take Me Alive**18 4005 3-8-11 68 ....(p) JohnFahy 6 73
(Clive Cox) *trckd ldrs: rdn over 2f out: chal jst over 1f out: styd on same pce ins fnl f* **16/1**

0-21 **5** *1 ½* **Palus San Marco (IRE)**27 3720 3-9-7 78 .... RobertHavlin 1 81
(Peter Chapple-Hyam) *trckd ldrs: rdn 3f out: nvr quite able to mount chal: kpt on same pce* **12/1**

2054 **6** *nse* **Hallmark Star**17 4067 3-9-7 78 .... RyanMoore 5 81
(Gerard Butler) *led after 1f: pushed along over 3f out: sn rdn: hdd over 2f out: kpt pressing wnr tl ent fnl f: no ex fnl 120yds* **7/2**[2]

2m 33.53s (0.53) **Going Correction** +0.10s/f (Slow) **6** Ran SP% **109.3**
Speed ratings (Par 102): **102,100,100,100,99 99**
toteswingers 1&2 £7.40, 1&3 £1.10, 2&3 £6.50 CSF £24.05 TOTE £5.50: £2.60, £2.40; EX 24.10.
Owner & Mrs F Cotton,& Mrs P Conway **Bred** Summerhill Bloodstock **Trained** Pulborough, W Sussex

FOCUS
A tight handicap. The pace was steady and the second ran into some trouble at a crucial stage. The third and fourth have been rated to their recent form.

4650 32REDBINGO.COM H'CAP 1m 2f (P)
5:40 (5:41) (Class 6) (0-60,60) 3-Y-O **£1,704** (£503; £251) **Stalls** Low

Form RPR
0032 **1** **Welsh Nayber**34 3469 3-9-6 59 ....(b) JimCrowley 1 69
(Amanda Perrett) *trckd ldrs: led 2f out: rdn clr and in command fnl f* **9/2**[1]

-401 **2** *1* **Norfolk Sky**13 4198 3-8-9 48 .... PaulHanagan 10 55
(Chris Wall) *mid-div: rdn and hdwy over 2f out: wnt 2nd ent fnl f: a being hld by wnr* **6/1**[2]

-366 **3** *hd* **Neige D'Antan**23 3847 3-8-12 51 .... ChrisCatlin 4 58
(Sir Mark Prescott Bt) *mid-div: rdn over 2f out: hdwy over 1f out: chal for 2nd ins fnl f: a being hld by wnr* **9/1**

0-50 **4** *3* **Supreme Rock**27 3736 3-9-7 60 ....(p) PatCosgrave 14 61
(Jim Boyle) *mid-div: rdn and stdy prog fr over 2f out: styd on fnl f: nvr trbld ldrs* **16/1**

056 **5** *3 ½* **Flamborough Breeze**12 4214 3-9-2 55 ....(tp) JoeFanning 9 49
(Ed Vaughan) *trckd ldrs: rdn over 2f out: kpt on same pce* **16/1**

6650 **6** *½* **Tigertoo (IRE)**14 4153 3-8-8 47 ....(t) WilliamCarson 2 40
(Stuart Williams) *w ldr: led wl over 2f out: sn rdn and hdd: no ex whn lost 2nd ent fnl f:* **12/1**

0000 **7** *¾* **Riviera Romance**4 4486 3-9-1 54 .... MircoDemuro 7 45
(J W Hills) *mid-div: rdn over 2f out: nvr any imp* **25/1**

2356 **8** *2 ½* **Song Of Joy (IRE)**9 4335 3-9-4 57 ....(p) WilliamBuick 8 43
(Paul D'Arcy) *trckd ldrs: rdn over 2f out: wknd jst over 1f out* **9/2**[1]

2000 **9** *¾* **Rocco Breeze (IRE)**14 4153 3-8-10 49 ow1 ......(v1) MircoMimmocchi 12 34
(Philip McBride) *hld up towards rr: rdn over 2f out: sme late prog but nvr any threat* **33/1**

0005 **10** *2 ½* **Here Comes Jeanie**29 3665 3-8-4 45 .... SimonPearce(3) 11 26
(Michael Madgwick) *mid-div: rdn over 2f out: wknd over 1f out* **25/1**

-005 **11** *shd* **Chocolat Chaud (IRE)**45 3122 3-8-13 52 .... SebSanders 6 31
(J W Hills) *hld up towards rr: rdn over 2f out: no imp on ldrs* **14/1**

6003 **12** *3 ½* **Wyebridge**19 3965 3-8-10 49 ....(b1) RyanMoore 13 21
(Gary Moore) *s.i.s: struggling 1/2-way: a towards rr* **15/2**[3]

0460 **13** *6* **You Got The Love**30 3620 3-8-7 45 ....(tp) JohnFahy 3 6
(Jeremy Gask) *mid-div: reminders over 4f out: rdn over 3f out: wknd over 1f out* **50/1**

0650 **14** *6* **Jimmy The Lollipop (IRE)**28 3713 3-8-13 57 .....(bt) CharlesBishop(5) 5 5
(Ian Williams) *led: rdn and hdd wl over 2f out: wknd over 1f out* **9/1**

2m 7.09s (0.49) **Going Correction** +0.10s/f (Slow) **14** Ran SP% **121.1**
Speed ratings (Par 98): **102,101,101,98,95 95,94,92,92,90 90,87,82,77**
toteswingers 1&2 £6.00, 1&3 £9.70, 2&3 £10.60 CSF £29.41 CT £239.28 TOTE £4.40: £1.30, £1.30, £6.40; EX 26.30.
Owner Coombelands Racing Syndicate **Bred** Usk Valley Stud **Trained** Pulborough, W Sussex

FOCUS
A minor handicap. It was run at a reasonable pace and the first three finished clear. The runner-up has been rated to her latest Yarmouth effort with the third close to her best form this year.
T/Plt: £20.40 to a £1 stake. Pool: £46477.20 - 1659.08 winning tickets T/Qpdt: £4.70 to a £1 stake. Pool: £4548.38 - 704.41 winning tickets TM

4152 WOLVERHAMPTON (A.W) (L-H)
Monday, July 30

OFFICIAL GOING: Standard
Wind: Fresh behind Weather: Cloudy with sunny spells

4651 HOTEL & CONFERENCING AT WOLVERHAMPTON MAIDEN FILLIES' STKS 5f 20y(P)
6:00 (6:01) (Class 5) 2-Y-O **£2,264** (£673; £336; £168) **Stalls** Low

Form RPR
4406 **1** **Excel Yourself (IRE)**29 3669 2-9-0 78 .... MartinDwyer 5 78
(James Tate) *mde virtually all: rdn and hung rt ins fnl f: r.o* **10/3**[3]

40 **2** *2* **Star Up In The Sky (USA)**40 3269 2-9-0 0 .... AmyRyan 8 71
(Kevin Ryan) *prom: jnd wnr 1/2-way: rdn over 1f out: styng on same pce whn nt clr run ins fnl f* **15/8**[1]

062 **3** *3* **Showtime Girl (IRE)**23 3844 2-9-0 0 .... DavidAllan 4 65+
(Tim Easterby) *prom: pushed along 1/2-way: sddle slipped sn after: rdr unable to assist but stl styd on for 3rd* **7/1**

3 **4** *1 ¾* **Clean Blow (USA)**28 3700 2-9-0 0 .... RichardMullen 9 54
(David Brown) *hld up: hdwy 1/2-way: rdn over 1f out: no ex fnl f* **11/4**[2]

5 *1* **Girl At The Sands (IRE)** 2-9-0 0 .... JamesSullivan 3 50
(James Given) *chsd ldrs: rdn over 1f out: no ex fnl f* **28/1**

2600 **6** *3* **Cymeriad**3 4545 2-9-0 59 .... GrahamGibbons 7 39
(Michael Easterby) *chsd ldrs: rdn 1/2-way: wknd over 1f out* **16/1**

5 **7** *1 ½* **Dashing Storm**27 3733 2-9-0 0 .... RobertWinston 6 37
(Jeremy Gask) *hld up: pushed along 1/2-way: sn wknd* **18/1**

66 **8** *9* **Star Maid**42 3217 2-9-0 0 .... DavidProbert 10
(Tony Carroll) *sn pushed along in rr: lost tch 1/2-way* **125/1**

9 *5* **Anna Isabella** 2-8-11 0 .... DaleSwift(3) 2
(Derek Shaw) *s.s: outpcd* **50/1**

1m 1.57s (-0.73) **Going Correction** -0.125s/f (Stan) **9** Ran SP% **114.4**
Speed ratings (Par 91): **100,96,92,89,87 82,80,66,58**
toteswingers 1&2 £1.60, 2&3 £3.80, 1&3 £3.50 CSF £9.80 TOTE £7.20: £2.70, £1.10, £2.10; EX 12.00 Trifecta £67.30 Pool: £224.05 - 2.46 winning units..
Owner Saif Ali **Bred** Rabbah Bloodstock Limited **Trained** Newmarket, Suffolk

FOCUS
This ordinary juvenile fillies' maiden was run at a decent pace, yet still it paid to race handily. The first two have been rated to form, with the third rated a length better than the bare form due to a slipping saddle.

NOTEBOOK
Excel Yourself(IRE) bounced back to form and ran out a ready winner on this AW debut. She flopped at Windsor last time out, but set the standard here with a mark of 78 and, despite lugging right under pressure late on, was always holding the runner-up inside the final furlong. She ought to make her presence felt in nurseries. (op 7-2 tchd 3-1)
Star Up In The Sky(USA) was always up there and made the winner work, but was held before that rival came across her late in the day. She finished a clear second-best and now qualifies for nurseries. (op 9-4 tchd 7-4)
Showtime Girl(IRE)'s rider continually looked down in the home straight as she coasted home for third. It later transpired the saddle had slipped after halfway, so this was a fair run in the circumstances. Official explanation: jockey said saddle slipped (op 5-1)
Clean Blow(USA) failed to build on her Windsor debut but wasn't helped by the wide draw. (op 3-1 tchd 7-2)
Girl At The Sands(IRE) ought to improve a deal for this initial experience. (op 25-1)

4652 FOLLOW US ON TWITTER @WOLVESRACES H'CAP 1m 4f 50y(P)
6:30 (6:30) (Class 6) (0-60,60) 3-Y-O+ **£1,704** (£503; £251) **Stalls** Low

Form RPR
6051 **1** **Honest Deal**14 4156 4-10-0 **60** .... RobertWinston 1 73+
(Alan Swinbank) *led 1f: trckd ldr: plld hrd: led 3f out: hung rt wl over 1f out: sn pushed clr: easily* **11/8**[1]

6-51 **2** *4 ½* **Layla's Boy**7 4402 5-9-12 **58** 6ex ....(bt) FrannyNorton 12 62
(John Mackie) *hld up: hdwy u.p over 1f out: styd on to go 2nd ins fnl f: no ch w wnr* **5/1**[3]

3642 **3** *2 ½* **White Deer (USA)**14 4156 8-9-9 **55** ....(v) SilvestreDeSousa 3 55
(Geoffrey Harker) *pushed along early and sn prom: chsd wnr over 2f out: rdn over 1f out: styd on same pce: lost 2nd ins fnl f* **4/1**[2]

-660 **4** *1 ¾* **Broughtons Swinger**19 3968 5-9-11 **57** .... StevieDonohoe 2 54
(Willie Musson) *chsd ldrs: rdn over 2f out: styd on same pce* **15/2**

4600 **5** *½* **Blue Cossack (IRE)**27 3734 4-9-13 **59** ....(v) DavidProbert 4 55
(Mark Usher) *hld up: hdwy u.p over 2f out: nvr on terms* **18/1**

06 **6** *9* **Squirrel Wood (IRE)**54 2821 4-9-13 **59** ....(b1) GeorgeBaker 7 41
(Mary Hambro) *hld up: hdwy over 3f out: sn rdn: wknd 2f out* **12/1**

-005 **7** *3 ¾* **Rajeh (IRE)**82 1991 9-10-0 **60** .... RobbieFitzpatrick 8 36
(Peter Grayson) *hld up: a in rr: bhd fnl 4f* **100/1**

5-00 **8** *2 ¾* **Silent Energy (IRE)**33 3483 3-7-13 **48** .... DarrenEgan(5) 6 20
(Ronald Harris) *mid-div: drvn along over 3f out: wknd over 2f out* **25/1**

0000 **9** *¾* **Breakheart (IRE)**12 4219 5-9-11 **57** ....(b1) MichaelStainton 9 27
(Paul Howling) *plld hrd: led after 1f: hdd 3f out: wknd 2f out* **18/1**

5400 **10** *15* **Redclue (IRE)**110 1303 3-8-9 **53** ....(p) MarcHalford 11
(Miss Louise Allan) *mid-div: pushed along over 5f out: wknd over 4f out: t.o* **33/1**

2m 39.15s (-1.95) **Going Correction** -0.125s/f (Stan)
WFA 3 from 4yo+ 12lb **10** Ran SP% **116.5**
Speed ratings (Par 101): **101,98,96,95,94 88,86,84,84,74**
toteswingers 1&2 £2.80, 2&3 £2.60, 1&3 £2.10 CSF £8.20 CT £22.55 TOTE £2.30: £1.10, £1.90, £1.90; EX 12.00 Trifecta £17.40 Pool: £226.25 - 9.60 winning units..

Owner Guy Reed **Bred** G Reed **Trained** Melsonby, N Yorks

FOCUS

A moderate handicap, run at an average pace. The runner-up has been rated as running 7lb below his improved effort at Southwell last time.

Blue Cossack(IRE) Official explanation: jockey said gelding missed the break

4653 LIKE US ON FACEBOOK WOLVERHAMPTON RACECOURSE H'CAP 5f 216y(P)

7:00 (7:00) (Class 6) (0-60,60) 3-Y-O+ **£1,704** (£503; £251) **Stalls** Low

Form | RPR

200- **1** **Elegant Muse**[286] 6938 4-9-5 **58** GeorgeBaker 13 65
(Michael Appleby) *led 5f out: hdd over 2f out: led again 1f out: drvn out* **14/1**

6660 **2** ½ **Mawjoodah**[4] 4495 4-9-2 **58** (v[1]) PaulPickard(3) 6 63+
(Brian Ellison) *hld up: rdn over 1f out: r.o: nt rch wnr* **13/2**

0100 **3** hd **Irie Ute**[20] 3949 4-9-4 **57** RichardHughes 3 62
(Sylvester Kirk) *a.p: rdn to chse wnr ins fnl f: r.o* **5/1**[3]

0053 **4** ½ **Imjin River (IRE)**[14] 4143 5-8-12 **56** AshleyMorgan(5) 5 59
(William Stone) *chsd ldrs: rdn over 1f out: r.o* **16/1**

3455 **5** ¾ **Invigilator**[14] 4146 4-9-2 **55** SilvestreDeSousa 4 56
(Derek Shaw) *hld up: hdwy over 1f out: sn rdn: styd on* **7/2**[1]

0006 **6** ½ **Juarla (IRE)**[101] 1497 4-8-12 **56** DarrenEgan(5) 12 55+
(Ronald Harris) *hld up: nt clr run over 1f out: rdn and r.o ins fnl f: nrst fin* **25/1**

3003 **7** shd **Glastonberry**[20] 3943 4-9-4 **57** MartinDwyer 7 56+
(Geoffrey Deacon) *hld up: hdwy over 1f out: r.o u.p ins fnl f: nt rch ldrs* **4/1**[2]

0000 **8** nse **Ace Of Spies (IRE)**[13] 4192 7-9-5 **58** HayleyTurner 1 57
(Conor Dore) *chsd ldrs: rdn over 2f out: styd on* **28/1**

3530 **9** nse **Rightcar**[90] 1734 5-9-1 **54** RobbieFitzpatrick 8 53
(Peter Grayson) *broke out of stalls sltly early: sn lost pl: r.o wl ins fnl f* **25/1**

5000 **10** nk **Men Don't Cry (IRE)**[20] 3943 3-9-0 **58** EddieAhern 10 56+
(Ed de Giles) *mid-div: sn drvn along: r.o ins fnl f: nvr trbld ldrs* **22/1**

5215 **11** ¾ **Almaty Express**[20] 3943 10-9-0 **60** (b) WilliamTwiston-Davies(7) 2 55
(John Weymes) *led early: chsd ldr: led again over 2f out: rdn and hdd 1f out: no ex wl ins fnl f* **15/2**

0016 **12** 2 **Aubrietia**[32] 3548 3-8-12 **56** IPoullis 9 45
(Alan McCabe) *hld up: rdn and edgd lft over 1f out: nvr trbld ldrs* **12/1**

6300 **13** ¾ **Nine Before Ten (IRE)**[16] 4087 4-8-11 **57** (tp) ThomasBrown(7) 11 43
(Charles Smith) *sn led: hdd 5f out: rdn over 1f out: wknd fnl f* **40/1**

1m 14.35s (-0.65) **Going Correction** -0.125s/f (Stan)
WFA 3 from 4yo+ 5lb **13 Ran SP% 122.2**
Speed ratings (Par 101): **99,98,98,97,96 95,95,95,95,95 94,91,90**
toteswingers 1&2 £19.90, 2&3 £5.00, 1&3 £12.30 CSF £98.30 CT £550.46 TOTE £21.40: £4.50, £3.00, £1.70; EX 155.60 TRIFECTA Not won..

Owner Terry Pryke **Bred** Genesis Green Stud Ltd **Trained** Danethorpe, Notts

FOCUS

This open-looking handicap was run at a decent pace and there was a bunched finish. The runner-up has been rated close to this year's best in the first-time visor, with the fourth also to form.

4654 DOWNLOAD OUR IPHONE APP MAIDEN STKS 5f 216y(P)

7:35 (7:35) (Class 5) 2-Y-O **£2,264** (£673; £336; £168) **Stalls** Low

Form | RPR

0 **1** **Intibaah**[30] 3634 2-9-3 0 TadhgO'Shea 11 87
(Brian Meehan) *a.p: chsd ldr 4f out: led over 2f out: sn rdn: hung lft ins fnl f: r.o wl* **7/2**[2]

233 **2** 2 **Rising Legend**[16] 4090 2-9-3 82 RichardHughes 6 81
(Richard Hannon) *led over 3f: rdn over 1f out: styd on same pce ins fnl f* **1/2**[1]

0 **3** 7 **Quiet Prayer**[47] 3040 2-9-3 0 HayleyTurner 7 58
(Ed Dunlop) *chsd ldrs: rdn over 2f out: styd on same pce fr over 1f out* **8/1**[3]

4 1 ¼ **Chelsea Grey (IRE)** 2-8-7 0 DarrenEgan(5) 10 49+
(Ronald Harris) *mid-div: rdn over 2f out: sn outpcd* **33/1**

04 **5** 2 ½ **Eyeline**[16] 4076 2-9-3 0 RussKennemore 4 46
(Reg Hollinshead) *sn pushed along and prom: rdn over 2f out: sn wknd* **40/1**

00 **6** ¾ **My Sweet Lord**[33] 3505 2-8-12 0 LeeNewnes(5) 12 43
(Mark Usher) *s.i.s: pushed along 1/2-way: nvr nrr* **80/1**

06 **7** hd **Plexolini**[32] 3545 2-9-3 0 J-PGuillambert 1 43
(Jo Hughes) *hld up: shkn up over 1f out: nvr nr to chal* **22/1**

8 1 **Top Town Boy** 2-9-3 0 AmirQuinn 3 39
(John Holt) *s.i.s: a in rr* **33/1**

0 **9** nk **Gambino (IRE)**[33] 3491 2-9-0 0 PaulPickard(3) 8 38
(Hugh McWilliams) *hld up: a in rr* **100/1**

0 **10** 2 ¾ **Cos I Can**[13] 4178 2-8-12 0 SilvestreDeSousa 5 25
(Derek Shaw) *chsd ldr 2f: rdn over 2f out: wknd wl over 1f out* **100/1**

11 2 ¾ **Pleasant Moment** 2-8-12 0 FrannyNorton 9 16
(Tom Dascombe) *hld up: a in rr* **14/1**

1m 14.29s (-0.71) **Going Correction** -0.125s/f (Stan) **11 Ran SP% 122.6**
Speed ratings (Par 94): **99,96,87,85,82 81,80,79,79,75 71**
toteswingers 1&2 £1.50, 2&3 £2.60, 1&3 £2.90 CSF £5.63 TOTE £3.40: £1.10, £1.02, £3.20; EX 9.20 Trifecta £18.90 Pool: £359.28 - 14.00 winning units..

Owner Hamdan Al Maktoum **Bred** Shadwell Estate Company Limited **Trained** Manton, Wilts

FOCUS

The two market leaders raced to the fore in this modest juvenile maiden and dominated from the home turn. The runner-up has been rated to form.

NOTEBOOK

Intibaah went for everything entering the home straight and mastered the runner-up to win readily. He was well beaten on his debut at Newmarket a month earlier, but that was a messy race and he had clearly come on a deal for the run. Another furlong should be within his range, but he's open to plenty of improvement over a stiff 6f and it will be interesting to see what mark he gets now. (tchd 3-1)

Rising Legend, placed on his previous three outings, was heavily backed to oblige on this switch to Polytrack. He set out to make all but was hassled throughout by the winner and ultimately found that rival too classy. He was nicely clear in second and deserves a change of fortune, but is clearly vulnerable to anything useful. (op 8-13 tchd 4-6)

Quiet Prayer did his best work late in the day on his debut over this trip at Kempton last month. He showed up more prominently this time, but was unable to live with the first pair and probably wants another furlong. (op 7-1 tchd 9-1)

Chelsea Grey(IRE) wasn't aided by the draw and, getting the hang of things when the race was effectively over, showed ability on her debut.

4655 HOLIDAY INN WOLVERHAMPTON FILLIES' H'CAP 5f 216y(P)

8:05 (8:05) (Class 4) (0-80,80) 3-Y-O+ **£4,204** (£1,251; £625; £312) **Stalls** Low

Form | RPR

-014 **1** **Bavarian Princess (USA)**[157] 686 4-9-4 **72** GeorgeBaker 2 78
(Mrs K Burke) *hld up in tch: rdn over 1f out: edgd lft: r.o to ld nr fin* **17/2**

3143 **2** shd **Fenella Fudge**[25] 3780 4-8-12 **66** (v[1]) MartinDwyer 3 72+
(Derek Shaw) *hld up: rdn over 1f out: r.o wl ins fnl f: jst failed* **11/1**

2646 **3** nse **Camache Queen (IRE)**[28] 3696 4-9-9 **77** EddieAhern 4 83
(Denis Coakley) *chsd ldrs: rdn over 1f out: edgd lft ins fnl f: r.o* **9/4**[1]

50-6 **4** nk **Gap Princess (IRE)**[40] 3272 8-8-13 **67** RobertWinston 1 72
(Geoffrey Harker) *led 1f: chsd ldrs: rdn over 2f out: r.o* **14/1**

230 **5** nk **Catflap (IRE)**[33] 3510 3-8-3 **62** NickyMackay 5 65
(Derek Haydn Jones) *led 5f out: rdn over 1f out: hdd nr fin* **33/1**

1603 **6** nk **My Own Way Home**[11] 4238 4-8-8 **62** SilvestreDeSousa 8 65
(David Evans) *hld up: hdwy over 1f out: r.o* **16/1**

0614 **7** ¾ **Piddie's Power**[33] 3500 5-9-5 **80** WilliamTwiston-Davies(7) 10 81
(Ed McMahon) *hld up: hdwy over 1f out: sn rdn: r.o* **13/2**[2]

06-0 **8** shd **Supreme Spirit (IRE)**[25] 3785 5-9-9 **77** RichardHughes 7 78
(Peter Makin) *hld up: r.o wl ins fnl f: nt clr run and eased nr fin* **8/1**

3420 **9** hd **Bouncy Bouncy (IRE)**[9] 4336 5-9-10 **78** (t) HayleyTurner 6 78
(Michael Bell) *hld up: pushed along 1/2-way: r.o ins fnl f: nvr rchd ldrs* **7/1**[3]

6262 **10** 4 **Kyanight (IRE)**[35] 3450 3-8-13 **72** AdamKirby 9 58
(Clive Cox) *prom: chsd ldr over 3f out: rdn over 1f out: wknd ins fnl f* **7/1**[3]

1m 14.11s (-0.89) **Going Correction** -0.125s/f (Stan)
WFA 3 from 4yo+ 5lb **10 Ran SP% 114.6**
Speed ratings (Par 102): **100,99,99,99,99 98,97,97,97,91**
toteswingers 1&2 £19.60, 2&3 £6.00, 1&3 £6.80 CSF £96.04 CT £254.60 TOTE £10.00: £3.10, £4.30, £1.10; EX 166.80 TRIFECTA Not won..

Owner The Sidney Club **Bred** Maura Gittens **Trained** Middleham Moor, N Yorks

FOCUS

There was a very tight finish to this competitive sprint handicap with the first nine closely covered. Ordinary form, with the front-running fifth outrunning her odds and the runner-up better over 7f.

Supreme Spirit(IRE) Official explanation: jockey said mare was denied a clear run

4656 THE BLACK COUNTRY'S ONLY RACECOURSE H'CAP 7f 32y(P)

8:35 (8:35) (Class 6) (0-55,55) 3-Y-O+ **£1,704** (£503; £251) **Stalls** High

Form | RPR

6505 **1** **Strong Man**[10] 4313 4-9-6 **55** (b) JamesSullivan 2 65
(Michael Easterby) *a.p: drvn along 1/2-way: rdn to ld ins fnl f: jst hld on* **10/1**

0646 **2** nk **July Days (IRE)**[20] 3949 6-9-6 **55** FrederikTylicki 4 64
(Brian Baugh) *chsd ldrs: rdn over 1f out: r.o* **8/1**

3264 **3** 2 **Gala Spirit (IRE)**[136] 932 5-9-2 **51** GrahamGibbons 5 55
(Michael Wigham) *led: rdn and hdd ins fnl f: no ex* **5/2**[1]

0041 **4** shd **Whitstable Native**[11] 4241 4-9-1 **55** DarrenEgan(5) 8 58
(Joseph Tuite) *hld up in tch: rdn over 1f out: r.o* **7/1**[3]

042U **5** ¾ **Volcanic Jack (IRE)**[33] 3497 4-9-4 **53** MichaelO'Connell 6 54
(Tony Carroll) *chsd ldr: rdn over 1f out: no ex ins fnl f* **8/1**

6045 **6** shd **Prince Of Passion (CAN)**[19] 3964 4-9-6 **55** (v[1]) SilvestreDeSousa 7 56
(Derek Shaw) *s.i.s: hld up: r.o ins fnl f: nvr nrr* **8/1**

6/00 **7** 2 ¾ **Hyde Lea Flyer**[14] 4158 7-9-5 **54** RussKennemore 12 48
(Barry Leavy) *hld up: rdn over 2f out: nvr trbld ldrs* **20/1**

0050 **8** hd **Hold The Star**[7] 4407 6-9-1 **55** AnnStokell(5) 1 48
(Ann Stokell) *chsd ldrs: pushed along over 2f out: edgd rt and wknd ins fnl f* **33/1**

0000 **9** 1 **Vhujon (IRE)**[42] 3229 7-9-6 **55** RobbieFitzpatrick 9 45
(Peter Grayson) *s.i.s: a in rr* **28/1**

00-0 **10** 2 **Born To Be Achamp (BRZ)**[199] 153 6-9-3 **52** FrannyNorton 11 37
(Geoffrey Harker) *hld up: nvr on terms* **33/1**

0054 **11** 15 **Maggie Mey (IRE)**[55] 2791 4-9-6 **55** GeorgeBaker 10
(Lawrence Mullaney) *prom: rdn 1/2-way: wknd over 2f out: eased* **7/2**[2]

1m 28.45s (-1.15) **Going Correction** -0.125s/f (Stan) **11 Ran SP% 119.8**
Speed ratings (Par 101): **101,100,98,98,97 97,94,93,92,90 73**
toteswingers 1&2 £13.50, 2&3 £4.30, 1&3 £8.50 CSF £85.21 CT £236.80 TOTE £10.80: £2.90, £5.00, £1.20; EX 130.40 TRIFECTA Not won..

Owner Mrs Jean Turpin **Bred** Mrs Jean Turpin **Trained** Sheriff Hutton, N Yorks

FOCUS

A tight handicap with 4lb covering the field. Straightforward form to rate, with the runner-up rated to her best form since her C&D win in February.

Maggie Mey(IRE) Official explanation: jockey said filly stopped quickly

4657 BOOK TICKETS ONLINE AT WOLVERHAMPTON-RACECOURSE.CO.UK H'CAP 1m 1f 103y(P)

9:05 (9:05) (Class 5) (0-75,75) 3-Y-O+ **£2,264** (£673; £336; £168) **Stalls** Low

Form | RPR

00-1 **1** **Noble Jack (IRE)**[28] 3712 6-9-5 **66** J-PGuillambert 10 76+
(Jo Hughes) *hld up: hdwy 4f out: rdn to chse ldr 2f out: r.o to ld post* **11/2**[3]

1-06 **2** shd **Spanish Plume**[59] 2661 4-9-13 **74** GrahamGibbons 7 84
(Reg Hollinshead) *chsd ldr: led 3f out: pushed clr 2f out: rdn ins fnl f: hdd post* **12/1**

63 **3** 3 **Majuro (IRE)**[18] 3994 8-10-0 **75** (t) RobbieFitzpatrick 5 79
(Charles Smith) *s.i.s: hld up: hdwy over 2f out: rdn over 1f out: styd on: nt rch ldrs* **14/1**

6605 **4** ¾ **I Confess**[14] 4155 7-9-6 **74** (v) JordanNason(7) 2 76
(Geoffrey Harker) *trckd ldrs: racd keenly: rdn over 1f out: styd on same pce fnl f* **20/1**

0-65 **5** 1 ¼ **Brigadoon**[11] 4243 5-9-11 **72** EddieAhern 9 72+
(William Jarvis) *hld up: r.o ins fnl f: nvr nrr* **12/1**

3260 **6** ½ **Scamperdale**[28] 3692 10-9-8 **69** (p) FrederikTylicki 1 67
(Brian Baugh) *mid-div: rdn over 1f out: styd on: nt trble ldrs* **20/1**

2/0- **7** 1 ½ **Matjar (IRE)**[8] 4381 9-9-6 **67** DiegoDias 3 62
(Joseph Quinn, Ire) *hld up: rdn over 1f out: n.d* **20/1**

0253 **8** hd **Spinning Ridge (IRE)**[14] 4155 7-9-4 **70** (b) DarrenEgan(5) 11 65+
(Ronald Harris) *hld up: plld hrd: rdn over 1f out: n.d* **25/1**

0/02 **9** nk **Encompassing (IRE)**[20] 3947 5-9-9 **70** (t) GeorgeBaker 13 64
(Sophie Leech) *s.i.s: hld up: hdwy and hung lft over 1f out: nvr trbld ldrs* **40/1**

01 **10** 3 ¾ **Nimble Thimble (USA)**[14] 4157 3-9-5 **75** JamesDoyle 6 61
(Roger Charlton) *trckd ldrs: rdn over 2f out: wknd over 1f out* **15/8**[1]

400 **11** 4 **Aragorn Rouge**[20] 3947 4-8-8 **60** AdamCarter(5) 12 38
(John Wainwright) *led over 6f: rdn and wknd over 1f out:* **66/1**

3600 **12** *11* **Yaa Salam**[25] 3792 3-9-5 **75**....................(vt) SilvestreDeSousa 4 30
(Mahmood Al Zarooni) *hld up in tch: rdn and wknd over 2f out* **4/1**[2]

1115 **13** *1/2* **Odd Ball (IRE)**[109] 1342 5-9-2 **63**.................... AmyRyan 8 17
(Lisa Williamson) *s.i.s: hld up: hdwy over 6f out: wknd over 2f out* **20/1**

2m 1.35s (-0.35) **Going Correction** -0.125s/f (Stan)
WFA 3 from 4yo+ 9lb **13** Ran SP% **119.0**
Speed ratings (Par 103): **96,95,93,92,91 91,89,89,89,85 82,72,72**
toteswingers 1&2 £20.20, 2&3 £62.90, 1&3 £7.50 CSF £61.68 CT £886.22 TOTE £9.70: £2.10, £2.90, £2.60; EX 173.40 TRIFECTA Not won..
Owner P J Hanly **Bred** Team Hogdala **Trained** Lambourn. Berks

FOCUS
They went a routine pace in this moderate handicap and there was a cracking finish between the first pair, who were clear. Probably not solid form, but it's been rated around the third to his latest form.
T/Jkpt: Not won. T/Plt: £26.10 to a £1 stake. Pool of £73634.85 - 2057.45 winning tickets.
T/Qpdt: £25.60 to a £1 stake. Pool of £5594.17 - 161.30 winning tickets. CR

4433 YARMOUTH (L-H)
Monday, July 30

OFFICIAL GOING: Good (good to soft in places on stands' side; 6.8)
Wind: medium, half against Weather: dry spells, light showers

4658 VISITENGLAND.COM MAIDEN AUCTION STKS 7f 3y
2:15 (2:15) (Class 6) 2-Y-O £1,617 (£481; £240; £120) **Stalls** Centre

Form RPR

1 **Cheektocheek (IRE)** 2-8-12 0.................... MartinHarley 3 71+
(Marco Botti) *s.i.s: hld up in tch: rdn: outpcd and looked btn over 1f out: rallied ins fnl f: str run fnl 100yds to ld cl home* **17/2**

5 **2** *nk* **Choral Prince (IRE)**[37] 3387 2-9-1 0.................... NeilCallan 4 73
(Mike Murphy) *t.k.h: chsd ldrs: rdn to chal over 1f out: led jst ins fnl f: edgd lft u.p: awkward hd carriage but kpt on tl hdd and no ex cl home* **9/2**[3]

0 **3** *1* **Muskat Link**[21] 3916 2-8-9 0.................... FergusSweeney 1 64
(Henry Candy) *chsd ldr tl led 2f out: rdn and hung lft over 1f out: hdd jst ins fnl f: styd on same pce after* **16/1**

2 **4** *1 1/4* **Jumeirah Moon**[20] 3948 2-9-1 0.................... MartinLane 6 67
(David Simcock) *hld up in tch: rdn and effrt whn edgd rt over 1f out: chal 1f out: unable qck and btn ins fnl f: wknd towards fin* **9/4**[1]

6444 **5** *2 3/4* **Northern Harbour (IRE)**[12] 4222 2-9-1 62..........(p) CathyGannon 10 60
(J S Moore) *in tch: rdn and unable qck whn hung rt over 1f out: btn 1f out and styd on same pce after* **20/1**

04 **6** *3* **Believe In Me**[46] 3084 2-8-3 0 ow2..........(p) AdamBeschizza(3) 8 42
(Julia Feilden) *led tl 2f out: sn rdn and unable qck: btn ent fnl f: wknd* **50/1**

05 **7** *2 3/4* **Orla's Rainbow (IRE)**[45] 3112 2-9-1 0.................... DarryllHolland 7 44
(John Berry) *in tch: rdn over 2f out: sn struggling: wknd over 1f out* **6/1**

8 *7* **Forceful Flame** 2-8-9 0.................... AndreaAtzeni 9 19
(Robert Eddery) *dwlt: hld up in rr: hdwy 1/2-way: rdn and struggling 3f out: wknd 2f out: bhd and eased ins fnl f* **7/2**[2]

9 *1* **Paige Flyer** 2-8-2 0 ow3.................... TobyAtkinson(5) 5 14
(Michael Quinn) *s.i.s: in tch: rdn and lost pl 1/2-way: bhd fnl 2f* **50/1**

1m 27.74s (1.14) **Going Correction** -0.25s/f (Firm) **9** Ran SP% **110.6**
Speed ratings (Par 92): **83,82,81,80,76 73,70,62,61**
toteswingers: 1&2 £6.60, 1&3 £16.90, 2&3 £12.20 CSF £43.27 TOTE £12.30: £2.40, £2.00, £6.10; EX 62.70.
Owner Giuliano Manfredini **Bred** Tally-Ho Stud **Trained** Newmarket, Suffolk

FOCUS
Not the strongest of juvenile maidens.

NOTEBOOK
Cheektocheek(IRE) overcame greenness to win narrowly. This colt, who fetched only 7,000gns at the Goffs Sales last year, was all at sea early on but he responded well to pressure in the final couple of furlongs and got up to win a shade cosily. He looks sure to improve for this experience and is definitely one to bear in mind for nurseries. (op 8-1 tchd 15-2 and 9-1)
Choral Prince(IRE) ran with promise on his debut at Lingfield and he appeared to post an improved display here. He looked certain to collect when striking the front but, despite sticking his neck out, was denied by the fast-finishing winner. He may struggle to find a maiden, but needs only one more run to qualify for a nursery mark. (op 7-1 tchd 15-2)
Muskat Link threw away his chance by veering across the track. He clearly has ability and is worthy of another chance with this experience behind him. (op 12-1 tchd 20-1)
Jumeirah Moon, weak in the market, raced keenly and was eventually run out of the places. He may benefit for a drop back to 6f. (op 6-4)
Orla's Rainbow(IRE) Official explanation: jockey said colt lost its action
Forceful Flame was always towards the rear and looks very limited. (op 7-1)

4659 WEDDINGS AT GREAT YARMOUTH RACECOURSE (S) STKS 6f 3y
2:45 (2:45) (Class 6) 2-Y-O £1,617 (£481; £240; £120) **Stalls** Centre

Form RPR

30 **1** **Reconsider Baby (IRE)**[45] 3126 2-8-6 0.................... MartinLane 2 58
(Mrs K Burke) *hld up in tch: effrt over 2f out: rdn to chal ent fnl f: led fnl 100yds: styd on wl* **9/2**

035 **2** *1* **Emperor's Daughter**[66] 2442 2-8-6 58..........(p) JimmyQuinn 8 55
(Tim Pitt) *t.k.h: chsd ldr tl led after 2f: rdn over 1f out: drvn 1f out: hdd and one pce fnl 100yds* **15/2**

5 **3** *2 1/4* **Hardy Blue (IRE)**[5] 4462 2-8-6 0.................... FergusSweeney 4 48
(Jamie Osborne) *chsd ldrs: rdn and effrt jst over 2f out: pressed ldrs wl over 1f out: no ex and flashed tail u.p jst ins fnl f: one pce after* **4/1**[3]

4442 **4** *1/2* **Wordsaplenty (IRE)**[6] 4421 2-8-6 58.................... CathyGannon 6 46
(J S Moore) *t.k.h: hld up in tch: rdn and effrt whn nt clr run and hmpd over 1f out: rallied and styd on ins fnl f: no threat to ldrs* **3/1**[1]

065 **5** *2 1/4* **Cernanova (IRE)**[34] 3465 2-7-13 41....................[1] NoelGarbutt(7) 1 39
(Hugo Palmer) *t.k.h: hld up in tch towards rr: rdn and nt qckn over 2f out: styd on and swtchd lft ins fnl f: no threat to ldrs* **33/1**

0001 **6** *4 1/2* **Grace Of Hearts**[5] 4462 2-8-11 58..........(v[1]) AndreaAtzeni 5 30
(Robert Eddery) *led for 2f: chsd ldr tl 2f out: fnd little u.p and sn struggling: wknd fnl f* **7/2**[2]

6130 **7** *1 3/4* **Suivez L'Argent**[5] 4462 2-8-11 58..........(v[1]) MartinHarley 7 24
(Joseph Tuite) *chsd ldrs: nt qckn u.p 2f out: sn btn and wknd over 1f out* **14/1**

0056 **8** *4* **Myzamour**[13] 4195 2-8-3 56..........(b[1]) RyanPowell(3) 9
(J S Moore) *wnt rt s and s.i.s: in tch in rr: rdn and struggling over 2f out: bhd over 1f out* **33/1**

3446 **9** *19* **Reberty Lee**[55] 2798 2-8-11 56.................... NeilCallan 3
(Noel Quinlan) *s.i.s and rdn along leaving stalls: in tch in rr: rdn and struggling over 2f out: lost tch 2f out* **22/1**

1m 14.07s (-0.33) **Going Correction** -0.25s/f (Firm) **9** Ran SP% **114.1**
Speed ratings (Par 92): **92,90,87,87,84 78,75,70,45**
toteswingers: 1&2 £7.60, 1&3 £5.00, 2&3 £7.60 CSF £36.49 TOTE £7.10: £2.00, £2.80, £1.10; EX 58.80.There was no bid for the winner.
Owner M Nelmes-Crocker **Bred** Liam Queally **Trained** Middleham Moor, N Yorks

FOCUS
A poor juvenile seller.

NOTEBOOK
Reconsider Baby(IRE) had hinted at ability on her debut before disappointing in this grade on softer ground at York last time, but she travelled better than most and knuckled down well in the closing stages. It's unlikely that this form amounts to a great deal, but she saw the trip out well and may be capable of slightly better. (op 11-2 tchd 13-2)
Emperor's Daughter made a bold bid from the front and was arguably a shade unlucky to find one too good. She had been off the track for 66 days and that may have aided her downfall as she refused to settle. That said, she took well to the first-time cheekpieces and shouldn't be written off in this company in the coming weeks, be it over this trip or when returning to the minimum. (tchd 7-1 and 9-1)
Hardy Blue(IRE) was handy throughout and kept on well enough without ever threatening. (op 7-1)
Wordsaplenty(IRE), having her seventh start, didn't get the clearest of runs. She had a good chance on these terms, but seems to have a habit of finding trouble. She should be given another chance, especially if upped to 7f. (op 5-2 tchd 9-4)

4660 MARTIN FOULGER MEMORIAL H'CAP 6f 3y
3:15 (3:16) (Class 4) (0-85,85) 3-Y-O+ £4,075 (£1,212; £606; £303) **Stalls** Centre

Form RPR

12 **1** **Minalisa**[28] 3698 3-8-10 **74**.................... NeilCallan 3 83+
(Rae Guest) *hld up in tch: hdwy over 2f out: rdn to chal over 1f out: led ins fnl f: r.o wl and holding rival towards fin* **2/1**[1]

0003 **2** *hd* **Peace Seeker**[19] 3960 4-8-10 **72**.................... DominicFox(3) 8 82
(Anthony Carson) *chsd ldr tl 1/2-way: rdn and ev ch over 1f out: clr w wnr ins fnl f: r.o but hld towards fin* **10/1**

1503 **3** *2 3/4* **Beat The Bell**[31] 3570 7-9-4 **77**..........(p) FergusSweeney 5 78
(Jamie Osborne) *chsd ldrs: wnt 2nd 1/2-way: rdn over 2f out: led over 1f out tl hdd and no ex jst ins fnl f: wknd fnl 75yds* **11/1**

420 **4** *1 3/4* **Paradise Spectre**[30] 3612 5-9-0 **73**.................... MartinHarley 1 68
(Mrs K Burke) *hld up in tch: hdwy over 2f out: rdn and chsd ldrs over 1f out: no ex and outpcd 1f out: no threat to ldrs and one pce fnl f* **10/3**[2]

0003 **5** *nk* **Five Star Junior (USA)**[6] 4437 6-9-11 **84**.................... DarryllHolland 4 78
(Linda Stubbs) *in tch in last trio: effrt and rdn over 2f out: no imp and btn 1f out: kpt on same pce after* **7/1**

2-2 **6** *2* **Soap Wars**[6] 4437 7-9-12 **85**.................... MartinLane 7 73
(Hugo Palmer) *led tl rdn and hdd over 1f out: btn 1f out: wknd fnl f* **9/2**[3]

0040 **7** *1 3/4* **Spin Again (IRE)**[10] 4302 7-8-7 **66** oh3.................... DaraghO'Donohoe 6 48
(John Ryan) *in tch in midfield: rdn and unable qck and lost pl 2f out: styng on same pce and wl hld whn eased fnl 75yds* **22/1**

5220 **8** *11* **Befortyfour**[18] 3993 7-8-9 **73**..........(p) MarkCoumbe(5) 2 20
(Charles Smith) *in tch: rdn and struggling 1/2-way: sn bhd: lost tch over 1f out* **28/1**

1m 12.15s (-2.25) **Going Correction** -0.25s/f (Firm)
WFA 3 from 4yo+ 5lb **8** Ran SP% **112.3**
Speed ratings (Par 105): **105,104,101,98,98 95,93,78**
toteswingers 1&2 £5.20, 1&3 £4.40, 2&3 £8.70 CSF £22.44 CT £174.25 TOTE £3.60: £1.70, £3.50, £3.40; EX 23.80.
Owner C J Mills **Bred** C J Mills **Trained** Newmarket, Suffolk

FOCUS
A competitive handicap and a smart effort from the lightly raced Minalisa, who bounced back to form to beat her brother in a driving finish. The winner was well in on the form of her debut win, while this was the runner-up's first decent effort on turf and he's been rated as running close to his Polytrack best.
Befortyfour Official explanation: jockey said gelding never travelled

4661 SHIRLEY GILL MEMORIAL H'CAP 7f 3y
3:50 (3:52) (Class 4) (0-80,80) 3-Y-O+ £4,075 (£1,212; £606; £303) **Stalls** Centre

Form RPR

6000 **1** **Zacynthus (IRE)**[104] 1431 4-9-7 **77**.................... PatrickHills(3) 5 91+
(Luca Cumani) *mde all and set stdy gallop: pushed along and qcknd wl over 1f out: in command fnl f: comf* **7/1**[3]

005 **2** *2 1/4* **Mr David (USA)**[11] 4255 5-9-8 **80**..........(b[1]) LeonnaMayor(5) 6 86
(Jamie Osborne) *t.k.h: hld up wl in tch: drvn and effrt over 1f out: styd on to go 2nd fnl 50yds: no ch w wnr* **9/1**

0534 **3** *hd* **Flynn's Boy**[25] 3790 4-9-8 **75**.................... NeilCallan 8 80
(Rae Guest) *chsd ldng pair: rdn to chse wnr over 1f out: unable qck w wnr ent fnl f: btn ins fnl f and lost 2nd fnl 50yds* **11/8**[1]

53-5 **4** *1 1/4* **Frognal (IRE)**[38] 3334 6-9-9 **76**..........(bt) CathyGannon 3 78
(Richard Guest) *taken down early: t.k.h: hld up in tch: rdn and effrt over 1f out: drvn and styd on same pce fnl f* **12/1**

1504 **5** *1/2* **Rough Rock (IRE)**[19] 3977 7-9-3 **73**.................... RaulDaSilva(3) 1 74
(Chris Dwyer) *taken down early: t.k.h: chsd wnr tl over 1f out: sn drvn and unable qck: styd on same pce fnl f* **11/2**[2]

0000 **6** *2* **Mubtadi**[17] 4068 4-9-5 **72**..........(v) RoystonFfrench 7 67
(Ismail Mohammed) *in tch in rr: niggled along 4f out: outpcd and rdn 2f out: one pce and no threat to ldrs after* **15/2**

041- **7** *7* **Red Bay**[225] 7808 3-9-2 **76**.................... KirstyMilczarek 2 50
(Jane Chapple-Hyam) *t.k.h: in tch: rdn and effrt over 2f out: wknd over 1f out: fdd fnl f* **14/1**

0060 **8** *11* **Dozy Joe**[19] 3963 4-9-6 **73**.................... MartinLane 9 20
(Ian Wood) *awkward leaving stalls: hld up in tch in rr: hdwy into midfield 1/2-way: rdn and unable qck 2f out: wknd over 1f out: eased ins fnl f* **12/1**

1m 28.19s (1.59) **Going Correction** -0.25s/f (Firm)
WFA 3 from 4yo+ 7lb **8** Ran SP% **113.8**
Speed ratings (Par 105): **80,77,77,75,75 72,64,52**
toteswingers: 1&2 £11.10, 1&3 £3.70, 2&3 £3.80 CSF £66.43 CT £135.65 TOTE £7.30: £2.80, £2.20, £1.10; EX 89.30.
Owner Mrs June Bownes **Bred** Keatly Overseas Ltd **Trained** Newmarket, Suffolk

FOCUS
An above-average handicap in which it paid to race handily. The third has been rated close to his recent C&D form, while the first two are well handicapped on their best form.

Red Bay Official explanation: jockey said gelding ran too freely

4662 HOLIDAY ON THE NORFOLK BROADS H'CAP 1m 3y
4:25 (4:25) (Class 5) (0-70,70) 3-Y-O+ £2,264 (£673; £336 ; £168) Stalls Centre

Form RPR
3460 1 **Brown Pete (IRE)**[7] 4405 4 -9-460..............................(e) CathyGannon 2 70
(Richard Guest) *hld up in tch in last pair: hdwy over 2f out: rdn to chse ldr over 1f out: drvn to ld fnl 100yds: r.o wl* 7/1[3]
-420 2 ¾ **Light Burst (USA)**[39] 3314 3 -8-1363........................ RoystonFfrench 4 69
(Ismail Mohammed) *in tch: rdn and effrt to press ldrs 2f out: led over 1f out: clr w wnr ins fnl f: hdd and one pce fnl 100yds* 17/2
052 3 3 ½ **Conducting**[9] 1333 4 -9-061.. NeilCallan 5 64
(Gay Kelleway) *chsd ldrs: rdn to ld 2f out: hdd over 1f out: outpcd and ldng pair 1f out: plugged on same pce after* 12/1
0421 4 5 **Saaboog**[7] 4407 3 -9-670 6ex... MartinLane 6 57
(James Tate) *in tch in midfield: rdn 3f out: 4th and no imp u.p over 1f out: wknd fnl f* 9/4[2]
0000 5 hd **Very Well Red**[11] 4242 9 -8-1052....................................... ShaneKelly 9 40
(Peter Hiatt) *led tl rdn and hdd over 1f out: sn struggling u.p: wknd u.p fnl f* 25/1
0262 6 2 ½ **Patriotic (IRE)**[19] 3976 4 -9-1170................................... RaulDaSilva(3) 10 53
(Chris Dwyer) *in tch in midfield: rdn over 3f out: struggling u.p 2f out: sn wknd: lame* 2/1[1]
0000 7 ¾ **Goal (IRE)**[16] 4089 4 -9-162......................................(tp) MarkCoumbe(5) 1 43
(Charles Smith) *stdd s: hld up in tch: rdn and effrt ent fnl 2f: racd awkwardly and no hdwy wl over 1f out: sn wknd* 25/1
0500 8 9 **Focail Eile**[17] 4068 7 -9-770.................................. GeorgeanBuckell(7) 12 30
(Tim Pitt) *chsd ldr tl ent fnl 2f: sn wknd: wl bhd and eased ins fnl f* 14/1
600 9 ¾ **Trulee Scrumptious**[73] 2249 3 -8-151 oh3.......................... JimmyQuinn 11
(Peter Charalambous) *hld up in tch in last quartet: rdn over 2f out: no hdwy and wknd wl over 1f out* 14/1

1m 40.14s (-0.46) **Going Correction** -0.25s/f (Firm)
WFA 3 from 4yo+ 8lb 9Ran SP% 115.8
Speed ratings (Par 103): **92,91,87,82,82 80,79,70,69**
toteswingers 1&2 £6.50, 1&3 £6.40, 2&3 £5.60 CSF £64.92 CT £695.31 TOTE £5.60 : £2.30, £2.30, £3.10 ; EX 64.70 .
Owner Rakebackmypoker.com **Bred** Jim Halligan **Trained** Stainforth, S Yorks

FOCUS
A modest handicap, run at an honest pace throughout. The winner has been rated a length up on this year's previous best effort and the runner-up has been rated pretty much to form.
Patriotic(IRE) Official explanation: trainer had no explanation for the poor form shown

4663 TRAFALGAR RESTAURANT AT GREAT YARMOUTH RACECOURSE H'CAP 5f 43y
4:55 (4:55) (Class 6) (0-65,64) 3-Y-O+ £1,617 (£481; £240 ; £120) Stalls Centre

Form RPR
5556 1 **Simple Rhythm**[11] 4237 6 -8-745.........................(p) DaraghO'Donohoe 2 55
(John Ryan) *chsd ldr: rdn to chal 2f out: led wl over 1f out: forged clr ins fnl f: r.o wl* 17/2
5056 2 1 ½ **Roy's Legacy**[6] 4428 3 -8-1355....................................... DarryllHolland 3 59
(Shaun Harris) *led tl wl over 1f out: drvn and stl ev ch ent fnl f: no ex and btn fnl 100yds: jst hld on for 2nd* 5/1[3]
1020 3 shd **Danzoe (IRE)**[9] 4332 5 -9-1062...................................... TomMcLaughlin 8 67
(Christine Dunnett) *sn rdn along on last pair: hdwy u.p to chse ldrs ent fnl f: styd on and almost snatched 2nd* 9/2[2]
0000 4 2 **Liberty Ship**[11] 4245 7 -9-863...(t) RyanClark(3) 5 60
(Mark Buckley) *chsd ldrs: pressed ldrs and unable qck u.p 1f out: wknd wl ins fnl f* 12/1
6000 5 nk **Bobby's Doll**[37] 3390 5 -9-964...................................... AdamBeschizza(3) 7 60
(Terry Clement) *s.i.s: sn rdn along in rr: plugged on steadily fnl f but nvr gng pce to chal* 8/1
610 6 1 ¾ **Catalyze**[75] 2173 4 -9-764...(t) MarkCoumbe(5) 11 54
(Charles Smith) *in tch: rdn 1/2-way: no imp u.p over 1f out: wknd fnl f* 9/2[2]
5544 7 2 **Samba Night (IRE)**[28] 3706 3 -9-362..........................(p) RaulDaSilva(3) 4 44
(James Eustace) *chsd ldrs: rdn and no rspnse 3f out: wknd over 1f out: bhd and eased ins fnl f* 5/2[1]

1m 4.65s (1.95) **Going Correction** -0.25s/f (Firm)
WFA 3 from 4yo+ 4lb 7Ran SP% 110.9
Speed ratings (Par 101): **74,71,71,68,67 64,61**
toteswingers 1&2 £2.80, 1&3 £5.70, 2&3 £2.10 CSF £46.91 CT £207.98 TOTE £12.80 : £4.20, £4.50; EX 10.40 .
Owner John Ryan Racing Partnership **Bred** P Quinlan **Trained** Newmarket, Suffolk

FOCUS
A modest sprint handicap. The runner-up has been rated as running a personal best on turf, while the third has been rated close to his recent best.

4664 INJURED JOCKEYS FUND H'CAP 2m
5:30 (5:30) (Class 6) (0-65,62) 4-Y-O+ £1,617 (£481; £240 ; £120) Stalls Centre

Form RPR
5024 1 **Mollyow (IRE)**[18] 4004 4 -8-1051..................................... CathyGannon 5 59
(Terry Clement) *in tch: rdn and upsides ldr 2f out: drvn to ld over 1f out: kpt on wl and a holding rival ins fnl f* 9/4[1]
/233 2 nk **Tae Kwon Do (USA)**[9] 3969 6 -8-748......................(t) FergusSweeney 3 55
(Tim Vaughan) *t.k.h: chsd ldrs: rdn to ld jst over 2f out: hdd over 1f out: kpt on u.p but a jst hld ins fnl f* 5/2[2]
-000 3 10 **Cookieshake**[20] 3939 4 -8-647....................................... KirstyMilczarek 4 42
(Peter Hiatt) *led: rdn over 3f out: hdd over 2f and sn outpcd by ldng pair: edgd rt u.p over 1f out: wl btn but hld on to modest 3rd fnl f* 16/1
3-35 4 shd **Ishismart**[9] 924 8 -8-849.. ShaneKelly 2 44
(Reg Hollinshead) *in tch: rdn and effrt over 2f out: outpcd by ldng pair and btn 2f out: battling for modest 3rd and plugged on fnl f* 7/1
1440 5 1 ½ **Cloudy Start**[40] 3283 6 -9-262...................................... LeonnaMayor(5) 6 55
(Jamie Osborne) *stdd s: hld up in rr: rdn and effrt over 2f out: outpcd and no ch w ldng pair wl over 1f out: wl btn 1f out* 4/1[3]
3-65 6 27 **Famagusta**[38] 1744 5 -8-445.......................................(v) JimmyQuinn 7
(Peter Charalambous) *chsd ldr: rdn over 3f out: lost 2nd over 2f out and sn struggling: wl bhd over 1f out: t.o* 13/2

3m 36.78s (4.38) **Going Correction** -0.25s/f (Firm) 6Ran SP% 111.1
Speed ratings (Par 101): **101,100,95,95,95 81**
toteswingers 1&2 £1.40, 1&3 £4.80, 2&3 £6.10 CSF £7.98 TOTE £5.70 : £3.90, £1.10 ; EX 5.90 .
Owner The Bill & Ben Partnership **Bred** J F Tuthill **Trained** Newmarket, Suffolk
■ Stewards' Enquiry : Fergus Sweeney two-day ban: used whip above permitted level (Aug 13-14)

FOCUS
A modest staying handicap run at a steady pace. The first two have been rated close to their Lingfield form from earlier in the month.

T/Plt: £7,012.50 to a £1 stake. Pool: £53026.69 - 5.52 winning tickets T/Qpdt: £178.20 to a £1 stake. Pool: £5907.09 - 24.52 w. tickets SP 4665a-4669a (Foreign Racing) See RI

4637 AYR (L-H)
Tuesday, July 31

OFFICIAL GOING: Good (good to soft in places; 0.9)
Wind: light to moderate, behind in straight Weather: sunny

4670 BEST ODDS GUARANTEED AT BETVICTOR.COM MAIDEN AUCTION STKS 5f
1:45 (1:45) (Class 6) 2-Y-O £1,704 (£503; £251) Stalls High

Form RPR
0 1 **Done Dreaming (IRE)**[10] 4344 2 -9-00......................... TonyHamilton 3 72
(Richard Fahey) *swtchd to rail s: racd keenly in tch: led wl over 1f out: sn rdn: hld on wl fnl f* 7/2[2]
02 2 ½ **Bogsnog (IRE)**[14] 4173 2 -8-130....................................... GrahamLee 5 69
(Linda Stubbs) *led against rail: edgd off rail 2f out and sn hdd: drvn over 1f out: kpt on but a jst hld* 4/1[3]
2040 3 1 ½ **Mount Seymour (IRE)**[24] 3844 2 -8-963.................. DeclanCannon(3) 4 63
(Nigel Tinkler) *trckd ldr: rdn 2f out: stl ev ch ins fnl f: no ex towards fin* 14/1
26 4 4 ½ **Cracking Choice (IRE)**[34] 3490 2 -8-120.................... PaulMulrennan 1 47
(Michael Dods) *hld up in tch: rdn over 2f out: sn btn* 11/8[1]
6224 5 2 ¾ **Pastoral Prey**[33] 3520 2 -8-1072.. PJMcDonald 2 35
(George Foster) *awkward s: hld up in tch: rdn 2f out: sn btn* 4/1[3]

1m 0.09s (0.69) **Going Correction** -0.075s/f (Good) 5Ran SP% 111.0
Speed ratings (Par 92): **91,90,87,80,76**
CSF £17.36 TOTE £5.20 : £2.50 , £3.80 ; EX 21.00 .
Owner Middleham Park Racing XXVIII **Bred** Pier House Stud **Trained** Musley Bank, N Yorks

FOCUS
Home bend out 8m from inner line and straight out 6m from inner line and Stands bend moved out 6m. 24yds added to races between 7f and 10f and 60yds to other races on Round course. The ground was gradually drying and it was officially good going into the first race. This looked an ordinary maiden. The runner-up has been rated close to his debut form, and the third to his recent best.

NOTEBOOK
Done Dreaming (IRE) took a marked step forward from what was nothing more than a modest first run. He was kept to the inside rail by his rider and, when the gap opened up, this Diamond Green colt picked up in good style to go by more experienced rivals and score. He has a pedigree that suggests he'll appreciate a little further in time. (op 5-1)
Bogsnog(IRE) had every chance but found the winner improving past him. He probably ran to a similar level as at Beverley last time. (op 11-4)
Mount Seymour (IRE) wasn't beaten far, which tends to hold the form down a bit, but he ran miles better than at Beverley last time where the soft ground clearly didn't suit. (op 12-1)
Cracking Choice (IRE) put up a dismal effort, having been expected to relish the better ground, but he was beaten by halfway. His career is going backwards at the moment.. Official explanation: trainer had no explanation for the poor form shown (tchd 6-4)

4671 BETVICTOR ON YOUR MOBILE H'CAP 5f
2:15 (2:16) (Class 4) (0-80,80) 3-Y-O £4,075 (£1,212; £606 ; £303) Stalls High

Form RPR
0102 1 **Decision By One**[5] 4496 3 -9-780..............................(t) RichardKingscote 4 88
(Tom Dascombe) *mde all: rdn over 1f out: a in command* 1/2[1]
6221 2 1 **One Kool Dude**[14] 4197 3 -8-766.......................................(v) LukeMorris 6 70
(Michael Bell) *chsd wnr: rdn 2f out: kpt on but a hld* 9/2[2]
5340 3 3 ½ **Rock Canyon (IRE)**[5] 4133 3 -8-062.............................(p) DeclanCannon(3) 2 53
(Linda Perratt) *sn chsd ldng pair: rdn 2f out: wknd ins fnl f* 20/1
055 4 1 ¼ **Artillery Train (IRE)**[5] 4144 3 -7-1161 oh11.................... NeilFarley(5) 5 48
(Tim Etherington) *in tch: pushed along and dropped towards rr 3f out: no threat after* 66/1
0-00 5 ½ **Lexington Spirit (IRE)**[43] 3234 3 -8-1170......................... TonyHamilton 3 55
(Richard Fahey) *sn pushed along towards rr: nvr threatened* 8/1[3]

58.69s (-0.71) **Going Correction** -0.075s/f (Good) 5Ran SP% 102.2
Speed ratings (Par 102): **102,100,94,92,92**
CSF £2.44 TOTE £1.40 : £1.10 , £1.20 ; EX 1.90 .
Owner The Half A Third Partnership **Bred** G E Amey **Trained** Malpas, Cheshire

FOCUS
The winner was well in following his Doncaster run and has been rated as running to a similar level, while the runner-up confirmed his back-to-form effort at Yarmouth.

4672 BETVICTOR FOR BEST PRICES NURSERY 7f 50y
2:45 (2:46) (Class 6) (0-65,65) 2-Y-O £1,704 (£503; £251) Stalls High

Form RPR
024 1 **Bonnie Lesley (IRE)**[38] 3378 2 -9-462......................... PaulMulrennan 6 69+
(Keith Dalgleish) *racd keenly: hld up: rdn and gd hdwy on outer over 1f out: led ins fnl f: sn wl in command* 7/2[3]
0462 2 2 ¼ **Out Of The Blocks**[6] 4450 2 -9-664.................................. PJMcDonald 8 64
(Ruth Carr) *trckd ldr: rdn to ld wl over 1f out: hdd ins fnl f: no ch w wnr* 11/4[2]
6000 3 3 ½ **Strasbourg Place**[6] 4450 2 -8-451.............................. DeclanCannon(3) 3 42
(Nigel Tinkler) *midfield: rdn 3f out: kpt on one pce* 40/1
0523 4 1 ½ **Sandy's Row (USA)**[6] 4450 2 -9-664................................ MircoDemuro 2 51
(Mark Johnston) *led: rdn 3f out: hdd wl over 1f out: wknd fnl f* 9/4[1]
0004 5 hd **Delores Rocket**[6] 4450 2 -9-664.. GrahamLee 5 50
(Kevin Ryan) *hld up: sn pushed along: rdn into midfield over 2f out: sn no imp on ldrs* 12/1
060 6 1 **Heliconia**[12] 4253 2 -9-361... LukeMorris 1 44
(Sir Mark Prescott Bt) *rdn along leaving stall: sn in midfield: wnt in snatches: briefly chsd ldrs 3f out: wknd over 1f out* 11/1
004 7 ¾ **Beadle**[17] 4083 2 -9-765... TonyHamilton 7 46
(Richard Fahey) *hld up: rdn 3f out: nvr threatened rr* 20/1
054 8 13 **Smooth Handle**[11] 4290 2 -8-751.................................(v[1]) RichardKingscote 4
(Tom Dascombe) *chsd ldrs: wknd qckly 3f out* 11/2

1m 33.08s (-0.32) **Going Correction** -0.225s/f (Firm) 8Ran SP% 118.3
Speed ratings (Par 92): **92,89,85,83,83 82,81,66**
toteswingers 1&2 £2.40, 2&3 £24.00, 1&3 £22.70 CSF £14.14 CT £331.01 TOTE £2.90 : £1.10 , £1.20, £11.50 ; EX 13.90 .
Owner Middleham Park Racing Iii **Bred** Peter & Sarah Fortune **Trained** Carluke, S Lanarks

FOCUS
This modest nursery was run at what looked like quite a strong pace. The runner-up sets the standard.

NOTEBOOK

Bonnie Lesley(IRE), who was stepping up in trip for this handicap debut, came from quite a way back despite being quite difficult to settle early. Paul Mulrennan timed his challenge to perfection in the closing stages as he swept down the outside whilst those in front were tiring. She may have been a little flattered in that the pace was so strong that the leaders came back, but she's an unexposed filly capable of further progress, especially if she can learn to settle better.

Out Of The Blocks ◆ ran a blinder in second as he chased the pace from the outset yet was still able to keep on stoutly to finish clear of the remainder. There must be a race for him off this sort of mark on this evidence. (tchd 5-2)

Strasbourg Place hadn't shown much in her career thus far and this definitely represented an improvement in her form. Whether she can go on from here remains to be seen. (op 66-1)

Sandy's Row(USA) was unable to keep up the gallop in the final couple of furlongs and paid for going too hard early. Official explanation: jockey said, regarding riding, that he was trying to look after the filly having made the running and would not have been third even if he had continued riding to the line. (op 11-4)

Smooth Handle bombed out completely and it's back to the drawing board with him. (op 8-1)

4673 BETVICTOR NUMBER 1 FOR FOOTBALL BETTING CLAIMING STKS 7f 50y

3:20 (3:20) (Class 6) 3-Y-0+ **£1,704** (£503; £251) **Stalls** High

Form RPR

0410 **1** **Tajneed (IRE)**[31] 3624 9-9-0 85 ShirleyTeasdale(7) 4 76
(David Nicholls) *trckd ldr: rdn to ld over 1f out: kpt on* **11/10**[1]

2-32 **2** 1 ¾ **Fishforcompliments**[186] 323 8-9-6 77 TonyHamilton 2 70
(Richard Fahey) *trckd ldrs: rdn over 2f out: kpt on one pce* **4/1**[3]

5455 **3** 2 **Daring Dream (GER)**[15] 4135 7-9-8 69 GrahamLee 6 67
(Jim Goldie) *hld up in rr: hdwy 2f out: sn rdn: kpt on one pce* **9/1**

4044 **4** 1 ½ **Polar Annie**[33] 3522 7-9-0 73 RachealKneller(5) 5 60
(Jim Goldie) *sn led: clr 5f out tl 2f out: hdd over 1f out: wknd ins fnl f* **8/1**

060 **5** 2 ½ **Pravda Street**[10] 4339 7-9-11 77 (p) AndrewElliott 1 59
(Brian Ellison) *hld up: pushed along over 4f out: nvr threatened* **3/1**[2]

2405 **6** 2 ½ **Spread Boy (IRE)**[18] 4042 5-9-7 48 PaddyAspell 3 48
(Alan Berry) *in tch: rdn over 3f out: sn wknd* **100/1**

1m 30.9s (-2.50) **Going Correction** -0.225s/f (Firm) **6** Ran SP% **114.7**
Speed ratings (Par 101): **105,103,100,99,96 93**
toteswingers 1&2 £2.10, 2&3 £2.20, 1&3 £2.80 CSF £6.18 TOTE £2.20: £1.90, £2.30; EX 5.80.
Owner Middleham Park Racing LIII & Partner **Bred** R Hodgins **Trained** Sessay, N Yorks

FOCUS
Not much depth here. It has been rated cautiously as there are doubts over the whole field and the form is muddling.

4674 BEST PREMIER LEAGUE PRICES AT BETVICTOR H'CAP 1m 2f

3:55 (3:55) (Class 4) (0-85,82) 3-Y-0+ **£4,075** (£1,212; £606; £303) **Stalls** Low

Form RPR

351 **1** **Royal Straight**[15] 4137 7-8-13 67 (t) RichardKingscote 6 81
(Linda Perratt) *hld up in tch: hdwy over 2f out: rdn to ld over 1f out: sn clr: easily* **7/1**

6006 **2** 9 **Staff Sergeant**[15] 4136 5-9-10 78 GrahamLee 7 74
(Jim Goldie) *hld up: rdn and hdwy 2f out: wnt 2nd 1f out: kpt on but no ch w wnr* **5/1**[2]

0030 **3** ½ **Sound Advice**[4] 4553 3-9-1 79 LukeMorris 4 74
(Keith Dalgleish) *midfield: pushed along 4f out: rn wd on bnd into st and brought stands' side: rdn 3f out: kpt on* **13/2**

0026 **4** ½ **Euston Square**[22] 3906 6-9-1 74 GarryWhillans(5) 3 68
(Alistair Whillans) *v.s.a: hld up in rr: rdn over 2f out: kpt on fnl 2f out: nvr threatened* **11/1**

6102 **5** 2 ¼ **Fourth Generation (IRE)**[39] 3337 5-9-8 76 AndrewElliott 9 66
(Alan Swinbank) *trckd ldr: rdn and ev ch 2f out: wknd ins fnl f* **2/1**[1]

3215 **6** 5 **Indepub**[15] 4136 3-9-4 82 TonyHamilton 5 62
(Kevin Ryan) *trckd ldr: rdn to ld over 2f out: hdd over 1f out: sn wknd* **5/1**[2]

105- **7** 2 ½ **Goldtrek (USA)**[65] 5303 5-9-4 77 LucyAlexander(5) 2 52
(N W Alexander) *midfield: wknd over 2f out* **33/1**

35 **8** ½ **Charpoy (USA)**[38] 3380 4-9-13 81 (p) PJMcDonald 8 55
(Ian Semple) *led: rdn whn hdd over 2f out: sn wknd* **6/1**[3]

2m 8.44s (-3.56) **Going Correction** -0.225s/f (Firm)
WFA 3 from 4yo+ 10lb **8** Ran SP% **118.1**
Speed ratings (Par 105): **105,97,97,97,95 91,89,88**
toteswingers 1&2 £6.30, 2&3 £5.70, 1&3 £10.80 CSF £43.15 CT £242.14 TOTE £9.10: £3.00, £1.30, £2.10; EX 42.10.
Owner Ken McGarrity **Bred** Brook Stud Bloodstock & Leydens Farm Stud **Trained** East Kilbride, S Lanarks

FOCUS
Quite a competitive little heat on paper, but it was turned into a rout. The level of form is a bit guessy, but the winner has been rated as running a personal best.

4675 LIVE IN-PLAY BETTING AT BETVICTOR.COM H'CAP 7f 50y

4:25 (4:25) (Class 4) (0-85,85) 3-Y-0 **£4,075** (£1,212; £606; £303) **Stalls** High

Form RPR

1213 **1** **Trail Blaze (IRE)**[18] 4075 3-9-7 85 GrahamLee 6 97
(Kevin Ryan) *mde all: rdn over 2f out: drvn and hld on wl towards fin* **5/2**[2]

3612 **2** ½ **Anton Chigurh**[8] 4401 3-9-2 80 RichardKingscote 7 91
(Tom Dascombe) *in tch: rdn 2f out: kpt on: nvr quite rch wnr* **5/4**[1]

2310 **3** 1 **Our Boy Jack (IRE)**[10] 4317 3-9-2 83 LeeTopliss(3) 3 93
(Richard Fahey) *hld up: rdn and hdwy over 1f out: kpt on: disputing 2nd whn short of room nr fin* **7/2**[3]

34P0 **4** ¾ **Chester Aristocrat**[10] 4329 3-8-2 66 LukeMorris 4 72
(Eric Alston) *chsd ldrs: rdn over 2f out: kpt on* **14/1**

6466 **5** ½ **Alkadi (IRE)**[12] 4256 3-8-4 68 MircoDemuro 1 73
(Mark Johnston) *hld up in tch: rdn and hdwy over 2f out: chsd wnr jst ins fnl f: no ex nr fin* **10/1**

4262 **6** 7 **Last Supper**[34] 3495 3-8-5 69 JimmyQuinn 5 63
(James Bethell) *trckd ldr: rdn over 2f out: already wkng whn short of room appr fnl f* **22/1**

1m 31.48s (-1.92) **Going Correction** -0.225s/f (Firm) **6** Ran SP% **115.3**
Speed ratings (Par 102): **101,100,99,98,97 89**
totewingers 1&2 £1.30, 2&3 £1.90, 1&3 £1.50 CSF £6.28 TOTE £3.30: £1.90, £1.10; EX 9.40.
Owner Mr & Mrs Julian And Rosie Richer **Bred** Edmond Kent **Trained** Hambleton, N Yorks

■ Stewards' Enquiry : Lee Topliss two-day ban: careless riding (Aug 14-15)
Mirco Demuro two-day ban: used whip above permitted level (Aug 14-15)

FOCUS
A few of these came here in good form. The winner and third have been rated as running small personal bests, with the runner-up rated to his latest Southwell run.

4676 PLAY CASINO ON YOUR MOBILE AT BETVICTOR.COM FILLIES' H'CAP 1m

4:55 (4:56) (Class 5) (0-70,68) 3-Y-0+ **£2,454** (£543; £543) **Stalls** Low

Form RPR

4134 **1** **Social Rhythm**[8] 4390 8-9-6 60 PJMcDonald 4 71
(Alistair Whillans) *dwlt: hld up: hdwy on outer over 2f out: rdn to ld over 1f out: kpt on to go clr ins fnl f* **10/1**

1533 **2** 3 ¾ **Emeralds Spirit (IRE)**[1] 4640 5-9-12 66 LukeMorris 8 68
(John Weymes) *in tch: rdn and ev ch over 1f out: kpt on but no ch w wnr* **9/2**

-012 **2** dht **Oddysey (IRE)**[15] 4134 3-9-2 67 LeeTopliss(3) 1 71+
(Michael Dods) *trckd ldr: short of room on rail 2f out: sn angled towards outer: r.o wl fnl 100yds* **15/8**[1]

3013 **4** nk **First Class Favour (IRE)**[14] 4177 4-9-12 66 DavidAllan 2 68
(Tim Easterby) *led: rdn 3f out: drvn whn hdd over 1f out: kpt on one pce* **10/3**[2]

4-44 **5** 3 ½ **Darling Lexi (IRE)**[18] 4057 3-9-0 62 TonyHamilton 7 54
(Richard Fahey) *trckd ldr: rdn and ev ch 2f out: hung lft and wknd ins fnl f* **7/2**[3]

-430 **6** 5 **Let's Face Facts**[8] 4389 5-8-13 53 (v) GrahamLee 6 35
(Jim Goldie) *hld up in tch: rdn over 2f out: sn btn* **14/1**

1m 41.69s (-2.11) **Going Correction** -0.225s/f (Firm)
WFA 3 from 4yo+ 8lb **6** Ran SP% **114.0**
Speed ratings (Par 100): **101,97,97,96,93 88**
PL: Emerald Spirit £1.80, Oddysey £0.90 EX: Social Rhythm/Emerald Spirit £19.10, SR/O £20.00, CSF: SR/ES £27.09, SR/O £14.97 TRI: SR/ES/O £60.87, SR/O/ES £42.93. totewingers: 1&ES £3.30, 1&O £3.90, ES&O £2.50 CT £49.23 TOTE £11.90: £5.20.
Owner Mrs L M Whillans **Bred** A And B Fairfields **Trained** Newmill-On-Slitrig, Borders

FOCUS
Reasonable form for the grade and a sound pace to boot. The winner has been rated close to her best form over the past two years.
T/Plt: £36.50 to a £1 stake. Pool of £34971.11 - 697.63 winning tickets. T/Qpdt: £20.10 to a £1 stake. Pool of £2881.08 - 105.70 winning tickets. AS

4395 BEVERLEY (R-H)

Tuesday, July 31

OFFICIAL GOING: Firm (good to firm in places; 9.9)
Wind: Light half behind Weather: overcast

4677 EBF HOLDERNESS PONY CLUB MAIDEN STKS 7f 100y

2:25 (2:26) (Class 5) 2-Y-0 **£3,169** (£943; £471; £235) **Stalls** Low

Form RPR

65 **1** **Linguine (FR)**[18] 4056 2-9-3 0 RobertWinston 4 76
(Charles Hills) *t.k.h early: led: rdn wl over 1f out: hdd and drvn ent fnl f: rallied gamely to ld again fnl 75yds* **11/4**[2]

3 **2** ½ **Excellent Mariner (IRE)**[7] 4427 2-8-12 0 FrannyNorton 5 69
(Mark Johnston) *trckd ldr: cl up 1/2-way: effrt to chal 2f out: slt ld ent fnl f: sn rdn: rn green: no ex and hdd last 75yds* **2/1**[1]

3 4 ½ **Sadfig** 2-9-3 0 KirstyMilczarek 3 63
(Clive Brittain) *trckd ldrs on inner: hdwy to chse ldng pair 3f out: rdn 2f out: kpt on same pce fr over 1f out* **18/1**

4 1 ¼ **He's A Striker (IRE)** 2-9-3 0 BarryMcHugh 7 60+
(Richard Fahey) *dwlt: hld up towards rr: hdwy to trck ldrs 1/2-way: pushed along on inner and sltly outpcd over 2f out: styd on appr fnl f* **7/1**

5 nk **Broughton (GER)** 2-8-12 0 AntiocoMurgia(5) 2 59+
(Mahmood Al Zarooni) *s.i.s and green in rr: hdwy on wd outside wl over 2f out: sn rdn and hung lft: green and wandered after: n.d* **4/1**[3]

6 ½ **Cape's Best** 2-9-3 0 MartinLane 10 58
(James Tate) *hld up in tch: hdwy wl over 2f out: sn rdn and wknd over 1f out* **11/1**

4 **7** 8 **Baraboy (IRE)**[84] 1955 2-8-12 0 DarylByrne(5) 8 38
(Tim Easterby) *chsd ldng pair: pushed along 3f out: sn rdn and wknd over 2f out* **33/1**

8 9 **Midnight Poet** 2-9-3 0 JamesSullivan 6 16
(James Given) *towards rr whn n.m.r and hmpd after 2f: a bhd* **28/1**

0 **9** 1 ¾ **Haaf'n Haaf**[46] 3126 2-9-3 0 DavidNolan 9 11
(Michael Easterby) *chsd ldrs to 1/2-way: sn wknd* **66/1**

1m 31.7s (-2.10) **Going Correction** -0.425s/f (Firm) **9** Ran SP% **114.0**
Speed ratings (Par 94): **95,94,89,87,87 86,77,67,65**
CSF £8.39 TOTE £3.60: £1.50, £1.40, £6.00; EX 9.50.
Owner Decadent Racing **Bred** Rupert Pflersch **Trained** Lambourn, Berks

FOCUS
All distances as advertised. This was an ordinary maiden and the order didn't change that much during the contest. The front pair pulled clear. It has been rated around the averages.

NOTEBOOK

Linguine(FR) had finished unplaced in his first two starts, but did show some ability and both races have since thrown up winners. Soon in front, he looked sure to be beaten when headed by the runner-up approaching the last furlong, but showed great courage to fight his way back to the front and saw it out well. He ought to have little difficulty in staying 1m and his battling qualities should continue to stand him in good stead. (op 7-2)

Excellent Mariner(IRE) ran green when third of six on her debut over a similar trip at Musselburgh seven days earlier, but looked more streetwise this time. She had every chance to get on top of the winner and looked like doing so over a furlong out, but she was just outbattled. She should soon go one better in a routine maiden. (op 3-1)

Sadfig, a 36,000gns colt out of a winner at around this trip, was always in about the same place but was forced to give best to a couple of rivals with previous experience. He should improve. (op 16-1 tchd 20-1)

He's A Striker(IRE), a £30,000 2yo and half-brother to three winners at up to 1m2f, took a keen grip in the middle of the field in the first half of the contest, but kept on and showed enough on this debut to believe he has a future, especially over a bit further. (op 8-1)

Broughton(GER), a 220,000euros colt out of a Group 2 Prix Robert Papin winner, proved weak in the market and did everything wrong on this debut, fluffing the start and then running green and hanging when trying to stay on up the straight. The experience shouldn't be lost on him. (op 5-2 tchd 9-4)

Cape's Best, a 34,000gns colt out of a four-time winner at up to 1m4f including at Group 3 level, was by no means disgraced, but his future probably lies over much further in due course. (op 9-1 tchd 12-1)

4678 FAMILY DAY TODAY (S) H'CAP — 1m 4f 16y

2:55 (2:55) (Class 6) (0-65,55) 3-Y-O — **£1,617** (£481; £240; £120) **Stalls** Low

Form — RPR

0405 **1** — **Fine Kingdom**[14] 4172 3-9-2 **50** .... BarryMcHugh 4 — 59
(Brian Ellison) *mde most: rdn 2f out: drvn over 1f out: styd on wl fnl f* **7/1**[3]

0512 **2** 3 1/2 **Emperors Waltz (IRE)**[15] 4147 3-9-7 **55** .... GrahamGibbons 1 — 58
(Rae Guest) *trckd wnr: effrt and cl up over 3f out: rdn to chal 2f out: ev ch tl drvn and one pce ent fnl f* **6/4**[1]

0440 **3** 1 3/4 **Hulwa (USA)**[8] 4399 3-8-11 **45** .... FrannyNorton 3 — 46
(Tracy Waggott) *trckd ldng pair on inner: effrt 3f out: rdn along wl over 1f out: kpt on same pce u.p fnl f* **15/2**

3354 **4** 1 **No Time To Cry**[14] 4172 3-9-3 **51** ....(p) JamesSullivan 5 — 50
(Ann Duffield) *chsd ldrs: rn wd bnd after 1 1/2f: chsd ldng pair whn hung lft and wd home turn: sn rdn and cl up wl over 1f out: drvn and one pce appr fnl f* **4/1**[2]

-056 **5** 1/2 **Little Red Minx (IRE)**[174] 472 3-9-7 **55** .... DanielTudhope 7 — 53
(David O'Meara) *trckd ldrs: hdwy 3f out: effrt 2f out: rdn and n.m.r over 1f out: sn no imp* **15/2**

0460 **6** 1/2 **Oops Caroline (IRE)**[13] 4210 3-8-5 **46** ....(v[1]) DavidBergin[(7)] 8 — 43+
(David O'Meara) *in tch: pushed along 4f out: rdn wl over 2f out: drvn and no imp fr wl over 1f out* **7/1**[3]

0000 **7** 3 1/2 **Bollin Nancy**[48] 3023 3-8-11 **45** .... DuranFentiman 6 — 37
(Tim Easterby) *a in rr: pushed along after 4f: rdn along 4f out: nvr a factor* **33/1**

0-00 **8** 88 **Serendipity Blue**[71] 2335 3-8-11 **45** .... MartinLane 2
(John Weymes) *towards rr: pushed along 1/2-way: outpcd and bhd over 4f out sn detached* **66/1**

2m 37.97s (-1.83) **Going Correction** -0.425s/f (Firm) — **8** Ran SP% **113.0**
Speed ratings (Par 98): **89,86,85,84,84 84,81,23**
toteswingers 1&2 £3.00, 2&3 £3.40, 1&3 £8.90 CSF £17.49 CT £80.91 TOTE £5.20: £1.60, £2.00, £1.30; EX 23.30.There was no bid for the winner.
Owner Keith Hanson & Steve Catchpole **Bred** A G Antoniades **Trained** Norton, N Yorks

FOCUS
Not a race to dwell on. It's been rated around the second and third.

4679 WILFORD WATTS MEMORIAL H'CAP — 1m 100y

3:30 (3:31) (Class 4) (0-85,82) 3-Y-O+ — **£4,204** (£1,251; £625; £312) **Stalls** Low

Form — RPR

0644 **1** — **Shadowtime**[8] 4398 7-8-13 **67** .... BarryMcHugh 3 — 76
(Tracy Waggott) *hld up in tch: hdwy 2f out: swtchd lft and rdn over 1f out: styd on strly fnl f to ld last 75yds* **7/1**[3]

-621 **2** 3/4 **Kaafel (IRE)**[38] 3384 3-9-1 **77** .... TadhgO'Shea 5 — 82+
(Charles Hills) *t.k.h: hld up in rr: stdy hdwy on outer wl over 2f out: rdn to chse ldrs over 1f out: drvn and kpt on fnl f* **9/2**[1]

502 **3** nk **Centrifugal (IRE)**[13] 4213 3-9-0 **76** .... FrannyNorton 8 — 80+
(Mark Johnston) *trckd ldrs: hdwy 1/2-way: cl up over 2f out: rdn to ld wl over 1f out: drvn ent fnl f: hdd and no ex last 75yds* **10/1**

6-22 **4** 2 3/4 **Next Edition (IRE)**[39] 3354 4-9-9 **82** .... ShaneBKelly[(5)] 4 — 82+
(Philip Kirby) *dwlt and in rr: hdwy over 2f out: sn nt clr run: swtchd lft to outer over 1f out: kpt on: nrst fin* **8/1**

3540 **5** hd **Desert Romance (IRE)**[34] 3493 6-9-12 **80** .... DanielTudhope 1 — 79
(David O'Meara) *cl up: led after 2f: jnd and rdn over 2f out: hdd wl over 1f out: kpt on same pce* **9/2**[1]

010 **6** 3/4 **Silverware (USA)**[6] 4474 4-9-10 **78** .... JamesSullivan 9 — 75
(Linda Stubbs) *in tch: hdwy to chse ldrs wl over 2f out: rdn wl over 1f out: no imp* **33/1**

0660 **7** 1 3/4 **Space War**[26] 3779 5-9-7 **75** .... DavidNolan 6 — 68
(Michael Easterby) *hld up: sme hdwy wl over 2f out: sn rdn and n.d* **5/1**[2]

-401 **8** 3 **Fastnet Storm (IRE)**[57] 2754 6-9-8 **76** ....(b[1]) GrahamGibbons 7 — 61
(David Barron) *t.k.h: chsd ldrs: rdn along wl over 2f out: sn wknd* **16/1**

6035 **9** 4 **Merchant Of Medici**[29] 3699 5-9-7 **75** .... MichaelO'Connell 11 — 50
(Micky Hammond) *s.i.s and swtchd rt s: a in rr* **14/1**

-111 **10** 1/2 **Eeny Mac (IRE)**[14] 4177 5-8-7 **64** .... JulieBurke[(3)] 2 — 38
(Neville Bycroft) *led 2f: cl up tl rdn along wl over 2f out and sn wknd* **5/1**[2]

1m 43.07s (-4.53) **Going Correction** -0.425s/f (Firm)
WFA 3 from 4yo+ 8lb — **10** Ran SP% **117.9**
Speed ratings (Par 105): **105,104,103,101,101 100,98,95,91,91**
toteswingers 1&2 £9.00, 2&3 £4.30, 1&3 £9.00 CSF £39.01 CT £327.97 TOTE £10.40: £3.20, £1.30, £2.80; EX 32.50.
Owner H Conlon **Bred** Darley **Trained** Spennymoor, Co Durham

FOCUS
A decent handicap featuring a few who normally like to force it, but there wasn't a contested lead which suggests a change of tactics for some. The runner-up has been rated to form, while the third has been rated to the best view of his maiden efforts.
Eeny Mac(IRE) Official explanation: jockey said gelding ran flat

4680 DALE SWIFT IS OUR SPONSORED JOCKEY H'CAP — 5f

4:05 (4:08) (Class 5) (0-75,81) 3-Y-O+ — **£2,264** (£673; £336; £168) **Stalls** Low

Form — RPR

6611 **1** — **Fear Nothing**[3] 4592 5-8-12 **69** 6ex .... DavidBergin[(7)] 7 — 78
(David O'Meara) *cl up travelling wl: led wl over 1f out: shkn up ent fnl f: kpt on* **11/10**[1]

0060 **2** 1 1/4 **Indian Trail**[2] 4631 12-9-6 **70** ....(b) AndrewMullen 4 — 75
(David Nicholls) *chsd ldrs: rdn over 1f out: styd on wl fnl f* **20/1**

0601 **3** nk **Last Sovereign**[8] 4400 8-9-10 **81** 6ex ....(b) JacobButterfield[(7)] 6 — 84
(Ollie Pears) *s.i.s and towards rr: hdwy wl over 1f out: rdn and squeezed through ent fnl f: fin wl* **12/1**

36 **4** 1/2 **Comptonspirit**[34] 3496 8-9-5 **74** .... JamesRogers[(5)] 2 — 76
(Brian Baugh) *led: rdn along 2f out: sn hdd: drvn and wknd fnl f* **20/1**

0060 **5** 1/2 **Nickel Silver**[8] 4400 7-9-6 **70** ....(v) RoystonFfrench 1 — 70
(Bryan Smart) *chsd ldrs: rdn along wl over 1f out: drvn and one pce appr fnl f* **18/1**

452 **6** 3 1/2 **Select Committee**[8] 4400 7-9-9 **73** ....(b) MichaelO'Connell 8 — 60
(John Quinn) *trckd ldrs: effrt on inner wl over 1f out: sn rdn and n.m.r: no imp fnl f* **8/1**[3]

3020 **7** 1 1/2 **Crimea (IRE)**[6] 4454 6-9-11 **75** ....(p) FrannyNorton 9 — 57
(David Nicholls) *cl up: rdn and ev ch 2f out: wknd appr fnl f* **20/1**

0333 **8** 1/2 **Tabaret**[5] 4495 9-9-4 **68** ....(v) AmyRyan 3 — 48
(Richard Whitaker) *chsd ldrs: rdn along wl over 1f out: sn wknd* **4/1**[2]

3011 **9** 2 1/4 **Red Cape (FR)**[13] 4207 9-9-9 **73** ....(b) JamesSullivan 10 — 45
(Ruth Carr) *wnt lft s: chsd ldrs on wd outside: rdn along 1/2-way: sn wknd* **9/1**

4036 **10** 7 **Just For Mary**[7] 4425 8-8-11 **66** ....(tp) MarkCoumbe[(5)] 5 — 13
(Daniel Mark Loughnane) *s.i.s: a in rr* **28/1**

1m 1.5s (-2.00) **Going Correction** -0.325s/f (Firm) — **10** Ran SP% **119.4**
Speed ratings (Par 103): **103,101,100,99,98 93,90,90,86,75**
toteswingers 1&2 £9.70, 2&3 £29.60, 1&3 £4.40 CSF £32.70 CT £193.39 TOTE £2.30: £1.10, £10.00, £4.30; EX 49.10.
Owner C Maxsted & Miss S Iggulden **Bred** Houghton Bloodstock Uk Ltd **Trained** Nawton, N Yorks
■ Stewards' Enquiry : James Rogers two-day ban: used whip above permitted level (Aug 14-15)

FOCUS
Five of these met in a similar event over C&D eight days earlier including the first three home. Indian Trail, who finished sixth then, fared best of the quintet this time. The winner was well in following his Newcastle success and didn't have to match that form to follow up, while the third has been rated close to his latest C&D effort.

4681 BEVERLEY ANNUAL BADGEHOLDERS MAIDEN AUCTION FILLIES' STKS — 5f

4:35 (4:36) (Class 5) 2-Y-O — **£2,264** (£673; £336; £168) **Stalls** Low

Form — RPR

3 **1** — **Scentpastparadise**[11] 4310 2-8-7 0 .... RoystonFfrench 5 — 73+
(Ann Duffield) *mde all: pushed clr wl over 1f out: rdn out* **5/6**[1]

60 **2** 5 **Palladius**[17] 4093 2-8-11 0 .... AmyRyan 1 — 62+
(Kevin Ryan) *chsd ldrs: rdn along and sltly outpcd 1/2-way: styd on u.p to chse wnr fnl f: no imp* **11/8**[2]

4 **3** 4 1/2 **Scoobys Girl (IRE)**[14] 4180 2-8-7 0 .... FrankieMcDonald 3 — 39
(Daniel Mark Loughnane) *cl up: rdn along 2f out: drvn and one pce fr over 1f out* **10/1**[3]

0 **4** 2 3/4 **Cool Sea (IRE)**[14] 4173 2-8-4 0 .... AndrewMullen 2 — 26
(Nigel Tinkler) *dwlt: a in rr* **16/1**

1m 3.05s (-0.45) **Going Correction** -0.325s/f (Firm) — **4** Ran SP% **111.6**
Speed ratings (Par 91): **90,82,74,70**
CSF £2.36 TOTE £1.60; EX 2.50.
Owner Mark Curtis **Bred** Brookridge Timber Ltd **Trained** Constable Burton, N Yorks

FOCUS
An uncompetitive fillies' maiden and ultimately a one-horse race. The time was modest and the form has been rated around the averages.

NOTEBOOK
Scentpastparadise showed plenty of ability when third of 14 in a 6f Pontefract maiden on her debut 11 days earlier and probably didn't need to improve much on that in order to run these rivals into the ground. The form means little, but she does appear to have an engine. (op Evens tchd 11-10)
Palladius showed good speed over 6f on her debut and had little chance in the Weatherbys Super Sprint last time. She found herself in a poor position stuck behind the two outsiders as the field crossed the intersection, just as the favourite was bounding clear. Although she plugged on, she never had a hope of getting on terms with her market rival. (op 5-4 tchd 6-4)
Scoobys Girl(IRE) had been well beaten on her debut and showed nothing here to make her of interest in the near future. (op 8-1 tchd 11-1)

4682 BEVERLEY MIDDLE DISTANCE SERIES H'CAP — 1m 4f 16y

5:10 (5:10) (Class 5) (0-75,69) 3-Y-O+ — **£2,587** (£770; £384; £192) **Stalls** Low

Form — RPR

0443 **1** — **Key Gold**[26] 3781 3-9-2 **69** .... FrannyNorton 1 — 82
(Mark Johnston) *hld up in tch: hdwy over 4f out: effrt over 2f out: rdn to chse ldr over 1f out: led ins fnl f: sn clr and kpt on strly* **5/4**[1]

3406 **2** 3 3/4 **Tribal Myth (IRE)**[14] 4179 5-9-5 **63** ....(p) JulieBurke[(3)] 8 — 70
(Kevin Ryan) *led 1 1/2f: cl up: rdn to ld wl over 1f out: drvn and hdd ins fnl f: kpt on same pce* **6/1**[3]

221 **3** 4 **Raleigh Quay (IRE)**[48] 3029 5-9-9 **69** .... ShaneBKelly[(5)] 5 — 70
(Micky Hammond) *trckd ldng pair: effrt over 2f out: sn rdn and kpt on same pce appr fnl f* **5/1**[2]

4000 **4** 2 **Ailsa Craig (IRE)**[12] 4249 6-9-11 **66** .... JamesSullivan 4 — 63
(Edwin Tuer) *hld up towards rr: hdwy over 3f out: rdn 2f out: no imp u.p appr fnl f* **15/2**

-065 **5** nse **Stanley Rigby**[15] 4138 6-9-2 **57** ....(b) BarryMcHugh 9 — 54
(Richard Fahey) *cl up: led after 1 1/2f: rdn along 3f out: hdd wl over 1f out and sn wknd* **14/1**

0010 **6** 7 **Maybeme**[44] 3180 6-9-2 **57** .... AmyRyan 2 — 43
(Neville Bycroft) *blind removed late and s.i.s: hdwy and in tch 1/2-way: rdn along over 3f out: sn wknd* **7/1**

3240 **7** 31 **Needwood Park**[38] 3402 4-8-12 **53** oh4 ....(p) AndrewMullen 6
(Ray Craggs) *chsd ldrs: rdn along over 3f out: sn wknd* **20/1**

2m 35.19s (-4.61) **Going Correction** -0.425s/f (Firm)
WFA 3 from 4yo+ 12lb — **7** Ran SP% **111.1**
Speed ratings (Par 103): **98,95,92,91,91 86,66**
toteswingers 1&2 £2.20, 2&3 £4.50, 1&3 £1.70 CSF £8.56 CT £26.07 TOTE £2.10: £1.10, £3.70; EX 9.90.
Owner Jaber Abdullah **Bred** Newsells Park Stud **Trained** Middleham Moor, N Yorks

FOCUS
An ordinary middle-distance handicap. The winner has been rated as running a personal best, with the runner-up to this year's form.
Maybeme Official explanation: jockey said, on first attempt, blindfold became stuck and mare was slowly away
Needwood Park Official explanation: trainer said gelding was unsuited by the track

4683 LADY JANE BETHELL MEMORIAL LADY RIDERS' H'CAP (FOR LADY AMATEUR RIDERS) — 1m 1f 207y

5:40 (5:40) (Class 6) (0-65,65) 3-Y-O+ — **£1,646** (£506; £253) **Stalls** Low

Form — RPR

0452 **1** — **Gold Rules**[14] 4179 5-10-7 **65** .... MissJCoward 12 — 81
(Michael Easterby) *hld up in midfield: smooth hdwy on inner to trck ldrs 1/2-way: led on bit 2f out: sn clr: easily* **7/2**[2]

0550 **2** 7 **Dean Iarracht (IRE)**[3] 4594 6-9-11 **55** ....(p) MrsCBartley 14 — 57
(Tracy Waggott) *hld up in rr: hdwy over 3f out: rdn 2f out: chsd wnr appr fnl f: sn no imp* **13/2**[3]

5301 **3** 7 **Kyle Of Bute**[43] 3236 6-10-5 **63** .... MissSBrotherton 2 — 51
(Brian Baugh) *chsd ldrs: hdwy 3f out: rdn over 2f out: kpt on same pce* **10/1**

0064 **4** 1/2 **Keys Of Cyprus**[7] 4432 10-10-4 **62** .... MrsAdeleMulrennan 3 — 49
(David Nicholls) *in tch: hdwy 3f out: rdn over 2f out: drvn and kpt on fnl f* **25/1**

-123 **5** 7 **Kathlatino**[37] 3416 5-9-9 **58** .... MissRSmith[(5)] 5 — 31
(Micky Hammond) *in rr: hdwy 3f out: plugged on fnl 2f: nvr a factor* **7/1**

-006 **6** 1 1/2 **Zennor**[11] 4311 5-10-2 **65** .... MissKMargarson[(5)] 8 — 35
(George Margarson) *cl up: led 1/2-way: rdn along and hdd 2f out: grad wknd* **33/1**

0043 **7** *hd* **General Tufto**[10] 4350 7-8-12 **47**............................(b) MissAliceMills(5) 13 17
(Charles Smith) *cl up on outer: wd st: rdn along over 2f out and grad wknd* **20/1**

6605 **8** *6* **Deep Applause**[8] 4389 4-8-13 **48**................................[1] MissJWalker(5) 4 6
(Michael Dods) *a towards rr* **20/1**

1411 **9** *2 3/4* **Tinseltown**[6] 4455 6-9-13 **60**.....................................(p) MissHBethell(3) 11 12
(Brian Rothwell) *led: hdd 1/2-way: cl up tl rdn along wl over 2f out: edgd lft and wknd* **7/4**[1]

402- **10** *5* **Wom**[63] 7113 4-9-8 **57**...(e[1]) MissBAndrews(5) 9
(Pam Sly) *cl up: rdn along 4f out: sn wknd* **28/1**

200- **11** *8* **Ivestar (IRE)**[273] 7216 7-9-6 **55**........................(bt) MissJoannaMason(5) 7
(Michael Easterby) *dwlt: a towards rr: bhd fnl 4f* **50/1**

2m 2.15s (-4.85) **Going Correction** -0.425s/f (Firm) **11** Ran SP% **115.2**
Speed ratings (Par 101): **102,96,90,90,84 83,83,78,76,72 66**
toteswingers 1&2 £5.90, 2&3 £9.10, 1&3 £6.20 CSF £22.97 CT £207.04 TOTE £4.80: £2.00, £2.30, £2.70; EX 33.10.
Owner B Padgett **Bred** Langham Hall Stud **Trained** Sheriff Hutton, N Yorks
■ Stewards' Enquiry : Mrs Adele Mulrennan six-day ban: used whip above permitted level down shoulder in the forehand (tbn)
Miss Alice Mills two-day ban: used whip above permitted level (tbn)

FOCUS
They went a strong pace in this moderate lady amateurs' handicap and the field finished well spread out. It was set up for a closer but the winner, who used to be a lot better than this as a 3yo, still impressed in the way he travelled through the race. The race has been rated through the runner-up to his recent C&D form.
Tinseltown Official explanation: jockey said gelding hung left
T/Jkpt: T/Plt: £29.50 to a £1 stake. Pool of £42564.35-1052.41 winning tickets. T/Qpdt: £12.40 to a £1 stake. Pool of £3332.00 - 197.36 winning tickets. JR

3338 GOODWOOD (R-H)
Tuesday, July 31

OFFICIAL GOING: Good (8.0)
Wind: fresh, against Weather: overcast, dry

4684 BET365.COM STKS (H'CAP) 1m 1f 192y
2:00 (2:00) (Class 2) 4-Y-O+
£28,012 (£8,388; £4,194; £2,097; £1,048; £526) **Stalls** Low

Form RPR

0011 **1** **Landaman (IRE)**[59] 2687 4-8-2 **90**................................ DarrenEgan(5) 17 104+
(Mark Johnston) *stmbld bdly leaving stalls: racd in midfield and styd wd early: stdy hdwy 1/2-way and chsd ldrs 4f out: led gng strly 3f out: sn rdn and qckd clr: in n.d after: pushed out fnl f:* **12/1**

0022 **2** *2 1/2* **Las Verglas Star (IRE)**[9] 4365 4-8-3 **86**......................... PaulHanagan 3 95
(Richard Fahey) *led for 1f: chsd ldr tl 6f out: chsd ldrs after: rdn and outpcd by wnr over 2f out: chsd clr wnr 1f out: kpt on but no threat to wnr* **7/1**[2]

4306 **3** *hd* **Start Right**[31] 3635 5-9-1 **98**.....................................(p) SilvestreDeSousa 9 107+
(Saeed Bin Suroor) *hld up in midfield: nt clr run and shuffled bk over 2f out: hdwy on inner over 1f out: styd on wl ins fnl f: no threat to wnr* **12/1**

1353 **4** *nk* **Retrieve (AUS)**[17] 4094 5-9-10 **107**................................. FrankieDettori 2 115
(Saeed Bin Suroor) *hld up in midfield: rdn and hdwy over 2f out: styng on whn edgd lft 1f out: kpt on wl fnl f: no threat to wnr* **7/1**[2]

0-50 **5** *3 1/2* **Kings Gambit (SAF)**[17] 4112 8-9-3 **100**......................... JamieSpencer 6 101
(Tom Tate) *chsd ldr tl led after 1f: hdd and rdn 3f out: sn outpcd by wnr and one pce: lost 2nd 1f out and wknd ins fnl f* **20/1**

1030 **6** *3/4* **Licence To Till (USA)**[17] 4112 5-8-12 **95**......................... JoeFanning 15 95
(Mark Johnston) *styd wd early: chsd ldrs: rdn and outpcd by wnr over 2f out: styd on same pce after tl wknd ins fnl f* **33/1**

-030 **7** *1* **Spanish Duke (IRE)**[38] 3372 5-8-13 **96**......................... EddieAhern 16 94
(John Dunlop) *in tch in midfield: rdn and unable qck wl over 2f out: plugged on but no ch w wnr fnl f* **16/1**

0300 **8** *shd* **Oceanway (USA)**[9] 4363 4-8-5 **88**................................. HayleyTurner 1 85
(Mark Johnston) *chsd ldrs: rdn and unable qck 3f out: no ch w wnr fnl 2f: wknd fnl f* **20/1**

011 **9** *1* **Danadana (IRE)**[57] 2773 4-9-5 **102**................................. KierenFallon 12 97
(Luca Cumani) *in tch in midfield: swtchd lft and effrt ent fnl 3f: sn unable qck and no ch w wnr: plugged on same pce after: eased wl ins fnl f* **4/1**[1]

0000 **10** *nse* **Nanton (USA)**[17] 4112 10-8-12 **95**................................. PhillipMakin 18 90
(Jim Goldie) *dwlt: bhd: rdn 3f out: styd on past btn horses fnl f: n.d* **50/1**

-440 **11** *3 3/4* **King Torus (IRE)**[41] 3268 4-9-8 **105**............................(b[1]) RyanMoore 14 93
(Richard Hannon) *hld up in rr: effrt on inner but stl plenty to do over 2f out: hung rt and no prog over 1f out: nvr trbld ldrs* **20/1**

3634 **12** *1* **Cai Shen (IRE)**[10] 4320 4-9-8 **105**............................. RichardHughes 10 91+
(Richard Hannon) *t.k.h: chsd ldrs early: grad stdd bk to r in midfield: rdn and no reponse 3f out: wl btn over 1f out* **7/1**[2]

1-06 **13** *1/2* **Kirthill (IRE)**[39] 3329 4-9-3 **100**... WilliamBuick 8 85+
(Luca Cumani) *racd in midfield: wd on bnd 5f out: rdn and effrt but stl plenty to do whn pushed lft over 2f out: no hdwy and wl hld after* **15/2**[3]

1020 **14** *3 1/4* **Silken Thoughts**[25] 3826 4-8-3 **86**................................. CathyGannon 11 64
(John Berry) *chsd ldrs tl 1/2-way: steadily lost pl: wknd u.p 3f out: wl btn over 1f out* **33/1**

405- **15** *1/2* **Specific Gravity (FR)**[339] 5466 4-8-12 **95**......................... TomQueally 4 72
(Sir Henry Cecil) *hld up in midfield: nt clr run 3f out: swtchd lft and rdn over 2f out: no rspnse and sn wl btn: wknd over 1f out* **25/1**

-000 **16** *1 3/4* **Pivotman**[17] 4112 4-8-5 **88**...(b[1]) MartinDwyer 5 62
(Amanda Perrett) *s.i.s: a in rr: bhd fnl 2f: eased wl ins fnl f* **28/1**

1060 **17** *3 1/4* **Right Step**[17] 4112 5-8-11 **94**... JimCrowley 7 61
(Alan Jarvis) *a in rr: wl bhd fnl 2f: eased wl ins fnl f* **25/1**

6031 **18** *22* **Don't Call Me (IRE)**[26] 3779 5-8-13 **96**......................(t) AdrianNicholls 13
(David Nicholls) *dwlt: a in rr: rdn and no hdwy over 3f out: t.o and eased ins fnl f* **25/1**

2m 6.84s (-1.26) **Going Correction** +0.15s/f (Good) **18** Ran SP% **127.6**
Speed ratings (Par 109): **111,109,108,108,105 105,104,104,103,103 100,99,99,96,96 94,92,74**
toteswingers 1&2 £7.50, 2&3 £18.30, 1&3 £26.70 CSF £84.18 CT £1063.87 TOTE £16.80: £3.00, £1.80, £3.50, £2.00; EX 85.20 Trifecta £2494.50 Pool: £3708.12 - 1.10 winning units..
Owner Sheikh Hamdan Bin Mohammed Al Maktoum **Bred** Darley **Trained** Middleham Moor, N Yorks

FOCUS
The running rail on the lower bend was dolled out 6yds from the 6f marker to the winning post, increasing race distances by 10yds, and the rail on the top bend was out 3yds, increasing distances by 5yds. A good-quality handicap run at no more than a fair gallop, with little getting into it from off the pace. It has been rated around the fourth to his Royal Ascot form.

NOTEBOOK
Landaman(IRE), who'd been off for 59 days after winning back-to-back races over this trip at Beverley, was up 9lb but did this in the style of a horse capable of ranking a good deal higher yet, especially when considering he was down on his nose having stumbled badly from what was already a pretty bad draw. He ought to follow up if reappearing in an apprentice handicap back here on Saturday (assuming the ground doesn't soften) and at this rate he'll probably end up in Group company before the season's end.
Las Verglas Star(IRE) was soon prominent and ran another solid race in defeat, doing well to hold on for a third consecutive second placing. His mark will rise again, however, so going one better in a good handicap will become tougher. (tchd 6-1 and 8-1)
Start Right, wearing first-time cheekpieces, didn't have a whole lot of room on the inside and should have been second, coming from further back than those around him. There's a decent handicap in him. (op 14-1)
Retrieve(AUS) was the supposed Godolphin first-string and he held a nice position throughout, but couldn't quite match the level of his Royal Ascot fifth from 1lb higher. (op 15-2 tchd 6-1)
Kings Gambit(SAF) ran better than the bare result at York the time before and it was no surprise to see him run well having been dropped 5lb. (op 25-1)
Licence To Till(USA) ran better but gives the impression the handicapper has a hold of him at present.
Spanish Duke(IRE) seemed to carry his head a touch high and lacked the necessary pace.
Danadana(IRE), who was on a hat-trick, looked far from happy on the track and may be worth another chance. (op 11-2 tchd 6-1)
King Torus(IRE) looked an awkward ride in the first-time blinkers. (op 25-1)
Cai Shen(IRE) failed to pick up having had to be reined back sharply at around halfway. (tchd 13-2)
Kirthill(IRE) endured a wide trip and can be given another chance. (op 8-1)
Specific Gravity(FR), gelded since last seen 339 days earlier, showed a bit in what was a competitive heat and should come on. (op 22-1)

4685 BET365 GORDON STKS (GROUP 3) 1m 4f
2:35 (2:35) (Class 1) 3-Y-O
£34,026 (£12,900; £6,456; £3,216; £1,614; £810) **Stalls** High

Form RPR

1122 **1** **Noble Mission**[39] 3327 3-9-0 110... TomQueally 7 115
(Sir Henry Cecil) *hld up but wl in tch: swtchd lft and gd hdwy over 2f out: rdn to ld over 1f out: strly chal for disp ld thrght fnl f: all out: won on nod* **11/4**[2]

21-1 **2** *nse* **Encke (USA)**[25] 3826 3-9-0 95.................................... MickaelBarzalona 4 115
(Mahmood Al Zarooni) *trckd ldrs: wnt 2nd over 5f out: pushed into ld 3f out: rdn whn hrd pressed sn after: hdd over 1f out: rallied gamely to dispute ld virtually thrght fnl f: all out: lost on nod* **8/1**

311 **3** *2 1/2* **Michelangelo**[31] 3630 3-9-0 111... WilliamBuick 2 111
(John Gosden) *little slowly away: trckd ldrs: rdn jst over 3f out: ev ch over 2f out tl over 1f out: styd on same pce* **6/4**[1]

043 **4** *3 1/4* **Girolamo (GER)**[30] 3683 3-9-0 114... AStarke 6 106
(P Schiergen, Germany) *cl up: wnt cl 3rd briefly 3f out: sn rdn: edgd lft over 1f out: styd on same pce* **9/2**[3]

1505 **5** *4* **Minimise Risk**[39] 3330 3-9-0 97.. JamieSpencer 1 99
(Andrew Balding) *led for over 1f: w ldr tl dropped to 3rd over 5f out: effrt wl over 2f out: no ex fnl f* **33/1**

15-4 **6** *19* **Farhaan (USA)**[73] 2275 3-9-0 104..................................... PaulHanagan 3 69
(John Dunlop) *hld up but wl in tch: rdn to chse ldrs over 2f out: hld whn short of room over 1f out* **14/1**

1103 **7** *nk* **Ed De Gas**[39] 3330 3-9-0 100... ChrisCatlin 5 68
(Rae Guest) *s.i.s: sn pushed along to sit w ldr: led wl after 1f: rdn and hdd 3f out: wknd wl over 1f out* **28/1**

2m 37.02s (-1.38) **Going Correction** +0.15s/f (Good) **7** Ran SP% **109.0**
Speed ratings (Par 110): **110,109,108,106,103 90,90**
toteswingers 1&2 £3.50, 2&3 £3.20, 1&3 £1.10 CSF £22.14 TOTE £3.70: £2.00, £3.70; EX 27.00.
Owner K Abdulla **Bred** Juddmonte Farms Ltd **Trained** Newmarket, Suffolk
■ Stewards' Enquiry : Mickael Barzalona four-day ban: used whip above permitted level (Aug 14-17)

FOCUS
Often a useful St Leger trial, with both Sixties Icon (2006) and Conduit ('08) winning en route to victory in the classic, and Arctic Cosmos finished third in 2010 before glory at Doncaster. Solid form for the grade, with the pace being even, and the progressive horses dominated. The form looks up to scratch with the winner rated to his King Edward VII run, the runner-up rated a stone higher than for his easy Sandown handicap win, and the third to form.

NOTEBOOK
Noble Mission improved for the step up to this trip when just denied by a stablemate in the King Edward VII at Royal Ascot and probably just stepped up on that form back down in grade, appearing to benefit from a more waiting ride on better ground. Whether Frankel's brother has the stamina for a St Leger remains to be seen, but he's still on the up (Cecil feels he's really come forward mentally and physically since Ascot) and how he fares in the Great Voltigeur at York next will likely decide whether he heads to Doncaster (best-priced 14-1). (op 10-3)
Encke(USA) was given a clever ride when winning narrowly from a mark of 90 on his reappearance at Sandown, and improvement always seemed likely up in trip back on faster ground. He battled on really well having been nicely placed throughout. Having only his fourth start, he's probably open to more improvement than the winner and shapes as though he'd stay the Leger trip (16-1 best, 14s generally). The Great Voltigeur will also be next for him. Incidentally, his rider was given a four-day whip ban. (op 10-1)
Michelangelo was disappointing, never convincing he was travelling like a winner. Although he'd won previously at the course, the return to a more conventional circuit will suit, as should the step up to 1m6f, and it's worth noting John Gosden's Arctic Cosmos was third in this prior to landing the Leger. (op 11-8 tchd 13-8)
Girolamo(GER) had been beaten just 1/2l in the German Derby last time behind impressive subsequent scorer Pastorius, but he surely failed to match that form here, being niggled at the top of the hill and proving one-paced. (op 4-1)
Minimise Risk didn't find for pressure, having appeared to travel quite well, but at least reversed Queen's Vase form with Ed De Gas. (tchd 50-1 in a place)
Farhaan(USA) had been off for 73 days since making a nice reappearance just behind the winner at Newmarket and proved laboured, continuing what has been a frustrating season for John Dunlop. (op 12-1)

4686 BET365 LENNOX STKS (GROUP 2) 7f
3:10 (3:10) (Class 1) 3-Y-O+
£79,394 (£30,100; £15,064; £7,504; £3,766; £1,890) **Stalls** Low

Form RPR

2-12 **1** **Chachamaidee (IRE)**[41] 3266 5-8-13 113......................... TomQueally 2 112+
(Sir Henry Cecil) *s.i.s: hld up in rr: smooth hdwy on outer over 2f out: rdn and qcknd to ld ent fnl f: in command and pushed out ins fnl f* **5/4**[1]

5011 **2** *1 ½* **Libranno**[31] 3633 4-9-2 110.. RichardHughes 5 111
(Richard Hannon) *chsd ldng pair: rdn and effrt whn short of room ent fnl f: swtchd rt and the lft ins fnl f: hdwy to chse wnr fnl 75yds: r.o wl but unable to chal* **11/2[2]**

04-3 **3** *shd* **Mac Love**[60] 2656 11-9-2 108.. JamesDoyle 6 111
(Roger Charlton) *hld up in last trio: rdn and effrt 2f out: sltly outpcd whn squeezed for room and shuffled bk 1f out: swtchd lft and rallied ins fnl f: r.o wl and battling for 2nd fnl 75yds* **40/1**

-202 **4** *2* **Firebeam**[17] 4092 4-9-2 109.. RyanMoore 4 106
(William Haggas) *chsd ldr: ev ch and rdn ent fnl 2f: drvn and chsd wnr jst ins fnl f: no imp and lost 2 pls fnl 75yds* **13/2[3]**

4-20 **5** *hd* **Foxtrot Romeo (IRE)**[42] 3209 3-8-9 114.. TomEaves 7 103
(Bryan Smart) *awkward leaving stalls and s.i.s: sn bustled along and rcvrd to r in midfield: rdn and unable qck whn edgd rt 1f out: one pce ins fnl f* **15/2**

3231 **6** *nk* **Majestic Myles (IRE)**[17] 4078 4-9-2 111.. PaulHanagan 3 104
(Richard Fahey) *led: rdn and qcknd 2f out: hdd and unable qck w wnr ent fnl f: outpcd and btn ins fnl f* **8/1**

4022 **7** *½* **Edinburgh Knight (IRE)**[10] 4321 5-9-2 109.. WilliamBuick 1 103
(Paul D'Arcy) *taken down early: hld up wl in tch in last trio: rdn and unable qck wl over 1f out: keeping on same pce and wl hld whn nt clr run towards fin* **13/2[3]**

1m 26.82s (-0.18) **Going Correction** +0.15s/f (Good)
WFA 3 from 4yo+ 7lb **7** Ran SP% **111.8**
Speed ratings (Par 115): **107,105,105,102,102 102,101**
toteswingers 1&2 £1.90, 2&3 £16.20, 1&3 £12.10 CSF £8.05 TOTE £2.50: £1.60, £2.30; EX 6.10.
Owner R A H Evans **Bred** Cheval Court Stud **Trained** Newmarket, Suffolk

FOCUS
Not a strong running of this Group 2 contest. Sectional times showed the pace gradually increased. The form is muddling, but the winner was best in at the weights and the runner-up and third ran as well as they were entitled to.

NOTEBOOK
Chachamaidee(IRE) would arguably have won the Windsor Forest Stakes at Royal Ascot last time had she not lost a few lengths at the start, but the stiff 1m found her out there after she had to work her way into contention and she finished runner-up for the second straight year. She again missed the kick here, but this represented a much less-demanding test and she swamped her rivals for pace when taken wide to ensure one continuous run in the straight. Her task was made easier by the runner-up being denied a clear run, but she did this easily. There's no doubt that speed rather than stamina is her main asset, and the Prix de la Foret could be her best opportunity to gain a first top-level success. (op 11-8 tchd 6-4 in places)
Libranno, last year's fourth, was on a hat-trick after victories in Listed and Group 3 company, but he was denied a clear run until inside the final furlong and that gave him no chance with the high-class winner. He didn't look an unlucky loser, but would have given the winner more to do had he enjoyed a better trip. (op 9-2)
Mac Love, who ran seventh in this race way back in 2006, had shown he retained plenty of ability when third in the Diomed Stakes at Epsom on his only previous start this season. Returning from a two-month break, he again reached a smart level, keeping on well after having to be switched, although he didn't look any better than third best. (op 33-1)
Firebeam was below form and probably found the ground too quick. (op 8-1 tchd 9-1 in a place)
Foxtrot Romeo(IRE), dropped back in trip after finishing sixth in the St James's Palace, seemed to recover okay from an awkward start, but he didn't produce his best. He can be given another chance. (op 6-1)
Majestic Myles(IRE), seventh in this race last year, found the competition a lot tougher than in the Listed event he won on soft at Chester last time.
Edinburgh Knight(IRE), a close second behind Libranno in the Group 3 Criterion Stakes before finishing runner-up off 104 in the hugely competitive International Stakes handicap at Ascot, was held up towards the inside and never had much room in the straight. He would probably have finished a bit closer with a clear run, and a stronger pace may also have helped. Official explanation: jockey said gelding was denied a clear run (op 11-1 tchd 14-1 in a place)

4687 BET365 MOLECOMB STKS (GROUP 3) 5f
3:45 (3:45) (Class 1) 2-Y-O
£22,684 (£8,600; £4,304; £2,144; £1,076; £540) **Stalls** High

Form RPR

1145 **1** **Bungle Inthejungle**[30] 3680 2-9-0 98.. MartinHarley 10 108
(Mick Channon) *taken down early: a.p helping force v str pce: rdn over 2f out: kpt on v bravely ins fnl f: led fnl strides* **14/1**

141 **2** *hd* **Morawij**[25] 3823 2-9-0 103.. NeilCallan 8 107
(Roger Varian) *trckd ldrs: rdn to ld over 1f out: kpt on u.str.p: hdd fnl strides* **2/1[1]**

2116 **3** *3 ¾* **Hototo**[17] 4093 2-9-0 102.. PhillipMakin 11 94
(Kevin Ryan) *taken down early: in tch: rdn over 2f out: kpt on to go 3rd ent fnl f: but nt gng pce to get on terms w front pair* **11/2[3]**

1100 **4** *½* **Lyric Ace (IRE)**[17] 4093 2-9-0 95.. RichardHughes 7 93+
(Richard Hannon) *hld up: nt clrest of runs whn rdn jst over 2f out: sn swtchd sltly rt: kpt on ins fnl f: wnt 4th nring fin* **8/1**

23 **5** *nk* **Dylanbaru (IRE)**[42] 3242 2-9-0 0..(t) WayneLordan 12 91
(T Stack, Ire) *in tch: rdn and sltly outpcd over 2f out: kpt on ins fnl f: nvr threatened* **12/1**

21 **6** *shd* **Dominate**[13] 4220 2-9-0 85.. RyanMoore 6 91+
(Richard Hannon) *hld up: rdn over 2f out: swtchd rt over 1f out: kpt on ins fnl f: nvr threatened ldrs* **7/1**

1321 **7** *¾* **Lady Ibrox**[18] 4045 2-8-11 91.. DaleSwift 4 85
(Alan Brown) *set v str pce: rdn 2f out: hdd over 1f out: no ex fnl 120yds* **25/1**

1153 **8** *½* **Jadanna (IRE)**[18] 4064 2-8-11 102.. FrankieDettori 5 83
(James Given) *little slowly away: mid-div: rdn over 2f out: kpt on same pce tl no ex fnl 140yds* **4/1[2]**

3110 **9** *11* **Bridge Night**[31] 3631 2-8-11 88.. WilliamBuick 2 43
(Eve Johnson Houghton) *chsd ldrs: rdn over 2f out: wknd fnl f* **33/1**

430 **10** *3 ½* **Sand And Deliver**[29] 3700 2-8-11 77.. EddieAhern 3 31
(Peter Crate) *little slowly away: sn mid-div in centre: struggling over 2f out: wknd over 1f out* **150/1**

58.22s (-1.98) **Going Correction** -0.20s/f (Firm) **10** Ran SP% **114.1**
Speed ratings (Par 104): **107,106,100,99,99 99,98,97,79,74**
toteswingers 1&2 £6.80, 2&3 £3.10, 1&3 £12.80 CSF £41.04 TOTE £18.50: £3.60, £1.20, £2.00; EX 77.40 Trifecta £263.00 Pool: £3131.34 - 8.81 winning units..
Owner Christopher Wright & Miss Emily Asprey **Bred** Stratford Place Stud **Trained** West Ilsley, Berks
■ Stewards' Enquiry : Neil Callan two-day ban: used whip above permitted level (Aug 14-15)

FOCUS
There was plenty of Royal Ascot form on show, including three of the first four from the Windsor Castle, and the fourth-placed finisher from the Norfolk. This result needs treating with caution, however, as the pace was with the high drawn runners and those close to the stands' rail looked to be at an advantage. The race has been rated up to scratch.

NOTEBOOK
Bungle Inthejungle managed only fifth in a Chantilly Group 3 following his fourth in the Windsor Castle, when he was behind Hototo and Dylanbaru. However, he was favourably drawn here and having the stands' rail to race against in the closing stages looked to make all the difference. The Flying Childers will apparently now be considered, but he'll do well to follow up. (tchd 12-1 and 16-1 in places)
Morawij, fourth in the Norfolk before winning a Sandown Listed event, travelled nicely and looked the winner when produced with his chance, but he didn't have the benefit of the stands' rail and was just held. He can yet do better and could now be stepped up to 6f, possibly for the Gimcrack. (op 9-4 tchd 5-2 in a place)
Hototo, the Windsor Castle winner who was sixth in the Super Sprint on his most recent start, simply lacked the pace of the front two but kept on well. He might be ready for 6f. (op 5-1)
Lyric Ace(IRE), seventh in the Super Sprint on his previous start, stayed on late but at no stage did he look like getting seriously competitive. He looks short of this level. (op 9-1)
Dylanbaru(IRE), third in the Windsor Castle on his previous start, kept on after being outpaced for much of the closing stages. (op 9-1 tchd 17-2)
Dominate, a Sandown maiden winner on his previous start, was the Hannon second string and duly finished behind his stablemate, but he looks better than the bare form as raced wider than those who finished ahead of him, away from the main pace. (op 8-1)
Lady Ibrox, who had a bit to find at this level, took the field along towards the stands' rail, but she had to work to get there from stall four and couldn't sustain her bid. (op 20-1 tchd 28-1)
Jadanna(IRE) was nowhere near the form she showed when fifth in the Queen Mary and third in the Cherry Hinton. Her draw didn't help, especially as she went right on leaving the stalls, and she was away from the main pace. Official explanation: jockey said filly ran flat (op 9-2 tchd 5-1 in places)

4688 CASINO AT BET365 EBF MAIDEN STKS (C&G) 6f
4:15 (4:18) (Class 2) 2-Y-O
£11,320 (£3,368; £1,683; £841) **Stalls** High

Form RPR

6 **1** **Blessington (IRE)**[31] 3637 2-9-0 0.. WilliamBuick 17 88
(John Gosden) *mde all and racd against stands' rail: rdn over 1f out: styd on wl fnl f: rdn out* **15/2[3]**

2 *1* **Vallarta (IRE)** 2-9-0 0.. MartinHarley 7 85+
(Mick Channon) *racd stands' side: stdd and dropped in after s: hld up towards rr: pushed along and hdwy over 2f out: carried rt over 1f out: styd on wl ins fnl f: wnt 2nd cl home* **50/1**

6 **3** *nk* **Saint Jerome (IRE)**[9] 4362 2-9-0 0.. HayleyTurner 3 85
(Marcus Tregoning) *led centre gp and prom whn gps merged over 2f out: chsd wnr and drvn jst over 1f out: kpt on same pce ins fnl f: lost 2nd cl home* **14/1**

3 **4** *1* **Garswood**[17] 4114 2-9-0 0.. PaulHanagan 5 81
(Richard Fahey) *racd in centre: in tch in midfield: rdn and effrt whn gps merged over 2f out: kpt on same pce u.p ins fnl f* **7/2[1]**

5 *¾* **Daylight** 2-9-0 0.. JimmyFortune 6 79+
(Andrew Balding) *racd in centre: stdd s: t.k.h and hld up in rr overall: hdwy whn gps merged over 2f out: chsd ldrs and drvn ent fnl f: no ex and no imp fnl 150yds* **25/1**

36 **6** *½* **Prince Regal**[46] 3123 2-9-0 0.. MichaelJMMurphy 13 77
(Alan Jarvis) *racd stands' side: chsd ldr tl edgd rt u.p over 1f out: wknd fnl 100yds* **50/1**

44 **7** *2 ¼* **Millers Wharf (IRE)**[11] 4283 2-9-0 0.. RichardHughes 1 70+
(Richard Hannon) *racd in centre: stdd s: hld up towards rr: hdwy whn gps merged over 2f out: pushed rt 2f out: no imp 1f out: wknd fnl 100yds* **6/1[2]**

8 *2* **Raging Bear (USA)** 2-9-0 0.. RyanMoore 9 64+
(Richard Hannon) *racd stands' side: s.i.s: bhd: rdn over 2f out: edging rt and hdwy over 1f out: kpt on wl ins fnl f: nvr trbld ldrs* **20/1**

9 *¾* **World Record (IRE)** 2-9-0 0.. PatDobbs 16 61
(Richard Hannon) *racd stands' side: s.i.s and short of room s: hld up towards rr: rdn ent fnl 2f: swtchd rt and hdwy over 1f out: kpt on but nvr trbld ldrs* **25/1**

2 **10** *¾* **Huntsmans Close**[14] 4194 2-9-0 0.. JamieSpencer 12 59+
(Michael Bell) *racd stands' side: stdd s: t.k.h and hld up towards rr: hdwy and swtchd rt over 2f: swtchd rt again and effrt 2f out: sn rdn and no imp: wl btn and eased fnl 100yds* **7/2[1]**

20 **11** *nse* **Sutton Sid**[71] 2330 2-9-0 0.. PatCosgrave 18 59
(George Baker) *racd nr stands' rail: chsd ldrs: rdn 1/2-way: wknd u.p over 1f out* **66/1**

23 **12** *½* **Whipper Snapper (IRE)**[22] 3916 2-9-0 0.. JimCrowley 10 57
(William Knight) *racd stands' side: chsd ldrs: rdn and unable qck over 2f out: wknd over 1f out* **16/1**

52 **13** *nk* **Nenge Mboko**[19] 3996 2-9-0 0.. FrankieDettori 2 56
(George Baker) *racd in centre: in tch overall: swtchd rt 1/2-way: rdn whn gps merged over 2f out: unable qck over 1f out: wknd ins fnl f* **10/1**

14 *1* **African Oil (FR)** 2-9-0 0.. MichaelHills 14 53
(Charles Hills) *racd stands' side: s.t.k.h: hld up towards rr: rdn and sme hdwy over 2f out: no imp and rn green over 1f out: sn wknd* **20/1**

15 *2* **Extrasolar** 2-9-0 0.. EddieAhern 4 47
(Amanda Perrett) *racd towards centre: in tch overall: swtchd lft to join stands' side gp 1/2-way: sn rdn and unable qck: wknd over 1f out* **66/1**

16 *8* **Addictive Nature (IRE)** 2-9-0 0.. AdamKirby 15 21
(Clive Cox) *racd stands' side: in tch: struggling and rdn 1/2-way: wknd ent fnl 2f: bhd fnl f* **25/1**

17 *11* **Keep Calm** 2-9-0 0.. SeanLevey 11
(Richard Hannon) *racd stands' side: in tch: rdn after 2f: struggling and losing pl 1/2-way: bhd and eased ins fnl f* **50/1**

1m 12.15s (-0.05) **Going Correction** -0.20s/f (Firm) **17** Ran SP% **122.1**
Speed ratings (Par 100): **92,90,90,88,87 87,84,81,80,79 79,78,78,77,74 63,49**
toteswingers 1&2 £88.00, 2&3 £132.80, 1&3 £19.40 CSF £349.54 TOTE £9.60: £3.00, £11.40, £4.60; EX 615.20 TRIFECTA Not won..
Owner H R H Princess Haya Of Jordan **Bred** David John Brown **Trained** Newmarket, Suffolk

FOCUS
Not exactly a maiden with a rich roll of honour and the form of this year's edition looks fairly ordinary. They raced in two groups until merging after 4f. The fourth has been rated to his debut effort while the sixth potentially anchors the form.

NOTEBOOK
Blessington(IRE) stepped up markedly on his debut effort (blew chance with a very slow start and then met trouble in running), leading against the stands' rail throughout and winning with something to spare. His trainer entered him in the Mill Reef and Middle Park on the morning of the race and he looks useful enough to take his chance in a higher grade, with the valuable 6f sales race at York in August an attractive option. (op 17-2 tchd 7-1)
Vallarta(IRE), whose dam was a 1m4f winner, is from a yard going well with its juveniles and he picked up nicely to make a pleasing debut. He's entitled to improve, especially upped to 7f.
Saint Jerome(IRE) made a good start at Ascot nine days earlier and he made the running in the centre-field group. He's bred to need further (dam a dual 1m2f winner) and can win his maiden. (tchd 12-1)
Garswood is seemingly thought a bit of and duly stepped up on his York debut, finishing well having raced centre-field. He can find a maiden back up north. (tchd 4-1 in places)

Daylight, a half-brother to five winners, including speedy pair Day By Day and Alexander Ballet, shaped with plenty of potential centre-field and should prove effective at 5f for now. (op 28-1)
Prince Regal is now eligible for nurseries and should find an opening. (op 66-1)
Millers Wharf(IRE) is another who will now get a mark. (op 11-2)
Huntsmans Close looked the best horse when worn down late over 7f on debut (soft ground; raced keenly) but he proved just as keen on this drop in trip and found little having been switched all the way to centre-field. He's clearly got talent but needs to learn to settle. (op 3-1 tchd 4-1 in places)
African Oil(FR), an 85,000euros 2yo who is a half-brother to sprinter Athwaab, looked green and should improve. (op 33-1)

4689 POKER AT BET365 STKS (H'CAP) 1m
4:50 (4:53) (Class 3) (0-90,91) 3-Y-O+ **£9,703** (£2,887; £1,443; £721) **Stalls** Low

Form RPR
1-04 **1** **Uppercut**[34] 3508 4-9-3 **80** .... NeilCallan 11 88
(Stuart Kittow) *mid-div: hdwy over 2f out: sn rdn: led jst over 1f out: hld on: all out* **16/1**
0-0 **2** *nk* **Bancnuanaheireann (IRE)**[31] 3647 5-9-12 **89** .... GeorgeBaker 4 97+
(Michael Appleby) *mid-div: smooth hdwy to trck ldrs wl over 1f out: nt clr run sn after: r.o wl whn swtchd rt jst ins fnl f: jst failed* **50/1**
2211 **3** *nk* **Jack's Revenge (IRE)**[18] 4068 4-9-11 **88** ....(bt) RyanMoore 7 95+
(George Baker) *hld up towards rr: hdwy over 2f out: weaved way through field over 1f out: rdn and r.o strly ins fnl f: nt best of runs fnl 75yds: clsng qckly at fin* **15/2**
-011 **4** *½* **Jacob Cats**[6] 4474 3-9-6 **91** 6ex .... RichardHughes 14 95
(Richard Hannon) *mid-div: swtchd out and hdwy 2f out: rdn to chal ent fnl f: kpt on but no ex fnl 120yds* **11/4**[1]
1550 **5** *nk* **Norse Blues**[34] 3508 4-9-12 **89** .... JamesDoyle 16 94+
(Sylvester Kirk) *hld up towards rr: nt clr run over 2f out: swtchd lft whn possible wl over 1f out: sn rdn: r.o strly ins fnl f* **20/1**
4003 **6** *1 ½* **Colour Guard**[3] 4578 4-9-7 **84** .... SilvestreDeSousa 18 86
(Mark Johnston) *chsd ldrs: rdn and ev ch 2f out tl ent fnl f: no ex fnl 120yds* **12/1**
0402 **7** *½* **Askaud (IRE)**[4] 4557 4-9-6 **83** ....(b) TomQueally 2 83
(Scott Dixon) *trckd ldrs: nt clr run jst over 1f out: rdn and kpt on whn gap appeared but nt gng pce to threaten* **6/1**[2]
2310 **8** *1* **Ree's Rascal (IRE)**[30] 3667 4-9-4 **81** .... PatCosgrave 6 79
(Jim Boyle) *towards rr: struggling 4f out: styd on fr over 1f out wout clrest of runs: fin wl* **25/1**
0433 **9** *½* **Shamdarley (IRE)**[20] 3963 4-9-3 **80** .... PhillipMakin 8 77
(Michael Dods) *mid-div: hdwy on rails 3f out: sn rdn: swtchd lft ent fnl f: kpt on but nt gng pce to get on terms* **7/1**[3]
3030 **10** *1 ¼* **Yojimbo (IRE)**[6] 4474 4-9-2 **79** .... MatthewDavies 9 73
(Mick Channon) *in tch: taking clsr order whn nt clr run over 2f out: sn rdn: kpt on same pce fnl f* **20/1**
0530 **11** *1 ¼* **Crown Counsel (IRE)**[4] 4557 4-9-8 **85** .... JoeFanning 20 76
(Mark Johnston) *prom: rdn to ld over 2f out: hdd over 1f out: wknd* **20/1**
0-03 **12** *nse* **Master Mylo (IRE)**[20] 3977 5-9-5 **82** .... FrederikTylicki 19 73
(Robert Cowell) *taken down early: mid-div on outside: rdn wl over 2f out: no imp* **33/1**
1035 **13** *½* **Starwatch**[4] 4529 5-9-13 **90** .... SeanLevey 13 80
(John Bridger) *mid-div: rdn wl over 2f out: nvr any imp* **20/1**
1-3 **14** *3 ¾* **War Singer (USA)**[18] 4060 5-9-13 **90** ....(t) EddieAhern 15 71
(David Pipe) *rdn over 3f out: a in rr* **40/1**
203- **15** *3* **Wilfred Pickles (IRE)**[214] 7922 6-9-6 **83** .... DaneO'Neill 3 57
(Jo Crowley) *nvr bttr than mid-div: wknd fnl f* **50/1**
16 *3 ½* **Spin Of A Coin (IRE)**[74] 2307 4-9-0 **82** .... AshleyMorgan(5) 1 48
(Pat Murphy) *s.i.s: a towards rr* **33/1**
0204 **17** *nk* **Snow Bay**[14] 4190 6-9-7 **84** .... AdrianNicholls 12 50
(David Nicholls) *led: rdn and hdd over 2f out: kpt chsng ldrs tl wknd ent fnl f* **20/1**
6060 **18** *3 ½* **Viva Ronaldo (IRE)**[10] 4317 6-9-9 **86** .... PaulHanagan 10 44
(Richard Fahey) *mid-div: swtchd lft and rdn over 2f out: sn wknd* **25/1**
1003 **19** *9* **Cruiser**[27] 3767 4-9-5 **82** .... MartinDwyer 17 19
(William Muir) *slowly away: sn swtchd rt: a towards rr* **33/1**
1405 **20** *2 ¾* **April Fool**[26] 3772 8-8-13 **81** ....(b) DarrenEgan(5) 5 12
(Ronald Harris) *prom: rdn to chse ldr over 3f out: sn lost pl and wknd* **33/1**

1m 39.52s (-0.38) **Going Correction** +0.15s/f (Good)
WFA 3 from 4yo+ 8lb **20** Ran SP% **128.4**
Speed ratings (Par 107): **107,106,106,105,105 104,103,102,102,100 99,99,99,95,92 88,88,85,76,73**
toteswingers 1&2 £154.90, 2&3 £61.70, 1&3 £27.10 CSF £659.57 CT £6505.04 TOTE £21.60: £4.50, £12.00, £1.80, £1.60; EX 965.80 TRIFECTA Not won..
Owner H A Cushing **Bred** The Hon Mrs R Pease **Trained** Blackborough, Devon

FOCUS
A competitive big-field handicap run at a good clip. The draw played no real part. The winner and fifth help set the standard, while a case can be made that the runner-up or third could/should have won.

NOTEBOOK
Uppercut had finished fourth behind the highly progressive Trade Commisioner (favourite for the Betfred Mile) at Salisbury last time and he hit a peak here, really gutting it out having edged ahead. There were a few with claims of being unlucky in behind, but he can yet rank higher, with a sound surface important. (tchd 18-1 in a place)
Bancnuanaheireann(IRE), picked up for just 2,500gns earlier this month, was always travelling well around the inside but had nowhere to go from 3f out to 1f out and just couldn't get there in time. Having just his sixth start, this 5yo clearly benefited from the sounder surface (all runs in Ireland on soft and heavy) and, although his mark will creep back into the 90s, he's a handicapper to monitor. (op 66-1)
Jack's Revenge(IRE), up 7lb, was another with claims for being unlucky. Having been dropped right out, he had to negotiate a tricky passage through the field and found the line coming too quickly. He remains on the up. (op 13-2 tchd 6-1)
Jacob Cats, the sole 3yo in the field reappearing just six days after winning again at Sandown, looked set to defy his penalty when switched 2f out, but couldn't pick up sufficiently. The race coming too soon, as well as him wanting genuine fast ground, are possible excuses and he's worth giving another chance to. (tchd 3-1 in places)
Norse Blues got no run when trying to switch 3f out and was left with too much ground to recoup once finally in the clear.
Colour Guard was forced to race wide from stall 18 and ran well, again suggesting he's nearing a win.
Askaud(IRE) had to wait for a gap but was by no means unlucky. Official explanation: jockey said filly was denied a clear run (op 13-2 tchd 7-1)
Ree's Rascal(IRE) didn't get much of a run while trying to stay on late.
Crown Counsel(IRE) used up too much juice from stall 20. (op 16-1)

4690 MOBILE AT BET365 STKS (H'CAP) 5f
5:25 (5:26) (Class 3) (0-90,90) 4-Y-O+ **£9,703** (£2,887; £1,443; £721) **Stalls** High

Form RPR
0-00 **1** **Time Medicean**[12] 4231 6-8-1 **73** ow1 .... RaulDaSilva(3) 14 81
(Tony Carroll) *racd in centre: bhd: stl plenty to do whn swtchd rt and effrt over 1f out: str run ins fnl f to ld last stride* **22/1**
0010 **2** *shd* **Le Toreador**[19] 4013 7-9-5 **88** ....(tp) PhillipMakin 1 96
(Kevin Ryan) *racd on far side thrght: pressed ldrs: led and edgd lft over 1f out: hdd ins fnl f: battled bk v gamely to ld again fnl 50yds: hdd last stride* **25/1**
1110 **3** *nk* **Valmina**[22] 3915 5-8-1 **75** ....(t) DarrenEgan(5) 10 82
(Tony Carroll) *racd in centre: bhd and sn pushed along: hdwy u.p over 1f out: styd on wl ins fnl f: wnt 3rd last strides* **33/1**
1000 **4** *nk* **Long Awaited (IRE)**[19] 4013 4-9-2 **85** ....(b1) RyanMoore 11 91
(David Barron) *racd centre to stands' side: in tch: rdn to chal over 1f out: led jst ins fnl f: drvn and hdd fnl 50yds: no ex* **16/1**
5121 **5** *nk* **Cruise Tothelimit (IRE)**[11] 4292 4-8-2 **74** .... RyanPowell(3) 5 79
(Ian Williams) *racd towards centre: chsd ldrs: rdn over 1f out: pressed ldrs ins fnl f: kpt on same pce towards fin* **12/1**
0003 **6** *½* **Arctic Feeling (IRE)**[17] 4077 4-8-13 **82** .... PaulHanagan 15 85
(Richard Fahey) *racd centre to stands' side: in tch: rdn and effrt to chse ldrs ent fnl f: styd on same pce fnl 100yds* **14/1**
0464 **7** *½* **Ganas (IRE)**[25] 3822 4-8-13 **82** .... AdamKirby 16 83+
(Clive Cox) *taken down early: racd towards stands' side: chsd ldr tl over 1f out: sn drvn: styd on same pce ins fnl f* **9/1**[3]
0006 **8** *nse* **Fitz Flyer (IRE)**[3] 4576 6-9-7 **90** .... AdrianNicholls 23 91
(David Nicholls) *racd towards stands' side: in tch in midfield: effrt and rdn over 1f out: styd on u.p ins fnl f: unable to chal* **7/1**[1]
31 **9** *shd* **Desert Strike**[5] 4508 6-8-5 **74** 6ex ....(p) MatthewChadwick 4 75
(Charles Hills) *taken down early: racd in centre and led: edgd lft 3f out: hdd over 1f out: sn rdn and no ex 1f out: wknd fnl 75yds* **16/1**
300- **10** *¾* **The Thrill Is Gone**[332] 5706 4-9-6 **89** .... MartinHarley 19 87
(Mick Channon) *racd stands' side: chsd ldrs: rdn wl over 1f out: kpt on same pce and no imp ins fnl f* **25/1**
0600 **11** *hd* **Hamoody (USA)**[31] 3608 8-8-8 **77** .... MartinDwyer 18 74
(David Nicholls) *racd towards stands' side: stdd s: hld up bhd: rdn and hdwy over 1f out: kpt on ins fnl f: nvr gng to rch ldrs* **10/1**
1211 **12** *1* **Silvanus (IRE)**[11] 4312 7-9-7 **90** .... RussKennemore 8 88+
(Paul Midgley) *taken down early: racd in centre: in tch: rdn and chsd ldrs ent fnl f: keeping on whn nt clr run fnl 100yds: lost all ch and eased* **16/1**
6000 **13** *¾* **Crown Choice**[39] 3336 7-8-13 **82** .... MickyFenton 22 73
(Paul Midgley) *taken down early: racd stands' side: bhd: effrt and hung rt over 1f out: styd on ins fnl f: nvr trbld ldrs* **40/1**
2344 **13** *dht* **Falasteen (IRE)**[5] 4501 5-8-13 **82** .... FrederikTylicki 17 73
(Milton Bradley) *racd stands' side: in tch: effrt and rdn over 1f out: kpt on same pce and no imp fnl f* **25/1**
0012 **15** *shd* **Noverre To Go (IRE)**[10] 4337 6-9-2 **85** .... JamesDoyle 6 76
(Ronald Harris) *racd in centre: chsd ldrs: unable qck u.p over 1f out: wknd ins fnl f* **7/1**[1]
1254 **16** *nk* **Kingsgate Choice (IRE)**[10] 4337 5-9-4 **87** .... TomQueally 13 76
(Ed de Giles) *racd centre to stands' side: in tch in midfield: rdn and effrt wl over 1f out: styd on same pce and no imp fnl f* **12/1**
0420 **17** *1 ¼* **Interakt**[22] 3915 5-8-3 **75** .... HarryBentley(3) 12 60
(Joseph Tuite) *racd towards stands' side: in tch in midfield: rdn 3f out: plugged on same pce and no threat to ldrs fnl 2f* **20/1**
6055 **18** *1 ¼* **Volcanic Dust (IRE)**[5] 4501 4-8-8 **77** .... CathyGannon 25 57
(Milton Bradley) *taken down early: racd against stands' rail: a towards rr: effrt u.p over 1f out: no real imp: n.d* **66/1**
0-00 **19** *1* **Invincible Lad (IRE)**[4] 4530 8-8-6 **75** .... MarcHalford 24 52
(Milton Bradley) *racd stands' side: bhd: effrt u.p and edgd rt over 1f out: no imp 1f out: n.d* **33/1**
00-6 **20** *½* **R Woody**[10] 4337 5-9-2 **85** .... JimCrowley 20 60
(Robert Cowell) *racd towards stands' side: towards rr: edging rt and effrt u.p 2f out: no prog and wknd 1f out* **8/1**[2]
2001 **21** *3 ¾* **Cadeaux Pearl**[97] 1602 4-9-6 **89** ....(b) KierenFallon 2 51
(Scott Dixon) *racd towards far side: midfield overall: hung rt to far side 1/2-way: wknd over 1f out: wl btn and eased fnl 100yds* **20/1**
506 **22** *6* **Bertoliver**[5] 4501 8-8-6 **75** .... JoeFanning 26 15
(Stuart Williams) *racd against stands' rail in tch: rdn and stuglling ent fnl 2f: wknd and bhd 1f out: eased ins fnl f* **33/1**
013 **23** *6* **Royal Bajan (USA)**[58] 2731 4-8-7 **76** .... MickaelBarzalona 21
(James Given) *racd towards stands' side: midfield: rdn and no prog wl over 1f out: wkng and towards rr whn sltly hmpd jst over 1f out: bhd and eased ins fnl f* **50/1**

58.22s (-1.98) **Going Correction** -0.20s/f (Firm) **23** Ran SP% **135.0**
Speed ratings (Par 107): **107,106,106,105,105 104,103,103,103,102 102,100,99,99,99 98,96,94,93,92 86,76,67**
toteswingers 1&2 £126.00, 2&3 not won. 1&3 not won. CSF £490.09 CT £16790.21 TOTE £30.70: £6.00, £8.70, £7.30, £5.10; EX 883.60 Trifecta £1703.60 Pool of £2532.48 - 1.10 winning units..
Owner A W Carroll **Bred** C A Cyzer **Trained** Cropthorne, Worcs

FOCUS
A fiercely competitive sprint handicap. Le Toreador, drawn in stall one, raced alone against the far rail through the early stages, but he ended up towards the middle of the track and that's where the main action developed. Those drawn high struggled to get competitive. The runner-up has been rated as running his best race since early 2010, while the fourth has been rated to form in the first-time blinkers.

NOTEBOOK
Time Medicean crept in at the bottom of the handicap and the race unfolded to suit, although he carried 1lb overweight and needed every yard to get on top. He's at his best off a strong pace and that's exactly what he got, enabling him to build on his first two efforts of the year with a fine late surge. It was around this time last season that he really came good and he could have more to offer when things drop right. Unsurprisingly, the greys race at the July course, which he won last term, is said to be the target once again. (tchd 25-1)
Le Toreador, who was fifth in this race in 2009, ran a blinder in defeat, only being collared in the final stride.
Valmina, the winner's stablemate, flopped on soft ground at Windsor last time, a run that followed three straight wins at Bath, but he bounced back with a career-best in defeat. (op 50-1)
Long Awaited(IRE) returned to form in first-time blinkers. Whether he will build on this remains to be seen, but easier ground will probably help. (tchd 18-1)
Cruise Tothelimit(IRE) continued his fine run of form, this effort coming off 6lb higher than when winning at Haydock on his previous start. (op 14-1)
Ganas(IRE) probably wasn't helped by racing more towards the stands' side than some, before hanging right. (op 7-1)
Fitz Flyer(IRE) wasn't helped by his high draw. (op 13-2 tchd 6-1)

Desert Strike found this tougher than the 6f seller he won last time. (op 25-1)
Silvanus(IRE) would have been a lot closer granted a clear run. Official explanation: jockey said gelding was denied a clear run
Noverre To Go (IRE)had looked revitalised lately, but he was well below form this time. (op 9-1)
T/Jkpt: Not won. T/Plt: £306.70 to a £1 stake. Pool of £255733.93 - 608.52 winning tickets.
T/Qpdt: £51.00 to a £1 stake. Pool of £12939.99 -187.75 winning tickets. SP

4691a, 4693a-4695a - (Foreign Racing) - See Raceform Interactive

4665 GALWAY (R-H)

Tuesday, July 31

OFFICIAL GOING: Soft

4692a TOPAZ MILE EUROPEAN BREEDERS FUND H'CAP — 1m 100y

5:35 (5:37) 3-Y-0+

£57,500 (£18,208; £8,625 ; £2,875 ; £1,916 ; £958)

RPR

1 **Vastonea (IRE)**[12] 4279 4 -9-0**89**.............................. DeclanMcDonogh 6 97
(Kevin Prendergast, Ire) *hld up in tch: cl 4th 1/2-way: pushed along to go 3rd ins fnl 2f: hrd rdn and swtchd lft ent fnl f and styd on wl to ld fnl 50yds: all out* **7/1**[3]

2 1/2 **Pintura**[52] 2910 5 -9-9**98**.. JPO'Brien 1 105
(Kevin Ryan) *attempted to make all: hdd over 3f out: regained ld 2f out on inner tl hdd fnl 50yds* **7/1**[3]

3 1 3/4 **Custom Cut (IRE)**[10] 4356 3 -9-3**105**......................... RonanWhelan(5) 4 107
(George J Kent, Ire) *cl up 3rd: wnt 2nd 2f out and almost on terms ent fnl f: no ex fnl 100yds* **10/1**

4 3/4 **Rock Critic (IRE)**[41] 3268 7 -9-12**101**................................ PatSmullen 8 103
(D K Weld, Ire) *chsd ldrs: carried wd early: hrd rdn in 5th under 2f out: kpt on u.p fnl f* **5/2**[1]

5 hd **Bold Thady Quill (IRE)**[28] 3743 5 -9-1**90**..........................(p) WJLee 16 91+
(K J Condon, Ire) *in rr: clsd gng wl into 6th 2f out: short of room disputing 4th ent fnl f: kpt on* **16/1**

6 3 3/4 **Miracle Cure (IRE)**[6] 4485 3 -8-4**87** oh1........................... RoryCleary 9 79
(J S Bolger, Ire) *sltly hmpd early: racd in mid-div: pushed along in 8th appr st: one pce fnl f* **12/1**

7 7 1/2 **Castle Bar Sling (USA)**[12] 4279 7 -8-4**84**..................(p) MACleere(5) 10 60
(T J O'Mara, Ire) *hld up towards rr: sme hdwy 3f out: kpt on fnl f* **14/1**

8 1 1/2 **Seanie (IRE)**[31] 3648 3 -8-11**94**.. FergalLynch 7 66
(David Marnane, Ire) *plld hrd in mid-div and edgd lft early: clsr in 4th bef 1/2-way: pushed along on outer and sn no imp fnl 2f* **11/1**

9 nk **Regulation (IRE)**[14] 4202 3 -8-9**92**.................................. ShaneFoley 13 63
(M Halford, Ire) *hld up towards rr: sme late hdwy: n.d* **10/1**

10 2 **One Fine Day (IRE)**[31] 3645 3 -8-0**88**........................ ConorHoban(5) 14 55
(Mrs John Harrington, Ire) *bhd: pushed along 1/2-way: nvr a factor* **12/1**

11 3 3/4 **Moran Gra (USA)**[51] 777 5 -9-11**100**......................(p) CO'Donoghue 2 60
(Ms Joanna Morgan, Ire) *cl up 2nd: led over 3f out: pushed along and hdd 2f out: sn wknd* **25/1**

12 8 **Spa's Dancer (IRE)**[24] 3878 5 -9-6**95**............................... ChrisHayes 5 37
(Ed de Giles) *slowly away: bhd and n.d fr over 2f out* **6/1**[2]

13 nk **Honourable Emperor (IRE)**[15] 1228 3 -8-13**96**................ FranBerry 3 36
(Noel Meade, Ire) *t.k.h on inner in 4th early: pushed along over 4f out and sn wknd* **16/1**

14 14 **Muck 'N' Brass (IRE)**[45] 4163 3 -8-5**91**...................... SamJames(3) 15 1
(Edward Lynam, Ire) *towards rr: n.d fr 3f out* **33/1**

1m 54.06s (3.86)
WFA 3 from 4yo+ 8lb **14**Ran SP% **135.0**
CSF £62.53 CT £519.12 TOTE £9.40 : £2.70 , £2.20 , £3.40 ; DF 62.80 .
Owner Norman Ormiston **Bred** Eyrefield Lodge Stud **Trained** Friarstown, Co Kildare

FOCUS
A very competitive renewal and a great finish. Again those up with the pace generally dominated. The runner-up and fourth help set the standard.

NOTEBOOK
Vastonea(IRE) was admirably tough under a patient ride. Declan McDonogh had to sit and wait at a crucial stage and he had around five horses ahead of him as they hit the final bend. However, he found more when, crucially, McDonogh pulled him to the centre of the track around a furlong out. At the finish, the lightly raced 4yo won a shade snugly. He likes easy ground and it will be interesting to see how he is campaigned. (op 7/1 tchd 13/2)
Pintura went 1-33 in-running and one wonders have those who backed at that price ever seen a race at Galway before. Given his weight and having been up there throughout, he was always going to be vulnerable off his career-high mark. He got a brilliant tactical ride, his jockey never panicking when headed, and ran a cracker. (op 15/2 tchd 8/1)
Custom Cut (IRE)has been one of the stories of the campaign and the next episode was nearly written. He was always going to find it tough to get an easy lead but his canny young rider knew that and there were no excuses. He is progressing remarkably well. (op 11/1 tchd 9/1)
Rock Critic (IRE)looked to have a tough task off his mark but he did not get the cleanest of runs and this was as good as he has ever run, all things considered. One imagines he will not run in a handicap again. Official explanation: trainer said gelding received an accidental bump in the straight. (op 11/4)
Bold Thady Quill (IRE)did best of those who came from off the pace and he deserves great credit as he had to do it the hard way from gate 16. He has had an excellent campaign.
Miracle Cure (IRE) touched off last time, was still 6lb higher here. She continues to progress. 14/1)
Castle Bar Sling (USA)s coming down the weights. This was more encouraging. (op 14/1 tchd 16/1)

4632 DEAUVILLE (R-H)

Tuesday, July 31

OFFICIAL GOING: Turf: good; fibresand: standard

4696a PRIX D'AVRANCHES (CONDITIONS) (2YO FILLIES) (TURF) — 6f

1:50 (12:00) 2-Y-0 **£14,166** (£5,666; £4,250 ; £2,833 ; £1,416)

RPR

1 **Wedge Trust (IRE)**[55] 2 -8-11**0** ow1.......................... ChristopheSoumillon 4 90
(J-C Rouget, France) **29/10**[2]

2 2 1/2 **Arena Sempione (FR)**[33] 3553 2 -8-10**0**......................... IoritzMendizabal 5 81
(J Heloury, France) **4/1**[3]

3 1 3/4 **Folle De Toi (FR)**[33] 2 -8-5**0**... MarcLerner(5) 6 75
(T Trapenard, France) **16/1**

4 1 **Tita Caty (FR)**[7] 2 -9-0**0**.. Christophe-PatriceLemaire 2 76
(M Boutin, France) **11/1**

5 2 **Sorry Woman (FR)**[14] 4205 2 -8-10**0**............................ MaximeGuyon 1 66
(H-A Pantall, France) **6/4**[1]

6 3 1/2 **Krupskaya (FR)**[22] 3909 2 -8-10**0**.................................. OlivierPeslier 3 54
(Mrs K Burke) *s.i.s: sn rdn to match pce of rivals: unable to go pce fr 1/2-way: given reminder 2 1/2f out: no ex: nvr a factor* **5/1**

1m 11.45s (0.45) **6**Ran SP% **116.5**
WIN (incl. 1 euro stake): 3.90. PLACES: 2.40, 2.20. SF: 14.50.
Owner Ecurie I M Fares **Bred** Scea Haras De Manneville **Trained** Pau, France

4684 GOODWOOD (R-H)

Wednesday, August 1

OFFICIAL GOING: Good (8.2)
Wind: virtually nil Weather: light cloud

4697 GOODWOOD STKS (H'CAP) — 2m 5f

2:00 (2:00) (Class 2) (0-95,95) 3-Y-0+

£18,675 (£5,592; £2,796 ; £1,398 ; £699 ; £351)

Form RPR

300 1 **Hurricane Higgins (IRE)**[25] 3857 4 -9-10**95**.................. JoeFanning 20 103
(Mark Johnston) *travelled wl: in tch: hdwy 4f out: wnt 2nd and clsng on ldr 3f out: rdn and ev ch over 1f out: led 1f out: forged to ld ins fnl f: hrd pressed and hld on towards fin: all out* **14/1**

050- 2 hd **Defence Of Duress (IRE)**[59] 7139 4 -8-7**78**.............. JamieSpencer 13 86
(T J Taaffe, Ire) *t.k.h: hld up in midfield: rdn and gd hdwy 3f out: chsd ldng trio and swtchd lft over 1f out: styd on strly ins fnl f: wnt 2nd and clsng on wnr towards fin: nt quite get up* **25/1**

1-00 3 3/4 **Never Can Tell (IRE)**[18] 4111 5 -9-10**95**...................... FrankieDettori 7 102
(Jamie Osborne) *chsd ldr: allowed ldr to go clr after 4f: pushed along and clsd 3f out: rdn to ld over 1f out: hdd 1f out: battled on gamely u.p tl no ex and btn fnl 75yds* **10/1**

/10- 4 1 3/4 **Beyond (IRE)**[275] 6690 5 -8-7**85** ow2............. WilliamTwiston-Davies(7) 5 91
(David Pipe) *led: wnt clr after 4f: 10 l clr 6f out: rdn over 2f out: hdd over 1f out: edgd lft and no ex ins fnl f* **9/1**

64/3 5 5 **Cape Express (IRE)**[22] 2474 7 -8-13**84**............................. NeilCallan 15 85
(Nicky Henderson) *hld up towards rr of midfield: rdn and gd hdwy on inner 3f out: chsd ldng quartet and swtchd lft wl over 1f out: no imp after* **7/1**[1]

1-06 6 3 1/2 **Seaside Sizzler**[39] 3373 5 -9-3**88**................................(bt) JimCrowley 17 86
(Ralph Beckett) *hld up in midfield: rdn and effrt over 3f out: hdwy u.p but stl plenty to do over 2f out: kpt on but no imp on ldrs fr over 1f out* **9/1**

6502 7 nk **Saborido (USA)**[33] 3572 6 -8-8**79**...................................... PatDobbs 12 77
(Amanda Perrett) *travelled wl: chsd ldrs: rdn and unable qck over 3f out: 6th and btn over 1f out: wknd* **33/1**

4-03 8 4 1/2 **Gordonsville**[11] 4326 9 -8-9**80**... ChrisCatlin 18 74
(Jim Goldie) *hld up in rr: hmpd and j. fallen rdr 12f out: wl bhd after: rdn and hdwy on outer over 3f out: plugged on but no ch w ldrs* **18/1**

06-0 9 6 **Sentry Duty (FR)**[13] 3241 10 -9-6**91**....................... SilvestreDeSousa 4 79
(Nicky Henderson) *hld up in rr: hdwy 8f out: rdn and effrt over 3f out: no imp 3f out and sn wknd* **25/1**

235 10 8 **Wild Desert (FR)**[15] 4176 7 -8-11**82**........................... RichardHughes 3 63
(Charlie Longsdon) *chsd ldrs: rdn and unable qck 4f out: sn outpcd and btn: no ch fnl 2f* **28/1**

4214 11 1 1/2 **Orsippus (USA)**[18] 4115 6 -8-11**82**............................... KierenFallon 14 62
(Michael Smith) *chsd ldrs: rdn and unable qck 4f out: wknd 3f out: wl btn 2f out* **15/2**[2]

3110 12 3 3/4 **Cloudy Spirit**[39] 3373 7 -8-10**81**....................................... LukeMorris 16 57
(Reg Hollinshead) *hld up in rr: hmpd bnd 12f out: rdn and hdwy on outer 4f out: no prog 3f out: sn wknd* **14/1**

4/53 13 1 1/2 **Nafaath (IRE)**[43] 3241 6 -9-3**88**....................................... SebSanders 1 63
(Neil King) *in tch: rdn and unable qck 4f out: sn struggling: wknd over 2f out* **11/1**

0-00 14 8 **Swingkeel (IRE)**[39] 3373 7 -9-10**95**..............................(p) TedDurcan 19 63
(John Dunlop) *a bhd: rdn and no real reponse over 4f out: t.o fnl 2f* **50/1**

0012 15 hd **Trovare (USA)**[14] 4215 5 -8-9**80**................................... HayleyTurner 10 48
(Amanda Perrett) *in tch: rdn and unable qck 4f out: wknd 3f out: wl bhd fnl f: t.o* **22/1**

206/ 16 11 **Akbabend**[61] 6715 6 -8-7**78**...(t) SamHitchcott 6 36
(Chris Gordon) *hld up in midfield: bdly hmpd on bnd 12f out: rdn and wknd 4f out: wl bhd and eased fnl f: t.o* **100/1**

2605 17 dist **Mica Mika (IRE)**[18] 4115 4 -8-12**83**.............................. PaulHanagan 9
(Richard Fahey) *a bhd: bdly hmpd on bnd 12f out: lost tch after: wl t.o and eased fnl 2f* **20/1**

/60- 18 1/2 **Font**[371] 4423 9 -8-11**82** ow1...(t) WilliamBuick 2
(Lawney Hill) *a bhd: sltly hmpd bnd 12f out: lost tch 8f out: wl t.o and eased fnl 2f* **40/1**

10-0 P **Veiled**[43] 3241 6 -9-9**94**.. EddieAhern 8
(Nicky Henderson) *in tch: rdn and unable qck 3f out: wkng whn lost action and eased 2f out: p.u and dismntd ins fnl f* **12/1**

0031 S **Romeo Montague**[12] 4284 4 -9-8**93**.................................. RyanMoore 11
(Ed Dunlop) *hld up in midfield tl slipped up on bnd 12f out* **8/1**[3]

4m 33.58s (2.58) **Going Correction** +0.075s/f (Good) **20**Ran SP% **127.7**
Speed ratings (Par 109): **98,97,97,96,95 93,93,91,89,86 86,84,84,80,80 76, , , ,**
toteswingers 1&2 £64.50, 1&3 £38.20, 2&3 £105.50 CSF £342.65 CT £3657.44 TOTE £17.30 : £3.60, £5.80 , £2.50 , £3.20 ; EX 374.60 TRIFECTA Not won. .
Owner A D Spence **Bred** Paul Nataf **Trained** Middleham Moor, N Yorks

FOCUS
Lower bend dolled out 6yds from 6f to the Winning Post increasing distances by about 10yds. Top bend dolled out 3yds adding about 5yds. The ground had reportedly dried a little overnight and remained good, unaffected by a few drops of rain which fell during the morning. A typical renewal of this historic stamina test, which sees the field head the opposite way up the home straight following a flip start. The pace appeared ordinary, set by fourth home Beyond, who soon compiled a clear lead, but the time was around ten seconds off the standard. Not many were able to get involved. The winner is rated close to last season's best, as is the runner-up.

NOTEBOOK
Hurricane Higgins (IRE)made smooth progress on the outer to lead, but needed to extend his neck to hold the runner-up. A classy performer at three who ran in the Gordon Stakes at the fixture last year, he had been inconsistent this season and had his stamina to prove, having not run at further than 1m6f, but he saw it out admirably. Further opportunities for him on the Flat will be in short supply though, as he has failed a stalls test. (op 12-1)
Defence Of Duress (IRE)who was having his first Flat run for Tom Taaffe, was the only one to make progress from further back in the main body. Once switched into daylight he took time to engage full stride, but he was staying on strongly near the finish. He saw out the longer trip well.

Never Can Tell(IRE) led the main body of the field before putting put her head in front briefly. She couldn't hold on for long, but this tough and genuine mare will no doubt head back to the Cesarewitch again with sound claims. (op 12-1 tchd 14-1 in places)

Beyond(IRE)'s lead was gradually whittled away in the straight, but he stuck on for a creditable fourth. He had not run since a hurdles outing in October, but lacked nothing in fitness. He was seventh in last year's Cesarewitch and that race would seem the logical target again. (op 10-1)

Cape Express(IRE), in the same ownership as the winner and carrying the second colours, has won two novice hurdles since his last Flat venture. Another upped in trip, he could not land a blow but was not beaten for lack of stamina.

Seaside Sizzler, last year's runner-up, ran a fair race off 6lb higher 12 months on, while \bSaborido\p raced in a similar position throughout without looking like winning. (op 8-1)

Gordonsville did well to reach his final position considering he was hampered by the faller. (op 14-1)

Orsippus(USA) came here in good heart, but didn't get home over this marathon trip. He had been a bit keen through the early stages. (tchd 7-1, 8-1 in places)

Cloudy Spirit Official explanation: trainer's rep said mare had been struck into off-fore

Veiled, last year's Ascot Stakes winner, was in the process of running well when sustaining a fatal injury. (op 14-1)

Romeo Montague came down at halfway, hampering several towards the back. (op 14-1)

4698 VEUVE CLICQUOT VINTAGE STKS (GROUP 2) 7f

2:35 (2:36) (Class 1) 2-Y-O

£34,026 (£12,900; £6,456; £3,216; £1,614; £810) **Stalls** Low

Form	Pos	Dist	Horse	RPR
121	**1**		**Olympic Glory (IRE)**[18] 4098 2-9-3 111 ...... RichardHughes 9 (Richard Hannon) *in tch in midfield: grad lost pl fr 1/2-way: swtchd rt and nt clr run over 1f out: 9th and stl plenty to do whn swtchd lft ent fnl f: qcknd and str run ins fnl f to ld cl home* **11/4**[2]	112+
3154	**2**	½	**Artigiano (USA)**[18] 4098 2-9-0 104 ...... FrankieDettori 1 (Mahmood Al Zarooni) *chsd ldrs: angling out lft and barging match w rival 3f out: hrd drvn and over 1f out: ev ch ins fnl f: styd on gamely to go 2nd last strides* **7/1**[3]	106
3310	**3**	hd	**Luhaif**[18] 4098 2-9-0 90 ...... SamHitchcott 5 (Mick Channon) *pushed along leaving stalls: led after 1f out: rdn over 2f out: drvn and hdd over 1f out: kpt on v gamely u.p: led again briefly wl ins fnl f: hdd and lost 2 pls cl home* **80/1**	106
411	**4**	hd	**Tha'Ir (IRE)**[39] 3368 2-9-0 98 ...... SilvestreDeSousa 2 (Saeed Bin Suroor) *led for 1f: chsd ldr after: rdn over 2f out: drvn to ld over 1f out: edgd lft ins fnl f: hdd and no ex wl ins fnl f* **8/1**	105
1	**5**	hd	**Ghurair (USA)**[19] 4066 2-9-0 0 ...... PaulHanagan 7 (John Gosden) *hld up in tch in midfield: rdn and swtchd rt over 1f out: rn green u.p ent fnl f: styd on strly fnl 100yds* **2/1**[1]	104+
10	**6**	1½	**Operation Chariot (IRE)**[18] 4098 2-9-0 0 ...... JimmyFortune 4 (Andrew Balding) *in tch in midfield: effrt u.p 2f out: drvn and unable qck over 1f out: styd on same pce ins fnl f* **100/1**	100
3112	**7**	1	**Birdman (IRE)**[18] 4098 2-9-0 108 ...... JamieSpencer 6 (David Simcock) *hld up in last trio: rdn and effrt on inner wl over 1f out: kpt on same pce ins fnl f* **15/2**	98
01	**8**	1	**Whipper's Boy (IRE)**[13] 4253 2-9-0 0 ...... KierenFallon 8 (Brian Meehan) *hld up in last trio: rdn and effrt wl over 1f out: no imp tl kpt on ins fnl f: nvr gng pce to chal ldrs* **22/1**	95
1515	**9**	1¾	**Chilworth Icon**[20] 4008 2-9-0 103 ...... MartinHarley 10 (Mick Channon) *s.i.s: hld up in last trio: rdn and effrt 2f out: sme hdwy over 1f out: no imp 1f out and wknd ins fnl f* **33/1**	90
113	**10**	1¼	**Maxentius (IRE)**[18] 4098 2-9-0 104 ...... WilliamBuick 3 (Peter Chapple-Hyam) *chsd ldrs: rdn whn bmpd and pushed lft over 2f out: wknd over 1f out* **8/1**	87

1m 27.7s (0.70) **Going Correction** +0.075s/f (Good) **10** Ran SP% **116.0**
Speed ratings (Par 106): **99,98,98,97,97 96,94,93,91,90**
toteswingers 1&2 £4.70, 1&3 £42.80, 2&3 £33.10 CSF £21.68 TOTE £3.60: £1.40, £3.00, £9.90; EX 25.30 Trifecta £954.50 Pool: £7,868.84 - 6.10 winning units..

Owner Mrs J Wood **Bred** Denis McDonnell **Trained** East Everleigh, Wilts

FOCUS

The first four from the Superlative Stakes were taken on by the once-raced Ghurair, and it was the maiden winner who was sent off favourite, but experience told in the end. Sectional times confirmed that the early pace was sedate and that the pace picked up in the final 3f. It's impossible to rate the race too highly, with a bunched finish involving two of the more exposed runners in the line-up filling the places. The third probably set the level with the pace nothing special, and the fourth is rated close to his Chesham form.

NOTEBOOK

Olympic Glory(IRE), a topical winner, defied his 3lb penalty for winning at Newmarket with a bit to spare, despite leaving it very late. He didn't handle the track that well, was checked by the favourite 2f out and had to be switched to the outer, and with a furlong to run he only had one rival behind him, but he picked up strongly from that point and finished so well that by the time he crossed the line he had won very cosily. Clearly a smart juvenile, a return to a more conventional course ought to suit him, and the Dewhurst is the obvious end-of-season target. He's a general 20-1 for next year's Guineas. (tchd 3-1 in places)

Artigiano(USA) finished closer to the winner than he did at Newmarket, albeit on 3lb better terms this time, and the quicker ground, coupled with a fairly prominent ride helped in that cause. He might be stepped up to a mile now. (op 10-1)

Luhaif didn't get home in the heavy ground at Newmarket, but ran a much better race on this sounder surface. He did, however, benefit from being allowed to set a steady early pace so was in the prime position to kick for home in the straight. (op 100-1 tchd 66-1, 150-1 in places)

Tha'Ir(IRE) won an ordinary Chesham at Royal Ascot and had a bit to prove at this level, but he ran well, albeit while benefiting from racing prominently in a race run at a steady early gallop. Official explanation: jockey said colt hung left

Ghurair(USA) didn't settle early and ran around a bit when coming under pressure. He was keeping on well at the finish, but the way the race was run didn't see him at his best and his lack of experience caught him out. He remains a colt of potential, and his trainer had mentioned that the Champagne Stakes could be next, although the Acomb in three weeks' time looks a suitable race. (op 9-4 tchd 5-2 in places)

Operation Chariot(IRE), beaten a long way in the Superlative, ran a better race here, but he could do with a drop in class to regain the winning thread. (op 66-1)

Birdman(IRE) couldn't repeat his excellent performance at Newmarket and probably needs more ease in the ground to be seen at his best. (op 8-1)

Whipper's Boy(IRE) never got involved from off the pace. (op 20-1 tchd 25-1)

Chilworth Icon was too keen early. (op 28-1)

Maxentius(IRE) was another who didn't settle through the early stages. He might be worth dropping back to 6f. (tchd 15-2, 9-1 in places)

4699 QIPCO SUSSEX STKS (BRITISH CHAMPIONS SERIES) (GROUP 1) 1m

3:10 (3:11) (Class 1) 3-Y-O+ **£179,487** (£68,047; £34,055; £16,964) **Stalls** Low

Form	Pos	Dist	Horse	RPR
1-11	**1**		**Frankel**[43] 3237 4-9-7 140 ...... TomQueally 3 (Sir Henry Cecil) *travelled strly: sn trcking pcemaker: cruised upsides 3f out: led 2f out: shkn up and readily qcknd clr over 1f out: eased towards fin: v easily* **1/20**[1]	138+
-132	**2**	6	**Farhh**[25] 3880 4-9-7 122 ...... FrankieDettori 4 (Saeed Bin Suroor) *broke wl: sn stdd bk and hld up in 3rd: rdn and sltly outpcd over 3f out: styd on to chse clr wnr over 1f out: no imp and wl hld after* **11/1**[2]	119
0215	**3**	3¼	**Gabrial (IRE)**[43] 3239 3-9-0 108 ...... PaulHanagan 1 (Richard Fahey) *stdd s: t.k.h early: hld up in rr: pushed along and effrt over 3f out: outpcd and wl btn 2f out: kpt on u.p and wnt modest 3rd ins fnl f* **80/1**[3]	110
0-46	**4**	½	**Bullet Train**[43] 3237 5-9-7 111 ...... IanMongan 2 (Sir Henry Cecil) *led: rdn and hdd 2f out: outpcd and immediately brushed aside by wnr over 1f out: lost modest 3rd ins fnl f* **150/1**	110

1m 37.56s (-2.34) **Going Correction** +0.075s/f (Good)
WFA 3 from 4yo+ 7lb **4** Ran SP% **105.5**
Speed ratings (Par 117): **114,108,104,104**
CSF £1.11 TOTE £1.10; EX 1.40.

Owner K Abdulla **Bred** Juddmonte Farms Ltd **Trained** Newmarket, Suffolk

FOCUS

The joint-smallest field since 1972. It seriously lacked depth too, without a miler as accomplished as Canford Cliffs in opposition this time. Frankel duly became the first dual winner of the Sussex Stakes, which was opened up to 4yos in 1960 and to horses aged five plus 15 years later. The winner did not need to run to form and the runner-up looked below his best.

NOTEBOOK

Frankel powered clear of his pursuers in trademark style for another thoroughly comprehensive victory. His winning margin did not come close to the eleven lengths by which he beat Excelebration in the Queen Anne, but he could have won by a much greater margin with Tom Queally only shaking up his mount and easing him close home once his rivals had been crushed. The colt won by a length more than he had beaten Canford Cliffs (from whom he received 8lb in weight for age) in 2011, and this year's time was just a tenth of a second slower. Frankel has proved himself far superior to his miling contemporaries over the last two seasons, but will step out of his comfort zone in next month's Juddmonte International at York, when his stamina will be tested over an extra two and a half furlongs. Now that he settles so well there seems no reason why he shouldn't stay, and if he does then a new cast of opponents will surely not be up to beating him. It will be interesting to see how many turn up to take him on, with Nathaniel, plus St Nicholas Abbey and Cirrus Des Aigles the standout names among the entries. (tchd 1-16 in places)

Farhh justified the sporting decision to run here rather than in the Jacques Le Marois at Deauville, winning more than three times what it cost to supplement him. Back at a mile for the first time since winning the Thirsk Hunt Cup, he was fitted with a rug down at the start but got away well and seems over the problems he has had with the stalls. Frankie Dettori was at him with 3f to go in an attempt to get to Frankel, but while he tried hard he failed to give the favourite any cause for concern. He has now been placed in three successive Group Ones and is an admirable colt capable of winning a race at this level, perhaps back at a mile and a quarter. His connections won't fight shy of taking on Frankel again at York. This was only his sixth run and he surely has more improvement in him. (op 14-1)

Gabrial(IRE) was the only representative of the younger generation. The St James's Palace Stakes fifth was anchored at the back before running past Bullet Train late on to pick up some cheap Group 1 black type. He is not up to this class, but is very smart and there was no repeat of the hanging he displayed at Chester and Haydock in the spring. He's likely to drop in grade now. (op 66-1)

Bullet Train did a fine job as pacemaker for his half-brother and work companion and tried hard to hold on for third once his main task was over. He finished closer to Frankel than he had in the Lockinge and Queen Anne. (op 100-1)

4700 UBS STKS (H'CAP) 1m 4f

3:45 (3:48) (Class 2) (0-105,93) 3-Y-O

£24,900 (£7,456; £3,728; £1,864; £932; £468) **Stalls** High

Form	Pos	Dist	Horse	RPR
2-01	**1**		**Sir Graham Wade (IRE)**[95] 1662 3-8-8 **80** ...... JoeFanning 14 (Mark Johnston) *racd wd: mid-div: hdwy fr over 2f out: rdn to ld wl over 1f out: drifted slghtly rt: styd on strly to assert fnl 120yds* **14/1**	92
-231	**2**	1¾	**Mawaqeet (USA)**[13] 4259 3-9-1 **87** ......(v) PaulHanagan 8 (Sir Michael Stoute) *hld up towards rr: hmpd after 2f: rdn 3f out: hdwy over 2f out: wnt 3rd ent fnl f: styd on to go 2nd towards fin* **16/1**	96
-310	**3**	½	**Cardinal Walter (IRE)**[19] 4072 3-8-12 **84** ...... JamieSpencer 1 (David Simcock) *hld up towards rr: bdly hmpd after 2f: hdwy and rough passage fr over 2f out tl swtchd lft jst over 1f: str run ins fnl f: unlucky* **16/1**	94+
1-33	**4**	½	**Goodwood Atlantis (IRE)**[25] 3882 3-8-8 **80** ...... TedDurcan 2 (John Dunlop) *hld up towards rr: hdwy 3f out: rdn to chse wnr over 1f out: no ex fnl 120yds* **8/1**[3]	87
6205	**5**	1½	**Trader Jack**[20] 4009 3-9-3 **89** ...... JamesDoyle 6 (Roger Charlton) *mid-div: travelling wl enough but yet to make move whn stuck bhd wkng horses on rails fr 2f out: styd on ins fnl f* **12/1**	94+
-124	**6**	shd	**Gassin Golf**[18] 4079 3-8-13 **85** ...... LukeMorris 16 (Sir Mark Prescott Bt) *slowly away and short of room sn after s: towards rr: hmpd after 2f: rdn over 2f out: sn short of room: styd on fnl f* **20/1**	90+
-402	**7**	1¼	**Misdemeanour (IRE)**[27] 3787 3-9-1 **87** ...... PatDobbs 9 (Richard Hannon) *in tch tl bdly squeezed up and lost pl 2f out: r.o ins fnl f but no ch after* **16/1**	90+
1-21	**8**	1	**Willie Wag Tail (USA)**[49] 3042 3-9-2 **88** ...... WilliamBuick 12 (Ed Walker) *hld up towards rr: hmpd after 2f: rdn over 2f out: no imp tl styd on wl fnl f* **13/2**[2]	89+
1211	**9**	nk	**Scatter Dice (IRE)**[4] 4575 3-9-2 **93** 6ex ...... DarrenEgan(5) 5 (Mark Johnston) *led for 4f: trckd ldrs: rdn over 2f out: styng on same pce whn bmpd in gp over 1f out: fdd fnl f* **8/1**[3]	94
0412	**10**	nse	**Handsome Man (IRE)**[41] 3296 3-9-2 **88** ...... FrankieDettori 11 (Saeed Bin Suroor) *mid-div: rdn to chse ldrs 2f out: fdd fnl f* **4/1**[1]	88
5211	**11**	3½	**Rule Book (IRE)**[35] 3509 3-9-4 **90** ...... RichardHughes 13 (Richard Hannon) *in tch: pushed along whn squeezed up bdly and dropped towards rr 2f out: nt a danger after* **10/1**	85+
1003	**12**	hd	**Singalat**[18] 4079 3-8-8 **80** ...... RoystonFfrench 7 (James Given) *prom: rdn to ld v briefly jst over 2f out: wknd ent fnl f* **50/1**	75
5361	**13**	3¼	**Trend Is My Friend (USA)**[25] 3882 3-8-9 **81** ...... EddieAhern 4 (Amanda Perrett) *trckd ldrs: travelling wl enough but nowhere to go bhd wkng horses on rails and lost pl: unable to mount chal* **16/1**	70+
3212	**14**	3¼	**Swnymor (IRE)**[16] 4151 3-8-12 **84** ...... JimCrowley 10 (William Haggas) *trckd ldrs: rdn and ev ch 2f out: squeezed up over 1f out: wknd fnl f* **11/1**	68+

2411 **15** 3/4 **Stature (IRE)**[20] 4009 3-9-7 **93** .... JimmyFortune 3 76
(Andrew Balding) *racd keenly: trckd ldrs: led 8f out: rdn and hdd over 2f out: wknd jst over 1f out* **14/1**

1631 **S** **Last Shadow**[16] 4151 3-9-0 **86** .... NeilCallan 15
(William Muir) *mid-div whn slipped up on bnd after 2f* **25/1**

2m 37.51s (-0.89) **Going Correction** +0.075s/f (Good) **16** Ran SP% **128.1**
Speed ratings (Par 106): **105,103,103,103,102 102,101,100,100,100 98,97,95,93,93**
toteswingers 1&2 £50.10, 1&3 £43.30, 2&3 £61.40 CSF £227.84 CT £3633.00 TOTE £16.10: £2.90, £4.00, £4.30, £2.90; EX 205.30 TRIFECTA Not won..
Owner Paul Dean **Bred** P D Savill **Trained** Middleham Moor, N Yorks

FOCUS
Nowhere near as high quality a race as the classification would indicate, with the top-weight rated 12lb below the ceiling. It was messy as well, with the pace steadying considerably during the middle part of the race, before a sprint finish. There was plenty of trouble in running. A personal-best from the winner, while the third and several just outside the frame were hampered and can be rated better than the bare form.

NOTEBOOK
Sir Graham Wade(IRE) ◆ avoided the early trouble caused by a faller as he raced fairly prominently, while racing towards the outer in the straight helped him avoid the trouble to his inside as the field bunched up. He can be counted fortunate on both counts, but he's well regarded and it'll be a surprise if he isn't capable of improving further still, especially when faced with a stiffer test of stamina. (op 11-1 tchd 10-1)
Mawaqeet(USA) had to take evasive action when Last Shadow fell in front of him early on, and did well to finish second following that incident. However, the slackening of the pace mid-race allowed him to make up the lost ground. Like the winner, he benefited from challenging wide of the trouble which occurred towards the inside. Official explanation: jockey said gelding was hampered by faller (tchd 14-1)
Cardinal Walter(IRE) ◆ was another who was hampered by the faller early on in the race. He also got involved in some scrimmaging approaching the furlong marker, and would probably have been second with a clear run. (tchd 20-1)
Goodwood Atlantis(IRE) was another who had a trouble-free run down the outside. He won't mind it if conditions dry out further in the coming weeks. (op 9-1)
Trader Jack had nowhere to go on the inside rail as the leader tired in front of him. He picked up well once he got some daylight, but it was all too late. Out of a half-sister to Al Kazeem, there should be better to come from him. (op 14-1)
Gassin Golf was another who came from the back of the field and didn't get much of a clear run. (op 28-1 tchd 33-1, 40-1 in a place)
Misdemeanour(IRE) found even more trouble and could only make any progress when finally in the clear inside the last. (op 20-1)
Willie Wag Tail(USA), towards the back and hampered by the faller early on, was another denied racing room on the inside rail in the final 2f. Snatched up, he was keeping on well past beaten horses late in the day. (op 15-2 tchd 8-1 in a place)
Scatter Dice(IRE), burdened with a 6lb penalty, may have found this coming a bit quick after her win at Ascot four days earlier. (op 13-2)
Handsome Man(IRE) was squeezed up a little late on but could still have been expected to do better. (op 7-1 tchd 8-1 in places)
Rule Book(IRE) ◆ can be given another chance as he was badly hampered when trying to squeeze through between horses inside the last 2f. Official explanation: jockey said colt suffered interference in running (op 8-1 tchd 15-2)
Trend Is My Friend(USA) ◆, whose rider had to sit and suffer as the colt was continually denied racing room and was hampered towards the inside, never got to show what he could do and this effort can be easily written off. Official explanation: jockey said colt was denied a clear run
Stature(IRE) Official explanation: jockey said gelding ran too free

4701 MARKEL INSURANCE MAIDEN FILLIES' STKS 6f
4:20 (4:20) (Class 2) 2-Y-O £11,320 (£3,368; £1,683; £841) **Stalls** Low

Form RPR

32 **1** **Pearl Sea (IRE)**[20] 4011 2-9-0 0 .... JamieSpencer 2 91+
(David Brown) *racd in far side to centre: mde all: rdn over 1f out: styd on strly and drew clr ins fnl f: readily* **11/8**[1]

4 **2** 3 **Malilla (IRE)**[82] 2020 2-9-0 0 .... AdamKirby 3 82
(Clive Cox) *racd far side to centre: chsd ldrs: edgd lft and chsd wnr 1/2-way: rdn 2f out: drvn and no ex ins fnl f* **28/1**

54 **3** 1 1/2 **Woodlandsway**[12] 4282 2-9-0 0 .... PatDobbs 18 77
(Richard Hannon) *racd stands' side to centre: a.p: chsd ldng pair 2f out: drvn over 1f out: no extra and btn ins fnl f* **12/1**

6 **4** 2 3/4 **Alhaarth Beauty (IRE)**[12] 4282 2-9-0 0 .... RichardHughes 15 68
(Richard Hannon) *racd towards stands' side: t.k.h: hld up in midfield: effrt to chse ldrs and edgd rt 2f out: outpcd and btn over 1f out: wl hld and one pce fnl f* **12/1**

5 3/4 **Tarara** 2-9-0 0 .... JimmyFortune 6 66+
(Andrew Balding) *racd in centre: hld up off the pce towards rr: pushed along and hdwy 2f out: styd on steadily under hands and heels riding fnl f: nvr trbld ldrs* **33/1**

4 **6** 1 1/4 **Red Four**[35] 3504 2-9-0 0 .... PatCosgrave 1 62
(George Baker) *racd far side to centre: s.i.s: sn in midfield: effrt u.p over 2f out: edgd rt and wknd over 1f out* **50/1**

7 1 1/4 **Arbaah (USA)** 2-9-0 0 .... PaulHanagan 10 58+
(John Dunlop) *s.i.s: racd centre to stands' side: bhd: kpt on fr over 1f out: nvr trbld ldrs* **25/1**

8 2 **Jida (IRE)** 2-9-0 0 .... JimCrowley 17 51
(Alan Jarvis) *racd towards stands' side: awkward leaving stalls and slowly away: hld up in midfield: rdn over 2f out: no prog and wknd over 1f out* **25/1**

0 **9** 1 1/4 **Delphica (IRE)**[42] 3269 2-9-0 0 .... TomQueally 5 47
(Gary Moore) *racd in centre: chsd ldrs: pushed lft and lost pl 1/2-way: sn rdn: wknd 2f out* **40/1**

4 **10** 3/4 **Hasbah (IRE)**[27] 3788 2-9-0 0 .... SilvestreDeSousa 14 45
(Peter Chapple-Hyam) *racd towards centre: t.k.h: hld up in tch: rdn and effrt over 2f out: no imp and btn over 1f out: wknd 1f out* **8/1**[2]

03 **11** 1/2 **Cut No Ice (IRE)**[27] 3783 2-9-0 0 .... ChrisCatlin 11 43
(Paul Cole) *racd in centre: in tch in midfield: rdn and struggling 1/2-way: wknd ent fnl 2f* **10/1**[3]

6 **12** 1 **Flywheel (IRE)**[14] 4217 2-9-0 0 .... FrankieDettori 12 40
(Brian Meehan) *racd towards stands' side: hld up towards rr: rdn and no prog over 2f out: n.d* **20/1**

13 3 1/4 **Avanzare** 2-9-0 0 .... MichaelHills 4 30
(Charles Hills) *racd in centre: s.i.s: rn green and a towards rr: lost tch over 1f out* **33/1**

63 **14** 1 **Cross Pattee (IRE)**[42] 3282 2-9-0 0 .... WilliamBuick 9 27
(John Gosden) *racd in centre: chsd wnr tl 1/2-way: sn lost pl: bhd over 1f out* **11/1**

6 **15** 2 1/4 **Bint Youmzain (IRE)**[20] 4002 2-9-0 0 .... MartinHarley 8 19
(Mick Channon) *racd towards centre: sn pushed along in midfield: struggling u.p 1/2-way: bhd over 1f out* **8/1**[2]

16 6 **Mill I Am (USA)** 2-9-0 0 .... AshleyMorgan 16
(Pat Murphy) *racd towards stands' side: s.i.s: a bhd* **100/1**

1m 11.2s (-1.00) **Going Correction** -0.225s/f (Firm) **16** Ran SP% **124.3**
Speed ratings (Par 97): **97,93,91,87,86 84,83,80,78,77 77,75,71,70,67 59**
toteswingers 1&2 £14.00, 1&3 £5.90, 2&3 £53.00 CSF £57.24 TOTE £2.30: £1.40, £6.90, £3.50; EX 56.90 Trifecta £840.00 Pool: £1,381.08 - 1.21 winning units..
Owner Pearl Bloodstock Ltd **Bred** D Noonan & Loughphilip Bloodstock **Trained** Averham Park, Notts
■ Stewards' Enquiry : Jamie Spencer two-day ban: careless riding (Aug 15-16)

FOCUS
This is often a decent fillies' maiden and half a dozen winners in the past decade have gone on to earn black type, among them Suez and Beyond Desire. At first the field split into two distinct groups, with 13 racing a little way off the stands' fence and just three isolated towards the centre. The groups had merged by halfway and the first two home came from the mini-group of three. The time was respectable and the form looks sound with the winner, third and fourth close to their marks.

NOTEBOOK
Pearl Sea(IRE) travelled well, probably showing in front overall throughout, and went on to score comfortably. The favourite set a good standard on her placings at Doncaster (a place behind subsequent winner Diaminda) and Newmarket (runner-up to the impressive Certify) and may not have needed to improve to take this. She holds entries in the Lowther and Cheveley Park and will presumably be shooting for some black type soon. (op 7-4 tchd 2-1 and 15-8 in places)
Malilla(IRE) had not been out since finishing last of four to three subsequent winners on her debut at Ascot in May. The extra furlong suited her here and she stuck on after chasing the favourite all the way. (op 33-1)
Woodlandsway, drawn on the opposite side of the track to the first two, led the main group and kept on at the one pace. She looks good enough to win a maiden, but connections have the option of moving her into nurseries now. (tchd 10-1)
Alhaarth Beauty(IRE) was well held in fourth, but this still represents a step up on her Ascot debut effort. (tchd 14-1)
Tarara was running on at the end and looks sure to step up on this with the experience to call on. She's a half-sister to several winners at sprint distances and this will probably be her trip.
Red Four, behind Princess Margaret fourth Jollification on her debut, may have benefited from chasing the first two home down the middle in the early stages. She's capable of finding a race at one of the minor tracks. (op 40-1)
Arbaah(USA) finished nicely from the rear of the field. She's a half-sister to decent performers Haatheq and Farhaan and she should be winning herself before long.
Hasbah(IRE) had made a promising debut against the colts at Yarmouth and this was disappointing in comparison. (tchd 7-1, 9-1 in a place)
Cross Pattee(IRE) could not build on her promising effort at Kempton. (op 10-1)

4702 BRITISH STALLION STUDS TURF CLUB EBF FILLIES' STKS (H'CAP) 1m 1f
4:55 (4:55) (Class 3) (0-95,90) 3-Y-O+
£9,337 (£2,796; £1,398; £699; £349; £175) **Stalls** Low

Form RPR

-320 **1** **My Queenie (IRE)**[11] 4319 3-9-4 **88** .... RichardHughes 13 98
(Richard Hannon) *mid-div: pushed along whn nt clr run over 1f out tl swtchd rt ins fnl f: str burst to ld fnl 75yds: r.o wl* **16/1**

-661 **2** nk **Strathnaver**[39] 3388 3-8-7 **77** .... SilvestreDeSousa 5 86
(Ed Dunlop) *towards rr of mid-div: nt clr run over 2f out: running on whn having to switch rt jst ins fnl f: sn pressing wnr: kpt on: hld nring fin* **10/1**

-520 **3** 1 3/4 **Oojooba**[25] 3882 3-8-11 **81** .... NeilCallan 15 86
(Roger Varian) *in tch: hdwy to ld wl over 1f out: sn rdn: kpt on but no ex whn hdd fnl 75yds* **10/1**

0-23 **4** nk **Epernay**[18] 4091 5-9-0 **76** ....(vt) JamieSpencer 17 81
(Ian Williams) *hld up towards rr: swtchd lft 2f out: sn rdn: styd on wl ins fnl f: wnt 4th towards fin* **16/1**

-223 **5** 1/2 **Ariyfa (IRE)**[19] 4068 4-9-6 **82** ....(t) WilliamBuick 6 86
(Noel Quinlan) *hld up towards rr: swtchd lft 2f out: sn rdn and hdwy: edgd rt ins fnl f: styd on* **7/1**[2]

4521 **6** shd **Chigun**[45] 3189 3-9-6 **90** .... TomQueally 7 94
(Sir Henry Cecil) *led: rdn and hdd wl over 1f out: styd on but no ex fnl 120yds* **7/1**[2]

33 **7** 2 1/4 **Savanna Days (IRE)**[19] 4062 3-8-10 **80** .... MartinHarley 2 79
(Mick Channon) *mid-div: rdn for effrt 2f out: styd on same pce fnl f* **10/1**

4-10 **8** hd **Amber Silk (IRE)**[36] 3476 3-8-11 **81** .... MichaelHills 12 79
(Charles Hills) *hld up towards rr: hdwy over 2f out: sn rdn: styd on same pce fnl f* **16/1**

-321 **9** 1 **Princess Caetani (IRE)**[50] 3013 3-8-10 **80** .... RoystonFfrench 4 76
(David Simcock) *towards rr of mid-div: rdn over 2f out: little imp* **8/1**[3]

0-1 **10** 1/2 **Valiant Girl**[40] 3340 3-9-1 **85** .... JamesDoyle 10 80
(Roger Charlton) *trckd ldrs: rdn to chal jst over 2f out: chsd wnr tl edgd lft and no ex fnl 100yds* **8/1**[3]

6024 **11** 2 3/4 **She's A Character**[20] 3991 5-9-0 **76** .... PaulHanagan 3 65
(Richard Fahey) *mid-div: rdn over 2f out: nt pce to chal: fdd ins fnl f* **33/1**

1100 **12** 3 1/2 **Stellar Express (IRE)**[33] 3563 3-9-1 **85** .... LukeMorris 11 66
(Michael Appleby) *mid-div: rdn 3f out: wknd ent fnl f* **50/1**

2460 **13** 1 1/2 **Way Too Hot**[25] 3879 3-9-6 **90** .... AdamKirby 18 68
(Clive Cox) *broke wl: sn settled in mid-div: rdn wl over 2f out: fading whn bmpd over 1f out* **40/1**

3041 **14** shd **Our Gal**[18] 4091 4-9-5 **81** .... ChrisCatlin 1 59
(Noel Quinlan) *sn prom: rdn 3f out: wknd wl over 1f out* **25/1**

-411 **15** 1 1/4 **Keene Dancer**[16] 4150 3-9-1 **85** .... FrankieDettori 9 60
(Sir Michael Stoute) *trckd ldrs: rdn over 2f out: wknd ent fnl f* **4/1**[1]

1035 **16** 30 **Miss Aix**[15] 4199 4-9-7 **83** .... HayleyTurner 8
(Michael Bell) *trckd ldrs: rdn over 2f out: wknd over 1f out: eased fnl f* **33/1**

1m 56.04s (-0.26) **Going Correction** +0.075s/f (Good)
WFA 3 from 4yo+ 8lb **16** Ran SP% **126.3**
Speed ratings (Par 104): **104,103,102,101,101 101,99,99,98,97 95,92,90,90,89 63**
toteswingers 1&2 £41.60, 1&3 £47.80, 2&3 £26.60 CSF £166.66 CT £1785.31 TOTE £22.10: £3.40, £2.20, £2.60, £3.70; EX 261.70 TRIFECTA Not won..
Owner N A Woodcock **Bred** Rathbarry Stud **Trained** East Everleigh, Wilts

FOCUS
A competitive fillies' handicap. The pace slackened halfway and the sectionals revealed that the last three furlongs were the fastest three splits of the race. Space was always going to be at a premium in a race like this. The fourth and fifth are rated close to their marks.

NOTEBOOK
My Queenie(IRE) had a poor effort at Ascot 11 days earlier to forgive, but she had appeared to be running into form before that and everything clicked into place here. Not that it was straightforward, as she had to thread her way through from the rear of the field from over a furlong out, but no-one rides this track better than Richard Hughes and he delivered her with precision timing. The longer trip was no problem. Official explanation: trainer said, regarding apparent improvement in form, that the filly was denied a clear run at Ascot and appreciated the step up in trip. (op 18-1)

Strathnaver was 6lb higher than when winning at Lingfield last time and up against much better rivals here, but she ran a blinder as she had no room to play with over a furlong out and had to be switched to the inside rail. She flew home and managed to nail the leader well inside the last, but unfortunately for her the winner finished even quicker. She saw the extra furlong out well enough. (tchd 9-1)

Oojooba hasn't got home in her previous tries beyond 1m, but looked all over the winner when sent to the front over a furlong out. However, her stamina then appeared to desert her again and she was run out of it. (op 16-1)

Epernay ◆ was the unlucky filly of the race. Held up well off the pace from the start, she was knocked back to last over a furlong from home and had to be switched wide. She finished like a train when out in the clear and very nearly got up for third, but she would surely have gone close to winning with a clear run. Official explanation: jockey said mare slipped 5f out (op 20-1 tchd 25-1)

Ariyfa(IRE), who 'won' the race on her side at Newmarket last time though only third overall, was tried in a tongue tie here. Having been held up in last place for much of the way, she appeared to be hanging when switched wide for her effort over a furlong from home and, although staying on, was never quite getting to the leaders. Official explanation: jockey said, regarding riding, that he eased filly before winning post to avoid clipping heels. (tchd 15-2)

Chigun, in her first handicap after making all to win a Salisbury maiden by ten lengths, wasn't allowed the luxury of an uncontested lead this time thanks to the attentions of \bOur Gal\p, so under the circumstances she did well to hang in there for as long as she did. This was only her fifth start, so she may still have some improvement left. (op 11-2)

Savanna Days(IRE) was travelling well behind the leaders coming to the last 2f and didn't have a lot of room at that stage, but only found the one pace when in the clear. (op 14-1)

Valiant Girl was proven over this C&D having narrowly won a maiden here on her reappearance in June, but although holding every chance she had no more to give inside the final furlong and found this too stiff a task on only her third outing. (op 7-1)

Keene Dancer was trying for a hat-trick off a 7lb higher mark following a couple of wins at Windsor, but despite holding a decent position early she was off the bridle a fair way out and dropped away disappointingly. (op 7-2 tchd 9-2 in a place)

4703 HARWOODS RACING CLUB H'CAP STKS (SPONSORED BY HARWOODS GROUP) 7f

5:30 (5:35) (Class 3) (0-90,92) 3-Y-0+ **£9,703** (£2,887; £1,443; £721) **Stalls** Low

Form				RPR
3006	**1**		**The Confessor**[21] 3977 5-9-6 **86** ... CathyGannon 8 (Henry Candy) *stmbld leaving stalls: t.k.h: hld up in tch: hdwy to join ldr 2f out: sn rdn to ld narrowly: sustained battle w runner-up after: r.o gamely u.p and asserted cl home* **12/1**[3]	96
5020	**2**	*nk*	**Santefisio**[39] 3380 6-9-5 **85** ... (b[1]) TomQueally 3 (Keith Dalgleish) *t.k.h: hld up in midfield: gd hdwy on inner to trck ldrs over 2f out: swtchd lft and forced way out to chal wl over 1f out: r.o u.p and sustained battle w wnr after: no ex cl home* **14/1**	94
4210	**3**	½	**Ducal**[11] 4321 4-9-8 **88** ... PatDobbs 1 (Mike Murphy) *t.k.h: hld up in midfield: nt clr run and swtchd rt 2f out: rdn and hdwy to chse ldng pair jst over 1f out: kpt on wl u.p fnl 100yds* **20/1**	96
2115	**4**	*2*	**Galician**[56] 2824 3-9-2 **88** ... JoeFanning 20 (Mark Johnston) *in tch: rdn and effrt to chse ldrs over 1f out: 4th and styd on same pce ins fnl f* **8/1**[2]	88+
-050	**5**	1 ½	**Rakaan (IRE)**[18] 4099 5-9-10 **90** ... JamieSpencer 2 (Jamie Osborne) *s.i.s and rdn along early: bhd: swtchd rt and hdwy over 1f out: styd on wl u.p fnl f: nvr gng to rch ldrs* **22/1**	88
1066	**6**	*nk*	**George Guru**[35] 3508 5-9-4 **89** ... MarkCoumbe[(5)] 15 (Michael Attwater) *hld up towards rr: rdn and effrt over 2f out: hdwy and edging rt over 1f out: styd on wl u.p fnl f: nt rch ldrs* **25/1**	87
1406	**7**	*2*	**Forceful Appeal (USA)**[40] 3348 4-9-7 **87** ... HayleyTurner 10 (Simon Dow) *t.k.h: hld up in midfield: rdn and effrt over 2f out: kpt on same pce and no imp fr over 1f out* **25/1**	79
0-01	**8**	*nk*	**Dubawi Sound**[4] 4589 4-9-9 **92** 6ex ... (t) HarryBentley[(3)] 4 (David Brown) *chsd ldng pair tl hdwy to ld over 3f out: rdn ent fnl 2f: hdd over 1f out and sn btn: wknd fnl f* **11/8**[1]	83
0645	**9**	3 ½	**North Star Boy (IRE)**[18] 4095 3-9-2 **88** ... KieranO'Neill 12 (Richard Hannon) *t.k.h: hld up in midfield: rdn and effrt on outer over 2f out: sme hdwy 2f out: no ex and wknd fnl f* **33/1**	68
4-04	**10**	2 ½	**Treadwell (IRE)**[67] 2489 5-9-9 **89** ... FergusSweeney 6 (Jamie Osborne) *t.k.h: hld up in midfield: n.m.r and shuffled bk over 2f out: swtchd lft and rdn over 1f out: kpt on but no ch* **14/1**	64
0160	**11**	¾	**Escape To Glory (USA)**[11] 4321 4-9-7 **87** ... (p) GeorgeBaker 9 (Mikael Magnusson) *chsd ldrs: rdn and unable qck ent fnl 2f: btn ent fnl f: no ch and eased wl ins fnl f* **25/1**	60
030-	**12**	*hd*	**Atlantis Star**[237] 7682 5-9-10 **90** ... JimmyFortune 18 (James Tate) *stdd s: hld up towards rr: effrt on outer over 2f out: no pogress over 1f out: wl hld and eased towards fin* **50/1**	63
-000	**13**	½	**Common Touch (IRE)**[18] 4110 4-9-10 **90** ... PaulHanagan 5 (Richard Fahey) *rdn along leaving stalls: in tch in midfield: rdn and hung rt over 2f out: no prog and wl hld after* **8/1**[2]	61
6014	**14**	1 ¾	**Duster**[26] 3812 5-9-6 **86** ... DarryllHolland 11 (Hughie Morrison) *stmbld leaving stalls: sn bustled along: a towards rr: rdn and no hdwy whn sltly hmpd jst over 2f out: n.d* **25/1**	53
303	**15**	1 ¼	**Celtic Sultan (IRE)**[13] 4252 8-9-2 **82** ... MickyFenton 19 (Paul Midgley) *broke wl to ld and crossed to inner: hdd over 3f out: lost pl qckly jst over 2f out: bhd 1f out: eased wl ins fnl f* **33/1**	45
1443	**16**	1 ¾	**Triple Charm**[42] 3281 4-9-5 **85** ... (p) WilliamBuick 17 (Jeremy Noseda) *hld up in rr: rdn and effrt over 2f out: no real prog: n.d* **12/1**[3]	43
1000	**17**	1 ¾	**Shifting Star (IRE)**[11] 4317 7-8-13 **86** ... (v) WilliamTwiston-Davies[(7)] 7 (John Bridger) *chsd ldr tl over 2f out: losing pl whn short of room 2f out: sn dropped out: bhd fnl f* **33/1**	40
-640	**18**	*15*	**Red Seventy**[41] 3294 3-9-4 **90** ... RichardHughes 13 (Richard Hannon) *stdd and dropped in bhd after s: hld up in rr: rdn and no hdwy 3f out: wl bhd and virtually p.u ins fnl f* **25/1**	

1m 26.29s (-0.71) **Going Correction** +0.075s/f (Good)
WFA 3 from 4yo+ 6lb **18** Ran SP% **132.2**
Speed ratings (Par 107): **107,106,106,103,102 101,99,99,95,92 91,91,90,88,87 85,83,66**
toteswingers 1&2 £29.00, 1&3 £39.50, 2&3 £59.60 CSF £156.32 CT £3449.30 TOTE £15.20: £2.90, £3.20, £3.90, £2.40; EX 132.10 TRIFECTA Not won..
Owner Six Too Many **Bred** Mrs C R D Wilson **Trained** Kingston Warren, Oxon

FOCUS

This handicap replaced the 0-95 classified stakes at the meeting over the same trip. The beaten favourite apart, this new race lacked progressive types, but it looks pretty solid form. The pace was brisk and the winner is rated to his best with the second to the best of his old form.

NOTEBOOK

The Confessor overcame a slow start to sit just off the speed and forced his head in front close home after a good duel with the runner-up, the pair having come together over a furlong from home. He had produced a number of commendable runs since his last win nearly two years ago and has a good record at Goodwood.

Santefisio has been placed on each of his four visits to Goodwood now, finding one too good three times. He had to rather force his way out as the winner held him in, but was in the clear in sufficient time and was just denied. First-time blinkers replaced cheekpieces on him. (tchd 12-1 and 16-1)

Ducal was running on turf for just the third time but this bold effort proved that he acts on the surface. From the inside draw he met some trouble, but he ran on well once in the clear. (op 28-1 tchd 33-1)

Galician had the highest draw and raced wide all the way, so this good run needs marking up. Her latest outing could have come too soon for her and she did best of the three from her age group who contested this. (op 10-1)

Rakaan(IRE) ran on well from the back of the field. He had been dropped a total of 8lb after three lowly efforts this year, while the return to better ground appeared to suit. (op 20-1)

George Guru ran creditably, running on from the back from a high draw on this return to 7f.

Forceful Appeal(USA) was by no means discredited, but remains vulnerable off this sort of mark.

Dubawi Sound, Saturday's Newcastle winner, looked to hold strong claims of following up under a 6lb penalty, with his talented rider offsetting half of that. Racing a shade keenly, he was in front by halfway, but he was pressed for the lead and was swallowed up in the straight. This may have come too soon for him. (op 7-4 tchd 2-1 in places and 15-8 in places)

Common Touch(IRE), runner-up in the equivalent classified stakes a year ago, was tackling 7f for the first time since. He could never get beyond mid-field.

Duster Official explanation: jockey said gelding stumbled leaving stalls

T/Jkpt: £58,791.50 to a £1 stake. Pool: £331220.03 - 4.0 winning tickets T/Plt: £745.20 to a £1 stake. Pool: £27,4463.53 - 268.84 winning tickets T/Qpdt: £93.20 to a £1 stake. Pool: £17013.19 - 135.03 winning tickets SP

4456 LEICESTER (R-H)

Wednesday, August 1

OFFICIAL GOING: Round course - good to firm (good in places); straight course - good (good to firm in places)

Wind: Fresh behind Weather: Cloudy with sunny spells

4704 HEINEKEN/BRITISH STALLION STUDS EBF MEDIAN AUCTION MAIDEN FILLIES' STKS 5f 218y

6:15 (6:15) (Class 5) 2-Y-0 **£3,234** (£962; £481; £240) **Stalls** High

Form				RPR
4	**1**		**El Manati (IRE)**[33] 3590 2-9-0 0 ... MartinDwyer 1 (James Tate) *plld hrd and prom: led 5f out: clr fr 1/2-way: easily* **4/5**[1]	92+
03	**2**	*9*	**Madame Elizabeth**[12] 4290 2-9-0 0 ... RussKennemore 7 (Reg Hollinshead) *hld up: rdn over 2f out: styd on fr over 1f out: no ch w wnr* **10/1**	61+
6	**3**	*nk*	**Icon Dance**[21] 3959 2-9-0 0 ... JohnFahy 12 (Ben De Haan) *prom: rdn over 2f out: styd on ins fnl f: nrst fin* **22/1**	60+
6	**4**	½	**Hayyona**[35] 3504 2-9-0 0 ... MatthewDavies 6 (Mick Channon) *led 1f: chsd wnr: rdn over 2f out: sn outpcd* **9/1**[3]	59
06	**5**	4 ½	**Her Royal Empress**[33] 3554 2-9-0 0 ... LiamJones 10 (James Unett) *sn pushed along in rr: rdn and swtchd rt over 1f out: nvr on terms* **33/1**	44
40	**6**	1 ¼	**Glen Ginnie (IRE)**[56] 2812 2-9-0 0 ... MatthewChadwick 9 (Charles Hills) *hld up: swtchd rt over 2f out: n.d* **8/1**[2]	40
0	**7**	4 ½	**Choral Rhythm (IRE)**[14] 4217 2-9-0 0 ... SeanLevey 3 (Richard Hannon) *hld up: pushed along and swtchd rt over 2f out: wknd over 1f out: hung lft fnl f* **11/1**	26
	8	½	**Sunny Hollow** 2-9-0 0 ... KirstyMilczarek 4 (James Toller) *chsd ldrs: rdn 1/2-way: wknd wl over 1f out* **14/1**	
35	**9**	4 ½	**Fruity Bun**[13] 4239 2-9-0 0 ... DaneO'Neill 8 (Matthew Salaman) *mid-div: rdn 1/2-way: wknd over 2f out* **50/1**	
06	**10**	½	**Vinifera (USA)**[27] 3788 2-9-0 0 ... FrederikTylicki 2 (Clive Brittain) *chsd ldrs: rdn over 2f out: wknd wl over 1f out* **22/1**	

1m 9.99s (-3.01) **Going Correction** -0.30s/f (Firm) 2y crse rec **10** Ran SP% **114.4**
Speed ratings (Par 91): **108,96,95,94,88 87,81,80,74,73**
toteswingers: 1&2 £3.80, 1&3 £10.90, 2&3 £24.80. CSF £8.68 TOTE £1.60: £1.10, £1.90, £5.90; EX 9.80 Trifecta £113.00 Pool: £274.93 - 1.80 winning units..
Owner Sheikh Rashid Dalmook Al Maktoum **Bred** Michael Downey & Roalso Ltd **Trained** Newmarket, Suffolk

FOCUS

Just an ordinary fillies' maiden, although Airwave did win it back in 2002. The winner scored easily while the second sets and possibly anchors the form.

NOTEBOOK

El Manati(IRE) ◆ won easily and broke the track record, admittedly helped by the following breeze. Strict reading of the form will probably give her a rating in the high-80s, but a recent Cheveley Park entry may not be wasted if she goes the right way from this, although she might need to settle better in future. (tchd 4-6)

Madame Elizabeth had stepped up on her debut when third at Haydock and the runner-up had scored since. However, she was unable to go the pace on this faster ground and by the time she got involved, the winner had long gone. She does qualify for nurseries now though. (tchd 11-1)

Icon Dance was another who ran on late having been outpaced and in the process built on her debut effort. (op 20-1 tchd 25-1)

Hayyona, a 145,000gns half-sister to a Group 2 performer, did best of those that tried to match strides with the winner but she paid for her efforts, losing two places in the last furlong. (op 8-1 tchd 15-2)

4705 FOSTERS SUPER CHILLED (S) STKS 7f 9y

6:45 (6:46) (Class 6) 3-Y-0 **£1,617** (£481; £240; £120) **Stalls** High

Form				RPR
-300	**1**		**Ebony Clarets**[21] 3952 3-8-7 64 ... FrederikTylicki 2 (Richard Fahey) *chsd ldr tl over 4f out: wnt 2nd again over 2f out: rdn to ld over 1f out: styd on wl* **13/8**[1]	58
50U2	**2**	*5*	**Mitie Mouse**[7] 4457 3-8-12 67 ... MartinDwyer 1 (Mike Murphy) *led: rdn and hdd over 1f out: no ex ins fnl f* **11/2**[3]	50
2300	**3**	*nk*	**Green Mountain (IRE)**[15] 4198 3-8-4 43 ... (t) RaulDaSilva[(3)] 4 (Philip McBride) *prom: chsd ldr over 4f out tl rdn over 2f out: styd on same pce fr over 1f out* **20/1**	44
6006	**4**	2 ¾	**Crown Dependency (IRE)**[41] 3311 3-8-5 84 ... RufusVergette[(7)] 11 (Richard Hannon) *prom: pushed along over 2f out: styd on same pce fr over 1f out* **9/4**[2]	42
-506	**5**	½	**Clowance Keys**[7] 4457 3-8-12 57 ... JamesMillman 5 (Rod Millman) *dwlt: hdwy over 4f out: rdn 1/2-way: styd on same pce fnl 2f* **14/1**	40
6	**6**	3 ½	**Giveherachance**[34] 3521 3-8-7 0 ... JohnFahy 9 (Ann Duffield) *hld up: rdn over 2f out: nvr on terms* **28/1**	26
25	**7**	*hd*	**Bajan Hero**[15] 4185 3-8-12 52 ... AndreaAtzeni 6 (David Evans) *prom: pushed along over 4f out: sn lost pl* **11/1**	30
0-00	**8**	*2*	**Pink Belini**[33] 3568 3-8-8 43 ow1 ... (vt) ShaneKelly 10 (Alan McCabe) *s.i.s: rdn 1/2-way: sn wknd* **80/1**	21

6-00 **9** *1 3/4* **Miss Granger**[64] 2577 3-8-7 43.. DavidProbert 8 15
(Ronald Harris) *mid-div: rdn over 4f out: wknd over 2f out* **33/1**
1m 24.27s (-1.93) **Going Correction** -0.30s/f (Firm) **9** Ran SP% **111.6**
Speed ratings (Par 98): **99,93,92,89,89 85,85,82,80**
toteswingers: 1&2 £2.50, 1&3 £6.60, 2&3 £5.50. CSF £10.12 TOTE £2.80: £1.60, £1.80, £8.00; EX 11.40 Trifecta £178.70 Pool: £377.67 - 1.56 winning units..There was no bid for the winner.
Owner The Matthewman Partnership **Bred** Michael E Broughton **Trained** Musley Bank, N Yorks

FOCUS
An uncompetitive seller and the form is rated negatively around the placed horses.

4706 JOHN SMITH'S EXTRA SMOOTH H'CAP 1m 1f 218y
7:15 (7:15) (Class 4) (0-80,80) 3-Y-0+ **£4,528** (£1,347; £673; £336) **Stalls** Low

Form RPR
-634 **1** **No Compromise**[27] 3785 3-8-12 **73**.................................... RobertHavlin 1 82
(Hughie Morrison) *hld up: hdwy and edgd rt over 1f out: shkn up to ld ins fnl f: r.o* **4/1**
0-06 **2** *2* **Pass Muster**[86] 1914 5-10-0 **80**.. FrederikTylicki 3 85
(Ollie Pears) *hld up: hdwy and edgd rt over 1f out: styd on same pce ins fnl f* **7/2[3]**
-060 **3** *1/2* **Superciliary**[29] 3736 3-8-3 **64** ow2.. MartinLane 9 68
(Ralph Beckett) *led: rdn over 1f out: hdd and unable qck ins fnl f* **22/1**
3-00 **4** *5* **The Cayterers**[44] 3226 10-9-6 **79**.............................. ThomasGarner(7) 11 73
(Tony Carroll) *prom: racd keenly: chsd ldr 2f out: sn rdn: no ex fnl f* **14/1**
26-0 **5** *1/2* **Wiggy Smith**[76] 2199 13-9-7 **73**.. DaneO'Neill 4 66
(Henry Candy) *prom: rdn over 1f out: styd on same pce* **16/1**
0321 **6** *1 3/4* **Hurakan (IRE)**[7] 4470 6-8-8 **67**..................(p) DanielMuscutt(7) 8 57
(Richard Price) *chsd ldr over 3f: remained handy: pushed along over 3f out: rdn whn rdr dropped whip over 1f out: wknd ins fnl f* **5/2[1]**
-000 **7** *1/2* **Alshazah**[23] 3920 4-9-1 **67**.. JamesMillman 7 56
(Rod Millman) *hld up: hdwy over 2f out: wknd over 1f out* **33/1**
23 **8** *4 1/2* **Barkis**[37] 3447 3-9-3 **78**.. KierenFallon 5 58
(Luca Cumani) *prom: chsd ldr over 6f out: pushed along over 4f out: n.m.r over 1f out: sn wknd* **3/1[2]**
2m 4.83s (-3.07) **Going Correction** -0.35s/f (Firm)
WFA 3 from 4yo+ 9lb **8** Ran SP% **115.6**
Speed ratings (Par 105): **98,96,96,92,91 90,89,86**
toteswingers: 1&2 £4.70, 1&3 £5.30, 2&3 £5.70. CSF £18.67 CT £271.46 TOTE £5.70: £1.60, £1.10, £10.20; EX 24.80 Trifecta £212.50 Part won. Pool: £287.23 - 0.10 winning units..
Owner Mouse Hamilton-Fairley **Bred** The Hon Mrs E J Wills **Trained** East Ilsley, Berks

FOCUS
Quite a competitive handicap although made less so by the withdrawals and the first two were held up at the back early on. a personal-best from the winner with the next two home helping to set the level.
Hurakan(IRE) Official explanation: jockey said gelding was denied a clear run

4707 NAVIGATION AT NEWARK/BRITISH STALLION STUDS EBF MAIDEN STKS 5f 218y
7:45 (7:45) (Class 4) 2-Y-0 **£4,334** (£1,289; £644; £322) **Stalls** High

Form RPR
330 **1** **Shahdaroba (IRE)**[18] 4093 2-9-3 87.................................... JamesMillman 9 83+
(Rod Millman) *chsd ldrs: rdn to ld over 1f out: hung lft ins fnl f: jst hld on: fin 1st: plcd 2nd* **5/2[2]**
5 **2** *shd* **Herbalist**[35] 3506 2-9-3 0.. DaneO'Neill 10 83+
(Henry Candy) *chsd ldrs: rdn and hung rt over 1f out: hmpd ins fnl f: r.o wl: fin 2nd: plcd 1st* **8/1**
322 **3** *nk* **Bold Prediction (IRE)**[4] 4604 2-9-3 0.................................... SeanLevey 1 82
(Richard Hannon) *led: rdn and hdd over 1f out: r.o* **2/1[1]**
4 *6* **Tarbawi (IRE)** 2-9-3 0.. MickaelBarzalona 2 64+
(Saeed Bin Suroor) *mid-div: drvn along 1/2-way: hdwy over 2f out: wknd fnl f* **6/1**
5 *3 1/4* **Penny Rose** 2-8-12 0.. FrannyNorton 3 51+
(Mark Johnston) *dwlt: outpcd: r.o ins fnl f: nvr nrr* **14/1**
00 **6** *3* **Winged Icarus (USA)**[48] 3074 2-9-3 0.. ShaneKelly 8 43
(Alan McCabe) *hld up: rdn over 2f out: sn wknd* **40/1**
05 **7** *nk* **Makinson Lane (IRE)**[20] 3989 2-9-3 0.............................. FrederikTylicki 5 42
(Richard Fahey) *prom: rdn over 2f out: wknd over 1f out* **33/1**
8 *5* **Duke Of Orange (IRE)** 2-9-3 0.. MatthewDavies 6 26+
(Mick Channon) *chsd ldrs tl wknd 2f out* **5/1[3]**
1m 10.92s (-2.08) **Going Correction** -0.30s/f (Firm) **8** Ran SP% **116.0**
Speed ratings (Par 96): **101,100,100,92,88 84,83,77**
toteswingers: 1&2 £4.10, 1&3 £2.00, 2&3 £2.10. CSF £28.83 TOTE £7.90: £1.80, £2.00, £1.60; EX 30.20 Trifecta £89.10 Pool: £284.44 - 2.36 winning units..
Owner The Links Partnership **Bred** Tinnakill Bloodstock & Forenaghts Stud **Trained** Kentisbeare, Devon

FOCUS
This maiden was run 0.91secs slower than the time recorded by the filly in the first race but the form looks sound enough.

NOTEBOOK
Shahdaroba(IRE) set a decent standard with a mark of 87, having shown sound form prior to not being beaten far in the Super Sprint. Back on a faster surface, he was never far away but wandered around under pressure before sticking his neck out to just hold on. He lost the race in the stewards' room, but that looked slightly harsh in view of current legislation and it will be no surprise if connections appeal. (tchd 11-4)
Herbalist had made a promising debut in a fair Salisbury maiden and stepped up on that here, being just denied before being awarded the race in the stewards' room. He tended to hang right in the closing stages, possibly feeling the ground, but his strong late effort only just failed and the winner did drift into him near the line. A half-brother to a 7f winner from the family of Gorse, he can win more races, possibly on a slightly easier surface. (op 12-1)
Bold Prediction(IRE), touched off on his two previous starts after racing up with the pace, he made the running but again came up just short. He tended to wander about under pressure and could not hold off the challengers, so it might be that racing on an easier track will enable him to get off the mark. (tchd 15-8 and 9-4)
Tarbawi(IRE) was noticeably green on this debut and weakened after getting upsides the leader over 2f out. From the family of Goldikova, he has ability and should have learnt a lot from the outing. (op 9-2)
Duke Of Orange(IRE), a 42,000gns half-brother to Society Rock, was coltish in the paddock and showed up early but dropped away in the second half of the race. (op 9-1)

4708 WOODMAN'S STROKE AT ROTHLEY H'CAP 5f 218y
8:15 (8:15) (Class 5) (0-70,70) 3-Y-0+ **£2,587** (£770; £384; £192) **Stalls** High

Form RPR
523 **1** **Links Drive Lady**[11] 4332 4-9-3 **63**.............................. PatrickHills(3) 16 74
(Dean Ivory) *hld up: hdwy over 2f out: rdn to ld 1f out: r.o* **4/1[1]**
5320 **2** *1 1/2* **Rio Cobolo (IRE)**[27] 3778 6-9-10 **67**..................(v) AdrianNicholls 18 73
(David Nicholls) *chsd ldrs: rdn to ld over 1f out: sn hdd: styd on same pce ins fnl f* **13/2**
560- **3** *nk* **Euroquip Boy (IRE)**[338] 5539 5-8-11 **59**.................... DavidKenny(5) 13 64
(Michael Scudamore) *chsd ldrs: led over 3f out: rdn and hdd over 1f out: styd on same pce ins fnl f* **33/1**
0056 **4** *1/2* **Jack My Boy (IRE)**[37] 3434 5-9-10 **67**..................(b) AndreaAtzeni 14 70
(David Evans) *sn pushed along and prom: rdn over 1f out: styd on same pce ins fnl f* **5/1[2]**
4000 **5** *3/4* **Methaaly (IRE)**[19] 4043 9-8-10 **53**..................(be) SeanQuinlan 1 54
(Michael Mullineaux) *hld up: hdwy over 2f out: rdn over 1f out: styd on* **28/1**
3241 **6** *3* **Bermondsey Bob (IRE)**[6] 4492 6-9-13 **70** 6ex.................. DaneO'Neill 8 61
(John Spearing) *led: hdd over 3f out: rdn over 1f out: no ex fnl f* **15/2**
3044 **7** *3/4* **Olynard (IRE)**[37] 3434 6-8-9 **52**.. JimmyQuinn 3 41
(Michael Mullineaux) *chsd ldrs: rdn over 2f out: no ex fnl f* **14/1**
6232 **8** *2 1/4* **Taizong (IRE)**[29] 3732 3-9-4 **65**.................................... StevieDonohoe 10 47
(Ian Williams) *mid-div: hdwy u.p over 2f out: eased whn btn ins fnl f* **11/2[3]**
0100 **9** *2 1/4* **Sairaam (IRE)**[22] 3949 6-9-10 **67**.. JohnFahy 11 42
(Charles Smith) *chsd ldrs: rdn over 2f out: wknd fnl f* **25/1**
4026 **10** *1/2* **Diamond Vine (IRE)**[46] 3139 4-9-12 **69**..................(p) DavidProbert 15 42
(Ronald Harris) *sn pushed along in rr: rdn over 2f out: n.d* **16/1**
5460 **11** *1 1/2* **Hatta Stream (IRE)**[42] 3281 6-9-2 **62**.......................... SimonPearce(3) 12 30
(Lydia Pearce) *hld up: rdn over 2f out: n.d* **11/1**
36/0 **12** *2 1/4* **Cheers Big Ears (IRE)**[34] 3544 6-8-2 **50** oh2........ MatthewLawson(5) 7
(Richard Price) *s.i.s: a in rr* **50/1**
0200 **13** *2* **Madame Kintyre**[19] 4059 4-9-6 **63**..................(b) JamesMillman 5
(Rod Millman) *prom: rdn over 2f out: sn wknd* **28/1**
-610 **14** *2* **Lucifers Shadow (IRE)**[71] 2374 3-8-10 **57**.......................... SeanLevey 6
(Sylvester Kirk) *hld up in tch: rdn and wknd over 2f out* **20/1**
1m 10.64s (-2.36) **Going Correction** -0.30s/f (Firm)
WFA 3 from 4yo+ 4lb **14** Ran SP% **118.4**
Speed ratings (Par 103): **103,101,100,99,98 94,93,90,87,87 85,82,79,76**
toteswingers: 1&2 £8.00, 1&3 £65.60, 2&3 £81.30. CSF £26.36 CT £582.59 TOTE £5.20: £2.20, £2.20, £14.90; EX 37.10 TRIFECTA Not won..
Owner It's Your Lucky Day **Bred** Peter Webb **Trained** Radlett, Herts

FOCUS
A modest but competitive sprint handicap and the runners were spread across the track, with those racing nearer the stands' rail coming out on top. The time was 0.65secs slower than the opening race and the form is straightforward but ordinary.
Taizong(IRE) Official explanation: jockey said colt moved poorly last 2f

4709 ROSE & CROWN HOUGHTON-ON-THE-HILL H'CAP 1m 60y
8:45 (8:45) (Class 6) (0-65,64) 3-Y-0 **£1,940** (£577; £288; £144) **Stalls** Low

Form RPR
505 **1** **Cape Explorer**[65] 2553 3-9-6 **63**.. MartinDwyer 3 78+
(James Tate) *led over 7f out: rdn over 1f out: styd on wl* **4/1[1]**
4230 **2** *3 3/4* **Casa Bex**[40] 3347 3-9-3 **63**..................................(tp) RaulDaSilva(3) 12 69
(Philip McBride) *s.i.s: rcvrd to chse wnr 7f out: rdn over 2f out: styd on same pce ins fnl f* **20/1**
04-0 **3** *3 1/2* **Lone Foot Laddie (IRE)**[29] 3735 3-9-6 **63**.......................... ShaneKelly 14 61
(Sylvester Kirk) *plld hrd and prom: rdn over 2f out: styd on same pce fr over 1f out* **14/1**
1502 **4** *nk* **Source Of Light (IRE)**[15] 4186 3-9-0 **57**.......................... StephenCraine 2 54
(Daniel Mark Loughnane) *prom: rdn over 2f out: styd on same pce appr fnl f* **11/1**
-050 **5** *1/2* **Wyndham Wave**[58] 2756 3-9-5 **62**.. JamesMillman 6 58
(Rod Millman) *hld up: hdwy over 3f out: rdn and hung rt fr over 2f out: nt rch ldrs* **10/1**
6510 **6** *2* **Lady Percy (IRE)**[31] 3665 3-9-2 **59**.................................... DavidProbert 11 51
(Mark Usher) *led 1f: chsd ldrs: rdn over 2f out: wknd fnl f* **8/1**
0400 **7** *3* **Capitol Gain (IRE)**[15] 4172 3-9-5 **62**..................(p) MickaelBarzalona 5 47
(Brian Meehan) *s.i.s: sn pushed along in rr: hdwy u.p over 1f out: eased ins fnl f* **7/1[3]**
006 **8** *nk* **Little Miss Mayhem (IRE)**[37] 3447 3-9-2 **59**.......... MircoMimmocchi 9 43
(Philip McBride) *hld up: rdn over 2f out: nvr on terms* **40/1**
0443 **9** *3/4* **Saint Irene**[15] 4186 3-8-11 **54**.. DaneO'Neill 1 36
(Michael Blanshard) *chsd ldrs: rdn over 2f out: wknd over 1f out* **13/2[2]**
1-30 **10** *7* **Hill Of Dreams (IRE)**[128] 1046 3-9-0 **60**.......................... PatrickHills(3) 8 26
(Dean Ivory) *hld up in tch: rdn over 2f out: wknd over 1f out* **25/1**
6-0 **11** *6* **Zafonic Star**[48] 3075 3-9-5 **62**.................................... StevieDonohoe 10 14
(Ian Williams) *hld up: rdn over 2f out: sn wknd* **12/1**
040 **12** *14* **Sir Lexington (IRE)**[16] 4157 3-9-5 **62**.................................... SeanLevey 4
(Richard Hannon) *hld up: rdn over 4f out: wknd 3f out: t.o* **8/1**
305 **13** *shd* **Charles Tyrwhitt**[62] 2626 3-9-7 **64**.................................... KierenFallon 13
(George Baker) *prom: lost pl over 6f out: shkn up over 2f out: sn wknd and eased: t.o* **8/1**
1m 42.59s (-2.51) **Going Correction** -0.35s/f (Firm) **13** Ran SP% **122.0**
Speed ratings (Par 98): **98,94,90,90,89 87,84,84,83,76 70,56,56**
toteswingers: 1&2 £17.50, 1&3 £12.90, 2&3 £11.20. CSF £93.17 CT £1073.23 TOTE £4.30: £1.80, £9.20, £2.50; EX 116.10 TRIFECTA Not won..
Owner Saif Ali **Bred** Highclere Stud **Trained** Newmarket, Suffolk

FOCUS
A really competitive 3-y-o handicap on paper, but it paid to be up with the pace as the first two held those positions virtually throughout. The runner-up sets the standard.
Cape Explorer Official explanation: trainer said, regarding apparent improvement in form, that the gelding had previously behaved badly but had now been gelded.
Wyndham Wave Official explanation: jockey said gelding hung right-handed
Hill Of Dreams(IRE) Official explanation: jockey said filly slipped on bend
T/Plt: £154.70 to a £1 stake. Pool: £75,619.38 - 356.70 winning tickets. T/Qpdt: £62.20 to a £1 stake. Pool: £5,758.00 - 68.40 winning tickets. CR

3401 REDCAR (L-H)
Wednesday, August 1
OFFICIAL GOING: Good (good to firm in places; 8.8)
Wind: fresh 1/2 behind Weather: fine, very breezy

4710 BRITISH STALLION STUDS SUPPORTING BRITISH RACING EBF MAIDEN STKS 6f
2:15 (2:19) (Class 5) 2-Y-0 **£3,135** (£925; £463) **Stalls** Centre

Form RPR
0 **1** **Ayasha**[57] 2790 2-8-12 0.. PaulMulrennan 11 70+
(Bryan Smart) *mde all: pushed along and kpt on wl fnl f: readily* **66/1**
0 **2** *1 1/4* **Izzy Boy (USA)**[10] 4362 2-9-3 0.. FrannyNorton 17 71
(Mark Johnston) *trckd wnr: upsides over 2f out: kpt on same pce fnl f* **11/4[1]**

4520 **3** *1 3/4* **Annie Gogh**47 3110 2-8-12 70........ DavidAllan 12 60
(Tim Easterby) *chsd ldrs: kpt on to take 3rd nr fin* **12/1**

43 **4** *nk* **Montcliffe**19 4069 2-9-3 0........ TonyHamilton 7 64
(Richard Fahey) *chsd ldrs: kpt on one pce appr fnl f* **12/1**

00 **5** *1 3/4* **Monsieur Royale**11 4344 2-9-0 0........ DaleSwift(3) 10 59+
(Geoffrey Oldroyd) *in rr and sn drvn along: hdwy over 1f out: styd on wl towards fin* **50/1**

0 **6** *nk* **Sharjah (IRE)**40 3346 2-9-3 0........ PJMcDonald 15 58
(Noel Quinlan) *mid-div: hdwy 2f out: kpt on ins fnl f* **7/1**

6 **7** *nse* **Grandorio (IRE)**18 4114 2-9-3 0........ DanielTudhope 5 58
(David O'Meara) *w ldrs: fdd over 1f out* **9/1**

8 *nk* **Star Request** 2-8-12 0........ AndrewMullen 8 52
(Keith Dalgleish) *chsd ldrs: wknd over 1f out* **50/1**

4 **9** *1/2* **Miss Perfect**39 3401 2-8-12 0........ MichaelO'Connell 9 50
(John Quinn) *chsd ldrs: drvn over 2f out: sn outpcd* **7/1**

10 *2 1/4* **Muharrib (IRE)** 2-9-3 0........ RobertHavlin 14 48
(Saeed Bin Suroor) *mid-div: effrt over 2f out: nvr a factor* **9/2**2

11 *1 3/4* **Shepherds Bow** 2-9-3 0........ JamesSullivan 4 42+
(Michael Easterby) *s.i.s: sme hdwy over 1f out: nvr a factor* **50/1**

12 *nk* **Returntobrecongill** 2-9-3 0........ MichaelStainton 2 41
(Sally Hall) *dwlt: sn chsng ldrs: lost pl over 1f out* **80/1**

13 *nk* **Lichen Angel** 2-8-12 0........ AmyRyan 3 35
(Richard Whitaker) *s.i.s: a towards rr* **66/1**

14 *nk* **Storma Norma** 2-8-12 0........ DuranFentiman 13 34
(Tim Easterby) *s.i.s: a in rr* **50/1**

2 **15** *3/4* **Lucy Minaj**72 2334 2-8-12 0........ TomEaves 6 32
(Bryan Smart) *trckd ldrs t.k.h: wknd over 1f out* **13/2**3

16 *1 1/4* **Artful Prince** 2-9-3 0........ GrahamLee 16 33
(James Given) *sn outpcd in rr: bhd fnl 3f* **50/1**

17 *hd* **Danehill Flyer (IRE)** 2-9-3 0........ RussKennemore 1 32
(Philip Kirby) *s.i.s: hdwy into mid-div after 3f: sn lost pl* **66/1**

1m 10.17s (-1.63) **Going Correction** -0.30s/f (Firm) **17** Ran SP% **124.1**
Speed ratings (Par 94): **98,96,94,93,91 90,90,90,89,86 84,84,83,83,82 80,80**
toteswingers 1&2 £77.50, 1&3 £76.60, 2&3 £8.00 CSF £244.34 TOTE £107.00: £22.90, £1.30, £3.20; EX 460.20.
Owner Crossfields Racing **Bred** Crossfields Bloodstock Ltd **Trained** Hambleton, N Yorks

FOCUS

Waterlogged areas at 6.5f on stands side and 7f on far side railed off. A big-field maiden and plenty of interesting types lined up.

NOTEBOOK

Ayasha didn't show much on her debut over C&D, but she proved a completely different proposition after almost two months off, probably running to a fair level. She's likely to find things tougher next time, but may progress again.

Izzy Boy(USA) ◆, a horse with plenty of size, had shown ability on his debut over 6f at Ascot and was well fancied to improve on that effort. He duly did so, but just couldn't go with the winner when it mattered. There should be a deal more to come. (op 7-2 tchd 5-2)

Annie Gogh, officially rated 70, was up to this trip for the first time. She seemed to run her race, but wasn't good enough. (op 9-1)

Montcliffe, dropped back in distance, didn't really build on his first two efforts, but nurseries are now an option. (op 14-1 tchd 11-1)

Monsieur Royale ◆, well held in a couple of 5f maidens, was under pressure a fair way out but ran on strongly. He's sprint bred, so it would probably be unwise to suggest he wants further and he probably just needs to wake up a bit. The way he finished suggests he's getting the idea and he'll be interesting if switching to a nursery next time. (op 33-1)

Sharjah(IRE) kept on nicely enough and we've probably yet to see the best of him. (op 6-1 tchd 9-1)

Grandorio(IRE) ◆, who shaped okay on his debut at York, should be capable of better. He showed pace more towards the far side than some and, as the card went on, it seemed that low-drawn runners were at a disadvantage in bid fields on the straight course. (op 14-1)

Star Request showed good pace on her debut.

Muharrib(IRE) never really featured. (tchd 4-1)

Shepherds Bow ◆ is a half-brother to Bow Bridge, a triple 5f juvenile winner (including Listed) for this owner/trainer combination, and the dam also won three times over sprint trips for the same connections. This was an eyecatching debut as he looked to have something to offer when a bit short of room for much of the closing stages, and he was not given a hard ride. There should be significantly better to come.

4711 CARIBBEAN CARNIVAL DAY SATURDAY 11TH AUGUST RATING RELATED MAIDEN STKS 7f

2:50 (2:50) (Class 5) 3-Y-0+ **£2,264** (£673; £336; £168) **Stalls** Centre

Form RPR

020- **1** **Diamond Belle**297 6725 3-8-12 67........ PJMcDonald 9 81
(Noel Quinlan) *wnt rt s: sn w ldrs: led 2f out: shkn up appr fnl f: forged wl clr* **9/1**

40-0 **2** *6* **Pearl War (USA)**31 3666 3-8-12 70........ PhillipMakin 8 65
(William Haggas) *chsd ldrs: rdn over 2f out: kpt on to take 2nd line* **4/1**2

4025 **3** *shd* **Tahnee Mara (IRE)**9 4401 3-8-12 66........ AmyRyan 6 64
(Kevin Ryan) *led: hdd 2f out: kpt on same pce appr fnl f* **10/1**

0034 **4** *2* **Nant Saeson (IRE)**22 3947 3-9-1 69........ MichaelO'Connell 7 62
(John Quinn) *chsd ldrs: drvn over 2f out: one pce* **5/1**

0500 **5** *2* **Decadence**11 4350 4-8-11 36........ DanielleMooney(7) 5 56?
(Nigel Tinkler) *chsd ldrs: outpcd after 2f: kpt on fnl 2f* **80/1**

233 **6** *1 3/4* **Legal Bond**25 3848 3-9-1 62........ TomEaves 1 52
(Bryan Smart) *trckd ldrs: t.k.h: rdn and outpcd over 2f out: kpt on ins fnl f* **7/1**

4323 **7** *2 1/2* **Gladsome**40 3333 4-9-4 69........ MichaelStainton 3 44
(Jason Ward) *chsd ldrs: outpcd over 3f out: wknd over 2f out* **9/2**3

-500 **8** *1 1/4* **Endless Applause**11 4348 3-8-12 52........ DavidAllan 2 39
(Richard Whitaker) *in rr and sn drvn along: nvr on terms* **50/1**

4-35 **9** *nk* **Alice Rose (IRE)**8 4436 3-8-12 67........ RobertWinston 4 38
(Rae Guest) *chsd ldrs: lost pl over 1f out* **3/1**1

5046 **10** *4 1/2* **Well Bank (IRE)**13 4263 3-8-12 57........ DaleSwift(3) 10 29
(Colin Teague) *carried rt s: in rr: rdn over 3f out: sn bhd* **50/1**

1m 21.84s (-2.66) **Going Correction** -0.30s/f (Firm)
WFA 3 from 4yo 6lb **10** Ran SP% **116.6**
Speed ratings (Par 103): **103,96,96,93,91 89,86,85,84,79**
toteswingers 1&2 £7.10, 1&3 £14.30, 2&3 £6.50 CSF £44.80 TOTE £12.30: £4.00, £1.90, £3.20; EX 67.90.
Owner Burns Farm Racing **Bred** Burns Farm Stud **Trained** Newmarket, Suffolk

FOCUS

A really weak maiden (the fifth-placed finisher came into this officially rated just 36) but the winner has potential. The three behind the winner were all close to their recent best.

Alice Rose(IRE) Official explanation: trainer's rep said filly ran flat

4712 HAPPY RETIREMENT HOWARD WRIGHT (S) STKS 1m 2f

3:25 (3:25) (Class 6) 3-Y-0+ **£1,704** (£503; £251) **Stalls** Low

Form RPR

-060 **1** **Valantino Oyster (IRE)**32 3628 5-9-5 58........(p) PatrickMathers 6 59
(Tracy Waggott) *dwlt: sn chsng ldrs: led over 2f out: edgd lft over 1f out: hld on towards fin* **9/2**3

5360 **2** *3/4* **Sinatramania**11 4350 5-9-2 53........ PaulPickard(3) 3 58
(Tracy Waggott) *dwlt: hld up in rr: hdwy over 3f out: upsides over 1f out: no ex last 50yds* **11/2**

3 *2 3/4* **Azrag (USA)**96 4-9-5 0........(v1) PaulMulrennan 9 52
(Gerard Butler) *swtchd lft after s: led after 1f: hdd 3f out: wandered and stmbld over 1f out: one pce* **6/1**

0-40 **4** *1 1/2* **Hoar Frost**4 4594 7-8-7 47........(p) GemmaTutty(7) 7 44
(Karen Tutty) *hld up in rr: swtchd outside over 3f out: styd on fnl f: tk 4th nr fin* **25/1**

0000 **5** *1/2* **Norton Girl**4 4594 4-9-0 40........ FrannyNorton 8 43
(Tracy Waggott) *hld up in rr: effrt over 3f out: kpt on fnl f: tk 4th last strides* **25/1**

5000 **6** *nk* **Yorksters Prince (IRE)**64 2588 5-9-5 64........(b) BarryMcHugh 1 47
(Tony Coyle) *rn in snatches: chsd ldrs: drvn to chal on ins over 2f out: wknd over 1f out: lost 2 pls nr line* **11/4**1

5000 **7** *1 1/2* **Henrys Gift (IRE)**24 3889 4-9-5 45........1 TomEaves 2 44
(Michael Dods) *dwlt: hld up in mid-div: effrt over 3f out: nvr a threat* **16/1**

100/ **8** *3 3/4* **Danehillsundance (IRE)**445 4450 8-8-12 80........(t) EvaMoscrop(7) 4 37
(Philip Kirby) *mid-div: drvn over 3f out: sn outpcd* **8/1**

1020 **9** *54* **Jack Dawkins (USA)**30 3692 7-9-10 68........ AdrianNicholls 5
(David Nicholls) *led 1f: trckd ldr: chal 3f out: sn heavily eased: eventually completed: tailed rt off* **4/1**2

2m 7.33s (0.23) **Going Correction** -0.125s/f (Firm) **9** Ran SP% **119.2**
Speed ratings (Par 101): **94,93,91,90,89 89,88,85,41**
toteswingers 1&2 £7.20, 1&3 £6.00, 2&3 £4.50 CSF £30.54 TOTE £4.50: £2.30, £2.00, £1.80; EX 22.10.There was no bid for the winner.
Owner Steve Sawley **Bred** Des Vere Hunt Farm Co And Jack Ronan **Trained** Spennymoor, Co Durham

FOCUS

A moderate seller in which the fourth, fifth and seventh set a moderate standard.

Valantino Oyster(IRE) Official explanation: Trainer said, regarding apparent improvement in form, that the gelding appreciated the better ground and drop in class.

Jack Dawkins(USA) Official explanation: jockey said gelding lost its action

4713 JOHN SMITH'S REDCAR STRAIGHT-MILE CHAMPIONSHIP STKS (QUALIFIER) (H'CAP) 1m

4:00 (4:00) (Class 4) (0-85,80) 3-Y-0 **£4,075** (£1,212; £606; £303) **Stalls** Centre

Form RPR

1343 **1** **Annie Walker (IRE)**22 3940 3-8-11 **70**........ AdrianNicholls 3 78
(David Nicholls) *w ldr: led over 2f out: styd on gamely fnl f* **4/1**3

-210 **2** *1* **Al Wajba (USA)**12 4298 3-9-4 **80**........ AdamBeschizza(3) 5 86
(William Haggas) *trckd ldrs: effrt over 2f out: upsides over 1f out: styd on same pce* **3/1**2

-011 **3** *3 1/2* **Kung Hei Fat Choy (USA)**15 4193 3-8-13 **72**........(b) GrahamLee 7 70
(James Given) *led: drvn over 3f out: hdd over 2f out: one pce over 1f out* **4/1**3

4110 **4** *1 1/2* **King Of Paradise (IRE)**13 4260 3-8-4 **70**........ JasonHart(7) 6 65
(Eric Alston) *hld up in last: effrt over 2f out: sn rdn: one pce* **6/1**

31 **5** *3/4* **Voice From Above (IRE)**36 3461 3-8-11 **70**........ DanielTudhope 4 63
(Patrick Holmes) *trckd ldrs: drvn over 2f out: one pce* **11/4**1

660- **6** *17* **Absolute Fun (IRE)**302 6611 3-8-2 **61** oh2........ DuranFentiman 1 15
(Tim Easterby) *sn trcking ldrs: drvn 3f out: sn lost pl: eased whn bhd* **25/1**

1m 35.1s (-2.90) **Going Correction** -0.30s/f (Firm) **6** Ran SP% **109.8**
Speed ratings (Par 102): **102,101,97,96,95 78**
toteswingers 1&2 £3.00, 1&3 £2.60, 2&3 £2.90 CSF £15.57 CT £45.47 TOTE £6.20: £3.70, £4.20; EX 18.90.
Owner D Nicholls & Mrs M C Jacobs **Bred** Round Hill Stud **Trained** Sessay, N Yorks

FOCUS

This was an uncompetitive and disappointing race for the class. The winner is rated to the best of her previous form.

4714 MARKET CROSS JEWELLERS H'CAP 1m 2f

4:35 (4:36) (Class 5) (0-75,73) 3-Y-0+ **£2,264** (£673; £336; £168) **Stalls** Low

Form RPR

0035 **1** **Kalk Bay (IRE)**13 4249 5-9-12 **71**........(t) JamesSullivan 7 85
(Michael Easterby) *mid-div: hdwy over 3f out: edgd lft and chal over 1f out: styd on to ld post* **7/1**2

2045 **2** *hd* **Daliance (IRE)**13 4254 3-9-1 **69**........ RichardKingscote 12 83
(Tom Dascombe) *trckd ldrs: led 3f out: jnd over 1f out: no ex and hdd last strides* **9/2**1

6053 **3** *4* **Chatterati (USA)**9 4391 3-8-3 **57**........ FrannyNorton 9 63
(Mark Johnston) *s.i.s: in rr: effrt on outer over 3f out: styd on over 1f out: tk 3rd nr fin* **7/1**2

6302 **4** *1/2* **Zaplamation (IRE)**14 4209 7-9-1 **60**........ MichaelO'Connell 4 65
(John Quinn) *s.i.s: sn chsng ldrs: drvn over 2f out: kpt on one pce* **7/1**2

225 **5** *2* **Cottam Donny**49 3021 4-9-4 **63**........ DavidAllan 10 64
(Mel Brittain) *hld up in rr: hdwy over 3f out: one pce fnl 2f* **9/1**

3606 **6** *6* **Law To Himself (IRE)**24 3891 5-9-7 **66**........ RobertWinston 1 55
(Alan Swinbank) *led 1f: chsd ldrs: drvn over 2f out: wknd and eased last 100yds* **10/1**

02U **7** *6* **Strike Force**30 3692 8-9-9 **68**........(t) TomEaves 3 45
(Alison Hutchinson) *chsd ldrs: effrt over 3f out: wknd 2f out* **20/1**

0066 **8** *nk* **Rock Of Deauville (IRE)**33 3577 5-9-1 **60**........(b1) GrahamLee 2 36
(Julie Camacho) *chsd ldrs: drvn over 3f out: wknd 2f out* **50/1**

4150 **9** *3/4* **Al Furat (USA)**6 4499 4-9-3 **67**........ ShaneBKelly(5) 5 42
(Ron Barr) *rel to r: sme hdwy on inner over 3f out: edgd rt: nvr a factor* **8/1**3

4-06 **10** *6* **Waltz Darling (IRE)**32 3628 4-9-12 **71**........ TonyHamilton 11 34
(Richard Fahey) *mid-div: t.k.h: lost pl and drvn over 4f out: wknd over 2f out* **10/1**

0536 **11** *6* **Goodness**28 3753 4-8-10 **62**........(v) DavidBergin(7) 6 13
(David O'Meara) *led after 1f: hdd 3f out: sn lost pl* **20/1**

6-31 **12** *1 1/2* **Xclaim**12 4314 4-9-12 **71**........ PJMcDonald 13 19
(Micky Hammond) *in rr: effrt on outside over 3f out: sn wknd* **10/1**

41-0 **13** *18* **Medieval Bishop (IRE)**[11] 4329 3-9-5 **73**.................... DuranFentiman 8
(Tim Walford) *trckd ldrs: drvn and lost pl 5f out: bhd whn eased 2f out: t.o* **40/1**

2m 5.05s (-2.05) **Going Correction** -0.125s/f (Firm)
WFA 3 from 4yo+ 9lb **13** Ran SP% **118.0**
Speed ratings (Par 103): **103,102,99,99,97 92,88,87,87,82 77,76,62**
toteswingers 1&2 £8.90, 1&3 £5.10, 2&3 £7.30 CSF £36.35 CT £232.67 TOTE £8.60: £3.00, £2.10, £3.10; EX 54.30.
Owner Mrs Jean Turpin **Bred** Wentworth Racing **Trained** Sheriff Hutton, N Yorks

FOCUS
A modest handicap run at a good pace, and two runners finished well clear. The third and fourth are rated close to recent marks and set the level.

4715 RACING UK ON CHANNEL 432 H'CAP (DIV I) 1m
5:05 (5:06) (Class 6) (0-65,65) 3-Y-O+ **£1,617** (£481; £240; £120) **Stalls** Centre

Form RPR

4205 **1** **Indian Giver**[13] 4260 4-9-5 **59**.................... PaulPickard(3) 12 68
(Hugh McWilliams) *towards rr: hdwy stands' side over 2f out: styd on to go 2nd last 100yds: led fnl strides* **22/1**

-233 **2** *hd* **Broctune Papa Gio**[40] 3356 5-9-10 **64**.................... DeclanCannon(3) 11 73
(Keith Reveley) *in rr: hdwy over 2f out: led over 1f out: hdd and no ex nr fin* **3/1**[1]

4 **3** *1 1/2* **Talent Scout (IRE)**[61] 2675 6-9-11 **62**.................... DuranFentiman 9 67
(Tim Walford) *led: 1f: w ldrs: led over 2f out: hdd over 1f out: kpt on same pce* **9/2**[2]

0423 **4** *3 1/4* **No Quarter (IRE)**[28] 3749 5-9-8 **59**.................... RobertWinston 10 57
(Tracy Waggott) *hld up in rr: hdwy over 2f out: chsng ldrs over 1f out: one pce* **12/1**

0326 **5** *shd* **Gadobout Dancer**[30] 3694 5-9-1 **52**.................... BarryMcHugh 8 49+
(Tony Coyle) *rrd s: sn trcking ldrs: one pce fnl 2f* **10/1**

30- **6** *8* **Cross The Boss (IRE)**[412] 3088 5-9-4 **55**....................(t) PJMcDonald 4 34
(Ben Haslam) *w ldrs: led after 2f: hdd over 2f out: lost pl over 1f out* **16/1**

5005 **7** *2 1/2* **Dream Win**[3] 4627 6-9-11 **65**.................... DaleSwift(3) 14 38
(Brian Ellison) *w ldrs: drvn over 2f out: wknd over 1f out* **9/2**[2]

003 **8** *nse* **Outlaw Torn (IRE)**[5] 4549 3-8-13 **57**....................(e) RobbieFitzpatrick 7 28
(Richard Guest) *mid-div: drvn over 2f out: wknd over 1f out* **12/1**

63 **9** *9* **El Dececy (USA)**[168] 562 8-9-6 **57**....................[1] StevieDonohoe 5
(John Butler) *dwlt: hdwy to ld after 1f: hdd after 2f: lost pl over 2f out* **8/1**[3]

0360 **10** *1 1/4* **Airmyles**[11] 4349 4-9-3 **54**.................... PatrickMathers 2
(Tracy Waggott) *chsd ldrs: lost pl 2f out* **66/1**

0330 **11** *5* **Border Abby**[36] 3469 4-9-0 **51**....................(b[1]) DavidAllan 3
(Rae Guest) *chsd ldrs: lost pl over 2f out* **12/1**

6-00 **12** *19* **Daffyd**[12] 4293 3-9-2 **60**.................... PhillipMakin 1
(Kevin Ryan) *w ldrs: wknd rapidly over 3f out: sn bhd: virtually p.u: t.o* **18/1**

1m 36.0s (-2.00) **Going Correction** -0.30s/f (Firm)
WFA 3 from 4yo+ 7lb **12** Ran SP% **121.6**
Speed ratings (Par 101): **98,97,96,93,92 84,82,82,73,72 67,48**
toteswingers 1&2 £12.50, 1&3 £9.80, 2&3 £4.10 CSF £89.51 CT £369.68 TOTE £35.70: £8.20, £1.10, £2.70; EX 136.50.
Owner J D Riches **Bred** M C Denning **Trained** Pilling, Lancs
■ Stewards' Enquiry : Declan Cannon two-day ban: used whip above permitted level (Aug 15-16)
Paul Pickard two-day ban: used whip above permitted level (Aug 15-16)

FOCUS
A moderate handicap in which the pace was probably a bit too strong, setting this up for a couple of runners from off the speed. The form looks straightforward with the placed horses rated close to last year's form in divisions of this contest.

4716 RACING UK ON CHANNEL 432 H'CAP (DIV II) 1m
5:40 (5:42) (Class 6) (0-65,64) 3-Y-O+ **£1,617** (£481; £240; £120) **Stalls** Centre

Form RPR

5011 **1** **Florio Vincitore (IRE)**[8] 4432 5-9-11 **64** 6ex....................(v) DaleSwift(3) 12 77
(Brian Ellison) *mid-div: drvn over 2f out: styd on to ld over 1f out: drvn clr* **15/8**[1]

0-40 **2** *4 1/2* **Tukitinyasok (IRE)**[9] 4398 5-9-7 **57**....................(p) TonyHamilton 13 60
(Clive Mulhall) *w ldrs: led over 2f out: hdd over 1f out: kpt on same pce* **16/1**

5012 **3** *1/2* **King Pin**[26] 3810 7-10-0 **64**....................(p) BarryMcHugh 3 66+
(Tracy Waggott) *hld up in rr: hdwy over 2f out: styd on same pce fnl f* **15/2**[3]

-000 **4** *1 1/4* **Whispered Times (USA)**[53] 2924 5-9-11 **64**....................(p) PaulPickard(3) 6 63+
(Tracy Waggott) *trckd ldrs: effrt over 2f out: kpt on same pce fnl f* **33/1**

0000 **5** *nk* **Final Drive (IRE)**[40] 3344 6-9-8 **58**....................(t) StevieDonohoe 9 56
(John Butler) *mid-div: hdwy over 2f out: one pce* **20/1**

5320 **6** *2 1/4* **Lean On Pete (IRE)**[47] 3111 3-9-3 **60**.................... TomEaves 7 51
(Ollie Pears) *mid-div: effrt over 2f out: kpt on fnl f* **9/1**

021 **7** *1* **Tazaamun (IRE)**[24] 3889 4-9-9 **59**.................... DanielTudhope 2 50
(David O'Meara) *trckd ldrs: effrt over 2f out: wknd over 1f out* **3/1**[2]

0540 **8** *1 1/2* **Maggie Mey (IRE)**[2] 4656 4-9-5 **55**.................... GrahamLee 5 42
(Lawrence Mullaney) *w ldrs: led over 3f out: hdd over 2f out: wknd over 1f out* **16/1**

2240 **9** *hd* **Silly Gilly (IRE)**[19] 4042 8-9-7 **62**.................... ShaneBKelly(5) 14 49
(Ron Barr) *s.i.s: sme hdwy 3f out: wknd over 1f out* **14/1**

6300 **10** *1 1/2* **Pilgrim Dancer (IRE)**[30] 3692 5-9-0 **50**.................... DavidNolan 8 33
(Tony Coyle) *trckd ldrs: drvn over 2f out: lost pl over 1f out* **50/1**

3435 **11** *1 1/2* **Georgebernardshaw (IRE)**[9] 4390 7-9-10 **60**.......... RobbieFitzpatrick 1 40
(Richard Guest) *mid-div: drvn over 2f out: sn btn* **16/1**

0050 **12** *8* **Hurricane Max (IRE)**[9] 4397 3-9-1 **58**.................... PaulMulrennan 11 18
(Chris Fairhurst) *dwlt: in rr: bhd fnl 2f* **14/1**

0500 **13** *nk* **Wolf Spirit (IRE)**[15] 4177 3-9-0 **57**....................(b) JamesSullivan 4 16
(Ruth Carr) *hld up in rr: drvn over 2f out: sn bhd* **40/1**

200 **14** *10* **Media Stars**[4] 4594 7-8-13 **52**....................(v[1]) LeeTopliss(3) 10
(Robert Johnson) *led: hdd over 3f out: sn lost pl: eased whn bhd* **50/1**

1m 35.25s (-2.75) **Going Correction** -0.30s/f (Firm)
WFA 3 from 4yo+ 7lb **14** Ran SP% **126.6**
Speed ratings (Par 101): **101,96,96,94,94 92,91,89,89,88 86,78,78,68**
toteswingers 1&2 £11.50, 1&3 £2.60, 2&3 £22.80 CSF £36.38 CT £205.81 TOTE £2.90: £1.50, £6.10, £2.00; EX 59.70.
Owner L S Keys & Kristian Strangeway **Bred** Newsells Park Stud **Trained** Norton, N Yorks

FOCUS
The winner of the second division of this handicap proved well ahead of his mark. The form is fluid although the third did well considering he raced far side.

4717 WIN A VIP DAY OUT AT REDCARRACING.CO.UK H'CAP 6f
6:10 (6:11) (Class 6) (0-65,65) 3-Y-O+ **£1,617** (£481; £240; £120) **Stalls** Centre

Form RPR

4041 **1** **Orwellian**[9] 4394 3-9-4 **61** 6ex.................... TomEaves 16 69
(Bryan Smart) *chsd ldrs: styd on to ld jst ins fnl f: hld on towards fin* **6/1**[3]

1-00 **2** *nk* **Emily Hall**[49] 3028 3-8-4 **47**.................... DuranFentiman 15 54
(Bryan Smart) *rrd s: in last: hdwy and swtchd stands' side 2f out: styd on to take 2nd last 50yds: no ex nr fin* **25/1**

3563 **3** *1* **Baybshambles (IRE)**[7] 4452 8-8-11 **55**.................... ShaneBKelly(5) 14 60
(Ron Barr) *w ldrs: kpt on same pce last 150yds* **11/1**

0-20 **4** *1 1/2* **Premier Choice**[38] 3421 3-9-5 **62**....................(p) DavidAllan 12 61
(Tim Easterby) *w ldrs: drvn over 2f out: kpt on same pce fnl f* **8/1**

3360 **5** *3/4* **Besty**[7] 4452 5-9-5 **58**.................... BarryMcHugh 10 56
(Paul Midgley) *chsd ldrs: rdn and hung lft over 1f out: kpt on same pce* **14/1**

0034 **6** *1/2* **Bay Of Fires (IRE)**[5] 4547 4-9-5 **65**....................(p) DavidBergin(7) 8 61
(David O'Meara) *mde most: hdd jst ins fnl f: wknd clsng stages* **5/1**[2]

-305 **7** *nk* **Karate Queen**[7] 4453 7-8-7 **46** oh1.................... AmyRyan 6 41+
(Ron Barr) *s.i.s: hdwy over 3f out: one pce over 1f out* **12/1**

6404 **8** *3/4* **Rio's Girl**[3] 4631 5-8-10 **56**.................... DavidSimmonson(7) 18 49
(Tony Coyle) *w ldrs: fdd appr fnl f* **18/1**

6010 **9** *1* **Ryedane (IRE)**[5] 4552 10-9-1 **61**....................(b) RachelRichardson(7) 13 51
(Tim Easterby) *in rr: hdwy over 1f out: edgd lft: nvr nr ldrs* **20/1**

0035 **10** *nk* **Blue Noodles**[24] 3893 6-8-8 **47**....................(p) PaddyAspell 20 36
(John Wainwright) *towards rr: kpt on fnl 2f: nvr a factor* **20/1**

4006 **11** *2* **Mango Music**[7] 4454 9-9-12 **65**....................(p) KellyHarrison 19 47
(David Thompson) *in rr: kpt on fnl 2f: nvr on terms* **33/1**

-363 **12** *1* **Lady Del Sol**[7] 4453 4-9-7 **60**....................(p) PhillipMakin 17 39
(Marjorie Fife) *dwlt: in rr: kpt on fnl 2f: nvr a factor* **10/1**

0634 **13** *1* **Green Warrior**[7] 4452 4-8-8 **50**....................(e) DeclanCannon(3) 2 26
(Richard Guest) *w ldrs: lost pl over 2f out* **20/1**

66U6 **14** *1/2* **Boga (IRE)**[16] 4134 5-8-0 **46** oh1....................(p) GemmaTutty(7) 5 20
(Karen Tutty) *in rr: nvr on terms* **25/1**

0000 **15** *1/2* **Roman Ruler (IRE)**[125] 1095 4-8-9 **48**....................(t) PaulMulrennan 4 21
(Chris Fairhurst) *mid-div: hdwy over 2f out: lost pl over 1f out* **33/1**

0000 **16** *nse* **Sleights Boy (IRE)**[7] 4452 4-8-9 **48**....................(e[1]) PatrickMathers 3 21
(Ian McInnes) *w ldrs: lost pl wl over 1f out* **40/1**

4411 **17** *5* **Novalist**[15] 4196 4-9-8 **61**....................(b) DanielTudhope 1 18
(Robin Bastiman) *swvd lft s: sn chsng ldrs on wd outside: lost pl over 2f out: sn bhd* **7/2**[1]

1m 10.07s (-1.73) **Going Correction** -0.30s/f (Firm)
WFA 3 from 4yo+ 4lb **17** Ran SP% **131.6**
Speed ratings (Par 101): **99,98,97,95,94 93,93,92,90,90 87,86,85,84,83 83,77**
toteswingers 1&2 £48.50, 1&3 £14.00, 2&3 £73.20 CSF £161.20 CT £1664.09 TOTE £6.20: £1.60, £7.30, £2.70, £2.80; EX 176.10.
Owner Just For Girls Partnership **Bred** Mrs Fiona Denniff **Trained** Hambleton, N Yorks

FOCUS
There was evidence earlier in the afternoon that a high draw may have provided an advantage in big fields on the straight course, and the first five home here came from double-figure stalls. The form looks fairly sound rated around the winner and third.
Novalist Official explanation: jockey said gelding missed the break
T/Plt: £436.00 to a £1 stake. Pool: £66720.81 - 111.71 winning tickets T/Qpdt: £28.60 to a £1 stake. Pool: £5224.83 - 134.76 winning tickets WG

4500 EPSOM (L-H)
Thursday, August 2

OFFICIAL GOING: Good (good to firm in places; 8.3)
Wind: Moderate across, towards stands Weather: Fine

4722 DOWNLOAD EPSOM'S ANDROID OR IPHONE APP NOW APPRENTICE H'CAP 1m 2f 18y
5:50 (5:50) (Class 5) (0-70,70) 4-Y-O+ **£2,587** (£770; £384; £192) **Stalls** Low

Form RPR

0302 **1** **Standpoint**[7] 4511 6-9-7 **70**.................... DavidKenny(3) 11 79
(Conor Dore) *trckd ldng trio: prog over 2f out: rdn to ld over 1f out: styd on wl* **8/1**[3]

0521 **2** *1 1/4* **Arashi**[7] 4504 6-9-0 **60** 6ex....................(v) AdamBeschizza 7 67
(Derek Shaw) *trckd ldrs: 5th st: rdn and effrt over 2f out: chsd ldng pair over 1f out: styd on to take 2nd last stride* **2/1**[1]

2206 **3** *nse* **Super Duplex**[21] 3999 5-9-0 **65**....................[1] JakePayne(5) 1 71
(Pat Phelan) *trckd ldng pair: clsd to ld over 2f out: rdn and hdd over 1f out: kpt on but lost 2nd last stride* **12/1**

4000 **4** *2* **Layline (IRE)**[15] 4216 5-9-5 **68**.................... DarrenEgan(3) 5 70
(Gay Kelleway) *dwlt: t.k.h: hld up: 8th st: hrd rdn and prog fr 2f out: hanging over 1f out: styd on fnl f: nrst fin* **11/4**[2]

0005 **5** *3 1/2* **Rosy Dawn**[14] 4241 7-7-12 **51** oh6.................... NoelGarbutt(7) 3 46
(John Bridger) *led to over 2f out: steadily fdd over 1f out* **50/1**

66-0 **6** *3 1/4* **Effigy**[83] 2051 8-9-4 **67**.................... AmyScott(3) 12 56
(Henry Candy) *hld up in rr: 10th st: no real prog over 2f out: kpt on fr over 1f out* **10/1**

10-0 **7** *nk* **Baan (USA)**[101] 1559 9-8-8 **61**.................... RyanTate(7) 4 49
(James Eustace) *sn detached in last pair: virtually t.o in 11th st: styd on fnl 2f: fin wl* **25/1**

6145 **8** *nk* **Bold Cross (IRE)**[36] 3485 9-9-4 **64**.................... MatthewCosham 13 52
(Edward Bevan) *nvr bttr than midfield: 7th st: effrt over 2f out: sn no prog: one pce* **12/1**

2000 **9** *6* **Barathea Dancer (IRE)**[23] 3940 4-9-3 **70**.................... MartinLeonard(7) 9 46
(Roger Teal) *wl in tch: 6th st: wknd wl over 2f out* **22/1**

0-50 **10** *1* **Phluke**[71] 2389 11-8-13 **62**.................... CharlesBishop(3) 6 36
(Eve Johnson Houghton) *chsd ldr to 3f out: sn wknd* **33/1**

0030 **11** *7* **Prince Of Thebes (IRE)**[50] 3043 11-8-5 **51** oh5.................... KierenFox 8 11
(Michael Attwater) *dwlt: nvr gng wl towards rr: 9th st: sn wknd and bhd* **28/1**

3243 **12** *3 1/4* **Count Ceprano (IRE)**[103] 1533 8-8-13 **66**.................... SophieSilvester(7) 10 19
(Lydia Pearce) *sn detached in last: t.o bef 1/2-way* **14/1**

2m 7.97s (-1.73) **Going Correction** -0.075s/f (Good) **12** Ran SP% **118.8**
Speed ratings (Par 103): **103,102,101,100,97 94,94,94,89,88 83,80**
toteswingers 1&2 £4.40, 1&3 £9.40, 2&3 £6.30 CSF £23.03 CT £199.01 TOTE £10.10: £2.80, £1.50, £3.40; EX 41.30 Trifecta £1091.90 Pool: £1,770.65 - 1.20 winning units..
Owner Mrs Jennifer Marsh **Bred** Juddmonte Farms Ltd **Trained** Hubbert's Bridge, Lincs

FOCUS
Inner configuration and all distances as advertised. Following a showery day, the ground was eased to "good, good to firm in places". A modest handicap run at an ordinary gallop and one in which those attempting to come from off the pace were at a disadvantage.
Count Ceprano(IRE) Official explanation: jockey said gelding was never travelling.

4723 KISS MIX H'CAP 6f
6:20 (6:21) (Class 4) (0-85,84) 3-Y-O **£4,528** (£1,347; £673; £336) **Stalls** High

Form RPR

0102 **1** **Orders From Rome (IRE)**^{10} 4412 3-8-7 **75** .... AmyScott(5) 5 87
(Eve Johnson Houghton) *declined frntic pce and wl bhd: last tl prog 2f out: edgd lft jst over 1f out: r.o to ld last 150yds: sn clr* **6/1**

6012 **2** 5 **Alice's Dancer (IRE)**^{14} 4234 3-9-4 **81** .... WilliamCarson 2 82+
(William Muir) *awkward s: hld up and wl off the pce: clsd fr 2f out: hmpd on inner 1f out: styd on fnl f to take 2nd last strides* **10/3^{2}**

035 **3** ¾ **Muhdiq (USA)**^{41} 3333 3-8-12 **75** .... DaneO'Neill 1 69+
(Mike Murphy) *disp ld at furious pce: def advantage st: hdd and brushed aside last 150yds: lost 2nd fnl strides* **8/1**

12-0 **4** 2 ½ **Billyrayvalentine (CAN)**^{68} 2509 3-9-2 **84** ....(tp) DavidKenny(5) 7 70
(George Baker) *awkward s: hld up and sn wl off the pce: wd and 6th ent st: tried to cl 2f out: one pce over 1f out* **12/1**

3654 **5** 1 ¼ **Le King Beau (USA)**^{7} 4489 3-8-3 **66** ....(v) KieranO'Neill 3 48
(John Bridger) *tried to trck ldng trio but sn outpcd by them: clsd 2f out: no prog whn bmpd 1f out* **20/1**

0461 **6** 2 ½ **Desert Philosopher**^{43} 3284 3-9-3 **80** .... JamieSpencer 8 54
(Kevin Ryan) *disp ld at furious pce and clr of rest: wd bnd ent st and lost grnd: stl pressing ldr 2f out: wandered and wknd jst over 1f out* **5/2^{1}**

3222 **7** 3 ¾ **Ghost Train (IRE)**^{8} 4468 3-8-8 **71** ....(p) NeilCallan 4 49
(Mark Johnston) *tried to match strides w ldng but could nt: 3rd st: tried to cl 2f out: btn whn hmpd 1f out and eased* **7/2^{3}**

1m 9.85s (0.45) **Going Correction** -0.075s/f (Good) **7** Ran SP% **111.7**
Speed ratings (Par 102): **94,87,86,83,81 78,73**
toteswingers 1&2 £5.80, 1&3 £7.20, 2&3 £5.90 CSF £24.99 CT £157.21 TOTE £8.80: £4.20, £1.50; EX 37.90 Trifecta £182.30 Pool: £3,660.04 - 14.85 winning units..
Owner G C Stevens **Bred** Bgd Breeders **Trained** Blewbury, Oxon
■ Stewards' Enquiry : Amy Scott five-day ban; careless riding (16th-20th Aug)

FOCUS
A useful handicap but an overly strong gallop set the race up for the finishers and this bare form doesn't look reliable.
Desert Philosopher Official explanation: trainer said colt was unsuited by the track.

4724 BRITISH STALLION STUDS SUPPORTING BRITISH RACING E B F MAIDEN STKS 7f
6:55 (6:55) (Class 5) 2-Y-O **£3,881** (£1,155; £577; £288) **Stalls** Low

Form RPR

2 **1** **Law Enforcement (IRE)**^{15} 4222 2-9-3 0 .... DaneO'Neill 2 79
(Richard Hannon) *dwlt: sn w ldr: shkn up 2f out: led over 1f out: rdn to assert ins fnl f: styd on wl* **8/11^{1}**

0 **2** ¾ **Lizzie Tudor**^{21} 4011 2-8-12 0 .... JimmyFortune 4 72
(Andrew Balding) *trckd ldng trio: rdn over 1f out: r.o fnl f to take 2nd nr fin and cl on wnr* **6/1^{3}**

06 **3** ¾ **Imperial Spirit**^{7} 4487 2-9-3 0 .... MatthewDavies 3 75
(Mick Channon) *narrow ldr: shkn up and hdd over 1f out: kpt on but lost 2nd nr fin* **25/1**

4 1 ¾ **Flow (USA)** 2-9-3 0 .... TomQueally 8 72+
(Sir Henry Cecil) *dwlt and veered rt s: in tch in rr: 6th st: prog on outer 2f out: rn green and one pce fr over 1f out: nt disgrcd* **9/2^{2}**

6 **5** 3 ¼ **Lamusawama**^{16} 4194 2-9-3 0 .... NeilCallan 9 62
(Ed Dunlop) *trckd ldrs: 5th and wl in tch st: no imp 2f out: fdd over 1f out* **16/1**

6 nk **Grey Blue (IRE)** 2-9-3 0 .... JoeFanning 5 61
(Mark Johnston) *trckd ldng pair: cl up 2f out: pushed along and wknd over 1f out* **7/1**

50 **7** 10 **Linda's Icon**^{10} 4408 2-8-7 0 .... CharlesBishop(5) 7 30
(Mick Channon) *dwlt: sn detached in rr: 7th st: struggling after* **33/1**

0 **8** 7 **Winslow Arizona (IRE)**^{12} 4340 2-9-3 0 .... JamieSpencer 1 17
(Michael Bell) *s.s: a in last: wl bhd fr 1/2-way* **20/1**

1m 23.69s (0.39) **Going Correction** -0.075s/f (Good) **8** Ran SP% **120.3**
Speed ratings (Par 94): **94,93,92,90,86 86,74,66**
toteswingers 1&2 £1.70, 1&3 £6.90, 2&3 £13.60 CSF £6.01 TOTE £1.70: £1.10, £1.90, £3.90; EX 6.70 Trifecta £74.10 Pool: £5,839.22 - 58.29 winning units..
Owner M S Al Shahi **Bred** Mrs E J O'Grady **Trained** East Everleigh, Wilts

FOCUS
A fair maiden but, while the gallop was ordinary, this race should throw up a winner or two. The form is straightforward with the winner the best guide.

NOTEBOOK
Law Enforcement(IRE) ◆, who created a pleasing impression on his debut, had the run of the race and didn't have to match that form after racing with the choke out to beat two rivals who had previously only shown modest form at best. However, he's in good hands, will be suited by 1m and is capable of better. (op 4-6)
Lizzie Tudor, who wasn't disgraced at Newmarket over 6f in soft ground on her debut, stepped up on that level over this longer trip on this quicker ground. She's likely to remain vulnerable against the better types in this grade but should be able to win a race at some point. (tchd 7-1)
Imperial Spirit, returned to 7f, is a progressive individual who had the run of the race and turned in his best effort yet. The switch to ordinary nursery company may provide him with his best chance of success.
Flow(USA) ◆ was too green to do himself justice but caught the eye at a course that didn't appear ideal on this debut and is the one to take from the race. This half-brother to the smart Ea is out of a Lowther winner and it wouldn't surprise to see him step up significantly on a more conventional track next time. (op 5-1 tchd 4-1)
Lamusawama failed to step up on his debut form in soft ground but he should be able to fare better over further once he's qualified for a handicap mark.
Grey Blue(IRE), a half-brother to useful Polytrack/turf 7f winner Baccarat, was fairly easy to back but showed ability for his in-form yard on this debut. It won't surprise to see him leave these bare facts behind at some point. (op 8-1)

4725 TRY TOTEQUICKPICK IF YOU'RE FEELING LUCKY CONDITIONS STKS 1m 2f 18y
7:30 (7:31) (Class 3) 3-Y-O+ **£6,847** (£2,050; £1,025; £512; £256) **Stalls** Low

Form RPR

-132 **1** **Cameron Highland (IRE)**^{33} 3630 3-8-8 **106** .... NeilCallan 5 103+
(Roger Varian) *led 3f: trckd ldr: shkn up to ld again 2f out: rdn and wl in command after* **6/4^{1}**

3020 **2** 4 ½ **Ottoman Empire (FR)**^{41} 3329 6-9-0 **102** .... JamieSpencer 4 91
(David Simcock) *chsd ldr: led after 3f: edgd rt and hdd 2f out: one pce and readily hld after* **5/2^{3}**

1 **3** 3 ¼ **Nadema Rose (IRE)**^{22} 3975 3-8-0 69 .... KieranO'Neill 2 80?
(Anthony Carson) *chsd ldng pair: clsd enough 3f out: shkn up and outpcd over 2f out: one pce after* **22/1**

253 **4** 3 ½ **Invisible Man**^{20} 4074 6-9-0 107 ....(b) SilvestreDeSousa 3 78
(Saeed Bin Suroor) *hld up in 4th: cl enough 3f out: sn rdn and nt qckn: wl btn fnl 2f* **2/1^{2}**

0636 **5** 12 **Thecornishcockney**^{23} 3946 3-8-5 68 .... DaraghO'Donohoe 1 54
(John Ryan) *dwlt: a in last: lost tch fr 1/2-way* **100/1**

2m 6.53s (-3.17) **Going Correction** -0.075s/f (Good)
WFA 3 from 6yo 9lb **5** Ran SP% **107.2**
Speed ratings (Par 107): **109,105,102,100,90**
CSF £5.27 TOTE £2.40: £1.30, £1.60; EX 5.10.
Owner H R H Sultan Ahmad Shah **Bred** Epona Bloodstock Ltd **Trained** Newmarket, Suffolk

FOCUS
Three smart performers in a decent conditions event but a modest gallop and the proximity of the 69-rated third means this bare form may not be entirely reliable.

NOTEBOOK
Cameron Highland(IRE), a progressive sort, was happy to take a lead and ran up to his best in a race run at just an ordinary gallop to win with something in hand. He's in good hands and, although this didn't really tell us anything new about him, he remains worth a try in minor Group company. (op Evens)
Ottoman Empire(FR) hadn't been seen to best effect in soft ground at Ascot but conditions here suited much better and he returned to form after enjoying the run of the race. He may not be easy to place in handicaps from his current mark, but should be able to win a similar event away from progressive sorts when conditions are in his favour. (op 11-4 tchd 3-1)
Nadema Rose(IRE), who caused a shock when winning a Yarmouth soft-ground maiden on her debut, ran well in the face of a very stiff task on this quicker ground over this longer trip against these much stronger rivals. Connections were obviously willing to blow what now looks a favourable mark and her short-term future in handicaps now depends on how the handicapper views this race. (op 20-1 tchd 25-1)
Invisible Man was disappointing, even allowing for the fact that a tactical race over this trip was never really going to play to his strengths. A truly run race over 1m on a sound surface are his requirements but he's not one to be taking too short a price about. (op 11-4)
Thecornishcockney, a 16-race maiden who had a very stiff task at the weights, was predictably outclassed.

4726 BRIDGET FILLIES' H'CAP 7f
8:00 (8:00) (Class 5) (0-75,75) 3-Y-O+ **£3,234** (£962; £481; £240) **Stalls** Low

Form RPR

1300 **1** **Avonrose**^{12} 4317 5-9-8 **69** ....(v) NeilCallan 9 77
(Derek Shaw) *trckd ldr 1f: cl 3rd st: led on inner 3f out: sn hrd pressed: edgd rt 1f out: drvn and styd on wl* **10/1**

1214 **2** 1 **Serene Oasis (IRE)**^{5} 4607 3-9-3 **75** ....(v) CharlesBishop(5) 11 78
(Mick Channon) *sn prom: cl 4th st: pressed wnr over 2f out: stl chalng 1f out: styd on but hld after* **3/1^{1}**

0012 **3** ¾ **Rum Punch**^{7} 4509 3-8-12 **65** .... JohnFahy 5 66+
(Eve Johnson Houghton) *nt as wl away as sme: in tch: sltly awkward downhill and 8th st: rdn over 2f out: prog over 1f out: r.o to take 3rd last strides* **5/1^{2}**

1134 **4** ½ **Dark Ages (IRE)**^{10} 4412 3-9-3 **75** ....(t) DavidKenny(5) 1 75
(Paul Burgoyne) *trckd ldrs: 5th st: chsd ldng trio wl over 2f out: styd on ins fnl f: nvr gng pce to chal* **7/1^{3}**

0014 **5** ¾ **National Hope (IRE)**^{14} 4238 4-8-12 **59** ....(tp) LukeMorris 2 59
(George Baker) *racd freely: led to 3f out: w wnr 2f out: fdd ins fnl f* **7/1^{3}**

1644 **6** 4 **Ermyn Flyer**^{21} 3998 3-8-0 **58** .... JemmaMarshall(5) 8 45
(Pat Phelan) *wl in tch: 6th st: pushed along and no imp on ldrs 2f out: eased whn hld ins fnl f* **10/1**

4010 **7** 1 **Jumeirah Palm Star**^{14} 4256 3-9-5 **72** .... DaneO'Neill 12 56
(Richard Hannon) *sn wl in rr: last st: nvr a factor but styd on fr over 1f out* **9/1**

6130 **8** 2 **Esprit Danseur**^{30} 3719 3-8-12 **65** .... PatCosgrave 3 44
(Jim Boyle) *awkward s: wl in rr: 9th st: sme prog on inner over 1f out: n.d* **12/1**

1010 **9** 2 ¼ **Silvee**^{12} 4332 5-9-3 **64** .... KieranO'Neill 4 39
(John Bridger) *hld up wl in rr: 10th st: pushed along over 2f out: no prog* **9/1**

3-20 **10** 13 **Rooknrasbryripple**^{167} 599 3-8-5 **58** .... WilliamCarson 6
(Ralph Smith) *in tch: 7th st: sn rdn and wknd: t.o* **33/1**

-100 **11** ½ **Poker Hospital**^{80} 2136 3-9-5 **72** ....(p) MatthewDavies 10
(John Stimpson) *prog to press ldr after 1f: lost 2nd and wknd rapidly jst over 3f out: t.o* **28/1**

1m 23.62s (0.32) **Going Correction** -0.075s/f (Good)
WFA 3 from 4yo+ 6lb **11** Ran SP% **118.9**
Speed ratings (Par 100): **95,93,93,92,91 87,85,83,81,66 65**
toteswingers 1&2 £6.50, 1&3 £13.70, 2&3 £2.30 CSF £40.54 CT £176.64 TOTE £11.30: £3.60, £1.50, £2.40; EX 37.00 Trifecta £1538.30 Pool: £2,972.84 - 1.43 winning units..
Owner Moorland Racing **Bred** Mrs Mary Taylor **Trained** Sproxton, Leics

FOCUS
A fair fillies' handicap run at just an ordinary gallop. This race favoured those who raced up with the pace and the first five pulled clear.
Avonrose Official explanation: trainer said regarding apparent improvement in form that mare was better suited by strong handling.

4727 CHALK LANE H'CAP 1m 114y
8:30 (8:30) (Class 4) (0-80,79) 3-Y-O+ **£4,528** (£1,347; £673; £336) **Stalls** Low

Form RPR

0300 **1** **Yojimbo (IRE)**^{2} 4689 4-10-0 **79** .... MatthewDavies 5 85
(Mick Channon) *trckd ldr: chal and upsides fr 3f out: impeded over 1f out: drvn and forged to ld last 75yds* **6/5^{1}**

0351 **2** ½ **Halling Dancer**^{13} 4288 3-9-3 **76** .... KierenFox 4 81
(Lee Carter) *led: upped the pce fr 1/2-way: drvn and hung rt over 1f out: hdd and no ex last 75yds* **15/8^{2}**

-646 **3** 1 ¼ **Saslong**^{22} 3976 3-8-8 **67** .... JoeFanning 1 69
(Mark Johnston) *chsd ldng pair: outpcd and rdn 3f out: no imp after tl styd on fnl f: nvr able to chal* **7/1^{3}**

1453 **4** 3 ½ **Final Delivery**^{8} 4457 3-8-7 **66** ....(v^{1}) LukeMorris 3 60
(George Baker) *hld up in last: outpcd fr 3f out: no ch after: tk 4th fnl f* **8/1**

6450 **5** 4 **Salient**^{28} 3774 8-8-6 **62** .... DavidKenny(5) 2 47
(Michael Attwater) *hld up in 4th: rdn and no prog 3f out: n.d after: wknd and eased fnl f* **16/1**

1m 46.46s (0.36) **Going Correction** -0.075s/f (Good)
WFA 3 from 4yo+ 8lb **5** Ran SP% **109.7**
Speed ratings (Par 105): **95,94,93,90,86**
CSF £3.66 TOTE £2.30: £1.50, £1.10; EX 3.60.
Owner Jon and Julia Aisbitt **Bred** Peter Kelly And Ms Wendy Daly **Trained** West Ilsley, Berks

FOCUS
Not a competitive handicap but one in which the two market leaders fought out the finish. The gallop was only a modest one.
T/Plt: £13.20 to a £1 stake. Pool: £57522.34 - 3166.33 winning tickets T/Qpdt: £3.10 to a £1 stake. Pool: £5741.25 - 1367.21 winning tickets JN

4419 FFOS LAS (L-H)
Thursday, August 2

OFFICIAL GOING: Good to soft (soft in places in back straight; 7.6)
Wind: fresh across Weather: cloudy

4728 STRADEY PARK HOTEL NURSERY 5f
5:40 (5:40) (Class 5) (0-75,74) 2-Y-O £2,264 (£673; £336; £168) Stalls Centre

Form RPR
6240 1 **Hot Secret**[13] 4282 2-8-7 67 ThomasBrown(7) 5 72
(Andrew Balding) *wnt to post early: trckd ldr: led wl over 1f out: sn in command: pushed out* 3/1[3]
4532 2 2 ¼ **Indian Affair**[14] 4230 2-9-7 74 IanMongan 6 71
(Milton Bradley) *chsd ldng trio: rdn along 1/2-way: carried sltly rt wl over 1f out: r.o to go 2nd ins fnl f: comf hld by wnr* 15/8[1]
4313 3 2 ¾ **Windforpower (IRE)**[14] 4230 2-9-3 70 (p) RobertWinston 2 57
(Ronald Harris) *chsd ldrs: pushed along 1/2-way: wnt 2nd wl over 1f out: sn rdn and hung rt: one pce and lost 2nd ins fnl f* 5/2[2]
2204 4 4 ½ **Golac**[87] 1904 2-8-11 64 SamHitchcott 7 35
(Mick Channon) *in rr: rdn along and sltly outpcd after 2f: styd on to go 4th towards fin* 9/1
4062 5 ½ **Frosted Off**[12] 4331 2-8-9 62 AdrianNicholls 3 32
(John Spearing) *taken to post early: led: rdn 2f out: sn hdd: hmpd and carried rt over 1f out: sn wknd* 13/2

1m 0.12s (1.82) **Going Correction** +0.25s/f (Good) 5 Ran SP% **111.7**
Speed ratings (Par 94): **95,91,87,79,79**
CSF £9.21 TOTE £2.40: £1.10, £1.70; EX 8.60.
Owner Hot To Trot Racing Club 1 **Bred** Whitsbury Manor Stud **Trained** Kingsclere, Hants

FOCUS
Just five stood their ground in this nursery and they kept a straight course down the middle of the track. The form is straightforward but lacks depth.

NOTEBOOK
Hot Secret didn't get home upped to 6f at Ascot last time and she relished the return to the minimum trip here to get off the mark at the fifth attempt. She showed a good cruising speed to track the leader before putting her seal on the race well over a furlong out and looks an out-and-out speed filly at this stage. Sharp tracks could prove her forte. (op 10-3)
Indian Affair kept on well without every really threatening the speedier winner. He has now run well in defeat in both handicap starts and ought to find a race at some point. (op 13-8 tchd 2-1)
Windforpower(IRE) looked an awkward ride as he hung under pressure but he wasn't good enough on the day anyway. (op 11-4)
Golac, back from an 87-day absence, was always struggling and could never get near the principals. (op 10-1)
Frosted Off dropped away tamely. Official explanation: jockey said gelding hung right-handed. (op 8-1 tchd 6-1)

4729 STRADEY PARK HOTEL MAIDEN STKS 5f
6:10 (6:11) (Class 5) 3-Y-O+ £2,264 (£673; £336) Stalls Centre

Form RPR
2 1 **Silken Express (IRE)**[17] 4144 3-8-12 0 IanMongan 2 73+
(Robert Cowell) *led early: trckd ldr: bmpd wl over 1f out: sn led: rdn and r.o wl* 11/10[1]
0-02 2 1 ½ **Blue Tiger**[31] 3702 3-9-3 72 (t) TedDurcan 4 72
(Saeed Bin Suroor) *trckd his two rivals: wnt 2nd over 1f out: sn rdn and nt run on: hld by wnr thrght fnl f* 11/10[1]
3 9 **Saunta** 3-8-12 0 MartinLane 1 35
(David Simcock) *taken to post early: s.i.s: sn led and racd keenly: edgd lft and bmpd wnr wl over 1f out: sn hdd and qckly in last: wknd* 6/1[2]

59.67s (1.37) **Going Correction** +0.25s/f (Good) 3 Ran SP% **109.5**
Speed ratings (Par 103): **99,96,82**
CSF £2.69 TOTE £2.00; EX 2.40.
Owner Malih Lahej Al Basti **Bred** Redpender Stud Ltd **Trained** Six Mile Bottom, Cambs

FOCUS
Just three runners but the form can be rated around the 72-rated runner-up Blue Tiger.

4730 AARTIC DRIVER CPC/BRITISH STALLION STUDS E B F MAIDEN STKS 6f
6:40 (6:42) (Class 4) 2-Y-O £4,528 (£1,347; £673; £336) Stalls Centre

Form RPR
1 **Bertie Royale** 2-9-3 0 DarryllHolland 7 79+
(J S Moore) *towards rr: nudged along 2f out: last but in tch over 1f out: sn swtchd lft: r.o wl to ld nr fin: readily* 40/1
4 2 ¾ **Dream Cast (IRE)**[14] 4239 2-9-3 0 StevieDonohoe 4 77
(David Simcock) *trckd ldrs: let down to ld over 1f out: rdn ins fnl f: edgd lft and hdd nr fin* 10/1
42 3 ¾ **Sorella Bella (IRE)**[7] 4494 2-8-12 0 SamHitchcott 9 70
(Mick Channon) *chsd ldrs: rdn 2f out: briefly in 2nd ent fnl f: kpt on* 5/2[1]
4 3 ¼ **Isis Blue** 2-9-3 0 JamesMillman 6 65+
(Rod Millman) *s.i.s: in rr: hdwy to chse ldrs over 2f out: sn rdn: kpt on same pce fnl f* 5/1[3]
2 5 1 ¼ **Vincentti (IRE)**[9] 4419 2-9-3 0 RobertWinston 2 61
(Ronald Harris) *cl up: led 2f out: sn hung lft u.p and hdd: fdd fnl f* 3/1[2]
42 6 ½ **Kodatish (IRE)**[17] 4148 2-9-3 0 IanMongan 5 60
(Ronald Harris) *led: rdn over 2f out: sn hdd: fdd fnl f* 16/1
7 1 ¼ **Titled Gent** 2-9-3 0 MartinLane 3 56
(Brian Meehan) *hld up towards rr: clsd over 2f out: ev ch wl over 1f out: sn carried lft and wknd* 5/2[1]

1m 11.89s (1.89) **Going Correction** +0.25s/f (Good) 7 Ran SP% **116.2**
Speed ratings (Par 96): **97,96,95,90,89 88,86**
toteswingers 1&2 £28.70, 1&3 £12.40, 2&3 £3.90 CSF £383.37 TOTE £37.30: £13.10, £1.60; EX 162.40.
Owner Ron Hull **Bred** D Hefin Jones **Trained** Upper Lambourn, Berks

FOCUS
Quite an interesting little maiden featuring a couple of runners with a decent level of form and some interesting newcomers. The form could be worth more than face value.

NOTEBOOK
Bertie Royale stormed through the final furlong from off the pace to make an impressive start to his career. He was still towards the rear as the field fanned out across the track entering the final furlong, but once switched to get a clear run this son of Bertolini picked up strongly to assert in the closing stages and ultimately prove well on top at the finish. He doesn't have any flashy entries but looks quite useful on this evidence. (op 33-1)
Dream Cast(IRE) looked to have put his seal on this when bursting through to take over inside the final furlong, but his run just flattened out close home and he was collared. This was definitely a big step forward from his debut run and he already looks good enough to pocket a maiden before going up in class. (op 15-2 tchd 7-1)
Sorella Bella(IRE), who brought the best form to the table courtesy of her second at Doncaster last time, had every chance having raced close to the pace and she kept battling away to post another solid effort. She qualifies for a mark now but she can win a maiden before going handicapping. (op 3-1 tchd 9-4)
Isis Blue was slowest from the stalls on this first start. He made some late progress and shaped like he'll improve for the experience, while a Mill Reef entry suggests connections are quite sweet on him at home. (op 9-2)
Vincentti(IRE) couldn't build on a promising first run and these easier conditions may have not been ideal. It's still early days and he can bounce back from this back on a sound surface. (op 7-2 tchd 4-1)
Kodatish(IRE) Official explanation: jockey said colt ran too freely.
Titled Gent has some lofty entries for the autumn but he proved a little disappointing, moving up smoothly to hold every chance on the outside before weakening when coming under pressure. He's from a yard whose juveniles tend to take a big step forward from first to second start so even though this wasn't the most promising of debuts, expect him to leave it behind next time. (op 3-1 tchd 7-2)

4731 RED LION AT LLANDYFAELOG KIDWELLY H'CAP 2m (R)
7:15 (7:15) (Class 4) (0-80,78) 4-Y-O+ £4,075 (£1,212; £606; £303) Stalls Low

Form RPR
-026 1 **L Frank Baum (IRE)**[22] 3953 5-9-4 75 MartinLane 6 84
(Bernard Llewellyn) *led after 100yds: qcknd 4f out: sn rdn: jnd 2f out: r.o wl u.p to hold on* 7/1
2304 2 nk **Sugar Hiccup (IRE)**[12] 4326 4-9-1 72 TedDurcan 1 80
(David Simcock) *trckd ldrs: rdn to chal 2f out: sn ev ch: jst hld by wnr* 11/4[1]
3352 3 6 **Ampleforth**[8] 4475 4-8-13 70 (b) StevieDonohoe 4 71
(Ian Williams) *in tch: rdn 4f out: sn outpcd by ldrs: kpt on one pce: wnt 3rd fnl 50yds* 9/2[3]
/212 4 ½ **Our Folly**[42] 3316 4-8-6 63 (t) AndreaAtzeni 7 63
(Stuart Kittow) *led early: trckd ldr: rdn over 2f out: one pce appr fnl f: lost 3rd fnl 50yds* 4/1[2]
0-00 5 8 **Spirit Of Adjisa (IRE)**[70] 2412 8-8-12 76 ThomasBrown(7) 5 67
(Andrew Balding) *forced stall open and s.s: racd keenly early: last but in tch: rdn and outpcd by ldrs over 3f out: wknd over 1f out* 14/1
0013 6 4 ½ **Sansili**[19] 4096 5-8-4 61 (tp) AdrianNicholls 2 46
(Peter Bowen) *hld up towards rr: rdn along over 4f out: sn outpcd by ldrs: wknd over 1f out* 4/1[2]
0-55 7 32 **Praxiteles (IRE)**[16] 4184 8-9-6 77 (tp) CathyGannon 8 24
(Rebecca Curtis) *midfield: dropped to rr after 3f: rdn 4f out: wknd over 2f out: t.o* 10/1

3m 37.75s (7.75) **Going Correction** +0.30s/f (Good) 7 Ran SP% **113.1**
Speed ratings (Par 105): **92,91,88,88,84 82,66**
toteswingers 1&2 £3.00, 1&3 £5.80, 2&3 £4.40 CSF £25.98 CT £95.92 TOTE £10.60: £3.40, £2.10; EX 30.10.
Owner Alex James **Bred** Ballymacoll Stud Farm Ltd **Trained** Fochriw, Caerphilly

FOCUS
The gallop didn't look very strong in this staying contest and that gave the front-running winner first run on his rivals as he lifted the pace on the home turn.

4732 TRUSTMARK DESIGN AND PRINT H'CAP 1m 4f (R)
7:45 (7:46) (Class 3) (0-90,90) 3-Y-O+ £6,792 (£2,021; £1,010; £505) Stalls Low

Form RPR
212 1 **Biographer**[15] 4216 3-9-1 88 TedDurcan 3 99+
(David Lanigan) *trckd ldrs: wnt 2nd 5f out: shkn up over 3f out: drvn 2f out: pressed ldr thrght fnl f: led last strides* 6/4[1]
0-43 2 shd **Ittirad (USA)**[50] 3036 4-9-11 87 AndreaAtzeni 4 98
(Roger Varian) *led: qcknd over 3f out: rdn over 1f out: sn hrd pressed: hdd last strides* 15/8[2]
2522 3 7 **Bayan (IRE)**[14] 4243 3-8-9 82 (b) MartinLane 8 82
(Brian Meehan) *hld up in 4th: rdn and outpcd by ldrs over 3f out: wnt 3rd appr fnl f: no imp on ldng pair* 9/2[3]
0-03 4 9 **Significant Move**[21] 3997 5-9-0 76 (tp) IanMongan 7 61
(Stuart Kittow) *racd keenly: last but in tch: wnt 3rd and rdn over 3f out: sn one pce: wknd and lost 3rd appr fnl f* 9/1
210/ 5 18 **Hunterview**[425] 6736 6-9-7 86 (p) SimonPearce(3) 5 43
(David Pipe) *trckd ldr 7f: rdn and relegated to last over 3f out: sn wknd: t.o* 14/1

2m 42.51s (5.11) **Going Correction** +0.30s/f (Good)
WFA 3 from 4yo+ 11lb 5 Ran SP% **109.6**
Speed ratings (Par 107): **94,93,89,83,71**
CSF £4.55 TOTE £2.70: £1.10, £2.00; EX 5.20.
Owner B E Nielsen **Bred** Bjorn E Nielsen **Trained** Upper Lambourn, Berks

FOCUS
Confidence in the strength of this form is slightly tempered by the fact that Ittirap was allowed to dictate at quite steady fractions and he looked to have given these the slip early in the straight when all of his rivals came off the bridle.

NOTEBOOK
Biographer knuckled down to his task well and deserves a lot of credit for running down the leader in the final strides. He shaped a with a deal of promise in defeat in a warm handicap on the all-weather last time and he took another step up the ladder in beating a decent yardstick who got first run on him here. Connections clearly think he has the potential to leave his current handicap mark well behind given his Great Voltigeur entry and this progressive son of Montjeu looks a Pattern-class performer in the making. (op 5-4)
Ittirad(USA) has some smart handicap form this season and, although he got the run of the race out in front, he has only found a potentially classy colt too strong, with the pair 7l clear. He will surely find a race soon off this sort of mark and he doesn't have to lead. (op 11-4)
Bayan(IRE) found coming from off the pace too tough an ask, but his form has been gradually progressive and connections will be able to find an opening for him soon. He might want better ground. (op 7-2)
Significant Move found this company too hot. (op 17-2)
Hunterview was backpedalling very early in the straight and was nowhere near his best returning from a lengthy absence. (tchd 16-1)

4733 DAVE LLEWELLYN MEMORIAL CELEBRATION H'CAP 1m 4f (R)
8:15 (8:15) (Class 5) (0-75,75) 4-Y-O+ £2,264 (£673; £336; £168) Stalls Low

Form RPR
0-06 1 **Transfer**[28] 3782 7-8-2 56 oh1 AndreaAtzeni 5 67
(Richard Price) *in tch: hdwy to trck ldrs 5f out: rdn 2f out: led ins fnl f: r.o wl* 22/1

3421 **2** *2* **Pandorica**[16] 4183 4-8-2 **63**........(p) DanielMuscutt(7) 7 71
(Bernard Llewellyn) *cl up: led 1/2-way: jnd over 2f out: sn rdn: hdd ins fnl f: sn no ex* **8/1**

13-2 **3** *4 1/2* **Dancing Primo**[20] 4061 6-9-2 **73**........ RyanClark(3) 11 74
(Mark Brisbourne) *trckd ldrs: chal 3f out: sn rdn and ev ch tl one pce fnl f* **2/1**[1]

5206 **4** *2 1/4* **Shabak Hom (IRE)**[4] 3187 5-8-11 **65**........ RichardThomas 4 62
(David Evans) *s.s: bhd: clsd 4f out: sn pushed along: styd on ins fnl f: gng on fin* **25/1**

1303 **5** *3 1/2* **Sand Skier**[8] 4460 5-9-0 **75**........ NicoleNordblad(7) 8 67
(Hans Adielsson) *led to 1/2-way: styd prom: rdn 3f out: sn one pce* **11/4**[2]

0-33 **6** *1 1/4* **Ice Nelly (IRE)**[7] 4505 4-8-12 **66**........ DarryllHolland 6 56
(Hughie Morrison) *a in similar position: rdn over 3f out: no imp on ldrs* **7/2**[3]

0660 **7** *4 1/2* **Sherman McCoy**[12] 4326 6-9-5 **73**........ JamesMillman 1 55
(Rod Millman) *a bhd: lost tch 2f out* **10/1**

0256 **8** *5* **Tijori (IRE)**[16] 4181 4-8-6 **60**........ CathyGannon 9 34
(Bernard Llewellyn) *chsd ldrs tl lost pl 1/2-way: rdn 4f out: wknd 3f out* **25/1**

2m 39.9s (2.50) **Going Correction** +0.30s/f (Good) **8** Ran SP% **114.5**
Speed ratings (Par 103): **103,101,98,97,94 94,91,87**
toteswingers 1&2 £14.60, 1&3 £9.60, 2&3 £4.20 CSF £180.61 CT £513.67 TOTE £45.40: £12.60, £2.30, £1.60; EX 145.80.
Owner G Ivall & R J Price **Bred** Kingsclere Stud **Trained** Ullingswick, H'fords

FOCUS
Run-of-the-mill handicap form but the pace looked reasonable.
Shabak Hom(IRE) Official explanation: trainers representative said gelding was unsuited by going (good to soft - soft in places).
Tijori(IRE) Official explanation: jockey said gelding hung left-handed.

4734 WALTERS UK H'CAP 6f
8:50 (8:51) (Class 6) (0-60,60) 3-Y-O **£1,617** (£481; £240; £120) **Stalls** Centre

Form RPR

-031 **1** **Verus Delicia (IRE)**[9] 4424 3-8-7 **51** 6ex........ MarkCoumbe(5) 10 59
(Daniel Mark Loughnane) *a.p: led wl over 2f out: sn rdn: hld on gamely fnl f* **6/4**[1]

0030 **2** *nk* **Yes It's The Boy (USA)**[31] 3706 3-9-7 **60**........(b) TedDurcan 1 67
(Ed Walker) *swtchd rt s: hld up in rr: hdwy over 2f out: drvn and ev ch fnl f: jst hld* **8/1**

40-0 **3** *1 3/4* **Roman Myst (IRE)**[21] 4003 3-9-0 **60**........ ThomasBrown(7) 3 61
(Sylvester Kirk) *chsd ldrs: ev ch over 1f out: sn one pce* **6/1**[3]

6-05 **4** *3/4* **Gypsy Rider**[36] 3489 3-9-2 **55**........ AdrianNicholls 9 54
(Bryn Palling) *racd keenly: in tch: swtchd lft over 1f out: r.o ins fnl f* **10/1**

0000 **5** *1 1/2* **Boragh Waters (IRE)**[9] 4424 3-8-7 **46** oh1........(t) MartinLane 12 40
(Brian Meehan) *sn chsng ldrs: rdn and unable qck 1/2-way: styd on ins fnl f* **33/1**

0004 **6** *1* **Compton Crofter**[16] 4185 3-8-6 **52**........(t) NicoleNordblad(7) 5 43
(Hans Adielsson) *in tch: outpcd by ldrs 1/2-way: kpt on same pce fnl 2f* **12/1**

7 *2 1/4* **Strategic Heights (IRE)**[27] 3841 3-8-7 **46** oh1........(b[1]) AndreaAtzeni 6 30
(Liam McAteer, Ire) *chsd ldrs tl wknd over 1f out* **20/1**

0-06 **8** *hd* **Princess Of Rock**[12] 4341 3-8-12 **51**........ SamHitchcott 13 34
(Mick Channon) *a towards rr* **9/2**[2]

4065 **9** *4 1/2* **Uncle Timmy**[16] 4197 3-8-12 **56**........(tp) NathanSweeney(5) 4 25
(David Evans) *led tl wl over 2f out: wknd over 1f out* **10/1**

4-00 **10** *2 1/4* **Hawaiian Freeze**[30] 3717 3-8-4 **46** oh1........ SimonPearce(3) 7
(John Stimpson) *midfield: rdn and dropped to rr 3f out: bhd fnl 2f* **40/1**

1m 11.66s (1.66) **Going Correction** +0.25s/f (Good) **10** Ran SP% **119.6**
Speed ratings (Par 98): **98,97,95,94,92 90,87,87,81,78**
toteswingers 1&2 £4.30, 1&3 £3.30, 2&3 £7.10 CSF £14.52 CT £61.04 TOTE £2.90: £1.60, £2.50, £1.50; EX 20.50.
Owner G J McGuinness & J Corcoran **Bred** R Fagan **Trained** Baldwin's Gate, Staffs

FOCUS
A weak handicap.
T/Plt: £419.50 to a £1 stake. Pool: £45350.31 - 78.90 winning tickets T/Qpdt: £81.70 to a £1 stake. Pool: £6177.42 - 55.90 winning tickets RL

4697 GOODWOOD (R-H)
Thursday, August 2

OFFICIAL GOING: Good (8.2)
Wind: fresh, against Weather: bright spells and showers

4735 BETFRED THE BONUS KING STKS (H'CAP) 1m 1f 192y
2:15 (2:17) (Class 2) 3-Y-O
£28,012 (£8,388; £4,194; £2,097; £1,048; £526) **Stalls** Low

Form RPR

4120 **1** **Grandeur (IRE)**[42] 3295 3-9-7 **99**........ WilliamBuick 16 109
(Jeremy Noseda) *t.k.h: hld up in tch: rdn and hdwy to press ldrs over 2f out: led over 1f out: clr and edgd rt ins fnl f: r.o wl* **8/1**

0400 **2** *1 3/4* **Switzerland (IRE)**[12] 4339 3-8-10 **88**........ NeilCallan 2 95
(Mark Johnston) *hld up in tch towards rr: nt clr run wl over 2f out: edging rt and hdwy 2f out: chsd ldrs 1f out: styd on wl to go 2nd cl home* **25/1**

32-1 **3** *shd* **Blue Surf**[31] 3703 3-8-7 **85** ow1........ PatDobbs 15 91
(Amanda Perrett) *in tch in midfield: wd and lost pl on bnd 5f out: hdwy on outer over 2f out: rdn ent fnl f: styd on wl to go 3rd last strides* **14/1**

1105 **4** *hd* **Fennell Bay (IRE)**[14] 4261 3-8-13 **91**........ JoeFanning 18 97
(Mark Johnston) *broke fast but awkwardly: chsd ldrs: rdn to chse ldr 3f out: led over 2f out tl 2f out: chsd wnr over 1f out: styd on one pce fnl f: lost 2 pls cl home* **16/1**

-353 **5** *1 1/2* **Devine Guest (IRE)**[33] 3606 3-7-10 **79**........ DarrenEgan(5) 9 82
(Mick Channon) *hld up in tch towards rr: rdn and effrt over 2f out: hdwy and edging rt over 1f out: kpt on ins fnl f: nt rch ldrs* **33/1**

0012 **6** *1/2* **Prussian**[5] 4596 3-8-11 **89**........ SilvestreDeSousa 1 91+
(Mark Johnston) *in tch towards rr: hdwy and edging rt 2f out: kpt on ins fnl f: nvr quite gng pce to chal ldrs* **15/2**[3]

0104 **7** *1 1/2* **Chapter Seven**[19] 4097 3-9-0 **92**........(p) PaulHanagan 11 91
(Richard Fahey) *bhd and sn pushed along: edging rt but hdwy past btn horses over 1f out: kpt on but no threat to ldrs fnl f* **25/1**

6551 **8** *nse* **Sheila's Buddy**[15] 4224 3-7-5 **76** oh1........ NoelGarbutt(7) 10 75
(J S Moore) *in tch: rdn and hdwy to press ldrs 3f out: led 2f out tl over 1f out: no ex ins fnl f: wknd fnl 100yds* **50/1**

2610 **9** *1 1/2* **Wrotham Heath**[42] 3295 3-9-3 **95**........ TomQueally 7 91
(Sir Henry Cecil) *stdd s: t.k.h: hld up in tch towards rr: hdwy in to midfield 5f out: rdn and effrt to chse ldrs over 2f out: wknd ent fnl f* **7/1**[2]

1154 **10** *6* **Pilgrims Rest (IRE)**[21] 4009 3-8-8 **86**........ JimCrowley 8 70
(Richard Hannon) *t.k.h: hld up wl in tch: rdn and effrt on inner to press ldrs 3f out: sn unable qck u.p: wknd over 1f out* **12/1**

2323 **11** *3/4* **Sir Mike**[15] 4223 3-8-3 **81**........(p) LukeMorris 4 63
(Amanda Perrett) *hld up in tch in midfield: swtchd rt and effrt on inner over 2f out: no ex 2f out: wknd over 1f out* **25/1**

2012 **12** *3 3/4* **Queen's Estate (GER)**[8] 4459 3-7-12 **76**........ NickyMackay 14 51
(Mark Johnston) *sn chsng ldr: rdn to ld ent fnl 3f: hdd over 2f out: sn wknd* **33/1**

-151 **13** *3 3/4* **Opinion (IRE)**[47] 3156 3-8-12 **90**........ RyanMoore 5 57+
(Sir Michael Stoute) *hld up in tch in midfield: stl gng wl enough whn short of room and hmpd ent fnl 2f: nt rcvr and n.d after* **8/1**

11-1 **14** *7* **Asatir (USA)**[32] 3667 3-9-2 **94**........ FrankieDettori 17 47
(Saeed Bin Suroor) *chsd ldrs: rdn and effrt to chal 3f out: struggling u.p: wknd 2f out: bhd and eased ins fnl f* **6/1**[1]

0152 **15** *2 1/4* **Beaufort Twelve**[32] 3668 3-9-1 **93**........ KierenFallon 3 42
(William Jarvis) *in tch towards rr: effrt on inner 3f out: no imp over 2f out: wl btn and eased ins fnl f* **10/1**

1311 **16** *2 1/4* **Hefner (IRE)**[13] 4287 3-8-12 **90**........ RichardHughes 12 34
(Richard Hannon) *chsd ldrs: effrt on inner and ev ch ent fnl 3f: struggling and losing pl whn hmpd ent fnl 2f: wl btn after: eased ins fnl f* **14/1**

2-12 **17** *3* **Hallings Comet**[20] 4068 3-8-5 **83**........ FrannyNorton 13 21
(Andrew Balding) *t.k.h: sn led and clr after 1f: hdd ent fnl 3f: sn dropped out and bhd: eased ins fnl f: t.o* **12/1**

0400 **18** *1 1/2* **Sir Glanton (IRE)**[8] 4473 3-8-2 **80**........ KieranO'Neill 6 15
(Amanda Perrett) *a in rr: rdn and no rspnse over 3f out: bhd and eased ins fnl f: t.o* **100/1**

2m 7.09s (-1.01) **Going Correction** +0.05s/f (Good) **18** Ran SP% **124.8**
Speed ratings (Par 106): **106,104,104,104,103 102,101,101,100,95 94,91,88,83,81 79,77,76**
toteswingers 1&2 £58.10, 1&3 £31.60, 2&3 £103.50 CSF £205.14 CT £2774.17 TOTE £9.30: £2.80, £6.60, £3.60, £5.60; EX 281.40 Trifecta £2267.40 Pool: £3,676.99 - 1.20 winning units..
Owner Miss Yvonne Jacques **Bred** Mrs Cherry Faeste **Trained** Newmarket, Suffolk

FOCUS
Lower bend dolled out 6yds from 6f to the Winning Post increasing distances by about 10yds. Top bend dolled out 3yds adding about 5yds. False rail up inside of track for last 3.5f removed to give 6m of fresh ground up straight. A decent handicap, run at a decent pace and the form should stack up. The third and fifth look the best guides to the level.

NOTEBOOK
Grandeur(IRE) probably found the softening ground against him in the Tercentenary Stakes at Royal Ascot last time, but was in decent form in handicaps before that, including a win over this C&D. He bounced right back to form here with an impressive success, especially considering his wide draw, but although he has now won here twice and once at Brighton, the way he hung to his right once in front inside the last furlong suggests he doesn't necessarily need an undulating track. He will probably have to move up into Listed company now, though the Cambridgeshire could be a possibility. (op 10-1)
Switzerland(IRE) was having his 12th start of 2012 and didn't convince in one previous try at the trip. He hadn't been in great form lately either, but he came from well off the pace to grab a fine second and fare best of the Johnston quartet, thereby confirming just how the stable's runners thrive on their racing. If he can repeat this, a decent handicap can be found. (tchd 33-1 in places)
Blue Surf had been gelded before overcoming a 310-day absence to make a winning handicap debut over this trip at Windsor last month. Raised 4lb for that and carrying another 1lb in overweight, he was another to come from well off the pace and made his effort wide. However, he was inclined to hang in behind his rivals when coming with his effort and was never quite getting there. This was only his fifth start, so he can be given the benefit of the doubt.
Fennell Bay(IRE) put some modest efforts behind him here having twice been well beaten since winning the King George V Handicap at Royal Ascot off 6lb lower. Another to make his effort out wide, having started from the outside stall, he had every chance until the winner pounced and came right back to his best.
Devine Guest(IRE) ◆ was making her handicap debut after showing some ability in three maidens over this trip and ran a blinder in this hot contest against several much more experienced rivals. She was given plenty to do, but stayed on well inside the final 2f, and with the possibility of further improvement, she can surely win a race before too long. (tchd 40-1 in places)
Prussian, another representing the Johnston yard and having his tenth start of 2012, didn't have a lot of room to play with from over 2f out and would have finished a bit closer otherwise. She is already due to go up another pound. (op 7-1)
Chapter Seven, sporting first-time cheekpieces, had finished well beaten in his only previous try over this far and seemed to be ridden with that in mind. Set plenty to do, he finished well but all too late, though in fairness he has looked best on softer ground. (op 33-1)
Sheila's Buddy, having his 18th career start, was off a 5lb higher mark than when winning narrowly at Sandown last month, but he ran well in this much better company and was in with a chance over a furlong from home before his effort flattened out.
Wrotham Heath went off too quick when well beaten in the Tercentenary Stakes at Royal Ascot last time (behind Grandeur), but was closely matched with that rival on previous Epsom running. On that basis he should have done better here, but he was held up this time and only made limited late headway. (op 8-1)
Asatir(USA) came into this 3-3 (never winning by more than half a length), with each appearance well spaced out, but this was his first try beyond 1m and he ran like a horse who failed to stay. (op 13-2)
Hallings Comet Official explanation: jockey said colt ran too free.

4736 AUDI RICHMOND STKS (GROUP 2) (C&G) 6f
2:45 (2:47) (Class 1) 2-Y-O
£39,697 (£15,050; £7,532; £3,752; £1,883; £945) **Stalls** High

Form RPR

1200 **1** **Heavy Metal**[21] 4008 2-9-0 95........ JoeFanning 5 110
(Mark Johnston) *chsd ldr tl led over 2f: drvn ent fnl f: styd on gamely fnl f* **9/1**

5101 **2** *1/2* **Master Of War**[20] 4058 2-9-0 99........ RichardHughes 2 108
(Richard Hannon) *t.k.h: hld up in tch in last trio: rdn and hdwy to chse wnr jst over 1f out: pressed wnr ins fnl f: r.o wl but a hld* **3/1**[2]

5116 **3** *2* **Cay Verde**[42] 3291 2-9-0 103........ WilliamBuick 7 102
(Mick Channon) *wanting to hang rt thrght: chsd ldrs and racd against stands' rail: rdn 2f out: chsd ldng pair and stl edging rt ins fnl f: styd on same pce* **4/1**[3]

21 **4** *nk* **Ginger Goose**[14] 4257 2-9-0 0........ TonyHamilton 3 101
(Richard Fahey) *in tch but sn niggled along: rdn and chsd ldrs over 1f out: no ex and styd on same pce fnl f* **16/1**

1414 **5** *1* **Euxton Hall (IRE)**[20] 4058 2-9-0 93........ PaulHanagan 8 99
(Richard Fahey) *led tl hdd and rdn over 2f out: no ex u.p over 1f out: one pce fnl f and wl hld whn short of room and eased nr fin* **14/1**

4204 **6** *1 1/4* **Top Boy**[19] 4093 2-9-0 101........ WilliamCarson 1 94
(Derek Shaw) *stdd s: t.k.h: hld up in rr: swtchd rt over 2f out: rdn and hdwy to chse ldrs over 1f out: no ex 1f out: wknd fnl 100yds* **14/1**

153 **7** *2* **Ahern**[21] 4008 2-9-0 107........ JamieSpencer 4 88
(David Barron) *hld up in last pair: swtchd rt and effrt u.p over 1f out: swtchd rt again and no prog 1f out: wl hld after and wl ins fnl f* **15/8**[1]

01 **8** *13* **Secret Sign**[33] 3638 2-9-0 75 .... KierenFallon 6 49
(Brian Meehan) *chsd ldrs tl over 2f out: sn lost pl: bhd 1f out: eased ins fnl f* **20/1**

1m 11.41s (-0.79) **Going Correction** -0.125s/f (Firm) **8** Ran SP% **113.8**
Speed ratings (Par 106): **100,99,96,96,94 93,90,73**
toteswingers 1&2 £5.60, 1&3 £7.00, 2&3 £3.10 CSF £35.84 TOTE £11.30: £2.60, £1.50, £1.80; EX 43.70 Trifecta £218.50 Pool: £6,202.59 - 20.99 winning units..

Owner Sheikh Hamdan Bin Mohammed Al Maktoum **Bred** Darley **Trained** Middleham Moor, N Yorks

FOCUS
An average running with, somewhat unusually, no unbeaten 2-y-o lining up. There was a solid enough pace on and the main action came just off the stands' rail late on. The placed horses, both Listed winners, set the level.

NOTEBOOK
Heavy Metal finished last behind the strongly fancied Ahern in the July Stakes 21 days earlier and had blown out in the Coventry the time before. This better ground was much more to his liking, however, and he landed a third career success in tenacious fashion. It's not simple to work out where this resurgence came from, but his uncomplicated running style was well suited to this course and his trainer's horses could hardly be in much better form (fourth winner of the meeting so far). This was obviously a personal-best effort and his attitude will continue to hold him in decent stead, but he's not going to prove simple to place successfully again from now on. (op 10-1)

Master Of War lacked the class of Richard Hannon's recent winners Harbour Watch and Libranno, but arrived at the top of his game after winning in Listed company at Newbury last time out. He threw down a serious challenge to the winner from the furlong marker, but was always just being held and, while he too recorded a personal best, this looks as good as he is. His trainer later added a seventh furlong is likely to see him peak, though. (op 10-3 tchd 7-2 in places)

Cay Verde was put in his place in the Norfolk Stakes at Royal Ascot on his previous outing, but his trainer's 2-y-os continue to go well and it was possible the extra furlong may bring about improvement. He travelled nicely against the stands' rail, but couldn't quicken sufficiently when asked for everything. This easy 6f was fine for him and he remains in good heart, but he too is not the easiest to place now. (tchd 9-2)

Ginger Goose, who won a maiden by a short-head at Hamilton a fortnight earlier, looked his stable's second string but didn't go without support on this big step up in class. He felt the pinch some way out wide of runners, but kept digging in under pressure and wasn't at all disgraced. His trainer can place him to resume winning ways before long. (op 20-1)

Euxton Hall(IRE), the choice of Paul Hanagan, has now been held behind the winner and runner-up both times he has met them. He therefore is another that helps to set the standard of this form. (tchd 12-1)

Top Boy posted a very creditable effort at Newbury in the Super Sprint last month and, while still a maiden, wasn't at all without hope according to official figures on this debut in Group company. He covered plenty of ground through the race and fully deserves to take advantage of a confidence-booster down in class. (tchd 16-1 in places)

Ahern set the standard on previous form and was well backed. Jamie Spencer buried him early on the stands' rail and angled him out for a challenge passing the 2f marker. It was soon apparent he was done with and surely something went amiss. (tchd 7-4 and 2-1)

Secret Sign is from a yard that has twice previously taken this event. He was firmly outclassed, but refusing to settle hampered his cause. (op 22-1 tchd 18-1, 25-1 in a place)

4737 ARTEMIS GOODWOOD CUP (BRITISH CHAMPIONS SERIES) (GROUP 2) 2m

3:15 (3:17) (Class 1) 3-Y-O+

£56,710 (£21,500; £10,760; £5,360; £2,690; £1,350) **Stalls** High

Form RPR

1-23 **1** **Saddler's Rock (IRE)**[42] 3293 4-9-7 114 ....(t) JohnnyMurtagh 10 115+
(John M Oxx, Ire) *chsd clr ldng pair: clsd 6f out: rdn to chse ldr over 2f out: led and drvn over 1f out: kpt on gamely u.p and a doing enough fnl f* **2/1**[1]

-654 **2** *1* **Askar Tau (FR)**[26] 3881 7-9-7 110 ....(v) GeorgeBaker 5 113
(Marcus Tregoning) *hld up wl off the pce in last trio: rdn and stl plenty to do 3f out: hdwy and hanging rt jst over 1f out: swtchd lft ins fnl f: styd on wl to chse wnr fnl 50yds* **25/1**

3-11 **3** *¾* **Colour Vision (FR)**[42] 3293 4-9-11 117 .... FrankieDettori 7 116
(Saeed Bin Suroor) *prom in main gp: rdn and effrt over 3f out: clsd on ldrs u.p over 1f out: chsd wnr fnl 100yds: hanging rt and one pce after: lost 2nd fnl 50yds* **5/2**[2]

1550 **4** *¾* **Electrolyser (IRE)**[26] 3881 7-9-7 108 .... AdamKirby 2 112
(Clive Cox) *chsd ldr and clr of field: rdn to ld over 3f out: hdd over 1f out: battled on wl but one pce after: lost 2 pls fnl 100yds* **66/1**

0-33 **5** *1 ¼* **Chiberta King**[26] 3881 6-9-7 108 ....(p) JimmyFortune 6 110
(Andrew Balding) *led and clr w rival: hdd and rdn over 3f out: 3rd and stl chsng ldrs over 1f out: no ex and one pce fnl f* **33/1**

0-11 **6** *¾* **Simenon (IRE)**[40] 3373 5-9-7 106 .... RyanMoore 8 109
(W P Mullins, Ire) *racd off the pce in midfield: rdn and effrt over 3f out: styd on u.p and chsng ldrs over 1f out: edgd rt 1f out and one pce fnl f* **4/1**[3]

5-44 **7** *nk* **Times Up**[63] 2639 6-9-7 109 .... EddieAhern 4 111+
(John Dunlop) *racd off the pce in midfield: rdn and effrt on inner over 3f out: kpt on u.p and chsng ldrs over 1f out: keeping on same pce whn nt clr run fnl 100yds* **16/1**

6-42 **8** *1 ¾* **Lost In The Moment (IRE)**[39] 3418 5-9-7 111 .....(p) SilvestreDeSousa 3 107
(Saeed Bin Suroor) *hld up wl off the pce in rr: 8th and stl wl off the pce over 2f out: hdwy and edging rt over 1f out: kpt on fnl f: nvr trbld ldrs* **8/1**

4-36 **9** *17* **Nehaam**[42] 3293 6-9-7 110 .... PaulHanagan 9 86
(John Gosden) *hld up wl off the pce in last trio: rdn and no hdwy 3f out: wl btn and edgd rt 2f out: eased fnl f* **16/1**

-042 **10** *32* **Aaim To Prosper (IRE)**[26] 3881 8-9-7 107 .... NeilCallan 1
(Brian Meehan) *awkward leaving stalls and slowly away: bhd tl hdwy 12f out: clsd to chse ldrs 6f out: rdn over 4f out: lost pl qckly over 3f out: losing tch whn hmpd 2f out: eased after: t.o* **50/1**

3m 30.83s (1.83) **Going Correction** +0.05s/f (Good) **10** Ran SP% **115.0**
Speed ratings (Par 115): **97,96,96,95,95 94,94,93,85,69**
toteswingers 1&2 £11.50, 1&3 £2.00, 2&3 £12.80 CSF £58.62 TOTE £3.20: £1.30, £5.50, £1.40; EX 58.10 Trifecta £151.20 Pool: £5,106.43 - 24.98 winning units..

Owner Michael O'Flynn **Bred** Rockfield Farm **Trained** Currabeg, Co Kildare

FOCUS
An absorbing Goodwood Cup. The early pace was decent and, while the leaders slowed up on the far side and the overall time was moderate, it provided a fair test. The second is rated to his old best while the third is not far off his Ascot mark under a penalty.

NOTEBOOK
Saddler's Rock(IRE) showed his true colours again and landed a career-best in ready fashion. He was undone by the tactical nature of the Gold Cup at Royal Ascot last time, but the early fractions back down in trip proved right up his street and Johnny Murtagh got the tactics spot on. He was ideally placed when the tempo became serious at the top of the home straight and was never in serious danger after taking it up near the final furlong. Interestingly, Murtagh later said he felt his mount was idling out in front. He's at his best on a sound surface and, still a 4-y-o, the best of him last likely still to be seen considering he's with a master trainer. The Lonsdale Cup at York next month now looks on the cards, and the Irish St Leger is also a possible target. John Oxx won the Prix Du Cadran with Alandi back in 2009 and he later nominated that race on Arc day at Longchamp in October as a likely race to sign off with this season. (op 7-4)

Askar Tau(FR) ran up to his best when coming from off the uneven pace in the Gold Cup, but was below that level down to Listed company at Sandown last time out. There was every chance he would bounce back on this suitably quicker ground, however, and he duly did so, coming from well back in the home straight. He deserves to find another opening, but does find winning hard these days.

Colour Vision(FR) was penalised 4lb for his extra-game success in the Gold Cup over another half mile when just ahead of Saddler's Rock in June, but he too was expected to enjoy this better ground. The race was run to suit, but he didn't appear too comfortable on the track turning for home and, despite rallying bravely, was always being held from 2f out. All considered it was another sterling effort and it will be fascinating to see who comes out on top should he re-oppose the winner, as is expected, later on this season. (op 3-1 tchd 10-3 in places)

Electrolyser(IRE) had found life hard, including when stuffed by Colour Vision on Polytrack, after a Listed success in April. However, he did finish second in this event two years earlier and he returned to near that sort of form with a brave effort.

Chiberta King, well beaten in this last season, had run two creditable races at Sandown since resuming this term, including when one place ahead of Asker Tau last time out. He likes to get on with it and got an aggressive ride, but was hassled throughout by Electrolyser. He gave his all late on and this is about as good as he is.

Simenon(IRE) was an impressive winner of both the Ascot Stakes and Queen Alexandra Stakes at Royal Ascot in June. He was well backed for this, but did have to find up to this class and his effort confirms Group company as being just beyond him. There's a strong chance he'll develop into a classy staying hurdler when reverting to jumps.

Times Up strictly ran close to his last-time-out form with Chiberta King at Sandown when last seen in May. He would have no doubt reversed that form and pushed for a place had he not found trouble on the far rail, though, and that wasn't the place to be so he must be rated better than the bare form. The 6-y-o needs a sound surface and, judging by the way he travelled here, his turn could be nearing again. (tchd 18-1)

Lost In The Moment(IRE) was just edged out by Opinion Poll in this event last season when finding a troubled passage. His running style dictated he found himself with plenty on turning for home and he was never going to trouble the principals. (tchd 9-1)

Nehaam was expected to enjoy reverting to quicker ground, but despite being handed a lot to do from off the pace back down in trip he ran flat. (op 20-1)

Aaim To Prosper(IRE) spoilt his chance by missing the kick as he slipped and then doing too much from halfway to recover into a prominent position. Official explanation: jockey said gelding slipped leaving stalls.

4738 ISHARES FILLIES' STKS (REGISTERED AS THE LILLIE LANGTRY STAKES) (GROUP 3) (F&M) 1m 6f

3:45 (3:49) (Class 1) 3-Y-O+

£31,190 (£11,825; £5,918; £2,948; £1,479; £742) **Stalls** High

Form RPR

150- **1** **Wild Coco (GER)**[350] 5220 4-9-5 113 .... TomQueally 5 109
(Sir Henry Cecil) *t.k.h: hld up in midfield: rdn and effrt to chse ldr 2f out: led over 1f out: clr and pushed out ins fnl f* **6/1**[2]

465- **2** *2 ¾* **Jehannedarc (IRE)**[27] 4-9-5 94 .... AntoineHamelin 8 105
(A De Royer-Dupre, France) *hld up off the pce in last quartet: rdn and gd hdwy on inner 2f out: chsd ldng trio ent fnl f: swtchd lft and styd on wl to snatch 2nd last strides: no threat to wnr* **25/1**

0-11 **3** *hd* **Estimate (IRE)**[41] 3330 3-8-9 105 .... RyanMoore 10 108
(Sir Michael Stoute) *in tch in midfield: rdn over 3f out: hdwy u.p to chse ldr over 2f out tl 2f out: chsd wnr ins fnl f: one pce and lost 2nd last strides* **3/1**[1]

61-1 **4** *1 ¼* **Hawaafez**[75] 2267 4-9-5 106 .... PaulHanagan 1 103
(Marcus Tregoning) *sn led: rdn and fnd ex 3f out: hdd and unable qck over 1f out: styd on same pce after* **3/1**[1]

6063 **5** *6* **Good Morning Star (IRE)**[21] 4007 3-8-6 92 .... JoeFanning 7 95
(Mark Johnston) *hld up in midfield: effrt on inner and n.m.r over 2f out: sn rdn and no imp: one pce and no threat to ldrs fr over 1f out* **22/1**

12 **6** *nse* **Midnight Soprano (IRE)**[32] 3678 5-9-5 103 .... RichardHughes 3 95
(P D Deegan, Ire) *in tch in midfield: hdwy over 3f out: rdn to chse ldrs over 2f out: no ex and btn jst over 1f out: wknd fnl f* **15/2**[3]

6440 **7** *¾* **Twin Soul (IRE)**[44] 3241 4-9-5 85 .... WilliamBuick 2 96
(Andrew Balding) *hld up in midfield: effrt and nt clr run over 2f out: nvr enough room after and lost any ch: kpt on ins fnl f* **40/1**

0341 **8** *¾* **Amaraja (GER)**[28] 3773 3-8-6 83 .... EddieAhern 12 93
(Sir Henry Cecil) *t.k.h: chsd ldr tl 3f out: sn rdn and struggling: btn 2f out: wknd over 1f out* **22/1**

-201 **9** *½* **Hazel Lavery (IRE)**[12] 4338 3-8-6 100 .... WilliamCarson 11 92
(Charles Hills) *hld up wl off the pce in rr: stl plenty to and effrt on outer ent fnl 2f: no real imp: wl btn over 1f out* **6/1**[2]

1012 **10** *½* **Quiz Mistress**[26] 3857 4-9-5 94 .... JimmyFortune 4 91
(Hughie Morrison) *s.i.s: hld up in last quartet: hdwy in to midfield and rdn 3f out: no ex u.p ent fnl 2f: wknd over 1f out* **12/1**

514 **11** *6* **Bolivia (GER)**[12] 4338 6-9-5 91 ....(t) JimCrowley 6 83
(Lucy Wadham) *chsd ldng pair: rdn to chse ldr 3f out tl over 2f out: sn wknd: bhd fnl f* **33/1**

1/5- **12** *62* **Clare Glen (IRE)**[40] 3411 6-9-5 95 .... JamieSpencer 9
(Sarah Dawson, Ire) *stdd s: hld up in last quartet: lost tch and virtually p.u fnl 2f: t.o* **66/1**

3m 3.39s (-0.21) **Going Correction** +0.05s/f (Good)
WFA 3 from 4yo+ 13lb **12** Ran SP% **117.4**
Speed ratings (Par 110): **102,100,100,99,96 96,95,95,95,94 91,55**
toteswingers 1&2 £36.60, 1&3 £5.00, 2&3 £18.90 CSF £152.37 TOTE £8.30: £2.70, £3.20, £1.60; EX 167.70 Trifecta £551.00 Pool: £5,898.24 - 7.92 winning units..

Owner Gestut Rottgen **Bred** Gestut Rottgen **Trained** Newmarket, Suffolk

FOCUS
A competitive staying prize for fillies, run at a sound pace and the form looks pretty solid.

NOTEBOOK
Wild Coco(GER) hadn't been seen since a couple of moderate efforts a year ago, including when an unplaced favourite in this event, but she was by far the best filly in the race on official ratings and, on this evidence, the absence has done her the world of good. Produced with her effort on the wide outside after crossing the intersection, she hit the front over a furlong out and powered clear. The Park Hill at the Doncaster St Leger meeting would seem the obvious target, which would give her a nice amount of time to get over this. (op 5-1)

Jehannedarc(IRE), a winner on heavy ground and Fibresand in France, didn't appear to have the form to figure in a race like this, but her trainer's fillies are always to be respected when he sends one over and she fully justified her place in the line up. Having made her move up the inside rail inside the last 2f, she had to take evasive action to avoid running into the back Hawaafez, but she still got up to grab second which is where she would have finished even with a clear run. (op 20-1)
Estimate(IRE) had improved plenty in all three previous starts and was impressive when winning the Queen's Vase by 5l at the Royal meeting, but that form is not really working out. She became slightly outpaced passing the half-mile pole, but her stamina came into play and she had every chance until outpaced by the winner inside the last furlong. It does seem that even this trip is too sharp for her. (tchd 7-2 and 11-4 in places)
Hawaafez came into this on a hat-trick after wins in a 1m4f Newmarket fillies' handicap and a 1m5f Newbury Listed event. Those successes came after much longer absences than the 75 days she had been away before this, so fitness was never going to be a worry, and although she didn't quite get home after trying to make most, it's unlikely that lack of sharpness was the reason. (op 10-3 tchd 7-2)
Good Morning Star(IRE) was handy early and plugged on again after getting outpaced. (op 25-1)
Midnight Soprano(IRE) proved a revelation when winning five on the bounce in Ireland between October and June (rising 24lb in the process) and lost nothing in defeat when runner-up in the Curragh Cup last time. Her stamina wasn't in doubt either and she looked a real threat when moving into contention starting up the home straight, but she was then done for foot. Perhaps she needs the ground deeper than this. (tchd 13-2)
Twin Soul(IRE), a triple winner on Polytrack, never got into it and is now 0-7 on turf, but she had a mountain to climb on these terms.
Amaraja(GER), the winner's stablemate, looked as though she would appreciate this extra 2f when winning an Epsom maiden last time. She dropped away after racing prominently to the 3f pole, but she is only rated 83 so was right up against it at this level. (op 33-1)
Hazel Lavery(IRE) gave every impression that she would relish this extra 2f when winning a Newmarket Listed event in impressive fashion last month, but having been held up at the back of the field she never got into the race at all and is better than this. (op 15-2 tchd 8-1)
Bolivia(GER) was later found to be in season. Official explanation: trainer said mare was in season. (op 40-1 tchd 50-1)

4739 E B F BRITISH STALLION STUDS NEW HAM MAIDEN FILLIES' STKS 7f

4:20 (4:24) (Class 2) 2-Y-O **£11,320** (£3,368; £1,683; £841) **Stalls** Low

Form				RPR
552	**1**		**Annie's Fortune (IRE)**[10] 4408 2-9-0 0 ... MichaelJMMurphy 13 (Alan Jarvis) *in tch in midfield on outer: rdn and pushed lft jst over 2f out: hdwy u.p over 1f out: led fnl 100yds: r.o strly* **25/1**	83
23	**2**	1 ¼	**Botanica (IRE)**[41] 3339 2-9-0 0 ... RichardHughes 4 (Richard Hannon) *pushed along leaving stalls to r in tch: hdwy u.p jst over 1f out: ev ch briefly fnl 100yds: outpcd by wnr after* **10/3**[2]	80
	3	½	**Arbeel** 2-9-0 0 ... WilliamBuick 20 (Peter Chapple-Hyam) *stdd after s: hld up in rr: stl plenty to do but hdwy whn edgd rt and rn green over 1f out: styng on whn swtchd lft ins fnl f: r.o strly fnl 100yds* **40/1**	78+
2	**4**	nk	**Living The Life (IRE)**[17] 4152 2-9-0 0 ... JamieSpencer 17 (Jamie Osborne) *in tch in outer: hdwy and edgd rt wl over 2f out: sn jnd ldrs and travelled strly: rdn over 1f out: drvn to ld jst ins fnl f: hdd and one pce fnl 100yds* **14/1**	78
4	**5**	1 ¾	**Supernova Heights (IRE)**[21] 4011 2-9-0 0 ... KierenFallon 8 (Brian Meehan) *led for 2f: chsd ldr after tl led again wl over 2f out: hrd drvn over 1f out: hdd jst ins fnl f: no ex and wknd fnl 75yds* **3/1**[1]	73
	6	1 ¼	**Squeeze My Brain (IRE)** 2-9-0 0 ... JimCrowley 1 (Ralph Beckett) *stdd s: t.k.h early and sn chsng ldrs: jnd ldr wl over 2f out: rdn 2f out: edgd lft u.p 1f out: no ex and edgd bk rt ins fnl f: wknd fnl 100yds* **7/1**	70+
	7	nk	**Talqaa** 2-9-0 0 ... MartinHarley 3 (Mick Channon) *in tch: rdn and effrt 2f out: styng on u.p and pressing ldrs whn squeezed for room and snatched up wl ins fnl f: nt rcvr* **33/1**	72+
	8	1	**Ghanaian (FR)** 2-9-0 0 ... MickaelBarzalona 12 (Mahmood Al Zarooni) *stdd after s: hld up in rr: rdn and stl plenty to do whn swtchd lft and rn green over 1f out: styd on wl ins fnl f: nvr trbld ldrs* **10/1**	66+
0	**9**	½	**Olympic Jule**[34] 3590 2-9-0 0 ... JamesDoyle 6 (John Dunlop) *in tch in midfield: rdn and pushed lft over 2f out: no imp over 1f out tl kpt on ins fnl f: unable to chal* **20/1**	65
	10	½	**Polly's Love (IRE)** 2-9-0 0 ... AdamKirby 5 (Clive Cox) *in tch: rdn and struggling to qckn whn wnt lft over 2f out: styd on same pce and no threat to ldrs fr over 1f out* **40/1**	64
3	**11**	¾	**Heading North**[13] 4297 2-9-0 0 ... RyanMoore 19 (Richard Hannon) *stdd s: t.k.h: hld up in rr: hanging rt and sme hdwy over 2f out: kpt on same pce ins fnl f: nvr trbld ldrs* **12/1**	62
	12	hd	**Golden Causeway** 2-9-0 0 ... MichaelHills 10 (Charles Hills) *stdd s: hld up in rr: pushed along 3f out: hdwy on inner rail over 1f out: styng on and chsng ldrs whn gap clsd and snatched up fnl 100yds: lost any ch and nt pushed after* **13/2**[3]	69+
	13	5	**Hermosa Vaquera (IRE)** 2-9-0 0 ... JimmyFortune 7 (Peter Chapple-Hyam) *in tch in midfield: rdn and unable qck ent fnl 2f: wknd over 1f out* **66/1**	48
	14	hd	**Rashfa** 2-9-0 0 ... PaulHanagan 15 (John Dunlop) *s.i.s: bhd: shkn up ent fnl 2f: kpt on same pce after: n.d* **40/1**	48
60	**15**	hd	**Open Letter (IRE)**[54] 2917 2-9-0 0 ... JoeFanning 9 (Mark Johnston) *chsd ldrs: losing pl u.p whn wnt lft jst over 2f out: wknd over 1f out* **25/1**	47
0	**16**	nk	**Sol Diva**[6] 4525 2-9-0 0 ... FrannyNorton 2 (Mick Channon) *dwlt: t.k.h and hdwy to ld after 2f: hdd and rdn wl over 2f out: sn losing pl: wknd wl over 1f out* **66/1**	47
	17	15	**My Gigi** 2-9-0 0 ... TomQueally 18 (Gary Moore) *t.k.h: hld up towards rr: dropped to last over 2f out: sn lost tch* **66/1**	8

1m 29.06s (2.06) **Going Correction** +0.05s/f (Good) **17** Ran SP% **124.6**
Speed ratings (Par 97): **90,88,88,87,85 84,83,82,82,81 80,80,74,74,74 74,56**
toteswingers 1&2 £19.70, 1&3 £54.90, 2&3 £46.60 CSF £102.52 TOTE £31.40: £6.40, £1.90, £11.90; EX 155.60 TRIFECTA Not won..
Owner Cedars Partnership **Bred** Summerhill Bloodstock **Trained** Twyford, Bucks

FOCUS

Often a decent fillies' maiden and previous experience told. The form looks reasonable rated around the second, fifth and ninth.

NOTEBOOK

Annie's Fortune(IRE) had already shown solid form in three 6f maidens and whilst it may be a little disappointing that a race like this was won by the most exposed filly, she did so purely on merit and also did well considering she took quite a bump coming to the last 2f. She produced a nice turn of foot to settle it late on and the longer trip obviously suited, but she will probably need to improve again when she tackles other previous winners. (op 22-1)
Botanica(IRE) had been placed in each of her previous two starts over shorter trips (form of both races working out well) and had every chance again, but she couldn't match the winner for finishing speed. She doesn't seem to be progressing, but now has the option of nurseries. (op 4-1 tchd 9-2 in places)
Arbeel ◆, a half-sister to four winners including the Listed winner Telwaar, is certainly one to take from the race as she was at the back of the field early having started from the worst draw, but she came home in taking style. She would surely finish ahead of the pair in front of her here were they to meet again. (tchd 33-1)
Living The Life(IRE), runner-up in a 6f Wolverhampton maiden on her debut last month despite running green, looked the one to beat when arriving with her effort on the wide outside around 2f from home travelling well, but she lacked a decisive finishing kick and was run out of it. Her Fillies' Mile entry looks optimistic, but she can certainly win races. (op 12-1 tchd 11-1)
Supernova Heights(IRE) finished a very promising fourth of 17 on her Newmarket debut last month and a couple of winners have come out of that race (including the runner-up here the previous day), but despite having every chance she didn't appear to see out the extra furlong. (op 11-4 tchd 7-2 and 4-1 in a place)
Squeeze My Brain(IRE) ◆, a 30,000gns half-sister to four winners at up to 1m6f (one also scored at up to 2m3f over hurdles), did well to hang in there for so long considering how hard she pulled early and it was only well inside the last furlong that she emptied. She is one to note, though her long-term future probably lies over much further. (op 9-1 tchd 13-2)
Talqaa ◆, a £70,000 yearling out of a 1m Listed winner in Canada, ran a promising debut and would have finished even closer had she not been chopped off against the inside rail half a furlong from home. (op 40-1)
Golden Causeway ◆'s effort can be marked up considerably, as she endured a nightmare passage against the inside rail from over 2f out and getting completely shut off well inside the last furlong was the final straw. A 60,000euros filly out of a winning half-sister to the St Leger winner Rule Of Law, she is in the Fillies' Mile and a lot more will be heard of her. (op 8-1)

4740 TATLER STKS (H'CAP) 7f

4:55 (4:56) (Class 2) (0-105,96) 3-Y-O

£12,450 (£3,728; £1,864; £932; £466; £234) **Stalls** Low

Form				RPR
3411	**1**		**Stirring Ballad**[8] 4473 3-8-7 **82** 6ex ... FrannyNorton 6 (Andrew Balding) *hld up wl off the pce in rr: swtchd rt and effrt on inner 2f out: gd hdwy over 1f out: chsd ldrs and swtchd arnd rival ins fnl f: led fnl 100yds: sn clr: r.o strly* **8/1**	97+
0036	**2**	2 ¼	**Arnold Lane (IRE)**[12] 4319 3-9-7 **96** ... MartinHarley 3 (Mick Channon) *hld up off the pce towards rr: hdwy in to midfield 4f out: chsd clr ldng pair wl over 2f out: hdwy u.p over 1f out: swtchd lft and clsd on ldrs over 1f out: pressed ldrs fnl 150yds: one pce after: wnt 2nd towards fin* **10/1**	105
3021	**3**	½	**My Sharona**[28] 3785 3-8-8 **83** ... JamesDoyle 1 (Sylvester Kirk) *chsd clr ldr and clr of field: jnd ldr and stl clr 2f out: rdn and ld jst over 1f out: hdd fnl 100yds and no ex fnl 100yds* **13/2**[2]	91
6512	**4**	nk	**Shamaal Nibras (USA)**[36] 3508 3-9-6 **95** ... RichardHughes 15 (Richard Hannon) *stdd and dropped in bhd after s: hld up wl off the pce: edging rt ent fnl 2f: rdn and hdwy over 1f out: swtchd lft and styd on ins fnl f* **11/2**[1]	102+
4535	**5**	1 ½	**Mr Red Clubs (IRE)**[20] 4063 3-9-6 **95** ... ShaneKelly 5 (Tim Pitt) *racd off the pce in midfield: rdn and effrt over 2f out: styd on u.p over 2f out: no imp ins fnl f* **16/1**	98
2-23	**6**	¾	**Jake's Destiny (IRE)**[19] 4097 3-9-1 **90** ... PatCosgrave 9 (George Baker) *hld up off the pce in midfield: drvn and effrt jst over 2f out: kpt on u.p fnl f: nvr gng pce to rch ldrs* **7/1**[3]	91
1311	**7**	1	**Dutch Rose (IRE)**[20] 4075 3-8-11 **86** ... DanielTudhope 12 (David O'Meara) *racd off the pce in midfield: effrt u.p over 2f out: kpt on fr over 1f out: nvr gng pce to chal ldrs* **10/1**	84
5400	**8**	1 ½	**Lord Ofthe Shadows (IRE)**[42] 3294 3-9-3 **92** ... PatDobbs 7 (Richard Hannon) *racd off the pce in midfield: rdn and effrt over 2f out: kpt on same pce fr over 1f out: nvr trbld ldrs* **16/1**	86
-010	**9**	1	**Hamza (IRE)**[42] 3294 3-9-0 **89** ... (b) TonyHamilton 4 (Kevin Ryan) *sn led and wnt clr: jnd but stl clr of field 2f out: drvn and hdd jst over 1f out: fdd ins fnl f* **25/1**	81
0002	**10**	shd	**Apostle (IRE)**[12] 4317 3-8-12 **92** ... LeonnaMayor(5) 14 (Michael Bell) *hld up wl off the pce in rr: rdn and effrt jst over 2f out: no real prog tl styd on ins fnl f: nvr trbld ldrs* **12/1**	83
00-0	**11**	6	**Diamondhead (IRE)**[20] 4063 3-9-1 **90** ... WilliamBuick 2 (Brian Meehan) *prom in main gp but wl off the pce: rdn and no hdwy over 2f out: wknd 2f out: bhd fnl f* **33/1**	65
6601	**12**	1 ¼	**Campanology**[40] 3393 3-9-0 **89** ... RyanMoore 16 (Richard Hannon) *hld up wl off the pce in rr: rdn and no hdwy over 2f out: n.d* **8/1**	61
5-40	**13**	¾	**Red Art (IRE)**[12] 4319 3-9-5 **94** ... MichaelHills 8 (Charles Hills) *hld up wl off the pce in rr: effrt on inner 3f out: no hdwy and squeezed for room 2f out: wl btn and nt pushed after* **25/1**	64
0050	**14**	1	**Alejandro (IRE)**[33] 3626 3-9-0 **89** ... PaulHanagan 11 (Richard Fahey) *racd off the pce in midfield: rdn and no hdwy over 2f out: sn wknd* **25/1**	56
0040	**15**	20	**Bayleyf (IRE)**[20] 4063 3-9-5 **94** ... LukeMorris 10 (John Best) *chsd clr ldng pair tl wl over 2f out: sn lost pl: wl bhd and eased fr over 1f out: t.o* **50/1**	
2-26	**16**	1 ¼	**Amazing Storm (IRE)**[106] 1457 3-9-2 **91** ... KierenFallon 13 (Jo Hughes) *racd off tha pce in midfield: rdn and no hdwy over 2f out: wknd and bhd 2f out: eased fnl f: t.o* **12/1**	

1m 25.89s (-1.11) **Going Correction** +0.05s/f (Good) **16** Ran SP% **125.2**
Speed ratings (Par 106): **108,105,104,104,102 101,100,99,97,97 90,89,88,87,64 63**
toteswingers 1&2 £17.20, 1&3 £15.00, 2&3 £14.90 CSF £83.16 CT £413.19 TOTE £8.80: £2.30, £2.90, £2.20, £1.90; EX 73.70 Trifecta £489.00 Pool: £2,368.12 - 3.58 winning units..
Owner George Strawbridge **Bred** George Strawbridge **Trained** Kingsclere, Hants

FOCUS

This was a highly competitive 3-y-o handicap. They went hard from the front and it proved a searching test of the distance. Rock-solid form.

NOTEBOOK

Stirring Ballad ◆ landed the hat-trick with an impressive display. She was penalised for her Sandown success last week and took a drift in the market near the off. She looked in trouble 2f out, but connections had worked out the last twice that coming through horses was key to her and ultimately the tricky passage was in her favour. She quickened smartly half a furlong out to seal the issue and is obviously a rapid improver. While the handicapper will now have his say, her trainer is looking forward to racing her back over an extra furlong and it's a decent bet she's not stopped winning yet. Indeed, she could end up Pattern class down the line. (op 6-1 tchd 17-2 and 9-1 in places)
Arnold Lane(IRE) was a sitting duck for the winner, but he moved sweetly through the race and this was an excellent effort under top weight. He's not simple to place, but certainly deserves to go one better again. (op 12-1)
My Sharona, 4lb higher, ran a blinder considering she did so much early on forcing the frantic pace. She has become really consistent and can find less competitive assignments again. (op 8-1)

Shamaal Nibras(USA) was second in a race working out well at Salisbury last time out and was 1lb higher. He wasn't helped by his draw and, with Richard Hughes taking a brave route on the inside, he found some trouble when the winner got the rail run just before him 2f out. He would have been placed for that and remains on an upward curve. (op 13-2 tchd 7-1 in places)
Mr Red Clubs(IRE) arrived in decent heart and this consistent 3yo ran another solid race in defeat. The handicapper probably has his measure now, though.
Jake's Destiny(IRE), well backed, had been placed on his two previous outings this season. He ran well, but ultimately shaped as though the drop back in trip was just too sharp. (op 8-1 tchd 13-2)
Dutch Rose(IRE) was bidding for a fifth success from six outings since resuming for her current yard this year and was up another 7lb. She wasn't disgraced from her double-figure stall and helps to give the form a decent look. (op 8-1)

4741 BETFRED MOBILE LOTTO STKS (H'CAP) 1m 3f
5:25 (5:31) (Class 3) (0-90,88) 3-Y-O

£9,337 (£2,796; £1,398; £699; £349; £175) **Stalls** Low

Form RPR
51-2 **1** **Silver Lime (USA)**[70] 2408 3-9-2 **83** JamesDoyle 10 96+
(Roger Charlton) *hld up towards rr: rdn and hdwy on outer over 2f out: chsd ldr and edgd rt wl over 1f out: str run fnl 100yds to ld last strides* **7/2**[1]

5302 **2** *hd* **Assizes**[12] 4347 3-9-3 **84** SilvestreDeSousa 4 96
(Mark Johnston) *in tch in midfield: hdwy to chse ldrs over 3f out: led over 2f out: rdn 2f out: drvn over 1f out: kpt on wl tl hdd and no ex last strides* **7/1**[2]

21 **3** *hd* **Marshgate Lane (USA)**[20] 4067 3-9-7 **88** MickaelBarzalona 9 100+
(Mahmood Al Zarooni) *s.i.s: hld up towards rr: c wd and hdwy u.p over 2f out: chsd ldng pair 1f out: r.o strly fnl 100yds: nt quite rch ldrs* **10/1**

2130 **4** *3 1/4* **Fortieth And Fifth (IRE)**[26] 3882 3-8-13 **80** LukeMorris 16 86
(Michael Bell) *hld up towards rr: c wd and drvn over 2f out: styd on u.p over 1f out: one pce ins fnl f* **50/1**

1224 **5** *3/4* **Prophesy (IRE)**[12] 4342 3-8-13 **80** DanielTudhope 8 85
(Declan Carroll) *in tch in midfield: hdwy to chse ldrs and rdn over 2f out: no ex over 1f out and btn 1f out: one pce fnl f* **20/1**

01 **6** *3* **Maria's Choice (IRE)**[23] 3946 3-9-2 **83** RyanMoore 6 82+
(Sir Michael Stoute) *hld up in midfield: rdn and effrt over 3f out: styd on same pce and no threat to ldrs fnl 2f* **11/1**

3341 **7** *shd* **Incendiary (IRE)**[24] 3920 3-8-11 **78** MichaelHills 11 77
(Hugo Palmer) *hld up in midfield: rdn and effrt whn squeezed for room and hmpd 2f out: no threat to ldrs and kpt on same pce after* **16/1**

0-11 **8** *1/2* **Clon Brulee (IRE)**[34] 3558 3-8-13 **80** GrahamGibbons 1 78
(David Barron) *in tch: hdwy on inner 3f out: rdn to chse ldrs over 2f out: no ex and btn over 1f out: wknd ent fnl f* **10/1**

31 **9** *hd* **Zamdy Man**[13] 4301 3-9-3 **84** EddieAhern 3 82+
(Venetia Williams) *chsd ldr for 2f: chsd ldrs after tl wnt 2nd again 5f out: rdn over 2f out: losing pl whn short of room and hmpd 2f out: one pce and n.d after* **14/1**

0-02 **10** *1 3/4* **Harlestone Wood**[28] 3786 3-9-2 **83** FrankieDettori 14 78
(John Dunlop) *in tch: rdn to chse ldrs and edgd lft u.p 2f out: struggling to qckn and hmpd wl over 1f out: sn wknd* **16/1**

4121 **11** *1/2* **Ruscello (IRE)**[30] 3737 3-9-0 **81** WilliamBuick 12 75+
(Ed Walker) *t.k.h: hld up in midfield: rdn and effrt whn squeezed for room and hmpd 2f out: no threat to ldrs after* **8/1**[3]

1-65 **12** *2 1/4* **Jupiter Storm**[70] 2408 3-8-11 **78** [1] ShaneKelly 7 68
(Gary Moore) *chsd ldrs tl wnt 2nd after 2f: led 5f out: rdn and hdd over 2f out: wknd wl over 1f out* **14/1**

2125 **13** *1* **Traveller's Tales**[26] 3882 3-8-9 **81** BrendanPowell[(5)] 5 69
(Richard Hannon) *in tch: rdn and unable qck whn short of room and hmpd 2f out: lost pl and wl hld after* **20/1**

012 **14** *2 1/2* **Sondeduro**[31] 3711 3-8-12 **79** FergusSweeney 2 63
(Jamie Osborne) *stdd and dropped out s: hld up in rr: rdn and no hdwy over 2f out: n.d* **25/1**

4212 **15** *1* **Cresta Star**[6] 4543 3-9-0 **81** RichardHughes 15 63
(Richard Hannon) *hld up in rr: switching rt and effrt over 2f out: no real prog: wl btn over 1f out* **14/1**

31- **16** *43* **Hurler And Farmer (IRE)**[261] 7422 3-8-12 **79** PaulHanagan 13
(Richard Fahey) *hdwy to ld after 1f: hdd 5f out: sn racing awkwardly and losing pl: bhd and virtually p.u fnl f* **33/1**

2m 27.91s (1.41) **Going Correction** +0.05s/f (Good) **16** Ran SP% **122.4**
Speed ratings (Par 104): **96,95,95,93,92 90,90,90,90,88 88,86,86,84,83 52**
CSF £23.88 CT £231.93 TOTE £4.00: £1.50, £2.40, £2.50, £10.20; EX 23.20 Trifecta £75.10 Pool: £2,766.39 - 27.23 winning units..
Owner K Abdulla **Bred** Millsec Ltd **Trained** Beckhampton, Wilts
■ Stewards' Enquiry : James Doyle one-day ban; careless riding (16th Aug).

FOCUS
A decent 3-y-o middle-distance handicap, though the pace through the first half-mile looked steady (backed up by the sectionals). The form looks solid with the first three clear.

NOTEBOOK
Silver Lime(USA) ◆ only just failed to get up over 1m1f on his reappearance in May, but given 70 days to get over that (had a bout of coughing) and with the extra 2f to help, he could hardly have left this any later. He still has scope and should develop into a nice middle-distance handicapper. (op 4-1)
Assizes was up 4lb after pulling clear of the third when runner-up at Ripon last month and all but defied the rise. He looked the likely winner when sent for home over 2f out, but despite trying hard he was caught on the line. He lacks the scope of the winner and third, but looks a typically tough sort from the yard and will win more races. (op 13-2)
Marshgate Lane(USA) seemed to improve for the step up to 1m2f when narrowly winning a Newmarket maiden last month and may have been a bit unlucky here as he was slow to break and then hampered early, finding himself with plenty to do. He eventually finished well down the wide outside and may have got there with a little further to go, but it shouldn't be long before he is winning again. (op 15-2 tchd 7-1)
Fortieth And Fifth(IRE) had to switch widest of all for his effort and although he was never getting on terms with the front three, this proved his terrible effort at Sandown last time to be all wrong.
Prophesy(IRE) didn't seem to improve for the step up to 1m2f when fourth of six at Newmarket last time, but he ran a decent race over this extra furlong, especially as he had to change positions a few times from over 2f out in order to see daylight.
Maria's Choice(IRE), back on turf for this handicap debut after justifying favouritism in a Wolverhampton maiden on his second start, was another not to see much daylight over the last couple of furlongs, but he lacked the speed to get himself out of trouble and by the time he did it was much too late. He looks to need an even stiffer test. (op 12-1)
Incendiary(IRE) was still in with some sort of chance prior to being hampered. (op 33-1)
Clon Brulee(IRE), 2-2 since being gelded, was bidding for a hat-trick off 7lb higher and had every chance against the inside rail a quarter of a mile out, but was then done for foot. He is already due another 2lb rise. (tchd 11-1)
Zamdy Man was disappointing as he was in a good position from the start, but looked one paced off the bridle. This was only his third start, however, so he's worth another chance. (op 12-1)
Harlestone Wood, making his handicap debut having been narrowly beaten by a subsequent winner in a 1m4f Newbury maiden last month, was close enough starting up the home straight but had run his race when hampered over a furlong from home. He looks to need more time. (op 14-1)
Sondeduro Official explanation: jockey said colt slipped leaving stalls.
Hurler And Farmer(IRE) Official explanation: jockey said gelding hung left.
T/Jkpt: Not won. T/Plt: £256.20 to a £1 stake. Pool: £286929.10 - 817.48 winning tickets T/Qpdt: £11.80 to a £1 stake. Pool: £15936.32 - 995.68 winning tickets SP

3074 NOTTINGHAM (L-H)
Thursday, August 2

OFFICIAL GOING: Good (good to firm in places in back straight; 8.5)
Wind: Light half against Weather: Cloudy with sunny periods

4742 IRISH STALLION FARMS EBF MAIDEN FILLIES' STKS 6f 15y
2:35 (2:37) (Class 5) 2-Y-O **£3,234** (£962; £481; £240) **Stalls** High

Form RPR
33 **1** **Indignant**[57] 2812 2-9-0 0 SeanLevey 6 84
(Richard Hannon) *led 2f: cl up: led again wl over 1f out: sn rdn and edgd rt: kpt on fnl f* **9/2**[3]

45 **2** *3* **Royal Steps (IRE)**[21] 4011 2-9-0 0 MartinDwyer 11 75
(James Tate) *cl up: led after 2f: rdn along 2f out: sn hdd and kpt on same pce* **10/3**[2]

3 **3** *1 1/2* **Elegant In Silk (USA)**[20] 4055 2-9-0 0 LiamJones 12 71
(William Haggas) *trckd ldrs: hdwy to chse ldng pair over 2f out: rdn and no imp appr fnl f* **17/2**

2 **4** *2* **Burning Dawn (USA)**[21] 3989 2-8-11 0 HarryBentley[(3)] 10 65
(David Brown) *trckd ldrs: pushed along and outpcd 1/2-way: rdn 2f out: sn no imp* **7/4**[1]

5 *3 1/4* **Best To Better (IRE)** 2-9-0 0 SebSanders 5 55
(Marco Botti) *chsd ldrs: rdn along over 2f out: no imp* **33/1**

35 **6** *hd* **Spiritual Girl**[54] 2938 2-9-0 0 HayleyTurner 3 54
(Michael Bell) *wnt bdly lft s and bhd: swtchd towards stands' rail 1/2-way: sn rdn and styd on strly appr fnl f* **20/1**

5 **7** *nk* **Uknowwhatushoulddo (IRE)**[13] 4282 2-8-11 0 RyanPowell[(3)] 4 53
(J S Moore) *towards rr: pushed along 1/2-way: hdwy on outer 2f out: sn rdn and kpt on fnl f* **17/2**

05 **8** *2 3/4* **Constant Dream**[45] 3217 2-9-0 0 GrahamLee 2 45
(James Given) *in tch: rdn along bef 1/2-way: sn wknd* **100/1**

9 *3/4* **Sand Grouse** 2-8-11 0 (b[1]) DominicFox[(3)] 7 43
(Marco Botti) *a towards rr* **25/1**

60 **10** *1 1/4* **Garmelow Girl**[13] 4310 2-9-0 0 PhillipMakin 8 39
(Kevin Ryan) *chsd ldrs to 1/2-way: sn wknd* **66/1**

11 *29* **True Ally** 2-9-0 0 PaddyAspell 9
(John Norton) *a towards rr* **250/1**

1m 13.96s (-0.94) **Going Correction** -0.15s/f (Firm) **11** Ran SP% **113.1**
Speed ratings (Par 91): **100,96,94,91,87 86,86,82,81,80 41**
toteswingers 1&2 £3.10, 1&3 £4.80, 2&3 £5.60 CSF £18.10 TOTE £4.90: £1.80, £1.50, £2.60; EX 21.50.
Owner Theakston Stud Syndicate **Bred** Theakston Stud **Trained** East Everleigh, Wilts

FOCUS
The ground had dried out, with it reckoned to be quicker in the back straight than the home straight. After the opener Liam Jones described it as 'good ground, no jar'. Probably a fair juvenile maiden and they raced stands' side. The placed horses set a sensible level.

NOTEBOOK
Indignant, third on the AW at Kempton on her second start in a race that is working out (second and fourth have won since), scored in convincing fashion and should progress further, especially if stepped up to 7f. (op 5-1 tchd 11-2)
Royal Steps(IRE), from a stable in flying form, showed plenty of pace and her turn will surely come. (tchd 3-1)
Elegant In Silk(USA) had finished third first time in a race at Newbury that is not working out at well. (op 7-1 tchd 9-1)
Burning Dawn(USA) was soon being shuffled along to go the pace. She stuck on in her own time and will be suited by a step up to 7f. (op 9-4 tchd 5-2)
Best To Better(IRE), out of an unraced mare, made a satisfactory debut and the experience will not be lost on her. (op 25-1)
Spiritual Girl, who swerved badly left leaving the stalls, kept on after being outpaced. She will be suited by a step up to 7f in nurseries. (op 14-1 tchd 12-1)
Uknowwhatushoulddo(IRE) completely failed to go the pace and already needs 7f or even 1m. (op 9-1 tchd 8-1)
True Ally Official explanation: jockey said filly hung left-handed.

4743 JOCKEY CLUB CATERING H'CAP 5f 13y
3:05 (3:06) (Class 5) (0-75,75) 3-Y-O+ **£2,264** (£673; £336; £168) **Stalls** High

Form RPR
3013 **1** **Triple Dream**[32] 3660 7-9-10 **73** (tp) RichardKingscote 5 81
(Milton Bradley) *cl up: led wl over 1f out: rdn ent fnl f: kpt on wl* **13/2**[3]

0360 **2** *hd* **Alpha Delta Whisky**[35] 3541 4-9-2 **65** MartinDwyer 11 72
(John Gallagher) *cl up: chal wl over 1f out: sn rdn: ev ch whn edgd persistently lft fnl f: jst hld* **9/2**[2]

6-10 **3** *2* **Bilash**[52] 2982 5-9-4 **67** TadhgO'Shea 6 67
(Reg Hollinshead) *dwlt and in rr: pushed along 1/2-way: hdwy 2f out: sn rdn and styd on strly fnl f* **10/1**

5-4 **4** *shd* **Moorhouse Girl**[41] 3357 5-9-4 **67** PhillipMakin 10 67
(David Brown) *led: rdn along 2f out: sn hdd: drvn and one pce whn n.m.r ins fnl f* **9/2**[2]

0600 **5** *3/4* **Divertimenti (IRE)**[4] 4631 8-9-0 **63** (b) RoystonFfrench 7 60
(Roy Bowring) *trckd ldrs: cl up 1/2-way: rdn and ev ch wl over 1f out: hld whn n.m.r ent fnl f: swtchd lft and one pce after* **7/1**

0356 **6** *shd* **Style And Panache (IRE)**[17] 4146 4-9-2 **65** (p) TomMcLaughlin 4 62
(David Evans) *trckd ldrs: effrt 2f out: sn rdn and no imp* **4/1**[1]

0-00 **7** *hd* **Gottcher**[4] 4631 4-8-11 **65** LMcNiff[(5)] 8 61
(David Barron) *chsd ldrs: rdn along 2f out: kpt on same pce appr fnl f* **14/1**

5300 **8** *5* **Master Of Disguise**[10] 4400 6-9-12 **75** DuranFentiman 3 53
(Brian Baugh) *chsd ldrs: rdn along over 2f out: sn wknd* **15/2**

-300 **9** *1 3/4* **Secret Venue**[6] 4552 6-9-3 **66** GrahamLee 1 38
(Jedd O'Keeffe) *in tch on wd outside: pushed along 1/2-way: wknd over 2f out* **14/1**

1m 0.61s (-0.39) **Going Correction** -0.15s/f (Firm) **9** Ran SP% **116.4**
Speed ratings (Par 103): **97,96,93,93,92 91,91,83,80**
toteswingers 1&2 £4.50, 1&3 £7.00, 2&3 £7.70 CSF £36.14 CT £294.18 TOTE £6.60: £2.20, £2.00, £2.40; EX 33.90.
Owner J M Bradley **Bred** Hesmonds Stud Ltd **Trained** Sedbury, Gloucs

FOCUS
A modest sprint handicap with good recent form thin on the ground.

Bilash Official explanation: jockey said horse was denied a clear run.

4744 JOY JORDAN 1960 ROME FINALIST H'CAP 2m 9y
3:40 (3:40) (Class 6) (0-65,60) 3-Y-O £1,617 (£481; £240 ; £120) Stalls Low

Form RPR
0-00 **1** **Phantom Ranch**[32] 3664 3 -8-8**47** HayleyTurner 10 61
(Hughie Morrison) *prom: trckd ldr after 4f: led 4f out: pushed along 3f out: rdn and edgd lft over 1f out: drvn ins fnl f and hld on gamely* **10/1**

0-10 **2** *nk* **Up Ten Down Two (IRE)** 4498 3 -9-6**59** (t) JamesSullivan 16 72
(Michael Easterby) *a.p: chsd wnr 3f out: rdn to chal 2f out and sn ev ch: drvn ins fnl f: kpt on* **10/3**[1]

0-00 **3** *3* **Zarosa (IRE)**[15] 4214 3 -8-7**46** RobertHavlin 7 56
(John Berry) *trckd ldrs: hdwy over 3f out: rdn to chse ldng pair whn n.m.r and swtchd rt over 1f out: sn drvn and kpt on same pce* **25/1**

-605 **4** *4* **Astonished Harry (GER)**[10] 4399 3 -8-12**51** RussKennemore 1 56
(Reg Hollinshead) *in rr: stdy hdwy over 5f out: effrt to chse ldrs 3f out: rdn 2f out: drvn and one pce appr fnl f* **12/1**

3024 **5** *2 1/2* **Vexillum (IRE)**[10] 4399 3 -9-3**56** SaleemGolam 8 58
(Mick Channon) *hld up in midfield: hdwy over 3f out: rdn to chse ldrs 2f out: sn drvn and kpt on same pce* **6/1**[2]

3336 **6** *1 1/4* **Angel Cake (IRE)**[6] 4538 3 -8-6**45** (p) JamieMackay 9 46
(Phil McEntee) *towards rr: hdwy 4f out: rdn to chse ldrs wl over 2f out: sn drvn and one pce* **16/1**

3601 **7** *2 1/4* **Madam Lilibet (IRE)**[30] 3729 3 -8-12**51** PaddyAspell 14 49
(Sharon Watt) *in rr: rdn along and sme hdwy 3f out: nvr nr ldrs* **12/1**

-605 **8** *9* **Altnaharra**[30] 3729 3 -8-1**45** NeilFarley(5) 2 32
(Jim Goldie) *nvr bttr than midfield* **8/1**[3]

300 **9** *1 1/4* **Native Eight (USA)**[13] 4293 3 -9-7**60** MichaelO'Connell 12 46
(Ian Williams) *swtchd lft s: hld up: a in rr* **14/1**

0005 **10** *shd* **Red Mystique (IRE)**[15] 4214 3 -9-2**55** TomMcLaughlin 13 40
(Ed Dunlop) *hld up: a towards rr* **8/1**[3]

5-36 **11** *2* **Serjeant Buzfuz**[45] 3232 3 -9-7**60** DavidNolan 5 43
(Richard Fahey) *trckd ldrs: effrt 4f out: rdn along 3f out: sn wknd* **14/1**

5606 **12** *1 1/2* **Desert Red (IRE)**[9] 4436 3 -8-10**49** ChrisCatlin 11 30
(Phil McEntee) *led 2f: prom tl rdn along 4f out and sn wknd* **25/1**

005 **13** *2* **Omega Omega**[16] 4188 3 -9-0**53** GrahamLee 15 32
(Julia Feilden) *prom: led after 2f: rdn along and hdd 4f out: wknd 3f out* **33/1**

-006 **14** *28* **Delishuss**[18] 3391 3 -8-2**48** ow3 JoshBaudains(7) 6
(Dominic Ffrench Davis) *a towards rr: bhd and eased fnl 3f* **100/1**

3m 38.25s (7.95) **Going Correction** +0.30s/f (Good) **14**Ran SP% **114.9**
Speed ratings (Par 98): **92,91,90,88,87 86,85,80,80,80 79,78,77,63**
toteswingers 1&2 £5.30, 1&3 £45.30, 2&3 £33.30 CSF £39.82 CT £819.10 TOTE £9.70 : £3.70, £1.10, £8.30 ; EX 33.80 .
Owner Mrs S Rowley-Williams **Bred** Pollards Stables **Trained** East Ilsley, Berks

FOCUS
There was a thunderstorm ahead of this low-grade 3yo stayers' handicap, which was run in heavy rain. Only two of these had previously run over 2m and many were taking a big step up in trip on their handicap bow. The pace was strong and it was a good test of stamina.
Phantom Ranch Official explanation: trainer's representative said regarding geldings apparent improvement in form, that gelding had benefited from a step up in trip in a poorer class of race.

4745 WIN £1000 ON TUESDAY 14TH AUGUST H'CAP 1m 2f 50y
4:15 (4:15) (Class 4) (0-85,85) 3-Y-0+ £4,075 (£1,212; £606 ; £303) Stalls Low

Form RPR
0011 **1** **Gala Casino Star (IRE)**[24] 3906 7 -9-1**79** (v) JordanNason(7) 3 93
(Geoffrey Harker) *trckd ldrs: smooth hdwy 3f out: led wl 2f out and sn clr: readily* **8/1**

3-44 **2** *9* **Minsky Mine (IRE)**[28] 826 5 -8-9**66** JamieMackay 11 63
(Michael Appleby) *cl up: pushed along and sltly outpcd 4f out: rdn and hdwy wl over 2f out: drvn and kpt on appr fnl f: no ch w wnr* **25/1**

1-06 **3** *3/4* **Attenborough (USA)**[70] 2408 3 -8-12**78** FrederikTylicki 2 73
(Jeremy Noseda) *dwlt and towards rr: hdwy 1/2-way: chsd ldrs 4f out: rdn wl over 2f out: kpt on same pce* **7/2**[2]

412 **4** *1/2* **Another For Joe**[24] 3906 4 -9-1**72** GrahamLee 1 67
(Jim Goldie) *sn led: rdn along 3f out: hdd 2f out: drvn over 1f out: kpt on same pce* **11/1**

-033 **5** *2 1/2* **Tamarrud**[14] 4254 3 -8-7**76** HarryBentley(3) 8 66
(Saeed Bin Suroor) *hld up in rr: hdwy on wd outside over 3f out: chsd ldrs over 2f out: sn rdn and btn* **9/4**[1]

-014 **6** *3/4* **Watered Silk**[55] 2887 4 -9-10**81** RichardMullen 7 69
(Marcus Tregoning) *s.i.s and in rr: hdwy on inner 4f out: rdn wl over 2f out: sn no imp* **17/2**

1336 **7** *4* **Amazing Blue Sky**[14] 4249 6 -9-8**79** JamesSullivan 4 60
(Ruth Carr) *prom: rdn along over 3f out: sn wknd* **16/1**

6313 **8** *3* **Paddyfrommenlo (IRE)**[13] 4289 3 -8-13**79** SebSanders 5 54
(J W Hills) *hld up in tch: hdwy to chse ldrs on outer 4f out: rdn along over 3f out: sn wknd* **13/2**[3]

5000 **9** *13* **West End Lad**[36] 3493 9 -9-8**79** (b) RoystonFfrench 10 29
(Roy Bowring) *prom: rdn along 4f out: wknd over 3f out* **22/1**

3/1- **10** *10* **Reality Show (IRE)**[334] 5738 5 -9-3**77** DominicFox(3) 9
(Michael Appleby) *s.i.s: a bhd* **33/1**

2m 13.34s (1.64) **Going Correction** +0.30s/f (Good)
WFA 3 from 4yo+ 9lb **10**Ran SP% **113.3**
Speed ratings (Par 105): **105,97,97,96,94 94,91,88,78,70**
toteswingers 1&2 £26.90, 1&3 £8.70, 2&3 £15.20 CSF £185.81 CT £821.80 TOTE £8.40 : £3.10, £7.90, £2.30 ; EX 191.50 .
Owner Mrs Tracy Nason **Bred** Glashare House Stud **Trained** Thirkleby, N Yorks

FOCUS
After the downpour the ground was reckoned to be on the slow side of good. Quite a competitive handicap, even though neither of the two confirmed front runners in the line-up were able to get to the head of affairs.
Watered Silk Official explanation: jockey said gelding was slowly away.
Reality Show (IRE) Official explanation: jockey said gelding was never travelling.

4746 DG TAXIS GETTING YOU HOME SAFELY MEDIAN AUCTION MAIDEN STKS 1m 75y
4:45 (4:46) (Class 6) 3-4-Y-O £1,617 (£481; £240 ; £120) Stalls Centre

Form RPR
34 **1** **The Baronet**[15] 4212 3 -9-3**0** ChrisCatlin 9 80
(Sir Mark Prescott Bt) *cl up: effrt to ld 2f out: sn rdn: styd on strly fnl f* **4/1**[2]

3660 **2** *1 3/4* **Dynamic Duo (IRE)**[8] 4474 3 -9-3**74** SeanLevey 8 76
(Richard Hannon) *trckd ldng pair: hdwy 3f out: rdn to chal 2f out: ev ch tl drvn and one pce ent fnl f* **13/8**[1]

2 **3** *nk* **Medici Music**[22] 3975 3 -9-3**0** KirstyMilczarek 2 75
(Luca Cumani) *trckd ldrs: pushed along and sltly outpcd 3f out: styng on whn n.m.r and swtchd rt ent fnl f: sn drvn and one pce* **4/1**[2]

0-05 **4** *2 3/4* **Sehnsucht (IRE)**[16] 4177 3 -9-5**72** ow2 (v[1]) PhillipMakin 4 71
(Alan McCabe) *led: rdn along 3f out: hdd 2f out: sn drvn and grad wknd* **11/1**

04- **5** *3/4* **Rock Song**[298] 6725 3 -9-3**0** GrahamLee 7 67
(Amanda Perrett) *trckd ldrs: hdwy over 3f out: rdn 2f out: wknd over 1f out* **13/2**[3]

05 **6** *1 1/2* **Cool As Cash**[13] 4301 3 -9-3**0** SebSanders 6 64
(Paul D'Arcy) *dwlt and in rr: hdwy over 3f out: rdn to chse ldrs over 2f out: sn one pce* **33/1**

7 *2 3/4* **Capacious** 3 -8-12**0** HayleyTurner 3 52+
(James Fanshawe) *dwlt: green and in rr tl sme late hdwy* **9/1**

60 **8** *1* **Summer Sun**[9] 4434 3 -8-5**0** DannyBrock(7) 1 50
(Phil McEntee) *towards rr: hdwy on wd outside 3f out: rdn over 2f out: sn wknd* **100/1**

9 *11* **Roger Thorpe** 3 -9-3**0** PaddyAspell 5 29
(Garry Woodward) *s.i.s: a in rr* **150/1**

1m 49.1s (3.50) **Going Correction** +0.30s/f (Good)
WFA 3 from 4yo 7lb **9**Ran SP% **114.4**
Speed ratings (Par 101): **94,92,91,89,88 86,84,83,72**
toteswingers 1&2 £3.00, 1&3 £2.80, 2&3 £3.00 CSF £10.76 TOTE £3.70 : £1.10 , £1.20 , £1.40 ; EX 13.50 .
Owner Charles C Walker - Osborne House **Bred** C C And Mrs D J Buckley **Trained** Newmarket, Suffolk
■ Stewards' Enquiry : Phillip Makin six-day ban; weight in 2lb ow (16th-21st Aug)
Danny Brock two-day ban; careless riding (16th,17th Aug)

FOCUS
A very ordinary maiden race but an unexposed winner who has the potential to go on to better things.

4747 BLACK & WHITE CHRISTMAS PARTY PACKAGES H'CAP 1m 75y
5:15 (5:15) (Class 5) (0-75,75) 3-Y-0+ £2,264 (£673; £336 ; £168) Stalls Centre

Form RPR
0032 **1** **Aerodynamic (IRE)**[21] 3994 5 -9-13**74** DavidNolan 2 86
(Michael Easterby) *hld up: hdwy over 3f out: chsd ldrs 2f out: rdn to ld ent fnl f: kpt on wl* **3/1**[2]

535 **2** *2* **Sir George (IRE)**[10] 4398 7 -9-7**68** BarryMcHugh 1 75
(Ollie Pears) *hld up: hdwy 3f out: chal 2f out: rdn to ld briefly over 1f out: hdd ent fnl f and kpt on same pce* **9/2**[3]

2 **3** *1 1/2* **Sir Trevor (IRE)**[10] 4398 3 -9-4**72** RichardKingscote 5 75+
(Tom Dascombe) *led over 3f: cl up tl led again wl over 2f out: sn rdn: hdd and drvn over 1f out: kpt on one pce fnl f* **2/1**[1]

0304 **4** *1 1/2* **Glenridding**[20] 4042 8 -9-13**74** GrahamLee 3 75
(James Given) *chsd ldrs on inner: rdn along 3f out: drvn wl over 1f out and kpt on same pce* **18/1**

4366 **5** *3/4* **Free Art**[10] 4391 4 -9-6**67** PJMcDonald 8 66
(Geoffrey Harker) *hld up: hdwy 1/2-way: rdn to chse ldrs over 2f out: drvn and no imp over 1f out* **14/1**

2622 **6** *1 1/2* **Mark Anthony (IRE)**[10] 4390 5 -8-4**56** oh3 LauraPike(5) 7 51
(Shaun Harris) *chsd ldr: led over 4f out: rdn along and hdd wl over 2f out: grad wknd* **14/1**

0153 **7** *1/2* **Nezami (IRE)**[17] 4141 7 -9-6**67** (b) RussKennemore 6 61
(Patrick Clinton) *dwlt: sn in tch: hdwy on outer to chse ldrs 3f out: rdn over 2f out and grad wknd* **28/1**

00-4 **8** *2* **High Five Society**[27] 3810 8 -9-7**68** (b) RoystonFfrench 10 58
(Roy Bowring) *s.i.s: a in rr* **33/1**

0-06 **9** *10* **So Wise (USA)**[12] 4345 4 -9-7**75** DavidBergin(7) 11 42
(David O'Meara) *in tch: hdwy on outer 4f out: rdn to chse ldrs 3f out: wknd over 2f out* **10/1**

1130 **10** *3/4* **Cono Zur (FR)**[10] 4398 5 -10-0**75** JamesSullivan 14 40
(Ruth Carr) *a towards rr* **9/1**

06/0 **11** *9* **Moorgate Lad**[24] 3913 5 -8-9**56** oh5 AndrewElliott 4
(Garry Woodward) *chsd ldng pair: rdn along wl over 3f out: sn wknd* **80/1**

1m 48.72s (3.12) **Going Correction** +0.30s/f (Good)
WFA 3 from 4yo+ 7lb **11**Ran SP% **121.8**
Speed ratings (Par 103): **96,94,92,91,90 88,88,86,76,75 66**
toteswingers 1&2 £3.90, 1&3 £3.00, 2&3 £3.70 CSF £17.54 CT £33.86 TOTE £5.00 : £1.50 , £2.50, £1.10 ; EX 19.90 .
Owner David Scott and Co (Pattern Makers) Ltd **Bred** Swettenham, Carradale, S Cosgrove & T Stack **Trained** Sheriff Hutton, N Yorks

FOCUS
There were several front runners in the line-up and the gallop was strong. The first two came from off the pace.
T/Plt: £46.60 to a £1 stake. Pool: £50286.55 - 787.45 winning tickets T/Qpdt: £9.50 to a £1 stake. Pool: £3068.12 - 238.79 w. tickets JR 4448a - 4450a (Foreign Racing) See RI

3886 OVREVOLL (R-H)
Thursday, August 2

OFFICIAL GOING: Turf: heavy

4751a POLAR CUP (GROUP 3) (3YO+) (TURF) 6f 187y
6:50 (12:00) 3-Y-0+ £32,292 (£10,764; £5,382 ; £3,229 ; £2,152)

RPR
1 **Silver Ocean (USA)**[19] 4 -9-4**0** Per-AndersGraberg 1
(Niels Petersen, Norway) *sn prom on outer: prog to ld over 2f out: c nr side in st: rdn 2f out: kpt on wl u.p ins fnl 1 1/2f: drvn out* **289/100**[2]

2 *1 1/2* **Giant Sandman (IRE)**[12] 5 -9-8**0** RafaelSchistl 2
(Rune Haugen, Norway) *midfield: rdn over 2f out: c nr side in st: r.o to go 2nd wl ins fnl f: kpt on wout matching wnr cl home* **11/10**[1]

3 *1/2* **Hansinger (IRE)**[42] 7 -9-4**0** CarlosLopez 6
(Cathrine Erichsen, Norway) *disp ld: led over 4f out: hdd over 2f out: rdn 2f out: styd far side in st: kpt on u.p ins fnl 1 1/2f: dropped to 3rd cl home* **9/1**

4 *2 1/2* **Tertio Bloom (SWE)**[34] 3603 7 -9-4**0** LennartHammer-Hansen 5
(Fabricio Borges, Sweden) *towards rr on outer: rdn and outpcd over 2f out: c nr side in st: r.o to go 4th wl ins fnl f* **36/5**

5 *1 1/2* **Tariq Too**[41] 3331 5 -9-4**0** ElioneChaves 3
(Amy Weaver) *pushed along to go early gallop: hld up in rr: rdn and brief effrt over 2f out: c nr side in st: sn outpcd and btn: plugged on* **29/10**[3]

6 ½ **Dingle View (IRE)**^{7} 4-9-1 0 .... JacobJohansen 4
(Bent Olsen, Denmark) *disp ld early: dropped in and trckd ldr on inner over 4f out: rdn over 2f out: styd far side in st: outpcd and btn over 1f out: plugged on* **157/10**

1m 23.7s (83.70) **6** Ran SP% **127.2**
PARI-MUTUEL (all including 1krone stakes): WIN 3.89 PLACE 2.24, 1.85; DF 4.87.
Owner Autoindustri AB **Bred** Sun Valley Farm **Trained** Norway

^{4486}BATH (L-H)

Friday, August 3

OFFICIAL GOING: Good (good to firm in places; 8.2)
Wind: Moderate across Weather: Sunny spells early

4752 OLDE ENGLISH MAIDEN AUCTION STKS 5f 161y
5:30 (5:30) (Class 5) 2-Y-O **£2,587** (£770; £384; £192) **Stalls** Centre

Form RPR
3332 **1** **Dream Maker (IRE)**^{9} [4471] 2-8-6 66 .... RichardKingscote 9 76+
(Tom Dascombe) *trckd ldrs: led and wnt lft over 1f out: pushed clr: readily* **10/11**^{1}
2 3 ½ **Clear Loch** 2-8-9 0 .... LiamJones 1 67
(John Spearing) *chsd ldrs: rdn: outpcd and swtchd rt over 2f out: styd on wl fnl f to take 2nd clsng stages but no imp on wnr* **33/1**
5 **3** 1 **Tregereth (IRE)**^{22} [4002] 2-8-4 0 .... WilliamCarson 5 60
(Jonathan Portman) *sn chsng ldr: rdn and hmpd over 1f out: rallied to chse wnr ins fnl f: no imp and lost 2nd clsng stages* **9/1**
4644 **4** 4 **Jimmy Elder**^{15} [4230] 2-8-13 68 .... SeanLevey 2 55
(Richard Hannon) *led: rdn: edgd rt and hdd over 1f out: wknd fnl f* **8/1**^{3}
2323 **5** 2 ½ **Boleyn**^{23} [3970] 2-8-4 68 .... FrankieMcDonald 7 38
(Richard Hannon) *sn rdn in rr: nvr gng pce to get into contention* **5/2**^{2}
4424 **6** ¾ **Wordsaplenty (IRE)**^{4} [4659] 2-8-1 58 ....(p^{1}) RyanPowell$^{(3)}$ 8 35
(J S Moore) *slowly away: sn rdn in rr: mod prog fnl f* **16/1**
7 hd **Mymazar** 2-8-9 0 .... J-PGuillambert 3 40
(Jo Hughes) *spd to 1/2-way* **25/1**
8 5 **Spreading** 2-8-4 0 .... JohnFahy 4 18
(Michael Blanshard) *a in rr* **33/1**

1m 11.53s (0.33) **Going Correction** -0.10s/f (Good) **8** Ran SP% **117.7**
Speed ratings (Par 94): **93,88,87,81,78 77,77,70**
toteswingers:1&2 £16.20, 2&3 £25.00, 1&3 £3.10 CSF £44.41 TOTE £2.10: £1.10, £7.40, £2.20; EX 29.80.
Owner Hot To Trot Racing Club 3 **Bred** D G Iceton **Trained** Malpas, Cheshire

FOCUS
The going was good, good to firm in places. 12.5 yards were added to any race distance that included the bottom bend. A fairly uncompetitive maiden run at a sound pace with the well-backed favourite drawing clear inside the final furlong. The form is rated at face value.

NOTEBOOK
Dream Maker(IRE) had acquitted herself well when runner-up in a 5f Sandown nursery off 66 last time and did not have to improve on that run to win here. The step up to 6f clearly suited although, with her chief market rival under performing, this contest took little winning. (op 13-8)
Clear Loch, a gelded son of Proclamation out of unraced half-sister to a 1m4f winner, had to be switched wide for his effort but, stayed on well on this debut. He showed definite signs of promise for the future, possibly over further, once handicapped. (op 25-1)
Tregereth(IRE), who showed ability when fifth of nine in a 5f Folkestone maiden on her debut, was always handily placed but ran as though finding this too sharp. (op 6-1)
Jimmy Elder, who was never dangerous off 68 on his nursery debut over 5f here last time, helped set the pace but faded inside the final furlong and is looking exposed. (op 7-1)
Boleyn held solid credentials coming into the race but she was most disappointing here. She was driven a long way from home with little response and this was not her running. Official explanation: jockey said that the filly was never travelling (tchd 9-4 and 11-4)
Wordsaplenty(IRE) Official explanation: jockey said that the filly was slowly away

4753 ADDLESTONES FILLIES' H'CAP 1m 5y
6:00 (6:00) (Class 4) (0-80,76) 3-Y-O+ **£4,851** (£1,443; £721; £360) **Stalls** Low

Form RPR
1-42 **1** **Rhagori**^{34} [3643] 3-9-7 76 .... RichardKingscote 5 87+
(Ralph Beckett) *hld up in rr: gd hdwy between horses over 2f out: sn pressing ldr: led appr fnl f: pushed out and a doing enough* **4/6**^{1}
6-22 **2** ½ **Miss Cap Estel**^{15} [4233] 3-9-6 75 .... FergusSweeney 2 83
(Andrew Balding) *trckd ldr: drvn to ld ins fnl 2f: hdd appr fnl f: kpt on but a hld by wnr* **3/1**^{2}
0-45 **3** 2 ¼ **Elbow Beach**^{13} [4329] 3-8-12 67 .... JamesMillman 3 70
(Rod Millman) *led: rdn and hdd ins fnl 2f: one pce fnl f* **25/1**
6321 **4** 5 **Represent (IRE)**^{8} [4506] 3-8-11 71 6ex .... CharlesBishop$^{(5)}$ 1 62
(Mick Channon) *plld hrd: moved clsr to ldrs over 3f out: rdn and btn over 2f out* **5/1**^{3}
50-0 **5** 6 **Farleaze**^{14} [4288] 3-8-10 65 .... SeanLevey 4 43
(Martyn Meade) *chsd ldrs: rdn over 3f out: sn btn* **40/1**
0200 **6** ¾ **Midas Moment**^{13} [4335] 4-9-3 65 ....(t) LiamJones 7 41
(William Muir) *in rr: hdwy on outside to chse ldrs 3f out: sn rdn and btn* **20/1**

1m 42.84s (2.04) **Going Correction** +0.20s/f (Good)
WFA 3 from 4yo 7lb **6** Ran SP% **112.7**
Speed ratings (Par 102): **97,96,94,89,83 82**
toteswingers:1&2 £1.20, 2&3 £6.00, 1&3 £2.90 CSF £2.87 TOTE £1.50: £1.10, £1.50; EX 2.90.
Owner Landmark Racing Limited **Bred** P T Tellwright **Trained** Kimpton, Hants

FOCUS
Not the strongest of handicaps, run at a steady pace, with the front two in the market asserting inside the final furlong. The winner looks value for more with the second setting the standard.

4754 BLACKTHORN H'CAP 1m 5y
6:35 (6:36) (Class 6) (0-60,60) 3-Y-O **£1,940** (£577; £288; £144) **Stalls** Low

Form RPR
0622 **1** **Authoritarian**^{8} [4490] 3-9-5 58 .... SeanLevey 2 64
(Richard Hannon) *sn prom: chsd ldr 3f out: chal 2f out: led over 1f out: drvn and hld on wl thrght fnl f* **11/4**^{1}
034 **2** nk **Zuzu Angel (IRE)**^{10} [4436] 3-8-13 57 ....^{1} DavidKenny$^{(5)}$ 13 62
(William Knight) *in rr: rdn and hdwy over 2f out: styd on u.p to take 3rd ins fnl f: pressed wnr clsng stages but a hld* **10/1**
0-00 **3** 1 **Refreshestheparts (USA)**^{33} [3665] 3-8-12 51 .... FrankieMcDonald 5 54
(George Baker) *in tch: rdn to chse ldrs 3f out: wnt 2nd ins fnl f but no imp on wnr: one pce into 3rd clsng stages* **50/1**
0350 **4** 1 ¾ **Inffiraaj (IRE)**^{27} [3847] 3-9-4 57 .... SamHitchcott 4 56
(Mick Channon) *chsd ldrs: led over 4f out: rdn 3f out: jnd 2f out: hdd over 1f out: no ex ins fnl f* **14/1**
0606 **5** nk **Rocquaine (IRE)**^{17} [4186] 3-8-9 48 .... RichardThomas 7 46
(David Evans) *chsd ldrs: rdn over 2f out: styd on same pce fr over 1f out* **33/1**
4015 **6** 1 ¼ **Titus Bolt (IRE)**^{15} [4256] 3-9-7 60 ....(v) PatCosgrave 15 55
(Jim Boyle) *in rr: hdwy on outside over 2f out: styd on same pce and no imp ins fnl f* **11/2**^{3}
3323 **7** 2 **One Last Dream**^{15} [4236] 3-8-10 49 .... WilliamCarson 12 40
(Ron Hodges) *broke wl: sn towards rr: rdn and hdwy on outside over 2f out: nvr rchd ldrs and styd on same pce* **8/1**
005 **8** 6 **Oceana Dreamer (IRE)**^{46} [3235] 3-8-11 50 .... FergusSweeney 6 27
(Andrew Balding) *in rr: rdn and sme hdwy on ins over 2f out: nvr rchd ldrs and wknd fnl f* **5/1**^{2}
0330 **9** 2 ½ **Welsh Royale**^{24} [3950] 3-9-3 56 .... LiamJones 10 27
(William Muir) *led tl hdd over 4f out: wknd u.p fr 3f out* **25/1**
20-4 **10** 1 ¾ **Sovereign Waters**^{15} [4232] 3-9-4 57 .... JohnFahy 8 24
(Eve Johnson Houghton) *in tch: rdn 3f out: nvr gng pce to get into contention and sn wknd* **10/1**
0006 **11** ½ **Fight (IRE)**^{15} [4232] 3-9-1 54 ....(b) MircoDemuro 1 20
(Jeremy Gask) *a in rr* **20/1**
0002 **12** 11 **Goodie Goodie**^{17} [4198] 3-8-6 52 ....(t) RufusVergette$^{(7)}$ 9
(Sylvester Kirk) *slowly away: a bhd* **12/1**
50-4 **13** 2 ¾ **Roman Senate (IRE)**^{67} [2548] 3-8-10 49 ....(b) RichardKingscote 3
(Martin Bosley) *chsd ldrs: rdn 3f out: wknd over 2f out: eased whn no ch fnl f* **12/1**

1m 42.4s (1.60) **Going Correction** +0.20s/f (Good) **13** Ran SP% **123.6**
Speed ratings (Par 98): **100,99,98,96,96 95,93,87,84,83 82,71,68**
toteswingers:1&2 £9.60, 2&3 £219.80, 1&3 £96.20 CSF £31.35 CT £1202.55 TOTE £3.10: £1.10, £5.30, £24.70; EX 35.10.
Owner Longview Stud & Bloodstock Ltd **Bred** Longview Stud & Bloodstock Ltd **Trained** East Everleigh, Wilts

FOCUS
An moderate wide open handicap, with only one of the 13 runners having won a race, run at a steady pace with another well-backed runner landing the prize. The form looks modest.
Refreshestheparts(USA) Official explanation: jockey said that the filly hung left
One Last Dream Official explanation: jockey said that the gelding hung right

4755 SIG H'CAP 1m 2f 46y
7:10 (7:11) (Class 4) (0-80,79) 3-Y-O **£4,851** (£1,443; £721; £360) **Stalls** Low

Form RPR
31- **1** **Future Security (IRE)**^{284} [7060] 3-9-7 79 .... PatCosgrave 1 85+
(Saeed Bin Suroor) *disp 2nd after 3f tl drvn and one pce over 2f out: styd on u.p on rails ins fnl f to ld clsng stages* **7/4**^{1}
-536 **2** nk **Drummond**^{32} [3703] 3-9-1 73 .... JohnFahy 6 78
(Clive Cox) *led: rdn and styd on wl whn jnd ins fnl 2f: stl narrow ld ins fnl f: hdd clsng stages* **9/1**
0042 **3** 2 ½ **Instrumentalist (IRE)**^{8} [4498] 3-8-11 69 .... LiamKeniry 4 69
(John Best) *chsd ldrs: drvn to chal ins fnl 2f: wknd fnl 120yds* **11/4**^{2}
0050 **4** ¾ **Good Of Luck**^{8} [4498] 3-9-0 72 .... SamHitchcott 5 71
(Mick Channon) *hld up in rr: hdwy fr 3f out: ev ch ins fnl 2f: wknd u.p ins fnl f* **11/1**
61-0 **5** 1 ¾ **Dreams Of Fire (USA)**^{86} [1973] 3-9-6 78 .... GeorgeBaker 3 73
(Sir Michael Stoute) *chsd ldr: rdn and ev ch ins fnl 2f: wknd ins fnl f* **4/1**^{3}
-030 **6** 7 **Alvitude (USA)**^{39} [3448] 3-8-12 70 .... EddieAhern 2 51
(Roger Charlton) *in rr but in tch: rdn over 2f out: sn btn* **8/1**

2m 12.47s (1.47) **Going Correction** +0.20s/f (Good) **6** Ran SP% **112.5**
Speed ratings (Par 102): **102,101,99,99,97 92**
toteswingers:1&2 £3.80, 2&3 £4.50, 1&3 £1.50 CSF £18.09 TOTE £2.10: £1.10, £5.40; EX 16.50.
Owner Godolphin **Bred** Mrs Vanessa Hutch **Trained** Newmarket, Suffolk

FOCUS
A fair handicap with some powerful stables represented, run at a steady pace with five nearly in a line passing the furlong pole. The runner-up sets the level but is likely to limit the form in the long run.

4756 L A CLARK H'CAP 2m 1f 34y
7:40 (7:40) (Class 5) (0-70,75) 4-Y-O+ **£2,587** (£770; £384; £192) **Stalls** Centre

Form RPR
5420 **1** **Sunny Future (IRE)**^{20} [4096] 6-9-1 64 .... TomMcLaughlin 7 72
(Malcolm Saunders) *hld up in rr: pushed along and hdwy over 2f out: chsd ldr appr fnl f: styd on wl to ld fnl 120yds: drvn out* **7/1**
111 **2** 1 ¼ **Callisto Moon**^{9} [4475] 8-9-12 75 6ex ....(p) J-PGuillambert 5 82
(Jo Hughes) *led: pushed along over 3f out: rdn over 1f out: one pce u.p ins fnl f: hdd and no ex fnl 120yds* **2/1**^{1}
130- **3** 1 **Whenever**^{10} [6722] 8-9-1 64 ....(v) FergusSweeney 3 69
(Richard Phillips) *chsd ldrs: rdn: outpcd and dropped to rr 3f out: styd on again fr over 1f out: tk 3rd fnl 75yds: no imp on ldng duo* **12/1**
5043 **4** 1 ¼ **Big Time Billy (IRE)**^{22} [4004] 6-8-13 62 ....(p) WilliamCarson 4 66
(Mike Hammond) *chsd ldrs: rdn along 4f out: wnt 2nd 3f out: sn hrd drvn: no imp on ldr fr 2f out: wknd fnl f* **7/2**^{3}
1355 **5** 5 **Handles For Forks (IRE)**^{20} [4096] 4-9-2 70 .... CharlesBishop$^{(5)}$ 1 68
(Mick Channon) *in rr but in tch: drvn and hdwy to cl on ldrs over 2f out but nvr on terms: wknd wl over 1f out* **13/2**
0003 **6** 1 ½ **Hidden Valley**^{35} [3572] 4-9-5 68 ....(v) LiamKeniry 6 64
(Andrew Balding) *sn chsng ldr: rdn and lost 2nd 3f out: wknd wl over 1f out* **3/1**^{2}

3m 53.71s (1.81) **Going Correction** +0.20s/f (Good) **6** Ran SP% **114.1**
Speed ratings (Par 103): **103,102,101,101,99 98**
toteswingers:1&2 £1.70, 2&3 £4.90, 1&3 £10.90 CSF £21.99 TOTE £9.30: £4.10, £1.10; EX 22.00.
Owner M S Saunders **Bred** Mrs G Stanga **Trained** Green Ore, Somerset

FOCUS
An uncompetitive staying handicap, run at a steady pace with the winner passing the field up the straight, to win under a well-timed ride. The form is a bit fluid with the runner-up probably the best guide.

4757 TRENT SERVICES H'CAP 5f 11y
8:10 (8:10) (Class 5) (0-75,75) 3-Y-O **£2,587** (£770; £384; £192) **Stalls** Centre

Form RPR
0023 **1** **Knocker Knowles (IRE)**^{25} [3919] 3-9-7 75 .... RichardKingscote 3 84
(David Evans) *mde all: rdn fnl f: hld on all out clsng stages* **6/1**
4464 **2** hd **Mister Musicmaster**^{16} [4221] 3-9-6 74 .... JamesMillman 6 82
(Rod Millman) *in rr: hdwy 2f out: chsd wnr ins fnl f: fin strly: nt quite get up* **6/1**
2303 **3** 5 **Ashpan Sam**^{37} [3486] 3-9-5 73 .... LiamJones 4 63
(John Spearing) *chsd ldrs: rdn over 2f out: styd on for wl-hld 3rd fnl f* **9/2**^{3}

6044 **4** 1 1/4 **Jinker Noble**[8] 4500 3-9-7 **75**....(p) JohnFahy 7 61
(Clive Cox) *chsd ldr: rdn over 2f out: wknd qckly fnl f* **7/1**
1301 **5** 1/2 **Trending (IRE)**[8] 4489 3-8-8 **62** 6ex....(b) MircoDemuro 1 46
(Jeremy Gask) *awkward s and s.i.s: rdn over 2f out but nvr gng pce to get into contention* **7/2**[1]
313 **6** 3 1/4 **Tinzapeas**[5] 4619 3-8-11 **70** 6ex....(v) CharlesBishop(5) 2 42
(Mick Channon) *chsd ldrs: rdn over 2f out: wknd qckly over 1f out* **4/1**[2]
50-4 **7** 7 **Cincinnati Kit**[9] 4467 3-8-4 **58**....(t) WilliamCarson 5
(Stuart Williams) *in tch whn rdn 1/2-way: sn btn* **8/1**

1m 1.65s (-0.85) **Going Correction** -0.10s/f (Good) **7** Ran SP% **112.6**
Speed ratings (Par 100): **102,101,93,91,90 85,74**
toteswingers:1&2 £6.30, 2&3 £10.10, 1&3 £1.80 CSF £39.72 TOTE £7.00: £1.80, £4.50; EX 79.60.
Owner Shropshire Wolves **Bred** Ballyhane Stud **Trained** Pandy, Monmouths
FOCUS
An open looking sprint handicap, run at a decent pace with the front two pulling clear and the winner making all, to win narrowly. The winner is getting back to his juvenile form.

4758 PROPERTY BUILDING MAINTENANCE CELEBRATING PAIGE'S 18TH H'CAP 5f 11y

8:40 (8:40) (Class 6) (0-60,63) 4-Y-O+ **£2,587** (£770; £384; £192) **Stalls** Centre

Form RPR
-641 **1** **Crimson Queen**[8] 4493 5-9-10 **63** 6ex....(b) ChrisCatlin 1 79
(Roy Brotherton) *mde all: drvn clr over 1f out: styd on wl: unchal* **5/4**[1]
0022 **2** 3 1/2 **Griffin Point (IRE)**[10] 4422 5-9-0 **53**....(b) WilliamCarson 3 56
(William Muir) *chsd ldrs: rdn over 2f out: kpt on to chse wnr appr fnl f but a readily hld* **8/1**
3434 **3** 1 3/4 **Even Bolder**[18] 4146 9-9-7 **60**.... GeorgeBaker 5 57
(Eric Wheeler) *in rr: pushed along over 2f out: styd on to take one pce 3rd fnl f* **11/2**[2]
3453 **4** shd **Trade Centre**[8] 4493 7-8-3 **49**.... DanielMuscutt(7) 4 46
(Milton Bradley) *in rr: rdn and hdwy fr 2f out: nvr nr wnr and btn appr fnl f* **16/1**
5000 **5** 2 **Fleetwoodsands (IRE)**[46] 3229 5-9-4 **57**....(t) RichardKingscote 7 47
(Milton Bradley) *chsd ldrs: rdn over 2f out: sn one pce* **12/1**
1232 **6** 2 **Autocracy**[10] 4439 5-9-6 **59**....(bt) FergusSweeney 9 41
(Daniel Kubler) *rdn over 2f out: one pce* **8/1**
4556 **7** 3 1/4 **Bateleur**[8] 4492 8-9-6 **59**.... MatthewDavies 6 30
(Mick Channon) *rdn over 2f out: outpcd* **12/1**
3123 **8** 1/2 **Spic 'n Span**[10] 4425 7-8-11 **50**....(b) MarcHalford 8 19
(Ronald Harris) *chsd ldrs tl wknd over 1f out* **7/1**[3]

1m 2.14s (-0.36) **Going Correction** -0.10s/f (Good) **8** Ran SP% **115.8**
Speed ratings (Par 101): **98,92,89,89,86 83,77,77**
toteswingers:1&2 £2.00, 2&3 £5.60, 1&3 £2.70 CSF £12.27 CT £42.20 TOTE £2.30: £1.10, £3.10, £2.20; EX 14.50.
Owner Arthur Clayton **Bred** Cheveley Park Stud Ltd **Trained** Elmley Castle, Worcs
FOCUS
A low grade sprint handicap run at a sound pace with the well-backed winner making all to win convincingly. The form looks sound enough through the second.
T/Plt: £99.10 to a £1 stake. Pool £41055.73 - 302.28 winning units. T/Qpdt: £96.90 to a £1 stake. Pool £4577.60 - 34.95 winning units. ST

4735 GOODWOOD (R-H)

Friday, August 3

OFFICIAL GOING: Good (overall 8.1; straight course: stands' 8.1; centre 8.3; far side 8.4)
Wind: fresh, against Weather: bright spells, breezy

4759 COUTTS GLORIOUS STKS (GROUP 3) 1m 4f

2:00 (2:00) (Class 1) 4-Y-O+
£34,026 (£12,900; £6,456; £3,216; £1,614; £810) **Stalls** High

Form RPR
-240 **1** **Quest For Peace (IRE)**[41] 3369 4-9-0 111.... KierenFallon 1 115
(Luca Cumani) *mde all and allowed to set stdy gallop: rdn and qcknd ent fnl 3f: hung lft but r.o wl fnl f* **5/1**[3]
3220 **2** 1 1/4 **Dandino**[22] 4010 5-9-0 106.... JohnnyMurtagh 2 113
(James Fanshawe) *t.k.h: hld up in tch: rdn and effrt on inner over 2f out: chsd wnr ins fnl f: r.o but nvr able to chal* **13/2**
-111 **3** 3/4 **Gatewood**[42] 3329 4-9-0 104.... WilliamBuick 5 111+
(John Gosden) *trckd ldng pair: effrt and rdn over 2f out: drvn and unable qck over 1f out: styd on same pce fnl f: wnt 3rd last strides* **9/4**[1]
1302 **4** hd **Songcraft (IRE)**[28] 3825 4-9-0 112.... FrankieDettori 7 111
(Saeed Bin Suroor) *chsd ldr: rdn 3f out: drvn and styd on same pce fr over 1f out: lost 2 pls ins fnl f* **11/4**[2]
1350 **5** 3 1/4 **Midsummer Sun**[41] 3372 4-9-0 96.... TomQueally 4 104
(Sir Henry Cecil) *s.i.s: t.k.h: hld up in last pair: rdn and hdwy over 2f out: outpcd and btn over 1f out: plugged on ins fnl f* **14/1**
-001 **6** nk **Dubai Prince (IRE)**[21] 4074 4-9-0 116.... AhmedAjtebi 3 104
(Mahmood Al Zarooni) *lw: hld up in last pair: rdn and hdwy over 2f out: no ex ent fnl f: wknd fnl 100yds* **7/1**
4-34 **7** 1 1/2 **Berling (IRE)**[34] 3632 5-9-0 99.... EddieAhern 6 101
(John Dunlop) *in tch: nt clr run 2f out: sn rdn and unable qck: wknd ent fnl f* **33/1**

2m 42.53s (4.13) **Going Correction** 0.0s/f (Good) **7** Ran SP% **109.5**
Speed ratings (Par 113): **86,85,84,84,82 82,81**
Tote Swingers: 1&2 £5.40, 1&3 £2.90, 2&3 £3.40 CSF £33.54 TOTE £6.40: £2.60, £3.20; EX 41.00.
Owner O T I Racing **Bred** Macquarie **Trained** Newmarket, Suffolk
FOCUS
Rail on top bend dolled out 3yds increasing distances by 5yds. Fresh ground on lower bend. This Group 3 has been won by several who have scored at a higher level such as Redwood and Alkaased, and has also been a jumping-off point for a number that have been given autumn international campaigns. Luca Cumani had won three of the previous ten renewals and improved his record. The early pace was very steady - they took over a minute to cover the first half-mile - and the overall time was slow. The form is therefore muddling and may not be reliable.
NOTEBOOK
Quest For Peace(IRE), back on a faster surface, was able to get an easy lead and dictated the gallop. He picked up really well when asked and was in control from over a furlong out. He's likely to be aimed at the Melbourne Cup now. (op 11-2)
Dandino has returned to something like his best for his new yard this season and stayed on pretty well, without ever looking likely to catch the winner. He is capable of taking a similar race, especially on a faster surface. (op 15-2 tchd 8-1)
Gatewood has progressed really well this season but was stepping up in both trip and grade here. He was made favourite and was always close to the steady pace, but could not pick up under pressure. He may not have quite got the extra distance but is reportedly being aimed at the Melbourne Cup. (op 15-8 tchd 5-2 in a place)
Songcraft(IRE) made an encouraging return over 1m2f at Sandown after a spell in Dubai, and was ridden close to the pace here. However, he was unable to respond when the winner committed for home and was just run out of the places. (op 3-1 tchd 5-2)
Midsummer Sun has struggled this season but the faster surface here was expected to be in his favour. However, he was held up off a steady gallop and was unable to pick up well enough to pose a threat. (op 16-1)
Dubai Prince(IRE), who returned to form at York last time, had the highest official rating. He was held up at the back before making good headway to challenge around 2f out but could not sustain the effort. He has never won beyond 1m1f and looked like a non-stayer, even at the slow gallop this race was run. (op 13-2)
Berling(IRE) was the outsider of the field but was travelling well 2f out, although a little short of room. However, he was left behind soon afterwards but was not far off previous course form with the runner-up.

4760 RSA THOROUGHBRED STKS (GROUP 3) 1m

2:35 (2:36) (Class 1) 3-Y-O
£21,507 (£21,507; £5,918; £2,948; £1,479; £742) **Stalls** Low

Form RPR
6-22 **1** **Archbishop (USA)**[55] 2951 3-9-0 107.... FrankieDettori 13 111
(Brian Meehan) *lw: in tch: effrt u.p over 2f out: ev ch over 1f out: drvn to ld 1f out: hdd ins fnl f: rallied gamely to join ldr on post* **10/1**
-140 **1** dht **Trumpet Major (IRE)**[69] 2514 3-9-4 114.... RichardHughes 3 115
(Richard Hannon) *in tch: hdwy to join ldrs on bit over 1f out: rdn 1f out: led narrowly ins fnl f: r.o u.p: jnd on post* **6/1**[2]
-413 **3** 3/4 **Aljamaaheer (IRE)**[44] 3265 3-9-0 107.... PaulHanagan 1 114+
(Roger Varian) *hld up in rr: hdwy on inner to chse ldrs whn nt clr run and hmpd wl over 1f out: no where to go after tl hdwy and swtchd lft and rt ins fnl f: r.o strly fnl 100yds: wnt 3rd towards fin* **7/2**[1]
1422 **4** 1/2 **Stipulate**[43] 3295 3-9-0 108.... TomQueally 2 110+
(Sir Henry Cecil) *hld up towards rr: sltly hmpd over 4f out: gd hdwy ent fnl 2f: chsng ldrs and running on whn nt clr run and swtchd lft 1f out: r.o wl fnl 100yds: nt rch ldrs* **6/1**[2]
0030 **5** 2 1/4 **Miblish**[13] 4319 3-9-0 95....(t) SilvestreDeSousa 11 103
(Clive Brittain) *lw: chsd ldr tl 5f out: styd chsng ldrs tl rdn to ld 2f out: drvn and hdd 1f out: no ex and wknd fnl 100yds* **100/1**
4603 **6** 1/2 **Saigon**[22] 4012 3-9-0 107....(b[1]) KirstyMilczarek 15 101
(James Toller) *hld up towards rr: rdn and effrt 3f out: kpt on same pce u.p ins fnl f* **28/1**
1-35 **7** 1/2 **Tales Of Grimm (USA)**[43] 3295 3-9-0 99.... RyanMoore 6 100+
(Sir Michael Stoute) *lw: dwlt: hld up in rr: rdn and effrt over 2f out: no imp over 1f out tl styd on ins fnl f: nvr gng pce to threaten ldrs* **16/1**
5030 **8** 2 3/4 **Red Duke (USA)**[44] 3265 3-9-0 109.... JohnnyMurtagh 4 94
(John Quinn) *chsd ldrs: rdn and jostling match on inner wl over 1f out: btn ent fnl f: wknd and wl hld whn eased wl ins fnl f* **9/1**[3]
5032 **9** 2 1/4 **Coupe De Ville (IRE)**[34] 3640 3-9-0 112.... DaneO'Neill 8 89+
(Richard Hannon) *t.k.h: hld up in midfield: lost pl and towards rr whn sltly hmpd over 4f out: rdn over 2f out: styd on past btn horses over 1f out: no ch* **12/1**
3-01 **10** 7 **Ewell Place (IRE)**[20] 4095 3-9-0 98.... StevieDonohoe 7 73
(Robert Mills) *t.k.h: hld up in tch in midfield: rdn and struggling 3f out: wknd 2f out* **66/1**
0622 **11** shd **Silverheels (IRE)**[20] 4095 3-9-0 97....(p) ChrisCatlin 12 72
(Paul Cole) *on toes: bhd: effrt u.p on outer over 2f out: no prog and wl hld whn hung rt 1f out* **66/1**
4050 **12** 3/4 **Ptolemaic**[44] 3265 3-9-0 107....(v) TomEaves 5 71
(Bryan Smart) *sn led: rdn and hdd 2f out: losing pl qckly whn hmpd wl over 1f out: sn bhd* **33/1**
1002 **13** 14 **Born To Surprise**[23] 3977 3-9-0 92.... JamieSpencer 14 39
(Michael Bell) *lw: t.k.h: hld up towards rr: hdwy to chse ldr 5f out tl over 2f out: sn dropped out: wl bhd and eased ins fnl f* **33/1**
5032 **14** 3/4 **Gregorian (IRE)**[33] 3681 3-9-0 114.... WilliamBuick 10 37
(John Gosden) *in tch in midfield: rdn 3f out: sn struggling and wknd 2f out: bhd and eased ins fnl f* **7/2**[1]

1m 37.53s (-2.37) **Going Correction** 0.0s/f (Good) **14** Ran SP% **119.0**
Speed ratings (Par 110): **111,111,110,109,107 107,106,103,101,94 94,93,79,78**Win: Trumpet Major £3.20 Archbishop £5.40 Place: TM £2.30 A £2.80 Aljamaaheer £1.90 Ex: TM-A £33.00 A-TM £29.20 CSF: TM-A £30.60 A-TM £32.81 Trifecta: 1-3-2 £104.50 3-1-2 £82.10. ToteSwinger: 1-2 £5.30 1-3 £8.20 2-3 £9.50. 27 Trifecta £Owner Catesby W Clay Bred.
Owner John Manley **Bred** John Cullinan **Trained** East Everleigh, Wilts
FOCUS
This race had been upgraded from Listed status since last year and it attracted a decent field, making for a competitive contest. They went a reasonable gallop and the time was 0.17 seconds quicker than the following Betfred Mile. The form looks decent, despite several hard-luck stories.
NOTEBOOK
Archbishop(USA) coped with the step up to Group 3 company when runner-up at Chantilly last time and showed he's still going the right way on his return from 55 days off. His task was made easier by the 4lb he received from Trumpet Major, as well as the third finding trouble, but he could keep improving. (tchd 5-1)
Trumpet Major(IRE) ◆ was forced to share the prize, and he'd have been given more to do had the third enjoyed a better trip, but he emerges as the best horse at the weights given he was conceding 4lb to all of his rivals. He was well beaten in the Irish Guineas when last season, but he had a legitimate excuse having been found to be coughing post-race. His earlier form suggested he could make one of the better 3yo milers as he'd defied a penalty in the Craven before finishing fourth in the Newmarket Guineas on ground softer than ideal. It was good to see him bounce back and the Celebration Mile back over C&D on August 25 could be a suitable target. (tchd 5-1)
Aljamaaheer(IRE) ◆, third in the Jersey on his previous start, was ridden patiently from inside draw on this first attempt at 1m and got no sort of run in the straight. The way he ran on when belatedly in the clear suggests he would have gone close to winning granted a better trip. He holds a number of Group entries, including the Celebration Mile, and there's a big race to be won with him. Official explanation: jockey said that the colt was denied a clear run (op 9-2 tchd 5-1 in a place)
Stipulate, dropped in trip after finishing runner-up in the Tercentenary at Royal Ascot, didn't get the clearest of runs after travelling well, and his chance was further compromised when he hung right late on. It's debatable whether he was anything other than fourth best, although Tom Queally reported the colt lost a shoe. Official explanation: jockey said that the colt lost a shoe (tchd 11-2)
Miblish, came into this rated just 95, but he's certainly not the first Clive Brittain horse to run better than expected in a Group race and it would be dangerous to think he holds the form down. He is entered in the Juddmonte International Stakes.
Saigon, in blinkers for the first time, ran with credit from an helpful draw. (op 33-1 tchd 25-1)
Tales Of Grimm(USA) was dropped in trip after his fifth in the Tercentenary Stakes, but he found this an insufficient test after missing the break. He was having only the fourth start of his career and remains capable of better. (op 14-1 tchd 12-1)

Red Duke(USA) seemed to be struggling when short of room in the straight and wasn't at his best. He looks like a horse in need of a confidence boost. (op 10-1)

Coupe De Ville(IRE) could probably have finished slightly closer with a clear run. (op 14-1)

Gregorian(IRE), who had been placed in Group 1s on his last two starts (third in the St James's Place and runner-up in the Jean Prat), ran no sort of race this time. Official explanation: jockey said that the colt ran flat (tchd 4-1)

4761 BETFRED MILE (HERITAGE H'CAP) 1m

3:10 (3:14) (Class 2) 3-Y-0+

£77,812 (£23,300; £11,650; £5,825; £2,912; £1,462) **Stalls** Low

Form RPR

0611 **1** **Fulbright**[6] 4598 3-8-13 **102** 6ex................................ SilvestreDeSousa 8 112+
(Mark Johnston) *lw: chsd ldrs: rdn and effrt over 2f out: led over 1f out: clr ins fnl f: kpt on: rdn out* **7/1**[2]

0300 **2** *1 ¼* **Mabait**[13] 4339 6-8-6 **95**................................ AliceHaynes(7) 10 102
(David Simcock) *swtg: hld up in tch: effrt and barging match 2f out: hdwy over 1f out: str run 1f out to chse wnr wl ins fnl f: nvr gng to rch wnr* **33/1**

0325 **3** *1 ¼* **Mister Music**[22] 4012 3-8-11 **100**................................ RichardHughes 17 103+
(Richard Hannon) *lw: stdd and dropped in bhd after s: hld up in rr: stuck bhd the whole field on inner 2f out: swtchd to outer over 1f out: edgd bk rt and hdwy 1f out: str run fnl f to go 3rd last strides* **25/1**

51-0 **4** *hd* **Boom And Bust (IRE)**[44] 3268 5-9-3 **99**................................ HayleyTurner 22 103+
(Marcus Tregoning) *lw: stdd s: hld up in rr: edgd rt and hdwy on inner over 1f out: gd hdwy ent fnl f: r.o wl ins fnl f* **20/1**

020 **5** *shd* **Excellent Guest**[13] 4321 5-9-2 **98**................................ TomQueally 3 101
(George Margarson) *in tch: rdn and chsd ldrs over 1f out: swtchd lft 1f out and drvn to chse clr wnr jst ins fnl f: styd on same pce: lost 3 pls wl ins fnl f* **8/1**[3]

004 **6** *¾* **Sir Reginald**[20] 4099 4-8-13 **95**................................ PaulHanagan 7 97
(Richard Fahey) *t.k.h: chsd ldr tl led over 2f out: rdn and hdd over 1f out: no ex ent fnl f: wknd fnl 100yds* **20/1**

-211 **7** *shd* **Swiftly Done (IRE)**[36] 3534 5-8-12 **94**................................ GrahamGibbons 1 95+
(Declan Carroll) *hld up in midfield: rdn and effrt 2f out: nt clr run and hmpd over 1f out: edgd rt and hdwy ins fnl f: r.o strly towards fin* **9/1**

2000 **8** *¾* **Belgian Bill**[20] 4099 4-9-3 **99**................................(t) JohnnyMurtagh 15 99
(George Baker) *hld up in rr: rdn and effrt on outer over 1f out: r.o ins fnl f: unable to chal* **16/1**

5322 **9** *½* **Vainglory (USA)**[13] 4339 8-8-10 **92**................................ MartinLane 9 91
(David Simcock) *lw: in tch in midfield: rdn and struggling to qckn over 2f out: pushed rt and nt clr run over 1f out: kpt on u.p fnl f: nvr able to chal* **16/1**

-215 **10** *shd* **Prince Of Johanne (IRE)**[5] 4628 6-9-5 **106**...............(p) DarrenEgan(5) 16 104
(Tom Tate) *in tch in midfield: effrt u.p over 2f out: unable qck over 1f out: styd on same pce fnl f* **16/1**

0401 **11** *1* **Field Of Dream**[13] 4321 5-9-6 **102** 3ex...............(b) JamieSpencer 13 104+
(Jamie Osborne) *lw: hld up towards rr: swtchd rt and effrt on inner 2f out: swtchd lft and hdwy over 1f out: chsng ldrs and styng on whn squeezed out and hmpd ins fnl f: lost any ch and nt pushed after* **12/1**

0404 **12** *½* **Bannock (IRE)**[5] 4628 3-9-4 **107**................................ JoeFanning 18 101
(Mark Johnston) *in tch in midfield: effrt to chse ldrs and rdn over 2f out: no ex over 1f out: wknd ins fnl f* **16/1**

1002 **13** *1 ¼* **Captain Bertie (IRE)**[20] 4099 4-8-11 **93**................................ MichaelHills 6 85+
(Charles Hills) *lw: t.k.h: chsd ldrs: rdn and unable qck ent 2f out: hmpd and lost pl over 1f out: styng on same pce and btn whn nt clr run and eased ins fnl f* **6/1**[1]

505 **14** *shd* **Albaqaa**[27] 3878 7-8-11 **93**................................ KieranO'Neill 5 85+
(P J O'Gorman) *swtg: s.i.s: t.k.h: hld up bhd: hdwy into midfield 1/2-way: wl in tch and gng wl whn nt clr run: hmpd and lost pl 2f out: swtchd lft over 1f out: styd on same pce after* **8/1**[3]

0310 **15** *½* **Memory Cloth**[20] 4112 5-9-0 **99**................................ DaleSwift(3) 20 90
(Brian Ellison) *swtg: hld up in tch: rdn and hdwy on outer over 2f out: edgd rt and no imp over 1f out: wknd ins fnl f* **28/1**

0-55 **16** *¾* **Decent Fella (IRE)**[20] 4099 6-9-0 **96**................................(vt) JimmyFortune 11 85
(Andrew Balding) *hld up in tch in midfield: effrt and n.m.r 2f out: sn rdn and no imp: plugged on same pce and wl hld after* **20/1**

1-50 **17** *hd* **Xilerator (IRE)**[69] 2472 5-8-13 **95**................................ AdrianNicholls 4 83
(David Nicholls) *on toes: led tl rdn and hdd over 2f out: no ex over 1f out: wknd fnl f* **25/1**

103- **18** *1* **Johnny Castle**[331] 5830 4-9-0 **96**................................ RyanMoore 19 82
(Amanda Perrett) *lw: hld up bhd: rdn and effrt on outer 2f out: no imp over 1f out: nvr trbld ldrs* **25/1**

0313 **19** *14* **Madam Macie (IRE)**[15] 4248 5-9-0 **96**................................ DanielTudhope 12 50
(David O'Meara) *lw: t.k.h: chsd ldrs tl over 2f out: sn dropped out: bhd and eased ins fnl f* **33/1**

0341 **20** *11* **Smarty Socks (IRE)**[69] 2505 8-9-4 **100**................................ KierenFallon 14 29
(David O'Meara) *lw: hld up towards rr: effrt on inner 2f out: midfield and no real hdwy whn nt clr run and hmpd over 1f out: nt pushed and wl btn after: eased: t.o* **22/1**

1m 37.7s (-2.20) **Going Correction** 0.0s/f (Good)

WFA 3 from 4yo+ 7lb **20** Ran SP% **129.7**

Speed ratings (Par 109): **111,109,108,108,108 107,107,106,106,106 105,104,103,103,102 101,101,100,86,75**

Tote Swingers: 1&2 £113.40, 1&3 £28.90, 2&3 £376.50 CSF £230.51 CT £5534.42 TOTE £7.40: £2.40, £8.40, £7.40, £4.10; EX 601.80 Trifecta £4710.90 Pool: £6,366.18 - 1.00 winning unit..

Owner Sheikh Hamdan Bin Mohammed Al Maktoum **Bred** R F And S D Knipe **Trained** Middleham Moor, N Yorks

■ Stewards' Enquiry : Graham Gibbons five-day ban: careless riding (17-21 Aug)
Jamie Spencer four-day ban: careless riding (17-20 Aug)

FOCUS

The usual big field and a hot race for this valuable handicap, and as normal there was several hard-luck stories. Mark Johnston had won this race twice in the previous three seasons, once with a 3-y-o, and, represented by two from that age group this time, he made it three from four. The form is relatively ordinary with several unlucky, bu the second and fourth help set the level.

NOTEBOOK

Fulbright has been on a rapid upward curve in recent weeks and completed the hat-trick on this step up in trip off 1lb lower (this was an early closing race) than when scoring the previous Saturday, despite a 6lb penalty. This was a third valuable success for connections, but once the handicapper has his say he will probably be unable to contest handicaps in the foreseeable future. However, he is relatively versatile regarding trip and can be ridden from the front, so might be up to winning Group races if the progression continues. (tchd 13-2)

Mabait ◆ has not won for over two years but has slipped to a reasonable mark and goes well for his apprentice rider. Held up off the pace, he got a split well over 1f out and came through to chase the winner, who was not stopping. He is capable of winning again soon on this evidence. (op 25-1)

Mister Music ◆ was one of the most unlucky horses in the race. Held up at the back, he was still last and short of room a furlong and a half from home, but then picked up really well once in the clear to pass most of his rivals, albeit too late to catch the winner. He was runner-up in the Britannia when beaten by another improver and he deserves to pick up a similar handicap. His ability to get 1m2f means he could be the sort to go well in the Cambridgeshire later on. (tchd 28-1)

Boom And Bust(IRE), who made all to win this from the rail draw last season, ran another terrific race from the wide outside berth, especially as he did not get the clearest of passages. His rider did well to get him onto the rail, but he was stacked up behind several looking for a route through and had to wait his turn. He finished really well to show he is back to somewhere near last season's form and a similar race could fall his way.

Excellent Guest is pretty reliable in these big handicaps and bounced back from a rare below-par effort. No doubt he will be aimed at a similar race at Ascot, where he goes so well. (tchd 9-1 in a place)

Sir Reginald ◆ is gradually finding his form following a long absence then a trip to Dubai, and was always in the leading group here. He could not sustain his effort and would be of interest dropped back to 6f.

Swiftly Done(IRE) had the rail draw but was yet another who did not get a clear run. He is progressing well of late and could be off to York next. (op 12-1)

Belgian Bill, another who has been competing well in similar races, appreciated the better ground this time and was yet another that finished well, having been held up, and was then short of room in the straight. (op 20-1)

Vainglory(USA) has been in good form but on softer ground that this. He ran on well having been held up but was passed by the much stronger-finishing third. He is still in good heart though.

Prince Of Johanne(IRE) is a really consistent performer in this sort of contest and he ran another fine race off 6lb higher than when winning the Royal Hunt Cup. A second Cambridgeshire will be on his agenda, and he might possibly follow last year's route by going to Doncaster in between.

Field Of Dream, the strong-finishing winner of a valuable Ascot handicap last time, was another held up and did not get the best of runs trying to get through near the rail. He will be seen to better effect back on a stiffer, possibly straight track. (op 11-1)

Captain Bertie(IRE) has been in good form and was ridden positively in a bid to improver on his Bunbury Cup second. He was unable to hold his pitch in the closing stages though, and might prefer softer ground and a more galloping track. (op 8-1)

Albaqaa Official explanation: jockey said that the gelding was denied a clear run

Smarty Socks(IRE), having his first run since May, was another who was faced with a wall of horses in the straight and was hampered over a furlong out before being eased. This should have blown the cobwebs away, setting him up for races at York and Doncaster in the next month or so, tracks where he has a good winning record. (op 20-1)

4762 GORDON'S KING GEORGE STKS (GROUP 2) 5f

3:45 (3:47) (Class 1) 3-Y-0+

£56,710 (£21,500; £10,760; £5,360; £2,690; £1,350) **Stalls** High

Form RPR

/104 **1** **Ortensia (AUS)**[20] 4100 7-9-5 **115**................................ WilliamBuick 13 121
(Paul Messara, Australia) *b: racd towards centre in stands' side gp: bhd: rdn and effrt 2f out: gd hdwy over 1f out: led ins fnl f: r.o strly: taken down early* **6/1**[1]

3254 **2** *1 ¼* **Spirit Quartz (IRE)**[27] 3877 4-9-1 **107**................................ FrankieDettori 7 112
(Robert Cowell) *racd in stands' side gp: midfield overall: hdwy u.p to chse ldrs ent fnl f: kpt on to go 2nd towards fin: 2nd of 11 in gp* **7/1**[3]

0-00 **3** *½* **Masamah (IRE)**[20] 4113 6-9-1 **110**................................ JamieSpencer 17 110
(Kevin Ryan) *racd in stands' side gp: chsd ldr tl led overall after 1f: rdn over 1f out: drvn and hdd ins fnl f: no ex and lost 2nd towards fin: 3rd of 11 in gp* **12/1**

5020 **4** *hd* **Confessional**[20] 4113 5-9-1 **106**................................(be) PaulHanagan 6 109
(Tim Easterby) *racd centre to far side gp: stdd s: hld up towards rr: rdn and hdwy over 1f out: kpt on same pce ins fnl f: 1st of 6 in gp* **20/1**

3-31 **5** *nk* **Angels Will Fall (IRE)**[41] 3375 3-8-9 **106**................................ RobertWinston 1 105
(Charles Hills) *racd in centre to far side gp: stdd s: hld up towards rr: hdwy over 2f out: rdn and chsd overall ldrs ent fnl f: hung lft and no ex ins fnl f: 2nd of 6 in gp* **13/2**[2]

3000 **6** *½* **Humidor (IRE)**[27] 3877 5-9-1 **104**................................(t) RichardHughes 9 107
(George Baker) *racd in stands' side gp: slowly away: wl bhd: sme hdwy and swtchd rt 2f out: hdwy and swtchd rt again 1f out: r.o wl: nvr trbld ldrs: 4th of 11 in gp: taken down early* **40/1**

6435 **7** *½* **Noble Storm (USA)**[14] 4299 6-9-1 **102**................................ RyanMoore 16 105
(Ed McMahon) *racd in stands' side gp: in tch: rdn 2f out: styd on same pce u.p fnl f: 5th of 11 in gp* **33/1**

1-00 **8** *1 ½* **Tangerine Trees**[45] 3238 7-9-1 **114**................................(v) TomEaves 3 99
(Bryan Smart) *racd far side to centre gp: led grooup and chsd ldrs overall tl edgd rt u.p over 1f out: wknd ins fnl f: 3rd of 6 in gp* **6/1**[1]

5-10 **9** *hd* **Stone Of Folca**[45] 3238 4-9-1 **100**................................ LukeMorris 2 99
(John Best) *racd far side to centre gp: chsd gp ldr and in tch overall: rdn and unable qck whn carried rt ent fnl f: wknd ins fnl f: 4th of 6 in gp: taken down early* **28/1**

1-40 **10** *nk* **Amour Propre**[45] 3238 6-9-1 **110**................................ DaneO'Neill 4 98
(Henry Candy) *racd far side to centre gp: hld up towards rr: swtchd lft 2f out: effrt u.p over 1f out: no imp fnl f: 5th of 6 in gp* **25/1**

-110 **11** *½* **Beyond Desire**[61] 2745 5-8-12 **107**................................ NeilCallan 10 93
(Roger Varian) *racd in stands' side gp: chsd ldrs: rdn and unable qck wl over 1f out: wknd ins fnl f: 6th of 11 in gp* **16/1**

-013 **12** *nk* **Excelette (IRE)**[41] 3375 3-8-9 **103**................................ RoystonFfrench 11 92
(Bryan Smart) *racd in stands' side gp: midfield overall: rdn and struggling 1/2-way: plugged on same pce and no threat to ldrs fr over 1f out: 7th of 11 in gp* **25/1**

0202 **13** *shd* **Pabusar**[20] 4113 4-9-1 **106**................................ JimCrowley 12 94
(Ralph Beckett) *lw: racd in stands' side gp: midfield overall: u.p 1/2-way: kpt on but no imp fr over 1f out: 8th of 11 in gp* **9/1**

0200 **14** *nk* **Stepper Point**[20] 4113 3-8-12 **108**................................(b[1]) MartinDwyer 5 93
(William Muir) *lw: racd far side to centre gp: midfield overall: rdn and struggling 2f out: wknd ent fnl f: 6th of 6 in gp* **40/1**

0301 **15** *1* **Hamish McGonagall**[20] 4113 7-9-1 **110**................................ DavidAllan 14 90
(Tim Easterby) *racd in stands' side gp: chsd ldr for 2f: sn rdn and struggling to hold pl: wknd over 1f out: 9th of 11 in gp: taken down early* **10/1**

-030 **16** *5* **Secret Asset (IRE)**[45] 3238 7-9-1 **110**................................ GeorgeBaker 15 72
(Jane Chapple-Hyam) *racd in stands' side gp: midfield overall for 2f: sn dropped to rr: bhd over 1f out: 10th of 11 in gp* **20/1**

6001 **17** *hd* **Elusivity (IRE)**[14] 4299 4-9-1 106......(b) EddieAhern 8 71
(Brian Meehan) *racd in centre tl jnd stands' side gp 3f out: midfield overall: rdn and struggling ent fnl 2f: wknd over 1f out: 11th of 11 in gp* **14/1**

57.24s (-2.96) **Going Correction** -0.25s/f (Firm)
WFA 3 from 4yo+ 3lb **17** Ran SP% **122.2**
Speed ratings (Par 115): **113,111,110,109,109 108,107,105,105,104 103,103,103,102,101 93,92**
Tote Swingers: 1&2 £6.00, 1&3 £14.00, 2&3 £17.00 CSF £41.08 TOTE £5.80: £1.90, £2.50, £5.40; EX 42.50 Trifecta £348.40 Pool: £5,207.81 - 11.06 winning unit..
Owner A D N Fraser, Miss A C N Fraser & Ms E J H Ridley **Bred** L D Rhodes **Trained** Australia

FOCUS
There were two main groups through the opening stages, with six runners racing up the middle and the majority positioned more towards the stands' side, and it was the larger bunch that provided the winner. Racing in between the two groups early on was Spirit Quartz, before he edged left. The runner-up and fourth set the standard.

NOTEBOOK
Ortensia(AUS) ♦ proved in a different league to her ordinary European rivals, despite carrying a 7lb penalty. Aside from the extra weight, there had to be a concern over whether or not she would have the speed to cope with this frantic 5f, and she was duly well behind early, but it was clear from some way out that she was going to be too good once fully into her stride. She hadn't been at her best in two runs since winning the Al Quoz Sprint in Dubai, but conditions hadn't been suitable on either occasion and the return to decent ground proved to be the key. The Nunthorpe is said to be her next target and she was a best-priced 7-1 shot for York straight after this race, but she'll surely be shorter on the day if conditions are in her favour. (tchd 13-2 in a place)
Spirit Quartz(IRE) did well to keep on for second. However, he had absolutely no chance of containing the winner's powerful finishing burst. (op 8-1)
Masamah(IRE), who made all in this race last year, hadn't been at his best so far in 2012 but this was a lot more encouraging. (op 10-1)
Confessional fared best of those who raced in the centre-field group from the off, a particularly creditable effort considering he probably would have preferred easier ground. (op 22-1 tchd 25-1)
Angels Will Fall(IRE) was second best of those who raced in the centre to far-side bunch, but this was tougher than the Ayr Listed race she won on her previous start. (op 8-1)
Humidor(IRE) didn't help himself with a slow start and had to be switched with his run more than once, but he was going on at the finish.
Tangerine Trees, kast season's Prix de l'Abbaye winner, should have found this less demanding than his first two starts of the year, but he was again below his best. (op 7-1)

4763 TELEGRAPH NURSERY 7f
4:20 (4:20) (Class 2) 2-Y-O
£9,703 (£2,887; £1,443; £721) **Stalls** Low

Form RPR
664 **1** **Aussie Reigns (IRE)**[15] 4253 2-7-10 **70**...... DarrenEgan(5) 7 74
(William Knight) *in tch in midfield: shuffled bk towards rr over 2f out: edging lft and rallied u.p over 1f out: gd hdwy ins fnl f: swtchd lft and str run wl ins fnl f to ld last strides* **20/1**
2122 **2** *nk* **Oasis Cannes**[7] 4540 2-8-11 **80**...... LukeMorris 1 83
(Sir Mark Prescott Bt) *b nr hind: led: rdn and fnd ex 2f out: hrd drvn ins fnl f: battled on gamely tl hdd and no ex last strides* **7/2**[1]
3211 **3** *nk* **Janoub Nibras (IRE)**[37] 3501 2-9-7 **90**...... RichardHughes 15 92
(Richard Hannon) *tall: lw: hld up in midfield: rdn and effrt 2f out: hdwy u.p jst ins fnl f: r.o wl fnl 100yds: nt quite rch ldr* **9/1**
1044 **4** *shd* **Party Royal**[7] 4526 2-8-9 **78**...... JoeFanning 2 80
(Mark Johnston) *coltish: chsd ldr: rdn ent fnl 2f: ev ch over 1f out: sltly outpcd 1f out: kpt on again fnl 100yds* **8/1**
451 **5** *hd* **Mystical Moment**[14] 4297 2-9-1 **84**...... RyanMoore 3 85
(Richard Hannon) *hld up in tch in midfield: effrt on inner 2f out: gd hdwy u.p 1f out: r.o wl towards fin: nt quite rch ldrs* **11/2**[2]
2100 **6** *nk* **Pay Freeze (IRE)**[20] 4093 2-9-4 **90**...... HarryBentley(3) 5 91
(Mick Channon) *in tch: rdn to chse ldrs 2f: no imp tl styd on fnl 100yds: nvr quite getting to ldrs* **13/2**[3]
400 **7** *nse* **Shafaani**[14] 4282 2-8-0 **69**...... (t) SilvestreDeSousa 4 70
(Clive Brittain) *chsd ldrs: rdn and unable qck over 1f out: rallied and kpt on again u.p ins fnl f* **40/1**
002 **8** *5* **Zanetto**[15] 4253 2-8-9 **78**...... LiamKeniry 12 66
(Andrew Balding) *stdd s: t.k.h: hld up in tch in rr: swtchd lft and effrt jst over 2f out: no prog and btn whn edgd rt 1f out* **12/1**
313 **9** *nse* **Glass Office**[14] 4283 2-9-4 **87**...... JamieSpencer 11 77
(David Simcock) *stdd after s: hld towards rr: hung lft and hdwy in centre 3f out: chsd ldrs and drvn over 1f out: no ex and btn ins fnl f: eased fnl 75yds* **14/1**
212 **10** *1 ¾* **Bircham (IRE)**[20] 4101 2-9-5 **88**...... FrankieDettori 9 71
(Mahmood Al Zarooni) *hld up in tch: rdn and unable qck ent fnl 2f: btn over 1f out: wknd fnl f* **8/1**
2630 **11** *3 ¾* **Strong Conviction**[34] 3637 2-8-7 **76**......(v[1]) MartinHarley 8 49
(Mick Channon) *hld up in rr: rdn and no hdwy 2f out: bhd over 1f out* **33/1**
221 **12** *4 ½* **Boom And Bloom (IRE)**[20] 4076 2-8-10 **79**...... PaulHanagan 10 40
(Richard Fahey) *awkward leaving stalls and s.i.s: a bhd: rdn and no hdwy over 2f out: bhd over 1f out* **14/1**
21 **13** *10* **A Certain Romance**[22] 3989 2-9-0 **83**...... WilliamBuick 6 18+
(Peter Chapple-Hyam) *chsd ldrs: rdn and losing pl whn hmpd over 2f out: bhd over 1f out: eased ins fnl f* **14/1**

1m 27.45s (0.45) **Going Correction** 0.0s/f (Good) **13** Ran SP% **121.0**
Speed ratings (Par 100): **97,96,96,96,95 95,95,89,89,87 83,78,66**
Tote Swingers: 1&2 £10.50, 1&3 £36.80, 2&3 £5.10 CSF £88.65 CT £722.57 TOTE £28.40: £5.20, £1.80, £2.70; EX 177.50 Trifecta £1211.50 Pool: £2,865.09 - 1.75 winning unit..
Owner The Old Brokers **Bred** S Connolly **Trained** Patching, W Sussex

FOCUS
Richard Hannon was doubly represented in his bid to win this highly competitive nursery for the third time in five years but he was unsuccessful, although his horses both performed well. The race produced a blanket finish and the second looks the best guide.

NOTEBOOK
Aussie Reigns(IRE) had shown modest form in three maidens on easy ground, but was making his handicap debut off just 70. He was held up and still eighth entering the final furlong, but he then picked up really well and burst through a gap to hit the front near the line. He should not go up much for this and, with his attitude, looks capable of going on from this. (op 25-1 tchd 28-1)
Oasis Cannes, a winner at this trip on Polytrack and a close second in three other races over the trip on varying ground, was ridden positively from his rail draw and went very close to making all the running. He ran on gamely in the face of a number of challenges and did not deserve to lose. (tchd 10-3 and 4-1 in places)
Janoub Nibras(IRE) ♦, a dual winner over 6f on Polytrack but with form on fast and soft turf prior to that, was up in trip here but stayed it well enough, keeping on but not as strongly as the winner. This was a good effort off top weight and from the outside draw. (op 8-1)
Party Royal, a winner at 6f on fast ground, was another stepping up in trip and ran his race, only to be squeezed out of the places late on. (tchd 9-1)
Mystical Moment, off the mark when making all over 7f on soft ground and with experience of this track, stuck to the inside in the straight and got a gap, but could not find the necessary change of gear in the last furlong. She probably needs a stiffer test at the trip. (op 5-1 tchd 6-1 in places)
Pay Freeze(IRE), a winner over 6f on fast ground but held in better races since, was taking a drop in grade and a step up in distance and had his chance, but maybe did not quite see it out. (op 8-1)
Shafaani had made a promising debut on fast ground but had then been held twice on softer since. Stepping up in trip for her handicap debut, she ran creditably if only able to find the one speed in the closing stages. (op 50-1)
Glass Office, a 6f Polytrack winner but with form on fast and easy ground on turf and at this trip, was held up before being pulled out wide to make an effort, only for it to peter out in the last furlong. (op 16-1)
Bircham(IRE), a winner on soft but beaten at long odds-on next time on heavy, was also up in trip. He was settled just behind the leaders after a good start, then came to have a chance before fading and being eased. (tchd 15-2)
Boom And Bloom(IRE), a winner over 5f at Chester on her third start, was up 2f in distance but missed the break and can be given another chance.
A Certain Romance Official explanation: jockey said that colt had lost a hind shoe and was unsuited by the track

4764 OAK TREE STKS (GROUP 3) (F&M) 7f
4:50 (4:52) (Class 1) 3-Y-O+
£31,190 (£11,825; £5,918; £2,948; £1,479; £742) **Stalls** Low

Form RPR
40-0 **1** **Regal Realm**[107] 1454 3-8-10 101......(p) RyanMoore 9 98+
(Jeremy Noseda) *hld up towards rr: rdn and hdwy over 1f out: str run fnl f to ld fnl 50yds: gng away at fin* **10/1**
40-0 **2** *¾* **Sunday Nectar (IRE)**[47] 4-9-2 0...... Roberto-CarlosMontenegro 3 98+
(X Thomas-Demeaulte, France) *lengthy: t.k.h: chsd ldrs: rdn and effrt over 1f out: drvn and ev ch ins fnl f: kpt on but outpcd by wnr fnl 50yds: wnt 2nd last strides* **16/1**
1014 **3** *hd* **Appealing (IRE)**[36] 3542 3-8-10 88...... MartinHarley 1 95
(Marco Botti) *hld up in tch: hdwy and swtchd lft over 1f out: sn chsng ldr: drvn and led jst ins fnl f: hdd and no ex fnl 50yds: lost 2nd last strides* **16/1**
2230 **4** *1 ½* **Moretta Blanche**[14] 4286 5-9-2 83......(bt[1]) JimCrowley 2 93
(Ralph Beckett) *hld up towards rr: gd hdwy on inner over 2f out: chsd ldrs whn nt clr run and swtchd lft over 1f out: styd on same pce ins fnl f* **33/1**
0622 **5** *nk* **Sioux Rising (IRE)**[21] 4070 6-9-2 100...... TonyHamilton 13 93
(Richard Fahey) *stdd and dropped in bhd after s: hld up in rr: hmpd bnd over 4f out: hdwy on inner and rdn 2f out: swtchd lft 1f out: kpt on fnl f* **16/1**
5265 **6** *hd* **Night Lily (IRE)**[7] 4527 6-9-2 85...... NeilCallan 8 92
(Paul D'Arcy) *hld up in midfield: rdn and effrt 2f out: no imp tl styd on ins fnl f: unable to chal* **25/1**
0310 **7** *½* **Dysphonia (AUS)**[44] 3266 6-9-2 108......(p) SilvestreDeSousa 11 91
(Saeed Bin Suroor) *in tch in midfield: rdn and unable qck over 2f out: kpt on but no threat to ldrs fr over 1f out* **12/1**
6140 **8** *1 ¾* **Inetrobil (IRE)**[21] 4070 3-8-10 100...... PhillipMakin 4 84
(Kevin Ryan) *chsd ldrs: rdn jst over 2f out: lost 2nd over 1f out: wknd ins fnl f* **20/1**
-152 **9** *½* **Survey (GER)**[34] 3653 3-8-13 105...... TomQueally 6 86
(Mario Hofer, Germany) *leggy: led: rdn and fnd ex ent fnl 2f: hdd jst ins fnl f: sn wknd* **5/1**[3]
0-11 **10** *2 ½* **Gamilati**[182] 418 3-8-10 115...... FrankieDettori 14 76
(Mahmood Al Zarooni) *hld up towards rr: swtchd lft and effrt 2f out: sn drvn and no hdwy: wl hld 1f out* **9/4**[1]
1320 **11** *2 ½* **Russian Rave**[6] 4579 6-9-2 89...... JamesDoyle 10 71
(Jonathan Portman) *hld up in rr: effrt on outer 2f out: no prog and wl hld 1f out* **16/1**
1 **12** *3 ½* **Gracia Directa (GER)**[21] 4070 4-9-5 102...... RobertWinston 12 65
(D Moser, Germany) *w'like: str: on toes: in tch in midfield: rdn and unable qck over 2f out: losing pl whn edgd rt and hmpd 2f out: bhd 1f out* **9/2**[2]
0035 **13** *½* **Sos Brillante (CHI)**[15] 4248 7-9-2 76......[1] DaneO'Neill 7 60
(Terry Clement) *hld up towards rr: rdn and no prog whn nt clr run 2f out: sn wknd* **150/1**
-410 **14** *hd* **Poisson D'Or**[36] 3542 3-8-10 85...... ChrisCatlin 5 58
(Rae Guest) *lw: chsd ldrs: rdn and struggling whn squeezed for room and hmpd 2f out: sn lost pl and bhd 1f out* **28/1**

1m 26.5s (-0.50) **Going Correction** 0.0s/f (Good)
WFA 3 from 4yo+ 6lb **14** Ran SP% **121.6**
Speed ratings (Par 113): **102,101,100,99,98 98,98,96,95,92 89,85,85,84**
Tote Swingers: 1&2 £20.70, 1&3 £35.10, 2&3 £45.00 CSF £152.46 TOTE £12.30: £3.40, £2.60, £5.90; EX 140.60 Trifecta £3596.60 Pool: £4,958.56 - 1.02 winning unit..
Owner Cheveley Park Stud **Bred** Cheveley Park Stud Ltd **Trained** Newmarket, Suffolk

FOCUS
A weak fillies and mares' Group 3 with the third, fourth and sixth all officially rated in the 80s coming into the race. The form is below standard for the grade.

NOTEBOOK
Regal Realm flopped in the Nell Gwyn on her only previous start this season, but she returned from her 107-day break with cheekpieces on for the first time and bounced back to form. This track very much suits as she won the Prestige Stakes on her only other start here and she's likely to face tougher challenges elsewhere, but she's entitled to come on for run. (op 8-1)
Sunday Nectar(IRE), who is trained in France, came into this off the back of a 1m Listed success in Italy. She was dismissed in the market but found only one too good despite being a bit keen. (tchd 20-1)
Appealing(IRE), lightly raced, was fourth in a Yarmouth Listed race last time and showed she's still improving, running well from her helpful draw. (op 25-1)
Moretta Blanche returned to form in first-time blinkers and would have finished a bit closer granted a better trip.
Sioux Rising(IRE) reversed recent 6f York form with the below-par Gracia Directa, but didn't really build on that effort. It can't have helped that she was hampered around 4f out. (op 14-1)
Night Lily(IRE) has shown her best form on Polytrack and came into this rated just 85 on turf, but she ran well. (op 33-1)
Survey(GER), a 1m Group 3 winner in Germany, seemed to make a slightly awkward start and gradually faded after going off quickly. She carried a 3lb penalty. (op 13-2)
Gamilati hadn't been seen since winning the UAE 1000 Guineas in February. She had to prove as effective on turf in a strongly run race, and failed to do so, although she looked a little uncomfortable on the track. (op 13-8)

Gracia Directa(GER), another German-trained runner, had a 3lb penalty for her victory in a 6f Group 3 on easy ground at York last time and she was nowhere near that form. Official explanation: jockey said that the filly was never travelling (op 15-2)

4765 BETFRED BONUS KING BINGO H'CAP 5f

5:25 (5:27) (Class 3) (0-95,93) 3-Y-O

£6,066 (£6,066; £1,398; £699; £349; £175) **Stalls** High

Form RPR

141 **1** **Lady Gibraltar**[8] 4500 3-8-4 **83** 6ex..................(v) MichaelJMMurphy(7) 4 92
(Alan Jarvis) *racd towards centre: midfield: rdn and hdwy over 1f out: led ins fnl f: r.o but ind on post* 16/1

31-1 **1** *dht* **Jwala**[37] 3486 3-9-2 **88**.. ShaneKelly 10 97
(Robert Cowell) *racd towards stands' side: chsd ldr: rdn to ld over 1f out: hrd drvn and hdd ins fnl f: battled on gamely to join ldr on post* 8/1

-050 **3** *1 ¼* **Tioman Legend**[48] 3165 3-9-6 **92**.......................... JamesDoyle 15 97
(Roger Charlton) *lw: racd against stands' rail: bhd: swtchd rt 3f out: hdwy over 1f out: kpt on wl ins fnl f* 14/1

2-1 **4** *hd* **Swan Song**[71] 2422 3-8-12 **84**.......................... JimmyFortune 16 88+
(Andrew Balding) *lw: racd towards stands' side: chsd ldrs: rdn over 1f out: kpt on same pce u.p fnl f* 7/1[3]

2103 **5** *hd* **Kyleakin Lass**[13] 4337 3-9-1 **87**.......................... RichardHughes 7 90+
(Ian Wood) *stdd s: swtchd lft to r towards stands' side sn after: hld up bhd: hdwy jst over 1f out: r.o wl ins fnl f: nt rch ldrs* 8/1

5531 **6** *¾* **Waseem Faris (IRE)**[7] 4558 3-8-12 **84** 6ex.................. MartinHarley 13 84
(Mick Channon) *racd towards stands' side: racd off the pce towards rr: hdwy u.p over 1f out: kpt on ins fnl f* 14/1

5- **7** *1 ½* **Harry Trotter (IRE)**[58] 2829 3-8-11 **83**.......................... TomQueally 18 78
(David Marnane, Ire) *racd against stands' rail sn pushed along and outpcd in rr: hdwy ent fnl f: styd on but nvr trbld ldrs* 8/1

-102 **8** *¾* **Larwood (IRE)**[7] 4530 3-8-7 **79**.......................... MartinDwyer 3 71
(Henry Candy) *stdd and short of room s: swtchd lft to r towards 'stands: hld up bhd: rdn and effrt jst over 1f out: kpt on but n.d* 5/1[2]

565 **9** *hd* **Signifer (IRE)**[8] 4500 3-8-6 **78**.......................... AdrianNicholls 9 70
(Mick Channon) *racd centre to stands' side: hld up towards rr: rdn 3f out: hdwy u.p over 1f out: no ex and wknd ins fnl f* 33/1

1-0P **10** *nk* **Heyward Girl (IRE)**[39] 3445 3-8-6 **81**.......................... HarryBentley(3) 11 71
(Robert Eddery) *racd towards stands' side: in tch: rdn and unable qck 1/2-way: wknd u.p jst ins fnl f* 25/1

13U1 **11** *nk* **Beau Mistral (IRE)**[21] 4044 3-8-11 **83**.......................... CathyGannon 8 72
(Paul Green) *lw: racd towards stands' side: in tch: rdn 2f out: struggling to qckn whn squeezed for room over 1f out: swtchd rt and one pce fnl f* 33/1

5031 **12** *¾* **Heartsong (IRE)**[16] 4221 3-8-13 **85**.......................... RobertWinston 2 72
(John Gallagher) *on toes: racd down centre: chsd ldrs: rdn 1/2-way: wknd fnl f* 25/1

0-03 **13** *¾* **Sandfrankskipsgo**[8] 4500 3-8-4 **76**.......................... JoeFanning 5 60
(Peter Crate) *racd down centre: in tch: rdn 1/2-way: wknd jst over 1f out* 16/1

2422 **14** *¾* **Place In My Heart**[21] 4063 3-9-7 **93**.......................... RyanMoore 12 74
(George Baker) *racd towards stands' side: sn pushed along in midfield: lost pl and bhd whn nt clr run ent fnl f: no ch after* 9/2[1]

0100 **15** *4 ½* **Powerful Wind (IRE)**[15] 4234 3-8-12 **89**.......................... DarrenEgan(5) 17 54
(Ronald Harris) *b.hind: swtg: racd against stands' rail: led tl hdd and rdn over 1f out: fdd fnl f* 33/1

57.83s (-2.37) **Going Correction** -0.25s/f (Firm) 15 Ran SP% **122.3**

Speed ratings (Par 104): **108,108,106,105,105 104,101,100,100,99 99,98,96,95,88**Win: Jwala £4.70 Lady Gibraltar £8.90 Place: J £2.80 LG £5.00 TL £5.80 Exacta: J-LG £61.47 LG-J £81.80 CSF: J-LG £61.47 LG-J £66.28 Tricast: J-LG-TL £897.08 LG-J-TL £941.24. Tote Swingers: J&LG £25.10, J&TL £25.20, LG&TL £37.00, £0.027, £OwnerBuckingham Flooring Bred Trifecta £Netherfield House Stud Trained Twyford, Bucks.

Owner Manor Farm Stud & Miss S Hoare **Bred** Manor Farm Stud (rutland) **Trained** Six Mile Bottom, Cambs

FOCUS

A good, competitive sprint handicap for 3yos. The time was a highly respectable 0.59 seconds slower than the earlier Group 3 King George Stakes. They raced middle to stands' side and there was no obvious track bias. The third is rated close to form and sets the level.

NOTEBOOK

Lady Gibraltar used to compromise her chance by hanging left, but she's really got her act together now and made it three wins from her last four starts, despite being 4lb wrong under the penalty for her recent Epsom success. She raced more towards the centre than most of the others for some of the way, but it didn't seem to make a difference.

Jwala was a winner at Bath on her reappearance and proved up to coping with a 7lb higher mark, completing a hat-trick that stretches back to a Wolverhampton maiden in December. This was only her seventh start in total and she could progress into a smart sprinter.

Tioman Legend seemed to appreciate the return to decent ground. The manner in which he kept on suggests he won't mind going back up to 6f - either that or a stiffer track at this distance.

Swan Song ◆ hadn't been seen since winning a Salisbury maiden on her reappearance in May. This was no easy task for just the third start of her career and it was a pleasing effort in the circumstances. She's bred to make a smart sprinter and is one to keep on-side. (op 13-2 tchd 6-1)

Kyleakin Lass kept on nicely from a fair way back and this was a creditable effort considering the ground was probably a little quicker than ideal. (op 10-1)

Waseem Faris(IRE) couldn't cope with a penalty for his recent York win. (op 20-1)

Harry Trotter(IRE) seemed unsuited by the drop in trip. (op 9-1 tchd 10-1)

Larwood(IRE) can be excused this. He was squeezed out at the start and was always behind over what was probably a sharp enough test. (tchd 11-2)

Place In My Heart had gone up a total of 8lb for finishing second on her last two starts. She wasn't at her best this time, but the Vet reported the filly lost a left hind and left front shoe. Official explanation: vet said the filly had lost a left hind and left front shoe (tchd 5-1)

T/Jkpt: Not won. T/Plt: £2,832.50 to a £1 stake. Pool: £290,507.85 - 74.87 winning tickets. T/Qpdt: £260.90 to a £1 stake. Pool: £21,233.44 - 60.22 winning tickets. SP

4426 MUSSELBURGH (R-H)

Friday, August 3

OFFICIAL GOING: Good (good to firm in places; 7.4)

Wind: Almost nil Weather: Overcast

4766 BLACKROCK AMATEUR RIDERS' H'CAP 1m 5f

6:10 (6:14) (Class 5) (0-70,74) 4-Y-O+ **£2,495** (£774; £386; £193) **Stalls** Low

Form RPR

3-00 **1** **Stormy Morning**[41] 3402 6-9-11 **55**..........................(p) MissHBethell(3) 8 62
(Philip Kirby) *prom: hdwy to ld over 1f out: pushed out fnl f* 20/1

0430 **2** *1 ½* **Sohcahtoa (IRE)**[13] 4326 6-11-0 **69**.......................... MissSBrotherton 3 73+
(David Barron) *t.k.h: hld up: outpcd over 2f out: swtchd rt and gd hdwy over 1f out: styd on to take 2nd towards fin: nt rch wnr* 3/1[1]

-101 **3** *nk* **Talk Of Saafend (IRE)**[13] 3116 7-10-2 **57**.......................... MissECSayer 5 61+
(Dianne Sayer) *in tch: lost pl 1/2-way: effrt on outside to chse wnr appr fnl f: one pce and lost 2nd towards fin* 10/1

0-31 **4** *1 ¼* **Houston Dynimo (IRE)**[10] 4429 7-11-2 **74** 6ex...... MissJRRichards(3) 7 76
(Nicky Richards) *sn w ldr: led after 3f: rdn and hdd over 1f out: kpt on same pce* 7/1

2044 **5** *¾* **Shy**[17] 4179 7-10-0 **60**..(b) MissPhillipaTutty(5) 6 61
(Karen Tutty) *t.k.h: led 3f: disp ld to over 3f out: edgd lft and one pce over 1f out* 6/1[3]

-202 **6** *¾* **Hi Dancer**[36] 3519 9-9-13 **54**.......................... MissJCoward 1 51
(Ben Haslam) *t.k.h: trckd ldrs: shkn up over 2f out: one pce over 1f out* 6/1[3]

0/05 **7** *¾* **Aggravation**[30] 3753 10-9-8 **52**.......................... SamanthaDrake(3) 11 51
(Chris Grant) *midfield: pushed along over 2f out: no imp over 1f out* 33/1

3332 **8** *1 ½* **Cadgers Brig**[11] 4391 4-10-5 **60**..........................(p) MrSWalker 10 57
(Keith Dalgleish) *hld up: stdy hdwy over 5f out: effrt over 2f out: carried hd high and no ex over 1f out* 9/2[2]

0102 **9** *13* **Vittachi**[10] 4431 5-10-3 **63**.......................... MrBCampbell(5) 2 40
(Alistair Whillans) *in tch: lost pl 1/2-way: effrt on outside over 3f out: wknd fnl 2f* 8/1

0003 **10** *19* **Purkab**[10] 4431 4-9-2 **50** oh5.......................... MrsICGoldie(7) 9
(Jim Goldie) *s.v.s: a wl bhd* 33/1

0 **11** *8* **Dimashq**[49] 3116 10-9-6 **50** oh5.......................... MissWGibson(3) 4
(Paul Midgley) *dwlt: hld up: hdwy on outside to chse ldrs over 5f out: rdn and wknd over 2f out* 33/1

2m 52.38s (0.38) **Going Correction** -0.025s/f (Good) 11 Ran SP% **118.0**

Speed ratings (Par 103): **97,96,95,95,94 94,93,92,84,73 68**

toteswingers:1&2 £20.00, 2&3 £8.20, 1&3 £25.60 CSF £77.50 CT £648.45 TOTE £34.30: £8.80, £1.70, £3.20; EX 124.60.

Owner Colin Fletcher & Ownaracehorse **Bred** Wellsummers Stud **Trained** Castleton, N Yorks

FOCUS

A modest amateur event. The gallop wasn't that strong until past halfway and it didn't pay to sit too far back, the second and third both better than the result, particularly the former. The fourth sets the level.

Stormy Morning Official explanation: trainer said, regarding the apparent improvement of form,that the gelding was better suited by the quicker ground

Purkab Official explanation: jockey said that the gelding missed the break

4767 WILKINSON & ASSOCIATES NURSERY 5f

6:45 (6:47) (Class 6) (0-65,65) 2-Y-O **£2,587** (£770; £384; £192) **Stalls** High

Form RPR

000 **1** **Mill End Dancer**[49] 3126 2-8-1 **45**.......................... JamesSullivan 4 50
(Michael Easterby) *prom: hdwy to ld appr fnl f: drvn and kpt on wl fnl f* 14/1

2524 **2** *1 ¼* **Perfect Words (IRE)**[30] 3748 2-9-2 **63**.......................... JulieBurke(3) 2 63
(Marjorie Fife) *chsd ldng gp on outside: effrt and rdn over 1f out: chsd wnr ins fnl f: r.o* 5/1[3]

2464 **3** *nk* **Therapeutic**[18] 4152 2-9-4 **62**..........................(p) MickyFenton 6 61
(Scott Dixon) *led tl rdn and hdd appr fnl f: kpt on ins fnl f* 11/4[1]

5550 **4** *½* **Someone's Darling**[11] 4387 2-9-4 **62**.......................... GrahamLee 8 60
(Jim Goldie) *hld up: nt clr run 1/2-way: effrt and rdn over 1f out: r.o fnl f: nt pce to chal* 5/1[3]

3203 **5** *nk* **Princess In Exile**[35] 3576 2-9-7 **65**.......................... BarryMcHugh 7 61
(George Foster) *trckd ldrs: effrt and drvn 2f out: kpt on same pce ins fnl f* 8/1

000 **6** *2 ¼* **Twinwood Star (IRE)**[14] 4310 2-7-13 **46**.......................... DeclanCannon(3) 5 34
(John Weymes) *disp ld: ev ch over 1f out: wknd ins fnl f* 16/1

1000 **7** *¾* **Vanessa**[9] 4450 2-9-2 **65**.......................... NeilFarley(5) 9 50
(Jim Goldie) *dwlt: sn rdn along in rr: shortlived effrt 2f out: sn btn* 20/1

640 **8** *1 ½* **Tiger Prince (IRE)**[24] 3948 2-8-6 **55**..........................(v[1]) ShaneBKelly(5) 3 35
(Ann Duffield) *s.i.s: towards rr: rdn and hung rt over 2f out: wknd wl over 1f out* 7/2[2]

000 **9** *16* **Cromwell Rose (IRE)**[13] 4344 2-8-6 **50**..........................(p) FrannyNorton 10
(John Weymes) *uns rdr and loose on way to s: sn drvn towards rr: lost tch fr 1/2-way: t.o* 16/1

1m 1.1s (0.70) **Going Correction** -0.10s/f (Good) 9 Ran SP% **116.5**

Speed ratings (Par 92): **90,88,87,86,86 82,81,79,53**

toteswingers:1&2 £9.50, 2&3 £2.30, 1&3 £11.50 CSF £83.17 CT £255.88 TOTE £23.00: £6.20, £2.60, £1.02; EX 106.40.

Owner W T Allgood **Bred** The Rt Hon Mary, Lady Manton **Trained** Sheriff Hutton, N Yorks

FOCUS

An ordinary sprint nursery, though it at least went to one of the unexposed sorts in the line-up. The winner and the fourth help set the level.

NOTEBOOK

Mill End Dancer was allotted a basement mark after finishing down the field in three qualifying runs and improved back from a break. She left the impression she was only doing what was required once hitting the front and will remain of interest from a mark which will only be in the low-50s even once reassessed. Official explanation: trainer could offer no explanation for the apparent improvement in form (op 16-1)

Perfect Words(IRE) bounced back to her very best on her second start for the yard, the return to a sounder surface probably suiting, though she already has a fairly exposed look about her. (op 4-1)

Therapeutic ran creditably in first-time cheekpieces but needs no excusing after leading against the rail. (op 5-2)

Someone's Darling ran just about her best race without ever threatening a serious blow. She's tried a few trips but 6f could suit ideally on this evidence. (op 7-1)

Princess In Exile was another to run her race whilst leaving the impression she has little obviously in hand of her opening mark. (op 10-1)

Tiger Prince(IRE) attracted market support down in trip on his nursery bow, but got warm beforehand and was never going in a first-time visor. He'll have a bit to prove next time. Official explanation: jockey said that the gelding hung right handed throughout (op 5-1)

4768 ISHARES H'CAP 1m 1f

7:20 (7:20) (Class 5) (0-70,73) 3-Y-O+ **£3,881** (£1,155; £577; £288) **Stalls** High

Form RPR

5101 **1** **Double Cee**[15] 4260 3-9-6 **70**.......................... DavidNolan 4 80
(Richard Fahey) *in tch: effrt over 2f out: hdwy and edgd lft over 1f out: edgd rt and led ins fnl f: drvn out* 11/2[3]

3501 **2** *1 ¼* **Call Of Duty (IRE)**[6] 4594 7-8-13 **60**.......................... LucyAlexander(5) 7 67
(Dianne Sayer) *hld up: gd hdwy on outside over 1f out: styd on to take 2nd nr fin: nt rch wnr* 5/1[2]

4002 **3** *¾* **Sangar**[10] 4426 4-9-7 **63**.......................... MichaelO'Connell 6 68
(Ollie Pears) *trckd ldr: led over 1f out to ins fnl f: kpt on same pce: lost 2nd towards fin* 5/1[2]

-523 **4** *1* **Christmas Light**[10] 4426 5-9-12 **68**.......................... BarryMcHugh 8 71
(Brian Ellison) *t.k.h: cl up: led over 2f out to over 1f out: one pce fnl f* 6/1

511 **5** *1 ½* **Royal Straight**[3] 4674 7-9-12 **73** 6ex............................(t) ShaneBKelly(5) 5 73
(Linda Perratt) *hld up towards rr: stdy hdwy over 2f out: effrt over 1f out: nt qckn* **3/1**[1]

04-0 **6** *1 ½* **Grand Diamond (IRE)**[36] 3519 8-8-10 **52**......................(p) GrahamLee 9 48
(Jim Goldie) *prom: rdn and outpcd wl over 2f out: rallied appr fnl f: no imp* **22/1**

6-43 **7** *3* **A Southside Boy (GER)**[10] 4429 4-8-4 **51** oh6................ NeilFarley(5) 2 41
(Jim Goldie) *t.k.h: hld up: rdn over 3f out: no imp fr 2f out* **40/1**

-000 **8** *hd* **Desert Vision**[13] 4325 8-9-12 **68**..............................(vt) JamesSullivan 10 57
(Michael Easterby) *t.k.h: led to over 2f out: wknd over 1f out* **13/2**

6262 **9** *6* **Mangham (IRE)**[4] 4643 7-8-7 **56**..........................(p) GeorgeChaloner(7) 3 32
(George Foster) *s.s: bhd: drvn 3f out: btn fnl 2f* **11/1**

1m 52.97s (-0.93) **Going Correction** -0.025s/f (Good)
WFA 3 from 4yo+ 8lb **9** Ran SP% **116.5**
Speed ratings (Par 103): **103,101,101,100,99 97,95,94,89**
toteswingers:1&2 £4.50, 2&3 £2.70, 1&3 £8.00 CSF £33.43 CT £147.12 TOTE £4.90: £1.90, £2.20, £1.50; EX 48.00.
Owner R A Fahey **Bred** Bearstone Stud **Trained** Musley Bank, N Yorks

FOCUS
A fair handicap and a good race for the grade, although it could be worth more as the placed horses are rated beklow their latest marks. Desert Vision ensured a sound enough pace but, typically round here, it still didn't pay to sit too far back.
Mangham(IRE) Official explanation: jockey said that the gelding missed the break

4769 TATTY BANKS BAGS A NAG TOMORROW H'CAP 7f 30y
7:50 (7:51) (Class 5) (0-75,75) 3-Y-O+ **£3,234** (£962; £481; £240) **Stalls** Low

Form RPR

2412 **1** **Cyflymder (IRE)**[9] 4469 6-9-0 **68**................................ LucyAlexander(5) 3 78
(David C Griffiths) *trckd ldrs: rdn to ld over 1f out: kpt on wl run-in* **2/1**[1]

-244 **2** *¾* **Springheel Jake**[42] 3354 3-9-6 **75**...................................... DavidNolan 1 81
(Ann Duffield) *t.k.h: trckd ldrs: nt clr run and swtchd lft over 1f out: hdwy to chse wnr ins fnl f: r.o* **7/2**[2]

5251 **3** *2 ½* **Soopacal (IRE)**[11] 4406 7-8-12 **61** 6ex.......................... BarryMcHugh 6 62
(Brian Ellison) *led: rdn over 2f out: hdd over 1f out: kpt on same pce fnl f* **9/2**[3]

6002 **4** *½* **Chookie Avon**[11] 4388 5-8-10 **64**..(p) LMcNiff(5) 9 64
(Keith Dalgleish) *hld up in tch: stdy hdwy over 2f out: rdn over 1f out: edgd rt and one pce fnl f* **6/1**

003 **5** *4 ½* **Berbice (IRE)**[10] 4432 7-8-11 **60**.................................... JamesSullivan 2 48
(Linda Perratt) *t.k.h: hld up in tch on ins: effrt over 2f out: btn fnl f* **16/1**

0006 **6** *2 ¼* **Shunkawakhan (IRE)**[4] 4643 9-8-4 **56** oh11........(tp) DeclanCannon(3) 5 38
(Linda Perratt) *prom: drvn over 2f out: wknd over 1f out* **40/1**

0450 **7** *1 ¼* **Long Lost Love**[38] 3471 3-8-5 **60**.................................... FrannyNorton 7 36
(Mark Johnston) *t.k.h: cl up: ev ch over 2f out to over 1f out: wknd ent fnl f* **12/1**

50-0 **8** *3* **Music Festival (USA)**[11] 4388 5-9-1 **64**............................ GrahamLee 8 34
(Jim Goldie) *hld up: drvn along over 2f out: sn outpcd* **16/1**

0040 **9** *nse* **Just The Tonic**[22] 3994 5-9-3 **69**.. JulieBurke(3) 4 39
(Marjorie Fife) *s.s: bhd: struggling wl over 2f out: sn btn* **14/1**

1m 29.49s (0.49) **Going Correction** -0.025s/f (Good)
WFA 3 from 5yo+ 6lb **9** Ran SP% **116.6**
Speed ratings (Par 103): **96,95,92,91,86 84,82,79,79**
toteswingers:1&2 £2.60, 2&3 £5.20, 1&3 £4.20 CSF £9.01 CT £27.87 TOTE £3.60: £2.20, £1.40, £1.50; EX 8.30.
Owner Steve Young **Bred** Miss Laura G F Ferguson **Trained** Bawtry, S Yorks

FOCUS
Another handicap in which they went a sound gallop but not many ever got in a serious blow. The third sets the level.
Just The Tonic Official explanation: jockey said that the mare missed the break

4770 BLACKROCK H'CAP 5f
8:20 (8:21) (Class 4) (0-80,80) 3-Y-O+ **£6,469** (£1,925; £962; £481) **Stalls** High

Form RPR

331- **1** **Queen Grace (IRE)**[33] 3677 5-8-13 **76**........................... ShaneGray(7) 4 88
(Michael J Browne, Ire) *hld up: smooth hdwy 1/2-way: rdn to ld ins fnl f: edgd rt: sn clr* **11/1**

6464 **2** *2 ¼* **Barney McGrew (IRE)**[7] 4554 9-9-8 **78**........................ BarryMcHugh 12 82
(Michael Dods) *taken early to post: midfield: hung rt thrght: outpcd 1/2-way: styd on wl fnl f to take 2nd cl home: no ch w wnr* **3/1**[1]

1-60 **3** *1* **We'll Deal Again**[6] 4591 5-9-2 **72**...............................(b) JamesSullivan 8 72
(Michael Easterby) *cl up: drvn over 2f out: kpt on same pce ins fnl f* **14/1**

115 **4** *hd* **Nomoreblondes**[9] 4451 8-9-0 **77**.................................(v) NedCurtis(7) 3 77
(Paul Midgley) *trckd ldr: drvn 1/2-way: one pce fnl f* **16/1**

253 **5** *½* **Diman Waters (IRE)**[34] 3608 5-9-1 **76**.......................... DarylByrne(5) 10 74
(Eric Alston) *hld up in tch: effrt over 1f out: no imp fnl f* **7/2**[2]

2003 **6** *hd* **Even Stevens**[6] 4591 4-9-8 **78**.......................................(p) MickyFenton 9 75
(Scott Dixon) *set str pce: led to ins fnl f: sn no ex* **9/1**

0610 **7** *hd* **Blown It (USA)**[4] 4638 6-8-9 **70** 6ex...................................... LMcNiff(5) 5 66
(Keith Dalgleish) *hld up: effrt and pushed along 2f out: kpt on fnl f: nvr able to chal* **25/1**

2160 **8** *1* **Rasaman (IRE)**[12] 4367 8-9-10 **80**...................................... GrahamLee 1 73+
(Jim Goldie) *hld up on outside: hdwy whn nt clr run ins fnl f: nvr on terms* **10/1**

335 **9** *1 ¼* **Diamond Blue**[63] 2674 4-8-8 **69**................................(v¹) ShaneBKelly(5) 2 57
(Richard Whitaker) *rrd s: bhd and drvn along: sme hdwy over 1f out: nvr on terms* **14/1**

321- **10** *2 ¼* **Idler (IRE)**[283] 7072 3-9-2 **75**... FrannyNorton 7 55
(Mark Johnston) *midfield: outpcd after 2f: n.d after* **4/1**[3]

13-0 **11** *3 ¾* **L'Astre De Choisir (IRE)**[76] 2264 4-8-9 **72**........ DavidSimmonson(7) 11 39
(Michael Easterby) *dwlt: a outpcd and bhd* **33/1**

59.2s (-1.20) **Going Correction** -0.10s/f (Good)
WFA 3 from 4yo+ 3lb **11** Ran SP% **120.6**
Speed ratings (Par 105): **105,101,99,99,98 98,98,96,94,90 84**
toteswingers: 1&2 £11.60, 2&3 £11.30, 1&3 £28.40 CSF £45.19 CT £491.98 TOTE £13.40: £3.10, £1.20, £8.50; EX 45.30.
Owner Michael J Browne **Bred** Michael J Woodlock **Trained** Cashel, Co. Tipperary

FOCUS
A one-sided handicap in the end and a step up from the winner with the second close to recent form.
Rasaman(IRE) Official explanation: jockey said that the gelding was denied a clear run
Diamond Blue Official explanation: jockey said that the filly reared as the stalls opened

4771 WILKINSON & ASSOCIATES H'CAP 1m
8:50 (8:50) (Class 6) (0-65,63) 3-Y-O **£1,940** (£577; £288; £144) **Stalls** Low

Form RPR

6-02 **1** **Dance For Georgie**[63] 2673 3-8-4 **49**............................... JulieBurke(3) 6 64
(Ben Haslam) *mde all: hrd pressed fr over 3f out: styd on strly to go clr fnl f* **6/1**[3]

0213 **2** *4 ½* **Miss Ella Jade**[17] 4172 3-8-8 **55**.................................... ShaneBKelly(5) 2 59
(Richard Whitaker) *t.k.h: hld up in tch on ins: effrt and drvn over 2f out: styd on to chse (clr) wnr ins fnl f: kpt on: no imp* **11/4**[1]

-003 **3** *½* **Kathleensluckylad (IRE)**[11] 4397 3-9-0 **56**...................... GrahamLee 7 59
(Kevin Ryan) *cl up: ev ch over 3f out: sn rdn: outpcd over 1f out: r.o ins fnl f* **7/1**

0640 **4** *1 ¾* **Sleepy Lucy**[88] 1918 3-8-0 **45**...................................... DeclanCannon(3) 1 44
(Richard Guest) *in tch: hdwy and ev ch over 1f out: edgd rt and no ex ins fnl f* **22/1**

6-54 **5** *½* **Gibraltar Road**[11] 4397 3-9-0 **56**.............................. MichaelO'Connell 12 54
(John Quinn) *t.k.h: hld up: hdwy and edgd lft over 2f out: kpt on fnl f: nvr able to chal* **9/2**[2]

0500 **6** *2 ¾* **Hikma (USA)**[15] 4263 3-8-13 **55**.. FrannyNorton 5 46
(Mark Johnston) *bhd: drvn and outpcd after 3f: hdwy 2f out: nvr able to chal* **9/1**

0064 **7** *2 ½* **La Salida**[23] 3952 3-8-13 **60**...(b¹) LMcNiff(5) 1 46
(David Barron) *trckd ldrs: rdn over 2f out: wknd over 1f out* **7/1**

0054 **8** *2* **Captain Baldwin**[31] 3727 3-7-12 **45**...............................(v) NeilFarley(5) 3 26
(Jim Goldie) *midfield: rdn and outpcd over 2f out: n.d after* **33/1**

0060 **9** *nk* **Windygoul Lad**[91] 1817 3-9-0 **56**..............................(p) JamesSullivan 10 36
(Keith Dalgleish) *t.k.h: hld up in tch on outside: struggling over 2f out: sn n.d* **20/1**

5030 **10** *5* **Divine Success (IRE)**[11] 4397 3-8-8 **50**......................... BarryMcHugh 8 19
(Richard Fahey) *towards rr: drvn along 1/2-way: btn fnl 2f* **12/1**

21-0 **11** *3 ¼* **Galilee Chapel (IRE)**[18] 4133 3-9-2 **63**...................... GarryWhillans(5) 9 24
(Alistair Whillans) *hld up on outside: struggling wl over 2f out: sn btn* **12/1**

0205 **12** *46* **Master Chipper**[42] 3352 3-9-2 **58**.................................(v¹) DavidNolan 13
(Michael Dods) *t.k.h and sn cl up on outside: rdn and wandered over 2f out: sn btn: t.o* **25/1**

1m 41.39s (0.19) **Going Correction** -0.025s/f (Good) **12** Ran SP% **125.4**
Speed ratings (Par 98): **98,93,93,91,90 88,85,83,83,78 74,28**
toteswingers:1&2 £5.60, 2&3 £6.40, 1&3 £4.50 CSF £23.11 CT £126.92 TOTE £7.60: £2.80, £1.10, £2.20; EX 14.70.
Owner Mrs Alison Royston **Bred** West Dereham Abbey Stud **Trained** Middleham Moor, N Yorks

FOCUS
Another wide-margin handicap winner while the placed horses set the standard.
T/Plt: £67.10 to a £1 stake. Pool £43791.06 - 475.78 winning units. T/Qpdt: £7.60 to a £1 stake. Pool £4552.38 - 439.30 winning units. RY

4595 NEWMARKET (R-H)
Friday, August 3

OFFICIAL GOING: Good to firm (8.2)
Wind: Light across Weather: Cloudy

4772 50 WILLOWS H'CAP 1m
5:50 (5:50) (Class 4) (0-80,80) 3-Y-O+ **£4,528** (£1,347; £673; £336) **Stalls** High

Form RPR

0210 **1** **Speedi Mouse**[35] 3589 3-8-3 **69**............................. NicoleNordblad(7) 12 79
(Philip McBride) *hld up: hdwy over 1f out: rdn to ld ins fnl f: r.o* **12/1**

4104 **2** *1* **Dixie's Dream (IRE)**[39] 3446 3-9-7 **80**................................ PatDobbs 11 88
(Richard Hannon) *hld up in tch: rdn and ev ch ins fnl f: edgd lft: styd on* **8/1**

-036 **3** *½* **Hurricane Lady (IRE)**[20] 4091 4-9-8 **74**......................... NickyMackay 7 82
(Mike Murphy) *s.i.s: hld up: hdwy over 1f out: rdn and edgd lft ins fnl f: r.o* **14/1**

601 **4** *½* **Mrs Greeley**[29] 3790 4-9-10 **76**.. TedDurcan 2 83+
(Eve Johnson Houghton) *hld up: rdn and r.o wl ins fnl f: nt rch ldrs* **5/1**[2]

4-60 **5** *1* **Early Applause**[69] 2473 4-9-8 **74**........................... MatthewChadwick 10 78
(Charles Hills) *led over 5f: rdn and n.m.r over 1f out: styd on* **14/1**

10 **6** *½* **Daruband**[13] 4345 4-9-11 **77**...(v) MickaelBarzalona 3 80
(Alan McCabe) *hld up: hdwy over 3f out: rdn over 1f out: no ex ins fnl f* **13/2**[3]

2500 **7** *1 ¾* **Mcbirney (USA)**[35] 3594 5-8-13 **72**.............................. LouisSteward(7) 5 71
(Paul D'Arcy) *s.i.s: sn prom: chsd ldr over 3f out: led over 2f out: rdn over 1f out: hdd and no ex ins fnl f* **14/1**

1-30 **8** *1* **Restaurateur (IRE)**[14] 4288 3-9-2 **75**............................. DarryllHolland 8 71
(Andrew Balding) *prom: chsd ldr over 5f out tl pushed along over 3f out: styd on same pce appr fnl f* **5/1**[2]

5004 **9** *2* **Chapter And Verse (IRE)**[33] 3667 6-9-11 **77**.............. StephenCraine 6 69
(Mike Murphy) *s.i.s: hld up: hdwy over 3f out: rdn over 1f out: wknd ins fnl f* **10/3**[1]

54 **10** *½* **Masters Blazing**[16] 4223 3-9-0 **73**........................... DaraghO'Donohoe 4 63
(John Ryan) *chsd ldr tl over 5f out: rdn over 3f out: n.m.r and lost pl over 2f out: n.d after* **16/1**

5045 **11** *1 ¼* **Rough Rock (IRE)**[4] 4661 7-9-2 **73**.............................. TobyAtkinson(5) 13 61
(Chris Dwyer) *prom: plld hrd: rdn over 2f out: wknd over 1f out* **16/1**

40-0 **12** *9* **Dashwood**[14] 4302 5-9-1 **74**.. SiobhanMiller(7) 1 42
(Anthony Carson) *in rr: pushed along over 3f out: sn wknd* **33/1**

1m 40.18s (0.18) **Going Correction** -0.025s/f (Good)
WFA 3 from 4yo+ 7lb **12** Ran SP% **123.3**
Speed ratings (Par 105): **98,97,96,96,95 94,92,91,89,89 88,79**
toteswingers:1&2 £14.70, 2&3 £8.80, 1&3 £36.30 CSF £108.94 CT £1384.99 TOTE £15.00: £3.20, £1.90, £3.20; EX 133.10 TRIFECTA Not won..
Owner P J McBride **Bred** Langham Hall Stud **Trained** Newmarket, Suffolk

FOCUS
Far side track used with stalls on far side except 12f: centre. The going was good to firm and there was a cross breeze on the track. They went a fair pace in this handicap. The first four all came from some way back and they were spread across the track at the finish. the third is rated her 3-y-o form.

4773 BRITISH STALLION STUDS SUPPORTING BRITISH RACING EBF MAIDEN STKS 6f
6:20 (6:21) (Class 4) 2-Y-O **£4,528** (£1,347; £673; £336) **Stalls** High

Form RPR
1 **Chief Inspector (IRE)** 2-9-3 0........ KierenFallon 7 86+
(Brian Meehan) *w ldr tl led over 3f out: hung rt over 1f out: sn rdn: edgd lft ins fnl f: styd on* **8/1**
2 ½ **Intrepid (IRE)** 2-9-3 0........ WilliamBuick 10 84+
(Jeremy Noseda) *a.p: pushed along and swtchd rt over 1f out: r.o wl ins fnl f: wnt 2nd towards fin: nt rch wnr* **7/1**[3]
3 1 ½ **Senator Bong** 2-9-3 0........ PadraigBeggy 11 79
(David Elsworth) *plld hrd and prom: rdn over 1f out: styd on same pce ins fnl f* **33/1**
0 **4** 1 **Rock Up (IRE)**[55] 2929 2-9-3 0........ TedDurcan 3 75
(David Elsworth) *hld up: hdwy over 2f out: rdn over 1f out: styd on same pce ins fnl f* **25/1**
00 **5** ¾ **Royal Caper**[21] 4066 2-9-3 0........ DaraghO'Donohoe 2 73+
(John Ryan) *sn led: hdd over 3f out: rdn over 1f out: styd on same pce* **150/1**
6 2 ¼ **George Cinq** 2-9-3 0........ HayleyTurner 8 66
(Michael Bell) *prom: rdn over 1f out: no ex ins fnl f* **20/1**
7 1 ¼ **Correggio** 2-9-3 0........ PatDobbs 4 62+
(Richard Hannon) *s.s: hgeld up: edgd lft over 2f out: nvr nrr* **14/1**
8 nk **Price Is Truth (USA)** 2-9-3 0........ MickaelBarzalona 5 61+
(Mahmood Al Zarooni) *rn green in rr: rdn over 2f out: hung lft ins fnl f: n.d* **15/8**[1]
9 nk **Daaree (IRE)** 2-9-3 0........(t) PaulHanagan 12 60
(Saeed Bin Suroor) *s.i.s: sn prom: rdn over 2f out: wknd over 1f out* **11/4**[2]
0 **10** 2 **Karr Wa Farr (IRE)**[13] 4340 2-9-3 0........ LukeMorris 1 53
(Ed Vaughan) *hld up: rdn over 2f out: a in rr* **25/1**
11 1 **Epic Battle (IRE)** 2-9-3 0........ DarryllHolland 9 50
(William Haggas) *rn green in mid-div: wknd over 2f out* **10/1**
12 1 **Hartwright** 2-9-3 0........ JamieSpencer 6 56+
(Michael Bell) *s.i.s: hld up: hmpd over 2f out: n.d* **20/1**

1m 15.67s (3.17) **Going Correction** -0.025s/f (Good) **12** Ran SP% **121.6**
Speed ratings (Par 96): **77,76,74,73,72 69,67,66,66,63 62,61**
toteswingers:1&2 £10.90, 2&3 £84.80, 1&3 £58.70 CSF £59.00 TOTE £9.60: £3.10, £3.10, £12.90; EX 82.10 TRIFECTA Not won..
Owner Bayardo **Bred** Castlemartin Sky & Skymarc Farm **Trained** Manton, Wilts

FOCUS
This is usually a hot maiden. Justineo went on to finish a respectable fourth in the Gimcrack after taking this last year and the most high-profile winner in recent years was 2003 scorer Haafhd who went on to win the 2000 Guineas and Champion Stakes the following year. This renewal was run at a steady pace and the two Godolphin market leaders were a bit disappointing, but the winner scored well and the second shaped with a huge amount of promise. Many of these should do better in time.

NOTEBOOK
Chief Inspector(IRE), a £55,000 half-brother to 8.5f juvenile winner Cloudracer out of an unraced half-sister to 1m2f Group 1 winner Chinese White, was always prominent and stayed on strongly to win with a bit in hand on this debut. A Kheleyf colt, he has plenty of size and scope and looked very professional on this first run. He holds entries in the Dewhurst and Royal Lodge and looks a useful prospect. (op 9-1)
Intrepid(IRE) ◆ got shuffled back in the pack and had to be switched wide, but he finished fast and almost gave the winner a scare. This was a very promising debut run from a 110,000euros yearling who is out of an unraced half-sister to Gimcrack/Middle Park winner Balmont. (tchd 13-2 and 8-1)
Senator Bong, out of a 2-y-o debut winner, was always near the pace and responded well to pressure in a good placed effort at a big price on his debut.
Rock Up(IRE) showed very little on his debut, but there was a lot to like about this staying-on effort from a £70,000 half-brother to three 5f-7f winners. (tchd 22-1)
Royal Caper, tailed off last in two previous starts, seemed to show a massive amount of improvement on his third run.
Price Is Truth(USA) cost $1,200,000 in March and was sent off a solid favourite, but he ran green and found some trouble out wide in a never dangerous run on this debut. (op 2-1 tchd 5-2)
Daaree(IRE) was prominent early on but hhe looked inexperienced when things got serious and faded. (op 3-1)

4774 FIRESTONE BUILDING PRODUCTS NOVICE STKS 7f
6:55 (6:55) (Class 4) 2-Y-O **£3,881** (£1,155; £577; £288) **Stalls** High

Form RPR
1 **Fantastic Moon** 2-9-0 0........ WilliamBuick 3 86+
(Jeremy Noseda) *hld up in tch: shkn up to ld over 2f out: rdn and edgd lft ins fnl f: r.o* **4/1**[3]
1 **2** ½ **Snowboarder (USA)**[37] 3499 2-9-5 0........ MickaelBarzalona 6 88
(Mahmood Al Zarooni) *chsd ldr tl over 5f out: remained handy: rdn and ev ch fr over 1f out: r.o* **5/4**[1]
0010 **3** nk **Glory Awaits (IRE)**[20] 4098 2-9-5 87........ SilvestreDeSousa 4 87
(Kevin Ryan) *led to 1/2-way: rdn 2f out: sn outpcd: rallied ins fnl f: r.o* **14/1**
1 **4** 2 ¾ **Here Comes When (IRE)**[33] 3658 2-9-5 0........ JamieSpencer 2 80
(Andrew Balding) *hld up: hdwy over 1f out: sn rdn: styd on same pce ins fnl f* **9/4**[2]
1330 **5** 3 ¾ **Baddilini**[45] 3240 2-9-5 87........ DarryllHolland 5 70
(Alan Bailey) *plld hrd: trckd ldr over 5f out: wnt centre and led 1/2-way: hdd over 2f out: sn rdn: wknd fnl f* **12/1**

1m 26.14s (0.44) **Going Correction** -0.025s/f (Good) **5** Ran SP% **109.6**
Speed ratings (Par 96): **96,95,95,91,87**
CSF £9.42 TOTE £4.60: £2.10, £1.10; EX 7.30.
Owner Saeed Suhail **Bred** Hascombe And Valiant Studs **Trained** Newmarket, Suffolk

FOCUS
They went a very steady pace in this novice event and a newcomer prevailed in a tight finish. The winner looks a nice prospect and the third is the key to the level.

NOTEBOOK
Fantastic Moon, a 215,000gns first foal of a 7f Listed/dual 1m winner Rhadegunda, gradually worked his way into a prominent position and showed a good attitude to fight off some useful experienced rivals. A Dalakhani colt who holds entries in the Royal Lodge and Champagne Stakes, he has plenty of scope for improvement and could stay quite a bit further than this in time. (op 9-2 tchd 5-1)
Snowboarder(USA), a winner of a 7f Kempton maiden on debut, was a hot favourite and travelled best for a long way but he couldn't get away from his rivals and was held by the battling winner. This was a slight setback but it was in a very slowly run contest and this $190,000 Raven's Pass colt remains an interesting prospect. (op 11-8)
Glory Awaits(IRE) bounced back with a brave bid back on fast ground but was just held. It has been all or nothing with him in five starts, but he has plenty of ability and the form of his 50-1 maiden win at Haydock received a major boost when the third went close in a Group 2 at Goodwood earlier in the week. (op 12-1)
Here Comes When(IRE), a 170,000euros Danehill Dancer colt who made a successful debut in a 7f Salisbury maiden last month, was prominent in the market but he couldn't land a blow from off the sedate pace. (tchd 2-1 and 5-2)
Baddilini pulled hard early on and had nothing left in the final furlong, stepped up to 7f on his return from a short break and gelding operation. Official explanation: jockey said that the gelding ran too free (op 8-1 tchd 14-1)

4775 GL EVENTS H'CAP 7f
7:30 (7:33) (Class 4) (0-85,85) 4-Y-O+ **£4,528** (£1,347; £505; £505) **Stalls** High

Form RPR
052 **1** **Mr David (USA)**[4] 4661 5-8-11 **80**........(b) LeonnaMayor(5) 10 94
(Jamie Osborne) *a.p: chsd ldr over 2f out: rdn to ld over 1f out: edgd rt ins fnl f: r.o wl* **7/1**[3]
-445 **2** 4 **Schoolmaster**[14] 4302 4-8-10 **74**........ SilvestreDeSousa 12 77
(Giles Bravery) *hld up in tch: rdn over 1f out: edgd rt and styd on same pce ins fnl f* **8/1**
0651 **3** 1 **Emkanaat**[18] 4155 4-9-2 **80**........[1] NeilCallan 8 81
(Roger Varian) *led: rdn: edgd rt and hdd over 1f out: no ex ins fnl f* **13/2**[2]
0226 **3** dht **Choral**[13] 4336 4-9-3 **81**........ PatDobbs 2 82+
(Richard Hannon) *hld up: hdwy u.p over 1f out: styd on: nt rch ldrs* **10/1**
3-31 **5** 1 ¾ **Forks**[14] 4302 5-8-8 **72**........ MickaelBarzalona 11 68
(Jane Chapple-Hyam) *sn chsng ldr: rdn over 1f out: no ex fnl f* **9/2**[1]
4133 **6** 1 ½ **Crew Cut (IRE)**[14] 4300 4-9-1 **79**........(p) PaulHanagan 3 71
(Jeremy Gask) *hld up: rdn over 2f out: hdwy over 1f out: wknd wl ins fnl f* **7/1**[3]
-030 **7** 2 ¼ **Ezdeyaad (USA)**[37] 3503 8-9-2 **80**........ WilliamBuick 6 66
(Ed Walker) *chsd ldrs: rdn over 2f out: wknd fnl f* **8/1**
0013 **8** ½ **Monzino (USA)**[11] 4405 4-7-9 **66**........(b[1]) NoelGarbutt(7) 1 50
(Michael Chapman) *dwlt: sn drvn along in rr: nvr on terms* **33/1**
-040 **9** 8 **Konstantin (IRE)**[29] 3772 4-9-0 **78**........ HayleyTurner 4 41
(Marcus Tregoning) *sn drvn along and a in rr* **8/1**
252 **10** nse **Offbeat Safaris (IRE)**[15] 4252 4-9-1 **79**........ LukeMorris 9 42
(Ronald Harris) *mid-div: rdn 1/2-way: hung lft and wknd over 1f out* **16/1**
0516 **11** ½ **Fathsta (IRE)**[6] 4589 7-9-7 **85**........ StevieDonohoe 7 46
(David Simcock) *plld hrd and prom: rdn over 2f out: sn wknd* **8/1**

1m 24.58s (-1.12) **Going Correction** -0.025s/f (Good) **11** Ran SP% **118.9**
Speed ratings (Par 105): **105,100,99,99,97 95,93,92,83,83 82**
PL: 2.00 (Choral), 0.80 (Emkanaat) Tricast: 193.31 (Emkanaat), 288.32 (Choral); toteswingers:1&2 £10.30, 2&C £10.30, 1&C £11.60, 2&E £6.10, 1&E £4.00 CSF £62.73 TOTE £8.80: £2.60, £2.90; EX 73.50 TRIFECTA Not won..
Owner K J P Gundlach **Bred** Mr & Mrs R David Randal **Trained** Upper Lambourn, Berks

FOCUS
A fair handicap in which the runner-up sets the standard. The winner surged clear from just off the pace and not many got involved.

4776 HYPHEN BLOODSTOCK H'CAP 1m 4f
8:00 (8:06) (Class 5) (0-70,69) 3-Y-O **£2,587** (£770; £384; £192) **Stalls** Centre

Form RPR
0012 **1** **Three Bards (IRE)**[4] 4649 3-9-7 **69** 6ex........ SilvestreDeSousa 7 83+
(Mark Johnston) *led: hdd over 10f out: chsd ldrs: nt clr run over 3f out: swtchd lft over 1f out: rdn to ld ins fnl f: hung rt: styd on wl* **2/1**[1]
-036 **2** 2 **Silver Samba**[48] 3142 3-8-13 **61**........ DarryllHolland 11 71+
(Andrew Balding) *led over 10f out: rdn over 1f out: hdd and unable qck ins fnl f* **9/2**[3]
040 **3** 6 **Kashgar**[39] 3448 3-9-5 **67**........ HayleyTurner 13 67
(Michael Bell) *s.s: hdwy to chse ldr over 9f out: rdn over 2f out: wknd ins fnl f* **12/1**
1005 **4** nk **Somemothersdohavem**[16] 4225 3-9-7 **69**........(b) DaraghO'Donohoe 3 69
(John Ryan) *hld up: hdwy over 2f out: rdn over 1f out: wknd fnl f* **14/1**
5300 **5** ½ **Porcini**[14] 4296 3-9-4 **66**........ LukeMorris 12 65
(Philip McBride) *hld up: hdwy over 3f out: rdn over 1f out: hung lft and wknd fnl f* **14/1**
0411 **6** 21 **Kaiser Wilhelm (IRE)**[8] 4510 3-9-3 **65** 6ex........(t) StevieDonohoe 1 30
(Paul Cole) *prom: rdn over 2f out: wknd over 1f out* **4/1**[2]
4305 **7** 1 ½ **Chrissycross (IRE)**[22] 3998 3-8-6 **59**........(b) MarkCoumbe(5) 2 22
(Roger Teal) *hld up: hdwy over 8f out: rdn and hung lft over 2f out: sn wknd* **20/1**
00-4 **8** 1 ¾ **Panettone (IRE)**[23] 3968 3-9-2 **64**........ NeilCallan 5 24
(Roger Varian) *s.i.s: hld up: hdwy over 4f out: rdn and hung lft over 2f out: sn wknd* **7/1**
-006 **9** 20 **Cape Rainbow**[14] 4288 3-8-9 **62**........ RachealKneller(5) 8
(Mark Usher) *s.i.s: hdwy 6f out: wknd over 3f out: t.o* **16/1**
2552 **10** 22 **Quixote**[17] 4200 3-9-4 **66**........ KierenFallon 9
(Clive Brittain) *hld up: hdwy 1/2-way: wknd over 2f out: t.o* **15/2**
0000 **P** **Wasabi (IRE)**[22] 3998 3-8-6 **54**........ MartinLane 4
(John Berry) *hld up: pushed along 1/2-way: lost tch fr over 4f out: p.u and dismntd over 1f out* **25/1**

2m 30.78s (-2.12) **Going Correction** -0.025s/f (Good) **11** Ran SP% **131.3**
Speed ratings (Par 100): **106,104,100,100,100 86,85,83,70,55**
toteswingers:1&2 £4.10, 2&3 £18.40, 1&3 £45.50 CSF £12.45 CT £97.21 TOTE £3.00: £1.20, £1.90, £5.40; EX 17.60 Trifecta £184.10 Pool £340.99 - 1.37 winning units..
Owner Sheikh Hamdan Bin Mohammed Al Maktoum **Bred** Thomas G Cooke **Trained** Middleham Moor, N Yorks

FOCUS
A competitive handicap in which the third and fourth are rated close to their marks. The favourite overcame trouble to score in good style and the first two pulled clear.
Kaiser Wilhelm(IRE) Official explanation: jockey said that the colt was unsuited by the good to firm ground.
Cape Rainbow Official explanation: jockey said that the gelding finished distressed
Quixote Official explanation: jockey said that the gelding lost his action
Wasabi(IRE) Official explanation: jockey said that the filly bled from the nose

4777 RACING UK H'CAP 6f
8:30 (8:34) (Class 5) (0-70,68) 3-Y-O **£2,587** (£770; £384; £192) **Stalls** High

Form RPR
0-00 **1** **Plum Bay**[33] 3665 3-8-6 **53**........ NickyMackay 6 64
(David Elsworth) *hld up: hdwy over 1f out: rdn to ld and edgd lft ins fnl f: r.o* **16/1**

4354 **2** *nk* **Kashmiri Star**[36] [3548] 3-8-5 **52**.................................. SilvestreDeSousa 4 62
(Michael Quinn) *w ldr tl led over 2f out: rdn over 1f out: hdd ins fnl f: r.o* **13/2**

2102 **3** *2 3/4* **Ooi Long**[17] [4197] 3-8-11 **63**...(t) TobyAtkinson(5) 1 64
(Mark Rimmer) *s.i.s: hld up: hdwy over 2f out: rdn over 1f out: styd on same pce ins fnl f* **5/1**[2]

6-00 **4** *2 1/4* **For Shia And Lula (IRE)**[70] [2459] 3-9-4 **65**....................... KierenFallon 2 59
(Daniel Mark Loughnane) *chsd ldrs: rdn over 1f out: styd on same pce fnl f* **6/1**

245 **5** *1 1/4* **Ficelle (IRE)**[15] [4235] 3-9-1 **62**.. LukeMorris 7 52
(Ronald Harris) *prom: pushed along 1/2-way: rdn over 1f out: no ex fnl f* **11/2**[3]

000 **6** *2 3/4* **Monymusk**[13] [4341] 3-9-1 **62**... PadraigBeggy 10 43
(David Elsworth) *s.i.s: hld up: hdwy u.p and hung lft over 1f out: wknd fnl f* **7/1**

0130 **7** *3 3/4* **Seventeen Seventy**[7] [4535] 3-9-3 **64**.................................. MartinLane 5 33
(Alan Coogan) *led over 3f: sn rdn: wknd ins fnl f* **11/1**

6106 **8** *3* **Sarah Berry**[17] [4197] 3-8-10 **57**... DarryllHolland 3 17
(Chris Dwyer) *prom: rdn over 2f out: wknd over 1f out* **7/1**

0-22 **9** *5* **Courtland Avenue (IRE)**[37] [3488] 3-9-7 **68**....................... TedDurcan 11
(Jonathan Portman) *chsd ldrs tl rdn and wknd over 1f out* **4/1**[1]

1m 12.7s (0.20) **Going Correction** -0.025s/f (Good) **9** Ran SP% **118.9**
Speed ratings (Par 100): **97,96,92,89,88 84,79,75,68**
toteswingers:1&2 £22.30, 2&3 £6.40, 1&3 £14.30 CSF £119.08 CT £610.44 TOTE £18.90: £5.10, £1.90, £2.10; EX 173.60 Trifecta £604.10 Part won. Pool £816.46 - 0.39 winning units..
Owner D R C Elsworth **Bred** K A Dasmal **Trained** Newmarket, Suffolk

FOCUS
A minor sprint handicap. The pace was fair and the winner came from some way back to reel in the long-time leader. The first two recorded personal-bests but there is little depth in behind.
Plum Bay Official explanation: trainer said, regarding the apparent improvement of form, that they had used different tactics and considered it a poor race
T/Plt: £426.40 to a £1 stake. Pool £61,923.98 - 106.01 winning units. T/Qpdt: £15.40 to a £1 stake. Pool £4816.05 - 230.50 winning units. CR

4545 THIRSK (L-H)

Friday, August 3

OFFICIAL GOING: Good to firm (good in places) changing to good (good to firm in places) after race 2 (2.25)
Wind: Virtually nil Weather: Cloudy

4778 THIRSKRACECOURSE.NET CLAIMING STKS — 7f
2:20 (2:21) (Class 4) 2-Y-O **£3,881** (£1,155; £577; £288) **Stalls** Low

Form RPR

3216 **1** **Yorkshire Icon**[9] [4450] 2-9-2 70...(p) GrahamLee 3 75
(Ann Duffield) *chsd ldrs: hdwy to chse ldr bnd over 4f out: led over 2f out: sn rdn clr: styd on* **5/2**[1]

4406 **2** *5* **Composed**[7] [4540] 2-9-5 69...(b[1]) PJMcDonald 10 64
(Paul Cole) *sn led: rdn along 3f out: hdd over 2f out and sn drvn: kpt on same pce* **8/1**

2141 **3** *1/2* **Mad Jazz**[42] [3351] 2-8-4 61.. ShaneBKelly(5) 9 54
(Tony Coyle) *trckd ldrs whn sltly hmpd and lost pl bnd over 4f out: rdn and hdwy 3f out: styd on u.p fnl 2f* **5/1**[3]

3 **4** *6* **Angels Calling**[36] [3533] 2-8-10 0............................. MichaelMetcalfe(3) 5 46+
(Mrs K Burke) *trckd ldrs whn bdly hmpd and almost lost rdr bnd over 4f out and bhd: hdwy on wd outside 3f out: sn rdn and styd on wl fnl 2f* **9/2**[2]

5 *2 1/4* **Darkside** 2-8-9 0..(b[1]) JamesSullivan 6 31+
(Michael Easterby) *dwlt: towards rr and keen early: hdwy whn hmpd bnd over 4f out: sn rcvrd to chse ldng pair: rdn 3f out: drvn 2f out and one pce* **33/1**

3100 **6** *5* **Captain Blue**[13] [4331] 2-8-9 60... RyanWhile(7) 7 25
(Bill Turner) *prom: sltly hmpd and lost pl bnd over 4f out: sn rdn along and n.d after* **50/1**

634 **7** *nk* **Chant (IRE)**[10] [4427] 2-9-0 0... FrannyNorton 11 22
(Ann Duffield) *dwlt and rr whn sltly hmpd bnd over 4f out: bhd after* **11/2**

00 **8** *hd* **Double Happiness**[38] [3457] 2-8-1 0.................................. NeilFarley(5) 8 14
(Brian Rothwell) *t.k.h: towards rr whn hmpd bnd over 4f out: bhd after* **200/1**

9 *18* **Little Squaw (IRE)** 2-8-5 0... DuranFentiman 2
(Tim Easterby) *dwlt and in rr whn hmpd bnd over 4f out: bhd after* **25/1**

6022 **P** **Blades Rose**[17] [4195] 2-8-2 57.. PatrickMathers 4
(Richard Fahey) *chsd ldr whn lost action: hung rt and p.u bnd over 4f out: sn dismntd* **6/1**

1m 28.96s (1.76) **Going Correction** +0.075s/f (Good) **10** Ran SP% **113.4**
Speed ratings (Par 96): **92,86,85,78,76 70,70,70,49,**
Tote Swingers: 1&2 £5.00, 1&3 £4.30, 2&3 £5.80 CSF £22.27 TOTE £4.50: £1.60, £3.20, £1.10; EX 21.00.
Owner Middleham Park Racing XXIX **Bred** G Hedley & Mike Channon Bloodstock Limited **Trained** Constable Burton, N Yorks
■ Stewards' Enquiry : Franny Norton jockey said that the gelding was carried wide on the bend

FOCUS
Following 3mm of rain overnight and drizzle leading up to the meeting, the ground had eased slightly and was now Good to firm, Good in places (from Good to firm). Not a bad juvenile claimer. The complex of the race changed completely when Blades Rosey suffered a pelvic injury at halfway, badly hampering several rivals, and leaving the front pair with a huge advantage. The form is modest and limited.

NOTEBOOK
Yorkshire Icon had excuses for his Catterick defeat last time after winning a Beverley maiden and had every chance on these terms. Well backed, his task was made easier by the mayhem that took place behind him on the home bend, which left him with only the runner-up to beat. He got on top of that rival over 2f from home and was never in any danger thereafter. (op 7-2 tchd 9-4)
Composed, blinkered for the first time, had the run of the race out in front but proved a sitting duck for the winner. Admittedly he had 8lb to find with his rival, but he does only look moderate. (op 9-1)
Mad Jazz, winner of a couple of sellers in her last three starts, was only getting there slowly and probably needs an easier surface. (op 9-2 tchd 4-1)
Angels Calling can be rated a good deal better than her final position as she was badly hampered at halfway which caused her rider to lose an iron. Under the circumstances she was far from disgraced, but this was the second time she hasn't been able to show what she is truly capable of and she is well worth another chance. (op 4-1 tchd 5-1)
Darkside, whose dam gained her only win over this C&D, had blinkers on for this debut and didn't perform that badly he missed the break, took a fierce hold, and was slightly hampered on the home bend. (op 28-1)
Chant(IRE) was already racing awkwardly at the back of the field when meeting interference on the bend. (op 15-2)
Blades Rose sadly suffered a pelvic injury at halfway, badly hampering several rivals. (op 9-2)

4779 THIRSK RACECOURSE PAVILION FOR WEDDINGS H'CAP (DIV I) — 7f
2:55 (2:58) (Class 5) (0-70,70) 3-Y-O+ **£3,234** (£962; £481; £240) **Stalls** Low

Form RPR

1006 **1** **It's A Mans World**[45] [3254] 6-8-7 **52**.............................. PaulPickard(3) 11 68+
(Brian Ellison) *in rr: hdwy and swtchd wd 3f out: rdn wl over 1f out: styd on strly fnl f to ld nr fin* **9/2**[2]

0351 **2** *nk* **Fayr Fall (IRE)**[24] [3950] 3-9-3 **65**..................................(b) DuranFentiman 7 78
(Tim Easterby) *trckd ldrs: hdwy 3f out: led 2f out: sn rdn and clr over 1f out: drvn ins fnl f: hdd and no ex nr fin* **7/1**

000 **3** *6* **Ryedale Dancer (IRE)**[8] [4495] 4-9-3 **59**.................... RobbieFitzpatrick 8 58
(Richard Guest) *in tch: hdwy to chse ldrs wl over 2f out: sn rdn: drvn and one pce appr fnl f* **14/1**

4565 **4** *1 1/2* **Fame Again**[17] [4175] 4-9-12 **68**.. PaddyAspell 12 63
(Michael Easterby) *stdd and swtchd lft s: hld up in rr: hdwy 3f out: sn swtchd wd and rdn 2f out: styd on wl u.p appr fnl f: nrst fin* **16/1**

0403 **5** *3/4* **Dhhamaan (IRE)**[11] [4388] 7-9-0 **56**................................(b) PJMcDonald 6 49+
(Ruth Carr) *led: rdn along and hdd 2f out: sn drvn and grad wknd* **7/2**[1]

0201 **6** *nse* **Chambles**[46] [3230] 3-9-8 **70**.. IanMongan 5 61
(Alan McCabe) *dwlt: sn in tch: effrt to chse ldrs over 3f out: rdn wl over 2f out: kpt on same pce* **9/1**

0000 **7** *2 1/4* **Mujaadel (USA)**[13] [4345] 7-10-0 **70**............................(p) AndrewMullen 13 57
(David Nicholls) *in rr: hdwy and in tch 1/2-way: rdn to chse ldrs over 2f out: kpt on same pce* **12/1**

0060 **8** *2 3/4* **Right Result (IRE)**[23] [3963] 3-9-8 **70**..............................(v[1]) GrahamLee 3 47
(James Bethell) *chsd ldrs on inner: rdn along wl over 2f out: grad wknd* **6/1**[3]

5445 **9** *4 1/2* **Whats For Pudding (IRE)**[18] [4134] 4-8-4 **51** oh5............ NeilFarley(5) 2 18
(Declan Carroll) *midfield: rdn along on inner 3f out: sn btn* **10/1**

0003 **10** *5* **Qeethaara (USA)**[32] [3709] 8-9-2 **65**..............................(p) JackDuern(7) 1 18
(Mark Brisbourne) *dwlt: hdwy and in tch 1/2-way: rdn along wl over 2f out and sn wknd* **14/1**

060 **11** *8* **Dubai Bay (FR)**[18] [4134] 4-9-7 **63**.................................(b[1]) MickyFenton 14
(Paul Midgley) *t.k.h: hdwy on outer and cl up after 1f: rdn along 3f out: sn wknd* **20/1**

000 **12** *2 1/4* **Nufoudh (IRE)**[10] [4432] 8-9-4 **60**...................................... FrannyNorton 9
(Tracy Waggott) *prom: rdn along 3f out: sn wknd* **20/1**

050 **13** *1 1/2* **Powerful Pierre**[8] [4495] 5-9-10 **66**...............................(b) FrederikTylicki 10
(Ian McInnes) *a in rr* **20/1**

1m 27.17s (-0.03) **Going Correction** +0.075s/f (Good)
WFA 3 from 4yo+ 6lb **13** Ran SP% **127.5**
Speed ratings (Par 103): **103,102,95,94,93 93,90,87,82,76 67,64,63**
Tote Swingers: 1&2 £12.50, 2&3 £9.10 CSF £37.66 CT £412.36 TOTE £8.90: £3.60, £2.90, £5.90; EX 111.90.
Owner Brian Ellison **Bred** Cheveley Park Stud Ltd **Trained** Norton, N Yorks
■ Stewards' Enquiry : Micky Fenton jockey said that the filly hung left
Ian Mongan jockey said that the filly suffered interference in running

FOCUS
A modest handicap.

4780 RACING UK MAIDEN STKS — 1m
3:30 (3:32) (Class 4) 3-Y-O+ **£4,528** (£1,347; £673; £336) **Stalls** Low

Form RPR

4 **1** **Quality Pearl (USA)**[55] [2935] 3-8-9 0............................... PatrickHills(3) 7 80+
(Luca Cumani) *trckd ldrs: hdwy wl over 2f out: rdn to ld jst over 1f out: styd on* **2/1**[1]

0-44 **2** *4* **All Time**[25] [3918] 4-9-5 68.. IanMongan 8 71
(Sir Henry Cecil) *awkward hd carriage and a edging lft: cl up: rdn to ld over 2f out and sn hung lft: drvn and hdd appr fnl f: sn one pce* **2/1**[1]

00 **3** *2 1/4* **Her Nibbs**[83] [2095] 3-8-12 0.. FrederikTylicki 10 65+
(Micky Hammond) *bhd: swtchd wd and hdwy 3f out: rdn 2f out: styd on wl u.p fnl f: nrst fin* **80/1**

6 **4** *1 1/4* **Eamaadd**[16] [4213] 3-9-0 0.. DominicFox(3) 3 67+
(Roger Varian) *hld up towards rr: hdwy 1/2-way: rdn to chse ldrs over 2f out: sn drvn and kpt on fnl f* **10/1**[3]

2-02 **5** *2 3/4* **Qannaas (USA)**[7] [4550] 3-9-3 80.. TadhgO'Shea 5 60
(Charles Hills) *sn led: rdn along and hdd over 2f out: sn drvn and wknd* **11/4**[2]

6 *2 1/4* **Albert Tatlock (IRE)** 3-9-0 0.............................. MichaelMetcalfe(3) 9 55
(David Nicholls) *midfield: hdwy and in tch over 3f out: rdn along over 2f out: sn no hdwy* **28/1**

0 **7** *8* **Wotsitgotodowithu (IRE)**[42] [3352] 4-9-7 0................(p) GaryBartley(3) 4 36
(Noel Wilson) *a towards rr* **100/1**

3 **8** *2 1/4* **Lieutenant Dan (IRE)**[7] [4551] 5-9-10 0........................... JamieMackay 6 31
(Michael Appleby) *in tch: rdn along bef 1/2-way: sn outpcd* **20/1**

0-0 **9** *3/4* **Cara's Delight (AUS)**[116] [1250] 5-9-5 0............................ PaddyAspell 12 24
(Frederick Watson) *chsd ldrs: rdn along 3f out: sn wknd* **200/1**

0 **10** *4* **Roc Fort**[7] [4551] 3-9-3 0... PJMcDonald 11 19
(Ruth Carr) *dwlt: a in rr* **28/1**

0 **11** *26* **Stars Legacy**[66] [2592] 3-8-12 0.. AndrewMullen 1
(George Moore) *dwlt: a bhd* **100/1**

0 **12** *23* **Shatin Spirit (IRE)**[15] [4259] 3-9-3 0................................ DuranFentiman 2
(Noel Wilson) *chsd ldrs: rdn along bef 1/2-way: sn wknd* **100/1**

1m 41.35s (1.25) **Going Correction** +0.075s/f (Good)
WFA 3 from 4yo+ 7lb **12** Ran SP% **118.8**
Speed ratings (Par 105): **96,92,89,88,85 83,75,73,72,68 42,19**
Tote Swingers: 1&2 £2.00, 1&3 £19.10, 2&3 £22.70 CSF £5.84 TOTE £3.40: £1.10, £1.10, £24.30; EX 7.40.
Owner Pearl Bloodstock Ltd **Bred** Nicholas Lotz & Rosemary Lotz **Trained** Newmarket, Suffolk

FOCUS
The ground was changed to Good, Good to firm in places before this race. Few could be fancied in this moderate older-horse maiden.

4781 JW 4X4 NORTHALLERTON FILLIES' H'CAP — 1m 4f
4:05 (4:06) (Class 5) (0-70,69) 3-Y-O **£3,234** (£962; £481; £240) **Stalls** Low

Form RPR

3031 **1** **Maybeagrey**[14] [4311] 3-9-7 **69**.. DuranFentiman 2 77
(Tim Easterby) *t.k.h early: trckd ldrs on inner: hdwy over 2f out: rdn to ld 1f out: drvn out* **4/1**[1]

0652 **2** *1* **Margo Channing**[16] [4210] 3-8-6 **54**.................................... PJMcDonald 8 60
(Micky Hammond) *hld up: hdwy on outer 3f out: rdn to chse ldrs 2f out: drvn to chse wnr ins fnl f: kpt on* **15/2**[2]

3040 **3** *1* **Lost Highway (IRE)**[46] [3212] 3-8-9 **57**.............................. RobertHavlin 4 62
(Mark Johnston) *t.k.h early: trckd ldrs: cl up over 3f out: led wl over 2f out and sn rdn: hdd 1f out: kpt on same pce* **8/1**[3]

0254 **4** ½ **Dorry K (IRE)**[15] 4250 3-9-0 **67**.. DeanHeslop(5) 7 71
(David Barron) *reminders s: hld up in rr: hdwy on wd outside wl over 2f out: rdn to chse ldrs over 1f out: drvn and kpt on fnl f* **9/1**

3420 **5** 2 **Rosie's Lady (IRE)**[32] 3697 3-8-0 **55**................................. DavidBergin(7) 5 56
(David O'Meara) *set stdy pce: hdd after 4f: cl up: effrt 3f out: rdn over 2f out and ev ch tl drvn and wknd over 1f out* **11/1**

0051 **6** 2¼ **Guiletta (IRE)**[27] 3847 3-9-3 **68**.. RyanClark(3) 1 65
(Rae Guest) *hld up: rdn along and outpcd 3f out: kpt on u.p fr over 1f out: n.d* **4/1**[1]

0005 **7** 2¾ **So Cheeky**[14] 4311 3-8-2 **53** ow3..........................(p) AdamBeschizza(3) 3 46
(Peter Salmon) *cl up: led after 4f: rdn along over 3f out: sn hdd & wknd over 2f out* **20/1**

534 **8** ¾ **Echo Of Footsteps**[15] 4259 3-9-3 **65**................................ PaddyAspell 10 57
(Michael Herrington) *chsd ldrs on outer: rdn along 3f out: drvn over 2f out: sn wknd* **22/1**

2m 40.9s (4.70) **Going Correction** +0.075s/f (Good) **8** Ran SP% **90.3**
Speed ratings (Par 97): **87,86,85,85,84 82,80,80**
Tote Swingers: 1&2 £4.10, 1&3 £8.50, 2&3 £9.00 CSF £20.33 CT £94.57 TOTE £2.60: £1.10, £1.70, £3.20; EX 17.80.
Owner Habton Farms **Bred** J K Beckitt And Son **Trained** Great Habton, N Yorks

FOCUS
An ordinary fillies' handicap that was weakened further when the favourite Cosmic Halo was withdrawn after going down in the stalls. They didn't go much of an early pace.

4782 THIRSK RACECOURSE CONFERENCE ROOMS MAIDEN FILLIES' STKS 7f
4:40 (4:43) (Class 5) 3-Y-0+ **£3,234** (£962; £481; £240) **Stalls** Low

Form RPR

2-36 **1** **Baheeja**[29] 3785 3-8-11 **71**.. DominicFox(3) 3 84+
(Roger Varian) *trckd ldrs: hdwy on inner and cl up 3f out: rdn and slt ld 2f out: drvn ent fnl f: styd on* **2/1**[1]

3035 **2** 1¾ **Gold Show**[8] 4505 3-9-0 **74**.. PJMcDonald 7 77
(Mick Channon) *trckd ldng pair: hdwy 3f out: chal 2f out: sn rdn and ev ch tl drvn and one pce fnl f* **9/4**[2]

3 3¼ **Ebble** 3-9-0 **0**.. RobertHavlin 9 68+
(John Gosden) *hld up in tch: hdwy on outer to chal 2f out and ev ch tl rdn: hung lft and one pce over 1f out* **9/2**[3]

-4 **4** 1¾ **Fairest (IRE)**[50] 3082 3-9-0 **0**.. RichardMullen 4 64
(Jeremy Noseda) *towards rr: hdwy over 3f out: rdn to chse ldrs 2f out: one pce appr fnl f* **8/1**

0 **5** 3½ **Eltiqaa (IRE)**[106] 1472 3-9-0 **0**.. TadhgO'Shea 2 54+
(John Gosden) *towards rr: rdn along 3f out: styd on u.p fnl 2f: nrst fin* **8/1**

5 **6** 3¾ **Symphony Of Stars**[7] 4550 3-9-0 **0**.. DuranFentiman 10 44
(Michael Appleby) *cl up: chal 3f out: led briefly over 2f out: sn hdd and grad wknd* **33/1**

7 ½ **Nurse Dominatrix (IRE)** 3-9-0 **0**.............................. RobbieFitzpatrick 6 43
(Richard Guest) *a towards rr* **66/1**

0-63 **8** 4 **Morna's Glory**[7] 4550 3-9-0 **0**.. MichaelStainton 11 32
(Jason Ward) *led: rdn along over 3f out: hdd jst over 2f out: sn drvn and wknd* **33/1**

9 6 **Under Ambition** 4-9-6 **0**.. PaddyAspell 12 18
(Frederick Watson) *s.i.s: a bhd* **200/1**

00- **10** 30 **Gorau Glas**[314] 6324 4-9-3 **0**.. RyanClark(3) 1
(Mark Brisbourne) *chsd ldrs to 1/2-way: sn wknd* **200/1**

1m 27.7s (0.50) **Going Correction** +0.075s/f (Good)
WFA 3 from 4yo 6lb **10** Ran SP% **112.9**
Speed ratings (Par 100): **100,98,94,92,88 84,83,78,72,37**
Tote Swingers: 1&2 £1.70, 1&3 £3.50, 2&3 £3.30 CSF £6.33 TOTE £2.80: £1.10, £1.10, £1.80; EX 7.20.
Owner Sheikh Ahmed Al Maktoum **Bred** Middle Park Stud Ltd **Trained** Newmarket, Suffolk
■ Stewards' Enquiry : Paddy Aspell jockey saidthat the filly missed the break

FOCUS
Another uncompetitive maiden, this time for older fillies.

4783 THIRSK RACECOURSE PAVILION FOR WEDDINGS H'CAP (DIV II) 7f
5:15 (5:15) (Class 5) (0-70,70) 3-Y-0+ **£3,234** (£962; £481; £240) **Stalls** Low

Form RPR

560 **1** **Muftarres (IRE)**[69] 2498 7-9-5 **61**..........................(b) RussKennemore 1 71
(Paul Midgley) *hld up in rr: gd hdwy 1/2-way: chsd ldrs 2f out: sn rdn and chal over 1f out: drvn to ld jst ins fnl f: kpt on wl* **12/1**

5-53 **2** nk **Tamara Bay**[32] 3694 4-9-1 **57**.. PJMcDonald 15 66
(John Davies) *dwlt and rcd wd early: hdwy and chsd ldrs 1/2-way: led wl over 2f out: rdn wl over 1f out: drvn and hdd jst ins fnl f: kpt on wl towards fin* **15/2**[3]

-350 **3** 2¼ **Tislaam (IRE)**[163] 652 5-9-11 **67**..........................(p) PatrickMathers 14 70
(Alan McCabe) *in rr: gd hdwy over 3f out: rdn to chse ldrs wl over 1f out: drvn and kpt on fnl f* **20/1**

0-05 **4** ½ **Dubai Celebration**[8] 4495 4-9-2 **58**.. PaddyAspell 7 60
(Julie Camacho) *hld up towards rr: hdwy over 3f out: rdn to chse ldrs 2f out: drvn and kpt on same pce fnl f* **12/1**

1052 **5** 2¾ **Ansells Pride (IRE)**[13] 4332 9-8-13 **62**..........................(p) JakePayne(7) 13 56
(Bill Turner) *prom: hdwy and cl up 3f out: rdn and ev ch over 2f out: drvn wl over 1f out and grad wknd* **14/1**

206 **6** 2 **Drive Home (USA)**[45] 3257 5-9-0 **59**..........................(p) GaryBartley(3) 11 48
(Noel Wilson) *hld up: hdwy on outer over 3f out: rdn to chse ldrs 2f out: sn drvn and no imp* **20/1**

0415 **7** 1¼ **Ptolemy**[35] 3555 3-9-4 **66**.. AndrewMullen 4 50
(David Barron) *chsd ldrs: rdn along 3f out: grad wknd* **4/1**[2]

1043 **8** shd **Steel Stockholder**[14] 4315 6-9-3 **66**.............................. RobertDodsworth(7) 8 51
(Mel Brittain) *prom: rdn along 2f out: drvn 2f out and grad wknd* **11/1**

5640 **9** shd **Crocodile Bay (IRE)**[11] 4406 9-8-9 **51** oh6..........(p) RobbieFitzpatrick 12 36
(Richard Guest) *chsd ldrs: rdn along and outpcd 1/2-way: kpt on fnl 2f: n.d* **40/1**

6502 **10** 3½ **Thrust Control (IRE)**[59] 2791 5-8-4 **53** oh2 ow2.. JacobButterfield(7) 10 29
(Tracy Waggott) *cl up: rdn along 3f out: sn wknd* **20/1**

0000 **11** 3¼ **Transmit (IRE)**[51] 3021 5-8-9 **51** oh1..........................(b) DuranFentiman 6 18
(Tim Easterby) *led: rdn along 3f out: sn hdd & wknd over 2f out* **20/1**

2103 **12** 5 **Viking Warrior (IRE)**[21] 4043 5-10-0 **70**.. RichardMullen 3 23
(Michael Dods) *trckd ldrs on inner: rdn along over 2f out: sn wknd* **5/2**[1]

0004 **13** 3½ **Moral Issue**[39] 3454 4-9-9 **65**.. FrederikTylicki 5 9
(Ian McInnes) *a in rr: outpcd and bhd fnl 3f* **10/1**

1m 28.48s (1.28) **Going Correction** +0.075s/f (Good)
WFA 3 from 4yo+ 6lb **13** Ran SP% **121.3**
Speed ratings (Par 103): **95,94,92,91,88 86,84,84,84,80 76,71,67**
Tote Swingers: 1&2 £13.60, 1&3 £43.50, 2&3 £37.80 CSF £92.49 CT £1861.59 TOTE £20.00: £4.90, £2.20, £7.90; EX 181.40.
Owner T W Midgley **Bred** Shadwell Estate Company Limited **Trained** Westow, N Yorks
■ Stewards' Enquiry : Richard Mullen jockey said that the gelding was never travelling

FOCUS
The main action unfolded down the centre of the track this time. The winning time was 1.31 seconds slower than the first division, though the ground had officially eased in the meantime.
Muftarres(IRE) Official explanation: trainer said, regarding the apparent improvement of form, that the gelding had benefited from the drop back in trip and being freshened up after a break

4784 COME RACING AT THIRSK TOMORROW APPRENTICE H'CAP 6f
5:45 (5:46) (Class 5) (0-70,69) 3-Y-0+ **£2,587** (£770; £384; £192) **Stalls** High

Form RPR

1244 **1** **Another Citizen (IRE)**[11] 4393 4-9-1 **64**..........................(b) GaryMahon(8) 4 75
(Tim Easterby) *trckd ldr: swtchd lft and hdwy 1/2-way: led over 2f out: rdn clr wl over 1f out: kpt on* **7/1**[3]

0100 **2** 4 **Ryedane (IRE)**[2] 4717 10-9-3 **61**..........................(b) RachelRichardson(3) 9 59
(Tim Easterby) *in rr: pushed along 1/2-way: hdwy 2f out: rdn and styd on wl fnl f* **8/1**

0432 **3** hd **Needy McCredie**[60] 2750 6-9-7 **62**.. JordanNason 2 60
(James Turner) *towards rr: hdwy 1/2-way: rdn to chse ldrs 2f out: drvn and kpt on fnl f* **6/1**[2]

5021 **4** 2¾ **Chosen One (IRE)**[5] 4631 7-9-4 **59** 6ex..............................[1] EvaMoscrop 3 48
(Ruth Carr) *led: rdn along 1/2-way: hdd over 2f out: sn drvn and wknd over 1f out* **5/2**[1]

0150 **5** ½ **Bandstand**[45] 3255 6-9-11 **69**.. PeterSword(3) 7 56
(Bryan Smart) *sn outpcd and bhd 1/2-way: hdwy 2f out: sn rdn and styd on wl fnl f: nrst fin* **15/2**

6314 **6** hd **Ice Trooper**[7] 4552 4-9-2 **65**..........................(p) GerJohnson(8) 6 52
(Linda Stubbs) *prom: rdn along over 2f out: sn edgd lft and grad wknd* **6/1**[2]

6130 **7** 1 **Secret City (IRE)**[14] 4315 6-10-0 **69**..........................(b) HannahNunn 8 52
(Robin Bastiman) *chsd ldrs: rdn along wl over 2f out: sn wknd* **10/1**

2-00 **8** 1¼ **Indieslad**[64] 2632 4-9-7 **67**..........................(p) KevinStott(5) 1 46
(Ann Duffield) *prom on outer: rdn along over 2f out: sn wknd* **12/1**

130 **9** 5 **Made In The Shade**[39] 3442 3-8-5 **55**.............................. DanielleMooney(5) 5 18
(Paul Midgley) *chsd ldrs: rdn along 1/2-way: sn wknd* **14/1**

1m 12.9s (0.20) **Going Correction** +0.125s/f (Good)
WFA 3 from 4yo+ 4lb **9** Ran SP% **116.0**
Speed ratings (Par 103): **103,97,97,93,93 92,91,89,83**
Tote Swingers: 1&2 £14.60, 1&3 £7.90, 2&3 £12.30 CSF £61.78 CT £359.44 TOTE £7.90: £2.00, £3.70, £1.20; EX 60.80.
Owner Middleham Park Racing V & Partners **Bred** Sandro Garavelli **Trained** Great Habton, N Yorks

FOCUS
The only contest on the straight track at the meeting and ultimately a one-horse race.
T/Plt: £402.00 to a £1 stake. Pool: £47,305.34 - 85.90 winning tickets. T/Qpdt: £29.70 to a £1 stake. Pool: £3,992.74 - 99.48 winning tickets. JR

4785 - 4789a (Foreign Racing) - See Raceform Interactive

4696 DEAUVILLE (R-H)
Friday, August 3

OFFICIAL GOING: Turf: very soft; fibresand: standard

4790a PRIX DU CERCLE (LISTED RACE) (3YO+) (TURF) 5f
2:55 (12:00) 3-Y-0+ **£21,666** (£8,666; £6,500; £4,333; £2,166)

RPR

1 **Monsieur Joe (IRE)**[20] 4113 5-9-5 **0**.. OlivierPeslier 9 112
(Robert Cowell) *broke fast fr wd draw: racd 2nd: chal for ld 1 1/2f out: led 1f out: r.o wl: wnt clr: nvr threatened* **47/10**[2]

2 1 **Gammarth (FR)**[26] 3901 4-9-5 **0**.............................. ChristopheSoumillon 7 109
(H-A Pantall, France) **7/2**[1]

3 hd **August Rush (SAF)**[42] 3366 6-9-5 **0**.......... Christophe-PatriceLemaire 6 108
(P Bary, France) **29/1**

4 1½ **Flash Mash (USA)**[104] 4-9-2 **0**.. GregoryBenoist 5 100
(X Nakkachdji, France) **15/2**

5 hd **Surfista**[37] 4-8-11 **0**.. IoritzMendizabal 2 94
(D Rabhi, France) **22/1**

6 ½ **B Fifty Two (IRE)**[12] 4367 3-8-11 **0**.. SebSanders 12 94
(J W Hills) *broke fast: racd midfield: rdn 1 1/2f out: no ex: wknd ins fnl f* **17/1**

7 nk **Chopouest (FR)**[26] 3901 5-9-1 **0**..........................(p) FredericSpanu 11 95
(T Castanheira, France) **22/1**

8 1 **Calahorra (FR)**[42] 3366 3-8-13 **0**.. StephanePasquier 10 91
(C Baillet, France) **17/1**

9 nk **Lisselan Diva (IRE)**[42] 3366 6-8-11 **0**..........................(p) WilliamsSaraiva 4 86
(Mme J Bidgood, France) **7/1**

10 1¼ **Mariol (FR)**[5] 9-9-5 **0**.. GeraldMosse 1 90
(Robert Collet, France) **10/1**

0 **Sabratah**[82] 2112 4-9-2 **0**.. MaximeGuyon 3
(H-A Pantall, France) **14/1**

0 **Sea Trial (FR)**[42] 3366 3-8-11 **0**.. JohanVictoire 8
(Mme C Head-Maarek, France) **63/10**[3]

57.88s (0.38)
WFA 3 from 4yo+ 3lb **12** Ran SP% **116.6**
WIN (incl. 1 euro stake): 5.70. PLACES: 2.20, 1.80, 6.60. DF: 8.50. SF: 20.10.
Owner Mrs Helen Checkley **Bred** Nicola And Eleanor Kent **Trained** Six Mile Bottom, Cambs

NOTEBOOK
Monsieur Joe(IRE) sat just off the leader before taking things up with a furlong to run and pulling clear. He handled the rain-softened ground well and could go for the Nunthorpe next, but longer term a return to Dubai is likely, as he seems more effective there than anywhere.
B Fifty Two(IRE) wasn't best drawn given the way the race developed, and the rain-softened ground wasn't in his favour either.

4494 DONCASTER (L-H)
Saturday, August 4

OFFICIAL GOING: Good to firm (firm in places on round course; 9.3)
Wind: Light, half-against Weather: Cloudy with sunny periods

4791 UNISON "FAIR PENSIONS FOR ALL" MAIDEN STKS (DIV I) 1m 2f 60y
1:40 (1:42) (Class 5) 3-4-Y-0 **£2,911** (£866; £432; £216) **Stalls** Low

Form RPR

5- **1** **Prince Of Orange (IRE)**[317] 6267 3-9-1 **0**.. AhmedAjtebi 9 86+
(Mahmood Al Zarooni) *hld up in rr: hdwy 3f out: chsd ldrs 2f out: str run to ld jst ins fnl f: sn rdn and kpt on wl* **9/2**

03 **2** *1 1/4* **Bedazzled**[72] 2430 3-8-10 0 SilvestreDeSousa 8 76+
(James Fanshawe) *hld up towards rr: hdwy on outer wl over 2f out: rdn to chse ldrs over 1f out: styd on u.p ins fnl f: nrst fin* **3/1**[2]

2 **3** *hd* **Infinite Hope (USA)**[43] 3340 3-8-10 0 KirstyMilczarek 7 76
(Luca Cumani) *trckd ldrs: hdwy 3f out: rdn to ld over 1f out: sn drvn and hdd jst ins fnl f: kpt on same pce* **9/4**[1]

5 **4** *1 3/4* **Caskelena (IRE)**[70] 2496 3-8-10 0 RichardMullen 5 73
(Sir Michael Stoute) *t.k.h: in tch: hdwy over 2f out: swtchd rt and rdn to chse ldrs over 1f out: carried hd high and sn one pce* **7/2**[3]

5 *3* **Wannabe Loved** 3-8-10 0 RobertHavlin 11 67+
(John Gosden) *wnt rt s: sn in tch on outer: hdwy 4f out: rdn along to chse ldrs over 2f out: sn drvn and one pce* **10/1**

00 **6** *hd* **Take The Stage (IRE)**[58] 2856 3-9-1 0 ShaneKelly 1 72
(Jeremy Noseda) *trckd ldrs: hdwy on inner and cl up 3f out: rdn along to ld over 2f out: sn drvn and hdd over 1f out: grad wknd* **33/1**

7 *1 1/4* **Italian Lady (USA)** 3-8-11 0 ow1 PhillipMakin 2 65
(Alan Jarvis) *trckd ldr: cl up 1/2-way: disp ld 3f out: rdn 2f out and grad wknd* **25/1**

06 **8** *8* **Regal Diva**[38] 3484 4-9-5 0 RussKennemore 6 49
(Reg Hollinshead) *hld up and bhd: sme hdwy over 3f out: sn rdn and wknd* **50/1**

0-0 **9** *16* **Royal Gig**[65] 2633 3-8-10 0 JohnFahy 4 19
(Tim Etherington) *led: rdn along 4f out: hdd 3f out and wknd qckly* **200/1**

0 **10** *5* **Doting**[29] 3809 3-9-1 0 RenatoSouza 3 14
(Peter Salmon) *prom: chsd ldr 1/2-way: rdn along 4f out: sn wknd* **200/1**

2m 10.06s (0.66) **Going Correction** -0.30s/f (Firm)
WFA 3 from 4yo 9lb **10** Ran SP% **115.0**
Speed ratings (Par 103): **85,84,83,82,80 79,78,72,59,55**
Tote Swingers 1&2 £3.90, 2&3 £1.10, 1&3 £2.80 CSF £17.79 TOTE £5.30: £1.70, £1.50, £1.50; EX 20.00.
Owner Godolphin **Bred** Darley **Trained** Newmarket, Suffolk

FOCUS
A fair maiden, but the pace was steady and the time was 3.70 seconds slower than the second leg. The form makes sense with the winner close to his debut form.

4792 UNISON "SERVING OUR COMMUNITIES" MAIDEN AUCTION STKS 7f
2:15 (2:17) (Class 5) 2-Y-O **£2,911** (£866; £432; £216) **Stalls** High

Form RPR

43 **1** **Dance With Dragons (IRE)**[17] 4222 2-8-13 0 ChrisCatlin 14 77+
(Paul Cole) *mde virtually all: rdn 2f out: clr jst over 1f out: edgd lft jst ins fnl f: sn drvn and jst hld on* **11/1**

02 **2** *hd* **Blue Nova**[31] 3764 2-8-11 0 ShaneKelly 5 74
(Jeremy Noseda) *a cl up: chal over 2f out: sn rdn and ev ch whn sltly outpcd over 1f out: swtchd rt and drvn ins fnl f: rallied and styd on wl nr fin: jst failed* **9/2**[2]

3 *2* **Secular Society** 2-9-2 0 RichardMullen 6 74+
(Brian Meehan) *towards rr: hdwy 1/2-way: trckd ldrs over 2f out: rdn to chse ldng pair wl over 1f out: kpt on fnl f* **25/1**

64 **4** *5* **Lady Marmelo (IRE)**[16] 4246 2-8-11 0 SamHitchcott 13 56
(Mick Channon) *chsd ldrs: rdn along over 2f out: drvn and one pce fr wl over 1f out* **6/1**[3]

6 **5** *hd* **Lady Vermeer**[23] 4011 2-8-8 0 SilvestreDeSousa 16 53
(Ralph Beckett) *hld up towards rr: hdwy over 2f out: rdn to chse ldrs and edgd lft wl over 1f out: sn one pce* **3/1**[1]

0 **6** *2 1/4* **Benoni**[17] 4222 2-8-9 0 CathyGannon 18 48
(Henry Candy) *hld up towards rr: hdwy on outer over 2f out: rdn and styd on appr fnl f* **20/1**

7 *nk* **Forced Family Fun** 2-8-11 0 JohnFahy 12 49+
(Michael Bell) *in rr: hdwy over 2f out: styd on appr fnl f* **28/1**

8 *1/2* **Mumeyez** 2-9-2 0 RobertHavlin 2 53+
(John Gosden) *dwlt and bhd: hdwy on outer over 2f out: styd on appr fnl f* **7/1**

0 **9** *3/4* **Blazeofenchantment (USA)**[21] 4114 2-9-2 0 MickyFenton 15 51+
(Paul Midgley) *chsd ldrs: rdn along wl over 2f out: sn wknd* **100/1**

640 **10** *1 1/2* **Annie Besant**[11] 4433 2-8-4 0 KirstyMilczarek 4 35
(David C Griffiths) *chsd ldrs: rdn along wl over 2f out: grad wknd* **50/1**

11 *2 1/4* **Attansky (IRE)** 2-8-6 0 DominicFox(3) 9 34
(Tim Easterby) *nvr bttr than midfield* **66/1**

12 *1* **Tobacco** 2-8-6 0 AdamCarter(5) 17 34
(Tim Easterby) *a towards rr* **28/1**

13 *1 3/4* **Substantivo (IRE)** 2-8-13 0 PhillipMakin 3 31
(Alan Jarvis) *a towards rr* **8/1**

642 **14** *7* **Notional Demand**[28] 3842 2-8-9 67 TedDurcan 10 9
(Tim Easterby) *in tch: rdn along 1/2-way: sn wknd* **14/1**

15 *2* **Everreadyneddy** 2-8-9 0 J-PGuillambert 8 4
(J S Moore) *midfield: pushed along 1/2-way: sn lost pl and bhd* **40/1**

16 *5* **Arch Ebony (USA)** 2-9-2 0 DavidNolan 1
(David O'Meara) *a in rr* **25/1**

66 **17** *3 1/4* **Lucky Prize**[26] 3909 2-7-11 0 RobertDodsworth(7) 11
(Mel Brittain) *chsd ldrs to 1/2-way: sn lost pl and bhd* **100/1**

1m 24.84s (-1.46) **Going Correction** -0.30s/f (Firm) **17** Ran SP% **123.3**
Speed ratings (Par 94): **96,95,93,87,87 84,84,84,83,81 78,77,75,67,65 59,56**
Tote Swingers 1&2 £17.30, 2&3 £25.80, 1&3 £33.50 CSF £55.22 TOTE £10.00: £2.90, £2.30, £9.60; EX 40.00.
Owner P F I Cole Ltd **Bred** Oak Lodge Bloodstock **Trained** Whatcombe, Oxon

FOCUS
A big-field juvenile maiden that should produce a few winners and the form looked better than average. They raced up the centre of the track.

NOTEBOOK
Dance With Dragons(IRE) was on quick ground for the first time and stepped up on the form of his two previous efforts, although he only just held on after looking set to win nicely. He should be competitive in nurseries. (op 12-1)
Blue Nova was beaten into second when favourite for a Polytrack maiden last time, but the winner that day, Roz, followed up in Listed company. She kept on strongly here and can find a similar race. (tchd 5-1)
Secular Society ◆, a 38,000gns gelding, is a half-brother to a 1m2f winner, out of a 1m winner. He did well to finish so close after a sluggish start and has plenty of ability. (tchd 28-1)
Lady Marmelo(IRE) kept on but wasn't good enough. Nurseries are now an option. (op 10-1)
Lady Vermeer didn't see her race out on this step up in trip, but she was having only her second start and is probably capable of better. (op 7-2 tchd 4-1 and 11-4)
Benoni showed ability and will be one to keep in mind once handicapped. (op 25-1)
Forced Family Fun, the first foal of Juniper Girl, who won the Northumberland Plate for these connections (also won over 7f at two), has already been gelded. He shaped nicely enough and is probably a long-term prospect. (op 25-1)
Mumeyez, a 42,000gns purchase, hinted at ability after starting slowly and running green. (op 11-2)
Blazeofenchantment(USA) ◆ did not receive a hard ride. (op 80-1)

4793 UNISON AND LV=FRIZZELL CAR INSURANCE FILLIES' H'CAP 6f
2:50 (2:53) (Class 5) (0-70,70) 3-Y-O+ **£2,911** (£866; £432; £216) **Stalls** High

Form RPR

/1-3 **1** **Willbeme**[8] 4547 4-9-3 **61** J-PGuillambert 4 78
(Neville Bycroft) *trckd ldrs: smooth hdwy and cl up over 2f out: led wl over 1f out: rdn and kpt on wl fnl f* **7/1**

0664 **2** *2* **Drift And Dream**[9] 4495 5-9-11 **69** TedDurcan 5 80
(Chris Wall) *trckd ldrs: hdwy 2f out: rdn to chse wnr over 1f out: drvn and no imp ins fnl f* **9/2**[1]

3300 **3** *1 1/2* **Code Six (IRE)**[8] 4547 3-9-1 **63** RichardMullen 6 68+
(Bryan Smart) *dwlt and bhd: swtchd to wd outside and hdwy 2f out: sn rdn and styd on strly fnl f: nrst fin* **20/1**

0031 **4** *shd* **Meandmyshadow**[8] 4547 4-9-6 **64** PhillipMakin 11 70
(Alan Brown) *cl up: rdn to chal over 2f out and ev ch tl drvn and one pce appr fnl f* **11/2**[3]

4243 **5** *1/2* **Art Form**[8] 4552 3-9-8 **70** (t) ShaneKelly 13 73
(Alan McCabe) *hld up in rr: hdwy over 2f out: rdn to chse ldrs over 1f out: drvn and one pce ent fnl f* **5/1**[2]

2123 **6** *3/4* **Demora**[17] 4208 3-9-6 **68** IanMongan 10 69
(Michael Appleby) *led: jnd and rdn along over 2f out: drvn and hdd wl over 1f out: edgd rt appr fnl f and grad wknd* **7/1**

5-61 **7** *1 1/4* **Trust Fund Babe (IRE)**[14] 4348 3-8-12 **60** RobertHavlin 12 57
(Tim Easterby) *chsd ldrs: rdn along over 2f out: sn drvn and wknd* **10/1**

66-0 **8** *1/2* **Adventure Story**[16] 4235 5-9-4 **62** KirstyMilczarek 1 58
(Tony Carroll) *chsd ldrs: rdn along over 2f out: grad wknd* **16/1**

5505 **9** *3/4* **Glenlini**[12] 4392 6-8-7 **51** oh1 ChrisCatlin 14 45
(Jim Goldie) *chsd ldrs: rdn along over 2f out: wknd wl over 1f out* **33/1**

-000 **9** *dht* **Sinai (IRE)**[8] 4547 3-9-5 **67** SilvestreDeSousa 8 60
(Geoffrey Harker) *chsd ldrs: rdn along and outpcd 1/2-way: sme late hdwy* **14/1**

6430 **11** *1 1/2* **Dolly Diva**[41] 3421 3-9-0 **62** MickyFenton 7 50
(Paul Midgley) *in tch: effrt over 2f out: sn rdn and wknd* **28/1**

3610 **12** *2* **Phoenix Clubs (IRE)**[8] 4558 3-9-8 **70** RussKennemore 15 52
(Paul Midgley) *in tch: rdn along over 2f out: sn outpcd* **12/1**

-000 **13** *4* **Majestic Bounty**[42] 3407 3-8-0 **51** oh6 DominicFox(3) 9
(Chris Fairhurst) *a in rr* **66/1**

0050 **14** *7* **Pindrop**[9] 4493 3-8-5 **53** JohnFahy 3
(Clive Cox) *a in rr* **40/1**

1m 11.49s (-2.11) **Going Correction** -0.30s/f (Firm)
WFA 3 from 4yo+ 4lb **14** Ran SP% **119.6**
Speed ratings (Par 100): **102,99,97,97,96 95,93,93,92,92 90,87,82,72**
Tote Swingers 1&2 £10.60, 2&3 £24.00, 1&3 £50.10 CSF £36.29 CT £466.00 TOTE £7.90: £2.60, £1.40, £7.90; EX 41.10.
Owner P D Burrow **Bred** Mrs J M Russell **Trained** Brandsby, N Yorks

FOCUS
The main action unfolded middle to stands' side. Just a modest fillies' handicap. The placed horses help set the level of the form.

4794 TRADE UNION UNISON AND THOMPSONS SOLICITORS LLP CONDITIONS STKS 6f
3:20 (3:22) (Class 3) 3-Y-O+
£8,092 (£2,423; £1,211; £605; £302; £152) **Stalls** High

Form RPR

-520 **1** **Artistic Jewel (IRE)**[48] 3190 3-8-7 102 RichardMullen 2 103
(Ed McMahon) *hld up: hdwy to trck ldrs 2f out: effrt over 1f out: rdn and slt ld ent fnl f: drvn and kpt on wl towards fin* **6/1**

4502 **2** *hd* **Royal Rock**[21] 4078 8-9-7 108 TedDurcan 6 113
(Chris Wall) *hld up in rr: swtchd lft to outer and gd hdwy 2f out: rdn to chal over 1f out and ev ch: drvn ins fnl f: no ex nr fin* **5/1**[3]

0204 **3** *1 3/4* **Boomerang Bob (IRE)**[27] 3901 3-8-9 106 SilvestreDeSousa 5 104+
(J W Hills) *trckd ldrs: effrt whn nt clr run and hmpd ent fnl f: kpt on to take 3rd last 100yds* **9/4**[1]

-440 **4** *1 1/4* **Bogart**[42] 3370 3-8-12 110 PhillipMakin 4 97
(Kevin Ryan) *led: rdn along and jnd 2f out: drvn and hdd ent fnl f: sn one pce* **7/2**[2]

2220 **5** *1/2* **Jimmy Styles**[42] 3370 8-8-13 105 (p) JohnFahy 1 94
(Clive Cox) *cl up: rdn to chal 2f out: ev ch tl drvn: edgd rt and wknd ent fnl f* **7/2**[2]

120- **6** *10* **Webbow (IRE)**[308] 6521 10-8-13 97 J-PGuillambert 7 62
(Julie Camacho) *chsd ldrs: rdn along over 2f out: sn wknd* **16/1**

-640 **7** *6* **West Leake Diman (IRE)**[78] 2236 3-8-9 103 MatthewChadwick 3 42
(Charles Hills) *cl up: rdn along wl over 2f out: sn wknd and bhd whn eased over 1f out* **28/1**

1m 10.36s (-3.24) **Going Correction** -0.30s/f (Firm)
WFA 3 from 8yo+ 4lb **7** Ran SP% **115.5**
Speed ratings (Par 107): **109,108,106,104,104 90,82**
Tote Swingers 1&2 £3.00, 2&3 £3.00, 1&3 £6.20 CSF £36.31 TOTE £7.10: £2.90, £2.70; EX 38.30.
Owner R L Bedding **Bred** Jim McDonald **Trained** Lichfield, Staffs

FOCUS
They raced stands' side. A decent conditions race.

NOTEBOOK
Artistic Jewel(IRE) gained her first success since landing a juvenile Listed event last October. She'll presumably be back in Pattern company next time and has more to offer. (tchd 7-1)
Royal Rock ran well considering he had 4lb to find with the winner. Like Artistic Jewel, he can be competitive back in Listed/Group races. (op 9-2)
Boomerang Bob(IRE) had insufficient room when trying to make his move. The way he ran on when belatedly in the open suggests he would have gone close to winning with a clear run. (op 10-3)
Bogart tends to hang right, so having the stands' rail to run against should have been beneficial, but he found disappointingly little for pressure. He hasn't gone on from a promising reappearance in the Duke of York. (op 9-2)
Jimmy Styles wasn't at his best. (op 3-1)

Webbow(IRE), who had a bit to do at the weights, shaped okay on his debut for a new yard after 308 days off. He travelled well to a point but became short of room when looking to challenge and was quickly held thereafter, being eased late on. (op 20-1)

4795 UNISON "SPEAKING UP FOR PUBLIC SERVICES" H'CAP — 1m 2f 60y

4:00 (4:01) (Class 2) (0-100,97) 3-Y-O+

£12,450 (£3,728; £1,864; £699; £699; £234) **Stalls** Low

Form — RPR

0313 **1** **Silvery Moon (IRE)**[21] 4110 5-9-6 **89** .... TedDurcan 6 — 94
(Tim Easterby) *chsd clr ldr: rdn along and hdwy 2f out: drvn ent fnl f: styd on gamely to ld nr line* **8/1**

11/ **2** *hd* **Conduct (IRE)**[676] 6447 5-9-13 **96** .... RichardMullen 8 — 100
(Sir Michael Stoute) *trckd ldrs: hdwy over 2f out: rdn over 1f out: drvn and kpt on ins fnl f: jst hld* **9/2**[1]

4460 **3** *hd* **Suits Me**[37] 3534 9-9-6 **89** .... SilvestreDeSousa 9 — 93
(David Barron) *led and sn clr: rdn and qcknd wl over 2f out: drvn over 1f out: hdd and no ex nr fin* **17/2**

0-01 **4** *hd* **Incendo**[38] 3502 6-9-2 **85** ....(t) ShaneKelly 3 — 89
(James Fanshawe) *hld up in midfield: hdwy 2f out: swtchd ins and rdn ent fnl f: styd on wl towards fin* **14/1**

0104 **4** *dht* **Cool Macavity (IRE)**[13] 4365 4-9-2 **85** .... IanMongan 4 — 89
(Charles Hills) *hld up in midfield: hdwy over 2f out: rdn to chse ldrs over 1f out: drvn and kpt on fnl f: nrst fin* **9/1**

5531 **6** *1/2* **Art Scholar (IRE)**[16] 4249 5-9-1 **84** .... JohnFahy 10 — 87
(Michael Appleby) *hld up and bhd: swtchd wd and hdwy 2f out: rdn to chse ldrs and edgd lft ins fnl f: kpt on: nrst fin* **8/1**

3404 **7** *1/2* **Calaf**[41] 3417 4-8-13 **82** .... PhillipMakin 7 — 84
(Brian Ellison) *chsd ldng pair: hdwy over 2f out: rdn over 1f out: kpt on same pce* **15/2**[3]

15-6 **8** *1 1/2* **Unex Michelangelo (IRE)**[101] 1604 3-9-3 **95** .... RobertHavlin 5 — 94
(John Gosden) *chsd ldrs: rdn over 2f out: drvn over 1f out: kpt on same pce* **10/1**

150- **9** *1 3/4* **Fulgur**[336] 5700 4-10-0 **97** .... J-PGuillambert 11 — 92
(Luca Cumani) *hld up in rr: sme hdwy 3f out: sn rdn and n.d* **11/2**[2]

4063 **10** *1 1/4* **Tinshu (IRE)**[13] 4365 6-9-2 **85** ....(p) CathyGannon 1 — 78
(Derek Haydn Jones) *in tch: effrt on inner: 3f out: rdn 2f out: wknd over 1f out* **8/1**

060 **11** *nk* **Dhaular Dhar (IRE)**[19] 4136 10-8-9 **78** .... ChrisCatlin 2 — 70
(Jim Goldie) *hld up towards rr: effrt and hdwy over 2f out: sn rdn and n.d* **28/1**

2m 7.12s (-2.28) **Going Correction** -0.30s/f (Firm)
WFA 3 from 4yo+ 9lb — **11 Ran SP% 118.4**
Speed ratings (Par 109): **97,96,96,96,96 96,95,94,93,92 91**
Tote Swingers 1&2 £15.90, 2&3 £7.30, 1&3 £4.90 CSF £44.21 CT £320.29 TOTE £6.80: £2.30, £1.80, £2.70; EX 32.10.
Owner R J Swinbourne **Bred** Colin Kennedy **Trained** Great Habton, N Yorks

FOCUS
Somewhat muddling form. Confirmed front-runner Suits Me took them along in a clear lead and for much of the closing stages it looked as though he had nicked this, but he emptied late on, leaving the field to close for a bunch finish. The form looks ordinary for the grade.

NOTEBOOK
Silvery Moon(IRE) had gained his first three wins over 1m and hadn't convinced on previous attempts at this distance, but he proved his stamina here. This was probably a career best and he'll have more options now. (op 7-1)
Conduct(IRE) looked highly promising when winning his first two starts in September 2010, the latter over this trip off 85, but he hadn't been seen since. Returning off 11lb higher, he showed he retains a lot of ability with a pleasing effort, keeping on all the way to the line. He can be expected to stay further, but is clearly fine at this trip. (op 5-1)
Suits Me could have been expected to see his race out better considering he was given so much rope in front. (tchd 8-1 and 9-1)
Cool Macavity(IRE) posted a solid effort, showing enough to suggest he can win off this mark. (op 12-1)
Incendo didn't come off the bridle when winning over 1m4f on Polytrack last time. Up 3lb, he again cruised through the race, but this time he didn't get the clearest of runs and failed to find extra when coming under pressure near the line. The impression is he remains well handicapped for when things drop just right. (op 12-1)
Fulgur ◆ had been off for 336 days and he can do better. (op 13-2 tchd 7-1)

4796 UNISON AND UIA HOME INSURANCE H'CAP — 1m 4f

4:35 (4:36) (Class 4) (0-85,84) 3-Y-O — **£5,175** (£1,540; £769; £384) **Stalls** Low

Form — RPR

-024 **1** **Al Saham**[38] 3509 3-9-7 **84** .... SilvestreDeSousa 2 — 94+
(Saeed Bin Suroor) *dwlt and sltly hmpd s: t.k.h early and hld up in rr: stdy hdwy 3f out: swtchd rt and rdn over 1f out: styd on wl to ld last 100yds* **7/2**[1]

6031 **2** *3/4* **Require**[29] 3813 3-9-7 **84** .... KirstyMilczarek 4 — 92
(Luca Cumani) *trckd ldng pair: hdwy to chse ldr over 2f out: sn rdn: drvn over 1f out: kpt on* **7/2**[1]

5131 **3** *3/4* **Flashman**[15] 4294 3-9-0 **77** .... DavidNolan 3 — 84
(Richard Fahey) *led: rdn along wl over 2f out: drvn over 1f out: hdd and no ex last 100yds* **7/2**[1]

0334 **4** *4 1/2* **Ex Oriente (IRE)**[14] 4323 3-9-5 **82** .... RobertHavlin 7 — 81
(John Gosden) *hld up in rr: hdwy on outer 3f out: rdn wl over 1f out: sn no imp* **4/1**[2]

6214 **5** *3 1/4* **Enery (IRE)**[12] 4396 3-8-11 **74** .... J-PGuillambert 8 — 68
(Mark Johnston) *prom: chsd ldr after 4f: cl up 4f out: sn rdn along: wknd over 2f out* **8/1**

2561 **6** *12* **Third Half**[14] 4325 3-8-9 **72** .... CathyGannon 5 — 47
(Tom Dascombe) *trckd ldrs: rdn along over 3f out: sn wknd* **6/1**[3]

-006 **7** *11* **Wise Venture (IRE)**[30] 3787 3-8-12 **75** .... PhillipMakin 6 — 32
(Alan Jarvis) *in tch: rdn along 3f out: sn wknd* **25/1**

2m 30.55s (-4.35) **Going Correction** -0.30s/f (Firm) — **7 Ran SP% 115.9**
Speed ratings (Par 102): **102,101,101,98,95 87,80**
Tote Swingers 1&2 £2.90, 2&3 £4.20, 1&3 £3.80 CSF £16.45 CT £45.41 TOTE £4.60: £3.10, £3.10; EX 13.30.
Owner Godolphin **Bred** Darley **Trained** Newmarket, Suffolk

FOCUS
A fair handicap and soundly run with the second running to his previous winning mark over C&D.

4797 UNISON "FAIR PENSIONS FOR ALL" MAIDEN STKS (DIV II) — 1m 2f 60y

5:10 (5:11) (Class 5) 3-4-Y-O — **£2,911** (£866; £432; £216) **Stalls** Low

Form — RPR

0-4 **1** **Blazing Speed**[43] 3349 3-9-1 0 .... ShaneKelly 1 — 93+
(James Fanshawe) *t.k.h: led 1f: trckd ldr: hdwy to ld 2f out: jnd and rdn ent fnl f: styd on strly and sn clr* **12/1**

2 *3 1/2* **Starfield** 3-9-1 0 ....(e[1]) RobertHavlin 6 — 87
(John Gosden) *hld up in midfield: stdy hdwy 3f out: chsd ldrs 2f out: chal appr fnl f and ev ch: sn rdn and one pce* **20/1**

3 *3 1/4* **Ustura (USA)** 3-9-1 0 ....(t) TedDurcan 3 — 81+
(Saeed Bin Suroor) *hld up towards rr: hdwy wl over 2f out: rdn over 1f out: styd on fnl f: nrst fin* **16/1**

05 **4** *4 1/2* **Malindi**[29] 3811 3-8-10 0 .... WilliamCarson 8 — 67
(James Given) *chsd ldrs: rdn along 3f out: plugged on one pce fnl 2f* **100/1**

22 **5** *2 1/2* **Ruwaiyan (USA)**[22] 4067 3-9-1 0 .... SilvestreDeSousa 11 — 67
(Mahmood Al Zarooni) *cl up: led after 1f: pushed along and jnd over 2f out: sn hdd and rdn: wknd over 1f out* **10/11**[1]

42 **6** *1 1/2* **Port Charlotte**[48] 3189 3-8-10 0 .... ChrisCatlin 2 — 59
(Hughie Morrison) *chsd ldrs: pushed along over 3f out: sn rdn and wknd over 2f out* **11/1**[3]

7 *1 1/4* **Muqantara (USA)** 3-8-10 0 .... RichardMullen 10 — 57+
(Sir Michael Stoute) *towards rr: pushed along 1/2-way: rdn along wl over 3f out: nvr a factor* **20/1**

05 **8** *1* **London Silver**[40] 3447 3-9-1 0 .... CathyGannon 5 — 60
(Henry Candy) *s.i.s: a in rr* **33/1**

02 **9** *2 1/2* **Checkpoint**[34] 3664 3-9-1 0 .... IanMongan 7 — 55
(Sir Henry Cecil) *trckd ldng pair: effrt over 3f out: sn rdn along and wknd wl over 2f out* **11/4**[2]

10 *8* **Matured** 3-8-10 0 ....[1] J-PGuillambert 9 — 35
(Ralph Beckett) *hld up: a towards rr* **25/1**

11 *2* **Vespasia** 3-8-10 0 .... JohnFahy 4 — 31
(Ed McMahon) *midfield: pushed along over 4f out: sn wknd* **33/1**

2m 6.36s (-3.04) **Going Correction** -0.30s/f (Firm) — **11 Ran SP% 121.2**
Speed ratings (Par 103): **100,97,94,91,89 87,86,86,84,77 76**
Tote Swingers 1&2 £11.80, 2&3 £41.30, 1&3 £20.60 CSF £227.18 TOTE £17.00: £3.70, £6.00, £7.20; EX 380.90.
Owner Dragon Gate **Bred** J Sankey **Trained** Newmarket, Suffolk

FOCUS
The form isn't as strong as it might have been with the front pair in the market both underperforming, but the time was the quickest of three races at the trip, including 3.70 seconds faster than the slowly run first division.
Ruwaiyan(USA) Official explanation: trainer's representative could offer no explanation for the colt's performance

4798 UNISON "CAMPAIGNING FOR A FAIRER SOCIETY" H'CAP — 5f

5:45 (5:45) (Class 5) (0-70,70) 3-Y-O — **£2,911** (£866; £432; £216) **Stalls** High

Form — RPR

0562 **1** **Roy's Legacy**[5] 4663 3-8-3 **52** ....(t) SilvestreDeSousa 4 — 63
(Shaun Harris) *mde all: rdn over 1f out: drvn ins fnl f: kpt on gamely towards fin* **8/1**

0440 **2** *nk* **Dartrix**[14] 4348 3-8-5 **54** ....(p) RoystonFfrench 11 — 64
(Michael Dods) *swtchd lft s and hld up: gd hdwy 2f out: sn chsng ldrs: rdn to chal ins fnl f: drvn and no ex towards fin* **12/1**

1214 **3** *2 1/2* **Just Like Heaven (IRE)**[8] 4558 3-9-4 **67** .... TedDurcan 5 — 68
(Tim Easterby) *cl up: rdn wl over 1f out: kpt on same pce ent fnl f* **2/1**[1]

4234 **4** *3/4* **Love Island**[9] 4496 3-9-0 **63** .... RussKennemore 3 — 61
(Richard Whitaker) *prom: rdn along 2f out: drvn and one pce ent fnl f* **9/2**[2]

0011 **5** *2 1/4* **Elusive Bonus (IRE)**[39] 3463 3-8-7 **63** .... DavidBergin[(7)] 6 — 53
(David O'Meara) *chsd ldrs: rdn and hung rt over 1f out: swtchd lft and drvn ent fnl f: no imp* **15/2**

1644 **6** *1/2* **Pettochside**[18] 4197 3-9-0 **63** ....(t) WilliamCarson 8 — 51
(Stuart Williams) *hld up and bhd: hdwy nr stands' rail whn nt clr run and sltly hmpd over 1f out: kpt on same pce after* **20/1**

-360 **7** *1/2* **Sky Crossing**[78] 2256 3-9-7 **70** .... PhillipMakin 1 — 57
(James Given) *dwlt: hdwy on wd outside and in tch over 2f out: sn rdn and wknd* **16/1**

056- **8** *hd* **Dream Whisperer**[292] 6919 3-8-12 **68** .... JoshBaudains[(7)] 10 — 54
(Dominic Ffrench Davis) *racd nr stands' rail: chsd ldrs: rdn along over 2f out: grad wknd* **20/1**

2-01 **9** *4 1/2* **Alnair (IRE)**[11] 4428 3-9-0 **63** .... DanielTudhope 9 — 33
(Declan Carroll) *chsd ldrs: rdn along 1/2-way: sn wknd* **11/2**[3]

5-06 **10** *6* **Selective Spirit**[64] 2680 3-8-6 **55** ....(be[1]) ChrisCatlin 2
(John Weymes) *chsd ldrs: rdn along wl over 2f out: sn wknd* **33/1**

0-05 **11** *7* **Absolute Bearing (IRE)**[63] 2695 3-8-2 **51** oh4 .... JohnFahy 7
(Tim Etherington) *chsd ldrs: rdn along 1/2-way: sn wknd* **33/1**

59.26s (-1.24) **Going Correction** -0.30s/f (Firm) — **11 Ran SP% 118.8**
Speed ratings (Par 100): **97,96,92,91,87 86,86,85,78,69 57**
Tote Swingers 1&2 £15.30, 2&3 £6.10, 1&3 £3.80 CSF £94.88 CT £271.08 TOTE £7.30: £1.90, £4.10, £1.30; EX 181.20.
Owner Karl Blackwell Steve Mohammed S A Harris **Bred** A Christou **Trained** Carburton, Notts

FOCUS
A moderate sprint handicap. They raced towards the stands' side and there were personal bests from the first two with the third to his latest mark.
T/Plt: £175.60 to a £1 stake. Pool £72,541.93. 301.40 winning tickets. T/Qpdt: £81.70 to a £1 stake. Pool £3,767.90. 34.10 winning tickets. JR

4759 GOODWOOD (R-H)

Saturday, August 4

OFFICIAL GOING: Good (round 7.9; straight 8.0 (stands' side 8.0, centre 8.1, far side 8.0))

Wind: Fresh, against Weather: showers clearing, cloudy with bright spells, breezy

4799 GET YOUR BET ON AT BLUESQ.COM STEWARDS' SPRINT STKS (H'CAP) — 6f

2:05 (2:06) (Class 2) 3-Y-O+

£18,675 (£5,592; £2,796; £1,398; £699; £351) **Stalls** High

Form — RPR

0416 **1** **Johannes (IRE)**[6] 4629 9-9-0 **89** .... GeorgeChaloner[(7)] 13 — 101
(Richard Fahey) *on toes: racd in centre: racd off the pce in midfield: swtchd rt and hdwy 2f out: styd on u.p to chal fnl 100yds: led fnl 50yds* **22/1**

2005 **2** *1/2* **Louis The Pious**[28] 3855 4-9-10 **92** ....(p) GrahamLee 6 — 102
(Kevin Ryan) *racd in centre: in tch: effrt u.p over 1f out: drvn to ld ins fnl f: r.o wl tl hdd and no ex fnl 50yds* **14/1**

2250 **3** *2* **Seeking Magic**[15] 4285 4-9-5 **87** ....(t) AdamKirby 2 — 91
(Clive Cox) *racd in far side trio: t.k.h: effrt and carried lft whn merged w centre gp over 2f out: kpt on ins fnl f* **25/1**

0000 **4** ½ **Valery Borzov (IRE)**[21] 4086 8-9-5 **87**................................(v) FranBerry 8 89+
(Richard Fahey) *racd in centre: in tch: squeezed for room and hmpd over 2f out: rdn over 1f out: swtchd rt and styd on ins fnl f* **25/1**

6050 **5** *hd* **El Viento (FR)**[7] 4611 4-9-6 **88**.......................................(b) EddieAhern 14 90
(Richard Fahey) *on toes: racd in centre: in tch: rdn ent fnl 2f: keeping on but unable qck whn sltly short of room jst ins fnl f: one pce after* **25/1**

201 **6** *nk* **Fair Value (IRE)**[9] 4501 4-9-8 **90** 6ex................................ HayleyTurner 7 91
(Simon Dow) *lw: racd in centre: overall ldr: rdn over 1f out: drvn 1f out: hdd ins fnl f: wknd fnl 75yds* **20/1**

6643 **7** *1* **Tax Free (IRE)**[7] 4611 10-9-10 **92**................................ AdrianNicholls 17 90
(David Nicholls) *racd in centre: chsd overall ldr: rdn and ev ch over 1f out: hung rt fr 1f out: wknd fnl 100yds* **10/1**[2]

5004 **8** ½ **Baby Strange**[15] 4286 8-8-10 **85**......................... MichaelJMMurphy(7) 25 81
(Derek Shaw) *awkward leaving stalls: bhd and racd towards stands' side: rdn and hdwy whn merged w centre gp over 2f out: styd on wl ins fnl f: nt rch ldrs* **25/1**

2/2- **9** *1* **Moscow Eight (IRE)**[16] 6-9-1 **86**................................. HarryBentley(3) 9 79
(E J O'Neill, France) *swtg: racd in centre: chsd ldrs: rdn and unable qck over 1f out: wknd ins fnl f* **33/1**

1001 **10** *shd* **Jarrow (IRE)**[29] 3822 5-8-9 **84**...................... WilliamTwiston-Davies(7) 10 76
(Milton Bradley) *racd in centre: chsd ldrs: rdn 2f out: keeping on whn short of room and swtchd lft jst ins fnl f: no ex and wknd fnl 100yds* **12/1**[3]

-404 **11** *nk* **Lutine Bell**[15] 4285 5-9-7 **89**.. JimmyFortune 18 81
(Mike Murphy) *lw: racd in centre: s.i.s and wl bhd: hdwy ent fnl f: styd on wl: nvr trbld ldrs* **14/1**

115 **12** ½ **Poole Harbour (IRE)**[15] 4286 3-9-3 **89**...................... RichardHughes 22 79
(Richard Hannon) *stdd s: bhd: swtchd to r in centre after 1f: swtchd rt and hdwy wl over 1f out: no prog 1f out: plugged on same pce after* **10/1**[2]

1306 **13** 1 ½ **Head Space (IRE)**[7] 4611 4-9-9 **91**................................ JamesSullivan 5 76
(Ruth Carr) *racd in centre: s.i.s: towards rr: hdwy u.p over 2f out: no ex 1f out and wknd ins fnl f* **8/1**[1]

004 **14** ¾ **Nasri**[7] 4611 6-9-6 **88**.. JimCrowley 20 71
(Milton Bradley) *racd in centre: in tch but sn rdn along: struggling 2f out: btn 1f out and wknd ins fnl f* **10/1**[2]

1140 **15** 1 ¼ **Klynch**[7] 4611 6-9-10 **92**...(b) AmyRyan 24 71
(Ruth Carr) *racd towards stands' side: in tch: merged w centre gp and rdn over 2f out: wknd 1f out* **33/1**

-300 **16** *shd* **Piazza San Pietro**[35] 3641 6-9-9 **91**.................................. NeilCallan 28 69
(Zoe Davison) *racd towards stands' side: midfield overall: edgd rt u.p and merged w centre gp over 2f out: no imp* **50/1**

000 **17** *shd* **Masked Dance (IRE)**[15] 4286 5-9-2 **84**.........................(bt) TomQueally 4 62
(Scott Dixon) *racd on far side: midfield overall: edgd lft and merged w centre over 2f out: drvn and wknd over 1f out* **66/1**

3614 **18** *1* **Jedward (IRE)**[13] 4367 5-9-4 **86** 6ex.............................. TonyHamilton 11 61
(Richard Fahey) *lw: racd in centre: in tch in midfield: rdn and struggling whn pushed lft over 2f out: wknd over 1f out* **14/1**

-020 **19** *nk* **Oneladyowner**[68] 2558 4-9-5 **87**.................................... WilliamBuick 16 61
(David Brown) *racd in centre: wl bhd: rdn and sme hdwy ent fnl f: kpt on: n.d* **16/1**

6600 **20** *nk* **Piscean (USA)**[11] 4437 7-8-13 **84**.................................. RyanClark(3) 3 57
(Tom Keddy) *s.i.s: swtchd lft to r in centre gp: wl bhd: modest late hdwy: n.d* **33/1**

0120 **21** ¾ **Noverre To Go (IRE)**[4] 4690 6-9-4 **86** 6ex....................... LukeMorris 23 57
(Ronald Harris) *b.hind: racd towards stands' side: chsd ldrs: edgd rt u.p to join centre gp over 2f out: wknd over 1f out* **33/1**

2360 **22** *nk* **Catfish (IRE)**[7] 4576 4-9-9 **91**................................ MickaelBarzalona 15 61
(Brian Meehan) *racd in centre: in tch: rdn and struggling over 2f out: wknd over 1f out: wl btn and eased ins fnl f* **14/1**

0230 **23** 1 ¾ **Novellen Lad (IRE)**[15] 4286 7-9-7 **89**............................ KierenFallon 21 53
(Willie Musson) *swtchd rt to r in centre gp s: midfield: rdn 1/2-way: wknd over 1f out: wl btn and eased ins fnl f* **25/1**

2264 **24** *hd* **Arctic Lynx (IRE)**[8] 4530 5-9-2 **84**................................ DavidProbert 12 47
(John Best) *edgy: swtg: racd in centre: midfield: effrt u.p over 2f out: no imp: wknd jst over 1f out* **33/1**

0000 **25** *2* **Shifting Star (IRE)**[3] 4703 7-9-6 **88**............................(v) KieranO'Neill 19 45
(John Bridger) *racd in centre gp: midfield: rdn over 3f out: edgd rt and wknd over 1f out* **66/1**

0500 **26** 3 ¾ **Dickie's Lad (IRE)**[42] 3374 4-9-9 **91**..............................(t) JamesDoyle 27 36
(Kevin Ryan) *swtg: racd towards stands' side: in tch in midfield: hung rt u.p 2f out: sn btn* **33/1**

0056 **27** *1* **Thunderball**[15] 4285 6-9-9 **91**......................................(p) RobertWinston 1 33
(Scott Dixon) *b: lw: led far side gp and chsd ldrs overall: edgd lft and jnd centre gp over 2f out: wknd over 1f out: eased ins fnl f* **40/1**

3210 **28** *3* **Chilli Green**[48] 3190 5-9-2 **89**......................................(p) DarrenEgan(5) 26 21
(Lee Carter) *racd towards stands' side: midfield: edgd rt and jnd centre gp over 2f out: wknd 2f out: wl bhd fnl f* **25/1**

1m 11.22s (-0.98) **Going Correction** +0.075s/f (Good)
WFA 3 from 4yo+ 4lb **28 Ran SP% 135.8**
Speed ratings (Par 109): **109,108,105,105,104 104,103,102,101,100 100,99,97,96,95 95,94,93,93,92 91,91,89,88,86 81,79,7**
Tote Swingers 1&2 £204.50, 2&3 £204.50, 1&3 £204.50 CSF £261.70 CT £7659.22 TOTE £36.40: £6.80, £5.20, £6.90, £7.00; EX 700.20 TRIFECTA Not won..
Owner John Nicholls Ltd/David Kilburn **Bred** Blue Bloodstock Limited **Trained** Musley Bank, N Yorks

FOCUS

There was 6mm of rain overnight but the ground remained good (Going Sick stands' side 8.0; centre 8.1; far side 8.0). Fresh ground was opened up on the top bend and all distances were as advertised. A typically competitive consolation race for those who missed the cut for the Stewards' Cup. They more or less avoided both rails and congregated up the centre of the track, and the action developed towards the far side of the bunch. The final split was slow and the third looks the best guide to the level.

NOTEBOOK

Johannes(IRE), who also won this race back in 2009, kept on strongest of all. One of the old men of the field, this quicker track suited him better than the stiff finish at Pontefract last time and he'll no doubt now try to follow up at York, where he has tasted success twice before. He won't find things easy off a higher mark, but is clearly at the top of his game right now. (op 20-1)

Louis The Pious, a four-time winner over 6f last term, was dropping back to his best distance for the first time this year and put up a much better effort. He should continue to run well off this sort of mark if kept to this trip. (tchd 16-1)

Seeking Magic settled better off this good gallop and put up a better display as a result. He's the type who needs others to set things up for him.

Valery Borzov(IRE), third in this race last year off 2lb lower, did win off a 1lb higher mark than this last September, so was feasibly treated. He ran a sound race but ideally could have done with a bit of cut in the ground. (tchd 33-1)

El Viento(FR), who recorded his best previous effort according to RPRs at this track over 7f, got slightly hampered inside the final furlong but it didn't make a huge amount of difference. (op 33-1)

Fair Value(IRE), carrying a penalty for her Epsom win over 5f, took them along for most of the way but just couldn't hold off this big field. She remains in top form and her new mark might not be beyond her in a smaller field where she can dominate. (op 25-1)

Tax Free(IRE) was 1lb well-in at the weights following his good run at York the previous week, but like the leader he got a bit tired in the closing stages having been up there the whole way. (tchd 9-1)

Baby Strange deserves credit as he was drawn high, which was away from where the main action developed, and he was the only one to make significant late headway towards the stands' rail. He's hinted on more than one occasion this season that he has a race in him off this sort of mark.

Moscow Eight(IRE), a winner in the French provinces in June, was another who was up there for a long way before tiring. He might not have much margin for error off his current mark.

Jarrow(IRE) looked good at Sandown and perhaps 5f is what he needs these days. (op 14-1)

Lutine Bell, again slowly away, was out the back for much of the race and got going all too late. He'll be suited by a return to a stiffer track.

Poole Harbour(IRE), who was switched to race up the centre after initially looking to race with a smaller group stands' side, simply kept on past weakening rivals without ever looking a serious threat. (op 12-1 tchd 9-1)

Head Space(IRE), who was 2lb well-in at the weights, was disappointing, failing to pick up as the leaders weakened. (op 10-1 tchd 11-1)

Nasri failed to build on his promising effort at York last time. (op 11-1)

Jedward(IRE) didn't see her race out over this extra furlong. (op 16-1)

Oneladyowner, who has good form at this track, was another who just couldn't pick up and proved disappointing. Official explanation: trainer said that the colt was unsuited by the good ground.

4800 TOYO TIRES PERFORMANCE STKS (H'CAP) 1m 6f

2:40 (2:40) (Class 2) (0-105,105) 3-Y-0+

£24,900 (£7,456; £3,728; £1,864; £932; £468) **Stalls** High

Form RPR

4-00 **1** **Motivado**[21] 4111 4-9-2 **93**.. LukeMorris 13 109
(Sir Mark Prescott Bt) *in rr: drvn and str hdwy whn edgd rt ins fnl 3f: led ins fnl 2f: drvn clr fnl f: won gng away* **11/2**[1]

-232 **2** *5* **A Boy Named Suzi**[22] 4072 4-9-4 **95**................................ GrahamLee 5 103
(James Eustace) *chsd ldrs: drvn over 2f out: styd on wl fnl f to take 2nd last stride but nvr any ch w wnr* **10/1**

3-56 **3** *shd* **Solar Sky**[94] 1750 4-9-12 **103**... EddieAhern 6 111
(Sir Henry Cecil) *lw: chsd ldrs: chal 3f out: sn ld: hdd ins fnl 2f: outpcd by wnr over 1f out: styd on but ct for 2nd last stride* **16/1**

0-20 **4** 3 ½ **Harlestone Times (IRE)**[42] 3372 5-9-8 **99**................. JimmyFortune 14 102
(John Dunlop) *towards rr: drvn and styd on fr over 2f out: kpt on fnl f but nvr any threat to ldrs* **12/1**

-012 **5** 3 ¾ **Life And Soul (IRE)**[43] 3341 5-9-2 **93**............................. WilliamBuick 1 91
(Amanda Perrett) *chsd ldrs: t.k.h: led 9f out: rdn and jnd 3f out: sn hdd: wknd 2f out* **8/1**[3]

1-00 **6** 1 ¾ **Petara Bay (IRE)**[35] 3625 8-10-0 **105**............................... JimCrowley 8 100
(Robert Mills) *lw: chsd ldrs: rdn over 3f out: wknd fr 2f out* **14/1**

0101 **7** *nk* **Vasily**[35] 3642 4-9-1 **92**.. AndreaAtzeni 10 87
(Robert Eddery) *chssed ldrs: rdn over 3f out: wknd over 2f out* **11/1**

-100 **8** *12* **Shubaat**[63] 2709 5-8-11 **88**... NeilCallan 4 66
(Roger Varian) *lw: led to 9f out: rdn 4f out: wknd 2f out* **12/1**

-002 **9** 2 ¾ **Late Telegraph (IRE)**[31] 3765 4-8-12 **89**......................... TomQueally 7 63
(Sir Henry Cecil) *chsd ldrs: rdn over 3f out: sn btn* **16/1**

42-2 **10** *4* **Roxy Flyer (IRE)**[31] 3766 5-9-4 **95**................................. RyanMoore 11 64
(Amanda Perrett) *a in rr* **8/1**[3]

0-30 **11** *4* **The Betchworth Kid**[35] 3625 7-9-4 **95**........................... HayleyTurner 3 58
(Alan King) *a in rr* **20/1**

-510 **12** *4* **Franciscan**[28] 3857 4-9-0 **91**... KierenFallon 12 48+
(Luca Cumani) *in tch: pushed along and bmpd ins fnl 3f: sn wknd* **7/1**[2]

2060 **13** 1 ½ **Spice Fair**[15] 4284 5-8-11 **88**.. DavidProbert 9 43
(Mark Usher) *in rr: wnt lft to r alone on stands' rail over 3f out and no ch after* **33/1**

3401 **14** *nse* **Very Good Day (FR)**[21] 4115 5-9-1 **92**....................... RichardHughes 2 47
(Mick Channon) *lw: towards rr: hdwy: sme hdwy over 4f out: wknd 3f out* **9/1**

3m 4.39s (0.79) **Going Correction** +0.125s/f (Good) **14 Ran SP% 119.1**
Speed ratings (Par 109): **102,99,99,97,94 93,93,86,85,83 80,78,77,77**
CSF £58.58 CT £837.70 TOTE £5.50: £2.70, £2.70, £6.20; EX 54.20 Trifecta £1996.40 Part won. Pool £2,697.94 - 0.84 winning units..
Owner Syndicate 2009 **Bred** Newsells Park Stud **Trained** Newmarket, Suffolk
■ Stewards' Enquiry : Luke Morris four-day ban: careless riding (18-21 Aug)

FOCUS

A stop-start gallop and several of the runners failed to give their running. A personal-best from the winner.

NOTEBOOK

Motivado ◆, who had only two behind running down the hill, fairly powered his way through (causing interference in the process) before storming clear in the manner of a stayer going places. Consistency has been an issue for the son of Motivator, who looked equally as good on occasions last season, but his poor run in the Northumberland Plate can be attributed to the heavy ground, and he'll surely head to the Ebor now with a major chance (should get in under a penalty) for which he is now 6-1 clear favourite. (op 6-1 tchd 13-2)

A Boy Named Suzi, who is hugely consistent, looked to run right to his best in second and gives the form a solid look. (op 9-1)

Solar Sky, making his handicap debut back from 94 days off, looked on a fair mark and he duly returned to form, just proving unable to quicken. It's hoped he goes on from this, although he'll remain tricky to place.

Harlestone Times(IRE) would have preferred a stronger gallop but this was still a step up on his latest effort. He continues to shapes like a horse with a decent handicap in him. (op 11-1)

Life And Soul(IRE) runs the course well but racing keenly through the early stages compromised his chance.

Petara Bay(IRE), last year's winner, was 2lb higher this time and remains below his best. (op 16-1)

Vasily's stamina didn't seem up to it and he can be given another chance return to proper fast ground. (op 12-1 tchd 14-1, 10-1 in places)

Shubaat hasn't progressed from April's Musselburgh win and it was surprising he didn't attempt to set a more even gallop. (op 14-1)

Late Telegraph(IRE) took a backward step, having chased home a rampant winner at Kempton the time before.

Roxy Flyer(IRE) is a dual winner here and had run well on her reappearance at Kempton, so there was presumably something amiss for her to run so poorly.

Franciscan was responding to pressure when badly hampered after Motivado bulldozed his way through. He's now had valid excuses each of he last twice and remains a horse of interest. (op 15-2 tchd 8-1 in a place)

Spice Fair Official explanation: jockey said that the gelding hung left

Very Good Day(FR), up 7lb and dropping 2f in trip, has run well over C&D on easy ground before, so this poor performance was hard to explain. Official explanation: trainer's representative said that the gelding was unsuited by the track (op 10-1)

4801 MARKEL INSURANCE NASSAU STKS (BRITISH CHAMPIONS SERIES) (GROUP 1) (F&M) 1m 1f 192y

3:15 (3:17) (Class 1) 3-Y-O+

£104,913 (£39,775; £19,906; £9,916; £4,976; £2,497) **Stalls** Low

Form				RPR
4132	**1**		**The Fugue**[44] 3292 3-8-11 111 ... RichardHughes 7 (John Gosden) *hld up in tch in last trio: swtchd lft and effrt jst over 1f out: qcknd smartly but edgd rt ins fnl f: led fnl 50yds: sn in command and eased cl home* **11/4**[2]	118+
0-40	**2**	1	**Timepiece**[79] 2209 5-9-6 110 ... TomQueally 1 (Sir Henry Cecil) *led and set stdy gallop: rdn and qcknd over 2f out: drvn and kpt on wl fnl f tl hdd and outpcd by wnr wl ins fnl f* **16/1**	115
314	**3**	1 ¾	**Was (IRE)**[13] 4378 3-8-11 113 ... RyanMoore 6 (A P O'Brien, Ire) *chsd ldr: rdn over 2f out: drvn and kpt on gamely fr over 1f out: one pce ins fnl f* **11/2**[3]	112
5-05	**4**	½	**Sea Of Heartbreak (IRE)**[23] 4010 5-9-6 107 ... JamesDoyle 3 (Roger Charlton) *awkward leaving stalls: hld up in rr: rdn and effrt on outer 2f out: no imp tl styd on wl ins fnl f* **33/1**	111
-530	**5**	nk	**Lay Time**[22] 4065 4-9-6 109 ... JimmyFortune 5 (Andrew Balding) *lw: wl in tch in midfield: rdn and effrt 2f out: drvn and outpcd over 1f out: kpt on same pce fnl f* **14/1**	110
-111	**6**	1	**Izzi Top**[34] 3676 4-9-6 115 ... WilliamBuick 8 (John Gosden) *swtg: edgy: t.k.h: chsd ldrs: rdn and effrt over 1f out: chsd ldr 1f out: no imp: lost 2nd fnl 100yds and immediately short of room and snatched up: eased towards fin* **7/4**[1]	111+
3-10	**7**	1 ½	**Clinical**[45] 3266 4-9-6 109 ... LukeMorris 4 (Sir Mark Prescott Bt) *t.k.h: hld up in last trio: rdn and effrt on inner over 2f out: no imp and swtchd lft over 1f out: wl hld after* **20/1**	105
12-0	**8**	2 ¼	**Nahrain**[45] 3266 4-9-6 117 ... NeilCallan 2 (Roger Varian) *lw: t.k.h: chsd ldrs: rdn and struggling to qckn 2f out: outpcd and btn jst over 1f out: eased whn wl hld ins fnl f* **13/2**	100

2m 9.61s (1.51) **Going Correction** +0.125s/f (Good)
WFA 3 from 4yo+ 9lb **8** Ran **SP% 112.0**
Speed ratings (Par 117): **98,97,95,95,95 94,93,91**
Tote Swingers 1&2 £8.70, 2&3 £7.90, 1&3 £2.90 CSF £42.82 TOTE £3.40: £1.40, £4.70, £1.80; EX 52.50 Trifecta £378.30 Pool £13,514.54 - 26.43 winning units..
Owner Lord Lloyd-Webber **Bred** Watership Down Stud **Trained** Newmarket, Suffolk
■ Stewards' Enquiry : Richard Hughes two-day ban: careless riding (Aug 18-19)

FOCUS
The pace was steady early and, despite a couple of the key older horses, most notably Izzi Top, failing to run up to their best, this still looked a good edition. The two 3-y-os looked to have plenty of upside still coming into the race, and they claimed first and third. The fourth and fifth are rated close to their marks and set the level.

NOTEBOOK
The Fugue finally gaining compensation for her unlucky Oaks third behind Was. Off since a 6l second on ground softer than ideal in the Ribblesdale, her participation here was still uncertain earlier in the afternoon, with the ground deemed to be on the slow side, but Richard Hughes appealed as the ideal jockey for her (Gosden reported he'd told Buick to ride Izzi Top) and the daughter of Dansili seemed to enjoy being held on to for as long as possible before asked to produce her burst, which was most telling. This will have restored any confidence lost following a rough passage suffered at Epsom and her trainer, who also houses Irish Oaks winner Great Heavens, indicated the Yorkshire Oaks would be next, with the Breeders' Cup Filly & Mare Turf, a race she looks tailor made for, the ultimate aim. (op 7-2 tchd 4-1)
Timepiece had performed well below last season's best (won Falmouth, twice placed in Group 1s in France) in a couple of starts behind Izzi Top this time round, but the return to more positive tactics clearly helped and she nearly triumphed under a well-judged ride. The winner was much classier overall, but she ought to be placed to winning advantage again before the season is out. (op 12-1 tchd 11-1)
Was(IRE) benefited from a good ride when winning the Oaks (prominent in a steadily run race) and would likely have placed in the Irish equivalent but for being hampered. She was done for speed this time, though, not proving able to quicken, and it was a surprise she didn't try to press on sooner. She'll likely return to 1m4f now for another crack at the winner in the Yorkshire Oaks. (op 15-2)
Sea Of Heartbreak(IRE), like the runner-up, had run poorly in two previous starts this year, but she put up a career-best effort this time. She benefited from a couple of the others underperforming to obtain her position, but is fresh for the time of year and this versatile sort can surely be found an opening. (op 28-1)
Lay Time, the Windsor Forest third, looked to appreciate the step up to 1m2f but has still to convince she's capable of winning a Group 1. (op 16-1)
Izzi Top, who got a little warm beforehand, has readily climbed the ranks this season, winning her first Group 1 in the Pretty Polly at the Curragh last time, but that wasn't a strong race for the grade and her chance was affected here by having to race wide without cover. She was beaten, but still in the mix for third, when squeezed up late on, and this seemed to confirm her winning stablemate is the superior of the pair. (op 13-8 tchd 6-4)
Clinical didn't look up to this and was readily held. (tchd 25-1)
Nahrain was again disappointing, being eased late on. The latter has now run poorly on both starts this season, and it's possible a hard race at last year's Breeders' Cup has left its mark. (op 5-1)

4802 BLUE SQUARE BET STEWARDS' CUP (HERITAGE H'CAP) 6f

3:55 (3:56) (Class 2) 3-Y-O+

£62,250 (£18,640; £9,320; £4,660; £2,330; £1,170) **Stalls** High

Form				RPR
0350	**1**		**Hawkeyethenoo (IRE)**[14] 4321 6-9-9 103 ... GrahamLee 4 (Jim Goldie) *lw: hld up in tch towards far side: gd hdwy fr 2f out: str chal fr ins fnl f tl led last stride* **9/1**[3]	112
03	**2**	nse	**Imperial Guest**[15] 4285 6-8-11 94 ... AshleyHamblett(3) 18 (George Margarson) *lw: chsd ldrs towards centre of crse: squeezed though to chal fr ins fnl 2f: edgd rt over 1f out: slt advantage fnl 120yds tl hdd last stride* **25/1**	103
1054	**3**	¾	**Lui Rei (ITY)**[22] 4073 6-9-2 101 ... DarrenEgan(5) 14 (Robert Cowell) *chsd ldrs towards centre of crse: chal fr 2f out tl led over 1f out: hdd fnl 120yds: kpt on wl* **20/1**	107
0042	**4**	½	**Waffle (IRE)**[42] 3371 6-9-9 103 ... FranBerry 6 (David Barron) *hld up towards rr far side: swtchd lft and hdwy towards centre fr 2f out: plenty to do over 1f out: str run ins fnl f: fin wl* **7/1**[1]	108+
3501	**5**	½	**Alben Star (IRE)**[28] 3860 4-9-3 97 ... TonyHamilton 22 (Richard Fahey) *chsd ldrs towards stands' side: edgd rt towards centre over 2f out: styd on strly fnl f* **14/1**	100+
-026	**6**	nse	**Jamesie (IRE)**[21] 4099 4-9-1 95 ... NeilCallan 9 (David Marnane, Ire) *prom far side: n.m.r ins fnl 2f: hmpd and swtchd rt 1f out: kpt on but nvr gng pce to press ldrs* **8/1**[2]	98
2200	**7**	nse	**Es Que Love (IRE)**[7] 4576 3-9-9 107 ... KierenFallon 17 (Mark Johnston) *pressed ldrs towards centre of crse: stl ev ch over 1f out: styd on same pce fnl 120yds* **16/1**	109
0021	**8**	hd	**Shropshire (IRE)**[15] 4285 4-9-1 100 6ex ... MatthewLawson(5) 21 (Charles Hills) *chsd ldrs centre of crse: pushed along 3f out: styd on to chse ldrs over 1f out: kpt on same pce fnl 120yds* **20/1**	102
2462	**9**	¾	**Borderlescott**[40] 3441 10-9-9 103 ... RobertWinston 11 (Robin Bastiman) *chsd ldrs towards centre of crse: rdn over 2f out: pushed rt over 1f out: kpt on same pce ins fnl f* **20/1**	103
100	**10**	nk	**Bajan Tryst (USA)**[7] 4576 6-9-4 101 ... JulieBurke(3) 1 (Kevin Ryan) *chsd ldrs towards far side: slt ld 2f out: hdd over 1f out: wknd fnl 120yds* **50/1**	100
3004	**11**	nk	**Advanced**[7] 4609 9-9-0 94 ... (t) AmyRyan 10 (Kevin Ryan) *chsd ldrs in centre of crse: chal over 1f out: wknd fnl 150yds* **66/1**	93
3100	**12**	½	**Atlantic Sport (USA)**[7] 4609 7-9-4 98 ... RichardHughes 7 (Mick Channon) *lw: hld up in rr towards far side: rdn and stl bhd appr fnl f: r.o clsng stages but nvr any ch* **20/1**	94
06	**13**	shd	**Lexi's Hero (IRE)**[35] 3641 4-9-3 97 ... (p) JamesDoyle 23 (Kevin Ryan) *pressed ldrs towards stands' side: rdn over 2f out: styd on same pce appr fnl f* **33/1**	93
5010	**14**	nse	**Grissom (IRE)**[7] 4611 6-9-2 96 6ex ... MickaelBarzalona 5 (Tim Easterby) *swtg: on toes: chsd ldrs far side: n.m.r ins fnl 2f and lost position: styd on again fnl 120yds* **33/1**	92+
3302	**15**	¾	**Mac's Power (IRE)**[15] 4285 6-9-3 97 ... (t) RyanMoore 16 (James Fanshawe) *hld up in rr towards centre of crse: drvn 2f out: styd on fnl f but nvr gng pce to get into contention* **11/1**	90
0020	**16**	½	**Swiss Cross**[7] 4611 5-9-0 94 ... (t) WilliamBuick 8 (Phil McEntee) *pressed ldrs towards far side: rdn and ev ch fr 2f out: n.m.r ins fnl f: eased clsng stages* **40/1**	86
-055	**17**	2 ½	**Dungannon**[13] 4367 5-9-3 97 ... JimmyFortune 24 (Andrew Balding) *lw: racd towards stands' side and bhd: edgd towards centre of crse fr 2f out but nvr gng pce to rch ldrs* **14/1**	81
1000	**18**	2 ½	**Oasis Dancer**[21] 4092 5-9-8 102 ... JimCrowley 12 (Ralph Beckett) *sn chsng ldrs towards far side: rdn over 2f out: wknd ins fnl f* **16/1**	78
1600	**19**	nse	**Seal Rock**[21] 4099 4-8-13 98 ... AmyScott(5) 15 (Henry Candy) *racd in midfield towards centre of crse: rdn 3f out and sn one pce* **12/1**	74
204	**20**	hd	**Whaileyy (IRE)**[7] 4576 4-9-0 94 ... (b) AdamKirby 27 (Marco Botti) *swtg: chsd ldrs towards stands' side: rdn 2f out and sn outpcd* **28/1**	69
3240	**21**	nk	**Esprit De Midas**[14] 4321 6-9-0 94 ... HayleyTurner 25 (Dean Ivory) *b.hind: racd towards stands' side and outpcd most of way* **66/1**	68
-002	**22**	1	**Victoire De Lyphar (IRE)**[16] 4258 5-8-12 92 ... AdrianNicholls 3 (David Nicholls) *bmpd s: racd towards far side and sn led: hdd over 2f out: wknd wl over 1f out* **12/1**	63
00P1	**23**	¾	**Elusive Prince**[21] 4077 4-9-0 94 6ex ... (b) GrahamGibbons 2 (David Barron) *wnt lft s: racd towards far side and sn pressing ldr: wknd ins fnl 2f: bmpd over 1f out* **16/1**	63
-000	**24**	½	**Breathless Kiss (USA)**[7] 4611 5-9-0 94 ... (b) DaraghO'Donohoe 10 (Kevin Ryan) *racd towards centreof crse: a outpcd* **66/1**	61
0410	**25**	12	**Palace Moon**[42] 3371 7-9-10 104 ... (t) TomQueally 20 (William Knight) *lw: s.i.s: racd towards centre of crse and a bhd* **25/1**	33
0400	**26**	1 ½	**Bayleyf (IRE)**[2] 4740 3-8-12 96 ... LukeMorris 28 (John Best) *racd towards stands' side: early spd: bhd fr 1/2-way* **66/1**	19
6/	**27**	hd	**Head Of Steam (USA)**[422] 5-9-3 97 ... EddieAhern 26 (Amanda Perrett) *b: b.hind: racd towards stands' side: a in rr* **66/1**	20

1m 11.27s (-0.93) **Going Correction** +0.075s/f (Good)
WFA 3 from 4yo+ 4lb **27** Ran **SP% 136.2**
Speed ratings (Par 109): **109,108,107,107,106 106,106,106,105,104 104,103,103,103,102 101,98,95,95,94 94,93,92,91,75 73**
Tote Swingers 1&2 £158.10, 2&3 £158.90, 1&3 £105.30 CSF £227.97 CT £4427.21 TOTE £9.40: £2.50, £5.60, £6.60, £2.30; EX 441.90 Trifecta £12537.10 Pool £112,468.61 - 6.63 winning units..
Owner Johnnie Delta Racing **Bred** S Leigh & R Leigh & Islandmore Stud **Trained** Uplawmoor, E Renfrews
■ Stewards' Enquiry : Ashley Hamblett two-day ban: use of whip (18-21)
Darren Egan two-day ban: use of whip (18-19 Aug)

FOCUS
They split into four groups to begin with but came together with 2f to run and there were any number in with a chance a furlong out. Just like in the Stewards' Sprint the winner was delivered towards the far side of the bunch. Sectional times reveal that they went 0.64sec slower through the first 2f than in the consolation race earlier on the card, but the final furlong was covered in a time 0.9sec quicker. The winning time was 1.14sec faster and the placed horses set the standard.

NOTEBOOK
Hawkeyethenoo(IRE) is a veteran of these big-field handicaps but had never run in this race before. Third in the Wokingham and fifth in the July Cup prior to a luckless run at Ascot last time, he had clearly been running well enough to go close here, and having travelled well into contention he found a nice turn of foot to pinch a lead on the far side, which he just about clung onto. He has the raw ability to win a Group race, but the way these big handicaps are run suit him much better, so it might not be so easy. His trainer said he could go for the Haydock Sprint Cup, though.
Imperial Guest travelled strongly into contention and quickened well between horses inside the final 2f, before putting his 7f stamina to good use and staying on strongly. Like the winner he's seen to best effect in this type of race, where he gets to sit off a strong gallop.
Lui Rei(ITY), who is suited by a sharp track, ran really well, but he had to go for home a fair way out and perhaps he could have done with being carried a little further into the race. His trainer mentioned that they might go pot hunting on the continent.
Waffle(IRE) was again well backed by the masochists, and he did what he does best and gave them a hard-luck story to take home with them. Switched from tracking the winner on the outer to the centre, he weaved his way through to make the places, and a flimsy case can be made that had he stayed where he was he might have gone close. (op 9-1)
Alben Star(IRE) ◆, one of the less exposed runners in the line-up, continues to improve, and this was another career-best. He seems to go on any ground and ought to continue to be a threat in these big sprint handicaps. Perhaps the Great St Wilfrid will come into consideration, as no doubt will the Ayr Gold Cup. (op 12-1)
Jamesie(IRE), back over 6f, coped with the drop back in distance fine and might have finished a little closer with a clearer run, but he's the type that will always need a bit of luck in running. He's another who'll no doubt be targeted at the Ayr Gold Cup, and his stamina for further will be a help there. (op 10-1)
Es Que Love(IRE), one of only two 3yos in the line-up, didn't run at all badly considering he raced more towards the stands' side and is on a stiff mark nowadays. His stable has been in cracking form at the meeting, though.
Shropshire(IRE) had Imperial Guest behind him when successful at Ascot last time, but his penalty meant he was 6lb worse off at the weights with that rival here. He wasn't able to confirm the form but was far from disgraced.

Borderlescott, who won this race back in 2006 and was placed the following two seasons, showed speed up the centre of the track, but was carried right in the closing stages, which didn't help his cause. (op 16-1)
Bajan Tryst(USA) was never far away on the far side but didn't see his race out. A strongly run 6f stretches his stamina a touch.
Advanced, one of the less likely contenders on paper, wasn't disgraced. (op 50-1)
Atlantic Sport(USA) struggled to pick up when initially asked, but was staying on at the finish. He could do with a return to 7f. (op 22-1)
Lexi's Hero(IRE) is at his best when he gets his own way out in front, which wasn't the case here.
Grissom(IRE) was denied racing room inside the final 2f and would probably have finished a little closer with a clear run. (op 50-1)
Mac's Power(IRE) was disappointing, carrying his head high and failing to repeat his performance in this race last year. (op 10-1)
Swiss Cross Official explanation: jockey said that the gelding suffered interference in running
jockey said that the gelding suffered interference in running
Dungonnon raced in the stands' side group early on, which wasn't the best place to be, but even so this was a tame effort.
Oasis Dancer travelled well through the first half of the race but got badly squeezed up with a furlong and a half to run and soon dropped back through the field. (op 20-1)
Seal Rock has lost his form a little of late and was never seen with a chance. (op 16-1)
Victoire De Lyphar(IRE) tried to make every yard on the far side but was under pressure some way out. (op 10-1)
Head Of Steam(USA) Official explanation: jockey said that the gelding was never travelling

4803 NAT WEST AHEAD FOR BUSINESS EBF MAIDEN STKS 7f
4:30 (4:31) (Class 2) 2-Y-O **£11,320** (£3,368; £1,683; £841) **Stalls** Low

Form				RPR
2	1		**Steeler (IRE)**[14] 4327 2-9-0 0 KierenFallon 12 (Mark Johnston) *athletic: lw: hld up in tch: hdwy over 3f out: chsd ldrs and edging rt over 1f out: swtchd lft and drvn 1f out: r.o wl to ld fnl 50yds* **10/3**[2]	87+
	2	¾	**Rock God (IRE)** 2-9-0 0 GrahamLee 3 (Eve Johnson Houghton) *tall: t.k.h: hld up in tch in midfield: effrt to chse ldr and rdn over 1f out: drvn to ld fnl 100yds: hdd and one pce fnl 50yds* **28/1**	83+
2	3	nk	**Improvisation (IRE)**[22] 4066 2-9-0 0 MickaelBarzalona 8 (Mahmood Al Zarooni) *chsd ldrs: rdn ent fnl 2f: hdwy u.p to chse ldng pair jst ins fnl f: kpt on towards fin* **3/1**[1]	82
	4	nk	**Kyllachy Rise** 2-9-0 0 TomQueally 14 (Sir Henry Cecil) *w'like: athletic: scope: t.k.h: hld up towards rr: edgd rt 3f out: swtchd bk lft over 2f out: hdwy and swtchd lft again jst over 1f out: styd on wl ins fnl f* **16/1**	81+
65	5	shd	**Colmar Kid (IRE)**[10] 4472 2-9-0 0 AdamKirby 2 (Richard Hannon) *led: rdn wl over 1f out: drvn ent fnl f: hdd fnl 100yds: no ex* **25/1**	81
	6	1	**Wentworth (IRE)** 2-9-0 0 RichardHughes 11 (Richard Hannon) *w'like: str: hld up in tch in midfield: shuffled bk and bhd over 2f out: swtchd lft and nt clr run 2f out: stl plenty to do and hdwy jst over 1f out: kpt on wl ins fnl f: nvr trbld ldrs* **10/3**[2]	81+
3	7	2 ½	**Hoarding (USA)**[35] 3634 2-9-0 0 WilliamBuick 6 (John Gosden) *w'like: attr: in tch: hdwy to chse ldrs over 2f out: rdn and unable qck 2f out: stl chsng ldrs and n.m.r over 1f out: rdn and no prog 1f out* **15/2**[3]	74
	8	1	**Gilded Frame** 2-9-0 0 HayleyTurner 15 (Marcus Tregoning) *attr: unf: hld up towards rr: rn green bnd 5f out: pushed rt 3f out: hdwy on inner over 1f out: kpt on ins fnl f: nvr able to chal* **66/1**	69+
	9	½	**Anjuna Beach (USA)** 2-9-0 0 RyanMoore 1 (Gary Moore) *w'like: tall: scope: stdd s: t.k.h and sn in tch in midfield: rdn and effrt over 1f out: unable qck and one pce after* **50/1**	68
	10	½	**The Gatling Boy (IRE)** 2-9-0 0 JamesDoyle 13 (Richard Hannon) *str: gd bodied: bit bkwd: rn green: towards rr and stuck wd: rdn 3f out: kpt on under hands and heels fr over 1f out: nvr trbld ldrs* **50/1**	67+
3	11	1	**Country Western**[14] 4340 2-9-0 0 MichaelHills 4 (Charles Hills) *unf: scope: t.k.h: chsd ldr tl over 1f out: wknd u.p ent fnl f* **8/1**	64
22	12	1	**Martial Art (IRE)**[30] 3770 2-9-0 0 DavidProbert 7 (Andrew Balding) *w'like: chsd ldrs: rdn and effrt ent fnl 2f: drvn and unable qck over 1f out: wknd 1f out* **12/1**	61
	13	3 ¼	**Work Ethic (IRE)** 2-9-0 0 LukeMorris 5 (Gerard Butler) *t.k.h: hld up towards rr: rdn and struggling 3f out: wknd over 1f out* **50/1**	53
	14	1	**Empiricist (IRE)** 2-9-0 0 JimCrowley 9 (Amanda Perrett) *w'like: lengthy: scope: stuck wd: in tch: lost pl 3f out: wknd 2f out: wl btn and edgd rt over 1f out* **66/1**	50
0	15	2	**Knight's Parade (IRE)**[9] 4507 2-9-0 0 EddieAhern 10 (Amanda Perrett) *w'like: leggy: bhd but in tch: hmpd over 2f out: sn struggling: bhd over 1f out* **100/1**	45

1m 28.87s (1.87) **Going Correction** +0.125s/f (Good) **15** Ran SP% **124.8**
Speed ratings (Par 100): **94,93,92,92,92 91,88,87,86,86 84,83,80,78,76**
Tote Swingers 1&2 £37.00, 2&3 £22.80, 1&3 £4.80 CSF £105.69 TOTE £4.70: £2.00, £5.30, £1.60; EX 239.00 Trifecta £501.80 Pool £1,871.62 - 2.76 winning units..
Owner Sheikh Hamdan Bin Mohammed Al Maktoum **Bred** Airlie Stud **Trained** Middleham Moor, N Yorks

FOCUS
An open-looking maiden, with many of the top yards represented, and the winner and sixth look the ones to take from the race. The form is rated close to the averages for the race of recent years.

NOTEBOOK
Steeler(IRE) was beaten through greenness on debut and looked more streetwise this time, challenging between horses and winning with more in hand than the bare margin. A horse with all the right entries, he has the physical attributes to continue to progress and ought to relish the step up to 1m. (op 13-2)
Rock God(IRE), half-brother to a useful 1m2f winner in France, was a bit keen but showed decent acceleration and fared best of the newcomers. Entered in the Group 2 Champagne Stakes, he too will benefit from 1m and should go one better in an ordinary maiden. (op 25-1)
Improvisation(IRE) probably ran to a similar level as on debut, again looking in need of a stiffer test. He should find an opening. (op 11-4 tchd 7-2 in places)
Kyllachy Rise, a half-brother to UAE Oaks winner Tamarillo, was keen and came from quite a way back. He was never getting there, but should improve.
Colmar Kid(IRE) has improved with each start and seemed to benefit from a more prominent ride this time. He's now qualified for nurseries. (op 33-1)
Wentworth(IRE) ◆, a half-brother to a quite useful 1m winner who cost 200,000gns, would surely have given the winner something to think about with normal luck in running, although it's doubtful he'd have won. He should improve once going 1m and is another ready-made maiden winner. (op 7-2 tchd 4-1 in places)
Hoarding(USA) was held when becoming short of room and may be more of a type for nurseries now. (op 8-1)
Gilded Frame, the second foal of an unraced dam, looked inexperienced but was noted keeping on nicely. He'll benefit from an extra furlong.
The Gatling Boy(IRE) was green and got caught wide, so can do better in time. (op 40-1)
Country Western failed to build on a promising start when third on soft ground at Newmarket, finding little having raced keenly. (op 15-2)
Martial Art(IRE), who'd been runner-up on both previous attempts, dropped away equally as tamely. (op 10-1)

4804 BET ON YOUR MOBILE AT BLUESQ.COM NURSERY (H'CAP) 6f
5:05 (5:05) (Class 2) 2-Y-O **£9,703** (£2,887; £1,443; £721) **Stalls** High

Form				RPR
2611	1		**Jamesbo's Girl**[24] 3951 2-8-9 75 TonyHamilton 4 (Richard Fahey) *chsd ldrs: rdn to ld over 1f out: kpt on wl u.p fnl f* **16/1**	81
1202	2	½	**New Pearl (IRE)**[37] 3532 2-9-4 87 HarryBentley[(3)] 7 (David Brown) *chsd ldr: rdn and ev ch over 1f out: sustained chal u.p tl no ex and hld towards fin* **14/1**	91
3210	3	1 ¾	**Jubilee Brig**[44] 3291 2-9-5 85 TomQueally 5 (Gary Moore) *on toes: awkward as stalls opened and slowly away: t.k.h: hld up in rr: hdwy over 1f out: drvn 1f out: chsd ldng pair and one pce fnl 100yds* **25/1**	84
542	4	¾	**Club House (IRE)**[40] 3452 2-8-12 78 StevieDonohoe 2 (Robert Mills) *sn led: rdn and hdd over 1f out: no ex 1f out and wknd fnl 100yds* **20/1**	75
5322	5	nk	**Indian Affair**[2] 4728 2-8-8 74 LukeMorris 1 (Milton Bradley) *chsd ldrs: rdn and effrt over 1f out: hung rt and styd on same pce ins fnl f* **20/1**	70
216	6	nk	**Dominate**[4] 4687 2-9-2 82 RichardHughes 6 (Richard Hannon) *stdd s: hld up in tch towards rr: clsd and gng wl but nt clr run 2f out: hmpd over 1f out: in the clr and kpt on ins fnl f: nvr able to chal* **2/1**[2]	80+
1	7	1	**Dutch Masterpiece**[25] 3937 2-9-0 80 RyanMoore 3 (Gary Moore) *str: taken down early: stdd s: t.k.h: hld up in tch: effrt and hanging rt 2f out: continued to hang bdly and unable to mount a chal: btn and eased wl ins fnl f* **15/8**[1]	74
3213	8	3 ¼	**Dansili Dual (IRE)**[8] 4526 2-8-12 78 KieranO'Neill 10 (Richard Hannon) *hld up in last trio: hdwy u.p over 1f out: no prog 1f out: hung rt and wknd fnl f* **8/1**[3]	60
2321	9	2 ½	**Super Simon (IRE)**[16] 4239 2-8-12 78 (v) NeilCallan 9 (Paul D'Arcy) *in tch: rdn and unable qck over 2f out: carried rt and btn 1f out: eased wl ins fnl f* **12/1**	56
0016	10	4	**Cuisine (IRE)**[49] 3138 2-8-12 78 DavidProbert 8 (Andrew Balding) *hld up in tch in midfield: rdn over 3f out: wknd 2f out: bhd whn eased wl ins fnl f* **33/1**	42

1m 12.66s (0.46) **Going Correction** +0.075s/f (Good) **10** Ran SP% **115.8**
Speed ratings (Par 100): **99,98,96,95,94 94,92,88,85,79**
Tote Swingers 1&2 £13.50, 2&3 £13.60, 1&3 £23.80 CSF £201.38 CT £5458.85 TOTE £12.70: £2.70, £3.40, £3.80; EX 249.50 Trifecta £1122.50 Part won. Pool £1,517.00 - 0.50 winning units..
Owner Hardisty Rolls **Bred** Lady Juliet Tadgell **Trained** Musley Bank, N Yorks

FOCUS
Very few got into this from off the pace but the form looks straightforward.

NOTEBOOK
Jamesbo's Girl, who was debuting for Richard Fahey having been claimed at Catterick last time, was previously trained by David Nicholls, who had been responsible for four of the last six winners of this nursery. She was never far off the pace, knuckled down well when she had to, and should have more to offer in nurseries. (op 12-1)
New Pearl(IRE) ran a better race back on a sounder surface and was rallying well at the finish. He should be up to winning something similar. (op 10-1)
Jubilee Brig ◆, racing over 6f for the first time, did best of those that were held up off the pace. Awkwardly away and a bit keen early, he was the only one to make any ground on leaders who weren't stopping, and he's probably capable of better. (op 14-1)
Club House(IRE), gelded since he last ran, was up there most of the way in a race in which the pace pretty much held up. He's probably a good guide to the level of the form. (op 14-1)
Indian Affair, the most exposed runner in the line-up, is another who acts as a marker for the form.
Dominate, beaten less than five lengths into sixth in the Molecomb four days earlier, looked to hold strong claims dropped in class and upped in trip, but he didn't come close to challenging for the win. He travelled well out the back, but was hampered as he went for his initial run and then found his path blocked inside the last furlong. While unlucky not to finish closer, he didn't exactly look to have loads left in the tank, and it might just be that he's a tricky ride. (op 5-2 tchd 11-4 in places)
Dutch Masterpiece didn't do much right as he raced keenly and then hung badly right, making him difficult to steer in the closing stages. His debut win came on the Fibresand and that form doesn't always translate to turf, but he deserves another chance on a flatter track. (op 5-2 tchd 11-4)
Dansili Dual(IRE) was another who didn't look at home on the track, as he too hung right in the closing stages. (tchd 9-1)

4805 QIPCO FUTURE STARS APPRENTICE STKS (H'CAP) (SUPPORTING SSAFA FORCES HELP) 1m 1f
5:40 (5:41) (Class 3) (0-90,96) 4-Y-O+ **£9,703** (£2,887; £1,443; £721) **Stalls** Low

Form				RPR
0111	1		**Landaman (IRE)**[4] 4684 4-9-9 96 6ex MichaelJMMurphy[(7)] 5 (Mark Johnston) *t.k.h: hld up in midfield: swtchd lft and smooth hdwy over 2f out: led over 1f out and sn clr: pushed out: easily* **11/8**[1]	109+
1-40	2	4	**Sakhee's Pearl**[45] 3278 6-8-4 75 NathanSweeney[(5)] 7 (Jo Crowley) *chsd ldrs: swtchd rt and rdn to chse ldr briefly 2f out: edgd rt u.p and outpcd over 1f out: plugged on to go 2nd wl ins fnl f* **33/1**	80
-424	3	¾	**Jawhar (IRE)**[22] 4068 4-8-9 75 [1] AdamBeschizza 3 (William Haggas) *lw: chsd ldr tl led over 2f out: rdn and hdd over 1f out: immediately brushed aside by wnr and one pce: lost 2nd wl ins fnl f* **9/1**	78
3055	4	¾	**Borug (USA)**[22] 4068 4-8-9 80 (p) WilliamTwiston-Davies[(5)] 6 (James Tate) *lw: s.i.s: hld up in tch: n.m.r 3f out: hdwy u.p 2f out: styd on fnl f: no ch w wnr* **13/2**[2]	81
4302	5	3 ½	**Karaka Jack**[19] 4136 5-9-2 82 HarryBentley 8 (David Nicholls) *chsd ldrs: effrt u.p ent fnl 2f: 5th and no hdwy over 1f out: wknd ins fnl f* **15/2**[3]	76
3521	6	3 ¾	**My Lord**[17] 4223 4-8-2 73 JakePayne[(5)] 12 (Luke Dace) *swtg: v.s.a: hld up in rr: effrt u.p on outer over 2f out: plugged on but n.d* **14/1**	58
0-62	7	¾	**Tuscania**[23] 3991 4-9-1 84 AshleyMorgan[(3)] 11 (Lucy Wadham) *taken down early: chsd ldrs tl over 2f out: sn struggling: no ch but rallied u.p whn edgd rt over 1f out* **25/1**	68
425	8	½	**Robemaker**[41] 3417 4-9-5 88 TobyAtkinson[(3)] 13 (John Gosden) *lw: hld up in last trio: rdn and hdwy 2f out: no imp and wl btn over 1f out: wknd ins fnl f* **12/1**	71

4550 **9** *hd* **Bloodsweatandtears**[15] 4287 4-8-4 **73** ow1............(b) DavidKenny(3) 14 55
(William Knight) *stdd after s: hld up towards rr: effrt u.p over 2f out: no prog 2f out and wl btn over 1f out* **25/1**

0500 **10** *1 3/4* **Perfect Cracker**[14] 4317 4-8-7 **78**............................ NicoleNordblad(5) 1 56
(Clive Cox) *b.hind: reluctant and led most of the way to post: t.k.h: hld up in midfield: rdn over 2f out: wknd u.p wl over 1f out* **25/1**

0100 **11** *4* **Megalala (IRE)**[13] 4365 11-9-2 **82**.......................... RyanPowell 2 52
(John Bridger) *led tl over 2f out: sn rdn and btn: wknd 2f out* **33/1**

25-0 **12** *8* **Little Black Book (IRE)**[125] 1156 4-8-9 **78**...............(t[1]) DarrenEgan(3) 9 30
(Gerard Butler) *hld up towards rr: rdn and hung rt 3f out: sn bhd* **14/1**

0063 **13** *2 1/4* **Switchback**[12] 4398 4-8-5 **71** oh1..................................(b[1]) AmyRyan 10 18
(Michael Easterby) *in tch on outer: rdn 3f out: sn wknd: wl bhd over 1f out* **22/1**

3050 **14** *1* **Prime Exhibit**[11] 4437 7-8-13 **82**.......................... MatthewLawson(3) 4 27
(Milton Bradley) *t.k.h: chsd ldr tl over 2f out: sn dropped out and bhd wl over 1f out* **40/1**

1m 55.36s (-0.94) **Going Correction** +0.125s/f (Good) **14 Ran SP% 122.4**
Speed ratings (Par 107): **109,105,104,104,101 97,97,96,96,94 91,84,82,81**
Tote Swingers 1&2 £21.90, 2&3 £53.90, 1&3 £4.40 CSF £68.79 CT £334.50 TOTE £2.40: £1.30, £9.50, £2.90; EX 72.60 Trifecta £1025.10 Pool £2,410.51 - 1.74 winning units..
Owner Sheikh Hamdan Bin Mohammed Al Maktoum **Bred** Darley **Trained** Middleham Moor, N Yorks

FOCUS
The pace was quite steady and the placed horses are rated a bit below their best form.

NOTEBOOK
Landaman(IRE) defied a 6lb penalty for Tuesday's success. A fine-looker who has improved rapidly since encountering a sound surface, he was tanking throughout and comfortably asserted for a fourth-straight victory. A Group performer in waiting, he was entitled to win like this and connections may opt to head straight into pattern-company, with his rating likely to be in the mid-100s once reassessed. (op 13-8)
Sakhee's Pearl was just 1lb higher than when winning on the Polytrack in December and he can count himself unfortunate to bump into the well-handicapped winner. (op 50-1)
Jawhar(IRE) seemed to run to form in the first-time hood and may be worth a try at 7f. (tchd 8-1)
Borug(USA) was probably unfortunate not to finish second, being slowly away and meeting interference in the run. He should be able to win from this mark. (op 7-1)
My Lord lost all chance at the start and ran fairly well considering. (op 12-1)
T/Jkpt: Not won. T/Plt: £6,069.40 to a £1 stake Pool £284,349.31. 34.20 winning tickets. T/Qpdt: £140.00 to a £1 stake. Pool £17,797.39. 94.05 winning tickets. SP

4257 HAMILTON (R-H)

Saturday, August 4

OFFICIAL GOING: Soft (7.3) (abandoned after race 2 (6.45) due to waterlogged track)
Wind: Almost nil Weather: Cloudy, heavy rain from 2nd race

4806 AVIA SIGNS NURSERY 6f 5y
6:15 (6:17) (Class 6) (0-65,68) 2-Y-O **£2,264** (£673; £336; £168) **Stalls** Low

Form RPR

0241 **1** **Bonnie Lesley (IRE)**[4] 4672 2-9-13 **68** 6ex.................. PaulMulrennan 2 79+
(Keith Dalgleish) *reluctant to enter stalls: trckd ldrs: hdwy to ld over 1f out: edgd lft and pushed clr fnl f* **5/4[1]**

3525 **2** *6* **Twilight Pearl**[15] 4310 2-8-13 **59**...................................... DarylByrne(5) 6 52
(Tim Easterby) *trckd ldrs: effrt and chsd wnr over 1f out: sn pushed along: no imp fnl f* **9/4[2]**

002 **3** *2* **Charlemagne Diva**[24] 3951 2-8-4 **52**........................ KevinStott(7) 5 39+
(Ann Duffield) *led: sddled sn slipped forward: rdn and hdd over 1f out: sn btn* **8/1[3]**

0033 **4** *2 1/4* **Stripped Bear (IRE)**[19] 4139 2-8-13 **54**................ RichardKingscote 3 34
(Tom Dascombe) *trckd ldrs tl rdn and wknd over 1f out* **12/1**

350 **5** *2* **Red Koko (IRE)**[76] 2309 2-8-2 **46**.......................... DeclanCannon(3) 1 20
(George Moore) *dwlt: bhd: rdn along over 2f out: nvr able to chal* **28/1**

650 **6** *5* **Kingsville**[25] 3937 2-8-9 **50**.. JimmyQuinn 4 9
(Mark Johnston) *bhd: struggling wl over 2f out: sn btn* **10/1**

6505 **7** *3 1/4* **Mace The Ace**[14] 4324 2-8-11 **59**.. IanBurns(7) 7 9
(David C Griffiths) *in tch: rdn and hung bdly rt wl over 1f out: sn btn* **25/1**

1m 15.16s (2.96) **Going Correction** +0.40s/f (Good) **7 Ran SP% 110.4**
Speed ratings (Par 92): **96,88,85,82,79 73,68**
Tote Swingers 1&2 £1.30, 2&3 £4.40, 1&3 £2.40 CSF £3.82 TOTE £2.20: £1.30, £1.20; EX 3.20.
Owner Middleham Park Racing Iii **Bred** Peter & Sarah Fortune **Trained** Carluke, S Lanarks

FOCUS
A weak nursery and a well-treated winner who scored easily.

NOTEBOOK
Bonnie Lesley(IRE) defied a penalty for Tuesday's win at Ayr with ease. She's clearly going the right way but the handicapper is sure to get his teeth into her after this and she'll face a much stiffer task on her hat-trick bid (won't be able to run again before being reassessed). (tchd 6-5, tchd 11-8 in a place)
Twilight Pearl probably matched her previous form but is starting to look exposed and was no match for the winner. (tchd 2-1 and 5-2)
Charlemagne Diva's rider had an uncomfortable time after his saddle slipped early, and this daughter of Holy Roman Emperor is probably worth another chance to show what she can do off a lowly opening handicap mark. Official explanation: jockey said that the filly's saddle slipped (op 17-2 tchd 15-2)
Stripped Bear(IRE) was well held in fourth and has yet to achieve much of worth on turf. (tchd 11-1 and 14-1)
Red Koko(IRE)'s form in sellers amounted to little and she never threatened on her nursery bow. (op 25-1)
Kingsville fared no better on this switch to turf/nurseries and looks one of his yard's lesser lights. (tchd 12-1)

4807 KANE GANG MAIDEN STKS 6f 5y
6:45 (6:47) (Class 5) 3-Y-0+ **£2,911** (£866; £432; £216) **Stalls** Low

Form RPR

2 **1** **Tahlia Ree (IRE)**[11] 4434 3-8-5 0.. IanBurns(7) 3 55+
(Michael Bell) *in tch: hdwy to ld appr fnl f: drew clr ins fnl f* **2/1[2]**

0 **2** *6* **Lady Bentinck (IRE)**[8] 4551 3-8-5 0................................ KevinStott(7) 4 37
(Alan Berry) *trckd ldrs: effrt and rdn over 1f out: chsd wnr ins fnl f: no imp* **100/1**

F056 **3** *3/4* **Dragon Spirit (IRE)**[21] 4084 3-8-10 40.......................... RossSmith(7) 6 40
(Linda Perratt) *led to appr fnl f: kpt on same pce last 100yds* **66/1**

00 **4** *2* **Bandy Bob**[17] 4211 3-8-12 0.................................. GarryWhillans(5) 11 34
(Iain Jardine) *bhd tl hdwy over 1f out: kpt on fnl f: nvr able to chal* **40/1**

0-0 **5** *1/2* **Lollypop Lady**[17] 4211 3-8-9 0..................................(p) DeclanCannon(3) 8 28
(Linda Perratt) *chsd ldrs tl rdn and wknd wl over 1f out* **50/1**

3242 **6** *2 3/4* **Elegant Girl (IRE)**[11] 4428 3-8-12 67........................(p) PaulMulrennan 2 19
(Tim Easterby) *rrd s: hld up towards rr: hdwy and edgd lft 2f out: nvr able to chal* **15/8[1]**

06- **7** *1 1/4* **Lady Of Edge**[414] 3123 3-8-7 0... LMcNiff(5) 5 16
(Keith Dalgleish) *prom tl rdn and wknd over 2f out* **33/1**

03 **8** *2 3/4* **Red Baron (IRE)**[10] 4456 3-9-3 0.................................... JimmyQuinn 12 12
(Eric Alston) *racd towards stands' rail: prom: rdn: hung lft and wknd over 1f out* **15/2**

00 **9** *1/2* **Libby's Lad**[26] 3913 3-9-3 0.. RichardKingscote 9 11
(David C Griffiths) *hld up: rdn and outpcd over 2f out: sn btn* **100/1**

10 *1/2* **Tayvallich (IRE)** 3-9-3 0.. JoeFanning 1
(Mark Johnston) *trckd ldrs: rdn over 2f out: wknd wl over 1f out* **7/2[3]**

5002 **11** *1 3/4* **Face East (USA)**[21] 4087 4-9-7 48..............................(b) PaddyAspell 7
(Alan Berry) *missed break: bhd and sn pushed along: shortlived effrt over 2f out: sn btn* **28/1**

12 *23* **Roseisle** 4-8-11 0.. DarylByrne(5) 10
(Linda Perratt) *s.s and wnt lft s: a wl bhd* **33/1**

1m 14.88s (2.68) **Going Correction** +0.40s/f (Good)
WFA 3 from 4yo 4lb **12 Ran SP% 119.3**
Speed ratings (Par 103): **98,90,89,86,85 82,80,76,76,75 73,42**
Tote Swingers 1&2 £51.90, 2&3 £91.40, 1&3 £22.30 CSF £210.67 TOTE £3.00: £1.20, £21.60, £12.60; EX 102.50.
Owner Paddy Barrett **Bred** Pendley Farm **Trained** Newmarket, Suffolk

FOCUS
A very weak maiden, rated around the third.
Elegant Girl(IRE) Official explanation: jockey said that the filly reared leaving the stalls

4808 FOLLOW @HAMILTONPARKRC ON TWITTER H'CAP 5f 4y
() (Class 5) (0-75,) 3-Y-0+ £

4809 BRITISH STALLION STUDS SUPPORTING BRITISH RACING EBF FILLIES' H'CAP 5f 4y
() (Class 4) (0-85,) 3-Y-0+ £

4810 BELL GROUP CAROLINA H'CAP 1m 65y
() (Class 5) (0-75,) 3-Y-0+ £

4811 HAMILTON-PARK.CO.UK H'CAP 1m 3f 16y
() (Class 5) (0-75,) 3-Y-0+ £

T/Plt: £2.20 to a £1 stake. Pool £44,386.00 - 14,571.34 winning tickets. RY

4644 LINGFIELD (L-H)

Saturday, August 4

OFFICIAL GOING: Turf course - good to firm (good in places 8.4); all-weather - standard
Wind: Fresh becoming moderate, behind Weather: Fine but cloudy

4812 LINGFIELDPARK.CO.UK APPRENTICE H'CAP 7f 140y
6:00 (6:01) (Class 6) (0-65,65) 3-Y-0+ **£2,181** (£644; £322) **Stalls** Centre

Form RPR

2651 **1** **Amba**[7] 4584 6-9-10 **65**.. DanielMuscutt(4) 2 77+
(Des Donovan) *taken down early: pressed ldr: chal over 2f out: shkn up to ld 1f out: styd on wl* **7/4[1]**

6315 **2** *1 1/4* **Paperetto**[32] 3723 4-9-7 **62**.. DanielCremin(4) 11 71
(Robert Mills) *racd against rail: sn trckd ldr: led over 2f out: rdn and hdd 1f out: styd on* **10/3[2]**

00-0 **3** *5* **Play The Blues (IRE)**[33] 3705 5-9-12 **63**..........................(t) NedCurtis 7 60
(Roger Curtis) *chsd ldrs: rdn 3f out: wnt 3rd over 1f out: no imp after* **20/1**

0000 **4** *2 3/4* **Prize Point**[16] 4236 6-8-5 **46** oh1..............................(t) RobertTart(4) 12 36
(Tom Gretton) *led to over 2f out: steadily wknd* **40/1**

041 **5** *3 1/2* **Jackie Love (IRE)**[16] 4240 4-9-3 **54**...............................(v) AliceHaynes 1 35
(Olivia Maylam) *nvr bttr than midfield: outpcd fr 3f out: n.d after* **8/1**

4310 **6** *nse* **Hierarch (IRE)**[43] 3344 5-9-10 **65**.............................. SiobhanMiller(4) 4 46+
(David Simcock) *hld up in last pair and wl off the pce: pushed along 2f out: styd on after: nrst fin* **5/1[3]**

050- **7** *1* **Hertford Street**[301] 6701 4-8-5 **46** oh1............................ JoeyHaynes(4) 5 24
(Eric Wheeler) *wl in rr: effrt against rail over 2f out: no real prog* **33/1**

00-5 **8** *4* **Grand Piano (IRE)**[79] 2207 5-9-10 **65**...................(v) JonathanWilletts(4) 9 33
(Andrew Balding) *chsd ldrs 3f: sn outpcd and btn* **15/2**

0040 **9** *nk* **Soldier Spy**[19] 4147 3-8-2 **46** oh1.................................(t[1]) RufusVergette 3 14
(David Flood) *racd wd: wl in rr: urged along and no ch whn bmpd over 2f out* **50/1**

0005 **10** *1/2* **Smarty Time**[7] 4602 5-8-13 **50**... NoelGarbutt 8 16
(John Bridger) *wl in rr: rdn whn swtchd sharply lft over 2f out: no prog* **20/1**

0660 **11** *12* **Jolie Etoile**[68] 2555 4-8-9 **46** oh1.................................. ThomasBrown 10
(Tony Carroll) *prom 3f: sn rdn and lost pl: wknd over 2f out* **33/1**

000- **12** *20* **George Tilehurst**[348] 5325 3-8-2 **46** oh1..................... SophieSilvester 6
(Geoffrey Deacon) *dwlt: sn t.o* **40/1**

1m 29.49s (-2.81) **Going Correction** -0.325s/f (Firm)
WFA 3 from 4yo+ 7lb **12 Ran SP% 121.2**
Speed ratings (Par 101): **101,99,94,92,88 88,87,83,83,82 70,50**
Tote Swingers 1&2 £2.60, 2&3 £16.10, 1&3 £9.80 CSF £6.92 TOTE £3.10: £1.10, £1.80, £5.30; EX 8.40.
Owner Mrs Jackie Cornwell **Bred** Mrs J A Cornwell **Trained** Exning, Suffolk

FOCUS
A modest apprentice handicap in which not too many could be seriously fancied and the form has little depth.
Jackie Love(IRE) Official explanation: jockey said that the filly had lost a front shoe

4813 BURRIDGE GOLF & RACING TROPHIES MEDIAN AUCTION MAIDEN STKS 7f 140y
6:30 (6:32) (Class 6) 2-Y-O **£2,181** (£644; £322) **Stalls** Centre

Form RPR

3 **1** **Dundonnell (USA)**[22] 4066 2-9-3 0................................... JamesDoyle 7 97+
(Roger Charlton) *trckd ldrs: wnt 2nd over 4f out: led wl over 1f out: shkn up and stormed clr* **1/4[1]**

2 *12* **Van Percy** 2-8-10 0... ThomasBrown(7) 12 66+
(Andrew Balding) *towards rr: n.m.r over 4f out: swtchd to outer 3f out: prog over 2f out: rn green but pushed along and styd on to take remote 2nd last strides* **20/1**

240 **3** ¾ **Hasanan**[23] 4011 2-8-12 82 (b[1]) BrettDoyle 4 59
(Clive Brittain) *racd freely: led at gd pce: hdd wl over 1f out: no ch w wnr after: wknd: eased briefly and lost 2nd last strides* **12/1**[3]

0 **4** 5 **Burlesque Star (IRE)**[30] 3783 2-8-12 0 SaleemGolam 1 47+
(Harry Dunlop) *hld up in rr: prog gng bttr than most over 3f out: shkn up over 2f out: kpt on one pce after* **40/1**

5 2½ **Arctic Admiral (IRE)** 2-9-3 0 SeanLevey 6 46+
(Richard Hannon) *wl in tch: chsd ldng pair 4f out but sn nt on terms: wknd over 1f out* **20/1**

03 **6** 2½ **Aint Got A Scooby (IRE)**[23] 3996 2-9-3 0 AdamKirby 9 40
(Clive Cox) *chsd ldr to over 4f out: rdn wl over 3f out: wknd over 1f out* **14/1**

50 **7** 3¼ **Kunzea (IRE)**[17] 4217 2-8-7 0 CharlesBishop(5) 8 28
(Mick Channon) *wl in rr: sme prog into midfield 3f out but no ch: wknd over 1f out* **66/1**

8 1 **Instigate (USA)** 2-9-3 0 GeorgeBaker 13 30
(Jeremy Noseda) *w ldrs 2f: sn lost pl: struggling fr 1/2-way* **16/1**

0 **9** 3¾ **Just Duchess**[8] 4532 2-8-9 0 SophieDoyle(3) 11 16
(Michael Blanshard) *spd 2f: sn lost pl: struggling in rr sn after 1/2-way* **150/1**

10 hd **Barefoot Sandy** 2-8-5 0 DanielMuscutt(7) 15 16
(Des Donovan) *spd 3f: sn lost pl: struggling sn after 1/2-way* **66/1**

11 2½ **Be Royale** 2-8-9 0 SimonPearce(3) 10 10
(Bryn Palling) *s.s: a in rr: struggling fr 1/2-way* **100/1**

12 8 **Oakham** 2-9-3 0 MickaelBarzalona 3
(Mahmood Al Zarooni) *t.o in last after 3f: no prog* **7/1**[2]

13 17 **Many Elements** 2-8-10 0 AccursioRomeo(7) 2
(Brett Johnson) *in tch in midfield on outer: wknd rapidly 3f out: t.o* **100/1**

1m 29.32s (-2.98) **Going Correction** -0.325s/f (Firm) 2y crse rec **13** Ran SP% **130.3**
Speed ratings (Par 92): **101,89,88,83,80 78,75,74,70,70 67,59,42**
Tote Swingers 1&2 £4.90, 2&3 £11.60, 1&3 £2.70 CSF £14.94 TOTE £1.30: £1.02, £5.30, £2.90; EX 14.30.
Owner K Abdulla **Bred** Juddmonte Farms Inc **Trained** Beckhampton, Wilts

FOCUS
An interesting juvenile maiden and an exciting performance. The winner could rate a lot higher.

NOTEBOOK
Dundonnell(USA) ◆ confirmed the promise of his debut to win with any amount in hand. He had shaped really well when third behind the highly-regarded Ghurair at Newmarket last month and looks a potentially smart recruit. He will have learnt plenty here, despite the wide margin of victory, and will surely be upped in class for his next start. He holds some lofty engagements later in the year and it would come as no surprise to see him take in something like the Champagne Stakes at Doncaster next month. A mile is likely to be his optimum trip. (op 2-5)
Van Percy finished off in taking fashion and he'll be of real interest next time. Juveniles from his yard tend to improve considerably from first to their second start and he's likely to want further. (op 16-1)
Hasanan, who set the standard judged on her official rating of 82, raced keenly in first-time blinkers and that ultimately cost her second. She hadn't been at all disgraced in Listed company on her second start and definitely gives the form some substance. This was the furthest she'd gone and it's likely that she'll have to come back down in trip in order to win a small race. (tchd 14-1)
Burlesque Star(IRE) did best of the remainder but her future surely lies in nurseries. (op 33-1)
Oakham was the big disappointment of the race. The son of Shirocco was not without each-way support but he was clueless through the early stages and was soon detached. He worryingly failed to make any ground and must surely have had something go amiss. (tchd 11-2)

4814 BIFFO'S BELATED 60TH BIRTHDAY H'CAP 7f
7:00 (7:02) (Class 5) (0-75,75) 3-Y-0+ **£3,067** (£905; £453) **Stalls** High

Form RPR

0160 **1** **Jungle Bay**[37] 3541 5-9-10 71 (p) MickaelBarzalona 1 84
(Jane Chapple-Hyam) *pressed ldrs: led 4f out: c across to rail over 2f out: clr over 1f out: styd on wl* **10/1**

0-31 **2** 3½ **Macchiara**[23] 3990 3-9-6 73 SebSanders 7 75
(Rae Guest) *s.i.s: pushed along in rr over 4f out: prog 3f out: styd on to take 2nd ins fnl f: no threat* **7/1**

-430 **3** ¾ **Fabled City (USA)**[16] 4233 3-9-5 72 (t) AdamKirby 5 72
(Clive Cox) *prom: rdn to chse wnr over 2f out: no imp: lost 2nd ins fnl f: kpt on* **12/1**

1410 **4** nse **Takitwo**[30] 3790 9-9-2 63 BrettDoyle 11 64
(Jonathan Portman) *wl in rr: pushed along in 9th bef 1/2-way: taken to outer 3f out: styd on fnl 2f: nrst fin* **8/1**

0-11 **5** ¾ **Scottish Glen**[73] 2399 6-9-6 67 GeorgeBaker 2 66+
(Patrick Chamings) *stdd s: hld up and wl off the pce: last tl jst pushed along and prog 2f out: styng on but no ch whn short of room and eased nr fin* **9/2**[1]

3450 **6** nse **Lunar Deity**[36] 3571 3-9-3 75 AmyScott(5) 6 72
(Eve Johnson Houghton) *chsd ldrs: edgd rt 4f out: wl in tch over 2f out: rdn and nt qckn over 1f out: kpt on* **8/1**

1066 **7** 4 **Shamrocked (IRE)**[9] 4517 3-9-6 73 MatthewDavies 4 59
(Mick Channon) *pressed ldr: w wnr 4f out to 3f out: wknd over 2f out* **5/1**[2]

460- **8** 1¾ **Dark Lane**[292] 6920 6-9-8 69 RichardThomas 10 53
(David Evans) *slowly away: t.k.h: hld up in last trio: shkn up over 2f out: no real prog* **50/1**

050 **9** 1 **Star Rover (IRE)**[14] 4317 5-9-12 73 TomMcLaughlin 3 54
(David Evans) *hld up in last trio and wl off the pce: shkn up over 2f out: no real prog* **25/1**

4400 **10** 4½ **Haadeeth**[7] 4602 5-9-9 70 SeanLevey 8 39
(David Evans) *led to 4f out: wknd over 2f out* **33/1**

2-11 **11** ½ **Eager To Bow (IRE)**[32] 3738 6-9-10 71 JimCrowley 9 39
(Patrick Chamings) *pushed along towards rr after 2f: struggling fr 1/2-way* **6/1**[3]

200 **12** hd **Forest Edge (IRE)**[37] 3541 3-9-0 67 JamesDoyle 13 32
(David Evans) *chsd ldrs: hmpd against rail 4f out: taken wd 3f out: no prog and btn 2f out: wknd and eased* **9/1**

1m 22.19s (-1.11) **Going Correction** -0.325s/f (Firm)
WFA 3 from 4yo+ 6lb **12** Ran SP% **119.4**
Speed ratings (Par 103): **93,89,88,88,87 87,82,80,79,74 73,73**
Tote Swingers 1&2 £9.00, 2&3 £10.80, 1&3 £22.60 CSF £77.76 CT £873.23 TOTE £13.30: £3.90, £3.00, £3.90; EX 54.10.
Owner S Brewster & D Charlesworth **Bred** Stowell Hill Ltd & Major & Mrs R B Kennard **Trained** Dalham, Suffolk

FOCUS
A fair 7f handicap, run at an honest pace and rated around the placed horses.
Scottish Glen Official explanation: jockey said that the gelding was denied a clear run
Lunar Deity Official explanation: vet said the gelding lost a shoe
Haadeeth Official explanation: jockey said that the gelding ran too free

4815 BEACHED BOYS H'CAP 6f
7:30 (7:31) (Class 6) (0-65,67) 3-Y-0+ **£2,181** (£644; £322) **Stalls** High

Form RPR

6036 **1** **My Own Way Home**[5] 4655 4-9-9 62 AdamKirby 5 72
(David Evans) *hld up in midfield: pushed along and prog over 2f out: clsd on ldrs over 1f out: drvn and r.o to ld last 100yds* **7/2**[1]

4230 **2** 1¼ **Perfect Honour (IRE)**[16] 4237 6-8-6 48 (p) AdamBeschizza(3) 12 54
(Des Donovan) *dwlt: rousted along and sn pressed ldr: rdn 2f out: stl upsides ins fnl f: nt qckn* **15/2**

4003 **3** hd **Miss Polly Plum**[11] 4439 5-9-0 53 (p) SaleemGolam 11 58
(Chris Dwyer) *led against rail: rdn 2f out: hanging lft after: hdd and no ex last 100yds* **7/1**[3]

00-6 **4** nk **Commandingpresence (USA)**[16] 4238 6-9-12 65 KieranO'Neill 2 69
(John Bridger) *pressed ldng pair: rdn 2f out: tried to chal 1f out: one pce fnl f* **25/1**

0002 **5** shd **Sermons Mount (USA)**[9] 4492 6-9-5 58 (p) TomMcLaughlin 7 62
(Paul Howling) *chsd ldrs: drvn on outer 2f out: tried to chal 1f out: one pce fnl f* **7/1**[3]

554 **6** nk **Ridgeway Sapphire**[9] 4492 5-8-8 47 (v) DavidProbert 1 50+
(Mark Usher) *hld up in last trio and cross to rail fr outside draw: rdn over 2f out: nt clr run briefly over 1f out: r.o fnl f: gaining at fin* **14/1**

6000 **7** 1½ **Jay Bee Blue**[53] 3002 3-9-5 62 (t) JamesDoyle 3 59
(Sean Curran) *chsd ldrs: rdn and cl enough 2f out: nt qckn and hld whn hung rt ins fnl f* **16/1**

0-00 **8** ½ **Adaeze (IRE)**[30] 3791 4-9-0 53 (p) MartinHarley 13 50
(Jonathan Portman) *chsd ldrs: cl up and hrd rdn 2f out: fdd jst over 1f out* **15/2**

0000 **9** nk **Seamus Shindig**[59] 2815 10-9-7 65 AmyScott(5) 10 61+
(Henry Candy) *hld up last: pushed along over 2f out: prog jst over 1f out: styd on but nvr gng pce to threaten* **6/1**[2]

0250 **10** 3¼ **Pose (IRE)**[14] 4332 5-8-11 50 (t) DaraghO'Donohoe 6 35
(Roger Ingram) *towards rr on outer: in tch 2f out: wknd over 1f out* **20/1**

0540 **11** 1½ **Sherjawy (IRE)**[10] 4467 8-8-10 52 SimonPearce(3) 14 33
(Zoe Davison) *chsd ldrs: u.p bef 1/2-way: wknd 2f out* **16/1**

0/0- **12** hd **Loved To Bits**[452] 1980 4-9-0 56 SophieDoyle(3) 4 36
(Eric Wheeler) *a in last trio: shkn up and no prog over 2f out* **28/1**

3-50 **13** 2 **Poseidon Grey (IRE)**[43] 3343 3-9-7 64 (t) GeorgeBaker 8 38
(Ian Williams) *tk fierce hold: hld up towards rr: no prog over 2f out: wknd over 1f out* **14/1**

1m 11.28s (0.08) **Going Correction** -0.325s/f (Firm)
WFA 3 from 4yo+ 4lb **13** Ran SP% **122.2**
Speed ratings (Par 101): **86,84,84,83,83 83,81,80,80,75 73,73,70**
Tote Swingers 1&2 £14.00, 2&3 £7.50, 1&3 £7.40 CSF £29.08 CT £185.99 TOTE £6.80: £2.60, £4.00, £1.90; EX 54.10.
Owner L Audus **Bred** Theresa Fitsall **Trained** Pandy, Monmouths

FOCUS
Only a modest sprint handicap but it served up an exciting finish. The form looks sound with the placed horses and fifth close to recent marks.
Jay Bee Blue Official explanation: jockey said that the gelding had a breathing problem
Sherjawy(IRE) Official explanation: jockey said that the gelding was unsuited by the good to firm, good in places going

4816 BRITISH STALLION STUDS SUPPORTING BRITISH RACING EBF MAIDEN STKS 5f (P)
8:00 (8:00) (Class 5) 2-Y-O **£3,816** (£1,135; £567; £283) **Stalls** High

Form RPR

3 **1** **Just Charlie**[35] 3617 2-9-3 0 DaneO'Neill 8 84
(Henry Candy) *mde all: rdn over 1f out: styd on wl and in command fnl f* **7/2**[2]

35 **2** ¾ **Nordikhab (IRE)**[16] 4257 2-9-3 0 JamesDoyle 1 81
(Kevin Ryan) *pressed wnr: rdn to chal over 1f out: nt qckn and readily hld fnl f* **2/1**[1]

2502 **3** 2¼ **Vestibule**[11] 4433 2-8-7 74 AmyScott(5) 9 68
(Eve Johnson Houghton) *racd on outer: chsd ldng trio: rdn over 2f out: styd on to take 3rd ins fnl f* **5/1**

0 **4** 1 **Royal Guinevere**[35] 3637 2-8-12 0 BrettDoyle 2 65
(Dean Ivory) *sn trckd ldng pair on inner: rdn 2f out: fdd ins fnl f* **12/1**

000 **5** ¾ **Melodee Princess (IRE)**[45] 3269 2-8-7 65 DarrenEgan(5) 3 62
(Ronald Harris) *chsd ldrs in 5th: pushed along 2f out: outpcd over 1f out: kpt on* **25/1**

232 **6** ¾ **Whistling Buddy**[9] 4487 2-9-3 75 SebSanders 7 64
(Peter Makin) *nt that wl away: sn in tch on inner: shkn up 2f out: fdd fnl f* **9/2**[3]

4 **7** 1¾ **Reinvigorate (IRE)**[11] 4419 2-8-12 0 SeanLevey 10 53
(Richard Hannon) *in tch on outer: pushed along 2f out: no prog over 1f out: fdd* **8/1**

05 **8** ½ **Borough Boy (IRE)**[19] 4148 2-9-3 0 StevieDonohoe 6 56
(Derek Shaw) *awkward and t.k.h s: restrained in last pair and sn adrift: pushed along bef 1/2-way: styd on quite takingly fnl f* **40/1**

0050 **9** 1¼ **Proventi**[24] 3971 2-9-3 67 (p) MartinHarley 5 52
(Alan McCabe) *in tch: racd awkwardly and reminder 1/2-way: no prog over 1f out: wknd* **50/1**

66 **10** 14 **Colourist**[7] 4604 2-9-3 0 GeorgeBaker 4 1
(Gary Moore) *slowly away: hld up and sn wl adrift in last pair: t.o* **16/1**

59.15s (0.35) **Going Correction** 0.0s/f (Stan) **10** Ran SP% **123.3**
Speed ratings (Par 94): **97,95,92,90,89 88,85,84,82,60**
Tote Swingers 1&2 £2.80, 2&3 £3.10, 1&3 £3.70 CSF £11.50 TOTE £3.60: £1.20, £1.50, £1.90; EX 15.30.
Owner Mrs A D Bourne/H Candy **Bred** Itchen Valley Stud **Trained** Kingston Warren, Oxon

FOCUS
An interesting juvenile maiden, run at a fast pace and the form looks strong through the runner-up, and could rate higher.

NOTEBOOK
Just Charlie ◆ built on his encouraging C&D debut. He had shown bright speed when third here in June, was again quick into stride and, despite pulling hard in the early stages, had more than enough in hand to fend off the favourite. He didn't have the best of draws and did well to wrestle the advantage away from the runner-up before halfway. He showed definite signs of greenness when lugging off the rail as they turned for home, but really stuck his neck out once straightened up. He clearly has an engine and should be competitive in nurseries for the remainder of the season. An easy 5f is probably ideal. (tchd 3-1)
Nordikhab(IRE) was the subject of some substantial late support but he came up just short. The form of his debut run at Ayr has worked out well and he looked to have plenty in his favour from stall one. However, he lacked the early pace of the winner and, despite travelling powerfully with 2f left to run, was never able to reel in the winner. This was his first try at 5f and he should be able to pick up a small race before too long. (op 5-2 tchd 3-1)

Vestibule, the most exposed of these, made the frame for the fourth time in seven starts. She was made to look a bit one-paced by the principals and is likely to benefit for a stiffer track or a return to 6f. (tchd 6-1)
Royal Guinevere didn't show a great deal at Windsor but improved on this, her AW debut. She was another to lack a change of gear late on but is entitled to come on again. (op 33-1)
Melodee Princess(IRE), out of her depth in the Queen Mary, stayed on towards the finish and could be of some interest in nurseries over further. (op 28-1)
Borough Boy(IRE) Official explanation: jockey said that the bit slipped through the colt's mouth
Colourist Official explanation: jockey said that the colt stumbled at the start

4817 LADBROKES GAME ON! H'CAP — 1m 2f (P)
8:30 (8:30) (Class 6) (0-55,55) 3-Y-O+ — **£2,181** (£644; £322) **Stalls** Low

Form — RPR
5140 **1** **Pindar (GER)**[15] 4296 8-9-3 **51** .... DaraghO'Donohoe 14 — 64
(Barney Curley) *racd wd: led after 1f: mostly dictated pce after: hdd briefly wl over 1f out: pushed along and sn qcknd clr: in n.d fnl f* **7/2**[1]
500/ **2** *2* **High 'n Dry (IRE)**[1218] 1122 8-8-9 **50** .... (t) NedCurtis(7) 12 — 59
(Roger Curtis) *stdd s: hld up in last: prog on outer fr 3f out: hanging bdly over 1f out: wnt 2nd ins fnl f: styd on but no hope of catching wnr* **25/1**
005 **3** *2 1/4* **Chasin' Rainbows**[32] 3721 4-9-0 **48** .... LiamKeniry 8 — 53
(Sylvester Kirk) *trckd ldrs: rdn over 2f out: outpcd wl over 1f out: styd on fnl f to take 3rd last strides* **14/1**
0503 **4** *hd* **Formidable Guest**[17] 4219 8-9-1 **54** .... HarryPoulton(5) 2 — 58
(Jamie Poulton) *t.k.h: hld up in rr: prog 2f out: rdn and styd on fnl f to take 4th last strides* **6/1**[2]
3614 **5** *hd* **Tinkerbell Will**[32] 3721 5-9-3 **51** .... RichardThomas 11 — 55
(John E Long) *trckd ldrs: rdn 3f out: nt qckn and lost pl over 1f out: styd on again ins fnl f* **13/2**[3]
4501 **6** *nk* **Minstrel Lad**[15] 4296 4-9-4 **55** .... SimonPearce(3) 4 — 58
(Lydia Pearce) *hld up in rr: prog on outer over 3f out: wnt 2nd jst over 2f out: drvn to ld briefly wl over 1f out: sn outpcd: wknd and lost pls ins fnl f* **7/2**[1]
5-00 **7** *2* **Crystal Sky (IRE)**[19] 4158 4-9-0 **48** .... JamesDoyle 13 — 47
(Natalie Lloyd-Beavis) *hld up in last trio: rdn wl over 2f out: sme late prog: nvr a factor* **40/1**
00-0 **8** *1 1/2* **Beat Up**[17] 4219 6-9-6 **54** .... GeorgeBaker 9 — 50
(Patrick Chamings) *trckd ldrs: shkn up wl over 2f out: nt qckn wl over 1f out: fdd* **13/2**[3]
060 **9** *3/4* **Divine Rule (IRE)**[33] 3701 4-9-4 **52** .... (b) AmirQuinn 5 — 47
(Laura Mongan) *t.k.h: hld up in midfield: lost pl on inner and in last trio over 2f out: effrt over 1f out: wknd fnl f* **25/1**
0600 **10** *1 1/4* **Holyfield Warrior (IRE)**[7] 4584 8-8-11 **50** .... MarkCoumbe(5) 1 — 42
(Michael Attwater) *t.k.h: hld up in rr: rdn over 2f out: no prog* **66/1**
52-0 **11** *3 3/4* **Galloping Queen (IRE)**[39] 3468 4-9-2 **50** .... DaneO'Neill 7 — 35
(Sheena West) *chsd ldrs: rdn 3f out: wknd wl over 1f out* **20/1**
-504 **12** *nk* **Corrib (IRE)**[49] 3137 9-8-10 **49** .... (p) DarrenEgan(5) 3 — 33
(Bryn Palling) *hld up towards rr: rdn on outer whn n.m.r briefly over 2f out: sn btn* **16/1**
-004 **13** *2 1/2* **Night Sky**[17] 4219 5-9-3 **51** .... JimCrowley 10 — 30
(Tony Carroll) *led 1f: w wnr to over 2f out: wknd qckly* **10/1**

2m 7.29s (0.69) **Going Correction** 0.0s/f (Stan) — **13 Ran SP% 123.4**
Speed ratings (Par 101): **97,95,93,93,93 93,91,90,89,88 85,85,83**
Tote Swingers 1&2 £30.50, 2&3 £35.80, 1&3 £37.60 CSF £107.48 CT £1129.26 TOTE £7.00: £2.60, £10.10, £4.50; EX 302.50.
Owner Curley Leisure **Bred** Gestut Schlenderhan **Trained** Newmarket, Suffolk

FOCUS
A moderate handicap, run at a sedate pace and the winner justified significant market confidence with the minimum of fuss. The form looks straightforward.
Pindar(GER) Official explanation: trainer's representative said, regarding the apparent improvement of form, that the gelding appeared to have benefited from a return to racing on an All Weather surface
Galloping Queen(IRE) Official explanation: two-day ban: careless riding (18-19 Aug)
T/Plt: £111.30 to a £1 stake. Pool £56,816.36. 372.45 winning tickets. T/Qpdt: £52.60 to a £1 stake. Pool £4,592.49. 64.50 winning tickets. JN

4772 NEWMARKET (R-H)
Saturday, August 4
OFFICIAL GOING: Good to firm changing to good after race 1 (1.45)
Wind: Light half-against Weather: Sunshine and showers

4818 ADNAMS BROADSIDE E B F MAIDEN FILLIES' STKS — 7f
1:45 (1:47) (Class 4) 2-Y-O — **£4,528** (£1,347; £673; £336) **Stalls** Low

Form — RPR
54 **1** **Everleigh**[24] 3959 2-9-0 0 .... PatDobbs 6 — 79
(Richard Hannon) *mde all: rdn over 1f out: edgd lft ins fnl f: r.o* **20/1**
3 **2** *3/4* **Ghostflower (IRE)**[17] 4217 2-9-0 0 .... FrankieDettori 8 — 77
(Mahmood Al Zarooni) *hld up: hdwy over 2f out: rdn over 1f out: edgd lft ins fnl f: r.o* **3/1**[2]
6 **3** *nk* **Trucanini**[57] 2892 2-9-0 0 .... SebSanders 9 — 76
(Chris Wall) *hld up: hdwy over 1f out: r.o: nt quite rch ldrs* **25/1**
242 **4** *2 1/4* **Strictly Silca**[14] 4318 2-9-0 88 .... MartinHarley 15 — 70
(Mick Channon) *hld up: hdwy 1/2-way: rdn and ev ch over 1f out: styd on same pce ins fnl f* **9/4**[1]
5 *1/2* **Rainbow Beauty** 2-9-0 0 .... FrannyNorton 3 — 69+
(Gerard Butler) *s.i.s: hld up: hdwy over 1f out: r.o: nvr nr to chal* **40/1**
6 *shd* **Our Obsession (IRE)** 2-9-0 0 .... LiamJones 5 — 68+
(William Haggas) *hld up: shkn up over 1f out: r.o ins fnl f: nrst fin* **16/1**
7 *3* **Cushion** 2-9-0 0 .... NickyMackay 13 — 61+
(John Gosden) *chsd ldrs: outpcd 2f out: styd on ins fnl f* **7/1**[3]
8 *3/4* **Oilinda** 2-9-0 0 .... JamieSpencer 2 — 59
(Michael Bell) *prom: shkn up over 1f out: wknd fnl f* **16/1**
0 **9** *shd* **Ottauquechee (IRE)**[39] 3474 2-9-0 0 .... SeanLevey 1 — 58
(Richard Hannon) *chsd ldrs: rdn over 1f out: wknd fnl f* **40/1**
10 *3/4* **Mar Mar (IRE)** 2-9-0 0 .... DaneO'Neill 11 — 56
(Saeed Bin Suroor) *s.s: rdn over 2f out: n.d* **12/1**
11 *1 1/2* **Kikonga** 2-8-11 0 .... PatrickHills(3) 10 — 53
(Luca Cumani) *hld up: hdwy over 2f out: wknd over 1f out* **20/1**
12 *1 1/2* **Wise Talk (USA)** 2-8-9 0 .... (t) AntiocoMurgia(5) 7 — 49
(Mahmood Al Zarooni) *hld up: swtchd rt over 2f out: rdn over 1f out: n.d* **14/1**
20 **13** *1 1/2* **Sadiigah**[31] 3764 2-9-0 0 .... MartinLane 16 — 45
(Clive Brittain) *chsd ldrs: rdn and ev ch over 1f out: wknd fnl f* **40/1**
14 *nk* **Kawaakib (USA)** 2-9-0 0 .... PaulHanagan 12 — 44
(John Dunlop) *prom: rn green: lost pl 4f out: sn bhd* **14/1**
00 **15** *4* **Hawsies Dream**[23] 4011 2-9-0 0 .... DarryllHolland 14 — 34
(Alan Bailey) *prom over 4f* **100/1**

1m 27.78s (2.08) **Going Correction** +0.025s/f (Good) — **15 Ran SP% 122.7**
Speed ratings (Par 93): **89,88,87,85,84 84,81,80,80,79 77,75,74,73,69**
toteswingers 1&2 £11.90, 1&3 £18.00, 2&3 £52.20 CSF £76.45 TOTE £30.80: £8.10, £1.60, £7.20; EX 103.90.
Owner Noodles Racing **Bred** Poulton Farm Stud **Trained** East Everleigh, Wilts

FOCUS
Far side track used with stalls on stands' side except 1m2f and 1m4f: centre. Following some heavy showers, the going was changed from good to firm to good after this opener. The first four home all the had the benefit of experience with the fourth the best guide to the level.

NOTEBOOK
Everleigh benefited from the step up to 7f, having shown a good amount of improvement with each start. Although by Bahamian Bounty, there is more stamina on the dam's side of Everleigh's pedigree and, having rallied over 6f at Kempton on her second start, she relished these conditions to race smoothly on the pace before finding plenty up the hill. She has a very progressive profile and looks a filly to keep on the right side of for now. (op 22-1)
Ghostflower(IRE) ◆ made good headway from midfield, and, although she hung left under pressure, she kept on well to confirm the promise of her all-weather debut. A maiden should be a formality for her. (op 9-2)
Trucanini, the fastest finisher, hadn't been seen since showing some promise behind Newfangled on her debut. She came home strongly from well off the pace and is another who looks well up to winning an average maiden. (op 33-1)
Strictly Silca easily set the standard from those with form, but she failed to live up to the promise of her latest second in Listed company. Her challenge petered out in the closing stages and it has to be a little disappointing that she couldn't fare better here. (op 5-2)
Rainbow Beauty finished with a flourish up the stands' side to shape encouragingly.
Our Obsession(IRE) ran on in the closing stages having been switched towards the stands' side. This was encouraging considering she has a pedigree that suggests stiffer tests will suit in time (dam won Cheshire Oaks).

4819 ADNAMS GHOST SHIP H'CAP — 7f
2:20 (2:21) (Class 3) (0-90,89) 3-Y-O — **£9,703** (£2,887; £1,443; £721) **Stalls** Low

Form — RPR
0633 **1** **Elusive Flame**[7] 4597 3-8-13 **81** .... DaneO'Neill 3 — 92
(David Elsworth) *mde all on stands' side: rdn over 1f out: styd on* **11/2**[2]
-053 **2** *1 1/4* **Princess Of Orange**[22] 4075 3-8-12 **80** .... SebSanders 5 — 88+
(Rae Guest) *racd stands' side: hld up in tch: edgd lft over 2f out: rdn and swtchd rt over 1f out: r.o wl* **20/1**
5142 **3** *1 1/2* **Hi There (IRE)**[14] 4329 3-8-4 **72** .... PaulHanagan 2 — 81+
(Richard Fahey) *racd stands' side tl swtchd to centre over 5f out: hld up: hdwy and nt clr run over 1f out: swtchd rt ins fnl f: r.o to go 3rd post: nt rch ldrs* **13/2**[3]
-340 **4** *shd* **Frog Hollow**[44] 3294 3-9-7 **89** .... GeorgeBaker 8 — 92
(Ralph Beckett) *racd centre: s.i.s: hld up: hdwy over 2f out: rdn over 1f out: hung rt ins fnl f: styd on* **5/2**[1]
2214 **5** *1/2* **Sir Fredlot (IRE)**[15] 4288 3-8-9 **77** .... DarryllHolland 6 — 79
(Charles Hills) *chsd wnr stands' side: edgd lft over 2f out: sn rdn: styd on same pce ins fnl f* **9/1**
04-5 **6** *nk* **Otto The Great**[99] 1645 3-9-3 **85** .... FrankieDettori 9 — 86
(Peter Chapple-Hyam) *chsd ldr centre tl led that gp over 1f out: sn rdn: no ex ins fnl f* **16/1**
063 **7** *2 1/4* **Sheikh The Reins (IRE)**[10] 4473 3-8-9 **77** .... LiamJones 10 — 72
(John Best) *led centre over 5f: no ex ins fnl f* **16/1**
1-05 **8** *3/4* **Usain Colt**[10] 4473 3-9-4 **86** .... PatDobbs 11 — 79
(Richard Hannon) *racd centre: hld up: hdwy over 2f out: rdn over 1f out: no ex fnl f* **7/1**
0300 **9** *4 1/2* **Semayyel (IRE)**[22] 4063 3-9-7 **89** .... MartinLane 13 — 70
(Clive Brittain) *s.i.s: hld up: racd centre: hdwy over 2f out: wknd fnl f* **33/1**
4004 **10** *6* **Cravat**[9] 4517 3-8-6 **74** .... FrannyNorton 14 — 39
(Mark Johnston) *racd centre: prom over 4f* **8/1**
3500 **11** *3 1/4* **Tidentime (USA)**[22] 4075 3-9-6 **88** .... MartinHarley 1 — 44
(Mick Channon) *racd stands' side: hld up: rdn and edgd lft over 2f out: wknd over 1f out* **12/1**
000 **12** *6* **Sans Loi (IRE)**[13] 4364 3-9-0 **82** .... (p) IPoullis 15 — 22
(Alan McCabe) *racd centre: prom tl wknd over 1f out* **40/1**

1m 25.11s (-0.59) **Going Correction** +0.025s/f (Good) — **12 Ran SP% 120.5**
Speed ratings (Par 104): **104,102,100,100,100 99,97,96,91,84 80,73**
toteswingers 1&2 £33.60, 1&3 £4.50, 2&3 £42.40 CSF £114.35 CT £556.53 TOTE £8.50: £2.40, £5.00, £2.40; EX 169.90 TRIFECTA Not won..
Owner J C Smith **Bred** Littleton Stud **Trained** Newmarket, Suffolk

FOCUS
A competitive 3yo handicap but the first three home all came up the stands' side, suggesting the rail was the place to be. Personal-bests from the first two.

NOTEBOOK
Elusive Flame, unlike all of her rivals,never once moved away from the rail as she made pretty much all the running. It was clear entering the rising ground that those in the middle were struggling to keep up with her, and she just kept rolling to bag her first race of the season. She had been shaping in recent starts like her turn was near and everything dropped into place this time. (op 13-2 tchd 7-1)
Princess Of Orange ◆, initially was one of the small group who followed Elusive Flame up the stands' rail. She wasn't making much headway having edged to the centre of the group, but once she came back towards the stands' rail she picked up in taking style. She has shown enough in her last couple of starts to suggest she is up to winning off this sort of mark.
Hi There(IRE) is one that might need upgrading a bit because he struggled to get a clear run down the middle and had to be switched to the stands' side to get a run. He didn't exactly fly at the finish but he is a horse who stays further, so he was never going to have an instant change of gear over this trip. (op 11-2 tchd 5-1)
Frog Hollow was disappointing when quite well fancied for the Britannia Stakes, but he's been freshened up since, and got his career back on track with a much more encouraging run here. He fared best of those to stay towards the centre and looks capable of winning a race like this. (op 9-2)
Sir Fredlot(IRE) had every chance but hung away from the rail under pressure. (op 8-1)
Otto The Great showed up well for a long way down the middle before fading in the closing stages. (op 14-1)

4820 ADNAMS BITTER FILLIES' NURSERY — 6f
2:55 (2:56) (Class 2) 2-Y-O — **£25,876** (£7,700; £3,848; £1,924) **Stalls** Low

Form — RPR
351 **1** **The Gold Cheongsam (IRE)**[8] 4539 2-9-7 **89** .... FrankieDettori 10 — 98+
(Jeremy Noseda) *racd stands' side: hld up: hdwy over 2f out: led over 1f out: edgd rt wl ins fnl f: rdn out* **3/1**[1]
431 **2** *1 1/2* **Califante**[12] 4408 2-8-12 **80** .... PatDobbs 5 — 85
(Richard Hannon) *racd stands' side: a.p: rdn and ev ch over 1f out: r.o: 2nd of 13 in gp* **6/1**[2]

1 **3** *nk* **Pure Excellence**18 4173 2-8-8 **76**.................................... FrannyNorton 4 83+
(Mark Johnston) *racd stands' side: prom: nt clr run and lost pl over 2f out: swtchd lft over 1f out: r.o ins fnl f: 3rd of 13 in gp* **12/1**

5330 **4** *1 ¾* **Effie B**42 3368 2-8-13 **81**.. MartinHarley 12 79
(Mick Channon) *racd stands' side: hld up: hdwy over 2f out: rdn and ev ch over 1f out: styd on same pce ins fnl f: 4th of 13 in gp* **20/1**

3121 **5** *hd* **Royal Rascal**21 4116 2-9-5 **87**... DavidAllan 13 85
(Tim Easterby) *racd stands' side: chsd ldr: rdn over 2f out: ev ch over 1f out: styd on same pce ins fnl f: 5th of 13 in gp* **8/1**3

5213 **6** *hd* **Momalorka**21 4093 2-9-6 **88**... KellyHarrison 6 85
(William Haggas) *racd stands' side: chsd ldrs: rdn over 1f out: edgd rt and styd on same pce ins fnl f: 6th of 13 in gp* **12/1**

342 **7** *nse* **Rio's Pearl**56 2917 2-8-10 **78**.. JamieSpencer 20 75
(Ralph Beckett) *led far side: clr of that gp 1/2-way: rdn over 1f out: no ex ins fnl f: 1st of 6 in gp* **8/1**3

362 **8** *¾* **Testamatta**16 4246 2-8-11 **79**.. MircoDemuro 3 74
(Marco Botti) *racd stands' side: s.i.s: hld up: hdwy over 1f out: nt rch ldrs: 7th of 13 in gp* **16/1**

1105 **9** *2* **Madam Mojito (USA)**21 4093 2-9-5 **87**.................... MichaelO'Connell 1 76
(John Quinn) *racd stands' side: hld up: nt clr run over 2f out: hdwy and nt clr run over 1f out: nvr trbld ldrs: 8th of 13 in gp* **16/1**

610 **10** *nse* **Mary's Daughter**43 3326 2-9-2 **84**................................. PaulHanagan 16 73
(Richard Fahey) *racd far side: prom: chsd clr ldr over 2f out: rdn over 1f out: styd on: n.d: 2nd of 6 in gp* **33/1**

122 **11** *1* **Rebel Magic**7 4574 2-9-6 **88**.. SeanLevey 19 74
(Richard Hannon) *racd far side: hld up: rdn over 2f out: nvr nrr: 3rd of 6 in gp* **16/1**

0221 **12** *¾* **Secret Destination**38 3491 2-8-7 **78** ow1........................ DaleSwift(3) 17 61
(Brian Ellison) *racd far side: chsd ldrs: rdn over 2f out: kpt on: 4th of 6 in gp* **25/1**

3534 **13** *1 ¼* **Ishi Honest**14 4324 2-8-5 **78**...................................... RachealKneller(5) 7 58
(Mark Usher) *racd stands' side: mid-div: hdwy over 2f out: rdn over 1f out: sn wknd 9th of 13 in gp* **50/1**

410 **14** *2* **Mandy Layla (IRE)**22 4064 2-8-9 **77**......................... RoystonFfrench 14 51
(Bryan Smart) *overall ldr stands'; side rdn and hdd over 1f out: wkng whn hmpd ins fnl f: 10 of 13 in gp* **25/1**

0104 **15** *½* **Dream Vale (IRE)**66 2603 2-8-9 **77**.................................. LiamKeniry 18 49
(Tim Easterby) *racd far side: chsd clr ld over 3f: wknd fnl f: 5th of 6 in gp* **50/1**

4020 **16** *2 ¾* **Woodland Mill (IRE)**21 4093 2-8-13 **84**...................... RaulDaSilva(3) 15 48
(Richard Fahey) *racd racd side: hld up: rdn and edgd rt over 2f out: wknd over 1f out: last of 6 in gp* **20/1**

1303 **17** *1 ¼* **All On Red (IRE)**22 4058 2-9-6 **88**...................................... MartinLane 2 48
(Tobias B P Coles) *racd stands' side: hld up: effrt over 2f out: wknd over 1f out: 11th of 13 in gp* **33/1**

14 **18** *4* **Strictly Ballroom (IRE)**21 4090 2-8-9 **77**........................ LiamJones 11 25
(Mark Johnston) *racd stands' side: chsd ldrs: rdn over 2f out: wknd fnl f: 12th of 13 in gp* **33/1**

313 **19** *6* **Dream Scenario**21 4116 2-8-9 **77** ow1............................ PatCosgrave 9 7
(Mel Brittain) *racd stands' side: s.i.s: a in rr: last of 13 in gp* **20/1**

1m 12.89s (0.39) **Going Correction** +0.025s/f (Good) **19** Ran SP% **129.3**
Speed ratings (Par 97): **98,96,95,93,93 92,92,91,89,88 87,86,84,82,81 77,76,70,62**
toteswingers 1&2 £8.50, 1&3 £8.80, 2&3 £42.20 CSF £17.07 CT £202.08 TOTE £3.30: £1.30, £1.80, £2.60, £6.60; EX 30.20 Trifecta £360.80 Pool £746.06 - 1.53 winning units..
Owner Arashan Ali **Bred** Tally-Ho Stud **Trained** Newmarket, Suffolk

FOCUS
The previous race bias towards the stands' rail didn't manifest in this contest. The fourth sets the level.

NOTEBOOK
The Gold Cheongsam(IRE) ♦ probably would have won wherever she had been on the track and she scored with plenty in hand despite top weight. The daughter of Red Clubs has always come with a tall reputation and she burst through towards the middle of the track to put her seal on the race entering the final furlong before edging over to towards the stands' side. She clearly won't be hanging around at this level given her Group race entries and is a class above this level. (op 10-3 tchd 7-2)
Califante was never far off the pace towards the stands' side and kept on well for pressure. She took another step forward here and looks more than capable of winning plenty more races. (tchd 13-2)
Pure Excellence won on her debut in a race that didn't look that great, but this filly looks useful and her run can be upgraded here. She had her momentum checked over a furlong out when trying to thread through, but finished well once in the clear. A nursery off this sort of mark looks her's for the taking even without the prospect of further progress. Official explanation: jockey said that the filly was denied a clear run (tchd 11-1)
Effie B ran with credit, keeping on from off the pace but couldn't get in a blow. (op 40-1)
Royal Rascal was unable to cope with a 9lb rise for her easy York win in what was a much stronger race. (tchd 15-2)
Rio's Pearl went quite hard from the front on the far side and couldn't keep it up.
Woodland Mill(IRE) Official explanation: jockey said that the filly was unsuited by the good ground

4821 ADNAMS TALLY HO H'CAP 1m 2f
3:25 (3:25) (Class 3) (0-90,89) 3-Y-O+ **£9,703** (£2,887; £1,443; £721) **Stalls** Centre

Form RPR

2264 **1** **Proud Chieftain**7 4596 4-9-9 **84**.. DarryllHolland 9 92
(Clifford Lines) *a.p: shkn up to ld over 1f out: sn rdn and edgd rt: styd on* **5/1**2

4415 **2** *1* **Odin (IRE)**9 4515 4-9-1 **76**.. DaneO'Neill 5 82
(David Elsworth) *hld up in tch: rdn: edgd rt and ev ch fr over 1f out: unable qck towards fin* **9/1**

0141 **3** *1* **Sheikhzayedroad**16 4243 3-8-13 **83**................................ JamieSpencer 6 87
(David Simcock) *stdd s: hld up: hdwy over 1f out: sn hung lft: rdn and hung rt ins fnl f: styng on same pce whn swvd rt nr fin* **7/4**1

164- **4** *1 ½* **Almagest**309 6497 4-9-11 **86**.......................................(b1) NickyMackay 7 87
(John Gosden) *hdwy to chse ldr 8f out: led over 2f out: rdn and hdd over 1f out: styd on same pce fnl f* **15/2**

3453 **5** *3* **Carragold**14 4347 6-9-1 **76**.. PatCosgrave 3 71
(Mel Brittain) *led over 7f: no ex fr over 1f out* **14/1**

505 **6** *4 ½* **Lyssio (GER)**29 3826 5-9-11 **86**...................................... PaulHanagan 8 72
(Michael Attwater) *prom: rdn over 2f out: wknd fnl f* **14/1**

1226 **7** *½* **Ginger Jack**21 4110 5-9-6 **84**.. DaleSwift(3) 4 69
(Geoffrey Harker) *prom: rdn over 2f out: wknd over 1f out* **6/1**3

0206 **8** *1* **Tameen**21 4112 4-10-0 **89**.. GeorgeBaker 2 72
(Ed Dunlop) *hld up: hdwy over 2f out: rdn and wknd over 1f out* **15/2**

06 **9** *9* **Provisional**22 4060 4-9-8 **83**.......................................(p) FergusSweeney 1 48
(Martyn Meade) *chsd ldr 2f: remained handy tl rdn over 2f out: wknd wl over 1f out* **50/1**

2m 9.24s (3.74) **Going Correction** +0.025s/f (Good)
WFA 3 from 4yo+ 9lb **9** Ran SP% **116.1**
Speed ratings (Par 107): **86,85,84,83,80 77,76,76,68**
toteswingers 1&2 £11.60, 1&3 £3.30, 2&3 £1.90 CSF £49.42 CT £108.84 TOTE £6.00: £2.40, £2.70, £1.10; EX 53.80.
Owner Prima Racing Partnership **Bred** John James **Trained** Exning, Suffolk

FOCUS
A very steady early gallop to this 1m2f handicap so no surprise it produced a slow overall time, and the form might not be that reliable.

NOTEBOOK
Proud Chieftain was a bit free through the early stages but he was still able to produce a turn of foot to lead inside the final furlong and win his third race on the July Course and his first of 2012. He had been in reasonable form this term without screaming that his turn was near again but a 4lb drop in the weights helped his cause, as did the slight easing of the ground as he doesn't want it rattling fast, and he clearly loves this uphill finish. (op 6-1)
Odin(IRE) hung his chance away at Salisbury last time but he proved much more tractable here, sticking on well having thrown down his challenge over a furlong out. (op 10-1 tchd 17-2)
Sheikhzayedroad probably would have won had he not been so errant in the closing stages. He will probably improve a good deal when headgear goes on. (op 2-1 tchd 9-4)
Almagest, having his first run since being gelded and in first time blinkers, shaped with encouragement in fourth without screaming that he was a much improved animal. He is entitled to come on for this fitness wise though. (op 11-2)
Carragold dropped away despite being allowed to set just modest early fractions and is in the grip of the handicapper.

4822 ADNAMS COPPER HOUSE DISTILLERY EBF CONDITIONS STKS 1m
4:05 (4:08) (Class 2) 4-Y-O+ **£12,450** (£3,728; £1,864; £932; £466) **Stalls** Low

Form RPR

4-65 **1** **Tazahum (USA)**29 3825 4-8-9 **109**.................................... PaulHanagan 3 103
(Sir Michael Stoute) *a.p: trckd ldr over 5f out: led over 2f out: shkn up over 1f out: rdn and r.o wl ins fnl f* **11/8**1

-000 **2** *1 ¾* **Balducci**170 587 5-8-9 **100**... JamieSpencer 5 99
(David Simcock) *trckd ldr tl over 5f out: remained handy: rdn to chse wnr over 1f out: styd on* **9/2**

0231 **3** *nk* **Dance And Dance (IRE)**16 4248 6-9-6 **110**..................... GeorgeBaker 2 109
(Ed Vaughan) *hld up: hdwy over 1f out: sn rdn: styd on* **7/2**3

0402 **4** *2 ¼* **Bridgefield (USA)**16 4248 4-8-9 **99**............................... FrankieDettori 1 92
(Mahmood Al Zarooni) *hld up: hdwy over 2f out: rdn over 1f out: no ex ins fnl f* **10/3**2

6561 **5** *hd* **Amoya (GER)**7 4578 5-8-4 **79**... RaulDaSilva 4 87
(Philip McBride) *led over 5f: sn rdn: styd on same pce fnl f* **14/1**

1m 40.4s (0.40) **Going Correction** +0.025s/f (Good) **5** Ran SP% **112.3**
Speed ratings (Par 109): **99,97,96,94,94**
CSF £8.16 TOTE £2.10: £1.10, £2.80; EX 8.80.
Owner Hamdan Al Maktoum **Bred** Shadwell Australia Ltd **Trained** Newmarket, Suffolk

FOCUS
A tricky little conditions race that always looked like it might become tactical, and so it proved, with an overall time 4secs outside of standard - slow for a race of this calibre. This isn't form to take too seriously and the beaten horses can easily be forgiven.

NOTEBOOK
Tazahum(USA)'s rider gained due reward for kicking for home first and his rivals were on the back foot thereafter. He hadn't been at his best this term, and although the drop in class did the trick, this race rather fell into his lap and it might be unwise to get carried away with him, especially as he'll probably go up to Listed or Group company next. (tchd 13-8 and 5-4 in a place)
Balducci, who won this race last year when with Andrew Balding, had been out of sorts in Dubai when last seen but this was a fairly encouraging start for David Simcock, given he was badly off at the weights with the winner and he too would have preferred a stronger pace to run at. (op 13-2 tchd 4-1)
Dance And Dance(IRE) wasn't disgraced but he was never going to be seen to his best in a race like this. He needs a much stronger pace to chase down and he struggled to get settled held up off this crawl. He fared okay in the circumstances and is much better than he was able to show. (tchd 4-1)
Bridgefield(USA) looked to have strong claims on his recent run behind Dance And Dance at Doncaster (weighted to reverse form) but he found disappointingly little when asked to quicken. Like all the beaten horses, it's probably unwise to read too much into this run though. (op 3-1 tchd 11-4 and 7-2 in places)
Amoya(GER) had no chance on these terms. (op 12-1)

4823 ADNAMS SOLE STAR H'CAP 1m 4f
4:40 (4:40) (Class 4) (0-85,85) 4-Y-O+ **£5,175** (£1,540; £769; £384) **Stalls** Centre

Form RPR

6-50 **1** **Braveheart Move (IRE)**72 2419 6-8-13 **77**.................(p) PaulHanagan 3 84
(Geoffrey Harker) *hld up and bhd: hdwy u.p over 1f out: r.o to ld wl ins fnl f* **9/1**

21-6 **2** *¾* **No Heretic**91 1850 4-9-2 **80**.. JamieSpencer 5 86
(David Simcock) *chsd clr ldrs: tk clsr order over 2f out: led over 1f out: hrd rdn and hdd wl ins fnl f* **7/2**2

-333 **3** *nk* **Knightly Escapade**29 3827 4-9-1 **79**............................. FrankieDettori 6 84
(John Dunlop) *s.i.s: hld up: hdwy over 2f out: rdn and ev ch ins fnl f: styd on* **11/4**1

246 **4** *nk* **O Ma Lad (IRE)**16 4251 4-9-2 **80**.................................... MartinHarley 9 85
(Sylvester Kirk) *hld up: hdwy over 3f out: rdn and hung rt over 1f out: styd on* **10/1**

4-00 **5** *¾* **Four Nations (USA)**72 2423 4-8-13 **77**............................ MartinLane 10 81
(Amanda Perrett) *chsd clr ldr tl led over 2f out: rdn and hdd over 1f out: styd on same pce ins fnl f* **14/1**

2332 **6** *7* **Arizona John (IRE)**9 4499 7-8-11 **75**............................ FrannyNorton 8 68
(John Mackie) *chsd clr ldrs: tk clsr order over 2f out: rdn over 1f out: wknd and eased ins fnl f* **9/2**3

30/0 **7** *½* **Stormy Weather (FR)**21 4111 6-9-4 **85**........................ DaleSwift(3) 4 77
(Brian Ellison) *chsd clr ldrs: rdn over 3f out: wknd over 1f out* **8/1**

1545 **8** *8* **Aldwick Bay (IRE)**22 4060 4-9-5 **83**................................... PatDobbs 1 62
(Richard Hannon) *hld up: rdn over 2f out: wknd over 1f out* **11/1**

013 **9** *46* **Ela Gonda Mou**44 3309 5-8-2 **66**...................................... NickyMackay 2
(Peter Charalambous) *led and sn wl clr: pushed along over 4f out: wknd and hdd over 2f out: t.o* **16/1**

2m 34.44s (1.54) **Going Correction** +0.025s/f (Good) **9** Ran SP% **118.2**
Speed ratings (Par 105): **95,94,94,94,93 88,88,83,52**
toteswingers 1&2 £13.30, 1&3 £8.80, 2&3 £3.60 CSF £41.58 CT £112.31 TOTE £13.20: £3.20, £1.60, £1.70; EX 59.40.
Owner C H McGhie **Bred** Moyglare Stud Farm Ltd **Trained** Thirkleby, N Yorks

FOCUS
A fair handicap with the runner-up close to his maiden form.

Braveheart Move(IRE) Official explanation: trainer said, regarding the apparent improvement of form, that the very strong pace of the race suited the gelding
Ela Gonda Mou Official explanation: jockey said that the mare bolted in the race

4824 ROBERT PALMER MEMORIAL H'CAP — 6f

5:15 (5:15) (Class 3) (0-90,89) 3-Y-O+ **£9,703** (£2,887; £1,443; £721) **Stalls** Low

Form RPR
2010 **1** **Trade Secret**[6] [4629] 5-9-4 **81** .... PatCosgrave 13 91
(Mel Brittain) *hld up: hdwy over 1f out: rdn and r.o to ld wl ins fnl f* **25/1**
-010 **2** *nk* **L'Ami Louis (IRE)**[52] [3049] 4-9-10 **87** .... DaneO'Neill 10 96
(Henry Candy) *trckd ldr tl led over 1f out: rdn and hdd wl ins fnl f* **12/1**
554 **3** *½* **My Son Max**[21] [0767] 4-9-0 **80** .... DarryllHolland 18 87
(P J O'Gorman) *hld up: hdwy and nt clr run over 1f out: r.o* **14/1**
0320 **4** *nk* **Apollo D'Negro (IRE)**[15] [4286] 4-9-1 **78** ....(v) LiamKeniry 19 84
(Clive Cox) *hld up: hdwy over 2f out: rdn over 1f out: r.o* **28/1**
263 **5** *hd* **Showboating (IRE)**[8] [4554] 4-9-2 **79** ....(tp) MartinHarley 11 85
(Alan McCabe) *a.p: rdn over 1f out: r.o* **9/1**[3]
10 **6** *1 ½* **Rocket Rob (IRE)**[23] [4013] 6-8-9 **72** .... JamieMackay 4 73+
(Willie Musson) *hld up: hdwy and hung lft fr over 1f out: styd on* **16/1**
0066 **7** *½* **Cheveton**[35] [3624] 8-9-2 **82** .... DaleSwift(3) 12 81
(Richard Price) *prom: rdn over 2f out: styd on same pce ins fnl f* **16/1**
-000 **8** *shd* **Expose**[13] [4367] 4-9-1 **78** .... LiamJones 6 77+
(William Haggas) *hld up: plld hrd: nt clr run fr over 2f out tl rdn over 1f out: r.o: nt rch ldrs* **40/1**
0300 **9** *2* **We Have A Dream**[15] [4286] 7-9-2 **79** .... MartinDwyer 5 72
(William Muir) *chsd ldrs: rdn over 2f out: edgd rt over 1f out: no ex wl ins fnl f* **33/1**
0120 **10** *nk* **Avonmore Star**[8] [4530] 4-9-3 **80** .... PatDobbs 15 72
(Richard Hannon) *hld up: rdn over 1f out: r.o towards fin: nvr nrr* **28/1**
5000 **11** *½* **Bravo Echo**[15] [4286] 6-9-0 **77** .... MartinLane 8 67
(Michael Attwater) *prom: rdn over 2f out: wknd fnl f* **50/1**
2651 **12** *nk* **Street Power (USA)**[15] [4286] 7-9-4 **84** .... RaulDaSilva(3) 14 73
(Jeremy Gask) *hld up: hdwy over 1f out: edgd rt and wknd ins fnl f* **8/1**[2]
2-21 **13** *½* **Cape Classic (IRE)**[68] [2558] 4-9-12 **89** .... FrankieDettori 3 77+
(William Haggas) *chsd ldrs: rdn over 2f out: wknd fnl f* **7/4**[1]
3001 **14** *1* **Perfect Pastime**[37] [3541] 4-8-13 **81** ....(p) NathanAlison(5) 20 65+
(Jim Boyle) *rrd s: bhd: rdn over 1f out: nt clr run and swtchd rt ins fnl f: nvr trbld ldrs* **20/1**
2410 **15** *nk* **Sacrosanctus**[7] [4611] 4-9-11 **88** .... MircoDemuro 2 71
(Scott Dixon) *chsd ldrs: rdn over 2f out: wkng whn n.m.r over 1f out* **14/1**
0205 **16** *½* **Button Moon (IRE)**[14] [4336] 4-8-9 **77** ....(p) AntiocoMurgia(5) 7 59
(Ian Wood) *led: rdn and hdd over 1f out: wknd ins fnl f* **25/1**
15 **17** *9* **Sir Pedro**[40] [3445] 3-9-2 **83** .... PaulHanagan 16 36+
(Charles Hills) *hld up: hdwy over 2f out: wknd and eased over 1f out* **8/1**[2]
-600 **18** *25* **Bless You**[36] [3571] 4-9-0 **77** ....[1] FergusSweeney 9
(Henry Candy) *sn outpcd: t.o* **20/1**

1m 12.62s (0.12) **Going Correction** +0.025s/f (Good)
WFA 3 from 4yo+ 4lb **18** Ran SP% **132.8**
Speed ratings (Par 107): **100,99,98,98,98 96,95,95,92,92 91,91,90,89,88 88,76,42**
toteswingers 1&2 £56.50, 1&3 £45.00, 2&3 £18.40 CSF £294.30 CT £4489.19 TOTE £38.10: £5.50, £3.40, £3.90, £5.40; EX 810.20.
Owner Mel Brittain **Bred** Whitsbury Manor Stud **Trained** Warthill, N Yorks

FOCUS
A competitive sprint handicap in which the action unfolded middle to far-side in the closing stages and there weren't any real excuses. The form is rated at face value around the third, fourth and fifth.

NOTEBOOK
Trade Secret can often blow his chance at the start but there were no problems this time and he found plenty to come home strongly from off the pace. He seems to appreciate a bit of cut in the ground, so the early showers would have helped and this has to go down as a personal best off a career-high mark.
L'Ami Louis(IRE) travelled smoothly into contention and, having hit the front just inside the final furlong, was only just run out of it in the closing stages. He showed here that he doesn't have to dominate to show his best, and he bounced back from a disappointing run in this grade last time. He is clearly up to winning at this level, especially on his favoured fast ground. (op 11-1 tchd 14-1)
My Son Max ideally wants a bit further than this and he shaped like that was the case, finishing nicely from well back and this marks him down as a major player back up to 7f next time.
Apollo D'Negro(IRE) fared better than at Ascot last time but just needs a touch more to score off this sort of mark.
Showboating(IRE) also kept on well once switched left and he's in good form.
Cape Classic(IRE) was a warm favourite and was in touch with the pace, but came under pressure some way out and found little. He is much better than this. (op 2-1 tchd 9-4 and 11-4 in a place)
Perfect Pastime Official explanation: jockey said that the gelding was slowly away
Sir Pedro Official explanation: jockey said that the colt became upset in the stalls
T/Plt: £89.30 to a £1 stake. Pool £70,647.23. 577.48 winning tickets. T/Qpdt: £8.80 to a £1 stake. Pool £4,575.00. 381.15 winning tickets. CR

[4778] THIRSK (L-H)

Saturday, August 4

OFFICIAL GOING: Good (good to firm in places; 9.4)
Wind: Light, across. Weather: changeable, showers

4825 BRITISH STALLION STUDS SUPPORTING BRITISH RACING EBF MAIDEN STKS — 5f

1:55 (1:56) (Class 4) 2-Y-O **£4,528** (£1,347; £673; £336) **Stalls** High

Form RPR
5 **1** **Shrimper Roo**[91] [1861] 2-9-3 0 .... DuranFentiman 9 75+
(Tim Easterby) *mid-div: drvn over 2f out: styd on over 1f out: led last 50yds: hld on nr fin* **12/1**
032 **2** *nk* **Shillito**[6] [4625] 2-9-3 0 .... BarryMcHugh 13 74
(Tony Coyle) *chsd ldrs: styd on fnl 100yds: jst hld* **2/1**[1]
03 **3** *2* **Mullit (IRE)**[17] [4220] 2-9-3 0 .... RichardKingscote 10 67
(Tom Dascombe) *led: hung bdly lft over 1f out: hdd last 50yds* **12/1**
4 *1 ½* **Time And Place** 2-9-3 0 .... FrederikTylicki 12 61+
(Richard Fahey) *s.v.s: hdwy to chse ldrs after 2f: edgd lft over 1f out: kpt on same pce ins fnl f* **3/1**[2]
0 **5** *nk* **Millkwood**[15] [4310] 2-9-3 0 .... PJMcDonald 6 60+
(John Davies) *mid-div: hdwy over 2f out: nt clr run and swtchd lft over 1f out: kpt on: nvr rchd ldrs* **50/1**
0 **6** *nk* **Passionate Poet**[40] [3436] 2-8-10 0 .... DavidSimmonson(7) 7 59
(Michael Easterby) *mid-div: sn drvn along: hdwy over 2f out: kpt on: nvr rchd ldrs* **28/1**
4 **7** *hd* **Ingleby Symphony (IRE)**[25] [3937] 2-8-7 0 .... ShaneBKelly(5) 8 54
(Richard Fahey) *dwlt: sn bhd: hdwy over 1f out: styd on wl towards fin* **16/1**
8 *¾* **Agripin (IRE)** 2-9-3 0 .... AndrewMullen 4 56
(David Barron) *swtchd rt s: w ldrs: wknd appr fnl f* **12/1**
6 **9** *1 ¼* **Dance Off (IRE)**[18] [4173] 2-8-9 0 .... LeeTopliss(3) 2 46
(Richard Fahey) *mid-div: hdwy on outer over 2f out: hung lft: wknd ins fnl f* **14/1**
10 *1 ¼* **Ridgeblade** 2-8-12 0 ow3 .... GaryBartley(3) 5 45
(Noel Wilson) *hld up towards rr: hung lft over 1f out: nvr on terms* **66/1**
3220 **11** *2 ¾* **Opt Out**[16] [4230] 2-9-3 72 .... JoeFanning 1 37
(Mark Johnston) *chsd ldrs on outer: lost pl over 1f out* **11/2**[3]
0 **12** *6* **Setfiretotherain**[75] [2330] 2-9-3 0 .... PaulMulrennan 3 15
(Kevin Ryan) *chsd ldrs: wknd over 1f out: eased whn bhd towards fin* **33/1**
0 **13** *2* **Anna Law (IRE)**[23] [4011] 2-8-12 0 .... WilliamCarson 11 7
(Charles Hills) *chsd ldrs: lost pl over 1f out: bhd whn eased clsng stages* **16/1**

1m 0.04s (0.44) **Going Correction** -0.05s/f (Good) **13** Ran SP% **125.1**
Speed ratings (Par 96): **94,93,90,87,87 86,86,85,83,81 77,67,64**
Tote Swingers 1&2 £2.20, 2&3 £9.40, 1&3 £48.50 CSF £37.21 TOTE £11.50: £3.20, £1.10, £4.60; EX 27.00.
Owner Reality Partnerships IV **Bred** Ercan Dogan **Trained** Great Habton, N Yorks

FOCUS
The first three home in this 2-y-o contest all had the benefit of a run. The form looks fluid with the runner-up the best guide.

NOTEBOOK
Shrimper Roo, who had shown clear ability on his debut here over C&D in May, had been gelded in the meantime and stuck to his task well. From an in-form yard he will stay further in due course. (op 10-1)
Shillito, well drawn here, again ran well and a similar contest should come his way. He looks straightforward and could also go down the nursery route. (op 5-2 tchd 11-4)
Mullit(IRE) travelled well and looked the winner entering the final furlong but hung badly left and threw his chance away. He has lots of speed and can shed his maiden tag if keeping straight. (op 14-1 tchd 11-1)
Time And Place ran a race full of promise, after missing the break badly he stayed on well from halfway and should improve plenty for this experience. (op 9-2)
Ingleby Symphony(IRE), having her second start, also stayed on well and can make her mark in due course. (op 20-1)
Dance Off(IRE) Official explanation: jockey said that the filly hung left throughout
Opt Out wasn't very well drawn here in stall 1 but in the end finished well beaten and is looking fairly exposed. (op 4-1)

4826 YORKSHIRE OUTDOORS ADVENTURE EXPERIENCES MAIDEN (S) STKS — 1m 4f

2:30 (2:30) (Class 5) 3-Y-O **£3,234** (£962; £481; £240) **Stalls** Low

Form RPR
-224 **1** **Scarlet Prince**[11] [4440] 3-8-12 57 .... BarryMcHugh 3 64
(Tony Coyle) *mid-div: hdwy 4f out: led over 1f out: forged clr* **9/2**[2]
0565 **2** *4* **Little Red Minx (IRE)**[4] [4678] 3-8-0 55 ....(p) DavidBergin(7) 12 53
(David O'Meara) *trckd ldrs: wnt 2nd over 3f out: led over 2f out: hdd over 1f out: one pce* **8/1**[3]
-462 **3** *nk* **Geanie Mac (IRE)**[9] [4510] 3-8-7 62 ....(b) JimmyQuinn 10 53
(Tim Pitt) *t.k.h: led: hdd over 2f out: one pce* **7/4**[1]
4 *nk* **Kealshore Again (IRE)** 3-8-12 0 .... PJMcDonald 7 57+
(George Moore) *s.i.s: reminders after s: in rr: hdwy 4f out: chsng ldrs over 2f out: kpt on one pce* **12/1**
-040 **5** *¾* **Baileys Over Ice**[8] [4549] 3-8-7 53 .... TomEaves 4 51
(James Given) *mid-div: hdwy over 3f out: sn chsng ldrs: one pce fnl 2f* **8/1**[3]
3544 **6** *shd* **No Time To Cry**[4] [4678] 3-8-7 51 ....(v) PatrickMathers 9 51
(Ann Duffield) *in tch: hdwy over 3f out: one pce fnl 2f* **8/1**[3]
-050 **7** *17* **Catramis**[14] [4349] 3-8-12 49 .... PaulMulrennan 2 28
(Geoffrey Oldroyd) *in rr: nvr on terms* **22/1**
0 **8** *1 ½* **Otto Nicolai**[40] [3447] 3-8-12 0 ....(b[1]) JoeFanning 8 26
(J S Moore) *chsd ldrs: wknd over 2f out* **25/1**
4606 **9** *5* **Oops Caroline (IRE)**[4] [4678] 3-8-7 46 .... DuranFentiman 5 13
(David O'Meara) *chsd ldrs: reminders after s: sn drvn along: lost pl 2f out* **18/1**
4403 **10** *4 ½* **Hulwa (USA)**[4] [4678] 3-8-6 44 ow2 .... PaulPickard(3) 13
(Tracy Waggott) *chsd ldrs: drvn over 4f out: wknd over 2f out* **14/1**
6-05 **11** *50* **Silent Ambition**[42] [3384] 3-8-7 40 .... RobbieFitzpatrick 11
(Mark Brisbourne) *mid-div: drvn and lost pl over 5f out: wl bhd and eased 3f out: hopelessly t.o: virtually p.u* **66/1**
00 **12** *11* **Lochluichart (IRE)**[37] [3521] 3-8-9 0 .... LeeTopliss(3) 6
(Ian Semple) *sn in rr: bhd 7f out: t.o 5f out: eased over 2f out: virtually p.u* **50/1**
000 **13** *35* **Connie Carlton**[17] [4211] 3-8-7 18 ....(b[1]) AndrewElliott 1
(David Thompson) *swvd lft s: sn bhd: t.o 5f out: eventually completed: virtually p.u* **80/1**

2m 36.17s (-0.03) **Going Correction** +0.10s/f (Good) **13** Ran SP% **120.4**
Speed ratings (Par 100): **104,101,101,100,100 100,89,88,84,81 48,41,17**
Tote Swingers 1&2 £11.70, 2&3 £2.40, 1&3 £1.50 CSF £39.11 TOTE £7.10: £2.00, £1.90, £1.60; EX 38.40.There was no bid for the winner.
Owner Mrs Nicola McGreavy **Bred** Southill Stud **Trained** Norton, N Yorks

FOCUS
This was a very ordinary 3yo seller run at a sound pace and highly unlikely to throw up many future winners. The first six pulled well clear of the remainder and the first two set the level.

4827 CONSTANT SECURITY NURSERY — 5f

3:05 (3:05) (Class 3) (0-95,93) 2-Y-O **£7,762** (£2,310; £1,154; £577) **Stalls** High

Form RPR
2512 **1** **Lucky Beggar (IRE)**[9] [4488] 2-9-5 **91** .... WilliamCarson 8 96
(Charles Hills) *trckd ldr: hmpd and dropped bk after 1f: sn drvn along: hdwy and swtchd lft 1f out: r.o to ld towards fin* **3/1**[2]
1150 **2** *nk* **Storm Moon (USA)**[44] [3291] 2-9-4 **90** .... JoeFanning 1 94
(Mark Johnston) *swvd lft s: led over 3f out: hdd and no ex clsng stages* **10/3**[3]
5414 **3** *1 ¼* **Mayfield Girl (IRE)**[7] [4614] 2-8-10 **82** .... PaulMulrennan 6 81
(Mel Brittain) *wnt lft s: chsd ldrs: drvn over 2f out: styd on same pce last 150yds* **11/2**
2151 **4** *¾* **Lady Poppy**[7] [4614] 2-8-9 **81** .... PJMcDonald 4 78
(George Moore) *bmpd s: led: swtchd rt to stands' rail after 1f: hdd over 3f out: drvn 2f out: kpt on same pce fnl f* **5/2**[1]
150 **5** *1 ½* **Rhagori Aur**[21] [4093] 2-8-7 **79** .... TomEaves 9 70
(Bryan Smart) *t.k.h in rr: hdwy over 2f out: one pce appr fnl f* **6/1**

0413 **6** *4* **Rat Catcher (IRE)**[22] 4045 2-8-5 77..........................(b) DuranFentiman 3 54
(Tim Easterby) *dwlt: sn trcking ldrs: effrt over 1f out: sn btn: eased clsng stages* **14/1**

58.88s (-0.72) **Going Correction** -0.05s/f (Good) **6** Ran SP% **113.0**
Speed ratings (Par 98): **103,102,100,99,96 90**
Tote Swingers 1&2 £2.90, 2&3 £9.00, 1&3 £5.30 CSF £13.55 CT £50.40 TOTE £3.60: £1.90, £2.10; EX 10.20.
Owner Hon Mrs Corbett, C Wright, Mrs B W Hills **Bred** Mrs Cherry Faeste **Trained** Lambourn, Berks

FOCUS
Despite three non-runners this nursery looked competitive and it was run at a sound tempo, backed up by the winning time. The third sets the level.

NOTEBOOK
Lucky Beggar(IRE) looked the part in the paddock and the strong pace suited him. He looks the type to improve next year and promises to stay further in due course. (op 5-2 tchd 10-3)
Storm Moon(USA) was taking a drop back in class and ran a solid race. He looks all about speed and with his trainer in top form at present it's highly likely he can win again. (op 3-1 tchd 11-4)
Mayfield Girl(IRE) may struggle to win from this mark. (op 7-1)
Lady Poppy, was up 6lb for her York success, appeared to have the race run to suit and while she has run a solid race the handicapper might be in charge. (op 11-4 tchd 9-4)

4828 TOTEPOOL.COM THIRSK SUMMER CUP (HANDICAP STKS) 1m
3:35 (3:35) (Class 3) (0-90,90) 3-Y-O+ **£19,407** (£5,775; £2,886; £1,443) **Stalls** Low

Form RPR
3026 **1** **Lord Aeryn (IRE)**[8] 4557 5-9-5 88................................ BarryMcHugh 16 95
(Richard Fahey) *hld up towards rr: hdwy on outer over 2f out: led last 75yds: jst hld on* **20/1**
2300 **2** *shd* **Al Muheer (IRE)**[7] 4589 7-8-13 89................................(b) JasonHart(7) 15 96
(Ruth Carr) *hld up in rr: hdwy on outer over 2f out: r.o fnl f: jst failed* **16/1**
-300 **3** *3/4* **Mont Ras (IRE)**[91] 1865 5-9-4 87.................................. DanielTudhope 4 92+
(David O'Meara) *trckd ldr: led over 3f out: drvn 2f out: hdd and no ex last 75yds* **9/2**[1]
-612 **4** *nk* **Venutius**[14] 4345 5-9-0 88.. ShaneBKelly(5) 11 92
(Ed McMahon) *trckd ldrs: t.k.h: kpt on same pce fnl f* **16/1**
4503 **5** *1* **Kyllachy Star**[14] 4339 6-9-5 88...................................... PatrickMathers 7 90
(Richard Fahey) *in tch: effrt on inner over 2f out: chsng ldrs 1f out: kpt on same pce* **12/1**
0200 **6** *3 1/4* **Classic Colori (IRE)**[28] 3878 5-9-4 87......................[1] DuranFentiman 10 82
(David O'Meara) *in rr: hdwy on outer over 2f out: kpt on same pce: nvr rchd ldrs* **16/1**
5300 **7** *1 1/4* **Crown Counsel (IRE)**[4] 4689 4-9-2 85............................. JoeFanning 13 77
(Mark Johnston) *mid-div: nt clr run 2f out: kpt on fnl f* **14/1**
5505 **8** *3/4* **Norse Blues**[4] 4689 4-9-6 89.. StephenCraine 6 79
(Sylvester Kirk) *mid-div: effrt over 2f out: edgd lft and one pce over 1f out* **7/1**[2]
-050 **9** *1 3/4* **Barren Brook**[49] 3164 5-9-3 86..................................... PaddyAspell 8 72+
(Michael Easterby) *mid-div: nt clr run on inner over 2f out: nvr a threat* **7/1**[2]
4050 **10** *2* **Orpsie Boy (IRE)**[7] 4609 9-9-2 85.................................. PJMcDonald 14 66+
(Ruth Carr) *in rr: sme hdwy and nt clr run on inner over 2f out: nvr a factor* **25/1**
4100 **11** *1/2* **Dubai Hills**[14] 4321 6-9-2 90....................................... JustinNewman(5) 9 70
(Bryan Smart) *mid-div on outer: effrt over 2f out: no threat* **33/1**
2000 **12** *hd* **Osteopathic Remedy (IRE)**[35] 3626 8-9-3 89.............. LeeTopliss(3) 2 69
(Michael Dods) *chsd ldrs: wknd over 1f out* **12/1**
5001 **13** *1 1/2* **Kiwi Bay**[43] 3354 7-9-3 86... TomEaves 12 62
(Michael Dods) *sn chsng ldrs: effrt over 2f out: sn wknd* **20/1**
4421 **14** *hd* **Corporal Maddox**[7] 4580 5-9-2 90.................................. LMcNiff(5) 17 66
(Patrick Morris) *s.i.s: nvr a factor* **8/1**[3]
3640 **15** *1* **Extraterrestrial**[19] 4136 8-9-3 86................................. FrederikTylicki 3 59
(Richard Fahey) *mid-div: nt clr run on inner over 2f out: sn wknd* **18/1**
2425 **16** *1/2* **Toto Skyllachy**[21] 4110 7-8-11 87................................. DavidBergin(7) 5 59
(David O'Meara) *s.i.s: sme hdwy on inner whn nt clr run over 2f out: sn wknd and eased* **16/1**
0-30 **17** *10* **Wannabe King**[91] 1865 6-9-5 88.................................... AndrewMullen 1
(Geoffrey Harker) *led tl over 3f out: lost pl over 1f out: heavily eased last 100yds* **20/1**
203 **18** *7* **Oriental Scot**[19] 4136 5-9-5 88..................................... WilliamCarson 18
(William Jarvis) *stmbld s: a in rr: eased fnl f* **16/1**

1m 39.33s (-0.77) **Going Correction** +0.10s/f (Good) **18** Ran SP% **132.1**
Speed ratings (Par 107): **107,106,106,105,104 101,100,99,97,95 95,95,93,93,92 91,81,74**
Tote Swingers 1&2 £62.30, 2&3 £31.80, 1&3 £28.70 CSF £311.48 CT £1768.50 TOTE £26.90: £6.00, £4.10, £2.20, £4.10; EX 646.30 Trifecta £484.50 Part won. Pool £654.74 - 0.20 winning units..
Owner Mrs H Steel **Bred** Woodhouse Syndicate **Trained** Musley Bank, N Yorks

FOCUS
A big field for this valuable 0-90 handicap which was run at a solid tempo in which the first five pulled well clear. The first two came widest of all but the form looks sound.

NOTEBOOK
Lord Aeryn(IRE) wasn't winning out of turn, sticking to his task well late on. Once the handicapper has his say it will require a career best to follow up.
Al Muheer(IRE) ran with credit and lost little in defeat. He might well have won in a couple more strides.
Mont Ras(IRE) was always up with the pace and ran up to form but is 13lb higher than his last winning mark. (op 5-1 tchd 11-2)
Venutius came here in top form and, after racing keenly, stuck to his task well. (op 20-1)
Kyllachy Star, a stable-companion of the winner, stayed on well and is slipping to a winning mark. (op 11-1 tchd 10-1)
Crown Counsel(IRE) ◆ is one to keep an eye on. He didn't get the run of the race and with his yard going very well at present he should be kept on-side. (op 16-1)
Orpsie Boy(IRE) Official explanation: jockey said that the gelding was denied a clear run
Extraterrestrial Official explanation: jockey said that the gelding was denied a clear run

4829 PETER BELL MEMORIAL H'CAP 6f
4:15 (4:16) (Class 4) (0-85,85) 3-Y-O+ **£5,175** (£1,540; £769; £384) **Stalls** High

Form RPR
4606 **1** **Lucky Numbers (IRE)**[8] 4554 6-9-3 76..................(e[1]) DanielTudhope 17 88
(David O'Meara) *reluctant to go to s: rrd and s.s: bhd: gd hdwy over 1f out: styd on strly to ld last 75yds* **13/2**[2]
3600 **2** *1 1/4* **Sound Amigo (IRE)**[63] 2697 4-9-5 78.......................... BarryMcHugh 15 86
(Ollie Pears) *mid-div stands' side: hdwy 2f out: led ins fnl f: sn hdd and no ex* **14/1**
3000 **3** *3/4* **Whozthecat (IRE)**[8] 4554 5-8-13 77.............................(v) NeilFarley(5) 10 83
(Declan Carroll) *led stands' side gp: hdd jst ins fnl f: kpt on same pce* **16/1**
1043 **4** *1 1/4* **Carambola**[15] 4312 6-9-0 80................................... RobertDodsworth(7) 14 82
(Mel Brittain) *chsd ldrs: kpt on same pce fnl f* **20/1**
5240 **5** *nk* **Green Park (IRE)**[8] 4554 9-8-13 79...........................(b) JasonHart(7) 16 80
(Declan Carroll) *chsd ldrs: sn drvn along: hung rt and kpt on same pce ins fnl f* **14/1**
0036 **6** *hd* **Cocktail Charlie**[8] 4554 4-9-2 75.......................................(p) TomEaves 1 75
(Tim Easterby) *chsd ldrs on outer: edgd rt and kpt on same pce fnl f* **17/2**[3]
6005 **7** *nk* **Illustrious Prince (IRE)**[8] 4552 5-8-6 72.................. LukeLeadbitter(7) 2 71
(Declan Carroll) *overall ldr far side: edgd rt over 1f out: hdd ins fnl f: no ex* **33/1**
0402 **8** *1/2* **Solar Spirit (IRE)**[6] 4629 7-9-5 83.............................. ShaneBKelly(5) 20 80
(Tracy Waggott) *in rr stands' side: hdwy 2f out: chsd ldrs 1f out: one pce whn slty hmpd 100yds out* **9/2**[1]
0460 **9** *3* **Saucy Brown (IRE)**[49] 3169 6-8-13 72........................ AndrewMullen 18 60
(David Nicholls) *mid-div: drvn over 2f out: wknd appr fnl f* **11/1**
500 **10** *3/4* **Gorgeous Goblin (IRE)**[12] 4400 5-8-6 72............(t) JacobButterfield(7) 9 57
(David C Griffiths) *swvd rt s: hld up in mid-div stands' side: kpt on fnl 2f: nvr a threat* **33/1**
202- **11** *1 1/4* **Jade**[324] 6094 4-9-2 78.. LeeTopliss(3) 4 59
(Ollie Pears) *dwlt: mid-div on outer: hdwy over 2f out: chsd ldrs over 1f out: wknd fnl 150yds* **20/1**
0-60 **12** *1 1/2* **Azzurra Du Caprio (IRE)**[35] 3612 4-9-9 82.................. PJMcDonald 7 59
(Ben Haslam) *chsd ldrs centre: wknd over 1f out* **16/1**
2600 **13** *1* **Little Jimmy Odsox (IRE)**[35] 3612 4-9-2 75...........(p) DuranFentiman 8 48
(Tim Easterby) *chsd ldrs towards centre: wknd over 1f out* **14/1**
1100 **14** *nk* **Choc'A'Moca (IRE)**[9] 4495 5-8-0 66..................(v) DanielleMooney(7) 12 38
(Paul Midgley) *chsd ldrs stands' side: wknd over 1f out* **33/1**
1203 **15** *1/2* **George Benjamin**[18] 4190 5-8-12 78............................... RyanWhile(7) 3 49
(Christopher Kellett) *chsd ldrs on outer: lost pl over 1f out* **25/1**
000- **16** *1 3/4* **Thirteen Shivers**[315] 6331 4-9-5 85..................... DavidSimmonson(7) 6 50
(Michael Easterby) *w ldrs centre: wknd over 1f out* **28/1**
3P40 **17** *6* **Toby Tyler**[8] 4554 6-9-3 76...(v) MickyFenton 5 22
(Paul Midgley) *s.s: towards rr on outer: bhd fnl 2f* **28/1**
3020 **18** *28* **Nubar Boy**[26] 3915 5-8-10 72...........................(v) MatthewCosham(3) 13
(David Evans) *mid-div on outer of stands' side gp: lost pl 2f out: bhd whn heavily eased ins fnl f: virtually p.u: t.o* **25/1**
3211 **19** *21* **Henry Bee**[15] 4291 3-9-1 78.. FrederikTylicki 19
(Richard Fahey) *s.s: reminders after 100yds: sn bhd: eased over 3f out: sn t.o: virtually p.u* **9/2**[1]

1m 11.62s (-1.08) **Going Correction** -0.05s/f (Good)
WFA 3 from 4yo+ 4lb **19** Ran SP% **133.3**
Speed ratings (Par 105): **105,103,102,100,100 100,99,98,94,93 92,90,88,88,87 85,77,40,12**
Tote Swingers 1&2 £39.90, 2&3 £49.90, 1&3 £29.40 CSF £88.49 CT £1432.95 TOTE £7.40: £1.80, £5.90, £5.40, £6.10; EX 139.50.
Owner Tom Tuohy & Tony Jafrate **Bred** Rory O'Brien **Trained** Nawton, N Yorks

FOCUS
Another big field for this 66-85 handicap which was run at a furious pace. They raced in two groups before converging into one group in the final furlong. The runner-up is rated to his best and sets the standard.
Henry Bee Official explanation: jockey said that the gelding missed the break and was never travelling thereafter

4830 MARKET CROSS JEWELLERS H'CAP 1m
4:50 (4:52) (Class 5) (0-70,73) 3-Y-O **£3,234** (£962; £481; £240) **Stalls** Low

Form RPR
431 **1** **Sweetnessandlight**[8] 4549 3-9-7 70......................... MichaelStainton 13 81+
(Jason Ward) *hld up: hdwy to trck ldrs over 3f out: led 2f out: kpt on wl* **13/2**[3]
6211 **2** *1 3/4* **Daddy Warbucks (IRE)**[12] 4397 3-9-5 68.................. AndrewMullen 15 75
(David Nicholls) *chsd ldrs: upsides 2f out: kpt on same pce* **6/1**[2]
5224 **3** *1/2* **Regal Acclaim (IRE)**[26] 3908 3-8-4 58............................ NeilFarley(5) 7 64
(Declan Carroll) *in rr: hdwy over 2f out: styd on same pce fnl f* **13/2**[3]
-005 **4** *2 1/2* **Blue Top**[12] 4397 3-8-5 54..(b) BarryMcHugh 12 54
(Tim Walford) *s.i.s: hdwy over 2f out: kpt on fnl f* **16/1**
5000 **5** *2 1/4* **Alabanda (IRE)**[12] 4397 3-8-6 55..............................(b[1]) DuranFentiman 17 50
(Tim Easterby) *mid-div: hdwy over 2f out: kpt on same pce* **20/1**
0026 **6** *nk* **Penang Pegasus**[64] 2673 3-8-3 52 oh2 ow1................... AndrewElliott 2 46+
(David O'Meara) *s.i.s: styd on fnl 2f: nt rch ldrs* **9/1**
3222 **7** *2 1/4* **Dream Walker (FR)**[12] 4397 3-9-3 66........................ PatrickMathers 11 55
(Ian McInnes) *chsd ldrs: sn drvn along: wknd fnl f* **10/1**
-650 **8** *nse* **First Glance**[16] 4250 3-7-13 51 oh5.............................. DominicFox(3) 6 40
(Michael Appleby) *w ldrs: led over 5f out: hdd 2f out: grad wknd* **20/1**
3261 **9** *7* **Raheeba**[11] 4426 3-9-10 73.. FrederikTylicki 3 46+
(Mark Johnston) *s.i.s: towards rr: hmpd and lost pl bnd over 4f out: kpt on fnl 2f: nvr on terms* **4/1**[1]
5150 **10** *8* **Bitaphon (IRE)**[14] 4329 3-9-0 68............................... JustinNewman(5) 4 22
(John Balding) *chsd ldrs: outpcd over 3f out: lost pl whn n.m.r on inner over 2f out* **25/1**
2503 **11** *3 3/4* **Berlusca (IRE)**[21] 4082 3-9-7 70............................ RobbieFitzpatrick 16 16
(Mark Brisbourne) *chsd ldrs: hung lft and lost pl over 2f out* **9/1**
2246 **12** *3/4* **Siouxies Dream**[130] 1058 3-8-6 55...............................(p) PJMcDonald 14
(Michael Appleby) *led tl over 5f out: wknd 2f out* **25/1**
0-63 **13** *2 1/4* **Simpson Millar**[27] 3892 3-7-13 51 oh2................. NataliaGemelova(3) 10
(Noel Wilson) *mid-div: lost pl over 3f out* **33/1**
040 **14** *20* **Running Reef (IRE)**[8] 4553 3-9-0 63................................. TomEaves 9
(Tracy Waggott) *in rr: bhd fnl 3f: t.o* **9/1**
300 **15** *59* **Pelican Rock (IRE)**[31] 3751 3-8-1 57 ow1.....................(t) JasonHart(7) 5
(Andrew Crook) *s.i.s: bhd: t.o 2f out: virtually p.u* **33/1**

1m 41.25s (1.15) **Going Correction** +0.10s/f (Good) **15** Ran SP% **126.7**
Speed ratings (Par 100): **98,96,95,93,91 90,88,88,81,73 69,68,66,46,**
Tote Swingers 1&2 £6.50, 2&3 £6.10, 1&3 £17.30 CSF £43.67 CT £280.67 TOTE £8.00: £3.30, £1.90, £3.30; EX 58.20.
Owner Mrs Jill Ward **Bred** Dxb Bloodstock Ltd **Trained** Middleham, N Yorks
■ Stewards' Enquiry : Robbie Fitzpatrick two-day ban: careless riding (18-19 Aug)

FOCUS
This 3-y-o handicap was run at a sound pace and it paid to race handily throughout. The first two are both going the right way.
Running Reef(IRE) Official explanation: jockey said that the gelding was struck into

Pelican Rock (IRE) Official explanation: jockey said that the gelding was never travelling

4831 SHIRLEY ANNE FAILL MEMORIAL H'CAP — 2m

5:25 (5:25) (Class 5) (0-75,75) 4-Y-0+ **£3,234** (£962; £481 ; £240) **Stalls** Low

Form				RPR
0055	1		**Bowdler's Magic**[14] 4326 5 -9-7**75**................................ FrederikTylicki 10	91+
			(Mark Johnston) *hld up in rr: hdwy 9f out: trckd ldrs over 3f out: shkn up to ld over 2f out: forged wl clr: eased towards fin* **2/1**[1]	
0111	2	9	**Waterford Star (IRE)**[32] 3734 4 -9-1**69**............................(v) TomEaves 2	74
			(Ian Williams) *hld up in mid-div: effrt over 3f out: wnt 2nd over 1f out: no ch w wnr* **5/1**[3]	
3-05	3	4½	**Native Colony**[17] 4216 4 -0 11**68**.........................(b[1]) DominicFox(3) 7	68
			(Roger Varian) *hld up in rr: effrt over 3f out: wnt 3rd over 1f out: one pce* **22/1**	
2140	4	11	**Corvette**[102] 1588 4 -8-6**60**.. PJMcDonald 3	47
			(Michael Appleby) *chsd ldrs: drvn over 3f out: wknd over 1f out* **28/1**	
2651	5	4	**Come Here Yew (IRE)** 4590 4 -8-11**70**......................... NeilFarley(5) 8	52
			(Declan Carroll) *trckd ldrs: chal over 3f out: wknd 2f out* **3/1**[2]	
0050	6	3¾	**Tiger Webb**[12] 4396 4 -8-5**59**... BarryMcHugh 6	36
			(Michael Easterby) *trckd ldr: led 9f out: hdd over 2f out: wknd over 1f out* **9/1**	
6-23	7	¾	**Finellas Fortune**[23] 3988 7 -8-2**56**................................. AndrewMullen 4	32
			(George Moore) *sn trcking ldrs: drvn over 3f out: wknd over 1f out* **9/1**	
406	8	33	**Bocamix (FR)**[20] 3437 6 -8-1**62**.......................................(t) JasonHart(7) 1	
			(Andrew Crook) *in rr: drvn 6f out: lost pl over 2f out: sn bhd and eased* **33/1**	
0314	9	16	**Spruzzo**[26] 3904 6 -8-10**64**... DuranFentiman 5	
			(Chris Fairhurst) *led tl 9f out: reminders over 7f out: lost pl over 4f out: t.o 3f out* **14/1**	
0/4-	10	125	**Royal Entourage**[111] 7413 7 -9-0**73**......................... JustinNewman(5) 11	
			(Philip Kirby) *stmbld s: in rr: drvn bnd after 6f: lost tch over 4f out: t.o whn virtually p.u over 3f out: eventually complered* **20/1**	

3m 29.77s (1.47)**Going Correction** +0.10s/f (Good) **10**Ran SP%**117.2**
Speed ratings (Par 103): **100,95,93,87,85 83,83,67,59,**
Tote Swingers 1&2 £3.50, 2&3 £15.70, 1&3 £9.70 CSF £11.62 CT £169.72 TOTE £2.90 : £1.90, £1.40, £3.50 ; EX 11.70 .
Owner Paul Dean **Bred** Miss K Rausing **Trained** Middleham Moor, N Yorks

FOCUS
An even tempo for this 56-75 handicap but the winner had dropped to a good mark and ran away with this.
T/Plt: £233.30 to a £1 stake. Pool £53,055.54. 165.98 winning tickets. T/Qpdt: £79.10 to a £1 stake. Pool £2,921.40. 27.32 winning tickets. WG

4832a, 4834a - 4835a - (Foreign Racing) - See Raceform Interactive

4785 GALWAY (R-H)

Saturday, August 4

OFFICIAL GOING: Soft to heavy

4833a LADBROKES MOBILE APP H'CAP (PREMIER HANDICAP) — 7f

4:00 (4:02) 3-Y-0+
£35,000 (£11,083; £5,250 ; £1,750 ; £1,166 ; £583)

			RPR
1		**Pintura**[4] 4692 5 -9-11**98**................... DeclanMcDonogh 12	108
		(Kevin Ryan) *trckd ldrs: travelled strly to cl 2f out: led home turn: pushed clr: hld on cl home* **5/1**[2]	
2	nk	**Battleoftheboyne (IRE)**[14] 4353 3 -7-13**83** oh2....... ConorHoban(5) 13	90+
		(Michael Mulvany, Ire) *hld up in rr: plenty to do appr home turn: styd on strly ins fnl f: jst failed* **20/1**	
3	2	**Sean Og Coulston (IRE)**[10] 4485 8 -8-9**82**.................. KevinManning 9	86
		(John J Coleman, Ire) *hld up: drvn to cl on ldrs 2f out: prog into 3rd ent fnl f: kpt on same pce fnl 100yds* **14/1**	
4	1½	**Northern Rocked (IRE)**[32] 3743 6 -9-7**94**......................(b) PatSmullen 2	94
		(D K Weld, Ire) *trckd ldrs: pushed along to maintain position appr home turn: kpt on same pce* **6/1**[3]	
5	3½	**Custom Cut (IRE)**[4] 4692 3 -9-7**105**......................... RonanWhelan(5) 11	94
		(George J Kent, Ire) *racd cl 2nd: sn ld: hdd by wnr appr home turn: wknd fnl f* **7/1**	
6	hd	**Winning Impact (IRE)**[14] 4356 5 -8-4**80**.....................(t) SamJames(3) 10	70
		(J G Coogan, Ire) *hld up towards rr: kpt on in st wout troubling ldrs* **12/1**	
7	1¼	**Bold Thady Quill (IRE)** 4692 5 -9-3**90**..........................(p) ShaneFoley 6	77
		(K J Condon, Ire) *hld up: pushed along bef home turn: nvr on terms* **6/1**[3]	
8	¾	**Lake George (IRE)**[4] 4694 4 -7-9**78** oh5 ow1.....(b) DylanRobinson(10) 8	63
		(James M Barrett, Ire) *trckd ldrs on outer tl wknd ins fnl 2f* **33/1**	
9	½	**Bendzoldan (IRE)**[13] 4382 4 -8-4**77** oh1..................(p) NGMcCullagh 5	60
		(Mrs John Harrington, Ire) *led early: racd in 2nd tl appr home turn: wknd* **8/1**	
10	2	**Footprint (IRE)**[16] 4278 5 -8-4**77**...(p) BenCurtis 7	55
		(Patrick Martin, Ire) *hld up in rr: nvr a threat* **8/1**	
11	½	**Bubbly Bellini (IRE)**[13] 4380 5 -8-10**86**..................(p) IJBrennan(3) 4	62
		(Adrian McGuinness, Ire) *trckd ldrs tl no imp ent fnl 2f: wknd* **9/1**	
12	1¼	**Flameoftheforest (IRE)**[35] 3648 5 -8-9**82**...................(p) ChrisHayes 3	55
		(Ed de Giles) *mostly mid-div: no imp appr home turn: eased* **9/2**[1]	
13	4¾	**Vale Of Clara (IRE)**[10] 4481 4 -8-13**86**.......................... WayneLordan 1	46
		(Edward Lynam, Ire) *hld up in rr: nvr a threat* **14/1**	

1m 28.9s (-2.70)
WFA 3 from 4yo+ 6lb **13**Ran SP%**136.9**
CSF £116.68 CT £1389.41 TOTE £6.00 : £2.30 , £5.50 , £4.20 ; DF 151.10 .
Owner Michael Beaumont **Bred** Dulverton Equine **Trained** Hambleton, N Yorks

FOCUS
One could say that Pintura deserved this having gone so close in the Topaz Mile earlier in the week. It just seemed a pity he had to do it at the expense of the consistent but luckless Battleoftheboyne and his equally luckless trainer Mick Mulvany. The level is set by the third and fourth.

NOTEBOOK
Pintura was always travelling best and went to the front turning into the straight which, as it turned out, was probably way too soon. There was a probably a mixture of idling and tiredness in the closing stages and in the end the winning post came just in time. He's a classy horse on this sort of ground and travels very well, but what this showed is that getting there too soon is probably not ideal. (op 9/2)
Battleoftheboyne(IRE) had spent the season running over sprint trips in a busy enough campaign, but he saw this out really well. He raced a bit keenly while being held up and started to make up his ground turning into the straight on the outside. Despite a slightly high head-carriage he sustained his run all the way to the line and was unfortunate not to get up. Both him and his trainer deserve a huge turnaround in the luck department. (op 20/1 tchd 22/1)
Sean Og Coulston (IRE)was held up in mid-division and stayed on to reasonable effect without threatening. (op 14/1 tchd 16/1)
Northern Rocked (IRE)took advantage of his good draw by jumping out and racing as close to the pace as possible. In the end he was one-paced in the straight and this might be as good as he is at the present time. (op 11/2)
Custom Cut (IRE)was ridden very positively, although he did race fairly keenly in front. He had little left when challenged and headed before the straight. His rider did well to get him across from his wide draw but he may well be too high in the handicap now and it can't be too long before they try him in stakes company. (op 7/1 tchd 8/1)
Bubbly Bellini (IRE) Official explanation: jockey said gelding stumbled on road crossing shorly after start.
Flameoftheforest(IRE) travelled behind the leaders for the first half of the race and appeared to have a wall of horses in front of him approaching the straight but he never really looked like threatening. (op 11/2)

4076 CHESTER (L-H)

Sunday, August 5

OFFICIAL GOING: Good to firm (good in places; 8.0) (racing abandoned after race 3 (3:05) due to a waterlogged track)
Wind: Light, half-against Weather: Sunny intervals, changing to torrential rain (3:30)

4836 LIVERPOOL ONE NURSERY — 6f 18y

2:00 (2:00) (Class 4) (0-85,85) 2-Y-0 **£4,851** (£1,443; £721 ; £360) **Stalls** Low

Form				RPR
3321	1		**Dream Maker (IRE)**[2] 4752 2 -8-9**73** 6ex................. RichardKingscote 3	84+
			(Tom Dascombe) *trckd ldrs: led over 1f out: r.o wl to draw clr fnl 100yds* **9/4**[1]	
3234	2	3¼	**The Sixties**[10] 4487 2 -9-0**78**...............................(v[1]) SamHitchcott 4	79
			(Mick Channon) *w ldr: led over 2f out: rdn and hdd over 1f out: outpcd by wnr fnl 100yds* **11/2**[3]	
0630	3	1¼	**Sylvia Pankhurst (IRE)**[9] 4574 2 -8-4**68**........................ FrannyNorton 2	65
			(David C Griffiths) *trckd ldrs: effrt over 1f out: kpt on same pce ins fnl f and no real imp* **8/1**	
204	4	1¼	**Starlight Angel (IRE)**[18] 4220 2 -8-2**71**.......................... DarrenEgan(5) 7	64
			(Ronald Harris) *s.i.s: in rr: stmbld 2f out: effrt over 1f out: hung lft ins fnl f: one pce* **16/1**	
2105	5	1	**Polski Max**[22] 4116 2 -9-4**85**... LeeTopliss(3) 6	75
			(Richard Fahey) *in tch on outer: clsd 3f out: sn hung rt: rdn and nt qckn over 1f out: wknd fnl 100yds* **4/1**[2]	
0021	6	3¾	**Penny Garcia**[27] 3909 2 -8-7**71**.. DavidAllan 5	50
			(Tim Easterby) *in rr: pushed along after 2f: outpcd over 1f out: nvr a threat: eased whn wl btn ins fnl f* **4/1**[2]	
0250	7	3	**Blue Clumber**[9] 4546 2 -8-13**77**................................... GrahamGibbons 1	47
			(Shaun Harris) *led: hdd over 2f out: wknd over 1f out: eased whn wl btn ins fnl f* **11/1**	

1m 15.82s (2.02)**Going Correction** +0.25s/f (Good) **7**Ran SP%**111.5**
Speed ratings (Par 96): **96,91,90,88,87 82,78**
toteswingers: 1&2 £2.20, 2&3 £7.50, 1&3 £4.20 CSF £14.16 TOTE £3.10 : £2.70 , £3.60 ; EX 9.60 .
Owner Hot To Trot Racing Club 3 **Bred** D G Iceton **Trained** Malpas, Cheshire

FOCUS
Rail moved out 3-6yds adding 37yds to all three races. There was 4mm of rain the previous day and the ground was given as good to firm, good in places (GoingStick 8.0). The early pace wasn't hectic here and it paid to race fairly handily; that said the form looks sound.

NOTEBOOK
Dream Maker (IRE)defied a penalty for winning at Bath two days earlier with a degree of ease. Travelling well tracking the pace, she quickened up well at the top of the straight and only had to be kept up to her work to score. The step up in trip of late has suited her and she has more to offer. (op 2-1)
The Sixties, who was visored for the first time, was free to post. Disputing the lead most of the way, he still had his chance turning in, but the winner just had too much in hand at these weights. He's a good guide to the level of the form. (op 6-1)
Sylvia Pankhurst (IRE) not for the first time, was keeping on when it was all over. A stronger gallop would probably have suited her. Official explanation: jockey said that the filly slipped turning in (tchd 17-2)
Starlight Angel (IRE)was another who could have done with them going quicker up front through the early part of the race, as she was slowly away. She also stumbled at the top of the straight, which didn't help. Official explanation: jockey said that the filly stumbled on the final bend (op 10-1)
Polski Max was caught wide throughout and didn't handle the bend into the straight at all. He can be given another chance back on a more conventional course. Official explanation: that the colt hung right throughout (op 5-1)
Penny Garcia was never travelling and perhaps needs easier ground than this. (op 5-1)

4837 M&S BANK EBF MAIDEN STKS — 7f 2y

2:30 (2:30) (Class 4) 2-Y-O **£4,851** (£1,443; £721 ; £360) **Stalls** Low

Form				RPR
242	1		**Black Monk (IRE)**[10] 4502 2 -9-3**75**...................................... SeanLevey 9	77
			(Richard Hannon) *mde all: moved across to ins rail after 1f: a gng strly: 2l clr 2f out: rdn ins fnl f: hld on wl towards fin* **5/2**[1]	
	2	nk	**Romantic Settings** 2 -8-12**0**.. PaulHanagan 8	71+
			(Richard Fahey) *s.i.s: hld up: hdwy over 1f out: r.o to take 2nd ins fnl f: clsd on wnr towards fin: promising* **9/1**	
6	3	2¼	**Signature Dish (IRE)**[39] 3505 2 -8-12**0**........................ JimmyFortune 7	65
			(Andrew Balding) *hld up: pushed along and hdwy 2f out: sn chsd ldrs on inner: styd on ins fnl f: outpcd and no imp on front two fnl 100yds* **5/1**[3]	
06	4	2	**Sennockian Star**[13] 4387 2 -9-3**0**...................................... JoeFanning 6	67+
			(Mark Johnston) *midfield: niggled along 4f out: nt clr run over 1f out: kpt on ins fnl f: nvr able to chal* **16/1**	
3	5	1¼	**Arlecchino (IRE)**[15] 4327 2 -9-3**0**................................... PaulMulrennan 3	62+
			(Ed McMahon) *in tch: pushed along over 4f out: chsd ldrs over 1f out: no ex fnl 100yds* **3/1**[2]	
2043	6	½	**Ouzinkie (IRE)**[8] 4587 2 -9-3**72**.. SamHitchcott 2	61
			(Mick Channon) *racd keenly: chsd ldrs: wnt 2nd over 3f out: no imp 2f out: lost 2nd and no ex ins fnl f* **10/1**	
	7	5	**Moorway (IRE)** 2 -9-3**0**.. GrahamGibbons 4	48+
			(Reg Hollinshead) *sn pushed along and a bhd* **33/1**	
62	8	3¼	**Zain Spirit (USA)**[13] 4404 2 -9-3**0**..................................... FrannyNorton 5	39
			(Gerard Butler) *midfield: hdwy 3f out: rdn and nt qckning whn hmpd 1f out: sn dropped away* **8/1**	
05	9	7	**Jawinski (IRE)**[19] 4194 2 -9-3**0**................................ SilvestreDeSousa 1	21
			(David Evans) *chsd wnr tl over 3f out: wknd over 2f out* **16/1**	

1m 28.79s (2.29)**Going Correction** +0.25s/f (Good) **9**Ran SP%**115.1**
Speed ratings (Par 96): **96,95,93,90,89 88,83,79,71**
toteswingers:1&2 £3.30, 2&3 £5.00, 1&3 £4.10 CSF £25.81 TOTE £4.10 : £1.10 , £2.80 , £2.40 ; EX 18.10 .
Owner Justin Dowley & Michael Pescod **Bred** Yeomanstown Stud **Trained** East Everleigh, Wilts

FOCUS
This maiden was won at the start and the winner sets the level.

NOTEBOOK
Black Monk(IRE) bounced out of the gates and was able to cross over from stall nine to make the running on the rail. Having got there he was able to steady things up before kicking again turning into the straight, and while things got a bit desperate close home as he tired and the runner-up closed him down, it was a well-earned victory. He had been a beaten favourite in each of his previous three starts, but this extra furlong suited him and there might be more to come in nurseries. (op 3-1)
Romantic Settings, a half-sister to 5f 2-y-o Listed winner Miss Work Of Art, was out the back for most of the way and had plenty of work to do turning in, but she picked up strongly once in line for home and closed the winner right down. This was a promising debut and she should have little difficulty going one better. (op 8-1)
Signature Dish(IRE) got a nice run through on the inside in the straight and showed improvement from her debut at Salisbury. She'll be one for nurseries after one more run. (tchd 6-1)
Sennockian Star had his path blocked at the top of the straight and gave the impression he'd have finished closer with a clear run. He'll be interesting when he steps up to a mile. (op 12-1)
Arlecchino(IRE), who holds Group race entries and is bred to stay very well, never looked happy and might be more effective back on a more galloping track. (tchd 5-2)
Ouzinkie(IRE), the most exposed runner in the line-up, is likely to remain vulnerable. (tchd 9-1)
Moorway(IRE), who is out of a half-sister to Mia's Boy, is from a stable not known for its debutant winners. He trailed for most of the race but ought to come on for the experience. (op 25-1)

4838 M&S BANK QUEENSFERRY STKS (LISTED RACE) 6f 18y
3:05 (3:06) (Class 1) 3-Y-0+
£18,714 (£7,095; £3,550; £1,768; £887; £445) **Stalls** Low

Form RPR
0101 **1** **Van Ellis**[8] 4611 3-8-10 106 .... JoeFanning 9 109
(Mark Johnston) *hld up in midfield: hdwy 3f out: led over 1f out: r.o gamely ins fnl f: a doing enough towards fin* **2/1**[1]
5560 **2** *nk* **Night Carnation**[29] 3877 4-8-9 102 .... JimmyFortune 4 104
(Andrew Balding) *racd keenly: chsd ldrs: effrt over 1f out: hung lft ins fnl f: r.o: gng on at fin* **3/1**[2]
1244 **3** *hd* **Hitchens (IRE)**[71] 2513 7-9-7 112 .... SilvestreDeSousa 7 115
(David Barron) *chsd ldr after 1f: chalng whn stmbld 2f out: continued to chal ins fnl f: r.o u.p: jst hld at fin* **9/2**[3]
0054 **4** *½* **Inxile (IRE)**[29] 3860 7-9-0 107 ....(p) AdrianNicholls 8 106
(David Nicholls) *chsd ldrs: led after 100yds: rdn and hdd over 1f out: stl ev ch ins fnl f: kpt on same pce fnl strides* **14/1**
-206 **5** *1 ¼* **Ponty Acclaim (IRE)**[22] 4113 3-8-5 104 .... DuranFentiman 3 96
(Tim Easterby) *missed break: midfield: hdwy to chse ldrs 2f out: styd on ins fnl f: nt pce to chal* **8/1**
4041 **6** *2 ¼* **Pale Orchid (IRE)**[12] 4423 3-8-5 86 .... SeanLevey 11 89
(David Evans) *hld up in rr: rdn over 1f out: kpt on ins fnl f: nvr able to chal* **50/1**
460 **7** *hd* **Googlette (IRE)**[127] 1129 4-8-9 87 ....(e[1]) PaulHanagan 2 90
(Ed Vaughan) *broke wl: led early: chsd ldrs after: outpcd and lost pl over 2f out: no imp after* **12/1**
3114 **8** *1 ¼* **Bogini (IRE)**[14] 4380 3-8-5 88 ....(b) FrannyNorton 5 85
(M D O'Callaghan, Ire) *in rr: hdwy into midfield whn stmbld 2f out: sn lost pl: n.d after* **16/1**
3662 **9** *10* **Sugar Beet**[15] 4336 4-8-9 92 .... DarrenEgan 6 54
(Ronald Harris) *hld up: pushed along and outpcd 2f out: nvr a threat* **16/1**

1m 14.93s (1.13) **Going Correction** +0.475s/f (Yiel)
WFA 3 from 4yo+ 4lb 9 Ran SP% **115.7**
Speed ratings (Par 111): **111,110,110,109,108 105,104,103,89**
toteswingers:1&2 £2.50, 2&3 £3.40, 1&3 £2.70 CSF £7.96 TOTE £2.90: £1.10, £1.50, £1.40; EX 9.90.
Owner Sheikh Hamdan Bin Mohammed Al Maktoum **Bred** D A Yardy **Trained** Middleham Moor, N Yorks

FOCUS
A low draw has been a big advantage in this race over the years. The placed horses set the standard but the form is limited by the proximity of the sixth and seventh.

NOTEBOOK
Van Ellis deserves plenty of credit for overcoming being drawn out in stall nine and suffering a wide trip. Consequently he deserves rating better than the bare form suggests, and this progressive colt deserves to take his chance in Group company now. He should be able to make his presence felt. (op 5-2)
Night Carnation was pretty keen early on and had her challenge delayed on the turn in as the winner denied her racing room, but she finished strongly down the outside in the straight. The trip isn't a problem for her over an easy 6f. (op 4-1)
Hitchens(IRE) stumbled on the turn in just as he was about to take the lead, which can't have helped. He wasn't beaten far and he'd have probably pushed Van Ellis even closer had that not happened. Official explanation: jockey said that the gelding slipped on the final bend (tchd 4-1)
Inxile(IRE) got to the front from stall eight and was able to dictate a pace to suit himself. He isn't as good as he once was, though, and just couldn't hold off the pack in the straight. (op 10-1)
Ponty Acclaim(IRE), who had a solid chance at the weights, kept on well enough from off the pace but couldn't really lay down a challenge to the first three. Perhaps had she settled better earlier on then she might have had more of a say in the finish.
Pale Orchid(IRE), who was dropped in from her poor draw, did best of those who looked to have it to do at the weights, although she was merely staying on past beaten horses at the finish. (op 33-1)
Googlette(IRE) had a good draw and showed some early pace. (op 16-1)
Bogini(IRE) raced keenly and stumbled on the turn in, but was ultimately outclassed. Official explanation: jockey said the filly slipped on the final bend (op 12-1)
Sugar Beet had plenty to prove at this level and being trapped wider than ideal throughout didn't help. (op 14-1)

4839 HALLIWELL JONES BMW MILE STKS (H'CAP) 7f 122y
() (Class 3) (0-95,) 3-Y-0+ £

4840 BRITISH STALLION STUDS SUPPORTING BRITISH RACING EBF CONDITIONS STKS (C&G) 6f 18y
() (Class 2) 2-Y-0 £

4841 NEW FASHIONED BANKING H'CAP 1m 4f 66y
() (Class 4) (0-85,) 3-Y-0+ £

4842 M&S BANK H'CAP 1m 2f 75y
() (Class 5) (0-75,) 3-Y-0 £

T/Plt: £3.00 to a £1 stake. Pool: £78,358.90 - 18,654.50 winning tickets T/Qpdt: £1.10 to a £1 stake. Pool: £5,462.45 - 4,166.05 winning tickets DO

[4090] NEWBURY (L-H)
Sunday, August 5

OFFICIAL GOING: Good to firm (good in places; 7.1)
Wind: Moderate across Weather: Sunny intervals

4843 MC SEAFOODS AMATEUR RIDERS' H'CAP (DIV I) 1m 2f 6y
1:40 (1:40) (Class 5) (0-70,70) 3-Y-0+ £2,183 (£677; £338; £169) **Stalls** Centre

Form RPR
0240 **1** **Hamilton Hill**[9] 4531 5-11-2 65 .... MissSBrotherton 11 75
(Dai Burchell) *chsd ldrs: t.k.h: led over 2f out: drvn out fnl f* **10/1**
2210 **2** *1 ½* **Tidal Run**[69] 2539 4-11-2 70 .... MissSMDoolan[(5)] 8 77
(Mick Channon) *chsd ldr: led 4f out: hdd over 2f out: styd on same pce u.p* **9/1**
0165 **3** *1 ¼* **Polar Auroras**[9] 4531 4-10-3 57 ....(t) MrCCarroll[(5)] 10 62
(Tony Carroll) *in rr: hdwy fr 4f out: drvn and styd on fr 2f out: hrd rdn to take 3rd fnl f: no imp on ldng duo* **16/1**
4630 **4** *2* **Merrjanah**[36] 3616 4-9-7 51 oh3 .... MrAFrench[(7)] 6 52
(John Wainwright) *wnt lft s: chsd ldrs: rdn over 2f out: styd on same pce* **25/1**
00-0 **5** *shd* **Tenessee**[35] 3659 5-11-4 67 .... MrSCrawford 7 67
(Jamie Osborne) *led to 4f out: styd chsng ldrs: lost 3rd and one pce fnl f* **12/1**
3-04 **6** *¾* **Danehill Dante (IRE)**[39] 3484 4-11-0 70 .... MrJoshuaNewman[(7)] 12 69
(Alan King) *in tch: rdn over 2f out: styd on fnl f: nvr gng pce to rch ldrs* **6/1**[3]
2421 **7** *½* **Cuckoo Rock (IRE)**[48] 3220 5-10-8 62 ....(p) MrJHarding[(5)] 3 60+
(Jonathan Portman) *in rr: pushed along and hdwy over 2f out: kpt on but nvr gng pce to rch ldrs* **4/1**[1]
5002 **8** *1 ¾* **Black Coffee**[19] 4183 7-10-10 62 ....(b) MissBeckyBrisbourne[(3)] 13 56
(Mark Brisbourne) *in rr: styd on fnl 2f: nvr a threat* **10/1**
-063 **9** *2 ½* **Gallego**[8] 4602 10-10-4 56 .... MrMPrice[(3)] 5 45
(Richard Price) *in rr tl styd on fr over 2f out: nvr a threat* **8/1**
3022 **10** *3 ½* **Entrance**[34] 3693 4-10-2 58 .... MrDeanSmith[(7)] 2 40
(Julia Feilden) *towards rr: mod prog whn bmpd appr fnl f* **11/2**[2]
4454 **11** *1 ½* **Mustajed**[52] 3073 11-10-0 54 ....(b) MrPMillman[(5)] 9 33
(Rod Millman) *chsd ldrs over 6f* **11/1**
006/ **12** *14* **Fool's Wildcat (USA)**[283] 7436 7-10-12 64 ....(tp) MissLAllan[(3)] 4 15
(Miss Louise Allan) *chsd ldrs 6f* **33/1**

2m 13.19s (4.39) **Going Correction** +0.20s/f (Good) 12 Ran SP% **117.7**
Speed ratings (Par 103): **90,88,87,86,86 85,85,83,81,78 77,66**
toteswingers: 1&2 £19.60, 2&3 £36.60, 1&3 £31.60 CSF £96.28 CT £1435.92 TOTE £10.30: £4.80, £1.70, £6.30; EX 130.60 TRIFECTA Not won..
Owner T G Price **Bred** Middleton Stud **Trained** Briery Hill, Blaenau Gwent

FOCUS
Rail realignment from 1m to 5f increased distances on Round course by 16m. As ever there was a varying degree of ability and experience amongst the amateur riders. It paid to be up with the pace and the runner-up sets the level.

4844 MC SEAFOODS AMATEUR RIDERS' H'CAP (DIV II) 1m 2f 6y
2:10 (2:10) (Class 5) (0-70,70) 3-Y-0+ £2,183 (£677; £338; £169) **Stalls** Centre

Form RPR
362 **1** **Laconicos (IRE)**[16] 4296 10-10-1 57 ....(t) MissCScott[(7)] 6 68
(William Stone) *in rr: hdwy over 2f out: styd on to chse ldr ins fnl f: kpt on wl to ld nr fin* **9/2**[1]
1210 **2** *¾* **The Ducking Stool**[17] 4251 5-10-8 62 .... MissSBirkett[(5)] 11 72
(Julia Feilden) *chsd ldrs: led 4f out: rdn and 4 l clr over 1f out: no ex and hdd nr fin* **5/1**[2]
0210 **3** *4 ½* **James Pollard (IRE)**[11] 4470 7-11-6 69 ....(t) MrSWalker 8 70
(Bernard Llewellyn) *chsd ldrs: wnt 2nd over 3f out: no imp and outpcd by ldr wl over 1f out: styd on same pce for 3rd fnl f* **9/2**[1]
0646 **4** *2 ¼* **Camrock Star (IRE)**[10] 4510 3-9-11 55 .... MrFWindsorClive 9 51
(David Evans) *chsd ldrs: rdn over 2f out: wknd ins fnl f* **12/1**
300- **5** *3* **Levantera (IRE)**[32] 7334 4-10-1 57 ....(t) MrJASavage[(7)] 3 47
(Jo Davis) *in rr: drvn and hdwy over 2f out: styd on fnl f but nvr a threat* **25/1**
520- **6** *1 ½* **Hernando Torres**[303] 6674 4-10-6 62 .... MissAHesketh[(7)] 13 49
(Michael Easterby) *s.i.s: in rr: styd on fnl 2f: nvr a threat* **15/2**[3]
666- **7** *nse* **Supa Seeker (USA)**[311] 6486 6-10-1 55 .... MrCCarroll[(5)] 2 42
(Tony Carroll) *in rr: styd on fr 2f out: nvr a threat* **14/1**
0400 **8** *6* **Quite A Catch (IRE)**[101] 1626 4-10-11 65 ....(v) MrJHarding[(5)] 4 40
(Jonathan Portman) *chsd ldrs: led briefly over 4f out: styd chsng ldrs tl wknd ins fnl 3f* **14/1**
3201 **9** *½* **Officer In Command (USA)**[15] 4333 6-11-0 66(p) MissSallyRandell[(3)] 7 40
(Paul Rich) *s.i.s: in rr: sme prog fnl 2f* **8/1**
0030 **10** *12* **Flag Of Glory**[19] 4179 5-10-6 62 .... MissMEdden[(7)] 5 12
(Peter Hiatt) *w ldr: chal over 4f out: wknd ins fnl 3f* **8/1**
020 **11** *1 ¾* **El Libertador (USA)**[10] 4504 6-10-0 52 ....(b) MrCMartin[(3)] 12
(Eric Wheeler) *a in rr* **14/1**
2/6- **12** *1 ¾* **Enchanting Smile (FR)**[509] 856 5-11-2 70 .... MrKevinJones[(5)] 1
(Mark Gillard) *led tl hdd appr fnl 4f: sn wknd* **50/1**

2m 13.39s (4.59) **Going Correction** +0.20s/f (Good)
WFA 3 from 4yo+ 9lb 12 Ran SP% **120.5**
Speed ratings (Par 103): **89,88,84,83,80 79,79,74,74,64 63,61**
toteswingers:1&2 £4.80, 2&3 £6.20, 1&3 £3.80 CSF £27.00 CT £109.51 TOTE £4.80: £1.90, £1.70, £1.40; EX 27.40 Trifecta £80.40 Pool £343.72 - 3.16 winning units..
Owner Miss Caroline Scott **Bred** Minch Bloodstock **Trained** West Wickham, Cambs

FOCUS
They went a more generous gallop in the second division of the amateur riders' handicap, however it still proved difficult to make up ground. The winner is rated to his best while the second continues to progress.

4845 ACADEMY INSURANCE IRISH EBF MAIDEN STKS (DIV I) 6f 8y
2:40 (2:42) (Class 4) 2-Y-0 £4,463 (£1,328; £663; £331) **Stalls** Centre

Form RPR
6 **1** **Derwent (USA)**[27] 3916 2-9-3 0 .... JamesDoyle 4 78+
(Roger Charlton) *mde virtually all but hrd pressed tl pushed along and asserted appr fnl f: won gng away fnl 120yds* **15/8**[1]
2 *2* **King Oliver** 2-9-3 0 .... RichardHughes 3 72+
(Richard Hannon) *hld up in tch: pushed along and hdwy fr 2f out: tk 2nd fnl 75yds but no ch w wnr* **9/2**[3]

0 **3** *nk* **Purcell (IRE)**[14] 4362 2-9-3 0 DavidProbert 11 71
(Andrew Balding) *pressed wnr: rdn and tk def 2nd fnl 120yds: no imp on wnr and one pce in to 3rd fnl 75yds* **11/4**[2]

4 *1 1/4* **Star Of Mayfair (USA)** 2-9-3 0 JimCrowley 8 68
(Alan Jarvis) *s.i.s: in rr: pushed along over 2f out: styd on wl clsng stages to take 4th last strides but nvr a threat to wnr* **20/1**

5 *nse* **Baltic Knight (IRE)** 2-9-3 0 PatDobbs 2 67+
(Richard Hannon) *chsd ldrs: rdn 2f out: styd on for 3rd ins fnl f: one pce fnl 75yds* **14/1**

6 *2 1/4* **Empowerment (IRE)** 2-9-3 0 DaneO'Neill 5 61+
(Richard Hannon) *in rr: pushed along 3f out: styd on fnl f: kpt on clsng stages* **14/1**

0 **7** *hd* **Overrider**[55] 2983 2-9-3 0 RobertWinston 9 60
(Charles Hills) *t.k.h: pressed ldrs and stl ev ch wl over 1f: wknd ins fnl f* **33/1**

50 **8** *1* **Hot Mustard**[9] 4539 2-9-3 0 HayleyTurner 12 57
(Michael Bell) *s.i.s: sn chsng ldrs: rdn and one pce fnl 2f* **14/1**

0 **9** *1* **Stormy Times (IRE)**[10] 4487 2-8-12 0 LukeMorris 10 49
(Mark Usher) *in rr: sn in tch: chsd ldrs 1/2-way: rdn 2f out: hung lft and wknd fnl f* **100/1**

0 **10** *6* **Run It Twice (IRE)**[81] 2164 2-9-3 0 KierenFallon 7 36
(Brian Meehan) *in rr: sn pushed along: a outpcd* **16/1**

0 **11** *hd* **Dawn Rock**[16] 4282 2-8-12 0 DarryllHolland 1 30
(Simon Dow) *chsd ldrs: wknd over 2f out* **100/1**

1m 16.12s (3.12) **Going Correction** +0.20s/f (Good) **11** Ran SP% **115.2**
Speed ratings (Par 96): **87,84,83,82,82 79,78,77,76,68 68**
toteswingers:1&2 £2.60, 2&3 £2.80, 1&3 £2.00 CSF £9.93 TOTE £2.30: £1.10, £1.70, £1.50; EX 10.10 Trifecta £28.40 Pool £711.61 - 18.51 winning units..
Owner K Abdulla **Bred** Juddmonte Farms Inc **Trained** Beckhampton, Wilts

FOCUS
The first division of the 6f 2-y-o maiden was run some 5.22secs above standard. It saw a substantial gamble on the winner. The form is fluid with the time modest.

NOTEBOOK
Derwent(USA) looked in trouble 2f out when he came under pressure with two rivals going better alongside him. He responded well, however, lengthening clear in the final 1f in the fashion of an above-average juvenile. Slowly away and green on debut, he'd clearly learned plenty and this half-brother to leading juvenile (for the same stable) and subsequent high-class older horse in the US, Three Valleys, can make up into a Pattern performer if he continues to improve. (op 7-4 tchd 9-4)
King Oliver, closely related to winning 2-y-o Wedding List, travelled well behind the leaders up to 2f out but was outpaced when the front three quickened. He ran on strongly when the penny dropped, not being given a hard time, and it will be a surprise if he doesn't go one better next time. (op 11-2)
Purcell(IRE) built on his debut with a much more professional performance without being any match for the winner. He can find a small maiden. (op 7-2 tchd 5-2)
Star Of Mayfair(USA) stayed on up the rail and being from the family of 1m US Grade 1 turf winner Never Return, will get further. (op 16-1 tchd 25-1)
Baltic Knight(IRE), the Hannon second string, shouldn't be forgotten having shown bright early speed. His dam was a dual 1m winner at two and there's plenty of class in the family. (tchd 12-1)
Hot Mustard couldn't sustain a mid-race move but has shown ability on all three starts. A half-brother to smart handicapper Horseradish (best with cut in the ground), he can make his mark in nurseries. (tchd 12-1, tchd 16-1 in a place)

4846 ACADEMY INSURANCE IRISH EBF MAIDEN STKS (DIV II) 6f 8y
3:15 (3:16) (Class 4) 2-Y-O **£4,463** (£1,328; £663; £331) **Stalls** Centre

Form RPR
30 **1** **Ceelo**[22] 4093 2-9-3 0 RichardHughes 3 79
(Richard Hannon) *mde all: pushed along and c clr fr 2f out: readily* **7/4**[1]

2 *2 1/4* **Grand Denial (IRE)** 2-9-3 0 AdamKirby 8 72+
(Clive Cox) *in tch: rdn over 2f out: sn swtchd rt: styd on wl fnl f to take 2nd clsng stages but no ch w wnr* **9/2**[3]

3 *1/2* **Lazarus Bell** 2-9-3 0 MartinDwyer 1 71+
(Brian Meehan) *sn chsng wnr towards centre of crse: rdn along 2f out: styd on fnl f but no imp: ct for 2nd clsng stages* **33/1**

0 **4** *1* **Lisa's Legacy**[36] 3638 2-9-3 0 DaneO'Neill 6 68
(Richard Hannon) *s.i.s: and bumper s: sn chsng ldrs: rdn 2f out: one pce ins fnl f* **20/1**

0 **5** *1 3/4* **Gracious George (IRE)**[23] 4056 2-9-3 0 EddieAhern 4 63
(Jimmy Fox) *chsd ldrs: disp 2nd 2f out: wknd ins fnl f* **14/1**

05 **6** *6* **Nine Iron (IRE)**[17] 4253 2-9-3 0 MatthewDavies 5 45
(Mick Channon) *chsd ldrs: rdn over 2f out: sn btn* **18/1**

7 *3 1/4* **Teolagi (IRE)** 2-9-3 0 DarryllHolland 7 35+
(J S Moore) *s.i.s and bmpd s: sn drvn along in rr: a outpcd* **16/1**

6 **8** *7* **Black Dave (IRE)**[74] 2384 2-9-3 0 JamesDoyle 9 14
(David Evans) *chsd ldrs tl rdn andbtn 2f out* **14/1**

9 *3/4* **Al Zein** 2-9-3 0 PatDobbs 10 12
(Richard Hannon) *spd over 3f* **9/1**

10 *3 1/2* **Red Invader (IRE)** 2-9-3 0 RobertWinston 11
(Charles Hills) *s.i.s: sn in tch: hung rt and wknd qckly 2f out* **4/1**[2]

1m 14.24s (1.24) **Going Correction** +0.20s/f (Good) **10** Ran SP% **116.7**
Speed ratings (Par 96): **99,96,95,94,91 83,79,70,69,64**
toteswingers:1&2 £2.60, 2&3 £33.50, 1&3 £11.20 CSF £9.42 TOTE £2.80: £1.20, £1.60, £5.60; EX 10.80 Trifecta £126.00 Pool £769.87 - 4.52 winning units..
Owner Andrew Tinkler **Bred** Colts Neck Stables Llc **Trained** East Everleigh, Wilts

FOCUS
They recorded a time 3.34secs above standard but it was still 1.88secs quicker than the first division. The winner is rated to his best and the first five were clear.

NOTEBOOK
Ceelo was sent off favourite on the back of finishing 16th in the Weatherbys Super Sprint (on heavy ground) here 22 days previously. Alertly away, he relished the fast ground, making all to win easily. By veteran leading fast-ground sprint sire Green Desert, out of an unraced sister to Breeders' Cup Turf winner Johar, he rates a stakes performer when getting similar ground conditions. (op 5-4)
Grand Denial(IRE), a 13,000euros yearling from the first crop of Thousand Words, made a taking debut. Settled in midfield, he had to be switched to start his run but came home with a wet sail. He displayed a high head carriage but if that was only down to greenness, he can also make up into a smart sort. (op 13-2)
Lazarus Bell, representing last year's winning stable, is the second foal of 1m4f winner Snake's Head. He shaped with plenty of encouragement, coming home strongly after initially being outpaced and, like most juveniles from this stable, will surely benefit from his debut.
Lisa's Legacy improved significantly on her debut when thrashed at Windsor. He'll be one for nurseries. (op 25-1)

Red Invader(IRE) was well backed but missed the break and, although he soon recovered, then hung and dropped away at the business end. Official explanation: jockey said that the colt hung right (op 13-2)

4847 GRUNDON RECYCLE NURSERY 7f (S)
3:50 (3:51) (Class 4) (0-85,80) 2-Y-O **£4,398** (£1,309; £654; £327) **Stalls** Centre

Form RPR
10 **1** **Pasaka Boy**[43] 3368 2-9-6 **79** MatthewDavies 4 90+
(Jonathan Portman) *trckd ldr 4f out: chal 3f out: led and c towards stands' side over 2f out: drvn over 1f out: forged clr fnl 120yds* **7/1**

616 **2** *4 1/2* **Front Page News**[9] 4526 2-9-1 **74** AndreaAtzeni 1 73
(Robert Eddery) *chsd ldrs: drvn and ev ch and c towards stands' side fr over 2f out: sn chsd wnr: outpcd fnl 120yds: hld on wl for 2nd nr fin* **7/2**[1]

210U **3** *shd* **Rated**[0] 4540 2-9-5 **78** MartinHarley 2 77
(Mick Channon) *stdd s: in rr: hdwy towards stands' side and n.m.r over 1f out: styd on to press for 2nd clsng stages but nvr any ch w wnr* **18/1**

5001 **4** *4* **Magic Channel (USA)**[9] 4540 2-8-7 **66** KieranO'Neill 5 55
(Richard Hannon) *led: c towards stands' side and hdd over 2f out: wknd fnl f* **7/2**[1]

052 **5** *3/4* **Poetic Verse**[43] 3387 2-7-13 **58** NickyMackay 7 45
(Rod Millman) *chsd ldrs: c sharply to stands' side over 2f out: one pce appr fnl f: styd on again cl home* **8/1**

022 **6** *1 1/4* **Ronaldinho (IRE)**[20] 4149 2-9-0 **73** RichardHughes 3 56
(Richard Hannon) *chsd ldrs: rdn over 2f out: wknd fnl f* **9/2**[2]

531 **7** *4* **Haatefina**[18] 4222 2-8-12 **71** DavidProbert 6 44
(Mark Usher) *in rr: styng on whn c to stands' side and hmpd 2f out: no ch after* **6/1**[3]

014 **8** *23* **Star Breaker**[30] 3823 2-9-7 **80** JamesDoyle 8
(Sylvester Kirk) *plld hrd: racd alone on stands' side after 2f: jnd and wknd over 2f out: eased whn no ch fnl f* **9/1**

1m 27.36s (1.66) **Going Correction** +0.20s/f (Good) **8** Ran SP% **115.8**
Speed ratings (Par 96): **98,92,92,88,87 85,81,55**
toteswingers:1&2 £6.20, 2&3 £9.20, 1&3 £9.80 CSF £32.15 CT £426.49 TOTE £9.30: £3.40, £1.50, £4.10; EX 38.40 TRIFECTA Not won..
Owner RWH Partnership **Bred** G Wickens And J Homan **Trained** Compton, Berks

FOCUS
An open-looking nursery which was turned into a procession. The form is rated at face value for now.

NOTEBOOK
Pasaka Boy, the first foal of the hardy multiple winning mare Shesha Bear (1m2f-1m4f), had been well-beaten in the Chesham Stakes at Royal Ascot after making a winning debut at Salisbury. Content to take a lead early, he burst clear over 1f out, leaving his rivals for dead. He'll be given a substantial rise but he seemed to relish the switch to fast ground and with scope for further improvement when he tackles 1m, he can win again. (op 10-1)
Front Page News had run creditably off a 2lb higher mark in an Ascot nursery nine days previously and looked likely to be suited by the step up to 7f. He travelled well but was left floundering by the winner and looks to be on about the right mark. (op 4-1 tchd 9-2)
Rated, having his seventh start, gave himself no chance of adding to his two wins racing far too freely throughout the early stages. He seems to have his quirks (ducked right unseating his rider at Newmarket last time out) but isn't short of ability and it's to his credit that he had the energy to come home strongly. (op 20-1 tchd 16-1)
Magic Channel(USA) didn't come close to following up his last-time-out win at Newmarket off a 4lb higher mark and it doesn't say much for that form. (op 9-2)
Haatefina Official explanation: jockey said hte filly been struck into left hind
Star Breaker tried to charter a lone path up the stands' rail but was beaten over 2f out and is going the wrong way. (op 10-1 tchd 8-1)

4848 BRITISH STALLION STUDS EBF CHALICE STKS (LISTED RACE) (F&M) 1m 4f 5y
4:20 (4:22) (Class 1) 3-Y-O+
£18,714 (£7,095; £3,550; £1,768; £887; £445) **Stalls** Centre

Form RPR
0-13 **1** **Ambivalent (IRE)**[15] 4338 3-8-6 94 AndreaAtzeni 5 106+
(Roger Varian) *hld up in rr: stdy hdwy fr 3f out: trckd ldr wl over 1f out: led ins fnl f: readily* **9/2**

6213 **2** *1 1/2* **Set To Music (IRE)**[29] 3856 4-9-6 105 HayleyTurner 7 107
(Michael Bell) *trckd ldrs: wnt 2nd over 4f out: led over 2f out: rdn over 1f out: hdd ins fnl f: sn outpcd* **2/1**[1]

0-11 **3** *4 1/2* **Khione**[40] 3476 3-8-6 90 KierenFallon 4 97
(Luca Cumani) *s.i.s: in rr: rdn over 4f out: hdwy and chsd ldrs fr over 2f out: styd on same pce over 1f out: sn fnd no ex* **3/1**[2]

0-33 **4** *shd* **Albamara**[17] 4261 3-8-6 89 LukeMorris 8 97
(Sir Mark Prescott Bt) *chsd ldr: led 5f out: rdn and hdd over 2f out: outpcd over 1f out* **7/2**[3]

4124 **5** *2 3/4* **Naseem Alyasmeen (IRE)**[17] 4261 3-8-6 96 MartinHarley 2 92
(Mick Channon) *chsd ldrs: rdn 2f out: wknd appr fnl f* **16/1**

0046 **6** *3 1/4* **Qushchi**[15] 4338 4-9-3 90 TomQueally 3 87
(William Jarvis) *in tch: rdn 3f out: sn btn* **18/1**

66-5 **P** **Zafarana**[36] 3632 4-9-3 88 [1] EddieAhern 1
(Roger Varian) *led tl hdd & wknd rapidly 5f out: p.u 4f out: dismntd and collapsed ins fnl f* **40/1**

2m 34.96s (-0.54) **Going Correction** +0.20s/f (Good)
WFA 3 from 4yo+ 11lb **7** Ran SP% **112.3**
Speed ratings (Par 111): **109,108,105,104,103 100,**
toteswingers:1&2 £2.60, 2&3 £2.00, 1&3 £2.70 CSF £13.43 TOTE £6.20: £2.20, £1.80; EX 19.80 Trifecta £73.70 Pool £1,505.11 - 15.11 winning units..
Owner Abdullah Saeed Belhab **Bred** Darley **Trained** Newmarket, Suffolk

FOCUS
The field was made up of entirely three and 4-y-os in the feature Listed race on the card. A modest early gallop resulted in a time 4.16secs over standard. The form makes sense rated through the second and fourth.

NOTEBOOK
Ambivalent(IRE) was backed off the boards when making a successful winning reappearance in a Nottingham handicap off 72. Her only subsequent run was when third in a Listed contest at Newmarket 15 days previously in which she was sent off favourite despite having plenty to find on ratings, so it is clear the regard connections hold her in. Settled in midfield here, she had to be niggled along to stay in contention 4f out but it was clear 2f out that she was going to take a hand in the finish. She took a while to master Set To Music but forged clear in the final 1f, wandering once hitting the front. She still has plenty of growing up to do, but it is clear she possesses a big engine. There are options for her at York and Doncaster in the near future. (op 13-2 tchd 7-1)
Set To Music(IRE) had to be withdrawn from her recent engagement at Newmarket having spread a plate but had previously won the Warwickshire Oaks and not been discredited in the Lancashire Oaks. Carrying a 3lb penalty for the former win and giving away 11lb weight-for-age to the winner, she ran another good race but is a galloper rather than a quickener. She seems to have found her level even if an end-to-end gallop would see her right at her best. (op 7-4 tchd 13-8)
Khione was last seen winning a handicap over 2f shorter here at the end of June. She could only plug on at the one pace but did gain some valuable black type. (op 11-4 tchd 10-3)

Albamara travelled strongly close to the pace to 2f out but seemed to be found out for stamina. (op 9-2)

4849 BATHWICK TYRES H'CAP — 5f 34y
4:55 (4:56) (Class 4) (0-85,84) 3-Y-O+ £5,175 (£1,540; £769 ; £384 Stalls Centre

Form RPR

03 **1** **Rowe Park**[9] 4530 9 -9-8[81] (p) SaleemGolam 7 89
(Linda Jewell) *chsd ldrs: rdn to ld 1f out: hld on wl u.p thrght fnl f* **15/2**

-000 **2** *hd* **Invincible Lad (IRE)**[7] 4690 8 -9-0[73] (p) LukeMorris 6 80
(Milton Bradley) *s.i.s: sn in tch: hdwy 2f out: str chal fr over 1f out: kpt pressing wnr u.p fnl f: no ex last strides* **16/1**

1524 **3** *nk* **Howyadoingnotsobad (IRE)**[36] 3618 4 -8-11[73] HarryBentley(3) 4 79
(Karen George) *trckd ldr: drvn to chal over 1f out: styd on strly fnl 120yds: no ex last strides* **9/2**[3]

-031 **4** *1/2* **Rebecca Romero**[17] 4231 5 -9-0[73] RichardHughes 2 77
(Denis Coakley) *hld up in rr stdy hdwy over 1f out: qcknd: nt clr run and swtchd lft fnl 120yds: fin wl: nt quite pce to chal* **4/1**[2]

3566 **5** *2 1/4* **Style And Panache (IRE)**[4] 4743 4 -8-8[67] oh1 ow1...(v[1]) ShaneKelly 8 63
(David Evans) *sn led: rdn: hung rt and hdd 1f out: sn btn* **9/1**

-004 **6** *nse* **Berberana (IRE)**[12] 4423 4 -9-2[75] RenatoSouza 5 71
(Jeremy Gask) *in rr: hdwy over 1f out: styd on fnl f but nvr gng pce to chal* **50/1**

0362 **7** *1 1/2* **O'Gorman**[23] 4044 3 -9-7[83] DaneO'Neill 3 74+
(Gary Brown) *stdd s: in rr: drvn over 1f out: kpt on fnl f but n.d* **3/1**[1]

40 **8** *1* **Estonia**[15] 4337 5 -8-8[67] AndreaAtzeni 12 54
(Michael Squance) *s.i.s: in tch 1/2-way: styd on same pce fr over 1f out* **40/1**

531 **9** *1/2* **Best Be Careful (IRE)**[5] 4530 4 -8-12[76] RachealKneller(5) 9 61
(Mark Usher) *bmpd s: in rr: in tch 1/2-way rdn and one pce fr over 1f out* **15/2**

305 **10** *1 3/4* **Tyfos**[8] 4591 7 -9-8[81] TomMcLaughlin 11 60
(Brian Baugh) *chsd ldrs over 3f* **16/1**

0550 **11** *5* **Volcanic Dust (IRE)**[7] 4690 4 -9-2[75] CathyGannon 10 36
(Milton Bradley) *bmpd s: a outpcd* **22/1**

1m 2.35s (0.95) **Going Correction** +0.20s/f (Good)
WFA 3 from 4yo+ 3lb 11Ran SP% 117.2
Speed ratings (Par 105): **100,99,99,98,94 94,92,90,89,87 79**
toteswingers:1&2 £24.20, 2&3 £12.40, 1&3 £8.10 CSF £117.35 CT £605.85 TOTE £10.50 : £3.10, £4.90 , £1.70 ; EX 136.30 TRIFECTA Not won.
Owner Mrs Sue Ashdown **Bred** J Baker **Trained** Hollingbourne, Kent

FOCUS
A fair sprint handicap run a strong gallop thanks to the trailblazing Style And Panache. The third and fourth are rated pretty much to form.
Volcanic Dust (IRE) Official explanation: jockey said that the filly was slowly away

4850 AJC PREMIER FILLIES' H'CAP — 1m 2f 6y
5:25 (5:25) (Class 5) (0-75,74) 3-Y-O £2,911 (£866; £432 ; £216 Stalls Centre

Form RPR

0-65 **1** **Scarlet Belle**[35] 3671 3 -8-11[64] [1] HayleyTurner 3 70
(Marcus Tregoning) *trckd ldr: drvn 2f out: styd on wl throighout fnl f to ld fnl 75yds: kpt on strly* **12/1**

3422 **2** *nk* **La Pampita (IRE)**[26] 3946 3 -8-11[67] HarryBentley(3) 7 72
(William Knight) *led: hrd drvn fnl f: hdd and nt qckn fnl 75yds* **15/2**

-023 **3** *3/4* **Kittens**[10] 4486 3 -8-5[58] MartinDwyer 2 62
(William Muir) *in rr: hdwy fr 4f out: rdn: over 2f out: styd on u.p fnl f: fin wl to take 3rd clsng stages but no imp on ldng duo* **14/1**

-053 **4** *3/4* **Srinagar Girl**[15] 4335 3 -9-3[70] TomQueally 5 72
(Sir Henry Cecil) *t.k.h towards rr: hdwy over 2f out: effrt to take 3rd ins fnl f: no imp on ldrs and dropped to 4th clsng stages* **9/2**[3]

0051 **5** *nk* **Bountiful Girl**[7] 4623 3 -9-5[72] 6ex FrederikTylicki 4 73
(Richard Fahey) *chsd ldrs: rdn over 2f out: one pce in 3rd fnl f: dropped two pls clsng stages* **7/2**[2]

010 **6** *4* **Lashyn (USA)**[15] 4335 3 -9-7[74] RyanMoore 8 67
(Sir Michael Stoute) *in rr: plld to outer and drvn over 3f out: hung lft over 2f out and no ch w ldrs sn after* **11/2**

15 **7** *12* **Selfsame (USA)**[40] 3476 3 -9-7[74] JimCrowley 9 43
(Amanda Perrett) *in rr: hdwy towards outer 3f out: rdn and edgd lft 2f out: sn wknd: eased fnl f* **3/1**[1]

4660 **8** *12* **Excellent News (IRE)**[10] 4510 3 -8-2[55] oh2 MatthewChadwick 6
(J W Hills) *chsd ldrs: rdn 3f out: wknd ins fnl 3f: eased fnl f* **50/1**

3-10 **9** *37* **Lady Arabella (IRE)**[65] 2679 3 -9-1[68] JamesDoyle 1
(Alastair Lidderdale) *t.k.h and sn chsng ldrs: wknd 3f out: eased whn no ch* **25/1**

0506 **10** *1 3/4* **Poly Pomona**[10] 4486 3 -8-12[65] RichardHughes 10
(Richard Hannon) *chsd ldrs: wknd over 2f out: eased whn btn* **25/1**

2m 11.16s (2.36) **Going Correction** +0.20s/f (Good) 10Ran SP% 116.6
Speed ratings (Par 97): **98,97,97,96,96 93,83,73,44,42**
toteswingers:1&2 £15.50, 2&3 £4.80, 1&3 £18.00 CSF £96.76 CT £1282.23 TOTE £12.90 : £2.40, £3.30 , £3.10 ; EX 76.30 Trifecta £355.50 Pool £961.07 - 2.00 winning units.
Owner The FOPS **Bred** Mr & Mrs A E Pakenham **Trained** Lambourn, Berks

FOCUS
A competitive fillies' handicap for 3-y-os with plenty of big stables represented, but this is not form to get carried away with. The field were taken along by La Pampita at no more than an average gallop and not form to rate too positively.
T/Jkpt: Part won. £53,958.70 to a £1 stake. Pool: £75,998.30 - 0.50 winning tickets. T/Plt: £112.30 to a £1 stake. Pool: £80959.73 - 526.15 winning tickets T/Qpdt: £11.90 to a £1 stake. Pool: £5983.89 - 369.75 w. tickets ST 4851a - 4860a (Foreign Racing) See RI

4790 DEAUVILLE (R-H)
Sunday, August 5

OFFICIAL GOING: Turf: very soft; fibresand: standard

4861a PRIX MAURICE DE GHEEST (GROUP 1) (3YO+) (TURF) — 6f 110y (S)
2:40 (12:00) 3-Y-O+ £119,041 (£47,625; £23,812 ; £11,895 ; £5,958)

RPR

1 **Moonlight Cloud**[43] 3370 4 -8-13[0] ThierryJarnet 9 127
(F Head, France) *broke wl: settled 3rd towards outside: qcknd wl to take ld 250yds out: sn wnt clr: extended advantage w ev stride: easily* **4/5**[1]

2 *5* **Wizz Kid (IRE)**[47] 3238 4 -8-13[0] GeraldMosse 6 112
(Robert Collet, France) *racd towards rr of field: swtchd to outside of field over 2f out: qcknd wl: wnt 2nd 1f out: r.o wl: clr 2nd* **10/1**

3 *1 3/4* **The Cheka (IRE)**[22] 4100 6 -9-2[0] (b) OlivierPeslier 10 110
(Eve Johnson Houghton) *broke wl: sn led: hdd over 250yds out: styd on wl ins fnl f: fin 4th: plcd 3rd* **16/1**

4 *hd* **American Devil (FR)**[36] 3657 3 -8-11[0] RonanThomas 4 110
(J Van Handenhove, France) *racd towards rr: swtchd towards outside 1 1/2f out: qcknd wl ins fnl f to take 3rd fnl strides: fin 3rd: plcd 4th (interference to The Cheka)* **40/1**

5 *hd* **Restiadargent (FR)**[43] 3370 3 -8-8[0] MaximeGuyon 8 106
(H-A Pantall, France) *broke fast to r in 2nd under restraint: hrd rdn 1f out: styd on wl fnl f* **5/1**[2]

6 *nk* **Lockwood**[28] 3901 3 -8-11[0] Pierre-CharlesBoudot 3 108
(A Fabre, France) *racd towards rr: swtchd to stands' rail 2 1/2f out: r.o wl fnl f: nrest at fin* **6/1**[3]

7 *3/4* **Kerasona (FR)**[44] 3366 3 -8-8[0] Christophe-PatriceLemaire 2 103
(J-C Rouget, France) *broke wl: a.p: unable qck ins fnl f: styd on* **16/1**

8 *2* **Marchand D'Or (FR)**[28] 3901 9 -9-2[0] DavyBonilla 5 100
(M Delzangles, France) *broke fast: racd cl up bhd ldrs u.str restraint: nt qckn 1 1/2f out: styd on* **16/1**

9 *12* **Kendam (FR)**[36] 3657 3 -8-8[0] StephanePasquier 1 62
(H-A Pantall, France) *prom early: fdd fr 2f out* **33/1**

1m 15.5s (-1.70) **Going Correction** +0.20s/f (Good)
WFA 3 from 4yo+ 4lb 9Ran SP% 118.6
Speed ratings: **117,111,109,111,108 108,107,105,91**
WIN (incl. 1 euro stake): 1.70. PLACES: 1.10, 2.30, 2.40. DF: 8.00. SF: 10.00
Owner George Strawbridge **Bred** George Strawbridge **Trained** France

FOCUS
This looked an up-to-standard renewal of this, the only Group 1 run over this in-between trip, but it proved something of a procession. The winner had her ideal conditions and has been rated to a 5lb personal best.

NOTEBOOK
Moonlight Cloud took this race in emphatic style 12 months previously but was perhaps even more impressive this time. Settled early, she was sent on inside the last 400m and soon put daylight between herself and the rest. Narrowly beaten by the unbeaten Australian superstar Black Caviar in the Diamond Jubilee, the softer ground played to her strengths here and she will be difficult to beat if aimed at the Prix de la Foret, especially as she scored over the C&D of that race on her reappearance.
Wizz Kid (IRE) who finished ahead of today's winner in the British Champions Sprint at Ascot last season, when the latter was admittedly unlucky, came through from the rear to chase the winner unavailingly. She would have been a clear-cut winner without that filly and posted her best effort at the top level. Another crack at Ascot's big autumn sprint looks on the cards, but she might contest the Abbaye beforehand, as she did last season.
The Cheka (IRE) had first-time blinkers replacing the first-time visor he had worn when a good second in a heavy ground July Cup. He made the running and kept on well for pressure, helped by his stamina for further. He has done really well for connections this season and looks capable of running well in a race like the Betfred Sprint Cup at Haydock next month.
American Devil (FR) fourth in the Porte Malliot when last seen, was taking a step back up in grade and ran with credit, if no match for the first two. He is up to winning a Group 3 on this evidence.
Restiadargent(FR) was the disappointment of the race, having finished just behind today's winner when third in the Diamond Jubilee. Her pacemaker Kendam was unable to get to the front, which might not have helped, but she still got a lead into the race only to be unable to react when the winner went for home. The ground should not have been an issue.
Lockwood had Marchand D'Or in third when taking the Group 3 Ris-Oranges last time, and the pair did not run far off that form, although neither was able to make a significant impact.
Kerasona(FR) had a stiff task stepping up from Listed company and was not up to the challenge at this stage of her career.
Marchand D'Or (FR) a three-time winner of this race at his peak, is doing well to compete at this level at the age of nine.

2746 DUSSELDORF (R-H)
Sunday, August 5

OFFICIAL GOING: Turf: good

4862a HENKEL-PREIS DER DIANA - DEUTSCHES STUTEN-DERBY (GROUP 1) (3YO FILLIES) (TURF) — 1m 3f
4:00 (4:02) 3-Y-O £191,666 (£75,000; £37,500 ; £20,833 ; £8,333)

RPR

1 **Salomina (GER)**[31] 3802 3 -9-2[0] FilipMinarik 5 110+
(P Schiergen, Germany) *taken bk and hld up in tch on inner: rdn to improve over 2 1/2f out: str run on rail to ld over 1 1/2f out: stretched clr ins fnl f: comf* **12/5**[1]

2 *3 1/2* **Nymphea (IRE)**[50] 3 -9-2[0] ASuborics 4 104
(P Schiergen, Germany) *prom on inner: swtchd to outer and rdn to improve over 2 1/2f out: r.o to go 2nd jst ins fnl f: kpt on wout matching wnr cl home* **114/10**

3 *3/4* **Waldtraut (GER)**[21] 4129 3 -9-2[0] JBojko 10 102
(A Wohler, Germany) *restrained early and hld up in last pair on outer: rdn in last over 2 1/2f out: styd on strly u.p to go 3rd wl ins fnl f: nvr able to chal* **129/10**

4 *2* **Rock My Heart (GER)**[41] 2522 3 -9-2[0] TedDurcan 6 99
(W Hickst, Germany) *hld up towards rr on inner: rdn to improve over 2 1/2f out: kpt on one pce u.p ins fnl 1 1/2f: wnt 4th ins fnl 100yds* **53/1**

5 *3/4* **High Heat (IRE)**[50] 3 -9-2[0] KKerekes 11 97
(W Figge, Germany) *rrd s and slow to stride: dropped in and hld up in last on inner: rdn to improve 2f out: kpt on one pce on rail ins fnl 1 1/2f: dropped to 5th ins fnl 100yds* **55/1**

6 *1/2* **Wilddrossel (GER)**[31] 3802 3 -9-2[0] MickaelBarzalona 8 97
(Markus Klug, Germany) *hld up towards rr on outer: rdn to maintain position over 5f out: outpcd over 3f out: plugged on under heavy press to go 6th cl home* **67/10**

7 *1* **Imagery (GER)**[21] 4129 3 -9-2[0] ADeVries 1 95
(J Hirschberger, Germany) *led tl hdd after 3f: trckd ldr in 2nd: rdn to chal over 2 1/2f out: sn outpcd by eventual wnr: kpt on tl no ex ins fnl f: fdd and dropped to 7th cl home* **33/10**[2]

8 *1* **Monami (GER)**[31] 3802 3 -9-2[0] EPedroza 3 93
(A Wohler, Germany) *prom: rdn 3f out: outpcd over 1 1/2f out: plugged on ins fnl f* **41/10**[3]

9 *1* **Omana (FR)**[70] 2531 3 -9-2[0] FabriceVeron 2 91
(H-A Pantall, France) *prom early: taken bk and settled in midfield after 2f: rdn over 2 1/2f out: outpcd and btn over 1f out: plugged on ins fnl f* **26/1**

10 *2 1/2* **Sworn Sold (GER)**[50] 3 -9-2[0] APietsch 7 87
(W Hickst, Germany) *midfield: rdn and dropped towards rr over 4f out: outpcd over 2f out: plugged on: n.d* **22/5**

11 *1* **Samba Brazil (GER)**[21] 4129 3-9-2 0.......................... MircoDemuro 12 85
(A Wohler, Germany) *midfield on outer early: prog to ld after 3f: rdn and strly pressed over 2 1/2f out: hdd over 1 1/2f out: sn btn and wknd* **40/1**

12 *18* **All For You (GER)**[21] 4129 3-9-2 0................................ RobertHavlin 13 52
(P Harley, Germany) *stmbld s: drvn to get across fr wd draw: sn prom: rdn and lost pl over 2 1/2f out: in rr and btn 1 1/2f out: eased ins fnl f* **52/1**

13 *3/4* **Ilena (GER)**[31] 3802 3-9-2 0.......................... LennartHammer-Hansen 9 51
(Dr A Bolte, Germany) *midfield: swtchd to outer and rdn to try and improve over 2 1/2f out: outpcd and btn 1 1/2f out: fdd: eased and dropped to last ins fnl f* **65/1**

2m 15.73s (135.73) **13** Ran SP% **132.2**
WIN (incl. 10 euro stake): 34. PLACES: 17, 32, 20. SF: 377.
Owner Gestut Bona **Bred** Gestut Bona **Trained** Germany

FOCUS
The race has been rated around the placed horses.

NOTEBOOK
Salomina(GER), held up in mid-division, saved ground on the inside and quickened up well in the straight before drawing clear in the closing stages. She has been sold to the Australian Bloodstock syndicate, and is likely to be trained by Antony Freedman down the road, but may remain with her current trainer until the end of the season.

KLAMPENBORG
Sunday, August 5

OFFICIAL GOING: Turf: firm

4863a LANWADES STUD SCANDINAVIAN OPEN CHAMPIONSHIP (GROUP 3) (3YO+) (TURF) 1m 4f
3:05 (12:00) 3-Y-0+ £33,707 (£11,235; £5,617; £3,370; £2,247)

RPR

1 **Bank Of Burden (USA)**[29] 3886 5-9-4 0.............. Per-AndersGraberg 9 101
(Niels Petersen, Norway) *settled towards rr: hdwy to trck ldng gp 3 1/2f out: c wd into st: qcknd u.p to ld towards stands' rail appr fnl f: drvn clr: won easing down: wore flexible blinkers* **9/5**[2]

2 *4* **Touch Of Hawk (FR)**[29] 3886 6-9-2 0.............................. EspenSki 7 93
(Wido Neuroth, Norway) *racd in midfield: moved up to r 3rd 1/2-way: pressed ldr 2 1/2f out: rdn and sltly outpcd ins fnl 2f: raon on u.p to go 2nd again over 1f out: styd on: nt pce of wnr* **7/1**

3 *1 1/2* **Peas And Carrots (DEN)**[61] 2807 9-9-2 0...................... FJohansson 8 90
(Lennart Reuterskiold Jr, Sweden) *prom: midfield on outer 1/2-way: scrubbed along to hold pl whn pce qcknd 2 1/2f out: 7th and rdn towards outside 2f out: styd on u.p to go 3rd 150yds out: run flattened out and jst hld 3rd* **69/10**[3]

4 *hd* **Without Fear (FR)**[29] 3886 4-9-2 0........................ JacobJohansen 4 90
(Arnfinn Lund, Norway) *settled towards rr: next to last and hrd rdn 2f out: kpt on u.p fnl f: jst missed 3rd: looked ill at ease on firm grnd* **8/5**[1]

5 *1 1/2* **Inspired Cry (USA)**[357] 4-9-2 0.................................(b) ElioneChaves 10 87
(Lennart Reuterskiold Jr, Sweden) *hld up toward rr: last and rdn 2 1/2f out: hdwy on rail 2f out: plugged on fnl f: nt pce to chal* **29/1**

6 *1* **Sir Henry (DEN)**[364] 4842 5-9-2 0.............................. RafaelSchistl 5 86
(Soren Jensen, Denmark) *a.p: pushed along and led 2 1/2f out: sn hrd rdn: hdd appr fnl f: grad wknd* **81/10**

7 *3/4* **Alnitak (USA)**[29] 3886 11-9-2 0.............................. MartinRodriguez 2 85
(Bent Olsen, Denmark) *chsd ldrs: 4th and scrubbed along over 2 1/2f out: styd prom tl wknd u.p over 1f out* **211/10**

8 *3* **Master Kid (DEN)**[364] 4842 7-9-2 0................................ CarlosLopez 6 80
(Bent Olsen, Denmark) *racd in mid-div: rdn and no imp fr 2f out: sn btn* **46/1**

9 *1 1/2* **Weald**[29] 3886 7-9-2 0.. DannyPatil 3 77
(Hans-Inge Larsen, Sweden) *settled last: short-lived effrt on outside over 2f out: sn btn: nvr a factor* **30/1**

10 *2* **East Meets West (IRE)**[42] 3-8-5 0.........................(b) ManuelMartinez 1 74
(Bent Olsen, Denmark) *led: hdd 2 1/2f out: wknd qckly* **25/1**

2m 23.0s (143.00)
WFA 3 from 4yo+ 11lb **10** Ran SP% **127.4**
PARI-MUTUEL (all including 1krone stakes): WIN 2.87; PLACE 1.41, 3.01, 2.37; SF 22.39.
Owner Stall Trick Or Treat **Bred** Bjarne Minde **Trained** Norway

4618 CARLISLE (R-H)
Monday, August 6

OFFICIAL GOING: Soft
Inside rail from Old Stable Bend up straight moved out adding 3yds to races of 7f and beyond.
Wind: Fairly strong, half-against Weather: Overcast, raining

4864 CARLISLE-RACES.CO.UK CLAIMING STKS (PRO-AM LADY RIDERS' RACE) 1m 1f 61y
6:05 (6:05) (Class 6) 3-Y-0+ £1,704 (£503; £251) Stalls Low

Form RPR

4014 1 **Kay Gee Be (IRE)**[8] 4620 8-10-7 85........................... LucyAlexander 15 87
(Richard Fahey) *prom: rdn over 3f out: rallied to ld appr fnl f: rdn out* **4/1**[2]

0346 2 *1 1/2* **Moheebb (IRE)**[8] 4620 8-9-13 70..........................(be) MissSBrotherton 1 76
(Ruth Carr) *dwlt: hld up: stdy hdwy into midfield 1/2-way: effrt on outside over 2f out: chsd wnr ins fnl f: r.o* **5/1**[3]

4115 3 *2* **Just Lille (IRE)**[8] 4621 9-10-2 85.......................................(p) AmyRyan 6 75
(Ann Duffield) *led: rdn: edgd rt and hdd appr fnl f: kpt on same pce* **3/1**[1]

5012 4 *3* **Call Of Duty (IRE)**[3] 4768 7-10-3 66........................... MissECSayer 12 69
(Dianne Sayer) *dwlt: hld up: hdwy over 3f out: edgd rt over 1f out: kpt on fnl f: nvr able to chal* **12/1**

00-0 5 *1* **Desert Creek (IRE)**[33] 3749 6-10-5 73................. MrsAdeleMulrennan 8 69
(David Nicholls) *t.k.h: cl up: wnt 2nd over 3f out: rdn and effrt 2f out: lost 2nd and wknd ins fnl f* **66/1**

1132 6 *3 1/4* **Rub Of The Relic (IRE)**[18] 4251 7-9-12 67............(v) MissHDukes(5) 16 60
(Paul Midgley) *bhd on outside: drvn along over 4f out: kpt on fr 2f out: nvr able to chal* **25/1**

4050 7 *3/4* **Monthly Medal**[8] 4620 9-9-9 56..............................(t) MissSMDoolan(5) 7 55
(Wilf Storey) *midfield: drvn along over 4f out: rallied over 2f out: nvr able to chal* **66/1**

1630 8 *5* **Veiled Applause**[40] 3494 9-10-4 81.. JulieBurke 9 48
(John Quinn) *in tch: rdn and outpcd over 3f out: n.d after* **7/1**

5130 9 *3 1/2* **Moody Tunes**[16] 4317 9-10-0 72.............................. MissALMurphy(5) 4 41
(Tom Dascombe) *chsd ldr to over 3f out: sn rdn and wknd* **12/1**

1130 10 *shd* **Benandonner (USA)**[16] 4317 9-10-0 76.................. MissMBryant(5) 11 41
(Paddy Butler) *hld up: drvn along on outside over 4f out: nvr able to chal* **28/1**

1060 11 *1 3/4* **Bold Marc (IRE)**[21] 4141 10-10-0 70................................ MrsCBartley 14 32
(Mrs K Burke) *in tch on outside: rdn over 3f out: wknd over 1f out* **50/1**

-0 12 *1 3/4* **Dancing Paddy (IRE)**[8] 4622 4-10-0 0.......................... MissRSmith(5) 13 33
(Alan Swinbank) *bhd: struggling whn hung lft over 4f out: nvr on terms* **40/1**

-410 13 *2 1/2* **Oneofapear (IRE)**[44] 3380 6-10-5 83.............................. RachaelGreen 3 28
(Alan Swinbank) *in tch tl rdn and wknd over 3f out* **11/2**

530- 14 *2 1/2* **Fremen (USA)**[320] 6262 12-9-0 70.............................. MissNHayes(5) 5 16
(David Nicholls) *prom tl rdn and wknd 3f out* **50/1**

6/0 15 *23* **Masra**[114] 1385 9-9-13 0.. MissCWalton 10
(David Thompson) *s.i.s: bhd: struggling over 5f out: nvr on terms: t.o* **100/1**

2m 2.05s (4.45) **Going Correction** +0.625s/f (Yiel) **15** Ran SP% **122.6**
Speed ratings (Par 101): **105,103,101,99,98 95,94,90,87,87 85,84,81,79,59**
Tote Swingers 1&2 £4.90, 2&3 £5.00, 1&3 £4.80 CSF £23.41 TOTE £5.40: £1.80, £2.40, £2.30; EX 30.90.
Owner G H Leatham & M A Leatham **Bred** Pursuit Of Truth Syndicate **Trained** Musley Bank, N Yorks

FOCUS
The second time this special ladies' night has taken place, in which all of the riders are females. The ground was changed to Soft after 11mm of rain during the day, and with a crosswind in the straight but the winning rider reported the ground was "not that bad." This was a very decent claimer based on official ratings, considering the prizemoney on offer, with good portion of the field rated 70-85, and it was dominated by those at the head of the market. The form is pretty sound, rated around the second and the fourth.

4865 INTEGRAL UK H'CAP (PRO-AM LADY RIDERS' RACE) 5f 193y
6:35 (6:37) (Class 6) (0-60,60) 4-Y-0+ £1,704 (£503; £251) Stalls Low

Form RPR

4056 1 **Spread Boy (IRE)**[6] 4673 5-9-9 48.............................. MissJRRichards 5 56
(Alan Berry) *chsd ldrs: effrt over 1f out: led wl ins fnl f: r.o* **10/1**

3053 2 *shd* **Distant Sun (USA)**[14] 4392 8-10-2 55..............................(p) AmyRyan 4 63
(Linda Perratt) *prom: hdwy to ld wl over 1f out: hdd wl ins fnl f: r.o* **14/1**

0040 3 *3/4* **Loukoumi**[11] 4495 4-10-7 60...(b) MissJCoward 3 65+
(Tim Easterby) *checked s: sn bhd: gd hdwy over 1f out: styd on fnl f: nrst fin* **11/4**[1]

-354 4 *shd* **Bridge Valley**[18] 4262 5-9-4 48.......................(b) MissFrancesHarper(5) 17 53
(Jason Ward) *racd towards stands' rail thrght: a cl up: effrt over 1f out: hung rt ins fnl f: r.o* **14/1**

-032 5 *1 1/2* **Isle Of Ellis (IRE)**[44] 3406 5-9-4 48.............................(v) MissRSmith(5) 6 48
(Ron Barr) *midfield: effrt over 2f out: kpt on fnl f: nvr able to chal* **16/1**

0440 6 *1 1/4* **Foreign Rhythm (IRE)**[10] 4547 7-10-1 59......................... MissVBarr(5) 10 55
(Ron Barr) *towards rr tl hdwy over 1f out: nvr able to chal* **14/1**

00-0 7 *hd* **Ivestar (IRE)**[6] 4683 7-9-11 55.........................(v) MissJoannaMason(5) 11 51
(Michael Easterby) *s.i.s: bhd tl hdwy 2f out: kpt on fnl f: no imp* **25/1**

345- 8 *1/2* **Lady Platinum Club**[370] 4647 4-10-0 58........................ MissMKeegan(5) 7 52
(Geoffrey Oldroyd) *cl up: ev ch over 2f out to over 1f out: wknd ins fnl f* **33/1**

6504 9 *3/4* **Reason To Believe (IRE)**[17] 4315 4-10-0 58........(p) KatieDowson(5) 12 50
(Ben Haslam) *in tch on wd outside: rdn over 2f out: no imp over 1f out* **7/1**[2]

4260 10 *2 1/2* **Hambleton**[92] 1881 5-9-10 49.. MrsCBartley 2 33
(Bryan Smart) *cl up far side tl rdn and wknd over 1f out* **25/1**

0350 11 *1 1/4* **Blue Noodles**[5] 4717 6-9-3 47.................................(p) EvaMoscrop(5) 16 27
(John Wainwright) *midfield: rdn 2f out: sn outpcd* **12/1**

1050 12 *hd* **Avoncreek**[54] 3026 8-9-9 48.....................................(v) MissSBrotherton 13 27
(Brian Baugh) *bhd and outpcd: no imp fr over 2f out* **25/1**

0440 13 *1* **Olynard (IRE)**[5] 4708 6-9-13 52....................................... KellyHarrison 9 28
(Michael Mullineaux) *prom on outside: hung lft 1/2-way: wknd over 1f out* **8/1**[3]

0336 14 *1 1/2* **Red Scintilla**[13] 4438 5-9-2 46.............................(p) DanielleMooney(5) 8 17
(Nigel Tinkler) *chsd ldrs tl rdn and wknd over 1f out* **12/1**

0050 15 *2 1/4* **Guilded Warrior**[34] 3723 9-9-13 57...............................(e[1]) MissMBryant(5) 1 21
(Paddy Butler) *overall ldr far side to over 1f out: sn btn* **33/1**

0020 16 *7* **Face East (USA)**[2] 4807 4-9-9 48..................................(b) LucyAlexander 14
(Alan Berry) *towards rr: struggling over 2f out: sn btn* **22/1**

1m 18.91s (5.21) **Going Correction** +0.675s/f (Yiel) **16** Ran SP% **122.4**
Speed ratings (Par 101): **92,91,90,90,88 87,86,86,85,81 80,79,78,76,73 64**
Tote Swingers 1&2 £47.20, 2&3 £11.60, 1&3 £2.10 CSF £130.42 CT £406.52 TOTE £9.50: £2.50, £3.00, £1.02, £4.50; EX 228.50.
Owner Alan Berry **Bred** Barry Murphy **Trained** Cockerham, Lancs

FOCUS
A moderate sprint handicap. The field came centre to stands' side in the straight. The runner-up is rated to last year's best form.
Loukoumi ◆ Official explanation: jockey said that the filly stumbled at the start
Lady Platinum Club Official explanation: jockey said that the filly's saddle slipped

4866 BEADLE & HILL H'CAP (PRO-AM LADY RIDERS' RACE) 5f 193y
7:05 (7:06) (Class 5) (0-75,72) 4-Y-0+ £3,881 (£1,155; £577; £288) Stalls Low

Form RPR

-500 1 **Nasharra (IRE)**[8] 4624 4-10-4 69.......................................(p) AmyRyan 5 80
(Kevin Ryan) *cl up: led over 3f out: clr over 1f out: kpt on wl: unchal* **25/1**

5601 2 *4* **Two Turtle Doves (IRE)**[10] 4535 6-9-8 59...................... KellyHarrison 3 57
(Michael Mullineaux) *chsd ldrs: effrt and wnt 2nd over 1f out: kpt on fnl f: nt pce of wnr* **14/1**

4323 3 *5* **Needy McCredie**[3] 4784 6-9-11 62.................................... JulieBurke 11 44
(James Turner) *s.i.s: hld up: stdy hdwy over 2f out: rdn over 1f out: sn no imp* **15/8**[1]

-252 4 *2 1/2* **Bid For Gold**[17] 4315 8-9-7 63.............................. MissEmmaBedford(5) 4 37
(Jedd O'Keeffe) *hld up in tch: drvn and outpcd 1/2-way: no imp wl over 1f out* **9/1**

0300 5 *2 1/4* **Black Annis Bower**[14] 4400 4-9-7 63..........(p) MissJoannaMason(5) 10 30
(Michael Easterby) *bmpd s: hld up in tch: rdn and effrt over 2f out: outpcd wl over 1f out* **20/1**

3630 6 *nk* **Insolenceofoffice (IRE)**[27] 3943 4-9-7 58..............(v[1]) LucyAlexander 7 24
(Richard Ford) *t.k.h: trckd ldrs to 2f out: sn wknd* **20/1**

40-0 7 *1 1/2* **Tongalooma**[34] 3730 6-9-10 66..................... MissRebeccaSparkes(5) 8 27
(James Moffatt) *wnt lft: bmpd and nrly uns rdr s: led to over 3f out: wknd wl over 1f out* **14/1**

-014 **8** *9* **Sir Mozart (IRE)**[34] 3738 9-10-2 **72**........................ MissSMStack(5) 12
(Barney Curley) *hld up: c alone to stands' side over 3f out: nvr on terms* **7/1**[3]
2513 **9** *7* **Soopacal (IRE)**[3] 4769 7-9-5 **61** ow1........................ MissJLambert(5) 9 +
(Brian Ellison) *rdr v slow to remove blindfold and s.v.s: t.o thrght* **3/1**[2]
20-6 **10** *½* **Feel The Heat**[10] 4552 5-10-5 **70**..............................(p) MrsCBartley 1
(Bryan Smart) *fly j. s: in tch tl rdn and wknd over 2f out* **9/1**
1m 17.26s (3.56) **Going Correction** +0.675s/f (Yiel) **10** Ran SP% **119.0**
Speed ratings (Par 103): **103,97,91,87,84 84,82,70,60,60**
Tote Swingers 1&2 £18.40, 2&3 £2.90, 1&3 £31.00 CSF £332.13 CT £1004.86 TOTE £31.20: £7.20, £2.60, £1.10; EX 124.80.
Owner Mr & Mrs Julian And Rosie Richer **Bred** P McCutcheon **Trained** Hambleton, N Yorks
■ Stewards' Enquiry : Miss J Lambert #140 fine: slow to remove the blind fold
Miss S M Stack ten-day ban: running and riding (20, 23, 25, 30, 31 Aug, 3, 25, 4, 9, 15 Oct)
FOCUS
This modest sprint was run 1.61secs faster than the moderate preceding contest. The level is fluid with the runner-up the best guide.
Nasharra(IRE) Official explanation: trainer said, regarding the apparent improvement of form,that the gelding was better suited by being ridden more positively in this race
Sir Mozart(IRE) Official explanation: jockey said regarding the running and riding,that her instructions were to keep on the outside where they thought the better ground was, and to do her best. She added that she had given the gelding a flick down the shoulder approaching the final furlong but she felt that the gelding was unsuited by the soft ground; trainer stated that he had told Miss Stack to keep on the outside on the better ground and to do her best; and that the gelding is quirky and is inconsistent.
Feel The Heat Official explanation: jockey said that the gelding hung right handed throughout

4867 LLOYD MINI H'CAP (PRO-AM LADY RIDERS' RACE) 2m 1f 52y
7:35 (7:35) (Class 6) (0-65,65) 4-Y-0+ **£1,617** (£481; £240; £120) **Stalls** Low

Form RPR
3-03 **1** **Bandanaman (IRE)**[68] 2599 6-10-2 **60**........................[1] RachaelGreen 9 68
(Alan Swinbank) *hld up: stdy hdwy 1/2-way: effrt over 2f out: styd on to ld towards fin* **9/1**
-030 **2** *nk* **Cool Baranca (GER)**[6] 3307 6-9-3 **47**........................ MissECSayer 11 54
(Dianne Sayer) *hld up: stdy hdwy over 7f out: led over 3f out: rdn and clr over 1f out: kpt on: hdd towards fin* **7/1**[3]
-633 **3** *¾* **Shirls Son Sam**[44] 3402 4-9-5 **49**.............................. KellyHarrison 16 55
(Chris Fairhurst) *prom: effrt and rdn over 2f out: edgd rt and kpt on fnl f: hld cl home* **12/1**
0214 **4** *5* **Jan Smuts (IRE)**[9] 4590 4-9-8 **57**........................(tp) MissSMDoolan(5) 7 58
(Wilf Storey) *midfield: rdn and lost pl over 5f out: rallied on outside over 2f out: styd on fnl f: nvr able to chal* **7/1**[3]
3645 **5** *2 ¾* **Stags Leap (IRE)**[9] 4590 5-10-0 **63**.................... MissEButterworth(5) 1 61
(Dianne Sayer) *prom: effrt over 3f out: no ex over 1f out: btn ins fnl f* **16/1**
-404 **6** *1* **Hoar Frost**[5] 4712 7-9-2 **46** oh1..............................(p) GemmaTutty 6 43
(Karen Tutty) *hld up: rdn along over 5f out: kpt on fr 2f out: no imp* **33/1**
-306 **7** *8* **Ritsi**[25] 3988 9-8-11 **46** oh1..............................(t) MissNHayes(5) 15 34
(Marjorie Fife) *hld up: stdy hdwy on outside and in tch over 4f out: wknd 2f out* **20/1**
4032 **8** *5* **Terenzium (IRE)**[25] 3988 10-9-0 **49**........................(p) MissRSmith(5) 17 31
(Micky Hammond) *hld up: checked after 5f: rdn and effrt over 4f out: nvr able to chal* **6/1**[2]
0215 **9** *2 ¾* **Tarantella Lady**[25] 3988 4-10-5 **63**........................(v) MissSBrotherton 10 42
(George Moore) *midfield: rdn and outpcd over 5f out: n.d after* **4/1**[1]
343- **10** *6* **Soprano (GER)**[142] 7105 10-9-12 **61**........................ MrsLGoldie(5) 5 34
(Jim Goldie) *hld up: pushed along over 6f out: nvr able to chal* **9/1**
0-00 **11** *6* **Front Rank (IRE)**[6] 3519 12-8-11 **46** oh1..........(p) MissRobynGray(5) 14 12
(Dianne Sayer) *cl up: led after 6f to over 3f out: wknd over 2f out* **50/1**
1/40 **12** *15* **Silk Drum (IRE)**[72] 2474 7-10-2 **65**........................(tp) MissNSayer(5) 8 15
(Dianne Sayer) *t.k.h: cl up tl rdn and wknd fr 3f out* **14/1**
60-0 **13** *11* **Leaving Alone (USA)**[33] 3752 5-9-4 **48**........................(p) MissADeniel 3
(Edwin Tuer) *midfield: struggling over 4f out: sn btn* **33/1**
04/0 **14** *2 ¾* **Border Tale**[14] 3988 12-8-13 **48** ow2..........(v) MissRebeccaSparkes(5) 13
(James Moffatt) *led 6f: cl up tl rdn and wknd over 5f out* **28/1**
-000 **15** *21* **Rare Coincidence**[16] 4138 11-9-2 **46** oh1.................. MissJRRichards 4
(Alan Berry) *towards rr: struggling over 5f out: sn btn* **50/1**
0-55 **16** *100* **Manager Mick (IRE)**[67] 2635 4-9-2 **46** oh1........................ AmyRyan 12
(John Norton) *midfield: lost pl 1/2-way: sn lost tch: t.o* **16/1**
4m 8.57s (15.57) **Going Correction** +0.625s/f (Yiel) **16** Ran SP% **123.4**
Speed ratings (Par 101): **88,87,87,85,83 83,79,77,75,73 70,63,58,56,46**
Tote Swingers 1&2 £17.00, 2&3 £16.20, 1&3 £19.30 CSF £66.93 CT £774.84 TOTE £10.40: £2.30, £2.00, £3.30, £2.60; EX 52.30.
Owner Miss J S Peat **Bred** Carradale Ltd & T Stack **Trained** Melsonby, N Yorks
FOCUS
A moderate stayers' handicap and a stiff test in the conditions. The winner is rated to his handicap best with the second to her Flat form.
Manager Mick(IRE) Official explanation: jockey said that the gelding was unsuited by the soft ground

4868 EDINBURGH WOOLLEN MILL STKS (PROFESSIONAL LADY RIDERS' H'CAP) 7f 200y
8:05 (8:07) (Class 4) (0-85,85) 3-Y-0+ **£4,851** (£1,443; £721; £360) **Stalls** Low

Form RPR
5016 **1** **Lady Chaparral**[20] 4175 5-9-9 **80**........................ KirstyMilczarek 3 87
(Michael Dods) *chsd ldrs: effrt and rdn over 2f out: led over 1f out: drvn out fnl f* **7/4**[1]
0206 **2** *¾* **Hot Rod Mamma (IRE)**[39] 3522 5-9-9 **85**.................. LucyAlexander(5) 2 90
(Dianne Sayer) *s.i.s: hld up: hdwy and swtchd lft over 2f out: effrt over 1f out: chsd wnr ins fnl f: r.o* **12/1**
3500 **3** *½* **Triple Eight (IRE)**[14] 4396 4-8-2 **66** oh5....................(b) EvaMoscrop(7) 5 70
(Philip Kirby) *hld up in tch: drvn and outpcd over 3f out: rallied over 1f out: kpt on ins fnl f* **28/1**
6626 **4** *nk* **Blues Jazz**[29] 3890 6-9-1 **79**........................ LauraBarry(7) 7 82
(Ian Semple) *t.k.h: cl up: rdn over 3f out: edgd rt over 1f out: kpt on ins fnl f* **12/1**
4121 **5** *¾* **Cyflymder (IRE)**[3] 4769 6-9-5 **76** 6ex........................ KellyHarrison 8 78
(David C Griffiths) *t.k.h: led tl edgd lft and hdd over 1f out: kpt on same pce ins fnl f* **5/1**[2]
5030 **6** *2 ¼* **Icy Blue**[16] 4345 4-8-9 **66**.. AmyRyan 1 63
(Richard Whitaker) *hld up in tch: effrt and rdn over 2f out: no ex over 1f out* **11/2**[3]
1503 **7** *8* **Exclusive Dancer**[16] 4329 3-8-0 **67**........................ JulieBurke(3) 4 45
(George Moore) *t.k.h: cl up tl rdn and wknd wl over 1f out* **13/2**
0342 **8** *½* **I'm Super Too (IRE)**[18] 4260 5-9-1 **77**........................ RachaelGreen(5) 6 54
(Alan Swinbank) *in tch on outside: rdn over 2f out: wknd over 1f out* **11/2**[3]
1m 44.86s (4.86) **Going Correction** +0.625s/f (Yiel)
WFA 3 from 4yo+ 7lb **8** Ran SP% **116.0**
Speed ratings (Par 105): **100,99,98,98,97 95,87,86**
Tote Swingers 1&2 £11.20, 2&3 £12.00, 1&3 £12.70 CSF £25.58 CT £440.63 TOTE £2.20: £1.10, £3.20, £11.00; EX 29.50.
Owner Geoff & Sandra Turnbull **Bred** Geoff & Sandra Turnbull **Trained** Denton, Co Durham
■ Stewards' Enquiry : Kirsty Milczarek two-day ban: excesive use of the whip (Aug 20-21)
FOCUS
The only race on the night confined solely to professional riders and it produced a good finish. The winner and third are the best guides to the level.

4869 LIVE MUSIC AFTER RACING TONIGHT H'CAP (PRO-AM LADY RIDERS' RACE) 1m 3f 107y
8:35 (8:39) (Class 6) (0-60,58) 4-Y-0+ **£1,704** (£503; £251) **Stalls** High

Form RPR
033 **1** **Bavarian Nordic (USA)**[29] 3891 7-10-5 **56**........................(v) AmyRyan 9 65
(Richard Whitaker) *cl up: led over 5f out: rdn over 4f out: hrd pressed fr over 1f out: drvn and hld on wl fnl f* **7/2**[1]
2056 **2** *1 ¼* **Petrocelli**[9] 4594 5-9-8 **50**..............................(t) MissSMDoolan(5) 14 57
(Wilf Storey) *prom: effrt and ev ch 2f out: edgd lft ins fnl f: kpt on: hld nr fin* **16/1**
1200 **3** *8* **Politbureau**[20] 4179 5-10-4 **55**..............................(p) MissSBrotherton 13 49
(Michael Easterby) *midfield: effrt over 3f out: chsd clr ldng pair over 1f out: sn no imp* **5/1**[3]
0-2 **4** *hd* **Tropenfeuer (FR)**[87] 2033 5-9-8 **50**.............. MissRebeccaSparkes(5) 10 44
(James Moffatt) *bhd tl styd on fr 2f out: nvr able to chal* **12/1**
0-62 **5** *¾* **Haka Dancer (USA)**[16] 4350 9-9-11 **47** ow1................(p) MissHBethell 8 41
(Philip Kirby) *t.k.h: hld up in tch: outpcd over 3f out: rallied and edgd rt 2f out: one pce fnl f* **11/2**
400 **6** *2* **Goodlukin Lucy**[20] 4179 5-9-10 **47**.............................. MissECSayer 2 36
(Dianne Sayer) *dwlt: t.k.h: hld up: effrt over 3f out: no imp fr 2f out* **15/2**
1013 **7** *2 ¾* **Talk Of Saafend (IRE)**[3] 4766 7-10-1 **57**............... MissRobynGray(5) 7 42
(Dianne Sayer) *cl up: pushed along over 3f out: wknd over 1f out* **9/2**[2]
00/0 **8** *1 ½* **Solis (GER)**[5] 4179 9-9-5 **47**..............................(e) MissEButterworth(5) 12 30
(Dianne Sayer) *hld up: struggling on outside wl over 3f out: sn btn* **11/1**
-010 **9** *1 ¾* **Idealism**[42] 3440 5-9-7 **49**........................ MissRSmith(5) 6 29
(Micky Hammond) *plld hrd: in tch tl outpcd over 3f out: n.d after* **16/1**
00-0 **10** *19* **Grethel (IRE)**[16] 3988 8-9-3 **45**........................ MissVBarr(5) 5
(Alan Berry) *dwlt: bhd: drvn over 4f out: sn btn: t.o* **33/1**
0564 **11** *9* **Ferney Boy**[21] 4145 6-9-3 **45**........................ MissEStead(5) 4
(Chris Fairhurst) *plld hrd: hld up on ins: checked after 3f: struggling over 5f out: sn btn: t.o* **9/1**
0/00 **12** *20* **Isitcozimcool (IRE)**[14] 3577 7-9-8 **45**........................(tp) JulieBurke 3
(Barry Murtagh) *t.k.h: led to over 5f out: wknd over 3f out: eased whn no ch fr over 1f out: t.o* **25/1**
2m 34.73s (11.63) **Going Correction** +0.625s/f (Yiel) **12** Ran SP% **128.8**
Speed ratings (Par 101): **82,81,75,75,74 73,71,70,68,54 48,33**
Tote Swingers 1&2 £6.60, 2&3 £7.20, 1&3 £3.50 CSF £66.20 CT £260.74 TOTE £4.20: £2.10, £5.80, £2.70; EX 46.20.
Owner Six Iron Partnership **Bred** Gainsborough Farm Llc **Trained** Scarcroft, W Yorks
■ Stewards' Enquiry : Miss Robyn Gray two day ban: use of whip (20, 25 Aug)
FOCUS
Only two mattered in the closing stages of this handicap. The first two set the level of the form.
T/Jkpt: Not won. T/Plt: £73.40 to a £1 stake. Pool £64,514.96. 641.21 winning tickets. T/Qpdt: £35.80 to a £1 stake. Pool £5,909.40. 122.05 winning tickets. RY

3958 KEMPTON (A.W) (R-H)
Monday, August 6

OFFICIAL GOING: Standard to slow
Wind: Light, half-behind Weather: mainly overcast

4870 LADIES DAY AT KEMPTON 08.09.2012 APPRENTICE H'CAP 1m 3f (P)
2:30 (2:30) (Class 6) (0-60,60) 3-Y-0 **£1,617** (£481; £240; £120) **Stalls** Low

Form RPR
-062 **1** **Attraction Ticket**[13] 4440 3-9-6 **59**........................ DarrenEgan 11 68+
(David Simcock) *stdd s: hld up off the pce in last quartet: gd hdwy over 2f out: nt clr run and swtchd lft 2f out: led jst ins fnl f: edgd lft but r.o wl: readily* **2/1**[1]
-504 **2** *3 ¼* **Supreme Rock**[7] 4650 3-9-7 **60**..............................(p) NathanAlison 8 63
(Jim Boyle) *chsd ldrs: rdn to chse ldr over 2f out: swtchd rt wl over 1f out: drvn to ld ent fnl f: hdd jst ins fnl f: styd on same pce after* **7/1**[3]
0-00 **3** *2 ¾* **Simply**[19] 4212 3-9-4 **57**.............................. AmyScott 2 55
(Eve Johnson Houghton) *racd in midfield: rdn and effrt 2f out: drvn 2f out: no ch w ldrs but plugged on to go 3rd ins fnl f: eased towards fin* **10/1**
0060 **4** *1 ¼* **Imperial Ruby**[53] 3088 3-9-2 **58**........................(v[1]) ThomasBrown(3) 9 54
(Joseph Tuite) *led after 1f: drvn and hdd ent fnl f: sn wknd* **33/1**
0023 **5** *½* **Smart Affair**[20] 4193 3-8-8 **52**........................(v) RobertTart(5) 7 47
(Alan Bailey) *s.i.s: bhd: styd on past btn horses fr over 1f out: nvr trbld ldrs* **10/1**
-005 **6** *½* **Sweet Liberta (IRE)**[18] 4263 3-8-13 **57**........................ DanielMuscutt(5) 6 51
(Andrew Balding) *trckd ldrs: rdn and effrt to press ldrs 2f out: sn struggling u.p: wknd over 1f out* **8/1**
0005 **7** *¾* **Fuzzy Logic (IRE)**[9] 4586 3-9-5 **58**........................ MatthewLawson 13 51
(William Muir) *racd off the pce in midfield: effrt u.p and swtchd lft over 2f out: plugged on but no imp* **8/1**
0005 **8** *3 ¾* **Castalian Spring (IRE)**[16] 4333 3-8-0 **46** oh1..... GeorgeanBuckell(7) 12 32
(Terry Clement) *hld up off the pce in last quartet: wd bnd 4f out: hung rt and rdn wl over 2f out: no prog* **33/1**
0300 **9** *6* **Green Legacy (USA)**[40] 3483 3-9-2 **55**........................ BrendanPowell 4 30
(Amanda Perrett) *racd off the pce in last quartet and sn pushed along: lost tch over 2f out* **7/1**[3]
0000 **10** *½* **Roman Around**[20] 4198 3-8-7 **46** oh1..............................(v) DavidKenny 1 20
(William Knight) *t.k.h: led for 1f: chsd ldr tl over 2f out: sn wknd* **28/1**
-005 **11** *1 ½* **Caledonian Lad**[20] 4189 3-9-0 **53**..............................(b[1]) AshleyMorgan 3 25
(Hughie Morrison) *t.k.h: chsd ldrs: wkng qckly whn hmpd over 2f out: bhd over 1f out* **13/2**[2]
00-0 **12** *½* **The Ploughman**[25] 3998 3-8-2 **46** oh1........................ NoelGarbutt(5) 10 17
(John Bridger) *chsd ldrs and stuck wd: rdn and lost pl 4f out: bhd over 2f out* **66/1**
2m 25.0s (3.10) **Going Correction** +0.275s/f (Slow) **12** Ran SP% **122.9**
Speed ratings (Par 98): **99,96,94,93,93 93,92,89,85,85 83,83**
Tote Swingers 1&2 £3.20, 2&3 £13.00, 1&3 £5.90 CSF £16.36 CT £120.59 TOTE £3.10: £1.80, £3.30, £5.20; EX 19.50.

Owner Oliver Brendon **Bred** The Kathryn Stud Ltd **Trained** Newmarket, Suffolk
FOCUS
Since the last Kempton meeting, the existing surface had been ameliorated with 844 tonnes of slightly modified Polytrack which has a higher percentage fibre and wax content. This was to invigorate the existing material and, in comparison to all new AW surfaces, it's expected to take a few weeks to settle down. Race times showed the surface was riding slow. A moderate apprentice handicap, run at a steady pace. The placed horses help to set the standard.
Roman Around Official explanation: vet said that the filly had lost a left-hind shoe

4871 BETFAIR CLAIMING STKS 1m (P)
3:00 (3:00) (Class 6) 3-Y-O £1,617 (£481; £240; £120) **Stalls** Low

Form RPR
0066 **1** **Venetian View (IRE)**[28] 3917 3-9-7 80..........(b) GeorgeBaker 2 81
(Gary Moore) *in tch: pushed along over 4f out: styd towards inner st and rdn to ld jst over 1f out: styd on wl and wnt clr fnl f* **7/5**[1]
0005 **2** *5* **Chalk And Cheese (USA)**[7] 4644 3-8-13 72..........(t) WilliamCarson 1 62
(Stuart Williams) *w ldr: rdn and edgd lft over 2f out: no ch w wnr and one pce fnl f* **13/2**
5224 **3** *2 ½* **It's A Privilege**[30] 3846 3-8-12 70..........(p) JimCrowley 3 55
(Ralph Beckett) *led and racd off inner rail: rdn and edgd lft over 1f out: 3rd and wknd 1f out* **15/8**[2]
0500 **4** *3 ¼* **Silkee Supreme**[10] 4534 3-9-1 68.......... RichardHughes 6 51
(Richard Hannon) *chsd ldrs: rdn over 3f out: 4th and wl btn over 1f out: eased ins fnl f* **6/1**[3]
6350 **5** *6* **Nic Nok**[97] 1726 3-8-9 46..........(vt[1]) FergusSweeney 7 30
(Joseph Tuite) *stdd s: hld up in rr: effrt and wd bnd 3f out: wknd over 2f out* **25/1**
00 **6** *5* **Medeeba**[16] 4334 3-9-0 0.......... JamieGoldstein 4 24
(Zoe Davison) *chsd ldrs: rdn 5f out: dropped to last over 3f out: lost tch wl over 2f out* **100/1**
1m 42.77s (2.97) **Going Correction** +0.275s/f (Slow) **6** Ran SP% **108.9**
Speed ratings (Par 98): **96,91,88,85,79 74**
Tote Swingers 1&2 £2.40, 2&3 £2.50, 1&3 £1.20 CSF £10.40 TOTE £2.00: £2.10, £1.20; EX 11.30.
Owner R A Green **Bred** J F Tuthill **Trained** Lower Beeding, W Sussex
FOCUS
Only a couple could be seriously fancied for this 3-y-o claimer. The winner is rated close to this year's handicap form.

4872 JIMMY MILLER LIFETIME IN RACING H'CAP (LONDON MILE QUALIFIER) 1m (P)
3:30 (3:30) (Class 5) (0-70,69) 3-Y-O+ **£2,264** (£673; £336; £168) **Stalls** Low

Form RPR
2530 **1** **Junket**[21] 4150 5-10-0 **69**.......... SeanLevey 10 84
(Dr Jon Scargill) *in tch: clsd on ldrs over 3f out: rdn to chse ldr wl over 1f out: led 1f out: sn clr: r.o wl: readily* **11/2**[3]
0042 **2** *5* **Guest Book (IRE)**[54] 3039 5-9-8 **68**..........(v[1]) DavidKenny(5) 8 71
(Michael Scudamore) *s.i.s: sn rcvrd and in midfield: rdn and effrt over 2f out: 3rd and no imp 1f out: wnt 2nd towards fin* **5/1**[2]
0100 **3** *1* **Spirit Of Gondree (IRE)**[26] 3958 4-9-7 **62**..........(b) CathyGannon 13 63
(Milton Bradley) *led and set gd gallop: clr wl over 2f out: drvn over 1f out: hdd 1f out: sn btn: wknd and lost 2nd towards fin* **14/1**
6331 **4** *nk* **Paphos**[12] 4469 5-9-11 **69**..........(v) RyanClark(3) 7 69
(Stuart Williams) *s.i.s and sn rdn along: wl off the pce in last quartet: styd on u.p fr over 1f out: no ch w wnr* **7/1**
6142 **5** *1 ¼* **Mr Fickle (IRE)**[34] 3719 3-9-5 **67**..........(b[1]) GeorgeBaker 1 64
(Gary Moore) *racd wl off the pce towards rr: swtchd rt and hdwy 2f out: styng on whn nt clr run and swtchd lft ins fnl f: nvr trbld ldrs* **11/4**[1]
-000 **6** *hd* **Bassett Road (IRE)**[17] 4302 4-9-5 **60**.......... StevieDonohoe 3 57
(Willie Musson) *wl bhd: pushed along over 2f out: styd on fnl f: nvr trbld ldrs* **33/1**
2404 **7** *hd* **Dvinsky (USA)**[12] 4469 11-9-8 **63**..........(b) RichardHughes 11 59
(Paul Howling) *t.k.h: chsd ldrs: rdn 2f out: no ex and btn over 1f out: wknd fnl f* **33/1**
0446 **8** *1 ½* **Bold Ring**[12] 4469 6-8-9 **57**.......... JoeyHaynes(7) 9 50
(Eric Wheeler) *chsd ldrs: rdn over 2f out: btn over 1f out: fdd fnl f* **33/1**
0620 **9** *2* **Khazium (IRE)**[11] 4517 3-9-1 **68**..........(p[1]) DarrenEgan(5) 5 56
(Pat Eddery) *racd wl off the pce in last quartet: rdn over 2f out: no real imp* **16/1**
2540 **10** *1 ½* **Hawk Moth (IRE)**[21] 4155 4-9-12 **67**.......... ChrisCatlin 4 52
(John Spearing) *a wl off the pce in rr: rdn and no prog on outer over 2f out* **14/1**
400 **11** *nse* **Peponi**[49] 3226 6-10-0 **69**..........(b[1]) DarryllHolland 2 54
(Peter Makin) *hld up in midfield: rdn and effrt over 2f out: no hdwy and wknd 2f out* **9/1**
30 **12** *14* **El Dececy (USA)**[5] 4715 8-9-12 **67**..........(p[1]) AdamKirby 6 19
(John Butler) *sn rdn along to press ldr: rdn over 3f out: lost pl over 2f out: wl bhd and eased ins fnl f* **15/2**
1m 41.74s (1.94) **Going Correction** +0.275s/f (Slow)
WFA 3 from 4yo+ 7lb **12** Ran SP% **121.0**
Speed ratings (Par 103): **101,96,95,94,93 93,93,91,89,88 88,74**
Tote Swingers 1&2 £5.00, 2&3 £14.40, 1&3 £18.00 CSF £33.39 CT £365.24 TOTE £3.60: £1.10, £1.40, £6.10; EX 37.50.
Owner Silent Partners **Bred** Cheveley Park Stud Ltd **Trained** Newmarket, Suffolk
FOCUS
A fair handicap, run at a strong pace, with the runner-up to latest C&D form.

4873 BETFAIR SUPPORTING GRASSROOTS RACING MEDIAN AUCTION MAIDEN STKS 6f (P)
4:00 (4:00) (Class 5) 2-Y-O **£2,264** (£673; £336; £168) **Stalls** Low

Form RPR
1 **Haafaguinea** 2-9-3 0.......... AdamKirby 1 86+
(Clive Cox) *dwlt: in tch: swtchd rt and effrt to chse ldr over 1f out: clr w ldr fnl f: sustained effrt and r.o wl to ld last strides* **25/1**
524 **2** *hd* **Letstalkaboutmoney (IRE)**[16] 4318 2-9-3 87.......... MartinHarley 7 85
(Mrs K Burke) *chsd ldr tl lft in ld 3f out: rdn over 1f out: clr w wnr fnl f: drvn fnl 150yds: hdd and no ex last strides* **10/11**[1]
020 **3** *6* **Secret Symphony**[17] 4310 2-9-3 79..........(t) PatDobbs 3 67
(Sylvester Kirk) *chsd ldrs: pushed lft bnd 3f out: rallied and chsd ldrs u.p wl over 1f out: wl btn but plugged on to go 3rd fnl 100yds* **14/1**
4 *1* **Spanish Art** 2-9-3 0.......... RichardHughes 6 64+
(Richard Hannon) *stdd s: rn green and pushed along at times in last pair: swtchd rt and hdwy to chse ldrs 2f out: no ex and btn over 1f out* **11/4**[2]
6033 **5** *1 ¾* **Bentleysoysterboy (IRE)**[16] 4324 2-9-3 71..........(p) DaneO'Neill 5 59
(David Elsworth) *t.k.h: led tl hung lft and hdd bnd 3f out: lost pl and bhd whn rdn 2f out: sn outpcd and no ch 1f out* **11/1**
64 **6** *nk* **Pearl Bounty (IRE)**[11] 4502 2-9-3 0.......... JimmyFortune 2 58
(Andrew Balding) *chsd ldrs: lft pressing ldr: ev ch and rdn 2f out: fnd little and btn jst over 1f out: wknd fnl f* **10/1**[3]
7 *4 ½* **Whiskey N Stout (IRE)** 2-9-3 0.......... FergusSweeney 4 44
(Jamie Osborne) *s.i.s: rn green in rr: hdwy on outer whn hmpd and pushed wdr bnd 3f out: wknd over 2f out* **40/1**
1m 15.47s (2.37) **Going Correction** +0.275s/f (Slow) **7** Ran SP% **109.4**
Speed ratings (Par 94): **95,94,86,85,83 82,76**
Tote Swingers 1&2 £6.10, 2&3 £3.40, 1&3 £11.50 CSF £44.78 TOTE £26.20: £7.80, £1.10; EX 80.90.
Owner Exors Of The Late Dennis Shaw **Bred** Bishop Wilton Stud **Trained** Lambourn, Berks
FOCUS
An interesting juvenile maiden and a likeable performance from the winner. The placed horses set the level.
NOTEBOOK
Haafaguinea showed a tremendous attitude to edge out the heavily backed favourite. The previously unraced son of Haafhd was clearly expected to need this given his lengthy odds but, despite showing early signs of greenness, was soon on the bridle and responded well to pressure. He required every inch of the trip to get on top but is entitled to sharpen up for this and looks an exciting prospect. With a 79-rated rival a long way back in third, it's likely he'll have a mark in the high-80s to contend with in nurseries. (op 20-1)
Letstalkaboutmoney(IRE) ran a blinder and could be considered unfortunate having come up against a clearly above-average newcomer. Dropping back to 6f for the first time, he was all the rage in the market and looked like justifying that confidence until the final couple of strides. He was far from disgraced in Listed company behind the highly regarded Toronado at Ascot last time and will surely go one better before too long.
Secret Symphony had travelled as well as anything until the 2f marker but was made to look very one-paced. He kept on without being knocked around, but is likely to remain vulnerable in maiden company and has a high enough nursery mark. (op 16-1 tchd 12-1)
Spanish Art ran with encouragement and should be a lot wiser next time. (op 5-2 tchd 3-1)
Bentleysoysterboy(IRE) failed to handle the bend but was plugging on again at the finish. (op 8-1)

4874 BETFAIR.COM MEDIAN AUCTION MAIDEN STKS 7f (P)
4:30 (4:33) (Class 5) 3-4-Y-O **£2,264** (£673; £336; £168) **Stalls** Low

Form RPR
06-5 **1** **Kinglami**[34] 3732 3-9-0 62.......... AdamBeschizza(3) 2 75
(Brian Gubby) *mde all: rdn and fnd ex to go clr 2f out: kpt on wl* **9/1**
3403 **2** *1 ½* **Admiralty**[19] 4211 3-9-3 67.......... RoystonFfrench 3 71
(Ismail Mohammed) *chsd ldrs: effrt u.p to chse ldr over 1f out: kpt on u.p ins fnl f: nvr gng to rch wnr* **4/1**[3]
62 **3** *1 ¼* **Ginger Monkey (IRE)**[26] 3972 3-9-3 0.......... JimmyFortune 7 69
(Peter Chapple-Hyam) *hld up in midfield: effrt towards inner and rdn to chse ldng pair over 1f out: drvn and styd on same pce fnl f* **2/1**[2]
4532 **4** *10* **Gunner Will (IRE)**[9] 4582 3-9-3 72.......... RichardHughes 5 41
(Jamie Osborne) *chsd ldr: rdn and unable qck 2f out: edgd lft u.p and wknd over 1f out: eased towards fin* **11/8**[1]
5 *4 ½* **Elusive Pursuit** 4-9-4 0.......... AdamKirby 9 23
(Clive Cox) *s.i.s: rn green and sn pushed along in last pair: clsd and jst in tch whn edgd lft bnd 3f out: wknd and lost tch jst over 2f out* **25/1**
6 *8* **Leonards Pride (IRE)** 3-9-3 0.......... WilliamCarson 6
(Daniel Mark Loughnane) *v.s.a: styd wd: bhd: clsd and jst in tch whn pushed lft and wd bnd 3f out: sn lost tch* **50/1**
0 **U** **Cluaindubhloch (IRE)**[19] 4212 4-9-9 0.......... JimCrowley 8
(Tony Carroll) *veered bdly lft and uns rdr leaving stalls* **100/1**
P **Good Mind (IRE)** 3-8-12 0.......... DaneO'Neill 1
(Don Cantillon) *chsd ldrs tl lost action and eased over 2f out: p.u and dismntd 2f out: fatally injured* **15/2**
1m 27.83s (1.83) **Going Correction** +0.275s/f (Slow)
WFA 3 from 4yo 6lb **8** Ran SP% **124.0**
Speed ratings (Par 103): **100,98,96,85,80 71, ,**
Tote Swingers 1&2 £4.10, 2&3 £2.60, 1&3 £3.90 CSF £48.18 TOTE £12.50: £2.20, £1.60, £1.40; EX 62.10.
Owner Brian Gubby **Bred** Cheveley Park Stud Ltd **Trained** Bagshot, Surrey
FOCUS
A modest maiden and the form is fluid, with the third to his latest Lingfield form the best guide.

4875 OLLY MURS 17.08.2012 FILLIES' H'CAP 1m 4f (P)
5:00 (5:03) (Class 5) (0-70,70) 3-Y-O+ **£2,264** (£673; £336; £168) **Stalls** Centre

Form RPR
2431 **1** **Fleur De La Vie (IRE)**[37] 3621 3-8-13 **66**.......... JimCrowley 7 77
(Ralph Beckett) *in tch in midfield: effrt and rdn to chal over 1f out: led 1f out: styd on wl to assert fnl 100yds* **6/4**[1]
361 **2** *1* **Madame St Clair (IRE)**[44] 3391 3-9-0 **67**.......... DaneO'Neill 10 76
(Roger Curtis) *in tch in midfield: rdn and effrt to chal 2f out: drvn to ld over 1f out: hdd 1f out: styd on same pce ins fnl f* **20/1**
6-20 **3** *nse* **Dora's Gift**[9] 4606 3-9-1 **68**.......... DarrylHolland 9 77
(Hughie Morrison) *chsd ldrs: wnt 2nd over 6f out: rdn and pressing ldrs whn edgd lft 2f out: ev ch over 1f out: styd on same pce ins fnl f* **7/1**[2]
140- **4** *4* **Deceptive**[277] 7255 4-10-0 **70**.......... RichardHughes 6 73
(Paul Webber) *hld up in last quartet: rdn and hdwy over 3f out: c v wd st: styd on fr over 1f out: no imp ins fnl f* **12/1**
006 **5** *½* **Raving Monsun**[32] 3773 3-8-9 **62**..........(b[1]) MartinHarley 8 64
(Marco Botti) *stdd s: t.k.h: hld up in rr: hdwy over 3f out: swtchd lft and rdn over 2f out: hdwy over 1f out: kpt on same pce ins fnl f* **16/1**
0026 **6** *2 ½* **Natasha Rostova**[21] 4153 3-8-7 **60**.......... DavidProbert 12 58
(Andrew Balding) *t.k.h: hdwy to ld after 1f: rdn ent fnl 2f: hdd over 1f out: fdd ins fnl f* **16/1**
6 **7** *2 ¾* **Vakiyla (FR)**[35] 3704 4-9-10 **66**.......... HayleyTurner 13 59
(David Simcock) *hld up in tch in rr: rdn and effrt towards inner over 1f out: no imp fnl 2f* **16/1**
3045 **8** *nk* **Broughton Sands**[26] 3979 4-9-9 **65**.......... StevieDonohoe 3 58
(Willie Musson) *hld up in midfield: rdn and effrt over 2f out: one pce and wl hld fnl 2f* **16/1**
2251 **9** *2 ½* **Our Phylli Vera (IRE)**[25] 4006 3-9-2 **69**.......... MickaelBarzalona 2 58
(Harry Dunlop) *t.k.h: hld up in rr: pushed along 5f out: rdn and struggling whn sltly hmpd over 2f out: n.d after* **11/1**
4105 **10** *1* **Talk Of The North**[16] 4335 3-9-3 **70**.......... MichaelHills 4 57
(Hugo Palmer) *t.k.h: chsd ldrs: rdn over 3f out: wknd 2f out: bhd fnl f* **15/2**[3]
1530 **11** *9* **The Blue Dog (IRE)**[20] 4189 5-9-9 **65**..........(v) WilliamCarson 5 38
(Michael Wigham) *led for 1f: chsd ldr tl over 6f out: rdn over 3f out: wknd over 2f out: wl bhd and eased ins fnl f* **20/1**

5304 12 ½ So Is She (IRE)[7] 4643 4-8-2 51 oh1..........................(be) RobertTart(7) 1 23
(Alan Bailey) t.k.h: in tch: rdn and wknd over 2f out: wl bhd fnl f 25/1

2m 37.02s (2.52) **Going Correction** +0.275s/f (Slow)
WFA 3 from 4yo+ 11lb 12 Ran SP% **117.2**
Speed ratings (Par 100): **102,101,101,98,98 96,94,94,92,92 86,85**
Tote Swingers 1&2 £10.30, 2&3 £22.70, 1&3 £3.50 CSF £38.81 CT £170.89 TOTE £1.70: £1.10, £6.80, £2.60; EX 35.80.
Owner Prime Of Life 3 **Bred** Edward & Scarlet Leatham **Trained** Kimpton, Hants

FOCUS
A fair handicap, run at a steady pace. The first three were clear and the fifth sets the level rated to her maiden form.
Our Phylli Vera(IRE) Official explanation: jockey said that the filly lost her action

4876 BETFAIR "DON'T SETTLE FOR LESS" H'CAP 7f (P)
5:30 (5:31) (Class 4) (0-80,80) 3-Y-O £4,075 (£1,212; £606; £303) Stalls Low

Form RPR
1044 1 Obliteright (IRE)[12] 4473 3-9-7 80.......................... JimCrowley 2 92+
(William Knight) hld up in tch: rdn and effrt on inner 2f out: led 1f out: r.o wl and gng away fnl 100yds 2/1[1]
-106 2 2¼ Don Libre[9] 4607 3-9-2 75.......................... RichardHughes 6 81
(Paul Cole) led: rdn and qcknd 2f out: drvn and hdd 1f out: btn and one pce fnl 100yds 8/1
342 3 nk Catwalk (IRE)[31] 3811 3-9-1 74.......................... HayleyTurner 1 79
(James Fanshawe) chsd ldrs: rdn and effrt 2f out: styd on same pce u.p fnl f 4/1[2]
2005 4 2¾ Lady Layla[11] 4497 3-9-1 74.......................... TomEaves 9 72
(Bryan Smart) chsd ldr tl rdn and unable qck 2f out: edgd lft and btn over 1f out: plugged on same pce fnl f 14/1
443 5 ¾ Bajan Story[9] 4605 3-8-9 68.......................... FergusSweeney 8 64
(Michael Blanshard) chsd ldrs on outer: rdn and unable qck 2f out: plugged on same pce and no threat to ldrs fr over 1f out 25/1
-000 6 nse Charitable Act (FR)[14] 4412 3-9-1 74.......................... MartinDwyer 5 70
(William Muir) in tch in rr: effrt 2f out: drvn and no imp fr over 1f out 18/1
3450 7 1 Compton Prince[38] 3566 3-8-8 67.......................... JohnFahy 7 60
(Clive Cox) in tch in rr: pushed along and hdwy on outer 4f out: struggling u.p over 2f out: wknd wl over 1f out 16/1
-404 8 1½ Spykes Bay (USA)[73] 2451 3-9-3 76.......................... MartinHarley 3 65
(Mrs K Burke) in tch in midfield: rdn over 1f out: unable qck u.p 2f out: wknd over 1f out 7/1
002 9 3 Shy Rosa (USA)[70] 2542 3-8-11 75..........................[1] KatiaScallan(5) 4 56
(Marcus Tregoning) t.k.h: hld up in midfield: lost pl and rdn over 2f out: no rspnse and bhd over 1f out 9/2[3]

1m 27.1s (1.10) **Going Correction** +0.275s/f (Slow) 9 Ran SP% **116.8**
Speed ratings (Par 102): **104,101,101,97,97 97,95,94,90**
Tote Swingers 1&2 £5.00, 2&3 £5.80, 1&3 £1.70 CSF £19.27 CT £60.10 TOTE £3.10: £1.30, £3.60, £2.30; EX 23.50.
Owner The Oil Men Partnership **Bred** Lodge Park Stud **Trained** Patching, W Sussex

FOCUS
A decent 7f handicap rated through the winner to form and backed up by the second.
T/Plt: £53.70 to a £1 stake. Pool £45,575.17. 618.83 winning tickets. T/Qpdt: £19.60 to a £1 stake. Pool £3,493.55. 131.80 winning tickets. SP

4343 RIPON (R-H)
Monday, August 6

OFFICIAL GOING: Good to soft (7.6)
Bend from back straight to home straight moved out 2m and 6yds added to races on Round course.
Wind: Moderate, half-behind Weather: fine, chance showers

4877 IRISH STALLION FARMS E B F MAIDEN STKS 6f
2:15 (2:17) (Class 5) 2-Y-O £3,557 (£1,058; £529; £264) Stalls High

Form RPR
220 1 Royal Aspiration (IRE)[23] 4093 2-9-3 90.......................... PaulHanagan 4 83
(William Haggas) w ldr: led over 2f out: edgd lft over 1f out: drvn out 2/5[1]
2 2½ Right Touch 2-9-3 0.......................... TonyHamilton 1 77+
(Richard Fahey) wnt rt s: chsd ldrs: wnt 2nd appr fnl f: kpt on same pce 11/1[3]
6250 3 2¼ Red Cobra (IRE)[8] 4618 2-9-3 76.......................... DavidAllan 7 69
(Tim Easterby) chsd ldrs: kpt on fnl f: tk 3rd last 75yds 16/1
5230 4 1½ Inchy Coo[20] 4173 2-8-12 70..........................(p) GrahamGibbons 9 60
(Tim Easterby) wnt rt s: led tl over 2f out: wknd fnl f 14/1
0 5 1½ Abraham Monro[10] 4545 2-9-3 0..........................[1] GrahamLee 3 60
(Kate Walton) wnt rt s: chsd ldrs: drvn and outpcd over 3f out: no threat after 100/1
4 6 2¼ Fantasy Invader (IRE)[20] 4178 2-9-3 0.......................... MichaelO'Connell 2 53
(John Quinn) sltly hmpd s: mid-div: outpcd over 2f out: nvr a threat 6/1[2]
7 6 Rich Forever (IRE) 2-9-3 0.......................... RobertWinston 8 39+
(James Bethell) s.v.s: a bhd 33/1
06 8 2¼ Joeluke[12] 4448 2-9-3 0.......................... MickyFenton 6 32
(Paul Midgley) dwlt: a outpcd and in rr: hung lft thrght 80/1
6 9 1½ Betzyoucan[11] 4512 2-8-12 0.......................... SilvestreDeSousa 5 34
(Mark Johnston) restless in stalls: mid-div: drvn 4f out: wknd and heavily eased over 1f out 12/1

1m 14.18s (1.18) **Going Correction** +0.025s/f (Good) 9 Ran SP% **119.5**
Speed ratings (Par 94): **93,89,86,84,82 79,71,68,66**
Tote Swingers 1&2 £2.00, 2&3 £13.60, 1&3 £3.40 CSF £6.67 TOTE £1.30: £1.10, £2.30, £3.20; EX 5.40 Trifecta £30.70 Pool £774.47 - 18.63 winning units..
Owner Scotney, Symonds, Asplin, Fisher **Bred** Patsy Byrne **Trained** Newmarket, Suffolk

FOCUS
Not a bad juvenile maiden that could be rated higher but the third looks the best guide for now.

NOTEBOOK
Royal Aspiration(IRE) shed his maiden tag and he duly took advantage, though he did prove rather hard work for the champion jockey. William Haggas's colt still proved much too good for his rivals, however, and the undulations of this course may not have been totally to his liking. The extra furlong proved no problem, indeed he looked better the further he went, and there should be a decent pot in him down the line. (op 4-11 tchd 1-3)
Right Touch ♦, from the outside stall, turned in a pleasing debut effort and was a clear second-best. He should improve plenty and looks a sure-fire future winner. (op 9-1 tchd 8-1)
Red Cobra(IRE) lacked the pace to go with the leaders early, but put in some decent work late on and returned to his previous best. His mark of 76 looks about right. (op 20-1)
Inchy Coo showed up early against the stands' rail and this was more encouraging again from her back on easier ground. A drop back to the minimum trip may suit ideally in the short-term. (op 16-1)
Fantasy Invader(IRE) ran with plenty of promise on his Beverley debut 20 days earlier when ahead of Red Cobra. He was faced with easier ground, but was in trouble before stamina became an issue and now has something to prove.
Joeluke Official explanation: jockey said the gelding hung left handed
Betzyoucan Official explanation: jockey said that the filly became upset in the stalls

4878 FOLLOW @RIPONRACES ON TWITTER (S) H'CAP 5f
2:45 (2:46) (Class 6) (0-65,65) 3-Y-O £2,045 (£603; £302) Stalls High

Form RPR
0115 1 Elusive Bonus (IRE)[2] 4798 3-8-12 63.......................... DavidBergin(7) 12 73
(David O'Meara) mde all: kpt on wl fnl f 5/2[1]
0605 2 1¾ Dazzlin Bluebell (IRE)[44] 3407 3-8-4 48..........................(b) DuranFentiman 10 52
(Tim Easterby) chsd ldrs: hung rt and kpt on to chse wnr ins fnl f: no imp 14/1
0430 3 1½ Come On Dave (IRE)[10] 4558 3-9-7 65.......................... AdrianNicholls 9 63
(David Nicholls) dwlt: hld up: hdwy over 2f out: upsides over 1f out: hung lft: kpt on same pce 3/1[2]
0420 4 shd Middleton Flyer (IRE)[19] 4207 3-8-11 62.......................... NedCurtis(7) 7 60
(Paul Midgley) chsd ldrs: kpt on same pce appr fnl f 8/1
4115 5 1 Tuibama (IRE)[13] 4428 3-9-1 64..........................(p) ShaneBKelly(5) 13 58
(Tracy Waggott) w ldrs: keeping on same pce whn hmpd 1f out 7/1[3]
-440 6 nk Pavers Star[44] 3407 3-7-11 46 oh1..........................(p) NeilFarley(5) 5 39
(Noel Wilson) w ldrs on outer: one pce over 1f out 28/1
0506 7 nk First Fast Now (IRE)[14] 4394 3-8-8 52.......................... SilvestreDeSousa 2 44
(Nigel Tinkler) chsd ldrs on outer: outpcd after 2f: hdwy over 2f out: hung lft and one pce over 1f out 14/1
34R0 8 2¼ Scrooby Doo[11] 4496 3-9-7 65.......................... TomQueally 8 49
(Scott Dixon) a outpcd and in rr 16/1
520 9 9 Kyllachy Dancer[8] 4631 3-9-2 60..........................(v) MichaelO'Connell 11 12
(John Quinn) swvd rt s: outpcd in rr: bhd fnl 2f 8/1
6000 10 2½ Knight Vision[19] 4211 3-8-13 57..........................(p) AndrewMullen 6
(David Nicholls) outpcd in rr: bhd fnl 2f 20/1

1m 0.8s (0.10) **Going Correction** +0.025s/f (Good) 10 Ran SP% **115.7**
Speed ratings (Par 98): **100,97,94,94,93 92,92,88,74,70**
Tote Swingers 1&2 £9.80, 2&3 £7.10, 1&3 £2.30 CSF £38.90 CT £109.96 TOTE £3.10: £1.30, £4.40, £1.10; EX 45.30 Trifecta £152.00 Pool £486.86 - 2.37 winning units..There was no bid for the winner.
Owner The Three County Partnership **Bred** T Jones **Trained** Nawton, N Yorks
■ Stewards' Enquiry : Adrian Nicholls one-day ban: careless riding (20 Aug)

FOCUS
A typically weak 3-y-o selling sprint handicap. The placed horses help set the level of the form.
First Fast Now(IRE) Official explanation: jockey said that the filly hung left handed

4879 CHILDREN'S DAY H'CAP 1m 1f 170y
3:15 (3:15) (Class 4) (0-85,85) 3-Y-O+ £4,410 (£1,320; £660; £330; £164) Stalls Low

Form RPR
450- 1 Universal (IRE)[415] 3182 3-8-13 79.......................... SilvestreDeSousa 1 94+
(Mark Johnston) sn chsng ldrs: drvn over 4f out: styd on to ld over 1f out: drvn clr ins fnl f 7/1[3]
0006 2 3¾ Demolition[9] 4596 8-9-8 82.......................... GaryBartley(3) 11 89
(Noel Wilson) trckd ldrs: wnt 2nd over 4f out: led over 2f out: hdd over 1f out: kpt on same pce 9/1
3350 3 1¼ Jo'Burg (USA)[51] 3167 8-9-6 77.......................... DanielTudhope 2 81
(David O'Meara) dwlt: mid-div: effrt on ins over 2f out: kpt on same pce to take 3rd 1f out 11/1
3035 4 ¾ Jonny Lesters Hair (IRE)[16] 4347 7-9-6 77.......................... DavidAllan 6 80
(Tim Easterby) led: hdd over 2f out: kpt on same pce 8/1
6544 5 2¼ Robert The Painter (IRE)[16] 4347 4-9-3 74.......................... TomQueally 5 72
(David O'Meara) hld up in rr: hdwy on outer over 2f out: hung rt over 1f out: one pce 6/1[2]
0111 6 8 Gala Casino Star (IRE)[4] 4745 7-9-7 85 6ex..........(v) JordanNason(7) 3 66
(Geoffrey Harker) trckd ldrs: drvn over 3f out: wknd over 1f out 15/8[1]
04-0 7 2 Auto Mac[14] 4398 4-8-9 66 oh2.......................... JamesSullivan 9 43
(Neville Bycroft) mid-div: sme hdwy over 3f out: wknd over 1f out 66/1
4160 8 3¾ Brockfield[14] 4396 6-9-2 73.......................... RobertWinston 4 42
(Mel Brittain) hld up in rr: effrt 4f out: nvr a factor 14/1
0-20 9 5 Always The Lady[82] 2180 4-9-12 83.......................... PaulHanagan 8 42
(Clive Cox) in rr: sn pushed along: bhd fnl 4f 15/2
6063 10 5 Imaginary World (IRE)[14] 4407 4-9-1 72..........(be) GrahamGibbons 7 20
(Alan McCabe) s.s: drvn and sme hdwy 4f out: wknd 2f out 25/1
-600 11 2½ Beaumont's Party (IRE)[28] 3911 5-10-0 85.......................... TonyHamilton 10 28
(Chris Grant) chsd ldrs: lost pl over 3f out 50/1

2m 4.23s (-1.17) **Going Correction** +0.025s/f (Good)
WFA 3 from 4yo+ 9lb 11 Ran SP% **116.7**
Speed ratings (Par 105): **105,102,101,100,98 92,90,87,83,79 77**
Tote Swingers 1&2 £11.80, 2&3 £18.70, 1&3 £11.90 CSF £67.09 CT £689.95 TOTE £10.50: £2.90, £3.10, £3.60; EX 75.10 Trifecta £496.70 Part won. Pool £671.32 - 0.20 winning units..
Owner Abdulla Al Mansoori **Bred** Grangecon Stud **Trained** Middleham Moor, N Yorks

FOCUS
A competitive handicap in which it paid to race handily. The runner-up sets the level.

4880 ARMSTRONG MEMORIAL H'CAP 6f
3:45 (3:45) (Class 3) (0-95,93) 3-Y-O+ £6,931 (£2,074; £1,037; £519; £258) Stalls High

Form RPR
0434 1 Caranbola[2] 4829 6-8-13 80.......................... SilvestreDeSousa 10 88
(Mel Brittain) chsd ldrs: styd on to ld wl ins fnl f 9/1
3011 2 ¾ Spinatrix[21] 4133 4-9-5 89..........................(p) LeeTopliss(3) 3 95
(Michael Dods) w ldr: led 2f out: hdd and no ex last 50yds 15/2
4165 3 ¾ Beckermet (IRE)[8] 4629 10-9-7 88.......................... PJMcDonald 11 91
(Ruth Carr) led: hdd 2f out: styd on same pce ins fnl f 9/1
1130 4 nk Powerful Presence (IRE)[9] 4611 6-9-11 92.......................... DanielTudhope 5 94
(David O'Meara) trckd ldrs: effrt over 1f out: kpt on same pce fnl f 5/1[2]
0160 5 hd Fast Shot[9] 4611 4-9-10 91.......................... DavidAllan 9 93
(Tim Easterby) chsd ldrs: styd on same pce fnl f 11/2[3]
0-05 6 1¼ Kellys Eye (IRE)[10] 4554 5-8-7 74.......................... RobertWinston 2 72
(David Brown) swtchd lft s: hdwy over 2f out: chsng ldrs over 1f out: kpt on same pce 11/4[1]
0350 7 ½ Another Wise Kid (IRE)[8] 4629 4-9-1 82.......................... MickyFenton 1 78
(Paul Midgley) dwlt: swtchd lft s: kpt on fnl 2f: nvr rchd ldrs 16/1
2040 8 2 Arganil (USA)[8] 4629 7-9-6 87..........................[1] PhillipMakin 6 77
(Kevin Ryan) in rr: kpt on fnl 2f: nvr a factor 25/1
1122 9 nse The Nifty Fox[13] 4430 8-9-0 81..........................(p) JamesSullivan 7 70
(Tim Easterby) mid-div: hdwy over 2f out: swtchd rt over 1f out: wknd last 150yds 8/1
34/0 10 5 Khawatim[82] 2177 4-9-5 93.......................... NedCurtis(7) 4 66
(Paul Midgley) chsd ldrs: lost pl over 2f out: sn bhd 25/1

0/0- **11** *24* **Jamaica Grande**[385] 4162 4-8-7 **74** oh29 PatrickMathers 8
(Terry Clement) *s.i.s: in rr: bhd fnl 3f: eased ins fnl f: t.o* **200/1**

1m 12.75s (-0.25) **Going Correction** +0.025s/f (Good) **11** Ran SP% **115.7**
Speed ratings (Par 107): **102,101,100,99,99 97,97,94,94,87 55**
Tote Swingers 1&2 £7.60, 2&3 £14.20, 1&3 £12.20 CSF £72.51 CT £639.81 TOTE £10.00: £3.40, £3.00, £3.10; EX 98.50 Trifecta £742.90 Pool £1,004.02 - 1.00 winning unit..
Owner Mel Brittain **Bred** T E Pocock **Trained** Warthill, N Yorks

FOCUS
A good sprint handicap. The main action came down the centre of the track late on and the form is solid.

NOTEBOOK
Caranbola, fourth at Thirsk two days earlier, was well placed 2f out and responded gamely when asked for everything passing the furlong marker. It looked as though the handicapper had her measure after her Beverley success in June, but she likes this course and it was reward for her consistency. Her form figures under Silvestra De Sousa now read 1121 as well. Another likely rise will probably find her out, though. (op 17-2)
Spinatrix was bidding for a hat-trick off a 5lb higher mark and made a bold bid under a positive ride, only getting picked off late in the day. She too likes this venue and is evidently still in top form as she ideally prefers genuinely soft ground. (op 7-1)
Beckermet(IRE) was back on suitably easier ground and ran right up to his best under his usual aggressive ride. He's now been placed on three of his four outings at this course and rates a sound benchmark. (op 11-1 tchd 12-1)
Powerful Presence(IRE) lacked the pace to land a telling blow widest of all and probably found this sharp enough. He still managed to narrowly reverse his last-time-out form with Fast Shot. (tchd 9-2)
Fast Shot made his way to the stands' rail 2f out and held every chance. This was another decent effort in defeat and, weighted to his best, he helps to give the form a good look. (tchd 6-1)
Kellys Eye(IRE) signalled a return to form on his second run back for the yard at York last time and was 3lb lower, thus looking on an attractive mark in relation to old form. A three-time winner here in 2010, he had his chance when brought stands' side nearing the final furlong, but tended to hang when asked for maximum effort and was somewhat disappointing. (op 7-2)

4881 AT THE RACES SKY 415 H'CAP — 5f
4:15 (4:16) (Class 4) (0-85,84) 3-Y-O **£4,528** (£1,347; £673; £336) **Stalls** High

Form RPR
1165 **1** **El McGlynn (IRE)**[10] 4558 3-7-12 **68** HannahNunn(7) 6 76
(Peter Salmon) *mde all: hld on wl* **11/2**
0245 **2** *½* **Chooseday (IRE)**[28] 3912 3-9-1 **78** (p) PhillipMakin 2 84
(Kevin Ryan) *hld up towards rr: hdwy 2f out: chsng ldrs 1f out: kpt on to take 2nd last 100yds: no ex* **5/2**[2]
3266 **3** *2* **Rusty Rocket (IRE)**[23] 4081 3-9-0 **77** SilvestreDeSousa 4 76
(Paul Green) *chsd ldrs on wd outside: rdn and outpcd over 2f out: edgd rt: kpt on and 2nd over 1f out: one pce ins fnl f* **4/1**[3]
2250 **4** *4½* **Sonko (IRE)**[24] 4044 3-9-2 **84** (b[1]) ShaneBKelly(5) 5 67
(Tim Pitt) *chsd ldrs: wknd over 1f out* **12/1**
2331 **5** *5* **Majestic Manannan (IRE)**[8] 4619 3-8-3 **66** 6ex AdrianNicholls 7 31
(David Nicholls) *w wnr: rdn 2f out: wknd over 1f out* **2/1**[1]
0-1 **6** *6* **Koolgreycat (IRE)**[73] 2460 3-7-11 **65** oh4 NeilFarley(5) 3
(Noel Wilson) *sn outpcd and drvn along: bhd fnl 2f* **16/1**

1m 0.47s (-0.23) **Going Correction** +0.025s/f (Good) **6** Ran SP% **110.9**
Speed ratings (Par 102): **102,101,98,90,82 73**
Tote Swingers 1&2 £3.30, 2&3 £1.80, 1&3 £3.30 CSF £19.10 TOTE £7.70: £5.50, £1.60; EX 24.90.
Owner Leods Contracts Limited **Bred** Michael Lyons Jnr **Trained** Kirk Deighton, W Yorks

FOCUS
A modest 3yo sprint handicap. There was no hanging about but the form is not strong for the grade.

4882 TOTEEXACTA MAIDEN STKS — 1m 4f 10y
4:45 (4:46) (Class 5) 3-Y-O+ **£2,587** (£770; £384; £192) **Stalls** Centre

Form RPR
2-22 **1** **Ace Of Valhalla**[19] 4224 3-9-3 79 TomQueally 9 87+
(Sir Henry Cecil) *trckd ldrs: chal over 2f out: shkn up to ld over 1f out: pushed out* **11/10**[1]
2 *1¼* **Chancery (USA)**[171] 4-10-0 0 DanielTudhope 3 85+
(David O'Meara) *s.i.s: hdwy 4f out: styd on to take 2nd ins fnl f: no real imp* **10/1**
2-33 **3** *5* **Pulverize (USA)**[36] 3663 3-9-3 82 PaulHanagan 10 77
(Sir Michael Stoute) *w ldrs: chal over 3f out: led over 2f out: hdd over 1f out: one pce* **7/2**[2]
22 **4** *3¼* **Roc De Prince**[18] 4259 3-9-3 0 TonyHamilton 7 72
(Richard Fahey) *chsd ldrs: one pce fnl 2f* **4/1**[3]
0- **5** *4½* **Mutarjim (USA)**[268] 7398 3-9-3 0 SilvestreDeSousa 2 65
(Saeed Bin Suroor) *hld up in mid-div: hdwy 5f out: sn rdn and outpcd: wknd fnl 2f* **14/1**
02 **6** *3¾* **Cottesmore (USA)**[12] 4464 3-9-3 0 AdrianNicholls 6 59
(Mark Johnston) *led after 2f: hdd over 2f out: wknd over 1f out* **12/1**
40 **7** *4* **Maska Pony (IRE)**[8] 4622 8-10-0 0 GrahamLee 1 52
(George Moore) *chsd ldrs: pushed along 6f out: outpcd and lost pl over 3f out* **50/1**
00 **8** *5* **Wotsitgotodowithu (IRE)**[3] 4780 4-9-11 0 GaryBartley(3) 5 44
(Noel Wilson) *led 2f: chsd ldrs drvn over 4f out: lost pl 3f out* **100/1**
9 *40* **Red Seal** 3-9-3 0 MickyFenton 4
(Tom Tate) *s.i.s: rn green and sn rousted along: bhd fnl 7f: t.o 2f out* **66/1**
10 *47* **Mr Tallyman**[11] 6-10-0 0 PJMcDonald 8
(Micky Hammond) *s.i.s: in rr: bhd fnl 4f: eased whn t.o 2f out: virtually p.u: sddle slipped* **100/1**

2m 37.06s (0.36) **Going Correction** +0.025s/f (Good)
WFA 3 from 4yo+ 11lb **10** Ran SP% **118.7**
Speed ratings (Par 103): **99,98,94,92,89 87,84,81,54,23**
Tote Swingers 1&2 £4.50, 2&3 £6.60, 1&3 £2.60 CSF £14.61 TOTE £2.40: £1.10, £2.70, £1.80; EX 11.50 Trifecta £101.40 Pool £1,025.45 - 7.48 winning units..
Owner I Wilson **Bred** Iain Wilson **Trained** Newmarket, Suffolk

FOCUS
Not a bad maiden. They went a routine sort of pace and the form should work out.
Mr Tallyman Official explanation: jockey said that the saddle slipped

4883 SIS LIVE H'CAP — 1m 4f 10y
5:15 (5:16) (Class 5) (0-70,71) 3-Y-O+ **£2,911** (£866; £432; £216) **Stalls** Centre

Form RPR
0224 **1** **Fossgate**[25] 3992 11-9-12 **68** GrahamLee 3 79
(James Bethell) *hld up towards rr: hdwy and 3rd over 2f out: hung rt and led over 1f out: idled ins fnl f: jst hld on* **9/2**[2]
0031 **2** *hd* **Song Of The Siren**[8] 4626 4-10-1 **71** 6ex DanielTudhope 8 78
(David O'Meara) *trckd ldr: chal 4f out: sn led: hdd over 1f out: rallied clsng stages: jst hld* **4/1**[1]
00-6 **3** *1½* **Major Domo (FR)**[14] 4396 4-9-6 **62** PJMcDonald 7 67
(Micky Hammond) *in rr: hdwy over 4f out: chsd ldrs over 1f out: kpt on same pce* **25/1**
0364 **4** *shd* **Saffa Hill (IRE)**[10] 4548 3-9-0 **67** DavidAllan 1 71
(Tim Easterby) *chsd ldng pair: drvn over 4f out: one pce over 1f out* **4/1**[1]
4540 **5** *½* **Authentication**[14] 4399 3-8-0 **53** SilvestreDeSousa 4 57
(Mark Johnston) *set str pce: hdd over 3f out: one pce fnl 2f* **9/2**[2]
11-5 **6** *3* **Sky High Diver (IRE)**[23] 4088 4-10-0 **70** RobertWinston 9 69
(Alan Swinbank) *in rr: kpt on fnl 2f: nvr a factor* **11/1**
-643 **7** *2¼* **Miss Blink**[20] 4199 5-10-0 **70** PhillipMakin 6 65
(Robin Bastiman) *hld up in rr: effrt 4f out: hdwy 2f out: nvr on terms: eased nr fin* **5/1**[3]
04-0 **8** *15* **Gosforth Park**[126] 1175 6-8-7 **56** RobertDodsworth(7) 2 27
(Mel Brittain) *in rr: hdwy wd outside over 6f out: lost pl over 2f out: sn bhd and eased: t.o* **20/1**
-436 **9** *7* **Moorside Magic**[20] 4177 3-8-2 **55** PatrickMathers 5 15
(Richard Fahey) *trckd 1st 3: drvn 5f out: lost pl over 3f out: bhd and eased 2f out* **25/1**

2m 39.34s (2.64) **Going Correction** +0.025s/f (Good)
WFA 3 from 4yo+ 11lb **9** Ran SP% **113.8**
Speed ratings (Par 103): **92,91,90,90,90 88,86,76,72**
Tote Swingers 1&2 £2.80, 2&3 £23.40, 1&3 £18.80 CSF £21.82 CT £394.20 TOTE £5.90: £1.80, £1.10, £8.50; EX 16.10 Trifecta £229.40 Pool £1,004.77 - 3.24 winning units..
Owner Mrs James Bethell **Bred** Mrs P A Clark **Trained** Middleham Moor, N Yorks
■ Stewards' Enquiry : David Allan caution: careless riding

FOCUS
The strong early pace teed up an amazing fifth win in the race for veteran Fossgate. The runner-up is rated to his latest Pontefract form and sets the standard.
T/Plt: £119.60 to a £1 stake. Pool £69,325.92. 422.97 winning tickets. T/Qpdt: £84.70 to a £1 stake. Pool £4,923.84. 43 winning tickets. WG

4651 WOLVERHAMPTON (A.W) (L-H)
Monday, August 6

OFFICIAL GOING: Standard
Wind: Light, behind Weather: Overcast

4884 FOLLOW US ON TWITTER @WOLVESRACES AMATEUR RIDERS' H'CAP — 1m 4f 50y(P)
6:20 (6:21) (Class 5) (0-75,75) 3-Y-O+ **£2,183** (£677; £338; £169) **Stalls** Low

Form RPR
3-00 **1** **Porgy**[47] 2887 7-10-7 **75** (b[1]) MrDLevey(7) 11 87+
(Brian Ellison) *hld up: hdwy over 5f out: led ins fnl f: pushed clr* **7/2**[2]
0000 **2** *4½* **Cape Safari (IRE)**[9] 4601 3-9-13 **74** (p) MissLMasterton(3) 10 79
(Alan Bailey) *sn prom: chsd ldr over 6f out: led over 5f out: rdn over 1f out: hdd and no ex ins fnl f* **18/1**
0-11 **3** *3* **Noble Jack (IRE)**[7] 4657 6-10-8 **72** 6ex MrCMartin(3) 7 72
(Jo Hughes) *s.i.s: hld up: hdwy over 4f out: rdn over 1f out: no ex fnl f* **5/2**[1]
1505 **4** *6* **Rockweiller**[17] 4296 5-10-1 **62** (v) MrSWalker 12 52
(Steve Gollings) *prom: chsd ldr over 3f out: rdn over 2f out: wknd fnl f* **9/2**[3]
2430 **5** *2¾* **Mediterranean Sea (IRE)**[32] 3769 6-10-9 **75** MrJSherwood(5) 8 61
(J R Jenkins) *hld up: hdwy over 5f out: rdn over 2f out: sn wknd* **12/1**
0450 **6** *10* **Sir Boss (IRE)**[27] 3945 7-10-8 **72** MissMMullineaux(3) 3 42
(Michael Mullineaux) *s.i.s: hld up: sme hdwy over 2f out: sn wknd* **15/2**
3630 **7** *5* **Sail Home**[16] 4335 5-10-4 **70** MissSBirkett(5) 5 32
(Julia Feilden) *chsd ldrs tl wknd 4f out: t.o* **12/1**
/-00 **8** *18* **Toledo Gold (IRE)**[14] 4391 6-9-4 **56** oh4 (t) MissAngelaBarnes(5) 9
(Maurice Barnes) *led over 10f out: hdd over 5f out: wknd over 3f out: t.o* **40/1**
25/0 **9** *2* **Leopard Hills (IRE)**[9] 4585 5-9-11 **58** JoshHamer 4
(Tony Carroll) *hld up: a in rr: bhd fnl 4f: t.o* **40/1**
624- **10** *5* **Resplendent Ace (IRE)**[252] 7564 8-9-12 **64** MissPhillipaTutty(5) 1
(Karen Tutty) *prom: lost pl 8f out: nt clr run over 5f out: wknd 4f out: t.o* **12/1**
100- **11** *52* **Diamond Vision (IRE)**[43] 4665 4-10-9 **75** (t) MissAliceMills(5) 2
(Carroll Gray) *led: hdd over 10f out: remained handy tl wknd over 4f out: t.o* **50/1**

2m 37.37s (-3.73) **Going Correction** -0.15s/f (Stan)
WFA 3 from 4yo+ 11lb **11** Ran SP% **115.9**
Speed ratings (Par 103): **106,103,101,97,95 88,85,73,71,68 33**
Tote Swingers 1&2 £18.60, 2&3 £9.30, 1&3 £2.60 CSF £62.65 CT £184.43 TOTE £4.60: £1.50, £7.00, £1.10; EX 97.80 Trifecta £408.70 Part won. Pool £552.33 - 0.40 winning units..
Owner A Barnes & C N Barnes **Bred** Juddmonte Farms Ltd **Trained** Norton, N Yorks

FOCUS
The pace picked up with a circuit to go and the field finished well strung out in this amateur riders' handicap. The winner is rated back to form.

4885 BETFRED MOBILE SPORTS H'CAP — 5f 20y(P)
6:50 (6:50) (Class 6) (0-65,65) 3-Y-O+ **£1,704** (£503; £251) **Stalls** Low

Form RPR
3140 **1** **Avonvalley**[11] 4495 5-9-4 **59** RobbieFitzpatrick 2 71
(Peter Grayson) *sn outpcd: gd hdwy to ld ins fnl f: r.o wl* **11/1**
6635 **2** *1½* **Mother Jones**[10] 4535 4-9-7 **65** MatthewCosham(3) 8 72
(David Evans) *hld up: hdwy over 1f out: rdn and ev ch ins fnl f: styd on same pce* **8/1**
1-02 **3** *1¼* **I See You**[59] 2869 3-9-6 **64** SebSanders 1 67
(Peter Makin) *hld up: hdwy u.p over 1f out: ev ch ins fnl f: no ex* **3/1**[2]
406 **4** *¾* **Decider (USA)**[13] 4422 9-9-1 **56** (b) LukeMorris 7 56
(Ronald Harris) *sn chsng ldr: led 1/2-way: rdn over 1f out: edgd rt: hdd and no ex ins fnl f* **25/1**
305 **5** *½* **Catflap (IRE)**[7] 4655 3-9-4 **62** NickyMackay 5 60
(Derek Haydn Jones) *prom: chsd ldr over 1f out: sn rdn: no ex ins fnl f* **6/1**[3]
6403 **6** *1¼* **Russian Bullet**[12] 4467 3-8-13 **62** LeonnaMayor(5) 10 56
(Jamie Osborne) *hld up in tch: rdn over 1f out: styd on same pce* **7/1**
0055 **7** *½* **Punching**[21] 4143 8-9-6 **64** RaulDaSilva(3) 4 56
(Conor Dore) *led early: chsd ldrs: drvn along 1/2-way: styd on same pce ins fnl f* **16/1**
6412 **8** *shd* **Ghazeer (IRE)**[8] 4619 3-9-2 **60** (v) JoeFanning 3 60+
(Derek Shaw) *hld up: rdn over 1f out: running on whn nt clr run and eased wl ins fnl f* **5/2**[1]
0060 **9** *2½* **Love Club**[21] 4154 4-8-5 **46** oh1 DuranFentiman 9 28
(Brian Baugh) *chsd ldrs: rdn 1/2-way: wknd fnl f* **40/1**

0400 10 1 ½ **Lucky Art (USA)**[8] 4245 6 -8-13**59** DavidKenny(5) 6 36
(Conor Dore) *sn led: hdd 1/2-way: rdn and wknd over 1f out* **14/1**

1m 1.4s (-0.90)**Going Correction** -0.15s/f (Stan)
WFA 3 from 4yo+ 3lb **10**Ran SP% **118.6**
Speed ratings (Par 101): **101,98,96,95,94 92,91,91,87,85**
Tote Swingers 1&2 £20.50, 2&3 £6.80, 1&3 £8.90 CSF £97.54 CT £342.53 TOTE £12.40 : £6.10 , £3.40, £3.40 ; EX 97.00 TRIFECTA Not won. .
Owner Richard Teatum **Bred** Ercan Dogan **Trained** Formby, Lancs

FOCUS
No hanging around in what looked an open sprint and the race set up for the closers. The form is sound rated around the first three.
Ghazeer(IRE) Official explanation: jockey said that the gelding was denied a clear run

4886 HOLIDAY INN WOLVERHAMPTON MAIDEN FILLIES' STKS 5f 216y (P)
7:20 (7:20) (Class 5) 2-Y-O **£2,264** (£673; £336 ; £168) **Stalls** Low

Form RPR
4 1 **Piper's Lass (IRE)**[7] 4646 2 -9-0**0** JoeFanning 6 75
(Mark Johnston) *chsd ldr tl led over 2f out: shkn up over 1f out: r.o* **6/5**[2]
3 2 1 **Contradict**[40] 3504 2 -9-0**0** KierenFallon 2 72
(Sir Michael Stoute) *s.i.s: sn chsng ldrs: rdn to go 2nd over 1f out: styd on* **10/11**[1]
3 3 ¼ **Lyric Piece** 2 -9-0**0** LukeMorris 5 62+
(Sir Mark Prescott Bt) *s.i.s: outpcd: r.o ins fnl f: nrst fin* **14/1**[3]
4 1 ¾ **Tristessa** 2 -9-0**0** AndreaAtzeni 1 57
(Derek Haydn Jones) *led over 3f: wknd ins fnl f* **40/1**
00 5 2 ¼ **Ceekay's Girl**[11] 4494 2 -8-11**0** MichaelMetcalfe(3) 3 50
(Mrs K Burke) *hld up: hdwy over 2f out: wknd ins fnl f* **33/1**
0 6 15 **Anna Isabella**[7] 4651 2 -8-11**0** DaleSwift(3) 4 5
(Derek Shaw) *prom: pushed along over 3f out: sn wknd* **100/1**

1m 14.91s (-0.09)**Going Correction** -0.15s/f (Stan) **6**Ran SP% **110.9**
Speed ratings (Par 91): **94,92,88,86,83 63**
Tote Swingers 1&2 £1.10, 2&3 £1.70, 1&3 £1.60 CSF £2.50 TOTE £3.00 : £1.20 , £1.10 ; EX 2.90 .
Owner Sheikh Hamdan Bin Mohammed Al Maktoum **Bred** Darley **Trained** Middleham Moor, N Yorks

FOCUS
Quite an interesting small-field maiden and the form looks decent for the track. The runner-up and fifth set a straightforward level.

NOTEBOOK
Piper's Lass (IRE)shaped with plenty of promise when fourth over 7f at Lingfield last week (may have been second but for late interference) and she had more than enough speed to cope with the drop to 6f. A nice-looker, she was always holding the favourite and could be one to keep on-side with nurseries in mind. (op 6-4)
Contradict again wasn't the best away but had her chance and simply wasn't good enough. She's capable of winning a maiden, with 7f likely to suit, but is clearly no star. (op 5-6)
Lyric Piece, half-sister to a pair of AW winners at further, wasn't the best away and ran green, typically of many newcomers from this yard, but she was going on nicely at the finish and should go in next time, with 7f sure to suit. (op 12-1)
Tristessa, half-sister to a 1m AW winner, seemed to know her job but may take a while to find her level.

4887 BETFRED MOBILE LOTTO H'CAP 5f 216y (P)
7:50 (7:53) (Class 5) (0-70,70) 3-Y-O+ **£2,264** (£673; £336 ; £168) **Stalls** Low

Form RPR
0456 1 **Prince Of Passion (CAN)**[5] 4656 4 -8-11**55** (v) JoeFanning 3 64
(Derek Shaw) *mid-div: rdn over 1f out: r.o ins fnl f: led post* **20/1**
2441 2 hd **Another Citizen (IRE)**[3] 4784 4 -9-8**66** (b) DuranFentiman 2 74
(Tim Easterby) *chsd ldrs: rdn to ld ins fnl f: hdd post* **6/4**[1]
5410 3 ¾ **Perlachy**[11] 4492 8 -9-4**67** (v) DarrenEgan(5) 4 73
(Ronald Harris) *mid-div: hdwy over 2f out: rdn ins fnl f: r.o* **18/1**
5012 4 1 **Going French (IRE)**[8] 4236 5 -9-3**66** AmyScott(5) 13 69
(Dai Burchell) *led 5f out: rdn and hung lft fr over 1f out: hdd and no ex ins fnl f* **14/1**
1216 5 nse **Full Shilling (IRE)**[13] 4420 4 -9-11**69** LiamJones 8 72+
(John Spearing) *s.i.s: hld up: rdn over 2f out: r.o ins fnl f: nrst fin* **14/1**
6602 6 ¾ **Efistorm**[11] 4508 11 -9-0**65** AliceHaynes(7) 1 65
(Joseph Tuite) *prom: rdn over 2f out: styd on same pce ins fnl f* **20/1**
0005 7 hd **Methaaly (IRE)**[5] 4708 9 -9-1**66** NatashaEaton(7) 9 66
(Michael Mullineaux) *hld up: rdn over 2f out: r.o ins fnl f: nvr nrr* **25/1**
2-00 8 nse **Ishetoo**[17] 4292 8 -9-8**66** RobbieFitzpatrick 5 65
(Peter Grayson) *led 1f: chsd ldr: rdn over 1f out: no ex fnl f* **40/1**
000 9 shd **Secret Queen**[11] 4492 5 -9-1**59** LukeMorris 7 58
(Martin Hill) *prom: rdn over 2f out: no ex ins fnl f* **33/1**
2431 10 ½ **Restless Bay (IRE)**[27] 3944 4 -9-9**70** (v) MichaelMetcalfe(3) 6 67
(Mrs K Burke) *s.i.s: hld up: rdn over 1f out: nvr on terms* **9/2**[2]
6602 11 ½ **Mawjoodah**[7] 4653 4 -8-9**56** (b) PaulPickard(3) 11 52
(Brian Ellison) *hld up: hdwy over 2f out: rdn over 1f out: styd on same pce* **10/1**
3223 12 1 ½ **Homeboy (IRE)**[12] 4469 4 -9-7**65** RichardMullen 12 56
(Marcus Tregoning) *hld up: hdwy 2f out: rdn and hung lft fr over 1f out: wknd ins fnl f* **5/1**[3]

1m 13.95s (-1.05)**Going Correction** -0.15s/f (Stan) **12**Ran SP% **121.3**
Speed ratings (Par 103): **101,100,99,98,98 97,97,97,96,96 95,93**
Tote Swingers 1&2 £9.80, 2&3 £10.30, 1&3 £45.00 CSF £48.93 CT £546.78 TOTE £31.40 : £7.00, £1.40 , £5.90 ; EX 113.10 TRIFECTA Not won. .
Owner Chris Hamilton **Bred** Majestic Thoroughbred Investments Inc **Trained** Sproxton, Leics

FOCUS
A tight handicap in which the third and fourth set the standard.

4888 DOWNLOAD OUR IPHONE APP MEDIAN AUCTION MDN STKS 1m 1f 103y (P)
8:20 (8:21)(Class 6) 3-4-Y-O **£1,704** (£503; £251) **Stalls** Low

Form RPR
4 1 **Intent (IRE)**[8] 4630 3 -8-12**0** HayleyTurner 2 79+
(Michael Bell) *chsd ldrs: led wl over 1f out: shkn up and r.o wl: readily* **15/8**[1]
33 2 3 ¾ **Christingle**[27] 3946 3 -8-12**0** LiamJones 10 71
(William Haggas) *chsd ldr tl led 3f out: rn wd: rdn and hdd wl over 1f out: styd on same pce fnl f* **11/2**
05 3 1 **Taglietelle**[11] 4516 3 -9-3**0** KierenFallon 4 74
(Andrew Balding) *hld up: hdwy over 6f out: rdn and hung lft fr over 1f out: styd on same pce fnl f* **3/1**[2]
0- 4 5 **Silken Satinwood (IRE)**[296] 6866 3 -8-12**0** RobertHavlin 3 59
(Peter Chapple-Hyam) *hld up in tch: plld hrd: rdn over 2f out: wknd over 1f out* **16/1**
44 5 ¾ **Eponastone (IRE)**[15] 4366 3 -8-12**0** LukeMorris 9 57
(Gerard Butler) *hld up: hdwy over 2f out: wknd over 1f out* **7/2**[3]
000 6 1 ¼ **Spanish Trail**[20] 4188 3 -8-5**40** DannyBrock(7) 5 54?
(Christopher Kellett) *chsd ldrs: rdn over 2f out: wknd wl over 1f out* **200/1**
06 7 1 **Merchants Return**[39] 3551 3 -9-3**0** SaleemGolam 7 57
(Lydia Pearce) *s.s: nvr nrr* **150/1**
5 8 3 **Lea Valley**[26] 3975 3 -8-9**0** AdamBeschizza(3) 11 46
(Julia Feilden) *hld up: rdn over 2f out: nvr on terms* **22/1**
03 9 4 **Kodiac Island**[42] 3453 3 -8-12**0** FrannyNorton 6 38
(Ed McMahon) *led over 6f: sn rdn: wknd wl over 1f out* **28/1**
034 10 7 **Stormont Bridge**[10] 4550 4 -9-11**63** (t) JimmyQuinn 1 28
(Maurice Barnes) *hld up: rdn over 3f out: wknd over 2f out* **50/1**
11 12 **Able Mabel**[22] 4 -9-6**0** SamHitchcott 8
(Charlie Longsdon) *hld up: a in rr: t.o* **50/1**

1m 59.99s (-1.71)**Going Correction** -0.15s/f (Stan)
WFA 3 from 4yo 8lb **11**Ran SP% **116.1**
Speed ratings (Par 101): **101,97,96,92,91 90,89,87,83,77 66**
Tote Swingers 1&2 £3.20, 2&3 £4.80, 1&3 £2.60 CSF £12.13 TOTE £3.50 : £1.60 , £1.40 , £1.40 ; EX 15.80 Trifecta £33.30 Pool £292.59 - 6.49 winning units. .
Owner The Royal Ascot Racing Club **Bred** L Queally **Trained** Newmarket, Suffolk

FOCUS
A fair maiden for the course rated around the placed horses.

4889 BETFRED MOBILE CASINO H'CAP 1m 141y (P)
8:50 (8:51) (Class 4) (0-85,80) 3-Y-O+ **£4,204** (£1,251; £625 ; £312) **Stalls** Low

Form RPR
2250 1 **Angelic Upstart (IRE)**[6] 4317 4 -9-9**75** MichaelStainton 8 87
(Andrew Balding) *hld up: hdwy over 1f out: rdn to ld ins fnl f: hung lft: r.o* **14/1**
1460 2 ¾ **Main Line**[38] 3594 3 -9-2**76** TedDurcan 10 86
(David Lanigan) *hld up: hdwy over 2f out: rdn and ev ch ins fnl f: styd on* **5/2**[1]
0040 3 ¾ **Kinloch Castle**[12] 4473 3 -9-3**77** FrannyNorton 11 85
(Mark Johnston) *sn outpcd: hdwy over 1f out: r.o: nt rch ldrs* **16/1**
0002 4 5 **Light From Mars**[44] 3405 7 -10-0**80** KierenFallon 7 77
(Patrick Morris) *chsd ldrs: led over 2f out: rdn over 1f out: hdd & wknd ins fnl f* **12/1**
1500 5 nk **Son Vida (IRE)**[21] 4141 4 -9-7**73** CathyGannon 4 69
(Alan Bailey) *chsd ldrs: rdn over 3f out: wknd ins fnl f* **66/1**
4022 6 1 ½ **Elijah Pepper (USA)**[7] 4313 7 -9-8**74** GrahamGibbons 2 67
(David Barron) *hld up: rdn over 2f out: nvr trbld ldrs* **9/1**[3]
0340 7 nse **Dolphin Rock**[16] 4345 5 -9-4**73** DaleSwift(3) 5 66
(Brian Ellison) *chsd ldrs: rdn over 4f out: sn lost pl: rallied over 1f out: wknd ins fnl f* **9/1**[3]
4004 8 2 **Alhaban (IRE)**[18] 4233 6 -9-9**75** LukeMorris 6 63
(Ronald Harris) *hld up: rdn over 2f out: n.d* **25/1**
3030 9 2 **California English (IRE)**[32] 3792 3 -9-5**79** (b[1]) AndreaAtzeni 3 62
(Marco Botti) *sn pushed along to chse ldr: led over 7f out: rdn and hdd over 2f out: wknd fnl f* **7/1**[2]
5654 10 1 ¼ **Fame Again**[3] 4779 4 -9-2**68** PaddyAspell 9 48
(Michael Easterby) *hld up: hdwy over 5f out: rdn over 2f out: wknd over 1f out* **16/1**
5023 11 16 **Centrifugal (IRE)**[6] 4679 3 -9-2**76** JoeFanning 1 20
(Mark Johnston) *led: hdd over 7f out: chsd ldr: rdn over 2f out: wknd wl over 1f out* **5/2**[1]

1m 47.87s (-2.63)**Going Correction** -0.15s/f (Stan)
WFA 3 from 4yo+ 8lb **11**Ran SP% **121.1**
Speed ratings (Par 105): **105,104,103,99,98 97,97,95,94,92 78**
Tote Swingers 1&2 £9.60, 2&3 £11.20, 1&3 £21.00 CSF £50.52 CT £492.93 TOTE £20.40 : £9.60, £1.60 , £7.70 ; EX 92.00 Trifecta £173.90 Part won. Pool £235.13 - 0.10 winning units. .
Owner Barry Burdett **Bred** Swordlestown Stud **Trained** Kingsclere, Hants

FOCUS
A good, competitive handicap (run at a fair gallop), featuring a few interesting 3-y-os, but it went to one of the older performers. The third is rated back to form.
Son Vida (IRE) Official explanation: jockey said that the gelding hung left-handed
Centrifugal(IRE) Official explanation: jockey said that the gelding stopped very quickly

4890 BETFRED "THE BONUS KING" H'CAP 1m 141y (P)
9:20 (9:20) (Class 6) (0-60,61) 3-Y-O+ **£1,704** (£503; £251) **Stalls** Low

Form RPR
4330 1 **Climaxfortackle (IRE)**[16] 4325 4 -9-12**60** (v) FrannyNorton 9 69
(Derek Shaw) *hld up: hdwy over 1f out: r.o to ld nr fin* **8/1**[3]
2 ½ **Heroine Chic (IRE)**[25] 4024 5 -9-6**57** (b) PaulPickard(3) 3 65
(Brian Ellison) *chsd ldrs: led over 1f out: sn rdn: hdd nr fin* **13/8**[1]
0550 3 1 ½ **Isingy Red (FR)**[44] 3388 4 -9-11**59** (p) JoeFanning 10 63
(Jim Boyle) *hld up: hdwy over 1f out: r.o: nt rch ldrs* **12/1**
4602 4 1 ½ **American Lover (FR)**[35] 3712 5 -8-13**47** PaddyAspell 7 48
(John Wainwright) *chsd ldrs: rdn over 2f out: ev ch over 1f out: styd on same pce fnl f* **16/1**
0000 5 2 ¾ **Perfect Outlook**[26] 3964 4 -9-3**54** RaulDaSilva(3) 2 49
(Jeremy Gask) *s.i.s: hld up: hdwy over 2f out: rdn over 1f out: no ex ins fnl f* **20/1**
4000 6 hd **Kielty's Folly**[27] 3950 8 -9-10**58** DuranFentiman 5 52
(Brian Baugh) *hld up: rdn over 2f out: styd on ins fnl f: nvr nrr* **25/1**
5030 7 ¾ **Poppy Golightly**[14] 4390 5 -8-6**47** JasonHart(7) 4 39
(Declan Carroll) *led: rdn and hdd over 1f out: wknd ins fnl f* **16/1**
5051 8 1 ¾ **Strong Man**[7] 4656 4 -9-13**61** 6ex (b) DavidNolan 6 49
(Michael Easterby) *trckd ldr: rdn and ev ch over 1f out: wknd ins fnl f* **4/1**[2]
4460 9 nk **Princess Gail**[38] 3559 4 -9-1**49** GrahamGibbons 11 37
(Mark Brisbourne) *hld up: racd keenly: hdwy over 5f out: rdn over 2f out: wknd fnl f* **12/1**
5100 10 ½ **Land Hawk (IRE)**[19] 4219 6 -9-11**59** SaleemGolam 1 46
(Lydia Pearce) *mid-div: stmbld over 7f out: n.m.r and lost pl over 6f out: n.d after* **8/1**[3]
0340 11 7 **Cristaliyev**[76] 2366 4 -9-1**52** (p) MatthewCosham(3) 8 22
(John Flint) *prom: rdn over 2f out: wknd wl over 1f out* **25/1**

1m 49.69s (-0.81)**Going Correction** -0.15s/f (Stan) **11**Ran SP% **119.9**
Speed ratings (Par 101): **97,96,95,93,91 91,90,89,88,88 82**
Tote Swingers 1&2 £3.50, 2&3 £6.50, 1&3 £10.90 CSF £21.21 CT £162.51 TOTE £15.00 : £3.70 , £1.02, £6.10 ; EX 29.40 Trifecta £168.40 Pool £323.29 - 1.42 winning units. .
Owner A Flint **Bred** Pat Fullam **Trained** Sproxton, Leics

FOCUS
More open than the market suggested. The winner is rated as having returned to her best form.
Land Hawk (IRE) Official explanation: jockey said that the gelding clipped heels entering the first bend

T/Plt: £37.00 to a £1 stake. Pool £69,805.91. 1,374.73 winning tickets. T/Qpdt: £9.10 to a £1 stake. Pool £6,352.36. 512.85 winning ticekts. CR

4891a - 4898a (Foreign Racing) - See Raceform Interactive

4752 BATH (L-H)

Tuesday, August 7

OFFICIAL GOING: Good (good to soft in places) changing to soft after race 6 (4.30)

Races utilising bottom bend increased in distance by about 12.5yds.

Wind: Moderate across Weather: Overcast with some rain

4899 FREEBETS.CO.UK MAIDEN AUCTION FILLIES' STKS 5f 161y

2:00 (2:00) (Class 6) 2-Y-O £1,811 (£539; £269 ; £134)Stalls Centro

Form RPR

0 1 **Entwined (IRE)**[15] 4408 2 -8-80 JohnFahy 3 72
(Clive Cox) *in rr but in tch: drvn and hdwy over 1f out: str run fnl f to ld fnl 120yds: won gng away* **14/1**

63 2 2 1/4 **Our Three Graces (IRE)**[9] 4645 2 -8-80 FergusSweeney 6 65
(Gary Moore) *sn led: narrowly hdd 2f out: styd pressing ldr and stl upsides tl outpcd by wnr fnl 120yds* **8/1**[3]

53 3 nk **Tregereth (IRE)**[4] 4752 2 -8-60 ChrisCatlin 2 62
(Jonathan Portman) *trckd ldrs: drvn to chal fr wl over 1f out tl outpcd by wnr fnl 120yds* **11/4**[2]

4 shd **Need You Now (IRE)** 2 -8-80 RobertHavlin 4 64
(Peter Chapple-Hyam) *t.k.h: sn trcking ldrs: slt ld 2f out but styd hrd pressed tl hdd fnl 120yds: one pce* **1/1**[1]

0 5 3 **Sarahmanda**[27] 3971 2 -8-80 (t) CathyGannon 5 54
(Peter Makin) *chsd ldrs: rdn over 2f out: outpcd fnl f* **28/1**

465 6 nk **Kryena's Rose**[11] 4532 2 -8-858 SamHitchcott 1 53
(Mick Channon) *towards rr: rdn and effrt over 2f out: nvr gng pce to rch ldrs and one pce appr fnl f* **11/1**

50 7 15 **Lady Calantha**[26] 3996 2 -8-120 RichardHughes 7
(Richard Hannon) *wnt rt s: sn in rr: shkn up over 2f out: sn btn: eased whn no ch* **20/1**

1m 13.14s (1.94)**Going Correction** +0.15s/f (Good) 7Ran SP%**111.0**

Speed ratings (Par 89): **93,90,89,89,85 85,65**

Tote Swingers: 1&2 £9.80, 1&3 £5.50, 2&3 £1.70 CSF £109.95 TOTE £19.60 : £4.20 , £2.90 ; EX 132.60.

Owner Loose Connections **Bred** J F Tuthill **Trained** Lambourn, Berks

FOCUS

The going was good, good to soft in places. A moderate fillies' maiden, run at a steady pace, with four in a line entering the final furlong. The form looks modest.

NOTEBOOK

Entwined(IRE), was badly drawn and outpaced when making her debut at Windsor and had learnt plenty from that, although this race took little winning. A half-sister to 5f 2yo winner Leftontheshelf (RPR 85) and 6.5f 2yo claiming winner Dearg (62), she was briefly outpaced 2f out but finished best of all and could well get further. (op 22-1 tchd 25-1)

Our Three Graces (IRE)had shown a willing attitude when third at Lingfield on her previous start and again responded well to pressure. She will be of interest in handicaps. (op 7-1)

Tregereth(IRE) travelled kindly on her second start in four days, but was another who was unable to quicken late on. She is now qualified for a mark and may well need a bit further in time. 3-1)

Need You Now (IRE)a half-sister to three winners, including 1m4f Irish Listed scorer Snippets and 2003 Cambrideshire fourth Applause, changed hands for 10,000gns in May and clearly looks to have a future. Her breeding suggests further will suit but she showed good pace early and was cantering over her rivals at the 2f pole, then was unable to pick up when asked. The ground may have been softer than ideal and she can certainly build on this. (op 11-10)

Kryena's Rose, the most experienced runner in the field, produced little for pressure and found this a bit too competitive and will have more of a chance in handicaps. (op 12-1 tchd 14-1)

4900 FREEBETS.CO.UK FREEBETS H'CAP 1m 5y

2:30 (2:30) (Class 6) (0-55,55) 3-Y-O £1,617 (£481; £240 ; £120) **Stalls** Low

Form RPR

1521 1 **Waspy**[19] 4232 3 -9-053 (t) RichardHughes 10 56+
(George Baker) *trckd ldrs: chal fr 2f out: slt ld fr 1f out: sn shkn up and a doing enough: comf* **11/8**[1]

4604 2 1/2 **High Five Prince (IRE)**[13] 4457 3 -8-347 RachealKneller(5) 2 49
(Mark Usher) *towards rr: hdwy over 2f out: drvn and chsd ldrs fnl f: kpt on to take 2nd clsng stages but no imp on wnr* **12/1**

4004 3 nk **Doc Hill**[43] 3433 3 -8-446 oh1 SophieDoyle(3) 6 47
(Michael Blanshard) *sn led: drvn and jnd fr over 2f out: narrowly hdd 1f out: styd pressing wnr but a hld: one pce and lost 2nd clsng stages* **16/1**

0020 4 hd **Goodie Goodie**[4] 4754 3 -8-1352 (t) LiamKeniry 12 53
(Sylvester Kirk) *trckd ldr: rdn to chal fr over 2f out tl ins fnl f: could nt qckn fnl 120yds* **10/1**[3]

0342 5 hd **Zuzu Angel (IRE)**[4] 4754 3 -8-1155 DavidKenny(5) 7 55
(William Knight) *s.i.s: in rr: pushed along 3f out: hdwy 2 out: styd on wl fnl f and gng on clsng stages but no imp on wnr* **7/4**[2]

600 6 1 1/2 **Alfie Joe**[22] 4154 3 -8-046 oh1 PhilipPrince(7) 1 43
(Ron Hodges) *in rr: hdwy over 2f out: chsd ldrs 1f out: one pce ins fnl f* **50/1**

-300 7 9 **Grande Illusion**[11] 4536 3 -8-746 oh1 (p) MartinLane 11 22
(J W Hills) *in rr but in tch: drvn and hdwy over 2f out: wknd over 1f out* **28/1**

0-30 8 2 1/2 **End Of May (IRE)**[11] 4542 3 -8-1049 JamesDoyle 9 19
(Peter Bowen) *in rr: drvn: hdwy and in tch over 2f out: wknd sn after* **20/1**

0000 9 nk **Can Do Les (IRE)**[40] 3543 3 -8-746 oh1 FergusSweeney 8 16
(Richard Phillips) *t.k.h and in tch: wknd fr 2f out* **40/1**

5506 10 3 1/2 **Norwood Lane**[12] 4508 3 -8-1150 (v[1]) JohnFahy 3 12
(Peter Hedger) *in tch: rdn 3f out: chsd ldrs over 2f out: wknd sn after* **28/1**

1m 45.34s (4.54)**Going Correction** +0.525s/f (Yiel) 10Ran SP%**117.2**

Speed ratings (Par 98): **98,97,97,97,96 95,86,83,83,80**

Tote Swingers: 1&2 £4.50, 1&3 £6.10, 2&3 £8.50 CSF £18.09 CT £198.61 TOTE £2.70 : £1.60 , £3.30, £5.80 ; EX 16.50 .

Owner Patrick Milmo **Bred** Jeremy Gompertz **Trained** Whitsbury, Hants

■ Stewards' Enquiry : Sophie Doyle two-day ban; used whip above permitted level (21st & 25th Aug).

FOCUS

This handicap, lacking any real depth, was run at a steady pace with the field racing up the centre of the track in the home straight. The placed horses help set the level of the form.

End Of May (IRE) Official explanation: jockey said filly lost her action.

4901 FREEBETS.CO.UK FREE MOBILE BETTING H'CAP 1m 5y

3:00 (3:00) (Class 5) (0-75,73) 3-Y-O £2,522 (£750; £375 ; £187) **Stalls** Low

Form RPR

603 1 **Dynastic**[37] 3664 3 -9-773 RichardHughes 6 78
(Richard Hannon) *trckd ldr: slt ld and pushed along fr 2f out: hrd pressed and rdn thrght fnl f: hld on wl* **7/2**[3]

0050 2 hd **Cockney Rhyme**[38] 3643 3 -8-1062 [1] DarryllHolland 1 67
(Heather Main) *stdd in rr: hdwy 2f out and sn rdn: styd on to chse wnr fnl 75yds: clsng at fin but nt quite get up* **11/1**

3204 3 3/4 **The Noble Ord**[15] 4413 3 -9-672 (t) LiamKeniry 7 75
(Sylvester Kirk) *chsd ldrs: rdn over 2f out: chal 1f out and sn edgd lft and one pce: kpt on to take 3rd fnl 50yds bit no imp on ldng duo* **2/1**[1]

053- 4 1 1/2 **Confirmed**[262] 7494 3 -9-672 AdamKirby 3 72
(Clive Cox) *t.k.h: chsd ldrs: rdn over 2f out: chal fnl f: no ex fnl 120yds: wknd fnl 50yds* **11/4**[2]

6-03 5 1/2 **I'm Harry**[10] 4583 3 -8-1365 PatCosgrave 5 63
(George Baker) *sn led: rdn and narrowly hdd 2f out: styd chalng to 1f out: wknd fnl 150yds* **7/2**[3]

1m 47.19s (6.39)**Going Correction** +0.525s/f (Yiel) 5Ran SP%**112.8**

Speed ratings (Par 100): **89,88,88,86,86**

CSF £35.48 TOTE £4.50 : £2.10 , £7.10 ; EX 33.50 .

Owner Andrew Tinkler **Bred** Castleton Lyons & Kilboy Estate **Trained** East Everleigh, Wilts

FOCUS

A modest if competitive handicap, run at a steady pace, with the field virtually in a line 100yards out. The third is the best guide backed up by the second.

4902 FREEBETS.CO.UK ONLINE BETTING H'CAP 5f 11y

3:30 (3:30) (Class 6) (0-55,55) 3-Y-O+ £1,704 (£503; £251)**Stalls** Centre

Form RPR

0222 1 **Griffin Point (IRE)**[4] 4758 5 -9-253 (b) RichardHughes 13 63
(William Muir) *trckd ldr: drvn to ld 1f out: rdn ins fnl f: kpt on wl clsng stages* **13/8**[1]

0230 2 1 3/4 **Kyllachy Storm**[43] 3434 8 -9-455 GeorgeBaker 8 59
(Ron Hodges) *in rr: rdn 2f out: hdwy ins fnl f: tk 2nd clsng stages but no ch w wnr* **13/2**

5-00 3 1/2 **Jawim**[76] 2388 3 -8-750 RaulDaSilva(3) 1 52
(Malcolm Saunders) *in tch: drvn and hdwy fr 2f out: chsd wnr ins fnl f: no imp and lost 2nd clsng stages* **25/1**

1230 4 hd **Spic 'n Span**[4] 4758 7 -8-1350 (b) JamesDoyle 2 51
(Ronald Harris) *led: rdn 2f out: hdd 1f out: lost 2nd ins fnl f: wknd clsng stages* **9/2**[3]

4534 5 2 **Trade Centre**[4] 4758 7 -8-1047 CathyGannon 5 41
(Milton Bradley) *in rr: rdn over 2f out: styd on over 1f out but no imp on ldrs and sn one pce* **7/2**[2]

-004 6 hd **La Sonadora**[14] 4424 3 -8-646 oh1 (b) SamHitchcott 7 39
(John Spearing) *unruly stalls: outpcd and rdn 1/2-way: mod prog u.p clsng stages* **33/1**

005 7 2 **Rupeetoups**[10] 4605 4 -8-946 oh1 FergusSweeney 12 32
(Henry Candy) *in rr: hdwy to take 3rd over 2f out: wknd appr fnl f* **16/1**

000 8 6 **White Shift (IRE)**[9] 4237 6 -8-946 oh1 JohnFahy 11
(tchd (Paul Howling) *chsd ldrs: rdn over 2f out: wknd fnl f: eased clsng stages* **12/1**

1m 3.65s (1.15)**Going Correction** +0.15s/f (Good)

WFA 3 from 4yo+ 3lb 8Ran SP%**112.2**

Speed ratings (Par 101): **96,93,92,92,88 88,85,75**

Tote Swingers: 1&2 £2.30, 1&3 £8.90, 2&3 £11.60 CSF £12.30 CT £183.96 TOTE £2.40 : £1.60 , £1.40, £6.60 ; EX 10.00 .

Owner F Hope **Bred** Vincent Dunne **Trained** Lambourn, Berks

FOCUS

Six runners were withdrawn prior to the start of this handicap, that was run at a solid pace. The winner is rated a slight improver on recent marks but in line with the level of his 2011 form.

4903 WINNING POST FILLIES' H'CAP 5f 11y

4:00 (4:00) (Class 5) (0-75,75) 3-Y-O+ £2,264 (£673; £336 ; £168)**Stalls** Centre

Form RPR

0405 1 **Cockney Fire**[14] 4420 3 -9-068 (v[1]) RichardHughes 1 76
(David Evans) *trckd ldrs: wnt 2nd and 3 l down 1f out: styd on wl fnl f: drvn to ld last strides* **8/1**

6411 2 hd **Crimson Queen**[4] 4758 5 -9-671 6ex (b) ChrisCatlin 2 79
(Roy Brotherton) *led: rdn and 3 l clr 1f out: wknd and hdd last strides* **11/8**[1]

2404 3 2 1/4 **Whitecrest**[11] 4535 4 -9-469 CathyGannon 7 69
(John Spearing) *chsd ldrs: rdn 3f out: styd on to take 3rd fnl f but no imp on ldng duo fnl 120yds* **4/1**[3]

00 4 4 **Bahama Spirit (IRE)**[38] 3613 3 -9-475 RaulDaSilva(3) 3 60
(Jeremy Gask) *ponied to s: chsd ldr: rdn and no imp over 1f out: wknd ins fnl f* **12/1**

0005 5 4 **Bobby's Doll**[8] 4663 5 -8-1364 DarryllHolland 4 35
(Terry Clement) *a towards rr: rdn and no ch fr 1/2-way* **28/1**

1133 6 1/2 **Ginzan**[19] 4235 4 -9-570 JamesDoyle 5 39
(Malcolm Saunders) *slowly away: rdn 1/2-way but nt rcvr and a outpcd* **11/4**[2]

1m 3.16s (0.66)**Going Correction** +0.15s/f (Good)

WFA 3 from 4yo+ 3lb 6Ran SP%**111.0**

Speed ratings (Par 100): **100,99,96,89,83 82**

Tote Swingers: 1&2 £2.30, 1&3 £3.70, 2&3 £1.90 CSF £19.18 CT £48.78 TOTE £10.60 : £2.80 , £1.70; EX 21.40 .

Owner G E Amey **Bred** G E Amey **Trained** Pandy, Monmouths

■ Stewards' Enquiry : Richard Hughes two-day ban; used whip above permitted level (21st & 25th Aug).

FOCUS

A decent sprint handicap run at a sound pace with the field once again coming over to the stands' side and the winner getting up right on the post, to give her jockey a four-timer. The runner-up is rated just below his latest course form.

Ginzan Official explanation: jockey said filly banged her head leaving stalls.

4904 FREEBETS.CO.UK FOOTBALL BETTING H'CAP 2m 1f 34y

4:30 (4:30) (Class 6) (0-60,60) 4-Y-O+ £1,617 (£481; £240 ; £120)**Stalls** Centre

Form RPR

4-50 1 **Eastern Magic**[12] 4491 5 -8-955 JackDuern(7) 3 64
(Reg Hollinshead) *chsd ldr: rdn over 5f out: hdd 4f out: styd in 2nd but looked hld whn ldr veered bdly lft fnl 120yds and lost momentum: styd on to ld last strides* **9/2**[3]

5002 **2** *hd* **Lucky Diva**[11] 4537 5-8-8 **54**..(p) JakePayne(7) 6 65+
(Bill Turner) *in rr tl gd hdwy on ins 4f out: led ins fnl 3f: rdn and over 2 l clr whn veered bdly lft and lost momentum fnl 120yds: sn jnd: hdd last strides* **15/2**
0355 **3** *4 1/2* **Josie's Dream (IRE)**[64] 2575 4-8-7 **46**............................ TadhgO'Shea 2 49
(Jo Hughes) *stdd in rr: hdwy over 3f out: styd on u.p to take 3rd ins fnl f but no ch w ldng duo* **8/1**
0241 **4** *3 1/4* **Mollyow (IRE)**[8] 4664 4-9-4 **57** 6ex.................................. CathyGannon 1 56+
(Terry Clement) *chsd ldrers: rdn and one pce over 3f out: styd on again for wl hld 4th cl home* **3/1**[1]
0003 **5** *nk* **Spinning Waters**[11] 4537 6-8-7 **46**.............................. KellyHarrison 13 45
(Dai Burchell) *chsd ldrs: led 4f out: hdd ins fnl 3f: styd chsng ldrs: wknd appr if out* **12/1**
0-00 **6** *3/4* **Party Palace**[54] 2575 8-8-0 **46** oh1.............................. NatashaEaton(7) 9 44
(Stuart Howe) *towards rr: drvn and hdwy over 3f out: one pce fnl 2f* **33/1**
5/00 **7** *3/4* **Ildiko (USA)**[35] 3734 5-8-0 **46** oh1.............................(t) DanielCremin(7) 4 43
(Dr Jeremy Naylor) *s.i.s: in rr: rdn 3f out: mod prog fr over 1f out* **66/1**
335 **8** *13* **Waldsee (GER)**[77] 2371 7-9-5 **58**.................................... JamesDoyle 8 40
(Sean Curran) *in tch 1/2-way: rdn and effrt over 3f out: chsd ldrs u.p over 2f out: wknd over 1f out* **11/2**
504- **9** *hd* **The Composer**[63] 4630 10-8-7 **46** oh1....................... FergusSweeney 12 27
(Michael Blanshard) *chsd ldrs: rdn 4f out: wknd ins fnl 3f* **20/1**
114/ **10** *31* **Kristallo (GER)**[20] 1087 7-9-7 **60**..............................(p) RichardHughes 7
(Peter Bowen) *in rr: hdwy on outside to cl on ldrs 7f out: wknd 3f out* **4/1**[2]
506/ **11** *nk* **Massachusetts**[8] 6257 5-8-2 **46** oh1..........................(v[1]) AmyScott(5) 10
(Dai Williams) *led tl hdd over 5f out: wknd 3f out* **50/1**
4m 3.55s (11.65) **Going Correction** +0.525s/f (Yiel) 11 Ran SP% **120.3**
Speed ratings (Par 101): **93,92,90,89,89 88,88,82,82,67 67**
Tote Swingers: 1&2 £8.90, 1&3 £8.40, 2&3 £13.20 CSF £37.94 CT £267.96 TOTE £5.50: £1.60, £2.20, £3.30; EX 39.50.
Owner Mrs Christine Stevenson **Bred** Mrs C A Stevenson **Trained** Upper Longdon, Staffs
FOCUS
A low-grade staying handicap that saw drama in the final furlong. The front two pulled clear and the third is rated close to form.

4905 FREEBETS.CO.UK FREE BINGO FILLIES' H'CAP 1m 5f 22y
5:00 (5:00) (Class 4) (0-80,80) 4-Y-0+ **£4,075** (£1,212; £606; £303) **Stalls** High

Form RPR
1140 **1** **Sula Two**[12] 4515 5-8-11 **77**.. PhilipPrince(7) 4 85
(Ron Hodges) *t.k.h and chsd ldrs in 3rd: rdn and disputing 2 l 2nd whn ent mist ins fnl 2f: in narrow ld and extending whn c bk into view fnl 120yds: styd on wl* **7/1**
4511 **2** *1* **Shades Of Grey**[25] 4061 5-9-7 **80**....................................... AdamKirby 5 86
(Clive Cox) *led at modest pce: stl in 2 l ld and pushed along whn ent mist ins fnl 2f: narrowly hdd and one pce whn bk into view fnl 120yds* **7/4**[1]
2502 **3** *3/4* **Reset City**[12] 4504 6-8-6 **65**... CathyGannon 1 70
(Ian Williams) *chsd ldrs: disputing 2nd whn ent mist ins fnl 2f: styng on same pce in 3rd whn bk into view fnl 120yds* **4/1**[3]
3315 **4** *1 1/2* **Asterales**[40] 3519 5-8-2 **61** oh4.. KellyHarrison 3 64
(Jo Hughes) *in rr: rdn along 4f out: styd on to dispute 2nd whn ent mist ins fnl 2f: wkng into 4th whn bk into view fnl 120yds* **16/1**
-420 **5** *42* **Dawn Gale (IRE)**[17] 4326 4-9-6 **79**................................. DarryllHolland 2
(Hughie Morrison) *chsd ldr to 5f out: wknd u.p fr 4f out: t.o* **2/1**[2]
3m 5.0s (13.00) **Going Correction** +0.525s/f (Yiel) 5 Ran SP% **108.1**
Speed ratings (Par 102): **81,80,79,79,53**
CSF £19.01 TOTE £7.10: £3.00, £1.60; EX 23.30.
Owner Richard Prince **Bred** D R Tucker **Trained** Charlton Mackrell, Somerset
FOCUS
The going changed to soft before the start of the race, with the mist restricting visibility down to 100 yards at points. A fairly competitive handicap despite the small field size, run at a steady pace with the field racing up the centre of the track in the home straight. The principals are rated close to their marks.
Dawn Gale(IRE) Official explanation: trainer said filly had a breathing problem.

4906 FREEBETS.CO.UK FOLLOW US ON TWITTER APPRENTICE H'CAP 1m 3f 144y
5:30 (5:30) (Class 5) (0-75,73) 3-Y-0 **£2,264** (£673; £336; £168) **Stalls** Low

Form RPR
0316 **1** **The Quarterjack**[17] 4323 3-8-10 **64**............................ DanielMuscutt(5) 5 75+
(Ron Hodges) *trckd ldrs in 3rd: wnt 2nd over 4f out: led over 2f out: rdn clr fnl f* **13/8**[1]
6110 **2** *3 3/4* **April Ciel**[20] 4225 3-9-6 **69**... DannyBrock 3 73
(Ronald Harris) *led tl hdd over 2f out: sn rdn: no imp on wnr: drvn out to hold 2nd* **10/3**[3]
-022 **3** *nk* **Hidden Justice (IRE)**[53] 3104 3-9-10 **73**......... WilliamTwiston-Davies 2 76
(Amanda Perrett) *hld up in rr: hdwy to take 3rd over 3f out: drvn and styd on fnl 2f: clsd on 2nd nr fin but nvr any ch w wnr* **5/2**[2]
000 **4** *7* **Flashy Star**[12] 4516 3-8-8 **62**.....................................(v) RobertTart(5) 4 53
(Mick Channon) *in rr but in tch: styd on for mod 4th ins fnl 3f: nvr any ch w ldrs and wl btn over 1f out* **10/1**
6031 **5** *9* **Arte Del Calcio**[27] 3965 3-8-13 **62**.............................. ThomasBrown 1 38
(Tony Carroll) *plld hrd and chsd ldrs: wnt 2nd over 4f out: rdn 3f out and wknd sn after* **15/2**
2m 38.54s (7.94) **Going Correction** +0.525s/f (Yiel) 5 Ran SP% **110.6**
Speed ratings (Par 100): **94,91,91,86,80**
CSF £7.39 TOTE £1.60: £2.40, £1.10; EX 8.80.
Owner P E Axon **Bred** Cheveley Park Stud Ltd **Trained** Charlton Mackrell, Somerset
FOCUS
A moderate apprentice handicap, run at a steady pace, with the field well strung out at the post. Muddling form with the third the best guide.
T/Jkpt: Not won T/Plt: £172.10 to a £1 stake. Pool: £62,564.90 - 265.26 winning tickets. T/Qpdt: £30.80 to a £1 stake. Pool: £5,901.19 - 141.50 winning tickets. ST

4448 CATTERICK (L-H)
Tuesday, August 7
OFFICIAL GOING: Good to firm (firm in places; 9.2)
Wind: virtually nil Weather: Cloudy, sunny periods

4907 IRISH STALLION FARMS E B F MAIDEN STKS 7f
2:20 (2:22) (Class 5) 2-Y-0 **£3,040** (£904; £452; £226) **Stalls** Centre

Form RPR
033 **1** **Medicoe**[10] 4612 2-9-3 78.. LukeMorris 1 77
(Sir Mark Prescott Bt) *mde all: jnd and rdn 2f out: drvn ent fnl f: kpt on wl* **4/6**[1]
32 **2** *2 1/2* **Excellent Mariner (IRE)**[7] 4677 2-8-12 0................ SilvestreDeSousa 8 68
(Mark Johnston) *n.m.r shortly after s: sn chsng ldrs: effrt to chal 2f out: rdn and ev ch whn edgd lft appr fnl f: one pce* **9/4**[2]
6340 **3** *2* **Chant (IRE)**[4] 4778 2-9-3 66.. PaulMulrennan 9 65
(Ann Duffield) *wnt lft s: chsd ldrs on inner: rdn 2f out: kpt on fnl f: wnt 3rd nr fin* **25/1**
0 **4** *1 1/4* **Star Request**[6] 4710 2-8-12 0.. AndrewMullen 2 56+
(Keith Dalgleish) *chsd ldrs: rdn 2f out: one pce: lost 3rd nr fin* **12/1**[3]
2 **5** *3* **Juana Belen**[13] 4449 2-8-12 0... GrahamGibbons 7 48
(David Barron) *chsd wnr: rdn over 2f out: sn wknd* **12/1**[3]
60 **6** *hd* **By A Wiska**[9] 4618 2-9-3 0..(t) PaddyAspell 3 53+
(Ann Duffield) *chsd ldrs: drvn over 2f out: grad wknd* **40/1**
23 **7** *9* **Vegas Belle**[21] 4191 2-8-12 0.. TomEaves 4 24
(Ollie Pears) *a towards rr* **18/1**
000 **8** *nk* **Vida Eterna (IRE)**[15] 4395 2-8-12 37........................... FrederikTylicki 5 23
(Ollie Pears) *s.i.s: a in rr* **100/1**
00 **9** *5* **Vision Of Judgment**[18] 4310 2-9-3 0.................................. GrahamLee 6 14
(Ollie Pears) *hmpd shortly after s: a in rr* **66/1**
1m 25.81s (-1.19) **Going Correction** -0.275s/f (Firm) 9 Ran SP% **120.2**
Speed ratings (Par 94): **95,92,89,88,85 84,74,74,68**
Tote Swingers: 1&2 £1.20, 1&3 £7.30, 2&3 £7.60 CSF £2.39 TOTE £1.60: £1.10, £1.10, £5.20; EX 2.00 Trifecta £10.40 Pool: £816.41 - 57.69 winning units..
Owner B Haggas **Bred** J B Haggas **Trained** Newmarket, Suffolk
FOCUS
The first pair dominated from two out and it is straightforward form, rated through the winner.
NOTEBOOK
Medicoe proved all the rage on this step up a furlong and duly obliged, getting off the mark at the fourth attempt. He had the plum draw and sensibly made full use of it, but was unable to get away from the pack early on. That saw him have to fend off challengers, but there was plenty to like about his attitude, especially in dispensing with the runner-up a furlong out. He wasn't doing a great deal in front, but looked better the further he went and has the scope to rate a deal higher as he matures. (op 4-5 tchd 8-13)
Excellent Mariner(IRE) had been placed on her two previous outings on contrasting ground despite running distinctly green on both occasions. She again proved green and is very much still learning her trade, but this was a decent effort considering her wide draw. Nurseries are now an option and she's well up to winning races when the penny drops. (op 2-1 tchd 5-2)
Chant(IRE), whose yard has a decent record in this event, dropped back as he failed to handle the turn all that well. He was coming back late in the day and this was better again. (op 28-1)
Star Request was well held on her Redcar debut over 6f last week and got warm beforehand here as she proved reluctant to enter the stalls. This was more encouraging and she shaped as though she would learn plenty again for the experience. Her brother Cara's Request prefers easier ground and it will be interesting to see what she does when getting her toe in.
Juana Belen was just thwarted in a C&D seller on her debut when well backed 13 days earlier. She duelled with the winner early, but was made to pay from 2f out and found this too hot.

4908 SSAFA FORCES HELP (S) STKS 1m 7f 177y
2:50 (2:50) (Class 6) 3-5-Y-0 **£2,045** (£603; £302) **Stalls** Centre

Form RPR
4623 **1** **Geanie Mac (IRE)**[3] 4826 3-8-2 62.......................(v[1]) SilvestreDeSousa 1 55
(Tim Pitt) *mde all: clr 1/2-way: jnd and rdn along 2f out: drvn fnl f: edgd lft and hld on towards fin* **1/1**[1]
5620 **2** *1/2* **Maid Of Meft**[9] 4626 5-9-9 62... MickyFenton 2 60
(Paul Midgley) *in tch: hdwy to chse wnr 7f out: tk clsr order 3f out: rdn to chal 2f out: ev ch tl drvn and one pce ins fnl f* **13/2**
3 *nk* **Camelopardalis** 3-7-9 0.. NoelGarbutt(7) 6 54
(Tobias B P Coles) *chsd ldrs: rdn along over 4f out: drvn and styd on fnl f: clsng on ldng pair whn n.m.r on inner nr fin* **16/1**
5003 **4** *20* **Commander Veejay**[20] 4209 4-9-1 50...........................(p) JasonHart(7) 4 35
(Brian Rothwell) *in tch: chsd ldrs 6f out: rdn over 3f out: wknd over 2f out* **16/1**
4000 **5** *12* **Redclue (IRE)**[8] 4652 3-8-8 53 ow1................................. MarcHalford 7 21
(Miss Louise Allan) *chsd wnr: pushed along 1/2-way: rdn over 5f out: sn wknd* **50/1**
6/ **6** *2 3/4* **Behtarini (IRE)**[11] 5508 5-9-8 79..................................(tp) GrahamLee 5 17
(Evan Williams) *chsd ldrs: rdn along over 5f out: sn lost pl and bhd* **11/2**[3]
-220 **7** *1 3/4* **Falcun**[9] 4626 5-9-8 58..(v) TomEaves 8 15
(Micky Hammond) *v.s.a: a bhd* **9/2**[2]
3m 26.51s (-5.49) **Going Correction** -0.275s/f (Firm)
WFA 3 from 4yo+ 15lb 7 Ran SP% **110.6**
Speed ratings (Par 101): **102,101,101,91,85 84,83**
Tote Swingers: 1&2 £1.60, 1&3 £5.70, 2&3 £8.00 CSF £7.49 TOTE £1.80: £1.40, £3.10; EX 7.30 Trifecta £70.30 Pool: £492.77 - 70.30 winning units..
Owner Drinkmore Stud **Bred** J Mulligan **Trained** Newmarket, Suffolk
FOCUS
This long-distance seller provided a decent test and there was a tight three-way finish. The form is weak.

4909 PIN POINT RECRUITMENT H'CAP 5f 212y
3:20 (3:20) (Class 5) (0-75,68) 3-Y-0+ **£2,264** (£673; £336; £168) **Stalls** Low

Form RPR
0-64 **1** **Gap Princess (IRE)**[8] 4655 8-9-11 **67**.......................(p) RobertWinston 1 76
(Geoffrey Harker) *in tch on inner: hdwy over 2f out: rdn to ld jst ins fnl f: sn edgd rt: kpt on* **7/1**[3]
3220 **2** *1* **Blue Shoes (IRE)**[11] 4547 3-9-2 **62**................................. DavidAllan 6 67
(Tim Easterby) *chsd ldr: hdwy on outer over 1f out: sn rdn: ev ch ins fnl f: kpt on* **9/1**
U21 **3** *1* **Oakbrook**[13] 4453 3-8-10 **56**... PaulMulrennan 7 58
(Ann Duffield) *in rr: swtchd rt and hdwy on outer 2f out: rdn and ch ins fnl f: sn drvn and one pce* **8/1**
6160 **4** *1* **Sophie's Beau (USA)**[20] 4207 5-8-6 **53**.................(bt) LeonnaMayor(5) 4 53
(Michael Chapman) *prom: effrt 2f out: rdn to ld over 1f out: hdd jst ins fnl f: kpt on same pce* **33/1**
3060 **5** *2* **See Clearly**[29] 3912 3-9-2 **67**.......................................(p) DarylByrne(5) 3 59
(Tim Easterby) *in rr: swtchd rt and hdwy 2f out: sn rdn: kpt on fnl f: nrst fin* **10/1**
3251 **6** *1/2* **Ferdy (IRE)**[13] 4452 3-8-11 **57**................................... SilvestreDeSousa 11 48
(Paul Green) *prom: rdn 2f out: edgd lft over 1f out: sn btn* **11/4**[1]
3500 **7** *2* **North Central (USA)**[22] 4134 5-9-4 **60**...........................(p) GrahamLee 5 45
(Jim Goldie) *in rr tl sme late hdwy* **10/1**
0602 **8** *1/2* **Indian Trail**[7] 4680 12-9-12 **68**.....................................(b) AndrewMullen 9 52
(David Nicholls) *in tch: effrt over 2f out: sn rdn and btn* **18/1**
0406 **9** *2 1/4* **Lady Kildare (IRE)**[11] 4547 4-9-4 **60**........................... AndrewElliott 8 36
(Jedd O'Keeffe) *a towards rr* **9/1**
0346 **10** *hd* **Bay Of Fires (IRE)**[6] 4717 4-9-10 **66**........................(p) DanielTudhope 2 42
(David O'Meara) *led: rdn wl over 2f out: hdwy over 1f out: sn wknd* **5/1**[2]

0-00 **11** *1 ¼* **Mr Wolf**[9] 4631 11-9-6 62..........................(p) TonyHamilton 10 34
(Paul Midgley) *cl up: rdn over 2f out: sn wknd* **33/1**

1m 11.49s (-2.11) **Going Correction** -0.275s/f (Firm)
WFA 3 from 4yo+ 4lb **11** Ran SP% **116.3**
Speed ratings (Par 103): **103,101,100,99,96 95,93,92,89,89 87**
Tote Swingers: 1&2 £15.40, 2&3 £7.50 CSF £67.76 CT £521.14 TOTE £4.30: £1.10, £4.20, £2.50; EX 84.20 Trifecta £346.30 Part won. Pool: £468.09 - 0.40 winning units..
Owner Northumbria Leisure Ltd & J L Harker **Bred** D Veitch And Musagd Abo Salim **Trained** Thirkleby, N Yorks

FOCUS
A moderate sprint handicap, run at a searching pace. The runner-up to his juvenile best with the third close to his previous C&D mark.
Ferdy(IRE) Official explanation: jockey said colt had no more to give.

4910 ABF THE SOLDIER'S CHARITY H'CAP 1m 5f 175y
3:50 (3:50) (Class 4) (0-85,79) 3-Y-0+ **£4,075** (£1,212; £606; £303) **Stalls** Low

Form RPR
1345 **1** **Bute Hall**[20] 4216 3-9-0 78..........................(b) SilvestreDeSousa 8 86
(Mark Johnston) *trckd ldr led 1/2-way: rdn over 2f out: drvn fnl f: kpt on* **6/5**[1]

213 **2** *2 ¼* **Raleigh Quay (IRE)**[7] 4682 5-8-13 69.......................... ShaneBKelly(5) 5 74
(Micky Hammond) *hld up in tch: hdwy to chse wnr over 4f out: rdn along 3f out: chal over 2f out: sn drvn and edgd persistently lft: no ex fnl 100yds* **8/1**

0053 **3** *2 ¾* **Meetings Man (IRE)**[12] 4499 5-8-11 67.......................... GarryWhillans(5) 4 68
(Micky Hammond) *prom: rdn along and sltly outpcd 5f out: styd on u.p fnl 2f* **2/1**[2]

4320 **4** *31* **Golden Future**[10] 4590 9-9-3 68.......................... TomEaves 2 26
(Peter Niven) *hld up in rr: sme hdwy 4f out: sn rdn and nvr a factor* **6/1**[3]

-220 **5** *13* **Oddsmaker (IRE)**[29] 3904 11-8-11 62 oh4..........................(t) PaulMulrennan 7
(Maurice Barnes) *led: hdd 1/2-way: sn wknd* **25/1**

2m 59.93s (-3.67) **Going Correction** -0.275s/f (Firm)
WFA 3 from 4yo+ 13lb **5** Ran SP% **108.0**
Speed ratings (Par 105): **99,97,96,78,71**
CSF £10.67 TOTE £1.90: £1.40, £3.60; EX 10.60 Trifecta £13.00 Pool: £406.69 - 23.14 winning units..
Owner Always Trying Partnership X **Bred** Southcourt Stud **Trained** Middleham Moor, N Yorks

FOCUS
This staying handicap was hit by non-runners. They went a sound pace, the runner-up up is rated to his recent best and the form should work out.

4911 17TH AUGUST IS LADIES' EVENING H'CAP 5f
4:20 (4:21) (Class 6) (0-60,56) 3-Y-0+ **£2,045** (£603; £302) **Stalls** Low

Form RPR
0-60 **1** **Piste**[13] 4452 6-8-10 45..........................(e) PaulMulrennan 2 57
(Tina Jackson) *in tch: hdwy 2f out: rdn to chse ldrs over 1f out: kpt on to ld last 100yds* **8/1**[3]

21 **2** *hd* **Irish Girls Spirit (IRE)**[33] 3791 3-9-2 54.......................... MickyFenton 8 64
(Paul Midgley) *chsd ldng pair: hdwy to ld 2f out: sn rdn: drvn ins fnl f: hdd and no ex last 100yds* **5/2**[1]

-040 **3** *hd* **Mr Mo Jo**[49] 3256 4-9-7 56.......................... DanielTudhope 12 66+
(Lawrence Mullaney) *cl up: carried bdly rt 1/2-way: sn rdn: ev ch ent fnl f: sn drvn: no ex last 100yds* **16/1**

-000 **4** *5* **Triskaidekaphobia**[64] 2748 9-8-11 46..........................(t) GrahamLee 1 38
(Wilf Storey) *chsd ldrs on inner: rdn and ch wl over 1f out: sn drvn and one pce* **14/1**

5350 **5** *½* **Gran Canaria Queen**[30] 3892 3-8-11 49.......................... TonyHamilton 7 38
(Ian Semple) *chsd ldrs: hdwy 2f out: sn prom and rdn: wknd ent fnl f* **11/1**

0045 **6** *2 ¼* **Duke Of Rainford**[10] 4592 5-8-12 47.......................... TomEaves 15 29
(Michael Herrington) *dwlt: towards rr: hdwy 1/2-way: sn rdn: kpt on fnl f* **16/1**

5000 **7** *¾* **On The High Tops (IRE)**[11] 4552 4-9-7 56..........................(b) PJMcDonald 3 36
(Ruth Carr) *led: hung bdly rt 1/2-way: sn hdd & wknd* **5/2**[1]

4000 **8** *1 ½* **Forever Janey**[55] 3025 3-8-4 45.......................... JulieBurke(3) 10 18
(Paul Green) *chsd ldrs to 1/2-way: sn wknd* **40/1**

-600 **9** *nse* **Peteron**[13] 4452 4-8-10 45.......................... PaddyAspell 5 19
(Colin Teague) *a towards rr* **20/1**

203 **10** *6* **Myjestic Melody (IRE)**[10] 4592 4-8-13 51 ow1..........(p) GaryBartley(3) 13
(Noel Wilson) *a towards rr* **5/1**[2]

004 **11** *1 ¼* **De Lesseps (USA)**[17] 4328 4-9-6 55.......................... JamesSullivan 14
(Alan Berry) *dwlt: a outpcd and bhd* **50/1**

59.38s (-0.42) **Going Correction** -0.275s/f (Firm)
WFA 3 from 4yo+ 3lb **11** Ran SP% **120.8**
Speed ratings (Par 101): **92,91,91,83,82 78,77,75,75,65 63**
Tote Swingers: 1&2 £7.10, 1&3 £18.10, 2&3 £9.30 CSF £28.66 CT £332.13 TOTE £7.40: £1.90, £1.60, £5.00; EX 43.50 Trifecta £117.10 Pool: £607.70 - 3.84 winning units..
Owner H L Thompson **Bred** Miss G Abbey **Trained** Liverton, Cleveland

FOCUS
A weak sprint handicap, run at a strong pace and few landed a serious blow as the principals fought out a blanket finish. The placed horses set the level of the form.
On The High Tops(IRE) Official explanation: jockey said gelding hung right handed throughout.

4912 GO RACING IN YORKSHIRE CLASSIFIED CLAIMING STKS 1m 3f 214y
4:50 (4:50) (Class 6) 3-Y-0+ **£2,045** (£603; £302) **Stalls** Centre

Form RPR
-265 **1** **Croftamie**[35] 3728 3-8-5 72.......................... SilvestreDeSousa 3 58
(Mark Johnston) *trckd ldrs: rn wd bnd after 3f: sn rcvrd: hdwy 3f out: cl up 2f out: rdn to ld over 1f out: drvn and edgd rt ins fnl f: kpt on* **6/4**[1]

2421 **2** *shd* **Eijaaz (IRE)**[20] 4209 11-9-1 59..........................(p) PJMcDonald 5 56
(Geoffrey Harker) *hld up in tch: hdwy 3f out: pushed along to chse ldr 2f out: rdn to chal over 1f out: ev ch whn hit in face by opponent's whip ins fnl f: kpt on* **7/4**[2]

4066 **3** *2* **Chookie Hamilton**[8] 4639 8-8-11 72..........................(b) GarryWhillans(5) 1 54
(Ian Semple) *led: clr 4f out: rdn over 2f out: hdd over 1f out: sn drvn and one pce* **5/1**[3]

0 **4** *2* **Dimashq**[4] 4766 10-9-0 44.......................... MickyFenton 7 49
(Paul Midgley) *s.i.s and bhd: hdwy 3f out: kpt on u.p fnl 2f: nrst fin* **40/1**

5006 **5** *½* **Rapturous Applause**[62] 2823 4-9-0 46.......................... FrederikTylicki 6 48
(Micky Hammond) *in tch: hdwy over 3f out: rdn along on outer to chse ldrs over 2f out: grad wknd* **28/1**

-630 **6** *12* **Lava Steps (USA)**[43] 3437 6-8-7 39..........................(b) DavidBergin(7) 2 29
(David O'Meara) *trckd ldng pair: rdn over 3f out: sn wknd* **16/1**

0460 **7** *24* **Cathcart Castle**[22] 4158 4-9-0 50..........................(p) DanielTudhope 4
(Simon West) *in tch on inner whn hmpd 7f out: in rr after* **14/1**

2m 37.43s (-1.47) **Going Correction** -0.275s/f (Firm)
WFA 3 from 4yo+ 11lb **7** Ran SP% **111.5**
Speed ratings (Par 101): **93,92,91,90,89 81,65**
Tote Swingers: 1&2 £1.40, 2&3 £2.00 CSF £4.10 TOTE £1.80: £1.10, £1.30; EX 4.50.The winner was claimed by Miss T. Waggott for £6,000.
Owner Mark Johnston Racing Ltd **Bred** Cheveley Park Stud Ltd **Trained** Middleham Moor, N Yorks

FOCUS
There was a solid pace on in this classified claimer and it served up a cracking finish. The winner was unimpressive, the second well off his best while the fourth and fifth limit the form.

4913 FOLLOW US ON TWITTER @CATTERICKRACES H'CAP 7f
5:20 (5:21) (Class 6) (0-65,65) 3-Y-0 **£2,045** (£603; £302) **Stalls** Centre

Form RPR
400- **1** **Come Hither**[384] 4194 3-9-0 58.......................... DanielTudhope 6 67+
(David O'Meara) *mde all: rdn over 1f out: clr fnl f* **4/1**[2]

-630 **2** *3 ¾* **Morna's Glory**[4] 4782 3-9-5 63.......................... PaddyAspell 4 62
(Jason Ward) *trckd wnr: hdwy 3f out: rdn and ch over 1f out: sn drvn and one pce* **14/1**

0225 **3** *nk* **Eastlands Lad (IRE)**[11] 4553 3-9-5 63..........................(p) PJMcDonald 7 61
(Micky Hammond) *prom: rdn 2f out: drvn and one pce appr fnl f* **2/1**[1]

0036 **4** *2 ¾* **Sir Windsorlot (IRE)**[13] 4452 3-9-1 59..........................(t) MichaelO'Connell 5 50
(John Quinn) *chsd ldrs: rdn over 2f out: sn drvn and one pce* **11/2**[3]

-604 **5** *nk* **Irrational**[13] 4453 3-8-13 57.......................... RoystonFfrench 1 47
(Bryan Smart) *towards rr: hdwy over 2f out: sn rdn and kpt on fnl f: nrst fin* **8/1**

00-0 **6** *4* **Goodfellows Quest (IRE)**[119] 1270 3-8-2 46 oh1.(v[1]) JamesSullivan 12 25
(Ann Duffield) *a towards rr* **33/1**

5255 **7** *nse* **Slenningford**[17] 4348 3-9-2 60.......................... GrahamLee 3 39
(Ollie Pears) *in tch on inner: effrt over 2f out: sn rdn and btn* **7/1**

-320 **8** *1 ¾* **Mad For Fun (IRE)**[15] 4397 3-8-8 52.......................... MickyFenton 10 26
(Paul Midgley) *chsd ldrs: rdn over 2f out: sn wknd* **10/1**

-304 **9** *8* **Becksies**[74] 2438 3-8-2 46 oh1.......................... PatrickMathers 2
(Paul Midgley) *towards rr: effrt and sme hdwy on outer over 2f out: sn rdn and wknd* **22/1**

5-00 **10** *48* **Come To Mind**[11] 4549 3-7-13 46 oh1..........................(b[1]) JulieBurke(3) 9
(Alan Berry) *s.i.s: a bhd* **100/1**

1m 24.94s (-2.06) **Going Correction** -0.275s/f (Firm) **10** Ran SP% **116.4**
Speed ratings (Par 98): **100,95,95,92,91 87,87,85,76,21**
Tote Swingers: 1&2 £13.50, 1&3 £3.60, 2&3 £9.00 CSF £56.96 CT £143.57 TOTE £2.70: £1.10, £6.50, £1.60; EX 67.90 Trifecta £392.30 Pool: £588.56 - 1.11 winning units..
Owner R S Cockerill (Farms) Ltd **Bred** R S Cockerill (farms) Ltd **Trained** Nawton, N Yorks

FOCUS
A weak 3-y-o handicap. It was run at a decent pace but still it paid to be handy. The placed horses off the best guide in a race with little depth.
Come To Mind Official explanation: jockey said gelding missed the break.
T/Plt: £12.30 to a £1 stake. Pool: £49,958.00 - 108.55 winning tickets. T/Qpdt: £9.00 to a £1 stake. Pool: £4,094.56 - 236.96 winning tickets. JR

4870 KEMPTON (A.W) (R-H)
Tuesday, August 7

OFFICIAL GOING: Standard to slow
Wind: Light, behind Weather: Cloudy

4914 BETFAIR CLASSIFIED STKS 1m (P)
5:55 (5:55) (Class 6) 3-Y-0+ **£1,617** (£481; £240; £120) **Stalls** Low

Form RPR
350- **1** **Scottish Lake**[301] 6775 4-9-4 61..........................(b[1]) KirstyMilczarek 14 71
(Olivia Maylam) *t.k.h: hld up bhd ldrs tl allowed to stride on into ld 5f out: mde rest: at least 2 l clr 1f out: clung on nr fin* **14/1**

523 **2** *nk* **Conducting**[8] 4662 4-9-4 64.......................... EddieAhern 6 70
(Gay Kelleway) *t.k.h: hld up in rr: rdn and prog on inner over 2f out: chsd wnr over 1f out: clsd at fin: jst hld* **6/1**[3]

6605 **3** *nk* **Divine Pamina (IRE)**[14] 4435 3-8-11 62.......................... TomQueally 2 68
(Jim Boyle) *sn in last and struggling to go the pce: rdn over 3f out: gd prog on outer fr 2f out: clsd 1f out: kpt on but a jst hld* **8/1**

0-26 **4** *4* **Kampai**[15] 4407 4-9-4 65.......................... PatCosgrave 4 60
(Julia Feilden) *in tch in midfield: rdn over 2f out: kpt on one pce fr over 1f out: n.d* **10/1**

5-20 **5** *1 ¾* **Tiberius Claudius (IRE)**[40] 3549 4-9-4 64.......................... IanMongan 7 56
(George Margarson) *cl up bhd ldrs: rdn over 2f out: disp 2nd briefly over 1f out: wknd* **25/1**

-514 **6** *½* **Autumn Fire**[51] 3193 3-8-11 62.......................... DavidProbert 10 54
(Andrew Balding) *towards rr: rdn 3f out: nt qckn and n.d fr 2f out: plugged on* **6/1**[3]

0-00 **7** *¾* **Comical**[12] 4504 3-8-11 65.......................... FrannyNorton 1 52
(Mark Johnston) *setted in rr: rdn 3f out: no prog and wl btn 2f out: sme late hdwy* **11/2**[2]

0200 **8** *2 ¾* **Swift Act**[12] 4486 3-8-6 65.......................... DarrenEgan(5) 8 46
(Ronald Harris) *led 3f: chsd ldr to over 1f out: wknd* **25/1**

0351 **9** *¾* **Darling Grace**[14] 4436 3-8-8 64..........................(p) AdamBeschizza(3) 13 44
(William Haggas) *nt that wl away but sn prom on outer: wknd wl over 2f out* **13/2**

0-02 **10** *½* **Foot Tapper**[88] 2045 3-8-11 65.......................... SebSanders 9 43
(Chris Wall) *trckd ldr 3f: styd prom tl wknd u.p over 2f out* **5/1**[1]

-005 **11** *11* **Greatest Dancer (IRE)**[19] 4232 3-8-11 65.......................... TedDurcan 3
(Jamie Osborne) *chsd ldrs: pushed along after 3f: wknd 3f out: eased and t.o* **20/1**

0460 **12** *9* **Avalon Bay**[21] 4193 4-9-4 47..........................(p[1]) DaneO'Neill 12
(Pat Eddery) *s.i.s: racd wd: rchd midfield after 3f: wd and wknd bnd 3f out: eased and t.o* **66/1**

1m 40.81s (1.01) **Going Correction** +0.125s/f (Slow)
WFA 3 from 4yo 7lb **12** Ran SP% **114.8**
Speed ratings (Par 101): **99,98,98,94,92 92,91,88,87,87 76,67**
Tote Swingers: 1&2 £14.80, 1&3 £31.80, 2&3 £13.00 CSF £88.89 TOTE £13.50: £5.80, £2.10, £3.30; EX 111.60 Trifecta £225.40 Part won. Pool: £304.65 - 0.20 winning units..
Owner Miss Olivia Maylam **Bred** Farmers Hill Stud **Trained** Epsom, Surrey

FOCUS
The second meeting since the track had been reworked and, like the previous day, it was riding on the slow side. This was a moderate contest and it proved hard work. The runner-up is rated close to his best with the third running a personal-best.
Darling Grace Official explanation: jockey said filly suffered interference leaving stalls.

Avalon Bay Official explanation: jockey said gelding hung left.

4915 BETFAIR SUPPORTING GRASSROOTS RACING H'CAP 1m 4f (P)
6:25 (6:27) (Class 6) (0-65,65) 3-Y-O+ **£1,617** (£481; £240; £120) **Stalls** Centre

Form RPR

0064 **1** **Sedgwick**[15] 4391 10-9-5 **63** MichaelJMMurphy(7) 5 72
(Shaun Harris) *stdd s: hld up in last trio: prog over 3f out: rdn wl over 2f out: clsd to ld over 1f out: styd on wl* **10/1**

3664 **2** *2* **Jalors (IRE)**[11] 4536 4-9-7 **63** DarrenEgan(5) 10 69
(Ronald Harris) *trckd ldrs: rdn and nt qckn 3f out: styd on fr 2f out to take 2nd last 100yds* **4/1**[2]

020 **3** *1 3/4* **Mount Abora (IRE)**[12] 4505 5-10-0 **65** IanMongan 12 68
(Laura Mongan) *hld up in rr: prog on outer fr 5f out: rdn to ld over 2f out: fnd nthing in front and hdd over 1f out: one pce after* **12/1**

600 **4** *nk* **Chemistry Master**[22] 4157 4-9-13 **64** DaneO'Neill 4 67
(Jeremy Gask) *stdd s: hld up in last trio: gng best over 3f out: rdn over 2f out and limited rspnse: kpt on fr over 1f out to press for 3rd nr fin* **11/2**[3]

0-06 **5** *2 1/4* **Pugnacious (IRE)**[13] 4465 3-8-11 **59** FrannyNorton 3 58
(Mark Johnston) *nt gng wl in last trio early: rdn in last 3f out and no prog: kpt on fr over 1f out* **8/1**

-250 **6** *1* **Phonic (IRE)**[27] 3961 5-9-11 **62** (b1) EddieAhern 6 60
(John Dunlop) *trckd ldr after 2f to wl over 2f out: steadily fdd* **13/2**

0053 **7** *3 3/4* **If I Were A Boy (IRE)**[27] 3962 5-10-0 **65** (p) TomQueally 2 57
(Dominic Ffrench Davis) *trckd ldr 2f: styd prom: rdn over 3f out: lost pl wl over 2f out: steadily wknd on inner* **3/1**[1]

4000 **8** *8* **Audacious**[21] 4199 4-10-0 **65** PatCosgrave 8 44
(Michael Quinn) *sn led at decent pce: hdd over 2f out: wknd qckly over 1f out* **25/1**

/60- **9** *6* **Rollin 'n Tumblin**[490] 1148 8-8-12 **54** MarkCoumbe(5) 1 23
(Michael Attwater) *planted himself on way to post: t.k.h early: cl up in over 3f out: wknd* **40/1**

0406 **10** *1 1/2* **Runaway Tiger (IRE)**[15] 4402 4-8-13 **50** (e1) SebSanders 13 17
(Paul D'Arcy) *slowly away: rousted along early then t.k.h and in tch: lost pl over 3f out: sn wknd* **14/1**

2m 36.63s (2.13) **Going Correction** +0.125s/f (Slow)
WFA 3 from 4yo+ 11lb **10** Ran SP% **114.6**
Speed ratings (Par 101): **97,95,94,94,92 92,89,84,80,79**
Tote Swingers: 1&2 £6.30, 1&3 £7.30, 2&3 £10.60 CSF £48.93 CT £490.18 TOTE £12.80: £3.20, £2.00, £3.40; EX 63.60 Trifecta £609.60 Part won. Pool: £823.91 - 0.80 winning units..
Owner Wilf Hobson **Bred** G And Mrs Middlebrook **Trained** Carburton, Notts

FOCUS
The winner, third, fourth and fifth were all held up early on, suggesting the pace was plenty fast enough on the slow surface. The winner is back to his Doncaster may form.

4916 BIG FISH TURNS 30 MEDIAN AUCTION MAIDEN STKS 1m 3f (P)
6:55 (6:57) (Class 6) 3-5-Y-O **£2,264** (£673; £336; £168) **Stalls** Low

Form RPR

6 **1** **Emerald Invader**[82] 2196 3-9-3 0 TedDurcan 7 76
(David Elsworth) *hld up in 5th: clsd on ldrs 2f out: drvn over 1f out: narrow ld ins fnl f: jst hld on* **7/1**[2]

5-2 **2** *nse* **Headline News (IRE)**[59] 2927 3-8-12 0 ChrisCatlin 4 71
(Rae Guest) *t.k.h early: hld up in tch: rdn and clsd on ldrs 2f out: styd on to chal last 100yds: jst pipped* **7/1**[2]

62-5 **3** *nk* **Moment Of Time**[50] 3219 4-9-8 89 JimmyFortune 1 71
(Andrew Balding) *trckd ldr 1f: styd handy: wnt 2nd again 3f out: rdn to ld 2f out but sn hrd pressed: hdd ins fnl f: tried to respond but one pce last 50yds* **1/2**[1]

00 **4** *3 1/2* **Keeping Time**[25] 4067 3-9-3 0 TomQueally 6 69
(Sir Henry Cecil) *trckd ldr after 1f: led over 3f out: drvn and hdd 2f out: one pce over 1f out* **14/1**

3 **5** *3* **Anychanceofabirdie (USA)**[78] 2339 3-9-3 0 MartinLane 5 64
(David Simcock) *hld up in last pair: outpcd 3f out: kpt on one pce fr 1f out: n.d* **10/1**[3]

6 *21* **Narapatisithu (FR)**[54] 5-9-13 0 JamieMackay 2 26
(K F Clutterbuck) *hld up in last pair: wknd over 3f out: t.o* **250/1**

0-00 **7** *41* **Time For A Tiger**[15] 4410 3-8-12 46 (b1) DaneO'Neill 3
(Henry Candy) *led to over 3f out: wknd rapidly: wl t.o* **66/1**

2m 23.03s (1.13) **Going Correction** +0.125s/f (Slow)
WFA 3 from 4yo+ 10lb **7** Ran SP% **109.3**
Speed ratings (Par 101): **100,99,99,97,95 79,49**
Tote Swingers: 1&2 £3.70, 1&3 £1.60, 2&3 £2.20 CSF £49.06 TOTE £9.70: £3.00, £3.10; EX 51.90.
Owner Mrs S Kelly & David Elsworth **Bred** Newsells Park Stud **Trained** Newmarket, Suffolk

FOCUS
The favourite looked to run well short of her official mark of 89 and the form is probably just fair, rated around the second and fifth.

4917 BETFAIR.COM MAIDEN STKS 7f (P)
7:25 (7:25) (Class 5) 2-Y-O **£2,264** (£673; £336; £168) **Stalls** Low

Form RPR

1 **Filfil (USA)** 2-9-3 0 AhmedAjtebi 4 81+
(Mahmood Al Zarooni) *chsd ldrs in 5th: shkn up over 2f out: prog to go 2nd jst over 1f out: r.o wl to ld last strides* **11/1**

2 **2** *nk* **Brave Command (USA)**[12] 4507 2-9-3 0 MickaelBarzalona 2 80+
(Mahmood Al Zarooni) *trckd ldr: led 2f out: shkn up and drew at least 3 l clr over 1f out: styd on but hdd last strides* **6/5**[1]

0 **3** *6* **Grilletto (USA)**[25] 4066 2-9-3 0 MartinDwyer 11 64
(James Tate) *chsd ldrs in 4th: rdn over 2f out: sn outpcd: kpt on to take 3rd wl ins fnl f* **33/1**

05 **4** *1 1/2* **Abraq**[17] 4340 2-9-3 0 GeorgeBaker 9 61+
(Ed Dunlop) *settled in 7th: last of those in tch 3f out: reminder 2f out: jst pushed along after and styd on steadily fnl f* **14/1**

4 **5** *nk* **Veturia (USA)**[19] 4247 2-8-12 0 (t) PhillipMakin 8 55
(Kevin Ryan) *rrd s but led: rdn and hdd 2f out: fdd fnl f* **5/1**[3]

6 *1* **Norphin** 2-9-3 0 EddieAhern 1 57
(Denis Coakley) *trckd ldng pair: gng wl enough over 2f out: shkn up and sn outpcd: fdd* **50/1**

7 *2 1/2* **Big Thunder** 2-9-3 0 LukeMorris 6 51+
(Sir Mark Prescott Bt) *s.s: wl in rr: 8th and off the pce over 2f out: pushed along and kpt on after: nt disgracd* **25/1**

8 *3 3/4* **Alcaeus** 2-9-3 0 ChrisCatlin 5 41
(Sir Mark Prescott Bt) *s.s: a wl in rr: pushed along and no real prog over 2f out* **40/1**

9 *1/2* **Echo Brava** 2-9-3 0 TedDurcan 12 40
(John Gallagher) *veered lft s: rn green and sn shoved along in rr: nvr a factor* **80/1**

10 *nk* **Derwentwater (IRE)** 2-9-3 0 WilliamBuick 13 39+
(John Gosden) *s.v.s: rn green and a in last pair* **11/1**

0 **11** *4* **Elhaame (IRE)**[25] 4066 2-9-3 0 KierenFallon 10 28
(Luca Cumani) *sn pushed along in 6th: no prog over 2f out: wknd qckly over 1f out* **9/2**[2]

1m 27.64s (1.64) **Going Correction** +0.125s/f (Slow) **11** Ran SP% **116.1**
Speed ratings (Par 94): **95,94,87,86,85 84,81,77,76,76 71**
Tote Swingers: 1&2 £5.20, 1&3 £57.00, 2&3 £8.60 CSF £23.63 TOTE £15.20: £3.30, £1.10, £10.40; EX 38.60 Trifecta £1017.10 Part won. Pool: £1,374.51 - 0.64 winning units..
Owner Godolphin **Bred** Fares Farm Llc **Trained** Newmarket, Suffolk

FOCUS
Some interesting nursery/long-term prospects among the beaten runners, but this only really concerned the two Mahmood Al Zarooni-trained colts, who are both sons of Kentucky Derby and Breeders' Cup Classic runner-up Hard Spun. The form is rated on the positive side.

NOTEBOOK
Filfil(USA) managed to claw back the favourite after being matched at 170 for pennies in running. The first foal of a 6f-1m dirt winner, he will have to prove as effective on turf, but he evidently has plenty of ability and is open to improvement. (op 16-1)
Brave Command(USA), a much more expensive purchase than his stablemate ($870,000 compared with 80,000gns), was looking to go one better than when runner-up at Folkestone on his debut. He didn't help himself by racing keenly, yet still found enough to pull well clear of the third. (op 10-11 tchd 5-6)
Grilletto(USA) improved on the form he showed when behind Elhaame (disappointing here) in a strong July course maiden on his debut.
Abraq caught the eye not being given a hard time on what was his third start. He can now switch to nurseries. (op 11-1)
Veturia(USA), a bit keen on her debut in a 6f novice event, could have settled better in front but she wasn't too bad. She wandered off a straight line under pressure, though, and it remains to be seen whether she's going to progress. An entry in the Fillies' Mile suggests she's shown plenty at home. (op 9-1)
Norphin is bred to want further (out of a 1m4f winner) but he showed up to a point on this racecourse debut and has ability.
Elhaame(IRE) shaped okay in a decent July course maiden on his debut, but was never going on this switch to Polytrack. (op 5-1)

4918 BETFAIR H'CAP 2m (P)
7:55 (7:55) (Class 5) (0-75,75) 3-Y-O **£2,264** (£673; £336; £168) **Stalls** Low

Form RPR

1-53 **1** **Awesome Pearl (USA)**[77] 2372 3-9-4 **75** HarryBentley(3) 1 83
(Sir Mark Prescott Bt) *pushed up to ld: mde all: urged along fr 1/2-way: drvn and hrd pressed 2f out: styd on stoutly and in command fnl f* **2/1**[2]

6613 **2** *2 1/4* **Byron Blue (IRE)**[20] 4225 3-9-4 **72** GeorgeBaker 4 77
(Jamie Osborne) *hld up in last pair: prog 5f out: wnt 2nd 3f out gng easily: rdn to chal 2f out: nt qckn over 1f out: flashed tail and wl hld fnl f* **7/4**[1]

4615 **3** *3/4* **Queen's Star**[11] 4537 3-8-7 **61** DavidProbert 2 65
(Andrew Balding) *hld up in tch: pushed along over 3f out: effrt on inner over 2f out: sn nt qckn u.p: kpt on fnl f* **13/2**[3]

4450 **4** *1/2* **Jorum**[18] 4311 3-9-3 **71** TomQueally 3 75
(Sir Henry Cecil) *cl up: trckd wnr after 7f: pushed along 4f out: lost 2nd 3f out: outpcd 2f out: kpt on* **15/2**

2500 **5** *1 1/2* **Ctappers**[3] 3087 3-7-11 **56** oh1 DarrenEgan(5) 6 58
(Mick Channon) *hld up in last pair: pushed along over 5f out: outpcd fr 4f out: n.d after: styd on fnl f* **8/1**

0000 **6** *57* **Saharan Air (IRE)**[49] 3246 3-8-7 **61** MickaelBarzalona 5
(Jim Boyle) *chsd wnr 7f: sn urged along: styd in tch tl wknd 4f out: wl t.o* **20/1**

3m 31.97s (1.87) **Going Correction** +0.125s/f (Slow) **6** Ran SP% **110.7**
Speed ratings (Par 100): **100,98,98,98,97 69**
Tote Swingers: 1&2 £1.50, 1&3 £1.80, 2&3 £1.90 CSF £5.71 TOTE £1.80: £1.10, £2.50; EX 7.60.
Owner Pearl Bloodstock Ltd **Bred** Centaur Farms Inc **Trained** Newmarket, Suffolk

FOCUS
A modest staying handicap in which the fifth could prove the best guide to the form.

4919 PATRICK BEACH MEMORIAL H'CAP 6f (P)
8:25 (8:27) (Class 4) (0-85,85) 3-Y-O **£4,075** (£1,212; £606; £303) **Stalls** Low

Form RPR

-631 **1** **Saloomy**[10] 4605 3-8-8 **72** WilliamBuick 4 86+
(David Simcock) *mde all: rdn 2f out: hrd pressed 1f out: styd on wl* **5/2**[1]

6053 **2** *1* **Intransigent**[19] 4234 3-9-7 **85** JimmyFortune 8 95
(Andrew Balding) *hld up in last: prog 2f out: chsd ldng pair 1f out: styd on to take 2nd last strides* **3/1**[3]

5221 **3** *hd* **Sir Maximilian (IRE)**[59] 2918 3-9-2 **80** KierenFallon 2 89
(Ed Dunlop) *t.k.h: hld up in 3rd: chsd wnr 2f out: chal on inner 1f out: hld last 100yds: lost 2nd post* **11/4**[2]

316- **4** *3 1/2* **Blackdown Fair**[408] 3429 3-9-2 **80** JamesMillman 6 78
(Rod Millman) *chsd wnr to 2f out: edgd lft and fdd over 1f out* **20/1**

-130 **5** *nk* **Fast Finian (IRE)**[16] 4364 3-8-8 **72** EddieAhern 7 69
(Paul D'Arcy) *racd on outer: trckd ldng trio: shkn up over 2f out: hanging over 1f out: sltly impeded sn after: no prog after* **7/1**

-005 **6** *2 1/2* **Gung Ho Jack**[15] 4412 3-8-13 **77** LukeMorris 5 66
(John Best) *in tch: rdn over 2f out: no prog and sn btn* **14/1**

50-0 **7** *1/2* **Elbe**[17] 4336 3-9-4 **82** TomQueally 1 70
(Sir Henry Cecil) *hld up in 6th: shkn up over 2f out: no prog* **10/1**

1m 13.01s (-0.09) **Going Correction** +0.125s/f (Slow) **7** Ran SP% **113.3**
Speed ratings (Par 102): **105,103,103,98,98 95,94**
Tote Swingers: 1&2 £2.20, 1&3 £1.10, 2&3 £2.90 CSF £10.10 CT £20.69 TOTE £2.90: £1.10, £2.90; EX 9.30 Trifecta £23.60 Pool: £431.59 - 13.48 winning units..
Owner Saleh Al Homaizi & Imad Al Sagar **Bred** D J And Mrs Deer **Trained** Newmarket, Suffolk

FOCUS
An interesting race and probably strong enough form for the grade. The winner looks an improver with the placed horses helping to back up the form.

4920 BETFAIR "BRINGS YOU BETTER VALUE" FILLIES' H'CAP 6f (P)
8:55 (8:55) (Class 5) (0-70,70) 3-Y-O+ **£2,264** (£673; £336; £168) **Stalls** Low

Form RPR

5225 **1** **Auntie Mabel**[12] 4493 3-8-9 **57** (v1) DavidProbert 3 67
(Andrew Balding) *chsd ldng trio: prog to chal 2f out: edgd lft but narrow ld jst over 1f out: drvn out* **6/1**

30 **2** *1/2* **Demoiselle Bond**[52] 3152 4-8-8 **52** RobertHavlin 1 61
(Lydia Richards) *taken down early: hanging lft thrght but led at str pce: hdd jst over 1f out: kpt on but hld ins fnl f* **16/1**

4115 **3** *1 1/4* **Lady Mango (IRE)**[11] 4533 4-9-4 **67** DarrenEgan(5) 4 72
(Ronald Harris) *outpcd and rdn in last trio: prog over 2f out: chsd ldng pair jst over 1f out: kpt on but nvr able to chal* **15/8**[1]

500 **4** 1 ½ **Flying Kitty**[37] 3670 3-8-3 **51** oh1 .... JamieMackay 2 50
(John Bridger) *dwlt: hld up but sn bdly outpcd and pushed along in last: prog over 1f out: kpt on fnl f but no threat* **33/1**

2050 **5** 4 ½ **Button Moon (IRE)**[3] 4824 4-9-5 **70** ....(p) WilliamTwiston-Davies(7) 5 56
(Ian Wood) *pressed ldr at str pce and forced to r quite wd: lost 2nd and wknd over 2f out* **4/1**[2]

-460 **6** ¾ **Topflight Princess**[20] 4218 3-9-5 **70** .... HarryBentley(3) 7 52
(Jeremy Gask) *chsd ldng pair: rdn to chal over 2f out: sn wknd* **17/2**

100 **7** ½ **By Invitation (USA)**[12] 4496 3-9-7 **69** .... JimCrowley 8 50
(Ralph Beckett) *chsd ldng quartet and in tch: rdn bef 1/2-way: wknd over 2f out* **11/2**[3]

222 **0** nk **Liberal Lady**[146] 890 4-9-3 **61** ....(e) LukeMorris 9 42
(Ralph Smith) *awkward s: outpcd in last trio: drvn and tried to cl on ldrs on inner 2f out: wknd over 1f out* **10/1**

1m 13.55s (0.45) **Going Correction** +0.125s/f (Slow)
WFA 3 from 4yo 4lb **8** Ran SP% **112.9**
Speed ratings (Par 100): **102,101,99,97,91 90,90,89**
Tote Swingers: 1&2 £4.20, 1&3 £7.60, 2&3 £9.30 CSF £90.54 CT £245.27 TOTE £10.50: £2.30, £2.10, £1.20; EX 86.40 Trifecta £494.20 Part won. Pool: £667.89 - 0.20 winning units..
Owner Kingsclere Racing CLub **Bred** R F Johnson Houghton **Trained** Kingsclere, Hants

FOCUS
A modest fillies' sprint run at a strong pace in which the first tow both recorded slight personal bests.
T/Plt: £301.20 to a £1 stake. Pool: £44,141.76 - 106.95 winning tickets. T/Qpdt: £19.60 to a £1 stake. Pool: £4,319.70 - 499.29 winning tickets. JN

4877 RIPON (R-H)
Tuesday, August 7

OFFICIAL GOING: Good (good to soft in places; 8.0)
Bend from back straight to home straight moved out 2m and 6yds added to races on Round course.
Wind: moderate 1/2 behind Weather: fine

4921 SILKS AND SADDLES BAR MAIDEN STKS 6f
6:05 (6:06) (Class 5) 2-Y-O £2,587 (£770; £384; £192) **Stalls** High

Form RPR

5 **1** **Melody Of Love**[17] 4344 2-8-12 0 .... PaulMulrennan 5 89+
(Ann Duffield) *trckd ldrs: effrt over 2f out: led appr fnl f: drvn clr* **6/1**[3]

3 **2** 4 **Moviesta (USA)**[9] 4625 2-9-3 0 .... TomEaves 6 82
(Bryan Smart) *t.k.h: w ldr: led after 2f: rdn and hung rt over 1f out: hdd appr fnl f: no ex* **7/4**[2]

4 **3** 5 **Darkening (IRE)**[46] 3346 2-9-3 0 .... SilvestreDeSousa 9 67
(Mahmood Al Zarooni) *led 2f: wknd over 1f out* **6/4**[1]

00 **4** ¾ **Aeronwyn Bryn (IRE)**[12] 4494 2-8-12 0 .... TonyHamilton 4 60
(Michael Dods) *dwlt: sn chsng ldrs: wknd over 1f out* **14/1**

5 9 **Elusive Thought (IRE)** 2-9-3 0 .... RobertWinston 7 38
(Tom Tate) *dwlt: sme hdwy on outside over 2f out: sn wknd* **9/1**

000 **6** 1 **Bollin Billy**[45] 3401 2-8-12 0 .... AdamCarter(5) 3 35
(Tim Easterby) *sn outpcd in rr: bhd fnl 3f* **100/1**

0 **7** ½ **Black Truffle (FR)**[9] 4625 2-9-3 0 .... AndrewElliott 2 33
(Michael Bell) *chsd ldrs: lost pl over 1f out* **33/1**

0 **8** 13 **Itsallinthemind**[11] 4545 2-8-12 0 .... DavidAllan 8
(Tim Easterby) *uns rdr leaving paddock: sn outpcd and in rr: bhd fnl 3f: eased ins fnl f* **50/1**

9 38 **Cazza** 2-8-12 0 .... AdrianNicholls 1
(David Nicholls) *s.v.s: a detached in last: wl bhd whn eased fnl f: hoplessly t.o* **33/1**

1m 12.43s (-0.57) **Going Correction** -0.225s/f (Firm) **9** Ran SP% **116.1**
Speed ratings (Par 94): **94,88,82,81,69 67,67,49,**
Tote Swingers: 1&2 £4.50, 1&3 £3.40, 2&3 £1.02 CSF £16.84 TOTE £5.20: £1.10, £1.40, £1.10; EX 21.20.
Owner Mrs P Good **Bred** Mrs P Good **Trained** Constable Burton, N Yorks

FOCUS
A dry night and day and the winning rider described the ground as "good", a comment backed up by the official time (within a second and a half of Racing Post Standard). A race won last year by the smart Mehdi and, although this winner has some way to go before reaching that level, there was plenty to like about the way she went about her business in this truly run race. The winner was impressive but the third and fourth were both below form.

NOTEBOOK
Melody Of Love ◆, who showed ability behind a potentially very useful sort over 5f at this course on her debut, stepped up a fair way on that level over this longer trip after attracting support. She'll have no problems with 7f, is open to further improvement and is the type to win again. (op 15-2 tchd 8-1)
Moviesta(USA) showed fair form, despite greenness, on his debut and took the eye in the preliminaries. He probably ran to a similar level despite racing with the choke out over this longer trip. He'll need to settle better than he did here if he is to progress but he's capable of winning races as he matures. (op 6-4)
Darkening(IRE) failed to match the form shown in softer ground in a stronger maiden than this on his debut at Newmarket. He doesn't have much in the way of physical scope but should be able to pick up an uncompetitive event at some point. (op 5-4 tchd Evens)
Aeronwyn Bryn(IRE) had shown modest form on his debut and probably ran to a similar level in what looked a fair maiden for the track. A move into ordinary nurseries and the step up to 7f and beyond should suit better and there's probably more to come. (op 20-1 tchd 25-1)
Elusive Thought(IRE), the first foal of a half-sister to winners from 5f-1m4f, attracted support at big odds but was always up against it after a tardy start and after running green. However, he should be all the better for this experience and will fare better granted a stiffer test of stamina. (op 20-1)

4922 CONSTANT SECURITY SERVICES NURSERY 5f
6:35 (6:36) (Class 5) (0-75,74) 2-Y-O £2,587 (£770; £384; £192) **Stalls** High

Form RPR

523 **1** **Dusty Storm (IRE)**[17] 4344 2-9-5 **72** .... AdrianNicholls 6 77
(Ed McMahon) *chsd ldng pair: drvn and outpcd over 2f out: styd on to ld jst ins fnl f: drvn out* **3/1**[1]

4561 **2** nk **La Sylphe**[28] 3936 2-9-2 **69** .... GrahamGibbons 5 73
(David Barron) *w ldr: led over 1f out: hdd jst ins fnl f: no ex nr fin* **13/2**

500 **3** ¾ **Sandsend (IRE)**[24] 4114 2-8-2 **55** .... PatrickMathers 2 56
(Richard Fahey) *sn drvn along and wl outpcd: hdwy 2f out: chsng ldrs 1f out: kpt on same pce clsng stages* **7/1**

034 **4** 1 ¾ **Teetotal (IRE)**[22] 4132 2-9-0 **67** .... SilvestreDeSousa 4 62
(Nigel Tinkler) *dwlt: sn drvn along and outpcd: hdwy over 2f out: chsng ldrs over 1f out: one pce* **7/2**[2]

104 **5** 1 ¼ **Projectisle (IRE)**[24] 4116 2-9-7 **74** .... AmyRyan 1 65
(Kevin Ryan) *in rr: drvn over 2f out: chsng ldrs over 1f out: one pce* **9/2**

0516 **6** 3 ½ **Our Diane (IRE)**[10] 4614 2-9-7 **74** .... DanielTudhope 7 52
(David O'Meara) *led: hdd over 1f out: sn wknd* **4/1**[3]

1m 0.28s (-0.42) **Going Correction** -0.225s/f (Firm) **6** Ran SP% **111.2**
Speed ratings (Par 94): **94,93,92,89,87 81**
Tote Swingers: 1&2 £2.30, 1&3 £3.00, 2&3 £3.90 CSF £21.87 TOTE £4.10: £2.40, £4.30; EX 18.40.
Owner R L Bedding **Bred** Yeomanstown Stud **Trained** Lichfield, Staffs

FOCUS
A fair nursery run at a decent gallop and the form appears sound with the first three close to their pre-race marks.

NOTEBOOK
Dusty Storm(IRE), who had shown fair form in maidens and whose last (course) run had been franked by the first winner on this card, got the perfect tow into the race and showed improved form on this nursery debut, despite not doing much in front. She's open to further improvement. (op 10-3 tchd 11-4)
La Sylphe ◆ deserves plenty of credit from this 6lb higher mark back on grass as she was harried for the lead throughout and stuck on determinedly to chase home an unexposed winner, who admittedly seemed to idle in front. She's capable of making amends over sprint distances. (op 8-1 tchd 6-1)
Sandsend(IRE) ◆ had hinted at ability in maidens (all at York) but turned in an improved effort after getting taken off his feet on this nursery debut. The step up to 6f will suit, he's in very good hands and is sure to pick up a race. (op 10-1)
Teetotal(IRE), who gave a bit of trouble once loaded into the stalls, had shown ability at a modest level over 6f and left the impression that the return to that trip and the return to a more conventional course would have suited. He's worth another chance. (op 3-1)
Projectisle(IRE) left the impression that the return to 6f and to a flatter track would have suited better and he is worth another chance. (tchd 11-2)
Our Diane(IRE) was again below her best after forcing too strong a gallop next to the favoured stands' rail, though it's worth remembering that the runner-up was upsides her throughout. She's best watched for now. (op 7-2 tchd 9-2)

4923 WASHROOM COMPANY H'CAP 1m 4f 10y
7:05 (7:06) (Class 4) (0-80,80) 3-Y-O £4,528 (£1,347; £673; £336) **Stalls** Centre

Form RPR

4432 **1** **Kunegunda**[18] 4311 3-9-5 **78** .... GrahamLee 4 87
(James Fanshawe) *hld up: effrt over 2f out: chsng ldr over 1f out: led last 100yds: drvn out* **11/4**[1]

106 **2** 2 **Modernism**[22] 4151 3-9-2 **75** .... NeilCallan 1 80
(Mark Johnston) *led: increased pce over 4f out: edgd lft and rt fnl f: hdd last 100yds: no ex* **9/1**

4023 **3** hd **Mizbah**[8] 4649 3-9-3 **76** ....(b[1]) SilvestreDeSousa 2 81
(Saeed Bin Suroor) *trckd ldrs: n.m.r on inner over 5f out: kpt on to chse ldrs over 2f out: nt clr run on inner and swtchd lft ins fnl f: styng on fin* **11/2**

1214 **4** 1 ¾ **Lady Kashaan (IRE)**[39] 3592 3-8-12 **71** .... AndrewElliott 6 73
(Alan Swinbank) *chsd ldrs: effrt 4f out: one pce appr fnl f* **3/1**[2]

0011 **5** 10 **Scarlet Whispers**[29] 3910 3-9-7 **80** .... MickyFenton 5 66
(Pam Sly) *w ldr: t.k.h: drvn over 3f out: lost pl over 2f out: eased over 1f out* **4/1**[3]

-552 **6** 24 **Linkable**[41] 3484 3-9-5 **78** .... MichaelHills 3 26
(Charles Hills) *chsd ldrs: pushed along 9f out: drvn and lost pl 4f out: sn bhd: eased fnl 2f: t.o* **6/1**

2m 34.89s (-1.81) **Going Correction** -0.125s/f (Firm) **6** Ran SP% **111.3**
Speed ratings (Par 102): **101,99,99,98,91 75**
Tote Swingers: 1&2 £3.80, 1&3 £2.60, 2&3 £6.00 CSF £26.14 TOTE £2.70: £2.40, £6.10; EX 34.80.
Owner Lord Halifax **Bred** Lord Halifax **Trained** Newmarket, Suffolk

FOCUS
A fair handicap but just an ordinary gallop until the pace lifted early in the straight. The form looks pretty solid.
Scarlet Whispers Official explanation: trainer said filly was unsuited by going (good - good to soft in places).
Linkable Official explanation: jockey said colt was never travelling.

4924 DAVID CHAPMAN MEMORIAL H'CAP 5f
7:35 (7:35) (Class 3) (0-95,93) 3-Y-O-£6,931 (£2,074; £1,037; £519; £258) **Stalls** High

Form RPR

30-6 **1** **Singeur (IRE)**[18] 4312 5-9-9 **92** .... DanielTudhope 12 101
(Robin Bastiman) *racd stands' side: hdwy over 2f out: r.o wl fnl f: led nr fin: 1st of 7 that gp* **9/2**[1]

1205 **2** ¾ **Oldjoesaid**[18] 4312 8-8-9 **78** .... RussKennemore 13 84
(Paul Midgley) *dwlt: racd stands' side: hdwy over 2f out: styd on wl: tk 2nd post: 2nd of 7 that gp* **20/1**

1110 **3** hd **Bosun Breese**[10] 4576 7-9-10 **93** .... GrahamGibbons 4 99
(David Barron) *overall ldr far side: hdd and no ex nr fin: 1st of 6 that gp* **9/1**

0060 **4** ¾ **Fitz Flyer (IRE)**[7] 4690 6-9-7 **90** .... AdrianNicholls 15 93
(David Nicholls) *led 6 others stands' side: kpt on same pce last 75yds: 3rd of 7 that gp* **9/2**[1]

2050 **5** nk **Defence Council (IRE)**[11] 4554 4-8-9 **78** .... SilvestreDeSousa 11 80
(Mel Brittain) *racd stands' side: w ldrs: edgd rt and kpt on same pce ins fnl f: 4th of 7 that gp* **17/2**[3]

1100 **6** shd **Best Trip (IRE)**[16] 4367 5-8-9 **78** .... GrahamLee 1 79
(Brian Ellison) *racd far side: chsd ldrs: kpt on same pce ins fnl f: 2nd of 6 that gp* **10/1**

2424 **7** shd **Haajes**[18] 4292 8-8-10 **79** ....(b) MickyFenton 14 80
(Paul Midgley) *w ldr stands' side: kpt on same pce last 150yds: 5th of 7 that gp* **20/1**

000 **8** ½ **Excel Bolt**[10] 4576 4-9-6 **89** .... TomEaves 5 88
(Bryan Smart) *racd far side: chsd ldrs: kpt on same pce fnl f: 3rd of 6 that gp* **11/1**

0136 **9** shd **Solemn**[26] 4013 7-9-7 **90** ....(b) NeilCallan 2 89
(Milton Bradley) *racd far side: chsd ldrs: edgd rt over 2f out: styd on same pce fnl f: 4th of 6 that gp* **16/1**

4221 **10** ¾ **Noodles Blue Boy**[10] 4591 6-8-11 **87** .... JacobButterfield(7) 7 83
(Ollie Pears) *swtchd rt s to r far side: sn chsng ldrs: fdd over 1f out: 5th of 6 that gp* **8/1**[2]

2610 **11** 1 **Hazelrigg (IRE)**[10] 4576 7-9-9 **92** .... DavidAllan 6 85
(Tim Easterby) *racd far side: hdwy on ins whn nt clr run over 2f out: swtchd lft: nvr trbld ldrs: last of 6 that gp* **12/1**

3-05 **12** ½ **Bonnie Charlie**[22] 4133 6-8-11 **80** .... AndrewMullen 10 71
(David Nicholls) *n.m.r sn after s on stands' side: sn in rr: nvr a factor: 6th of 7 that gp* **8/1**[2]

-0 **13** 2 ¾ **Perfect Blossom**[73] 2507 5-8-12 **84**.................................. DaleSwift(3) 8 65
(Ian McInnes) *racd stands' side: chsd ldrs: lost pl over 1f out: last of 7 that gp* **40/1**

58.66s (-2.04) **Going Correction** -0.225s/f (Firm) **13** Ran SP% **122.1**
Speed ratings (Par 107): **107,105,105,104,103 103,103,102,102,101 99,98,94**
Tote Swingers: 1&2 £37.60, 1&3 £8.30, 2&3 £49.20 CSF £105.61 CT £819.37 TOTE £4.10: £2.50, £4.00, £3.10; EX 155.30.
Owner Ms M Austerfield **Bred** Patrick Cassidy **Trained** Cowthorpe, N Yorks

FOCUS
Exposed performers in a very useful handicap. The pace was sound and there was no advantage in the draw or with racing on any part of the track. The form looks straightforward rated around the placed horses.

NOTEBOOK
Singeur(IRE), who wasn't at his best in testing ground on his reappearance, confirmed himself a very useful sprinter back on this better surface. He won't be going up much for this, will be suited by the return to 6f and will be an interesting runner if returned to this track for the Great St Wilfrid later in the month. (op 5-1 tchd 11-2)
Oldjoesaid has only won once since last spring but he's bordering on useful when things drop for him and he matched the pick of his form from this season. He's suited by coming off a fast pace and will be one to look out for when a strong gallop is on the cards. (op 28-1)
Bosun Breese, an improved performer this year who reportedly slipped leaving the stalls when below his best at Ascot last time, had the run of the race and ran as well as he ever has done to emerge in front of the group that raced on the far side. He should continue to give a good account. (op 7-1)
Fitz Flyer(IRE) extended his run of creditable efforts, despite edging right under pressure but, while he's capable of winning from this sort of mark, a record of only one win from 27 turf starts confirms he's not really one to be going in head down for. (op 5-1 tchd 4-1)
Defence Council(IRE) has won only one of his 24 career starts and, while the return to 6f may be more to his liking, his record this year suggests he wouldn't be sure to step up on this next time. (op 16-1)
Best Trip(IRE)'s form looked to have levelled out on his last couple of starts but, while he ran creditably after racing against the far rail, he'll have to raise his game to win a similarly competitive handicap from this mark. (op 16-1)
Haajes hasn't won for nearly a year but extended his run of creditable efforts with the headgear refitted (for first time in over three years) and there'll be easier assignments from this mark than this one. He should continue to give a good account. (op 14-1)

4925 SIS LIVE H'CAP — 2m
8:05 (8:05) (Class 4) (0-85,83) 3-Y-0+ **£4,528** (£1,347; £673; £336) **Stalls** High

Form RPR
35-0 **1** **Body Language (IRE)**[17] 4326 4-9-3 **72**...............(p) SilvestreDeSousa 1 83
(Ian Williams) *mde all: drvn 4f out: hld on gamely* **7/1**
-502 **2** ½ **Gabrial's Star**[11] 4548 3-8-7 **77** ow1...................................... TomEaves 2 87
(Bryan Smart) *sn chsng ldrs: wnt 2nd over 2f out: kpt on same pce last 50yds* **11/4**[1]
2534 **3** 11 **Anna's Arch (IRE)**[9] 4626 5-9-1 **70**................................ RobertWinston 5 67
(Alan Swinbank) *mid-div: hdwy over 4f out: kpt on same pce fnl 2f: tk modest 3rd nr fin* **8/1**
0006 **4** ½ **Becausewecan (USA)**[10] 4575 6-10-0 **83**............................ NeilCallan 3 80
(Mark Johnston) *chsd wnr: drvn over 3f out: one pce fnl 2f* **6/1**[3]
4132 **5** hd **Choisan (IRE)**[17] 4346 3-8-9 **79**... DavidAllan 4 75
(Tim Easterby) *chsd ldrs: drvn 6f out: one pce fnl 2f* **7/2**[2]
6-46 **6** 3 **Petella**[21] 4176 6-8-10 **65**... PJMcDonald 6 58
(George Moore) *in rr: shkn up 8f out: outpcd 4f out: hdwy over 2f out: wknd towards fin* **17/2**
-620 **7** 8 **Riptide**[45] 3373 6-9-9 **78**...(p) JamieGoldstein 9 61
(Michael Scudamore) *sn chsng ldrs: reminders over 6f out: lost pl over 2f out* **10/1**
350 **8** 10 **Wild Desert (FR)**[6] 4697 7-9-13 **82**.................................... GrahamLee 7 53
(Charlie Longsdon) *hld up in rr: effrt 4f out: lost pl over 2f out* **12/1**
-004 **9** 8 **Hollins**[40] 3535 8-9-5 **74**.. FrederikTylicki 8 36
(Micky Hammond) *in rr: lost pl over 4f out: sn wl bhd* **33/1**

3m 27.71s (-4.09) **Going Correction** -0.125s/f (Firm)
WFA 3 from 4yo+ 15lb **9** Ran SP% **117.0**
Speed ratings (Par 105): **105,104,99,99,98 97,93,88,84**
Tote Swingers: 1&2 £2.90, 1&3 £11.00, 2&3 £6.40 CSF £26.98 CT £160.37 TOTE £9.00: £2.60, £1.20, £2.20; EX 38.30.
Owner Farranamanagh **Bred** Michael Morrissey **Trained** Portway, Worcs

FOCUS
A useful handicap in which the first two pulled a long way clear. The gallop was an ordinary one unil picking up around the 4f pole. The first two were clear and the winner is rated to her best.

4926 RACING AGAIN 18TH AUGUST MAIDEN STKS — 1m 1f 170y
8:35 (8:35) (Class 5) 3-4-Y-0 **£2,587** (£770; £384; £192) **Stalls** Low

Form RPR
03 **1** **Zanotti**[15] 4410 3-9-3 0...(t) NeilCallan 4 87+
(Roger Varian) *trckd ldrs: nt clr run on inner over 2f out: shkn up to ld over 1f out: styd on strly: eased nr fin* **8/13**[1]
66 **2** 2 **Mama Quilla (USA)**[16] 4366 3-8-12 0....................... SilvestreDeSousa 6 73
(William Haggas) *w ldr: drvn to chal 4f out: led 3f out: hdd over 1f out: kpt on same pce* **11/4**[2]
25 **3** 7 **Madame Blavatsky (FR)**[19] 4259 4-9-7 0......................... GrahamLee 7 58
(Karen McLintock) *trckd ldrs: effrt over 3f out: edgd rt over 2f out: one pce* **16/1**
0- **4** 3 ¾ **Dark Ruler (IRE)**[298] 6836 3-8-12 0............................ GarryWhillans(5) 2 55
(Alan Swinbank) *chsd ldrs: outpcd 6f out: one pce whn hung rt over 1f out* **25/1**
4 **5** 8 **Generous Dream**[59] 2927 4-9-0 0......................... RobertDodsworth(7) 8 34
(Mel Brittain) *in rr and sn pushed along: bhd fnl 6f* **33/1**
04 **6** 7 **Revelette (USA)**[42] 3461 3-8-12 0...................................... MichaelHills 1 19
(Charles Hills) *led: hdd 3f out: weakning whn hmpd over 2f out: bhd whn eased 1f out* **10/1**[3]
00 **R** **Shavalley (USA)**[9] 4630 3-8-12 0.................................. AdrianNicholls 3
(David Nicholls) *ref to r* **66/1**

2m 4.55s (-0.85) **Going Correction** -0.125s/f (Firm)
WFA 3 from 4yo 9lb **7** Ran SP% **111.8**
Speed ratings (Par 103): **98,96,90,87,81 75,**
Tote Swingers: 1&2 £1.10, 1&3 £3.40, 2&3 £2.90 CSF £2.31 TOTE £1.30: £1.10, £2.20; EX 2.90.

Owner Saleh Al Homaizi & Imad Al Sagar **Bred** Saleh Al Homaizi & Imad Al Sagar **Trained** Newmarket, Suffolk

FOCUS
An uncompetitive maiden run at just a modest gallop but fair form from the winner, who won with plenty in hand. The form is a bit fluid with the first two clear and nothing solid behind.
T/Plt: £13.40 to a £1 stake. Pool: £59,268.00 - 3,223.39 winning tickets. T/Qpdt: £8.50 to a £1 stake. Pool: £5,738.00 - 499.29 winning tickets. WG

4884 WOLVERHAMPTON (A.W) (L-H)
Tuesday, August 7

OFFICIAL GOING: Standard
Wind: Fresh behind Weather: Overcast

4927 £32 BONUS AT 32RED.COM FILLIES' NURSERY — 5f 20y(P)
2:10 (2:11) (Class 5) (0-75,73) 2-Y-0 **£2,385** (£704; £352) **Stalls** Low

Form RPR
204 **1** **Not Now Blondie**[14] 4433 2-8-8 60.................................. AndreaAtzeni 1 60
(Chris Dwyer) *chsd ldrs: rdn over 1f out: r.o to ld post* **5/1**[2]
043 **2** shd **Jet Acclaim (IRE)**[10] 4581 2-8-12 64 .... MircoDemuro 5 64
(Marco Botti) *led: rdn over 1f out: edgd lft wl ins fnl f: hdd post* **7/1**
00 **3** hd **Modern Lady**[11] 4545 2-8-0 55.................................. DeclanCannon(3) 9 54
(Richard Guest) *sn chsng ldrs: rdn and ev ch ins fnl f: r.o* **8/1**
0352 **4** ½ **Emperor's Daughter**[8] 4659 2-8-6 58..........................(p) JimmyQuinn 2 55
(Tim Pitt) *s.i.s: hld up: hdwy over 1f out: sn rdn: r.o* **13/2**[3]
6400 **5** 2 ¼ **Until It Sleeps**[13] 4450 2-8-1 53.. FrannyNorton 6 42
(Alan McCabe) *hld up: outpcd over 3f out: r.o u.p ins fnl f: nvr nrr* **40/1**
014 **6** 1 **Senora Lobo (IRE)**[14] 4421 2-8-5 57.......................... RoystonFfrench 7 43
(Lisa Williamson) *chsd ldr: rdn and ev ch over 1f out: no ex ins fnl f* **16/1**
404 **7** 2 ½ **Red Star Lady (IRE)**[12] 4512 2-8-9 61........................... MartinHarley 3 38
(Mrs K Burke) *chsd ldrs: rdn over 1f out: wknd fnl f* **5/2**[1]
5310 **8** 3 ¼ **Snow Angel (IRE)**[12] 4488 2-9-7 73.............................. SebSanders 4 38
(J W Hills) *prom: rdn over 1f out: sn wknd* **5/1**[2]
644 **9** 1 ¾ **Summer Isles**[47] 3313 2-9-7 73.. JoeFanning 8 32
(Ed Dunlop) *hld up: rdn and wknd 2f out* **15/2**

1m 1.8s (-0.50) **Going Correction** -0.10s/f (Stan) **9** Ran SP% **118.9**
Speed ratings (Par 91): **100,99,99,98,95 93,89,84,81**
Tote Swingers: 1&2 £6.70, 1&3 £8.20, 2&3 £13.50 CSF £41.09 CT £281.30 TOTE £10.00: £3.00, £1.50, £4.30; EX 41.90.
Owner Not Now Partnership **Bred** Mrs Shelley Dwyer **Trained** Six Mile Bottom, Cambs

FOCUS
A fair fillies' nursery, run at a decent pace and it served up a thrilling finish.

NOTEBOOK
Not Now Blondie had hinted at ability on a couple of occasions in maidens, including on her debut at Yarmouth when she finished an encouraging second. However, this was a definite step forward on what she'd achieved previously and she deserves plenty of credit having been one of the first under pressure. This trip looks a bare minimum for her and she's likely to be even more effective once returning to 6f. She's unlikely to be too harshly dealt with for this success and could well reappear at Lingfield next week under a penalty. (op 6-1)
Jet Acclaim(IRE) broke smartly and looked set for an all-the-way victory until being headed in the very last stride. She had shown some useful bits of form in three AW races before this and clearly goes well on the surface. This track appeared to suit more than Lingfield last time and I'd expect her to remain competitive at this kind of level in the coming weeks. Like the winner, this was her nursery debut and she by no means looks badly treated on this evidence. (op 9-2)
Modern Lady, fitted with a rug on entry to the stalls, ran a mighty race and was perhaps the hard luck story of the race. She was keener than ideal in the early stages and was forced to make her effort about five horses wide on the home turn. She found herself isolated down the centre and would surely have won with a smoother passage. (op 10-1)
Emperor's Daughter gave definite reasons for encouragement. This was a step up on her latest selling defeat and she would surely have finished even closer had she not lost valuable ground at the start. She was another to race against the far rail in the straight and is worthy of another chance. (op 7-1)
Red Star Lady(IRE) produced a bitterly disappointing run. She appeared to be travelling better than anything through halfway but found nil off the bridle. This had looked a good opportunity on paper and it would come as no surprise to see headgear applied next time. (op 9-2)

4928 32REDBET.COM H'CAP (DIV I) — 5f 216y(P)
2:40 (2:41) (Class 6) (0-60,60) 3-Y-0+ **£1,704** (£503; £251) **Stalls** Low

Form RPR
2000 **1** **Flaxen Lake**[14] 4438 5-8-10 46 oh1.........................(p) RichardKingscote 6 57
(Milton Bradley) *sn chsng ldr: led over 1f out: rdn out* **9/2**[2]
4555 **2** 2 ½ **Invigilator**[8] 4653 4-9-5 55...(t) JoeFanning 9 58
(Derek Shaw) *s.i.s: hld up: hdwy over 1f out: r.o to go 2nd post: nt rch wnr* **11/4**[1]
2150 **3** shd **Almaty Express**[8] 4653 10-9-10 60..................................(b) KieranO'Neill 7 62
(John Weymes) *led: rdn and hdd over 1f out: no ex ins fnl f: lost 2nd post* **6/1**[3]
5300 **4** 1 ½ **Rightcar**[8] 4653 5-9-4 54.. RobbieFitzpatrick 1 52
(Peter Grayson) *hld up: hdwy u.p over 1f out: r.o: nrst fin* **6/1**[3]
-600 **5** ½ **Yungaburra (IRE)**[28] 3943 8-9-0 50...............................(tp) FrannyNorton 2 46
(David C Griffiths) *chsd ldrs: rdn over 2f out: no ex fnl f* **10/1**
0460 **6** 1 ¼ **Royal Envoy (IRE)**[42] 3477 9-9-0 50.......................... MichaelStainton 4 42
(Paul Howling) *prom: rdn over 2f out: sn outpcd* **11/1**
4646 **7** 3 ¼ **Memphis Man**[17] 4332 9-8-13 49................................. RichardThomas 5 31
(David Evans) *sn pushed along and prom: rdn over 2f out: wknd over 1f out* **8/1**
0020 **8** 2 ¾ **Bold Diva**[19] 4240 7-8-10 46...(v) LiamJones 3 19
(Tony Carroll) *prom: rdn over 2f out: wknd over 1f out* **11/1**

1m 14.35s (-0.65) **Going Correction** -0.10s/f (Stan) **8** Ran SP% **110.3**
Speed ratings (Par 101): **100,96,96,94,93 92,87,84**
Tote Swingers: 1&2 £3.30, 1&3 £5.00, 2&3 £2.30 CSF £16.00 CT £67.79 TOTE £5.00: £4.20, £1.30, £2.30; EX 14.90.
Owner Asterix Partnership **Bred** R Hollinshead And M Johnson **Trained** Sedbury, Gloucs

FOCUS
A modest sprint handicap, run at a strong pace and a convincing victory. The form looks straightforward and makes sense.
Flaxen Lake Official explanation: trainers representative said regarding apparent improvement in form that the yard was possibly coming back into form.

4929 32REDBET.COM H'CAP (DIV II) — 5f 216y(P)
3:10 (3:10) (Class 6) (0-60,60) 3-Y-0+ **£1,704** (£503; £251) **Stalls** Low

Form RPR
005 **1** **Jerry Ellen (IRE)**[64] 2774 3-8-6 46 oh1...................(b[1]) DuranFentiman 1 55
(Tim Easterby) *a.p: rdn to ld ins fnl f: r.o* **8/1**
0000 **2** 1 **Dingaan (IRE)**[57] 2973 9-8-11 47........................... RobbieFitzpatrick 3 53
(Peter Grayson) *hld up: gd hdwy and hung lft ins fnl f: r.o: nt rch wnr* **16/1**
0000 **3** hd **Botanist**[35] 3717 5-8-13 49....................................(be) RichardKingscote 2 54
(Milton Bradley) *hld up: hdwy over 1f out: rdn and n.m.r ins fnl f: r.o* **8/1**
66 **4** 1 ½ **Pinball (IRE)**[19] 4262 6-9-0 50..(v) BarryMcHugh 9 51
(Lisa Williamson) *chsd ldrs: rdn to ld and hung rt ins fnl f: sn hdd: styd on same pce* **11/1**

6500 **5** *nk* **One Way Or Another (AUS)** 4531 9 -9-1060.....(t) RichardThomas 6 60
(David Evans) *s.i.s: hld up: r.o ins fnl f: nvr nrr* **5/1**[3]
0000 **6** *1* **Not Bad For A Boy (IRE)**[18] 4592 3 -9-559..................(b[1]) SeanLevey 4 54
(Barry Leavy) *chsd ldr: rdn and ev ch fr over 1f out tl edgd rt and no ex ins fnl f* **9/2**[2]
1003 **7** *½* **Irie Ute**[8] 4653 4 -9-757.. ShaneKelly 7 52
(Sylvester Kirk) *chsd ldrs: rdn over 2f out: styng on same pce whn nt clr run ins fnl f* **5/1**[1]
0050 **8** *½* **Replicator**[13] 4467 7 -8-746 oh1......................................(e) RyanClark(3) 8 39
(Patrick Gilligan) *led: rdn over 2f out: hdd & wknd ins fnl f* **16/1**
0020 **9** *1 ½* **Little Perisher**[43] 3456 5 -9-151..(p) MichaelStainton 5 44
(Paul Howling) *chsd ldrs: rdn over 2f out: wkng whn nt clr run ins fnl f* **8/1**
1m 14.8s (-0.20)**Going Correction** -0.10s/f (Stan)
WFA 3 from 4yo+ 4lb **9**Ran SP% **116.9**
Speed ratings (Par 101): **97,95,95,93,93 91,91,90,88**
Tote Swingers: 1&2 £20.20, 1&3 £22.20, 2&3 £54.00 CSF £126.47 CT £762.37 TOTE £9.40 : £1.70, £10.10 , £2.30 ; EX 116.00 .
Owner Con Harrington **Bred** Mrs Chris Harrington **Trained** Great Habton, N Yorks

FOCUS
A messy race rated around those in the frame behind the winner.
Jerry Ellen (IRE) Official explanation: trainer said regarding apparent improvement in form that the gelding had benefited from 1st time blinkers.
Pinball(IRE) Official explanation: jockey said mare hung right handed throughout.
One Way Or Another (AUS) Official explanation: jockey said gelding missed the break.

4930 32RED.COM H'CAP 1m 5f 194y (P)
3:40 (3:40) (Class 4) (0-80,78) 3-Y-O **£4,528** (£1,347; £673 ; £336) **Stalls** Low

Form RPR
121 **1** **Courtesy Call (IRE)**[20] 4215 3 -9-778................................ JoeFanning 4 88
(Mark Johnston) *chsd ldrs: rdn over 2f out: r.o to ld wl ins fnl f* **9/4**[2]
3146 **2** *½* **Cape Savannah**[39] 3592 3 -9-677.................................... HayleyTurner 5 86
(David Simcock) *led: rdn and jnd over 1f out: hdd wl ins fnl f* **11/4**[3]
1121 **3** *1 ¾* **Bridgehampton**[12] 4513 3 -9-374.................................. JamieSpencer 6 82
(Michael Bell) *sn chsng ldr: ev ch over 1f out: sn hrd rdn: styd on same pce ins fnl f* **13/8**[1]
0546 **4** *8* **Hallmark Star**[8] 4649 3 -9-778... BarryMcHugh 3 73
(Gerard Butler) *hld up: rdn over 2f out: sn wknd* **11/1**
0040 **5** *12* **Hyson**[9] 4626 3 -8-1067..(p) RussKennemore 2 46
(Reg Hollinshead) *prom: rdn over 3f out: wknd over 2f out* **33/1**
3m 4.66s (-1.34)**Going Correction** -0.10s/f (Stan) **5**Ran SP% **106.8**
Speed ratings (Par 102): **99,98,97,93,86**
CSF £8.20 TOTE £3.40 : £2.40, £1.10 ; EX 11.60 .
Owner A D Spence **Bred** Mrs James Wigan **Trained** Middleham Moor, N Yorks

FOCUS
A decent staying handicap and a strong performance. The runner-up sets the standard.

4931 32RED CASINO MAIDEN FILLIES' STKS 1m 141y (P)
4:10 (4:11) (Class 5) 3-Y-O+ **£2,587** (£770; £384 ; £192) **Stalls** Low

Form RPR
0350 **1** *½* **Junior Diary (USA)**[12] 3476 3 -9-071................................ ShaneKelly 7 62+
(Brian Meehan) *chsd wnr: rdn over 1f out: chalng whn hmpd ins fnl f: styd on: fin 2nd: awrdd the r* **10/3**[3]
04-2 **2** **Sigurwana (USA)**[69] 2601 3 -9-070.................................... LiamJones 4 63+
(William Haggas) *mde all: rdn over 1f out: hung rt ins fnl f: styd on u.p: fin 1st: disqualified and plcd 2nd* **11/4**[2]
5 **3** *½* **Any Other Day**[20] 4213 3 -9-00... JimCrowley 1 60+
(William Knight) *hld up: hdwy over 1f out: nt clr run ins fnl f: r.o* **12/1**
56 **4** *½* **We Used To Wait (USA)**[8] 3918 3 -9-00.......................... AndreaAtzeni 8 59
(Peter Chapple-Hyam) *chsd ldrs: rdn over 2f out: styd on* **10/1**
00 **5** *¾* **Suedehead**[20] 4213 3 -9-00..................................... StevieDonohoe 3 57
(William Muir) *prom: rdn over 2f out: styd on u.p* **40/1**
6 *1 ¼* **Boonga Roogeta** 3 -8-90.. TobyAtkinson(5) 9 54
(Peter Charalambous) *hld up: rdn over 1f out: r.o ins fnl f: nt trble ldrs* **50/1**
00 **7** *hd* **Blue Dune**[9] 4630 3 -9-00.. JoeFanning 6 54
(Mark Johnston) *chsd ldrs: rdn over 1f out: no ex wl ins fnl f* **12/1**
8 *6* **Maria Vezzera** 3 -9-00.. MircoDemuro 5 40+
(Marco Botti) *s.s: hdwy 5f out: shkn up and wknd over 1f out* **6/4**[1]
6-00 **9** *10* **Midnite Motivation**[137] 1016 3 -9-00................................... JimmyQuinn 2 17
(Derek Shaw) *hld up: wknd over 2f out* **100/1**
1m 49.02s (-1.48)**Going Correction** -0.10s/f (Stan) **9**Ran SP% **119.6**
Speed ratings (Par 100): **101,102,101,100,100 98,98,93,84**
Tote Swingers: 1&2 £3.60, 1&3 £5.40, 2&3 £2.60 CSF £13.46 TOTE £4.20 : £1.10 , £1.20 , £3.90 ; EX 14.00 .
Owner Mrs Lucinda Freedman **Bred** Cliveden Stud Ltd **Trained** Manton, Wilts

FOCUS
A dramatic end to this fillies' maiden. There was only a pound between the first two home on ratings and they appeared to run close to form with just a half-length separating them at the line and the result reversed after an enquiry. That pair set the level of the form.

4932 32REDBINGO.COM H'CAP 1m 141y (P)
4:40 (4:41) (Class 6) (0-55,55) 3-Y-O **£1,617** (£481; £240 ; £120) **Stalls** Low

Form RPR
3050 **1** **Exceedexpectations (IRE)**[12] 4506 3 -9-255.......................... HayleyTurner 7 70
(Michael Bell) *chsd ldrs: rdn to ld and hung rt ins fnl f: sn clr* **7/1**[2]
6506 **2** *4 ½* **Tigertoo (IRE)**[8] 4650 3 -8-847..................................... WilliamCarson 10 52
(Stuart Williams) *chsd ldr tl led over 2f out: rdn over 1f out: edgd rt and hdd ins fnl f: no ex* **8/1**
0000 **3** *¾* **Riviera Romance**[8] 4650 3 -8-1251.................................. MircoDemuro 13 54
(J W Hills) *hld up: rdn over 1f out: r.o ins fnl f: nrst fin* **25/1**
00 **4** *1 ½* **Stag Hill (IRE)**[21] 4198 3 -9-053.. ShaneKelly 2 53
(Sylvester Kirk) *chsd ldrs: rdn over 2f out: styd on same pce fr over 1f out* **7/1**[2]
5005 **5** *½* **Tooley Woods (IRE)**[15] 4403 3 -8-1049................................. AndreaAtzeni 5 48
(Alan McCabe) *s.i.s: sn pushed along and prom: rdn over 2f out: styd on same pce appr fnl f* **33/1**
000 **6** *1 ½* **Regalo Rosado**[16] 4366 3 -9-154.. KieranO'Neill 12 49
(Mike Murphy) *dwlt: hld up: rdn over 3f out: styd on ins fnl f: nvr nrr* **3/1**[1]
000 **7** *½* **Trulee Scrumptious**[8] 4662 3 -8-448.............................. TobyAtkinson(5) 9 42
(Peter Charalambous) *mid-div: hdwy 5f out: rdn over 2f out: wknd over 1f out* **50/1**
3602 **8** *hd* **Remember Rocky**[11] 4549 3 -9-053.......................................(p) LiamJones 8 47
(Steve Gollings) *mid-div: rdn over 3f out: wknd over 1f out* **15/2**[3]
-360 **9** *nk* **No Plan B (IRE)**[19] 3275 3 -9-053.. JimCrowley 3 46
(Noel Quinlan) *led 6f: sn rdn: wknd fnl f* **12/1**

0004 **10** *nk* **Miss Socialite**[36] 3712 3 -8-1150... MartinHarley 6 42
(Jeremy Gask) *hld up: rdn over 2f out: n.d* **10/1**
2000 **11** *2 ½* **Lithograph (USA)**[27] 3966 3 -9-255.. JoeFanning 4 41
(Mark Johnston) *hld up: effrt over 2f out: nvr on terms* **25/1**
6-35 **12** *1 ½* **Capriska**[41] 3483 3 -8-1352... StevieDonohoe 11 35
(Willie Musson) *s.i.s: pushed along over 3f out: a in rr* **17/2**
1050 **13** *¾* **Compton Target (IRE)**[14] 4438 3 -9-053..............(t) RichardKingscote 1 34
(Milton Bradley) *mid-div: rdn over 3f out: wknd over 2f out* **9/1**
1m 48.8s (-1.70)**Going Correction** -0.10s/f (Stan) **13**Ran SP% **122.8**
Speed ratings (Par 98): **103,99,98,97,96 95,94,94,94,94 91,90,89**
Tote Swingers: 1&2 £10.60, 1&3 £23.60, 2&3 £23.30 CSF £61.65 CT £1393.18 TOTE £14.20 : £3.40, £3.40 , £8.70 ; EX 55.60 .
Owner Malcolm Caine **Bred** R S Cockerill (farms) Ltd & Peter Dodd **Trained** Newmarket, Suffolk

FOCUS
A moderate handicap, run at fair pace and the form looks sound, rated through the runner-up.
Exceedexpectations(IRE) Official explanation: trainer said regarding apparent improvement in form that gelding had appreciated the step up in trip and surface.
Regalo Rosado Official explanation: jockey said filly ran green.

4933 32RED FILLIES' H'CAP 7f 32y (P)
5:10 (5:11) (Class 4) (0-85,82) 3-Y-O+ **£4,528** (£1,347; £673 ; £336) **Stalls** High

Form RPR
1041 **1** **Dance Company**[8] 4647 3 -9-882 6ex............................... JimCrowley 2 89+
(William Knight) *chsd ldrs: rdn to ld wl ins fnl f: r.o: edgd rt nr fin* **1/1**[1]
0-00 **2** *¾* **Al Mayasah (IRE)**[17] 4336 4 -9-479.............................. AliceHaynes(7) 1 86
(David Simcock) *hld up: hdwy over 1f out: r.o wl ins fnl f: nt rch wnr* **9/1**
661 **3** *¾* **Flashbang**[34] 3761 4 -8-1069..................................(tp) AshleyMorgan(5) 8 74
(Paul Cole) *chsd ldr tl led over 1f out: rdn and hdd ins fnl f: edgd lft: styd on same pce* **14/1**
1432 **4** *1* **Fenella Fudge**[8] 4655 4 -8-1266...............................(v) StevieDonohoe 4 68
(Derek Shaw) *rrd s: hld up: rdn and r.o ins fnl f: nt rch ldrs* **15/2**[3]
-100 **5** *½* **Safe House (IRE)**[5] 4388 3 -8-1272.................................. JoeFanning 5 72
(Mark Johnston) *led: rdn and hdd over 1f out: styng on same pce whn n.m.r ins fnl f* **11/1**
1463 **6** *shd* **Bint Alzain (IRE)**[8] 4647 3 -8-1275...........................(tp) DominicFox(3) 3 74
(Gerard Butler) *prom: rdn over 1f out: styd on same pce fnl f* **7/1**[2]
000- **7** *2 ¼* **Cheers For Thea (IRE)**[297] 3757 7 -9-1280...........(t) DuranFentiman 6 75
(Tim Easterby) *s.i.s: hld up: rdn over 1f out: nvr trbld ldrs* **22/1**
0141 **8** *4* **Bavarian Princess (USA)**[8] 4655 4 -9-378 6ex........ ConorHarrison(7) 7 62
(Mrs K Burke) *prom: rdn over 2f out: edgd rt wl over 1f out: sn wknd* **11/1**
1m 28.97s (-0.63)**Going Correction** -0.10s/f (Stan)
WFA 3 from 4yo+ 6lb **8**Ran SP% **111.9**
Speed ratings (Par 102): **99,98,97,96,95 95,92,88**
Tote Swingers: 1&2 £3.50, 1&3 £5.40, 2&3 £14.50 CSF £10.25 CT £77.58 TOTE £1.90 : £1.40 , £3.10, £4.00 ; EX 10.50 .
Owner Mrs P G M Jamison **Bred** David Jamison Bloodstock **Trained** Patching, W Sussex
■ Stewards' Enquiry : Ashley Morgan two-day ban; careless riding (21st & 25th Aug)

FOCUS
A decent fillies' handicap, run at a sedate pace and best rated around the placed horses.

4934 32REDPOKER.COM NURSERY 7f 32y (P)
5:40 (5:40) (Class 5) (0-75,75) 2-Y-O **£2,264** (£673; £336 ; £168) **Stalls** High

Form RPR
000 **1** **Sekumkum (IRE)**[19] 4253 2 -8-256..............................(bt) AndreaAtzeni 4 63+
(Marco Botti) *hld up: hdwy 2f out: rdn to ld 1f out: r.o wl* **11/2**[3]
5053 **2** *2 ¾* **This Is Nice (IRE)**[15] 4408 2 -9-371........................... RichardKingscote 7 71
(Tom Dascombe) *chsd ldr tl led 2f out: rdn and hdd 1f out: styd on same pce* **13/8**[1]
004 **3** *½* **Marguerite St Just**[35] 3733 2 -8-458................................ JimmyQuinn 8 57
(Olivia Maylam) *s.i.s: hld up: pushed along over 2f out: r.o ins fnl f: nrst fin* **16/1**
0065 **4** *½* **Getaway Car**[24] 4102 2 -8-660.......................................(p) BarryMcHugh 2 57
(Gerard Butler) *prom: rdn over 1f out: styd on same pce fnl f* **10/1**
324 **5** *1* **Red Refraction (IRE)**[11] 4555 2 -9-775.................................. SeanLevey 5 70
(Richard Hannon) *prom: rdn and ev ch over 1f out: no ex ins fnl f* **9/4**[2]
4046 **6** *1* **Tough Lady (IRE)**[7] 4331 2 -8-1266.................................... JoeFanning 6 58
(Mark Johnston) *chsd ldrs: rdn over 1f out: no ex fnl f* **18/1**
000 **7** *3* **Whitford (IRE)**[33] 3788 2 -7-1356...................................... RyanPowell(3) 3 40
(Chris Dwyer) *hld up: effrt over 1f out: wknd fnl f* **28/1**
6053 **8** *12* **Little Miss Zuri (IRE)**[7] 4331 2 -7-1252 oh3.................. KieranO'Neill 1
(Sylvester Kirk) *led: hung rt over 2f out: sn hdd: wknd and eased fnl f* **12/1**
1m 29.34s (-0.26)**Going Correction** -0.10s/f (Stan) **8**Ran SP% **115.6**
Speed ratings (Par 94): **97,93,93,92,91 90,87,73**
Tote Swingers: 1&2 £2.20, 1&3 £10.00, 2&3 £5.70 CSF £15.06 CT £136.57 TOTE £7.70 : £1.70, £1.10, £5.50 ; EX 17.80 .
Owner Sultan Ali **Bred** Epona Bloodstock Ltd **Trained** Newmarket, Suffolk

FOCUS
An interesting nursery turned into a procession.

NOTEBOOK
Sekumkum(IRE) made a mockery of his modest rating. He had shown only limited promise in three maiden starts (all at Grade 1 tracks) but he looked a very different proposition on this, his nursery debut, as he scampered clear for a wide-margin success. Blinkered as early as his second start, he clearly isn't straightforward and can carry his head awkwardly. However, the style in which he put this race to bed was impressive and would probably have won even easier had the early pace been stronger. He holds entries at both Lingfield and Kempton in the coming week and will surely bid to follow-up under a penalty before being reassessed. Official explanation: trainers representative said regarding apparent improvement in form that colt had possibly benefited from the application of a tongue strap. (op 10-1)
This Is Nice (IRE)for whom there was plenty of money around, performed creditably, despite being no match for the winner. Tom Dascombe's filly had finished third off a 1lb higher mark at Windsor last time and appeared to run up to form. She will remain vulnerable to better handicapped horses however. (op 11-8 tchd 7-4)
Marguerite St Just ◆ is worth putting in the notebook, having made significant late headway. She conceded valuable ground at the start and ought to be able to win off this sort of mark, especially if tried over a mile. (op 12-1)
Red Refraction (IRE) supported into 9-4 from 11-4, was one of the first off the bridle and never really looked like landing the gamble. She did keep finding in the straight but was made to look very one-paced. (op 3-1)
Tough Lady (IRE)has run poorly both starts since qualifying for a mark and is clearly one of Mark Johnston's lesser lights. (op 16-1)
Little Miss Zuri (IRE)made the running but was heavily eased once beaten. (op 10-1)
T/Plt: £335.90 to a £1 stake. Pool: £49,958.00 - 108.55 winning tickets. T/Qpdt: £79.10 to a £1 stake. Pool: £ - 141.50 w. tickets CR

4935a (Foreign Racing) See RI

4237 BRIGHTON (L-H)

Wednesday, August 8

OFFICIAL GOING: Good to soft (good in places; 7.2)

Races utilising bottom bend increased in distance by about 12.5yds.

Wind: Virtually nil Weather: Low cloud, misty

4936 MAISON MAURICE NURSERY 5f 59y

2:20 (2:20) (Class 5) (0-75,75) 2-Y-O **£2,264** (£673; £336; £168) **Stalls** Centre

Form RPR

0401 **1** **Danz Choice (IRE)**[14] 4471 2-9-0 **68** RichardHughes 2 73+
(Richard Hannon) *stdd s: hld up in tch: rdn over 2f out: hdwy over 1f out: edgd lft but led fnl 100yds: r.o wl* **6/4**[1]

2401 **2** ¾ **Hot Secret**[6] 4728 2-8-12 **73** 6ex ThomasBrown(7) 5 74
(Andrew Balding) *taken down early: pressed ldr: drvn to ld over 1f out: edgd lft u.p 1f out: hdd and one pce fnl 100yds* **9/4**[2]

0501 **3** 1 ½ **Khefyn (IRE)**[15] 4421 2-8-10 **64** MarcHalford 4 60
(Ronald Harris) *chsd ldrs: styd on inner 3f out: stl pressing ldrs and drvn over 1f out: no ex and btn fnl 100yds* **11/1**

3610 **4** 1 ½ **Pixilated**[50] 3242 2-9-6 **74** NeilCallan 1 64
(Gay Kelleway) *led: drvn and hdd over 1f out: wknd ins fnl f* **11/2**[3]

5120 **5** 1 ¼ **Bheleyf (IRE)**[12] 4526 2-9-4 **75** HarryBentley(3) 3 61
(Joseph Tuite) *dwlt: a in last: rdn and no hdwy 2f out: plugged on same pce after* **13/2**

1m 4.39s (2.09) **Going Correction** +0.175s/f (Good) 5 Ran SP% **107.8**

Speed ratings (Par 94): **90,88,86,84,82**

CSF £4.86 TOTE £2.40: £1.40, £3.00; EX 3.80.

Owner Dragon Gate **Bred** J & J Waldron **Trained** East Everleigh, Wilts

FOCUS

With 6-7mm of rain in the morning the going was changed to good to soft, good in places before racing. Richard Hughes, who won the opener, reported it was "more or less soft." A competitive nursery, despite the small field, and the majority came stands' side. The form looks straightforward and appears sound.

NOTEBOOK

Danz Choice(IRE) had come from last to first to score last time and similar tactics were employed. He appeared in trouble 2f out but picked up really well for pressure and won cosily. He should not go up much for this and a hat-trick looks on the cards if kept to this sort of level. (op 7-4)

Hot Secret had won her maiden on easy ground and was given a positive ride, but after getting the better of the leader was left vulnerable to the late run of the favourite. (tchd 11-4)

Khefyn(IRE) was dropping in trip after scoring over 6f on his previous start, but he had hung badly left on that occasion and his rider was keen to keep the rail on his left, so stuck to the far side. He was not beaten far, suggesting there was no major track bias at this stage. (op 10-1 tchd 12-1)

Pixilated, whose win came on fast ground, made the running but was given no peace in front and faded in the last furlong and a half. She would have preferred it quicker. (op 6-1 tchd 13-2)

Bheleyf(IRE) missed the break and was always at the back. His C&D win was on fast ground and he looked far less effective on this surface. (op 11-2 tchd 5-1)

4937 ALICE RYAN MEMORIAL H'CAP 5f 213y

2:50 (2:50) (Class 6) (0-55,54) 3-Y-O **£1,617** (£481; £240; £120) **Stalls** Centre

Form RPR

3542 **1** **Kashmiri Star**[5] 4777 3-9-2 **52** PatCosgrave 10 64
(Michael Quinn) *chsd ldrs: rdn 3f out: racd against stands' rail fr over 2f out: drvn to ld over 1f out: drew clr fnl 100yds: eased cl home* **15/8**[1]

0160 **2** 1 ¾ **Aubrietia**[9] 4653 3-8-7 **50** (b) WilliamTwiston-Davies(7) 6 56
(Alan McCabe) *hld up in tch: hdwy to 2f out: drvn and chsd wnr over 1f out: edgd lft fnl f: outpcd and btn fnl 100yds* **9/2**[2]

40 **3** 2 ¼ **Copper Falls**[42] 3489 3-9-2 **52** KirstyMilczarek 8 51
(Brendan Powell) *taken down early: dwlt: hld up in rr: hdwy over 2f out: drvn and chsd ldrs over 1f out: no ex and wknd fnl 100yds* **8/1**

4600 **4** 1 ¼ **Indiana Guest (IRE)**[56] 3050 3-9-1 **51** IanMongan 7 46
(George Margarson) *in tch in last trio: hdwy u.p over 1f out: styd on same pce ins fnl f* **10/1**

2666 **5** ½ **First Rebellion**[22] 4185 3-8-9 **45** (v[1]) DavidProbert 1 39
(Tony Carroll) *taken down early: led: styd on inner rail over 2f out: rdn and hdd over 1f out: wknd ins fnl f* **7/1**[3]

0-00 **6** 1 **Rain Dance**[64] 2788 3-9-3 **53** (b[1]) NeilCallan 3 43
(Eve Johnson Houghton) *chsd ldr: rdn 2f out: nt qckn and struggling over 1f out: wknd and wl hld whn eased wl ins fnl f* **25/1**

0000 **7** 1 ½ **Men Don't Cry (IRE)**[9] 4653 3-9-2 **52** LiamKeniry 11 38
(Ed de Giles) *in tch in midfield: rdn and effrt 3f out: no hdwy 2f out: wl btn and edgd lft ins fnl f* **12/1**

-000 **8** 4 **Triple Salchow**[20] 4237 3-9-2 **52** JohnFahy 9 25
(Alastair Lidderdale) *in tch in midfield: rdn and struggling over 2f out: wknd and bhd over 1f out* **66/1**

300- **9** nk **Kaylee**[294] 6942 3-9-4 **54** TomQueally 2 26
(Gary Moore) *t.k.h: chsd ldrs: rdn and fnd little 2f out: sn wknd: bhd fnl f* **8/1**

4005 **10** 1 ¼ **Tenderly Place**[15] 4424 3-8-6 **47** (t) DavidKenny(5) 5 15
(William Knight) *taken down early: hld up in rr: effrt and rdn 2f out: wknd over 1f out: bhd fnl f* **16/1**

1m 12.1s (1.90) **Going Correction** +0.175s/f (Good) 10 Ran SP% **115.7**

Speed ratings (Par 98): **94,91,88,87,86 85,83,77,77,75**

toteswingers: 1&2 £2.80, 1&3 £3.00, 2&3 £4.30. CSF £9.79 CT £53.95 TOTE £2.90: £1.40, £2.00, £2.30; EX 13.20.

Owner M Quinn **Bred** Pendley Farm **Trained** Newmarket, Suffolk

FOCUS

A moderate 3-y-o sprint handicap, and again all bar one came to the stands' side in the straight. The finish was dominated by fillies and the form is a bit fluid with few solid.

4938 CALEDONIAN FLYING SCOTSMAN BRITISH STALLION STUDS E B F MAIDEN STKS 6f 209y

3:20 (3:20) (Class 5) 2-Y-O **£3,169** (£943; £471; £235) **Stalls** Centre

Form RPR

2332 **1** **Rising Legend**[9] 4654 2-9-3 82 RichardHughes 5 81
(Richard Hannon) *chsd ldr after 1f: upsides ldr and racd against stands' rail fr 3f out: pushed into ld over 1f out: rdn and drew clr ins fnl f: comf* **9/4**[2]

4 **2** 2 ¼ **Canadian Run (IRE)**[14] 4463 2-9-3 0 StevieDonohoe 1 75
(Robert Mills) *t.k.h: hld up in tch: effrt and rdn over 1f out: drvn ins fnl f: sn outpcd by wnr but kpt on to go 2nd fnl 50yds* **9/1**

4 **3** ½ **Hazzaat (IRE)**[22] 4194 2-9-3 0 NeilCallan 4 74
(Roger Varian) *rn green: led: rdn and jnd 3f out: hdd over 1f out: no ex and one pce ins fnl f: lost 2nd fnl 50yds* **2/1**[1]

0 **4** ¾ **Roman Order (IRE)**[14] 4472 2-9-3 0 MartinDwyer 2 72
(Brian Meehan) *in tch: rdn and unable qck 2f out: edgd lft ent fnl f: styd on same pce fnl f* **4/1**[3]

0 **5** 15 **Corn Snow (USA)**[55] 3074 2-9-3 0 MickaelBarzalona 3 40
(Mahmood Al Zarooni) *t.k.h: chsd ldrs: sltly hmpd over 5f out: short of room 2f out: wknd over 1f out: wl bhd and eased ins fnl f* **5/1**

1m 25.23s (2.13) **Going Correction** +0.175s/f (Good) 5 Ran SP% **110.8**

Speed ratings (Par 94): **94,91,90,90,72**

CSF £20.48 TOTE £2.20: £1.50, £3.70; EX 16.30.

Owner M S Al Shahi **Bred** Cheveley Park Stud Ltd **Trained** East Everleigh, Wilts

FOCUS

A fair juvenile maiden that usually falls to a representative of one of the major yards, and it went to the most experienced runner. The winner is the best guide, rated to his mark.

NOTEBOOK

Rising Legend had been placed in all four previous starts, although the worst of those efforts was on easy ground. Never far away, he grabbed the stands' rail and, once he got the better of his tussle with the favourite, was always going to hold on. Rated 82, he sets the standard and, with no fancy entries, will now have to take his chance in handicaps. (op 15-8)

Canadian Run(IRE), a half-brother to a useful juvenile winner but out of a half-sister to Group 1 winning milers, has a Derby entry. He was held up before staying on late and, still looking as if he has some maturing to do, ran another encouraging race. (op 12-1)

Hazzaat(IRE), who was green and didn't handle the ground on his debut, was unlucky that the going probably went against him here. He made the running but could not get the rail and eventually lost out in a protracted battle with the winner. He can do better on a sounder surface. (op 9-4)

Roman Order(IRE) got the rail behind the winner but as a result had nowhere to go from over 2f out. He did not pick up when a gap appeared though and might do better given time and a switch to handicaps. (op 9-2 tchd 5-1)

Corn Snow(USA), who was keen and whose saddle slipped on his debut, again refused to settle early on and finished well held. He needs to show a lot more if he is to remain with current connections. (tchd 9-2)

4939 JOHN SMITH'S BRIGHTON MILE CHALLENGE TROPHY (H'CAP) 7f 214y

3:50 (3:50) (Class 4) (0-80,80) 3-Y-O+

£9,337 (£2,796; £1,398; £699; £349; £175) **Stalls** Centre

Form RPR

0502 **1** **Frozen Over**[19] 4302 4-8-7 **63** MickaelBarzalona 1 73
(Stuart Kittow) *in tch in midfield: rdn over 4f out: styd towards inner 3f out: drvn and chsd ldr over 1f out: led ins fnl f: kpt on wl: rdn out* **9/1**

3111 **2** nk **Chosen Character (IRE)**[12] 4531 4-9-3 **80** (vt) NatashaEaton(7) 11 89
(Tom Dascombe) *t.k.h: chsd ldr: styd towards inner 3f out: rdn over 1f out: hdd ins fnl f: kpt on wl but a jst hld* **6/1**[3]

0443 **3** shd **Satwa Laird**[16] 4413 6-8-8 **69** DavidKenny(5) 12 78
(Conor Dore) *hld up towards rr of main gp: c towards stands' side 3f out: hdwy u.p and nt clr run over 1f out tl 1f out: r.o wl ins fnl f: nt quite rch ldrs* **16/1**

1154 **4** 3 ¼ **Methayel (IRE)**[20] 4255 4-9-5 **75** MartinDwyer 13 77
(Clive Brittain) *in tch: c towards stands' side 3f out: effrt 2f out: unable qck u.p over 1f out: styd on same pce fnl f* **8/1**

0520 **5** ½ **Ocean Legend (IRE)**[26] 4043 7-9-0 **70** JimCrowley 16 70
(Tony Carroll) *in tch: c towards stands' side 3f out: chsd ldrs u.p 2f out: no ex ent fnl f: one pce and wl hld after* **22/1**

1165 **6** ½ **Xinbama (IRE)**[11] 4607 3-9-0 **77** SebSanders 9 76
(J W Hills) *hld up in rr of main gp: c stands' side 3f out: drvn whn nt clr run and swtchd rt over 1f out: styd on wl fnl f: nvr trbld ldrs* **22/1**

40-0 **7** 2 **You've Been Mowed**[17] 4365 6-9-2 **77** MatthewLawson(5) 2 72
(Richard Price) *led: styd towards inner 3f out: drvn and hdd over 1f out: wknd fnl f* **25/1**

4424 **8** ¾ **Great Shot**[18] 4317 4-9-5 **75** RichardHughes 8 68
(Sylvester Kirk) *in tch in midfield: c towards stands' side 3f out: effrt and jostled over 2f out: no ex u.p over 1f out: wknd fnl f* **2/1**[1]

0601 **9** 1 ¼ **Rossetti**[11] 4603 4-9-4 **74** TomQueally 10 64
(Ian Williams) *in tch in midfield: styd in centre 3f out: drvn and no imp over 1f out: wknd fnl f* **7/2**[2]

420 **10** 1 ¼ **Perfect Mission**[13] 4503 4-9-2 **72** (v) DavidProbert 4 59
(Andrew Balding) *in tch in midfield: styd in centre 3f out: edgd lft u.p and no hdwy over 1f out: wknd fnl f* **20/1**

-000 **11** ½ **Green Earth (IRE)**[175] 570 5-8-0 **61** JemmaMarshall(5) 15 47
(Pat Phelan) *chsd ldrs: c towards stands' side 3f out: struggling u.p 2f out: wknd over 1f out* **12/1**

0000 **12** 1 ¼ **Rulesn'regulations**[13] 4503 6-9-0 **77** (p[1]) ThomasGarner(7) 7 60
(Matthew Salaman) *stdd after s: hld up in rr: styd towards centre 3f out: no hdwy u.p over 1f out: sn wknd* **50/1**

002- **13** 4 **Mountrath**[237] 7764 5-8-7 **70** (v) WilliamTwiston-Davies(7) 5 44
(Gary Moore) *t.k.h: in tch: c towards stands' side 3f out: wknd qckly u.p over 1f out* **33/1**

1300 **14** 1 ½ **Esprit Danseur**[6] 4726 3-7-11 **65** NathanAlison(5) 3 36
(Jim Boyle) *rrd leaving stalls and slowly away: a in rr: styd towards inner 3f out: no prog* **40/1**

60-0 **15** 23 **Roy The Boy (USA)**[12] 4541 4-9-0 **70** (v) CathyGannon 6
(Alan Bailey) *chsd ldrs: losing pl and c towards stands' side 3f out: bhd over 1f out: wl bhd and eased ins fnl f: t.o* **40/1**

1m 36.34s (0.34) **Going Correction** +0.175s/f (Good)

WFA 3 from 4yo+ 7lb 15 Ran SP% **131.6**

Speed ratings (Par 105): **105,104,104,101,100 100,98,97,96,95 94,93,89,87,64**

toteswingers: 1&2 £8.50, 1&3 £10.00, 2&3 £15.20. CSF £61.74 CT £913.22 TOTE £12.60: £4.10, £2.40, £4.80; EX 77.90.

Owner P A & M J Reditt **Bred** Manor Farm Packers Ltd **Trained** Blackborough, Devon

■ Stewards' Enquiry : Natasha Eaton two-day ban: use of whip (25 Aug & TBA)

FOCUS

One of the feature races of Brighton's season and it produced a big field and looked competitive on paper. The runners again split into two groups and those who stayed far side came out on top. The winner is rated back to his best.

Esprit Danseur Official explanation: jockey said that the filly was slowly away

4940 LAINES BEST H'CAP 1m 1f 209y

4:20 (4:21) (Class 6) (0-55,55) 3-Y-O+ **£1,617** (£481; £240; £120) **Stalls** Centre

Form RPR

053 **1** **Chasin' Rainbows**[4] 4817 4-9-0 **48** RichardHughes 6 57
(Sylvester Kirk) *hld up in tch in last quartet: hdwy over 2f out: rdn to chse ldr over 1f out: chal ins fnl f: kpt on wl to ld fnl 50yds* **3/1**[1]

42U5 **2** nk **Volcanic Jack (IRE)**[9] 4656 4-9-5 **53** JimCrowley 1 61
(Tony Carroll) *hld up in last quartet: hdwy 3f out: led and edgd rt u.p wl over 1f out: hrd pressed and kpt on u.p ins fnl f: hdd and no ex fnl 50yds* **7/1**[3]

3005 **3** 2¼ **Bondi Mist (IRE)**[13] 4510 3-8-9 **55** ... HarryBentley(3) 8 59
(Jonathan Portman) *in tch: styd towards inner 3f out: rdn and ev ch wl over 1f out: hung rt 1f out but pressing ldrs 1f out: wknd fnl 100yds* **9/1**

363 **4** 3 **Thecornishcowboy**[22] 4198 3-8-10 **53** ... (tp) BrettDoyle 10 51+
(John Ryan) *hld up in tch: effrt whn nt clr run and hmpd ent fnl 2f: swtchd lft and rallied u.p over 1f out: no ex and wknd ins fnl f* **5/1**[2]

6620 **5** 1 **Ermyntrude**[13] 4505 5-9-6 **54** ... IanMongan 2 50
(Pat Phelan) *bustled along leaving stalls: in tch in midfield: hdwy to chse ldrs 2f out: drvn and carried rt over 1f out: no ex and btn 1f out: wknd* **8/1**

3400 **6** 2¼ **Regal Rave (USA)**[13] 4511 5-9-0 **48** ... (v) JohnFahy 9 39
(Peter Hedger) *stdd s: hld up in rr: hdwy over 4f out: chsd ldrs: edgd lft u.p and no ex over 1f out: wknd fnl f* **11/1**

0055 **7** 9 **Rosy Dawn**[6] 4722 7-8-12 **46** oh1 ... KieranO'Neill 12 19
(John Bridger) *chsd ldr tl led 1/2-way: hdd over 2f out: btn over 1f out: fdd fnl f* **14/1**

0300 **8** ¾ **Sir Dylan**[12] 4534 3-8-9 **52** ... MarcHalford 13 24
(Ronald Harris) *stdd and dropped in bhd after s: hld up in rr: styd towards inner 3f out: no hdwy and hung rt 2f out: hung bk lft over 1f out: eased fnl f* **50/1**

026 **9** 4½ **Young Jackie**[41] 3552 4-8-13 **47** ... SebSanders 5 10
(George Margarson) *chsd ldrs: hdwy to join ldr 1/2-way: rdn to ld and edgd rt jst over 2f out: hdd wl over 1f out: btn over 1f out: wknd* **8/1**

406 **10** ½ **Jumeirah Liberty**[21] 4219 4-9-6 **54** ... JamieGoldstein 11 16
(Zoe Davison) *in tch: hdwy to join ldrs 1/2-way: rdn whn carried rt jst over 2f out: drvn and no hdwy whn n.m.r over 1f out: sn wknd* **20/1**

11 13 **Tadjena (GER)**[384] 5-8-12 **46** oh1 ... DaneO'Neill 7
(Tony Newcombe) *t.k.h: sn led: hdd 1/2-way: styd towards inner 3f out: wknd 2f out and sn eased: t.o fnl f* **12/1**

6/20 **12** 6 **Devon Diva**[36] 3721 6-9-1 **49** ... LiamKeniry 3
(David Bridgwater) *in tch: pushed along whn hmpd and lost pl over 4f out: lost tch 2f out: t.o and eased fnl f* **20/1**

2m 5.47s (1.87) **Going Correction** +0.175s/f (Good)
WFA 3 from 4yo+ 9lb — **12** Ran SP% **120.6**
Speed ratings (Par 101): **99,98,96,94,93 91,84,84,80,80 69,64**
toteswingers: 1&2 £6.60, 1&3 £6.50, 2&3 £10.40. CSF £23.59 CT £174.64 TOTE £4.50: £2.30, £2.10, £3.90; EX 27.40.
Owner J B J Richards **Bred** J B J Richards **Trained** Upper Lambourn, Berks

FOCUS
A moderate but tightly knit handicap and another winner for Richard Hughes. The time was reasonable and the form appears sound.
Sir Dylan Official explanation: jockey said that the gelding hung right

4941 CALEDONIAN DEUCHARS IPA (S) H'CAP — 1m 3f 196y
4:50 (4:52) (Class 6) (0-55,55) 3-Y-0+ — £1,617 (£481; £240; £120) Stalls Centre

Form — RPR

3436 **1** **Bengal Tiger**[42] 3498 6-9-5 **50** ... JimCrowley 4 59
(Tony Carroll) *hld up towards rr: hdwy to trck ldrs 4f out: hrd drvn and ev ch over 1f out: led ins fnl f: asserted fnl 100yds: rdn out* **13/2**[2]

5204 **2** 1 **Lisselan Pleasure (USA)**[22] 4183 5-9-1 **53** ... (t) DanielMuscutt(7) 1 60
(Bernard Llewellyn) *chsd ldrs: wnt 2nd over 5f out tl led over 3f out: rdn and hrd pressed over 1f out: hdd ins fnl f: no ex and btn fnl 100yds* **12/1**

0/ **3** 1¼ **Chapter Nine (IRE)**[159] 780 6-9-1 **46** oh1 ... LiamKeniry 10 51
(Seamus Mullins) *fly-jmpd leaving stalls and slowly away: bhd: hdwy over 4f out: chsd ldng pair and rdn wl over 1f out: styd on same pce fnl f* **16/1**

00-5 **4** 1 **Saloon (USA)**[77] 2394 8-9-7 **52** ... (p) RichardHughes 3 56
(Jane Chapple-Hyam) *stdd and dropped out in rr: clsd over 3f out: hdwy but hld hd high over 1f out: chsd ldng trio 1f out: kpt on but nvr looked a threat to ldrs* **9/1**[3]

-430 **5** 6 **Isobella**[13] 4510 3-8-12 **54** ... (p) DarryllHolland 8 48
(Hughie Morrison) *sn pushed along in midfield and nvr gng wl: hdwy to chse ldrs 4f out: rdn and nt qckn 3f out: edgd lft and wknd ent fnl f* **3/1**[1]

0/0- **6** 5 **Weybridge Light**[9] 911 7-9-4 **49** ... (b) TomQueally 6 35
(Jim Best) *chsd ldr: reminders 6f out: lost 2nd over 5f out: drvn and struggling 3f out: wknd wl over 1f out* **3/1**[1]

5122 **7** 9 **Emperors Waltz (IRE)**[8] 4678 3-8-13 **55** ... MartinDwyer 2 27
(Rae Guest) *led tl over 3f out: rdn and struggling over 2f out: wknd wl over 1f out* **3/1**[1]

6066 **8** 5 **Rather Cool**[13] 4504 4-9-2 **47** ... (t) KieranO'Neill 9 11
(John Bridger) *in tch: rdn and struggling 4f out: bhd fnl 2f* **16/1**

0540 **9** 45 **Ladram Bay (IRE)**[12] 4537 3-8-4 **46** oh1 ... NickyMackay 5
(Jonathan Portman) *chsd ldrs tl rdn and lost pl 4f out: wl t.o fnl 2f: eased fnl f* **40/1**

0060 **10** 16 **Delishuss**[6] 4744 3-8-4 **46** oh1 ... (t) JohnFahy 7
(Dominic Ffrench Davis) *chsd ldrs tl lost pl and no rspnse u.p 6f out: bhd fnl 4f: wl t.o and eased fnl f* **80/1**

2m 36.13s (3.43) **Going Correction** +0.175s/f (Good)
WFA 3 from 4yo+ 11lb — **10** Ran SP% **121.5**
Speed ratings (Par 101): **95,94,93,92,88 85,79,76,46,35**
toteswingers: 1&2 £8.70, 1&3 £18.80, 2&3 £17.20. CSF £84.94 CT £1213.13 TOTE £5.80: £2.00, £4.50, £6.50; EX 94.60.
Owner A W Carroll **Bred** Kingsclere Stud **Trained** Cropthorne, Worcs

FOCUS
Not much between the majority of the field in this selling handicap and it produced a decent finish. The winner is rated in line with the best of his spring form.

4942 BAR PULSE - IN MEMORY OF CHRISTINE HANCOCK FILLIES' H'CAP — 6f 209y
5:20 (5:20) (Class 5) (0-70,69) 3-Y-0+ — £2,264 (£673; £336; £168) Stalls Centre

Form — RPR

0433 **1** **Little Rainbow**[39] 3619 3-9-1 **64** ... AdamKirby 6 74
(Clive Cox) *t.k.h: chsd ldr tl led over 1f out: rdn clr ent fnl f: kpt on wl* **9/2**[2]

-004 **2** 2 **Renoir's Lady**[53] 3152 4-8-4 **50** oh2 ... HarryBentley(3) 8 57
(Simon Dow) *chsd ldrs: rdn 2f out: chsd clr wnr and hung lft ins fnl f: styd on same pce* **14/1**

53 **3** 2½ **Dundrum Dancer (IRE)**[20] 4242 5-9-1 **65** ... ThomasGarner(7) 3 65
(Alex Hales) *s.i.s: hld up towards rr: hdwy u.p over 1f out: no imp fnl 150yds* **9/1**

2-00 **4** 1½ **Leelu**[36] 3738 6-9-0 **57** ... LiamKeniry 5 53
(David Arbuthnot) *led: rdn and hdd over 1f out: btn and lost 2nd ins fnl f: wknd fnl 100yds* **14/1**

415 **5** ½ **Jackie Love (IRE)**[4] 4812 4-8-6 **54** ... (v) LauraPike(5) 1 49
(Olivia Maylam) *chsd ldrs: rdn and unable qck 2f out: drvn and plugged on same pce fr over 1f out* **11/2**[3]

0000 **6** 1½ **Findeln**[13] 4490 3-8-3 **52** ... (b[1]) JohnFahy 2 41
(Eve Johnson Houghton) *t.k.h: hld up in tch towards rr: hdwy into midfield 4f out: drvn and no hdwy wl over 1f out: wknd ent fnl f* **66/1**

040- **7** nse **Malekat Jamal (IRE)**[324] 6214 3-9-2 **65** ... MartinDwyer 4 54
(David Simcock) *t.k.h: hld up in midfield: rdn and unable qck wl over 1f out: plugged on same pce but no threat to ldrs fr over 1f out* **8/1**

2552 **8** nk **Viking Rose (IRE)**[15] 4436 4-9-5 **69** ... DannyBrock(7) 7 60+
(James Eustace) *in tch: rdn and unable qck 2f out: btn over 1f out: eased fnl f: sddle slipped* **11/4**[1]

1366 **9** 1¾ **The New Black (IRE)**[11] 4583 3-9-2 **65** ... (v) CathyGannon 12 49
(Gay Kelleway) *s.i.s: in tch in rr: rdn and no hdwy wl over 1f out: n.d* **12/1**

404 **10** nk **Cheers**[14] 4468 4-9-7 **64** ... (t) FrankieMcDonald 10 49
(Oliver Sherwood) *in tch in midfield: rdn and nt qckn wl over 1f out: wknd ent fnl f* **8/1**

0040 **11** ½ **Bedibyes**[42] 3485 4-8-4 **52** ... DavidKenny(5) 11 36
(Richard Mitchell) *in tch in midfield: lost pl and pushed along 4f out: flashed tail u.p and wknd wl over 1f out* **16/1**

1m 24.43s (1.33) **Going Correction** +0.175s/f (Good)
WFA 3 from 4yo+ 6lb — **11** Ran SP% **120.9**
Speed ratings (Par 100): **99,96,93,92,91 90,90,89,87,87 86**
toteswingers: 1&2 £9.80, 1&3 £9.30, 2&3 £20.70. CSF £67.99 CT £567.13 TOTE £6.00: £2.40, £5.00, £3.10; EX 80.30.
Owner Trevor Fox **Bred** Mrs Sandra Fox **Trained** Lambourn, Berks

FOCUS
This fillies' handicap had been dominated by course specialist Lady Florence, who had taken the previous three renewals. The winner is rated in line with the best view of her latest form.
Viking Rose(IRE) Official explanation: jockey said that the saddle slipped

4943 HEINEKEN UK MAIDEN H'CAP — 5f 213y
5:50 (5:50) (Class 6) (0-65,62) 3-Y-0+ — £1,617 (£481; £240; £120) Stalls Centre

Form — RPR

3054 **1** **Langley Vale**[36] 3732 3-9-7 **62** ... AdamKirby 3 69
(Roger Teal) *restless in stalls: awkward s and slowly away: in tch in rr: swtchd lft and hdwy over 1f out: ev ch fnl f: led wl ins fnl f: r.o wl* **9/2**

2625 **2** ½ **Marah Music**[36] 3719 3-9-4 **59** ... (p) DarryllHolland 7 64
(Peter Makin) *chsd ldrs tl n.m.r and shuffled bk 2f out: swtchd lft and hdwy to chal 1f out: kpt on same pce towards fin* **7/2**[3]

-005 **3** nk **Ever The Optimist (IRE)**[55] 3076 4-9-4 **55** ... DaneO'Neill 4 60
(Tony Newcombe) *racd keenly: led tl wl over 1f out: drvn and led again 1f out: hdd and one pce wl ins fnl f* **3/1**[2]

2065 **4** 2¾ **Jemimaville (IRE)**[22] 4196 5-8-8 **45** ... (v) LiamJones 5 41
(Giles Bravery) *in tch: rdn and effrt 2f out: pressed ldrs and unable qck jst over 1f out: edgd lft jst ins fnl f: wknd fnl 100yds* **16/1**

004 **5** 3¾ **Depden (IRE)**[20] 4237 4-8-3 **47** ow2 ... DanielMuscutt(7) 8 31
(Richard Price) *hld up in tch in last pair: pushed along and nt clr run over 2f out: rdn and no imp whn edgd lft over 1f out: wknd fnl f* **14/1**

4326 **6** 1¼ **Pharoh Jake**[14] 4467 4-8-11 **48** ... KieranO'Neill 2 28
(John Bridger) *chsd ldrs tl led wl over 1f out: sn rdn: hdd 1f out: wkng whn pushed lft jst ins fnl f: hung lft and fdd fnl 150yds* **11/4**[1]

0-03 **7** hd **The Wonga Coup (IRE)**[20] 4240 5-8-3 **45** ... JemmaMarshall(5) 1 25
(Pat Phelan) *taken down early: pressed ldr: rdn and fnd little over 1f out: wknd 1f out* **8/1**

1m 12.4s (2.20) **Going Correction** +0.175s/f (Good)
WFA 3 from 4yo+ 4lb — **7** Ran SP% **115.7**
Speed ratings (Par 101): **92,91,90,87,82 80,80**
toteswingers: 1&2 £2.10, 1&3 £2.09, 2&3 £3.10. CSF £21.11 CT £54.31 TOTE £4.80: £1.70, £3.60; EX 10.90.
Owner Miss Brooke Sanders **Bred** Miss Brooke Sanders **Trained** Ashtead, Surrey

FOCUS
A moderate maiden handicap that was dominated by the top weights. The runner-up is rated close to his best.
T/Plt: £423.90 to a £1 stake. Pool: £52,662.59 - 90.68 winning tickets. T/Qpdt: £371.40 to a £1 stake. Pool: £3,764.34 - 7.50 winning tickets. SP

4914 KEMPTON (A.W) (R-H)
Wednesday, August 8

OFFICIAL GOING: Standard to slow
Wind: Light, across Weather: Fine, warm

4944 WIN BIG WITH BETDAQ MULTIPLES APPRENTICE H'CAP — 1m 3f (P)
6:00 (6:04) (Class 4) (0-85,85) 4-Y-0+ — £4,075 (£1,212; £606; £303) Stalls Low

Form — RPR

-130 **1** **Kuda Huraa (IRE)**[21] 4216 4-9-5 **80** ... DarrenEgan 4 89+
(Roger Varian) *pressed ldr: led 3f out: sn 2 l clr: shkn up over 1f out: readily* **6/4**[1]

0010 **2** 2¼ **Beat Route**[34] 3782 5-8-6 **70** ... IanBurns(3) 7 75
(Michael Attwater) *trckd ldrs: rdn over 2f out: chsd wnr over 1f out: styd on but no imp* **8/1**

3110 **3** 2¼ **Hurricane Spirit (IRE)**[39] 3654 8-9-1 **79** ... NicoleNordblad(3) 3 80
(Hans Adielsson) *dwlt and stdd s: t.k.h and hld up in last pair: prog over 2f out: rdn over 1f out: kpt on one pce to take 3rd ins fnl f* **5/2**[2]

160 **4** 1¼ **St Ignatius**[37] 3703 5-8-10 **76** ... (p) RobertTart(5) 6 75
(Alan Bailey) *led to 3f out: one pce after: lost 2 pls fr over 1f out* **8/1**

0220 **5** 6 **Urban Space**[37] 3703 6-8-9 **70** ... DeanHeslop 2 58
(John Flint) *settled in tch: rdn over 2f out: no prog and sn wknd* **10/1**

0000 **6** 4½ **Admirable Duque (IRE)**[26] 4061 6-9-7 **85** ... (be) JoshBaudains(3) 1 65
(Dominic Ffrench Davis) *hld up: prog on wd outside 5f out: lost grnd bnd 3f out: sn wknd* **16/1**

2-03 **7** 1 **On Khee**[23] 4150 5-9-1 **79** ... WilliamTwiston-Davies(3) 8 57
(David Pipe) *racd wd mostly: cl up: lost grnd bnd 3f out: sn wknd* **6/1**[3]

2m 23.06s (1.16) **Going Correction** +0.05s/f (Slow) — **7** Ran SP% **120.1**
Speed ratings (Par 105): **97,95,93,92,88 85,84**
toteswingers: 1&2 £4.20, 1&3 £2.10, 2&3 £2.20. CSF £15.77 CT £30.15 TOTE £2.50: £1.30, £4.30; EX 19.30 Trifecta £39.80 Pool: £163.91 - 3.04 winning units..
Owner Mrs Fitri Hay **Bred** Healing Music Partnership **Trained** Newmarket, Suffolk

FOCUS
The going on the newly relaid surface was standard to slow. Plenty of interest was taken out of this apprentice handicap when the well-backed Rawaki burst through the stalls and had to be withdrawn. This contest was run at a steady pace and it paid to race handy. The runner-up sets the standard in a muddling race.

4945 BACK OR LAY AT BETDAQ.COM H'CAP — 1m 3f (P)
6:30 (6:30) (Class 5) (0-75,73) 3-Y-O — £2,264 (£673; £336; £168) Stalls Low

Form — RPR

0032 **1** **Gallipot**[28] 3968 3-9-7 **73** ... WilliamBuick 7 91
(John Gosden) *trckd ldng trio: pushed along and prog over 3f out: led wl over 2f out: rdn and steadily drew clr fr over 1f out* **7/4**[1]

0566 **2** *6* **Sky Khan**[13] 4498 3-9-2 **68**................ FrankieDettori 5 75
(Ed Dunlop) *sn settled into 3rd: chsd ldr over 3f out: upsides whn wnr wnt by wl over 2f out: steadily lft bhd* **11/4**[2]

3443 **3** *2* **Exning Halt**[21] 4224 3-9-5 **71**................ HayleyTurner 1 74
(James Fanshawe) *hld up in 5th: prog 3f out: rdn over 2f out: disp 2nd on inner over 1f out: one pce* **11/2**

2-15 **4** *2* **Bold Cuffs**[19] 4289 3-9-6 **72**................ SebSanders 2 72
(Sir Mark Prescott Bt) *sn pushed up to ld: urged along 4f out and tried to kick on: hung bdly lft bnd 3f out: sn hdd and dropped to 4th: one pce after* **5/1**[3]

5042 **5** *22* **Supreme Rock**[2] 4870 3-8-3 **60**................(p) NathanAlison(5) 4 20
(Jim Boyle) *tk fierce hold: stmbld sltly after 150yds: bmpd rival over 9f out: in tch tl wknd over 3f out: t.o* **12/1**

1050 **6** *11* **Northern Territory (IRE)**[20] 4256 3-8-9 **61**................ PatCosgrave 6
(Jim Boyle) *sn chsd ldr: wknd rapidly over 3f out: t.o* **33/1**

0533 **7** *1* **Chatterati (USA)**[7] 4714 3-9-3 **69**................ NeilCallan 3
(Mark Johnston) *settled in rr: bmpd and swvd lft bnd over 9f out: nvr gng wl after: wknd over 3f out: t.o* **16/1**

2m 20.33s (-1.57) **Going Correction** +0.05s/f (Slow) **7** Ran SP% **111.6**
Speed ratings (Par 100): **107,102,101,99,83 75,75**
toteswingers: 1&2 £1.90, 1&3 £3.40, 2&3 £3.40. CSF £6.33 CT £19.45 TOTE £2.90: £1.30, £1.90; EX 8.00 Trifecta £31.60 Pool: £308.79 - 7.23 winning units..
Owner Lady Rothschild **Bred** Kincorth Investments Inc **Trained** Newmarket, Suffolk

FOCUS
Quite a competitive handicap, run at a sound pace with the front four pulling a long way clear. The form looks solid rated around the placed horses.
Supreme Rock Official explanation: jockey saicd that the gelding ran too free

4946 BETDAQ MOBILE APPS/BRITISH STALLION STUDS E B F MAIDEN FILLIES' STKS 7f (P)
7:00 (7:00) (Class 5) 2-Y-O **£3,234** (£962; £481; £240) **Stalls** Low

Form RPR
23 **1** **Pompeia**[20] 4246 2-9-0 0................ JimCrowley 7 78
(Ralph Beckett) *pressed ldr: chal over 2f out: rdn to take narrow ld jst over 1f out: hld on* **15/8**[2]

2 *hd* **Miss Marjurie (IRE)** 2-9-0 0................ EddieAhern 5 77
(Denis Coakley) *dwlt: trckd ldrs in 6th gng wl: effrt 2f out: shkn up to cl on wnr 1f out: r.o to take 2nd nr fin: jst failed* **16/1**

4 **3** *nk* **Naalatt (IRE)**[27] 4002 2-9-0 0................ MickaelBarzalona 6 77
(Mahmood Al Zarooni) *prom: shkn up to chal over 2f out: w ldrs over 1f out: nt qckn fnl f* **6/1**[3]

4 *1* **Alwilda** 2-9-0 0................ SebSanders 10 74+
(Sir Mark Prescott Bt) *prom but rn green and pushed along at various stages: tried to chal fr 2f out: styd on but a hld fnl f* **18/1**

5 *½* **Thiqa (IRE)** 2-9-0 0................ FrankieDettori 4 73
(Saeed Bin Suroor) *led: shkn up and pressed over 2f out: hdd jst over 1f out: fdd last 75yds* **11/8**[1]

6 *5* **Emotionalblackmail (IRE)** 2-9-0 0................ HayleyTurner 9 60
(Joseph Tuite) *settled wl in rr: lft bhd by ldrs fr 3f out: wnt modest 6th wl over 1f out: pushed along and kpt on steadily* **33/1**

7 *13* **Wild Diamond (IRE)** 2-8-7 0................ TimClark(7) 2 36+
(Sir Mark Prescott Bt) *dwlt: rn green and bhd in last pair: nvr a factor but passed a few stragglers fnl 2f: likely to do bttr in time* **40/1**

8 *1 ½* **Afro** 2-9-0 0................ StevieDonohoe 1 22
(Peter Hedger) *in tch in midfield tl wknd 3f out: t.o* **100/1**

9 *2 ¼* **Privacy Order** 2-8-9 0................[1] RosieJessop(5) 11 16
(Sir Mark Prescott Bt) *slowly away: rapid prog on outer to press ldrs after 2f: wknd rapidly over 2f out: t.o* **33/1**

10 *2 ¼* **Daneglow (IRE)** 2-9-0 0................ ShaneKelly 13 10+
(Mike Murphy) *s.s: wl in rr: brief effrt over 3f out: sn wknd: t.o* **40/1**

11 *5* **Phoebe's Perfect** 2-9-0 0................ JamesMillman 14
(Rod Millman) *s.s: t.o after 3f* **66/1**

1m 28.06s (2.06) **Going Correction** +0.05s/f (Slow) **11** Ran SP% **115.6**
Speed ratings (Par 91): **90,89,89,88,87 82,67,65,62,60 54**
toteswingers: 1&2 £5.60, 1&3 £3.00, 2&3 £12.80. CSF £28.61 TOTE £3.10: £1.10, £4.70, £2.70; EX 27.50 Trifecta £267.40 Pool: £625.32 - 1.73 winning units..
Owner J L Rowsell **Bred** Ashbrittle Stud **Trained** Kimpton, Hants

FOCUS
Quite an interesting fillies' maiden that was run at a steady pace, with the front five pulling a long way clear. Once again, it paid to race handy and the form is rated around the winner and race averages.

NOTEBOOK
Pompeia, the most experienced runner in the field, put that to good use with a hard-fought success, confirming the promise she had shown when runner-up in a decent Newbury maiden on her debut. Her breeding suggests she will want further in time and nurseries look her next step. (op 7-4 tchd 2-1)
Miss Marjurie(IRE), bought for 42,000gns in April, is out of a half-sister to leading miler Soviet Song. She ran a most encouraging race on her debut for a yard who have not had a juvenile winner here, from 21 runners, in the last five seasons. (op 20-1)
Naalatt(IRE) was the lesser fancied of the Godolphin pair, judged on the betting, but she stepped up on her debut when fourth of nine at Folkestone (5f) over this longer trip and looks capable of landing a maiden. (op 5-1)
Alwilda, a half-sister to Albamara, an 8.5f winner at two and Listed-placed over 1m2f at three, ran a most promising race on her debut. She did not look the finished article prior to the start and had to be niggled to remain competitive entering the straight but kept on in style. She looks an exciting long-term prospect and can easily land a maiden. (op 16-1 tchd 20-1)
Thiqa(IRE), a half-sister to winners Northern Spy (7f-8.5f, RPR 90), Skyfire (7f, 83) and Arch Of Colours (8.6f AW, 73), was well backed on her debut but was unable to pick up once driven, having travelled kindly in front. One can expect her to improve for this. (op 7-4 tchd 15-8)
Emotionalblackmail(IRE), a half-sister to a Norwegian sprint winner and a 1m1f winner in France, was held up early and made some late progress suggesting she possesses some ability.

4947 BETDAQ CASINO GAMES NURSERY 6f (P)
7:30 (7:31) (Class 4) (0-85,85) 2-Y-O **£3,428** (£1,020; £509; £254) **Stalls** Low

Form RPR
5005 **1** **Masarah (IRE)**[11] 4574 2-8-3 **67**................ KirstyMilczarek 1 73
(Clive Brittain) *trckd ldng pair: clsd to chal 2f out: shkn up to ld jst over 1f out: edgd lft but styd on wl* **7/2**[3]

146 **2** *2* **London Citizen (USA)**[25] 4098 2-9-7 **85**................ WilliamBuick 3 85
(Mrs K Burke) *led at mod pce: jnd and shkn up over 2f out: hdd jst over 1f out: kpt on but readily hld after* **6/5**[1]

033 **3** *4* **Blazing Knight (IRE)**[13] 4502 2-8-8 **72**................(v[1]) JimCrowley 8 60
(Ralph Beckett) *pressed ldr: chal over 2f out: rdn: edgd lft and nt qckn wl over 1f out: sn lost 2nd and btn* **3/1**[2]

351 **4** *3 ½* **Stupenda**[28] 3971 2-8-2 **66**................ TadhgO'Shea 2 44
(Denis Coakley) *pushed along in last bef 1/2-way: lost tch w ldrs over 2f out: tk modest 4th fnl f* **6/1**

006 **5** *4 ½* **Harrogate Fair**[36] 3733 2-7-12 **62** oh4................ JamieMackay 5 26
(Michael Squance) *s.i.s: hld up in 4th: rdn and lost tch w ldrs over 2f out: wknd over 1f out* **20/1**

1m 13.81s (0.71) **Going Correction** +0.05s/f (Slow) **5** Ran SP% **111.7**
Speed ratings (Par 96): **97,94,89,84,78**
toteswinger: 1&2 £6.00. CSF £8.33 TOTE £5.40: £2.40, £1.10; EX 9.30 Trifecta £19.40 Pool: £266.14 - 10.13 winning units..
Owner Mohammed Al Nabouda **Bred** Rabbah Bloodstock Limited **Trained** Newmarket, Suffolk

FOCUS
Not the strongest of nurseries, run at a sound pace with the field well strung out crossing the line. The form has a solid feel rated around the first two.

NOTEBOOK
Masarah(IRE) had been outclassed in two Group 2 contests before running well enough in a hot Ascot nursery last time and she appreciated this easier assignment to win well. She was ideally positioned behind the leaders and saw it out gamely up the home straight. She holds entries in the Group 1 Fillies' Mile and Cheveley Park Stakes, but this looks her level. Official explanation: trainer's representative said, regarding the apparent improvement of form, that this race was a drop in class for the filly (op 9-2)
London Citizen(USA) was well backed returning to the scene of his impressive debut C&D victory, but despite travelling kindly could not pick up as well as the winner, with the slower surface possibly not suiting. (tchd 5-4)
Blazing Knight(IRE), wearing a first-time visor and switched to the AW for his nursery debut, travelled strongly but came widest of the three principals up the straight and he rates capable of better. (op 7-2 tchd 11-4)
Stupenda got the better of a bunched finish at Lingfield last time but struggled here on her handicap debut. She made some late progress, having been outpaced entering the straight, and may be worth trying over further. (op 5-1 tchd 13-2)

4948 DOWNLOAD RACING PLUS APP MAIDEN STKS 1m (P)
8:00 (8:01) (Class 5) 3-Y-O+ **£2,264** (£673; £336; £168) **Stalls** Low

Form RPR
00 **1** **Magma**[19] 4301 3-8-12 0................ DavidProbert 7 80
(Andrew Balding) *chsd ldrs: rdn over 2f out: wnt 2nd over 1f out: sn clsd and drvn to ld 150yds out: hld on after* **66/1**

0-5 **2** *½* **Dubawi Island (FR)**[30] 3913 3-9-3 0................(b) MartinDwyer 10 84
(James Tate) *led after 2f: kicked on over 2f out: hanging rt and nrly hit rail wl over 1f out: idled and hdd 150yds out: styd on but nt qckn after* **20/1**

3 *2 ¼* **Claude Monet (BRZ)** 3-8-5 0................ MickaelBarzalona 11 66+
(Jeremy Noseda) *dwlt: rcvrd on wd outside and trckd ldr after 2f: shkn up over 2f out: one pce and lost 2nd over 1f out* **7/2**[2]

63 **4** *3 ¾* **Narcissist (IRE)**[21] 4213 3-9-3 0................ RichardHughes 6 69
(Ed Dunlop) *w.w towards rr: shkn up jst over 2f out: nt qckn and no ch w ldrs after: plugged on* **6/1**

5 *½* **A'Juba** 3-9-3 0................ FrankieDettori 5 68+
(Saeed Bin Suroor) *rn v green and sn in last: urged along and sme prog over 2f out but ldrs already long gone: kpt on fnl f* **7/4**[1]

6 *4* **Tribal I D (IRE)** 3-9-3 0................ PatCosgrave 4 58
(Jim Boyle) *slowly away: wl in rr and rn green: no ch fr over 2f out but a little late hdwy* **40/1**

0 **7** *12* **No No Cardinal (IRE)**[51] 3227 3-9-3 0................ AdamKirby 1 30
(Peter Hedger) *wl in tch tl pushed along and wknd qckly over 2f out: t.o* **100/1**

8 *2 ¾* **Kept** 3-9-3 0................ HayleyTurner 12 23+
(James Fanshawe) *slowest away: rn v green and wl in rr: nvr a factor* **12/1**

534 **9** *2 ½* **Register (IRE)**[64] 2800 3-9-3 85................(t) NeilCallan 3 17
(William Muir) *led 2f: chsd ldng pair tl wknd qckly over 2f out: t.o* **9/2**[3]

225- **10** *4* **Sir Francis Drake**[422] 3001 4-9-10 79................ AndreaAtzeni 8
(Robert Eddery) *racd wd: prom 5f: wknd rapidly: t.o* **8/1**

1m 39.4s (-0.40) **Going Correction** +0.05s/f (Slow)
WFA 3 from 4yo 7lb **10** Ran SP% **119.5**
Speed ratings (Par 103): **104,103,101,97,97 93,81,78,75,71**
toteswingers: 1&2 £41.70, 1&3 £39.90, 2&3 £21.50. CSF £995.07 TOTE £71.60: £11.10, £6.60, £1.90; EX 319.70 TRIFECTA Not won..
Owner A H Robinson **Bred** H & Mrs C Robinson **Trained** Kingsclere, Hants

FOCUS
Not the strongest of maidens, run at a steady pace, with the far-side rail looking the place to be and very few coming from behind. Not much depth formwise and fluid.

4949 SPORTINGLIFE.COM H'CAP (LONDON MILE QUALIFIER) 1m (P)
8:30 (8:32) (Class 4) (0-85,85) 3-Y-O **£4,075** (£1,212; £606; £303) **Stalls** Low

Form RPR
2140 **1** **Henry Clay**[14] 4474 3-8-11 **75**................ NeilCallan 7 84
(Mark Johnston) *mde all: drifted lft fr jst over 2f out: ended up towards nr side rail but decisive ld 1f out: styd on* **15/2**

1-00 **2** *1 ¾* **Asifa (IRE)**[60] 2930 3-9-7 **85**................(v[1]) FrankieDettori 6 90
(Saeed Bin Suroor) *hld up in midfield: prog wl over 2f out: rdn and tk 2nd 1f out: styd on but nvr able to chal* **9/2**[3]

-206 **3** *½* **Grizzle**[55] 3063 3-9-4 **82**................ MickaelBarzalona 3 86
(Mahmood Al Zarooni) *prom: shkn up and nt qckn over 2f out: styd on fr over 1f out to take 3rd nr fin* **9/1**

2265 **4** *nse* **Tight Lipped (IRE)**[44] 3446 3-8-10 **74**................ RichardHughes 1 78
(James Eustace) *chsd wnr 2f: styd prom: drvn wl over 2f out: kpt on to chse ldng pair fnl f: lost 3rd nr fin* **20/1**

4345 **5** *2 ¾* **Scrupul (IRE)**[13] 4498 3-8-10 **74**................ KierenFallon 8 72
(Luca Cumani) *trckd wnr after 2f: trying to chal whn impeded jst over 2f out and again over 1f out: lost momentum and sn wknd* **3/1**[1]

2626 **6** *hd* **Presburg (IRE)**[26] 4068 3-9-5 **83**................ LiamKeniry 5 80
(Joseph Tuite) *dwlt: hld up in rr: gng wl enough whn short of room briefly 3f out: effrt over 2f out: rdn and one pce after* **12/1**

3-15 **7** *shd* **Mugazala (IRE)**[25] 4091 3-9-2 **80**................ TadhgO'Shea 9 77
(Ed Dunlop) *t.k.h early: hld up in midfield: pushed up on outer to chse ldrs over 3f out: hanging over 2f out: nt qckn and n.d after* **20/1**

11U6 **8** *6* **Viscount Vert (IRE)**[21] 4223 3-9-4 **82**................ DavidProbert 2 65
(Andrew Balding) *reluctant to enter stalls: dwlt: sn chsd ldrs: rdn over 3f out: losing pl whn no room on inner over 2f out: wknd* **12/1**

621 **9** *1 ½* **Niger (IRE)**[21] 4213 3-8-13 **77**................ WilliamBuick 4 57
(Jeremy Noseda) *rrd in stalls: slowest away: wl in rr: shkn up and no prog over 2f out* **4/1**[2]

0305 **10** *nk* **Responsive**[26] 4062 3-9-4 **82**................(b) DarryllHolland 10 61
(Hughie Morrison) *hld up in rr: last and lost tch 3f out: no ch after* **16/1**

01- **11** *5* **Knave Of Clubs (IRE)**[278] 7258 3-9-0 **78**........................ SebSanders 11 45
(Peter Makin) *in tch: rdn over 3f out: wknd qckly over 2f out* **33/1**

1m 39.87s (0.07) **Going Correction** +0.05s/f (Slow) **11** Ran SP% **118.7**
Speed ratings (Par 102): **101,99,98,98,95 95,95,89,88,87 82**
toteswingers: 1&2 £8.00, 1&3 £13.00, 2&3 £8.60. CSF £40.53 CT £314.49 TOTE £10.40: £2.70, £2.30, £2.30; EX 47.20 Trifecta £110.70 Pool: £363.64 - 2.43 winning units..
Owner Sheikh Hamdan Bin Mohammed Al Maktoum **Bred** Rabbah Bloodstock Limited **Trained** Middleham Moor, N Yorks

FOCUS
This looked a decent enough handicap, run at a steady pace with the front-runner making all despite hanging to his right all the way up the straight, finishing near to the stands' rail. Again it proved hard to make ground from the rear but the form looks straightforward.
Niger(IRE) Official explanation: jockey said that the colt reared in the stalls
Responsive Official explanation: jockey said that the filly did not face the kickback

4950 SPORTINGLIFE.COM RACING H'CAP — 1m (P)
9:00 (9:01) (Class 6) (0-65,65) 3-Y-O+ — **£1,617** (£481; £240; £120) **Stalls** Low

Form — RPR

-405 **1** **Saharia (IRE)**[27] 3995 5-9-11 **65**..(v) ShaneKelly 7 76+
(Michael Attwater) *free to post: hld up in last trio: cruising over 2f out: weaved way through fnl 2f to ld on bit 100yds out: easily* **28/1**

2302 **2** *1 ¾* **Casa Bex**[7] 4709 3-8-13 **63**...(tp) RaulDaSilva(3) 8 69
(Philip McBride) *pressed ldr at str pce: led wl over 2f out: sn drvn: styd on wl but hdd and brushed aside last 100yds* **9/2**[2]

320 **3** *2 ½* **West Leake (IRE)**[37] 3705 6-9-6 **60**.................................... LiamKeniry 3 61
(Paul Burgoyne) *hld up in midfield gng easily: effrt on outer over 2f out: nt qckn wl over 1f out: kpt on to take 3rd fnl f* **16/1**

040 **4** *2 ¼* **Saucy Buck (IRE)**[13] 4511 4-9-6 **60**.................................(t) NeilCallan 12 56
(Jamie Poulton) *prom: drvn to chse ldr 2f out: lost 2nd and fdd 1f out* **12/1**

2235 **5** *1 ¼* **Douze Points (IRE)**[28] 3958 6-9-11 **65**.................. AdamKirby 11 58
(John Butler) *hld up and sn last: rdn 3f out: prog past tiring rivals fr 2f out: nvr gng pce to threaten* **12/1**

0651 **6** *½* **Abriachan**[28] 3964 5-9-8 **62**... RichardHughes 6 54
(Noel Quinlan) *hld up towards rr: tried to make prog on outer 2f out: limited rspnse and kpt on one pce after* **15/8**[1]

-141 **7** *¾* **Shaunas Spirit (IRE)**[42] 3497 4-9-1 **62**............................ PaulBooth(7) 5 52
(Dean Ivory) *v s.i.s: t.k.h in last trio: prog 3f out to chse ldrs 2f out: wknd fnl f* **6/1**[3]

0-66 **8** *¾* **Rafella (IRE)**[20] 4240 4-9-4 **58**.................................... HayleyTurner 9 47
(Michael Scudamore) *chsd ldrs: rdn 1/2-way: struggling after but only grad fdd* **33/1**

3000 **9** *4* **Gallantry**[21] 4219 10-9-4 **58**... AmirQuinn 14 37
(Paul Howling) *chsd ldrs: rdn on outer in 5th over 3f out: lost pl over 2f out: wknd* **33/1**

3230 **10** *1* **Blue Deer (IRE)**[16] 4413 4-9-8 **62**.............................. SebSanders 10 39
(Lee Carter) *prom in strly run contest tl wknd over 2f out* **9/1**

0-45 **11** *12* **Resuscitator (USA)**[29] 3947 5-9-11 **65**..........................(v) EddieAhern 2 15
(Linda Stubbs) *led at str pce: hdd wl over 2f out: wknd rapidly and eased wl over 1f out: t.o* **12/1**

1m 39.85s (0.05) **Going Correction** +0.05s/f (Slow)
WFA 3 from 4yo+ 7lb **11** Ran SP% **115.5**
Speed ratings (Par 101): **101,99,96,94,93 92,92,91,87,86 74**
toteswingers: 1&2 £20.40, 1&3 £83.50, 2&3 £17.70. CSF £145.82 CT £2104.53 TOTE £29.20: £6.30, £1.50, £3.60; EX 384.60 Trifecta £243.60 Part won. Pool: £329.21 - 0.20 winning units..
Owner The Attwater Partnership **Bred** Woodcote Stud Ltd **Trained** Epsom, Surrey

FOCUS
An open-looking contest run at a steady gallop with the winner the only one to have come from off the pace on the whole card. The form looks sound if limited.
T/Plt: £199.70 to a £1 stake. Pool: £50,002.13 - 182.75 winning tickets. T/Qpdt: £101.00 to a £1 stake. Pool: £4,477.74 - 32.80 winning tickets. JN

4587 NEWCASTLE (L-H)
Wednesday, August 8

OFFICIAL GOING: Good (good to soft in places) changing to good after race 1 (2.10).
Wind: Breezy, half behind Weather: Cloudy, warm

4951 CARLING NURSERY — 7f
2:10 (2:10) (Class 4) (0-85,82) 2-Y-O — **£3,428** (£1,020; £509; £254) **Stalls** Centre

Form — RPR

003 **1** **Salutation (IRE)**[14] 4448 2-8-9 **70**..................................... FrannyNorton 8 77
(Mark Johnston) *mde all: rdn over 2f out: drifted lft ins fnl f: kpt on strly* **6/1**

0641 **2** *2* **Charlie Em**[14] 4450 2-8-8 **69**... TonyHamilton 7 71
(Richard Fahey) *chsd ldrs: rdn and outpcd wl over 1f out: styd on fnl f to take 2nd nr fin: nt rch wnr* **13/2**

10U3 **3** *nk* **Rated**[3] 4847 2-9-3 **78**... SamHitchcott 6 79
(Mick Channon) *t.k.h: hld up: hdwy to chse wnr over 1f out: rdn and hung lft ins fnl f: one pce and lost 2nd towards fin* **5/1**[3]

052 **4** *3 ¾* **Marhaba Malayeen (IRE)**[15] 4427 2-8-10 **71**.................... TomEaves 2 62
(Kevin Ryan) *t.k.h: cl up: rdn over 2f out: outpcd fnl f* **14/1**

4622 **5** *shd* **Out Of The Blocks**[8] 4672 2-8-5 **66**............................. JamesSullivan 9 57
(Ruth Carr) *hld up: rdn and effrt over 2f out: kpt on fnl f: nvr able to chal* **7/1**

303 **6** *2 ½* **Requested**[13] 4507 2-9-4 **79**... SilvestreDeSousa 1 64
(Mahmood Al Zarooni) *trckd ldrs: rdn wl over 1f out: edgd lft: wknd fnl f* **3/1**[1]

0252 **7** *1 ¼* **Old Man Clegg**[25] 4116 2-8-4 **68**...................................... DominicFox(3) 4 51
(Michael Easterby) *slowly away: hld up: drvn over 2f out: nvr able to chal* **4/1**[2]

105 **8** *5* **Cumbrian Craic**[67] 2688 2-9-2 **77**................................. DuranFentiman 5 45
(Tim Easterby) *prom: drvn fr 1/2-way: wknd over 1f out* **18/1**

1m 25.86s (-1.94) **Going Correction** -0.25s/f (Firm) **8** Ran SP% **113.7**
Speed ratings (Par 96): **101,98,98,94,93 91,89,83**
toteswingers: 1&2 £8.90, 1&3 £6.20, 273 £6.30. CSF £43.80 CT £208.30 TOTE £6.20: £1.90, £2.90, £1.50; EX 48.70.
Owner Sheikh Hamdan Bin Mohammed Al Maktoum **Bred** Foursome Thoroughbreds, Muir & Waldron **Trained** Middleham Moor, N Yorks

FOCUS
On a bright summer's day the ground was drying out all the time and after the opener it was reckoned to be good, if a little on the slow side. A wide-open nursery handicap but ultimately a decisive winner. The form has a solid feel.

NOTEBOOK
Salutation(IRE), a strong, well-made individual had shown improved form on his third start when third over 6f. He made every yard and, despite drifting left towards the far side, he kept up the gallop to win going away. He will be hard to beat if turned out under a penalty. (op 11-2 tchd 13-2)
Charlie Em, 3lb higher than when narrowly accounting for Out Of the Blocks at Catterick, may lack size and scope but her heart is certainly in the right place. (op 6-1)
Rated, third at Newbury three days earlier, travelled strongly but his effort petered out near the line and he just missed out on second spot. This was this tough sorts eighth outing. (op 11-2 tchd 6-1)
Marhaba Malayeen(IRE), runner-up in a maiden at Musselburgh on his third start, seemed to find this stiffer track against him on his nursery bow. (tchd 16-1)
Out Of The Blocks, having his tenth start, was unable to reproduce his Catterick form with Charlie Em. (tchd 13-2)
Requested lacks scope and tended to hang left-handed. He does not look to be progressing. (op 7-2 tchd 4-1)
Old Man Clegg, raised 2lb after finishing runner-up over 6f at York, walked out of the stalls and never got competitive. A big type, he is well worth another chance. (tchd 7-2)

4952 COBRA MEDIAN AUCTION MAIDEN STKS — 6f
2:40 (2:43) (Class 6) 2-Y-O — **£1,617** (£481; £240; £120) **Stalls** Centre

Form — RPR

2342 **1** **The Sixties**[3] 4836 2-9-3 **78**..(v) SamHitchcott 6 77
(Mick Channon) *cl up: rdn to ld appr fnl f: hld on wl towards fin* **2/1**[1]

5552 **2** *nk* **Grievous Angel (IRE)**[14] 4448 2-8-12 **68**.......................... GrahamLee 9 71
(Ann Duffield) *trckd ldrs: effrt and rdn over 1f out: chsd wnr ins fnl f: r.o* **7/1**[2]

30 **3** *4* **Bapak Bangsawan**[80] 2308 2-9-3 **0**.................................... AmyRyan 7 65
(Kevin Ryan) *led to appr fnl f: lost 2nd and outpcd ins fnl f* **33/1**

40 **4** *1 ¾* **Miss Perfect**[7] 4710 2-8-12 **0**... JimmyQuinn 1 54
(John Quinn) *dwlt: hld up: rdn along over 2f out: no imp over 1f out* **25/1**

0 **5** *2* **Chloe's Image**[13] 4494 2-8-12 **0**.. PaddyAspell 5 48
(Philip Kirby) *trckd ldrs: outpcd and rdn over 2f out: r.o fnl f: no imp* **100/1**

6 *2 ½* **Major Parkes** 2-9-3 **0**... MichaelO'Connell 8 45
(John Quinn) *dwlt: hld up in tch: rdn over 2f out: btn fnl f* **22/1**[3]

00 **7** *27* **Elusive Shadow**[16] 4395 2-8-12 **0**...................................... MickyFenton 4
(Alan Brown) *t.k.h: prom tl rdn and wknd over 2f out* **100/1**

1m 14.21s (-0.39) **Going Correction** -0.25s/f (Firm) **7** Ran SP% **58.9**
Speed ratings (Par 92): **92,91,86,83,81 77,41**
toteswingers: 1&2 £1.10, 1&3 £3.60, 2&3 £4.60. CSF £2.47 TOTE £1.60: £1.10, £1.10; EX 3.30.
Owner Bargate **Bred** Imperial & Mike Channon Bloodstock Ltd **Trained** West Ilsley, Berks

FOCUS
Plenty of drama ahead of this 2-y-o maiden. The first two set an ordinary level. The withdrawal of both Hoofalong and Al Manaal resulted in a Rule 4 deduction of 50p in the pound.

NOTEBOOK
The Sixties, with two of the market leaders withdrawn, had a golden opportunity to open his account at the eighth attempt. Beaten favourite three times and runner-up in a nursery at Chester just three days earlier, he did just enough. (op 7-4)
Grievous Angel(IRE), who had 5lb to find with the winner, travelled strongly but was just held. She was having her fifth start but is still on the upgrade. (op 13-2)
Bapak Bangsawan, a half-brother to three winners, took them along on his third start. He still looked inexperienced and is now qualified for a nursery mark.
Miss Perfect was never going the pace and will need a return to 7f or 1m in nurseries.
Chloe's Image showed a fraction more than on her debut but will need to improve a good deal if she is to make her presence felt outside selling company.
Major Parkes, from a speedy family, gave away ground at the start. There ought to be a fair bit better to come. (op 20-1)
Elusive Shadow Official explanation: jockey said that the filly lost her action

4953 COORS LIGHT H'CAP — 5f
3:10 (3:11) (Class 5) (0-75,75) 3-Y-O — **£2,264** (£673; £336; £168) **Stalls** Centre

Form — RPR

222 **1** **Wild Sauce**[13] 4500 3-9-1 **74**...(p) JustinNewman(5) 4 83
(Bryan Smart) *sweating and edgy in preliminaries: mde all: rdn over 1f out: pricked ears ins fnl f: kpt on wl* **3/1**[2]

1 **2** *1 ½* **Phebes Wish (IRE)**[33] 3837 3-9-2 **70**.............................(t) JamesSullivan 2 74
(John C McConnell, Ire) *trckd ldrs: effrt and wnt 2nd over 1f out: kpt on same pce ins fnl f* **11/4**[1]

0046 **3** *¾* **I'll Be Good**[11] 4591 3-9-0 **75**...................................(p) DavidSimmonson(7) 6 76
(Robert Johnson) *cl up: rdn 2f out: kpt on same pce fnl f* **12/1**

43-0 **4** *¾* **Headstight (IRE)**[22] 4174 3-8-2 **56**................................ DuranFentiman 3 54
(Paul Midgley) *t.k.h: cl up tl rdn and one pce appr fnl f* **16/1**

1501 **5** *1 ¼* **Baltic Bomber (IRE)**[11] 4593 3-8-9 **63**.......................... MichaelO'Connell 8 57
(John Quinn) *hld up in tch: rdn over 2f out: edgd lft over 1f out: no imp fnl f* **6/1**

136 **6** *3 ¾* **Tinzapeas**[5] 4757 3-8-13 **67**..(v) SamHitchcott 9 47
(Mick Channon) *hld up in tch: rdn over 2f out: nvr able to chal* **6/1**

2212 **7** *2 ¼* **One Kool Dude**[8] 4671 3-8-7 **66**....................................(v) ShaneBKelly(5) 1 38
(Michael Bell) *half rrd and wnt lft s: sn drvn in rr: no imp fr 1/2-way* **9/2**[3]

54-0 **8** *15* **Make Up**[16] 4394 3-8-4 **58**.. JimmyQuinn 7
(Noel Wilson) *dwlt: t.k.h in rr: struggling over 2f out: sn lost tch* **33/1**

59.84s (-1.26) **Going Correction** -0.25s/f (Firm) **8** Ran SP% **114.9**
Speed ratings (Par 100): **100,97,96,95,93 87,83,59**
toteswingers: 1&2 £2.40, 1&3 £6.90, 2&3 £7.30. CSF £11.79 CT £83.97 TOTE £4.50: £1.30, £1.10, £2.70; EX 13.10.
Owner Richard Page **Bred** Ashbrittle Stud **Trained** Hambleton, N Yorks

FOCUS
What looked a competitive 3-y-o sprint handicap was turned into a procession by the speedy winner. The first two recorded persoanal-bests with the third to his mark.
One Kool Dude Official explanation: jockey said that the gelding missed the break and was never travelling

4954 CAFFREYS H'CAP — 7f
3:40 (3:42) (Class 5) (0-75,74) 3-Y-O+ — **£2,264** (£673; £336; £168) **Stalls** Centre

Form — RPR

623 **1** **Discression**[13] 4496 3-9-6 **74**... GrahamLee 10 84
(Kevin Ryan) *in tch: rdn over 2f out: led ent fnl f: kpt on strly* **4/1**[2]

0165 **2** *2* **Main Beach**[34] 3790 5-9-8 **70**...(p) MickyFenton 9 77
(Paul Midgley) *hld up: rdn and hdwy 2f out: chsd wnr ins fnl f: kpt on: no imp* **9/2**[3]

-000 **3** *1 ¼* **Stilettoesinthemud (IRE)**[16] 4398 4-8-7 **55**...............[1] JamesSullivan 5 58
(James Given) *hld up in tch: hdwy over 1f out: kpt on ins fnl f* **66/1**

4234 **4** *nk* **No Quarter (IRE)**[7] 4715 5-8-11 **59**.............................. FrannyNorton 12 61
(Tracy Waggott) *hld up: rdn and hdwy over 1f out: r.o fnl f* **11/1**

2113 **5** *shd* **Eastward Ho**[18] 4345 4-9-8 **70**.. TonyHamilton 3 72
(Jason Ward) *prom: rdn and ev ch over 2f out to over 1f out: kpt on same pce* **7/2**[1]

44-0 **6** *nk* **Who's Shirl**[74] 2487 6-9-10 **72**....... DuranFentiman 7 73
(Chris Fairhurst) *hld up in midfield: hdwy over 2f out: kpt on same pce ins fnl f* **25/1**
0004 **7** *¾* **Whispered Times (USA)**[7] 4716 5-9-2 **64**.......(p) PaddyAspell 8 63
(Tracy Waggott) *prom: hdwy to ld over 2f out: hdd ent fnl f: sn outpcd* **22/1**
-052 **8** *4* **Amoure Medici**[10] 4624 3-9-2 **70**....... SilvestreDeSousa 11 57
(Ann Duffield) *hld up: rdn over 2f out: hdwy over 1f out: no imp* **7/2**[1]
0-00 **9** *9* **Music Festival (USA)**[5] 4769 5-8-10 **63**....... ShaneBKelly(5) 14 27
(Jim Goldie) *hld up: rdn over 3f out: no imp fnl 2f* **20/1**
10 *5* **Mcmonagle (USA)**[65] 2778 4-9-6 **68**....... JimmyQuinn 4 19
(Alan Brown) *prom tl rdn and wknd over 2f out* **40/1**
006 **11** *10* **Henry Morgan**[13] 4495 5-9-0 **62**.......(p) TomEaves 6
(Bryan Smart) *hld up bhd ldng gp: struggling over 2f out: sn btn* **20/1**
0005 **12** *4* **Oil Strike**[27] 3993 5-9-3 **72**....... DavidSimmonson(7) 2
(Michael Easterby) *led to over 2f out: sn rdn and wknd* **20/1**
10R5 **13** *8* **Nadeen (IRE)**[15] 4432 5-9-4 **66**.......(v[1]) AndrewMullen 1
(Michael Smith) *s.v.s: t.o thrght* **50/1**

1m 26.34s (-1.46) **Going Correction** -0.25s/f (Firm)
WFA 3 from 4yo+ 6lb **13** Ran SP% **119.3**
Speed ratings (Par 103): **98,95,94,93,93 93,92,88,77,72 60,56,46**
toteswingers: 1&2 £5.60, 1&3 £62.90, 2&3 £98.50. CSF £19.63 CT £1038.65 TOTE £4.90: £1.60, £1.80, £21.20; EX 29.70.
Owner T G & Mrs M E Holdcroft, K MacPherson **Bred** Bearstone Stud **Trained** Hambleton, N Yorks

FOCUS
A wide-open 7f handicap and there was little between the first seven home at the line. The runner-up ran to his best turf form with the third and fourth to their marks.

4955 WORTHINGTON H'CAP 1m 6f 97y
4:10 (4:10) (Class 5) (0-70,67) 3-Y-O+ **£2,264** (£673; £336; £168) **Stalls** Low

Form RPR
1 **Passion Planet (IRE)**[67] 2724 4-9-5 **58**....... JamesSullivan 4 68
(John C McConnell, Ire) *hld up in midfield: hdwy to ld 2f out: sn rdn and edgd lft: hld on wl fnl f* **16/1**
500- **2** *1 ½* **Maybe I Wont**[63] 6918 7-9-6 **62**....... LucyAlexander(3) 6 70
(James Moffatt) *hld up and bhd: hdwy 3f out: chsd wnr over 1f out: r.o fnl f* **18/1**
0 **3** *2 ¾* **Jawaab (IRE)**[109] 1525 8-9-0 **60**....... JasonHart(7) 2 64
(Philip Kirby) *hld up in tch on ins: rdn over 4f out: rallied over 2f out: kpt on ins fnl f* **5/1**[2]
416 **4** *2 ½* **Madrasa (IRE)**[11] 4590 4-10-0 **67**.......(bt) TomEaves 8 68
(Keith Reveley) *t.k.h: hld up: smooth hdwy to chse ldrs over 2f out: sn rdn: one pce over 1f out* **13/2**
3521 **5** *7* **Red Tyke (IRE)**[21] 4210 3-8-3 **55**....... JimmyQuinn 13 46
(John Quinn) *hld up towards rr: struggling over 3f out: plugged on fr 2f out: no imp* **10/1**
2312 **6** *3 ¾* **Mr Snoozy**[10] 4626 3-8-8 **60**....... DuranFentiman 9 46
(Tim Walford) *cl up: rdn over 3f out: wknd wl over 1f out* **11/4**[1]
45 **7** *1 ¼* **Asteroid Belt (IRE)**[11] 4594 3-8-4 **56**....... AmyRyan 1 40
(Chris Grant) *cl up: rdn 3f out: wknd wl over 1f out* **7/1**
000 **8** *1* **Media Stars**[7] 4716 7-8-8 **50**.......(p) DominicFox(3) 5 32
(Robert Johnson) *s.i.s: hld up: effrt wl over 2f out: wknd over 1f out* **66/1**
1005 **9** *1 ¾* **Quiet Appeal (IRE)**[11] 4585 3-8-9 **61**....... FrannyNorton 7 41
(Mark Johnston) *led tl rdn and hdd 2f out: sn wknd* **10/1**
0-00 **10** *9* **Sea Change (IRE)**[18] 4326 5-9-12 **65**....... GrahamLee 3 32
(Jim Goldie) *trckd ldrs tl wknd qckly over 2f out* **6/1**[3]
106 **11** *2 ¼* **Ad Value (IRE)**[69] 2635 4-9-9 **62**....... AndrewElliott 10 26
(Alan Swinbank) *midfield on outside: struggling over 3f out: sn btn* **14/1**
00-0 **12** *47* **Cat O' Nine Tails**[19] 4311 5-9-6 **59**....... PaddyAspell 12
(Brian Rothwell) *towards rr: struggling over 5f out: lost tch fnl 3f* **50/1**

3m 8.83s (-2.47) **Going Correction** -0.15s/f (Firm)
WFA 3 from 4yo+ 13lb **12** Ran SP% **122.9**
Speed ratings (Par 103): **101,100,98,97,93 91,90,89,88,83 82,55**
toteswingers: 1&2 £22.50, 1&3 £20.50, 2&3 £21.80. CSF £284.24 CT £1664.62 TOTE £20.80: £5.20, £5.40, £2.80; EX 173.00.
Owner Derek Kierans **Bred** Irish National Stud **Trained** Stamullen, Co Meath

FOCUS
The pace was strong in this modest stayers' handicap and those that raced up with the pace paid a heavy price. The first five home came from off the pace. The winner is rated close to his irish best with the runner-up to last year's Flat form.
Sea Change(IRE) Official explanation: jockey said that the gelding hung left in the final six furlongs

4956 CARLING CHROME H'CAP (DIV I) 6f
4:40 (4:40) (Class 6) (0-65,63) 3-Y-O+ **£1,617** (£481; £240; £120) **Stalls** Centre

Form RPR
0410 **1** **Circuitous**[54] 3115 4-9-12 **63**.......(v) GrahamLee 4 71
(Keith Dalgleish) *mde all: rdn 2f out: hld on wl fnl f* **12/1**
213 **2** *¾* **Oakbrook**[1] 4909 3-9-1 **56**....... SilvestreDeSousa 6 62
(Ann Duffield) *in tch: effrt and drvn over 2f out: styd on to take 2nd nr fin: r.o* **9/4**[1]
-023 **3** *¾* **Ypres**[18] 4348 3-9-5 **60**....... PaddyAspell 3 63
(Jason Ward) *hld up in tch: rdn over 1f out: chsd wnr ins fnl f tl nr fin: one pce* **7/2**[2]
3050 **4** *1 ¼* **Karate Queen**[7] 4717 7-8-8 **45**....... AmyRyan 1 44
(Ron Barr) *hld up: hdwy and cl up over 1f out: one pce ins fnl f* **12/1**
-002 **5** *1* **Emily Hall**[7] 4717 3-8-6 **47**....... DuranFentiman 7 43
(Bryan Smart) *taken early to post: dwlt: t.k.h in rr: rdn and hdwy over 1f out: kpt on: nrst fin* **5/1**[3]
5020 **6** *9* **Thrust Control (IRE)**[5] 4783 5-8-12 **49**....... FrannyNorton 8 16
(Tracy Waggott) *cl up tl rdn and wknd over 1f out* **5/1**[3]
0000 **7** *2 ½* **Sleights Boy (IRE)**[7] 4717 4-8-9 **46**....... TomEaves 2
(Ian McInnes) *hld up on outside: rdn over 2f out: btn over 1f out* **40/1**
6600 **8** *10* **Kieron's Rock (IRE)**[12] 4549 3-8-5 **46** ow1.......(b) AndrewElliott 5
(Jedd O'Keeffe) *cl up tl rdn and wknd over 2f out* **33/1**
4062 **9** *1 ½* **Cross Of Lorraine (IRE)**[11] 4593 9-9-7 **58**.......(b) TonyHamilton 9
(Chris Grant) *hld up: drvn over 2f out: btn over 1f out* **9/1**

1m 13.6s (-1.00) **Going Correction** -0.25s/f (Firm)
WFA 3 from 4yo+ 4lb **9** Ran SP% **117.1**
Speed ratings (Par 101): **96,95,94,92,91 79,75,62,60**
toteswingers: 1&2 £4.20, 1&3 £7.80, 2&3 £3.00. CSF £39.88 CT £119.25 TOTE £18.40: £4.90, £1.10, £1.20; EX 55.60.
Owner A R M Galbraith **Bred** Deepwood Farm Stud **Trained** Carluke, S Lanarks

FOCUS
A modest sprint handicap won from the front and rated around the placed horses pretty much to their form.
Circuitous Official explanation: trainer could offer no explanation for the apparent improvement of form
Cross Of Lorraine(IRE) Official explanation: jockey said that the gelding stopped quickly

4957 CARLING CHROME H'CAP (DIV II) 6f
5:10 (5:11) (Class 6) (0-65,63) 3-Y-O+ **£1,617** (£481; £240; £120) **Stalls** Centre

Form RPR
-352 **1** **Ursus**[14] 4453 7-8-11 **49**.......(p) SilvestreDeSousa 3 59
(Christopher Wilson) *cl up: led 2f out: hrd pressed ins fnl f: hld on gamely u.p* **3/1**[1]
-601 **2** *nk* **Piste**[1] 4911 6-8-13 **51** 6ex.......(e) DuranFentiman 4 60
(Tina Jackson) *hld up in tch: hdwy to dispute ld ent fnl f: sn rdn: kpt on: hld nr fin* **9/2**[3]
5500 **3** *5* **Brave Battle**[13] 4495 4-8-12 **55**....... ShaneBKelly(5) 1 48
(Ron Barr) *t.k.h: prom: effrt 2f out: kpt on same pce appr fnl f* **7/1**
0320 **4** *½* **Bartley**[27] 3994 3-9-7 **63**.......(p) TomEaves 7 54
(Bryan Smart) *cl up: drvn and effrt over 2f out: nt qckn over 1f out* **9/2**[3]
3360 **5** *¾* **Red Scintilla**[2] 4865 5-8-8 **46**.......(p) AndrewMullen 5 35
(Nigel Tinkler) *led to 2f out: sn rdn and kpt on same pce* **6/1**
0050 **6** *3* **King Laertis (IRE)**[28] 3952 3-8-3 **45**....... FrannyNorton 6 24
(Tracy Waggott) *trckd ldrs tl rdn and wknd 2f out* **33/1**
1346 **7** *½* **Celestial Dawn**[14] 4461 3-9-5 **61**....... JamesSullivan 8 39
(John Weymes) *hld up bhd ldng gp: drvn along 1/2-way: btn over 1f out* **7/2**[2]
0560 **8** *5* **Queen's Princess**[18] 4348 4-8-7 **45**.......(p) MichaelStainton 2
(John Wainwright) *trckd ldrs tl rdn and wknd over 2f out* **22/1**

1m 13.5s (-1.10) **Going Correction** -0.25s/f (Firm)
WFA 3 from 4yo+ 4lb **8** Ran SP% **117.7**
Speed ratings (Par 101): **97,96,89,89,88 84,83,76**
toteswingers: 1&2 £4.20, 1&3 £5.50, 2&3 £7.80. CSF £17.41 CT £87.71 TOTE £4.40: £1.70, £2.40, £1.60; EX 27.00.
Owner Mrs J Wilson (durham) **Bred** Mrs Andrea Bartlett **Trained** Manfield, N Yorks

FOCUS
Part two of a modest sprint handicap. The winner is rated close to his 2010 best with the runner-up matching her form of the previous day.

4958 CARLING ZEST APPRENTICE H'CAP 1m 2f 32y
5:40 (5:40) (Class 6) (0-60,60) 3-Y-O+ **£1,617** (£481; £240; £120) **Stalls** Low

Form RPR
3-00 **1** **Pattern Mark**[30] 3914 6-9-6 **55**....... JacobButterfield(3) 3 61
(Ollie Pears) *hld up in tch: pushed along over 4f out: hdwy over 2f out: styd on wl fnl f: led towards fin* **3/1**[1]
0003 **2** *1* **Sally Friday (IRE)**[11] 4594 4-9-0 **53**.......(p) KevinStott(7) 5 57
(Edwin Tuer) *t.k.h: led at stdy gallop: rdn 2f out: kpt on fnl f: hdd nr fin* **5/1**[2]
5000 **3** *nk* **Downtown Boy (IRE)**[14] 4453 4-9-0 **46** oh1.......(p) GeorgeChaloner 2 49
(Ray Craggs) *t.k.h: disp ld: rdn 2f out: no ex wl ins fnl f* **22/1**
0243 **4** *1 ¼* **Snooker (GER)**[14] 4455 6-10-0 **60**....... HarryChalloner 4 61
(Rose Dobbin) *prom: effrt over 2f out: edgd rt over 1f out: kpt on same pce fnl f* **3/1**[1]
0560 **5** *2* **Time To Excel**[12] 4549 3-8-0 **48**.......(p) ConnorNichol(7) 11 45
(Michael Dods) *hld up: rdn and hdwy over 2f out: kpt on fnl f: nvr able to chal* **22/1**
6-04 **6** *10* **Think**[18] 4349 5-8-12 **47**.......(t) DavidSimmonson(3) 6 24
(Clive Mulhall) *trckd ldrs tl rdn and wknd over 2f out* **11/2**[3]
1403 **7** *¾* **Kian's Joy**[19] 4313 3-8-8 **49**.......(p) JasonHart 1 24
(Jedd O'Keeffe) *cl up: drvn over 4f out: wknd over 2f out* **6/1**
-005 **8** *3 ¾* **Bedlam**[12] 4549 3-9-0 **55**.......(b) DarylByrne 8 23
(Tim Easterby) *hld up: struggling over 4f out: sn btn* **10/1**
040- **9** *shd* **Karmarouge (IRE)**[224] 2239 4-8-11 **46** oh1.......(tp) ConorHarrison(3) 10 14
(Brian Rothwell) *in tch: drvn and struggling over 3f out: sn wknd* **50/1**

2m 14.38s (2.48) **Going Correction** -0.15s/f (Firm)
WFA 3 from 4yo+ 9lb **9** Ran SP% **116.1**
Speed ratings (Par 101): **84,83,82,81,80 72,71,68,68**
toteswingers: 1&2 £4.00, 1&3 £15.30, 2&3 £16.40. CSF £17.91 CT £277.39 TOTE £5.20: £2.40, £1.80, £8.20; EX 22.60.
Owner David Scott and Co (Pattern Makers) Ltd **Bred** D Scott **Trained** Norton, N Yorks

FOCUS
A rock-bottom apprentice handicap run at a very steady pace until the final 4f. The placed horses are rated to their recent marks.
T/Jkpt: £109,291.50 to a £1 stake. Pool: £230,897.56 - 1.50 winning tickets. T/Plt: £201.60 to a £1 stake. Pool: £86,424.72 - 312.80 winning tickets. T/Qpdt: £89.90 to a £1 stake. Pool: £5,073.04 - 41.75 winning tickets. RY

4625 PONTEFRACT (L-H)
Wednesday, August 8

OFFICIAL GOING: Good to firm (8.7)
Wind: Light half behind Weather: Fine and dry

4959 PONTEFRACT GENTLEMEN'S H'CAP (FOR GENTLEMAN AMATEUR RIDERS) 1m 2f 6y
2:30 (2:30) (Class 5) (0-75,72) 3-Y-O+ **£2,183** (£677; £338; £169) **Stalls** Low

Form RPR
-260 **1** **A Little Bit Dusty**[34] 3775 4-10-9 **65**....... MrFMitchell(5) 1 75
(Reg Hollinshead) *mde all: rdn wl over 1f out: edgd rt ent fnl f: sn drvn and kpt on wl* **9/1**
2102 **2** *¾* **The Ducking Stool**[3] 4844 5-10-11 **62**....... MrPCollington 5 70
(Julia Feilden) *trckd ldrs: hdwy on outer over 3f out: cl up 2f out: rdn to chal over 1f out: drvn and ev ch ins fnl f: no ex last 100yds* **13/8**[1]
5323 **3** *3 ½* **Skyfire**[18] 4325 5-11-2 **67**....... MrSWalker 8 68
(Nick Kent) *cl up: rdn to chal 2f out: drvn over 1f out: n.m.r and swtchd lft ent fnl f: sn one pce* **7/4**[2]
5000 **4** *1 ½* **Betteras Bertie**[10] 4627 9-10-7 **63**....... MrAaronJames(5) 3 61
(Tony Coyle) *hld up in rr: hdwy 2f out: rdn over 1f out: kpt on fnl f: nt rch ldrs* **12/1**
6210 **5** *2 ¾* **Hail Promenader (IRE)**[19] 4296 6-11-0 **72**.......(p) MrGrahamCarson(7) 7 65
(Anthony Carson) *hld up in rr: hdwy over 2f out: rdn wl over 1f out: sn no imp* **11/2**[3]
-060 **6** *3* **Rowan Lodge (IRE)**[22] 4179 10-9-11 **53** oh1.......(b) MrNSlatter(5) 6 40
(Ollie Pears) *t.k.h: trckd ldrs: effrt over 2f out: sn rdn and wknd wl over 1f out* **40/1**

00 7 6 **Mystified (IRE)**[16] 3310 9-10-2 **53** oh8...................... MrFWindsorClive 4 28
(Alan Berry) *trckd ldng pair on inner: rdn along 3f out: sn wknd* **66/1**

2m 15.37s (1.67) **Going Correction** -0.30s/f (Firm)
WFA 3 from 4yo+ 9lb 7 Ran SP% **111.5**
Speed ratings (Par 103): **81,80,77,76,74 71,67**
toteswingers: 1&2 £2.80, 1&3 £4.00, 2&3 £1.10. CSF £22.92 CT £36.83 TOTE £9.90: £3.10, £1.80; EX 30.10 Trifecta £78.60 Pool: £689.41 - 6.49 winning units..
Owner John P Evitt **Bred** T O C S Limited **Trained** Upper Longdon, Staffs

FOCUS
A typically moderate race of its type. It was run at an steady early pace and, as a result, the leaders were not for catching in the home straight. A personal-best from the winner with the second slightly below her latest form.

4960 IRISH STALLION FARMS E B F MAIDEN STKS 6f
3:00 (3:00) (Class 4) 2-Y-O £4,398 (£1,309; £654; £327) **Stalls** Low

Form RPR
4 1 **Kamchatka**[12] 4545 2-9-3 0.. RobertWinston 1 80+
(Alan Swinbank) *mde all: rdn clr over 1f out: edgd rt ins fnl f: styd on strly* **5/2**[1]

2 3 **Polish Crown** 2-8-12 0.. JoeFanning 9 67+
(Mark Johnston) *dwlt: n.m.r and green s: in rr: pushed along and hdwy on outer over 2f out: rdn over 1f out: styd on wl fnl f* **9/1**

0 3 nk **New Rich**[25] 4114 2-9-3 0.. PaulMulrennan 10 70
(Michael Dods) *in tch: hdwy on inner 2f out: rdn over 1f out: styd on fnl f: nrst fin* **10/1**

0 4 ¾ **Duke Of Orange (IRE)**[7] 4707 2-9-3 0............................ MartinHarley 7 68
(Mick Channon) *n.m.r s and in rr: pushed along and hdwy over 2f out: rdn to chse ldrs over 1f out: kpt on fnl f* **14/1**

5 5 ½ **Bapak Pesta (IRE)**[12] 4545 2-9-3 0.................................. PhillipMakin 3 66
(Kevin Ryan) *trckd ldrs: hdwy over 2f out: rdn wl over 1f out: kpt on same pce* **3/1**[2]

33 6 ½ **Titus Titan (IRE)**[22] 4178 2-9-0 0.................................. PaulPickard(3) 4 70+
(Brian Ellison) *hmpd s and in rr: hdwy 2f out: swtchd rt and rdn over 1f out: nt clr run and swtchd rt to outer ins fnl f: styd on: nrst fin* **5/1**[3]

7 2 **Silkelly** 2-8-5 0.. DavidBergin(7) 6 54
(David O'Meara) *wnt rt s: cl up: rdn along and ev ch 2f out: wknd appr fnl f* **40/1**

46 8 nse **Fantasy Invader (IRE)**[2] 4877 2-9-3 0.......................... BarryMcHugh 2 59
(John Quinn) *trckd ldrs on inner: rdn along over 2f out: wknd over 1f out* **14/1**

6 9 12 **Amirah (IRE)**[13] 4494 2-8-12 0.................................... GrahamGibbons 5 18
(Alan McCabe) *wnt lft s: cl up: rdn along wl over 2f out: sn wknd* **8/1**

1m 15.87s (-1.03) **Going Correction** -0.30s/f (Firm) 9 Ran SP% **116.2**
Speed ratings (Par 96): **94,90,89,88,87 87,84,84,68**
toteswingers: 1&2 £4.70, 1&3 £6.50, 2&3 £10.10. CSF £26.13 TOTE £3.30: £1.40, £2.60, £3.40; EX 26.10 Trifecta £143.60 Pool: £829.04 - 4.27 winning units..
Owner S P C Woods **Bred** Whitsbury Manor Stud **Trained** Melsonby, N Yorks

FOCUS
They went a sound pace in this modest juvenile maiden and there was a blanket finish behind the taking winner. The form is a bit messy behind but the winner looks useful.

NOTEBOOK
Kamchatka had run well when fourth on the far side over 5f at Thirsk first time out 12 days earlier and had the plum draw upped to 6f here. He was given a no-nonsense ride and came right away from the field when asked to win the race approaching the final furlong. There was still slight signs of greenness near the finish and he obviously relished this stiffer test on the quick surface. He wasn't cheap and rates a very useful prospect. (op 11-4 tchd 3-1)
Polish Crown ◆ proved very easy to back for her debut. She took time to get organised well off the pace, but stayed on pleasingly when taken to the outer after straightening for home and looks sure to come on a bundle. She's also bred to appreciate another furlong or so and should soon be winning. (tchd 8-1)
New Rich, who didn't go unbacked, was ridden a lot more positively than had been the case on his York debut last month and he ran on well once getting a clear passage on the inside late on. He has scope and is evidently going the right way. (op 16-1)
Duke Of Orange(IRE) ◆ showed the benefit of his debut experience at Leicester and was doing all of his best work at the finish. He's entered in the Royal Lodge and, while that is too fanciful, a step up in trip should see him off the mark. (op 16-1)
Bapak Pesta(IRE) was one place behind the winner at Thirsk 12 days earlier when racing on the other side of the track. Well backed, he had his chance but failed to see out the extra furlong and his Group 1 entries are too ambitious (tchd 11-4 and 10-3)
Titus Titan(IRE) set the standard on his previous third at Beverley. He endured a troubled passage from the start and deserves another chance. Nurseries are now an option. (op 4-1 tchd 11-2)

4961 BIG FELLAS NIGHTCLUB H'CAP 1m 4y
3:30 (3:30) (Class 4) (0-80,77) 3-Y-O £4,075 (£1,212; £606; £303) **Stalls** Low

Form RPR
4665 1 **Alkadi (IRE)**[8] 4675 3-8-12 **68**.. JoeFanning 1 77
(Mark Johnston) *mde all: rdn wl over 1f out: drvn ins fnl f: styd on* **13/2**[3]

01 2 1 ¼ **Watt Broderick (IRE)**[64] 2802 3-8-7 **63**............................ FrederikTylicki 4 69+
(Ian Williams) *t.k.h early: hld up: swtchd ins and hdwy 2f out: rdn over 1f out: drvn and styd on to chse wnr ins fnl f: no imp towards fin* **11/4**[1]

-123 3 nk **Miss Ellany (IRE)**[12] 4553 3-9-7 **77**.............................. DanielTudhope 5 82
(David O'Meara) *trckd ldng pair on outer: effrt over 2f out: rdn wl over 1f out: drvn and one pce fnl f* **11/4**[1]

030 4 2 ¼ **Green Mitas (ITY)**[25] 4082 3-8-0 **59**.............................. JulieBurke(3) 2 59
(Frank Sheridan) *cl up: rdn along 2f out: drvn and kpt on same pce fnl f* **16/1**

-112 5 2 ¼ **Sabhan (IRE)**[32] 3882 3-9-6 **76**...................................... RobertWinston 6 71
(Geoffrey Harker) *hld up towards rr: effrt and sme hdwy over 2f out: sn rdn and btn* **3/1**[2]

-210 6 12 **Iffraam (IRE)**[16] 4388 3-9-5 **75**......................................(p) PaulMulrennan 7 42
(Michael Dods) *hld up in rr: effrt over 2f out: sn rdn and nvr a factor* **9/1**

0120 7 8 **Dansili Dutch (IRE)**[12] 4553 3-8-11 **67**.............................. TedDurcan 3 16
(Andrew Crook) *trckd ldrs on inner: pushed along over 3f out: rdn over 2f out: sn wknd* **20/1**

1m 42.83s (-3.07) **Going Correction** -0.30s/f (Firm) 7 Ran SP% **112.3**
Speed ratings (Par 102): **103,101,101,99,96 84,76**
toteswingers: 1&2 £4.10, 1&3 £3.70, 2&3 £2.30. CSF £23.81 TOTE £7.50: £3.50, £1.50; EX 28.10.
Owner Sheikh Hamdan Bin Mohammed Al Maktoum **Bred** Darley **Trained** Middleham Moor, N Yorks

FOCUS
This ordinary 3yo handicap was another example of how this track benefits those ridden positively. The placed horses are rated to form at face value.
Sabhan(IRE) Official explanation: jockey said that the colt had been struck into
Iffraam(IRE) Official explanation: jockey said that the colt was unsuited by the good to firm going
Dansili Dutch(IRE) Official explanation: jockey said that the filly was unsuited by the good to firm going

4962 FAMILY DAY ON SUNDAY 19TH AUGUST H'CAP 1m 4f 8y
4:00 (4:01) (Class 3) (0-95,89) 3-Y-O+
£6,411 (£1,919; £959; £479; £239; £120) **Stalls** Low

Form RPR
-011 1 **Sir Graham Wade (IRE)**[7] 4700 3-9-0 **86** 6ex.................. JoeFanning 7 103+
(Mark Johnston) *trckd ldrs: smooth hdwy over 2f out: chal over 1f out: rdn to ld ent fnl f: sn clr and styd on strly* **11/10**[1]

0115 2 4 ½ **Edmaaj (IRE)**[26] 4072 4-9-11 **86**.................................. DanielTudhope 8 93
(David O'Meara) *prom: led after 3f: rdn along 2f out: drvn and hdd ent fnl f: kpt on: no ch w wnr* **11/1**

6602 3 1 ¼ **Northside Prince (IRE)**[10] 4621 6-9-5 **85**.................. GarryWhillans(5) 4 90
(Alan Swinbank) *a.p: cl up over 2f out: sn rdn and kpt on same pce* **15/2**[3]

2-06 4 ½ **Spifer (IRE)**[60] 2933 4-10-0 **89**...................................... KierenFallon 3 93
(Luca Cumani) *hld up in rr: hdwy to trck ldrs over 3f out: rdn 2f out: sn one pce* **11/4**[2]

6164 5 1 ¼ **Tartan Gigha (IRE)**[12] 4543 7-9-10 **85**.......................... RobertWinston 1 87
(Geoffrey Harker) *chsd ldrs: rdn along wl over 2f out: sn drvn and wknd* **33/1**

5015 6 5 **Bollin Greta**[18] 4338 7-9-12 **87**...................................... DavidAllan 5 81
(Tim Easterby) *hld up in rr: sme hdwy wl over 2f out: nvr nr ldrs* **16/1**

103- 7 10 **Samarkand (IRE)**[300] 6822 4-9-11 **86**.......................... PaulMulrennan 2 64
(Sir Mark Prescott Bt) *led 3f: cl up: rdn along over 2f out: wknd wl over 1f out* **11/1**

6460 8 ¾ **All The Winds (GER)**[6] 3766 7-9-3 **78**.......................... RussKennemore 6 55
(Shaun Lycett) *in tch: rdn along 5f out: sn wknd* **50/1**

2m 35.81s (-4.99) **Going Correction** -0.30s/f (Firm)
WFA 3 from 4yo+ 11lb 8 Ran SP% **113.5**
Speed ratings (Par 107): **104,101,100,99,99 95,89,88**
toteswingers: 1&2 £2.90, 1&3 £3.00, 2&3 £7.30. CSF £14.86 CT £63.03 TOTE £2.20: £1.10, £2.40, £1.50; EX 12.60 Trifecta £49.80 Pool: £1,065.92 - 15.82 winning units..
Owner Paul Dean **Bred** P D Savill **Trained** Middleham Moor, N Yorks

FOCUS
This decent middle-distance handicap was all about Sir Graham Wade and he didn't disappoint, following up his Goodwood success a week earlier under a penalty. he looks progressive and is backed up but the efforts of the placed horses.

NOTEBOOK
Sir Graham Wade(IRE) ◆'s stable could hardly be in better form at present, indeed it won the preceding 3-y-o handicap on the card, and he looked a 3-y-o going places when adding to his maiden success at the Glorious meeting last week. This was his first outing against older horses, but he was confidently ridden and didn't have to be fully extended to seal the issue when hitting the front 1f out. This track probably wasn't ideal for him as he's an imposing performer and, while the handicapper will now have his say, surely there is more to come. A step up in trip in due course also promises to see him peak and don't rule out him turning out quickly again this weekend at either Ascot or Haydock in search of the four-timer. (op Evens tchd 10-11 and 6-5 in a place)
Edmaaj(IRE), who sweated up beforehand, lined up with previous course form figures reading 221 and he got a positive ride. He travelled just about best through the race and, while no match for the winner late on, this was a decent effort in defeat. He's a decent benchmark. (op 7-1)
Northside Prince(IRE), another to get warm, stayed on well at Carlisle last time and went off the same mark. He was a sitting duck for the winner when that rival asserted, but kept on gamely and his form figures around here now read 31233. (op 8-1)
Spifer(IRE) was down in grade and attracted support. He tried to go with the winner into the home turn, but was soon in trouble and proved laboured. He may not have totally enjoyed this circuit and wasn't given too hard a time when his chance became apparent, but he is in danger of becoming frustrating. (op 3-1)
All The Winds(GER) Official explanation: jockey said that the gelding hung right throughout

4963 CHAPLINS CLUB H'CAP 5f
4:30 (4:30) (Class 5) (0-75,75) 3-Y-O+ £2,264 (£673; £336; £168) **Stalls** Low

Form RPR
0012 1 **Sunny Side Up (IRE)**[12] 4547 3-8-5 **66**.......................... LauraBarry(7) 6 76
(Richard Fahey) *cl up: led over 2f out: rdn wl over 1f out: kpt on wl fnl f* **2/1**[1]

4040 2 1 ¼ **Rio's Girl**[7] 4717 5-8-5 **56**.. BarryMcHugh 4 62
(Tony Coyle) *led: rdn along and hdd over 2f out: drvn over 1f out: kpt on u.p fnl f* **11/2**[3]

4206 3 1 **Wicked Wilma (IRE)**[14] 4451 8-8-11 **65**........................ JulieBurke(3) 10 68
(Alan Berry) *prom: rdn along 2f out: drvn over 1f out: kpt on u.p fnl f* **25/1**

210 4 ½ **Commanche Raider (IRE)**[9] 4638 5-9-8 **73**............(b) PaulMulrennan 9 74
(Michael Dods) *in tch: hdwy on inner to chse ldrs 1/2-way: rdn wl over 1f out: kpt on same pce* **15/2**

5104 5 ½ **Steelcut**[16] 4400 8-9-7 **72**..(p) FrederikTylicki 1 72
(Mark Buckley) *chsd ldrs: rdn along 2f out: drvn over 1f out: kpt on one pce* **9/2**[2]

-005 6 1 ¾ **Media Jury**[10] 4631 5-8-5 **56** oh6.................................(v) PatrickMathers 5 50
(John Wainwright) *chsd ldrs: rdn along over 2f out: drvn wl over 1f out: sn one pce* **40/1**

3000 7 nk **Master Of Disguise**[6] 4743 6-9-8 **73**............................ DanielTudhope 11 66
(Brian Baugh) *a towards rr* **8/1**

00-0 8 nk **Major Muscari (IRE)**[16] 4400 4-8-13 **67**.............................[1] DaleSwift(3) 3 59
(Geoffrey Oldroyd) *s.i.s: a in rr* **20/1**

64 9 ½ **Comptonspirit**[8] 4680 8-9-4 **74**.................................... JamesRogers(5) 8 64
(Brian Baugh) *sltly hmpd s: a in rr* **9/1**

0000 10 1 ¼ **Wildcat Wizard (USA)**[12] 4554 6-9-3 **75**........................ NedCurtis(7) 12 61
(Paul Midgley) *a towards rr* **20/1**

1m 2.1s (-1.20) **Going Correction** -0.30s/f (Firm)
WFA 3 from 4yo+ 3lb 10 Ran SP% **115.6**
Speed ratings (Par 103): **97,95,93,92,91 89,88,88,87,85**
toteswingers: 1&2 £3.70, 1&3 £14.70, 2&3 £16.00. CSF £12.06 CT £214.76 TOTE £3.50: £2.00, £1.80, £4.20; EX 15.50 Trifecta £217.60 Pool: £785.45 - 2.67 winning units..
Owner Jim McGrath, Roger & Dianne Trevitt **Bred** Jim McGrath & Reg Griffin **Trained** Musley Bank, N Yorks

FOCUS
A moderate sprint handicap. It was run at a decent tempo and once again those to the fore dominated. A personal-best from the winner with the second rated to form.
Steelcut Official explanation: jockey said that the gelding lost a front shoe

4964 MATTY BOWN VETERANS H'CAP 1m 4y
5:00 (5:03) (Class 4) (0-80,80) 6-Y-O+ £4,075 (£1,212; £606; £303) **Stalls** Low

Form RPR
1115 1 **Woolston Ferry (IRE)**[20] 4233 6-8-12 **71**.......................... MartinHarley 3 80
(Henry Candy) *trckd ldrs on inner: swtchd rt and hdwy 2f out: rdn to chal over 1f out: led jst ins fnl f: styd on* **6/1**[3]

3306 **2** 1 ½ **Striker Torres (IRE)**[16] 4398 6-8-8 **67**..............................(v) DavidAllan 6 73
(Ian McInnes) *in tch: hdwy over 2f out: rdn to chse ldrs and edgd lft over 1f out: styd on wl fnl f* **16/1**

40 **3** 1 ¼ **Just Bond (IRE)**[12] 4557 10-9-2 **78**.................................. DaleSwift(3) 10 81
(Geoffrey Oldroyd) *hld up and bhd: hdwy on wd outside wl over 1f out: sn rdn and styd on strly fnl f* **20/1**

3 **4** 1 ¼ **Talent Scout (IRE)**[7] 4715 6-8-0 **62**................................. JulieBurke(3) 5 62
(Tim Walford) *chsd ldr: hdwy 3f out: rdn 2f out and ev ch tl drvn and wknd fnl f* **7/1**

2213 **5** ¾ **Horatio Carter**[10] 4624 7-8-6 **72**...................................... DavidBergin(7) 4 70
(David O'Meara) *trckd ldrs: hdwy wl over 2f out: rdn to dispute ld over 1f out: sn drvn and wknd fnl f* **5/1**[2]

5405 **6** ¾ **Desert Romance (IRE)**[8] 4679 6-9-7 **80**..................(v) DanielTudhope 1 76
(David O'Meara) *led: rdn along 2f out: drvn and hdd appr fnl f: grad wknd* **3/1**[1]

352 **7** *shd* **Sir George (IRE)**[6] 4747 7-8-9 **68**.................................. PaulMulrennan 8 64
(Ollie Pears) *hld up: effrt and sme hdwy 2f out: sn rdn and no imp fr over 1f out* **8/1**

0014 **8** *nk* **Pendragon (USA)**[14] 4474 9-9-6 **79**............................... BarryMcHugh 9 74
(Brian Ellison) *in tch: rdn along 2f out: no imp* **6/1**[3]

-000 **9** 7 **One Scoop Or Two**[52] 3185 6-9-2 **75**..................(p) RussKennemore 11 54
(Reg Hollinshead) *a in rr* **40/1**

4010 **10** 19 **Fastnet Storm (IRE)**[8] 4679 6-9-3 **76**......................(b) GrahamGibbons 2 12
(David Barron) *chsd ldr: rdn along over 3f out: wknd over 2f out* **9/1**

1m 42.38s (-3.52) **Going Correction** -0.30s/f (Firm) **10** Ran SP% **116.9**
Speed ratings: **105,103,102,101,100 99,99,99,92,73**
toteswingers: 1&2 £21.90, 1&3 £25.50, 2&3 £55.40. CSF £96.91 CT £1837.64 TOTE £7.50: £2.40, £5.40, £7.20; EX 132.00 TRIFECTA Not won..
Owner Ms L Burns **Bred** Tim Taylor **Trained** Kingston Warren, Oxon

FOCUS
An open-looking handicap. There was a strong early pace on, with jockeys surely mindful of the pace bias, and for the first time on the afternoon the placed horses came from out the back. The runner-up sets the level.
Just Bond(IRE) Official explanation: jockey said, regarding the running and riding, that his instructions were to drop the gelding out, but that the gelding, who is a difficult ride, became significantly detached in rear. He added that the gelding was able to run on once he hit the rising ground, passing tired horses in what was a fast-run race. He further stated that the gelding would not have finished closer for more vigorous riding in the early stages

4965 KEITH HAMMILL MEMORIAL H'CAP 6f
5:30 (5:30) (Class 5) (0-75,75) 3-Y-O £2,264 (£673; £336; £168) Stalls Low

Form RPR

-600 **1** **Taffe**[12] 4558 3-9-7 **75**... FrederikTylicki 3 86
(James Given) *cl up: chal 2f out: led wl over 1f out: sn rdn and styd on wl* **16/1**

1534 **2** 2 ½ **Half A Billion (IRE)**[25] 4081 3-9-4 **75**.............................. LeeTopliss(3) 1 78
(Michael Dods) *led: rdn along over 2f out: hdd wl over 1f out: drvn and kpt on fnl f* **9/4**[2]

0020 **3** 1 ¾ **Ambitious Boy**[51] 3218 3-8-9 **63** ow2.......................... GrahamGibbons 8 60
(Reg Hollinshead) *hld up: hdwy to chse ldng pair over 2f out: rdn wl over 1f out: sn one pce* **16/1**

3130 **4** 3 ½ **Sujet Bellagio**[21] 4218 3-9-7 **75**... JoeFanning 7 61
(Brian Meehan) *chsd ldng pair: rdn along 2f out: sn drvn and wknd ent fnl f* **4/1**[3]

-516 **5** 1 ¾ **Holy Angel (IRE)**[10] 4619 3-8-7 **61** ow1............................... DavidAllan 4 42
(Tim Easterby) *bmpd s: in rr: effrt over 2f out: sn rdn and n.d* **9/1**

0431 **6** 22 **Charity Box**[41] 3547 3-9-3 **71**.. TedDurcan 5
(Chris Wall) *wnt lft s: trckd ldrs: rdn along wl over 2f out: sn wknd* **13/8**[1]

1m 15.23s (-1.67) **Going Correction** -0.30s/f (Firm) **6** Ran SP% **110.6**
Speed ratings (Par 100): **99,95,93,88,86 57**
toteswingers: 1&2 £6.40, 1&3 £9.90, 2&3 £4.80. CSF £50.63 CT £571.99 TOTE £25.80: £6.20, £2.10; EX 46.70 Trifecta £405.30 Pool: £898.38 - 1.64 winning units..
Owner Ingram Racing **Bred** Graham Wilson **Trained** Willoughton, Lincs

FOCUS
This ordinary 3-y-o sprint handicap was yet another race on the card where those racing positively held sway and they finished in Indian file. The winner is ratred a slight improver on his juvenile form with the second to his recent best.
Charity Box Official explanation: jockey said that the filly was never travelling
T/Plt: £128.50 to a £1 stake. Pool: £49,332.78 - 280.25 winning tickets. T/Qpdt: £29.10 to a £1 stake. Pool: £3,635.75 - 92.20 winning tickets. JR

4658 YARMOUTH (L-H)
Wednesday, August 8

OFFICIAL GOING: Good to soft changing to good after race 2 (5.45)
Wind: Light across Weather: Fine and sunny

4966 GEORGE DARLING MEMORIAL APPRENTICE H'CAP 7f 3y
5:15 (5:16) (Class 5) (0-70,68) 4-Y-O+ £2,264 (£673; £336; £168) Stalls Centre

Form RPR

100- **1** **Dannios**[310] 6587 6-9-9 **67**...(t) NoelGarbutt 7 76
(Ed Walker) *hld up: pushed along over 2f out: hdwy over 1f out: rdn and edgd lft ins fnl f: styd on to ld nr fin* **4/1**[3]

5350 **2** ½ **Batgirl**[13] 4517 5-9-5 **66**... HannahNunn(3) 10 74
(John Berry) *hld up: hdwy 1/2-way: led on bit over 1f out: sn rdn: edgd lft ins fnl f: hdd nr fin* **7/2**[2]

0000 **3** 2 ½ **Mishrif (USA)**[41] 3549 6-9-10 **68**...........................(b) MichaelJMMurphy 9 69
(J R Jenkins) *trckd ldrs: rdn and ev ch over 1f out: styd on same pce ins fnl f* **10/3**[1]

0400 **4** 2 ½ **Spin Again (IRE)**[9] 4660 7-8-12 **63**............................ BradleyBosley(7) 3 57
(John Ryan) *plld hrd and prom: shkn up over 1f out: no ex fnl f* **7/2**[2]

-060 **5** 4 **Primo Lady**[14] 4469 4-9-6 **64**...(v) RufusVergette 5 47
(Gay Kelleway) *prom: rdn over 2f out: wknd over 1f out* **8/1**

0500 **6** 1 ¾ **Rasteau (IRE)**[22] 4196 4-8-0 **49** oh4............................ DanielCremin(5) 1 28
(Tom Keddy) *chsd ldrs: pushed along over 2f out: rdn and wknd wl over 1f out* **50/1**

0564 **7** ½ **See The Storm**[15] 4439 4-8-1 **52** oh3 ow3...........(v) MatthewMcGhee(7) 2 29
(Lisa Williamson) *plld hrd: sn led: pushed along and hdd over 1f out: sn wknd* **10/1**

1m 27.33s (0.73) **Going Correction** -0.175s/f (Firm) **7** Ran SP% **109.7**
Speed ratings (Par 103): **88,87,84,81,77 75,74**
toteswingers: 1&2 £2.10, 1&3 £3.70, 2&3 £2.50. CSF £16.79 CT £46.05 TOTE £7.40: £2.80, £1.80; EX 8.20.
Owner Mrs T Walker **Bred** Roseland Thoroughbreds Ltd **Trained** Newmarket, Suffolk

FOCUS
A feature of the opening apprentice handicap was the pedestrian gallop set by See The Storm. The winner is a course specialist while the runner-up is rated to recent marks and sets the level.

4967 ASCO/PERENCO UK MAIDEN AUCTION STKS 7f 3y
5:45 (5:45) (Class 6) 2-Y-O £1,617 (£481; £240; £120) Stalls Centre

Form RPR

5 **1** **Indigo Lady**[13] 4494 2-8-7 0... RobertHavlin 5 74+
(Peter Chapple-Hyam) *mde all: shkn up over 1f out: rdn out* **1/1**[1]

4 **2** 1 ½ **Poor Duke (IRE)**[29] 3948 2-8-12 0..................................... LukeMorris 11 74
(Jamie Osborne) *chsd wnr: j. path over 5f out: rdn over 1f out: hung lft ins fnl f: styd on* **9/2**[2]

3 3 **Red Delilah (IRE)** 2-8-6 0... MartinLane 8 60+
(David Simcock) *hld up: hdwy over 2f out: rdn over 1f out: styd on same pce fnl f* **8/1**

4 **4** 2 ¼ **Just A Pound (IRE)**[37] 3708 2-8-9 0................................ KellyHarrison 6 57
(Jo Hughes) *prom: nt clr run and hung lft over 2f out: sn rdn: no ex whn hung lft fnl f* **11/1**

0 **5** 2 ¼ **Silk Fairy (IRE)**[19] 4297 2-8-6 0... ChrisCatlin 3 48
(Noel Quinlan) *plld hrd and prom: hmpd over 5f out: rdn over 1f out: wknd fnl f* **11/2**[3]

6 2 ¼ **Luv U Whatever** 2-8-9 0.. J-PGuillambert 2 47
(Jo Hughes) *chsd ldrs: pushed along 1/2-way: rdn and wknd over 1f out: eased* **16/1**

7 ¾ **Helamis** 2-8-4 0.. WilliamCarson 4 38
(Stuart Williams) *dwlt: hld up: swtchd lft over 2f out: wknd over 1f out* **18/1**

1m 27.88s (1.28) **Going Correction** -0.175s/f (Firm) **7** Ran SP% **114.2**
Speed ratings (Par 92): **85,83,79,77,74 72,71**
toteswingers: 1&2 £1.80, 1&3 £1.60, 2&3 £4.80. CSF £5.75 TOTE £1.60: £1.10, £2.60; EX 7.30.
Owner C S C Hancock **Bred** West Lodge Stud **Trained** Newmarket, Suffolk

FOCUS
A maiden auction lacking strength in depth. The runner-up looks the guide to the level.

NOTEBOOK
Indigo Lady made a promising debut when fifth at Doncaster 13 days previously and built on that here to record a straightforward victory. A mark in the mid-70s should prove workable. (op 5-4)
Poor Duke(IRE) was well beaten by a subsequent Listed-placed filly on his debut at Wolverhampton last month, but he did show a degree a promise that day. He still appeared green (jumped path), but picked up in style to chase the winner home. He's one for nurseries after another run. (op 4-1)
Red Delilah(IRE) came home first of the newcomers but to say this was any more than a fair effort would be overplaying it. (op 9-1)
Silk Fairy(IRE) failed to build on her debut and is modest. (op 8-1 tchd 17-2)

4968 MOULTON NURSERIES FILLIES' H'CAP 7f 3y
6:20 (6:20) (Class 4) (0-85,80) 3-Y-O+ £4,075 (£1,212; £606) Stalls Centre

Form RPR

2222 **1** **Rivas Rhapsody (IRE)**[19] 4300 4-9-3 **78**........... MichaelJMMurphy(7) 4 88
(Ian Wood) *hld up in tch: rdn to ld wl ins fnl f: r.o* **9/4**[2]

2142 **2** 1 ¾ **Serene Oasis (IRE)**[6] 4726 3-9-0 **74**..................................(v) ChrisCatlin 2 77
(Mick Channon) *set stdy pce tl qcknd 2f out: rdn and hdd wl ins fnl f: edgd lft: styd on same pce* **4/1**[3]

1- **3** *nk* **Albaspina (IRE)**[336] 5819 3-9-6 **80**..................................... LukeMorris 1 82
(Sir Mark Prescott Bt) *trckd ldr: rdn and ev ch over 1f out: styd on same pce ins fnl f* **4/5**[1]

1m 28.75s (2.15) **Going Correction** -0.175s/f (Firm)
WFA 3 from 4yo 6lb **3** Ran SP% **106.3**
Speed ratings (Par 102): **80,78,77**
CSF £8.68 TOTE £3.10; EX 7.20.
Owner D Hefin Jones **Bred** D Hefin Jones **Trained** Upper Lambourn, Berks

FOCUS
After the second race the ground was changed to good all round. Just the three runners but an interesting contest. The runner-up is a rated just off her mark with the third to her debut form.

4969 EASTANGLIANAMBULANCE.ORG.UK H'CAP 6f 3y
6:50 (6:51) (Class 5) (0-70,69) 3-Y-O+ £2,264 (£673; £336; £168) Stalls Centre

Form RPR

2140 **1** **Big Wave (IRE)**[27] 4003 4-9-11 **68**................................... RobertHavlin 2 79
(Alison Hutchinson) *trckd ldr tl led over 1f out: rdn and edgd lft ins fnl f: jst hld on* **6/1**

-001 **2** *hd* **Elusive Hawk (IRE)**[15] 4438 8-9-9 **66**...................... DaraghO'Donohoe 4 76
(Barney Curley) *sn pushed along in rr: hdwy over 2f out: rdn to chse wnr over 1f out: edgd lft wl ins fnl f: r.o* **9/4**[1]

4055 **3** 4 ½ **Thereabouts (USA)**[12] 4544 3-9-8 **69**............................ MircoDemuro 6 65
(Marco Botti) *sn outpcd: hdwy over 1f out: r.o to go 3rd wl ins fnl f: nt rch ldrs* **8/1**

022 **4** ¾ **Arch Walker (IRE)**[10] 4631 5-9-2 **59**................................(v[1]) LukeMorris 3 52
(John Weymes) *led: clr 4f out: rdn and hdd over 1f out: wknd ins fnl f* **11/4**[2]

-021 **5** 2 ¾ **Amosite**[41] 3546 6-9-1 **65**...(p) MichaelJMMurphy(7) 5 49
(J R Jenkins) *prom: pushed along over 2f out: wknd over 1f out* **4/1**[3]

0203 **6** ¾ **Danzoe (IRE)**[9] 4663 5-9-5 **62**.. WilliamCarson 1 44
(Christine Dunnett) *chsd ldrs: rdn over 2f out: wknd over 1f out* **11/1**

1m 13.33s (-1.07) **Going Correction** -0.175s/f (Firm)
WFA 3 from 4yo+ 4lb **6** Ran SP% **111.2**
Speed ratings (Par 103): **100,99,93,92,89 88**
toteswingers: 1&2 £1.30, 1&3 £5.70, 2&3 £4.60. CSF £19.51 TOTE £9.30: £4.50, £1.50; EX 27.50.
Owner Philip Carney **Bred** P De Vere Hunt **Trained** Exning, Suffolk

FOCUS
A small field featuring modest sorts.

4970 3 SUN H'CAP 5f 43y
7:20 (7:20) (Class 6) (0-60,60) 3-Y-O £1,617 (£481; £240; £120) Stalls Centre

Form RPR

1060 **1** **Sarah Berry**[5] 4777 3-9-4 **57**.. MircoDemuro 6 61
(Chris Dwyer) *hld up: hdwy 1/2-way: rdn over 1f out: r.o to ld wl ins fnl f* **10/3**[3]

0006 **2** ¾ **Roundelay**[53] 3141 3-8-7 **46** oh1...................................... WilliamCarson 5 47
(Anthony Carson) *a.p: rdn and ev ch fr over 1f out: r.o* **11/4**[1]

-000 **3** *hd* **Theresnoneedfordat (IRE)**[26] 4043 3-9-2 **60**.......(b) AshleyMorgan(5) 1 61
(Stuart Williams) *chsd ldrs: swtchd lft over 1f out: sn rdn: r.o* **3/1**[2]

6-00 **4** *shd* **Kara's Vision**[37] 3706 3-8-10 **49**.. LukeMorris 4 49
(Robert Cowell) *chsd ldr tl led 1/2-way: rdn over 1f out: hdd and unable qck wl ins fnl f* **6/1**

0-60 5 6 **Ottavino (IRE)**[23] 4144 3 -8-3[49] oh1 ow3..................(p) LewisWalsh(7) 2 28
(Jane Chapple-Hyam) *led to 1/2-way: rdn over 1f out: wknd ins fnl f* **9/1**
326- 6 7 **Stans Deelyte**[323] 6237 3 -8-13[52]................................ RoystonFfrench 3
(Lisa Williamson) *hld up: pushed along 1/2-way: rdn and wknd over 1f out* **15/2**
1m 4.17s (1.47) **Going Correction** -0.175s/f (Firm) 6Ran SP% **110.8**
Speed ratings (Par 98): **81,79,79,79,69 58**
toteswingers: 1&2 £2.60, 1&3 £3.00, 2&3 £2.60. CSF £12.54 TOTE £4.40 : £2.20 , £1.60 ; EX 12.90.
Owner Strawberry Fields Stud **Bred** F B B White **Trained** Six Mile Bottom, Cambs
FOCUS
A low-grade contest for 3-y-os over the minimum trip and a bunched finish.
Sarah Berry Official explanation: trainer said, regarding the apparent improvement of form,that the filly was much calmer and settled better.

4971 GUIDE DOGS FOR THE BLIND H'CAP 1m 3f 101y
7:50 (7:51) (Class 6) (0-65,65) 3-Y-O £1,617 (£481; £240 ; £120) Stalls Low

Form RPR
000- 1 **Authora (IRE)**[266] 7432 3 -8-9[56]..............................[1] AshleyHamblett(3) 2 65
(Peter Chapple-Hyam) *plld hrd and prom: stdd and lost pl over 9f out: hdwy over 2f out: led over 1f out: edgd rt: styd on wl: eased nr fin* **16/1**
3465 2 2 **Aliante**[19] 4294 3 -9-7[65]..(v[1]) MircoDemuro 5 70
(Mark Johnston) *hld up: hdwy 2f out: rdn over 1f out: hmpd ins fnl f: styd on to go 2nd post: nt rch wnr* **5/1**[3]
-023 3 nk **Grand Liaison**[51] 3228 3 -8-9[53]...................................... RobertHavlin 10 58
(John Berry) *hld up: hdwy over 3f out: nt clr run over 1f out: sn rdn: styd on same pce ins fnl f* **13/8**[1]
0235 4 1 1/2 **Smart Affair**[2] 4870 3 -8-4[48]..(v) WilliamCarson 7 50
(Alan Bailey) *s.s and looked reluctant: hdwy to ld 10f out: rdn and hdd over 1f out: hung rt and no ex ins fnl f* **6/1**
0010 5 3/4 **Al Karlovyyh (IRE)**[2] 4198 3 -8-7[54]................................ RyanPowell(3) 6 55
(Clive Brittain) *led: hdd 10f out: chsd ldr: rdn over 1f out: hmpd and no ex ins fnl f* **9/1**
4060 6 5 **Roughlyn**[21] 4210 3 -8-5[49]..(p) RoystonFfrench 8 42
(Lisa Williamson) *prom: rdn over 3f out: wknd over 1f out* **25/1**
5000 7 nse **Scripturist**[13] 4510 3 -8-2[46] oh1..(v[1]) MartinLane 9 38
(William Jarvis) *prom: rdn over 4f out: wknd 2f out* **50/1**
4133 8 2 3/4 **Astroscarlet**[23] 4153 3 -9-1[59].. ChrisCatlin 4 47
(Mark H Tompkins) *chsd ldrs: rdn over 3f out: wknd 2f out* **7/2**[2]
2m 32.12s (3.42) **Going Correction** -0.175s/f (Firm) 8Ran SP% **113.0**
Speed ratings (Par 98): **80,78,78,77,76 73,73,71**
toteswingers: 1&2 £13.50, 1&3 £6.30, 2&3 £3.90. CSF £91.25 CT £203.03 TOTE £17.10 : £4.00 , £1.80, £1.20 ; EX 106.80 .
Owner Woodcote Stud Ltd **Bred** Woodcote Stud Ltd **Trained** Newmarket, Suffolk
FOCUS
A moderate 3-y-o handicap with the runner-up close to her best and the third to form.

4972 BANHAM POULTRY H'CAP 1m 6f 17y
8:20 (8:20) (Class 5) (0-75,75) 3-Y-O+ £2,264 (£673; £336 ; £168) Stalls High

Form RPR
2434 1 **Suzi's A Class Act**[11] 4585 4 -9-2[66]......................(p) AdamBeschizza(3) 2 86
(James Eustace) *sn pushed along to chse ldrs: led over 3f out: rdn clr fr over 1f out* **8/1**
0054 2 16 **Somemothersdohavem**[5] 4776 3 -8-9[69]............(p) DaraghO'Donohoe 1 67
(John Ryan) *hld up: hdwy over 2f out: rdn to chse wnr over 1f out: sn outpcd* **11/1**
2413 3 4 1/2 **Seven Veils (IRE)**[11] 4585 3 -9-1[75]...................................... LukeMorris 5 66
(Sir Mark Prescott Bt) *chsd ldr: led wl over 3f out: sn rdn and hdd: hung lft over 2f out: wknd over 1f out* **11/10**[1]
4522 4 2 1/2 **Jennifer J**[37] 3697 3 -8-7[67].. ChrisCatlin 6 55
(Mark H Tompkins) *hld up in tch: racd keenly: rdn over 3f out: wknd over 2f out* **11/4**[2]
1030 5 11 **Hyperlink (IRE)**[18] 4323 3 -8-11[71].................................(v[1]) MircoDemuro 4 43
(Mark Johnston) *led: hdd wl over 3f out: wknd over 2f out: t.o* **11/2**[3]
00-2 6 16 **Echo Of Dream**[22] 4188 3 -8-9[69]..............................(p) RoystonFfrench 3 19
(Ismail Mohammed) *hld up: reminders 8f out: rdn and wknd over 3f out: t.o* **28/1**
3m 4.02s (-3.58) **Going Correction** -0.175s/f (Firm)
WFA 3 from 4yo 13lb 6Ran SP% **112.6**
Speed ratings (Par 103): **103,93,91,89,83 74**
toteswingers: 1&2 £9.20, 1&3 £1.70, 2&3 £1.20. CSF £83.12 TOTE £9.80 : £2.20 , £5.00 ; EX 53.40.
Owner Greenstead Hall Racing Ltd **Bred** East Burrow Farm **Trained** Newmarket, Suffolk
■ Stewards' Enquiry : Adam Beschizza four-day ban: use of whip (25-18 Aug)
FOCUS
The pace was fair and it produced a clear-cut winner, with the winner worth more at face value.
T/Plt: £60.80 to a £1 stake. Pool: £39,086.34 - 468.56 winning tickets. T/Qpdt: £28.20 to a £1 stake. Pool: £4,744.30 - 124.25 w. tickets CR

4973a - 4979a (Foreign Racing) - See RI

4936 BRIGHTON (L-H)
Thursday, August 9

OFFICIAL GOING: Good (7.5)
Races utilising bottom bend increased in distance by about 12.5yds.
Wind: Light against Weather: Mist, clearing last race

4980 JOIN 888SPORT, GET £88 IN FREE BETS! H'CAP 5f 59y
2:20 (2:20) (Class 5) (0-75,75) 4-Y-O+ £2,264 (£673; £336 ; £168) Stalls Centre

Form RPR
530- 1 **Peter Island (FR)**[394] 3940 9 -9-0[68]...............................(v) DarryllHolland 5 77
(John Gallagher) *mde all: rdn jst over 1f out: kpt on wl fnl f* **16/1**
4200 2 1 3/4 **Interakt**[9] 4690 5 -9-7[75].. RichardHughes 3 78
(Joseph Tuite) *in tch: hdwy to chse wnr 2f out: styd on same pce u.p fnl f* **11/8**[1]
1111 3 shd **Scommettitrice (IRE)**[16] 4425 4 -8-8[62]......................(p) AndreaAtzeni 2 65
(David Evans) *chsd ldrs: rdn 1/2-way: styd on same pce u.p fr over 1f out* **7/4**[2]
0136 4 6 **Billy Red**[31] 3919 8 -9-6[74]...(b) FergusSweeney 4 56
(J R Jenkins) *s.i.s: a struggling in rr: c centre 1/2-way: wknd over 1f out: wl btn and edgd lft 1f out* **8/1**
3020 5 17 **Osiris Way**[14] 4501 10 -9-7[75].. GeorgeBaker 6
(Patrick Chamings) *chsd ldr tl 1/2-way: c to r centre after: wknd over 1f out: bhd and heavily eased fnl 100yds: collapsed fatally after fin* **5/1**[3]
1m 3.13s (0.83) **Going Correction** +0.075s/f (Good) 5Ran SP% **112.1**
Speed ratings (Par 103): **96,93,93,83,56**
CSF £39.61 TOTE £18.30 : £7.40 , £1.10 ; EX 32.50 .
Owner C R Marks (banbury) **Bred** Earl Elevage De La Source **Trained** Chastleton, Oxon
FOCUS
Not many lined up for this fair sprint handicap but the pace was strong and this was a good effort from Peter Island, who defied a lengthy absence on his return from retirement. The placed horses are rated a bit below recent marks.
Billy Red Official explanation: jockey said gelding was slowy away.

4981 VILLAGE MARQUEE COMPANY (S) H'CAP 6f 209y
2:50 (2:51) (Class 6) (0-60,59) 3-Y-O+ £1,617 (£481; £240 ; £120) Stalls Centre

Form RPR
4005 1 **Community (USA)**[105] 1625 4 -8-11[51]......................... LeonnaMayor(5) 3 59
(Jamie Osborne) *chsd ldr tl led over 2f out: rdn wl over 1f out: hrd pressed towards fin: hld on* **17/2**
654 2 hd **Dana's Present**[14] 4490 3 -8-13[54]................................ RichardHughes 10 59
(George Baker) *hld up in last trio: gd hdwy over 1f out: swtchd lft and styd on strly u.p ins fnl f: pressed wnr towards fin: nt quite get up* **7/2**[1]
000 3 nse **Whinging Willie (IRE)**[4] 4506 3 -9-0[55]......................... JamesDoyle 9 60
(Gary Moore) *in tch in midfield: effrt u.p over 1f out: styd on u.p to chse wnr fnl 100yds: lost 2nd but clsng on wnr cl home* **12/1**
-030 4 1 **The Wonga Coup (IRE)**[4] 4943 5 -8-5[45]............... JemmaMarshall(5) 8 49
(Pat Phelan) *taken down early: t.k.h: hld up in midfield: hdwy u.p to chse wnr 1f out tl fnl 100yds: one pce after* **25/1**
4400 5 3 1/4 **Rainbow Riches (IRE)**[4] 3141 3 -8-1[45]..................(p) RyanPowell(3) 13 38
(Roger Curtis) *chsd ldrs: rdn 2f out: no ex u.p 1f out: wknd ins fnl f* **16/1**
2066 6 2 1/2 **Pearl Opera**[30] 3947 4 -9-1[50].. KierenFallon 11 39
(Denis Coakley) *in tch in midfield: effrt u.p 2f out: no prog fr over 1f out* **9/2**[2]
0600 7 1 1/2 **Lana (IRE)**[23] 4185 3 -8-11[52].. AndreaAtzeni 1 35
(David Evans) *chsd ldrs: wnt 2nd 2f out tl 1f out: wknd fnl f* **33/1**
0000 8 3/4 **Peg Peg**[15] 4457 3 -8-1[45].. RaulDaSilva(3) 12 26
(Nerys Dutfield) *stdd s: hld up in rr: effrt 2f out: no imp over 1f out: btn whn edgd lft ins fnl f* **80/1**
10-5 9 1 3/4 **Olney Lass**[79] 2362 5 -9-7[59].. SimonPearce(3) 6 37
(Lydia Pearce) *a towards rr: no hdwy whn nt clr run and hmpd over 1f out: n.d* **13/2**
40 10 1/2 **Toms River Tess (IRE)**[4] 4508 4 -8-10[45]......................... MircoDemuro 5 21
(Zoe Davison) *in tch in midfield: edgd lft bnd over 4f out: wknd over 1f out* **50/1**
354 11 2 **Basle**[23] 4196 5 -9-9[58]... EddieAhern 4 29
(Gay Kelleway) *dwlt: sn in tch in midfield: squeezed for room and bdly hmpd bnd over 4f out: wknd wl over 1f out* **11/2**[3]
5332 12 8 **Baby Driver**[21] 4241 4 -9-4[53]..(b[1]) FergusSweeney 2
(Tony Newcombe) *racd v freely: sn led: hdd and drvn over 2f out: sn dropped out: wl bhd and heavily eased ins fnl f* **13/2**
1m 23.82s (0.72) **Going Correction** +0.075s/f (Good)
WFA 3 from 4yo+ 6lb 12Ran SP% **116.5**
Speed ratings (Par 101): **98,97,97,96,92 90,88,87,85,84 82,73**
toteswingers 1&2 £2.90, 1&3 £20.60, 2&3 £7.90 CSF £35.24 CT £321.68 TOTE £10.30 : £3.50 , £1.10, £3.50 ; EX 56.00 .There was no bid for the winner.
Owner Steve Jakes **Bred** Brereton C Jones **Trained** Upper Lambourn, Berks
FOCUS
A poor selling handicap, run at a strong pace on drying ground. The form is sound for the grade rated through the runner-up.

4982 FREDDIE FROST AND THE DREAM DEALS MAIDEN AUCTION STKS 7f 214y
3:20 (3:20) (Class 5) 2-Y-O £2,264 (£673; £336 ; £168) Stalls Centre

Form RPR
024 1 **Noble Bull (IRE)**[9] 4327 2 -9-0[75]................................... DarryllHolland 2 73
(Charles Hills) *chsd ldr tl led 2f out: rdn and hdd over 1f out: rallied gamely u.p ins fnl f: styd on wl to ld fnl 50yds* **9/4**[2]
4 2 1/2 **Emell**[24] 4149 2 -9-1[0]... RichardHughes 5 73
(Richard Hannon) *t.k.h early: chsd ldrs: effrt and hung lft 2f out: led over 1f out but continued to hang lft: drvn ins fnl f: hdd and no ex fnl 50yds* **10/11**[1]
000 3 13 **Kalahari Breeze (IRE)**[14] 4487 2 -8-9[61] ow2................. EddieAhern 4 37
(William Muir) *chsd ldrs: effrt u.p over 2f out: btn over 1f out: wknd fnl f* **20/1**
50 4 16 **Persian Wave**[23] 4194 2 -9-2[0].. MartinDwyer 1 7
(James Tate) *led: rdn and hdd over 2f out: struggling whn pushed lft 2f out: sn wknd: wl bhd and eased ins fnl f* **7/2**[3]
1m 36.85s (0.85) **Going Correction** +0.075s/f (Good) 4Ran SP% **110.1**
Speed ratings (Par 94): **98,97,84,68**
CSF £4.83 TOTE £4.40 ; EX 4.60 .
Owner John C Grant & Ray Harper **Bred** Ogham Bloodstock **Trained** Lambourn, Berks
■ Stewards' Enquiry : Eddie Ahern three-day ban; weight in 2lb over (25th-27th Aug).
FOCUS
A modest juvenile maiden rated around the winner and the time.
NOTEBOOK
Noble Bull (IRE) raced with the choke out early on and looked booked for second when becoming outpaced with a quarter of the mile to run. However, he knuckled down tenaciously and was able force his head back in front where it mattered. Relatively well beaten on all three previous starts, it remains to be seen what he actually achieved, but he clearly relished this step up to 1m and ought to be capable of even better once tackling middle-distances. (op 7-4)
Emell had shaped with promise on debut and was clearly expected to improve on that with him backed into a shade of odds-on. Victory looked guaranteed as he swept clear but, lugging onto the far rail, he was running on empty when the winner renewed his effort. Nursed along for the much of the straight, he looks the type who'll come on again for this experience. A switch to an easier track may help. (op 5-4 tchd 11-8)
Kalahari Breeze (IRE) carrying 2lb overweight, was outclassed. (op 12-1)
Persian Wave helped set the early pace but weakened rapidly and was all but pulled up. (op 4-1 tchd 9-2)

4983 FROSTS4CARS.CO.UK BRIGHTON CHALLENGE CUP H'CAP 1m 3f 196y
3:50 (3:50) (Class 4) (0-80,79) 3-Y-O+
£9,337 (£2,796; £1,398 ; £699 ; £349 ; £175) Stalls Centre

Form RPR
45-4 1 **Ethics Girl (IRE)**[35] 3774 6 -9-6[75]..............................(t) DarryllHolland 1 84
(John Berry) *midfield: 9th 4f out: c to stands' side st: in ld fnl 100yds: styd on wl* **14/1**
154 2 1 **Fleeting Image**[20] 4294 3 -8-1[74]............................(p) NatashaEaton(7) 12 81
(Alan Bailey) *led: hdd and one pce fnl 100yds* **18/1**
6055 3 nse **Iron Condor**[29] 3961 5 -9-3[72].. JamesDoyle 10 79
(James Eustace) *hld up towards rr: 10th 4f out: pressing ldrs and one pce fnl 100yds* **16/1**

0624 **4** *1 ¾* **Hawaana (IRE)**[21] 4243 7-8-12 **70** DeclanCannon(3) 11 74
(Gay Kelleway) *in tch in midfield: 7th 4f out: chsng ldrs and styd on same pce fnl 100yds* **16/1**

6564 **5** *½* **Kings Troop**[21] 4251 6-8-12 **67** (v) FergusSweeney 4 70
(Alan King) *chsd ldrs: 4th 4f out: chsng ldrs and styd on same pce fnl 100yds* **25/1**

2053 **6** *nk* **Maastricht (IRE)**[19] 4346 3-8-12 **78** KierenFallon 6 81
(Mark Johnston) *in tch: 5th and pushed along 4f out: c to stands' side st: btn and kpt on same pce fnl 100yds* **7/2**[2]

0004 **7** *3* **Layline (IRE)**[7] 4722 5-8-13 **68** EddieAhern 8 66
(Gay Kelleway) *chsd ldrs: 3rd 4f out: c centre st: 7th and btn whn hung lft fnl 100yds* **8/1**[3]

0245 **8** *7* **Filun**[37] 3722 7-8-7 **69** ow1 WilliamTwiston-Davies(7) 3 56
(Anthony Middleton) *hld up towards rr: 11th 4f out: no ch w ldrs ins fnl f* **33/1**

2000 **9** *2* **Super Duplex**[7] 4722 5-8-5 **65** JemmaMarshall(5) 14 49
(Pat Phelan) *taken down early: stdd s: hld up in rr: 12th 4f out: wl btn fnl 100yds* **20/1**

1033 **10** *17* **Steely**[12] 4606 4-9-1 **70** PatCosgrave 2 26
(Gary Moore) *taken down early: chsd ldr: rdn 4f out: wl bhd fnl 100yds* **11/1**

0220 **11** *17* **Dubai Glory**[47] 3400 4-9-3 **75** HarryBentley(3) 13
(Sheena West) *in tch: 8th and rdn 4f out: t.o fnl 100yds* **8/1**[3]

122 **12** *5* **Varnish**[27] 4057 3-8-12 **78** RichardHughes 9
(Richard Hannon) *in tch: 6th and losing pl 4f out: c towards stands' side st: t.o fnl 100yds* **5/2**[1]

435/ **P** **Higgy's Ragazzo (FR)**[83] 6813 5-9-10 **79** GeorgeBaker 5
(Roger Ingram) *sn detached in last: p.u between 10f out and 4f out* **25/1**

2m 31.93s (-0.77) **Going Correction** +0.075s/f (Good)
WFA 3 from 4yo+ 11lb **13** Ran SP% **120.4**
Speed ratings (Par 105): **105,104,104,103,102 102,100,95,94,83 71,68,**
toteswingers 1&2 £66.60, 1&3 £118.60, 2&3 £63.10 CSF £232.62 CT £4038.03 TOTE £14.10: £3.60, £6.40, £5.00; EX 371.70.
Owner The 1997 Partnership **Bred** Newsells Park Stud **Trained** Newmarket, Suffolk

FOCUS
A strong renewal of this handicap. Visibility was considerably worse than at any other stage during the afternoon and there was a difference of opinion as to where the quickest ground would be in the straight. The winner came near side and she deserves plenty of credit for that given that the second, third, fourth, fifth and sixth had all headed to the far side. The form is sound rated around the winner and third.
Varnish Official explanation: jockey said filly was never tavelling.
Higgy's Ragazzo(FR) Official explanation: jockey said gelding lost its action.

4984 NUMBER ONE DEALER IN SUSSEX, FROSTS CHEVROLET FILLIES' H'CAP 1m 1f 209y
4:20 (4:21) (Class 4) (0-85,83) 3-Y-0+ **£4,075** (£1,212; £606; £303) **Stalls** Centre

Form RPR

0352 **1** **Sound Hearts (USA)**[15] 4458 3-8-9 **76** DominicFox(3) 1 91
(Roger Varian) *chsd clr ldr but clr of field: in clr ld ins fnl f: styd on wl* **9/2**[3]

6606 **2** *6* **Cochabamba (IRE)**[62] 2890 4-10-0 **83** GeorgeBaker 2 86
(Roger Teal) *led: clr 4f out: 2nd and no ch w wnr ins fnl f: kpt on for clr 2nd* **8/1**

6013 **3** *6* **Forgive**[12] 4579 3-8-13 **77** RichardHughes 3 68
(Richard Hannon) *racd in midfield: modest 4th and rdn 4f out: 3rd and wl btn ins fnl f* **11/4**[2]

6-43 **4** *½* **Yojojo (IRE)**[44] 3461 3-8-0 **64** oh1 NickyMackay 5 54
(Gay Kelleway) *hld up wl off the pce in last pair: modest 5th and rdn 4f out: 4th and wl btn ins fnl f* **16/1**

0500 **5** *2 ¾* **Abishena (IRE)**[14] 4505 3-8-6 **70** KierenFallon 4 55
(Mark Johnston) *chsd ldng pair but nvr on terms: 5th and wl btn ins fnl f* **6/1**

-146 **6** *4 ½* **Shestheman**[44] 3476 3-9-3 **81** JamesDoyle 7 57
(David Lanigan) *a in last: nvr on terms* **15/8**[1]

2m 1.87s (-1.73) **Going Correction** +0.075s/f (Good)
WFA 3 from 4yo 9lb **6** Ran SP% **110.9**
Speed ratings (Par 102): **109,104,99,99,96 93**
toteswingers 1&2 £4.60, 1&3 £2.10, 2&3 £4.60 CSF £36.90 TOTE £6.60: £3.20, £5.90; EX 46.80.
Owner Y Masuda **Bred** M A Co , Ltd **Trained** Newmarket, Suffolk

FOCUS
A decent fillies' handicap, run in terrible visibility. The form looks fluid in view of the extended distances.

4985 THISTLE HOTEL BRIGHTON H'CAP 5f 213y
4:50 (4:50) (Class 5) (0-75,75) 3-Y-0 **£2,264** (£673; £336; £168) **Stalls** Centre

Form RPR

3125 **1** **Picture Dealer**[22] 4221 3-9-7 **75** JamesDoyle 3 84+
(Gary Moore) *hld up in tch: pushed and chalng 1f out: led ins fnl f: r.o wl: readily* **1/1**[1]

3150 **2** *1 ½* **Millibar (IRE)**[12] 4598 3-9-6 **74** (p) DarryllHolland 1 78
(Nick Littmoden) *dwlt: rcvrd to ld after 1f: hrd pressed and drvn 1f out: hdd and styd on same pce ins fnl f* **13/2**

3033 **3** *nk* **Ashpan Sam**[6] 4757 3-8-12 **73** WilliamTwiston-Davies(7) 5 76
(John Spearing) *t.k.h: hld up in tch: 3rd and pressing ldrs u.p 1f out: styd on same pce ins fnl f* **5/1**[3]

0533 **4** *4 ½* **Generalyse**[18] 4364 3-9-4 **72** (p) KieranO'Neill 4 61
(Ben De Haan) *led for 1f: chsd ldr after: 5th and btn 1f out: wknd ins fnl f* **9/2**[2]

2066 **5** *½* **Uncle Roger (IRE)**[13] 4534 3-8-10 **64** (b) EddieAhern 2 51
(Eve Johnson Houghton) *chsd ldrs: 4th and unable qck 1f out: wknd ins fnl f* **8/1**

1m 10.99s (0.79) **Going Correction** +0.075s/f (Good) **5** Ran SP% **109.3**
Speed ratings (Par 100): **97,95,94,88,87**
CSF £7.81 TOTE £2.30: £2.20, £2.40; EX 8.10.
Owner R A Green **Bred** L Ellinas & Old Mill Stud **Trained** Lower Beeding, W Sussex

FOCUS
A fair 3-y-o handicap, run at a steady pace and rated around the placed horses.

4986 PIPER HEIDSIECK H'CAP 7f 214y
5:20 (5:20) (Class 6) (0-60,60) 3-Y-0+ **£1,617** (£481; £240; £120) **Stalls** Centre

Form RPR

-520 **1** **Daffydowndilly**[13] 4533 4-9-12 **60** (t) DarryllHolland 2 71
(Hughie Morrison) *taken down early: chsd ldrs: rdn and ev ch over 1f out: led ins fnl f: styd on wl* **4/1**[1]

0210 **2** *1 ½* **Rockme Cockney**[27] 4043 3-9-2 **60** (p) RaulDaSilva(3) 11 67
(Jeremy Gask) *chsd ldr: drvn and ev ch over 1f out: no ex and styd on same pce ins fnl f* **6/1**

-000 **3** *1 ¼* **No Larking (IRE)**[12] 4584 4-9-11 **59** FergusSweeney 10 64
(Henry Candy) *led early: chsd ldrs 5f out: rdn to ld 2f out: hdd ins fnl f: wknd towards fin* **9/2**[2]

5530 **4** *¾* **Gazboolou**[23] 4193 8-8-9 **48** AmyScott(5) 4 51
(Henry Candy) *racd off the pce in midfield: chsng ldrs u.p over 1f out: plugged on same pce ins fnl f* **12/1**

0465 **5** *2 ¾* **Netley Marsh**[12] 4603 3-8-11 **59** (b) WilliamTwiston-Davies(7) 3 55
(Richard Hannon) *pushed along leaving stalls: racd off the pce towards rr: sme hdwy u.p over 1f out: kpt on: nvr trbld ldrs* **7/1**

0-43 **6** *hd* **Trust Me Boy**[21] 4241 4-8-9 **46** oh1 SimonPearce(3) 7 42
(John E Long) *racd off the pce towards rr: stl plenty to do u.p over 1f out: kpt on ins fnl f: nvr trbld ldrs* **25/1**

3015 **7** *1* **Percythepinto (IRE)**[58] 3014 3-9-3 **58** (t) PatCosgrave 6 51
(George Baker) *hld up off the pce towards rr: hdwy 4f out: drvn and no imp over 1f out: wknd ins fnl f* **9/1**

0001 **8** *2 ½* **Cha Ching (IRE)**[14] 4490 3-9-5 **60** MircoDemuro 8 47
(J W Hills) *sn wl detached in last: styd on u.p fnl f: nvr trbld ldrs* **11/2**[3]

0-00 **9** *6* **Yanbu (USA)**[16] 4435 7-9-1 **52** DeclanCannon(3) 5 26
(Michael Murphy) *racd off the pce in midfield: wknd u.p 2f out: bhd fnl f* **40/1**

5243 **10** *3 ¾* **Putin (IRE)**[17] 4406 4-8-10 **47** (bt) RyanPowell(3) 9 13
(Phil McEntee) *broke fast but awkwardly: chsd ldrs tl led 5f out: hdd 2f out: edgd lft u.p and wknd over 1f out* **11/2**[3]

1m 36.39s (0.39) **Going Correction** +0.075s/f (Good)
WFA 3 from 4yo+ 7lb **10** Ran SP% **119.7**
Speed ratings (Par 101): **101,99,98,97,94 94,93,91,85,81**
toteswingers 1&2 £3.40, 1&3 £4.50, 2&3 £8.70 CSF £29.00 CT £116.46 TOTE £5.70: £1.90, £2.20, £2.10; EX 21.30.
Owner Lady Blyth **Bred** D Curran **Trained** East Ilsley, Berks

FOCUS
A modest handicap, run at a strong pace. The winner is rated to his old turf best with the third to this year's form and it appears sound enough.
Trust Me Boy Official explanation: jockey said gelding lost its action.

4987 GAY KELLEWAY FUNOWNERSHIP WITH SMILESWITHHISEYES.CO.UK LADY AMATEUR RIDERS' H'CAP 1m 1f 209y
5:55 (5:55) (Class 5) (0-70,70) 3-Y-0+ **£2,183** (£677; £338; £169) **Stalls** Centre

Form RPR

2102 **1** **Tidal Run**[4] 4843 4-10-5 **70** MissSMDoolan(5) 1 79+
(Mick Channon) *chsd ldr tl 7f out: styd chsng ldrs: rdn to go 2nd again 2f out: led over 1f out: clr and styd on wl fnl f: rdn out* **7/4**[1]

3604 **2** *3 ½* **Iguacu**[14] 4504 8-9-5 **51** oh2 (p) MissSBrotherton 3 53
(Richard Price) *chsd ldng trio: effrt and rdn 2f out: plugged on u.p to go 2nd ins fnl f: no imp on wnr* **7/2**[2]

0066 **3** *5* **Zennor**[9] 4683 5-10-0 **65** MissKMargarson(5) 4 57
(George Margarson) *chsd ldrs tl wnt 2nd 7f out: rdn and ev ch 3f out: led over 2f out: hung lft 2f out: hdd over 1f out: wknd fnl f* **7/1**

4516 **4** *nk* **Jordaura**[12] 4586 6-10-9 **69** MissZoeLilly 5 60
(Gay Kelleway) *t.k.h: hld up in last trio: clsd on ldrs over 3f out: rdn 2f out: plugged on but no ch w wnr fnl f* **7/1**

2U0 **5** *nk* **Strike Force**[8] 4714 8-10-5 **68** (t) MissALHutchinson(3) 6 59
(Alison Hutchinson) *hld up off the pce in last pair: stl plenty to do and pushed along over 1f out: plugged on fnl f: no ch* **12/1**

4201 **6** *3* **Ostentation**[12] 4586 5-10-1 **66** (b) MissSBirkett(5) 7 51
(Gay Kelleway) *stdd s: hld up off the pce in rr: clsd 3f out: rdn and hdwy over 2f out: no imp ent fnl f: wknd fnl 100yds* **5/1**[3]

0500 **7** *10* **Guilded Warrior**[3] 4865 9-9-7 **58** ow1 (e) MissMBryant(5) 2 23
(Paddy Butler) *led tl over 2f out: wknd and bhd over 1f out: fdd fnl f* **28/1**

2m 4.51s (0.91) **Going Correction** +0.075s/f (Good) **7** Ran SP% **111.4**
Speed ratings (Par 103): **99,96,92,91,91 89,81**
toteswingers 1&2 £3.10, 1&3 £4.70, 2&3 £3.00 CSF £7.49 TOTE £3.30: £1.60, £2.00; EX 8.20.
Owner M Channon **Bred** Barry Walters Farms **Trained** West Ilsley, Berks

FOCUS
A fair lady riders' handicap, run at a decent pace and the winner did not need to improve on this year's form to score.
Jordaura Official explanation: jockey said saddle slipped.
T/Plt: £1,150.00 to a £1 stake. Pool: £50273.15 - 31.91 winning tickets T/Qpdt: £113.80 to a £1 stake. Pool: £4630.63 - 30.10 winning tickets SP

4531 CHEPSTOW (L-H)
Thursday, August 9

OFFICIAL GOING: Good to soft (5.5)
Wind: Virtually nil Weather: Sunny early, getting dark

4988 FREEBETS.CO.UK H'CAP (FOR LADY AMATEUR RIDERS) 1m 14y
5:15 (5:17) (Class 5) (0-70,71) 3-Y-0+ **£2,183** (£677; £338; £169) **Stalls** Centre

Form RPR

0304 **1** **Shomberg**[29] 3974 3-8-10 **52** MrsAlexDunn(3) 2 61
(Dai Burchell) *pressed ldrs and upsides fr over 2f out: str chal fnl f: narrowly on top last strides* **12/1**

6004 **2** *shd* **Tanforan**[76] 2464 10-9-1 **50** MissMMullineaux(3) 1 59
(Brian Baugh) *pressed ldrs tl slt advantage over 3f out but styd hrd pressed and jnd fnl 2f: narrowly hdd last strides* **14/1**

2401 **3** *1 ¾* **Hamilton Hill**[4] 4843 5-10-6 **71** 6ex MissCBoxall(5) 9 76+
(Dai Burchell) *in rr: stl plenty to do whn hdwy over 2f out: styd on to take 3rd fnl f: fin wl but nt rch ldng duo* **5/2**[1]

2305 **4** *7* **Marvo**[29] 3967 8-9-11 **64** MissSLewis(7) 7 53
(Dai Burchell) *wnt lft s: sn in tch: rdn to press ldrs over 2f out: wknd and lost 3rd fnl f* **9/1**

0-63 **5** *¾* **Astragal**[30] 3942 4-8-13 **50** MissAngelaBarnes(5) 5 37
(Shaun Lycett) *chsd ldrs: rdn and outpcd over 2f out: styd on again ins fnl f* **6/1**[3]

2603 **6** *2 ¾* **Temuco (IRE)**[13] 4531 3-10-0 **67** MrsEEvans 8 48
(David Evans) *in rr and t.k.h: sn prom: chal 4f out to 3f out: wknd 2f out* **3/1**[2]

0050 **7** *1 ¼* **Mr Udagawa**[13] 4531 6-9-11 **60** (p) MissSallyRandell(3) 4 38
(Bernard Llewellyn) *slt ld to 1/2-way: wknd over 2f out* **6/1**[3]

-000 **8** *nk* **Barista (IRE)**[162] 736 4-10-2 **67** MissJBuck(5) 12 44
(Brian Forsey) *s.i.s: in rr: hdwy 1/2-way: in tch and rdn 3f out: wknd over 2f out* **16/1**

000/ **9** *hd* **Arch Event**[918] 389 7-9-1 **50** oh5 MissLMasterton(3) 6 27
(Bernard Llewellyn) *bhd most of way* **28/1**
0-50 **10** *3 1/4* **Nicky Nutjob (GER)**[54] 3143 6-9-1 **50** oh5 (v) MissRachelKing(3) 10 19
(John O'Shea) *chsd ldrs 5f* **33/1**
212/ **11** *12* **Boomtown**[10] 360 7-10-4 **69** (t) MissAliceMills(5) 3 11
(Claire Dyson) *in rr: lost tch fr 1/2-way* **25/1**
1m 37.33s (1.13) **Going Correction** +0.10s/f (Good)
WFA 3 from 4yo+ 7lb 11 Ran SP% **122.6**
Speed ratings (Par 103): **98,97,96,89,88 85,84,84,83,80 68**
toteswingers 1&2 £20.50, 1&3 £16.80, 2&3 £13.70 CSF £170.84 CT £572.02 TOTE £12.40: £3.80, £2.20, £1.50; EX 127.50.
Owner T R Pearson **Bred** Dullingham Park & Ian I ochhead **Trained** Briery Hill, Blaenau Gwent
■ Stewards' Enquiry : Mrs E Evans four-day ban; used whip above permitted levels (tbd)

FOCUS
A modest handicap for lady amateurs to open the card. The form is not solid, although rated around the first three.

4989 FREEBETS.CO.UK FREE BETS FILLIES' H'CAP 1m 14y
5:50 (5:51) (Class 5) (0-75,74) 3-Y-O+ **£2,264** (£673; £336; £168) **Stalls** Centre

Form RPR
2104 **1** **Silvas Romana (IRE)**[19] 4329 3-9-4 **74** RyanClark(3) 3 82
(Mark Brisbourne) *trckd ldr: led ins fnl 3f: drvn and hrd pressed ins fnl f: hld on all out* **5/2**[1]
6326 **2** *nse* **Lady Sylvia**[12] 4602 3-8-8 **66** DarrenEgan(5) 2 74
(Joseph Tuite) *chsd ldrs: wnt 2nd over 2f out hrd drvn and styd on fnl f: chal clsng stages: jst failed* **6/1**[3]
300 **3** *1 1/2* **Ashkalara**[61] 2915 5-8-11 **57** CathyGannon 1 62
(Stuart Howe) *in rr but in tch: hdwy to chse ldrs 3f out: distpued 2nd and rdn over 1f out: one pce ins fnl f* **10/3**[2]
4 *6* **Guess Who (IRE)**[19] 4355 4-8-9 **55** oh1 (t) MichaelHussey 5 47
(Peter McCreery, Ire) *in tch: rdn 3f out: hung lft fr 2f out and sn btn* **8/1**
0451 **5** *9* **Shes Rosie**[13] 4533 4-9-7 **72** MarkCoumbe(5) 7 43
(John O'Shea) *sn led: hdd ins fnl 3f and sn btn* **5/2**[1]
6 *41* **Golden Acorn (IRE)**[34] 3841 3-8-11 **64** NeilCallan 6
(Nigel Hawke) *prom 4f: sn btn: eased whn no ch: t.o* **14/1**
1m 36.25s (0.05) **Going Correction** +0.10s/f (Good)
WFA 3 from 4yo+ 7lb 6 Ran SP% **112.3**
Speed ratings (Par 100): **103,102,101,95,86 45**
toteswingers 1&2 £3.00, 1&3 £2.20, 2&3 £3.40 CSF £17.78 TOTE £2.90: £1.10, £4.70; EX 21.90.
Owner The Bourne Connection **Bred** Limetree Stud **Trained** Great Ness, Shropshire

FOCUS
Six fillies lined up for this handicap and the third sets the level rated to this year's form.

4990 FREEBETS.CO.UK FREE MOBILE BETTING MEDIAN AUCTION MAIDEN FILLIES' STKS 5f 16y
6:20 (6:23) (Class 5) 2-Y-O **£2,264** (£673; £336; £168) **Stalls** Centre

Form RPR
1 **Scatty Cat (IRE)**[15] 4479 2-9-0 0 MichaelHussey 4 78
(Peter McCreery, Ire) *unruly stalls entry and v warm: chsd ldrs: drvn and styd on to take 2nd fnl 120yds: hrd rdn and kpt on to ld last strides* **14/1**
2 **2** *shd* **Smart Daisy K**[43] 3487 2-9-0 0 ShaneKelly 6 78
(Reg Hollinshead) *trckd ldrs: wnt 2nd over 2f out: led wl over 1f out: rdn ins fnl f no ex clsng stages and hdd last strides* **13/8**[1]
3 **3** *4 1/2* **Dawn Catcher**[14] 4487 2-9-0 0 KirstyMilczarek 8 61
(Tony Carroll) *led: rdn over 2f out: hdd wl over 1f out: no ch w wnr fnl f: wknd and dropped to 3rd fnl 120yds* **2/1**[2]
40 **4** *3 3/4* **Silver Arny**[17] 4408 2-9-0 0 RichardMullen 5 48
(Brendan Powell) *in rr: in tch 1/2-way: sn rdn: styd on same pce fnl 2f* **8/1**[3]
5 *1/2* **Baltic Sea (IRE)** 2-8-11 0 MatthewCosham(3) 1 46
(David Evans) *bdly outpcd after 2f and wl bhd: styd on fr over 1f out: gng on clsng stages* **14/1**
4 **6** *nk* **Chelsea Grey (IRE)**[10] 4654 2-8-9 0 DarrenEgan(5) 2 45
(Ronald Harris) *chsd ldrs: rdn over 2f out: no ch after* **8/1**[3]
000 **7** *7* **Jackpot**[28] 4002 2-8-9 45 BrendanPowell(5) 3 20
(Brendan Powell) *chsd ldrs to 1/2-way* **33/1**
0440 **8** *2 1/4* **Shirley's Pride**[36] 3747 2-9-0 56 NeilCallan 7 12
(John Holt) *racd in 3rd to 1/2-way: wknd ins fnl 2f* **25/1**
59.89s (0.59) **Going Correction** +0.10s/f (Good) 8 Ran SP% **113.8**
Speed ratings (Par 91): **99,98,91,85,84 84,73,69**
toteswingers 1&2 £3.30, 1&3 £4.60, 2&3 £1.40 CSF £36.93 TOTE £21.80: £4.80, £1.10, £1.40; EX 50.50.
Owner All For The Crack Syndicate **Bred** Mrs Fiona McStay **Trained** Clane, Co Kildare
■ Stewards' Enquiry : Michael Hussey eight-day ban: excessive use of whip (23th-30th Aug).

FOCUS
Another fillies' contest. This time a median auction maiden for 2-y-os over the minimum trip and the form looks solid at the level.

NOTEBOOK
Scatty Cat(IRE) came through late to collar the favourite. The Irish raider, who was well-beaten in a Naas maiden on her debut, got awash with sweat in the preliminaries and took some time before consenting to go into the stalls. She was far more straightforward in the race and came home very strongly. She's likely to appreciate another 1f and, if going the right way mentally, will be a nice filly. (op 12-1)
Smart Daisy K had shown good speed when runner-up on her debut at Bath over 6f. Never far off the speed, she looked the winner when pushed into the lead 1f out but had nothing left when the winner challenged. She can be found a race. (op 11-10 tchd 7-4)
Dawn Catcher, third over 6f on her debut at Bath, looked set to appreciate this drop back to 5f. She did but still failed to see it out and is a pure speedball. Connections need to find an easier 5f. (op 3-1)

4991 FREEBETS.CO.UK NURSERY 6f 16y
6:50 (6:50) (Class 5) (0-70,69) 2-Y-O **£2,264** (£673; £336; £168) **Stalls** Centre

Form RPR
4020 **1** **Must Be Me**[12] 4574 2-9-1 **63** CathyGannon 5 76+
(Eve Johnson Houghton) *t.k.h: hld up in tch: stdy hdwy over 1f out: led ins fnl f sn pushed along to assert: easily* **4/1**[3]
15 **2** *6* **Risky Rizkova**[19] 4331 2-9-7 **69** MatthewDavies 6 64
(Jonathan Portman) *sn led: drvn along and pressed 2f out: hdd u.p ins fnl f and sn no ch w wnr but kpt on wl for 2nd* **8/1**
6236 **3** *2 1/2* **Mrs Warren**[12] 4574 2-9-3 **65** DavidProbert 1 53
(Charles Hills) *in tch: hdwy to chse ldrs 2f out: no ch w ldng duo fnl f and wl hld fnl f* **11/4**[1]
0451 **4** *nk* **Windsor Rose (IRE)**[19] 4343 2-8-10 **58** ShaneKelly 2 45
(Mark Brisbourne) *chsd ldr: rdn over 2f out: btn over 1f out: sn hung lft and no ch after* **11/1**
0505 **5** *3/4* **Kwanto**[21] 4230 2-7-7 **46** oh1 KatiaScallan(5) 3 30
(Malcolm Saunders) *in rr: drvn along over 3f out: sme prog fr 2f out but nvr any ch* **8/1**
4013 **6** *4 1/2* **Lucky Suit (IRE)**[16] 4421 2-8-7 **60** DarrenEgan(5) 7 31
(Ronald Harris) *chsd ldrs over 3f* **8/1**
605 **7** *1 1/4* **Spivey Cove**[26] 4114 2-9-3 **65** RichardMullen 4 32
(Ed McMahon) *t.k.h: chsd ldrs over 3f* **7/2**[2]
1m 12.86s (0.86) **Going Correction** +0.10s/f (Good) 7 Ran SP% **110.6**
Speed ratings (Par 94): **98,90,86,86,85 79,77**
toteswingers 1&2 £1.60, 1&3 £6.10, 2&3 £30.80 CSF £32.59 TOTE £8.80: £6.10, £3.60; EX 32.00.
Owner Eden Racing Club **Bred** Mrs R F Johnson Houghton **Trained** Blewbury, Oxon

FOCUS
An open nursery but an impressive winner who can go on to better things.

NOTEBOOK
Must Be Me met trouble in running when not beaten far on her nursery debut over 7f at Ascot. She made amends here, travelling strongly until being unleashed 2f out, when she showed a smart turn-of-foot to quicken right away and can hold her own in a higher grade. (op 9-2 tchd 5-1)
Risky Rizkova travelled strongly but was no match for the winner in the final 1f and looks high enough in the weights. (op 7-1 tchd 13-2)
Mrs Warren, with David Probert taking over in the saddle, travelled strongly but isn't finishing her races off. A drop back to 5f will suit, however she's 0-6 now. (op 3-1 tchd 5-2)
Windsor Rose(IRE) won a small-field seller last time out and couldn't build on that stepped into nursery company. (op 7-1)
Spivey Cove, a strapping colt, attracted support stepping into nurseries but was far too free and was beaten early. (op 6-1)

4992 CHEPSTOW ANNUAL MEMBERS MAIDEN STKS 7f 16y
7:25 (7:26) (Class 5) 3-Y-O+ **£2,264** (£673; £336; £168) **Stalls** Centre

Form RPR
253 **1** **Keyaadi**[22] 4212 3-9-3 78 [1] NeilCallan 16 73+
(Roger Varian) *trckd ldrs: led appr fnl 2f: jnd fnl f: edgd lft sn after and narrowly hdd fnl 120yds: drvn to ld again clsng stages* **4/5**[1]
546- **2** *nk* **Peak Storm**[289] 7080 3-8-12 73 DarrenEgan(5) 1 72
(John O'Shea) *in tch: hdwy 3f out: chsd wnr 2f out: chal fnl f: sn pushed lft and narrow ld fnl 120yds: hdd and no ex clsng stages* **3/1**[2]
3 *3* **Another Squeeze** 4-9-1 0 RyanClark(3) 13 61
(Peter Hiatt) *s.i.s: in rr tl gd prog ins fnl 3f: styd on to take 3rd appr fnl f: no imp and edgd rt fnl 120yds* **33/1**
0 **4** *3 1/2* **My Stroppy Poppy**[20] 4293 3-8-12 0 (t) CathyGannon 12 49
(Frank Sheridan) *in rr: rdn 3f out: styd on fr ins fnl 2f: nvr gng pce to rch ldrs* **16/1**
5 *2 1/2* **Brown Volcano (IRE)** 3-8-12 0 MarkCoumbe(5) 15 48
(John O'Shea) *in rr: hdwy and rdn over 2f out: kpt on but nvr any ch* **80/1**
03 **6** *2 1/4* **Aureolin Gulf**[42] 3539 3-8-10 0 JackDuern(7) 8 42
(Reg Hollinshead) *chsd ldrs: rdn over 3f out: wknd ins fnl 2f* **12/1**
7 *3 1/2* **Trevose (IRE)** 3-9-3 0 KirstyMilczarek 14 32
(Roy Brotherton) *in rr: mod prog fnl 2f* **50/1**
8 *nk* **Bov La Raconteuse** 3-8-5 0 PhilipPrince(7) 5 26
(Carroll Gray) *a towards rr* **100/1**
0 **9** *1 3/4* **Vivacious Way**[18] 4366 3-8-12 0 DavidProbert 6 22
(Andrew Balding) *chsd ldrs over 4f* **7/1**[3]
5- **10** *shd* **Cityar (FR)**[134] 222 8-9-4 0 NathanSweeney(5) 7 28
(John O'Shea) *in tch 4f* **50/1**
0- **11** *1/2* **Make Me Smyle**[279] 7257 3-9-3 0 MatthewDavies 9 25
(Stuart Kittow) *chsd ldrs 4f* **20/1**
1m 24.55s (1.35) **Going Correction** +0.10s/f (Good)
WFA 3 from 4yo+ 6lb 11 Ran SP% **120.5**
Speed ratings (Par 103): **96,95,92,88,85 82,78,78,76,76 75**
toteswingers 1&2 £1.60, 1&3 £6.10, 2&3 £30.80 CSF £3.16 TOTE £1.60: £1.10, £1.80, £7.10; EX 3.80.
Owner Sheikh Ahmed Al Maktoum **Bred** Mrs J A Chapman **Trained** Newmarket, Suffolk

FOCUS
A maiden for older horses lacking any strength in depth. The winner is rated to previous form.
Bov La Raconteuse Official explanation: jockey said filly hung left.

4993 HAPPY 50TH BIRTHDAY ANDY SMITH H'CAP 7f 16y
8:00 (8:01) (Class 6) (0-65,59) 3-Y-O+ **£1,617** (£481; £240; £120) **Stalls** Centre

Form RPR
6460 **1** **Memphis Man**[2] 4928 9-9-2 **52** MatthewCosham(3) 7 61
(David Evans) *in rr: hrd drvn and hdwy over 2f out: styd on wl appr fnl f: led fnl 100yds: readily* **12/1**
4065 **2** *1 1/4* **Bashama**[45] 3430 4-9-2 **49** (p) DavidProbert 4 55
(Nikki Evans) *chsd ldrs: slt ld ins fnl 2f: kpt on fnl f tl hdd and outpcd fnl 100yds* **20/1**
304 **3** *1/2* **Greyemkay**[21] 4236 4-8-5 **45** DanielMuscutt(7) 3 49
(Richard Price) *chsd ldr: slt ld over 2f out: hdd sn after: styd chsng ldr tl ins fnl f: one pce fnl 120yds* **10/1**
2300 **4** *hd* **Cadmium Loch**[30] 3950 4-9-4 **58** (p) JackDuern(7) 9 62
(Reg Hollinshead) *in rr: hdwy over 2f out: disp 2nd over 1f out: one pce ins fnl f* **10/1**
160 **5** *nk* **Loyal N Trusted**[14] 4517 4-9-10 **57** (p) KirstyMilczarek 14 60
(Richard Price) *s.i.s: in rr: drvn and hdwy over 1f out: styd on fnl f: no ex clsng stages* **6/1**[1]
-554 **6** *4* **Set To Go**[78] 2385 5-8-12 **50** (b) BrendanPowell(5) 2 42
(Brendan Powell) *sn slt ld: hdd over 3f out: styd front rnk tl wknd fnl f* **6/1**[1]
0066 **7** *3/4* **Juarla (IRE)**[10] 4653 4-9-4 **56** DarrenEgan(5) 15 46
(Ronald Harris) *in rr: rdn and hdwy 2f out: no prog u.p fr over 1f out* **9/1**[3]
0004 **8** *nk* **Prize Point**[5] 4812 6-8-5 **45** (t) RobertTart(7) 5 34
(Tom Gretton) *chsd ldrs: slt ld over 3f out: hdd over 2f out: wknd appr fnl f* **16/1**
0300 **9** *2* **Huzzah (IRE)**[19] 4332 7-9-12 **59** MichaelHussey 1 43
(Paul Howling) *chsd ldrs: rdn and btn 2f out* **7/1**[2]
0005 **10** *2 3/4* **Fleetwoodsands (IRE)**[6] 4758 5-9-10 **57** (t) NeilCallan 10 33
(Milton Bradley) *in rr: hdwy over 2f out and sn rdn: wknd over 1f out* **9/1**[3]
3450 **11** *2 1/2* **The Jailer**[14] 4492 9-8-13 **51** (p) MarkCoumbe(5) 12 21
(John O'Shea) *chsd ldrs over 4f* **16/1**
6600 **12** *3 1/4* **Petrarchan**[30] 3949 4-9-2 **49** (b[1]) CathyGannon 6
(Milton Bradley) *slowly in to stride: in rr: sme hdwy over 2f out: sn btn* **16/1**
6-04 **13** *1* **Crucis Abbey (IRE)**[21] 4240 4-9-2 **49** (b[1]) ShaneKelly 13
(Mark Brisbourne) *a outpcd* **10/1**
1m 24.79s (1.59) **Going Correction** +0.10s/f (Good) 13 Ran SP% **118.4**
Speed ratings (Par 101): **94,92,92,91,91 86,86,85,83,80 77,73,72**
toteswingers 1&2 £109.40, 1&3 £45.20, 2&3 £33.90 CSF £228.98 CT £2482.50 TOTE £16.90: £4.80, £8.50, £5.00; EX 516.00.
Owner Mrs I M Folkes **Bred** R T And Mrs Watson **Trained** Pandy, Monmouths

FOCUS
A wide-open 7f handicap run at a breakneck gallop. The form is straightforward rated around the third and fourth.

4994 FREEBETS.CO.UK H'CAP 1m 4f 23y
8:30 (8:30) (Class 6) (0-60,60) 3-Y-O+ **£1,617** (£481; £240; £120) **Stalls** Low

Form RPR
3455 **1** **Taste The Wine (IRE)**[13] 4536 6-9-11 **60**............................ NeilCallan 6 71
(Bernard Llewellyn) *in tch: hdwy over 3f out: led over 2f out: gng clr whn edgd lft fnl f easily* **11/2**[2]
2-02 **2** *3 ¼* **Captain Oats (IRE)**[62] 2872 9-8-12 **54**........................ GemmaTutty(7) 9 59
(Pam Ford) *slowly in to stride: in rr: hdwy over 2f out: styd on to chse wnr over 1f out but nvr any ch* **9/1**[3]
6/46 **3** *1 ½* **Bazart**[13] 4536 10-9-3 **59**..(tp) AliceHaynes(7) 1 62
(Bernard Llewellyn) *chsd ldrs: rdn over 2f out: styd on same pce for wl hld 3rd fnl f* **14/1**
2623 **4** *3 ¼* **Mayan Flight (IRE)**[66] 2769 4-9-0 **54**...................... BrendanPowell(5) 12 51
(Tony Carroll) *hld up in rr: stdy hdwy fr 3f out: rdn 2f out: hung rt and wknd sn after* **7/2**[1]
4050 **5** *4 ½* **Onertother**[14] 4510 3-8-11 **57**....................................... MatthewDavies 8 47
(Joseph Tuite) *chsd ldr: led over 3f out: hdd over 2f out and sn btn* **11/2**[2]
0002 **6** *3 ½* **Femme Royale**[23] 4181 4-8-5 **47**................................ DanielMuscutt(7) 7 32
(Richard Price) *chsd ldrs: rdn 3f out: sn btn* **11/2**[2]
/50- **7** *shd* **Highland Cadett**[288] 7107 5-8-8 **46** oh1.............. MatthewCosham(3) 10 30
(Pam Ford) *led tl hdd over 3f out: wknd over 2f out* **25/1**
300- **8** *6* **Boogie Dancer**[18] 4703 8-8-11 **46** oh1............................ CathyGannon 3 21
(Stuart Howe) *in rr: rdn and sme hdwy on ins 4f out: wknd 3f out* **16/1**
-030 **9** *7* **Dangerous To Know**[22] 4214 3-8-6 **52**......................... RichardMullen 5 16
(Hughie Morrison) *chsd ldrs: rdn and wknd over 2f out* **7/2**[1]

2m 46.83s (7.83) **Going Correction** +0.70s/f (Yiel)
WFA 3 from 4yo+ 11lb **9** Ran SP% **117.0**
Speed ratings (Par 101): **101,98,97,95,92 90,90,86,81**
toteswingers 1&2 £10.90, 1&3 £8.10, 2&3 £20.10 CSF £54.58 CT £661.19 TOTE £8.80: £2.50, £5.00, £6.10; EX 84.40.
Owner Alan J Williams **Bred** Trevor Reilly **Trained** Fochriw, Caerphilly

FOCUS
A moderate line-up for this closing 1m4f handicap, but fairly sound form rated around the first two.
Onertother Official explanation: jockey said gelding hung violently right.
Dangerous To Know Official explanation: jockey said filly lost her action behind on home turn.
T/Plt: £202.20 to a £1 stake. Pool: £30842.27 - 111.32 winning tickets T/Qpdt: £24.50 to a £1 stake. Pool: £3696.72 - 111.4 winning tickets ST

4324 HAYDOCK (L-H)
Thursday, August 9

OFFICIAL GOING: Good (8.5)
All races on Inner home straight and distances on Round course decreased by 5yds.
Wind: Light, half against Weather: Hot and Sunny

4995 TRC CHARITY RACEDAY MAIDEN STKS 1m
2:10 (2:10) (Class 5) 2-Y-O **£2,264** (£673; £336; £168) **Stalls** Low

Form RPR
1 **Authorship (IRE)** 2-9-3 0... SilvestreDeSousa 5 74+
(Mahmood Al Zarooni) *trckd ldrs: pushed along and lost pl over 4f out: rn green: rallied wl over 2f out: hung lft over 1f out: sn swtchd rt: r.o ins fnl f: got up to ld fnl strides* **9/1**
53 **2** *hd* **Disclaimer**[23] 4194 2-9-3 0.. TomQueally 4 74
(Sir Henry Cecil) *racd keenly: w ldr: led over 3f out: pressed over 2f out: plld out more 1f out: hdd fnl strides* **1/1**[1]
4 **3** *1* **Lightning Launch (IRE)**[15] 4472 2-9-3 0....................... MartinHarley 6 72
(Mick Channon) *a.p: racd on outer: chalng and upsides over 2f out: nt qckn 1f out: kpt on u.p ins fnl f: hld towards fin* **11/4**[2]
4 *2* **Northern Star (IRE)** 2-8-12 0............................... RichardKingscote 1 62
(Tom Dascombe) *hld up bhd ldrs: effrt over 2f out: rn green: one pce ins fnl f* **10/1**
0 **5** *3* **Rhombus (IRE)**[12] 4595 2-9-3 0.. DanielTudhope 3 60
(William Haggas) *led: hdd over 3f out: sn rdn and lost pl: wknd over 1f out* **7/1**[3]
6 *2 ¾* **Perfect Pasture** 2-9-3 0.. JamesSullivan 2 54
(Michael Easterby) *dwlt: in rr: pushed along and outpcd over 2f out: lft bhd over 1f out* **50/1**

1m 43.87s (0.17) **Going Correction** -0.325s/f (Firm) **6** Ran SP% **110.2**
Speed ratings (Par 94): **86,85,84,82,79 77**
toteswingers 1&2 £1.70, 1&3 £1.40, 2&3 £1.50 CSF £18.01 TOTE £5.90: £2.80, £1.90; EX 14.10.
Owner Godolphin **Bred** Mrs Eithne Hamilton **Trained** Newmarket, Suffolk

FOCUS
Quite likely this was a decent maiden, two Group-entered horses with previous experience being run down late by a well-bred newcomer. The third looks the best guide to the level.

NOTEBOOK
Authorship(IRE), a 150,000euros half-brother to the yard's smart performer Dubai Prince, was weak in the betting and displayed obvious signs of greenness, but had enough about him to deny the favourite and, although he lacks any significant entries, is a horse to keep on-side. (op 6-1)
Disclaimer got warm and was again keen but that didn't appear to stop him running his race. He's not up to fulfilling his multiple Group entries, but should go one better in a maiden and also has the option of nurseries.
Lightning Launch(IRE) confirmed the promise of his 7f Sandown debut, travelling strongly without proving able to quicken. He's related to the yard's formerly smart Halicarnassus and should continue to progress. (op 3-1 tchd 7-2)
Northern Star(IRE), a half-sister to Group-placed French 1m-1m1f winner Slow Down, made a pleasing start and should benefit from the experience. She can win a standard maiden. (op 8-1)
Rhombus(IRE) was readily swept aside and looks more of a handicap prospect. (op 12-1)
Perfect Pasture, out of a 5f-6f winner, is clearly thought to have plenty of stamina, to be starting off at this trip, and he showed enough to suggest there'll be races in him. (tchd 66-1)

4996 JOHN GREAVES & DEREK WILSON SUPPORTS TRC FILLIES' H'CAP 1m
2:40 (2:41) (Class 5) (0-75,71) 3-Y-O+ **£2,264** (£673; £336; £168) **Stalls** Low

Form RPR
0122 **1** **Oddysey (IRE)**[9] 4676 3-8-13 **67**.. LeeTopliss(3) 1 81+
(Michael Dods) *chsd ldrs: wnt 2nd 4f out: led over 2f out: rdn over 1f out: styd on wl and in control ins fnl f* **11/4**[2]
1341 **2** *3* **Social Rhythm**[9] 4676 8-9-7 **65** 6ex.............................. PaulMulrennan 4 72
(Alistair Whillans) *hld up: hdwy over 3f out: 2nd 2f out: kpt on u.p and no imp on wnr fr over 1f out* **7/1**
2051 **3** *2* **Indian Giver**[8] 4715 4-9-7 **65** 6ex... TomEaves 7 67
(Hugh McWilliams) *in tch: rdn and outpcd 2f out: kpt on u.p ins fnl f: nvr able to chal* **14/1**
315 **4** *nk* **Voice From Above (IRE)**[8] 4713 3-9-5 **70**.................. DanielTudhope 8 70
(Patrick Holmes) *hld up: rdn 2f out: hdwy to chse ldrs over 1f out: one pce fnl 110yds* **9/1**
031 **5** *nse* **Elegant Flight**[13] 4553 3-8-13 **71**......................(v) MichaelJMMurphy(7) 2 71
(Alan Jarvis) *hld up: effrt on inner 2f out: one pce over 1f out: nvr able to chal* **9/4**[1]
3230 **6** *¾* **Gladsome**[8] 4711 4-9-11 **69**.. TonyHamilton 3 68
(Jason Ward) *chsd ldr to 4f out: rdn and one pce over 1f out: no ex towards fin* **16/1**
3414 **7** *1 ¾* **Grey Seal (IRE)**[29] 3976 3-9-5 **70**.................................... HayleyTurner 6 64+
(James Fanshawe) *in tch: lost pl 3f out: nt clr run over 2f out and under 2f out: sn outpcd: nvr a threat* **9/2**[3]
30-0 **8** *15* **Fairlie Dinkum**[40] 3615 4-9-10 **71**.................................. GaryBartley(3) 5 32
(Andrew Crook) *led: hdd over 2f out: rdn and wknd over 1f out* **66/1**

1m 41.41s (-2.29) **Going Correction** -0.325s/f (Firm)
WFA 3 from 4yo+ 7lb **8** Ran SP% **112.2**
Speed ratings (Par 100): **98,95,93,92,92 91,90,75**
toteswingers 1&2 £3.10, 1&3 £7.80, 2&3 £5.60 CSF £21.39 CT £224.27 TOTE £3.60: £1.10, £2.80, £4.90; EX 26.80.
Owner Pearson, Lowthian & Coburn **Bred** Darling Smile Syndicate **Trained** Denton, Co Durham

FOCUS
Fair form for the grade and rated on the positive side, with the third the best guide.

4997 LORDSHIP STUD SUPPORTS TRC H'CAP 1m
3:10 (3:10) (Class 3) (0-95,92) 3-Y-O **£6,663** (£1,982; £990; £495) **Stalls** Low

Form RPR
240 **1** **Van Der Art**[19] 4321 3-8-13 **91**.............................. MichaelJMMurphy(7) 1 99
(Alan Jarvis) *dwlt: in rr: nt travelling wl over 3f out: hdwy u.p over 1f out: led ins fnl f: a doing enough fnl strides* **6/1**[3]
0253 **2** *hd* **Jack Who's He (IRE)**[12] 4607 3-8-13 **84**................. SilvestreDeSousa 5 91
(David Evans) *midfield: niggled along over 4f out: outpcd over 2f out: swtchd rt and hdwy over 1f out: chalng wl ins fnl f: kpt on u.p: jst hld* **12/1**
5-40 **3** *1 ½* **Compton**[26] 4097 3-9-7 **92**...................................... RichardKingscote 8 96
(Ralph Beckett) *racd keenly: in tch: chalng over 3f out: led over 1f out: hdd ins fnl f: no ex towards fin* **6/1**[3]
-516 **4** *3 ¾* **Andalieb**[26] 4097 3-8-8 **79**... MartinLane 4 74
(David Simcock) *stdd s: hld up bhd: hdwy on inner over 2f out: rdn and edgd rt to chse ldrs over 1f out: one pce fnl 100yds* **10/1**
4311 **5** *3 ½* **Touch Gold (IRE)**[35] 3792 3-9-2 **87**................................ TomQueally 7 74
(Sir Henry Cecil) *sn prom: rdn and chalng fr 2f out tl ins fnl f: wknd fnl 100yds* **15/8**[1]
5121 **6** *¾* **Satanic Beat (IRE)**[31] 3911 3-9-2 **87**........................... PaulMulrennan 6 73
(Jedd O'Keeffe) *led: pressed fr 2f out: hdd over 1f out: wknd fnl 110yds* **9/2**[2]
6400 **7** *¾* **Just Fabulous**[13] 4553 3-8-6 **77**.. AndrewElliott 2 61
(George Moore) *hld up in midfield: pushed along and outpcd over 2f out: wl btn ins fnl f* **12/1**
21-0 **8** *4 ½* **Ellaal**[112] 1468 3-9-0 **85**... TadhgO'Shea 3 59
(Charles Hills) *prom: lost pl over 3f out: wknd 2f out* **11/1**

1m 40.02s (-3.68) **Going Correction** -0.325s/f (Firm) **8** Ran SP% **114.3**
Speed ratings (Par 104): **105,104,103,99,96 95,94,90**
toteswingers 1&2 £8.20, 1&3 £5.30, 2&3 £7.40 CSF £73.33 CT £452.35 TOTE £6.30: £1.90, £3.60, £2.00; EX 71.60.
Owner Market Avenue Racing Club Ltd **Bred** Natton House Thoroughbreds & Mark Woodall **Trained** Twyford, Bucks
■ Stewards' Enquiry : Michael J M Murphy two-day ban; used whip above permitted level (25th-26th Aug).

FOCUS
Plenty of pace on in this 3-y-o handicap and those coming from off the speed benefited. The first two help set the level.

NOTEBOOK
Van Der Art was dropping in grade and appreciated the decent gallop, picking up strongly having looked to be struggling 3f out. She shouldn't go up much and can continue to give a good account. (op 7-1)
Jack Who's He(IRE) is holding his form well and appreciated the step back up in trip, but he remains winless since his early 2-y-o days. (op 14-1 tchd 11-1)
Compton, fourth from this mark in the Britannia on his reappearance, appreciated the return to better ground and wasn't far from that form here. (op 11-2 tchd 5-1)
Andalieb sweated up badly when blowing out at Newmarket the time before, and this was better, although he didn't exactly look in love with the drying ground (Doncaster win was on soft). (op 16-1)
Touch Gold(IRE), up 10lb for this hat-trick bid, pushed too strong a pace on this slight drop in trip and was quickly beaten once headed. (op 7-4 tchd 2-1)
Satanic Beat(IRE), up 5lb, went too hard in front and was eased off late. He can be given another chance. Official explanation: jockey said gelding ran flat. (tchd 4-1 and 5-1)

4998 PROFESSIONAL FOOTBALLERS' ASSOCIATION SUPPORTS TRC H'CAP (DIV I) 6f
3:40 (3:40) (Class 4) (0-85,85) 3-Y-O+ **£4,204** (£1,251; £625; £312) **Stalls** Centre

Form RPR
0650 **1** **Chiswick Bey (IRE)**[32] 3890 4-9-3 **79**.................... AdamBeschizza(3) 8 88
(Peter Salmon) *mde all: rdn over 1f out: fnd ex ins fnl f: kpt on wl towards fin* **4/1**[1]
-006 **2** *¾* **Mount Hollow**[20] 4315 7-9-0 **73**...(p) TomQueally 6 80
(Reg Hollinshead) *hld up in rr: rdn and hdwy over 1f out: styd on to take 2nd towards fin: nvr able to chal wnr* **11/1**
3333 **3** *½* **Jack Luey**[43] 3496 5-9-4 **77**...[1] DanielTudhope 4 82
(Lawrence Mullaney) *chsd ldrs: effrt 2f out: kpt on u.p ins fnl f* **6/1**[3]
0044 **4** *2 ½* **Coolminx (IRE)**[19] 4336 5-9-2 **82**........................... LauraBarry(7) 3 79
(Richard Fahey) *w ldr: rdn and nt qckn over 1f out: no ex ins fnl f* **6/1**[3]
03-0 **5** *1 ¼* **Galatian**[118] 1354 5-9-4 **77**.. JamesMillman 5 70
(Rod Millman) *hld up: rdn over 1f out: kpt on one pce ins fnl f: nvr able to chal* **12/1**
4004 **6** *2 ¼* **Dickie Le Davoir**[12] 4591 8-8-12 **71**.........................(v) RobbieFitzpatrick 9 57
(Richard Guest) *hld up: rdn over 1f out: no imp* **20/1**
3100 **7** *1 ½* **Barkston Ash**[13] 4554 4-8-8 **74**.. JasonHart(7) 2 55
(Eric Alston) *cl up: rdn over 3f out: wknd ins fnl f* **4/1**[1]
3500 **8** *1 ¾* **Another Wise Kid (IRE)**[3] 4880 4-9-9 **82**.................. MickyFenton 10 58
(Paul Midgley) *prom: rdn and lost pl over 1f out: wknd fnl f* **9/2**[2]

0310 **9** 4½ **Barons Spy (IRE)**[20] 4286 11-9-12 **85**........................ SilvestreDeSousa 7 46
(Richard Price) *midfield: rdn over 3f out: outpcd fnl 2f* **14/1**

1m 14.26s (0.46) **Going Correction** +0.125s/f (Good) 9 Ran SP% **114.2**
Speed ratings (Par 105): **101,100,99,96,94 91,89,87,81**
toteswingers 1&2 £14.50, 1&3 £5.80, 2&3 £8.30 CSF £47.68 CT £261.26 TOTE £5.10: £1.80, £5.60, £1.20; EX 75.20.
Owner Two Ladies And A Gentleman **Bred** Mrs Kay Egan **Trained** Kirk Deighton, W Yorks

FOCUS
The early pace was steady in division one of this modest sprint handicap (time 0.46secs slower than division two) and there seemed an advantage in racing prominently. The winner is rated close to the balance of his form, backed up by the second.
Barons Spy(IRE) Official explanation: jockey said gelding ran flat.

4999 PROFESSIONAL FOOTBALLERS' ASSOCIATION SUPPORTS TRC H'CAP (DIV II) 6f

4:10 (4:11) (Class 4) (0-85,84) 3-Y-0+ **£4,204** (£1,251; £625; £312) **Stalls** Centre

Form RPR

0600 **1** **Another Try (IRE)**[13] 4554 7-8-13 **78**.................. MichaelJMMurphy(7) 6 90
(Alan Jarvis) *midfield early: towards rr over 4f out: rdn over 2f out: hdwy over 1f out: r.o to ld wl ins fnl f: in command cl home* **5/1**[2]

1215 **2** 1¼ **Cruise Tothelimit (IRE)**[9] 4690 4-8-11 **74**................ CharlesBishop(5) 3 82
(Ian Williams) *chsd ldrs: burst through gap to chal ins fnl f: sn led briefly: hld cl home* **7/2**[1]

3202 **3** 1¾ **Rio Cobolo (IRE)**[8] 4708 6-8-9 **67**...............................(v) AdrianNicholls 4 69
(David Nicholls) *prom: rdn over 1f out: chalng ent fnl f: kpt on same pce fnl 100yds* **6/1**[3]

1141 **4** nk **Julius Geezer (IRE)**[13] 4554 4-9-12 **84**.................. RichardKingscote 7 85
(Tom Dascombe) *midfield: rdn over 2f out: effrt to chse ldrs and wanted to lugg lft over 1f out: kpt on ins fnl f: nt quite pce to chal* **7/2**[1]

2405 **5** ¾ **Green Park (IRE)**[5] 4829 9-9-2 **79**.................................(b) NeilFarley(5) 8 78
(Declan Carroll) *hld up: rdn and hdwy over 1f out: styd on towards fin: nvr able to mount serious chal* **10/1**

10 **6** 1 **Desert Strike**[9] 4690 6-9-2 **74**...............................(p) MatthewChadwick 9 69
(Charles Hills) *led: rdn 2f out: hdd over 1f out: stl chalng ent fnl f: no ex fnl 100yds* **12/1**

0001 **7** ½ **Sleepy Blue Ocean**[14] 4495 6-8-13 **71**......................(p) RobertWinston 5 65
(John Balding) *chsd ldrs: led over 1f out: hdd ins fnl f: fdd towards fin* **9/1**

5316 **8** 4 **Captain Scooby**[20] 4292 6-9-5 **77**............................ RobbieFitzpatrick 1 58
(Richard Guest) *bhd: outpcd 3f out: hung rt u.p over 1f out: nvr a threat* **40/1**

0035 **9** 1 **Five Star Junior (USA)**[10] 4660 6-9-10 **82**...................(p) TomEaves 10 60
(Linda Stubbs) *hld up: rdn over 2f out: no imp* **12/1**

-044 **10** 1 **Silver Wind**[14] 4508 7-8-7 **72**.......................................(p) NoraLooby(7) 2 47
(Alan McCabe) *a bhd* **33/1**

1m 13.8s **Going Correction** +0.125s/f (Good) 10 Ran SP% **115.3**
Speed ratings (Par 105): **105,103,101,100,99 98,97,92,90,89**
toteswingers 1&2 £5.00, 1&3 £7.10, 2&3 £4.70 CSF £22.56 CT £107.08 TOTE £4.60: £1.60, £1.20, £2.40; EX 26.90.
Owner The Twyford Partnership **Bred** Jarvis Associates **Trained** Twyford, Bucks

FOCUS
This was run in a time 0.46secs faster than the first division. Sound form for the level rated around the third and fourth.

5000 BETFAIR SUPPORTS THOROUGHBRED REHABILITATION CENTRE H'CAP (BETFAIR SPRINT FLAT SERIES QUALIFIER) 6f

4:40 (4:41) (Class 5) (0-70,69) 3-Y-0 **£3,234** (£962; £481; £240) **Stalls** Centre

Form RPR

4P04 **1** **Chester Aristocrat**[9] 4675 3-8-11 **66**............................... JasonHart(7) 5 74
(Eric Alston) *a.p: rdn to ld wl over 1f out: kpt on wl towards fin* **7/1**

3165 **2** nk **Duke Of Aricabeau (IRE)**[14] 4496 3-9-7 **69**.............. RobertWinston 6 76
(Mrs K Burke) *racd keenly: hld up: hdwy over 1f out: chalng ins fnl f: kpt on: hld towards fin* **7/2**[2]

-204 **3** ¾ **Premier Choice**[8] 4717 3-9-0 **62**..................................(p) DanielTudhope 7 67
(Tim Easterby) *hld up: hdwy 2f out: chsd ldrs over 1f out: chalng wl ins fnl f: styd on same pce towards fin* **13/2**

0252 **4** 1½ **Ambitious Icarus**[19] 4348 3-9-0 **62**.........................(e) RobbieFitzpatrick 9 62
(Richard Guest) *hld up: rdn and hdwy 2f out: chalng ins fnl f: no ex towards fin* **14/1**

0411 **5** 2¾ **Orwellian**[8] 4717 3-9-4 **66** 6ex.. TomEaves 4 57
(Bryan Smart) *chsd ldrs: rdn over 1f out: no ex fnl 100yds* **3/1**[1]

0520 **6** 1¾ **Dear Ben**[63] 2862 3-8-2 **50**...................................... MatthewChadwick 3 35
(Brian Baugh) *led: rdn and hdd wl over 1f out: wknd ins fnl f* **33/1**

0044 **7** 8 **Star Kingdom (IRE)**[12] 4592 3-8-6 **54**.............................. BarryMcHugh 2 14
(Brian Ellison) *midfield: rdn over 2f out: no imp: wknd fnl f* **5/1**[3]

5400 **8** ¾ **Alpha Arion (IRE)**[21] 4263 3-8-7 **55**........................... DuranFentiman 10 12
(Tim Easterby) *prom: rdn 3f out: wknd over 2f out* **33/1**

000- **9** ¾ **Electrickery**[327] 6154 3-8-8 **56**... TonyHamilton 8 11
(Mark Buckley) *midfield: rdn and outpcd 2f out: wl btn ins fnl f* **40/1**

06 **10** 20 **Gabrial's Gift (IRE)**[19] 4329 3-9-6 **68**..................... SilvestreDeSousa 1
(Patrick Morris) *dwlt: in rr: rdn over 2f out: no imp: eased whn btn wl over 1f out* **7/1**

1m 15.09s (1.29) **Going Correction** +0.125s/f (Good) 10 Ran SP% **117.2**
Speed ratings (Par 100): **96,95,94,92,88 86,75,74,73,47**
toteswingers 1&2 £5.10, 1&3 £7.90, 2&3 £6.00 CSF £31.49 CT £169.65 TOTE £6.90: £2.90, £1.50, £3.10; EX 31.40.
Owner Buist, Long, Thompson **Bred** J A E Hobby **Trained** Longton, Lancs

FOCUS
A competitive sprint in which several held their chance and the form looks sound enough, rated around the first three.

5001 JOCKEY CLUB SUPPORTS THE THOROUGHBRED REHABILITATION CENTRE H'CAP (BETFAIR 10F SERIES QUALIFIER) 1m 2f 95y

5:10 (5:12) (Class 5) (0-70,71) 3-Y-0+ **£3,234** (£962; £481; £240) **Stalls** High

Form RPR

2414 **1** **The Lock Master (IRE)**[15] 4460 5-9-13 **69**............ SilvestreDeSousa 11 78
(Michael Appleby) *trckd ldrs: wnt 2nd 2f out: rdn to ld ins fnl f: hld on wl cl home* **7/1**

5306 **2** nk **Change The Subject (USA)**[14] 4499 4-9-11 **70**(vt[1]) AdamBeschizza(3) 6 78
(Peter Salmon) *in rr: swtchd rt and pushed along under 3f out: hdwy over 1f out: r.o ins fnl f: clsng on wnr cl home* **20/1**

4521 **3** ½ **Gold Rules**[9] 4683 5-10-1 **71** 6ex.. DavidNolan 9 78
(Michael Easterby) *hld up: hdwy over 1f out: r.o ins fnl f: nt quite to get to wnr* **3/1**[2]

4110 **4** nk **Tinseltown**[9] 4683 6-9-5 **68**...(p) JasonHart(7) 12 74
(Brian Rothwell) *led: rdn over 2f out: hdd ins fnl f: no ex towards fin* **11/1**

13 **5** 1 **Nadema Rose (IRE)**[7] 4725 3-9-4 **69**.................................. MartinHarley 3 74
(Anthony Carson) *hld up: pushed along over 3f out: hdwy to chse ldrs over 2f out: kpt on u.p ins fnl f* **5/2**[1]

405 **6** 9 **Tallevu (IRE)**[14] 4511 3-8-10 **61**............................ RichardKingscote 2 48
(Tom Dascombe) *chsd ldr: rdn to chal over 2f out: wknd over 1f out* **9/2**[3]

5-4 **7** 3 **Dicey Vows (USA)**[134] 1065 4-9-2 **65**................ MichaelJMMurphy(7) 10 47
(Alan Jarvis) *midfield: rdn 2f out: wknd over 1f out* **12/1**

4025 **8** 3½ **The Lodge Road (IRE)**[20] 4314 4-9-11 **67**.................. PaulMulrennan 5 42
(Martin Todhunter) *midfield: pushed along over 2f out: sn bhd* **33/1**

0-00 **9** 5 **Oriental Cavalier**[14] 4499 6-9-9 **65**..................................(v) TomQueally 1 31
(Mark Buckley) *in tch: rdn over 3f out: wknd wl over 1f out* **40/1**

2m 11.39s (-4.11) **Going Correction** -0.325s/f (Firm)
WFA 3 from 4yo+ 9lb 9 Ran SP% **110.4**
Speed ratings (Par 103): **103,102,102,102,101 94,91,88,84**
toteswingers 1&2 £19.30, 1&3 £3.30, 2&3 £12.20 CSF £126.74 CT £481.00 TOTE £7.40: £2.10, £6.50, £1.90; EX 115.00.
Owner K G Kitchen **Bred** Patrick F Kelly **Trained** Danethorpe, Notts

FOCUS
A moderate handicap run at a fairly ordinary gallop. The winner, second and fourth set the level.
Tinseltown Official explanation: jockey said gelding ran too freely.

5002 THOROUGHBRED REHABILITATION CENTRE H'CAP 1m 6f

5:45 (5:45) (Class 4) (0-80,79) 4-Y-0+ **£4,204** (£1,251; £625; £312) **Stalls** Low

Form RPR

0222 **1** **Daring Indian**[15] 4460 4-9-2 **74**.................................. RichardKingscote 2 79
(Tom Dascombe) *hld up: hdwy gng wl over 2f out: r.o to ld wl ins fnl f: rdr dropped whip fnl 50yds: r.o* **5/1**[3]

10 **2** shd **Hawkeshead**[43] 3494 5-9-4 **76**.. MichaelO'Connell 8 81
(Ian Williams) *led: rdn over 2f out: hdd wl over 1f out: rallied gamely and stl chalng ins fnl f: r.o* **16/1**

2321 **3** hd **Cape Rising (IRE)**[19] 4326 5-9-7 **79**.......................... RobertWinston 6 83
(Alan Swinbank) *in tch: wnt 2nd over 2f out: led wl over 1f out: hdd u.p wl ins fnl f: r.o u.p* **3/1**[1]

-354 **4** hd **Blazing Field**[26] 4096 4-9-6 **78**.. JohnFahy 3 82
(Clive Cox) *in tch: rdn 2f out: nt qckn over 1f out: prog wl ins fnl f: r.o towards fin* **8/1**

4440 **5** 1¾ **Jonny Delta**[26] 4115 5-9-0 **72**... GrahamLee 9 74
(Jim Goldie) *awkward s: hld up in rr: effrt to chse ldrs over 1f out: styd on ins fnl f: nvr able to chal* **7/1**

3466 **6** nk **The Bells O Peover**[12] 4613 4-9-4 **76**..................(b) SilvestreDeSousa 5 77+
(Mark Johnston) *chsd ldrs: nt clr run on inner over 2f out: unable to mount serious chal: kpt on same pce fnl f* **7/2**[2]

400/ **7** 13 **Maxwil**[647] 6634 7-8-9 **70** ow1..................................... MichaelMetcalfe(3) 7 53
(Mrs K Burke) *hld up: rdn and sme hdwy over 2f out: no imp: wknd wl over 1f out* **40/1**

-445 **8** 15 **Ashiri (IRE)**[28] 3992 4-9-3 **78**... AdamBeschizza(3) 1 40
(David Simcock) *hld up in rr: rdn over 3f out: no imp 2f out: wl btn fnl f: collapsed after fin* **6/1**

6000 **9** 4 **English Summer**[19] 4326 5-8-10 **68**.. TomQueally 4 24
(Patrick Morris) *chsd ldr: pushed along over 3f out: lost 2nd over 2f out: sn wknd* **16/1**

3m 0.44s (-1.56) **Going Correction** -0.325s/f (Firm) 9 Ran SP% **116.0**
Speed ratings (Par 105): **91,90,90,90,89 89,82,73,71**
toteswingers 1&2 £16.50, 1&3 £2.80, 2&3 £10.10 CSF £80.46 CT £281.18 TOTE £6.90: £2.20, £4.50, £1.20; EX 69.90.
Owner Denarius Consulting Ltd **Bred** Juddmonte Farms Ltd **Trained** Malpas, Cheshire

FOCUS
Few got into this from off the pace and it wasn't a thorough test at the trip. The form looks ordinary.
T/Plt: £299.20 to a £1 stake. Pool: £47695.35 - 116.36 winning tickets T/Qpdt: £67.50 to a £1 stake. Pool: £3730.80 - 40.90 winning tickets DO

4512 SANDOWN (R-H)

Thursday, August 9

OFFICIAL GOING: Sprint course - good (good to firm in places; 8.3); round course - good to firm (good in places; 8.5)
Round course dolled out up to 6yds from 7f to 2f increasing distances by about 8yds. Sprint track dolled in 3yds from far side rail.
Wind: Almost nil Weather: Sunny, very warm

5003 SLUG AND LETTUCE CANARY WHARF EBF MAIDEN FILLIES' STKS 5f 6y

5:40 (5:42) (Class 5) 2-Y-0 **£3,234** (£962; £481; £240) **Stalls** Low

Form RPR

1 **Winning Express (IRE)** 2-9-0 0.. RyanMoore 2 83+
(Ed McMahon) *broke on terms but n.m.r early and taken bk to 6th: plld out wd and gd prog over 1f out: rdn and r.o to ld last 50yds* **2/1**[1]

04 **2** ½ **New Fforest**[14] 4488 2-9-0 0... JimmyFortune 8 80
(Andrew Balding) *led and racd against rail: rdn and r.o fnl f: mown down last 50yds* **9/4**[2]

3 2 **Melbourne Memories** 2-9-0 0.. AdamKirby 7 73
(Clive Cox) *chsd ldrs: shkn up 2f out: effrt to take 3rd ins fnl f: styd on but no imp* **9/1**

4 2¾ **Chasing Dreams** 2-9-0 0... PhillipMakin 6 63+
(Kevin Ryan) *nt that wl away: t.k.h and chsd ldr over 3f out: lost 2nd and fdd jst ins fnl f* **14/1**

5 ¾ **Chorister Choir (IRE)** 2-9-0 0.. DaneO'Neill 4 60
(David Elsworth) *s.s: hld up in last: sme prog 2f out: plld out wd over 1f out: kpt on fnl f* **15/2**

6 nk **Elusive Gold (IRE)** 2-9-0 0.. SebSanders 9 59
(J W Hills) *racd on outer: chsd ldrs: rdn to chal for 2nd 1f out: fdd fnl f* **25/1**

04 **7** 2¾ **Take The Lead**[17] 4408 2-9-0 0... WilliamBuick 3 49
(Richard Hannon) *racd against rail: chsd ldr to over 3f out: styd handy tl wknd over 1f out* **11/2**[3]

05 **8** 3½ **Katy Spirit (IRE)**[16] 4419 2-9-0 0.. JimmyQuinn 5 37
(Michael Blanshard) *racd on outer: a in last trio: wknd over 1f out* **66/1**

9 10 **Royal Betty** 2-9-0 0... SeanLevey 1
(Brett Johnson) *s.i.s: rn green in last trio: wknd 2f out: sn wl bhd: t.o* **40/1**

1m 2.01s (0.41) **Going Correction** -0.125s/f (Firm) 9 Ran SP% **115.7**
Speed ratings (Par 91): **91,90,87,82,81 80,76,70,54**
toteswingers: 1&2 £1.60, 1&3 £5.00, 2&3 £2.80 CSF £6.60 TOTE £3.30: £1.50, £1.50, £2.60; EX 9.80 Trifecta £95.70 Pool: £710.42 - 5.49 winning units..

Owner Milton Express Limited **Bred** Yeomanstown Stud **Trained** Lichfield, Staffs

FOCUS

A dry and warm run up to a meeting on ground that was on the quick side. More than half the field were newcomers but this looked a fair maiden in which the first two pulled a couple of lengths clear. The gallop was reasonable and the impressive winner can do better.

NOTEBOOK

Winning Express(IRE) ◆, who cost 16,000GBP and is a half-sister to 6f-7f winner Reason To Believe out of a winning sprinter in Italy, attracted plenty of support and showed a good turn of foot after running green to get off the mark on this racecourse debut. She should prove effective over 6f and is the sort to win more races. (op 7-2 tchd 15-8)

New Fforest, who showed fair form in a race that has been franked at Bath on her previous start, stepped up again on that level - despite racing with the choke out - and she's the best guide to the worth of this form. She's capable of making amends in similar company, especially at tracks that place more of an emphasis on speed. (op 7-4)

Melbourne Memories, a 2,200GBP first foal of a useful 6f Polytrack winner and from the yard that won the corresponding race last year, shaped with promise on this racecourse debut and can be expected to improve. She'll be at least as good over 6f and is capable of winning races. (tchd 8-1 and 10-1)

Chasing Dreams cost 23,000gns this year and is out of an unraced half-sister to a stack of winners, showed ability after a tardy start and after taking a good hold. She'll be better for this experience and there will be easier opportunities in the north than this one. (op 16-1 tchd 12-1)

Chorister Choir(IRE), the second foal of a maiden half-sister to five winners caught the eye under a considerate ride on this racecourse debut. She's open to plenty of improvement, will be suited by the step up to 6f and is one to keep an eye on. (op 13-2 tchd 8-1)

Elusive Gold(IRE), a 12,000GBP half-sister to this year's smart dual 1m winner Duntle, isn't from a yard normally associated with debut winners in this grade but she showed up well for a long way on this racecourse debut and can be expected to improve for the experience. (tchd 33-1)

Take The Lead Official explanation: jockey said filly hung right.

5004 SLUG AND LETTUCE 02 ARENA H'CAP — 7f 16y

6:10 (6:15) (Class 4) (0-85,86) 3-Y-0+ — **£4,075** (£1,212; £606; £303) Stalls Low

Form	Pos	Dist	Horse	Jockey	RPR
-320	**1**		**Rustic Deacon**[40] 3615 5-9-4 **77** (Willie Musson) *trckd ldng pair: squeezed through on inner to ld over 1f out: sn 2 l clr: drvn out* **8/1**	PhillipMakin 2	89
0006	**2**	*1 ½*	**Golden Tempest (IRE)**[21] 4233 4-9-4 **77** (Eve Johnson Houghton) *hld up in 7th: shkn up over 2f out: prog on outer over 1f out: r.o to take 2nd fnl 100yds: unable to chal* **20/1**	JimmyFortune 6	85
0202	**3**	*nk*	**Santefisio**[8] 4703 6-9-12 **85** (Keith Dalgleish) *dwlt: hld up in 8th: effrt over 2f out: nt clr run wl over 1f out: r.o fnl f to take 3rd nr fin* **4/1**[2]	(b) WilliamBuick 1	92+
5310	**4**	*1*	**Johnno**[15] 4473 3-9-5 **84** (J W Hills) *led at decent pce: rdn and hdd over 1f out: one pce* **15/2**	SebSanders 5	86
4-53	**5**	*1 ¾*	**Bajan Bear**[14] 4517 4-8-11 **70** (Michael Blanshard) *trckd ldrs in 5th: prog on outer to chal over 1f out: nt qckn w wnr: wknd fnl 100yds* **14/1**	DaneO'Neill 7	70
22	**6**	*nse*	**Gaul Wood (IRE)**[12] 4580 3-9-5 **84** (Tom Dascombe) *chsd ldng trio: sltly outpcd and pushed along 3f out: nt qckn whn asked to cl 2f out: one pce after* **9/4**[1]	RyanMoore 9	82+
0521	**7**	*1 ¼*	**Mr David (USA)**[6] 4775 5-9-8 **86** 6ex (Jamie Osborne) *trckd ldrs in 6th: shkn up 2f out: clsng to chal for a pl whn no room on inner last 150yds: eased* **5/1**[3]	(b) LeonnaMayor(5) 4	91+
1200	**8**	*1*	**Focail Maith**[12] 4596 4-8-9 **75** (Tim Pitt) *hld up: detached in last after 2f: styd there tl r.o fr over 1f out* **33/1**	GeorgeanBuckell(7) 10	69
3100	**9**	*1 ½*	**Emman Bee (IRE)**[42] 3542 3-8-12 **77** (John Gallagher) *pressed ldr to wl over 1f out: wknd and eased* **16/1**	RichardHughes 8	64
-060	**10**	*nk*	**Rondeau (GR)**[14] 4503 7-9-7 **80** (Patrick Chamings) *taken steadily to post: dwlt: hld up in 9th: shkn up over 2f out and no prog: n.d after* **25/1**	SeanLevey 3	69
0000	**11**	*2*	**Elna Bright**[20] 4285 7-9-8 **81** (Peter Crate) *stdd fr wd draw and hld up: a in last pair: nvr remotely involved* **25/1**	JimmyQuinn 11	64

1m 29.0s (-0.50) **Going Correction** +0.075s/f (Good)

WFA 3 from 4yo+ 6lb — **11** Ran SP% **118.3**

Speed ratings (Par 105): **105,103,102,101,99 99,98,97,95,95 92**

toteswingers: 1&2 £48.40, 1&3 £7.60, 2&3 £19.80 CSF £159.73 CT £750.16 TOTE £8.20: £3.10, £4.80, £1.70; EX 172.10 TRIFECTA Not won..

Owner Mrs Rita Brown **Bred** P V Jackson **Trained** Newmarket, Suffolk

FOCUS

A useful handicap in which the gallop was soon sound. The form appears reasonably solid.

Rustic Deacon Official explanation: trainer said regarding apparent improvement in form that gelding was suited by good ground.

5005 SLUG AND LETTUCE HAPPY MONDAYS EBF MAIDEN STKS — 1m 14y

6:40 (6:43) (Class 5) 2-Y-0 — **£3,234** (£962; £481; £240) Stalls Low

Form	Pos	Dist	Horse	Jockey	RPR
	1		**Excess Knowledge** 2-9-3 0 (John Gosden) *nvr appeared in paddock: dwlt: w.w disputing 5th: hld together tl pushed along firmly and clsd to ld 1f out: shkn up and styd on wl* **9/2**[3]	WilliamBuick 5	79+
	2	*½*	**Nichols Canyon** 2-9-3 0 (John Gosden) *nvr appeared in paddock: dwlt: rn green in last pair: pushed along and no prog over 2f out: picked up wl jst over 1f out: r.o to take 2nd last 75yds: clsd on wnr at fin* **7/1**	FrankieDettori 7	75+
0	**3**	*1 ¼*	**Evangelist**[27] 4066 2-9-3 0 (Sir Michael Stoute) *trckd ldng pair: pushed along over 2f out: styd on but nvr quite pce to chal* **10/3**[2]	RyanMoore 2	72
0	**4**	*shd*	**Raging Bear (USA)**[9] 4688 2-9-3 0 (Richard Hannon) *pressed ldr: led over 2f out but sn jnd: hdd and outpcd 1f out* **3/1**[1]	RichardHughes 3	72
5	**5**	*2 ¼*	**Constans (IRE)**[40] 3611 2-9-3 0 (Clive Cox) *trckd ldng pair: effrt to dispute ld over 2f out: hanging and flashed tail whn shkn up wl over 1f out: wknd fnl f* **9/2**[3]	AdamKirby 4	67
0	**6**	*nk*	**Star Of Missouri**[27] 4066 2-9-3 0 (Mark H Tompkins) *mde most at stdy pce to over 2f out: nt qckn after: fdd fnl f* **20/1**	KierenFallon 1	66
	7	*13*	**Kubera (IRE)** 2-9-3 0 (J S Moore) *tk fierce hold: hld up in last pair: wknd rapidly over 2f out* **28/1**	SeanLevey 6	36
	8	*33*	**Soviet Rock (IRE)** 2-9-3 0 (Andrew Balding) *green in preliminaries: in tch disputing 5th: cl enough over 2f out: fading whn hung violently lft across crse over 1f out: virtually p.u* **10/1**	JimmyFortune 8	

1m 45.92s (2.62) **Going Correction** +0.075s/f (Good) — **8** Ran SP% **114.2**

Speed ratings (Par 94): **89,88,87,87,84 84,71,38**

toteswingers: 1&2 £4.00, 1&3 £4.40, 2&3 £7.60 CSF £35.61 TOTE £5.70: £1.90, £2.10, £1.60; EX 13.90 Trifecta £70.10 Pool: £486.23 - 5.13 winning units.

Owner K Abdulla **Bred** Juddmonte Farms Ltd **Trained** Newmarket, Suffolk

■ Stewards' Enquiry : William Buick £280.00 fine; failed to enter parade ring.

Frankie Dettori £280.00 fine; failed to enter parade ring.

FOCUS

A race that usually throws up a decent sort and, although an ordinary early gallop meant that the first four finished in a bit of a heap, this year's winner looks the sort to hold his own in stronger company. The form cannot be rated higher but more can be expected from the principals.

NOTEBOOK

Excess Knowledge ◆, a half-brother to very useful Rain Mac out of a 1m4f Listed winner, created a good impression in a race run at just an ordinary gallop on this racecourse debut. This Royal Lodge and Derby entry will be suited by a much stiffer test of stamina in due course and he appeals strongly as the sort to hold his own in better company. (tchd 4-1 and 5-1)

Nichols Canyon ◆, a 48,000gns first foal of an unraced half-sister to Group 3 Winter Derby winner Nideeb and a stable companion of the winner, also created a good impression on this racecourse debut. A better overall gallop would have suited this Derby/Champagne Stakes entry and he's sure to win a similar event at the very least. (op 8-1)

Evangelist, the first foal of a Group 2 Park Hill winner, attracted support and left his debut form well behind on this first run on quicker ground. He'd have been suited but a stiffer test over this trip, he's open to improvement and should pick up a race in this grade. (op 7-2 tchd 3-1)

Raging Bear(USA) showed only modest form on his debut over 6f, but duly improved for the step up to this trip after enjoying the run of the race. He is in very good hands and is sure to win a race or two. (tchd 11-4 and 10-3)

Constans(IRE) showed ability at a modest level on his debut and at least matched that effort in this stronger event. He's open to further progress and there will be easier opportunities in maiden company than this one. (op 4-1)

Star Of Missouri was beaten a long way in soft ground on his debut, but fared better after getting the run of the race. There's better to come but he looks more a nursery type than a ready made winner of a maiden in this part of the country. (op 22-1 tchd 25-1)

Soviet Rock(IRE), an 180,000gns brother to Listed winner Anna's Rock, travelled well for a long way but hung violently across the track in the closing stages on this racecourse debut. At this stage it's probably best to put this down to greenness but he'll be one to watch next time. Official explanation: jockey said colt hung left in straight. (op 9-1 tchd 8-1)

5006 SLUG AND LETTUCE LONDON EYE H'CAP — 1m 2f 7y

7:15 (7:17) (Class 3) (0-90,90) 3-Y-0 — **£6,663** (£1,982; £990; £495) Stalls Low

Form	Pos	Dist	Horse	Jockey	RPR
4-15	**1**		**Initiator**[48] 3327 3-9-1 **84** (Jeremy Noseda) *ponied to s: t.k.h: trckd ldr for 2f then restrained in tch: prog to chse ldr over 1f out: hrd rdn and str chal fnl f: led fnl 75yds* **10/1**	JimmyFortune 7	95
2104	**2**	*½*	**Niceofyoutotellme**[27] 4046 3-8-12 **81** (Ralph Beckett) *hld up early: prog to trck ldrs 4f out: led gng strly over 2f out: hrd pressed fnl f: hdd fnl 75yds* **9/1**	JamesDoyle 10	91
1	**3**	*¾*	**Royal Empire (IRE)**[22] 4212 3-9-7 **90** (Saeed Bin Suroor) *trckd ldrs: rdn 2f out: styd on fr over 1f out to take 3rd nr fin: nvr quite pce to chal* **15/8**[1]	FrankieDettori 4	98+
421	**4**	*½*	**Angel Gabrial (IRE)**[14] 4515 3-9-0 **83** (Ian Williams) *t.k.h: hld up in rr: pushed along and no prog over 2f out: rdn over 1f out: styd on to take 4th last strides* **15/2**[3]	KierenFallon 3	90+
2041	**5**	*hd*	**Deia Sunrise (IRE)**[15] 4459 3-9-7 **90** (John Gosden) *led at fair pce: hdd 3f out: kpt trying and cl up tl no ex fnl 100yds* **4/1**[2]	WilliamBuick 5	97
622	**6**	*1*	**Courage (IRE)**[17] 4410 3-9-0 **83** (Sir Michael Stoute) *trckd ldrs: rdn and cl enough 2f out: nt qckn over 1f out: one pce after* **8/1**	RyanMoore 6	88
01-	**7**	*2 ¾*	**Mazeydd**[320] 6334 3-8-13 **82** (Roger Varian) *hld up towards rr: rdn 2f out: nvr gng pce to threaten* **12/1**	AndreaAtzeni 9	82
2105	**8**	*2 ¼*	**Come On Blue Chip (IRE)**[12] 4600 3-9-2 **85** (Paul D'Arcy) *s.i.s: hld up in rr: shkn up over 2f out: no real prog wl over 1f out: wl hld after* **16/1**	(b) SebSanders 2	80
	9	*5*	**Naael (USA)**[34] 3838 3-8-0 **72** (Luke Dace) *mostly in last pair: shkn up and no prog over 2f out: no ch after* **50/1**	HarryBentley(3) 1	57
0155	**10**	*2 ½*	**Educate**[19] 4342 3-8-12 **81** (Ismail Mohammed) *restless in stalls: trckd ldr after 2f: led 3f out to over 2f out: wkng whn hmpd over 1f out: eased* **16/1**	(v) AhmedAjtebi 8	61

2m 9.65s (-0.85) **Going Correction** +0.075s/f (Good) — **10** Ran SP% **118.2**

Speed ratings (Par 104): **106,105,105,104,104 103,101,99,95,93**

toteswingers: 1&2 £17.30, 1&3 £3.40, 2&3 £5.30 CSF £97.79 CT £244.57 TOTE £14.90: £3.40, £2.10, £1.40; EX 114.90 TRIFECTA Not won..

Owner Cheveley Park Stud **Bred** D D & Mrs J P Clee **Trained** Newmarket, Suffolk

FOCUS

A useful handicap in which a modest gallop only picked up around the 2f pole and this bare form doesn't look entirely reliable. The second is getting back to earlier form on this better ground.

NOTEBOOK

Initiator, who didn't get home over 1m4f in soft ground at Royal Ascot, again took a good hold but fared considerably better back over this trip returned to a sound surface on this first run since being gelded. He really needs to learn to settle but he did show a willing attitude and he's almost certainly capable of better. (op 12-1)

Niceofyoutotellme hadn't been at his best with give in the ground on his last two starts, but he had the run of the race and ran as well as he ever has done back on a sound surface. These conditions could be the key to him and he's lightly raced enough to be open to a bit of improvement. (op 8-1 tchd 10-1)

Royal Empire(IRE), the least exposed member of this field, deserves plenty of credit on this handicap and turf debut. He shaped as though a stiffer overall test of stamina would have suited, he's open to plenty of improvement and remains capable of winning more races. (op 5-2 tchd 7-4 and 11-4 in a place)

Angel Gabrial(IRE) is a steadily progressive individual who was far from disgraced from this 5lb higher mark returned to the scene of his recent victory. A stronger gallop would have been more beneficial and he should continue to give a good account. (op 6-1 tchd 8-1)

Deia Sunrise(IRE), who was allowed an easy lead when scoring at Leicester, again got his own way in front and was far from disgraced from this 6lb higher mark in this better event. He doesn't have much in the way of a turn of foot and he's worth a try over a bit further. (op 5-1)

Courage(IRE), who showed useful form over this trip on good ground on his final start in maiden company, failed to build on that effort on this handicap debut. However he's a well-bred sort who is in good hands and may be capable of better. (op 7-1 tchd 13-2)

Mazeydd, who created a favourable impression when scoring in easy ground at Haydock last autumn, wasn't disgraced on this quicker ground on this first run since. He'll be suited by a stiffer test of stamina in due course and is well worth another chance.

5007 SLUG AND LETTUCE 2-4-1 COCKTAILS H'CAP — 1m 2f 7y

7:50 (7:51) (Class 4) (0-80,80) 3-Y-O+ £4,075 (£1,212; £606; £303) Stalls Low

Form			Horse	RPR
4543	1		**Cactus Valley (IRE)**[13] 4548 3-9-2 78 ... JamesDoyle 1 (Roger Charlton) *hld up abt 8th: shkn up on outer over 2f out: gd prog over 1f out: r.o wl to ld fnl 100yds* 10/3[1]	86+
1344	2	¾	**Scottish Star**[14] 4499 4-9-8 75 ... AndreaAtzeni 4 (James Eustace) *led: hrd pressed fr over 2f out: battled on wl tl hdd and outpcd fnl 100yds* 11/2[3]	81
5216	3	nk	**My Lord**[5] 4805 4-9-6 73 ...[1] RichardHughes 10 (Luke Dace) *dropped out in last: stl there 2f out: rapid prog jst over 1f out: r.o wl to take 3rd fnl 75yds: clsng fin but no real ch to chal* 13/2	78+
2600	4	1 ½	**Glass Mountain (IRE)**[12] 4602 4-9-5 72 ... KierenFallon 7 (Ian Williams) *hld up in midfield: prog fr over 4f out: chsd ldr over 2f out and sn chalng: upsides 150yds out: wknd* 25/1	74
0-02	5	¾	**Jewelled**[19] 4335 6-9-7 74 ... SebSanders 2 (Lady Herries) *hld up in last trio: prog on inner fr 2f out: styd on fnl f: nvr gng pce to chal* 16/1	75
3320	6	¾	**Choral Festival**[15] 4474 6-9-9 76 ... KieranO'Neill 6 (John Bridger) *trckd ldng pair for 4f: styd handy: rdn over 2f out: cl enough over 1f out: one pce* 16/1	75
3045	7	¾	**Laughing Jack**[50] 3278 4-9-4 74 ... RaulDaSilva(3) 3 (Tony Carroll) *trckd ldr to over 4f out: styd cl up: nt qckn over 2f out: hld whn n.m.r and eased fnl 100yds* 12/1	73
0301	8	1	**Keepax**[14] 4498 3-9-3 79 ... GeorgeBaker 5 (Chris Wall) *hld up in midfield: lost pl 2f out: nt clr run wl over 1f out and dropped to rr: hmpd sn after and no ch: kpt on nr fin* 4/1[2]	75+
6-05	9	¾	**Wiggy Smith**[8] 4706 13-9-6 73 ... DaneO'Neill 9 (Henry Candy) *hld up in last trio: rdn on outer over 2f out: no real prog* 20/1	67
0-45	10	1	**Top Billing**[35] 3786 3-9-3 79 ...(b[1]) WilliamBuick 11 (John Gosden) *trckd ldrs: prog to chse ldr over 4f out to over 2f out: sn wknd* 13/2	71
0010	11	1 ¾	**Franco Is My Name**[21] 4249 6-9-13 80 ...(p) AdamKirby 8 (Peter Hedger) *hld up in midfield: effrt over 2f out: rdn to chse ldrs over 1f out: wknd rapidly fnl f* 14/1	69

2m 11.98s (1.48) **Going Correction** +0.075s/f (Good)
WFA 3 from 4yo+ 9lb — 11 Ran SP% 119.9
Speed ratings (Par 105): **97,96,96,94,94 93,93,92,91,90 89**
toteswingers: 1&2 £7.30, 1&3 £17.10, 2&3 £9.40 CSF £22.09 CT £115.80 TOTE £4.60: £1.60, £2.40, £3.30; EX 31.30 Trifecta £297.40 Part won. Pool: £401.93 - 0.94 winning units..

Owner H R H Sultan Ahmad Shah **Bred** Gerrardstown House Stud **Trained** Beckhampton, Wilts

■ Stewards' Enquiry : Richard Hughes one-day ban: careless riding (Aug 26)
James Doyle two-day ban: careless riding (Aug 25-26)

FOCUS
A fair handicap run at just an ordinary gallop. The runner-up sets the standard.

Keepax Official explanation: jockey said gelding was denied a clear run.

5008 SLUG AND LETTUCE BOOK NOW FOR XMAS H'CAP — 1m 14y

8:20 (8:22) (Class 5) (0-75,75) 3-Y-O+ £2,264 (£673; £336; £168) Stalls Low

Form			Horse	RPR
2632	1		**Hip Hip Hooray**[35] 3774 6-9-2 63 ... RichardHughes 1 (Luke Dace) *hld up in last quartet in strly run r: gd prog over 1f out: r.o to ld fnl 100yds: drvn out* 9/2[2]	71
0660	2	½	**Push Me (IRE)**[22] 4223 5-9-9 70 ... JamesDoyle 11 (Jamie Poulton) *hld up in last in strly run r: gd prog on outer over 1f out: chal 100yds out: styd on but hld after* 7/1	77
6-14	3	½	**Malih**[21] 4256 3-9-4 72 ... FergusSweeney 2 (Jamie Osborne) *led at str pce: hrd pressed over 2f out: drvn ahd again over 1f out: hdd fnl 150yds: styd on* 8/1	77+
0006	4	nk	**May's Boy**[29] 3958 4-8-9 59 ...(p) HarryBentley(3) 9 (Mark Usher) *hld up in midfield: prog wl over 1f out: drvn to ld 150yds out: sn hdd and nt qckn* 25/1	64
5046	5	2	**Rock Anthem (IRE)**[15] 4474 8-9-3 64 ... KieranO'Neill 7 (Mike Murphy) *hld up in last quartet in strly run r: prog on inner 2f out: clsd and looked dangerous 1f out: one pce fnl f* 15/2	64
3623	6	1	**Cathedral**[19] 4341 3-9-7 75 ...(b[1]) FrankieDettori 8 (Brian Meehan) *s.i.s: pushed along to rcvr and rchd 5th after 3f: rdn 2f out: nt qckn over 1f out: one pce after* 9/4[1]	72
0000	7	2 ¾	**Uncle Fred**[17] 4413 7-9-13 74 ... GeorgeBaker 10 (Patrick Chamings) *hld up in last quartet in strly run r: effrt on outer over 2f out: no real prog over 1f out* 16/1	66
2-45	8	1 ¾	**Beauchamp Zorro**[12] 4584 4-9-1 62 ... DaneO'Neill 4 (Henry Candy) *trckd ldng pair: rdn to chse ldr over 1f out: hung rt and wknd 1f out* 6/1[3]	50
030	9	3 ¾	**Calypso Magic (IRE)**[17] 4413 4-9-1 62 ...(t) SebSanders 5 (Olivia Maylam) *trckd ldr: chal and upsides 3f out: btn 2f out: wkng whn short of room over 1f out* 12/1	41
0000	10	5	**Barathea Dancer (IRE)**[7] 4722 4-9-9 70 ...(v[1]) AdamKirby 3 (Roger Teal) *chsd ldng pair: rdn over 2f out: wknd rapidly wl over 1f out* 20/1	38

1m 43.81s (0.51) **Going Correction** +0.075s/f (Good)
WFA 3 from 4yo+ 7lb — 10 Ran SP% 120.8
Speed ratings (Par 103): **100,99,99,98,96 95,92,91,87,82**
toteswingers: 1&2 £9.00, 1&3 £12.70, 2&3 £29.60 CSF £37.56 CT £255.67 TOTE £5.40: £2.00, £2.80, £2.10; EX 53.30 Trifecta £144.40 Pool: £357.87 - 1.83 winning units.

Owner M C S D Racing Partnership **Bred** Mrs R S Evans **Trained** Five Oaks, W Sussex

FOCUS
A fair handicap in which the gallop was soon reasonable. The winner is rated to his turf best with the runner-up pretty much to form.

Beauchamp Zorro Official explanation: jockey said gelding hung right.

T/Jkpt: Not won. T/Plt: £149.70 to a £1 stake. Pool: £61,003.60 - 297.33 winning tickets T/Qpdt: £33.60 to a £1 stake. Pool: £4221.20 - 92.70 winning tickets JN

4401 SOUTHWELL (L-H)

Thursday, August 9

OFFICIAL GOING: Standard
Wind: Light behind Weather: Fine and dry

5009 MIRROR PUNTERS CLUB NURSERY — 7f (F)

4:55 (4:55) (Class 6) (0-65,65) 2-Y-O £2,045 (£603; £302) Stalls Low

Form			Horse	RPR
046	1		**Vino Collapso (IRE)**[28] 3989 2-9-7 65 ... JamesSullivan 5 (James Given) *led 2f: cl up: chal 2f out: rdn to ld appr fnl f: sn drvn: edgd rt towards fin and jst hld on* 10/1	68
6603	2	shd	**Brazilian Clown (IRE)**[24] 4140 2-9-7 65 ... FrannyNorton 7 (Tom Dascombe) *trckd ldrs on outer: hdwy 1/2-way: cl up over 2f out: rdn to ld wl over 1f out: hdd appr fnl f: sn drvn and kpt on: n.m.r and no ex nr fin* 15/2	68
1413	3	1 ¾	**Mad Jazz**[6] 4778 2-8-12 61 ... ShaneBKelly(5) 6 (Tony Coyle) *in tch: pushed along 1/2-way: hdwy over 2f out: sn rdn and kpt on fnl f: nrst fin* 3/1[2]	59
406	4	6	**Marabout (IRE)**[20] 4310 2-9-3 61 ... DavidAllan 8 (Mel Brittain) *pushed along to chse ldrs: led after 2f: rdn over 2f out: hdd wl over 1f out and sn one pce* 7/2[3]	44
01	5	1 ¾	**Bear Totem (IRE)**[15] 4449 2-8-13 57 ... J-PGuillambert 4 (Jo Hughes) *sn pushed along in rr: rdn and sme hdwy 1/2-way: drvn over 2f out: nvr a factor* 11/2	35
003	6	13	**Holding Fast (IRE)**[17] 4404 2-8-10 54 ow1 ...(p) StevieDonohoe 2 (Tobias B P Coles) *a in rr: outpcd and bhd fr over 2f out* 33/1	
5234	7	12	**Sandy's Row (USA)**[9] 4672 2-9-7 65 ... JoeFanning 1 (Mark Johnston) *cl up on inner: ev ch over 2f out: sn rdn and wknd* 11/4[1]	

1m 30.06s (-0.24) **Going Correction** -0.075s/f (Stan) — 7 Ran SP% 113.1
Speed ratings (Par 92): **98,97,95,89,87 72,58**
toteswingers: 1&2 £5.90, 1&3 £7.80, 2&3 £7.60 CSF £78.25 CT £280.23 TOTE £17.60: £7.00, £2.90; EX 41.50.

Owner Simply Racing Limited **Bred** Ciaran Mac Ferran **Trained** Willoughton, Lincs

FOCUS
A modest nursery and the two horses drawn widest were non-runners. The placed horses set a solid but unspectacular level.

NOTEBOOK
Vino Collapso(IRE) had run better on his second of his three previous starts recording an RPR of 61 when fourth in maiden company at Ripon. Making his nursery bow from a mark of 65, he drifted into the whip but in the end did just enough. (op 14-1)

Brazilian Clown(IRE), gelded after his third run, returned to finish a well-beaten third over this C&D. Another making his handicap bow, he took plenty of stoking up but in the end was just held. (op 12-1)

Mad Jazz, winner of two sellers and third in a claimer, was another making her handicap bow on her first taste of Fibresand. She shapes as if a stiffer test will now be in her favour. (op 4-1)

Marabout(IRE), very warm beforehand, helped take them along but he does not look to be progressing at all. (op 4-1 tchd 9-2)

Bear Totem(IRE), winner of a Catterick seller, was hard at work at halfway and soon dropped away. (op 6-1 tchd 5-1)

Sandy's Row(USA), who had run respectably in nurseries at Catterick and Ayr, stuck to the inner. She dropped right away 2f out and was eased in the end. It was disappointing because her sire Street Cry has an excellent record on this surface. Official explanation: jockey said filly ran flat. (op 13-8)

5010 FREEBETS.CO.UK MAIDEN AUCTION STKS — 6f (F)

5:25 (5:29) (Class 5) 2-Y-O £2,393 (£712; £355; £177) Stalls Low

Form			Horse	RPR
24	1		**Jumeirah Moon**[10] 4658 2-8-12 0 ... RoystonFfrench 5 (David Simcock) *dwlt: in tch: gd hdwy 1/2-way: chal 2f out: rdn to ld appr fnl f: drvn out* 11/4[2]	70
4020	2	1 ¼	**Relight My Fire**[15] 4450 2-8-9 64 ...(b[1]) DavidAllan 8 (Tim Easterby) *cl up: led after 1f: rdn 2f out: hdd appr fnl f: sn drvn and kpt on* 15/8[1]	63
34	3	3 ½	**Ace Pearl (USA)**[79] 2370 2-8-11 0 ... FrannyNorton 3 (David Brown) *in tch: hdwy on inner 1/2-way: rdn to chse ldrs 2f out: sn drvn and one pce* 6/1	55
35	4	shd	**Red Gift (IRE)**[23] 4173 2-8-11 0 ... PaulPickard(3) 2 (Brian Ellison) *led 1f: cl up: rdn along over 2f out: sn one pce* 10/3[3]	57
060	5	7	**Plexolini**[10] 4654 2-8-11 0 ... J-PGuillambert 7 (Jo Hughes) *chsd ldrs: rdn along over 2f out: sn drvn and wknd* 16/1	33
00	6	2	**Precision Strike**[12] 4587 2-8-12 0 ... AndrewMullen 9 (Richard Guest) *dwlt: sn chsng ldrs: rdn along wl over 2f out: sn outpcd* 20/1	28
	7	½	**Inherited** 2-9-1 0 ... ChrisCatlin 1 (Sir Mark Prescott Bt) *slowly in to stride: rn green: sn outpcd and bhd tl styd on fnl 2f* 16/1	30+
0400	8	6	**Only For You**[66] 2770 2-8-4 37 ... JamesSullivan 4 (Alan Brown) *a in rr: outpcd and bhd fnl 2f* 66/1	1

1m 16.3s (-0.20) **Going Correction** -0.075s/f (Stan) — 8 Ran SP% 116.8
Speed ratings (Par 94): **98,96,91,91,82 79,78,70**
toteswingers: 1&2 £1.20, 1&3 £3.30, 2&3 £3.00 CSF £8.54 TOTE £2.00: £1.10, £1.30, £3.10; EX 6.70.

Owner Khalifa Dasmal **Bred** K A Dasmal **Trained** Newmarket, Suffolk

FOCUS
A modest juvenile maiden rated around the first three.

NOTEBOOK
Jumeirah Moon, who ran over 7f on his first two starts, is out of a mare that won over 5f at two. He travelled strongly but in the end had to be kept right up to his work to hold the renewed effort of the runner-up. He should be competitive in nurseries from a mark in the low-70s. (op 6-4)

Relight My Fire, narrowly beaten in nursery from a mark of 60, failed to see out 7f when returned to turf. In first-time blinkers, he overcame his outside draw and was soon taking them along. He fought back all the way to the line but is now rated 64. (op 3-1 tchd 7-4)

Ace Pearl(USA), having his third outing after a break, misbehaved and had to be led riderless to the start. He is not progressing and is one to have reservations about now. Franny Norton reported that the gelding had hung right. Official explanation: jockey said gelding hung right. (op 9-2)

Red Gift(IRE)was having his third start and this relatively unexposed type is a likely nursery sort. (op 8-1)

Inherited, stoutly bred on his dams' side, was clueless. Soon hopelessly adrift in last, he will no doubt show his true colours over middle-distances at three. (op 12-1)

5011 FREEBETS.CO.UK FREE BETS MEDIAN AUCTION MAIDEN STKS 7f (F)
6:00 (6:00) (Class 5) 2-Y-O **£2,393** (£712; £355) **Stalls** Low

Form RPR
2 **1** **Mocenigo (IRE)**[10] 4646 2-9-3 0 RobertHavlin 3 81+
(Peter Chapple-Hyam) *mde all: cruised clr over 2f out: unchal* **1/25**[1]
0 **2** *11* **Chamtille (IRE)**[30] 3948 2-8-12 0 JoeFanning 2 40
(Derek Haydn Jones) *trckd other duo: pushed along and outpcd 3f out: sn rdn and styd on fr over 1f out to take remote 2nd nr fin* **25/1**[3]
3 *3/4* **Sylvia's Diamond** 2-8-12 0 AndrewMullen 1 38
(Richard Guest) *sn chsng wnr: rdn along wl over 2f out: sn one pce and lost remote 2nd towards fin* **20/1**[2]
1m 31.97s (1.67) **Going Correction** -0.075s/f (Stan) 3 Ran SP% **104.8**
Speed ratings (Par 94): **87,74,73**
CSF £2.12 TOTE £1.02; EX 2.20.
Owner Eledy Srl **Bred** Eledy S R L **Trained** Newmarket, Suffolk

FOCUS
A total non-event and hard to gauge the performance of the winner.

NOTEBOOK
Mocenigo(IRE), who recorded a RPR of 80 when pipped on his debut on the all-weather at Lingfield ten days earlier, holds Royal Lodge and Champagne Stakes entries. He was never out of fourth gear and would have done more in a spin in the morning. (op 1-20)
Chamtille(IRE), who has quite a stout pedigree did just enough to secure a distant second spot.
Sylvia's Diamond, whose dam won over 6f at two, looked very inexperienced but at least enjoyed a pay day on her debut.

5012 FREE BETTING WITH FREEBETS.CO.UK H'CAP 1m 3f (F)
6:30 (6:30) (Class 5) (0-70,70) 4-Y-O+ **£2,264** (£673; £336; £168) **Stalls** Low

Form RPR
3021 **1** **Standpoint**[7] 4722 6-9-7 **70** HayleyTurner 9 86
(Conor Dore) *a.p: cl up 4f out: chal wl over 2f out: rdn to ld over 1f out: drvn ins fnl f: hld on wl* **6/1**[3]
0511 **2** *hd* **Honest Deal**[10] 4652 4-9-3 **66** 6ex AndrewElliott 11 82
(Alan Swinbank) *cl up: led after 3f: pushed along 3f out: rdn over 2f out: hdd over 1f out: drvn and rallied ins fnl f: edgd rt and no ex towards fin* **2/1**[1]
3024 **3** *4 1/2* **Bring Sweets (IRE)**[17] 4402 5-8-7 **56** AmyRyan 6 64
(Brian Ellison) *midfield: hdwy 5f out: trckd ldng pair 3f out: rdn wl over 1f out: drvn and one pce ent fnl f* **10/1**
4220 **4** *2 1/2* **Tobrata**[11] 4626 6-8-12 **61** DavidAllan 3 64
(Mel Brittain) *in tch: hdwy 5f out: rdn to chse ldrs wl over 2f out: drvn and no imp appr fnl f* **12/1**
3350 **5** *7* **Doctor Zhivago**[72] 2593 5-9-0 **66** DaleSwift(3) 5 56
(Ian McInnes) *reminders s and outpcd in rr: hdwy over 4f out: sn rdn along: styd on fnl 2f: nvr nr ldrs* **16/1**
-512 **6** *1* **Layla's Boy**[10] 4652 5-9-2 **65** (bt) FrannyNorton 10 54
(John Mackie) *sn outpcd and bhd: hdwy 4f out: rdn over 3f out: plugged on fnl 2f: n.d* **7/1**
0002 **7** *5* **Lakeman (IRE)**[17] 4402 6-8-6 **58** ow1 (b) PaulPickard(3) 8 38
(Brian Ellison) *chsd ldrs: hdwy and cl up 1/2-way: rdn along over 3f out: grad wknd* **25/1**
2260 **8** *4* **Favorite Girl (GER)**[28] 3992 4-9-5 **68** JoeFanning 2 40
(Michael Appleby) *awkward s: towards rr: hdwy 5f out: rdn along over 3f out: chsd ldrs over 2f out: sn wknd* **5/1**[2]
-310 **9** *4 1/2* **Dispol Diva**[10] 4639 6-8-10 **66** ow1 (v) NedCurtis(7) 7 30
(Paul Midgley) *a in rr* **25/1**
2011 **10** *nk* **Kingaroo (IRE)**[23] 4189 6-8-12 **61** ChrisCatlin 4 25
(Garry Woodward) *led 1f: cl up: rdn along 1/2-way: wknd 4f out* **12/1**
-054 **11** *16* **Persian Herald**[29] 3015 4-9-1 **64** StevieDonohoe 1
(William Muir) *reminders s: cl up: led after 1f: hdd after 3f: sn drvn along and lost pl: bhd fr 1/2-way* **25/1**
2m 25.42s (-2.58) **Going Correction** -0.075s/f (Stan) 11 Ran SP% **118.7**
Speed ratings (Par 103): **106,105,102,100,95 94,91,88,85,84 73**
toteswingers: 1&2 £1.60, 1&3 £7.60, 2&3 £14.00 CSF £18.07 CT £115.81 TOTE £10.80: £4.20, £1.10, £4.60; EX 17.70.
Owner Mrs Jennifer Marsh **Bred** Juddmonte Farms Ltd **Trained** Hubbert's Bridge, Lincs

FOCUS
No hanging about here and they came home well strung out. The runner-up is rated back to his best with the third to form.

5013 FOLLOW US ON TWITTER @SOUTHWELL_RACES (S) STKS 5f (F)
7:05 (7:05) (Class 6) 3-Y-O+ **£1,704** (£503; £251) **Stalls** High

Form RPR
4303 **1** **Come On Dave (IRE)**[3] 4878 3-9-3 65 AndrewMullen 1 69
(David Nicholls) *qckly away: clr 1/2-way: rdn over 1f out: kpt on* **11/8**[1]
1055 **2** *1 3/4* **Fol Hollow (IRE)**[15] 4454 7-9-12 70 AdrianNicholls 6 69
(David Nicholls) *prom: effrt to chse wnr 2f out: rdn over 1f out: kpt on fnl f* **4/1**[2]
5560 **3** *nk* **Argentine (IRE)**[11] 4631 8-9-12 62 (b) RoystonFfrench 7 68
(Ian Semple) *trckd ldrs: effrt over 1f out: sn rdn and kpt on fnl f* **5/1**[3]
2060 **4** *4* **Scarlet Rocks (IRE)**[13] 4547 4-9-1 57 DavidAllan 3 43
(Ron Barr) *towards rr: hdwy wl over 1f out: kpt on fnl f: nvr nr ldrs* **9/1**
360 **5** *2 1/4* **Just For Mary**[9] 4680 8-9-6 65 StephenCraine 5 40
(Daniel Mark Loughnane) *dwlt and in rr: swtchd wd and hdwy 2f out: sn rdn and n.d* **14/1**
230 **6** *nk* **The Magic Of Rio**[23] 4187 6-8-10 45 ShaneBKelly(5) 8 33
(John Balding) *cl up: rdn along over 2f out: wknd wl over 1f out* **9/1**
0250 **7** *1 3/4* **Brunswick Vale (IRE)**[19] 4348 3-8-12 52 (b) RussKennemore 12 27
(Paul Midgley) *a towards rr* **16/1**
500- **8** *4 1/2* **Tyre Giant Dot Com**[294] 6975 3-9-0 60 DaleSwift(3) 11 16
(Geoffrey Oldroyd) *prom: rdn along 1/2-way: sn wknd* **28/1**
5000 **9** *2 3/4* **Fathey (IRE)**[73] 2555 6-9-1 42 NathanAlison(5) 9
(Charles Smith) *blind removed after stalls opened and lost many l s: a bhd* **100/1**
0005 **10** *nse* **Vogarth**[24] 4141 8-8-13 39 (b) DannyBrock(7) 10
(Michael Chapman) *chsd ldrs: rdn along 1/2-way: sn wknd* **50/1**
5/00 **11** *nse* **Berrymead**[51] 3243 7-8-10 45 AnnStokell(5) 4
(Ann Stokell) *a towards rr* **100/1**
59.05s (-0.65) **Going Correction** -0.10s/f (Stan)
WFA 3 from 4yo+ 3lb 11 Ran SP% **118.7**
Speed ratings (Par 101): **101,98,97,91,87 87,84,77,72,72 72**
toteswingers: 1&2 £2.00, 1&3 £2.50, 2&3 £4.40 CSF £6.70 TOTE £3.20: £1.40, £1.60, £1.60; EX 8.90.There was no bid for the winner.
Owner Middleham Park Racing XLIV **Bred** Mrs Eithne Hamilton **Trained** Sessay, N Yorks

FOCUS
The leaders went off very fast, few got in to it, and the first three home were in the leading group throughout. The winner is rated to this year's marks with the third the key to the level.
The Magic Of Rio Official explanation: trainer said mare bled from nose.
Fathey(IRE) Official explanation: jockey said gelding missed the break.

5014 MEMBERSHIP AVAILABLE AT SOUTHWELL GOLF CLUB H'CAP 7f (F)
7:40 (7:42) (Class 6) (0-55,55) 3-Y-O **£1,704** (£503; £251) **Stalls** Low

Form RPR
0030 **1** **Jay Kay**[17] 4397 3-9-0 **53** ChrisCatlin 3 59
(Danielle McCormick) *in tch: hdwy to chse ldrs 2f out: sn swtchd rt to outer and sn rdn: drvn ent fnl f and styd on strly to ld last 75yds* **10/1**
00 **2** *1 1/2* **Choice Pearl (USA)**[16] 4434 3-9-2 **55** (t) JoeFanning 4 57
(Tobias B P Coles) *hld up: hdwy over 2f out: rdn to chse ldrs over 1f out: kpt on fnl f* **18/1**
0050 **3** *hd* **Brailsford (IRE)**[14] 4506 3-9-0 **53** (v) RoystonFfrench 11 54
(Ismail Mohammed) *led: rdn 2f out: drvn over 1f out: edgd rt fnl f: hdd and one pce fnl 75yds* **9/1**
2430 **4** *nk* **Red Shadow**[17] 4397 3-9-0 **53** MartinLane 8 54
(Alan Brown) *cl up: rdn 2f out and ev ch tl drvn ins fnl f: one pce fnl 100yds* **12/1**
6015 **5** *1 1/4* **Majestic Breeze (IRE)**[13] 4547 3-8-10 **52** PaulPickard(3) 5 49
(Brian Ellison) *cl up: rdn along over 2f out: drvn over 1f out: wknd ent fnl f* **9/2**[2]
4000 **6** *1 1/2* **Sweet Grace**[23] 4189 3-8-7 **46** oh1 (t) FrannyNorton 2 39
(David Brown) *hld up: hdwy on inner 2f out: rdn to chse ldrs over 1f out: drvn and no imp fnl f* **20/1**
5302 **7** *1 3/4* **Big Sylv (IRE)**[23] 4185 3-8-9 **48** LiamJones 6 36
(James Unett) *nvr bttr than midfield* **10/1**
400 **8** *3/4* **Charmel's Delight**[13] 4550 3-8-10 **52** DaleSwift(3) 9 38
(Geoffrey Oldroyd) *dwlt and towards rr: rdn and sme hdwy 2f out: n.d* **33/1**
6400 **9** *1 3/4* **Elusive Island (USA)**[15] 4452 3-8-9 **48** PatrickMathers 1 30
(Ann Duffield) *s.i.s: a towards rr* **12/1**
016 **10** *5* **Military Green (FR)**[17] 4397 3-8-13 **52** DuranFentiman 10 20
(Tim Easterby) *nvr nr ldrs* **3/1**[1]
0003 **11** *2 1/4* **Great Nicanor (IRE)**[17] 4394 3-8-13 **52** (p) TomEaves 12 14
(Ian Semple) *chsd ldrs: rdn and hung rt 2f out: sn wknd* **16/1**
5054 **12** *3* **Magic Bounty**[13] 4549 3-8-11 **50** (p) DavidAllan 14
(Tim Easterby) *cl up on outer: rdn along 1/2-way: sn wknd* **7/1**[3]
6404 **13** *1/2* **Sleepy Lucy**[6] 4771 3-8-8 **47** oh1 ow1 RobbieFitzpatrick 7
(Richard Guest) *chsd ldrs: n.m.r and lost pl bef 1/2-way: bhd fnl 2f* **20/1**
1m 31.2s (0.90) **Going Correction** -0.075s/f (Stan) 13 Ran SP% **122.9**
Speed ratings (Par 98): **91,89,89,88,87 85,83,82,80,75 72,69,68**
toteswingers: 1&2 £28.90, 1&3 £14.20, 2&3 £41.80 CSF £177.17 CT £1744.12 TOTE £22.50: £6.50, £5.20, £5.70; EX 125.80.
Owner John Kenny **Bred** Miss S E Hall **Trained** Westhead, Lancs

FOCUS
A wide-open low-grade 3-y-o handicap. The form is a bit shaky with the third the best guide.
Military Green(FR) Official explanation: trainers representative said gelding was never travelling.

5015 DOWNLOAD OUR IPHONE APP H'CAP 1m (F)
8:10 (8:10) (Class 6) (0-55,58) 3-Y-O+ **£1,704** (£503; £251) **Stalls** Low

Form RPR
0061 **1** **It's A Mans World**[6] 4779 6-9-8 **58** 6ex PaulPickard(3) 5 71+
(Brian Ellison) *midfield: gd hdwy on outer to chse ldrs 3f out: rdn to ld wl over 1f out: drvn out* **11/10**[1]
-006 **2** *1 1/2* **Tresabella**[41] 3575 3-8-5 **45** (b[1]) FrannyNorton 12 54
(Michael Appleby) *prom: hdwy and cl up 3f out: rdn to ld briefly 2f out: hdd wl over 1f out and sn drvn: kpt on fnl f* **25/1**
0500 **3** *4* **Meydan Style (USA)**[15] 4453 6-8-13 **46** JoeFanning 13 46
(Richard Ford) *in tch: hdwy on outer 3f out: rdn to chse ldrs 2f out: styd on same pce* **18/1**
3265 **4** *4 1/2* **Gadobout Dancer**[8] 4715 5-9-0 **52** [1] ShaneBKelly(5) 3 42
(Tony Coyle) *towards rr: hdwy over 2f out: sn rdn and styd on appr fnl f: nvr nr ldrs* **8/1**[3]
/000 **5** *3 1/2* **Hyde Lea Flyer**[10] 4656 7-9-7 **54** RussKennemore 6 36
(Barry Leavy) *trckd ldrs on inner: hdwy over 2f out: sn rdn and no imp* **10/1**
-630 **6** *nk* **Orpen Wide (IRE)**[23] 4193 10-8-7 **47** (bt) DannyBrock(7) 2 28
(Michael Chapman) *led: rdn 3f out: drvn and hdd 2f out: grad wknd* **20/1**
-001 **7** *5* **Applaude**[17] 4405 7-9-4 **51** (b) MichaelStainton 1 21
(Chris Bealby) *cl up on inner: rdn along over 2f out: sn wknd* **9/2**[2]
0350 **8** *2* **Nicholas Pocock (IRE)**[4] 3047 6-9-2 **49** PatrickMathers 7 14
(Ian McInnes) *s.i.s: a in rr: t.o 1/2-way: sme late hdwy* **22/1**
0000 **9** *3/4* **Kata Rock (USA)**[20] 4314 5-9-1 **48** BarryMcHugh 4
(Brian Rothwell) *chsd ldrs: rdn along over 3f out and sn wknd* **20/1**
6066 **10** *2* **Amber Moon**[17] 4406 7-8-7 **45** (b) AnnStokell(5) 10
(Ann Stokell) *a in rr* **50/1**
6400 **11** *15* **Crocodile Bay (IRE)**[6] 4783 9-8-12 **45** (b) J-PGuillambert 9
(Richard Guest) *cl up: rdn along 3f out: sn wknd* **20/1**
1m 43.12s (-0.58) **Going Correction** -0.075s/f (Stan)
WFA 3 from 4yo+ 7lb 11 Ran SP% **115.7**
Speed ratings (Par 101): **99,97,93,89,85 85,80,78,77,75 60**
toteswingers: 1&2 £11.50, 1&3 £11.30, 2&3 £20.70 CSF £41.75 CT £346.87 TOTE £2.20: £1.30, £9.20, £3.60; EX 48.90.
Owner Brian Ellison **Bred** Cheveley Park Stud Ltd **Trained** Norton, N Yorks

FOCUS
A weak handicap with the winner rated back to his old best.
Gadobout Dancer Official explanation: jockey said mare reared as gates opened.
Nicholas Pocock(IRE) Official explanation: jockey said gelding was slowly away.

T/Plt: £200.90 to a £1 stake. Pool: £23,945.74 - 87.01 winning tickets T/Qpdt: £9.30 to a £1 stake. Pool: £2754.97, 218.71 winning tickets JR

[4966] YARMOUTH (L-H)

Thursday, August 9

OFFICIAL GOING: Good (good to firm in places; 7.2)

Wind: Light across Weather: Sunny

5016 BRITISH STALLION STUDS SUPPORTING BRITISH RACING EBF MAIDEN STKS — 6f 3y

2:30 (2:30) (Class 5) 2-Y-0 — **£3,234** (£962; £481; £240) **Stalls** Centre

Form — RPR

1 **Taayel (IRE)** 2-9-3 0 .... PaulHanagan 2 90+
(John Gosden) *chsd ldrs: shkn up to ld over 1f out: r.o wl* **15/8**[1]

205 2 2¾ **Living Desert**[27] [4058] 2-9-3 89 .... RobertHavlin 3 82
(James Toller) *led: rdn and hdd over 1f out: styd on same pce ins fnl f* **5/1**

3 *nk* **Raskova (USA)** 2-8-12 0 .... MickaelBarzalona 5 76
(William Jarvis) *s.i.s: sn pushed along in rr: hdwy 2f out: rdn and ev ch over 1f out: styd on same pce ins fnl f* **16/1**

4 4 *1* **Exotic Guest**[18] [4362] 2-9-3 0 .... IanMongan 1 78
(George Margarson) *trckd ldrs: racd keenly: led over 1f out: sn rdn and hdd: no ex wl ins fnl f* **4/1**[3]

0 5 2½ **Emerald Sea**[28] [4011] 2-8-12 0 .... TedDurcan 6 66
(Chris Wall) *trckd ldrs: plld hrd: rdn and ev ch over 1f out: edgd lft and wknd ins fnl f* **9/4**[2]

0 6 2½ **Misty Secret (IRE)**[22] [4217] 2-8-12 0 .... BrettDoyle 4 58
(Jane Chapple-Hyam) *chsd ldr tl rdn and wknd over 1f out* **100/1**

1m 15.07s (0.67) **Going Correction** -0.15s/f (Firm) 6 Ran SP% **109.1**
Speed ratings (Par 94): **89,85,84,83,80 76**
toteswingers 1&2 £2.00, 1&3 £2.70, 2&3 £4.10 CSF £10.97 TOTE £2.80: £2.70, £2.00; EX 12.10.

Owner Hamdan Al Maktoum **Bred** Corrin Stud **Trained** Newmarket, Suffolk

FOCUS
An interesting juvenile maiden that threw up a promising debut winner. The form is rated at face value through the runner-up.

NOTEBOOK
Taayel(IRE) ◆, a newcomer whose dam was useful at sprint distances in Italy, won with the minimum of fuss. He quickened away nicely, needing only hands-and-heels riding to do so, and looks a decent prospect. It will be a surprise if he fails to collect again. (op 3-1)
Living Desert, three-times raced over this trip and officially rated 90, is probably flattered by that mark. He ran well nonetheless and should not take long to find an opportunity to score at this level. (op 10-3)
Raskova(USA), a debutante who cost 130,000gns, was green in the early stages, needing to be nudged along in order to keep tabs on the rest. She began to get the hang of things before halfway, though, and was briefly second. She should improve for this run and ought to win a maiden soon. (op 17-2)
Exotic Guest, fourth in a decent 6f maiden at Ascot on his only previous run, chased the pace for 3f. He was unable to quicken in the second half of the race, however, and did not take a significant step forward following his encouraging debut. (op 7-2)
Emerald Sea, ninth of 17 on her Newmarket debut behind a potentially smart prospect, attracted plenty of support beforehand. It appeared she might make an impact in the race, too, but after figuring prominently 2f out, she faded quite tamely. (op 3-1)
Misty Secret(IRE) had shown little when eighth of ten on her AW debut and was out of her depth in this company. She was towards the front in the early stages, but could muster no response when the principals engaged a higher gear. (op 66-1)

5017 NORFOLK AND SUFFOLK ANIMAL TRUST MAIDEN H'CAP — 6f 3y

3:00 (3:00) (Class 6) (0-65,65) 3-Y-0+ — **£1,617** (£481; £240; £120) **Stalls** Centre

Form — RPR

1 **Jouster (IRE)**[64] [2831] 4-9-11 64 ....[1] IanMongan 6 72
(M D O'Callaghan, Ire) *hld up: hdwy over 2f out: rdn to ld wl ins fnl f: styd on* **7/2**[2]

4466 2 ½ **Miakora**[16] [4434] 4-8-6 50 .... TobyAtkinson(5) 8 56
(Michael Quinn) *a.p: led over 1f out: sn rdn: edgd lft and hdd wl ins fnl f: styd on* **20/1**

0-00 3 ½ **Scarabocio**[69] [2680] 3-9-4 64 .... AshleyHamblett(3) 3 67
(Peter Chapple-Hyam) *a.p: rdn and edgd lft ins fnl f: styd on* **11/1**

44-6 4 2¾ **Elite**[155] [827] 3-9-8 65 .... SamHitchcott 2 62
(Mick Channon) *chsd ldrs: effrt and nt clr run over 1f out: rdn and hmpd ins fnl f: nvr able to chal* **6/1**[3]

0000 5 ¾ **Itum**[23] [4187] 5-8-7 46 .... BrettDoyle 9 39
(Christine Dunnett) *hld up in tch: led over 2f out: rdn and hdd over 1f out: no ex ins fnl f* **28/1**

0302 6 2¼ **Yes It's The Boy (USA)**[7] [4734] 3-9-3 60 ....(b) TedDurcan 11 45
(Ed Walker) *hld up: effrt over 1f out: n.m.r and wknd ins fnl f* **11/4**[1]

5603 7 3¾ **Choice Words (USA)**[64] [2809] 4-9-9 62 .... PaulHanagan 1 36
(Natalie Lloyd-Beavis) *led: rdn: hung lft and hdd over 2f out: wknd fnl f* **11/4**[1]

3365 8 9 **Conowen**[14] [4509] 3-9-8 65 .... LiamKeniry 10
(William Jarvis) *chsd ldr: rdn and ev ch over 2f out: wknd over 1f out* **16/1**

-000 9 19 **Pink Belini**[8] [4705] 3-8-3 46 oh1 ....(bt[1]) KellyHarrison 7
(Alan McCabe) *s.i.s: sn pushed along in rr: wknd 1/2-way: t.o* **50/1**

1m 14.25s (-0.15) **Going Correction** -0.15s/f (Firm)
WFA 3 from 4yo+ 4lb 9 Ran SP% **114.2**
Speed ratings (Par 101): **95,94,93,90,89 86,81,69,43**
toteswingers 1&2 £10.80, 1&3 £5.50, 2&3 £15.60 CSF £70.05 CT £695.70 TOTE £4.60: £1.50, £4.90, £4.50; EX 75.40 TRIFECTA Not won..

Owner Michael O'Callaghan **Bred** Keith Wills **Trained** Rathangan, Co. Kildare

■ Stewards' Enquiry : Toby Atkinson two-day ban; used whip above permitted level (25th-26th Aug).
Ashley Hamblett two-day ban; careless riding (25th-26th Aug).\n\x\x four-day ban; used whip above permitted level (27th-30th Aug)

FOCUS
A typically weak maiden handicap with the winner to the balance of his irish form and the second to her latest maiden mark.
Jouster(IRE) Official explanation: trainers representative said regarding apparent improvement in form that gelding is very nervous and benefited from the application of a hood.

5018 GOLDEN MILE GREAT YARMOUTH (S) STKS — 1m 3y

3:30 (3:30) (Class 6) 3-Y-0 — **£1,617** (£481; £240; £120) **Stalls** Centre

Form — RPR

4000 1 **Capitol Gain (IRE)**[8] [4709] 3-9-3 62 ....(p) MickaelBarzalona 5 71
(Brian Meehan) *trckd ldrs: led and c towards stands' side over 2f out: rdn clr fr over 1f out* **13/2**[3]

3560 2 8 **Song Of Joy (IRE)**[10] [4650] 3-8-12 57 .... LukeMorris 6 48
(Paul D'Arcy) *s.i.s: hld up: hdwy over 3f out: sn rdn: wnt 2nd over 1f out: styd on same pce* **12/1**

6640 3 1¼ **Poetic Power (IRE)**[12] [4606] 3-9-3 68 .... LiamKeniry 3 50
(David Elsworth) *led over 5f: sn rdn: wknd over 1f out* **15/8**[2]

6-41 4 1½ **Future Wonder (IRE)**[15] [4457] 3-9-3 65 .... PaulHanagan 4 46
(Rae Guest) *trckd ldr: plld hrd: rdn over 2f out: wknd over 1f out* **1/1**[1]

0-00 5 35 **Dine Out**[57] [3048] 3-8-12 52 ....(p) TedDurcan 2
(Mark H Tompkins) *s.i.s: rdn 1/2-way: sn wknd: t.o* **40/1**

1m 41.38s (0.78) **Going Correction** -0.15s/f (Firm) 5 Ran SP% **108.2**
Speed ratings (Par 98): **90,82,80,79,44**
CSF £62.94 TOTE £6.70: £2.80, £4.20; EX 42.90.There was no bid for the winner. Future Wonder was claimed by Mr Brian Ellison for £4,500. Poetic Power was claimed by Mr S. D. Petty for £4,500.

Owner N Attenborough,Mrs L Mann,M Wilmshurst **Bred** Pier House Stud **Trained** Manton, Wilts

FOCUS
An ordinary 3-y-o seller with the winner rated to previous form, despite scoring by a wide margin.

5019 BETTERBET FILLIES' H'CAP — 1m 3y

4:00 (4:00) (Class 5) (0-75,75) 3-Y-0 — **£2,264** (£673; £336; £168) **Stalls** Centre

Form — RPR

141 1 **Shena's Dream (IRE)**[12] [4583] 3-9-5 73 .... LiamJones 1 84+
(William Haggas) *sn led: j. path after 5f out: rdn over 1f out: edgd rt ins fnl f: styd on gamely* **5/4**[1]

063 2 ½ **Feelthedifference**[20] [4288] 3-9-1 69 .... IanMongan 3 79
(Sir Henry Cecil) *hld up: hdwy over 2f out: rdn to chse wnr over 1f out: edgd lft and ev ch ins fnl f: styd on* **9/4**[2]

3-34 3 ½ **Fulney**[35] [3792] 3-9-7 75 .... LukeMorris 5 84
(James Eustace) *led early: chsd wnr: shkn up over 2f out: rdn over 1f out: styd on u.p* **9/2**[3]

422- 4 5 **Silke Top**[328] [6131] 3-9-6 74 .... MickaelBarzalona 7 71
(William Jarvis) *prom: racd keenly: rdn over 2f out: wknd fnl f* **14/1**

25-0 5 8 **Lady Bellatrix**[20] [4314] 3-8-11 65 .... TedDurcan 4 44
(Mark H Tompkins) *hld up: hdwy over 2f out: rdn and wknd over 1f out* **33/1**

0003 6 19 **Confluence**[29] [3975] 3-8-6 60 .... PaulHanagan 2
(Clifford Lines) *prom: rdn over 2f out: sn wknd: t.o* **12/1**

1m 39.5s (-1.10) **Going Correction** -0.15s/f (Firm) 6 Ran SP% **110.7**
Speed ratings (Par 97): **99,98,98,93,85 66**
toteswingers 1&2 £1.80, 1&3 £2.00, 2&3 £2.00 CSF £4.11 TOTE £2.10: £1.10, £2.50; EX 4.80.

Owner Miss Pat O'Kelly **Bred** Kilcarn Stud **Trained** Newmarket, Suffolk

FOCUS
A moderate 3-y-o fillies' handicap. The winner should do even better, while the third is rated to her best juvenile form.

5020 BBC RADIO NORFOLK H'CAP — 5f 43y

4:30 (4:30) (Class 4) (0-80,77) 3-Y-0+ — **£4,075** (£1,212; £606; £303) **Stalls** Centre

Form — RPR

20 1 **Tom Sawyer**[23] [4174] 4-8-6 59 ....(b[1]) LukeMorris 7 69
(Julie Camacho) *a.p: chsd ldr 2f out: sn rdn: edgd rt and led ins fnl f: styd on u.p* **13/2**

0424 2 2 **Ryan Style (IRE)**[10] [4638] 6-9-5 72 ....(v) PaulHanagan 5 75
(Lisa Williamson) *hld up: hdwy 1/2-way: rdn over 1f out: styd on to go 2nd wl ins fnl f: nt trble wnr* **3/1**[1]

5650 3 ¾ **Signifer (IRE)**[6] [4765] 3-9-7 77 .... SamHitchcott 2 76
(Mick Channon) *w ldr tl led over 3f out: rdn over 1f out: hdd and unable qck ins fnl f* **7/2**[2]

5610 4 *nk* **The Strig**[20] [4300] 5-8-13 66 .... SaleemGolam 1 65
(Stuart Williams) *led: hdd over 3f out: chsd ldr tl pushed along 2f out: styd on same pce ins fnl f* **8/1**

44 5 2 **Moorhouse Girl**[7] [4743] 5-9-0 67 .... TedDurcan 3 59
(David Brown) *s.i.s: plld hrd and sn prom: rdn over 1f out: no ex fnl f* **3/1**[1]

-640 6 ½ **Magical Speedfit (IRE)**[19] [4317] 7-9-2 69 .... IanMongan 4 59
(George Margarson) *sn outpcd* **6/1**[3]

1m 3.01s (0.31) **Going Correction** -0.15s/f (Firm)
WFA 3 from 4yo+ 3lb 6 Ran SP% **111.0**
Speed ratings (Par 105): **91,87,86,86,82 82**
toteswingers 1&2 £3.50, 1&3 £3.30, 2&3 £1.90 CSF £25.49 TOTE £7.70: £5.20, £1.50; EX 20.80.

Owner Bolingbroke J Howard FAO Mersey R & Ptns **Bred** Newsells Park Stud **Trained** Norton, N Yorks

FOCUS
An ordinary sprint handicap rated around the first two to recent form.

5021 NORFOLK CHAMBER OF COMMERCE H'CAP — 1m 1f

5:00 (5:00) (Class 6) (0-65,65) 3-Y-0+ — **£1,617** (£481; £240; £120) **Stalls** Low

Form — RPR

-030 1 **Critical Point**[31] [3907] 3-8-1 46 oh1 ....(b[1]) LukeMorris 9 59
(Sir Mark Prescott Bt) *s.i.s: rcvrd to ld 8f out: hdd 6f out: led again 4f out: sn pushed along: rdn clr and edgd rt fr over 1f out: styd on wl* **7/1**

0-00 2 3 **Dandarrell**[19] [4349] 5-8-10 47 .... FrederikTylicki 8 53
(Julie Camacho) *led 1f: chsd ldr tl led again 6f out: hdd 4f out: sn rdn: styd on same pce appr fnl f* **6/1**

0-64 3 3 **Twin Shadow (IRE)**[16] [4435] 3-9-3 62 .... MickaelBarzalona 6 61
(James Fanshawe) *s.i.s: hld up: pushed along 5f out: hdwy over 2f out: sn rdn: no ex fnl f* **7/2**[2]

/612 4 ¾ **King's Masque**[17] [4409] 6-9-7 65 .... RobertWilliams(7) 2 63
(Bernard Llewellyn) *prom: rdn over 2f out: no ex fnl f* **9/2**[3]

0205 5 3½ **Kelpie Blitz (IRE)**[21] [4242] 3-9-5 64 .... PaulHanagan 7 54
(Seamus Durack) *chsd ldrs: rdn over 2f out: wknd over 1f out* **11/4**[1]

0550 6 *nk* **Zenarinda**[40] [3609] 5-9-9 60 .... TedDurcan 5 49
(Mark H Tompkins) *hld up: rdn over 2f out: n.d* **9/1**

0000 7 24 **Ayaarah (IRE)**[21] [4242] 4-8-4 46 oh1 .... DavidKenny(5) 3
(William Knight) *hld up: a in rr: rdn and wknd over 2f out: t.o* **25/1**

630- 8 3¼ **Concrete Jungle (IRE)**[351] [5394] 4-9-10 61 .... IanMongan 4
(Natalie Lloyd-Beavis) *chsd ldrs: rdn over 3f out: sn wknd: t.o* **25/1**

1m 54.11s (-1.69) **Going Correction** -0.15s/f (Firm)
WFA 3 from 4yo+ 8lb 8 Ran SP% **111.5**
Speed ratings (Par 101): **101,98,95,95,91 91,70,67**
toteswingers 1&2 £5.90, 1&3 £3.50, 2&3 £5.50 CSF £45.83 CT £167.89 TOTE £10.20: £2.30, £2.20, £1.20; EX 54.00 Trifecta £264.30 Part won. Pool: £357.27 - 0.73 winning units..

Owner G Moore - Osborne House **Bred** Lofts Hall, M Philipson & Cheveley Park **Trained** Newmarket, Suffolk

FOCUS
A weak handicap in which it paid to race handily. The form is best rated around the second and fourth.

5022 SCROBY SANDS WINDFARM H'CAP 1m 6f 17y
5:30 (5:31) (Class 6) (0-58,57) 3-Y-O+ £1,617 (£481; £240 ; £120) Stalls High

Form RPR
0245 1 **Vexillum (IRE)**[7] 4744 3 -8-12[56] SamHitchcott 4 69
(Mick Channon) *hld up: hdwy 6f out: led over 2f out: edgd lft: drvn out* **4/1**[3]
/6-0 2 5 **Akula (IRE)**[117] 452 5 -9-9[54] TedDurcan 2 60
(Mark H Tompkins) *chsd ldrs: rdn over 2f out: styd on same pce fnl f* **11/4**[2]
-003 3 2 **Zarosa (IRE)**[7] 4744 3 -8-2[46] LukeMorris 7 49
(John Berry) *led 1f: chsd ldr: rdn over 2f out: wandered over 1f out: no ex fnl f* **6/4**[1]
0503 4 6 **Satwa Ballerina**[24] 4147 4 -9-4[54] (b) TobyAtkinson(5) 9 49
(Mark Rimmer) *hld up: bhd and rdn 5f out: styd on fnl f: nvr nrr* **22/1**
3454 5 2 **Barbirolli**[21] 4244 10 -8-9[45] LauraPike(5) 6 37
(William Stone) *hld up: bhd 5f out: sn rdn: styd on fnl f: nvr on terms* **16/1**
0-30 6 1 **Skyblue**[16] 4440 3 -7-10[45] (b) RosieJessop(5) 3 36
(Tobias B P Coles) *s.i.s: hdwy and hmpd after 1f: pushed along to ld 4f out: sn rdn: edgd rt and hdd over 2f out: sn wknd* **18/1**
050 7 22 **Flaming Telepath**[24] 4157 4 -9-0[45] (p) IanMongan 1
(Christine Dunnett) *hld up: a in rr: bhd fnl 5f: t.o* **50/1**
1/06 8 22 **Giant Sequoia (USA)**[14] 4200 8 -9-12[57] (t) DaraghO'Donohoe 5
(Barney Curley) *slowly in to stride: sn pushed along: hdwy to ld and edgd lft after 1f: clr 10f out: hdd & wknd 4f out: t.o* **14/1**
-060 9 36 **Hal Of A Lover**[38] 3712 4 -9-0[45] (p) FrederikTylicki 8
(Lisa Williamson) *prom 8f: t.o* **28/1**

3m 6.45s (-1.15) **Going Correction** -0.15s/f (Firm)
WFA 3 from 4yo+ 13lb 9Ran SP% 114.2
Speed ratings (Par 101): **97,94,93,89,88 87,75,62,42**
toteswingers 1&2 £2.90, 1&3 £2.70, 2&3 £2.10 CSF £14.94 CT £22.87 TOTE £5.60 : £1.40, £1.10, £1.40 ; EX 16.40 Trifecta £36.00 Pool: £310.84 - 6.38 winning units.
Owner Insignia Racing (Roundel) **Bred** Rathasker Stud **Trained** West Ilsley, Berks

FOCUS
A low-grade finale rated through the winner back to his best form. The early pace was steady.
T/Plt: £273.80 to a £1 stake. Pool: £42233.35 - 112.60 winning tickets T/Qpdt: £101.60 to a £1 stke Pool: £3744.70 - 27.25 w. tckts CR 5023a-5026a, 5028a-5029a (Foreign Racing) See RI

[4518] LEOPARDSTOWN (L-H)
Thursday, August 9
OFFICIAL GOING: Good to soft (good in places)

5027a BALLYROAN STKS (GROUP 3) 1m 4f
7:30 (7:33) 3-Y-O+ £31,145 (£9,104; £4,312 ; £1,437)

RPR
1 **Galileo's Choice (IRE)**[21] 4280 6 -9-9[110] PatSmullen 4 111+
(D K Weld, Ire) *trckd ldrs: 5th 1/2-way: prog to ld over 2f out: styd on wl* **9/4**[1]
2 1 1/2 **Massiyn (IRE)**[31] 3926 3 -8-12[102] (t) JohnnyMurtagh 7 109+
(M Halford, Ire) *trckd ldrs: led over 3f out: hdd and dropped to 3rd 2f out: r.o wl fnl f to take 2nd cl home* **6/1**
3 nk **Bible Belt (IRE)**[14] 2525 4 -9-6[111] FranBerry 1 106
(Mrs John Harrington, Ire) *hld up in tch: prog over 3f out: 2nd 2f out: short of room ins fnl f: lost 3rd cl home* **6/1**
4 1 **Treasure Beach**[26] 4117 4 -9-9[115] CO'Donoghue 5 107
(A P O'Brien, Ire) *trckd ldrs: 4th 1/2-way: 3rd 2f out: no ex fnl f* **3/1**[2]
5 3 3/4 **Blue Corner (IRE)**[25] 4126 3 -8-12 ShaneFoley 3 101
(M Halford, Ire) *bhd: 8th over 3f out: kpt on fnl 2f* **16/1**
6 1 3/4 **Light Heavy (IRE)**[40] 3651 3 -9-3[109] (tp) KevinManning 2 103
(J S Bolger, Ire) *trckd ldrs: 4th over 1f out: no ex fnl f* **7/2**[3]
7 2 1/2 **Steps To Freedom (IRE)**[21] 4280 6 -9-9[109] (t) DeclanMcDonogh 8 94
(Mrs John Harrington, Ire) *bhd: 2nd over 3f out: wknd st* **11/1**
8 11 **Bob Le Beau (IRE)**[21] 4280 5 -9-9[104] EmmetMcNamara 6 77
(Mrs John Harrington, Ire) *led: hdd & wknd over 3f out* **40/1**

2m 34.82s (-0.48) **Going Correction** +0.225s/f (Good)
WFA 3 from 4yo+ 11lb 8Ran SP% 123.2
Speed ratings: **110,109,108,108,105 104,102,95**
CSF £18.10 TOTE £3.10 : £1.20 , £1.60 , £2.00 ; DF 27.70 .
Owner Dr R Lambe, Dr M Smurfit, D Keough & Newtown Anner **Bred** Patrick F Kelly **Trained** The Curragh, Co Kildare
■ Stewards' Enquiry : Pat Smullen caution (reduced from two-day ban on appeal): careless riding

FOCUS
A good renewal of this Group 3 rated around the runner-up and fifth to fair personal bests.

NOTEBOOK
Galileo's Choice (IRE) booked his place in the Irish St Leger line-up by responding well for pressure to give trainer Dermot Weld a fourth consecutive win in this event and his eighth success overall. After tracking the leaders, he went for his race off the final bend, edging left over 2f out and again under pressure inside the final furlong to win driven out. The winner has proved himself versatile in terms of distance, having won over 1m2f, 1m6f and 2m1f in addition to twice scoring over hurdles. (op 5/2)
Massiyn(IRE) had looked unlucky when beaten a short head in a Listed event over this trip at Roscommon on his previous start when bidding for a hat-trick. The better ground here was expected to suit and he produced a good effort, going to the front over 3f out and staying on again inside the final furlong to take second close home after being headed turning for home. (op 11/2 tchd 13/2)
Bible Belt (IRE) a smart performer last year and having only her second start of the season, was held up before getting a nice run through on the inside to dispute the lead into the straight. She came under pressure before finding herself short of room on the winner's inside early in the final furlong and, while she could not be considered an unlucky loser, she was unlucky not to have finished second.
Treasure Beach, last year's Irish Derby winner, had been globetrotting since that victory and had not won since landing the Secretariat Stakes at Arlington a year ago. He had been to Dubai, Hong Kong and the US this year and had run moderately at Belmont Park last month. He raced a bit keenly but moved into third place one and a half furlongs out before his effort flattened out. 5/2)
Blue Corner (IRE) the least experienced in the race and having only his third run, was going up in trip and class. He raced in rear before staying on over the last 2f without ever posing a threat.
Light Heavy (IRE) was well placed for much of the journey but was being ridden along and making little impression when he was hampered by the winner off the final bend. (op 6/1)

CLAIREFONTAINE (R-H)
Thursday, August 9
OFFICIAL GOING: Turf: heavy

5030a PRIX LE GRAND ORDRE DU TROU NORMAND (PRIX DE BROCOTTE) (CONDITIONS) (4YO+) (TURF) 1m 4f
6:40 (12:00) 4-Y-O+ £10,000 (£4,000; £3,000 ; £2,000 ; £1,000)

RPR
1 **Fair Boss (IRE)**[102] 1700 4 -8-11[0] MaximeGuyon 1 85
(W Hickst, Germany) **18/5**[2]
2 1/2 **Regamonti (FR)**[410] 5 -8-11[0] GeraldMosse 4 84
(W Hefter, Germany) **11/1**
3 3/4 **Roatan**[57] 7 -8-11[0] StephanePasquier 5 83
(P Bary, France) **2/1**[1]
4 1 3/4 **Ranthambore (FR)**[32] 6 -9-0[0] AlexisBadel 2 86
(J-M Beguigne, France) **7/1**
5 nse **Achalas (IRE)**[15] 4460 4 -8-13[0] MatthieuAutier(3) 6 82
(Heather Main) *hld up towards rr on ins: rdn bef st: swtchd away fr rails and r.o u.p ent fnl f: fin wl: jst failed to get up for 4th* **32/1**
6 3 1/2 **Aspasia De Mileto**[18] 4386 4 -8-10[0] OlivierPeslier 3 76
(C Laffon-Parias, France) **19/5**[3]
7 1/2 **Staros (IRE)**[100] 4 -9-0[0] Pierre-CharlesBoudot 9 75
(E Lellouche, France) **63/10**
8 3 **Voie Romaine (FR)**[32] 5 -8-7[0] JulienGuillochon(6) 7 74
(Mme V Seignoux, France) **33/1**
9 snk **Young Poli (FR)**[99] 5700 9 -8-11[0] NadegeOuakli 8 72
(Robert Collet, France) **44/1**

2m 42.5s (4.60) 9Ran SP% 118.6
WIN (incl. 1 euro stake): 4.60. PLACES: 1.90, 2.50, 1.40. DF: 34.80. SF: 86.40 .
Owner WH Sport International **Bred** Stall Parthenaue **Trained** Germany

[4669] DEL MAR (L-H)
Thursday, August 9
OFFICIAL GOING: Polytrack: fast

5031a SORRENTO STKS (GRADE 3) (2YO FILLIES) (POLYTRACK) 6f 110y
1:10 (12:00) 2-Y-O £58,064 (£19,354; £11,612 ; £5,806 ; £1,935)

RPR
1 **Executiveprivilege (USA)**[26] 2 -8-11[0] RBejarano 6 104
(Bob Baffert, U.S.A) **2/5**[1]
2 1 1/4 **Speedinthruthecity (USA)**[26] 2 -8-7[0] (b) JTalamo 5 96
(Peter Miller, U.S.A) **77/10**[3]
3 2 1/2 **Switch To The Lead (USA)** 2 -8-7[0] (b) YuichiFukunaga 7 89
(Patrick L Biancone, U.S.A) **103/10**
4 hd **Renee's Titan (USA)** 2 -8-6[0] ow1 CNakatani 2 88
(Doug O'Neill, U.S.A) **141/10**
5 2 3/4 **Somethingabouther (USA)** 2 -8-7[0] MESmith 4 81
(James Cassidy, U.S.A) **39/1**
6 2 1/4 **Wittgenstein (IRE)**[36] 3764 2 -8-5[0] MGarcia 3 72
(Brian Meehan) *taken bk and hld up last in detached fnl pair: rdn to try and improve over 2f out: stl last 1f out: plugged on to go 6th cl home: nvr a factor* **37/1**
7 1 **O Happy Gray (USA)**[36] 2 -8-7[0] (b) VEspinoza 1 71
(Mike Harrington, U.S.A) **46/1**
8 6 3/4 **Bares Tripper (USA)** 2 -8-5[0] GKGomez 8 50
(Peter Miller, U.S.A) **68/10**[2]

1m 16.98s (76.98) 8Ran SP% 118.5
PARI-MUTUEL (all including $2 stakes): WIN 2.80; PLACE (1-2) 2.20, 4.40; SHOW (1-2-3) 2.10, 3.40, 4.00; DF 5.80 SF 7.60 .
Owner Karl Watson, Michael E Pegram & Paul Weitman **Bred** Betz, D J Stable et al **Trained** USA

[4980] BRIGHTON (L-H)
Friday, August 10
OFFICIAL GOING: Good to firm (good in places; 7.6)
Rail dolled out from 6f to 4.5f but distances as advertised.
Wind: light, across Weather: sunny and warm

5032 BRITISH STALLION STUDS SUPPORTING BRITISH RACING E B F MAIDEN STKS 5f 213y
2:10 (2:10) (Class 5) 2-Y-O £3,169 (£943; £471 ; £235)Stalls Centre

Form RPR
53 1 **Hajam**[27] 4101 2 -9-3[0] MartinDwyer 7 93+
(James Tate) *chsd ldng pair: pushed along and hdwy over 2f out: led over 1f out: sn clr and r.o wl: easily* **13/2**[3]
063 2 7 **Imperial Spirit**[8] 4724 2 -9-3[0] MatthewDavies 1 70
(Mick Channon) *dwlt: sn rcvrd to chse ldr: rdn and pressing ldrs whn sltly squeezed over 1f out: chsd clr wnr and wl hld after: plugged on* **10/3**[2]
24 3 2 1/4 **Bornean (IRE)**[41] 3611 2 -9-3[0] MickaelBarzalona 4 62
(Mahmood Al Zarooni) *sn dropped to last trio: pushed along and nvr gng wl: rdn and sme hdwy 2f out: hanging lft fr over 1f out: wnt modest 3rd ins fnl f: nvr trbld ldrs* **11/10**[1]
3235 4 3 3/4 **Boleyn**[7] 4752 2 -8-9[68] HarryBentley(3) 5 45
(Richard Hannon) *chsd ldng pair tl over 2f out: sn hanging rt u.p: wknd and no ch fnl 2f* **9/1**
3203 5 1 **Dust Whirl**[25] 4148 2 -9-3[81] (b[1]) PatDobbs 6 47
(Richard Hannon) *led and racd freely in clr ld: rdn and hdd over 1f out: immediately btn and fdd fnl f* **9/1**
0 6 2 1/2 **Whiskey N Stout (IRE)** 4873 2 -9-3[0] FergusSweeney 2 39
(Jamie Osborne) *s.i.s: a bhd: nvr on terms* **50/1**
00 7 6 **Karr Wa Farr (IRE)** 4773 2 -9-3[0] TedDurcan 3 20
(Ed Vaughan) *sn outpcd in last trio: wl bhd fnl 2f* **25/1**

1m 9.58s (-0.62) **Going Correction** -0.05s/f (Good) 7Ran SP% 109.8
Speed ratings (Par 94): **102,92,89,84,83 80,72**
Tote Swingers: 1&2 £4.70, 1&3 £2.50, 2&3 £1.20 CSF £26.08 TOTE £11.10 : £3.90 , £2.00 ; EX 29.30.

Owner Saif Ali **Bred** Rabbah Bloodstock Limited **Trained** Newmarket, Suffolk

FOCUS

A modest juvenile maiden but the winner scored easily and could be rated 5lb higher.

NOTEBOOK

Hajam got stuck in the mud when disappointing at Haydock on his second start, but this son of Exceed And Excel was a different proposition on the better ground and he was in no danger through the final furlong. He looks a big, scopey colt and his rider reported afterwards that he didn't really handle the track, so he looks capable of plenty more improvement on a galloping track. (op 15-2 tchd 6-1)

Imperial Spirit is a fair guide to the strength of the form. He had every chance but was blown away in the final furlong and lacks the scope of the winner. (op 9-2)

Bornean(IRE) had the form to win this, but he could never get in a blow from off the pace and the writing was on the wall some way out for his backers. He didn't look very happy on the track but he has run here before so it might not pay to make too many excuses. (op 10-11)

Boleyn isn't progressing and is going to remain vulnerable in this company. (op 17-2 tchd 8-1)

Dust Whirl went off way too fast in the first time blinkers and unsurprisingly didn't get home. (op 17-2)

5033 CHECKATRADE H'CAP — 5f 59y

2:40 (2:40) (Class 6) (0-60,59) 3-Y-O+ — **£1,617** (£481; £240; £120) **Stalls** Centre

Form — RPR

5466 **1** **Imaginary Diva**^{17} 4439 6-9-1 **56** RyanPowell$^{(3)}$ 6 — 64
(George Margarson) *hld up in tch in last: rdn and hdwy over 1f out: drvn and ev ch ins fnl f: r.o wl to ld last stride* **6/1**^{3}

4362 **2** *shd* **Funcheon Vale (IRE)**^{15} 4489 3-9-3 **58** DarryllHolland 2 — 65
(Hughie Morrison) *taken down early: led: rdn over 1f out: hrd pressed: drvn and battled on gamely fnl f tl hdd last stride* **13/8**^{1}

11-6 **3** *3/4* **Lucky Royale**^{210} 148 4-9-4 **59** RaulDaSilva$^{(3)}$ 1 — 64
(Jeremy Gask) *t.k.h: chsd ldrs: wnt 2nd 2f out: rdn and ev ch 1f out: no ex and btn fnl 50yds* **3/1**^{2}

0650 **4** *1 1/2* **Uncle Timmy**^{8} 4734 3-9-1 **56** (vt^{1}) NeilCallan 4 — 55
(David Evans) *in tch: rdn over 2f out: chsd ldng trio and styd on same pce u.p fnl f* **17/2**

5561 **5** *4 1/2* **Simple Rhythm**^{11} 4663 6-8-13 **51** 6ex (p) DaraghO'Donohoe 5 — 35
(John Ryan) *chsd ldrs: rdn ent fnl 2f: unable qck and drvn over 1f out: wknd fnl f* **13/2**

3305 **6** *1/2* **Chicarito**^{43} 3540 3-8-7 **55** (p) WilliamTwiston-Davies$^{(7)}$ 3 — 36
(John Gallagher) *chsd ldr tl 2f out: rdn and no ex over 1f out: wknd fnl f* **11/1**

1m 2.82s (0.52) **Going Correction** -0.05s/f (Good) — **6** Ran SP% **109.6**
WFA 3 from 4yo+ 3lb
Speed ratings (Par 101): **93,92,91,89,82 81**
Tote Swingers: 1&2 £1.20, 1&3 £3.60, 2&3 £1.40 CSF £15.47 TOTE £4.90: £2.70, £1.40; EX 15.60.
Owner Graham Lodge Partnership **Bred** Norcroft Park Stud **Trained** Newmarket, Suffolk

FOCUS

A weak sprint handicap but the form is straightforward with the first three close to their marks.

5034 JIMMY HEAL MEMORIAL (S) STKS — 5f 213y

3:10 (3:10) (Class 6) 3-Y-O+ — **£1,617** (£481; £240; £120) **Stalls** Centre

Form — RPR

6026 **1** **Efistorm**^{4} 4887 11-9-2 71 DarrenEgan$^{(5)}$ 3 — 64
(Joseph Tuite) *chsd ldrs: rdn to ld over 1f out: edgd rt ins fnl f: styd on and a doing enough towards fin* **11/4**^{2}

0000 **2** *nk* **Stonecrabstomorrow (IRE)**^{22} 4238 9-8-11 58 MarkCoumbe$^{(5)}$ 5 — 58
(Michael Attwater) *s.i.s: sn detached in last: hdwy u.p over 1f out: pressing wnr and carried sltly rt ins fnl f: kpt on but hld towards fin* **20/1**^{3}

400 **3** *2 1/2* **Toms River Tess (IRE)**^{1} 4981 4-8-8 38 SimonPearce$^{(3)}$ 2 — 45
(Zoe Davison) *led: rdn over 2f out: drvn and hdd over 1f out: no ex and btn fnl 100yds* **50/1**

6103 **4** *1/2* **Kingswinford (IRE)**^{15} 4508 6-9-0 80 WilliamTwiston-Davies$^{(7)}$ 4 — 53
(David Evans) *chsd ldr: upsides over 2f out: drvn and nt qckn over 1f out: plugged on same pce fnl f* **1/1**^{1}

0064 **5** *4* **Crown Dependency (IRE)**^{9} 4705 3-8-12 84 PatDobbs 1 — 36
(Richard Hannon) *stdd s: hld up in tch: effrt on inner over 1f out: rdn and fnd little ent fnl f: wknd ins fnl f* **11/4**^{2}

1m 10.33s (0.13) **Going Correction** -0.05s/f (Good) — **5** Ran SP% **110.1**
WFA 3 from 4yo+ 4lb
Speed ratings (Par 101): **97,96,93,92,87**
CSF £40.98 TOTE £4.40: £2.00, £2.10; EX 23.90.The winner was bought in for 5,500gns.
Owner Andrew Liddiard **Bred** E Duggan And D Churchman **Trained** Great Shefford, Berks

FOCUS

A weak seller in which the time and the third set a very moderate standard.

Kingswinford(IRE) Official explanation: trainer's rep said gelding was unsuited by the track

5035 TALK TO VICTOR BRIGHTON BULLET H'CAP — 5f 213y

3:40 (3:40) (Class 4) (0-80,80) 3-Y-O+ **£6,301** (£1,886; £943; £472; £235) **Stalls** Centre

Form — RPR

4-22 **1** **Prodigality**^{14} 4554 4-9-5 **78** DarrenEgan$^{(5)}$ 3 — 91+
(Ronald Harris) *hld up in tch and travelled wl: hdwy to chse ldrs over 1f out: rdn and effrt to chal ins fnl f: led fnl 75yds: r.o wl and gng away at fin* **2/1**^{1}

4540 **2** *2* **Yurituni**^{22} 4231 5-9-7 **75** (b) CathyGannon 1 — 82
(Eve Johnson Houghton) *taken down early: led: rdn over 1f out: hdd fnl 75yds: sn outpcd and brushed aside by wnr: kpt on for clr 2nd* **20/1**

5050 **3** *1 3/4* **Courageous (IRE)**^{19} 4367 6-9-10 **78** MircoDemuro 9 — 79
(Milton Bradley) *stdd after s: hld up in last quartet: effrt on outer jst over 1f out: styd on wl fnl f to go 3rd towards fin: no threat to wnr* **10/1**^{3}

0-64 **4** *nk* **Commandingpresence (USA)**^{6} 4815 6-8-11 **65** KieranO'Neill 15 — 65
(John Bridger) *in tch: effrt u.p over 1f out: kpt on to go 3rd ins fnl f: no imp after: lost 3rd towards fin* **40/1**

5021 **5** *1 1/4* **Night Trade (IRE)**^{17} 4420 5-9-5 **76** (p) RaulDaSilva$^{(3)}$ 11 — 72+
(Ronald Harris) *hld up in last trio: switching to inner and hdwy wl over 1f out: nt clr run 1f out: kpt on but no threat to wnr fnl f* **16/1**

1200 **6** *nse* **Avonmore Star**^{6} 4824 4-9-5 **80** WilliamTwiston-Davies$^{(7)}$ 2 — 76
(Richard Hannon) *chsd ldrs tl wnt 2nd over 2f out: upsides ldr and gng wl 2f out: rdn and unable qck over 1f out: wknd fnl 150yds* **11/1**

4412 **7** *3/4* **Another Citizen (IRE)**^{4} 4887 4-8-9 **63** (b) TedDurcan 5 — 56
(Tim Easterby) *in tch in midfield: drvn and unable qck over 1f out: styd on same pce and wl hld fnl f* **3/1**^{2}

3000 **8** *1* **We Have A Dream**^{6} 4824 7-9-11 **79** MartinDwyer 10 — 69
(William Muir) *chsd ldr tl wl over 2f out: sn drvn and unable qck: wknd fnl f* **18/1**

640- **9** *1* **Billion Dollar Kid**^{241} 7130 7-8-9 **68** (t) MarkCoumbe$^{(5)}$ 4 — 55
(Jo Davis) *in tch in midfield: rdn over 2f out: no imp u.p over 1f out: wknd fnl f* **40/1**

1130 **10** *1 1/4* **Legal Legacy**^{58} 3045 6-9-8 **76** AmirQuinn 13 — 59
(Richard Rowe) *hld up in rr: effrt and sme hdwy on inner over 1f out: no imp 1f out: wknd ins fnl f* **20/1**

1323 **11** *shd* **Aye Aye Digby (IRE)**^{29} 4000 7-9-9 **77** HayleyTurner 14 — 60
(Patrick Chamings) *in tch in midfield: lost pl and towards rr whn rdn 2f out: no imp* **10/1**^{3}

3040 **12** *2 1/4* **Dasho**^{42} 3557 4-9-4 **72** (b^{1}) NeilCallan 8 — 48
(Gay Kelleway) *chsd ldrs: rdn and unable qck 2f out: btn and lost pl over 1f out: wknd fnl f* **20/1**

2140 **13** *2 3/4* **Drawnfromthepast (IRE)**^{127} 1204 7-9-9 **77** FergusSweeney 7 — 44
(Jamie Osborne) *hld up towards rr: rdn and effrt 2f out: no prog: wknd and bhd fnl f* **20/1**

0060 **14** *7* **Mac Gille Eoin**^{30} 2060 [illegible] **77** DarryllHolland 12 — 21
(John Gallagher) *styd wd: dwlt: a in rr and struggling: rdn and no rspnse over 2f out: bhd and eased fnl f* **16/1**

1m 9.1s (-1.10) **Going Correction** -0.05s/f (Good) — **14** Ran SP% **125.8**
Speed ratings (Par 105): **105,102,100,99,97 97,96,95,94,92 92,89,85,76**
Tote Swingers: 1&2 £15.40, 1&3 £6.10, 2&3 £25.60 CSF £54.08 CT £356.87 TOTE £2.40: £1.20, £6.90, £3.40; EX 57.30 Trifecta £569.80 Pool: £1,178.24 - 1.53 winning units..
Owner Paul Moulton **Bred** Darley **Trained** Earlswood, Monmouths

FOCUS

A competitive race and a progressive winner who can do better, while the runner-up sets the standard.

Mac Gille Eoin Official explanation: jockey said horse was unsettled and hung left throughout

5036 AMPLICON DIRECTORS' H'CAP — 7f 214y

4:10 (4:10) (Class 5) (0-70,70) 3-Y-O — **£2,264** (£673; £336; £168) **Stalls** Centre

Form — RPR

-021 **1** **Dance For Georgie**^{7} 4771 3-8-3 **55** 6ex DeclanCannon$^{(3)}$ 5 — 70+
(Ben Haslam) *mde all: rdn and readily wnt clr wl over 1f out: wl in command after: eased towards fin: comf* **9/4**^{1}

031 **2** *4* **Siouxperhero (IRE)**^{14} 4544 3-9-4 **67** MartinDwyer 8 — 72
(William Muir) *chsd wnr thrght: rdn over 2f out: outpcd by wnr wl over 1f out: no ch w wnr but kpt on to hold 2nd fnl f* **8/1**

-356 **3** *1* **Gold Sceptre (FR)**^{15} 4511 3-9-5 **68** (b) PatDobbs 1 — 71
(Richard Hannon) *chsd ldrs: rdn ent fnl 2f: hrd rdn in 3rd and no ch w wnr over 1f out: plugged on same pce after* **13/2**

5502 **4** *1 1/4* **Al's Memory (IRE)**^{13} 4583 3-9-4 **67** ShaneKelly 7 — 67
(David Evans) *t.k.h: hld up in tch: rdn and effrt over 2f out: outpcd wl over 1f out: wl btn 1f out: plugged on u.p fnl f* **6/1**^{3}

1645 **5** *1/2* **Manomine**^{73} 2583 3-9-3 **66** (b) NeilCallan 2 — 65
(Clive Brittain) *in tch: rdn and unable qck over 2f out: outpcd and btn wl over 1f out: plugged on same pce after* **11/1**

5220 **6** *1* **Good Luck Charm**^{18} 4413 3-9-6 **69** FergusSweeney 6 — 65
(Gary Moore) *stdd s: t.k.h: hld up in last trio: swtchd rt wl over 2f out: effrt u.p 2f out: 4th and btn 1f out: plugged on same pce after* **11/4**^{2}

0000 **7** *9* **Invincible Dream (IRE)**^{30} 3966 3-7-13 **53** JemmaMarshall$^{(5)}$ 3 — 29
(Pat Phelan) *stdd s: hld up in rr: hdwy on outer over 3f out: sn rdn: hld hd high and no hdwy 2f out: wknd over 1f out* **33/1**

2005 **8** *4 1/2* **Oratorian (IRE)**^{21} 4288 3-9-7 **70** CathyGannon 4 — 35
(Sylvester Kirk) *hld up in last trio: rdn and effrt over 2f out: sn struggling: wknd over 1f out: bhd fnl f* **18/1**

1m 34.97s (-1.03) **Going Correction** -0.05s/f (Good) — **8** Ran SP% **112.7**
Speed ratings (Par 100): **103,99,98,96,96 95,86,81**
Tote Swingers: 1&2 £2.50, 1&3 £3.80, 2&3 £4.90 CSF £20.32 CT £101.12 TOTE £3.10: £1.40, £1.60, £1.70; EX 14.60 Trifecta £33.30 Pool: £1,317.07 - 29.22 winning units..
Owner Mrs Alison Royston **Bred** West Dereham Abbey Stud **Trained** Middleham Moor, N Yorks

FOCUS

A moderate handicap and straightforward form rated around the placed horses.

5037 RENDEZVOUS CASINO BRIGHTON MARINA H'CAP — 1m 1f 209y

4:40 (4:41) (Class 6) (0-60,60) 3-Y-O — **£1,617** (£481; £240; £120) **Stalls** Centre

Form — RPR

0606 **1** **Scarlett Fever**^{15} 4490 3-8-11 **50** (b^{1}) ShaneKelly 7 — 59
(Marcus Tregoning) *hld up towards rr: swtchd to outer and effrt whn sltly hmpd 2f out: ev ch u.p ins fnl f: drvn and kpt on to ld on post* **16/1**

-055 **2** *nse* **Operation Tracer**^{13} 4583 3-9-5 **58** HayleyTurner 13 — 67
(Michael Bell) *stdd s: hld up towards rr: rdn and hdwy whn swtchd lft over 1f out: styd on u.p and ev ch ins fnl f: hrd drvn to ld towards fin: hdd on post* **4/1**^{1}

0-00 **3** *hd* **Frosty Secret**^{43} 3543 3-9-7 **60** MartinDwyer 3 — 68
(Jane Chapple-Hyam) *in tch in midfield: effrt u.p on inner over 2f out: drvn to ld ins fnl f: kpt on wl tl hdd and no ex towards fin* **16/1**

-050 **4** *4* **Garzoni**^{13} 4586 3-9-7 **60** NeilCallan 5 — 60
(Sir Mark Prescott Bt) *led: rdn 2f out: edgd rt u.p jst over 1f out: hdd fnl 150yds: sn btn and wknd towards fin* **6/1**^{2}

00-0 **5** *nk* **Awesome Rock (IRE)**^{43} 3548 3-8-2 **46** oh1 DarrenEgan$^{(5)}$ 2 — 46
(Louise Best) *t.k.h: hld up in rr: stl last 2f out: hdwy over 1f out: styd on ins fnl f: nvr trbld ldrs* **50/1**

3634 **6** *nk* **Thecornishcowboy**^{2} 4940 3-9-0 **53** (tp) DaraghO'Donohoe 1 — 52
(John Ryan) *in tch in midfield: rdn 3f out: no imp u.p over 1f out: styd on same pce and wl hld fnl f* **4/1**^{1}

0550 **7** *3 1/2* **Bramshill Lass**^{20} 4335 3-9-5 **58** (v) DarryllHolland 6 — 50
(Amanda Perrett) *in tch in midfield: rdn and effrt to press ldrs 3f out: nt qckning and wandering u.p 2f out: wkng whn pushed lft and hmpd over 1f out: no ch fnl f* **12/1**

0635 **8** *1* **Essell**^{15} 4490 3-9-6 **59** PatCosgrave 8 — 49
(Mick Channon) *t.k.h: chsd ldr for 2f: styd in tch: rdn and chsd ldr again over 2f out tl no ex u.p over 1f out: fdd ins fnl f* **8/1**^{3}

6-0 **9** *9* **Gucci D'Oro (USA)**^{85} 2197 3-9-5 **58** MartinLane 4 — 30+
(David Simcock) *t.k.h: hld up in midfield: dropped to rr and rdn over 2f out: no prog and wknd over 1f out: wl btn and eased ins fnl f* **4/1**^{1}

0005 **10** *2* **Denton Dancer**^{17} 4440 3-9-1 **54** CathyGannon 12 — 22
(James Eustace) *t.k.h: chsd ldrs: wnt 2nd 8f out tl 5f out: rdn over 2f out: styng on same pce and btn whn hmpd jst over 1f out: btn and eased fnl f* **16/1**

0500 **11** *14* **Petersboden**^{22} 4232 3-8-11 **50** (p) FergusSweeney 9
(Michael Blanshard) *t.k.h: hld up in tch: rdn over 2f out: wknd qckly over 1f out: wl bhd and eased fnl f: t.o* **33/1**

-050 **12** *1 1/2* **Dark Celt (IRE)**^{101} 1726 3-8-4 **46** oh1 RyanPowell$^{(3)}$ 11
(Michael Madgwick) *stdd s: t.k.h: hld up in rr tl hdwy to chse ldr 5f out tl over 2f out: sn dropped out: wl bhd and eased fnl f: t.o* **22/1**

2m 3.13s (-0.47) **Going Correction** -0.05s/f (Good) — **12** Ran SP% **120.0**
Speed ratings (Par 98): **99,98,98,95,95 95,92,91,84,82 71,70**
Tote Swingers: 1&2 £13.30, 1&3 £31.20, 2&3 £17.70 CSF £78.83 CT £1072.64 TOTE £18.10: £3.90, £1.60, £6.10; EX 75.70 TRIFECTA Not won..
Owner The O D's **Bred** Heather Raw **Trained** Lambourn, Berks

FOCUS
A messy race and not that convincing, despite the first three running close to their maiden form.
Scarlett Fever Official explanation: trainer's rep said, regarding apparent improvement in form, that the filly had benefited for the first time blinkers and step up in trip.
Denton Dancer Official explanation: jockey said gelding ran too free
Dark Celt(IRE) Official explanation: jockey said gelding ran too free

5038 TEENAGE CANCER TRUST H'CAP — 1m 3f 196y
5:10 (5:13) (Class 6) (0-65,65) 3-Y-O+ — **£1,617** (£481; £240; £120) **Stalls** Centre

Form / RPR

241 **1** **Laser Blazer**[15] 4491 4-9-10 **61**....(p) MircoDemuro 2 68+
(Jeremy Gask) *v.s.a: wl detached in last but grad clsd: in tch 5f out: rdn and effrt jst over 2f out: 5th and stl plenty to 1f out: styd on strly to ld fnl 50yds* **13/8**[1]

-650 **2** ½ **Squad**[15] 4504 6-9-10 **61**....(v) NeilCallan 6 67
(Simon Dow) *hld up in tch: rdn and effrt in centre over 2f out: pressing ldrs ins fnl f: edgd rt but styd on to go 2nd towards fin* **9/1**

5003 **3** 1 **Thundering Home**[22] 4244 5-9-4 **55**.... HayleyTurner 8 59
(Richard Mitchell) *stdd s: hld up in rr of main gp: rdn and hdwy on inner over 2f out: drvn to ld jst over 1f out: hdd and ex fnl 50yds* **9/1**

4201 **4** 1¾ **Before Bruce**[14] 4536 5-9-7 **65**....(b[1]) ThomasGarner(7) 7 67
(Brendan Powell) *chsd ldr tl led 9f out: rdn jst over 2f out: drvn and hdd jst over 1f out: wknd fnl 100yds* **11/1**

646- **5** 3¼ **Soundbyte**[12] 7363 7-9-5 **63**.... WilliamTwiston-Davies(7) 3 59
(John Gallagher) *hld up in tch: reminders over 4f out: sn rdn and struggling: no ch but plugged on past btn horses fnl f* **10/1**

45/0 **6** 2¼ **Beggar's Opera (IRE)**[11] 3620 5-9-13 **64**....(t) PatCosgrave 4 57
(Jim Best) *led tl 9f out: styd on chsng ldrs: rdn over 3f out: drvn and btn jst over 1f out: wknd fnl f* **28/1**

32-0 **7** 15 **Astroleo**[15] 4491 6-8-13 **50**.... DarryllHolland 10 19
(Mark H Tompkins) *chsd ldrs: rdn to chse ldr over 3f out tl ent fnl 2f: sn wknd: wl btn and eased ins fnl f* **9/2**[2]

-300 **8** 5 **Penang Cinta**[45] 3468 9-9-6 **57**....(v) CathyGannon 1 18
(David Evans) *in tch: rdn and fnd little over 2f out: sn bhd: wl btn and eased ins fnl f* **8/1**[3]

100 **9** 19 **Autarch (USA)**[15] 4504 3-9-2 **64**....(p) MartinDwyer 9
(Amanda Perrett) *chsd ldrs: wnt 2nd 8f out tl over 3f out: sn dropped out u.p: t.o and virtually p.u ins fnl f* **9/1**

2m 32.54s (-0.16) **Going Correction** -0.05s/f (Good)
WFA 3 from 4yo+ 11lb — **9** Ran SP% **118.3**
Speed ratings (Par 101): **98,97,97,95,93 92,82,78,66**
Tote Swingers: 1&2 £4.50, 1&3 £4.40, 2&3 £13.10 CSF £17.96 CT £105.54 TOTE £2.70: £1.30, £2.90, £3.20; EX 19.30 Trifecta £288.00 Pool: £1,381.94 - 3.55 winning units..
Owner Calne Engineering Ltd **Bred** Edward J G Young **Trained** Sutton Veny, Wilts

FOCUS
An uninspiring contest rated at face value, although the winner rates value for a good deal further.
T/Jkpt: Not won. T/Plt: £420.00 to a £1 stake. Pool: £62,753.03 - 109.05 winning tickets. T/Qpdt: £51.00 to a £1 stake. Pool: £4,869.02 - 70.62 winning tickets. SP

4995 HAYDOCK (L-H)
Friday, August 10

OFFICIAL GOING: Good (good to firm in places; 8.7)
Stands Side track used with Stalls on Far Side except 10f: Centre.
Wind: Nil Weather: Hot and Fine

5039 BETDAQ HAYDOCK PARK APPRENTICE TRAINING SERIES H'CAP (PART OF THE RACING EXCELLENCE INITIATIVE) — 1m 3f 200y
5:50 (5:50) (Class 5) (0-75,73) 4-Y-O+ — **£2,264** (£673; £336; £168) **Stalls** High

Form / RPR

0124 **1** **Call Of Duty (IRE)**[4] 4864 7-9-3 **66**.... GarryWhillans 5 73
(Dianne Sayer) *racd keenly: hld up: hdwy over 3f out: sn chalng: led over 2f out: rdn and edgd rt over 1f out: strly pressed wl ins fnl f: all out* **15/8**[2]

3-23 **2** shd **Dancing Primo**[8] 4733 6-9-7 **73**.... JackDuern(3) 1 80
(Mark Brisbourne) *trckd ldrs: lost pl over 3f out: swtchd rt over 2f out: rallied and edgd rt wl over 1f out: wnt 2nd 1f out: str chal wl ins fnl f: r.o: jst denied* **13/8**[1]

6430 **3** 4½ **Amir Pasha (UAE)**[16] 4455 7-8-5 **54**....(p) ShaneBKelly 4 54
(Micky Hammond) *led after 1f at slow pce: increased tempo 3f out: rdn and hdd over 2f out: sn hung rt: stl ch over 1f out: no ex fnl 75yds* **17/2**

5254 **4** 2 **Tenhoo**[12] 4627 6-9-2 **68**.... DarylByrne(3) 2 65
(Eric Alston) *hld up: rdn wl over 1f out: no imp: one pce fnl f* **7/2**[3]

000/ **5** 7 **Lean Burn (USA)**[11] 7958 6-8-2 **54** oh9.... NatashaEaton(3) 6 39
(Barry Leavy) *led at slow pce for 1f: remained prom: chalng over 2f out: sn n.m.r and lost pl: wknd over 1f out* **22/1**

2m 34.15s (0.35) **Going Correction** -0.475s/f (Firm) — **5** Ran SP% **110.0**
Speed ratings (Par 103): **79,78,75,74,69**
CSF £5.31 TOTE £2.60: £1.50, £1.20; EX 4.10.
Owner T W Rebanks **Bred** Gainsborough Stud Management Ltd **Trained** Hackthorpe, Cumbria
■ Stewards' Enquiry : Garry Whillans two-day ban: used whip above permitted level (Aug 25-26)

FOCUS
Sunny, dry conditions for day two of this three-day fixture, with the inner home straight deployed in all six races and changes to the advertised race distances of all bar the 6f contest as a result. This modest apprentice handicap was run over 15 yards further than usual, and with Stock Hill Fair a late withdrawal it took even less winning than it might. The first two are rated to their best.

5040 JAY BUXTON STRIDES EQUESTRIAN 21ST CELEBRATION IRISH E B F MAIDEN STKS — 6f
6:20 (6:20) (Class 5) 2-Y-O — **£3,234** (£962; £481; £240) **Stalls** Centre

Form / RPR

1 **Ribaat (IRE)** 2-9-3 0.... PaulHanagan 7 86+
(Roger Varian) *racd keenly: hld up: clsd into midfield 3f out: effrt and r.o to chal whn hung lft fr jst over 1f out: led ins fnl f: readily* **6/4**[1]

0 **2** 2¼ **Seven Of Clubs (IRE)**[14] 4539 2-9-3 0.... PJMcDonald 5 76
(Noel Quinlan) *trckd ldrs: rdn to chal 2f out: led jst over 1f out: hdd ins fnl f: outpcd by wnr fnl 75yds* **8/1**

0 **3** 2¼ **Caramack**[35] 3824 2-9-3 0.... RichardHughes 1 70
(Richard Hannon) *led: rdn and hdd jst over 1f out: no ex ins fnl 100yds* **10/3**[2]

4 1½ **Layla's Oasis** 2-8-12 0.... StephenCraine 9 60+
(Kevin Ryan) *prom: chalng 2f out: rdn and nt qckn over 1f out: checked whn sltly intimidated ins fnl f: kpt on same pce after* **25/1**

5 nk **Dutiful Son (IRE)** 2-9-3 0.... MartinHarley 10 64+
(Jeremy Noseda) *midfield: hdwy 3f out: rdn to chal 2f out: kpt on same pce ins fnl f* **11/2**[3]

30 **6** 1¾ **Municipal (IRE)**[14] 4545 2-9-3 0.... TonyHamilton 4 59
(Michael Dods) *midfield: rdn 2f out: outpcd over 1f out: nvr able to chal* **20/1**

5 **7** nk **Mysterious Wonder**[51] 3271 2-9-3 0.... RenatoSouza 8 58
(Peter Salmon) *hld up: niggled along 3f out: kpt on ins fnl f: nvr able to get competitive* **9/1**

8 5 **Noble Bacchus (IRE)** 2-9-3 0.... RichardKingscote 11 43
(Tom Dascombe) *in rr: rdn 2f out: nvr a threat* **14/1**

0 **9** ½ **Hidden Asset**[24] 4173 2-9-3 0.... JoeFanning 3 41
(Michael Appleby) *prom: rdn 2f out: sn wknd* **40/1**

00 **10** 6 **Gambino (IRE)**[11] 4654 2-9-0 0.... PaulPickard(3) 2 23
(Hugh McWilliams) *hld up: effrt over 2f out: nvr able to get on terms w ldrs: wl btn over 1f out: eased ins fnl f* **200/1**

0 **11** 47 **Hazard Warning (IRE)**[20] 4344 2-9-3 0.... DavidAllan 6
(Tim Easterby) *s.i.s: sn hung bdly lft: wl bhd: hung rt over 4f out: hung lft again 2f out: eased over 1f out: t.o* **66/1**

1m 13.21s (-0.59) **Going Correction** -0.225s/f (Firm) — **11** Ran SP% **119.3**
Speed ratings (Par 94): **94,91,88,86,85 83,82,76,75,67 4**
toteswingers: 1&2 £3.20, 1&3 £2.00, 2&3 £5.70 CSF £14.24 TOTE £2.60: £1.30, £2.80, £1.40; EX 17.60.
Owner Hamdan Al Maktoum **Bred** F Dunne **Trained** Newmarket, Suffolk

FOCUS
A maiden which proved a good test at the trip, with a deal of pace on from the outset. The race is rated around the time and race averages.

NOTEBOOK
Ribaat(IRE) was securing Roger Varian a fourth winner from as many juvenile runners at this venue, and this extensively entered-up individual duly obliged while still looking a little way off the finished article. Nicely covered up until inside the final 2f, this 280,000gns (yearling) son of Invincible Spirit hung markedly towards the inner once seeing clear daylight, crossing the outpaced Layla's Oasis and getting close to Seven Of Clubs, but nevertheless created a taking impression in winning going away. Connections noted afterwards that he may prefer conditions a little less lively underfoot. (tchd 13-8)

Seven Of Clubs(IRE) ◆ raced closer to the speed than on his Newmarket debut a fortnight earlier and looked wiser for that initial experience here, too. A routine sprint maiden looks a formality on this evidence. (op 10-1 tchd 11-1)

Caramack will need further than this in time, but his conspicuous display of early speed here suggests his immediate prospects remain best over sprint distances. (op 4-1 tchd 9-2)

Layla's Oasis got outpaced entering the final third of this contest.

Dutiful Son(IRE) didn't quite seem to know how to convert a promising position 2f out into a strong finish, but the experience won't be lost on this 150,000euros yearling purchase. (op 5-1)

Mysterious Wonder, turned over at 4-6 on his racecourse debut and sole start for Kevin Ryan, never looked at ease and has even more to prove now. (op 8-1 tchd 14-1 and 12-1 early)

5041 COUNTRYWIDE FREIGHT NURSERY — 6f
6:55 (6:56) (Class 4) (0-80,79) 2-Y-O — **£3,881** (£1,155; £577; £288) **Stalls** Centre

Form / RPR

3341 **1** **Capo Rosso (IRE)**[25] 4152 2-9-6 **78**.... RichardKingscote 4 84
(Tom Dascombe) *a.p: rdn over 2f out: led over 1f out: r.o gamely ins fnl f: kpt finding more towards fin* **4/1**[2]

4661 **2** nk **Tussie Mussie**[25] 4139 2-8-7 **65**.... JoeFanning 1 70
(Mark Johnston) *led: rdn and hdd over 1f out: continued to chal gamely ins fnl f: hld towards fin* **9/2**[3]

365 **3** 2¼ **Sejalaat (IRE)**[14] 4539 2-9-5 **77**.... PaulHanagan 6 75
(John Dunlop) *racd keenly: hld up: hdwy 2f out: chsd ldrs over 1f out: no ex fnl 50yds* **5/2**[1]

264P **4** nk **Cappadocia (IRE)**[15] 4502 2-8-10 **68**.... MartinHarley 7 65
(Mick Channon) *hld up: effrt 2f out: sn chsd ldrs: kpt on ins fnl f: nt pce to chal front two* **9/2**[3]

0200 **5** 2¼ **Amelia Jay**[11] 4637 2-8-6 **64** ow2.... PJMcDonald 8 55
(Danielle McCormick) *in rr: pushed along 2f out: kpt on for press towards fin: nvr able to trble ldrs* **33/1**

154 **6** 1¼ **Ingleby Royale**[71] 2630 2-9-3 **75**.... TonyHamilton 9 62
(Richard Fahey) *dipped at s: midfield: rdn 2f out: no imp over 1f out: one pce fnl f* **13/2**

0120 **7** 1¾ **Blue Lotus (IRE)**[13] 4614 2-9-7 **79**.... DavidAllan 2 62
(Tim Easterby) *prom: outpcd over 1f out: wl btn ins fnl f: eased fnl 50yds* **10/1**

5050 **8** 12 **Mace The Ace**[6] 4806 2-8-1 **59**....(b[1]) JamieMackay 5 5
(David C Griffiths) *plld hrd: trckd ldrs to 1/2-way: bhd fnl 2f* **50/1**

1m 13.75s (-0.05) **Going Correction** -0.225s/f (Firm) — **8** Ran SP% **112.3**
Speed ratings (Par 96): **91,90,87,87,84 82,80,64**
toteswingers 1&2 £3.90, 1&3 £4.00, 2&3 £1.80 CSF £21.46 CT £52.62 TOTE £5.20: £1.70, £1.70, £1.10; EX 28.90.
Owner Deva Racing Red Clubs Partnership **Bred** Michael Wiley **Trained** Malpas, Cheshire

FOCUS
A fairly competitive nursery, run at a fair pace initially but won in a time just over half a second slower than the preceding maiden. The form looks sound with the first two clear.

NOTEBOOK
Capo Rosso(IRE) translated his AW improvement back onto a natural surface with a gutsy display. Wresting a share of the lead having sat handy throughout proved the easy bit, but it took all his fighting reserves to battle the tenacious runner-up into submission. He can land another of these, with 6f continuing to look as far as he wants. (tchd 10-3)

Tussie Mussie had similarly come good switched to synthetics on her last outing, albeit over Southwell's Fibresand and in nursery company. She once again exhibited a tremendous appetite for a scrap, keeping Capo Rosso right to his work up to the line despite having helped cut out the early pace. Her bravery alone ought to secure her another one of these before long. (op 4-1)

Sejalaat(IRE) proved restless buried behind horses early on and showing more inclination to go left than forwards once asked to pick up with over a furlong to go. His handicap mark looks feasible enough, but this display leaves questions of temperament to answer now. (tchd 3-1)

Cappadocia(IRE), evidently none the worse for having pulled up and dismounted at Epsom a fortnight earlier, was closest at the finish. A seventh furlong looks required for him. (tchd 4-1)

Ingleby Royale has proven gently regressive since a winning debut, albeit set some stiff tasks. Even allowing for a nod at the start here, he may struggle off what looks a tough enough opening mark. (op 8-1)

Blue Lotus(IRE) offered insufficient immediate-term encouragement that this sixth furlong is what he needs to progress now. (op 11-1 tchd 12-1)

5042 BRITISH STALLION STUDS CHRIS FAYLE MEMORIAL E B F NOVICE STKS 7f
7:25 (7:25) (Class 4) 2-Y-0 **£4,528** (£1,347; £673; £336) **Stalls** Low

Form RPR
12 **1** **Tickle Time (IRE)**[22] 4247 2-9-4 0 GrahamGibbons 5 93
(David Barron) *racd w ldr: led narrowly 4f out: rdn and pressed ins fnl f: r.o gamely* **11/4**[2]
210 **2** ½ **Miss You Too**[15] 4514 2-8-13 87 [1] SamHitchcott 3 87
(Mick Channon) *racd keenly: trckd ldrs: checked whn n.m.r and trying to chal ins fnl 100yds: r.o cl home* **14/1**
3 *hd* **Twary (USA)** 2-8-10 0 PaulHanagan 4 83+
(Roger Varian) *s.i.s: rn green in rr: clsd to sit bhd ldrs over 4f out: effrt to chal over 1f out: r.o for press ins fnl f: jst hld* **5/1**[3]
1 **4** *nk* **Professor**[21] 4290 2-9-4 0 RichardHughes 1 91
(Richard Hannon) *racd keenly: led: hdd narrowly 4f out: continued to r w wnr: rdn whn stl chalng ins fnl f: no ex fnl strides* **4/6**[1]

1m 27.62s (-3.08) **Going Correction** -0.475s/f (Firm) 2y crse rec **4** Ran SP% **110.0**
Speed ratings (Par 96): **98,97,97,96**
CSF £26.32 TOTE £4.00; EX 23.40.
Owner Miss N J Barron **Bred** Pier House Stud **Trained** Maunby, N Yorks

FOCUS
A decent-looking novice event won in a new juvenile course record for 7f, albeit the race distance was closer to 6f 215yd. The early pace hadn't looked that exceptional despite the eventual quick time, and a rather messy finish ensued. Despite that the form looks reasonably straightforward.

NOTEBOOK
Tickle Time(IRE) avoided the worst of the problems around him to hold on, despite edging slightly left towards the runner-up in the dying strides. A half-brother to Angelic Upstart, a 2-y-o winner over a mile as well as today's trip, rider Graham Gibbons is in no doubt that the Kheleyf gelding will need the additional furlong. (op 3-1)

Miss You Too ◆ was tanking with around two and a half to travel, but 2f later the gap to get her past or round the winner and eventual fourth still hadn't come. That she was still finding plenty once finally seeing daylight only adds to the impression that this was a luckless run and in all probability a winning chance gone begging. She is, at least, plainly up to striking in similar company next time. (op 10-1)

Twary(USA), the first foal of a 7f Group 2-winning dirt performer and entered in both the Champagne Stakes and Redcar's Two-Year-Old Trophy, overcame a tardy start and initial greenness to find plenty when asked late on. This was a good debut and it shouldn't be a problem to find him a maiden at this trip or even a furlong further. (tchd 6-1)

Professor seemed agitated by Richard Hughes taking a tug leaving the back straight, and while travelling strongly again halfway up the straight fell back through the field close home. He can prove better than this when allowed his own way again in future. (op 4-5)

5043 BETVICTOR.COM FILLIES' H'CAP 1m
8:00 (8:01) (Class 2) (0-100,92) 3-Y-O£9,955 (£2,979; £1,489; £745; £371) **Stalls** Low

Form RPR
-105 **1** **Lady Macduff (IRE)**[13] 4579 3-8-11 82 JoeFanning 6 91
(Mark Johnston) *chsd ldr: led over 1f out: sn rdn: kpt on ins fnl f: a doing enough towards fin* **9/1**
1162 **2** ¾ **Burke's Rock**[16] 4474 3-8-12 83 RichardHughes 4 90
(Jeremy Noseda) *chsd ldrs: rdn to chse wnr over 1f out: ev ch and styd on ins fnl f: a looked hld* **5/2**[1]
-620 **3** *1* **Tuscania**[6] 4805 4-9-6 84 FrederikTylicki 5 90
(Lucy Wadham) *midfield: rdn and hdwy over 1f out: styd on ins fnl f: nt quite able to chal ldrs* **16/1**
6211 **4** 2¼ **Magic Destiny**[29] 3991 3-8-9 80 MartinHarley 9 80
(Mrs K Burke) *hld up: nt clr run 3f out: rdn whn nt clr run over 2f out: effrt to chse ldrs over 1f out: styd on: no imp ins fnl f* **5/1**[3]
1000 **5** 1½ **Stellar Express (IRE)**[9] 4702 3-9-0 85 (p) GrahamGibbons 1 81
(Michael Appleby) *led: hdd over 1f out: sn rdn: hld whn n.m.r fnl 110yds: no ex* **25/1**
2235 **6** 2¼ **Ariyfa (IRE)**[9] 4702 4-9-4 82 PaulHanagan 8 73
(Noel Quinlan) *racd keenly in midfield: lost pl 2f out: no imp whn hung lft ins fnl f* **3/1**[2]
0050 **7** *5* **Fillionaire**[15] 4497 3-9-0 85 SamHitchcott 3 65
(Mick Channon) *chsd ldrs: pushed along over 3f out: rdn over 2f out: wknd over 1f out* **33/1**
5300 **8** *4* **Roger Sez (IRE)**[14] 4557 3-9-7 92 (p) DavidAllan 2 63
(Tim Easterby) *s.i.s: bhd: u.p fr 5f out: nvr a threat: wl btn fnl f* **20/1**
-025 **R** **Miss Azeza**[13] 4597 3-9-5 90 RichardKingscote 10
(David Simcock) *ref to r* **14/1**

1m 39.02s (-4.68) **Going Correction** -0.475s/f (Firm) course record
WFA 3 from 4yo 7lb **9** Ran SP% **104.3**
Speed ratings (Par 96): **104,103,102,100,98 96,91,87,**
toteswingers 1&2 £2.20, 1&3 £20.50, 2&3 £9.50 CSF £25.55 CT £259.93 TOTE £9.80: £2.20, £1.20, £3.70; EX 21.50.
Owner Sheikh Hamdan Bin Mohammed Al Maktoum **Bred** Mrs E Thompson **Trained** Middleham Moor, N Yorks

FOCUS
A competitive 0-100 fillies handicap, but at the same time one diminished by Miss Azeza's refusal to leave the stalls and Askaud's withdrawal after getting upset in them. The pace was good and the winning time fast, though this again was a race run over five yards shorter than usual. The form is rated slightly positively through the runner-up.

NOTEBOOK
Lady Macduff(IRE) was happy to take a tow from Stellar Express until committing with over a furlong to run and always answering Joe Fanning's every call thereafter. Her dam's side errs more towards sub-1m trips and, although not exactly stopping close home here, connections feel a drop back down to 7f wouldn't inconvenience. (op 8-1)

Burke's Rock never quite looked about to overhaul a rival in irresistible mood but posted a solid runner-up effort for the second race running nevertheless. Things went badly awry for her tried over 1m2f three starts previously, but splitting the difference and seeing if 1m1f can bring about a little further improvement might be the way to go now. (op 2-1)

Tuscania avenged the previous month's half-length Doncaster defeat by Magic Destiny on 5lb better terms, and may additionally have run first two home closer had she not been short of room inside the final furlong. This is an effort to mark up a touch.

Magic Destiny met with traffic issues of her own without them looking the difference between victory and defeat. Nevertheless, this is almost certainly as well as she's ever run away from her preferred easier surfaces. (op 11-2 tchd 6-1)

Ariyfa(IRE) under-performed here after pulling too hard early on. (op 9-2)

5044 LIVERPOOL ONE H'CAP 1m 3f 200y
8:30 (8:31) (Class 4) (0-80,80) 3-Y-O **£4,204** (£1,251; £625; £312) **Stalls** High

Form RPR
5221 **1** **Brockwell**[36] 3775 3-9-3 76 RichardKingscote 2 87
(Tom Dascombe) *in tch: wnt 2nd over 2f out: sn rdn: led jst ins fnl f: r.o and in command cl home* **11/4**[1]
-452 **2** ¾ **Aazif (IRE)**[13] 4601 3-9-7 80 PaulHanagan 8 89
(John Dunlop) *chsd ldrs: wnt 2nd over 4f out: led 3f out: rdn over 2f out: hdd jst ins fnl f: stl ev ch after: no ex cl home* **3/1**[2]
6242 **3** 2¾ **Deepsand (IRE)**[28] 4046 3-9-6 79 DavidAllan 3 84
(Tim Easterby) *hld up: rdn over 2f out: swtchd rt over 1f out: styd on ins fnl f: tk 3rd fnl 75yds: nt trble ldrs* **9/2**
0401 **4** 1½ **Now My Sun**[21] 4289 3-9-2 75 RichardHughes 4 78
(Mrs K Burke) *plld hrd: hld up: rdn 2f out: hdwy to chse ldrs over 1f out: no imp ins fnl f* **4/1**[3]
201- **5** 1½ **Snowed In (IRE)**[7] 7582 3-8-11 70 JoeFanning 1 70
(Jennie Candlish) *chsd ldr tl over 4f out: rdn and outpcd 2f out: wl btn fnl 100yds* **20/1**
1216 **6** *shd* **Dovils Date**[23] 4225 3-8-13 72 JamesMillman 7 72
(Rod Millman) *hld up in rr: outpcd over 3f out: kpt on ins fnl f: nvr able to trble ldrs* **8/1**
642 **7** 1¼ **Petaluma**[29] 4005 3-8-13 72 MartinHarley 5 70
(Mick Channon) *led: rdn and hdd 3f out: wknd over 1f out* **12/1**

2m 29.32s (-4.48) **Going Correction** -0.475s/f (Firm) **7** Ran SP% **113.4**
Speed ratings (Par 102): **95,94,92,91,90 90,89**
toteswingers: 1&2 £2.80, 1&3 £4.80, 2&3 £1.10 CSF £11.09 CT £34.35 TOTE £4.00: £2.20, £2.20; EX 13.40.
Owner South Wind Racing 3 **Bred** South Wind Bloodstock **Trained** Malpas, Cheshire

FOCUS
Another decent handicap for its grade and, like the opening apprentice race on the card, run over 15 yards further than usual. Following an early pace no worse than fair, the winner clocked in 4.8 seconds quicker than the earlier event. The third sets the standard backed up by the fourth.
T/Plt: £19.80 to a £1 stake. Pool: £47,588.61. 1,747.11 winning tickets. T/Qpdt: £12.90 to a £1 stake. Pool: £4,328.17. 246.60 winning tickets. DO

4812 LINGFIELD (L-H)
Friday, August 10

OFFICIAL GOING: Standard
Wind: Almost nil Weather: Sunny, very warm

5045 GREASE NIGHT HERE TOMORROW! NOVICE STKS 5f (P)
2:20 (2:20) (Class 5) 2-Y-O **£2,385** (£704; £352) **Stalls** High

Form RPR
1230 **1** **Hairy Rocket**[40] 3680 2-9-0 96 RyanMoore 5 98+
(Richard Hannon) *trckd ldr: led wl over 1f out: sn clr: rdn out* **1/5**[1]
1422 **2** 4½ **Ask The Guru**[28] 4045 2-9-5 95 (b[1]) JamesDoyle 1 88
(Ralph Beckett) *awkward s: in tch in last: shkn up 2f out: rdn to chse wnr jst over 1f out: no imp and pushed along last 100yds* **9/2**[2]
51 **3** *10* **Coconut Kisses**[118] 1388 2-8-7 70 JakePayne(7) 2 46
(Bill Turner) *led to wl over 1f out: wknd rapidly* **25/1**[3]

58.97s (0.17) **Going Correction** +0.175s/f (Slow) **3** Ran SP% **105.4**
Speed ratings (Par 94): **105,97,81**
CSF £1.37 TOTE £1.30; EX 1.10.
Owner Rockcliffe Stud **Bred** Rockcliffe Stud **Trained** East Everleigh, Wilts

FOCUS
This was straightforward for Hairy Rocket, who was basically much too good for her two rivals. The race could be 6lb out either way.

NOTEBOOK
Hairy Rocket had been highly tried since winning a Windsor maiden by 5l on her debut, most recently contesting a French Group 3 (beaten favourite, reportedly unsuited by quick ground), and this was her easiest task to date. A step back up in class awaits and she could be competitive in Pattern company provided conditions aren't too fast. (op 4-11)
Ask The Guru had to concede 5lb to the decent winner, but even so it's questionable whether he ran right up to his official mark of 95, the first-time blinkers seemingly not helping on this his Polytrack debut. (op 11-4)
Coconut Kisses looked a proper early season type when winning a Wolverhampton maiden on her second start in April, so it was a worry she'd been off since. According to her trainer she'd had "a cough and one or two niggles", and she showed little on this return to action. (op 16-1 tchd 28-1)

5046 FOLLOW US ON TWITTER @LINGFIELDPARK FILLIES' (S) STKS 6f (P)
2:50 (2:52) (Class 6) 2-Y-O **£1,704** (£503; £251) **Stalls** Low

Form RPR
0054 **1** **Alexandrakollontai (IRE)**[16] 4462 2-8-12 49 (b) LiamKeniry 9 55
(J S Moore) *pressed ldr: drvn over 1f out: styd on to ld last 100yds: jst hld on* **10/1**
00 **2** *hd* **Kimvara**[11] 4646 2-8-12 0 (b[1]) ChrisCatlin 7 54
(Joseph Tuite) *prog on outer to press ldrs after 2f: drvn 2f out: chal fnl f: styd on but jst hld* **33/1**
2305 **3** *1* **Napinda**[25] 4152 2-8-12 58 DavidProbert 2 51
(Des Donovan) *trckd ldrs: cl up 2f out: swtchd lft 1f out: kpt on to take 3rd nr fin* **5/2**[1]
53 **4** *nk* **Hardy Blue (IRE)**[11] 4659 2-8-7 0 LeonnaMayor(5) 5 51
(Jamie Osborne) *chsd ldrs: cl enough 2f out: nt qckn and drifted lft over 1f out: kpt on: fin 5th: plcd 4th* **11/4**[2]
0654 **5** *12* **Madam Moreton**[18] 4395 2-8-12 44 IanMongan 3 15
(George Margarson) *s.i.s: t.k.h: hld up: wknd 2f out: eased and t.o: fin 6th: plcd 5th* **25/1**
4 **6** 3¾ **Hippie Chick**[77] 2462 2-8-5 0 JakePayne(7) 6
(Bill Turner) *s.i.s: t.k.h and hld up: wknd 1/2-way: t.o: fin 7th: plcd 6th* **16/1**
006 **7** *31* **Casta Diamante**[13] 4581 2-8-7 40 (b[1]) JamesRogers(5) 8
(Ralph Beckett) *s.i.s: sn outpcd and bhd: wl t.o: fin 8th: plcd 7th* **25/1**
0016 **D** ½ **Grace Of Hearts**[11] 4659 2-9-3 59 (p) AndreaAtzeni 4 54
(Robert Eddery) *led: hrd pressed 2f out: drifted rt over 1f out: hdd & wknd last 100yds: fin 4th: disqualified and plcd last* **5/1**[3]

1m 14.08s (2.18) **Going Correction** +0.175s/f (Slow) **8** Ran SP% **97.5**
Speed ratings (Par 89): **92,91,90,89,73 68,27,89**
Tote Swingers: 1&2 £23.90, 1&3 £4.00, 2&3 £16.30 CSF £189.95 TOTE £8.80: £2.10, £7.80, £1.10; EX 157.40.No bid for the winner.
Owner Norton Common Farm Racing **Bred** Sean O'Sullivan **Trained** Upper Lambourn, Berks
■ Stewards' Enquiry : Andrea Atzeni three-day ban: failed to weigh-in (Aug 25-27)

FOCUS
A moderate contest, as you'd expect for a juvenile fillies' seller and not form to dwell on.

NOTEBOOK

Alexandrakollontai(IRE) was behind Grace Of Hearts over C&D last time, but she reversed that form and gained her first victory on her seventh start. She could struggle to defy a penalty at this level. (op 14-1)

Kimvara, dropped in grade and trip, plus fitted with blinkers for the first time, just failed after being forced to go widest of all into the straight. She might win a similar race. (op 28-1)

Napinda was possibly unlucky not to fight out the finish with the first two as she failed to find a gap between the winner and fourth inside the final furlong and was forced to switch. (op 3-1)

Hardy Blue(IRE) had to switch to the inside with her challenge in the straight and might be capable of a little better. (op 3-1 tchd 7-2)

Grace Of Hearts struggled under the penalty she was carrying for her C&D success (today's winner behind) in a claimer the previous month. She was subsequently disqualified from fourth place after Andrea Atzeni failed to weigh in. (op 9-2 tchd 4-1 and 6-1)

5047 MARRY ME EITHNE! H'CAP — 6f (P)
3:20 (3:21) (Class 6) (0-60,60) 3-Y-O+ **£1,704** (£503; £251) **Stalls** Low

Form | | | | RPR
55-6 **1** **For Life (IRE)**[86] 2171 10-9-4 **58** NataliaGemelova(3) 2 — 66
(John E Long) *mde all: 2 l clr 1/2-way: pushed along 2f out: a holding on* **17/2**

0534 **2** ¾ **Imjin River (IRE)**[11] 4653 5-9-2 **56** AdamBeschizza(3) 1 — 62
(William Stone) *chsd wnr: drvn 2f out: grad clsd fnl f: a hld* **9/2**[3]

2200 **3** ¾ **Mary's Pet**[20] 4332 5-9-9 **60** (v[1]) SebSanders 6 — 64+
(Lee Carter) *s.i.s: hld up in last pair: taken wd bef 1/2-way: effrt over 2f out: styd on to take 3rd ins fnl f: nrst fin* **4/1**[2]

-040 **4** ¾ **Bahri Sheen (IRE)**[17] 4438 4-9-6 **57** JamesDoyle 5 — 58
(John Best) *sn in last: pushed along bef halfwy: prog over 1f out: styd on same pce fnl f* **4/1**[2]

5400 **5** 1 ¾ **Sherjawy (IRE)**[6] 4815 8-9-3 **54** KirstyMilczarek 8 — 50
(Zoe Davison) *chsd ldrs: lost pl over 2f out: one pce and struggling after* **14/1**

5305 **6** nk **Illustrious Lad (IRE)**[17] 4438 3-9-2 **57** TomQueally 4 — 52
(Jim Boyle) *hld up on inner: effrt 2f out: no imp on ldrs 1f out: fdd* **3/1**[1]

0601 **7** 2 **Speedyfix**[17] 4439 5-9-6 **57** (t) JimmyQuinn 9 — 45
(Christine Dunnett) *t.k.h: hld up in tch: prog to chse ldng pair wl over 1f out: wknd ins fnl f* **11/1**

-200 **8** 8 **Rooknrasbryripple**[8] 4726 3-9-3 **58** ChrisCatlin 7 — 21
(Ralph Smith) *hld up: prog on wd outside 1/2-way to chse ldng pair briefly 2f out: wknd qckly over 1f out* **20/1**

1m 13.33s (1.43) **Going Correction** +0.175s/f (Slow)
WFA 3 from 4yo+ 4lb — **8** Ran SP% **113.5**
Speed ratings (Par 101): **97,96,95,94,91 91,88,77**
Tote Swingers: 1&2 £3.80, 1&3 £2.90, 2&3 £4.40 CSF £45.69 CT £178.72 TOTE £7.00: £2.80, £1.30, £1.80; EX 47.30.
Owner Brian C Oakley **Bred** R N Auld **Trained** Caterham, Surrey

FOCUS

A moderate sprint handicap in which For Life was allowed to dominate, as he likes to, and found plenty after racing in a clear lead. The winner is rated an improver on his winter form with the runner-up to his latest mark.

5048 LINGFIELD MARRIOTT HOTEL & COUNTRY CLUB MAIDEN STKS — 1m 5f (P)
3:50 (3:52) (Class 5) 3-Y-O+ **£2,385** (£704; £352) **Stalls** Low

Form | | | | RPR
0-5 **1** **Fleur De Cactus (IRE)**[51] 3279 3-8-10 0 RyanMoore 3 — 89+
(Sir Michael Stoute) *trckd ldr 4f: styd handy: rdn over 2f out: wnt 2nd again wl over 1f out: clsd to ld 150yds out: styd on wl and sn clr* **5/1**[2]

452 **2** 4 **Dr Yes (FR)**[14] 4542 3-9-1 84 TomQueally 1 — 88+
(Sir Henry Cecil) *led: stretched field fr 5f out: drvn 2f out: hdd and one pce last 150yds* **8/11**[1]

2235 **3** 4 **Bank Bonus**[20] 4323 3-9-1 80 JimmyFortune 10 — 82
(Andrew Balding) *t.k.h: cl up: pushed along 5f out: sn outpcd: styd on again fr 2f out to snatch 3rd nr fin* **6/1**[3]

00 **4** nk **Sanctioned**[14] 4542 3-9-1 0 JamesDoyle 13 — 82
(Roger Charlton) *prog on outer to trck ldr after 4f: rdn to chal over 2f out: lost 2nd wl over 1f out: wknd and lost 3rd nr fin* **25/1**

0-0 **5** hd **Maria Letizia**[18] 4410 3-8-10 0 RobertHavlin 9 — 76+
(John Gosden) *trckd ldrs: outpcd and rdn 5f out: n.m.r briefly over 4f out: struggling 3f out: styd on wl again fr over 1f out* **25/1**

0 **6** 7 **Addazero**[18] 4410 3-9-1 0 JohnFahy 5 — 71
(Alastair Lidderdale) *settled wl in rr: lft bhd by ldrs 5f out: prog fr 3f out: shkn up and styd on to take modest 6th fnl f: nt disgracd* **100/1**

02 **7** 2 ¾ **City Of Canton (IRE)**[16] 4465 3-8-12 0 PatrickHills(3) 12 — 67
(Luca Cumani) *dwlt: rcvrd into midfield after 4f: outpcd by ldrs fr 5f out: steadily fdd* **12/1**

0204 **8** nse **Coplow**[14] 4542 3-8-10 79 SebSanders 2 — 62
(Richard Hannon) *dwlt: t.k.h and sn prom: rdn and outpcd fr 5f out: steadily fdd* **9/1**

2 **9** 12 **Maid Of Silk (IRE)**[16] 4182 6-9-8 0 (t) AdamKirby 6 — 44
(Neil Mulholland) *hld up wl in rr: lft bhd 5f out: taken out wd and rdn over 3f out: no prog: t.o* **66/1**

10 2 ½ **Fairview Sue**[12] 8-9-8 0 ChrisCatlin 11 — 40
(Graeme McPherson) *dwlt: towards rr: urged along after 5f: lft bhd fr 5f out: t.o* **100/1**

5 **11** 1 ½ **Variety Show (IRE)**[66] 2794 3-8-10 0 IanMongan 8 — 38
(Sir Henry Cecil) *t.k.h: sn prom on outer: rdn and wknd fr 5f out: t.o* **33/1**

00 **12** 1 ½ **Oh So Charming**[18] 4410 3-9-1 0 JimmyQuinn 7 — 40
(Andy Turnell) *a wl in rr: lft bhd fr 5f out: t.o* **66/1**

60 **13** 20 **Ice Apple**[16] 4464 4-9-8 0 RichardThomas 4 — 5
(John E Long) *pushed along in last after 3f: nvr a factor: wl t.o* **150/1**

2m 45.5s (-0.50) **Going Correction** +0.175s/f (Slow)
WFA 3 from 4yo+ 12lb — **13** Ran SP% **122.8**
Speed ratings (Par 103): **108,105,103,102,102 98,96,96,89,87 86,85,73**
Tote Swingers: 1&2 £1.10, 1&3 £2.40, 2&3 £2.20 CSF £8.93 TOTE £4.20: £1.20, £1.30, £1.60; EX 14.30.
Owner Ballymacoll Stud **Bred** Ballymacoll Stud Farm Ltd **Trained** Newmarket, Suffolk

FOCUS

Just a fair maiden and the form is rated cautiously. The early pace was steady and a few of these were keen.

Variety Show(IRE) Official explanation: jockey said filly ran too free

5049 BOOTLEG BEATLES HERE NEXT SATURDAY H'CAP (DIV I) — 7f (P)
4:20 (4:21) (Class 6) (0-60,60) 3-Y-O+ **£1,704** (£503; £251) **Stalls** Low

Form | | | | RPR
640 **1** **Duke Of Destiny (IRE)**[43] 3539 3-8-13 **58** JimmyFortune 5 — 69+
(Ed Walker) *hld up in tch: prog on outer over 2f out: rdn to ld 1f out: styd on wl* **6/4**[1]

5503 **2** 1 ½ **Isingy Red (FR)**[4] 4890 4-9-6 **59** (p) JamesDoyle 4 — 66
(Jim Boyle) *chsd ldrs: drvn to go 3rd over 2f out: chal u.p and upsides 1f out: styd on same pce after* **11/4**[2]

0400 **3** 2 **Bedibyes**[2] 4942 4-8-8 **52** DavidKenny(5) 1 — 54
(Richard Mitchell) *dwlt: hld up last: stl there over 2f out: prog over 1f out: styd on to take 3rd last strides* **16/1**

000 **4** nk **Local Singer (IRE)**[15] 4517 4-9-5 **58** IanMongan 6 — 59
(Paul Howling) *chsd ldr 2f: drvn 1/2-way: tried to rally over 1f out: kpt on one pce* **9/1**

640- **5** 1 **Lord Deevert**[384] 4337 7-8-6 **52** JakePayne(7) 8 — 50
(Bill Turner) *led: drvn and hdd 1f out: wknd* **25/1**

0465 **6** 2 **Louphole**[15] 4508 10-8-11 **50** SebSanders 3 — 43
(J R Jenkins) *dwlt: hld up in last trio: pushed along 2f out: nvr involved* **12/1**

0312 **7** ½ **Ereka (IRE)**[72] 2607 4-9-3 **56** TomQueally 2 — 47
(John Best) *hld up in rr: shuffled along fr 2f out: nvr nr ldrs* **15/2**[3]

-640 **8** hd **Reginald Claude**[16] 4469 4-9-2 **60** LeeNewnes(5) 7 — 51
(Mark Usher) *trckd ldr after 2f: upsides 2f out gng easily: wknd rapidly over 1f out* **8/1**

0000 **9** 2 ½ **Cuthbert (IRE)**[22] 4240 5-8-8 **47** KirstyMilczarek 9 — 31
(Michael Attwater) *dwlt: racd wd: in tch: struggling fr 1/2-way: wknd over 2f out* **25/1**

1m 26.39s (1.59) **Going Correction** +0.175s/f (Slow)
WFA 3 from 4yo+ 6lb — **9** Ran SP% **120.8**
Speed ratings (Par 101): **97,95,93,92,91 89,88,88,85**
Tote Swingers: 1&2 £2.20, 1&3 £8.60, 2&3 £9.90 CSF £5.93 CT £45.56 TOTE £2.70: £1.10, £1.20, £4.00; EX 9.00.
Owner Dubai Thoroughbred Racing **Bred** John O'Connor **Trained** Newmarket, Suffolk

FOCUS

A moderate contest with the runner-up back to form.

5050 BOOTLEG BEATLES HERE NEXT SATURDAY H'CAP (DIV II) — 7f (P)
4:50 (4:50) (Class 6) (0-60,60) 3-Y-O+ **£1,704** (£503; £251) **Stalls** Low

Form | | | | RPR
600 **1** **Precision Five**[29] 4001 3-7-12 **46** oh1 (p) DominicFox(3) 10 — 54
(Jeremy Gask) *hld up in last trio: pushed along on outer 3f out: gd prog over 1f out: drvn and r.o to ld last 75yds* **20/1**

0006 **2** 1 **Not My Choice (IRE)**[15] 4493 7-9-1 **54** (t) J-PGuillambert 6 — 59
(Paul Howling) *slowest away: rcvrd arnd outer to go 2nd after 1f and sn clr w ldr: led 2f out: hrd rdn over 1f out: hdd and one pce last 75yds* **16/1**

2243 **3** shd **Chandrayaan**[80] 2366 5-8-7 **49** (v) SimonPearce(3) 3 — 54
(John E Long) *trckd clr ldng pair after 2f: clsd over 1f out: drvn and nt qckn fnl f* **4/1**[2]

0203 **4** 1 ¼ **King's Future**[30] 3972 3-8-13 **58** KierenFox 9 — 58
(Lee Carter) *led: clr w one rival after 2f: hdd 2f out: fdd ins fnl f* **6/1**

3540 **5** ¾ **Basle**[1] 4981 5-9-4 **57** (t) DavidProbert 2 — 57
(Gay Kelleway) *hld up in last trio: effrt and taken wd 2f out: styd on fnl f: nvr any threat* **9/2**[3]

-326 **6** nk **Patavium Prince (IRE)**[18] 4413 9-9-7 **60** IanMongan 1 — 59
(Jo Crowley) *hld up in midfield: effrt over 2f out: one pce and nvr able to chal* **7/4**[1]

00-0 **7** 3 ¾ **Style Margi (IRE)**[30] 3972 4-9-6 **59** JohnFahy 8 — 48
(Ed de Giles) *chsd ldr 1f: reminders over 4f out: styd in tch tl wknd over 1f out* **25/1**

5650 **8** hd **Grand Honour (IRE)**[38] 3717 6-8-7 **47** oh2 JimmyQuinn 7 — 34
(Paul Howling) *hld up: gng wl enough whn appeared to be hanging over 2f out: n.m.r wl over 1f out: wknd* **28/1**

0026 **9** 2 ½ **Captainrisk (IRE)**[22] 4241 6-8-13 **52** (v) SebSanders 4 — 33
(Christine Dunnett) *stdd s: hld up in last: rdn 3f out: no prog* **9/1**

1m 26.68s (1.88) **Going Correction** +0.175s/f (Slow)
WFA 3 from 4yo+ 6lb — **9** Ran SP% **116.8**
Speed ratings (Par 101): **96,94,94,93,92 92,87,87,84**
Tote Swingers: 1&2 £44.00, 1&3 £13.00, 2&3 £12.00 CSF £293.80 CT £1553.54 TOTE £36.30: £4.50, £3.90, £1.40; EX 476.00.
Owner Calne Engineering Ltd **Bred** Edward J G Young **Trained** Sutton Veny, Wilts

FOCUS

The time was 0.29 seconds slower than the first division. This was a weak race that was run at a strong pace thanks to King's Future, who was closely pursued by Not My Choice, with the pair clear after a furlong or so. The third sets the initial standard.

Precision Five Official explanation: trainer's rep said, regarding apparent improvement in form, that the filly had ran green in its previous races.

5051 "DO IT FOR DAD" FUN RUN H'CAP — 2m (P)
5:20 (5:20) (Class 5) (0-75,81) 4-Y-O+ **£2,385** (£704; £352) **Stalls** Low

Form | | | | RPR
0551 **1** **Bowdler's Magic**[6] 4831 5-9-6 **81** 6ex MichaelJMMurphy(7) 2 — 89+
(Mark Johnston) *dwlt: hld up in tch: trckd ldng pair over 4f out: plld out and swiftly moved ahd over 1f out: sn clr: easily* **30/100**[1]

2414 **2** 8 **Mollyow (IRE)**[3] 4904 4-8-4 **58** 6ex ow1 ChrisCatlin 4 — 56
(Terry Clement) *trckd ldr: led over 5f out: hrd pressed and drvn 2f out: hdd over 1f out: easily outpcd* **11/2**[2]

041/ **3** 3 **Bugsy's Boy**[62] 6775 8-8-11 **70** (p) DavidKenny(5) 5 — 64
(George Baker) *hld up: pressed ldng pair 6f out: chal and upsides 2f out: sltly short of room and btn sn after* **14/1**

6/00 **4** 36 **Curacao**[13] 4606 6-9-1 **69** SebSanders 1 — 20
(Amanda Perrett) *led to over 5f out: last fr 4f out: t.o* **10/1**[3]

3m 34.36s (8.66) **Going Correction** +0.175s/f (Slow) — **4** Ran SP% **108.1**
Speed ratings (Par 103): **85,81,79,61**
CSF £2.35 TOTE £1.20; EX 2.10.
Owner Paul Dean **Bred** Miss K Rausing **Trained** Middleham Moor, N Yorks

FOCUS

A deeply uncompetitive staying handicap run at a slow gallop (time over 18 seconds above standard) courtesy of Curacao, who offered nothing when joined by the runner-up and third down the back straight. The winner did not need to improve on last year's form to score.

5052 LADBROKES GAME ON! H'CAP — 1m 2f (P)
5:55 (5:57) (Class 6) (0-65,65) 3-Y-O+ **£1,704** (£503; £251) **Stalls** Low

Form | | | | RPR
0253 **1** **Top Frock (IRE)**[13] 4586 3-9-4 **64** (b) AdamKirby 9 — 72
(Clive Cox) *trckd ldr: rdn to ld wl over 1f out: styd on wl* **4/1**[2]

0321 **2** 1 ½ **Welsh Nayber**[11] 4650 3-9-5 **65** 6ex (b) JimmyFortune 11 — 70
(Amanda Perrett) *trckd ldrs: rdn over 2f out: chsd wnr over 1f out: kpt on but no imp* **7/2**[1]

3663 **3** nk **Neige D'Antan**[11] 4650 3-8-5 **51** ChrisCatlin 1 — 56+
(Sir Mark Prescott Bt) *awkward s: racd in last pair tl effrt on wd outside fr 3f out: drvn and styd on fr over 1f out: tk 3rd nr fin* **9/2**[3]

6423 **4** ½ **Warden Bond**[25] 4158 4-9-6 **57**.......................................(p) TomQueally 4 61
(William Stone) *in tch but pushed along early: prog on inner over 2f out: rdn to chse ldng pair briefly ins fnl f: kpt on* **10/1**

3-00 **5** ¾ **Greeley House**[57] 3081 4-9-9 **60**.............................. GeorgeBaker 13 62
(Chris Wall) *dwlt: hld up in midfield and racd on outer: effrt and wd bnd 2f out: rdn and kpt on same pce after: nvr able to chal* **8/1**

6436 **6** 1¼ **Storm Runner (IRE)**[25] 4158 4-9-5 **56**.............................. IanMongan 7 56
(George Margarson) *wl in tch: shkn up over 2f out: styd on same pce fr over 1f out: nvr able to threaten* **14/1**

2060 **7** 3¾ **D'Urberville**[25] 4142 5-9-13 **64**.............................. KirstyMilczarek 6 56
(J R Jenkins) *racd freely: led at gd pce: hdd & wknd wl over 1f out* **16/1**

2000 **8** 3½ **Diamond Twister (USA)**[13] 4594 6-8-4 **46** oh1......(t) CharlesBishop(5) 3 31
(Lisa Williamson) *dwlt: hld up in last: lost tch w main gp over 3f out: nvr on terms after* **40/1**

5045 **9** 4 **Edgewater (IRE)**[71] 2637 5-10-0 **65**.............................. SebSanders 2 42
(Lee Carter) *hld up towards rr: rdn and effrt to chse ldrs wl over 1f out: sn wknd* **8/1**

4100 **10** 9 **Always Eager**[13] 4586 3-9-3 **63**.............................. RobertHavlin 14 22
(Mark Johnston) *trckd ldrs to 3f out: wknd: eased wl over 1f out* **14/1**

0-44 **11** 9 **Goodwood Starlight (IRE)**[14] 4409 7-9-2 **60**.........(t) AprilKitchener(7) 8
(Jim Best) *chsd ldrs to 1/2-way: sn dropped out: t.o 3f out* **33/1**

2m 6.91s (0.31) **Going Correction** +0.175s/f (Slow)
WFA 3 from 4yo+ 9lb **11** Ran SP% **116.3**
Speed ratings (Par 101): **105,103,103,103,102 101,98,95,92,85 78**
Tote Swingers 1&2 £3.30, 2&3 £3.90, 1&3 £5.40 CSF £18.16 CT £65.26 TOTE £7.30: £2.20, £1.50, £1.70; EX 24.90.
Owner A McIver **Bred** Alberto Panetta **Trained** Lambourn, Berks

FOCUS
A moderate handicap but interesting nonetheless. The placed horses set the level to their latest C&D marks.
T/Plt: £122.80 to a £1 stake. Pool: £48,311.99 - 286.97 winning tickets. T/Qpdt: £52.00 to a £1 stake. Pool: £4,378.88 - 62.29 winning tickets. JN

4766 MUSSELBURGH (R-H)

Friday, August 10

OFFICIAL GOING: Good to firm (8.0)
All distances as advertised.
Wind: Breezy, half against Weather: Sunny, hot

5053 SLI MAIDEN AUCTION STKS 5f
2:00 (2:00) (Class 5) 2-Y-O £2,587 (£770; £384; £192) **Stalls** Centre

Form RPR

3 **1** **American Impact (USA)**[17] 4433 2-8-11 0.................. BarryMcHugh 2 67+
(Tony Coyle) *w ldr: rdn wl over 1f out: led ins fnl f: kpt on wl towards fin* **1/1**[1]

05 **2** shd **Multisure**[12] 4625 2-8-10 0.............................. PatrickMathers 3 66
(Richard Fahey) *led: rdn 2f out: hdd ins fnl f: rallied: hld cl home* **5/2**[2]

0403 **3** 3¼ **Mount Seymour (IRE)**[10] 4670 2-8-10 63.............................. GrahamLee 4 54
(Nigel Tinkler) *cl up: drvn over 2f out: rallied: outpcd ins fnl f* **10/3**[3]

00 **4** 1¾ **I'Ve No Money (IRE)**[73] 2587 2-8-10 0.........(t) FrannyNorton 5 49+
(David C Griffiths) *trckd ldrs: drvn 2f out: no ex fnl f* **16/1**

1m 0.28s (-0.12) **Going Correction** -0.25s/f (Firm) **4** Ran SP% **107.5**
Speed ratings (Par 94): **90,89,84,81**
CSF £3.72 TOTE £1.60; EX 3.10.
Owner Matt & Lauren Morgan **Bred** Dr Harold Fishman & W S Farish **Trained** Norton, N Yorks

FOCUS
With no Racing Post bonus on offer this was a weak 2-y-o maiden. The form is not straightforward and could be too high, but can be given a chance.

NOTEBOOK
American Impact(USA), who recorded an RPR of 64 when third first time over 6f at Yarmouth, is quite a laid back individual. He had to work hard to get the better of the runner-up, but was always just doing enough late on. His rider chanced his arm not riding him out all the way to the line, though. A step back up in trip in nursery company beckons. (op 11-10 tchd 10-11)
Multisure, having his third start, knew his job this time. Only edged out near the line he too looks a likely nursery type. (op 3-1)
Mount Seymour(IRE), with an official rating of 63, is looking fully exposed. (op 5-2 tchd 7-2)
I'Ve No Money(IRE), who showed next to nothing on his first two starts, shaped much better in a first-time tongue tie. However, his expected nursery mark around 60 will do him no favours. (op 18-1)

5054 CORNHILL BUILDERS H'CAP 1m 4f 100y
2:30 (2:30) (Class 6) (0-65,69) 3-Y-O+ £2,587 (£770; £384; £192) **Stalls** Low

Form RPR

5342 **1** **Arley Hall**[11] 4642 3-9-0 **65**.............................. LeeTopliss(3) 4 79
(Richard Fahey) *prom: hdwy to ld over 2f out: clr whn edgd rt ins fnl f: kpt on strly* **5/2**[1]

2040 **2** 4½ **Coax**[12] 4626 4-9-9 **60**.............................. DuranFentiman 10 67
(Patrick Holmes) *hld up: hdwy to chse (clr) wnr over 1f out: kpt on fnl f: no imp* **22/1**

2323 **3** 1½ **Schmooze (IRE)**[11] 4642 3-8-6 **54**.............................. JamesSullivan 6 59
(Linda Perratt) *hld up: pushed along over 2f out: hdwy over 1f out: kpt on fnl f: nvr able to chal* **9/2**[3]

2111 **4** 2½ **Luctor Emergo (IRE)**[11] 4642 3-9-7 **69** 6ex.............(p) PaulMulrennan 2 70
(Keith Dalgleish) *led after 2f: rdn and hdd over 3f out: outpcd fnl 2f* **7/2**[2]

-625 **5** ½ **Haka Dancer (USA)**[4] 4869 9-8-12 **49** ow2..........(p) RussKennemore 8 49
(Philip Kirby) *t.k.h: chsd ldrs: drvn and edgd rt over 2f out: sn no imp* **9/1**

3000 **6** 2¼ **Polurrian (IRE)**[50] 3310 5-9-11 **62**.............................(p) DanielTudhope 7 59
(David O'Meara) *led 2f: cl up: led over 3f out to over 2f out: wknd over 1f out* **14/1**

4051 **7** 3½ **Fine Kingdom**[10] 4678 3-8-8 **56** 6ex.............................. BarryMcHugh 9 47
(Brian Ellison) *hld up in midfield on ins: effrt over 2f out: wknd wl over 1f out* **7/1**

0026 **8** 1¼ **Border Bandit (USA)**[12] 4627 4-9-9 **60**.............................. PaddyAspell 1 49
(Tracy Waggott) *in tch on ins: outpcd over 5f out: btn fnl 2f* **11/1**

4600 **9** 3 **Cathcart Castle**[3] 4912 4-8-6 **50**.............................(v) ShirleyTeasdale(7) 5 35
(Simon West) *hld up: shortlived effrt over 3f out: btn fnl 2f* **50/1**

046 **10** 7 **Laybach (IRE)**[22] 4259 8-8-11 **48**.............................. GrahamLee 3 22
(Jim Goldie) *hld up: struggling over 3f out: sn btn* **33/1**

2m 42.01s (0.01) **Going Correction** -0.15s/f (Firm)
WFA 3 from 4yo+ 11lb **10** Ran SP% **115.7**
Speed ratings (Par 101): **93,90,89,87,87 85,83,82,80,75**
Tote Swingers: 1&2 £1.90, 1&3 £1.80, 2&3 £1.10 CSF £62.58 CT £238.41 TOTE £3.80: £1.40, £5.50, £1.50; EX 69.20.
Owner Mrs E Armstrong & R Marshall **Bred** Plantation Stud **Trained** Musley Bank, N Yorks

FOCUS
A modest handicap run at just a steady pace, but there was a progressive winner. The form looks pretty sound rated around the first four.
Fine Kingdom Official explanation: jockey said gelding hung right

5055 BRITISH STALLION STUDS E B F CONDITIONS STKS 5f
3:00 (3:01) (Class 3) 2-Y-O £7,762 (£2,310; £1,154; £577) **Stalls** Centre

Form RPR

10 **1** **Cosmic Chatter**[52] 3242 2-9-2 0.............................. GrahamGibbons 1 98
(David Barron) *cl up: led after 1f: rdn 2f out: styd on strly to draw clr fnl f* **4/1**[2]

3001 **2** 3 **Liber**[15] 4488 2-9-2 97.............................. LukeMorris 4 87
(Sir Mark Prescott Bt) *led 1f: chsd wnr: drvn and outpcd over 2f out: rallied over 1f out: no imp fnl f* **1/4**[1]

31 **3** 4 **Findog**[18] 4395 2-8-13 72.............................. PaulMulrennan 3 70
(Linda Perratt) *t.k.h: cl up tl rdn and outpcd by ldng pair fnl f* **20/1**[3]

5166 **4** 3¾ **Our Diane (IRE)**[3] 4922 2-8-12 74 ow1.............................. DanielTudhope 5 56
(David O'Meara) *in tch: rdn over 2f out: sn n.d* **20/1**[3]

056 **5** 3¼ **Lothian Countess**[41] 3604 2-8-8 68.............................. JamesSullivan 2 40
(George Foster) *t.k.h: in tch: rdn over 2f out: edgd rt and wknd wl over 1f out* **66/1**

58.51s (-1.89) **Going Correction** -0.25s/f (Firm) **5** Ran SP% **111.0**
Speed ratings (Par 98): **105,100,93,87,82**
CSF £5.56 TOTE £4.40: £1.20, £1.10; EX 6.50.
Owner Highclere T'Bred Racing & David Barron **Bred** Harrowgate Bloodstock Ltd **Trained** Maunby, N Yorks

FOCUS
A match on paper but it did not go as the betting suggested. The runner-up was below form with the third and fourth the guides to the level.

NOTEBOOK
Cosmic Chatter ◆, who created a good impression when winning on his debut at Haydock in June, became unsettled at the start when only 11th in the Windsor Castle at Royal Ascot. Calm and well behaved this time, he took the race in smart style, quickening right away in the final furlong. The Listed Roses Stakes at York looks very tempting. (tchd 9-2)
Liber was firmly put in his place, so whether he ran to his official rating is open to doubt. (op 2-5)
Findog, claimed for £10,000 after taking a claimer at Beverley on his second start, is rated just 72. He ran surprisingly well and was certainly not knocked about. His rating might shoot up, however. (op 14-1)
Our Diane(IRE), who dropped out rapidly in a nursery at Ripon just three days earlier, was held up this time. She is not really progressing. (op 12-1)
Lothian Countess, a winner first time out at Redcar in April, behaved badly at Chester on her previous start. She was on better terms with herself this time, but raced keenly and looks her own worst enemy.

5056 CRUDEN GROUP H'CAP 2m
3:30 (3:30) (Class 5) (0-70,69) 4-Y-O+ £3,881 (£1,155; £577; £288) **Stalls** Centre

Form RPR

4302 **1** **Sohcahtoa (IRE)**[7] 4766 6-9-2 **69**.............................. LMcNiff(5) 3 76
(David Barron) *hld up: rdn over 3f out: hdwy over 2f out: styd on wl u.p to ld last stride* **9/4**[2]

43-4 **2** shd **Royal Bonsai**[149] 392 4-8-11 **59**.............................. MichaelO'Connell 2 66
(John Quinn) *chsd clr ldr: smooth hdwy to ld over 2f out: sn rdn: kpt on u.p fnl f: hdd last stride* **9/2**[3]

4603 **3** 1 **Bradbury (IRE)**[13] 4590 4-9-6 **68**.............................(p) GrahamLee 4 74
(James Bethell) *chsd ldrs: rdn 3f out: effrt wl over 1f out: ch ins fnl f: kpt on same pce last 75yds* **2/1**[1]

3140 **4** 4½ **Spruzzo**[6] 4831 6-9-2 **64**.............................. DuranFentiman 6 64
(Chris Fairhurst) *led and sn wl clr: rdn over 3f out: hdd over 2f out: rallied: wknd ins fnl f* **13/2**

0-00 **5** 11 **Spiders Star**[7] 2698 9-7-11 **52** ow2.............................. ShirleyTeasdale(7) 5 39
(Simon West) *dwlt: bhd: lost tch 1/2-way: sme hdwy and edgd rt over 2f out: nvr on terms* **33/1**

056 **6** 18 **Artisan**[12] 4626 4-9-3 **65**.............................. BarryMcHugh 1 31
(Brian Ellison) *hld up in tch: struggling over 3f out: sn btn* **9/2**[3]

3m 29.37s (-4.13) **Going Correction** -0.15s/f (Firm) **6** Ran SP% **116.7**
Speed ratings (Par 103): **104,103,103,101,95 86**
Tote Swingers: 1&2 £1.90, 1&3 £1.80, 2&3 £1.10 CSF £13.44 TOTE £3.00: £2.40, £2.40; EX 13.50.
Owner Douglas Pryde Jim Beaumont **Bred** Knockainey Stud **Trained** Maunby, N Yorks

FOCUS
No hanging about in this modest 2m handicap and the form is straightforward, if ordinary.
Artisan Official explanation: jockey said gelding ran flat

5057 EDGEN MURRAY EUROPE LTD H'CAP 7f 30y
4:00 (4:01) (Class 3) (0-90,89) 3-Y-O+ £7,762 (£2,310; £1,154; £577) **Stalls** Low

Form RPR

4130 **1** **Able Master (IRE)**[13] 4609 6-9-7 **84**.............................. DanielTudhope 3 95
(David O'Meara) *t.k.h early: chsd ldr: effrt 2f out: led ins fnl f: rdn out* **7/1**[3]

0614 **2** 1½ **Vito Volterra (IRE)**[27] 4110 5-9-3 **80**.............................. AndrewMullen 8 87
(Michael Smith) *chsd ldrs: rdn to ld over 2f out: edgd rt over 1f out: hdd ins fnl f: kpt on same pce* **9/1**

5101 **3** 2¼ **Copperwood**[14] 4541 7-8-11 **74**.............................. FrannyNorton 5 75
(Mark Johnston) *t.k.h early: trckd ldrs: effrt and rdn over 2f out: edgd rt over 1f out: one pce fnl f* **8/1**

-132 **4** shd **Green Howard**[35] 3812 4-9-6 **83**.............................. LukeMorris 10 84
(Robin Bastiman) *s.i.s: sn pushed along in rr: hdwy fnl 2f: nrst fin* **11/4**[1]

4020 **5** nk **Solar Spirit (IRE)**[6] 4829 7-9-6 **83**.............................. GrahamLee 9 83
(Tracy Waggott) *hld up towards rr: smooth hdwy over 2f out: rdn over 1f out: sn no imp* **8/1**

3300 **6** 4 **Clockmaker (IRE)**[34] 3855 6-9-10 **87**.............................. DuranFentiman 2 76
(Tim Easterby) *taken early to post: hld up in tch: rdn 3f out: edgd rt and outpcd wl over 1f out* **8/1**

0250 **7** 4 **Polish World (USA)**[13] 4589 8-9-7 **84**.............................. MickyFenton 7 62
(Paul Midgley) *led: rdn and clr over 3f out: hdd over 2f out: wknd over 1f out* **22/1**

3002 **8** ¾ **Al Muheer (IRE)**[6] 4828 7-9-12 **89**.............................(b) JamesSullivan 6 65
(Ruth Carr) *taken early to post: s.i.s: bhd: drvn and outpcd wl over 2f out: nvr on terms* **7/2**[2]

-000 **9** 2¼ **Imperator Augustus (IRE)**[12] 4629 4-9-3 **80**.................. PaddyAspell 1 50
(Patrick Holmes) *hld up on ins: effrt and rdn over 2f out: wknd over 1f out* **11/1**

1m 26.56s (-2.44) **Going Correction** -0.15s/f (Firm) **9** Ran SP% **117.4**
Speed ratings (Par 107): **107,105,102,102,102 97,93,92,89**
Tote Swingers: 1&2 £6.90, 1&3 £8.50, 2&3 £8.20 CSF £69.05 CT £521.75 TOTE £8.50: £2.90, £3.20, £2.20; EX 81.70.
Owner Direct Racing Club **Bred** Scuderia Miami Di Sandro Guerra And Co **Trained** Nawton, N Yorks

FOCUS
A very competitive 7f handicap, run at a furious pace. The runner-up helps set the standard.
NOTEBOOK
Able Master(IRE) made the running in the past but here he was happy to accept a lead. He got a fine ride and, rated 20lb higher at his peak, he should continue to give a good account of himself. (tchd 15-2)
Vito Volterra(IRE), who often makes the running, took charge but the winner was only biding his time. He is better suited by courses with a stiffer finish. (op 7-1)
Copperwood has already won five times in 2012 but has only gone up 7lb in the ratings. He found 7f his bare minimum, especially on quick ground. (op 7-1 tchd 13-2)
Green Howard, drawn wide, was soon struggling in the rear. He was staying on in good style at the finish and can return to winning ways when the ground eases once more. (op 7-2)
Solar Spirit(IRE) travels strongly but doesn't always find much for pressure. Catterick, the scene of his last four wins, is his happy hunting ground. (op 7-1)
Clockmaker(IRE), back after a break, was paying his first visit here. He is another who prefers give in the ground. (op 9-1)
Al Muheer(IRE), narrowly denied over a mile at Thirsk six days earlier, never figured. No doubt he will soon bounce back. Connections reported that he was unsuited by the quick ground. Official explanation: trainer said gelding was unsuited by the good to firm ground (op 4-1)

5058 FIVE-A-DAY CLAIMING STKS 5f
4:30 (4:31) (Class 6) 3-Y-0+ **£1,940** (£577; £288; £144) **Stalls** Centre

Form RPR
0002 **1** **Partner (IRE)**[16] 4454 6-9-10 87 ....(b) GrahamLee 2 88+
(Kevin Ryan) *in tch: stdy hdwy 1/2-way: rdn to ld ins fnl f: kpt on wl* **11/10**[1]
526 **2** ¾ **Select Committee**[10] 4680 7-8-12 75 ....(v) MichaelO'Connell 3 73
(John Quinn) *trckd ldrs: hdwy gng wl over 1f out: ev ch ins fnl f: sn rdn: kpt on* **3/1**[2]
0200 **3** 2¾ **Crimea (IRE)**[10] 4680 6-8-9 70 ....(p) ShirleyTeasdale(7) 5 67
(David Nicholls) *trckd ldrs: n.m.r and lost pl over 1f out: kpt on fnl f: nt rch first two* **5/1**[3]
0035 **4** ½ **Berbice (IRE)**[7] 4769 7-9-3 59 .... JulieBurke(3) 7 64
(Linda Perratt) *slowly away: bhd: effrt and rdn over 1f out: no imp fnl f: fin 5th: plcd 4th* **14/1**
00/ **5** 12 **The Bear**[693] 6140 9-9-2 65 .... PaulMulrennan 4
(Linda Perratt) *walked to s: led to 1/2-way: rdn and wknd over 1f out: fin 6th: plcd 5th* **20/1**
0-63 **D** 1½ **Arriva La Diva**[51] 3276 6-8-1 58 .... JamesSullivan 1 47
(Linda Perratt) *w ldr: led 1/2-way to ins fnl f: edgd rt and sn btn: disqualified and plcd last* **11/1**

58.22s (-2.18) **Going Correction** -0.25s/f (Firm) **6** Ran SP% **109.0**
Speed ratings (Par 101): **107,105,101,98,79 99**
Tote Swingers: 1&2 £2.10, 1&3 £2.00, 2&3 £2.40 CSF £4.22 TOTE £2.10: £1.40, £1.30; EX 5.10.Partner (IRE) claimed by Mr N. Wilson for £12,000.
Owner Dr Marwan Koukash **Bred** Miss Joan Murphy **Trained** Hambleton, N Yorks
■ Stewards' Enquiry : James Sullivan three-day ban: failed to weigh-in (Aug 25-27)
FOCUS
The two leaders went off very fast in this 5f claimer setting it up for the closers. The winner is better than this grade and neither he or the second needed to run to their best.

5059 SCOTTISH RACING APPRENTICE H'CAP 1m
5:00 (5:00) (Class 5) (0-70,70) 4-Y-0+ **£3,234** (£962; £481; £240) **Stalls** Low

Form RPR
5003 **1** **Triple Eight (IRE)**[4] 4868 4-8-8 **61** ....(b) EvaMoscrop(7) 3 76
(Philip Kirby) *chsd clr ldr: hdwy to ld over 1f out: edgd lft: pushed clr fnl f* **9/2**[2]
423 **2** 6 **Military Call**[11] 4643 5-8-7 **58** ....(p) JasonHart(5) 5 59
(Alistair Whillans) *bhd: rdn over 3f out: gd hdwy on outside over 1f out: chsd (clr) wnr ins fnl f: no imp* **7/2**[1]
1066 **3** 1 **Cannon Bolt (IRE)**[17] 4432 4-8-10 **56** ....(b) JulieBurke 8 55
(Robin Bastiman) *led and sn clr: rdn and hdd over 1f out: outpcd fnl f* **11/1**
003 **4** ¾ **Byron Bear (IRE)**[69] 2692 4-8-5 **51** oh2 .... AmyRyan 6 48
(Paul Midgley) *hld up towards rr: rdn over 3f out: hdwy on outside over 2f out: no imp over 1f out* **9/2**[2]
0010 **5** 1½ **Collateral Damage (IRE)**[18] 4398 9-9-8 **68** ....(t) LucyAlexander 9 62
(Tim Easterby) *dwlt: sn in tch on outside: drvn 3f out: no ex over 1f out* **11/1**
0650 **6** ½ **Goldenveil (IRE)**[18] 4396 4-8-9 **55** .... LeeTopliss 7 48
(Richard Fahey) *prom: drvn 3f out: edgd rt and no ex over 1f out* **11/2**[3]
0000 **7** 1½ **Mujaadel (USA)**[7] 4779 7-9-5 **70** ....(p) ShirleyTeasdale(5) 1 59
(David Nicholls) *dwlt: bhd: drvn along 1/2-way: nvr on terms* **12/1**
201 **8** 11 **Last Destination (IRE)**[18] 4398 4-8-8 **57** .... LMcNiff(3) 2 21
(Nigel Tinkler) *hld up on ins: struggling over 3f out: sn btn* **9/2**[2]

1m 39.21s (-1.99) **Going Correction** -0.15s/f (Firm) **8** Ran SP% **116.5**
Speed ratings (Par 103): **103,97,96,95,93 93,91,80**
Tote Swingers: 1&2 £4.00, 1&3 £10.10, 2&3 £9.90 CSF £21.09 CT £165.18 TOTE £3.60: £1.50, £1.10, £2.00; EX 24.80.
Owner C B Construction (Cleveland) Limited **Bred** Moyglare Stud Farm Ltd **Trained** Castleton, N Yorks
FOCUS
The clear leaders soon had them strung out in this apprentice handicap. The winner confirmed his recent return to form but the form overall is somewhat fluid.
T/Plt: £40.20 to a £1 stake. Pool: £39,669.09 - 719.20 winning tickets. T/Qpdt: £10.80 to a £1 stake. Pool: £3,103.82 - 211.30 winning tickets. RY

4818 NEWMARKET (R-H)
Friday, August 10
OFFICIAL GOING: Good to firm (8.0)
Wind: Nil Weather: Warm and sunny

5060 PIPER-HEIDSIECK NURSERY 7f
5:40 (5:40) (Class 4) (0-85,82) 2-Y-0 **£3,881** (£1,155; £577; £288) **Stalls** High

Form RPR
1222 **1** **Oasis Cannes**[7] 4763 2-9-7 **82** .... WilliamBuick 5 88
(Sir Mark Prescott Bt) *mde all: rdn over 1f out: edgd rt wl ins fnl f: styd on gamely* **13/8**[1]
51 **2** hd **Makafeh**[24] 4194 2-9-4 **79** .... KierenFallon 4 84+
(Luca Cumani) *chsd wnr 1f: wnt 2nd again 3f out: rdn over 1f out: ev ch ins fnl f: styd on* **10/3**[2]
033 **3** 6 **Freeport**[40] 3658 2-9-2 **77** .... FrankieDettori 1 67
(Brian Meehan) *chsd wnr 6f out tl pushed along 3f out: rdn and hung lft over 1f out: sn wknd* **9/2**[3]
0U33 **4** 1½ **Rated**[2] 4951 2-9-3 **78** .... MatthewDavies 6 64
(Mick Channon) *prom: rdn and wknd wl over 1f out* **10/1**
01 **5** 2¼ **Rafale**[15] 4487 2-9-3 **78** .... RyanMoore 3 58
(Richard Hannon) *s.i.s: hld up: rdn over 2f out: sn wknd* **5/1**
330 **6** 1¾ **Red Adair (IRE)**[46] 3444 2-9-3 **78** .... DaneO'Neill 2 54
(Richard Hannon) *sn pushed along and prom: rdn and wknd over 2f out* **20/1**

1m 25.63s (-0.07) **Going Correction** -0.05s/f (Good) **6** Ran SP% **109.9**
Speed ratings (Par 96): **98,97,90,89,86 84**
toteswingers: 1&2 £1.40, 1&3 £2.10, 2&3 £3.10 CSF £6.87 TOTE £2.40: £1.50, £2.30; EX 7.50.
Owner J L C Pearce **Bred** J L C Pearce **Trained** Newmarket, Suffolk
■ Stewards' Enquiry : William Buick caution: careless riding
FOCUS
Probably not much depth to this nursery, but the front two are both likeable types and came clear of the rest. The winner did give the second a slight nudge near the line but it would be hard to argue it made much difference. The form looks straightforward.
NOTEBOOK
Oasis Cannes gained reward for a string of good efforts since going into nurseries, making the running again and pulling out a bit more when it looked like he was going to be swamped by the runner-up towards the finish. He could go up a fair bit for this with the front two pulling clear, but his attitude is sure to continue to hold him in good stead and there's the potential for better still when he tackles 1m. (tchd 6-4 and 15-8)
Makafeh duly built on his soft-ground Yarmouth maiden success, clearly having no problem with the much quicker conditions here. Like the winner, he'll be suited by 1m and there's definitely more to come from him, the fact he holds a Royal Lodge entry suggesting connections hold him in high regard. (op 3-1 tchd 11-4)
Freeport clearly has a fair level of ability, but an opening mark of 77 looked stiff enough beforehand and he was no match for the leading pair in the final 2f. (op 5-1)
Rated perhaps found this coming a bit quick just a couple of days after Newcastle as he probably not quite at his best. (tchd 11-1)
Rafale had left the impression he'd be well suited by this sort of trip when getting up late in a 5.7f Bath maiden last month so this was a bit disappointing, never a threat after a slowish start. (op 11-2 tchd 9-2)
Red Adair(IRE)'s best effort in maidens came on soft ground and he never threatened to land a serious blow on his nursery bow (op 16-1)

5061 COLLEGE OF WEST ANGLIA (S) STKS 7f
6:10 (6:10) (Class 5) 2-Y-0 **£3,234** (£962; £481; £240) **Stalls** High

Form RPR
0 **1** **Super Cookie**[21] 4297 2-8-5 0 .... HarryBentley(3) 7 60
(Philip McBride) *chsd ldrs: rdn over 1f out: led ins fnl f: styd on wl: eased nr fin* **11/2**[3]
6444 **2** 1¾ **Jimmy Elder**[7] 4752 2-8-13 68 .... RyanMoore 1 60
(Richard Hannon) *led: rdn over 1f out: hdd and unable qck ins fnl f* **9/4**[2]
0436 **3** 1½ **Ouzinkie (IRE)**[5] 4837 2-8-13 72 ....(v) MatthewDavies 8 56
(Mick Channon) *hld up in tch: racd keenly: jnd ldrs over 2f out: sn rdn: hung rt fr over 1f out: styd on same pce ins fnl f* **2/1**[1]
4 ½ **Silk Scarf (IRE)** 2-8-8 0 .... KierenFallon 3 50
(Mark H Tompkins) *s.i.s: hld up: pushed along 1/2-way: outpcd over 2f out: styd on ins fnl f* **11/2**[3]
5 ½ **Alpine Jerry (IRE)** 2-8-8 0 .... TadhgO'Shea 5 49
(J S Moore) *s.s: in rr: hdwy and hung lft over 1f out: nt trble ldrs* **16/1**
4445 **6** 1¾ **Northern Harbour (IRE)**[11] 4658 2-8-13 62 ....(p) LiamKeniry 4 49
(J S Moore) *chsd ldrs: rdn and ev ch over 2f out: no ex ins fnl f* **10/1**
400 **7** 1¼ **Rio Cato**[15] 4494 2-8-3 42 .... AshleyMorgan(5) 6 41
(Ed Dunlop) *chsd ldrs: rdn over 2f out: wknd* **25/1**
0 **8** 10 **Paige Flyer**[11] 4658 2-8-8 0 .... RichardMullen 2 15
(Michael Quinn) *wnt rt s: hld up: hld up: hdwy 1/2-way: rdn and wknd over 1f out* **50/1**

1m 27.95s (2.25) **Going Correction** -0.05s/f (Good) **8** Ran SP% **115.7**
Speed ratings (Par 94): **85,83,81,80,80 78,76,65**
toteswingers: 1&2 £2.70, 1&3 £2.90, 2&3 £1.50 CSF £18.55 TOTE £7.60: £2.20, £1.10, £1.10; EX 20.90 Trifecta £50.10 Pool: £657.07 - 9.69 winning units..The winner was bought in for £8,000.
Owner The Honorable Earle I Mack **Bred** Earle I Mack **Trained** Newmarket, Suffolk
FOCUS
Just modest form in this seller. It was steadily run until halfway and the form is typical of the grade.
NOTEBOOK
Super Cookie had shown up well for a fair way in a maiden here last month and proved more than good enough down in grade, asserting inside the last. She'll be suited by 1m and appeals as the type to do well in nurseries, as the handicapper can hardly go overboard with her on this. (op 15-2)
Jimmy Elder ran his race dropped into a seller, dictating up in trip but having no answer to the winner inside the last. This is his level. (tchd 5-2)
Ouzinkie(IRE) is thoroughly exposed and had no excuses dropped into a seller with a visor refitted. (tchd 9-4)
Silk Scarf(IRE), a daughter of Windsor Knot, showed ability and will be of interest next time kept to this sort of grade. She was outpaced here when the tempo increased but kept on at the finish. There's of plenty of stamina on the dam's side of her pedigree and she'll be well suited by 1m. (op 15-2 tchd 5-1)
Alpine Jerry(IRE) was a cheaply bought daughter of Jeremy but did show ability by the finish and should be wiser next time. (op 14-1 tchd 12-1)
Northern Harbour(IRE)'s form in maidens gave him claims and he clearly wasn't close to his best. (op 8-1)

5062 NGK SPARK PLUGS MAIDEN STKS 7f
6:45 (6:47) (Class 4) 2-Y-0 **£4,528** (£1,347; £673; £336) **Stalls** High

Form RPR
1 **Ashdan** 2-9-3 0 .... WilliamBuick 15 90+
(John Gosden) *a.p: led over 1f out: shkn up and r.o wl: readily* **7/2**[1]
2 2¼ **Mutazamen** 2-9-3 0 .... TadhgO'Shea 9 81+
(Richard Hannon) *led: edgd rt and hdd over 1f out: styd on same pce ins fnl f* **18/1**
3 1 **Zurbriggen** 2-9-3 0 .... MickaelBarzalona 13 79+
(Mahmood Al Zarooni) *chsd ldrs: rdn over 1f out: styd on same pce ins fnl f* **5/1**[3]
4 1 **Tamarkuz (USA)** 2-9-3 0 .... FrankieDettori 12 76+
(Saeed Bin Suroor) *hld up: hdwy over 2f out: swtchd rt over 1f out: no imp ins fnl f* **9/2**[2]
5 2 **Rangi** 2-9-3 0 .... SaleemGolam 7 71+
(John Gosden) *s.s: hld up: hung rt over 2f out: styd on fr over 1f out: nvr trbld ldrs* **14/1**
6 1 **Etijaah (USA)** 2-9-3 0 .... MichaelHills 10 68+
(Brian Meehan) *mid-div: pushed along over 2f out: styd on ins fnl f: nvr nrr* **25/1**

7 1 **Lancelot Du Lac (ITY)** 2 -9-3 0 BrettDoyle 6 66+
(Dean Ivory) *hld up: shkn up over 1f out: styd on ins fnl f: nvr nrr* 40/1
8 1/2 **Lionheart** 2 -9-3 0 (t) KierenFallon 14 64+
(Luca Cumani) *prom: rdn over 1f out: wknd ins fnl f* 12/1
9 1 **Pearl Castle (IRE)** 2 -9-0 0 HarryBentley(3) 1 62
(Andrew Balding) *hld up: pushed along 1/2-way: n.d* 9/1
10 3/4 **Camp Floyd (USA)** 2 -9-3 0 AhmedAjtebi 11 60
(Mahmood Al Zarooni) *prom: lost pl over 5f out: hdwy over 2f out: rdn and hung lft over 1f out: wknd fnl f* 9/1
11 1 3/4 **Rhyolite (IRE)** 2 -9-3 0 AndreaAtzeni 3 55
(Marco Botti) *chsd ldrs: pushed along over 2f out: wknd over 1f out* 28/1
12 3/4 **King Of Kudos (IRE)** 2 -9-3 0 RyanMoore 2 53
(Richard Hannon) *w ldr tl pushed along over 2f out: wknd over 1f out* 15/2
13 2 **The Scuttler (IRE)** 2 -9-3 0 MatthewDavies 4 48
(Mick Channon) *prom tl rdn and wknd over 1f out* 25/1
14 5 **Snoqualmie Chief** 2 -9-3 0 TedDurcan 5 35
(David Elsworth) *hld up: wknd over 2f out* 25/1

1m 26.58s (0.88) **Going Correction** -0.05s/f (Good) 14Ran SP% **125.9**
Speed ratings (Par 96): **92,89,88,87,84 83,82,82,80,80 78,77,74,69**
toteswingers: 1&2 £20.70, 1&3 £4.90, 2&3 £24.00 CSF £69.24 TOTE £4.90 : £2.10 , £5.30 , £2.00; EX 89.50 Trifecta £281.40 Pool: £570.51 - 1.50 winning units.
Owner K Abdulla **Bred** Juddmonte Farms Ltd **Trained** Newmarket, Suffolk

FOCUS
Plenty of well-bred sorts from top yards here and probably a race that will throw up a few winners.

NOTEBOOK
Ashdan ◆, a brother to the Prestige winner Sense Of Joy and a half-brother to the smart Day Flight, holds entries in some Pattern races this autumn and could well prove up to that sort of level as this was a most encouraging start, quickening nicely clear for one slap inside the final furlong.
Mutazamen, a son of Sakhee's Secret, knew his job but this was still a pleasing debut. Time may show he ran into a good one in the winner and he shouldn't be long in going one better. (op 6-1)
Zurbriggen, a Raven's Pass colt who cost 170,000gns as a foal, displayed ability on this debut and should improve. (op 6-1 tchd 7-1)
Tamarkuz(USA), a $325,00 foal, shaped nicely on his first outing and is promising. (op 5-1)
Rangi ◆, a stablemate of the winner, holds an entry in the Champagne at Doncaster and shaped quite encouragingly by the finish, missing the break and keeping on without being unduly punished. A half-brother to a couple of smart sorts, he can only improve. (op 16-1)
Etijaah(USA) showed clear ability by the finish and, in common with most from the yard, is likely to do better with this initial experience behind him. (op 28-1)
Lancelot Du Lac (ITY) ◆, a son of Shamardal who cost 45,000 gns earlier this year, shaped with a bit of promise amidst greenness and might be one to bear in mind for a maiden at one of the smaller tracks, particularly as his relatively unfashionable connections should ensure he goes off a reasonable price, keeping on without being subjected to an unduly hard time at any stage. (tchd 50-1)
Lionheart, a son of Zamindar out of a mare from a good family, was better than the result and will leave this bare form behind in due course, prominent for a long way and not knocked about as he faded. (op 9-1)
King Of Kudos (IRE) an Acclamation colt, faded right out of it in the end after being prominent for a long way but is in the right hands to progress. (op 8-1)

5063 WALKER TRANSPORT H'CAP 1m 2f
7:15 (7:16) (Class 5) (0-75,74) 3-Y-O+ £2,587 (£770; £384 ; £192) Stalls Centre

Form RPR
6-14 1 **Sammy Alexander**[56] 3101 4 -9-13 73 WilliamBuick 7 82+
(David Simcock) *hld up: hdwy 2f out: rdn to ld and edgd lft wl ins fnl f* 11/4[2]
6645 2 3/4 **Larkrise Star**[18] 4411 5 -9-0 63 PatrickHills(3) 4 70
(Dean Ivory) *chsd ldr: led over 1f out: sn rdn: hdd wl ins fnl f* 9/2[3]
030 3 2 3/4 **Nave (USA)**[37] 3766 5 -10-0 74 MartinLane 2 76
(David Simcock) *s.i.s: sn prom: rdn and ev ch over 2f out: styd on same pce fnl f* 7/4[1]
6-06 4 3 1/2 **Effigy**[8] 4722 8 -9-2 67 AmyScott(5) 8 62
(Henry Candy) *hld up in tch: rdn over 1f out: wknd fnl f* 7/1
305- 5 7 **Spyder**[282] 7236 4 -9-12 72 (p) BrettDoyle 6 53
(Jane Chapple-Hyam) *led: rdn and hdd over 1f out: wknd fnl f* 8/1
0-00 6 4 1/2 **Galletto (IRE)**[20] 4341 3 -7-11 55 oh7 DominicFox(3) 5 27
(Terry Clement) *hld up: rdn over 4f out: wknd over 2f out* 25/1
3210 7 12 **My Guardian Angel**[42] 3558 3 -9-5 74 TedDurcan 1 22
(Mark H Tompkins) *chsd ldrs tl rdn and wknd over 2f out: t.o* 5/1

2m 6.55s (1.05) **Going Correction** -0.05s/f (Good)
WFA 3 from 4yo+ 9lb 7Ran SP% **125.3**
Speed ratings (Par 103): **93,92,90,87,81 78,68**
toteswingers 1&2 £1.30, 1&3 £4.00, 2&3 £3.70 CSF £17.60 CT £28.67 TOTE £3.30 : £2.10 , £2.40; EX 17.40 Trifecta £57.50 Pool: £669.54 - 8.61 winning units.
Owner Mrs T A Foreman **Bred** Mrs T A Foreman **Trained** Newmarket, Suffolk

FOCUS
Not a particularly competitive handicap for the course. The runner-up sets an ordinary standard.
My Guardian Angel Official explanation: jockey said gelding ran flat

5064 PIPER-HEIDSIECK CONDITIONS STKS 1m 2f
7:50 (7:50) (Class 3) 3-Y-O £7,470 (£2,236; £1,118) Stalls Centre

Form RPR
0320 1 **Coupe De Ville (IRE)** 4760 3 -9-0 112 RyanMoore 2 100+
(Richard Hannon) *trckd ldr: shkn up to ld over 1f out: sn rdn and edgd rt: r.o u.p* 10/11[1]
-132 2 1 1/2 **Kingsdesire (IRE)**[62] 2920 3 -9-0 102 (t) FrankieDettori 1 97+
(Marco Botti) *hld up: hdwy to chse wnr over 1f out: sn rdn and edgd lft: eased whn hld nr fin* 11/8[2]
4014 3 3 **Clare Island Boy (IRE)**[14] 4529 3 -9-0 88 WilliamBuick 3 91
(Richard Hannon) *led: rdn and hdd over 1f out: no ex ins fnl f* 7/1[3]

2m 8.58s (3.08) **Going Correction** -0.05s/f (Good) 3Ran SP% **107.0**
Speed ratings (Par 104): **85,83,81**
CSF £2.45 TOTE £1.90 ; EX 2.40 .
Owner Macdonald,Wright,Creed,Smith & Jiggins **Bred** Flor Ryan **Trained** East Everleigh, Wilts

FOCUS
A useful effort from the winner to take this small-field conditions event. Predictably the gallop wasn't strong and the first two are rated below their best.

NOTEBOOK
Coupe De Ville (IRE) was found a good opportunity to get back to winning ways and made no mistake, proving himself at the trip into the bargain, though the emphasis was hardly on stamina. Chances are he might find the odd one too good again when he goes back up in grade, but he'll never owe connections anything after that valuable sales race success last season. (op 6-5)
Kingsdesire(IRE) had a bit to find with the winner and ran at least as well as previously after two months off. He's only had five career starts so he should find a bit more improvement at some stage. Official explanation: vet said colt lost its off-fore shoe (op Evens)
Clare Island Boy (IRE) had a fair bit to find at the weights and was readily brushed aside in the end. Connections will be hoping the handicapper doesn't take a literal reading of this form. (tchd 13-2 and 8-1)

5065 PIPER-HEIDSIECK H'CAP 6f
8:20 (8:21) (Class 3) (0-95,94) 3-Y-O+ £7,115 (£2,117; £1,058 ; £529) Stalls High

Form RPR
5521 1 **Picabo (IRE)**[17] 4437 4 -9-1 83 DaneO'Neill 4 98+
(Henry Candy) *dwlt: hld up: hdwy to ld 1f out: edgd lft: r.o wl* 9/2[2]
0040 2 3 **Joe Packet**[20] 4321 5 -9-12 94 MatthewDavies 9 99+
(Jonathan Portman) *hld up: hdwy and nt clr run over 1f out: swtchd rt: r.o to go 2nd post: nt rch wnr* 4/1[1]
0635 3 hd **Fratellino**[13] 4576 5 -9-9 91 (t) FrankieDettori 5 95
(Alan McCabe) *chsd ldrs: rdn and ev ch 1f out: styd on same pce* 11/2[3]
3400 4 hd **Sohraab**[13] 4576 8 -9-5 87 (b[1]) RyanMoore 1 91
(Hughie Morrison) *hld up: rdn and r.o wl ins fnl f: nrst fin* 10/1
0314 5 1 3/4 **Cheworee**[63] 2894 3 -8-8 80 LiamKeniry 10 78+
(David Elsworth) *chsd ldrs: ev ch 1f out: no ex ins fnl f* 12/1
4100 6 1 1/2 **Sacrosanctus**[6] 4824 4 -9-6 88 MircoDemuro 7 81
(Scott Dixon) *chsd ldrs: rdn adn ev ch 1f out: wknd wl ins fnl f* 11/1
0200 7 1 3/4 **Swiss Cross**[6] 4802 5 -9-7 94 (t) LeonnaMayor(5) 11 82
(Phil McEntee) *disp ld tl rdn and hdd 1f out: wknd ins fnl f* 8/1
0003 8 hd **Whozthecat (IRE)**[6] 4829 5 -8-4 77 (v) NeilFarley(5) 3 64
(Declan Carroll) *sn pushed along to dispute ld: rdn and hdd 1f out: sn wknd* 6/1
0400 9 1/2 **Rafaaf (IRE)**[21] 4300 4 -8-9 77 AndreaAtzeni 6 62
(Robert Eddery) *hld up: effrt and nt clr run over 1f out: wknd ins fnl f* 16/1
400- 10 8 **Harrison George (IRE)**[308] 6672 7 -9-7 92 (t) HarryBentley(3) 8 52
(P J O'Gorman) *hld up: rdn and wknd over 1f out* 10/1

1m 11.06s (-1.44) **Going Correction** -0.05s/f (Good)
WFA 3 from 4yo+ 4lb 10Ran SP% **119.1**
Speed ratings (Par 107): **107,103,102,102,100 98,95,95,94,84**
toteswingers: 1&2 £4.50, 1&3 £1.50, 2&3 £2.40 CSF £23.43 CT £104.76 TOTE £5.40 : £2.00 , £1.90, £2.10 ; EX 26.00 Trifecta £31.70 Pool: £1,043.63 - 24.33 winning units.
Owner Tom Ford **Bred** A B Mulholland **Trained** Kingston Warren, Oxon

FOCUS
A fairly useful sprint which was soundly run and the third, fourth and fifth help set the standard in a race which is rated on the positive side.

NOTEBOOK
Picabo(IRE) ◆, whose form has taken off since fitted with a hood, defied an 8lb rise for Yarmouth with ease. She'll be in for another fair hike, but it may not stop her the way she's progressing at present and connections are considering a tilt at the Great St Wilfrid at Ripon. (tchd 4-1 and 5-1)
Joe Packet underlined he's back in good form and won't always run into one as well treated as Picabo. He took a bit of time to pick up under pressure but finished well. (op 9-2 tchd 7-2)
Fratellino ran a third successive good race and is likely to remain competitive. (op 9-2 tchd 6-1)
Sohraab will probably pop up from this sort of mark at some stage, but he is increasingly becoming the sort that needs things to fall right, getting going too late here in first-time blinkers. (op 8-1 tchd 7-1)
Cheworee is still unexposed and could be worth a try over 5f before long, travelling as well as any for a long way here. (op 9-1)
Sacrosanctus fared a little better than of late but essentially appears in the handicapper's grip for now. (op 16-1)
Whozthecat(IRE) is on a long losing run and failed to repeat the form of last weekend's third at Thirsk. He faded having cut out the running. (op 13-2 tchd 7-1)
T/Plt: £29.40 to a £1 stake. Pool: £56,413.78. 1,396.53 winning tickets. T/Qpdt: £21.00 to a £1 stake Pool £4,356.10 153.20 w. tckts CR 5066a, 5068a-5072a (Foreign Racing) See RI

[4441] TIPPERARY (L-H)
Friday, August 10

OFFICIAL GOING: Soft to heavy (soft in places)

5067a ABERGWAUN STKS (LISTED RACE) 5f
6:00 (6:00) 3-Y-O+ £21,666 (£6,333; £3,000 ; £1,000)

RPR
1 **Inxile (IRE)**[5] 4838 7 -9-9 (p) AdrianNicholls 6 113
(David Nicholls) *led: rdn over 2f out: responded wl to press to repel chalrs appr fnl f: styd on wl cl home: gamely* 5/1[2]
2 1 1/2 **Nocturnal Affair (SAF)**[32] 1146 6 -9-9 113 (t) FergalLynch 4 108
(David Marnane, Ire) *chsd ldrs: 4th 1/2-way: rdn sn after to chse ldr: styd on wl but hld fnl f* 6/1[3]
3 shd **My Girl Anna (IRE)**[8] 4070 5 -9-3 100 RoryCleary 2 102+
(Muredach Kelly, Ire) *cl up bhd ldrs: 5th 1/2-way: sn rdn to chal: wnt 3rd ins fnl f: r.o wl* 6/1[3]
4 1 **Katla (IRE)**[16] 4482 4 -9-3 99 (t) WJLee 5 98
(J F Grogan, Ire) *cl up bhd ldrs: 6th 1/2-way: rdn and impr appr fnl f: r.o same pce cl home* 14/1
5 1/2 **After (IRE)**[8] 4749 3 -9-0 101 SeamieHeffernan 9 95+
(A P O'Brien, Ire) *in rr: rdn to chse ldrs after 1/2-way: nt qckn but styd on same pce fnl f* 7/1
6 1 1/2 **Bogini (IRE)**[5] 4838 3 -9-0 88 (b) PatSmullen 8 90+
(M D O'Callaghan, Ire) *sltly detached in rr early: rdn after 1/2-way: nvr nr to chal but r.o fnl f* 18/1
7 shd **Arctic (IRE)**[26] 4123 5 -9-6 105 (t) MichaelHussey 1 93
(Tracey Collins, Ire) *chsd ldrs on outer: 3rd 1/2-way: sn rdn to chal: no ex appr fnl f* 6/1[3]
8 3/4 **Santo Padre (IRE)**[26] 4123 8 -9-9 106 CO'Donoghue 7 94
(David Marnane, Ire) *chsd ldrs: reminders after 2f: rdn sn after and no ex* 10/1
9 4 3/4 **Free Zone**[34] 3877 3 -9-3 TomEaves 3 73
(Bryan Smart) *chsd ldr: 2nd 1/2-way: rdn to chal over 2f out: no ex and wknd fnl f* 3/1[1]

1m 2.84s (3.84)
WFA 3 from 4yo+ 3lb 9Ran SP% **118.0**
CSF £35.88 TOTE £5.00 : £2.30 , £2.10 , £2.50 ; DF 47.90 .
Owner Mrs Jackie Love & David Nicholls **Bred** Denis And Mrs Teresa Bergin **Trained** Sessay, N Yorks

FOCUS
After Wayne Lordan's successful manoeuvre in the opener, they all veered towards the stands' side rail. Some were inconvenienced by the move, most notably Arctic, who never landed a blow on the far side of the group. Afterwards, the winning rider described the ground as "deep" and that's probably why Inxile was sent off at such a big price to defend his crown. The third is the best guide, while the fourth and sixth support the level.

NOTEBOOK
Inxile(IRE), who 12 months previously landed this prize on good to firm ground, had had ten unsuccessful attempts since and folded pretty tamely on his last two starts. As normal, he blasted from the stalls and his rider gradually increased the tempo from halfway. He kept finding and won going away. (op 11/2 tchd 6/1 amd 9/2)
Nocturnal Affair(SAF), back on home soil, ran well considering he would have detested the ground. He travelled quite well and, while he couldn't peg back the winner, this was a nice prep for the Nunthorpe.
My Girl Anna(IRE) tends to travel sweetly but she was further back than ideal with 2f to run. She stayed on well to almost snatch second but was left with too much to do and may have benefited from racing closer to the stands' side rail.
Katla(IRE) briefly looked a threat 2f out but flattered to deceive somewhat. Her finishing effort was pretty tame and she's not quite the force she was in these type of events.
After(IRE) seems to need further than this and lacked the instant acceleration needed to get involved.

[4935] DEAUVILLE (R-H)

Friday, August 10

OFFICIAL GOING: Turf: good to soft; fibresand: standard

5073a PRIX D'AUQUAINVILLE (CLAIMER) (2YO COLTS & GELDINGS) (FIBRESAND) 6f 110y

2:20 (12:00) 2-Y-0 **£11,250** (£4,500; £3,375; £2,250; £1,125)

RPR
1 **Kalicamix**[14] 4539 2-9-2 0 ..... OlivierPeslier 4 85
(Paul Cole) *broke wl: racd cl 2nd: tk ld 2 1/2f out: r.o wl u.p whn chal 1 1/2f out: hld on wl u.p fnl 100yds* **33/10**[2]
2 ½ **Pont Marie (FR)**[13] 2-8-13 0 ..... (b) GregoryBenoist 7 81
(F Chappet, France) **9/1**
3 3 **Gottingen (FR)** 2-8-13 0 ..... ChristopheSoumillon 5 72
(J-C Rouget, France) **3/1**[1]
4 4½ **Prince Eliot (FR)**[7] 2-8-9 0 ..... (b) Christophe-PatriceLemaire 8 56
(M Boutin, France) **21/1**
5 shd **Kukurun (FR)**[17] 2-8-9 0 ..... AlexisBadel 9 56
(Mme M Bollack-Badel, France) **17/1**
6 1¼ **Haring (SPA)**[28] 2-8-2 0 ..... SoufyaneMoulin(7) 1 52
(C Boutin, France) **52/1**
7 4½ **Litian Rocket (FR)**[14] 2-9-3 0 ..... GeraldMosse 3 48
(M Boutin, France) **12/1**
8 nk **T'Choupi Chop (FR)**[17] 2-9-3 0 ..... (b) IoritzMendizabal 2 47
(A De Watrigant, France) **3/1**[1]
9 15 **Royaleo (FR)**[33] 2-8-9 0 ..... (p) ThierryThulliez 6
(E Libaud, France) **11/2**[3]

1m 20.8s (80.80) **9** Ran SP% **118.3**
WIN (incl. 1 euro stake): 4.30. PLACES: 2.00, 2.60, 1.70. DF: 27.60. SF: 38.40.
Owner P F I Cole Ltd **Bred** Whatton Manor Stud **Trained** Whatcombe, Oxon

NOTEBOOK
Kalicamix, second in a 6f auction maiden at Newmarket last time out, has been rated as taking another small step forward to win this, with the runner-up a fair guide to the level in behind.

5074a PRIX DE LA PEGASERIE (CLAIMER) (3YO) (FIBRESAND) 1m 4f

3:25 (12:00) 3-Y-0 **£9,583** (£3,833; £2,875; £1,916; £958)

RPR
1 **Kreousa**[17] 3-8-7 0 ..... RudyPimbonnet(8) 2 84
(C Laffon-Parias, France) **9/2**[2]
2 1½ **Kamate (FR)**[232] 3-8-11 0 ..... GregoryBenoist 5 78
(F Rohaut, France) **5/1**[3]
3 ½ **Milord De Reward (FR)**[37] 3-8-11 0 ..... GaetanMasure 8 77
(D Bressou, France) **17/1**
4 7 **Fani (FR)** 3-8-11 0 ..... (p) TonyPiccone 12 66
(N Bertran De Balanda, France) **30/1**
5 hd **Abayo (USA)**[7] 3-9-4 0 ..... (p) UmbertoRispoli 1 72
(C Boutin, France) **15/1**
6 4 **Lac Sacre (FR)**[122] 3-8-13 0 ..... EddyHardouin(5) 14 66
(Robert Collet, France) **54/1**
7 2½ **Jigsaw (FR)**[37] 3-8-11 0 ..... ThierryThulliez 7 55
(S Wattel, France) **10/1**
8 ½ **El Casco (FR)**[35] 3-8-11 0 ..... ThomasHuet 13 54
(S Cerulis, France) **9/1**
9 shd **Hot Wired** 3-8-11 0 ..... (p) TheoBachelot 3 54
(S Wattel, France) **25/1**
10 12 **Alatasarai (IRE)** 3-8-11 0 ..... ChristopheSoumillon 11 35
(J-C Rouget, France) **23/10**[1]
0 **Tokyo Brown (USA)**[65] 2818 3-8-11 0 ..... StephanePasquier 9
(Heather Main) *broke wl: racd cl 2nd: tk ld briefly 4f out: hdd bef st: unable to go pce: wknd* **30/1**
0 **March Avril (FR)**[14] 3-9-1 0 ..... OlivierPeslier 10
(J Boisnard, France) **14/1**
0 **Lucario (FR)**[30] 3-9-1 0 ..... Francois-XavierBertras 6
(J-P Carvalho, Germany) **22/1**
0 **Lucky Du Verger (FR)** 3-8-6 0 ..... (b¹) ChristopherGrosbois(5) 4
(J-M Gatteau, France) **71/1**

2m 39.8s (159.80) **14** Ran SP% **120.6**
WIN (incl. 1 euro stake): 5.50. PLACES: 2.10, 1.90, 3.90. DF: 11.80. SF: 17.00.
Owner Leonidas Marinopoulos **Bred** Stilvi Compania Finaciera S A **Trained** Chantilly, France

[4574] ASCOT (R-H)

Saturday, August 11

OFFICIAL GOING: Good to firm (straight course 10.1; round course 9.8)
Round Course rail positioned 4yds in from 12f to 2f increasing distances of Old Mile by 8yds, 12f and 2m by 16yds.
Wind: Virtually nil Weather: Sunny

5075 LES AMBASSADEURS CASINO SHERGAR CUP MILE (H'CAP) 1m (R)

12:55 (1:01) (Class 2) (0-100,100) 4-Y-0+

£14,754 (£5,166; £2,361; £1,842; £1,623; £1,182) **Stalls** Low

Form RPR
1-04 1 **Boom And Bust (IRE)**[8] 4761 5-9-9 **99** ..... KierenFallon 1 109
(Marcus Tregoning) *trckd ldr: led over 5f out: drvn over 1f out: hrd pressed fnl 120yds: styd on wl and a jst doing enough* **3/1**[1]
4-00 2 nk **Trade Storm**[52] 3268 4-9-4 **94** ..... MatthewChadwick 4 103
(David Simcock) *in rr: hdwy on outer 2f out: str run to chse wnr 1f out: chal fnl 120yds: no ex clsng stages* **16/1**
-200 3 2¼ **Boogie Shoes**[52] 3268 4-9-5 **95** ..... HayleyTurner 2 99
(Roger Varian) *chsd ldrs: wnt 2nd 2f out: sn drvn and no imp on wnr: lost 2nd 1f out and sn outpcd by ldng duo* **8/1**
2001 4 1¼ **Mull Of Killough (IRE)**[21] 4339 6-9-10 **100** ..... AGryder 11 101
(Jane Chapple-Hyam) *led tl hdd over 5f out: chsd wnr to 2f out: edging rt and styd on same pce fnl f* **9/1**
2125 5 2 **Dubai Dynamo**[15] 4557 7-9-7 **97** ..... JamesDoyle 3 94
(Ruth Carr) *in rr: hdwy on ins 3f out: disp 3rd ins fnl 2f: no ex and btn* **9/1**
0-02 6 nk **Bancnuanaheireann (IRE)**[11] 4689 5-9-2 **92** ..... EmmaJayneWilson 12 88
(Michael Appleby) *in rr: rdn 2f out: hdwy over 1f out: kpt on fnl f: nvr gng pce to rch ldrs* **7/1**[3]
3200 7 4 **Mawaakef (IRE)**[28] 4099 4-9-3 **93** ..... JohnnyMurtagh 7 80
(J R Jenkins) *t.k.h: chsd ldrs: rdn over 2f out: wknd over 1f out* **16/1**
3603 8 4½ **Imperial Djay (IRE)**[14] 4609 7-9-5 **95** ..... CristianDemuro 6 71
(Ruth Carr) *in rr: sme prog on outside 3f out: nvr rchd ldrs and wknd fnl 2f* **20/1**
1-10 9 13 **Arabian Star (IRE)**[52] 3268 4-9-2 **92** ..... FrankieDettori 9 39
(Andrew Balding) *chsd ldrs: rdn towards outside 3f out: wknd fr 2f out* **5/1**[2]

1m 40.33s (-0.37) **Going Correction** -0.05s/f (Good) **9** Ran SP% **101.8**
Speed ratings (Par 109): **99,98,96,95,93 92,88,84,71**
toteswingers: 1&2 £9.00, 1&3 £2.90, 2&3 £43.30. CSF £41.43 CT £242.68 TOTE £2.90: £1.40, £4.80, £2.10; EX 46.70 Trifecta £534.00 Part won. Pool: £721.66 - 0.69 winning units..
Owner Jas Singh **Bred** Duncan A McGregor **Trained** Lambourn, Berks

FOCUS
The rail was positioned 4yds in from the 1m4f start to the 2f pole, increasing distances by 8yds in the 1m race and 16yds in the 1m4f and 2m races. As ever with this novelty meeting, there were plenty of jockeys who were alien to the track, so the form may not be too reliable. A decent handicap, although the pace was ordinary and those who raced prominently were favoured, with the placed horses the best guide.

NOTEBOOK
Boom And Bust(IRE)'s victory can be owed to a fine tactical ride by Kieren Fallon. An eyecatcher at Goodwood eight days earlier, he held on well having kicked off the final bend and was undoubtedly helped by having the rail to race against. He'll be rated in the low-100s following this, but is clearly still on the up and should remain competitive in top handicaps. (op 11-4)
Trade Storm looked interesting from this mark on the pick of his form and his effort needs upgrading, having come from off the pace. He appeared to be coming with a winning run over 1f out, but just flattened out late and was always being held. (op 11-1)
Boogie Shoes, with the hood left off this time, was keen on the inside, but at least raced prominently and this represented a return to something like his best. (op 9-1)
Mull Of Killough(IRE), up 3lb for his soft-ground Newmarket win, was always up there and ran well considering the quick ground was probably to his disadvantage. (op 8-1)
Dubai Dynamo, 9lb above his last winning mark, would have preferred a stronger pace to chase. (op 10-1 tchd 8-1)
Bancnuanaheireann(IRE), probably unlucky not to win at Goodwood, received no cover from a wide draw here and was never involved having had to be dropped right out. He deserves another chance. (tchd 8-1)
Arabian Star(IRE) was clearly below form, dropping out as though something may have been amiss. (op 7-1)

5076 REDSTONE SHERGAR CUP STAYERS (H'CAP) 2m

1:30 (1:32) (Class 2) (0-100,97) 4-Y-0+

£14,754 (£5,166; £2,361; £1,842; £1,623; £1,182) **Stalls** Low

Form RPR
02 1 **Address Unknown**[14] 4575 5-9-11 **94** ..... (vt) ASuborics 2 102
(Ian Williams) *chsd ldrs: wnt 2nd jst ins fnl 2f: rdn to ld appr fnl f: pushed out: readily* **9/2**[1]
-565 2 ½ **Woolfall Treasure**[50] 3341 7-9-5 **88** ..... (v) MatthewChadwick 11 94
(Gary Moore) *sn led: jnd over 6f out tl qcknd over 3f out: rdn over 2f out: hdd appr fnl f: sn outpcd by wnr but kpt on to wl to hold 2nd* **16/1**
-054 3 1¾ **Mystery Star (IRE)**[15] 4528 7-9-8 **91** ..... FrankieDettori 7 95
(Mark H Tompkins) *chsd ldrs: drvn and styd on to take 3rd appr fnl f: nvr gng pce to rch ldng duo* **12/1**
0-03 4 2¾ **Lyric Street (IRE)**[28] 4111 4-9-11 **94** ..... EmmaJayneWilson 4 95
(Ed Dunlop) *chsd ldrs on outer: chal fr 6f out tl over 3f out: sn rdn: styd on same pce to take 4th ins fnl f* **11/2**[3]
0064 5 1¼ **Becausewecan (USA)**[4] 4925 6-9-0 **83** ..... YutakaTake 5 82
(Mark Johnston) *chsd ldrs in 3rd fr 1/2-way: rdn to dispute 2nd 2f out: wknd appr fnl f* **10/1**
-000 6 ¾ **Bernie The Bolt (IRE)**[49] 3373 6-9-6 **89** ..... HayleyTurner 1 87
(Andrew Balding) *in rr: rdn over 2f out: mod prog fnl f: nvr gng pce to get into contention* **5/1**[2]
00 7 ¾ **Astral Thunder (ARG)**[29] 4072 5-10-0 **97** ..... (b¹) ChantalSutherland 3 94
(Marco Botti) *in rr: racd towards outside: rdn over 3f out: nvr in contention: mod late prog* **25/1**
-300 8 ¾ **The Betchworth Kid**[7] 4800 7-9-9 **92** ..... (p) KierenFallon 12 88
(Alan King) *rdn along 3f out and a struggling towards rr* **10/1**
0053 9 1½ **Montaff**[15] 4528 6-9-7 **90** ..... JohnnyMurtagh 8 85
(Mick Channon) *rdn over 2f out: a towards rr* **11/2**[3]
42-0 10 nk **Ermyn Lodge**[63] 2933 6-9-12 **95** ..... (v) AGryder 9 89
(Pat Phelan) *chsd ldrs: rdn 3f out: wknd over 2f out* **6/1**

3m 32.62s (3.62) **Going Correction** -0.05s/f (Good) **10** Ran SP% **115.5**
Speed ratings (Par 109): **88,87,86,85,84 84,84,83,83,82**
toteswingers: 1&2 £15.90, 1&3 £7.40, 2&3 £29.60. CSF £75.73 CT £808.05 TOTE £5.40: £2.00, £4.60, £2.40; EX 87.90 Trifecta £1015.90 Part won. Pool: £1,372.89 - 0.30 winning units..

Owner Dr Marwan Koukash **Bred** Juddmonte Farms Ltd **Trained** Portway, Worcs
■ Stewards' Enquiry : Chantal Sutherland four-day ban: used whip above permitted level (25-28)

FOCUS
The pace was steady until past halfway in this staying handicap. The form is not the strongest for the grade despite the first three being close to their marks.

NOTEBOOK
Address Unknown was just denied by a progressive 3-y-o over 1m4f at the course recently, and his extra speed was a telling factor. His resurgence in form has coincided with the return to faster ground and he'll run in the Ebor if he can get in. (op 5-1 and 6-1 in places)
Woolfall Treasure was finishing runner-up in this event for a third consecutive year. He was 7lb lower than last year and benefited from a fine front-running ride, simply finding the winner too pacey. (op 11-1 tchd 10-1)
Mystery Star(IRE) has run good races back-to-back over this C&D and remains fairly treated on old form. (op 14-1 tchd 11-1)
Lyric Street(IRE) ran well on this step up in trip considering he had no cover wide and was a little keen. He can leave this form behind in time. (op 9-2)
Becausewecan(USA), making a quick reappearance, has never convinced with his stamina for this trip. (op 12-1)
Bernie The Bolt(IRE), winner of this in 2010, was always going to struggle for pace in being held up off the steady gallop. (op 13-2)
Montaff found little and was disappointing. (tchd 6-1 in a place)
Ermyn Lodge, fourth last year, has now run poorly on both starts this season. (op 13-2 tchd 7-1)

5077 BARCLAYS SHERGAR CUP DASH (H'CAP) 5f
2:05 (2:06) (Class 2) (0-105,105) 3-Y-0+

£14,754 (£5,166; £2,361; £1,842; £1,623; £1,182) **Stalls** High

Form				RPR
0200	**1**		**Desert Law (IRE)**[14] 4576 4-9-10 **101** .... CristianDemuro 11 (Andrew Balding) *hld up in tch: hdwy to trck ldrs 2f out and sn str chal: stl upsides ins fnl f: drvn to ld last strides* **11/2**[3]	110
4312	**2**	*shd*	**Taajub (IRE)**[14] 4576 5-9-9 **100** .... MatthewChadwick 4 (Peter Crate) *chsd ldrs: slt ld ins fnl 2f but styd hrd pressed and jnd ins fnl f: hdd last strides* **7/1**	109
10-5	**3**	*nk*	**Ahtoug**[78] 2446 4-9-5 **96** .... YutakaTake 8 (Mahmood Al Zarooni) *hld up in rr but in tch: stdy hdwy over 1f out: str run ins fnl f: fin wl: nt quite catch ldng duo* **10/1**	104
0531	**4**	*1*	**Steps (IRE)**[21] 4337 4-9-4 **95** ....(b) HayleyTurner 12 (Roger Varian) *in rr: hdwy over 1f out: styd on wl fnl f to take 4th clsng stages but nt rch ldng trio* **6/1**	99+
0543	**5**	*1 ¼*	**Lui Rei (ITY)**[7] 4802 6-9-12 **103** .... KierenFallon 2 (Robert Cowell) *pressed ldrs: drvn 2f out: styd on same pce ins fnl f* **8/1**	102
-033	**6**	*1 ¼*	**Zero Money (IRE)**[14] 4576 6-9-9 **100** ....(b) ChantalSutherland 6 (Roger Charlton) *chsd ldrs: rdn over 2f out: one pce over 1f out: wknd ins fnl f* **9/2**[1]	95
2652	**7**	*nk*	**Elnawin**[22] 4299 6-10-0 **105** .... FrankieDettori 9 (Richard Hannon) *in rr: rdn and sme prog towards outer 2f out: nvr rchd ldrs and sn wknd* **5/1**[2]	99
-100	**8**	*4 ½*	**Stone Of Folca**[8] 4762 4-9-9 **100** .... EmmaJayneWilson 3 (John Best) *sn led: hdd & wknd ins fnl 2f* **16/1**	78
1200	**9**	*3 ¾*	**Judge 'n Jury**[20] 4367 8-9-13 **104** ....(t) JamesDoyle 7 (Ronald Harris) *pressed ldrs 3f* **10/1**	68
0506	**10**	*1 ¼*	**B Fifty Two (IRE)**[8] 4790 3-9-6 **100** .... ASuborics 10 (J W Hills) *outpcd* **16/1**	60

58.53s (-1.97) **Going Correction** -0.275s/f (Firm)
WFA 3 from 4yo+ 3lb **10** Ran SP% **118.1**
Speed ratings (Par 109): **104,103,103,101,99 97,97,90,84,82**
toteswingers: 1&2 £4.00, 1&3 £18.80, 2&3 £57.00. CSF £44.39 CT £387.10 TOTE £7.10: £2.30, £2.20, £3.90; EX 38.70 Trifecta £219.10 Pool: £1,362.09 - 4.60 winning units..
Owner J C Smith **Bred** Littleton Stud **Trained** Kingsclere, Hants
■ Stewards' Enquiry : Cristian Demuro four-day ban: used whip above permitted level (Aug 25-28)

FOCUS
A good-quality sprint handicap, with the first three worth keeping on-side.

NOTEBOOK
Desert Law(IRE) looked a shade unlucky not to win the 'Dash' on Derby Day, and had excuses for his two subsequent defeats. This race worked out perfectly for him, getting a nice tow through, and he could easily make the jump to Pattern level. (op 13-2 tchd 7-1)
Taajub(IRE) brought strong recent form at the course into this race and posted another career-best in defeat, being denied right on the line. He's progressing all the time and is another who could make the jump to Pattern level at some stage. (op 11-2)
Ahtoug fared better than the bare result on his most recent outing at Goodwood, 78 days earlier, and the return to 5f on fast ground was very much to his liking. He may well have won had his rider got him going sooner. (op 8-1)
Steps(IRE), up 5lb for his soft-ground Newmarket win, took too long to pick up back on this faster surface, but the way he finished suggests he's still progressing. (tchd 13-2)
Lui Rei(ITY), third in the Stewards' Cup, ran another solid race without having the necessary pace returning to 5f on quicker ground.
Zero Money(IRE), just behind Taajub over C&D last time, couldn't quite match that form. (op 11-2 tchd 4-1)
Elnawin was always likely to prove vulnerable under top weight over this trip on fast ground. (tchd 6-1 in places)

5078 TITANIC BELFAST SHERGAR CUP CLASSIC (H'CAP) 1m 4f
2:40 (2:40) (Class 3) (0-95,95) 3-Y-0

£14,754 (£5,166; £2,361; £1,842; £1,623; £1,182) **Stalls** Low

Form				RPR
-312	**1**		**Sun Central (IRE)**[21] 4323 3-9-2 **85** .... JamesDoyle 5 (William Haggas) *hld up in rr: hdwy towards outside 3f out: str run and drvn to ld appr fnl f: kpt on wl* **2/1**[1]	98+
2431	**2**	*1*	**Ahzeemah (IRE)**[20] 4365 3-9-9 **92** ....(p) YutakaTake 4 (Saeed Bin Suroor) *hld up in rr: hdwy fr 2f out: str run to chse wnr fnl 120yds: a readily hld* **8/1**	101
2110	**3**	*2*	**Scatter Dice (IRE)**[10] 4700 3-9-10 **93** .... ChantalSutherland 9 (Mark Johnston) *chsd ldrs: drvn to dispute 2nd fr 2f out and stl disputing that position fnl 120yds whn nt pce of ldng duo but hld on wl for narrow 3rd last strides* **12/1**	99
22-2	**4**	*shd*	**Repeater**[35] 3859 3-9-12 **95** .... CristianDemuro 8 (Sir Mark Prescott Bt) *in rr: hdwy on ins fr 2f out: styd on wl thrght fnl f to press for 3rd clsng stages but no imp on wnr* **8/1**	101+
1132	**5**	*nse*	**Ruacana**[28] 4079 3-9-6 **89** .... EmmaJayneWilson 1 (Michael Bell) *in rr: drvn over 2f out: styd on fnl f to press for 3rd last strides but no ch w ldng duo* **16/1**	95+
0126	**6**	*½*	**Prussian**[9] 4735 3-9-7 **90** .... JohnnyMurtagh 3 (Mark Johnston) *sn led: rdn appr fnl 2f: hdd appr fnl f: outpcd fnl 120yds* **7/1**[2]	95
2110	**7**	*1 ¼*	**Rule Book (IRE)**[10] 4700 3-9-7 **90** .... FrankieDettori 12 (Richard Hannon) *chsd ldrs: rdn and ev ch 2f out: wknd fnl 120yds* **10/1**	93
1054	**8**	*2 ¼*	**Fennell Bay (IRE)**[9] 4735 3-9-10 **93** .... ASuborics 10 (Mark Johnston) *chsd ldr: rdn over 2f out: wknd appr fnl f* **15/2**[3]	93
4020	**9**	*2 ½*	**Misdemeanour (IRE)**[10] 4700 3-9-4 **87** .... AGryder 2 (Richard Hannon) *rdn along over 3f out: a towards rr* **9/1**	83
631S	**10**	*2 ¾*	**Last Shadow**[10] 4700 3-9-3 **86** .... KierenFallon 11 (William Muir) *in rr: rdn towards outside over 3f out: sn no prog and btn* **14/1**	77

2m 31.48s (-1.02) **Going Correction** -0.05s/f (Good) **10** Ran SP% **119.2**
Speed ratings (Par 104): **101,100,99,98,98 98,97,96,94,92**
toteswingers: 1&2 £5.40, 1&3 £1.90, 2&3 £5.00. CSF £18.91 CT £158.42 TOTE £3.10: £1.60, £2.80, £2.40; EX 23.10 Trifecta £303.40 Pool: £1,906.55 - 4.65 winning units..
Owner Lael Stable **Bred** Lael Stables **Trained** Newmarket, Suffolk
■ Stewards' Enquiry : Yutaka Take four-day ban: used whip above permitted level (Aug 25-28)

FOCUS
Although going steady early, the pace increased from a long way out in this useful-looking 3yo handicap, which hadn't been the case in earlier contests, and the form looks solid. The time was 1.69secs slower than the following older horse handicap.

NOTEBOOK
Sun Central(IRE) ◆'s recent course second (handicap debut; still looked green), had been given a notable boost when the winner that day followed up at Haydock earlier in the afternoon, and he was backed as though defeat was out of the question. Despite being caught wide and racing a little keenly, he got nicely on top once when unleashed down the straight and it took his rider a while to pull him up. He's bred to stay well and should relish 1m6f, marking him down as a horse to keep on-side. (op 3-1 early tchd 5-2 in a place)
Ahzeemah(IRE), up 6lb, promised to improve for extra 2f and was duly running on strongly at the finish. He remains capable of better still. (op 9-1 tchd 10-1)
Scatter Dice(IRE), a C&D winner two starts ago, bounced back from an average effort at Goodwood (race perhaps came too soon), keeping on again to grab third. She still has more to offer. (op 11-1)
Repeater was keen early under restraint and couldn't quite reach the leaders. He'd have benefited from a stronger gallop and may be ready for a longer trip. (op 7-1 tchd 9-1)
Ruacana wasn't well positioned considering he was dropping in trip, getting going all too late. (op 14-1)
Prussian, whose stamina was far from guaranteed stepping back up in trip, was asked to go too fast from quite a way out and can be given another chance. (tchd 15-2)
Rule Book(IRE) was a little disappointing, even though reversing Goodwood form with stablemate Misdemeanour. (op 9-1)
Fennell Bay(IRE), winner of the King George V handicap over C&D at the Royal meeting, failed to build on a solid Goodwood run. (op 8-1 tchd 9-1)
Misdemeanour(IRE) looked to run flat. (op 8-1)
Last Shadow, who slipped up at Goodwood, needs soft ground. (op 16-1)

5079 MICHAEL PAGE INTERNATIONAL SHERGAR CUP CHALLENGE (H'CAP) 1m 4f
3:15 (3:16) (Class 3) (0-95,95) 4-Y-0+

£14,754 (£5,166; £2,361; £1,842; £1,623; £1,182) **Stalls** Low

Form				RPR
-141	**1**		**Viking Storm**[24] 4216 4-9-8 **89** .... AGryder 8 (Harry Dunlop) *in tch: drvn and hdwy on ins over 2f out: wnt 2nd 1f out: styd on wl to ld fnl 150yds: readily* **5/1**[3]	100
-432	**2**	*½*	**Ittirad (USA)**[9] 4732 4-9-9 **90** .... JohnnyMurtagh 12 (Roger Varian) *chsd ldrs: wnt 2nd over 3f out: rdn to ld over 1f out: hdd and nt qckn fnl 150yds* **11/4**[1]	100
4212	**3**	*½*	**John Biscuit (IRE)**[14] 4578 4-9-3 **84** .... HayleyTurner 7 (Andrew Balding) *s.i.s: in rr: hdwy over 2f out: rdn to take 3rd fnl 120yds but no imp on ldng duo* **4/1**[2]	93
-311	**4**	*2 ¾*	**Star Commander**[77] 2474 4-9-4 **85** .... CristianDemuro 5 (Mark H Tompkins) *chsd ldrs: rdn over 2f out: styd on same pce to take 4th clsng stages* **11/1**	90
211	**5**	*1*	**John Louis**[28] 4103 4-9-7 **88** .... EmmaJayneWilson 9 (Philip McBride) *led: shkn up over 2f out: rdn and hdd over 1f out: wknd ins fnl f* **6/1**	91
0000	**6**	*1*	**Nanton (USA)**[11] 4684 10-9-9 **90** .... JamesDoyle 11 (Jim Goldie) *in rr: rdn and sme hdwy towards outer over 2f out: nvr gng pce to rch ldrs* **12/1**	92
0125	**7**	*2 ¾*	**Life And Soul (IRE)**[7] 4800 5-9-12 **93** .... YutakaTake 6 (Amanda Perrett) *in rr: hdwy towards outer 3f out: effrt over 2f out: nvr nr ldrs and sn wknd* **17/2**	90
0010	**8**	*1 ½*	**Rock A Doodle Doo (IRE)**[20] 4363 5-10-0 **95** .... ChantalSutherland 3 (William Jarvis) *in rr: pushed along and n.m.r bnd ins fnl 3f: no ch after* **14/1**	90
04/0	**9**	*½*	**Too Much Trouble**[146] 6-9-12 **93** .... MatthewChadwick 10 (Ed Vaughan) *chsd ldr tl over 3f out: wknd ins fnl 2f* **20/1**	87
2006	**10**	*10*	**Classic Colori (IRE)**[7] 4828 5-9-4 **85** .... ASuborics 1 (David O'Meara) *in rr: drvn and sme prog ins fnl 3f: nvr rchd ldrs and wknd 2f out* **14/1**	63

2m 29.79s (-2.71) **Going Correction** -0.05s/f (Good) **10** Ran SP% **122.3**
Speed ratings (Par 107): **107,106,106,104,103 103,101,100,100,93**
toteswingers: 1&2 £2.10, 1&3 £4.90, 2&3 £3.20. CSF £20.18 CT £62.72 TOTE £5.80: £2.00, £1.40, £2.20; EX 21.40 Trifecta £73.40 Pool: £1,950.67 - 19.66 winning units..
Owner Be Hopeful Partnership **Bred** Charlie Wyatt **Trained** Lambourn, Berks

FOCUS
This was run at a good, solid pace and ultimately dominated by in-form horses. Strong form. The time was 1.69secs faster than the previous 3yo handicap.

NOTEBOOK
Viking Storm, a dual AW winner this year whose turf defeat came over 1m6f (strong race, not quite get home), looked fairly treated off a 4lb higher mark and, despite getting shuffled back somewhat rounding the final bend, proved good enough to recoup the situation. A soundly run 1m4f is ideal and he can yet rate higher still. (tchd 9-2 and 11-2)
Ittirad(USA), up 3lb, ran another good race in defeat and deserves extra credit when considering he's missed engagements due to fast ground in the past. Another rise will follow, however. (op 4-1 tchd 5-2)
John Biscuit(IRE), up 2lb having just missed out over 1m2f at the course last time, saw out the longer trip well, having got a bit far back, and continues to go the right way. (tchd 9-2)
Star Commander, up 7lb, hadn't run in 77 days and couldn't quicken on this slight drop in trip. He should be sharper next time and remains capable of better. (op 10-1 tchd 9-1)
John Louis, a dual soft-ground winner at Newmarket this summer, has twice missed engagements due to fast ground, so all things considering ran well from this 5lb higher mark. (op 7-1 tchd 8-1)
Nanton(USA) got going late from the rear, but never threatened. (tchd 11-1)

Life And Soul(IRE) faded disappointingly having briefly made a forward move. (op 8-1 tchd 9-1)

5080 DUBAI DUTY FREE SHERGAR CUP SPRINT (H'CAP) 6f
3:50 (3:50) (Class 2) (0-100,98) 3-Y-O

£14,754 (£5,166; £2,361; £1,842; £1,623; £1,182) **Stalls** High

Form RPR

2100 **1** **Mince**[29] 4063 3-9-10 **94** MatthewChadwick 1 103
(Roger Charlton) *mde virtually all: rdn fnl f: edgd rt clsng stages: comf* **6/1**[3]

1154 **2** ½ **Galician**[10] 4703 3-9-4 **88** ChantalSutherland 7 95+
(Mark Johnston) *in rr: hdwy 2f out: drvn to chse ldrs 1f out: styd on to take 2nd fnl 120yds but no imp on wnr* **4/1**[1]

3606 **3** ¾ **Lady Gorgeous**[14] 4598 3-10-0 **98** HayleyTurner 11 103
(Mick Channon) *in rr: rdn over 2f out: styd on u.p to take 3rd clsng stages and gaining on 2nd but no imp on wnr* **8/1**

3633 **4** ½ **Heeraat (IRE)**[14] 4598 3-9-5 **89** ASuborics 2 92
(William Haggas) *chsd ldrs: rdn to go 2nd over 1f out but no imp on wnr: styd on for one pce 4th ins fnl f* **4/1**[1]

2064 **5** 2 ½ **Big Note (IRE)**[29] 4063 3-9-10 **94** FrankieDettori 10 89
(Andrew Balding) *chsd ldrs: rdn over 2f out: sn one pce: wknd ins fnl f* **8/1**

-260 **6** ½ **Amazing Storm (IRE)**[9] 4740 3-9-5 **89** CristianDemuro 3 83
(Jo Hughes) *chsd ldrs: rdn over 2f out: wknd fnl f* **25/1**

0600 **7** 1 **Accession (IRE)**[14] 4598 3-9-8 **92** (p) JohnnyMurtagh 8 83
(Clive Cox) *in rr: rdn over 2f out: nvr gng pce to get into contention and no ch after* **9/1**

3021 **8** nk **Springinmystep (IRE)**[14] 4588 3-9-7 **91** JamesDoyle 4 81
(Michael Dods) *in tch: rdn and effrt to cl on ldrs 2f out: sn wknd* **5/1**[2]

-452 **9** 1 **Kool Henry (IRE)**[15] 4558 3-9-6 **90** KierenFallon 6 76
(David O'Meara) *chsd ldrs 4f* **12/1**

6644 **10** 14 **Fanrouge (IRE)**[23] 4234 3-9-2 **86** AGryder 5 28
(Malcolm Saunders) *rdn over 2f out: a outpcd* **16/1**

1m 11.5s (-3.00) **Going Correction** -0.275s/f (Firm) course record **10** Ran SP% **120.6**
Speed ratings (Par 106): **109,108,107,106,103 102,101,100,99,80**
toteswingers: 1&2 £7.60, 1&3 £10.10, 2&3 £15.60. CSF £31.38 CT £202.14 TOTE £6.60: £2.30, £2.30, £2.30; EX 20.10 Trifecta £405.00 Pool: £58,936.70 - 107.66 winning units..
Owner Lady Rothschild **Bred** The Rt Hon Lord Rothschild **Trained** Beckhampton, Wilts

FOCUS
Few got into this sprint handicap, which despite appearing not to be run at an overly fast pace, produced a course record time, perhaps emphasising just how fast the ground was. Mince very much had the run of the race.

NOTEBOOK
Mince, who'd twice disappointed since winning off 3lb lower at Newmarket in May, was very much gifted an easy lead and clearly benefited from the change in tactics. She may yet develop into a Pattern filly (certainly has the size to progress), but it's doubtful a race will work out as kindly again. (op 7-1)
Galician would surely have won had she been ridden more forward, as has often been the case in the past, on this drop in trip. She finished strongly, having found herself nearer last with 2f to run, and is yet another tough Mark Johnston 3-y-o firmly on the up. (op 9-2)
Lady Gorgeous, down 2lb, ran another solid race, reversing Newmarket form with Heeraat, but like the runner-up found the winner was away and gone by the time she got going. (tchd 15-2)
Heeraat(IRE) had few excuses, failing to build on his last-time-out Newmarket third. (tchd 5-1 in a place)
Big Note(IRE) isn't straightforward and would have found this ground fast enough. (op 7-1)
Amazing Storm(IRE) ran a more encouraging race and will be of some interest once eased in the weights. (op 16-1)
Springinmystep(IRE) found the combination of a 6lb rise in a better race too much. (op 11-2 tchd 13-2)
T/Jkpt: Not won. T/Plt: £137.00 to a £1 stake. Pool: £165,716.89 - 882.79 winning tickets. T/Qpdt: £23.30 to a £1 stake. Pool: £11,059.48 - 350.89 winning tickets. ST

4670 AYR (L-H)
Saturday, August 11

OFFICIAL GOING: Good to firm (9.3)
Home bend, Stand bend and both straights all moved out 8metres adding 24yds to races between 7f & 10f and 66yds to 1m 5f race.
Wind: Breezy, half behind Weather: Cloudy, warm

5081 GAS SURE & JAMES FREW 101 YEAR H'CAP 1m
5:35 (5:35) (Class 6) (0-65,64) 3-Y-O+ **£2,070** (£616; £307; £153) **Stalls** Low

Form RPR

4060 **1** **Glenluji**[12] 4643 7-9-2 **52** (p) GrahamLee 12 61
(Jim Goldie) *hld up in midfield: rdn over 2f out: gd hdwy over 1f out: led ins fnl f: kpt on strly* **14/1**

1141 **2** 1 ½ **Cheeky Wee Red**[12] 4643 4-9-1 **58** (p) LauraBarry(7) 10 64
(Richard Fahey) *cl up chsng gp: wnt 2nd over 3f out: effrt and rdn over 2f out: led over 1f out to ins fnl f: kpt on same pce* **9/4**[1]

0063 **3** nk **Kwik Time**[78] 2463 4-8-2 **45** JasonHart(7) 9 50
(Robin Bastiman) *prom: rdn and outpcd over 2f out: rallied over 1f out: kpt on ins fnl f* **9/1**

0151 **4** ¾ **Mr Chocolate Drop (IRE)**[19] 4390 8-9-9 **59** (t) RussKennemore 3 63
(Mandy Rowland) *s.i.s: t.k.h in rr: rdn and hdwy wl over 1f out: kpt on: nrst fin* **4/1**[3]

6226 **5** 1 **Mark Anthony (IRE)**[9] 4747 5-8-10 **53** ShirleyTeasdale(7) 11 54
(Shaun Harris) *led and sn wl clr: rdn and hdd over 1f out: kpt on same pce* **7/2**[2]

440 **6** hd **Cheers Buddy (IRE)**[19] 4389 4-9-5 **55** (e) PJMcDonald 7 56
(Ian Semple) *hld up in rr: rdn and hdwy on outside over 1f out: edgd rt over 1f out: r.o fnl f* **14/1**

2025 **7** ¾ **Sabratha (IRE)**[12] 4640 4-10-0 **64** GrahamGibbons 4 63
(Linda Perratt) *hld up: rdn over 2f out: hdwy over 1f out: nvr able to chal* **12/1**

0066 **8** 1 ½ **Shunkawakhan (IRE)**[8] 4769 9-8-12 **48** ow3 (tp) PaddyAspell 6 44
(Linda Perratt) *t.k.h: prom tl rdn and no ex fr over 1f out* **40/1**

0000 **9** ½ **Champagne Valley**[19] 4390 3-8-3 **46** ow1 AmyRyan 1 41
(Sharon Watt) *bhd: rdn over 3f out: hdwy over 1f out: nvr on terms* **50/1**

-00 **10** 9 **Noinformation (IRE)**[171] 653 5-8-9 **45** (b) AndrewElliott 5 19
(Mark Michael McNiff, Ire) *hld up towards rr: struggling over 2f out: sn btn* **28/1**

-006 **11** 2 ¾ **Fleetwoodmaxi (USA)**[59] 3052 5-8-13 **49** PaulMulrennan 8 16
(Keith Dalgleish) *chsd clr ldr to over 3f out: rdn and wknd over 2f out* **12/1**

1m 40.87s (-2.93) **Going Correction** -0.30s/f (Firm)
WFA 3 from 4yo+ 7lb **11** Ran SP% **119.6**
Speed ratings (Par 101): **102,100,100,99,98 98,97,96,95,86 83**
toteswingers 1&2 £3.50, 2&3 £5.60, 1&3 £21.00 CSF £45.98 CT £279.32 TOTE £12.20: £3.60, £1.60, £2.50; EX 84.90 Trifecta £226.70 Pool: £392.15 - 1.28 winning units..
Owner J S Goldie **Bred** Jim Goldie **Trained** Uplawmoor, E Renfrews

FOCUS
After a dry spell the ground had dried out and after the opener it was described as "good, fast ground" by Graham Lee and "quick" by Russ Kennemore. Both bends had been moved out adding 24 yards to races between 7f and 1m2f and 66yds to the 1m5f race. A low-grade opener and the clear leaders went off too fast.
Fleetwoodmaxi(USA) Official explanation: jockey said gelding hung right-handed in straight

5082 JOCKEYJAN.CO.UK JAN WILSON MEMORIAL APPRENTICE H'CAP 6f
6:05 (6:05) (Class 5) (0-75,73) 3-Y-O+ **£2,911** (£866; £432; £216) **Stalls** Centre

Form RPR

5603 **1** **Argentine (IRE)**[2] 5013 8-9-1 **61** (v) ShirleyTeasdale 11 70
(Ian Semple) *hld up in tch: hdwy stands' rail to ld over 1f out: pushed out fnl f* **9/1**

204 **2** ½ **Paradise Spectre**[12] 4660 5-9-8 **71** ConorHarrison(3) 4 78
(Mrs K Burke) *slowly away: sn prom: hdwy and ev ch over 1f out: edgd rt and kpt on fnl f* **2/1**[1]

0444 **3** 2 ¼ **Polar Annie**[11] 4673 7-9-10 **70** DarylByrne 3 70
(Jim Goldie) *prom: drvn and outpcd 2f out: kpt on fnl f: nt rch first two* **8/1**

1/00 **4** shd **Jinky**[12] 4638 4-9-7 **72** RossSmith(5) 10 72
(Linda Perratt) *slt ld to over 1f out: edgd lft and sn one pce* **11/1**

21-0 **5** 2 ¼ **Idler (IRE)**[8] 4770 3-9-9 **73** GeorgeChaloner 7 66
(Mark Johnston) *disp ld: rdn and hung lft over 1f out: sn outpcd* **3/1**[2]

0230 **6** 2 **Dotty Darroch**[17] 4453 4-8-9 **55** oh1 JasonHart 9 41
(Robin Bastiman) *prom: drvn and outpcd 2f out: sn n.d* **7/1**[3]

6100 **7** nk **Blown It (USA)**[8] 4770 6-9-1 **68** PaulHainey(7) 2 53
(Keith Dalgleish) *hld up in tch: rdn over 2f out: btn fnl f* **10/1**

5206 **8** 5 **Weetentherty**[12] 4638 5-8-6 **55** oh1 (p) LauraBarry(3) 1 24
(Linda Perratt) *hld up: rdn and outpcd over 2f out: n.d after* **25/1**

-000 **9** 2 ¾ **Sheedal (IRE)**[19] 4390 4-8-4 **55** oh10 (e) PaulMcGiff(5) 5 16
(Ian Semple) *bhd: struggling over 3f out: sn btn* **80/1**

1m 10.75s (-1.65) **Going Correction** -0.20s/f (Firm)
WFA 3 from 4yo+ 4lb **9** Ran SP% **114.4**
Speed ratings (Par 103): **103,102,99,99,96 93,93,86,82**
toteswingers 1&2 £2.00, 2&3 £2.80, 1&3 £3.60 CSF £27.12 CT £154.39 TOTE £9.60: £3.20, £1.10, £2.80; EX 42.00 TRIFECTA Not won..
Owner Jim Hampson, Robert Reid **Bred** Tony Hirschfeld & L K Piggott **Trained** Carluke, S Lanarks

FOCUS
A modest apprentice sprint handicap.
Dotty Darroch Official explanation: trainer said filly was unsuited by the good to firm ground

5083 CHAMPAGNE G.H. MUMM CUVEE R. LALOU/E.B.F. MAIDEN STKS 7f 50y
6:35 (6:35) (Class 5) 2-Y-O **£3,881** (£1,155; £577; £288) **Stalls** High

Form RPR

1 **Bee Brave** 2-8-12 0 PaddyAspell 2 68
(Sharon Watt) *noisy in paddock: hld up: rdn and hdwy over 1f out: styd on wl fnl f: led last stride* **50/1**

0 **2** nse **Orions Hero (IRE)**[56] 3168 2-9-3 0 PatrickMathers 8 73
(Richard Fahey) *chsd ldrs on outside: effrt and rdn 2f out: led ins fnl f: kpt on wl: hdd last stride* **12/1**

5 **3** 1 ¾ **Causeway Foot (USA)**[19] 4387 2-9-3 0 PJMcDonald 1 68
(Jedd O'Keeffe) *t.k.h early: trckd ldrs: drvn over 2f out: kpt on ins fnl f* **12/1**

02 **4** hd **Izzy Boy (USA)**[10] 4710 2-9-3 0 FrannyNorton 7 68
(Mark Johnston) *led: rdn 2f out: hdd ins fnl f: kpt on same pce* **11/8**[1]

52 **5** 1 ¾ **Emperatriz**[37] 3776 2-8-12 0 RussKennemore 6 58
(John Holt) *t.k.h: cl up: rdn over 2f out: wknd ins fnl f* **6/1**[3]

0 **6** ½ **Khelac**[15] 4555 2-9-3 0 AndrewElliott 10 62
(Alan Swinbank) *s.i.s: t.k.h: hld up: checked over 5f out: rdn over 2f out: kpt on fnl f: nvr able to chal* **50/1**

04 **7** nk **Foolbythepool**[19] 4387 2-9-3 0 PaulMulrennan 3 63+
(Keith Dalgleish) *hld up on ins: pushed along over 2f out: no imp fnl f* **20/1**

6 **8** hd **Funding Deficit (IRE)**[23] 4257 2-9-3 0 GrahamGibbons 5 61
(David Barron) *plld hrd early: hld up in tch: effrt whn nt clr run: hmpd and stmbld over 1f out: sn btn* **25/1**

3 **9** 3 **Greeleys Love (USA)**[19] 4387 2-9-3 0 AmyRyan 4 53
(Kevin Ryan) *s.i.s: hmpd after 1f: hld up: hdwy on outside and prom after 3f: rdn and hung lft over 2f out: wknd over 1f out* **3/1**[2]

44 **10** 10 **Fife Jo**[12] 4637 2-9-3 0 GrahamLee 9 27
(Jim Goldie) *hld up in tch: drvn over 2f out: sn wknd* **12/1**

1m 32.4s (-1.00) **Going Correction** -0.30s/f (Firm) **10** Ran SP% **117.0**
Speed ratings (Par 94): **93,92,90,90,88 88,87,87,84,72**
toteswingers 1&2 £51.80, 2&3 £23.30, 1&3 £97.90 CSF £543.48 TOTE £18.10: £4.60, £3.60, £3.00; EX 458.00 TRIFECTA Not won..
Owner Major E J Watt **Bred** Psb Holdings Ltd **Trained** Brompton-on-Swale, N Yorks
■ Stewards' Enquiry : Patrick Mathers two-day ban: used whip above permitted level (Aug 25-26)

FOCUS
Probably a fair 2-y-o maiden by this track's standards but the picture changed dramatically late on. The field were quite well bunched at the finish and the form may prove limited.

NOTEBOOK
Bee Brave is a half-sister to two winners but the family have on the whole have needed plenty of time. Last to break, she came from last to first despite meeting traffic problems in the final 2f. She will be even better suited by a mile and could progress and prove decent. (op 66-1)
Orions Hero(IRE), favourite when last in soft ground on his debut at York, has plenty of size and scope. He worked hard to get his head in front only to be mugged on the line. He will make an even better 3-y-o but can surely lose the maiden tag this season. (op 16-1)
Causeway Foot(USA), whose dam has already bred three winners, stepped up on his debut effort. He should improve again.
Izzy Boy(USA), who recorded a RPR of 74 when runner-up on his second start over 6f at Redcar, set the pace and looked in charge at one stage. He tied up in the closing stages and, up in the air at present, 6f may suit him better for the time being. (op 11-10)
Emperatriz, runner-up in soft ground over 6f at Haydock, tired badly in the final furlong and may not have appreciated the much quicker ground. Official explanation: jockey said filly lost its action (op 11-2 tchd 5-1)
Khelac, tailed off last on his debut at York, showed a lot more and will improve again.
Foolbythepool again showed ability on his third start and looks likely nursery material.
Funding Deficit(IRE) Official explanation: jockey said gelding clipped heels

Greeleys Love(USA), the paddock pick, found himself posted wide after a tardy start from his outside draw. He hung left and weakened over a furlong out and may not have appreciated the much quicker ground. His rider reported that he suffered interference shortly after the start, so he must not be written off yet. Official explanation: jockey said colt suffered interference shortly after start (op 4-1)

5084 UNISON'S AYRSHIRE & ARRAN HEALTH BRANCH H'CAP — 7f 50y

7:05 (7:05) (Class 5) (0-70,70) 3-Y-O+ — **£2,911** (£866; £432; £216) **Stalls** High

Form — RPR

6-16 **1** — **Burnwynd Boy**[19] 4388 7-8-9 **53** .... PJMcDonald 3 — 61
(Ian Semple) *hld up: smooth hdwy whn nt clr run over 2f out: shkn up to ld ins fnl f: pushed out* **4/1**[3]

0-00 **2** *½* **Carrie's Magic**[14] 4592 5-8-7 **51** oh2 .... AndrewElliott 9 — 57
(Alistair Whillans) *t.k.h: cl up: led over 2f out to ins fnl f: rallied: hld nr fin* **16/1**

4063 **3** *nk* **Chookie Royale**[19] 4393 4-9-9 **67** ....(p) PaulMulrennan 7 — 72
(Keith Dalgleish) *in tch: hdwy to chse ldrs over 1f out: kpt on fnl f: hld towards fin* **7/2**[2]

0510 **4** *1 ¼* **Strong Man**[5] 4890 4-9-2 **60** ....(b) PaddyAspell 1 — 62
(Michael Easterby) *plld hrd early: prom: effrt and rdn over 2f out: kpt on same pce fnl f* **6/1**

4450 **5** *1* **Whats For Pudding (IRE)**[8] 4779 4-8-2 **51** oh6 .... NeilFarley(5) 5 — 50
(Declan Carroll) *trckd ldrs: rdn and outpcd 3f out: rallied over 1f out: no imp fnl f* **9/1**

-660 **6** *1 ¼* **Hills Of Dakota**[26] 4133 4-9-12 **70** .... GrahamGibbons 4 — 66
(David Barron) *hld up: rdn and swtchd rt over 2f out: no imp fnl f* **10/3**[1]

2U10 **7** *5* **Goninodaethat**[18] 4432 4-9-0 **58** .... GrahamLee 2 — 41
(Jim Goldie) *t.k.h: led to over 2f out: wknd over 1f out* **9/2**

1m 30.74s (-2.66) **Going Correction** -0.30s/f (Firm) — **7** Ran SP% **113.7**
Speed ratings (Par 103): **103,102,102,100,99 98,92**
toteswingers 1&2 £5.80, 2&3 £12.70, 1&3 £3.10 CSF £60.16 CT £243.21 TOTE £4.80: £2.50, £4.40; EX 77.10 Trifecta £173.50 Part won. Pool: £234.49 - 0.50 winning units..
Owner Robert Reid **Bred** Mrs A F Tullie **Trained** Carluke, S Lanarks

FOCUS
They went very steady to the halfway mark and there was little between the first five at the line.
Burnwynd Boy Official explanation: trainer said, regarding apparent improvement in form, that the gelding was better suited by faster ground.

5085 CHAMPAGNE G.H. MUMM BLANC DE BLANC H'CAP — 1m 2f

7:35 (7:36) (Class 5) (0-75,76) 3-Y-O+ — **£2,911** (£866; £432; £216) **Stalls** Low

Form — RPR

00U2 **1** — **King Of Windsor (IRE)**[12] 4641 5-10-1 **76** ....(p) PaulMulrennan 6 — 84
(Keith Dalgleish) *prom: smooth hdwy over 2f out: rdn and ev ch over 1f out: led wl ins fnl f: r.o* **9/4**[1]

5061 **2** *nk* **Watts Up Son**[54] 3213 4-9-7 **75** ....(bt) JasonHart(7) 7 — 82
(Declan Carroll) *led: rdn and qcknd bnd over 3f out: jnd over 1f out: hdd wl ins fnl f: jst hld* **8/1**

0264 **3** *1 ¼* **Euston Square**[11] 4674 6-9-12 **73** .... PJMcDonald 3 — 78
(Alistair Whillans) *s.i.s: hld up: hdwy on outside and edgd lft over 1f out: kpt on ins fnl f* **13/2**[3]

0250 **4** *1 ½* **Hawdyerwheesht**[12] 4641 4-8-11 **58** .... GrahamLee 4 — 60
(Jim Goldie) *hld up: rdn over 2f out: styd on fnl f: nvr able to chal* **10/1**

4420 **5** *hd* **High Resolution**[12] 4641 5-9-1 **62** .... GrahamGibbons 1 — 63
(Linda Perratt) *dwlt: hld up: hdwy 2f out: rdn and no imp fnl f* **12/1**

1326 **6** *2 ¼* **Rub Of The Relic (IRE)**[5] 4864 7-8-13 **67** ....(v) NedCurtis(7) 10 — 64
(Paul Midgley) *chsd ldr: drvn and outpcd over 2f out: no imp fr over 1f out* **13/2**[3]

0251 **7** *nk* **Painted Tail (IRE)**[13] 4627 5-9-5 **71** .... GarryWhillans(5) 2 — 67
(Alan Swinbank) *hld up in tch: drvn and outpcd over 2f out: sn n.d* **9/2**[2]

0-05 **8** *13* **Northern Jewel (IRE)**[15] 4548 3-8-0 **56** ....(p) PatrickMathers 8 — 26
(Richard Fahey) *t.k.h: cl up tl rdn and wknd 2f out* **22/1**

0000 **9** *1 ½* **Fighter Boy (IRE)**[15] 4557 5-10-0 **75** .... PaddyAspell 5 — 42
(Michael Easterby) *dwlt: t.k.h: hld up: hdwy on outside and cl up over 4f out: rdn and wknd 2f out* **8/1**

2m 8.73s (-3.27) **Going Correction** -0.30s/f (Firm)
WFA 3 from 4yo+ 9lb — **9** Ran SP% **119.0**
Speed ratings (Par 103): **101,100,99,98,98 96,96,85,84**
toteswingers 1&2 £5.50, 2&3 £12.30, 1&3 £4.20 CSF £21.89 CT £105.35 TOTE £3.40: £1.40, £3.20, £1.80; EX 22.30 Trifecta £187.50 Pool: £253.39 - 1.00 winning units..
Owner Gordon McDowall **Bred** Shadwell Estate Company Limited **Trained** Carluke, S Lanarks

Fighter Boy(IRE) Official explanation: jockey said gelding hung right-handed in straight

5086 Q T S GROUP H'CAP — 1m 7f

8:05 (8:06) (Class 6) (0-65,66) 4-Y-O+ — **£2,070** (£616; £307; £153) **Stalls** Low

Form — RPR

6464 **1** — **Forrest Flyer (IRE)**[12] 4639 8-9-7 **62** .... GrahamLee 4 — 70
(Jim Goldie) *led: rdn and hdd over 2f out: styd upsides: regained ld ins fnl f: kpt on gamely* **4/1**[3]

1020 **2** *1* **Vittachi**[8] 4766 5-9-7 **62** .... PaulMulrennan 2 — 69
(Alistair Whillans) *cl up: chal over 5f out: led over 2f out: hdd ins fnl f: kpt on same pce towards fin* **9/2**

5 **3** *2 ½* **Shisha Threesixty (IRE)**[11] 4391 4-8-11 **57** ....(b) LMcNiff(5) 5 — 61
(Lucinda Russell) *t.k.h: in tch: hdwy over 3f out: outpcd over 2f out: kpt on fnl f: no imp* **16/1**

2413 **4** *3* **Nay Secret**[33] 3904 4-8-5 **51** .... NeilFarley(5) 1 — 51
(Jim Goldie) *in tch: drvn and outpcd over 3f out: rallied fnl f: no imp* **11/4**[2]

-031 **5** *½* **Bandanaman (IRE)**[5] 4867 6-9-6 **66** 6ex .... GarryWhillans(5) 3 — 65
(Alan Swinbank) *prom: outpcd and hung lft wl over 2f out: sn no imp* **7/4**[1]

2-00 **U** — **Rhyton (IRE)**[18] 4431 5-8-11 **52** .... PJMcDonald 7
(Brian Storey) *rrd and uns rdr leaving stalls* **25/1**

3m 23.03s (2.63) **Going Correction** -0.30s/f (Firm) — **6** Ran SP% **110.9**
Speed ratings (Par 101): **80,79,78,76,76**
toteswingers 1&2 £3.20, 2&3 £11.20, 1&3 £8.20 CSF £21.35 TOTE £5.40: £2.30, £2.30; EX 16.50 TRIFECTA Not won..
Owner Mrs Camille Macdonald **Bred** Philip Lau **Trained** Uplawmoor, E Renfrews

FOCUS
The first two took each other on from the halfway mark and they were always in pole position.
Bandanaman(IRE) Official explanation: jockey said gelding hung left-handed

5087 CHAMPAGNE G.H. MUMM CORDON ROUGE H'CAP — 5f

8:35 (8:40) (Class 6) (0-55,58) 3-Y-O+ — **£2,070** (£616; £307; £153) **Stalls** Centre

Form — RPR

4604 **1** — **Imperial Legend (IRE)**[18] 4428 3-8-10 **54** ....(p) ShirleyTeasdale(7) 5 — 63
(David Nicholls) *mde all: rdn and edgd rt over 1f out: edgd lft and hld on wl towards fin* **12/1**

0 **2** *½* **Strategic Heights (IRE)**[9] 4734 3-8-9 **46** oh1 ....(b) PJMcDonald 2 — 53
(Liam McAteer, Ire) *cl up on outside: effrt and rdn over 1f out: kpt on ins fnl f: hld towards fin* **25/1**

212 **3** *nk* **Irish Girls Spirit (IRE)**[4] 4911 3-9-3 **54** .... MickyFenton 10 — 60
(Paul Midgley) *cl up: drvn and edgd lft over 1f out: kpt on ins fnl f* **15/8**[1]

0532 **4** *½* **Distant Sun (USA)**[5] 4865 8-9-0 **55** ....(p) JasonHart(7) 16 — 59
(Linda Perratt) *hld up stands' side: rdn and edgd lft over 2f out: styd on fnl f: nrst fin* **8/1**[3]

3505 **5** *hd* **Gran Canaria Queen**[4] 4911 3-8-5 **49** ....(v) GeorgeChaloner(7) 3 — 53
(Ian Semple) *t.k.h: cl up: rdn over 2f out: kpt on ins fnl f* **16/1**

2022 **6** *1* **Missile Attack (IRE)**[26] 4154 4-9-0 **53** ....(p) GarryWhillans(5) 15 — 53
(Ian Semple) *cl up stands' rail: rdn 2f out: kpt on same pce ins fnl f* **12/1**

/005 **7** *hd* **Jebel Tara**[12] 4638 7-8-12 **51** ....(bt) NeilFarley(5) 6 — 50
(Ian Semple) *s.i.s: bhd and outpcd: hung lft 1/2-way: styd on fnl f: nvr able to chal* **20/1**

000 **8** *nk* **Busy Bimbo (IRE)**[15] 4547 3-8-9 **46** oh1 ....(b) AmyRyan 9 — 44
(Alan Berry) *hld up: rdn over 2f out: kpt on fnl f: nt gng pce to chal* **33/1**

6023 **9** *2* **Amno Dancer (IRE)**[14] 4593 5-9-0 **48** ....(p) PaddyAspell 11 — 39
(Ian Semple) *hld up: rdn along 2f out: no imp fnl f* **14/1**

5621 **10** *1 ¾* **Roy's Legacy**[7] 4798 3-9-7 **58** ....(t) GrahamLee 12 — 43
(Shaun Harris) *prom: rdn and outpcd 2f out: n.d after* **5/1**[2]

0563 **11** *nse* **Dragon Spirit (IRE)**[7] 4807 3-8-9 **46** oh1 .... FrannyNorton 13 — 31
(Linda Perratt) *dwlt and hld up towards stands' side: rdn over 2f out: btn fnl f* **16/1**

00- **12** *2 ¼* **Yo Credo (IRE)**[301] 6880 3-8-9 **46** oh1 ....[1] GrahamGibbons 7 — 22
(John Carr) *cl up: rdn and hung lft 2f out: sn btn* **20/1**

500 **13** *3* **Little Thief**[13] 4620 5-8-12 **46** oh1 .... AndrewElliott 4 — 12
(Iain Jardine) *in tch tl rdn and wknd over 2f out* **20/1**

6-04 **14** *nk* **Findhornbay**[19] 4394 3-9-4 **55** .... PaulMulrennan 14 — 20
(Keith Dalgleish) *prom: drvn along over 2f out: sn btn* **12/1**

58.29s (-1.11) **Going Correction** -0.20s/f (Firm)
WFA 3 from 4yo+ 3lb — **14** Ran SP% **125.1**
Speed ratings (Par 101): **100,99,98,97,97 96,95,95,92,89 89,85,80,80**
toteswingers 1&2 £78.60, 2&3 £20.80, 1&3 £10.60 CSF £295.44 CT £848.03 TOTE £11.10: £2.90, £11.30, £1.70; EX 305.60.
Owner Pinnacle Mujadil Partnership **Bred** Newlands House Stud **Trained** Sessay, N Yorks
■ Stewards' Enquiry : Shirley Teasdale two-day ban: careless riding (Aug 25-26)

FOCUS
They covered two thirds of the track in this rock-bottom sprint handicap.
T/Plt: £2,779.30 to a £1 stake. Pool of £46068.83 - 12.10 winning tickets. T/Qpdt: £782.10 to a £1 stake. Pool of £4016.42, 3.80 winning tickets. RY

5039 HAYDOCK (L-H)

Saturday, August 11

OFFICIAL GOING: Good to firm (8.9)
All races on Outer home straight and races on Round course increased in distance by about 51yds.
Wind: Light, half behind Weather: Fine

5088 JOHN BUDWORTH HUGHES MEMORIAL NURSERY — 5f

1:45 (1:46) (Class 3) (0-95,94) 2-Y-O — **£7,439** (£2,213; £1,106; £553) **Stalls** High

Form — RPR

2531 **1** — **Barracuda Boy (IRE)**[23] 4230 2-8-2 **75** .... SilvestreDeSousa 6 — 81
(Tom Dascombe) *a.p: led 2f out: r.o ins fnl f: in command towards fin* **6/1**[3]

106 **2** *1 ¼* **The Taj (USA)**[16] 4488 2-9-2 **89** .... TadhgO'Shea 8 — 91
(Richard Hannon) *a.p: rdn 2f out: kpt on to take 2nd wl ins fnl f: no imp on wnr* **9/2**[2]

4100 **3** *1* **Mandy Layla (IRE)**[7] 4820 2-8-2 **75** .... JoeFanning 5 — 73
(Bryan Smart) *led: hdd 2f out: sn rdn: stl cl up chsng wnr over 1f out: lost 2nd and no ex wl ins fnl f* **12/1**

15 **4** *hd* **Normal Equilibrium**[16] 4488 2-8-9 **85** .... HarryBentley(3) 1 — 82
(Roger Varian) *hld up: hdwy to chse ldrs over 1f out: styd on same pce and no imp ins fnl f* **4/1**[1]

3434 **5** *shd* **Regal Dan (IRE)**[57] 3117 2-8-5 **78** .... WilliamCarson 4 — 75
(Charles Hills) *hld up: hdwy to chse ldrs over 1f out: styd on same pce ins fnl f* **14/1**

2041 **6** *nk* **Equitania**[21] 4331 2-8-10 **83** .... RyanMoore 11 — 79
(Richard Hannon) *chsd ldrs: rdn and nt qckn over 1f out: kpt on same pce ins fnl f* **13/2**

413 **7** *1 ¾* **Botanic Garden**[36] 3823 2-9-7 **94** .... JamieSpencer 10 — 83
(William Haggas) *in rr: pushed along 2f out: kpt on ins fnl f: nvr able to trble ldrs: eased fnl 50yds* **8/1**

15 **8** *nse* **Secret Look**[23] 4247 2-8-9 **82** .... FrannyNorton 9 — 71
(Ed McMahon) *hld up: rdn over 1f out: one pce ins fnl f: nt trble ldrs* **9/1**

5432 **9** *2 ¼* **Millie N Aire**[21] 4324 2-7-5 **71** oh5 .... NoelGarbutt(7) 7 — 52
(Danielle McCormick) *hld up: effrt 2f out: no imp over 1f out: wl btn fnl 100yds* **50/1**

513 **10** *2 ½* **Blackdown Spirit**[16] 4488 2-9-2 **89** .... JamesMillman 3 — 66
(Rod Millman) *prom tl rdn and wknd over 1f out: eased whn wl btn fnl 100yds* **11/1**

0010 **11** *2 ½* **Starbotton**[29] 4071 2-7-13 **72** .... JimmyQuinn 2 — 35
(James Bethell) *chsd ldrs: pushed along 2f out: wknd over 1f out* **50/1**

58.56s (-2.24) **Going Correction** -0.475s/f (Firm) 2y crse rec — **11** Ran SP% **113.5**
Speed ratings (Par 98): **98,96,94,94,93 93,90,90,86,82 78**
toteswingers: 1&2 £6.80, 1&3 £17.20, 2&3 £13.90. CSF £31.89 CT £309.73 TOTE £7.80: £2.40, £1.40, £4.30; EX 31.90.
Owner Laurence A Bellman **Bred** Mount Coote Partnership **Trained** Malpas, Cheshire

FOCUS
Those that headed the weights brought some good performances into this contest, so the form should be reliable, with the third the best guide.

NOTEBOOK
Barracuda Boy(IRE) was up in class after winning at Bath but found that no barrier to success. Faced with fast ground for the first time, he stormed to the front over 1f out and won in fair style. An entry in the DBS Premier Yearling Stakes at York later this month is likely to be taken up all being well. (op 13-2)
The Taj(USA) raced a shade keenly towards the head of affairs and didn't do too badly, considering he was giving 14lb away to the horses either side of him. He remains a useful sprinting prospect. (op 7-2)
Mandy Layla(IRE), trying 5f for the first time, showed a lot of speed and, considering her owner, will surely be seen whizzing round Chester at some stage. (op 16-1)
Normal Equilibrium came with a group of three closest to the far-side rail, which didn't look the place to be. He should be allowed another chance. (op 9-2)

Regal Dan(IRE) ◆, absent since mid-June, had a nice line of form involving Bungle Inthejungle but didn't get away the quickest, hampering his chances. He made nice progress late on, however, and will be of interest next time. (op 12-1)

5089 NATIONWIDEVEHICLECONTRACTS.CO.UK LEVY BOARD H'CAP 1m 3f 200y

2:20 (2:20) (Class 2) 3-Y-O

£31,125 (£9,320; £4,660; £2,330; £1,165; £585) **Stalls** High

Form RPR

3-11 **1** **Gospel Choir**[21] 4323 3-9-1 **90** RyanMoore 6 104+
(Sir Michael Stoute) *chsd ldr: rdn to chal wl over 2f out: led over 1f out: jnd fnl 110yds: gamley fnd ex towards fin* **5/2**[1]

-421 **2** ½ **Stencive**[15] 4542 3-8-13 **88** TomQueally 1 101+
(William Haggas) *in tch: clsd 3f out: swtchd rt wl over 1f out: wnt 2nd 1f out: upsides and str chal fnl 110yds: hld cl home* **8/1**

0111 **3** 2 **Sir Graham Wade (IRE)**[3] 4962 3-9-5 **94** 6ex JoeFanning 7 104
(Mark Johnston) *in tch: effrt 3f out: hung lft and no imp on ldrs over 1f out: styd on to take 3rd fnl 75yds: unable to chal front pair* **11/4**[2]

11-6 **4** 1¼ **Anjaz (USA)**[14] 4608 3-8-13 **88** SilvestreDeSousa 5 96
(Saeed Bin Suroor) *racd keenly: chsd ldrs: effrt 3f out: led over 2f out: hdd over 1f out: no ex fnl 75yds* **14/1**

0121 **5** 1½ **Three Bards (IRE)**[8] 4776 3-8-2 **77** FrannyNorton 9 83
(Mark Johnston) *led at stdy pce: rdn and hdd over 2f out: one pce 1f out: no ex fnl 100yds* **10/1**

1201 **6** 4 **Gabrial The Great (IRE)**[35] 3859 3-9-4 **93** JamieSpencer 8 92
(Michael Bell) *hld up in rr: checked whn nt clr run over 2f out and sn after: rdn and no imp over 1f out: nvr threatened: wl btn ins fnl f* **7/1**

4-11 **7** 16 **Rosslyn Castle**[94] 1978 3-9-7 **96** GeorgeBaker 4 70
(Roger Charlton) *hld up: rdn over 2f out: lft bhd fnl f* **5/1**[3]

2m 32.87s (-0.93) **Going Correction** -0.15s/f (Firm) **7** Ran SP% **111.3**
Speed ratings (Par 106): **97,96,95,94,93 90,80**
toteswingers: 1&2 £4.40, 1&3 £2.10, 2&3 £5.10. CSF £21.44 CT £55.39 TOTE £2.90: £2.20, £3.40; EX 17.50 Trifecta £55.60 Pool: £716.26 - 9.52 winning units..
Owner Cheveley Park Stud **Bred** Cheveley Park Stud Ltd **Trained** Newmarket, Suffolk
■ Stewards' Enquiry : Tom Queally caution: careless riding.

FOCUS
It would be surprising if a few subsequent winners didn't emerge from this. The form looks strong and has been rated positively, with the third and fifth the best guides.

NOTEBOOK
Gospel Choir ◆ has quickly developed into a very useful performer. One of the first off the bridle, he looked sure to be beaten as runners closed up but he found plenty for pressure to gain success. He doesn't have any fancy entries, so it'll be interesting to see where connections head with him next. (tchd 11-4)
Stencive ◆ came into this off the back of a maiden victory and ran a cracker despite being worn down inside the final half a furlong by Gospel Choir. The way the Haggas-trained colt travels suggests he's a classy type. (op 15-2 tchd 7-1)
Sir Graham Wade(IRE), a C&D winner, was going for a fourth success in a row (he won his first handicap off a mark of 80), but never really looked like achieving it. He shaped as though a try over further could be helpful now. (op 3-1 tchd 5-2)
Anjaz(USA) showed little on her seasonal return but was up in trip for this and did a lot better despite being a bit free early. (op 16-1)
Gabrial The Great(IRE), a C&D winner in July, got short of room when moving nicely about 2f out and wasn't able to get back into the mix after losing a position or two. He appeared to be going as well as the runner-up when meeting trouble. (op 13-2)
Rosslyn Castle, off since beating Gabrial The Great at Chester in May and gelded in the interim, was really disappointing but is entitled to come on for this effort. Roger Charlton reported that the gelding was unsuited by the good to firm going. Official explanation: trainer said gelding was unsuited by the good to firm ground (op 11-2)

5090 TALK TO VICTOR ROSE OF LANCASTER STKS (GROUP 3) 1m 2f 95y

2:55 (2:56) (Class 1) 3-Y-O+ **£31,190** (£11,825; £5,918; £2,948; £1,479) **Stalls** Centre

Form RPR

630 **1** **Hunter's Light (IRE)**[49] 3369 4-9-3 110 SilvestreDeSousa 1 116
(Saeed Bin Suroor) *chsd ldr: led over 2f out: rdn over 1f out: r.o wl and in command fnl f* **3/1**[3]

1134 **2** 2 **Jet Away**[14] 4610 5-9-3 112 TomQueally 5 112
(Sir Henry Cecil) *chsd ldrs: rdn 2f out: wnt 2nd wl over 1f out: no imp on wnr fnl f* **15/8**[1]

2153 **3** 4 **Gabrial (IRE)**[10] 4699 3-8-8 108 JamieSpencer 4 108
(Richard Fahey) *plld hrd: hld up: rdn and hung lft over 1f out and wnt 3rd: no imp on ldrs: kpt on same pce ins fnl f: eased fnl 75yds* **9/4**[2]

-055 **4** 6 **Ransom Note**[14] 4610 5-9-3 110 (p) RyanMoore 2 93
(Charles Hills) *led: rdn and hdd over 2f out: wknd over 1f out* **9/2**

/2-4 **5** 91 **Self Employed**[23] 4248 5-9-3 75 WilliamCarson 3
(Garry Woodward) *bustled along briefly jst after s: plld hrd: hld up in last pl: hung rt ent st wl over 4f out: sn lost tch: t.o fnl 3f* **80/1**

2m 11.73s (-3.77) **Going Correction** -0.15s/f (Firm)
WFA 3 from 4yo+ 9lb **5** Ran SP% **110.0**
Speed ratings (Par 113): **109,107,104,99,26**
CSF £9.03 TOTE £3.80: £1.80, £1.60; EX 9.60.
Owner Godolphin **Bred** Darley **Trained** Newmarket, Suffolk

FOCUS
Tactics were always going to play a part in such a small field and one felt that Silvestre De Sousa got everything right on his mount. The form is not the most solid but the winner is rated a slight improver with the placed horses a similar amount below their marks.

NOTEBOOK
Hunter's Light(IRE), who'd missed his last engagement due to fast ground, has a decent record in small fields (3-5 in races with eight or less runners) and was gaining an overdue first Group success by taking this. The jockey said afterwards that he felt his mount could handle a step back up in class again. (op 9-2)
Jet Away looked to have every chance but couldn't get to the winner once he'd quickened. He's basically a Listed-class performer on what we have seen to-date. (op 7-4)
Gabrial(IRE), the only 3-y-o in the line-up, was a shade keen early and hung left (something he has done previously) behind Jet Away with about 1f to go. He is better than he showed here. (tchd 5-2 in places)
Ransom Note, wearing cheekpieces for the first time, was allowed to dictate so this has to be a disappointing effort. However, he is starting to edge down the weights and maybe quality handicaps might come into the reckoning again if continuing to run below par. (op 4-1)

5091 BETVICTOR.COM H'CAP 1m 2f 95y

3:25 (3:26) (Class 2) (0-105,94) 3-Y-O+ **£12,938** (£3,850; £1,924; £962) **Stalls** Centre

Form RPR

1510 **1** **Opinion (IRE)**[9] 4735 3-9-1 **90** RyanMoore 8 96+
(Sir Michael Stoute) *a.p: rdn 2f out: led jst over 1f out: pressed ins fnl f: r.o gamely towards fin* **4/1**[2]

0410 **2** ¾ **Fork Handles**[14] 4608 4-9-4 **84** GeorgeBaker 1 89
(Mick Channon) *trckd ldrs: effrt 2f out: chalng fr over 1f out: nt qckn and hld towards fin* **20/1**

5-1 **3** ½ **Invisible Hunter (USA)**[16] 4516 3-9-5 **94** (t) SilvestreDeSousa 6 98+
(Saeed Bin Suroor) *led: rdn 2f out: hdd jst over 1f out: stl ch ins fnl f: no ex fnl 50yds* **11/4**[1]

5316 **4** ¾ **Art Scholar (IRE)**[7] 4795 5-9-4 **84** TomQueally 4 86+
(Michael Appleby) *hld up in rr: rdn and hdwy over 1f out: styd on and hung lft ins fnl f: nt quite able to get to ldrs* **7/1**

3-53 **5** 3¾ **Haylaman (IRE)**[15] 4529 4-9-7 **87** JamieSpencer 5 82
(David Simcock) *hld up: rdn over 2f out: one pce fnl f: nvr able to chal* **11/2**

0500 **6** 1½ **Barren Brook**[7] 4828 5-9-4 **84** DavidNolan 2 76
(Michael Easterby) *dwlt: racd keenly: hld up: rdn over 1f out: no imp* **9/2**[3]

0306 **7** hd **Licence To Till (USA)**[11] 4684 5-10-0 **94** JoeFanning 3 86
(Mark Johnston) *prom: rdn whn chalng over 2f out: wknd over 1f out* **8/1**

-062 **8** ¾ **Spanish Plume**[12] 4657 4-8-13 **79** J-PGuillambert 7 69
(Reg Hollinshead) *trckd ldrs: pushed along 3f out: rdn and wknd over 1f out* **25/1**

2m 13.53s (-1.97) **Going Correction** -0.15s/f (Firm)
WFA 3 from 4yo+ 9lb **8** Ran SP% **112.5**
Speed ratings (Par 109): **101,100,100,99,96 95,95,94**
toteswingers: 1&2 £10.00, 1&3 £2.00, 2&3 £5.00. CSF £73.65 CT £252.24 TOTE £4.40: £2.00, £2.80, £1.30; EX 59.40.
Owner Highclere Thoroughbred Racing-Herring **Bred** Ballylinch Stud **Trained** Newmarket, Suffolk

FOCUS
The early fractions didn't look frenetic but the winner ground out victory rather than quicken away. The third and fourth help set the level.

NOTEBOOK
Opinion(IRE), down the field after being hampered in a hot race at the Glorious Goodwood meeting just over a week previously, appeared to gallop his rivals in to submission once in front. A half-brother to horses that stayed at least 1m4f, including the ill-fated Fox Hunt, it wouldn't be a surprise to see him up in distance next time. (op 5-1)
Fork Handles, without a visor, was reunited with George Baker (previously 1-1 on her) and went really well for him. The partnership clearly works, so she's one to be interested in when this rider is booked. (op 14-1)
Invisible Hunter(USA), up in trip, was making his handicap debut and ran nicely after leading. A drop in trip again wouldn't hurt his chances, although he didn't seem to have many problems with this distance. (op 3-1 tchd 10-3)
Art Scholar(IRE) stayed on strongly, despite hanging late on, after coming round runners from the rear to make his challenge. He's holding his form remarkably well. (op 9-1)
Barren Brook has come down the weights to a fair mark but never threatened after racing keenly in rear. He'll no doubt hit top form at some stage before the end of the season (op 5-1)

5092 BRITISH STALLION STUDS DICK HERN EBF FILLIES' STKS (LISTED RACE) 1m

4:00 (4:00) (Class 1) 3-Y-O+

£21,549 (£8,170; £4,088; £2,036; £1,022; £513) **Stalls** Low

Form RPR

2326 **1** **Ladys First**[13] 4628 3-8-7 100 BarryMcHugh 5 106
(Richard Fahey) *mde virtually all: pressed over 2f out: r.o gamely fnl f* **13/2**

-101 **2** ¾ **Dank**[14] 4579 3-8-7 98 RyanMoore 8 105
(Sir Michael Stoute) *midfield: effrt 3f out: wnt 2nd over 1f out: ev ch ins fnl f: hld towards fin* **9/4**[1]

4013 **3** 3 **Moone's My Name**[15] 4527 4-9-0 97 JamieSpencer 2 99
(Ralph Beckett) *chsd wnr: str chal and jnd wnr briefly over 2f out: lost 2nd over 1f out: styd on same pce ins fnl f* **6/1**[3]

0501 **4** ½ **Rhythm Of Light**[21] 4328 4-9-0 103 RichardKingscote 1 97
(Tom Dascombe) *hld up: rdn 2f out: kpt on ins fnl f: nvr able to chal* **11/2**[2]

6462 **5** 1½ **Villeneuve**[15] 4527 3-8-7 94 SilvestreDeSousa 6 93
(William Muir) *chsd ldrs: rdn over 2f out: btn over 1f out* **16/1**

-150 **6** nk **Neutrafa (IRE)**[86] 2211 4-9-0 93 StephenCraine 4 93
(John Mackie) *in tch: effrt over 2f out: one pce 1f out: no ex fnl 100yds* **50/1**

1034 **7** 8 **Irish History (IRE)**[29] 4065 3-8-7 106 AhmedAjtebi 7 74
(Mahmood Al Zarooni) *hld up: rdn over 2f out: no imp over 1f out: wl btn ins fnl f* **9/4**[1]

1m 41.94s (-1.76) **Going Correction** -0.15s/f (Firm)
WFA 3 from 4yo 7lb **7** Ran SP% **112.4**
Speed ratings (Par 108): **102,101,98,97,96 95,87**
toteswingers: 1&2 £2.80, 1&3 £4.90, 2&3 £1.90. CSF £20.79 TOTE £7.30: £3.90, £1.60; EX 24.40.
Owner Mrs H Steel **Bred** Sparsholt Stud **Trained** Musley Bank, N Yorks

FOCUS
This looked up to the sort of standard you'd hope to see for Listed company, and it produced a likeable performance from the winner. The form makes sense with the third and fifth close to their latest Ascot form.

NOTEBOOK
Ladys First rallied bravely after losing the clear lead to get back to the front and hold on. The Atalanta Stakes at Sandown, now a Group 3, could be ideal for her next. (op 7-1 tchd 15-2)
Dank ◆ was one of the least exposed of these and shaped nicely up in grade. She seemed a little green still under full pressure, so presumably there is a bit more to come. (op 11-4)
Moone's My Name was unlucky last time at Ascot after losing plenty of ground exiting the stalls, but had every chance here under what appeared to be ideal conditions and wasn't good enough. (op 11-2)
Rhythm Of Light didn't have a great deal of room when making her bid, although it's fair to say the jockey didn't need to stop riding while in traffic. (op 7-2)
Villeneuve, who has often run well at Listed and Group 3 level, finished in front of Moone's My Name last time, but couldn't confirm positions. The representative of William Muir reported that the filly ran flat. Official explanation: trainer's rep said filly ran flat
Neutrafa(IRE) travelled strongly for quite a while and will obviously be most interesting when finding ease in the ground. (op 40-1)
Irish History(IRE) had contested and run well in Group 1 races on her last two outings, so this was a poor effort. Ahmed Ajtebi reported that the filly ran flat. Official explanation: jockey said filly ran flat (op 11-4)

5093 DUKE OF LANCASTER'S OWN YEOMANRY H'CAP 6f

4:30 (4:40) (Class 5) (0-70,71) 3-Y-O+ **£3,234** (£962; £481; £240) **Stalls** High

Form RPR

1-31 **1** **Willbeme**[7] 4793 4-9-9 **67** J-PGuillambert 3 83+
(Neville Bycroft) *racd keenly w ldr: led over 2f out: rdn over 1f out: r.o wl and in command fnl f* **5/2**[1]

543 **2** 2½ **Sole Danser (IRE)**[15] 4535 4-9-11 **69** RichardKingscote 7 77
(Milton Bradley) *hld up in midfield: hdwy over 1f out: styd on to take 2nd wl ins fnl f: no imp on wnr* **11/2**[3]

2516 **3** 2 **Ferdy (IRE)**[4] 4909 3-8-12 **60** JoeFanning 11 62
(Paul Green) *chsd ldrs: rdn and edgd lft over 2f out: no imp on wnr over 1f out: styd on same pce ins fnl f* **8/1**

2023 **4** nk **Rio Cobolo (IRE)**[2] 4999 6-9-10 **68** (v) AndrewMullen 13 69
(David Nicholls) *chsd ldrs: rdn over 2f out: nt qckn over 1f out: styd on same pce ins fnl f* **7/2**[2]

-603 **5** 3 **We'll Deal Again**[8] 4770 5-9-13 **71** (b) DavidNolan 10 62
(Michael Easterby) *led: pushed along and hdd over 2f out: wknd fnl f* **16/1**

0050 **6** 3/4 **Methaaly (IRE)**[5] 4887 9-8-5 **52** HarryBentley(3) 4 41
(Michael Mullineaux) *outpcd and bhd: rdn 2f out: styd on ins fnl f wout troubling ldrs* **12/1**

000- **7** 3 **Sir Nod**[281] 7265 10-9-6 **67** PaulPickard(3) 1 46
(Julie Camacho) *chsd ldrs: pushed along over 4f out: sn outpcd: no imp after* **50/1**

3054 **8** nk **Sally's Swansong**[17] 4461 6-8-8 **52** (b) JimmyQuinn 14 30
(Eric Alston) *towards rr: sn niggled along: impr into midfield over 3f out: outpcd over 1f out: n.d after* **25/1**

3000 **9** 3 **Secret Venue**[9] 4743 6-9-5 **63** BarryMcHugh 2 31
(Jedd O'Keeffe) *hld up in mdfield: outpcd over 2f out: sn bhd* **66/1**

0100 **10** 3/4 **Daunt (IRE)**[14] 4588 3-9-8 **70** GeorgeBaker 5 36+
(John Quinn) *hld up in rr: nt clr run and checked over 2f out: sn swtchd lft: hung lft and no imp over 1f out* **20/1**

2416 **11** nse **Bermondsey Bob (IRE)**[10] 4708 6-9-6 **64** SilvestreDeSousa 6 42+
(John Spearing) *dwlt: towards rr: outpcd 4f out: rdn 2f out: hdwy into midfield over 1f out: eased whn n.d ins fnl f* **7/1**

1000 **12** nk **Stevie Gee (IRE)**[17] 4468 8-9-3 **66** (v) JamesRogers(5) 8 31
(Mark Buckley) *in tch: rdn and wkng whn edgd rt over 2f out* **25/1**

1m 11.76s (-2.04) **Going Correction** -0.475s/f (Firm)
WFA 3 from 4yo+ 4lb 12 Ran SP% **119.3**
Speed ratings (Par 103): **94,90,88,87,83 82,78,78,74,73 73,72**
toteswingers: 1&2 £4.20, 1&3 £5.80, 2&3 £9.90. CSF £15.44 CT £99.56 TOTE £3.50: £1.40, £2.40, £2.90; EX 16.40.
Owner P D Burrow **Bred** Mrs J M Russell **Trained** Brandsby, N Yorks

FOCUS
With We'll Deal Again going off at a strong pace, not many got into this. The form looks sound rated around those in the frame behind the winner.

5094 READ HAYLEY AT RACINGUK.COM EVERY FRIDAY H'CAP 1m
5:05 (5:05) (Class 3) (0-95,91) 3-Y-O+ **£8,409** (£2,502; £1,250; £625) **Stalls** Low

Form RPR

133 **1** **Postscript (IRE)**[17] 4474 4-9-2 **79** JamieSpencer 6 95
(Ian Williams) *midfield: hdwy over 2f out: rdn to ld over 1f out: r.o ins fnl f: in command towards fin* **7/1**[2]

1241 **2** 2 **Famous Poet (IRE)**[31] 3963 3-9-7 **91** SilvestreDeSousa 10 102
(Saeed Bin Suroor) *chsd ldrs: led over 2f out: sn edgd lft: rdn and hdd over 1f out: stl ch ins fnl f: no ex fnl 50yds* **3/1**[1]

6200 **3** 1 1/4 **Lucky Henry**[21] 4319 3-9-1 **85** AdamKirby 13 92+
(Clive Cox) *chsd ldrs: effrt to chal over 2f out: edgd rt and nt qckn over 1f out: styd on same pce ins fnl f* **9/1**[3]

1300 **4** 1 **Weapon Of Choice (IRE)**[20] 4365 4-9-13 **90** TomQueally 12 96
(Stuart Kittow) *midfield: hdwy 3f out: rdn 2f out: styd on ins fnl f: nt rch ldrs* **11/1**

2120 **5** 1 1/4 **Razorbill (USA)**[30] 4009 3-9-4 **88** RyanMoore 7 90
(Charles Hills) *midfield: hdwy 3f out: chalng 2f out: rdn and nt qckn over 1f out: no ex ins fnl f* **3/1**[1]

6400 **6** shd **Extraterrestrial**[7] 4828 8-9-7 **84** (p) BarryMcHugh 2 87
(Richard Fahey) *hld up: rdn over 2f out: impr into midfield over 1f out: styd on ins fnl f: one pce towards fin* **25/1**

5031 **7** 3/4 **Mirrored**[13] 4620 6-9-9 **86** DuranFentiman 4 87
(Tim Easterby) *hld up: rdn over 2f out: plugged on at one pce fr over 1f out: no imp* **12/1**

-366 **8** 7 **Estrela**[14] 4579 3-9-4 **88** (p) GeorgeBaker 1 72
(Roger Charlton) *chsd ldr: lost 2nd and losing pl whn n.m.r and bmpd over 2f out: wknd over 1f out* **11/1**

2040 **9** 2 **Snow Bay**[11] 4689 6-9-5 **82** AndrewMullen 9 62
(David Nicholls) *led: hdd over 2f out: sn n.m.r and hmpd whn losing pl: wknd over 1f out* **20/1**

215- **10** 1 **Icebuster**[320] 6409 4-9-5 **82** JamesMillman 11 60
(Rod Millman) *s.s: a bhd: nvr on terms* **25/1**

4305 **11** nk **First Post (IRE)**[17] 4474 5-9-0 **80** HarryBentley(3) 5 57
(Derek Haydn Jones) *hld up: n.m.r and hmpd on bnd under 6f out: rdn over 2f out: nvr on terms w ldrs: wl btn over 1f out* **16/1**

0/0- **12** 5 **Marine Boy (IRE)**[463] 1849 6-9-13 **90** (t) RichardKingscote 8 56
(Tom Dascombe) *hld up: pushed along over 3f out: wl btn over 1f out* **22/1**

1m 40.96s (-2.74) **Going Correction** -0.15s/f (Firm)
WFA 3 from 4yo+ 7lb 12 Ran SP% **119.5**
Speed ratings (Par 107): **107,105,103,102,101 101,100,93,91,90 90,85**
toteswingers: 1&2 £2.90, 1&3 £6.90, 2&3 £6.60. CSF £26.94 CT £195.60 TOTE £6.80: £2.70, £1.70, £3.00; EX 21.90.
Owner Dr Marwan Koukash **Bred** Darley **Trained** Portway, Worcs

FOCUS
A race that was run at a strong pace early. The form looks sound with the placed horses the best guides.

NOTEBOOK
Postscript(IRE), a previous C&D winner, has been hugely consistent this season and got back to winning ways when the gaps opened up nicely down the home straight. He's versatile with regards to underfoot coniditons, and clearly relishes chasing a strong gallop. (op 6-1)

Famous Poet(IRE), raised 6lb for his Kempton success, was trying 1m on turf for the first time and did well despite edging a bit to his left late on. He ought to have a bit more to come but the winner had his measure inside the final furlong. (op 4-1)

Lucky Henry, who ran a cracker over C&D in the Silver Bowl back in May, was done no favours here when the runner-up went towards the inside rail. Forced to switch round that rival about 1f out, he can be rated almost upsides the Godolphin horse. (tchd 10-1)

Weapon Of Choice(IRE) ran as though he was being anchored by his weight. He has an excellent record of 112 when raced over 1m1f, so a return to that distance would be eyecatching. (op 9-1)

Razorbill(USA) was unexposed in comparison to the majority of his rivals but didn't see it out after holding every chance. (tchd 10-3)

Extraterrestrial, with cheekpieces on for the first time since September 2008, made late progress from the rear.

T/Plt: £94.80 to a £1 stake. Pool: £86,916.00 - 668.83 winning tickets. T/Qpdt: £9.70 to a £1 stake. Pool: £5,885.06 - 448.50 winning tickets. DO

5045 LINGFIELD (L-H)
Saturday, August 11

OFFICIAL GOING: Turf course - good to firm; all-weather - standard
Wind: Moderate, across (away from stands) Weather: Fine but cloudy, warm

5095 ASHURSTWOOD H'CAP (TURF) 7f 140y
5:45 (5:45) (Class 6) (0-60,60) 3-Y-O **£2,181** (£644; £322) **Stalls** Centre

Form RPR

4-04 **1** **Classic Falcon (IRE)**[16] 4506 3-9-2 **58** AdamBeschizza(3) 7 74+
(William Haggas) *trckd ldng pair: rdn over 2f out: led wl over 1f out: sn clr: eased last 75yds* **7/2**[1]

4204 **2** 3 1/2 **Collectable**[15] 4533 3-8-12 **51** (t) MatthewDavies 12 55
(Jonathan Portman) *settled in 7th: looking for room over 2f out: prog over 1f out: r.o to take 2nd wl ins fnl f: no ch w wnr* **9/2**[3]

3504 **3** 1 3/4 **Inffiraaj (IRE)**[8] 4754 3-9-3 **56** SamHitchcott 8 56
(Mick Channon) *racd against rail: led or disp to wl over 1f out: sn outpcd* **6/1**

0200 **4** 2 3/4 **Artful Lady (IRE)**[44] 3547 3-8-6 **48** RyanPowell(3) 11 41+
(George Margarson) *towards rr: wl off the pce whn taken to outer over 2f out: nt clr run briefly sn after: styd on fr over 1f out: nvr nrr* **25/1**

0000 **5** 1 1/2 **Johnny Splash (IRE)**[12] 4644 3-8-4 **50** (p) MartinLeonard(7) 6 39
(Roger Teal) *led or disp to wl over 1f out: wknd fnl f* **33/1**

250 **6** 1/2 **Bajan Hero**[10] 4705 3-8-11 **50** ShaneKelly 15 38
(David Evans) *racd against rail: chsd ldng trio: hrd rdn over 2f out: wknd over 1f out* **20/1**

4430 **7** hd **Saint Irene**[10] 4709 3-8-13 **52** FergusSweeney 5 39
(Michael Blanshard) *wl in rr: taken to outer and drvn over 2f out: kpt on but nvr a threat* **17/2**

5-00 **8** 1 **Sea Anemone**[15] 4533 3-8-8 **50** SimonPearce(3) 3 35
(Andrew Balding) *chsd ldng trio: rdn over 2f out: wknd wl over 1f out* **25/1**

-600 **9** 1 **Sanad (IRE)**[54] 3218 3-9-4 **60** (p) DominicFox(3) 1 42
(Anthony Carson) *racd on outer in rr: struggling over 2f out: last whn hmpd jst over 1f out: modest late prog* **33/1**

0-00 **10** 3/4 **Royale Ransom**[21] 4332 3-9-6 **59** JamesDoyle 10 39
(Sylvester Kirk) *a towards rr: rdn and no great prog 3f out: wl btn fnl 2f* **20/1**

442 **11** 1 **La Confession**[41] 3665 3-9-0 **53** ChrisCatlin 14 31
(Rae Guest) *chsd ldng trio: rdn over 3f out: wknd over 2f out* **4/1**[2]

5030 **12** nse **Enthrall (IRE)**[45] 3489 3-8-7 **46** oh1 CathyGannon 9 24
(Denis Coakley) *a in rr: rdn and no prog 3f out* **20/1**

-066 **13** 1 3/4 **Willow Beauty**[16] 4509 3-8-7 **46** oh1 (v[1]) JamieMackay 2 19
(J R Jenkins) *racd on outer: struggling in rr fr 1/2-way* **50/1**

-400 **14** 2 3/4 **Allegra Byron**[16] 4506 3-9-1 **54** (p) BrettDoyle 13 21
(Jonathan Portman) *awkward s: sn rdn: a wl in rr and struggling* **25/1**

1m 30.5s (-1.80) **Going Correction** -0.20s/f (Firm) 14 Ran SP% **118.9**
Speed ratings (Par 98): **101,97,95,93,91 91,90,89,88,88 87,87,85,82**
totseswingers: 1&2 £3.80, 1&3 £5.20, 2&3 £11.30 CSF £15.74 CT £92.96 TOTE £4.40: £1.90, £2.10, £3.00; EX 24.00.
Owner Sheikh Hamdan Bin Maktoum Al Maktoum **Bred** Robert Berns **Trained** Newmarket, Suffolk

FOCUS
Handicaps dont come much weaker than this and most of these will struggle to win races.
La Confession Official explanation: trainer's rep said filly has a breathing problem

5096 LINGFIELDPARK.CO.UK MAIDEN STKS (TURF) 6f
6:15 (6:15) (Class 5) 3-Y-O+ **£3,067** (£905; £453) **Stalls** High

Form RPR

243 **1** **Palmette**[18] 4434 3-8-12 70 (b[1]) MartinDwyer 4 78
(John Gosden) *mde virtually all: crossed to nr side rail over 4f out: shkn up 2f out: in command and pushed out fnl f* **5/1**[3]

-302 **2** 1 3/4 **Al Janadeirya**[43] 3568 4-8-13 70 AshleyHamblett(3) 7 73+
(Peter Chapple-Hyam) *racd against rail: seem disconcerted whn wnr crossed in front over 4f out and lost a little grnd: shkn up 2f out: nvr much room but styd on to take 2nd last stride: no ch to chal* **11/8**[1]

0-5 **3** shd **Dawn Glory**[21] 4341 3-8-12 0 JamesDoyle 5 72
(Roger Charlton) *prom: mostly chsd wnr fr over 4f out: rdn 2f out: wl hld fnl f: lost 2nd last stride* **10/3**[2]

-022 **4** 4 1/2 **Blue Tiger**[9] 4729 3-9-3 73 (t) MickaelBarzalona 3 62
(Saeed Bin Suroor) *hld up in 4th: moved up on outer to dispute 2nd 2f out to over 1f out: wknd fnl f* **10/3**[2]

00 **5** 7 **Litmus (USA)**[63] 2935 3-8-12 0 FergusSweeney 2 35
(Simon Dow) *chsd ldrs tl wknd over 2f out* **40/1**

6 4 **Scary Canary**[253] 4-9-4 0 RyanPowell(3) 8 28
(George Margarson) *struggling to stay in tch after 2f: bhd over 2f out* **80/1**

00 **7** 2 1/4 **I Stand Corrected**[18] 4434 3-8-12 0 MartinLane 6 15
(Ed Walker) *scratchy to post: dwlt: a in last: wl bhd fr 1/2-way* **25/1**

1m 9.46s (-1.74) **Going Correction** -0.20s/f (Firm)
WFA 3 from 4yo 4lb 7 Ran SP% **112.4**
Speed ratings (Par 103): **103,100,100,94,85 79,76**
toteswingers 1&2 £1.50, 2&3 £2.40, 1&3 £1.70 CSF £11.94 TOTE £5.20: £2.70, £1.20; EX 13.90.
Owner K Abdulla **Bred** Juddmonte Farms Ltd **Trained** Newmarket, Suffolk

FOCUS
A 1-2-3 for sire Oasis Dream, but this is probably not great maiden form,

5097 HAPPY BIRTHDAY LIN PURVEY H'CAP (TURF) 6f
6:45 (6:45) (Class 5) (0-75,75) 3-Y-O+ **£3,067** (£905; £453) **Stalls** High

Form RPR

6636 **1** **Rash Judgement**[22] 4300 7-9-9 **72** FergusSweeney 11 82
(Stuart Kittow) *racd against rail: no room after 1f: trckd ldrs after: waited tl gap appeared over 1f out: plld out and r.o to ld nr fin* **13/2**

2632 **2** hd **Rambo Will**[17] 4461 4-9-9 **72** PatDobbs 9 81
(J R Jenkins) *racd against rail: trckd ldr: clsd to ld jst over 1f out gng strly: rdn fnl f: hdd nr fin* **9/2**[2]

106 **3** 1 3/4 **Rocket Rob (IRE)**[7] 4824 6-9-9 **72** (b) StevieDonohoe 4 76
(Willie Musson) *dwlt: wl in rr: rdn on outer 2f out: styd on fr over 1f out to take 3rd nr fin* **5/2**[1]

0603 **4** 1 **Swendab (IRE)**[17] 4461 4-9-4 **72** (v) BrendanPowell(5) 5 73
(John O'Shea) *s.s: rousted along to rcvr: rdn bef 1/2-way: prog on outer 2f out: kpt on same pce fnl f* **16/1**

106 **5** 1/2 **Desert Strike**[2] 4999 6-9-11 **74** (p) JamesDoyle 8 73
(Charles Hills) *taken down early: led and sn crossed to rail: hdd and fdd jst over 1f out* **5/1**[3]

1-24 **6** *shd* **Oh So Spicy**[77] 2493 5-9-10 **73** .... TedDurcan 1 72
(Chris Wall) *chsd ldrs: rdn and nt qckn 2f out: fdd over 1f out* **7/1**

0000 **7** *½* **Seamus Shindig**[7] 4815 10-8-9 **63** .... AmyScott[(5)] 3 60
(Henry Candy) *racd wdst of all: sn in last: effrt 2f out: no real prog* **20/1**

-636 **8** *1* **Belle Bayardo (IRE)**[15] 4535 4-9-3 **66** .... LukeMorris 10 60
(Ronald Harris) *chsd ldrs: u.p sn after 1/2-way: lost pl and btn 2f out* **8/1**

0200 **9** *nk* **Nubar Boy**[7] 4829 5-9-7 **70** .... ShaneKelly 6 63
(David Evans) *chsd ldng pair: rdn over 2f out: wknd wl over 1f out* **33/1**

3-00 **10** *8* **Foxtrot India (IRE)**[15] 4530 3-9-8 **75** .... RenatoSouza 2 42
(Jeremy Gask) *chsd ldrs tl wknd 2f out: eased fnl f: t.o* **40/1**

1m 10.3s (-0.90) **Going Correction** -0.20s/f (Firm)
WFA 3 from 4yo+ 4lb **10** Ran SP% **116.4**
Speed ratings (Par 103): **98,97,95,94,93 93,92,91,90,80**
toteswingers 1&2 £5.50, 2&3 £2.70, 1&3 £4.70 CSF £35.07 CT £94.85 TOTE £9.00: £2.20, £1.90, £1.70; EX 38.80.
Owner Reg Gifford **Bred** D R Tucker **Trained** Blackborough, Devon

FOCUS
They went a good gallop here and the field fanned across the track in the final furlong.

5098 BRITISH STALLION STUDS SUPPORTING BRITISH RACING E B F MAIDEN STKS 1m (P)

7:15 (7:15) (Class 5) 2-Y-O **£3,816** (£1,135; £567; £283) **Stalls** Low

Form RPR

02 **1** **Blue Wave (IRE)**[14] 4595 2-9-3 0 .... MickaelBarzalona 6 76
(Mahmood Al Zarooni) *racd in 5th: pushed along after 2f despite slow pce: prog 1/2-way: rdn 2f out: responded and r.o to ld wl ins fnl f* **8/11**[1]

3 **2** *nk* **Lord Of Leitrim (IRE)**[17] 4463 2-9-3 0 .... ShaneKelly 1 75
(Brian Meehan) *led at slow pce for 1f: trckd ldr to over 3f out: styd cl up: effrt to ld on inner 1f out: styd on but hdd wl ins fnl f* **7/2**[2]

0 **3** *½* **Astrosapphire**[43] 3590 2-8-12 0 .... TedDurcan 2 69
(Mark H Tompkins) *wl in tch: rdn on wd outside 2f out: styd on fnl f: nvr quite able to chal* **25/1**

0 **4** *¾* **Fair Comment**[19] 4408 2-8-12 0 .... FergusSweeney 4 67
(Michael Blanshard) *cl up: trckd ldr over 3f out: chal 2f out: nt qckn over 1f out: hld whn impeded nr fin* **33/1**

0 **5** *1 ¾* **Shiatsu**[20] 4362 2-9-3 0 .... PatDobbs 5 68
(Richard Hannon) *stdd s: keen and allowed to ld after 1f but maintained modest pce: tried to kick on 2f out: hdd and outpcd 1f out* **8/1**

6 *6* **Man From Seville** 2-9-3 0 .... LukeMorris 3 57+
(Sir Mark Prescott Bt) *dwlt: rn green and a struggling in last* **11/2**[3]

1m 42.2s (4.00) **Going Correction** +0.10s/f (Slow) **6** Ran SP% **113.4**
Speed ratings (Par 94): **84,83,83,82,80 74**
toteswingers 1&2 £1.10, 2&3 £11.10, 1&3 £5.90 CSF £3.66 TOTE £1.30: £1.50, £1.10; EX 3.10.
Owner Godolphin **Bred** Tom Darcy And Vincent McCarthy **Trained** Newmarket, Suffolk

FOCUS
This turned into a bit of a sprint after they dawdled through the first half of the contest and the form isn't strong, with the winner rated below the form of his second run.

NOTEBOOK
Blue Wave(IRE) was having to be niggled from an early stage despite the slow pace, but he began to respond and was within striking distance by the home turn where he stayed on well enough to see off main rival. He didn't have to run any better than he did when only just beaten at Newmarket on his second start, so we didn't really learn a great deal about him here, but at least he's got his head in front. (tchd 4-6 and 4-5)
Lord Of Leitrim(IRE) stepped up on his debut run here and, although this was a messy little affair, he looks to have enough ability to win races. (tchd 4-1)
Astrosapphire finished strongly down the outside and clearly wasn't suited by the way this panned out. Her pedigree suggests she will want further in time (dam won over 1m6f), so a dawdle then a sprint over this trip was never going to help her. She can do much better when getting a stiffer test of stamina and is arguably the one to take from the race.
Shiatsu was too keen early and we surely didn't see best of her. She might need dropping back in trip as her pedigree is mostly speed. (tchd 10-1)
Man From Seville was a bit clueless and needs more time. (op 7-1)

5099 BOOTLEG BEATLES HERE NEXT SATURDAY H'CAP 7f (P)

7:45 (7:45) (Class 5) (0-75,75) 3-Y-O **£3,067** (£905; £453) **Stalls** Low

Form RPR

-361 **1** **Baheeja**[8] 4782 3-9-4 **75** .... DominicFox[(3)] 2 85
(Roger Varian) *trckd ldrs: clsd over 2f out: led wl over 1f out: hrd pressed fnl f: hld on gamely* **11/4**[1]

-241 **2** *hd* **Jack Of Diamonds (IRE)**[31] 3972 3-9-7 **75** .... JamesDoyle 8 84
(Roger Teal) *racd on outer: in tch: rdn 2f out: wnt 2nd jst over 1f out: str chal fnl f: nt qckn nr fin* **11/4**[1]

1-36 **3** *3 ½* **Lucky Money**[31] 3952 3-9-5 **73** .... (b) LukeMorris 3 73
(Sir Mark Prescott Bt) *in tch: nt qckn 2f out: styd on to take 3rd ins fnl f: no imp* **10/3**[2]

5024 **4** *2 ¾* **Al's Memory (IRE)**[1] 5036 3-8-13 **67** .... ShaneKelly 4 59
(David Evans) *sn in last pair: pushed along 3f out: struggling over 2f out: styd on over 1f out: tk 4th nr fin* **5/1**[3]

5002 **5** *1 ¼* **Adranian (IRE)**[12] 4644 3-9-7 **75** .... (v) TedDurcan 1 64
(David C Griffiths) *trckd ldr: led over 2f out gng strly: hdd and no rspnse wl over 1f out: wknd fnl f* **16/1**

0660 **6** *1 ¼* **Shamrocked (IRE)**[7] 4814 3-9-3 **71** .... MatthewDavies 5 56
(Mick Channon) *led to over 2f out: wknd over 1f out* **10/1**

00-0 **7** *12* **Silence Is Easy**[124] 1256 3-8-9 **63** .... MartinDwyer 6 16
(William Muir) *stdd s: hld up in last: shkn up 3f out: wknd 2f out: t.o* **16/1**

1m 25.39s (0.59) **Going Correction** +0.10s/f (Slow) **7** Ran SP% **113.9**
Speed ratings (Par 100): **100,99,95,92,91 89,76**
toteswingers 1&2 £2.00, 2&3 £3.80, 1&3 £2.40 CSF £10.42 CT £24.82 TOTE £3.50: £1.50, £2.30; EX 9.40.
Owner Sheikh Ahmed Al Maktoum **Bred** Middle Park Stud Ltd **Trained** Newmarket, Suffolk

FOCUS
Just ordinary handicap form.

5100 LADBROKES GAME ON! MEDIAN AUCTION MAIDEN STKS 1m 2f (P)

8:15 (8:16) (Class 6) 3-4-Y-O **£2,181** (£644; £322) **Stalls** Low

Form RPR

1 **Dr Houseman** 3-9-3 0 ....[1] EddieAhern 7 69+
(Amanda Perrett) *dwlt: mostly last of main gp tl prog on outer over 3f out: clsd on ldrs 2f out: rdn to ld jst over 1f out: styd on wl: readily* **5/1**[3]

2 *2 ¼* **Tiger Cliff (IRE)** 3-9-3 0 .... IanMongan 1 66+
(Sir Henry Cecil) *trckd ldrs: pushed along 3f out: nt clr run as r unfolded over 2f out: shkn up and r.o fnl f to take 2nd nr fin* **2/1**[1]

05 **3** *nk* **Comedy House**[19] 4410 4-9-12 0 .... JamieGoldstein 2 64
(Michael Madgwick) *trckd ldng pair: chal on ins wl over 1f out: styd on same pce after* **16/1**

0605 **4** *nk* **Princess Willow**[56] 3152 4-9-4 47 .... SimonPearce[(3)] 6 58?
(John E Long) *trckd ldng trio: clsd over 2f out: rdn to ld briefly over 1f out: one pce after* **10/1**

0 **5** *7* **Elsie Bay**[20] 4366 3-8-12 0 .... LiamKeniry 3 44
(Mark Usher) *in tch: rdn over 4f out: prog to chse ldrs over 2f out: wknd over 1f out* **12/1**

-304 **6** *6* **Edraaq**[26] 4157 3-9-3 67 .... (t) TadhgO'Shea 8 37
(Brian Meehan) *dwlt: rcvrd to ld after 3f: hdd & wknd rapidly over 1f out* **7/2**[2]

60 **7** *2 ½* **Yogic Flyer**[14] 4582 3-8-12 0 .... MartinDwyer 4 27
(Gay Kelleway) *a towards rr: lost tch wl over 2f out* **40/1**

65 **8** *2 ¼* **Mariet**[26] 4157 3-8-12 0 .... DavidProbert 5 23
(Andrew Balding) *led 3f: w ldr to 1/2-way: wknd over 3f out* **7/2**[2]

0 **9** *1 ¾* **Peace In Our Time**[22] 4301 3-9-0 0 .... DominicFox[(3)] 9 24
(Anthony Carson) *slowly away and tk sme persuading to r properly: a detached in last* **33/1**

2m 6.89s (0.29) **Going Correction** +0.10s/f (Slow)
WFA 3 from 4yo 9lb **9** Ran SP% **122.5**
Speed ratings (Par 101): **102,100,99,99,94 89,87,85,84**
toteswingers 1&2 £3.90, 2&3 £15.30, 1&3 £6.10 CSF £16.45 TOTE £8.00: £2.30, £1.20, £3.70; EX 20.30.
Owner Normandie Stud Ltd **Bred** Normandie Stud Ltd **Trained** Pulborough, W Sussex

FOCUS
Those who had experience were no great shakes, so hardly a surprise that the first two home were nicely bred newcomers and both posted performances of some potential.
Princess Willow Official explanation: jockey said filly hung right throughout
Mariet Official explanation: jockey said filly ran too free
T/Plt: £14.80 to a £1 stake. Pool of £57336.57 - 2821.72 winning tickets. T/Qpdt: £6.20 to a £1 stake. Pool of £5007.96 - 590.28 winning tickets. JN

5060 NEWMARKET (R-H)

Saturday, August 11

OFFICIAL GOING: Good to firm
Stands Side track used with Stalls on Stands Side except 10f & 12f and 2m: Centre
Wind: Light behind Weather: Fine and sunny

5101 RACEBETS.COM - BIGGEST RACING OFFER WORLDWIDE H'CAP 1m 2f

2:25 (2:25) (Class 2) (0-100,97) 3-Y-O+ **£12,938** (£3,850; £1,924; £962) **Stalls** Centre

Form RPR

10 **1** **Sir John Hawkwood (IRE)**[28] 4097 3-9-0 **92** .... RichardHughes 9 103+
(Sir Michael Stoute) *hld up: hdwy over 2f out: rdn to ld wl ins fnl f: styd on wl* **4/1**[2]

6000 **2** *1 ¾* **Man Of Action (USA)**[52] 3268 5-10-0 **97** .... MickaelBarzalona 10 104
(Saeed Bin Suroor) *hld up: hdwy to ld over 2f out: rdn over 1f out: hdd and unable qck wl ins fnl f* **8/1**

3022 **3** *nk* **Assizes**[9] 4741 3-8-5 **90** .... MichaelJMMurphy[(7)] 5 96+
(Mark Johnston) *a.p: rdn and ev ch fr over 1f out tl no ex wl ins fnl f* **7/2**[1]

3003 **4** *6* **Ghost Protocol (IRE)**[21] 4342 3-8-7 **85** .... EddieAhern 7 79
(David Simcock) *hld up: hdwy over 3f out: edgd rt 2f out: sn rdn: wknd ins fnl f* **11/1**

1-43 **5** *3 ¾* **Raasekha**[98] 1851 4-9-11 **94** .... PaulHanagan 2 81
(Charles Hills) *trckd ldrs: racd keenly: led 3f out: hdd over 2f out: rdn and wknd over 1f out* **20/1**

04-0 **6** *2 ¾* **Daghash**[114] 1468 3-8-0 **78** .... KieranO'Neill 3 59
(Clive Brittain) *plld hrd and prom: rdn over 3f out: hung lft and wknd over 2f out* **33/1**

0103 **7** *6* **Flaxen Flare (IRE)**[21] 4319 3-8-2 **80** .... (v) DavidProbert 4 49
(Andrew Balding) *chsd ldrs: rdn over 3f out: wknd over 2f out* **16/1**

4321 **8** *nk* **Unex El Greco**[14] 4596 4-9-10 **93** .... RobertHavlin 6 62
(John Gosden) *led: hdd 4f out: rdn and hmpd 2f out: wknd over 1f out* **9/2**[3]

0554 **9** *1 ½* **Borug (USA)**[7] 4805 4-8-10 **79** .... (b[1]) MartinDwyer 1 45
(James Tate) *s.i.s: sn drvn along to chse ldr: led 4f out: sn hdd: rdn: hung lft and wknd over 2f out* **8/1**

-005 **10** *17* **Classic Punch (IRE)**[14] 4596 9-9-7 **90** .... IanMongan 11 22
(David Elsworth) *chsd ldrs: rdn over 4f out: wknd 2f out: eased: t.o* **9/1**

2m 4.94s (-0.56) **Going Correction** +0.15s/f (Good)
WFA 3 from 4yo+ 9lb **10** Ran SP% **114.5**
Speed ratings (Par 109): **108,106,106,101,98 96,91,91,90,76**
toteswingers 1&2 £6.50, 2&3 £4.20, 1&3 £35.37 CT £121.70 TOTE £5.00: £2.00, £2.80, £1.50; EX 46.60 Trifecta £123.40 Pool: £428.64 - 2.57 winning units..
Owner Ballymacoll Stud **Bred** Ballymacoll Stud Farm Ltd **Trained** Newmarket, Suffolk

FOCUS
A good handicap and this looks strong form amongst the front three, who drew clear.

NOTEBOOK
Sir John Hawkwood(IRE) ◆ looked decent when making a winning debut at Windsor (1m2f, soft), but struggled badly next time on heavy ground here. This was his first try on a quick surface and it evidently suited, the colt travelling well and then outstaying the runner-up having briefly been outpaced by that rival. In defying a mark of 92 he ran to a smart level and he looks a Group horse in the making, possibly over further in due course. (op 5-1)
Man Of Action(USA) had only previously raced beyond 1m in last year's Cambridgeshire when he got no sort of run, so he was worth a try at this distance, but he's not straightforward. Without any headgear after 52 days off, he missed the break and didn't travel for much of the contest, but then suddenly took off inside the final 3f, surging to the lead. Quite improbably, though, it meant he ended up in front too soon, and it wasn't any fault of his jockey. He has more talent than his current mark suggests and will be worth another go at this trip, but he's one to tread carefully with. Maybe the headgear will go back on next time. (op 9-1)
Assizes has shot up in the weights without winning, including being 6lb higher than when a close second at Goodwood the previous week, and it seemed he was beaten by a couple of better-handicapped rivals. (op 4-1)
Ghost Protocol(IRE) travelled well to a point but wasn't good enough. (op 12-1 tchd 14-1)
Raasekha, the only filly in the line-up, didn't prove her stamina on this handicap debut, although the vet reported the filly had been struck into. Official explanation: vet said filly had been struck into
Unex El Greco was disappointing off 4lb higher than when winning over C&D on his previous start. (op 4-1 tchd 5-1)

Classic Punch(IRE), 4lb lower than when winning this last year (his most recent success), was kept towards the stands' rail in the straight, away from the others who were just off the fence, but the pace of the race had been too strong for him to really dominate as he likes to. (op 8-1)

5102 BADEN-RACING.COM H'CAP 7f

3:00 (3:00) (Class 2) (0-105,102) 3-Y-O+

£12,450 (£3,728; £1,864; £932; £466; £234) **Stalls** Low

Form				RPR
1115	**1**		**Highland Colori (IRE)**[21] 4321 4-8-10 **88** DavidProbert 1 (Andrew Balding) *a.p: nt clr run and hit over hd by rivals whip over 1f out: sn rdn: r.o to ld nr fin* **3/1**[1]	99+
1040	**2**	*nk*	**Quick Wit**[14] 4609 5-9-10 **102** MickaelBarzalona 7 (Saeed Bin Suroor) *mid-div: pushed along 4f out: hdwy over 1f out: rdn and ev ch ins fnl f: r.o* **14/1**	110
13-5	**3**	*hd*	**Zumbi (IRE)**[115] 1453 3-9-3 **101** PatDobbs 6 (Sir Michael Stoute) *hld up: nt clr run over 1f out: n.m.r and r.o wl ins fnl f: jst failed* **11/1**	108+
0305	**4**	*3/4*	**Citrus Star (USA)**[14] 4609 5-9-1 **93** TedDurcan 10 (Chris Wall) *hld up: hdwy over 1f out: rdn to ld ins fnl f: hdd nr fin* **12/1**	98
-000	**5**	*nk*	**Castles In The Air**[21] 4321 7-9-0 **92** PaulHanagan 11 (Richard Fahey) *mid-div: pushed along over 2f out: hdwy u.p over 1f out: ev ch ins fnl f: no ex nr fin* **16/1**	97
4000	**6**	*nk*	**Redact (IRE)**[52] 3265 3-9-2 **100** RichardHughes 5 (Richard Hannon) *hld up: hdwy and nt clr run over 1f out: r.o: nvr able to chal* **25/1**	102
-300	**7**	*3/4*	**Democretes**[51] 3294 3-8-3 **87** KieranO'Neill 14 (Richard Hannon) *led: hdd over 5f out: chsd ldr tl led again over 2f out: sn rdn: hdd and no ex ins fnl f* **14/1**	87
100	**8**	*1 1/4*	**Mississippi**[51] 3294 3-8-4 **88** MartinDwyer 8 (Brian Meehan) *hld up in tch: hmpd after 1f: rdn and ev ch whn hung rt over 1f out: hung lft and no ex ins fnl f* **11/2**[2]	84
002	**9**	*hd*	**White Frost (IRE)**[14] 4609 4-9-0 **92** [1] RobertWinston 4 (Charles Hills) *chsd ldrs: rdn and edgd lft over 1f out: no ex ins fnl f* **11/2**[2]	90
-210	**10**	*1 1/2*	**Cape Classic (IRE)**[7] 4824 4-8-11 **89** JimCrowley 3 (William Haggas) *hld up: swtchd lft over 2f out: hdwy and hmpd over 1f out: eased ins fnl f* **8/1**[3]	83+
5460	**11**	*3*	**Hadaj**[31] 3977 3-8-2 **86** (b) KirstyMilczarek 9 (Clive Brittain) *plld hrd and prom: rdn and ev ch whn hmpd over 1f out: wknd ins fnl f* **18/1**	70
60	**12**	*6*	**Noble Citizen (USA)**[14] 4609 7-8-7 **90** (b) LauraPike(5) 13 (David Simcock) *hld up: rdn over 2f out: wknd over 1f out* **20/1**	60
3000	**13**	*16*	**King Of Jazz (IRE)**[28] 4099 4-9-3 **95** (v) LukeMorris 12 (Michael Bell) *led over 5f out: rdn and hdd over 2f out: sn wknd and eased: t.o* **25/1**	21

1m 25.45s (-0.25) **Going Correction** +0.15s/f (Good)
WFA 3 from 4yo+ 6lb **13** Ran **SP% 119.8**
Speed ratings (Par 109): **107,106,106,105,105 104,104,102,102,100 97,90,72**
toteswingers 1&2 £8.40, 2&3 £17.10, 1&3 CSF £46.76 CT £409.98 TOTE £4.00: £1.70, £4.90, £3.30; EX 67.80 Trifecta £785.30 Pool: £1,167.36 - 1.10 winning units..
Owner Evan M Sutherland **Bred** Rathbarry Stud **Trained** Kingsclere, Hants

FOCUS

A good, competitive handicap run at a decent enough pace. The runners raced towards the stands' rail for much of the way and room was at a premium in the closing stages, but they were spread out across the track at the line. The winner is improving, the second is rated back to his best, while the fifth and sixth help to set the level.

NOTEBOOK

Highland Colori(IRE) made it four victories from his last five starts, his winning sequence only interrupted by a good fifth in the International Stakes at Ascot last time. He might have missed out had the third got in the clear sooner, but Andrew Balding's runner found plenty of trouble himself (including being hit on the head with a whip) and his effort is all the more creditable considering David Probert felt the ground didn't suit. There should be more to come from a horse who was having just his tenth start. (op 9-2 tchd 5-1 in a place)

Quick Wit was never really travelling, but the rising ground helped him and he enjoyed a clearer run than some. He won over 1m2f in Dubai earlier in the year and might benefit from a step back up in distance.

Zumbi(IRE) ◆, absent since finishing fifth off this mark in the Free Handicap in April, travelled as well as any under a hold-up ride, but didn't find a gap until it was too late. He probably would have won had he got in the clear sooner, even allowing for the winner having also found trouble, but regardless this was clearly a promising return to action and he can be expected to progress. (op 8-1)

Citrus Star(USA) was taken wide with his challenge, more towards the far rail than any of the others, and that might not have been ideal, albeit he enjoyed a clear run as a result. (op 13-2)

Castles In The Air had his chance but didn't pick up well enough. He's yet to hit peak form this year.

Redact(IRE) was taking a significant drop in grade having contested races like the Guineas and (most recently) the Jersey, and he ran well after 52 days off. He didn't get the clearest of runs, but it didn't seem to cost him and he appeared suited by running on past beaten horses.

White Frost(IRE) couldn't match the form he showed when runner-up off 6lb lower at York last time, seemingly not taking to the first-time hood. (op 5-1)

Cape Classic(IRE) was another who became a bit short of room in the closing stages, but while that exaggerated the beaten margin, he had appeared unlikely to take a hand in the finish, not picking up after travelling well. He looks better at 6f. Official explanation: jockey said colt was denied a clear run (op 7-1)

King Of Jazz(IRE) Official explanation: jockey said gelding ran too free

5103 GERMAN-THOROUGHBRED.COM SWEET SOLERA STKS (GROUP 3) (FILLIES) 7f

3:35 (3:35) (Class 1) 2-Y-O

£25,519 (£9,675; £4,842; £2,412; £1,210; £607) **Stalls** Low

Form				RPR
1	**1**		**Certify (USA)**[30] 4011 2-8-12 0 MickaelBarzalona 3 (Mahmood Al Zarooni) *s.i.s: plld hrd and sn prom: led over 1f out: pushed out* **11/8**[1]	105+
11	**2**	*1*	**Sky Lantern (IRE)**[68] 2780 2-8-12 0 RichardHughes 2 (Richard Hannon) *a.p: rdn to chse wnr fnl f: edgd lft: styd on* **2/1**[2]	101+
1	**3**	*2 3/4*	**Reyaadah**[43] 3590 2-8-12 0 PaulHanagan 1 (Charles Hills) *hld up: racd keenly: hdwy and nt clr run over 1f out: r.o to go 3rd wl ins fnl f: nt rch ldrs* **8/1**[3]	94
212	**4**	*1/2*	**Savanna La Mar (USA)**[16] 4514 2-8-12 92 LukeMorris 4 (Sir Mark Prescott Bt) *led: rdn over 2f out: sn hdd: styng on same pce whn hung lft ins fnl f* **16/1**	93
11	**5**	*nk*	**Redressthebalance (IRE)**[14] 4574 2-8-12 84 JimCrowley 7 (Ralph Beckett) *hld up: hdwy over 1f out: styd on same pce ins fnl f* **9/1**	92
2136	**6**	*3/4*	**Momalorka**[7] 4820 2-8-12 87 KellyHarrison 5 (William Haggas) *chsd ldr: rdn to ld 2f out: hdd over 1f out: no ex fnl f* **25/1**	90
3211	**7**	*1 1/2*	**Dream Maker (IRE)**[6] 4836 2-8-12 72 JimmyFortune 8 (Tom Dascombe) *hld up: hdwy over 1f out: sn rdn: wknd ins fnl f* **20/1**	86
315	**8**	*7*	**Fantacise**[29] 4064 2-8-12 92 (b) RobertWinston 6 (Brian Meehan) *chsd ldrs: rdn over 2f out: wknd over 1f out* **28/1**	67

1m 27.15s (1.45) **Going Correction** +0.15s/f (Good) **8** Ran **SP% 114.5**
Speed ratings (Par 101): **97,95,92,92,91 90,89,81**
toteswingers 1&2 £1.60, 2&3 £3.90, 1&3 £3.20 CSF £4.10 TOTE £2.00: £1.10, £1.10, £2.40; EX 4.60 Trifecta £15.50 Pool: £2,106.01 - 100.09 winning units..
Owner Godolphin **Bred** Hurstland Farm Inc Et Al **Trained** Newmarket, Suffolk

FOCUS

There have been some high-class winners of the Sweet Solera, including the likes of Soviet Song and Maids Causeway, and it's a contest Godolphin target these days. Indeed, they were landing the race for the fourth straight season, the last two having now gone to a Mahmood Al Zarooni-trained runner after Saeed Bin Suroor supplied the winner in both 2009 and 2010. They raced stands' side and the early pace didn't appear overly strong, but a couple of smart types pulled clear of a promising sort in third. The winner built on her debut but the form is limited by those in behind.

NOTEBOOK

Certify(USA) impressed when winning a 6f maiden on soft at the July meeting and had no problems with the different conditions this time, confirming herself a really decent juvenile. She was a touch keen early, but it was nothing to be worried about and she ran on strongly after coming off the bridle before the runner-up. Presumably she'll now be aimed at the May Hill and/or the Fillies' Mile, and while she'll have to prove her stamina for 1m, she ought to stay. She's now around a 16-1 shot for the 1000 Guineas. (op 6-4 tchd 13-8, 7-4 in a place)

Sky Lantern(IRE) had to wait for a clear run, allowing the winner to get a start on her, but it made no difference to the result. She had been absent since winning a 6f Listed race at Naas in early June, so it's reasonable to expect there will be more to come, perhaps back over shorter. (op 15-8)

Reyaadah ◆ looks capable of better than the result might imply. The winner of a 6f maiden here on her only previous start, she was a bit keen under restraint and was left with a lot to do when not getting the clearest of runs, still looking green throughout. It wouldn't surprise to see her make significant progress from this run and she could give the winner more to do should they meet again. (op 10-1)

Savanna La Mar(USA) found this tougher than the Sandown Listed race in which she was runner-up last time.

Redressthebalance(IRE) was up in significantly in class after winning off 75 at Ascot on her previous outing. (op 8-1 tchd 15-2)

Momalorka didn't prove her stamina or her ability to cope with this grade.

5104 WATCH GERMAN RACES LIVE AT GERMAN-TOTE.COM MAIDEN FILLIES' STKS 7f

4:10 (4:10) (Class 4) 2-Y-O

£4,528 (£1,347; £673; £336) **Stalls** Low

Form				RPR
	1		**Winsili** 2-9-0 0 RobertHavlin 8 (John Gosden) *chsd ldrs: led over 1f out: shkn up and r.o wl* **4/1**[2]	87+
	2	*3 1/2*	**Jabhaat (USA)** 2-9-0 0 PaulHanagan 2 (Ed Dunlop) *chsd ldr tl led 3f out: rdn and hdd over 1f out: styd on same pce ins fnl f* **10/1**	76+
	3	*1/2*	**Alnawiyah** 2-9-0 0 TedDurcan 10 (John Dunlop) *hld up: rdn over 2f out: swtchd lft over 1f out: nt clr run and swtchd rt ins fnl f: shkn up and r.o wl: wnt 3rd nr fin* **33/1**	77+
	4	*3/4*	**Solace (USA)** 2-9-0 0 MarcHalford 4 (John Gosden) *s.i.s: hld up: nt clr run over 1f out: r.o ins fnl f: nrst fin* **40/1**	73+
	5	*1 1/4*	**Zero Game (IRE)** 2-9-0 0 LukeMorris 12 (Michael Bell) *hld up: nt clr run over 1f out: r.o ins fnl f: nvr nrr* **22/1**	70+
	6	*hd*	**Neamour** 2-9-0 0 EddieAhern 9 (David Simcock) *chsd ldrs: rdn over 1f out: edgd rt ins fnl f: no ex* **25/1**	68
	7	*nk*	**Savvy Chic (USA)** 2-9-0 0 JimmyFortune 14 (Jeremy Noseda) *wnt rt s: hld up: hdwy over 1f out: shkn up ins fnl f: wknd towards fin* **7/1**	67
	8	*1*	**Thwart** 2-9-0 0 JimCrowley 3 (Ralph Beckett) *led 4f: rdn over 1f out: wknd ins fnl f* **8/1**	65
	9	*3/4*	**Downhill Dancer (IRE)** 2-9-0 0 RichardMullen 6 (Brian Meehan) *mid-div: pushed along over 2f out: hdwy and hmpd over 1f out: sn wknd* **22/1**	64
	10	*shd*	**Stresa** 2-9-0 0 SaleemGolam 7 (John Gosden) *hld up in tch: rdn over 1f out: wknd ins fnl f* **20/1**	62
	11	*1 1/2*	**Tilstarr (IRE)** 2-9-0 0 DaneO'Neill 13 (Richard Hannon) *dwlt: hld up: kpt on ins fnl f: nvr nrr* **22/1**	58
	12	*2 3/4*	**Followeveryrainbow** 2-9-0 0 RichardHughes 11 (Richard Hannon) *mid-div: rdn over 2f out: wknd over 1f out* **9/2**[3]	51
	13	*2 1/2*	**Valley Of Queens (IRE)** 2-9-0 0 MickaelBarzalona 1 (Mahmood Al Zarooni) *trckd ldrs: nt clr run: swtchd lft and bmpd rival over 1f out: cl up and styng on whn hmpd and eased ins fnl f* **7/2**[1]	71+

1m 29.11s (3.41) **Going Correction** +0.15s/f (Good) **13** Ran **SP% 120.1**
Speed ratings (Par 93): **86,82,81,80,79 78,78,77,76,76 74,71,68**
toteswingers 1&2 £12.30, 2&3 £39.80, 1&3 £36.50 CSF £39.07 TOTE £5.20: £1.90, £3.40, £10.10; EX 55.30 Trifecta £636.50 Part won. Pool: £860.14 - 0.50 winning units..
Owner K Abdulla **Bred** Juddmonte Farms Ltd **Trained** Newmarket, Suffolk

FOCUS

A maiden for unraced fillies and there were plenty of interesting types on show. They went a steady pace (time was almost 2secs slower than the Sweet Solera) and the action unfolded towards the stands' rail, meaning a few of these found trouble as the race began to get serious. The winner looks sure to do better, as should the placed horses.

NOTEBOOK

Winsili ◆, the first foal of a decent dual 1m2f winner, was always travelling easily and drew clear without needing the whip. Her task was made easier by a few of her rivals meeting trouble, but she looks pretty smart. She doesn't hold any Group-race entries in Britain or Ireland, so perhaps her connections will be taking it steady with her this year. (op 7-2)

Jabhaat(USA), a half-sister to Motheeba, placed over 1m in Italy (Listed, RPR 87), was green throughout. She had her ears pricked from an early stage, taking it all in, and should know a lot more next time. (op 20-1)

Alnawiyah ◆ put up a promising debut. She's a sister to Mubaraza, a recent 1m5f winner here off 79 for these connections, out of a 1m4f winner for the same team, but she looks to have a bit of speed. Having been caught wide early after missing the break, she was then dropped in well off the pace and was denied a clear run until it was too late. The way she finished suggests she was probably second best on the day and she really should build on this. (op 25-1)

Solace(USA), out of 1m Group 3 winner in France who stayed well, she travelled nicely but was short of room at a crucial stage. She kept on when in the clear and is open to plenty of improvement. (op 33-1)

Zero Game(IRE) ◆, the only runner in the line-up with an entry in the Fillies' Mile, was another to finish nicely having been short of room when first trying to get going. A half-sister to a 1m winner, out of a successful sprinter, she should do a lot better. (op 16-1)

Neamour, the first foal of a 1m4f winner, showed up to a point out wide.

Savvy Chic(USA), a $220,000 purchase, had to challenge wider than ideal and should improve plenty. (op 11-2)

Thwart showed pace and was a bit short of room when weakening out of contention. (tchd 15-2)
Downhill Dancer(IRE), a half-sister to the stable's Racing Post Trophy winner Crowded House (down the field over C&D on his debut), didn't have the smoothest of trips. She wasn't unlucky, but should improve a good deal. (op 20-1 tchd 25-1)
Valley Of Queens(IRE) had a pretty rough introduction, her rider not impressing with his handling of a newcomer. Having been hard ridden in the direction of a gap between rivals inside the final couple of furlongs, she soon had to be switched and was then badly hampered on more than one occasion, before eventually being eased. It remains to been seen which way she'll go. (op 9-2 tchd 5-1)

5105 WT'S SNOOKER AND SPORTING CLUB MAIDEN STKS 1m 4f
4:45 (4:45) (Class 5) 3-Y-0+ **£3,234** (£962; £481; £240) **Stalls** Centre

Form				RPR
54	1		**Castilo Del Diablo (IRE)**[19] 4410 3-9-1 0 ... PaulHanagan 3 (David Simcock) *hld up: racd keenly: hdwy over 2f out: led and hung lft over 1f out: rdn out* **12/1**	80
4-	2	2 ¾	**Enthusiastic**[336] 5911 4-9-7 0 ... DarrenEgan(5) 6 (Michael Murphy) *hld up in tch: pushed along over 2f out: rdn and ev ch over 1f out: styd on same pce ins fnl f* **14/1**	85
	3	1 ¼	**Perfect Heart** 3-9-1 0 ... RobertHavlin 7 (John Gosden) *chsd ldrs: rdn and ev ch over 1f out: styd on same pce fnl f* **8/1**[3]	83
	4	1 ¼	**Spiritoftomintoul** 3-9-1 0 ... EddieAhern 4 (Sir Henry Cecil) *s.s: hld up: hdwy over 4f out: rdn over 2f out: styd on same pce fr over 1f out* **16/1**	81
4-34	5	3	**Toptempo**[21] 4346 3-8-10 83 ... RobertWinston 8 (Mark H Tompkins) *hld up: pushed along 4f out: hdwy u.p over 2f out: wknd fnl f* **11/2**[2]	71
	6	½	**Malekov (IRE)** 3-9-1 0 ... IanMongan 2 (Sir Henry Cecil) *s.i.s: sn prom: rdn over 2f out: wknd over 1f out* **8/1**[3]	75
-240	7	4	**Uriah Heep (FR)**[51] 3296 3-9-1 89 ... RichardHughes 1 (Sir Michael Stoute) *chsd ldr tl led over 3f out: rdn and hdd over 1f out: wknd and eased ins fnl f* **4/7**[1]	69
	8	19	**Tiermore Lass (IRE)**[83] 9-9-2 0 ... HarryPoulton(5) 5 (Terry Clement) *led over 8f: rdn and wknd over 2f out: t.o* **100/1**	34

2m 33.21s (0.31) **Going Correction** +0.15s/f (Good)
WFA 3 from 4yo+ 11lb **8 Ran SP% 122.5**
Speed ratings (Par 103): **104,102,101,100,98 98,95,82**
toteswingers 1&2 £11.30, 2&3 £11.60, 1&3 £9.00 CSF £171.26 TOTE £16.60: £2.50, £3.30, £2.20; EX 130.40 Trifecta £479.10 Pool: £1,449.89 - 5.18 winning units..
Owner Sir Robert Ogden **Bred** Ennistown Stud **Trained** Newmarket, Suffolk

FOCUS
An interesting maiden and the form looks fair, but muddlign with the form horses disappointing.
Toptempo Official explanation: jockey said filly hung right

5106 MICKEY FLYNN'S AMERICAN POOL HALL H'CAP 2m 24y
5:20 (5:21) (Class 3) (0-90,88) 3-Y-0+ **£9,703** (£2,887; £1,443; £721) **Stalls** Centre

Form				RPR
4015	1		**Mubaraza (IRE)**[16] 4513 3-8-10 85 ... PaulHanagan 1 (John Dunlop) *hld up: hdwy over 4f out: chsd ldr over 2f out: edgd lft and styd on u.p to ld wl ins fnl f* **3/1**[2]	98
2513	2	1 ½	**Moon Trip**[14] 4601 3-8-0 80 ... DarrenEgan(5) 7 (Mark Johnston) *sn chsng ldr: led 4f out: clr over 2f out: rdn and hdd wl ins fnl f* **11/4**[1]	91+
0120	3	5	**Trovare (USA)**[10] 4697 5-9-5 79 ... RichardHughes 6 (Amanda Perrett) *hld up and bhd: hdwy over 2f out: rdn and hung lft fr over 1f out: no ex ins fnl f* **16/1**	84
-020	4	¾	**Dazinski**[14] 4613 6-10-0 88 ... RobertWinston 11 (Mark H Tompkins) *hld up: hdwy over 3f out: sn rdn: outpcd whn nt clr run over 1f out: styd on ins fnl f* **12/1**	92
4134	5	5	**Winner's Wish**[16] 4513 3-8-7 82 ... RichardMullen 5 (Jeremy Noseda) *prom: rdn over 2f out: hmpd and wknd over 1f out* **11/2**[3]	80
3-04	6	1 ¼	**Sirius Superstar**[17] 4475 4-9-1 75 ...(p) DavidProbert 8 (Andrew Balding) *mid-div: hdwy 6f out: rdn over 3f out: wknd over 2f out* **25/1**	72
5020	7	2 ½	**Saborido (USA)**[10] 4697 6-9-4 78 ... JimCrowley 4 (Amanda Perrett) *prom: rdn over 3f out: wknd over 1f out* **16/1**	72
1112	8	2 ¼	**Waterford Star (IRE)**[7] 4831 4-8-9 69 ...(v) PatCosgrave 10 (Ian Williams) *chsd ldrs tl rdn and wknd over 1f out* **12/1**	60
3433	9	63	**Purification (IRE)**[22] 4284 4-9-11 85 ...(b) RobertHavlin 12 (John Gosden) *prom: swtchd to r alone far side over 7f out: bhd fnl 3f: t.o* **8/1**	
-134	10	11	**Rockfella**[22] 4284 6-9-7 81 ... EddieAhern 13 (Denis Coakley) *led 12f: sn rdn: wknd and eased fnl 3f* **14/1**	
4250	11	8	**Mohanad (IRE)**[28] 4096 6-9-2 76 ... IanMongan 3 (Sheena West) *chsd ldrs: rdn over 3f out: wknd 2f out: virtuall p.u ins fnl f: t.o* **16/1**	

3m 25.53s (-1.47) **Going Correction** +0.15s/f (Good)
WFA 3 from 4yo+ 15lb **11 Ran SP% 121.7**
Speed ratings (Par 107): **109,108,105,105,102 102,101,99,68,62 58**
toteswingers 1&2 £3.90, 2&3 £9.10, 1&3 £12.90 CSF £12.18 CT £116.56 TOTE £3.90: £1.70, £1.60, £4.50; EX 15.60 Trifecta £207.10 Pool: £1,449.89 - 5.18 winning units..
Owner Hamdan Al Maktoum **Bred** Shadwell Estate Company Limited **Trained** Arundel, W Sussex

FOCUS
A decent enough staying handicap in which the third sets the standard, rated close to recent form and his mark in this race in 2011.

NOTEBOOK
Mubaraza(IRE) did well to win as the runner-up very much got first run, briefly appearing to have kicked into a decisive lead. He was reversing recent Sandown form with Winner's Wish, proving well suited by the step up to 2m, and should have more to offer at this distance. (op 9-2)
Moon Trip was well ridden by his apprentice, only being clawed back by the strong-staying winner with the pair clear. (op 9-4 tchd 4-1 in a place)
Trovare(USA), 3lb lower than when third in this last year, travelled well under a patient ride, but ruined his chance by hanging badly left under pressure, eventually ending up against the far rail. Official explanation: jockey said gelding hung left (op 14-1)
Dazinski carried his head a touch awkwardly and could make no real impression. (op 10-1)
Winner's Wish failed to prove her stamina. (op 7-1 tchd 8-1)
Rockfella Official explanation: jockey said gelding was unsuited by the good to firm ground
Mohanad(IRE) Official explanation: jockey said gelding had no more to give

5107 EUROPEAN BREEDERS' FUND FILLIES' H'CAP 1m
5:55 (5:55) (Class 4) (0-80,82) 3-Y-0+ **£5,175** (£1,540; £769; £384) **Stalls** Low

Form				RPR
0532	1		**Princess Of Orange**[7] 4819 3-9-9 82 ... SebSanders 5 (Rae Guest) *hld up: swtchd rt and hdwy to ld 1f out: shkn up and qcknd clr* **6/1**[3]	96
032	2	4 ½	**Four Leaves (IRE)**[41] 3666 3-9-3 76 ... AndreaAtzeni 8 (Marco Botti) *chsd ldrs: rdn to ld over 1f out: sn hdd: styd on same pce* **17/2**	80
-102	3	4	**Rugosa**[14] 4579 3-9-5 78 ... RobertWinston 2 (Charles Hills) *hld up: hdwy over 2f out: sn rdn: styd on to go 3rd wl ins fnl f* **9/2**[2]	73
00-3	4	½	**Soho Rocks**[18] 4436 3-8-10 69 ... KirstyMilczarek 7 (James Toller) *led: racd keenly: hdd over 1f out: no ex ins fnl f* **16/1**	63
4-46	5	1 ¾	**Gifted Dancer**[15] 4533 3-8-9 68 ... DaneO'Neill 3 (Henry Candy) *chsd ldr: rdn and ev ch over 1f out: wknd ins fnl f* **10/1**	58
4422	6	1 ¼	**Roedean (IRE)**[15] 4544 3-8-3 67 ow1 ...(tp) LauraPike(5) 6 (William Stone) *prom: pushed along over 2f out: wknd ins fnl f* **12/1**	54
0221	7	8	**Sputnik Sweetheart**[77] 2483 3-9-2 75 ... RichardHughes 1 (Richard Hannon) *hld up: racd keenly: hdwy 2f out: sn rdn and hung lft: wknd and eased fnl f* **13/8**[1]	43
-033	8	15	**Afnoon (USA)**[15] 4544 3-8-12 71 ... PaulHanagan 4 (John Dunlop) *trckd ldrs: rdn over 2f out: hung rt and wknd over 1f out: eased: t.o* **7/1**	

1m 40.61s (0.61) **Going Correction** +0.15s/f (Good)
WFA 3 from 4yo 7lb **8 Ran SP% 116.3**
Speed ratings (Par 102): **102,97,93,93,91 90,82,67**
toteswingers: 1&2 £9.10, 1&3 £4.10, 2&3 £5.30 CSF £56.16 CT £254.05 TOTE £7.10: £2.40, £2.70, £1.90; EX 55.20 Trifecta £245.20 Pool: £672.90 - 2.03 winning units..
Owner Colin Joseph **Bred** Cheveley Park Stud Ltd **Trained** Newmarket, Suffolk

FOCUS
A fair fillies' handicap in which the winner was impressive and the second sets the level, rated close to her maiden form.
Afnoon(USA) Official explanation: jockey said filly lost its action
T/Plt: £278.90 to a £1 stake. Pool of £88182.96 - 230.78 winning tickets. T/Qpdt: £58.70 to a £1 stake. Pool of £4549.58 - 57.3 winning tickets. CR

4710 REDCAR (L-H)
Saturday, August 11

OFFICIAL GOING: Good to firm (firm in places; 9.1)
Wind: moderate across Weather: Cloudy

5108 RACING UK ON CHANNEL 432 (S) STKS 6f
2:00 (2:02) (Class 6) 2-Y-0 **£2,045** (£603; £302) **Stalls** Centre

Form				RPR
301	1		**Reconsider Baby (IRE)**[12] 4659 2-8-9 61 ... MichaelMetcalfe(3) 4 (Mrs K Burke) *trckd ldng pair: pushed along to chse ldr whn carried lft 2f out: sn led and clr ent fnl f* **11/10**[1]	68+
5335	2	6	**Dil Laney (IRE)**[32] 3936 2-8-13 62 ow2 ... DanielTudhope 1 (David O'Meara) *trckd ldrs: hdwy over 2f out: sn rdn and styd on to take 2nd ins fnl f* **3/1**[2]	50
6006	3	½	**Cymeriad**[12] 4651 2-8-6 50 ... JamesSullivan 6 (Michael Easterby) *trckd ldrs: hdwy 1/2-way: rdn along 2f out: kpt on one pce* **10/1**[3]	41
0	4	2 ½	**Little Squaw (IRE)**[8] 4778 2-8-8 0 ow2 ...(b[1]) DavidAllan 3 (Tim Easterby) *sn led: rdn along and edgd lft 2f out: sn hdd & wknd appr fnl f* **18/1**	35
	5	4 ½	**Big Spender (IRE)** 2-8-11 0 ow3 ... DaleSwift(3) 7 (Ian McInnes) *dwlt: a in rr* **12/1**	27
005	6	1 ¼	**Poppy's Purse**[17] 4449 2-8-6 0 ...(b[1]) RoystonFfrench 2 (Ollie Pears) *in tch: effrt over 2f out: sn rdn and n.d* **50/1**	15
003	7	4 ½	**Special Report (IRE)**[17] 4449 2-8-11 54 ... TomEaves 5 (Nigel Tinkler) *a towards rr* **10/1**[3]	5
0	8	8	**Cazza**[4] 4921 2-8-6 0 ... AdrianNicholls 8 (David Nicholls) *chsd ldr: rdn along 1/2-way: sn wknd* **16/1**	

1m 12.0s (0.20) **Going Correction** -0.175s/f (Firm) **8 Ran SP% 111.6**
Speed ratings (Par 92): **91,83,82,79,73 71,65,54**
toteswingers 1&2 £1.50, 2&3 £3.70, 1&3 £3.30 CSF £4.08 TOTE £1.80: £1.10, £1.40, £2.40; EX 4.20.The winner was bought in £8,800.
Owner M Nelmes-Crocker **Bred** Liam Queally **Trained** Middleham Moor, N Yorks

FOCUS
This was a desperately weak juvenile contest, although the winner could be value for a little more.

NOTEBOOK
Reconsider Baby(IRE), the only previous scorer in the race, proved far too strong. She landed one of these at Yarmouth 12 days earlier and had been found a cracking opportunity here. Once switched to the far rail for her effort she soon put the race to bed and is evidently a deal better than this grade. The handicapper will probably hike up up in the ratings after this, though. She was retained for £8,800. (op Evens tchd 10-11)
Dil Laney(IRE), second on his only previous outing at this venue, lined up officially rated 1lb higher than the winner and was getting 1lb from that rival. He bounced back from a couple of disappointing efforts back down in class and helps to set the level, but his mark needs looking at. (op 4-1 tchd 9-2)
Cymeriad lacked the pace to land a serious blow, but did some fair work late on and this was a return to something like her debut form back in May. (op 11-1 tchd 12-1)
Little Squaw(IRE) was quickly dropped in grade after showing next to nothing on her debut over 7f at Thirsk and went in first-time blinkers. The headgear lit her up and she was the only serious rival to the winner 1f out, but ultimately got firmly put in her place. (op 22-1)

5109 WIN A VIP DAY OUT AT REDCARRACING.CO.UK NURSERY 6f
2:35 (2:35) (Class 4) (0-85,82) 2-Y-0 **£3,752** (£1,116; £557; £278) **Stalls** Centre

Form				RPR
31	1		**Scentpastparadise**[11] 4681 2-9-2 77 ... RoystonFfrench 4 (Ann Duffield) *cl up: led 1/2-way: rdn over 1f out: drvn ins fnl f: hld on gamely* **8/1**	79
036	2	shd	**Team Challenge**[45] 3491 2-8-4 65 ... JamesSullivan 2 (Tim Easterby) *trckd ldrs: hdwy wl over 2f out: rdn to chal over 1f out: ev ch ins fnl f: drvn and no ex nr fin* **16/1**	67
1	3	1 ½	**Diggory Delvet**[35] 3844 2-9-2 77 ... TonyHamilton 6 (Richard Fahey) *trckd ldng pair: hdwy and cl up over 2f out: rdn and ev ch over 1f out tl drvn and no ex ins fnl f* **2/1**[1]	74

41 **4** 1 ½ **Yourartisonfire**[37] 3777 2-9-4 **82** .... MichaelMetcalfe(3) 7 75
(Mrs K Burke) *trckd ldrs: effrt and cl up 2f out: sn rdn and ev ch tl drvn and one pce fnl f* **9/4**[2]

214 **5** nk **Megamunch (IRE)**[17] 4471 2-9-0 **75** .... TomEaves 1 67
(Linda Stubbs) *wnt lft s: trckd ldrs on outer: effrt over 2f out: sn rdn and wknd over 1f out* **13/2**[3]

0415 **6** nk **Lucky Lodge**[29] 4071 2-8-12 **73** .... DavidAllan 3 64
(Mel Brittain) *led: pushed along and hdd 1/2-way: rdn 2f out: grad wknd* **17/2**

000 **7** 2 ¼ **Stand N Applaude**[55] 3182 2-8-6 **67** .... AdrianNicholls 5 51
(David Nicholls) *hld up: effrt over 2f out: sn rdn and no imp appr fnl f* **16/1**

1m 12.3s (0.50) **Going Correction** -0.175s/f (Firm) **7 Ran SP% 110.0**
Speed ratings (Par 96): **89,88,86,84,84 84,81**
toteswingers 1&2 £29.70, 2&3 £6.60, 1&3 £3.00 CSF £109.85 TOTE £8.10: £3.90, £9.40; EX 142.50.
Owner Mark Curtis **Bred** Brookridge Timber Ltd **Trained** Constable Burton, N Yorks

FOCUS
A modest nursery, but three last-time-out maiden winners were in attendance and the form is straightforward, rated around the principals, and fair for the class.

NOTEBOOK
Scentpastparadise comfortably made all in a Beverley maiden 11 days previously and she followed up on this nursery debut in brave fashion. She looked to have started in this sphere on a tricky mark, but she clearly improved for the extra furlong and, despite a likely rise, a bold bid for the hat-trick should be expected while she's in such form. (op 7-1 tchd 6-1)
Team Challenge bombed out at Carlisle on bad ground last time, but had previously looked a fair sort in the making when placed there the time before. He went off bottom weight on this handicap debut and very nearly got off the mark, but the winner proved that bit too resolute. A rise is now inevitable, but he's obviously up to winning races. (tchd 18-1)
Diggory Delvet won on his debut at Beverley last month and hails from a powerful yard that has a decent record in this contest. He had his chance over this stiffer test, but couldn't quicken sufficiently and perhaps he wants returning to softer ground. (tchd 15-8 and 9-4)
Yourartisonfire overcame trouble in running when off the mark at Haydock last time out and, with his yard having won the opening event on this card with a 2-y-o, he came in for strong support. He was conceding upwards of 5lb all round, but it looked to be the quicker surface that found him out and he's not one to abandon yet. (op 10-3 tchd 2-1)
Megamunch(IRE), easy to back, was expected to enjoy stepping up in trip but he's yet another here that looked inconvenienced by the switch to a quicker surface. (op 9-2 tchd 7-1)

5110 STAN PLUMPTON CELEBRATING HIS RETIREMENT H'CAP 7f
3:10 (3:11) (Class 4) (0-85,84) 3-Y-O+ **£4,398** (£1,309; £654; £327) **Stalls** Centre

Form RPR

4-04 **1** **Roninski (IRE)**[12] 4640 4-9-3 **80** .... JustinNewman(5) 13 92
(Bryan Smart) *hld up towards rr: hdwy 1/2-way: cl up over 2f out: rdn to ld 1 1/2f out: edgd lft ins fnl f: kpt on wl towards fin* **11/1**

6002 **2** 1 ¼ **Sound Amigo (IRE)**[7] 4829 4-9-8 **80** .... TomEaves 5 89
(Ollie Pears) *trckd ldrs: effrt over 2f out and sn pushed along: hdwy over 1f out: rdn to chal ins fnl f: ev ch tl drvn and no ex last 50yds* **10/1**

2050 **3** 1 ¼ **Mon Brav**[13] 4629 5-9-3 **78** .... DaleSwift(3) 7 83
(Brian Ellison) *towards rr: hdwy over 2f out: sn rdn and styd on fnl f: nrst fin* **12/1**

5221 **4** nk **Pearl Nation (USA)**[16] 4496 3-9-2 **80** .... FrederikTylicki 4 82
(Brian Baugh) *hld up: hdwy on outer over 2f out: sn rdn and styd on fnl f: nrst fin* **3/1**[1]

6040 **5** ½ **Boris Grigoriev (IRE)**[29] 4075 3-9-2 **80** .... JamesSullivan 9 81
(Michael Easterby) *cl up: led after 1f: rdn along over 2f out: hdd 1 1/2f out: grad wknd* **20/1**

030 **6** 1 **Celtic Sultan (IRE)**[10] 4703 8-9-8 **80** .... MickyFenton 1 80
(Paul Midgley) *cl up: rdn along wl over 2f out: grad wknd* **18/1**

6000 **7** 1 **Little Jimmy Odsox (IRE)**[7] 4829 4-9-0 **72** ....(p) TonyHamilton 3 70
(Tim Easterby) *towards rr: hdwy wl over 2f out: rdn to chse ldrs over 1f out: sn no imp* **14/1**

0200 **8** ½ **Fred Willetts (IRE)**[13] 4629 4-9-7 **84** ....(b) ShaneBKelly(5) 10 80
(Tony Coyle) *hld up towards rr: hdwy 1/2-way: rdn to chse ldrs 2f out: grad wknd* **9/1**

P400 **9** ½ **Toby Tyler**[7] 4829 6-9-2 **74** .... RoystonFfrench 12 69
(Paul Midgley) *in rr: hdwy wl over 2f out: sn rdn along and n.d* **33/1**

0050 **10** nse **Illustrious Prince (IRE)**[7] 4829 5-8-12 **70** .... DanielTudhope 6 65
(Declan Carroll) *dwlt and in rr: hdwy 3f out: rdn over 2f out: n.d* **5/1**[2]

0000 **11** 1 ¼ **Ralphy Boy (IRE)**[14] 4588 3-9-1 **82** .... JulieBurke(3) 11 71
(Kevin Ryan) *chsd ldrs: rdn along wl over 2f out: grad wknd* **14/1**

00-0 **12** 10 **Thirteen Shivers**[7] 4829 4-9-4 **83** .... DavidSimmonson(7) 8 47
(Michael Easterby) *wnt rt s: a towards rr* **33/1**

0015 **13** ½ **Indego Blues**[22] 4291 3-8-12 **76** .... AdrianNicholls 2 37
(David Nicholls) *led 1f: cl up: rdn along 3f out: sn wknd* **18/1**

4116 **14** 22 **Act Your Shoe Size**[23] 4261 3-9-5 **83** .... DavidAllan 14
(Keith Dalgleish) *chsd ldrs: rdn along over 3f out: sn wknd and in rr whn eased and bhd fnl 2f* **15/2**[3]

1m 23.38s (-1.12) **Going Correction** -0.175s/f (Firm)
WFA 3 from 4yo+ 6lb **14 Ran SP% 123.1**
Speed ratings (Par 105): **99,97,96,95,95 94,92,92,91,91 90,78,78,53**
toteswingers 1&2 £21.40, 2&3 £18.30, 1&3 £32.10 CSF £116.92 CT £1389.42 TOTE £12.90: £3.90, £3.60, £5.80; EX 105.70.
Owner Ron Hull **Bred** Peter Hodgson And Star Pointe Limited **Trained** Hambleton, N Yorks

FOCUS
This was a competitive handicap. There was an average pace on and there were any amount in with a chance 2f out.
Roninski(IRE) Official explanation: trainer's rep said, regarding apparent improvement in form, that the gelding was better suited by the stronger pace and quicker ground.
Boris Grigoriev(IRE) ◆ Official explanation: jockey said gelding hung left
Illustrious Prince(IRE) Official explanation: jockey said gelding missed the break
Act Your Shoe Size Official explanation: trainer's rep said filly boiled over prior to race

5111 JOHN SMITH'S REDCAR STRAIGHT-MILE CHAMPIONSHIP (H'CAP) (QUALIFIER) 1m
3:45 (3:46) (Class 4) (0-85,83) 3-Y-O+ **£4,398** (£1,309; £654; £327) **Stalls** Centre

Form RPR

3503 **1** **Jo'Burg (USA)**[5] 4879 8-9-6 **77** .... DanielTudhope 6 88
(David O'Meara) *dwlt and towards rr: smooth hdwy over 3f out: chsd ldrs 2f out: rdn to ld over 1f out: clr ins fnl f* **6/1**[2]

1300 **2** 1 ¾ **Cono Zur (FR)**[9] 4747 5-9-3 **74** .... JamesSullivan 14 81
(Ruth Carr) *chsd ldr: rdn along over 2f out: drvn and ev ch over 1f out: kpt on u.p fnl f* **28/1**

3312 **3** nk **Hakuna Matata**[63] 2922 5-9-2 **73** ....(p) TomEaves 5 79+
(Michael Dods) *midfield: hdwy to chse ldrs over 2f out: rdn wl over 1f out: kpt on fnl f* **11/1**

23 **4** hd **Sir Trevor (IRE)**[9] 4747 3-8-8 **72** .... DavidAllan 4 77
(Tom Dascombe) *led: rdn along wl over 2f out: drvn and hdd over 1f out: kpt on one pce* **11/4**[1]

2-00 **5** 1 **Alakhan (IRE)**[37] 3779 6-9-12 **83** .... MichaelO'Connell 10 87
(Ian Williams) *chsd ldrs: rdn along over 2f out: drvn and one pce appr fnl f* **14/1**

-224 **6** 1 ¾ **Next Edition (IRE)**[11] 4679 4-9-6 **82** .... ShaneBKelly(5) 2 82
(Philip Kirby) *trckd ldrs: hdwy over 2f out: rdn wl over 1f out and kpt on same pce* **10/1**

0400 **7** ¾ **Aquarian Spirit**[56] 3167 5-9-0 **74** .... LeeTopliss(3) 9 72
(Richard Fahey) *chsd ldrs: rdn along and outpcd over 3f out: kpt on u.p fnl f* **18/1**

106 **8** 3 **Silverware (USA)**[11] 4679 4-9-5 **76** .... TonyHamilton 8 67
(Linda Stubbs) *prom: rdn along wl over 2f out: grad wknd* **25/1**

2332 **9** 1 ¾ **Broctune Papa Gio**[10] 4715 5-8-7 **67** .... DeclanCannon(3) 1 54
(Keith Reveley) *nvr nr ldrs* **13/2**[3]

403 **10** 1 ½ **Just Bond (IRE)**[3] 4964 10-9-4 **78** .... DaleSwift(3) 11 61
(Geoffrey Oldroyd) *towards rr: sme hdwy wl over 2f out: sn rdn and n.d* **8/1**

5110 **11** 1 ¾ **Oratory (IRE)**[28] 4110 6-9-11 **82** .... MickyFenton 7 61
(Paul Midgley) *in tch: rdn along over 3f out: sn wknd* **16/1**

0215 **12** 1 ¼ **Ingleby Exceed (IRE)**[21] 4345 4-9-2 **80** .... DavidBergin(7) 13 57
(David O'Meara) *chsd ldrs on wd outside: rdn along over 3f out: sn wknd* **11/1**

0003 **13** ¾ **City Of The Kings (IRE)**[13] 4620 7-9-8 **79** ....(p) FrederikTylicki 12 54
(Ollie Pears) *a in rr* **16/1**

1m 35.58s (-2.42) **Going Correction** -0.175s/f (Firm)
WFA 3 from 4yo+ 7lb **13 Ran SP% 122.1**
Speed ratings (Par 105): **105,103,102,102,101 100,99,96,94,93 91,90,89**
toteswingers 1&2 £30.40, 2&3 £25.00, 1&3 £5.00 CSF £165.21 CT £1872.41 TOTE £8.80: £1.90, £8.70, £3.60; EX 146.00.
Owner Richard Walker **Bred** Tim Cooper **Trained** Nawton, N Yorks

FOCUS
This looked wide-open. It was run at a sound pace.

5112 MARKET CROSS JEWELLERS CLAIMING STKS 1m
4:20 (4:20) (Class 6) 3-Y-O **£2,045** (£603; £302) **Stalls** Centre

Form RPR

3001 **1** **Ebony Clarets**[10] 4705 3-8-7 64 ow1 .... FrederikTylicki 1 56
(Richard Fahey) *cl up: led over 3f out: rdn over 1f out: drvn ins fnl f: hld on wl* **11/4**[2]

0560 **2** nk **Icewan**[23] 4250 3-8-11 52 ....(b[1]) MickyFenton 6 59
(Paul Midgley) *s.i.s and bhd: rdn along and sme hdwy over 2f out: drvn and hung rt over 1f out: str run on wd outside ent fnl f: kpt on* **33/1**

3431 **3** 1 ½ **Annie Walker (IRE)**[10] 4713 3-9-1 75 .... AdrianNicholls 4 60
(David Nicholls) *cl up: effrt to dispute ld over 2f out: sn rdn: drvn and ev ch ent fnl f: sn one pce* **8/11**[1]

5100 **4** 5 **Lady Advocate (IRE)**[35] 3847 3-8-0 60 ....(b) JamesSullivan 3 33
(Tim Easterby) *led: pushed along 1/2-way: sn hdd & wknd wl over 1f out* **12/1**

1505 **5** 1 **Priestley's Reward (IRE)**[29] 4046 3-9-8 70 ....(v) MartinHarley 5 53
(Mrs K Burke) *in tch: hdwy to chse ldrs 3f out: sn rdn and no imp* **6/1**[3]

0000 **6** 15 **Majestic Bounty**[7] 4793 3-8-0 42 ow3 .... DeclanCannon(3) 2
(Chris Fairhurst) *chsd ldrs: rdn along 1/2-way: outpcd and bhd fnl 3f* **80/1**

1m 36.94s (-1.06) **Going Correction** -0.175s/f (Firm) **6 Ran SP% 110.7**
Speed ratings (Par 98): **98,97,96,91,90 75**
.Ebony Clarets was claimed by L. A. Perratt for £8000.\n\x\x
Owner The Matthewman Partnership **Bred** Michael E Broughton **Trained** Musley Bank, N Yorks

FOCUS
There was a cracking finish to this moderate 3-y-o claimer.

5113 FOLLOW REDCARRACING ON FACEBOOK & TWITTER MEDIAN AUCTION MAIDEN STKS 7f
4:55 (4:56) (Class 5) 3-4-Y-O **£2,587** (£770; £384; £192) **Stalls** Centre

Form RPR

6 **1** **Ever Fortune (USA)**[14] 4582 3-9-3 0 .... DavidAllan 9 69+
(Rae Guest) *in tch: pushed along 3f out: hdwy over 2f out: sn rdn: styd on strly fnl f to ld nr line* **7/2**[2]

2362 **2** hd **Sabore**[15] 4551 3-8-12 67 .... TonyHamilton 6 64
(Richard Fahey) *led: rdn 2f out: drvn: carried hd high and edgd lft ins fnl f: hdd and no ex nr line* **5/4**[1]

0-0 **3** 3 ½ **Jack Barker**[26] 4144 3-9-3 0 .... DanielTudhope 5 59
(Robin Bastiman) *t.k.h early: trckd ldrs: hdwy 1/2-way: rdn to chal 2f out and ev ch tl drvn and one pce ent fnl f* **33/1**

0004 **4** 3 **Benidorm**[15] 4551 4-9-4 52 ....(v) AdamCarter(5) 4 53
(John Wainwright) *cl up: rdn along over 2f out: wknd wl over 1f out* **12/1**

2230 **5** 1 ¾ **Bond Style**[55] 3184 3-9-3 60 ....(e[1]) TomEaves 7 46
(Bryan Smart) *chsd ldrs: rdn along 3f out: wknd over 2f out* **15/2**[3]

0 **6** 3 **Vera Richardson (IRE)**[36] 3811 3-8-9 0 .... LeeTopliss(3) 10 33
(Michael Dods) *in rr tl sme late hdwy* **9/1**

0060 **7** 1 ¾ **Medecis Mountain**[15] 4549 3-8-12 41 ....(p) ShaneBKelly(5) 3 33
(John Wainwright) *a towards rr* **100/1**

0 **8** ¾ **Under Ambition**[8] 4782 4-9-4 0 .... FrederikTylicki 2 28
(Frederick Watson) *a in rr* **100/1**

9 8 **Midnami** 3-9-3 0 .... JamesSullivan 1
(Linda Stubbs) *racd wd: a towards rr* **22/1**

04 **10** 3 ¼ **Dream On Paddy**[49] 3384 3-9-0 0 .... DaleSwift(3) 8
(Ian McInnes) *chsd ldrs: rdn along 1/2-way: sn outpcd and bhd* **9/1**

1m 24.5s **Going Correction** -0.175s/f (Firm)
WFA 3 from 4yo 6lb **10 Ran SP% 115.4**
Speed ratings (Par 103): **93,92,88,85,83 79,77,77,67,64**
toteswingers: 1&2 £2.10, 1&3 £18.00, 2&3 £6.80 CSF £7.96 TOTE £5.80: £1.50, £1.10, £8.10; EX 13.40.
Owner Fung Lok Li **Bred** Lantern Hill Farm Llc **Trained** Newmarket, Suffolk

FOCUS
A very weak maiden.
Dream On Paddy Official explanation: trainer said gelding was unsuited by the good to firm (firm in places) ground

5114 LADIES' & GENTS' EVENING 25TH AUGUST H'CAP (DIV I) 1m 6f 19y
5:30 (5:30) (Class 6) (0-60,60) 3-Y-O+ **£1,940** (£577; £288; £144) **Stalls** Low

Form RPR

5502 **1** **Dean Iarracht (IRE)**[11] 4683 6-9-7 **53** ....(p) FrederikTylicki 5 59
(Tracy Waggott) *dwlt: hld up in rr: hdwy 4f out: chsd ldng pair over 2f out: rdn wl over 1f out: styd on to ld ins fnl f: drvn out* **5/2**[1]

5652 **2** ½ **Little Red Minx (IRE)**[7] 4826 3-8-1 **53**.......................... DavidBergin(7) 8 58
(David O'Meara) *trckd ldng pair: hdwy to ld 3f out: rdn 2f out: drvn and edgd rt ent fnl f: sn hdd: kpt on* **11/4**[2]

30-2 **3** 1 **Sheila's Castle**[17] 4455 8-9-5 **58**.......................... JackDuern(7) 6 62
(Sean Regan) *hld up in tch: hdwy 4f out: cl up 3f out: rdn 2f out and ev ch tl drvn: n.m.r and one pce ins fnl f* **3/1**[3]

6050 **4** 12 **Deep Applause**[11] 4683 4-8-7 **46** oh1.......................... ConnorNichol(7) 4 33
(Michael Dods) *trckd ldrs: hdwy over 3f out: rdn along over 2f out: sn one pce* **9/1**

0-00 **5** 7 **Donna Elvira**[19] 3310 5-8-9 **46** oh1..........................(p) ShaneBKelly(5) 7 23
(Edwin Tuer) *led: rdn along 4f out: hdd over 3f out and sn wknd* **14/1**

46-0 **6** 2 ½ **Andorn (GER)**[68] 2775 8-9-7 **60**.......................... EvaMoscrop(7) 1 34
(Philip Kirby) *hld up in rr: rdn along 4f out: sn outpcd* **7/1**

0-00 **7** 6 **Willy McBay**[19] 4399 3-8-1 **46** oh1.......................... JamesSullivan 9 12
(George Moore) *cl up: rdn along 4f out: wknd 3f out* **33/1**

3m 5.95s (1.25) **Going Correction** -0.175s/f (Firm)
WFA 3 from 4yo+ 13lb **7** Ran SP% **112.3**
Speed ratings (Par 101): **89,88,88,81,77 75,72**
toteswingers 1&2 £3.20, 2&3 £1.90, 1&3 £2.40 CSF £9.30 CT £19.90 TOTE £3.30: £2.00, £1.10; EX 8.30.
Owner Michael Howarth **Bred** Ken Carroll **Trained** Spennymoor, Co Durham

FOCUS
An ordinary staying handicap.
Andorn(GER) Official explanation: trainer said horse finished distressed

5115 LADIES' & GENTS' EVENING 25TH AUGUST H'CAP (DIV II) 1m 6f 19y
6:00 (6:00) (Class 6) (0-60,63) 3-Y-0+ **£1,940** (£577; £288; £144) **Stalls** Low

Form RPR

6343 **1** **Dr Irv**[19] 4399 3-8-2 **54** ow2.......................... DavidBergin(7) 5 67+
(Kate Walton) *trckd ldrs: smooth hdwy 4f out: led on bit over 2f out: sn shkn up and edgd rt: sn rdn and styd on wl fnl f* **5/2**[2]

2026 **2** 2 ½ **Hi Dancer**[8] 4766 9-9-4 **53**.......................... DeclanCannon(3) 9 61
(Ben Haslam) *led: rdn along 3f out: hdd over 2f out: rallied u.p appr fnl f: kpt on same pce* **7/1**[3]

0-50 **3** 1 ¼ **Sweet Fairnando**[19] 4399 3-8-9 **54**..........................(p) DavidAllan 6 60
(Tim Easterby) *cl up: rdn 3f out and ev ch tl drvn and one pce fr over 1f out* **8/1**

2241 **4** 10 **Scarlet Prince**[7] 4826 3-9-1 **63**.......................... DaleSwift(3) 8 55
(Tony Coyle) *hld up towards rr: hdwy over 3f out: sn rdn along and nvr nr ldrs* **2/1**[1]

0-0 **5** 3 ¼ **Erycina (IRE)**[38] 3753 4-8-13 **48** oh1 ow2.......................... GaryBartley(3) 4 36
(Noel Wilson) *in tch: effrt over 3f out: sn rdn along and nvr a factor* **50/1**

0/00 **6** nk **Prairie Hawk (USA)**[14] 4590 7-9-1 **47**..........................(t) TomEaves 1 34
(Brian Rothwell) *hld up: a in rr* **20/1**

0040 **7** 1 **Brasingaman Espee**[19] 4399 3-8-1 **46** oh1.......................... JamesSullivan 2 32
(George Moore) *chsd ldrs: rdn along over 4f out: sn wknd* **11/1**

-001 **8** 10 **Stormy Morning**[8] 4766 6-9-6 **59**..........................(p) EvaMoscrop(7) 3 31
(Philip Kirby) *chsd ldrs: rdn along and lost pl over 5f out: sn bhd* **7/1**[3]

3m 3.4s (-1.30) **Going Correction** -0.175s/f (Firm)
WFA 3 from 4yo+ 13lb **8** Ran SP% **113.1**
Speed ratings (Par 101): **96,94,93,88,86 86,85,79**
toteswingers 1&2 £3.10, 2&3 £11.30, 1&3 £6.20 CSF £19.91 CT £119.87 TOTE £4.30: £2.00, £2.50, £2.70; EX 27.20.
Owner Irvine Lynch **Bred** Whitsbury Manor Stud & Pigeon House Stud **Trained** Middleham Moor, N Yorks

FOCUS
The second division of the ordinary staying handicap. The form makes sense.
Scarlet Prince Official explanation: jockey said gelding ran too free early stages
T/Plt: £576.00 to a £1 stake. Pool of £41797 - 52.97 winning tickets. T/Qpdt: £51.20 to a £1 stake. Pool of £3819.96 - 55.16 winning tickets. JR

5073 DEAUVILLE (R-H)
Saturday, August 11
OFFICIAL GOING: Turf: good; fibresand: standard

5116a PRIX DE POMONE - HARAS D'ETREHAM (GROUP 2) (3YO+ FILLIES & MARES) (TURF) 1m 4f 110y
1:00 (12:00) 3-Y-0+ **£61,750** (£23,833; £11,375; £7,583; £3,791)

RPR

1 **La Pomme D'Amour**[20] 4386 4-9-4 0.......................... MaximeGuyon 2 111
(A Fabre, France) *settled 4th: rdn 1 1/2f out: qcknd wl ins fnl f: tk ld 100yds out: wnt clr: comf* **43/10**[2]

2 2 **Shimmering Surf (IRE)**[35] 3856 5-9-4 0.......................... NeilCallan 3 108
(Roger Varian) *sn led: u.p 1 1/2f out: r.o wl: hdd 100yds out: styd on wl* **6/1**[3]

3 ½ **Dalkala (USA)**[55] 3203 3-8-6 0.......................... Christophe-PatriceLemaire 4 107
(A De Royer-Dupre, France) *settled cl 2nd alongside ldr: rdn ent fnl 1 1/2f: no ex: styd on wl fnl f* **23/10**[1]

4 ¾ **Solemia (IRE)**[75] 2570 4-9-8 0.......................... OlivierPeslier 1 110
(C Laffon-Parias, France) *settled 3rd on ins: rdn 1 1/2f out: no ex: styd on fnl f* **43/10**[2]

5 shd **Haya Landa (FR)**[75] 2570 4-9-4 0.......................... ThierryThulliez 8 106
(Mme L Audon, France) *racd midfield: styd on u.p fnl 1 1/2f: nt rch ldrs* **33/1**

6 ¾ **Pirika (IRE)**[20] 4386 4-9-4 0.......................... Pierre-CharlesBoudot 5 105
(A Fabre, France) *settled towards rr: r.o u.p fnl f: clst at fin* **8/1**

7 1 ½ **Gloomy Sunday (FR)**[28] 4119 3-8-6 0.......................... JohanVictoire 6 103
(C Ferland, France) *settled midfield: rdn 1 1/2f out: no ex: styd on fnl f* **13/1**

8 nk **Sarah Lynx (IRE)**[244] 7729 5-9-4 0..........................(b) ChristopheSoumillon 7 102
(J E Hammond, France) *a towards rr: no ex in st* **9/1**

9 1 ¾ **Brasileira**[67] 2805 4-9-4 0.......................... AlexisBadel 9 100
(J-M Beguigne, France) *a at rr: no prog in st* **31/1**

2m 42.2s (-4.20)
WFA 3 from 4yo+ 11lb **9** Ran SP% **116.6**
WIN (incl. 1 euro stake): 5.30. PLACES: 1.90, 2.00, 1.50. DF: 18.00. SF: 36.90.
Owner Guy Reed **Bred** G Reed **Trained** Chantilly, France

NOTEBOOK
La Pomme D'Amour enjoyed a couple of confidence-boosters before finishing second in a Listed race at Maisons-Laffite last time, and she built on that with a convinicing win upped in grade and distance here.
Shimmering Surf(IRE), runner-up to Great Heavens in the Lancashire Oaks last time, was allowed to dictate here own pace out in front but couldn't cope with the winner's turn of speed late on. She ran right up to her best in defeat.
Dalkala(USA), upped in trip, probably ran to a similar level as when fifth in the Prix de Diane.

5117a PRIX GONTAUT-BIRON - HONG KONG JOCKEY CLUB (GROUP 3) (4YO+) (TURF) 1m 2f
1:30 (12:00) 4-Y-0+ **£33,333** (£13,333; £10,000; £6,666; £3,333)

RPR

1 **Don Bosco (FR)**[24] 4229 5-8-11 0.......................... GregoryBenoist 1 108
(D Smaga, France) *sn led: r.o wl u.p 1f out: all out to hold runner-up fnl 50yds* **99/10**

2 ¾ **Sagramor**[72] 2640 4-8-11 0.......................... DarrylHolland 6 107
(Hughie Morrison) *settled at rr: chkn up ent fnl 1 1/2f: r.o strly fnl f: nt rch ldr* **5/1**[2]

3 1 ¼ **Saga Dream (FR)**[46] 3482 6-8-11 0.......................... ThierryJarnet 4 104
(F Lemercier, France) *racd midfield: u.p 1f out: styd on wl: got up for 3rd cl home* **9/1**

4 snk **Abdel (FR)**[22] 4316 4-8-9 0.......................... AnthonyCrastus 2 102
(C Laffon-Parias, France) *settled 3rd on ins: u.p ent fnl f: no ex fnl 100yds: lost 3rd cl home* **10/1**

5 nk **Maxios**[69] 2744 4-8-11 0.......................... StephanePasquier 3 103
(J E Pease, France) *racd cl 2nd: ev ch but nt qckn ent fnl f: nt hrd rdn fnl 50yds whn ch gone* **4/5**[1]

6 10 **Mighty Mouse (GER)**[61] 2989 4-8-9 0.......................... JohanVictoire 7 81
(P Vovcenko, Germany) *settled 4th: rdn and u.p bef st: grad wknd: eased ins fnl f* **34/1**

7 6 **Da Paolino (FR)**[55] 5-8-9 0.......................... PaulineProd'homme 5 69
(D Prod'Homme, France) *settled towards rr: swung wd ent straght: rdn but fnd no ex: nvr a factor* **68/10**[3]

2m 6.29s (-3.91) **7** Ran SP% **116.2**
WIN (incl. 1 euro stake): 10.90. PLACES: 2.80, 2.80. SF: 66.00.
Owner Omar El Sharif **Bred** Haras D'Etreham, Vision Bloodstock Ltd **Trained** Lamorlaye, France

NOTEBOOK
Don Bosco(FR) didn't have to go too quick out in front and that meant he had something in hand to repel the challenge of Sagramor late on.
Sagramor could have done with a stronger pace as he was never quite able to catch the winner from the back of the field. His rider thought that a little ease in the ground would have been in his favour as well.

5118a PRIX DE MARIVEL (CONDITIONS) (4YO+) (LADY RIDERS) (FIBRESAND) 7f 110y
3:10 (12:00) 4-Y-0+ **£11,666** (£4,666; £3,500; £2,333; £1,166)

RPR

1 **Orife (IRE)**[239] 5-8-9 0.......................... DelphineSantiago 7 89
(C Ferland, France) **29/10**[2]

2 1 ½ **Curro Perote (FR)**[13] 5-8-9 0.......................... CelineHerissondeBeauvoir 5 85
(L A Urbano-Grajales, France) **5/2**[1]

3 1 ½ **Casa Ingrid (FR)**[44] 5-8-5 0.......................... MlleMarylineVeillat(5) 8 82
(Y De Nicolay, France) **23/1**

4 2 **Glad Sky**[55] 3205 6-8-9 0.......................... NadegeOuakli 2 76
(J-L Pelletan, France) **12/1**

5 1 ¼ **Burj Alzain (IRE)**[343] 4-8-4 0.......................... MlleAmelieFoulon(5) 3 73
(Gerard Butler) *awkward s and slowly away: sn rcvrd to be prom on inner: t.k.h: rdn to chal 2f out: led briefly over 1f out: sn hdd and fdd ins fnl f* **13/1**

6 ¾ **Istimlaak (IRE)**[73] 5-8-9 0.......................... CarlaO'Halloran 12 71
(J E Hammond, France) **12/1**

7 nk **Planet Elder**[28] 4-8-8 0 ow4.......................... PaulineProd'homme(5) 1 75
(P Bary, France) **6/1**[3]

8 nk **Private Jet (FR)**[40] 3716 4-8-10 0..........................(p) MlleAngelaLeCorre(8) 13 79
(P Monfort, France) **14/1**

9 1 ¾ **Clever Man**[86] 4-8-9 0..........................(b) KarenBeaumard 9 65
(P Vovcenko, Germany) **41/1**

10 4 **Action Chope (FR)**[37] 4-8-7 0 ow1..........................(p) MlleNathalieDesoutter 11 53
(D Guillemin, France) **15/2**

0 **Thyan (FR)**[73] 5-8-9 0.......................... MlleAudeDuporte 4
(P Capelle, France) **86/1**

0 **Nova Neyev (FR)**[158] 814 4-8-9 0.......................... AnnaWyszynska 10
(P Capelle, France) **45/1**

0 **Crystal High**[36] 4-8-0 0.......................... MlleEmilieLalaouna(6) 6
(Mme J Bidgood, France) **73/1**

1m 30.6s (90.60) **13** Ran SP% **120.7**
PMU (all including 1 euro stake): WIN 3.90; PLACE 1.60, 1.50, 4.20; DF 5.50; SF 11.10.
Owner Simon Springer **Bred** Lagartijo S L **Trained** France

4506 FOLKESTONE (R-H)
Sunday, August 12
OFFICIAL GOING: Good to firm (watered; round course 8.2; straight course: stands' side 9.3, far side 8.5)
Wind: light, across Weather: dry and sunny

5119 GOOD LUCK IN TAMPA PAUL OSBORNE MEDIAN AUCTION MAIDEN STKS 7f (S)
2:00 (2:00) (Class 6) 2-Y-0 **£2,181** (£644; £322) **Stalls** High

Form RPR

0 **1** **Complexity**[17] 4487 2-9-3 0.......................... MatthewChadwick 1 78
(Charles Hills) *mde all and sn crossed to r against stands' rail: gng best 2f out: rdn fnl f: kpt on and a gng to hold on* **15/2**[3]

0 **2** nk **Master Ming (IRE)**[18] 4472 2-9-3 0.......................... HayleyTurner 4 77
(Brian Meehan) *trckd ldng pair: rdn to chse wnr over 2f out: drvn and no imp over 1f out: styd on fnl 100yds: nvr quite getting to wnr* **11/10**[1]

56 **3** 10 **Stiff Upper Lip (IRE)**[24] 4253 2-9-3 0.......................... RichardHughes 3 50
(Richard Hannon) *chsd wnr but sn niggled along and nvr gng wl: reminders 4f out: rdn and lost 2nd over 2f out: wknd over 1f out* **5/4**[2]

0 **4** nk **Xerxes (IRE)**[34] 3916 2-8-12 0.......................... MartinLane 2 44
(Hugo Palmer) *stdd and dropped in bhd after s: clsd 3f out: rdn and unable qck over 2f out: wknd over 1f out* **20/1**

1m 26.35s (-0.95) **Going Correction** -0.125s/f (Firm) **4** Ran SP% **108.6**
Speed ratings (Par 92): **100,99,88,87**
CSF £16.45 TOTE £7.20; EX 10.30.
Owner Robert Ng **Bred** Allseasons Bloodstock **Trained** Lambourn, Berks

FOCUS
A modest small-field maiden, the winner making all against the favoured stands' rail. The form is fluid with the second and fourth likely to dictate the level.

NOTEBOOK
Complexity, soon behind on his 5.5f Bath debut, showed plenty of early pace over this longer trip, soon having his rivals out of their comfort zone, and saw it out nicely under a well-judged ride from Matthew Chadwick, who'd impressed at the previous day's Shergar Cup meeting. This colt is reportedly been a slow learner and is expected to improve further. (op 13-2)
Master Ming(IRE) improved markedly on the form of his Sandown debut, drawing clear of the third but always being held. He's likely to want 1m before long. (op 6-5 tchd 5-4)
Stiff Upper Lip(IRE) was the first in trouble and has gone backwards in a trio of starts. She now has the option of nurseries. (op 6-4)
Xerxes(IRE) was ultimately outpaced, but showed ability and should have a future in handicaps. (op 12-1)

5120 VEGAS BETTING GURKHA CUP H'CAP 7f (S)
2:30 (2:30) (Class 4) (0-80,78) 3-Y-O+ **£4,528** (£1,347; £673; £336) **Stalls** High

Form RPR
0400 **1** **Konstantin (IRE)**[9] 4775 4-9-11 **77**.................................... HayleyTurner 5 89
(Marcus Tregoning) *hld up in tch: rdn and effrt 2f out: chsd ldr 1f out: drvn to ld fnl 100yds: styd on wl: drvn out* **7/1**[3]
1400 **2** *nk* **Maverik**[86] 2257 4-9-12 **78**.................................... JimCrowley 2 89
(Ralph Beckett) *chsd ldr: grad crossed to r against stands' rail and led 1/2-way: rdn 2f out: hdd fnl 100yds: kpt on u.p but a hld after* **7/4**[1]
4301 **3** *1 1/4* **Annes Rocket (IRE)**[17] 4517 7-8-10 **67**....................(p) KatiaScallan(5) 8 75
(Jimmy Fox) *stdd s: t.k.h: hld up towards rr: hdwy over 2f out: chsng ldrs and n.m.r whn swtchd rt 1f out: styd on same pce fnl 100yds* **8/1**
5526 **4** *1 1/2* **Emiratesdotcom**[17] 4503 6-9-9 **75**.................................... LiamKeniry 1 79
(Milton Bradley) *t.k.h: hld up in tch: effrt and rdn jst over 2f out: chsng ldrs over 1f out: no ex and one pce ins fnl f* **16/1**
1423 **5** *3/4* **Abigails Angel**[24] 4255 5-9-6 **72**.................................... DavidProbert 7 74
(Brett Johnson) *chsd ldrs: rdn to chse ldr over 2f out tl 1f out: wknd fnl 100yds* **9/2**[2]
5000 **6** *1 3/4* **Space Station**[38] 3772 6-9-9 **75**....................................(b) SebSanders 9 72
(Simon Dow) *in tch: rdn and wanting to edgd rt over 2f out: no ex over 1f out: wknd fnl f* **15/2**
60-0 **7** *1* **Dark Lane**[8] 4814 6-9-1 **67**.................................... RichardThomas 10 61
(David Evans) *hld up in rr: struggling u.p 3f out: sme hdwy over 1f out: no imp fnl f* **33/1**
1300 **8** *8* **Legal Legacy**[2] 5035 6-9-10 **76**.................................... IanMongan 4 49
(Richard Rowe) *chsd ldrs: rdn and struggling over 2f out: wknd over 1f out* **14/1**
4000 **9** *2* **Haadeeth**[8] 4814 5-9-1 **67**.................................... StevieDonohoe 6 34
(David Evans) *taken down early: led tl 1/2-way losing pl u.p over 1f out: bhd fnl f* **28/1**
41-0 **10** *42* **Red Bay**[13] 4661 3-9-3 **75**.................................... KirstyMilczarek 3
(Jane Chapple-Hyam) *stdd s: t.k.h: hld up in rr: lost tch 1/2-way: t.o and eased fnl f* **20/1**

1m 26.18s (-1.12) **Going Correction** -0.125s/f (Firm)
WFA 3 from 4yo+ 6lb **10** Ran SP% **113.6**
Speed ratings (Par 105): **101,100,99,97,96 94,93,84,82,34**
toteswingers 1&2 £3.40, 2&3 £4.90, 1&3 £8.20 CSF £18.64 CT £102.52 TOTE £10.40: £2.90, £1.10, £2.80; EX 24.10 Trifecta £79.10 Pool: £671.75 - 6.28 winning units..
Owner Lady Tennant **Bred** Miss Annmarie Burke **Trained** Lambourn, Berks

FOCUS
For some reason the rail was shunned for the first half of the race, with Jim Crowley aboard runner-up Maverik being the only one shrewd enough to take advantage.
Red Bay Official explanation: trainer said gelding lost an off-fore and near-hind shoe; vet said gelding returned lame; jockey said gelding suffered interference in running

5121 LISA WILSON SCHOLARSHIP FUND E B F MAIDEN STKS 6f
3:00 (3:00) (Class 5) 2-Y-O **£3,299** (£981; £490; £245) **Stalls** High

Form RPR
5 **1** **Brazen**[64] 2934 2-9-3 0.................................... JimCrowley 4 82+
(David Simcock) *pressed ldr tl led 1/2-way: mde rest: rdn clr ent fnl f: r.o wl: easily* **10/11**[1]
04 **2** *6* **Lisa's Legacy**[7] 4846 2-9-3 0.................................... RichardHughes 2 63
(Richard Hannon) *stdd s: in tch in rr: swtchd rt and effrt 2f out: outpcd and btn 1f out: plugged on to go 2nd fnl 100yds* **5/2**[2]
0 **3** *2 1/4* **Hartwright**[9] 4773 2-9-3 0.................................... JamieSpencer 1 56
(Michael Bell) *chsd ldrs: chsd ldr over 2f out and sn rdn: no ex and btn ent fnl f: wknd fnl 100yds* **7/2**[3]
4 *3 1/4* **Somoud (IRE)** 2-9-3 0.................................... IanMongan 3 45
(J R Jenkins) *chsd ldrs: 3rd and rdn wl over 1f out: no ex and btn jst over 1f out: wknd fnl f* **28/1**
60 **5** *5* **Black Dave (IRE)**[7] 4846 2-9-3 0.................................... RichardThomas 5 29
(David Evans) *taken down early: t.k.h and racd awkwardly: led tl 1/2-way: sn struggling u.p: bhd fnl f* **20/1**

1m 11.63s (-1.07) **Going Correction** -0.125s/f (Firm) **5** Ran SP% **111.4**
Speed ratings (Par 94): **102,94,91,86,80**
CSF £3.52 TOTE £1.60: £1.10, £1.90; EX 3.30.
Owner H E Sheikh Sultan Bin Khalifa Al Nahyan **Bred** Lostford Manor Stud Ltd **Trained** Newmarket, Suffolk

FOCUS
Little depth to this juvenile maiden, although the winner was impressive. The second was a little below previous form.

NOTEBOOK
Brazen coasted to an easy success. He had shaped nicely at Newmarket on his debut and, despite slight concerns over the faster going, he was never in any danger. He could be the right type to contest sales races. (op 6-5 tchd 5-4 and 5-6)
Lisa's Legacy struggled to stay in touch early, perhaps finding the ground a bit lively, but he did stay on and should benefit from further once handicapping. (op 7-4)
Hartwright's Group 2 Champagne entry is clearly pie in the sky stuff judging by what we've seen of him in two starts to-date. He'll be one to watch out for in low-grade nurseries. (op 5-1 tchd 13-2)
Black Dave(IRE) Official explanation: jockey said colt hung right throughout

5122 SMP LARGE FORMAT FILLIES' H'CAP 6f
3:30 (3:31) (Class 5) (0-70,70) 3-Y-O+ **£2,726** (£805; £201; £201) **Stalls** High

Form RPR
231 **1** **Links Drive Lady**[11] 4708 4-9-10 **68**.................................... RichardHughes 3 76
(Dean Ivory) *in tch: swtchd rt and effrt to chal ent fnl f: rdn ins fnl f: led last stride* **4/5**[1]
0205 **2** *shd* **Amazon Twilight**[23] 4300 4-9-11 **69**.................................... DavidProbert 1 77
(Brett Johnson) *styd wd early: chsd ldr: rdn over 2f out: drvn and styd on to ld 1f out: kpt on wl u.p tl hdd last stride* **12/1**
0361 **3** *1 1/4* **My Own Way Home**[8] 4815 4-9-8 **66**.................................... StevieDonohoe 2 70
(David Evans) *t.k.h: chsd ldng pair: rdn over 2f out: chsd ldrs u.p 1f out: styd on same pce ins fnl f* **7/1**[3]
5164 **3** *dht* **Maria Montez**[17] 4509 3-8-10 **58**.................................... MartinLane 6 61
(J W Hills) *in tch: swtchd rt arnd wkng rival and nt clr run 1f out: kpt on u.p fnl 100yds* **25/1**
2525 **5** *nk* **Ocean Myth**[17] 4489 3-9-2 **64**.................................... JimCrowley 8 66
(Jonathan Portman) *t.k.h: hld up in tch in last trio: swtchd rt and effrt over 1f out: styd on same pce ins fnl f* **6/1**[2]
-500 **6** *2 1/4* **Saskia's Dream**[23] 4302 4-9-5 **70**....................................(b[1]) LewisWalsh(7) 5 66
(Jane Chapple-Hyam) *led: rdn and clr over 2f out: hdd 1f out: btn whn jostled fnl 150yds: wknd after* **10/1**
6503 **7** *1/2* **Judas Jo (FR)**[17] 4509 3-8-13 **68**.................................... NatashaEaton(7) 7 61
(Gay Kelleway) *stdd s: hld up in last trio: swtchd rt and effrt 2f out: no imp 1f out: wknd ins fnl f* **11/1**
60 **8** *nse* **Sweet Ovation**[25] 4218 3-9-2 **64**.................................... HayleyTurner 4 57
(Mark Usher) *stdd s: hld up in tch in rr: switching rt and hdwy wl over 1f out: no prog 1f out* **20/1**

1m 11.89s (-0.81) **Going Correction** -0.125s/f (Firm)
WFA 3 from 4yo 4lb **8** Ran SP% **116.1**
CSF £Owner CT £It's Your Lucky Day TOTE £Bred: £Peter Webb, £Trained, £Radlett, Herts.

FOCUS
More competitive than the market suggested.

5123 NATASHA AND LAURA OSBORNE GIRL GUIDES H'CAP 5f
4:00 (4:00) (Class 5) (0-75,81) 3-Y-O+ **£3,067** (£905; £453) **Stalls** High

Form RPR
2620 **1** **Clear Praise (USA)**[16] 4530 5-9-8 **74**.................................... HayleyTurner 5 83
(Simon Dow) *taken down early: hld up wl in tch: gng wl but nt clr run over 1f out: swtchd rt and hdwy 1f out: str chal ins fnl f: r.o wl to ld towards fin* **7/2**[2]
-030 **2** *nk* **Sandfrankskipsgo**[9] 4765 3-9-6 **75**.................................... SebSanders 3 82
(Peter Crate) *chsd ldr: rdn ent fnl 2f: drvn to ld ent fnl f: r.o wl tl hdd and no ex towards fin* **6/1**[3]
0044 **3** *3 1/4* **Love You Louis**[26] 4187 6-9-2 **68**....................................(v) IanMongan 6 64
(J R Jenkins) *led: rdn wl over 1f out: hdd jst ins fnl f: wknd fnl 100yds* **3/1**[1]
3602 **4** *nk* **Alpha Delta Whisky**[10] 4743 4-9-3 **69**.................................... TadhgO'Shea 4 64
(John Gallagher) *hld up in rr: effrt and swtchd rt ent fnl 2f: hdwy and chsng ldrs over 1f out: no ex and btn fnl 150yds: wknd towards fin* **13/2**
0131 **5** *2* **Triple Dream**[10] 4743 7-9-5 **78**....................................(tp) DanielMuscutt(7) 2 66
(Milton Bradley) *hld up in tch: pushed along 1/2-way: effrt and edging lft over 1f out: wknd ins fnl f* **7/1**
0231 **6** *6* **Knocker Knowles (IRE)**[9] 4757 3-9-12 **81**.................................... RichardHughes 1 46
(David Evans) *taken down early: chsd ldrs: pushed along 1/2-way: drvn and unable qck 2f out: wknd ent fnl f* **3/1**[1]

58.7s (-1.30) **Going Correction** -0.125s/f (Firm)
WFA 3 from 4yo+ 3lb **6** Ran SP% **112.3**
Speed ratings (Par 103): **105,104,99,98,95 86**
toteswingers 1&2 £3.70, 2&3 £6.10, 1&3 £3.90 CSF £23.98 TOTE £3.50: £2.20, £2.90; EX 25.60.
Owner Chua, Moore, Goalen & Warner **Bred** Juddmonte Farms Inc **Trained** Epsom, Surrey

FOCUS
The front pair pulled clear in what was an ordinary sprint handicap.

5124 ROSE AND CROWN AT STELLING MINNIS H'CAP 1m 4f
4:30 (4:30) (Class 5) (0-70,70) 3-Y-O+ **£3,067** (£905; £453) **Stalls** Low

Form RPR
0400 **1** **Mazij**[14] 4626 4-9-9 **65**.................................... HayleyTurner 9 73
(Peter Hiatt) *led tl over 7f out: chsd ldr after tl led again over 2f out: drvn 2f out: kpt on wl fnl f* **14/1**
6-04 **2** *1* **Peachez**[16] 4538 4-9-10 **66**....................................(p) RichardHughes 4 72
(Alastair Lidderdale) *hld up in last trio: effrt on inner 2f out: rdn to chse wnr 1f out: drvn and styd on same pce ins fnl f* **5/2**[2]
4/06 **3** *2* **Moose Moran (USA)**[18] 4475 5-10-0 **70**....................(v) KirstyMilczarek 6 73
(Olivia Maylam) *chsd wnr tl 8f out: rdn to chse wnr again 2f out tl 1f out: one pce after* **25/1**
0-00 **4** *1 3/4* **Kaylena**[16] 4538 3-8-8 **61**.................................... JamieSpencer 3 61
(Jeremy Noseda) *t.k.h: hld up in midfield: rdn 2f out: sme hdwy to chse ldng trio ent fnl f: no imp after* **7/2**[3]
3035 **5** *6* **The Calling Curlew**[17] 4491 4-9-1 **62**....................................(b[1]) AmyScott(5) 8 53
(Henry Candy) *t.k.h: chsd ldrs tl led over 7f out: hdd over 2f out: sn rdn and hld hd high: fnd nil: hung rt and wknd over 1f out* **9/1**
064 **6** *13* **Romantic (IRE)**[17] 4498 3-8-12 **65**....................................(b) IanMongan 1 35
(Sir Henry Cecil) *t.k.h: chsd ldrs: rdn and fnd nil ent fnl 2f: wkng whn carried rt over 1f out* **13/8**[1]
5-00 **7** *10* **Scotsbrook Cloud**[8] 4464 7-9-8 **67**.................................... RichardEvans(3) 5 21
(David Evans) *a in rr: rdn and lost tch 3f out* **20/1**

2m 38.29s (-2.61) **Going Correction** -0.225s/f (Firm)
WFA 3 from 4yo+ 11lb **7** Ran SP% **114.2**
Speed ratings (Par 103): **99,98,97,95,91 83,76**
toteswingers 1&2 £6.10, 2&3 £8.30, 1&3 £13.30 CSF £48.98 CT £885.61 TOTE £12.50: £4.50, £1.80; EX 29.80 Trifecta £368.80 Part won. Pool: £498.44 - 0.10 winning units..
Owner P W Hiatt **Bred** The Hill Stud **Trained** Hook Norton, Oxon

FOCUS
Moderate handicap form.

5125 LEASCLIFFHALL.CO.UK FILLIES' H'CAP 1m 1f 149y
5:00 (5:00) (Class 5) (0-70,70) 3-Y-O+ **£2,726** (£805; £402) **Stalls** Centre

Form RPR
044 **1** **Cape Joy (IRE)**[17] 4486 3-8-12 **63** ow1.................................... RichardHughes 4 73
(Richard Hannon) *mde all: rdn and fnd ex ent fnl 2f: clr over 1f out: eased towards fin* **11/8**[1]
4-21 **2** *2 1/4* **Sigurwana (USA)**[5] 4931 3-9-5 **70**.................................... LiamJones 7 73
(William Haggas) *chsd wnr thrght: rdn over 2f out: edgd rt u.p and no imp fr over 1f out* **15/8**[2]
6-04 **3** *4 1/2* **Zaahya (IRE)**[23] 4314 3-8-12 **63**.................................... TadhgO'Shea 2 57
(John Dunlop) *chsd ldng pair thrght: rdn and outpcd 2f out: wl hld after* **3/1**[3]
000 **4** *7* **Wishformore (IRE)**[32] 3964 5-8-8 **53**.................................... RyanPowell(3) 8 32
(Zoe Davison) *chsd ldng trio: pushed along after 2f: clsd and in tch 4f out: rdn and outpcd over 2f out: wl btn fnl 2f* **20/1**

3000 **5** 1 3/4 **Vena Amoris (USA)**[33] 3939 3-8-0 **51** oh3...................... JamieMackay 6 26
(Richard Rowe) *a same position: clsd and in tch over 4f out: rdn 3f out: sn btn* **33/1**

0306 **6** 77 **Hubood**[31] 4006 4-8-10 **52**.. KirstyMilczarek 3
(Zoe Davison) *s.i.s: a detached in last: t.o fnl 4f* **20/1**

2m 2.6s (-2.30) **Going Correction** -0.225s/f (Firm)
WFA 3 from 4yo+ 9lb **6** Ran SP% **114.4**
Speed ratings (Par 100): **100,98,94,89,87 26**
toteswingers 1&2 £1.30, 2&3 £1.70, 1&3 £1.40 CSF £4.26 CT £5.65 TOTE £2.50: £2.00, £1.10; EX 5.10 Trifecta £7.50 Pool: £817.25 - 79.97 winning units..
Owner Mrs John Lee **Bred** L Mulryan & M C Fahy **Trained** East Everleigh, Wilts

FOCUS
This concerned only three and Richard Hughes put on an exhibition in race-riding.
T/Plt: £310.70 to a £1 stake. Pool of £58450.24 - 137.32 winning tickets. T/Qpdt: £17.30 to a £1 stake. Pool of £5622.49 - 239.46 winning tickets. SP

[4704] LEICESTER (R-H)

Sunday, August 12

OFFICIAL GOING: Good to firm (9.8)
Wind: Almost nil Weather: Overcast

5126 BRITISH STALLION STUDS SUPPORTING BRITISH RACING E B F MAIDEN STKS 7f 9y

2:15 (2:17) (Class 4) 2-Y-O **£4,398** (£1,309; £654; £327) **Stalls** High

Form RPR

1 **Tamayuz Star (IRE)** 2-9-3 0.. PatDobbs 5 79+
(Richard Hannon) *chsd ldrs: pushed along over 2f out: rdn over 1f out: led ins fnl f: edgd rt: r.o* **11/1**

4 **2** nk **Flow (USA)**[10] 4724 2-9-3 0... TomQueally 9 78+
(Sir Henry Cecil) *chsd ldr tl led over 2f out: rdn and hdd ins fnl f: r.o* **5/4**[1]

0 **3** 2 1/4 **Shebebi (USA)**[64] 2929 2-9-3 0... TedDurcan 2 72
(John Dunlop) *hld up: hdwy over 2f out: rdn over 1f out: styd on same pce ins fnl f* **12/1**

3 **4** nk **Lord Of The Garter (IRE)**[16] 4539 2-9-3 0...................... MartinDwyer 1 71
(Brian Meehan) *trckd ldrs: rdn over 1f out: styd on same pce ins fnl f* **5/2**[2]

5 2 **Unmoothaj** 2-9-3 0.. PaulHanagan 6 66+
(Charles Hills) *dwlt: hld up: pushed along over 2f out: nvr trbld ldrs* **4/1**[3]

0 **6** 3/4 **Ivanhoe**[18] 4472 2-9-3 0.. FergusSweeney 8 64
(Michael Blanshard) *led over 4f: wknd ins fnl f* **66/1**

00 **7** 2 1/4 **Run It Twice (IRE)**[7] 4845 2-9-3 0.................................... RichardMullen 4 58
(Brian Meehan) *hld up: rdn over 2f out: wknd fnl f* **50/1**

1m 26.31s (0.11) **Going Correction** -0.325s/f (Firm) 7 Ran SP% **112.5**
Speed ratings (Par 96): **86,85,83,82,80 79,77**
toteswingers 1&2 £3.50, 2&3 £4.00, 1&3 £6.00 CSF £24.54 TOTE £9.60: £2.50, £1.70; EX 30.40.
Owner Abdulla Al Mansoori **Bred** John Malone **Trained** East Everleigh, Wilts

FOCUS
A fair juvenile maiden and the winner could be worth more in time.

NOTEBOOK
Tamayuz Star(IRE) produced a neat turn of foot to get on top inside the final furlong and ran out a ready debut winner. He has plenty of speed in his pedigree, but clearly stays well and looks to have a bright future for his top yard. (op 12-1)
Flow(USA), an encouraging fourth on his debut at Epsom, bagged the stands' rail and appeared the one to beat on nearing the final furlong. He got caught out by the winner's turn of foot, however, and as he rallied to come back at that rival the line came just too soon. Had his rider kicked on earlier he may well have come out on top and he remains a useful prospect. (op 11-8)
Shebebi(USA) proved distinctly green on his debut at Newmarket in June and again showed his inexperience here. However, he was doing some good work late in the day and is evidently on an upward curve. (tchd 10-1)
Lord Of The Garter(IRE) shaped as though this trip would benefit him when placed over 6f on his initial outing at Newmarket 16 days earlier. He had his chance, but failed to see it out like the principals. (op 2-1)
Unmoothaj, who has two future Group entries, was the choice of Paul Hanagan. He proved too green to do himself full justice and ought to learn plenty. (op 5-1)

5127 RUTLAND (S) STKS 7f 9y

2:45 (2:48) (Class 6) 3-4-Y-O **£2,070** (£616; £307; £153) **Stalls** High

Form RPR

0055 **1** **Tooley Woods (IRE)**[5] 4932 3-8-5 49.......................... SilvestreDeSousa 9 52
(Alan McCabe) *chsd ldrs: rdn over 2f out: led over 1f out: jst hld on* **9/2**[2]

0000 **2** nk **Barista (IRE)**[3] 4988 4-8-11 67.................................... CharlesBishop(5) 8 58
(Brian Forsey) *a.p: rdn over 2f out: r.o* **11/4**[1]

0- **3** nk **Pull The Pin (IRE)**[253] 7627 3-8-7 0........................ AdamBeschizza(3) 5 55?
(William Kinsey) *chsd ldrs: rdn over 1f out: r.o* **33/1**

0U22 **4** 8 **Mitie Mouse**[11] 4705 3-8-10 63.. MartinDwyer 7 34
(Mike Murphy) *led to 1/2-way: led again over 2f out: rdn and hdd over 1f out: wknd ins fnl f* **11/4**[1]

0 **5** 3 1/4 **Nurse Dominatrix (IRE)**[9] 4782 3-8-2 0...................... DeclanCannon(3) 2 10
(Richard Guest) *hld up: rdn and wknd over 2f out* **13/2**[3]

506 **6** 1 **Bajan Hero**[1] 5095 3-8-10 50... CathyGannon 3 22
(David Evans) *dwlt: outpcd* **15/2**

5065 **7** 3 1/2 **Clowance Keys**[11] 4705 3-8-12 50 ow2.....................(b[1]) JamesMillman 6 15
(Rod Millman) *dwlt: sn chsng ldrs: led 1/2-way: rdn and hdd over 2f out: wknd over 1f out* **10/1**

-056 **8** 15 **Aglaja**[113] 1530 3-8-5 42...(t) MircoDemuro 4
(Frank Sheridan) *sn outpcd: t.o* **20/1**

1m 26.58s (0.38) **Going Correction** -0.325s/f (Firm)
WFA 3 from 4yo 6lb 8 Ran SP% **113.4**
Speed ratings (Par 101): **84,83,83,74,70 69,65,48**
toteswingers 1&2 £3.20, 2&3 £15.60, 1&3 £14.30 CSF £17.00 TOTE £5.30: £1.80, £1.30, £5.90; EX 21.70.There was no bid for the winner.
Owner Hodgson, Jarvis, Louch **Bred** Mount Coote Stud & M & W Bell Racing **Trained** Averham Park, Notts

FOCUS
A weak seller in which the principals came clear.
Bajan Hero Official explanation: jockey said gelding had no more to give

5128 LEICESTER MERCURY FAMILY FUN DAY H'CAP 5f 218y

3:15 (3:16) (Class 3) (0-90,87) 3-Y-O **£8,191** (£2,451; £1,225; £613; £305) **Stalls** High

Form RPR

0416 **1** **Pale Orchid (IRE)**[7] 4838 3-9-6 **86**.................................. CathyGannon 6 95
(David Evans) *a.p: rdn to chse ldr over 1f out: r.o to ld nr fin* **12/1**

2331 **2** 1/2 **Ihtifal**[19] 4434 3-9-7 **87**..(t) SilvestreDeSousa 1 94
(Saeed Bin Suroor) *ponied to s: led: rdn and hung rt ins fnl f: hdd nr fin* **2/1**[1]

6450 **3** 2 1/4 **North Star Boy (IRE)**[11] 4703 3-9-6 **86**.................................. PatDobbs 2 86
(Richard Hannon) *s.i.s: hld up: swtchd lft and hdwy over 1f out: rdn and hung rt ins fnl f: r.o: could nt rch ldrs* **12/1**

121 **4** 1/2 **Minalisa**[13] 4660 3-8-12 **78**... ChrisCatlin 7 77
(Rae Guest) *hld up: racd keenly: hdwy over 1f out: sn rdn: styd on same pce ins fnl f* **5/2**[2]

1000 **5** 2 **Dishy Guru**[48] 3445 3-8-11 **77**... FergusSweeney 4 69
(Michael Blanshard) *chsd ldrs: rdn over 1f out: no ex ins fnl f* **33/1**

630 **6** 3/4 **Sheikh The Reins (IRE)**[8] 4819 3-8-11 **77**...................... PaulHanagan 5 67
(John Best) *hld up: pushed along over 2f out: styd on ins fnl f: nvr on terms* **7/1**

1021 **7** 1 **Decision By One**[12] 4671 3-9-5 **85**.................................(t) StephenCraine 3 72
(Tom Dascombe) *chsd ldr tl rdn over 1f out: wknd ins fnl f* **11/2**[3]

150 **8** 9 **Ivor's Princess**[15] 4607 3-8-9 **82** ow2........(b) WilliamTwiston-Davies(7) 8 40
(Rod Millman) *sn pushed along in rr: lost tch fr over 2f out* **20/1**

1m 10.37s (-2.63) **Going Correction** -0.325s/f (Firm) 8 Ran SP% **112.9**
Speed ratings (Par 104): **104,103,100,99,97 96,94,82**
toteswingers 1&2 £3.00, 2&3 £6.10, 1&3 £10.40 CSF £35.50 CT £301.90 TOTE £16.10: £3.30, £1.90, £2.80; EX 38.10.
Owner A F O'Callaghan **Bred** Mrs A J Donnelly **Trained** Pandy, Monmouths

FOCUS
A fair 3yo handicap. It was run at a sound enough pace and the first pair dominated inside the final furlong.

NOTEBOOK
Pale Orchid(IRE) was produced nearing the furlong marker and responded gamely to master the runner-up near the finish. She wasn't disgraced in Listed company at Chester a week earlier and had won on a handicap at Ffos Las off 3lb lower the time before, so it was surprising she proved so easy to back. She deserves credit as the winner carried her right when hanging and it was her fifth success in 2012. Her trainer later said she will probably now head to Newmarket next weekend. (op 9-1)
Ihtifal broke her duck in good style at Yarmouth, on her first outing as a sprinter, and she again set out to make all on this handicap debut. She made them all go, but has shown temperament in the past and didn't help her cause when hanging right into the whip when put under maximum pressure. That suggests she resented being given a smack and was again ponied to the start here, so while she's open to progression over sprint trips she evidently needs things to go all her own way. (op 5-2 tchd 7-4)
North Star Boy(IRE) was well held by the first two, but this was much more encouraging returned to quicker ground and dropped back a furlong. He's now on a more workable mark.
Minalisa made it two wins from three career outings on her handicap debut at Yarmouth 13 days earlier and was up 4lb. She proved keen under restraint and probably wasn't helped by making her effort widest of all from halfway. This lightly raced filly remains capable of rating a little higher as she matures. (tchd 3-1)

5129 THURMASTON H'CAP 1m 1f 218y

3:45 (3:47) (Class 4) (0-85,85) 3-Y-O+ **£5,175** (£1,540; £769; £384) **Stalls** Low

Form RPR

5051 **1** **Cape Explorer**[11] 4709 3-8-4 **70**... MartinDwyer 8 79+
(James Tate) *chsd ldr tl led 8f out: rdn over 1f out: jst hld on* **10/3**[1]

0146 **2** nk **Watered Silk**[10] 4745 4-9-9 **80**... RichardMullen 7 88
(Marcus Tregoning) *stmbld s: chsd ldrs: rdn over 2f out: hung rt ins fnl f: r.o* **14/1**

003 **3** 1 1/2 **Fadhaa (IRE)**[17] 4515 4-9-13 **84**... PaulHanagan 4 89
(Charles Hills) *led: hdd 8f out: ev ch over 2f out: sn rdn: styd on same pce ins fnl f* **6/1**

5015 **4** 5 **Refractor (IRE)**[80] 2419 4-9-4 **75**.. PatDobbs 6 70
(James Fanshawe) *hld up: hdwy over 2f out: rdn over 1f out: styd on same pce* **6/1**

-523 **5** 1 **Kenyan Cat**[24] 4249 5-9-4 **82**.......................... WilliamTwiston-Davies(7) 9 75
(Ed McMahon) *hld up: hdwy over 3f out: rdn over 2f out: styd on same pce fr over 1f out* **5/1**[2]

4-40 **6** 1/2 **Spensley (IRE)**[15] 4606 6-9-1 **72**... TomQueally 1 64
(James Fanshawe) *hld up: rdn over 2f out: nvr on terms* **17/2**

3550 **7** 1/2 **Chelsea Mick**[17] 4498 3-7-9 **68** ow1.................................... IanBurns(7) 5 59
(John Mackie) *chsd ldrs: rdn over 2f out: wknd fnl f* **18/1**

2552 **8** 10 **Shavansky**[25] 4223 8-10-0 **85**....................................... JamesMillman 10 56
(Rod Millman) *s.s: a in rr* **10/1**

-142 **9** 1 1/2 **Night And Dance (IRE)**[17] 4515 4-10-0 **85**....................... AdamKirby 3 53
(Clive Cox) *prom: rdn over 2f out: wknd over 1f out: eased ins fnl f* **11/2**[3]

0100 **10** 22 **Flying Applause**[74] 2606 7-9-2 **76**................................(b) LeeTopliss(3) 2
(Roy Bowring) *s.i.s: hld up: hdwy over 3f out: wknd over 2f out: t.o* **50/1**

2m 3.74s (-4.16) **Going Correction** -0.275s/f (Firm)
WFA 3 from 4yo+ 9lb 10 Ran SP% **117.2**
Speed ratings (Par 105): **105,104,103,99,98 98,97,89,88,71**
toteswingers 1&2 £10.30, 2&3 £14.00, 1&3 £4.00 CSF £53.13 CT £272.41 TOTE £4.10: £1.60, £3.60, £2.50; EX 52.60.
Owner Saif Ali **Bred** Highclere Stud **Trained** Newmarket, Suffolk

FOCUS
Another fair handicap. It paid to race handily as the hold-up horses struggled.
Shavansky Official explanation: jockey said gelding was slowly away
Night And Dance(IRE) Official explanation: trainer said filly was unsuited by the good to firm ground
Flying Applause Official explanation: trainer said gelding finished sore having lost a front shoe

5130 LEICESTER MERCURY WEEKEND EDITION H'CAP 5f 218y

4:15 (4:15) (Class 5) (0-70,67) 3-Y-O **£2,911** (£866; £432; £216) **Stalls** High

Form RPR

000 **1** **Forest Edge (IRE)**[8] 4814 3-9-4 **64**..............................(b[1]) CathyGannon 2 77
(David Evans) *chsd ldr tl rdn to ld wl over 1f out: styd on wl* **25/1**

4350 **2** 2 3/4 **Cynthia Calhoun**[13] 4647 3-9-5 **65**...................................... AdamKirby 1 69
(Clive Cox) *w ldrs: rdn over 1f out: styd on same pce ins fnl f* **11/1**

2212 **3** shd **Marinus (IRE)**[17] 4506 3-8-11 **57**... PatDobbs 5 61
(Sylvester Kirk) *hld up: hdwy over 1f out: r.o: nt rch ldrs* **3/1**[2]

0600 **4** 1 1/2 **Right Result (IRE)**[9] 4779 3-9-7 **67**..................................(v) TedDurcan 3 66
(James Bethell) *hld up: rdn over 1f out: no ex ins fnl f* **12/1**

00-1 **5** hd **Come Hither**[5] 4913 3-9-4 **64** 6ex.. DanielTudhope 4 62
(David O'Meara) *prom: rdn and swtchd rt over 2f out: no ex fnl f* **11/8**[1]

5421 **6** 1/2 **Kashmiri Star**[4] 4937 3-9-3 **63** 6ex.................................... PatCosgrave 8 60
(Michael Quinn) *led: rdn and hdd wl over 1f out: no ex fnl f* **6/1**[3]

-004 **7** 1 1/4 **For Shia And Lula (IRE)**[9] 4777 3-9-3 **63**...................... StephenCraine 6 56
(Daniel Mark Loughnane) *hld up: pushed along over 2f out: n.d* **16/1**

1m 10.66s (-2.34) **Going Correction** -0.325s/f (Firm) 7 Ran SP% **113.7**
Speed ratings (Par 100): **102,98,98,96,95 95,93**
toteswingers 1&2 £15.50, 2&3 £5.20, 1&3 £9.40 CSF £255.54 CT £1072.26 TOTE £25.10: £6.10, £5.30; EX 91.20.

Owner Peter Swinnerton **Bred** Alberto Panetta **Trained** Pandy, Monmouths
FOCUS
A weak 3-y-o sprint handicap.
Forest Edge(IRE) Official explanation: trainer said, regarding apparent improvement in form, that the gelding was better suited by being able to dominate.

5131 ROTHERBY H'CAP 5f 2y
4:45 (4:45) (Class 6) (0-65,65) 3-Y-0+ **£2,070** (£616; £307; £153) **Stalls** High

Form RPR
605 **1** **Maltease Ah**[69] 2762 3-8-4 **48**.................................... SilvestreDeSousa 1 57
(Alan McCabe) *mde all: rdn over 1f out: jst hld on* **9/1**
2-00 **2** *nk* **Irish Boy (IRE)**[26] 4187 4-9-3 **65**.. NeilCurtis(7) 9 70
(Paul Midgley) *hld up in tch: rdn and hung rt over 1f out: sn ev ch: styd on* **11/4**[2]
6012 **3** *4* **Two Turtle Doves (IRE)**[6] 4866 6-9-4 **59**...................... KellyHarrison 2 53
(Michael Mullineaux) *chsd ldrs: pushed along 1/2-way: rdn and ev ch 1f out: wknd wl ins fnl f* **13/8**[1]
0004 **4** *2 ¼* **Liberty Ship**[13] 4663 7-9-3 **61**..(t) RyanClark(3) 3 47
(Mark Buckley) *hld up: hdwy over 1f out: wknd ins fnl f* **12/1**
0605 **5** *½* **Portrush Storm**[69] 2761 7-8-5 **46** oh1............................. MircoDemuro 8 30
(Ray Peacock) *chsd ldrs: rdn over 1f out: hung rt and wknd ins fnl f* **16/1**
6005 **6** *hd* **Divertimenti (IRE)**[10] 4743 8-9-4 **62**............................(b) LeeTopliss(3) 5 45
(Roy Bowring) *chsd ldrs: rdn 1/2-way: wknd ins fnl f* **11/2**[3]
3440 **7** *7* **Miserere Mei (IRE)**[15] 4592 3-7-13 **46** oh1...........(p) DeclanCannon(3) 6
(Richard Guest) *hld up: pushed along 1/2-way: wknd over 1f out* **10/1**

59.63s (-0.37) **Going Correction** -0.325s/f (Firm)
WFA 3 from 4yo+ 3lb **7** Ran SP% **112.8**
Speed ratings (Par 101): **89,88,82,78,77 77,66**
toteswingers 1&2 £5.00, 2&3 £2.00, 1&3 £3.30 CSF £33.05 CT £60.55 TOTE £8.40: £3.00, £1.50; EX 49.60.
Owner A S Reid **Bred** A S Reid **Trained** Averham Park, Notts
FOCUS
A weak handicap.
Liberty Ship Official explanation: jockey said saddle slipped

5132 BOOK YOUR CHRISTMAS PARTY AT LEICESTER H'CAP 1m 60y
5:15 (5:15) (Class 5) (0-75,75) 3-Y-0+ **£2,911** (£866; £432; £216) **Stalls** Low

Form RPR
2332 **1** **Mayo Lad (IRE)**[15] 4603 3-9-7 **75**.. PatDobbs 1 80+
(Richard Hannon) *hld up: hdwy over 2f out: rdn over 1f out: r.o to ld last strides* **6/4**[1]
1-61 **2** *½* **May Be Some Time**[31] 3999 4-9-12 **73**.....................(t) FergusSweeney 2 74
(Stuart Kittow) *a.p: chsd ldrs and rdn over 1f out: styd on to ld wl ins fnl f: hdd last strides* **9/4**[2]
0504 **3** *½* **Indian Art (IRE)**[24] 4252 6-9-13 **74**.................................... TomQueally 5 74
(Sylvester Kirk) *chsd ldrs: rdn over 2f out: r.o* **11/2**[3]
5010 **4** *½* **Foursquare Funtime**[20] 4398 3-9-2 **70**.............................. AdamKirby 6 68
(Reg Hollinshead) *led: rdn over 1f out: hdd and unable qck wl ins fnl f* **18/1**
2010 **5** *7* **My Boy Ginger**[16] 4531 3-9-2 **70**.. JamesMillman 4 52
(Rod Millman) *chsd ldr: rdn over 2f out: wknd ins fnl f* **8/1**
22-0 **6** *2 ¼* **Cristal Gem**[66] 2846 3-8-11 **72**...................... WilliamTwiston-Davies(7) 3 48
(Alan McCabe) *hld up: hdwy over 3f out: rdn and wknd fnl f* **11/1**

1m 44.91s (-0.19) **Going Correction** -0.275s/f (Firm)
WFA 3 from 4yo+ 7lb **6** Ran SP% **110.9**
Speed ratings (Par 103): **89,88,88,87,80 78**
toteswingers 1&2 £1.40, 2&3 £2.50, 1&3 £2.00 CSF £4.92 TOTE £2.50: £1.20, £1.40; EX 5.60.
Owner Middleham Park Racing IX & James Pak **Bred** Redpender Stud Ltd **Trained** East Everleigh, Wilts
FOCUS
This was a tight-looking handicap and it threw up a close four-way finish, but the winner is value for further.
T/Jkpt: Not won. T/Plt: £2,231.90 to a £1 stake. Pool of £94476.53 - 30.90 winning tickets. T/Qpdt: £916.30 to a £1 stake. Pool of £7182.1 - 5.80 winning tickets. CR

5133 - (Foreign Racing) - See Raceform Interactive

4375 CURRAGH (R-H)
Sunday, August 12
OFFICIAL GOING: Yielding changing to soft after race 1 (2.20)

5134a KEENELAND ROYAL WHIP STKS (GROUP 2) 1m 2f
2:50 (2:52) 3-Y-0+ **£47,625** (£15,041; £7,125; £2,375)

RPR
1 **Famous Name**[17] 4521 7-9-10 116...................................... PatSmullen 3 119
(D K Weld, Ire) *settled in 2nd: clsd appr 3f out and led gng wl over 2f out: pushed along appr fnl f and sn extended advantage: easily* **Evs**[2]
2 *6 ½* **Born To Sea (IRE)**[43] 3651 3-9-1 118.......................... JohnnyMurtagh 4 106+
(John M Oxx, Ire) *t.k.h in 3rd: tk clsr order 3f out and pushed along in 2nd 2f out: sn no ch w wnr: kpt on* **10/11**[1]
3 *13* **Warwick Avenue (IRE)**[28] 4126 3-9-1 98.............................. JPO'Brien 2 90+
(A P O'Brien, Ire) *w.w and settled in rr: wnt 3rd under 2f out and sn hrd rdn to cl: no imp appr fnl f: eased* **12/1**[3]
4 *4 ½* **Bob Le Beau (IRE)**[3] 5027 5-9-10 104..........................(b[1]) ShaneFoley 1 71
(Mrs John Harrington, Ire) *broke wl to ld: hdd appr 2f out and sn dropped away* **33/1**

2m 19.39s (5.09) **Going Correction** +0.475s/f (Yiel)
WFA 3 from 5yo+ 9lb **4** Ran SP% **113.0**
Speed ratings: **98,92,82,78**
CSF £2.38 TOTE £2.10; DF 2.80.
Owner K Abdulla **Bred** Juddmonte Farms Ltd **Trained** The Curragh, Co Kildare
FOCUS
A small field in which only two made any serious appeal. The winner has been rated to the best view of his recent form.
NOTEBOOK
Famous Name has now won 19 of his 36 races, 11 of them at Group 3 level. He proved far too good for the Irish Derby runner-up, Born To Sea, on the day, and after he went to the front over 2f out it was soon obvious there was only going to be one result. He stretched clear over the final furlong and ran out an easy winner. While he has been placed a few times in Group 1 company, it will be interesting whether he continues his season in Group 2s or Group 3s, or if connections will give him another shot at the Irish Champion Stakes. (op 11/10 tchd 8/11)
Born To Sea(IRE) raced without the hood he wore in the Irish Guineas, the St James's Palace Stakes and the Irish Derby. The ground cannot really be put forward as an excuse and it was disappointing that he failed to muster a better effort over a trip that should have suited him. He was a little keen early in the race and, after moving into second almost 2f out, he was soon under pressure and was already beaten when he edged right in behind the winner over 1f out. (op 9/10 tchd 11/10)
Warwick Avenue(IRE), winner of a maiden over the course and trip and a 'winners' race over the distance at Fairyhouse, was stepping up quite a bit in class here and never really threatened to get into serious contention. (op 12/1 tchd 14/1)
Bob Le Beau(IRE), last of eight behind Galileo's Choice in a 1m4f Group 3 event at Leopardstown three days previously, again made the running but was done with once headed by the winner over 2f out.

5135a KEENELAND DEBUTANTE STKS (GROUP 2) (FILLIES) 7f
3:20 (3:21) 2-Y-0 **£51,458** (£15,041; £7,125; £2,375)

RPR
1 **My Special J'S (USA)**[24] 4276 2-9-0 .... CO'Donoghue 4 105
(John Patrick Shanahan, Ire) *chsd ldrs: stl travelling wl over 2f out and pushed along to sn ld: almost jnd appr fnl f: hrd rdn and kpt on wl to jst hold on* **12/1**[3]
2 *nk* **Harasiya (IRE)**[24] 4276 2-9-0 .... JohnnyMurtagh 8 104
(John M Oxx, Ire) *settled in 3rd: qcknd on nr side to almost get on terms ent fnl f: rdn and high hd carriage: kpt on u.p: jst hld* **2/5**[1]
3 *2 ½* **Diamond Sky (IRE)**[12] 4693 2-9-0 .... KevinManning 2 98+
(J S Bolger, Ire) *hld up in rr: swtchd rt to far side over 2f out: chal 1 1/2f out: sn no ex ent fnl f: kpt on* **16/1**
4 *3 ¾* **Roseraie (IRE)**[24] 4276 2-9-0 .... ChrisHayes 3 88
(Kevin Prendergast, Ire) *hld up towards rr: pushed along over 2f out on nr side: rdn in rr appr fnl f: kpt on to go 4th 150yds out wout ever threatening principals* **12/1**[3]
5 *¾* **Nandiga (USA)**[69] 2780 2-9-0 .... DeclanMcDonogh 6 86
(P J Prendergast, Ire) *cl up in 2nd: disp ld over 2f out: sn rdn and one pce ent fnl f* **25/1**
6 *1 ¾* **Magical Dream (IRE)**[12] 4693 2-9-1 ow1........................... JPO'Brien 7 82
(A P O'Brien, Ire) *led: rdn and hdd over 2f out: no imp and wknd ent fnl f* **3/1**[2]

1m 34.61s (3.81) **Going Correction** +0.475s/f (Yiel) **6** Ran SP% **121.5**
Speed ratings: **97,96,93,89,88 86**
CSF £19.27 TOTE £11.50: £3.50, £1.02; DF 32.00.
Owner M R Ziegler & Thistle Bloodstock Limited **Bred** Double Eagle Thoroughbreds **Trained** Danesfort, Co. Kilkenny
FOCUS
The winner reversed the form with the runner-up, but there's no reason to doubt the form.
NOTEBOOK
My Special J'S(USA) had shown plenty of ability in finishing second on her two previous starts, the more recent of which saw her beaten two and a half lengths by Harasiya in a Group 3 event over this trip at Leopardstown. She reversed placings with that filly here and battled gamely to do so having raced prominently and gone to the front over 2f out. She had it put up to her inside the final furlong but stuck her head out and never flinched. (op 8/1)
Harasiya(IRE) started odds-on to make it three from three. She began her effort 2f out, soon had every chance and, although carrying her head a bit high, stuck to her task without quite getting to the winner. There appeared to be no obvious excuses and Johnny Murtagh didn't offer any. (op 8/13)
Diamond Sky(IRE) had finished second over this trip on her debut at the Galway festival. Held up in rear, she moved up in the centre of the course to begin her effort over 2f out and soon had every chance before failing to make much impression from over 1f out. (op 14/1)
Roseraie(IRE) had finished third behind Harasiya and My Special J's at Leopardstown on her previous start when she finished well having been outpaced. Held up, she was ridden to try to close 2f out but never picked up enough to mount a serious challenge. (op 10/1)
Nandiga(USA), a winner over 6f on good ground on her debut in May, was tackling this trip and slow ground for the first time on her return from a break. She raced prominently and was vying for the lead over 2f out before finding no extra soon afterwards.
Magical Dream(IRE) had won the Galway maiden in which Diamond Sky ran third but she was unable to confirm that form and, after making the running, she was done with quickly after being headed 2f out. (op 3/1 tchd 5/2)

5136a KEENELAND PHOENIX STKS (GROUP 1) (ENTIRE COLTS & FILLIES) 6f
3:50 (3:57) 2-Y-0 **£91,833** (£30,083; £14,250; £4,750; £3,166)

RPR
1 **Pedro The Great (USA)**[43] 3649 2-9-3 98................ SeamieHeffernan 2 105
(A P O'Brien, Ire) *hld up bhd ldrs: 5th 3f out: swtchd rt and qcknd on outer to ld under 1 1/2f out: rdn and drew clr ins fnl f: comf* **10/1**
2 *2 ¾* **Leitir Mor (IRE)**[19] 4445 2-9-3 95................................(p) KevinManning 3 97
(J S Bolger, Ire) *cl up: rdn in 3rd and edgd lft appr fnl f: sn wnt 2nd and kpt on wl clsng stages: no ch w wnr* **12/1**
3 *1 ¾* **Lottie Dod (IRE)**[27] 4159 2-9-0 90.. PatSmullen 8 89
(Charles O'Brien, Ire) *dislodged rdr on way to s: rrd and lost grnd s: settled in rr: swtchd rt under 2f out and kpt on wl to go mod 3rd fnl 50yds* **25/1**
4 *½* **Probably (IRE)**[43] 3649 2-9-3 106...................................... WayneLordan 5 90
(David Wachman, Ire) *trckd ldr in 2nd: clsd to get on terms gng wl over 2f out: led briefly: sn no ex and kpt on same pce ins fnl f: denied 3rd fnl 50yds* **5/4**[1]
5 *23* **Bungle Inthejungle**[12] 4687 2-9-3 .... MartinHarley 4 21
(Mick Channon) *rrd in stalls bef s: broke wl to ld: pushed along appr fnl 2f and sn hdd: wknd qckly and detached in rr whn hmpd 1f out* **7/1**[3]
S **Cristoforo Colombo (USA)**[43] 3649 2-9-3 112.................... JPO'Brien 6 97+
(A P O'Brien, Ire) *hld up in tch: n.m.r and swtchd lft to stands' rail whn clipped heels and slipped up 1f out* **6/4**[2]

1m 19.05s (3.55) **Going Correction** +0.85s/f (Soft) **6** Ran SP% **117.6**
Speed ratings: **102,98,96,95,64**
CSF £113.85 TOTE £16.20: £4.50, £5.20; DF 71.00.
Owner Derrick Smith & Mrs John Magnier & Michael Tabor **Bred** Hascombe Stud **Trained** Ballydoyle, Co Tipperary
FOCUS
By no means the strongest renewal of this race with the field reduced to six because of three withdrawals due to the ground, which was changed to soft - slower than that according to some jockeys - after the first race. The third, who has been rated to her best, is the most solid guide.
NOTEBOOK
Pedro The Great(USA) had easily landed a maiden over this trip at Leopardstown on his second start but had finished ten lengths adrift of Probably in the Railway Stakes. Having been held up, he began his effort on the outside 2f out. In front well over 1f out, he ran on well and, taking everything into account, there was probably no element of fluke about his superiority on the day.
Leitir Mor(IRE) has been kept busy and had only once finished out of the first three, when a respectable seventh in the Coventry Stakes. He had every chance from 2f out and kept on inside the final furlong without ever troubling the winner. (op 12/1 tchd 14/1)

Lottie Dod(IRE), unseated Johnny Murtagh leaving the parade ring, causing him to be replaced by Pat Smullen. Like the runner-up, she is a maiden and the decision to run her in the hope of earning black type was justified despite her missing the break.
Probably(IRE) had handled testing ground when winning the Railway Stakes. He got to the front 2f out but came under pressure and could raise no extra when headed by the winner. (op 13/8)
Bungle Inthejungle, racing over the trip for the first time, made the running until 2f out before dropping out quickly and being eased to finish tailed off. (op 6/1)
Cristoforo Colombo(USA) clipped heels and fell about 1f out when trying to find room to begin his challenge. (op 11/8 tchd 13/8)

5137a PATRICK P. O'LEARY MEMORIAL PHOENIX SPRINT STKS (GROUP 3) 6f
4:20 (4:28) 3-Y-O+ **£32,500** (£9,500; £4,500; £1,500)

RPR
1 **Fire Lily (IRE)**[29] 41UU 3-9-3 110 WayneLordan 6 113
(David Wachman, Ire) *hld up in tch: in rr 1/2-way: impr into 3rd under 2f out: wnt 2nd ins fnl f and styd on wl u.p to ld fnl 50yds: all out* **5/2**[2]
2 ½ **Gordon Lord Byron (IRE)**[28] 4123 4-9-7 104 ShaneFoley 3 112
(T Hogan, Ire) *chsd ldrs on outer: 4th 1/2-way: impr to ld under 2f out: chal wl ins fnl f and hdd fnl 50yds* **6/1**[3]
3 3 ½ **Definightly**[29] 4092 6-9-10 (b) KevinManning 2 104
(Roger Charlton) *broke wl and settled in 3rd: clsd to dispute 2f out: sn rdn and no ex ent fnl f: kpt on* **9/4**[1]
4 4 ¾ **Invincible Ash (IRE)**[84] 2326 7-9-4 111 (p) PatSmullen 8 83
(M Halford, Ire) *dwlt: cl 5th 1/2-way swtchd rt 2f out and pushed along ent fnl f: kpt on into nvr threatening 4th fnl 100yds* **12/1**
5 1 **Norville (IRE)**[183] 527 5-9-7 89 (b) MarcMonaghan 5 82
(Lee Smyth, Ire) *cl up: 2nd 1/2-way: pushed along appr fnl 2f and sn no imp* **40/1**
6 13 **Starspangledbanner (AUS)**[708] 5744 6-9-7 115 JPO'Brien 9 41
(A P O'Brien, Ire) *broke wl on nr side to sn ld: pushed along over 2f out and hdd: wknd qckly* **9/4**[1]

1m 17.54s (2.04) **Going Correction** +0.85s/f (Soft)
WFA 3 from 4yo+ 4lb 6 Ran SP% **114.5**
Speed ratings: **112,111,106,100,99 81**
CSF £18.02 TOTE £3.20: £1.80, £2.00; DF 17.30.
Owner Michael Tabor & Mrs John Magnier & Derrick Smith **Bred** Beauty Is Truth Syndicate **Trained** Goolds Cross, Co Tipperary

FOCUS
This was run in a good time, and the runner-up seemed to produce a persoanl best.

NOTEBOOK
Fire Lily(IRE), who has been Group 1-placed, struggled in very heavy ground when only seventh in the July Cup last month but, down in class here, came from behind to deliver her challenge from over 1f out and ran on under pressure to hit the front close home. (op 9/4 tchd 11/4)
Gordon Lord Byron(IRE), a four-time winner who had been placed at Listed level, was running in his first Group contest and he ran a cracking race on ground he handles, going to the front 2f out and only giving best near the finish. (op 6/1 tchd 5/1)
Definightly, returning here following a below-par run at Newbury on his previous start, had won a Group 3 over 5f over the course in June. Always close up, he was second and under pressure over 1f out before failing to find any extra. (op 2/1)
Invincible Ash(IRE), a nine-time winner at 5f and this trip, is possibly better suited by the minimum trip. More certain is her preference for better ground and, on her first run since contesting a Group 1 in Kranji in May, she made some headway around halfway but was unable to make any impression inside the last 2f. (op 10/1)
Starspangledbanner(AUS), the Golden Jubilee Stakes and July Cup winner of two years ago, was back on the track for the first time since September 2010 having encountered fertility problems at stud. He dropped out quickly after leading for 4f, being eased when his chance had gone, and his rider reported that the six-year-old had got very tired having failed to handle the testing conditions. Official explanation: jockey said horse did not act on the soft ground (op 11/4 tchd 2/1)

5138 - 5139a (Foreign Racing) - See Raceform Interactive

5116 DEAUVILLE (R-H)
Sunday, August 12
OFFICIAL GOING: Turf: good; fibresand: standard

5140a PRIX FRANCOIS BOUTIN (LISTED RACE) (2YO) (TURF) 7f
1:30 (12:00) 2-Y-O **£22,916** (£9,166; £6,875; £4,583; £2,291)

RPR
1 **Style Vendome (FR)**[18] 4476 2-9-2 0 ThierryThulliez 8 100
(N Clement, France) **8/1**
2 ¾ **One Word More (IRE)**[20] 4387 2-9-2 0 WilliamCarson 5 98
(Charles Hills) *racd 3rd: rdn 1 1/2f out: r.o wl u.p fnl f* **16/1**
3 ¾ **Avantage (FR)**[31] 2-9-2 0 GregoryBenoist 7 96
(Mme Pia Brandt, France) **16/1**
4 1 ¼ **Deauville Prince (FR)**[22] 4327 2-9-2 0 RichardKingscote 3 93
(Tom Dascombe) *sn led on stands' rail: hdd 1 1/2f out: no ex u.p: styd on* **16/1**
5 ¾ **San Marino Grey (FR)**[21] 2-9-2 0 MaximeGuyon 1 91
(A Fabre, France) **10/3**[2]
6 3 **Kamran (FR)**[29] 4118 2-9-2 0 OlivierPeslier 6 83
(F Head, France) **13/2**[3]
7 ½ **El Trastolillo (IRE)**[42] 3680 2-9-2 0 (b[1]) IoritzMendizabal 4 82
(P Bary, France) **9/1**
U **Havana Gold (IRE)**[23] 4283 2-9-2 0 RyanMoore 2 103+
(Richard Hannon) *racd in midfield: plld hrd: swtchd to outside over 1 1/2f out: qcknd wl to ld 1f out: sddle slipped and uns rdr 100yds out* **11/10**[1]

1m 23.9s (-4.40) **Going Correction** -0.40s/f (Firm) 8 Ran SP% **122.8**
Speed ratings: **109,108,107,105,105 101,101,**
WIN (incl. 1 euro stake): 13.30. PLACES: 4.00, 5.40, 5.40. DF: 75.40. SF: 165.00.
Owner Comte Andre de Ganay **Bred** Guy Pariente **Trained** Chantilly, France

NOTEBOOK
Style Vendome(FR), who won his maiden here over 5.5f last time out, was the beneficiary of Havana Gold's misfortune.
One Word More(IRE) ran well on this step up in class and should get a mile in time on this evidence.
Deauville Prince(FR), who won easily at Haydock last time, has been rated as running a little better on this step up in grade.
Havana Gold(IRE) looked set to win when hitting the front a furlong out, but his saddle slipped inside the last and Moore was unshipped. He would have won, and has been rated as doing so, and the Racing Post Trophy was mentioned as a likely end-of-season target.

5141a PRIX DU HARAS DE FRESNAY-LE-BUFFARD - JACQUES LE MAROIS (GROUP 1) (3YO+) (TURF) 1m (R)
2:40 (12:00) 3-Y-O+ **£285,700** (£114,300; £57,150; £28,550; £14,300)

RPR
1 **Excelebration (IRE)**[54] 3237 4-9-4 0 ChristopheSoumillon 11 126+
(A P O'Brien, Ire) *prom thrght: rdn over 2 1/2f out: swtchd out and r.o to chal over 1f out: led jst ins fnl f: drvn out* **5/2**[1]
2 1 ¼ **Cityscape**[36] 3880 6-9-4 0 JamesDoyle 1 123
(Roger Charlton) *trckd ldr: rdn to chal over 2 1/2f out: wnt 2nd jst ins fnl f: kpt on wout matching wnr after* **12/1**
3 nk **Elusive Kate (USA)**[14] 4633 3-8-8 0 FrankieDettori 7 119
(John Gosden) *led on nr side rail: rdn and strly pressed fr over 2 1/2f out: hdd jst ins fnl f: kpt on wl for 3rd cl home* **9/1**
4 hd **Moonlight Cloud**[7] 4861 4-9-1 0 ThierryJarnet 4 120+
(F Head, France) *hld up towards rr: stdy prog and stl gng wl whn bdly hmpd and lost pl over 2 1/2f out: in rr and rdn over 2f out: r.o to go 4th cl home: gng on at fin: unlucky* **3/1**[2]
5 snk **Caspar Netscher**[42] 3681 3-8-11 0 ShaneKelly 5 120
(Alan McCabe) *hld up towards rr on inner: rdn to improve over 2 1/2f out: wnt 4th over 1 1/2f out: kpt on ins fnl f: dropped to 5th cl home* **50/1**
6 5 **Tin Horse (IRE)**[35] 3900 4-9-4 0 Christophe-PatriceLemaire 8 110+
(D Guillemin, France) *hld up towards rr on outer: rdn and outpcd over 2 1/2f out: plugged on to go 6th cl home: n.d* **14/1**
7 ¾ **Golden Lilac (IRE)**[14] 4633 4-9-1 0 MaximeGuyon 10 105+
(A Fabre, France) *plld hrd: midfield and looking for cover early: swtchd out and allowed to stride on after 3f: sn prom on outer: rdn over 2f out: sn btn and fdd* **10/1**
8 2 **Immortal Verse (IRE)**[14] 4633 4-9-1 0 GeraldMosse 6 100+
(Robert Collet, France) *hld up in last: swtchd to rail and rdn to try and improve over 2 1/2f out: laboured prog u.p and edgd rt once in the clr ins fnl f: eased cl home: nvr a factor* **14/1**
9 ½ **Indomito (GER)**[54] 3237 6-9-4 0 OlivierPeslier 2 102
(A Wohler, Germany) *midfield on inner: rdn over 3f out: sn outpcd and btn: fdd* **40/1**
10 1 ½ **Fallen For You**[51] 3328 3-8-8 0 WilliamBuick 9 95
(John Gosden) *t.k.h: midfield on outer: rdn and outpcd over 2 1/2f out: sn btn and fdd* **10/1**
11 dist **Most Improved (IRE)**[54] 3239 3-8-11 0 KierenFallon 3 +
(Brian Meehan) *plld hrd: midfield: rdn over 4f out: lost pl rapidly over 2 1/2f out: in rr and btn over 1f out: heavily eased ins fnl f* **7/1**[3]

1m 34.6s (-6.20) **Going Correction** -0.40s/f (Firm)
WFA 3 from 4yo+ 7lb 11 Ran SP% **119.7**
Speed ratings: **115,113,113,113,113 108,107,105,104,103**
WIN (incl. 1 euro stake): 3.20. PLACES: 1.70, 5.40, 2.00. DF: 59.30. SF: 74.60.
Owner Derrick Smith & Mrs John Magnier & Michael Tabor **Bred** Owenstown Stud **Trained** Ballydoyle, Co Tipperary

FOCUS
The strongest renewal of the Prix Jacques Le Marois for many a year, with all of Europe's top milers bar Frankel lining up. Frankie Dettori dictated a modest gallop on recent Prix Rothschild winner Elusive Kate resulting in plenty of the runners racing too freely. It paid to be prominent, while those held up and/or racing wide were at a disadvantage. The fifth limits the form given the tight finish.

NOTEBOOK
Excelebration(IRE) was sensibly kept close to the pace by Christophe Soumillon (replacing the injured Ryan Moore) and, although he took a while to master the pacesetter, once he hit the front victory was never in doubt. He's seen the rear end of Frankel on both starts since winning his comeback at the Curragh this season but this proves he's just as good at four as he was at three. Now Frankel is being stepped up to 1m2f, he has Europe's remaining Group 1 1m events at his mercy.
Cityscape ran slightly below form when fourth, beaten over 8l in the Eclipse on his last start, but connections believed then that he didn't see out the 1m2f trip. They were proved spot-on here, as it could be argued this was a career best. He was at an advantage being prominently placed, but had plenty of multiple Group 1 winners in behind.
Elusive Kate(USA), taking on colts for the first time, lost nothing in defeat and she'll be a warm order if returning to taking on her own sex in the Sun Chariot.
Moonlight Cloud, impressive winner of the Prix Maurice du Gheest, was ridden to get the trip and came home best of all to just be denied a place after meeting intereference when Most Improved dropped away quickly. Connections will have learnt something about her stamina limitations from this.
Caspar Netscher has smart form over 7f this season and wouldn't have been inconvenienced by the lack of pace. This was still an excellent performance as he came home strongly from off the pace to dispute the places. He may still have to drop down to Group 2 company to return to winning ways, though.
Tin Horse(IRE), although previously a Group 1 winner, has yet to prove he's up to winning a race of this quality.
Golden Lilac(IRE) hasn't convinced with her attitude in her last three starts now, racing far too freely again. Perhaps connections will employ the use of a pacemaker next time.
Immortal Verse(IRE) hasn't returned the same filly this year but deserves another chance when getting her favoured soft ground.
Fallen For You, who was surprisingly chosen by Buick ahead of Elusive Kate, who appeared to have the stronger form of the two, refused to settle on the outside of the pack and finished well beaten.
Most Improved(IRE) finished tailed off last having been ridden along from an early stage. He seems a rhythm horse and the slow gallop didn't suit at all. Perhaps connections will try making the running with him next time as he seemed to be at his most fluent when being sent on early at Ascot. That said, there's plenty of evidence now that the 3yo colts in the miling division are particularly weak this year.

5142a PRIX MINERVE (GROUP 3) (3YO FILLIES) (TURF) 1m 4f 110y
3:10 (12:00) 3-Y-O **£33,333** (£13,333; £10,000; £6,666; £3,333)

RPR
1 **Forces Of Darkness (IRE)**[56] 3203 3-8-9 0 GregoryBenoist 3 102
(F Vermeulen, France) *racd midfield on inner: swtchd away fr rails 1 1/2f out: qcknd wl into spce 1f out: fin strly to get up fnl strides* **6/1**[3]
2 snk **Nobilis**[29] 4119 3-8-9 0 Pierre-CharlesBoudot 2 102
(A Fabre, France) *racd 4th on ins: swtchd away fr rails early in st: qcknd wl whn swtchd bk to ins 1f out: led 100yds out: r.o wl: hdd fnl strides* **12/1**
3 ½ **La Conquerante**[37] 3-8-9 0 IoritzMendizabal 9 101
(J-C Rouget, France) *racd towards rr: shkn up early in st: qcknd wl ent fnl f: r.o wl fnl 100yds: nt rch ldrs* **15/2**

4 1 1/4 **Biscaya Bay**46 3-8-9 0 MaximeGuyon 1 99
(A Fabre, France) *hld up towards rr: mde gd prog through field 1 1/2f out: r.o wl ins fnl f* **8/1**

5 snk **Marina Piccola (IRE)**29 4119 3-8-9 0 ThierryThulliez 10 99
(N Clement, France) *racd midfield: cl up bhd ldrs 1 1/2f out: rdn but no ex fnl 100yds: styd on* **10/3**2

6 hd **Preferential**15 3-8-9 0 StephanePasquier 4 99
(Mme C Head-Maarek, France) *hld up at rr of field: swtchd to wd outside ent st: picked up wl 1 1/2f out: looked threatening ent fnl f: rdn but no ex fr 50yds out* **6/1**3

7 nk **Mandistana (FR)**49 3423 3-8-9 0 Christophe-PatriceLemaire 6 98
(A De Royer-Dupre, France) *racd 3rd bhd her pacemaker: ahead of ldr into st: tk ld 1 1/2f out: rdn but no ex: hdd 100yds out: wknd* **5/2**1

8 3 1/2 **Gold For Tina (FR)**19 3-8-9 0 RonanThomas 11 93
(J Van Handenhove, France) *hld up towards rr: rdn early in st: no ex: wknd* **33/1**

9 20 **Bit By Bit**29 4119 3-8-9 0 ChristopheSoumillon 7 63
(D Smaga, France) *racd midfield: rdn but no ex in st: wknd* **10/1**

10 hd **Registara (GER)**28 4129 3-8-9 0 JamesDoyle 8 63
(Markus Klug, Germany) *hld up at rr for 3f then rushed up to ld after 4f: wnt clr: sn rdn in st: hdd 1 1/2f out: no ex: wknd* **25/1**

11 dist **Darayya (IRE)**29 4119 3-8-9 0 FreddyDiFede 5
(A De Royer-Dupre, France) *led for 4f: racd 2nd tl end of bk st: grad fdd: eased in st* **40/1**

2m 40.7s (-5.70) **Going Correction** -0.40s/f (Firm) 11 Ran SP% **129.1**
Speed ratings: **101,100,100,99,99 99,99,97,84,84**
WIN (incl. 1 euro stake): 7.60. PLACES: 2.50, 3.70, 2.40. DF: 50.80. SF: 72.20.
Owner Gerard Augustin-Normand **Bred** Keatly Overseas Ltd **Trained** France

FOCUS
With seven in a line a furlong out the form is hard to rate highly.

NOTEBOOK
Forces Of Darkness(IRE), a surprise fourth in the Prix de Diane, appreciated the step up in distance and got up in the final strides to register a narrow win.

4359 JAGERSRO (R-H)
Sunday, August 12

OFFICIAL GOING: Dirt: standard

5143a MARGARETA WETTERMARKS MINNESLOPNING (LISTED RACE) (3-5YO FILLIES & MARES) (DIRT) 1m 143y(D)
2:01 (12:00) 3-5-Y-0 **£28,089** (£9,363; £4,681; £2,808; £1,872)

RPR

1 **Golden Memory (DEN)**413 4-9-6 0 Per-AndersGraberg 2 92
(Niels Petersen, Norway) **27/10**2

2 1/2 **White Cheek Fox (USA)**74 5-9-6 0 ElioneChaves 8 91
(Lennart Reuterskiold Jr, Sweden) **25/1**

3 5 **Girl From Ipanema (SWE)** 3-8-13 0 CarlosLopez 6 81
(Patrick Wahl, Sweden) **162/10**

4 5 **Vuvuzela (USA)** 5-9-6 0 (b) MartinRodriguez 1 69
(Jessica Long, Sweden) **25/1**

5 nk **Minnie McGinn (USA)**17 5-9-6 0 OliverWilson 7 68
(Annike Bye Hansen, Norway) **11/2**

6 hd **Geordie Iris (IRE)**336 5982 4-9-6 0 FJohansson 9 68
(Wido Neuroth, Norway) **29/10**3

7 2 **Truly Charming (GER)**22 4359 3-8-13 0 ManuelMartinez 5 64
(Fredrik Reuterskiold, Sweden) **144/10**

8 1 3/4 **The Sydney Arms (IRE)**17 4-9-6 0 RafaeldeOliveira 3 59
(Morten Arnesen, Norway) **27/1**

9 20 **Bittersweet (SWE)** 5-9-6 0 EspenSki 4 15
(Pal Jorgen Nordbye, Norway) **137/10**

10 5 **Gooseberry Fool**43 3653 3-8-13 0 JacobJohansen 10 5
(Sir Mark Prescott Bt) *racd in midfield on outside fr wd draw: 5th and scrubbed along whn lost pl over 3f out: sn wl bhd: t.o* **13/5**1

1m 48.3s (108.30)
WFA 3 from 4yo+ 8lb 10 Ran SP% **126.2**
PARI-MUTUEL (all including 1sek stake): WIN 3.70; PLACE 1.58, 5.94, 4.26; SF 49.95.
Owner Nordic Girl Power **Bred** Berner Olsen **Trained** Norway

5144a IKC FONDER SOFIEROLOPNING (CONDITIONS) (3YO) (DIRT) 1m 143y(D)
3:53 (12:00) 3-Y-0 **£12,632** (£6,316; £3,031; £2,021; £1,263)

RPR

1 **Holly Martins**18 4466 3-9-4 0 GeorgeBaker 4
(Hans Adielsson) *hdd main pack bhd clr ldr: prog to r on ldr's quarters fr 2f out: led 1 1/2f out: r.o wl u.p fnl f: a in command* **6/5**1

2 1/2 **Glad Bear (GER)**59 3-9-4 0 ValmirDeAzeredo 11
(Fredrik Reuterskiold, Sweden) **68/10**

3 1/2 **Notnowhoney**59 3-9-4 0 (b) Per-AndersGraberg 9
(Niels Petersen, Norway) **61/10**3

4 1 1/4 **Cassano (DEN)**84 3-9-4 0 FJohansson 3
(Wido Neuroth, Norway) **18/5**2

5 hd **Latitude (SWE)** 3-9-1 0 EspenSki 1
(Vanja Sandrup, Sweden) **174/10**

6 4 **Vox** 3-9-4 0 ManuelMartinez 6
(Jessica Long, Sweden) **30/1**

7 3 **Just A Cat (SWE)** 3-9-4 0 (b) JacobJohansen 8
(Lennart Reuterskiold Jr, Sweden) **32/1**

8 6 **Puyol (SWE)**49 3-9-4 0 (p) ElioneChaves 5
(Henrik Engblom, Sweden) **13/2**

9 5 **Jonny No Nose (SWE)** 3-9-4 0 (b) OliverWilson 10
(Lennart Reuterskiold Jr, Sweden) **42/1**

10 6 **Glen Ellen (SWE)** 3-9-1 0 DannyPatil 12
(Hans-Inge Larsen, Sweden) **67/1**

11 2 **Absolute Soul (IRE)** 3-9-4 0 RafaelSchistl 7
(Francisco Castro, Sweden) **33/1**

1m 48.8s (108.80) 11 Ran SP% **125.9**
PARI-MUTUEL (all including 1sek stake): WIN 2.22; PLACE 1.26, 2.29, 2.15; SF 18.17.
Owner The Third Man **Bred** Biddestone Stud **Trained** Kingston Lisle, Oxon

4636 MUNICH (L-H)
Sunday, August 12

OFFICIAL GOING: Turf: good

5145a WETTKONTOR MUNCHEN-GROSSER PREIS VON BAYERN (EX RHEINLAND-POKAL) (GROUP 1) (3YO+) (TURF) 1m 4f
3:20 (3:25) 3-Y-0+ **£83,333** (£25,000; £12,500; £5,833; £2,500)

RPR

1 **Temida (IRE)**43 3652 4-9-3 0 FilipMinarik 6 113
(M G Mintchev, Germany) *hld up in last pair: rdn to improve over 3f out: r.o to ld over 1 1/2f out: styd on strly under hands and heels to go clr ins fnl f: eased cl home: comf* **135/10**

2 2 **Feuerblitz (GER)**14 4636 3-8-9 0 ASuborics 2 113
(M Figge, Germany) *t.k.h: trckd ldr on inner: rdn to ld 2f out: hdd over 1 1/2f out: kpt on wout matching wnr ins fnl f* **77/10**

3 3 **Earl Of Tinsdal (GER)**21 4383 4-9-6 0 EPedroza 4 108
(A Wohler, Germany) *sn led: rdn and hdd 2f out: sn outpcd by ldng pair: plugged on for 3rd ins fnl f* **11/10**1

4 4 **Caitania (IRE)**38 3802 3-8-6 0 AStarke 5 99
(U Stoltefuss, Germany) *hld up in last: rdn over 2 1/2f out: wnt 4th over 1f out: plugged on: n.d* **67/10**

5 4 **Baltic Rock (IRE)**42 3683 3-8-9 0 GHind 3 95
(J D Hillis, Germany) *trckd ldr on outer: rdn and outpcd over 2 1/2f out: sn btn and fdd* **18/5**3

P **Atempo (GER)**40 3746 4-9-6 0 ADeVries 1
(J Hirschberger, Germany) *hld up in tch: rdn over 3 1/2f out: sing to improve whn broke down bdly on turn into st: fatally injured* **31/10**2

2m 26.83s (146.83)
WFA 3 from 4yo 11lb 6 Ran SP% **125.1**
WIN (incl. 10 euro stake): 145. PLACES: 43, 39. SF: 1,541.
Owner Litex Commerce Ad **Bred** Anne & Gerard Corry **Trained** Germany

NOTEBOOK
Temida(IRE) didn't really have the previous form to take this but she won easily in a course record time. She will run once more, probably in the Grosser Preis von Baden, before being retired to stud in England.
Feuerblitz(GER) had finished behind Baltic Rock last time they met but easily reversed that form here. He'll have a short break now and probably run in the Preis von Europa.
Earl Of Tinsdal(GER) was disappointing but probably didn't like the quick ground.
Caitania(IRE) chased home the subsequent German Oaks winner last time but never featured here.

4728 FFOS LAS (L-H)
Monday, August 13

OFFICIAL GOING: Good to soft changing to soft after race 1 (2:20)
Wind: moderate across Weather: heavy rain race 1, sunny spells later

5146 32RED BRITISH STALLION STUDS E B F MAIDEN FILLIES' STKS 6f
2:20 (2:22) (Class 5) 2-Y-O **£3,881** (£1,155; £577; £288) **Stalls** Centre

Form RPR

1 **Orpha** 2-9-0 0 MartinHarley 10 84+
(Mick Channon) *hld up in tch: smooth hdwy 2f out: shkn up to ld appr fnl f: sn rdn clr: comf* **2/1**1

5 2 2 1/2 **Tarara**12 4701 2-9-0 0 DavidProbert 6 77
(Andrew Balding) *cl up: led 3f out tl appr fnl f: unable qck but kpt on for 2nd* **9/2**3

632 3 2 3/4 **It's Taboo**31 4055 2-9-0 79 JohnFahy 3 68
(Mark Usher) *midfield: pushed along and hdwy to chse ldrs over 2f out: one pce ins fnl f* **17/2**

2044 4 1 1/4 **Starlight Angel (IRE)**8 4836 2-8-9 71 DarrenEgan(5) 4 65
(Ronald Harris) *t.k.h: trckd ldrs: outpcd by principals 2f out: kpt on u.p ins fnl f* **20/1**

2 5 2 **Jubilant Queen**32 4002 2-9-0 0 AdamKirby 1 59
(Clive Cox) *t.k.h early: trckd ldrs: rdn 2f out: sn one pce* **11/2**

20 6 5 **Solvanna**17 4525 2-8-9 0 CharlesBishop(5) 8 44
(Heather Main) *trckd ldrs: rdn over 2f out: wknd over 1f out* **33/1**

2 7 1 1/4 **Almalekiah (IRE)**17 4532 2-9-0 0 TadhgO'Shea 2 40
(J S Moore) *s.i.s: in rr: sme hdwy 3f out: sn hung lft u.p: wknd over 1f out* **4/1**2

0 8 2 **Shades Of Light**16 4604 2-9-0 0 JamesDoyle 5 34
(Peter Makin) *taken to post early: pushed along 1/2-way: a towards rr* **50/1**

540 9 3/4 **Lilly May (IRE)**45 3590 2-8-9 52 LeonnaMayor(5) 9 32
(Phil McEntee) *sn outpcd: a in rr* **100/1**

5023 10 3 3/4 **Vestibule**9 4816 2-9-0 71 CathyGannon 7 20
(Eve Johnson Houghton) *slt ld tl hdd 3f out: wknd wl over 1f out* **10/1**

1m 12.4s (2.40) **Going Correction** +0.175s/f (Good) 10 Ran SP% **117.2**
Speed ratings (Par 91): **91,87,84,82,79 73,71,68,67,62**
toteswingers 1&2 £3.90, 1&3 £5.10, 2&3 £6.80 CSF £10.81 TOTE £4.70: £1.90, £2.80, £4.20; EX 15.90 Trifecta £66.60 Pool: £563.09 - 6.25 winning units..
Owner Prince A A Faisal **Bred** Nawara Stud Co Ltd **Trained** West Ilsley, Berks

FOCUS
Steady rain arrived shortly before racing commenced, on what was already easy ground, and it looked pretty hard work in the opener. There wasn't all that much strength in depth to this 2yo fillies' maiden, but the winner looks a decent prospect and the first pair were clear.

NOTEBOOK
Orpha, a well backed newcomer, came out best. This venue hadn't previously been a happy hunting ground for trainer Mick Channon (1-39), but there was plenty of confidence behind his choicely bred debutante and she got her career off to the perfect start. She travelled kindly in midfield before making stealthy headway, but her rider had to get stuck into her to master the runner-up inside the final furlong. That may have been down to the holding surface, or possibly her inexperience, and she was well on top at the business end. Future entries in the Group 1 Moyglare and Fillies' Mile indicate how highly she is regarded, and bigger and better things likely await her. (op 13-8 tchd 9-4)
Tarara ◆ stepped up on her debut fifth at Goodwood and made the winner work hard late on. She finished a clear second-best, evidently appreciates some cut underfoot and ought to be going one better before long. (op 11-2 tchd 6-1)
It's Taboo made her challenge nearest to the far rail and probably can close to her last-time-out form at Newbury, so helps to set the level even though a mark of 79 looks high enough for her. (op 10-1 tchd 12-1 and 8-1)

Starlight Angel(IRE), back on easy ground, hit a flat spot before staying on again and she too likely ran close enough to her previous level. (op 16-1)
Jubilant Queen failed to see out the extra furlong that well, but probably found the ground turn against her. (op 6-1 tchd 9-2)
Almalekiah(IRE) just missed out on her Chepstow debut 17 days earlier, but after making a tardy start she looked all at sea on this contrasting surface and never remotely threatened. Official explanation: jockey said filly hung left (tchd 7-2)

5147 32RED CASINO MEDIAN AUCTION MAIDEN STKS 1m (R)
2:50 (2:50) (Class 5) 3-5-Y-O **£2,264** (£673; £336; £168) **Stalls** Low

Form RPR
222 **1** **Miss Cap Estel**[10] 4753 3-8-12 75 DavidProbert 5 81
(Andrew Balding) *trckd ldr: drvn 2f out: led over 1f out: rdn out ins fnl f* **1/1**[1]
0352 **2** *1 ½* **Gold Show**[10] 4782 3-8-12 71 MartinHarley 3 77
(Mick Channon) *led: brought field to centre of trck st 4f out: drvn over 2f out: hdd over 1f out: kpt on but a hld by wnr* **9/4**[2]
3350 **3** *8* **Trusting (IRE)**[18] 4486 3-8-12 57 (b[1]) CathyGannon 1 59
(Eve Johnson Houghton) *trckd ldrs: rdn 3f out: ev ch 2f out: wknd appr fnl f* **16/1**
53-4 **4** *21* **Typography**[32] 4001 3-9-3 70 JamesDoyle 2 16
(William Muir) *in last but in tch: drvn over 2f out: sn wknd: no ch whn hung rt over 1f out: sn eased: t.o* **10/3**[3]

1m 48.81s (7.81) **Going Correction** +0.70s/f (Yiel) **4** Ran SP% **109.7**
Speed ratings (Par 103): **88,86,78,57**
CSF £3.60 TOTE £1.10; EX 2.20.
Owner J L C Pearce **Bred** J L C Pearce **Trained** Kingsclere, Hants

FOCUS
The rain continued to fall and predictably the going was officially changed to soft, good to soft in places after the first race. This was a tight little maiden and they went an ordinary pace, resulting in something of a sprint for home passing 3f out. Straightforward form.
Typography Official explanation: jockey said gelding hung right

5148 IWEC ELECTRICAL H'CAP 1m (R)
3:20 (3:21) (Class 6) (0-65,62) 3-Y-O+ **£1,617** (£481; £240; £120) **Stalls** Low

Form RPR
6464 **1** **Camrock Star (IRE)**[8] 4844 3-8-11 **55** MatthewCosham[(3)] 10 63
(David Evans) *hld up: rdn and hdwy over 2f out: hung lft over 1f out: r.o to ld fnl 50yds* **9/2**[2]
1-52 **2** *1 ¾* **Croeso Mawr**[59] 3096 6-9-7 **55** CathyGannon 2 60+
(John Spearing) *led 1f: cl up: led again over 1f out tl hdd u.p fnl 50yds: no ex* **11/4**[1]
2430 **3** *3* **Putin (IRE)**[4] 4986 4-8-8 **47** (bt) LeonnaMayor[(5)] 1 45
(Phil McEntee) *led after 1f: rdn over 2f out: hdd over 1f out: one pce* **15/2**
5106 **4** *2 ¼* **Lady Percy (IRE)**[12] 4709 3-9-3 **58** DavidProbert 3 50
(Mark Usher) *midfield: rdn 3f out: styd on u.p: nvr trbld ldrs* **6/1**[3]
-520 **5** *¾* **Sasheen**[16] 4602 5-10-0 **62** (p) MircoDemuro 8 53
(Jeremy Gask) *trckd ldrs: rdn over 3f out: sn one pce* **8/1**
-300 **6** *1 ¼* **End Of May (IRE)**[6] 4900 3-8-8 **49** MartinHarley 6 36
(Peter Bowen) *towards rr: rdn 3f out: styd on one pce* **33/1**
-505 **7** *1* **Inniscastle Boy**[60] 3068 3-9-7 **62** (p) JamesDoyle 4 47
(William Muir) *chsd ldrs: rdn 3f out: wknd wl over 1f out* **9/2**[2]
-500 **8** *13* **Phluke**[11] 4722 11-9-12 **60** (b[1]) JohnFahy 5 16
(Eve Johnson Houghton) *cl up 2f: dropped to rr over 4f out: lost tch 3f out: t.o* **14/1**
262/ **9** *9* **Ceto**[916] 473 5-9-10 **58** AdamKirby 7
(Phil McEntee) *t.k.h: hld up in tch: drvn 3f out: sn wknd: t.o* **14/1**

1m 47.37s (6.37) **Going Correction** +0.70s/f (Yiel)
WFA 3 from 4yo+ 7lb **9** Ran SP% **116.5**
Speed ratings (Par 101): **96,94,91,89,88 87,86,73,64**
toteswingers 1&2 £4.70, 1&3 £8.60, 2&3 £5.70 CSF £17.46 CT £91.34 TOTE £5.60: £2.70, £1.30, £2.30; EX 23.10 Trifecta £183.90 Pool: £440.14 - 1.77 winning units..
Owner Dukes Head Racing **Bred** N Ormiston **Trained** Pandy, Monmouths

FOCUS
A moderate handicap. It was run at a fair pace and there was a slow-motion finish on the taxing surface. The winner is rated back to her best.

5149 THREE RIVERS H'CAP 5f
3:50 (3:53) (Class 6) (0-65,62) 3-Y-O+ **£1,617** (£481; £240; £120) **Stalls** Centre

Form RPR
-032 **1** **My Meteor**[20] 4425 5-9-10 **62** JohnFahy 7 72
(Tony Newcombe) *towards rr: briefly n.m.r 2f out: smooth hdwy over 1f out: r.o to ld ins fnl f: drvn out towards fin* **7/2**[2]
455 **2** *1* **Ficelle (IRE)**[10] 4777 3-9-1 **61** DarrenEgan[(5)] 1 66
(Ronald Harris) *in rr: rdn after 2f: hdwy over 1f out: briefly ev ch ins fnl f: sn one pce* **4/1**[3]
2304 **3** *1 ¾* **Spic 'n Span**[6] 4902 7-8-12 **50** (v) MarcHalford 9 50
(Ronald Harris) *prom: led after 2f: clr over 1f out: sn edgd lft and rdn: hdd and no ex ins fnl f* **6/1**
0/0- **4** *½* **Rowayton**[327] 6261 6-8-10 **48** MartinHarley 2 46
(Muredach Kelly, Ire) *led early: styd prom: one pce appr fnl f* **5/1**
3360 **5** *1* **Cape Royal**[17] 4535 12-9-10 **62** (tp) CathyGannon 3 56
(Milton Bradley) *sn led: hdd after 2f: rdn 2f out: wknd over 1f out* **14/1**
435 **6** *shd* **Ishiamiracle**[146] 977 3-9-1 **61** (p) LeonnaMayor[(5)] 4 54
(Phil McEntee) *s.i.s: in rr: kpt on ins fnl f: nt trble ldrs* **25/1**
5012 **7** *8* **Red Rhythm**[17] 4535 5-9-6 **58** (v) JamesDoyle 8 23
(David Evans) *cl up: rdn 2f out: sn wknd* **5/2**[1]

1m 1.36s (3.06) **Going Correction** +0.65s/f (Yiel)
WFA 3 from 5yo+ 3lb **7** Ran SP% **112.3**
Speed ratings (Par 101): **101,99,96,95,94 94,81**
toteswingers 1&2 £3.60, 1&3 £3.10, 2&3 £4.90 CSF £17.16 CT £78.79 TOTE £5.90: £3.70, £1.60; EX 18.90 Trifecta £113.60 Pool: £668.14 - 4.35 winning units..
Owner A G Newcombe **Bred** M P B Bloodstock Ltd **Trained** Yarnscombe, Devon

FOCUS
A weak sprint handicap, but it looked competitive enough for the class. Unsurprisingly there was no hanging about and that suited the closers. The form makes some sense.

5150 £32 BONUS AT 32RED.COM H'CAP 6f
4:20 (4:20) (Class 5) (0-75,75) 3-Y-O+ **£1,468** (£1,468; £336; £168) **Stalls** Centre

Form RPR
5500 **1** **Masai Moon**[16] 4580 8-9-9 **73** (b) JamesMillman 5 80
(Rod Millman) *disp ld tl relegated to 2nd over 1f out: rallied u.p to join ldr on post* **7/1**
26 **1** *dht* **Rigolleto (IRE)**[15] 4624 4-9-10 **74** MartinHarley 1 81
(Mick Channon) *disp ld: def advantage over 1f out: rdn ins fnl f: jnd post* **7/2**[2]
0564 **3** *1* **Jack My Boy (IRE)**[12] 4708 5-9-2 **66** (b) JamesDoyle 2 70
(David Evans) *chsd ldrs: sltly outpcd over 1f out: r.o ins fnl f* **5/2**[1]
6045 **4** *1 ½* **Mambo Spirit (IRE)**[32] 4000 8-9-5 **69** AdamKirby 9 69
(Tony Newcombe) *in tch: hdwy over 1f out: r.o ins fnl f* **9/1**
6360 **5** *2* **Belle Bayardo (IRE)**[2] 5097 4-9-2 **66** MarcHalford 3 60
(Ronald Harris) *s.s: t.k.h: sn trcking ldrs: wknd fnl f* **6/1**
0260 **6** *hd* **Diamond Vine (IRE)**[12] 4708 4-8-13 **68** (p) DarrenEgan[(5)] 8 61
(Ronald Harris) *t.k.h: in tch tl wknd over 1f out* **9/1**
045 **7** *3* **Beach Candy (IRE)**[20] 4437 3-9-5 **73** DavidProbert 7 57
(Phil McEntee) *sed awkwardly: in rr: hdwy to chse ldrs 3f out: wknd over 1f out* **11/2**[3]

1m 13.9s (3.90) **Going Correction** +0.65s/f (Yiel)
WFA 3 from 4yo+ 4lb **7** Ran SP% **113.0**
Speed ratings (Par 103): **100,100,98,96,94 93,89**WIN: Masai Moon £4.40 Rigolleto £3.40 PL: MM £2.80, R £2.80 EX: MM/R £20.80 R/MM £16.40 CSF: MM/R £15.40 R/MM £13.49. T/C: MM/R/JMB £38.80, R/MM/JMB £35.05. TRIFECTA Pool of £422.28; 2-3-9 £35.50 - 4.40 winning units,27 Owner.
Owner Rod Millman Racing Club **Bred** Mrs B A Matthews **Trained** Kentisbeare, Devon

FOCUS
This was a moderate sprint handicap and a tight affair. The first two were up there there from the off and fought out a bobbing finish, resulting in a dead-heat. The form is rated on the negative side.

5151 32RED H'CAP 1m 4f (R)
4:50 (4:50) (Class 4) (0-80,75) 3-Y-O+ **£4,075** (£1,212; £606; £303) **Stalls** Low

Form RPR
6635 **1** **Little Dutch Girl**[26] 4224 3-9-3 **75** (b) AdamKirby 11 83
(Clive Cox) *mde all: qcknd pce over 3f out: rdn over 1f out: hung rt wl ins fnl f: kpt on* **5/1**[2]
2064 **2** *nk* **Shabak Hom (IRE)**[11] 4733 5-8-12 **62** MatthewCosham[(3)] 6 70
(David Evans) *prom: rdn over 3f out: chsd wnr over 2f out: styng on u.p whn carried rt and bmpd wl ins fnl f: jst hld* **12/1**
0011 **3** *2* **Astra Hall**[27] 4181 3-8-4 **62** DavidProbert 2 73+
(Ralph Beckett) *hld up in tch: swtchd lft and hdwy over 2f out: rdn appr fnl f: sn n.m.r: cl 3rd whn hmpd wl ins fnl f: nt rcvr* **5/4**[1]
425 **4** *¾* **One For Joules (IRE)**[72] 2698 5-9-6 **67** JamieGoldstein 3 70+
(John Flint) *hld up in last: travelling wl and n.m.r 2f out: r.o to chse ldrs appr fnl f: nvr nrr* **12/1**
0000 **5** *½* **Toughness Danon**[16] 4578 6-9-5 **71** DarrenEgan[(5)] 4 73
(Brendan Powell) *chsd ldrs: rdn 3f out: sn one pce* **10/1**
4013 **6** *1 ½* **Hamilton Hill**[4] 4988 5-9-3 **71** 6ex RobertWilliams[(7)] 5 71
(Dai Burchell) *in tch: hdwy to chse ldrs 3f out: nt run on over 1f out: wknd ent fnl f* **10/1**
4212 **7** *5* **Pandorica**[11] 4733 4-8-12 **66** (p) DanielMuscutt[(7)] 7 58
(Bernard Llewellyn) *cl up tl rdn over 3f out: wknd over 1f out* **9/1**
5636 **8** *2 ½* **Mezzanisi (IRE)**[17] 4543 7-10-0 **75** MartinHarley 9 63
(Peter Bowen) *towards rr: rdn 3f out: nvr trbld ldrs* **28/1**
3213 **9** *2 ½* **Circle Of Angels**[15] 4627 4-9-3 **64** JamesDoyle 1 48
(Ian Williams) *hld up in rr: sme hdwy over 2f out: sn wknd* **15/2**[3]

2m 47.07s (9.67) **Going Correction** +0.70s/f (Yiel)
WFA 3 from 4yo+ 11lb **9** Ran SP% **119.9**
Speed ratings (Par 105): **95,94,93,92,92 91,88,86,84**
toteswingers 1&2 £9.90, 1&3 £2.80, 2&3 £6.50 CSF £65.26 CT £120.37 TOTE £4.40: £1.10, £2.60, £2.40; EX 65.20 Trifecta £418.50 Part won. Pool: £565.60 - 0.63 winning units..
Owner Mrs Hugh Maitland-Jones **Bred** Mrs Hugh Maitland-Jones **Trained** Lambourn, Berks

FOCUS
A modest handicap. It was run at a steady early pace, which suited those racing handily, and there was a desperate finish. The form should be treated with caution but the winner rates a 4lb personal best. The third was unlucky.

5152 32REDPOKER.COM H'CAP 1m 2f (R)
5:20 (5:22) (Class 6) (0-65,65) 3-Y-O **£1,617** (£481; £240; £120) **Stalls** Low

Form RPR
54-2 **1** **Alborz (IRE)**[23] 3483 3-9-7 **65** CathyGannon 1 77+
(Tim Vaughan) *mde all: rdn 3f out: clr ent fnl f: styd on strly* **4/1**[2]
2 *3 ½* **Filatore (IRE)**[39] 3800 3-8-11 **62** DanielMuscutt[(7)] 9 66
(Bernard Llewellyn) *in tch towards rr: clsd 4f out: sn chsng wnr: kpt on u.p fnl 2f but a being hld* **11/8**[1]
4-00 **3** *15* **Present Day**[43] 3666 3-9-0 **58** (v[1]) AdamKirby 4 32
(Clive Cox) *chsd ldrs: rdn 4f out: wknd over 2f out: plugged on for remote 3rd* **15/2**
0505 **4** *½* **Wyndham Wave**[12] 4709 3-9-2 **60** JamesMillman 2 33
(Rod Millman) *chsd wnr to over 3f out: rdn and wknd over 2f out* **7/1**[3]
0430 **5** *6* **Aiaam Al Wafa (IRE)**[45] 3592 3-8-9 **58** (p) DarrenEgan[(5)] 5 19
(Phil McEntee) *in rr: pushed along 4f out: wknd over 2f out: t.o* **16/1**
4501 **6** *1 ¼* **Anginola (IRE)**[28] 4147 3-8-11 **60** NathanSweeney[(5)] 8 19
(David Evans) *in tch tl wknd 3f out: t.o* **7/1**[3]

2m 16.88s (7.48) **Going Correction** +0.70s/f (Yiel) **6** Ran SP% **104.8**
Speed ratings (Par 98): **98,95,83,82,78 77**
toteswingers 1&2 £1.70, 1&3 £2.60, 2&3 £2.80 CSF £8.62 CT £27.35 TOTE £2.40: £1.10, £2.30; EX 10.40 Trifecta £42.10 Pool: £448.72 - 7.88 winning units..
Owner Diamond Racing Ltd **Bred** Darley **Trained** Aberthin, Vale of Glamorgan

FOCUS
This ordinary 3yo handicap was run at an average pace and the first pair came a long way clear from 2f out. Weakish form but it has been taken at something like face value.
Wyndham Wave Official explanation: trainer said gelding was unsuited by the soft ground
T/Plt: £105.70 to a £1 stake. Pool: £53854.73 - 371.60 winning tickets T/Qpdt: £50.50 to a £1 stake. Pool: £4,456.90 - 65.18 winning tickets RL

[4944]KEMPTON (A.W) (R-H)
Monday, August 13

OFFICIAL GOING: Standard to slow
Wind: mild breeze behind Weather: overcast with rain at times

5153 BETFAIR. DON'T SETTLE FOR LESS MEDIAN AUCTION MAIDEN FILLIES' STKS 7f (P)
2:30 (2:32) (Class 6) 2-Y-O **£1,617** (£481; £240; £120) **Stalls** Low

Form RPR
3420 **1** **Rio's Pearl**[9] 4820 2-9-0 78 JimCrowley 6 75
(Ralph Beckett) *mde all: rdn over 1f out: 1 l up ent fnl 100yds: jst hld on* **8/11**[1]
032 **2** *shd* **Madame Elizabeth**[12] 4704 2-9-0 62 RussKennemore 4 75
(Reg Hollinshead) *trckd ldrs: rdn over 2f out: no imp tl r.o ins fnl f: only jst failed* **25/1**

423 **3** *nk* **Sorella Bella (IRE)**[11] 4730 2-9-0 72 SamHitchcott 5 74
(Mick Channon) *trckd ldrs: rdn over 2f out: sn hung rt: no imp tl r.o fnl 120yds* **7/1**[3]

64 **4** *4* **Alhaarth Beauty (IRE)**[12] 4701 2-9-0 0 RichardHughes 1 64
(Richard Hannon) *prom: rdn and ev ch fr wl over 1f out tl fdd and lost 2 pls fnl 100yds fnl 100yds* **5/2**[2]

5 *1 1/2* **Poitin** 2-9-0 0 SilvestreDeSousa 2 60
(Harry Dunlop) *hld up wl in tch: rdn over 2f out: kpt on but nt pce to threaten* **20/1**

0 **6** *18* **Be Very Careful**[21] 4408 2-9-0 0 SeanLevey 7 13
(Richard Hannon) *sn pushed along bhd ldrs: rdn over 3f out: wknd over 2f out* **50/1**

7 *6* **Multi Fours** 2-9-0 0 MartinDwyer 3
(Daniel Kubler) *s.i.s: racd green: a detached in last* **20/1**

1m 27.67s (1.67) **Going Correction** +0.10s/f (Slow) **7** Ran SP% **114.3**
Speed ratings (Par 89): **94,93,93,88,87 66,59**
toteswingers 1&2 £3.40, 1&3 £1.70, 2&3 £4.00 CSF £26.84 TOTE £1.80: £1.10, £7.80; EX 15.10.
Owner Pearl Bloodstock Ltd **Bred** Downfield Cottage Stud **Trained** Kimpton, Hants

FOCUS
Just an ordinary maiden, the winner probably not quite running up to the pick of her previous form as she scraped home. The gallop was just modest until the straight.

NOTEBOOK
Rio's Pearl certainly doesn't lack for speed and only just lasted home over this longer trip. She showed she can be competitive off her current mark in a hot Newmarket nursery last time and her rating shouldn't go up for this win. (op 4-5 tchd 10-11 and Evens in a place)
Madame Elizabeth's previous form didn't amount to a great deal (beaten 9l into second last time) and this undoubtedly represents an improvement, the longer trip being much in her favour and only just failing to peg back the winner. Further still will suit her. (op 20-1)
Sorella Bella(IRE) at least matched her turf form switched to the AW, going down only narrowly despite wandering about a bit under pressure. She leaves the impression she'll stay 1m. (tchd 6-1 and 15-2)
Alhaarth Beauty(IRE) had shaped as if she'd be suited by this trip, so this was a shade disappointing, backing out of it rather tamely in the end. It's clearly still early days, though, and she could hardly be in better hands. (op 11-4 tchd 3-1)
Poitin, a daughter of Kheleyf out of an unraced half-sister to several winners, showed ability and is entitled to improve for the experience, though it's hardly an effort which suggests she's likely to go close at a similar level next time. (tchd 16-1)
Be Very Careful looks one of her yard's lesser lights at this stage.
Multi Fours gave a bit of trouble down at the start and trailed throughout after missing the break. (tchd 16-1)

5154 BETTER PRICES ON BETFAIR MOBILE MEDIAN AUCTION MAIDEN FILLIES' STKS 1m 4f (P)
3:00 (3:00) (Class 6) 3-5-Y-O £1,617 (£481; £240; £120) **Stalls** Centre

Form RPR
402 **1** **Caphira**[14] 4648 3-8-12 79 RichardHughes 5 82
(William Knight) *prom early: trckd ldr: rdn for str chal fr 2f out: led fnl 120yds: drvn out* **9/4**[1]

2 **2** *nk* **Altaria**[44] 3622 3-8-12 0 IanMongan 8 81
(Amanda Perrett) *trckd ldrs: rdn to ld 2f out: sn hrd pressed: hdd fnl 120yds: kpt on but no ex* **11/4**[2]

2435 **3** *13* **Idyllic Star (IRE)**[18] 4486 3-8-12 66 DarryllHolland 6 60
(J S Moore) *hld up: swtchd lft wl over 2f out: sn rdn into 3rd but no ch w ldng pair* **5/1**

525 **4** *2 3/4* **Broadway Babe (IRE)**[46] 3551 3-8-12 69 SilvestreDeSousa 1 56
(Harry Dunlop) *led: rdn and hdd 2f out: sn lost 3rd: one pce after* **11/2**

5 *nk* **Shea** 3-8-12 0 RichardThomas 2 56
(Ralph Beckett) *trckd ldrs: rdn in disp 3rd over 2f out: sn one pce* **16/1**

0-54 **6** *2 3/4* **Buzkashi (IRE)**[23] 4335 3-8-12 74 DaneO'Neill 7 51
(David Lanigan) *in tch: rdn to dispute cl 3rd wl over 2f out: wknd over 1f out* **9/2**[3]

7 *nk* **Magic In Motion**[20] 5-9-9 0 (t) EddieAhern 4 51
(Neil Mulholland) *dwlt: in last trio: rdn wl over 2f out: nvr any imp on ldrs* **50/1**

8 *3 3/4* **Ridiyka (IRE)** 3-8-12 0 SamHitchcott 3 45
(Seamus Mullins) *s.i.s: in last trio: rdn 3f out: wknd over 1f out* **50/1**

2m 35.13s (0.63) **Going Correction** +0.10s/f (Slow)
WFA 3 from 5yo 11lb **8** Ran SP% **117.5**
Speed ratings (Par 98): **101,100,92,90,90 88,88,85**
toteswingers 1&2 £2.70, 1&3 £3.50, 2&3 £1.90 CSF £8.95 TOTE £4.20: £2.20, £1.40, £1.90; EX 10.60.
Owner Bluehills Racing Limited **Bred** Hesmonds Stud Ltd **Trained** Patching, W Sussex

FOCUS
No depth to this maiden, but the leading pair still deserve some credit for pulling well clear once the race began in earnest. The winner confirmed her latest Lingfield improvement.

5155 BETFAIR SUPPORTS GRASSROOTS RACING AT KEMPTON NURSERY 1m (P)
3:30 (3:31) (Class 5) (0-75,74) 2-Y-O £2,264 (£673; £336; £168) **Stalls** Low

Form RPR
406 **1** **Quintilian (IRE)**[23] 4340 2-9-5 72 SilvestreDeSousa 5 80+
(Mahmood Al Zarooni) *s.i.s: pushed along in rr early: swtchd lft and rdn over 2f out: str run to ld jst over 1f out: styd on wl to draw clr* **7/1**[3]

0014 **2** *3 1/2* **Magic Channel (USA)**[8] 4847 2-8-13 66 RichardHughes 1 66
(Richard Hannon) *hld up: pushed along over 5f out: rdn wl over 2f out: swtchd lft and hdwy over 1f out: ev ch briefly jst over 1f out: styd on same pce* **9/2**[1]

0456 **3** *3/4* **Walter White (IRE)**[19] 4472 2-9-3 70 JimmyFortune 8 68
(Andrew Balding) *trckd ldrs: rdn over 2f out: ch briefly over 1f out: kpt on same pce* **5/1**[2]

630 **4** *1/2* **Tuffan (USA)**[16] 4595 2-9-2 69 (t) BrettDoyle 6 66
(Clive Brittain) *mid-div: rdn over 2f out: no imp tl styd on ins fnl f: wnt 4th fnl stride* **16/1**

553 **5** *nse* **Mowhoob**[47] 3499 2-9-5 72 EddieAhern 7 69
(John Gosden) *trckd ldr: rdn to ld 2f out: sn edgd lft: hdd jst over 1f out: styd on same pce* **5/1**[2]

553 **6** *3 1/4* **Eastern Dragon (IRE)**[58] 3168 2-8-9 62 ow1 DarryllHolland 2 51
(Michael Scudamore) *trckd ldrs: effrt over 2f out: ch over 1f out: fdd fnl f* **8/1**

0432 **7** *4* **Bix (IRE)**[28] 4140 2-8-11 71 (b) MichaelJMMurphy(7) 9 51
(Brian Meehan) *s.i.s: sn pushed along to trck ldrs: rdn for brief chal over 2f out: qckly btn* **9/2**[1]

522 **8** *3/4* **New Falcon (IRE)**[17] 4546 2-9-7 74 MartinDwyer 4 53
(James Tate) *led: rdn and hdd 2f out: wknd fnl f* **7/1**[3]

505 **9** *24* **Unidexter (IRE)**[15] 4618 2-9-1 68 SamHitchcott 3
(Mick Channon) *hld up: rdn over 4f out: wknd 2f out* **25/1**

1m 40.26s (0.46) **Going Correction** +0.10s/f (Slow) **9** Ran SP% **115.5**
Speed ratings (Par 94): **101,97,96,96,96 92,88,88,64**
toteswingers 1&2 £4.50, 1&3 £6.00, 2&3 £4.30 CSF £38.53 CT £173.64 TOTE £8.20: £2.80, £1.20, £3.00; EX 57.90.
Owner Godolphin **Bred** Mrs C Regalado-Gonzalez **Trained** Newmarket, Suffolk

FOCUS
The gallop didn't look that strong, but the race still provided a test of stamina for juveniles at this time of year, the principals all coming from the back. Straightforward, solid enough form.

NOTEBOOK
Quintilian(IRE) hadn't looked to be going forward in turf maidens, but was firmly back on track here, being well suited by the increased test of stamina (dam half-sister to Saddler's Rock) despite not going with that much fluency in rear for a long way, but powering up the straight. Connections will presumably try and get him out under a penalty as he's going to go up a fair bit for this. (op 12-1)
Magic Channel(USA), as expected, proved well suited by the step up to 1m and won't always bump into one so far ahead of his mark as the winner. (tchd 5-1)
Walter White(IRE) matched his previous best switched to AW for the first time without suggesting he has anything in hand of his mark, sticking to his task up in trip. (op 15-2)
Tuffan(USA) offered a bit more than previously fitted with a tongue tie on his nursery/AW bow, seeing the trip out well after being ridden with more restraint on this occasion. (op 14-1)
Mowhoob wasn't disgraced on his nursery debut, faring best of those who raced close to the pace, but doesn't look one of his yard's many progressive types at this stage. (op 7-2)
Eastern Dragon(IRE) didn't find any improvement for a switch of yard and step up in trip. (op 9-1)
Bix(IRE) was a bit too keen for his own good in the second-time headgear, not running close to the form he showed at Southwell last time. (op 4-1)
New Falcon(IRE) hails from a yard going well, but was below her maiden form switched to a nursery, leaving the impression the trip stretched her at this stage, weakening after cutting out a lot of the running. (op 6-1)

5156 BETFAIR BOOSTS PRIZE MONEY AT KEMPTON FILLIES' H'CAP 7f (P)
4:00 (4:00) (Class 5) (0-75,74) 3-Y-O £2,264 (£673; £336; £168) **Stalls** Low

Form RPR
2346 **1** **Saratoga Slew (IRE)**[14] 4647 3-8-13 71 TobyAtkinson(5) 6 78+
(Marco Botti) *in tch: rdn wl over 2f out: running on whn swtchd rt jst over 1f out: kpt on wl to ld fnl stride* **9/2**[2]

404 **2** *shd* **Majestic Zafeen**[73] 2672 3-9-7 74 DaneO'Neill 2 81
(Alastair Lidderdale) *led: rdn 2f out: kpt on: hdd fnl stride* **6/1**

0212 **3** *1* **Purley Queen (IRE)**[20] 4424 3-8-6 59 MartinDwyer 1 63
(Sylvester Kirk) *trckd ldrs: rdn 3f out: kpt on ins fnl f* **8/1**

4-44 **4** *1 3/4* **Norlander**[42] 3702 3-8-7 60 RichardThomas 8 60
(Ralph Beckett) *hld up in last pair: rdn wl over 2f out: no imp tl r.o ins fnl f: no ch w ldrs* **9/1**

530 **5** *3/4* **Princess Steph (IRE)**[86] 2273 3-9-3 70 JimmyFortune 4 68
(Heather Main) *trckd ldrs: rdn over 2f out: one pce fr over 1f out* **8/1**

0100 **6** *nse* **Jumeirah Palm Star**[11] 4726 3-9-7 74 RichardHughes 7 71
(Richard Hannon) *chsd ldr: rdn over 3f out: fdd fnl f* **5/2**[1]

0002 **7** *2 1/2* **Macy Anne (IRE)**[25] 4232 3-8-4 57 SilvestreDeSousa 3 48
(Robert Mills) *in tch: rdn to chse ldrs over 2f out: fdd fnl f* **11/2**[3]

60-0 **8** *7* **Ice Missile**[47] 3507 3-8-2 58 RyanPowell(3) 5 30
(Sylvester Kirk) *s.i.s: rdn 3f out: a towards rr* **20/1**

1m 27.14s (1.14) **Going Correction** +0.10s/f (Slow) **8** Ran SP% **113.4**
Speed ratings (Par 97): **97,96,95,93,92 92,89,81**
toteswingers 1&2 £5.90, 1&3 £5.20, 2&3 £8.80 CSF £30.92 CT £208.50 TOTE £5.80: £1.70, £2.60, £2.50; EX 29.60.
Owner Dachel Stud **Bred** Old Carhue Stud **Trained** Newmarket, Suffolk

FOCUS
A fair handicap. The gallop wasn't that strong, the winner probably deserving of a little extra credit if anything after coming from quite a long way back. The time was modest and the runner-up sets the standard.
Macy Anne(IRE) Official explanation: jockey said filly had no more to give

5157 SCOTT MILLS & STOOSHE LIVE 07.09.12 H'CAP 6f (P)
4:30 (4:30) (Class 5) (0-70,65) 3-Y-O+ £2,264 (£673; £336; £168) **Stalls** Low

Form RPR
4561 **1** **Prince Of Passion (CAN)**[7] 4887 4-9-7 60 6ex (v) SilvestreDeSousa 7 71
(Derek Shaw) *mde all: rdn over 1f out: in command fnl f: eased towards fin* **9/2**[3]

001 **2** *1 1/2* **Plum Bay**[10] 4777 3-9-2 59 DaneO'Neill 1 65+
(David Elsworth) *hld up in cl 5th: pushd along whn swtchd out 2f out: sn rdn: wnt 3rd over 1f out: kpt on to go 2nd fnl 75yds: a being hld by wnr* **9/4**[1]

4003 **3** *1 1/2* **Hoover**[19] 4468 4-9-12 65 (t) EddieAhern 3 66
(Jim Boyle) *cl up: rdn over 2f out: chsd wnr over 1f out: lost 2nd ins fnl f: kpt on same pce* **3/1**[2]

5451 **4** *6* **Hannibal Hayes (USA)**[19] 4467 3-9-6 63 RichardHughes 5 45
(Jeremy Noseda) *trckd wnr: rdn wl over 2f out: wknd ent fnl f* **9/4**[1]

4200 **5** *4 1/2* **Waterloo Dock**[19] 4468 7-9-7 65 (v) TobyAtkinson(5) 6 33
(Michael Quinn) *chsd ldr: rdn wl over 2f out: wknd over 1f out* **20/1**

1m 13.16s (0.06) **Going Correction** +0.10s/f (Slow)
WFA 3 from 4yo+ 4lb **5** Ran SP% **109.5**
Speed ratings (Par 103): **103,101,99,91,85**
CSF £14.77 TOTE £3.10: £2.40, £1.50; EX 14.30.
Owner Chris Hamilton **Bred** Majestic Thoroughbred Investments Inc **Trained** Sproxton, Leics

FOCUS
Not a strong sprint handicap by any mean, but the time was good and the winner deserves a bit of credit.
Waterloo Dock Official explanation: vet said gelding lost a right-front shoe

5158 OLLY MURS LIVE HERE ON FRIDAY H'CAP 2m (P)
5:00 (5:00) (Class 4) (0-80,80) 4-Y-O+ £4,075 (£1,212; £606; £303) **Stalls** Low

Form RPR
516 **1** **Jamarjo (IRE)**[23] 4326 5-9-1 74 RichardHughes 3 85
(Steve Gollings) *trckd ldrs in chsng gp: chal 2f out: sn shkn up to ld: styd on wl* **9/4**[1]

005 **2** *2 1/2* **Twice Bitten**[33] 3962 4-9-5 78 GeorgeBaker 5 86
(James Toller) *hld up: stdy prog w gp fr 4f out: rdn to chse wnr over 1f out: styd on but hld fnl 100yds* **7/2**[2]

240P **3** *6* **Taikoo**[24] 4284 7-9-7 80 DarryllHolland 6 81
(Hughie Morrison) *trckd clr ldr: steadily clsd on ldr fr 4f out: led over 2f out: sn rdn: hdd over 1f out: fdd fnl f* **6/1**

6025 **4** *2 1/2* **Lady of Burgundy**[19] 4475 6-8-6 65 SilvestreDeSousa 2 63
(Mark Usher) *hld up: stdy prog fr 4f out: rdn to chse ldrs whn swtchd rt 2f out: fdd fnl f* **7/1**

06/0 **5** *13* **Akbabend**[12] 4697 6-9-0 **73**.....(t) SamHitchcott 1 55
(Chris Gordon) *trckd clr ldr tl rdn 5f out: wknd over 2f out* **16/1**
45-6 **6** *21* **Alsadaa (USA)**[26] 4216 9-9-7 **80**..... IanMongan 7 37
(Laura Mongan) *led: sn wl clr: rdn and hdd over 2f out: wknd qckly* **4/1**[3]
1034 **7** *13* **Frederick William**[26] 4215 4-8-11 **70** ow1.....(p) DaneO'Neill 4
(Chris Gordon) *in tch in chsng gp: pushedf along over 5f out: sn bhd* **12/1**

3m 30.15s (0.05) **Going Correction** +0.10s/f (Slow) 7 Ran SP% **113.4**
Speed ratings (Par 105): **103,101,98,97,91 80,74**
toteswingers 1&2 £2.80, 1&3 £3.50, 2&3 £4.50 CSF £10.06 TOTE £3.70: £2.40, £1.10; EX 11.30.
Owner Northern Bloodstock Racing **Bred** Frank Dunne **Trained** Scamblesby, Lincs

FOCUS
A modest staying event. The form is taken at face value, rated through the second to his Polytrack best.
Alsadaa(USA) Official explanation: jockey said gelding ran too freely

5159 LADIES DAY WITH TOBY ANSTIS 08.09.12 H'CAP 1m 3f (P)
5:30 (5:30) (Class 5) (0-75,72) 3-Y-O+ **£2,264** (£673; £336; £168) **Stalls** Low

Form RPR
-655 **1** **Brigadoon**[14] 4657 5-9-7 **72**..... MichaelJMMurphy(7) 6 82
(William Jarvis) *mid-div: hdwy fr 3f out: rdn 2f out: led ent fnl f: hld on wl whn strly chal fnl 120yds: all out* **7/2**[2]
1252 **2** *shd* **Spartan Spirit (IRE)**[21] 4411 4-9-8 **66**..... RichardHughes 8 76
(Hughie Morrison) *hld up: trckd wnr through fr over 2f out: rdn for str chal ins fnl f: jst hld* **7/4**[1]
6426 **3** *4 ½* **Tilsworth Glenboy**[22] 4365 5-10-0 **72**..... DarryllHolland 7 74
(J R Jenkins) *hld up: hdwy wl over 1f out: sn rdn: swtchd to far rails and styd on to go 3rd ins fnl f* **4/1**[3]
-000 **4** *1 ½* **Height Of Summer (IRE)**[17] 4538 4-10-0 **72**..... GeorgeBaker 5 71
(Chris Wall) *trckd ldr: led over 2f out: sn rdn: hdd jst over 1f out: fdd fnl 120yds* **10/1**
1306 **5** *hd* **Passion Play**[16] 4585 4-9-6 **64**..... JimmyFortune 1 63
(William Knight) *led: rdn and hdd over 2f out: wknd fnl f* **7/1**
0300 **6** *hd* **Azerodegree (IRE)**[18] 4499 3-9-0 **68**.....(b[1]) JimmyQuinn 2 66
(Marco Botti) *little s.i.s: sn rousted along to trck ldrs: rdn over 3f out: wknd fnl f* **12/1**
3140 **7** *10* **Bennelong**[16] 4585 6-9-10 **68**..... IanMongan 3 48
(Richard Rowe) *mid-div: rdn over 2f out: wknd over 1f out* **12/1**

2m 24.06s (2.16) **Going Correction** +0.10s/f (Slow)
WFA 3 from 4yo+ 10lb 7 Ran SP% **115.6**
Speed ratings (Par 103): **96,95,92,91,91 91,84**
toteswingers 1&2 £3.70, 1&3 £3.20, 2&3 £1.70 CSF £10.30 CT £24.64 TOTE £6.10: £3.60, £1.10; EX 13.20.
Owner James Bowditch **Bred** Biddestone Stud **Trained** Newmarket, Suffolk

FOCUS
This was steadily run, which means the leading pair deserve a fair bit of credit for being able to quicken so far clear. The winner is rated to his best.
T/Plt: £117.40 to a £1 stake. Pool: £43573.82 - 270.78 winning tickets T/Qpdt: £43.80 to a £1 stake. Pool: £3577.35 - 60.36 winning tickets TM

5095 LINGFIELD (L-H)
Monday, August 13

OFFICIAL GOING: Standard
Wind: light, half behind Weather: overcast

5160 32REDPOKER.COM NURSERY 6f (P)
2:10 (2:10) (Class 6) (0-65,65) 2-Y-O **£1,874** (£553; £276) **Stalls** Low

Form RPR
10 **1** **Somethingboutmary**[87] 2252 2-9-4 65..... JulieBurke(3) 7 70
(Kevin Ryan) *mde all: rdn over 1f out: styd on wl to assert ins fnl f: rdn out* **11/4**[1]
656 **2** *1* **Meet Me Halfway**[21] 4408 2-9-4 62..... TedDurcan 5 64
(Chris Wall) *chsd ldrs: effrt and rdr dropped whip over 1f out: chsd wnr fnl 75yds: kpt on same pce* **11/4**[1]
6400 **3** *¾* **Annie Besant**[9] 4792 2-8-3 50..... HarryBentley(3) 6 50
(David C Griffiths) *dwlt: bustled along leaving stalls and sn rcvrd to chse ldrs: rdn and unable qck over 1f out: styd on same pce fnl f* **12/1**
404 **4** *nk* **Moonlit Dancer (IRE)**[16] 4581 2-9-3 61.....(t) PatDobbs 3 60
(J W Hills) *hld up in last pair: rdn and effrt on inner over 1f out: kpt on same pce fnl 100yds* **8/1**
050 **5** *shd* **Borough Boy (IRE)**[9] 4816 2-9-7 65..... NeilCallan 1 63
(Derek Shaw) *t.k.h: swtchd rt and effrt over 1f out: styd on same pce ins fnl f* **15/2**
004 **6** *1 ½* **Iris Blue**[14] 4645 2-9-3 61..... SaleemGolam 4 55
(John Gosden) *hld up in last pair: stl travelling wl enough but switching lft and rt looking for run over 1f out: nvr enough room and unable to chal* **5/1**[2]
505 **7** *nse* **Persian Marvel (IRE)**[23] 4330 2-8-12 56..... JoeFanning 2 50
(Jim Boyle) *pressed wnr on inner: rdn wl over 1f out: no ex 1f out: lost 2nd fnl 75yds: sn eased* **11/2**[3]

1m 13.91s (2.01) **Going Correction** +0.125s/f (Slow) 7 Ran SP% **116.0**
Speed ratings (Par 92): **91,89,88,88,88 86,86**
toteswingers 1&2 £2.40, 1&3 £5.80, 2&3 £7.50 CSF £10.50 TOTE £3.10: £1.60, £2.50; EX 10.70.
Owner Wildcard Racing Syndicate **Bred** Stuart Thom & Paul Rock **Trained** Hambleton, N Yorks

FOCUS
A low-grade nursery in which all seven runners were racing in a handicap for the first time. A weak race, lacking improvers.

NOTEBOOK
Somethingboutmary, a winner on Fibresand on debut, was thought good enough to contest a Listed race at York last time, so although well beaten that day a mark of 65 always had the potential to underestimate her ability, and she bounced back to form. She broke well and was always well placed before kicking early in the straight and she saw out the extra furlong with no problem to make it two wins from three starts. Although she didn't win with masses in hand, she remains open to improvement and will probably prove competitive off slightly higher marks. (tchd 7-2)
Meet Me Halfway had not really progressed in three maiden runs, but she fared slightly better this time, keeping on well enough despite her rider dropping his whip to suggest there may be a small race in her at some stage. (op 7-2)
Annie Besant has looked pretty hopeless so far, but this was easily her best run as she made good headway down the middle without ever really threatening. She should stay further on pedigree and the way she raced here suggests she's worth stepping back up in trip. (tchd 14-1)
Moonlit Dancer(IRE) kept on from off the pace without ever being able to challenge and she looks fairly modest. She needs to step up if she is to win in this company. (op 15-2)
Borough Boy(IRE) was too keen around the inside and again failed to deliver any significant promise. (op 10-1 tchd 13-2)

5161 32REDBET.COM NURSERY 7f (P)
2:40 (2:40) (Class 6) (0-60,60) 2-Y-O **£1,874** (£553; £276) **Stalls** Low

Form RPR
0000 **1** **Whitford (IRE)**[6] 4934 2-9-3 56..... AndreaAtzeni 6 62+
(Chris Dwyer) *chsd ldng pair tl clsd qckly to ld 2f out: sn clr and in command: rdn out* **7/1**[3]
045 **2** *2 ¾* **Spithead**[34] 3948 2-9-4 60..... AdamBeschizza(3) 7 59
(William Haggas) *t.k.h: hld up in midfield: nt clr run 2f out tl swtchd lft and hdwy over 1f out: sn chsng clr wnr: styd on but nvr able to chal* **5/2**[1]
500 **3** *2 ¾* **Linda's Icon**[11] 4724 2-9-6 59..... NeilCallan 5 51
(Mick Channon) *sn wl outpcd in rr and swtchd to r wd: hdwy u.p bnd 2f out: styd on fnl f to snatch 3rd on post: no ch w wnr* **14/1**
400 **4** *nse* **Ana Shababiya (IRE)**[18] 4507 2-9-1 54..... RoystonFfrench 1 46
(Ismail Mohammed) *racd in midfield: rdn and outpcd over 2f out: no ch w wnr but styd on to 3rd ins fnl f: lost 3rd on post* **9/1**
500 **5** *1 ½* **Kunzea (IRE)**[9] 4813 2-8-13 52..... ChrisCatlin 3 40
(Mick Channon) *sn wl outpcd in last and swtchd to r wd: styd on past btn horses fnl f: n.d* **8/1**
600 **6** *shd* **Garmelow Girl**[11] 4742 2-8-10 52..... JulieBurke(3) 2 39
(Kevin Ryan) *sn outpcd and bhd in last trio: sme hdwy and swtchd rt 1f out: kpt on but n.d* **9/1**
006 **7** *6* **Birdy Boy (USA)**[18] 4502 2-8-6 45.....(b[1]) JoeFanning 4 17
(Mark Johnston) *led: rdn and hdd 2f out: immediately outpcd and btn: wkng whn edgd rt over 1f out: fdd fnl f* **11/4**[2]
4060 **8** *1 ¼* **Lawful**[25] 4230 2-9-7 60.....(e[1]) FrankieMcDonald 9 29
(Paul Fitzsimons) *chsd ldr: rdn and outpcd by wnr 2f out: wkng whn pushed rt over 1f out: fdd fnl f* **14/1**
655 **9** *5* **Cernanova (IRE)**[14] 4659 2-7-13 45..... NoelGarbutt(7) 8
(Hugo Palmer) *racd in midfield: rdn and struggling wl over 2f out: wknd 2f out: wl bhd fnl f* **20/1**

1m 27.36s (2.56) **Going Correction** +0.125s/f (Slow) 9 Ran SP% **116.9**
Speed ratings (Par 92): **90,86,83,83,81 81,74,73,67**
toteswingers 1&2 £5.30, 1&3 £24.70, 2&3 £8.60 CSF £25.20 CT £243.16 TOTE £7.00: £2.70, £1.40, £4.00; EX 50.20.
Owner R S G Jones **Bred** Newtown Stud **Trained** Six Mile Bottom, Cambs

FOCUS
A candidate for worst nursery of the season so far and half the field were flat to the boards and struggling to stay in touch by halfway, although that might partly be because Birdy Boy looked to set what looked quite a strong pace. The winner impressed, but the time was slow and the form is not rated positively.

NOTEBOOK
Whitford(IRE) blew the race apart on the turn for home where he swept clear in quite devastating style, and although his lead was slightly diminished in the final 50yds or so, the prize was already in the bag. It's hard to know where his improvement has come from given he was beaten around 9l over this trip at Wolverhampton on handicap debut, where he didn't appear to get home, but he was a different horse this time and a mark of 56 clearly underestimates him if this can be taken literally. He'd have to be of strong interest if out quickly under a penalty. Official explanation: trainer said, regarding apparent improvement in form, that the colt suffered interference in running on its last start and benefited from a more positive ride. (op 12-1)
Spithead was ridden with a little more restraint than last time and he kept plugging away for clear cut second. He shaped here like he'd do better for a slightly stiffer test of stamina and his pedigree backs that up. (op 2-1 tchd 15-8)
Linda's Icon made some headway from well back but wasn't really closing on the second in the final half furlong.
Ana Shababiya(IRE)
Kunzea(IRE) couldn't go the gallop early, but stayed on in the manner of a filly that can do better over further, albeit at a lowly level. (op 9-1)
Birdy Boy(USA), who was well backed, took them along at a good clip in the first-time headgear, but dropped away tamely in the final 2f and continues to disappoint. (tchd 5-2)

5162 32RED CASINO MAIDEN STKS 7f (P)
3:10 (3:12) (Class 5) 2-Y-O **£2,587** (£770; £384; £192) **Stalls** Low

Form RPR
62 **1** **Labienus**[19] 4463 2-9-3 0..... TedDurcan 8 76+
(David Lanigan) *chsd ldng pair: effrt to chse ldr 2f out: led 1f out: in command and pushed out ins fnl f: readily* **3/1**[2]
6 **2** *1 ¼* **Grey Blue (IRE)**[11] 4724 2-9-3 0..... JoeFanning 5 71
(Mark Johnston) *led: rdn 2f out: hdd and unable qck 1f out: styd on same pce after* **5/2**[1]
3 *¾* **Concise** 2-8-12 0..... PaulHanagan 1 64+
(Ed Dunlop) *in tch in last trio: rn green ent fnl 2f: hdwy over 1f out: styd on to go 3rd fnl 100yds: clsng on ldrs towards fin* **8/1**
4 *¾* **Mishaal (IRE)** 2-9-3 0..... NeilCallan 6 67+
(Roger Varian) *in tch in midfield: rdn and effrt 2f out: rn green: hung lft and no imp over 1f out: kpt on again ins fnl f* **5/1**[3]
6 **5** *½* **Empowerment (IRE)**[8] 4845 2-9-3 0..... PatDobbs 3 66
(Richard Hannon) *chsd ldr tl 2f out: sn u.p and unable qck: kpt on same pce after* **11/2**
0 **6** *6* **Big Thunder**[6] 4917 2-9-3 0..... ChrisCatlin 7 50
(Sir Mark Prescott Bt) *dwlt: in tch towards rr: rdn and struggling 3f out: bhd 2f out: no ch but styd on fnl f* **16/1**
00 **7** *nk* **Progenitor (IRE)**[19] 4463 2-9-3 0..... FrankieMcDonald 4 49
(David Lanigan) *t.k.h: chsd ldng trio: rdn and losing pl wl over 2f out: bhd fnl 2f: no ch but plugged on fnl f* **66/1**
8 *1 ½* **Admirable Art (IRE)** 2-9-3 0..... AndreaAtzeni 2 45
(Marco Botti) *s.i.s: early reminder and flashed tail: rn green in last trio: hdwy and swtchd rt over 2f out: rdn and btn over 1f out: fdd fnl f* **12/1**

1m 27.22s (2.42) **Going Correction** +0.125s/f (Slow) 8 Ran SP% **111.8**
Speed ratings (Par 94): **91,89,88,87,87 80,80,78**
toteswingers 1&2 £2.30, 1&3 £4.30, 2&3 £3.40 CSF £10.40 TOTE £5.40: £1.60, £1.30, £3.00; EX 8.50.
Owner B E Nielsen **Bred** Mrs S L Gibson Fleming **Trained** Upper Lambourn, Berks

FOCUS
This should turn out to be reasonable maiden form with the first four home all looking like they could be above average. The winner should improve again.

NOTEBOOK
Labienus finished in front of two horses here last time (Lord of Leitrim and Canadian Run) who have both run well in defeat since and he backed the form up with a smart effort of his own here to get off the mark. The son of Compton Place was always in a handy position in behind the leader and although that rival tried to stretch early in the straight, Labienus wasn't hard pressed to reel him in before putting daylight between him and his rivals to win with a good bit left in the locker. He should be able to make his mark in nurseries provided he isn't overly burdened and has the potential to make into a stakes horse at some stage. (op 7-4)

Grey Blue(IRE) pointed his toe nicely out in front and stepped up on his debut run for sure. His dam was useful over this sort of trip and it won't be long before this grey colt gets off the mark before going on to better things. (op 7-2 tchd 9-4)

Concise ◆, the only filly in the race, made strong late headway down the outside to mark herself down as one to be very interested in next time. She is entered in several of the Tattersalls Million races and she could be useful. (op 10-1 tchd 7-1)

Mishaal(IRE) was able to lie-up a bit handier than third home Concise and he shaped with a good deal of promise too, without his rider getting overly serious. He looks another winner in waiting. (op 11-2 tchd 6-1)

Empowerment(IRE) was a touch free through the early stages and didn't finish his race. He might need dropping back to 6f. (op 6-1)

Big Thunder was struggling at the back a long way out, but the penny began to drop in the closing stages where he passed a couple of rivals, and he looks more of a long-term project. (op 14-1)

Admirable Art(IRE) Official explanation: jockey said colt was slowly away

5163 32RED H'CAP — 1m 2f (P)

3:40 (3:41) (Class 4) (0-80,79) 3-Y-O — £4,528 (£1,347; £673; £336) Stalls Low

Form				RPR
-123	1		**Watheeq (USA)**[18] 4498 3-9-2 74 ... PaulHanagan 1 (Roger Varian) *t.k.h: chsd ldr for 2f: styd handy: rdn and qcknd through on inner to ld wl over 1f out: idling but a doing enough ins fnl f: rdn out* **7/4**[1]	81+
4336	2	1	**Corsetry (USA)**[41] 3737 3-9-3 75 ... TomQueally 3 (Sir Henry Cecil) *hld up in tch: nt clr run over 2f out: hdwy and followed wnr through on inner wl over 1f out: kpt on u.p and chsd wnr ins fnl f: no imp fnl 75yds* **3/1**[2]	80
2-14	3	nse	**Westwiththenight (IRE)**[59] 3106 3-9-7 79 ... ChrisCatlin 5 (William Haggas) *stdd s: hld up in tch in last: rdn and effrt on outer bnd 2f out: kpt on wl u.p ins fnl f: wnt 3rd on post* **11/2**[3]	84+
0423	4	nse	**Instrumentalist (IRE)**[10] 4755 3-9-2 74 ... TedDurcan 6 (John Best) *in tch: pushed along briefly 5f out: gd hdwy on outer over 2f out: ev ch u.p 2f out: unable qck over 1f out: styd on same pce fnl f* **7/1**	79
3512	5	14	**Halling Dancer**[11] 4727 3-9-1 76 ... AdamBeschizza(3) 4 (Lee Carter) *led: rdn and hdd wl over 1f out: btn over 1f out: fdd fnl f* **10/1**	53
51-0	6	nk	**Intuition**[89] 2182 3-9-5 77 ...(b[1]) PatDobbs 2 (Richard Hannon) *t.k.h: chsd ldrs: rdn and lost pl jst over 2f out: bhd over 1f out* **14/1**	53
350	7	7	**Parley (USA)**[35] 3906 3-9-6 78 ... JoeFanning 7 (Mark Johnston) *chsd ldrs: hdwy to chse ldr 7f out tl over 2f out: sn struggling and losing pl whn short of room 2f out: wl bhd after* **8/1**	40

2m 6.31s (-0.29) **Going Correction** +0.125s/f (Slow) 7 Ran SP% **116.1**

Speed ratings (Par 102): **106,105,105,105,93 93,88**

toteswingers 1&2 £1.70, 1&3 £3.30, 2&3 £4.90 CSF £7.37 CT £23.16 TOTE £2.70: £1.50, £2.90; EX 7.60.

Owner Hamdan Al Maktoum **Bred** Shadwell Farm LLC **Trained** Newmarket, Suffolk

FOCUS

A reasonable handicap run at a decent pace. The form makes sense with the second and fourth setting the standard.

5164 32REDBINGO.COM H'CAP — 1m 4f (P)

4:10 (4:11) (Class 6) (0-60,60) 3-Y-O+ — £1,704 (£503; £251) Stalls Low

Form				RPR
0621	1		**Attraction Ticket**[7] 4870 3-8-13 59 ... AdamBeschizza(3) 9 (David Simcock) *racd in midfield: clsd on ldrs 8f out: chsd ldrs over 3f out: rdn to ld wl over 1f out: flashed tail u.p 1f out: idling ins fnl f: hung rt towards fin: a gng to hold on* **5/6**[1]	72+
516	2	1/2	**Melodrama (IRE)**[60] 3088 3-9-3 60 ...(b) TedDurcan 5 (David Lanigan) *hld up in midfield: clsd on ldrs 8f out: hdwy and wnt clr w ldng quartet 3f out: rdn and fnd little over 1f out: chsd wnr and swtchd lft ins fnl f: kpt on* **8/1**[2]	72
0306	3	2 1/2	**Celtic Charlie (FR)**[65] 2937 7-9-1 52 ... JemmaMarshall(5) 4 (Pat Phelan) *led: stdd gallop 8f out: qcknd over 3f out: rdn and hdd wl over 1f out: one pce and btn ins fnl f* **16/1**	60
0042	4	4	**Secret Era**[26] 4219 5-9-11 57 ... NeilCallan 7 (William Muir) *t.k.h early: chsd ldrs: wnt 2nd 4f out: rdn and unable qck whn squeezed for room 2f out: 4th and wl btn fnl f* **11/1**[3]	59
2010	5	3/4	**Rodrigo De Freitas (IRE)**[18] 4504 5-9-11 57 ...(v) PaulHanagan 11 (Jim Boyle) *stdd s: t.k.h and hld up in rr: rdn and hdwy into modest 6th over 2f out: plugged on but nvr trbld ldrs* **14/1**	57
0624	6	2	**Beneath**[18] 4491 5-9-12 58 ...(bt) TomQueally 2 (Neil Mulholland) *sn niggled along towards rr: travelling bttr and clsd whn gallop stdd 8f out: rdn and past btn horses to go modest 6th 2f out: no imp* **20/1**	55
6604	7	8	**Maccabees**[51] 3391 3-8-9 57 ... MatthewLawson(5) 8 (Roger Curtis) *stdd s: t.k.h: hld up in rr: hdwy 8f out: 5th and struggling u.p wl over 2f out: sn btn and wknd 2f out* **14/1**	41
0050	8	nk	**Castalian Spring (IRE)**[7] 4870 3-7-10 46 oh1 ... NatashaEaton(7) 3 (Terry Clement) *chsd ldrs: rdn and losing pl 4f out: wl btn fnl 2f* **66/1**	30
0000	9	13	**Breakheart (IRE)**[14] 4652 5-9-9 55 ...(p) TomMcLaughlin 1 (Paul Howling) *in tch in midfield rdn and struggling 4f out: lost tch 3f out: t.o* **50/1**	18
-065	10	17	**Pugnacious (IRE)**[6] 4915 3-9-2 59 ... JoeFanning 10 (Mark Johnston) *sn niggled along towards rr: rdn and toiling over 4f out: wl bhd fnl 3f: t.o* **8/1**[2]	
0050	11	nk	**Moonshine Ruby**[17] 4536 6-9-4 50 ... WilliamCarson 6 (Peter Hiatt) *chsd ldr tl 4f out: sn dropped out u.p: wl bhd fnl 2f: t.o* **33/1**	

2m 32.77s (-0.23) **Going Correction** +0.125s/f (Slow)

WFA 3 from 5yo+ 11lb 11 Ran SP% **115.5**

Speed ratings (Par 101): **105,104,103,100,99 98,93,92,84,72 72**

toteswingers 1&2 £3.00, 1&3 £4.60, 2&3 £20.80 CSF £7.26 CT £63.84 TOTE £1.80: £1.10, £2.10, £4.70; EX 9.40.

Owner Oliver Brendon **Bred** The Kathryn Stud Ltd **Trained** Newmarket, Suffolk

■ Stewards' Enquiry : Adam Beschizza one-day ban: careless riding (Aug 29)

FOCUS

A weak handicap with no depth, but it was sound run and the best time on the card. A step up from the winner.

Castalian Spring(IRE) Official explanation: jockey said filly hung right

5165 32RED.COM H'CAP — 5f (P)

4:40 (4:41) (Class 4) (0-85,84) 3-Y-O+ — £4,528 (£1,347; £673; £336) Stalls High

Form				RPR
000	1		**Gorgeous Goblin (IRE)**[9] 4829 5-9-0 77 ...(t) HarryBentley(3) 4 (David C Griffiths) *w ldrs: rdn and ev ch 2f out: drvn ent fnl f: kpt on wl to ld towards fin: all out* **16/1**	84
-012	2	shd	**Tango Sky (IRE)**[30] 4081 3-9-5 82 ...(p) JimCrowley 3 (Ralph Beckett) *w ldrs on inner tl led 4f out: rdn 2f out: drvn over 1f out: hdd and no ex towards fin* **6/4**[1]	88
3440	3	nse	**Falasteen (IRE)**[13] 4690 5-8-13 73 ... ChrisCatlin 5 (Milton Bradley) *w ldrs on outer: rdn and sltly outpcd over 1f out: rallied u.p and kpt on wl fnl 100yds* **7/1**	79
0000	4	3/4	**Expose**[9] 4824 4-9-0 77 ... AdamBeschizza(3) 1 (William Haggas) *hld up wl in tch: effrt on inner over 1f out: drvn and chsd ldrs 1f out: styd on same pce u.p fnl 100yds* **10/3**[2]	81
0001	5	shd	**Proper Charlie**[19] 4468 4-8-13 73 ... NeilCallan 7 (William Knight) *stdd s: sn pushed along but in tch in rr: swtchd rt and hdwy bnd 2f out: kpt on u.p ins fnl f* **9/2**[3]	76
1400	6	3/4	**Pucon**[43] 3670 3-7-9 65 oh5 ... IanBurns(7) 2 (Roger Teal) *t.k.h: hld up wl in tch: rdn and effrt over 1f out: nt clr run and swtchd lft 1f out: styd on same pce ins fnl f* **33/1**	65
0002	7	3 1/4	**Invincible Lad (IRE)**[8] 4849 8-9-10 84 ...(p) TomQueally 6 (Milton Bradley) *in tch: wd and dropped to rr bnd 2f out: no prog: wknd fnl f* **12/1**	73

59.41s (0.61) **Going Correction** +0.125s/f (Slow)

WFA 3 from 4yo+ 3lb 7 Ran SP% **110.3**

Speed ratings (Par 105): **100,99,99,98,98 97,92**

toteswingers 1&2 £5.90, 1&3 £13.70, 2&3 £3.00 CSF £37.82 CT £179.31 TOTE £16.90: £5.50, £1.60; EX 52.00.

Owner K Humphries & Sons Roofing Contractors **Bred** S & L Humphries **Trained** Bawtry, S Yorks

FOCUS

A bunch finish to this muddling sprint. Ordinary form at best, and not the most convincing.

5166 £32 BONUS AT 32RED.COM MAIDEN FILLIES' STKS — 1m (P)

5:10 (5:12) (Class 5) 3-Y-O — £2,587 (£770; £384; £192) Stalls High

Form				RPR
5533	1		**Khazeena**[22] 4366 3-9-0 79 ... PaulHanagan 6 (William Haggas) *led after 1f: mde rest: rdn and wnt clr 2f out: in command 1f out: eased cl home* **30/100**[1]	81+
	2	3	**Be My Rock** 3-8-9 0 ... JamieJones(5) 3 (Rae Guest) *broke wl: stdd and hld up in tch: rdn 2f out: wnt 3rd over 1f out: kpt on to go 2nd wl ins fnl f: no threat to wnr* **12/1**[3]	71
	3	1	**Merry Jaunt (USA)** 3-9-0 0 ... TomQueally 1 (John Gosden) *chsd ldrs: chsd wnr 3f out: rdn and unable qck 2f out: btn ent fnl f: styd on same pce and lost 2nd wl ins fnl f* **4/1**[2]	68
06	4	11	**Shahrazad (IRE)**[26] 4212 3-9-0 0 ... JamieMackay 2 (Patrick Gilligan) *t.k.h: flashed tail leaving stalls: led for 1f: chsd wnr after tl 3f out: wknd over 1f out* **33/1**	42
00	5	6	**Venetias Dream (IRE)**[20] 4434 3-9-0 0 ...(t) WilliamCarson 4 (Stuart Williams) *hld up in tch: rdn and struggling over 2f out: sn btn and bhd over 1f out* **66/1**	28
	6	31	**Rosa Lottie** 3-9-0 0 ... TomMcLaughlin 5 (David C Griffiths) *s.i.s: in tch in rr: rdn and struggling over 3f out: lost tch 3f out: t.o* **40/1**	

1m 38.89s (0.69) **Going Correction** +0.125s/f (Slow) 6 Ran SP% **111.5**

Speed ratings (Par 97): **101,98,97,86,80 49**

toteswingers 1&2 £1.70, 1&3 £1.10, 2&3 £1.40 CSF £5.07 TOTE £1.30: £1.02, £3.80; EX 5.30.

Owner Hamdan Al Maktoum **Bred** Sheikh Abdulla Bin Isa Al-Khalifa **Trained** Newmarket, Suffolk

FOCUS

No depth to this maiden but the winner is rated value for a bit extra and the form is rated around her.

Venetias Dream(IRE) Official explanation: jockey said filly lost its action

T/Plt: £10.30 to a £1 stake. Pool: £44191.51 - 3131.58 winning tickets T/Qpdt: £4.70 to a £1 stake. Pool: £4325.91 - 677.80 winning tickets SP

4825 THIRSK (L-H)

Monday, August 13

OFFICIAL GOING: Good to firm (good in places; 10.4)

Wind: Light half behind Weather: Cloudy

5167 LADIES DAY ON SATURDAY 8TH SEPTEMBER H'CAP — 5f

5:50 (5:50) (Class 4) (0-85,81) 3-Y-O — £4,528 (£1,347; £673; £336) Stalls High

Form				RPR
2344	1		**Love Island**[9] 4798 3-8-2 62 ... PaulQuinn 6 (Richard Whitaker) *trckd ldrs: swtchd lft and hdwy over 1f out: rdn to chal jst ins fnl f: led last 100yds: kpt on* **11/1**	74
-136	2	3/4	**Dreaming Of Rubies**[65] 2928 3-8-11 71 ...(t) PJMcDonald 8 (Ben Haslam) *led: rdn along over 1f out: drvn ent fnl f: hdd and no ex last 100yds* **8/1**	80
1236	3	1 1/4	**Demora**[9] 4793 3-8-7 67 ... MartinLane 7 (Michael Appleby) *prom: pushed along 1/2-way: rdn and edgd rt over 1f out: kpt on u.p fnl f* **8/1**	72
3144	4	1/2	**Gowanharry (IRE)**[15] 4619 3-8-7 67 ...(p) PaulMulrennan 3 (Michael Dods) *cl up: effrt 2f out: sn rdn and ev ch tl drvn and one pce ent fnl f* **14/1**	70
4110	5	shd	**Lupin Pooter**[17] 4558 3-9-5 79 ...(b[1]) GrahamGibbons 4 (David Barron) *cl up: rdn wl over 1f out: drvn whn sltly hmpd appr fnl f: sn wknd* **10/3**[1]	81
1151	6	nse	**Elusive Bonus (IRE)**[7] 4878 3-8-2 69 6ex ... DavidBergin(7) 5 (David O'Meara) *trckd ldrs: swtchd lft and hdwy 2f out: rdn and ch over 1f out: one pce fnl f* **10/1**	71
-600	7	1	**Amadeus Denton (IRE)**[68] 2824 3-8-8 75 ... ConnorNichol(7) 10 (Michael Dods) *chsd ldrs on inner: rdn along wl over 1f out: grad wknd* **33/1**	74
2-20	8	4	**Master Bond**[87] 2256 3-9-0 79 ... JustinNewman(5) 1 (Bryan Smart) *sltly hmpd and wnt lft s: a towards rr* **14/1**	63
2143	9	1/2	**Just Like Heaven (IRE)**[9] 4798 3-8-7 67 ... DuranFentiman 9 (Tim Easterby) *chsd ldrs: rdn along 2f out: sn wknd* **5/1**[3]	49
6046	U		**Pea Shooter**[17] 4558 3-9-7 81 ... AmyRyan 2 (Kevin Ryan) *stmbld and uns rdr s* **4/1**[2]	

58.07s (-1.53) **Going Correction** -0.25s/f (Firm) 10 Ran SP% **115.7**

Speed ratings (Par 102): **102,100,98,98,97 97,96,89,88,**

Tote Swingers: 1&2 £12.60, 1&3 £5.70, 2&3 £22.40 CSF £95.09 CT £747.95 TOTE £16.30: £3.00, £3.30, £2.20; EX 155.80.

Owner J Barry Pemberton **Bred** Hellwood Farm And J B Pemberton **Trained** Scarcroft, W Yorks

FOCUS
The rail was moved out 3-4 yards on both bends onto fresh ground, adding around 12 yards to races over 7f and 1m and around 20 yards to races over further. Several vied for the lead and the pace was generous if not overly strong. The form looks modest but sound, rated around the placed horses.

5168 BRITISH STALLION STUDS SUPPORTING BRITISH RACING EBF MAIDEN STKS 5f
6:20 (6:20) (Class 4) 2-Y-O £4,528 (£1,347; £673; £336) Stalls High

Form RPR
3 **1** **Stand Of Glory (USA)**[20] 4419 2-9-3 0 .... MartinLane 7 76+
(David Simcock) *dwlt: sn led: shkn up over 1f out: sn clr* 4/11[1]
60 **2** 2 ½ **Dance Off (IRE)**[9] 4825 2-8-9 0 .... LeeTopliss(3) 3 59
(Richard Fahey) *chsd ldrs: rdn and edgd rt wl over 1f out: kpt on fnl f* 9/1[3]
0 **3** nse **Fidget**[51] 3381 2-8-12 0 .... RobertWinston 6 59
(David Brown) *trckd ldrs: effrt wl over 1f out: sn rdn and kpt on fnl f* 10/1
0 **4** 1 ¾ **Megaleka**[23] 4344 2-8-12 0 .... DuranFentiman 5 53
(Chris Fairhurst) *chsd ldrs: rdn and edgd lft wl over 1f out: kpt on same pce ins fnl f* 66/1
00 **5** 1 **Lady Of Seville (IRE)**[24] 4290 2-8-12 0 .... GrahamGibbons 4 49
(Tom Tate) *cl up: rdn along 2f out: wknd appr fnl f* 33/1
05 **6** 3 **Unassailable**[24] 4290 2-9-3 0 .... AmyRyan 2 44
(Kevin Ryan) *wnt bdly lft s: in tch: rdn along bef 1/2-way and sn outpcd* 15/2[2]
0 **7** 6 **Shepherds Bow**[12] 4710 2-9-3 0 .... JamesSullivan 1 27+
(Michael Easterby) *hmpd s: a outpcd and bhd* 33/1

59.93s (0.33) **Going Correction** -0.25s/f (Firm) 7 Ran SP% **111.5**
Speed ratings (Par 96): **87,83,82,80,78 73,64**
Tote Swingers: 1&2 £1.40, 1&3 £1.70, 2&3 £5.60 CSF £4.10 TOTE £1.40: £1.50, £1.10; EX 3.50.

Owner H E Sheikh Sultan Bin Khalifa Al Nahyan **Bred** Nursery Place Llc **Trained** Newmarket, Suffolk

FOCUS
This proved easy for the hot favourite who strolled home in a time around 1.8secs slower than the previous 3-y-o handicap. A weak race, the runner-up and poor time helping with the level.

NOTEBOOK
Stand Of Glory(USA) had shown ability when looking likely to improve for his debut run at Ffos Las last month, and although that race had not worked out too well so far, this 160,000gns purchase faced an easier task this time. Using his early pace, he made full use of his rail draw to dictate matters, and none of the others could go with him. This was quite impressive, although the competition was not that tough. (op 2-5)
Dance Off(IRE) was taken off her feet early over C&D last time, before making brief late headway, and once again she was niggled at halfway before keeping on. She had to race in the middle of the track, which did not help, and she could be better over further in time. (op 10-1 tchd 8-1)
Fidget tracked the winner against the rail but despite keeping on could make no impression on the winner. She had shown some early pace before running out of steam on her debut over 5f in soft ground at Haydock in June and improved on that run here. (op 12-1)
Megaleka Official explanation: jockey said filly hung left
Unassailable, racing with his head characteristically to one side, went left on exiting the stalls and was always struggling. Official explanation: jockey said colt hung left (op 8-1)

5169 TURFTV.CO.UK MAIDEN AUCTION STKS 7f
6:50 (6:50) (Class 5) 2-Y-O £2,587 (£770; £384; £192) Stalls Low

Form RPR
2 **1** **Kolonel Kirkup**[14] 4637 2-8-9 0 .... PaulMulrennan 9 70+
(Michael Dods) *trckd ldr: hdwy and cl up 1/2-way: rdn to ld over 1f out: drvn ins fnl f: hld on wl* 7/2[3]
022 **2** hd **Dr Phibes (IRE)**[15] 4618 2-8-12 78 .... AndrewElliott 3 73
(Alan Swinbank) *trckd ldrs: hdwy 3f out: chal wl over 1f out: drvn and ev ch ins fnl f: jst failed* 6/4[1]
5203 **3** 1 ½ **Annie Gogh**[12] 4710 2-8-7 67 .... DavidAllan 4 64
(Tim Easterby) *led: rdn along 3f out: hdd over 1f out: sn drvn and kpt on fnl f* 3/1[2]
0 **4** 1 ½ **Attansky (IRE)**[9] 4792 2-8-4 0 .... DarylByrne(5) 5 62
(Tim Easterby) *in tch: hdwy on inner 3f out: rdn 2f out: kpt on appr fnl f: nrst fin* 28/1
6 **5** 5 **Lexington Blue**[28] 4140 2-8-9 0 .... GrahamGibbons 2 52
(David O'Meara) *chsd ldng pair on inner whn n.m.r after 2f: rdn along 3f out: wknd 2f out* 11/1
04 **6** 2 ¼ **Byron's Dream**[15] 4618 2-8-9 0 .... FrederikTylicki 7 43
(Jedd O'Keeffe) *t.k.h early: in tch: hdwy to chse ldrs 3f out: sn rdn and wknd 2f out* 10/1
04 **7** 1 ¼ **Cool Sea (IRE)**[13] 4681 2-8-4 0 .... AndrewMullen 8 35
(Nigel Tinkler) *dwlt: a in rr* 50/1
8 4 ½ **Fake Or Fortune (IRE)** 2-8-9 0 .... DuranFentiman 6 28
(Tim Walford) *s.i.s and in rr: sme hdwy 3f out: sn rdn and wknd* 25/1

1m 27.99s (0.79) **Going Correction** 0.0s/f (Good) 8 Ran SP% **113.9**
Speed ratings (Par 94): **95,94,93,91,85 83,81,76**
Tote Swingers: 1&2 £2.20, 1&3 £2.70, 2&3 £1.70 CSF £8.97 TOTE £5.60: £1.60, £1.10, £1.50; EX 6.70.
Owner Kevin Kirkup **Bred** Newsells Park Stud **Trained** Denton, Co Durham

FOCUS
The first two had to dig deep in a protracted battle to the line, and four finished clear. The winner stepped forward and the second was close to his mark.

NOTEBOOK
Kolonel Kirkup had shown some ability on his debut in a 6f Ayr maiden last month when he looked likely to improve for a step up in trip. He raced freely up with the pace early on, but held a good position to deliver a challenge, and found more when challenged to just keep hold of the advantage near the line. (tchd 4-1)
Dr Phibes(IRE) came under pressure early but finished strongly over 6f last time at Carlisle, so the step up to 7f looked sure to suit. Making a mid-race move, he knuckled down to battle it out with the winner and just lost out. This was a creditable performance as the tight turn did not play to his strengths. (op 5-4 tchd 13-8)
Annie Gogh showed early speed and got a good position against the rail. She kept on to run a fair race considering she had a bit to find on the ratings. (op 7-2 tchd 4-1)
Attansky(IRE), a stablemate of the third, raced in mid-division against the rail and was doing his best work at the finish. He never featured at big odds on his debut in a Doncaster maiden the previous week, but this run suggests there is some latent ability to build on. (op 33-1)

5170 CALVERTS CARPETS H'CAP 1m
7:20 (7:20) (Class 5) (0-75,74) 3-Y-O £3,234 (£962; £481; £240) Stalls Low

Form RPR
2112 **1** **Daddy Warbucks (IRE)**[9] 4830 3-9-3 70 .... AdrianNicholls 7 80
(David Nicholls) *mde all: qcknd over 2f out: rdn over 1f out: styd on strly* 5/2[1]
5600 **2** 3 **Sardanapalus**[18] 4498 3-9-3 70 ....(b[1]) PaulMulrennan 3 73
(Kevin Ryan) *plld hrd: hld up in rr: hdwy on outer 3f out: rdn to chse wnr over 1f out: drvn and hung lft ins fnl f: sn one pce* 13/2
0054 **3** 2 ½ **Blue Top**[9] 4830 3-8-2 55 oh3 ....(p) DuranFentiman 4 52
(Tim Walford) *chsd ldrs: rdn along and sltly outpcd wl over 2f out: kpt on u.p appr fnl f* 11/1
000 **4** 1 ¼ **Endless Applause**[12] 4711 3-8-2 55 oh5 .... PaulQuinn 2 49
(Richard Whitaker) *chsd ldrs: rdn along 3f out: drvn 2f out: sn one pce* 40/1
-500 **5** ½ **Mitchum**[89] 2182 3-9-2 74 .... LMcNiff(5) 9 67
(David Barron) *stdd s: hld up in rr: hdwy over 2f out: sn rdn along: drvn and n.m.r wl over 1f out: sn no imp* 11/2[3]
0-02 **6** nse **Poontoon (IRE)**[25] 4263 3-8-6 59 .... BarryMcHugh 1 52
(Richard Fahey) *towards rr: rdn along and hdwy on inner over 2f out: drvn wl over 1f out: no imp* 6/1
2243 **7** 3 ¼ **Regal Acclaim (IRE)**[9] 4830 3-8-1 59 ....(t) NeilFarley(5) 5 45
(Declan Carroll) *chsd ldrs: hdwy on outer 1/2-way: rdn along 3f out: edgd rt and wknd wl over 1f out* 5/1[2]
4150 **8** 18 **Ptolemy**[10] 4783 3-8-11 64 .... GrahamGibbons 6
(David Barron) *chsd wnr: rdn along 3f out: sn drvn and wknd* 11/2[3]

1m 39.77s (-0.33) **Going Correction** 0.0s/f (Good) 8 Ran SP% **114.4**
Speed ratings (Par 100): **101,98,95,94,93 93,90,72**
Tote Swingers: 1&2 £4.80, 1&3 £5.20, 2&3 £11.50 CSF £19.28 CT £150.67 TOTE £4.10: £1.10, £3.90, £3.90; EX 29.20.
Owner Martin Love **Bred** Edmond Kent **Trained** Sessay, N Yorks

FOCUS
There was a recent handle on previous form as three of these had met in a Class 5 handicap over C&D earlier in the month.
Regal Acclaim(IRE) Official explanation: jockey said gelding hung left

5171 THIRSK RACECOURSE PAVILION FOR WEDDING RECEPTIONS (S) H'CAP 1m
7:50 (8:34) (Class 6) (0-65,65) 3-Y-O+ £2,587 (£770; £384; £192) Stalls Low

Form RPR
0000 **1** **Mahadee (IRE)**[21] 4411 7-10-0 65 ....(b) FrederikTylicki 5 77
(Ed de Giles) *bhd: pushed along 3f out: hdwy 2f out: rdn and str run ent fnl f: led fnl 50yds* 5/1[2]
0206 **2** 1 ¾ **Thrust Control (IRE)**[5] 4956 5-8-12 49 ....(p) MichaelO'Connell 7 57
(Tracy Waggott) *slt ld: rdn over 2f out: drvn and edgd rt ent fnl f: hdd and no ex fnl 50yds* 25/1
0030 **3** nk **Outlaw Torn (IRE)**[12] 4715 3-8-9 56 ....(e) DeclanCannon(3) 6 62
(Richard Guest) *midfield: hdwy on wd outside 2f out: sn rdn and styd on wl fnl f: nrst fin* 11/1
5060 **4** 1 ¾ **Fortunate Bid (IRE)**[42] 3712 6-9-4 55 ....(p) JamesSullivan 15 58
(Linda Stubbs) *hld up in rr: gd hdwy on inner 2f out: rdn to chse ldrs over 1f out: styd on same pce fnl f* 16/1
4-00 **5** 1 **Auto Mac**[7] 4879 4-9-13 64 ....(b) MartinLane 14 65
(Neville Bycroft) *cl up: effrt over 2f out: sn rdn and evc hance whn edgd rt ent fnl f: sn drvn and wknd* 10/1[3]
0045 **6** nk **Boy The Bell**[19] 4452 5-9-1 59 .... JacobButterfield(7) 17 59
(Ollie Pears) *chsd ldrs: rdn along wl over 2f out: kpt on same pce appr fnl f* 10/1[3]
0660 **7** 1 ½ **Rock Of Deauville (IRE)**[12] 4714 5-8-13 50 ....(v[1]) BarryMcHugh 13 47
(Julie Camacho) *stdd s and hld up in rr: hdwy wl over 2f out: rdn to chse ldrs over 1f out: sn no imp* 12/1
040 **8** nk **Praxios**[21] 4390 4-9-0 54 ....(b[1]) GaryBartley(3) 18 50
(Noel Wilson) *in tch: hdwy to chse ldng pair 3f out: rdn to chal over 2f out and ev ch tl wknd over 1f out* 33/1
0040 **9** ¾ **Whispered Times (USA)**[5] 4954 5-9-12 63 ....(p) RobertWinston 8 57
(Tracy Waggott) *trckd ldrs: hdwy to chse ldng pair wl over 2f outer: sn rdn and wknd over 1f out* 7/2[1]
6024 **10** ½ **American Lover (FR)**[7] 4890 5-8-11 48 .... PaddyAspell 12 41
(John Wainwright) *a towards rr* 14/1
034 **11** ½ **Byron Bear (IRE)**[3] 5059 4-8-12 49 .... PaulQuinn 3 50
(Paul Midgley) *midfield: hdwy 3f out: chsd ldrs 2f out: swtchd rt and styng on whn nt clr run and hmpd ent fnl f: nt rcvr* 5/1[2]
0040 **12** 2 ¼ **Moral Issue**[10] 4783 4-9-11 65 .... DaleSwift(3) 4 52
(Ian McInnes) *a in rr* 25/1
3600 **13** 3 **Airmyles**[12] 4715 4-8-13 50 .... PatrickMathers 9 30
(Tracy Waggott) *a towards rr* 50/1
1600 **14** 6 **Sky Diamond (IRE)**[21] 4402 4-9-1 52 ....(b) GrahamGibbons 10 18
(John Mackie) *chsd ldng pair: rdn along 3f out: sn wknd* 12/1
0-30 **15** 3 ¾ **Red Mercury (IRE)**[23] 4349 4-8-11 48 ....(b) PaulMulrennan 1
(Ollie Pears) *chsd ldrs on inner: rdn along 3f out: sn wknd* 12/1

1m 39.76s (-0.34) **Going Correction** 0.0s/f (Good)
WFA 3 from 4yo+ 7lb 15 Ran SP% **130.3**
Speed ratings (Par 101): **101,99,98,97,96 95,94,94,93,92 92,90,87,81,77**
Tote Swingers 1&2 £45.80, 2&3 £36.30, 1&3 £20.10 CSF £139.16 CT £1365.98 TOTE £8.10: £3.10, £9.30, £2.70; EX 169.20.No bid for the winner.
Owner 2 1/2 - 3 1/2 Club **Bred** Darley **Trained** Ledbury, H'fords
■ Stewards' Enquiry : Jacob Butterfield two-day ban: careless riding (Aug 27-28)

FOCUS
A moderate selling handicap, though the time was fractionally quicker than the earlier Class 5 handicap. After a lengthy delay, due to a racegoer needing medical attention, this was run in near-darkness. A few had made it to the start before the delay and that seemed to be an advantage. The placed horses set the level.
Byron Bear(IRE) Official explanation: jockey said gelding suffered interference in running

5172 RACING AGAIN NEXT MONDAY - 20TH AUGUST H'CAP 2m
8:20 (8:56) (Class 6) (0-65,64) 4-Y-O+ £1,940 (£577; £288; £144) Stalls Low

Form RPR
5-52 **1** **Dr Finley (IRE)**[16] 4590 5-9-4 64 .... SimonPearce(3) 3 72
(Lydia Pearce) *trckd ldrs: pushed along over 3f out: hdwy over 2f out: rdn to chal over 1f out: led ins fnl f: sn drvn and jst hld on* 13/5[1]
-322 **2** shd **Bijou Dan**[40] 3750 11-9-0 57 .... PJMcDonald 13 65
(George Moore) *trckd ldng pair: hdwy over 3f out: rdn 2f out: drvn over 1f out: styd on and ev ch ins fnl f: jst hld* 9/2[2]
6550 **3** 1 ¼ **Descaro (USA)**[16] 4590 6-8-12 62 ....(v) DavidBergin(7) 6 68
(David O'Meara) *led 4f: chsd clr ldr tl led again wl over 2f out: rdn wl over 1f out: drvn and hdd ins fnl f: kpt on* 9/2[2]
4-04 **4** 2 **Grand Art (IRE)**[45] 3577 8-8-11 54 ....(p) GrahamGibbons 11 58
(Noel Wilson) *in tch: hdwy to chse ldrs 5f out: rdn over 2f out: drvn over 1f out: kpt on same pce* 25/1
-005 **5** ½ **Spiders Star**[3] 5056 9-8-0 50 .... ShirleyTeasdale(7) 5 53
(Simon West) *hld up and bhd: stdy hdwy over 3f out: rdn over 2f out: styd on fnl f: nrst fin* 7/1[3]

0320 **6** 3 ¼ **Terenzium (IRE)**[7] 4867 10-8-6 **49**............................(p) JamesSullivan 10 48
(Micky Hammond) *hld up and bhd: hdwy 3f out: rdn along over 2f out: sn no imp* **12/1**

/006 **7** 1 **Prairie Hawk (USA)**[2] 5115 7-8-4 **47**..........................(t) PatrickMathers 7 45
(Brian Rothwell) *trckd ldrs: hdwy 1/2-way: chsd ldng pair 3f out and sn rdn: drvn 2f out and grad wknd* **18/1**

604 **8** 4 **Jim Tango (FR)**[15] 4622 8-9-5 **62**..........................(bt) PaulMulrennan 12 55
(Brian Storey) *hld up and bhd tl sme late hdwy* **28/1**

6306 **9** ¾ **Lava Steps (USA)**[6] 4912 6-8-2 **45**...........................(b) DuranFentiman 1 38
(David O'Meara) *prom: led after 4f and sn clr: rdn along over 3f out: hdd wl over 2f out and sn wknd* **20/1**

010- **10** 3 ½ **Miss Ferney**[311] 6666 8-9-4 **04**....................................... PaulPickard[(3)] 8 52+
(Alan Kirtley) *hld up in rr: sme hdwy 3f out: rdn over 2f out: n.d* **12/1**

5453 **11** 4 **Lady Gargoyle**[45] 3579 4-7-11 **45**................................... NeilFarley[(5)] 9 29
(Jim Goldie) *chsd ldrs: rdn along over 4f out: sn wknd* **8/1**

00/0 **12** 42 **Super Smile (IRE)**[34] 3946 4-8-2 **45**.............................. AndrewMullen 4
(Michael Appleby) *t.k.h: chsd ldng trio: rdn along over 4f out: sn wknd* **40/1**

3m 37.46s (9.16) **Going Correction** 0.0s/f (Good) **12** Ran SP% **122.9**
Speed ratings (Par 101): **77,76,76,75,75 73,72,70,70,68 66,45**
Tote Swingers 1&2 £1.50, 2&3 £3.80, 1&3 £7.80 CSF £13.71 CT £52.76 TOTE £3.60: £1.70, £1.80, £2.00; EX 12.70.
Owner Killarney Glen **Bred** Darley **Trained** Newmarket, Suffolk

FOCUS
It was touch and go whether this could be run at all in the descending gloom. After a sedate early pace the tempo gradually increased and in the end it produced a tight finish. The form makes sense rated around the first two.
T/Jkpt: £11,363.40 to a £1 stake. Pool: £184,055.59 - 11.50 winning tickets. T/Plt: £58.80 to a £1 stake. Pool: £66,180.06 - 820.66 winning tickets. T/Qpdt: £10.70 to a £1 stake. Pool: £6,676.88 - 456.90 winning tickets. JR

4927 WOLVERHAMPTON (A.W) (L-H)
Monday, August 13

OFFICIAL GOING: Standard
Wind: light across Weather: overcast

5173 HOLIDAY INN WOLVERHAMPTON APPRENTICE H'CAP 2m 119y(P)
5:40 (5:40) (Class 6) (0-65,60) 4-Y-0+ **£1,704** (£503; £251) **Stalls** Low

Form RPR

1404 **1** **Corvette**[9] 4831 4-9-10 **60**.. TimClark 6 65
(Michael Appleby) *sn trcking ldrs: chal 3f out: led over 1f out: hld on towards fin* **11/4**[2]

4046 **2** ½ **Hoar Frost**[7] 4867 7-8-9 **45**...(p) GemmaTutty 2 49
(Karen Tutty) *hld up in last: hdwy over 5f out: sn chsng ldrs: styd on ins fnl f: no ex towards fin* **15/2**

/5-3 **3** ¾ **Arctic Wings (IRE)**[43] 465 8-8-10 **49**................................ RyanTate[(3)] 5 52
(Tony Carroll) *trckd ldrs: t.k.h: led over 5f out: edgd rt and hdd over 1f out: kpt on same pce last 100yds* **85/40**[1]

0304 **4** 5 **Sacco D'Oro**[10] 4537 6-8-7 **48**..........................(v) JordanNason[(5)] 1 45
(Michael Mullineaux) *dwlt: sn trcking ldrs: drvn 6f out: wknd last 150yds* **3/1**[3]

0/0- **5** 9 **Feeling Peckish (USA)**[23] 1153 8-8-4 **45**...............(t) RichardOld[(5)] 3 31
(Michael Chapman) *led: hdd over 5f out: lost pl over 3f out* **40/1**

30/0 **6** 8 **Mujamead**[121] 366 8-9-0 **57**.................................... AidenBlakemore[(7)] 4 34
(Tony Carroll) *trckd ldrs: t.k.h: effrt over 3f out: sn lost pl* **8/1**

3m 46.26s (4.46) **Going Correction** -0.125s/f (Stan) **6** Ran SP% **109.0**
Speed ratings (Par 101): **84,83,83,81,76 73**
Tote Swingers: 1&2 £3.00, 1&3 £2.20, 2&3 £3.30 CSF £21.28 TOTE £6.30: £2.40, £3.00; EX 17.60.
Owner Tom Cunnane **Bred** Newsells Park Stud **Trained** Danethorpe, Notts

FOCUS
A low-grade handicap run at a steady gallop and in a slow time. The first three pulled clear and the winner came down the centre in the straight. He has tentatively been rated to form.

5174 GREAT OFFERS AT WOLVERHAMPTON-RACECOURSE.CO.UK (S) STKS 1m 4f 50y(P)
6:10 (6:10) (Class 6) 3-Y-0+ **£1,704** (£503; £251) **Stalls** Low

Form RPR

-022 **1** **Locum**[39] 3794 7-9-7 57.. KierenFallon 6 62
(Mark H Tompkins) *trckd ldrs: drvn over 5f out: kpt on to ld last 75yds* **11/4**[1]

2 1 **Goldmadchen (GER)**[19] 4-9-2 78.................................... JamieSpencer 2 55
(Philip Hobbs) *trckd ldr: led over 2f out: hdd ins fnl f: no ex* **10/1**

0663 **3** 2 **Chookie Hamilton**[6] 4912 8-9-2 70..........................(b) GarryWhillans[(5)] 3 57
(Ian Semple) *led: qcknd pce over 5f out: hdd over 2f out: hung rt and fdd fnl f* **11/4**[1]

0060 **4** ¾ **Tartan Gunna**[18] 4499 6-9-7 65.. GrahamLee 8 56
(James Given) *hld up towards rr: drvn over 5f out: one pce fnl 2f: nvr trbld ldrs* **4/1**[2]

5164 **5** ½ **Jordaura**[4] 4987 6-9-12 64... PhillipMakin 7 60
(Gay Kelleway) *hld up in rr: effrt over 3f out: one pce fnl 2f* **9/2**[3]

6 6 **Ilewin Dundee**[41] 6-9-2 0.. LeeNewnes[(5)] 1 46
(Gary Brown) *dwlt: in rr: reminders 5f out: outpcd 4f out: no threat after* **20/1**

7 14 **Rye Park**[126] 6-9-2 0... LiamKeniry 4 18
(J S Moore) *trckd ldrs: drvn 4f out: wknd 2f out: sn bhd: t.o* **33/1**

2m 39.97s (-1.13) **Going Correction** -0.125s/f (Stan) **7** Ran SP% **108.3**
Speed ratings (Par 101): **98,97,96,95,95 91,81**
Tote Swingers: 1&2 £3.00, 1&3 £2.20, 2&3 £3.30 CSF £27.59 TOTE £4.80: £1.70, £5.40; EX 16.90 Trifecta £40.80 Pool: £211.51 - 3.83 winning units..There was no bid for winner. Goldmadchen (GER) was claimed by K. W. Dalgleish for £6,000.
Owner Ray Smith and Partners **Bred** Cheveley Park Stud Ltd **Trained** Newmarket, Suffolk

FOCUS
A mixed bag in an ordinary seller. The gallop was a muddling one and the winner came down the centre. He is worth a bit more at face value, but the time was slow.

5175 LIKE US ON FACEBOOK WOLVERHAMPTON RACECOURSE H'CAP 1f 103y(P)
6:40 (6:41) (Class 6) (0-60,60) 3-Y-0+ **£1,704** (£503; £251) **Stalls** Low

Form RPR

0450 **1** **My Mate Jake (IRE)**[15] 4627 4-9-8 **56**...............................(b) GrahamLee 8 72
(James Given) *trckd ldrs: wnt 2nd over 1f out: led last 150yds: pushed clr: readily* **8/1**

0-51 **2** 4 ½ **Mac Tiernan (IRE)**[28] 4158 5-9-8 **56**.................................... LiamKeniry 6 63
(Ed de Giles) *trckd ldrs: led 3f out: sn drvn clr: hdd and no ex ins fnl f* **3/1**[1]

1456 **3** 1 ½ **King's Road**[25] 4244 7-9-10 **58**..(t) KierenFallon 11 61
(Anabel K Murphy) *mid-div: sn pushed along: hdwy 3f out: kpt on to take 3rd last 100yds* **16/1**

0360 **4** 4 ½ **Avison (IRE)**[31] 4048 4-9-9 **57**.......................................[1] TonyHamilton 13 51
(Richard Fahey) *sn chsng ldrs: one pce fnl 3f* **16/1**

0205 **5** ½ **Harrys Yer Man**[20] 3236 8-9-3 **51**...................................... ShaneKelly 12 44
(Mark Brisbourne) *in rr: hdwy over 2f out: kpt on fnl f* **16/1**

0004 **6** 1 ¾ **Imperial Wave (IRE)**[26] 4214 3-9-0 **56**........................(b) RichardMullen 4 45
(David Lanigan) *chsd ldrs: one pce fnl 3f* **7/2**[2]

1653 **7** ½ **Polar Auroras**[8] 4843 4-9-9 **57**...(t) PhillipMakin 5 45
(Tony Carroll) *hld up towards rr: effrt over 3f out: nvr a factor* **10/1**

-600 **8** 2 ¼ **Bubbly Bounty**[31] 4067 3-8-8 **50**.. LiamJones 7 33
(Alan Bailey) *mid-div: drvn over 3f out: one pce* **40/1**

5000 **9** 5 **Just Five (IRE)**[14] 4643 6-9-10 **58**.................................(v) LukeMorris 2 31
(John Weymes) *chsd ldrs: drvn over 3f out: sn wknd: eased whn bhd ins fnl f* **20/1**

0440 **10** 4 ½ **Athletic**[18] 4490 3-9-4 **60**..(p) FrannyNorton 3 24
(Alan McCabe) *led: hdd 3f out: wknd and eased over 1f out* **11/1**

0500 **11** 70 **Rufus Stone (USA)**[17] 4541 4-9-5 **53**..........................(p) JamieSpencer 9
(Jane Chapple-Hyam) *sn detached last and pushed along: virtually p.u 2f out: eventually completed: t.o* **11/2**[3]

1m 59.15s (-2.55) **Going Correction** -0.125s/f (Stan)
WFA 3 from 4yo+ 8lb **11** Ran SP% **116.0**
Speed ratings (Par 101): **106,102,100,96,96 94,94,92,87,83 21**
Tote Swingers: 1&2 £5.60, 1&3 £44.90, 2&3 £12.90 CSF £31.70 CT £380.56 TOTE £7.00: £2.40, £2.90, £7.50; EX 42.10 TRIFECTA Not won..
Owner Alex Owen **Bred** Crandon Park Stud **Trained** Willoughton, Lincs

FOCUS
A moderate handicap run at a reasonable gallop. The winner was another to race down the centre. He's rated back to something like last year's form.

5176 IRISH STALLION FARMS E B F MAIDEN STKS 5f 216y(P)
7:10 (7:11) (Class 5) 2-Y-0 **£3,137** (£933; £466; £233) **Stalls** Low

Form RPR

0 **1** **Titled Gent**[11] 4730 2-9-3 0.. KierenFallon 9 81+
(Brian Meehan) *trckd ldrs: led 2f out: pushed out: readily* **15/8**[2]

0 **2** 1 ½ **Excuse To Linger**[22] 4362 2-9-3 0... ShaneKelly 5 75
(Jeremy Noseda) *trckd ldrs: trapped on inner over 2f out: chsd wnr over 1f out: no imp* **11/10**[1]

0 **3** 5 **Gravitational (IRE)**[31] 4066 2-9-3 0...................................... GrahamLee 7 59+
(Ed Dunlop) *in tch: hdwy 3f out: tk 3rd 1f out: hung lft and kpt on* **12/1**

0 **4** 4 **Annalova**[15] 4625 2-8-12 0.. TonyHamilton 6 41
(Richard Fahey) *s.i.s: in rr: hdwy over 2f out: kpt on fnl f: too modest 4th nr fin* **50/1**

5 nk **Bapak Sayang (USA)** 2-9-3 0.. PhillipMakin 1 45
(Kevin Ryan) *w ldr: ledover 3f out: hdd 2f out: wknd fnl f* **7/1**[3]

0 **6** hd **Red Eclipse (IRE)**[66] 2892 2-8-12 0................................... FrannyNorton 3 40
(Alan Bailey) *led: hdd over 3f out: wknd appr fnl f* **14/1**

7 32 **Wicked Tara** 2-8-9 0.. RaulDaSilva[(3)] 4
(Frank Sheridan) *dwlt: sn bhd: t.o* **40/1**

1m 14.0s (-1.00) **Going Correction** -0.125s/f (Stan) **7** Ran SP% **113.7**
Speed ratings (Par 94): **101,99,92,87,86 86,43**
Tote Swingers: 1&2 £1.50, 1&3 £4.50, 2&3 £2.40 CSF £4.21 TOTE £2.80: £2.10, £1.10; EX 5.40 Trifecta £22.90 Pool: £273.29 - 8.80 winning units..
Owner Lanesborough **Bred** Whatton Manor Stud **Trained** Manton, Wilts

FOCUS
Little strength in depth but fair form from the two market leaders, who pulled clear in the closing stages. The gallop was a reasonable one and the winner edged towards the far rail in the closing stages.

NOTEBOOK
Titled Gent, who disappointed when favourite on his debut, turned in a much-improved effort on this AW debut. While his Dewhurst entry looks optimistic, he looks sure to win again over this trip or over 7f. (op 13-8 tchd 2-1)
Excuse To Linger, who showed fair form at Ascot on his debut, matched that effort against the well-regarded winner on this AW debut after attracting support. He pulled clear of the remainder and is sure to win a similarly uncompetitive event. (op 11-8 tchd 6-4)
Gravitational(IRE), well beaten over 7f in soft ground on his debut, was no match for the first two but bettered that level back in trip on this AW debut. The return to further should suit and he looks more a nursery type. Official explanation: jockey said colt hung left-handed (op 28-1)
Annalova shaped as though a much stiffer test of stamina would suit in due course and she'll be one to take into nurseries. (op 40-1)
Bapak Sayang(USA), who cost 60,000GBP and who is related to a couple of winners in the US, showed ability before getting tired on this racecourse debut and is entitled to improve for the experience. (op 11-1)
Red Eclipse(IRE) was well beaten in a stronger race (form worked out well) on her debut but showed up for a long way on this AW debut and may do better in nurseries. (op 9-1)
Wicked Tara Official explanation: jockey said filly was slowly away

5177 DOWNLOAD OUR IPHONE APP MAIDEN STKS 5f 20y(P)
7:40 (7:40) (Class 5) 3-4-Y-0 **£2,264** (£673; £336; £168) **Stalls** Low

Form RPR

0 **1** **Havin' A Good Time (IRE)**[53] 3312 3-8-12 0................[1] AndreaAtzeni 4 63+
(Roger Varian) *chsd ldrs: effrt and nt clr run over 1f out: swtchd ins and sn 2nd: styd on to ld post* **5/2**[3]

3064 **2** hd **Asian Trader**[14] 4644 3-9-3 69...(t) LiamJones 6 67
(William Haggas) *trckd ldr: led travelling best over 1f out: rdn and mugged nr line* **9/4**[2]

0226 **3** 3 ¼ **Missile Attack (IRE)**[2] 5087 4-9-1 56......................... GarryWhillans[(5)] 1 58
(Ian Semple) *led: hdd over 1f out: one pce* **2/1**[1]

\- **4** 1 ¼ **My Time** 3-9-3 0.. SeanQuinlan 7 53
(Michael Mullineaux) *s.s: in rr: hdwy over 2f out: kpt on fnl f* **28/1**

0666 **5** ¾ **Too Ambitious**[18] 4489 3-8-12 46...................................... RussKennemore 3 45
(Reg Hollinshead) *chsd ldrs: one pce fnl 2f* **14/1**

0 **6** nse **Stoneacre Hull (IRE)**[56] 3235 3-8-12 0....................... RobbieFitzpatrick 2 45
(Peter Grayson) *mid-div: hdwy over 2f out: kpt on one pce* **40/1**

600 **7** 20 **Mrs Bridges**[33] 3972 3-8-12 45... LiamKeniry 8
(Roger Ingram) *mid-div: lost pl 2f out: eased ins fnl f: t.o* **50/1**

8 2 **My Honychurch** 3-8-9 0.. RaulDaSilva[(3)] 5
(Frank Sheridan) *s.i.s: reminders and sn bhd: t.o 3f out* **18/1**

1m 1.46s (-0.84) **Going Correction** -0.125s/f (Stan)
WFA 3 from 4yo 3lb **8** Ran SP% **112.5**
Speed ratings (Par 103): **101,100,95,93,92 92,60,57**
Tote Swingers: 1&2 £1.20, 1&3 £2.30, 2&3 £1.10 CSF £8.20 TOTE £3.00: £1.10, £1.10, £1.10; EX 8.40 Trifecta £20.30 Pool: £272.61 - 9.90 winning units..
Owner A D Spence **Bred** Twelve Oaks Stud Establishment **Trained** Newmarket, Suffolk

FOCUS
A modest and uncompetitive maiden in which the pace was sound throughout. The winner raced against the far rail in the closing stages. The form is rated around the second.
My Honychurch Official explanation: jockey said filly was slowly away

5178 BOOK TICKETS ONLINE AT WOLVERHAMPTON-RACECOURSE.CO.UK NURSERY 7f 32y(P)
8:10 (8:10) (Class 4) (0-80,84) 2-Y-0 **£4,204** (£1,251; £625; £312) **Stalls** High

Form RPR
0024 **1** **Pippy**[15] 4625 2-8-10 **68** RichardKingscote 3 69
(Tom Dascombe) *hld up in last: effrt 3f out: styd on wl last 150yds: led last stride* **13/2**
452 **2** *hd* **Royal Steps (IRE)**[11] 4742 2-9-4 **76** MartinDwyer 1 76
(James Tate) *trckd ldrs: t.k.h: effrt 3f out: led on ins over 1f out: hdd post* **6/4**[1]
030 **3** *hd* **Wellingrove (IRE)**[19] 4472 2-8-11 **69** FrannyNorton 2 69
(Mark Johnston) *led: increased pce over 3f out: swung wd off bnd wl over 1f out: sn hdd: edgd lft and rallied last 50yds: jst hld* **9/4**[2]
3304 **4** *2 3/4* **Effie B**[9] 4820 2-9-7 **79** MatthewDavies 4 72
(Mick Channon) *w ldr: drvn 3f out: one pce over 1f out* **3/1**[3]
1m 28.91s (-0.69) **Going Correction** -0.125s/f (Stan) **4 Ran SP% 109.1**
Speed ratings (Par 96): **98,97,97,94**
CSF £16.67 TOTE £15.10; EX 17.40.
Owner Mr & Mrs W Rooney **Bred** Cranford Bloodstock-Houghton Bloodstock **Trained** Malpas, Cheshire

FOCUS
A fair, tight nursery run at an ordinary gallop. The winner came down the centre in the straight and can probably improve again.
NOTEBOOK
Pippy proved well suited by the step up to this trip and turned in his best effort to get off the mark on this AW debut. A stronger overall gallop would have suited and, given he's unlikely to be raised much for this, may well be capable of better. (op 6-1 tchd 11-2)
Royal Steps(IRE), switched to Polytrack for her AW debut, ran as well as she ever has and is sure to win a race, though she'll have to settle better than she did here if she is to progress. (tchd 11-8)
Wellingrove(IRE) didn't help his chance by racing freely or hanging but he posted an improved effort on this AW debut and may do better as he matures. (op 7-2)
Effie B, the most experienced member of this field, didn't improve for the return to this trip in the anticipated manner on this nursery debut. The drop back to 6f in a more truly run race may suit best but she may not have much in hand from her current mark. (op 9-4)

5179 BOOK NOW FOR CHRISTMAS H'CAP 7f 32y(P)
8:40 (8:43) (Class 5) (0-70,69) 3-Y-0+ **£2,264** (£673; £336; £168) **Stalls** High

Form RPR
4433 **1** **Satwa Laird**[5] 4939 6-9-12 **69** HayleyTurner 11 79
(Conor Dore) *chsd ldrs: effrt and swtchd ins wl over 1f out: led last 75yds: hld on towards fin* **5/2**[1]
4346 **2** *nk* **Unlimited**[16] 4584 10-9-7 **64** J-PGuillambert 8 73
(Tony Carroll) *chsd ldrs: led over 1f out: hdd ins fnl f: no ex towards fin* **16/1**
1423 **3** *2 3/4* **Know No Fear**[16] 4584 7-9-4 **66** AmyScott[(5)] 7 68
(Alastair Lidderdale) *sn chsng ldrs: styd on same pce fnl f* **4/1**[3]
6005 **4** *3/4* **Yungaburra (IRE)**[6] 4928 8-8-7 **50** (t) FrannyNorton 5 50
(David C Griffiths) *mid-div: effrt over 2f out: kpt on fnl f* **25/1**
0130 **5** *hd* **Monzino (USA)**[10] 4775 4-9-8 **65** (b) RussKennemore 10 64
(Michael Chapman) *s.i.s: sn chsng ldrs: outpcd over 2f out: styd on ins fnl f* **12/1**
0560 **6** *nk* **Whitechapel**[21] 4413 5-9-8 **65** MartinDwyer 4 63
(Daniel Kubler) *rr-div: hdwy over 2f out: kpt on fnl f* **15/2**
3044 **7** *1* **Glenridding**[11] 4747 8-9-11 **68** GrahamLee 12 64
(James Given) *led: hdd over 1f out: wknd ins fnl f* **7/2**[2]
0000 **8** *3 1/4* **Ace Of Spies (IRE)**[14] 4653 7-9-0 **57** LiamKeniry 2 44
(Conor Dore) *trckd ldrs: effrt over 2f out: wknd wl over 1f out* **50/1**
00-0 **9** *3/4* **Mistress Shy**[53] 3317 5-8-4 **50** oh5 (t) DominicFox[(3)] 3 35
(Michael Appleby) *in rr: nvr a factor* **100/1**
0050 **10** *3 1/4* **Fleetwoodsands (IRE)**[4] 4993 5-9-8 **65** (t) RichardKingscote 1 41
(Milton Bradley) *a in rr: bhd fnl 2f* **11/1**
0404 **11** *4 1/2* **Arachnophobia (IRE)**[34] 3943 6-9-3 **60** (v) LukeMorris 9 24
(Martin Bosley) *s.i.s: in rr: bhd fnl 2f* **14/1**
1m 28.39s (-1.21) **Going Correction** -0.125s/f (Stan) **11 Ran SP% 117.9**
Speed ratings (Par 103): **101,100,97,96,96 96,94,91,90,86 81**
Tote Swingers: 1&2 £6.80, 1&3 £3.60, 2&3 £8.20 CSF £45.70 CT £159.48 TOTE £3.70: £1.90, £2.90, £2.00; EX 67.20 Trifecta £358.30 Part won. Pool: £484.20 - 0.78 winning units..
Owner Mrs Jennifer Marsh **Bred** The Policy Setters **Trained** Hubbert's Bridge, Lincs

FOCUS
A moderate handicap run at a reasonable gallop but one in which those held up could never get competitive. The winner raced towards the far rail in the straight. The form seems sound enough.
Fleetwoodsands(IRE) Official explanation: jockey said gelding ran flat
T/Plt: £212.50 to a £1 stake. Pool: £44,975.00 - 154.48 winning tickets. T/Qpdt: £36.00 to a £1 stake. Pool: £6,274.00 - 128.80 winning tickets. WG

5180 - 5183a (Foreign Racing) - See Raceform Interactive

5081 AYR (L-H)
Tuesday, August 14

OFFICIAL GOING: Good to firm (9.3)
Wind: Almost nil Weather: Cloudy

5184 CAPTAIN MORGAN SPICED/IRISH E B F MAIDEN FILLIES' STKS 7f 50y
2:20 (2:20) (Class 4) 2-Y-0 **£4,398** (£1,309; £654; £327) **Stalls** High

Form RPR
1 **Asgardella (IRE)** 2-9-0 0 TonyHamilton 4 73+
(Richard Fahey) *hld up in tch: effrt whn nt clr run over 1f out: styd on wl ins fnl f: led nr fin* **9/2**[3]
2 *nse* **Reggae Star** 2-9-0 0 JoeFanning 5 71
(Mark Johnston) *cl up: led gng wl over 2f out: rdn and hdd ins fnl f: rallied: kpt on wl: jst hld* **14/1**
33 **3** *hd* **Elegant In Silk (USA)**[12] 4742 2-9-0 0 PhillipMakin 2 70
(William Haggas) *dwlt: t.k.h: prom: rdn to ld ins fnl f: pricked ears: idled and hdd nr fin* **7/2**[2]
4 *4* **Al Thumama** 2-9-0 0 AmyRyan 3 60
(Kevin Ryan) *led: rdn and hdd over 2f out: hung lft over 1f out: wknd ins fnl f* **20/1**
4 **5** *1 1/2* **Alwilda**[6] 4946 2-9-0 0 PaulMulrennan 1 56
(Sir Mark Prescott Bt) *trckd ldrs: effrt and rdn over 2f out: wknd fnl f* **8/13**[1]
1m 32.48s (-0.92) **Going Correction** -0.30s/f (Firm) **5 Ran SP% 113.8**
Speed ratings (Par 93): **93,92,92,88,86**
CSF £52.24 TOTE £3.90: £3.00, £6.20; EX 50.70.
Owner Middleham Park Racing XLVII **Bred** Ruskerne Ltd **Trained** Musley Bank, N Yorks

FOCUS
Home bend and both straights moved out 8m and 24yds added to races between 7f & 10f and 66yds to 13f race. Just the five runners in this fillies' maiden and the early pace was steady, but it produced a thrilling finish. The time was slow and the form is rated tentaively through the third.
NOTEBOOK
Asgardella(IRE) was settled in last place, but travelled well. She didn't have much room to play with coming to the last furlong, but proved brave when asked to go through the gap and maintained her run to hit the front right on the line. A 40,000gns half-sister to a 1m Polytrack winner, out of a half-sister to the high-class Magistretti from the family of Damister, she ought to get another furlong at least and should go on from this. (op 5-1)
Reggae Star was ridden to the front over 2f out and battled back gamely after being headed inside the last. Out of a dual 1m2f winner, she started a big price for a debutante from the yard, which suggests that not a great deal was expected, so this was a good initial effort and she ought to improve, especially when put over further. (tchd 12-1)
Elegant In Silk(USA) looked the likely winner when hitting the front down the outside inside the last, but she was worried out of it. She had the advantage of previous experience on her two main rivals and has now finished third in all three starts, so doesn't seem to be progressing. (op 4-1 tchd 10-3)
Al Thumama, a 10,000gns half-sister to a Group 3-placed mare in Italy and a 1m Polytrack winner, out of a 1m4f winner, set the early fractions until done for speed over the last 2f. She looked as though the experience would do her good. (tchd 16-1)
Alwilda finished a promising fourth of 11 on her Kempton debut six days earlier, despite running green, and was sent off at very skinny odds here, but she was the first of the quintet off the bridle and, although a little short of room late on, was well beaten by then. This was very disappointing and perhaps the race came too soon. (op 8-11 tchd 4-5)

5185 JACK DANIELS TENNESSEE HONEY H'CAP 7f 50y
2:50 (2:52) (Class 6) (0-65,64) 3-Y-0+ **£1,704** (£503; £251) **Stalls** High

Form RPR
0024 **1** **Chookie Avon**[11] 4769 5-9-12 **64** (p) JoeFanning 5 75
(Keith Dalgleish) *hld up in midfield: hdwy and shkn up over 1f out: led ins fnl f: rdn out* **6/1**[3]
50-6 **2** *1/2* **Giorgio's Dragon (IRE)**[18] 4553 3-9-1 **59** TonyHamilton 7 67
(Richard Fahey) *t.k.h: led: jnd over 2f out: hdd ins fnl f: kpt on: hld nr fin* **3/1**[1]
0631 **3** *2 1/4* **Star City (IRE)**[27] 4211 3-9-6 **64** (be) PaulMulrennan 9 66
(Michael Dods) *pressed ldr: ev ch over 2f out to over 1f out: kpt on same pce ins fnl f* **7/2**[2]
4505 **4** *nk* **Whats For Pudding (IRE)**[3] 5084 4-8-2 **45** NeilFarley[(5)] 2 48
(Declan Carroll) *trckd ldrs: drvn over 2f out: rallied: one pce ins fnl f* **6/1**[3]
0050 **5** *2 1/4* **Jebel Tara**[3] 5087 7-8-13 **51** (bt) RobertWinston 6 48
(Ian Semple) *t.k.h in rr: rdn and hdwy over 1f out: no imp fnl f* **10/1**
0660 **6** *1 3/4* **Shunkawakhan (IRE)**[3] 5081 9-8-7 **45** (tp) AmyRyan 13 37
(Linda Perratt) *hld up: effrt on outside over 2f out: hung lft: no imp over 1f out* **20/1**
5000 **7** *1/2* **North Central (USA)**[7] 4909 5-9-8 **60** (v[1]) GrahamLee 11 51
(Jim Goldie) *hld up: rdn over 2f out: no imp fnl f* **16/1**
0250 **8** *nk* **Sabratha (IRE)**[3] 5081 4-9-5 **64** PaulNorton[(7)] 14 54
(Linda Perratt) *hld up: pushed along on outside over 2f out: nvr able to chal* **9/1**
6302 **9** *1 3/4* **Morna's Glory**[7] 4913 3-9-3 **61** PaddyAspell 1 35
(Jason Ward) *t.k.h: trckd ldrs tl rdn and wknd over 1f out* **8/1**
-240 **10** *1 3/4* **Carnival Dream**[49] 3460 7-8-8 **46** JamesSullivan 4 27
(Hugh McWilliams) *plld hrd in midfield: struggling 2f out: sn btn* **20/1**
0040 **11** *17* **De Lesseps (USA)**[7] 4911 4-9-0 **55** JulieBurke[(3)] 8
(Alan Berry) *t.k.h: hld up in tch: struggling over 2f out: sn btn: eased fnl f* **100/1**
1m 31.12s (-2.28) **Going Correction** -0.30s/f (Firm)
WFA 3 from 4yo+ 6lb **11 Ran SP% 122.4**
Speed ratings (Par 101): **101,100,97,97,94 92,92,92,90,88 68**
toteswingers 1&2 £6.80, 2&3 £5.70, 1&3 £6.60 CSF £24.90 CT £75.55 TOTE £7.00: £3.10, £2.10, £1.10; EX 31.90 Trifecta £146.60 Pool: £368.53 - 1.86 winning units..
Owner Gordon McDowall **Bred** D And J Raeburn **Trained** Carluke, S Lanarks

FOCUS
A moderate handicap in which few got into the race from off the pace. The form makes sense though.

5186 TENNENT'S LAGER H'CAP 1m
3:20 (3:24) (Class 3) (0-90,89) 3-Y-0+ **£6,663** (£1,982; £990; £495) **Stalls** Low

Form RPR
-300 **1** **Wannabe King**[10] 4828 6-9-1 **83** (v) JordanNason[(7)] 4 95
(Geoffrey Harker) *in tch: stdy hdwy to ld over 1f out: edgd lft ins fnl f: pushed out* **20/1**
3000 **2** *2 1/4* **Crown Counsel (IRE)**[10] 4828 4-9-8 **83** JoeFanning 2 90
(Mark Johnston) *chsd ldr: effrt over 2f out: wnt 2nd ins fnl f: could nt rch wnr* **5/1**[2]
4250 **3** *1 3/4* **Toto Skyllachy**[10] 4828 7-9-10 **85** DanielTudhope 8 88
(David O'Meara) *led: rdn over 2f out: hdd over 1f out: one pce and lost 2nd ins fnl f* **12/1**
2023 **4** *shd* **Santefisio**[5] 5004 6-9-13 **88** (b) PaulMulrennan 7 91+
(Keith Dalgleish) *t.k.h: hld up: hdwy over 2f out: kpt on fnl f: could nt rch prom rrs* **7/1**
4330 **5** *1 1/4* **Shamdarley (IRE)**[14] 4689 4-9-5 **80** PhillipMakin 10 80+
(Michael Dods) *hld up: rdn over 2f out: hdwy over 1f out: kpt on: nvr able to chal* **9/2**[1]
1653 **6** *3/4* **Beckermet (IRE)**[8] 4880 10-9-12 **87** JamesSullivan 9 85
(Ruth Carr) *hld up in midfield: effrt over 2f out: no imp fnl f* **16/1**
1135 **7** *4 1/2* **Eastward Ho**[6] 4954 4-8-9 **70** RobertWinston 1 58
(Jason Ward) *cl up tl rdn: edgd rt and wknd 2f out* **5/1**[2]
6264 **8** *hd* **Blues Jazz**[8] 4868 6-9-4 **79** PJMcDonald 11 66
(Ian Semple) *midfield: drvn and outpcd over 2f out: sn btn* **14/1**
0003 **9** *1/2* **Take It To The Max**[18] 4557 5-9-7 **89** GeorgeChaloner[(7)] 12 75
(Richard Fahey) *slowly away and rrd s: t.k.h: hld up on outside: rdn over 2f out: sn btn* **13/2**[3]
1000 **10** *9* **Northern Fling**[24] 4317 8-8-10 **71** GrahamLee 5 37
(Jim Goldie) *hld up: rdn over 2f out: sn btn* **25/1**
0600 **11** *40* **Dhaular Dhar (IRE)**[10] 4795 10-8-9 **75** NeilFarley[(5)] 6
(Jim Goldie) *s.i.s: hld up: struggling over 3f out: sn btn: t.o* **25/1**
1m 38.82s (-4.98) **Going Correction** -0.30s/f (Firm) **11 Ran SP% 110.0**
Speed ratings (Par 107): **112,109,108,107,106 105,101,101,100,91 51**
toteswingers 1&2 £17.40, 2&3 £9.60, 1&3 £22.60 CSF £97.29 CT £950.56 TOTE £34.50: £8.40, £2.80, £3.70; EX 164.30 TRIFECTA Not won..
Owner Mr & Mrs H Nensey, Saif Nensey **Bred** Chippenham Lodge Stud Ltd **Trained** Thirkleby, N Yorks

FOCUS
The best contest on the card by far and they went a decent early gallop, but something of a shock result. This was another race where it proved hard to come from off the pace. The winner was well in on last year's form and is worth a few pounds more at face value.

NOTEBOOK
Wannabe King had been on the downgrade since winning off 12lb higher on his reappearance last season, but this is his ground and he was given a good ride by his apprentice, never being far away until sent for home out in the middle of the track 1f out. If he has truly turned the corner, he will still be off a good mark after being reassessed, but he would be of obvious interest under a penalty. Official explanation: trainer said, regarding apparent improvement in form, that the gelding was suited by the reapplication of a visor
Crown Counsel(IRE) came into this on a losing run of 16, but he's on a good mark now and had hinted at a return to form couple of times in his recent outings. Always close to the pace, he had every chance and things will surely fall right for him before too long. (op 9-2 tchd 4-1)
Toto Skyllachy was back off the same mark as when pipped in the Carlisle Bell last month and he ran another good race from the front, but he remains 3lb above his highest winning mark.
Santefisio, up 3lb after a couple of solid placed efforts in the past fortnight, ran a blinder to finish where he did as he gave himself an awful lot to do in a race where you had to be handy. The only worry is that, despite his consistency, he has only managed to win one of his last 25 starts. (op 5-1)
Shamdarley(IRE) hasn't been at his very best so far this season, but he too can be forgiven this as he found himself stuck in the rear group early and was never getting there in time. (op 6-1)
Beckermet(IRE) was racing over 1m for the first time since his only two previous tries over the trip at Nad Al Sheba early in 2008. He ran creditably, but could never land a blow. (op 22-1)
Eastward Ho has twice been held off this mark since his two wins in June and was up against much better rivals here, but he got himself into a sweat and faded after racing prominently early. (op 7-1 tchd 15-2)
Take It To The Max signalled a return to form when third of 11 in a stronger handicap at York last time, but it's probably best to put a line through this effort as he completely fluffed the start and that proved fatal in this contest. Official explanation: jockey said gelding reared leaving stalls (op 8-1)

5187 COORS LIGHT H'CAP — 1m 2f
3:50 (3:50) (Class 6) (0-60,58) 3-Y-0+ — **£1,704** (£503; £251) **Stalls** Low

Form				RPR
0266	**1**		**Penang Pegasus**[10] 4830 3-8-8 **49** ... RobertWinston 7 (David O'Meara) *prom: effrt whn nt clr run over 2f out: swtchd rt and led over 1f out: edgd lft ins fnl f: pushed out* **9/4**[2]	59
2504	**2**	2	**Hawdyerwheesht**[3] 5085 4-9-12 **58** ... GrahamLee 4 (Jim Goldie) *hld up on ins: hdwy over 2f out: rdn and ev ch over 1f out: kpt on fnl f: could nt rch wnr* **13/8**[1]	64
4-06	**3**	1 ½	**Grand Diamond (IRE)**[11] 4768 8-9-5 **51** ...(p) DanielTudhope 3 (Jim Goldie) *led: rdn and hdd over 1f out: kpt on same pce ins fnl f* **9/1**	54
5605	**4**	5	**Time To Excel**[6] 4958 3-8-0 **48** ...(p) ConnorNichol(7) 1 (Michael Dods) *t.k.h: cl up: rdn and ev ch over 2f out to over 1f out: wknd ins fnl f* **16/1**	41
0540	**5**	nk	**Captain Baldwin**[11] 4771 3-7-13 **45** ...(v) NeilFarley(5) 8 (Jim Goldie) *hld up in tch: drvn and outpcd over 2f out: n.d after* **28/1**	37
5446	**6**	½	**No Time To Cry**[10] 4826 3-8-9 **50** ...(p) PaulMulrennan 5 (Ann Duffield) *pressed ldr: drvn over 3f out: edgd lft and wknd 2f out* **7/1**[3]	41
035/	**7**	14	**Kai Broon (IRE)**[13] 5360 5-9-6 **55** ... LucyAlexander(3) 2 (Lucinda Russell) *s.i.s: hld up: struggling 4f out: sn btn* **10/1**	18
0-00	**8**	4 ½	**Born To Be Achamp (BRZ)**[15] 4656 6-9-3 **49** ... JoeFanning 6 (Geoffrey Harker) *dwlt: hld up: rdn over 3f out: struggling fnl 2f* **14/1**	

2m 9.54s (-2.46) **Going Correction** -0.30s/f (Firm)
WFA 3 from 4yo+ 9lb — **8** Ran SP% **116.5**
Speed ratings (Par 101): **97,95,94,90,89 89,78,74**
toteswingers 1&2 £2.60, 2&3 £4.90, 1&3 £5.10 CSF £6.44 CT £25.65 TOTE £2.70: £1.80, £1.02, £3.30; EX 7.30 Trifecta £43.40 Pool: £490.33 - 8.36 winning units..
Owner Mrs A K H Ooi **Bred** Mrs A K H Ooi **Trained** Nawton, N Yorks

FOCUS
A moderate handicap and not form to dwell on. It is rated around the second.

5188 COCA-COLA H'CAP — 1m 5f 13y
4:20 (4:20) (Class 5) (0-75,75) 3-Y-0+ — **£2,264** (£673; £336; £168) **Stalls** Low

Form				RPR
6045	**1**		**Ukrainian (IRE)**[20] 4466 3-8-9 **68** ...(b1) JoeFanning 3 (Mark Johnston) *chsd ldr: led 3f out: sn rdn: clr whn edgd lft over 1f out: kpt on fnl f: unchal* **3/1**[1]	80+
3233	**2**	3 ¼	**Schmooze (IRE)**[4] 5054 3-7-12 **57** oh1 ... JamesSullivan 5 (Linda Perratt) *hld up in tch: smooth hdwy to chse (clr) wnr over 2f out: rdn over 1f out: kpt on fnl f* **5/1**[3]	64
1410	**3**	5	**La Bacouetteuse (FR)**[17] 4613 7-9-3 **71** ...(p) GeorgeChaloner(7) 6 (Iain Jardine) *hld up: rdn over 3f out: plugged on ins fnl f: nt gng pce of first two* **7/1**	71
-000	**4**	shd	**Sea Change (IRE)**[6] 4955 5-9-4 **65** ... DanielTudhope 1 (Jim Goldie) *hld up: rdn and edgd lft over 3f out: no imp fnl 2f* **16/1**	64
1025	**5**	hd	**Fourth Generation (IRE)**[14] 4674 5-10-0 **75** ...[1] RobertWinston 4 (Alan Swinbank) *hld up: rdn and hdwy over 2f out: sn no imp* **7/2**[2]	74
132	**6**	11	**Raleigh Quay (IRE)**[7] 4910 5-9-8 **69** ... PJMcDonald 8 (Micky Hammond) *chsd ldrs tl rdn and wknd over 2f out* **5/1**[3]	52
6515	**7**	1	**Come Here Yew (IRE)**[10] 4831 4-9-4 **70** ... NeilFarley(5) 7 (Declan Carroll) *led to 3f out: sn rdn and wknd* **11/2**	51

2m 51.29s (-2.71) **Going Correction** -0.30s/f (Firm)
WFA 3 from 4yo+ 12lb — **7** Ran SP% **114.3**
Speed ratings (Par 103): **96,94,90,90,90 83,83**
toteswingers 1&2 £3.50, 2&3 £7.20, 1&3 £4.60 CSF £18.27 CT £95.31 TOTE £4.10: £1.70, £4.50; EX 16.70 Trifecta £416.90 Part won. Pool: £563.50 - 0.84 winning units..
Owner Sheikh Majid Bin Mohammed al Maktoum **Bred** Mrs Fiona McStay **Trained** Middleham Moor, N Yorks

FOCUS
An ordinary staying handicap dominated by the two 3yos, but a true test at the trip. The winner more than matched his AW form.
Fourth Generation(IRE) Official explanation: trainer's rep said gelding was unsuited by the good to firm ground
Raleigh Quay(IRE) Official explanation: jockey said gelding ran flat

5189 COURVOISIER VSOP H'CAP — 6f
4:50 (4:52) (Class 5) (0-75,75) 3-Y-0+ — **£2,264** (£673; £336; £168) **Stalls** Centre

Form				RPR
1032	**1**		**Frequency**[15] 4640 5-9-11 **74** ...(b) JoeFanning 10 (Keith Dalgleish) *hld up in tch: hdwy whn nt clr run briefly over 1f out: led ins fnl f: pushed out* **5/1**	84
33	**2**	1 ½	**Majuro (IRE)**[15] 4657 8-9-12 **75** ... RobbieFitzpatrick 8 (Charles Smith) *led: rdn 2f out: hdd ins fnl f: kpt on same pce* **9/2**[3]	80
/004	**3**	1 ½	**Jinky**[3] 5082 4-9-9 **72** ... PhillipMakin 9 (Linda Perratt) *trckd ldrs: effrt and rdn 2f out: kpt on same pce ins fnl f* **6/1**	72
5001	**4**	2 ¼	**Nasharra (IRE)**[8] 4866 4-9-8 **71** 6ex ...(p) AmyRyan 4 (Kevin Ryan) *dwlt: sn prom: ev ch over 2f out to over 1f out: wknd ins fnl f* **3/1**[1]	64
0352	**5**	½	**Namwahjobo (IRE)**[15] 4638 4-9-11 **74** ...(v) DanielTudhope 2 (Jim Goldie) *bhd: rdn and outpcd 1/2-way: styd on fnl f: nvr able to chal* **10/3**[2]	65
3403	**6**	8	**Rock Canyon (IRE)**[14] 4671 3-8-7 **60** ...(p) PJMcDonald 1 (Linda Perratt) *cl up: rdr lost iron briefly sn after s: rdn and wknd 2f out* **22/1**	26
66-6	**7**	3	**Eilean Mor**[15] 4640 4-8-13 **62** ... DuranFentiman 7 (R Mike Smith) *cl up to 1/2-way: sn struggling* **66/1**	18
0-36	**8**	1 ¾	**Monel**[103] 1799 4-8-2 **56** oh2 ... NeilFarley(5) 3 (Jim Goldie) *missed break: bhd and drvn along: nvr on terms* **14/1**	

1m 10.54s (-1.86) **Going Correction** -0.30s/f (Firm)
WFA 3 from 4yo+ 4lb — **8** Ran SP% **109.7**
Speed ratings (Par 103): **100,98,96,93,92 81,77,75**
toteswingers 1&2 £4.30, 2&3 £5.80, 1&3 £6.20 CSF £24.23 CT £97.10 TOTE £7.70: £3.00, £1.50, £2.40; EX 26.50 Trifecta £151.30 Pool: £478.55 - 2.34 winning units..
Owner Mrs Francesca Mitchell **Bred** Manor Farm Stud (rutland) **Trained** Carluke, S Lanarks

FOCUS
A modest sprint handicap. It was sound run and the second sets the standard.

5190 KOPPARBERG NAKED APPLE H'CAP — 5f
5:25 (5:31) (Class 6) (0-65,65) 3-Y-0+ — **£1,704** (£503; £251) **Stalls** Centre

Form				RPR
6041	**1**		**Imperial Legend (IRE)**[3] 5087 3-8-9 **60** 6ex ...(p) ShirleyTeasdale(7) 5 (David Nicholls) *hmpd s: sn cl up: led 1/2-way: clr whn edgd rt over 1f out: kpt on strly ins fnl f* **11/4**[1]	76
2063	**2**	3 ¾	**Wicked Wilma (IRE)**[6] 4963 8-9-7 **65** ... JulieBurke(3) 11 (Alan Berry) *cl up: effrt and chsd wnr 1/2-way: kpt on fnl f: nt gng pce to chal* **13/2**	68
2344	**3**	1 ¼	**Here Now And Why (IRE)**[22] 4392 5-9-3 **58** ...(p) RobertWinston 7 (Ian Semple) *wnt lft s: in tch: hdwy and rdn 2f out: kpt on same pce fnl f* **5/1**[3]	56
5324	**4**	½	**Distant Sun (USA)**[3] 5087 8-9-0 **55** ...(p) AmyRyan 9 (Linda Perratt) *bhd tl hdwy over 1f out: kpt on fnl f: nrst fin* **6/1**	51+
0551	**5**	1	**Mecca's Team**[18] 4552 4-9-3 **65** ...(p) DavidSimmonson(7) 12 (Michael Dods) *w ldr: drvn 1/2-way: no ex fr over 1f out* **4/1**[2]	58
5446	**6**	½	**Angelo Poliziano**[21] 4430 6-9-8 **63** ...(p) DuranFentiman 6 (George Foster) *hmpd s: towards rr: hdwy over 1f out: kpt on fnl f: nvr able to chal* **11/1**	54
5050	**7**	nk	**Glenlini**[10] 4793 6-8-8 **49** ... JoeFanning 2 (Jim Goldie) *bhd: rdn 1/2-way: kpt on fnl f: nvr able to chal* **14/1**	39
2060	**8**	nk	**Weetentherty**[3] 5082 5-8-13 **54** ...(p) GrahamLee 1 (Linda Perratt) *bhd and sn pushed along: sme late hdwy: nvr on terms* **16/1**	43
0250	**9**	1 ¼	**Saxonette**[15] 4638 4-9-0 **55** ...(p) PJMcDonald 10 (Linda Perratt) *prom: drvn over 2f out: wknd over 1f out* **20/1**	39
-600	**10**	1 ¾	**Running Water**[71] 2748 4-8-5 **46** oh1 ... JamesSullivan 3 (Hugh McWilliams) *in tch: drvn 1/2-way: wknd over 1f out* **80/1**	24
0/6	**11**	1 ¼	**The Bear**[4] 5058 9-9-10 **65** ... PaulMulrennan 8 (Linda Perratt) *led to 1/2-way: rdn and wknd wl over 1f out* **25/1**	38

57.89s (-1.51) **Going Correction** -0.30s/f (Firm)
WFA 3 from 4yo+ 3lb — **11** Ran SP% **121.7**
Speed ratings (Par 101): **100,94,92,91,89 88,88,87,85,83 81**
toteswingers 1&2 £5.40, 2&3 £5.80, 1&3 £2.70 CSF £21.44 CT £89.80 TOTE £2.90: £1.10, £3.20, £1.60; EX 22.00 Trifecta £351.40 Pool: £607.98 - 1.98 winning units..
Owner Pinnacle Mujadil Partnership **Bred** Newlands House Stud **Trained** Sessay, N Yorks

FOCUS
Another moderate sprint handicap in which seven of the 11 runners were sporting cheekpieces. A clear personal best from the winner.
T/Plt: £229.00 to a £1 stake. Pool of £52933.42 - 168.70 winning tickets. T/Qpdt: £84.60 to a £1 stake. Pool of £6303.97 - 55.10 winning tickets. RY

4899 BATH (L-H)
Tuesday, August 14

OFFICIAL GOING: Good (good to soft in places; 6.6)
Wind: bright and dry Weather: fresh breeze half across

5191 BREEZE RADIO H'CAP — 5f 161y
2:00 (2:00) (Class 6) (0-55,55) 3-Y-0+ — **£1,617** (£481; £240; £120) **Stalls** Centre

Form				RPR
2302	**1**		**Kyllachy Storm**[7] 4902 8-9-0 **55** ... PhilipPrince(7) 10 (Ron Hodges) *mid-div: pushed along and hdwy 2f out: led fnl 130yds: r.o wl: pushed out* **7/2**[1]	64
0003	**2**	1 ¼	**Botanist**[7] 4929 5-9-1 **49** ...(be) LiamKeniry 7 (Milton Bradley) *stdd s: sn in tch: rdn to chse ldr over 1f out: ev ch briefly fnl 130yds: kpt on same pce* **14/1**	54
060-	**3**	½	**Till Dawn (IRE)**[39] 3836 4-8-13 **47** ... JimmyFortune 17 (Rodger Sweeney, Ire) *hld up towards rr: rdn over 2f out: stdy prog over 1f out: styd on fnl f: wnt 3rd towards fin* **7/1**	50
2643	**4**	1	**Gala Spirit (IRE)**[15] 4656 5-9-3 **51** ...(p) ShaneKelly 13 (Michael Wigham) *mid-div: rdn over 2f out: styd on ins fnl f: wnt 4th towards fin* **5/1**[2]	51
1503	**5**	1	**Almaty Express**[7] 4928 10-9-3 **51** ...(b) ChrisCatlin 6 (John Weymes) *led: rdn 2f out: hdd fnl 130yds: no ex* **12/1**	48
5345	**6**	1 ½	**Trade Centre**[7] 4902 7-8-6 **47** ... DanielMuscutt(7) 12 (Milton Bradley) *trckd ldrs: rdn over 2f out: sn one pce* **11/2**[3]	39
025	**7**	3 ¼	**Brandywell Boy (IRE)**[19] 4492 9-9-1 **49** ... DarryllHolland 16 (Dominic Ffrench Davis) *towards rr: sme late prog: nvr a danger* **8/1**	30
064	**8**	nk	**Decider (USA)**[8] 4885 9-8-8 **47** ...(b) DarrenEgan(5) 2 (Ronald Harris) *wnt to s early: trckd ldr: rdn over 2f out: wknd over 1f out* **16/1**	27
00	**9**	1	**London Avenue (IRE)**[26] 4236 4-8-7 **46** oh1 ... CharlesBishop(5) 14 (Neil Mulholland) *s.i.s: chsd ldrs after 1f: rdn over 2f out: wknd over 1f out* **40/1**	23
600-	**10**	4 ½	**Gwilym (GER)**[412] 3512 9-9-7 **55** ...(p) AdamKirby 11 (Tony Newcombe) *pushed along whn short of room briefly wl over 2f out: a in rr* **25/1**	17

403 **11** *dist* **Copper Falls**[6] 4937 3-9-0 **52** .... KirstyMilczarek 9
(Brendan Powell) *wnt to s early: ref to leave stalls and missed break completely: cantered bk: t.o* **6/1**

1m 12.26s (1.06) **Going Correction** +0.025s/f (Good)
WFA 3 from 4yo+ 4lb **11** Ran SP% **118.7**
Speed ratings (Par 101): **93,91,90,89,88 86,81,81,79,73**
toteswingers 1&2 £11.70, 2&3 £23.60, 1&3 £6.80 CSF £55.86 CT £338.02 TOTE £4.30: £1.60, £2.90, £3.00; EX 61.70.
Owner Mrs Angela Hart **Bred** Sir Eric Parker **Trained** Charlton Mackrell, Somerset

FOCUS
The winning jockey in the first described it as "lovely ground, just on the good side of soft" and the time for the opener was 2.46sec slower than standard, confirming that the ground wasn't riding fast. This low-grade sprint was rendered less competitive by half a dozen non-runners and the recalcitrance of Copper Falls. The form is straightforward. Races utilising bottom bend increased in distance by about 12.5yds.

5192 WINNING CONNECTIONS CLUB MAIDEN AUCTION STKS 5f 161y
2:30 (2:31) (Class 5) 2-Y-O **£2,264** (£673; £336; £168) **Stalls** Centre

Form RPR
1 **Alcando (IRE)** 2-8-11 0 .... ShaneKelly 2 74+
(Denis Coakley) *trckd ldr: sltly hmpd after 1f: led over 1f out: r.o wl: pushed out* **3/1**[2]
2 *2 ¾* **Miss Mocca** 2-8-3 0 .... AmyScott(5) 5 62
(Ian Wood) *chsd ldrs: upsides 3f out: sn rdn: kpt on same pce fnl f* **14/1**
426 **3** *¾* **Kodatish (IRE)**[12] 4730 2-8-11 73 .... DarrenEgan(5) 1 67
(Ronald Harris) *hung rt thrght: led: rdn and hdd over 1f out: drifted to stands' side rails: kpt on same pce* **5/2**[1]
05 **4** *nk* **Sarahmanda**[7] 4899 2-8-4 0 .... JohnFahy 6 54
(Peter Makin) *trckd ldrs: rdn over 2f out: kpt on same pce* **9/1**
5 *1 ¾* **Beam Of Light** 2-8-1 0 .... LeonnaMayor(5) 7 51+
(Jamie Osborne) *hld up: rdn and kpt on fnl 2f but nvr gng pce to get on terms* **16/1**
3 **6** *9* **Cashel's Missile (IRE)**[28] 4180 2-8-9 0 .... ChrisCatlin 4 24
(John Spearing) *wnt sltly rt leaving stalls: chsd ldrs: rdn wl over 2f out: wknd over 1f out* **7/2**[3]
400 **7** *2* **Lobelia**[53] 3339 2-8-4 54 .... CathyGannon 3 12
(Brian Meehan) *s.i.s: sn pushed along to rcvr: prom 3f out: rdn sn after: wknd over 1f out* **11/2**

1m 12.04s (0.84) **Going Correction** +0.025s/f (Good) **7** Ran SP% **113.7**
Speed ratings (Par 94): **95,91,90,89,87 75,72**
CSF £41.53 TOTE £4.90: £1.90, £5.50; EX 50.70.
Owner The Good Mixers **Bred** E O'Gorman **Trained** West Ilsley, Berks

FOCUS
A pretty weak maiden with little depth. The winner could possibly do a good deal better.

NOTEBOOK
Alcando(IRE), one of three newcomers in the field, was on top when edging to his right late on. He looked a little green and it's fair to assume he can improve on this with the experience behind him. Nurseries are likely to be the way forward. (op 7-2 tchd 4-1)
Miss Mocca, another debutante, stuck on against the rail late on. Out of a mare who won over 1m2f, she should get a little further. (op 12-1)
Kodatish(IRE) was drawn nearest the inside but hung badly to his right and ended up near the stands' rail. He would have finished much closer had he kept straight, but he is not progressing. Official explanation: jockey said colt hung right (op 9-4 tchd 15-8)
Sarahmanda, without the tongue-tie she wore last time, plugged on for fourth and is now eligible for nurseries. Her yard has had a lean season and is yet to get off the mark with its juveniles. (op 11-1 tchd 12-1)
Beam Of Light, who played up in the preliminaries, soon found herself trailing after veering to her right leaving the stalls. She made late progress without being knocked about and can be expected to improve on this. (op 11-1)
Cashel's Missile(IRE) could not build on a reasonably promising debut effort, racing keenly and soon burning himself out out. (op 9-2)
Lobelia came in for support, but she appeared to have no obvious excuse. (op 7-1)

5193 LANGRIDGE H'CAP 1m 5y
3:00 (3:01) (Class 5) (0-70,70) 3-Y-O+ **£2,264** (£673; £336; £168) **Stalls** Low

Form RPR
1-00 **1** **Cyril The Squirrel**[25] 4295 8-9-4 **60** .... DarryllHolland 5 68+
(Karen George) *squeezed up s: sn trcking ldrs: rdn 2f out: r.o to ld narrowly fnl 40yds: on top at fin* **7/2**[2]
5205 **2** *nk* **Ocean Legend (IRE)**[6] 4939 7-10-0 **70** .... MichaelO'Connell 3 77
(Tony Carroll) *prom: led wl over 2f out: sn rdn: no ex whn hdd fnl 40yds* **5/2**[1]
-000 **3** *7* **Bidable**[18] 4533 8-9-0 **61** .... DarrenEgan(5) 1 52
(Bryn Palling) *wnt to s early: hld up: rdn wl over 2f out: stdy prog over 1f out: styd on but nvr any ch* **9/1**
5065 **4** *1 ¼* **Muhandis (IRE)**[26] 4238 4-9-6 **62** .... ChrisCatlin 6 50
(Nick Littmoden) *cl up: rdn to chse ldng pair wl over 2f out: fdd ent fnl f* **5/1**
-01 **5** *1* **Fire King**[17] 4602 6-9-6 **67** ....(p) BrendanPowell(5) 8 53
(Natalie Lloyd-Beavis) *hld up: rdn 3f out: nvr any imp on ldrs* **9/2**[3]
-550 **6** *1 ¾* **Sweet Secret**[57] 3230 5-9-11 **67** ....(p) AdamKirby 2
(Jeremy Gask) *led for 2f: chsd ldrs: rdn over 3f out: wknd jst over 1f out* **11/2**
0600 **7** *11* **Striking Willow**[71] 2760 4-8-9 **51** oh6 ....(p) CathyGannon 4
(Nikki Evans) *trckd ldrs: led after 2f: rdn and hdd wl over 2f out: wknd over 1f out* **50/1**

1m 43.16s (2.36) **Going Correction** +0.10s/f (Good) **7** Ran SP% **113.0**
Speed ratings (Par 103): **92,91,84,83,82 80,69**
toteswingers 1&2 £2.00, 2&3 £5.20, 1&3 £6.40 CSF £12.38 CT £69.63 TOTE £4.10: £2.00, £2.30; EX 12.40.
Owner R E Baskerville **Bred** R E Baskerville **Trained** Higher Eastington, Devon

FOCUS
They went a reasonable pace in this very modest handicap. The first two came clear and the winner was close to his progressive winter 2010/11 AW form.

5194 BATH BUSINESS AWARDS 2012 NURSERY 5f 11y
3:30 (3:30) (Class 6) (0-65,65) 2-Y-O **£1,617** (£481; £240; £120) **Stalls** Centre

Form RPR
446 **1** **Spray Tan**[48] 3487 2-8-13 **57** .... KirstyMilczarek 4 58
(Tony Carroll) *led for jst over 2f: pressed ldr: rdn wl over 1f out: led narrowly ent fnl f: kpt on gamely* **8/1**
5013 **2** *¾* **Khefyn (IRE)**[6] 4936 2-9-1 **64** .... DarrenEgan(5) 6 63
(Ronald Harris) *trckd ldrs: rdn wl over 1f out: chsd wnr fnl 120yds: kpt on but a being hld* **3/1**[2]
0006 **3** *¾* **Twinwood Star (IRE)**[11] 4767 2-8-4 **48** ow3 .... ChrisCatlin 5 44
(John Weymes) *outpcd in rr: hdwy jst over 1f out: styd on to go 3rd ins fnl f: fin wl* **14/1**
3524 **4** *1 ¾* **Emperor's Daughter**[7] 4927 2-9-0 **58** ....(p) ShaneKelly 1 48
(Tim Pitt) *prom: led wl over 2f out: sn rdn: hdd narrowly ent fnl f: fdd fnl 120yds* **7/2**[3]
404 **5** *3 ¾* **Mixed Message (IRE)**[40] 3776 2-9-4 **62** .... RichardMullen 3 39
(Ed McMahon) *trckd ldrs: rdn wl over 2f out: wknd ins fnl f* **6/4**[1]
6546 **6** *5* **Madam Moreton**[4] 5046 2-7-12 **45** .... RyanPowell(3) 7 3
(George Margarson) *chsd ldrs: rdn over 2f out: wknd ent fnl f* **16/1**

1m 3.7s (1.20) **Going Correction** +0.025s/f (Good) **6** Ran SP% **110.9**
Speed ratings (Par 92): **91,89,88,85,79 71**
toteswingers 1&2 £1.80, 2&3 £5.90, 1&3 £5.00 CSF £31.18 TOTE £8.50: £3.40, £3.60; EX 35.30.
Owner Lady Whent **Bred** Lady Whent **Trained** Cropthorne, Worcs

FOCUS
Not much of a nursery. The second, third and time set the level.

NOTEBOOK
Spray Tan was never far from the pace and she stepped up on her efforts in maiden and claiming company to get off the mark. Presumably another nursery will be next for her, and things will be tougher off her revised mark. (op 7-1)
Khefyn(IRE), the only previous winner in the race, came through for second. He kept straight enough this time but did give the impression he wasn't quite putting it all in. (tchd 7-2)
Twinwood Star(IRE), racing from effectively 6lb wrong, finished quite well for third. She's worth another try at 6f. (op 16-1)
Emperor's Daughter broke well this time and showed good pace, but could not fend off the closers. (tchd 4-1)
Mixed Message(IRE) seemed fairly treated for this handicap debut and things looked in place for a good run, but she did not get the best of breaks and was never travelling with much fluency afterwards. Perhaps she needs 6f after all. (tchd 11-8 and 13-8)

5195 BATH BUILDING SOCIETY H'CAP 5f 11y
4:00 (4:00) (Class 4) (0-80,79) 3-Y-O **£4,528** (£1,347; £673; £336) **Stalls** Centre

Form RPR
1160 **1** **Cats Eyes**[18] 4558 3-9-0 **72** .... ShaneKelly 1 81
(Robert Cowell) *mde all: rdn 2f out: kpt on wl ins fnl f* **5/1**[3]
1502 **2** *1 ¼* **Millibar (IRE)**[5] 4985 3-9-2 **74** ....(p) DarryllHolland 3 78
(Nick Littmoden) *chsd ldrs: rdn whn outpcd over 2f out: styd on fnl f: wnt 2nd fnl 75yds* **5/1**[3]
4051 **3** *¾* **Cockney Fire**[7] 4903 3-9-2 **74** 6ex ....(v) AdamKirby 7 75
(David Evans) *trckd wnr: rdn over 2f out: lost 2nd whn no ex fnl 75yds: jst hld on for 3rd* **5/1**[3]
4642 **4** *shd* **Mister Musicmaster**[11] 4757 3-9-7 **79** .... JamesMillman 5 79
(Rod Millman) *s.i.s: pushed along in last: swtchd lft wl over 1f out: styd on: wnt 4th wl ins fnl f: nvr gng pce to threaten* **7/2**[2]
6503 **5** *1 ½* **Signifer (IRE)**[5] 5020 3-9-4 **76** .... ChrisCatlin 9 71
(Mick Channon) *stdd bk to last pair sn after s: cl enough but nt clrest of runs 2f out: sn rdn: nt gng pce to get involved* **5/1**[3]
241 **6** *3 ¾* **Supreme Quest**[20] 4456 3-9-1 **78** .... BrendanPowell(5) 6 60
(Roger Charlton) *trckd ldrs: rdn 2f out: wknd ent fnl f* **3/1**[1]

1m 2.35s (-0.15) **Going Correction** +0.025s/f (Good) **6** Ran SP% **113.9**
Speed ratings (Par 102): **102,100,98,98,96 90**
toteswingers 1&2 £4.20, 2&3 £5.70, 1&3 £1.90 CSF £29.96 CT £130.37 TOTE £5.30: £2.90, £2.70; EX 22.20.
Owner Manor Farm Stud (rutland) **Bred** Manor Farm Stud & Mrs A J Ralli **Trained** Six Mile Bottom, Cambs

FOCUS
As the prices suggest this was a very competitive handicap, despite the small field. The form looks pretty sound.

5196 WESTERN H'CAP 2m 1f 34y
4:30 (4:30) (Class 6) (0-60,60) 3-Y-O+ **£1,617** (£481; £240; £120) **Stalls** Centre

Form RPR
/5-6 **1** **Knox Overstreet**[128] 1240 4-9-7 **58** .... CharlesBishop(5) 7 66
(Mick Channon) *hld up bhd: rdn and stdy prog fr over 2f out: swtchd rt to chal over 1f out: sn led: styd on wl* **10/1**
3553 **2** *1 ½* **Josie's Dream (IRE)**[7] 4904 4-8-9 **46** .... JemmaMarshall(5) 12 52
(Jo Hughes) *hld up towards rr: stdy hdwy fr 8f out: rdn to chse ldrs over 2f out: led narrowly jst over 1f out: sn hdd: kpt on but no ex* **7/1**[3]
0422 **3** *hd* **Galiotto (IRE)**[42] 3734 6-9-9 **60** ....(v) DarrenEgan(5) 1 66
(Gary Moore) *mid-div: nudged along and c wdst on bnd over 3f out: sn rdn: hdwy 2f out: ev ch ent fnl f: styd on but no ex* **9/2**[2]
0022 **4** *1* **Lucky Diva**[7] 4904 5-9-1 **54** ....(p) JakePayne(7) 6 59
(Bill Turner) *hld up bhd: clr passage on inner and gd hdwy on bnd over 3f out: sn trcking ldrs: rdn 2f out: ev ch ent fnl f: no ex* **2/1**[1]
000 **5** *6* **Scribe (IRE)**[11] 4536 4-9-1 **47** ....[1] AdamKirby 11 45
(David Evans) *mid-div: rdn to chse ldrs 3f out: wknd jst over 1f out* **14/1**
435 **6** *¾* **Dream Catcher (SWE)**[29] 4145 9-9-9 **60** ....(p) BrendanPowell(5) 8 57
(Jonjo O'Neill) *trckd ldrs: rdn to chal over 2f out tl fdd ent fnl f* **8/1**
050- **7** *2 ¾* **Annelko**[356] 5379 5-9-12 **58** .... JimmyFortune 9 54
(Michael Blake) *led for 4f: prom: led 7f out: rdn over 2f out: hdd over 1f out: wknd and eased ins fnl f* **12/1**
0035 **8** *9* **Spinning Waters**[7] 4904 6-9-0 **46** .... KellyHarrison 4 29
(Dai Burchell) *mid-div: rdn over 2f out: wknd over 1f out* **14/1**
0003 **9** *23* **Cookieshake**[15] 4664 4-9-0 **46** oh1 ....(b) KirstyMilczarek 5
(Peter Hiatt) *in tch: led after 4f tl 7f out: rdn 3f out: sn wknd: eased over 1f out* **14/1**
00-5 **10** *13* **Levantera (IRE)**[9] 4844 4-9-6 **57** ....(t) AshleyMorgan(5) 10
(Jo Davis) *trckd ldrs tl over 6f out: sn in rr: eased fr over 1f out* **25/1**
04-0 **11** *dist* **The Composer**[7] 4904 10-9-0 **46** oh1 .... LiamKeniry 3
(Michael Blanshard) *chsd ldrs tl rdn 3f out: wknd qckly: virtually p.u* **40/1**

3m 53.09s (1.19) **Going Correction** +0.10s/f (Good) **11** Ran SP% **118.2**
Speed ratings (Par 101): **101,100,100,99,96 96,95,91,80,74**
toteswingers 1&2 £13.10, 2&3 £4.30, 1&3 £9.40 CSF £78.74 CT £364.64 TOTE £12.70: £3.10, £2.20, £1.90; EX 102.20.
Owner M Channon **Bred** Bearstone Stud **Trained** West Ilsley, Berks

FOCUS
The principals came from the rear in this lowly staying handicap, which was run in a slow time. Ordinary form at best, with the well-in favourite disappointing.

5197 LINDLEY CATERING H'CAP 1m 2f 46y
5:00 (5:01) (Class 5) (0-75,75) 3-Y-O+ **£2,385** (£704; £352) **Stalls** Low

Form RPR
0332 **1** **Highland Duke (IRE)**[25] 4289 3-9-0 **70** .... AdamKirby 5 80+
(Clive Cox) *trckd ldr: pushed along to ld over 2f out: styd on wl ins fnl f: rdn out* **9/4**[1]

2103 **2** 2 ½ **James Pollard (IRE)**[9] 4844 7-9-1 **69**....................(t) RobertWilliams(7) 8 72
(Bernard Llewellyn) *in tch: hdwy 3f out: sn rdn: disp 2nd over 1f out: kpt on same pce fnl f* **8/1**

56 **3** *nk* **Amistress**[20] 4470 4-9-2 **63**.. JimmyFortune 1 65
(Eve Johnson Houghton) *trckd ldrs: rdn over 2f out: disp 2nd over 1f out: kpt on same pce fnl f* **9/2**[2]

4005 **4** *3* **Cool Hand Luke (IRE)**[43] 3711 3-8-1 **60**.....................(t) RyanPowell(3) 7 56
(Ian Williams) *trckd ldrs: rdn over 3f out: one pce fnl 2f* **7/1**[3]

-001 **5** *1 ¼* **Croquembouche (IRE)**[19] 4511 3-9-5 **75**......................... LiamKeniry 2 69
(Ed de Giles) *led: rdn and hdd over 2f out: wknd fnl f* **9/2**[2]

0/03 **6** *½* **Gavi**[25] 4293 6-9-1 **62**.. DarryllHolland 9 55
(Karen George) *stdd s: in last pair: rdn over 3f out: nvr a danger* **10/1**

4000 **7** *1 ¼* **Highlife Dancer**[22] 4411 4-8-12 **59**................................ ChrisCatlin 3 49
(Mick Channon) *hld up in last trio: rdn wl over 2f out: nvr any imp* **10/1**

0630 **8** *2 ½* **Gallego**[9] 4843 10-8-9 **56**... KellyHarrison 6 41
(Richard Price) *stdd s: rdn over 2f out: nvr any imp: a in last* **25/1**

2m 12.87s (1.87) **Going Correction** +0.10s/f (Good)
WFA 3 from 4yo+ 9lb **8** Ran SP% **112.8**
Speed ratings (Par 103): **96,94,93,91,90 89,88,86**
toteswingers 1&2 £3.10, 2&3 £3.60, 1&3 £2.80 CSF £20.45 CT £73.52 TOTE £2.90: £1.10, £2.40, £2.00; EX 17.60.
Owner Highland Thoroughbred Ltd **Bred** Philip Brady **Trained** Lambourn, Berks

FOCUS
A modest handicap run at an ordinary pace. Sound form with the second and third setting the standard.

5198 AVON H'CAP — 1m 3f 144y
5:30 (5:33) (Class 6) (0-55,54) 3-Y-0+ **£1,704** (£503; £251) **Stalls** Low

Form RPR

0/3 **1** **Chapter Nine (IRE)**[6] 4941 6-9-1 **45**................................... LiamKeniry 4 61+
(Seamus Mullins) *s.i.s: bhd: smooth hdwy over 3f out: sat w ldr travelling the bttr fr wl over 2f out: shkn up to ld over 1f out: sn in command: easily* **11/4**[1]

2042 **2** *3 ½* **Lisselan Pleasure (USA)**[6] 4941 5-9-2 **53**...........(t) RobertWilliams(7) 3 60
(Bernard Llewellyn) *hld up towards rr: hdwy over 4f out: led over 2f out: sn rdn: hdd over 1f out: kpt on for clr 2nd but sn hld by wnr* **3/1**[2]

00/0 **3** *5* **Arch Event**[5] 4988 7-8-8 **45**.. DanielMuscutt(7) 5 44
(Bernard Llewellyn) *mid-div: rdn wl over 2f out: styd on same pce wnt 3rd ins fnl f* **16/1**

-050 **4** *1* **Duneen Dream (USA)**[43] 3713 7-9-1 **45**........................ DarryllHolland 9 42
(Nikki Evans) *led: c wd ent st over 3f out: rdn and hdd over 2f out: styd on same pce* **14/1**

040 **5** *9* **Shakespeare Dancer**[29] 4157 3-8-4 **45**.......................... KellyHarrison 2 27
(James Evans) *t.k.h in mid-div: lost pl on bnd over 4f out: nt a danger after* **33/1**

0-05 **6** *1* **Awesome Rock (IRE)**[4] 5037 3-7-13 **45**........................ DarrenEgan(5) 8 25
(Louise Best) *mid-dvision: hdwy 5f out: rdn to chal 3f out: sn btn* **9/2**[3]

0455 **7** *2 ¼* **Armiger**[20] 4457 3-8-2 **46**.. RyanPowell(3) 1 22
(William Muir) *rdn 4f out: a towards rr* **22/1**

0-00 **8** *11* **True Prince (USA)**[56] 3246 3-8-7 **48**..............................(p) SeanLevey 10
(Amanda Perrett) *trckd ldrs: rdn over 3f out: sn wknd* **12/1**

-406 **9** *15* **Indian Blossom**[61] 3080 3-8-11 **52**................................. JohnFahy 11
(Harry Dunlop) *trckd ldrs: rdn over 3f out: wknd over 2f out: t.o* **7/1**

0026 **10** *15* **Femme Royale**[5] 4994 4-9-3 **47**...................................... AdamKirby 7
(Richard Price) *chsd ldrs tl wknd over 3f out: t.o* **9/1**

2m 33.62s (3.02) **Going Correction** +0.10s/f (Good)
WFA 3 from 4yo+ 11lb **10** Ran SP% **119.9**
Speed ratings (Par 101): **93,90,87,86,80 80,78,71,61,51**
toteswingers 1&2 £3.60, 2&3 £10.70, 1&3 £12.50 CSF £11.47 CT £112.78 TOTE £3.10: £1.10, £2.00, £6.70; EX 8.80.
Owner Seamus Mullins **Bred** Mrs M Regan **Trained** Wilsford-Cum-Lake, Wilts

FOCUS
A low-grade handicap run at a reasonable pace, and the field fanned across the track in the home straight. The first two met in a Brighton selling handicap last week. Weak but sound form, with the field strung out.
T/Plt: £1,243.70 to a £1 stake. Pool of £58611.04 - 34.40 winning tickets T/Qpdt: £122.30 to a £1 stake. Pool of £4900.14 - 29.64 winning tickets. TM

4742 NOTTINGHAM (L-H)
Tuesday, August 14

OFFICIAL GOING: Good to firm (8.9)
Wind: Almost nil Weather: fine and sunny

5199 SIMPLY CARTONS COMMERCIAL APPRENTICE H'CAP — 1m 2f 50y
5:20 (5:20) (Class 6) (0-65,64) 4-Y-0+ **£1,617** (£481; £240; £120) **Stalls** Low

Form RPR

1450 **1** **Bold Cross (IRE)**[12] 4722 9-9-8 **62**................................. ThomasBrown 1 69
(Edward Bevan) *hld up and bhd: gd hdwy over 3f out: swtchd lft and trckd ldrs 2f out: swtchd rt and rdn appr fnl f: fin strly to ld nr line* **11/1**

3024 **2** *nk* **Zaplamation (IRE)**[13] 4714 7-9-5 **59**................ WilliamTwiston-Davies 3 65
(John Quinn) *trckd ldrs: hdwy on inner 3f out: led wl over 1f out: sn rdn: hdd and no ex nr line* **4/1**[2]

5-45 **3** *½* **Finch Flyer (IRE)**[16] 3220 5-8-12 **52**.........................(p) NicoleNordblad 7 57
(Aytach Sadik) *trckd ldrs: hdwy 3f out: rdn wl over 1f out: kpt on ins fnl f: nrst fin* **16/1**

1253 **4** *1* **Mighty Clarets (IRE)**[31] 4080 5-9-7 **64**................ JacobButterfield(3) 11 67
(Barry Leavy) *led 3f: led again over 2f out: sn rdn and hdd wl over 1f out: kpt on same pce fnl f* **4/1**[2]

2012 **5** *1* **Honoured (IRE)**[16] 4627 5-9-6 **63**..................................(t) NedCurtis(3) 10 64
(Michael Appleby) *cl up: effrt and ev ch 3f out: rdn 2f out: kpt on same pce fnl f* **9/4**[1]

0-50 **6** *1 ½* **Naledi**[77] 1831 8-8-7 **47**.. DannyBrock 5 45
(Richard Price) *t.k.h: cl up: led after 3f: rdn along 3f out: sn hdd and grad wknd* **28/1**

0633 **7** *1 ½* **Market Puzzle (IRE)**[24] 4349 5-8-7 **47**..............................(p) IanBurns 8 43
(Mark Brisbourne) *hld up: a towards rr* **7/1**[3]

0020 **8** *1* **Black Coffee**[9] 4843 7-9-3 **62**..................................... RobertTart(5) 4 56
(Mark Brisbourne) *hld up: a towards rr* **16/1**

0152 **9** *nk* **Harare**[29] 4138 11-9-7 **64**...(v) GemmaTutty(3) 9 57
(Karen Tutty) *plld hrd: hdwy to chse ldrs after: rdn 4f out: sn wknd* **16/1**

2m 19.51s (7.81) **Going Correction** -0.35s/f (Firm) **9** Ran SP% **112.7**
Speed ratings (Par 101): **54,53,53,52,51 50,49,48,48**
Tote Swingers 1&2 £12.00, 2&3 £11.80, 1&3 £27.20 CSF £53.21 CT £705.14 TOTE £13.70: £2.90, £2.50, £4.50; EX 85.80 TRIFECTA Not won..
Owner E G Bevan **Bred** M Hosokawa **Trained** Ullingswick, H'fords

FOCUS
A low-grade apprentice handicap. With no confirmed front-runner the pace was very steady until the final 3f and as a result several were very keen. The form is rated around the first three.

5200 SIMPLY RACING LTD H'CAP — 1m 6f 15y
5:50 (5:50) (Class 3) (0-90,87) 3-Y-0+ **£6,411** (£1,919; £959; £479) **Stalls** Low

Form RPR

-442 **1** **Gosbeck**[44] 3661 4-9-5 **83**... DaneO'Neill 3 89
(Henry Candy) *trckd ldng pair: smooth hdwy 3f out: led 2f out: rdn clr ent fnl f: styd on* **9/4**[2]

3200 **2** *3 ¼* **Lexington Bay (IRE)**[45] 3625 4-9-8 **86**.......................... BarryMcHugh 5 87+
(Richard Fahey) *trckd ldng pair: effrt on inner 3f out: swtchd rt and rdn 2f out: kpt on fnl f: tk 2nd nr line* **4/1**[3]

-P60 **3** *hd* **Kazbow (IRE)**[17] 4613 6-9-8 **86**.................................... PaulHanagan 2 87
(Chris Grant) *led: rdn along 4f out: hdd 2f out: kpt on same pce: lost 2nd nr line* **10/1**

-330 **4** *44* **Palazzo Bianco**[45] 3625 4-9-7 **85**................................. WilliamBuick 1 24
(John Gosden) *trckd ldr: pushed along 4f out: sn rdn and wknd: sn eased and bhd: t.o: lame bhd* **11/10**[1]

3m 5.01s (-1.29) **Going Correction** -0.35s/f (Firm) **4** Ran SP% **107.5**
Speed ratings (Par 107): **89,87,87,61**
CSF £10.59 TOTE £3.20; EX 10.10 TRIFECTA Cancelled due to number of non-runners..
Owner Major M G Wyatt **Bred** Dunchurch Lodge Stud Co **Trained** Kingston Warren, Oxon

FOCUS
A depleted field on account of the quick ground. The pace was very steady until once in line for home. The form is not rated the most reliable but the winner rates a small personal best.

NOTEBOOK
Gosbeck, the only filly in the line-up, had finished runner-up to a subsequent winner when stepped up to 1m6f at Salisbury. Winner of just one of her nine previous starts, she travelled strongly and had this won in a matter of strides. Eased down in the final 50yds, she should continue to give a good account of herself. (tchd 5-2)
Lexington Bay(IRE), absent since the Northumberland Plate, won three times in 2011. He challenged on the inner 3f out but carried his head high and had to be switched. He took second near the line, but clearly wears a sheepskin noseband for a reason. (op 9-2 tchd 5-1)
Kazbow(IRE), virtually pulled up in two of his three previous starts this time, had finished runner-up from a 4lb higher mark a year ago. He set just a steady pace and though this was better the quick ground and small field suited him. (op 15-2)
Palazzo Bianco, upsides Lexington Bay down the field at Newcastle, doesn't have the smoothest of actions. He was completely tapped for toe when the pace increased and was behind when heavily eased over 2f out. He has something to prove after this. He was later reported to have finished lame on his right hind leg. Official explanation: vet said colt returned lame right-hind (op 6-5 tchd Evens)

5201 E B F SIMPLY CARTONS SALES NOVICE STKS — 6f 15y
6:20 (6:21) (Class 5) 2-Y-0 **£3,234** (£962; £481; £240) **Stalls** High

Form RPR

1 **1** **Flyman**[60] 3123 2-9-5 0.. BarryMcHugh 1 97
(Richard Fahey) *w ldr: t.k.h: led over 2f out: rdn and hdd over 1f out: rdn ins fnl f: kpt on wl to ld nr fin* **5/1**[3]

1 **2** *hd* **Odooj (IRE)**[80] 2469 2-9-5 0... PaulHanagan 2 96
(William Haggas) *led: hdd over 2f out: rdn to ld again over 1f out: drvn ins fnl f: hdd and no ex nr line* **13/2**

120 **3** *2* **Mister Marc (IRE)**[54] 3291 2-9-5 0................................ RichardHughes 4 90
(Richard Hannon) *trckd ldng pair: effrt 2f out: sn rdn and kpt on same pce fnl f* **9/4**[2]

1 **4** *1* **Exceptionelle**[69] 2812 2-9-0 0.. WilliamBuick 3 84
(Roger Varian) *plld hrd: trckd ldng pair: effrt over 2f out: sn rdn and kpt on same pce ent fnl f* **1/1**[1]

1m 12.1s (-2.80) **Going Correction** -0.35s/f (Firm) **4** Ran SP% **110.8**
Speed ratings (Par 94): **104,103,101,99**
CSF £29.92 TOTE £11.30; EX 18.30.
Owner George Murray **Bred** Coln Valley Stud **Trained** Musley Bank, N Yorks

FOCUS
All four previous winners and the first two home had won their only previous starts. Decent form with the first two improving on their previous efforts.

NOTEBOOK
Flyman, who had created a good impression when winning over 5f in soft ground at York in June, was quite keen upsides. After taking charge he had to dig deep to repel the runner-up's renewed challenge. He will be even better with a lead and less firm ground. A step up to seven will not be a problem. (op 9-2 tchd 4-1)
Odooj(IRE), a smart winner at Chester in May, was keen to grab the stands' side rail. He fought back when headed and just missed out at the line. He lost nothing in defeat. (op 9-2 tchd 7-1)
Mister Marc(IRE), who chased home Dawn Approach at Naas, didn't shine in the 5f Norfolk Stakes. Tucked in on the rail behind the leader, he could never land a blow. (op 3-1)
Exceptionelle, the only filly in the line-up, had looked potentially smart when winning first time at Kempton. The next four home have won since and she has been given a Cheveley Park entry. Steadied leaving the stalls, she simply would not settle and folded completely near the line. She will need to learn to settle if she is to live up to expectations. (op 5-4 tchd 10-11)

5202 SIMPLY CARTONS PRODUCTION NURSERY — 6f 15y
6:50 (6:52) (Class 5) (0-75,75) 2-Y-0 **£2,264** (£673; £336; £168) **Stalls** High

Form RPR

2240 **1** **Echion (IRE)**[18] 4526 2-9-4 **72**...................................... RichardHughes 7 76+
(Richard Hannon) *trckd ldrs: hdwy over 2f out: rdn to ld ins fnl f: kpt on* **4/1**[2]

2500 **2** *½* **Ryedale Valley**[18] 4545 2-7-9 **52** oh1.............................. DominicFox(3) 6 54
(Tim Easterby) *led: rdn wl over 1f out: hdd ins fnl f: edgd rt: kpt on* **25/1**

401 **3** *½* **Ziggy's Secret**[16] 4625 2-9-6 **74**.................................... EddieAhern 10 75
(Lucy Wadham) *trckd ldrs: hdwy 2f out: rdn over 1f out: n.m.r ins fnl f: kpt on* **11/4**[1]

430 **4** *hd* **Ighraa (IRE)**[46] 3560 2-9-4 **72**...................................... PaulHanagan 5 71
(Brian Meehan) *cl up: rdn and ev ch over 2f out: drvn and one pce ins fnl f* **11/1**

51 **5** *hd* **Beau Select (IRE)**[52] 3387 2-8-12 **66**............................ AndreaAtzeni 8 65
(Robert Eddery) *trckd ldrs: effrt 2f out: sn swtchd lft and rdn: ev ch tl one pce ins fnl f* **11/2**

3225 **6** *1 ½* **Indian Affair**[10] 4804 2-9-4 **72**...................................... RussKennemore 9 66
(Milton Bradley) *cl up: rdn 2f out: wknd appr fnl f: btn whn n.m.r ins fnl f* **7/1**

0064 **7** *3* **We Are City**[17] 4574 2-8-8 **62**....................................... JamieSpencer 2 47
(Michael Bell) *hld up towards rr: hdwy on outer over 2f out: rdn over 1f out: sn wknd and eased* **9/2**[3]

620 **8** *6* **Man In The Arena**[18] 4539 2-8-11 **65**............................. FrannyNorton 11 32
(Dr Jon Scargill) *a in rr* **25/1**

004 **9** *2* **Our Golden Girl**27 4217 2-8-2 **56**.......................... CathyGannon 3 17
(Mark Usher) *wnt lft s: a in rr* **16/1**
1m 13.45s (-1.45) **Going Correction** -0.35s/f (Firm) **9** Ran SP% **114.6**
Speed ratings (Par 94): **95,94,93,93,93 91,87,79,76**
Tote Swingers 1&2 £10.40, 2&3 £17.60, 1&3 £3.90 CSF £93.93 CT £316.78 TOTE £2.40: £1.10, £9.00, £1.20; EX 90.30 TRIFECTA Not won..
Owner Titan Assets **Bred** Howard Barton Stud **Trained** East Everleigh, Wilts

FOCUS
A nursery run at a steady pace to halfway and little to choose between the first five home at the line. Straightforward form.

NOTEBOOK
Echion(IRE), dropped 3lb on his third start in nursery company, travelled sweetly and in the end scored with a fraction in hand. He should continue to give a good account of himself at this level and a drop back to 5f will not be a problem. (op 7-2 tchd 10-3)
Rydale Valley, 1lb out of the weights, had finished runner-up first time at Southwell. He hasn't progressed since but here under a determined ride kicked for home from the front and at the line only the winner took his measure. That said he looked only third best. (op 33-1)
Ziggy's Secret, off the mark at the 3rd attempt when dropped to 5f at Pontefract, looked unlucky not to at least give the winner more of a race. Tucked in on the inner she met serious traffic problems and was reeling back the first two at the line. She deserves compensation. (op 4-1 tchd 9-2)
Ighraa(IRE), forced to race wide, put a poor effort in maiden company behind her on her nursery debut, but she looks on about the right sort of mark. (tchd 9-1)
Beau Select(IRE), off the mark in a very ordinary 7f maiden at Lingfield, stuck on after being outpaced and needs a stiffer test. (op 4-1)

5203 SIMPLY SPORTS MANAGEMENT H'CAP 6f 15y
7:20 (7:23) (Class 6) (0-60,60) 3-Y-O+ **£1,617** (£481; £240; £120) **Stalls** High

Form RPR
0005 **1** **Amis Reunis**47 3547 3-9-3 **60**.......................... DominicFox(3) 3 66+
(Anthony Carson) *towards rr: swtchd lft to outer and hdwy 2f out: sn rdn: styd on strly ent fnl f: edgd rt and led nr fin* **15/2**3
0-30 **2** *nk* **Aussie Blue (IRE)**74 2675 8-9-9 **59**.......................... MichaelStainton 13 65
(Charles Pogson) *trckd ldr: led wl over 1f out: sn rdn: drvn ins fnl f: hdd and no ex nr fin* **33/1**
-610 **3** *hd* **Trust Fund Babe (IRE)**10 4793 3-9-6 **60**.......................... DavidAllan 12 64
(Tim Easterby) *chsd ldrs: hdwy over 2f out: sn rdn: styd on fnl f: nrst fin* **8/1**
605 **4** *hd* **Loyal N Trusted**5 4993 4-9-7 **57**..........................(p) AndreaAtzeni 8 62+
(Richard Price) *s.i.s: towards rr: hdwy 2f out: chsd ldrs: n.m.r and swtchd lft ins fnl f: kpt on towards fin* **3/1**1
0000 **5** *½* **Jay Bee Blue**10 4815 3-9-6 **60**..........................(t) JamesDoyle 11 62
(Sean Curran) *chsd ldng pair: hdwy wl over 1f out: rdn and ev ch ent fnl f: kpt on* **12/1**
5546 **6** *½* **Ridgeway Sapphire**10 4815 5-8-11 **47**..........................(v) RichardHughes 16 50+
(Mark Usher) *hld up: hdwy over 2f out: sn chsng ldrs: rdn and styng on whn n.m.r ent fnl f: one pce* **11/2**2
0025 **7** *hd* **Sermons Mount (USA)**10 4815 6-9-8 **58**..........................(p) TomMcLaughlin 9 59
(Paul Howling) *in tch: hdwy over 2f out: rdn and ch over 1f out: sn drvn and one pce* **12/1**
0060 **8** *¾* **Dancing Maite**33 3994 7-9-4 **59**..........................(b) MarkCoumbe(5) 14 57
(Roy Bowring) *led: rdn along over 2f out: hdd wl over 1f out: grad wknd* **20/1**
6261 **9** *1* **George Fenton**144 1010 3-8-11 **51**..........................(p) J-PGuillambert 4 45+
(Richard Guest) *towards rr: rdn along 1/2-way: hdwy and n.m.r over 1f out: n.d* **12/1**
000 **10** *2* **Steel City Boy (IRE)**56 3256 9-8-11 **52**.......................... LMcNiff(5) 2 41
(Garry Woodward) *prom: rdn over 2f out: grad wknd* **28/1**
030 **11** *3½* **First Voice (IRE)**39 3809 3-9-5 **59**.......................... RoystonFfrench 15 36
(James Given) *a towards rr* **20/1**
3605 **12** *1¼* **Besty**13 4717 5-9-0 **57**.......................... NedCurtis(7) 10 31
(Paul Midgley) *in tch: rdn along over 2f out: sn wknd* **8/1**
3200 **13** *¾* **Whiteoak Lady (IRE)**24 4332 7-8-12 **55**.......................... GemmaTutty(7) 5 26
(Karen Tutty) *alwars in rr* **16/1**
-000 **14** *20* **Regency Art (IRE)**71 2758 5-9-9 **59**..........................(b) RussKennemore 7
(Milton Bradley) *a in rr: bhd fnl 2f: t.o* **66/1**
1m 12.57s (-2.33) **Going Correction** -0.35s/f (Firm)
WFA 3 from 4yo+ 4lb **14** Ran SP% **120.7**
Speed ratings (Par 101): **101,100,100,100,99 98,98,97,96,93 88,87,86,59**
Tote Swingers 1&2 £49.70, 2&3 £29.20, 1&3 £15.10 CSF £246.59 CT £2101.10 TOTE £10.10: £2.90, £15.90, £2.10; EX 438.30 Trifecta £268.10 Part won. Pool £362.41 - 0.64 winning units..
Owner Peter Alderson & Willie Carson **Bred** Paddock Space **Trained** Newmarket, Suffolk

FOCUS
A rock bottom sprint handicap. They raced in one group towards the stands' side rail and there was little between the first nine at the line. The winner enjoyed a trouble free passage on the outer, but there were traffic problems towards the rail. Ordinary form.
Regency Art(IRE) Official explanation: jockey said gelding felt wrong behind

5204 SIMPLY CARTONS LTD CONDITIONS STKS 5f 13y
7:50 (7:50) (Class 3) 3-Y-O+ **£6,411** (£1,919; £959; £479; £239) **Stalls** High

Form RPR
6053 **1** **Dinkum Diamond (IRE)**25 4299 4-8-11 **103**.......................... CathyGannon 1 103
(Henry Candy) *chsd ldng pair: hdwy wl over 1f out: rdn to challnge ent fnl f: led last 100yds: styd on* **11/2**
003 **2** *½* **Masamah (IRE)**11 4762 6-9-5 **108**.......................... JamieSpencer 5 109
(Kevin Ryan) *led: rdn over 1f out: drvn ins fnl f: hdd and no ex last 100yds* **6/4**1
-556 **3** *1½* **Doctor Parkes**52 3374 6-8-11 **90**.......................... DavidAllan 2 96
(Eric Alston) *cl up: rdn over 1f out: ev ch tl drvn and one pce ins fnl f* **16/1**
1-00 **4** *nk* **Move In Time**72 2745 4-9-0 **101**.......................... PaulHanagan 4 98
(Bryan Smart) *hld up: hdwy on wd outside over 1f out: sn rdn: styd on towards fin* **11/4**2
4350 **5** *2½* **Noble Storm (USA)**11 4762 6-8-11 **103**.......................... RichardHughes 3 86
(Ed McMahon) *chsd ldrs: rdn over 1f out: drvn and wknd ins fnl f* **4/1**3
57.71s (-3.29) **Going Correction** -0.35s/f (Firm) course record **5** Ran SP% **107.9**
Speed ratings (Par 107): **112,111,108,108,104**
CSF £13.72 TOTE £3.30: £3.70, £1.10; EX 15.00.
Owner Eight Star Syndicate **Bred** Ms H W Topping **Trained** Kingston Warren, Oxon

FOCUS
A class 3 sprint and on quick ground the winner lowered a 12-year-old track record. The first three ended up towards the far side.

NOTEBOOK
Dinkum Diamond(IRE), who relishes a fast pace and quick ground, had everything in his favour and seized his chance. (op 9-2)
Masamah(IRE), the 2011 King George winner at Goodwood, had finished third this time. Lumbered with a 5lb penalty he showed all his usual dash and to his credit was coming back for more at the line. He is entitled to have another crack at the Nunthorpe now. (tchd 11-8 and 13-8)
Doctor Parkes ran out of his skin bearing in mind he would have met the winner on 13lb better terms and the runner-up on 10lb better terms in a handicap. Connections will be hoping his mark is unchanged. It was, after all, his 30th career start. (op 25-1)
Move In Time, who was isolated towards the stands' side, had contested a Group 2 in France on his previous start. This was his first outing for ten weeks and he should be sharper next time. (op 9-2 tchd 5-2)
Noble Storm(USA), without a win since May 2011, continues off the boil. At the weights he ought to have reversed Goodwood placings with Masamah but he never threatened. (op 11-4 tchd 5-2)

5205 SIMPLY CARTONS OPERATIONS H'CAP 5f 13y
8:20 (8:20) (Class 5) (0-70,68) 3-Y-O+ **£2,264** (£673; £336; £168) **Stalls** High

Form RPR
4042 **1** **Selfara**21 4420 3-9-7 **68**..........................(bt) JamesDoyle 9 81+
(Roger Charlton) *racd alone stands' rail: prom: lod wl over 1f out: clr ins fnl f* **11/8**1
6446 **2** *3¼* **Pettochside**10 4798 3-9-0 **61**..........................(t) DaneO'Neill 2 60
(Stuart Williams) *chsd ldrs: rdn along 2f out: drvn and kpt on fnl f* **14/1**
0056 **3** *½* **Divertimenti (IRE)**2 5131 8-8-13 **62**..........................(b) MarkCoumbe(5) 7 61
(Roy Bowring) *hmpd s: in tch: rdn wl over 1f out: kpt on fnl f* **11/1**
3146 **4** *hd* **Ice Trooper**11 4784 4-9-9 **67**..........................(p) CathyGannon 8 65
(Linda Stubbs) *chsd ldrs: rdn wl over 1f out: kpt on same pce* **17/2**
0605 **5** *1¼* **Nickel Silver**14 4680 7-9-10 **68**..........................(v) PaulHanagan 3 61
(Bryan Smart) *wnt rt s: led: rdn and hdd wl over 1f out: wknd fnl f* **15/2**3
-103 **6** *3¾* **Bilash**12 4743 5-9-9 **67**.......................... RussKennemore 1 47
(Reg Hollinshead) *in tch: effrt and rdn 2f out: sn no imp* **8/1**
445 **7** *1¼* **Moorhouse Girl**5 5020 5-9-8 **66**.......................... JamieSpencer 4 41
(David Brown) *hmpd s: a bhd* **4/1**2
58.84s (-2.16) **Going Correction** -0.35s/f (Firm) course record
WFA 3 from 4yo+ 3lb **7** Ran SP% **110.5**
Speed ratings (Par 103): **103,97,97,96,94 88,86**
Tote Swingers 1&2 £7.80, 2&3 £16.00, 1&3 £8.10 CSF £20.91 CT £141.94 TOTE £2.40: £1.70, £8.20; EX 25.30 Trifecta £276.80 Part won. Pool £374.14 - 0.10 winning units..
Owner K Abdulla **Bred** Juddmonte Farms Ltd **Trained** Beckhampton, Wilts

FOCUS
A modest sprint handicap. The first three home raced towards the stands' side. The form is taken at face value and the winner is likely to take a hit for this.
Moorhouse Girl Official explanation: jockey said mare suffered interference at start
T/Plt: £1,278.00 to a £1 stake. Pool £36,677.24. 20.95 winning tickets T/Qpdt: £90.70 to a £1 stake. Pool £5,396.6. 44.0 winning tickets JR

5173 WOLVERHAMPTON (A.W) (L-H)
Tuesday, August 14

OFFICIAL GOING: Standard
Wind: Fresh, behind Weather: Cloudy with sunny spells

5206 32REDBET.COM NURSERY 1m 141y(P)
2:10 (2:11) (Class 6) (0-60,60) 2-Y-O **£1,704** (£503; £251) **Stalls** Low

Form RPR
0560 **1** **Myzamour**15 4659 2-8-12 51..........................(b) AndreaAtzeni 3 52
(J S Moore) *a.p: racd keenly: led over 2f out: sn rdn: styd on* **25/1**
006 **2** *nk* **Alpine Mysteries (IRE)**20 4463 2-9-4 57.......................... TedDurcan 10 57
(John Dunlop) *s.i.s: swtchd lft sn after s: hld up: hdwy over 2f out: swtchd rt wl over 1f out: rdn: edgd lft and ev ch ins fnl f: styd on* **6/1**
6506 **3** *1½* **Kingsville**10 4806 2-8-9 48.......................... SilvestreDeSousa 8 45
(Mark Johnston) *prom: chsd ldr over 5f out tl rdn over 2f out: styd on* **17/2**
006 **4** *½* **Tomway**27 4222 2-9-5 58.......................... RichardKingscote 1 53
(Tom Dascombe) *chsd ldrs: rdn over 2f out: styd on same pce ins fnl f* **3/1**1
0606 **5** *hd* **Heliconia**14 4672 2-9-6 59.......................... LukeMorris 4 54
(Sir Mark Prescott Bt) *sn drvn along to chse ldrs: led over 6f out: rdn and hdd over 2f out: styd on* **9/2**2
4020 **6** *1¼* **Sojoum**17 4574 2-9-7 60..........................1 MartinHarley 7 52
(Mick Channon) *hld up: hdwy over 1f out: sn rdn: no ex ins fnl f* **5/1**3
5016 **7** *¾* **Lucy Bee**27 4324 2-9-5 58.......................... AndrewMullen 6 48
(Keith Dalgleish) *prom: rdn over 2f out: styd on same pce fnl f* **7/1**
0600 **8** *¾* **Icanboogie**19 4487 2-8-10 49.......................... FrannyNorton 9 38
(Karen George) *hld up: rdn over 2f out: n.d* **20/1**
6606 **9** *19* **Schottische**29 4152 2-8-6 45.......................... FrankieMcDonald 2
(Derek Haydn Jones) *led: hdd over 6f out: chsd ldrs: rdn over 3f out: wknd wl over 2f out* **20/1**
1m 51.96s (1.46) **Going Correction** 0.0s/f (Stan) **9** Ran SP% **110.5**
Speed ratings (Par 92): **93,92,91,90,90 89,89,88,71**
Tote Swingers 1&2 £22.10, 2&3 £5.90, 1&3 £13.10 CSF £157.00 CT £1343.72 TOTE £21.70: £5.50, £2.30, £2.10; EX 124.50.
Owner Ray Styles **Bred** Easton Park Stud **Trained** Upper Lambourn, Berks
■ Stewards' Enquiry : Andrea Atzeni four-day ban: used whip above permitted level (Aug 28-31)

FOCUS
A weak nursery in which all the runners were stepping up to this trip for the first time. There were few well treated or interesting sorts on view.

NOTEBOOK
Myzamour had been beaten in sellers on her last three starts but, being by Azamour, she would have appreciated this stiffer test of stamina (sire's progeny seem to stay well) and she had enough in the locker to hold on, despite running around a bit in the final furlong. She could well improve again for going 1m2f, but this isn't form to get carried away with. Official explanation: trainer said, regarding apparent improvement in form, that the filly was better suited by the step up in trip and the all-weather surface. (op 16-1)
Alpine Mysteries(IRE), who was the slowest away, came with what looked like a winning challenge in the final half furlong but she just couldn't get by the more experienced winner. This was a step in the right direction, though, and a small race looks within his capabilities. (op 7-1)
Kingsville clearly didn't like soft ground last time but he fared much better here and appeared to see the longer trip out no problem. (op 9-1 tchd 10-1)
Tomway had every chance around the inside, having raced prominently, and had no excuses. This was still a step forward, though, and he doesn't need to improve much more to get off the mark. (op 4-1)
Heliconia is still too green and looks a slow learner at this stage. There is ability there but she looks one for further down the line. (op 5-1 tchd 11-2)

Sojourn travelled well towards the back and was close enough to mount a serious challenge turning in but she didn't really pick up when push came to shove. (op 7-2 tchd 10-3 and 11-2)

5207 £32 BONUS AT 32RED.COM MAIDEN AUCTION STKS 1m 141y(P)
2:40 (2:40) (Class 6) 2-Y-O £1,704 (£503; £251) Stalls Low

Form				RPR
6600	1		**Lea Valley Black**[20] 4450 2-8-12 65 RichardKingscote 3 (Tom Dascombe) *chsd ldr tl over 6f out: remained handy: rdn to go 2nd over 1f out: styd on u.p to ld wl ins fnl f* 5/1	68
44	2	1 1/4	**Just A Pound (IRE)**[6] 4967 2-8-9 0 FrannyNorton 5 (Jo Hughes) *a.p: chsd ldr over 6f out: led over 5f out: hdd 3f out: led again 2f out: rdn and hung lft over 1f out: hdd wl ins fnl f* 4/1[2]	62
	3	hd	**Buckstay (IRE)** 2-9-1 0 JamieSpencer 4 (Peter Chapple-Hyam) *s.s: hld up: rdn over 2f out: r.o ins fnl f: nrst fin* 9/2[3]	68+
	4	3/4	**Rakticate (IRE)** 2-8-4 0 AndreaAtzeni 2 (J S Moore) *prom: rdn over 1f out: styd on same pce fnl f* 16/1	55
0	5	2 3/4	**Sioux Chieftain (IRE)**[17] 4595 2-8-12 0 SilvestreDeSousa 1 (Tim Pitt) *led 3f: chsd ldr tl led again 3f out: rdn and hdd 2f out: no ex fnl f* 3/1[1]	57
	6	4	**Brick Rising** 2-8-12 0 WilliamBuick 6 (Andrew Balding) *mid-div: sn pushed along: rdn and wknd over 2f out* 8/1	48
4456	7	3/4	**Northern Harbour (IRE)**[4] 5061 2-8-12 64 TedDurcan 8 (J S Moore) *hld up: rdn over 2f out: sn wknd* 7/1	47
	8	6	**Canadian Red** 2-8-12 0 StephenCraine 7 (Tom Dascombe) *dwlt: rn green in rr: lost tch fr over 2f out* 12/1	33

1m 51.55s (1.05) **Going Correction** 0.0s/f (Stan) 8 Ran SP% **117.0**
Speed ratings (Par 92): **95,93,93,93,90 87,86,81**
Tote Swingers 1&2 £1.60, 2&3 £3.40, 1&3 £6.00 CSF £25.96 TOTE £3.20: £1.10, £4.50, £1.60; EX 23.20.
Owner London Market Racing Club **Bred** A J Coleing **Trained** Malpas, Cheshire

FOCUS
A pretty weak maiden and the form can be based around the 65-rated winner and the poor time.

NOTEBOOK
Lea Valley Black was having his fifth start. Experience and professionalism probably won him the day, but in the longer term a couple of those in behind might turn out to be better. He had shaped at Catterick (7f) on handicap debut as though he would appreciate going further and he confirmed that here. He looks well worth a try back in handicap-company off this sort of mark, due to being unexposed at the trip. (op 7-2)
Just A Pound(IRE) stepped up on his two runs over 7f and still has scope to do better. Official explanation: jockey said gelding hung left in home straight (op 5-1)
Buckstay(IRE) made a promising debut and is definitely one that can progress past the sort of rating the winner holds. He didn't look to be going anywhere 3f out, but the penny really dropped in the closing stages and he came home strongly. He looks a surefire improver for this experience. (tchd 4-1 and 5-1)
Rakticate(IRE) shaped with promise and is entitled to build on this. (op 18-1 tchd 20-1 and 14-1)
Sioux Chieftain(IRE) displayed quite a pronounced knee action and might be one to do better when he encounters slow turf. (op 6-1)

5208 32RED CASINO MEDIAN AUCTION MAIDEN STKS 1m 4f 50y(P)
3:10 (3:10) (Class 6) 3-4-Y-O £1,704 (£503; £251) Stalls Low

Form				RPR
06	1		**Any Given Dream (IRE)**[45] 3622 3-9-2 0 MartinLane 4 (David Simcock) *chsd ldrs: led over 1f out: sn rdn: swished tail and hung lft: styd on* 7/4[1]	62+
360	2	1 1/2	**Plus Fours (USA)**[16] 4630 3-9-2 62 AndreaAtzeni 5 (Charles Smith) *hld up: hdwy over 2f out: rdn and ev ch over 1f out: kpt on* 4/1	59+
3366	3	4 1/2	**Angel Cake (IRE)**[12] 4744 3-8-11 42 (p) SilvestreDeSousa 3 (Phil McEntee) *led: racd keenly: clr fr over 6f out tl 3f out: rdn and hdd over 1f out: wknd ins fnl f* 7/2[3]	47
0-4	4	4 1/2	**Silken Satinwood (IRE)**[8] 4888 3-8-11 0 WilliamBuick 1 (Peter Chapple-Hyam) *trckd ldr: plld hrd: rdn over 2f out: sn ev ch: wknd fnl f* 11/4[2]	40
0U	5	16	**Cluaindubhloch (IRE)**[8] 4874 4-9-13 0 StephenCraine 2 (Tony Carroll) *prom tl rdn and wknd over 2f out* 66/1	19
	6	40	**Blackamoor Harry** 3-9-2 0 AndrewMullen 6 (Richard Ford) *s.s: hld up: plld hrd: rdn and wknd over 3f out: t.o* 25/1	

2m 41.49s (0.39) **Going Correction** 0.0s/f (Stan)
WFA 3 from 4yo 11lb 6 Ran SP% **110.6**
Speed ratings (Par 101): **98,97,94,91,80 53**
Tote Swingers 1&2 £1.50, 2&3 £2.20, 1&3 £2.30 CSF £8.89 TOTE £2.00: £1.10, £2.60; EX 8.70.
Owner Malcolm Caine & Bob Michaelson **Bred** Edward Nuzum **Trained** Newmarket, Suffolk

FOCUS
A poor maiden with the exposed 42-rated third not beaten far. The winner is rated up 6lb.
Silken Satinwood(IRE) Official explanation: jockey said filly ran too freely

5209 32RED H'CAP 1m 1f 103y(P)
3:40 (3:40) (Class 3) (0-95,95) 3-Y-O £7,115 (£2,117; £1,058; £529) Stalls Low

Form				RPR
5300	1		**Prince Alzain (USA)**[24] 4319 3-9-7 95 JamieSpencer 4 (Gerard Butler) *chsd ldr tl led after 1f: hung rt wl over 1f out: sn rdn: edgd lft ins fnl f: eased towards fin* 4/1[2]	104
50-1	2	2 3/4	**Universal (IRE)**[8] 4879 3-8-11 85 6ex SilvestreDeSousa 3 (Mark Johnston) *led 1f: chsd wnr: rdn over 2f out: hmpd wl over 1f out: hung lft and no ex ins fnl f* 2/5[1]	88
330	3	3 3/4	**Savanna Days (IRE)**[13] 4702 3-8-7 81 MartinHarley 5 (Mick Channon) *hld up: hdwy over 1f out: wknd ins fnl f* 8/1[3]	76
-550	4	7	**Zimira (IRE)**[17] 4608 3-8-10 84 (b[1]) TedDurcan 1 (Ed Dunlop) *chsd ldrs: rdn 2f out: wknd and eased fnl f* 22/1	65

2m 0.56s (-1.14) **Going Correction** 0.0s/f (Stan) 4 Ran SP% **106.9**
Speed ratings (Par 104): **105,102,99,93**
CSF £6.11 TOTE £2.10; EX 7.00.
Owner Asaad Al Banwan **Bred** Dermot Cantillon & Patrick Hayes **Trained** Newmarket, Suffolk

FOCUS
A good little handicap, despite there being just the four runners, but the form is not the most solid. The winner got an easy lead and is better on Polytrack than turf.

NOTEBOOK
Prince Alzain(USA) made it 3-3 at this track in comprehensive style. Although hanging markedly to his right as he came into the straight, taking the runner-up with him, he saw it out well and the runner-up couldn't be described as unlucky. He was, perhaps surprisingly, sent into the lead by Jamie Spencer, where he settled well, and despite his deviation from a true course, he found plenty for pressure. He is a smart performer on this surface. (tchd 5-1)
Universal(IRE), although he might well have been slightly inconvenienced by being taken wide early in the straight by the winner, probably didn't quite match the exploits of his return to action last week. It was always going to be a tough ask just eight days later but still ran well in defeat and remains a colt of some potential. (op 4-7)
Savanna Days(IRE) ran well up to a point but couldn't land a blow in the straight and will find more suitable opportunities. (op 5-1)
Zimira(IRE) was eased off when her chance had gone in the straight, but this was stiill much more encouraging than at York last time. She remains lightly-raced and capable of better. (op 14-1)

5210 32REDPOKER.COM MAIDEN AUCTION FILLIES' STKS 5f 216y(P)
4:10 (4:10) (Class 6) 2-Y-O £1,704 (£503; £251) Stalls Low

Form				RPR
4	1		**Need You Now (IRE)**[7] 4899 2-8-6 0 SilvestreDeSousa 1 (Peter Chapple-Hyam) *sn chsng ldrs: rdn and hung lft fr over 2f out: styd on to ld wl ins fnl f* 4/11[1]	62
000	2	1/2	**Hawsies Dream**[10] 4818 2-7-11 45 NatashaEaton(7) 3 (Alan Bailey) *chsd ldr tl led wl over 1f out: sn rdn and edgd lft: hdd wl ins fnl f* 20/1[3]	58
43	3	5	**Scoobys Girl (IRE)**[14] 4681 2-8-6 0 FrankieMcDonald 4 (Daniel Mark Loughnane) *prom: racd keenly: rdn over 2f out: sn outpcd* 25/1	44
2223	4	3/4	**Throwing Roses**[49] 3457 2-8-4 67 PatrickMathers 2 (Ollie Pears) *led: rdn and hdd wl over 1f out: wknd fnl f* 3/1[2]	40

1m 15.74s (0.74) **Going Correction** 0.0s/f (Stan) 4 Ran SP% **106.9**
Speed ratings (Par 89): **95,94,87,86**
CSF £8.32 TOTE £1.50; EX 8.00.
Owner Franconson Partners **Bred** John M Weld **Trained** Newmarket, Suffolk

FOCUS
The winner did not really impress in winning a weak race.

NOTEBOOK
Need You Now(IRE) faced a penalty kick on paper, but she made very hard work of it and almost threw it away. She was hanging and lugging all the way up the straight and only just managed to get up and collar the 45-rated runner-up. On the plus side, she did pretty much everything wrong and still won, whereas the runner-up did everything right and was still beaten. Highly regarded, she is much better than she was able to show here and it's still a learning curve for her. (tchd 2-5)
Hawsies Dream posted easily her best run so far and the drop in class and switch to Polytrack showed her in a much more favourable light. She is always going to be vulnerable in maiden company, though. (op 14-1)
Scoobys Girl(IRE) probably showed marginal improvement but that isn't saying much given the standard of her first two runs. Official explanation: jockey said filly hung right-handed on bend (op 20-1)
Throwing Roses is becoming disappointing. (tchd 10-3)

5211 32RED.COM H'CAP 1m 5f 194y(P)
4:40 (4:40) (Class 4) (0-80,81) 3-Y-O+ £4,204 (£1,251; £625; £312) Stalls Low

Form				RPR
2134	1		**Venegazzu (IRE)**[17] 4601 3-8-13 77 (v) JamieSpencer 4 (Peter Chapple-Hyam) *hld up in tch: swtchd rt ins fnl f: r.o to ld nr fin* 6/4[1]	86
-001	2	nk	**Porgy**[8] 4884 7-9-13 81 6ex (b) PaulPickard(3) 3 (Brian Ellison) *hld up: hdwy on outer over 2f out: led ins fnl f: edgd lft: hdd nr fin* 3/1[3]	89
2145	3	1/2	**Enery (IRE)**[10] 4796 3-9-1 79 SilvestreDeSousa 1 (Mark Johnston) *chsd ldr: shkn up over 2f out: rdn to ld over 1f out: edgd lft and hdd ins fnl f: kpt on* 5/2[2]	86
6600	4	2 1/4	**Sherman McCoy**[12] 4733 6-9-6 71 TedDurcan 5 (Rod Millman) *set stdy pce tl qcknd over 3f out: hdd over 1f out: styng on same pce whn n.m.r ins fnl f: eased* 16/1	76
0002	5	3/4	**Cape Safari (IRE)**[8] 4884 3-8-3 74 (p) NatashaEaton(7) 2 (Alan Bailey) *chsd ldrs: pushed along over 2f out: no ex ins fnl f* 9/1	77

3m 5.65s (-0.35) **Going Correction** 0.0s/f (Stan)
WFA 3 from 5yo+ 13lb 5 Ran SP% **109.5**
Speed ratings (Par 105): **101,100,100,99,98**
CSF £6.22 TOTE £3.00: £1.40, £4.80; EX 6.40.
Owner Eledy Srl **Bred** Pat And Mrs O'Donovan **Trained** Newmarket, Suffolk

FOCUS
A competitive little heat but the pace was steady and all five runners had every chance at the top of the straight. Muddling form which is perhaps not sound.

5212 32REDBINGO.COM H'CAP 1m 141y(P)
5:10 (5:10) (Class 6) (0-55,54) 3-Y-O+ £1,704 (£503; £251) Stalls Low

Form				RPR
4336	1		**Avon Supreme**[49] 3470 4-8-8 48 NatashaEaton(7) 4 (Gay Kelleway) *a.p: pushed along over 2f out: r.o to ld wl ins fnl f: jst hld on* 5/1[2]	54
0-40	2	nse	**Roman Senate (IRE)**[11] 4754 3-8-8 49 (tp) MartinLane 3 (Martin Bosley) *hld up: rdn over 1f out: r.o wl ins fnl f: jst failed* 10/1	55
0565	3	1	**Flamborough Breeze**[15] 4650 3-8-11 52 (bt[1]) TedDurcan 11 (Ed Vaughan) *chsd ldr tl led over 1f out: rdn and hdd wl ins fnl f* 6/1	56
04	4	1 3/4	**Stag Hill (IRE)**[7] 4932 3-8-12 53 SilvestreDeSousa 9 (Sylvester Kirk) *prom: rdn over 2f out: styd on same pce fnl f* 5/2[1]	53
4600	5	1 3/4	**Princess Gail**[8] 4890 4-8-13 49 RyanClark(3) 7 (Mark Brisbourne) *s.i.s: hld up: racd keenly: hdwy over 4f out: rdn over 2f out: styd on same pce fnl f* 11/2[3]	45
0030	6	nk	**Godwit**[28] 4193 4-8-5 45 JoshBaudains(7) 1 (Eugene Stanford) *chsd ldrs: rdn over 2f out: styd on same pce fnl f* 9/1	40
-0	7	1	**Echo Knight (IRE)**[223] 38 3-8-13 54 MartinHarley 10 (C Moore, Ire) *led: rdn and hdd over 1f out: no ex ins fnl f* 7/1	47
0000	8	2 1/4	**Can Do Les (IRE)**[7] 4900 3-8-1 45 (b) SimonPearce(3) 5 (Richard Phillips) *hld up: rdn over 3f out: nvr on terms* 40/1	33
000	9	2 3/4	**Blackthorn Stick (IRE)**[47] 3539 3-8-4 45 FrankieMcDonald 6 (John Butler) *hld up: pushed along over 5f out: nvr on terms* 25/1	26
005-	10	3 1/2	**Blackamoor Zara**[287] 7210 3-8-4 45 AndrewMullen 8 (Richard Ford) *prom: racd keenly: rdn over 2f out: wknd over 1f out* 25/1	18

1m 51.52s (1.02) **Going Correction** 0.0s/f (Stan)
WFA 3 from 4yo 8lb 10 Ran SP% **116.6**
Speed ratings (Par 101): **95,94,94,92,90 90,89,87,85,82**
Tote Swingers 1&2 £8.00, 2&3 £7.80, 1&3 £4.40 CSF £52.68 CT £314.68 TOTE £4.60: £1.50, £3.80, £2.50; EX 75.30.
Owner Brian C Oakley **Bred** Catridge Farm Stud And Mrs J Hall **Trained** Exning, Suffolk

FOCUS
A poor-quality handicap in which the first four were all maidens coming into it. The gallop looked reasonable and the finish was dominated by two horses who came from off the pace. The winner is rated to the balance of this year's form.
T/Plt: £191.80 to a £1 stake. Pool of £39596.33 - 150.64 winning tickets. T/Qpdt: £24.70 to a £1 stake. Pool of £3887.26 - 116.25 winning tickets. CR

5016 YARMOUTH (L-H)

Tuesday, August 14

OFFICIAL GOING: Good to firm (7.4)

Wind: Light, against Weather: dry

5213 BRITISH STALLION STUDS SUPPORTING BRITISH RACING E B F MEDIAN AUCTION MAIDEN STKS 6f 3y

5:05 (5:05) (Class 6) 2-Y-O £2,587 (£770; £384; £192) Stalls Centre

Form RPR

366 1 **Prince Regal**[14] 4688 2-8-10 78 MichaelJMMurphy(7) 2 75
(Alan Jarvis) *stdd s: hld up in tch: hdwy over 2f out: effrt and hung lft over 1f out: led 1f out: in command ins fnl f: kpt on wl* 5/4[1]

2 1 ½ **Speedfit Boy (IRE)** 2-9-3 0 TomQueally 1 71+
(George Margarson) *rn green and pushed along early: in tch: rdn and outpcd wl over 1f out: swtchd rt and rallied 1f out: styd on wl to go 2nd towards fin: no threat to wnr* 10/1

3 1 **Ostralegus** 2-9-3 0 FrederikTylicki 6 68+
(Richard Fahey) *chsd ldrs tl jnd ldr 4f out: led 2f out: sn rdn: hdd 1f out: styd on same pce: lost 2nd towards fin* 3/1[2]

05 4 8 **Silk Fairy (IRE)**[6] 4967 2-8-12 0 WilliamCarson 3 39
(Noel Quinlan) *in tch: rdn and effrt over 2f out: drvn and btn over 1f out: fdd fnl f* 28/1

46 5 ½ **Oscars Journey**[18] 4539 2-9-3 0 RyanMoore 5 42
(J R Jenkins) *chsd ldr tl lft in ld 4f out: rdn and hdd 2f out: btn ent fnl f: fdd* 4/1[3]

6300 6 27 **Strong Conviction**[11] 4763 2-9-3 75 (v) SamHitchcott 4
(Mick Channon) *rein broke sn after s: led: edgd to far rail and hdd 4f out: dropped out and sn bhd: t.o over 1f out* 9/1

1m 14.9s (0.50) **Going Correction** +0.075s/f (Good) 6 Ran SP% **112.0**

Speed ratings (Par 92): **99,97,95,85,84 48**

Tote Swingers 1&2 £2.10, 2&3 £4.70, 1&3 £1.20 CSF £14.84 TOTE £2.00: £1.40, £2.50; EX 8.50.

Owner T&J Partnership **Bred** Mrs Ann Jarvis **Trained** Twyford, Bucks

FOCUS

The main action unsurprisingly developed down the centre of the track in this modest juvenile maiden and the form should work out. The winner is rated to his mark.

NOTEBOOK

Prince Regal took advantage of the drop in class and shed his maiden tag at the fourth time of asking. His previous experience was a notable asset, but he looks well up to his official mark of 78 and should make his presence felt in nurseries when getting similarly quick ground. (op 6-5 tchd 11-10 and 11-8)

Speedfit Boy(IRE) ◆ is from a good family his trainer knows all about. He was motoring at the finish once the penny dropped and looks like being the one that should get his stable off the mark with its juveniles this year. (tchd 17-2)

Ostralegus knew his job and made the winner work a furlong out, but flattened out nearing the finish and shaped as though he would come on for this initial outing. It was an encouraging introduction. (tchd 5-2 and 7-2)

Silk Fairy(IRE) looks moderate but now has the option of nurseries.

Oscars Journey was disappointing as his previous level gave him a chance in this company, but he now also becomes eligible for a mark. (op 5-1)

Strong Conviction, back down in trip, raced solo towards the far side. However, his tack had gone wrong and he held no chance as a result. Official explanation: jockey said rein broke just after start (op 10-1 tchd 12-1 and 8-1)

5214 GREAT YARMOUTH TOURIST AUTHORITY H'CAP 7f 3y

5:35 (5:37) (Class 5) (0-75,75) 3-Y-O+ £2,264 (£673; £336; £168) Stalls Centre

Form RPR

00-1 1 **Dannios**[6] 4966 6-8-11 67 (t) NoelGarbutt(7) 3 79
(Ed Walker) *dwlt: bhd: rdn over 2f out: hdwy ent fnl f: led ins fnl f: r.o wl and sn clr* 2/1[2]

0355 2 2 ½ **Sunley Pride**[18] 4534 3-9-2 71 SamHitchcott 6 74
(Mick Channon) *chsd ldrs: rdn over 2f out: drvn and hdwy to press ldrs ent fnl f: styd on same pce after: wnt 2nd towards fin* 4/1[3]

20 3 nk **Jonnie Skull (IRE)**[28] 4192 6-8-10 59 (vt) KierenFallon 1 63
(Phil McEntee) *led: rdn wl over 1f out: hdd ins fnl f: styd on same pce after: lost 2nd towards fin* 9/1

-164 4 3 ¼ **Performing Pocket (USA)**[153] 897 3-9-1 73 AdamBeschizza(3) 5 67
(David Simcock) *t.k.h: hld up wl in tch: rdn 2f out: edgd rt and no prog 1f out: wknd ins fnl f* 12/1

5230 5 shd **Great Expectations**[40] 3790 4-9-10 73 RyanMoore 2 68
(J R Jenkins) *trckd ldr: rdn and fnd nil over 1f out: wknd ins fnl f* 6/4[1]

1m 27.06s (0.46) **Going Correction** +0.075s/f (Good)

WFA 3 from 4yo+ 6lb 5 Ran SP% **111.0**

Speed ratings (Par 103): **100,97,96,93,92**

CSF £10.31 TOTE £2.60: £1.30, £1.90; EX 10.60.

Owner Mrs T Walker **Bred** Roseland Thoroughbreds Ltd **Trained** Newmarket, Suffolk

FOCUS

This was weakened by the non-runners but it still wasn't a bad handicap for the grade. They went a fair pace and the form looks straightforward enough. The winner has a fine record here.

5215 INJURED JOCKEYS FUND H'CAP 7f 3y

6:05 (6:10) (Class 6) (0-55,55) 3-Y-O £1,617 (£481; £240; £120) Stalls Centre

Form RPR

6004 1 **Indiana Guest (IRE)**[6] 4937 3-8-12 51 (b[1]) TomQueally 10 59
(George Margarson) *hld up wl in tch: rdn to chse ldr jst over 1f out: led ins fnl f: styd on wl: rdn out* 14/1

0-00 2 1 ¾ **New Romantic**[70] 2795 3-8-10 49 (p) LukeMorris 12 52
(Julie Camacho) *t.k.h: chsd ldrs tl wnt 2nd 5f out tl over 1f out: outpcd ent fnl f: rallied u.p and styd on again fnl 100yds* 14/1

0-06 3 1 ¼ **Dark Orchid**[47] 3539 3-9-2 55 RyanMoore 14 55+
(Peter Chapple-Hyam) *t.k.h: hld up towards rr: hdwy and swtchd lft over 1f out: chsd ldrs and drvn ins fnl f: kpt on same pce fnl 100yds* 4/1[1]

5503 4 nse **Arrow Lake (FR)**[19] 4506 3-9-2 55 FrederikTylicki 11 54
(Noel Quinlan) *chsd ldr tl led after 2f: rdn wl over 1f out: hdd ins fnl f: no ex and one pce after* 4/1[1]

00-0 5 nse **Silent Laughter**[123] 1357 3-8-10 52 HarryBentley(3) 13 51
(Jonathan Portman) *hld up in tch in midfield: rdn and no imp over 1f out tl styd on wl u.p fnl 100yds: nvr enough pce to rch ldrs* 12/1[3]

0050 6 4 **Tenderly Place**[6] 4937 3-8-4 48 ow1 (t) DavidKenny(5) 3 37
(William Knight) *stdd and dropped in bhd s: swtchd rt and effrt over 2f out: no imp u.p fnl f* 33/1

000 7 1 ½ **Hoonose**[29] 4144 3-8-7 46 oh1 WilliamCarson 15 31
(Pat Eddery) *stdd s: hld up in rr: effrt u.p over 2f out: styd on same pce and no prog fnl f* 18/1

60 8 3 ¼ **Joy To The World (IRE)**[58] 3193 3-8-10 49 HayleyTurner 6 25
(Paul Cole) *t.k.h: hld up in tch towards rr: rdn over 2f out: no imp wl over 1f out: sn wknd* 8/1[2]

306 9 shd **Coach Montana (IRE)**[70] 2802 3-8-13 52 BrettDoyle 16 27
(Jane Chapple-Hyam) *towards rr: rdn and effrt wl over 2f out: no prog whn swtchd lft over 1f out: no ch after* 14/1

00 10 nk **Selinda**[19] 4489 3-8-8 47 SaleemGolam 5 22
(Mick Channon) *in tch in midfield: rdn and struggling over 2f out: wknd over 1f out* 33/1

-060 11 6 **Princess Of Rock**[12] 4734 3-8-12 51 SamHitchcott 2
(Mick Channon) *in tch in midfield: rdn and lost pl ent fnl 2f: bhd and wl btn over 1f out* 16/1

0500 12 5 **Hurricane Max (IRE)**[13] 4716 3-9-2 55 (p) GeorgeBaker 7
(Ian McInnes) *led for 2f: chsd ldrs after tl wknd u.p over 1f out: bhd and eased wl ins fnl f* 8/1[2]

0600 13 1 ½ **Canning Vale**[47] 3548 3-8-4 46 oh1 AdamBeschizza(3) 9
(Julia Feilden) *chsd ldrs: rdn 1/2-way: steadily lost pl: bhd over 1f out* 66/1

000 14 3 ¾ **Ebtisama (USA)**[53] 3340 3-8-9 48 (b[1]) TadhgO'Shea 4
(Marcus Tregoning) *in tch in midfield: rdn 3f out: sn btn: bhd and eased ins fnl f* 16/1

1m 27.61s (1.01) **Going Correction** +0.075s/f (Good) 14 Ran SP% **114.3**

Speed ratings (Par 98): **97,95,93,93,93 88,87,83,83,83 76,70,68,64**

Tote Swingers 1&2 £34.80, 2&3 £20.10, 1&3 £12.90 CSF £175.99 CT £813.26 TOTE £10.80: £2.70, £3.10, £1.30; EX 188.10.

Owner John Guest Racing **Bred** D And Mrs D Veitch **Trained** Newmarket, Suffolk

■ Sleepy Lucy was withdrawn (12/1, ref to ent stalls). Deduct 5p in the £ under R4.

FOCUS

A weak 3-y-o handicap and it was wide open. There was an average pace on and the first five came clear. The second and fourth look the best guides to the level. A 6lb personal best from the winner.

5216 SIDEGATE MOTORS H'CAP 1m 3y

6:35 (6:39) (Class 6) (0-60,61) 3-Y-O+ £1,617 (£481; £240; £120) Stalls Centre

Form RPR

-206 1 **Enriching (USA)**[25] 4296 4-9-4 52 StevieDonohoe 7 59
(Lydia Pearce) *w ldrs: rdn wl over 1f out: drvn to ld jst ins fnl f: forged ahd fnl 100yds: rdn out* 9/2[2]

6000 2 ½ **Sanad (IRE)**[3] 5095 3-9-5 60 (b[1]) WilliamCarson 8 65
(Anthony Carson) *hld up wl in tch in rr: swtchd rt ent fnl 2f: hdwy over 1f out: drvn and pressing wnr whn hung lft ins fnl f: one pce towards fin* 14/1

6060 3 ½ **Desert Red (IRE)**[12] 4744 3-8-5 46 oh1 (b[1]) JimmyQuinn 5 50
(Phil McEntee) *stdd s: hld up in tch in rr: hdwy to chse ldrs and hung lft 2f out: swtchd rt jst over 1f out: ev ch and drvn ins fnl f: no ex fnl 100yds* 40/1

5-00 4 ½ **Arabic**[75] 2624 3-9-5 60 TomQueally 1 63
(James Fanshawe) *in tch: rdn over 1f out: kpt on u.p ins fnl f: nvr quite gng pce to chal* 11/2[3]

0663 5 2 ¼ **Exopuntia**[21] 4435 6-9-0 51 AdamBeschizza(3) 3 50
(Julia Feilden) *dwlt: sn rcvrd to chse ldrs: led 6f out: rdn over 1f out: hdd jst ins fnl f: sn btn and wknd fnl 100yds* 6/1

0501 6 2 **Exceedexpectations (IRE)**[7] 4932 3-9-6 61 6ex HayleyTurner 2 54
(Michael Bell) *led for 2f: chsd ldr after: rdn ent fnl 2f: unable qck over 1f out: wknd ins fnl f* 11/8[1]

0060 7 8 **Little Miss Mayhem (IRE)**[13] 4709 3-9-2 57 (t) MircoMimmocchi 6 32
(Philip McBride) *t.k.h: hld up wl in tch: rdn over 2f out: sn struggling: wknd over 1f out* 18/1

020 8 31 **Danceyourselfdizzy (IRE)**[43] 3712 4-8-12 46 oh1 KierenFallon 9
(Phil McEntee) *in tch: rdn and no rspnse over 2f out: wknd wl over 1f out: eased fnl f: t.o* 10/1

1m 40.97s (0.37) **Going Correction** +0.075s/f (Good)

WFA 3 from 4yo+ 7lb 8 Ran SP% **113.4**

Speed ratings (Par 101): **101,100,100,99,97 95,87,56**

Tote Swingers 1&2 £9.00, 2&3 £54.40, 1&3 £3.40 CSF £62.37 CT £2197.00 TOTE £3.40: £1.20, £4.70, £11.20; EX 88.30.

Owner Franconson Partners **Bred** Adena Springs **Trained** Newmarket, Suffolk

FOCUS

A moderate handicap that resulted in a tight finish. Sound if limited form.

Exceedexpectations(IRE) Official explanation: trainer's rep had no explanation for the poor form shown

5217 RACING WELFARE H'CAP 5f 43y

7:05 (7:07) (Class 6) (0-55,55) 3-Y-O+ £1,617 (£481; £240; £120) Stalls Centre

Form RPR

050 1 **Whiskey Junction**[28] 4196 8-9-1 52 LukeMorris 5 61
(Michael Quinn) *chsd ldr tl over 3f out: styd chsng ldrs: rdn over 1f out: kpt on u.p to ld fnl 75yds: styd on wl* 5/1

0033 2 1 **Miss Polly Plum**[10] 4815 5-9-3 54 (p) SaleemGolam 8 59
(Chris Dwyer) *dwlt: t.k.h: chsd ldr over 3f out: rdn over 1f out: led ins fnl f: hdd and no ex fnl 75yds* 7/2[2]

2-04 3 nk **Excellent Aim**[21] 4438 5-8-11 55 RichardOld(7) 9 59
(George Margarson) *hld up in tch: rdn along and hdwy jst over 1f out: hanging lft and chsd ldrs ins fnl f: kpt on towards fin* 10/3[1]

5004 4 nk **Fantasy Fighter (IRE)**[172] 687 7-8-9 46 oh1 JimmyQuinn 1 50
(John E Long) *hld up in tch: chsd ldrs and rdn ent fnl f: kpt on same pce fnl 100yds* 15/2

0005 5 ¾ **Silver Linnet (IRE)**[21] 4439 5-9-2 53 (b) TomQueally 2 54
(John Butler) *led: rdn ent fnl f: hdd ins fnl f: no ex and wknd towards fin* 13/2

000 6 32 **One Bid Too Many (USA)**[22] 4405 3-8-3 46 oh1 (v) RaulDaSilva(3) 3
(Derek Shaw) *taken down early: in tch: rdn and lost pl 1/2-way: lost tch 2f out* 20/1

-000 7 132 **Adaeze (IRE)**[10] 4815 4-8-11 51 (p) HarryBentley(3) 4
(Jonathan Portman) *hd stuck over neighbouring stall as stalls opened: lost all ch and t.o thrght* 4/1[3]

1m 4.09s (1.39) **Going Correction** +0.075s/f (Good)

WFA 3 from 4yo+ 3lb 7 Ran SP% **111.8**

Speed ratings (Par 101): **91,89,88,88,87 36,**

Tote Swingers 1&2 £4.40, 2&3 £3.90, 1&3 £5.20 CSF £21.73 CT £64.63 TOTE £5.50: £2.80, £2.30; EX 28.70.

Owner Steven Astaire **Bred** Mrs I A Balding **Trained** Newmarket, Suffolk

FOCUS

This low-grade sprint handicap saw another tight finish.

Adaeze(IRE) Official explanation: jockey said filly got its head stuck in adjoining stall and he was unable to correct until runners had gone half a furlong

5218 WEDDINGS AT GREAT YARMOUTH RACECOURSE FILLIES' H'CAP 1m 1f

7:35 (7:35) (Class 4) (0-80,79) 3-Y-O+ **£4,075** (£1,212; £606; £303) **Stalls** Low

Form RPR

0046 **1** **Nemushka**[19] 4497 3-9-2 **75**.......................................(p) FrederikTylicki 3 85
(Richard Fahey) *in tch in rr: hdwy on inner 3f out: chsd ldr 2f out: rdn to chal ent fnl f: led fnl 150yds: styd on wl* **8/1**

5615 **2** ¾ **Amoya (GER)**[10] 4822 5-9-11 **79**.................................. RaulDaSilva(3) 2 87
(Philip McBride) *led: wnt clr 1/2-way: rdn ent fnl 2f: drvn and chal ent fnl f: hdd fnl 150yds: kpt on gamely but a hld after* **7/1**[3]

0511 **3** ¾ **Consider Yourself (USA)**[21] 4435 5-9-8 **73**.............(p) WilliamCarson 1 80
(Anthony Carson) *chsd ldrs: wnt 2nd 6f out tl 2f out: kpt on same pce u.p fr over 1f out* **14/1**

45-1 **4** 4 **Coco Rouge (IRE)**[42] 3735 4-9-7 **72**.............................. HayleyTurner 6 70
(James Fanshawe) *t.k.h: chsd ldr tl 6f out: rdn and unable qck ent fnl 2f: 4th and wknd 1f out* **9/1**

-502 **5** 2¼ **Isatis**[16] 4630 3-8-13 **72**... TomQueally 8 65
(Sir Henry Cecil) *hld up in tch: effrt on outer over 2f out: edgd lft u.p and no hdwy over 1f out: sn wknd* **4/1**[2]

1-05 **6** 1¼ **Dreams Of Fire (USA)**[11] 4755 3-9-2 **75**........................ RyanMoore 5 65
(Sir Michael Stoute) *hld up in tch: rdn and effrt over 2f out: no prog u.p 2f out: wknd over 1f out* **8/1**

0-10 **7** 2¾ **Maz**[70] 2801 4-8-11 **62**.. LukeMorris 7 46
(Alan Bailey) *in tch in midfield: rdn and unable qck 3f out: wknd 2f out* **40/1**

0500 **8** 2¼ **Ellie In The Pink (IRE)**[25] 4287 4-9-2 **74**........... MichaelJMMurphy(7) 4 53
(Alan Jarvis) *bhd: rdn and no rspnse 4f out: sn btn and no ch fnl 2f* **8/1**

3411 **9** 6 **Play Street**[19] 4486 3-9-1 **77**... HarryBentley(3) 9 43
(Jonathan Portman) *in tch: rdn and unable qck 3f out: wknd 2f out: bhd and eased ins fnl f* **9/4**[1]

1m 53.83s (-1.97) **Going Correction** -0.25s/f (Firm)
WFA 3 from 4yo+ 8lb **9** Ran SP% **115.7**
Speed ratings (Par 102): **98,97,96,93,91 90,87,85,80**
Tote Swingers 1&2 £14.30, 2&3 £16.00, 1&3 £16.30 CSF £62.79 CT £571.93 TOTE £9.00: £2.40, £2.90, £2.90; EX 94.10.
Owner The G-Guck Group **Bred** Avenue Farm Stud **Trained** Musley Bank, N Yorks

FOCUS

A fair fillies' handicap, run at a solid pace and the principals were clear at the finish. The form seems sound enough despite the two at the head of the market disappointing.
Nemushka Official explanation: trainer's rep had no explanation for the apparent improvement in form
Play Street Official explanation: jockey said filly never travelled

5219 GUIDE DOGS FOR THE BLIND H'CAP 1m 3f 101y

8:05 (8:06) (Class 5) (0-70,67) 3-Y-O **£2,264** (£673; £336; £168) **Stalls** Low

Form RPR

500 **1** **Between Us**[20] 4466 3-9-3 **63**.. LukeMorris 5 84+
(Sir Mark Prescott Bt) *mde all: rdn and clr 2f out: styd on strly: eased towards fin* **9/1**

-560 **2** 5 **Aleksandar**[53] 3345 3-9-6 **66**.. KierenFallon 2 76+
(Luca Cumani) *in tch in midfield: pushed along 5f out: rdn and hdwy to go 3rd 2f out: plugged on u.p to chse wnr ins fnl f: nvr a threat* **5/2**[1]

6103 **3** 4 **Curly Come Home**[33] 4005 3-9-7 **67**................................ GeorgeBaker 6 73+
(Chris Wall) *hld up in last trio: hdwy 4f out: chsd wnr over 2f out: rdn and no hdwy 2f out: wl btn 1f out: lost 2nd ins fnl f: eased towards fin* **4/1**[2]

0004 **4** 1¾ **Flashy Star**[7] 4906 3-9-2 **62**......................................(v) SamHitchcott 10 62
(Mick Channon) *t.k.h: hld up in last trio: rdn and swtchd rt over 2f out: wnt modest 4th jst over 1f out: nvr trbld ldrs* **16/1**

0403 **5** 5 **Kashgar**[11] 4776 3-9-5 **65**... HayleyTurner 3 57
(Michael Bell) *t.k.h: chsd wnr tl over 3f out: wknd u.p 2f out* **6/1**[3]

000 **6** ½ **Albonny (IRE)**[22] 4410 3-8-10 **63**......................... MichaelJMMurphy(7) 8 54
(Alan Jarvis) *in tch in midfield: rdn and fnd little over 2f out: wknd 2f out* **20/1**

0540 **7** 2¼ **Rogue Reporter (IRE)**[22] 4411 3-9-1 **61**..................... WilliamCarson 1 48
(Stuart Williams) *chsd ldrs: wnt 2nd over 3f out tl over 2f out: losing pl whn short of room ent fnl 2f: sn wknd* **7/1**

6-00 **8** 6 **Hawkino (IRE)**[22] 4399 3-8-2 **48** oh3.................................(v) JimmyQuinn 7 25
(Derek Shaw) *stdd s: a wl bhd: nvr on terms* **66/1**

505 **9** 25 **Hummingbird**[16] 4630 3-9-5 **65**......................................(b[1]) RyanMoore 4
(William Haggas) *t.k.h: chsd ldrs tl lost pl 5f out: rdn and lost tch 3f out: t.o* **6/1**[3]

2m 25.9s (-2.80) **Going Correction** -0.25s/f (Firm) **9** Ran SP% **111.8**
Speed ratings (Par 100): **100,96,93,92,88 88,86,82,64**
Tote Swingers 1&2 £7.50, 2&3 £4.00, 1&3 £6.90 CSF £30.41 CT £103.72 TOTE £13.90: £2.30, £1.10, £2.50; EX 50.40.
Owner Cheveley Park Stud **Bred** Cheveley Park Stud Ltd **Trained** Newmarket, Suffolk

FOCUS

A moderate 3yo handicap on paper, but there were potential improvers lurking. It was another race run at a good pace, but few landed a serious blow. The form is rated on the positive side around the placed horses.
Hawkino(IRE) Official explanation: jockey said gelding moved poorly throughout
T/Jkpt: Not won. T/Plt: £1,333.80 to a £1 stake. Pool £53,263.38. 29.15 winning tickets T/Qpdt: £159.10 to a £1 stake. Pool £7,592.55. 35.3 winning tickets SP

4677 BEVERLEY (R-H)

Wednesday, August 15

OFFICIAL GOING: Good to firm changing to good to firm (firm in places) after race 1 (2.15)

Wind: fresh 1/2 behind Weather: fine but breezy, overcast and rain race 2 onwards, heavy race 3 onwards

5220 JOURNAL CLASSIFIED CLAIMING STKS 7f 100y

2:15 (2:15) (Class 6) 3-Y-O+ **£1,811** (£539; £269; £134) **Stalls** Low

Form RPR

601 **1** **Muftarres (IRE)**[12] 4783 7-8-13 65.....................(b) RussKennemore 11 73
(Paul Midgley) *swtchd rt s: hld up in rr: hdwy on ins over 2f out: nt clr run and swtchd rt over 1f out: burst through to ld 100yds out: drvn clr* **12/1**

-000 **2** 2½ **Brocklebank (IRE)**[25] 4347 3-9-4 75.....................(tp) PhillipMakin 9 77
(Kevin Ryan) *led: hdd and no ex last 100yds* **14/1**

2560 **3** nk **Sunnyside Tom (IRE)**[25] 4345 8-9-2 73......................... TonyHamilton 3 69
(Richard Fahey) *drvn to chse ldrs: chal 1f out: kpt on same pce last 100yds* **7/2**[1]

5232 **4** ¾ **Abidhabidubai**[17] 4620 4-9-1 72.............................. DavidSimmonson(7) 7 74
(John Quinn) *trckd ldrs: effrt outside over 3f out: chsng ldrs 2f out: kpt on same pce last 150yds* **9/1**[3]

2230 **5** 1½ **Lindoro**[25] 4317 7-9-2 69.. BarryMcHugh 8 64
(Brian Ellison) *trckd ldrs: chal over 2f out: one pce fnl f* **7/2**[1]

0240 **6** hd **River Ardeche**[17] 4620 7-8-11 61................................. ShaneBKelly(5) 5 64
(Tracy Waggott) *trckd ldrs: fdd last 100yds* **33/1**

-000 **7** 2¼ **Indieslad**[12] 4784 4-9-2 64...(p) PaulMulrennan 2 58
(Ann Duffield) *t.k.h in rr: hdwy over 2f out: nvr a threat* **16/1**

3462 **8** 1½ **Moheebb (IRE)**[0] 4004 8-8-12 60...............................(be) JamesSullivan 4 51
(Ruth Carr) *in rr and sn drvn along: sme hdwy over 3f out: lost pl 2f out* **7/2**[1]

2162 **9** ½ **Violent Velocity (IRE)**[29] 4177 9-9-3 75................................. LMcNiff(5) 6 60
(John Quinn) *dwlt: hdwy on outside 4f out: sn outpcd: hdwy to chse ldrs 2f out: hung rt and wknd fnl f* **6/1**[2]

0-06 **10** 10 **Lady Gar Gar**[63] 3021 4-8-9 57.....................................(b[1]) DaleSwift(3) 10 26
(Geoffrey Oldroyd) *chsd ldrs: hung rt and lost pl over 1f out: bhd whn eased towards fin* **25/1**

1m 30.74s (-3.06) **Going Correction** -0.35s/f (Firm)
WFA 3 from 4yo+ 6lb **10** Ran SP% **118.0**
Speed ratings (Par 101): **103,100,99,98,97 97,94,92,92,80**
toteswingers 1&2 £12.50, 1&3 £8.80, 2&3 £14.80 CSF £168.76 TOTE £14.30: £3.90, £2.20, £2.00; EX 234.30.Abidhabidubai was claimed by Michael Wigham for £9,000.
Owner T W Midgley **Bred** Shadwell Estate Company Limited **Trained** Westow, N Yorks

FOCUS

The rail around the bottom bend was moved in, adding 19yds to all races on the round course. A dry run up to a meeting staged on fast ground. A fair event of its type but a moderate early gallop saw several fail to settle early on.
Indieslad Official explanation: jockey said gelding ran too free
Moheebb(IRE) Official explanation: trainer had no explanation for the poor form shown

5221 HULL DAILY MAIL/IRISH STALLION FARMS EBF MAIDEN STKS 7f 100y

2:45 (2:45) (Class 5) 2-Y-O **£3,428** (£1,020; £509; £254) **Stalls** Low

Form RPR

6 **1** **Claim (IRE)**[18] 4595 2-9-3 0.. RichardMullen 3 78
(Sir Michael Stoute) *dwlt: sn drvn to ld: hdd over 4f out: led 3f out: hld on gamely* **3/1**[1]

54 **2** nk **Athman (IRE)**[41] 3770 2-9-3 0.................................... SilvestreDeSousa 4 77
(Mahmood Al Zarooni) *led early: trckd ldrs: chal over 1f out: no ex nr fin* **3/1**[1]

3 3½ **Bahamamay** 2-9-3 0... TonyHamilton 2 69+
(Richard Fahey) *tk fierce hold: trckd ldrs: led over 4f out: hdd 3f out: fdd fnl f* **13/2**[3]

0 **4** 3 **Danehill Flyer (IRE)**[14] 4710 2-9-3 0.......................... MichaelO'Connell 1 62
(Philip Kirby) *chsd ldrs: kpt on same pce fnl 2f* **33/1**

5 1 **Mudaawem (USA)** 2-9-3 0.. TadhgO'Shea 10 59
(Mark Johnston) *chsd ldrs: one pce fnl 2f* **10/1**

0 **6** 2½ **Red Eight (USA)**[19] 4555 2-9-3 0.. TomQueally 9 56+
(John Quinn) *dwlt: hld up in mid-divsion: hdwy over 1f out: kpt on* **9/1**

63 **7** hd **Signature Dish (IRE)**[10] 4837 2-8-12 0............................. MartinDwyer 6 48
(Andrew Balding) *dwlt: mid-div: drvn over 2f out: nvr nr ldrs: eased clsng stages* **4/1**[2]

00 **8** 6 **Juhaina (IRE)**[19] 4546 2-8-12 0... GrahamLee 8 34
(Ann Duffield) *in rr: nvr a factor* **80/1**

9 nk **Hurricane John (IRE)** 2-9-3 0...................................... AdrianNicholls 11 38
(David Nicholls) *dwlt and wnt lft s: in rr: effrt on outside over 2f out: hung lft and sn wknd* **16/1**

00 **10** 23 **Symphonic Air (IRE)**[36] 3948 2-8-12 0............................. PhillipMakin 7
(John Weymes) *s.i.s: in rr: bhd fnl 3f: eased fnl f: t.o* **80/1**

1m 31.45s (-2.35) **Going Correction** -0.35s/f (Firm) **10** Ran SP% **113.7**
Speed ratings (Par 94): **99,98,94,91,90 87,87,80,79,53**
toteswingers 1&2 £2.50, 1&3 £6.80, 2&3 £5.70 CSF £11.38 TOTE £4.20: £1.50, £1.30, £2.20; EX 14.30.
Owner Robert Ng **Bred** Raysiza Partnership **Trained** Newmarket, Suffolk

FOCUS

A fair maiden and, although the gallop was an ordinary one, this race should throw up a couple of winners. The runner-up helps with the level of the form.

NOTEBOOK

Claim(IRE) duly stepped up on a pleasing debut effort and showed a willing attitude to get off the mark. He'll have no problems with a bit further, he's in very good hands, and is open to further progress. (op 11-4 tchd 5-2)
Athman(IRE) is a steadily progressive individual who had the run of the race and turned in his best effort. He's sure to pick up a similar event away from the more progressive sorts. (tchd 10-3)
Bahamamay ◆, the second foal of an unraced half-sister to several decent types, including smart stayer Bosham Mill, is the one to take from the race. After attracting plenty of support, he did well to finish as close as he did given he refused to settle and this scopey sort is sure to improve and win races. (op 15-2)
Danehill Flyer(IRE) stepped up appreciably on the form shown on his debut but, while he was probably flattered in a race run at just an ordinary gallop and while he is likely to remain vulnerable in this grade, he'll be of more interest once switched to nurseries. (op 28-1)
Mudaawem(USA), out of a 7f winner and a half-brother to a 7f winner, was fairly easy to back and showed ability at an ordinary level on this racecourse debut. A stiffer test of stamina could suit and he should be able to step up on these bare facts. (op 17-2)
Red Eight(USA) again had his limitations exposed in this type of event, but is the type to fare better once qualified for a nursery mark. (op 14-1)
Signature Dish(IRE) failed by a long chalk to confirm the promise shown at Chester on her previous start. However she's in good hands and will be worth another chance at some point. (op 7-2 tchd 3-1)

5222 EAST RIDING MAIL MAIDEN AUCTION STKS 5f

3:15 (3:15) (Class 5) 2-Y-O **£2,264** (£673; £336; £168) **Stalls** Low

Form RPR

05 **1** **Tumblewind**[56] 3286 2-8-6 0.. AmyRyan 8 67+
(Richard Whitaker) *chsd ldrs: led over 1f out: drvn out* **5/1**[3]

022 **2** ¾ **Bogsnog (IRE)**[15] 4670 2-9-1 72.. GrahamLee 6 73
(Linda Stubbs) *led tl over 2f out: upsides over 1f out: kpt on same pce last 150yds* **5/4**[1]

0 **3** 7 **Storma Norma**[14] 4710 2-8-12 0.. DavidAllan 7 45
(Tim Easterby) *dwlt: hdwy 2f out: kpt on to take modest 3rd nr line* **7/1**

20 **4** ½ **Lucy Minaj**[14] 4710 2-8-10 0... RichardMullen 4 41
(Bryan Smart) *chsd ldrs: drvn 2f out: one pce* **5/2**[2]

0505 **5** nk **Sound Affects**[75] 2663 2-8-6 0.................................... PatrickMathers 2 36
(Alan Brown) *w ldr: led over 2f out: hdd over 1f out: sn wknd* **33/1**

0 **6** 3 ¾ **Knockamany Bends (IRE)**[17] 4625 2-9-2 0 ow1........... PaddyAspell 3 32
(John Wainwright) *dwlt: outpcd and bhd: kpt on fnl 100yds* **33/1**

0 **7** ¾ **Shesnotforturning (IRE)**[42] 3747 2-8-8 0....................... PJMcDonald 5 22
(Ben Haslam) *mid-div: effrt over 2f out: lost pl over 1f out* **16/1**

00 **8** 1 **Nifty Nadine (IRE)**[37] 3909 2-8-6 0........................ AndrewMullen 1 16
(Nigel Tinkler) *chsd ldrs: outpcd and lost pl over 3f out: sn bhd* **25/1**

1m 1.27s (-2.23) **Going Correction** -0.50s/f (Hard) **8** Ran SP% **117.8**
Speed ratings (Par 94): **97,95,84,83,83 77,76,74**
toteswingers 1&2 £2.60, 1&3 £4.70, 2&3 £3.10 CSF £11.90 TOTE £8.40: £2.30, £1.02, £2.50; EX 15.90.
Owner Nice Day Out Partnership **Bred** Hellwood Stud Farm **Trained** Scarcroft, W Yorks

FOCUS
A modest and uncompetitive maiden run in driving rain. The gallop was sound and the first two pulled clear in the last furlong. Sound but limited form.

NOTEBOOK
Tumblewind has improved with every run and posted her best effort to get off the mark at the third attempt. She should be equally at home over 6f and may do better in ordinary nursery company. (op 6-1)
Bogsnog(IRE) again finished second but wasn't far off his best and looks a reasonable guide to the level of this form. He pulled clear of the rest and remains capable of winning a similarly uncompetitive event. (op 10-11)
Storma Norma stepped up on the form shown on her debut and she'll be of interest over further once qualified for a nursery mark. (op 10-1)
Lucy Minaj attracted support and got a good tow into the race but her response for pressure was fairly limited and she was again a fair way below the form shown on her debut at Redcar. She looks best watched for now. (op 10-3 tchd 7-2)
Sound Affects showed a bit of toe and a bit of improvement but she'll have to raise her game a fair way again before she's a solid betting proposition. (op 28-1 tchd 25-1)

5223 RAWFIELD AND PARAGON DATA H'CAP 5f
3:50 (3:50) (Class 5) (0-75,75) 3-Y-0+ **£3,234** (£962; £481; £240) **Stalls** Low

Form RPR

6100 **1** **Six Wives**[121] 1417 5-9-9 74.. TomQueally 7 86
(Scott Dixon) *mde all: kpt on wl fnl f: drvn out* **16/1**

0622 **2** 2 **Waking Warrior**[19] 4552 4-8-13 71..............................(tp) KevinStott(7) 5 76
(Kevin Ryan) *in rr-div: effrt whn nt clr run and swtchd lft over 1f out: styd on wl to take 2nd nr fin* **6/1**[3]

262 **3** nk **Select Committee**[5] 5058 7-9-3 75...................(v) DavidSimmonson(7) 8 79
(John Quinn) *chsd wnr: kpt on same pce fnl f* **12/1**

0366 **4** nse **Cocktail Charlie**[11] 4829 4-9-9 74..........................(p) DanielTudhope 14 78
(Tim Easterby) *in rr-div: hdwy on outer 2f out: kpt on same pce ins fnl f* **5/2**[2]

6111 **5** 1 ¼ **Fear Nothing**[15] 4680 5-9-1 73...................................... DavidBergin(7) 9 72
(David O'Meara) *chsd wnr: drvn over 1f out: wknd towards fin* **9/4**[1]

6020 **6** 1 ¼ **Indian Trail**[8] 4909 12-9-5 70.......................................(b) PaulQuinn 11 65
(David Nicholls) *swtchd rt s: in rr: kpt on fnl 2f: swtchd lft jst ins fnl f: nvr a factor* **14/1**

000 **7** hd **Ingleby Star (IRE)**[23] 4400 7-8-11 67..............................(p) LMcNiff(5) 3 61
(Ian McInnes) *mid-div: effrt and hung lft over 2f out: nvr trbld ldrs* **25/1**

5-00 **8** 1 **Mey Blossom**[17] 4631 7-8-11 62..................................... TonyHamilton 1 53
(Richard Whitaker) *in rr: hdwy on ins over 1f out: nvr a factor* **25/1**

3433 **9** 1 **Belinsky (IRE)**[17] 4631 5-8-10 64..................................(v) DaleSwift(3) 10 51
(Julie Camacho) *chsd ldrs: rdn and hung rt 2f out: fdd fnl f* **17/2**

640 **10** 4 **Comptonspirit**[7] 4963 8-9-8 73.................................. DuranFentiman 13 46
(Brian Baugh) *mid-div: effrt on outer over 2f out: lost pl over 1f out* **28/1**

1000 **11** 3 ¼ **Choc'A'Moca (IRE)**[11] 4829 5-8-13 64........................(v) MickyFenton 6 25
(Paul Midgley) *mid-div: drvn over 2f out: sn lost pl* **25/1**

0056 **12** 10 **Media Jury**[7] 4963 5-8-5 56 oh6...............................(v) PatrickMathers 12
(John Wainwright) *slipped slowly: a detached in last* **50/1**

1m 0.61s (-2.89) **Going Correction** -0.50s/f (Hard) **12** Ran SP% **121.3**
Speed ratings (Par 103): **103,99,99,99,97 95,94,93,91,85 80,64**
toteswingers 1&2 £15.10, 1&3 £13.60, 2&3 £10.10 CSF £105.45 CT £1220.34 TOTE £17.10: £4.00, £2.20, £3.60; EX 103.90.
Owner Sexy Six Partnership **Bred** Cheveley Park Stud Ltd **Trained** Babworth, Notts

FOCUS
A fair handicap run at a sound pace but only a couple figured. Solid, straightfiorward form.
Ingleby Star(IRE) Official explanation: jockey reported gelding hung left
Belinsky(IRE) Official explanation: jockey reported gelding hung right
Media Jury Official explanation: jockey reported gelding slipped leaving stalls

5224 WOLD CONSTRUCTION BRIAN AND IAN MEMORIAL H'CAP (DIV I) 1m 1f 207y
4:25 (4:25) (Class 4) (0-85,85) 3-Y-0+ **£4,528** (£1,347; £673; £336) **Stalls** Low

Form RPR

0351 **1** **Kalk Bay (IRE)**[14] 4714 5-9-6 77...............................(t) PaulMulrennan 9 92
(Michael Easterby) *trckd ldrs: led and wnt rt 2f out: rdn clr fnl f* **5/1**[3]

0350 **2** 4 ½ **Merchant Of Medici**[15] 4679 5-9-2 73............................ PJMcDonald 1 78
(Micky Hammond) *mid-div: effrt over 2f out: chsd wnr appr fnl f: no imp* **14/1**

1645 **3** 1 ¾ **Tartan Gigha (IRE)**[7] 4962 7-10-0 85.......................(p) DanielTudhope 7 86
(Geoffrey Harker) *hld up in rr: effrt and edgd lft over 2f out: kpt on to take 3rd last 100yds* **6/1**

4550 **4** 2 ¼ **Tres Coronas (IRE)**[27] 4249 5-9-13 84............................ PhillipMakin 2 81
(David Barron) *dwlt: hld up in rr: hdwy over 2f out: kpt on one pce: tk 4th last 100yds* **7/2**[1]

6000 **5** 4 **Unknown Rebel (IRE)**[13] 3610 4-9-0 74......................(p) JulieBurke(3) 4 63
(Kevin Ryan) *led: hdd 2f out: wknd fnl 150yds* **11/1**

420 **6** 6 **Certral**[18] 4608 4-9-2 80... JacobButterfield(7) 6 57
(Brian Ellison) *dwlt: mid-div: effrt over 2f out: hung rt and wknd over 1f out* **9/2**[2]

1600 **7** 3 ¼ **Brockfield**[9] 4879 6-9-2 73....................................... SilvestreDeSousa 5 43
(Mel Brittain) *chsd ldrs: rdn to chal over 2f out: wknd over 1f out: heavily eased fnl 75yds* **7/1**

3360 **8** 2 ¼ **Amazing Blue Sky**[13] 4745 6-9-6 77............................... JamesSullivan 8 43
(Ruth Carr) *chsd ldrs: drvn over 3f out: wknd 2f out* **8/1**

/1-0 **9** 37 **Reality Show (IRE)**[13] 4745 5-8-11 73 ow1............. JustinNewman(5) 3
(Michael Appleby) *rrd s: in rr: bhd and drvn 4f out: t.o whn eased clsng stages* **20/1**

2m 2.18s (-4.82) **Going Correction** -0.35s/f (Firm) **9** Ran SP% **114.7**
Speed ratings (Par 105): **105,101,100,98,95 90,87,85,56**
toteswingers 1&2 £10.20, 1&3 £5.00, 2&3 £12.80 CSF £71.01 CT £428.26 TOTE £4.10: £1.20, £5.30, £2.30; EX 82.70.
Owner Mrs Jean Turpin **Bred** Wentworth Racing **Trained** Sheriff Hutton, N Yorks

FOCUS
Exposed performers in a fairly useful handicap. The gallop was soon sound and the rain hadn't got into the ground judging by the winning time. Straightforward form.
Brockfield Official explanation: jockey reported gelding had no more to give

5225 BEVERLEY ADVERTISER H'CAP 1m 1f 207y
4:55 (4:55) (Class 5) (0-70,70) 3-Y-0+ **£2,264** (£673; £336; £168) **Stalls** Low

Form RPR

1553 **1** **Saint Thomas (IRE)**[23] 4396 5-9-4 63................................ DaleSwift(3) 7 71
(John Mackie) *chsd ldrs: effrt on outside over 2f out: styd on to ld last 50yds: hld on nr fin* **4/1**[1]

0506 **2** hd **Tiger Webb**[11] 4831 4-9-0 56..................................... PaulMulrennan 14 64+
(Michael Easterby) *in rr: hdwy over 2f out: styd on wl on outside appr fnl f: tk 2nd nr fin: jst hld* **13/2**

4062 **3** 1 ½ **Tribal Myth (IRE)**[15] 4682 5-9-5 64..............................(p) JulieBurke(3) 9 69
(Kevin Ryan) *led 2f: chsd ldrs: ev ch jst ins fnl f: kpt on same pce* **9/2**[2]

3602 **4** nse **Sinatramania**[14] 4712 5-8-13 55.................................... FrederikTylicki 6 60
(Tracy Waggott) *trckd ldrs: drvn 3f out: styd on appr fnl f: kpt on towards fin* **17/2**

0430 **5** 1 ¼ **Count Bertoni (IRE)**[44] 3699 5-9-13 69..................(b) DanielTudhope 11 72
(David O'Meara) *w ldr: led after 2f: hdd & wknd last 50yds* **16/1**

4-16 **6** ½ **Forster Street (IRE)**[17] 4623 3-9-0 65............................... DavidAllan 13 67
(Tim Easterby) *slipped s: in rr: hdwy on inner over 2f out: nt clr run appr fnl f: styd on one pce last 100yds* **7/1**

3062 **7** ½ **Striker Torres (IRE)**[7] 4964 6-9-11 67.........................(v) GrahamLee 5 68
(Ian McInnes) *in tch: effrt over 2f out: sn chsng ldrs: fdd last 50yds* **6/1**[3]

0004 **8** 6 **Ailsa Craig (IRE)**[15] 4682 6-9-7 63................................ TonyHamilton 4 52
(Edwin Tuer) *mid-div: effrt on ins over 2f out: sn chsng ldrs: wknd jst ins fnl f* **13/2**

0-04 **9** 25 **Peadar Miguel**[20] 685 5-9-8 64...................................... SeanQuinlan 2
(Daniel Mark Loughnane) *s.i.s: in rr: bhd fnl 3f: t.o whn eased nr fin* **28/1**

600- **10** 52 **Above Standard (IRE)**[249] 7716 4-9-7 70......... DavidSimmonson(7) 12
(Michael Easterby) *trckd ldrs on outer: drvn over 3f out: sn lost pl: wl bhd whn eased ins fnl f: hopelessly t.o* **25/1**

2m 4.39s (-2.61) **Going Correction** -0.35s/f (Firm)
WFA 3 from 4yo+ 9lb **10** Ran SP% **115.3**
Speed ratings (Par 103): **96,95,94,94,93 93,92,88,68,26**
toteswingers 1&2 £7.60, 1&3 £5.40, 2&3 £7.60 CSF £29.71 CT £121.17 TOTE £5.20: £1.80, £2.00, £1.50; EX 36.80.
Owner P Riley **Bred** S Coughlan **Trained** Church Broughton , Derbys

FOCUS
A modest handicap in which an ordinary gallop increased turning for home. Straightforward form, the fourth and fifth setting the level.
Forster Street(IRE) Official explanation: jockey reported gelding slipped leaving stalls
Above Standard(IRE) Official explanation: trainer's rep reported gelding had breathing problem

5226 PROPERTY GUIDE H'CAP (PART OF THE BEVERLEY MIDDLE DISTANCE SERIES) 1m 4f 16y
5:25 (5:25) (Class 6) (0-65,65) 3-Y-0+ **£2,587** (£770; £384; £192) **Stalls** Low

Form RPR

4652 **1** **Aliante**[7] 4971 3-9-3 65..(v) SilvestreDeSousa 2 76+
(Mark Johnston) *drvn early to chse ldrs: led appr fnl f: styd on strly: eased towards fin* **4/1**[2]

5212 **2** 3 **Arashi**[13] 4722 6-9-8 62..(v) DaleSwift(3) 6 67
(Derek Shaw) *t.k.h in mid-div: effrt over 2f out: nt clr run over 1f out: styd on to take 2nd last 50yds* **7/2**[1]

0655 **3** ½ **Stanley Rigby**[15] 4682 6-9-4 55..................................(b) BarryMcHugh 5 59
(Richard Fahey) *hld up in rr: drvn over 3f out: chsng ldrs over 1f out: edgd rt and kpt on same pce last 100yds* **12/1**

-043 **4** 2 **Pinotage**[17] 4626 4-9-11 62.. GrahamLee 1 63
(Peter Niven) *led 3f: w ldr: led over 3f out: hdd appr fnl f: wknd towards fin* **4/1**[2]

0106 **5** 1 ¼ **Maybeme**[15] 4682 6-9-5 56.. MichaelO'Connell 4 55+
(Neville Bycroft) *hood removed after s: s.s: hdwy over 3f out: chsng ldrs over 1f out: one pce whn hmpd wl ins fnl f* **9/1**

6000 **6** 2 **Kieron's Rock (IRE)**[7] 4956 3-7-13 47 oh1 ow1........ DuranFentiman 10 43
(Jedd O'Keeffe) *stdd s: t.k.h in rr: hdwy on ins over 2f out: nt clr run over 1f out: one pce fnl 150yds* **50/1**

0550 **7** 7 **Sharp Sovereign (USA)**[29] 4179 6-9-1 57......................... LMcNiff(5) 8 43
(Ian McInnes) *w ldr: led after 3f: hdd over 3f out: wknd over 1f out* **20/1**

255 **8** 2 ¼ **Cottam Donny**[14] 4714 4-9-10 61...................................... DavidAllan 11 44
(Mel Brittain) *chsd ldrs on outer: drvn over 3f out: lost pl over 1f out: eased towards fin* **5/1**[3]

0000 **9** 2 ½ **Mr Perceptive (IRE)**[17] 4627 4-9-11 62.......................(p) PJMcDonald 7 41
(Micky Hammond) *in rr: drvn 3f out: nvr a factor* **16/1**

2003 **10** 7 **Politbureau**[9] 4869 5-9-4 55.......................................(b) PaulMulrennan 3 23
(Michael Easterby) *chsd ldrs: lost pl over 2f out* **14/1**

2m 36.37s (-3.43) **Going Correction** -0.35s/f (Firm)
WFA 3 from 4yo+ 11lb **10** Ran SP% **115.9**
Speed ratings (Par 101): **97,95,94,93,92 91,86,85,83,78**
toteswingers 1&2 £3.30, 1&3 £5.90, 2&3 £7.00 CSF £18.28 TOTE £3.90: £1.40, £1.90, £3.70; EX 12.20.
Owner Miss K Rausing **Bred** Miss K Rausing And Mrs S M Rogers **Trained** Middleham Moor, N Yorks

FOCUS
A modest handicap run at an ordinary gallop. A personal best from the winner and the form looks sound enough in behind.
Maybeme Official explanation: jockey reported blindfold stuck under mare's bridle and unable to remove at first attempt

5227 WOLD CONSTRUCTION BRIAN AND IAN MEMORIAL H'CAP (DIV II) 1m 1f 207y
6:00 (6:00) (Class 4) (0-85,84) 3-Y-0+ **£4,528** (£1,347; £673; £336) **Stalls** Low

Form RPR

4535 **1** **Carragold**[11] 4821 6-9-3 73.................................... SilvestreDeSousa 5 82
(Mel Brittain) *trckd ldrs: wnt 2nd over 6f out: drvn over 3f out: led wl over 1f out: kpt on* **5/2**[1]

0515 **2** 1 **Bountiful Girl**[10] 4850 3-8-7 72..................................... BarryMcHugh 8 79
(Richard Fahey) *trckd ldr: t.k.h: stdd over 6f out: effrt over 3f out: chsd wnr 1f out: styd on same pce* **6/1**

005 **3** 1 ½ **Granston (IRE)**[19] 4543 11-9-4 74................................... GrahamLee 1 78
(James Bethell) *stmbld s: hld up in rr: hdwy over 4f out: swtchd lft over 1f out: kpt on same pce last 100yds* **11/2**

0354 **4** 2 ¾ **Jonny Lesters Hair (IRE)**[9] 4879 7-9-7 77......................... DavidAllan 7 76
(Tim Easterby) *slipped s: led: hdd wl over 1f out: wknd last 100yds* **3/1**[2]

0605 **5** 8 **Pravda Street**[15] 4673 7-9-1 74...............................[1] DaleSwift(3) 2 58
(Brian Ellison) *trckd ldrs: pushed along 6f out: sn lost pl: bhd fnl 3f* **12/1**

642 **6** *4 ½* **Judicious**^{76} 2620 5-9-12 **82**.................... MickyFenton 6 57
(Paul Midgley) *hld up: hdwy over 5f out: sn chsng ldrs: wknd 2f out: bhd whn eased ins fnl f* **4/1**^{3}

2m 4.67s (-2.33) **Going Correction** -0.35s/f (Firm)
WFA 3 from 4yo+ 9lb **6** Ran SP% **110.9**
Speed ratings (Par 105): **95,94,93,90,84 80**
toteswingers 1&2 £3.30, 1&3 £3.00, 2&3 £3.60 CSF £17.19 CT £70.49 TOTE £3.50: £1.50, £2.40; EX 16.40.
Owner Mel Brittain **Bred** Darley **Trained** Warthill, N Yorks

FOCUS
Exposed sorts in a fair handicap. The gallop was just an ordinary one and the form makes sense.
Jonny Lesters Hair(IRE) Official explanation: jockey reported gelding slipped leaving stalls
Judicious Official explanation: trainer's rep reported gelding unsuited by good to firm, firm in places going
T/Jkpt: Not won. T/Plt: £126.10 to a £1 stake. Pool: £77254.32, 447.08 winning tickets T/Qpdt: £15.20 to a £1 stake. Pool: £6656.74, 323.7 winning tickets WG

5153 KEMPTON (A.W) (R-H)
Wednesday, August 15

OFFICIAL GOING: Standard to slow
Wind: Fresh, half behind Weather: Fine

5228 WIN BIG WITH BETDAQ MULTIPLES APPRENTICE H'CAP 1m 3f (P)
5:35 (5:35) (Class 4) (0-80,80) 3-Y-O **£4,075** (£1,212; £606; £303) **Stalls** Low

Form RPR
2-30 **1** **Yanabeeaa (USA)**^{70} 2826 3-9-4 **77**....................(v^{1}) DarrenEgan 3 81
(Sir Michael Stoute) *trckd ldr: rdn to chal 2f out and upsides after: edgd rt and bmpd nr fin: led last stride* **8/1**^{3}
341 **2** *shd* **The Baronet**^{13} 4746 3-9-3 **76**.................... RosieJessop 4 80+
(Sir Mark Prescott Bt) *hd over anther stall as they opened and slowly away: sn ct up in modestly run r: brought wd and rdn 2f out: styd on and grad clsd fnl f: jst failed* **6/4**^{1}
-323 **3** *nse* **Daneking**^{20} 4513 3-9-4 **80**.................... WilliamTwiston-Davies$^{(3)}$ 2 84
(John Gosden) *led: set modest pce tl past 1/2-way: sed dash for home wl over 1f out whn pressed: edgd lft after: bmpd nr fin: hdd last stride* **6/4**^{1}
-161 **4** *¾* **Moment In Time (IRE)**^{64} 2999 3-9-2 **75**.................... BrendanPowell 1 78
(David Simcock) *dwlt: trckd ldr: rdn to chal wl over 1f out: stl rt there ins fnl f: no ex nr fin* **5/1**^{2}

2m 25.32s (3.42) **Going Correction** +0.125s/f (Slow) **4** Ran SP% **107.8**
Speed ratings (Par 102): **92,91,91,91**
CSF £20.16 TOTE £11.30; EX 29.10.
Owner Hamdan Al Maktoum **Bred** Pollock Farms **Trained** Newmarket, Suffolk

FOCUS
With the new surface gradually bedding in, the ground was still officially standard to slow. A small field for this fair apprentice handicap with all the runners from major yards. They went a really pedestrian gallop and it turned into a sprint up the straight. All four had a chance entering the last furlong and only a length separated them at the line.

5229 BACK OR LAY AT BETDAQ.COM H'CAP 7f (P)
6:05 (6:06) (Class 6) (0-65,68) 3-Y-O **£1,617** (£481; £240; £120) **Stalls** Low

Form RPR
-245 **1** **Silver Lace (IRE)**^{71} 2803 3-9-1 **59**.................... TedDurcan 14 70
(Chris Wall) *dropped in fr wdst draw and hld up in last trio: prog on inner over 2f out: wnt 2nd jst ins fnl f: hrd rdn and styd on to ld last strides* **12/1**
6-51 **2** *nk* **Kinglami**^{9} 4874 3-9-7 **68** 6ex.................... AdamBeschizza$^{(3)}$ 2 79+
(Brian Gubby) *led: drvn for home over 2f out and sn 4 l clr: wknd fnl f: hdd last strides* **5/2**^{1}
3004 **3** *1* **Raffinn**^{28} 4218 3-9-7 **65**.................... LiamKeniry 6 73
(Sylvester Kirk) *trckd ldrs: rdn over 2f out: prog and wnt 2nd briefly 1f out: styd on but nvr able to chal* **10/1**^{3}
6-00 **4** *1* **Abhaath (USA)**^{74} 2689 3-9-7 **65**.................... LukeMorris 12 70
(Ronald Harris) *hld up in last trio: prog over 2f out: clsd to press for a pl 1f out: styd on same pce after* **20/1**
0-50 **5** *3* **Salutary**^{25} 4341 3-9-1 **59**.................... BrettDoyle 3 56
(Jane Chapple-Hyam) *chsd ldr: rdn and outpcd over 2f out: no imp after: wknd ins fnl f* **20/1**
4202 **6** *1 ½* **Light Burst (USA)**^{16} 4662 3-9-7 **65**....................(p) RoystonFfrench 13 58
(Ismail Mohammed) *racd on outer: chsd ldr: outpcd over 2f out: no imp after: wknd fnl f* **10/1**^{3}
2000 **7** *hd* **Swift Act**^{8} 4914 3-9-2 **65**.................... DarrenEgan$^{(5)}$ 10 57
(Ronald Harris) *hld up in rr: prog over 2f out: one of many trying to cl 1f out: wknd ins fnl f* **40/1**
-300 **8** *1 ¾* **Hill Of Dreams (IRE)**^{14} 4709 3-9-0 **58**.................... ShaneKelly 8 46
(Dean Ivory) *prom: rdn and lost pl over 2f out: struggling after* **20/1**
3022 **9** *shd* **Casa Bex**^{7} 4950 3-9-2 **63**....................(tp) RaulDaSilva$^{(3)}$ 11 50
(Philip McBride) *racd wd in rr: lost grnd bnd 3f out: n.d after* **11/2**^{2}
0046 **10** *1 ½* **Compton Crofter**^{13} 4734 3-7-12 **49**....................(t) NicoleNordblad$^{(7)}$ 1 32
(Hans Adielsson) *hld up: n.m.r after 2f and dropped to last: stl there and nudged along over 1f out: modest late prog* **25/1**
0003 **11** *4 ½* **Poetry Writer**^{20} 4490 3-9-1 **59**.................... FergusSweeney 5 30
(Michael Blanshard) *a towards rr: rdn and no prog over 2f out: wknd over 1f out* **25/1**
6545 **12** *¾* **Le King Beau (USA)**^{13} 4723 3-9-6 **64**....................(v) SeanLevey 7 33
(John Bridger) *nvr bttr than midfield: rdn over 2f out: wknd over 1f out* **14/1**
4620 **13** *8* **Moody Dancer**^{20} 4506 3-9-4 **62**.................... GeorgeBaker 9 10
(William Muir) *racd wd: chsd ldrs: lost grnd bnd 3f out: sn wknd: t.o* **16/1**

1m 26.94s (0.94) **Going Correction** +0.125s/f (Slow) **13** Ran SP% **106.8**
Speed ratings (Par 98): **99,98,97,96,92 91,91,89,88,87 82,81,72**
toteswingers 1&2 £9.50, 2&3 £8.30, 1&3 £12.30 CSF £30.35 CT £243.19 TOTE £10.70: £6.20, £1.02, £3.20; EX 57.90 TRIFECTA Not won..
Owner The Equema Partnership **Bred** Liam Queally **Trained** Newmarket, Suffolk

FOCUS
A maximum field for this modest 3yo handicap and it fell to the filly drawn on the wide outside.
Moody Dancer Official explanation: jockey reported filly had no more to give

5230 BETDAQ MOBILE APPS MEDIAN AUCTION MAIDEN STKS 7f (P)
6:35 (6:35) (Class 5) 2-Y-O **£2,264** (£673; £336; £168) **Stalls** Low

Form RPR
1 **Georgian Bay (IRE)** 2-9-3 0.................... MartinHarley 3 83+
(Mrs K Burke) *trckd ldng trio: prog to go 2nd 2f out: shkn up and sn chalng: rdn to ld last 150yds: rn green in front but styd on wl* **12/1**^{2}
622 **2** *¾* **Tropical Song**^{21} 4472 2-9-3 84.................... WilliamBuick 2 81
(John Gosden) *trckd ldng pair: smooth prog to ld over 2f out: pressed and shkn up wl over 1f out: hdd and nt qckn last 150yds* **2/13**^{1}
3 *3 ¼* **Marmot Bay (IRE)** 2-8-12 0.................... FergusSweeney 7 68
(Jamie Osborne) *trckd ldr to over 2f out: shkn up and styd on one pce after* **33/1**
4 *1* **Subtle Difference** 2-8-12 0.................... DavidProbert 5 65
(Andrew Balding) *s.s: rn green in last: prog to take 4th over 1f out: styd on but n.d* **16/1**^{3}
5 *9* **Red Catkin** 2-8-9 0.................... RyanPowell$^{(3)}$ 1 42
(George Margarson) *in tch in 5th: wknd over 2f out* **40/1**
0 **6** *1* **Caramel Sundae**^{36} 3948 2-8-7 0.................... TobyAtkinson$^{(5)}$ 6 39
(Marco Botti) *dwlt: in tch in 6th but rn green: wknd over 2f out* **16/1**^{3}
0 **7** *½* **Fossa**^{51} 3444 2-9-3 0.................... TedDurcan 4 43
(Dean Ivory) *led to over 2f out: wknd* **25/1**

1m 28.31s (2.31) **Going Correction** +0.125s/f (Slow) **7** Ran SP% **115.3**
Speed ratings (Par 94): **91,90,86,85,75 73,73**
toteswingers 1&2 £1.60, 2&3 £5.10, 1&3 £6.70 CSF £14.75 TOTE £9.40: £2.00, £1.10; EX 18.70.
Owner P O'Grady **Bred** Old Carhue & Grange Bloodstock **Trained** Middleham Moor, N Yorks

FOCUS
Just a fair maiden but the winner looks a nice recruit.

NOTEBOOK
Georgian Bay(IRE), a newcomer related to winners from five to 1m2f, was never far away from the favourite and was produced to challenge entering the last furlong. He displayed his greenness and jinked into the favourite when hitting the front, so can be expected to know more next time. He has a bit of scope and hopefully can go on from this. (op 10-1)
Tropical Song had what looked a fair opportunity to get off the mark against inexperienced rivals and everything appeared to be going to plan when he was produced to lead over 2f out. However, he could not put the race to bed and was run down by the newcomer inside the last furlong. He was given a nudge by that rival late on but it did not affect the result. A return to a sound surface on turf might enable him to pick up better. (op 2-11)
Marmot Bay(IRE), a sister to the very useful juvenile Hestian, was never far away and, although unable to go with the principals in the closing stages, showed a fair degree of promise on this debut.
Subtle Difference missed the break and was being nudged along on the home turn, but stayed on quite nicely and can be expected to benefit from this experience.
Caramel Sundae Official explanation: jockey reported filly slowly away
Fossa Official explanation: jockey reported gelding had no more to give

5231 BETDAQ CASINO GAMES H'CAP (LONDON MILE QUALIFIER) 1m (P)
7:05 (7:07) (Class 5) (0-70,70) 3-Y-O **£2,264** (£673; £336; £168) **Stalls** Low

Form RPR
00-4 **1** **Storm King**^{25} 4341 3-9-2 **65**.................... BrettDoyle 8 86+
(Jane Chapple-Hyam) *reluctant to enter stalls: led for 1f: trckd ldng pair: wnt 2nd 3f out: clsd to ld wl over 1f out: shkn up and sn clr: eased last 100yds* **7/2**^{2}
3503 **2** *6* **Trusting (IRE)**^{2} 5147 3-8-8 **57**....................(b) JohnFahy 9 61
(Eve Johnson Houghton) *trckd ldrs: prog 2f out: styd on to take 2nd last 150yds: no ch w wnr* **9/1**
4302 **3** *1 ¼* **Travelling**^{22} 4435 3-9-5 **68**.................... MartinHarley 2 69
(Marco Botti) *settled in last: pushed along 1/2-way: prog over 2f out: styd on to take 3rd last 100yds: no ch* **4/1**^{3}
2630 **4** *1 ½* **Graylyn Valentino**^{26} 4296 3-8-11 **63**.................... HarryBentley$^{(3)}$ 6 61
(Robin Dickin) *led after 1f: kicked on 3f out: hdd wl over 1f out: no ch w wnr: wknd fnl f* **6/1**
54-3 **5** *¾* **Breaking The Bank**^{27} 4233 3-9-7 **70**.................... GeorgeBaker 4 68
(William Muir) *hld up in midfield: effrt over 2f out: shkn up to dispute 3rd over 1f out but no ch: nt qckn and wknd ins fnl f* **3/1**^{1}
0502 **6** *hd* **Cockney Rhyme**^{8} 4901 3-8-13 **62**.................... EddieAhern 3 57
(Heather Main) *hld up in 7th: sme prog 2f out: shkn up and one pce over 1f out: fdd* **10/1**
0-25 **7** *9* **Scouting For Girls**^{20} 4506 3-8-8 **57**.................... ShaneKelly 1 32
(Jim Boyle) *pressed ldr after 1f to 3f out: sn wknd qckly* **15/2**
6365 **8** *9* **Thecornishcockney**^{13} 4725 3-9-5 **68**....................(t^{1}) DaraghO'Donohoe 7 22
(John Ryan) *rousted along early: sn chsd ldrs on outer: wknd over 2f out: t.o* **25/1**

1m 39.63s (-0.17) **Going Correction** +0.125s/f (Slow) **8** Ran SP% **116.2**
Speed ratings (Par 100): **105,99,97,96,95 95,86,77**
toteswingers 1&2 £5.60, 2&3 £6.40, 1&3 £4.20 CSF £35.24 CT £132.68 TOTE £4.70: £2.30, £2.60, £1.20; EX 50.10 Trifecta £173.60 Pool: £335.52 - 1.43 winning units..
Owner Norcroft Park Stud **Bred** Norcroft Park Stud And D Laidlaw **Trained** Dalham, Suffolk

FOCUS
A modest but fairly open-looking handicap that was turned into a procession by the winner.

5232 RACING PLUS ONLINE, MOBILE AND APP NURSERY 6f (P)
7:35 (7:35) (Class 3) (0-95,90) 2-Y-O **£5,602** (£1,677; £838; £419) **Stalls** Low

Form RPR
3130 **1** **Glass Office**^{12} 4763 2-9-4 **87**.................... WilliamBuick 1 91+
(David Simcock) *sn trckd ldng pair: clsd on inner to ld over 1f out: hung lft fnl f: r.o wl last 100yds* **5/6**^{1}
521 **2** *1 ¾* **Hipster**^{34} 3996 2-8-12 **81**....................(p) JimCrowley 3 81
(Ralph Beckett) *pushed along in last over 3f out: rdn and clsd on outer fr 2f out: wnt 2nd 1f out: intimidated by wnr ins fnl f: sn outpcd* **2/1**^{2}
4035 **3** *½* **Ocean Applause**^{32} 4098 2-9-7 **90**.................... BrettDoyle 2 87
(John Ryan) *chsd ldr: rdn to chal 2f out: upsides over 1f out: sn outpcd* **7/1**^{3}
016 **4** *1* **Claude Greenwood**^{25} 4318 2-8-12 **81**.................... JimmyFortune 4 75
(Sylvester Kirk) *led: rdn and hdd over 1f out: fdd* **10/1**

1m 14.43s (1.33) **Going Correction** +0.125s/f (Slow) **4** Ran SP% **109.5**
Speed ratings (Par 98): **96,93,93,91**
CSF £2.80 TOTE £2.50; EX 3.20.
Owner Mrs Fitri Hay **Bred** Bloomsbury Stud **Trained** Newmarket, Suffolk

FOCUS
A decent nursery despite the small field but weakened by the withdrawal of the forecast favourite. The winner is very well suited by the surface and the third helps with the level.

NOTEBOOK
Glass Office, whose only previous try on this track had been successful, was dropping in trip and tracked the pace then got a good split at the cut-away to the straight. However, he went sharply left across his rivals in the final furlong, a manoeuvre that particularly affected the runner-up, but always looked like holding on. This trip and surface clearly suits him best at present. (op 11-10)
Hipster, a winner on soft ground at Epsom on his previous start, was trying the surface for the first time but seemed to have more trouble handling the right-handed bend into the straight. He picked up well for pressure and looked set to give the winner a fight when that rival went across his bow and caused him to lose momentum. He should be able to gain compensation before long. (op 15-8)

Ocean Applause has generally had stiff tasks since his debut, running in Group and Listed company. This looked a better option for him, but he was still not good enough. (op 6-1)
Claude Greenwood, whose previous success had been on Polytrack, made the running but could not pick up when the race began in earnest. (op 9-1)

5233 PHIL TONER (FAUCETS) RETIREMENT H'CAP 6f (P)
8:05 (8:05) (Class 4) (0-85,85) 3-Y-0+ **£4,075** (£1,212; £606; £303) **Stalls** Low

Form RPR
0532 **1** **Intransigent**[8] 4919 3-9-8 **85** .... JimmyFortune 1 98+
(Andrew Balding) *trckd ldng pair: clsd to ld over 1f out: pushed clr: comf* **6/4**[1]
1200 **2** 2 1/4 **Noverre To Go (IRE)**[11] 4799 6-9-11 **84** .... LukeMorris 3 90
(Ronald Harris) *trckd ldrs in 5th: effrt and nt clr run briefly over 1f out: styd on to take 2nd ins fnl f: no ch w wnr* **5/1**[2]
2642 **3** 1 **Midnight Rider (IRE)**[48] 3541 4-9-8 **81** .... GeorgeBaker 4 84
(Chris Wall) *stdd s: hld up in last pair: pushed along and prog 2f out: reminder and styd on to take 3rd last 75yds: no ch* **11/2**[3]
613 **4** 1 1/4 **Flashbang**[8] 4933 4-8-5 **69** .... (tp) AshleyMorgan(5) 8 68
(Paul Cole) *pressed ldr: led 2f out to over 1f out: fdd fnl f* **12/1**
2220 **5** 3/4 **Ghost Train (IRE)**[13] 4723 3-8-8 **71** .... FrannyNorton 5 66
(Mark Johnston) *led to 2f out: nt qckn over 1f out: lost pl fnl f* **8/1**
3000 **6** 3/4 **Diamond Charlie (IRE)**[20] 4501 4-9-9 **82** .... SebSanders 6 76
(Simon Dow) *sltly awkward s: plld hrd early and hld up: rdn over 2f out: nt qckn on outer wl over 1f out: btn after* **25/1**
0003 **7** 3/4 **Tagula Night (IRE)**[26] 4286 6-9-9 **82** .... (b) TedDurcan 10 74
(Dean Ivory) *hld up towards rr: shkn up and no prog 2f out: one pce after* **8/1**
6205 **8** 1/2 **Bella Ophelia (IRE)**[32] 4081 3-9-1 **78** .... WilliamBuick 7 67
(Hughie Morrison) *chsd ldng trio: rdn over 2f out and edgd lft: sn btn* **14/1**
0200 **9** 2 1/2 **Lastkingofscotland (IRE)**[58] 3230 6-9-0 **73** .... (b) HayleyTurner 9 56
(Conor Dore) *sn pushed along in last: struggling fr 1/2-way* **20/1**

1m 12.71s (-0.39) **Going Correction** +0.125s/f (Slow)
WFA 3 from 4yo+ 4lb **9** Ran SP% **117.2**
Speed ratings (Par 105): **107,104,102,101,100 99,98,97,94**
toteswingers 1&2 £3.10, 2&3 £5.60, 1&3 £2.50 CSF £9.18 CT £33.19 TOTE £1.70: £1.10, £2.40, £2.10; EX 11.70 Trifecta £37.60 Pool: £315.56 - 6.21 winning units..
Owner Kingsclere Racing CLub **Bred** Kingsclere Stud **Trained** Kingsclere, Hants

FOCUS
A competitive sprint handicap but it went just as the market suggested.

5234 SPORTINGLIFE.COM RACING H'CAP 7f (P)
8:35 (8:36) (Class 5) (0-75,75) 3-Y-0+ **£2,264** (£673; £336; £168) **Stalls** Low

Form RPR
50-1 **1** **Scottish Lake**[8] 4914 4-9-4 **67** 6ex .... (b) KirstyMilczarek 3 77
(Olivia Maylam) *led after 1f: kicked on over 2f out: rdn and pressed over 1f out: styd on wl* **5/2**[1]
0-30 **2** 1 **Afkar (IRE)**[128] 1262 4-9-5 **68** .... (b) SebSanders 9 75
(Clive Brittain) *prom: chsd wnr 4f out: rdn over 2f out: kpt pressing but readily hld fnl f* **5/1**[3]
353- **3** 3 3/4 **Sunshine Always (IRE)**[339] 5970 6-8-12 **66** .... MarkCoumbe(5) 5 63
(Michael Attwater) *chsd ldrs: rdn over 2f out: tk 3rd wl over 1f out: one pce and no imp* **11/1**
-004 **4** 1 **Leelu**[7] 4942 6-9-0 **63** .... LiamKeniry 2 58
(David Arbuthnot) *led at a brisk pce for 1f: chsd ldng pair 4f out to wl over 1f out where outpcd: n.d after* **10/1**
0600 **5** 1/2 **Dozy Joe**[16] 4661 4-9-5 **75** .... MichaelJMMurphy(7) 1 68
(Ian Wood) *s.s: outpcd in last: rousted along and prog on wd outside bnd 4f out to 3f out: no imp on ldrs fnl 2f* **10/3**[2]
-060 **6** 3 1/4 **Airborne Again (IRE)**[20] 4496 3-9-3 **72** .... HayleyTurner 4 55
(Harry Dunlop) *chsd ldrs: rdn over 2f out: wknd over 1f out* **7/1**
-000 **7** 2 1/2 **Clearing House**[19] 4541 7-8-0 **56** oh2 .... NatashaEaton(7) 6 34
(John Ryan) *dwlt and n.m.r s: a towards rr: outpcd over 2f out: no ch after* **40/1**
-000 **8** hd **Regal Approval**[20] 4503 4-9-12 **75** .... (bt1) PatCosgrave 7 53
(Jim Boyle) *chsd ldrs: lost pl wl over 2f out and immediately btn* **16/1**
6 **9** 7 **Gracie's Games**[34] 3993 6-8-2 **56** oh1 .... (v) DarrenEgan(5) 8 16
(Richard Price) *sn rdn: outpcd and a in last pair* **10/1**

1m 26.09s (0.09) **Going Correction** +0.125s/f (Slow)
WFA 3 from 4yo+ 6lb **9** Ran SP% **115.7**
Speed ratings (Par 103): **104,102,98,97,96 93,90,90,82**
toteswingers 1&2 £4.60, 2&3 £12.70, 1&3 £8.70 CSF £15.24 CT £115.93 TOTE £3.10: £1.10, £2.40, £3.80; EX 18.90 Trifecta £446.70 Part won. Pool of £603.70 - 0.60 winning units..
Owner Miss Olivia Maylam **Bred** Farmers Hill Stud **Trained** Epsom, Surrey

FOCUS
This handicap was run 0.85secs faster than the two earlier races over the trip.
T/Plt: £89.60 to a £1 stake. Pool of £46043.80 - 375.04 winning tickets. T/Qpdt: £6.70 to a £1 stake. Pool of £6256.12 - 682.92 winning tickets. JN

4602 SALISBURY (R-H)
Wednesday, August 15

OFFICIAL GOING: Good to soft changing to soft after race 1 (2.30)
Wind: mild brezze against, quiet strong after Race 3 Weather: overcast

5235 BRITISH STALLION STUDS EBF MOLSON COORS MAIDEN STKS 6f
2:30 (2:30) (Class 4) 2-Y-0 **£4,237** (£1,260; £630; £315) **Stalls** Low

Form RPR
63 **1** **Saint Jerome (IRE)**[15] 4688 2-9-3 0 .... HayleyTurner 5 84+
(Marcus Tregoning) *trckd ldrs: rdn over 1f out: led ent fnl f: r.o strly* **13/8**[1]
04 **2** 1 1/2 **Rock Up (IRE)**[12] 4773 2-9-3 0 .... TedDurcan 7 80
(David Elsworth) *trckd ldr: rdn to ld 2f out: sn edgd rt: hdd jst over 1f out: kpt on but sn hld by wnr* **18/1**
03 **3** 3/4 **Digress**[25] 4330 2-9-3 0 .... RyanMoore 9 78
(Sir Michael Stoute) *bmpd leaving stalls: towards rr: hdwy whn nt clr run and swtchd lft over 1f out: r.o ins fnl f: wnt 3rd towards fin: nt rch ldrs* **10/1**
4 1/2 **Music Master** 2-9-3 0 .... DaneO'Neill 2 76+
(Henry Candy) *hld up towards rr: hdwy 2f out: swtchd rt whn nt clr run over 1f out: rdn and r.o fnl f* **9/2**[3]
440 **5** 2 3/4 **Millers Wharf (IRE)**[15] 4688 2-9-3 79 .... PatDobbs 8 68
(Richard Hannon) *wnt lft leaving stalls: mid-div: hdwy over 2f out: rdn to chse ldrs over 1f out: one pce fnl f* **9/1**
65 **6** 3 1/4 **Red Dragon (IRE)**[20] 4512 2-9-3 0 .... MatthewChadwick 6 58
(Charles Hills) *led: rdn and hdd 2f out: wknd ins fnl f* **40/1**
7 2 1/4 **Desert Command** 2-9-3 0 .... JimmyFortune 1 51
(Andrew Balding) *chsd ldrs: rdn over 2f out: wknd ent fnl f* **10/1**
00 **8** hd **Elvin**[21] 4463 2-9-3 0 .... EddieAhern 3 50
(Amanda Perrett) *mid-div: hdwy 2f out: sn rdn: wknd fnl f* **66/1**
9 hd **Blue Twister** 2-9-3 0 .... LiamKeniry 14 50
(Andrew Balding) *hmpd leaving stalls: a towards rr* **25/1**
2 **10** 3/4 **King Oliver**[10] 4845 2-9-3 0 .... RichardHughes 12 48
(Richard Hannon) *mid-div: rdn over 2f out: wknd over 1f out* **4/1**[2]
0 **11** 3 **Lyrical Vibe**[18] 4604 2-8-12 0 .... CathyGannon 10 34
(David Evans) *hmpd leaving stalls: a towards rr* **100/1**
12 4 **Astrum** 2-9-3 0 .... JamesMillman 4 27
(Rod Millman) *prom tl rdn over 3f out* **66/1**

1m 17.15s (2.35) **Going Correction** +0.35s/f (Good) **12** Ran SP% **120.0**
Speed ratings (Par 96): **98,96,95,94,90 86,83,83,82,81 77,72**
toteswingers 1&2 £8.10, 1&3 £3.90, 2&3 £9.20 CSF £36.79 TOTE £2.60: £1.30, £4.00, £3.20; EX 15.40 Trifecta £159.80 Pool £1,045.56 - 4.84 winning units..
Owner Lady Tennant **Bred** P Turley **Trained** Lambourn, Berks

FOCUS
Considerable morning rain eased the ground from the overnight Good to firm. The time for the opener was 4.75secs slower than standard and the jockeys reported the ground to be riding "soft". The paper favourite was an absentee, but this still looked a decent maiden and one that contained future winners. The runners came down the centre of the track. The winner is capable of better, whatever the true level of this form turns out to be.

NOTEBOOK
Saint Jerome(IRE) built on the promise of his second run at Glorious Goodwood. He ran on strongly once in front and there's more to come from him when he's stepped up in trip. The ease in the ground suited him and his trainer thinks he might be the type for sales races in the autumn. (op 5-2 tchd 11-4)
Rock Up(IRE), fourth in what may have been a warm Newmarket maiden on his second outing, put in another good run although he did wander around in front. This scopey colt should soon get off the mark. (op 16-1)
Digress ◆, like the first two, was having his third outing. Down in trip and again held up at the back, he found his path blocked for a while, but finished his race in good style. He's well related and should certainly win a maiden. (op 9-1)
Music Master ◆, a half-brother to the Candy stable's useful handicapper The Confessor, came on for support on his debut, and while he could not reward his supporters he still shaped with a good deal of promise. He looks a sure future winner. (tchd 5-1)
Millers Wharf(IRE) set the standard with a BHA mark of 79, but was apparently the Hannon second string. He travelled well for a while before being put in his place by the principals and finished further behind Saint Jerome than he had at Goodwood. (op 12-1)
Red Dragon(IRE) raced prominently this time and, although fading out of it, this still looked a step up.
Desert Command, a brother to his stable's recent Shergar Cup winner Desert Law, should improve with the run behind him. (tchd 9-1 and 11-1)
Blue Twister, a speedily-bred newcomer who was very coltish in the preliminaries, can step up on this. (tchd 22-1)
King Oliver's trainer has won five divisions of this race since 2008 but this one, the choice of Richard Hughes, could not enhance that record. Easy to back, the colt could not reproduce his Newbury effort and probably failed to act on the ground. (op 11-4 tchd 5-2)
Astrum was reported to have jumped the path. Official explanation: jockey reported gelding jumped path

5236 STEVENS GARNIER LTD NURSERY 6f 212y
3:00 (3:00) (Class 5) (0-75,81) 2-Y-0 **£2,587** (£770; £384; £192) **Stalls** Centre

Form RPR
036 **1** **Aint Got A Scooby (IRE)**[11] 4813 2-8-6 **60** .... JohnFahy 2 65
(Clive Cox) *stmbld leaving stalls: trckd ldrs: rdn to ld 2f out: styd on: rdn out* **4/1**[2]
435 **2** 1 **Pira Palace (IRE)**[20] 4507 2-9-0 **68** .... RyanMoore 5 70
(Sir Michael Stoute) *trckd ldr tl lost pl and short of room jst over 3f out: sn rdn: styd on to go 2nd ins fnl f: a being hld fnl 120yds* **4/1**[2]
0525 **3** 1 1/4 **Poetic Verse**[10] 4847 2-8-4 **58** .... NickyMackay 7 57
(Rod Millman) *trckd ldrs: rdn to chal 2f out: kpt on same pce fnl f* **8/1**
2421 **4** 5 **Black Monk (IRE)**[10] 4837 2-9-13 **81** 6ex .... RichardHughes 1 67
(Richard Hannon) *trckd ldrs: wnt 2nd over 3f out: rdn and ev ch 2f out: wknd ins fnl f* **6/4**[1]
5633 **5** 4 **It's Only Business**[39] 3858 2-8-5 **66** .... RyanWhile(7) 4 42
(Bill Turner) *chsd ldrs: struggling over 3f out: sn btn* **7/1**[3]
0160 **6** hd **Cuisine (IRE)**[11] 4804 2-9-7 **75** .... (v1) DavidProbert 6 50
(Andrew Balding) *led: rdn and hdd 2f out: wknd qckly* **12/1**

1m 31.41s (2.81) **Going Correction** +0.35s/f (Good) **6** Ran SP% **111.3**
Speed ratings (Par 94): **97,95,94,88,84 83**
toteswingers 1&2 £2.40, 1&3 £5.00, 2&3 £3.70 CSF £19.70 TOTE £4.50: £3.00, £1.50; EX 24.30.
Owner Exors Of The Late Dennis Shaw **Bred** D Veitch & R O'Callaghan **Trained** Lambourn, Berks

FOCUS
Just an ordinary nursery. The first three home handles the ground better than the others and their form looks sound enough.

NOTEBOOK
Aint Got A Scooby(IRE) slipped and stumbled his way out of the stalls, but did it quite well in the end, appearing to score with a bit to spare. He handled the ground better than most and this track suited him more than Epsom or Lingfield had. (op 5-1 tchd 6-1)
Pira Palace(IRE) dropped to the rear of the field before rallying quite well. This was a fair run, but she's not necessarily progressing. (op 7-2)
Poetic Verse had her chance and kept on once her measure had been taken. She handled this different ground well enough. (op 9-1 tchd 10-1)
Black Monk(IRE) was 2lb badly in under the penalty for his Chester win. Racing keenly in the early stages and appearing to resent not being given his head, he found little at the business end. He might appreciate dropping back to 6f. (op 5-4)
It's Only Business does not convince that 7f and soft ground is an ideal combination for him. (op 17-2 tchd 9-1)
Cuisine(IRE) did too much in the first-time visor and seems to be going the wrong way. (op 11-1)

5237 GOLDRING SECURITY SERVICES PEMBROKE CUP (H'CAP) 1m
3:35 (3:35) (Class 4) (0-85,84) 3-Y-0 **£4,851** (£1,443; £721; £360) **Stalls** Low

Form RPR
01-0 **1** **Knave Of Clubs (IRE)**[7] 4949 3-9-1 **78** .... SebSanders 5 84
(Peter Makin) *s.i.s: sn trcking ldr: rdn over 3f out: styd on gamely u.str.p to ld fnl 70yds: jst hld on* **33/1**
2251 **2** hd **Juvenal (IRE)**[23] 4413 3-9-0 **77** .... (p) RyanMoore 1 83+
(Richard Hannon) *hld up in rr of midfield: rdn wl over 2f out: hdwy ent fnl f: swtchd lft whn nt best of runs fnl 80yds: fin strly: jst failed* **9/2**[2]
2-11 **3** 1/2 **Discoverer (IRE)**[189] 471 3-9-7 **84** .... NickyMackay 6 89
(John Gosden) *led: rdn wl over 1f out: styd on gamely tl hdd fnl 70yds: no ex* **9/2**[2]

6212 **4** 3/4 **Kaafel (IRE)**[15] 4679 3-9-3 80 PaulHanagan 8 83
(Charles Hills) *trckd ldrs: nudged along over 4f out: rdn over 2f out: nvr quite able to chal: styd on same pce fnl f* **7/2**[1]

3601 **5** hd **Verse Of Love**[19] 4534 3-9-0 77 CathyGannon 7 80
(David Evans) *mid-div: rdn over 2f out: hdwy ent fnl f: styd on but nt clrest of runs fnl 70yds* **12/1**

3230 **6** shd **Sir Mike**[13] 4735 3-9-3 80 (p) JimCrowley 2 82
(Amanda Perrett) *mid-div: rdn over 2f out: hdwy ent fnl f: styd on same pce fnl 120yds* **6/1**[3]

-300 **7** 1/2 **Restaurateur (IRE)**[12] 4772 3-8-10 73 (v[1]) JimmyFortune 4 74
(Andrew Balding) *trckd ldrs: rdn to press ldr fr 2f out tl hung lft sn after: styng on at same pce whn jockey dropped whip 1f out: fdd fnl 60yds* **8/1**

-030 **8** 21 **Dance With Me (IRE)**[46] 3630 3-8-12 75 DavidProbert 9 30
(Jonathan Geake) *v.s.a: a towards rr: wknd over 1f out: eased* **28/1**

40-2 **9** 2 3/4 **Dare To Dream**[88] 2272 3-9-6 83 RichardHughes 11 32
(Richard Hannon) *hld up towards rr: rdn over 2f out: nvr any imp: eased whn btn* **9/2**[2]

1m 45.73s (2.23) **Going Correction** +0.35s/f (Good) **9** Ran SP% **116.2**
Speed ratings (Par 102): **102,101,101,100,100 100,99,78,76**
toteswingers 1&2 £17.60, 1&3 £20.80, 2&3 £4.60 CSF £176.93 CT £821.34 TOTE £49.50: £7.30, £2.60, £1.60; EX 331.60 TRIFECTA Not won..
Owner J P Carrington **Bred** Bakewell Bloodstock **Trained** Ogbourne Maisey, Wilts

FOCUS
The ground had eased further by this stage and was officially described as Soft now. This was a fair handicap, but they finished in a bunch and the form does not look the most solid.
Restaurateur(IRE) Official explanation: jockey reported colt hung left
Dance With Me(IRE) Official explanation: jockey reported gelding slow away

5238 EUROPEAN BREEDERS' FUND UPAVON FILLIES' STKS (LISTED RACE) 1m 1f 198y
4:05 (4:06) (Class 1) 3-Y-0+
£23,818 (£9,030; £4,519; £2,251; £1,129; £567) **Stalls** Low

Form RPR
6-40 **1** **Opera Gal (IRE)**[54] 3329 5-9-0 95 JimmyFortune 3 97+
(Andrew Balding) *mde all: jnd 3f out: rdn clr 2f out: styd on strly fnl f* **3/1**[2]

5203 **2** 2 1/4 **Oojooba**[14] 4702 3-8-5 82 AndreaAtzeni 9 93+
(Roger Varian) *hld up: hdwy over 2f out: sn rdn: styd on to chse wnr ent fnl f: a being hld* **9/1**[3]

0410 **3** 3 **Rumh (GER)**[32] 4115 4-9-0 99 JimCrowley 6 87+
(Saeed Bin Suroor) *trckd wnr: jnd wnr 3f out: sn rdn: hld 2f out: lost 2nd ent fnl f: styd on same pce* **10/1**

-234 **4** 2 3/4 **Epernay**[14] 4702 5-9-0 77 (vt) JamesDoyle 8 82
(Ian Williams) *trckd ldrs: effrt to chal 3f out: styd on same pce fnl 2f* **25/1**

-041 **5** 2 1/2 **Qaadira (USA)**[82] 2453 3-8-5 82 PaulHanagan 4 77
(John Gosden) *led by handler most of way to s: racd keenly early: hld up: rdn over 2f out: nvr any imp* **20/1**

1222 **6** 4 **Love Your Looks**[19] 4529 4-9-0 90 RichardHughes 7 71
(Mike Murphy) *trckd ldrs: rdn to dispute cl 2nd over 2f out: wknd ent fnl f* **10/1**

612 **7** 11 **Emirates Queen**[19] 4556 3-8-6 109 ow1 KierenFallon 5 50
(Luca Cumani) *hld up: pushed along over 5f out: nvr any imp: wknd 2f out* **10/11**[1]

2m 8.91s (-0.99) **Going Correction** +0.175s/f (Good)
WFA 3 from 4yo+ 9lb **7** Ran SP% **114.2**
Speed ratings (Par 108): **110,108,105,103,101 98,89**
toteswingers 1&2 £3.70, 1&3 £4.30, 2&3 £6.70 CSF £29.26 TOTE £3.10: £1.70, £3.80; EX 24.80 Trifecta £129.80 Pool £1,137.36 - 1.94 winning units..
Owner J C Smith **Bred** Littleton Stud **Trained** Kingsclere, Hants

FOCUS
Not a strong edition of this Listed race, run in soft ground, and with the favourite not giving her running the form is not strong.

NOTEBOOK
Opera Gal(IRE) produced a commendable effort, the mare making all and staying on determinedly to go one better than she had behind Primevere 12 months ago. Last year she went on to take a similar event at Windsor later in the month, but she will be allowed a second crack at a Group race now, probably at Baden-Baden. (op 5-1)
Oojooba, back up in grade, ran on from the rear for second without threatening the winner. She's out of Guineas heroine Ameerat and this black type makes her even more valuable. (op 12-1)
Rumh(GER), by the same sire as the runner-up, was dropping back from 2m. She had her chance, but lacked a change of pace and is not especially consistent. (op 8-1 tchd 11-1)
Epernay, unlucky in a Goodwood handicap last time, when just behind today's runner-up Oojooba, ran a creditable race on this rise in grade. She's a reliable mare. (tchd 33-1)
Qaadira(USA), off since winning a maiden in late May and re-equipped with a hood, was led down to post. She could make just minor progress from the rear of the field. (op 18-1)
Love Your Looks travelled strongly, but her stamina ebbed away in this ground once she was let down. This admirable filly deserves another crack at this grade. (op 15-2 tchd 7-1)
Emirates Queen's neck second to Barefoot Lady in this grade at York was the best form on offer, and she had 10lb in hand of her rivals here on BHA figures. However, it was clear from an early stage that she was not travelling with any fluency and she never picked up from the rear. The ground is an obvious excuse, while she has her quirks and was again walked to the start before being installed early. The Stewards considered her running and noted the trainer's representative's explanation that the filly was unsuited by the soft ground. They ordered the filly to be routine tested. Official explanation: trainer's rep explained to stewards filly unsuited by soft ground (op 5-6 tchd Evens, 8-11 early in places)

5239 CHAMPAGNE JOSEPH PERRIER H'CAP 1m 1f 198y
4:40 (4:41) (Class 5) (0-70,70) 3-Y-0+ **£2,587** (£770; £384; £192) **Stalls** Low

Form RPR
2-00 **1** **Oetzi**[56] 3278 4-9-4 67 MichaelJMMurphy[(7)] 7 77
(Alan Jarvis) *unsettled stalls: hld up in last: swtchd lft and hdwy over 2f out: sn rdn: jockey lost whip sn after: veered bdly lft jst over 1f out: kpt on wl: pushed out* **4/1**[3]

3-02 **2** 1/2 **Monopoli**[20] 4505 3-9-1 66 JimCrowley 9 75
(Ralph Beckett) *hld up towards rr: hdwy into midfield over 5f out: rdn and edgd rt over 2f out: ev ch but no ex fnl 75yds* **5/2**[1]

254/ **3** 1 1/2 **Presto Volante (IRE)**[726] 5256 4-9-6 62 HayleyTurner 4 69
(Amanda Perrett) *hld up towards rr: struggling over 5f out: hdwy 2f out: mounting chal and ev ch whn bdly hmpd jst over 1f out: kpt on but no ch after* **7/1**

5333 **4** 1 3/4 **South Cape**[21] 4470 9-9-9 65 RyanMoore 2 70
(Gary Moore) *in tch: pushed along fr over 3f out: mounting chal whn bdly squeezed up jst over 1f out: no ch after: kpt on same pce* **11/4**[2]

0000 **5** 5 **Alshazah**[14] 4706 4-9-6 62 (p) JamesMillman 8 55
(Rod Millman) *sn trcking ldrs: wnt 2nd after 3f: rdn to ld 2f out: hdd whn sltly hmpd jst over 1f out: wknd* **16/1**

445/ **6** 3 3/4 **Star Hill**[649] 7338 5-9-5 61 DaneO'Neill 1 47
(Alan King) *trckd ldrs: rdn over 2f out: wknd ent fnl f* **12/1**

2300 **7** 1 1/4 **Blue Deer (IRE)**[7] 4950 4-9-11 67 SebSanders 14 51
(Lee Carter) *led: rdn and hdd 2f out: wknd ent fnl f* **25/1**

452- **8** 47 **Langley**[141] 6785 5-9-0 63 DanielMuscutt[(7)] 3
(Tim Vaughan) *trckd ldrs: rdn over 3f out: sn wknd: t.o* **15/2**

2m 10.69s (0.79) **Going Correction** +0.175s/f (Good)
WFA 3 from 4yo+ 9lb **8** Ran SP% **116.9**
Speed ratings (Par 103): **103,102,101,100,96 93,92,54**
toteswingers 1&2 £3.30, 1&3 £5.00, 2&3 £5.00 CSF £14.83 CT £67.83 TOTE £4.40: £1.60, £1.70, £2.10; EX 15.80 Trifecta £307.20 Pool £805.50 - 1.94 winning units..
Owner Allen B Pope & Jarvis Associates **Bred** Jarvis Associates **Trained** Twyford, Bucks

FOCUS
A modest handicap which was hit by non-runners. The principals came from the rear and things got rough in the latter stages with the winner the culprit.

5240 CGA RACING EXCELLENCE APPRENTICE H'CAP (WHIPS SHALL BE CARRIED BUT NOT USED) 6f 212y
5:10 (5:11) (Class 5) (0-70,67) 3-Y-0+ **£2,587** (£770; £384; £192) **Stalls** Centre

Form RPR
0-40 **1** **King Vahe (IRE)**[82] 2449 3-9-6 66 MichaelJMMurphy 5 75+
(Alan Jarvis) *mde all: wandered whn pushed along over 2f out: kpt on wl ins fnl f* **17/2**

4655 **2** 2 1/2 **Netley Marsh**[6] 4986 3-8-8 59 (b) MeganWhitehead[(5)] 9 61
(Richard Hannon) *s.i.s: mid-div: pushed along over 2f out: hdwy over 1f out: styd on to chse wnr fnl 120yds: a being hld* **4/1**[2]

0024 **3** 1 1/4 **George Thisby**[18] 4602 6-9-4 63 (p) DanielMuscutt[(5)] 6 64
(Rod Millman) *chsd ldrs: pushed along over 2f out: nvr able to mount chal: styd on same pce* **3/1**[1]

5-00 **4** 3/4 **Batchworth Blaise**[193] 422 9-8-4 49 oh4 (b) JoeyHaynes[(5)] 1 48
(Eric Wheeler) *racd keenly: prom: pushed along to chse wnr over 2f out tl no ex and lost 2 pls fnl 120yds* **28/1**

3520 **5** 1 **The Name Is Frank**[18] 4602 7-9-8 62 IanBurns 13 58
(Mark Gillard) *little slowly away: racd keenly: mid-div: pushed along 3f out: one pce fnl 2f* **9/2**[3]

0-44 **6** 3 1/4 **Mulberry Brite**[18] 4582 4-9-2 56 DannyBrock 10 44
(Alastair Lidderdale) *mid-div: hdwy over 3f out: effrt over 2f out: fdd fnl f* **7/1**

3000 **7** 8 **Grande Illusion**[8] 4900 3-8-3 49 oh4 (p) JakePayne 3 14
(J W Hills) *prom tl 2f out: wknd over 1f out* **33/1**

000- **8** 2 3/4 **Realt Na Mara (IRE)**[352] 5539 9-8-6 51 RyanTate[(5)] 12 11
(Hughie Morrison) *in last pair and struggling fr 4f out: wknd over 1f out* **14/1**

0-00 **9** 1 1/4 **Eye For The Girls**[18] 4584 6-8-6 49 oh1 (t) NoelGarbutt[(3)] 7 6
(William Knight) *v awkward leaving stalls: a towards rr* **16/1**

0-50 **10** nk **Grand Piano (IRE)**[11] 4812 5-9-4 63 (v) AdamMcLean[(5)] 8 19
(Andrew Balding) *s.i.s: sn chsng ldrs: dropped away tamely 3f out* **7/1**

1m 31.77s (3.17) **Going Correction** +0.35s/f (Good)
WFA 3 from 4yo+ 6lb **10** Ran SP% **117.6**
Speed ratings (Par 103): **95,92,90,89,88 85,75,72,71,70**
toteswingers 1&2 £4.60, 1&3 £6.60, 2&3 £3.60 CSF £42.90 CT £128.06 TOTE £10.20: £3.00, £2.00, £2.10; EX 52.60 Trifecta £302.70 Pool £1,080.11 - 2.63 winning units..
Owner Cedars Partnership **Bred** Hong Kong Breeders Club **Trained** Twyford, Bucks

FOCUS
A weak apprentice handicap run at just a steady pace, and not form to treat too seriously.
T/Plt: £204.00 to a £1 stake. Pool: £76111.85 - 272.23 winning tickets T/Qpdt: £46.10 to a £1 stake. Pool: £6198.80 - 99.30 winning tickets TM

5009 SOUTHWELL (L-H)
Wednesday, August 15

OFFICIAL GOING: Standard
Wind: virtually nil Weather: Heavy cloud and heavy showers

5241 PLAY GOLF AT SOUTHWELL GOLF CLUB AMATEUR RIDERS' H'CAP 1m 6f (F)
5:15 (5:16) (Class 6) (0-65,65) 4-Y-0+ **£1,646** (£506; £253) **Stalls** Low

Form RPR
/603 **1** **Veloso (FR)**[30] 4145 10-10-4 60 oh6 MissKBannon[(5)] 5 78
(Noel Wilson) *hld up in tch: smooth hdwy to trck ldrs over 4f out: chal on bit over 2f out: led wl over 1f out: sn pushed clr easily* **10/1**

4540 **2** 12 **Mustajed**[10] 4843 11-10-4 60 oh6 (v) MrPMillman[(5)] 13 60
(Rod Millman) *hld up towards rr: stdy hdwy over 5f out: chsd ldrs 3f out: rdn and styd on inner fnl 2f: no ch w wnr* **25/1**

4060 **3** 1 3/4 **Bocamix (FR)**[11] 4831 6-10-9 60 oh1 (t) MrsCBartley 6 58
(Andrew Crook) *prom: led 1/2-way: rdn along and hdd 3f out: sn drvn and kpt on same pce* **17/2**

-340 **4** 2 1/2 **Decana**[35] 3961 4-10-9 65 MrRPooles[(5)] 9 59
(Hughie Morrison) *prom: led 3f out: rdn and hdd wl over 1f out: sn drvn and wknd appr fnl f* **7/2**[2]

0020 **5** hd **Lakeman (IRE)**[6] 5012 6-10-4 60 oh3 (b) MrJohnWilley[(5)] 14 54
(Brian Ellison) *prom on outer: effrt and cl up over 4f out: rdn along wl over 2f out: grad wknd* **9/1**

0160 **6** 6 **William's Way**[51] 3449 10-10-6 60 oh4 (tp) MrCMartin[(3)] 4 46
(Ian Wood) *hld up towards rr: stdy hdwy 6f out: chsd ldrs over 3f out: swtchd rt to outer and drvn wl over 1f out: sn wknd* **8/1**[3]

0012 **7** 2 **Omid**[30] 4145 4-10-12 63 (vt) MrSWalker 12 47
(Nicky Vaughan) *trckd ldrs: pushed along after 5f: sn rdn and lost pl: bhd fr 1/2-way* **5/4**[1]

6005 **8** 3 3/4 **Blue Cossack (IRE)**[16] 4652 4-10-2 60 oh3 MrsRWilson[(7)] 3 39
(Neil King) *led: pushed along and hdd 1/2-way: rdn and lost pl over 5f out: sn bhd* **14/1**

350/ **9** 13 **Mix N Match**[22] 4300 8-10-9 60 oh7 MissGAndrews 10 22
(Christopher Kellett) *dwlt: a in rr* **50/1**

05-0 **10** 22 **Stadium Of Light (IRE)**[136] 1154 5-10-9 60 oh9 (tp) MissADeniel 1
(Shaun Harris) *in tch on inner: pushed along 1/2-way: rdn and wknd over 5f out: sn bhd* **25/1**

3m 8.46s (0.16) **Going Correction** -0.075s/f (Stan) **10** Ran SP% **123.7**
Speed ratings (Par 101): **96,89,88,86,86 83,82,79,72,59**
toteswingers 1&2 £26.70, 2&3 £14.50, 1&3 £15.10 CSF £238.44 CT £2228.92 TOTE £15.70: £4.10, £7.30, £3.10; EX 238.90.
Owner Brian Morton **Bred** Jean Louis Pariente **Trained** Middleham, N Yorks

FOCUS
There was very heavy rain before racing, and riders repored the kickback to be among the worst ever here. The majority of runners were out of the weights in this amateur riders' handicap. The favourite was very disappointing but the winner hammered his rivals. He was very well in on old form.
Omid Official explanation: jockey reported gelding never travelling

5242 COME JUMPING ON THE 19TH AUGUST MAIDEN STKS 5f (F)
5:45 (5:46) (Class 5) 2-Y-O £2,587 (£770; £384; £192) Stalls High

Form RPR
5 **1** **Girl At The Sands (IRE)**[16] 4651 2-8-12 0 JoeFanning 7 68
(James Given) *cl up: chal 2f out: rdn to ld ins fnl f: kpt on* **10/1**
303 **2** *2* **Bapak Bangsawan**[7] 4952 2-9-3 0 AmyRyan 3 66
(Kevin Ryan) *led: rdn along wl over 1f out: hdd ins fnl f: kpt on same pce* **11/2**
5424 **3** *nk* **Club House (IRE)**[11] 4804 2-9-3 77 (p) StevieDonohoe 11 65
(Robert Mills) *chsd ldrs: rdn along 2f out: kpt on u.p fnl f* **3/1**[2]
4 *¾* **Look On By** 2-9-3 0 AdrianNicholls 10 62+
(Ed McMahon) *green and outpcd: rdn along 1/2-way: swtchd rt to stands' rail wl over 1f out: styd on appr fnl f: nrst fin* **8/1**
6 **5** *2 ¾* **First Serve (IRE)**[25] 4344 2-8-12 0 GrahamGibbons 6 48
(David Barron) *cl up: pushed along 1/2-way: sn rdn and wknd wl over 1f out* **5/2**[1]
6 *1* **Tartania** 2-8-12 0 RobertWinston 1 44
(Scott Dixon) *prom on wd outside: rdn along 2f out: wknd fnl f* **16/1**
3000 **7** *½* **Simply Dreaming**[22] 4433 2-8-12 45 JamieMackay 8 42
(Michael Squance) *chsd ldrs: rdn along 1/2-way: sn wknd* **66/1**
60 **8** *2 ¾* **Grandorio (IRE)**[14] 4710 2-9-3 0 IanMongan 4 39
(David O'Meara) *sn outpcd and a bhd* **4/1**[3]
40 **9** *nk* **Ingleby Symphony (IRE)**[11] 4825 2-8-7 0 ShaneBKelly[(5)] 9 31
(Richard Fahey) *sn outpcd and a bhd* **10/1**
06 **10** *9* **Anna Isabella**[9] 4886 2-8-12 0 MartinDwyer 2
(Derek Shaw) *dwlt: a outpcd and bhd* **66/1**

1m 0.17s (0.47) **Going Correction** +0.025s/f (Slow) **10** Ran SP% **127.1**
Speed ratings (Par 94): **97,93,93,92,87 86,85,80,80,66**
toteswingers 1&2 £10.10, 2&3 £4.20, 1&3 £5.40 CSF £70.09 TOTE £20.30: £7.10, £1.30, £2.70; EX 58.40.
Owner Peter Swann **Bred** Rossenarra Bloodstock Limited **Trained** Willoughton, Lincs

FOCUS
Two of the three market leaders were disappointing in this weak maiden, perhaps due to the kickback, but a market springer scored in good style. She improved on her debut effort.

NOTEBOOK
Girl At The Sands(IRE) was supported at biggish prices and travelled well down the centre of the track before forging clear for a comfortable success. A first foal of a 5f 2yo winner, this was a big step forward on her 28-1 fifth at Wolverhampton on debut and this speedy filly has quite a bit of potential for further progress. (op 12-1)
Bapak Bangsawan, placed behind a 78-rated winner in a 6f Newcastle maiden last time, gave it a good shot under a positive ride back but was overhauled in the closing stages back at 5f on his Fibresand debut. He is a half-brother to winners at up to 1m6f but seems to have plenty of speed and is out of a fairly useful 5f 2yo winner.
Club House(IRE) set the standard on his 3l fourth off a mark of 78 on his nursery debut at Goodwood last time, but he hit a flat spot at a crucial stage before staying on after the winner had got away on his Fibresand debut. (op 5-2)
Look On By looked inexperienced but shaped with plenty of promise staying on strongly from some way back. A gelded half-brother to connections' 6f Listed winner Now Look Here and fairly useful 6f/7f winner Look Here's Carol, he is a scopey type who should improve next time. (op 12-1)
First Serve(IRE), a promising 25-1 sixth behind a couple of subsequent winners in a decent 5f Ripon maiden on debut, was laboured as favourite switched to Fibresand.
Tartania Official explanation: jockey reported filly hung left
Grandorio(IRE) was prominent in the market but he was detached at a relatively early stage and was never travelling and was on his third start. (op 5-1)

5243 BOOK TICKETS ONLINE AT SOUTHWELL-RACECOURSE.CO.UK H'CAP 1m (F)
6:15 (6:15) (Class 4) (0-80,86) 3-Y-O+ £4,204 (£1,251; £625; £312) Stalls Low

Form RPR
2122 **1** **Henry Allingham**[19] 4553 3-9-2 78 DominicFox[(3)] 3 90+
(Roger Varian) *trckd ldrs: hdwy on inner 2f out: rdn to chal ent fnl f: drvn to ld last 75yds: eased nr line* **11/4**[1]
-055 **2** *½* **Position**[41] 3787 3-9-7 80 ChrisCatlin 5 90
(Sir Mark Prescott Bt) *led: rdn along wl over 1f out: jnd and drvn ent fnl f: hdd last 75yds: no ex towards fin* **9/2**[2]
0311 **3** *4 ½* **Myboyalfie (USA)**[61] 3099 5-9-11 77 (v) IanMongan 6 78
(J R Jenkins) *trckd ldng pair: hdwy over 2f out: rdn wl over 1f out: drvn and edgd lft ent fnl f: one pce* **13/2**[3]
0141 **4** *1* **Kay Gee Be (IRE)**[9] 4864 8-10-1 86 6ex ShaneBKelly[(5)] 8 84
(Richard Fahey) *chsd ldrs: rdn along over 2f out: sn drvn and no imp fr over 1f out* **8/1**
1013 **5** *2 ¼* **Copperwood**[5] 5057 7-9-12 78 JoeFanning 7 71
(Mark Johnston) *cl up: rdn along over 2f out: sn drvn and grad wknd* **9/2**[2]
0403 **6** *8* **Follow The Flag (IRE)**[23] 4401 8-9-11 77 (v) StephenCraine 2 52
(Alan McCabe) *sn rdn along and outpcd in rr: bhd 1/2-way: wd st: styd on fnl 2f: nvr nr ldrs* **10/1**
4214 **7** *8* **Saaboog**[16] 4662 3-8-13 72 MartinDwyer 11 27
(James Tate) *cl up on outer: rdn along over 2f out: sn drvn and wknd* **13/2**[3]
265/ **8** *¾* **El Bravo**[306] 6-9-6 79 ShirleyTeasdale[(7)] 12 34
(Shaun Harris) *a towards rr* **50/1**
0630 **9** *2 ½* **Imaginary World (IRE)**[9] 4879 4-9-6 72 (be) WilliamCarson 4 21
(Alan McCabe) *in tch: rdn along 1/2-way: sn wknd* **33/1**
3363 **10** *7* **Regal Swain (IRE)**[17] 4622 4-9-6 72 RobertWinston 1 5
(Alan Swinbank) *in tch: rdn along 1/2-way: sn wknd* **10/1**
6014 **11** *5* **Flying Pickets (IRE)**[23] 4401 3-8-10 69 (be) IPoullis 10
(Alan McCabe) *dwlt: a in rr: bhd fr 1/2-way* **25/1**

1m 40.09s (-3.61) **Going Correction** -0.075s/f (Stan)
WFA 3 from 4yo+ 7lb **11** Ran SP% **127.7**
Speed ratings (Par 105): **115,114,110,109,106 98,90,90,87,80 75**
toteswingers 1&2 £4.70, 2&3 £6.20, 1&3 £3.50 CSF £16.23 CT £79.40 TOTE £2.20: £1.10, £1.90, £2.20; EX 19.00.
Owner J Collins, N Horsfall & N O'Sullivan **Bred** Red House Stud **Trained** Newmarket, Suffolk

FOCUS
A decent handicap. It was run at a fair pace and a pair of 3yos pulled clear. The winner is progressive and the form appeals as sound, despite the conditions.

5244 FOLLOW US ON TWITTER @SOUTHWELL_RACES MAIDEN STKS 7f (F)
6:45 (6:46) (Class 5) 3-Y-O+ £2,264 (£673; £336; £168) Stalls Low

Form RPR
026- **1** **Layla's King**[266] 7515 4-9-9 59 MartinDwyer 8 70
(David C Griffiths) *trckd ldrs: hdwy to chse ldr over 2f out: rdn over 1f out: styd on to ld last 75yds* **13/2**[3]
-000 **2** *1* **Greek Islands (IRE)**[21] 4469 4-9-9 64 (v[1]) ChrisCatlin 3 67
(Ed de Giles) *cl up: led 1/2-way: rdn wl over 1f out: drvn and edgd rt ins fnl f: hdd and no ex last 75yds* **10/1**
-044 **3** *6* **Parisian Princess (IRE)**[19] 4534 3-8-12 75 JoeFanning 7 47
(Hughie Morrison) *in tch: rdn along bef 1/2-way: swtchd wd wl over 2f out: styd on appr fnl f: n.d* **4/5**[1]
-00 **4** *2* **Fauran (IRE)**[71] 2800 3-8-12 0 RobertWinston 4 42
(Clive Brittain) *chsd ldrs: rdn along 3f out: sn one pce* **16/1**
5 *2 ¾* **Audeamus (IRE)** 3-8-12 0 StevieDonohoe 2 34
(Tobias B P Coles) *dwlt and bhd tl sme late hdwy* **20/1**
202 **6** *6* **Queen Cassiopeia**[51] 3453 3-8-12 62 IanMongan 6 19
(J R Jenkins) *chsd ldrs: rdn along over 2f out: sn drvn and wknd* **10/3**[2]
7 *11* **Rockzanda (IRE)**[91] 2190 3-8-12 0 AmyRyan 5
(Kevin Ryan) *a in rr* **12/1**
8 *5* **Lady Oz (IRE)** 5-9-4 0 GrahamGibbons 1
(Michael Easterby) *led: hdd 1/2-way: sn rdn along and wknd* **14/1**

1m 30.45s (0.15) **Going Correction** -0.075s/f (Stan)
WFA 3 from 4yo+ 6lb **8** Ran SP% **126.1**
Speed ratings (Par 103): **96,94,88,85,82 75,63,57**
toteswingers 1&2 £7.70, 2&3 £2.40, 1&3 £2.50 CSF £75.19 TOTE £6.00: £1.80, £2.60, £1.02; EX 58.50.
Owner Norcroft Park Stud **Bred** Norcroft Park Stud **Trained** Bawtry, S Yorks

FOCUS
The odds-on favourite was disappointing in this modest maiden which was won by an exposed performer. The bad kickback was perhaps a factor but this was not a race to be making excuses in.
Queen Cassiopeia Official explanation: jockey reported filly never travelling

5245 FIND US ON FACEBOOK SOUTHWELL RACECOURSE H'CAP 6f (F)
7:15 (7:16) (Class 5) (0-75,75) 3-Y-O+ £2,264 (£673; £336; £168) Stalls Low

Form RPR
6010 **1** **Pick A Little**[30] 4155 4-9-5 71 RyanClark[(3)] 2 81
(Brian Ellison) *cl up: rdn along 2f out: drvn over 1f out: styd on u.p ins fnl f to ld nr fin* **7/1**
0-50 **2** *nk* **Opus Dei**[23] 4388 5-9-1 67 (p) GaryBartley[(3)] 8 76
(Noel Wilson) *chsd ldrs on outer: cl up 1/2-way: led 2f out and sn rdn: drvn ins fnl f: hdd and no ex nr fin* **12/1**
0253 **3** *4* **Tahnee Mara (IRE)**[14] 4711 3-8-13 66 (b[1]) AmyRyan 6 62
(Kevin Ryan) *chsd ldrs: rdn along 2f out: drvn over 1f out: kpt on same pce* **13/2**[3]
1161 **4** *2* **Only Ten Per Cent (IRE)**[23] 4401 4-9-12 75 IanMongan 3 66+
(J R Jenkins) *chsd ldrs on inner: rdn along 2f out: drvn over 1f out and sn one pce* **6/4**[1]
0550 **5** *shd* **Punching**[9] 4885 8-9-1 64 JoeFanning 1 55
(Conor Dore) *led: pushed along and hdd 1/2-way: sn rdn and wknd over 1f out* **12/1**
3045 **6** *1 ¾* **Whisky Bravo**[18] 4588 3-9-6 73 MichaelStainton 5 59
(David Brown) *sn rdn along: a towards rr* **7/4**[2]
000 **7** *½* **Elhamri**[21] 4468 8-8-4 58 ow1 DavidKenny[(5)] 7 42
(Conor Dore) *a towards rr* **28/1**
360 **8** *¾* **Greenhead High**[18] 4592 4-9-7 70 AdrianNicholls 4 52
(David Nicholls) *cl up: led 1/2-way: rdn and hdd 2f out: sn wknd* **20/1**

1m 15.68s (-0.82) **Going Correction** -0.075s/f (Stan)
WFA 3 from 4yo+ 4lb **8** Ran SP% **125.8**
Speed ratings (Par 103): **102,101,96,93,93 91,90,89**
toteswingers 1&2 £11.00, 2&3 £12.90, 1&3 £10.40 CSF £93.33 CT £592.62 TOTE £6.10: £2.20, £2.00, £1.70; EX 163.10.
Owner The K A C Partnership **Bred** D R Tucker **Trained** Norton, N Yorks

FOCUS
The first two pulled clear in this sprint handicap and two market leaders were laboured. Quite straightforward form.
Opus Dei Official explanation: two-day ban: used whip above permitted level (Aug 29-30)
Whisky Bravo Official explanation: jockey reported gelding slow away

5246 JOIN NOTTINGHAMSHIRE RACING PARTNERSHIP H'CAP 7f (F)
7:45 (7:45) (Class 6) (0-55,55) 3-Y-O+ £1,704 (£503; £251) Stalls Low

Form RPR
000 **1** **Decimate**[72] 2761 4-9-6 54 GrahamGibbons 4 68+
(Alan McCabe) *mde all: rdn clr wl over 1f out: easily* **8/1**
0504 **2** *5* **My New Angel (IRE)**[30] 4142 3-8-8 48 (be) JamieMackay 2 48
(Paul Green) *in rr: hdwy on inner 2f out: sn rdn and kpt on wl fnl f to take 2nd nr fin: no ch w wnr* **5/1**[2]
6-20 **3** *½* **Chez Vrony**[82] 2464 6-8-12 46 oh1 WilliamCarson 5 45
(Dave Morris) *towards rr: wd st: hdwy 2f out: sn rdn and styd on fnl f: nrst fin* **10/1**
002 **4** *hd* **Choice Pearl (USA)**[6] 5014 3-9-1 55 (t) JoeFanning 10 53
(Tobias B P Coles) *chsd ldrs: effrt over 2f out: sn rdn and kpt on same pce* **10/3**[1]
2460 **5** *1 ¼* **Siouxies Dream**[11] 4830 3-8-13 53 IanMongan 12 48
(Michael Appleby) *towards rr: wd st: hdwy 2f out: sn rdn and kpt on: nrst fin* **8/1**
04 **6** *2 ¼* **Gracie's Gift (IRE)**[36] 3941 10-9-3 51 (v) J-PGuillambert 7 40
(Richard Guest) *chsd ldng pair: rdn along 3f out: drvn 2f out and sn one pce* **15/2**[3]
4333 **7** *hd* **Rapid Water**[29] 4192 6-9-1 54 (p) DavidKenny[(5)] 3 43
(Pat Eddery) *towards rr: hdwy wl over 2f out: rdn to chse ldrs over 1f out: sn wknd* **5/1**[2]
0060 **8** *4* **Sapphire Seeker**[22] 4438 3-8-13 53 (b[1]) ChrisCatlin 9 31
(Des Donovan) *dwlt: sn swtchd wd and rdn along: n.d* **16/1**
1330 **9** *1 ¾* **Tenancy (IRE)**[27] 4237 8-9-4 52 (b) RobertWinston 11 26
(Shaun Harris) *cl up: rdn along over 2f out: drvn wl over 1f out: grad wknd* **9/1**
-354 **10** *2 ¼* **Coastal Passage**[89] 2225 4-9-0 48 RobbieFitzpatrick 1 16
(Charles Smith) *nvr nr ldrs* **16/1**
3400 **11** *15* **Bond Blade**[29] 4193 4-8-11 52 JacobButterfield[(7)] 14
(Suzzanne France) *chsd ldrs: rdn along 3f out: sn wknd* **25/1**

3040 **12** *10* **Becksies**[8] 4913 3-8-6 **46** oh1 MartinDwyer 13
(Paul Midgley) *midfield: rdn along 1/2-way: sn wknd* **40/1**

1m 28.76s (-1.54) **Going Correction** -0.075s/f (Stan)
WFA 3 from 4yo+ 6lb 12 Ran SP% **127.5**
Speed ratings (Par 101): **105,99,98,98,97 94,94,89,87,85 67,56**
toteswingers 1&2 £16.60, 2&3 £15.20, 1&3 £24.70 CSF £51.56 CT £423.33 TOTE £8.90: £2.70, £1.60, £2.20; EX 102.00.
Owner A S Reid **Bred** A S Reid **Trained** Averham Park, Notts

FOCUS
This looked a competitive handicap but the winner powered clear under a prominent ride and hardly anything got involved from off the pace on a night where the kickback was bad. The winner is rated back to his best.
Rapid Water Official explanation: jockey reported gelding missed break
Coastal Passage Official explanation: jockey reported gelding's saddle slipped

5247 MEMBERSHIP AVAILABLE AT SOUTHWELL GOLF CLUB H'CAP 5f (F)
8:15 (8:17) (Class 6) (0-60,60) 3-Y-O **£1,704** (£503; £251) **Stalls** Low

Form				RPR
0233	**1**		**Ypres**[7] 4956 3-9-7 **60** PaddyAspell 3 (Jason Ward) *chsd ldrs: hdwy 2f out: rdn to chal ent fnl f: kpt on to ld last 100yds* **9/4**[1]	66
004	**2**	*1 1/4*	**Kara's Vision**[7] 4970 3-8-10 **49** (p) JoeFanning 1 (Robert Cowell) *dwlt: sn prom on wd outside: rdn to ld over 1f out: jnd and drvn ent fnl f: hdd and no ex last 100yds* **8/1**	51
6052	**3**	*hd*	**Dazzlin Bluebell (IRE)**[9] 4878 3-8-9 **48** (b) DuranFentiman 4 (Tim Easterby) *led: rdn along 2f out: hdd over 1f out: drvn and kpt on fnl f* **7/1**	49
4-00	**4**	*1/2*	**Make Up**[7] 4953 3-9-2 **58** GaryBartley(3) 13 (Noel Wilson) *in tch: hdwy 2f out: sn rdn and kpt on fnl f: nrst fin* **16/1**	57
2500	**5**	*1 1/4*	**Brunswick Vale (IRE)**[6] 5013 3-8-13 **52** (b) RussKennemore 2 (Paul Midgley) *towards rr: hdwy 2f out: sn rdn and kpt on fnl f: nrst fin* **16/1**	47
2145	**6**	*1 1/4*	**Medam**[30] 4154 3-8-8 **54** ShirleyTeasdale(7) 5 (Shaun Harris) *chsd ldr: rdn along 1/2-way: sn drvn and grad wknd* **13/2**	44
-004	**7**	*3/4*	**Derek The Diamond**[63] 3024 3-8-9 **51** (p) DominicFox(3) 9 (Michael Appleby) *nvr bttr than midfield* **10/1**	39
0105	**8**	*nk*	**Kai**[65] 2972 3-9-4 **57** (be[1]) GrahamGibbons 6 (Alan McCabe) *hmpd s: a towards rr* **6/1**[3]	43
4120	**9**	*nk*	**Ghazeer (IRE)**[9] 4885 3-9-7 **60** (v) MartinDwyer 10 (Derek Shaw) *rdn along sn after s: a in rr* **9/2**[2]	45
-060	**10**	*8*	**Rock Of Monet**[38] 3892 3-9-4 **57** (v) StevieDonohoe 12 (Michael Bell) *a in rr* **14/1**	14
0000	**11**	*2 1/2*	**Forever Janey**[8] 4911 3-8-7 **46** oh1 AmyRyan 11 (Paul Green) *chsd ldrs: rdn along bef 1/2-way: sn wknd* **40/1**	
000	**12**	*hd*	**Libby's Lad**[11] 4807 3-8-7 **46** oh1 AdrianNicholls 8 (David C Griffiths) *a in rr* **50/1**	

1m 0.44s (0.74) **Going Correction** +0.025s/f (Slow) 12 Ran SP% **132.1**
Speed ratings (Par 98): **95,93,92,91,89 87,86,86,85,72 68,68**
toteswingers 1&2 £11.80, 2&3 £28.60, 1&3 £7.00 CSF £24.14 CT £116.06 TOTE £3.40: £2.00, £3.50, £2.60; EX 37.30.
Owner Pear Tree Partnership **Bred** Philip Graham Harvey **Trained** Middleham, N Yorks

FOCUS
They were spread across the track in this weak sprint handicap and the favourite delivered with a bit in hand. He was amongst the best treated on recent form.
T/Plt: £784.50 to a £1 stake. Pool: £52435.82 - 48.79 winning tickets. T/Qpdt: £72.30 to a £1 stake. Pool of £9178.87 - 93.90 winning tickets. JR

5140 DEAUVILLE (R-H)
Wednesday, August 15
OFFICIAL GOING: Turf: good to soft; fibresand: standard

5248a PRIX DE LA VALLEE D'AUGE (LISTED RACE) (2YO) (TURF) 5f
1:35 (12:00) 2-Y-O **£22,916** (£9,166; £6,875; £4,583; £2,291)

			RPR
1		**Faithfilly (IRE)**[29] 4205 2-8-10 0 MaximeGuyon 9 (Ed Walker) *broke fast on outside: racd 2nd: rdn 1 1/2f out: qcknd to ld 150yds out: r.o wl* **42/10**[3]	97
2	*3/4*	**Rime A Rien**[13] 2-8-10 0 ThierryJarnet 3 (F Rohaut, France) **9/1**	94
3	*2*	**Plaza Mayor (FR)** 2-8-10 0 FranckBlondel 4 (F Rossi, France) **19/5**[2]	87
4	*shd*	**Via Chope (FR)**[24] 4384 2-8-10 0 IoritzMendizabal 10 (Y Barberot, France) **20/1**	87
5	*nk*	**Tricky Week (FR)**[13] 2-8-10 0 UmbertoRispoli 2 (C Baillet, France) **13/1**	86
6	*nk*	**Lily Merrill**[22] 2-8-10 0 RonanThomas 8 (T Lemer, France) **18/1**	85
7	*snk*	**To My Valentine (FR)**[24] 4384 2-8-11 0 ow1 ChristopheSoumillon 7 (F-H Graffard, France) **5/2**[1]	85
8	*1 1/4*	**Wingate**[15] 2-9-0 0 GregoryBenoist 6 (J-P Gallorini, France) **83/10**	84
9	*2 1/2*	**Lasdramad (FR)**[29] 4205 2-8-10 0 OlivierPeslier 1 (Y Durepaire, Spain) **17/1**	71
10	*3*	**Black Whip (IRE)**[37] 2-8-10 0 SylvainRuis 5 (Mlle M Henry, France) **29/1**	60

57.6s (0.10) 10 Ran SP% **115.4**
WIN (incl. 1 euro stake): 5.20. PLACES: 1.60, 2.80, 2.10. DF: 23.60. SF: 45.20.
Owner Laurence A Bellman **Bred** Deer Forest Stud **Trained** Newmarket, Suffolk

FOCUS
The form is probably a bit below average for the grade.

NOTEBOOK
Faithfilly(IRE) fought off successive challenges to make virtually every yard. She had chased home Bailey's Jubilee at Vichy last month before this latest success and seems to be improving. She could come back to France for the Prix d'Arenberg at Chantilly next month.

5249a PRIX DE LIEUREY (GROUP 3) (3YO FILLIES) (TURF) 1m (R)
2:05 (12:00) 3-Y-O **£33,333** (£13,333; £10,000; £6,666; £3,333)

			RPR
1		**Sarkiyla (FR)**[19] 4573 3-8-11 0 Christophe-PatriceLemaire 4 (A De Royer-Dupre, France) *racd midfield: shkn up 1 1/2f out: picked up wl 1f out: tk ld 150yds out: r.o wl: jst hld on* **9/4**[1]	108
2	*hd*	**Foreign Tune**[19] 4573 3-8-11 0 OlivierPeslier 8 (C Laffon-Parias, France) *hld up towards rr: qcknd wl on outside 1f out: r.o strly u.p fnl 100yds: jst failed* **12/1**	107
3	*1 1/4*	**Dream Clover**[23] 3-8-11 0 (b) ThierryJarnet 6 (F Head, France) *racd 2nd: rdn 1 1/2f out: tk ld 250yds out: hdd 150yds out: styd on wl* **18/1**	104
4	*3/4*	**Poupee Flash (USA)**[45] 3682 3-8-11 0 StephanePasquier 2 (P Bary, France) *hld up towards rr: gd prog ent fnl f: fin wl: clst at fin* **12/1**	103
5	*2*	**Regatta (FR)**[45] 3682 3-8-11 0 ChristopheSoumillon 3 (E Lellouche, France) *hld up towards rr on ins: pulling freely: gd prog 1 1/2f out: nt qckn ins fnl f: styd on* **11/1**	98
6	*1*	**Arsaadi (IRE)**[39] 3879 3-8-11 0 (b) WilliamBuick 10 (William Haggas) *broke wl to r 2nd: sent to ld after 1f: rdn 1 1/2f out: hdd 250yds out: no ex: styd on fnl f* **10/1**	96
7	*2 1/2*	**Naruko (USA)**[33] 3-8-11 0 MaximeGuyon 1 (A Fabre, France) *hld up at rr of field: mde little prog in st: nvr a factor* **10/1**	90
8	*nse*	**Bugie D'Amore**[18] 4616 3-8-11 0 AntoineHamelin 5 (A De Royer-Dupre, France) *racd midfield: ev ch 1 1/2f out: rdn but no ex: fdd* **3/1**[2]	90
9	*2*	**Cherry Danon (IRE)**[46] 3653 3-9-2 0 AStarke 7 (P Schiergen, Germany) *led for 1f: settled 3rd: rdn early in st: no ex: wknd* **9/2**[3]	90
10	*nse*	**Sydarra (FR)**[10] 3-8-11 0 FlavienPrat 9 (F Head, France) *racd midfield on outside of field: rdn early in st: no ex: wknd* **16/1**	85

1m 42.7s (1.90) 10 Ran SP% **127.0**
WIN (incl. 1 euro stake): 3.50. PLACES: 1.60, 3.90, 4.10. DF: 18.00. SF: 35.40.
Owner H H Aga Khan **Bred** S A Aga Khan **Trained** Chantilly, France

NOTEBOOK
Sarkiyla(FR) rewarded her owner for supplementing her with a hard-fought success over Foreign Tune, as she extended her record to four wins from five starts. She could be aimed at the Prix Daniel Wildenstein.
Arsaadi(IRE) set out to make all but was unable to hold back the tide of challengers in the straight. Her rider thought she might need a return to further.

5250a PRIX GUILLAUME D'ORNANO - HARAS DU LOGIS SAINT-GERMAIN (GROUP 2) (3YO) (TURF) 1m 2f
2:35 (12:00) 3-Y-O **£190,000** (£73,333; £35,000; £23,333; £11,666)

			RPR
1		**Saint Baudolino (IRE)**[32] 4121 3-9-2 0 MaximeGuyon 8 (A Fabre, France) *hld up in midfield: qcknd wl to chse clr ldrs 1 1/2f out: tk ld 150yds out: sn wnt clr: easily* **13/8**[1]	119+
2	*3*	**Aesop's Fables (USA)**[45] 3681 3-9-2 0 Pierre-CharlesBoudot 6 (A Fabre, France) *settled 3rd: chsd ldrs early in st: dropped bk into midfield 1 1/2f out: rallied wl u.p ent fnl f: fin wl to get up for 2nd on line* **7/2**[3]	111
3	*nse*	**Ashkiyr (FR)**[22] 3-9-2 0 Christophe-PatriceLemaire 4 (A De Royer-Dupre, France) *hld up towards rr: mde gd prog ent fnl f: r.o wl: wnt 2nd 50yds out: lost 2nd on line* **11/4**[2]	111
4	*3/4*	**Starboard**[24] 4385 3-9-2 0 WilliamBuick 5 (John Gosden) *racd in 2nd: rdn to share ld early in st: r.o wl u.p to ld 1 1/2f out: hdd 150yds out: lost 2nd 50yds out: styd on* **10/1**	109
5	*hd*	**Smoking Sun (USA)**[23] 4418 3-9-2 0 StephanePasquier 1 (P Bary, France) *racd midfield: r.o u.p in st: styd on wl fnl f* **7/1**	109
6	*shd*	**Gris De Reve (FR)**[23] 4418 3-9-2 0 AntoineHamelin 2 (J-P Gauvin, France) *racd towards rr on ins: r.o wl fnl f: nvr rchd ldrs* **14/1**	109
7	*1 3/4*	**Rewarded**[34] 4007 3-9-2 0 KirstyMilczarek 7 (James Toller) *sn led: jnd in ld early in st: r.o: hdd 1 1/2f out: no ex ins fnl f: styd on one pce* **25/1**	105
8	*4*	**Anakin Skywalker (GER)**[24] 3-9-2 0 AStarke 9 (P Vovcenko, Germany) *v.s.a: a in rr: nvr a factor* **50/1**	97
9	*1 1/4*	**Loi (IRE)**[24] 4385 3-9-2 0 (b[1]) OlivierPeslier 3 (J-M Beguigne, France) *racd midfield: no ex whn rdn 1 1/2f out: wknd* **25/1**	95

2m 7.7s (-2.50) 9 Ran SP% **124.9**
WIN (incl. 1 euro stake): 2.10 (Saint Baudolino coupled with Aesop's Fables). PLACES: 1.20, 1.90, 1.50. DF: 5.00. SF: 6.80.
Owner Godolphin SNC **Bred** Darley Stud Management Co Ltd **Trained** Chantilly, France

NOTEBOOK
Saint Baudolino(IRE) thrust himself into the Arc picture with an impressive display, which saw his price among bookmakers tumble. He had previously finished runner-up in the Prix du Jockey Club and then a close third in the Grand Prix de Paris. Guyon was content to sit just off the pace and, turning for home, even allowed them a little extra rope before rousting his mount. (op 7-4)
Starboard was never far away but, after leading halfway up the straight, was run out of the places late on.
Rewarded made the running before fading and is probably not quite up to this level.

5251 - (Foreign Racing) - See Raceform Interactive

SAN SEBASTIAN (R-H)
Wednesday, August 15
OFFICIAL GOING: Turf: good

5252a PREMIO COPA DE ORO DE SAN SEBASTIAN (CONDITIONS) (3YO+) (TURF) 1m 4f
6:05 (12:00) 3-Y-O+ **£33,333** (£13,333; £6,666; £3,333)

			RPR
1		**Pazifiksturm (GER)**[731] 5-9-4 0 Jean-BaptisteHamel 3 (Mlle A Imaz-Ceca, France) **19/10**[1]	
2	*3 1/2*	**Phuket (SPA)** 3-8-7 0 JoseLuisBorrego 7 (J L De Salas, Spain) **34/1**	
3	*nse*	**Australia Day (IRE)**[25] 3502 9-9-4 0 DarryllHolland 4 (Paul Webber) *broke wl and led: hdd over 3f out: 2nd and rdn as pressed on both sides 2f out: rallied and kpt on gamely u.p fnl f: lost 2nd on line* **208/10**	
4	*1/2*	**Fortun (IRE)** 3-8-7 0 CharlesNora 1 (J L Maroto, Spain) **61/10**	
5	*nse*	**Entre Copas**[836] 8-9-4 0 JeremyCrocquevieille 6 (J-M Osorio, Spain) **23/10**[3]	
6	*1 1/2*	**High Jo**[24] 4-9-4 0 PhilippeSogorb 2 (E Lellouche, France) **7/1**	

7 ¾ **Achtung (SPA)** 4-9-4 0 .... JulienGrosjean 8
(R Lopez Gallego, Spain) **213/10**

8 3 **Dunnboinee (IRE)**[79] 4-9-4 0 .... MlleGloriaMaderoParayre 5
(Mlle A Imaz-Ceca, France) **19/10**[1]

P **Esles (FR)**[32] 4-9-4 0 .... Jean-BernardEyquem 9
(C Laffon-Parias, France) **21/10**[2]

2m 38.28s (158.28)
WFA 3 from 4yo+ 11lb **9** Ran SP% **170.0**
WIN (incl. 1 euro stake): 2.90 (coupled with Dunnboinee). PLACES: 2.70, 13.60. SF: 49.60..
Owner Cuadra Martul **Bred** Gestut Karlshof **Trained** France

NOTEBOOK
Australia Day(IRE), whose saddle moved a little as he exited the stalls, was just denied second. He'll stay on the continent now to be prepared for another run at San Sebastian in September.

5220 BEVERLEY (R-H)
Thursday, August 16

OFFICIAL GOING: Good to firm (firm in places; 8.5)
Wind: Fresh across Weather: Fine and dry

5253 HOLD YOUR CHRISTMAS PARTY HERE (S) H'CAP — 1m 4f 16y
2:30 (2:30) (Class 6) (0-60,60) 3-Y-O+ **£1,617** (£481; £240; £120) **Stalls** Low

Form RPR

0601 **1** **Valantino Oyster (IRE)**[15] 4712 5-9-7 **58** ....(p) ShaneBKelly(5) 3 65
(Tracy Waggott) led: hdd over 7f out: cl up: rdn to ld appr fnl f: drvn and kpt on wl towards fin **6/1**[2]

5021 **2** ¾ **Dean Iarracht (IRE)**[5] 5114 6-9-13 **59** 6ex ....(p) FrederikTylicki 4 65
(Tracy Waggott) hld up in rr: hdwy 4f out: effrt 2f out: n.m.r and swtchd lft over 1f out: sn rdn and styd on to chse wnr ins fnl f: no imp towards fin **7/4**[1]

0445 **3** 1 ¼ **Shy**[13] 4766 7-9-7 **60** ....(b) GemmaTutty(7) 2 64
(Karen Tutty) trckd ldrs: hdwy over 3f out: rdn wl over 1f out: kpt on fnl f **6/1**[2]

2300 **4** 1 ½ **Kames Park (IRE)**[19] 4594 10-9-5 **51** .... RobbieFitzpatrick 11 52
(Richard Guest) dwlt and in rr: hdwy on outer 3f out: rdn 2f out: styd on fnl f: nrst fin **8/1**[3]

0065 **5** nse **Rapturous Applause**[9] 4912 4-9-0 **46** .... PJMcDonald 1 47
(Micky Hammond) chsd ldrs: hdwy on inner over 2f out and sn rdn: drvn over 1f out: kpt on same pce **10/1**

0006 **6** 1 **Yorksters Prince (IRE)**[15] 4712 5-9-12 **58** ....(b) BarryMcHugh 12 58
(Tony Coyle) cl up: led 7f out: rdn along over 2f out: drvn and hdd appr fnl f: grad wknd **18/1**

/300 **7** ¾ **Gulf Coast**[22] 4455 7-9-4 **50** ....(p) GrahamGibbons 5 49
(Tim Walford) chsd ldrs: rdn along over 2f out: sn one pce **10/1**

0R **8** 1 ¾ **Sinnamara (IRE)**[23] 4431 4-9-9 **60** ....(p) AdamCarter(5) 6 56
(John Wainwright) trckd ldrs: hdwy and cl up 1/2-way: chal 2f out: sn rdn and wknd over 1f out **14/1**

0034 **9** 1 **Commander Veejay**[9] 4908 4-8-11 **50** ....(p) JasonHart(7) 8 44
(Brian Rothwell) a in rr **14/1**

3500 **10** 12 **Nicholas Pocock (IRE)**[7] 5015 6-9-3 **49** .... GrahamLee 10 24
(Ian McInnes) a in rr **40/1**

50-0 **11** 41 **Lady Lyricist**[21] 4486 3-8-12 **54** .... ChrisCatlin 7
(Reg Hollinshead) midfield: pushed along and lost pl after 5f: sn bhd **66/1**

2m 37.14s (-2.66) **Going Correction** -0.35s/f (Firm)
WFA 3 from 4yo+ 10lb **11** Ran SP% **116.8**
Speed ratings (Par 101): **94,93,92,91,91 90,90,89,88,80 53**
toteswingers 1&2 £2.70, 2&3 £2.90, 1&3 £7.10 CSF £16.65 CT £66.95 TOTE £8.80: £2.10, £1.20, £2.60; EX 11.30.The winner was bought by A McCardle for £4000.
Owner Steve Sawley **Bred** Des Vere Hunt Farm Co And Jack Ronan **Trained** Spennymoor, Co Durham

FOCUS
A rock-bottom selling handicap. The winner was one of three pacesetters and trainer Tracy Waggott enjoyed a one-two. Rail realignment around bottom bend increased distances by about 19ys except 5f races.

5254 RACING UK ON SKY 432 NURSERY — 7f 100y
3:05 (3:06) (Class 5) (0-75,75) 2-Y-O **£2,264** (£673; £336; £168) **Stalls** Low

Form RPR

41 **1** **Hunting Rights (USA)**[24] 4404 2-9-5 **73** .... SilvestreDeSousa 1 83+
(Mark Johnston) chsd clr ldr: hdwy 3f out: cl up 2f out: sn led and clr: rdn ent fnl f and kpt on wl **7/4**[1]

6032 **2** 4 **Brazilian Clown (IRE)**[7] 5009 2-8-11 **65** .... FrannyNorton 2 65
(Tom Dascombe) chsd ldng pair: hdwy over 2f out: rdn to chse wnr over 1f out: drvn and no imp fnl f **13/2**[3]

2161 **3** ¾ **Yorkshire Icon**[13] 4778 2-9-7 **75** ....(p) PaulMulrennan 4 73
(Ann Duffield) hld up in rr: hdwy on wd outside 2f out: sn rdn and styd on fnl f: nrst fin **13/2**[3]

554 **4** 2 ½ **Sleepy Haven (IRE)**[30] 4173 2-8-12 **66** .... GrahamGibbons 5 58
(David Barron) midfield: hdwy on inner 2f out and sn rdn: drvn and no imp ent fnl f **10/1**

0201 **5** 2 ¾ **Must Be Me**[7] 4991 2-9-1 **69** 6ex .... GrahamLee 3 55
(Eve Johnson Houghton) chsd ldrs: rdn along over 2f out: sn drvn and no hdwy **9/2**[2]

000 **6** 3 ½ **If You Can (IRE)**[35] 3989 2-7-12 **52** .... DuranFentiman 11 30
(Tim Easterby) led and sn clr at str pce: rdn along and jnd 2f out: sn hdd & wknd **25/1**

3643 **7** 1 ¾ **Bayan Kasirga (IRE)**[19] 4574 2-9-1 **69** .... TonyHamilton 7 43
(Richard Fahey) s.i.s and swtchd rt s: in rr tl sme hdwy 3f out: sn rdn and nvr a factor **7/1**

0005 **8** 5 **Clock On Tom**[22] 4450 2-8-1 **55** .... JamesSullivan 6 17
(Michael Easterby) chsd ldrs: rdn along 3f out: sn drvn and wknd **20/1**

0003 **9** 5 **Strasbourg Place**[16] 4672 2-7-13 **53** oh6 ow1 .... AndrewMullen 8 3
(Nigel Tinkler) a in rr **50/1**

0006 **10** 3 ¾ **Bollin Billy**[9] 4921 2-7-9 **52** oh7 .... DominicFox(3) 9
(Tim Easterby) a in rr: bhd fr 1/2-way **40/1**

1m 31.62s (-2.18) **Going Correction** -0.35s/f (Firm) **10** Ran SP% **115.8**
Speed ratings (Par 94): **98,93,92,89,86 82,80,74,69,64**
toteswingers 1&2 £2.50, 2&3 £5.80, 1&3 £3.70 CSF £12.77 CT £60.57 TOTE £2.80: £1.10, £2.80, £1.80; EX 13.00.
Owner Sheikh Hamdan Bin Mohammed Al Maktoum **Bred** Darley **Trained** Middleham Moor, N Yorks

FOCUS
The leader went off at a break-neck pace and the field was soon well strung out. The winner was the only one to keep tabs on the leader. He has been given full form credit, with the next two close to their marks.

NOTEBOOK
Hunting Rights(USA), off the mark at the second attempt over 7f on the all-weather at Southwell, made his nursery debut from a mark of just 73. Ideally drawn, he went to the front full of running and had only to be kept up to his work. A grand type, he should improve again and will be hard to beat under a penalty. (op 5-2)
Brazilian Clown(IRE), who showed improved form to finish third in a maiden and runner-up in a nursery on the AW at Southwell, looks equally effective on turf. (op 8-1)
Yorkshire Icon, who found himself way off the pace, came through late to secure third spot despite showing a tendency to hang right. Rated 75, another claimer could be tempting. (op 11-2)
Sleepy Haven(IRE), making his nursery bow, didn't really improve for the step up in trip. (op 17-2)
Must Be Me, hammered with a 12lb weight rise after her wide-margin win over 6f in the mud at Chepstow, struggled under her penalty on totally different ground. (op 10-3 tchd 3-1)
If You Can(IRE), who showed little in three maidens, was soon setting a fast pace from his outside draw. On a track with an uphill finish, it was just a question of time before he began to flag. (op 28-1)

5255 E B F BEVERLEY ANNUAL BADGEHOLDERS MAIDEN FILLIES' STKS — 5f
3:35 (3:35) (Class 5) 2-Y-O **£3,428** (£1,020; £509; £254) **Stalls** Low

Form RPR

43 **1** **March**[36] 3959 2-9-0 0 .... SilvestreDeSousa 4 80+
(Marco Botti) trckd ldrs: nt clr run and swtchd lft wl over 1f out: sn chsng ldr: rdn and edgd rt appr fnl f: styd on wl to ld last 75yds **5/4**[2]

32 **2** 1 ½ **Avec Rose**[20] 4545 2-8-11 0 .... LeeTopliss(3) 2 73+
(Richard Fahey) led: rdn clr wl over 1f out: drvn ins fnl f: hdd & wknd last 75yds **10/11**[1]

000 **3** 11 **Elusive Shadow**[8] 4952 2-8-11 0 .... DaleSwift(3) 3 33
(Alan Brown) cl up: rdn and edgd rt wl over 2f out: sn drvn and one pce **200/1**

4 ¾ **Hit The Note** 2-9-0 0 .... GrahamLee 8 31+
(Ann Duffield) in rr: pushed along 1/2-way: sme hdwy 2f out: n.d **33/1**

2500 **5** hd **Blue Clumber**[11] 4836 2-9-0 77 .... RobertWinston 1 30
(Shaun Harris) cl up: rdn along 2f out: sn drvn and wknd **16/1**

6 ½ **St Mary De Castro** 2-9-0 0 .... JamesSullivan 7 28+
(Michael Easterby) a outpcd in rr **66/1**

7 3 **Equinox** 2-9-0 0 .... RoystonFfrench 5 17
(Bryan Smart) chsd ldrs: rdn along 1/2-way: sn wknd **14/1**[3]

1m 2.88s (-0.62) **Going Correction** -0.125s/f (Firm) **7** Ran SP% **114.3**
Speed ratings (Par 91): **99,96,79,77,77 76,71**
toteswingers 1&2 £1.02, 2&3 £38.90, 1&3 £38.90 CSF £2.68 TOTE £2.50: £1.10, £1.60; EX 2.70.
Owner H E Sheikh Sultan Bin Khalifa Al Nahyan **Bred** T K & Mrs P A Knox **Trained** Newmarket, Suffolk

FOCUS
Almost certainly an above-average maiden 2yo fillies' event for this track, the first two a long way clear. They both showed improved form, but the rest were well beaten off.

NOTEBOOK
March, significantly backed to overturn the favourite, was back to 5f after two tries over six. She travelled very strongly and, when pulled out for racing room, showed a bright turn of foot to cut down the leader. She is well worth a chance at Listed class after this. (op 13-8)
Avec Rose, runner-up in a strong maiden at Thirsk run in a fast time, looked to have taken a winning advantage soon after halfway but was cut down in ruthless fashion by the winner. She will certainly find a race. (op 5-6 tchd 11-10)
Elusive Shadow, who had failed to beat a rival in two starts in maiden company and one in a claimer, was not surprisingly left for dead by the first two. (op 150-1)
Hit The Note, whose dam won over a mile at two, will have learnt something from this introduction and will be suited by a step up in trip. (tchd 28-1)
Blue Clumber, 100-1 when runner-up in the Hilary Needler here on her fourth start, has gone backwards since and, after a peck at the start, she faded badly in the final quarter-mile. Official explanation: jockey said filly slipped on leaving stalls (op 14-1 tchd 12-1)

5256 JACKSON'S YORKSHIRE CHAMPION BREAD H'CAP — 2m 35y
4:10 (4:10) (Class 4) (0-85,80) 3-Y-O+ **£4,075** (£1,212; £606) **Stalls** Low

Form RPR

5132 **1** **Moon Trip**[5] 5106 3-9-0 **80** .... SilvestreDeSousa 3 94
(Mark Johnston) trckd ldng pair: smooth hdwy to chse ldr over 2f out: led over 1f out: sn rdn clr and styd on strly **1/2**[1]

-252 **2** 8 **Yours Ever**[17] 4639 3-8-10 **76** .... ChrisCatlin 2 80
(Sir Mark Prescott Bt) led: pushed along 4f out: rdn over 2f out: hdd over 1f out: sn one pce and eased **3/1**[2]

224 **3** 72 **Mojolika**[19] 4613 4-9-9 **75** .... GrahamGibbons 4
(Tim Easterby) sn trcking ldr: pushed along over 3f out: rdn wl over 2f out: sn wknd and heavily eased **13/2**[3]

3m 31.14s (-8.66) **Going Correction** -0.35s/f (Firm)
WFA 3 from 4yo 14lb **3** Ran SP% **105.0**
Speed ratings (Par 105): **107,103,67**
CSF £2.16 TOTE £1.40; EX 1.80.
Owner Sheikh Hamdan Bin Mohammed Al Maktoum **Bred** Darley **Trained** Middleham Moor, N Yorks

FOCUS
Just three runners but the gallop was unrelenting and a wide margin, highly progressive young stayer.
Mojolika Official explanation: trainer said gelding lost a front shoe

5257 BULLET DAY IS ON 1 SEPTEMBER FILLIES' H'CAP — 5f
4:45 (4:47) (Class 5) (0-70,69) 3-Y-O+ **£2,264** (£673; £336; £168) **Stalls** Low

Form RPR

350 **1** **Diamond Blue**[13] 4770 4-9-8 **67** ....(p) AmyRyan 1 76
(Richard Whitaker) hld up: effrt and nt clr run wl over 1f out: hdwy ent fnl f: sn rdn: qcknd wl to ld nr fin **3/1**[1]

6100 **2** ½ **Phoenix Clubs (IRE)**[12] 4793 3-9-8 **69** .... PJMcDonald 5 76
(Paul Midgley) trckd ldrs: hdwy over 1f out: sn rdn and styd on wl fnl f **8/1**

3 **3** shd **Ingenti**[73] 2748 4-8-6 **51** .... SilvestreDeSousa 10 58
(Christopher Wilson) cl up on outer: led over 1f out: rdn ins fnl f: hdd and no ex nr fin **5/1**[3]

3162 **4** 1 **Pivotal Prospect**[41] 3815 4-9-4 **63** .... RobertWinston 6 66
(Tracy Waggott) blind removed late: slowly away and in rr: hdwy whn n.m.r over 1f out: rdn and styd on fnl f: nrst fin **15/2**

0632 **5** 1 ¼ **Wicked Wilma (IRE)**[2] 5190 8-9-3 **65** .... JulieBurke(3) 9 64
(Alan Berry) trckd ldrs: n.m.r and swtchd lft 2f out: sn rdn and kpt on same pce fnl f **9/2**[2]

0402 **6** 3 ½ **Rio's Girl**[8] 4963 5-8-10 **55** .... BarryMcHugh 8 41
(Tony Coyle) led to 1/2-way: cl up: rdn wl over 1f out: grad wknd **9/2**[2]

3005 **7** 2 ½ **Black Annis Bower**[10] 4866 4-9-4 **63** ....(b[1]) JamesSullivan 4 40
(Michael Easterby) t.k.h: chsd ldrs: rdn 2f out: sn edgd rt and wknd **22/1**

0000 **8** *nse* **Nearly A Gift (IRE)**43 3751 3-8-13 **60**..............................(t) DavidAllan 3 37
(Tim Easterby) *cl up on inner: led 1/2-way: rdn and hdd over 1f out: sn wknd* **14/1**

1m 2.87s (-0.63) **Going Correction** -0.125s/f (Firm)
WFA 3 from 4yo+ 2lb **8** Ran SP% **111.9**
Speed ratings (Par 100): **100,99,99,97,95 89,85,85**
toteswingers 1&2 £5.70, 2&3 £6.00, 1&3 £3.20 CSF £26.39 CT £114.10 TOTE £3.90: £1.70, £2.20, £1.70; EX 29.40.
Owner Mrs Jane Newett **Bred** Hellwood Stud Farm **Trained** Scarcroft, W Yorks

FOCUS
A very modest fillies' sprint handicap. The three leaders took each other on setting the race up for a closer.
Pivotal Prospect Official explanation: jockey said filly became fractious and was leaning on side of stalls causing him to be slow on removing blindfold and it was slowly away
Rio's Girl Official explanation: jockey said he was slow to remove blindfold as he had become distracted by behaviour of filly in adjoining stall

5258 WHITE ROSE SADDLERY AMATEUR RIDERS' H'CAP (DIV I) 1m 100y
5:15 (5:15) (Class 6) (0-65,65) 4-Y-0+ **£1,559** (£483; £241; £121) **Stalls** Low

Form RPR
460- **1** **Meglio Ancora**374 4869 5-10-1 **52**.................................... MissZoeLilly 8 60
(Alastair Lidderdale) *in tch: hdwy over 3f out: chal wl over 1f out: sn rdn and styd on to ld wl ins fnl f* **16/1**
435 **2** *nk* **Special Mix**59 3232 4-11-0 **65**.. MissJCoward 5 73
(Michael Easterby) *hld up in midfield: hdwy over 2f out: rdn to chse ldrs over 1f out: swtchd rt and styd on strly towards fin* **7/1**
2654 **3** *nk* **Gadobout Dancer**7 5015 5-10-0 **51**................................. MissADeniel 4 58
(Tony Coyle) *trckd ldrs: hdwy 1/2-way: led wl over 1f out: sn rdn: drvn and hdd wl ins fnl f: kpt on* **17/2**
4000 **4** *nk* **Kheskianto (IRE)**120 1436 6-9-6 **46** oh1......................... MrCMartin(3) 7 52
(Michael Chapman) *hld up towards rr: hdwy over 3f out: chsd ldrs 2f out: sn rdn and styd on fnl f: nrst fin* **40/1**
2 **5** *¾* **Heroine Chic (IRE)**10 4890 5-10-3 **57**.....................(b) MissHBethell(3) 9 62
(Brian Ellison) *trckd ldrs on inner: effrt over 2f out: sn rdn and ev ch tl one pce ent fnl f* **9/4**1
2400 **6** *½* **Silly Gilly (IRE)**15 4716 8-10-4 **60**.................................(p) MissVBarr(5) 6 63
(Ron Barr) *prom: led 1/2-way: rdn along and hdd wl over 1f out: kpt on same pce fnl f* **12/1**
6304 **7** *2¾* **Merrjanah**11 4843 4-9-4 **48**... MrAFrench(7) 1 45
(John Wainwright) *s.i.s and bhd: stdy hdwy 3f out: rdn 2f out: styd on fnl f: nrst fin* **12/1**
2632 **8** *hd* **Potentiale (IRE)**19 4602 8-10-5 **63**....................(v) MrEdwardSibbick(7) 2 60
(J W Hills) *hld up towards rr: hdwy over 2f out: sn rdn and n.d* **6/1**3
3013 **9** *1* **Kyle Of Bute**16 4683 6-10-12 **63**.............................. MissSBrotherton 11 57
(Brian Baugh) *hld up towards rr: hdwy on outer 3f out: sn rdn and n.d* **11/2**2
6000 **10** *2½* **Wiseman's Diamond (USA)**18 4627 7-10-6 **62**....(b) MissHDukes(5) 14 51
(Paul Midgley) *hld up: a towards rr* **25/1**
5040 **11** *shd* **Desert Hunter (IRE)**80 2535 9-9-7 **49**..................(p) MissRSmith(5) 12 37
(Micky Hammond) *prom: rdn along wl over 3f out: grad wknd* **28/1**
0-00 **12** *1¼* **Thoroughly Red (IRE)**30 4189 7-9-4 **46**.............. MrAaronJames(5) 10 31
(Suzzanne France) *led: rdn along and hdd 1/2-way: sn wknd* **40/1**
0-00 **13** *27* **Ivestar (IRE)**10 4865 7-9-9 **53**...............................(v) MrsKristaBrown(7) 13
(Michael Easterby) *lost many l at s: a wl bhd* **40/1**

1m 46.41s (-1.19) **Going Correction** -0.35s/f (Firm) **13** Ran SP% **119.3**
Speed ratings (Par 101): **91,90,90,90,89 88,86,85,84,82 82,81,54**
toteswingers 1&2 £13.00, 2&3 £7.20, 1&3 £14.90 CSF £118.31 CT £1024.27 TOTE £13.80: £3.50, £2.90, £3.20; EX 144.70.
Owner C S J Beek **Bred** Mrs R Pease **Trained** Lambourn, Berks

FOCUS
Part one of a very modest amateur riders' handicap and plenty in with a shout coming to the final furlong spread right across the track.

5259 WHITE ROSE SADDLERY AMATEUR RIDERS' H'CAP (DIV II) 1m 100y
5:45 (5:50) (Class 6) (0-65,65) 4-Y-0+ **£1,559** (£483; £241; £121) **Stalls** Low

Form RPR
4233 **1** **Know No Fear**3 5179 7-10-9 **65**...............................(p) MissSBirkett(5) 10 76
(Alastair Lidderdale) *sn led: clr after 3f: rdn over 1f out: styd on* **11/4**1
020 **2** *3¾* **Iulus**45 3699 4-10-3 **61**... MrOJPimlott(7) 6 63
(John Quinn) *chsd ldrs: rdn along over 2f out: styd on fnl f* **11/1**
0006 **3** *1* **Xpres Maite**64 3022 9-10-1 **55**.................................(b) MrCMartin(3) 7 55
(Roy Bowring) *hld up: hdwy to chse ldrs 3f out: rdn 2f out: styd on appr fnl f* **17/2**3
0346 **4** *nk* **Iceblast**51 3460 4-10-2 **58**.................................. MissJoannaMason(5) 4 57
(Michael Easterby) *prom early: sn lost pl and towards rr 1/2-way: hdwy over 2f out: sn rdn: styd on same pce fnl f* **9/2**2
20-6 **5** *½* **Hernando Torres**11 4844 4-10-4 **62**............................ MissAHesketh(7) 3 60
(Michael Easterby) *hld up and bhd: swtchd wd and hdwy over 2f out: sn rdn and styd on wl fnl f: nrst fin* **17/2**3
0010 **6** *2¼* **Applaude**7 5015 7-9-7 **51**.................................(b) MissFrancesHarper(7) 8 44
(Chris Bealby) *midfield: hdwy to chse wnr 1/2-way: rdn along over 2f out: drvn and wknd over 1f out* **16/1**
0 **7** *1½* **Ra Junior (USA)**34 4042 6-9-9 **49**.................................. MissWGibson(3) 1 39
(Paul Midgley) *chsd wnr: rdn along 1/2-way: wknd wl over 2f out* **11/1**
-0 **8** *4* **Tropical Duke (IRE)**90 2239 6-9-4 **46** oh1........................ MissVBarr(5) 14 26
(Ron Barr) *dwlt: rapid hdwy on outer after 2f: chsd wnr 1/2-way: rdn wl over 2f out: grad wknd* **12/1**
6306 **9** *½* **Orpen Wide (IRE)**7 5015 10-9-10 **47**...................(bt) MrFWindsorClive 5 26
(Michael Chapman) *chsd ldrs to 1/2-way: sn wknd* **33/1**
0044 **10** *1½* **Benidorm**5 5113 4-9-8 **52**..(v) MrAFrench(7) 13 28
(John Wainwright) *a towards rr* **20/1**
0005 **11** *3* **Stamp Duty (IRE)**45 3712 4-9-7 **49**.......................... MrAaronJames(5) 2 18
(Suzzanne France) *a in rr* **14/1**
0030 **12** *5* **Qeethaara (USA)**13 4779 8-10-9 **63**...........(p) MissBeckyBrisbourne(3) 9 20
(Mark Brisbourne) *a towards rr* **18/1**

1m 46.2s (-1.40) **Going Correction** -0.35s/f (Firm) **12** Ran SP% **115.8**
Speed ratings (Par 101): **93,89,88,87,87 85,83,79,79,77 74,69**
toteswingers 1&2 £9.20, 2&3 £18.20, 1&3 £4.90 CSF £33.08 TOTE £3.50: £1.70, £3.70, £3.00; EX 27.70.
Owner Trinity TT Racing Partnerships **Bred** B Bargh **Trained** Lambourn, Berks
■ Stewards' Enquiry : Miss A Hesketh two-day ban: used whip above permitted level (Aug 30-31)

FOCUS
Part two and very few of these came into this in any sort of form.
T/Plt: £26.50 to a £1 stake. Pool of £42535.14 - 1170.41 winning tickets. T/Qpdt: £16.30 to a £1 stake. Pool of £2996.56 -135.46 winning tickets. JR

4988 CHEPSTOW (L-H)
Thursday, August 16

OFFICIAL GOING: Soft (5.3)
Wind: Light, against Weather: muggy and overcast, shower race 5

5260 32RED.COM/IRISH STALLION FARMS E B F MAIDEN STKS 5f 16y
5:20 (5:20) (Class 5) 2-Y-0 **£3,169** (£943; £471; £235) **Stalls** Centre

Form RPR
4 **1** **Vectis**19 4604 2-9-3 0.. CathyGannon 3 79+
(Harry Dunlop) *slow away and rousted along early: in rr: rdn and carried hd awkwardly over 2f out: pressed ldr 1f out: styd on wl to ld fnl 100yds: sn wnt clr* **5/1**2
25 **2** *2¾* **Vincentti (IRE)**14 4730 2-9-3 0... LukeMorris 6 69
(Ronald Harris) *trckd ldrs: pushed along to ld 2f out: clr w wnr ins fnl f: drvn and hdd fnl 100yds: nt gng pce of wnr* **6/1**3
062 **3** *3½* **Silverrica (IRE)**19 4581 2-8-12 70............................. TomMcLaughlin 4 51
(Malcolm Saunders) *led: hdd 2f out: drvn over 1f out: grad wknd ins fnl f* **5/1**2
42 **4** *7* **Dream Cast (IRE)**14 4730 2-9-3 0...................................... MartinLane 7 31
(David Simcock) *hld up: slt bump shortly after s: pushed along over 2f out: drvn and nt qckn over 1f out: sn btn* **4/5**1
20 **5** *2* **Bamurru (IRE)**61 3140 2-9-3 0.......................................(b1) SebSanders 5 24
(Peter Makin) *cl up: urged along 3f out: str reminders over 2f out: fnd little and hung lft: btn fnl f* **14/1**

1m 3.6s (4.30) **Going Correction** +0.525s/f (Yiel) **5** Ran SP% **109.8**
Speed ratings (Par 94): **86,81,76,64,61**
CSF £31.80 TOTE £7.60: £3.40, £2.10; EX 36.40.
Owner The Bow Wave Partnership **Bred** Mrs P M Ignarski **Trained** Lambourn, Berks

FOCUS
About an inch of rain fell in the 24 hours up to racing and the runners also faced a stiff headwind in the straight. A fair maiden on paper but one that didn't take as much winning with the market leader under-performing. The winner still impressed. The gallop was reasonable.

NOTEBOOK
Vectis, was down in trip and tackling very different ground to that on his debut but this was a fair test in the conditions and, although still looking green, turned in an improved performance. He'll be suited by the return to further and may do better in ordinary nurseries. (op 6-1 tchd 13-2)
Vincentti(IRE) hadn't been at his best over 6f last time but fared better back in trip and left the impression that he may do better on a sounder surface. He's in good hands and is capable of picking up a small event. (op 8-1)
Silverrica(IRE) had improved with every run on a sound surface but failed to match her previous run on this first run in soft ground. She'll be suited by the return to quicker ground. (op 10-3)
Dream Cast(IRE) was a long way below the form shown in softish ground over 6f at Ffos Las. However he has plenty to recommend him on looks and he'll be worth another chance in due course. Official explanation: trainer's rep said colt becamed unbalanced on the soft ground (op Evens tchd 4-6)
Bamurru(IRE), having his first run for two months and his first since being gelded, was again a long way below debut form on this first run in soft ground and in first-time blinkers. Quicker ground may help but he has something to prove at present. (op 12-1)

5261 32RED CASINO H'CAP 1m 14y
5:50 (5:50) (Class 6) (0-55,55) 3-Y-0+ **£1,617** (£481; £240; £120) **Stalls** Centre

Form RPR
0042 **1** **Tanforan**7 4988 10-9-2 **50**.. KellyHarrison 1 59
(Brian Baugh) *t.k.h: disp ld tl clr advantage 4f out: pushed along 3f out: extended clr ins fnl 2f: clr but kpt up to work ins fnl f* **11/4**2
2U52 **2** *2¼* **Volcanic Jack (IRE)**8 4940 4-9-4 **52**.................................. LukeMorris 3 56
(Tony Carroll) *slow away: in rr: hdwy 4f out: chsd wnr 3f out: drvn and one pce 2f out: plugged on but no hope of catching wnr fnl f* **6/4**1
6006 **3** *nk* **Alfie Joe**9 4900 3-7-13 **46** oh1....................................... PhilipPrince(7) 10 49
(Ron Hodges) *hld up: urged along 4f out: drvn and unable qck 3f out: plodded on one pce fnl 2f: tk mod 3rd ins fnl f* **8/1**3
6000 **4** *6* **Petrarchan**7 4993 4-9-1 **49**...................................(bt) RichardKingscote 9 38
(Milton Bradley) *t.k.h: cl up: pressed ldr 4f out: drvn along 3f out: one pce and no hope of catching wnr ins fnl 2f: lost 3rd ins fnl f* **9/1**
630 **5** *5* **One For The Girls**27 4293 3-8-10 **50**......................(t) RussKennemore 2 28
(Nicky Vaughan) *midfield: urged along 3f out: sn drvn and fnd little: btn fnl 2f* **9/1**
6/00 **6** *1¼* **Cheers Big Ears (IRE)**15 4708 6-8-7 **46** oh1........ MatthewLawson(5) 8 21
(Richard Price) *t.k.h: duelled for ld tl drvn and hdd 4f out: sn struggling and btn fnl 2f* **16/1**
0000 **7** *10* **Bridal Medic**24 4406 3-8-6 **46** oh1...................................... MartinLane 12
(John Mackie) *hld up: urged along 4f out: drvn and no hdwy fnl 3f: sn btn* **12/1**

1m 42.7s (6.50) **Going Correction** +0.525s/f (Yiel)
WFA 3 from 4yo+ 6lb **7** Ran SP% **111.4**
Speed ratings (Par 101): **88,85,85,79,74 73,63**
toteswingers 1&2 £1.50, 1&3 £6.00, 2&3 £4.20 CSF £6.85 CT £25.31 TOTE £3.00: £2.60, £1.50; EX 5.20 Trifecta £81.10 Pool: £109.64 - 1.00 winning units..
Owner Miss S M Potts **Bred** Bearstone Stud **Trained** Audley, Staffs

FOCUS
A depleted field for this moderate handicap. The gallop was an ordinary one.
One For The Girls Official explanation: jockey said gelding hung left

5262 32RED FILLIES' H'CAP 1m 14y
6:20 (6:20) (Class 5) (0-75,73) 3-Y-0+ **£2,264** (£673; £336; £168) **Stalls** Centre

Form RPR
-522 **1** **Croeso Mawr**3 5148 6-8-9 **55**.. CathyGannon 3 64
(John Spearing) *taken to post early: mde all: set sedate pce: urged over 2f out and qcknd pce: wnt clr over 1f out: kpt on gamely ins fnl f: gd ride* **5/2**2
146 **2** *2¼* **Autumn Fire**9 4914 3-8-10 **62**... MartinDwyer 5 65
(Andrew Balding) *in tch: chsd wnr 2f out: pushed along and nt qckn w wnr ins fnl 2f: one pce but hld on wl for 2nd* **13/2**3
-540 **3** *2¼* **Valley Queen**20 4538 3-9-1 **67**...1 LukeMorris 7 65
(Mark Usher) *midfield: drvn along 3f out: no ch w wnr 2f out: plugged on one pce: tk 3rd ins fnl f* **20/1**
3102 **4** *1½* **Supaheart**20 4531 3-9-7 **73**.. DarryllHolland 4 67
(Hughie Morrison) *taken to post early: cl up: urged along 4f out: drvn and no hdwy ins fnl 3f: wknd fnl f* **5/2**2
-424 **5** *4½* **Santarini (IRE)**55 3340 3-9-6 **72**................................... RichardHughes 6 56
(Richard Hannon) *hld up: dropped to last over 3f out: urged along over 2f out: rdn and looked awkward over 1f out: no ch after* **2/1**1

0666 6 *18* **Basantee**[37] 3940 3-8-10 **62** .... RichardKingscote 2
(Tom Dascombe) *in tch: drvn and wknd 3f out: sn eased* **9/1**

1m 40.8s (4.60) **Going Correction** +0.525s/f (Yiel)
WFA 3 from 4yo+ 6lb 6 Ran SP% **118.6**
Speed ratings (Par 100): **98,95,93,92,87 69**
toteswingers: 1&2 £12.40, 1&3 £15.80, 2&3 £2.50 CSF £19.96 TOTE £4.20: £2.20, £2.40; EX 15.50.
Owner Mrs Richard Evans **Bred** Richard Evans Bloodstock **Trained** Kinnersley, Worcs

FOCUS
A fair fillies' handicap run at just an ordinary gallop in the conditions.
Santarini(IRE) Official explanation: trainer said filly was unsuited by the soft ground

5263 32REDPOKER.COM MAIDEN H'CAP 6f 16y
6:50 (6:50) (Class 6) (0-65,65) 3-Y-O £1,617 (£481; £240; £120) **Stalls** Centre

Form RPR
3230 1 **One Last Dream**[13] 4754 3-8-2 **49** ow1 .... (b[1]) RaulDaSilva(3) 4 65
(Ron Hodges) *mde all: rdn clr 2f out: in n.d fnl f* **5/1[2]**
0-03 2 *5* **Roman Myst (IRE)**[14] 4734 3-9-2 **60** .... RichardHughes 2 60
(Sylvester Kirk) *urged along into midfield early: pushed along and hdwy over 2f out: drvn over 1f out: plugged on and wnt 2nd 1f out but nvr any hope of catching wnr* **15/2**
3 *2 ¼* **Dark Danger (IRE)**[6] 5071 3-8-5 **49** .... (p) LukeMorris 5 42
(David Peter Nagle, Ire) *chsd wnr: rdn along ins fnl 3f: nt pce of wnr 2f out: wknd and lost poor 2nd 1f out* **4/1[1]**
0005 4 *3* **Jay Bee Blue**[2] 5203 3-8-13 **60** .... (t) SophieDoyle(3) 3 43
(Sean Curran) *cl up: drvn and outpcd over 2f out: looked awkward u.p and btn fnl f* **11/2[3]**
0006 5 *¾* **Findeln**[8] 4942 3-8-8 **52** .... (b) JohnFahy 6 33
(Eve Johnson Houghton) *slow away: in rr: drvn 3f out: no ch 2f out: plugged on u.p past btn rivals fnl f: nvr any threat* **33/1**
6252 6 *¾* **Marah Music**[8] 4943 3-9-1 **59** .... (p) SebSanders 1 37
(Peter Makin) *midfield: rdn along 3f out: effrt 2f out: drvn and btn fnl f* **4/1[1]**
0445 7 *2 ¼* **Bitter Lemon**[28] 4237 3-8-7 **51** .... FergusSweeney 11 22
(Tony Newcombe) *in tch: urged along 3f out: drvn over 2f out: grad wknd after: btn fnl f* **18/1**
-054 8 *2* **Gypsy Rider**[14] 4734 3-8-5 **54** .... DarrenEgan(5) 12 19
(Bryn Palling) *hld up: drvn 3f out: struggling fnl 2f: dropped rt away fnl f* **10/1**
4-64 9 *1 ½* **Elite**[7] 5017 3-9-7 **65** .... PatCosgrave 7 25
(Mick Channon) *in tch: rdn 3f out: drvn and btn fnl 2f* **10/1**
-003 10 *8* **Jawim**[9] 4902 3-8-6 **50** .... CathyGannon 9
(Malcolm Saunders) *in rr: drvn 3f out: sn floundering and dropped rt away: t.o* **12/1**

1m 15.31s (3.31) **Going Correction** +0.525s/f (Yiel) 10 Ran SP% **117.9**
Speed ratings (Par 98): **98,91,88,84,83 82,79,76,74,64**
toteswingers: 1&2 £9.50, 1&3 £5.10, 2&3 £14.70 CSF £42.85 CT £166.05 TOTE £6.40: £2.00, £3.60, £2.00; EX 26.60 TRIFECTA Not won..
Owner P E Axon **Bred** P E Axon **Trained** Charlton Mackrell, Somerset

FOCUS
A modest handicap run at a decent gallop.

5264 LISWERRY AND NASH CONSTITUTIONAL CLUB MAIDEN H'CAP 2m 2f
7:20 (7:20) (Class 6) (0-65,62) 3-Y-O+ £1,617 (£481; £240; £120) **Stalls** Low

Form RPR
5005 1 **Ctappers**[9] 4918 3-8-0 **55** .... DarrenEgan(5) 4 63
(Mick Channon) *hld up: pushed along 5f out: surged through on outer to ld 3f out: clr ins fnl f: rdn out* **11/4[2]**
30-4 2 *3 ½* **Kahsabelle (FR)**[29] 3316 7-9-9 **62** .... HarryChalloner(5) 6 66
(Venetia Williams) *in tch: drvn and outpcd 6f out: plugged on one pce 3f out: kpt on to take 2nd cl home but no hope of catching wnr* **6/1**
0033 3 *hd* **Zarosa (IRE)**[7] 5022 3-7-13 **49** .... JimmyQuinn 3 53
(John Berry) *t.k.h: hld up: hdwy 4f out: swept through and wnt clr w wnr 3f out: drvn ins fnl 2f: wknd and tired fnl f: lost 2nd cl home* **7/2[3]**
0030 4 *14* **Cookieshake**[2] 5196 4-9-0 **48** oh3 .... (b) LukeMorris 1 36
(Peter Hiatt) *led: jinked 8f out: urged along 6f out: rdn and hdd 3f out: sn dropped away* **10/1**
2332 5 *6* **Tae Kwon Do (USA)**[17] 4664 6-9-2 **50** .... (t) RichardHughes 5 47
(Tim Vaughan) *dropped rt out in last: stl plenty to do and rdn 4f out: no real hdwy fnl 3f: dropped away and eased fnl f* **7/4[1]**
0-0 P **Bold Identity (IRE)**[56] 3316 6-10-0 **62** .... (b[1]) FergusSweeney 7
(Richard Phillips) *chsd ldr: urged along 5f out: drvn but would nt overtake ldr over 4f out: wknd and dropped away 2f out: t.o and wnt wrong whn p.u 1f out* **25/1**

4m 24.1s (20.50) **Going Correction** +0.75s/f (Yiel)
WFA 3 from 4yo+ 16lb 6 Ran SP% **112.5**
Speed ratings (Par 101): **84,82,82,76,73**
toteswingers: 1&2 £3.40, 1&3 £2.40, 2&3 £4.30 CSF £19.17 CT £57.30 TOTE £2.50: £1.50, £2.00; EX 15.90 Trifecta £40.20 Pool: £156.51 - 2.87 winning units..
Owner Peter Taplin **Bred** Imperial & Mike Channon Bloodstock Ltd **Trained** West Ilsley, Berks

FOCUS
A modest handicap run at a reasonable gallop.
Bold Identity(IRE) Official explanation: vet said gelding pulled up distressed

5265 £32 BONUS AT 32RED.COM H'CAP 1m 4f 23y
7:50 (7:50) (Class 6) (0-60,66) 3-Y-O+ £1,617 (£481; £240; £120) **Stalls** Low

Form RPR
6010 1 **Madam Lilibet (IRE)**[14] 4744 3-8-10 **52** .... PaulQuinn 6 62
(Sharon Watt) *hld up: smooth prog on outer 4f out: pushed along to chse ldr 2f out: kpt on wl to ld ins fnl f: kpt on wl* **5/1[2]**
4551 2 *1* **Taste The Wine (IRE)**[7] 4994 6-9-13 **66** 6ex .... RobertWilliams(7) 5 74
(Bernard Llewellyn) *midfield: hdwy 4f out: drvn to ld 2f out: hdd and edgd lft ins fnl f: nt pce of wnr* **5/1[2]**
/463 3 *3 ¼* **Bazart**[7] 4994 10-9-6 **59** .... (tp) DanielMuscutt(7) 11 62
(Bernard Llewellyn) *cl up: led 4f out: drvn and hdd 2f out: wknd ins fnl f: one pce* **14/1**
0500 4 *nk* **David's Folly (IRE)**[20] 4537 3-8-8 **50** .... LukeMorris 7 52
(Bryn Palling) *hld up: pushed along and hdwy to chse ldrs 4f out: drvn and one pce 2f out: plugged on* **25/1**
500- 5 *9* **Neighbourhood (USA)**[336] 6087 4-8-13 **48** .... RaulDaSilva(3) 9 36
(James Evans) *led: drvn and hdd 4f out: ev ch tl wknd over 2f out: one pce fnl f* **25/1**
-500 6 *¾* **Pelham Crescent (IRE)**[21] 4491 9-9-7 **58** .... DarrenEgan(5) 10 45
(Bryn Palling) *slow away: hld up: rdn 5f out: no imp fnl 2f: one pce* **14/1**
00 7 *1 ½* **Gucci D'Oro (USA)**[6] 5037 3-9-2 **58** .... MartinLane 3 42
(David Simcock) *hld up: pushed along 5f out: brief effrt 4f out: no imp fnl 3f* **7/1**
0233 8 *21* **Kittens**[11] 4850 3-9-2 **58** .... MartinDwyer 8
(William Muir) *in tch: pushed along and effrt over 4f out: drvn and stopped qckly 2f out: sn btn: t.o* **2/1[1]**
1455 9 *5* **Delagoa Bay (IRE)**[50] 3498 4-9-5 **51** .... RichardHughes 2
(Sylvester Kirk) *cl up: pressed ldr 6f out: pushed along over 4f out: grad lost pl ins fnl 3f: eased fnl f: t.o* **11/2[3]**
0/ 10 *12* **Bull Market (IRE)**[204] 6669 9-9-13 **59** .... JamieGoldstein 4
(Alan Jones) *a in rr: no imp fnl 4f: wl t.o* **66/1**

2m 50.69s (11.69) **Going Correction** +0.75s/f (Yiel)
WFA 3 from 4yo+ 10lb 10 Ran SP% **117.1**
Speed ratings (Par 101): **91,90,88,87,81 81,80,66,63,55**
toteswingers: 1&2 £5.70, 1&3 £13.50, 2&3 £4.10 CSF £29.83 CT £330.83 TOTE £6.70: £2.60, £2.00, £2.70; EX 38.40 Trifecta £136.40 Pool: £200.96 - 1.09 winning units..
Owner D H Montgomerie **Bred** Mrs Clodagh McStay **Trained** Brompton on Swale, N Yorks

FOCUS
No more than a modest handicap but the winner is progressive. The gallop was an ordinary one but this was a good test in the conditions.

5266 32REDBINGO.COM H'CAP 1m 2f 36y
8:20 (8:22) (Class 6) (0-55,59) 3-Y-O+ £1,617 (£481; £240; £120) **Stalls** Low

Form RPR
0053 1 **Bondi Mist (IRE)**[8] 4940 3-8-13 **55** .... RichardKingscote 4 68
(Jonathan Portman) *cl up: rdn to chse ldrs over 3f out: drvn to ld over 1f out: sn wnt clr and in n.d ins fnl f: easy* **7/2[2]**
5040 2 *12* **Corrib (IRE)**[12] 4817 9-8-9 **46** .... (p) RaulDaSilva(3) 12 35
(Bryn Palling) *in tch: rdn to ld over 3f out: drew clr w wnr 2f out: hdd over 1f out: sn no ch w wnr: eased but hld on for 2nd* **10/1**
005 3 *1 ¼* **Very Well Red**[17] 4662 9-9-1 **49** .... KirstyMilczarek 10 36
(Peter Hiatt) *led: urged along 4f out: hdd over 3f out: drvn and one pce fnl 2f: kpt battling on and jst hld on for 3rd* **20/1**
-030 4 *hd* **My Sister**[51] 3468 5-8-12 **46** oh1 .... MartinDwyer 2 32
(Mark Usher) *in tch: drvn and one pce over 3f out: swtchd to outer and r.o to press for pls ins fnl f* **16/1**
3000 5 *½* **Sir Dylan**[8] 4940 3-8-5 **52** .... (p) DarrenEgan(5) 1 37
(Ronald Harris) *cl up: rdn and hdwy on outer over 3f out: drvn and one pce fnl 2f* **16/1**
0301 6 *½* **Critical Point**[7] 5021 3-8-9 **51** 6ex .... (b) LukeMorris 7 35
(Sir Mark Prescott Bt) *cl up: drvn 4f out: wknd 2f out: btn fnl f* **6/4[1]**
0 7 *4* **Tadjena (GER)**[8] 4940 5-8-12 **46** oh1 .... JohnFahy 3 22
(Tony Newcombe) *in rr and nvr figured: pushed along 5f out: one pce fnl 3f* **50/1**
2-03 8 *½* **Oliver's Gold**[27] 4314 4-9-0 **55** .... ShirleyTeasdale(7) 13 30
(Shaun Harris) *in tch: hdwy 5f out: drvn along 3f out: one pce and no imp fnl 2f* **10/1**
5506 9 *6* **Mighty Motive**[45] 3712 3-8-2 **51** .... DanielMuscutt(7) 15 14
(John Mackie) *in rr: rdn and hanging lft over 5f out: rdr nt looking comfortable after: sn no ch t.o* **5/1[3]**
2-00 10 *17* **Vergrigio (IRE)**[38] 3920 3-8-10 **55** .... (b) SimonPearce(3) 6
(David Pipe) *nvr a threat: drvn and struggling fnl 6f: t.o* **25/1**
11 *22* **Top Spin (FR)**[276] 5-9-1 **49** .... PaulQuinn 16
(Nikki Evans) *a in rr: struggling 7f out: hopelessly t.o* **25/1**

2m 17.64s (7.04) **Going Correction** +0.75s/f (Yiel)
WFA 3 from 4yo+ 8lb 11 Ran SP% **123.3**
Speed ratings (Par 101): **101,91,90,90,89 89,86,85,81,67 49**
toteswingers 1&2 £9.60, 1&3 £5.90, 2&3 £10.70 CSF £38.58 CT £633.84 TOTE £4.10: £1.20, £1.90, £9.40; EX 49.20 TRIFECTA Not won..
Owner Looks A Bright Prospect Racing **Bred** Akoya Syndicate **Trained** Compton, Berks

FOCUS
A moderate but one-sided handicap in which the market leader disappointed.
T/Plt: £281.80 to a £1 stake. Pool: £41,242.72. 106.81 winning tickets. T/Qpdt: £47.30 to a £1 stake. Pool: £5,490.34. 85.80 winning tickets. CS

5101 NEWMARKET (R-H)
Thursday, August 16

OFFICIAL GOING: Good to firm (watered; 8.1)
Wind: fresh, half behind Weather: dry

5267 RACING UK MEDIAN AUCTION MAIDEN FILLIES' STKS 6f
2:10 (2:10) (Class 5) 2-Y-O £3,234 (£962; £481; £240) **Stalls** High

Form RPR
1 **Fearless Jacq (IRE)** 2-9-0 0 .... RichardMullen 2 83+
(David Simcock) *in tch: shkn up and effrt to chal jst over 1f out: rdn to ld fnl 100yds: rn green in front but styd on wl* **12/1**
2 *1 ¼* **Sherinn** 2-9-0 0 .... AndreaAtzeni 6 79
(Roger Varian) *wnt rt at s: chsd ldrs: pushed along wl over 2f out: rdn and hdwy to chal jst over 1f out: ev ch ins fnl f: styd on same pce fnl 100yds* **10/1**
030 3 *1* **Cut No Ice (IRE)**[15] 4701 2-9-0 **77** .... PaulHanagan 4 76
(Paul Cole) *wnt rt s: led: rdn 2f out: hrd pressed and drvn ent fnl f: hdd and one pce fnl 100yds* **7/1**
403 4 *2 ¼* **Frege (USA)**[17] 4646 2-9-0 **74** .... FrankieDettori 10 70
(Brian Meehan) *taken down early and ponied to s: w ldr: rdn 3f out: unable qck over 1f out: btn 1f out: wknd ins fnl f* **9/2[3]**
5 *5* **Lady Of The Vine (USA)** 2-9-0 0 .... LiamKeniry 11 55
(Andrew Balding) *t.k.h: chsd ldrs: rdn and pressing ldrs whn rn green and edgd lft over 1f out: btn ent fnl f: fdd fnl f* **4/1[2]**
05 6 *1 ½* **Girl Of Cadiz**[21] 4487 2-9-0 0 .... RyanMoore 1 50
(Richard Hannon) *in tch in midfield: rdn over 2f out: unable qck and outpcd wl over 1f out: wl hld fnl f* **12/1**
40 7 *½* **Rosie Future (IRE)**[20] 4539 2-9-0 0 .... TomQueally 8 49+
(Rae Guest) *short of room and hmpd s: slowLy into stride and pushed along early: in tch: rdn and struggling over 2f out: wknd over 1f out* **50/1**
00 8 *7* **Choral Rhythm (IRE)**[15] 4704 2-9-0 0 .... SeanLevey 9 28
(Richard Hannon) *in tch in midfield: lost pl u.p and in rr 3f out: bhd over 1f out* **50/1**
9 *4 ½* **Jazz On The Beach** 2-9-0 0 .... KierenFallon 3 14
(Luca Cumani) *dwlt and short of room leaving stalls: in tch towards rr but sn pushed along: wknd over 2f out: bhd over 1f out* **15/2**
5 10 *15* **Chorister Choir (IRE)**[7] 5003 2-9-0 0 .... TedDurcan 5
(David Elsworth) *plld hrd: in tch tl sddle slipped and drifted to far rail 4f out: wl bhd fnl 2f: t.o* **10/3[1]**

1m 12.73s (0.23) **Going Correction** +0.125s/f (Good) 10 Ran SP% **113.9**
Speed ratings (Par 91): **103,101,100,97,90 88,87,78,72,52**
toteswingers: 1&2 £23.00, 2&3 £5.70, 1&3 £10.40 CSF £122.90 TOTE £13.00: £2.90, £3.20, £2.30; EX 79.50 Trifecta £407.60 Part won. Pool: £550.82 - 0.63 winning units..

Owner Daniel Pittack **Bred** Ballylinch Stud **Trained** Newmarket, Suffolk

FOCUS

The runners came centre-field down the straight throughout the afternoon. A fairly ordinary fillies' maiden by course standards, with two of the newcomers coming to the fore. The third and fourth help with the level. Far side track used with stalls on Far side except 10f: Centre. Repositioned bend into home straight increased distance of 10f races by about 15m.

NOTEBOOK

Fearless Jacq(IRE), a half-sister to eight winners including the Group 1-placed Coliseum, appeared to know her job and travelled strongly before finding nicely for pressure to assert. Winning with a bit in hand for her in-form trainer, she looks a useful prospect and should have no trouble with 7f. (op 10-1 tchd 9-1)

Sherinn, who is related to a host of smart middle-distance performers, showed surprising speed but should still appreciate a step up in trip. There's probably a small maiden in her. (op 17-2)

Cut No Ice(IRE) put her experience to use and ran an improved race on what was the fastest ground she's tackled so far. (op 15-2 tchd 8-1)

Frege(USA), who was ponied to the start early, is a good-looker but doesn't appear to be progressing, the drop to 6f not helping. (op 4-1)

Lady Of The Vine(USA), a $60,000 2yo who is a half-sister to numerous winners in the US, was well backed but she couldn't race on having proved a little too enthusiastic through the early stages. Better was clearly expected and she should improve. (op 6-1 tchd 13-2)

Girl Of Cadiz now has the option of nurseries and should be found an opening, with a step up to 7f/1m likely to help. (tchd 10-1)

Jazz On The Beach, first foal of an unraced half-sister to Izzi Top, is from a yard whose juveniles often need a run, but it would still have been nice to see her show a little more, never featuring after a sluggish start. (op 8-1)

Chorister Choir(IRE), fifth over 5f on her Sandown debut seven days earlier, had no chance to build on that after her saddle slipped not long after the start. Official explanation: jockley said saddle slipped (op 7-2 tchd 4-1)

5268 HISCOX CHAIRMAN'S H'CAP (BETFAIR 10 FURLONG FLAT SERIES QUALIFIER) 1m 2f

2:40 (2:40) (Class 4) (0-85,85) 3-Y-O+ **£5,175** (£1,540; £769; £384) **Stalls** Centre

Form				RPR
-621	**1**		**Sequence (IRE)**[20] 4548 3-9-6 **85** .... RyanMoore 12 *(Sir Michael Stoute) mde all and allowed to bowl along in front: clr fr 8f out: stl wl clr and nudged along over 1f out: styd on strly: eased towards fin: unchal* **9/4**[1]	104
4152	**2**	*9*	**Odin (IRE)**[12] 4821 4-9-7 **78** .... LiamKeniry 5 *(David Elsworth) prom in main gp: rdn and chsd clr wnr over 2f out: won battle for 2nd ins fnl f and kpt on u.p: no ch w wnr* **7/1**[3]	79
1301	**3**	*1 ¾*	**Kuda Huraa (IRE)**[8] 4944 4-9-4 **80** .... DarrenEgan(5) 13 *(Roger Varian) stdd s: t.k.h: sn prom in main gp: rdn and ev ch of 2nd 2f out: no imp on wnr and styd on same pce fnl f: nvr a threat to wnr* **3/1**[2]	78
-403	**4**	*1 ½*	**Ellemujie**[19] 4596 7-9-12 **83** ....(p) TomQueally 3 *(Dean Ivory) t.k.h early: hld up in midfield: rdn over 2f out: styd on u.p to go 4th 1f out: kpt on fnl f: no ch w wnr* **17/2**	78
2-02	**5**	*¾*	**Looking On**[22] 4470 4-9-3 **74** .... EddieAhern 1 *(Henry Candy) chsd clr ldr tl over 2f out: sn struggling to qckn u.p: plugged on same pce fnl 2f: nvr a threat to the wnr* **10/1**	67
0-0	**6**	*shd*	**Aquilonius (IRE)**[19] 4600 3-9-3 **82** .... WilliamCarson 8 *(Stuart Williams) stdd s: t.k.h: hld up in midfield but nvr on terms w wnr: rdn and hung lft fr 2f out: plugged on but no ch* **40/1**	75
0403	**7**	*3 ¾*	**Kinloch Castle**[10] 4889 3-8-12 **77** .... FrankieDettori 2 *(Michael Wigham) stdd bk towards rr after s: t.k.h: hld up in rr: rdn 3f out: no imp: nvr on terms* **17/2**	62
4-46	**8**	*nk*	**Abbraccio**[21] 4516 4-9-4 **75** .... PaulHanagan 11 *(James Fanshawe) t.k.h early: hld up in midfield but nvr on terms w wnr: rdn and lost pl wl over 2f out: no ch after* **9/1**	60
20-0	**9**	*3 ½*	**Hot Spice**[117] 1513 4-9-7 **78** .... TedDurcan 4 *(John Dunlop) hld up in rr: rdn and no prog over 2f out: nvr on terms* **16/1**	56

2m 6.97s (1.47) **Going Correction** +0.125s/f (Good)
WFA 3 from 4yo+ 8lb **9** Ran SP% **116.7**
Speed ratings (Par 105): **99,91,90,89,88 88,85,85,82**
toteswingers 1&2 £4.20, 2&3 £4.90, 1&3 CSF £18.91 CT £48.19 TOTE £3.30: £1.60, £1.90, £1.40; EX 15.60 Trifecta £132.90 Pool: £902.26 - 5.02 winning units..

Owner The Queen **Bred** His Highness The Aga Khan's Studs S C **Trained** Newmarket, Suffolk

FOCUS

A farce of a race with Ryan Moore aboard the favourite Sequence, who'd won over 2f further the time before, being gifted several-lengths lead and never coming back. Back to school for the riders of those who watched her effortlessly glide clear without reacting.

5269 HISCOX PROPERTY H'CAP 7f

3:15 (3:15) (Class 4) (0-85,85) 3-Y-O+ **£4,528** (£1,347; £673; £336) **Stalls** High

Form				RPR
0000	**1**		**Common Touch (IRE)**[15] 4703 4-9-12 **85** ....(p) PaulHanagan 11 *(Richard Fahey) wnt sharply rt at s: chsd ldrs: pressed ldr over 1f out: rdn and ev ch ent fnl f: led fnl 75yds: styd on wl* **5/1**[2]	93
0001	**2**	*½*	**Zacynthus (IRE)**[17] 4661 4-9-12 **85** .... KierenFallon 5 *(Luca Cumani) led: rdn 2f out: kpt on wl u.p tl hdd and styd on same pce fnl 75yds* **7/1**	92
1042	**3**	*shd*	**Dixie's Dream (IRE)**[13] 4772 3-9-4 **82** .... RyanMoore 8 *(Richard Hannon) hld up wl in tch in rr: rdn and effrt over 1f out: drvn ins fnl f: styd on wl fnl 100yds: could nt quite rch ldrs* **5/1**[2]	87
1112	**4**	*½*	**Chosen Character (IRE)**[8] 4939 4-9-0 **80** ....(vt) NatashaEaton(7) 9 *(Tom Dascombe) sltly hmpd s: chsd ldrs: rdn and edgd lft ent fnl f: styd on same pce u.p ins fnl f* **4/1**[1]	85
4430	**5**	*½*	**Triple Charm**[15] 4703 4-9-9 **82** ....(v[1]) FrankieDettori 10 *(Jeremy Noseda) stdd s: hld up in tch: chsng ldrs and nt clr run ent fnl f: in the clr and rdn ins fnl f: kpt on same pce towards fin* **15/2**	86
0450	**6**	*¾*	**Rough Rock (IRE)**[13] 4772 7-8-12 **71** .... AndreaAtzeni 6 *(Chris Dwyer) chsd ldrs: rdn 2f out: drvn and unable qck ent fnl f: styd on same pce after* **25/1**	73
0062	**7**	*¾*	**Golden Tempest (IRE)**[7] 5004 4-9-4 **77** .... TomQueally 7 *(Eve Johnson Houghton) hld up wl in tch in rr: rdn over 1f out: swtchd lft and hdwy ins fnl f: kpt on but nvr gng pce to chal* **6/1**[3]	77
53-0	**8**	*hd*	**Dominium (USA)**[20] 4554 5-9-3 **76** ....(bp) EddieAhern 1 *(Jeremy Gask) t.k.h early: hld up wl in tch: rdn and unable qck wl over 1f out: styd on same pce u.p fnl f* **20/1**	75
0304	**9**	*1 ¼*	**Aldermoor (USA)**[21] 4503 6-9-3 **76** .... WilliamCarson 4 *(Stuart Williams) chsd ldr tl no ex u.p ent fnl f: wknd ins fnl f* **22/1**	72
0000	**10**	*4*	**Lowther**[19] 4580 7-9-4 **77** .... IanMongan 3 *(Brett Johnson) in tch in rr: shkn up briefly 1/2-way: rdn and no prog wl over 1f out* **25/1**	62
2646	**11**	*5*	**Royal Reyah**[25] 4364 3-8-9 **73** .... LiamKeniry 2 *(Stuart Kittow) in tch: rdn 2f out: sn lost pl u.p: bhd ins fnl f* **18/1**	43

1m 25.69s (-0.01) **Going Correction** +0.125s/f (Good)
WFA 3 from 4yo+ 5lb **11** Ran SP% **113.9**
Speed ratings (Par 105): **105,104,104,103,103 102,101,101,99,95 89**
toteswingers 1&2 £8.70, 2&3 £4.40, 1&3 £5.00 CSF £36.11 CT £184.42 TOTE £5.50: £2.30, £3.10, £1.40; EX 42.20 Trifecta £236.80 Pool: £1078.78 - 3.37 winning units..

Owner Nicholas Wrigley & Kevin Hart **Bred** Overbury Stallions Ltd And D Boocock **Trained** Musley Bank, N Yorks

FOCUS

A competitive handicap, but the pace was fairly steady and probably not form to get carried away with.

5270 LIBERTY MUTUAL INSURANCE CONDITIONS STKS 7f

3:45 (3:45) (Class 2) 2-Y-O **£7,762** (£2,310; £1,154; £577) **Stalls** High

Form				RPR
1	**1**		**Al Waab (IRE)**[26] 4340 2-9-1 0 .... TomQueally 1 *(Sir Henry Cecil) hld up in tch: swtchd rt and effrt over 1f out: qcknd to ld 1f out: in command and rdn out hands and heels ins fnl f: comf* **3/1**[2]	103+
261	**2**	*2*	**Ask Dad**[50] 3505 2-9-1 97 .... RyanMoore 3 *(Richard Hannon) hld up in tch: rdn and effrt wl over 1f out: drvn and chsd wnr jst ins fnl f: styd on same pce and no imp after* **10/3**[3]	97
1	**3**	*1*	**Timoneer (USA)**[19] 4595 2-9-1 0 .... FrankieDettori 2 *(Mahmood Al Zarooni) led: rdn wl over 1f out: hdd and unable qck 1f out: styd on same pce after* **15/8**[1]	94
3103	**4**	*5*	**Luhaif**[15] 4698 2-9-1 105 .... SamHitchcott 4 *(Mick Channon) pushed along leaving stalls: chsd ldr: rdn 2f out: unable qck and lost pl jst over 1f out: wknd fnl f* **10/3**[3]	81

1m 27.14s (1.44) **Going Correction** +0.125s/f (Good) **4** Ran SP% **105.9**
Speed ratings (Par 100): **96,93,92,86**
CSF £12.00 TOTE £3.70; EX 13.50.

Owner Mubarak Al Naemi **Bred** Aunt Julia Syndicate **Trained** Newmarket, Suffolk

FOCUS

The pace was pretty steady for this conditions event and the time wasn't great, but this looks a race to be positive about. The winner is awarded large improvement.

NOTEBOOK

Al Waab(IRE) picked up nicely to win in the style of a very useful juvenile. A C&D winner on his debut (soft ground), he had no trouble with the faster conditions and one would expect him to take up one of his several Group-race engagements, with next month's Champagne Stakes or Royal Lodge the most likely (also entered in Dewhurst and Racing Post Trophy). He should have no trouble with 1m. (op 11-4)

Ask Dad had been given a short break since breaking his maiden and he posted a career-best on this first try at 7f. He can win something similar, although would make plenty of appeal if taking his place in next month's valuable sales race at Doncaster. (op 4-1)

Timoneer(USA) overcame early interference to make a winning debut over C&D, but he proved vulnerable here having set just a steady gallop. His dam's a half-sister to Raven's Pass and he should benefit from 1m. (op 9-4, tchd 5-2 in a place)

Luhaif set the standard on form, having finished third to Olympic Glory in a Group 2 at Goodwood, but he very much enjoyed the run of the race that day and was unable to reproduce it back down in grade. (op 9-4)

5271 CLIMATE ENERGY GROUP H'CAP 7f

4:20 (4:20) (Class 2) (0-100,98) 3-Y-O **£10,350** (£3,080; £1,539; £769) **Stalls** High

Form				RPR
1101	**1**		**I'm So Glad**[19] 4597 3-8-10 **92** .... CharlesBishop(5) 1 *(Mick Channon) mde all: rdn and qcknd clr wl over 1f out: drvn and tiring ins fnl f: a gng to hold on: rdn out* **9/1**	101
0-02	**2**	*¾*	**Nawwaar (USA)**[19] 4600 3-8-10 **87** .... PaulHanagan 2 *(John Dunlop) chsd ldrs: chsd wnr ent fnl 3f: rdn and outpcd wl over 1f out: kpt on again u.p ins fnl f: nvr quite getting bk to wnr* **5/1**[3]	94
1232	**3**	*1 ¾*	**Dutch Supreme**[22] 4473 3-8-13 **90** .... TedDurcan 5 *(David Lanigan) in tch: effrt to chse ldng pair wl over 2f out: rdn and unable qck over 1f out: kpt on ins fnl f* **9/2**[2]	92
411-	**4**	*nk*	**Strictly Silver (IRE)**[299] 7021 3-8-7 **84** .... KierenFallon 3 *(Alan Bailey) stdd s: hld up in tch in rr: hdwy u.p but edging lft over 1f out: kpt on but nvr gng pce to rch wnr* **8/1**	85
-064	**5**	*2*	**Diala (IRE)**[19] 4579 3-8-13 **90** .... RyanMoore 4 *(William Haggas) hld up in tch: effrt jst over 2f out: hdwy u.p but edging lft over 1f out: one pce and no imp fnl f* **5/2**[1]	86
3004	**6**	*2 ¼*	**Eastern Sun (IRE)**[35] 4012 3-9-7 **98** .... RobertHavlin 6 *(John Gosden) hld up wl in tch in last trio: effrt u.p but hung lft 2f out: no prog and wl hld over 1f out* **14/1**	88
0020	**7**	*2 ¼*	**Apostle (IRE)**[14] 4740 3-9-1 **92** .... TomQueally 8 *(Michael Bell) chsd wnr tl over 5f out: styd chsng ldrs tl rdn and lost pl qckly wl over 1f out: wknd ent fnl f* **9/1**	76
-120	**8**	*33*	**Hallings Comet**[14] 4735 3-8-7 **84** ow1 .... LiamKeniry 7 *(Andrew Balding) taken down early: plld hrd: hld up in midfield: hung lft to far rail and hdwy to chse wnr over 5f out tl ent fnl 3f: sn dropped out: t.o over 1f out* **8/1**	

1m 25.91s (0.21) **Going Correction** +0.125s/f (Good) **8** Ran SP% **112.3**
Speed ratings (Par 106): **103,102,100,99,97 94,92,54**
toteswingers 1&2 £6.00, 2&3 £3.60, 1&3 £5.40 CSF £51.36 CT £231.74 TOTE £7.90: £2.10, £1.70, £1.90; EX 37.90 Trifecta £144.50 Pool: £937.39 - 4.80 winning units..

Owner Chris Wright & The Hon Mrs J M Corbett **Bred** Stratford Place Stud **Trained** West Ilsley, Berks

FOCUS

The pace was steady and few were able to get into the race, making the form questionable. The race is rated a little cautiously.

NOTEBOOK

I'm So Glad was granted an easy lead, as had been the case when winning over C&D from 2lb lower the time before, and always looked to be holding on. She's now won four of her last five and continues to progress. (op 5-1)

Nawwaar(USA) was never far away, but he was dropping from 1m and just couldn't quicken in time. He'd probably have won granted a stronger gallop. (op 11-2 tchd 6-1)

Dutch Supreme was caught flat-footed at halfway and was another who found the line coming too soon. He remains on the up. (op 4-1)

Strictly Silver(IRE) ran well after 299 days off. Bidding for a hat-trick off a 3lb higher mark, she was given little chance the way the race unfolded and should come on. (op 17-2 tchd 9-1)

Diala(IRE) was keen off the steady pace and wasn't seen to best effect, but the fact remains she's become a little disappointing for a filly her highly respected trainer felt good enough to contest the 1,000 Guineas. (op 10-3 tchd 7-2)

Eastern Sun(IRE) always seemed likely to find this mark beyond him. (op 11-1)

Hallings Comet, dropping in trip to try and get settled, started to pull soon after the start and, taken to the far rail, dropped right out. (op 10-1)

5272 TURFTV H'CAP 5f
4:55 (4:56) (Class 4) (0-80,76) 3-Y-O+ **£4,528** (£1,347; £673; £336) **Stalls** High

Form RPR

0121 **1** **Sunny Side Up (IRE)**[8] 4963 3-8-11 **72** 6ex................. LauraBarry(7) 11 80
(Richard Fahey) *chsd ldrs: rdn over 1f out: chal ins fnl f: r.o wl to ld towards fin* **3/1**[1]

0022 **2** *nk* **Macdillon**[27] 4292 6-9-5 **71**.. LiamKeniry 5 78
(Stuart Kittow) *in tch in midfield: rdn and effrt whn bmpd 1f out: drvn ins fnl f: styd on strly fnl 100yds: wnt 2nd last stride* **11/2**[3]

3523 **3** *shd* **Ring For Baileys**[46] 3670 3-9-0 **68**.. JoeFanning 4 75
(Chris Dwyer) *jostled s: chsd ldrs: effrt u.p over 1f out: drvn to ld 1f out: kpt on u.p tl hdd and lost 2 pls towards fin* **11/1**

0314 **4** *½* **Rebecca Romero**[11] 4849 5-9-7 **73**.................................... EddieAhern 8 78
(Denis Coakley) *hld up towards rr: pushed along and effrt ent fnl f: rdn out hands and heels and r.o wl ins fnl f: nvr quite getting to ldrs* **6/1**

154 **5** *1* **Nomoreblondes**[13] 4770 8-9-3 **76**...................................(v) NedCurtis(7) 9 77
(Paul Midgley) *led: rdn over 1f out: hdd 1f out: no ex ins fnl f* **16/1**

01 **6** *½* **Tom Sawyer**[7] 5020 4-8-13 **65** 6ex................................(b) PaulHanagan 7 65
(Julie Camacho) *chsd ldr tl jst over 1f out: edgd lft u.p and bmpd rival 1f out: wknd wl ins fnl f* **11/1**

535 **7** *1 ½* **Diman Waters (IRE)**[13] 4770 5-9-9 **75**............................ KierenFallon 3 69
(Eric Alston) *jostled s and sn dropped to rr: rdn 1/2-way: hdwy u.p but edging lft wl over 1f out: no prog 1f out* **7/2**[2]

310 **8** *hd* **Best Be Careful (IRE)**[11] 4849 4-9-5 **76**...................... LeeNewnes(5) 10 69
(Mark Usher) *in tch in midfield: rdn 2f out: unable qck over 1f out: wknd ins fnl f* **16/1**

1045 **9** *2 ½* **Steelcut**[8] 4963 8-9-6 **72**...(p) TomQueally 1 56
(Mark Buckley) *in tch in midfield: short of room: squeezed and lost pl wl over 1f out: styd on same pce and no imp fr over 1f out* **25/1**

5600 **10** *2 ¾* **Matsunosuke**[45] 3707 10-9-4 **70**.. FrankieDettori 6 45
(Alan Coogan) *hld up in rr: rdn wl over 1f out: no hdwy: n.d* **40/1**

0210 **11** *1 ¼* **Sir Geoffrey (IRE)**[22] 4461 6-9-8 **74**..................................(p) IanMongan 2 44
(Scott Dixon) *in tch: rdn 1/2-way: wknd u.p jst over 1f out* **16/1**

59.15s (0.05) **Going Correction** +0.125s/f (Good)
WFA 3 from 4yo+ 2lb **11** Ran SP% **117.5**
Speed ratings (Par 105): **104,103,103,102,100 100,97,97,93,89 87**
toteswingers 1&2 £4.00, 2&3 £9.80, 1&3 £7.70 CSF £19.57 CT £163.67 TOTE £4.00: £1.60, £2.20, £2.60; EX 24.40 Trifecta £284.50 Pool: £792.00 - 2.06 winning units..
Owner Jim McGrath, Roger & Dianne Trevitt **Bred** Jim McGrath & Reg Griffin **Trained** Musley Bank, N Yorks

FOCUS
Plenty of exposed sorts in this sprint handicap, and no surprise to see it go to one of the 3yos.

5273 NEWMARKETRACECOURSES.CO.UK H'CAP 1m 2f
5:25 (5:28) (Class 2) (0-100,93) 3-Y-O **£10,221** (£3,041; £1,519; £759) **Stalls** Centre

Form RPR

214 **1** **Angel Gabrial (IRE)**[7] 5006 3-8-11 **83**................................. KierenFallon 4 96
(Ian Williams) *t.k.h: hld up in tch: rdn and effrt over 2f out: ev ch and drvn 1f out: led fnl 100yds: hld on wl u.p* **3/1**[2]

233 **2** *nk* **Suegioo (FR)**[20] 4542 3-8-9 **81**... MircoDemuro 7 93
(Marco Botti) *awkward leaving stalls: t.k.h: chsd ldrs: wnt 2nd 5f out: rdn and ev ch 2f out: drvn to ld jst ins fnl f: sn hdd: kpt on wl but a hld* **7/2**[3]

315 **3** *3 ½* **Fluctuate (USA)**[27] 4287 3-9-4 **90**...................................... NickyMackay 5 95
(John Gosden) *led: rdn 2f out: hrd pressed jst over 1f out: hdd jst ins fnl f: no ex and sn btn* **7/2**[3]

1540 **4** *2 ¾* **Pilgrims Rest (IRE)**[14] 4735 3-8-13 **85**............................. RyanMoore 3 85
(Richard Hannon) *chsd ldrs: rdn and effrt over 2f out: unable qck over 1f out and btn 1f out* **11/4**[1]

31-0 **5** *3 ¾* **Hurler And Farmer (IRE)**[14] 4741 3-8-7 **79**................ WilliamCarson 1 71
(Richard Fahey) *hld up in tch in rr: rdn over 3f out: hanging lft and outpcd over 2f out: wknd wl over 1f out* **20/1**

1520 **6** *shd* **Beaufort Twelve**[14] 4735 3-9-4 **93**................................ HarryBentley(3) 2 85
(William Jarvis) *in tch: rdn and struggling to qckn whn outpcd and sltly short of room over 2f out: wknd over 1f out* **6/1**

2m 7.77s (2.27) **Going Correction** +0.125s/f (Good) **6** Ran SP% **115.2**
Speed ratings (Par 106): **95,94,91,89,86 86**
toteswingers 1&2 £2.60, 2&3 £1.70, 1&3 £2.60 CSF £14.36 TOTE £4.90: £2.60, £2.50; EX 15.00.
Owner Dr Marwan Koukash **Bred** K And Mrs Cullen **Trained** Portway, Worcs

FOCUS
Not a particularly strong race for the grade. The pace was a steady one until past halfway.

NOTEBOOK
Angel Gabrial(IRE) is taking his racing well and saw the race out nicely when considering he was keen early. He continues to shape as though a step up to 1m4f would bring further improvement and can rate higher still. (op 7-2 tchd 4-1)
Suegioo(FR), making his handicap debut, was again forced to settle for a place, being a shade unfortunate after starting awkwardly and then racing keenly with no cover. He'll be bumped up the wrights for this. (op 10-3)
Fluctuate(USA) had no obvious excuses and isn't going to find it easy from this mark. Perhaps he'll be tried back at 1m. (op 10-3 tchd 3-1)
Pilgrims Rest(IRE) arguably brought the best form into this, but he'd been below par at Goodwood the time before and ran rather flat here. (op 10-3 tchd 5-2)
Hurler And Farmer(IRE) showed more than on his reappearance, but doesn't look to be near winning form at present. Official explanation: jockey said gelding hung left (op 25-1 tchd 28-1)
Beaufort Twelve was another unable to bounce back from a disappointing run at Goodwood. Official explanation: jockey said colt hung left (tchd 7-1)
T/Plt: £246.00 to a £1 stake. Pool of £66822.54 - 198.26 winning tickets. T/Qpdt: £25.60 to a £1 stake. Pool of £4380.42 - 126.21 winning tickets. SP

5235 SALISBURY (R-H)
Thursday, August 16

OFFICIAL GOING: Soft (good to soft in places) changing to good to soft (soft in places) after race 1 (1.50)
Wind: quite strong against Weather: cloudy with sunny periods

5274 K J PIKE & SONS LTD MAIDEN AUCTION STKS (DIV I) 6f 212y
1:50 (1:50) (Class 5) 2-Y-O **£2,587** (£770; £384; £192) **Stalls** Centre

Form RPR

42 **1** **Annecdote**[51] 3473 2-8-4 0.. JohnFahy 11 76+
(Jonathan Portman) *in tch: qcknd up to ld over 1f out: sn rdn and hrd pressed: edgd sltly rt but hld on wl fnl f: all out* **6/1**

232 **2** *hd* **Botanica (IRE)**[14] 4739 2-8-11 82.................................. RichardHughes 7 82+
(Richard Hannon) *mid-div: hdwy 2f out: rdn for str chal over 1f out: ev ch thrght fnl f: kpt on: jst hld* **9/4**[1]

4233 **3** *1 ¾* **Sorella Bella (IRE)**[3] 5153 2-8-6 72................................. SaleemGolam 4 73
(Mick Channon) *trckd ldrs: led 2f out: sn rdn: hdd over 1f out: hld in cl 3rd whn short of room ins fnl f* **9/1**

2 **4** *4* **Laudate Dominum (IRE)**[27] 4310 2-8-4 0.................. PatrickMathers 10 61
(Richard Fahey) *mid-div: rdn 3f out: chsd ldrs 2f out: nt pce of ldrs fnl f* **7/1**

0 **5** *1 ¾* **Gilded Frame**[12] 4803 2-8-9 0.. HayleyTurner 1 61
(Marcus Tregoning) *little slowly away: towards rr: effrt to cl on ldrs 2f out: one pce fr over 1f out* **9/2**[3]

50 **6** *nse* **Rioja Day (IRE)**[82] 2480 2-8-13 0.. SebSanders 9 65
(J W Hills) *struggling in rr 1/2-way: sme prog over 1f out: nvr gng to trble ldrs* **50/1**

0 **7** *1 ¼* **Felix Fabulla**[22] 4472 2-8-11 0... DarryllHolland 5 60
(Hughie Morrison) *hld up: swtchd rt and rdn 2f out: nt gng pce to get on terms* **7/2**[2]

6 **8** *¾* **Captain McCaw**[21] 4507 2-9-2 0.. ShaneKelly 8 63
(Brian Meehan) *led main gp but overall 2nd: rdn and ev ch 2f out: wknd jst over 1f out* **20/1**

05 **9** *3 ¼* **Day In Day Out**[17] 4646 2-9-2 0... JimCrowley 3 54
(Ralph Beckett) *overall ldr: racd alone nrest far rails: jnd main gp and rdn wl over 2f out: sn hdd: wknd jst over 1f out* **25/1**

0 **10** *7* **Pink Mischief**[22] 4463 2-8-4 0.. DavidProbert 2 24
(Harry Dunlop) *chsd ldrs tl 2f out: wknd* **66/1**

1m 28.65s (0.05) **Going Correction** +0.025s/f (Good) **10** Ran SP% **120.0**
Speed ratings (Par 94): **100,99,97,93,91 91,89,88,85,77**
Tote Swingers 1&2 £4.30, 2&3 £2.90, 1&3 £5.80 CSF £19.94 TOTE £7.50: £2.00, £1.90, £2.50; EX 24.60.
Owner Tom Edwards & Partners **Bred** The Hon Mrs R Pease **Trained** Compton, Berks

FOCUS
The ground had dried up a little from the previous day's meeting and was Soft, Good to soft in places (from Soft). The inside rail was out 20ft from the turn for home to the winning post to take out ground cut up by the runners at Wednesday's meeting. This first division of the maiden auction wasn't as competitive as the numbers would suggest, but a few of these had already shown decent form and they filled the first four places. The runners came up the nearside rail, which set the trend for subsequent races, and the winning time was 2.65 seconds outside standard. The form is straightforward rated through the third.

NOTEBOOK
Annecdote had chased home the subsequent Cherry Hinton second and Princess Margaret winner Maureen at Newbury in her previous start and stepped up again from that. She showed a good attitude when produced with her effort against the stands' rail, battling on well to force her nose in front at the line despite edging away to her right. There should be more to come. (op 7-1)
Botanica(IRE), rated 82 having been already been placed in three much better races than this, was produced from the back of the field to hold every chance, but yet again she managed to find one to beat her. She doesn't appear to do much wrong and deserves to get her head in front. (op 15-8 tchd 7-4)
Sorella Bella(IRE), rated 72 having made the frame in her first four starts, had every chance when sent to the front passing the 2f pole, but was already looking held when slightly short of room between the front pair well inside the last. She is proving consistent, but remains vulnerable to an improver in races like this and may be better off in a nursery. (op 7-1)
Laudate Dominum(IRE), just ahead of a dual subsequent winner when runner-up on her Pontefract debut, was being shoved along to stay in touch at halfway, despite the extra furlong, and may be worth stepping up in trip again. (op 8-1)
Gilded Frame showed promise in a much better maiden on his Goodwood debut, but could never get into this following a slow start. He remains capable of better. (op 6-1 tchd 13-2)
Felix Fabulla, green when well beaten on his Sandown debut, was never in it and still looks to need more time. (op 6-1)

5275 K J PIKE & SONS LTD MAIDEN AUCTION STKS (DIV II) 6f 212y
2:20 (2:21) (Class 5) 2-Y-O **£2,587** (£770; £384; £192) **Stalls** Centre

Form RPR

0 **1** **The Gatling Boy (IRE)**[12] 4803 2-9-2 0........................ RichardHughes 8 82
(Richard Hannon) *trckd ldrs: rdn to ld ent fnl f: r.o wl to assert fnl 75yds* **5/1**[3]

02 **2** *¾* **Swift Cedar (IRE)**[26] 4330 2-8-4 0..................... MichaelJMMurphy(7) 11 75
(Alan Jarvis) *bhd: hdwy 4f out: rdn over 2f out: chal ent fnl f: kpt on but hld fnl 75yds* **7/2**[2]

03 **3** *2 ¾* **Muskat Link**[17] 4658 2-8-9 0... FergusSweeney 4 66
(Henry Candy) *led: rdn 2f out: hdd ent fnl f: no ex* **18/1**

0 **4** *2 ¼* **Storming (IRE)**[19] 4604 2-9-2 0.. DavidProbert 7 67+
(Andrew Balding) *mid-div: hdwy over 2f out: sn rdn to chse ldrs: one pce fnl f* **14/1**

5 *3 ¾* **Sakhee's Rose** 2-8-6 0... RichardKingscote 9 47
(Roger Charlton) *mid-div: hdwy over 2f out: sn rdn: fdd fnl f* **16/1**

2 **6** *hd* **Vallarta (IRE)**[16] 4688 2-8-13 0.. MartinHarley 6 54
(Mick Channon) *mid-div: nt clr run over 2f out: sn rdn: nt pce to get on terms: fdd fnl f* **10/11**[1]

7 *nk* **North Weald (IRE)** 2-8-11 0.. SebSanders 3 51
(J W Hills) *towards rr: rdn wl over 2f out: little imp on ldrs* **50/1**

00 **8** *¾* **Just Duchess**[12] 4813 2-8-1 0.. SophieDoyle(3) 2 42
(Michael Blanshard) *mid-div: rdn over 2f out: wknd fnl f* **250/1**

9 *1* **Sovereign Power** 2-9-2 0... JimCrowley 5 51
(Paul Cole) *mid-div tl dropped to last trio 4f out: rdn 3f out: wknd fnl f* **33/1**

10 *15* **Lucky Black Star (IRE)** 2-8-13 0.. PatCosgrave 1 9
(George Baker) *chsd ldrs: rdn wl over 2f out: sn wknd* **33/1**

1m 29.14s (0.54) **Going Correction** +0.025s/f (Good) **10** Ran SP% **117.3**
Speed ratings (Par 94): **97,96,93,90,86 85,85,84,83,66**
Tote Swingers 1&2 £3.30, 2&3 £3.80, 1&3 £9.30 CSF £22.70 TOTE £7.70: £1.80, £1.50, £2.40; EX 24.20.
Owner Kennet Valley Thoroughbreds I **Bred** Sean Collins **Trained** East Everleigh, Wilts

FOCUS
The ground was officially changed to Good to soft, Soft in places before this race. This didn't look quite as strong as the first division, but again a handful had already shown some good form. Again they came stands' side and the winning time was around half a second slower than the first leg. The placed horses set the level.

NOTEBOOK
The Gatling Boy(IRE) had run green and didn't enjoy the ideal trip when unplaced in a stronger maiden on his Goodwood debut, but with that experience under his belt everything clicked into place this time and he saw it out gamely after leading a furlong out. He can improve again and, as there is plenty of stamina on the dam's side of his pedigree, should have no problem getting 1m. (op 6-1)

Swift Cedar(IRE) showed ability when runner-up at Lingfield on his second start and might have been unfortunate not to go one better here. He was forced to concede his starting position against the stands' rail with a slow break and therefore had to switch to the wide outside to make his run, so did very well to get into a position where he held every chance inside the last furlong. He now gets a mark and should gain compensation before too long. (tchd 9-2)
Muskat Link still looked green when third at Yarmouth on his second start (just ahead of a subsequent winner), but was given every chance from the front here and just came up against two better rivals from the furlong pole. He also now gets a mark. (op 14-1)
Storming(IRE), well beaten on his debut here last month, ran better this time and may be the type for nurseries after one more run. (op 16-1 tchd 12-1)
Sakhee's Rose, a 15,000GBP filly out of a 6f winner, fared best of the four newcomers and should have learnt from the experience.
Vallarta(IRE) ran a most promising race when runner-up in a stronger maiden on his Goodwood debut (third and sixth have won since), but was never travelling at all here and ran a shocker. Perhaps he didn't like the ground. Official explanation: jockey said colt never travelled (op Evens tchd 5-4 in places)

5276 MARY WORT MEMORIAL MAIDEN STKS — 6f 212y
2:50 (2:55) (Class 5) 3-4-Y-0 — **£3,234** (£962; £481; £240) **Stalls** Centre

Form — RPR
2402 **1** **Dream Tune**[21] 4516 3-9-3 87 ... JamesDoyle 10 — 89+
(Clive Cox) *mde all: rdn clr over 1f out: comf* **1/1**[1]
3 **2** *4* **Ebble**[13] 4782 3-8-12 0 ... WilliamBuick 5 — 73
(John Gosden) *trckd ldrs: rdn to chse wnr over 1f out but a being comf hld* **13/2**
3 **3** *3* **Love Tatoo (IRE)**[118] 1501 3-8-12 0 ... JimmyFortune 1 — 65+
(Andrew Balding) *v.s.a: towards rr: pushed along and hdwy fr 3f out: wnt 3rd ent fnl f: styd on: nvr any ch w front pair* **9/2**[3]
0- **4** *4* **Mary Frith**[302] 6946 3-8-12 0 ... JimCrowley 7 — 54
(William Knight) *trckd wnr tl rdn over 1f out: fdd ins fnl f* **28/1**
62 **5** *1 1/4* **Gold Edition**[29] 4212 3-9-3 0 ... (v) RichardHughes 11 — 56
(Jeremy Noseda) *taken down early: wnt lft at s: trckd ldrs: rdn over 2f out: sn hld: wknd fnl f* **4/1**[2]
6 *nse* **Morning Call** 3-9-3 0 ... DaneO'Neill 9 — 56+
(Henry Candy) *s.i.s: towards rr: rdn over 2f out: styd on fnl f wout ever threatening to trble ldrs* **28/1**
0 **7** *2* **Maligned (USA)**[19] 4582 3-8-12 0 ... PatDobbs 3 — 45
(Richard Hannon) *mid-div: rdn over 2f out: wknd over 1f out* **50/1**
0 **8** *1 1/4* **Garrisson (IRE)**[26] 4341 3-9-3 0 ... MichaelHills 13 — 47
(Charles Hills) *trckd ldrs: rdn over 2f out: wknd over 1f out* **20/1**
9 *8* **Sambirano** 3-9-3 0 ... DarryllHolland 4 — 25
(William Knight) *mid-div: rdn over 2f out: sn wknd* **40/1**
0/ **10** *3* **Gladstone (IRE)**[671] 6883 4-9-3 0 ... (e1) KatiaScallan(5) 12 — 17
(Jim Allen) *v unruly leaving paddock: led to s by handler: s.i.s and hmpd s: sn mid-div: wknd 2f out* **80/1**
11 *21* **Need A Rave** 4-9-3 0 ... JamieJones(5) 8
(Mark Hoad) *taken down early: s.i.s: sn struggling in rr: t.o fnl 2f* **150/1**

1m 27.93s (-0.67) **Going Correction** +0.025s/f (Good)
WFA 3 from 4yo 5lb — **11** Ran SP% **119.5**
Speed ratings (Par 103): **104,99,96,91,90 89,87,86,77,73 49**
Tote Swingers 1&2 £3.10, 2&3 £2.90, 1&3 £2.30 CSF £7.93 TOTE £1.90: £1.10, £1.60, £1.50; EX 9.10.
Owner H E Sheikh Sultan Bin Khalifa Al Nahyan **Bred** Aislabie Bloodstock Ltd **Trained** Lambourn, Berks

FOCUS
This maiden lacked strength in depth.

5277 EBF BILL WHEELER 70TH BIRTHDAY FILLIES' H'CAP — 1m 4f
3:25 (3:26) (Class 4) (0-80,80) 3-Y-0+ — **£5,175** (£1,540; £769; £384) **Stalls** Low

Form — RPR
1-03 **1** **Saytara (IRE)**[22] 4459 3-9-1 77 ... DaneO'Neill 4 — 86
(Saeed Bin Suroor) *trckd ldrs: rdn 2f out: styd on wl ent fnl f: led towards fin* **7/2**[2]
245 **2** *nk* **Infinitum**[20] 4542 3-9-1 77 ... WilliamBuick 2 — 86
(John Gosden) *trckd ldrs: rdn wl over 1f out: led jst ins fnl f: hrd drvn whn hdd towards fin* **4/1**[3]
0523 **3** *1 1/2* **Napoleon's Muse (IRE)**[19] 4608 3-8-9 71 ... JimCrowley 3 — 77
(Ralph Beckett) *led: rdn 2f out: hdd jst ins fnl f: no ex* **3/1**[1]
1250 **4** *3 3/4* **Traveller's Tales**[14] 4741 3-9-3 79 ... RichardHughes 6 — 79
(Richard Hannon) *mid-div: creeping clsr whn nt clr run wl over 3f out: swtchd rt and rdn to chse ldrs over 2f out: kpt on same pce fnl f* **7/1**
521 **5** *2* **Adeste**[30] 4182 3-9-2 78 ... PatDobbs 5 — 75
(Noel Quinlan) *trckd ldr: rdn over 2f out: wknd fnl f* **14/1**
0243 **6** *2 1/4* **Shesha Bear**[28] 4251 7-9-9 75 ... (p) JamesDoyle 1 — 68
(Jonathan Portman) *mid-div: rdn over 2f out: nt pce to get on terms: wknd fnl f* **10/1**
0350 **7** *3/4* **Miss Aix**[15] 4702 4-10-0 80 ... HayleyTurner 7 — 72
(Michael Bell) *hld up in last pair: swtchd to centre whn rdn wl over 2f out: flattered briefly over 1f out: wknd fnl f* **20/1**
442 **8** *11* **Urban Daydream (IRE)**[18] 4622 3-8-8 70 ... NeilCallan 8 — 45
(Roger Varian) *wnt lft s: hld up last: rdn 3f out: nvr any imp: wknd over 1f out* **11/2**

2m 38.81s (0.81) **Going Correction** +0.125s/f (Good)
WFA 3 from 4yo+ 10lb — **8** Ran SP% **115.6**
Speed ratings (Par 102): **102,101,100,98,96 95,94,87**
Tote Swingers 1&2 £3.90, 2&3 £3.60, 1&3 £3.10 CSF £18.18 CT £46.15 TOTE £3.60: £1.20, £2.00, £1.60; EX 18.80.
Owner Godolphin **Bred** Peter Savill **Trained** Newmarket, Suffolk

FOCUS
They only went an ordinary pace in these fillies' handicap and it was dominated by the 3-y-os.

5278 TOTEPOOL.COM SOVEREIGN STKS (GROUP 3) (C&G) — 1m
3:55 (3:56) (Class 1) 3-Y-0+
£31,190 (£11,825; £5,918; £2,948; £1,479; £742) **Stalls** Low

Form — RPR
1113 **1** **Tullius (IRE)**[26] 4320 4-9-0 112 ... JimmyFortune 7 — 116
(Andrew Balding) *trckd ldr: rdn 2f out: sn chalng ldrs: v awkward hd carriage but kpt on to ld fnl 100yds: drvn rt out* **11/4**[2]
2101 **2** *1/2* **Sovereign Debt (IRE)**[35] 4012 3-8-8 106 ... HayleyTurner 1 — 114
(Michael Bell) *trckd ldr: rdn to chal wl over 1f out: led jst ins fnl f: hrd drvn and hdd fnl 100yds: kpt on* **3/1**[3]
0131 **3** *nk* **Highland Knight (IRE)**[18] 4628 5-9-0 110 ... (t) DavidProbert 4 — 114
(Andrew Balding) *wnt lft s: led: rdn 2f out: hdd ent fnl f: kpt on but no ex fnl 100yds* **10/1**
0-63 **4** *3* **Set The Trend**[18] 4628 6-9-0 107 ... JimCrowley 2 — 107
(David O'Meara) *chsd ldrs: rdn over 2f out: swtchd rt over 1f out: styd on same pce fnl f* **11/1**
-434 **5** *3 3/4* **Mehdi (IRE)**[131] 1216 3-8-8 100 ... (bt1) ShaneKelly 8 — 98
(Brian Meehan) *trckd ldr tl rdn 2f out: wknd ent fnl f* **40/1**
1-40 **6** *3 1/4* **Rockinante (FR)**[109] 1698 3-8-8 107 ... RichardHughes 6 — 90
(Richard Hannon) *hmpd leaving stalls: trcking ldrs whn crowded out and lost pl after 1f: in last pair tl moved prom whn switching to centre over 4f out: rdn over 2f out: wknd ent fnl f* **11/1**
1311 **7** *1 1/4* **Trade Commissioner (IRE)**[40] 3878 4-9-0 105 ... WilliamBuick 9 — 88
(John Gosden) *hld up last: tk clsr order 4f out: nt clr run whn swtchd rt over 2f out: sn rdn: nt pce to mount serious chal: wknd ent fnl f* **15/8**[1]

1m 41.84s (-1.66) **Going Correction** +0.025s/f (Good)
WFA 3 from 4yo+ 6lb — **7** Ran SP% **114.6**
Speed ratings (Par 113): **109,108,108,105,101 98,96**
Tote Swingers 1&2 £2.40, 2&3 £3.00, 1&3 £3.30 CSF £11.54 TOTE £4.00: £1.90, £2.40; EX 14.70.
Owner Kennet Valley Thoroughbreds VI **Bred** Sc Archi Romani **Trained** Kingsclere, Hants

FOCUS
The 13th running of Salisbury's most prestigious race and the ninth time as a Group 3. Older horses held the advantage over the 3yos by nine wins to three in the previous 12 runnings and they provided the winner again this time. The pace was sensible in the conditions.

NOTEBOOK
Tullius(IRE), whose stable had won this twice since 2003 including last year, was the highest-rated runner in the field having won a handicap and a couple of soft-ground Listed events before finishing a close third in the Group 2 Summer Mile at Ascot last time. He was ridden with plenty of confidence here and showed real determination when brought to challenge inside the last, putting it all in under strong pressure. He doesn't possess the most attractive of head-carriages, but there is no doubting his courage. (op 5-2)
Sovereign Debt(IRE) was unlucky in the Jersey, but did it nicely in a couple of nice soft-ground events either side and had every chance having been up with the pace from the off. He was only just outbattled in a driving finish and did much the best of the three 3-y-os, but although his Queen Elizabeth II Stakes entry looks optimistic he can certainly win a Group race. (op 9-2)
Highland Knight(IRE), the winner's stablemate, looked better than ever when winning a Pontefract Listed contest last month and made a brave bid to make all (especially as he was kept honest up front by Mehdi in the early stages) and wasn't collared until well inside the last. His very best form has come on a sounder surface, so this was a cracking effort back up in class. (tchd 11-1)
Set The Trend had 2l to find with former stablemate Highland Knight on last month's Pontefract running (sent off favourite) and ran close to that form with his old rival. It's still early days for him with his new yard. (op 9-1)
Rockinante(FR), whose stable had won three of the previous 12 runnings of this race, hadn't been seen since finishing well beaten in the Italian 2000 Guineas back in April, but he did win at this level as a juvenile. He was switched to race wide, away from his rivals, after getting messed around after 2f and that may not have helped, as he was going nowhere from over 2f out. (op 14-1 tchd 16-1)
Trade Commissioner(IRE) had a few pounds to find on these terms, but had been improving fast lately and looked good in winning a couple of hot handicaps both here and at Sandown. However, having tried to move closer at halfway his rider was soon sending out distress signals and it was clear that this wasn't going to be his day. He holds some fancy entries later in the season which now look optimistic, but it's too early to be giving up on him. His rider reported that the gelding had lost his action. Official explanation: jockey said gelding never travelled (op 9-5 tchd 13-8, 2-1 in a place)

5279 BILL GARNETT MEMORIAL FILLIES' H'CAP — 6f
4:30 (4:30) (Class 5) (0-70,70) 3-Y-0+ — **£2,587** (£770; £384; £192) **Stalls** Low

Form — RPR
3214 **1** **Represent (IRE)**[13] 4753 3-9-2 65 ... MartinHarley 2 — 73
(Mick Channon) *hld up: trcking ldrs whn nt clr run fr wl over 1f out: qcknd up wl whn gap appeared ent fnl f: rdn to ld fnl 110yds: readily* **2/1**[1]
0040 **2** *1 1/2* **Red Mischief (IRE)**[20] 4533 3-9-2 65 ... HayleyTurner 1 — 68
(Harry Dunlop) *prom: rdn to chal over 1f out: led jst ins fnl f: hdd fnl 110yds: nt pce of wnr* **15/2**
5255 **3** *2* **Ocean Myth**[4] 5122 3-9-1 64 ... JimCrowley 8 — 61
(Jonathan Portman) *led: rdn whn chal 2f out: kpt on gamely tl hdd jst ins fnl f: no ex fnl 100yds* **7/2**[3]
0200 **4** *1* **Amber Heights**[51] 3466 4-8-12 58 ... DaneO'Neill 5 — 51
(Henry Candy) *racd keenly: trckd ldrs: rdn 2f out: kpt on same pce fnl f* **13/2**
0-00 **5** *3/4* **One Cool Chick**[21] 4492 4-8-7 53 ... KieranO'Neill 6 — 44
(John Bridger) *s.i.s: trckd ldrs: rdn over 2f out: one pce fr over 1f out* **25/1**
2165 **6** *2 3/4* **Full Shilling (IRE)**[10] 4887 4-9-9 69 ... JamesDoyle 3 — 51
(John Spearing) *wnt rt s: cl up: effrt over 1f out: fdd fnl 140yds* **10/3**[2]
4-00 **7** *5* **Red Hot Secret**[73] 2757 3-9-4 70 ... (b1) RaulDaSilva(3) 7 — 36
(Jeremy Gask) *wnt rt s: trckd ldrs: rdn 2f out: wknd over 1f out* **16/1**

1m 15.05s (0.25) **Going Correction** +0.025s/f (Good)
WFA 3 from 4yo 3lb — **7** Ran SP% **113.5**
Speed ratings (Par 100): **99,97,94,93,92 88,81**
Tote Swingers 1&2 £3.70, 2&3 £4.70, 1&3 £2.40 CSF £17.56 CT £48.82 TOTE £2.80: £1.60, £2.80; EX 16.40.
Owner Insignia Racing (Ensign) **Bred** Whatton Manor Stud **Trained** West Ilsley, Berks

FOCUS
A modest fillies' sprint handicap.
Red Hot Secret Official explanation: trainer said filly scoped badly on return

5280 KEVIN HALL & PAT BOAKES MEMORIAL H'CAP — 1m 6f 21y
5:05 (5:05) (Class 5) (0-70,72) 3-Y-0+ — **£2,587** (£770; £384; £192)

Form — RPR
4341 **1** **Suzi's A Class Act**[8] 4972 4-10-0 72 6ex ... (p) AdamBeschizza(3) 5 — 85
(James Eustace) *mde all: styd on v gamely fnl 2f: rdn out* **4/1**[1]
-142 **2** *3 1/4* **Abundantly**[20] 4536 3-8-11 64 ... HayleyTurner 6 — 72
(Hughie Morrison) *hld up bhd: grabbed stands' side rail over 5f out: rdn 3f out: no imp tl styd on fr 2f out: wnt 2nd ins fnl f: no ch w wnr* **4/1**[1]
0134 **3** *2 3/4* **Zowaina**[27] 4311 3-9-2 69 ... [1] NeilCallan 3 — 73
(Roger Varian) *mid-div: swtchd to centre and rdn over 3f out: hdwy to chse wnr over 2f out: lost 2nd whn no ex ins fnl f* **4/1**[1]
2/04 **4** *6* **Gordon Flash**[42] 3782 5-9-4 59 ... MichaelHills 10 — 55
(Charles Hills) *mid-div: hdwy over 3f out: sn rdn: one pce fnl 2f* **9/1**
050 **5** *1/2* **Call Me April**[50] 3485 4-8-11 52 ... KirstyMilczarek 12 — 47
(Karen George) *tk str hold: in chsng gp tl plld wd and hdwy to join clr ldr after 5f: rdn 3f out: hld fr 2f out* **40/1**
0-00 **6** *3* **The Ploughman**[10] 4870 3-7-12 51 oh6 ... KieranO'Neill 11 — 42
(John Bridger) *chsd clr ldr for 5f: styd 3rd: rdn over 3f out: nt pce to chal ldrs: fdd ins fnl f* **100/1**
2451 **7** *3 1/2* **Vexillum (IRE)**[7] 5022 3-8-8 61 6ex ... MartinHarley 4 — 47
(Mick Channon) *hld up towards rr: hdwy u.p 3f out: wknd over 1f out* **7/1**[3]

004 8 9 **Chella Thriller (SPA)**[22] 4465 3 -8-11**64** DavidProbert 9 37
(Alastair Lidderdale) *hld up towards rr: effrt wl over 3f out: wknd 2f out* **16/1**

-450 9 51 **Tantamount**[61] 3142 3 -8-13**66** JamesDoyle 7
(Roger Charlton) *mid-div: swtchd to centre and effrt over 3f out: sn hung rt to far side rail: wknd 2f out: virtually p.u* **12/1**

22 P **Grandad Mac**[36] 3979 4 -9-10**65** RichardHughes 1
(Jane Chapple-Hyam) *racd keenly early: trckd ldr in chsng gp tl lost action over 5f out: immediately eased: p.u over 3f out* **5/1**[2]

3m 10.48s (3.08) **Going Correction** +0.125s/f (Good)
WFA 3 from 4yo+ 12lb **10**Ran SP% **116.2**
Speed ratings (Par 103): **96,94,92,89,88 87,85,80,50,**
Tote Swingers 1&2 £3.80, 2&3 £6.00, 1&3 £6.30 CSF £19.66 CT £67.84 TOTE £5.40 : £1.90 , £1.30, £1.80 ; EX 25.10 .
Owner Greenstead Hall Racing Ltd **Bred** East Burrow Farm **Trained** Newmarket, Suffolk

FOCUS
A modest staying handicap and quite a test in the ground, but it became a very one-sided affair. With a couple of rivals in Grandad Mac (pulled up) and Tantamount (hung right over to the far rail) not running their races, it's hard to know how strong the form is, but the winner could hardly have done it any easier.\n
Call Me April Official explanation: jockey said filly hung left and ran too freely
Grandad Mac Official explanation: vet said gelding pulled up lame left-fore
T/Plt: £48.80 to a £1 stake. Pool of £50657.06 - 757.65 winning tickets. T/Qpdt: £9.20 to a £1 stake.Pool of £4888.62 - 392.38 w. tckts TM 5281a-5285a, 5287a (Foreign Racing) See RI

[5023] LEOPARDSTOWN (L-H)
Thursday, August 16
OFFICIAL GOING: Soft

5286a DESMOND STKS (GROUP 3) 1m
7:25 (7:25) 3-Y-O+ **£31,145** (£9,104; £4,312 ; £1,437)

RPR
1 **Duntle (IRE)**[57] 3270 3 -9-0**110** WayneLordan 8 110+
(David Wachman, Ire) *hld up in tch: clsd gng wl into 4th appr st: pushed along in 3rd 2f out and impr to ld fnl 150yds: kpt on wl* **5/2**[2]

2 ¾ **Ballybacka Lady (IRE)**[31] 4521 4 -9-6**102** FranBerry 4 109
(Mrs John Harrington, Ire) *chsd ldrs: cl 2nd into st and rdn to ld under 2f out: hdd fnl 150yds: kpt on* **14/1**

3 1 ½ **Requisition (IRE)**[116] 1548 3 -9-3**105** JPO'Brien 6 108
(A P O'Brien, Ire) *broke wl to ld: pushed along on inner into st and hdd under 2f out: sn n.d: kpt on ins fnl f* **5/1**

4 5 **Aloof (IRE)**[50] 3516 3 -9-0**92** WJLee 3 94
(David Wachman, Ire) *chsd ldrs: cl up 4th on inner under 3f out: rdn in 5th and no imp ent fnl 2f: kpt on to go 4th ins fnl f* **33/1**

5 ¾ **Penitent**[81] 2533 6 -10-0 DanielTudhope 10 101
(David O'Meara) *w.w towards rr: brought wd into st and sn rdn: kpt on wout ever threatening principals fnl f* **3/1**[3]

6 2 ½ **Marvada (IRE)**[14] 4749 4 -9-9**101** KevinManning 11 90
(K J Condon, Ire) *chsd ldrs: pushed along disputing 3rd into st: no imp fnl 2f* **16/1**

7 2 ¼ **Banna Boirche (IRE)**[64] 3055 6 -9-9**106** ShaneFoley 5 85
(M Halford, Ire) *hld up in rr: n.d fr after 1/2-way* **20/1**

8 12 **Takar (IRE)**[26] 4354 3 -9-6**108** (t) NGMcCullagh 9 59
(John M Oxx, Ire) *hld up in tch: t.k.h: cl 5th 3f out and sn rdn: one pce fnl 2f: eased* **9/4**[1]

1m 46.26s (5.06) **Going Correction** +0.975s/f (Soft)
WFA 3 from 4yo+ 6lb **8**Ran SP% **121.3**
Speed ratings: **113,112,110,105,105 102,100,88**
CSF £39.31 TOTE £3.40 : £1.10 , £2.20 , £1.60 ; DF 50.20 .
Owner Niarchos Family **Bred** Airlie Stud **Trained** Goolds Cross, Co Tipperary

FOCUS
Duntle, who won the Sandringham Stakes Handicap at Royal Ascot in June, was having her first race since and made it three wins from five starts with a first Group race victory here. The form fits the race averages.

NOTEBOOK
Duntle(IRE) ◆ has progressed well since landing a maiden by 18 lengths at Dundalk early in the season and won here despite her connections' reservations about the soft ground. Held up in touch, she began her effort early in the straight and picked up for pressure to lead about 150 yards from the finish. There should be more improvement to come. (op 100/30 tchd 7/2)
Ballybacka Lady (IRE) had run well on her reappearance here last month when second to easy winner Famous Name in the Meld Stakes. This was her first experience of soft ground and she handled it quite well, racing prominently and leading early in the straight. She stuck to her task, although the winner had too much for her in the closing stages. (op 12/1)
Requisition(IRE) ◆ had not been seen since landing a 7f Listed event at the Curragh in April. He had plenty of use made of him and led until headed under 2f out. With this run behind him he can be expected to improve next time. (op 11/2)
Aloof(IRE) needed to improve to figure seriously here, but having kept in touch she was unable to make any impression from well over 1f out.
Penitent was having his first run since failing to perform in a Group 1 in France in May. Held up, he was asked to try and close early in the straight, and while he kept on he never posed any sort of threat. (op 7/2)
Takar(IRE) had shown that he handles this sort of ground. However, he ran well below expectations here and was later reported to have lost his action due to being struck into. Official explanation: jockey said colt lost its action; vet said colt was struck into in running (op 7/4 tchd 5/2)

[5030] CLAIREFONTAINE (R-H)
Thursday, August 16
OFFICIAL GOING: Turf: very soft

5288a PRIX PARIS-TURF (PRIX DE VAUVILLE) (MAIDEN) (2YO FILLIES) (TURF) 7f
11:30 (12:00) 2-Y-O **£10,000** (£4,000; £3,000 ; £2,000 ; £1,000)

RPR
1 **Khadima (FR)**[19] 4615 2 -9-0**0** IoritzMendizabal 4 83+
(J-C Rouget, France) **2/5**[1]

2 1 ¼ **Agence Belge (FR)**[18] 2 -9-0**0** MorganDelalande 1 80
(Y Barberot, France) **15/1**

3 2 **Dauphine Russe (FR)** 2 -9-0**0** ThomasHuet 8 75
(F Doumen, France) **21/1**

4 ¾ **Emotionalblackmail (IRE)**[8] 4946 2 -9-0**0** ChristopheSoumillon 3 73
(Joseph Tuite) *broke smartly: racd in 2nd: swtchd to stands' rail early in st: rdn 1 1/2f out: no ex: styd on fnl f* **19/1**

5 1 **Bintisultan (FR)**[25] 2 -9-0**0** FlavienPrat 2 70
(T Clout, France) **44/1**

6 3 **Aylin (FR)**[35] 2 -9-0**0** ThierryThulliez 5 62
(N Clement, France) **16/1**

7 nk **Spellbound (FR)** 2 -8-8**0** KevinAubree[(6)] 7 62
(H Hotger, Germany) **72/1**

8 1 ½ **Rebecca's Filly (FR)**[85] 2 -8-8**0** EddyHardouin[(6)] 10 57
(Robert Collet, France) **65/1**

8 nk **Falcolina (IRE)**[20] 2 -9-0**0** OlivierPeslier 11 57
(F Head, France) **10/1**[3]

10 2 ½ **Red Shot (FR)**[20] 2 -9-0**0** MaximeGuyon 9 50
(H-A Pantall, France) **9/1**[2]

0 **Holzer (SPA)** 2 -8-10**0** AntoineCoutier[(4)] 6
(S Cerulis, France) **75/1**

1m 28.4s (88.40) **11**Ran SP% **118.6**
WIN (incl. 1 euro stake): 1.40. PLACES: 1.10, 1.70, 2.00. DF: 5.90. SF: 6.00
Owner H H Aga Khan **Bred** S A Aga Khan **Trained** Pau, France

NOTEBOOK
Emotionalblackmail(IRE) improved on her debut effort and handled the soft ground.

[4907] CATTERICK (L-H)
Friday, August 17
OFFICIAL GOING: Good (8.6)
Wind: moderate half behind Weather: steady drizzle before racing, but soon cleared up

5290 PIN POINT RECRUITMENT AMATEUR RIDERS' H'CAP 1m 3f 214y
5:35 (5:35) (Class 5) (0-75,76) 3-Y-O+ **£2,183** (£677; £338 ; £169) **Stalls** Centre

Form RPR
0001 1 **Pertuis (IRE)**[46] 3692 6 -9-9**60** MissRSmith[(5)] 6 68
(Micky Hammond) *hld up in tch: hdwy to trck ldng pair 1/2-way: rdn 2f out: led appr fnl f: kpt on wl* **8/1**

1021 2 2 ¾ **Tidal Run**[8] 4987 4 -10-11**76** 6ex MissSMDoolan[(5)] 4 79
(Mick Channon) *trckd ldrs: rdn to ld narrowly over 1f out: sn hdd: kpt on but a hld* **7/2**[2]

3266 3 1 ½ **Rub Of The Relic (IRE)**[6] 5085 7 -10-2**67** (v) MissHDukes[(5)] 5 68
(Paul Midgley) *trckd ldr: pressed ldr 1/2-way: rdn and ev ch over 1f out: sn outpcd: plugged on ins fnl f* **12/1**

1104 4 ¾ **Tinseltown**[8] 5001 6 -10-8**68** (p) MrSWalker 7 68
(Brian Rothwell) *led: rdn 2f out: hdd over 1f out: sn one pce and btn* **11/4**[1]

1500 5 1 ¼ **Al Furat (USA)**[16] 4714 4 -9-13**64** MissVBarr[(5)] 2 63
(Ron Barr) *slowly away: hld up in tch: rdn over 2f out: sme hdwy on inner over 1f out: no further imp fnl f: short of room nr fin* **7/1**

1241 6 2 ¼ **Call Of Duty (IRE)**[6] 5039 7 -10-6**66** MissECSayer 8 60
(Dianne Sayer) *hld up in tch: hdwy on outer over 2f out: sn rdn: wknd appr fnl f* **5/1**[3]

0/3- 7 12 **Maneki Neko (IRE)**[468] 1908 10 -10-12**72** MissSBrotherton 3 47
(Edwin Tuer) *hld up in tch: rdn over 2f out: wknd over 1f out* **6/1**

2m 38.02s (-0.88) **Going Correction** +0.025s/f (Good) **7**Ran SP% **111.1**
Speed ratings (Par 103): **103,101,100,99,98 97,89**
toteswingers 1&2 £5.50, 1&3 £14.10, 2&3 £10.10 CSF £33.94 CT £323.84 TOTE £9.80 : £4.20 , £2.30; EX 43.40 .
Owner M D Hammond **Bred** Killeen Castle Stud **Trained** Middleham Moor, N Yorks
■ Stewards' Enquiry : Mr S Walker one-day ban: careless riding (tbn)

FOCUS
A fair middle-distance amateur riders' handicap. They appeared to go an even pace on ground officially described as good. The form appears sound.
Al Furat (USA) Official explanation: jockey said saddle slipped

5291 GO RACING IN YORKSHIRE (S) STKS 7f
6:05 (6:07) (Class 6) 2-Y-O **£2,045** (£603; £302) **Stalls** Centre

Form RPR
4246 1 **Wordsaplenty (IRE)**[14] 4752 2 -8-6**59** DavidAllan 1 51
(J S Moore) *hld up in tch: pushed along 3f out: hdwy 2f out: kpt on fnl f: led post* **3/1**[2]

030 2 nse **Special Report (IRE)**[6] 5108 2 -8-4**54** DanielleMooney[(7)] 3 56
(Nigel Tinkler) *led: rdn over 2f out: drvn over 1f out: kpt on: hdd post* **12/1**

40 3 1 ¾ **Baraboy (IRE)**[17] 4677 2 -8-6**0** DarylByrne[(5)] 8 51
(Tim Easterby) *in tch on outer: rdn 2f out: kpt on* **13/2**[3]

25 4 shd **Juana Belen**[10] 4907 2 -8-6**0** JoeFanning 6 46
(David Barron) *trckd ldr: rdn over 1f out: kpt on one pce* **6/4**[1]

3505 5 4 ½ **Red Koko (IRE)**[13] 4806 2 -8-6**40** AndrewMullen 5 34
(George Moore) *trckd ldr: rdn and outpcd over 2f out: wknd fnl f* **20/1**

6 4 **Annabella Milbanke** 2 -8-6**0** JimmyQuinn 7 29+
(John Holt) *hld up in rr: pushed along 1/2-way: wl bhd tl sme hdwy over 1f out: eased jnside fnl f* **12/1**

5 7 ½ **Big Spender (IRE)**[6] 5108 2 -8-6**0** NeilFarley[(5)] 4 28
(Ian McInnes) *in tch: rdn and outpcd over 2f out: wknd over 1f out* **20/1**

2044 8 44 **Golac**[15] 4728 2 -8-11**60** RoystonFfrench 2
(Mick Channon) *in tch: rdn 1/2-way: sn dropped to rr: eased over 1f out* **8/1**

1m 28.27s (1.27) **Going Correction** +0.025s/f (Good) **8**Ran SP% **114.4**
Speed ratings (Par 92): **93,92,90,90,85 81,80,30**
toteswingers 1&2 £8.80, 1&3 £2.70, 2&3 £16.80 CSF £38.10 TOTE £3.70 : £1.10 , £6.20 , £4.00 ; EX 41.40 .There was no bid for the winner. Baraboy was claimed by Mr F. P. Murtagh for £5,000.
Owner The Moore The Merrier **Bred** Peter Kelly **Trained** Upper Lambourn, Berks
■ Stewards' Enquiry : David Allan 18-day ban (takes into account previous offences): improper use of the whip - above permitted level (Aug 31 - Sep 17)

FOCUS
A modest juvenile seller and the winner did not need to match her very best efforts. The runner-up helps anchor the form.

NOTEBOOK
Wordsaplenty(IRE) has done well to win having not really made use of a helpful low draw. She ended up being held up just off the pace and narrowly managed to prevail by getting up in the shadow of the post. She was the one to beat according to adjusted official ratings on these favourable terms and may have more to offer in this lowly grade over 1m. In all honesty, though, it was no surprise to see that there was no bid for her in the subsequent auction. (op 11-4 tchd 10-3)
Special Report (IRE) ran a game race from the front and may be able to pick up a similarly weak affair in this grade. (op 9-1)

Baraboy(IRE) managed to build on his previous two distinctly modest efforts and this trip looks suitable. He was claimed by Barry Murtagh after the race. (op 8-1 tchd 9-1)
Juana Belen once again took the eye in the paddock, but is becoming frustrating to follow. (op 15-8 tchd 2-1)
Golac Official explanation: jockey said colt lost its action

5292 SUZANNE GILL MILLINERY NURSERY 5f 212y
6:35 (6:35) (Class 4) (0-85,72) 2-Y-O £3,881 (£1,155; £577; £288) Stalls Low

Form RPR
6303 1 **Sylvia Pankhurst (IRE)**[12] 4836 2-9-2 68 JoeFanning 5 72+
(David C Griffiths) *in tch: rdn 2f out: led ins fnl f: kpt on wl* 11/2[3]
11 2 1 ½ **Lady Moonlight (IRE)**[30] 4206 2-9-6 72 GrahamLee 7 71
(Ann Duffield) *dwlt: racd keenly: hld up: rdn and hdwy on outer over 1f out: kpt on fnl f: wnt 2nd nr fin* 6/4[1]
5612 3 nk **La Sylphe**[10] 4922 2-9-3 69 AndrewMullen 4 67
(David Barron) *racd keenly: trckd ldr: led narrowly 2f out: hdd ins fnl f: one pce: lost 2nd nr fin* 4/1[2]
5411 4 nk **Lord Avonbrook**[31] 4191 2-9-6 72 AndrewElliott 6 69
(Andrew Crook) *in tch: rdn over 2f out: kpt on one pce* 10/1
050 5 1 ¼ **Makinson Lane (IRE)**[16] 4707 2-9-6 72 TonyHamilton 2 66
(Richard Fahey) *led: hdd over 2f out: rdn 2f out: sn dropped to 5th: one pce fnl f: sltly short of room nr fin* 6/1
2304 6 13 **Inchy Coo**[11] 4877 2-9-4 70 (p) DavidAllan 3 23
(Tim Easterby) *dwlt: sn in tch: rdn over 2f out: sn wknd* 8/1
1m 14.01s (0.41) **Going Correction** +0.025s/f (Good) 6 Ran SP% **109.9**
Speed ratings (Par 96): **98,96,95,95,93 76**
toteswingers 1&2 £1.80, 1&3 £3.30, 2&3 £1.70 CSF £13.64 TOTE £6.10: £1.60, £1.70; EX 15.20.
Owner Norton Common Farm Racing **Bred** T Cahalan & D Cahalan **Trained** Bawtry, S Yorks

FOCUS
A fair nursery handicap. Pretty straightforward form rated around the principals.

NOTEBOOK
Sylvia Pankhurst(IRE) reportedly slipped turning in when a very respectable third in a better nursery over this trip on good to firm ground at Chester this month. She is a consistent performer who looked an interesting contender beforehand, on a similar track on decent ground. She picked up well in the home straight and looks capable of further success under similar conditions. (op 5-1 tchd 6-1)
Lady Moonlight(IRE) looked the one to beat on form, but also vunerable dropped back in trip on good ground from her soft-ground 7f success here the previous month. She has a tendency to start slowly and a return to 7f with cut in the ground will be of benefit to her. (tchd 5-4 and 13-8 in a place)
La Sylphe took it up in the home straight, but always looked likely to be caught after racing a tad freely earlier in the contest. A return to 5f now beckons. (op 9-2 tchd 5-1)
Lord Avonbrook was unable to dominate from a wide draw attempting to record a hat-trick on his first start for new trainer Andrew Cook, after two claiming successes for Bill Turner previously. There will be better opportunities ahead. (op 9-1)
Makinson Lane(IRE) appears a tad high in the weights on the evidence of this handicap debut. (op 7-1)

5293 KELLY CLARKE COUTURE MAIDEN STKS 1m 3f 214y
7:10 (7:11) (Class 5) 3-Y-O+ £2,264 (£673; £336; £168) Stalls Centre

Form RPR
0-02 1 **Galleon**[44] 3763 3-9-2 82 RobertWinston 5 92+
(Sir Michael Stoute) *trckd ldng pair: led 2f out: pushed clr fnl f: comf* 10/11[1]
026 2 3 ½ **Cottesmore (USA)**[11] 4882 3-9-2 0 JoeFanning 3 83
(Mark Johnston) *led: rdn whn hdd 2f out: kpt on but no ch w wnr* 3/1[2]
3 5 **The Tiddly Tadpole**[14] 7-9-12 0 AndrewElliott 2 75
(Simon West) *in tch: rdn 3f out: wnt 3rd 2f out: kpt on but no threat ldng pair* 20/1
0- 4 5 **Roubiliac (USA)**[431] 3001 5-9-12 0 GrahamLee 10 43
(Paul Webber) *in tch: rdn over 7f out: sn lost pl and btn: fin 5th: plcd 4th* 9/1
0- 5 nse **Muzey's Princess**[14] 6504 6-9-7 0 (t) SeanQuinlan 6 38
(Michael Mullineaux) *hld up: nvr threatened: fin sixth: plcd 5th* 100/1
6 38 **Father Shine (IRE)**[33] 9-9-12 0 (bt) PaulMulrennan 8
(Shaun Harris) *trckd ldrs: rdn and lost pl qckly over 7f out: t.o: fin seventh: plcd sixth* 20/1
0 7 24 **Showmehow**[56] 3352 4-9-7 0 PaddyAspell 1
(Ray Craggs) *hld up: a bhd: fin eighth: plcd seventh* 100/1
00 8 11 **Shatin Spirit (IRE)**[14] 4780 3-8-13 0 GaryBartley(3) 7
(Noel Wilson) *hld up in midfield: rdn over 7f out: sn dropped to rr and bhd: fin ninth: plcd eight* 100/1
0-24 D 15 **Al Mamzar (IRE)**[23] 4464 3-9-2 75 RoystonFfrench 9 51
(David Simcock) *prom: rdn 3f out: sn wknd: fin 4th: disqualified and plcd last* 4/1[3]
2m 37.29s (-1.61) **Going Correction** +0.025s/f (Good)
WFA 3 from 4yo+ 10lb 9 Ran SP% **119.9**
Speed ratings (Par 103): **106,103,100,87,86 61,45,38,90**
toteswingers 1&2 £1.60, 2&3 £7.90, 1&3 £6.30 CSF £3.90 TOTE £2.00: £1.10, £1.10, £5.60; EX 3.90.
Owner The Queen **Bred** The Queen **Trained** Newmarket, Suffolk
■ Stewards' Enquiry : Royston Ffrench three-day ban: failed to weigh in (Aug 31-Sep 2)

FOCUS
A fair middle-distance maiden for 3yos and up although one with little depth. The form makes some sense.
Muzey's Princess Official explanation: trainer said mare ran without tongue strap which became adrift and could not be re-fitted.

5294 MAD HATTER TEA COMPANY H'CAP 5f
7:45 (7:46) (Class 6) (0-65,64) 3-Y-O+ £2,045 (£603; £302) Stalls Low

Form RPR
0000 1 **On The High Tops (IRE)**[10] 4911 4-9-2 56 PJMcDonald 3 66+
(Ruth Carr) *half rrd s: hld up in tch: hdwy towards outer over 1f out: kpt on: led fnl 100yds* 10/1
4406 2 ½ **Pavers Star**[11] 4878 3-7-12 45 (p) NeilFarley(5) 9 53
(Noel Wilson) *w ldr: rdn to ld narrowly over 1f out: kpt on: hdd fnl 100yds* 33/1
-463 3 nk **Hadrians Rule (IRE)**[46] 3706 3-9-1 57 DavidAllan 1 64
(Tim Easterby) *trckd ldrs: rdn and ev ch over 1f out: kpt on* 9/2[1]
0403 4 shd **Mr Mo Jo**[10] 4911 4-9-2 56 DanielTudhope 15 63+
(Lawrence Mullaney) *sn prom on outer: rdn 2f out: kpt on* 10/1
4204 5 1 ½ **Middleton Flyer (IRE)**[11] 4878 3-8-13 62 (b[1]) NedCurtis(7) 10 63
(Paul Midgley) *in tch: rdn 1/2-way: kpt on one pce* 16/1
552 6 2 **Spirit Of Coniston**[29] 4245 9-9-1 55 RussKennemore 4 49
(Paul Midgley) *in tch: rdn 1/2-way: one pce: nvr threatened ldrs* 8/1
6012 7 nse **Piste**[9] 4957 6-8-11 51 6ex (e) PaulMulrennan 13 45
(Tina Jackson) *hld up in tch: sn pushed along: nvr threatened* 5/1[2]
0214 8 ¾ **Chosen One (IRE)**[14] 4784 7-9-4 58 JamesSullivan 14 49
(Ruth Carr) *hld up on outer: nvr threatened* 13/2
00-6 9 hd **Francis Albert**[120] 1483 6-9-1 55 SeanQuinlan 12 45
(Michael Mullineaux) *dwlt: hld up: nvr threatened* 40/1
3462 10 1 ½ **Ballarina**[20] 4592 6-9-2 56 JimmyQuinn 7 43
(Eric Alston) *led: rdn whn hdd over 1f out: wknd* 6/1[3]
-000 11 nk **Gottcher**[15] 4743 4-9-10 64 AndrewMullen 6 48
(David Barron) *in tch: rdn 1/2-way: wknd over 1f out* 16/1
061 12 1 **Kyzer Chief**[23] 4454 7-9-5 64 ShaneBKelly(5) 2 58+
(Ron Barr) *midfield on inner: sltly short of room over 2f out: sn rdn: sltly short of room again ins fnl f: nvr threatened* 9/1
-060 13 19 **Selective Spirit**[13] 4798 3-8-9 51 (b) DuranFentiman 5
(John Weymes) *dwlt: a in rr: eased over 1f out* 66/1
58.25s (-1.55) **Going Correction** -0.275s/f (Firm)
WFA 3 from 4yo+ 2lb 13 Ran SP% **119.3**
Speed ratings (Par 101): **101,100,99,99,97 93,93,92,92,89 89,87,57**
toteswingers 1&2 £78.00, 1&3 £15.80, 2&3 £60.90 CSF £311.90 CT £1747.38 TOTE £13.50: £3.30, £8.70, £2.20; EX 361.00.
Owner Paul Saxton & The Bottom Liners **Bred** Mrs Clodagh McStay **Trained** Huby, N Yorks

FOCUS
A modest sprint handicap for 3yos and up. It was significantly the best comparative winning time on the card and the form makes sense.
Spirit Of Coniston Official explanation: jockey said gelding hung left
Kyzer Chief Official explanation: jockey said gelding was denied a clear run

5295 RACING AGAIN ON 29TH AUGUST H'CAP 7f
8:15 (8:16) (Class 6) (0-60,66) 3-Y-O+ £2,045 (£603; £302) Stalls Centre

Form RPR
3630 1 **Lady Del Sol**[16] 4717 4-9-10 60 [1] DanielTudhope 8 69
(Marjorie Fife) *w ldr: led over 4f out: rdn over 2f out: drvn over 1f out: kpt on wl* 11/1
3521 2 2 **Ursus**[9] 4957 7-9-5 55 6ex (p) PaddyAspell 1 58
(Christopher Wilson) *trckd ldrs: rdn over 2f out: kpt on* 9/1
2344 3 shd **No Quarter (IRE)**[9] 4954 5-9-8 58 RobertWinston 14 61
(Tracy Waggott) *hld up in tch: rdn over 2f out: hdwy to chse ldr over 1f out: kpt on* 5/1[2]
-532 4 1 ½ **Tamara Bay**[14] 4783 4-9-10 60 PJMcDonald 4 59
(John Davies) *prom: rdn over 2f out: no ex ins fnl f* 5/4[1]
6460 5 ½ **Hoppy's Flyer (FR)**[35] 4043 4-9-8 58 RussKennemore 11 56
(Paul Midgley) *hld up in tch: rdn over 2f out: sme hdwy over 1f out: one pce fnl f* 15/2
400 6 3 ¼ **Thats Molly (IRE)**[28] 4293 3-9-0 55 JimmyQuinn 5 44
(Eric Alston) *hld up: nvr threatened* 20/1
0000 7 1 ½ **Darrow (IRE)**[27] 4334 3-9-5 60 GrahamLee 6 45
(Wilf Storey) *hld up: nvr threatened* 25/1
0456 8 ½ **Boy The Bell**[4] 5171 5-9-9 59 (p) TomEaves 7 42
(Ollie Pears) *dwlt: sn chsd ldrs: rdn over 2f out: wknd over 1f out* 7/1[3]
000 9 8 **Nufoudh (IRE)**[14] 4779 8-9-7 57 JoeFanning 3 19
(Tracy Waggott) *restless stall: led narrowly: hdd over 4f out: sn dropped to midfield: wknd over 2f out: eased fnl f* 22/1
1m 26.89s (-0.11) **Going Correction** +0.025s/f (Good)
WFA 3 from 4yo+ 5lb 9 Ran SP% **116.7**
Speed ratings (Par 101): **101,98,98,96,96 92,90,90,81**
toteswingers 1&2 £11.90, 1&3 £12.60, 2&3 £8.60 CSF £102.20 CT £564.07 TOTE £17.10: £4.30, £2.60, £1.50; EX 131.10.
Owner Mrs Sue Johnson **Bred** Bond Thoroughbred Corporation **Trained** Stillington, N Yorks

FOCUS
A modest handicap for 3yos and up. The winner is rated back to her 3yo best.
T/Plt: £418.80 to a £1 stake. Pool: £37,979.60 - 66.20 winning tickets T/Qpdt: £36.60 to a £1 stake. Pool: £4,162.89 - 84 winning tickets AS

5228 KEMPTON (A.W) (R-H)
Friday, August 17

OFFICIAL GOING: Standard to slow
Wind: Light, half behind Weather: Sunny, very warm

5296 PIPER-HEIDSIECK H'CAP 5f (P)
5:45 (5:54) (Class 5) (0-75,74) 3-Y-O+ £2,264 (£673; £336; £168) Stalls Low

Form RPR
5243 1 **Howyadoingnotsobad (IRE)**[12] 4849 4-9-6 73 HarryBentley(3) 9 83
(Karen George) *mde virtually all: rdn and jnd jst over 1f out: forged ahd again fnl f: styd on wl* 2/1[2]
0353 2 1 ¼ **Muhdiq (USA)**[15] 4723 3-9-8 74 RichardHughes 6 80
(Mike Murphy) *chsd ldrs in 5th: pushed along 1/2-way: rdn and nt qckn over 1f out: r.o fnl f to take 2nd last 50yds* 15/8[1]
6504 3 ½ **Uncle Timmy**[7] 5033 3-8-0 55 oh2 (vt) SophieDoyle(3) 7 59
(David Evans) *prom on outer: rdn and nt qckn over 1f out: styd on fnl f: tk 3rd nr fin* 20/1
2220 4 ¾ **Liberal Lady**[10] 4920 4-8-11 61 (e) LukeMorris 2 62
(Ralph Smith) *mostly chsd wnr: chal on ins and upsides jst over 1f out: fdd ins fnl f* 11/1
5500 5 2 ½ **Volcanic Dust (IRE)**[12] 4849 4-9-9 73 RichardKingscote 3 65
(Milton Bradley) *slowest away: hld up in last pair: reminders over 1f out: styd on fnl f: nvr involved* 10/1
-500 6 ½ **Poseidon Grey (IRE)**[13] 4815 3-8-8 60 SilvestreDeSousa 4 51
(Ian Williams) *t.k.h: hld up in 6th: effrt on inner over 1f out: sn no prog* 14/1
0010 7 1 **Jack Smudge**[19] 4631 4-9-7 71 (b) GeorgeBaker 5 58
(James Given) *prom: rdn and wknd over 1f out* 9/2[3]
56-0 8 1 **Dream Whisperer**[13] 4798 3-8-13 65 JimmyFortune 8 48
(Dominic Ffrench Davis) *a in last pair: shkn up and no prog over 1f out* 16/1
1m 0.43s (-0.07) **Going Correction** +0.025s/f (Slow)
WFA 3 from 4yo+ 2lb 8 Ran SP% **121.0**
Speed ratings (Par 103): **101,99,98,97,93 92,90,89**
toteswingers 1&2 £1.10, 1&3 £8.50, 2&3 £10.40 CSF £6.64 CT £57.37 TOTE £2.30: £1.10, £1.80, £6.00; EX 4.20.
Owner Ten Four Fun **Bred** J G Reid **Trained** Higher Eastington, Devon

FOCUS
A few of these were out of form and this wasn't that comepetitive. Being on or close to the speed has always been important on the 5f course at Kempton and the winner was given an easy lead. He earns a length personal best.

5297 SCOTT MILLS & STOOSHE LIVE 07.09.12 MAIDEN STKS 1m 2f (P)
6:15 (6:21) (Class 4) 3-Y-O £4,075 (£1,212; £606; £303) Stalls Low

Form RPR
3 **1** **Ustura (USA)**[13] 4797 3-9-0 0 (t) HarryBentley(3) 9 87+
(Saeed Bin Suroor) *hld up in midfield: prog on outer 4f out: chsd ldr 2f: drvn and looked hld 1f out: styd on wl to ld last strides* **5/2**[1]
4- **2** *hd* **Ruban (IRE)**[297] 7083 3-9-3 0 SilvestreDeSousa 11 86
(Mahmood Al Zarooni) *dwlt: sn rcvrd to chse ldr: led jst over 2f out: drvn and kpt on wl fr over 1f out: hdd last strides* **5/1**[3]
6602 **3** *3 ¾* **Dynamic Duo (IRE)**[15] 4716 3-9-3 70 RichardHughes 12 78
(Richard Hannon) *a in 3rd: drvn and cl up bhd ldng pair over 1f out: outpcd fnl f* **7/1**
3-0 **4** *2* **Mossbrae**[90] 2271 3-9-3 0 JimCrowley 3 74+
(Roger Varian) *towards rr: nt clr run briefly over 2f out: prog to chse ldng trio over 1f out: kpt on but no imp* **14/1**
223 **5** *3* **Sir Quintin (IRE)**[29] 4259 3-9-3 85 JimmyFortune 1 68+
(Andrew Balding) *hld up in rr: stl only 10th jst over 2f out: prog over 1f out: tk 5th ins fnl f: no ch* **3/1**[2]
6 *1 ¼* **Mutaaleq (IRE)** 3-9-3 0 PaulHanagan 4 66+
(Roger Varian) *chsd ldrs in 5th: in tch whn nt clr run briefly 2f out: wknd over 1f out* **10/1**
03 **7** *4 ½* **Cape Alex**[77] 2665 3-8-12 0 (b[1]) LukeMorris 6 52
(Clive Brittain) *s.s: rdn and green in last pair early: rcvrd and in tch 6f out: wknd wl over 1f out* **33/1**
050 **8** *nse* **Chapelle du Roi (USA)**[56] 3349 3-9-3 0 IanMongan 5 56
(David Lanigan) *nvr bttr than midfield: rdn 3f out: wknd wl over 1f out* **16/1**
0 **9** *7* **Broughtons Maxim**[25] 4410 3-9-3 0 StevieDonohoe 2 42
(Willie Musson) *hld up and sn in last: detached fr rest and pushed along 3f out: nvr in it* **200/1**
10 *¾* **Sands Of Fortune (IRE)** 3-9-3 0 RyanMoore 10 41+
(Sir Michael Stoute) *dwlt: chsd ldng trio but urged along after 2f: maintained pl for press tl wknd over 2f out* **8/1**
0 **11** *11* **My Espoir**[88] 2344 3-8-12 0 PatCosgrave 8 14
(Clive Cox) *led to jst over 2f out: sltly short of room whn wkng rapidly wl over 1f out: t.o* **66/1**

2m 7.33s (-0.67) **Going Correction** +0.025s/f (Slow) 11 Ran SP% **120.4**
Speed ratings (Par 102): **103,102,99,98,95 94,91,91,85,85 76**
toteswingers 1&2 £4.60, 1&3 £6.20, 2&3 £2.60 CSF £15.70 TOTE £3.50: £1.70, £2.30, £1.50; EX 17.70.
Owner Godolphin **Bred** Darley **Trained** Newmarket, Suffolk

FOCUS
This might turn out to be useful maiden form with nearly all the field being well-bred sorts from top Newmarket yards. It proved difficult for anything to make an impact from off the pace so extra credit probably needs to go to the winner. The third sets a solid standard.

5298 LADIES DAY WITH TOBY ANSTIS 08.09.12 CLASSIFIED CLAIMING STKS 6f (P)
6:45 (6:48) (Class 6) 3-5-Y-O £1,617 (£481; £240; £120) Stalls Low

Form RPR
4636 **1** **Bint Alzain (IRE)**[10] 4933 3-9-0 74 (tp) LukeMorris 7 78
(Gerard Butler) *dwlt: hld up in last: gd prog on outer over 1f out: drvn to press ldr ins fnl f: styd on to ld last 50yds* **6/1**
0025 **2** *nk* **Adranian (IRE)**[6] 5099 3-8-8 75 (b) HarryBentley(3) 3 74
(David C Griffiths) *pressed ldr: led over 2f out: hrd rdn over 1f out: hdd last 50yds: kpt on* **7/2**[2]
6352 **3** *hd* **Mother Jones**[11] 4885 4-8-8 65 ow1 StevieDonohoe 5 67
(David Evans) *blindfold off sltly late and dwlt: hld up in last trio: rdn and prog towards inner 2f out: chal ins fnl f: kpt on nr fin* **12/1**
0565 **4** *3 ¼* **Chevise (IRE)**[44] 3761 4-9-4 71 JimCrowley 6 67
(Steve Woodman) *settled in last trio: rdn and no prog over 2f out: n.d after: plugged on to take 4th nr fin* **16/1**
3503 **5** *¾* **Tislaam (IRE)**[14] 4783 5-8-10 75 (p) RyanMoore 4 57
(Alan McCabe) *chsd ldrs in 4th: rdn and nt qckn over 2f out: sn lost pl and btn* **6/4**[1]
1105 **6** *4* **Mercers Row**[25] 4400 5-8-11 74 SilvestreDeSousa 1 45
(Noel Wilson) *t.k.h: chsd ldng trio: hrd rdn over 2f out: wknd over 1f out* **9/2**[3]
6030 **7** *7* **Choice Words (USA)**[8] 5017 4-8-13 67 RichardHughes 2 24
(Natalie Lloyd-Beavis) *led to over 2f out: wknd over 1f out: eased* **12/1**

1m 12.78s (-0.32) **Going Correction** +0.025s/f (Slow)
WFA 3 from 4yo+ 3lb 7 Ran SP% **116.0**
Speed ratings (Par 101): **103,102,102,98,97 91,82**
toteswingers 1&2 £5.00, 1&3 £8.20, 2&3 £6.70 CSF £27.96 TOTE £6.50: £3.00, £3.10; EX 34.30.
Owner Asaad Al Banwan **Bred** Philip Brady **Trained** Newmarket, Suffolk

FOCUS
Just an ordinary claimer, but the pace was strong. The form is rated around the third.
Mercers Row Official explanation: jockey said gelding had no more to give

5299 KEMPTON.CO.UK MEDIAN AUCTION MAIDEN FILLIES' STKS 7f (P)
7:20 (7:21) (Class 6) 3-5-Y-O £1,617 (£481; £240; £120) Stalls Low

Form RPR
0 **1** **Fever Few**[26] 4366 3-9-0 0 SilvestreDeSousa 9 77
(Jane Chapple-Hyam) *prog on outer to chse ldr 4f out: rdn to ld 2f out: kpt on wl fnl f* **7/1**
26 **2** *2* **Medhyaar**[37] 3975 3-9-0 0 (t) PaulHanagan 4 72
(William Haggas) *dwlt: in tch in rr: prog 3f out: hrd rdn to chse wnr over 1f out: one pce and no imp* **2/1**[1]
635 **3** *2 ¼* **Shore Performer (IRE)**[20] 4582 3-9-0 68 RyanMoore 8 66
(William Haggas) *led after 2f: shkn up and hdd 2f out: nt qckn and sn btn* **3/1**[2]
0- **4** *8* **Widow Flower (IRE)**[371] 5011 3-9-0 0 LukeMorris 1 44
(Michael Bell) *in tch: drvn and effrt over 2f out: sn no hdwy: wl btn 4th fr over 1f out* **16/1**
50 **5** *6* **Bazron (IRE)**[49] 3568 4-9-2 0 RyanPowell(3) 3 30
(Des Donovan) *led 2f: pushed along 1/2-way: wknd over 2f out* **33/1**
0 **6** *4 ½* **Who's That Chick (IRE)**[22] 4516 3-9-0 0 MartinHarley 2 16
(Ralph Smith) *t.k.h: chsd ldrs: wknd qckly over 2f out* **13/2**
7 *7* **Stoneacre Thirsk (IRE)** 3-9-0 0 RobbieFitzpatrick 6
(Peter Grayson) *rn green and sn detached in last pair: nvr a factor* **50/1**
8 *14* **Cowslip** 3-9-0 0 RichardHughes 5
(Richard Hannon) *s.s: v green and t.o after 2f* **4/1**[3]

1m 26.31s (0.31) **Going Correction** +0.025s/f (Slow)
WFA 3 from 4yo 5lb 8 Ran SP% **115.0**
Speed ratings (Par 98): **99,96,94,85,78 73,65,49**
toteswingers 1&2 £1.90, 1&3 £7.80, 2&3 £2.20 CSF £21.57 TOTE £11.30: £2.00, £1.10, £1.30; EX 30.40.
Owner Redgate Bloodstock & Mrs Zara Wise **Bred** Redgate Bloodstock Ltd & Mrs Z Wise **Trained** Dalham, Suffolk

FOCUS
A modest fillies' maiden in which the field came home at quite long intervals and this probably isn't a race that will throw up many winners. Slightly shaky form with the second and third having disappointed on their previous starts.

5300 BRITISH STALLION STUDS SUPPORTING BRITISH RACING E B F MAIDEN FILLIES' STKS 7f (P)
7:55 (7:56) (Class 5) 2-Y-O £3,234 (£962; £481; £240) Stalls Low

Form RPR
1 **Love Magic** 2-9-0 0 RyanMoore 3 79+
(Sir Michael Stoute) *led 2f: sn dropped to 3rd: effrt again towards inner over 2f out: urged into ld over 1f out: drvn and hld on wl despite swishing tail* **4/1**[3]
30 **2** *nk* **Heading North**[15] 4739 2-9-0 0 RichardHughes 2 78
(Richard Hannon) *t.k.h: chsd ldr over 4f out: rdn to chal on outer over 1f out: pressed wnr fnl f: jst hld* **4/1**[3]
3 *1 ¾* **Centred (IRE)** 2-9-0 0 DavidProbert 1 73+
(Sir Michael Stoute) *cl up: chsd ldng trio 3f out: shkn up and styd on to take 3rd last 100yds: nvr able to chal* **14/1**
022 **4** *1 ¾* **Blue Nova**[13] 4792 2-9-0 75 ShaneKelly 7 69
(Jeremy Noseda) *led after 2f: rdn and hdd over 1f out: fdd fnl f* **9/4**[1]
5 *2 ¼* **Snow Rose (USA)** 2-9-0 0 SilvestreDeSousa 6 63+
(Mahmood Al Zarooni) *dwlt: prog to chse ldng trio 1/2-way: sn hanging and rdn and lost pl: n.d over 2f out: plugged on* **5/2**[2]
0 **6** *1 ¾* **Sand Grouse**[15] 4742 2-9-0 0 (b) MartinHarley 8 59
(Marco Botti) *dwlt: towards rr: sme prog and chsd ldrs over 2f out: nt on terms and no hdwy after* **28/1**
0 **7** *3 ¾* **Duchess Of Gazeley (IRE)**[28] 4297 2-9-0 0 StevieDonohoe 10 49
(Lydia Pearce) *racd wd: a towards rr: rdn and struggling 3f out: sn bhd* **50/1**
8 *1 ¾* **Kiwani Bay** 2-9-0 0 JimmyFortune 5 44
(J W Hills) *in tch to 1/2-way: sn wknd* **25/1**
0 **9** *2* **Privacy Order**[9] 4946 2-9-0 0 LukeMorris 4 39
(Sir Mark Prescott Bt) *dropped to rr 1/2-way: wl btn over 2f out* **25/1**
0 **10** *1 ¼* **Barefoot Sandy**[13] 4813 2-9-0 0 AdamKirby 9 36
(Des Donovan) *v s.i.s: mostly last: wl bhd fnl 2f* **100/1**

1m 27.05s (1.05) **Going Correction** +0.025s/f (Slow) 10 Ran SP% **120.1**
Speed ratings (Par 91): **95,94,92,90,88 86,81,79,77,76**
toteswingers 1&2 £4.90, 1&3 £4.60, 2&3 £14.50 CSF £20.12 TOTE £5.90: £2.00, £1.60, £3.90; EX 30.20.
Owner Lady Rothschild **Bred** Kincorth Investments Inc **Trained** Newmarket, Suffolk

FOCUS
This looked a fair fillies' juvenile maden. The form is rated around the second.

NOTEBOOK
Love Magic, who is out of a Cheveley Park winner, made a cracking debut and she looks a lovely prospect. Although a little free early on, she showed a terrific attitude in the final furlong to see off more experienced rivals and the form can be rated around the fourth-placed filly, who is rated 75 and seemingly ran her race. (op 11-2)
Heading North had excuses at Goodwood last time, but this was a real step back in the right direction after her promising Newmarket debut last month. She had every chance in the final furlong but bumped into an above-average winner. A race like this is clearly hers for the taking on this evidence. (op 11-2 tchd 6-1)
Centred(IRE) ◆, a beautifully-bred filly, stayed on really nicely to finish in front of the standard-setter Blue Nova. She has to go down as a winning in waiting given the promise of this run. (op 10-1)
Blue Nova had every chance, but found the front three too good. She still looks capable of winning a maiden. (op 7-4)
Snow Rose(USA), a sister to Raven's Pass, was too green to do herself justice but she definitely shaped with some promise and is sure to learn plenty from this first outing. Official explanation: jockey said filly had no more to give (op 11-4)

5301 BYRNE GROUP "LONDON MILE" H'CAP (QUALIFIER) 1m (P)
8:25 (8:26) (Class 3) (0-95,93) 3-Y-O+
£6,411 (£1,919; £959; £479; £239; £120) Stalls Low

Form RPR
4002 **1** **Switzerland (IRE)**[15] 4735 3-8-10 **90** MichaelJMMurphy(7) 12 99
(Mark Johnston) *prom: wnt 2nd over 5f out: led over 2f out: sn rdn: hrd pressed fr over 1f out: jst hld on* **2/1**[1]
-645 **2** *shd* **Loving Spirit**[37] 3977 4-9-8 **89** PatCosgrave 8 98+
(James Toller) *hld up wl in rr: gd prog on wd outside fr 2f out: clsd fnl f: drifted lft but styd on: jst failed* **8/1**
3-24 **3** *shd* **Double Dealer**[97] 2082 4-9-11 **92** SilvestreDeSousa 9 101
(Mahmood Al Zarooni) *prom: rdn to chse wnr 2f out: sustained chal fnl f: styd on but lost 2nd last stride* **13/2**[3]
0040 **4** *1 ¾* **Chapter And Verse (IRE)**[14] 4772 6-9-1 **82** JimmyFortune 4 87
(Mike Murphy) *t.k.h early: chsd ldr to over 5f out: styd prom: drvn and tried to chal fr 2f out: one pce fnl f* **16/1**
2512 **5** *¾* **Takeitfromalady (IRE)**[27] 4319 3-9-0 **87** (b) JimCrowley 3 89+
(Ralph Beckett) *dwlt: rcvrd into midfield after 3f: rdn and prog on inner over 2f out: chsd ldrs 1f out: one pce after* **9/2**[2]
0350 **6** *1 ½* **Starwatch**[17] 4689 5-9-8 **89** KieranO'Neill 6 89
(John Bridger) *t.k.h early: chsd ldrs: rdn sn after 1/2-way: nvr able to make any prog but kpt on* **28/1**
5-60 **7** *hd* **Unex Michelangelo (IRE)**[13] 4795 3-9-6 **93** RobertHavlin 2 91
(John Gosden) *chsd ldrs: rdn over 2f out and cl enough: no imp over 1f out: fdd* **16/1**
2210 **8** *¾* **Mingun Bell (USA)**[20] 4580 5-9-9 **90** LiamKeniry 10 88
(Ed de Giles) *broke on terms w ldrs on outer but restrained after 100yds to rr: effrt again on outer 5f out: drvn over 2f out: no prog* **25/1**
-026 **9** *½* **Bancnuanaheireann (IRE)**[6] 5075 5-9-11 **92** GeorgeBaker 13 88
(Michael Appleby) *hld up and wl in rr: shkn up on outer over 2f out: nvr a factor but kpt on fnl f* **14/1**
600- **10** *1 ½* **Shamir**[295] 7127 5-9-6 **87** IanMongan 7 80
(Jo Crowley) *wl in tch in midfield: rdn over 3f out: sn lost pl: wl in rr 2f out: trying to keep on but no ch whn hmpd 1f out* **16/1**
0005 **11** *nk* **Final Drive (IRE)**[16] 4716 6-9-5 **86** (p) StevieDonohoe 14 78
(John Butler) *hld up and sn in last: rdn and no prog 2f out: n.d after* **33/1**

1000 **12** ½ **Sinfonico (IRE)**[37] 3963 4-9-2 **83**............................(e) RichardHughes 11 74
(Richard Hannon) *hld up in last pair: shkn up 2f out: no prog and nvr a factor* **20/1**

2311 **13** *nk* **Lockantanks**[27] 4345 5-9-12 **93**.. LukeMorris 1 83
(Michael Appleby) *sn wl in rr: rdn sn after 1/2-way: effrt on inner over 2f out: sn no prog: fdd* **8/1**

0040 **14** *nk* **Bay Knight (IRE)**[69] 2919 6-9-8 **92**.............................. SophieDoyle[(3)] 5 82
(Sean Curran) *led at decent pce to over 2f out: sn wknd* **50/1**

1m 38.9s (-0.90) **Going Correction** +0.025s/f (Slow) **14** Ran SP% **128.3**

WFA 3 from 4yo+ 6lb

Speed ratings (Par 107): **105,104,104,103,102 100,100,99,99,97 97,97,96,96**

toteswingers 1&2 £8.50, 1&3 £6.50, 2&3 £11.70 CSF £10.60 CT £07.06 TOTE £2.80: £1.80, £3.00, £2.40; EX 27.80.

Owner Sheikh Majid Bin Mohammed al Maktoum **Bred** Rabbah Bloodstock Limited **Trained** Middleham Moor, N Yorks

■ Stewards' Enquiry : Michael J M Murphy two-day ban: used whip above permitted level (Aug 31-Sep 1)

FOCUS

A really competitive handicap, but the pace was steady and it paid to be handy when the sprint began over 2f out. The form makes sense though.

NOTEBOOK

Switzerland(IRE) was asked to race a bit closer to the pace down the back as his rider realised the tempo was only steady, but he wasn't rushed up. He was asked to gradually work himself into a better position and that proved a key manoeuvre as he was ideally placed to kick early in the straight. He had enough guts to see it out and build on the promise of his recent second at Goodwood. He clearly loves this surface and took his record to three wins from four starts on Polytrack. Like most from his yard, he is back in the groove now having been quiet for the last couple of months. (op 11-4)

Loving Spirit's effort has to go down as a blinding performance given how much further back in the field he was in comparison to the winner when the pace quickened. He was therefore trying to make up a lot of ground on a horse who wasn't stopping and very nearly did it. He hasn't won since his debut but this has to go down as one of his best runs and he can clearly win off this sort of mark. (op 15-2)

Double Dealer tracked the leader around the outside and threw down a strong challenge in the final furlong but just couldn't quite get there. This was a rock solid run and although he hasn't won since his sole start success in 2010 the margins are often fine when you keep this sort of company regularly and his day will come again if maintaining this level of form. (op 6-1 tchd 7-1)

Chapter And Verse(IRE), given how free he was early, deserves credit for keepinng on for fourth, although he never threw down a serious challenge. He is better chasing down a strong pace but his win record is poor nowadays in any case. (tchd 20-1)

Takeitfromalady(IRE), making his all-weather debut, made some late headway from off the pace but couldn't get into it and wasn't seen at his best because of how things panned out.

Shamir Official explanation: jockey said gelding was denied a clear run

5302 BYRNE GROUP H'CAP 7f (P)

8:55 (8:55) (Class 4) (0-80,86) 3-Y-O **£4,075** (£1,212; £606; £303) **Stalls** Low

Form RPR

1305 **1** **Fast Finian (IRE)**[10] 4919 3-8-6 **72**...................... MichaelJMMurphy[(7)] 4 81
(Paul D'Arcy) *t.k.h: sltly hmpd after 2f: hld up in tch: rdn and prog to chse clr ldr 2f out: styd on fnl f to ld last strides* **8/1**

1062 **2** ¾ **Don Libre**[11] 4876 3-9-2 **75**.. RichardHughes 8 82
(Paul Cole) *t.k.h: hld up tl allowed to stride on into ld over 4f out: clr 2f out: hrd rdn over 1f out: wknd fnl f: hdd last strides* **13/2**

0441 **3** *nk* **Oblitereight (IRE)**[11] 4876 3-9-13 **86** 6ex.......................... JimCrowley 7 92+
(William Knight) *hld up in last pair: plenty to do after injection of pce 1/2-way: drvn 2f out: prog jst over 1f out: styd on fnl f: nrst fin* **13/8**[1]

4500 **4** *hd* **Compton Prince**[11] 4876 3-8-1 **67**..................................(b[1]) RyanTate[(7)] 5 73+
(Clive Cox) *hld up in last pair: plenty to do after pce lifted 1/2-way: rdn 2f out: prog fnl f: styd on wl nr fin* **20/1**

1422 **5** 4 **Serene Oasis (IRE)**[9] 4968 3-9-4 **77**...........................(v) MartinHarley 2 72
(Mick Channon) *hld up towards rr: rdn and effrt over 2f out: no imp over 1f out: wl hld after* **8/1**

0-51 **6** 3 **Catherine Laboure (IRE)**[20] 4582 3-9-1 **74**................. JimmyFortune 3 61
(Eve Johnson Houghton) *led at mod pce to over 4f out: sltly impeded sn after: rdn over 2f out: wknd jst over 1f out* **5/1**[3]

0306 **7** 3 **Dubai Sunshine (IRE)**[28] 4291 3-9-5 **78**............................ AdamKirby 1 57
(Michael Bell) *towards rr: pushed along 1/2-way: no prog over 2f out: sn btn* **10/1**

-363 **8** ½ **Lucky Money**[6] 5099 3-9-0 **73**..(b) LukeMorris 6 50
(Sir Mark Prescott Bt) *plld hrd: prog to press ldr over 4f out: rdn and wknd 2f out* **9/2**[2]

1m 26.4s (0.40) **Going Correction** +0.025s/f (Slow) **8** Ran SP% **122.4**

Speed ratings (Par 102): **98,97,96,96,92 88,85,84**

toteswingers 1&2 £9.90, 1&3 £4.10, 2&3 £3.20 CSF £62.74 CT £129.50 TOTE £8.00: £2.00, £2.70, £1.20; EX 61.40.

Owner John W Kennedy **Bred** N Hartery **Trained** Newmarket, Suffolk

FOCUS

Messy form because they crawled early, but kicked for home fully 3f out. A length personal best from the winner.

Don Libre Official explanation: jockey said colt ran too free

T/Plt: £114.90 to a £1 stake. Pool: £39997.43 - 254.08 winning tickets T/Qpdt: £25.50 to a £1 stake. Pool: £4119.99 - 119.1 winning tickets JN

4843 NEWBURY (L-H)

Friday, August 17

OFFICIAL GOING: Good (6.7)

Wind: Moderate across Weather: Sunny spells

5303 DON DEADMAN MEMORIAL EUROPEAN BREEDERS' FUND MAIDEN STKS (DIV I) 7f (S)

1:50 (1:53) (Class 4) 2-Y-O **£4,463** (£1,328; £663; £331) **Stalls** Centre

Form RPR

1 **Glean** 2-9-3 0.. PatDobbs 1 85+
(Richard Hannon) *trckd ldrs: shkn up and qcknd to chse ldr 1f out: led fnl 150yds: readily* **18/1**

3 **2** ½ **Intimidate**[81] 2550 2-9-3 0.. RyanMoore 4 84
(Jeremy Noseda) *trckd ldr: led over 2f out: rdn over 1f out: hdd fnl 150yds: kpt on u.p* **4/1**[2]

3 7 **Altharoos (IRE)** 2-9-3 0... PaulHanagan 9 68+
(Sir Michael Stoute) *s.i.s: in rr: gd hdwy 2f out: green but styd on strly to take wl hld 3rd fnl 120yds* **6/1**[3]

4 1 ½ **So Beloved** 2-9-3 0.. JamesDoyle 3 64+
(Roger Charlton) *chsd ldrs: wnt 2nd and rdn 2f out: wknd appr fnl f* **9/1**

5 **5** 2 ½ **Newtown Cross (IRE)**[20] 4604 2-9-3 0............................ KieranO'Neill 8 55
(Jimmy Fox) *in tch and pushed along 1/2-way: styd on same pce fnl 2f* **16/1**

6 ¾ **Mizyen (IRE)** 2-9-3 0... MartinDwyer 6 53+
(James Tate) *led tl hdd over 2f out: wknd and hung lft fnl f* **33/1**

0 **7** ½ **Rutherglen**[20] 4604 2-9-3 0...................................... PatCosgrave 13 52
(George Baker) *in tch: rdn and no prog fnl 2f* **100/1**

8 ¾ **Code Of Honor** 2-9-3 0.. DaneO'Neill 10 50+
(Henry Candy) *in rr: pushed along 1/2-way: styd on ins fnl f* **33/1**

9 ½ **Another Cocktail** 2-9-3 0.. DarryllHolland 5 49
(Hughie Morrison) *s.i.s: in rr: hdwy 1/2-way: wknd 2f out* **25/1**

10 1 **A Ladies Man (IRE)** 2-9-3 0.................................... RichardHughes 11 46
(Richard Hannon) *chsd ldrs: drvn over 2f out: sn wknd* **5/4**[1]

11 3 ½ **Imperial Glance** 2-9-3 0... DavidProbert 2 37
(Andrew Balding) *bhd fr 1/2-way* **25/1**

12 1 ¼ **Muthafar (IRE)** 2-9-3 0.. JimmyFortune 7 34
(John Dunlop) *s.i.s: outpcd* **25/1**

13 ½ **Damian One** 2-9-3 0.. LiamKeniry 12 33
(Joseph Tuite) *sn bhd* **100/1**

1m 26.99s (1.29) **Going Correction** +0.15s/f (Good) **13** Ran SP% **119.3**

Speed ratings (Par 96): **98,97,89,87,84 84,83,82,82,80 76,75,74**

toteswingers 1&2 £13.30, 1&3 £24.90, 2&3 £5.80 CSF £84.23 TOTE £25.20: £4.70, £1.70, £1.90; EX 117.60 Trifecta £543.00 Part won. Pool: £733.88 - 0.74 winning units..

Owner Lady Rothschild **Bred** The Rt Hon Lord Rothschild **Trained** East Everleigh, Wilts

FOCUS

Rail realignment between 8f and 5f on Round course added about 10m to distances on that course. The ground had dried out as a result a brisk crosswind, and the jockeys reported it was "beautiful ground". This has proved a good maiden, having been won by the subsequent Champagne Stakes winner Saamidd and the Breeders' Cup Juvenile Turf winner Pounced in recent runnings. Only three of the field had run before and just one of those was amongst the four at the head of the market. Richard Hannon was responsible for the well-touted hot favourite here, but it was the lesser fancied stable companion who prevailed. The first two pulled clear and the form is rated around the race averages.

NOTEBOOK

Glean ◆, the first foal of the Listed 1m winner Harvest Queen from the family of Golan, tracked his stable companion but moved up going notably better around 2f out and showed a good attitude to get the better of the more experienced runner-up. He looks capable of going on to better things. (op 16-1)

Intimidate had shown promise on his debut at Leicester in May (6f) but, despite the winner having been subsequently Group 2 placed, the form of that race has not really worked out. He was always in the front rank here and tried to assert inside the last quarter-mile, but the winner proved too strong. He was clear of the rest and should be up to winning before long. (op 5-1 tchd 11-2)

Altharoos(IRE) ◆, the first foal of an unraced half-sister to Tazahum, was held up out the back before making good late headway. A Derby entry, he should come on for the experience and will appreciate longer trips in time. (op 13-2 tchd 7-1)

So Beloved, a sizeable sibling to six winners including Cantabria and Deportivo, tracked the pace and had every chance around 2f out, but then faded under pressure. He is probably a bit weak at present but should make up into a nice 3-y-o. (tchd 8-1)

Newtown Cross(IRE), had shown promise on his debut last month when finding a troubled passage, but was being ridden along some way from home before keeping on late. (op 20-1 tchd 25-1)

Mizyen(IRE), a 38,000gns half-brother to a couple of winners, soon pulled his way to the front and was quite keen. He did well to keep going once headed and this Racing Post Trophy entry can be expected to build on this if learning to settle. (op 40-1)

Another Cocktail ◆, an 85,000gns first foal of a winning sister to Fame And Glory, is bred to stay a good deal further and so this was a promising effort, finishing in the pack without being given too hard a time. (tchd 20-1)

A Ladies Man(IRE), a 220,000gns half-brother to three winners from the family of Myself, was disappointing considering his starting price. He tracked the pace but was being ridden along 2f out and failed to pick up, being allowed to come home in his own time once beaten. He is surely better than this effort indicates. (op 6-5 tchd 11-10)

5304 DON DEADMAN MEMORIAL EUROPEAN BREEDERS' FUND MAIDEN STKS (DIV II) 7f (S)

2:20 (2:23) (Class 4) 2-Y-O **£4,463** (£1,328; £663; £331) **Stalls** Centre

Form RPR

42 **1** **Related**[21] 4555 2-9-3 0.. AdamKirby 13 81
(Clive Cox) *sn led: rdn and styd on gamely whn hrd pressed fr ins fnl f: hld on wl clsng stages* **8/1**

3 **2** *hd* **Pythagorean**[35] 4056 2-9-3 0.. JamesDoyle 2 80+
(Roger Charlton) *t.k.h and hld up in rr: gd hdwy over 2f out: drvn and stl green over 1f out: chal fr ins fnl f: nt qckn clsng stages* **9/4**[2]

0 **3** 1 ¼ **Erodium**[23] 4472 2-9-3 0... PatDobbs 12 77+
(Richard Hannon) *towards rr but in tch: rdn and hdwy over 2f out: styd on wl u.p to take 3rd last strides but no imp on ldng duo* **11/1**

0 **4** *shd* **Empiricist (IRE)**[13] 4803 2-9-3 0................................... IanMongan 10 77
(Amanda Perrett) *wnt rt s: sn chsng ldrs: chsd wnr wl over 1f out but no imp: one pce ins fnl f: lost 3rd last strides* **80/1**

5 1 ½ **Sanjuro (IRE)** 2-9-3 0.. MartinHarley 9 73+
(Mick Channon) *in rr: rdn: hung lft and green fr 2f out: kpt on wl fnl f: gng on clsng stages* **40/1**

0 **6** 2 ¾ **Ersaal**[20] 4595 2-9-3 0... PaulHanagan 5 66
(Roger Varian) *chsd ldrs: rdn over 2f out: wknd fnl f* **3/1**[3]

2 **7** ½ **Sea Shanty (USA)**[26] 4362 2-9-3 0............................... RichardHughes 6 65
(Richard Hannon) *trckd ldrs: shkn up 2f out: swtchd lft and sn btn* **2/1**[1]

0 **8** 4 ½ **El Mirage (IRE)**[49] 3590 2-8-12 0................................. ShaneKelly 3 48
(Dean Ivory) *chsd wnr: rdn 2f out: wknd over 1f out* **66/1**

9 2 **Codebreaker** 2-9-3 0... DarryllHolland 8 48
(Hughie Morrison) *in rr: shkn up and wknd over 2f out* **28/1**

10 7 **Polhem** 2-9-3 0.. RyanMoore 4 30
(John Dunlop) *bhd fr 1/2-way* **25/1**

11 7 **Hanga Roa (IRE)** 2-9-3 0.. GeorgeBaker 11 11
(Gary Moore) *bmpd s: racd alone towards stands' side and a towards rr* **66/1**

1m 26.92s (1.22) **Going Correction** +0.15s/f (Good) **11** Ran SP% **122.5**

Speed ratings (Par 96): **99,98,97,97,95 92,91,86,84,76 68**

toteswingers 1&2 £4.10, 1&3 £22.40, 2&3 £50.90 CSF £26.73 TOTE £10.80: £2.10, £1.10, £2.80; EX 31.80 Trifecta £496.80 Part won. Pool: £671.42 - 0.20 winning units..

Owner H E Sheikh Sultan Bin Khalifa Al Nahyan **Bred** Laundry Cottage Stud Farm **Trained** Lambourn, Berks

FOCUS

The second division of this good maiden was run fractionally faster that the first. Good, solid form with limitations.

NOTEBOOK

Related, a half-brother to Wootton Bassett, had shown promise in maidens at 6f-7f on a sound surface, and the race he finished fourth in on his debut had seen the second, third and fifth go on to score subsequently. He made the running and, after looking likely to be run down by the second inside the final furlong, found extra to hold on. He looks open to further improvement. (op 10-1)

Pythagorean, out of a 1m4f winning sister to Oaks second Flight Of Fancy, had shown promise when third on his debut over this C&D on soft ground, and the second, fourth, fifth and seventh in that contest had won since. Held up out the back, he made his ground well and had every chance, but just found the winner too strong. His turn should not be far away. (op 2-1 tchd 11-4)

Erodium, held on his debut in a 7f maiden at Sandown, built on that effort and should make up into a fair handicapper in time. (op 10-1 tchd 12-1)

Empiricist(IRE), well beaten at Goodwood earlier in the month, stepped up considerably this time, having been in the front rank throughout. He should be up to winning races. (op 100-1 tchd 66-1)

Sanjuro(IRE) ◆, a 45,000euros half-brother to three winners at up to 1m, made an encouraging debut and this Derby entry can be expected to build on this. (op 50-1)

Ersaal slowly away on his debut in a race that had produced a couple of winners, ran reasonably again without getting seriously involved and might be the sort to do better next season. (op 5-1)

Sea Shanty(USA), first foal of a 6f-1m winner, including at Listed level, had been a strong-finishing second on his debut in a 6f newcomers' race at Ascot. He was the second successive favourite from the yard to disappoint. (op 9-4 tchd 5-2 in a place)

5305 CHRISTOPHER SMITH ASSOCIATES CLAIMING STKS — 7f (S)

2:50 (2:52) (Class 5) 3-Y-0+ — £2,587 (£770; £384; £192) **Stalls** Centre

Form				RPR
0500	1		**Prime Exhibit**[13] 4805 7-9-4 77.....(t) RichardKingscote 3 (Milton Bradley) *stdd in rr: hdwy 1/2-way: trckd ldr appr fnl f: drvn to ld fnl 150yds: kpt on wl clsng stages* **7/1**	82
0300	2	*nk*	**Ezdeyaad (USA)**[14] 4775 8-9-2 79.....GeorgeBaker 5 (Ed Walker) *trckd ldrs: led over 2f out: rdn and hdd fnl 150yds: no ex clsng stages* **7/1**	79
0140	3	*2*	**Duster**[16] 4703 5-9-9 85.....RyanMoore 9 (Hughie Morrison) *mde most tl rdn and hdd over 2f out: styd on one pce 3rd fnl f* **2/1**[1]	81
0036	4	*2 ¼*	**Caterina**[21] 4531 3-8-10 62.....(b) RichardHughes 2 (Richard Hannon) *in rr: drvn and hdwy over 2f out: no imp on ldng trio fnl f* **18/1**	65
1034	5	*3 ¾*	**Kingswinford (IRE)**[7] 5034 6-8-11 80.....MatthewCosham(3) 11 (David Evans) *chsd ldrs: rdn over 2f out: sn one pce: wknd fnl f* **12/1**	56
1002	6	*½*	**Bawaardi (IRE)**[46] 3709 6-8-12 78.....SilvestreDeSousa 10 (David Evans) *in tch: rdn and sme hdwy 2f out: nvr rchd ldrs: wknd fnl f* **6/1**[3]	53
5043	7	*1 ½*	**Indian Art (IRE)**[5] 5132 6-9-1 74.....JamesDoyle 12 (Sylvester Kirk) *in rr: rdn and no prog fr over 2f out* **15/2**	51
0030	8	*2 ½*	**Irie Ute**[10] 4929 4-8-13 55.....LiamKeniry 8 (Sylvester Kirk) *pushed along 2f out: a in rr* **66/1**	43
-322	9	*1 ¾*	**Fishforcompliments**[17] 4673 8-8-13 77.....PaulHanagan 7 (Richard Fahey) *in tch: rdn over 2f out and sn btn* **9/2**[2]	38
0	10	*5*	**Captain Hero (IRE)**[20] 4582 5-9-4 0.....IanMongan 1 (Laura Mongan) *pressed ldr: rdn over 3f out: wknd 2f out* **250/1**	30

1m 26.92s (1.22) **Going Correction** +0.15s/f (Good)
WFA 3 from 4yo+ 5lb — **10** Ran SP% **117.4**
Speed ratings (Par 103): **99,98,96,93,89 88,87,84,82,76**
toteswingers 1&2 £13.40, 1&3 £7.90, 2&3 £5.70 CSF £55.70 TOTE £8.20: £2.10, £2.50, £1.80; EX 58.00 Trifecta £200.00 Pool: £616.33 - 2.28 winning units..Ezdeyaad was claimed by Mrs Joanna Hughes for £8,000.

Owner Dab Hand Racing **Bred** Matthews Breeding And Racing Ltd **Trained** Sedbury, Gloucs

FOCUS

A decent and quite competitive claimer for the prizemoney, but the time was identical to the second division of the maiden that preceded it. Given the grade the form is rated a bit cautiously.

Bawaardi(IRE) Official explanation: jockey said gelding moved poorly

5306 PUNTER SOUTHALL TRANSACTION SERVICES H'CAP — 1m 5f 61y

3:25 (3:25) (Class 3) (0-90,88) 3-Y-0+ — £6,663 (£1,982; £990; £495) **Stalls** Low

Form				RPR
0151	1		**Lily In Pink**[23] 4460 4-10-0 **88**.....JamesDoyle 2 (Jonathan Portman) *in tch: hdwy over 3f out: chsd ldr 2f out: rdn to ld over 1f out: edgd rt u.p ins fnl f: drvn out* **12/1**	97
32/	2	*nk*	**Monte Cavallo (SAF)**[162] 6276 7-9-4 **78**.....GeorgeBaker 6 (Rebecca Curtis) *s.i.s: hld up in rr: stdy hdwy on outer fr over 2f out: chsd wnr over 1f out: kpt on u.p fnl f but a jst hld* **25/1**	86
464	3	*2*	**O Ma Lad (IRE)**[13] 4823 4-9-6 **80**.....RichardHughes 7 (Sylvester Kirk) *hld up in rr: hdwy over 2f out: n.m.r over 1f out: styd on fnl f to take 3rd clsng stages: nt rch ldng duo* **20/1**	86+
30-0	4	*½*	**Tuscan Gold**[59] 3241 5-9-9 **83**.....IanMongan 15 (Laura Mongan) *chsd ldrs tl wnt 2nd 5f out: led over 3f out: sn rdn: hdd u.p over 1f out: sn one pce: lost 3rd clsng stages* **50/1**	87
-004	5	*½*	**Sandbanks Sizzler (IRE)**[35] 4060 4-9-3 **77**.....(t) JimCrowley 13 (Ralph Beckett) *in rr: hdwy on outer over 2f out: styd on fnl f but nvr gng pce to get into contention* **33/1**	81
332-	6	*1*	**Valid Reason**[181] 6707 5-9-11 **85**.....ShaneKelly 1 (Dean Ivory) *chsd ldrs: rdn over 2f out: kpt on same pce fr over 1f out* **14/1**	87
2-11	7	*hd*	**Grandiloquent**[78] 2634 3-8-13 **84**.....RyanMoore 9 (Sir Michael Stoute) *chsd ldrs: rdn over 2f out: nvr gng pce to chal: wknd fnl f* **15/8**[1]	86
0312	8	*¾*	**Require**[13] 4796 3-9-0 **85**.....KirstyMilczarek 8 (Luca Cumani) *in rr hdwy 4f out: drvn to chse ldrs 2f out but nvr gng pce to chal: wknd fnl f* **5/1**[2]	86
1104	9	*1 ¼*	**Maydream**[20] 4606 5-8-9 **69**.....[1] KieranO'Neill 10 (Jimmy Fox) *slowly away: in rr: hdwy 3f out: sn rdn and nvr gng pce to get into contention: no ch fnl 2f* **16/1**	68+
3002	10	*10*	**Dunhoy (IRE)**[42] 3827 4-9-8 **82**.....DaneO'Neill 12 (Tony Newcombe) *in tch rdn over 3f out: sn btn* **22/1**	66
0600	11	*2 ¼*	**Spice Fair**[13] 4800 5-9-12 **86**.....DavidProbert 16 (Mark Usher) *slowly away: rdn and no rspnse 3f out* **40/1**	66
340-	12	*2 ½*	**Ardlui (IRE)**[156] 6333 4-9-11 **85**.....JimmyFortune 11 (Alan King) *chsd ldrs over 11f* **8/1**[3]	62
0100	13	*1*	**Kangaroo Court (IRE)**[21] 4528 8-9-5 **79**.....MickyFenton 4 (Emma Lavelle) *chsd ldr: led 6f out: racd towards outside and hdd over 3f out: sn wknd* **28/1**	54
11	14	*12*	**Asker (IRE)**[31] 4184 4-9-8 **87**.....(b) KatiaScallan(5) 5 (Marcus Tregoning) *s.i.s: in rr: sme hdwy on ins over 3f out: nvr in contention and sn wknd* **8/1**[3]	44
4000	15	*78*	**Eye Of The Tiger (GER)**[34] 4103 7-9-1 **75**.....LiamKeniry 3 (Barney Curley) *led: hdd 6f out: sn btn: eased fnl 3f: t.o* **50/1**	

2m 53.99s (1.99) **Going Correction** +0.05s/f (Good)
WFA 3 from 4yo+ 11lb — **15** Ran SP% **119.6**
Speed ratings (Par 107): **95,94,93,93,92 92,92,91,91,84 83,81,81,73,25**
toteswingers 1&2 £81.90, 1&3 £73.10, 2&3 £56.90 CSF £285.11 CT £5807.27 TOTE £11.50: £3.30, £8.60, £3.40; EX 441.50 TRIFECTA Not won..

Owner Mrs S L Morley **Bred** J Ford & Peter J Skinner **Trained** Compton, Berks

FOCUS

A good handicap that often falls to an improver, but some of the progressive runners here disappointed and this looks ordinary form.

NOTEBOOK

Lily In Pink ◆ has progressed well this season and took another step forward. She looks capable of making her mark at a higher level, and perhaps connections might consider something like the Mallard handicap at Doncaster, or alternatively look to earn some black type with her. (op 9-1)

Monte Cavallo(SAF), absent since winning over hurdles in March, had not run on the Flat since 2010. He put up a fine display, coming from off the pace to challenge until his effort flattened out inside the last furlong. He looks more than capable of winning on the level.

O Ma Lad(IRE) seems to handle most surfaces and finished well here, having been held up. He might be in the handicapper's grip now, but perhaps some form of headgear could extract a little more from him. The Veterinary Officer reported that the gelding was lame on his right fore. Official explanation: vet said gelding finished lame right-fore (tchd 16-1)

Tuscan Gold ◆, well beaten in the Ascot Stakes when last seen following a spell over hurdles, ran creditably on this return from a break, having been in the front rank from the start and then having kicked for home 2f out. He can be placed to win a staying handicap this autumn. (op 40-1)

Sandbanks Sizzler(IRE) ◆ is lightly raced and was trying this trip for the first time. He was staying on when short of room over a furlong out, but picked up again once switched and can make his mark at this sort of distance.

Valid Reason, having his first run on the Flat since October, having had a successful hurdling campaign in the meantime, performed well on this comeback over a trip that is probably on the short side for him. He could be one to consider for one of the big staying handicaps this autumn, although he might struggle to get into a race like the Cesarewitch. (tchd 16-1)

Grandiloquent tracked the pace throughout but was unable to pick up under pressure, He might have needed the run after 11 weeks off. (op 5-2)

Require's effort flattened out on the last furlong and a half and she might prefer a little more cut. Kirsty Milczarek reported that the filly stumbled coming out of the stalls. Official explanation: jockey said filly stumbled leaving stalls (op 6-1)

Spice Fair's rider reported that the gelding hung left. Official explanation: jockey said gelding hung left

Asker(IRE), whose trainer had won this twice in the preceding ten years and who was previously unbeaten, was always out the back and failed to pick up in the straight. The faster ground here might have been an issue, although he won his bumper on a similar surface. (op 7-1)

5307 BATHWICK TYRES ST HUGH'S STKS (LISTED RACE) — 5f 34y

4:00 (4:00) (Class 1) 2-Y-0

£13,043 (£4,945; £2,474; £1,232; £618; £310) **Stalls** Centre

Form				RPR
1	1		**Rosdhu Queen (IRE)**[27] 4344 2-8-12 0.....RyanMoore 5 (William Haggas) *trckd ldr: drvn to ld wl over 1f out: edgd rt u.p fnl 120yds: hld on: kpt on wl clsng stages* **11/10**[1]	99+
61	2	*¾*	**Sound Of Guns**[24] 4433 2-8-12 82.....LukeMorris 3 (Ed Walker) *s.i.s: sn in tch: chsd wnr and drvn jst ins fnl f: hrd rdn and hung rt fnl 120yds: nt qckn clsng stages* **7/1**[3]	96
122	3	*1*	**Sandreamer (IRE)**[20] 4577 2-8-12 99.....MartinHarley 6 (Mick Channon) *in tch: rdn 2f out: styd on to take 3rd ins fnl f: kpt on clsng stages: nt pce of ldng duo* **4/1**[2]	94
1023	4	*2 ¼*	**Miss Diva**[20] 4599 2-8-12 88.....RichardHughes 4 (Richard Hannon) *led: rdn 2f out: hdd wl over 1f out: wknd ins fnl f* **14/1**	85
042	5	*¾*	**New Fforest**[8] 5003 2-8-12 0.....JimmyFortune 2 (Andrew Balding) *s.i.s: in rr: hdwy over 1f out: styd on fnl f but nvr gng pce to rch ldrs* **9/1**	82
614	6	*1 ¼*	**Jollification (IRE)**[20] 4577 2-8-12 91.....PatCosgrave 1 (George Baker) *chsd ldrs: rdn 1/2-way: wknd 1f out* **22/1**	77
1062	7	*5*	**Lasilia (IRE)**[42] 3823 2-8-12 92.....PaulHanagan 7 (Kevin Ryan) *chsd ldrs: rdn 1/2-way: wknd over 1f out* **12/1**	59
4061	8	*15*	**Excel Yourself (IRE)**[18] 4651 2-8-12 79.....MartinDwyer 11 (James Tate) *racd w sole rival on stands' side and no ch fr 1/2-way* **50/1**	5+
1100	9	*hd*	**Bridge Night**[17] 4687 2-8-12 88.....SilvestreDeSousa 9 (Eve Johnson Houghton) *racd w sole rival stands' side and no ch fr 1/2-way* **50/1**	5+
4215	10	*13*	**Three Crowns**[20] 4614 2-8-12 83.....JamesDoyle 10 (Ian Wood) *rrd stalls: v.s.a and a bhd* **50/1**	

1m 1.2s (-0.20) **Going Correction** +0.15s/f (Good) — **10** Ran SP% **114.7**
Speed ratings (Par 102): **107,105,104,100,99 97,89,65,65,44**
toteswingers 1&2 £2.40, 1&3 £1.60, 2&3 £4.50 CSF £8.82 TOTE £1.90: £1.10, £2.80, £1.50; EX 10.30 Trifecta £40.50 Pool: £1,016.00 - 18.53 winning units..

Owner Clipper Logistics **Bred** Old Carhue & Graeng Bloodstock **Trained** Newmarket, Suffolk

FOCUS

Two of the previous four winners of this Listed race went on to take the Group 2 Flying Childers Stakes at Doncaster. The speedy winner built on her impressive debut win, with the fourth and fifth and the race averages helping with the level.

NOTEBOOK

Rosdhu Queen(IRE) ◆ had impressed when beating three subsequent winners on her debut at Ripon, and was well backed to make a successful step up in grade. Always in the front rank, she had to work hard to hold off the second but showed the right attitude. A tilt at the Flying Childers would be fully justified after this, especially as the time was comparatively the fastest of the day. (op 11-8)

Sound Of Guns ◆, who beat two subsequent winners when taking her maiden over 6f at Yarmouth, was down in trip but handled it well and gave the winner a good race. (op 8-1 tchd 9-1)

Sandreamer(IRE) had the highest official rating of these, having finished runner-up in the Princess Margaret Stakes. However, she was dropping in trip here and was caught out having to switch around the fading Lasilia just as the leaders kicked for home. She finished well and a return to 6f, for something like the Firth Of Clyde takes at Ayr, could see her score at this level. (op 3-1)

Miss Diva made the running but had nothing more to offer once the principals took her on. She is a reliable type and helps set the level of the form. (op 12-1)

New Fforest, the only maiden in the field, ran creditably and is getting her act together. A half-sister to six winners, including Border Patrol and Eisteddfod, a win and black type will increase her potential paddock value even more. (op 12-1)

Three Crowns's rider reported that the filly reared as the stalls opened. Official explanation: jockey said filly reared as stalls opened

5308 SALLY, NATASHA, LOUIS MONEM H'CAP — 6f 8y
4:30 (4:30) (Class 4) (0-80,79) 3-Y-O — £4,528 (£1,347; £673; £336) Stalls Centre

Form — RPR

-011 **1** **Take A Note**[30] 4218 3-8-13 **71** .... JimCrowley 3 — 81
(Patrick Chamings) *chsd ldrs: drvn and wnt 2nd over 1f out: led fnl 120yds: kpt on wl u.p* **5/1**[3]

0444 **2** *1 1/4* **Jinker Noble**[14] 4757 3-9-1 **73** .... (b[1]) AdamKirby 4 — 79
(Clive Cox) *led: rdn over 1f out: hdd fnl 120yds: sn edgd lft and one pce* **10/1**

5334 **3** *1 3/4* **Generalyse**[8] 4985 3-9-0 **72** .... (p) PaulHanagan 5 — 72
(Ben De Haan) *chsd ldrs: rdn 2f out: styd on same pce for 3rd fnl f* **16/1**

-153 **4** *3/4* **Delft**[28] 4300 3-9-7 **79** .... RyanMoore 1 — 77
(Jeremy Noseda) *in rr and sn outpcd: rdn 2f out: hdwy to take 4th u.p 1f out: no further prog and sn btn* **13/8**[1]

1530 **5** *3 3/4* **Willies Wonder (IRE)**[22] 4496 3-9-3 **75** .... DavidProbert 8 — 61
(Charles Hills) *chsd ldrs: rdn and hld whn bmpd ins fnl 2f: sn wknd* **8/1**

3-51 **6** *3* **Byton**[49] 3568 3-9-2 **74** .... DaneO'Neill 6 — 50
(Henry Candy) *chsd ldrs: rdn and edgd rt ins fnl 2f: sn btn* **3/1**[2]

1344 **7** *2* **Dark Ages (IRE)**[15] 4726 3-8-12 **75** .... (t) DavidKenny[(5)] 9 — 45
(Paul Burgoyne) *chsd ldrs to 1/2-way* **14/1**

16- **8** *1/2* **Trumpet Voluntary (IRE)**[336] 6111 3-9-3 **75** .... MartinHarley 2 — 43
(Nicky Vaughan) *stdd s: in rr: sme hdwy 2f out: nvr rchd ldrs and sn wknd* **20/1**

1m 13.5s (0.50) **Going Correction** +0.15s/f (Good) — **8** Ran SP% **115.9**
Speed ratings (Par 102): **102,100,98,97,92 88,85,84**
toteswingers 1&2 £6.00, 1&3 £7.70, 2&3 £9.00 CSF £62.55 CT £893.20 TOTE £7.80: £2.30, £3.60, £4.90; EX 65.70 Trifecta £418.00 Pool: £1,079.14 - 1.91 winning units..
Owner The Foxford House Partnership **Bred** P J L Wright **Trained** Baughurst, Hants

FOCUS
A tight little sprint handicap whose best recent winner was the subsequent Ayr Gold Cup hero Jimmy Styles. It was strong run and the winner carried over his recent AW progress.
Byton Official explanation: jockey said filly never travelled
Trumpet Voluntary(IRE) Official explanation: vet said gelding lost both front shoes

5309 RIDGEWAY MAIDEN FILLIES' STKS — 1m 2f 6y
5:05 (5:08) (Class 5) 3-Y-O+ — £2,587 (£770; £384; £192) Stalls Low

Form — RPR

4-03 **1** **Bana Wu**[41] 3879 3-8-13 100 .... DavidProbert 5 — 85+
(Andrew Balding) *chsd ldrs: rdn and edgd lft over 2f out: styd on u.p to chse ldr over 1f out: led fnl 120yds: drvn out* **2/5**[1]

4-55 **2** *1 1/4* **Miracle Maid**[49] 3565 3-8-13 75 .... AdamKirby 3 — 82
(Clive Cox) *led: rdn 2f out: hdd and no ex fnl 120yds* **4/1**[2]

0-0 **3** *5* **Still I'm A Star (IRE)**[118] 1532 3-8-13 0 .... MartinHarley 7 — 72+
(David Simcock) *chsd ldr: rdn and no imp fr 2f out: wknd and lost 2nd over 1f out* **25/1**

4 *7* **Entitlement** 3-8-13 0 ....[1] ShaneKelly 4 — 58+
(James Fanshawe) *s.i.s: sn in mid-div but nvr nr ldr: rdn and no ch fnl 2f* **10/1**[3]

5 *3 3/4* **Miss Fortywinks** 3-8-13 0 .... LiamKeniry 9 — 51
(Paul Henderson) *hmpd s and s.i.s: in rr: pushed along and outpcd over 3f out: mod prog fnl 2f* **50/1**

50 **6** *7* **Caphene**[103] 1893 3-8-13 0 .... DaneO'Neill 2 — 37
(John Dunlop) *a in rr* **12/1**

00 **7** *2 3/4* **Divea**[26] 4366 3-8-13 0 .... MartinDwyer 1 — 31
(Charles Hills) *chsd ldrs: rdn 4f out: sn btn* **12/1**

0 **8** *11* **Orla (IRE)**[87] 2368 4-9-0 0 .... JoshBaudains[(7)] 8
(Dominic Ffrench Davis) *in tch: rdn: hung rt and wknd 4f out* **66/1**

9 *55* **Mystic Melody (IRE)** 3-8-8 0 .... AshleyMorgan[(5)] 6
(Paul Cole) *a in rr: t.o fnl 3f* **33/1**

2m 8.22s (-0.58) **Going Correction** +0.05s/f (Good)
WFA 3 from 4yo 8lb — **9** Ran SP% **126.1**
Speed ratings (Par 100): **104,103,99,93,90 84,82,73,29**
toteswingers 1&2 £1.10, 1&3 £8.40, 2&3 £14.30 CSF £2.75 TOTE £1.40: £1.10, £1.10, £5.90; EX 2.70 Trifecta £33.50 Pool: £1,577.75 - 34.82 winning units..
Owner G B Russell **Bred** Equine Breeding Ltd **Trained** Kingsclere, Hants

FOCUS
An ordinary looking fillies' maiden and the winner did not need to match her best.

5310 POLAR JEST APPRENTICE H'CAP (IN MEMORY OF JACK COLLING) — 1m 1f
5:40 (5:40) (Class 5) (0-70,75) 4-Y-O+ — £2,587 (£770; £384; £192) Stalls Low

Form — RPR

0203 **1** **Mount Abora (IRE)**[10] 4915 5-8-9 **60** .... CharlotteJenner[(5)] 14 — 69
(Laura Mongan) *in rr: hdwy on outer fr 3f out: styd on to ld appr fnl f: kpt on wl* **25/1**

0450 **2** *1 1/2* **Edgewater (IRE)**[7] 5052 5-8-12 **65** .... AaronChave[(7)] 10 — 70
(Lee Carter) *chsd ldrs: led ins fnl 3f: hdd ins fnl 2f: styd chsng ldrs: one pce appr 1f out: rallied to take 2nd fnl 100yds but no imp on wnr* **18/1**

0305 **3** *1/2* **Ssafa**[23] 4470 4-9-7 **67** .... LeonnaMayor 13 — 71
(J W Hills) *racd on outside and wd into st: hdwy fr 4f out: led ins fnl 2f: hdd appr fnl f: no ex and lost 2nd fnl 100yds* **18/1**

0004 **4** *1/2* **Having A Ball**[87] 2366 8-8-5 **51** oh4 .... MatthewLawson 15 — 54+
(Jonathan Portman) *in rr: racd wd: hdwy over 2f out: styd on wl fnl f to take 4th clsng stages: nt rch ldrs* **20/1**

0530 **5** *3/4* **If I Were A Boy (IRE)**[10] 4915 5-9-2 **65** .... (p) JoshBaudains[(3)] 9 — 66
(Dominic Ffrench Davis) *sn led: hdd ins fnl 3f: styd chsng ldrs u.p: one pce fnl 2f* **18/1**

4331 **6** *2 1/2* **Satwa Laird**[4] 5179 6-10-1 **75** 6ex .... DavidKenny 8 — 70
(Conor Dore) *in rr: hdwy 3f out: chsd ldrs 2f out: wknd fnl f* **13/2**[2]

605 **7** *nk* **Stylistickhill (IRE)**[21] 4538 4-8-6 **57** .... (t) JordanUys[(5)] 11 — 52
(Scott Dixon) *in rr: hdwy on outside over 2f out: nvr gng pce to chal and one pce fr over 1f out* **16/1**

6104 **8** *1 3/4* **Cane Cat (IRE)**[60] 3220 5-8-13 **64** .... (t) RyanTate[(5)] 7 — 55
(Tony Carroll) *in rr: hdwy on ins to chse ldrs fr 3f out: wknd ins fnl 2f* **20/1**

-064 **9** *1* **Effigy**[7] 5063 8-9-2 **65** .... ThomasBrown[(3)] 12 — 54
(Henry Candy) *rdn 3f out: sme hdwy over 2f out: wknd sn after* **12/1**

6330 **10** *2 1/2* **Market Puzzle (IRE)**[3] 5199 5-8-0 **51** oh4 .... (p) GemmaTutty[(5)] 16 — 34
(Mark Brisbourne) *chsd ldr to 6f out: wknd 3f out* **33/1**

0313 **11** *2 1/4* **Matavia Bay (IRE)**[43] 3782 4-9-3 **66** .... MichaelJMMurphy[(3)] 2 — 44
(Alan Jarvis) *chsd ldrs: t.k.h: wnt 2nd 6f out: rdn over 2f out and sn btn* **15/8**[1]

3010 **12** *1/2* **Osgood**[33] 3213 5-9-10 **70** .... CharlesBishop 5 — 47
(Mick Channon) *in rr: hdwy 4f out: chsd ldrs 3f out: wknd over 2f out* **10/1**

0050 **13** *1/2* **Smarty Time**[13] 4812 5-8-0 **51** oh3 .... NoelGarbutt[(5)] 1 — 27
(John Bridger) *chsd ldrs: rdn over 3f out: wknd 2f out* **50/1**

5000 **14** *2* **Menadati (USA)**[50] 3544 4-9-0 **60** .... AshleyMorgan 6 — 32
(Peter Hiatt) *hmpd ss: a towards rr* **16/1**

0045 **15** *3 3/4* **Blue Maisey**[25] 4413 4-9-5 **65** .... BrendanPowell 4 — 28
(Peter Makin) *chsd ldrs tl wknd 3f out* **7/1**[3]

0024 **16** *7* **Victorian Number (FR)**[32] 4158 4-8-10 **56** .... JamesRogers 3
(Geoffrey Deacon) *chsd ldrs to 3f out* **25/1**

1m 55.23s (-0.27) **Going Correction** +0.05s/f (Good) — **16** Ran SP% **127.1**
Speed ratings (Par 103): **103,101,101,100,100 97,97,96,95,92 90,90,90,88,84 78**
toteswingers 1&2 £52.00, 1&3 £50.10, 2&3 £104.10 CSF £408.62 CT £8065.41 TOTE £49.20: £7.20, £4.70, £3.90, £4.60; EX 1002.90 TRIFECTA Not won..
Owner Condover Racing **Bred** Dr M V O'Brien **Trained** Epsom, Surrey

FOCUS
A modest apprentice handicap and any number were in with a chance entering the last quarter-mile. Straightforward form.
T/Plt: £848.50 to a £1 stake. Pool: £66,661.89 - 57.35 winning tickets T/Qpdt: £120.30 to a £1 stake. Pool: £5,250.94 - 32.30 winning tickets ST

4951 NEWCASTLE (L-H)
Friday, August 17

OFFICIAL GOING: Good to soft (good in places) changing to good to soft (soft in places) after race 4 (3.35)
Wind: Fresh, half behind Weather: Cloudy

5311 BRITISH STALLION STUDS E.B.F./WATERAID MAIDEN STKS — 7f
2:00 (2:03) (Class 5) 2-Y-O — £3,234 (£962; £481; £240) Stalls Centre

Form — RPR

4 **1** **Al Mukhdam**[20] 4595 2-9-3 0 .... PaulMulrennan 5 — 75+
(Peter Chapple-Hyam) *trckd ldrs: shkn up to ld over 2f out: hung rt ins fnl f: rdn out* **5/4**[1]

2 *1 1/4* **Mister Marcasite** 2-9-3 0 .... DavidAllan 10 — 72+
(Mel Brittain) *dwlt: sn prom: hdwy to chse wnr appr fnl f: kpt on: nt rch wnr* **25/1**

65 **3** *1/2* **Lamusawama**[15] 4724 2-9-3 0 .... GrahamLee 9 — 71+
(Ed Dunlop) *hld up: effrt whn nt clr run briefly over 2f out: hdwy over 1f out: kpt on ins fnl f* **12/1**[3]

4 *nk* **Wyldfire (IRE)** 2-9-3 0 .... TonyHamilton 1 — 70+
(Richard Fahey) *missed break: bhd: rdn and hdwy over 2f out: kpt on fnl f: nt pce to chal* **9/2**[2]

0 **5** *4 1/2* **Returntobrecongill**[16] 4710 2-9-3 0 .... MichaelStainton 2 — 59
(Sally Hall) *in tch: rdn and effrt over 2f out: outpcd appr fnl f* **100/1**

50 **6** *1* **Salvatore Fury (IRE)**[25] 4387 2-9-3 0 .... JoeFanning 14 — 56
(Keith Dalgleish) *prom: hdwy to chse wnr briefly over 1f out: wknd ins fnl f* **66/1**

52 **7** *1 3/4* **Dark Ocean (IRE)**[25] 4387 2-9-3 0 .... AndrewElliott 11 — 52
(Jedd O'Keeffe) *t.k.h: cl up: led after 2f to over 2f out: edgd lft and wknd over 1f out* **9/2**[2]

8 *1/2* **Apache Rising** 2-9-3 0 .... TomEaves 8 — 51+
(Bryan Smart) *prom: rdn over 2f out: wknd over 1f out* **25/1**

05 **9** *2 1/2* **Noosa Sound**[21] 4546 2-8-12 0 .... PJMcDonald 6 — 39
(John Davies) *led 2f: cl up tl rdn and wknd over 1f out* **25/1**

10 *1 1/4* **Beautifulwildthing** 2-8-12 0 .... AndrewMullen 13 — 36
(David Barron) *noisy and green in paddock: midfield: drvn over 2f out: sn btn* **16/1**

04 **11** *2* **Captain's Dream (IRE)**[20] 4587 2-9-3 0 .... BarryMcHugh 3 — 36
(Jedd O'Keeffe) *bhd: drvn along and outpcd after 3f: nvr on terms* **40/1**

5 **12** *1 1/4* **Reggie Bond**[62] 3168 2-9-0 0 .... DaleSwift[(3)] 12 — 33
(Geoffrey Oldroyd) *dwlt: sn rdn towards rr: effrt u.p 3f out: sn btn* **12/1**[3]

00 **13** *3 1/4* **French Revolution**[20] 4587 2-9-3 0 .... JamesSullivan 4 — 25
(Jedd O'Keeffe) *missed break: bhd and sn outpcd: nvr on terms* **100/1**

14 *13* **Indies Gold** 2-9-3 0 .... PaddyAspell 7
(Ann Duffield) *dwlt: hld up: struggling over 3f out: sn btn* **66/1**

1m 29.31s (1.51) **Going Correction** +0.05s/f (Good) — **14** Ran SP% **121.0**
Speed ratings (Par 94): **93,91,91,90,85 84,82,81,78,77 75,73,70,55**
toteswingers 1&2 £12.60, 1&3 £3.90, 2&3 £41.50 CSF £46.22 TOTE £2.20: £1.20, £7.40, £2.30; EX 51.90.
Owner Ziad A Galadari **Bred** Galadari Sons Stud Company Limited **Trained** Newmarket, Suffolk

FOCUS
After 17mm of rain the previous night and a further 8mm in a mid-morning deluge, the ground was changed to good to soft, good in places. After the opener it was described as "slow, soft ground" by Paul Mulrennan, who brought up 50 winners for the season aboard the winner. A 2yo maiden with a couple holding big-race entries. Routine form but the first four were clear.

NOTEBOOK
Al Mukhdam, a promising fourth first time at Newmarket, holds a Champagne Stakes entry. He travelled strongly on the outer but once in front hung right and ended up near the stands' side rail. He will need a big step on this if he is to hold his own at a much higher level. (tchd 11-10 and 11-8)
Mister Marcasite, a half-brother to six winners, ran much better than the betting forecast on his debut and looks sure to go one better at some stage.
Lamusawama, who cost 180,000gns, was having his third run. He shaped really well without being in any way knocked about and is one to note in nursery company. (tchd 11-1)
Wyldfire(IRE), another Champagne entry, missed a beat at the start. He stayed on nicely to finish clear of the remainder and will be a different proposition with this outing under his belt. (op 11-2 tchd 7-1)
Returntobrecongill showed a lot more than on his first outing, showing good speed until tiring late on.
Salvatore Fury(IRE), having his third start, was another seemingly to show vast improvement. This may well have blown a lenient nursery mark out of the water.
Dark Ocean(IRE), runner-up on his second start on heavy ground at Ayr, was disappointing, racing freely before dropping right away. (op 4-1)

5312 GOWLAND AND DAWSON H'CAP — 1m 2f 32y
2:30 (2:31) (Class 5) (0-75,73) 3-Y-O — £2,264 (£673; £336; £168) Stalls Low

Form — RPR

-635 **1** **Buster Brown (IRE)**[29] 4250 3-8-11 **66** .... DaleSwift[(3)] 3 — 75
(James Given) *hld up in last pl: plenty to do whn nt clr run over 3f out: gd hdwy 2f out: styd on wl to ld cl home* **6/1**

0552 **2** *shd* **Operation Tracer**[7] 5037 3-8-6 **58** .... JamesSullivan 6 — 67
(Michael Bell) *plld hrd in midfield: effrt and rdn over 2f out: edgd lft and chsd wnr appr fnl f: led briefly cl home: jst hld* **5/1**[3]

3443 **3** *1* **Party Line**[35] 4048 3-9-6 **72** .... JoeFanning 4 — 79
(Mark Johnston) *chsd clr ldr: hdwy over 3f out: rdn to ld over 1f out: kpt on: hdd and no ex cl home* **7/2**[1]

1045 **4** *7* **Almuftarris (USA)**[20] 4601 3-9-7 **73**........................(b[1]) PaulMulrennan 7 66
(Ed Dunlop) *t.k.h: led and sn clr: hdd over 1f out: sn btn* **4/1**[2]

6300 **5** *2 ½* **Night Flash (GER)**[49] 3558 3-8-13 **65**................................ GrahamLee 2 53
(James Given) *hld up on ins: rdn over 3f out: no imp fr 2f out* **20/1**

0244 **6** *½* **Vital Calling**[21] 4553 3-9-2 **73**.. LMcNiff(5) 8 60
(David Barron) *plld hrd: hld up in tch on outside: effrt 3f out: edgd lft and wknd over 1f out* **13/2**

0303 **7** *2 ½* **Outlaw Torn (IRE)**[4] 5171 3-8-1 **56**........................(e) DeclanCannon(3) 9 38
(Richard Guest) *taken early to post: s.i.s: hld up: rdn over 3f out: btn fnl 2f* **12/1**

60-6 **8** *27* **Absolute Fun (IRE)**[16] 4713 3-8-3 **55**.......................... DuranFentiman 5
(Tim Easterby) *hld up: struggling over 3f out: sn btn: t.o* **50/1**

0445 **9** *6* **Artistic Dawn (IRE)**[19] 4622 3-8-12 **64**............................ TomEaves 10
(John Weymes) *dwlt: sn cl up: rdn over 3f out: sn wknd* **50/1**

-640 **P** **Spirit Na Heireann (IRE)**[79] 2605 3-8-8 **60**.................. TonyHamilton 1
(Richard Fahey) *prom in chsng gp: rdn whn p.u lame wl over 2f out* **7/1**

2m 12.27s (0.37) **Going Correction** +0.05s/f (Good) **10** Ran SP% **115.4**
Speed ratings (Par 100): **100,99,99,93,91 91,89,67,62,**
toteswingers 1&2 £7.60, 1&3 £5.00, 2&3 £2.40 CSF £35.10 CT £120.07 TOTE £4.80: £2.30, £2.30, £1.70; EX 45.10.
Owner Mrs Linda P Fish **Bred** Yeguada De Milagro Sa **Trained** Willoughton, Lincs

FOCUS
The clear leader went off very fast, setting up this for a closer. The winner is rated back to his 2yo form.
Buster Brown(IRE) Official explanation: trainer said, regarding apparent improvement in form, that the colt was suited by the change of tactics.
Spirit Na Heireann(IRE) Official explanation: vet said filly pulled up lame right-hind

5313 ESH CONSTRUCTION NURSERY 5f
3:00 (3:13) (Class 6) (0-65,65) 2-Y-O £1,617 (£481; £240; £120) Stalls Centre

Form RPR
5003 **1** **Sandsend (IRE)**[10] 4922 2-8-11 **55**................................ TonyHamilton 4 61
(Richard Fahey) *t.k.h: cl up: smooth hdwy to ld over 1f out: pushed along and kpt on wl fnl f* **15/8**[1]

264 **2** *1* **Cracking Choice (IRE)**[17] 4670 2-9-6 **64**..............(p) PaulMulrennan 11 66
(Michael Dods) *led tl rdn and hdd over 1f out: kpt on fnl f: hld towards fin* **9/2**[3]

060 **3** *1 ½* **Grand Jipeck (IRE)**[21] 4545 2-8-12 **56**.......................(t) PatrickMathers 3 53
(Ian McInnes) *s.i.s: bhd and outpcd: hdwy 2f out: kpt on fnl f: nt pce of first two* **16/1**

4000 **4** *4* **Betty Boo (IRE)**[21] 4545 2-8-1 **52**........................... ShirleyTeasdale(7) 7 34
(Shaun Harris) *prom: rdn and outpcd 2f out: no imp fnl f* **16/1**

2035 **5** *3* **Princess In Exile**[14] 4767 2-9-5 **63**............................... BarryMcHugh 2 34
(George Foster) *w ldr tl rdn and wknd appr fnl f* **12/1**

003 **6** *1 ½* **Modern Lady**[10] 4927 2-8-8 **55**.................................. DeclanCannon(3) 9 21
(Richard Guest) *taken early to post: t.k.h: hld up in tch: rdn over 2f out: wknd over 1f out* **3/1**[2]

3004 **7** *nk* **Hellolini**[49] 3576 2-8-12 **56** ow1.....................................(p) DanielTudhope 6 21
(Robin Bastiman) *t.k.h: cl up tl rdn and wknd over 1f out* **10/1**

0246 **8** *1 ½* **Sulky Sheila (IRE)**[25] 4395 2-8-3 **47**........................... DuranFentiman 12 7
(Tim Easterby) *sn drvn along in tch: struggling over 2f out: edgd lft and sn btn* **20/1**

6000 **9** *¾* **Royal Jenray**[63] 3123 2-8-11 **55**................................(b[1]) AndrewElliott 10 12
(Jedd O'Keeffe) *s.i.s: bhd and outpcd: no ch fr 1/2-way* **20/1**

1m 2.66s (1.56) **Going Correction** +0.05s/f (Good) **9** Ran SP% **116.0**
Speed ratings (Par 92): **89,87,85,78,73 71,70,68,67**
toteswingers 1&2 £2.90, 1&3 £7.90, 2&3 £10.60 CSF £10.56 CT £98.24 TOTE £2.70: £1.20, £1.50, £4.10; EX 8.70.
Owner A Rhodes Haulage And P Timmins **Bred** Lisieux Stud **Trained** Musley Bank, N Yorks

FOCUS
There was a brisk, heavy shower ahead of this low-grade nursery. The second and third set the level.

NOTEBOOK
Sandsend(IRE), narrowly denied from the same mark at Ripon, was much happier on this more galloping track. He travelled best and scored in decisive fashion. There may be even better to come. (op 11-4)
Cracking Choice(IRE), the paddock pick, wore cheekpieces for the first time on his nursery bow. He showed ahead for a short while but was always coming to come off second best. His trainer feels he would be better in less soft ground. (op 7-2 tchd 5-1)
Grand Jipeck(IRE), run off his feet in the early stages, kept on to finish clear of the remainder and will be better suited by 6f. (op 18-1 tchd 14-1)
Betty Boo(IRE) has gone backwards since her debut and the eyeshields she wore on her previous start were discarded. (op 22-1)
Princess In Exile showed bags of speed to take them along but may be more effective on much faster ground and a sharper track. (op 11-1)
Modern Lady, a close third at Wolverhampton from a this mark, and a pund well in here, did not reproduce that effort back on turf. (tchd 11-4 and 10-3)
Royal Jenray Official explanation: jockey said colt never travelled

5314 JN BENTLEY'S 40TH ANNIVERSARY H'CAP 7f
3:35 (3:39) (Class 4) (0-85,90) 3-Y-O+ £4,075 (£1,212; £454; £454) Stalls Centre

Form RPR
231 **1** **Discression**[9] 4954 3-9-3 **80** 6ex... GrahamLee 6 96
(Kevin Ryan) *in tch: hdwy to ld 2f out: rdn clr fnl f: readily* **5/2**[1]

1301 **2** *5* **Able Master (IRE)**[7] 5057 6-10-4 **90** 6ex......................... DanielTudhope 2 93
(David O'Meara) *in tch: effrt and rdn over 2f out: hdwy to chse (clr) wnr last 100yds: kpt on: no imp* **8/1**

0031 **3** *2* **Triple Eight (IRE)**[7] 5059 4-8-0 **65** oh4......................(b) EvaMoscrop(7) 9 63
(Philip Kirby) *t.k.h: cl up: led after 3f to 2f out: sn one pce* **9/2**[2]

500 **3** *dht* **Ted's Brother (IRE)**[56] 3334 4-8-12 **70**......................... J-PGuillambert 4 68
(Richard Guest) *hld up: effrt and hdwy 2f out: kpt on fnl f: nt pce to chal* **14/1**

6-50 **5** *1* **Holy Roman Warrior (IRE)**[22] 4498 3-8-4 **67**.............. BarryMcHugh 1 61
(Richard Fahey) *hld up: stdy hdwy over 2f out: sn rdn: kpt on fnl f: nvr able to chal* **25/1**

2606 **6** *¾* **Dance The Rain**[32] 4135 3-9-0 **77**..................................(v[1]) TomEaves 3 69
(Bryan Smart) *dwlt: t.k.h and sn cl up: ev ch over 2f out to wl over 1f out: outpcd fnl f* **20/1**

1613 **7** *1* **Dr Red Eye**[22] 4503 4-9-6 **81**.....................................(p) DeclanCannon(3) 7 71
(Scott Dixon) *t.k.h: cl up: rdn over 2f out: wknd ex wl over 1f out* **5/1**[3]

1000 **8** *10* **Ashva (USA)**[44] 3767 4-9-8 **80**..[1] PaulMulrennan 5 43
(Michael Dods) *hld up: struggling over 3f out: sn no ch* **10/1**

1643 **9** *3 ¾* **Fieldgunner Kirkup (GER)**[32] 4135 4-9-0 **77**.................. LMcNiff(5) 11 30
(David Barron) *swtchd to r alone stands' side: cl up tl rdn and wknd over 2f out* **13/2**

046 **10** *15* **China Excels**[21] 4550 5-8-8 **66**.. PJMcDonald 10
(Sue Smith) *t.k.h: led 3f: rdn and wknd 3f out: t.o* **12/1**

1m 27.2s (-0.60) **Going Correction** +0.05s/f (Good)
WFA 3 from 4yo+ 5lb **10** Ran SP% **119.9**
Speed ratings (Par 105): **105,99,97,97,95 95,93,82,78,61**
PL: Ted's Brother £2.70, Triple Eight £1.10. toteswingers 1&2 £2.40, 2&TB £10.60, 1&TB £5.40, 2&TE £2.50, 1&TE £1.80 CSF £24.10 TOTE £3.30: £1.10, £2.70; EX 13.10.
Owner T G & Mrs M E Holdcroft, K MacPherson **Bred** Bearstone Stud **Trained** Hambleton, N Yorks

FOCUS
More rain ahead of this competitive handicap. The time was decent and the winner impressed again.
Ted's Brother(IRE) Official explanation: jockey said, regarding riding, that the gelding hung right and became unbalanced inside final half furlong, but never stopped riding out to line

5315 FASTFLOW PIPELINE SERVICES MAIDEN STKS (DIV I) 1m 2f 32y
4:10 (4:13) (Class 5) 3-Y-O+ £2,264 (£673; £336; £168) Stalls Low

Form RPR
4 **1** **White Nile (IRE)**[70] 2895 3-9-3 0.. GrahamLee 9 84+
(David Simcock) *in tch: stdy hdwy on outside over 3f out: effrt 2f out: edgd lft appr fnl f: led wl ins fnl f: styd on* **6/5**[1]

5-3 **2** *nk* **Noble Silk**[19] 4630 3-9-3 0... PaulMulrennan 2 83
(Lucy Wadham) *midfield on ins: smooth hdwy to ld over 2f out: rdn over 1f out: hdd wl ins fnl f: kpt on: hdd nr fin* **15/8**[2]

23 **3** *8* **Medici Music**[15] 4746 3-9-3 0.. J-PGuillambert 1 67
(Luca Cumani) *chsd ldrs: niggled fr 5f out: effrt and drvn 3f out: outpcd by first two appr fnl f* **7/2**[3]

4 *½* **Smart Ruler (IRE)**[72] 6-9-8 0................................... LucyAlexander(3) 12 66
(James Moffatt) *s.i.s: hld up: hdwy over 2f out: kpt on fnl f: nvr nr ldrs* **20/1**

00 **5** *15* **Nowdoro**[19] 4630 3-9-3 0.. BarryMcHugh 3 36
(Julie Camacho) *hld up in tch: drvn and outpcd 3f out: btn fnl 2f* **66/1**

00 **6** *1* **Miss Matiz**[21] 4550 5-9-3 0.. PaulPickard(3) 8 29
(Alan Kirtley) *t.k.h: led to over 2f out: rdn and wknd over 1f out* **100/1**

45 **7** *1 ¾* **Generous Dream**[10] 4926 4-8-13 0................... RobertDodsworth(7) 6 26
(Mel Brittain) *towards rr: struggling over 4f out: nvr on terms* **33/1**

06 **8** *5* **Miss Mohawk (IRE)**[48] 3606 3-8-9 0..................................... DaleSwift(3) 10 16
(Alan Brown) *in tch tl rdn and wknd over 3f out* **100/1**

9 *1 ¼* **Lord Aratan (GER)**[126] 5-9-11 0... PJMcDonald 11 18
(George Moore) *s.i.s: towards rr: struggling over 4f out: nvr on terms* **25/1**

U **10** *33* **Josie Lennon**[90] 2288 3-8-12 0....................................... PatrickMathers 7
(Robert Johnson) *s.i.s: plld hrd in rr: wknd over 4f out: t.o* **100/1**

00 **11** *1 ½* **Roc Fort**[14] 4780 3-9-3 0... JamesSullivan 4
(Ruth Carr) *reluctant to enter stalls: t.k.h: cl up tl rdn and wknd over 3f out: t.o* **66/1**

2m 13.81s (1.91) **Going Correction** +0.05s/f (Good)
WFA 3 from 4yo+ 8lb **11** Ran SP% **120.0**
Speed ratings (Par 103): **103,102,96,95,83 83,81,77,76,50 49**
toteswingers 1&2 £1.20, 1&3 £2.00, 2&3 £1.80 CSF £3.55 TOTE £2.20: £1.10, £1.02, £1.40; EX 3.30.
Owner Sir Robert Ogden **Bred** Super Gift Syndicate **Trained** Newmarket, Suffolk

FOCUS
The ground was changed to good to soft, soft in places after more heavy rain. No strength in depth at all in division one of this maiden and the first three in the betting filled the first three places. The gallop was just steady in the ever-deteriorating conditions. The first two were clear.
Lord Aratan(GER) Official explanation: trainer's rep said gelding finished lame left-fore

5316 FASTFLOW PIPELINE SERVICES MAIDEN STKS (DIV II) 1m 2f 32y
4:40 (4:42) (Class 5) 3-Y-O+ £2,264 (£673; £336; £168) Stalls Low

Form RPR
54 **1** **Caskelena (IRE)**[13] 4791 3-8-12 0....................................... GrahamLee 8 74
(Sir Michael Stoute) *t.k.h: prom: effrt and rdn and sltly outpcd over 2f out: rallied over 1f out: led wl ins fnl f: styd on wl* **11/8**[1]

662 **2** *nk* **Mama Quilla (USA)**[10] 4926 3-8-12 **68**........................ DanielTudhope 2 73
(William Haggas) *led 1f: cl up: led over 2f out: sn rdn: edgd rt and hdd wl ins fnl f: kpt on: hld nr fin* **2/1**[2]

2 **3** *1 ¼* **Fly Solo**[32] 4157 3-9-3 0.. AndrewElliott 11 75
(Alan Swinbank) *trckd ldrs: effrt and rdn over 2f out: kpt on ins fnl f* **17/2**

4 **4** *11* **Quiet Route (IRE)**[13] 3913 3-9-0 0................................ PaulPickard(3) 5 53+
(Brian Ellison) *hld up: rdn along 3f out: kpt on fnl f: nvr able to chal* **9/1**

0/5- **5** *1* **Oakwell (IRE)**[27] 4018 4-9-11 **37**.................................. MichaelStainton 6 51
(Sally Hall) *hld up on ins: rdn and outpcd 3f out: rallied over 1f out: no imp* **33/1**

45 **6** *2 ¼* **Beggar's Banquet (IRE)**[146] 1031 3-9-3 0......................... TomEaves 9 47+
(Ed Vaughan) *t.k.h in midfield: rdn and edgd lft over 2f out: sn wknd* **11/2**[3]

0-0 **7** *1* **There's No Rules**[72] 2826 3-9-0 0.............................. DeclanCannon(3) 10 45
(Richard Guest) *plld hrd: led after 1f to over 2f out: wknd over 1f out* **100/1**

30 **8** *5* **Punta Baluarte**[183] 581 6-9-6 0... BarryMcHugh 4 30
(Julie Camacho) *t.k.h: cl up tl rdn and wknd fr 2f out* **80/1**

9 *26* **Brenkley Melani** 4-8-13 0... EvaMoscrop(7) 7
(Tim Fitzgerald) *s.i.s: towards rr: lost tch fr 4f out: t.o* **100/1**

10 *17* **Lady Ongar** 4-9-6 0.. JamesSullivan 3
(Alan Kirtley) *hld up on ins: struggling over 5f out: lost tch fr 4f out: t.o* **100/1**

11 *dist* **Toepaz** 3-9-3 0.. PaddyAspell 12
(Alan Berry) *s.i.s: sn t.o* **100/1**

2m 13.72s (1.82) **Going Correction** +0.275s/f (Good)
WFA 3 from 4yo+ 8lb **11** Ran SP% **119.5**
Speed ratings (Par 103): **103,102,101,92,92 90,89,85,64,51**
toteswingers 1&2 £1.40, 1&3 £3.20, 2&3 £3.40 CSF £4.33 TOTE £2.50: £1.10, £1.10, £3.40; EX 4.50.
Owner Nurlan Bizakov **Bred** Berend Van Dalfsen **Trained** Newmarket, Suffolk

FOCUS
Part two and more of the same with Newmarket-trained horses dominating the market and finishing one-two. A similar time to the first division and the first three were clear, with the winner rated 4lb off her Doncaster run.

5317 NORTHUMBRIAN WATER H'CAP 6f
5:15 (5:15) (Class 6) (0-65,65) 3-Y-O+ £1,617 (£481; £240; £120) Stalls Centre

Form RPR
0314 **1** **Meandmyshadow**[13] 4793 4-9-8 **64**................................ DaleSwift(3) 11 73
(Alan Brown) *trckd ldrs: rdn over 2f out: hdwy to ld 1f out: edgd lft: drvn out* **13/8**[1]

3204 **2** *1 ½* **Bartley**[9] 4957 3-9-2 **63**...(v[1]) JustinNewman(5) 4 67
(Bryan Smart) *cl up: led over 2f out to 1f out: kpt on same pce ins fnl f* **7/1**

0060 **3** 2 ½ **Mango Music**[16] 4717 9-9-9 **62** .... BarryMcHugh 6 58
(David Thompson) *hld up: effrt and rdn 2f out: kpt on fnl f: nt pce of first two* **12/1**

5400 **4** ½ **Maggie Mey (IRE)**[16] 4716 4-9-0 **53** ....[1] DuranFentiman 10 48
(Lawrence Mullaney) *t.k.h: led to over 2f out: sn rdn and edgd lft: rallied over 1f out: no imp ins fnl f* **7/2**[2]

5005 **5** 7 **Decadence**[16] 4711 4-8-8 **47** oh1 ow1 .... TomEaves 9 19
(Nigel Tinkler) *dwlt: hld up in tch: drvn over 2f out: wknd over 1f out* **11/1**

034 **6** 2 **Cataract**[20] 4593 3-8-4 **46** oh1 ....(v) JamesSullivan 8 12
(John Weymes) *prom tl rdn and wknd wl over 1f out* **22/1**

0640 **7** nse **La Salida**[14] 4771 3-8-8 **57** .... ShelleyTeasdale(7) 1 23
(David Barron) *dwlt: t.k.h and sn cl up on outside: shkn up and wknd over 1f out* **4/1**[3]

0-00 **8** nk **Cara's Delight (AUS)**[14] 4780 5-8-7 **46** oh1 .... AmyRyan 3 11
(Frederick Watson) *hld up in tch: struggling over 2f out: sn btn* **25/1**

1m 16.58s (1.98) **Going Correction** +0.275s/f (Good)
WFA 3 from 4yo+ 3lb **8** Ran SP% **117.0**
Speed ratings (Par 101): **97,95,91,91,81 79,78,78**
toteswingers 1&2 £3.10, 1&3 £4.50, 2&3 £8.40 CSF £14.35 TOTE £2.80: £1.30, £1.50, £3.90; EX 9.60.
Owner G Morrill **Bred** M J Dawson **Trained** Yedingham, N Yorks

FOCUS
A modest sprint handicap, the first four clear in the end. The winner is probably the best guide to the form.
Maggie Mey(IRE) Official explanation: jockey said filly hung left-handed
Cara's Delight(AUS) Official explanation: jockey said mare hung left-handed

5318 WATERAID H'CAP 5f
5:50 (5:50) (Class 5) (0-70,67) 3-Y-O **£2,264** (£673; £336; £168) **Stalls** Centre

Form RPR

061 **1** **Planetex (IRE)**[58] 3289 3-9-5 **65** .... MichaelO'Connell 9 81
(John Quinn) *prom: smooth hdwy to ld over 1f out: sn pushed along: hung rt ins fnl f: kpt on strly: eased cl home* **10/3**[1]

126 **2** 4 ½ **Lord Buffhead**[20] 4593 3-8-8 **57** .... DeclanCannon(3) 6 57
(Richard Guest) *plld hrd: chsd ldrs: rdn and effrt over 1f out: sn outpcd: rallied to chse (clr) wnr towards fin: no imp* **7/1**

1155 **3** ¾ **Tuibama (IRE)**[11] 4878 3-9-1 **64** ....(p) DaleSwift(3) 2 61
(Tracy Waggott) *t.k.h: led: hdd over 1f out: kpt on same pce fnl f: lost 2nd towards fin* **8/1**

4402 **4** 2 **Dartrix**[13] 4798 3-8-13 **59** ....(p) TomEaves 4 49
(Michael Dods) *in tch: effrt and rdn 2f out: outpcd fnl f* **7/2**[2]

3600 **5** nk **Sky Crossing**[13] 4798 3-9-7 **67** .... JamesSullivan 7 56
(James Given) *plld hrd: prom: rdn and outpcd over 2f out: kpt on fnl f: no imp* **5/1**[3]

2360 **6** ¾ **Untold Melody**[21] 4547 3-9-4 **64** ....(tp) AmyRyan 5 50
(Kevin Ryan) *chsd ldrs: n.m.r and stmbld sn after s: rdn and outpcd 2f out: n.d after* **7/2**[2]

5060 **7** 1 **First Fast Now (IRE)**[11] 4878 3-8-6 **52** .... BarryMcHugh 1 35
(Nigel Tinkler) *hld up in tch: effrt on outside 1/2-way: wknd over 1f out* **16/1**

1m 2.26s (1.16) **Going Correction** +0.05s/f (Good) **7** Ran SP% **113.7**
Speed ratings (Par 100): **101,93,92,89,88 87,86**
CSF £26.31 CT £170.75 TOTE £5.10: £2.70, £2.80; EX 18.60.
Owner Ross Harmon **Bred** Mrs Diane Williams **Trained** Settrington, N Yorks
■ Stewards' Enquiry : Declan Cannon one-day ban: careless riding (Aug 31)

FOCUS
A modest 3yo sprint handicap but an unexposed winner who produced another step up.
Untold Melody Official explanation: jockey said filly suffered interference in running
T/Plt: £3.70 to a £1 stake. Pool: £60,790.65 - 11,823.26 winning tickets T/Qpdt: £1.70 to a £1 stake. Pool: £5,385.14 - 2,332.30 winning tickets RY

5267 NEWMARKET (R-H)
Friday, August 17
OFFICIAL GOING: Good to firm (8.5)
Wind: fresh, half behind Weather: dry

5319 FRAGS MEDIAN AUCTION MAIDEN STKS 7f
5:25 (5:26) (Class 5) 2-Y-O **£3,234** (£962; £481; £240) **Stalls** High

Form RPR

024 **1** **Ajmany (IRE)**[20] 4612 2-9-3 81 .... KierenFallon 5 81
(Luca Cumani) *led tl over 5f out: chsd ldr after: rdn 3f out: drvn to ld over 1f out: idling in front and drvn out fnl f* **15/8**[1]

0 **2** 1 ¾ **World Record (IRE)**[17] 4688 2-9-3 0 .... SeanLevey 16 76
(Richard Hannon) *hld up in tch: rdn and hdwy on far rail over 2f out: chsd wnr jst over 1f out: kpt on u.p but a hld* **5/1**[2]

6 **3** 2 ½ **Magical Rose (IRE)**[52] 3473 2-8-12 0 .... SebSanders 15 65
(Paul D'Arcy) *in tch towards rr: rdn and hdwy 2f out: swtchd rt over 1f out: styd on to go 3rd nr fin: no threat to ldng pair* **11/1**

0 **4** ½ **Forceful Flame**[18] 4658 2-9-3 0 .... AndreaAtzeni 4 69
(Robert Eddery) *t.k.h: chsd ldr tl led over 5f out: rdn and hdd over 1f out: wknd ins fnl f: lost 3rd nr fin* **50/1**

25 **5** ½ **French Press (IRE)**[27] 4327 2-9-3 0 .... RichardMullen 13 67
(David Brown) *stdd and awkward leaving stalls: t.k.h and sn chsng ldrs: rdn 2f out: outpcd ent fnl f: styd on same pce after* **14/1**

53 **6** nk **Typhon (USA)**[45] 3733 2-9-3 0 .... TedDurcan 11 67
(David Lanigan) *chsd ldrs: rdn ent fnl 2f: sme hdwy u.p over 1f out: styd on same pce fnl f* **16/1**

7 2 ½ **Carlarajah** 2-9-3 0 .... JamesDoyle 12 60
(Michael Bell) *in tch in midfield: rdn and unable qck 2f out: outpcd and btn over 1f out: wknd ins fnl f* **9/1**[3]

8 2 ¾ **Mouth Piece** 2-9-3 0 .... FrannyNorton 14 53
(Sir Michael Stoute) *in tch in midfield: rdn 4f out: sn struggling: plugged on but no threat to ldrs fnl f* **12/1**

0 **9** 5 **Intrigo**[20] 4604 2-9-3 0 .... PatDobbs 2 40
(Richard Hannon) *chsd ldrs: rdn 2f out: struggling and pushed rt over 1f out: sn wknd* **33/1**

10 2 ¾ **Depict** 2-9-3 0 .... MichaelHills 3 33
(Charles Hills) *awkward leaving stalls and slowly away: bhd: clsd and in tch 1/2-way: wknd 2f out* **16/1**

11 2 ¾ **Star Of Broadway** 2-9-3 0 .... FrankieDettori 9 26
(Mahmood Al Zarooni) *stdd s: hld up in rr: rdn and wknd over 2f out* **5/1**[2]

0 **12** 6 **Wild Diamond (IRE)**[9] 4946 2-8-12 0 .... ChrisCatlin 6 5
(Sir Mark Prescott Bt) *a in rr: lost tch 3f out* **50/1**

1m 26.82s (1.12) **Going Correction** +0.10s/f (Good) **12** Ran SP% **119.4**
Speed ratings (Par 94): **97,95,92,91,91 90,87,84,78,75 72,65**
toteswingers 1&2 £4.20, 1&3 £7.40, 2&3 £7.60 CSF £10.60 TOTE £2.70: £1.30, £1.90, £3.20; EX 15.10 Trifecta £191.10 Pool: £609.59 - 2.36 winning units.
Owner Sheikh Mohammed Obaid Al Maktoum **Bred** Rockfield Farm **Trained** Newmarket, Suffolk

FOCUS
Far Side track used with Stalls on Far Side except 10f: Centre. Repositioned bend into home straight increased distance of 1f races by about 15m. The forecast rain didn't arrive and 3mm of water was put on the track in the morning. There was a strong tail wind down the course and the going was good to firm. The leading form contender had to work quite hard but scored with something in hand in this maiden. The winner is rated to his pre-race form.

NOTEBOOK
Ajmany(IRE) set the standard on his best form, notably a close second behind subsequent wide-margin conditions winner Hasopop in a 6f Yarmouth maiden two runs back. He was niggled along in a prominent position some way out but he kept responding and justified favouritism with something to spare on his fourth start. Out of a well-related 1m4f winner, he should continue to improve as he goes up in trip and looks fairly treated off a current mark of 81. (op 2-1 tchd 9-4)
World Record(IRE) stayed on well on the far side and nearly gave the winner a scare on his second run. He is a Choisir half-brother to 1m2f Listed winner Dance Partner and prolific 7f-1m winner Kindlelight Debut and could take some stopping in a similar race next time. (op 13-2)
Magical Rose(IRE) didn't show much on her debut at Newbury but she stayed on steadily out wide in this promising second run. (op 10-1 tchd 12-1)
Forceful Flame was disappointing when a big market springer on his debut but this half-brother to numerous winners at 6f-1m showed ability under a prominent ride here. (op 40-1)
French Press(IRE) couldn't land a blow from off the pace. He has not built on his debut 33-1 second at Doncaster in two subsequent starts but he is a half-brother to Group 3 juvenile winner Percolator and could be interesting switched to nurseries. (tchd 16-1)
Typhon(USA) got tapped for speed before plugging on switched to turf for the first time. He doesn't look entirely straightforward but has had only three starts and will face more realistic assignments in nurseries.
Star Of Broadway, a 35,000gns colt who is out of a triple 1m3f/1m4f winner, attracted support but he ran green and was never involved before finishing out the back on his debut. (op 4-1 tchd 7-2)

5320 TALK NIGHT CLUB H'CAP (BETFAIR SPRINT FLAT SERIES QUALIFIER) 6f
5:55 (6:02) (Class 4) (0-85,85) 3-Y-O+ **£5,175** (£1,540; £769; £384) **Stalls** High

Form RPR

3123 **1** **Goldream**[28] 4291 3-9-7 **83** .... KierenFallon 8 93
(Luca Cumani) *in tch in midfield: rdn 2f out: drvn and hdwy ent fnl f: chsd ldr fnl 150yds: styd on u.p to ld nr fin* **9/2**[1]

6013 **2** shd **Last Sovereign**[17] 4680 8-9-1 **81** ....(b) JacobButterfield(7) 2 90
(Ollie Pears) *led: rdn over 1f out: kpt on wl tl hdd and no ex towards fin* **14/1**

0406 **3** 1 **Lujeanie**[42] 3822 6-9-5 **78** ....(p) TedDurcan 6 84
(Dean Ivory) *stdd s: t.k.h: hld up in midfield: rdn and hdwy over 1f out: drvn and kpt on ins fnl f* **10/1**

6000 **4** hd **Piscean (USA)**[13] 4799 7-9-5 **81** ....(b) RyanClark(3) 19 86
(Tom Keddy) *in tch in midfield: rdn and effrt over 1f out: kpt on u.p ins fnl f: nt rch ldrs* **22/1**

042 **5** shd **Paradise Spectre**[6] 5082 5-8-12 **71** ....(v) JamesDoyle 16 76
(Mrs K Burke) *awkward leaving stalls: t.k.h and sn chsng ldrs: rdn and unable qck over 1f out: styd on same pce ins fnl f* **9/2**[1]

1103 **6** hd **Valmina**[17] 4690 5-9-0 **78** ....(t) ConorHoban(5) 5 82
(Tony Carroll) *t.k.h: hld up in tch towards rr: hdwy u.p over 1f out: kpt on ins fnl f* **16/1**

543 **7** 1 ¾ **My Son Max**[13] 4824 4-9-8 **81** .... DarryllHolland 12 80
(P J O'Gorman) *stdd s: t.k.h: hld up in tch in rr: rdn and hdwy over 1f out: styd on same pce and no imp fnl f* **5/1**[2]

23 **8** 3 ¼ **My Kingdom (IRE)**[19] 4629 6-9-12 **85** ....(t) WilliamCarson 14 73
(Stuart Williams) *t.k.h: hld up in tch in midfield: rdn and unable qck 2f out: wknd 1f out* **8/1**

-0P0 **9** shd **Heyward Girl (IRE)**[14] 4765 3-9-2 **78** .... AndreaAtzeni 10 66
(Robert Eddery) *chsd ldr: rdn over 2f out: drvn and no ex over 1f out: wknd ins fnl f* **10/1**

1601 **10** 1 ¾ **Jungle Bay**[13] 4814 5-9-5 **78** ....(p) FrankieDettori 3 60
(Jane Chapple-Hyam) *chsd ldrs: rdn ent fnl 2f: unable qck over 1f out: btn ins fnl f: eased fnl 75yds* **11/2**[3]

4324 **11** ¾ **Fenella Fudge**[10] 4933 4-8-8 **67** ....(v) FrannyNorton 15 47
(Derek Shaw) *stdd s: plld hrd and hld up in tch in rr: rdn 2f out: no prog: n.d* **16/1**

0-00 **12** 7 **Dashwood**[14] 4772 5-8-11 **70** .... SaleemGolam 9 27
(Anthony Carson) *hld up in last pair: rdn and no hdwy 2f out: wknd over 1f out* **33/1**

1m 12.26s (-0.24) **Going Correction** +0.10s/f (Good)
WFA 3 from 4yo+ 3lb **12** Ran SP% **123.4**
Speed ratings (Par 105): **105,104,103,103,103 102,100,96,96,93 92,83**
toteswingers 1&2 £13.70, 1&3 £21.80, 2&3 £54.90 CSF £71.61 CT £616.33 TOTE £5.30: £2.30, £3.00, £4.40; EX 77.60 Trifecta £273.20 Part won. Pool: £369.28 - 0.06 winning units..
Owner Tsega Horses **Bred** Tsega Breeding Limited **Trained** Newmarket, Suffolk
■ Camache Queen was withdrawn (14/1, broke out of stalls). Deduct 5p in the £ under R4.

FOCUS
A fair sprint handicap, though it was weakened by a number of non-runners and Camache Queen was withdrawn after getting loose in the preliminaries. They went a fair pace and the favourite scored from some way back.
Jungle Bay Official explanation: jockey said gelding hung left

5321 STAR AMUSEMENTS, SOUTHEND E B F MAIDEN STKS 1m
6:25 (6:29) (Class 4) 2-Y-O **£4,528** (£1,347; £673; £336) **Stalls** High

Form RPR

0 **1** **Altruism (IRE)**[23] 4472 2-8-12 0 .... AntiocoMurgia(5) 7 83
(Mahmood Al Zarooni) *mde all: set stdy gallop tl stretched clr 5f out: stl clr and rdn over 1f out: kpt on: rdn out: unchal* **12/1**

2 1 ¾ **Tarikhi (USA)** 2-9-3 0 .... FrankieDettori 6 79+
(Saeed Bin Suroor) *chsd ldng pair: rdn ent fnl 2f: chsd clr wnr over 1f out: styd on ins fnl f: clsng towards fin but nvr gng to rch wnr* **9/4**[1]

3 3 ¼ **Squire Osbaldeston (IRE)** 2-9-3 0 .... TomQueally 8 72+
(Sir Henry Cecil) *hld up in last trio: rdn and hdwy 3f out: chsd ldng pair u.p ent fnl f: one pce and no imp after* **5/1**[3]

4 ¾ **Cat O'Mountain (USA)** 2-9-3 0 .... KierenFallon 4 70+
(Mahmood Al Zarooni) *rn green: towards rr and sn pushed along: rdn and hdwy 3f out: struggling and looked wkng over 1f out: edgd lft and rallied ins fnl f: kpt on and gng on steadily at fin* **11/2**

5 ½ **Ennistown** 2-9-3 0 JamesDoyle 1 69+
(Mahmood Al Zarooni) *wnt rt and stdd s: hld up in rr: swtchd rt and hdwy 3f out: no imp on wnr over 1f out tl kpt on ins fnl f* **12/1**

42 6 1 ¾ **Glory City (IRE)**[27] 4340 2-9-3 0 SebSanders 10 65
(Marco Botti) *chsd wnr: rdn and no imp ent fnl 2f: lost 2nd and btn over 1f out: wknd ins fnl f* **3/1**[2]

7 1 ¾ **East Texas Red (IRE)** 2-9-3 0 PatDobbs 11 61
(Richard Hannon) *in tch: rdn and unable qck over 2f out: no imp and btn over 1f out: wknd ent fnl f* **14/1**

06 8 2 ¼ **Sharjah (IRE)**[16] 4710 2-9-3 0 RichardMullen 3 55
(Noel Quinlan) *stdd s: grad moved across to far rail: hld up towards rr: rdn and struggling over 2f out: wknd u.p over 1f out* **18/1**

005 9 1 ½ **Royal Caper**[14] 4773 2-9-3 0 DaraghO'Donohoe 5 52
(John Ryan) *in tch in midfield: lost pl and rdn wl over 2f out: bhd ent fnl f* **66/1**

1m 40.41s (0.41) **Going Correction** +0.10s/f (Good) **9** Ran SP% **116.6**
Speed ratings (Par 96): **101,99,96,95,94 93,91,89,87**
toteswingers 1&2 £7.00, 1&3 £10.00, 2&3 £1.30 CSF £39.72 TOTE £16.30: £3.40, £1.50, £1.80; EX 43.70 TRIFECTA Not won..
Owner Godolphin **Bred** Kevin & Meta Cullen **Trained** Newmarket, Suffolk

FOCUS
This is usually a hot maiden. Subsequent Derby hero Motivator won this race in 2004, and in 2010 the mighty Frankel held off subsequent King George/ Eclipse winner Nathaniel with this year's Royal Ascot Gold Cup winner Colour Vision back in eleventh of 12. This looked a fair renewal but not many got involved in a steadily run race and a runner that looked the Godolphin fourth-string caused a surprise. The bare form is probably worth no more but several of these have improvement in them.

NOTEBOOK
Altruism(IRE) didn't show a great deal at Sandown on his debut and was sent off at 12-1 here but he set the pace and put in a strong galloping display to run his rivals into submission in a much-improved second run. A scopey Authorized colt who has a middle-distance pedigree and a six-figure price-tag, he still looked a bit inexperienced and has plenty of potential for further progress. (op 16-1)
Tarikhi(USA), a Derby-entered half-brother to Lincoln winner Expresso Star and two middle-distance winners, was sent off favourite on his debut and ran a promising race but couldn't to grips with the front-running winner. This was a decent start and he should improve for the experience. (op 2-1 tchd 5-2)
Squire Osbaldeston(IRE), a 100,000gns Mr Greeley colt out of a Group-placed 1m4f winning sister to Racing Post Trophy/St Leger winner Brian Boru, ran green before staying on steadily in an encouraging debut run. He should know a lot more next time and is a well-regarded type who holds entries in the Royal Lodge and Dewhurst. (op 4-1)
Cat O'Mountain(USA), a half-brother to Ribblesdale winner Michita and useful 1m2f-1m4f winner Willing Foe, looked in trouble when his move out wide seemed to dissolve but he rallied again and finished the race off well on his debut. (op 6-1 tchd 5-1)
Ennistown, a first foal of dual 6f/7f Group 1 winner/1,000 Guineas third Saoirse Abu, started slowly and looked inexperienced before making some late headway out wide. (op 14-1 tchd 11-1)
Glory City(IRE), a close second as favourite in a soft-ground 7f maiden here last time, set the standard but he didn't find much before fading switched to fast ground. (op 4-1)

5322 NOVAE BLOODSTOCK INSURANCE H'CAP 1m
7:00 (7:01) (Class 5) (0-75,75) 3-Y-O+ **£2,587** (£770; £384; £192) **Stalls** High

Form RPR

2101 1 **Speedi Mouse**[14] 4772 3-8-13 **73** NicoleNordblad(7) 13 82
(Philip McBride) *hld up in tch in rr: rdn and gd hdwy on far rail wl over 1f out: rdn to ld 1f out: styd on wl: rdn out* **9/2**[2]

040- 2 ¾ **Amelia May**[312] 6757 3-9-6 **73** DaraghO'Donohoe 8 80
(Ed Vaughan) *stdd s: hld up in tch: rdn 3f out: hdwy u.p to ld jst over 1f out: sn hdd: kpt on u.p fnl f but a hld* **28/1**

-605 3 1 ½ **Early Applause**[14] 4772 4-9-11 **72** MichaelHills 6 77
(Charles Hills) *in tch: rdn and effrt over 2f out: drvn and pressing ldrs ent fnl f: styd on same pce fnl f* **7/1**

6-04 4 nk **Buzz Law (IRE)**[28] 4295 4-9-8 **69** JamesDoyle 10 75+
(Mrs K Burke) *stdd s: hld up in rr: hdwy on bit over 1f out: chsng ldrs and effrt whn nt clr run ins fnl f: swtchd lft and kpt on same pce fnl 100yds* **6/1**[3]

6002 5 1 ¾ **McCool Bannanas**[21] 4541 4-9-3 **64** LiamJones 11 64
(James Unett) *hld up in tch: hdwy to chse ldrs gng wl 3f out: rdn and led over 1f out: sn hdd and unable qck: plugged on same pce fnl f* **7/1**

4350 6 ½ **Georgebernardshaw (IRE)**[16] 4716 7-8-11 **58** KellyHarrison 18 57
(Richard Guest) *stdd s: t.k.h and sn pressing ldrs: led 6f out: edgd rt u.p and hdd over 1f out: btn and styd on same pce fnl f* **18/1**

2105 7 nk **Hail Promenader (IRE)**[9] 4959 6-9-11 **72** (p) WilliamCarson 2 70
(Anthony Carson) *w ldrs: ev ch u.p over 1f out: unable qck 1f out: outpcd ins fnl f* **12/1**

0010 8 8 **Mazovian (USA)**[25] 4401 4-8-5 **59** JacobButterfield(7) 12 39
(Michael Chapman) *in tch: rdn and struggling over 2f out: wknd over 1f out* **28/1**

540 9 ½ **Masters Blazing**[14] 4772 3-9-5 **72** BrettDoyle 1 50
(John Ryan) *hld up in rr: effrt and sme hdwy wl over 1f out: no prog and btn ent fnl f: wknd* **22/1**

0-63 10 1 ¾ **Buaiteoir (FR)**[38] 3947 6-9-9 **70** KierenFallon 3 45
(Amy Weaver) *hld up towards rr: effrt and sme hdwy whn nt clr run ent fnl f: no ch after and eased ins fnl f* **16/1**

203 11 nk **Jonnie Skull (IRE)**[3] 5214 6-8-12 **59** (vt) ChrisCatlin 9 33
(Phil McEntee) *t.k.h: chsd ldrs: rdn and struggling over 2f out: wknd over 1f out* **25/1**

3541 12 3 ¼ **Elkhart (IRE)**[20] 4600 3-9-6 **73** FrankieDettori 7 40
(Michael Wigham) *led for 2f: chsd ldr tl 2f out: sn lost pl u.p: bhd fnl f* **11/4**[1]

1m 40.03s (0.03) **Going Correction** +0.10s/f (Good)
WFA 3 from 4yo+ 6lb **12** Ran SP% **118.1**
Speed ratings (Par 103): **103,102,100,100,98 98,97,89,89,87 87,84**
toteswingers 1&2 £13.50, 1&3 £7.40, 2&3 £41.20 CSF £131.38 CT £881.07 TOTE £4.50: £1.50, £5.20, £1.90; EX 172.70 TRIFECTA Not won..
Owner P J McBride **Bred** Langham Hall Stud **Trained** Newmarket, Suffolk
■ Stewards' Enquiry : Daragh O'Donohoe one-day ban: careless riding (Aug 31)

FOCUS
There were stacks of non-runners in this handicap but it was still competitive and the winner completed a double. The form looks sound.

5323 NGK SPARK PLUGS H'CAP 1m 2f
7:35 (7:36) (Class 5) (0-70,70) 3-Y-O+ **£2,587** (£770; £384; £192) **Stalls** Centre

Form RPR

006 1 **Semeen**[25] 4410 3-9-1 **65** KierenFallon 20 74+
(Luca Cumani) *in tch: rdn over 2f out: hdwy to chse ldrs over 1f out: ev ch ins fnl f: led fnl 75yds: styd on wl* **13/2**[3]

0000 2 ¾ **Audacious**[10] 4915 4-9-9 **65** AndreaAtzeni 6 72
(Michael Quinn) *led: rdn and fnd ex wl over 1f out: hdd and no ex fnl 75yds* **40/1**

-061 3 1 **Calculated Risk**[29] 4250 3-9-2 **66** JamieMackay 8 71+
(Willie Musson) *hld up in tch in midfield: rdn and hdwy over 1f out: chsd ldrs ins fnl f: styd on same pce fnl 100yds* **9/2**[2]

6244 4 ½ **Hawaana (IRE)**[8] 4983 7-10-0 **70** NeilCallan 7 74+
(Gay Kelleway) *hld up in tch: hdwy to chse ldrs whn nt clr run and swtchd lft jst ins fnl f: nt clr run and swtchd bk rt: kpt on towards fin* **9/1**

5125 5 ½ **Eagle Nebula**[43] 3782 8-10-0 **70** SeanLevey 5 73
(Brett Johnson) *in tch in midfield: rdn and effrt over 2f out: hdwy u.p over 1f out: kpt on same pce ins fnl f* **20/1**

621 6 ½ **Laconicos (IRE)**[12] 4844 10-9-2 **63** 6ex (t) LauraPike(5) 11 65
(William Stone) *t.k.h: chsd ldrs: swtchd lft and rdn over 1f out: styd on same pce ins fnl f* **14/1**

5000 7 2 ¼ **Mcbirney (USA)**[14] 4772 5-9-7 **70** LouisSteward(7) 14 68
(Paul D'Arcy) *chsd ldr tl unable qck u.p over 1f out: wknd ins fnl f* **16/1**

56U4 8 hd **Inpursuitoffreedom**[25] 4407 5-8-13 **62** NicoleNordblad(7) 13 59
(Philip McBride) *stdd s: hld up in rr: swtchd sharply lft and hdwy 2f: chsd ldrs but hung lft over 1f out: wknd ins fnl f* **20/1**

2430 9 3 ½ **Count Ceprano (IRE)**[15] 4722 8-9-2 **65** SophieSilvester(7) 4 55
(Lydia Pearce) *hld up towards rr: swtchd lft wl over 2f out: rdn and effrt but n.m.r over 1f out: no prog and wl hld fnl f* **50/1**

0542 10 ½ **Spey Song (IRE)**[21] 4538 4-9-10 **66** (b) FrankieDettori 12 60
(James Bethell) *stdd s: hld up towards rr: hdwy and swtchd lft over 2f out: chsd ldrs and drvn 2f out: wknd ent fnl f: eased fnl 100yds* **4/1**[1]

5016 11 1 ¾ **Minstrel Lad**[13] 4817 4-8-10 **55** SimonPearce(3) 18 41
(Lydia Pearce) *in tch in midfield: rdn and no prog over 1f out: wknd 1f out* **8/1**

1305 12 1 ¼ **Monzino (USA)**[4] 5179 4-9-6 **62** (b) ChrisCatlin 2 45
(Michael Chapman) *t.k.h: hld up in rr: swtchd lft and sme hdwy u.p over 2f out: wknd over 1f out* **33/1**

0-54 13 2 ¾ **Saloon (USA)**[9] 4941 8-8-3 **52** (p) LewisWalsh(7) 15 30
(Jane Chapple-Hyam) *in tch in midfield: rdn over 3f out: no prog and sltly hmpd 2f out: sn wknd* **20/1**

0542 14 4 **Somemothersdohavem**[9] 4972 3-9-4 **68** (p) DaraghO'Donohoe 16 38
(John Ryan) *in tch in midfield: rdn and struggling over 2f out: wknd wl over 1f out* **14/1**

4662 15 1 ¾ **Darnathean**[52] 3475 3-9-3 **67** (e) FrannyNorton 3 33
(Paul D'Arcy) *t.k.h: hld up in midfield: shuffled bk towards rr 3f out: rdn and no rspnse over 2f out: bhd fnl f* **20/1**

2030 16 10 **Mafi (IRE)**[37] 3962 4-9-8 **69** (v1) JamieJones(5) 17 15
(Mark Hoad) *chsd ldrs tl lost pl u.p over 3f: wl bhd fnl f* **25/1**

2m 6.84s (1.34) **Going Correction** +0.10s/f (Good)
WFA 3 from 4yo+ 8lb **16** Ran SP% **122.1**
Speed ratings (Par 103): **98,97,96,96,95 95,93,93,90,90 88,87,85,82,81 73**
toteswingers 1&2 £78.00, 1&3 £15.80, 2&3 £60.90 CSF £254.85 CT £1304.35 TOTE £5.80: £1.70, £5.20, £1.90, £2.80; EX 260.60 TRIFECTA Not won..
Owner Sheikh Mohammed Obaid Al Maktoum **Bred** Darley **Trained** Newmarket, Suffolk

FOCUS
They went a fair pace and an unexposed 3yo scored on his handicap debut. The form looks sound enough.
Semeen Official explanation: trainer said, regarding apparent improvement in form, that having lost its action last time, this was a fair reflection of the colt's ability.

5324 CAKES BY MOI FILLIES' H'CAP 7f
8:05 (8:05) (Class 3) (0-95,94) 3-Y-O+ **£7,762** (£2,310; £1,154; £577) **Stalls** High

Form RPR

0122 1 **Alice's Dancer (IRE)**[15] 4723 3-8-8 **81** WilliamCarson 7 68+
(William Muir) *stdd s: t.k.h: hld up in tch in rr: swtchd rt and effrt 2f out: str run u.p ins fnl f to ld fnl 50yds* **8/1**

6331 2 ¾ **Elusive Flame**[13] 4819 3-9-0 **87** TedDurcan 6 72+
(David Elsworth) *led: rdn over 1f out: kpt on gamely u.p tl hdd and no ex fnl 50yds* **6/4**[1]

000 3 ½ **Trulee Scrumptious**[10] 4932 3-7-11 **75** oh30 (b1) RosieJessop(5) 10 59?
(Peter Charalambous) *chsd ldrs: rdn: unable qck over 1f out: kpt on again ins fnl f* **25/1**

0031 4 hd **Shesastar**[22] 4497 4-9-6 **88** FrankieDettori 5 73+
(David Barron) *hld up in tch in last pair: rdn and effrt 2f out: ev ch fnl f: no ex towards fin* **7/4**[2]

21 5 2 **Tahlia Ree (IRE)**[13] 4807 3-7-9 **75** IanBurns(7) 2 53+
(Michael Bell) *chsd ldr: rdn over 1f out: unable qck 1f out: styd on same pce and hld fnl f* **4/1**[3]

1m 27.45s (1.75) **Going Correction** +0.10s/f (Good)
WFA 3 from 4yo+ 5lb **5** Ran SP% **111.3**
Speed ratings (Par 104): **94,93,92,92,90**
CSF £20.85 TOTE £7.40: £2.10, £1.60; EX 16.70 TRIFECTA Part won. Pool: £404.42 - 0.49 winning units..
Owner Perspicacious Punters Racing Club **Bred** Rathasker Stud **Trained** Lambourn, Berks

FOCUS
Another race decimated by non-runners. The pace was steady but there was an exciting finish. The third was a long way out of the weights and is a big doubt, but the other four was seemed close to their mark.

NOTEBOOK
Alice's Dancer(IRE) travelled well in rear before finding a sustained burst out wide to snatch the prize on this step back up to 7f. She can start slowly and has seen quite a bit of action but she has form figures of 1221 in an improved spell since a hood has been applied. (op 6-1)
Elusive Flame put in a dominant display against the stands' rail over C&D 13 days earlier. She tried to repeat the trick off 6lb higher but was worn down in the closing stages. Her saddle seemed to slip forward. (op 13-8 tchd 7-4)
Trulee Scrumptious ran a huge race with blinkers applied from 30lb out of the weights, but she may have been flattered by her proximity in a steadily run race and this could ruin her handicap mark. (op 14-1)
Shesastar ran respectably off 4lb higher than her narrow win in a 0-90 handicap at Doncaster last time. Her battle with the handicapper looks finely balanced but she has shaped like worth another try at 1m recently and could find a bit extra at that trip. (op 2-1)
Tahlia Ree(IRE), a runaway winner of a 6f Hamilton maiden last time, lacked the street smarts of some of her rivals in this muddling event on her handicap debut and just third run. (tchd 7-2)
T/Jkpt: Not won. T/Plt: £107.60 to a £1 stake. Pool: £71298.96 - 483.39 winning tickets T/Qpdt: £24.00 to a £1 stake. Pool: £5281.04 - 162.8 winning tickets SP

5199 NOTTINGHAM (L-H)

Friday, August 17

OFFICIAL GOING: Good (good to firm in places) changing to good after race 2 (2:40)

Wind: Moderate against Weather: Grey cloud

5325 BRITISH STALLION STUDS SUPPORTING BRITISH RACING E B F MAIDEN STKS — 6f 15y

2:10 (2:11) (Class 5) 2-Y-O £3,234 (£962; £481; £240) Stalls High

Form RPR

2 **1** **Cour Valant**[20] 4612 2-9-3 0 .... NeilCallan 4 89+
(Noel Quinlan) *mde all: rdn clr appr fnl f: kpt on wl* **15/8**[1]

33 **2** 2 3/4 **Bravo Youmzain (IRE)**[20] 4604 2-9-3 0 .... AndreaAtzeni 7 80
(Marco Botti) *trckd ldrs: hdwy 2f out: rdn to chse wnr over 1f out: sn no imp* **9/2**[2]

30 **3** 4 **Hoarding (USA)**[13] 4803 2-9-3 0 .... RobertHavlin 13 68
(John Gosden) *trckd ldrs on outer: hdwy over 2f out: rdn to chse ldng pair over 1f out: kpt on same pce* **9/2**[2]

4 **4** 3/4 **Bartack (IRE)**[50] 3545 2-9-3 0 .... KierenFallon 12 66
(Luca Cumani) *chsd wnr: rdn along 2f out: wknd appr fnl f* **7/1**

5 1/2 **Double Your Money (IRE)** 2-9-3 0 .... FrannyNorton 9 64
(Mark Johnston) *in tch: hdwy to chse ldrs over 2f out: rdn wl over 1f out: kpt on same pce* **13/2**[3]

6 2 3/4 **Shore Step (IRE)** 2-9-3 0 .... SamHitchcott 6 56
(Mick Channon) *wnt lft s: chsd ldrs: rdn along over 2f out: grad wknd* **33/1**

7 3/4 **Smart Eighteen** 2-9-3 0 .... SebSanders 3 54+
(Paul D'Arcy) *towards rr: hdwy wl over 2f out: green and pushed along wl over 1f out: n.d* **14/1**

8 1 **Alfie's Rose** 2-9-3 0 .... LiamJones 5 51
(William Haggas) *dwlt and sltly hmpd s: green and in rr tl sme late hdwy* **20/1**

04 **9** 1/2 **Order Of Service**[35] 4069 2-9-3 0 .... RichardMullen 8 49
(David Brown) *a towards rr* **50/1**

0 **10** 6 **Artful Prince**[16] 4710 2-9-3 0 .... FrederikTylicki 11 31
(James Given) *chsd ldrs: rdn along bef 1/2-way: sn wknd* **100/1**

5 **11** 1/2 **Baltic Sea (IRE)**[8] 4990 2-8-12 0 .... CathyGannon 10 25
(David Evans) *a in rr* **66/1**

1m 14.1s (-0.80) **Going Correction** -0.275s/f (Firm) **11** Ran SP% **115.8**

Speed ratings (Par 94): **94,90,85,84,83 79,78,77,76,68 68**

toteswingers 1&2 £2.60, 1&3 £7.10, 2&3 £5.10 CSF £9.57 TOTE £3.30: £1.20, £1.60, £2.00; EX 11.30.

Owner David F O'Rourke **Bred** Plantation Stud **Trained** Newmarket, Suffolk

FOCUS

Two useful types drew clear in what was probably a decent maiden. The form could be rated a little higher.

NOTEBOOK

Cour Valant was undone by greenness on debut, but he'd clearly improved and always looked in control, winning with something to spare. He's not the biggest, but is clearly useful and it will be interesting to see what mark he's given with nurseries in mind. (tchd 7-4 and 2-1)

Bravo Youmzain(IRE) reportedly found the ground too firm when beaten at Salisbury and this was more like the level of form shown on debut. Clear of the remainder, he can win a maiden before going handicapping.

Hoarding(USA) was again readily held but should find an opening now qualified for nurseries. (op 5-1)

Bartack(IRE) ran to a similar level as on debut and doesn't look up to winning a maiden. He's needs one more run for a mark. (op 8-1)

Double Your Money(IRE), a half-brother to several winners, including the useful Bikini Babe (effective from 7f-1m2f), looked in need of the experience as well as a longer trip. He should improve enough to win a maiden. (op 11-2 tchd 7-1)

Shore Step(IRE), a half-brother to useful 6f performer Balty Boys, made a brief forward move and should improve for the experience.

Smart Eighteen, half-brother to a 1m-1m2f winner, showed promise despite running green. (tchd 16-1)

Alfie's Rose, whose dam is a half-sister to 5f-6f performer River Falcon, showed ability. (op 16-1)

5326 1STSECURITYSOLUTIONS.CO.UK FILLIES' H'CAP (BETFAIR SPRINT FLAT SERIES QUALIFIER) — 6f 15y

2:40 (2:46) (Class 4) (0-80,80) 3-Y-0+ £5,175 (£1,540; £769; £384) Stalls High

Form RPR

02-0 **1** **Jade**[13] 4829 4-9-5 **76** .... LeeTopliss(3) 6 86
(Ollie Pears) *prom: cl up 1/2-way: led over 2f out: rdn over 1f out: jnd and drvn ent fnl f: hld on gamely towards fin* **6/1**[3]

6140 **2** nk **Piddie's Power**[18] 4655 5-9-11 **79** .... SeanLevey 8 88
(Ed McMahon) *trckd ldrs: smooth hdwy over 2f out: rdn to chal over 1f out: drvn and ev ch ins fnl f: no ex nr line* **14/1**

2102 **3** 2 **Dancheur (IRE)**[22] 4497 3-9-7 **78** .... TomQueally 5 81+
(Mrs K Burke) *trckd ldrs: rdn along and outpcd 1/2-way: styd on u.p fr wl over 1f out* **9/4**[1]

0215 **4** 3/4 **Night Trade (IRE)**[7] 5035 5-9-3 **76** ....(p) DarrenEgan(5) 11 76
(Ronald Harris) *hld up: hdwy over 2f out: rdn to chse ldng pair over 1f out: kpt on same pce* **9/1**

3001 **5** 3 **Avonrose**[15] 4726 5-9-5 **73** ....(v) NeilCallan 4 64
(Derek Shaw) *cl up: led 1/2-way: sn hdd and rdn along: wknd over 1f out* **12/1**

3613 **6** 1 1/2 **My Own Way Home**[5] 5122 4-8-12 **66** .... MartinLane 9 52
(David Evans) *in tch: effrt to chse ldrs over 2f out: sn rdn and one pce* **14/1**

3321 **7** 3 3/4 **School Fees**[29] 4235 3-9-7 **78** .... FergusSweeney 12 52
(Henry Candy) *in tch on wd outside: rdn along wl over 2f out: sn btn* **5/1**[2]

-551 **8** 1 1/2 **Lollina Paulina**[70] 2894 3-9-6 **80** .... JulieBurke(3) 2 49
(Kevin Ryan) *cl up: disp ld 1/2-way: rdn along 2f out: sn drvn and wknd* **8/1**

00-1 **9** 3 **Elegant Muse**[18] 4653 4-8-4 **61** .... DominicFox(3) 1 20
(Michael Appleby) *awkward s: sn cl up on outer: rdn along wl over 2f out and sn wknd* **22/1**

5402 **10** 15 **Yurituni**[7] 5035 5-9-7 **75** ....(b) CathyGannon 3
(Eve Johnson Houghton) *led: rdn along and hdd 1/2-way: sn wknd* **12/1**

1m 15.1s (0.20) **Going Correction** 0.0s/f (Good)

WFA 3 from 4yo+ 3lb **10** Ran SP% **115.9**

Speed ratings (Par 102): **98,97,94,93,89 87,82,80,76,56**

toteswingers 1&2 £20.50, 1&3 £5.40, 2&3 £14.10 CSF £85.58 CT £244.91 TOTE £4.30: £2.90, £3.90, £1.10; EX 111.80.

Owner L C Sigsworth **Bred** Brook Stud Bloodstock Ltd **Trained** Norton, N Yorks

■ Stewards' Enquiry : Sean Levey two-day ban: used whip above permitted level (Aug 31-Sep 1)

FOCUS

No hanging around in this and the front pair had it to themselves from over 1f out. Ordinary fillies' form, the winner rated back to her best.

Jade Official explanation: trainer's rep said, regarding apparent improvement in form, that the filly had improved for its first run previously following a long break.

5327 1STSECURITYSOLUTIONS.CO.UK H'CAP — 5f 13y

3:15 (3:16) (Class 6) (0-60,60) 3-Y-0+ £1,617 (£481; £240; £120) Stalls High

Form RPR

1602 **1** **Aubrietia**[9] 4937 3-8-1 **49** ....(b) DavidBergin(7) 2 61
(Alan McCabe) *mde most: rdn and hung rt ent fnl f: kpt on* **7/1**[3]

224 **2** 1 1/4 **Arch Walker (IRE)**[9] 4969 5-9-1 **59** ....(b) DarrenEgan(5) 5 67
(John Weymes) *hmpd s: sn trcking prom: hdwy to chse wnr over 1f out: sn rdn and kpt on same pce* **5/2**[1]

0456 **3** 2 1/4 **Duke Of Rainford**[10] 4911 5-8-8 **47** .... SamHitchcott 12 46+
(Michael Herrington) *dwlt and in rr: rdn and hdwy 2f out: styd on strly appr fnl f: nrst fin* **16/1**

6010 **4** nk **Speedyfix**[7] 5047 5-9-4 **57** ....(t) JimmyQuinn 7 55
(Christine Dunnett) *hmpd s: in tch: hdwy to chse ldrs 2f out: sn rdn and kpt on same pce fnl f* **25/1**

123 **5** 2 1/4 **Irish Girls Spirit (IRE)**[6] 5087 3-8-13 **54** .... RussKennemore 3 44
(Paul Midgley) *cl up: effrt 2f out: sn rdn and hld whn sltly hmpd ent fnl f: sn wknd* **5/2**[1]

0132 **6** hd **Ladydolly**[127] 1343 4-9-0 **56** ....(p) RaulDaSilva(3) 13 46
(Roy Brotherton) *chsd ldrs: rdn along 2f out: sn no imp* **8/1**

6-00 **7** 1 1/2 **Adventure Story**[13] 4793 5-9-0 **60** .... WilliamTwiston-Davies(7) 11 44
(Tony Carroll) *a towards rr* **11/2**[2]

0 **8** 2 **Canadian Danehill (IRE)**[43] 3791 10-9-2 **55** ....(p) NeilCallan 8 32
(Robert Cowell) *racd nr stands' rail: prom: rdn along 1/2-way: sn wknd* **22/1**

0005 **9** 3/4 **Itum**[8] 5017 5-8-4 **46** ....(p) DominicFox(3) 4 20
(Christine Dunnett) *wnt rt s: in tch: rdn along 1/2-way: sn wknd* **33/1**

0050 **10** 1/2 **Rupeetoups**[10] 4902 4-8-7 **46** oh1 .... FergusSweeney 10 18
(Henry Candy) *a in rr* **33/1**

1m 0.79s (-0.21) **Going Correction** 0.0s/f (Good)

WFA 3 from 4yo+ 2lb **10** Ran SP% **116.1**

Speed ratings (Par 101): **101,99,95,94,91 91,88,85,84,83**

CSF £23.75 CT £274.53 TOTE £9.00: £3.00, £1.40, £5.00; EX 30.50.

Owner Mrs M J McCabe **Bred** C J Murfitt **Trained** Averham Park, Notts

FOCUS

A low-grade sprint handicap. The form has been taken at face value.

Irish Girls Spirit(IRE) Official explanation: jockey said filly ran flat

Ladydolly Official explanation: trainer said filly was unsuited by the good ground

5328 COCO DOLLY AND GLADSTONIAN FILLIES' H'CAP — 1m 2f 50y

3:50 (3:51) (Class 4) (0-85,84) 3-Y-O £4,075 (£1,212; £606; £303) Stalls Low

Form RPR

1 **1** **Surprise Moment (IRE)**[25] 4410 3-9-6 **83** .... FrederikTylicki 6 93+
(Saeed Bin Suroor) *dwlt and towards rr: hdwy on wd outside 3f out: rdn to chse ldrs wl over 1f out: drvn and styd on wl fnl f to ld nr fin* **15/8**[1]

3521 **2** 1/2 **Sound Hearts (USA)**[8] 4984 3-9-2 **82** 6ex .... DominicFox(3) 9 89
(Roger Varian) *trckd ldr: hdwy 3f out: led over 2f out: rdn wl over 1f out: drvn and edgd rt ins fnl f: hdd and no ex nr fin* **11/2**[2]

320 **3** 1 **Red Hand (USA)**[103] 1887 3-9-0 **77** .... RobertHavlin 1 82
(John Gosden) *hld up towards rr: hdwy wl over 2f out: rdn to chse ldrs over 1f out: kpt on fnl f* **28/1**

3210 **4** 1 1/2 **Princess Caetani (IRE)**[16] 4702 3-9-0 **80** .... AdamBeschizza(3) 4 82
(David Simcock) *hld up in rr: effrt 3f out and sn pushed along: rdn 2f out: kpt on fnl f: nrst fin* **7/1**

5031 **5** 1 **Candycakes (IRE)**[21] 4538 3-8-10 **78** .... DarrenEgan(5) 5 78
(Michael Bell) *led: rdn along over 3f out: hdd over 2f out: sn drvn and grad wknd* **9/1**

06 **6** nk **Silver Sycamore (USA)**[28] 4287 3-9-6 **83** .... TadhgO'Shea 7 82
(David Lanigan) *trckd ldng pair: hdwy 3f out: rdn 2f out: drvn and one pce appr fnl f* **14/1**

0014 **7** 1 1/4 **Popular**[20] 4608 3-9-4 **81** .... TomQueally 8 78
(Sir Henry Cecil) *chsd ldrs: hdwy 3f out: rdn 2f out: grad wknd* **13/2**[3]

6341 **8** 17 **No Compromise**[16] 4706 3-8-9 **79** ow1 .... WilliamTwiston-Davies(7) 3 44
(Hughie Morrison) *a in rr* **13/2**[3]

-350 **9** 12 **Lacily (USA)**[59] 3252 3-9-7 **84** .... NeilCallan 10 26
(Mahmood Al Zarooni) *hld up in rr: sme hdwy on outer 3f out: sn rdn and btn* **20/1**

2m 12.69s (0.99) **Going Correction** +0.05s/f (Good) **9** Ran SP% **114.2**

Speed ratings (Par 99): **98,97,96,95,94 94,93,79,70**

toteswingers 1&2 £4.50, 1&3 £18.50, 2&3 £11.70 CSF £11.94 CT £211.21 TOTE £3.10: £1.30, £2.20, £3.50; EX 12.40.

Owner Godolphin **Bred** Darley **Trained** Newmarket, Suffolk

FOCUS

A good, competitive fillies' handicap that was run at a steady pace early before increasing markedly towards the end of the back straight. This rating could still underplay the unexposed winner.

5329 DOUBLE M CATERING CHALLENGE MAIDEN STKS — 1m 75y

4:20 (4:21) (Class 5) 3-Y-O £2,264 (£673; £336; £168) Stalls Centre

Form RPR

24 **1** **Estebsaal (IRE)**[22] 4516 3-9-3 0 .... TadhgO'Shea 2 87+
(John Dunlop) *prom: trckd ldr 1/2-way: cl up 3f out: sn led: rdn wl over 1f out: clr ent fnl f: kpt on strly* **3/1**[1]

-046 **2** 7 **Almaas (USA)**[21] 4548 3-9-3 76 ....(t) RobertHavlin 11 70
(Saeed Bin Suroor) *hld up: hdwy on outer 3f out: rdn to chse ldrs 2f out: drvn and kpt on fnl f: no ch w wnr* **5/1**[3]

3 3/4 **Roger Ramjet (IRE)** 3-9-3 0 ....(t) SamHitchcott 8 69
(Brian Meehan) *chsd ldrs: hdwy 3f out: rdn 2f out: drvn and kpt on same pce fnl f* **14/1**

03 **4** nk **Positively**[45] 3735 3-8-12 0 .... NeilCallan 12 63
(Sir Michael Stoute) *hld up in tch: hdwy to trck ldrs 1/2-way: rdn along wl over 2f out: drvn wl over 1f out and sn one pce* **3/1**[1]

5 2 1/4 **Shawka** 3-8-12 0 .... MatthewChadwick 7 58
(Charles Hills) *led: jnd and rdn 3f out: sn hdd and grad wknd* **17/2**

6 1 3/4 **Mohair** 3-8-12 0 ....[1] CathyGannon 10 54+
(James Fanshawe) *stdd s and hld up in rr: sme hdwy wl over 2f out: sn rdn and nvr nr ldrs* **18/1**

0 **7** 3 1/2 **Siena Street**[20] 4582 3-8-12 0 .... FergusSweeney 1 46
(Henry Candy) *chsd ldrs: rdn along 3f out: sn wknd* **50/1**

6 **8** 2 1/2 **Leonards Pride (IRE)**[11] 4874 3-9-3 0 .... StephenCraine 3 42
(Daniel Mark Loughnane) *dwlt: a towards rr* **50/1**

00 **9** *1 ¼* **Al Qatari (USA)**[56] 3349 3-9-0 0..........................(b[1]) AdamBeschizza(3) 9 39
(William Haggas) *a in rr* **20/1**

0 **D** *1 ¼* **Italian Lady (USA)**[13] 4791 3-8-12 0.................................. MartinLane 6 43
(Alan Jarvis) *chsd ldrs: rdn along 3f out: sn wknd* **7/2**[2]

1m 50.14s (4.54) **Going Correction** +0.05s/f (Good) **10** Ran SP% **120.0**
Speed ratings (Par 100): **79,72,71,70,68 66,63,59,58,62**
toteswingers 1&2 £6.00, 1&3 £7.70, 2&3 £9.00 CSF £18.74 TOTE £4.60: £4.60, £1.02, £5.60; EX 19.40.
Owner Hamdan Al Maktoum **Bred** Shadwell Estate Company Limited **Trained** Arundel, W Sussex

FOCUS
Little depth to this maiden, with the runner-up perhaps not worth his rating, and the time was slow, but the winner impressed and the form has been rated at face value.

5330 NOTTINGHAM RACECOURSE BLACK & WHITE CHRISTMAS PARTY H'CAP 1m 6f 15y
4:55 (4:55) (Class 6) (0-60,60) 3-Y-O £1,617 (£481; £240; £120) Stalls Low

Form RPR

4104 **1** **Foster's Road**[22] 4511 3-9-7 **60**.. SamHitchcott 9 71
(Mick Channon) *hld up towards rr: stdy hdwy 5f out: chsd ldrs wl over 2f out: swtchd rt and rdn to ld 1 1/2f out: styd on strly* **8/1**

6054 **2** *3 ¾* **Astonished Harry (GER)**[15] 4744 3-8-11 **50**............ RussKennemore 2 56+
(Reg Hollinshead) *t.k.h: a.p: hdwy to ld wl over 2f out: rdn and hdd 1 1/2f out: sn drvn and kpt on same pce* **4/1**[2]

606 **3** *7* **Seagoing**[19] 4622 3-9-7 **60**.. TadhgO'Shea 5 56
(Tim Easterby) *in rr: rdn along 6f out: hdwy 3f out: styd on appr fnl f: tk modest 3rd nr line* **14/1**

3431 **4** *hd* **Dr Irv**[6] 5115 3-8-12 **58** 6ex.. DavidBergin(7) 12 54
(Kate Walton) *trckd ldrs: hdwy over 3f out: rdn along over 2f out: drvn and one pce fr wl over 1f out: lost modest 3rd nr line* **13/8**[1]

0050 **5** *3* **Omega Omega**[15] 4744 3-8-6 **48**.................................. AdamBeschizza(3) 4 39
(Julia Feilden) *midfield: sme hdwy over 3f out: sn rdn along and nvr a factor* **33/1**

-500 **6** *1 ¾* **Istan Star (USA)**[32] 4153 3-8-7 **46** oh1........................(v[1]) CathyGannon 1 35
(Julie Camacho) *led 5f: prom: rdn along wl over 4f out: drvn over 3f out and sn wknd* **25/1**

003 **7** *6* **Joyful Motive**[54] 3420 3-8-10 **52**...................................... DominicFox(3) 3 33
(Tom Tate) *chsd ldrs: rdn along and hdwy to chse ldr 6f out: drvn 4f out: sn wknd* **16/1**

4205 **8** *1 ½* **Rosie's Lady (IRE)**[14] 4781 3-9-0 **53**................................. DavidNolan 6 32
(David O'Meara) *chsd ldrs: led after 6f: rdn along over 3f out: sn hdd and drvn: wknd fnl 2f* **6/1**[3]

-060 **9** *28* **Hunting Gonk**[45] 3729 3-9-1 **54**.. FrederikTylicki 8
(James Given) *a towards rr: bhd fnl 4f* **16/1**

0-00 **10** *49* **Royal Gig**[13] 4791 3-8-2 **46** oh1... DarrenEgan(5) 11
(Tim Etherington) *a in rr: bhd fnl 4f* **80/1**

0050 **S** **Red Mystique (IRE)**[15] 4744 3-8-11 **50**........................(b[1]) JackMitchell 7
(Ed Dunlop) *hld up towards rr: hdwy and in tch 6f out: chsd ldrs whn slipped up over 4f out* **14/1**

3m 7.4s (1.10) **Going Correction** +0.05s/f (Good) **11** Ran SP% **116.6**
Speed ratings (Par 98): **98,95,91,91,90 89,85,84,68,40**
toteswingers 1&2 £3.90, 1&3 £7.80, 2&3 £7.80 CSF £39.17 CT £446.97 TOTE £6.70: £2.70, £1.10, £4.30; EX 37.70.
Owner Dave and Gill Hedley **Bred** G Hedley & Mike Channon Bloodstock Limited **Trained** West Ilsley, Berks

FOCUS
Plenty of pace on and the race set up for the closers. Modest form, the winner rated back to his 2yo best.
T/Plt: £39.50 to a £1 stake. Pool: £55,648.20 - 1,028.060 winning tickets T/Qpdt: £9.50 to a £1 stake. Pool: £3,238.77 - 249.72 winning tickets JR

4836 CHESTER (L-H)
Saturday, August 18

OFFICIAL GOING: Good (good to firm in places) changing to good after race 2 (2.25)
Wind: Light, across Weather: Cloudy

5331 SHARE IN THE SUCCESS AT MANORHOUSESTABLES.COM MAIDEN AUCTION STKS 7f 2y
1:50 (1:50) (Class 4) 2-Y-O £5,175 (£1,540; £769; £384) Stalls Low

Form RPR

04 **1** **Mandeville (IRE)**[22] 4555 2-8-8 0... SeanLevey 3 74
(Richard Hannon) *chsd ldr: pushed along 3f out: led 2f out: r.o wl to draw clr fnl 100yds* **2/1**[1]

2 *5* **White Coppice** 2-9-1 0.. BarryMcHugh 6 68+
(Richard Fahey) *s.i.s: in rr: pushed along and hdwy 3f out: styd on to take 2nd ins fnl f: nt trble wnr: should improve* **11/2**[3]

3 *2* **Uncle Bernie (IRE)** 2-8-7 0... PaulPickard(3) 7 58
(Reg Hollinshead) *midfield: hdwy on outer 2f out: chsd ldrs over 1f out: kpt on same pce ins fnl f* **16/1**

0 **4** *½* **Moorway (IRE)**[13] 4837 2-8-12 0................................... StevieDonohoe 9 59+
(Reg Hollinshead) *in rr: struggling to go pce 3f out: styd on and wanted to lugg lft ins fnl f: nvr nrr* **25/1**

4000 **5** *2 ¼* **Only For You**[9] 5010 2-8-4 32... FrannyNorton 1 45
(Alan Brown) *chsd ldrs: outpcd by front pair 2f out: one pce fnl f* **66/1**

032 **5** *dht* **Surround Sound**[21] 4587 2-8-9 71...................................... JoeFanning 2 50
(Tim Easterby) *racd keenly: led: hdd 2f out: unable to go w wnr over 1f out: wknd fnl 150yds* **9/4**[2]

0 **7** *1* **Inherited**[9] 5010 2-8-9 0... RosieJessop(5) 5 52
(Sir Mark Prescott Bt) *dwlt: hld up in rr: pushed along over 1f out: nvr able to trble ldrs* **16/1**

0 **8** *3 ¾* **Mirlo Blanco (IRE)**[22] 4555 2-9-1 0.............................. PatrickMathers 4 44
(Richard Fahey) *chsd ldrs tl rdn and wknd 2f out* **20/1**

4 **9** *9* **Ella Motiva (IRE)**[22] 4546 2-8-11 0 ow1.......................... TomMcLaughlin 8 16
(Mark Brisbourne) *racd 3 wd: chsd ldrs: hung rt 5f out: sn lost pl: struggling over 2f out: bhd fnl f* **11/2**[3]

1m 28.32s (1.82) **Going Correction** -0.075s/f (Good) **9** Ran SP% **116.7**
Speed ratings (Par 96): **86,80,78,77,74 74,73,69,59**
Tote Swingers: 1&2 £3.60, 1&3 £6.40, 2&3 £15.40 CSF £13.48 TOTE £2.50: £1.40, £1.30, £3.70; EX 14.10.
Owner Andrew Tinkler **Bred** Noel O'Callaghan **Trained** East Everleigh, Wilts

FOCUS
Rail at innermost position and all distances as advertised. This didn't look the strongest of Chester maidens with the 32-rated Only For You finishing uncomfortably close, but the winner did it nicely. The time also limits the form.

NOTEBOOK
Mandeville(IRE) improved from her debut to dead-heat for fourth at York on her second start and that form was franked by the subsequent success of the runner-up. Although always handy, she was having to be shoved along at halfway but to her credit she responded and once getting the better of the leader inside the last 2f, the prize was hers. With her market rival running poorly, the form may not add up to much but she should still have a future in nurseries. (op 11-4 tchd 3-1 in a place)
White Coppice, a 30,000gns colt out of a sister to a French Group 3 winner, looked badly in need of the experience as he missed the break and was needing to be niggled along throughout, but he showed definite signs of promise as the race developed and stayed on for a clear second. He should build on this, especially on a more conventional track. (op 5-1)
Uncle Bernie(IRE) also showed ability by keeping on to the line and this 6,000GBP 2yo, who is a brother to a 1m4f winner and half-brother to four other winners at up to the same trip, will surely come into his own when presented with a stiffer test. (tchd 14-1)
Moorway(IRE) stayed on in the latter stages having been well behind early and this was an improvement on his debut effort, but he will need to progress again in order to win races. He looks one for handicaps later on. (op 22-1)
Surround Sound had improved in each of his first three starts and his mark of 71 provided the benchmark, but having set the pace he was all too easily picked off by the winner off the home bend and this was bitterly disappointing. His rider reported that the colt hung left handed. Official explanation: jockey said colt hung left-handed (op 5-2)

5332 ROUGE RECRUITMENT NURSERY 5f 16y
2:25 (2:25) (Class 3) (0-95,93) 2-Y-O £7,762 (£2,310; £1,154; £577) Stalls Low

Form RPR

1003 **1** **Mandy Layla (IRE)**[7] 5088 2-8-3 **75**................................. FrannyNorton 6 81
(Bryan Smart) *displayed gd pce s: mde all: rdn over 1f out: r.o wl* **11/2**

6542 **2** *1 ¾* **Bispham Green**[21] 4614 2-8-0 **72**................................... PatrickMathers 3 72
(Richard Fahey) *chsd wnr: rdn over 2f out: nt qckn over 1f out: no imp ins fnl f* **5/1**

2126 **3** *1 ¾* **Forray**[36] 4071 2-8-9 **81**... RichardMullen 5 75
(Ed McMahon) *hld up: pushed along 2f out: sn outpcd: styd on for press towards fin: nt quite pce to get to ldrs* **9/2**[3]

4012 **4** *½* **Hot Secret**[10] 4936 2-7-13 **74**.. SimonPearce(3) 2 66
(Andrew Balding) *chsd ldrs: pushed along 2f out: nt qckn over 1f out: lost 3rd pl towards fin* **5/1**

1502 **5** *hd* **Storm Moon (USA)**[14] 4827 2-9-7 **93**................................ JoeFanning 7 84
(Mark Johnston) *sweating: hld up: pushed along over 1f out: styd on ins fnl f: nvr able to rch ldrs* **4/1**[2]

313 **6** *7* **Uncomplicated**[24] 4471 2-8-5 **77**... SeanLevey 1 43
(Jim Boyle) *chsd ldrs: pushed along over 2f out: rdn and wknd over 1f out* **7/2**[1]

1040 **7** *1 ¼* **Dream Vale (IRE)**[14] 4820 2-8-3 **75**.................................... AmyRyan 4 36
(Tim Easterby) *sn outpcd and wl bhd: nvr on terms* **10/1**

1m 0.83s (-0.17) **Going Correction** -0.075s/f (Good) **7** Ran SP% **118.2**
Speed ratings (Par 98): **98,95,92,91,91 80,78**
Tote Swingers: 1&2 £5.40, 1&3 £7.70, 2&3 £4.70 CSF £34.34 TOTE £9.30: £3.30, £3.20; EX 49.00.
Owner Dr Marwan Koukash **Bred** Mrs E J O'Grady **Trained** Hambleton, N Yorks

FOCUS
A tight nursery according to the market, but this race was almost decided at the stalls as the front pair held those positions throughout. The form makes sense.

NOTEBOOK
Mandy Layla(IRE) possesses plenty of speed and, despite being drawn towards the outside of the field, she pinged the gates, got across to the rail and was soon bowling along in front. Keeping on for pressure, she never looked like being caught and will continue to be a potent rival when able to dominate on a quick surface. (tchd 6-1)
Bispham Green was the only maiden in the field, but had improved plenty since switched to nurseries the last twice and tried hard to get on terms with the winner, having been her closest rival throughout. It's only a matter of time before he wins one of these. (tchd 9-2)
Forray was having his was his first try on ground faster than Good to soft. He seemed to fine everything happening too quickly for him, but deserves credit for doing best of those that tried to come from off the pace and a return to an easier surface and/or a stiffer track should help him. His rider reported that the colt hung right handed. Official explanation: jockey said colt hung right-handed (op 8-1)
Hot Secret had a good draw, but wasn't able to hold her position early and though soon in touch with the front pair, was forced to make her effort wider than ideal off the home bend. She may also want a bit more cut in the ground. (op 4-1 tchd 7-2)
Storm Moon(USA), who got himself into quite a lather, raced wide from the outside stall and didn't look to be handling the track rounding the home bend. He is worth another chance back on a straight track. (tchd 7-2)
Uncomplicated was withdrawn from the Listed contest at Newbury the previous day because of the ground (had raced mainly on soft ground before this) and she was in trouble at halfway. It may be best to forgive her this effort and she is worth another chance back on an easier surface. The trainer's representative reported that the filly was unsuited by the track. Official explanation: trainer's rep said filly was unsuited by the track (op 4-1)
Dream Vale(IRE) was taken off her feet from the start. Her rider reported that the filly was wrong behind. Official explanation: jockey said filly was wrong behind (tchd 12-1)

5333 GROSVENOR SHOPPING CENTRE H'CAP 1m 4f 66y
3:00 (3:00) (Class 2) (0-105,99) 3-Y-O+ £16,172 (£4,812; £2,405; £1,202) Stalls Low

Form RPR

3443 **1** **Communicator**[35] 4103 4-8-13 **84**..................................... RichardMullen 5 101
(Andrew Balding) *hld up: hdwy on bit 3f out: led jst over 2f out: r.o wl to draw clr over 1f out: in command after: eased cl home* **11/2**[3]

2240 **2** *9* **Local Hero (GER)**[28] 4103 5-9-2 **87**................................(p) JackMitchell 3 89
(Steve Gollings) *bustled along s: bhd: rdn to go pce over 2f out: swtchd rt over 1f out: styd on ins fnl f: tk 2nd towards fin: no ch w wnr* **11/2**[3]

021 **3** *¾* **Address Unknown**[7] 5076 5-10-0 **99**..........................(vt) FrannyNorton 7 100
(Ian Williams) *in tch: effrt over 2f out: wnt 2nd over 1f out: no ch w wnr: lost 2nd towards fin* **9/2**[2]

6050 **4** *4 ½* **Mica Mika (IRE)**[17] 4697 4-8-12 **83**............................(p) BarryMcHugh 2 77
(Richard Fahey) *chsd ldrs: rdn over 2f out: wknd over 1f out* **6/1**

0600 **5** *7* **Kiama Bay (IRE)**[35] 4111 6-9-7 **92**................................... StevieDonohoe 4 75
(John Quinn) *bustled along s: sn led: rdn and hdd jst over 2f out: wknd over 1f out* **9/2**[2]

1103 **6** *14* **Scatter Dice (IRE)**[7] 5078 3-8-12 **93**.................................. JoeFanning 8 53
(Mark Johnston) *led early: chsd ldr: rdn 5f out: lost pl 3f out: wknd 2f out: eased whn wl btn over 1f out* **2/1**[1]

2m 35.6s (-2.90) **Going Correction** 0.0s/f (Good)
WFA 3 from 4yo+ 10lb **6** Ran SP% **114.8**
Speed ratings (Par 109): **109,103,102,99,94 85**
Tote Swingers: 1&2 £3.20, 1&3 £5.00, 2&3 £4.50 CSF £35.51 CT £147.19 TOTE £11.60: £5.60, £1.40; EX 49.70.
Owner Lady Davis **Bred** Lady Davis **Trained** Kingsclere, Hants

FOCUS
A decent middle-distance handicap, but the leaders may have gone off too quick and set the race up for the closers. The impressive winner deserves credit and produced a clear best.

NOTEBOOK

Communicator had consistently been finding a couple to beat him since joining his current yard, but proved a revelation here, sitting off the strong pace early before sweeping around the outside to lead on the home bend and pulling right away from his toiling rivals. To an extent this race may have fallen into his lap and the handicapper will hit him hard, but it may be that his new connections have found the key to him. (op 5-1)

Local Hero(GER), back on the Flat after winning a Listed handicap hurdle at Market Rasen, was soon settled in last place and was caught on heels when the winner made his move starting the home turn, but his stamina eventually kicked in and he stayed on to finish a clear, if remote, second. This ground would have been quick enough for him. (tchd 5-1)

Address Unknown was 5lb higher than when winning the Shergar Cup Stayers' over 2m at Ascot last time and therefore appeared to have it do in order to reverse earlier form with Scatter Dice. However, he was another to benefit from being given a patient ride, though he was slightly caught in a pocket when the winner made his move turning in and he lacked the pace to go with him once in the clear. A return to further looks to be in order. (op 5-1)

Mica Mika(IRE) started off the season well, including a C&D success, but things have gone wrong lately and connections reached for the cheekpieces. He raced handily for a long way, but was easily shaken off and the headgear didn't seem to have much effect. (op 7-1)

Kiama Bay(IRE) hadn't hit his very best form in three previous starts this year, but adopted the role of pacemaker here, being hard ridden to lead early and staying there until swamped by the winner rounding the home bend. (op 5-1)

Scatter Dice(IRE) is already a four-time winner this season and looked to hold sound claims, but her rider was getting anxious a good 5f from home and she eventually stopped to nothing. Perhaps chasing the strong pace counted against her, but this was still very disappointing. The stewards noted that the trainer's representative could offer no explanation for the filly's performance and they ordered her to be routine tested. Official explanation: trainer's rep had no explanation for the poor form shown (op 9-4)

5334 FOZ ELECTRICAL H'CAP — 7f 122y

3:35 (3:35) (Class 2) (0-105,98) 3-Y-O **£32,345** (£9,625; £4,810; £2,405) **Stalls** Low

Form — RPR

4111 **1** **Stirring Ballad**[16] 4740 3-8-12 **89** .... FrannyNorton 1 104+
(Andrew Balding) *in tch: effrt 2f out: prog over 1f out: led ins fnl f: r.o wl and in command towards fin* **11/4**[1]

2131 **2** 1 ¾ **Trail Blaze (IRE)**[18] 4675 3-8-10 **87** .... AmyRyan 10 95
(Kevin Ryan) *led: rdn over 2f out: hdd ins fnl f: no ex towards fin* **8/1**

0500 **3** *shd* **Alejandro (IRE)**[16] 4740 3-8-10 **87** .... BarryMcHugh 4 94
(Richard Fahey) *a.p: rdn over 2f out: chalng fr over 1f out: nt qckn ins fnl f* **12/1**

3103 **4** 3 ¾ **Our Boy Jack (IRE)**[18] 4675 3-8-1 **85** ow1 .... LauraBarry(7) 11 83+
(Richard Fahey) *hld up: rdn and hdwy on inner over 1f out: styd on ins fnl f: no trble ldrs* **10/1**

1051 **5** 2 **Lady Macduff (IRE)**[8] 5043 3-8-9 **86** .... JoeFanning 3 79
(Mark Johnston) *stmbld sltly s: hld up: hdwy over 2f out: kpt on same pce fr over 1f out: no imp on ldrs* **7/2**[2]

5124 **6** *nk* **Shamaal Nibras (USA)**[16] 4740 3-9-4 **95** .... SeanLevey 5 87
(Richard Hannon) *hld up: rdn and hdwy 2f out: one pce fnl f* **9/2**[3]

0603 **7** 1 ¾ **Bible Black (IRE)**[58] 3322 3-9-7 **98** .... GaryCarroll 7 86
(G M Lyons, Ire) *prom: rdn 2f out: unable to go w ldrs over 1f out: wknd ins fnl f* **14/1**

5035 **8** 3 ¼ **Gatepost (IRE)**[21] 4598 3-9-5 **96** .... StevieDonohoe 6 76
(Richard Fahey) *chsd ldrs tl rdn over 2f out: sn wknd* **8/1**

4600 **9** 2 **Hadaj**[7] 5102 3-8-4 **84** .... RyanPowell(3) 9 59
(Clive Brittain) *in tch: pushed along and wknd over 2f out: sn bhd* **20/1**

1m 32.71s (-1.09) **Going Correction** 0.0s/f (Good) **9** Ran SP% **117.5**

Speed ratings (Par 106): **105,103,103,99,97 97,95,92,90**

Tote Swingers: 1&2 £7.20, 1&3 £7.10 CSF £26.01 CT £231.14 TOTE £4.50: £1.10, £2.90, £4.50; EX 21.00.

Owner George Strawbridge **Bred** George Strawbridge **Trained** Kingsclere, Hants

FOCUS

This was a hot contest, run at a true pace, and the winner completed a valuable handicap double on the card for the Andrew Balding stable. Not many were at their best but the form still looks sound.

NOTEBOOK

Stirring Ballad, who had two of these behind her when scoring at Goodwood last time, was 7lb higher in her bid for a four-timer, but she is a filly at the top of her game. She settled well enough in midfield early after threatening to take a hold, before moving up smoothly on the approach to the home turn. She then found plenty once switched out wide, quickening up nicely to lead inside the last and eventually winning with a bit in hand. Another hike in her mark awaits, but given her race of progression connections might consider a tilt for some black type with her. (op 9-4 tchd 2-1)

Trail Blaze(IRE) had never failed to place in nine starts since his racecourse debut, winning four. All those wins had come from the front and he was soon able to gain the early advantage from his wide draw again here. He ran his socks off and was just unlucky to come up against a most-progressive filly inside the last furlong. He is proving a credit to connections. (op 15-2)

Alejandro(IRE) ◆ had proved disappointing since an encouraging seasonal reappearance and finished a long way behind a couple of these at Goodwood last time, but this was much better. Always handy, he was presented with every chance when the runner-up hung off the inside rail starting up the straight, but didn't quite have the speed to make the most of it. He is much better handicapped now and is one to watch out for. (op 16-1 tchd 20-1)

Our Boy Jack(IRE), closely matched with Trail Blaze on last month's Ayr running, was up to a new career-high mark and, with the overweight, was 6lb higher than when winning over C&D three starts back. Dropped out from the outside stall, he stayed on late against the inside rail but never had a hope of getting on terms with the leading trio. (op 8-1)

Lady Macduff(IRE), raised 4lb for her recent Haydock success, could never get involved but was having only her sixth start and runners from her yard can never be written off. (op 9-2)

Shamaal Nibras(USA) finished fourth behind Stirring Ballad at Goodwood last time and was 7lb better off for a beating of just over 3l having been drawn much worse than his rival there, but he could make no impression once off the bridle and should have done better. (op 5-1)

Bible Black(IRE) was making his handicap debut having mainly contested Pattern events during the past year, but although in a good position early he was on the retreat well over a furlong from home. Perhaps this ground was quick enough. (op 12-1)

5335 BET AT SPORTSBOOK-UK.COM MAIDEN STKS — 7f 2y

4:05 (4:06) (Class 4) 3-Y-O+ **£5,175** (£1,540; £769; £384) **Stalls** Low

Form — RPR

1 **An Cat Dubh (IRE)**[37] 4021 3-9-3 0 .... FrannyNorton 10 81
(Ian Williams) *w ldr: kicked clr w rival over 2f out: led wl over 1f out: asserted fnl 150yds* **7/2**[2]

2333 **2** 3 ¼ **Shaleek**[25] 4420 3-8-12 73 ....(b) JackMitchell 1 67
(Roger Varian) *led: kicked clr w rival over 2f out: hdd wl over 1f out: no ex fnl 150yds* **6/4**[1]

3 5 **Zenafire** 3-9-0 0 .... PaulPickard(3) 3 59+
(Reg Hollinshead) *dwlt: hld up: nt clr run over 2f out: hdwy over 1f out: styd on to take 3rd wl ins fnl f: nt trble front two* **16/1**

63 **4** 3 ¼ **Mexican Mick**[37] 3990 3-9-3 0 .... StevieDonohoe 2 50
(Ian Williams) *pushed along early: midfield: u.p whn n.m.r and hmpd 3f out: outpcd over 2f out: plugged on at one pce fnl f: no imp* **4/1**[3]

3622 **5** *nse* **Sabore**[7] 5113 3-8-12 65 ....(p) BarryMcHugh 8 45
(Richard Fahey) *awkward s: midfield: hdwy 3f out: outpcd by front two over 2f out: no ex wl ins fnl f* **5/1**

02 **6** ½ **Lady Bentinck (IRE)**[14] 4807 3-8-5 0 .... KevinStott(7) 11 43
(Alan Berry) *hld up: effrt on wd outer over 2f out: one pce over 1f out: no imp* **66/1**

0 **7** 10 **Smirfys Emerald (IRE)**[29] 4293 4-9-8 0 .... RichardMullen 9 23
(Michael Mullineaux) *awkward s: pushed along in rr: wl outpcd over 2f out: nvr able to get on terms w ldrs* **66/1**

0-3 **8** ¾ **Pull The Pin (IRE)**[6] 5127 3-9-3 0 .... AmyRyan 6 19
(William Kinsey) *chsd ldrs tl rdn and wknd over 2f out* **12/1**

0/6 **9** *shd* **Heart Beat Song**[50] 3580 4-9-8 0 .... PatrickMathers 4 21
(Alan Berry) *midfield: hdwy to chse ldrs over 3f out: outpcd by front two over 2f out: wl btn ins fnl f* **66/1**

6-0 **10** 13 **House Of Mirrors (USA)**[208] 273 4-9-8 0 .... TomMcLaughlin 5
(Mark Brisbourne) *racd keenly: chsd ldrs tl rdn and wknd over 2f out* **20/1**

1m 27.39s (0.89) **Going Correction** 0.0s/f (Good)

WFA 3 from 4yo 5lb **10** Ran SP% **121.7**

Speed ratings (Par 105): **94,90,84,80,80 80,68,67,67,52**

Tote Swingers: 1&2 £2.50, 1&3 £10.00, 2&3 £15.60 CSF £9.44 TOTE £4.50: £1.90, £1.10, £4.70; EX 12.80.

Owner Paul Wildes **Bred** Kildare Racing Syndicate **Trained** Portway, Worcs

FOCUS

This was a pretty weak maiden, the front two were at the sharp end from the start and the pair had the race to themselves from a long way out. This is not form to take too seriously, but the winner deserves some credit.

5336 PERFECT CLAIMS MANAGEMENT CLASSIFIED CLAIMING STKS — 1m 2f 75y

4:40 (4:41) (Class 4) 3-Y-O **£5,175** (£1,540; £769; £384) **Stalls** High

Form — RPR

-445 **1** **Darling Lexi (IRE)**[18] 4676 3-8-4 60 .... FrannyNorton 1 67
(Richard Fahey) *a bit awkward gng to s: mde all: rdn 2f out: edgd rt ins fnl f: pressed: hld on wl cl home* **7/2**[2]

5152 **2** *nk* **Bountiful Girl**[3] 5227 3-8-8 72 .... BarryMcHugh 2 70
(Richard Fahey) *chsd ldrs: effrt to go 2nd 2f out: trying to chal whn sltly intimidated by wnr wl ins fnl f: styd on but a hld cl home* **1/2**[1]

6455 **3** 2 ½ **Manomine**[8] 5036 3-8-3 65 .... RyanPowell(3) 4 64
(Clive Brittain) *in rr: pushed along briefly wl over 7f out: shkn up 4f out: rdn to take 3rd over 1f out: no imp ins fnl f* **7/1**[3]

5030 **4** 14 **Berlusca (IRE)**[14] 4830 3-8-11 70 .... TomMcLaughlin 3 42
(Mark Brisbourne) *plld hrd: chsd wnr: rdn and ev ch 3f out: lost 2nd 2f out: wknd over 1f out: eased whn wl btn ins fnl f* **10/1**

2m 11.1s (-0.10) **Going Correction** 0.0s/f (Good) **4** Ran SP% **110.5**

Speed ratings (Par 102): **100,99,97,86**

CSF £5.95 TOTE £3.20; EX 7.30.Bountiful Girl claimed by Ms Julie French for £12,000.

Owner Dr Marwan Koukash **Bred** Georgestown Stud **Trained** Musley Bank, N Yorks

FOCUS

A moderate claimer which provided a 1-2 for trainer Richard Fahey, though not in the order most would have expected. The time was respectable.

5337 CRUISE NIGHTSPOT H'CAP — 6f 18y

5:15 (5:16) (Class 3) (0-90,90) 3-Y-O **£12,938** (£3,850; £1,924; £962) **Stalls** Low

Form — RPR

2452 **1** **Chooseday (IRE)**[12] 4881 3-8-11 **80** ....(p) AmyRyan 5 89
(Kevin Ryan) *chsd ldr: led over 1f out: r.o ins fnl f: in command fnl 100yds* **11/2**[3]

5-0 **2** 2 **Harry Trotter (IRE)**[15] 4765 3-8-13 **82** .... RichardMullen 2 85
(David Marnane, Ire) *chsd ldrs: rdn over 1f out: swtchd lft ins fnl f: styd on to take 2nd towards fin: no imp on wnr* **15/8**[1]

3U10 **3** *hd* **Beau Mistral (IRE)**[15] 4765 3-9-0 **83** .... JoeFanning 3 85
(Paul Green) *led: rdn and hdd over 1f out: edgd rt ins fnl f: no ex and lost 2nd towards fin* **15/2**

3211 **4** 1 ¾ **Economic Crisis (IRE)**[30] 4262 3-7-11 **71** oh4 .... NeilFarley(5) 7 67
(Alan Berry) *chsd ldrs: rdn over 2f out: one pce fr over 1f out* **20/1**

5316 **5** *shd* **Waseem Faris (IRE)**[15] 4765 3-9-1 **84** .... StevieDonohoe 6 80
(Mick Channon) *hld up: rdn over 1f out: kpt on ins fnl f: nvr able to chal* **13/2**

4024 **6** 1 ¾ **Kimbali (IRE)**[33] 4135 3-9-1 **84** .... FrannyNorton 1 74+
(Richard Fahey) *s.i.s: in rr: sn pushed along: wl outpcd fr 1/2-way: nvr able to get on terms* **2/1**[2]

1m 14.38s (0.58) **Going Correction** 0.0s/f (Good) **6** Ran SP% **113.4**

Speed ratings (Par 104): **96,93,93,90,90 88**

Tote Swingers 1&2 £3.70, 2&3 £3.50, 1&3 £6.60 CSF £16.59 TOTE £8.30: £3.20, £3.70; EX 19.60.

Owner Mrs S J Barker **Bred** Jerry O'Sullivan **Trained** Hambleton, N Yorks

FOCUS

A valuable sprint handicap for 3yos to end the card, but just the six runners. Ordinary form for the grade.

NOTEBOOK

Chooseday(IRE) had been beaten ten times since his successful racecourse debut and was put up 2lb for his recent narrow defeat at Ripon, but he seemed to enjoy this return to 6f, quickening up nicely to lead over a furlong out and scoring with a bit in hand. He can win again. (op 13-2 tchd 7-1)

Harry Trotter(IRE), back up to his optimum trip, travelled well behind the leaders but the winner rather got first run on him and all he could do was stay on into second. (op 9-4 tchd 5-2)

Beau Mistral(IRE), already a dual winner over 5f on soft ground here this term, tried to make all the running but the sixth furlong just appeared to find her out. (op 5-1)

Economic Crisis(IRE) was weak in the market, but wasn't entirely disgraced as she was forced to race wide from the outside stall and, being 4lb wrong, was 8lb higher in her bid for a hat-trick following two wins in testing ground at Hamilton. (op 9-1)

Waseem Faris(IRE) ought to have found the return to 6f on this sharp track a help, but he was given plenty to do and never managed to get into the race at all. (op 6-1 tchd 11-2)

Kimbali(IRE) was always trailing following a slow break and his rider was looking down over a furlong from home. (op 5-2)

T/Plt: £563.00 to a £1 stake. Pool: £39,0128.90 - 50.59 winning tickets. T/Qpdt: £41.60 to a £1 stake. Pool: £2,571.08 - 45.72 winning tickets. DO

[4791]DONCASTER (L-H)

Saturday, August 18

OFFICIAL GOING: Good (8.6)

Wind: Light against Weather: Overcast and warm

5338 ROYAL BRITISH LEGION POPPY H'CAP (DIV I) 7f

1:35 (1:36) (Class 5) (0-70,72) 3-Y-0+ **£2,911** (£866; £432; £216) **Stalls** High

Form RPR

236 **1** **First Class**[29] 4302 4-8-13 **57** DavidProbert 7 68
(Rae Guest) *trckd ldrs: hdwy over 2f out: rdn to ld wl over 1f out: drvn ins fnl f and styd on wl* **5/1**[3]

1321 **2** *1 ¼* **Hayek**[20] 4624 5-9-5 **68** (b) AdamCarter(5) 12 76
(Tim Easterby) *dwlt: hld up in rr: hdwy over 2f out: chsd ldrs over 1f out: sn rdn and styd on to chal ins fnl f: drvn and no ex last 75yds* **4/1**[2]

6651 **3** *2* **Alkadi (IRE)**[10] 4961 3-9-9 **72** SilvestreDeSousa 11 72
(Mark Johnston) *cl up on stands' rail: led 3f out: rdn and hdd wl over 1f out: drvn and one pce fnl f* **11/4**[1]

1652 **4** *1 ¾* **Main Beach**[10] 4954 5-10-0 **72** (p) MickyFenton 10 70
(Paul Midgley) *hld up towards rr: hdwy 2f out: sn rdn and kpt on fnl f: nrst fin* **13/2**

6215 **5** *1 ½* **Red Trump (IRE)**[37] 3994 3-9-5 **68** MatthewChadwick 6 59
(Charles Hills) *trckd ldrs: rdn along and sltly outpcd 3f out: kpt on u.p fr over 1f out* **8/1**

1000 **6** *hd* **Sairaam (IRE)**[17] 4708 6-9-8 **66** AndreaAtzeni 8 59
(Charles Smith) *led: rdn along 1/2-way: sn hdd and grad wknd* **25/1**

-000 **7** *hd* **Music Festival (USA)**[10] 4954 5-9-0 **61** GaryBartley(3) 9 53
(Jim Goldie) *a towards rr* **28/1**

4310 **8** *shd* **Restless Bay (IRE)**[12] 4887 4-9-5 **70** (p) ConorHarrison(7) 2 62
(Mrs K Burke) *cl up: rdn along wl over 2f out: grad wknd* **12/1**

40-0 **9** *½* **Louis Hull**[103] 1916 3-8-9 **58** (p) PJMcDonald 5 47
(Garry Moss) *towards rr: sme hdwy on outer 1/2-way: sn rdn along and wknd* **50/1**

500 **10** *¾* **Powerful Pierre**[15] 4779 5-9-4 **65** (b) DeclanCannon(3) 1 54
(Ian McInnes) *in tch: pushed along 1/2-way: rdn wl over 2f out: sn wknd* **50/1**

00 **11** *1 ¾* **Ellies Image**[51] 3549 5-8-13 **57** TomEaves 4 41
(Brian Baugh) *a towards rr* **22/1**

03 **12** *8* **Ryedale Dancer (IRE)**[15] 4779 4-9-0 **58** (p) J-PGuillambert 3 20
(Richard Guest) *s.i.s and bhd: hdwy on outer to chse ldrs 1/2-way: rdn along wl over 2f out: sn wknd and bhd* **16/1**

1m 27.35s (1.05) **Going Correction** -0.05s/f (Good)
WFA 3 from 4yo+ 5lb 12 Ran SP% 116.9
Speed ratings (Par 103): **92,90,88,86,84 84,84,84,83,82 80,71**
toteswingers 1&2 £6.90, 1&3 £2.80, 2&3 £3.00 CSF £23.51 CT £66.34 TOTE £6.50: £1.90, £2.00, £1.50; EX 32.10.
Owner Brian Cooper And Miss Elaine Reffo **Bred** Amethyst Stud **Trained** Newmarket, Suffolk

FOCUS

The first division of a fair handicap for 3yos and up. They went an even pace on ground officially described as Good. The ground appeared loose on top. It was the slower division and has been rated around the winner to his recent form.

Ryedale Dancer(IRE) Official explanation: jockey said filly stumbled leaving stalls

5339 CROWN HOTEL BAWTRY LEGER PREVIEW DINNER IRISH EBF MAIDEN FILLIES' STKS 1m (S)

2:05 (2:10) (Class 5) 2-Y-0 **£3,816** (£1,135; £567; £283) **Stalls** High

Form RPR

02 **1** **Lizzie Tudor**[16] 4724 2-9-0 0 DavidProbert 8 76
(Andrew Balding) *hld up towards rr: swtchd lft to outer and hdwy 3f out: effrt to chse ldrs wl over 1f out: rdn to chal appr fnl f: styd on wl to ld last 75yds* **6/1**[3]

0 **2** *½* **Ghanaian (FR)**[16] 4739 2-9-0 0 SilvestreDeSousa 15 75
(Mahmood Al Zarooni) *mde most: rdn wl over 1f out: drvn ins fnl f: hdd and no ex last 75yds* **3/1**[1]

0 **3** *½* **Willowing (USA)**[29] 4297 2-8-9 0 AntiocoMurgia(5) 1 74
(Mahmood Al Zarooni) *trckd ldrs on outer: hdwy and cl up over 2f out: sn rdn to chal and ev ch tl one pce wl ins fnl f* **6/1**[3]

2 **4** *1 ¼* **Romantic Settings**[13] 4837 2-9-0 0 DavidNolan 2 71
(Richard Fahey) *midfield: hdwy to trck ldrs over 2f out: rdn over 1f out: kpt on same pce fnl f* **5/1**[2]

5 *3 ¾* **Spieta (IRE)** 2-9-0 0 J-PGuillambert 11 65+
(Luca Cumani) *trckd ldrs: rdn along over 2f out: sn one pce* **25/1**

3 **6** *¾* **Iberis**[22] 4546 2-9-0 0 IanMongan 3 60
(Sir Henry Cecil) *trckd ldrs: cl up 1/2-way: rdn to chal wl over 1f out: ev ch tl wknd appr fnl f* **6/1**[3]

7 *2 ¾* **Granule** 2-9-0 0 ChrisCatlin 12 54
(Peter Chapple-Hyam) *in tch: pushed along and lost pl bef 1/2-way and towards rr: sme hdwy fnl 2f: n.d* **16/1**

5 **8** *1 ¾* **Color Shades**[53] 3474 2-9-0 0 JohnFahy 16 50
(Clive Cox) *cl up: rdn along 3f out: grad wknd fnl 2f* **6/1**[3]

0 **8** *dht* **Kat Moon**[22] 4546 2-9-0 0 PJMcDonald 10 50
(Tim Easterby) *cl up: rdn along 3f out: wknd over 2f out* **33/1**

10 *7* **Angilina** 2-9-0 0 TomEaves 6 34
(Kevin Ryan) *a towards rr* **22/1**

0 **11** *3 ¼* **Santa Fe Stinger**[53] 3457 2-8-9 0 DarylByrne(5) 17 27
(Tim Easterby) *chsd ldrs to 1/2-way: sn wknd* **100/1**

12 *9* **Marble Silver (IRE)** 2-9-0 0 PaddyAspell 4 6
(Tim Easterby) *dwlt: a in rr* **50/1**

0 **13** *5* **Hadeeya**[24] 4463 2-9-0 0 BrettDoyle 13
(Clive Brittain) *in tch: rdn along 3f out: sn wknd* **50/1**

1m 40.51s (1.21) **Going Correction** -0.05s/f (Good) 13 Ran SP% 120.7
Speed ratings (Par 91): **91,90,90,88,85 84,81,79,79,72 69,60,55**
toteswingers 1&2 £3.80, 1&3 £11.90, 2&3 £8.00 CSF £23.28 TOTE £7.40: £2.50, £1.60, £2.90; EX 29.50.
Owner Ms Karen Gough **Bred** Mickley Stud & Richard Kent **Trained** Kingsclere, Hants

■ Stewards' Enquiry : David Probert four-day ban: used whip above permitted level (Sep 1-4)
Antioco Murgia four-day ban: used whip above permitted level (Sep 1-4)

FOCUS

A fair juvenile fillies' maiden. They went an even pace up the centre of the course and the winner and fourth set the level.

NOTEBOOK

Lizzie Tudor progressed markedly to finish a close second over 7f on good ground at Epsom on her second start this month and this extra furlong was always going to suit the way she was finishing on that occasion. She came with a withering run to get up late in this contest. She appears suited by this 1m trip on decent ground and is a fair handicapper in the making. (op 5-1 tchd 9-2)

Ghanaian(FR) didn't appreciate the gradients over 1f shorter on good ground at Goodwood on debut this month and found progression on this second start. She was sent about her business plenty soon enough and looked likely to prevail until the winner appeared on the scene inside the final 100 yards. She should be able to win a similar contest. (op 9-2)

Willowing(USA) made it a two-three for trainer Mahmood Al Zarooni, who won the previous two runnings of this contest. She looked well beforehand and has progressed markedly from a modest 7f soft-ground debut at Newmarket the previous month. She is a half-sister to two winners in the USA and is out of a well-related dam. She looks capable of winning a similar contest and going on to better things than her stablemate in second. (op 14-1)

Romantic Settings ran well over 7f at Chester on good to firm ground on debut this month and appears to have reproduced a similar level of display over this extra furlong on good ground. She may be able to land a similar contest but looks a fair prospect over this trip in handicaps in any case. (op 9-2)

Spieta(IRE) is certainly one to note from this contest. She cost 40,000gns as a yearling and came home really well once the penny dropped here on debut. She looks a nice, middle-distance prospect for next year and may land a similar contest in the meantime. (op 20-1)

Iberis didn't go on from a fair 7f debut on good to firm ground at Thirsk the previous month. (op 13-2 tchd 11-2)

Hadeeya Official explanation: jockey said filly suffered interference in running

5340 ROBINSONS OF BAWTRY MAIDEN STKS 6f

2:40 (2:40) (Class 5) 3-4-Y-0 **£2,911** (£866; £432; £216) **Stalls** High

Form RPR

2-26 **1** **Signor Sassi**[42] 3876 3-9-3 77 AndreaAtzeni 4 88+
(Roger Varian) *trckd ldrs: smooth hdwy over 2f out: rdn to ld jst ins fnl f: styd on* **5/2**[2]

22 **2** *1 ¾* **Stir Trader (IRE)**[21] 4605 3-9-3 0 KieranO'Neill 1 80
(Roger Charlton) *cl up: rdn to chal wl over 1f out: led briefly 1f out: sn hdd and kpt on same pce* **11/4**[3]

6 **3** *¾* **Enrol**[52] 3507 3-8-12 0 DavidProbert 9 73
(Sir Michael Stoute) *trckd ldr: cl up 1/2-way: led over 2f out: rdn wl over 1f out: hdd and drvn 1f out: one pce* **15/8**[1]

4 *4* **Avon Breeze** 3-8-12 0 TomEaves 10 60
(Richard Whitaker) *s.i.s and bhd: hdwy over 2f out: rdn and styd on appr fnl f: nrst fin* **25/1**

5 *2* **Never Forever** 3-9-3 0 PJMcDonald 5 59
(George Moore) *dwlt: a in rr* **16/1**

6 *6* **Gilly The Filly** 3-8-12 0 MartinLane 8 35
(Hugo Palmer) *t.k.h: chsd ldrs: rdn along over 2f out: sn wknd* **10/1**

56- **7** *1 ¼* **Wood Nymph (IRE)**[330] 6291 3-8-7 0 DarylByrne(5) 6 31
(Tim Easterby) *led: rdn along wl over 2f out: sn hdd & wknd* **33/1**

1m 12.37s (-1.23) **Going Correction** -0.05s/f (Good) 7 Ran SP% 111.8
Speed ratings (Par 103): **106,103,102,97,94 86,85**
toteswingers 1&2 £1.50, 1&3 £1.70, 2&3 £2.40 CSF £9.35 TOTE £2.90: £1.60, £2.10; EX 10.00.
Owner P D Smith **Bred** D G Hardisty Bloodstock **Trained** Newmarket, Suffolk

FOCUS

A fair maiden in which the form trio came clear. Improvement from the winner.

5341 ROYAL BRITISH LEGION POPPY H'CAP (DIV II) 7f

3:15 (3:15) (Class 5) (0-70,70) 3-Y-0+ **£2,911** (£866; £432; £216) **Stalls** High

Form RPR

0633 **1** **Chookie Royale**[7] 5084 4-9-10 **68** (p) TomEaves 3 78
(Keith Dalgleish) *trckd ldrs: hdwy 2f out: chal jst over 1f out: rdn to ld jst ins fnl f: kpt on* **7/1**

0430 **2** *½* **Steel Stockholder**[15] 4783 6-9-0 **65** RobertDodsworth(7) 5 74
(Mel Brittain) *led: rdn along 2f out: drvn and hdd jst ins fnl f: kpt on wl u.p towards fin* **14/1**

-054 **3** *2 ¾* **Dubai Celebration**[15] 4783 4-8-12 **56** PaddyAspell 11 58
(Julie Camacho) *trckd ldrs: hdwy 2f out: sn rdn to chse ldng pair over 1f out: drvn and one pce fnl f* **6/1**[3]

010 **4** *2 ¼* **Last Destination (IRE)**[8] 5059 4-8-13 **57** SilvestreDeSousa 10 53
(Nigel Tinkler) *hld up in rr: hdwy 2f out: rdn over 1f out: kpt on fnl f: nrst fin* **15/2**

003 **5** *½* **Ted's Brother (IRE)**[1] 5314 4-9-12 **70** J-PGuillambert 7 64
(Richard Guest) *hld up in rr: hdwy over 2f out: rdn wl over 1f out: no imp fnl f* **4/1**[1]

-535 **6** *shd* **Bajan Bear**[9] 5004 4-9-11 **69** DavidProbert 12 63
(Michael Blanshard) *in tch: hdwy to chse ldrs 2f out: sn rdn and no imp fnl f* **5/1**[2]

-054 **7** *1 ½* **Sehnsucht (IRE)**[16] 4746 3-9-7 **70** (v) JohnFahy 2 58
(Alan McCabe) *trckd ldrs: sn chsng ldng pair: rdn along 3f out: sn wknd* **14/1**

-402 **8** *1* **Tukitinyasok (IRE)**[17] 4716 5-8-13 **57** (p) PJMcDonald 1 44
(Clive Mulhall) *trckd ldr: effrt over 2f out: sn rdn and wknd* **5/1**[2]

30-5 **9** *1 ¾* **Summer Dancer (IRE)**[103] 1917 8-9-9 **67** MickyFenton 4 49
(Paul Midgley) *stdd s and hld up in rr: swtchd lft and sme hdwy over 2f out: sn rdn and btn* **11/1**

5000 **10** *½* **Hurricane Max (IRE)**[4] 5215 3-8-6 **55** (b[1]) AndrewElliott 9 34
(Ian McInnes) *in tch: rdn along wl over 2f out: sn wknd* **40/1**

1m 25.64s (-0.66) **Going Correction** -0.05s/f (Good)
WFA 3 from 4yo+ 5lb 10 Ran SP% 116.0
Speed ratings (Par 103): **101,100,97,94,94 94,92,91,89,88**
toteswingers 1&2 £12.20, 1&3 £6.30, 2&3 £17.10 CSF £99.23 CT £638.90 TOTE £6.70: £2.40, £3.60, £2.70; EX 101.80.
Owner Raeburn Brick Limited **Bred** D And J Raeburn **Trained** Carluke, S Lanarks

FOCUS

The second division of a fair handicap for 3yos and up. The winning time was significantly faster than the first instalment. The winner is rated to last year's turf best.

Summer Dancer(IRE) Official explanation: jockey said gelding clipped heels shortly after start

5342 LINDSEY CLOSE BUILDING SERVICES H'CAP 7f

3:50 (3:51) (Class 2) (0-105,99) 3-Y-0+ **£12,938** (£3,850; £1,924; £962) **Stalls** High

Form RPR

-401 **1** **Go Dutch (IRE)**[23] 4503 3-8-8 **86** AndreaAtzeni 3 100+
(Roger Varian) *trckd ldrs: hdwy wl over 1f out: n.m.r and chal over 1f out: sn led: rdn and styd on wl fnl f* **9/2**[2]

4040 **2** *¾* **Lutine Bell**[14] 4799 5-9-0 **87** JohnFahy 12 100
(Mike Murphy) *hld up: gd hdwy on outer wl over 1f out: sn rdn and str run to chal ins fnl f: ev ch tl drvn and no ex last 50yds* **12/1**

3003 **3** *3 1/2* **Mont Ras (IRE)**[14] 4828 5-9-0 **87**................................ SilvestreDeSousa 4 91
(David O'Meara) *trckd ldrs: hdwy 2f out: rdn to dispute ld over 1f out: sn drvn and one pce ins fnl f* **4/1**[1]

4210 **4** *nk* **Corporal Maddox**[14] 4828 5-8-10 **90**.................. MichaelJMMurphy(7) 6 93
(Patrick Morris) *towards rr: hdwy on wd outside 2f out: sn rdn and edgd rt jst ins fnl f: nereat fin* **10/1**

1000 **5** *3/4* **Atlantic Sport (USA)**[14] 4802 7-9-9 **96**........................... IanMongan 10 97
(Mick Channon) *trckd ldrs: hdwy over 2f out: sn rdn: drvn and kpt on same pce appr fnl f* **16/1**

1151 **6** *nk* **Highland Colori (IRE)**[7] 5102 4-9-4 **91**.................. DavidProbert 15 91+
(Andrew Balding) *chsd ldrs: rdn along 2f out: drvn and one pce fr over 1f out* **5/1**[3]

0104 **7** *1 3/4* **Sam Nombulist**[33] 4136 4-8-12 **85**.................................(v) PaddyAspell 5 80
(Richard Whitaker) *led: rdn along wl over 2f out: drvn and hdd over 1f out: sn edgd lft: wkng whn hmpd jst ins fnl f* **33/1**

0350 **8** *1/2* **Balty Boys (IRE)**[21] 4598 3-9-7 **99**....................... MatthewChadwick 11 92
(Charles Hills) *prom: effrt over 2f out: sn rdn and wknd over 1f out* **8/1**

046 **9** *hd* **Sir Reginald**[15] 4761 4-9-6 **93**... DavidNolan 17 86
(Richard Fahey) *in tch: pushed along and sltly outpcd 3f out: rdn and hdwy 2f out: sn drvn and no imp* **9/1**

0010 **10** *3/4* **Kiwi Bay**[14] 4828 7-8-13 **86**.. TomEaves 2 77
(Michael Dods) *bhd: sme hdwy 2f out: sn rdn and n.d* **33/1**

036 **11** *1 1/2* **Greensward**[21] 4609 6-9-0 **87**... KieranO'Neill 8 74
(Mike Murphy) *midfield: sme hdwy wl over 1f out: rdn and no imp whn sltly hmpd jst ins fnl f* **28/1**

1255 **12** *1 1/4* **Dubai Dynamo**[7] 5075 7-9-8 **95**....................................... PJMcDonald 13 79
(Ruth Carr) *in tch: rdn along wl over 2f out: sn wknd* **16/1**

5210 **13** *2 1/4* **Mr David (USA)**[9] 5004 5-9-1 **88**................................(b) J-PGuillambert 9 66
(Jamie Osborne) *chsd ldrs: rdn along over 2f out: grad wknd* **20/1**

/50- **14** *1 1/2* **Swift Gift**[350] 5699 7-9-9 **96**.. ChrisCatlin 16 70
(Ed Dunlop) *a towards rr* **33/1**

661- **15** *2 1/2* **Diescentric (USA)**[371] 5059 5-9-3 **90**.............................. MickyFenton 14 57
(Julie Camacho) *nvr bttr than midfield* **50/1**

3006 **16** *hd* **Clockmaker (IRE)**[8] 5057 6-8-7 **85**.............................. DarylByrne(5) 18 52
(Tim Easterby) *chsd ldrs: rdn along 3f out: sn wknd* **33/1**

0113 **17** *3 1/4* **King Of Eden (IRE)**[21] 4589 6-9-2 **89**................................ JimmyQuinn 7 47
(Eric Alston) *s.i.s: a in rr* **20/1**

2300 **18** *2 1/2* **Novellen Lad (IRE)**[14] 4799 7-9-0 **87**............................. JamieMackay 1 38
(Willie Musson) *in rr fr 1/2-way* **40/1**

1m 24.33s (-1.97) **Going Correction** -0.05s/f (Good)
WFA 3 from 4yo+ 5lb **18** Ran SP% **133.6**
Speed ratings (Par 109): **109,108,104,103,102 102,100,100,99,98 97,95,93,91,88 88,84,81**
toteswingers 1&2 £16.40, 1&3 £4.80, 2&3 £9.70 CSF £56.06 CT £254.96 TOTE £6.70: £2.00, £2.90, £1.50, £2.50; EX 85.20.
Owner K Allen, R Marchant, G Moss & G Jarvis **Bred** Wiji Bloodstock & Gerry Mullins **Trained** Newmarket, Suffolk

FOCUS
A good-class handicap for 3yos and up. It was well run and the form is pretty sound.

NOTEBOOK
Go Dutch(IRE) represented trainer Roger Varian, who now has a 45% strike-rate in similar handicaps here in recent seasons, and his jockey Andrea Atzeni now has a 31%strike-rate when riding for this stable this year. He appreciated the good to firm ground when winning over this 7f trip at Epsom off 5lb lower the previous month and he showed a very willing attitude to follow up under similar conditions. This specialist trip appears important to him and he may be able to continue improving under these conditions. (op 11-2)
Lutine Bell has shown signs of a revival in his last two starts and may be able to land a handicap off a mark in the mid-80s this term on this encouraging evidence.
Mont Ras(IRE) ran well over 1f further at Thirsk on good ground this month. He will remain of interest if returned to that trip. (op 5-1)
Corporal Maddox appeared to hold every chance if good enough. (op 8-1)
Atlantic Sport(USA) is a pretty solid hook for the form in fifth and performed respectably off joint top-weight.
Highland Colori(IRE) had won four of his previous five starts and there may be more to come if stepped back up to 1m after another decent display. (tchd 9-2)
King Of Eden(IRE) Official explanation: jockey said gelding reared as gates opened

5343 70TH BIRTHDAY KEITH BOWNES H'CAP 5f
4:25 (4:27) (Class 3) (0-95,94) 3-Y-O+ **£8,409** (£2,502; £1,250; £625) **Stalls** High

Form RPR

403- **1** **Face The Problem (IRE)**[301] 7018 4-8-13 **90**... MichaelJMMurphy(7) 18 101
(Patrick Morris) *hld up: hdwy 2f out: rdn to chse ldrs over 1f out: styd on ent fnl f to ld last 100yds* **12/1**

2540 **2** *3/4* **Kingsgate Choice (IRE)**[18] 4690 5-9-2 **86**..................... KieranO'Neill 9 94
(Ed de Giles) *in tch: hdwy wl over 1f out: sn rdn and styd on wl fnl f* **14/1**

-002 **3** *nk* **Master Rooney (IRE)**[24] 4451 6-9-1 **85**.............................. TomEaves 6 92
(Bryan Smart) *led: rdn along wl over 1f out: drvn ent fnl f: hdd and no ex last 100yds* **12/1**

1002 **4** *3/4* **Pearl Blue (IRE)**[37] 4013 4-9-6 **90**.. IanMongan 2 94
(Chris Wall) *hld up: hdwy wl over 1f out: rdn and styd on strly fnl f: nrst fin* **7/1**

4640 **5** *1 1/4* **Ganas (IRE)**[18] 4690 4-8-12 **82**... JohnFahy 10 82
(Clive Cox) *prom: rdn along 2f out: drvn over 1f out: kpt on same pce* **5/1**[2]

300 **6** *nse* **Burning Thread (IRE)**[21] 4576 5-9-7 **91**........................ MickyFenton 13 91
(Tim Etherington) *chsd ldrs: rdn whn sltly hmpd over 1f out: one pce after* **20/1**

0036 **7** *1/2* **Arctic Feeling (IRE)**[18] 4690 4-8-9 **82**........................... LeeTopliss(3) 3 80
(Richard Fahey) *in rr: hdwy wl over 1f out: sn rdn and styd on fnl f: nrst fin* **12/1**

0021 **8** *hd* **Partner (IRE)**[8] 5058 6-9-0 **87**.. GaryBartley(3) 5 84
(Noel Wilson) *midfield: styd on appr fnl f: n.d* **16/1**

0000 **9** *shd* **Marine Commando**[42] 3845 4-8-13 **83**............................... PJMcDonald 4 80
(Ruth Carr) *dwlt and in rr tl styd on fnl 2f: nrst fin* **40/1**

2210 **10** *nk* **Noodles Blue Boy**[11] 4924 6-8-10 **87**.................... JacobButterfield(7) 1 83
(Ollie Pears) *chsd ldrs: rdn over 1f out: wknd fnl f* **20/1**

0010 **11** *hd* **Cadeaux Pearl**[18] 4690 4-8-11 **88**................................(b) JordanUys(7) 14 83
(Scott Dixon) *cl up: rdn and hung lft over 1f out: sn wknd* **40/1**

1360 **12** *3/4* **Solemn**[11] 4924 7-9-5 **89**..(b) MatthewChadwick 19 81
(Milton Bradley) *in tch: rdn along 2f out: grad wknd* **20/1**

0010 **13** *nse* **Jarrow (IRE)**[14] 4799 5-9-0 **84**.. DavidProbert 20 76
(Milton Bradley) *chsd ldrs: rdn along wl over 1f out: grad wknd* **13/2**[3]

1600 **14** *3/4* **Rasaman (IRE)**[15] 4770 8-8-10 **80**.. ChrisCatlin 12 69
(Jim Goldie) *a towards rr* **20/1**

6100 **15** *2 3/4* **Hazelrigg (IRE)**[11] 4924 7-9-7 **91**...................................... DavidNolan 17 70
(Tim Easterby) *dwlt: a in rr* **20/1**

0 **16** *shd* **Quality Art (USA)**[37] 4013 4-9-0 **84**.............................. J-PGuillambert 8 63
(Richard Guest) *prom: rdn along 2f out: sn wknd* **20/1**

6353 **17** *nk* **Fratellino**[8] 5065 5-9-7 **91**...(t) SilvestreDeSousa 15 69
(Alan McCabe) *chsd ldrs: rdn along 1/2-way: sn wknd* **9/2**[1]

59.34s (-1.16) **Going Correction** -0.05s/f (Good)
WFA 3 from 4yo+ 2lb **17** Ran SP% **129.8**
Speed ratings (Par 107): **107,105,105,104,102 102,101,100,100,100 99,98,98,97,93 92,92**
toteswingers 1&2 £33.10, 1&3 £20.10, 2&3 £40.90 CSF £157.14 CT £2154.90 TOTE £12.90: £3.10, £4.10, £2.20, £2.00; EX 300.80.
Owner Dr Marwan Koukash **Bred** J Joyce **Trained** Tarporley, Cheshire
■ Stewards' Enquiry : Kieran O'Neill one-day ban: careless riding (Sep 1)

FOCUS
A good-class sprint handicap in which little became involved from the rear. The winner is rated back to something like his 2yo best.

NOTEBOOK
Face The Problem(IRE) was returning from a ten-month break on his first start for new trainer Patrick Morris since leaving Charlie Hills, and had been gelded in the meantime. He benefited from yet another fine ride by 7lb-claiming jockey Michael Murphy. He had dropped to a mark just 1lb above the last of three successes in July 2010, over this trip on good to firm ground at Thirsk. He clearly goes well fresh and may be able to remain competitive if given time to get over these exertions once reassessed. (op 9-1)
Kingsgate Choice(IRE) appears to be finding some form and may be able to find a race off a mark in the mid-80s under these conditions this term. (op 16-1)
Master Rooney(IRE) ran another solid race in third.
Pearl Blue(IRE) is a solid hook for the form as a previous C&D winner who arrived in decent form. She came home strongly into a never-nearer fourth. (op 9-1)
Ganas(IRE) performed perfectly respectably from an always prominent position. (op 6-1)
Burning Thread(IRE) wasn't beaten far and was slightly hampered over 1f out. (op 12-1)
Arctic Feeling(IRE) ran well under suitable conditions and has dropped to a competitive mark.
Marine Commando was making his debut for new trainer Ruth Carr, since leaving Richard Fahey, returning from a six-week break. He may be able to build on this display. (op 33-1)
Hazelrigg(IRE) Official explanation: jockey said gelding anticipated start
Fratellino came into the race in good form but proved very disappointing on this occasion. Official explanation: trainer's rep said horse ran flat (op 4-1)

5344 PARK HILL HOSPITAL H'CAP 1m 6f 132y
5:00 (5:00) (Class 4) (0-85,85) 3-Y-O+ **£5,175** (£1,540; £769; £384) **Stalls** Low

Form RPR

0536 **1** **Maastricht (IRE)**[9] 4983 3-8-7 **77**................................ SilvestreDeSousa 5 91
(Mark Johnston) *mde all: rdn 2f out: sn jnd and drvn ins fnl f: kpt on gamely towards fin* **7/2**[2]

1246 **2** *1/2* **Gassin Golf**[17] 4700 3-9-1 **85**.. ChrisCatlin 3 98
(Sir Mark Prescott Bt) *hld up in tch: smooth hdwy on inner 3f out: chsd wnr 2f out: rdn to chal over 1f out and ev ch tl drvn ins fnl f and no ex towards fin* **2/1**[1]

0313 **3** *13* **Getabuzz**[35] 4115 4-9-11 **82**.. TomEaves 1 77
(Tim Easterby) *trckd ldrs on inner: smooth hdwy 4f out: rdn over 2f out: sn drvn and kpt on same pce: tk mod 3rd nr line* **7/1**[3]

3164 **4** *nk* **Art Scholar (IRE)**[7] 5091 5-9-13 **84**.............................. PaulMulrennan 9 79
(Michael Appleby) *hld up in rr: hdwy on outer over 3f out: rdn to chse ldng pair wl over 1f out: drvn and one pce appr fnl f: wknd and lost 3rd nr fin* **8/1**

-050 **5** *3* **Harvey's Hope**[22] 3564 6-8-6 **68**.................................... ShaneBKelly(5) 8 59
(Keith Reveley) *hld up: hdwy to chse ldrs over 3f out: sn rdn along and n.d* **14/1**

2221 **6** *5* **Daring Indian**[9] 5002 4-9-2 **76**...................................... RossAtkinson(3) 10 60
(Tom Dascombe) *rrd s and s.i.s: a in rr* **9/1**

-005 **7** *5* **Four Nations (USA)**[14] 4823 4-9-5 **76**................................. MartinLane 4 53
(Amanda Perrett) *chsd ldrs: rdn along over 4f out: sn wknd* **10/1**

5635 **8** *3 1/4* **Bollin Felix**[28] 3953 8-8-10 **74**.................................(p) RachelRichardson(7) 6 47
(Tim Easterby) *chsd ldrs: rdn along over 4f out: sn wknd* **25/1**

31 **9** *4 1/2* **Stock Hill Fair**[38] 3979 4-9-2 **73**.. PJMcDonald 7 40
(Brendan Powell) *trckd wnr: rdn along over 3f out and sn wknd* **10/1**

3m 4.53s (-2.87) **Going Correction** -0.05s/f (Good)
WFA 3 from 4yo+ 13lb **9** Ran SP% **117.9**
Speed ratings (Par 105): **105,104,97,97,96 93,90,88,86**
CSF £11.17 CT £46.32 TOTE £4.80: £2.00, £1.60, £1.70; EX 17.20.
Owner Sheikh Hamdan Bin Mohammed Al Maktoum **Bred** A G Antoniades **Trained** Middleham Moor, N Yorks
■ Stewards' Enquiry : Chris Catlin two-day ban: used whip above permitted level (Sep 1-2)

FOCUS
A decent staying handicap for 3yos and up. The first two pulled a long way clear and the winner clocked significantly the best comparative time on the card. Improvement from the first two.

5345 DC TRAINING APPRENTICE H'CAP 1m 2f 60y
5:35 (5:35) (Class 5) (0-75,77) 4-Y-O+ **£2,911** (£866; £432; £216) **Stalls** Low

Form RPR

0211 **1** **Standpoint**[9] 5012 6-9-12 **77**.. DavidKenny 6 85
(Conor Dore) *trckd ldrs: hdwy over 2f out: rdn to chal over 1f out: led ins fnl f: drvn out* **8/1**[3]

124 **2** *1/2* **Another For Joe**[16] 4745 4-9-4 **72**................................. DarylByrne(3) 4 79
(Jim Goldie) *sn led: rdn wl over 2f out: drvn over 1f out: hdd ins fnl f: no ex towards fin* **9/1**

0125 **3** *1* **Honoured (IRE)**[4] 5199 5-8-7 **63**.............................. DanielMuscutt(5) 10 68
(Michael Appleby) *a.p: trckd ldr over 4f out: rdn along to chal 2f out: ev ch tl drvn and one pce ent fnl f* **8/1**[3]

5445 **4** *1* **Robert The Painter (IRE)**[12] 4879 4-9-2 **72**..............(p) DavidBergin(5) 1 75
(David O'Meara) *hld up: hdwy to chse ldrs 3f out: rdn wl over 1f out: kpt on same pce u.p fnl f* **3/1**[1]

0260 **5** *1 1/4* **Border Bandit (USA)**[8] 5054 4-8-8 **59**............................ GarryWhillans 9 60
(Tracy Waggott) *hld up in rr: hdwy 3f out: swtchd lft to inner and chsd ldrs 2f out: sn rdn and no imp appr fnl f* **25/1**

120 **6** *2* **Bright Applause**[20] 4621 4-9-6 **71**.................................... ShaneBKelly 8 68
(Tracy Waggott) *chsd ldrs: rdn along over 2f out: grad wknd* **11/1**

-034 **7** *3 3/4* **Librettela**[26] 4411 4-8-12 **66**.................................... MichaelJMMurphy(3) 3 56
(Alan Jarvis) *in tch: effrt over 3f out: sn rdn along and n.d* **9/2**[2]

-134 **8** *1 1/4* **Hydrant**[36] 4048 6-9-6 **71**.. MatthewLawson 5 58
(Peter Salmon) *a towards rr* **11/1**

4036 **9** *nk* **Follow The Flag (IRE)**[3] 5243 8-9-0 **68**..................(be) NoraLooby(3) 12 55
(Alan McCabe) *hld up in rr: sme hdwy over 3f out: sn rdn and nvr a factor* **16/1**

0641 **10** *1/2* **Sedgwick**[11] 4915 10-9-0 **68**... ShirleyTeasdale(3) 2 54
(Shaun Harris) *a in rr* **14/1**

6000 **11** *8* **Brockfield**[3] 5224 6-9-1 **73**...................................... RobertDodsworth(7) 7 44
(Mel Brittain) *dwlt and in rr: rapid hdwy on outer to chse ldr after 2f: rdn along over 4f out and sn wknd* **16/1**

550 **12** *18* **Woteva**[37] 3994 6-8-9 **60**....(p) TobyAtkinson 14
(Nigel Tinkler) *a towards rr* **25/1**
2306 **13** *2 ½* **Gladsome**[9] 4996 4-9-2 **67**.... AdamCarter 11
(Jason Ward) *chsd ldrs: rdn along 3f out: sn wknd* **28/1**
2m 9.07s (-0.33) **Going Correction** -0.05s/f (Good) **13** Ran SP% **121.6**
Speed ratings (Par 103): **99,98,97,97,96 94,91,90,90,89 83,68,66**
toteswingers 1&2 £14.30, 1&3 £20.40, 2&3 £13.50 CSF £77.89 CT £606.63 TOTE £8.50: £2.90, £2.50, £3.20; EX 66.40.
Owner Mrs Jennifer Marsh **Bred** Juddmonte Farms Ltd **Trained** Hubbert's Bridge, Lincs
■ Stewards' Enquiry : David Kenny four-day ban: used whip above permitted level (Sep 1-4)
FOCUS
A fair apprentice riders' handicap for older horses. The first three were always prominent. The winner is rated close to his old turf best.
Librettela Official explanation: jockey said gelding was unsuited by the good ground
Sedgwick Official explanation: jockey said gelding slipped on bend
T/Plt: £134.90 to a £1 stake. Pool: £72,205.05 - 390.58 winning tickets T/Qpdt: £26.00 to a £1 stake. Pool: £3,864.54 - 109.66 winning tickets JR

5160 LINGFIELD (L-H)

Saturday, August 18

OFFICIAL GOING: Turf - good to firm (8.5); all-weather - standard
Wind: Almost nil Weather: Sunny and hot

5346 COLIN & LUCY SHEER TERROR APPRENTICE JOCKEYS TRAINING SERIES H'CAP (RACING EXCELLENCE INITIATIVE) 6f

5:30 (5:30) (Class 5) (0-70,68) 4-Y-0+ **£3,067** (£905; £453) **Stalls** High

Form RPR
-644 **1** **Commandingpresence (USA)**[8] 5035 6-9-7 **65**.... IanBurns 4 73
(John Bridger) *led tl 2f out: led again ins fnl f: rdn out* **6/1**[3]
54-0 **2** *1* **Leadenhall Lass (IRE)**[129] 1300 6-9-3 **61**.... JakePayne 8 66
(Pat Phelan) *chsd ldr: led 2f out tl ins fnl f: kpt on same pce* **5/1**[2]
4343 **3** *½* **Even Bolder**[15] 4758 9-8-10 **59**.... JoeyHaynes(5) 7 62
(Eric Wheeler) *hld up in 6th: hdwy 2f out: wnt 3rd over 1f out: kpt on* **5/1**[2]
0000 **4** *½* **Secret Queen**[12] 4887 5-8-11 **55**.... JoshBaudains 5 57
(Martin Hill) *chsd ldrs: rdn 3f out: styd on same pce* **8/1**
6400 **5** *2 ¾* **Reginald Claude**[8] 5049 4-8-13 **57**.... RachealKneller 1 50
(Mark Usher) *hld up in rr: swtchd towards centre and effrt wl over 1f out: unable to chal* **12/1**
2000 **6** *1 ¼* **Nubar Boy**[7] 5097 5-9-10 **68**....(v) ThomasBrown 2 57
(David Evans) *chsd ldrs towards centre 4f* **11/1**
3152 **7** *nk* **Paperetto**[14] 4812 4-9-1 **64**.... DanielCremin(5) 3 52
(Robert Mills) *chsd ldrs: rdn 3f out: wknd 2f out* **6/4**[1]
1m 9.5s (-1.70) **Going Correction** -0.35s/f (Firm) **7** Ran SP% **114.8**
Speed ratings (Par 103): **97,95,95,94,90 89,88**
toteswingers:1&2 £5.30, 2&3 £1.80, 1&3 £5.60 CSF £35.84 CT £161.03 TOTE £6.60: £2.90, £1.90; EX 39.40 Trifecta £84.60 Pool £260.83 - 2.28 winning units..
Owner Mrs Liz Gardner **Bred** Lazy Lane Farms Inc **Trained** Liphook, Hants
FOCUS
As usual here, there appeared to be an advantage in racing close to the stands' rail, but the winner was racing one wide of the runner-up. The time was only modest.

5347 PAULINE, ELLIE & NETTIE HAPPY BIRTHDAY (S) STKS 6f

6:00 (6:00) (Class 6) 3-Y-0+ **£2,181** (£644; £322) **Stalls** High

Form RPR
0525 **1** **Ansells Pride (IRE)**[15] 4783 9-8-13 62....(p) JakePayne(7) 1 72
(Bill Turner) *mde all: rdn and hld on wl fnl 2f* **7/1**[3]
5033 **2** *1 ¾* **Beat The Bell**[19] 4660 7-9-6 76....(p) FergusSweeney 2 66
(Jamie Osborne) *chsd wnr: hrd rdn over 1f out: kpt on same pce* **4/6**[1]
3523 **3** *1* **Mother Jones**[1] 5298 4-8-12 67.... MatthewCosham(3) 5 58
(David Evans) *hld up in 4th: effrt and wnt 3rd over 2f out: one pce* **5/2**[2]
003 **4** *6* **Toms River Tess (IRE)**[8] 5034 4-8-10 41.... LiamKeniry 4 34
(Zoe Davison) *last most of way: outpcd fr 1/2-way* **40/1**
0645 **5** *½* **Crown Dependency (IRE)**[8] 5034 3-8-5 72.... RufusVergette(7) 3 37
(Richard Hannon) *chsd ldng pair tl wknd and edgd lft over 2f out* **12/1**
1m 8.4s (-2.80) **Going Correction** -0.35s/f (Firm)
WFA 3 from 4yo+ 3lb **5** Ran SP% **111.2**
Speed ratings (Par 101): **104,101,100,92,91**
CSF £12.54 TOTE £6.30: £2.60, £1.10; EX 13.10.
Owner Ansells Of Watford **Bred** E Lonergan **Trained** Sigwells, Somerset
■ Stewards' Enquiry : Jake Payne two-day ban: careless riding (Sep 1-2)
FOCUS
The first two set a fair standard for the grade - the winner on his form of several years ago, and the runner-up on his current mark of 76. The winner's best form since late 2009.

5348 THEO MICRO TOON BRITISH STALLION STUDS EBF NOVICE STKS 7f

6:30 (6:30) (Class 5) 2-Y-0 **£2,098** (£2,098) **Stalls** High

Form RPR
3441 **1** **Ayaar (IRE)**[23] 4507 2-9-5 90.... MartinHarley 3 90
(Mick Channon) *trckd ldr: drvn to chal ins fnl f: drew level fnl 25yds* **6/4**[2]
12 **1** *dht* **Snowboarder (USA)**[15] 4774 2-9-5 0.... FrankieDettori 2 90
(Mahmood Al Zarooni) *led: shkn up 2f out: kpt on u.p fnl f: jnd by sole rival fnl 25yds* **1/2**[1]
1m 21.1s (-2.20) **Going Correction** -0.35s/f (Firm) **2** Ran SP% **106.7**
Speed ratings (Par 94): **98,98**
WIN: Ayaar £1.10, Snowboarder £0.70.
Owner Godolphin **Bred** Fares Farm Llc **Trained** Newmarket, Suffolk
Owner Sheikh Mohammed Bin Khalifa Al Maktoum **Bred** Blue Bloodstock Ltd **Trained** West Ilsley, Berks
FOCUS
A remarkable result from which it is hard to draw any hard-and-fast conclusions. The form surprisingly does make sense.
NOTEBOOK
Ayaar(IRE) has already run in Group 2 company and looks a useful sort, with 1m likely to suit. (op 4-7)
Snowboarder(USA)'s attempt to dictate terms and make all was half-thwarted, but he is still a horse of some potential. (op 4-7)

5349 TOONS FAMILY AND FRIENDS H'CAP 7f 140y

7:00 (7:01) (Class 6) (0-65,64) 3-Y-0+ **£2,181** (£644; £322) **Stalls** Centre

Form RPR
3314 **1** **Paphos**[12] 4872 5-9-4 **55**....(e[1]) SaleemGolam 13 66
(Stuart Williams) *hld up in midfield: rdn and hdwy over 1f out: r.o to ld ins fnl f: readily* **5/1**[3]
5304 **2** *2* **Gazboolou**[9] 4986 8-8-10 **47**.... FergusSweeney 7 53
(Henry Candy) *in tch: trckd ldrs 2f out: wnt 2nd ins fnl f: nt qckn* **5/1**[3]
0001 **3** *1* **Capitol Gain (IRE)**[9] 5018 3-9-7 **64**....(p) FrankieDettori 6 67+
(Brian Meehan) *w ldrs tl no ex fnl f* **7/2**[1]
-630 **4** *hd* **My Scat Daddy (USA)**[30] 4241 3-8-9 **52** ow1.... ShaneKelly 10 54
(Brett Johnson) *sn led: rdn over 2f out: hdd and no ex ins fnl f* **14/1**
-600 **5** *1 ½* **Red Yarn**[172] 732 5-9-7 **58**....(b) EddieAhern 8 57
(Daniel Kubler) *dwlt: towards rr: rdn 4f out: nvr rchd ldrs* **20/1**
404 **6** *¾* **Saucy Buck (IRE)**[10] 4950 4-9-5 **59**.... NataliaGemelova(3) 12 56
(Jamie Poulton) *bhd tl sme late hdwy* **11/1**
3064 **7** *nk* **Catchanova (IRE)**[28] 4333 5-9-13 **64**....(b[1]) JimmyFortune 1 61
(Eve Johnson Houghton) *in tch: rdn 3f out: outpcd fnl 2f* **8/1**
6042 **8** *2 ¼* **High Five Prince (IRE)**[11] 4900 3-8-0 **48**.... RachealKneller(5) 11 38
(Mark Usher) *nvr beyond midfield* **12/1**
0000 **9** *1* **Green Earth (IRE)**[10] 4939 5-9-8 **59**.... RyanMoore 3 48
(Pat Phelan) *dwlt: bhd: sme hdwy in centre 2f out: no imp* **4/1**[2]
40-5 **10** *2 ¼* **Lord Deevert**[8] 5049 7-8-6 **50**.... JakePayne(7) 4 33
(Bill Turner) *prom tl wknd 2f out* **25/1**
00 **11** *18* **Cliffords Reprieve**[24] 4468 4-8-12 **52**....(p) SophieDoyle(3) 9
(Eric Wheeler) *chsd ldr tl wknd qckly 2f out* **25/1**
5600 **12** *10* **Dichoh**[88] 2364 9-8-10 **47**....(v) LiamKeniry 5
(Michael Madgwick) *outpcd in rr: no ch fnl 2f* **50/1**
1m 29.2s (-3.10) **Going Correction** -0.35s/f (Firm)
WFA 3 from 4yo+ 6lb **12** Ran SP% **123.8**
Speed ratings (Par 101): **101,99,98,97,96 95,95,93,92,89 71,61**
toteswingers:1&2 £7.10, 2&3 £3.60, 1&3 £4.50 CSF £30.35 CT £103.84 TOTE £5.50: £1.30, £2.20, £2.30; EX 35.30 Trifecta £65.80 Pool £530.23 - 5.95 winning units..
Owner Stuart C Williams **Bred** L Ellinas And Old Mill Stud Ltd **Trained** Newmarket, Suffolk
FOCUS
A modest handicap in which the winner stayed close to the rail despite arriving from behind. The second set the standard.

5350 ANABELLE & EVIE LITTLE LOVELIES CLAIMING STKS 1m (P)

7:30 (7:32) (Class 6) 3-Y-0 **£2,181** (£644; £322) **Stalls** High

Form RPR
1550 **1** **Rockgoat (IRE)**[72] 2860 3-9-1 68.... MartinHarley 7 73
(Marco Botti) *chsd ldrs: led and hung lft over 1f out: drvn out* **4/1**[2]
2034 **2** *3* **King's Future**[8] 5050 3-8-6 57.... AdamBeschizza(3) 8 59
(Lee Carter) *trckd ldr: led 3f out tl over 1f out: nt qckn* **8/1**[3]
0050 **3** *11* **Here Comes Jeanie**[19] 4650 3-7-13 41.... NatashaEaton(7) 3 30
(Michael Madgwick) *hld up in 5th: rdn and struggling 3f out: passed btn horses to take 3rd ins fnl f* **33/1**
4-12 **4** *2* **Pawprints (IRE)**[22] 4533 3-8-12 70.... RyanMoore 4 31
(William Haggas) *t.k.h: prom: rdn 3f out: sn outpcd* **8/13**[1]
00 **5** *4 ½* **Anniesuella (IRE)**[72] 2865 3-8-8 0.... LiamKeniry 6 16
(Martin Bosley) *s.i.s: a towards rr: outpcd and n.d fnl 3f* **33/1**
6 *1 ½* **Sweet Mystery (IRE)**[13] 4858 3-9-0 69.... MatthewCosham(3) 1 22
(David Evans) *a in rr: lost tch over 3f out* **8/1**[3]
0161 **7** *2 ¾* **Moment In The Sun**[81] 2580 3-8-13 65....(b) NataliaGemelova(3) 2 14
(David Flood) *led tl 3f out: wknd 2f out* **8/1**[3]
1m 38.89s (0.69) **Going Correction** +0.075s/f (Slow) **7** Ran SP% **121.1**
Speed ratings (Par 98): **99,96,85,83,78 77,74**
toteswingers:1&2 £4.80, 2&3 £16.20, 1&3 £13.20 CSF £37.72 TOTE £4.50: £2.10, £3.30; EX 34.00 TRIFECTA Not won..Rockgoat was claimed by I. W. McInnes for £9000.
Owner Giuliano Manfredini **Bred** Tullpark Limited **Trained** Newmarket, Suffolk
FOCUS
A weak race with no strength in depth. The runner-up looks the best guide.

5351 TOONER GO LARGE PUNTERS! H'CAP 1m 2f (P)

8:00 (8:00) (Class 6) (0-62,68) 3-Y-0+ **£2,181** (£644; £322) **Stalls** Low

Form RPR
-003 **1** **Royal Dutch**[29] 4296 3-9-5 **61**.... EddieAhern 5 76+
(Denis Coakley) *chsd ldrs: wnt cl 2nd over 2f out: led over 1f out: rdn clr* **9/4**[2]
5506 **2** *4* **Zenarinda**[9] 5021 5-9-4 **57**.... HarryPoulton(5) 1 64+
(Mark H Tompkins) *in tch: bmpd over 2f out: r.o to take 2nd ins fnl f: nt trble wnr* **25/1**
6145 **3** *2 ½* **Tinkerbell Will**[14] 4817 5-9-2 **50**.... RichardThomas 13 52
(John E Long) *hld up towards rr: wd on home turn and gd hdwy fr over 1f out: nrst fin* **10/1**
0000 **4** *½* **Irons On Fire (USA)**[46] 3738 4-9-12 **60**.... AmirQuinn 7 61
(Lee Carter) *hld up in tch: smooth hdwy on outer over 3f out: led over 2f out tl over 1f out: hrd rdn: no ex* **7/1**[3]
1236 **5** *¾* **Ryedale Lass**[26] 4411 4-10-0 **62**.... LiamKeniry 3 62+
(Joseph Tuite) *s.i.s: hld up towards rr: nt clr rn appr st: pshd along and styd on fnl 2f: nvr nrr* **20/1**
4-03 **6** *½* **Lone Foot Laddie (IRE)**[17] 4709 3-9-6 **62**.... ShaneKelly 11 61+
(Sylvester Kirk) *w ldrs tl 3f out: wknd over 1f out* **10/1**
0300 **7** *2 ¼* **Prince Of Thebes (IRE)**[16] 4722 11-8-9 **48**.... MarkCoumbe(5) 10 42
(Michael Attwater) *s.s: towards rr and wd: hdwy over 2f out: no ex over 1f out* **33/1**
200 **8** *nk* **El Libertador (USA)**[13] 4844 6-9-13 **61**....(b) JimmyFortune 8 54
(Eric Wheeler) *bhd: rdn 2f out: nt rch ldrs* **28/1**
5034 **9** *2 ¾* **Formidable Guest**[14] 4817 8-9-5 **53**.... MartinHarley 2 41
(Jamie Poulton) *mid-div: n.m.r over 2f out: sn rdn and outpcd* **14/1**
6304 **10** *6* **Choral Bee**[24] 4458 3-9-1 **57**.... FergusSweeney 9 33
(Henry Candy) *broke wl: sn chsng ldrs: wknd 3f out* **16/1**
441 **11** *10* **Cape Joy (IRE)**[6] 5125 3-9-12 **68** 6ex.... RyanMoore 14 24
(Richard Hannon) *mde most tl wknd over 2f out* **15/8**[1]
004 **12** *14* **Wishformore (IRE)**[6] 5125 5-9-5 **53**.... JamieGoldstein 12
(Zoe Davison) *chsd ldr tl 3f out: wknd quickly over 2f out* **40/1**
2m 7.35s (0.75) **Going Correction** +0.075s/f (Slow)
WFA 3 from 4yo+ 8lb **12** Ran SP% **126.2**
Speed ratings (Par 101): **100,96,94,94,93 93,91,91,89,84 76,65**
toteswingers:1&2 £19.90, 2&3 £65.50, 1&3 £8.40 CSF £69.76 CT £509.07 TOTE £3.80: £1.60, £9.90, £2.80; EX 88.00 Trifecta £306.70 Pool £414.58 - 1.00 winning unit..
Owner Chris Van Hoorn **Bred** Sir Eric Parker **Trained** West Ilsley, Berks
■ Stewards' Enquiry : Amir Quinn four-day ban: used whip above permitted level (Sep 1-4)

FOCUS
A routine race of its type, but with a progressive winner. The early pace was fast, which eventually put paid to those who had helped to set it.
Ryedale Lass Official explanation: jockey said filly was denied a clear run
Prince Of Thebes(IRE) Official explanation: jockey said blindfold was tucked in tightly under bridle on left-hand side, causing him to slightly misjudge its removal and gelding was slowly away.
Wishformore(IRE) Official explanation: trainer said mare bled from the nose
T/Plt: £175.10 to a £1 stake. Pool £38,039.98 - 158.50 winning units T/Qpdt: £21.20 to a £1 stake. Pool £4,545.79 - 158.50 winning units LM

5303 NEWBURY (L-H)
Saturday, August 18

OFFICIAL GOING: Good to firm (7.1)
Wind: Virtually nil Weather: Suny spells

5352 BETFRED "THE HOME OF GOALS GALORE" EBF MAIDEN FILLIES' STKS (DIV I) 6f 8y
1:30 (1:33) (Class 4) 2-Y-0 **£4,528** (£1,010; £1,010; £336) **Stalls** Centre

Form RPR
1 **Tantshi (IRE)** 2-8-11 0 DominicFox(3) 4 81+
(Roger Varian) *trckd ldrs: drvn and swtchd rt to get stands' rail ins fnl f: qcknd wl clsng stages to ld last strides* **9/1**
45 2 *hd* **Supernova Heights (IRE)**[16] 4739 2-9-0 0 FrankieDettori 2 80
(Brian Meehan) *led: hrd pressed and rdn fr over 1f out: kpt slt advantage thrght fnl f tl hdd last strides* **11/4**[1]
2 *dht* **Secretly** 2-9-0 0 FergusSweeney 3 80+
(Henry Candy) *chsd ldrs: strly chal fr over 1f out and stl upsides thrght fnl f: nt quite pce of wnr last strides* **20/1**
0 4 1 ½ **Talqaa**[16] 4739 2-9-0 0 SamHitchcott 1 76
(Mick Channon) *chsd ldrs: rdn and ev ch fr 2f out: one pce fnl 120yds* **7/1**[3]
5 ½ **Evoke (IRE)** 2-9-0 0 JimmyFortune 6 74
(Jeremy Noseda) *in tch: drvn and hdwy over 1f out: styd on wl fnl 120yds: nt pce to rch ldrs* **12/1**
6 *shd* **Abated** 2-9-0 0 RichardKingscote 8 76+
(Roger Charlton) *hld up in rr: shkn up and gd hdwy wl over 1f out: swtchd rt and styng on wl whn nt clr run ins fnl f: r.o again clsng stages* **11/4**[1]
7 1 ½ **Victrix Ludorum (IRE)** 2-9-0 0 RyanMoore 5 69
(Richard Hannon) *slowly in to stride: in rr hdwy to chse ldrs 1/2-way: ev ch 2f out: wknd fnl f* **13/2**[2]
5 8 2 ¼ **Sinaadi (IRE)**[44] 3783 2-9-0 0 SebSanders 7 62
(Clive Brittain) *chsd ldrs: rdn 2f out: wknd over 1f out* **12/1**
0 9 *nk* **Equitissa (IRE)**[53] 3474 2-9-0 0 DarryllHolland 10 62
(Richard Hannon) *in rr but in tch: pushed along 2f out: nvr gong pce to get into contention* **40/1**
10 ½ **Pivotal Silence** 2-9-0 0 AdamKirby 11 60
(Amanda Perrett) *s.i.s: outpcd most of way* **50/1**

1m 14.88s (1.88) **Going Correction** 0.0s/f (Good) **10** Ran SP% **113.7**
Speed ratings (Par 93): **87,86,86,84,84 83,81,78,78,77**PL: £2.90, Secretly £3.60, Supernova Heights £1.60 Tote Exacta: Tantshi, Secretly £103.20, Tantshi, Supernova Heights £19.20 CSF: Tantshi, Secretly £83.54, Tantshi, Supernova Heights £16.30. Tote Swingers: 1&S £47.80, 1&SH £4.70, S&SH £10.80 TOTE £11.30: £027, £Owner, £Sheikh Ahmed Al Maktoum, £BredDarley Trained Trifecta £Newmarket, Suffolk.

FOCUS
The rail between 1m and 5f had been moved in since the previous day's meeting, and the course was consequently six metres longer than standard on the round course. An interesting fillies' maiden (four of these hold Group 1 entries), but they didn't seem to go that quick and gradually edged over to the stands' rail, resulting in a bunch finish. The form is rated at the bottom end of the race averages.

NOTEBOOK
Tantshi(IRE), who's in the Cheveley Park, was keen early but travelled well for a long way and picked up nicely once switched onto the stands' rail in the closing stages. She's a half-sister to, among others, 7f Listed winner Toolain, and is obviously a decent prospect. (op 8-1)
Secretly, a 54,000gns purchase, is a half-sister to a couple of 6f winners, and her dam was successful over 7f-1m in New Zealand. She showed plenty of pace and kept on well, a particularly creditable effort considering she was stuck a touch wider than might have been ideal. (op 3-1)
Supernova Heights(IRE), a beaten favourite when upped to 7f at Goodwood on her second start, ran her race under a forward ride but wasn't good enough. (op 3-1)
Talqaa, two places behind Supernova Heights when making her debut over 7f (met trouble), showed plenty of pace on this drop in trip but came up short. (op 8-1)
Evoke(IRE), a 30,000euros half-sister to a few winners over a variety of trips, is out of a 1m2f winner. She showed ability and is from a stable with a fine record with second-time out 2yos. (op 14-1)
Abated ◆ is a sister to high-class sprinter Bated Breath, and a half-sister to Group 1-winning miler Cityscape, and she's in the Fillies' Mile. She had plenty of cover but still raced keenly, and then didn't get the clearest of runs without looking unlucky. There should be significantly more to come, especially if she settles better. (op 9-4)
Victrix Ludorum(IRE) ◆, who cost 75,000gns wasn't helped by being stuck widest and was given a sympathetic introduction. She should improve a good deal. (op 7-1)

5353 DENFORD STUD STKS (REGISTERED AS THE WASHINGTON SINGER STAKES) (LISTED RACE) 7f (S)
2:00 (2:04) (Class 1) 2-Y-0 **£13,043** (£4,945; £2,474; £1,232; £618) **Stalls** Centre

Form RPR
1 1 **Just The Judge (IRE)**[53] 3474 2-8-9 0 MichaelHills 4 100+
(Charles Hills) *stdd s: hld up in rr: smooth hdwy over 1f out: led ins fnl f: pushed along and qcknd to assert fnl 75yds* **3/1**[3]
1 2 1 **Excess Knowledge**[9] 5005 2-9-0 0 FrankieDettori 3 102
(John Gosden) *sn led: drvn and qcknd over 1f out: hdd ins fnl f but styd pressing wnr tl edgd lft and outpcd fnl 75yds* **11/4**[2]
1 3 1 ½ **Ninjago**[22] 4532 2-9-0 0 RyanMoore 1 98
(Richard Hannon) *t.k.h: trckd ldr: drvn and ev ch over 1f out: edgd lft and wknd fnl 75yds* **2/1**[1]
2102 4 4 **Miss You Too**[8] 5042 2-8-9 86 SamHitchcott 2 82
(Mick Channon) *chsd ldrs and t.k.h: rdn 2f out: hung lft and wknd over 1f out* **12/1**
101 5 8 **Pasaka Boy**[13] 4847 2-9-0 89 RichardKingscote 5 65
(Jonathan Portman) *chsd ldrs: rdn over 2f out: wknd wl over 1f out* **5/1**

1m 26.23s (0.53) **Going Correction** 0.0s/f (Good) **5** Ran SP% **109.4**
Speed ratings (Par 102): **96,94,93,88,79**
CSF £11.37 TOTE £4.00: £2.20, £1.90; EX 7.00.
Owner Sangster Family & Matthew Green **Bred** Mrs J Dempsey **Trained** Lambourn, Berks

FOCUS
A Listed contest for 2yos who had not won a Pattern race, and whose sire won over at least 1m2f. It's often a good race and the best winner in the last decade was Haafhd, who subsequently landed five Group 1s. They raced up the middle. The pace looked just modest. The first two both built on their maiden wins.

NOTEBOOK
Just The Judge(IRE), who stayed on well having been held up, was following up a C&D maiden win that has worked out well enough and looks pretty smart. There should be more to come when she gets a stronger pace and/or more distance to cover, and she looks the type who will come into her own next year. In the shorter term, she's entered in the Moyglare Stud Stakes and the Fillies' Mile. (op 9-4)
Excess Knowledge ◆, whose trainer had won this three times in the last seven years, was dropped in trip after winning a 1m maiden at Sandown on his debut, but he's bred for middle-distances. This was a solid performance in defeat and he can reach a higher level when faced with more of a test. He's in the Royal Lodge and the Racing Post Trophy. (op 10-3)
Ninjago, who won a 6f Chepstow maiden on his debut, was keen without cover early on and simply found a couple of decent types too strong. (op 9-4 tchd 5-2)
Miss You Too pulled far too hard and can't have run to her best. (op 11-1 tchd 10-1)
Pasaka Boy was nowhere near the form he showed when winning a C&D nursery off 79 last time. (op 11-2 tchd 6-1)

5354 BETFRED "THE BONUS KING" GEOFFREY FREER STKS (GROUP 3) 1m 5f 61y
2:30 (2:30) (Class 1) 3-Y-0+
£31,190 (£11,825; £5,918; £2,948; £1,479; £742) **Stalls** Low

Form RPR
4-11 1 **Mount Athos (IRE)**[35] 4111 5-9-4 116 RyanMoore 7 121
(Luca Cumani) *hld up in 5th and wl bhd ldng duo tl stdy hdwy fr 4f out to trck ldrs 3f out: led 2f out: drvn and qcknd clr fnl f: readily* **5/4**[1]
-410 2 3 ¼ **Brown Panther**[28] 4322 4-9-4 118 RichardKingscote 1 116
(Tom Dascombe) *s.i.s: racd in 4th and wl bhd ldng duo tl hdwy fr 4f out: chsd ldrs 3f out: chal 2f out: sn chsng wnr: edgd lft u.p appr fnl f: sn outpcd* **9/4**[2]
0-46 3 4 **Modun (IRE)**[37] 4010 5-9-4 110 FrankieDettori 5 110
(Saeed Bin Suroor) *racd in last pl wl bhd ldng duo: hdwy over 2f out: styd on to take 3rd appr fnl f but nvr any ch* **8/1**
-030 4 4 ½ **Masked Marvel**[28] 4322 4-9-4 114 JimmyFortune 4 103
(John Gosden) *chsd ldr and wl clr of 3rd: led appr fnl 3f: rdn and hdd 2f out: sn btn* **3/1**[3]
2530 5 10 **Dartford (USA)**[88] 2372 3-8-7 74 SaleemGolam 6 88?
(John Gosden) *led: sn 6 l clr of 2nd and wl clr of main gp: hdd appr fnl 3f: sn btn* **150/1**
102- 6 12 **Arrigo (GER)**[233] 4-9-4 114 MartinDwyer 2 70
(Ibrahim Saeed Al Malki, Qatar) *chsd ldrs in 3rd: rdn 4f out: hung bdly lft and btn over 3f out* **25/1**

2m 49.2s (-2.80) **Going Correction** -0.125s/f (Firm)
WFA 3 from 4yo+ 11lb **6** Ran SP% **115.8**
Speed ratings (Par 113): **103,101,98,95,89 82**
Tote Swingers: 1&2 £1.10, 1&3 £3.50, 2&3 £1.60 CSF £4.59 TOTE £2.30: £1.30, £1.80; EX 5.20.

Owner Dr Marwan Koukash **Bred** David Magnier And Cobra Bloodstock **Trained** Newmarket, Suffolk

FOCUS
Not form to get carried away with, but it's hard to fault the winner who is not far off the leading stayers. The pace was stong and the field were soon spread out.

NOTEBOOK
Mount Athos(IRE) was more at home on the quick ground than his nearest rival. He was following up a couple of smart handicap victories (gained off 103 and 108) and is evidently progressing to a really smart level. The Melbourne Cup, for which he's now around 14-1, will be much more competitive, but he goes there with a chance. (op 2-1)
Brown Panther, who was also runner-up in this race last year, didn't look totally comfortable on the quick ground in the closing stages and it's doubtful he ran to his absolute best. The Irish St Leger had been mentioned as a possible target and there seems to no reason why that race couldn't still be on the agenda. (tchd 5-2)
Modun(IRE) ran better than on soft ground at the July meeting last time, but just wasn't good enough. (tchd 7-1)
Masked Marvel may have gone off too fast behind his pacemaker Dartford. However, he just hasn't looked the same horse this year and was beaten almost as soon as he came under pressure. (op 5-2 tchd 7-2)
Dartford(USA) was the pacemaker.
Arrigo(GER) Official explanation: trainer's rep said colt had a breathing problem

5355 BETFRED HUNGERFORD STKS (GROUP 2) 7f (S)
3:05 (3:05) (Class 1) 3-Y-0+
£51,039 (£19,350; £9,684; £4,824; £2,421; £1,215) **Stalls** Centre

Form RPR
2342 1 **Lethal Force (IRE)**[28] 4328 3-8-12 107 (b[1]) AdamKirby 4 116
(Clive Cox) *mde all: sn clr: 5 l ahd 3f out and stl holding that advantage wl over 1f out: hrd drvn fnl f: hld on all out* **25/1**
0-00 2 *nk* **Strong Suit (USA)**[35] 4100 4-9-3 123 RyanMoore 10 117+
(Richard Hannon) *in tch but stl 5 l off all-the-way wnr ins fnl 2f whn drvn: styd on strly thrght fnl f: fin wl: nt quite get up* **9/4**[2]
-310 3 1 ½ **Alanza (IRE)**[36] 4065 4-9-0 108 NGMcCullagh 9 110
(John M Oxx, Ire) *bmpd s: in rr: hdwy over 1f out: styd on wl to take 3rd jst ins fnl f: nvr gng pce to trble ldng duo* **9/1**
2316 4 ½ **Majestic Myles (IRE)**[18] 4686 4-9-3 110 FrederikTylicki 7 111
(Richard Fahey) *bmpd s: in rr: drvn and hdwy over 1f out: styd on to cl on 3rd wl ins fnl f but no imp on ldng duo* **16/1**
6102 5 2 ¼ **Pastoral Player**[28] 4320 5-9-3 113 DarryllHolland 1 105
(Hughie Morrison) *in rr: rdn over 2f out: styd on fnl f but nvr gng pce to get into contention* **11/2**[3]
0641 6 *shd* **Soul (AUS)**[35] 4092 5-9-3 117 FrankieDettori 6 105
(Saeed Bin Suroor) *awkward leaving stalls: in tch w main gp: hdwy to dispute 2nd 2f out but nvr nr all-the-way wnr: wknd fnl f* **2/1**[1]
1400 7 2 ¼ **Red Jazz (USA)**[28] 4320 5-9-3 110 MichaelHills 2 99
(Charles Hills) *racd towards hd of main gp but nvr nr all-the-way wnr: disp 2nd 2f out: wknd over 1f out* **20/1**
0220 8 ½ **Edinburgh Knight (IRE)**[18] 4686 5-9-3 109 SebSanders 8 98
(Paul D'Arcy) *hmpd s: rdn 2f out: a towards rr* **18/1**

0112 **9** 3 1/2 **Libranno**[18] 4686 4-9-3 110 .... JimmyFortune 3 88
(Richard Hannon) *racd in 2nd but nvr nr all-the-way wnr: wknd ins fnl 2f* **10/1**

1m 22.96s (-2.74) **Going Correction** 0.0s/f (Good)
WFA 3 from 4yo+ 5lb **9** Ran SP% **118.3**
Speed ratings (Par 115): **115,114,112,112,109 109,107,106,102**
Tote Swingers: 1&2 £68.70, 1&3 £60.30, 2&3 £14.80 CSF £83.33 TOTE £23.10: £3.80, £1.70, £2.40; EX 117.60 Trifecta £1323.60 Part won. Pool: £1,323.60 - 0.68 winning units..
Owner Alan G Craddock **Bred** Declan Johnson **Trained** Lambourn, Berks

FOCUS
This is muddling form. Tactics very much won the day with Adam Kirby excelling aboard Lethal Force, in contrast to Ryan Moore on the runner-up. However the time was good and the surprise winner has been given credit.

NOTEBOOK
Lethal Force(IRE) raced in a clear lead up the middle of the track, and with the first-time blinkers (replacing cheekpieces) very much doing the trick, as well as Kirby getting the fractions spot-on, he just held off the confidently ridden second. It's worth pointing out Clive Cox's runner, who was the only 3yo in the line-up, is a pretty smart sort, but he had 16lb to find with Strong Suit on official figures. Whether the headgear will work as well next time remains to be seen, and he surely won't be allowed such an easy lead again any time soon. (op 22-1 tchd 20-1)
Strong Suit(USA)'s rider wasn't helped by how events unfolded. It made sense to find cover on a horse who was racing keenly, and in doing so he could have done with others closing down the leader. However, while Strong Suit was always going to struggle to produce his best under these circumstances, he was still travelling easily passing the two-furlong pole and was asked to challenge too late. He can do better back in a more conventionally run race. (tchd 5-2)
Alanza(IRE) was a bit short of room on leaving the stalls, but it didn't look to cost her and she kept on at the one pace. (op 8-1)
Majestic Myles(IRE) was squeezed out at the start and then travelled enthusiastically. He needed a stronger pace to aim at and might be worth another try over 6f. (op 18-1)
Pastoral Player was another unsuited by how the race unfolded. He's easily excused. (op 6-1)
Soul(AUS) won a 6f Group 3 here last time, but the ground was heavy. He couldn't run to the same form back on a quick surface over this longer trip, and going right on leaving the stalls probably didn't matter. The Vet reported the horse lost a front shoe. Official explanation: vet said gelding lost a front shoe (op 3-1)
Red Jazz(USA) continues to go the wrong way. (op 16-1)
Edinburgh Knight(IRE) lost his chance when squeezed out at the start. (op 16-1 tchd 20-1)
Libranno failed to give his true running. (op 8-1)

5356 BETFRED MOBILE SPORTS LADIES DAY H'CAP 7f (S)
3:40 (3:42) (Class 3) (0-95,94) 3-Y-0+
£9,337 (£2,796; £1,398; £699; £349; £175) **Stalls** Centre

Form RPR
0104 **1** **Emilio Largo**[28] 4339 4-9-9 **91** .... TomQueally 12 100
(Sir Henry Cecil) *in tch: drvn and hdwy appr fnl f: str run fnl 150yds to ld last strides* **5/1**[2]
040 **2** *hd* **Nasri**[14] 4799 6-9-4 **86** .... RichardKingscote 1 94
(Milton Bradley) *led and racd alone tl jnd main gp 3f out: drvn and narrowly hdd appr fnl f: rallied to ld again sn after: kpt on tl hdd last strides* **12/1**
0114 **3** 3/4 **Jacob Cats**[18] 4689 3-9-5 **92** .... RyanMoore 2 96+
(Richard Hannon) *towards rr: hdwy 2f out: swtchd lft and str run ins fnl f: fin wl: nt rch ldng duo* **5/2**[1]
6/0 **4** *nse* **Head Of Steam (USA)**[14] 4802 5-9-10 **92** .... FrankieMcDonald 6 98
(Amanda Perrett) *chsd ldrs: rdn over 1f out: styd wl there thrght fnl f tl nt qckn clsng stages* **40/1**
4000 **5** *hd* **Lord Ofthe Shadows (IRE)**[16] 4740 3-9-3 **90** .... MartinDwyer 8 93
(Richard Hannon) *in rr: drvn and no imp appr fnl f: rdn and rallied fnl 120yds: fin strly* **20/1**
5050 **6** *1* **Norse Blues**[14] 4828 4-9-7 **89** .... DarryllHolland 9 92
(Sylvester Kirk) *chsd ldrs: rdn over 2f out: kpt on wl u.p fnl f but nvr quite gng pce to chal* **10/1**
0004 **7** *hd* **Valery Borzov (IRE)**[14] 4799 8-9-4 **86** ....(v) FrederikTylicki 3 88
(Richard Fahey) *chsd ldrs: rdn and slt ld appr fnl f: hdd sn after: styd chalelngig tl wknd fnl 100yds* **12/1**
0505 **8** *nse* **Rakaan (IRE)**[17] 4703 5-9-8 **90** .... FrankieDettori 7 92
(Jamie Osborne) *s.i.s: in rr: drvn and hdwy 2f out: pressed ldrs 1f out: wknd fnl 120yds* **7/1**[3]
0666 **9** 3/4 **George Guru**[17] 4703 5-9-2 **89** .... MarkCoumbe(5) 10 89
(Michael Attwater) *chsd ldrs: rdn over 2f out: wknd fnl 120yds* **14/1**
3025 **10** *nse* **Karaka Jack**[14] 4805 5-9-0 **82** .... TadhgO'Shea 15 82
(David Nicholls) *s.i.s: in rr: pushed along over 1f out: styd on ins fnl f: gng on cl home* **11/1**
-040 **11** 3 1/4 **Treadwell (IRE)**[17] 4703 5-9-5 **87** .... FergusSweeney 13 78
(Jamie Osborne) *chsd ldrs: rdn over 2f out: sn hung rt: btn over 1f out* **16/1**
6000 **12** 3/4 **Kakatosi**[49] 3641 5-9-4 **86** .... JimmyFortune 11 75
(Andrew Balding) *chsd ldrs: rdn over 2f out: btn sn after* **20/1**
5341 **13** *1* **Redvers (IRE)**[28] 4317 4-9-8 **90** ....(b) LiamJones 14 76
(Ed Vaughan) *in tch: rdn 2f out: nvr seeing much daylight and wknd over 1f out* **16/1**
1500 **14** *11* **Bronze Prince**[28] 4321 5-9-12 **94** .... SebSanders 16 51
(Michael Attwater) *stdd s and t.k.h: rdn over 2f out and nvr any ch: eased ins fnl f* **16/1**

1m 24.47s (-1.23) **Going Correction** 0.0s/f (Good)
WFA 3 from 4yo+ 5lb **14** Ran SP% **126.8**
Speed ratings (Par 107): **107,106,105,105,105 104,104,104,103,103 99,98,97,85**
Tote Swingers: 1&2 £19.50, 1&3 £3.50, 2&3 £20.20 CSF £66.13 CT £195.64 TOTE £7.20: £2.50, £5.00, £1.90; EX 105.80 Trifecta £764.20 Pool: £1,136.10 - 1.10 winning units..
Owner Malcolm C Denmark **Bred** Mrs M Chaworth-Musters **Trained** Newmarket, Suffolk

FOCUS
A good, competitive handicap, if lacking improvers. A length personal best from the winner. They raced up the middle of the track, although Nasri was kept apart from the others through the opening stages.

NOTEBOOK
Emilio Largo travelled strongly but had to wait for a clear run and did well to win. He could defy a rise. (op 13-2)
Nasri, who was back up in trip, stuck on strongly when meeting up with the main group and was just collared. (op 16-1)
Jacob Cats ◆ took too long to pick up and ended up having to challenge towards the outer of the field. He was strong at the line and should be suited by a return to 1m. (op 3-1 tchd 10-3 in a place)
Head Of Steam(USA) offered much more than at Goodwood on his British debut. (op 33-1)
Lord Ofthe Shadows(IRE) finished strongly and might both be suited by this back over 1m. (op 25-1)
Norse Blues carried his head a touch high and couldn't sustain his bid. (tchd 9-1)
Karaka Jack missed the break and was doing his best work late. (tchd 12-1)
Treadwell(IRE) Official explanation: vet said horse lost a right-fore shoe
Redvers(IRE), 6lb higher than when winning a valuable big-field ladies' race at Ascot last time, looked a bit awkward. (op 9-1)
Bronze Prince Official explanation: trainer said gelding was unsuited by the good to firm ground

5357 BETFRED "THE HOME OF GOALS GALORE" EBF MAIDEN FILLIES' STKS (DIV II) 6f 8y
4:20 (4:21) (Class 4) 2-Y-O
£4,528 (£1,347; £673; £336) **Stalls** Centre

Form RPR
42 **1** **Malilla (IRE)**[17] 4701 2-9-0 0 .... AdamKirby 2 85
(Clive Cox) *racd wd and w ldrs tl jnd main gp and upsides fr 2f out: chal appr fnl f tl narrow led fnl 120yds: drvn out* **7/2**[3]
220 **2** *hd* **Jillnextdoor (IRE)**[59] 3269 2-9-0 89 .... SamHitchcott 4 84
(Mick Channon) *trckd ldrs: led appr fnl 2f: jnd appr fnl f: narrowly hdd fnl 120yds: no ex clsng stages* **7/4**[1]
3 3 3/4 **Talent** 2-9-0 0 .... RichardThomas 6 73+
(Ralph Beckett) *s.i.s: in rr: pushed along and green 2f out: kpt on wl to take 3rd fnl 120yds but no ch w ldng duo* **14/1**
4 1 3/4 **Floating Along (IRE)** 2-9-0 0 .... LiamJones 10 68+
(William Haggas) *in rr: pushed along and hdwy fr 2f out: kpt on fnl f but nvr gng pce to rch ldrs* **3/1**[2]
30 **5** *nk* **Something Magic**[45] 3764 2-9-0 0 .... MartinDwyer 5 67
(Sylvester Kirk) *sn led: hdd approachin fnl 2f: wknd over 1f out* **33/1**
6 3/4 **Valais Girl** 2-8-9 0 .... KatiaScallan(5) 1 64
(Marcus Tregoning) *chsd ldrs: pushed along over 2f out: wknd over 1f out* **16/1**
7 3/4 **Greenery (IRE)** 2-9-0 0 .... RichardKingscote 3 62
(Roger Charlton) *in tch: pushed along 2f out to try an cl on ldrs: no imp and sn btn* **16/1**
8 2 1/2 **Tippotina** 2-9-0 0 .... TomQueally 7 55
(Brian Meehan) *s.i.s: outpcd most of way* **33/1**
03 **9** *3* **Glossy Posse**[37] 4002 2-9-0 0 .... RyanMoore 8 46
(Richard Hannon) *in rr but in tch whn rdn: hung rt and btn over 2f out* **10/1**
10 *3* **So Lyrical** 2-9-0 0 .... DarryllHolland 9 37
(Peter Makin) *sn green and rdn: a in rr* **33/1**

1m 13.56s (0.56) **Going Correction** 0.0s/f (Good) **10** Ran SP% **119.9**
Speed ratings (Par 93): **96,95,90,88,88 87,86,82,78,74**
Tote Swingers: 1&2 £2.40, 1&3 £9.20, 2&3 £7.50 CSF £10.18 TOTE £4.00: £1.50, £1.20, £4.30; EX 11.80.
Owner Mrs T L Cox **Bred** Tally-Ho Stud **Trained** Lambourn, Berks

FOCUS
The time was 1.32 seconds quicker than the modestly run first division. They raced up the middle of the track, although Malilla was positioned away from the others through the opening exchanges. The form looks fairly solid.

NOTEBOOK
Malilla(IRE) had produced an improved effort at Goodwood on her second start and showed she's very much going the right way with a game effort. She could progress to a decent level. (tchd 4-1)
Jillnextdoor(IRE), runner-up on her first two starts before a respectable effort in the Queen Mary, was up to 6f for the first time. She ran to a useful level once again, and there might be more to come considering she'd been off for two months, although she didn't totally convince she was really knuckling down with her effort. (op 2-1)
Talent, a half-sister to Listed-placed miler Skilful, out of a 1m4f winner, fared best of the newcomers. She clearly has plenty of ability. (op 12-1)
Floating Along(IRE) ◆, a 400,000gns purchase, is from a family the trainer knows well, notably being a half-sister to the stable's Prix Maurice de Gheest winner King's Apostle. She's in the Cheveley Park, but was too green to do herself justice and only got the idea late on. There should be significantly more to come. (op 7-2)
Something Magic was well held last time but here she went some way to confirming her debut promise. (op 20-1)
Valais Girl, who cost 80,000gns, showed ability and can be expected to improve. (op 20-1)

5358 BETFRED BIGGER ODDS ON GOALS GALORE H'CAP 1m 2f 6y
4:55 (4:55) (Class 4) (0-85,85) 3-Y-O **£5,175** (£1,540; £769; £384) **Stalls** Low

Form RPR
-236 **1** **Rose Season**[36] 4067 3-8-10 **77** .... DominicFox(3) 3 85
(Roger Varian) *chsd ldrs: drvn to ld 2f out: strly chal and edging lft ins fnl f: hld on all out* **12/1**
-221 **2** *hd* **Commend**[20] 4622 3-9-6 **84** .... RyanMoore 10 94+
(Sir Michael Stoute) *trckd ldrs: nt clr run fr 2f out tl squeezed through on rails ins fnl f but stl n.m.r: upsides fnl 75yds but nt qckn last strides* **5/4**[1]
0-10 **3** *nse* **Valiant Girl**[17] 4702 3-9-5 **83** .... TomQueally 11 93+
(Roger Charlton) *hld up in rr: nt clr run fr 2f out and stl no room ins fnl f: edgd rt and str run fnl 50yds: fin fast: unlucky* **6/1**[2]
3535 **4** 1 1/4 **Devine Guest (IRE)**[16] 4735 3-9-1 **79** .... SamHitchcott 5 84
(Mick Channon) *in tch: chsd ldrs over 2f out: rdn to chal over 1f out: outpcd fnl 120yds* **8/1**[3]
6266 **5** 1/2 **Presburg (IRE)**[10] 4949 3-9-5 **83** .... MartinDwyer 9 87
(Joseph Tuite) *chsd ldrs: drvn over 2f out: styd on same pce fnl f* **16/1**
1500 **6** *2* **Freddy Q (IRE)**[23] 4515 3-9-5 **83** .... JimmyFortune 2 83
(Richard Hannon) *towards rr: rdn and sme hdwy over 2f out: nvr quite gng pce to press ldrs: wknd fnl f* **11/1**
11-2 **7** 3 3/4 **Docs Legacy (IRE)**[20] 4623 3-8-9 **73** .... FrederikTylicki 1 66
(Richard Fahey) *chsd ldrs: rdn over 2f out: wkng on rails whn n.m.r appr fnl f* **6/1**[2]
5362 **8** *7* **Drummond**[15] 4755 3-8-12 **76** .... RichardKingscote 4 55
(Clive Cox) *led: rdn 3f out: hdd 2f out: sn btn* **14/1**
1030 **9** *9* **Minstrels Gallery (IRE)**[70] 2930 3-9-2 **80** .... DarryllHolland 7 41
(J R Jenkins) *in rr: rdn 3f out: sn dropped away* **28/1**

2m 6.88s (-1.92) **Going Correction** -0.125s/f (Firm) **9** Ran SP% **116.1**
Speed ratings (Par 102): **102,101,101,100,100 98,95,90,83**
Tote Swingers: 1&2 £21.00, 1&3 £24.60, 2&3 £3.20 CSF £27.62 CT £105.34 TOTE £15.90: £3.40, £1.20, £2.50; EX 40.50.
Owner Sultan Ali **Bred** Cliveden Stud Ltd **Trained** Newmarket, Suffolk

FOCUS
The pace was steady and this was a messy race. The second and third were the chief sufferers.
Minstrels Gallery(IRE) Official explanation: trainer said colt was unsuited by the good to firm ground

5359 BETFRED "BONUS KING BINGO" LADIES DERBY H'CAP (FOR LADY AMATEUR RIDERS) 1m 4f 5y
5:25 (5:25) (Class 4) (0-80,81) 3-Y-0+ **£4,991** (£1,548; £773; £387) **Stalls** Low

Form RPR
3161 **1** **The Quarterjack**[11] 4906 3-9-1 **69** .... MissSBrotherton 8 78
(Ron Hodges) *chsd ldrs: wnt 2nd 5f out: pushed along and grad clsd on ldr thrght fnl f: led last stride* **15/8**[1]

1022 **2** *hd* **The Ducking Stool**[10] 4959 5-9-1 **64**............................ MissSBirkett(5) 9 72
(Julia Feilden) *sn led: rdn 2f out: styd on fnl f: hdd last stride* **6/1**[3]

5550 **3** *5* **Saint Helena (IRE)**[38] 3962 4-10-3 **75**.............................. MissEJJones 6 75
(Harry Dunlop) *chsd ldrs: rdn and no ch w ldng duo fr over 2f out* **10/1**

1300 **4** *8* **Benandonner (USA)**[12] 4864 9-9-9 **72**...................... MissMBryant(5) 5 59
(Paddy Butler) *in rr: pushed along fr 3f out: mod prog into wl btn 4th ins fnl f* **25/1**

0300 **5** *3/4* **Almail (USA)**[85] 2447 6-10-4 **79**............................ MissHayleyMoore(3) 2 65
(Jamie Osborne) *in rr: hung bdly rt to r alone in centre crse fr over 3f out and nvr any ch after* **14/1**

-600 **6** *2* **Mons Calpe (IRE)**[53] 3472 6-9-1 **64**.....................(p) MissAliceMills(5) 11 47
(Paul Cole) *s.i.s: sn rcvrd to chse ldrs: wknd fr 6f out* **10/1**

5112 **7** *4* **Shades Of Grey**[11] 4905 5-10-6 **81**............................ MissRachelKing(3) 4 58
(Clive Cox) *rdn over 3f out: a in rr* **5/2**[2]

0136 **8** *2* **Hamilton Hill**[5] 5151 5-9-11 **72**...................................... MrsAlexDunn(3) 1 45
(Dai Burchell) *s.i.s: in rr: sme hdwy over 3f out: sn wknd* **10/1**

0006 **9** *21* **Admirable Duque (IRE)**[10] 4944 6-9-3 **66** ow1.......(v1) MissCBoxall(5) 7
(Dominic Ffrench Davis) *racd wd: mod prog 4f out: sn wknd* **16/1**

2m 36.93s (1.43) **Going Correction** -0.125s/f (Firm)
WFA 3 from 4yo+ 10lb **9** Ran SP% **121.3**
Speed ratings (Par 105): **90,89,86,81,80 79,76,75,61**
Tote Swingers 1&2 £2.30, 2&3 £18.50, 1&3 £7.60 CSF £14.69 CT £94.00 TOTE £2.70: £1.40, £1.80, £2.70; EX 13.90.
Owner P E Axon **Bred** Cheveley Park Stud Ltd **Trained** Charlton Mackrell, Somerset

FOCUS
A forward ride was a must in this slowly run handicap for lady amateurs. The first two finished clear and showed improvement.
T/Plt: £23.00 to a £1 stake. Pool: £98,279.21 - 3,106.15 winning tickets. T/Qpdt: £9.30 to a £1 stake. Pool: £6,368.01 - 503.38 winning tickets. ST

5319 NEWMARKET (R-H)

Saturday, August 18

OFFICIAL GOING: Good to firm changing to good to firm (firm in places) after race 4 (3.20)
Wind: Nil Weather: Sunny

5360 BARTON STUD EBF MAIDEN STKS 6f
1:40 (1:41) (Class 4) 2-Y-O **£5,175** (£1,540; £769; £384) **Stalls** High

Form RPR

0020 **1** **Zanetto**[15] 4763 2-9-3 78.. LiamKeniry 4 79
(Andrew Balding) *racd centre: mde all: rdn and edgd lft fr over 1f out: styd on* **15/2**

2 *1 3/4* **Coincidently** 2-8-5 0.. NatashaEaton(7) 6 69
(Alan Bailey) *racd centre: chsd wnr: rdn and ev ch over 1f out: sn hung lft: styd on: 2nd of 6 in gp* **20/1**

3 *nk* **Noble Deed** 2-9-0 0... AdamBeschizza(3) 7 73
(William Haggas) *racd centre: a.p: pushed along 1/2-way: rdn over 1f out: styd on: 3rd of 6 in gp* **14/1**

0 **4** *2 1/4* **Inka Surprise (IRE)**[120] 1499 2-9-3 0.................................. JimCrowley 8 66+
(Ralph Beckett) *led far side: rdn over 1f out: stayng on same pce whn hmpd ins fnl f: 1st of 3 in gp* **11/4**[2]

5 **5** *hd* **Shamaheart (IRE)**[49] 3637 2-9-3 0.. PatDobbs 2 66
(Richard Hannon) *racd centre: hld up: hdwy over 2f out: rdn and hung lft fr over 1f out: styd on same pce ins fnl f: 4th of 6 in gp* **9/1**

2424 **6** *6* **Strictly Silca**[14] 4818 2-8-12 85....................................... MartinHarley 10 43+
(Mick Channon) *racd far side: chsd ldrs: rdn over 2f out: wknd over 1f out: 2nd of 3 in gp* **5/1**[3]

2 **7** *1 3/4* **Intrepid (IRE)**[15] 4773 2-9-3 0... ShaneKelly 9 42+
(Jeremy Noseda) *chsd ldr far side: rdn over 2f out: wknd over 1f out: last of 3 in gp* **7/4**[1]

0 **8** *6* **The Obvious Choice**[51] 3545 2-9-3 0................................. JamesDoyle 1 24
(Stuart Williams) *racd centre: chsd ldrs tl rdn and wknd over 2f out: 5th of 6 in gp* **100/1**

9 *13* **Dumbarton Rock** 2-9-3 0... WilliamCarson 5
(William Jarvis) *racd centre: s.i.s: outpcd: hung lft fnl 4f: t.o: last of 6 in gp* **33/1**

1m 11.63s (-0.87) **Going Correction** -0.20s/f (Firm) **9** Ran SP% **116.8**
Speed ratings (Par 96): **97,94,94,91,91 83,80,72,55**
Tote Swingers: 1&2 £28.70, 1&3 £48.50, 2&3 £22.50 CSF £138.59 TOTE £8.70: £1.50, £8.20, £3.70; EX 180.20 Trifecta £265.80.
Owner Mick and Janice Mariscotti **Bred** Aislabie Bloodstock Ltd **Trained** Kingsclere, Hants
■ Stewards' Enquiry : Natasha Eaton one-day ban: careless riding (Sep 1)

FOCUS
Stands' side track used with stalls on far except 1m2f & 1m4f centre. With 6mm of water applied to the course after the previous evening's racing the going was Good to firm. The jockeys reported it was either "fast" or "beautiful ground." This maiden has tended to produce useful handicappers in general, although Young Pretender went on to win and place at Group level. The field split into two groups early before drifting towards the far rail, those that raced in the centre for most of the way filled the first three places, suggesting that it was quicker there than on the far side. The winner is rated to form.

NOTEBOOK
Zanetto had run his best previous race when making the running and pulled to hard when held up in a Goodwood nursery on his previous start. Allowed to go on here, he set a reasonable pace and found plenty up the hill when asked. This is clearly the way to ride him and he is probably the best guide to the level of the form. (tchd 8-1)
Coincidently, a 77,000gns breeze-up purchase with a speedy pedigree, showed up throughout on this debut and stuck to her task despite drifting away to the far side. She has a Lowther Stakes entry so is obviously well thought-of, but that race may come too soon for her. (op 22-1 tchd 18-1)
Noble Deed ◆ is closely related to Peeress and Entitled but was relatively unfancied for this debut. However, he made a nice start, keeping on steadily in the closing stages without being given a particularly hard time, and could be the one to take out of the race.
Inka Surprise(IRE), not seen since going off joint favourite for a hot maiden at Newbury in April, made the running towards the far side but was struggling when hampered by the runner-up in the closing stages. He did by far the best of those to race on that part of the track. (op 7-2 tchd 4-1)
Shamaheart(IRE) ran a similar race to on his debut in June, finishing not far behind the placed horses. He should benefit from a step up in trip. (op 8-1)
Strictly Silca, rated 85 having been already placed in Listed company, was dropping in trip but possibly suffered from the track bias and was in trouble a good way from home. (op 6-1)
Intrepid(IRE) had run promisingly here earlier in the month and can be given another chance having probably raced on the slower part of the track. (op 6-4)
Dumbarton Rock's rider reported that the colt was slowly away and slow into stride. Official explanation: jockey said colt was slowly away

5361 BET AT BLUESQ.COM FILLIES' NURSERY 7f
2:15 (2:16) (Class 2) 2-Y-O **£10,350** (£3,080; £1,539; £769) **Stalls** High

Form RPR

10 **1** **Light Up My Life (IRE)**[57] 3326 2-9-5 **83**............................ EddieAhern 3 96+
(Richard Hannon) *led to 1/2-way: led again over 2f out: shkn up and r.o wl* **14/1**

01 **2** *3 3/4* **Dusky Queen (IRE)**[30] 4246 2-8-13 **77**............................ JamesDoyle 7 80+
(Richard Fahey) *hld up: hdwy over 2f out: rdn over 1f out: hung lft ins fnl f: styd on same pce* **9/1**[3]

21 **3** *nk* **Fleeting Smile (USA)**[22] 4626 2-9-7 **86**............................ PaulHanagan 11 87
(Richard Hannon) *chsd wnr tl led 1/2-way: hdd over 2f out: sn rdn: styd on same pce fnl f* **11/4**[2]

1 **4** *hd* **Waterway Run (USA)**[21] 4604 2-9-0 **78**............................ JimCrowley 6 80
(Ralph Beckett) *chsd ldrs: rdn and hung lft over 1f out: styd on same pce* **15/8**[1]

13 **5** *6* **Elle Woods (IRE)**[30] 4247 2-9-3 **81**.................................. ShaneKelly 12 67
(Michael Dods) *s.i.s: hdwy over 4f out: rdn and wknd over 1f out* **10/1**

3514 **6** *2* **Stupenda**[10] 4947 2-7-13 **63**.. NickyMackay 4 44
(Denis Coakley) *hld up: rdn 1/2-way: wknd over 1f out* **40/1**

01 **7** *1* **Ishigunnaeatit**[20] 4618 2-9-0 **78**...................................... CathyGannon 5 57
(Mrs K Burke) *hld up: plld hrd: rdn over 2f out: sn wknd* **25/1**

051 **8** *1 1/2* **Starlight Symphony (IRE)**[23] 4494 2-8-12 **76**........... MickaelBarzalona 10 51
(Eve Johnson Houghton) *prom tl rdn and wknd over 1f out* **12/1**

541 **9** *6* **Everleigh**[14] 4818 2-9-4 **82**... PatDobbs 9 41
(Richard Hannon) *chsd ldrs: rdn over 2f out: sn wknd* **12/1**

15 **10** *2* **Columella**[48] 3669 2-8-10 **77**............................... AdamBeschizza(3) 2 31
(William Haggas) *s.i.s: hld up: rdn and wknd over 2f out* **16/1**

2210 **11** *12* **Boom And Bloom (IRE)**[15] 4763 2-9-0 **78**................. WilliamCarson 1
(Richard Fahey) *hld up: rdn and wknd over 2f out: t.o* **22/1**

1m 23.57s (-2.13) **Going Correction** -0.20s/f (Firm) 2y crse rec **11** Ran SP% **119.1**
Speed ratings (Par 97): **104,99,99,99,92 90,88,87,80,78 64**
Tote Swingers: 1&2 £40.80, 1&3 £4.80, 2&3 £4.30 CSF £132.78 CT £465.39 TOTE £16.90: £3.00, £1.70, £1.50; EX 143.30 Trifecta £386.70 Pool: £689.93 - 1.32 winning units..
Owner D Boocock **Bred** D Boocock **Trained** East Everleigh, Wilts

FOCUS
The subsequent Listed winner and Rockfel runner-up Pimpernel took this fillies' nursery in 2001. This year's contest looked competitive judged on official ratings, with the majority of the runners in a 9lb weight range, but was won in good style by the Hannon third-string, judged on jockey bookings. The first four pulled clear, suggesting the form is sound rated around the third and fourth.

NOTEBOOK
Light Up My Life(IRE) had been the stable second-string when taking her maiden from three subsequent winners, but had failed to handle the soft ground at Ascot next time. Down in class and back in fast going, she made the running and picked up well when headed by her stablemate to pull nicely clear up the hill. She has no fancy entries by looks capable of winning more good races this season. (op 12-1)
Dusky Queen(IRE) improved from her debut run to score narrowly next time over this trip and this looked another step up, as she did best of those to come from off the pace, although she had no chance with the winner. (op 10-1 tchd 11-1)
Fleeting Smile(USA) was up with the pace for most of the way and kicked on over 2f out. However, the winner responded and once headed she could only keep on at the one pace. With an entry in the Fillies' Mile she was obviously considered potentially a Group-class filly, and it may be that she ran into one could be in the same league here. (op 10-3 tchd 5-2 after early 4-1)
Waterway Run(USA) ◆ had beaten more experienced rivals on her debut and was stepping up in trip. She was never far away but was outpaced running into the Dip before keeping on again. She will have learnt from this. (op 9-4 tchd 5-2)
Elle Woods(IRE)'s form coming into this looked pretty solid; she had beaten two subsequent winners, one at Listed level, on her debut. She was never far away but those in the frame drew away from her up the hill. Shane Kelly reported that the filly was unsuited by the good to firm ground. (tchd 9-1)

5362 BLUE SQUARE BET GREY HORSE H'CAP (FOR GREY HORSES ONLY) 6f
2:45 (2:46) (Class 4) (0-85,84) 3-Y-O+
£12,450 (£3,728; £1,864; £932; £466; £234) **Stalls** High

Form RPR

0050 **1** **Medici Time**[22] 4554 7-9-4 **78**..(v) EddieAhern 12 88
(Tim Easterby) *chsd ldrs: led over 1f out: edgd rt ins fnl f: r.o* **10/1**

1000 **2** *1 1/4* **Emman Bee (IRE)**[9] 5004 3-8-12 **75**.................... MickaelBarzalona 4 81
(John Gallagher) *chsd ldrs: rdn and ev ch over 1f out: styd on* **12/1**

5611 **3** *nse* **Dream Catcher (FR)**[29] 4315 4-9-0 **74**........................ CathyGannon 3 80
(Henry Candy) *a.p: rdn and ev ch over 1f out: edgd lft ins fnl f: styd on* **9/2**[1]

4524 **4** *3* **Silver Rime (FR)**[26] 4388 7-8-12 **72**.................................... JimCrowley 7 68
(Linda Perratt) *s.i.s: sn prom: rdn over 1f out: styd on same pce fnl f* **15/2**[3]

0003 **5** *hd* **Red Avalanche (IRE)**[23] 4492 5-7-12 **58** oh1................. NickyMackay 2 54
(Tony Newcombe) *chsd ldrs: rdn over 1f out: styd on same pce fnl f* **9/1**

4241 **6** *1* **Rylee Mooch**[24] 4461 4-8-10 **77**...............................(e) JasonHart(7) 13 69
(Richard Guest) *led: rdn and hdd over 1f out: no ex ins fnl f* **16/1**

1336 **7** *shd* **Crew Cut (IRE)**[15] 4775 4-9-5 **79**...................................(p) GeorgeBaker 8 71
(Jeremy Gask) *hld up: hdwy and nt clr run over 1f out: swtchd lft ins fnl f: nt trble ldrs* **7/1**[2]

000 **8** *2 3/4* **Masked Dance (IRE)**[14] 4799 5-8-13 **80**(bt) WilliamTwiston-Davies(7) 19 63
(Scott Dixon) *chsd ldrs: rdn over 1f out: wknd fnl f* **28/1**

3035 **9** *nse* **Sutton Veny (IRE)**[22] 4530 6-9-7 **84**........................ RaulDaSilva(3) 11 67
(Jeremy Gask) *prom: rdn over 2f out: wknd fnl f* **10/1**

-001 **10** *1 1/4* **Time Medicean**[18] 4690 6-8-12 **77**........................... ConorHoban(5) 17 56
(Tony Carroll) *dwlt: hld up: nt clr run fr over 1f out: nvr on terms* **7/1**[2]

0355 **11** *1* **Berbice (IRE)**[8] 5058 7-8-1 **64** ow2.................... AdamBeschizza(3) 1 40
(Linda Perratt) *hld up: hdwy over 2f out: wknd fnl f* **25/1**

443- **12** *1/2* **Witchry**[277] 7425 10-8-4 **64**...................................... KirstyMilczarek 6 38
(Tony Newcombe) *hld up: plld hrd: hld up: rdn and wknd over 1f out* **20/1**

0100 **13** *3/4* **Silvee**[16] 4726 5-7-10 **63**.. IanBurns(7) 9 35
(John Bridger) *mid-div: sn pushed along: wknd 2f out* **33/1**

0432 **14** *hd* **Speightowns Kid (USA)**[45] 3761 4-8-3 **68**.............. AshleyMorgan(5) 10 39
(Jeremy Gask) *prom: rdn over 2f out: wkng whn nt clr run over 1f out* **14/1**

130 **15** *7* **Royal Bajan (USA)**[18] 4690 4-8-13 **73**.......................... WilliamCarson 14 22
(James Given) *mid-div: rdn over 2f out: wknd over 1f out* **33/1**

1m 10.86s (-1.64) **Going Correction** -0.20s/f (Firm)
WFA 3 from 4yo+ 3lb **15** Ran SP% **121.3**
Speed ratings (Par 105): **102,100,100,96,96 94,94,90,90,89 87,87,86,85,76**
Tote Swingers: 1&2 £34.40, 1&3 £9.20, 2&3 £12.10 CSF £116.62 CT £634.68 TOTE £9.90: £3.60, £4.30, £1.70; EX 147.30 Trifecta £608.80 Part won. Pool: £822.71 - 0.50 winning units..

Owner Mrs C A Hodgetts **Bred** Mrs Fiona Denniff **Trained** Great Habton, N Yorks

FOCUS

This annual sprint confined to greys produced a big field, despite four absentees that spoilt the each-way terms, with the two previous winners, Witchry and Time Medicean taking part. They surprisingly went towards the far side early on, but three that raced more towards the centre in the closing stages drew away from the rest. The form looks sound.

5363 NEWMARKET EQUINE HOSPITAL STKS (H'CAP) 6f

3:20 (3:21) (Class 2) (0-105,98) 3-Y-O

£24,900 (£7,456; £3,728; £1,864; £932; £468) **Stalls** High

Form				RPR
0100	**1**		**Hamza (IRE)**[16] 4740 3-8-11 **88**........(b) JimCrowley 4 (Kevin Ryan) *chsd ldrs: led over 3f out: rdn out* **14/1**	103
-126	**2**	1 ¾	**Gabriel's Lad (IRE)**[30] 4234 3-8-9 **86**........ EddieAhern 5 (Denis Coakley) *hld up: plld hrd: hdwy over 1f out: rdn to chse wnr ins fnl f: styd on* **14/1**	95+
150	**3**	1 ¼	**Poole Harbour (IRE)**[14] 4799 3-8-11 **88**........ PatDobbs 13 (Richard Hannon) *led: hdd over 3f out: remained handy: rdn over 1f out: styd on same pce ins fnl f* **10/1**	93
4241	**4**	hd	**Amadeus Wolfe Tone (IRE)**[21] 4607 3-8-10 **87**........(p) ShaneKelly 8 (Jamie Osborne) *hmpd s: hld up: nt clr run: swtchd lft and hdwy over 1f out: rdn whn rdr dropped reins ins fnl f: styd on same pce* **6/1**[2]	91+
1542	**5**	¾	**Galician**[7] 5080 3-9-0 **91**........ RobertHavlin 6 (Mark Johnston) *chsd ldrs: rdn over 2f out: outpcd and n.m.r over 1f out: r.o ins fnl f* **5/2**[1]	93+
1112	**6**	1 ¼	**Show Flower**[21] 4588 3-9-3 **94**........ MartinHarley 15 (Mick Channon) *hld up: hdwy over 2f out: sn rdn: no ex ins fnl f* **10/1**	92
26-0	**7**	nk	**Gold City (IRE)**[70] 2916 3-9-7 **98**........(t) MickaelBarzalona 2 (Saeed Bin Suroor) *s.i.s: sn prom: rdn and edgd lft over 1f out: no ex fnl f* **8/1**[3]	95
5355	**8**	2 ¼	**Mr Red Clubs (IRE)**[16] 4740 3-8-10 **94**...(p) WilliamTwiston-Davies(7) 11 (Tim Pitt) *chsd ldrs: rdn over 1f out: wknd ins fnl f* **12/1**	84
1021	**9**	nk	**Orders From Rome (IRE)**[16] 4723 3-7-12 **82**........ NicoleNordblad(7) 14 (Eve Johnson Houghton) *hld up: shkn up over 1f out: nvr trbld ldrs* **18/1**	71
4161	**10**	nk	**Pale Orchid (IRE)**[6] 5128 3-9-2 **93** 6ex........ CathyGannon 7 (David Evans) *w ldrs: rdn over 1f out: wknd ins fnl f* **20/1**	81
0503	**11**	4	**Tioman Legend**[15] 4765 3-9-2 **93**........ JamesDoyle 12 (Roger Charlton) *s.i.s: sn prom: rdn over 1f out: sn wknd* **8/1**[3]	68
15-4	**12**	7	**Alaskan Bullet (IRE)**[84] 2509 3-9-1 **92**........ WilliamCarson 1 (Michael Bell) *wnt rt s: hld up plld hrd: wknd over 2f out* **25/1**	45

1m 10.42s (-2.08) **Going Correction** -0.20s/f (Firm) **12** Ran SP% **118.2**

Speed ratings (Par 106): **105,102,101,100,99 98,97,94,94,93 88,79**

Tote Swingers: 1&2 £31.70, 1&3 £13.80, 2&3 £36.50 CSF £195.29 CT £2084.94 TOTE £13.50: £4.10, £3.90, £2.90; EX 229.40 Trifecta £871.40 Pool: £1,177.65 - 1.00 winning units..

Owner Mubarak Al Naemi **Bred** Castlemartin Stud And Skymarc Farm **Trained** Hambleton, N Yorks

FOCUS

Subsequent Group 1 winner King's Apostle was the best recent winner of this strong, competitive sprint handicap for 3yos. It was run at a sound pace and the time was 0.44 secs faster than the preceding greys' race. Again, those that raced in the centre of the track dominated the finish. The form is not rated too positively.

NOTEBOOK

Hamza(IRE) made all when scoring in first-time blinkers over 7f in May, the last time he raced on fast ground, and repeated the trick. He did not appear to be doing much in front and, having established an advantage in the Dip, found plenty up the hill. There might be more to come on this sort of ground. (op 12-1)

Gabriel's Lad(IRE) was held up at the back and did best of those to come from off the pace. He was racing on fast ground for the first time but handled it well enough, although he was unable to reel in the winner. (op 16-1)

Poole Harbour(IRE) had run reasonably in two all-aged handicaps on his last two starts but fared better against his own age group, despite the fact that he raced more towards the far rail than most. He seems best suited by a forward ride. (tchd 9-1)

Amadeus Wolfe Tone(IRE) ◆, raised 5lb for his narrow success over 7f last time, was arguably the most unlucky horse in the race. Held up at the back, he was faced with a wall of horses in the Dip and had to switch right around them to get a run. He narrowly missed out on third place and can gain compensation given a better run. (op 5-1 tchd 13-2)

Galician has progressed well this season but was 3lb higher than when narrowly beaten at Ascot the previous weekend. However, his main problem here was that he got involved in some scrimmaging just as the race was developing and had to be switched to get a run. He powered up the hill to suggest that, despite a fair rise in the weights, he is still on an upward curve. (op 11-4 tchd 9-4, 3-1 in a place)

Show Flower has been in fine form on varying ground this season, and ran creditably again. However, she has risen 20lb in the weights as a result and the handicapper looks to have her measure now. (op 9-1)

Gold City(IRE), back on fast ground and down in trip following a ten-week break, was fitted with a tongue tie and given a good lead into the race by the winner, but could not sustain his effort up the hill. (op 11-1)

Alaskan Bullet(IRE)'s rider reported that the gelding ran too free. Official explanation: jockey said gelding ran too free (op 16-1)

5364 SIR PERCY CONDITIONS STKS 1m 2f

3:55 (3:56) (Class 2) 3-Y-O+ **£12,450** (£3,728; £1,864; £932; £466) **Stalls** Centre

Form				RPR
-220	**1**		**Laajooj (IRE)**[161] 877 4-9-1 107........ MickaelBarzalona 2 (Mahmood Al Zarooni) *a.p: styd stands' side over 7f out tl merged w centre gp over 5f out: rdn to ld ins fnl f: r.o* **15/8**[1]	106
236-	**2**	2	**Calvados Blues (FR)**[427] 3153 6-9-1 116........ JamesDoyle 6 (Mahmood Al Zarooni) *led: styd stands' side over 7f out: sn hung lft: jnd centre gp over 5f out: rdn over 1f out: hdd and unable qck ins fnl f* **5/1**	102
3253	**3**	hd	**Mister Music**[15] 4761 3-8-10 100........ PatDobbs 4 (Richard Hannon) *hld up: wnt centre over 7f out: hdwy over 1f out: hmpd sn after: styd on: nt trble ldrs: fin 4th: promoted to 3rd* **7/2**[3]	105+
5-46	**4**	½	**Farhaan (USA)**[18] 4685 3-8-7 104........ PaulHanagan 1 (John Dunlop) *chsd ldr tl wnt centre and led that trio over 7f out tl gps merged over 5f out: stl w ldr: rdn over 2f out: ev ch over 1f out: sn swtchd rt: styd on same pce: fin 3rd: disqualified and plcd 4th* **10/3**[2]	101
2641	**5**	2 ¾	**Proud Chieftain**[14] 4821 4-9-1 89........ EddieAhern 5 (Clifford Lines) *chsd ldrs: wnt centre over 7f out: rdn over 2f out: no ex fnl f* **7/1**	95?

2m 7.39s (1.89) **Going Correction** -0.20s/f (Firm)

WFA 3 from 4yo+ 8lb 5 Ran SP% **109.3**

Speed ratings (Par 109): **84,82,81,82,79**

CSF £11.21 TOTE £2.60: £1.70, £1.50; EX 8.50.

Owner Godolphin **Bred** Kildaragh Stud **Trained** Newmarket, Suffolk

FOCUS

The going was changed to Good to firm, firm in places before this race. A conditions race that could have easily passed for a Listed race judged on the ratings of most of the contenders, although slightly weakened by the withdrawal of Fury. The pace was very steady early on and did not really pick up until the last half-mile. The form is muddling and limited by the fifth.

NOTEBOOK

Laajooj(IRE), a Listed winner over this distance ion the Rowley Mile last season, was returning from a break having last run at Meydan in March. He got a good lead into the race and found plenty for pressure up the hill to score. He has not had much racing and there are Group races to be won with him on a sound surface, either here or back in Dubai. (op 2-1 tchd 7-4 and 9-4 in places)

Calvados Blues(FR) was clear top on official ratings but had not been seen since Royal Ascot in 2011. He made the running and gave a lead to his stable companion, then responded to pressure when headed by that rival. Much will depend on how he comes out of this, but he could pick up a Group race at around 1m4f given good or easy ground this autumn. (op 9-2)

Mister Music, a generally consistent sort, managed to find trouble in running despite the small field. He was held up and still appeared to be going well 2f out, but he got stuck behind the third and had to take evasive action more than once to get in the clear. By then the race was virtually over and he was rightly awarded third place in the stewards' room. (op 3-1)

Farhaan(USA) has been competing in Group and Listed company since winning twice at around this time last season. He appeared to have every chance by wandered about under pressure and could not cope with his older rivals. He was demoted to fourth as a result of interefering with the run of Mister Music. (op 7-2)

Proud Chieftain, a C&D winner last time off 84, had a lot to find on official ratings and did well to finish as close as he did. Hopefully, the handicapper will not take the form at face value, or the gelding's handicap mark will suffer. (op 13-2 tchd 6-1)

5365 HORSEFLIES H'CAP 1m

4:30 (4:30) (Class 4) (0-85,87) 3-Y-O **£5,175** (£1,540; £769; £384) **Stalls** High

Form				RPR
1-66	**1**		**Kiz Kulesi**[23] 4515 3-9-3 **81**........ JamesDoyle 1 (Mahmood Al Zarooni) *chsd ldr tl led over 3f out: rdn over 1f out: hung lft: r.o* **5/1**[2]	93
-221	**2**	2 ½	**Zaeem**[60] 3248 3-9-3 **81**........ MickaelBarzalona 9 (Mahmood Al Zarooni) *a.p: rdn to chse wnr over 1f out: styd on same pce* **4/1**[1]	87
0303	**3**	1 ¼	**Nelson's Bay**[21] 4600 3-9-1 **79**........(t) EddieAhern 7 (Brian Meehan) *chsd ldrs: rdn over 2f out: styd on same pce fnl f* **15/2**	82
2532	**4**	nk	**Jack Who's He (IRE)**[9] 4997 3-9-9 **87**........ CathyGannon 6 (David Evans) *hld up: pushed along over 2f out: r.o ins fnl f: nvr nrr* **13/2**	89
6206	**5**	1	**Strada Facendo (USA)**[21] 4600 3-9-0 **78**........ KirstyMilczarek 3 (Luca Cumani) *hld up: rdn over 1f out: r.o ins fnl f: nvr rchd ldrs* **10/1**	78
0500	**6**	2 ¼	**Fillionaire**[8] 5043 3-8-11 **80**........ CharlesBishop(5) 2 (Mick Channon) *led over 4f: sn pushed along: sddle slipped over 2f out: eased ins fnl f* **16/1**	75+
-266	**7**	2 ¼	**Levi Draper**[33] 4155 3-8-4 **68**........ PaulHanagan 8 (James Fanshawe) *hld up: rdn over 1f out: wknd fnl f* **11/1**	58
15	**8**	9	**Falcon In Flight**[103] 1938 3-9-5 **83**........ ShaneKelly 5 (Jeremy Noseda) *chsd ldrs: rdn over 2f out: wknd over 1f out* **5/1**[2]	52
5-26	**9**	½	**Ruby Night (IRE)**[29] 4298 3-9-6 **84**........ GeorgeBaker 4 (Michael Bell) *hld up: a in rr: wknd over 1f out: eased* **11/2**[3]	52

1m 38.18s (-1.82) **Going Correction** -0.20s/f (Firm) **9** Ran SP% **117.1**

Speed ratings (Par 102): **101,98,97,96,95 93,91,82,81**

Tote Swingers: 1&2 £6.70, 1&3 £13.70, 2&3 £6.30 CSF £25.73 CT £151.15 TOTE £7.20: £2.80, £2.00, £2.20; EX 25.90 Trifecta £228.70 Pool: £507.04 - 1.64 winning units..

Owner Godolphin **Bred** Darley **Trained** Newmarket, Suffolk

FOCUS

A tightly knit 3yo handicap that has often fallen to a lightly raced improver and that was more or less the case again. The winner recorded a personal best with the third to recent form.

Strada Facendo(USA) Official explanation: jockey said colt was reluctant leaving stalls

Fillionaire Official explanation: jockey said saddle slipped

5366 DODSON & HORRELL H'CAP 1m 4f

5:05 (5:06) (Class 4) (0-85,84) 3-Y-O+ **£5,175** (£1,540; £769; £384) **Stalls** Centre

Form				RPR
3344	**1**		**Ex Oriente (IRE)**[14] 4796 3-9-1 **81**........ NickyMackay 3 (John Gosden) *s.i.s: hld up: hdwy over 4f out: rdn to chse ldr and hung rt over 1f out: led ins fnl f: styd on u.p* **11/2**[3]	92
2415	**2**	3 ¾	**Spanish Wedding**[49] 3614 3-9-2 **82**........(b) MickaelBarzalona 1 (Marco Botti) *prom: rdn over 2f out: ev ch over 1f out: styd on same pce* **8/1**	87
062	**3**	½	**Modernism**[11] 4923 3-8-10 **76**........ RobertHavlin 5 (Mark Johnston) *chsd ldr tl led over 3f out: rdn over 1f out: hdd and no ex ins fnl f* **11/2**[3]	80
6240	**4**	¾	**Hurricane In Dubai (IRE)**[28] 4323 3-8-9 **75**........ EddieAhern 6 (Denis Coakley) *hld up: hdwy over 2f out: rdn over 1f out: styd on same pce fnl f* **8/1**	78
-131	**5**	nk	**Arch Villain (IRE)**[19] 4649 3-8-10 **76**........ PatDobbs 7 (Amanda Perrett) *chsd ldrs: rdn over 2f out: no ex fnl f* **5/1**[2]	78
1325	**6**	12	**Bathwick Street**[21] 4606 3-8-4 **70**........ CathyGannon 8 (David Evans) *chsd ldrs: rdn over 2f out: wknd over 1f out* **8/1**	53
24	**7**	27	**Gabrial The Hero (USA)**[49] 3605 3-9-4 **84**........ GeorgeBaker 4 (David Simcock) *s.v.s: sme hdwy 2f out: sn wknd and eased: t.o* **4/1**[1]	24
0113	**8**	8	**Ultimate Destiny**[37] 3992 3-8-10 **76**........ JimCrowley 2 (Ralph Beckett) *led over 8f: sn rdn: wknd 2f out: t.o* **11/2**[3]	
115	**9**	38	**Royal Straight**[15] 4768 7-9-1 **76**........(t) CharlesBishop(5) 9 (Linda Perratt) *hld up: plld hrd: hdwy over 4f out: wknd 3f out: t.o* **20/1**	

2m 28.72s (-4.18) **Going Correction** -0.20s/f (Firm)

WFA 3 from 7yo 10lb **9** Ran SP% **120.9**

Speed ratings (Par 105): **105,102,102,101,101 93,75,70,44**

Tote Swingers 1&2 £17.20, 2&3 £13.00, 1&3 £9.90 CSF £51.22 CT £258.88 TOTE £6.60: £1.80, £2.90, £2.50; EX 63.90 Trifecta £270.50 Pool: £833.48 - 2.28 winning units..

Owner Nicholas Cooper & Rachel Hood **Bred** Mrs Vanessa Hutch **Trained** Newmarket, Suffolk

FOCUS

Only one older horse took on the 3-y-os in this fair handicap and he finished well beaten. The form looks solid rated around the first three.

Modernism Official explanation: jockey said colt ran minus a shoe

Gabrial The Hero(USA) Official explanation: jockey said colt stopped quickly

T/Plt: £3,456.50 to a £1 stake. Pool: £80,138.87 - 16.92 winning tickets. T/Qpdt: £101.30 to a £1 stake. Pool: £6,138.45 - 44.80 winning tickets. CR

4921 RIPON (R-H)

Saturday, August 18

OFFICIAL GOING: Good (good to soft in places; 7.9)

Wind: light 1/2 behind Weather: fine and sunny, very warm

5367 FROM EPSOM TO RIPON ALL DONE MAIDEN AUCTION STKS 6f

1:45 (1:48) (Class 5) 2-Y-O **£3,234** (£962; £481; £240) **Stalls** High

Form RPR

0 **1** **Grey Street**[70] 2917 2-8-6 0 ... JimmyQuinn 3 75
(Richard Fahey) *hmpd s: hdwy on wd outside over 2f out: r.o to ld last 50yds* **25/1**

3024 **2** *1¼* **Balinka**[28] 4344 2-7-13 66 ... NeilFarley(5) 6 69
(Mel Brittain) *t.k.h: led: hdd and no ex wl ins fnl f* **12/1**

352 **3** *shd* **Nordikhab (IRE)**[14] 4816 2-9-3 81 ... GrahamLee 8 82
(Kevin Ryan) *trckd ldr: upsides and rdn 1f out: kpt on same pce last 50yds* **7/2**[2]

4225 **4** *3* **Bachotheque (IRE)**[21] 4612 2-8-11 79 ... DavidAllan 2 67
(Tim Easterby) *swtchd lft sn after s: sn chsng ldrs: drvn over 2f out: one pce over 1f out* **13/8**[1]

0 **5** *1¼* **Pipers Note**[28] 4344 2-8-11 0 ... RussKennemore 1 63
(Richard Whitaker) *carried rt s: sn chsng ldrs on outer: wandered bdly over 2f out: swtchd rt over 1f out: kpt on* **66/1**

0 **6** *1¾* **Rich Forever (IRE)**[12] 4877 2-9-1 0 ... NeilCallan 5 62
(James Bethell) *dwlt: outpcd and lost pl over 3f out: hdwy over 1f out: kpt on* **33/1**

2 **7** *1* **Baron Run**[23] 4512 2-8-8 0 ... MichaelMetcalfe(3) 11 55
(Mrs K Burke) *dwlt: hld up in mid-div: effrt over 2f out: wknd over 1f out* **5/1**[3]

8 *3½* **Heaven's Guest (IRE)** 2-9-3 0 ... TonyHamilton 4 50
(Richard Fahey) *wnt rt s: sn chsng ldrs: wknd over 1f out* **9/1**

05 **9** *8* **Abraham Monro**[12] 4877 2-8-11 0 ... PaulMulrennan 9 20
(Kate Walton) *chsd ldrs: drvn and lost pl over 3f out: hung rt and sn bhd* **40/1**

0 **10** *3* **Silkelly**[10] 4960 2-8-6 0 ... DuranFentiman 7 6
(David O'Meara) *chsd ldrs: lost pl over 3f out: bhd fnl 2f* **33/1**

11 *shd* **Mujadora (IRE)** 2-8-10 0 ... KellyHarrison 10 10
(William Haggas) *in rr: bhd fnl 2f* **11/1**

12 *26* **Troy Boy** 2-8-13 0 ow2 ... DanielTudhope 12
(Robin Bastiman) *dwlt: sn detached in last: reminders after 2f: sn t.o* **25/1**

1m 13.5s (0.50) **Going Correction** +0.05s/f (Good) **12 Ran SP% 120.5**

Speed ratings (Par 94): **98,96,96,92,90 88,86,82,71,67 67,32**

toteswingers 1&2 Not won, 1&3 £28.10, 2&3 £8.90 CSF £284.60 TOTE £24.20: £5.40, £4.10, £1.70; EX 208.60.

Owner Havelock Racing **Bred** Whitsbury Manor Stud And Mrs M E Slade **Trained** Musley Bank, N Yorks

FOCUS

Rail at innermost position and all distances as advertised. The ground was described by the winning jockey in the first as "on the easy side of good", and the time for the opener was 2.5sec outside standard. This was effectively a valuable race of its type, the whole field being eligible for the £10,000 Racing Post Yearling Bonus, but in truth it was a pretty ordinary event for the grade with a couple of the form horses failing to deliver. However the time was decent and the form makes sense around the second and third.

NOTEBOOK

Grey Street swept through late on the outside after racing towards the back for most of the trip. She had also been slowly away on her debut back in June, when finishing last, but this half-sister to a couple of Listed winners was more clued up here. A nursery will presumably be next for her.

Balinka made most of the running and showed a willing attitude as she tried to hold on. The return to 6f suited. (op 10-1)

Nordikhab(IRE), back up in trip, held every chance racing alongside the stands' rail. (op 4-1 tchd 10-3)

Bachotheque(IRE)'s trainer has a fine recent record in this event but this one was somewhat disappointing. It could have been that he did not really act on the track. (op 5-2)

Pipers Note had missed the break on his debut here behind Bachotheque and finished considerably closer to that horse now. He did wander quite badly not long after halfway. (op 50-1)

Rich Forever(IRE) was not quite as slowly away as he had been on his debut over C&D, and ran a better race. (op 40-1)

Baron Run, second to the useful Pearl Acclaim on his debut, was a little reluctant to load then lacked a change of gear at the business end of the race. (op 4-1)

Heaven's Guest(IRE), the winner's shorter-priced stablemate, showed enough to suggest he'll win a race or two in time. (op 10-1)

Abraham Monro Official explanation: jockey said gelding hung right

5368 WILLIAM HILL SILVER TROPHY H'CAP (CONSOLATION RACE FOR THE WILLIAM HILL GREAT ST WILFRID STKS) 6f

2:20 (2:21) (Class 2) 3-Y-O+

£12,450 (£3,728; £1,864; £932; £466; £234) **Stalls** High

Form RPR

0505 **1** **El Viento (FR)**[14] 4799 4-9-6 87 ...(b) TonyHamilton 4 98
(Richard Fahey) *racd far side: led that gp last 75yds: jst hld on: 1st of 10 that gp* **12/1**

-221 **2** *shd* **Prodigality**[8] 5035 4-9-5 86 ... GrahamLee 18 97+
(Ronald Harris) *racd stands' side: trckd ldrs: led that gp jst ins fnl f: r.o wl: jst failed: 1st of 9 that gp* **5/2**[1]

0112 **3** *1¼* **Spinatrix**[12] 4880 4-9-6 90 ...(p) LeeTopliss(3) 8 97
(Michael Dods) *racd far side: w ldrs: styd on same pce last 150yds: 2nd of 10 that gp* **9/1**[3]

6054 **4** *¾* **Damika (IRE)**[20] 4629 9-9-5 86 ...(v) MichaelStainton 7 90
(David Brown) *led 9 others far side: hdd last 75yds: no ex: 3rd of 10 that gp* **20/1**

0102 **5** *2* **L'Ami Louis (IRE)**[14] 4824 4-9-8 89 ... FranBerry 10 87+
(Henry Candy) *swtchd rt s to r far side: in rr: hdwy over 2f out: styd on same pce fnl f: 4th of 10 that gp* **15/2**[2]

6536 **6** *½* **Beckermet (IRE)**[4] 5186 10-9-3 87 ... DaleSwift(3) 3 83
(Ruth Carr) *dwlt: racd far side: mid-div: effrt over 2f out: one pce fnl f* **20/1**

6331 **7** *nk* **Ballista (IRE)**[19] 4640 4-9-2 90 ... RyanTate(7) 19 85
(Tom Dascombe) *led 8 others stands' side: hdd that gp jst ins fnl f: no ex: 2nd of 9 that gp* **14/1**

4341 **8** *¾* **Caranbola**[12] 4880 6-9-2 83 ... DuranFentiman 20 76
(Mel Brittain) *racd stands' side: chsd ldrs: kpt on one pce over 1f out: 3rd of 9 that gp* **20/1**

4101 **9** *hd* **Tajneed (IRE)**[18] 4673 9-8-11 85 ... ShirleyTeasdale(7) 16 77
(David Nicholls) *racd stands' side: hld up in mid-div: effrt over 2f out: kpt on: nvr a threat: 4th of 9 that gp* **12/1**

0000 **10** *nk* **Capaill Liath (IRE)**[21] 4611 4-9-6 90 ...(p) JulieBurke(3) 15 81
(Kevin Ryan) *racd stands' side: towards rr: kpt on fnl 2f: nvr a factor: 5th of 9 that gp* **22/1**

4060 **11** *hd* **Parisian Pyramid (IRE)**[21] 4609 6-9-4 85 ... NeilCallan 14 76
(Patrick Morris) *racd stands' side: chsd ldrs: wknd appr fnl f: 6th of 9 that gp* **25/1**

1605 **12** *1¼* **Fast Shot**[12] 4880 4-9-9 90 ... DavidAllan 6 77
(Tim Easterby) *racd far side: in rr: kpt on fnl 2f: nvr a factor: 6th of 10 that gp* **14/1**

4201 **13** *1* **Mappin Time (IRE)**[84] 2488 4-9-6 87 ...(p) DanielTudhope 5 70
(Tim Easterby) *racd far side: in rr: swtchd lft over 1f out: nvr on terms: 7th of 10 that gp* **20/1**

1006 **14** *3¼* **Sacrosanctus**[8] 5065 4-9-2 86 ...(p) HarryBentley(3) 11 59
(Scott Dixon) *swtchd lft and racd stands' side: chsd ldrs on outer: wknd over 1f out: 7th of 9 that gp* **33/1**

0205 **15** *hd* **Solar Spirit (IRE)**[8] 5057 7-8-11 83 ... ShaneBKelly(5) 9 55
(Tracy Waggott) *racd far side: in rr-div: nvr a factor: 8th of 10 that gp* **25/1**

4/00 **16** *½* **Khawatim**[12] 4880 4-9-1 89 ... NedCurtis(7) 12 60
(Paul Midgley) *racd stands' side: chsd ldrs: wknd over 1f out: 8th of 9 that gp* **50/1**

3060 **17** *1¼* **Head Space (IRE)**[14] 4799 4-9-10 91 ... JamesSullivan 1 58
(Ruth Carr) *racd far side: a in rr: 9th of 10 that gp* **16/1**

0604 **18** *8* **Fitz Flyer (IRE)**[11] 4924 6-9-8 89 ... AdrianNicholls 2 30
(David Nicholls) *racd far side: w ldrs: lost pl over 2f out: eased over 1f out: last of 10 that gp* **16/1**

0101 **19** *14* **Trade Secret**[14] 4824 5-9-3 84 ... PatCosgrave 13
(Mel Brittain) *racd stands' side: in rr: wl bhd fnl 2f: last of 9 that gp* **16/1**

1m 12.05s (-0.95) **Going Correction** +0.05s/f (Good) **19 Ran SP% 132.7**

Speed ratings (Par 109): **108,107,106,105,102 101,101,100,100,99 99,97,96,92,91 91,89,78,60**

toteswingers 1&2 £5.10, 1&3 £69.10, 2&3 £7.20 CSF £38.45 CT £317.56 TOTE £12.90: £3.50, £1.50, £1.90, £4.80; EX 58.00.

Owner John Nicholls Ltd/David Kilburn **Bred** Ballykilbride Stud **Trained** Musley Bank, N Yorks

FOCUS

The first running of this consolation race for the Great St Wilfrid, and a highly competitive handicap in its own right. The field divided into two similar sized groups and five of the first six home raced on the far side, with the unlucky runner-up the exception. The time was only a fraction slower than the main event. The winner is rated back to his best.

NOTEBOOK

El Viento(FR) burst between horses to lead inside the last, but while this was a meritorious effort he was fortunate that the narrow runner-up was drawn on the wrong side. The winner's last victory had been over C&D in July last year, and he was back down to the same mark today. (op 10-1 tchd 9-1)

Prodigality ◆ came in for solid support and he can be considered an unlucky loser, as he needed another stride after motoring through the final furlong. He finished the best part of 5l ahead of the next nearest in the group of nine who raced down the stands' side and remains a progressive sprinter with more to offer. Unfortunately he will be up considerably in the weights for this, but he may be able to overcome that. He has one more opportunity to race off this mark at Ffos Las on Friday, and would take all the beating if he goes there. (op 7-2 tchd 4-1)

Spinatrix has thrived since being fitted with cheekpieces and she ran another solid race, always up with the pace in the far-side group. (op 10-1 tchd 11-1)

Damika(IRE), the 2010 Great St Wilfrid winner, is now 8lb lower than when recording that victory. He led his group, and the race overall, with two to run, but could not hold on inside the last.

L'Ami Louis(IRE) continues to run well although the ease in the ground would not have been entirely in his favour. (op 9-1)

Beckermet(IRE) was happier over this trip than he had been at a mile at Ayr a few days earlier.

Ballista(IRE), second in the group to race near the stands' fence, had made the running on that side. He was 6lb higher than when winning over 7f at Ayr last time.

Caranbola, whose immediate victims when winning over C&D last time finished third and sixth here, was keeping on late up the less favoured flank. (op 18-1)

5369 VW VAN CENTRE (WEST YORKSHIRE) H'CAP 1m

2:55 (2:56) (Class 3) (0-90,90) 3-Y-O-**£8,821** (£2,640; £1,320; £660; £329) **Stalls** Low

Form RPR

0310 **1** **Mirrored**[7] 5094 6-9-9 85 ... DuranFentiman 3 97
(Tim Easterby) *trckd ldrs gng wl: trckd ldr over 2f out: shkn up to ld appr fnl f: edgd rt and drvn clr: v readily* **7/1**

6142 **2** *4* **Vito Volterra (IRE)**[8] 5057 5-9-6 82 ... AndrewMullen 7 85
(Michael Smith) *led after 1f: wnt clr over 5f out: hdd appr fnl f: no ex* **7/1**

2062 **3** *2½* **Hot Rod Mamma (IRE)**[12] 4868 5-9-4 85 ... ShaneBKelly(5) 4 82
(Dianne Sayer) *mid-div: hdwy to trck ldrs over 3f out: 3rd 2f out: styd on same pce appr fnl f* **13/2**[3]

5031 **4** *1¼* **Jo'Burg (USA)**[7] 5111 8-9-5 81 ... DanielTudhope 11 75+
(David O'Meara) *dwlt: swtchd rt after s: hld up in rr: hdwy over 3f out: styd on to take 4th nr fin* **6/1**[2]

0020 **5** *½* **Al Muheer (IRE)**[8] 5057 7-10-0 90 ...(b) JamesSullivan 10 83
(Ruth Carr) *t.k.h midfield: hdwy over 3f out: chsng ldrs and edgd rt 1f out: one pce* **16/1**

5035 **6** *2¼* **Kyllachy Star**[14] 4828 6-9-11 87 ... NeilCallan 8 79+
(Richard Fahey) *sn trcking ldrs: nt clr run on inner over 2f out: wknd over 1f out: hmpd ins fnl f: eased* **9/2**[1]

3-00 **7** *½* **L'Astre De Choisir (IRE)**[15] 4770 4-8-9 71 oh1 ... DavidAllan 1 58
(Michael Easterby) *t.k.h in rr: hdwy 3f out: nt clr run: one pce fnl 2f* **50/1**

1100 **8** *1¼* **Oratory (IRE)**[7] 5111 6-8-11 80 ... NedCurtis(7) 5 64
(Paul Midgley) *hood removed late: s.v.s: hdwy over 2f out: nvr a factor* **18/1**

0500 **9** *hd* **Orpsie Boy (IRE)**[14] 4828 9-9-5 84 ... DaleSwift(3) 6 67
(Ruth Carr) *mid-div: hdwy over 3f out: one pce fnl 2f* **20/1**

0-00 **10** *½* **You've Been Mowed**[10] 4939 6-8-8 75 ... MatthewLawson(5) 12 57
(Richard Price) *hld up in rr: effrt over 4f out: one pce fnl 2f* **33/1**

05-0 **11** *6* **Tiger Reigns**[35] 4110 6-9-12 88 ... PaulMulrennan 9 56
(Michael Dods) *t.k.h in rr: bhd fnl 3f* **10/1**

2506 **12** *6* **Majestic Dream (IRE)**[28] 4317 4-9-0 76 ...(b) GrahamLee 2 31
(Michael Easterby) *t.k.h: led 1f: chsd ldrs: wknd 2f out: sn bhd* **9/2**[1]

1m 40.18s (-1.22) **Going Correction** +0.05s/f (Good) **12 Ran SP% 118.9**

Speed ratings (Par 107): **108,104,101,100,99 97,97,95,95,95 89,83**

toteswingers 1&2 £37.00, 1&3 £37.00, 2&3 £5.00 CSF £54.52 CT £338.74 TOTE £7.30: £2.10, £2.70, £2.70; EX 66.80.

Owner Middleham Park Racing XXX **Bred** Millsec Limited **Trained** Great Habton, N Yorks

■ Stewards' Enquiry : James Sullivan two-day ban: careless riding (Sep 1-2)

FOCUS

They went a brisk pace in this fair handicap and not many became involved. The winner's best form since he was a 3yo.

NOTEBOOK

Mirrored drew clear with the runner-up from the two pole and shrugged off his rival to win in clear-cut style. He's not entirely straightforward but is largely consistent all the same. (op 8-1)

Vito Volterra(IRE) faced early competition for the lead but had gone clear turning in. He was put firmly in his place by the winner in the end, but this was another creditable showing. (op 8-1 tchd 9-1)
Hot Rod Mamma(IRE) ran a solid race without seriously threatening the first two and remains well handicapped on her best form of last season. (op 6-1 tchd 11-2 and 7-1)
Jo'Burg(USA), a recent Redcar winner, was dropped in from his wide draw and held up at the back. He ran on, but too late to get involved. (op 4-1)
Al Muheer(IRE) took a hold early and hung a little when put under pressure, so ran respectably in the circumstances. (op 12-1)
Kyllachy Star would certainly have been closer had he enjoyed a clear run, but can't be classed as unlucky. (op 11-2)
Oratory(IRE) Official explanation: jockey said blindfold was tucked in tightly under bridle, he was unable to remove it at first attempt and gelding was slowly away.
Majestic Dream(IRE) did rather too much early and ended up plumb last. (op 7-1)

5370 WILLIAM HILL GREAT ST WILFRID STKS (H'CAP) 6f
3:30 (3:32) (Class 2) 3-Y-0+
£43,575 (£13,048; £6,524; £3,262; £1,631; £819) **Stalls** High

Form RPR
-600 **1** **Pepper Lane**[56] 3371 5-9-1 **99**....................[1] DanielTudhope 10 111
(David O'Meara) *smartly away and swtchd rt to ld 9 others far side: drvn clr over 1f out: kpt on wl: 1st of 10 that gp* **20/1**
6430 **2** *1 ½* **Tax Free (IRE)**[14] 4799 10-8-8 **92**.................... AdrianNicholls 18 99
(David Nicholls) *racd stands' side: chsd ldrs: led that gp over 1f out: edgd rt and styd on ins fnl f: 1st of 10 that gp* **20/1**
0052 **3** *1 ¾* **Louis The Pious**[14] 4799 4-8-13 **97**....................(p) GrahamLee 7 99
(Kevin Ryan) *racd far side: hld up in rr: hdwy over 2f out: styd on to take 2nd that side last 150yds: 2nd of 10 that gp* **8/1**[3]
-003 **4** *½* **Captain Ramius (IRE)**[35] 4099 6-9-2 **100**.................... PatCosgrave 5 100
(Kevin Ryan) *racd far side: drvn along to sn chse ldrs: kpt on same pce fnl f to take 3rd that side last 100yds: 3rd of 10 that gp* **20/1**
4161 **5** *½* **Johannes (IRE)**[14] 4799 9-8-5 **96**.................... GeorgeChaloner[(7)] 17 94+
(Richard Fahey) *racd stands' side: in rr: hdwy over 2f out: edgd rt and styd on wl fnl f: 2nd of 10 that gp* **16/1**
0-61 **6** *shd* **Singeur (IRE)**[11] 4924 5-8-12 **96**.................... DuranFentiman 13 94
(Robin Bastiman) *racd stands' side: chsd ldrs: kpt on one pce over 1f out: 3rd of 10 that gp* **12/1**
0061 **7** *1* **Barnet Fair**[21] 4576 4-8-7 **91**.................... KierenFox 6 86
(Richard Guest) *racd far side: in rr: hdwy 2f out: kpt on same pce fnl f: 4th of 10 that gp* **11/1**
5015 **8** *hd* **Alben Star (IRE)**[14] 4802 4-8-13 **97**.................... TonyHamilton 3 91
(Richard Fahey) *racd far side: chsd ldrs: wnt 2nd that side over 1f out: fdd last 100yds: 5th of 10 that gp* **5/1**[1]
6363 **9** *¾* **Regal Parade**[28] 4328 8-9-4 **102**.................... MichaelO'Connell 14 94
(Milton Bradley) *racd stands' side: chsd ldrs: one pce over 1f out: 4th of 10 that gp* **28/1**
1400 **10** *hd* **Klynch**[14] 4799 6-8-8 **92**....................(b) JamesSullivan 16 83
(Ruth Carr) *racd stands' side: in rr: kpt on fnl 2f: nvr a factor: 5th of 10 that gp* **40/1**
0100 **11** *¾* **Grissom (IRE)**[14] 4802 6-8-9 **93**.................... DavidAllan 4 82
(Tim Easterby) *racd far side: chsd ldrs: hung lft fdd last 150yds: 6th of 10 that gp* **22/1**
0403 **12** *hd* **Bertiewhittle**[28] 4321 4-8-6 **93**.................... HarryBentley[(3)] 1 81
(David Barron) *racd far side: mid-div: sn drvn along: n.m.r on ins and swtchd lft over 1f out: nvr a threat: 7th of 10 that gp* **7/1**[2]
60 **13** *¾* **Lexi's Hero (IRE)**[14] 4802 4-8-11 **95**....................(b) NeilCallan 20 81
(Kevin Ryan) *led 9 others stands' side: hdd over 1f out: sn wknd: 6th of 10 that gp* **10/1**
0420 **14** *hd* **Secret Witness**[27] 4367 6-9-5 **106**....................(b) DaleSwift[(3)] 11 91
(Ronald Harris) *swtchd lft s and racd stands' side: mid-div on outer: effrt over 2f out: nvr trbld ldrs: 7th of 10 that gp* **28/1**
0015 **15** *hd* **Colonel Mak**[21] 4611 5-8-12 **101**.................... LMcNiff[(5)] 12 85
(David Barron) *racd stands' side: chsd ldrs: wknd over 1f out: 8th of 10 that gp* **12/1**
1263 **16** *2 ½* **Our Jonathan**[35] 4078 5-9-10 **108**.................... StephenCraine 19 84
(Kevin Ryan) *s.s: racd stands' side: a in rr: 9th of 10 that gp* **12/1**
6000 **17** *hd* **Seal Rock**[14] 4802 4-8-12 **96**.................... PaulMulrennan 15 72
(Henry Candy) *racd stands' side: in rr-div: effrt over 2f out: nvr a threatlast of 10 that gp* **16/1**
0P10 **18** *1 ¾* **Elusive Prince**[14] 4802 4-8-4 **93**....................(b) DeanHeslop[(5)] 8 63
(David Barron) *racd far side: a in rr: 8th of 10 that gp* **20/1**
1103 **19** *2 ¼* **Bosun Breese**[11] 4924 7-8-10 **94**.................... AndrewMullen 2 57
(David Barron) *racd far side: chsd ldrs: lost pl over 1f out: 9th of 10 that gp* **25/1**
2000 **20** *5* **Es Que Love (IRE)**[14] 4802 3-9-6 **107**.................... FranBerry 9 54
(Mark Johnston) *racd far side: chsd ldrs: wknd 2f out: last of 10 that gp* **12/1**

1m 11.95s (-1.05) **Going Correction** +0.05s/f (Good)
WFA 3 from 4yo+ 3lb **20** Ran SP% **136.8**
Speed ratings (Par 109): **109,107,104,104,103 103,101,101,100,100 99,99,98,97,97 94,93,91,88,81**
toteswingers 1&2 £24.20, 2&3 £64.70, 1&3 £200.50 CSF £367.34 CT £3554.44 TOTE £33.50: £7.00, £4.80, £2.50, £6.90; EX 661.70 Trifecta £10643.10 Pool: £10,643.10 - 2.80 winning units..
Owner Mrs Lynne Lumley & K Nicholson **Bred** Conor J C Parsons & Brian M Parsons **Trained** Nawton, N Yorks

FOCUS
An up-to-scratch edition of this historic handicap, but one that was missing leading ante-post fancies Fulbright and Van Ellis, both from the Mark Johnston yard. Stewards' Cup second Imperial Guest was another absentee, but half of this field ran in either the big Goodwood sprint or its consolation race. They split into two equally sized groups and the far side came out on top, but the runner-up raced on the opposite flank and in truth there was no real advantage either way. A personal best from Pepper Lane.

NOTEBOOK
Pepper Lane, successful off 4lb lower 12 months ago, became a rare dual winner of this event. A year ago she made all up the stands' side, but this time, drawn down the middle in stall 10, she joined the far-side group. Equipped with a hood for the first time, she broke better than she had been doing and was nicely on top from the furlong pole. She had chased black type on her first two runs this year and blew the start back in a handicap in the Wokingham.
Tax Free(IRE)'s trainer has a fine record in this event with two victories since 2005, and the 10-y-o ran a big race. Edging to his right in the latter stages, he could not peg back the mare but still beat the rest on his side decisively enough. (tchd 25-1)
Louis The Pious, runner-up in Goodwood's consolation race latest, raced a few lengths off the inside rail and ran on for third. This was a sound run off a career-high mark. (op 10-1)
Captain Ramius(IRE), another to race on the far side, followed up his Bunbury Cup third with another sound effort. This trip is on the sharp side for him though.
Johannes(IRE), the Stewards' Sprint winner, was finishing to good effect after drifting towards the centre of the course. He's not rated out of things at present.
Singeur(IRE) won here earlier in the month and would appear to like Ripon, but he is more effective over 5f. The intermediate trip of the Portland at Doncaster could suit him, however. (op 10-1 tchd 8-1)
Barnet Fair ran just respectably off a 3lb higher mark than when winning at Ascot, with this track not best suiting his come-from-behind style. (op 10-1 tchd 12-1)
Alben Star(IRE) had run well in the Stewards' Cup and in the Wokingham before that, but he faded here after racing up with the pace. (op 7-1)
Grissom(IRE) Official explanation: jockey said gelding hung left throughout
Bertiewhittle probably found this too sharp and was a well beaten twelfth, but still did best of the trainer's four runners. Harry Bentley reported that the gelding was denied a clear run. Official explanation: jockey said gelding was denied a clear run (op 9-1)
Our Jonathan, last year's runner-up, was the class act in this field, but he was always struggling after missing the break.

5371 RIPON HORN BLOWER CONDITIONS STKS 6f
4:00 (4:01) (Class 3) 2-Y-0 **£7,561** (£2,263; £1,131; £566; £282) **Stalls** High

Form RPR
21 **1** **Pearl Acclaim (IRE)**[23] 4512 2-9-2 0.................... HarryBentley[(3)] 1 98+
(Richard Hannon) *chsd ldr on outer: led jst ins fnl f: styd on wl: readily* **3/1**[2]
21 **2** *2 ¼* **Ashaadd (IRE)**[33] 4149 2-9-5 0.................... NeilCallan 4 91
(Roger Varian) *hmpd s: led: rdn and edgd rt over 1f out: hdd jst ins fnl f: no ex* **11/8**[1]
301 **3** *1 ½* **King Dragon (IRE)**[40] 3916 2-9-5 90.................... FranBerry 2 87
(Brian Meehan) *hmpd at s: chsd ldrs: drvn over 2f out: kpt on same pce over 1f out* **4/1**[3]
1 **4** *2 ¼* **Luck (IRE)**[46] 3725 2-9-5 0.................... GrahamLee 7 80
(Kevin Ryan) *chsd ldrs stands' rail: drvn 3f out: one pce* **9/2**
0200 **5** *5* **Woodland Mill (IRE)**[14] 4820 2-9-0 84.................... TonyHamilton 5 60
(Richard Fahey) *wnt rt s: in tch: effrt over 2f out: lost pl over 1f out* **14/1**
00 **6** *10* **Blazeofenchantment (USA)**[14] 4792 2-9-0 0.......... RussKennemore 3 33
(Paul Midgley) *hmpd s: in rr: reminders over 3f out: lost pl 2f out: sn bhd* **100/1**

1m 13.22s (0.22) **Going Correction** +0.05s/f (Good) **6** Ran SP% **112.9**
Speed ratings (Par 98): **100,97,95,92,85 72**
toteswingers 1&2 £1.20, 1&3 £2.50, 2&3 £2.00 CSF £7.66 TOTE £5.00: £2.40, £1.20; EX 7.40.
Owner Pearl Bloodstock Ltd **Bred** Awbeg Stud **Trained** East Everleigh, Wilts

FOCUS
A good edition of this conditions event, which was won in 2010 by this year's July Cup winner Mayson. Listed quality form, with the winner progressing from his easy Sandown victory.

NOTEBOOK
Pearl Acclaim(IRE) went down to his smart stablemate Havana Gold on his debut before winning second time up at Sandown. The runner-up there, Baron Run, didn't exactly boost the form in the opener on this card, but Pearl Acclaim did this well after mastering the runner-up. His rider thought the colt was not at home on the track's undulations, which makes this performance more creditable. He holds Group-race entries later in the season but a Listed assignment could make more sense first. (tchd 10-3)
Ashaadd(IRE)'s Windsor win in the mud has not been working out. Hampered leaving the traps, he tried to make all, but edged to his right when the pressure was on and the winner proved much too strong inside the last. This looks as good as he is. (op 13-8)
King Dragon(IRE), another testing-ground Windsor winner, in a race that has been working out well, stayed on for pressure and might be ready for a seventh furlong. (op 7-2 tchd 9-2)
Luck(IRE), an easy Hamilton maiden winner, had the benefit of the rail to race alongside but was found wanting in this higher grade. The better ground was presumably not a problem. (tchd 4-1 and 5-1)
Woodland Mill(IRE) went to her right leaving the stalls and was never really in it. It was a little disappointing she could not finish closer. (tchd 11-1)
Blazeofenchantment(USA) was done no favours in the early strides and trailed throughout, but he may do better when in handicap company.

5372 BRITISH STALLION STUDS SUPPORTING BRITISH RACING EBF FILLIES' H'CAP 1m 1f 170y
4:35 (4:36) (Class 4) (0-80,80) 3-Y-0+ **£5,670** (£1,697; £848; £424; £211) **Stalls** Low

Form RPR
1233 **1** **Miss Ellany (IRE)**[10] 4961 3-9-3 **77**.................... DanielTudhope 2 89+
(David O'Meara) *mde all: increased pce over 3f out: styd on strly fnl 2f: drvn out: unchal* **4/1**[2]
5134 **2** *2 ½* **Lady Loch**[28] 4319 3-9-4 **78**....................(b) TonyHamilton 4 84
(Richard Fahey) *trckd ldrs: drvn and outpcd over 3f out: styd on fnl f: tk 2nd post* **4/1**[2]
4415 **3** *hd* **Anya**[36] 4057 3-8-12 **72**.................... NeilCallan 9 78
(Ed Walker) *swtchd rt s: hld up towards rr: hdwy and 3rd 2f out: wnt 2nd last 100yds: lost 2nd post* **12/1**
0023 **4** *3 ½* **Sangar**[15] 4768 4-9-0 **66**.................... MichaelO'Connell 6 65
(Ollie Pears) *chsd ldrs: wnt 2nd over 2f out: wknd last 150yds* **9/1**
2610 **5** *7* **Raheeba**[14] 4830 3-8-13 **73**.................... FranBerry 8 57
(Mark Johnston) *hld up towards rr: hdwy 4f out: sn drvn: one pce fnl 2f* **10/1**
00-0 **6** *shd* **Cheers For Thea (IRE)**[11] 4933 7-9-12 **78**....................(t) DuranFentiman 1 62
(Tim Easterby) *s.s: nvr a factor* **20/1**
0134 **7** *4 ½* **First Class Favour (IRE)**[18] 4676 4-9-0 **66**.................... DavidAllan 7 40
(Tim Easterby) *sn trcking ldrs: t.k.h: wknd over 1f out* **16/1**
-402 **8** *4* **Sakhee's Pearl**[14] 4805 6-9-5 **76**.................... NathanSweeney[(5)] 5 42
(Jo Crowley) *mid-div: lost pl over 3f out: hdwy on ins whn nt clr run over 2f out: wknd over 1f out* **6/1**[3]
41 **9** *20* **Intent (IRE)**[12] 4888 3-9-6 **80**.................... GrahamLee 3
(Michael Bell) *trckd ldrs: wknd over 2f out: bhd whn eased 1f out: t.o* **3/1**[1]

2m 5.04s (-0.36) **Going Correction** +0.05s/f (Good)
WFA 3 from 4yo+ 8lb **9** Ran SP% **116.7**
Speed ratings (Par 102): **103,101,100,98,92 92,88,85,69**
toteswingers 1&2 £1.80, 1&3 £8.30, 2&3 £10.50 CSF £20.67 CT £176.90 TOTE £5.70: £2.30, £1.50, £3.70; EX 19.60.
Owner W O'Brien **Bred** Miss Debbie Kitchin **Trained** Nawton, N Yorks

FOCUS
A fair distaff handicap. The winner was probably in the best place in front but this still rates a clear personal best.
Intent(IRE) Official explanation: jockey said filly ran flat

5373 SIS LIVE H'CAP 1m 4f 10y
5:10 (5:11) (Class 5) (0-75,74) 3-Y-0 **£3,234** (£962; £481; £240) **Stalls** Centre

Form RPR
0305 **1** **Hyperlink (IRE)**[10] 4972 3-9-0 **67**.................... FranBerry 2 74
(Mark Johnston) *led 2f: t.k.h: trckd ldr: led over 3f out: styd on fnl f: hld on wl* **13/2**

0311 **2** *1 1/4* **Maybeagrey**[15] 4781 3 -9-5[72] .... DuranFentiman 3 77
(Tim Easterby) *mid-div: effrt over 3f out: wnt 2nd over 1f out: almost upsides jst ins fnl f: styd on same pce* **3/1**[1]

-660 **3** *1/2* **Millymonkin**[89] 2336 3 -8-7[60] .... (t) JamesSullivan 7 64
(Michael Easterby) *in rr: reminder over 4f out: hdwy over 2f out: styd on fnl f: tk 3rd post* **14/1**

0414 **4** *shd* **Cellist**[31] 4225 3 -9-7[74] .... NeilCallan 5 78
(William Haggas) *trckd ldrs: nt clr run and swtchd lft over 2f out: styd on ins fnl f: tk 4th nr fin* **5/1**[3]

3421 **5** *1* **Arley Hall**[8] 5054 3 -9-7[74] .... TonyHamilton 8 76
(Richard Fahey) *w ldrs: led after 2f: hdd over 3f out: wknd last 100yds* **4/1**[2]

6522 **6** *2 1/2* **Margo Channing**[15] 4781 3 -8-2[55] .... KellyHarrison 6 55
(Micky Hammond) *chsd ldrs: effrt over 4f out: hung rt and one pce whn hmpd and eased ins fnl f* **10/1**

5000 **7** *18* **Finbar**[23] 4498 3 -9-4[71] .... GrahamLee 4 41
(James Given) *trckd ldrs: lost pl over 2f out: bhd whn eased ins fnl f: t.o* **11/2**

1056 **8** *15* **Bob's World**[47] 3711 3 -9-5[72] .... StephenCraine 1 18
(Jennie Candlish) *s.s: in rr: bhd fnl 3f: eased over 1f out: t.o* **7/1**

2m 39.45s (2.75) **Going Correction** +0.05s/f (Good) **8**Ran SP% **118.6**
Speed ratings (Par 100): **92,91,90,90,90 88,76,66**
toteswingers 1&2 £5.90, 1&3 £21.20, 2&3 Not won CSF £27.43 CT £270.10 TOTE £8.00 : £2.40, £1.40, £4.90 ; EX 39.40 .
Owner Sheikh Hamdan Bin Mohammed Al Maktoum **Bred** Airlie Stud **Trained** Middleham Moor, N Yorks

FOCUS
A modest handicap run at just an ordinary pace. The winner is rated back to form.
Margo Channing Official explanation: jockey said filly hung right
T/Jkpt: Not won. T/Plt: £346.80 to a £1 stake. Pool: £81,131.03 - 170.74 winning tickets T/Qpdt: £48.70 to a £1 stake Pool: £5,102.00 - 77.50 w. tckts WG 5373a (Foreign Racing) See RI

ARLINGTON PARK (L-H)

Saturday, August 18

OFFICIAL GOING: Turf: good

5374a AMERICAN ST. LEGER STKS (CONDITIONS) (3YO+) (TURF) 1m 5f 110y
9:14 (9:17) 3-Y-O+

£150,193 (£50,064; £25,032 ; £12,516 ; £7,509 ; £5,006)

RPR

1 **Jakkalberry (IRE)**[56] 3369 6 -8-7[0] .... CO'Donoghue 5 114+
(Marco Botti) **8/5**[1]

2 *2 1/4* **Ioya Bigtime (USA)**[35] 5 -8-11[0] .... JASanchez 8 115
(Chris Block, U.S.A) **14/5**[2]

3 *6 1/4* **Zuider Zee (GER)**[56] 3373 5 -8-7[0] .... WilliamBuick 7 102
(John Gosden) **11/2**

4 *1* **Lake Drop (USA)**[90] 2323 4 -8-9[0] .... RADominguez 4 102
(H Graham Motion, U.S.A) **39/10**[3]

5 *1/2* **Lemonade Kid (USA)**[41] 7 -8-7[0] .... (b) FTorres 2 99
(Anthony Mitchell, U.S.A) **38/1**

6 *3 3/4* **Helicopter (USA)**[622] 6 -8-7[0] .... (b) BMeier 1 94
(Larry Rivelli, U.S.A) **27/1**

7 *7 3/4* **Lumberyard Jack (USA)**[20] 4 -8-7[0] .... MGutierrez 3 82
(Doug O'Neill, U.S.A) **138/10**

8 *3 3/4* **Lethal (USA)**[16] 4 -8-7[0] .... (b) JEFelix 6 77
(John Haran, U.S.A) **56/1**

9 *7* **Bridge Of Gold (USA)**[58] 3293 6 -8-7[0] .... KierenFallon 9 66
(Mikael Magnusson) **141/10**

2m 49.01s (169.01) **9**Ran SP% **121.8**
PARI-MUTUEL (all including $2 stakes): WIN 5.20; PLACE (1-2) 3.20, 3.60; SHOW (1-2-3) 2.40, 2.80, 3.20; SF 19.40 .
Owner ATB Jakkalberry Sy, Porter & Duke **Bred** Azienda Agricola Allevamento Deni **Trained** Newmarket, Suffolk

FOCUS
The first running of the American St Leger and British-based challengers made up a third of the field. There's not much depth to the form, but it's likely the race will earn graded status in due course and grow in popularity.

NOTEBOOK
Jakkalberry(IRE), who didn't use Lasix for this US debut, was the clear form pick (Group 1 winner in Italy) and was also getting 4lb from Ioya Bigtime, but he still did well to win so readily considering the runner-up had everything go his way. The step back up in trip suited and he won well under a straightforward ride. He's reportedly owned by an Australian syndicate and is being aimed at the Melbourne Cup.
Ioya Bigtime (USA) was allowed an easy lead and set just modest fractions, going 25.11 for the first quarter, 50.82 for the half, and 1.15.43 at the 6f point. A recent Grade 3 winner over 1m4f here, he stuck on well to finish clear of the remainder and this was a good effort conceding weight all round, but he did have the run of the race.
Zuider Zee (GER) who was on first-time Lasix, hit a flat spot, and wasn't totally at home on the tight track or the quick ground. The horse wasn't at his best, but this still a respectable showing.
Lake Drop (USA) last seen winning an Italian Group 3 on easy ground in May, was set a lot to do on his US debut and never threatened.
Bridge Of Gold (USA) reportedly missed training earlier in the week owing to an elevated temperature. He used Lasix for this US debut, but ran no sort of race (took keen hold early) and has lost his way.

5375a SECRETARIAT STKS (GRADE 1) (3YO) (TURF) 1m 2f
9:48 (9:53) 3-Y-O

£189,677 (£63,225; £31,612 ; £15,806 ; £9,483 ; £6,322)

RPR

1 **Bayrir (FR)**[27] 4385 3 -8-9[0] .... Christophe-PatriceLemaire 7 113
(A De Royer-Dupre, France) **16/5**[3]

2 *1 1/4* **Finnegans Wake (USA)**[27] 3 -8-7[0] .... JLezcano 4 109
(Dale Romans, U.S.A) **17/2**

3 *1 1/4* **Summer Front (USA)**[27] 3 -8-11[0] .... RADominguez 2 110
(Christophe Clement, U.S.A) **13/5**[2]

4 *2* **Handsome Mike (USA)**[20] 4635 3 -8-7[0] .... (b) MGutierrez 1 102
(Doug O'Neill, U.S.A) **196/10**

5 *nse* **Silver Max (USA)**[27] 3 -9-0[0] .... RAlbarado 8 109
(Dale Romans, U.S.A) **2/1**[1]

6 *1/2* **Cozzetti (USA)**[35] 3 -8-11[0] .... SXBridgmohan 3 105
(Dale Romans, U.S.A) **199/10**

7 *hd* **All Stormy (USA)**[35] 3 -8-7[0] .... RosemaryBHomeisterJr 5 101
(Greg Geier, U.S.A) **44/1**

8 *7 1/4* **Daddy Long Legs (USA)**[34] 2514 3 -8-11[0] .... (b[1]) CO'Donoghue 6 90
(A P O'Brien, Ire) **58/10**

2m 2.92s (1.28) **8**Ran SP% **122.0**
PARI-MUTUEL (all including $2 stakes): WIN 8.40; PLACE (1-2) 4.80, 6.40; SHOW (1-2-3) 3.60, 3.60, 3.40; SF 55.60 .
Owner H H Aga Khan **Bred** S A Aga Khan **Trained** Chantilly, France

FOCUS
This looked a decent enough edition of the Secretariat.

NOTEBOOK
Bayrir(FR) ◆, who had been given plenty of time to get into his stride, picked up smartly. He only made his debut in May, but came here after winning the Group 2 Prix Eugene Adam and was improving his career record to 4-5. A straightforward individual who should be suited by further, he could progress into a high-class type and the Breeders' Cup Turf has been mentioned as a possible target. He didn't use Lasix.
Finnegans Wake (USA) has a progressive profile and this was another career-best. He can make his mark at the top level when he doesn't have European competition to worry about.
Summer Front (USA) was unbeaten in five turf starts at up to 1m, but obviously had stamina to prove. He did well to last so long considering he raced freely, and he has more to offer back over shorter and/or if relaxing at this sort of distance.
Handsome Mike (USA) ran okay on this return to turf and probably still has a bit more to offer.
Silver Max (USA) who had won his last seven turf starts from the front, went to the lead and he was able to set comfortable enough opening fractions of 24.65, 48.94, and 1.13.25 for 6f. However, he was then hassled by Summer Front, before being passed by Daddy Long Legs, who made a big move around 3f out.
Daddy Long Legs (USA) who sported blinkers for the first time, ran an uneven race, his connections perhaps fearing the strong front-runner Silver Max. Having raced further back than usual, he was then rushed up to lead well before the turn, his rider presumably wanting to avoid an early pace duel whilst also ensuring the leader couldn't nick the race. However, the tactics blatantly didn't work.

5376a BEVERLY D. STKS (GRADE 1) (3YO+ FILLIES & MARES) (TURF) 1m 1f 110y
11:02 (11:03) 3-Y-O+

£278,709 (£92,903; £46,451 ; £23,225 ; £13,935 ; £9,290)

RPR

1 **I'm A Dreamer (IRE)**[48] 3676 5 -8-11[0] .... HayleyTurner 2 114
(David Simcock) **63/10**

2 *hd* **Marketing Mix (CAN)**[41] 4 -8-11[0] .... JRLeparoux 8 114+
(Thomas F Proctor, U.S.A) **17/5**[2]

3 *3/4* **Joviality**[36] 4065 4 -8-11[0] .... WilliamBuick 10 112
(John Gosden) **13/2**

4 *1 3/4* **Kapitale (GER)**[300] 7047 4 -8-11[0] .... MircoDemuro 1 109
(A Wohler, Germany) **26/1**

5 *hd* **Upperline (USA)**[35] 5 -8-11[0] .... (b) JamesGraham 4 108
(Michael Stidham, U.S.A) **206/10**

6 *1/2* **Up (IRE)**[27] 4376 3 -8-5[0] .... CO'Donoghue 6 109
(A P O'Brien, Ire) **13/1**

7 *1 3/4* **Romacaca (USA)**[35] 6 -8-11[0] .... (b) FTorres 3 104
(Danny L Miller, U.S.A) **105/10**

8 *nse* **Mystical Star (USA)**[49] 4 -8-11[0] .... JLezcano 5 104
(Christophe Clement, U.S.A) **42/10**[3]

9 *nk* **Stars To Shine (USA)**[27] 5 -8-11[0] .... ASolis 9 103
(Mark Frostad, Canada) **201/10**

10 *3 1/2* **Aruna (USA)**[49] 5 -8-11[0] .... RADominguez 7 96
(H Graham Motion, U.S.A) **33/10**[1]

1m 55.29s (-0.18)
WFA 3 from 4yo+ 7lb **10**Ran SP% **121.2**
PARI-MUTUEL (all including $2 stakes): WIN 14.60; PLACE (1-2) 7.40, 4.60; SHOW (1-2-3) 4.40, 3.40, 5.00; SF 67.60 .
Owner St Albans Bloodstock LLP **Bred** Sean Murphy **Trained** Newmarket, Suffolk

FOCUS
An ordinary running of the Beverly D. The pace was solid with Romacaca recording splits of 23.67, 48.40 and 1.12.54 at the 6f stage.

NOTEBOOK
I'm A Dreamer (IRE) who raced on Lasix, was suited by the fair gallop and picked up well to get first run on the second, before just holding on for her first top-level success. She was runner-up in the E P Taylor at Woodbine last year, her only previous start in North America, and it would make sense if that race was again on her agenda. This victory earned her an automatic berth into the Breeders' Cup Filly & Mare Turf.
Marketing Mix (CAN) came into this with a 6-8 record on turf, including graded victories, and she just failed after allowing the winner to get a bit of a start on her
Joviality, who won the Windsor Forest on decent ground before failing to handle soft in the Falmouth, deserves credit for finishing so close. Racing with the aid of Lasix, she was a touch keen without cover early on, and her rider had his whip knocked from his hand turning into the straight, yet she was still best of those who raced handily.
Kapitale(GER) ran with real credit considering she'd been off since October.
Up(IRE) went on a fair way out and briefly looked like skipping clear, but she had done plenty of running and probably isn't up to this level.
Aruna(USA) seemed to stumble on leaving the stalls and was always behind.

5377a ARLINGTON MILLION STKS (GRADE 1) (3YO+) (TURF) 1m 2f
11:44 (11:47) 3-Y-O+

£367,741 (£122,580; £45,967 ; £45,967 ; £18,387 ; £12,258)

RPR

1 **Little Mike (USA)**[48] 5 -9-0[0] .... RADominguez 4 119
(Dale Romans, U.S.A) **39/10**[2]

2 *1 1/2* **Afsare**[21] 4610 5 -9-0[0] .... KierenFallon 3 115+
(Luca Cumani) **56/10**[3]

3 *1 1/2* **Rahystrada (USA)**[35] 8 -9-0[0] .... JRLeparoux 1 112+
(Byron G Hughes, U.S.A) **157/10**

3 *dht* **Colombian (IRE)**[59] 3267 4 -9-0[0] .... WilliamBuick 5 112
(John Gosden) **96/10**

5 *nse* **Crackerjack King (IRE)**[42] 3880 4 -9-0[0] .... CO'Donoghue 9 112
(Marco Botti) **7/2**[1]

6 *1/2* **Treasure Beach**[9] 5027 4 -9-0[0] .... JamieSpencer 6 111+
(A P O'Brien, Ire) **94/10**

7 *nse* **Wigmore Hall (IRE)**[21] 4610 5 -9-0[0] .... HayleyTurner 8 111
(Michael Bell) **18/1**

8 *1 1/2* **Willcox Inn (USA)**[27] 4 -9-0[0] .... (b) JamesGraham 7 108
(Michael Stidham, U.S.A) **122/10**

9 *3/4* **Boisterous (USA)**[35] 5 -9-0[0] .... JLezcano 2 106
(Claude McGaughey III, U.S.A) **39/10**[2]

10 *nk* **Cherokee Lord (USA)**[35] 5 -9-0[0] .... FTorres 10 106
(Charlie Livesay, U.S.A) **52/1**

11 3 3/4 **Vertiformer (USA)**[35] 5 -9-00 .... JASanchez 11 98
(Wayne Catalano, U.S.A) **26/1**
2m 2.44s (0.80) **11**Ran SP% **121.4**
PARI-MUTUEL (all including $2 stakes): WIN 9.80; PLACE (1-2) 5.60, 6.60; SHOW (1-2-3) 4.40, 4.80, 4.40 (Rahystrada), 3.80 (Colombian); SF 63.40 .
Owner Priscilla Vaccarezza **Bred** Carlo E Vaccarezza **Trained** USA

FOCUS
The 2012 Arlington Million didn't look a strong race beforehand. The winner set a slow pace and the time was only fractionally faster than the earlier stayers' race.

NOTEBOOK
Little Mike (USA) a confirmed front-runner, was allowed a totally uncontested lead and set a dawdling pace. Unproven over quite this far, his stamina was not tested and he could hardly fail to win. He already had three triple-digit Beyer figures to his name, all of them earned from the front, the most recent when taking a 1m1f Grade 1.
Afsare finished very strongly, surprisingly considering he got worked up in the preliminaries. He raced on Lasix.
Rahystrada(USA) had come up short in this race for the last two years and did so again, but this was a creditable effort. He likes it around Arlington.
Colombian(IRE), for whom the drying ground probably wasn't ideal, sat handier than most and that helped.
Crackerjack King (IRE)faced an impossible task from off the slow pace, and so too did Treasure Beach and Wigmore Hall.
Treasure Beach, who was unsuited by the steady gallop, could now head for the Northern Dancer at Woodbine ahead of the Canadian International, and Aidan O'Brien's runner did at least offer a bit more than of late.
Wigmore Hall (IRE)was another who needed a better pace and could also head for the Northern Dancer, a race he won last year.

5248 DEAUVILLE (R-H)
Saturday, August 18
OFFICIAL GOING: Turf: good: fibresand: standard

5378a PRIX DU MONT CANISY (CLAIMER) (2YO COLTS & GELDINGS) (FIBRESAND) 7f 110y
11:30 (12:00) 2-Y-O **£9,583** (£3,833; £2,875 ; £1,916 ; £958)

RPR
1 **Composed**[15] 4778 2 -9-20 .... ChristopheSoumillon 6 80
(Paul Cole) *racd midfield: proged to 4th bef st: qcknd to ld 1 1/2f out: sn wnt clr: easily* **19/10**[1]
2 2 1/2 **Freestyler (FR)**[22] 2 -8-90 .... TheoBachelot 5 67
(Mario Hofer, Germany) **10/1**[3]
3 2 1/2 **Medipearl (FR)**[15] 2 -8-40 .... (p) AntoineCoutier(5) 8 61
(F Chappet, France) **5/1**[2]
4 2 **Haring (SPA)**[8] 5073 2 -8-20 .... SoufyaneMoulin(7) 14 57
(C Boutin, France) **56/1**
5 snk **Mister Black (FR)**[15] 2 -8-130 .... AlexisBadel 13 60
(F Sanchez, France) **13/1**
6 hd **Back To Capri (IRE)**[15] 2 -8-80 .... (b) NicolasLarenaudie(8) 1 63
(G Collet, France) **10/1**[3]
7 shd **Emir De La Vis (FR)**[8] 2 -9-00 .... IoritzMendizabal 7 60
(D Windrif, France) **19/1**
8 1/2 **Contesurmoi (FR)** 2 -8-130 .... RonanThomas 4 58
(A Bonin, France) **11/1**
9 1 1/2 **Prince Eliot (FR)**[8] 5073 2 -8-130 .... (b) GregoryBenoist 10 55
(M Boutin, France) **20/1**
10 1/2 **Secret Taboo (FR)**2 -8-100 .... EddyHardouin(6) 2 57
(Robert Collet, France) **16/1**
0 **Anatolien (FR)**[112] 2 -8-90 .... JulienAuge 3
(J-L Gay, France) **70/1**
0 **Telmo (FR)**[24] 4476 2 -8-130 .... FabienLefebvre 12
(A Lamotte D'Argy, France) **34/1**
0 **Allez (FR)**[21] 2 -8-100 .... MarcLerner(6) 11
(A Lamotte D'Argy, France) **11/1**
U **Houghton Hill (FR)**2 -8-90 .... JohanVictoire 9
(Mme C Head-Maarek, France) **36/1**
1m 33.0s (93.00) **14**Ran SP% **117.5**
WIN (incl. 1 euro stake): 2.90. PLACES: 1.50, 2.50, 1.50. DF: 16.30. SF: 24.80 .
Owner P F I Cole Ltd **Bred** E J Harper & Whitsbury Manor Stud **Trained** Whatcombe, Oxon

NOTEBOOK
Composed, having his first start on synthetics since his debut, took this in emphatic style.

5379a PRIX DU CALVADOS - HARAS DES CAPUCINES (GROUP 3) (2YO FILLIES) (TURF) 7f
1:30 (12:00) 2-Y-O **£33,333** (£11,666; £11,666 ; £6,666 ; £3,333)

RPR
1 **Purr Along**[23] 4514 2 -8-110 .... UmbertoRispoli 12 103
(William Muir) *prom fr s: wnt 2nd at 1/2-way: tk ld 150yds out: r.o wl u.p: jst hld on* **168/10**
2 snk **Premier Steps (IRE)**[36] 4064 2 -8-110 .... MaximeGuyon 11 103
(Tom Dascombe) *racd bhd ldrs: rdn 1 1/2f out: r.o wl u.p fnl 100yds: wnt 2nd 25yds out: jnd in 2nd on line* **14/1**
2 dht **Sara Lucille**[27] 4384 2 -8-110 .... ThierryJarnet 1 103
(F Head, France) *hld up towards rr: swtchd towards outside 1 1/2f out: r.o wl fnl 100yds: got up to share 2nd on line* **8/1**
4 hd **City Image (IRE)**[36] 4064 2 -8-110 .... GeraldMosse 8 102
(Richard Hannon) *racd midfield: rdn 1 1/2f out: r.o wl fnl 150yds: nt quite rch ldrs* **17/2**
5 1/2 **Califante**[14] 4820 2 -8-110 .... OlivierPeslier 9 101
(Richard Hannon) *racd midfield: styd on wl u.p fnl f* **14/1**
6 1/2 **More Than Sotka (FR)**[23] 2 -8-110 .... RonanThomas 3 99
(F-H Graffard, France) *racd 3rd on stands' rail: dropped towards rr over 1 1/2f out: picked up wl u.p ent fnl f: styd on wl* **20/1**
7 1/2 **Koonunja (IRE)**[45] 2 -8-110 .... StephanePasquier 5 98
(D Prod'Homme, France) *racd midfield: rdn but no ex 1 1/2f out: r.o u.p fnl f* **19/1**
8 1 **Morning Frost (IRE)**[16] 2 -8-110 .... JulienAuge 6 96
(C Ferland, France) *racd towards rr: swtchd to wd outside 2f out: r.o wl ent fnl f: no ex fnl 100yds* **33/10**[1]
9 1/2 **Wedge Trust (IRE)**[18] 4696 2 -8-110 .... ChristopheSoumillon 4 94
(J-C Rouget, France) *broke poorly: sn racd midfield: mde prog 1f out: no ex u.p ent fnl 100yds: styd on* **13/2**[3]
10 3/4 **Shingueti (FR)**[27] 2 -8-110 .... JohanVictoire 2 92
(C Baillet, France) *a in rr: sme late prog: nvr a factor* **19/1**
0 **Discernable**[21] 4615 2 -8-110 .... IoritzMendizabal 10
(Mark Johnston) *sn led on stands' rail: u.p 1 1/2f out: no ex: fdd* **19/5**[2]
0 **Aksil (FR)**[23] 2 -8-110 .... GregoryBenoist 7
(R Martens, France) *racd midfield: no ex u.p 2f out: sn wknd* **31/1**
1m 24.9s (-3.40) **12**Ran SP% **115.9**
WIN (incl. 1 euro stake): 17.80. PLACES: 5.50, 3.40, 3.70. DF: 49.10. SF: 98.80 .
Owner Muir Racing Partnership - Manchester **Bred** Moyns Park Estate And Stud Ltd **Trained** Lambourn, Berks

FOCUS
They finished in a heap in a steady time and the form has been rated at the bottom end of the race averages, which still sees all the principals improving.

NOTEBOOK
Purr Along provided her trainer with a first winner at Deauville and in the process earned her passage for the country's premier 2-y-o race for fillies on Arc day. She got the better of a blanket finish, finishing a short neck ahead of the dead-heating Premier Steps and Sara Lucille. The rider was enjoying his first Group success in France but said he was in front too soon and that he'd have won by further if he'd waited a bit longer.
Premier Steps (IRE)had made the frame in the Albany and Cherry Hinton and represents a fair guide to the level of the form.

5380a - 5381a (Foreign Racing) See RI

4959 PONTEFRACT (L-H)
Sunday, August 19
OFFICIAL GOING: Good to firm (8.1)
Wind: virtually nil Weather: Cloudy

5382 BRITISH STALLION STUDS EBF TREVOR WOODS MEMORIAL MAIDEN STKS 5f
2:15 (2:17) (Class 4) 2-Y-O **£5,369** (£1,597; £798 ; £399) **Stalls** Low

Form RPR
4 1 **Time And Place**[15] 4825 2 -9-30 .... TonyHamilton 5 77+
(Richard Fahey) *trckd ldrs: rdn 2f out: kpt on: led post* **6/1**
2 2 shd **Polish Crown**[11] 4960 2 -8-120 .... JoeFanning 2 72
(Mark Johnston) *led narrowly: rdn over 2f out: kpt on: hdd post* **4/1**[3]
05 3 1 1/2 **Millkwood**[15] 4825 2 -9-30 .... PJMcDonald 4 71
(John Davies) *w ldr: rdn 2f out: ev ch tl no ex fnl 75yds* **40/1**
0 4 nk **Dream Ally (IRE)**[30] 2330 2 -9-30 .... TomEaves 9 70
(Jedd O'Keeffe) *trckd ldrs: pushed along and outpcd over 2f out: rdn over 1f out: swtchd rt ins fnl f: kpt on* **50/1**
2046 5 1/2 **Top Boy**[17] 4736 2 -9-0100 .... DaleSwift(3) 8 68
(Derek Shaw) *racd keenly: hld up in tch: rdn 2f out: kpt on one pce: nvr threatened ldrs* **9/4**[1]
0322 6 1 3/4 **Shillito**[15] 4825 2 -9-375 .... BarryMcHugh 7 62
(Tony Coyle) *prom towards outer: rdn 2f out: wknd ins fnl f* **17/2**
7 1 1/2 **Ready (IRE)** 2 -9-30 .... FrederikTylicki 3 57
(Garry Moss) *dwlt: hld up in tch on inner: pushed along 2f out: nvr threatened* **66/1**
8 1 3/4 **Robot Boy (IRE)**2 -9-30 .... FrankieDettori 12 50+
(David Barron) *hld up in tch on outer: pushed along 2f out: edgd lft over 1f out: sn no imp: eased towards fin* **3/1**[2]
9 4 1/2 **Bitusa (USA)** 2 -9-30 .... PaulMulrennan 13 34
(Alan Swinbank) *wnt rt s and s.i.s: a towards rr* **50/1**
10 46 **Partner's Gold (IRE)**2 -9-30 .... PaddyAspell 10
(Alan Berry) *v.s.a: a wl bhd* **100/1**
1m 3.28s (-0.02)**Going Correction** -0.25s/f (Firm) **10**Ran SP% **109.4**
Speed ratings (Par 96): **90,89,87,86,86 83,80,78,70,**
Tote Swingers: 1&2 £4.60, 1&3 £38.50, 2&3 £22.50 CSF £26.44 TOTE £7.10 : £2.00 , £1.60 , £9.60; EX 24.50 Trifecta £591.60 Part won. Pool: £799.54 - 0.30 winning tickets. .
Owner Mel Roberts & Ms Nicola Meese 1 **Bred** Worksop Manor Stud **Trained** Musley Bank, N Yorks

FOCUS
An open-looking maiden on paper and it produced a thrilling finish. Improved form from the first two.

NOTEBOOK
Time And Place, fourth on his debut at Thirsk when slowly away, was keen early but once settled travelled powerfully coming into the straight, and once moved to the outside he stayed on well to just pass the long-time leader. He will be effective stepped up in trip and has a future in handicaps. (op 7-1)
Polish Crown was only denied in the final strides. She didn't look to need a drop in trip judged on her good debut effort over 6f and will be winning races over further in time. (op 9-2 tchd 5-1)
Millkwood stepped up on recent efforts with a solid display, holding every chance 1f out, and now qualifies for a mark. (op 50-1)
Dream Ally (IRE)ran well considering he was posted out wide and got outpaced soon after halfway. He should have races in him. (tchd 40-1)
Top Boy has been mixing it in Group company this season but proved slightly disappointing back this grade. He was too free from the outset and the handicap mark of 100 does now look to flatter him. (op 2-1 tchd 5-2)
Robot Boy (IRE)came in for support but he never looked like landing a blow. The jockey wasn't hard on him once beaten and he can be given another chance. (op 5-2 tchd 10-3, tchd 9-4 in places)

5383 TOTEPOOL.COM H'CAP 1m 4f 8y
2:45 (2:45) (Class 3) (0-90,89) 3-Y-O+
£8,092 (£2,423; £1,211 ; £605 ; £302 ; £152) **Stalls** Low

Form RPR
2144 1 **Lady Kashaan (IRE)**[12] 4923 3 -7-1370 oh1 .... JimmyQuinn 5 79+
(Alan Swinbank) *hld up in tch: rdn and hdwy towards outer over 2f out: led over 1f out: kpt on wl* **13/2**[3]
3326 2 2 **Arizona John (IRE)**[15] 4823 7 -9-075 .... FrannyNorton 6 81
(John Mackie) *hld up in tch: rdn and hdwy on inner over 1f out: sn chsd ldr: kpt on one pce* **10/1**
4431 3 shd **Key Gold**[19] 4682 3 -8-576 .... JoeFanning 1 82
(Mark Johnston) *in tch: rdn to chse ldr wl over 1f out: kpt on one pce* **9/4**[2]
1020 4 5 **Dark Dune (IRE)**[21] 4621 4 -9-479 .... DavidAllan 3 77
(Tim Easterby) *hld up in rr: rdn over 2f out: minor late hdwy: nvr threatened* **9/1**
2212 5 3/4 **Muntasir (IRE)**[24] 4513 3 -9-489 .... FrankieDettori 7 86
(Saeed Bin Suroor) *trckd ldr: pushed along to ld wl over 2f out: rdn whn hdd over 1f out: sn wkndl* **13/8**[1]

2510 **6** 3¾ **Painted Tail (IRE)**[8] 5085 5-8-10 **71**................................ AndrewElliott 2 62
(Alan Swinbank) *trckd ldr on inner: briefly short of room and lost pl over 2f out: sn rdn: wknd over 1f out* **16/1**

3041 **7** 22 **Alsahil (USA)**[47] 3728 6-8-9 **75**.................................... GarryWhillans(5) 4 30
(Micky Hammond) *led: hdd wl over 2f out: sn wknd* **20/1**

2m 35.64s (-5.16) **Going Correction** -0.25s/f (Firm)
WFA 3 from 4yo+ 10lb 7 Ran SP% **111.9**
Speed ratings (Par 107): **107,105,105,102,101 99,84**
Tote Swingers: 1&2 £4.50, 1&3 £3.20, 2&3 £2.70 CSF £63.60 CT £188.43 TOTE £5.90: £2.40, £3.00; EX 51.90 Trifecta £262.70 Pool: £539.74 - 1.52 winning units..
Owner G Brogan **Bred** Corduff Stud Ltd & J Corcoran **Trained** Melsonby, N Yorks

FOCUS
A fair handicap run at a good pace (just 0.14sec outside Racing Post standard).

NOTEBOOK
Lady Kashaan(IRE) was returning to winning form after two decent efforts at Newmarket and Ripon and extended the good run of 3yos in the race. Jimmy Quinn sat off the pace and was in no hurry until caught a bit flat-footed half a mile out. However, Lady Kashaan responded to Quinn's urgings and stayed on best of all in the straight, looking value for more than the margin of victory. Having started the season on a mark of 49, she won here off 70 (1lb out of the handicap) and looks capable of further progression and appears capable of staying further than this 1m4f. (op 7-1 tchd 8-1)
Arizona John(IRE) travelled well, went for a run up the rail rounding the home turn and looked to briefly hit the front before the winner quickened on the outside. He stayed on stoutly to fill the runner-up spot, but was no match for the winner. He helps set the level of the form. (op 15-2)
Key Gold was another to be caught for pace rounding the home turn, but was still in contention in the straight. However, the 7lb she was raised for winning at Beverley last month was enough to blunt her finish. (op 3-1)
Dark Dune(IRE) was a course winner back in June when coming from the rear and David Allan tried repeat tactics here. However, the leaders had quickened by the time he got into contention and he could only stay on for fourth. (op 8-1)
Muntasir(IRE) proved a disappointing favourite. He was never far away, but had to be ridden to lead before turning into the straight and faded once challenged. (op 7-4 tchd 6-4)
Painted Tail(IRE) Official explanation: jockey said mare was denied a clear run

5384 TANNIES RACEDAY H'CAP — 2m 1f 22y
3:15 (3:16) (Class 5) (0-70,66) 3-Y-0+ **£2,911** (£866; £432; £216) **Stalls** Low

Form RPR

6202 **1** **Maid Of Meft**[12] 4908 5-9-10 **62**.. MickyFenton 2 71
(Paul Midgley) *hld up in midfield: pushed along over 4f out: hdwy over 2f out: sn chsd ldr: led ins fnl f: styd on* **18/1**

3211 **2** nk **Solar View (IRE)**[23] 4537 3-8-11 **63**.................................... ChrisCatlin 8 76+
(Sir Mark Prescott Bt) *trckd ldr: led over 3f out: rdn 3 to 4 l clr 2f out: idled over 1f out: hdd ins fnl f: styd on but a jst hld* **15/8**[1]

-466 **3** 7 **Petella**[12] 4925 6-9-11 **63**.. PJMcDonald 3 64
(George Moore) *hld up: pushed along 4f out: rdn and hdwy over 2f out: chsd ldng pair over 1f out: no ex ins fnl f* **6/1**

5503 **4** ½ **Descaro (USA)**[6] 5172 6-9-10 **62**..................................(v) DanielTudhope 7 62
(David O'Meara) *trckd ldr: rdn 4f out: sn one pce* **11/2**[3]

0055 **5** ½ **Spiders Star**[6] 5172 9-8-2 **47**.................................. ShirleyTeasdale(7) 10 47
(Simon West) *midfield: rdn over 4f out: plugged on: nvr threatened ldrs* **16/1**

6333 **6** 1½ **Shirls Son Sam**[13] 4867 4-8-12 **50**.................................. KellyHarrison 5 48
(Chris Fairhurst) *sn led: rdn whn hdd over 3f out: wknd over 1f out* **12/1**

5-61 **7** 5 **Knox Overstreet**[5] 5196 4-9-7 **64** 6ex.............................. CharlesBishop(5) 4 57
(Mick Channon) *s.i.s: hld up in rr: rdn 4f out: sn no imp* **4/1**[2]

2-00 **8** 1¾ **Tanjung Agas (IRE)**[22] 4585 4-8-11 **54**.................(v¹) MarkCoumbe(5) 9 45
(Christopher Kellett) *midfield: rdn over 3f out: sn wknd* **66/1**

1130 **9** ½ **Blackstone Vegas**[33] 4176 6-9-7 **66**............ WilliamTwiston-Davies(7) 6 56
(Derek Shaw) *hld up in midfield: rdn 4f out: wknd over 2f out* **10/1**

3m 48.77s (4.17) **Going Correction** -0.25s/f (Firm)
WFA 3 from 4yo+ 14lb 9 Ran SP% **113.9**
Speed ratings (Par 103): **80,79,76,76,76 75,73,72,71**
Tote Swingers: 1&2 £6.20, 1&3 £14.00, 2&3 £3.10 CSF £51.42 CT £236.28 TOTE £22.20: £5.70, £1.30, £2.20; EX 80.20 Trifecta £363.50 Pool: £736.91 - 1.50 winning units..
Owner David Mann **Bred** Ian Murray Tough **Trained** Westow, N Yorks

FOCUS
A steady pace early in this staying handicap and it paid to race close to the pace. The front two drew well clear.
Knox Overstreet Official explanation: jockey said gelding ran flat

5385 BRITISH STALLION STUDS EBF FLYING FILLIES' STKS (LISTED RACE) — 6f
3:45 (3:56) (Class 1) 3-Y-0+
£21,266 (£8,062; £4,035; £2,010; £1,008; £506) **Stalls** Low

Form RPR

1001 **1** **Mince**[8] 5080 3-8-11 **100**.. FrankieDettori 11 107
(Roger Charlton) *prom: led 4f out: hdd over 2f out: rdn to ld again appr fnl f: kpt on wl* **9/4**[1]

0341 **2** 2 **Ultrasonic (USA)**[29] 4336 3-8-11 **102**.................................... PatDobbs 7 101+
(Sir Michael Stoute) *hld up: hdwy over 2f out: rdn over 1f out: kpt on fnl f: wnt 2nd towards fin* **7/1**[2]

5201 **3** ½ **Artistic Jewel (IRE)**[15] 4794 3-8-11 **102**.................... RichardMullen 14 99
(Ed McMahon) *in tch: rdn over 2f out: kpt on* **15/2**[3]

-010 **4** ½ **La Fortunata**[22] 4576 5-9-0 **88**.. CharlesBishop 2 97?
(Eve Johnson Houghton) *led: hdd 4f out: led again over 2f out: rdn whn hdd appr fnl f: edgd rt ins fnl f: no ex and lost 2 pls fnl 100yds* **28/1**

6063 **5** ¾ **Lady Gorgeous**[8] 5080 3-8-11 **99**...................................... MartinHarley 8 95
(Mick Channon) *trckd ldng pair: rdn over 2f out: one pce* **9/1**

224- **6** 2¼ **Miss Work Of Art**[330] 6337 3-8-11 **103**.......................... FrederikTylicki 3 88+
(Richard Fahey) *midfield on inner: pushed along whn briefly tight for room over 2f out: kpt on one pce fr over 1f out* **7/1**[2]

4020 **7** 3 **Switcher (IRE)**[39] 3987 3-8-11 **96**..........................(v) RichardKingscote 9 78
(Tom Dascombe) *hld up: rdn over 2f out: sn no imp* **14/1**

066 **8** nse **Perfect Tribute**[78] 2710 4-9-0 **95**.. AdamKirby 4 78
(Clive Cox) *restless in stall: in tch on inner: rdn over 2f out: wknd appr fnl f* **10/1**

6225 **9** ½ **Sioux Rising (IRE)**[16] 4764 6-9-0 **98**............................ TonyHamilton 12 76
(Richard Fahey) *midfield on outer: rdn over 2f out: sn wknd* **12/1**

634 **10** 8 **Colorful Notion (IRE)**[24] 4497 3-8-11 **87**...................... AndreaAtzeni 13 51
(Marco Botti) *dwlt: swtchd lft s: hld up in rr: pushed along over 3f out: a towards rr* **40/1**

0-46 **11** 6 **Golden Delicious**[63] 3190 4-9-0 **88**...................................... ChrisCatlin 5 32
(Hughie Morrison) *hld up: rdn over 2f out: sn wknd* **22/1**

3140 **12** 98 **Haamaat (IRE)**[22] 4609 4-9-0 **92**...................................... TadhgO'Shea 10
(William Haggas) *virtually ref to r: a t.o* **14/1**

1m 14.2s (-2.70) **Going Correction** -0.25s/f (Firm)
WFA 3 from 4yo+ 3lb 12 Ran SP% **117.9**
Speed ratings (Par 108): **108,105,104,104,103 100,96,95,95,84 76,**
Tote Swingers: 1&2 £5.20, 1&3 £6.70, 2&3 £9.10 CSF £16.92 TOTE £3.30: £1.70, £2.40, £2.00; EX 15.70 Trifecta £126.90 Pool: £1,659.41 - 9.67 winning units..
Owner Lady Rothschild **Bred** The Rt Hon Lord Rothschild **Trained** Beckhampton, Wilts

FOCUS
One of the major races run at this track during the season, although not the strongest Listed contest, but a good-sized field.

NOTEBOOK
Mince had threatened to be a Pattern-class filly at the start of this season and she bounced back to that sort of form last time out when breaking the course record at Ascot in a handicap on Shergar Cup day carrying 9st 10lb. That performance once again suggested she was capable of something special and she continued her progress, making light work of her rivals and winning in Listed company for the first time with the minimum of fuss. With black type secured connections can maybe look at winning a Group race with her while the ground remains fast. (op 3-1)
Ultrasonic(USA), perhaps the unlucky horse in the race, unlike the others involved in the finish, raced with only one behind through the early stages. She was ridden before the turn but, as she began to make her move on the home bend, was caught short of room, had her stride broken and was forced to quicken again. The fact she did was impressive and, while it would be a stretch to suggest she would have beaten the winner, she too could be up to winning a Group 3. (op 13-2 tchd 6-1)
Artistic Jewel(IRE) raced widest of all, forfeiting ground to her rivals. However she had a trouble-free passage and a similar race should not be beyond her. (op 8-1)
La Fortunata took on Mince for the early lead and was still in there fighting with a furlong to go, but while the winner found more, she faded. (op 33-1)
Lady Gorgeous, who finished behind today's winner at Ascot but was worse off here, was given a well-judged ride and was perfectly placed to feature, but she just lacked the class to get involved in the finish. (tchd 10-1)
Miss Work Of Art finished clear of the remainder. She had the highest official rating in the field but was making her first appearance since finishing fourth in the Cheveley Park Stakes last September. She fell back through the field as the race unfolded before staying on again at the end and the outing should bring her on. (op 8-1 tchd 13-2)

5386 CGC EVENTS FOR CONFERENCE & BANQUETING H'CAP — 1m 4y
4:15 (4:22) (Class 3) (0-95,93) 3-Y-0
£8,092 (£2,423; £1,211; £605; £302; £152) **Stalls** Low

Form RPR

4311 **1** **Sweetnessandlight**[15] 4830 3-8-1 **76**............................ DominicFox(3) 4 85+
(Jason Ward) *hld up in tch: stl only 5th 1f out: r.o strly to ld towards fin* **9/2**[3]

0015 **2** ½ **Croquembouche (IRE)**[5] 5197 3-8-5 **77**.............................. ChrisCatlin 6 85
(Ed de Giles) *sn led: rdn 2f out: drvn and one pce ins fnl f: hdd towards fin* **12/1**

1-10 **3** ½ **Asatir (USA)**[17] 4735 3-9-7 **93**.. FrankieDettori 1 100
(Saeed Bin Suroor) *in tch: pushed along over 2f out: rdn to chse ldr 1f out: sn ev ch: drvn and one pce fnl 100yds* **11/4**[1]

4004 **4** 3¼ **Nameitwhatyoulike**[22] 4588 3-8-8 **80**........................... PaulMulrennan 2 79+
(Michael Easterby) *hld up: rdn 2f out: kpt on fnl f: no threat ldng trio* **5/1**

-231 **5** 2¾ **Warcrown (IRE)**[21] 4630 3-8-6 **78**................................. BarryMcHugh 5 71
(Richard Fahey) *prom: rdn over 2f out: drvn over 1f out: wknd ins fnl f* **3/1**[2]

1216 **6** ¾ **Satanic Beat (IRE)**[10] 4997 3-9-1 **87**.................................... TomEaves 7 78
(Jedd O'Keeffe) *trckd ldrs: rdn over 2f out: wknd fnl f* **6/1**

1150 **7** 1¼ **Ardmay (IRE)**[22] 4600 3-9-1 **87**.. AmyRyan 8 75
(Kevin Ryan) *in tch on outer: rdn 3f out: wknd over 1f out* **7/1**

1m 42.66s (-3.24) **Going Correction** -0.25s/f (Firm) 7 Ran SP% **121.0**
Speed ratings (Par 104): **106,105,105,101,99 98,97**
Tote Swingers: 1&2 £9.50, 1&3 £3.10, 2&3 £5.60 CSF £58.07 CT £179.00 TOTE £6.80: £2.60, £4.10; EX 75.50 Trifecta £303.50 Pool: £824.48 - 2.01 winning units..
Owner Mrs Jill Ward **Bred** Dxb Bloodstock Ltd **Trained** Middleham, N Yorks

FOCUS
As expected, there was a battle for the early lead and the runner-up deserves great credit for the way he sustained the gallop. It was a truly-run affair and that played into the hands of the winner, who swooped late to score.

NOTEBOOK
Sweetnessandlight is a filly in form and she managed to defy a 6lb rise following her recent Thirsk triumph. She was held up but caught the eye travelling as well as anything on the outside of the pack with 3f to run. She briefly looked short of room early in the home straight, which allowed the runner-up to get first run, but once daylight appeared the acceleration was immediate and she won a shade more snugly than the winning margin suggests. (op 6-1 tchd 13-2)
Croquembouche(IRE) needed to fight for early supremacy and, once he got to the front, he was keener than ideal. He managed to quicken again around 2f out and looked to have a winning lead entering the final furlong, but the winner was able to reel him in. It was a fine effort and compensation should be possible when he manages to secure an easier lead. (op 14-1 tchd 11-1)
Asatir(USA) put his disappointing Goodwood date behind him with a much-improved display off top weight. He was drawn in stall one but dwelt slightly which forced his rider to deploy waiting tactics. He improved on the inside to go in pursuit of the winner with 1f to run but never looked like getting there. He gave the impression that a return to further would suit. (op 2-1)
Nameitwhatyoulike was held up at the back but was being shoved along before the home turn and just plugged on at the one pace. (op 17-2)
Warcrown(IRE), the disappointment of the race, wasn't able to assume his customary front-running role and seemed to struggle as a result. He was beaten early in the home straight. (op 4-1)

5387 IN LOVING MEMORY OF ALISON CLARK MAIDEN STKS — 1m 4y
4:45 (4:45) (Class 4) 3-Y-0+ **£5,175** (£1,540; £769; £384) **Stalls** Low

Form RPR

2-2 **1** **Sunnybridge Boy (IRE)**[30] 4293 3-8-11 0............ MichaelMetcalfe(3) 2 87+
(Mrs K Burke) *trckd ldr: rdn over 2f out: drvn over 1f out: kpt on: led post* **10/3**[2]

6-32 **2** shd **Alraased (USA)**[30] 4301 3-9-0 75...................................... TadhgO'Shea 5 86+
(John Dunlop) *trckd ldr: led wl over 2f out: rdn over 1f out: drvn and kpt on fnl f: hdd post* **5/2**[1]

-442 **3** 4½ **All Time**[16] 4780 4-9-1 68.. IanMongan 1 71
(Sir Henry Cecil) *racd keenly: in tch: pushed along to chse ldr over 2f out: drvn and hung jst lft ins fnl f: sn wknd* **5/2**[1]

6020 **4** 2 **Cool Sky**[24] 4516 3-8-9 75.. DavidKenny(5) 3 71
(William Knight) *s.i.s: hld up in tch: rdn over 2f out: no imp* **6/1**

64 **5** 6 **Eamaadd**[16] 4780 3-9-0 0.. AndreaAtzeni 4 57
(Roger Varian) *hld up: rdn 3f out: nvr threatened* **11/2**[3]

0 **6** *39* **Lady Oz (IRE)**[4] 5244 5-8-10 0 ow2........................ DavidSimmonson(7) 7
(Michael Easterby) *sn led: hdd wl over 2f out: sn wknd* **12/1**
1m 42.74s (-3.16) **Going Correction** -0.25s/f (Firm)
WFA 3 from 4yo+ 6lb **6** Ran SP% **117.6**
Speed ratings (Par 105): **105,104,100,98,92 53**
Tote Swingers: 1&2 £1.40, 1&3 £2.50, 2&3 £1.90 CSF £12.86 TOTE £4.30: £1.90, £1.60; EX 11.70.
Owner Keep Racing **Bred** Edmond Kent **Trained** Middleham Moor, N Yorks
FOCUS
A fair maiden with a strong suspicion beforehand that some of these weren't progressing despite having some promising efforts to their names. The first two home are certainly going the right way though, and put daylight between themselves and the remainder.

5388 NOVA DISPLAY H'CAP (DIV I) 6f
5:15 (5:16) (Class 5) (0-75,74) 3-Y-O+ **£2,911** (£866; £432; £216) **Stalls** Low

Form RPR
0110 **1** **Johnny Cavagin**[24] 4496 3-9-6 **71**..(t) TomEaves 4 84
(Richard Guest) *stdd s: racd keenly hld up: hdwy to trck ldng pair over 2f out: angled to outer over 1f out: rdn to ld ins fnl f: kpt on wl* **9/2**[3]
1000 **2** *2 1/4* **Available (IRE)**[24] 4496 3-9-7 **72**.. FrannyNorton 5 78
(John Mackie) *w ldr: rdn over 2f out: led 1f out: sn hdd: kpt on but no ch w wnr* **8/1**
0010 **3** *2 1/2* **Sleepy Blue Ocean**[10] 4999 6-9-9 **71**........................(p) DanielTudhope 1 69
(John Balding) *led narrowly: rdn 2f out: hdd 1f out: grad wknd* **5/2**[1]
300- **4** *hd* **Cornus**[299] 7074 10-9-12 **74**..(be) MartinHarley 6 71
(Alan McCabe) *in tch: rdn over 2f out: kpt on one pce* **14/1**
-005 **5** *4 1/2* **Lexington Spirit (IRE)**[19] 4671 3-9-1 **66**........................ BarryMcHugh 3 49
(Richard Fahey) *dwlt: hld up: pushed along 1/2-way: nvr threatened* **7/1**
0000 **6** *5* **Wildcat Wizard (USA)**[11] 4963 6-9-8 **70**........................(p) MickyFenton 9 37
(Paul Midgley) *hld up: rdn over 2f out: sn btn* **20/1**
2265 **7** *2 1/4* **Mark Anthony (IRE)**[8] 5081 5-8-0 **55** oh3.............. ShirleyTeasdale(7) 7 15
(Shaun Harris) *prom on outer: wknd over 2f out* **7/2**[2]
1m 15.44s (-1.46) **Going Correction** -0.25s/f (Firm)
WFA 3 from 5yo+ 3lb **7** Ran SP% **104.0**
Speed ratings (Par 103): **99,96,92,92,86 79,76**
Tote Swingers: 1&2 £4.80, 1&3 £2.30, 2&3 £3.80 CSF £31.83 CT £79.63 TOTE £4.40: £2.20, £4.20; EX 20.60 Trifecta £50.90 Pool: £604.38 - 8.77 winning units..
Owner A Bell **Bred** A Bell **Trained** Stainforth, S Yorks
FOCUS
The defection of Planetex left this modest sprint handicap wide open.
Mark Anthony(IRE) Official explanation: jockey said gelding became upset in stalls

5389 NOVA DISPLAY H'CAP (DIV II) 6f
5:45 (5:50) (Class 5) (0-75,72) 3-Y-O+ **£2,911** (£866; £432; £216) **Stalls** Low

Form RPR
54-6 **1** **Above The Stars**[21] 4631 4-9-2 **67**................................ ShaneBKelly(5) 3 75
(Richard Fahey) *s.i.s: hld up in tch: briefly short of room on inner 2f out: rdn and gd hdwy appr fnl f: led fnl 100yds: hld on all out* **11/4**[1]
5320 **2** *hd* **Consistant**[24] 4495 4-9-3 **63**.. DuranFentiman 9 70
(Brian Baugh) *w ldr: rdn over 2f out: led narrowly over 1f out: sn drvn: edgd rt: hdd fnl 100yds: kpt on: jst hld* **5/1**
4000 **3** *shd* **Toby Tyler**[8] 5110 6-9-11 **71**..(p) MickyFenton 2 78
(Paul Midgley) *hld up: pushed along over 2f out: rdn and hdwy towards outer over 1f out: kpt on fnl f* **7/2**[2]
0560 **4** *3/4* **Media Jury**[4] 5223 5-8-7 **53** oh3................................(v) PatrickMathers 1 58
(John Wainwright) *chsd ldrs: rdn over 2f out: kpt on* **25/1**
4110 **5** *1 3/4* **Novalist**[18] 4717 4-9-1 **61**..(b) DanielTudhope 7 60
(Robin Bastiman) *led narrowly: rdn over 2f out: hdd over 1f out: wknd ins fnl f* **9/2**[3]
000 **6** *3/4* **Powerful Pierre**[1] 5338 5-9-2 **65**................................(b) DaleSwift(3) 5 62
(Ian McInnes) *midfield: rdn over 2f out: one pce and nvr threatened ldrs* **12/1**
104 **7** *3 1/2* **Commanche Raider (IRE)**[11] 4963 5-9-12 **72**.........(b) PaulMulrennan 8 57
(Michael Dods) *trckd ldrs: rdn over 2f out: wknd appr fnl f* **7/1**
0440 **8** *2 1/2* **Silver Wind**[10] 4999 7-9-0 **67**..(p) NoraLooby(7) 4 44
(Alan McCabe) *hld up: pushed along 1/2-way: a towards rr* **10/1**
1m 15.99s (-0.91) **Going Correction** -0.25s/f (Firm) **8** Ran SP% **116.9**
Speed ratings (Par 103): **96,95,95,94,92 91,86,83**
Tote Swingers: 1&2 £4.20, 1&3 £3.50, 2&3 £4.30 CSF £17.28 CT £49.37 TOTE £3.90: £1.70, £2.10, £1.70; EX 19.40 Trifecta £87.10 Pool: £649.94 - 5.52 winning units..
Owner Miss K R Harrison **Bred** Manor Farm Stud (rutland) **Trained** Musley Bank, N Yorks
FOCUS
The second leg of this modest sprint was run 0.55secs slower than the first.
T/Plt: £709.10 to a £1 stake. Pool: £81,896.96 - 84.30 winning tickets. T/Qpdt: £21.50 to a £1 stake. Pool: £7,217.58 - 247.54 winning tickets. AS

5390 - 5396a (Foreign Racing) - See Raceform Interactive

4159 DUNDALK (A.W) (L-H)
Sunday, August 19
OFFICIAL GOING: Standard

5397a IRISH STALLION FARMS EUROPEAN BREEDERS FUND AUGUST H'CAP (PREMIER HANDICAP) 1m 2f 150y(P)
6:10 (6:35) 3-Y-O+ **£24,375** (£7,125; £3,375; £1,125)

RPR
1 **Muck 'N' Brass (IRE)**[19] 4692 3-9-3 **91**........................ WayneLordan 6 100+
(Edward Lynam, Ire) *t.k.h: chsd ldrs: 4th 3f out: gng wl appr fnl 2f whn n.m.r: sn clsd to ld 1f out: veered rt cl home: jst hld on* **14/1**
2 *hd* **Sindjara (USA)**[23] 4562 3-9-5 **93**................................ NGMcCullagh 3 102
(John M Oxx, Ire) *chsd ldrs: pushed along and n.m.r up inner under 2f out: sn chal and ev ch: kpt on wl ins fnl f: jst failed* **7/2**[1]
3 *1 1/4* **Iron Major (IRE)**[17] 4748 5-9-1 **84**................................(p) SamJames(3) 5 90
(Edward Lynam, Ire) *mid-div: 8th 3f out: prog to chal ins fnl f: no ex whn sltly hmpd in 3rd cl home* **25/1**
4 *3/4* **Barrow Island (IRE)**[34] 4163 5-9-2 **87**........................(p) ConorHoban(5) 1 91
(M Halford, Ire) *hld up towards rr: 9th 3f out: short of room on inner appr fnl f: kpt on u.p to go 4th wl ins fnl f* **10/1**
5 *1/2* **Back Burner (IRE)**[31] 4279 4-9-12 **92**................................ FranBerry 9 95
(Mrs John Harrington, Ire) *cl up 2nd: pushed along to ld briefly under 2f out: outpcd ent fnl f* **7/2**[1]
6 *nk* **Brendan Brackan (IRE)**[25] 4483 3-9-1 **92**......... EmmetMcNamara(3) 10 96
(G M Lyons, Ire) *hld up towards rr: sme hdwy fnl 2f: kpt on wl* **8/1**
7 *3/4* **Super Say (IRE)**[50] 3647 6-9-12 **92**................................ ChrisHayes 12 93
(A Oliver, Ire) *hld up in rr of mid-div: 10th under 3f out: rdn and sme hdwy: kpt on same pce fnl 2f* **12/1**
8 *1/2* **Strait Of Zanzibar (USA)**[34] 4163 3-8-13 **87**........................(p) WJLee 8 88
(K J Condon, Ire) *chsd ldrs: stl gng wl into st whn nt clr run: kpt on same pce fnl f* **16/1**
9 *1/2* **Colour Guard**[19] 4689 4-9-4 **84**.. JPO'Brien 11 83
(Mark Johnston) *chsd ldrs: pushed along in 3rd appr st: no ex ent fnl f* **4/1**[2]
10 *shd* **Miracle Cure (IRE)**[19] 4692 3-8-12 **86**............................ KevinManning 4 86
(J S Bolger, Ire) *hld up towards rr: rdn and swtchd lft appr fnl f: kpt on: nvr a threat* **14/1**
11 *3 1/4* **Suehail**[34] 4163 3-8-12 **86**.. FergalLynch 2 80
(David Marnane, Ire) *slowly away and settled towards rr: rdn and swtchd rt 2f out: no imp ins fnl f* **9/1**
12 *3/4* **Certerach (IRE)**[84] 2526 4-9-10 **90**................................ ShaneFoley 7 81
(M Halford, Ire) *mid-div: n.d fnl 2f* **13/2**[3]
13 *2* **Akasaka (IRE)**[31] 4279 5-9-7 **87**........................(p) DeclanMcDonogh 14 74
(Edward Lynam, Ire) *sn led: chal and hdd under 2f out: wknd* **16/1**
14 *3/4* **Solo Performer (IRE)**[23] 4565 7-9-4 **84**........................(b) PatSmullen 13 70
(H Rogers, Ire) *v.s.a and a in rr* **25/1**
2m 13.03s (133.03)
WFA 3 from 4yo+ 9lb **14** Ran SP% **148.5**
CSF £77.06 CT £1329.71 TOTE £23.90: £6.90, £1.70, £7.90; DF 201.10.
Owner Edward Lynam **Bred** Holborn Trust Co **Trained** Dunshaughlin, Co Meath
FOCUS
The winner had been very unlucky on his previous visit here, running out when looking in command, and he duly atoned here. The standard is set by the third, fourth, fifth and sixth.
NOTEBOOK
Muck 'N' Brass(IRE), after having to wait for an opening, hit the front entering the final furlong before jinking right and almost losing the race close home. He should go on from this. (op 14/1 tchd 16/1)
Sindjara(USA) got a run through on the inside from 2f out and stayed on well for pressure inside the final furlong. (op 4/1)
Iron Major(IRE) ran his best race for some time. He made headway from 2f out and kept on quite well although he looked held when slightly hampered close home.
Barrow Island(IRE) was held up and stayed on in the straight despite encountering a spot of traffic trouble. (op 12/1)
Back Burner(IRE), 7lb higher than when scoring over 1m1f at Leopardstown last month, raced prominently and went to the front early in the straight. He was unable to raise his game sufficiently when challenged for the lead entering the final furlong. (op 4/1 tchd 5/1)
Strait Of Zanzibar(USA) Official explanation: jockey said gelding got no run in straight
Colour Guard, a three-time winner on Southwell's all-weather, raced close up and was being ridden along in third turning for home. He was soon struggling. (op 4/1 tchd 7/2)
T/Jkpt: Not won. T/Plt: @77.00. Pool of @20,979.76 - 204.16 winning units. BF

5378 DEAUVILLE (R-H)
Sunday, August 19
OFFICIAL GOING: Turf: good: fibresand: standard

5398a DARLEY PRIX MORNY (GROUP 1) (2YO COLTS & FILLIES) (TURF) 6f
1:30 (12:00) 2-Y-O **£166,658** (£66,675; £33,337; £16,654; £8,341)

RPR
1 **Reckless Abandon**[28] 4384 2-9-0 0................................ GeraldMosse 8 115
(Clive Cox) *qckly across and mde virtually all against nr side rail: rdn over 2f out: skipped clr ent fnl f: kpt on wl u.p to maintain advantage cl home* **6/4**[1]
2 *3/4* **George Vancouver (USA)**[34] 4159 2-9-0 0........................ RyanMoore 4 113
(A P O'Brien, Ire) *hld up towards rr: rdn 2 1/2f out: briefly outpcd over 1 1/2f out: styd on thrght fnl f: wnt 2nd fnl strides* **13/2**[2]
3 *snk* **Parliament Square (IRE)**[26] 4442 2-9-0 0....................(p) WilliamBuick 9 112
(A P O'Brien, Ire) *hld up towards rr: rdn over 2f out: r.o to go 2nd ins fnl 50yds: immediately jnd and dropped to 3rd fnl strides* **20/1**
4 *3/4* **Sir Prancealot (IRE)**[28] 4384 2-9-0 0........................ StephanePasquier 5 110
(Richard Hannon) *trckd ldr on inner: rdn to chal 2f out: swtchd out and r.o to go 2nd 1f out: kpt on tl no ex and fdd wl ins fnl f: dropped to 4th cl home* **7/1**[3]
5 *1/2* **Moohaajim (IRE)**[28] 4362 2-9-0 0................................ MaximeGuyon 1 109+
(Marco Botti) *hld up in last: swtchd to wd outside and rdn to improve over 2f out: rn green u.p: kpt on to go 5th ins fnl f: do bttr* **16/1**
6 *1* **Mazameer (IRE)**[21] 4632 2-9-0 0........................ ChristopheSoumillon 7 106
(F Head, France) *prom: rdn over 2f out: kpt on tl no ex and fdd ins fnl f* **15/2**
7 *nk* **Pearl Flute (IRE)**[21] 4632 2-9-0 0............... Christophe-PatriceLemaire 3 105
(F-H Graffard, France) *midfield on inner: rdn over 2f out: sn outpcd: plugged on to go 7th ins fnl 100yds* **20/1**
8 *1/2* **Zenji (USA)**[36] 4118 2-9-0 0.. Pierre-CharlesBoudot 6 103
(A Fabre, France) *midfield: rdn over 2f out: outpcd over 1f out: fdd and dropped to 8th ins fnl 100yds* **12/1**
9 *shd* **Snowday (FR)**[28] 4384 2-9-0 0.. OlivierPeslier 2 103
(C Laffon-Parias, France) *hld up towards rr on inner: rdn and outpcd in last 2f out: swtchd out and plugged on ins fnl f: n.d* **16/1**
10 *1 1/2* **Penny's Picnic (IRE)**[28] 4384 2-9-0 0........................ ThierryJarnet 11 98
(D Guillemin, France) *trckd ldr in 2nd on outer: rdn to chal 2f out: no ex and btn 1f out: fdd* **14/1**
11 *snk* **Alhebayeb (IRE)**[38] 4008 2-9-0 0................................ PaulHanagan 10 98
(Richard Hannon) *midfield on outer: rdn 2 1/2f out: outpcd and lost pl over 1f out: fdd and dropped to last ins fnl f* **8/1**
1m 9.6s (-1.40) **Going Correction** -0.025s/f (Good) **11** Ran SP% **124.4**
Speed ratings: **108,107,106,105,105 103,103,102,102,100 100**
WIN (incl. 1 euro stake): 2.40. PLACES: 1.50, 4.60, 5.80. DF: 25.00. SF: 31.50.
Owner Miss J Deadman & S Barrow **Bred** Car Colston Hall Stud **Trained** Lambourn, Berks
FOCUS
Possibly a weak renewal, with the home team contributing little. The winner essentially reproduced his Prix Robert Papin defeat of the fourth.

NOTEBOOK

Reckless Abandon gave Clive Cox his second big winner of the weekend and extended his unbeaten record to four starts when making all for Gerald Mosse. He continued his rise through the grades, with the Morny coming on top of a brace of Group 2 wins in the Norfolk at Royal Ascot, and Prix Robert Papin last time out at Maisons-Laffitte. Although not without his quirks, the colt has an abundance of talent, and once Mosse got over to the rail from stall eight, the race was effectively over, as the jockey dictated the pace then kicked again with a furlong to go. The rail helped keep Reckless Abandon straight as a die, as he did not hang as he had at Ascot, although he did get a bit stirred up at the start. Presumably connections will look at the Middle Park for him now.

George Vancouver(USA), winner of a Dundalk maiden last time on his third start, coped well with the step up in grade, keeping on late.

Parliament Square(IRE), a 5f Listed winner on his previous start, also did well up in grade.

Sir Prancealot(IRE), runner-up in the Papin, looked as if he did not get home and the Flying Childers or Cornwallis might offer better opportunities.

Moohaajim(IRE) ◆ was taking a big step up after winning an Ascot newcomers' race on his debut and fared pretty well on that basis, still looking green but keeping on late.

Alhebayeb(IRE), who won the July Stakes on his previous outing, dropped away as if something was amiss.

5399a DARLEY PRIX JEAN ROMANET (GROUP 1) (4YO+ FILLIES & MARES) (TURF) 1m 2f

2:40 (12:00) 4-Y-0+ **£119,041** (£47,625; £23,812; £11,895; £5,958)

			RPR
1		**Snow Fairy (IRE)**[280] 7410 5-9-0 0 .... RyanMoore 8 (Ed Dunlop) *hld up towards rr: mde gd prog towards outside 2f out: qcknd wl 1f out: squeezed for room 150yds out: r.o determinedly to ld 75yds out* **4/1**[3]	119+
2	¾	**Izzi Top**[15] 4801 4-9-0 0 .... WilliamBuick 9 (John Gosden) *hld up towards rr: qcknd wl early in st: led 1f out: wandered off st line squeezing eventual wnr: hdd 75yds out: r.o wl* **6/1**	117+
3	½	**Galikova (FR)**[56] 3424 4-9-0 0 .... OlivierPeslier 7 (F Head, France) *followed pcemaker: tk ld 2f out: rdn 1 1/2f out: hdd 1f out: rallied u.p: styd on wl fnl f to take 3rd cl home* **11/4**[2]	116
4	snk	**Timepiece**[15] 4801 5-9-0 0 .... TomQueally 3 (Sir Henry Cecil) *racd in 3rd: tk ld briefly 1 1/2f out: wandered off st line u.p: hdd 1f out: styd on wl: lost 3rd cl home* **8/1**	116
5	nk	**Siyouma (IRE)**[37] 4065 4-9-0 0 .... GeraldMosse 4 (F Doumen, France) *racd in midfield: rdn 1 1/2f out: styd on wl fnl f: nrest at fin* **14/1**	115
6	1 ½	**Giofra**[37] 4065 4-9-0 0 .... ChristopheSoumillon 6 (A De Royer-Dupre, France) *settled in 4th: mde gd prog early in st: rdn over 1 1/2f out: nt qckn: styd on fnl f* **9/4**[1]	112
7	2	**Sea Of Heartbreak (IRE)**[15] 4801 5-9-0 0 .... JamesDoyle 2 (Roger Charlton) *settled towards rr: rdn early in st: no ex: styd on fnl 1 1/2f* **33/1**	108
8	5	**Sortilege (IRE)**[69] 2989 4-9-0 0 .... MaximeGuyon 5 (A Wohler, Germany) *bkmarker fr s: no prog u.p in st: nvr a factor* **50/1**	98
9	1 ½	**Tempura (GER)**[83] 2570 4-9-0 0 ....(b) FlavienPrat 1 (C Laffon-Parias, France) *led fr s: qcknd tempo bef end of bk st: rdn and hdd 2f out: sn wknd* **100/1**	95

2m 6.3s (-3.90) **Going Correction** -0.025s/f (Good) **9** Ran SP% **115.4**

Speed ratings: **114,113,113,112,112 111,109,105,104**

WIN (incl. 1 euro stake): 5.10. PLACES: 2.20, 2.10, 1.70. DF: 18.00. SF: 29.20.

Owner Anamoine Ltd **Bred** Windflower Overseas Holdings Inc **Trained** Newmarket, Suffolk

FOCUS

The fourth running of this race as a Group 1. Despite it falling just 15 days after the Nassau, and only four days before the Yorkshire Oaks, as well as it bizarrely being restricted to 4yos and above, there was a strong line-up. However, the pacemaker set a modest gallop (first 1000m went by in 1.05.6) and the first five were covered by fewer than 2l at the line. The form makes sense.

NOTEBOOK

Snow Fairy(IRE) produced a special performance to land a star-studded Prix Jean Romanet on her first start for 280 days. Having overcome a serious injury setback, she was settled towards the rear by Ryan Moore and showed a good turn of foot and all her trademark battling qualities. Tight for room in the straight, she battled all the way to the line with Izzi Top. The win further enhanced Snow Fairy's perfect record under Moore, making it six Group 1 wins in six starts. Bookmakers reacted by cutting her to 20-1 for the Arc, a race she finished third in last year.

Izzi Top bounced back from a below-par effort in the Nassau, and like the winner came wide and late, momentarily taking the lead before the older mare ground her down in the closing stages. The Prix de l'Opera looks a natural target for her.

Galikova(FR) was well positioned throughout sat on the quarters of her pacemaker Tempura, but she didn't quicken as well as her two British rivals.

Timepiece was ridden positively and ran well but was run out of the places near the finish.

5400a DARLEY PRIX KERGORLAY (GROUP 2) (3YO+) (TURF) 1m 7f

3:10 (12:00) 3-Y-0+ **£61,750** (£23,833; £11,375; £7,583; £3,791)

			RPR
1		**Joshua Tree (IRE)**[38] 4010 5-9-4 0 .... RyanMoore 2 (Marco Botti) *led on settling: hdd bef end of st: rdn and r.o wl 1 1/2f out: led 1f out: styd on wl* **9/2**[3]	108+
2	1	**Brigantin (USA)**[17] 5-9-4 0 .... Pierre-CharlesBoudot 4 (A Fabre, France) *hld up towards rr: r.o wl u.p 1 1/2f out: styd on wl to go 2nd cl home* **9/2**[3]	107
3	snk	**Shahwardi (FR)**[36] 4120 6-9-4 0 .... OlivierPeslier 5 (A De Royer-Dupre, France) *settled in midfield: swtchd to ins rail 1f out: r.o wl to go 2nd 100yds out: styd on wl: lost 2nd cl home* **11/1**	107
4	shd	**Vadamar (FR)**[36] 4120 4-9-6 0 .... Christophe-PatriceLemaire 3 (M Delzangles, France) *in rr fr s: sent up to go cl 2nd passing stands first time: nt qckn udner press early in st: rallied and styd on wl fnl f* **9/4**[1]	108
5	½	**Flamingo Fantasy (GER)**[21] 4634 7-9-4 0 ....(p) StephanePasquier 7 (S Smrczek, Germany) *hld up at rr of field tl end of bk st whn rushed to ld on ins 2 1/2f out: hdd 1f out: r.o but wknd fnl 100yds* **16/1**	106
6	2	**Americain (USA)**[113] 1686 7-9-6 0 .... GeraldMosse 1 (A De Royer-Dupre, France) *racd in midfield on ins: rdn but nt qckn 2f out: rallied and r.o wl tl 100yds out* **7/2**[2]	105
7	2 ½	**Tres Rock Danon (FR)**[21] 4634 6-9-4 0 ....(p) JohanVictoire 6 (W Hickst, Germany) *amongst early ldrs fr s: relegated to midfield down bk st: rdn but nt qckn in st: styd on* **12/1**	100

3m 17.7s (-1.40) **Going Correction** -0.025s/f (Good) **7** Ran SP% **111.3**

Speed ratings: **102,101,101,101,101 100,98**

WIN (incl. 1 euro stake): 3.70. PLACES: 2.50, 2.90. SF: 21.40.

Owner K K Al Nabooda & K Albahou **Bred** Castlemartin Stud And Skymarc Farm **Trained** Newmarket, Suffolk

FOCUS

A bit of a bunch finish given the race distance.

NOTEBOOK

Joshua Tree(IRE), a good second in the Princess of Wales's' Stakes last time, made most of the running and rallied well when challenged. He looks a natural for the Prix Royal-Oak, although the Irish St Leger might also be a possibility..

5401 - (Foreign Racing) - See Raceform Interactive

4862 DUSSELDORF (R-H)

Sunday, August 19

OFFICIAL GOING: Turf: good

5402a GROSSER SPARKASSENPREIS - PREIS DER STADTSPARKASSE DUSSELDORF (GROUP 3) (3YO) (TURF) 1m 2f 110y

3:40 (12:00) 3-Y-0

£26,666 (£9,166; £4,583; £2,500; £1,666; £1,250)

			RPR
1		**Andolini (GER)**[49] 3683 3-9-0 0 .... EPedroza 6 (A Wohler, Germany) *trckd ldr in 2nd on outer: rdn to chal over 2f out: led ent fnl f: drvn out* **11/5**[2]	104
2	2	**Raheb**[70] 3-9-2 0 .... FredericSpanu 2 (Carmen Bocskai, Switzerland) *hld up in last: rdn to improve 2 1/2f out: styd on to go 2nd last strides: nvr able to chal* **14/5**[3]	102+
3	hd	**Salon Soldier (GER)**[49] 3683 3-9-2 0 .... AStarke 5 (P Schiergen, Germany) *led: rdn and strly pressed fr over 2f out: hdd ent fnl f: no ex and fdd: dropped to 3rd last strides* **13/10**[1]	102
4	1 ½	**Nexius (IRE)**[35] 4171 3-9-2 0 .... APietsch 1 (W Hickst, Germany) *racd in 3rd on inner: rdn over 2f out: sn outpcd: dropped to 4th ins fnl f: plugged on* **48/10**	99
5	1 ¾	**Nostro Amico (GER)**[49] 3683 3-9-2 0 .... THellier 4 (Mario Hofer, Germany) *racd in 4th in outer: rdn and outpcd over 2f out: dropped to last over 1f out: plugged on* **11/2**	95

2m 8.88s (128.88) **5** Ran SP% **133.7**

WIN (incl. 10 euro stake): 32. PLACES: 18, 18. SF: 173.

Owner T Gehrig **Bred** Th Gehrig **Trained** Germany

5296 KEMPTON (A.W) (R-H)

Monday, August 20

OFFICIAL GOING: Standard to slow

Wind: Virtually nil Weather: Bright early, getting darker

5403 FAST ERIC NURSERY (SUPPORTED BY BETFAIR) 5f (P)

6:20 (6:22) (Class 6) (0-60,60) 2-Y-0 **£1,617** (£481; £240; £120) **Stalls** Low

Form				RPR
0334	1		**Stripped Bear (IRE)**[16] 4806 2-8-11 **50** .... RichardKingscote 8 (Tom Dascombe) *sn chsng ldr: led wl over 1f out and sn clr: pushed out* **5/1**[3]	62
535	2	3 ¾	**Hardy Blue (IRE)**[10] 5046 2-9-0 **53** .... FergusSweeney 11 (Jamie Osborne) *chsd ldrs: rdn and styd on fr 2f out: tk 2nd fnl 140yds but nvr any ch w wnr* **9/2**[2]	52
000	3	nk	**Prince Of Prophets (IRE)**[63] 3224 2-8-6 **45** ....(t) WilliamCarson 6 (Stuart Williams) *s.i.s: in rr: sme hdwy whn hmpd bnd 2f out: swtchd rt and drvn wl over 1f out: str run to take 3rd fnl f and gaining on 2nd cl home but no ch w wnr* **8/1**	44
0340	4	3 ¼	**Jamnean**[47] 3748 2-9-2 **55** .... AmirQuinn 10 (John Holt) *in rr: rdn 3f out: hdwy over 1f out: styd on to take 4th ins fnl f but nvr any ch* **20/1**	41
5244	5	2 ¼	**Emperor's Daughter**[6] 5194 2-8-12 **58** ....(b[1]) NoelGarbutt[(7)] 3 (Tim Pitt) *sn led: hdd wl over 1f out: wknd qckly fnl f* **7/2**[1]	36
050	6	¾	**Persian Marvel (IRE)**[7] 5160 2-9-3 **56** .... PatCosgrave 2 (Jim Boyle) *s.i.s: sn rdn and in tch but nvr nr ldrs: wknd fr 2f out* **7/1**	31
004	7	hd	**I'Ve No Money (IRE)**[10] 5053 2-9-3 **56** ....(t) TedDurcan 5 (David C Griffiths) *s.i.s and bhd: hdwy and nt clr run on ins wl over 1f out and again whn hdwy ins fnl f: kpt on: nt rcvr* **14/1**	34
0050	8	1 ¼	**Tough Question**[26] 4463 2-8-3 **45** ....(v[1]) SimonPearce[(3)] 12 (Michael Madgwick) *racd on outer thrght: rdn and no ch fr 1/2-way* **33/1**	15
4400	9	1 ¾	**Shirley's Pride**[11] 4990 2-8-13 **52** .... KieranO'Neill 1 (John Holt) *s.i.s: sn rcvrd and in tch: rdn 1/2-way: wknd over 1f out* **10/1**	15
040	10	8	**Purple Day**[22] 4625 2-9-7 **60** ....(p) AdamKirby 4 (Pam Sly) *chsd ldrs to 1/2-way: sn wknd* **5/1**[3]	

1m 1.22s (0.72) **Going Correction** +0.025s/f (Slow) **10** Ran SP% **120.8**

Speed ratings (Par 92): **95,89,88,83,79 78,78,76,73,60**

toteswingers: 1&2 £3.30, 1&3 £15.40, 2&3 £11.60 CSF £28.93 CT £182.05 TOTE £6.80: £2.90, £1.70, £5.00; EX 27.40.

Owner The MHS 4x10 Partnership **Bred** Tally-Ho Stud **Trained** Malpas, Cheshire

FOCUS

A low-grade nursery in which the gallop was a strong one. The winner chased the front-running favourite and proved much too good for her rivals. The second and third help set a modest level.

NOTEBOOK

Stripped Bear(IRE) had previously shown her best form on Fibresand but this was a good performance on her second start on Polytrack. She showed plenty of pace and, although she was tiring near the line, she had already done enough to secure the win when quickening clear entering the final furlong. (op 4-1)

Hardy Blue(IRE) was dropping down in trip and making her handicap debut after showing only fair form in three plating-class events. She was forced to race wide from her high draw and this was a solid effort, leaving the impression she'd be suited by a step back up in trip. (op 6-1 tchd 4-1)

Prince Of Prophets(IRE) was ridden with restraint and finished strongly on this handicap debut despite being hampered entering the straight. His breeding suggests he'll want further than this and judging by this run he can improve given a stiffer test. Official explanation: jockey said gelding was denied a clear run (op 12-1)

Jamnean did some good late work on this nursery debut.

Emperor's Daughter, with first-time blinkers replacing cheekpieces, was expected to be suited by the return to Polytrack but set too strong a gallop and was a spent force entering the final furlong. (op 11-4 tchd 5-2)

I'Ve No Money(IRE), with the tongue-tie retained, was slowly away on this handicap/Polytrack debut but had his run repeatedly blocked in the straight. He can be rated higher. Official explanation: jockey said colt was denied a clear run (tchd 16-1)

5404 BONNEVILLE MEDIAN AUCTION MAIDEN STKS 1m 2f (P)
6:50 (6:50) (Class 5) 3-5-Y-O **£2,264** (£673; £336; £168) **Stalls** Low

Form RPR

6023 **1** **Dynamic Duo (IRE)**[3] 5297 3-9-3 78 KieranO'Neill 3 82
(Richard Hannon) *chsd ldrs in 3rd: wnt 2nd over 3f out: drvn to ld over 1f out: edgd rt and pressed ins fnl f: kpt on wl clsng stages* **13/8**[2]

2- **2** *½* **Revered Citizen (USA)**[374] 5011 3-9-3 0 TedDurcan 2 81
(Sir Michael Stoute) *towards rr but in tch: hdwy to take 3rd 3f out: chsd wnr over 1f out: effrt to chal on inner fnl f but nvr quite upsides: no ex and hld fnl 100yds* **5/4**[1]

44 **3** *7* **Iz She**[33] 4213 4-9-6 0 DarryllHolland 4 62
(William Knight) *led: rdn over 2f out: hdd over 1f out: wknd qckly fnl f* **7/1**[3]

0 **4** *3 ¾* **Rokcella**[29] 4366 3-8-12 0 RichardKingscote 7 55
(Clive Cox) *chsd ldrs: rdn wknd 3f out* **16/1**

4 **5** *7* **Balcary Bay**[40] 3975 3-9-3 0 AndreaAtzeni 8 46
(James Eustace) *chsd ldr tl wknd over 3f out* **10/1**

6 **6** *20* **Tribal I D (IRE)**[12] 4948 3-9-3 0 PatCosgrave 1
(Jim Boyle) *plld hrd: in tch tl hung lft and wknd fr 4f out: t.o* **33/1**

7 *16* **Refute (IRE)** 3-9-3 0 AdamKirby 6
(Harry Dunlop) *slowly away: sn rdn and green: a wl bhd: t.o* **20/1**

2m 8.52s (0.52) **Going Correction** +0.025s/f (Slow)
WFA 3 from 4yo 8lb **7** Ran SP% **117.7**
Speed ratings (Par 103): **98,97,92,89,83 67,54**
toteswingers: 1&2 £1.40, 1&3 £2.50, 2&3 £1.70 CSF £4.23 TOTE £2.60: £1.70, £1.10; EX 4.20.

Owner Mrs J Wood **Bred** Mrs O M E McKeever **Trained** East Everleigh, Wilts

FOCUS
An interesting maiden in which the gallop was a moderate one. The winner raced centre-to-far-side in the straight and the first two pulled clear in an ordinary time. The winner looks the best guide.

Tribal I D(IRE) Official explanation: jockey said gelding ran too free

5405 SOUTHERN CLASSIC BIKE SHOW H'CAP (SUPPORTED BY BETFAIR) 1m 2f (P)
7:20 (7:21) (Class 5) (0-70,70) 3-Y-O+ **£2,264** (£673; £336; £168) **Stalls** Low

Form RPR

4501 **1** **My Mate Jake (IRE)**[7] 5175 4-9-6 **62** 6ex (b) RichardKingscote 9 71
(James Given) *trckd ldrs: wnt 2nd 4f out: drvn to take narrow appr fnl f: edgd rt and hrd pressed ins fnl f: hld on all out* **7/2**[2]

5662 **2** *shd* **Sky Khan**[12] 4945 3-9-4 **68** (v[1]) MickaelBarzalona 8 77
(Ed Dunlop) *racd on outer: hdwy 7f out: led 5f out: rdn and narrowly hdd appr fnl f: styd chalng and edgd lft ins fnl f: kpt on: jst failed off* **15/8**[1]

003 **3** *1 ½* **Ashkalara**[11] 4989 5-9-1 **57** CathyGannon 6 67+
(Stuart Howe) *s.i.s towards rr: hdwy fr 3f out: styd on to take 3rd over 1f out: chal between horses and no room thrght fnl f: eased clsng stages: nt rcvr* **20/1**

5005 **4** *1 ¾* **Abishena (IRE)**[11] 4984 3-9-1 **65** AdamKirby 7 67
(Mark Johnston) *sn led: hdd 5f out: rdn over 3f out: styd on same pce fr over 1f out* **10/1**

5054 **5** *½* **Rockweiller**[14] 4884 5-9-5 **61** (v) DarryllHolland 2 62
(Steve Gollings) *chsd ldr to 5f out: rdn and wd bnd over 2f out: rallied u.p and kpt on again clsng stages* **13/2**

1425 **6** *¾* **Mr Fickle (IRE)**[14] 4872 3-9-3 **67** (b) GeorgeBaker 3 67
(Gary Moore) *rr: rdn 4f out: styd on fr over 1f out: nvr a threat* **5/1**[3]

3206 **7** *6* **Island Melody (IRE)**[32] 4250 3-9-6 **70** (p) LiamKeniry 5 58
(J S Moore) *chsd ldrs: rdn and wknd over 2f out* **10/1**

0006 **8** *21* **Regalo Rosado**[13] 4932 3-8-2 **52** KieranO'Neill 4
(Mike Murphy) *a in rr: no ch fnl 4f: t.o* **8/1**

000- **9** *14* **Miss Boops (IRE)**[435] 2964 4-9-0 **56** JamieGoldstein 1
(Zoe Davison) *bhd fr 1/2-way: t.o* **50/1**

2m 8.33s (0.33) **Going Correction** +0.025s/f (Slow)
WFA 3 from 4yo+ 8lb **9** Ran SP% **123.0**
Speed ratings (Par 103): **99,98,97,96,95 95,90,73,62**
toteswingers: 1&2 £1.90, 1&3 £5.80, 2&3 £5.70 CSF £11.27 CT £119.41 TOTE £5.70: £2.00, £1.10, £4.10; EX 14.10.

Owner Alex Owen **Bred** Crandon Park Stud **Trained** Willoughton, Lincs

FOCUS
A fair handicap, the pace was moderate and the winner was ridden prominently. The form is rated around the winner who was close to his old best.

Ashkalara Official explanation: jockey said mare was denied a clear run

5406 NORTON JAP CLAIMING STKS (SUPPORTED BY BETFAIR) 7f (P)
7:50 (7:51) (Class 5) 3-Y-O **£2,264** (£673; £336; £168) **Stalls** Low

Form RPR

401 **1** **Ziefhd**[21] 4644 3-8-8 76 (p) CathyGannon 3 68
(David Evans) *mde all: rdn and hrd pressed ins fnl f: hld on all out* **15/8**[2]

0060 **2** *hd* **Marford Missile (IRE)**[40] 3960 3-9-6 75 RichardKingscote 4 80
(Tom Dascombe) *chsd ldrs: wnt 2nd 2f out: drvn to chal ins fnl f: styd pressing wnr tl no ex last strides* **7/2**[3]

0661 **3** *1 ¾* **Venetian View (IRE)**[14] 4871 3-9-7 82 (b) GeorgeBaker 1 76
(Gary Moore) *in rr: rdn along 3f out: hdwy to take 3rd over 1f out: styd on same pce ins fnl f* **6/4**[1]

00 **4** *6* **Joy To The World (IRE)**[6] 5215 3-8-8 49 (t[1]) LiamKeniry 5 47
(Paul Cole) *s.i.s: rdn over 2f out: mod prog to take 4th last strides* **33/1**

3056 **5** *nk* **Illustrious Lad (IRE)**[10] 5047 3-8-11 55 WilliamCarson 8 49
(Jim Boyle) *chsd ldr rdn over 2f out: sn dropped to 3rd: wknd fnl f* **20/1**

0300 **6** *6* **Enthrall (IRE)**[9] 5095 3-8-4 43 (v[1]) TadhgO'Shea 2 26
(Denis Coakley) *chsd ldrs: rdn and wknd 2f out* **25/1**

1610 **7** *11* **Moment In The Sun**[2] 5350 3-9-2 65 (b) MickaelBarzalona 6
(David Flood) *s.i.s: rdn over 3f out: a bhd* **10/1**

1m 26.1s (0.10) **Going Correction** +0.025s/f (Slow) **7** Ran SP% **117.6**
Speed ratings (Par 100): **100,99,97,90,90 83,71**
toteswingers: 1&2 £2.20, 1&3 £1.70, 2&3 £1.70 CSF £9.13 TOTE £4.60: £4.10, £1.10; EX 10.90.The winner was claimed by Mr T D McCarthy for £8,000.

Owner Mrs E Evans **Bred** Deepwood Farm Stud **Trained** Pandy, Monmouths

FOCUS
Very little strength in depth to this claimer and the market got it wrong with the winner proving easy to back. The form is rated a bit cautiously and the winner only needed to run to his latest.

5407 LAND SPEED RECORD MAIDEN STKS (SUPPORTED BY BETFAIR) 1m (P)
8:20 (8:21) (Class 5) 2-Y-O **£2,264** (£673; £336; £168) **Stalls** Low

Form RPR

1 **Cap O'Rushes** 2-9-3 0 SilvestreDeSousa 3 85+
(Mahmood Al Zarooni) *led after 1f: wnt lft 5f out: pushed along 2f out: c reaily clr wl over 1f out: v easily* **3/1**[2]

5 **2** *8* **Arctic Admiral (IRE)**[16] 4813 2-9-3 0 KieranO'Neill 6 68
(Richard Hannon) *trckd wnr: pushed lft 5f out: rdn and readily outpcd fr 2f out: eased whn no ch clsng stages and jst hld on for 2nd* **8/1**

00 **3** *shd* **Shooting Jacket (USA)**[30] 4340 2-8-12 0 AntiocoMurgia[(5)] 4 66
(Mahmood Al Zarooni) *in tch: pushed along to take 3rd 2 out: styd on to cl on eased down 2nd clsng stages but nvr any ch w wnr* **7/1**[3]

0 **4** *3 ½* **Dark Templar**[23] 4595 2-9-3 0 GeorgeBaker 5 58+
(Ed Vaughan) *towards rr: pushed along and kpt on fnl 2f but nvr a threat* **10/1**

5 *3* **Bountiful Bess** 2-8-12 0 LiamKeniry 2 46+
(Pam Sly) *s.i.s: in rr: styd on fnl 2f: nvr a threat* **33/1**

03 **6** *¾* **Grilletto (USA)**[13] 4917 2-9-3 0 MartinDwyer 9 49
(James Tate) *chsd ldrs and bmpd 5f out: styd wl there tl wknd 2f out* **11/4**[1]

00 **7** *2* **Knight's Parade (IRE)**[16] 4803 2-9-3 0 MartinLane 7 45
(Amanda Perrett) *pushed along 3f out: a towards rr* **25/1**

8 *6* **Raven's Tower (USA)** 2-9-3 0 MickaelBarzalona 10 31
(Mahmood Al Zarooni) *chsng ldrs whn bmpd 5f out: styd in tch and rdn over 3f out: sn wknd* **11/4**[1]

6 **9** *nk* **Man From Seville**[9] 5098 2-9-3 0 ChrisCatlin 6 30
(Sir Mark Prescott Bt) *slowly away: a in rr* **16/1**

10 *2 ¾* **Positive Parenting (IRE)** 2-8-12 0 WilliamCarson 1 19
(Stuart Williams) *chsd ldrs: wknd ins fnl 3f* **33/1**

1m 40.3s (0.50) **Going Correction** +0.025s/f (Slow) **10** Ran SP% **126.6**
Speed ratings (Par 94): **98,90,89,86,83 82,80,74,74,71**
toteswingers: 1&2 £8.90, 1&3 £3.80, 2&3 £11.30 CSF £29.64 TOTE £4.90: £1.10, £5.30, £2.30; EX 32.80.

Owner Godolphin **Bred** Darley **Trained** Newmarket, Suffolk

FOCUS
This looked a decent maiden but one in which the gallop was only moderate, and that suited those ridden prominently. The winner impressed and is worth his place in better class.

NOTEBOOK
Cap O'Rushes, a half-brother to eight winners from 7f-2m1f, was allowed to dictate steady fractions. He caught the eye in the preliminaries, as did he in the race, and it was hard not to be impressed with the style in which he lengthened clear inside the final furlong. He can only improve for the experience, which was backed up by his jockey after the race, and he looks to have a bright future, possibly over middle distances. (op 7-2)
Arctic Admiral(IRE) was the only runner to serve up any challenge to the impressive winner but he was easily brushed aside in the straight. He was eased close home and just held on for second, but this was a step up on his debut run. His jockey, Kieran O'Neill, reported that the saddle slipped. Official explanation: jockey said saddle slipped
Shooting Jacket(USA), a stablemate of the winner, had been well held in his two previous starts but this was an improved effort stepping up in trip. He nearly snatched second on the line and looks sure to win races. (op 8-1)
Dark Templar fared okay given that he was ridden with restraint in this steadily run maiden. He was still travelling well on the bend into the straight and and made some eyecatching late progress suggesting he can make his mark in ordinary handicaps. (op 12-1 tchd 9-1)
Bountiful Bess, out of a winning stayer, was another noted to be staying on up the straight. She is entitled to improve for this experience but her future may be over further.
Grilletto(USA) didn't show any improvement over this longer trip and was well below the form of his previous placed run at this track over 7f. (op 7-2)
Raven's Tower(USA), fifth foal of a high-class performer in the US, herself a sister to dual Breeders' Cup winner Tiznow, was the market fancy of the three Godolphin runners. He took a bump before halfway and was forced to race wide from his high draw but this was a disappointing debut. It is hoped that he can improve for the experience. (op 5-2 tchd 3-1)

5408 KEMPTON AUTOJUMBLE H'CAP 1m 4f (P)
8:50 (8:50) (Class 6) (0-60,60) 3-Y-O **£1,617** (£481; £240; £120) **Stalls** Centre

Form RPR

162 **1** **Melodrama (IRE)**[7] 5164 3-9-7 **60** (b) TedDurcan 11 72
(David Lanigan) *trckd ldrs: c lft to r wd fr 2f out: led appr fnl f: hrd drvn: hld on all out* **7/4**[1]

4012 **2** *shd* **Norfolk Sky**[21] 4650 3-8-7 **49** HarryBentley[(3)] 5 61
(Chris Wall) *towards rr: hdwy 4f out: c towards stands' side fr 2f out: styd to chse wnr ins fnl f: gng on clsng stages: nt quite get up* **9/2**[3]

6633 **3** *2 ¼* **Neige D'Antan**[10] 5052 3-8-13 **52** ChrisCatlin 3 60
(Sir Mark Prescott Bt) *chsd ldrs: drvn to chse wnr over 1f out: no imp and lost 2nd ins fnl f: kpt on same pce* **3/1**[2]

0606 **4** *7* **Roughlyn**[12] 4971 3-8-7 **46** oh1 (p) KieranO'Neill 7 43
(Lisa Williamson) *mid-div: rdn 4f out: styd on fnl 2f tk mod 4th fnl 100yds* **33/1**

0505 **5** *3 ¼* **Onertother**[11] 4994 3-9-1 **54** LiamKeniry 12 46
(Joseph Tuite) *trckd ldr: led over 3f out: rdn 2f out: hdd appr fnl f: sn wknd: lost 3rd fnl 100yds* **7/1**

060 **6** *½* **Merchants Return**[14] 4888 3-9-1 **57** SimonPearce[(3)] 4 48
(Lydia Pearce) *s.i.s: in rr: drvn along over 4f out: mod last prog* **16/1**

0-05 **7** *6* **Farleaze**[17] 4753 3-9-5 **58** FergusSweeney 1 39
(Martyn Meade) *a towards rr* **25/1**

6600 **8** *6* **Excellent News (IRE)**[15] 4850 3-9-7 **60** SebSanders 2 32
(J W Hills) *in tch: rdn 3f out: sn wknd* **20/1**

-000 **9** *nk* **Karistar (IRE)**[27] 4440 3-8-6 **48** RyanClark[(3)] 9 19
(Tom Keddy) *a towards rr* **33/1**

0400 **10** *1 ¾* **Sir Lexington (IRE)**[19] 4709 3-9-0 **60** WilliamTwiston-Davies[(7)] 6 29
(Richard Hannon) *chsd ldrs: rdn 5f out: wknd 3f out* **20/1**

0000 **11** *28* **Lithograph (USA)**[13] 4932 3-8-11 **50** SilvestreDeSousa 10
(Mark Johnston) *led: rdn 4f out: hdd over 3f out: wknd over 2f out: eased whn no ch fnl f* **14/1**

2m 34.56s (0.06) **Going Correction** +0.025s/f (Slow) **11** Ran SP% **123.8**
Speed ratings (Par 98): **100,99,98,93,91 91,87,83,83,81 63**
toteswingers: 1&2 £1.70, 1&3 £2.10, 2&3 £2.60 CSF £9.65 CT £23.22 TOTE £2.50: £1.02, £1.80, £2.20; EX 11.50.

Owner Mrs John Magnier & Bob Lanigan **Bred** Tullamaine Castle Stud And Orpendale **Trained** Upper Lambourn, Berks

■ Stewards' Enquiry : Ted Durcan three-day ban: failed to give filly time to respond to whip (Sep 3-5)

FOCUS
A modest handicap in which the pace was steady and several were in with a chance entering the straight. The winner came down the centre of the track. The first three came clear in a decent time and the winner ran to her Lingfield form.

5409 FLAT TRACK CORNER FILLIES' H'CAP 7f (P)
9:20 (9:20) (Class 4) (0-85,85) 3-Y-O **£4,075** (£1,212; £606; £303) **Stalls** Low

Form RPR
212 **1** **Subtle Knife**[21] 4647 3-8-11 **75**.. WilliamCarson 6 85
(Giles Bravery) *in rr: drvn 3f out: c towards centre crse and styd on wl fr 2f out to ld 1f out: drvn out* **3/1**[3]
20-1 **2** *1 1/4* **Diamond Belle**[19] 4711 3-8-12 **76**.. JamesDoyle 3 83
(Noel Quinlan) *trckd ldr: drvn to ld over 1f out: sn hdd: styd on fnl f but nt pce of wnr* **11/4**[2]
4600 **3** *1 1/2* **Way Too Hot**[19] 4702 3-9-7 **85**.. AdamKirby 7 88
(Clive Cox) *in rr: hdwy on ins to chse ldrs over 2f out: sn rdn: styd on same pce fnl f* **9/4**[1]
-312 **4** *shd* **Macchiara**[16] 4814 3-8-9 **73**.. SilvestreDeSousa 4 75
(Rae Guest) *in tch: drvn to chse ldrs over 2f out: ev ch over 1f out: sn one pce* **6/1**
0-00 **5** *3 3/4* **Self Centred**[23] 4597 3-9-2 **80**.. DarryllHolland 2 72
(Charles Hills) *sn led: rdn over 2f out: hdd over 1f out: wknd ins fnl f* **20/1**
3000 **6** *5* **Semayyel (IRE)**[16] 4819 3-9-7 **85**.. SebSanders 5 64
(Clive Brittain) *chsd ldrs: rdn 3f out: wknd fr 2f out* **11/1**
0550 **7** *6* **More Than Words (IRE)**[51] 3619 3-8-4 **68**.................... KieranO'Neill 1 30
(Richard Hannon) *chsd ldrs: rdn over 3f out: wknd ins fnl 2f* **14/1**

1m 26.15s (0.15) **Going Correction** +0.025s/f (Slow) **7** Ran SP% **116.5**
Speed ratings (Par 99): **100,98,96,96,92 86,79**
toteswingers: 1&2 £2.20, 1&3 £1.50, 2&3 £2.40 CSF £12.14 TOTE £6.00: £4.00, £1.80; EX 10.00.
Owner D B Clark & Russel Grant **Bred** Mrs F Bravery **Trained** Newmarket, Suffolk

FOCUS
A decent fillies' handicap in which the gallop was sound. The winner was ridden with restraint and raced up the centre in the straight. The form is taken at fave value.
T/Plt: £21.50 to a £1 stake. Pool: £52,709.97. 1,781.72 winning tickets. T/Qpdt: £9.20 to a £1 stake. Pool: £4,475.43. 357.88 winning tickets. ST

5167 THIRSK (L-H)
Monday, August 20

OFFICIAL GOING: Good (good to soft in places; 9.1)
Wind: Virtually nil Weather: White cloud

5410 BRITISH STALLION STUDS SUPPORTING BRITISH RACING E B F MAIDEN STKS 6f
2:00 (2:02) (Class 4) 2-Y-O **£4,528** (£1,347; £673; £336) **Stalls** High

Form RPR
1 **Beach Club** 2-9-3 0.. RichardMullen 8 80+
(David Brown) *sn led: rdn over 1f out: sn hung bdly lft to far rail: kpt on* **5/1**[3]
2 *1 1/2* **George Rooke (IRE)** 2-9-3 0.. AmyRyan 10 78+
(Kevin Ryan) *chsd ldrs: hdwy on outer over 2f out: rdn and ev ch whn carried bdly lft over 1f out: hmpd and swtchd rt ins fnl 100yds: kpt on* **6/1**
4 **3** *2 1/4* **Bond Club**[39] 3989 2-9-0 0.. DaleSwift(3) 14 69
(Geoffrey Oldroyd) *cl up: effrt 2f out: rdn and ev ch whn hmpd over 1f out: kpt on same pce* **4/1**[1]
4 *3/4* **Anderton (IRE)** 2-9-3 0.. PaulHanagan 11 67
(Richard Fahey) *trckd ldrs on inner: effrt 2f out: sn rdn and kpt on same pce* **9/2**[2]
4 **5** *2* **Hit The Lights (IRE)**[26] 4448 2-9-3 0.. BarryMcHugh 1 61
(Ollie Pears) *cl up: rdn 2f out: wkng whn sltly hmpd over 1f out* **9/1**
0 **6** *1/2* **Just Paul (IRE)**[23] 4587 2-9-3 0.. MichaelO'Connell 15 59
(Kate Walton) *chsd ldrs: rdn along 2f out: grad wknd* **11/1**
7 *2 1/2* **Multifact** 2-9-0 0.. LeeTopliss(3) 12 52
(Michael Dods) *s.i.s and sn pushed along: hdwy into midfield after 2f: rdn to chse ldrs over 2f out: sn one pce* **22/1**
0 **8** *3/4* **Mash Potato (IRE)**[110] 1753 2-9-3 0.. TomEaves 17 50
(Michael Dods) *dwlt and in rr: sme hdwy fnl 2f: n.d* **11/1**
5 **9** *3* **Pour La Victoire (IRE)**[60] 3303 2-9-3 0.. AndrewMullen 3 41
(Nigel Tinkler) *a towards rr* **33/1**
0 **10** *8* **Pleasant Moment**[21] 4654 2-8-12 0.. DavidAllan 6 12
(Tom Dascombe) *a towards rr* **40/1**
65 **11** *1/2* **Lexington Blue**[7] 5169 2-9-3 0.. DanielTudhope 16 15
(David O'Meara) *a towards rr* **16/1**
0 **12** *1 1/2* **Fake Or Fortune (IRE)**[7] 5169 2-9-3 0.. DuranFentiman 9 11
(Tim Walford) *chsd ldrs: rdn along 1/2-way: sn wknd* **100/1**
13 *1/2* **Misu Mac** 2-8-12 0.. AndrewElliott 7 4
(Neville Bycroft) *sn outpcd and a in rr* **66/1**
14 *8* **Faither** 2-9-3 0.. AdrianNicholls 5
(David Nicholls) *sn outpcd and bhd* **28/1**
00 **15** *30* **Shepherds Bow**[7] 5168 2-8-10 0.. DavidSimmonson(7) 2
(Michael Easterby) *v s.i.s and lost many l s: a wl bhd* **100/1**

1m 14.09s (1.39) **Going Correction** +0.025s/f (Good) **15** Ran SP% **118.3**
Speed ratings (Par 96): **91,89,86,85,82 81,78,77,73,62 62,60,59,48,8**
toteswingers 1&2 £6.20, 1&3 £5.30, 2&3 £6.40 CSF £32.49 TOTE £7.20: £2.70, £2.70, £2.10; EX 43.10 TRIFECTA Not won..
Owner J C Fretwell **Bred** Mill House Stud **Trained** Averham Park, Notts
■ Stewards' Enquiry : Richard Mullen two-day ban: careless riding (Sep 3-4)

FOCUS
Rail on both bends moved out 3-4yds adding about 12yds 7f & 8f races and 20yds to distances over a mile. After overnight rain the ground was described as good to soft, good in places. After the opener it was reported as "easy side of good" by champion Paul Hanagan. Probably just an ordinary 2yo maiden, but the winner is clearly speedy. The fifth and sixth help with the level.

NOTEBOOK
Beach Club, a 30,000gns yearling purchase, is a half-brother to a 2yo 5f winner. A sharp type, he made every yard but hung violently left in the final furlong and a half, ending up racing towards the far side rail. It is to be hoped that it was just inexperience that caused him to deviate. (op 7-1 tchd 9-2)
George Rooke(IRE), a son of Rock of Gibraltar, is a sturdy individual. He raced towards the outside of the leaders and was crossed and forced to check by the errant winner near the line. He should improve for the outing and looks sure to go one better. (op 7-1)
Bond Club confirmed the promise of his debut effort. A similar event should come his way. (tchd 9-2)
Anderton(IRE), the paddock pick, cost £90,000. Racing against the stands' side rail just behind the winner, he could never land a telling blow. The experience will not be lost on him. (op 7-2)
Hit The Lights(IRE), keen to post, had the worst of the draw. He was impeded by the winner, but will need to settle if he is to progress. Official explanation: jockey said colt ran too free (op 8-1 tchd 15-2)
Just Paul(IRE) settled much better than on his debut and looks a likely nursery type with another outing under his belt. (op 20-1 tchd 22-1)
Shepherds Bow Official explanation: jockey said colt missed the break

5411 THIRSK RACECOURSE CONFERENCE CENTRE CLAIMING STKS 5f
2:30 (2:31) (Class 4) 2-Y-O **£3,881** (£1,155; £577; £288) **Stalls** High

Form RPR
023 **1** **Charlemagne Diva**[16] 4806 2-8-9 52.. PJMcDonald 8 61
(Ann Duffield) *cl up: led over 1f out: sn rdn and kpt on wl towards fin* **9/1**
513 **2** *1 1/4* **Coconut Kisses**[10] 5045 2-8-3 69.. JakePayne(7) 4 58
(Bill Turner) *cl up: effrt to chal wl over 1f out: sn rdn and ev ch tl drvn and no ex wl ins fnl f* **5/1**[3]
0400 **3** *1* **Dream Vale (IRE)**[2] 5332 2-8-13 75.. DuranFentiman 9 57
(Tim Easterby) *hld up in tch: hdwy on inner wl over 1f out: sn rdn and kpt on fnl f* **5/2**[2]
052 **4** *1* **Autumn Shadow (IRE)**[28] 4395 2-8-10 60.................... TonyHamilton 6 50
(Richard Fahey) *hld up in tch: hdwy 2f out: sn rdn and one pce fnl f* **7/1**
01 **5** *1* **Done Dreaming (IRE)**[20] 4670 2-9-7 74.. PaulHanagan 3 58
(Richard Fahey) *dwlt and swtchd rt s: in rr: hdwy 2f out sn rdn and no imp* **13/8**[1]
00 **6** *1 1/2* **Setfiretotherain**[16] 4825 2-9-0 0.. AmyRyan 7 45
(Kevin Ryan) *led: pushed along 2f out: sn rdn and hdd overe1f out: grad wknd* **40/1**
4033 **7** *4 1/2* **Mount Seymour (IRE)**[10] 5053 2-8-9 65................ DanielleMooney(7) 2 31
(Nigel Tinkler) *chsd ldrs on outer: rdn along 1/2-way: sn wknd* **33/1**

1m 0.77s (1.17) **Going Correction** +0.025s/f (Good) **7** Ran SP% **111.2**
Speed ratings (Par 96): **91,89,87,85,84 81,74**
toteswingers 1&2 £7.20, 1&3 £3.40, 2&3 £3.30 CSF £49.86 TOTE £14.30: £4.50, £3.10; EX 63.80 Trifecta £191.40 Pool: £470.85 - 1.82 winning units..
Owner Taylor, Simpson & Barlow **Bred** Marston Stud And Fleming Thoroughbreds **Trained** Constable Burton, N Yorks

FOCUS
A moderate claimer, and the runner with the least chance on official ratings came out on top. Not a race to dwell on, with the winner the key to the form.

NOTEBOOK
Charlemagne Diva, rated just 52 after four previous starts, had the stands' side rail to assist her and, firmly in command at the line, there was certainly no fluke about this. She clearly appreciated the give underfoot. (op 15-2)
Coconut Kisses, having her second start in ten days after four months on the sidelines, had 16lb in hand of the winner on official ratings. She raced wider and looks all speed. (op 8-1)
Dream Vale(IRE), top-rated on official ratings, was drawn hard against the stands' side rail. She stayed on after struggling to go the pace on her second start in three days. She had finished last of seven in a nursery at Chester and will continue to struggle from a mark of 75. (op 11-4 tchd 3-1)
Autumn Shadow(IRE), runner-up in a claimer at Beverley on her previous start, struggled to go the pace and needs a stiffer test. (op 11-2)
Done Dreaming(IRE), winner of a modest maiden at Ayr, was asked to give weight away all round and was not up to the task. (op 15-8)
Setfiretotherain again showed plenty of toe to take them along, but at this stage he looks something of a short-runner. (op 28-1)

5412 WELCOME TO YORKSHIRE, YORKSHIRE CHAMPIONS H'CAP 5f
3:00 (3:01) (Class 4) (0-80,80) 4-Y-O+ **£4,528** (£1,347; £673; £336) **Stalls** High

Form RPR
0030 **1** **Whozthecat (IRE)**[10] 5065 5-8-10 **76**..(b) JasonHart(7) 6 88
(Declan Carroll) *cl up stands' side: led 2f out: sn rdn and kpt on wl fnl f* **8/1**
4240 **2** *2* **Haajes**[13] 4924 8-9-5 **78**..(b) MickyFenton 9 83
(Paul Midgley) *racd towards stands' side: in tch: hdwy 2f out: rdn and ev ch whn edgd lft ent fnl f: kpt on same pce: 2nd of 11 in gp* **16/1**
6222 **3** *hd* **Waking Warrior**[5] 5223 4-8-5 **71**..(tp) KevinStott(7) 13 75
(Kevin Ryan) *trckd ldrs stands' side: hdwy 2f out: sn rdn and kpt on same pce fnl f: 3rd of 11 in gp* **9/2**[2]
0505 **4** *3/4* **Defence Council (IRE)**[13] 4924 4-9-4 **77**.................... PaulHanagan 15 78
(Mel Brittain) *chsd ldrs stands' side: rdn wl over 1f out: kpt on same pce: 4th of 11 in gp* **11/2**[3]
1115 **5** *1 1/2* **Fear Nothing**[5] 5223 5-8-7 **73**..(v) DavidBergin(7) 14 69
(David O'Meara) *prom stands' side: rdn along over 2f out: grad wknd: 5th of 11 in gp* **7/2**[1]
0655 **6** *1 1/2* **Bronze Beau**[27] 4430 5-9-4 **77**..(tp) AmyRyan 3 68
(Linda Stubbs) *led far side gp: cl up: rdn along and ev ch over 1f out: wknd ins fnl f: 1st of 3 in gp* **28/1**
0050 **7** *1* **Mandalay King (IRE)**[24] 4554 7-9-0 **73**.................... (p) DanielTudhope 8 60
(Marjorie Fife) *dwlt and bhd stands' side tl styd on appr fnl f: nrst fin: 6th of 11 in gp* **16/1**
610 **8** *2 1/4* **Kyzer Chief**[3] 5294 7-8-5 **64**.. BarryMcHugh 1 43
(Ron Barr) *blind removed late: cl up far side: rdn along 2f out and sn wknd: 2nd of 3 in gp* **33/1**
6005 **9** *nk* **Beauty Pageant (IRE)**[45] 3815 5-9-4 **77**.................... RichardMullen 11 55
(Ed McMahon) *overall ldr stands' side: rdn along and hdd 2f out: sn wknd: 7th of 11 in gp* **11/1**
4642 **10** *nk* **Barney McGrew (IRE)**[17] 4770 9-9-7 **80**.................... TomEaves 10 57
(Michael Dods) *dwlt: a towards rr stands' side: 8th of 11 in gp* **9/1**
2101 **11** *3 1/4* **Dispol Grand (IRE)**[100] 2084 6-8-10 **76**.. NedCurtis(7) 7 41
(Paul Midgley) *chsd ldrs stands' side: rdn along 2f out: sn wknd: 9th of 11 in gp* **14/1**
200- **12** *3 1/2* **Pavershooz**[353] 5680 7-9-4 **80**..(t) GaryBartley(3) 4 32
(Noel Wilson) *racd far side: cl up: rdn wl over 1f out and sn wknd 3rd of 3 in gp: b.b.v* **16/1**
0206 **13** *1 1/4* **Indian Trail**[5] 5223 12-8-11 **70**..(b) AdrianNicholls 12 18
(David Nicholls) *a towards rr stands' side: 10th of 11 in gp* **28/1**
0401 **14** *3/4* **Lost In Paris (IRE)**[26] 4451 6-9-6 **79**..(p) DavidAllan 5 24
(Tim Easterby) *cl up stands' side: rdn along 1/2-way: sn wknd: 11th of 11 in gp* **16/1**

59.07s (-0.53) **Going Correction** +0.025s/f (Good) **14** Ran SP% **125.3**
Speed ratings (Par 105): **105,101,101,100,97 95,93,90,89,89 84,78,76,75**
toteswingers 1&2 £22.00, 1&3 £14.60, 2&3 £14.90 CSF £132.49 CT £676.04 TOTE £9.30: £3.40, £4.40, £2.10; EX 157.30 TRIFECTA Not won..
Owner Ninerus **Bred** Liam Queally **Trained** Sledmere, E Yorks
■ Stewards' Enquiry : Jason Hart 21-days (takes into account previous offences): improper use of the whip - above permitted level (Aug 31-Sep 20)

FOCUS
Three elected to race on the far side, but the first five home stuck to the stands' side. The winner is rated to his best form of the past year.

Whozthecat(IRE) Official explanation: trainer said, regarding apparent improvement in form, that the gelding had benefited from the re-application of blinkers.
Kyzer Chief Official explanation: jockey said, just before gates opened, the gelding lunged forward causing him to be unable to remove blindfold at first attempt.
Pavershooz Official explanation: vet said gelding bled from the nose
Indian Trail Official explanation: trainer's rep said gelding was unsuited by the good to soft (good in places) ground

5413 THIRSK RACECOURSE PAVILION FOR WEDDING RECEPTIONS FILLIES' H'CAP 1m 4f

3:30 (3:30) (Class 5) (0-70,71) 3-Y-O+ **£3,234** (£962; £481; £240) **Stalls** Low

Form RPR

2544 **1** **Dorry K (IRE)**[17] 4781 3-9-0 **66** ShaneKelly 4 73
(David Barron) *sn pushed along and towards rr: hdwy on outer 1/2-way and sn cl up: led wl over 2f out and sn rdn clr: drvn ins fnl f and hld on gamely* **13/2**

2332 **2** ½ **Mistress Of Rome**[32] 4250 3-9-1 **70** (p) LeeTopliss(3) 3 76
(Michael Dods) *prom on outer whn carried wd on bnd after 2f: chsd ldng pair: rdn along and outpcd over 3f out: hdwy 2f out: drvn to chse wnr ent fnl f: kpt on wl towards fin* **7/2**[2]

00-1 **3** hd **Authora (IRE)**[12] 4971 3-8-9 **61** PaulHanagan 12 67
(Peter Chapple-Hyam) *hld up towards rr: pushed wd on bnd after 2f: hdwy 3f out: rdn to chse ldrs wl over 1f out: drvn and styd on wl fnl f* **6/1**[3]

3-33 **4** 6 **Neil's Pride**[105] 1915 3-8-5 **57** BarryMcHugh 8 53
(Richard Fahey) *hld up: hdwy on outer wl over 2f out: rdn to chse ldrs wl over 1f out: sn no imp* **9/4**[1]

4530 **5** hd **Lady Gargoyle**[7] 5172 4-8-4 **51** oh6 (p) NeilFarley(5) 1 47
(Jim Goldie) *led: rn wd bnd after 2f: rdn along and hdd wl over 2f out: grad wknd* **66/1**

5340 **6** 2 ½ **Echo Of Footsteps**[17] 4781 3-8-10 **62** TonyHamilton 9 54
(Michael Herrington) *in tch: hdwy on inner to chse ldrs over 2f out: sn rdn along and kpt on same pce* **28/1**

5151 **7** 14 **Silver Tigress**[38] 4048 4-9-7 **63** PJMcDonald 6 33
(George Moore) *hld up in tch: hdwy over 3f out: rdn over 2f out: sn btn* **8/1**

4001 **8** 5 **Mazij**[8] 5124 4-9-10 **71** 6ex JustinNewman(5) 11 33
(Peter Hiatt) *chsd ldr: rdn along over 3f out: grad wknd* **14/1**

0040 **9** 4 **Morilles**[88] 2424 3-8-12 **64** (p) TomEaves 2 19
(Clive Cox) *chsd ldrs: rdn along over 3f out: sn wknd* **9/1**

600 **10** 5 **Isolde's Return**[49] 3697 3-7-13 **51** oh6 AndrewMullen 10
(George Moore) *a in rr: bhd fr 1/2-way: t.o fnl 3f* **150/1**

1004 **11** shd **Lady Advocate (IRE)**[9] 5112 3-8-7 **59** (b) DavidAllan 7
(Tim Easterby) *a in rr: bhd fr 1/2-way: t.o fnl 3f* **33/1**

2m 40.64s (4.44) **Going Correction** +0.325s/f (Good)
WFA 3 from 4yo+ 10lb **11** Ran SP% **116.9**
Speed ratings (Par 100): **98,97,97,93,93 91,82,79,76,73 73**
toteswingers 1&2 £10.90, 1&3 £7.80, 2&3 £3.40 CSF £28.87 CT £145.60 TOTE £8.80: £2.80, £2.50, £1.30; EX 47.00 Trifecta £283.80 Pool: £475.72 - 1.24 winning units..
Owner Twinacre Nurseries Ltd **Bred** Twinacre Nurseries Ltd **Trained** Maunby, N Yorks

FOCUS
A modest 1m4f fillies' handicap run at a sound pace. The first three finished clear but there are doubts over the form.

5414 WELCOMETOHERRIOTCOUNTRY.COM H'CAP 1m

4:00 (4:01) (Class 4) (0-80,79) 3-Y-O+ **£4,528** (£1,347; £673; £336) **Stalls** Low

Form RPR

0611 **1** **It's A Mans World**[11] 5015 6-8-9 **64** PaulPickard(3) 6 80
(Brian Ellison) *hld up in midfield: smooth hdwy on inner over 1f out: swtchd rt and chal wl over 1f out: sn led: rdn and edgd rt ent fnl f: kpt on wl* **17/2**

2245 **2** ¾ **Prophesy (IRE)**[18] 4741 3-9-2 **79** NeilFarley(5) 4 92
(Declan Carroll) *dwlt: hdwy into midfield 1/2-way: effrt to chse ldrs over 2f out: rdn and ev ch over 1f out: drvn and one pce ins fnl f* **6/1**[2]

0400 **3** 8 **Snow Bay**[9] 5094 6-9-13 **79** AdrianNicholls 11 75
(David Nicholls) *led: rdn along over 2f out: hdd wl over 1f out: kpt on same pce* **11/1**

34 **4** 1 ½ **Talent Scout (IRE)**[12] 4964 6-8-10 **62** DuranFentiman 8 54
(Tim Walford) *towards rr: hdwy on inner over 2f out: sn rdn and styd on fnl f* **18/1**

0105 **5** 3 **Collateral Damage (IRE)**[10] 5059 9-9-1 **67** (t) DavidAllan 3 52
(Tim Easterby) *cl up: rdn along over 2f out: sn wknd* **14/1**

2135 **6** 1 ¼ **Horatio Carter**[12] 4964 7-9-6 **72** DanielTudhope 9 54
(David O'Meara) *hld up: hdwy wl over 2f out: sn rdn and no imp* **8/1**[3]

50 **7** nk **The Osteopath (IRE)**[64] 3185 9-9-10 **76** PJMcDonald 12 58
(John Davies) *in rr tl sme late hdwy* **12/1**

5423 **8** 2 ½ **My Single Malt (IRE)**[31] 4302 4-9-8 **74** PaulHanagan 2 50
(Julie Camacho) *trckd ldrs: effrt wl over 2f out: sn rdn and wknd* **7/2**[1]

0306 **9** ½ **Icy Blue**[14] 4868 4-8-12 **64** AmyRyan 5 39
(Richard Whitaker) *chsd ldrs: rdn along over 3f out: sn wknd* **8/1**[3]

1-00 **10** shd **Medieval Bishop (IRE)**[19] 4714 3-8-4 **69** GemmaTutty(7) 14 43
(Tim Walford) *a in rr* **66/1**

4553 **11** 1 **Daring Dream (GER)**[20] 4673 7-9-0 **69** GaryBartley(3) 16 41
(Jim Goldie) *racd wd: prom: rdn along 1/2-way: sn wknd* **14/1**

106 **12** 6 **Daruband**[17] 4772 4-9-10 **76** (be) ShaneKelly 10 34
(Alan McCabe) *a towards rr* **16/1**

6200 **13** 6 **Seldom (IRE)**[28] 4398 6-8-11 **63** TomEaves 13
(Mel Brittain) *a in rr* **20/1**

00-0 **14** 12 **Silver Bullitt**[135] 1220 4-9-9 **75** RobertHavlin 7
(Mark Johnston) *bhd fr 1/2-way* **20/1**

1m 41.64s (1.54) **Going Correction** +0.325s/f (Good)
WFA 3 from 4yo+ 6lb **14** Ran SP% **120.8**
Speed ratings (Par 105): **105,104,96,94,91 90,90,87,87,87 86,80,74,62**
toteswingers 1&2 £6.90, 1&3 £15.50, 2&3 £16.20 CSF £57.67 CT £591.00 TOTE £6.10: £1.40, £2.50, £3.20; EX 65.00 Trifecta £299.90 Pool: £555.25 - 1.37 winning units..
Owner Brian Ellison **Bred** Cheveley Park Stud Ltd **Trained** Norton, N Yorks
■ Stewards' Enquiry : Paul Pickard two-day ban: careless riding (Sep 3-4)

FOCUS
A wide-open handicap, but in the end the first two pulled well clear. Both showed improved form.
My Single Malt(IRE) Official explanation: jockey said gelding never travelled

5415 THIRSKRACECOURSE.NET H'CAP 7f

4:30 (4:31) (Class 5) (0-75,74) 3-Y-O **£3,234** (£962; £481; £240) **Stalls** Low

Form RPR

1310 **1** **Mick Slates (IRE)**[27] 4432 3-8-2 **62** JasonHart(7) 4 70
(Declan Carroll) *hmpd s and keen in rr: hdwy over 2f out: swtchd rt over 1f out: rdn to chal ent fnl f: kpt on wl u.p to ld nr fin* **7/1**

3512 **2** ¾ **Fayr Fall (IRE)**[17] 4779 3-9-3 **70** (b) DuranFentiman 5 76
(Tim Easterby) *trckd ldrs: hdwy on outer over 3f out: cl up 2f out: rdn to ld appr fnl f: sn drvn: hdd and no ex towards fin* **13/8**[1]

4134 **3** nk **Fine Altomis**[22] 4623 3-8-12 **68** LeeTopliss(3) 2 73
(Michael Dods) *trckd ldrs: hdwy 2f out: swtchd lft and rdn over 1f out: drvn to chal ins fnl f: no ex towards fin* **6/1**[3]

441 **4** 2 ¾ **Evanescent (IRE)**[24] 4550 3-9-7 **74** ShaneKelly 10 72
(Alan McCabe) *sn chsng ldr: hdwy to ld wl over 2f out: drvn and hdd over 1f out: wknd fnl f* **14/1**

6313 **5** 1 **Star City (IRE)**[6] 5185 3-8-11 **64** (be) TomEaves 7 59
(Michael Dods) *sn led: rdn along and hdd wl over 2f out: grad wknd fr over 1f out* **7/1**

2430 **6** ¾ **Regal Acclaim (IRE)**[7] 5170 3-8-1 **59** (t) NeilFarley(5) 3 52
(Doolan Carroll) *plld hrd: chsd ldrs: rdn along wl over 2f out: wknd over 1f out* **11/2**[2]

1005 **7** 5 **Safe House (IRE)**[13] 4933 3-9-4 **71** RobertHavlin 11 51
(Mark Johnston) *chsd ldrs on outer: rdn along 3f out: sn wknd* **10/1**

0301 **8** 1 ½ **Jay Kay**[11] 5014 3-8-3 **56** AndrewMullen 1 31
(Danielle McCormick) *cl up on inner: rdn along 3f out: wknd over 2f out* **18/1**

3000 **9** ¾ **Loyal Master (IRE)**[55] 3460 3-9-3 **70** PJMcDonald 6 43
(Garry Moss) *prom 2f: sn lost pl and bhd fr 1/2-way* **8/1**

1m 29.6s (2.40) **Going Correction** +0.325s/f (Good) **9** Ran SP% **124.9**
Speed ratings (Par 100): **99,98,97,94,93 92,86,85,84**
toteswingers 1&2 £5.40, 1&3 £9.80, 2&3 £3.30 CSF £20.43 CT £78.68 TOTE £8.30: £3.00, £1.10, £2.80; EX 32.60 TRIFECTA Part won. Pool: £340.76 - 0.74 winning units..
Owner Ormskirk **Bred** Peter McCutcheon **Trained** Sledmere, E Yorks

FOCUS
There was plenty of pace in this 7f 3yo-only handicap. Pretty straightforward form.

5416 THIRSK RACES FAMILY DAY FRIDAY 31ST AUGUST LADY AMATEUR RIDERS' H'CAP 6f

5:00 (5:02) (Class 5) (0-70,67) 3-Y-O+ **£1,871** (£580; £290; £145) **Stalls** High

Form RPR

0605 **1** **See Clearly**[13] 4909 3-10-1 **64** (p) MissJCoward 10 75
(Tim Easterby) *trckd ldrs: hdwy 2f out: led over 1f out: rdn ins fnl f and kpt on wl* **4/1**[1]

00-0 **2** 1 ¼ **Sir Nod**[9] 5093 10-9-11 **64** MissLWilson(7) 8 71
(Julie Camacho) *hld up: hdwy wl over 1f out: rdn to chse wnr ins fnl f: sn no imp* **28/1**

4406 **3** 1 ¼ **Foreign Rhythm (IRE)**[14] 4865 7-9-7 **58** MissVBarr(5) 17 61
(Ron Barr) *hld up: hdwy wl over 1f out: sn rdn: swtchd lft ins fnl f: kpt on wl towards fin* **11/1**

4060 **4** 1 ½ **Lady Kildare (IRE)**[13] 4909 4-9-4 **57** MissEmmaBedford(7) 13 55
(Jedd O'Keeffe) *hld up towards rr: hdwy wl over 1f out: rdn and styd on wl fnl f: nrst fin:* **12/1**

0-60 **5** 1 ½ **Feel The Heat**[14] 4866 5-10-7 **67** (v) MrsCBartley 14 60
(Bryan Smart) *racd nr stands' rail: led: rdn along 2f out: hdd over 1f out: grad wknd fnl f* **10/1**

1604 **6** 1 **Sophie's Beau (USA)**[13] 4909 5-9-1 **52** (bt) MissAliceMills(5) 5 42
(Michael Chapman) *cl up: rdn along and ev ch over 1f out: wknd ent fnl f* **20/1**

0005 **7** ½ **Red Roar (IRE)**[26] 4461 5-10-4 **67** MissJRRichards(3) 12 56
(Alan Berry) *midfield: rdn along wl over 1f out: kpt on fnl f:* **14/1**

5633 **8** ½ **Baybshambles (IRE)**[19] 4717 8-9-5 **56** MissRSmith(5) 6 43
(Ron Barr) *towards rr: hdwy wl over 1f out: styd on ins fnl f: nrst fin* **10/1**

030 **9** 1 **Overwhelm**[152] 985 4-9-9 **55** (t) MissZoeLilly 1 39
(Alan McCabe) *racd wd: hdwy 2f out: swtchd lft and rdn wl over 1f out: sn one pce* **12/1**

45-0 **10** nse **Lady Platinum Club**[14] 4865 4-9-3 **56** MissMKeegan(7) 3 40
(Geoffrey Oldroyd) *racd wd: cl up: rdn along wl over 1f out: wknd ent fnl f: sddle slipped* **25/1**

0-65 **11** ½ **Hernando Torres**[4] 5259 4-9-8 **61** (p) MissAHesketh(7) 16 43
(Michael Easterby) *a bhd* **5/1**[2]

0506 **12** ½ **Methaaly (IRE)**[9] 5093 9-9-1 **50** (be) MissMMullineaux(3) 2 30
(Michael Mullineaux) *a bhd* **16/1**

-043 **13** shd **Excellent Aim**[6] 5217 5-9-4 **55** MissKMargarson(5) 4 35
(George Margarson) *racd wd: prom: rdn along 2f out: sn wknd* **9/1**

6050 **14** hd **Besty**[6] 5203 5-9-8 **57** MissWGibson(3) 18 36
(Paul Midgley) *a towards rr* **8/1**[3]

-000 **R** **Ivestar (IRE)**[4] 5258 7-9-3 **56** ow3 (v) MrsKristaBrown(7) 9
(Michael Easterby) *ref to r tk no part* **40/1**

1m 14.05s (1.35) **Going Correction** +0.025s/f (Good)
WFA 3 from 4yo+ 3lb **15** Ran SP% **126.7**
Speed ratings (Par 103): **92,90,88,86,84 83,82,82,80,80 79,79,79,78,**
toteswingers 1&2 £22.00, 1&3 £5.70, 2&3 £68.50 CSF £132.65 CT £1211.23 TOTE £5.00: £2.70, £13.10, £5.40; EX 184.50 Trifecta £252.10 Part won. Pool: £340.76 - 0.39 winning units..
Owner Ryedale Partners No 4 **Bred** Rabbah Bloodstock Limited **Trained** Great Habton, N Yorks

FOCUS
Three chose to race wide, the remainder raced towards the stands' side. The winner was down to a good mark on her 2yo form.
Lady Platinum Club Official explanation: jockey said saddle slipped
T/Jkpt: Not won T/Plt: £425.40 to a £1 stake. Pool: £63367.81 - 108.73 winning tickets T/Qpdt: £18.90 to a £1 stake. Pool: £4470.00 - 174.86 winning tickets JR

4408 WINDSOR (R-H)

Monday, August 20

OFFICIAL GOING: Good to firm (9.0)
Wind: Moderate, behind Weather: Fine, warm

5417 DAVISBAKERYCARIBBEAN.COM APPRENTICE H'CAP 1m 2f 7y

5:30 (5:30) (Class 5) (0-75,75) 4-Y-O+ **£2,264** (£673; £336; £168) **Stalls** Centre

Form RPR

5305 **1** **If I Were A Boy (IRE)**[3] 5310 5-8-7 **63** (p) JoshBaudains(5) 4 73
(Dominic Ffrench Davis) *mde all: kicked on over 3f out: at leasy 3 l clr after: styd on wl* **11/4**[1]

3206 **2** 4 ½ **Choral Festival**[11] 5007 6-9-5 **75** WilliamTwiston-Davies(5) 6 76
(John Bridger) *hld up in 5th: prog 3f out gng wl: rdn 2f out: chsd wnr 1f out: one pce and no imp* **4/1**[2]

4U10 **3** nk **Edgeworth (IRE)**[65] 3154 6-9-8 **73** AdamBeschizza 2 73
(David Bridgwater) *mostly chsd wnr: rdn 3f out: no imp after: lost 2nd 1f out: kpt on* **15/2**

014U **4** *6* **Royal Etiquette (IRE)**[28] 4411 5-8-12 **66**................. BrendanPowell(3) 5 54
(Lawney Hill) *hld up in last trio: rdn and prog on outer 3f out: ch of a pl over 1f out: wknd* **11/2**

-025 **5** *2 ½* **Jewelled**[11] 5007 6-9-5 **73**.. DavidKenny(3) 7 56+
(Lady Herries) *dwlt: hld up in last trio: effrt whn sltly hmpd 2f out and stmbld bdly sn after: no ch to rcvr* **5/1**[3]

020- **6** *½* **Uncle Dermot (IRE)**[219] 7425 4-8-11 **65**................ MatthewLawson(3) 8 47
(Brendan Powell) *awkward s: hld up in last trio: rdn 4f out: sn btn* **28/1**

6004 **7** *½* **Glass Mountain (IRE)**[11] 5007 4-9-7 **72**.......................... RyanPowell 3 53
(Ian Williams) *t.k.h: prom: disp 2nd fr 6f out to over 2f out: sn wknd* **15/2**

/135 **8** *2* **Reaction**[18] 4400 6-8-6 **61**..(p) MartinLeonard(7) 1 41
(Sheena West) *dwlt: pushed up to chse ldng trio: rdn 4f out: wknd 3f out* **16/1**

2m 4.6s (-4.10) **Going Correction** -0.50s/f (Hard) 8 Ran SP% **111.6**
Speed ratings (Par 103): **96,92,92,87,85 84,84,82**
toteswingers 1&2 £3.60, 1&3 £5.10, 2&3 £6.70 CSF £13.00 CT £69.75 TOTE £4.00: £1.80, £1.60, £2.40; EX 17.70 Trifecta £128.10 Pool: £4,591.27 - 26.50 winning units..
Owner R F Haynes **Bred** Kilco Builders **Trained** Lambourn, Berks

FOCUS
Inner of straight dolled out 10yds at 6f and 2yds at winning post. Top bend dolled out 2yds from normal configuration adding 11yds to races beyond a mile. An apprentice handicap which few ever got into. Modest form, not rated too positively.
Jewelled Official explanation: vet said mare sustained injury to left-fore fetlock

5418 E B F ROYAL BERKSHIRE ODDFELLOWS MAIDEN STKS 6f
6:00 (6:01) (Class 5) 2-Y-O **£3,299** (£981; £490; £245) **Stalls** Low

Form RPR

655 **1** **Colmar Kid (IRE)**[16] 4803 2-9-3 83.. DaneO'Neill 4 79
(Richard Hannon) *racd against rail: pressed ldng pair: shkn up to ld over 1f out: styd on and holding rivals fnl f* **5/2**[1]

0 **2** *½* **African Oil (FR)**[20] 4688 2-9-3 0.. MichaelHills 11 78
(Charles Hills) *w ldr: upsides over 1f out: chsd wnr after: styd on but a hld* **13/2**

00 **3** *hd* **Overrider**[15] 4845 2-9-3 0.. JamesDoyle 8 77
(Charles Hills) *trckd ldrs: gng bttr than most over 2f out: rdn over 1f out: styd on to press for 2nd nr fin* **33/1**

4 *1 ¼* **Wayfoong Express (IRE)** 2-9-3 0.. NeilCallan 2 73+
(William Muir) *dwlt: rcvrd into midfield after 2f: rdn and swtchd out wd over 1f out: kpt on but nvr able to threaten* **20/1**

03 **5** *¾* **Purcell (IRE)**[15] 4845 2-9-3 0.. JimmyFortune 7 71
(Andrew Balding) *trckd ldrs: rdn up over 1f out: nt qckn and no imp fnl f* **10/3**[2]

6 *2 ½* **Birdlover** 2-8-12 0.. RichardThomas 6 58
(Ralph Beckett) *pushed along in last trio early and rn green: sme prog fr 1/2-way: no hdwy over 1f out* **20/1**

7 *2* **Marju Prince** 2-9-3 0.. RyanMoore 5 57
(Sir Michael Stoute) *s.s: detached in last and rn green: pushed along and kpt on fr over 1f out* **9/2**[3]

0 **8** *nk* **Extrasolar**[20] 4688 2-9-3 0.. EddieAhern 9 57+
(Amanda Perrett) *mde most to over 1f out: shkn up and wknd qckly* **20/1**

9 *½* **Global Icon** 2-9-3 0.. PatDobbs 1 55
(Richard Hannon) *in tch in midfield: rdn and no prog 2f out: wknd over 1f out* **8/1**

0 **10** *8* **Imperial Oak**[56] 3444 2-9-3 0.. JohnFahy 10 31
(Eve Johnson Houghton) *in tch on outer: shkn up and wknd rapidly 2f out: t.o* **50/1**

06 **11** *1 ¾* **Whiskey N Stout (IRE)**[10] 5032 2-9-3 0.. SeanQuinlan 3 26
(Jamie Osborne) *s.s: rn green and a detached in last pair: t.o* **50/1**

1m 11.27s (-1.73) **Going Correction** -0.375s/f (Firm) 11 Ran SP% **115.4**
Speed ratings (Par 94): **96,95,95,93,92 89,86,86,85,74 72**
toteswingers 1&2 £1.90, 1&3 £24.50, 2&3 £30.90 CSF £16.83 TOTE £3.30: £1.30, £2.50, £5.10; EX 17.30 Trifecta £203.50 Pool: £3,743.53 - 13.61 winning units..
Owner The Heffer Syndicate **Bred** Mr & Mrs G Middlebrook **Trained** East Everleigh, Wilts

FOCUS
Fair form from the principals in this maiden, with the second and third the key.

NOTEBOOK
Colmar Kid(IRE)'s Goodwood form set the standard and, with the drop back to 6f as expected suiting, he was able to get off the mark at the fourth time of asking, nicely enough on top in the end. A current BHA mark of 83 wouldn't obviously leave him thrown in for nurseries, but it would be a brave call to say we've seen the best of him yet given the yard he hails from. (op 2-1 tchd 11-4)
African Oil(FR) ◆ was clearly all the better for last month's Goodwood debut and shouldn't be long in going one better, always being to the fore here. (op 11-2 tchd 7-1)
Overrider will get a higher handicap mark than might have been the case but is another who is obviously heading in the right direction, settling better on this occasion which enabled him to see his race out.
Wayfoong Express(IRE), an Acclamation colt who cost 50,000gns earlier this year, made a nice debut in the end as he clearly needed this first experience (slowly into stride), keeping on well inside the final furlong. He should improve. (op 25-1)
Purcell(IRE) had finished in front of Overrider at Newbury so might have been expected to do a bit better, particularly the form his yard has been in over the last few days. He didn't have any obvious excuses but it's clearly still early days and nurseries are also an option now. (op 7-2 tchd 3-1)
Birdlover, a newcomer by Byron, showed ability and is likely to improve. (op 16-1 tchd 25-1)
Marju Prince was another who showed ability. He was prominent in the betting but clearly needed the experience (slowly away and not unduly knocked about). (op 7-1 tchd 4-1)
Extrasolar has more ability than his two starts to date suggest, travelling well up with the pace until over 1f out before hanging left as he weakened. He wouldn't get much of a mark with another similar run to this. (op 28-1)
Global Icon, a stable-companion of the winner, didn't look any great shakes on debut but is in top hands and is entitled to progress. (op 15-2 tchd 6-1)

5419 MIRROR PUNTERS CLUB (S) STKS 1m 3f 135y
6:30 (6:30) (Class 6) 3-Y-O+ **£1,617** (£481; £240; £120) **Stalls** Centre

Form RPR

6124 **1** **King's Masque**[11] 5021 6-9-8 62.. RobertWilliams(7) 7 69
(Bernard Llewellyn) *hld up in last pair: prog to chse ldr over 1f out: rdn to ld jst ins fnl f: idled but hld on* **5/1**[3]

-050 **2** *½* **Hawridge Song**[28] 4411 4-9-10 62..(b) JamesMillman 1 63
(Rod Millman) *trckd ldr 5f: wnt 2nd again 3f out: rdn to ld over 2f out: hdd jst ins fnl f: kpt on wl but jst hld* **5/1**[3]

2560 **3** *3 ½* **Tijori (IRE)**[18] 4733 4-9-10 57..(b[1]) NeilCallan 5 57
(Bernard Llewellyn) *led: hrd rdn and hdd over 2f out: nt qckn and sn outpcd: plugged on* **20/1**

0061 **4** *2 ¾* **Into The Wind**[28] 4409 5-9-10 60.. IanMongan 6 53
(Rod Millman) *in tch in last pair: rdn 3f out: sn lft bhd and btn* **9/2**[2]

5016 **5** *¾* **Anginola (IRE)**[7] 5152 3-9-0 60.. EddieAhern 4 51
(David Evans) *prom: chsd ldr after 5f to 3f out: wknd* **9/1**

5-0 **6** *3* **Cityar (FR)**[11] 4992 8-9-5 0.. BrendanPowell(5) 3 46
(John O'Shea) *cl up: rdn 3f out: hung lft and wknd 2f out* **50/1**

2205 **U** **Urban Space**[12] 4944 6-9-10 73.. KierenFox 2
(John Flint) *stmbld leaving stalls and uns rdr* **5/4**[1]

2m 27.81s (-1.69) **Going Correction** -0.50s/f (Hard)
WFA 3 from 4yo+ 10lb 7 Ran SP% **112.7**
Speed ratings (Par 101): **85,84,82,80,80 78,**
toteswingers: 1&2 £4.80, 1&3 £14.00, 2&3 £13.70 CSF £28.94 TOTE £5.10: £2.50, £3.00; EX 35.20.There was no bid for the winner. Urban Space was claimed by Mr J M Curran for £5,000.
Owner B J Llewellyn **Bred** Deerfield Farm **Trained** Fochriw, Caerphilly
■ Robert Williams' first winner since turning professional.

FOCUS
The complexion of this seller clearly changed quite a bit when the short-priced favourite stumbled and unseated leaving the stalls. Weakish form, the winner rated up 4lb on this year's best.

5420 DAVISBAKERYCARIBBEAN.COM FILLIES' H'CAP 1m 67y
7:00 (7:00) (Class 4) (0-85,85) 3-Y-O+ **£4,204** (£1,251; £625; £312) **Stalls** Low

Form RPR

1622 **1** **Burke's Rock**[10] 5043 3-9-8 **85**..(p) RyanMoore 2 97+
(Jeremy Noseda) *mostly trckd ldng pair: gap appeared and produced to ld jst ins fnl f: rdn and qckly asserted* **15/8**[1]

0133 **2** *1 ¾* **Forgive**[11] 4984 3-9-0 **77**.. PatDobbs 9 85
(Richard Hannon) *pressed ldr at str pce fr wd draw: rdn to ld jst over 2f out: edgd rt briefly: hdd jst ins fnl f: styd on* **10/1**

1203 **3** *2 ¼* **The Giving Tree (IRE)**[38] 4057 3-9-1 **78**.. JamesDoyle 8 81
(Sylvester Kirk) *hld up in midfield: effrt 2f out: rdn and styd on to take 3rd ins fnl f: nvr able to chal* **10/1**

6203 **4** *nk* **Tuscania**[10] 5043 4-9-13 **84**.. EddieAhern 7 87+
(Lucy Wadham) *trckd ldrs: lost pl and dropped to 8th 3f out but stl gng wl: looking for room after: jst shkn up whn in the clr fnl f: r.o but no ch* **8/1**[3]

6612 **5** *½* **Strathnaver**[19] 4702 3-9-4 **81**.. FrankieDettori 5 82
(Ed Dunlop) *trckd ldrs: cl up 2f out: rdn and nt qckn over 1f out: fdd ins fnl f* **3/1**[2]

-100 **6** *1* **Amber Silk (IRE)**[19] 4702 3-9-3 **80**.. MichaelHills 3 79
(Charles Hills) *hld up in last trio: prog on outer over 3f out: rdn and tried to cl wl over 1f out: fdd fnl f* **8/1**[3]

5520 **7** *6* **Viking Rose (IRE)**[12] 4942 4-8-9 **69**.. AdamBeschizza(3) 4 55
(James Eustace) *hld up in last trio: pushed along 1/2-way: effrt on wd outside u.p 3f out: wknd 2f out* **12/1**

1041 **8** *¾* **Silvas Romana (IRE)**[11] 4989 3-8-12 **78**.. RyanClark(3) 1 61
(Mark Brisbourne) *led at gd pce but pressed: hdd jst over 2f out: short of room sn after and wknd qckly* **16/1**

4-00 **9** *1 ¾* **Sugarformyhoney (IRE)**[26] 4474 3-9-1 **78**.. JimmyFortune 6 57
(Seamus Durack) *hld up: a in last: wknd over 2f out* **50/1**

1m 40.29s (-4.41) **Going Correction** -0.50s/f (Hard)
WFA 3 from 4yo 6lb 9 Ran SP% **115.7**
Speed ratings (Par 102): **102,100,98,97,97 96,90,89,87**
toteswingers: 1&2 £6.20, 1&3 £9.60, 2&3 £11.20 CSF £22.14 CT £151.79 TOTE £2.50: £1.10, £3.90, £4.10; EX 29.30 Trifecta £218.50 Pool: £3,847.45 - 13.03 winning units..
Owner S E Construction (Kent) Ltd **Bred** Brook Stud Bloodstock Ltd **Trained** Newmarket, Suffolk

FOCUS
A competitive enough race of its type. The gallop looked sound enough, too, so there's no reason why the form won't hold up. The runner-up sets the standard.

5421 SKYBET MOBILE FOR IPHONE & ANDROID MAIDEN STKS 1m 67y
7:30 (7:30) (Class 5) 3-4-Y-O **£2,264** (£673; £336; £168) **Stalls** Low

Form RPR

2-5 **1** **My Body Is A Cage (IRE)**[108] 1824 3-8-12 0.. JimmyFortune 3 78
(Jeremy Noseda) *sn trckd ldng pair: clsd to ld 3f out and crossed to nr side rail: drvn and styd on wl fnl 2f* **8/1**

4333 **2** *2 ¼* **Engrossing**[24] 4544 3-9-3 73.. PatDobbs 2 78
(Richard Hannon) *hld up in 5th: prog over 2f out: chsd wnr wl over 1f out: sn rdn and nt qckn* **4/1**[3]

3 *2* **Surreal (IRE)**[124] 1458 3-8-12 0..[1] RyanMoore 4 68+
(Sir Michael Stoute) *dwlt: off the pce in last pair: pushed along 1/2-way: prog on outer over 2f out: styd on to take 3rd fnl f* **9/2**

3 **4** *2* **Tonle Sap (IRE)**[50] 3666 3-8-12 0.. JohnFahy 8 63
(Clive Cox) *trckd ldng trio: effrt and rdn to dispute 2nd briefly wl over 1f out: nt qckn and sn btn* **11/4**[1]

00 **5** *4* **Italian Lady (USA)**[3] 5329 3-8-5 0.. MichaelJMMurphy(7) 6 53
(Alan Jarvis) *led after 1f: rdn and hdd 3f out: steadily wknd fnl 2f* **16/1**

00 **6** *1* **Fly On By**[105] 1937 3-9-3 0.. DaneO'Neill 7 56
(Henry Candy) *led 1f: trckd ldr: upsides 3f out: steadily wknd fnl 2f* **33/1**

7 *7* **Tabib (IRE)** 3-9-3 0.. FrankieDettori 5 39
(Saeed Bin Suroor) *settled in 6th: pushed along and no prog 3f out: wknd over 1f out: eased* **7/2**[2]

8 *19* **Kalily** 3-9-3 0.. J-PGuillambert 1
(Luca Cumani) *s.s: rn green and sn detached in last: t.o fr 1/2-way* **10/1**

1m 40.8s (-3.90) **Going Correction** -0.50s/f (Hard) 8 Ran SP% **116.1**
Speed ratings (Par 103): **99,96,94,92,88 87,80,61**
toteswingers: 1&2 £8.90, 1&3 £8.40, 2&3 £5.60 CSF £40.62 TOTE £8.80: £2.20, £2.00, £2.70; EX 49.50 Trifecta £167.80 Pool: £3,847.45 - 11.20 winning units..
Owner Joseph Barton **Bred** Mrs T V Ryan **Trained** Newmarket, Suffolk

FOCUS
Fair form in this maiden, the runner-up a good yardstick and rated back to his best. They went a stronger gallop than is often the case in races of this nature.
Tonle Sap(IRE) Official explanation: jockey said filly lost a shoe
Kalily Official explanation: jockey said colt lost a shoe

5422 SKYBET.COM H'CAP 5f 10y
8:00 (8:00) (Class 4) (0-85,85) 3-Y-O **£4,204** (£1,251; £625; £312) **Stalls** Low

Form RPR

166 **1** **Blanc De Chine (IRE)**[25] 4500 3-8-11 **75**.. JimmyFortune 6 82
(Peter Makin) *anticipated s and fast away: mde all and sn crossed to nr side rail: drvn to hold on last 100yds* **7/1**

21 **2** *nk* **Silken Express (IRE)**[18] 4729 3-8-9 **73**.. RyanMoore 5 79
(Robert Cowell) *pressed ldng pair on outer: rdn wl over 1f out: styd on to take 2nd ins fnl f: clsd on wnr but jst hld* **6/4**[1]

0310 **3** *¾* **Heartsong (IRE)**[17] 4765 3-9-7 **85**.. NeilCallan 4 88
(John Gallagher) *chsd wnr: rdn wl over 1f out: nt qckn and lost 2nd ins fnl f: one pce* **12/1**

3620 **4** ½ **O'Gorman**[15] 4849 3-9-5 **83** DaneO'Neill 7 85+
(Gary Brown) *dwlt: in last pair tl prog on wd outside over 1f out: tried to cl on ldrs fnl f: one pce last 100yds* **8/1**
416 **5** 1¾ **Supreme Quest**[6] 5195 3-9-0 **78** JamesDoyle 3 73
(Roger Charlton) *chsd ldrs: drvn and nt qckn wl over 1f out: no imp after* **4/1**[2]
16-4 **6** 1¾ **Blackdown Fair**[13] 4919 3-9-0 **78** JamesMillman 2 67
(Rod Millman) *settled in last pair: rdn over 1f out: one pce and no prog whn short of room briefly ins fnl f* **8/1**
5035 **7** 1½ **Signifer (IRE)**[6] 5195 3-8-12 **76** [1] PatCosgrave 1 60
(Mick Channon) *in tch: drvn wl over 1f out: edgd rt jst ins fnl f: wknd* **6/1**[3]

59.16s (-1.14) **Going Correction** -0.375s/f (Firm) **7** Ran SP% **116.7**
Speed ratings (Par 102): **94,93,92,91,88 85,83**
toteswingers 1&2 £3.40, 1&3 £16.90, 2&3 £3.50 CSF £18.65 TOTE £7.90: £3.50, £1.20; EX 22.80.
Owner R P Marchant & Mrs E Lee **Bred** Newlands House Stud **Trained** Ogbourne Maisey, Wilts

FOCUS
They went a good gallop but it still proved hard to get into the race from off the pace. The front three were handy throughout. The time was ordinary and the form may not prove too reliable.
T/Plt: £135.90 to a £1 stake. Pool: £59,419.97. 319.13 winning tickets. T/Qpdt: £38.50 to a £1 stake. Pool: £5,977.17. 114.60 winning tickets. JN

5206 WOLVERHAMPTON (A.W) (L-H)

Monday, August 20

OFFICIAL GOING: Standard
Wind: Light behind Weather: Cloudy

5423 DOWNLOAD OUR IPHONE APP MEDIAN AUCTION MAIDEN STKS 5f 20y(P)
2:20 (2:20) (Class 6) 2-Y-O £1,704 (£503; £251) Stalls Low

Form RPR
0 **1** **Welliesinthewater (IRE)**[22] 4618 2-9-3 0 JoeFanning 3 74
(Derek Shaw) *a.p: led over 1f out: r.o: eased nr fin* **13/2**[3]
522 **2** ¾ **Grievous Angel (IRE)**[12] 4952 2-8-12 71 (v[1]) GrahamLee 4 66
(Ann Duffield) *s.i.s: sn pushed along in rr: hdwy 1/2-way: chsd wnr ins fnl f: sn rdn: r.o* **5/4**[1]
052 **3** 3 **Multisure**[10] 5053 2-9-3 70 FrederikTylicki 1 60
(Richard Fahey) *prom: rdn over 1f out: styd on same pce fnl f* **15/8**[2]
0500 **4** hd **Mace The Ace**[10] 5041 2-8-12 51 FrannyNorton 5 54
(David C Griffiths) *led: rdn and hdd over 1f out: no ex ins fnl f* **40/1**
00 **5** 1¾ **Stormy Times (IRE)**[15] 4845 2-8-12 0 [1] DavidProbert 6 48
(Mark Usher) *prom: pushed along 1/2-way: rdn and edgd lft over 1f out: styd on same pce* **25/1**
50 **6** nk **Dashing Storm**[21] 4651 2-8-12 0 RobertWinston 2 50+
(Jeremy Gask) *chsd ldr to 1/2-way: sn rdn: no ex fnl f* **14/1**
040 **7** 3¼ **Baltic Prince (IRE)**[54] 3491 2-9-3 55 CathyGannon 8 40
(Paul Green) *sn pushed along in rr: rdn over 1f out: nvr on terms* **25/1**

1m 3.25s (0.95) **Going Correction** -0.10s/f (Stan) **7** Ran SP% **109.4**
Speed ratings (Par 92): **88,86,82,81,78 78,73**
Tote Swingers 1&2 £1.60, 2&3 £1.40, 1&3 £2.10 CSF £13.81 TOTE £6.80: £2.00, £1.20; EX 17.30.
Owner The Whiteman Partnership **Bred** Brendan Ryan **Trained** Sproxton, Leics

FOCUS
A modest juvenile maiden and the front pair, although ending up nearer the stands' side, were able to pull clear. Straightforward form.

NOTEBOOK
Welliesinthewater(IRE) showed promise despite having not been the best away on last month's Carlisle debut over 6f, and he showed the benefit of that experience in this lesser race. He had no trouble with the drop to 5f and looks an obvious type for nurseries. (op 8-1)
Grievous Angel(IRE) wasn't the best away in the first-time visor, but ultimately had her chance and is now 0-6. She'll remain vulnerable in maidens. (op 6-4)
Multisure looked ideally berthed in stall one considering he made the running last time, but Frederik Tylicki failed to take advantage and his race was over once the field came around him towards the end of the back straight. He's probably in need of 6f. (op 6-4)
Mace The Ace, rated just 51, got to the front early and finished close enough to hold the form down.

5424 BOOK HOSPITALITY AT WOLVERHAMPTON RACECOURSE CLAIMING STKS 5f 216y(P)
2:50 (2:50) (Class 6) 2-Y-O £1,704 (£503; £251) Stalls Low

Form RPR
1 **Queen Aggie (IRE)** 2-9-1 0 GrahamLee 1 75+
(Richard Fahey) *slowly in to stride: hld up: hdwy over 1f out: led ins fnl f: r.o wl: comf* **8/1**
0541 **2** 4 **Alexandrakollontai (IRE)**[10] 5046 2-8-5 58 (b) AndreaAtzeni 2 50
(J S Moore) *sn pushed along and prom: rdn and n.m.r over 1f out: styd on same pce* **7/1**
3053 **3** nk **Napinda**[10] 5046 2-8-5 55 DavidProbert 11 49
(Des Donovan) *led 1f: remained w ldr tl pushed along to ld 2f out: rdn over 1f out: hdd and no ex ins fnl f* **10/1**
5204 **4** 1¼ **Baltic Gin (IRE)**[30] 4331 2-8-9 59 CathyGannon 6 49
(Malcolm Saunders) *chsd ldrs: rdn over 1f out: no ex ins fnl f* **8/1**
002 **5** 1 **Kimvara**[10] 5046 2-8-11 57 (b) LiamKeniry 5 48
(Joseph Tuite) *chsd ldrs: rdn and ev ch over 1f out: no ex ins fnl f* **16/1**
000 **6** 1¾ **Gowertonian (IRE)**[58] 3387 2-8-5 0 DarrenEgan(5) 10 42
(Ronald Harris) *s.i.s: hld up: styd on ins fnl f: nvr nrr* **66/1**
40 **7** nk **Reinvigorate (IRE)**[16] 4816 2-9-5 0 KieranO'Neill 7 50
(Richard Hannon) *hld up: rdn over 1f out: hung lft ins fnl f: nvr on terms* **6/1**[3]
00 **8** shd **Black Truffle (FR)**[13] 4921 2-8-6 0 HayleyTurner 8 37
(Michael Bell) *led 5f out tl rdn and hdd 2f out: wknd ins fnl f* **14/1**
0063 **9** 1¼ **Cymeriad**[9] 5108 2-8-11 55 JamesSullivan 12 38
(Michael Easterby) *hdwy over 2f out: rdn over 1f out: wknd fnl f* **33/1**
4005 **10** 1¼ **Until It Sleeps**[13] 4927 2-8-1 50 JimmyQuinn 3 24
(Mandy Rowland) *s.i.s: hld up: rdn over 1f out: a in rr* **20/1**
5 **11** ½ **Beluckyformammy (IRE)**[35] 4161 2-8-1 0 [1] SilvestreDeSousa 9 23
(S Donohoe, Ire) *prom: pushed along over 4f out: rdn over 2f out: wknd over 1f out* **9/2**[2]
34 **12** 1¼ **Angels Calling**[17] 4778 2-9-1 0 MartinHarley 4 33
(Mrs K Burke) *prom: rdn over 2f out: wknd over 1f out* **3/1**[1]

1m 14.87s (-0.13) **Going Correction** -0.10s/f (Stan) **12** Ran SP% **123.0**
Speed ratings (Par 92): **96,90,90,88,87 84,84,84,82,81 80,78**
Tote Swingers 1&2 £6.70, 2&3 £8.90, 1&3 £17.70 CSF £64.52 TOTE £10.10: £2.80, £2.90, £3.60; EX 80.70.Alexandrakollontai was claimed by Mr A. C. Whillans for £5,000. Queen Aggie was claimed by Mr P. D. Evans for £10,000.
Owner Dr Marwan Koukash **Bred** Mrs Marion Daly **Trained** Musley Bank, N Yorks

FOCUS
What had looked quite a competitive claimer was won in dominant fashion by the newcomer Queen Aggie, who is basically better than the grade. Typically poor form in behind.

NOTEBOOK
Queen Aggie(IRE) caught the eye beforehand, representing top connections, and won well. Related to three winners up to 1m, she wasn't the best away, but Graham Lee bided his time and the response was quite impressive, considering the grade, when asked to win her race. She's undoubtedly better than this level and it will be interesting to see what mark she's given with nurseries in mind. She was claimed by David Evans. (op 17-2 tchd 9-1)
Alexandrakollontai(IRE), narrow winner of a seller over the trip at Lingfield, was a length in front of Napinda that day and the pair ran to form without proving a match for the winner. He was claimed by Alistair Whillans. (op 13-2)
Napinda again ran well without being able to reverse Lingfield form with the runner-up. (op 11-1 tchd 12-1)
Baltic Gin(IRE), dropping in grade for the first-time, looked a big threat off the final bend, but didn't see it out. A return to 5f may help.
Kimvara had split the second and third at Lingfield, when wearing first-time blinkers, and the headgear evidently didn't work as well a second time. (op 14-1)
Gowertonian(IRE) offered more on this drop in grade, but is clearly still limited. (op 80-1 tchd 50-1)
Reinvigorate(IRE) was conceding weight all round and never featured on this drop in grade. (op 13-2 tchd 11-2)
Black Truffle(FR) showed a bit more, but is clearly very moderate. (op 18-1)
Beluckyformammy(IRE) had no cover out wide in the first-time hood and failed to perform. Official explanation: jockey said filly ran flat (tchd 4-1 and 5-1)
Angels Calling looked short in the market for what she'd actually achieved and was well held on this drop in trip. (op 4-1 tchd 9-2)

5425 FOSTERFORBIRMINGHAM.COM MAIDEN FILLIES' STKS 5f 216y(P)
3:20 (3:21) (Class 5) 2-Y-O £2,264 (£673; £336; £168) Stalls Low

Form RPR
1 **Bottle Blonde** 2-9-0 0 FrannyNorton 4 76
(Ed McMahon) *sn pushed along towards rr: hdwy over 4f out: hmpd wl over 1f out: led 1f out: shkn up and r.o wl* **25/1**
45 **2** 2 **Veturia (USA)**[13] 4917 2-9-0 0 (t) PaulMulrennan 6 70
(Kevin Ryan) *racd keenly: led 5f out: rdn and hung rt wl over 1f out: hdd 1f out: styd on same pce* **2/1**[1]
3 **3** ½ **Lyric Piece**[14] 4886 2-9-0 0 ChrisCatlin 1 69
(Sir Mark Prescott Bt) *s.i.s: sn pushed along in rr: r.o ins fnl f: nvr nrr* **4/1**[2]
630 **4** 1½ **Cross Pattee (IRE)**[19] 4701 2-9-0 77 WilliamBuick 2 64
(John Gosden) *chsd ldrs: lost pl over 4f out: rdn over 1f out: no imp fnl f* **2/1**[1]
3420 **5** 1¼ **Mandy Lexi (IRE)**[30] 4324 2-9-0 77 GrahamLee 3 60
(Patrick Morris) *led 1f: racd keenly: trckd ldrs: rdn over 1f out: wknd ins fnl f* **7/1**[3]
6 ¾ **Wildcrafting** 2-9-0 0 HayleyTurner 5 58
(Michael Bell) *prom: chsd ldr over 4f out: hmpd wl over 1f out: wknd ins fnl f* **12/1**

1m 15.38s (0.38) **Going Correction** -0.10s/f (Stan) **6** Ran SP% **110.7**
Speed ratings (Par 91): **93,90,89,87,86 85**
Tote Swingers 1&2 £6.60, 2&3 £1.60, 1&3 £6.20 CSF £73.15 TOTE £35.20: £9.70, £1.80; EX 49.90.
Owner HFL Racing Partnership **Bred** M A L Evans **Trained** Lichfield, Staffs

FOCUS
A fair maiden for the track, with the form potentially 6lb better than rated.

NOTEBOOK
Bottle Blonde, related to a couple of 2yo winners, one of them speedy, is from a yard always respected with its juveniles and her extra pace was a difference maker. According to her trainer she'd already visited the track for experience and she'll presumably take the nursery route now. (op 14-1)
Veturia(USA) is in the Group 1 Fillies' Mile, but she'd disappointed over 7f at Kempton the time before and was again beaten with no excuses. Nurseries are now an option. (op 7-2)
Lyric Piece performed similarly to her debut, missing the break before staying on all too late. She should learn again from the experience and is a maiden winner in waiting once granted a stiffer test. (tchd 7-2 and 9-2)
Cross Pattee(IRE) was shuffled back a bit early and then found herself unable to quicken having been switched inside down the straight. Ordinary nurseries should be more her thing. (tchd 13-8)
Mandy Lexi(IRE) is exposed and didn't see it out having raced keenly. (op 9-2)
Wildcrafting, half-sister to a 7f 2yo winner (later won at 1m4f), fared better than the bare result, displaying some pace, so expect better next time. (op 17-2)

5426 FOLLOW US ON TWITTER @WOLVESRACES FILLIES' H'CAP 7f 32y(P)
3:50 (3:50) (Class 5) (0-75,75) 3-Y-O+ £2,264 (£673; £336; £168) Stalls High

Form RPR
4042 **1** **Majestic Zafeen**[7] 5156 3-9-6 **74** MartinHarley 4 83
(Alastair Lidderdale) *chsd ldr tl led 2f out: edgd lft ins fnl f: rdn out* **5/1**
0054 **2** 1½ **Lady Layla**[14] 4876 3-9-4 **72** GrahamLee 6 77
(Bryan Smart) *s.i.s: hld up: hdwy over 2f out: rdn to go 2nd ins fnl f: r.o: no ch w wnr* **4/1**[2]
-400 **3** nk **Solfilia**[23] 4598 3-9-7 **75** HayleyTurner 8 79
(Hughie Morrison) *prom: outpcd 2f out: swtchd lft and styd on ins fnl f* **9/2**[3]
40-0 **4** nk **Malekat Jamal (IRE)**[12] 4942 3-8-8 **62** LiamKeniry 9 65
(David Simcock) *s.i.s: hld up: hdwy over 1f out: r.o: nt rch ldrs* **16/1**
-100 **5** 1½ **Maz**[6] 5218 4-9-3 **66** DavidProbert 10 67
(Alan Bailey) *hld up: hdwy over 1f out: r.o: nvr nrr* **25/1**
000 **6** nk **Obligada (IRE)**[26] 4474 4-9-10 **73** (b) MartinLane 1 73
(Tobias B P Coles) *led: rdn and hdd 2f out: no ex ins fnl f* **8/1**
-660 **7** nk **Quick Bite (IRE)**[65] 3156 3-9-7 **75** MartinDwyer 7 73
(Hugo Palmer) *s.i.s: hld up: hdwy over 1f out: sn rdn: nvr trbld ldrs* **7/2**[1]
2-06 **8** 5 **Cristal Gem**[8] 5132 3-9-4 **72** SilvestreDeSousa 12 56
(Alan McCabe) *trckd ldrs: plld hrd: rdn over 2f out: wknd fnl f: eased* **20/1**
4133 **9** hd **Lady Bayside**[53] 3541 4-9-8 **71** TomMcLaughlin 3 57
(Malcolm Saunders) *chsd ldrs: rdn over 2f out: wknd over 1f out* **6/1**
1000 **10** 1¼ **Poker Hospital**[18] 4726 3-8-8 **67** (v[1]) DarrenEgan(5) 2 47
(John Stimpson) *hld up: rdn over 2f out: nt clr run over 1f out: n.d* **25/1**

1m 28.41s (-1.19) **Going Correction** -0.10s/f (Stan)
WFA 3 from 4yo 5lb **10** Ran SP% **120.8**
Speed ratings (Par 100): **102,100,99,99,97 97,97,91,91,89**
Tote Swingers 1&2 £4.40, 2&3 £5.10, 1&3 £5.40 CSF £25.66 CT £97.10 TOTE £5.80: £3.40, £2.30, £1.20; EX 23.10.
Owner Lambourn Valley Racing II **Bred** Mike Channon Bloodstock Ltd **Trained** Lambourn, Berks

FOCUS
They didn't appear to go overly quick but the time was reasonable. A step up from the winner on her latest form.

Lady Bayside Official explanation: trainer had no explanation for the poor form shown

5427 BOOK HORIZONS RESTAURANT AT WOLVERHAMPTON H'CAP (DIV I) 7f 32y (P)

4:20 (4:21) (Class 6) (0-65,65) 3-Y-0+ **£1,704** (£503; £251) **Stalls** High

Form RPR
-004 **1** **Abhaath (USA)**[5] 5229 3 -9-265 DarrenEgan(5) 3 73
(Ronald Harris) *chsd ldrs: nt clr run wl over 1f out: rdn to ld wl ins fnl f: edgd lft: eased last strides* **3/1**[1]
0654 **2** *nk* **Muhandis (IRE)**[6] 5193 4 -9-962 ChrisCatlin 11 71
(Nick Littmoden) *dwlt: hld up: rdn over 1f out: str run and hung lft ins fnl f: nt quite rch wnr* **11/1**
5400 **3** *3/4* **Hawk Moth (IRE)**[14] 4872 4 -9-1265 CathyGannon 12 72
(John Spearing) *hld up: hdwy over 1f out: r.o* **17/2**
-020 **4** *hd* **Foot Tapper**[13] 4914 3 -9-563 GeorgeBaker 8 67
(Chris Wall) *prom: chsd ldr over 5f out: led over 1f out: rdn: edgd lft and hdd wl ins fnl f: unable qck* **11/2**[3]
3004 **5** *2 1/4* **Cadmium Loch**[11] 4993 4 -9-558 (p) RussKennemore 1 58
(Reg Hollinshead) *led 1f: chsd ldrs: rdn over 1f out: styd on same pce ins fnl f* **10/1**
4101 **6** *1 1/4* **Circuitous**[12] 4956 4 -9-255 (v) GrahamLee 10 52
(Keith Dalgleish) *sn prom: rdn over 1f out: no ex fnl f* **5/1**[2]
0006 **7** *1/2* **Kielty's Folly**[14] 4890 8 -9-356 FrederikTylicki 9 52
(Brian Baugh) *hld up in tch: rdn over 1f out: no ex ins fnl f* **18/1**
5556 **8** *3/4* **Landaho**[24] 4549 3 -8-246 oh1 JamesSullivan 7 38
(Hugh McWilliams) *mid-div: rdn over 2f out: n.d* **50/1**
6100 **9** *hd* **Lucifers Shadow (IRE)**[19] 4708 3 -8-1357 WilliamBuick 2 48
(Sylvester Kirk) *led 6f out: rdn and hdd over 1f out: wknd ins fnl f* **6/1**
5606 **10** *3/4* **Whitechapel**[7] 5179 5 -9-1265 (v[1]) MartinDwyer 4 56
(Daniel Kubler) *hld up: rdn over 2f out: n.d* **8/1**

1m 29.12s (-0.48) **Going Correction** -0.10s/f (Stan)
WFA 3 from 4yo+ 5lb **10**Ran SP% **117.6**
Speed ratings (Par 101): **98,97,96,96,94 92,92,91,90,90**
Tote Swingers 1&2 £8.60, 2&3 £16.70, 1&3 £7.60 CSF £38.25 CT £262.26 TOTE £5.70 : £2.30, £4.10, £2.00 ; EX 50.80 .
Owner Anisska Racing Limited **Bred** Santa Rosa Partners **Trained** Earlswood, Monmouths

FOCUS
The first leg of a moderate handicap, run at an ordinary enough gallop, and no surprise to see it go to one of the 3yos. It was slightly the faster division. The winner is rated pretty much to his 2yo form.
Whitechapel Official explanation: vet said gelding lost its near-fore shoe

5428 BOOK HORIZONS RESTAURANT AT WOLVERHAMPTON H'CAP (DIV II) 7f 32y (P)

4:50 (4:50) (Class 6) (0-65,65) 3-Y-0+ **£1,704** (£503; £251) **Stalls** High

Form RPR
6462 **1** **July Days (IRE)**[21] 4656 6 -9-659 FrederikTylicki 4 66
(Brian Baugh) *mde all: rdn over 1f out: edgd rt ins fnl f: jst hld on* **9/1**
3464 **2** *nk* **Iceblast**[4] 5259 4 -9-558 JamesSullivan 11 64
(Michael Easterby) *chsd ldrs: rdn 1/2-way: styd on u.p* **11/2**[2]
2123 **3** *3/4* **Marinus (IRE)**[8] 5130 3 -9-462 WilliamBuick 1 64
(Sylvester Kirk) *chsd ldrs: rdn over 2f out: ev ch over 1f out: styd on* **11/4**[1]
4032 **4** *shd* **Admiralty**[14] 4874 3 -9-765 (v[1]) RoystonFfrench 9 67
(Ismail Mohammed) *hld up: hdwy over 4f out: rdn over 1f out: styd on* **11/2**[2]
3301 **5** *nse* **Climaxfortackle (IRE)**[14] 4890 4 -9-1164 (v) FrannyNorton 10 68+
(Derek Shaw) *s.s: hld up: rdn and r.o wl ins fnl f: nt rch ldrs* **10/1**
4406 **6** *hd* **Cheers Buddy (IRE)**[9] 5081 4 -9-053 (e) PaulMulrennan 5 56
(Ian Semple) *hld up: hdwy over 1f out: sn rdn: r.o* **16/1**
0004 **7** *1* **Tiradito (USA)**[30] 4334 5 -9-765 (p) MarkCoumbe(5) 3 66
(Michael Attwater) *a.p: rdn over 2f out: styd on* **20/1**
0051 **8** *1* **Jerry Ellen (IRE)**[13] 4929 3 -8-650 (b) JoeFanning 6 46
(Tim Easterby) *chsd wnr: rdn over 1f out: no ex ins fnl f* **6/1**[3]
056 **9** *1 3/4* **Cool As Cash**[18] 4746 3 -9-462 SebSanders 7 53
(Paul D'Arcy) *hld up: rdn over 1f out: nvr on terms* **15/2**
1150 **10** *2* **Odd Ball (IRE)**[21] 4657 5 -9-161 ShirleyTeasdale(7) 12 49
(Lisa Williamson) *s.s: hld up: n.d* **20/1**
06-0 **11** *6* **Lady Of Edge**[16] 4807 3 -7-1146 DarrenEgan(5) 8 15
(Keith Dalgleish) *prom: rdn 1/2-way: sn wknd* **22/1**
5000 **12** *1/2* **Sienna Blue**[24] 4533 4 -8-1352 (t) JimmyQuinn 2 22
(Simon Hodgson) *hld up: nt clr run 1/2-way: wknd over 2f out* **66/1**

1m 29.49s (-0.11) **Going Correction** -0.10s/f (Stan)
WFA 3 from 4yo+ 5lb **12**Ran SP% **123.8**
Speed ratings (Par 101): **96,95,94,94,94 94,93,92,90,87 80,80**
Tote Swingers 1&2 £13.20, 2&3 £4.50, 1&3 £5.40 CSF £57.88 CT £180.18 TOTE £11.90 : £2.90, £1.80, £2.00 ; EX 70.70 .
Owner S Holmes **Bred** Deer Forest Stud **Trained** Audley, Staffs

FOCUS
Probably the weaker of the two divisions, and the slowest of the three C&D times. Little got into it from off the pace, with the early gallop being steady. The winner is possibly the best guide.

5429 MIRROR PUNTERS CLUB H'CAP 1m 141y (P)

5:20 (5:22) (Class 4) (0-85,85) 3-Y-0+ **£4,204** (£1,251; £625 ; £312) **Stalls** Low

Form RPR
03-4 **1** **Star Links (USA)**[18] 4748 6 -9-172 (b) RobertWinston 7 84
(S Donohoe, Ire) *chsd ldrs: rdn over 2f out: led 1f out: edgd lft: styd on u.p* **14/1**
0552 **2** *2 1/4* **Position**[5] 5243 3 -9-280 ChrisCatlin 11 87
(Sir Mark Prescott Bt) *sn pushed along and prom: chsd ldr over 5f out: led 4f out: rdn and hdd 1f out: styd on same pce* **9/4**[1]
0000 **3** *1/2* **One Scoop Or Two**[12] 4964 6 -8-1168 (p) RussKennemore 6 73
(Reg Hollinshead) *hld up: hdwy over 1f out: r.o: nt rch ldrs* **25/1**
0U21 **4** *1/2* **King Of Windsor (IRE)**[5] 5085 5 -9-374 (p) JoeFanning 8 78+
(Keith Dalgleish) *hld up: pushed along over 2f out: hdwy over 1f out: rdn and edgd lft ins fnl f: r.o* **11/2**
-002 **5** *1 1/2* **Asifa (IRE)**[12] 4949 3 -9-785 (v) SilvestreDeSousa 2 86
(Saeed Bin Suroor) *chsd ldrs: rdn over 2f out: no ex ins fnl f* **4/1**[2]
0024 **6** *2 1/2* **Light From Mars**[14] 4889 7 -9-778 GrahamLee 1 73
(Patrick Morris) *chsd ldrs: rdn and ev ch over 2f out: wknd ins fnl f* **10/1**
6-1 **7** *1 3/4* **The Tiger**[42] 3913 4 -9-879 WilliamBuick 3 70+
(Ed Dunlop) *s.i.s: hld up: rdn over 1f out: nvr on terms* **9/2**[3]
6600 **8** *shd* **Space War**[20] 4679 5 -9-172 (b[1]) PaulMulrennan 5 63
(Michael Easterby) *hmpd sn after s: hld up: rdn over 1f out: n.d* **14/1**
00-0 **9** *7* **Apache Glory (USA)**[23] 4608 4 -9-278 DarrenEgan(5) 4 53
(John Stimpson) *hld up: wknd over 2f out* **66/1**
3002 **10** *5* **Cono Zur (FR)**[9] 5111 5 -9-374 JamesSullivan 10 37
(Ruth Carr) *led over 4f: rdn and wknd over 2f out* **20/1**
350 **11** *7* **Charpoy (USA)**[20] 4674 4 -9-879 (b[1]) RoystonFfrench 9 26
(Ian Semple) *chsd ldrs: rdn over 3f out: wknd over 2f out* **25/1**

1m 48.12s (-2.38) **Going Correction** -0.10s/f (Stan)
WFA 3 from 4yo+ 7lb **11**Ran SP% **120.7**
Speed ratings (Par 105): **106,104,103,103,101 99,98,97,91,87 81**
Tote Swingers 1&2 £10.10, 2&3 £20.80, 1&3 £44.20 CSF £45.31 CT £834.19 TOTE £13.60 : £4.40, £1.50 , £9.10 ; EX 61.90 .
Owner Gerry Dolan & Mrs Marie E Dolan **Bred** Shell Bloodstock **Trained** Cootehill Road, Co Cavan

FOCUS
Several wanted the lead early, but the pace eventually slowed. The winner was on a good mark on his winter form here.

5430 FIND US ON FACEBOOK WOLVERHAMPTON RACECOURSE H'CAP 1m 4f 50y (P)

5:50 (5:51) (Class 6) (0-75,75) 3-Y-0+ **£2,264** (£673; £336 ; £168) **Stalls** Low

Form RPR
4311 **1** **Fleur De La Vie (IRE)**[7] 4875 3 -9-172 JimCrowley 10 83
(Ralph Beckett) *a.p: chsd ldr 4f out: rdn to ld over 1f out: styd on wl* **2/1**[1]
5112 **2** *3 1/4* **Honest Deal**[11] 5012 4 -9-1172 RobertWinston 2 78
(Alan Swinbank) *led: rdn and hdd over 1f out: styd on same pce* **4/1**[3]
4-52 **3** *1/2* **Rysbrack (USA)**[42] 3920 6 -10-075 WilliamBuick 6 80
(Paul Webber) *a.p: rdn over 1f out: styd on* **11/4**[2]
4 *nse* **Hootie (IRE)**[43] 3897 4 -8-956 oh2 (b) PaulMulrennan 4 61
(S Donohoe, Ire) *hld up: hdwy 6f out: rdn over 1f out: styd on* **12/1**
2606 **5** *1 1/2* **Scamperdale**[21] 4657 10 -9-667 FrederikTylicki 8 70
(Brian Baugh) *s.i.s: hld up: hdwy over 2f out: rdn over 1f out: wknd ins fnl f* **22/1**
1114 **6** *2 3/4* **Luctor Emergo (IRE)**[10] 5054 3 -8-1168 (p) JoeFanning 9 66
(Keith Dalgleish) *s.i.s: hld up: hdwy over 4f out: rdn over 2f out: wknd over 1f out* **10/1**
-343 **7** *nk* **Switched Off**[186] 582 7 -9-1273 RoystonFfrench 3 71
(Ed McMahon) *hld up: rdn over 2f out: hdwy over 1f out: wknd fnl f* **20/1**
0000 **8** *12* **English Summer**[11] 5002 5 -9-465 (p) GrahamLee 1 44
(David Simcock) *chsd ldr 8f: rdn over 2f out: wknd wl over 1f out* **10/1**
4550 **9** *9* **Delagoa Bay (IRE)**[3] 5265 4 -8-656 oh2 RaulDaSilva(3) 7 20
(Sylvester Kirk) *chsd ldrs: pushed along 7f out: rdn over 4f out: wknd over 3f out* **33/1**

2m 37.66s (-3.44) **Going Correction** -0.10s/f (Stan)
WFA 3 from 4yo+ 10lb **9**Ran SP% **117.9**
Speed ratings (Par 101): **107,104,104,104,103 101,101,93,87**
Tote Swingers 1&2 £2.40, 2&3 £3.20, 1&3 £4.00 CSF £10.22 CT £22.10 TOTE £3.30 : £1.60 , £1.40, £1.50 ; EX 9.60 .
Owner Prime Of Life 3 **Bred** Edward & Scarlet Leatham **Trained** Kimpton, Hants

FOCUS
English Summer and Honest Deal were duelling for the lead from an early stage and the pace seemed quite generous. Strong form for a Class 6 handicap, with the winner continuing on the up.
Delagoa Bay (IRE) Official explanation: jockey said filly never travelled
T/Plt: £211.20 to a £1 stake. Pool: £52122.52 - 180.11 winning tickets T/Qpdt: £30.30 to a £1 stake. Pool: £3660.23 - 89.36 w. tckts CR 5431a - 5438a (Foreign Racing) See RI

5032 BRIGHTON (L-H)

Tuesday, August 21

OFFICIAL GOING: Good to firm
Wind: Fresh, against Weather: Mainly cloudy

5439 BRITISH STALLION STUDS SUPPORTING BRITISH RACING E B F MEDIAN AUCTION MAIDEN STKS 6f 209y

2:15 (2:15) (Class 5) 2-Y-0 **£3,169** (£943; £471) **Stalls** Low

Form RPR
5 **1** **Mirsaale**[39] 4066 2 -9-30 MartinDwyer 2 81+
(James Tate) *trckd ldr: led over 1f out: pushed clr: comf* **4/11**[1]
033 **2** *3 1/4* **Branson (IRE)**[36] 4152 2 -9-372 PatDobbs 3 72
(Richard Hannon) *led tl over 1f out: sn outpcd* **6/1**[3]
3 *22* **House Of Orange (IRE)** 2 -9-30 JoeFanning 1 20
(Mark Johnston) *s.s: a last: rdn over 2f out: lost tch wl over 1f out* **4/1**[2]

1m 26.25s (3.15) **Going Correction** +0.025s/f (Good) **3**Ran SP% **107.6**
Speed ratings (Par 94): **83,79,54**
CSF £2.89 TOTE £1.60 ; EX 2.20 .
Owner Saif Ali **Bred** Mr & Mrs A E Pakenham **Trained** Newmarket, Suffolk

FOCUS
The rail was dolled out from 6f to 3.5f by four yards, adding nine yards to race distances. A slow time, and not form to trust implicitly. The winner is clearly on the up.

NOTEBOOK
Mirsaale showed plenty of ability when fifth in a strong July course maiden on his debut (7f, soft) and is entered in the Racing Post Trophy. This was considerably easier and he won as expected. A step up in class now awaits. (op 8-13)
Branson(IRE), upped to 7f for the first time, had his chance but ran into a potentially decent sort. (op 4-1)
House Of Orange (IRE) is a half-brother to a few winners, notably 1000 Guineas third Vista Bella, but he missed the break on this debut and didn't convince the track suited, being eased in the closing stages. (op 3-1)

5440 HARDINGSCATERING.CO.UK SUPPORTING ABF THE SOLDIERS CHARITY H'CAP 6f 209y

2:45 (2:45) (Class 5) (0-70,70) 3-Y-0+ **£2,264** (£673; £336 ; £168) **Stalls** Low

Form RPR
-110 **1** **Eager To Bow (IRE)**[17] 4814 6 -9-967 GeorgeBaker 7 75
(Patrick Chamings) *hld up in rr: hdwy over 1f out: r.o to ld on line* **17/2**
0123 **2** *nse* **Aciano (IRE)**[24] 4603 4 -9-1068 (tp) SebSanders 8 76
(Brendan Powell) *trckd ldr: led over 1f out: hrd rdn fnl f: ct on line* **8/1**
5005 **3** *1 1/2* **One Way Or Another (AUS)**[13] 4929 9 -9-159 (t) RichardThomas 2 63
(David Evans) *hld up towards rr: pushed along and r.o fr over 1f out: gng on at fin* **33/1**
0261 **4** *1/2* **Efistorm**[11] 5034 11 -9-770 MarkCoumbe(5) 10 72
(Joseph Tuite) *in tch on outer: chsd ldrs over 2f out: styd on same pce* **20/1**
0014 **5** *1* **Comadoir (IRE)**[24] 4584 6 -8-1362 (p) NathanSweeney(5) 6 62
(Jo Crowley) *led tl over 1f out: no ex fnl f* **9/2**[2]
4500 **6** *1/2* **Justbookie Dot Com (IRE)**[36] 4155 4 -9-166 (b) WilliamTwiston-Davies(7) 9 64
(David Evans) *mid-div to rr: outpcd 2f out: styd on fnl f* **14/1**
3000 **7** *4* **Esprit Danseur**[13] 4939 3 -9-063 PatCosgrave 3 49
(Jim Boyle) *t.k.h: chsd ldrs: rdn over 2f out: wknd over 1f out* **16/1**

4104 **8** 3¼ **Takitwo**[17] 4814 9-9-5 **63** HayleyTurner 1 42
(Jonathan Portman) *mid-div: rdn 5f out: wknd over 2f out* **11/2**[3]

4331 **9** 2¼ **Little Rainbow**[13] 4942 3-9-5 **68** AdamKirby 4 39
(Clive Cox) *plld hrd: in tch tl hrd rdn and wknd 2f out* **13/8**[1]

660- **10** ½ **Rohlindi**[297] 7173 4-9-4 **62** CathyGannon 5 33
(Eve Johnson Houghton) *s.i.s: outpcd: a bhd* **33/1**

1m 24.37s (1.27) **Going Correction** +0.025s/f (Good)
WFA 3 from 4yo+ 5lb **10** Ran SP% **116.5**
Speed ratings (Par 103): **93,92,91,90,89 88,84,80,78,77**
Tote Swingers 1&2 £9.80, 2&3 £42.00, 1&3 £67.20 CSF £72.71 CT £2160.98 TOTE £7.30: £3.00, £2.60, £9.00; EX 53.60.
Owner Mrs J E L Wright **Bred** Stone Ridge Farm **Trained** Baughurst, Hants

FOCUS
Just a modest handicap. The winner matched his recent AW best.
Little Rainbow Official explanation: jockey said filly ran too free; vet said filly had been struck into
Rohlindi Official explanation: jockey said filly stumbled 6f out

5441 JOHN "JACK" BRODRICK MEMORIAL H'CAP 1m 1f 209y
3:15 (3:16) (Class 5) (0-70,66) 3-Y-0+ **£2,264** (£673; £336; £168) **Stalls** High

Form RPR

2055 **1** **Kelpie Blitz (IRE)**[12] 5021 3-9-2 **62** (t) MickyFenton 3 74
(Seamus Durack) *a gng wl: trckd ldrs: led over 1f out: shkn up and sn clr: easily* **14/1**

30-4 **2** 3½ **Swift Blade (IRE)**[138] 1205 4-10-0 **66** (p) SebSanders 9 71
(Lady Herries) *s.i.s: hld up in rr: rdn and hdwy fnl 2f: styd on to take 2nd fnl strides* **9/1**[3]

3212 **3** *nk* **Welsh Nayber**[11] 5052 3-9-6 **66** (b) PatDobbs 7 70
(Amanda Perrett) *in tch: rdn to chse ldrs 2f out: hung lft over 1f out: nt qckn* **7/2**[2]

0056 **4** 1¼ **Sweet Liberta (IRE)**[15] 4870 3-8-8 **54** DavidProbert 2 56
(Andrew Balding) *hld up in rr: rdn 3f out: hdwy 2f out: no imp fnl f* **11/1**

563 **5** 2¼ **Amistress**[7] 5197 4-9-11 **63** CathyGannon 5 60
(Eve Johnson Houghton) *in tch: rdn 4f out: outpcd and btn over 2f out* **3/1**[1]

420 **6** 1¼ **La Confession**[10] 5095 3-8-0 **53** NoelGarbutt(7) 10 48
(Rae Guest) *t.k.h: prom tl hrd rdn and wknd over 1f out* **12/1**

6205 **7** ½ **Ermyntrude**[13] 4940 5-9-0 **52** (v[1]) IanMongan 4 46
(Pat Phelan) *t.k.h: chsd ldr: led over 2f out tl wknd over 1f out* **10/1**

5330 **8** 8 **Chatterati (USA)**[13] 4945 3-8-10 **56** JoeFanning 1 34
(Mark Johnston) *dwlt: sn led: hdd & wknd over 2f out: eased whn no ch 1f out* **7/2**[2]

4266 **9** 18 **Santadelacruze**[25] 4544 3-9-5 **65** (p) GeorgeBaker 6
(Gary Moore) *plld hrd: in tch: wknd 3f out: sn bhd: eased whn no ch* **20/1**

2m 4.61s (1.01) **Going Correction** +0.025s/f (Good)
WFA 3 from 4yo+ 8lb **9** Ran SP% **116.0**
Speed ratings (Par 103): **96,93,92,91,90 89,88,82,67**
Tote Swingers 1&2 £11.90, 2&3 £5.70, 1&3 £10.20 CSF £133.14 CT £543.64 TOTE £15.20: £3.90, £3.70, £1.40; EX 132.50.
Owner Mrs Anne Cowley **Bred** Irish National Stud **Trained** Baydon, Wilts

FOCUS
A modest contest. The form is rated around the third, the winner finally matching his Yarmouth April figure.
Santadelacruze Official explanation: jockey said colt stopped quickly

5442 LOTHBURY PENDIL H'CAP 1m 3f 196y
3:45 (3:45) (Class 5) (0-70,74) 3-Y-0 **£2,264** (£673; £336; £168) **Stalls** High

Form RPR

001 **1** **Between Us**[7] 5219 3-9-4 **69** 6ex ChrisCatlin 3 85+
(Sir Mark Prescott Bt) *mde all: drvn 2 l clr 2f out: styd on wl: rdn out* **11/10**[1]

0014 **2** 6 **Dont Take Me Alive**[22] 4649 3-9-2 **67** (p) AdamKirby 4 73
(Clive Cox) *hld up in 4th: rdn 4f out: chsd wnr fnl 2f: no imp* **10/1**

0451 **3** 2 **Ukrainian (IRE)**[7] 5188 3-9-9 **74** 6ex (b) JoeFanning 5 77
(Mark Johnston) *chsd wnr tl 2f out: sn outpcd* **11/4**[2]

-651 **4** 1½ **Scarlet Belle**[16] 4850 3-9-3 **68** HayleyTurner 1 69
(Marcus Tregoning) *chsd ldng pair tl rdn and btn over 3f out* **4/1**[3]

0504 **5** 13 **Good Of Luck**[18] 4755 3-9-4 **69** SamHitchcott 2 49
(Mick Channon) *s.s: hld up in rr: effrt on outer 3f out: wkng whn hung lft fr 2f out* **14/1**

2m 32.78s (0.08) **Going Correction** +0.025s/f (Good) **5** Ran SP% **110.0**
Speed ratings (Par 100): **100,96,94,93,85**
CSF £12.60 TOTE £1.50: £1.10, £2.80; EX 12.60.
Owner Cheveley Park Stud **Bred** Cheveley Park Stud Ltd **Trained** Newmarket, Suffolk

FOCUS
An ordinary race but an improving winner in the shape of Between Us, who was allowed an uncontested lead and had her rivals strung out. She's rated similarly to her Yarmouth win.

5443 THERMOLAST ROOFING AND GRANDSTAND SOLUTIONS H'CAP 7f 214y
4:15 (4:16) (Class 6) (0-65,65) 3-Y-0 **£1,617** (£481; £240; £120) **Stalls** Low

Form RPR

0460 **1** **Compton Crofter**[6] 5229 3-7-12 **49** (t) NicoleNordblad(7) 9 52
(Hans Adielsson) *hld up and bhd in detached last: gd hdwy over 1f out: r.o to ld nr fin* **28/1**

5004 **2** ½ **Silkee Supreme**[15] 4871 3-9-7 **65** (b[1]) PatDobbs 4 67
(Richard Hannon) *trckd ldrs: led gng wl 2f out and wnt 3 l clr: hrd rdn fnl f: ct nr fin* **25/1**

0003 **3** *nk* **Whinging Willie (IRE)**[12] 4981 3-8-13 **57** AdamKirby 5 58
(Gary Moore) *in tch: rdn 3f out: chsd ldr jst over 1f out: r.o u.p* **7/1**[3]

3406 **4** ¾ **Saint Boniface**[22] 4644 3-9-3 **61** FergusSweeney 8 60
(Peter Makin) *hld up in rr: rdn and hdwy 2f out: kpt on fnl f* **33/1**

3660 **5** *hd* **The New Black (IRE)**[13] 4942 3-9-5 **63** (v) SebSanders 6 62
(Gay Kelleway) *towards rr: rdn 3f out: hdwy over 1f out: styd on same pce ins fnl f* **20/1**

012 **6** 3¾ **Watt Broderick (IRE)**[13] 4961 3-9-6 **64** JoeFanning 2 54
(Ian Williams) *s.i.s: hld up in rr of midfield: rdn 3f out: hdwy to press ldrs 2f out: wknd jst over 1f out* **10/11**[1]

5211 **7** 3¾ **Waspy**[14] 4900 3-8-13 **57** (t) PatCosgrave 11 39+
(George Baker) *towards rr: n.m.r over 2f out: hrd rdn over 1f out: n.d* **6/1**[2]

-000 **8** 1¾ **Sea Anemone**[10] 5095 3-8-3 **47** DavidProbert 7 25
(Andrew Balding) *chsd ldr tl 2f out: hrd rdn: wknd over 1f out* **28/1**

0043 **9** 2¼ **Doc Hill**[14] 4900 3-8-2 **46** CathyGannon 3 19
(Michael Blanshard) *prom tl wknd and n.m.r 2f out* **16/1**

2102 **10** 2½ **Rockme Cockney**[12] 4986 3-9-1 **62** (p) RaulDaSilva(3) 10 29
(Jeremy Gask) *led tl 2f out: 4th and fading whn n.m.r over 1f out* **7/1**[3]

3650 **11** 1½ **Conowen**[12] 5017 3-9-4 **62** HarryBentley 1 25
(William Jarvis) *chsd ldrs tl wknd over 2f out* **25/1**

1m 37.08s (1.08) **Going Correction** +0.025s/f (Good) **11** Ran SP% **119.8**
Speed ratings (Par 98): **95,94,94,93,93 89,85,84,81,79 77**
Tote Swingers 1&2 £54.50, 2&3 £21.90, 1&3 £25.40 CSF £560.51 CT £5431.85 TOTE £43.60: £8.60, £6.20, £3.00; EX 585.80.
Owner Erik Penser **Bred** Redmyre Bloodstock And Stuart McPhee **Trained** Kingston Lisle, Oxon

FOCUS
A moderate but competitive handicap. Limited form, rated through the runner-up.
Watt Broderick(IRE) Official explanation: trainer's rep said gelding was unsuited by the track

5444 THERMOLAST ROOFING LTD H'CAP 5f 213y
4:45 (4:46) (Class 6) (0-60,58) 3-Y-0+ **£1,617** (£481; £240; £120) **Stalls** Low

Form RPR

0002 **1** **Stonecrabstomorrow (IRE)**[11] 5034 9-9-2 **58** MarkCoumbe(5) 9 66
(Michael Attwater) *dwlt: hld up in rr: rdn and hdwy 2f out: r.o to ld fnl 120yds: pushed out* **15/2**

3120 **2** ¾ **Ereka (IRE)**[11] 5049 4-8-4 **46** TobyAtkinson(5) 2 52
(John Best) *chsd ldrs: edgd rt and rdn fr 2f out: r.o to take 2nd on line* **6/1**[3]

0030 **3** *nse* **Baby Dottie**[73] 2943 5-9-6 **57** IanMongan 7 62
(Pat Phelan) *led: hrd rdn fnl f: hdd and nt qckn fnl 120yds* **7/1**

4036 **4** 3 **Russian Bullet**[15] 4885 3-9-0 **54** FergusSweeney 8 50
(Jamie Osborne) *chsd ldr tl no ex ins fnl f* **8/1**

5466 **5** ½ **Ridgeway Sapphire**[7] 5203 5-8-10 **47** (v) DavidProbert 10 41
(Mark Usher) *in tch: rdn and outpcd 2f out: hung lft: styd on fnl f* **7/2**[1]

4601 **6** 2½ **Memphis Man**[12] 4993 9-9-2 **56** MatthewCosham(3) 1 42
(David Evans) *hld up in midfield: n.m.r on rail over 4f out: rdn over 2f out: nvr nr to chal* **7/1**

000 **7** *hd* **White Shift (IRE)**[14] 4902 6-8-8 **45** KierenFox 6 31
(Paul Howling) *chsd ldrs: hrd rdn 2f out: sn btn* **28/1**

460 **8** 3¼ **Fonterutoli (IRE)**[35] 4196 5-9-1 **52** (v) AdamKirby 5 27
(Roger Ingram) *s.s: towards rr: mod effrt 3f out: sn btn* **8/1**

0200 **9** 1¾ **Little Perisher**[14] 4929 5-8-10 **47** (p) CathyGannon 4 17
(Paul Howling) *prom tl wknd over 2f out* **20/1**

060- **10** 21 **La Passionata**[251] 7757 3-8-3 **46** RaulDaSilva(3) 3
(Jeremy Gask) *walked to post: dwlt: plld hrd towards rr: no ch and eased fnl 2f* **11/2**[2]

1m 11.64s (1.44) **Going Correction** +0.025s/f (Good)
WFA 3 from 4yo+ 3lb **10** Ran SP% **119.1**
Speed ratings (Par 101): **91,90,89,85,85 81,81,77,75,47**
Tote Swingers 1&2 £10.10, 2&3 £10.80, 1&3 £10.90 CSF £53.20 CT £340.95 TOTE £8.30: £2.30, £2.00, £4.00; EX 47.80.
Owner The Attwater Partnership **Bred** P Dillon **Trained** Epsom, Surrey

FOCUS
A moderate sprint handicap. The winner is rated a length off last year's best.
La Passionata Official explanation: jockey said filly ran too free

5445 THERMOLASTROOFING.CO.UK H'CAP 5f 59y
5:15 (5:15) (Class 6) (0-65,63) 3-Y-0+ **£1,617** (£481; £240; £120) **Stalls** Low

Form RPR

4006 **1** **Pucon**[8] 5165 3-8-13 **60** MarkCoumbe(5) 6 68
(Roger Teal) *in tch: effrt 2f out: led jst over 1f out: pushed out* **17/2**

4661 **2** ½ **Imaginary Diva**[11] 5033 6-9-2 **59** RyanPowell(3) 3 65
(George Margarson) *hld up in 6th: hdwy over 1f out: r.o to take 2nd ins fnl f* **17/2**

1113 **3** 1 **Scommettitrice (IRE)**[12] 4980 4-9-1 **62** (p) WilliamTwiston-Davies(7) 5 65
(David Evans) *prom: chal over 1f out: one pce fnl f* **3/1**[2]

051 **4** 1½ **Maltease Ah**[9] 5131 3-8-12 **54** 6ex DavidProbert 2 52
(Alan McCabe) *led tl over 1f out: no ex* **11/2**

1023 **5** ½ **Ooi Long**[18] 4777 3-9-2 **63** TobyAtkinson(5) 1 59
(Mark Rimmer) *chsd ldrs: led briefly over 1f out: wknd ins fnl f* **4/1**[3]

2326 **6** 1¼ **Autocracy**[18] 4758 5-9-5 **59** (bt) FergusSweeney 4 50
(Daniel Kubler) *hld up in rr: rdn 2f out: nvr able to chal* **9/1**

3622 **7** ¾ **Funcheon Vale (IRE)**[11] 5033 3-9-4 **60** GeorgeBaker 7 49
(Hughie Morrison) *pressed ldr tl wknd over 1f out* **11/4**[1]

1m 3.93s (1.63) **Going Correction** +0.025s/f (Good)
WFA 3 from 4yo+ 2lb **7** Ran SP% **115.3**
Speed ratings (Par 101): **87,86,84,82,81 79,78**
Tote Swingers 1&2 £18.80, 2&3 £5.00, 1&3 £7.30 CSF £106.78 TOTE £24.40: £7.30, £5.80; EX 137.30.
Owner J A Redmond **Bred** J Redmond **Trained** Ashtead, Surrey

FOCUS
A moderate sprint handicap which has been rated cautiously.
Maltease Ah Official explanation: jockey said filly hung right
Autocracy Official explanation: trainer said gelding finished distressed
Funcheon Vale(IRE) Official explanation: jockey said filly stopped quickly
T/Plt: £1,260.80 to a £1 stake. Pool of £47758.17 - 27.65 winning tickets. T/Qpdt: £90.10 to a £1 stake. Pool of £4721.17 -38.75 winning tickets. LM

3539 WARWICK (L-H)
Tuesday, August 21
OFFICIAL GOING: Good (good to soft in places in back straight; 7.5)
Wind: Light behind becoming fresher Weather: Overcast

5446 ENTERTAIN CLIENTS AT WARWICK RACECOURSE APPRENTICE H'CAP 6f
5:00 (5:00) (Class 6) (0-65,65) 3-Y-0 **£1,617** (£481; £240; £120) **Stalls** Low

Form RPR

6021 **1** **Aubrietia**[4] 5327 3-8-13 **57** 6ex (b) DavidBergin(3) 1 70
(Alan McCabe) *chsd ldrs: rdn to ld over 1f out: r.o* **9/4**[1]

2610 **2** 1½ **George Fenton**[7] 5203 3-8-10 **51** (p) JoshBaudains 2 59
(Richard Guest) *chsd ldr tl led 4f out: rdn and hdd over 1f out: styd on same pce ins fnl f* **8/1**

032 **3** 3¾ **Gladiatrix**[61] 3312 3-9-5 **65** DanielMuscutt(5) 3 61+
(Rod Millman) *hld up: nt clr run over 3f out: hdwy over 1f out: sn rdn: styd on: nt rch ldrs* **9/2**[2]

6665 **4** 1½ **First Rebellion**[13] 4937 3-8-1 **47** oh1 ow1 RobertTart(5) 11 38
(Tony Carroll) *chsd ldrs: rdn over 2f out: no ex fnl f* **25/1**

3300 **5** ½ **Lord Paget**[64] 3218 3-8-13 **59** EvaMoscrop(5) 6 49
(Reg Hollinshead) *hld up: hdwy over 2f out: rdn over 1f out: wknd ins fnl f* **25/1**

2251 **6** 1½ **Auntie Mabel**[14] 4920 3-8-13 **61** (v) JoeyHaynes(7) 12 46
(Andrew Balding) *prom: rdn over 2f out: wknd ins fnl f* **6/1**[3]

552 7 4½ **Ficelle (IRE)**[8] 5149 3-9-1 61 .... RyanTate(5) 9 32
(Ronald Harris) *led 2f: rdn 1/2-way: wknd over 1f out* **7/1**
3020 8 1 **Big Sylv (IRE)**[12] 5014 3-8-7 48 .... IanBurns 8 15
(James Unett) *s.i.s: sn pushed along in rr: rdn over 2f out: nvr on terms* **12/1**
-630 9 2¼ **Simpson Millar**[17] 4830 3-8-6 47 .... DarylByrne 10 7
(Noel Wilson) *stmbld s: sn outpcd* **22/1**
10 ¾ **Oh So Quaint (IRE)**[89] 2434 3-9-10 65 .... JakePayne 5 23
(A L T Moore, Ire) *plld hrd and prom: rdn over 2f out: wknd and eased over 1f out* **16/1**
-000 11 10 **Red All Over (IRE)**[25] 4550 3-7-12 46 oh1 .... KevinStott(7) 4
(Alan Berry) *chsd ldrs: lost pl over 3f out: sn bhd* **100/1**

1m 10.35s (-1.45) **Going Correction** -0.20s/f (Firm) 11 Ran SP% 113.5
Speed ratings (Par 98): **101,99,94,92,91 89,83,82,79,78 64**
toteswingers:1&2 £8.20, 2&3 £10.20, 1&3 £2.10 CSF £18.98 CT £73.95 TOTE £2.90: £1.20, £2.90, £1.80; EX 25.30 Trifecta £125.10 Part won. Pool £169.09 - 0.64 winning units..
Owner Mrs M J McCabe **Bred** C J Murfitt **Trained** Averham Park, Notts

FOCUS
Stables bend out 2yds which increased distances on Round course by about 20yds. A moderate 3yo sprint for apprentices and the first two, who came from the lowest stalls, had it to themselves in the straight and the time was decent, helped by a tailwind in the straight. The winner is thriving and the second helps set the standard.
Simpson Millar Official explanation: vet said gelding lost a right-fore shoe

5447 ALLINSON PRINT (S) STKS 6f
5:30 (5:34) (Class 6) 3-Y-0+ **£1,617** (£481; £240; £120) **Stalls** Low

Form RPR
0/0- 1 **Basilica**[23] 1361 4-8-6 80 .... JakePayne(7) 3 78
(Bill Turner) *mde all: set stdy pce tl qcknd over 2f out: rdn and hung rt ins fnl f: r.o: comf* **12/1**
000 2 2¾ **Blue Jack**[32] 4312 7-8-13 90 .... (v) FrannyNorton 6 69
(Tom Dascombe) *trckd ldrs: plld hrd: wnt 2nd 2f out: shkn up fnl f: no imp* **1/1**[1]
1065 3 1½ **Desert Strike**[10] 5097 6-9-5 73 .... (p) RobertWinston 5 70
(Charles Hills) *hld up: racd keenly: hdwy over 2f out: shkn up ins fnl f: styd on same pce* **5/1**[3]
0154 4 1¾ **Sarangoo**[26] 4493 4-8-3 65 .... MatthewLawson(5) 4 54
(Malcolm Saunders) *s.i.s: hld up: rdn over 2f out: hung lft and styd on ins fnl f: nt trble ldrs* **4/1**[2]
500- 5 3½ **Ave Sofia**[321] 6628 3-8-2 50 .... DominicFox(3) 7 43
(John Holt) *chsd wnr tl rdn 2f out: wknd over 1f out* **40/1**
4600 6 1½ **Athaakeel (IRE)**[42] 3943 6-8-3 50 .... (b) DarrenEgan(5) 1 38
(Ronald Harris) *hld up: rdn and wknd over 2f out* **16/1**
5665 7 2¼ **Style And Panache (IRE)**[16] 4849 4-8-8 64 .... (p) StevieDonohoe 2 31
(David Evans) *plld hrd and prom: rdn and wknd over 1f out* **7/1**
00 8 16 **Icing Sugar**[25] 4550 4-8-8 0 .... PatrickMathers 8
(Mike Sowersby) *prom: rdn 1/2-way: sn wknd* **100/1**

1m 10.7s (-1.10) **Going Correction** -0.20s/f (Firm)
WFA 3 from 4yo+ 3lb 8 Ran SP% 116.2
Speed ratings (Par 101): **99,95,93,91,86 84,81,60**
toteswingers:1&2 £5.10, 2&3 £1.50, 1&3 £4.80 CSF £24.99 TOTE £19.00: £4.40, £1.02, £2.20; EX 29.10 Trifecta £166.50 Pool £558.20 - 2.48 winning units..There was no bid for the winner. Blue Jack was claimed by A. J. McCabe for £6,000. Desert Strike was claimed by C. R. Dore for £6,000.
Owner Anthony Knott **Bred** B Minty **Trained** Sigwells, Somerset

FOCUS
Mixed levels of ability in this seller, and the time was 0.35 secs slower than the opening race. The form is rated cautiously.
Style And Panache(IRE) Official explanation: vet said filly lost a front shoe

5448 BRITISH STALLION STUDS SUPPORTING BRITISH RACING EBF MAIDEN FILLIES' STKS 5f 110y
6:00 (6:03) (Class 5) 3-4-Y-0 **£3,234** (£962; £481; £240) **Stalls** Low

Form RPR
3022 1 **Al Janadeirya**[10] 5096 4-9-3 70 .... RyanMoore 3 75
(Peter Chapple-Hyam) *mde all: shkn up and c clr fr over 1f out: easily* **1/4**[1]
0-4 2 9 **Mary Frith**[5] 5276 3-9-0 0 .... JimCrowley 7 45
(William Knight) *chsd wnr: rdn over 2f out: swished tail and outpcd fr over 1f out* **5/1**[2]
5425 3 ¾ **Script**[23] 4619 3-9-0 46 .... PatrickMathers 5 43
(Alan Berry) *prom: rdn 1/2-way: outpcd fr over 1f out: edgd lft ins fnl f* **50/1**
4 3½ **Alderton (IRE)** 3-9-0 0 .... JamesDoyle 2 31
(Martyn Meade) *chsd ldrs: rdn over 2f out: wknd over 1f out* **33/1**
00 5 3 **Vivacious Way**[12] 4992 3-9-0 0 ....[1] JimmyFortune 1 21
(Andrew Balding) *prom: lost pl 1/2-way: sn bhd* **12/1**[3]
6 1 **Nic's Rebel** 3-9-0 0 .... LiamJones 4 18
(James Unett) *hld up: pushed along 3f out: wknd 2f out* **50/1**
56 U **Symphony Of Stars**[18] 4782 3-8-11 0 .... DominicFox(3) 6
(Michael Appleby) *rrd and uns rdr s* **25/1**

1m 5.02s (-0.88) **Going Correction** -0.20s/f (Firm)
WFA 3 from 4yo 2lb 7 Ran SP% 115.1
Speed ratings (Par 100): **97,85,84,79,75 74,**
toteswingers:1&2 £1.30, 2&3 £7.50, 1&3 £6.00 CSF £1.90 TOTE £1.10: £1.10, £1.90; EX 2.20.
Owner Allan Belshaw **Bred** Times Of Wigan Ltd **Trained** Newmarket, Suffolk

FOCUS
A weak sprint maiden. The winner was a few grades above the rest and didn't need to improve.

5449 BRITISH STALLION STUDS SUPPORTING BRITISH RACING EBF MAIDEN STKS 5f
6:30 (6:33) (Class 5) 2-Y-0 **£3,234** (£962; £481; £240) **Stalls** Low

Form RPR
2205 1 **Fletcher Christian**[43] 3916 2-9-3 75 .... NeilCallan 4 73
(John Gallagher) *chsd ldr: rdn over 1f out: hung lft ins fnl f: styd on to ld nr fin* **4/1**[3]
34 2 nk **Clean Blow (USA)**[22] 4651 2-8-12 0 .... RichardMullen 1 67
(David Brown) *led: rdn over 1f out: hung lft ins fnl f: hdd nr fin* **3/1**[2]
2 3 3¾ **Tanghan (IRE)**[67] 3123 2-9-3 0 .... DavidNolan 2 58
(Richard Fahey) *sn pushed along to chse ldrs: rdn over 1f out: hung rt and no ex fnl f* **1/1**[1]
0 4 ½ **Top Town Boy**[22] 4654 2-9-3 0 .... RussKennemore 3 57
(John Holt) *prom: pushed along 1/2-way: riidden over 1f out: no ex fnl f* **66/1**
5 3 **Cross My Heart** 2-8-12 0 .... RyanMoore 5 41
(William Haggas) *chsd ldrs: pushed along over 3f out: wknd 1/2-way* **10/1**
6 4½ **Speed Date** 2-8-12 0 .... JimCrowley 7 25
(Ralph Beckett) *s.i.s and wnt rt s: outpcd* **10/1**
00 7 8 **Cos I Can**[22] 4654 2-8-12 0 ....[1] FrannyNorton 6
(Derek Shaw) *sn pushed along in rr: bhd fnl 3f* **50/1**

59.32s (-0.28) **Going Correction** -0.20s/f (Firm) 7 Ran SP% 116.6
Speed ratings (Par 94): **94,93,87,86,81 74,61**
toteswingers:1&2 £2.50, 2&3 £1.70, 1&3 £1.80 CSF £17.02 TOTE £6.20: £1.90, £1.60; EX 25.10.
Owner C R Marks (banbury) **Bred** H G And J R Dutfield **Trained** Chastleton, Oxon

FOCUS
This maiden contained some interesting sorts from major yards but the form is still modest, with the winner rated to his mark.

NOTEBOOK
Fletcher Christian set a fair standard in this juvenile maiden and put his experience to good use on his first start since being gelded and got the better of a good tussle with the runner-up. (op 7-1)
Clean Blow(USA), who had subsequent winners behind on both her previous starts, jumped well from the inside draw and made the running but, despite rallying after being headed by the winner, had to just give best. She looks well up to winning races and now qualifies for a handicap mark. (op 4-1)
Tanghan(IRE) had made a promising debut on easy ground at York in June but was the greenest of all going to post and, although appearing close enough turning for home, tended to hang right under pressure and could not pick up. He has questions to answer now. David Nolan reported that the colt hung badly right. Official explanation: jockey said colt hung badly right (op 4-5 tchd 11-10)
Top Town Boy improved considerably on his Polytrack debut here, although he looked somewhat unco-ordinated under pressure. He could be interesting on a straight track, possibly in nurseries after another outing. (op 50-1 tchd 80-1)
Cross My Heart, who was difficult to load, was too green to make an impression on her debut. (op 17-2)
Speed Date also proved green. (op 11-1 tchd 12-1)

5450 RACING UK NURSERY 5f
7:00 (7:01) (Class 4) (0-85,79) 2-Y-O **£3,428** (£1,020; £509; £254) **Stalls** Low

Form RPR
646 1 **Monkey Bar Flies (IRE)**[24] 4612 2-8-11 69 .... TonyHamilton 6 71
(Richard Fahey) *chsd ldr tl led over 1f out: rdn and hung rt ins fnl f: jst hld on* **3/1**[1]
5231 2 shd **Dusty Storm (IRE)**[14] 4922 2-9-3 75 .... AdrianNicholls 4 77
(Ed McMahon) *a.p: chsd wnr over 1f out: rdn: hung rt and ev ch ins fnl f: r.o* **7/2**[2]
4011 3 1 **Danz Choice (IRE)**[13] 4936 2-9-0 72 .... RyanMoore 3 70+
(Richard Hannon) *sn pushed along in rr: hdwy over 1f out: r.o: nt rch ldrs* **3/1**[1]
3133 4 1½ **Windforpower (IRE)**[19] 4728 2-8-10 68 .... (p) JamesDoyle 8 61
(Ronald Harris) *prom: rdn over 1f out: styd on same pce ins fnl f* **12/1**
033 5 shd **Mullit (IRE)**[17] 4825 2-8-10 68 .... FrannyNorton 9 61
(Tom Dascombe) *sn led: hung rt 1/2-way: rdn and hdd over 1f out: styd on same pce* **11/2**
610 6 2 **Knight Charm**[38] 4093 2-9-7 79 .... JohnFahy 2 64
(Eve Johnson Houghton) *hld up in tch: rdn over 1f out: no ex ins fnl f* **9/2**[3]
6150 7 2 **Majestic Red (IRE)**[26] 4488 2-9-0 72 .... TomMcLaughlin 7 50
(Malcolm Saunders) *sn pushed along in rr: rdn 1/2-way: n.d* **25/1**
510 8 7 **Harleys Rocket**[51] 3669 2-8-5 68 .... DavidKenny(5) 1 21
(Brendan Powell) *free to post: hld up: racd keenly: rdn 1/2-way: sn wknd* **25/1**

59.15s (-0.45) **Going Correction** -0.20s/f (Firm) 8 Ran SP% 121.2
Speed ratings (Par 96): **95,94,93,90,90 87,84,73**
toteswingers:1&2 £3.80, 2&3 £2.30, 1&3 £3.90 CSF £14.77 CT £33.85 TOTE £4.40: £1.70, £2.00, £1.10; EX 26.90 Trifecta £74.30 Pool £607.93 - 6.05 winning units..
Owner Penman Bond Partnership **Bred** Mrs Sheila O'Ryan **Trained** Musley Bank, N Yorks

FOCUS
A competitive nursery run 0.17secs faster than the preceding maiden. Pace held up well through the card, which counted against the third.

NOTEBOOK
Monkey Bar Flies(IRE) had taken part in some decent maidens, coming up against the likes of Reckless Abandon and Royal Ascot winner Hototo, and was well backed on this nursery debut. He jumped well and came through to lead over a furlong out before just holding off the runner-up, helped by ending up on the stands' rail. (op 4-1)
Dusty Storm(IRE) is going the right way and, raised 3lb after her Ripon success, ran well and was only just touched off. (op 4-1 tchd 5-1)
Danz Choice(IRE) had finished strongly from behind when winning his previous two races but, with the track showing a pace bias, coming from behind was always going to be difficult. He was struggling on the turn but picked up well, although too late to reel in the principals. He still looks on an upward curve and a stiffer test will be in his favour next time. (op 7-2 tchd 11-4)
Windforpower(IRE) ran his race without threatening to win, but probably helps set the level of the form. (op 14-1)
Mullit(IRE), who had made the running then hung left in his two previous starts, went off quickly but went right this time and that spoilt his chance. Franny Norton reported that the colt hung right. Official explanation: jockey said colt hung right (op 6-1 tchd 7-1)
Knight Charm, a C&D winner on soft ground in June, did not look entirely happy on the drying ground and could never land a blow. (op 7-2)
Harleys Rocket Official explanation: jockey said filly ran too freely to post

5451 CHIEFTAIN FABRICS H'CAP 1m 2f 188y
7:30 (7:30) (Class 4) (0-85,83) 3-Y-O **£4,075** (£1,212; £606; £303) **Stalls** Low

Form RPR
1401 1 **Henry Clay**[13] 4949 3-9-4 80 .... NeilCallan 3 88
(Mark Johnston) *mde all: rdn and hung rt fr over 1f out: styd on gamely* **4/1**[2]
4-06 2 hd **Daghash**[10] 5101 3-8-12 74 .... RobertWinston 1 82
(Clive Brittain) *sn pushed along and prom: rdn to chse wnr over 1f out: swvd rt ins fnl f: styd on* **5/1**[3]
5431 3 3½ **Cactus Valley (IRE)**[12] 5007 3-9-7 83 .... JamesDoyle 5 84+
(Roger Charlton) *hld up: hdwy over 2f out: rdn over 1f out: hung lft ins fnl f: styd on same pce* **15/8**[1]
660 4 6 **Falcon's Reign (FR)**[26] 4498 3-8-5 70 .... DominicFox(3) 6 60
(Michael Appleby) *hld up: plld hrd: effrt over 2f out: wknd over 1f out* **25/1**
1102 5 2¾ **April Ciel**[14] 4906 3-8-1 68 .... DarrenEgan(5) 4 53
(Ronald Harris) *chsd wnr: rdn over 2f out: wknd over 1f out* **4/1**[2]
2120 S **Cresta Star**[19] 4741 3-9-5 81 .... RyanMoore 2
(Richard Hannon) *sn pushed along to chse ldrs: disputing 4th whn n.m.r and slipped up over 2f out* **5/1**[3]

2m 19.97s (-1.13) **Going Correction** -0.05s/f (Good) 6 Ran SP% 112.0
Speed ratings (Par 102): **102,101,99,94,92**
toteswingers:1&2 £11.80, 2&3 £1.02, 1&3 £4.20 CSF £23.54 TOTE £6.10: £4.90, £3.20; EX 30.30.
Owner Sheikh Hamdan Bin Mohammed Al Maktoum **Bred** Rabbah Bloodstock Limited **Trained** Middleham Moor, N Yorks

FOCUS
A fair 3yo handicap that was run at a steady gallop, indicated by most of the field taking a strong hold early on. Several of the field wandered around in the straight. The stewards and jockeys subsequently inspected the bend where Cresta Star came down and sand was put down before the final race of the evening. The winner is worth more at face value but this form is rated a bit cautiously.

5452 FOLLOW US ON TWITTER @WARWICKRACES H'CAP — 1m 2f 188y
8:00 (8:07) (Class 6) (0-60,60) 3-Y-0+ £1,617 (£481; £240; £120) Stalls Low

Form RPR
0005 1 **Hyde Lea Flyer**[12] 5015 7-8-12 **46** oh1 RussKennemore 2 53
(Barry Leavy) *mde all: rdn over 1f out: edgd rt ins fnl f: styd on wl* **16/1**
6506 2 2 1/4 **Goldenveil (IRE)**[11] 5059 4-9-5 **53** [1] TonyHamilton 3 56
(Richard Fahey) *chsd ldrs: rdn over 1f out: styd on same pce ins fnl f* **7/2**[1]
-003 3 nk **Simply**[15] 4870 3-8-12 **55** NeilCallan 6 57
(Eve Johnson Houghton) *chsd wnr tl rdn over 1f out: styd on same pce ins fnl f* **4/1**[2]
300 4 2 3/4 **Nolecce**[31] 4350 5-9-9 **57** (p) RobbieFitzpatrick 13 54
(Richard Guest) *prom: rdn over 2f out: styd on same pce fr over 1f out* **18/1**
2500 5 2 **Musically**[26] 4486 3-8-7 **55** CharlesBishop(5) 10 48+
(Mick Channon) *hld up: rdn over 2f out: styd on fr over 1f out: nt trble ldrs* **9/2**[3]
0-50 6 3/4 **Mabel's Song**[29] 4410 3-9-3 **60** DaneO'Neill 1 52
(Henry Candy) *chsd ldrs: rdn over 2f out: wknd fnl f* **4/1**[2]
300 7 2 1/2 **Gallego**[7] 5197 10-9-2 **55** RachealKneller(5) 7 42+
(Richard Price) *s.s: hld up: nvr nrr* **12/1**
0-63 8 1 1/2 **Spring Secret**[35] 4183 6-9-7 **60** DarrenEgan(5) 5 44
(Bryn Palling) *hld up in tch: plld hrd: rdn over 2f out: wknd over 1f out* **5/1**
0000 9 7 **Can Do Les (IRE)**[7] 5212 3-8-0 **46** oh1 (b) SimonPearce(3) 11 17
(Richard Phillips) *hld up: a in rr: wknd over 2f out* **66/1**

2m 23.46s (2.36) **Going Correction** -0.05s/f (Good)
WFA 3 from 4yo+ 9lb 9 Ran SP% **117.4**
Speed ratings (Par 101): **89,87,87,85,83 83,81,80,75**
toteswingers:1&2 £8.80, 2&3 £4.10, 1&3 £10.60 CSF £72.67 CT £276.09 TOTE £22.00: £4.50, £1.90, £1.30; EX 100.70 Trifecta £384.50 Part won. Pool £519.66 - 0.99 winning units..
Owner Mrs J McVay **Bred** Hesmonds Stud Ltd **Trained** Forsbrook, Staffs

FOCUS
This moderate handicap was run even more slowly than the preceding race, the time being 3.49secs slower than the previous 3yo contest. The field waited until they were into the straight before racing in earnest, and the winner made all with the next three always prominent too. The form is rated loosley around the third.
T/Plt: £34.80 to a £1 stake. Pool £33,186.53 - 695.68 winning units. T/Qpdt: £30.90 to a £1 stake. Pool £3,457.66 - 82.55 winning units. CR

5213 YARMOUTH (L-H)
Tuesday, August 21

OFFICIAL GOING: Good to firm (7.3)
Wind: light, half against Weather: dry and sunny

5453 VISIT ENGLAND.COM MEDIAN AUCTION MAIDEN STKS — 6f 3y
2:05 (2:06) (Class 6) 3-Y-0 £1,617 (£481; £240; £120) Stalls Centre

Form RPR
-330 1 **Salacia (IRE)**[62] 3281 3-8-12 79 RoystonFfrench 3 83+
(Ismail Mohammed) *w ldr tl led over 3f out: shkn up and qckmd clr jst over 1f out: v easily* **11/10**[1]
0 2 7 **Sushi**[134] 1257 3-8-12 0 WilliamBuick 5 58
(Rae Guest) *hld up in tch: rdn and effrt over 2f out: outpcd by wnr and btn 1f out: plugged on to go 2nd towards fin* **7/2**[3]
4 3 1 **Bull Bay**[27] 4456 3-9-3 0 MickaelBarzalona 4 60
(Jane Chapple-Hyam) *chsd ldrs: rdn over 3f out: drvn to chse wnr over 1f out: sn outpcd and btn: lost 2nd towards fin* **9/4**[2]
6 4 2 3/4 **Jermatt**[112] 1739 3-8-10 0 JasonHart(7) 1 51
(J R Jenkins) *led tl over 3f out: rdn over 2f out: lost 2nd and btn over 1f out: wknd ins fnl f* **12/1**
0 5 42 **Fierecilla**[62] 3279 3-8-9 0 RyanClark(3) 2
(Tom Keddy) *in tch: rdn 4f out and sn struggling: t.o and heavily eased ins fnl f* **40/1**

1m 12.58s (-1.82) **Going Correction** -0.025s/f (Good) 5 Ran SP% **110.7**
Speed ratings (Par 98): **111,101,100,96,40**
CSF £5.41 TOTE £2.30: £1.10, £2.40; EX 5.60.
Owner Abdullah Saeed Belhab **Bred** Darley **Trained** Newmarket, Suffolk

FOCUS
The track had missed any showers and the going was reckoned to be good to firm, with William Buick confirming it to be "pretty quick." A very weak maiden. The winner's best run since she was a 2yo.

5454 PLEASUREWOOD HILLS MAIDEN H'CAP — 6f 3y
2:35 (2:36) (Class 5) (0-70,70) 3-Y-0+ £2,264 (£673; £336; £168) Stalls Centre

Form RPR
0203 1 **Ambitious Boy**[13] 4965 3-8-12 **61** ShaneKelly 9 71
(Reg Hollinshead) *hld up in tch in last trio: hdwy over 2f out: rdn to chal and edgd lft over 1f out: rdn to ld 1f out: drvn and hld on fnl 100yds* **10/1**
4662 2 nk **Miakora**[12] 5017 4-8-6 **52** AndreaAtzeni 7 61
(Michael Quinn) *led: rdn 2f out: drvn and hdd 1f out: kpt on u.p but a jst hld fnl f* **16/1**
0003 3 hd **Theresnoneedfordat (IRE)**[13] 4970 3-8-11 **60** (b) WilliamCarson 10 68
(Stuart Williams) *t.k.h: hld up in tch: swtchd rt and hdwy u.p over 1f out: chsd ldng pair 1f out: kpt on u.p fnl 100yds* **12/1**
0553 4 4 1/2 **Thereabouts (USA)**[13] 4969 3-9-5 **68** (b[1]) MartinHarley 6 62
(Marco Botti) *chsd ldrs: rdn 2f out: drvn and outpcd ent fnl f: one pce and no threat to ldrs fnl f* **6/1**[3]
-003 5 nk **Scarabocio**[12] 5017 3-9-2 **65** RobertHavlin 1 58
(Peter Chapple-Hyam) *taken down early: hld up in tch in rr: rdn and hdwy over 1f out: no imp 1f out and wl hld fnl f* **17/2**
205 6 3/4 **Tiberius Claudius (IRE)**[14] 4914 4-9-2 **62** TomQueally 2 53
(George Margarson) *dwlt: swtchd rt sn after s: bhd tl hdwy to chse ldrs after 2f: rdn and nt qckning whn sltly short of room over 1f out: wknd 1f out* **16/1**
0-65 7 2 1/2 **Black Douglas**[27] 4456 3-9-4 **67** (t) MartinLane 5 50
(William Jarvis) *s.i.s: t.k.h: hld up in tch in last trio: shkn up and effrt ent fnl 2f: no imp over 1f out: wknd 1f out* **20/1**
0036 8 1 1/2 **Confluence**[12] 5019 3-8-8 **57** EddieAhern 8 35
(Clifford Lines) *in tch: rdn and wandered u.p 2f out: wknd over 1f out* **33/1**
0-62 9 2 3/4 **Excellent Jem**[47] 3790 3-9-7 **70** [1] MickaelBarzalona 3 39
(Jane Chapple-Hyam) *in tch: effrt and sme hdwy u.p over 2f out: drvn and no hdwy 2f out: wknd over 1f out* **13/8**[1]
000 10 1 3/4 **Blue Dune**[14] 4931 3-8-8 **57** SilvestreDeSousa 4 20
(Mark Johnston) *chsd ldr for 2f: lost pl and dropped to rr over 2f out: bhd over 1f out* **5/1**[2]

1m 14.11s (-0.29) **Going Correction** -0.025s/f (Good)
WFA 3 from 4yo 3lb 10 Ran SP% **115.8**
Speed ratings (Par 103): **100,99,99,93,92 91,88,86,82,80**
Tote Swingers 1&2 £17.30, 2&3 £13.10, 1&3 £17.70 CSF £155.99 CT £1283.51 TOTE £10.30: £3.60, £4.20, £2.60; EX 136.60 Trifecta £322.70 Part won. Pool: £436.17 - 0.10 winning units.
Owner C W Wardle & Mrs J E Wardle **Bred** Cecil W Wardle & Mrs Janet E Wardle **Trained** Upper Longdon, Staffs

FOCUS
A very modest maiden 3yo handicap run in a relatively slow time. The race developed on the stands' side of the main bunch.
Black Douglas Official explanation: jockey said gelding hung badly left
Excellent Jem Official explanation: jockey said colt never travelled

5455 GRANGE HOTEL ORMESBY ST MARGARET H'CAP — 1m 3f 101y
3:05 (3:05) (Class 3) (0-95,85) 3-Y-0 £6,663 (£1,982; £990; £495) Stalls Low

Form RPR
1210 1 **Ruscello (IRE)**[19] 4741 3-9-2 80 WilliamBuick 4 89
(Ed Walker) *stdd after s: hld up in last: c towards centre st: rdn and clsd on ldrs 2f out: led over 1f out: hld hd high but asserted fnl 100yds: styd on* **5/2**[2]
1215 2 1 1/4 **Three Bards (IRE)**[10] 5089 3-8-13 77 SilvestreDeSousa 3 84
(Mark Johnston) *led: styd on far rail st: rdn and hdd over 3f out: stl ev ch whn unbalanced 2f out: battled on wl tl no ex and one pce fnl 100yds* **6/4**[1]
0-14 3 3 1/2 **Inthar (USA)**[51] 3668 3-9-7 85 FrankieDettori 5 86
(Saeed Bin Suroor) *chsd ldr: c to centre st: rdn to ld over 3f out: hdd over 1f out: no ex and wknd ins fnl f* **5/2**[2]
-020 4 nk **Harlestone Wood**[19] 4741 3-9-3 81 TomQueally 1 82
(John Dunlop) *hld up in 3rd: c to centre st: rdn 4f out: drvn and no imp 2f out: outpcd and btn 1f out: plugged on same pce fnl f* **15/2**[3]

2m 27.93s (-0.77) **Going Correction** +0.05s/f (Good) 4 Ran SP% **108.9**
Speed ratings (Par 104): **104,103,100,100**
CSF £6.68 TOTE £3.40; EX 7.90.
Owner Laurence A Bellman **Bred** Ballymacoll Stud Farm Ltd **Trained** Newmarket, Suffolk

FOCUS
A decent 3yo handicap run at a sound pace. Three Bards stuck to the far side in the home straight. The runner-up set the standard.

NOTEBOOK
Ruscello(IRE), whose two previous victories this year were on Polytrack, is a keen sort and pulled hard after being dropped in at the start. He moved upsides travelling smoothly and had only to be shaken up to go clear in the closing stages. He was reckoned unsuited by the track when unplaced at Goodwood on his previous start. (op 9-4)
Three Bards(IRE), a winner three-time this year, with the last two coming from a much lower mark, was left to race alone in the home straight. He never gave up trying but could not match the winner for foot ultimately. (op 15-8)
Inthar(USA), out of a Ribblesdale winner, was stepping up in trip. He looked to be travelling strongly when striking for home over 3f out but had been headed and had no more to give when Frankie Dettori, aboard his only booked ride of the day, dropped his whip just inside the final furlong. (tchd 3-1)
Harlestone Wood, down the field alongside Ruscello at Goodwood, was made to look paceless. (op 6-1)

5456 INJURED JOCKEYS FUND MAIDEN H'CAP — 1m 6f 17y
3:35 (3:35) (Class 5) (0-70,70) 3-Y-0+ £2,264 (£673; £336; £168) Stalls High

Form RPR
2545 1 **Mafeteng**[23] 4626 4-9-5 **61** TomQueally 7 69
(John Dunlop) *hld up in tch in rr: hdwy towards centre 4f out: rdn to ld 2f out: asserted u.p ins fnl f: styd on wl* **11/2**
5565 2 1 3/4 **Bohemian Rhapsody (IRE)**[22] 4648 3-9-2 **70** (p) MartinLane 3 76
(J W Hills) *led and set stdy gallop: rdn over 3f out: drvn and hdd 2f out: battled on wl and ev ch after tl no ex and btn fnl 100yds* **10/1**
6420 3 1/2 **Petaluma**[11] 5044 3-9-2 **70** MartinHarley 6 75
(Mick Channon) *t.k.h: hld up in tch: rdn and effrt over 3f out: chsd ldrs and drvn over 1f out: kpt on same pce fnl f* **11/2**
5405 4 1 3/4 **Authentication**[15] 4883 3-7-12 **52** SilvestreDeSousa 5 54
(Mark Johnston) *t.k.h early: chsd ldrs: rdn to chse ldr over 3f out tl 2f out: one pce fr over 1f out* **5/2**[1]
4353 5 11 **Idyllic Star (IRE)**[8] 5154 3-8-12 **66** (p) DarryllHolland 2 53
(J S Moore) *t.k.h: rdn and effrt over 3f out: wknd u.p over 1f out* **9/2**[3]
060 6 hd **Regal Diva**[17] 4791 4-9-3 **59** ShaneKelly 1 46
(Reg Hollinshead) *t.k.h: hld up in tch: effrt on far rail over 3f out: drvn and no imp 2f out: wknd over 1f out* **28/1**
0253 7 1 **Finity Run (GER)**[46] 3813 3-9-2 **70** MircoDemuro 4 55
(Mark Johnston) *chsd ldr tl over 3f out: sn struggling u.p: bhd over 1f out* **7/2**[2]

3m 7.63s (0.03) **Going Correction** +0.05s/f (Good)
WFA 3 from 4yo 12lb 7 Ran SP% **112.3**
Speed ratings (Par 103): **101,100,99,98,92 92,91**
Tote Swingers 1&2 £5.30, 2&3 £8.60, 1&3 £3.50 CSF £54.56 TOTE £8.10: £2.40, £10.10; EX 59.70.
Owner Mrs Jane Poulter **Bred** Mrs J A M Poulter **Trained** Arundel, W Sussex
■ Stewards' Enquiry : Tom Queally caution: careless riding.

FOCUS
This was run at a steady pace until the final 4f. Modest form with the winner rated back to her old best.

5457 BANHAM POULTRY H'CAP — 7f 3y
4:05 (4:06) (Class 4) (0-80,77) 3-Y-0+ £4,075 (£1,212; £606; £303) Stalls Centre

Form RPR
-302 1 **Afkar (IRE)**[6] 5234 4-9-1 **66** (b) SilvestreDeSousa 7 77
(Clive Brittain) *mde all: set stdy gallop tl rdn and qckmd 2f out: clr ins fnl f: r.o wl: eased cl home* **7/2**[2]
4506 2 1 1/2 **Rough Rock (IRE)**[5] 5269 7-9-6 **71** AndreaAtzeni 6 77
(Chris Dwyer) *hld up in tch: rdn and effrt ent fnl 2f: drvn and chsd clr wnr jst ins fnl f: kpt on but no real imp* **5/1**[3]

6014 **3** *1* **Mrs Greeley**[18] 4772 4 -9-11**76**........ WilliamCarson 4 79
(Eve Johnson Houghton) *stdd s: hld up in tch in rr: rdn and effrt over 1f out: kpt on u.p ins fnl f: nvr gng pce to threaten wnr* **11/4**[1]

3040 **4** *nse* **Aldermoor (USA)**[5] 5269 6 -9-4**76**........ ThomasBrown(7) 5 79
(Stuart Williams) *chsd wnr tl 4f out: chsd wnr again 3f out: rdn ent fnl 2f: styd on same pce fr over 1f out: lost 2 pls ins fnl f* **10/1**

030 **5** *3/4* **Jonnie Skull (IRE)**[7] 5322 6 -8-1**59**........(vt) DannyBrock(7) 1 60
(Phil McEntee) *t.k.h: stdd s: hld up towards rr: rdn ent fnl 2f: drvn over 1f out: swtchd rt and kpt on ins fnl f: no threat to wnr* **25/1**

-315 **6** *2* **Forks**[18] 4775 5 -9-7**72**........ MickaelBarzalona 3 68
(Jane Chapple-Hyam) *chsd ldrs: wnt 2nd 4f out tl 3f out: wknd u.p ent fnl f* **7/2**[2]

-060 **7** *35* **Imelda Mayhem**[47] 3785 3 -9-7**77**........(p) DarrylHolland 2
(J S Moore) *hld up in tch: rdn and effrt over 2f out: no imp and btn whn rdr looking down and eased fr over 1f out* **15/2**

1m 26.88s (0.28) **Going Correction** -0.025s/f (Good)
WFA 3 from 4yo+ 5lb **7**Ran SP% **112.5**
Speed ratings (Par 105): **97,95,94,94,93 90,50**
Tote Swingers 1&2 £3.10, 2&3 £2.40, 1&3 £2.60 CSF £20.46 TOTE £4.20 : £1.60 , £3.80 ; EX 14.60.
Owner C E Brittain **Bred** Jaykayenn Syndicate **Trained** Newmarket, Suffolk

FOCUS
A fine front-running ride by Silvestre de Sousa aboard a long-standing maiden. The winner is still potentially on a good mark.
Imelda Mayhem Official explanation: trainer said filly was in season

5458 HOLIDAY ON NORFOLK BROADS H'CAP 7f 3y
4:35 (4:37) (Class 6) (0-60,60) 3-Y-O **£1,617** (£481; £240 ; £120 **Stalls** Centre

Form RPR
-000 **1** **Mount Mayday (IRE)**[73] 2927 3 -8-12**51**........(t) MickaelBarzalona 10 63
(Stuart Williams) *chsd ldr tl led over 2f out: rdn clr 2f out: in command after and r.o wl: readily* **15/2**

0041 **2** *4* **Indiana Guest (IRE)**[7] 5215 3 -9-2**55** 6ex........(b) TomQueally 11 56
(George Margarson) *hld up in tch in midfield: effrt u.p to chse ldrs 2f out: chsd clr wnr and hrd drvn jst over 1f out: no imp* **4/1**[2]

-032 **3** *1/2* **Roman Myst (IRE)**[5] 5263 3 -9-7**60**........ SilvestreDeSousa 4 60+
(Sylvester Kirk) *chsd ldrs: rdn 3f out: drvn and chsd clr wnr over 2f out: no imp: 3rd and kpt on same pce fnl f* **7/2**[1]

00-0 **4** *3* **Silent Mistress**[61] 3312 3 -8-7**46** oh1........ JamieMackay 8 38
(J R Jenkins) *stdd s: t.k.h: hld up in rr: sme hdwy u.p over 1f out: kpt on but no threat to ldrs fnl f* **40/1**

0005 **5** *1/2* **Boragh Waters (IRE)**[9] 4734 3 -8-7**46** oh1........(t) MartinLane 5 36
(Brian Meehan) *hld up in last trio: hdwy u.p over 1f out: kpt on fnl f: nvr trbld ldrs* **33/1**

0506 **6** *nk* **Tenderly Place**[7] 5215 3 -8-7**46** oh1........(t) AndreaAtzeni 3 36
(William Knight) *taken down early: t.k.h: hld up in tch in midfield: rdn and little rspnse over 2f out: wl hld and one pce fr over 1f out* **16/1**

4040 **7** *2* **Sleepy Lucy**[12] 5014 3 -8-4**46** oh1........ DeclanCannon(3) 12 30
(Richard Guest) *t.k.h: hld up in tch: hdwy to chse ldrs and rdn over 2f out: btn over 1f out: wknd fnl f* **20/1**

0603 **8** *2 3/4* **Desert Red (IRE)**[7] 5216 3 -8-7**46** oh1........(b) JimmyQuinn 9 23
(Phil McEntee) *stdd s: t.k.h: hld up in midfield: lost pl and bhd whn swtchd rt and drvn 2f out: no prog and wknd over 1f out* **12/1**

0002 **9** *6* **Sanad (IRE)**[7] 5216 3 -9-4**57**........(p) WilliamCarson 7 18
(Anthony Carson) *chsd ldrs: rdn and no rspnse over 2f out: wknd over 1f out: wl btn and eased ins fnl f* **7/2**[1]

-605 **10** *11* **Ottavino (IRE)**[13] 4970 3 -8-2**46** oh1 ow2........ LewisWalsh(7) 1
(Jane Chapple-Hyam) *led tl over 2f out: wknd qckly wl over 1f out: wl bhd fnl f* **50/1**

3-00 **11** *3 1/4* **Sweet Ophelia**[26] 4516 3 -9-7**60**........ TedDurcan 2
(George Baker) *in tch: rdn and no rspnse over 3f out: sn bhd: eased ins fnl f: t.o* **9/2**[3]

1m 26.75s (0.15) **Going Correction** -0.025s/f (Good) **11**Ran SP% **120.1**
Speed ratings (Par 98): **98,93,92,89,88 88,86,83,76,63 59**
Tote Swingers 1&2 £9.50, 2&3 £2.50, 1&3 £8.90 CSF £37.24 CT £128.81 TOTE £8.20 : £2.50 , £1.60, £1.50 ; EX 59.10 Trifecta £152.70 Pool: £1021.61 - 4.95 winning units.
Owner Paul W Stevens **Bred** Tullamaine Castle Stud **Trained** Newmarket, Suffolk

FOCUS
A rock-bottom handicap but a clear-cut winner. The race developed on the stands' side of the main bunch. The winner's first real sound form.
Mount Mayday (IRE) Official explanation: trainer said, regarding apparent improvement in form, that this was the gelding's first run in a handicap, raced in a more settled manner and benefited from the firmer surface.

5459 BBC RADIO NORFOLK APPRENTICE TRAINING SERIES H'CAP (PART OF THE RACING EXCELLENCE INITIATIVE) 1m 3y
5:05 (5:07) (Class 6) (0-60,59) 3-Y-O+ **£1,617** (£481; £240 ; £120 **Stalls** Centre

Form RPR
-055 **1** **Siberian Belle (IRE)**[22] 4643 3 -8-6**45**........(p) LauraBarry 4 52
(Richard Fahey) *in tch: pushed along and hdwy to chse ldrs 4f out: led over 2f out: rn green ins fnl f: styd on to assert fnl 100yds: rdn out* **11/2**[3]

0150 **2** *1 3/4* **Percythepinto (IRE)**[12] 4986 3 -9-0**56**........(t) TimClark(3) 7 59
(George Baker) *stdd s: hld up in rr: hdwy over 3f out: rdn and ev ch 2f out: no ex and btn fnl 100yds* **9/1**

4303 **3** *5* **Putin (IRE)**[8] 5148 4 -8-9**47**........(bt) SiobhanMiller(5) 2 40
(Phil McEntee) *chsd ldrs: rdn over 2f out: no ex ent fnl f: wknd fnl 150yds* **9/1**

0633 **4** *2 1/4* **Kwik Time**[10] 5081 4 -8-12**45**........(t) JasonHart 6 32
(Robin Bastiman) *led tl over 5f out: chsd ldr tl led again over 3f out tl over 2f out: sn struggling: 4th and wl hld over 1f out* **7/2**[2]

0151 **5** *5* **Archina (IRE)**[51] 3665 3 -9-6**59**........ ThomasBrown 3 34
(Chris Wall) *hld up in tch: rdn over 3f out: struggling u.p over 2f out: wknd 2f out* **2/1**[1]

3003 **6** *13* **Green Mountain (IRE)**[20] 4705 3 -8-7**46**........(t) ShirleyTeasdale 1
(Philip McBride) *hld up on rr: rdn over 3f out: lost tch and wandering wl over 2f out* **12/1**

5602 **7** *1 1/4* **Song Of Joy (IRE)**[7] 5018 3 -8-6**50**........ LouisSteward(5) 9
(Paul D'Arcy) *in tch: lost pl and rdn over 3f out: lost tch wl over 2f out* **8/1**

4000 **8** *1 1/4* **Crocodile Bay (IRE)**[2] 5015 9 -8-12**45**........(p) NoraLooby 5
(Richard Guest) *t.k.h: chsd ldr tl led over 5f out: hdd over 3f out: dropped out rapidly over 2f out: wl bhd over 1f out* **28/1**

200 **9** *1 1/2* **Danceyourselfdizzy (IRE)**[7] 5216 4 -8-12**45**........ DannyBrock 8
(Phil McEntee) *c to r on stands' rail in tch in midfield: struggling u.p 1/2-way: lost tch over 2f out* **33/1**

1m 40.03s (-0.57) **Going Correction** -0.025s/f (Good)
WFA 3 from 4yo+ 6lb **9**Ran SP% **116.1**
Speed ratings (Par 101): **101,99,94,92,87 74,72,71,70**
Tote Swingers 1&2 £8.60, 2&3 £9.20, 1&3 £9.30 CSF £54.15 CT £442.53 TOTE £5.00 : £1.40 , £1.70, £2.20 ; EX 83.80 Trifecta £635.30 Part won. Pool of £858.59 - 0.64 winning units.
Owner Wildcard Racing Syndicate X1 **Bred** Alma Partnership **Trained** Musley Bank, N Yorks

FOCUS
A low-grade handicap confined to apprentices. The first pair were clear but this is not a race to be positive about.
Siberian Belle (IRE) Official explanation: trainer's rep said filly benefited from wearing the first-time cheek pieces.
Crocodile Bay (IRE) Official explanation: jockey said gelding ran too freely
T/Plt: £922.50 to a £1 stake. Pool of £57109.87 - 45.19 winning tickets. T/Qpdt: £85.40 to a £1 stake. Pool of £3948.60- 34.20 wi. tickets SP 5460a -5470a (Foreign Racing) See RI

[5398] DEAUVILLE (R-H)
Tuesday, August 21
OFFICIAL GOING: Turf: good; fibresand: standard

5471a CRITERIUM DU FONDS EUROPEEN DE L'ELEVAGE (LISTED RACE) (2YO) (TURF) 1m (R)
1:50 (12:00) 2-Y-O **£50,833** (£20,333; £15,250 ; £10,166 ; £5,083)

RPR
1 **Meneas (FR)**[48] 2 -8-11**0**........ OlivierPeslier 11 100
(C Laffon-Parias, France) **41/10**[3]

2 *1 1/2* **Morandi (FR)**[67] 2 -8-11**0**........ ChristopheSoumillon 6 97
(J-C Rouget, France) **23/10**[1]

3 *3/4* **Local Lover (FR)**[13] 2 -8-11**0**........ MaximeGuyon 3 95
(H-A Pantall, France) **11/1**

4 *snk* **Kensea (FR)**[18] 2 -8-8**0**........ FabriceVeron 9 91
(H-A Pantall, France) **27/1**

5 *1/2* **Meri Shika (FR)**[25] 2 -8-8**0**........ ThierryJarnet 5 90
(J Bertran De Balanda, France) **36/1**

6 *nk* **Sir Patrick Moore (FR)**[38] 4118 2 -8-11**0**........ IoritzMendizabal 10 93
(Harry Dunlop) *broke fast: sn led: hdd 250yds out: r.o u.p: no ex fnl 100yds* **7/2**[2]

7 *3/4* **Bottoms Up (IRE)**[22] 2 -8-11**0**........ GeraldMosse 1 91
(Robert Collet, France) **16/1**

8 *snk* **Northern Star (IRE)**[12] 4995 2 -8-8**0**........ RichardKingscote 2 88
(Tom Dascombe) *broke wl: settled in 2nd on ins: rdn over 1 1/2f out: no ex: styd on one pce fnl f* **44/1**

9 *1/2* **Gengis (FR)**[11] 2 -8-11**0**........ StephanePasquier 7 89
(G Doleuze, France) **9/1**

10 *1 1/4* **Windsea (IRE)**[24] 2 -8-11**0**........ GregoryBenoist 4 87
(Y Barberot, France) **33/1**

11 **Courcy (FR)**[24] 2 -8-11**0**........ Christophe-PatriceLemaire 8
(J-C Rouget, France) **9/1**

1m 43.0s (2.20) **11**Ran SP% **117.8**
WIN (incl. 1 euro stake): 5.10. PLACES: 1.90, 1.60, 2.80. DF: 9.70. SF: 23.90
Owner Leonidas Marinopoulos **Bred** Janus Bloodstock Inc & Stilvi Compania Financiera **Trained** Chantilly, France

NOTEBOOK
Sir Patrick Moore (FR) found the ground a little quicker than ideal according to his trainer.

5472a PRIX DE LA NONETTE - SHADWELL (GROUP 2) (3YO FILLIES) (TURF) 1m 2f
2:20 (12:00) 3-Y-O **£61,750** (£23,833; £11,375 ; £7,583 ; £3,791)

RPR
1 **Romantica**[24] 4616 3 -9-0**0**........ MaximeGuyon 5 110
(A Fabre, France) *settled 5th: rdn 2f out: qcknd wl ent fnl 1 1/2f: led 1f out: r.o wl: wnt clr fnl 100yds: comf* **37/10**[2]

2 *1 1/2* **Leaupartie (IRE)**[24] 4616 3 -9-0**0**........ GregoryBenoist 2 107
(F Chappet, France) *settled 4th on ins: rdn 1 1/2f out: r.o wl to go 2nd 1f out: styd on wl u.p to jst hold pl cl home* **7/1**[3]

3 *snk* **Trois Lunes (FR)**[55] 3203 3 -9-0**0**........ Francois-XavierBertras 1 107
(F Rohaut, France) *settled in 2nd: rdn 2f out: r.o wl ent fnl 300yds: styd on wl u.p fnl f: wnt 3rd fnl 50yds: jst missed 2nd cl home* **12/1**

4 *nk* **Dark Orchid (USA)**[24] 4616 3 -9-0**0**........ Pierre-CharlesBoudot 3 106
(A Fabre, France) *hld up towards rr: rdn over 1 1/2f out: r.o wl ent fnl f: fin wl: nt rch ldrs: clst at fin* **23/1**

5 *hd* **Ridasiyna (FR)**[51] 3682 3 -9-0**0**........ Christophe-PatriceLemaire 7 106
(M Delzangles, France) *followed pcemaker fr s: then relegated to 3rd after 2f: rdn early in st: led 1 1/2f out: no ex ent fnl f: hdd 1f out: wknd 100yds out* **3/5**[1]

6 *2* **Chutney Flight (FR)**[31] 4361 3 -9-0**0**........ ArnaudBourgeais 4 102
(N Leenders, France) *missed break: hld up at rr: mde prog on outside 1 1/2f out: no ex: styd on one pce fnl 150yds* **23/1**

7 *8* **Parisham (FR)**[29] 3 -9-0**0**........(b) ThierryJarnet 6 86
(M Delzangles, France) *led fr s: rdn 2 1/2f out: no ex: sn wknd* **20/1**

2m 6.2s (-4.00) **7**Ran SP% **117.1**
WIN (incl. 1 euro stake): 4.70. PLACES: 2.50, 2.90. SF: 15.90
Owner K Abdulla **Bred** Juddmonte Farms Ltd **Trained** Chantilly, France

NOTEBOOK
Romantica proved well suited by the gallop set by Ridasiyna's pacemaker and won quite comfortably in the end, reversing previous form with Leaupartie and Ridasiyna in the process. She's progressive, ought to get further, and the Prix Vermeille was mentioned as her likely target.
Leaupartie(IRE), winner of the Group 3 Prix de Psyche last time out when having Romantica half a length back in second, was keeping on well at the finish but didn't have the winner's acceleration.
Ridasiyna(FR) was disappointing, her rider claiming that she didn't relax at all and had nothing left in the final 100 metres.

5473a PRIX DE BONNEBOSQ - ETALON SAKHEE (CLAIMER) (3YO) (FIBRESAND) 6f 110y
3:55 (12:00) 3-Y-O **£11,250** (£4,500; £3,375 ; £2,250 ; £1,125)

RPR
1 **Saint Louet (FR)**[21] 3 -8-6**0**........(b) AntoineCoutier(5) 4 94
(F Chappet, France) **136/10**

2 1 1/4 **Larga Charla (IRE)**[16] 3-9-2 0....................(b) UmbertoRispoli 15 96
(G Botti, Italy) **68/10**[3]
3 2 **Happy Sun Percy**[21] 3-8-11 0.................... MaximeGuyon 2 85
(G Doleuze, France) **12/1**
4 snk **Dampierre**[14] 3-8-11 0.................... ThierryThulliez 11 85
(A De Mieulle, France) **14/1**
5 hd **Noble Fantasy (GER)**[332] 6371 3-8-8 0....................(b) TheoBachelot 13 81
(Mario Hofer, Germany) **24/1**
6 1 **Boots And Spurs**[41] 3952 3-8-11 0....................(b) JulienAuge 7 81
(Mrs K Burke) *hld up towards rr: mde gd prog ent fnl f: fin wl: nt rch ldrs* **11/1**
7 snk **Mephala (FR)**[127] 3-8-3 0.................... MarcLerner(5) 9 78
(C Baillet, France) **22/1**
8 shd **That's The Spirit (FR)**[90] 3-8-11 0.................... OlivierPeslier 14 80
(P Bary, France) **5/1**[1]
9 2 **Star Seed (FR)**[28] 3-8-13 0.................... EddyHardouin(3) 12 80
(M Rolland, France) **19/1**
10 nse **Louvain (FR)**[16] 3-9-4 0....................(p) ChristopheSoumillon 3 81
(P Demercastel, France) **73/10**
0 **Whip My Heart (IRE)**[25] 3-8-11 0....................(b) GeraldMosse 5
(U Suter, France) **28/1**
0 **Antalia (FR)**[25] 3-8-8 0.................... IoritzMendizabal 8
(J-C Rouget, France) **13/2**[2]
0 **Fuscano (GER)**[48] 3-8-11 0....................(p) JohanVictoire 16
(W Hickst, Germany) **10/1**
0 **Hamamba (USA)**[166] 3-8-8 0....................(p) WilliamsSaraiva 1
(Mme J Bidgood, France) **50/1**
0 **Garajonay (FR)**[151] 3-9-2 0.................... StephanePasquier 10
(F Rodriguez Puertas, Spain) **22/1**
0 **Le Maltais (FR)** 3-8-8 0....................(p) AnthonyCaramanolis(3) 6
(P Azzopardi, France) **78/1**

1m 19.8s (79.80) **16** Ran SP% **117.9**
WIN (incl. 1 euro stake): 14.60. PLACES: 4.60, 3.10, 4.60. DF: 58.60. SF: 147.70.
Owner Gerard Augustin-Normand **Bred** Gerard Samain **Trained** France

5403 KEMPTON (A.W) (R-H)
Wednesday, August 22

OFFICIAL GOING: Standard to slow
Wind: Moderate across Weather: Sunny getting dark

5474 SCOTT MILLS & STOOSHE LIVE 07.09.12 FILLIES' H'CAP 1m 3f (P)
5:50 (5:50) (Class 4) (0-85,82) 3-Y-0+ **£4,075** (£1,212; £606; £303) **Stalls** Low

Form RPR
0321 1 **Gallipot**[14] 4945 3-9-5 82.................... RobertHavlin 9 100
(John Gosden) *led 1f: trckd ldr: led 5f out: drvn over 2f out: hrd pressed ins fnl f: kpt on u.p and a doing enough* **1/1**[1]
032 2 1/2 **Bedazzled**[18] 4791 3-8-13 76....................[1] HayleyTurner 7 93
(James Fanshawe) *chsd ldrs: wnt 2nd over 3f out: drvn 2f out: pressed wnr ins fnl f but nvr quite upsides: nt qckn fnl 100yds but wl clr of 3rd* **6/1**[2]
0-10 3 9 **Livia's Dream (IRE)**[32] 4325 3-8-10 73.................... MartinLane 4 74
(Ed Walker) *in rr: hdwy over 3f out: drvn and styd on fnl 2f to take wl hld 3rd fnl f* **9/1**[3]
-143 4 9 **Westwiththenight (IRE)**[9] 5163 3-9-2 79.................... ChrisCatlin 3 64
(William Haggas) *hld up in rr: stdy hdwy to trck ldrs 3f out: rdn to take mod 3rd over 2f out: nvr any ch w ldng duo and wknd into poor 4th over 1f out* **6/1**[2]
2542 5 6 **Kathleen Frances**[41] 3997 5-9-9 77.................... DarryllHolland 2 51
(Mark H Tompkins) *rdn 4f out: mod hdwy over 2f out: sn wknd* **14/1**
5023 6 8 **Reset City**[15] 4905 6-8-11 65....................(t) SilvestreDeSousa 8 25
(Ian Williams) *chsd ldrs: rdn 4f out: wknd u.p over 2f out* **14/1**
-041 7 6 **Hayaku (USA)**[32] 4335 4-9-10 78....................(t) RichardKingscote 1 27
(Ralph Beckett) *led after 1f: hdd 5f out: sn rdn: wknd ins fnl 3f* **14/1**
000 8 10 **Zaina (IRE)**[25] 4608 3-9-2 82....................(p) DominicFox(3) 6
(Gerard Butler) *in tch: rdn 4f out: wknd over 3f out* **10/1**

2m 18.99s (-2.91) **Going Correction** +0.025s/f (Slow)
WFA 3 from 4yo+ 9lb **8** Ran SP% **117.7**
Speed ratings (Par 102): **111,110,104,97,93 87,83,75**
Tote Swingers: 1&2 £2.70, 1&3 £3.90, 2&3 £4.00 CSF £7.74 CT £36.52 TOTE £2.10: £1.02, £3.70, £2.00; EX 8.80 Trifecta £103.00 Pool: £465.05 - 3.34 winning units..
Owner Lady Rothschild **Bred** Kincorth Investments Inc **Trained** Newmarket, Suffolk
■ Stewards' Enquiry : Hayley Turner two-day ban: used whip above permitted level (Sep 5-6)

FOCUS
A decent Polytrack race, but dominated by the first two, both of whom look progressive. The pace was good, which accentuated their superiority. Another step up from the winer, who has really got her act together.
Reset City Official explanation: jockey said mare had no more to give

5475 WIN BIG WITH BETDAQ MULTIPLES NURSERY 6f (P)
6:20 (6:20) (Class 5) (0-75,75) 2-Y-0 **£2,264** (£673; £336; £168) **Stalls** Low

Form RPR
0226 1 **Ronaldinho (IRE)**[17] 4847 2-9-3 71.................... PatDobbs 6 80
(Richard Hannon) *trckd ldrs: drvn to take 2nd over 1f out: chal ins fnl f: led fnl 150yds: sn drew clr: readily* **8/1**
241 2 3 **Jumeirah Moon**[13] 5010 2-9-3 71.................... HayleyTurner 2 71
(David Simcock) *in rr: hdwy over 2f out: styd on wl fnl f to takle 2nd last stride but no ch w wnr* **7/4**[1]
010 3 nse **Secret Sign**[20] 4736 2-9-5 73....................(v[1]) MartinLane 5 73
(Brian Meehan) *trckd ldr: led 3f out: rdn 2f out: jnd 1f out: hdd fnl 150yds: sn btn: lost 2nd last stride* **9/2**[2]
063 4 2 **Secretori**[37] 4149 2-8-12 66.................... LiamKeniry 8 60
(Matthew Salaman) *chsd ldrs: rdn and styd on same pce fnl 2f* **20/1**
0236 5 3/4 **Hardy Red (IRE)**[29] 4419 2-9-5 73.................... AdamKirby 9 65
(Jamie Osborne) *in tch: rdn and one pce appr fnl 2f: styd on again u.p ins fnl f* **12/1**
0040 6 1 1/4 **Our Golden Girl**[8] 5202 2-8-2 56.................... DavidProbert 4 44
(Mark Usher) *in rr: rdn along fr 3f out: mod prog fnl f* **20/1**
145 7 hd **Megamunch (IRE)**[11] 5109 2-9-7 75.................... TomEaves 3 62
(Linda Stubbs) *t.k.h in rr: rdn and stl last over 2f out: kpt on fnl f* **10/1**
0001 8 2 **Whitford (IRE)**[9] 5161 2-8-7 61 6ex.................... AndreaAtzeni 1 42
(Chris Dwyer) *sn led: hdd and rdn 3f out: wknd over 1f out* **5/1**[3]
0203 9 1/2 **Secret Symphony**[16] 4873 2-9-7 75....................(t) JimmyFortune 7 55
(Sylvester Kirk) *bmpd 4f out: rdn and effrt on outside over 2f out: nvr gng pce to rch ldrs* **14/1**

1m 14.1s (1.00) **Going Correction** +0.025s/f (Slow) **9** Ran SP% **115.3**
Speed ratings (Par 94): **94,90,89,87,86 84,84,81,81**
Tote Swingers: 1&2 £3.90, 1&3 £3.50, 2&3 £2.10 CSF £22.35 CT £71.02 TOTE £7.30: £2.30, £1.10, £2.70; EX 31.60 Trifecta £111.40 Pool: £419.87 - 2.78 winning units..
Owner Macdonald,Wright,Creed,Smith & Jiggins **Bred** J Fallon **Trained** East Everleigh, Wilts

FOCUS
Not a bad nursery, with some fair juvenile form on show. The pace was testing, which suited the winner, but it did no favours to the pair who set it. The second and third offer a good guide to the form.

NOTEBOOK
Ronaldinho(IRE) had looked useful on turf but this switch to Polytrack brought out the best in him and he should go on from here. He didn't appear to stay 7f last time, and the drop back to sprinting paid dividends, but the manner of his success suggested that the extra furlong shouldn't be a problem after all. (op 10-1)
Jumeirah Moon has run well at 6f and 7f, and on turf, Fibresand and Polytrack, so he is nothing if not versatile. This mark looks stiff enough, but he should improve again. (tchd 6-4 and 15-8)
Secret Sign ran with credit on this Polytrack debut, but the first-time visor made him do too much too early. In the circumstances he did well to hang on for third. (op 4-1)
Secretori ran reasonably well on this AW debut but needs to improve a bit to win off this opening handicap mark.
Hardy Red(IRE), stepped up from 5f, just seemed to have too much weight on this nursery debut. (op 11-1 tchd 10-1)
Our Golden Girl would be more at home at 7f in lesser company. (op 28-1)
Whitford(IRE) looked suited by 7f last time, so rattling along in front at 6f pace wasn't ideal. (op 6-1 tchd 13-2)

5476 BETDAQ MOBILE APPS/BRITISH STALLION STUDS EBF MAIDEN STKS 7f (P)
6:50 (6:52) (Class 5) 2-Y-0 **£3,169** (£943; £471; £235) **Stalls** Low

Form RPR
40 1 **Royal Prize**[47] 3824 2-9-3 0.................... RichardKingscote 6 75
(Ralph Beckett) *in tch: hdwy over 2f out: chsd ldr over 1f out: drvn to ld ins fnl f: pushed out* **5/1**[2]
0 2 1 1/4 **Mission Approved**[61] 3346 2-9-3 0.................... RichardMullen 9 72
(Sir Michael Stoute) *in tch: hdwy to chse ldr ins fnl 3f: drvn to ld over 1f out: hdd ins fnl f: sn outpcd by wnr but styd clr of 3rd* **11/10**[1]
0 3 4 **Keep Calm**[22] 4688 2-9-3 0.................... PatDobbs 2 62
(Richard Hannon) *chsd ldrs: disp 2nd and rdn over 3f out: styd on for one pce 3rd appr fnl f* **7/1**[3]
0 4 7 **Alcaeus**[15] 4917 2-9-3 0.................... LukeMorris 1 43+
(Sir Mark Prescott Bt) *in rr: rdn: edgd lft and green over 2f out: mod prog fnl f* **16/1**
5 3/4 **Atalanta Bay (IRE)** 2-8-12 0.................... HayleyTurner 4 36+
(Marcus Tregoning) *s.i.s: in rr and green: drvn over 2f out: mod prog fnl f* **17/2**
6 1 1/4 **Flying Tempo** 2-9-3 0.................... JackMitchell 7 38
(Ed Dunlop) *sn rdn and green in rr: mod prog fnl f* **20/1**
6 7 1 **Dark Justice (IRE)**[26] 4525 2-8-12 0.................... RobertHavlin 8 31
(Tim Pitt) *s.i.s: sn led: 5 l clr over 3f out: fading fr 2f out: hdd over 1f out and wknd rapidly* **8/1**
8 14 **Last Chance Ranch** 2-9-3 0.................... DaneO'Neill 11
(Derek Shaw) *s.i.s: sn in tch: rdn and wknd 3f out* **33/1**
9 2 3/4 **Aphrodite's Dream** 2-8-12 0.................... SilvestreDeSousa 3
(Derek Shaw) *t.k.h: chsd ldr to 3f out: wknd qckly* **16/1**

1m 27.91s (1.91) **Going Correction** +0.025s/f (Slow) **9** Ran SP% **117.9**
Speed ratings (Par 94): **90,88,84,76,75 73,72,56,53**
Tote Swingers: 1&2 £2.30, 1&3 £5.20, 2&3 £2.50 CSF £11.09 TOTE £5.20: £1.30, £1.02, £2.80; EX 12.40 Trifecta £126.30 Pool: £450.62 - 2.64 winning units..
Owner J C Smith **Bred** Littleton Stud **Trained** Kimpton, Hants

FOCUS
A strongly-run maiden with some late developers, many of whom will come into their own over longer trips when they get the opportunity. The pace was strong. Improved form from the winner.

NOTEBOOK
Royal Prize found this more to his liking than the two Sandown maidens he had contested previously. He handled the Polytrack well and a greater test of stamina is certain to suit him later in his career. (op 6-1)
Mission Approved stepped up on his turf debut with a solid performance that suggests he can win a similar race. Well supported here, he is likely to improve again. (op 4-5)
Keep Calm, last of 17 on his debut, on turf, put that behind him with a creditable AW debut. 7f suits him better than 6f, and he should be placed to win in the coming months. (tchd 15-2)
Alcaeus is one to keep an eye on, particularly when he gets his handicap mark after one more run. He will stay much further as he matures. (op 25-1)
Atalanta Bay(IRE), a 10,000euros half-sister to a 1m7f winner, needed the experience and looks a late-season nursery sort. (op 14-1)
Flying Tempo will be sharper for the outing but probably needs at least 1m. (tchd 16-1)
Dark Justice(IRE) gave herself no chance by going off so fast. (op 10-1 tchd 11-1)

5477 BACK OR LAY AT BETDAQ.COM MEDIAN AUCTION MAIDEN STKS 1m 4f (P)
7:20 (7:23) (Class 6) 3-5-Y-0 **£1,617** (£481; £240; £120) **Stalls** Centre

Form RPR
0-02 1 **Hesperides**[27] 4486 3-8-9 61.................... DavidProbert 6 76
(Harry Dunlop) *mde virtually all: drvn and qcknd fr 3f out: styd on wl fnl 2f: unchal* **7/1**[2]
22 2 3 3/4 **Altaria**[9] 5154 3-8-9 0.................... PatDobbs 1 70
(Amanda Perrett) *trckd ldrs: wnt 2nd over 3f out: rdn and wandered over 2f out: no ch of getting to wnr after* **1/6**[1]
U050 3 23 **Who Loves Ya Baby**[60] 3400 4-9-10 45.................... AdamKirby 5 38
(Peter Charalambous) *chsd wnr after 3f: riddnand dropped to 3rd over 3f out: sn no ch: hld on all out for distant 3rd* **16/1**[3]
4 1/2 **Aunt Ger (IRE)** 3-8-2 0.................... NoelGarbutt(7) 4 32
(Hugo Palmer) *racd in 4th and drvn along fr 6f out: styd on u.p to disp distant 3rd fnl f* **33/1**

2m 34.91s (0.41) **Going Correction** +0.025s/f (Slow)
WFA 3 from 4yo 10lb **4** Ran SP% **107.0**
Speed ratings (Par 101): **99,96,81,80**
CSF £8.98 TOTE £8.10; EX 7.10.
Owner Bluehills Racing Limited **Bred** Hesmonds Stud Ltd **Trained** Lambourn, Berks

FOCUS
This was a weakly contested maiden with a shock result. Unconvincing form, although the winner was entitled to improve.

5478 BETDAQ CASINO GAMES MEDIAN AUCTION MAIDEN STKS 1m (P)
7:50 (7:51) (Class 6) 2-Y-O **£1,617** (£481; £240; £120) **Stalls** Low

Form RPR

6 **1** **Red Runaway**[26] 4555 2-9-3 0 HayleyTurner 7 77+
(Ed Dunlop) *trckd ldr: wnt 2nd 2f out: drvn and styd on to ld fnl 120yds: r.o strly* **7/2**[2]

0 **2** 2½ **Anjuna Beach (USA)**[18] 4803 2-9-3 0 AdamKirby 1 71
(Gary Moore) *led: rdn over 3f out: kpt on: hdd and one pce fnl 120yds* **11/4**[1]

3 4½ **Entrapping** 2-9-3 0 PatDobbs 5 61+
(Richard Hannon) *s.i.s: in rr: pushed along over 2f out: hdwy appr fnl f: styd on fnl 120yds to take wl-hld 3rd last stride* **11/1**[3]

03 **4** nse **Age Of Bronze**[28] 4462 2-9-3 0 SeanLevey 2 61
(Richard Hannon) *chsd ldr until rdn 3f out: one pce fnl 2f: kpt on to dispute wl 3rd clsng stages* **11/1**[3]

52 **5** nk **Choral Prince (IRE)**[23] 4658 2-9-3 0 MartinDwyer 6 60
(Mike Murphy) *in tch: rdn over 2f out: styd on to dispute wl hld 3rd fnl 120yds* **7/2**[2]

6 ¾ **Le Talisman (IRE)** 2-9-3 0 SilvestreDeSousa 8 58
(Mahmood Al Zarooni) *chsd ldrs in 3rd: rdn wl over 2f out: styd on same pce fnl f* **7/2**[2]

7 2¼ **Black Eyed Girl (IRE)** 2-8-12 0 LiamKeniry 4 48
(J S Moore) *s.i.s: in rr: effrt on outer over 2f out: nvr gng pce to get into contention and sn btn* **20/1**

1m 40.9s (1.10) **Going Correction** +0.025s/f (Slow) **7** Ran SP% **114.8**
Speed ratings (Par 92): **95,92,88,87,87 86,84**
Tote Swingers: 1&2 £3.50, 1&3 £5.60, 2&3 £6.80 CSF £13.68 TOTE £4.50: £2.20, £2.20; EX 23.80 Trifecta £250.10 Part won. Pool: £338.09 - 0.39 winning units..
Owner R J Arculli **Bred** Lofts Hall, M Philipson & Cheveley Park **Trained** Newmarket, Suffolk

FOCUS
The presence of some top stables and lack of experience among the runners made this an interesting maiden, although it wouldn't be wise to get too carried away by it. The winner should build on this.

NOTEBOOK
Red Runaway was green on his debut at York and this drop in grade did the trick. There is some stamina in the family and this 50,000gns son of Medicean has long-term prospects. (op 9-2)
Anjuna Beach(USA), not beaten far on his debut, took the switch to Polytrack in his stride. A $40,000 yearling, he should win a similar event. (op 10-3 tchd 7-2)
Entrapping, a 18,000gns half-brother to a 6f AW winner, made an encouraging debut and should be placed to good effect in the last few months of the season. (op 12-1)
Age Of Bronze is now qualified for a handicap mark and his form is good enough for nurseries to be a possibility when connections have discovered his best trip. (op 10-1 tchd 12-1)
Choral Prince(IRE) found this tougher than the Yarmouth maiden last time, but he should find a race at the right level. (op 3-1)
Le Talisman(IRE), half-brother to two smart performers at 1m1f-plus, showed early speed but was hard at work some way out and needs to do more. (op 5-2)

5479 RACING PLUS ONLINE, MOBILE AND APP H'CAP 1m (P)
8:20 (8:20) (Class 6) (0-60,60) 3-Y-O **£1,617** (£481; £240; £120) **Stalls** Low

Form RPR

-003 **1** **Refreshestheparts (USA)**[19] 4754 3-8-12 **51** PatCosgrave 9 64
(George Baker) *broke wl: stdd in rr: swtchd lft and hdwy 2f out: led appr fnl f: drvn clr* **20/1**

0003 **2** 3¾ **Riviera Romance**[15] 4932 3-8-11 **50** MircoDemuro 2 54
(J W Hills) *in tch: hdwy 2f out: styd on to chse wnr appr fnl f: sn no imp but styd on wl for 2nd* **6/1**[3]

-643 **3** 3¼ **Twin Shadow (IRE)**[13] 5021 3-9-7 **60** HayleyTurner 4 57
(James Fanshawe) *chsd ldrs: drvn ins fnl 3f: kpt on same pce for 3rd fnl f* **7/2**[1]

5054 **4** hd **Wyndham Wave**[9] 5152 3-9-7 **60** JamesMillman 12 56
(Rod Millman) *chsd ldrs: rdn over 2f out: styd on same pce for 4th fnl f* **16/1**

0506 **5** 1 **Northern Territory (IRE)**[14] 4945 3-9-5 **58** (t) RobertHavlin 14 52
(Jim Boyle) *chsd ldrs: rdn over 2f out: styd on one pce fr over 1f out* **20/1**

0024 **6** ½ **Choice Pearl (USA)**[7] 5246 3-9-2 **55** (t) HarryBentley 13 48
(Tobias B P Coles) *disp ld tl def advantage wl over 2f out: hdd appr fnl f: wknd fnl 150yds* **12/1**

-000 **7** nse **Alnoomaas (IRE)**[34] 4232 3-9-1 **54** TomMcLaughlin 1 47
(Luke Dace) *in tch: chsd ldrs and rdn over 2f out: wknd fnl f* **9/1**

00-0 **8** 2¾ **Kaylee**[14] 4937 3-8-13 **52** ShaneKelly 6 38
(Gary Moore) *in rr: swtchd rt to ins and hdwy to chse ldrs ins fnl 2f: wknd over 1f out* **33/1**

0-00 **9** ½ **Perfect Example (IRE)**[76] 2864 3-9-5 **58** (p) RoystonFfrench 11 43
(Ismail Mohammed) *in rr: rdn 3f out: styd on fnl f: nvr a threat* **33/1**

0-30 **10** 4½ **Mitch Rapp (USA)**[35] 4219 3-9-6 **59** FergusSweeney 5 34
(Jamie Osborne) *chsd ldrs: rdn over 2f out: hung rt and sn btn* **10/1**

005 **11** 1¼ **Blissamore**[76] 2865 3-8-13 **52** DarryllHolland 8 24
(Hughie Morrison) *s.i.s: bhd most of way* **7/1**

3300 **12** 2½ **Welsh Royale**[19] 4754 3-9-1 **54** MartinDwyer 10 20
(William Muir) *chsd ldrs: rdn over 3f out wknd sn after* **25/1**

5440 **13** ½ **Samba Night (IRE)**[23] 4663 3-9-7 **60** LukeMorris 3 25
(James Eustace) *rdn and bhd fr 1/2-way* **12/1**

5032 **14** 9 **Trusting (IRE)**[7] 5231 3-9-4 **57** (b) CathyGannon 7
(Eve Johnson Houghton) *disputed ld tl hdd wl over 2f out: sn btn* **9/2**[2]

1m 39.94s (0.14) **Going Correction** +0.025s/f (Slow) **14** Ran SP% **126.8**
Speed ratings (Par 98): **100,96,93,92,91 91,91,88,88,83 82,79,79,70**
Tote Swingers: 1&2 £17.50, 1&3 £23.90, 2&3 £9.50 CSF £135.39 CT £550.40 TOTE £28.80: £6.90, £2.00, £2.20; EX 158.60 TRIFECTA Not won..
Owner Michel de Carvalho **Bred** Lazy Lane Farms Inc **Trained** Whitsbury, Hants

FOCUS
A modest race, with few of the runners in top form beforehand. Another clear best from the winner.

5480 LADIES DAY WITH TOBY ANSTIS 08.09.12 H'CAP (LONDON MILE QUALIFIER) 1m (P)
8:50 (8:51) (Class 4) (0-80,84) 3-Y-O+ **£4,075** (£1,212; £606; £303) **Stalls** Low

Form RPR

5-00 **1** **Little Black Book (IRE)**[18] 4805 4-9-8 **76** (b[1]) HarryBentley 13 84
(Gerard Butler) *chsd ldrs: led appr fnl 2f: styd on wl u.p fnl f: hld on wl* **14/1**

1-3 **2** nk **Albaspina (IRE)**[14] 4968 3-9-6 **80** LukeMorris 8 87
(Sir Mark Prescott Bt) *chsd ldrs: wnt 2nd ins fnl f: hrd rdn but a jst hld clsng stages* **7/2**[2]

2501 **3** nk **Angelic Upstart (IRE)**[16] 4889 4-9-11 **79** JimmyFortune 10 86
(Andrew Balding) *in tch: hdwy 2f out: styd on u.p to take 3rd fnl 120yds: nt quite rch ldng duo* **15/2**[3]

1221 **4** 1 **Henry Allingham**[7] 5243 3-9-7 **84** 6ex DominicFox[(3)] 1 93+
(Roger Varian) *chsd ldrs: hdwy: nt clr run and wnt rt ins fnl f: swtchd lft and r.o clsng stages: nt rcvr* **9/4**[1]

6040 **5** ½ **Fantasy Gladiator**[25] 4580 6-9-11 **79** (p) JimmyQuinn 14 83
(Robert Cowell) *toon t.k.h: chsd ldrs: rdn over 1f out: no ex ins fnl f* **25/1**

301 **6** nk **Junket**[16] 4872 5-9-10 **78** SeanLevey 11 81+
(Dr Jon Scargill) *in rr: hdwy on outside over 2f out: styd on u.p fnl f: nt rch ldrs* **20/1**

2413 **7** ½ **Good Authority (IRE)**[25] 4580 5-9-10 **78** DarryllHolland 9 80
(Karen George) *s.i.s: in rr: hdwy and rdn over 1f out: kpt on clsng stages: nvr gng pce to get into contention* **12/1**

4051 **8** nk **Saharia (IRE)**[14] 4950 5-9-5 **73** (v) ShaneKelly 2 74
(Michael Attwater) *s.i.s: hld up in rr: stdy hdwy 2f out: shkn up and one pce fnl f* **16/1**

0300 **9** nse **California English (IRE)**[16] 4889 3-9-4 **78** (b) AdamKirby 5 78
(Marco Botti) *led after 1f: hdd appr fnl 2f: wkng on rail whn hmpd ins fnl f* **8/1**

-030 **10** 1 **Master Mylo (IRE)**[22] 4689 5-9-11 **79** SilvestreDeSousa 4 81+
(Robert Cowell) *plld hrd: led 1f: styd chsng ldrs: rdn over 2f out: weaking whn hmpd on rails ins fnl f* **10/1**

301- **11** hd **Orthodox Lad**[143] 6748 4-9-5 **73** LiamKeniry 6 71
(Ed de Giles) *towards rr most of way* **33/1**

1103 **12** 3 **Hurricane Spirit (IRE)**[14] 4944 8-9-3 **78** NicoleNordblad[(7)] 3 69
(Hans Adielsson) *in rr: sme hdwy on inner over 2f out: nvr rchd ldrs and sn wknd* **14/1**

1m 40.72s (0.92) **Going Correction** +0.025s/f (Slow)
WFA 3 from 4yo+ 6lb **12** Ran SP% **123.4**
Speed ratings (Par 105): **96,95,95,94,93 93,93,92,92,91 91,88**
Tote Swingers: 1&2 £19.50, 1&3 £21.80, 2&3 £8.90 CSF £63.83 CT £415.00 TOTE £24.10: £5.30, £1.20, £2.20; EX 89.30 TRIFECTA Not won..
Owner A D Spence **Bred** Rabbah Bloodstock Limited **Trained** Newmarket, Suffolk

FOCUS
A competitive heat containing some in-form runners, with all but one of them involved in the finish. It was not strong run and was quite a messy race. The winner ran close to his best.
T/Plt: £82.50 to a £1 stake. Pool: £48,304.00 - 427.09 winning tickets. T/Qpdt: £64.00 to a £1 stake. Pool: £4,136.00 - 47.78 winning tickets. ST

5346 LINGFIELD (L-H)
Wednesday, August 22

OFFICIAL GOING: Good to firm (firm in places in back straight; 8.5)
Wind: Moderate, across towards stands Weather: Fine but cloudy

5481 DOLPHIN SQUARE H'CAP 1m 2f
2:15 (2:15) (Class 6) (0-55,55) 4-Y-O+ **£1,704** (£503; £251) **Stalls** Low

Form RPR

0304 **1** **The Wonga Coup (IRE)**[13] 4981 5-8-4 **46** oh1 SimonPearce[(3)] 5 54
(Pat Phelan) *hld up in last: nt clr run briefly over 2f out: sn swtchd to outer and rapid prog over 1f out: wnt 2nd jst ins fnl f: styd on wl to ld last strides* **20/1**

1365 **2** nk **Spiritual Art**[27] 4504 6-9-1 **54** (v) StephenCraine 1 61
(Luke Dace) *mde most: drew clr over 3f out: stl gng strly 2f out: rdn and 3 l up 1f out: tired and hdd last strides* **6/1**

6234 **3** 1½ **Mayan Flight (IRE)**[13] 4994 4-9-0 **53** MichaelO'Connell 4 57
(Tony Carroll) *hld up in last trio: prog on inner over 2f out: chsd clr ldr over 1f out to jst ins fnl f: kpt on* **11/2**[3]

0531 **4** 1 **Chasin' Rainbows**[14] 4940 4-8-13 **52** LiamKeniry 12 54
(Sylvester Kirk) *hld up in last pair: looking for room over 2f out: prog after: rdn to dispute 2nd over 1f out: kpt on one pce* **7/2**[2]

-635 **5** 3¼ **Astragal**[13] 4988 4-8-4 **48** RosieJessop[(5)] 9 44
(Shaun Lycett) *prom on outer: rdn over 2f out: disp 2nd wl over 1f out: wknd ins fnl f* **14/1**

0422 **6** 3 **Lisselan Pleasure (USA)**[8] 5198 5-8-8 **54** (t) DanielMuscutt[(7)] 3 44
(Bernard Llewellyn) *t.k.h: trckd ldng pair: chsd clr ldr 3f out to over 1f out: wknd* **3/1**[1]

-030 **7** 3 **Oliver's Gold**[6] 5266 4-9-2 **55** (p) SilvestreDeSousa 7 39
(Shaun Harris) *hld up in midfield: rdn over 2f out: no prog: wknd over 1f out* **6/1**

0003 **8** 1 **Gee Major**[56] 3497 5-8-7 **46** (p) LukeMorris 11 28
(Nicky Vaughan) *w ldr to 1/2-way: lost 2nd 3f out: wknd 2f out* **14/1**

50-0 **9** 1¾ **Hertford Street**[18] 4812 4-8-0 **46** oh1 JoeyHaynes[(7)] 8 24
(Eric Wheeler) *hld up in midfield: rdn and no prog over 2f out: wknd wl over 1f out* **40/1**

350 **10** 6 **Pastoral Jet**[71] 3006 4-8-8 **47** JohnFahy 2 13
(Richard Rowe) *trckd ldrs tl wknd qckly jst over 2f out* **20/1**

2m 10.13s (-0.37) **Going Correction** -0.125s/f (Firm) **10** Ran SP% **116.5**
Speed ratings (Par 101): **96,95,94,93,91 88,86,85,84,79**
Tote Swingers: 1&2 £18.70, 1&3 £19.20, 2&3 £6.60 CSF £132.65 CT £764.16 TOTE £23.90: £6.10, £1.50, £2.20; EX 237.20.
Owner Celtic Contractors Limited **Bred** Harry Sweeney **Trained** Epsom, Surrey

FOCUS
A moderate handicap, run at a steady pace on the fast ground. Not an easy race to assess, but the form is taken at something like face value.
Oliver's Gold Official explanation: jockey said gelding stumbled approaching 3f out

5482 OILFIELD INSURANCE AGENCIES LTD H'CAP 1m 2f
2:45 (2:45) (Class 5) (0-75,73) 3-Y-O **£2,385** (£704; £352) **Stalls** Low

Form RPR

0-44 **1** **Cayuga**[58] 3447 3-9-7 **73** RichardMullen 4 87+
(Sir Michael Stoute) *trckd ldr 4f and again over 3f out: pushed into ld 2f out: steadily drew clr* **5/4**[1]

0603 **2** 2¾ **Superciliary**[21] 4706 3-8-11 **63** SebSanders 6 69
(Ralph Beckett) *led at gd pce: rdn and hdd wl over 1f out: one pce* **5/2**[2]

6061 **3** 1 **Scarlett Fever**[12] 5037 3-8-3 **55** (b) HayleyTurner 1 59
(Marcus Tregoning) *hld up in last pair: wnt 3rd 2f out: reminders and nt qckn over 1f out: pushed along and couldn't overtake runner-up fnl f* **7/1**

300 **4** 6 **Rei D'Oro (USA)**[43] 3945 3-9-4 **70** MartinLane 2 62
(David Simcock) *hld up in last pair: rdn over 3f out and no prog: wknd 2f out* **5/1**[3]

5 shd **Hail Hail (USA)**[43] 3-9-7 **73** SilvestreDeSousa 5 65
(Paul Cole) *prom: chsd ldr after 4f to over 3f out: sn rdn: wknd 2f out* **10/1**

2m 8.8s (-1.70) **Going Correction** -0.125s/f (Firm) 5 Ran SP% **111.3**
Speed ratings (Par 100): **101,98,98,93,93**
CSF £4.68 TOTE £2.60: £3.30, £1.40; EX 5.80.

Owner K Abdulla **Bred** Juddmonte Farms Ltd **Trained** Newmarket, Suffolk

FOCUS

A fair handicap, but it lacked depth. It was run at an even pace and the form is taken at face value.

5483 HELP FOR HEROES H'CAP 1m 3f 106y
3:20 (3:20) (Class 6) (0-60,60) 3-Y-O+ £1,704 (£503; £251) Stalls High

Form RPR

4260 1 **Pahente**[26] 4536 4-8-12 **46** oh1 (p) MichaelO'Connell 4 55
(Tony Carroll) *t.k.h: trckd ldng trio: wnt 2nd 1/2-way: led over 4f out: drvn and kpt on fnl 2f* **4/1**[2]

0105 2 2 3/4 **Rodrigo De Freitas (IRE)**[9] 5164 5-9-9 **57** (v) PatCosgrave 1 61
(Jim Boyle) *slowly away: drvn and reminders early: travelled bttr in rr after 3f: prog 5f out: rdn to chse wnr 2f out: no imp fnl f* **13/2**

0/03 3 7 **Arch Event**[8] 5198 7-8-5 **46** oh1 DanielMuscutt(7) 6 38
(Bernard Llewellyn) *trckd ldrs: rdn 4f out: chsd wnr 3f out to 2f out: wknd fnl f* **17/2**

564 4 7 **We Used To Wait (USA)**[15] 4931 3-9-3 **60** RobertHavlin 3 41
(Peter Chapple-Hyam) *snatched up after 1f and dropped to rr: wl in tch: outpcd over 3f out: rdn and no imp over 2f out: wl btn after* **2/1**[1]

5/06 5 1 **Beggar's Opera (IRE)**[12] 5038 5-9-5 **60** (t) AprilKitchener(7) 7 39
(Jim Best) *mde most to over 4f out: wknd 3f out* **22/1**

0005 6 12 **Vena Amoris (USA)**[10] 5125 3-8-5 **48** JamieMackay 8
(Richard Rowe) *settled in rr: shkn up and no imp on ldrs over 3f out: wknd over 2f out: eased* **33/1**

5500 7 54 **Bramshill Lass**[12] 5037 3-8-13 **56** DarryllHolland 2
(Amanda Perrett) *rousted along early to join ldng pair: wknd rapidly 1/2-way: wl t.o* **13/2**

5330 8 71 **Taqaat (USA)**[27] 4511 4-9-9 **57** [1] LukeMorris 5
(Tim McCarthy) *w ldr to 1/2-way: drvn and dropped out rapidly: t.o whn virtually p.u 3f out* **5/1**[3]

2m 29.72s (-1.78) **Going Correction** -0.125s/f (Firm)
WFA 3 from 4yo+ 9lb 8 Ran SP% **114.5**
Speed ratings (Par 101): **101,99,93,88,88 79,40,**
Tote Swingers: 1&2 £4.30, 1&3 £6.10, 2&3 £5.90 CSF £30.05 CT £208.25 TOTE £3.90: £1.20, £1.80, £2.50; EX 27.00.

Owner Mayden Stud **Bred** Mayden Stud, J A And D S Dewhurst **Trained** Cropthorne, Worcs

FOCUS

A weak handicap and questionable third with the winner and third wrong at the weights. Unconvincing form.

Taqaat(USA) Official explanation: jockey said gelding lost its action

5484 HORSEBACK UK NURSERY 7f
3:55 (3:56) (Class 5) (0-70,68) 2-Y-O £2,385 (£704; £352) Stalls High

Form RPR

0452 1 **Spithead**[9] 5161 2-8-13 **60** LiamJones 5 62
(William Haggas) *mde all and racd against nr side rail: drvn and hrd pressed over 1f out: hld on wl* **5/1**[3]

64P4 2 nk **Cappadocia (IRE)**[12] 5041 2-9-0 **66** CharlesBishop(5) 9 67
(Mick Channon) *trckd ldrs: wnt 2nd over 2f out: pressed wnr over 1f out: nt qckn ins fnl f* **11/4**[1]

4045 3 1 1/2 **Mixed Message (IRE)**[8] 5194 2-9-1 **62** RichardMullen 4 59
(Ed McMahon) *t.k.h: hld up in 6th: prog over 2f out: chsd ldng pair over 1f out: nt qckn* **16/1**

4044 4 shd **Moonlit Dancer (IRE)**[9] 5160 2-9-0 **61** (t) SebSanders 8 58
(J W Hills) *wnt lft s: trckd ldrs on rails: pushed along fr over 2f out: nt clr run tl ins fnl f: styd on nr fin* **20/1**

0206 5 1/2 **Sojoum**[8] 5206 2-8-11 **58** SamHitchcott 1 54+
(Mick Channon) *awkward s: dropped in fr wd draw: hld up in last and off the pce: drvn 2f out: styd on fr over 1f out: nrst fin* **25/1**

536 6 3/4 **Curl (IRE)**[74] 2917 2-9-7 **68** PatDobbs 6 62
(Richard Hannon) *dwlt then nudged sn after s: off the pce in last trio: effrt on outer over 2f out: bmpd over 1f out: tried to cl u.p fnl f: one pce* **11/4**[1]

056 7 4 1/2 **Sakhee's Ichigou**[23] 4646 2-8-8 **55** LukeMorris 3 37
(Michael Blanshard) *chsd ldrs but urged along after 2f: lost pl fr 1/2-way* **25/1**

632 8 2 3/4 **Our Three Graces (IRE)**[15] 4899 2-9-4 **65** FergusSweeney 2 40
(Gary Moore) *chsd wnr to over 2f out: wknd wl over 1f out: eased* **10/1**

200 9 3 1/4 **Sutton Sid**[22] 4688 2-9-5 **66** (p) PatCosgrave 7 32
(George Baker) *bmpd s: off the pce in last trio: taken wd and drvn over 2f out: bmpd over 1f out: wknd* **9/2**[2]

1m 22.1s (-1.20) **Going Correction** -0.30s/f (Firm) 9 Ran SP% **115.6**
Speed ratings (Par 94): **94,93,91,91,91 90,85,82,78**
Tote Swingers: 1&2 £3.50, 1&3 £9.90, 2&3 £10.00 CSF £18.66 CT £200.93 TOTE £6.20: £2.80, £1.40, £4.80; EX 24.00.

Owner Mrs Charles Cyzer **Bred** C A Cyzer **Trained** Newmarket, Suffolk

FOCUS

A weak, low-grade nursery, run at a modest pace and dominated by those that raced against the stands' side rail.

NOTEBOOK

Spithead just came out on top in a driving finish. The 2yo broke well from his stall and, having grabbed the rail and the lead, soon had many of his rivals in trouble. He ran gun-barrel straight under pressure and had just enough in hand to repel the late challenge of the runner-up. He had been slightly disappointing when beaten on the AW track at this venue last time, but was given a much more positive ride on this occasion and clearly benefited. It's unlikely he'll be too harshly penalised for this success and he should remain competitive in the coming weeks. (op 9-2 tchd 4-1)

Cappadocia(IRE) atracted plenty of support and he only just failed to justify the confidence. He tracked the winner through before being pulled out to challenge, but could never quite get by. He lost very little in defeat, though is now beginning to look exposed. (op 7-2)

Mixed Message(IRE) had done all of her running over 5f and 6f and may not quite have got home here, despite filling out third. (op 14-1)

Moonlit Dancer(IRE) had shaped well on her nursery debut over 6f last time and again performed creditably over this longer trip. (tchd 18-1)

Sojoum caught the eye by making excellent late progress from the rear. She was awkwardly away and should be up to winning a small race off this kind of mark. (op 20-1)

Curl(IRE) wasn't entirely disgraced, but she hung badly right under pressure. She wasn't suited by how the race developed and was asked to make ground on the unfavourable part of the track. (op 3-1)

5485 OILFIELD OFFSHORE UNDERWRITING LTD MAIDEN AUCTION STKS 6f
4:30 (4:31) (Class 6) 2-Y-O £1,704 (£503; £251) Stalls High

Form RPR

0 1 **Cardmaster (IRE)**[72] 2983 2-9-0 0 JimmyFortune 6 71
(Eve Johnson Houghton) *pushed along in last trio and off the pce: clsd fr 1/2-way: drvn and r.o to ld jst over 1f out: sn in command* **8/1**

4000 2 1 3/4 **Marvelino**[39] 4093 2-9-0 73 DaneO'Neill 3 66
(Pat Eddery) *led and sn crossed to nr side rail: rdn and hdd jst over 1f out: nt qckn* **9/4**[2]

6 3 1 **Daisie Cutter**[29] 4433 2-8-2 0 SimonPearce(3) 4 54+
(Lydia Pearce) *fractious bef ent stalls: dwlt: off the pce in last and pushed along: prog on outer 2f out: styd on to take 3rd wl ins fnl f* **14/1**

4003 4 1 1/4 **Annie Besant**[9] 5160 2-8-5 50 MartinDwyer 5 50
(David C Griffiths) *awkward s: pushed along in last trio and off the pce: prog fr 2f out but stl racing awkwardly: nvr able to threaten* **8/1**

5 5 2 1/4 **Little Indian**[29] 4433 2-8-12 0 FergusSweeney 1 51
(J R Jenkins) *disp 2nd pl for much of way tl wknd over 1f out* **7/1**[3]

0 6 1 1/4 **Many Elements**[18] 4813 2-9-3 0 KierenFox 8 52
(Brett Johnson) *racd against rail: disp 2nd early: chsd along bef 1/2-way: wknd over 2f out* **20/1**

04 7 13 **Burlesque Star (IRE)**[18] 4813 2-8-11 0 LukeMorris 7
(Harry Dunlop) *prom but sn pushed along: lost pl and struggling bef 1/2-way: t.o* **2/1**[1]

00 8 4 1/2 **Stockholm**[26] 4532 2-8-11 0 JamesMillman 2
(Rod Millman) *disp 2nd to 1/2-way: wknd rapidly: t.o* **33/1**

1m 10.09s (-1.11) **Going Correction** -0.30s/f (Firm) 8 Ran SP% **113.2**
Speed ratings (Par 92): **95,92,91,89,86 85,67,61**
Tote Swingers: 1&2 £3.50, 1&3 £9.10, 2&3 £6.50 CSF £25.86 TOTE £10.00: £3.20, £1.10, £4.40; EX 27.30.

Owner Henry Marsh & Charlie Crossley Cooke **Bred** Tally-Ho Stud **Trained** Blewbury, Oxon

FOCUS

Very little in the way of strength or depth to this maiden. The form is straightforward.

NOTEBOOK

Cardmaster(IRE) impressed with the way he got the job done. He had shown virtually nothing when finishing last of 13 on soft ground at Windsor on his debut, but he left that form a long way behind on this much quicker surface. Badly outpaced early on, he made rapid progress in the final 2f and came through to win with seemingly plenty in hand and deserves extra credit having made his move down the unfavoured centre of the track. It's hard to know what he actually achieved here, but he lacks nothing in size and scope and ought to be capable of much better. (op 10-1)

Marvelino set the standard on ratings and appeared to have the race wrapped up when kicking clear against the stands' rail. He was made to look very one-paced by the winner late on, but may simply have bumped into an above-average type. He possess plenty of early pace and should be able to find a small race, be it over this trip or when returning to 5f. (op 15-8)

Daisie Cutter was all at sea early on, but she stayed on powerfully and is definitely one for the notebook. She was fractious in the preliminaries, but should be up to winning races providing her temperament doesn't get the better of her.

Annie Besant appeared to post a career-best effort. However, it's unlikely this will have done her nursery mark much good and it remains to be seen if she can continue to go forward. (op 13-2 tchd 6-1)

Burlesque Star(IRE) attracted solid market support, but ran abysmally. She's now qualified for a nursery mark, but will need to improve dramatically if she's to make an impression in that sphere. (op 7-2)

5486 RESOURCE GROUP H'CAP 6f
5:05 (5:05) (Class 4) (0-80,80) 3-Y-O+ £4,075 (£1,212; £454; £454) Stalls High

Form RPR

6642 1 **Drift And Dream**[18] 4793 5-9-0 **70** HarryBentley 10 82
(Chris Wall) *chsd ldng pair and racd against rail: plld out over 1f out: clsd to ld jst ins fnl f: drvn out: decisively* **2/1**[1]

3230 2 2 1/4 **Aye Aye Digby (IRE)**[12] 5035 7-9-5 **75** DaneO'Neill 9 80
(Patrick Chamings) *racd against nr side rail: led to over 4f out: pressed ldr tl led again 2f out: hdd and outpcd jst ins fnl f* **13/2**[3]

4506 3 nk **Lunar Deity**[18] 4814 3-9-0 **73** (p) JohnFahy 4 77
(Eve Johnson Houghton) *racd on outer in midfield: drvn over 2f out: kpt on fr over 1f out: nvr able to chal* **14/1**

4-02 3 dht **Leadenhall Lass (IRE)**[4] 5346 6-8-5 **61** CathyGannon 3 65
(Pat Phelan) *in tch in midfield: rdn over 2f out: styd on fr over 1f out: nvr able to chal* **10/1**

0004 5 1 1/4 **Expose**[9] 5165 4-9-7 **77** LiamJones 2 77
(William Haggas) *spd fr wd draw to press ldr: led over 4f out to 2f out: lost 2nd and wknd 1f out* **16/1**

2154 6 hd **Night Trade (IRE)**[5] 5326 5-9-6 **76** (p) LukeMorris 8 75
(Ronald Harris) *pushed along in last trio early: n.m.r against rail over 3f out: effrt 2f out: one pce* **9/1**

0503 7 1 1/2 **Courageous (IRE)**[12] 5035 6-9-8 **78** WilliamCarson 1 73
(Milton Bradley) *stdd s and dropped in fr wd draw: mostly in last pair: pushed along and sme inroads 2f out: no hdwy fnl f: eased nr fin* **12/1**

4121 8 3 **Jocasta Dawn**[30] 4412 3-9-5 **78** FergusSweeney 6 63
(Henry Candy) *chsd ldrs: rdn over 2f out: sn wknd* **9/2**[2]

3-05 9 2 1/2 **Galatian**[13] 4998 5-9-5 **75** (b) JamesMillman 7 52
(Rod Millman) *dwlt: bdly outpcd fr the s and t.o after 2f: pushed along and lost no further grnd fr 1/2-way* **9/1**

1m 8.64s (-2.56) **Going Correction** -0.30s/f (Firm)
WFA 3 from 4yo+ 3lb 9 Ran SP% **114.2**
Speed ratings (Par 105): **105,102,101,101,99 99,97,93,90**Place: Lunar Deity £2.50, Leadenhall Lass £1.80. Tricast: Drift And Dream, Aye Aye Digby, Lunar Deity £71.01, Drift And Dream, Aye Aye Digby, Leadenhall Lass £52.08. Tote Swingers: DAD,AAD £4.00 AAD, LD £5.90 AAD, LL £5.90 DAD,LD £4.70 DAD,LL £2.60. CSF £14.9427 CT £Owner TOTE £Lady Juliet Tadgell: £Bred, £Lady Juliet Tadgell, £Trained, £Newmarket, Suffolk .

FOCUS

A decent sprint handicap, run at a fair pace. The winner is rated close to her old best.

Galatian Official explanation: jockey said gelding never travelled

T/Plt: £181.50 to a £1 stake. Pool: £59,095.20 - 237.60 winning tickets. T/Qpdt: £46.20 to a £1 stake. Pool: £4,889.20 - 464.21 winning tickets. JN

4608 YORK (L-H)

Wednesday, August 22

OFFICIAL GOING: Good to firm (good in places; 8.1)

Wind: fresh 1/2 against Weather: fine but breezy

5487 SYMPHONY GROUP STKS (H'CAP) 5f 89y

2:00 (2:01) (Class 2) (0-105,104) 3-Y-0+£25,876 (£7,700; £3,848; £1,924) Stalls Centre

Form				RPR
4302	1		**Tax Free (IRE)**[4] 5370 10-9-0 92 AdrianNicholls 11 (David Nicholls) *chsd ldrs: hung lft and led over 1f out: hld on towards fin* 7/1[3]	101
2532	2	nk	**Mass Rally (IRE)**[31] 4367 5-9-0 92 (b) PaulMulrennan 18 (Michael Dods) *s.i.s: hdwy and nt clr run over 1f out: styd on wl towards fin* 12/1	100
6040	3	nk	**Fitz Flyer (IRE)**[4] 5368 6-8-11 89 (v) JoeFanning 15 (David Nicholls) *s.i.s: effrt and n.m.r 2f out: styd on ins fnl f* 20/1	96+
3530	4	nk	**Fratellino**[4] 5343 5-8-13 91 (t) RobertWinston 13 (Alan McCabe) *chsd ldrs: nt clr run 2f out: styd on wl ins fnl f* 20/1	97
-060	5	nse	**Kaldoun Kingdom (IRE)**[25] 4611 7-9-1 93 PaulHanagan 12 (Richard Fahey) *mid-div: hdwy 2f out: kpt on same pce ins fnl f* 12/1	99
000	6	3/4	**Ancient Cross**[40] 4073 8-9-3 95 (t) KierenFallon 5 (Michael Easterby) *in rr: hdwy over 2f out: kpt on same pce* 11/1	98
2065	7	nse	**Ponty Acclaim (IRE)**[17] 4838 3-9-7 101 TedDurcan 2 (Tim Easterby) *mid-div: hdwy to chse ldrs over 1f out: no ex* 16/1	104
5563	8	1 1/4	**Doctor Parkes**[8] 5204 6-8-12 90 EddieAhern 1 (Eric Alston) *in rr: hdwy and n.m.r over 1f out: kpt on same pce* 11/1	89
00-0	9	hd	**The Thrill Is Gone**[22] 4690 4-8-10 88 MartinHarley 9 (Mick Channon) *led: hdd over 1f out: wknd ins fnl f* 25/1	86
0336	10	hd	**Zero Money (IRE)**[11] 5077 6-9-8 100 (b) JamesDoyle 6 (Roger Charlton) *chsd ldrs: fdd fnl 150yds* 13/2[2]	97
-514	11	hd	**Rex Imperator**[25] 4598 3-9-10 104 GeorgeBaker 20 (Roger Charlton) *hld up: hdwy and nt clr run over 2f out tl ins fnl f: no ch* 9/2[1]	100+
060	12	1 3/4	**Chunky Diamond (IRE)**[25] 4611 3-9-3 97 WilliamBuick 17 (Peter Chapple-Hyam) *in rr: hdwy over 1f out: nvr a threat* 20/1	87
5000	13	hd	**Dickie's Lad (IRE)**[18] 4799 4-8-10 88 (t[1]) GrahamLee 19 (Kevin Ryan) *mid-div: hdwy over 1f out: nvr nr ldrs* 16/1	78
-650	14	nk	**Captain Dunne (IRE)**[81] 2704 7-9-10 102 DuranFentiman 8 (Tim Easterby) *prom: wknd over 1f out* 25/1	91
1000	15	3/4	**Hazelrigg (IRE)**[4] 5343 7-8-13 91 DavidAllan 7 (Tim Easterby) *chsd ldrs: wknd over 1f out* 25/1	77
006	16	2 1/2	**Burning Thread (IRE)**[4] 5343 5-8-13 91 GrahamGibbons 10 (Tim Etherington) *nvr bttr than mid-div* 20/1	68
2110	17	2	**Silvanus (IRE)**[22] 4690 7-8-12 90 RussKennemore 16 (Paul Midgley) *mid-div: wknd over 1f out* 20/1	60
13-0	18	3/4	**Mister Manannan (IRE)**[137] 1219 5-9-5 97 AndrewMullen 3 (David Nicholls) *a towards rr* 33/1	65
0102	19	1/2	**Le Toreador**[22] 4690 7-8-13 91 (tp) PhillipMakin 14 (Kevin Ryan) *chsd ldrs: lost pl over 1f out* 16/1	57

1m 2.98s (-1.12) **Going Correction** -0.025s/f (Good)
WFA 3 from 4yo+ 2lb **19 Ran SP% 132.0**
Speed ratings (Par 109): **107,106,106,105,105 104,104,102,101,101 101,98,98,97,96 92,89,88,87**
Tote Swingers: 1&2 £14.10, 1&3 £37.70, 2&3 £62.20 CSF £79.02 CT £1695.16 TOTE £8.20: £1.90, £3.10, £5.50, £6.40; EX 118.80 Trifecta £2691.70 Part won. Pool: £3,637.53 - 0.10 winning units..

Owner Ian Hewitson **Bred** Denis And Mrs Teresa Bergin **Trained** Sessay, N Yorks

■ Stewards' Enquiry : Adrian Nicholls six-day ban: used whip above permitted level, down shoulder in the forehand (Sep 5-10)

FOCUS

Races on traditional line and distances as advertised. There was 7mm of rain overnight. The ground was good to firm, good in places and the assistant clerk of the course reported that "it is nice fast ground with no jar." A hot sprint handicap run over an intermediate trip. They were spread across the track in a strongly run race and there didn't seem to be any track or pace bias. The time was 0.02 seconds faster than standard. Straightforward form, Tax Free confirming his Ripon latest.

NOTEBOOK

Tax Free(IRE) had been beaten less than 3l in six hot handicaps this season, including when runner-up in the Great St Wilfrid on Saturday. He was always well positioned just behind the leaders and produced a surging run to score despite drifting to the left. This was just his second win since May 2009 but it was a 16th career success from this admirable veteran who still retains a huge amount of ability and enthusiasm. His mark will move back into the mid 90s after this but he will remain well treated on old form and should continue to be a force in top sprint handicaps. (op 8-1)

Mass Rally(IRE) who had a hood added to blinkers, travelled well tucked away at the back on the near side before finishing fast but he was just held in his second consecutive near-miss. He is 0-23 since his last win in November 2009 but he has a high cruising speed and should continue to be very dangerous if things go his way in hot handicaps.

Fitz Flyer(IRE), well beaten in the consolation race for the Great St Wilfrid on Saturday, had to wait to find a gap before finishing well to snatch third. (op 25-1)

Fratellino was laboured at Doncaster on Saturday but he bounced back with a strong finishing effort back over this slightly longer trip. He is on a workable mark but the slight negative is that he has an ordinary strike-rate of 3-32 for a horse of his ability.

Kaldoun Kingdom(IRE) stayed on steadily but couldn't land a major blow over a trip a bit sharper than ideal. His losing run dates back to March 2010 but he is well handicapped and it is worth noting that four of his five wins have been at 6f on good or slower ground during September and October.

Ancient Cross took a while to get going but he stayed on well in his best run of the season. His slow starting style makes him a bit risky but he is on the same mark as his Newcastle win last summer.

Ponty Acclaim(IRE) travelled smoothly into contention down the centre of the track and kept battling in a promising run dropped back to handicap company. (op 18-1)

Doctor Parkes ran respectably on the far side but he has lacked a bit of finishing spark this season. (op 10-1)

The Thrill Is Gone faded in the closing stages after setting a decent pace on her second run back from ten months off. (op 20-1)

Zero Money(IRE) attracted support but he got a bit warm in the preliminaries and couldn't sustain his effort on the far side. (op 10-1)

Rex Imperator, a big market mover in the morning, got trapped behind several rivals on the stands' side and it was all over by the time he got in the clear. This was an unlucky run for a lightly raced 3yo who is a strong traveller with some potential for further improvement. Official explanation: jockey said gelding was denied a clear run (tchd 5-1 in a place)

5488 PINSENT MASONS LLP ACOMB STKS (GROUP 3) 7f

2:30 (2:31) (Class 1) 2-Y-O £31,190 (£11,825; £5,918; £2,948; £1,479) Stalls Low

Form				RPR
31	1		**Dundonnell (USA)**[18] 4813 2-9-0 0 JamesDoyle 3 (Roger Charlton) *trckd ldrs: smooth hdwy to ld over 2f out: edgd lft: drvn and edgd rt ins fnl f: drvn out* 15/8[1]	111+
21	2	3/4	**Steeler (IRE)**[18] 4803 2-9-0 0 KierenFallon 5 (Mark Johnston) *sn chsng ldrs: drvn over 2f out: chsd wnr over 1f out: r.o: hld whn impeded nr line* 5/1	109+
4	3	1/2	**Afonso De Sousa (USA)**[27] 4518 2-9-0 0 JPO'Brien 2 (A P O'Brien, Ire) *led: hdd over 2f out: rallied over 1f out: styd on same pce last 150yds* 11/4[3]	108
1	4	3 1/2	**Ebn Arab (USA)**[26] 4555 2-9-0 0 PaulHanagan 4 (Charles Hills) *trckd ldrs: effrt 2f out: sn upsides: fdd fnl f* 9/4[2]	98
31	5	18	**American Impact (USA)**[12] 5053 2-9-0 72 BarryMcHugh 1 (Tony Coyle) *lost pl 4f out: sn bhd* 66/1	50

1m 23.88s (-1.42) **Going Correction** -0.175s/f (Firm) **5 Ran SP% 110.4**
Speed ratings (Par 104): **101,100,99,95,75**
CSF £11.49 TOTE £2.60: £1.50, £1.70; EX 10.40.

Owner K Abdulla **Bred** Juddmonte Farms Inc **Trained** Beckhampton, Wilts

FOCUS

The Acomb Stakes has been won by some high-class types over the years, including subsequent Classic winners King's Best (1999) and Rule Of Law (2003), but it was only awarded Group 3 status 2006 and wasn't run at all in 2008. Only five runners this season, but it was an interesting race and the front two look particularly nice prospects. The sectionals told a story of a slow-fast-slow pace. Here they are in full: 14.52, 11.67, 11.68, 10.88, 10.88, 11.43, 12.24. The overall time was good and it's a race to be positive about. The impressive winner has more to offer.

NOTEBOOK

Dundonnell(USA) won despite the race not unfolding to suit, confirming the good impression he made when bolting up in a Lingfield maiden on his second start. He was a bit keen off the steady early pace, but James Doyle understandably didn't want to let the others get a start on him and his mount ended up getting there soon enough after tanking into contention. While Dundonnell was ultimately made to work by the Johnston runner, he looked to be idling and it was noticeable he took a while to pull up after the line. The small field didn't help a colt who should be seen to even better effect in a truly run race and he's potentially high class. He deserves his chance in a Group 1, with the Dewhurst and Racing Post Trophy obvious possible targets, and in the longer term Ladbrokes make him a generous 25-1 shot for the Guineas. (op 2-1 tchd 7-4)

Steeler(IRE) looks a fine long-term prospect. He was green on his first two starts, most recently winning a Goodwood maiden, but he's getting the idea and kept on strongly, proving himself already up to Pattern class. Out of a Park Hill winner, he can be fully expected to keep improving with time and distance. (op 9-2 tchd 11-2)

Afonso De Sousa(USA) was responsible for setting the pace, but he had finished behind Dundonnell in a July course maiden before winning when dropped to 6f at Leopardstown, and he just didn't look good enough. It's fair to say Aidan O'Brien doesn't tend to target this race with his best juveniles. (op 3-1)

Ebn Arab(USA) looked good when winning a C&D maiden by 5l on his debut, and the form had already been boosted, but he failed to prove up to this class. Better was expected. (op 5-2)

American Impact(USA) had only three rivals when winning a modest 5f maiden at Musselburgh last time and this was an awful lot tougher.

5489 NEPTUNE INVESTMENT MANAGEMENT GREAT VOLTIGEUR STKS (GROUP 2) (C&G) 1m 4f

3:05 (3:05) (Class 1) 3-Y-O £89,871 (£33,990; £16,987; £8,486) Stalls Centre

Form				RPR
2143	1		**Thought Worthy (USA)**[61] 3327 3-8-12 106 WilliamBuick 6 (John Gosden) *led: qcknd over 4f out: kpt on wl: hld on towards fin* 9/1	117
1124	2	nk	**Main Sequence (USA)**[39] 4121 3-8-12 115 TedDurcan 3 (David Lanigan) *dwlt: hld up: hdwy to trck ldrs 7f out: effrt over 3f out: chsng wnr over 1f out: styd on same pce last 50yds* 13/8[1]	116
1-12	3	2	**Encke (USA)**[22] 4685 3-8-12 112 MickaelBarzalona 5 (Mahmood Al Zarooni) *trckd wnr: t.k.h: rdn and edgd lft over 1f out: kpt on same pce* 7/1	113
1221	4	1/2	**Noble Mission**[22] 4685 3-8-12 113 TomQueally 2 (Sir Henry Cecil) *t.k.h: effrt on outside over 3f out: chsng ldrs over 2f out: kpt on same pce over 1f out* 9/2[3]	112
-511	5	2	**Thomas Chippendale (IRE)**[61] 3327 3-9-1 108 PaulHanagan 4 (Sir Henry Cecil) *t.k.h: effrt over 3f out: one pce fnl 2f* 4/1[2]	112+
-241	6	4 1/2	**Energizer (GER)**[62] 3295 3-8-12 112 FrankieDettori 1 (Mahmood Al Zarooni) *hld up in last: effrt over 3f out: nvr a threat: eased ins fnl f* 8/1	102

2m 35.96s (2.76) **Going Correction** -0.025s/f (Good) **6 Ran SP% 109.9**
Speed ratings (Par 112): **89,88,87,87,85 82**
Tote Swingers: 1&2 £3.70, 1&3 £8.00, 2&3 £3.00 CSF £23.19 TOTE £11.30: £5.00, £1.30; EX 34.70.

Owner George Strawbridge **Bred** George Strawbridge **Trained** Newmarket, Suffolk

FOCUS

A hugely competitive Group 2 with all the runners rated between 106 and 115. This has been a key trial for the St Leger and Rule Of Law (2004) and Lucarno (2007) have both completed the double in recent years, while Mastery went on to win the St Leger after being well held in this race in 2009 and last year's winner Sea Moon finished third at Doncaster. The winner put in a brave performance under a shrewd tactical ride but the downside to the form is that the early pace was very steady and couple of runners compromised their chance by taking a strong hold. The time was 6.36 seconds slower than standard. The form has been taken at face value with Thought Worthy earning a 5lb personal best, Main Sequence to his Derby form and the next two pretty much to Gordon form.

NOTEBOOK

Thought Worthy(USA), a close third behind two of these rivals in the King Edward VII Stakes at Ascot last time, set a steady pace but he had several of his rivals in trouble when attacking around the final bend and showed a gritty attitude to hold off the favourite in the closing stages. A brother to Lucarno who completed the Great Voltigeur and St Leger double in 2007, he looks a strong stayer who is effective on any ground and a step up to an extended 1m6f will suit him more than most in the St Leger. He should give it a good shot at Doncaster and received quotes of around 10-1, but he will have some work to do to hold off Triple Crown seeker Camelot who finished 11l ahead of him in the Derby. (op 8-1)

Main Sequence(USA) set the standard on his second in the Derby and luckless fourth in the Group 1 Grand Prix de Paris at Longchamp last time. Sent off a strong favourite, he got a bit caught out when the winner quickened but he knuckled down well and was just held in his bid to improve his record to 5-7. This was a creditable effort in a race where the other hold-up runners found things tough. His running style and elements of his pedigree suggest that he could find another jolt of improvement at 1m6f and he should run well if taking his chance in the St Leger. (op 7-4 t hd 15-8)

Encke(USA) ran a huge race stepped up to Group company when just denied by Noble Mission in the Gordon Stakes at Goodwood last time, a performance that resulted in his mark shooting up from 95 to 112. Always well positioned just behind the pace, he battled well and managed to turn his latest form around but he couldn't pose a big threat to the all-the-way winner. This was another decent run and he seems to have a bit more staying power than his 1m2f Group 3 winning brother Genius Beast. (op 13-2)

Noble Mission put a dent in his chance by pulling hard off the steady pace with a hood removed for the first time since his debut and couldn't make an impact behind the trailblazing winner. This was a slight setback for a horse who had looked increasingly professional on his last couple of starts but he does deserve credit for fighting on and was not beaten far in the end. He will always be overshadowed by his superstar brother Frankel and this performance adds some doubt about whether he will stay further than this, but he is a smart middle-distance performer who could bounce back if getting a stronger pace to aim at in a similar race next time. (tchd 5-1)

Thomas Chippendale(IRE) came out on top in a three-way finish against Noble Mission and Thought Worthy in a Group 2 at Royal Ascot when last seen in June. However, he had more to do conceding 3lb on his return and was keen off the sedate pace and never looked particularly comfortable on the fast ground. (op 9-2 tchd 5-1)

Energizer(GER) improved for a hood and a step up to 1m2f when winning a Group 3 in good style at Royal Ascot last time. He had been bought by Godolphin since then and was having his first try at 1m4f but he was in trouble before stamina became an issue and may not have handled the fast ground on his return from two months off. (op 7-1)

5490 JUDDMONTE INTERNATIONAL STKS (BRITISH CHAMPIONS SERIES) (GROUP 1) 1m 2f 88y

3:40 (3:41) (Class 1) 3-Y-O+

£411,147 (£155,875; £78,010; £38,860; £19,502; £9,787) **Stalls** Low

Form				RPR
-111	**1**		**Frankel**[21] 4699 4-9-5 140 .... TomQueally 7 (Sir Henry Cecil) *dwlt: hld up in rr: smooth hdwy on wd outside over 3f out: led over 2f out: shkn up and wnt clr over 1f out: impressive* **1/10**[1]	142+
1322	**2**	7	**Farhh**[21] 4699 4-9-5 122 .... FrankieDettori 4 (Saeed Bin Suroor) *trckd ldrs: hdwy over 3f out: chsng ldrs over 2f out: kpt on to take 2nd nr fin* **10/1**[3]	126
2213	**3**	*nse*	**St Nicholas Abbey (IRE)**[32] 4322 5-9-5 124 .... JPO'Brien 3 (A P O'Brien, Ire) *trckd ldng trio: led briefly wl over 2f out: sn hdd: kpt on same pce over 1f out* **5/1**[2]	126
-233	**4**	6	**Twice Over**[46] 3880 7-9-5 118 .... IanMongan 9 (Sir Henry Cecil) *hld up in rr: hdwy over 3f out: kpt on same pce to take modest 4th ins fnl f* **12/1**	114
-464	**5**	*nk*	**Bullet Train**[21] 4699 5-9-5 108 .... EddieAhern 6 (Sir Henry Cecil) *led 1f: chsd ldng pair: one pce fnl 3f* **50/1**	113
6501	**6**	2	**Sri Putra**[25] 4610 6-9-5 116 .... (b) NeilCallan 2 (Roger Varian) *hld up towards rr: effrt over 3f out: one pce fnl 2f* **20/1**	109
-330	**7**	3 ¾	**Planteur (IRE)**[63] 3267 5-9-5 117 .... WilliamBuick 8 (Marco Botti) *hld up in rr: drvn over 3f out: hmpd over 2f out: wknd over 1f out* **25/1**	102
3600	**8**	15	**Robin Hood (IRE)**[32] 4322 4-9-5 99 .... (v) SeamieHeffernan 5 (A P O'Brien, Ire) *led after 1f: hdd wl over 2f out: sn lost pl and bhd* **100/1**	72
6545	**9**	11	**Windsor Palace (IRE)**[27] 4521 7-9-5 106 .... (v) CO'Donoghue 1 (A P O'Brien, Ire) *chsd ldr after 1f: rdn 3f out: sn edgd rt and lost pl* **100/1**	50

2m 6.59s (-5.91) **Going Correction** -0.025s/f (Good) **9** Ran SP% **136.9**
Speed ratings (Par 117): **122,116,116,111,111 109,106,94,85**
Tote Swingers: 1&2 £1.80, 1&3 £1.60, 2&3 £2.20 CSF £4.18 TOTE £1.10: £1.02, £2.40, £1.30; EX 4.30 Trifecta £8.90 Pool: £26,193.49 - 2,168.11 winning units..
Owner K Abdulla **Bred** Juddmonte Farms Ltd **Trained** Newmarket, Suffolk
■ Stewards' Enquiry : Eddie Ahern four-day ban: used whip above permitted level (Sep 5-7,9)

FOCUS

Frankel faced a new challenge racing beyond 1m for the first time but there was the same outcome with Sir Henry Cecil's great colt proving just as effective over this longer trip. He earned a provisional RPR of 142, equalling his previous best which came in the Queen Anne in June, and this form was arguably more solid with the second and third pretty much to form.

NOTEBOOK

Frankel faced a proper test at the trip with Aidan O'Brien's Robin Hood taking the field along at a good gallop, closely pursued by stablemate Windsor Palace with Frankel's usual lead horse Bullet Train not far behind. The sectionals to the 3f pole (ignoring the first 88 yards) were 12.03, 11.61, 11.78, 11.97, 12.11, 12.46, 12.33, at which point Frankel took over and set the race's quickest split of 11.05 before coming home in 11.45 and 12.10. The final time was 3.40 seconds faster than the later Class 2 handicap.The field raced stands' side in the straight, and Tom Queally was brave in challenging between St Nicholas Abbey and the rail, but Frankel cruised through. He briefly looked set to win on the bridle, but as always he was asked to show off his brilliance and he didn't disappoint, drawing well clear. It was noticeable he had made a sluggish start, not obviously through design, but he was soon travelling nicely with the good gallop helping him to settle as well as ever. The form in behind is nothing special - it can be argued the runner-up and in particular the third did not have their optimum conditions - but Frankel has yet to meet a rival who can truly test him, and in proving his versatility trip-wise he has only enhanced his reputation as one of the greatest racehorses of all time. This was the ninth Group 1 win of his career and he's now 13-13. His aggregate winning margin now stands at 74.5l, while his average winning margin is 5.7l. It would be great to see him face another fresh challenge in something like the Arc and/or at the Breeders' Cup, but his connections, who have handled him brilliantly to this point, have always been keen on a return to Ascot in October for Qipco British Champions Day. (tchd 1-7 in places)

Farhh was beaten a length further by Frankel than when chasing him home in the Sussex Stakes, but this was a highly respectable effort on ground that was probably quicker than ideal. He's now 0-4 in Group 1 company, but can surely be placed to find a race at the top level.

St Nicholas Abbey(IRE) had the ground to suit, but his last three Group 1 wins have been gained over 1m4f and he didn't have sufficient speed to even slightly bother the winner. A return to further surely awaits.

Twice Over, a stablemate of the winner, won this last year (also runner-up in 2010), but he doesn't quite have the legs these days and was short of his best. (op 14-1)

Bullet Train, a close relation to Frankel and so often his pacemaker, didn't have to lead this time and kept on admirably, although it was unfortunate to hear his rider picked up four-day whip ban. He's a smart sort in his own right. (op 66-1 tchd 100-1)

Sri Putra won the Group 2 York Stakes over C&D last time, when he had a hood added to blinkers for the first time, but he's never been one to trust and looked in a thoroughly mulish mood throughout. (op 25-1)

Planteur(IRE) presumably found the ground too fast.

5491 BETVICTOR.COM STKS (H'CAP) 2m 88y

4:15 (4:15) (Class 2) (0-100,100) 4-Y-O+**£16,172** (£4,812; £2,405; £1,202) **Stalls** Low

Form				RPR
	1		**Olympiad (IRE)**[19] 4786 4-8-10 89 .... PatSmullen 11 (D K Weld, Ire) *trckd ldrs: led 2f out: edgd lft and styd on wl fnl f* **9/2**[1]	98+
4010	**2**	1 ½	**Very Good Day (FR)**[18] 4800 5-8-12 91 .... NeilCallan 10 (Mick Channon) *in rr: hdwy over 3f out: nt clr run 2f out: styd on wl ins fnl f: tk 2nd nr fin* **16/1**	97
0204	**3**	½	**Dazinski**[11] 5106 6-8-9 88 .... PaulHanagan 7 (Mark H Tompkins) *prom: chsng ldrs over 2f out: styd on same pce last 150yds* **8/1**[3]	93
0543	**4**	¾	**Mystery Star (IRE)**[11] 5076 7-9-0 93 .... KierenFallon 2 (Mark H Tompkins) *rn in snatches: mid-div: chsng ldrs 3f out: one pce over 1f out* **25/1**	98
-503	**5**	1	**Itlaaq**[25] 4613 6-8-12 91 .... (t) GrahamGibbons 15 (Michael Easterby) *hld up in rr: hdwy whn nt clr run 2f out: styd on ins fnl f* **20/1**	94
-342	**6**	1	**Eagle Rock (IRE)**[25] 4613 4-8-3 82 .... FrannyNorton 14 (Tom Tate) *trckd ldrs: effrt over 2f out: one pce* **8/1**[3]	84
2365	**7**	*nk*	**High Office**[25] 4575 6-8-8 87 .... FrederikTylicki 3 (Richard Fahey) *chsd ldrs: effrt over 3f out: one pce fnl 2f* **16/1**	89
4/35	**8**	4 ½	**Cape Express (IRE)**[21] 4697 7-8-0 84 .... DarrenEgan(5) 17 (Nicky Henderson) *hld up in rr: effrt over 3f out: sn drvn and outpcd* **9/1**	80
3120	**9**	1	**Reem Star**[25] 4613 4-8-9 88 .... AmyRyan 12 (Kevin Ryan) *hld up in rr: hdwy on outer 11f out: wknd 2f out* **33/1**	83
-003	**10**	1 ¾	**Never Can Tell (IRE)**[21] 4697 5-9-7 100 .... FrankieDettori 5 (Jamie Osborne) *led: hdd 2f out: wknd last 150yds* **11/1**	93
0605	**11**	2	**Deauville Flyer**[25] 4613 6-8-10 89 .... (p) DavidAllan 9 (Tim Easterby) *in rr: drvn over 3f out: nvr a factor* **12/1**	80
-240	**12**	*shd*	**French Hollow**[25] 4613 7-8-2 81 .... JamesSullivan 1 (Tim Fitzgerald) *in rr: n.m.r ins bnd over 4f out: nvr a factor* **40/1**	72
3201	**13**	1 ½	**Herostatus**[25] 4613 5-8-8 87 .... (p) WilliamBuick 13 (David O'Meara) *sn chsng ldrs: drvn over 3f out: wkng whn hmpd over 1f out: eased clsng stages* **12/1**	76
612	**14**	¾	**Western Prize**[26] 4528 4-8-11 90 .... JimCrowley 4 (Ralph Beckett) *trckd ldrs: effrt over 3f out: wkng whn hmpd over 1f out* **6/1**[2]	78+
00-0	**15**	*hd*	**Ashbrittle**[64] 3241 5-8-8 87 .... (b) GrahamLee 6 (David Pipe) *s.v.s: detached in last: nvr on terms* **14/1**	75
42-0	**16**	2	**Downhiller (IRE)**[25] 4575 7-8-6 85 .... EddieAhern 8 (John Dunlop) *mid-div: drvn over 3f out: sn btn* **10/1**	70

3m 32.89s (-1.61) **Going Correction** -0.025s/f (Good) **16** Ran SP% **129.9**
Speed ratings (Par 109): **103,102,102,101,101 100,100,98,97,96 95,95,95,94,94 93**
Tote Swingers: 1&2 £27.70, 1&3 £8.00, 2&3 £38.90 CSF £80.98 CT £588.04 TOTE £5.90: £1.90, £5.00, £2.40, £4.90; EX 155.90 Trifecta £1037.00 Pool: £4,008.00 - 2.86 winning units..
Owner Sir Robert Ogden **Bred** Mrs C L Weld **Trained** The Curragh, Co Kildare

FOCUS

A decent staying handicap but one lacking improvers. Straightforward form. Never Can Tell, who is better over further, took them along at a modest gallop before the pace increased over half a mile out.

NOTEBOOK

Olympiad(IRE) an Irish-trained colt, wasn't a sure stayer on breeding - he's a brother to the trainer's Irish 1000 Guineas winner Nightime - but he proved suited by this step up in trip, as well as the switch to better ground. He's lightly raced and open to plenty more improvement. (op 15-2 tchd 8-1 in a place)

Very Good Day(FR) was reported to have been unsuited by the track when below form at Goodwood last time. Prior to that he'd won over C&D and this represented a return to form. He didn't get the clearest of runs late on, but wasn't unlucky. (op 20-1)

Dazinski ran a decent race off a mark only 1lb higher than when winning this race last year. (op 15-2)

Mystery Star(IRE) seemed to up his recent level, but he doesn't have much in hand off this rating.

Itlaaq goes well here and he would have been closer with a clear run. He still reversed last-time out course form with Eagle Rock.

Eagle Rock(IRE) didn't go on from his recent second.

Cape Express(IRE) didn't improve as might have been expected for the drop in trip. (tchd 10-1)

Herostatus was reported to have lost his action. Official explanation: jockey said gelding lost its action (op 14-1 tchd 11-1)

Western Prize, a previously progressive type, wasn't picking up well enough when becoming short of room in the straight. The beaten margin was exaggerated, but he was going nowhere at the time. Official explanation: jockey said gelding suffered interference (op 5-1)

Ashbrittle, returning from two months off, lost his chance with a very slow start. (op 16-1)

5492 TALK TO VICTOR STKS (H'CAP) 1m 2f 88y

4:50 (4:52) (Class 2) (0-105,101) 3-Y-O+**£16,172** (£4,812; £2,405; £1,202) **Stalls** Low

Form				RPR
0110	**1**		**Danadana (IRE)**[22] 4684 4-10-0 101 .... KierenFallon 2 (Luca Cumani) *s.i.s: mid-div: hdwy over 2f out: styd on wl fnl f: led last 50yds* **7/1**[3]	114
3511	**2**	1 ½	**Kalk Bay (IRE)**[7] 5224 5-8-10 83 6ex .... (t) PaulMulrennan 4 (Michael Easterby) *mid-div: smooth hdwy over 3f out: led over 1f out: hdd and no ex clsng stages* **12/1**	93
3060	**3**	1 ½	**Licence To Till (USA)**[11] 5091 5-9-5 92 .... JoeFanning 11 (Mark Johnston) *trckd ldrs: n.m.r over 1f out: kpt on wl ins fnl f* **25/1**	99+
0300	**4**	*nk*	**Spanish Duke (IRE)**[22] 4684 5-9-7 94 .... EddieAhern 1 (John Dunlop) *towards rr whn hmpd bnd after 1f: hdwy over 3f out: edgd lft over 1f out: kpt on wl ins fnl f* **16/1**	100+
4603	**5**	½	**Suits Me**[18] 4795 9-9-2 89 .... TomQueally 9 (David Barron) *led: hdd and edgd rt over 1f out: kpt on one pce* **25/1**	94
1261	**6**	*shd*	**Hajras (IRE)**[26] 4529 3-9-1 96 .... PaulHanagan 13 (Mark Johnston) *mid-div: effrt over 3f out: kpt on fnl f* **6/1**[2]	101
0202	**7**	1	**Ottoman Empire (FR)**[20] 4725 6-9-12 99 .... JamieSpencer 10 (David Simcock) *trckd ldrs: edgd lft over 1f out: one pce* **20/1**	102
101	**8**	*shd*	**Sir John Hawkwood (IRE)**[11] 5101 3-9-3 98 .... WilliamBuick 14 (Sir Michael Stoute) *hld up towards rr: effrt over 2f out: pushed lft over 1f out: styng on whn hmpd ins fnl f* **2/1**[1]	104+
3063	**9**	2 ¼	**Start Right**[22] 4684 5-9-13 100 .... (p) FrankieDettori 17 (Saeed Bin Suroor) *s.i.s: in rr: effrt over 3f out: kpt on fnl f* **11/1**	99
0222	**10**	¾	**Las Verglas Star (IRE)**[22] 4684 4-9-2 89 .... TonyHamilton 8 (Richard Fahey) *trckd ldrs: ev ch tl wknd over 1f out* **16/1**	86
1044	**11**	2 ¼	**Cool Macavity (IRE)**[18] 4795 4-8-12 85 .... RobertWinston 16 (Charles Hills) *in rr: effrt over 3f out: nvr a factor* **20/1**	78
3321	**12**	*shd*	**Maven**[25] 4608 4-8-12 85 .... DavidAllan 7 (Tim Easterby) *hld up in rr: effrt on wd outside over 2f out: sn wknd* **11/1**	77
4102	**13**	1	**Fork Handles**[11] 5091 4-8-13 86 .... MartinHarley 5 (Mick Channon) *trckd ldrs: drvn 3f out: wknd over 1f out: eased towards fin* **33/1**	76
401	**14**	¾	**Van Der Art**[13] 4997 3-8-7 95 .... MichaelJMMurphy(7) 15 (Alan Jarvis) *slowly into s: in rr whn n.m.r on bnd after 1f: effrt on ins over 3f out: wknd and eased over 1f out* **10/1**	84
0321	**15**	9	**Aerodynamic (IRE)**[20] 4747 5-8-9 82 oh2 .... JamesSullivan 3 (Michael Easterby) *in rr whn n.m.r bnd after 1f: bhd fnl 2f* **66/1**	53

4400 **16** *11* **King Torus (IRE)**[22] 4684 4-9-13 **100** (b) JimCrowley 12 49
(Richard Hannon) *trckd ldrs: effrt over 3f out: wknd 2f out: sn eased* **33/1**

2m 9.99s (-2.51) **Going Correction** -0.025s/f (Good)
WFA 3 from 4yo+ 8lb **16** Ran SP% **129.9**
Speed ratings (Par 109): **109,107,106,106,105 105,105,105,103,102 100,100,99,99,92 83**
Tote Swingers: 1&2 £22.60, 1&3 £42.10, 2&3 £71.50 CSF £86.82 CT £2041.73 TOTE £8.70: £2.40, £2.80, £4.50, £3.50; EX 99.00 Trifecta £2768.30 Pool: £5,835.87 - 1.56 winning units..
Owner Sheikh Mohammed Obaid Al Maktoum **Bred** Darley **Trained** Newmarket, Suffolk

FOCUS
A highly competitive handicap. The early pace was not very strong and the action unfolded in the centre to far side.The time was 3.40 seconds slower than the International Stakes. Solid form, with a clear personal best from Danadana

NOTEBOOK
Danadana(IRE) hit a new form high when winning the Zetland Gold Cup off 7lb lower in June and didn't look entirely comfortable on the track when well held as favourite at Goodwood last time. Prominent in the market again, he negotiated his way past some traffic problems before producing a strong run out wide to improve his strike-rate to 4-10. A generally progressive 4yo who seems ideally suited by a strongly run 1m2f on fast ground, he has the potential to develop into a Group performer. (tchd 15-2 abd 13-2)
Kalk Bay(IRE) powered clear when completing a double in a 0-85 handicap at Beverley last week. He had a penalty to deal with in this stronger race but ran a huge race and was just overhauled by a faster finisher. (op 10-1)
Licence To Till(USA) looked like he was on the retreat in the final furlong but he showed a feisty attitude to rally for third. He has looked in the grip of the handicapper since his Chester win in June but he is sliding back down the weights and he bounced back with consecutive wins last autumn.
Spanish Duke(IRE) finished well switched to the far rail in his best run since his closing third at Epsom in June. He should appreciate a step back up to 1m4f. (op 14-1)
Suits Me, a close third off the same mark in a similar handicap at Doncaster last time, gave it another good shot under usual trailblazing tactics but couldn't repel some finishers.
Hajras(IRE) improved his record to 3-5 when justifying favouritism in a 1m2f Ascot handicap last time, but he got a bit tapped for speed off 6lb higher in this steadily run race and got going too late. He could resume his progress off a stronger gallop next time and his running style suggests a step up to 1m4f could work for him. (op 7-1)
Ottoman Empire(FR) had every chance but he looked a bit awkward and hung left under pressure on ground probably faster than ideal. (tchd 25-1)
Sir John Hawkwood(IRE) bounced back from a disappointment in the mud when scoring with something in hand in a 1m2f handicap at Newmarket last time. Heavily-backed in his bid to defy a 6lb rise and a wide draw, he was ridden patiently but there were warning signs early in the straight and he couldn't land a blow.This was a bit disappointing but the steady pace was probably against him and he would have finished closer if he wasn't hampered in the closing stages.A very lightly raced 3yo still has scope for further improvement and should be suited by stepping up in trip.
Official explanation: jockey said colt was denied a clear run (op 9-4)
Start Right stayed on steadily from some way back in a race that didn't really set up for his closing style. (op 12-1)
Las Verglas Star(IRE), runner-up in 1m1f/1m2f handicaps on good or slower ground on his last three runs, was well positioned for a long way but his effort petered out on ground quicker than ideal. (op 14-1)
T/Jkpt: £31,532.60 to a £1 stake. Pool: £66,718.19 - 1.50 winning tickets. T/Plt: £167.70 to a £1 stake. Pool: £267,848.20 - 1,165.56 winning tickets. T/Qpdt: £22.00 to a £1 stake. Pool: £13,857.47 - 1.50 winning tickets. WG

5493 - 5500a (Foreign Racing) - See Raceform Interactive

5191 BATH (L-H)

Thursday, August 23

OFFICIAL GOING: Good (good to soft in places)
Wind: Virtually nil Weather: White cloud

5501 SATELLITE INFORMATION SERVICES H'CAP — 1m 5y
1:50 (1:50) (Class 5) (0-70,71) 3-Y-O **£2,264** (£673; £336; £168) **Stalls** Low

Form RPR
0006 **1** **Charitable Act (FR)**[17] 4876 3-9-7 **70** DarryllHolland 11 80
(William Muir) *mde virtually all: qcknd fr 3f out: rdn and jnd appr fnl f: kpt on wl u.p and a jst doing enough* **12/1**
0021 **2** *nk* **Multi Bene**[56] 3548 3-9-5 **68** SeanLevey 12 77
(Ed McMahon) *in tch: hdwy towards outside fr 3f out: drvn to press wnr appr fnl f: kpt chalng but a jst hld* **9/4**[1]
312 **3** *2 ½* **Siouxperhero (IRE)**[13] 5036 3-9-4 **67** StevieDonohoe 5 70
(William Muir) *towards rr: rdn and hdwy fr 3f out: styd on fnl f to take 3rd clsng stages* **6/1**[3]
3041 **4** *1* **Shomberg**[14] 4988 3-8-8 **57** KellyHarrison 4 58
(Dai Burchell) *t.k.h: chsd ldrs: rdn over 2f out: styd on same pce fnl f: lost 3rd clsng stages* **7/1**
-100 **5** *1* **Golden Jubilee (USA)**[58] 3475 3-8-9 **65** WilliamTwiston-Davies(7) 9 64
(Richard Hannon) *chsd ldrs: rdn over 2f out: styd on same pce* **14/1**
6350 **6** *¾* **Essell**[13] 5037 3-8-8 **57** SamHitchcott 7 54
(Mick Channon) *prom: chsd wnr 3f out: sn rdn: wknd fnl f* **12/1**
6036 **7** *½* **Temuco (IRE)**[14] 4988 3-9-1 **67** MatthewCosham(3) 10 63
(David Evans) *s.i.s: in rr: pushed along and hdwy towards outside over 2f out: kpt on fnl f but nvr gng pce to get into contention* **8/1**
4435 **8** *½* **Bajan Story**[17] 4876 3-9-2 **65** FergusSweeney 1 60
(Michael Blanshard) *in rr: hdwy on ins over 1f out: nvr gng pce to rch ldrs* **12/1**
0041 **9** *2 ¼* **Abhaath (USA)**[3] 5427 3-9-3 **71** 6ex DarrenEgan(5) 8 60
(Ronald Harris) *in rr: rdn and sme hdwy towards outside 2f out: nvr gng pce to rch ldrs* **5/1**[2]

1m 43.94s (3.14) **Going Correction** +0.40s/f (Good) **9** Ran SP% **115.1**
Speed ratings (Par 100): **100,99,97,96,95 94,93,93,91**
toteswingers 1&2 £10.10, 1&3 £9.70, 2&3 £3.40 CSF £39.17 CT £184.53 TOTE £21.20: £4.60, £1.70, £1.90; EX 68.40.
Owner Muir Racing Partnership - Chester **Bred** Aleyrion Bloodstock Ltd **Trained** Lambourn, Berks

FOCUS
Races utilising bottom bend increased in distances by about 12.5yds. There was 25mm of rain since last week's meeting and the going was good, good to soft in places. A competitive handicap, involving three last-time-out winners, but it was run at a steady pace and a surprise winner made all. The winner had slipped to a good mark on his 2yo best.

5502 MATTHEW CLARK H'CAP — 5f 161y
2:20 (2:23) (Class 5) (0-75,75) 3-Y-O+ **£2,264** (£673; £336; £168) **Stalls** Centre

Form RPR
6000 **1** **Divine Call**[49] 3778 5-9-6 **71** ShaneKelly 8 78
(Milton Bradley) *in rr: hdwy on outer over 1f out: str run ins fnl f to ld last stride* **16/1**
6034 **2** *hd* **Swendab (IRE)**[12] 5097 4-9-0 **72** (v) WilliamTwiston-Davies(7) 12 78
(John O'Shea) *chsd ldrs: chal 2f out: led wl over 1f out: drvn and kpt on fnl f: hdd last strides* **16/1**
1336 **3** *shd* **Ginzan**[16] 4903 4-9-5 **70** TomMcLaughlin 17 76
(Malcolm Saunders) *chsd ldrs: drvn to chal 1f out: styd on wl fnl f: jst failed* **14/1**
0000 **4** *nk* **Rulesn'regulations**[15] 4939 6-9-7 **72** (b) PatCosgrave 7 79+
(Matthew Salaman) *broke wl: sn towards rr: hdwy over 1f out: sn nt clr run: str run fnl 120yds: fin wl* **16/1**
2606 **5** *shd* **Diamond Vine (IRE)**[10] 5150 4-9-3 **68** (p) KierenFox 13 73
(Ronald Harris) *towards rr and r on outside: hdwy appr fnl f: str rn fnl f: fin wl* **33/1**
0124 **6** *1 ¼* **Going French (IRE)**[17] 4887 5-9-1 **66** KellyHarrison 4 67
(Dai Burchell) *chsd ldrs: rdn over 2f out: ev ch 1f out: wknd clsng stages* **14/1**
0513 **7** *¾* **Cockney Fire**[9] 5195 3-9-5 **73** (v) CathyGannon 10 71
(David Evans) *chsd ldrs: drvn along 2f out: wknd fnl 100yds* **14/1**
4103 **8** *¾* **Perlachy**[17] 4887 8-8-10 **66** (v) DarrenEgan(5) 9 62
(Ronald Harris) *in rr: racd on outer and hdwy over 1f out: chsd ldrs ins fnl f: wknd fnl 120yds* **16/1**
3021 **9** *shd* **Kyllachy Storm**[9] 5191 8-8-3 **64** 6ex PhilipPrince(7) 3 56
(Ron Hodges) *chsd ldrs: rdn over 2f out: styd on same pce fnl f* **8/1**[3]
5264 **10** *¾* **Emiratesdotcom**[11] 5120 6-9-10 **75** LiamKeniry 15 68+
(Milton Bradley) *in rr: sme hdwy whn nt clr run jst ins fnl f: no ch after* **8/1**[3]
0-00 **11** *nk* **Victorian Bounty**[89] 2482 7-9-10 **75** DaneO'Neill 5 67
(Tony Newcombe) *nvr gng pce to get into contention* **20/1**
6000 **12** *2 ½* **Matsunosuke**[7] 5272 10-9-5 **70** MartinLane 16 54
(Alan Coogan) *stdd s: in rr: sme late hdwy fr way off pce* **50/1**
004 **13** *shd* **Bahama Spirit (IRE)**[16] 4903 3-9-1 **72** RaulDaSilva(3) 11 55
(Jeremy Gask) *chsd ldrs: rdn over 2f out: wknd fnl f* **20/1**
1133 **14** *½* **Scommettitrice (IRE)**[2] 5445 4-8-6 **62** (p) NathanSweeney(5) 1 44
(David Evans) *spd to 1/2-way* **14/1**
1400 **15** *2* **Drawnfromthepast (IRE)**[13] 5035 7-9-9 **74** FergusSweeney 2 49
(Jamie Osborne) *chsd ldrs 3f* **22/1**
4112 **16** *7* **Crimson Queen**[16] 4903 5-9-10 **75** (b) ChrisCatlin 14 27
(Roy Brotherton) *led: jst led again 2f out: hdd over 1f out: sn wknd* **9/2**[2]
4442 **17** *12* **Jinker Noble**[6] 5308 3-8-12 **73** (v[1]) RyanTate(7) 6
(Clive Cox) *led after 1f: hdd 2f out: wknd qckly over 1f out* **4/1**[1]

1m 12.54s (1.34) **Going Correction** +0.15s/f (Good)
WFA 3 from 4yo+ 3lb **17** Ran SP% **129.4**
Speed ratings (Par 103): **97,96,96,96,96 94,93,92,92,91 90,87,87,86,84 74,58**
toteswingers 1&2 £103.00, 1&3 £31.00, 2&3 £67.40 CSF £248.19 CT £3792.88 TOTE £24.40: £4.50, £5.10, £2.80, £3.50; EX 734.90.
Owner E A Hayward **Bred** Cheveley Park Stud Ltd **Trained** Sedbury, Gloucs

FOCUS
It was fast and furious in this sprint handicap. The two market leaders got involved in a destructive battle up front and the winner came from a long way back to prevail in a bunch finish. The third and fifth help set the standard.
Divine Call Official explanation: trainer said, regarding the apparent improvement of form, that the gelding has improved in his condition since his last run and benefitted from the change in tactics

5503 FESTIVAL RACING MEDIAN AUCTION MAIDEN STKS — 5f 11y
2:50 (2:52) (Class 6) 2-Y-O **£1,617** (£481; £240; £120) **Stalls** Centre

Form RPR
263 **1** **Kodatish (IRE)**[9] 5192 2-9-3 73 KierenFox 5 72
(Ronald Harris) *chsd ldrs: rdn along fr 3f out: styd on 1f out: stl 3 l off wnr but sn in pursuit: styd on wl fnl 75yds to ld cl home* **6/1**
33 **2** *½* **Dawn Catcher**[14] 4990 2-8-9 0 RaulDaSilva(3) 2 65
(Tony Carroll) *led: sn clr and stl 3 l clr 1f out: sn hrd drvn: no ex and hdd cl home* **7/2**[3]
0632 **3** *2 ½* **Imperial Spirit**[13] 5032 2-9-3 75 SamHitchcott 7 61
(Mick Channon) *in tch: drvn and hdwy to briefly chse wnr 1f out: sn dropped to 3rd and styd on same pce fnl 120yds* **10/3**[2]
605 **4** *2 ½* **Black Dave (IRE)**[11] 5121 2-9-3 0 RichardThomas 4 52
(David Evans) *in rr: sn pushed along: styd on fnl f to take one pce 4th fnl 75yds* **33/1**
5 *¾* **Tagalaka (IRE)** 2-9-3 0 CathyGannon 8 50
(Eve Johnson Houghton) *s.i.s: in rr: pushed along 3f out: hdwy fnl f: kpt on clsng stages but nvr any threat* **7/1**
2326 **6** *2 ¼* **Whistling Buddy**[19] 4816 2-9-3 73 SebSanders 1 41
(Peter Makin) *chsd ldr: rdn and no imp fr over 2f out: lost 2nd and wknd 1f out* **11/4**[1]
7 *1 ¼* **Shes Ellie** 2-8-7 0 MarkCoumbe(5) 3 32
(John O'Shea) *outpcd in rr tl mod late prog* **66/1**
043 **8** *3 ¾* **Pal Of The Cat**[28] 4512 2-8-12 67 DarrenEgan(5) 6 23
(Brian Gubby) *racd on outer: bhd fr 1/2-way* **8/1**

1m 4.16s (1.66) **Going Correction** +0.15s/f (Good) **8** Ran SP% **114.3**
Speed ratings (Par 92): **92,91,87,83,82 78,76,70**
toteswingers 1&2 £3.30, 1&3 £5.50, 2&3 £3.70 CSF £27.26 TOTE £4.50: £1.80, £1.10, £2.10; EX 33.20.
Owner J Hatherell & Ridge House Stables **Bred** Lynn Lodge Stud **Trained** Earlswood, Monmouths

FOCUS
There was an open market for this maiden. Very few got involved but there was an exciting finish as the 73-rated winner reeled in the long-time leader close home. The form is rated around the first two.

NOTEBOOK
Kodatish(IRE) hung right throughout when below-par as favourite at 5.7f here last time but there no wayward signs this time and he showed plenty of determination to snatch the prize on his fifth start. He is still relatively unexposed and hits the ground quite hard, so may prove ideally suited by a slow surface. (op 11-2)
Dawn Catcher showed plenty of speed when third in a pair of maidens here and at Chepstow on her first two starts. She didn't hold back again and opened up a clear lead turning in but she was just caught near the line. A Bertolini filly who seems effective on fast and slow ground, she looks all about speed and could take some catching in a 5f nursery on a sharp track. (op 4-1 tchd 9-2)
Imperial Spirit had leading claims on his placed efforts at Epsom and Brighton on his last two runs but the drop back to 5f was against him and he was under pressure some way out and couldn't pose a threat. (op 7-2)
Black Dave(IRE), tailed off on the last two of his three runs, bounced back with a fair staying-on effort dropped back to 5f. He is quite a scopey type and may be able to build on this in nurseries. (op 28-1)
Tagalaka(IRE), a 10,000euros half-brother to a modest ten-race maiden over hurdles, showed some promise on his debut and should improve for the experience. (op 12-1)

Whistling Buddy tracked the leader but he didn't find much and cut out quickly. He might ideally want a sharp 5f on fast ground but this was a second below-par run from this 73-rated colt and he has a bit to prove.

5504 BEAUFORT MAINTENANCE LTD CONVEYORS H'CAP 5f 11y
3:25 (3:26) (Class 6) (0-60,59) 4-Y-0+ **£1,617** (£481; £240; £120) **Stalls** Centre

Form RPR
0660 1 **Juarla (IRE)**[14] 4993 4-8-10 **53** DarrenEgan(5) 13 68
(Ronald Harris) *in tch: gd hdwy 2f out to ld appr fnl f: drvn and styd on strly fnl 120yds* **9/2**[2]
2221 2 2 1/4 **Griffin Point (IRE)**[16] 4902 5-9-6 **58** (b) StevieDonohoe 12 65
(William Muir) *chsd ldrs towards outside: rdn 2f out: chal appr fnl f: sn chsng wnr but no imp but wl clr of 3rd* **5/1**[3]
2242 3 6 **Arch Walker (IRE)**[6] 5327 5-9-7 **59** (b) DarryllHolland 10 44
(John Weymes) *pressed ldrs: chal fr over 2f out tl appr fnl f sn outpcd by ldng duo but kpt on for 3rd* **13/8**[1]
/0 0 4 3/4 **Loved To Bits**[19] 4815 4-8-13 **54** SophieDoyle(3) 3 37
(Eric Wheeler) *in rr: hdwy on outer over 1f out: styd on fnl f: nvr a threat* **33/1**
1326 5 1 3/4 **Ladydolly**[6] 5327 4-9-4 **56** (p) ChrisCatlin 6 32
(Roy Brotherton) *w ldr tl led 2f out: hdd appr fnl f and sn wknd* **11/1**
6 1/2 **Fiona's Spirit (IRE)**[43] 3982 5-8-4 **47** ow2 (tp) MarkCoumbe(5) 11 22
(Daniel Mark Loughnane) *towards rr: hdwy 1/2-way: chsd ldrs and hrd rdn over 1f out: one pce* **33/1**
0032 7 3/4 **Botanist**[9] 5191 5-8-12 **50** (be) LiamKeniry 8 22
(Milton Bradley) *s.i.s: in rr: hdwy 3f out: rdn over 2f out: sn outpcd* **15/2**
0000 8 3/4 **Adaeze (IRE)**[9] 5217 4-8-13 **51** DaneO'Neill 1 20
(Jonathan Portman) *chsd ldrs: rdn 2f out: wknd 1f out: eased whn btn ins fnl f* **20/1**
60 9 nse **Quadra Hop (IRE)**[35] 4236 4-8-7 **45** CathyGannon 9 14
(Bryn Palling) *in tch: n.m.r fr 2f out to 1f out: rdn and no prog fnl f* **25/1**
000 10 2 3/4 **Wishbone (IRE)**[65] 3243 5-8-13 **51** J-PGuillambert 5
(Jo Hughes) *hmpd sn after s: outpcd most of way* **22/1**
0001 11 1/2 **Flaxen Lake**[16] 4928 5-8-11 **52** (p) RaulDaSilva(3) 2
(Milton Bradley) *sn led: hdd 2f out: eased whn no ch fnl f* **12/1**

1m 3.02s (0.52) **Going Correction** +0.15s/f (Good) 11 Ran SP% 119.6
Speed ratings (Par 101): **101,97,87,86,83 83,81,80,80,76 75**
toteswingers 1&2 £7.80, 1&3 £6.40, 2&3 £2.40 CSF £25.70 CT £51.27 TOTE £4.20: £1.40, £2.50, £1.20; EX 39.00.
Owner Robert & Nina Bailey **Bred** D And Mrs D Veitch **Trained** Earlswood, Monmouths

FOCUS
The winner landed a gamble in smooth style in this handicap and the runner-up finished a long way clear of the rest. The pick of the three C&D times and the winner was close to his 3yo best.
Adaeze(IRE) Official explanation: trainer said that the filly was unsuited by the going which was good, good to soft in places

5505 RACING AT BATH MAIDEN STKS 5f 11y
4:00 (4:00) (Class 5) 3-4-Y-0 **£2,264** (£673; £336; £168) **Stalls** Centre

Form RPR
32 1 **Angelito**[29] 4456 3-9-3 0 SeanLevey 3 68+
(Ed McMahon) *chsd ldr: chal 2f out: sn led: drvn out fnl f* **1/1**[1]
0642 2 1 1/2 **Asian Trader**[10] 5177 3-9-3 69 (t) LiamJones 1 65+
(William Haggas) *trckd ldrs: nt clr run over 1f out: swtchd rt and r.o to chse wnr ins fnl f but no imp: hld on all out for 2nd* **7/2**[3]
5 3 nse **Brown Volcano (IRE)**[14] 4992 3-8-12 0 MarkCoumbe(5) 4 63
(John O'Shea) *chsd ldrs: rdn over 2f out: kpt on fnl f to press for 2nd clsng stages but no imp on wnr* **33/1**
3056 4 3 3/4 **Chicarito**[13] 5033 3-9-3 52 (p) FergusSweeney 6 49
(John Gallagher) *sn led: jnd 2f out: sn hdd: wknd fnl f* **28/1**
2230 5 hd **Homeboy (IRE)**[17] 4887 4-9-5 61 [1] ShaneKelly 7 49
(Marcus Tregoning) *in rr: rdn over 2f out: a outpcd* **5/2**[2]
6 6 28 **Multiply**[26] 4605 3-9-3 0 (b[1]) SebSanders 5
(Peter Makin) *sn rdn and bdly outpcd: t.o* **28/1**

1m 3.41s (0.91) **Going Correction** +0.15s/f (Good)
WFA 3 from 4yo 2lb 6 Ran SP% 110.6
Speed ratings (Par 103): **98,95,95,89,89 44**
toteswingers 1&2 £1.40, 1&3 £4.10, 2&3 £9.30 CSF £4.66 TOTE £1.70: £1.10, £1.40; EX 4.60.
Owner Least Moved Partners **Bred** Least Moved Partners **Trained** Lichfield, Staffs

FOCUS
The favourite had to work but cashed in on a good opportunity in this modest maiden. The winner did not need to match his latest form.

5506 LINDLEY CATERING H'CAP 1m 2f 46y
4:35 (4:36) (Class 6) (0-65,71) 3-Y-0+ **£1,617** (£481; £240; £120) **Stalls** Low

Form RPR
0000 1 **Belle Park**[27] 4536 5-8-9 **46** DarryllHolland 9 56
(Karen George) *stdd s: hld up in rr: drvn and hdwy on outer over 3f out: chal fr 2f out: rdn to ld wl over 1f out: styd on wl* **14/1**
6042 2 1/2 **Iguacu**[14] 4987 8-8-12 **49** (p) AndreaAtzeni 1 58
(Richard Price) *chsd ldrs: rdn 4f out: styd on chse wnr fnl f: gng on clsng stages but a hld* **15/2**
2534 3 3 1/2 **Mighty Clarets (IRE)**[9] 5199 5-9-6 **64** WilliamTwiston-Davies(7) 10 66
(Barry Leavy) *chsd ldrs: rdn 3f out: styd on u.p to take one pce 3rd ins fnl f* **4/1**[1]
3425 4 1 1/4 **Zuzu Angel (IRE)**[16] 4900 3-8-8 **58** DavidKenny(5) 8 58
(William Knight) *in rr: rdn 4f out: styd on fnl 2f: nvr gng pce to rch ldrs* **5/1**[2]
2331 5 1/2 **Know No Fear**[7] 5259 7-9-13 **71** 6ex (p) SemiraPashai(7) 4 70
(Alastair Lidderdale) *t.k.h: led 7f out: sn clr: jnd 2f out: hdd wl over 1f out: wknd fnl f* **13/2**
0-05 6 1/2 **Tenessee**[18] 4843 5-10-0 **65** ChrisCatlin 6 63
(Jamie Osborne) *led tl hdd 7f out: styd chsng ldr: rdn 3f out: wknd appr fnl f* **6/1**
4450 7 16 **Sir Bruno (FR)**[27] 4531 5-9-9 **65** DarrenEgan(5) 3 31
(Bryn Palling) *chsd ldrs: rdn 3f out: wknd 2f out* **8/1**
1532 8 11 **Ishikawa (IRE)**[26] 4586 4-10-0 **65** FergusSweeney 5
(Alan King) *in tch: rdn 4f out: effrt 3f out: wknd qckly 2f out* **11/2**[3]
000/ 9 6 **Gouranga**[445] 186 9-8-6 **46** oh1 SophieDoyle(3) 2
(Tony Carroll) *chsd ldrs: rdn and wknd 4f out: t.o* **66/1**
000 10 11 **Autarch (USA)**[13] 5038 3-9-3 **62** IanMongan 7
(Amanda Perrett) *in rr: rdn and no rspnse 4f out: t.o* **25/1**

2m 14.58s (3.58) **Going Correction** +0.40s/f (Good)
WFA 3 from 4yo+ 8lb 10 Ran SP% 114.6
Speed ratings (Par 101): **101,100,97,96,96 96,83,74,69,60**
toteswingers 1&2 £11.80, 1&3 £8.60, 2&3 £5.90 CSF £112.85 CT £502.83 TOTE £14.00: £3.90, £3.50, £2.10; EX 156.30.
Owner R A Bimson **Bred** C A Green **Trained** Higher Eastington, Devon

FOCUS
They went a decent pace in this handicap. Modest form with the second looking the best guide.

5507 LANSDOWN H'CAP 1m 5f 22y
5:05 (5:05) (Class 5) (0-70,70) 4-Y-0+ **£2,385** (£704; £352) **Stalls** High

Form RPR
065 1 **Passion Play**[10] 5159 4-8-10 **64** DavidKenny(5) 6 73
(William Knight) *chsd ldr: led over 2f out: rdn and chal fr over 1f out: narrowly hdd fnl 120yds: rallied to ld again sn after: drvn out* **12/1**
-042 2 hd **Peachez**[11] 5124 4-8-12 **66** (p) AmyScott(5) 11 74
(Alastair Lidderdale) *s.i.s: hld up in rr: hdwy on outside over 2f out: edgd lft sn after: drvn to chal over 1f out: narrow ld fnl 120yds: sn hdd: nt qckn* **9/2**[2]
4-05 3 1 3/4 **Castlemorris King**[61] 3400 4-8-10 **64** MarkCoumbe(5) 9 70
(Michael Attwater) *hld up in rr: hdwy on outside fr 2f out and sn bmpd: tk 3rd 1f out: one pce u.p* **9/2**[2]
411 4 5 **Laser Blazer**[13] 5038 4-9-3 **66** (p) IanMongan 3 64
(Jeremy Gask) *hld up in rr: t.k.h: hdwy on ins over 3f out: drvn and swtchd rt to outer over 2f out: sn rdn: styd on same pce ins fnl f* **3/1**[1]
-046 5 3/4 **Danehill Dante (IRE)**[18] 4843 4-9-5 **68** FergusSweeney 8 65
(Alan King) *chsd ldrs: rdn to chse ldrs in 3rd fr ins fnl 3f: no imp fr 2f out: wknd fnl f* **7/1**
3555 6 3/4 **Handles For Forks (IRE)**[20] 4756 4-9-6 **69** SamHitchcott 2 65
(Mick Channon) *sn led: rdn and hdd over 2f out: wknd over 1f out* **15/2**
-061 7 8 **Transfer**[21] 4733 7-8-13 **62** AndreaAtzeni 4 46
(Richard Price) *in tch: rdn 3f out: wknd 2f out* **11/2**[3]
0- 8 5 **Parhelion**[100] 6893 5-9-7 **70** (t) DaneO'Neill 5 46
(Derek Haydn Jones) *chsd ldrs: rdn 3f out: wknd over 3f out* **33/1**

2m 58.43s (6.43) **Going Correction** +0.40s/f (Good) 8 Ran SP% 111.6
Speed ratings (Par 103): **96,95,94,91,91 90,85,82**
toteswingers 1&2 £9.60, 1&3 £8.90, 2&3 £5.60 CSF £61.98 CT £278.38 TOTE £14.00: £3.00, £2.80, £1.50; EX 87.20.
Owner Mascalls Stud **Bred** Mascalls Stud **Trained** Patching, W Sussex
■ Stewards' Enquiry : Amy Scott one-day ban: careless riding (6 Sep)

FOCUS
A competitive handicap. It was run at just a fair pace and there was a tight finish. The first three came clear and may be on fair marks.

5508 PEGGOTY APPRENTICE H'CAP 1m 3f 144y
5:35 (5:35) (Class 6) (0-55,55) 3-Y-0+ **£1,617** (£481; £240; £120) **Stalls** Low

Form RPR
0005 1 **Sir Dylan**[7] 5266 3-8-8 **49** [1] DarrenEgan 12 57
(Ronald Harris) *t.k.h: hld up in rr: hdwy 2f out: rdn and styd on to ld fnl 140yds: hung rt u.p: drvn out* **10/1**
-506 2 1 3/4 **Naledi**[9] 5199 8-8-13 **47** DannyBrock(3) 10 52
(Richard Price) *t.k.h: hld up in rr: drvn and hdwy fr 2f out: styd on far rail and r.o fnl f to take 2nd last stride: no imp on wnr* **25/1**
-453 3 nse **Finch Flyer (IRE)**[9] 5199 5-9-4 **52** (p) NicoleNordblad(3) 1 57
(Aytach Sadik) *chsd ldrs: chal fr over 2f out tl led over 1f out: hdd fnl 120yds: carried rt and one pce sn after: lost 2nd last stride* **8/1**[3]
-022 4 3/4 **Captain Oats (IRE)**[14] 4994 9-9-7 **55** RachealKneller(3) 4 59
(Pam Ford) *in tch: chsd ldrs 4f out: chal fr 3f out: slt ld sn after: narrowly hdd over 2f out: stl ev ch 1f out: carried rt and one pce fnl 120yds* **15/2**[2]
5500 5 2 1/2 **Lady Romanza (IRE)**[36] 4214 3-9-0 **55** MatthewLawson 13 54
(Brendan Powell) *chsd ldrs: rdn 4f out: slt ld over 2f out: hdd over 1f out: btn whn carried rt fnl 120yds* **20/1**
0/31 6 1 1/4 **Chapter Nine (IRE)**[9] 5198 6-9-3 **51** 6ex WilliamTwiston-Davies(3) 6 48
(Seamus Mullins) *hld up in rr: stdy hdwy 4f out to chal wl over 2f out: wknd fnl f* **5/4**[1]
506 7 3/4 **Belleau (IRE)**[28] 4491 4-9-9 **54** CharlesBishop 8 50
(Matt Sheppard) *s.i.s: in rr: hdwy on outside over 3f out: to chal fr wl over 2f out tl over 1f out: sn wknd* **10/1**
00/4 8 7 **Mossmann Gorge**[112] 1770 10-9-1 **46** oh1 (p) AshleyMorgan 2 30
(Anthony Middleton) *in rr: rdn and hdwy on ins over 2f out: nvr rchd ldrs and wknd over 1f out* **33/1**
0604 9 4 1/2 **Imperial Ruby**[17] 4870 3-8-11 **55** (v) ThomasBrown(3) 11 31
(Joseph Tuite) *chsd ldr: rdn and wknd over 2f out* **14/1**
3606 10 1/2 **Blue Pencil**[27] 4537 3-8-2 **46** oh1 JoshBaudains(3) 5 22
(Roger Curtis) *t.k.h: in tch: rdn 3f out: wknd sn after* **33/1**
50-0 11 9 **Highland Cadett**[14] 4994 5-9-1 **46** oh1 LeonnaMayor 9
(Pam Ford) *sn led: hdd & wknd ins fnl 3f* **50/1**
040 12 1/2 **Cash Injection**[57] 3483 3-8-9 **50** (t) DavidKenny 7
(Karen George) *chsd ldrs: sddle slipped 6f out: upsides ins fnl 3f: sn wknd and eased* **11/1**
000 13 9 **Pass The Time**[80] 2757 3-8-3 **47** NoelGarbutt(3) 3
(Neil Mulholland) *chsd ldrs to 5f out: sn wknd* **33/1**

2m 38.23s (7.63) **Going Correction** +0.40s/f (Good)
WFA 3 from 4yo+ 10lb 13 Ran SP% 119.9
Speed ratings (Par 101): **90,88,88,88,86 85,85,80,77,77 71,70,64**
toteswingers 1&2 £9.90, 1&3 £6.50, 2&3 £9.40 CSF £245.09 CT £2100.78 TOTE £10.90: £2.30, £6.00, £1.80; EX 306.90.
Owner David & Gwyn Joseph/Ridge House Stables **Bred** Cavendish Bloodstock **Trained** Earlswood, Monmouths
■ Stewards' Enquiry : Matthew Lawson four-day ban: use of whip (6, 8, 9 & 10 Sep)

FOCUS
The hot favourite was a bit disappointing in this apprentice handicap and the action unfolded down the middle of the track.
Chapter Nine(IRE) Official explanation: trainer said that the gelding ran flat
Cash Injection Official explanation: jockey said that his saddle slipped
T/Plt: £148.00 to a £1 stake. Pool: £47527.42 - 234.33 winning tickets T/Qpdt: £6.10 to a £1 stake. Pool: £4235.13 - 512.88 winning tickets ST

5119 FOLKESTONE (R-H)
Thursday, August 23

OFFICIAL GOING: Good to firm (firm in places)
Wind: Moderate, half against Weather: Sunny becoming cloudy

5509 LADBROKES.COM AMATEUR RIDERS' H'CAP 1m 4f
5:10 (5:10) (Class 5) (0-70,70) 3-Y-0+ **£2,305** (£709; £354) **Stalls** High

Form RPR
-613 1 **Bouggatti**[28] 4504 4-11-0 **70** MrSWalker 4 78
(Lady Herries) *chsd clr ldr after 2f: clsd 2f out: drvn to ld over 1f out: sn clr* **5/6**[1]

4142 **2** *3½* **Mollyow (IRE)**[13] 5051 4-9-5 **54** MrGrahamCarson(7) 3 56
(Terry Clement) *led 1f: prom in chsng gp: rdn 2f out: styd on to take 2nd ent fnl f* **8/1**

6300 **3** *½* **Sail Home**[17] 4884 5-10-12 **68** MrRBirkett 5 70
(Julia Feilden) *hld up in 5th: rdn 3f out: styd on to take 3rd ins fnl f* **7/1**[3]

0550 **4** *2¼* **Rosy Dawn**[15] 4940 7-9-2 **51** oh6 MrAJones(7) 2 49
(John Bridger) *led after 1f: sn clr: 10 l ld 7f out: wknd and hdd over 1f out* **20/1**

6502 **5** *½* **Squad**[13] 5038 6-10-3 **64** (v) MrJCoffill-Brown(5) 1 61
(Simon Dow) *prom in chsng gp: rdn over 2f out: no imp* **9/2**[2]

4545 **6** *16* **Barbirolli**[14] 5022 10-9-4 **51** oh6 (p) MissCScott(5) 6 23
(William Stone) *hld up in rr: n.d fnl 3f* **20/1**

440- **7** *20* **Croix Rouge (USA)**[260] 7654 10-9-10 **57** MissKMargarson(5) 7
(Ralph Smith) *t.k.h in rr: wd in bk st and on home turn: no ch fnl 3f* **20/1**

2m 38.75s (-2.15) **Going Correction** -0.10s/f (Good) **7** Ran SP% **110.6**
Speed ratings (Par 103): **103,100,100,98,98 87,74**
toteswingers 1&2 £1.10, 1&3 £3.20, 2&3 £4.00 CSF £7.35 TOTE £1.50: £1.40, £3.80; EX 10.10.
Owner Lady Sarah Clutton **Bred** Chippenham Lodge Stud **Trained** Patching, W Sussex
■ Stewards' Enquiry : Miss C Scott five-day ban: use of whip (25 Sep, 4, 9, 15 & 19 Oct)

FOCUS
After a dry night and a bright, breezy morning, the ground was officially good to firm (firm in places). GoingStick readings were: round course 8.5, straight course 8.9, far side 9.2, stands' side. A modest amateurs' event with the form limited by the fourth.

5510 LADBROKESGAMES.COM MAIDEN STKS 1m 1f 149y
5:40 (5:42) (Class 5) 3-Y-O+ **£2,385** (£704; £352) **Stalls** Centre

Form RPR

23 **1** **Infinite Hope (USA)**[19] 4791 3-8-12 [1] KirstyMilczarek 4 72
(Luca Cumani) *mainly 2nd tl jnd ldr 2f out: rdn into narrow ld jst ins fnl f: hld on wl* **5/4**[1]

0- **2** *nk* **Opera Box**[461] 2257 4-9-6 GeorgeBaker 6 71
(Marcus Tregoning) *prom: led 7f out: jnd by wnr 2f out: hdd jst ins fnl f: kpt on wl* **14/1**

00- **3** *1½* **Multilateral (USA)**[339] 6216 3-9-3 [1] EddieAhern 1 73
(Amanda Perrett) *trckd ldrs: rdn 2f out: styd on fnl f* **22/1**

05 **4** *¾* **Miss Dashwood**[62] 3340 3-8-12 MickaelBarzalona 3 66
(James Fanshawe) *t.k.h: in tch: rdn 2f out: kpt on fr over 1f out* **6/1**[3]

5354 **5** *4* **Devine Guest (IRE)**[5] 5358 3-8-12 **79** MatthewDavies 9 58
(Mick Channon) *hld up in tch: effrt on outer 3f out: wknd over 1f out* **6/4**[2]

0 **6** *1½* **Symfony (IRE)**[81] 2734 3-8-12 JamesDoyle 5 55
(Clive Cox) *led tl 7f out: chsd ldrs tl wknd 2f out* **16/1**

5 **7** *11* **Ahuqd (IRE)**[29] 4464 3-8-9 RyanPowell(3) 8 32
(Clive Brittain) *a bhd* **33/1**

8 *3½* **Wood Meister** 4-9-11 DavidProbert 7 29
(Brett Johnson) *s.i.s: towards rr: hrd rdn and lost tch over 3f out* **66/1**

9 *1½* **Icebreaker Two** 3-9-0 SimonPearce(3) 2 26
(John E Long) *a bhd: no ch fnl 3f* **66/1**

2m 4.02s (-0.88) **Going Correction** -0.10s/f (Good)
WFA 3 from 4yo 8lb **9** Ran SP% **121.6**
Speed ratings (Par 103): **99,98,97,96,93 92,83,80,79**
toteswingers 1&2 £3.30, 1&3 £3.20, 2&3 £6.50 CSF £21.29 TOTE £2.20: £1.10, £3.80, £5.80; EX 19.50 Trifecta £262.20 Pool: £435.88 - 1.23 winning units..
Owner Miss Sarah J Leigh **Bred** Sarah J Leigh **Trained** Newmarket, Suffolk

FOCUS
Few of these had an obvious chance on form in this modest maiden. The form is rated a bit cautiously.
Icebreaker Two Official explanation: jockey said that the colt lost action on the bend

5511 LADIES LOVE KMFM MAIDEN AUCTION STKS 7f (S)
6:10 (6:12) (Class 6) 2-Y-O **£1,704** (£503; £251) **Stalls** High

Form RPR

5 **1** **Beam Of Light**[9] 5192 2-8-7 ow1 EddieAhern 2 73
(Jamie Osborne) *pressed ldrs: led 3f out: hrd rdn over 1f out: edgd rt: hld on wl* **5/1**

644 **2** *1* **Alhaarth Beauty (IRE)**[10] 5153 2-8-8 PatDobbs 1 71
(Richard Hannon) *hld up in tch: rdn to chal over 1f out: kpt on: nt qckn fnl 100yds* **9/4**[1]

3 *1½* **Firstkissoflove** 2-8-4 DavidProbert 7 63+
(Clive Cox) *hld up: rdn over 3f out: hdwy to press wnr on stands' rail over 2f out: one pce appr fnl f* **9/2**[3]

4 *10* **Paddy's Saltantes (IRE)** 2-8-9 KieranO'Neill 5 42
(J S Moore) *dwlt: outpcd and bhd: passed btn horses fnl 2f* **10/1**

04 **5** *3½* **Xerxes (IRE)**[11] 5119 2-8-6 MircoDemuro 4 30
(Hugo Palmer) *led tl 3f out: wknd 2f out* **10/1**

50 **6** *8* **Double Jeopardy**[44] 3948 2-8-9 (b[1]) SaleemGolam 3 12
(Dr Jon Scargill) *plld hrd and hung rt: in tch tl 1/2-way* **50/1**

655 **7** *6* **Sally Bruce**[119] 1629 2-7-12 **55** ow1 JenniferFerguson(7) 6
(Louise Best) *s.s: a towards rr: drvn along and n.d fnl 3f* **33/1**

8 *dist* **Night's Watch** 2-8-13 WilliamCarson 8
(William Jarvis) *plld hrd and hung bdly rt: dwlt: w ldr after 1f: wknd 3f out: veered rt and virtually p.u 2f out* **5/2**[2]

1m 26.62s (-0.68) **Going Correction** -0.35s/f (Firm) **8** Ran SP% **117.3**
Speed ratings (Par 92): **89,87,86,74,70 61,54,**
toteswingers 1&2 £2.80, 1&3 £5.10, 2&3 £2.10 CSF £17.17 TOTE £4.80: £2.30, £1.10, £1.90; EX 13.00 Trifecta £79.50 Pool: £533.39 - 4.96 winning units..
Owner The Beam Of Light Partnership **Bred** J A E Hobby **Trained** Upper Lambourn, Berks

FOCUS
A modest juvenile maiden, with little solid form to assess, but made more interesting by a clutch of newcomers. The first three finished clear.

NOTEBOOK
Beam Of Light, fifth at Bath on her only previous outing, took a significant step forward to take this prize. Always disputing the lead, she had the advantage of racing close to the stands' rail. Nothing should detract from her gameness, though, as she fought hard to hold off the more experienced runner-up. (op 9-2)
Alhaarth Beauty(IRE), officially rated 72 but well below that level last time out, posted a solid effort in defeat. Never too far off the pace, she tried hard in the closing stages, but could not quite match the winner. (op 11-8)
Firstkissoflove, a newcomer from a stable bang in form, showed promise, staying on nicely in the final furlong. She is unlikely to turn into a star, but should improve when stepped up in distance. (op 7-2 tchd 11-2)
Paddy's Saltantes(IRE), a 6,000gns yearling purchase, attracted money at each-way prices on his debut. He could never get into contention, however, after starting slowly and struggling for early pace. (op 16-1 tchd 8-1)
Xerxes(IRE) had finished last on both her previous starts, so this has to go down as an improvement. It seems doubtful, though, that she would be able to notch a victory in the majority of maidens. (op 12-1 tchd 14-1 and 9-1)
Double Jeopardy, fitted with first-time blinkers, was always towards the rear. (op 33-1)
Night's Watch, a first-time-out half-brother to several winners, was well backed. He was very keen early on, however, and threw his head about wildly as if he had a problem with his tack. Official explanation: jockey said that the colt's bit slipped (op 7-1 tchd 15-2)

5512 ANNA BUSBRIDGE'S MEMORIAL H'CAP 7f (S)
6:40 (6:40) (Class 4) (0-80,80) 3-Y-O **£4,851** (£1,443; £721; £360) **Stalls** High

Form RPR

3611 **1** **Baheeja**[12] 5099 3-9-4 **80** DominicFox(3) 4 93+
(Roger Varian) *trckd ldr: led over 1f out: pushed out: comf* **15/8**[1]

4303 **2** *2* **Fabled City (USA)**[19] 4814 3-8-13 **72** (t) AdamKirby 6 78
(Clive Cox) *t.k.h: chsd ldrs: rdn over 2f out: kpt on to take 2nd fnl 100yds* **7/1**

?210 **3** *¾* **Sputnik Sweetheart**[12] 5107 3-9-2 **75** PatDobbs 1 79
(Richard Hannon) *led: hrd rdn and hdd over 1f out: one pce fnl f* **4/1**[2]

4225 **4** *1* **Serene Oasis (IRE)**[6] 5302 3-9-3 **76** (v) MatthewDavies 7 77
(Mick Channon) *hld up in rr: swtchd outside and wnt prom 3f out: no ex fnl f* **9/2**[3]

2145 **5** *1½* **Sir Fredlot (IRE)**[19] 4819 3-9-3 **76** (b[1]) WilliamCarson 5 73
(Charles Hills) *plld hrd: in tch: drvn along over 2f out: no imp over 1f out* **4/1**[2]

04-5 **6** *9* **Rock Song**[21] 4746 3-8-11 **70** EddieAhern 2 43
(Amanda Perrett) *chsd ldrs 4f: sn bhd* **12/1**

1m 24.41s (-2.89) **Going Correction** -0.35s/f (Firm) **6** Ran SP% **113.2**
Speed ratings (Par 102): **102,99,98,97,96 85**
toteswingers 1&2 £3.80, 1&3 £3.20, 2&3 £6.30 CSF £15.85 TOTE £3.60: £2.10, £3.20; EX 16.70.
Owner Sheikh Ahmed Al Maktoum **Bred** Middle Park Stud Ltd **Trained** Newmarket, Suffolk

FOCUS
A seemingly competitive handicap in which the successful top-weight was rated 80. The form looks sound, with the winner perhaps value for extra.

5513 WW ELECTRICAL H'CAP 6f
7:15 (7:15) (Class 6) (0-65,65) 3-Y-O **£1,704** (£503; £251) **Stalls** High

Form RPR

0050 **1** **Strategic Action (IRE)**[28] 4506 3-8-6 **50** (tp) SaleemGolam 6 57
(Linda Jewell) *trckd ldrs: led on stands' rail over 1f out: rdn out and hld on wl* **16/1**

0412 **2** *nk* **Indiana Guest (IRE)**[2] 5458 3-8-8 **55** 6ex (b) RyanPowell(3) 1 61
(George Margarson) *hld up in 5th: effrt and n.m.r over 1f out: r.o to press wnr ins fnl f: jst hld* **9/2**[3]

0033 **3** *hd* **Theresnoneedfordat (IRE)**[2] 5454 3-9-2 **60** (b) WilliamCarson 2 65+
(Stuart Williams) *missed break and lost 5 l: bhd: hdwy and nt clr run over 1f out: swtchd rt: clsng on first 2 fnl 100yds* **3/1**[2]

123 **4** *2¼* **Rum Punch**[21] 4726 3-9-7 **65** EddieAhern 5 63
(Eve Johnson Houghton) *led: edgd rt off stands' rail and hdd over 1f out: no ex fnl f* **11/10**[1]

004 **5** *3½* **Flying Kitty**[16] 4920 3-8-6 **50** KieranO'Neill 3 37
(John Bridger) *chsd ldr tl over 2f out: wknd over 1f out* **20/1**

0601 **6** *6* **Sarah Berry**[15] 4970 3-9-2 **60** MircoDemuro 4 28
(Chris Dwyer) *hld up in tch on outer: rdn over 2f out: wknd over 1f out* **10/1**

1m 12.03s (-0.67) **Going Correction** -0.35s/f (Firm) **6** Ran SP% **110.5**
Speed ratings (Par 98): **90,89,89,86,81 73**
toteswingers 1&2 £13.90, 1&3 £10.40, 2&3 £2.40 CSF £81.36 TOTE £47.30: £7.50, £3.20; EX 168.70.
Owner M J Boutcher **Bred** Martin O'Hanlon **Trained** Hollingbourne, Kent

FOCUS
A very modest handicap, with the top weight rated 65, but it produced an exciting finish. The winner is rated to his latest form.
Strategic Action(IRE) Official explanation: trainer said, regarding the apparent improvement of form, hat the gelding had benefitted from a tongue strap and the first time over six furlongs.

5514 EASTWELL MANOR H'CAP 5f
7:45 (7:45) (Class 5) (0-75,74) 3-Y-O+ **£2,385** (£704; £352) **Stalls** High

Form RPR

0421 **1** **Selfara**[9] 5205 3-9-10 **74** 6ex (bt) JamesDoyle 3 84
(Roger Charlton) *s.i.s: hdwy 2f out: styd on to ld fnl 50yds* **8/11**[1]

0443 **2** *½* **Love You Louis**[11] 5123 6-9-6 **68** (v) PatDobbs 5 76
(J R Jenkins) *led: rdn over 1f out: hdd and nt qckn fnl 50yds* **7/1**

002 **3** *1¾* **Irish Boy (IRE)**[11] 5131 4-9-3 **65** MickyFenton 4 67
(Paul Midgley) *prom: hrd rdn over 1f out: one pce* **5/1**[2]

0046 **4** *1½* **Berberana (IRE)**[18] 4849 4-9-7 **72** RaulDaSilva(3) 6 68
(Jeremy Gask) *dwlt: in rr: rdn over 2f out: styd on fr over 1f out* **13/2**[3]

6104 **5** *nk* **The Strig**[14] 5020 5-9-3 **65** (b[1]) WilliamCarson 1 60
(Stuart Williams) *swtchd rt s and racd alone far side: chsd ldrs: no ex appr fnl f* **14/1**

0-00 **6** *1¾* **Monessa (IRE)**[42] 4003 3-8-6 **56** (tp) SaleemGolam 7 45
(Linda Jewell) *a towards rr* **25/1**

2000 **7** *1¼* **Rooknrasbryripple**[13] 5047 3-8-5 **55** (e[1]) KieranO'Neill 2 39
(Ralph Smith) *prom tl wknd 2f out* **40/1**

59.04s (-0.96) **Going Correction** -0.35s/f (Firm)
WFA 3 from 4yo+ 2lb **7** Ran SP% **113.4**
Speed ratings (Par 103): **93,92,89,87,86 83,81**
toteswingers 1&2 £2.00, 1&3 £1.70, 2&3 £2.80 CSF £6.43 TOTE £1.40: £1.10, £3.50; EX 4.90.
Owner K Abdulla **Bred** Juddmonte Farms Ltd **Trained** Beckhampton, Wilts

FOCUS
A finale in which the only last-time-out winner dominated the betting and came home in front. She's possibly a bit better than the bare form.
T/Plt: £35.20 to a £1 stake. Pool: £36,013.72 -746.20 winning tickets T/Qpdt: £17.90 to a £1 stake. Pool: £4,302.34 - 177.77 winning tickets LM

5487 YORK (L-H)
Thursday, August 23

OFFICIAL GOING: Good to firm (good in places) changing to good after race 4 (3.40)
Wind: light 1/2 behind Weather: overcast, showers, rain race 3 and 4

5515 DBS PREMIER YEARLING STKS 6f
2:00 (2:01) (Class 2) 2-Y-O
£147,736 (£59,118; £29,559; £14,749; £7,389; £7,389) **Stalls** Centre

Form RPR

1163 **1** **Hototo**[23] 4687 2-9-2 **100** PhillipMakin 17 102
(Kevin Ryan) *w ldrs towards stands' side: styd on to ld nr fin* **10/1**[3]

2341 **2** *nk* **Well Acquainted (IRE)**[49] 3770 2-8-11 81........................... JohnFahy 4 96
(Clive Cox) *chsd ldrs far side: edgd rt over 1f out: led last 50yds: hdd nr fin* **33/1**

6111 **3** *½* **Body And Soul (IRE)**[40] 4093 2-8-11 88........................... DavidAllan 9 95
(Tim Easterby) *w ldrs: led over 1f out: hdd last 50yds: no ex clsng stages* **8/1[2]**

0012 **4** *1 ½* **Liber**[13] 5055 2-8-11 97... LukeMorris 14 90
(Sir Mark Prescott Bt) *trckd ldrs: kpt on same pce fnl f* **10/1[3]**

2110 **5** *½* **Dream Maker (IRE)**[12] 5103 2-8-6 85............................. FrannyNorton 7 84
(Tom Dascombe) *mid-div: effrt and outpcd over 2f out: kpt on fnl f* **33/1**

110 **6** *1* **Indian Jade**[65] 3240 2-9-2 92.. GrahamLee 6 91
(Kevin Ryan) *towards rr: hdwy over 1f out: kpt on ins fnl f* **16/1**

5311 **7** *nse* **Barracuda Boy (IRE)**[12] 5088 2-8-11 83................. RichardKingscote 5 86
(Tom Dascombe) *w ldrs towards far side: hmpd over 1f out: one pce* **14/1**

3301 **8** *1* **Shahdaroba (IRE)**[22] 4707 2-8-11 85........................... JamesMillman 3 82
(Rod Millman) *in rr towards far side: hdwy over 2f out: kpt on fnl f* **40/1**

1203 **9** *shd* **Mister Marc (IRE)**[9] 5201 2-8-11 0.............................. RichardHughes 15 82
(Richard Hannon) *mid-div: effrt over 2f out: kpt on fnl f* **8/1[2]**

1514 **10** *nk* **Lady Poppy**[19] 4827 2-8-6 81... PJMcDonald 19 76
(George Moore) *w ldrs stands' side: one pce over 1f out* **50/1**

2005 **11** *¾* **Woodland Mill (IRE)**[5] 5371 2-8-6 84............................. PaulHanagan 8 74
(Richard Fahey) *chsd ldrs: wknd over 1f out* **66/1**

1055 **12** *nk* **Polski Max**[18] 4836 2-8-11 83....................................... TonyHamilton 10 78
(Richard Fahey) *t.k.h in rr: hmpd and lost pl over 3f out: swtchd stands' side over 1f out: styd on wl ins fnl f* **66/1**

3305 **13** *½* **Baddilini**[20] 4774 2-8-11 87... FrankieDettori 12 79
(Alan Bailey) *in rr: effrt over 2f out: n.m.r over 1f out: edgd lft: nvr a factor* **50/1**

631 **14** *½* **Saint Jerome (IRE)**[8] 5235 2-8-11 0............................. HayleyTurner 11 75
(Marcus Tregoning) *in rr: kpt on fnl 2f: nvr a factor* **12/1**

41 **15** *nk* **Carlton Blue (IRE)**[27] 4526 2-8-11 81...................... SilvestreDeSousa 1 74
(Paul Cole) *led overall towards far side: hdd over 1f out: wknd jst ins fnl f* **33/1**

2022 **16** *4 ½* **New Pearl (IRE)**[19] 4804 2-8-11 91.............................. JamieSpencer 20 61
(David Brown) *dwlt: mid-div stands' side: drvn over 2f out: lost pl and eased over 1f out* **12/1**

311 **17** *5* **Scentpastparadise**[12] 5109 2-8-6 81.......................... RoystonFfrench 2 41
(Ann Duffield) *lost pl far side over 4f out: sn bhd eased towards fin* **40/1**

12 **18** *1* **Rocky Ground (IRE)**[26] 4599 2-8-11 0.............................. NeilCallan 16 43
(Roger Varian) *t.k.h: dwlt: sn mid-div: effrt over 2f out: wknd over 1f out: eased towards fin* **3/1[1]**

2101 **19** *¾* **Annunciation**[54] 3604 2-8-11 100................................. JimmyFortune 18 40
(Richard Hannon) *chsd ldrs stands' side: lost pl over 2f out: eased whn bhd* **10/1[3]**

1m 10.48s (-1.42) **Going Correction** -0.125s/f (Firm) **19** Ran SP% **123.0**
Speed ratings (Par 100): **104,103,102,100,100 98,98,97,97,97 96,95,94,94,93 87,81,79,78**
toteswingers 1&2 £76.10, 1&3 £5.20, 2&3 £69.60 CSF £323.39 TOTE £12.20: £3.50, £11.00, £2.10; EX 468.90 Trifecta £1874.40 Part won. Pool: £2,532.98 - 0.63 winning units..
Owner Kenneth Macpherson **Bred** B P Hammond **Trained** Hambleton, N Yorks

FOCUS

Races on traditional line and distances as advertised. Following a dry night the ground remained good to firm, good in places (GoingStick 8.2). After the opener a couple of the jockeys reported it to be riding on the firm side. A typically hot renewal of this very valuable sales race and a contest that has been won by some classy 2yos within the past ten years, with Somnus (2002), Dark Angel (2007) and Wootton Bassett (2010) all going on to record successes at Group 1 level, the latter pair in their juvenile seasons. Sectional times suggested that they went hard early, as apart from the first furlong (from a standing start) each subsequent furlong was run progressively slower, but the winning time was only 0.08 seconds outside standard. The field raced centre-to-stands' side with Carlton Blue disputing the advantage towards the far side and Lady Poppy against the stands' rail, while the winner was to the fore in the centre. The fact that the other two faded out of it makes the winner's performance even better. The form looks straightforward, although the placed horses were big improvers.

NOTEBOOK

Hototo, representing last year's winning stable, was stepping up to 6f for the first time and had a 5lb penalty to carry for his success in the Windsor Castle, but he relished the extra yardage and, having always been up there, kept on pulling out more to assert close to the line. He has already done his connections proud, but looks a tough colt and there seems no reason why he cannot add another decent prize or two. He seems likely to try and emulate last year's winner Bogart by adding Redcar's Totepool Two-Year-Old Trophy to this success. (op 11-1)

Well Acquainted(IRE) seemed to see the 7f out well when winning an Epsom maiden last month, but a strongly run race over this trip wasn't a problem. Always handy towards the far side, he hung about under pressure when brought to challenge inside the last 2f, but stuck at it and was only just denied. He would have been a stone better off with the winner in a nursery, so this was a smart effort and he deserved to win a nice prize.

Body And Soul(IRE) had four of these behind when completing the hat-trick in the Weatherbys Super Sprint, but faced a stiff task trying to confirming that form on these different terms and this was her first try at 6f. Under the circumstances she ran a blinder, holding every chance until the last few strides, and it would seem fair to say that she did get the extra furlong. (tchd 15-2)

Liber had a bit to prove after being beaten at odds of 1-4 at Musselburgh last time and didn't quite seem to see out 6f in his only previous try in the Woodcote, but he ran right up to form here, staying on well after being switched right over a furlong from home if lacking the speed to trouble the front three. (op 12-1)

Dream Maker(IRE) found a combination of Group 3 company and the step up to 7f too much when bidding for a hat-trick in the Sweet Solera last time, but she was staying on late from the middle of the field here and may be worth another crack at the longer trip in less-exalted company.

Indian Jade ◆, the winner's stablemate, was last seen finishing a creditable eighth in the Coventry and, like him, had a 5lb penalty to shoulder. Given plenty to do, he was finishing to some effect and, in a race otherwise dominated by prominent racers, this effort can be marked up. He is one to watch.

Barracuda Boy(IRE) came into this on a hat-trick after winning a couple of nurseries, but didn't stay this trip in one previous try. However, he was far from out of it when given a hefty bump by the runner-up inside the last 2f, but for which he would have finished closer.

Shahdaroba(IRE), who finished behind four of these in the Weatherbys Super Sprint, was well behind towards the far side of the field early, but was noted making up plenty of late ground and is worth keeping an eye on.

Mister Marc(IRE) was a little disappointing in two starts since chasing home the subsequent Coventry winner Dawn Approach in a Naas Listed event, and never managed to get involved this time either. (op 9-1)

Baddilini's rider reported that the gelding was denied a clear run. Official explanation: jockey said that the gelding was denied a clear run

New Pearl(IRE)'s trainer reported that the colt was unsuited by the ground. Official explanation: trainer said that the colt was unsuited by the going which was good/firm, good in places (tchd 14-1)

Rocky Ground(IRE) was narrowly beaten at odds-on last time, but was the least exposed in the field and the market suggested that much better was expected. He was up with the pace until weakening over a furlong from home, but his lofty entries later in the season, including in the Middle Park and Dewhurst, suggest that he is held in some regard and it's too early to be giving up on him. His rider reported that the colt moved poorly. Official explanation: jockey said that the colt moved poorly. (tchd 7-2)

5516 JAGUAR CARS LOWTHER STKS (GROUP 2) (FILLIES) 6f

2:30 (2:32) (Class 1) 2-Y-O

£62,381 (£23,650; £11,836; £5,896; £2,959; £1,485) **Stalls** Centre

Form RPR

11 **1** **Rosdhu Queen (IRE)**[6] 5307 2-8-12 0......................... RichardHughes 3 105
(William Haggas) *mde all: rdn and edgd rt 1f out: hld on wl* **9/2[2]**

0312 **2** *1 ¾* **Baileys Jubilee**[25] 4632 2-8-12 103.............................. KierenFallon 2 100
(Mark Johnston) *chsd wnr on outer: ev ch jst ins fnl f: kpt on same pce* **12/1**

1215 **3** *hd* **Royal Rascal**[19] 4820 2-8-12 86.. DavidAllan 4 99
(Tim Easterby) *chsd ldrs: kpt on wl ins fnl f* **33/1**

221 **4** *1 ½* **City Girl (IRE)**[24] 4645 2-8-12 78...................................... JimCrowley 8 95
(Ralph Beckett) *hld up stands' side: hdwy over 2f out: sn chsng ldrs: kpt on same pce over 1f out* **40/1**

321 **5** *½* **Pearl Sea (IRE)**[22] 4701 2-8-12 93................................. JamieSpencer 9 93
(David Brown) *hld up stands' side: hdwy over 2f out: sn chsng ldrs: kpt on same pce appr fnl f* **15/2**

223 **6** *shd* **Sandreamer (IRE)**[6] 5307 2-8-12 99............................... MartinHarley 5 93
(Mick Channon) *hdwy over 2f out: sn chsng ldrs: kpt on same pce appr fnl f* **12/1**

300 **7** *1 ¾* **Threes Grand**[41] 4064 2-8-12 83...................................... TomQueally 7 88
(Scott Dixon) *dwlt: hld up in rr: effrt over 2f out: edgd lft over 1f out: nvr a factor* **100/1**

1 **8** *2 ¾* **Badr Al Badoor (IRE)**[55] 3560 2-8-12 0......................... HayleyTurner 1 80
(James Fanshawe) *hld up on outside: hdwy over 2f out: lost pl over 1f out* **7/1[3]**

2210 **9** *25* **All Fur Coat**[64] 3269 2-8-12 87.......................................(b[1]) JoeFanning 6
(Jo Hughes) *chsd ldrs: drvn over 2f out: sn lost pl and bhd: virtually p.u: t.o* **66/1**

11 **P** **Newfangled (USA)**[62] 3326 2-8-12 0............................. WilliamBuick 11
(John Gosden) *chsd ldrs: p.u and dismntd over 4f out: lame* **1/1[1]**

1m 11.75s (-0.15) **Going Correction** +0.10s/f (Good) **10** Ran SP% **115.7**
Speed ratings (Par 103): **105,102,102,100,99 99,97,93,60,**
toteswingers 1&2 £6.50, 1&3 £13.60, 2&3 £18.40 CSF £54.69 TOTE £6.20: £1.80, £2.50, £4.90; EX 50.40 Trifecta £1237.90 Pool: £6,976.11 - 4.17 winning units..
Owner Clipper Logistics **Bred** Old Carhue & Graeng Bloodstock **Trained** Newmarket, Suffolk

FOCUS

This was run in heavy rain and Joe Fanning felt the ground to be riding loose on top. Much of the interest was lost when impressive Albany winner Newfangled went wrong after about a furlong. The bare form is ordinary for the grade, held down by the third and fourth.

NOTEBOOK

Rosdhu Queen(IRE) put up a good effort just six days after winning a 5f Listed race at Newbury, but isn't one to get carried away with long term. Soon in front, she raced a little keenly, but wasn't expending much energy under Hughes, and the pair were always doing enough. The step up to 6f was clearly no problem, but it's quite possible she'll revert to 5f for the Flying Childers before a crack at the Cheveley Park. She's not a Guineas filly. (op 5-1 tchd 11-2)

Baileys Jubilee has been helped of late by the more restrained tactics and this has to go down as a career-best, her having to switch not affecting the result.

Royal Rascal, fifth from a mark of 87 on her recent nursery debut, holds the form back. She's clearly progressing but isn't going to be easy to place now. (tchd 25-1)

City Girl(IRE), rated just 78, bettered the form of her recent maiden win, keeping on despite Sandreamer having briefly edged into her. She'll presumably keep hunting for black type. (op 33-1)

Pearl Sea(IRE) raced more towards the stands' side and had her chance, failing to step up on her Goodwood maiden win. (op 8-1)

Sandreamer(IRE) was beaten twice as far by the winner as she had been at Newbury six days earlier, not improving as much as expected for the return to 6f. (op 11-1 tchd 10-1)

Badr Al Badoor(IRE) is seemingly well thought-of, but she'd met with a setback after winning on her debut, and didn't look to be striding out properly late on here. (op 13-2 tchd 8-1)

Newfangled(USA), a hot favourite here, went wrong after about a furlong and was quickly pulled up. She'd changed her legs a few times and sadly it later emerged that she'd fractured her pelvis. Attempts were made to save her but the following day she had to be put down. Official explanation: trainer's representative said that the filly was lame (op 11-10 tchd 6-5 in places)

5517 BETFAIR. DON'T SETTLE FOR LESS STKS (H'CAP) 1m

3:05 (3:08) (Class 2) 3-Y-O+

£46,687 (£13,980; £6,990; £3,495; £1,747; £877) **Stalls** Low

Form RPR

-002 **1** **Trade Storm**[12] 5075 4-9-1 **98**... JamieSpencer 1 109
(David Simcock) *hld up in mid-div: effrt over 2f out: swtchd lft over 1f out: led jst ins fnl f: drvn out* **12/1**

11-4 **2** *1 ¼* **Strictly Silver (IRE)**[7] 5271 3-7-12 **87** oh3..................... JimmyQuinn 12 95
(Alan Bailey) *s.i.s: sn mid-div: hdwy over 2f out: led briefly 1f out: kpt on same pce clsng stages* **16/1**

3504 **3** *1 ¼* **Indian Jack (IRE)**[26] 4578 4-8-4 **87**.............................. HayleyTurner 9 92
(Luca Cumani) *in rr: drvn over 3f out: styd on wl over 1f out: nrst fin* **11/1**

5410 **4** *1* **Navajo Chief**[40] 4112 5-9-1 **105**......................... MichaelJMMurphy[(7)] 11 108+
(Alan Jarvis) *mid-div: hdwy and edgd lft over 2f out: kpt on fnl f* **8/1[2]**

0002 **5** *½* **Crown Counsel (IRE)**[9] 5186 4-8-0 **83**.............................. LukeMorris 2 85
(Mark Johnston) *w ldr: led over 2f out: hdd 1f out: fdd last 100yds* **10/1**

3220 **6** *¾* **Vainglory (USA)**[20] 4761 8-8-4 **92**................................. LauraPike[(5)] 20 92
(David Simcock) *hld up in rr: styd on fnl 2f: nt rch ldrs* **25/1**

0261 **7** *¾* **Lord Aeryn (IRE)**[19] 4828 5-8-7 **90**............................... BarryMcHugh 3 88
(Richard Fahey) *chsd ldrs: drvn over 2f out: one pce* **20/1**

5211 **8** *1* **Anderiego (IRE)**[27] 4557 4-8-10 **93**............................... KierenFallon 6 89
(David O'Meara) *chsd ldrs: edgd rt over 2f out: fdd appr fnl f* **5/1[1]**

205 **9** *hd* **Excellent Guest**[20] 4761 5-9-0 **97**................................. TomQueally 17 92+
(George Margarson) *in rr-div: hdwy whn hmpd over 2f out: swtchd lft over 1f out: kpt on* **14/1**

0234 **10** *nse* **Santefisio**[9] 5186 6-8-5 **88**.......................................(b) AndrewMullen 16 83
(Keith Dalgleish) *swtchd lft s: t.k.h in midfield: effrt 3f out: one pce* **33/1**

2534 **11** *1 ½* **Invisible Man**[21] 4725 6-9-7 **104**.............................(v[1]) FrankieDettori 18 96+
(Saeed Bin Suroor) *dwlt: in rr: sme hdwy whn hmpd 2f out: nt clr run over 1f put: nvr a factor* **14/1**

0515 **12** *shd* **Lady Macduff (IRE)**[5] 5334 3-7-12 **87** oh1.................. NickyMackay 15 79
(Mark Johnston) *n.m.r s: sn chsng ldrs: drvn over 2f out: wknd fnl f* **25/1**

0-00 **13** *¾* **Diamondhead (IRE)**[21] 4740 3-7-12 **87** oh1...............(t) JamieMackay 5 77
(Brian Meehan) *led: hdd over 2f out: wknd fnl f* **66/1**

0205 **14** *½* **Al Muheer (IRE)**[5] 5369 7-8-7 **90**.................................(b) JamesSullivan 7 79
(Ruth Carr) *in rr: sme hdwy whn hmpd over 1f out: nvr a factor* **50/1**

1331 **15** *nk* **Postscript (IRE)**[12] 5094 4-8-2 **85**.................................. FrannyNorton 19 73+
(Ian Williams) *mid-div: effrt stands' side whn hmpd over 2f out: no threat after* **9/1**[3]

2150 **16** *hd* **Prince Of Johanne (IRE)**[20] 4761 6-9-8 **105**...................(p) JohnFahy 8 93+
(Tom Tate) *mid-div: hmpd over 2f out: sn lost pl* **16/1**

1400 **17** *1* **Sandagiyr (FR)**[39] 4130 4-9-10 **107**........................ SilvestreDeSousa 10 92
(Saeed Bin Suroor) *trckd ldrs: edgd rt and hmpd over 2f out: sn wknd* **25/1**

6030 **18** *3* **Imperial Djay (IRE)**[12] 5075 7-8-11 **94**............................ PJMcDonald 4 72
(Ruth Carr) *a towards rr: sme hdwy over 2f out: lost pl over 1f out* **33/1**

0021 **19** *1* **Switzerland (IRE)**[6] 5301 3-8-7 **96** 6ex............................ JoeFanning 14 72
(Mark Johnston) *in rr: sme hdwy over 3f out: no imp whn hmpd over 3f out* **16/1**

-146 **20** *25* **Kahruman (USA)**[63] 3294 3-8-9 **98**................................ PaulHanagan 13 17+
(William Haggas) *trckd ldrs: drvn over 3f out: losing pl whn sltly hmpd over 2f out: eased whn bhd: virtually p.u: t.o* **8/1**[2]

1m 37.47s (-1.53) **Going Correction** +0.10s/f (Good)
WFA 3 from 4yo+ 6lb **20** Ran SP% **130.6**
Speed ratings (Par 109): **111,109,108,107,107 106,105,104,104,104 102,102,101,101,101 100,99,96,95,70**
toteswingers 1&2 £57.90, 1&3 £22.30, 2&3 £51.50 CSF £183.18 CT £2251.64 TOTE £15.30: £3.20, £4.30, £3.80, £2.40; EX 305.50 TRIFECTA Pool: £5,401.19 - 1.80 winning units..
Owner Universal Racing **Bred** G T Lucas **Trained** Newmarket, Suffolk
■ Stewards' Enquiry : Silvestre De Sousa four day ban: careless riding (6, 8, 9 10 Sep)
Kieren Fallon two-day ban: careless riding (6 - 7 Sep)

FOCUS
Horses aged four or under have dominated recent runnings of this hot handicap and that trend continued. The evidence of the eye (backed up by the sectional times) was that the pace didn't pick up significantly until past halfway. As a result room became tight and several met traffic problems. The runners came centre-to-stands' side on reaching the home straight with the principals tended to race away from the stands' rail. Personal bests from the first two with the next pair close to form.

NOTEBOOK
Trade Storm had been raised 4lb for his recent narrow defeat in the Shergar Cup Mile, but that effort signalled a return to form and he built on the Ascot run by going one better under a well-judged ride. Having been held up early, he made up his ground gradually more towards the centre of the track, in doing so missing the trouble that unfolded towards the nearside, and produced a tidy turn of foot to score. Now that he is back in the groove, he could well win again. (tchd 11-1)
Strictly Silver(IRE) ◆, 3lb wrong here, didn't run at all badly after 299 days off at Newmarket a week earlier and was a prime candidate to bounce, but there was none of that and he was produced to hold every chance entering the last furlong before the winner pounced. He will head into the autumn fresher than most and can surely find a nice handicap.
Indian Jack(IRE), back down to his optimum trip, slipstreamed the winner starting up the home straight, but his rival got away from him coming to the last furlong and by the time he got going again it was too late. He is just 2lb above his last winning mark and should remain competitive.
Navajo Chief has a good record at York and was 2lb higher than when winning this race in 2011, but he didn't have a lot of room to play with between the 3f and 2f poles and had too much ground to make up when out in the clear. (op 9-1)
Crown Counsel(IRE) was always up with the pace and had every chance once leading over a furlong out, but he couldn't get clear and was soon overhauled. He is already due to go up 2lb and this took his losing run to 18. (op 11-1)
Vainglory(USA), the winner's stablemate, tried to come from last place having started from the outside stall so did well to finish where he did, but he would have done well to win a race as hot as this at the age of eight. (op 28-1)
Lord Aeryn(IRE), raised 2lb for his narrow Thirsk success earlier this month, was produced to hold a chance coming to the last furlong, but could then only find the one pace.
Anderiego(IRE) was sent off a well-supported favourite to complete a C&D hat-trick off a 6lb higher mark. He was never far off the pace, but caused problems for a few, including Postscript and Sandagiyr, when moving across to the stands' rail over 2f out. He had every chance at that point, but his effort then flattened out and whether he was in the ideal position against the rail is debatable. (op 7-1)
Excellent Guest is still 10lb higher than for his last win, but has run several cracking races in similarly hot handicaps since then. He was another to meet plenty of trouble coming to the last 2f and had too much ground to make up once switched out to his left to find daylight. (op 16-1)
Invisible Man, consistent over this trip though winless since taking last year's Royal Hunt Cup in first-time blinkers, had a first-time visor on here, but he endured a nightmare, repeatedly getting stopped in his run from well over 2f from home. He passed the line full of running and there will surely be another day for him. Official explanation: jockey said that the gelding was denied a clear run
Prince Of Johanne(IRE), still 5lb higher than when winning the Royal Hunt Cup, ran into traffic problems coming to the last 2f and his chance was soon gone. A line can be put through this.
Switzerland(IRE), carrying a 6lb penalty for his recent Kempton success which took his record on Polytrack to 3-4, is now 0-12 on turf but he had yet to be played when getting seriously hampered coming to the last 2f. His fine effort in defeat at Glorious Goodwood showed that he can do it on this surface. (tchd 20-1)
Kahruman(USA) raced prominently in a wide position early, but already looked to be feeling the pinch when squeezed out over 2f from home after which he was eased right off.

5518 DARLEY YORKSHIRE OAKS (BRITISH CHAMPIONS SERIES) (GROUP 1) (F&M) 1m 4f

3:40 (3:40) (Class 1) 3-Y-O+

£175,801 (£66,650; £33,356; £16,616; £8,339; £4,185) **Stalls** Centre

Form RPR

-322 **1** **Shareta (IRE)**[60] 3424 4-9-7 117.................. Christophe-PatriceLemaire 7 119
(A De Royer-Dupre, France) *trckd ldr: drvn over 2f out: styd on wl to ld towards fin* **2/1**[2]

1321 **2** *nk* **The Fugue**[19] 4801 3-8-11 116... WilliamBuick 2 118
(John Gosden) *hld up: hdwy over 2f out: led 1f out: drvn and edgd rt: hdd and no ex nr fin* **7/4**[1]

3143 **3** *1 ¾* **Was (IRE)**[19] 4801 3-8-11 113.................................. SeamieHeffernan 4 115
(A P O'Brien, Ire) *led: increased pce over 4f out: hdd 1f out: keeping on same pce whn hit over hd by rdr of runner-up's whip then hmpd clsng stages* **11/2**[3]

2232 **4** *3 ¼* **Shirocco Star**[32] 4378 3-8-11 112................................ RichardHughes 6 110
(Hughie Morrison) *stdd s: hld up in last: hdwy over 3f out: kpt on one pce fnl 2f* **7/1**

2-43 **5** *3* **Bible Belt (IRE)**[14] 5027 4-9-7 110... FranBerry 1 105
(Mrs John Harrington, Ire) *trckd ldrs: effrt over 3f out: wknd over 1f out* **12/1**

1-16 **6** *16* **Coquet**[83] 2658 3-8-11 103.. RobertHavlin 5 79
(Hughie Morrison) *trckd ldrs: effrt over 3f out: lost pl over 2f out: sn bhd* **14/1**

2m 33.87s (0.67) **Going Correction** +0.10s/f (Good)
WFA 3 from 4yo 10lb **6** Ran SP% **111.9**
Speed ratings (Par 117): **101,100,99,97,95 84**
toteswingers 1&2 £1.80, 1&3 £2.60, 2&3 £2.60 CSF £5.87 TOTE £2.30: £1.40, £1.50; EX 5.20.
Owner H H Aga Khan **Bred** His Highness The Aga Khan's Studs S C **Trained** Chantilly, France

FOCUS
The rain had set in quite heavily again by the time of this contest. The gallop was steady for much of the first half of the race, but strong form nonetheless, and the runners came stands' side in the straight. Barring Punctilious in 2005, this is a race that only top-class older horses have won in recent years and that was again the case. This is perhaps the weakest renewal since the 2005 one, Shareta a bit off her Arc form. The Fugue and Was are rated to their Nassau and Oaks marks.

NOTEBOOK
Shareta(IRE) gained a first win at the highest level. Last year's surprise Arc runner-up hadn't won in a year, but returned to something like her previous best when second of four in a race contested by subsequent Group 1 scorers Meandre and Danedream (King George) at Saint-Cloud last time, and she outstayed The Fugue here under a well-judged ride. The Arc is presumably the aim once more, depending on her getting reasonable ground, with her first having the option of the Vermeille, or possibly the Foy (to avoid the same owner's Valyra), on Arc trials weekend. (op 9-4 tchd 5-2)
The Fugue, impressive winner of the Musidora at the course back in May, gained her first Group 1 win with an impressive burst of speed in a steadily run Nassau and she again travelled like the best filly, but probably saw daylight plenty soon enough and couldn't quite hold on. She got on particularly well with Richard Hughes at Goodwood and one would expect to see her held on to for longer next time. The Breeders' Cup Filly & Mare Turf, a race that should really suit her strengths, remains the long-term aim. (tchd 13-8)
Was(IRE) benefited from a good ride when winning the Oaks, from an unlucky looking The Fugue, and she wasn't able to confirm the form, despite things very much going her way once more. A truly run 1m2f would probably suit best but, despite her Epsom triumph, she continues to look short of top class. (op 6-1)
Shirocco Star has proven highly consistent this season, finishing runner-up in both the Epsom and Irish Oaks, but the drop-out tactics employed by Hughes weren't suited to the way the race was run and she could never get close enough. The Group 2 Park Hill Stakes, over 1m61/2f at next month's St Leger meeting, could prove a suitable target. (tchd 13-2)
Bible Belt(IRE) was unable to reproduce the sort of form that saw her finish second to Dancing Rain at last season's Champions Day meeting. (tchd 14-1)
Coquet, unlucky in the Oaks and off since, having not taken the race too well, had missed a few pieces of work due to pulling off a shoe and her trainer feared she wouldn't be fit enough. She was the first beaten and ran too poorly for fitness to be blamed. (op 12-1 tchd 16-1)

5519 BRITISH STALLION STUDS SUPPORTING BRITISH RACING EBF GALTRES STKS (LISTED RACE) (F&M) 1m 4f

4:15 (4:15) (Class 1) 3-Y-O+

£22,684 (£8,600; £4,304; £2,144; £1,076; £540) **Stalls** Centre

Form RPR

1 **Pale Mimosa (IRE)**[20] 4787 3-8-8 0.................................... PatSmullen 5 107
(D K Weld, Ire) *trckd ldrs: effrt 3f out: sn upsides: styd on to ld last 75yds* **9/4**[2]

6211 **2** *2 ½* **Sequence (IRE)**[7] 5268 3-8-8 88.................................. RichardHughes 1 103
(Sir Michael Stoute) *trckd ldrs: effrt 4f out: rdn over 2f out: kpt on fnl f: tk 2nd post* **13/8**[1]

244- **3** *shd* **Cracking Lass (IRE)**[341] 6149 5-9-4 104........................ TonyHamilton 6 103
(Richard Fahey) *dwlt: detached in last: sn pushed along: hdwy on inner over 3f out: led over 2f out: hdd and no ex last 75yds* **10/1**

021 **4** *1* **Bite Of The Cherry**[26] 4601 3-8-8 88.............................. HayleyTurner 2 101
(Michael Bell) *trckd ldrs: effrt over 3f out: outpcd over 2f out: kpt on fnl f: styng on wl at fin* **15/2**[3]

-351 **5** *1 ¼* **Aniseed (IRE)**[24] 4648 3-8-8 88... KierenFallon 4 99
(William Haggas) *stdd s: t.k.h towards rr: drvn 4f out: outpcd over 2f out: kpt on fnl f* **16/1**

3-05 **6** *16* **Firdaws (USA)**[27] 4556 3-8-8 97....................................... PaulHanagan 7 74
(Roger Varian) *led: qcknd pce over 5f out: hdd over 2f out: wknd wl over 1f out* **15/2**[3]

7 *32* **Dane Street (USA)**[57] 3516 3-8-8 90............................... WilliamBuick 3 22
(Mrs John Harrington, Ire) *sn trcking ldrs: drvn over 3f out: lost pl 2f out: sn bhd and eased: t.o* **20/1**

2m 31.98s (-1.22) **Going Correction** +0.10s/f (Good)
WFA 3 from 5yo 10lb **7** Ran SP% **112.1**
Speed ratings (Par 111): **108,106,106,105,104 94,72**
toteswingers 1&2 £1.70, 1&3 £5.50, 2&3 £4.20 CSF £6.03 TOTE £3.40: £2.00, £1.60; EX 5.90.
Owner Dr R Lambe **Bred** Irish National Stud **Trained** The Curragh, Co Kildare

FOCUS
The rain had got into the ground and was changed to good before this race. The Galtres has gone to some high-class fillies during the past ten years with Mezzo Soprano (2003) and Kastoria (2005) going on to win at Group 1 level. Subsequent Group-race winners Alexander Three D (2002) and Anna Pavlova (2006) were also successful, but since then only last year's winner Set To Music has managed to win another race after this. However, this year's winner has scope and looks set for better things. She has quickly made up into a smart performer and is rated up a stone on her maiden win. Despite what looked an ordinary early pace (fastest sectional came between 3f and 2f out) and the ground having eased in the meantime, the winning time was still 1.89 seconds faster than the Yorkshire Oaks.

NOTEBOOK
Pale Mimosa(IRE) was having just her second start and returning from a 293-day absence when justifying odds-on by 15l in a heavy ground Galway maiden over this trip earlier in the month. Always close to the pace, once produced with her effort over 2f from home she always looked like getting the better of her two nearest rivals and seems just the type that can go on from here. The Park Hill looks the obvious option now, while she could be even better next year as a 4-y-o. (op 2-1 tchd 5-2 in a place)
Sequence(IRE), up in class in her hat-trick bid following two handicap successes (the most recent by 9l when allowed to dominate at Newmarket seven days earlier), had to be content with a stalking role this time, but stuck at it after coming off the bridle a fair way out. She looks a stayer and may be able to find a race at this level when presented with a proper test. (op 2-1)
Cracking Lass(IRE), runner-up in this race last year, was returning from almost a year off this time though she did win on her reappearance last term. She didn't seem to take much of an interest in the first half of the contest and raced in snatches at the back of the field, but travelled more kindly once into the straight and had every chance until outpaced by the winner in the latter stages. This was a good effort against the 3-y-os following such a long absence, but she has already run moderately in three previous tries over longer trips, including in last year's Park Hill, so it would be a surprise if she took the winner on again there. (op 9-1 tchd 12-1)
Bite Of The Cherry had a bit to do strictly on official ratings, but she could hardly have done it any easier on her handicap debut over a furlong further at Newmarket last time and that form has been well boosted since. She was staying on again at the line after getting outpaced here and a return to further will help her. (op 9-1)
Aniseed(IRE), back up into more exalted company after landing the odds in a Lingfield Polytrack maiden, also had plenty to find on BHA ratings and, although she plugged on after coming under a pressure a long way out, this looked too tall an order.

Firdaws(USA) hadn't reached the heights in two previous starts this year that seemed possible at the end of her juvenile campaign, but she has always hinted that the step up to 1m4f would suit, as her breeding would suggest. Soon sent to the front, the way she was easily picked off over 2f from home was disappointing and, although the rain may not have been welcome for her, this was still a poor effort. (tchd 8-1)
Dane Street(USA), having her first try at 1m4f, was close enough towards the nearside coming to the last 2f, but soon dropped away and was eased right off as though something was amiss. The trainer's representative reported that the filly was unsuited by the ground. Official explanation: trainer's representative said the filly was unsuited going which was good/firm, good in places (op 16-1)

5520 EVENTMASTERS.CO.UK E B F FILLIES' STKS (H'CAP) 7f
4:50 (4:51) (Class 2) (0-100,92) 3-Y-O+ **£16,172** (£4,812; £2,405; £1,202) **Stalls** Low

Form				RPR
3110	**1**		**Dutch Rose (IRE)**[21] 4740 3-9-1 **86** DanielTudhope 8 (David O'Meara) *chsd ldr: led over 5f out: kpt on wl fnl f: hld on gamely* **13/2**[2]	96
-042	**2**	1 1/4	**Whimsical (IRE)**[26] 4607 3-8-12 **83** RichardHughes 7 (Richard Hannon) *stdd s: hld up in rr: hdwy 2f out: styd on to take 2nd nr fin* **8/1**	89+
0-04	**3**	1/2	**Instance**[26] 4597 4-9-9 **89** WilliamBuick 10 (Jeremy Noseda) *chsd ldrs: kpt on same pce fnl f* **8/1**	95
0314	**4**	3/4	**Shesastar**[6] 5324 4-9-8 **88** GrahamGibbons 14 (David Barron) *dwlt: in rr: hdwy on wd outside 3f out: sn chsng ldrs: kpt on same pce fnl f* **12/1**	92
2446	**5**	nk	**Honeymead (IRE)**[45] 3911 4-9-5 **85** PaulHanagan 13 (Richard Fahey) *in rr: hdwy to chse ldrs over 2f out: kpt on same pce appr fnl f* **11/1**	88
1305	**6**	1/2	**No Poppy (IRE)**[26] 4589 4-9-4 **84** DavidAllan 1 (Tim Easterby) *chsd ldrs: lost pl on bnd over 4f out: hdwy over 2f out: one pce over 1f out* **33/1**	86
1320	**7**	1	**Misplaced Fortune**[26] 4611 7-9-8 **91** DaleSwift(3) 9 (Nigel Tinkler) *hld up in rr: hdwy and nt clr run over 1f out: nvr threatened* **25/1**	90
2-01	**8**	3/4	**Jade**[6] 5326 4-8-13 **82** 6ex LeeTopliss(3) 5 (Ollie Pears) *trckd ldrs: t.k.h: fdd fnl f* **20/1**	79
-312	**9**	1/2	**Ladyship**[34] 4286 3-9-7 **92** FrankieDettori 11 (Sir Michael Stoute) *hld up: hdwy and repeatedly denied clr over 2f out tl over 1f out: kpt on same pce fnl f* **2/1**[1]	87+
	10	6	**Swerve**[75] 2947 3-9-5 **90** KierenFallon 2 (Alan McCabe) *led over 1f: chsd ldrs: lost pl over 1f out: eased clsng stages* **16/1**	69
6314	**11**	3 1/4	**Bunraku**[38] 4150 3-8-9 **80** MichaelHills 6 (Charles Hills) *mid-div: hung lft over 2f out: nt clr run and lost pl over 1f out: eased whn bhd* **12/1**	50
3110	**12**	6	**Shabora (IRE)**[138] 1221 3-9-4 **89** NeilCallan 3 (Roger Varian) *mid-div: effrt and edgd rt over 2f out: sn wknd: eased whn bhd* **16/1**	43
2122	**13**	4	**Riot Of Colour**[26] 4597 3-8-13 **84** (b[1]) JimCrowley 12 (Ralph Beckett) *upset in stalls: hld up in rr: hmpd over 2f out: lost pl over 1f out: bhd whn eased* **15/2**[3]	27

1m 23.84s (-1.46) **Going Correction** -0.05s/f (Good)
WFA 3 from 4yo+ 5lb **13** Ran SP% **127.7**
Speed ratings (Par 96): **106,104,104,103,102 102,101,100,99,92 89,82,77**
toteswingers 1&2 £11.50, 1&3 £9.50, 2&3 £12.10 CSF £60.66 CT £439.02 TOTE £7.20: £2.70, £3.30, £3.30; EX 63.10 Trifecta £453.20 Pool: £4,640.20 - 7.57 winning units..
Owner Favourites Racing XXIV **Bred** Joseph Kennedy **Trained** Nawton, N Yorks

FOCUS
Not many got involved from off the pace in what had looked an open fillies' handicap. A personal best from the progressive winner with the third and fourth setting the standard.

NOTEBOOK
Dutch Rose(IRE), under a well-judged ride, galloped on strongly to win her fifth race of the season, bouncing back from a below-par effort when drawn wide at Goodwood in the process. A previous C&D winner, she's versatile with regards to tactics, goes on most ground, and will probably end up taking her chance in Pattern company before long. (op 8-1)
Whimsical(IRE), up 4lb for an unfortunate defeat at Salisbury, did best of those coming from behind but never had a chance of reeling in the winner. She may be nudged up the weights again, so winning won't become any easier.
Instance ◆ did best of the older horses, confirming the promise of her last-time-out Newmarket fourth. She's back on track and has something similar in her. (tchd 7-1)
Shesastar, last year's winner, making a quick reappearance, appreciated the return to a larger field and ran to something like her best out wide. (tchd 13-1 in a place)
Honeymead(IRE) ran well enough and is on a reasonable mark, although hasn't won since her juvenile days. (op 16-1)
No Poppy(IRE) has gone well off this mark in the past and she ran about as well as could have been expected against several more progressive types. (op 28-1)
Misplaced Fortune had no room when needed but ultimately proved one-paced.
Jade was too keen and found little. (op 25-1)
Ladyship, up 6lb following her narrow miss over 6f at Ascot, endured a troubled passage, but didn't appear to have much more to give once in the clear late anyway, so one doubt's whether she'd have beaten the winner. She can be given another chance, possibly back at 6f. (op 9-4 tchd 11-4 and 5-2 in places)
Bunraku was cut up on more than one occasion and looked awkward. (op 16-1)
Shabora(IRE) was weak in the market and could have done without the rain. (op 20-1 tchd 25-1)
Riot Of Colour, wearing first-time blinkers, was eased right off having been squeezed out. Jim Crowley reported she'd become upset in the stalls. Official explanation: jockey said the filly became upset in the stalls and missed the break. (op 7-1)
T/Jkpt: Not won T/Plt: £378.40 to a £1 stake. Pool: £251,796.90 - 485.67 winning tickets T/Qpdt: £14.10 to a £1 stake. Pool: £17,692.80 - 926.69 winning tickets WG

5521 - 5522a (Foreign Racing) - See Raceform Interactive

5066 TIPPERARY (L-H)
Thursday, August 23

OFFICIAL GOING: Soft to heavy

5523a FAIRY BRIDGE STKS (GROUP 3) (F&M) 7f 100y
6:20 (6:21) 3-Y-O+ **£31,145** (£9,104; £4,312; £1,437)

			RPR
1		**Lady Wingshot (IRE)**[21] 4749 3-9-0 101 KevinManning 10 (J S Bolger, Ire) *hld up in mid-div: 6th 1/2-way: smooth hdwy to go 3rd early st: rdn to ld jst over 1f out: styd on wl fnl f: eased fnl 50yds* **7/1**	108+
2	1/2	**Yellow Rosebud (IRE)**[21] 4749 3-9-3 107 (b) ShaneFoley 1 (D K Weld, Ire) *hld up in mid-div: 7th 1/2-way: rdn to go 4th under 2f out: kpt on wl u.p to chse wnr ins fnl f: clsng nr fin* **2/1**[1]	110+
3	2 3/4	**Boastful (IRE)**[41] 4070 4-9-5 MartinHarley 8 (Mrs K Burke) *chsd ldrs: 3rd 1/2-way: rdn to ld briefly under 2f out: hdd over 1f out: styd on same pce u.p* **11/2**[3]	102
4	3/4	**Coolnagree (IRE)**[108] 1943 3-9-0 98 DeclanMcDonogh 5 (W McCreery, Ire) *hld up in rr: rdn 3f out and prog to go 5th over 1f out: r.o wl fnl f* **7/1**	98
5	3/4	**Radio Gaga**[41] 4070 3-9-0 RichardMullen 6 (Ed McMahon) *chsd ldrs: 4th 1/2-way: rdn over 2f out and sn one pce* **5/1**[2]	96
6	1	**After (IRE)**[13] 5067 3-9-0 100 CO'Donoghue 4 (A P O'Brien, Ire) *hld up in rr of mid-div: 8th 1/2-way: rdn in st: wnt 6th over 1f out and styd on same pce* **9/1**	94
7	1	**Empowering (IRE)**[29] 4482 4-9-5 98 JPO'Brien 3 (A P O'Brien, Ire) *hld up in rr of mid-div: 9th 1/2-way: rdn and c wd st: no imp* **9/1**	93
8	nk	**One Fine Day (IRE)**[23] 4692 3-9-0 87 EmmetMcNamara 2 (Mrs John Harrington, Ire) *in rr: detached fr main field early: stl last appr st: rdn and sme prog fr 2f out: nvr nrr* **33/1**	90
9	1/2	**Caprella**[21] 4749 3-9-0 97 NGMcCullagh 7 (P D Deegan, Ire) *chsd ldr: 2nd 1/2-way: rdn to ld briefly early st: hdd under 2f out and grad wknd* **14/1**	89
10	1/2	**Singing Bird (IRE)**[21] 4749 3-9-0 93 WayneLordan 9 (David Wachman, Ire) *chsd ldrs: 5th 1/2-way: rdn appr st and no imp: wknd* **12/1**	88
11	nk	**Redoutable (IRE)**[11] 5138 3-9-0 80 (b[1]) ChrisHayes 11 (Kevin Prendergast, Ire) *led: 3 l clr 1/2-way: rdn appr st: hdd early st and wknd* **33/1**	87?

1m 38.16s (98.16)
WFA 3 from 4yo 5lb **11** Ran SP% **130.6**
CSF £23.84 TOTE £15.10: £2.70, £1.02, £2.10; DF 23.30.
Owner Ballylinch Stud **Bred** C J Foy **Trained** Coolcullen, Co Carlow

FOCUS
The winner looks to be on the upgrade and the eighth might be the best guide to the level.

NOTEBOOK
Lady Wingshot(IRE) just about confirmed her superiority over Yellow Rosebud from their meeting at Galway on slightly worse terms. Settled in mid-division, she made her challenge on the outside and quickened that bit more effectively than the runner-up when it mattered as she just got a vital length or two a furlong out. She looks progressive having had a slow start to the season and there's every reason to hope that the best is still to come. (op 11/2)
Yellow Rosebud(IRE) had the perfect inside draw but it's only a perfect draw on a horse that is ridden handily. She was slightly restrained but was struggling a little to make up her ground entering the straight and from a furlong out she just stayed on. Even on ground like this she definitely wants a mile as she just didn't possess enough tactical speed to get towards the front when she needed to or to cope with the extra foot the winner possesses. (op 15/8 tchd 9/4)
Boastful(IRE) raced close to the pace for most of the way but in the end she probably paid for it a bit as the first two drew away from her inside. It's probably about as good as she is. (op 7/1)
Coolnagree(IRE) might well be a filly that will win a half-decent race before the season is out. This was her first run since May and she travelled well just off the pace but didn't have the toe to get into it, keeping on well late. One imagines she might just progress from this. (op 13/2)
Radio Gaga was off the bridle before they turned in and to her credit she stuck to her task well. She just wasn't good enough. (op 7/1 tchd 8/1)
After(IRE) briefly threatened to get into it but was eventually one-paced. (op 10/1)
One Fine Day(IRE) didn't run at all badly considering she got left a few lengths at the start.

5524 - 5526a (Foreign Racing) - See Raceform Interactive

5146 FFOS LAS (L-H)
Friday, August 24

OFFICIAL GOING: Flat course - soft (7.0); jumps course - good to soft changing to good to soft (soft in places) after race 6 (4.30)
Wind: Fresh, behind Weather: breezy, showers

5527 BET TOTEPLACEPOT TEXT TOTE TO 89660 NURSERY 6f
1:40 (1:40) (Class 4) (0-85,84) 2-Y-O **£3,428** (£1,020; £509; £254) **Stalls** Centre

Form				RPR
01	**1**		**Intibaah**[25] 4654 2-9-7 **84** TadhgO'Shea 5 (Brian Meehan) *pressed ldr tl led and gng best over 2f out: pushed along and wnt clr 2f out: in command and nudged along fnl f: comf* **5/4**[1]	88+
61	**2**	1 3/4	**Derwent (USA)**[19] 4845 2-9-7 **84** GeorgeBaker 2 (Roger Charlton) *led tl over 2f out: sn rdn and unable qck: kpt on same pce u.p fnl f* **7/4**[2]	82
3044	**3**	1/2	**Effie B**[11] 5178 2-9-2 **79** MartinHarley 1 (Mick Channon) *trckd ldrs: effrt and drvn 2f out: kpt on same pce and no threat to wnr fnl f* **11/2**[3]	75
6323	**4**	nk	**It's Taboo**[11] 5146 2-9-2 **79** DaneO'Neill 3 (Mark Usher) *in tch: rdn over 2f out: sn drvn: kpt on but no threat to wnr fnl f* **7/1**	74

1m 13.46s (3.46) **Going Correction** +0.475s/f (Yiel) **4** Ran SP% **108.7**
Speed ratings (Par 96): **95,92,92,91**
CSF £3.74 TOTE £2.20; EX 4.30.
Owner Hamdan Al Maktoum **Bred** Shadwell Estate Company Limited **Trained** Manton, Wilts

FOCUS
The ground was cutting up and riding soft. It was interesting to see how two last-time-out maiden winners would fare off the same weight in a handicap. Thrun could be rated higher but this looks a sensible starting point.

NOTEBOOK
Intibaah had stayed on well to beat an odds-on favourite in a Wolverhampton maiden at the end of last month earning a RPR of 87, which suggested that he could be well treated off a mark of 84 for his first foray into handicaps. On his toes in the paddock and with two handlers, he settled well once leaving the stalls, helped set the pace and pulled clear in a professional manner. He has a good cruising speed, a healthy attitude and should continue to progress. (tchd 6-5 and 11-8)
Derwent(USA) landed a gamble at Newbury earlier this month, earning a RPR of 81. That suggested he had something to find with today's winner. He ran a similar race here, once again getting outpaced, but he stayed on well enough though he was no match for the winner and did not act as well on the ground. He was relaxed in the paddock but was not as taking as the winner either.
Effie B had form on soft ground and indeed kept on well enough without ever getting to the front two. She is now 1-9 and looks exposed. (op 5-1 tchd 6-1)

It's Taboo has not been able to win a maiden and was up against a potentially well handicapped rival here, but she has ability although she looks vulnerable on soft ground. (op 9-1)

5528 FOLLOW MECCA SWANSEA ON FACEBOOK H'CAP 1m 2f (R)

2:10 (2:13) (Class 5) (0-70,71) 3-Y-0+ **£2,264** (£673; £336; £168) **Stalls** Low

Form RPR

-453 **1** **Elbow Beach**[21] 4753 3-9-1 **65** .... JamesMillman 3 73
(Rod Millman) *mde all: rdn 3f out: kpt on u.p fr over 1f out: a holding rival fnl f* **9/1**

-154 **2** ¾ **Bold Cuffs**[16] 4945 3-9-6 **70** .... ChrisCatlin 5 76
(Sir Mark Prescott Bt) *stdd s: hld up in tch in rr: hdwy 5f out: rdn to chse wnr 4f out: drvn and kpt on fnl 2f: a hld fnl f* **9/4**[2]

4-21 **3** 7 **Alborz (IRE)**[11] 5152 3-9-7 71 6ex .... CathyGannon 4 63
(Tim Vaughan) *chsd wnr tl 4f out: sn outpcd u.p: 3rd and wl hld fnl 2f* **6/4**[1]

1032 **4** 5 **James Pollard (IRE)**[10] 5197 7-9-5 **68** ....(t) RobertWilliams(7) 1 50
(Bernard Llewellyn) *hld up wl in tch: rdn and effrt over 3f out: sn outpcd and struggling: wl btn fnl 2f* **9/2**[3]

-630 **5** nk **Spring Secret**[3] 5452 6-8-13 **60** .... DarrenEgan(5) 2 41
(Bryn Palling) *t.k.h: chsd ldrs: rdn and struggling over 3f out: wl btn fnl 2f* **10/1**

2m 21.17s (11.77) **Going Correction** +1.275s/f (Soft)
WFA 3 from 6yo+ 8lb **5** Ran SP% **108.0**
Speed ratings (Par 103): **103,102,96,92,92**
CSF £28.24 TOTE £9.40: £2.60, £1.80; EX 29.40.
Owner David Brocklehurst **Bred** D Brocklehurst **Trained** Kentisbeare, Devon

FOCUS
Rain had begun to fall quite heavily and a strong breeze had picked up shortly before this race, which made this a testing affair. The form is rated cautiously given the conditions.

5529 INTEGRAL GEOTECHNIQUE/IRISH STALLION FARMS EBF MAIDEN FILLIES' STKS 1m (R)

2:45 (2:48) (Class 4) 3-Y-0+ **£5,175** (£1,540; £769; £384)

Form RPR

3522 **1** **Gold Show**[11] 5147 3-8-12 71 .... MartinHarley 4 76
(Mick Channon) *chsd ldr tl led on bit over 2f out: rdn over 1f out: kpt on: rdn out* **1/1**[1]

2 **2** ¾ **Be My Rock**[11] 5166 3-8-7 0 .... JamieJones(5) 5 74
(Rae Guest) *chsd ldng pair: chsd wnr ent fnl 2f: rdn over 1f out: kpt on but a hld ins fnl f* **15/8**[2]

0020 **3** 15 **Virginia Galilei (IRE)**[31] 4435 3-8-12 70 .... DaneO'Neill 2 40
(David Lanigan) *tk keen old: hld up in last: rdn and effrt over 2f out: edgd lft u.p and sn struggling: wknd over 1f out* **4/1**[3]

/ **4** 1 **Fairy Trader (IRE)**[28] 5-9-4 0 ....(t) LiamKeniry 1 37
(Keith Goldsworthy) *led tl rdn and hdd over 2f out: sn struggling: wknd over 1f out* **33/1**

1m 51.13s (10.13) **Going Correction** +1.275s/f (Soft)
WFA 3 from 5yo 6lb **4** Ran SP% **107.7**
Speed ratings (Par 102): **100,99,84,83**
CSF £3.13 TOTE £2.10; EX 2.70.
Owner Jaber Abdullah **Bred** Mr & Mrs A E Pakenham **Trained** West Ilsley, Berks

FOCUS
There was a flip start for this maiden to avoid having to drag the stalls across the jumps track on the wettest part of the course. This was a weak race. The winner is rated to recent form.

5530 TOTEPOOL MOBILE TEXT TOTE TO 89660 H'CAP 6f

3:20 (3:21) (Class 2) (0-100,88) 3-Y-O£9,955 (£2,979; £1,489; £745; £371) **Stalls** Centre

Form RPR

113 **1** **Khubala (IRE)**[37] 4221 3-9-3 **84** ....(b) ChrisCatlin 9 94
(Ed Dunlop) *hld up in tch in last trio: rdn and hdwy to chal jst over 1f out: led ins fnl f: r.o wl* **12/1**[3]

2212 **2** nk **Prodigality**[6] 5368 4-9-3 **86** .... DarrenEgan(5) 11 95
(Ronald Harris) *in tch: hdwy to join ldrs 2f out: rdn and ev ch over 1f out: sltly outpcd and edgd lft u.p ins fnl f: rallied and kpt on towards fin but a hld* **8/11**[1]

4004 **3** ¾ **Sohraab**[14] 5065 8-9-9 **87** ....(b) JohnFahy 8 94
(Hughie Morrison) *led for 1f: styd prom: rdn to ld again wl over 1f out: hdd ins fnl f: no ex fnl 100yds* **20/1**

261 **4** 2 ¾ **Rigolleto (IRE)**[11] 5150 4-9-2 **80** 6ex .... MartinHarley 3 78
(Mick Channon) *w ldr tl led after 1f: rdn and hdd wl over 1f out: btn ent fnl f: plugged on same pce after* **16/1**

2260 **5** hd **Gouray Girl (IRE)**[27] 4597 5-9-9 **87** .... DaneO'Neill 6 85
(Henry Candy) *v.s.a: rcvrd and in tch in rr after 1f: rdn and effrt 2f out: sme hdwy u.p over 1f out: kpt on but nvr gng pce to threaten ldrs* **14/1**

0660 **6** nk **Cheveton**[20] 4824 8-9-3 **81** .... SaleemGolam 10 78
(Richard Price) *in tch: rdn and unable qck whn n.m.r 2f out: styd on same pce u.p fr over 1f out* **8/1**[2]

0000 **7** 1 ¼ **Masked Dance (IRE)**[6] 5362 5-9-2 **80** ....(bt) JamesMillman 1 73
(Scott Dixon) *dwlt: sn pushed along and rcvrd to join ldr after 1f: rdn ent fnl 2f: wknd ent fnl f* **20/1**

3212 **8** shd **First In Command (IRE)**[33] 4380 7-8-11 **78** ....(t) MarkCoumbe(3) 7 70
(Daniel Mark Loughnane) *in tch in midfield: rdn and unable qck ent fnl 2f: wknd jst over 1f out* **16/1**

200 **9** nse **Bathwick Bear (IRE)**[33] 4367 4-9-7 **85** .... CathyGannon 5 77
(David Evans) *pressed ldrs: rdn and unable qck jst over 2f out: wknd u.p ent fnl f* **20/1**

6160 **10** ¾ **Flameoftheforest (IRE)**[20] 4833 5-9-2 **80** ....(p) LiamKeniry 4 70
(Ed de Giles) *stdd s: hld up in tch in rr: rdn and no hdwy ent fnl 2f: wl hld whn swtchd rt over 1f out* **12/1**[3]

1m 11.79s (1.79) **Going Correction** +0.475s/f (Yiel)
WFA 3 from 4yo+ 3lb **10** Ran SP% **117.1**
Speed ratings (Par 109): **107,106,105,101,101 101,99,99,99,98**
Tote Swingers 1&2 £1.10, 2&3 £6.90, 1&3 £11.00 CSF £20.62 CT £181.92 TOTE £12.80: £2.40, £1.10, £4.80; EX 23.10.
Owner Miss P Araci **Bred** James F Hanly **Trained** Newmarket, Suffolk

FOCUS
A fair handicap despite the top weights being 13lb below the ceiling for this race, but there was only one horse in it as far as the market was concerned, especially when forecast second favourite Priceless Jewel became a non-runner, although things did not go according to plan. The winner resumed his progress back at 6f.

NOTEBOOK
Khubala(IRE) kept tabs on the favourite in the early stages before coming through to win quite comfortably. He had swept past his rivals to land a Doncaster handicap in June, but the drop back to 5f next time did not pay off. Although this was a marked step up from that level the soft ground and flat track was in his favour, and he looks progressive with a commendable win ratio. (op 8-1 tchd 7-1)

Prodigality narrowly failed to get up on the line when favourite for the consolation race for the Great St Wilfred at Ripon six days ago. Able to run off the same mark here and once again making use of Darren Egan's claim, as they had when successful at Brighton the time before, he was well supported once again. However, after travelling comfortably he began to struggle from 2f out and could not match the winner's pace in the testing ground. (op Evens)

Sohraab is not as good as he was but blinkers had some effect at Newmarket a fortnight previously and they were retained. It helped him break well and race up with the pace, and he remained right there until just fading as the line approached. (op 14-1)

Rigolleto(IRE) showed early speed but was up against it carrying a penalty for dead-heating in a Class 5 handicap over C&D 11 days earlier, and eventually it proved too much. (tchd 20-1)

Gouray Girl(IRE) ran better than the bare form as she missed the break and lost several lengths, but stayed on in ground that suits.

Cheveton's last win came in the Ayr Silver Cup last September, and he also won the Bronze Cup the year before. As usual, he has yet to hit form this summer and has dropped down the weights, and he could have done with a decent run here to move back up if a repeat bid is to be his target, but he could make no real impression. (op 7-1)

4799 GOODWOOD (R-H)

Friday, August 24

OFFICIAL GOING: Good (good to firm in places) changing to good after race 3 (6.15)

Wind: Moderate, across (away from stands') Weather: Overcast, drizzly

5531 CHICHESTER OBSERVER APPRENTICE STKS (H'CAP) 6f

5:10 (5:10) (Class 5) (0-70,70) 3-Y-0+ **£3,234** (£962; £481; £240) **Stalls** High

Form RPR

0500 **1** **Illustrious Prince (IRE)**[13] 5110 5-9-2 **69** .... LukeLeadbitter(7) 6 78
(Declan Carroll) *pushed along early to chse ldrs: rdn and prog on outer to ld over 1f out: sn hrd pressed: kpt on wl nr fin* **7/2**[2]

1544 **2** ½ **Sarangoo**[3] 5447 4-9-2 **65** .... MatthewLawson(3) 3 72
(Malcolm Saunders) *sltly slowly away: off the pce in last pair: gd prog on wd outside over 2f out: jnd wnr jst over 1f out: no ex last 75yds* **11/1**

0000 **3** ½ **Seamus Shindig**[13] 5097 10-8-12 **61** .... AmyScott(3) 2 66
(Henry Candy) *settled off the pce in last trio: stdy prog jst over 2f out: hrd rdn and tk 3rd fnl f: styd on but nvr quite able to chal* **8/1**

0015 **4** 3 ¼ **Proper Charlie**[11] 5165 4-9-1 **64** .... DavidKenny(3) 4 59
(William Knight) *w.w in 7th: clsd on ldrs on outer over 2f out: rdn and cl up in 3rd over 1f out: wknd fnl f* **12/1**

2301 **5** ¾ **One Last Dream**[8] 5263 3-8-5 **54** 6ex ....(b) RaulDaSilva 5 47
(Ron Hodges) *pressed ldrs: rdn over 2f out: wknd jst over 1f out* **2/1**[1]

10 **6** nk **Jake The Snake (IRE)**[57] 3544 11-9-7 **70** .... BrendanPowell(3) 8 62
(Tony Carroll) *s.s: off the pce in last pair: shkn up and hanging fr 2f out: styd on fr over 1f out: nrst fin* **15/2**[3]

3266 **7** nse **Pharoh Jake**[16] 4943 4-8-0 **51** oh4 .... IanBurns(5) 1 42
(John Bridger) *led after 1f on outer: rdn and hdd over 1f out: wknd* **33/1**

00-0 **8** 2 ¾ **Indian Shuffle (IRE)**[43] 4003 4-9-4 **67** .... CharlesBishop(3) 10 50
(Jonathan Portman) *racd against nr side rail: led 1f: lost pl 1/2-way: struggling after* **25/1**

3433 **9** 1 ¼ **Even Bolder**[6] 5346 9-8-6 **59** .... JoeyHaynes(3) 9 38
(Eric Wheeler) *awkward s: rcvrd to chse ldrs and racd against nr side rail: lost pl fr over 2f out* **20/1**

2146 **10** 9 **Cocohatchee**[43] 4000 4-9-4 **69** .... JakePayne(5) 7 19
(Pat Phelan) *pressed ldrs to 1/2-way: sn wknd qckly: t.o* **15/2**[3]

1m 11.37s (-0.83) **Going Correction** -0.45s/f (Firm)
WFA 3 from 4yo+ 3lb **10** Ran SP% **117.8**
Speed ratings (Par 103): **87,86,85,81,80 79,79,76,74,62**
Tote Swingers 1&2 £12.90, 2&3 £19.80, 1&3 £7.40 CSF £40.92 CT £291.67 TOTE £5.00: £2.60, £4.50, £3.20; EX 54.60.
Owner Ray Flegg **Bred** Rathbarry Stud **Trained** Sledmere, E Yorks
■ Luke Leadbitter's first winner on just his third ride.

FOCUS
Lower bend dolled out 5yds adding 8yds to distances on that course. The going was good, good to firm in places. They went off fast in this apprentice handicap. The first three came from off the pace down the centre of the track and pulled clear of the rest.

5532 GREENE KING NURSERY 6f

5:40 (5:40) (Class 5) (0-75,75) 2-Y-O **£3,408** (£1,006; £503) **Stalls** High

Form RPR

2200 **1** **Opt Out**[20] 4825 2-9-2 **70** .... FrannyNorton 8 81
(Mark Johnston) *racd towards nr side rail: trckd ldr: nt asked for effrt 2f out: led over 1f out: pushed clr* **6/1**[3]

000 **2** 4 ½ **Michael's Song (IRE)**[29] 4487 2-8-0 **57** .... SophieDoyle(3) 4 54
(Mick Channon) *chsd ldng pair: rdn to chal 2f out: chsd wnr jst over 1f out: easily lft bhd* **8/1**

152 **3** nk **Risky Rizkova**[15] 4991 2-9-0 **68** .... MatthewDavies 5 64
(Jonathan Portman) *led: rdn over 2f out: hdd over 1f out: sn lost 2nd and outpcd* **9/2**[2]

106 **4** nse **Belle Intrigue**[36] 4230 2-9-0 **68** .... JimCrowley 7 64
(Amanda Perrett) *taken down early: awkward s: chsd ldrs: shkn up wl over 1f out: styd on towards nr side rail ins fnl f* **8/1**

050 **5** 1 **Katy Spirit (IRE)**[15] 5003 2-7-12 **55** .... RaulDaSilva(3) 1 48
(Michael Blanshard) *settled in last pair: prog on outer 1/2-way: clsd on ldrs wl over 1f out: sn outpcd* **14/1**

3030 **6** 1 **Cio Cio San (IRE)**[27] 4574 2-8-13 **67** .... KieranO'Neill 2 57
(Richard Hannon) *chsd ldrs: pushed along 1/2-way: effrt and cl up 2f out: nt qckn over 1f out: fdd* **7/4**[1]

3306 **7** 4 ½ **Red Adair (IRE)**[14] 5060 2-9-6 **74** .... PatCosgrave 3 50
(Richard Hannon) *a in rr: rdn and effrt over 2f out: wknd over 1f out* **6/1**[3]

1m 11.84s (-0.36) **Going Correction** -0.45s/f (Firm) **7** Ran SP% **112.0**
Speed ratings (Par 94): **84,78,77,77,76 74,68**
Tote Swingers 1&2 £7.40, 2&3 £19.80, 1&3 £12.90 CSF £49.37 CT £233.57 TOTE £6.30: £1.70, £3.60; EX 42.60.
Owner Sheikh Hamdan Bin Mohammed Al Maktoum **Bred** Darley **Trained** Middleham Moor, N Yorks

FOCUS
All of the runners in this nursery had been beaten 4l or more on their previous start and most of them failed to reverse that trend behind the emphatic winner. The form has been rated conservatively but this was still a useful, improved effort from Opt Out.

NOTEBOOK
Opt Out arrived with a patchy record of 0-7 but he blasted back to form with a runaway win on this step back up to 6f. The form does not look strong and he will face a sharp rise in mark but the style was impressive and this Pivotal half-brother to seven winners could find further improvement. (tchd 13-2)

Michael's Song(IRE) ran respectably on her nursery debut. She was beaten quite a long way but she is an unexposed half-sister to plenty of winners and has been generally progressive in four runs. (tchd 15-2)
Risky Rizkova raced near the pace but had no answer when the winner surged past him near the stands' rail. (op 4-1)
Belle Intrigue travelled well out the back before staying on steadily against the stands' rail. She has not gone on from her debut win in a three-runner soft-ground Brighton maiden in June but she rates a bit better than this bare form. (tchd 15-2)
Katy Spirit(IRE) looked dangerous out wide but her effort flattened out on her nursery debut. (op 10-1)
Cio Cio San(IRE) didn't get home over 7f last time and was a strong favourite switched back to sprinting but she didn't travel with much fluency and was a spent force approaching the final furlong. (op 11-4)

5533 CHICHESTER CITY STKS (H'CAP) 1m 4f
6:15 (6:15) (Class 4) (0-80,79) 3-Y-O **£4,528** (£1,347; £673; £336) **Stalls** High

Form RPR
623 **1** **Modernism**[6] 5366 3-9-4 **76**.......... FrannyNorton 7 87
(Mark Johnston) *mde all: rdn and pressed jst over 2f out: r.o wl to draw clr fr over 1f out* **6/4**[1]
0223 **2** *4* **Hidden Justice (IRE)**[17] 4906 3-9-0 **72**.......... JimCrowley 1 77
(Amanda Perrett) *dwlt: pushed up to chse ldng pair: chal on inner jst over 2f out: outpcd over 1f out* **9/2**[2]
3010 **3** *1 3/4* **Keepax**[15] 5007 3-9-7 **79**.......... SebSanders 5 81
(Chris Wall) *hld up in tch: 5th 1/2-way: shkn up and prog 3f out: chal jst over 2f out: one pce over 1f out* **9/2**[2]
1-36 **4** *1 1/2* **Moderator**[189] 596 3-9-6 **78**.......... FergusSweeney 2 77
(Gary Moore) *hld up in last: prog to take 4th 2f out: rdn and sn outpcd* **14/1**
4312 **5** *3 3/4* **Jane Lachatte (IRE)**[36] 4254 3-9-2 **74**.......... MickaelBarzalona 6 67
(Stuart Williams) *hld up: prog after 4f: rdn wl over 2f out: steadily wknd fnl 2f* **5/1**[3]
0516 **6** *7* **Guiletta (IRE)**[21] 4781 3-8-10 **68**.......... PatCosgrave 4 50
(Rae Guest) *chsd wnr to wl over 2f out: wknd* **10/1**

2m 41.32s (2.92) **Going Correction** +0.15s/f (Good) **6** Ran SP% **108.8**
Speed ratings (Par 102): **96,93,92,91,88 84**
Tote Swingers 1&2 £2.50, 2&3 £3.20, 1&3 £2.00 CSF £7.87 TOTE £2.90: £2.40, £2.80; EX 9.00.
Owner Sheikh Hamdan Bin Mohammed Al Maktoum **Bred** Darley **Trained** Middleham Moor, N Yorks

FOCUS
Some rain had arrived and the going was changed to good. This looked a competitive handicap but the well-backed winner powered clear under a front-running ride.

5534 GREENE KING MAIDEN STKS 1m
6:45 (6:46) (Class 4) 2-Y-O **£4,528** (£1,347; £673; £336) **Stalls** Low

Form RPR
0 **1** **Pearl Castle (IRE)**[14] 5062 2-9-3 0.......... FrannyNorton 3 80
(Andrew Balding) *mde all: kicked on over 3f out: rdn and clr over 1f out: styd on wl* **9/2**[3]
03 **2** *2* **Astrosapphire**[13] 5098 2-8-12 0.......... JimCrowley 1 70
(Mark H Tompkins) *cl up: chsd wnr 3f out: no imp fr 2f out: styd on* **12/1**
3 *1 3/4* **Restraint Of Trade (IRE)** 2-9-3 0.......... MickaelBarzalona 2 71+
(Mahmood Al Zarooni) *dwlt: rn green in last pair: rdn and struggling over 3f out: plld wd over 2f out: hung lft after but r.o to take 3rd ins fnl f* **11/8**[1]
43 **4** *3 1/2* **Lightning Launch (IRE)**[15] 4995 2-9-3 0.......... MatthewDavies 6 63
(Mick Channon) *t.k.h: hld up in 4th: prog to chse ldng pair 2f out: no imp: wknd fnl f* **7/2**[2]
5 *3/4* **Lord Provost (IRE)** 2-8-12 0.......... AntiocoMurgia(5) 5 61+
(Mahmood Al Zarooni) *s.i.s: rn green in last pair: taken wd 1/2-way: edgd lft and no prog 2f out: wl btn after* **9/2**[3]
0 **6** *2 3/4* **Sovereign Power**[8] 5275 2-9-3 0.......... PatCosgrave 4 55
(Paul Cole) *mostly chsd wnr to 3f out: sn wknd* **33/1**

1m 41.55s (1.65) **Going Correction** +0.15s/f (Good) **6** Ran SP% **111.3**
Speed ratings (Par 96): **97,95,93,89,89 86**
Tote Swingers 1&2 £5.00, 2&3 £2.70, 1&3 £1.60 CSF £50.46 TOTE £5.80: £2.60, £3.90; EX 41.20.
Owner Pearl Bloodstock Ltd **Bred** Mogeely Stud **Trained** Kingsclere, Hants

FOCUS
Some rain had arrived and the going was changed to good. They went a steady pace in this fair maiden and the winner made all off a soft lead. The form makes sense but may not prove that reliable.

NOTEBOOK
Pearl Castle(IRE), a never dangerous ninth of 14 in a 7f Newmarket maiden two weeks ago, looked a lot more streetwise switched to positive tactics on his second start and showed a good attitude to run his rivals into submission. He did have the run of the race but there was still a lot to like about the performance. A 150,000gns Montjeu first foal of a 6f winner, he is a scopey type with plenty of potential for further improvement. (op 7-2 tchd 3-1)
Astrosapphire, a close third in a 1m AW maiden at Lingfield last time, stuck to her task well in a solid third run. A Manduro filly out of a 1m6f winner, she is open to progress and could find her niche over middle-distances next season. (op 7-1)
Restraint Of Trade(IRE) was heavily backed, but he did a lot wrong on his debut. He started slowly and pulled hard off the sedate pace for a long way, but he deserves plenty of credit for finishing well when switched very wide in the straight. This was not a bad start in the circumstances by a 100,000gns half-brother to four 1m-1m4f Listed/Group winners and he could find significant improvement next time. (op 9-4)
Lightning Launch(IRE) set a fair standard on his two frame efforts in 7f/1m maidens at Sandown and Haydock, but he took a strong hold and couldn't find a response when the winner attacked. (tchd 10-3 and 4-1)
Lord Provost(IRE) who looked the Godolphin second-string, travelled well into contention out wide but he couldn't pick up and faded. He should improve for the experience and is a half-brother to hugely progressive five-time 1m1f-1m2f handicapper winner Landaman. (op 6-1 tchd 13-2)

5535 PORTSMOUTH NEWS STKS (H'CAP) 1m 1f
7:20 (7:20) (Class 3) (0-90,89) 3-Y-O+
£7,470 (£2,236; £1,118; £559; £279; £140) **Stalls** Low

Form RPR
004 **1** **The Cayterers**[23] 4706 10-8-13 **77**.......... RaulDaSilva(3) 2 85
(Tony Carroll) *s.s: hld up in last: plld out wd and gd prog jst over 2f out: swooped to ld jst ins fnl f: r.o wl to hold on nr fin* **25/1**
5032 **2** *hd* **Jungle Beat (IRE)**[35] 4288 3-9-6 **88**.......... (b) NickyMackay 3 96
(John Gosden) *t.k.h: trckd ldrs: prog to take narrow ld over 2f out: hdd jst ins fnl f: r.o but jst hld* **4/1**[3]
3340 **3** *3 3/4* **Stage Attraction (IRE)**[48] 3878 4-9-3 **85**.......... DanielMuscutt(7) 7 84
(Andrew Balding) *trckd ldr after 2f: rdn to chal over 2f out: nt qckn over 1f out: outpcd after* **3/1**[2]
3001 **4** *1 1/2* **Yojimbo (IRE)**[22] 4727 4-9-6 **81**.......... MatthewDavies 5 77
(Mick Channon) *led to over 2f out: kpt pressing new ldr tl wknd jst over 1f out* **10/1**
-041 **5** *2* **Uppercut**[24] 4689 4-9-9 **84**.......... JimCrowley 6 76
(Stuart Kittow) *hld up in 7th: prog to trck ldrs 2f out: swtchd lft sn after: rdn and nt qckn over 1f out: lft bhd fnl f* **11/4**[1]
3100 **6** *nk* **Ree's Rascal (IRE)**[24] 4689 4-9-6 **81**.......... PatCosgrave 1 72
(Jim Boyle) *hld up in tch: rdn and effrt to chal on inner 3f out: wknd over 1f out* **8/1**
3506 **7** *2 1/4* **Starwatch**[7] 5301 5-10-0 **89**.......... KieranO'Neill 4 75
(John Bridger) *chsd ldr 2f: rdn 4f out: tried to chal on inner 3f out: sing to lose pl whn squeezed out jst over 2f out: no ch after* **16/1**
4233 **8** *1 1/4* **Save The Bees**[25] 4641 4-8-11 **72**.......... FergusSweeney 8 55
(Declan Carroll) *racd on outer: trckd ldrs: rdn 3f out: wknd 2f out* **15/2**

1m 55.98s (-0.32) **Going Correction** +0.15s/f (Good)
WFA 3 from 4yo+ 7lb **8** Ran SP% **113.4**
Speed ratings (Par 107): **107,106,103,102,100 100,98,97**
Tote Swingers 1&2 £9.80, 2&3 £2.00, 1&3 £6.80 CSF £120.09 CT £398.31 TOTE £33.50: £5.40, £1.70, £1.30; EX 106.10.
Owner R D Willis and M C Watts **Bred** Acrum Lodge Stud **Trained** Cropthorne, Worcs
■ Stewards' Enquiry : Pat Cosgrave two day ban: failed to ride out a horse (7 and 8 Sept)
Nicky Mackay two-day ban: use of whip (7 and 9 Sept)

FOCUS
They went a fair pace in this decent handicap and there was a surprise result as a veteran came from last to first to land the prize.

NOTEBOOK
The Cayterers was slowly away and had plenty of work to do turning in but he finished fast to record a first Flat win since July 2009. He is not the force he used to be and is not certain to back this up off a higher mark next time but this admirable veteran still retains plenty of ability and enthusiasm and has a record that includes ten Flat wins at 6f-1m2f and also a couple of hurdle wins. (op 20-1 tchd 16-1)
Jungle Beat(IRE) went close in an handicap at Ascot last time and it was similar story here for this lightly raced 3yo who was a bit unlucky to run into a revitalised rival. His mark will probably re-enter the 90s after this clear second but he has done well since blinkers have been applied and this Galileo colt has scope for further progress. (op 3-1)
Stage Attraction(IRE) was heavily backed and travelled smoothly for a long way but he didn't find as much as expected when pressure was applied on his first run beyond 1m. (op 9-2)
Yojimbo(IRE) showed a good attitude to score in a small-field handicap at Epsom last time but he was comfortably overhauled off 2lb higher in this stronger race. (op 12-1 tchd 14-1)
Uppercut prevailed in a bunch finish to a 1m handicap here last month on just his third run of the season. He was solid in the market off 4lb higher here but he ran into some trouble and couldn't pick up when he got a clear run. (tchd 3-1)

5536 LEOPARDSTOWN RACECOURSE MEMBERS STKS (H'CAP) 5f
7:50 (7:50) (Class 5) (0-75,75) 3-Y-O **£3,234** (£962; £481; £240) **Stalls** High

Form RPR
-023 **1** **I See You**[18] 4885 3-8-10 **64**.......... (p) JimCrowley 3 73
(Peter Makin) *chsd ldrs: wnt 2nd over 1f out: str chal and upsides fnl f: jst prevailed* **5/1**
0302 **2** *shd* **Sandfrankskipsgo**[12] 5123 3-9-7 **75**.......... SebSanders 7 84
(Peter Crate) *racd against rail: mde most: jnd fnl f: jst pipped last strides* **4/1**[3]
4255 **3** *2* **Welease Bwian (IRE)**[63] 3350 3-8-11 **65**.......... (e[1]) MickaelBarzalona 5 67
(Stuart Williams) *chsd ldrs: rdn to take cl 3rd 1f out: one pce ins fnl f* **10/3**[2]
1652 **4** *3 3/4* **Duke Of Aricabeau (IRE)**[15] 5000 3-9-1 **72**.......... RaulDaSilva(3) 6 60
(Mrs K Burke) *off the pce in last pair: effrt 2f out: no hdwy 1f out: fdd* **2/1**[1]
6210 **5** *3 3/4* **Roy's Legacy**[13] 5087 3-8-4 **58**.......... (t) FrannyNorton 4 33
(Shaun Harris) *w ldr tl over 1f out: wknd qckly* **9/1**
0030 **6** *6* **Jawim**[8] 5263 3-8-2 **56** oh7.......... NickyMackay 2
(Malcolm Saunders) *outpcd in last pair: brief effrt over 1f out: wknd qckly* **25/1**
1366 **P** **Tinzapeas**[16] 4953 3-8-12 **66**.......... (v) MatthewDavies 1
(Mick Channon) *chsd ldrs early: wknd suddenly and p.u over 1f out: suffered fatal heart attack* **12/1**

57.93s (-2.27) **Going Correction** -0.45s/f (Firm) **7** Ran SP% **114.6**
Speed ratings (Par 100): **100,99,96,90,84 75,**
Tote Swingers 1&2 £6.90, 2&3 £3.70, 1&3 £3.60 CSF £25.28 TOTE £5.50: £3.00, £1.60; EX 16.00.
Owner Mrs C C Regalado-Gonzalez **Bred** Lilac Bloodstock & Redmyre Bloodstock **Trained** Ogbourne Maisey, Wilts

FOCUS
It was raining hard and visibility was poor for this sprint handicap.
T/Plt: £658.50 to a £1 stake. Pool: £46366.83 - 51.40 winning tickets T/Qpdt: £38.70 to a £1 stake. Pool: £4317.70 - 82.46 winning tickets JN

4806 HAMILTON (R-H)
Friday, August 24

OFFICIAL GOING: Soft (heavy in places; 7.1)
Wind: Virtually nil Weather: overcast

5537 RACING UK NURSERY 6f 5y
5:35 (5:36) (Class 5) (0-75,74) 2-Y-O **£3,234** (£962; £481; £240) **Stalls** High

Form RPR
0216 **1** **Penny Garcia**[19] 4836 2-9-2 **69**.......... DuranFentiman 4 79
(Tim Easterby) *hld up in tch: angled to outer over 1f out: sn rdn and hdwy: led 1f out: kpt on wl to draw clr* **5/1**
1045 **2** *3 3/4* **Projectisle (IRE)**[17] 4922 2-9-2 **72**.......... JulieBurke(3) 2 71
(Kevin Ryan) *chsd ldr: pushed along 1/2-way: rdn to ld narrowly over 1f out: hdd 1f out: one pce and sn no ch w wnr* **7/1**
112 **3** *nk* **Lady Moonlight (IRE)**[7] 5292 2-9-2 **72**.......... DaleSwift(3) 1 70
(Ann Duffield) *racd keenly: in tch on outer: rdn and ev ch over 1f out: one pce fnl f* **7/4**[1]
01 **4** *6* **Ayasha**[23] 4710 2-9-2 **74**.......... JustinNewman(5) 6 54
(Bryan Smart) *prom: rdn over 2f out: wknd fnl f* **4/1**[2]
5242 **5** *1 3/4* **Perfect Words (IRE)**[21] 4767 2-8-6 **64**.......... JasonHart(5) 7 39
(Marjorie Fife) *in tch: rdn over 2f out: wknd over 1f out* **12/1**
641 **6** *12* **Flighty Clarets (IRE)**[30] 4448 2-9-4 **71**.......... FrederikTylicki 3 10
(Richard Fahey) *led: rdn whn hdd over 1f out: wknd and eased* **9/2**[3]

1m 16.42s (4.22) **Going Correction** +0.50s/f (Yiel) **6** Ran SP% **111.4**
Speed ratings (Par 94): **91,86,85,77,75 59**
Tote Swingers 1&2 £4.60, 2&3 £4.10, 1&3 £1.60 CSF £37.18 TOTE £5.50: £1.90, £3.90; EX 41.10.
Owner Jim & Helen Bowers **Bred** J Bowers **Trained** Great Habton, N Yorks

FOCUS
Rail realignment around the loop added about 25yds to distances on Round course. This card was run on testing ground and they came home quite well strung out for a 6f race. Straightforward form around the second and third.

NOTEBOOK
Penny Garcia had shown a clear liking for easy conditions prior to disappointing on fast ground at Chester last time (after which she was dropped 2lb) and she came from last to first down the outside to storm clear up the hill and win in emphatic style. This more conventional track suited her and she remains a progressive juvenile when conditions are in her favour. (tchd 9-2 and 11-2)

Projectisle(IRE) kept plugging away and fared best of the rest, but was no match for the winner. This was her first run on slow ground and she seemed to handle it fine, but she has now been fairly well beaten in three nurseries, so is clearly vulnerable off this sort of mark. (op 13-2)

Lady Moonlight(IRE) probably saw a bit too much daylight out wide and was a bit too keen. She could only keep on at the one pace in the final furlong and probably ran a little below par. (op 2-1)

Ayasha had every chance, but dropped away and conditions could easily be an excuse given both previous runs had been on a sound surface.

Flighty Clarets(IRE) Official explanation: trainer said that the filly was unsuited by the ground (soft, heavy in places)

5538 VARIETY CLUB H'CAP — 6f 5y
6:05 (6:05) (Class 6) (0-65,71) 3-Y-O — **£2,045** (£603; £302) **Stalls** High

Form / RPR

3460 **1** **Celestial Dawn**[16] 4957 3-9-1 **59** ..... JamesSullivan 2 — 69
(John Weymes) *slowly away: sn pushed along in rr: reminders 1/2-way: stl last jst ins fnl f: r.o strly towards stands' rail to ld nr fin* **20/1**

2202 **2** 3/4 **Blue Shoes (IRE)**[17] 4909 3-9-6 **64** ..... DuranFentiman 1 — 72
(Tim Easterby) *trckd ldr: rdn to ld appr fnl f: kpt on: hdd nr fin* **6/1**[3]

0214 **3** 1/2 **Lord Franklin**[25] 4642 3-8-6 **55** ..... JasonHart(5) 10 — 61
(Eric Alston) *hld up in tch: rdn over 2f out: hdwy over 1f out: kpt on fnl f* **3/1**[2]

2042 **4** 1 1/4 **Bartley**[7] 5317 3-8-13 **62** ..... (v) JustinNewman(5) 3 — 64
(Bryan Smart) *midfield on outer: pushed along 1/2-way: drvn over 1f out: kpt on* **8/1**

2524 **5** 1/2 **Ambitious Icarus**[15] 5000 3-9-4 **62** ..... (e) RobbieFitzpatrick 4 — 63
(Richard Guest) *hld up: hdwy 2f out: pushed along whn n.m.r over 1f out: one pce ins fnl f: nvr threatened ldrs* **12/1**

0600 **6** nk **Windygoul Lad**[21] 4771 3-8-9 **53** ..... AndrewMullen 5 — 53
(Keith Dalgleish) *in tch: pushed along over 2f out: sn one pce and nvr threatened ldrs* **50/1**

0000 **7** 1/2 **Sinai (IRE)**[20] 4793 3-8-13 **64** ..... (p) JordanNason(7) 9 — 62
(Geoffrey Harker) *trckd ldr: pushed along over 1f out: outpcd jst ins fnl f: no threat after* **8/1**

11 **8** 1 3/4 **Planetex (IRE)**[7] 5318 3-9-13 **71** 6ex ..... MichaelO'Connell 8 — 64
(John Quinn) *led narrowly: rdn whn hdd appr fnl f: grad wknd* **7/4**[1]

4036 **9** 2 1/4 **Rock Canyon (IRE)**[10] 5189 3-8-11 **60** ..... (p) ShaneBKelly(5) 6 — 45
(Linda Perratt) *prom: rdn and ev ch appr fnl f* **20/1**

1m 15.5s (3.30) **Going Correction** +0.50s/f (Yiel) — 9 Ran SP% **117.0**
Speed ratings (Par 98): **98,97,96,94,94 93,92,90,87**
Tote Swingers 1&2 £8.30, 2&3 £5.00, 1&3 £17.50 CSF £134.11 CT £473.38 TOTE £16.60: £4.30, £2.20, £1.80; EX 47.60 Trifecta £309.40 Part won. Pool £418.24 - 0.40 winning units..
Owner Grange Park Racing **Bred** The Welcome Alliance **Trained** Middleham Moor, N Yorks

FOCUS
This was run at quite a strong pace, which only served to set it up for a closer. A slightly positive view has been taken of the form.

Celestial Dawn Official explanation: trainer's representative said reagarding the apparent improvement of form, that the filly was better suited by the softer ground

Planetex(IRE) Official explanation: trainer's representative said that the gelding was unsuited by the ground (soft, heavy in places).

5539 DOWNLOAD THE LADBROKES MOBILE APP H'CAP — 6f 5y
6:35 (6:36) (Class 4) (0-85,85) 3-Y-O+ — **£5,175** (£1,540; £769; £384) **Stalls** High

Form / RPR

0000 **1** **Amenable (IRE)**[39] 4133 5-9-3 **78** ..... AndrewMullen 4 — 90
(David Nicholls) *mde all: pushed along over 2f out: drvn over 1f out: kpt on wl* **20/1**

1000 **2** 3/4 **Barkston Ash**[15] 4998 4-8-7 **73** ..... (p) JasonHart(5) 7 — 83
(Eric Alston) *rrd s and slowly away: hld up: rdn over 2f out: hdwy over 1f out: chsd wnr jst ins fnl f: kpt on* **11/1**

1006 **3** 1 1/2 **Best Trip (IRE)**[17] 4924 5-8-13 **77** ..... PaulPickard(3) 9 — 82
(Brian Ellison) *trckd ldrs: stl gng wl over 1f out: rdn to chse wnr appr fnl f: one pce ins fnl f* **13/2**[3]

6654 **4** 1 3/4 **Jeannie Galloway (IRE)**[57] 3524 5-9-4 **79** ..... (v1) JoeFanning 1 — 78
(Keith Dalgleish) *in tch: rdn over 2f out: one pce fnl f* **6/1**[2]

5324 **5** 3/4 **Roker Park (IRE)**[27] 4589 7-9-10 **85** ..... DanielTudhope 6 — 82
(David O'Meara) *hld up: pushed along over 2f out: kpt on ins fnl f: nrst fin* **3/1**[1]

01 **6** 3/4 **Breezolini**[49] 3815 4-9-0 **75** ..... DuranFentiman 10 — 69
(Geoffrey Harker) *prom: rdn and outpcd over 1f out: kpt on again fnl 100yds* **9/1**

5331 **7** 1 **Crimson Knot (IRE)**[31] 4430 4-9-3 **81** ..... LucyAlexander(3) 5 — 72
(Alan Berry) *in tch: rdn over 2f out: wknd ins fnl f* **8/1**

2442 **8** 3/4 **Springheel Jake**[21] 4769 3-8-13 **77** ..... GrahamLee 2 — 66
(Ann Duffield) *trckd wnr: rdn 2f out: wknd appr fnl f* **7/1**

4443 **9** hd **Polar Annie**[13] 5082 7-8-3 **71** ow2 ..... JordanNason(7) 11 — 59
(Jim Goldie) *stdd s: hld up in tch: pushed along over 2f out: nvr threatened ldrs* **20/1**

1220 **10** 1 1/2 **The Nifty Fox**[18] 4880 8-9-6 **81** ..... (p) JamesSullivan 8 — 64
(Tim Easterby) *hld up in tch: rdn over 2f out: nvr threatened* **16/1**

10-0 **11** 1/2 **Pelmanism**[111] 1868 5-9-1 **79** ..... DaleSwift(3) 3 — 61
(Brian Ellison) *s.i.s: hld up: drvn over 1f out: a towards rr* **20/1**

5510 **12** 3/4 **Lollina Paulina**[7] 5326 3-8-13 **80** ..... (p) JulieBurke(3) 12 — 59
(Kevin Ryan) *prom: rdn over 2f out: wknd appr fnl f* **16/1**

1m 15.55s (3.35) **Going Correction** +0.70s/f (Yiel)
WFA 3 from 4yo+ 3lb — 12 Ran SP% **120.6**
Speed ratings (Par 105): **105,104,102,99,98 97,96,95,95,93 92,91**
Tote Swingers 1&2 £43.00, 2&3 £19.70, 1&3 £19.60 CSF £222.50 CT £1611.11 TOTE £31.80: £7.50, £5.50, £1.20; EX 271.70 TRIFECTA Not won..
Owner Turton Brown Williams Lindley **Bred** Michael Downey & Roalso Ltd **Trained** Sessay, N Yorks

■ Stewards' Enquiry : Andrew Mullen two-day ban: use of whip (7 and 9 Sep)

FOCUS
A wide-open sprint handicap and once again the pace looked strong, but the bare time was moderate. The winner is rated to last year's best.

5540 LADBROKES LANARK SILVER BELL (H'CAP) — 1m 4f 17y
7:05 (7:05) (Class 3) (0-90,90) 3-Y-O+ — **£15,525** (£4,620; £2,308; £1,154) **Stalls** Low

Form / RPR

1152 **1** **Edmaaj (IRE)**[16] 4962 4-9-8 **88** ..... DanielTudhope 8 — 98
(David O'Meara) *trckd ldrs: pushed along to ld over 2f out: rdn over 1f out: strly pressed ins fnl f: kpt on wl u.str.p: jst hld on* **8/1**

-506 **2** nse **Scrapper Smith (IRE)**[42] 4072 6-9-3 **86** ..... JulieBurke(3) 4 — 96
(Alistair Whillans) *slowly away: hld up in rr: pushed along and hdwy over 2f out: chsd ldr over 1f out: ev ch ins fnl f: kpt on wl: jst failed* **12/1**

2423 **3** 1 1/4 **Deepsand (IRE)**[14] 5044 3-8-3 **79** ..... JamesSullivan 9 — 87
(Tim Easterby) *midfield: rdn and hdwy over 2f out: chsd wnr over 1f out: chal strly ins fnl f: no ex towards fin* **12/1**

0610 **4** 1 3/4 **Moidore**[34] 4323 3-8-4 **80** ..... AndrewMullen 5 — 85
(John Quinn) *in tch: rdn and outpcd over 2f out: rallied over 1f out: styd on ins fnl f* **7/1**[3]

4040 **5** 1 **Calaf**[20] 4795 4-8-12 **81** ..... DaleSwift(3) 6 — 85
(Brian Ellison) *racd keenly: hld up: gd hdwy 2f out: rdn and ev ch jst ins fnl f: wknd fnl 100yds* **17/2**

2300 **6** 2 3/4 **Hillview Boy (IRE)**[41] 4112 8-9-10 **90** ..... GrahamLee 14 — 89
(Jim Goldie) *hld up: pushed along over 2f out: rdn over 1f out: nvr threatened ldrs* **6/1**[2]

2002 **7** 1 3/4 **Lexington Bay (IRE)**[10] 5200 4-9-6 **86** ..... FrederikTylicki 13 — 82
(Richard Fahey) *midfield: hdwy over 3f out: sn prom: rdn over 2f out: wknd appr fnl f* **10/1**

3213 **8** 4 1/2 **Cape Rising (IRE)**[15] 5002 5-8-9 **80** ..... GarryWhillans(5) 7 — 69
(Alan Swinbank) *trckd ldrs: rdn over 2f out: wknd over 1f out* **9/1**

0223 **9** 3/4 **Assizes**[13] 5101 3-8-9 **90** ..... JasonHart(5) 15 — 78
(Mark Johnston) *hld up in midfield: hdwy over 3f out: sn prom: rdn over 2f out: wknd over 1f out* **9/2**[1]

0062 **10** 5 **Staff Sergeant**[24] 4674 5-8-6 **77** ..... ShaneBKelly(5) 12 — 57
(Jim Goldie) *hld up in midfield: rdn over 2f out: sn no imp: wknd over 1f out* **25/1**

0006 **11** 3/4 **Merchant Of Dubai**[35] 4284 7-9-0 **83** ..... (p) LucyAlexander(3) 11 — 62
(Jim Goldie) *trckd ldrs: rdn 4f out: sn lost pl and struggling* **16/1**

0645 **12** nk **Becausewecan (USA)**[13] 5076 6-9-1 **81** ..... JoeFanning 10 — 59
(Mark Johnston) *led for 2f: prom: led again over 3f out: hdd over 2f out: sn wknd* **17/2**

1201 **13** 4 **Pokfulham (IRE)**[57] 3535 6-8-13 **79** ..... (v) DuranFentiman 3 — 51
(Jim Goldie) *pushed along and reminders leaving stall: led after 2f: hdd over 3f out: sn wknd* **25/1**

2m 45.47s (6.87) **Going Correction** +0.75s/f (Yiel)
WFA 3 from 4yo+ 10lb — 13 Ran SP% **125.2**
Speed ratings (Par 107): **107,106,106,104,104 102,101,98,97,94 93,93,91**
Tote Swingers 1&2 £14.00, 2&3 £41.00, 1&3 £16.00 CSF £105.46 CT £1161.16 TOTE £8.40: £1.60, £4.50, £5.50; EX 105.00 Trifecta £166.70 Part won. Pool £225.39 - 0.50 winning units..
Owner K Nicholson **Bred** Airlie Stud **Trained** Nawton, N Yorks

■ Stewards' Enquiry : Julie Burke four-day ban: use of whip (7, 9 10, 11 Sep)

FOCUS
A really competitive handicap run at a sound pace and a cracking finish.

NOTEBOOK
Edmaaj(IRE) just held on from the late thrust of Scrapper Smith. He settled well just in behind the pace and travelled smoothly before moving to the fore early in the straight and finding plenty for pressure to repel all the challengers and defy a career-high mark. David O'Meara's charge has been progressive since being stepped up in trip this season and he loves ground like this. He clearly stays this trip well and could still be capable of better. (op 7-1)

Scrapper Smith(IRE) didn't help his cause by losing ground at the start but once in the straight he began to make headway and he finished best of all to swoop late and only fail by the narrowest of margins. He can probably go down as unlucky given he made up so much ground on the winner, but that rival had used up a lot more petrol by sitting closer to the speed, so it's not clear-cut that the runner-up would reverse this form on another day. (op 9-1)

Deepsand(IRE) must have run somewhere near a career best and he ran a blinder at a trip he was not proven over. His losing run now goes back nearly 12 months, but this surely signals his turn is near. (op 14-1)

Moidore, having his first run for John Quinn, rallied in the closing stages having got outpaced and looks more of a stayer than some of these. He is lightly raced compared to many of these and has the potential to improve further, especially over staying trips. (op 8-1)

Calaf caught the eye as he made smooth progress towards the far side of the field in the straight, but his effort flattened out in the closing stages and he might just have paid for being a little free early. (op 11-1 tchd 12-1)

Hillview Boy(IRE) couldn't get in a blow from off the pace and appears to have lost his way a little bit. (tchd 5-1)

Assizes found this too much of a stamina test having come strongly before dropping away in the final furlong. (op 11-2)

5541 LADBROKES MOBILE TEXT MOBILE TO 86131 OPEN MAIDEN STKS — 1m 1f 36y
7:40 (7:41) (Class 5) 3-4-Y-O — **£3,234** (£962; £481; £240) **Stalls** Low

Form / RPR

0262 **1** **Cottesmore (USA)**[7] 5293 3-9-3 78 ..... JoeFanning 7 — 77+
(Mark Johnston) *mde all: pushed clr over 1f out: kpt on: comf* **4/5**[1]

0-4 **2** 3 1/4 **Dark Ruler (IRE)**[17] 4926 3-8-12 0 ..... GarryWhillans(5) 4 — 70
(Alan Swinbank) *trckd ldr: rdn over 1f out: briefly jinked lft: kpt on ins fnl f: no ch w wnr* **12/1**

46-2 **3** 7 **Peak Storm**[15] 4992 3-9-3 73 ..... DanielTudhope 1 — 54
(John O'Shea) *trckd ldr: rdn over 1f out: wknd ins fnl f* **9/4**[2]

4 4 1/2 **Donatia** 3-8-12 0 ..... AndrewMullen 6 — 40
(David Nicholls) *rn green: hld up in tch: pushed along over 3f out: rdn over 2f out: nvr threatened* **15/2**[3]

5 9 **Speedy Star (IRE)** 3-9-3 0 ..... JamesSullivan 3 — 25
(Tina Jackson) *s.i.s: midfield: rdn over 2f out: sn wknd* **25/1**

6 hd **Tilthefatladysings** 3-8-12 0 ..... RobbieFitzpatrick 5 — 19
(Richard Guest) *slowly away: hld up: rdn over 3f out: a bhd* **33/1**

2m 7.8s (8.10) **Going Correction** +0.75s/f (Yiel) — 6 Ran SP% **112.6**
Speed ratings (Par 103): **94,91,84,80,72 72**
Tote Swingers 1&2 £1.40, 2&3 £2.90, 1&3 £1.80 CSF £12.24 TOTE £1.40: £1.20, £3.40; EX 8.10.
Owner Sheikh Hamdan Bin Mohammed Al Maktoum **Bred** Wind Hill Farm **Trained** Middleham Moor, N Yorks

FOCUS
A modest little maiden.

5542 HAMILTON-PARK.CO.UK H'CAP 5f 4y
8:10 (8:10) (Class 6) (0-60,66) 3-Y-O+ £1,940 (£577; £288; £144) Stalls Centre

Form RPR
6301 **1** **Lady Del Sol**[7] 5295 4-9-13 **66** 6ex................................ DanielTudhope 8 73
(Marjorie Fife) *trckd ldr: pushed along over 2f out: led ins fnl f: kpt on to go clr fnl 100yds* **2/1**[1]
0-05 **2** *2 ¾* **Lollypop Lady**[20] 4807 3-8-5 **46** oh1................................(p) JoeFanning 4 43
(Linda Perratt) *hld up: rdn and hdwy over 2f out: led appr fnl f: hdd ins fnl f: no match for wnr fnl 100yds* **18/1**
4400 **3** *2 ½* **Miserere Mei (IRE)**[12] 5131 3-8-5 **46** oh1.................(e) JamesSullivan 2 34
(Richard Guest) *chsd ldr: rdn 2f out: sn one pce and no threat to ldng pair* **10/1**
0600 **4** *nk* **Weetentherty**[10] 5190 5-0-13 **52**.......................................(p) GrahamLee 3 39
(Linda Perratt) *hld up: pushed along over 2f out: kpt on one pce ins fnl f: nvr threatened* **4/1**[3]
0120 **5** *nk* **Piste**[7] 5294 6-9-2 **55**..(e) FrederikTylicki 6 41
(Tina Jackson) *chsd ldrs: rdn over 2f out: lost pl over 1f out: one pce ins fnl f* **7/2**[2]
3244 **6** *1 ¾* **Distant Sun (USA)**[10] 5190 8-8-13 **57**........................(p) ShaneBKelly(5) 1 37
(Linda Perratt) *hld up: rdn over 2f out: nvr threatened* **6/1**
000 **7** *3 ¾* **Busy Bimbo (IRE)**[13] 5087 3-8-2 **46** oh1.........................(b) JulieBurke(3) 7
(Alan Berry) *in tch: pushed along and lost pl 1/2-way: wknd over 1f out* **9/1**
5630 **8** *1* **Dragon Spirit (IRE)**[13] 5087 3-8-5 **46** oh1.................... DuranFentiman 5
(Linda Perratt) *led: clr 4f out tl 2f out: hdd appr fnl f: wknd* **16/1**

1m 3.7s (3.70) **Going Correction** +0.70s/f (Yiel)
WFA 3 from 4yo+ 2lb **8** Ran SP% **120.1**
Speed ratings (Par 101): **98,93,89,89,88 85,79,78**
Tote Swingers 1&2 £11.70, 2&3 £11.80, 1&3 £5.10 CSF £43.71 CT £308.11 TOTE £3.50: £1.20, £3.20, £1.80; EX 29.10 Trifecta £187.90 Pool £286.98 - 1.13 winning units.
Owner Mrs Sue Johnson **Bred** Bond Thoroughbred Corporation **Trained** Stillington, N Yorks
FOCUS
A weak sprint handicap, but they went hard up front.
T/Plt: £2,411.40 to a £1 stake. Pool: £46247.59 - 14.00 winning tickets T/Qpdt: £81.00 to a £1 stake. Pool: £5199.44 - 47.46 winning tickets AS

5311 NEWCASTLE (L-H)
Friday, August 24

OFFICIAL GOING: Good (good to firm in places final 3f on straight course; good to soft in places on round course; 7.2)
Wind: Light, half-behind Weather: overcast

5543 ALAN SHEARER FOUNDATION SUPPORTING CHUF "HANDS AND HEELS" APPRENTICE SERIES H'CAP 6f
4:45 (4:48) (Class 6) (0-65,65) 3-Y-O+ £3,234 (£962; £481; £240) Stalls Low

Form RPR
4302 **1** **Steel Stockholder**[6] 5341 6-9-8 **65**....................... RobertDodsworth(5) 7 73
(Mel Brittain) *chsd ldrs: led over 2f out: hld on towards fin* **9/2**[2]
3360 **2** *hd* **Bygones For Coins (IRE)**[27] 4594 4-8-6 **49**................. KevinStott(5) 14 56
(Robert Johnson) *hld up in mid-div: hdwy over 2f out: styd on to take 2nd last 50yds: no ex* **14/1**
5104 **3** *2* **Strong Man**[13] 5084 4-9-8 **60**.................................(b) DavidSimmonson 3 61
(Michael Easterby) *trckd ldrs: wnt 2nd over 2f out: kpt on same pce fnl f* **9/1**
1002 **4** *¾* **Ryedane (IRE)**[21] 4784 10-9-6 **61**......................(b) RachelRichardson(3) 8 60
(Tim Easterby) *in rr: hdwy 2f out: styd on fnl f: tk 4th towards fin* **16/1**
2062 **5** *¾* **Thrust Control (IRE)**[11] 5171 5-8-10 **48**...............(p) JacobButterfield 10 44
(Tracy Waggott) *chsd ldrs: kpt on same pce appr fnl f* **10/1**
5130 **6** *4* **Soopacal (IRE)**[18] 4866 7-9-3 **60**............................... ShereeGlover(5) 13 43
(Brian Ellison) *in rr: swtchd stands' side over 3f out: kpt on fnl 2f: nvr a factor* **17/2**[3]
3300 **7** *hd* **Tenancy (IRE)**[9] 5246 8-8-11 **52**................................(b) EvaMoscrop(3) 4 35
(Shaun Harris) *half-rrd s: led tl over 2f out: fdd appr fnl f* **20/1**
262 **8** *shd* **Lord Buffhead**[7] 5318 3-9-2 **57**................................... JoshBaudains 1 39
(Richard Guest) *racd far side: hdwy over 2f out: nvr nr ldrs* **16/1**
5003 **9** *1 ¾* **Brave Battle**[16] 4957 4-9-2 **54**..................................... GemmaTutty 12 31
(Ron Barr) *mid-div: effrt over 2f out: one pce* **12/1**
0603 **10** *½* **Mango Music**[7] 5317 9-9-10 **62**... NoelGarbutt 5 37
(David Thompson) *mid-div: effrt over 2f out: one pce* **25/1**
3500 **11** *2 ½* **Blue Noodles**[18] 4865 6-8-5 **46** oh1..............................(v[1]) KevinLundie(3) 2 13
(John Wainwright) *racd far side: chsd ldrs: wknd 2f out* **33/1**
3233 **12** *½* **Needy McCredie**[18] 4866 6-9-8 **60**..................................... NedCurtis 16 26
(James Turner) *hld up towards rr: sme hdwy over 2f out: nvr a factor* **3/1**[1]
2460 **13** *¾* **Hellbender (IRE)**[32] 4389 6-9-4 **59**................................ BTTreanor(3) 9 22
(George Foster) *chsd ldrs: wknd over 1f out* **18/1**
1540 **14** *4 ½* **Qubuh (IRE)**[41] 4087 4-9-5 **62**.................................. GerJohnson(5) 11 11
(Linda Stubbs) *mid-div: wknd over 1f out* **25/1**
0500 **15** *10* **Saktoon (USA)**[119] 1638 4-8-13 **51**.........................(v) ShirleyTeasdale 15
(Derek Shaw) *mid-div: lost pl over 3f out: sn bhd* **25/1**

1m 13.64s (-0.96) **Going Correction** -0.30s/f (Firm)
WFA 3 from 4yo+ 3lb **15** Ran SP% **123.4**
Speed ratings (Par 101): **94,93,91,90,89 83,83,83,81,80 77,76,75,69,56**
Tote Swingers 1&2 £29.40, 2&3 £60.60, 1&3 £5.50 CSF £62.43 CT £572.04 TOTE £4.50: £1.70, £9.10, £3.30; EX 88.60.
Owner Mel Brittain **Bred** Mrs Joan M Langmead **Trained** Warthill, N Yorks
FOCUS
Rail moved on Round course to give fresh ground. A modest apprentice handicap, run at a good pace on rain-softened ground.
Needy McCredie Official explanation: jockey said that the mare was never travelling

5544 KATHERINE JENKINS AT CLOSE HOUSE SUPPORTING CHUF NURSERY 5f
5:20 (5:21) (Class 5) (0-75,73) 2-Y-O £3,234 (£962; £481; £240) Stalls Low

Form RPR
330 **1** **Dark Opal (IRE)**[27] 4612 2-9-4 **70**....................................... AmyRyan 10 75
(John Weymes) *trckd ldr towards centre: hdwy over 1f out: r.o wl to ld towards fin* **7/1**
6123 **2** *½* **La Sylphe**[7] 5292 2-9-5 **71**.. GrahamGibbons 1 74
(David Barron) *overall ldr on far side: hdd and no ex last 50yds* **5/2**[1]
2642 **3** *1* **Cracking Choice (IRE)**[7] 5313 2-8-12 **64**...................(p) BarryMcHugh 2 64
(Michael Dods) *chsd ldrs far side: edgd rt ins fnl f: kpt on same pce* **7/2**[2]
1050 **4** *hd* **Cumbrian Craic**[16] 4951 2-9-7 **73**....................................... DavidNolan 8 72
(Tim Easterby) *led two others in centre of crse tl over 1f out: edgd lft and one pce ins fnl f* **12/1**
4320 **5** *½* **Millie N Aire**[13] 5088 2-8-13 **65**... PJMcDonald 7 62
(Danielle McCormick) *sn outpcd far side: hdwy over 2f out: kpt on same pce fnl f* **5/1**[3]
344 **6** *1 ½* **Teetotal (IRE)**[17] 4922 2-8-13 **65**.................................... KellyHarrison 9 58
(Nigel Tinkler) *trckd ldr centre: led that gp over 1f out: one pce and hld whn hmpd nr fin* **7/1**
0505 **7** *3 ½* **Borough Boy (IRE)**[11] 5160 2-8-13 **65**............................ PaddyAspell 5 44
(Derek Shaw) *stdd s: racd far side: nvr a factor* **20/1**
0100 **8** *12* **Starbotton**[13] 5088 2-9-3 **60**...(b[1]) AndrewElliott 4 5
(James Bethell) *chsd ldrs far side: lost pl over 2f out: sn bhd* **8/1**

1m 0.35s (-0.75) **Going Correction** -0.30s/f (Firm) **8** Ran SP% **116.0**
Speed ratings (Par 94): **94,93,91,91,90 88,82,63**
Tote Swingers 1&2 £4.70, 2&3 £2.30, 1&3 £3.90 CSF £25.30 CT £73.04 TOTE £6.50: £2.10, £2.60, £1.30; EX 37.60.
Owner Scothern,Leadbetter,Morley & Partners **Bred** M S And C S Griffiths **Trained** Middleham Moor, N Yorks
FOCUS
An interesting nursery, run at a blistering gallop. Improvement from the winner and solid form from the second.
NOTEBOOK
Dark Opal(IRE), making her nursery debut, is bred to appreciate longer trips and she clearly saw this out well, charging down the centre of the track to score with something in hand. Reverting to the minimum distance having raced over 6f on her last two starts, she looks sure to go on from this and ought to be capable of defying a penalty. Her trainer isn't renowned for his successes with his juveniles but she's already looking good value having cost only 5,000 euros as a yearling. Official explanation: trainer said, reagrding the apparent improvement of form, that the filly had benefited from the slower ground on this occasion (op 8-1)
La Sylphe ◆ ran a blinder and was arguably a shade unfortunate not to have held on for a first win on turf. Having raced keenly last time, she was allowed to roll along in front here and was clear of her field until the final 100 yards. She ought to have no problem winning off this kind of mark, especially on a sharper track. (op 11-4 tchd 3-1)
Cracking Choice(IRE) could never get near the lead but was keeping on nicely at the finish. She possesses a long, raking stride and may well have appreciated quicker ground. (tchd 10-3)
Cumbrian Craic, whom there was plenty to like about the way in which he finished off, had been slightly disappointing since winning by a wide margin on his debut and he was more at home on this easier surface. (op 14-1)
Borough Boy(IRE) Official explanation: jockey said, regarding the running and riding, that his instructions were to drop in last as the colt had been running keen in his previous races to try to get him to settle. He added that due to the fast early pace he quickly found himself detached and as he was already flat out he was unable to make up any ground

5545 SPEEDFLEX (EUROPE) LTD SUPPORTING CHUF H'CAP 7f
5:50 (5:52) (Class 5) (0-75,75) 3-Y-O £3,234 (£962; £481; £240) Stalls Low

Form RPR
6415 **1** **Lolita Lebron (IRE)**[41] 4082 3-9-0 **73**............................... DarylByrne(5) 5 80+
(Lawrence Mullaney) *hld up: smooth hdwy over 3f out: shkn up to ld appr fnl f: pushed out* **7/2**[2]
300 **2** *1* **Dolly Diva**[20] 4793 3-8-6 **60** ow1.. PJMcDonald 7 62
(Paul Midgley) *hld up in rr: effrt 3f out: chsng ldrs 1f out: tk 2nd last 75yds: no imp* **20/1**
-301 **3** *½* **Dutch Heritage**[25] 4638 3-9-7 **75**.. DavidNolan 6 76
(Richard Fahey) *s.s: swtchd lft after s: sn chsng ldrs: drvn over 3f out: nt clr run on ins and swtchd rt over 1f out: kpt on same pce* **13/8**[1]
554 **4** *1 ¾* **Artillery Train (IRE)**[24] 4671 3-7-11 **56** oh6................. NeilFarley(5) 8 52
(Tim Etherington) *sn drvn along and detached in last: reminders after 1f: hdwy in centre and hung rt over 1f out: kpt on to take 4th last 50yds* **33/1**
-545 **5** *1 ¼* **Gibraltar Road**[21] 4771 3-8-2 **56** oh1................................ JimmyQuinn 3 49
(John Quinn) *chsd ldrs: effrt 3f out: one pce over 1f out* **11/2**[3]
4400 **6** *2 ¼* **Dark Falcon (IRE)**[32] 4401 3-8-13 **67**.............................. GrahamGibbons 4 54
(James Tate) *t.k.h: led 1f: w ldrs: led wl over 1f out: hdd appr fnl f: wknd last 150yds* **17/2**
6103 **7** *2 ¼* **Trust Fund Babe (IRE)**[10] 5203 3-8-6 **60**....................... BarryMcHugh 1 41
(Tim Easterby) *chsd ldrs: drvn over 2f out: edgd rt and wknd over 1f out* **6/1**
0463 **8** *4* **I'll Be Good**[16] 4953 3-8-13 **74**.............................(p) DavidSimmonson(7) 2 44
(Robert Johnson) *t.k.h: w ldr: led after 1f: hdd wl over 1f out: wknd fnl f* **12/1**

1m 27.56s (-0.24) **Going Correction** -0.30s/f (Firm) **8** Ran SP% **115.9**
Speed ratings (Par 100): **89,87,87,85,83 81,78,74**
Tote Swingers 1&2 £10.30, 2&3 £7.50, 1&3 £2.20 CSF £68.34 CT £153.77 TOTE £4.80: £3.00, £8.30, £1.10; EX 73.90.
Owner Ian Buckley **Bred** Epona Bloodstock Ltd **Trained** Great Habton, N Yorks
■ Stewards' Enquiry : David Nolan two-day ban: use of whip (7 and 9 Sep)

5546 "HAVE A HEART" TROPHY H'CAP 1m 4f 93y
6:25 (6:25) (Class 4) (0-80,80) 4-Y-O+ £6,469 (£1,925; £962; £481) Stalls Low

Form RPR
-016 **1** **Full Toss**[62] 3380 6-9-0 **76** ow1.................................... GaryBartley(3) 12 83
(Jim Goldie) *trckd ldr: led over 2f out: 3 l clr 1f out: hld on towards fin* **14/1**
0/00 **2** *nk* **Stormy Weather (FR)**[20] 4823 6-9-7 **80**......................(b) MickyFenton 13 87+
(Brian Ellison) *hld up in rr: hdwy over 1f out: wnt 2nd 100yds out: styd on wl: nt quite rch wnr* **10/1**
1505 **3** *2 ½* **Achalas (IRE)**[15] 5030 4-9-3 **76**.................................. GrahamGibbons 5 79
(Heather Main) *chsd ldrs: effrt over 2f out: kpt on same pce fnl f: tk 3rd last strides* **16/1**
164 **4** *hd* **Madrasa (IRE)**[16] 4955 4-8-0 **66**...................................(bt) DavidBergin(7) 2 68
(Keith Reveley) *hld up in rr: hdwy on ins 3f out: sn chsng ldrs: 3rd last 150yds: lost 3rd last strides* **5/1**[2]
03-0 **5** *nk* **Samarkand (IRE)**[16] 4962 4-9-7 **80**................................ PaulMulrennan 8 82+
(Sir Mark Prescott Bt) *hld in mid-div: gng wl whn nt clr run over 2f out tl swtchd rt jst ins fnl f: r.o: lft w too much too do* **7/2**[1]
6300 **6** *1 ½* **Veiled Applause**[18] 4864 9-8-13 **79**............................. KevinLundie(7) 14 78
(John Quinn) *mid-div: drvn over 4f out: kpt on one pce fnl 2f* **20/1**
2643 **7** *nk* **Euston Square**[13] 5085 6-9-0 **73**..................................... PJMcDonald 3 72
(Alistair Whillans) *chsd ldrs: one pce fnl 2f* **16/1**
5042 **8** *nk* **Hawdyerwheesht**[10] 5187 4-7-11 **61** oh3.......................... NeilFarley(5) 6 59+
(Jim Goldie) *hld up in rr: hdwy on inner over 2f out: nt clr run over 1f out: keeping on same pce whn n.m.r 75yds out* **10/1**

1206 **9** *3/4* **Bright Applause**[6] 5345 4-8-12 **71**.............................. RoystonFfrench 1 68
(Tracy Waggott) *chsd ldrs: one pce whn nt clr run and swtchd rt jst ins fnl f* **14/1**

2000 **10** *1* **Lucky Windmill**[34] 4347 5-9-2 **75**.............................. AndrewElliott 4 71
(Alan Swinbank) *led: hdd over 2f out: wkng whn hmpd and eased 100yds out* **12/1**

0312 **11** *7* **Song Of The Siren**[18] 4883 4-9-0 **73**.............................. TomEaves 11 57
(David O'Meara) *trckd ldrs: t.k.h: drvn 3f out: lost pl over 1f out* **8/1**[3]

400 **12** *3 3/4* **Steuben (GER)**[30] 4460 6-9-7 **80**.............................. JimmyQuinn 9 58
(Barney Curley) *t.k.h in mid-div: effrt over 4f out: lost pl over 2f out* **25/1**

4141 **13** *6* **The Lock Master (IRE)**[15] 5001 5-8-11 **73**............ DeclanCannon(3) 15 42
(Michael Appleby) *v awkward s: sn chsng ldrs: drvn over 3f out: lost pl over 2f out* **8/1**[3]

2241 **14** *2 1/2* **Fossgate**[18] 4883 11-9-0 **73**.............................. AmyRyan 10 38
(James Bethell) *in rr: hdwy on outer over 7f out: drvn over 4f out: sn lost pl and bhd* **16/1**

2m 42.24s (-3.36) **Going Correction** -0.15s/f (Firm) **14** Ran SP% **126.6**
Speed ratings (Par 105): **105,104,103,103,102 101,101,101,100,100 95,93,89,87**
Tote Swingers 1&2 £21.30, 2&3 £34.90, 1&3 £35.30 CSF £154.83 TOTE £16.30: £6.00, £3.90, £6.40; EX 158.50.

Owner J S Goldie **Bred** The Queen **Trained** Uplawmoor, E Renfrews

FOCUS
A competitive handicap, run at a fair pace.

5547 MAMMA MIA AT CLOSE HOUSE SUPPORTING CHUF H'CAP 1m 3y(S)
6:55 (6:57) (Class 5) (0-70,70) 3-Y-0+ **£3,234** (£962; £481; £240) **Stalls** Low

Form RPR

0500 **1** **Monthly Medal**[18] 4864 9-8-7 **54**.............................. (t) DominicFox(3) 8 62
(Wilf Storey) *hld up towards rr: hdwy over 2f out: wnt 3rd over 1f out: styd on to ld last 100yds: drvn out* **18/1**

0123 **2** *3/4* **King Pin**[23] 4716 7-9-6 **64**.............................. (p) RoystonFfrench 14 70
(Tracy Waggott) *hld up in mid-div: smooth hdwy to chse ldr over 2f out: led over 1f out: hdd and no ex last 100yds* **10/1**

-026 **3** *1 3/4* **Poontoon (IRE)**[11] 5170 3-8-9 **59**.............................. BarryMcHugh 15 61
(Richard Fahey) *racd stands' side tl swtchd lft after 1f: in rr: hdwy over 2f out: wnt 4th over 1f out: kpt on to take 3rd last 50yds* **6/1**[2]

5450 **4** *3/4* **Amethyst Dawn (IRE)**[39] 4150 6-8-13 **64**.............. DavidBergin(7) 12 64
(Alan McCabe) *w ldr: led 4f out: hdd over 1f out: wknd last 75yds* **9/4**[1]

3015 **5** *4* **Climaxfortackle (IRE)**[4] 5428 4-9-6 **64**.............. (v) JimmyQuinn 9 55
(Derek Shaw) *s.i.s: in rr: hdwy over 2f out: wnt modest 5th 1f out* **12/1**

2550 **6** *7* **Cottam Donny**[9] 5226 4-9-3 **61**.............................. (t) PaulMulrennan 6 36
(Mel Brittain) *chsd ldrs: lost pl over 1f out* **7/1**[3]

1055 **7** *1 1/2* **Collateral Damage (IRE)**[4] 5414 9-9-9 **67**.......... (t) GrahamGibbons 5 39
(Tim Easterby) *chsd ldrs: drvn over 3f out: wknd over 1f out* **9/1**

2620 **8** *3/4* **Mangham (IRE)**[21] 4768 7-8-9 **58**.............................. NeilFarley(5) 1 28
(George Foster) *in rr and sn drvn along: sme hdwy over 2f out: wknd over 1f out* **33/1**

5602 **9** *1 1/4* **Icewan**[13] 5112 3-8-12 **62**.............................. (b) MickyFenton 2 29
(Paul Midgley) *in rr and drvn along: detached over 4f out: sn rdn: kpt on fnl 2f: nvr on terms* **33/1**

253 **10** *2 1/4* **Madame Blavatsky (FR)**[17] 4926 4-9-3 **61**.............. TomEaves 7 23
(Karen McLintock) *chsd ldrs: drvn over 2f out: wknd over 1f out* **16/1**

0300 **11** *nk* **Koo And The Gang (IRE)**[46] 3911 5-9-5 **70**........ JacobButterfield(7) 13 31
(Brian Ellison) *led tl 4f out: wknd over 2f out* **7/1**[3]

60-0 **12** *8* **Artlana**[26] 4623 3-8-4 **54** ow1.............................. AmyRyan 11
(Julie Camacho) *chsd ldrs: lost pl 2f out: sn bhd* **50/1**

3506 **13** *11* **Georgebernardshaw (IRE)**[7] 5322 7-9-0 **58**.............. KellyHarrison 16
(Richard Guest) *lft to r alone stands' side: lost pl over 2f out: sn bhd: eased* **10/1**

1m 40.3s (-3.10) **Going Correction** -0.30s/f (Firm)
WFA 3 from 4yo+ 6lb **13** Ran SP% **124.9**
Speed ratings (Par 103): **103,102,100,99,95 88,87,86,85,83 82,74,63**
Tote Swingers 1&2 £51.50, 2&3 £9.40, 1&3 £35.00 CSF £193.59 CT £1265.58 TOTE £26.90: £7.00, £3.10, £2.20; EX 353.50.

Owner Gremlin Racing **Bred** G S Shropshire **Trained** Muggleswick, Co Durham

FOCUS
A fair handicap, run at a strong pace and it served up a good finish.

5548 TSG.COM SUPPORTING CHUF EBF FILLIES' H'CAP 6f
7:30 (7:32) (Class 5) (0-75,75) 3-Y-0+ **£4,528** (£1,347; £673; £336) **Stalls** Low

Form RPR

5053 **1** **Midnight Dynamo**[25] 4638 5-8-12 **63**.............................. AndrewElliott 7 73
(Jim Goldie) *unruly in stalls: dwlt: drvn and outpcd over 3f out: hdwy and swtchd rt 1f out: styd on strly to ld nr fin* **9/1**

1410 **2** *1* **Bavarian Princess (USA)**[17] 4933 4-9-2 **74**.......... ConorHarrison(7) 8 81
(Mrs K Burke) *hld up towards rr: hdwy over 2f out: led 1f out: hdd and no ex nr fin* **14/1**

1624 **3** *1 1/4* **Pivotal Prospect**[8] 5257 4-8-12 **63**.............................. RoystonFfrench 6 66
(Tracy Waggott) *trckd ldrs: wnt 2nd jst ins fnl f: styd on same pce* **15/2**

3240 **4** *3* **Fenella Fudge**[7] 5320 4-9-2 **67**.............................. (v) GrahamGibbons 3 60
(Derek Shaw) *dwlt: hld up: effrt over 2f out: kpt on fnl f: tk 4th nr fin* **13/2**

3003 **5** *nk* **Code Six (IRE)**[20] 4793 3-8-9 **63**.............................. TomEaves 5 55
(Bryan Smart) *led: hdd 1f out: fdd last 150yds* **6/1**

1401 **6** *1* **Big Wave (IRE)**[16] 4969 4-9-8 **73**.............................. MickyFenton 1 62
(Alison Hutchinson) *w ldr: fdd last 150yds* **9/2**[2]

2541 **7** *1/2* **Dora's Sister (IRE)**[51] 3751 3-8-10 **64**.............................. BarryMcHugh 2 52
(John Quinn) *trckd ldrs: effrt over 2f out: fdd fnl f* **3/1**[1]

0360 **8** *1/2* **Ballinargh Girl (IRE)**[25] 4638 4-8-13 **64**.............................. PJMcDonald 4 50
(Danielle McCormick) *chsd ldrs: drvn over 2f out: fdd fnl f* **14/1**

0 **9** *1/2* **Gracie's Games**[9] 5234 6-8-4 **62** ow2.............. (v) JacobButterfield(7) 10 46
(Richard Price) *dwlt: a outpcd in last: kpt on fnl 100yds: nvr a factor* **5/1**[3]

1m 13.63s (-0.97) **Going Correction** -0.30s/f (Firm)
WFA 3 from 4yo+ 3lb **9** Ran SP% **122.6**
Speed ratings (Par 100): **94,92,91,87,86 85,84,83,83**
Tote Swingers 1&2 £6.00, 2&3 £15.60, 1&3 £4.90 CSF £132.52 CT £1006.95 TOTE £11.30: £3.60, £4.90, £3.60; EX 85.90.

Owner Lorimer Racing **Bred** E W Hyslop **Trained** Uplawmoor, E Renfrews

FOCUS
A fair fillies' handicap, run at a strong pace.

5549 CHRISTMAS PARTIES AT CLOSE HOUSE SUPPORTING CHUF MAIDEN STKS 7f
8:00 (8:01) (Class 5) 3-4-Y-O **£3,234** (£962; £481; £240) **Stalls** Low

Form RPR

2446 **1** **Vital Calling**[7] 5312 3-9-3 73.............................. GrahamGibbons 5 72
(David Barron) *hld up: hdwy to chse ldr 2f out: sn led and rdn 2 l clr: hld on all out at fin* **11/10**[1]

203- **2** *1/2* **Snooky**[336] 6300 3-9-3 75.............................. DavidNolan 6 71
(Richard Fahey) *trckd ldrs: led 2f out: sn hdd: kpt on wl last 100yds: a hld* **11/4**[2]

3 *5* **Spanish Legacy** 3-8-12 0.............................. BarryMcHugh 10 52
(Julie Camacho) *hld up towards rr: effrt over 2f out: kpt on fnl f: tk modest 3rd towards fin* **10/1**

0440 **4** *1 1/4* **Benidorm**[8] 5259 4-9-3 54.............................. (v) AdamCarter(5) 4 56
(John Wainwright) *led: hdd 2f out: edgd lft and lost 3rd nr fin* **25/1**

5 *2 1/4* **Touching History (IRE)** 3-9-3 0.............................. AndrewElliott 3 48
(Tim Etherington) *w ldrs: drvn over 3f out: one pce fnl 2f* **40/1**

5 **6** *1 1/4* **Never Forever**[6] 5340 3-9-3 0.............................. PJMcDonald 7 44
(George Moore) *hld up towards rr: effrt over 2f out: nvr a threat* **4/1**[3]

05 **7** *3/4* **Nurse Dominatrix (IRE)**[12] 5127 3-8-9 0.............. DeclanCannon(3) 8 37
(Richard Guest) *t.k.h in rr: sme hdwy over 2f out: nvr nr ldrs* **28/1**

0005 **8** *1 1/2* **Skiddaw View**[27] 4593 4-9-3 39.............................. (t) PaulMulrennan 2 33
(Maurice Barnes) *dwlt: hld up in rr: effrt over 2f out: nvr trbld ldrs* **100/1**

9 *1 3/4* **Carla Allegra** 3-8-7 0.............................. NeilFarley(5) 9 29
(Jim Goldie) *dwlt: towards rr: hdwy over 3f out: wknd 2f out* **16/1**

0R0 **10** *13* **Idarose (IRE)**[137] 1250 3-8-5 0.............................. VictorSantos(7) 1
(Hugh McWilliams) *sn chsng ldrs: edgd lft and lost pl over 2f out: sn bhd* **200/1**

1m 28.17s (0.37) **Going Correction** -0.30s/f (Firm)
WFA 3 from 4yo 5lb **10** Ran SP% **120.5**
Speed ratings (Par 103): **85,84,78,77,74 73,72,70,68,53**
Tote Swingers 1&2 £1.30, 2&3 £16.50, 1&3 £7.20 CSF £4.28 TOTE £2.10: £1.10, £1.10, £3.40; EX 7.40.

Owner John Raper **Bred** J Raper **Trained** Maunby, N Yorks

FOCUS
Not many could be seriously fancied for this maiden and the market proved the best guide.
T/Plt: £5,312.10 to a £1 stake. Pool: £48027.21- 6.60 winning tickets T/Qpdt: £1,086.30 to a £1 stake. Pool: £4697.58- 3.20 winning tickets WG

5360 NEWMARKET (R-H)
Friday, August 24

OFFICIAL GOING: Good to firm
Wind: Light, across Weather: Cloudy with sunny spells

5550 EBF PIPER-HEIDSIECK MAIDEN FILLIES' STKS (DIV I) 7f
1:20 (1:20) (Class 4) 2-Y-O **£4,528** (£1,347; £673; £336) **Stalls** High

Form RPR

1 **Desert Blossom (IRE)** 2-9-0 0.............................. MickaelBarzalona 10 84+
(Mahmood Al Zarooni) *hld up: hdwy over 2f out: rdn to ld 1f out: r.o* **4/1**[1]

0 **2** *1/2* **Valley Of Queens (IRE)**[13] 5104 2-9-0 0.............................. AhmedAjtebi 2 83+
(Mahmood Al Zarooni) *hld up: hdwy over 2f out: led over 1f out: sn rdn and hdd: r.o* **4/1**[1]

5 **3** *3* **Rainbow Beauty**[20] 4818 2-9-0 0.............................. LukeMorris 8 75
(Gerard Butler) *chsd ldrs: led 3f out: rdn and hdd over 1f out: styd on same pce fnl f* **5/1**[2]

0 **4** *4* **Dali's Lover (IRE)**[50] 3783 2-9-0 0.............................. WilliamCarson 6 65
(Charles Hills) *chsd ldrs: rdn and ev ch over 1f out: wknd fnl f* **16/1**

3 **5** *1 1/4* **Raskova (USA)**[15] 5016 2-9-0 0.............................. JimCrowley 11 62
(William Jarvis) *chsd ldrs: rdn over 2f out: ev ch over 1f out: wknd fnl f* **5/1**[2]

6 *3 3/4* **Star Pearl (USA)** 2-9-0 0.............................. AndreaAtzeni 1 52
(Roger Varian) *s.i.s and wnt rt s: hld up: hdwy over 2f out: rdn and wknd over 1f out* **7/1**[3]

7 *1 1/4* **Funky Cold Medina** 2-9-0 0.............................. RobertHavlin 12 49
(Peter Chapple-Hyam) *led 4f: rdn and wknd over 1f out* **9/1**

644 **8** *nk* **Lady Marmelo (IRE)**[20] 4792 2-9-0 74.............................. SamHitchcott 4 48
(Mick Channon) *chsd ldrs: rdn over 2f out: wknd wl over 1f out* **9/1**

60 **9** *7* **Flywheel (IRE)**[23] 4701 2-9-0 0.............................. MartinDwyer 9 30
(Brian Meehan) *w ldr tl pushed along 1/2-way: wknd wl over 1f out* **25/1**

10 *1 1/4* **Pennyweight** 2-8-11 0.............................. AdamBeschizza(3) 5 26
(James Eustace) *dwlt: outpcd* **100/1**

11 *2 3/4* **Planchette** 2-8-7 0.............................. LewisWalsh(7) 7 19
(Jane Chapple-Hyam) *s.i.s: sn prom: pushed along over 4f out: rdn and wknd 2f out* **40/1**

1m 25.57s (-0.13) **Going Correction** -0.125s/f (Firm) **11** Ran SP% **119.0**
Speed ratings (Par 93): **95,94,91,86,85 80,79,78,70,69 66**
Tote Swingers 1&2 £1.90, 2&3 £30.40, 1&3 £7.90 CSF £19.65 TOTE £4.50: £1.90, £1.90, £2.50; EX 12.80.

Owner Godolphin **Bred** Gerry Flannery Developments **Trained** Newmarket, Suffolk

FOCUS
Stands' side track used with stalls on far side except 12f: centre. The first division of a fair juvenile fillies' maiden. They went an honest gallop on watered ground, officially Good to firm, but the winning time was nearly three seconds slower than standard. The form is rated to the mid point of the race averages.

NOTEBOOK
Desert Blossom(IRE) ◆ increased in value every time she went through a sales ring and was a 100,000gns purchase in April. She is a half-sister to several winners, including useful 5f/6f winner Taqseem and 7f/1m2f winner Aqraan, and her dam was a Group-placed 7f 2yo winner. She came through with a sustained challenge up the far rail from about 2f out and kept on nicely under jockey Mickael Barzalona, who has won with one in every three horses he has ridden for Mahmood Al Zarooni on this course this season. She looks a nice prospect at up to 1m. (op 7-2 tchd 10-3)
Valley Of Queens(IRE) came home strongly into second up the middle of the track. She is a half-sister to a French 1m2f winner out of a French extended 1m2f Group 3 winner. She produced respectable form after a nightmare passage in a decent 7f maiden here on debut this month and has stepped up on that display. She has a decent future at up to 1m2f. (op 15-2)
Rainbow Beauty ◆ ran on into a never-nearer fifth over this C&D on good to firm ground on debut this month and has progressed on that display. She looks capable of winning a similar contest. (tchd 11-2)
Dali's Lover(IRE) was returning from a seven-week break since her modest debut seventh over 6f on good to soft ground at Newbury the previous month. This was a better effort.

Raskova(USA) produced a fair third over 6f at Yarmouth on good ground on debut this month and may have regressed slightly on that display. (tchd 11-2)

5551 EBF PIPER-HEIDSIECK MAIDEN FILLIES' STKS (DIV II) 7f
1:50 (1:52) (Class 4) 2-Y-O **£4,528** (£1,347; £673; £336) **Stalls** High

Form RPR

1 **Music Chart (USA)** 2-9-0 0 MickaelBarzalona 8 80+
(Mahmood Al Zarooni) *s.i.s: sn pushed along and prom: rn green: rdn to ld wl ins fnl f: styd on* **8/1**

2333 2 ½ **Sorella Bella (IRE)**[8] 5274 2-9-0 72 SamHitchcott 6 79
(Mick Channon) *chsd ldr tl led 4f out: rdn over 1f out: hdd wl ins fnl f: styd on* **10/1**

0 3 5 **Kikonga**[20] 4818 2-9-0 0 KirstyMilczarek 11 66
(Luca Cumani) *chsd ldrs: ev ch over 2f out: sn rdn: no ex fnl f* **33/1**

2 4 ¾ **Flawless Beauty**[28] 4525 2-9-0 0 MichaelHills 2 64
(Hugo Palmer) *hld up: hdwy 1/2-way: rdn over 1f out: no ex fnl f* **11/4**[2]

5 1 **Qawaafy (USA)** 2-9-0 0 AndreaAtzeni 4 61
(Roger Varian) *prom: shkn up over 2f out: styd on same pce fr over 1f out* **5/1**[3]

6 nk **Divergence (IRE)** 2-9-0 0 HayleyTurner 10 61
(Michael Bell) *prom: rdn over 2f out: styd on same pce appr fnl f* **28/1**

7 2 ¼ **Azelle** 2-9-0 0 SeanLevey 5 55
(Richard Hannon) *hld up: rdn over 2f out: n.d* **25/1**

8 7 **Missed Call (IRE)** 2-9-0 0 IanMongan 1 37
(Sir Henry Cecil) *s.s: hld up: rdn 1/2-way: wknd over 2f out* **12/1**

0 9 8 **Golden Causeway**[22] 4739 2-9-0 0 WilliamCarson 12 29
(Charles Hills) *led 3f: sn pushed along: wknd 2f out: eased* **15/8**[1]

1m 25.91s (0.21) **Going Correction** -0.125s/f (Firm) **9** Ran SP% **116.2**
Speed ratings (Par 93): **93,92,86,85,84 84,81,73,64**
Tote Swingers 1&2 £11.10, 2&3 £48.10, 1&3 £32.90 CSF £82.26 TOTE £8.40: £2.80, £3.20, £12.70; EX 51.50.

Owner Godolphin **Bred** Bedford Bloodstock Llc **Trained** Newmarket, Suffolk

FOCUS

The second division of a fair juvenile fillies' maiden. They went an even pace and the winning time was slower than the first instalment of this maiden. The first piar were clear but the race is only rated to the bottom end of the race averages.

NOTEBOOK

Music Chart(USA) ◆ was a $230,000 yearling purchase and is the second foal out of Conchita, who is a half-sister to Fillies' Mile winner White Moonstone. She started slowly on this debut and raced green but came through to win readily enough. She is entered in a valuable sales contest over an extended 6f at Doncaster in September and that looks a viable target. She looks a nice 7f/1m prospect for the future in any case. (op 6-1 tchd 11-2)

Sorella Bella(IRE) was easily the most experienced contender beforehand and brought a BHA rating of 73 into this contest. She ran well here under conditions which suit.

Kikonga stepped up on her debut effort over this C&D this month but looks a future middle-distance handicapper.

Flawless Beauty ran well on debut over 7f on firm ground at Ascot the previous month but looks to have regressed slightly on that display on this occasion. (op 3-1 tchd 5-2)

Qawaafy(USA), out of Oaks winner Eswarah, holds an entry in the Fillies' Mile here in September but will need to step up significantly on the bare form of this debut display to continue to entertain such lofty aspirations. (op 11-2 tchd 13-2)

Divergence(IRE) was a 120,000GBP purchase as a yearling but looks a handicap prospect over further for the future. (op 25-1)

Golden Causeway simply failed to find the form of her very encouraging Goodwood debut this month and there must have been something amiss with her. She was later found to be in season. Official explanation: trainer's representative could offer no explanation for the poor performance shown (op 9-4 tchd 5-2)

5552 HEMIHELP NURSERY 1m
2:20 (2:20) (Class 4) (0-80,79) 2-Y-O **£3,881** (£1,155; £577; £288) **Stalls** High

Form RPR

21 1 **Law Enforcement (IRE)**[22] 4724 2-9-6 78 SeanLevey 1 88
(Richard Hannon) *chsd ldrs: rdn to ld over 1f out: edgd lft ins fnl f: r.o* **9/4**[2]

4061 2 1 **Quintilian (IRE)**[11] 5155 2-9-6 78 6ex MickaelBarzalona 3 86
(Mahmood Al Zarooni) *dwlt: hld up: swtchd rt over 2f out: hdwy over 1f out: rdn to chse wnr ins fnl f: r.o* **9/2**[3]

651 3 1 ¼ **Linguine (FR)**[24] 4677 2-9-4 76 WilliamCarson 4 81
(Charles Hills) *led: rdn and hdd over 1f out: styd on same pce ins fnl f* **10/1**

6641 4 6 **Aussie Reigns (IRE)**[21] 4763 2-9-2 74 JimCrowley 5 65
(William Knight) *prom: rdn over 2f out: wknd over 1f out* **6/1**

411 5 3 ¼ **Hunting Rights (USA)**[8] 5254 2-9-7 79 6ex FrannyNorton 6 63
(Mark Johnston) *chsd ldr: pushed along over 2f out: wknd over 1f out* **13/8**[1]

1m 39.14s (-0.86) **Going Correction** -0.125s/f (Firm) **5** Ran SP% **110.4**
Speed ratings (Par 96): **99,98,96,90,87**
CSF £12.41 TOTE £3.40: £2.00, £2.50; EX 16.40.

Owner M S Al Shahi **Bred** Mrs E J O'Grady **Trained** East Everleigh, Wilts

FOCUS

A fair nursery handicap. They went an honest gallop despite the small field. Sound form, with improved efforts from the first two.

NOTEBOOK

Law Enforcement(IRE) progressed slightly on his fair 7f soft-ground Sandown debut the previous month when landing his maiden over 7f at Epsom on good ground this month. He appeared to take a more significant step forward here, in winning this nursery handicap off a BHA rating of 78, stepping up to 1m. He looks progressive in this sort of company under these conditions. (op 7-2)

Quintilian(IRE) was carrying a 6lb penalty for winning a similar 1m contest at Kempton off a mark of 72 this month and gives this form real substance in second. He appears equally happy on a decent turf surface and is bred to get further than 1m. (op 5-1)

Linguine(FR) attempted to make all on this handicap debut, fresh from winning his maiden at the third time of asking over an extended 7f at Beverley on firm ground the previous month, and held every chance if good enough. (op 15-2)

Aussie Reigns(IRE) did not appear to get home on this stiffer track over a longer trip. (op 9-2)

Hunting Rights(USA), carrying a penalty for his beverley success, dropped away up the hill. (op 6-4 tchd 7-4)

5553 EBF PIPER-HEIDSIECK MAIDEN STKS (C&G) 7f
2:55 (2:55) (Class 4) 2-Y-O **£4,528** (£1,347; £673; £336) **Stalls** High

Form RPR

3 1 **Lazarus Bell**[19] 4846 2-9-0 0 MartinDwyer 3 86+
(Brian Meehan) *chsd ldr tl led over 2f out: shkn up ins fnl f: r.o wl* **1/1**[1]

44 2 2 ¾ **Exotic Guest**[15] 5016 2-9-0 0 IanMongan 2 78
(George Margarson) *trckd ldrs: plld hrd: shkn up over 2f out: rdn to chse wnr fnl f: no imp* **7/2**[3]

3 1 **Sicur** 2-9-0 0 J-PGuillambert 4 76
(Luca Cumani) *in tch but rn green: shkn up over 2f out: rdn over 1f out: styd on same pce ins fnl f* **3/1**[2]

05 4 1 **Shiatsu**[13] 5098 2-9-0 0 SeanLevey 1 73
(Richard Hannon) *wnt rt s: plld hrd and sn led: hdd over 2f out: rdn over 1f out: no ex ins fnl f* **15/2**

1m 28.95s (3.25) **Going Correction** -0.125s/f (Firm) **4** Ran SP% **109.0**
Speed ratings (Par 96): **76,72,71,70**
CSF £4.80 TOTE £2.00; EX 3.30.

Owner Lanesborough **Bred** Blackman, Bladon & Phillips **Trained** Manton, Wilts

FOCUS

A fair small-field juvenile maiden for colts and geldings. They went a steady gallop and the winning time was over six seconds slower than standard. The winner did it wel but it will take time to gauge the true merit of this.

NOTEBOOK

Lazarus Bell finished a fair third over 6f at Newbury on good to firm ground on his debut this month. He showed his potential here, in quickening up off an admittedly modest pace, and stretching clear of his field over this extra furlong. He looks a decent prospect at up to 1m but will have to prove it off a stronger tempo in the future. (op 5-6)

Exotic Guest pulled hard in behind the modest gallop and failed to make any impression on the winner from the furlong marker. A drop back to 6f in nursery handicaps may suit. (op 3-1 tchd 11-4)

Sicur attracted late market support on this debut but ran green and will know more next time. (op 13-2)

Shiatsu failed to build on a fair Lingfield debut on Polytrack this month, after pulling hard and being sent to the front early in the race. (op 11-2)

5554 GRANTS WHISKY H'CAP 1m 4f
3:30 (3:32) (Class 4) (0-85,85) 3-Y-O+ **£4,528** (£1,347; £673; £336) **Stalls** Centre

Form RPR

542 1 **Fleeting Image**[15] 4983 3-8-3 77 (p) NatashaEaton(7) 7 86
(Alan Bailey) *mde virtually all: clr 9f out tl rdn over 1f out: edgd lft and rt ins fnl f: styd on* **22/1**

016 2 1 **Maria's Choice (IRE)**[22] 4741 3-9-1 **82** JimCrowley 1 89
(Sir Michael Stoute) *hld up: hdwy over 2f out: sn rdn: styd on to go 2nd post: nt rch wnr* **8/1**[2]

5361 3 nk **Maastricht (IRE)**[6] 5344 3-9-2 **83** 6ex FrannyNorton 8 90
(Mark Johnston) *chsd ldrs: rdn to go 2nd over 2f out: styd on u.p: lost 2nd post* **4/1**[1]

06-2 4 ½ **Huff And Puff**[44] 3962 5-9-8 **79** AdamKirby 9 85
(Amanda Perrett) *hld up: pushed along over 7f out: hdwy u.p over 2f out: styd on* **14/1**

3333 5 7 **Knightly Escapade**[20] 4823 4-9-8 **79** IanMongan 6 74
(John Dunlop) *s.s: hld up: hdwy over 2f out: rdn over 1f out: wknd ins fnl f* **10/1**[3]

0050 6 19 **Classic Punch (IRE)**[13] 5101 9-9-7 **85** WilliamTwiston-Davies(7) 4 50
(David Elsworth) *chsd ldr tl rdn over 2f out: wknd over 1f out* **14/1**

611 7 17 **The High Man**[29] 4499 4-9-13 **84** HayleyTurner 3 21
(Ed Walker) *prom: racd keenly: rdn over 3f out: wknd over 2f out: eased: t.o* **4/1**[1]

2m 29.62s (-3.28) **Going Correction** -0.125s/f (Firm)
WFA 3 from 4yo+ 10lb **7** Ran SP% **77.9**
Speed ratings (Par 105): **105,104,104,103,99 86,75**
Tote Swingers 1&2 £7.40, 2&3 £3.30, 1&3 £1.10 CSF £80.97 CT £251.44 TOTE £16.30: £4.20, £2.60; EX 83.90.

Owner P T Tellwright **Bred** P T Tellwright **Trained** Newmarket, Suffolk

■ Gassin Golf was withdrawn (13/8F, spread a placte). Deduct 35p in the £ under R4.

FOCUS

A decent middle-distance handicap for 3-y-os and up. The gallop was a searching one and produced the best comparative winning time on the card. A 5lb personal best from the winner.

The High Man Official explanation: jockey said that the gelding stopped quickly

5555 TULLAMORE DEW IRISH WHISKEY MAIDEN STKS 1m
4:05 (4:07) (Class 5) 3-Y-O+ **£3,234** (£962; £481; £240) **Stalls** High

Form RPR

0 1 **Mawhub**[127] 1467 3-9-3 0 TedDurcan 2 79+
(Saeed Bin Suroor) *mid-div: hdwy 1/2-way: led 2f out: rdn edgd lft and hdd ins fnl f: rallied to ld post* **6/4**[1]

5 2 nse **A'Juba**[16] 4948 3-9-3 0 RobertHavlin 5 79+
(Saeed Bin Suroor) *a.p: led over 3f out: rdn and hdd 2f out: rallied to ld ins fnl f: hung rt towards fin: hdd post* **8/1**

3 3 ¼ **Qanan** 3-9-0 0 PatrickHills(3) 1 71+
(Luca Cumani) *s.i.s: hld up: hdwy over 2f out: styd on: nt trble ldrs* **20/1**

4 4 1 ¾ **Spring Tonic**[35] 4301 3-9-3 0 J-PGuillambert 11 67+
(Luca Cumani) *hld up in tch: nt clr run and lost pl 3f out: r.o fnl f* **14/1**

43-0 5 ½ **Rawaafed (IRE)**[99] 2196 3-9-3 84 MartinDwyer 6 66
(Brian Meehan) *chsd ldrs: rdn over 2f out: no ex fnl f* **3/1**[2]

6 6 1 ½ **Boonga Roogeta**[17] 4931 3-8-7 0 RosieJessop(5) 3 57
(Peter Charalambous) *prom: racd keenly: rdn over 1f out: wknd fnl f* **25/1**

7 hd **All On Black** 3-9-3 0 LukeMorris 12 62+
(James Eustace) *s.i.s: hld up: sme hdwy over 1f out: n.d* **50/1**

0 8 ½ **Capacious**[22] 4746 3-8-12 0 HayleyTurner 10 55
(James Fanshawe) *chsd ldrs tl rdn and wknd over 1f out* **12/1**

5 9 10 **Audeamus (IRE)**[9] 5244 3-8-12 0 StevieDonohoe 4 31
(Tobias B P Coles) *bhd and rdn 1/2-way: nvr on terms* **80/1**

00 10 9 **Garrisson (IRE)**[8] 5276 3-9-3 0 WilliamCarson 7 15
(Charles Hills) *prom: plld hrd: rdn and wknd over 2f out* **28/1**

3-4 11 1 ¾ **Caitlin**[119] 1649 3-8-12 0 DavidProbert 8
(Andrew Balding) *led over 5f: rdn and wknd over 2f out* **11/2**[3]

6 12 18 **Scary Canary**[13] 5096 4-9-9 0 IanMongan 9
(George Margarson) *plld hrd: trckd ldrs: rdn and wknd over 2f out: t.o* **100/1**

1m 39.75s (-0.25) **Going Correction** -0.125s/f (Firm)
WFA 3 from 4yo 6lb **12** Ran SP% **122.1**
Speed ratings (Par 103): **96,95,92,90,90 88,88,88,78,69 67,49**
Tote Swingers 1&2 £3.20, 2&3 £5.30, 1&3 £3.40 CSF £14.27 TOTE £2.30: £1.10, £2.10, £5.60; EX 16.00.

Owner Godolphin **Bred** Darley **Trained** Newmarket, Suffolk

■ Stewards' Enquiry : Robert Havlin two-day ban: use of whip (7 and 9 Sep)

FOCUS
A fair maiden for 3-y-os and up. They went an honest gallop and the winning time was over 3 secs slower than standard. The Bin Suroor first pair were both up a stone+ on their debuts.

5556 GLENFIDDICH H'CAP 7f
4:40 (4:40) (Class 3) (0-90,89) 3-Y-O £7,115 (£2,117; £1,058; £529) Stalls High

Form RPR
4-56 **1** **Otto The Great**[20] 4819 3-9-1 **83**.. ShaneKelly 9 93
(Peter Chapple-Hyam) *mde all: rdn over 1f out: styd on u.p* **9/2**[3]
6010 **2** 1 ¾ **Campanology**[22] 4740 3-9-0 **89**.................... WilliamTwiston-Davies(7) 1 94
(Richard Hannon) *chsd wnr: rdn: hung lft and ev ch over 1f out: styd on same pce ins fnl f* **4/1**[2]
2102 **3** 2 ¾ **Al Wajba (USA)**[23] 4713 3-8-12 **83**......................(b[1]) AdamBeschizza(3) 3 81
(William Haggas) *hld up: hdwy over 1f out: sn rdn: no ex ins fnl f* **8/1**
02 **4** 1 ½ **Swing Alone (IRE)**[35] 4298 3-9-6 **88**.............................. DavidProbert 7 82
(Gay Kelleway) *chsd ldrs: rdn over 2f out: sn outpcd: styd on ins fnl f* **4/1**[2]
1000 **5** ½ **Mississippi**[13] 5102 3-9-4 **86**..(b[1]) HayleyTurner 4 78
(Brian Meehan) *hld up: hdwy over 1f out: wknd ins fnl f* **11/4**[1]
003 **6** 1 ¼ **Trulee Scrumptious**[7] 5324 3-7-11 **70** oh25............(b) RosieJessop(5) 2 59
(Peter Charalambous) *chsd ldrs: rdn over 2f out: wknd over 1f out* **28/1**
6002 **7** 5 **Sardanapalus**[11] 5170 3-8-2 **70**...(b) LukeMorris 8 46
(Kevin Ryan) *chsd ldrs: rdn over 2f out: sn wknd* **6/1**

1m 25.9s (0.20) **Going Correction** -0.125s/f (Firm) **7 Ran SP% 113.7**
Speed ratings (Par 104): **93,91,87,86,85 84,78**
Tote Swingers 1&2 £5.20, 2&3 £5.70, 1&3 £6.00 CSF £22.45 TOTE £4.70: £3.10, £2.80; EX 22.70.
Owner Mrs Doreen M Swinburn **Bred** Genesis Green Stud **Trained** Newmarket, Suffolk

FOCUS
A decent 3-y-o handicap. They went a modest gallop and the winning time was over 3secs slower than standard. There's a chance this form is worth more.

NOTEBOOK
Otto The Great was drawn next to the far-side rail and duly kept things simple by making all the running. He ran respectably over this C&D on good ground off 2lb higher this month and he looks a typical 7f specialist, who can be placed to advantage over this distance going forward. (op 4-1 tchd 7-2)
Campanology bounced back from a disappointing Goodwood display this month and he looks capable of further success over this 7f trip off marks in the mid-to-high 80s. (op 7-2)
Al Wajba(USA) sported first-time blinkers here but she was unable to pick up inside the final furlong. (op 5-1)
Swing Alone(IRE) needs a stronger gallop over this trip or a return to 1m on this evidence. (op 11-2)
Mississippi was tried in first-time blinkers, after losing his form on turf since a 1m Kempton success in April. He weakened again inside the final furlong. (op 4-1)

5557 PIPER-HEIDSIECK H'CAP (BETFAIR SPRINT FLAT SERIES QUALIFIER) 6f
5:15 (5:15) (Class 4) (0-85,85) 3-Y-O+ £5,175 (£1,540; £769; £384) Stalls High

Form RPR
0004 **1** **Piscean (USA)**[7] 5320 7-9-3 **81**......................................(b) RyanClark(3) 1 93
(Tom Keddy) *hld up: nt clr run over 2f out: swtchd rt over 1f out: str run to ld wl ins fnl f: sn clr* **16/1**
2635 **2** 2 ½ **Showboating (IRE)**[20] 4824 4-9-4 **79**............................(tp) SeanLevey 10 83+
(Alan McCabe) *hld up: nt clr run over 1f out: r.o ins fnl f: wnt 2nd post* **13/2**
1600 **3** hd **Escape To Glory (USA)**[23] 4703 4-9-10 **85**...................... IanMongan 5 88
(Mikael Magnusson) *chsd ldrs: rdn over 2f out: led over 1f out: hdd wl ins fnl f: lost 2nd post* **14/1**
4063 **4** ½ **Lujeanie**[7] 5320 6-9-3 **78**..(p) TedDurcan 11 80
(Dean Ivory) *chsd ldrs: rdn over 1f out: ev ch ins fnl f: styd on same pce* **8/1**
4301 **5** nse **Orbit The Moon (IRE)**[26] 4629 4-9-2 **80**.....................(tp) LeeTopliss(3) 8 82
(Michael Dods) *led 5f out: rdn and hdd over 1f out: styd on same pce ins fnl f* **11/2**[3]
1414 **6** 1 **Julius Geezer (IRE)**[15] 4999 4-9-9 **84**............... RichardKingscote 6 82
(Tom Dascombe) *led 1f: chsd ldrs: rdn over 1f out: styd on same pce ins fnl f* **5/1**[2]
0200 **7** shd **Oneladyowner**[20] 4799 4-9-10 **85**...................................... HayleyTurner 4 83
(David Brown) *hld up: hdwy u.p over 1f out: nt rch ldrs* **10/1**
560 **8** nk **Caldercruix (USA)**[35] 4286 5-9-5 **80**...(v) LukeMorris 7 77
(James Evans) *prom: rdn over 2f out: no ex ins fnl f* **16/1**
063 **9** nse **Rocket Rob (IRE)**[13] 5097 6-8-11 **72**..............................(b) JamieMackay 9 71+
(Willie Musson) *hld up: hdwy over 1f out: nt clr run thrght fnl f: nvr able to chal* **8/1**
-050 **10** 1 ¾ **Bonnie Charlie**[17] 4924 6-9-3 **78**...................................(t) AdrianNicholls 3 69
(David Nicholls) *s.i.s: hld up: hdwy u.p over 1f out: wknd ins fnl f* **4/1**[1]
2036 **11** 1 ¼ **Danzoe (IRE)**[16] 4969 5-8-5 **66** oh5.. KierenFox 2 53
(Christine Dunnett) *chsd ldrs: rdn over 1f out: wknd ins fnl f* **33/1**
2000 **12** 2 ¾ **Fred Willetts (IRE)**[13] 5110 4-9-7 **82**.............................. DavidProbert 12 61
(David C Griffiths) *chsd ldrs: rdn over 2f out: wknd fnl f* **16/1**
641 **13** 3 ¼ **Gap Princess (IRE)**[17] 4909 8-8-11 **72**............................(p) RobertHavlin 13 40
(Geoffrey Harker) *s.i.s: hdwy 4f out: wknd over 1f out: eased* **16/1**

1m 12.35s (-0.15) **Going Correction** -0.125s/f (Firm) **13 Ran SP% 129.8**
Speed ratings (Par 105): **96,92,92,91,91 90,90,89,89,87 85,82,77**
Tote Swingers 1&2 £25.60, 2&3 £19.40, 1&3 £61.30 CSF £126.60 CT £1592.17 TOTE £15.00: £3.80, £2.10, £6.80; EX 153.60.
Owner Andrew Duffield **Bred** Connie And John Iacuone **Trained** Newmarket, Suffolk

FOCUS
A decent sprint handicap. They went a sound pace. The winner was back towards his old turf best.
T/Plt: £1,844.80 to a £1 stake. Pool: £38,513.48 - 15.24 winning tickets T/Qpdt: £166.40 to a £1 stake. Pool: £3,005.92 - 13.36 winning tickets CR

5515 YORK (L-H)
Friday, August 24

OFFICIAL GOING: Good (7.4)
Wind: Light, across Weather: Cloudy with sunny periods

5558 SKY BET MOBILE STKS (H'CAP) 1m 4f
2:00 (2:00) (Class 2) (0-100,98) 3-Y-O+ £19,407 (£5,775; £2,886; £1,443) Stalls Centre

Form RPR
-060 **1** **Kirthill (IRE)**[24] 4684 4-10-0 **98**.. KierenFallon 17 109
(Luca Cumani) *hld up in rr: gd hdwy 3f out: rdn to chal and edgd rt over 1f out: led ent fnl f: sn rdn and hung lft: styd on* **11/1**
5-63 **2** ½ **Martin Chuzzlewit (IRE)**[107] 1978 3-8-8 **88**..................(v[1]) NeilCallan 14 98
(Sir Michael Stoute) *chsd ldrs: hdwy 4f out: cl up 3f out: rdn to ld 2f out: drvn: edgd lft and hdd ent fnl f: kpt on wl* **10/1**[3]
0136 **3** hd **Tropical Beat**[33] 4363 4-9-8 **92**....................................... WilliamBuick 3 102
(John Gosden) *hld up towards rr: hdwy on wd outside over 2f out: rdn wl over 1f out: styd on strly fnl f* **14/1**
210 **4** ¾ **Willie Wag Tail (USA)**[23] 4700 3-8-8 **88**...................... JamieSpencer 4 99+
(Ed Walker) *hld up towards rr: hdwy over 3f out: swtchd lft and str run over 2f out: rdn to chse ldng pair and ev ch whn n.m.r and hmpd jst over 1f out: swtchd lft and styng on whn n.m.r towards fin* **9/2**[1]
0006 **5** ¾ **Nanton (USA)**[13] 5079 10-9-3 **87**....................................... GrahamLee 13 94
(Jim Goldie) *hld up in rr: hdwy over 3f out: swtchd lft and rdn over 2f out: styng on strly whn n.m.r and swtchd rt ins fnl f: nrst fin* **25/1**
6205 **6** 2 ¼ **Bridle Belle**[27] 4608 4-9-0 **84**.. PaulHanagan 15 88
(Richard Fahey) *in tch: trckd ldrs 1/2-way: effrt to chse ldrs 3f out: sn rdn: drvn and one pce fr over 1f out* **16/1**
4123 **7** 2 ¾ **Rio's Rosanna (IRE)**[42] 4072 5-9-6 **90**.............................. AmyRyan 9 89
(Richard Whitaker) *chsd ldrs: lost pl and towards rr 1/2-way: hdwy wl over 2f out: sn swtchd lft and rdn: kpt on: nt rch ldrs* **10/1**[3]
0020 **8** ½ **Late Telegraph (IRE)**[20] 4800 4-9-4 **88**.......................... EddieAhern 20 87
(Sir Henry Cecil) *in tch: hdwy on outer to chse ldrs over 4f out: rdn along 3f out and no imp* **40/1**
1-21 **9** ½ **Silver Lime (USA)**[22] 4741 3-8-11 **91**.......................... JamesDoyle 16 89
(Roger Charlton) *midfield: pushed along outer 1/2-way: sme hdwy 3f out: rdn along over 2f out and no imp* **11/2**[2]
2404 **10** 3 **Stand To Reason (IRE)**[41] 4112 4-9-11 **95**..............(p) RichardHughes 2 88
(Mikael Magnusson) *midfield: sme hdwy over 3f out: sn rdn and n.d* **14/1**
2123 **11** nk **John Biscuit (IRE)**[13] 5079 4-9-3 **87**.............................. JimmyFortune 6 80
(Andrew Balding) *t.k.h: chsd ldrs: rdn along over 3f out: wkng whn n.m.r wl over 1f out* **14/1**
3131 **12** 1 **Silvery Moon (IRE)**[20] 4795 5-9-7 **91**............................... DavidAllan 12 82
(Tim Easterby) *cl up: disp ld 4f out: sn rdn along and wknd wl over 2f out* **20/1**
-021 **13** 2 ¼ **Expert Fighter (USA)**[28] 4543 3-8-12 **92**...................... FrankieDettori 18 79
(Saeed Bin Suroor) *trckd ldrs: hdwy over 3f out: led wl over 2f out: sn rdn and hdd 2f out: sn drvn and grad wknd* **16/1**
0-06 **14** 7 **Samsons Son**[63] 3341 8-9-1 **85**... RobertWinston 8 61
(Terry Clement) *midfield: hdwy over 3f out: sn rdn and wknd over 2f out* **66/1**
1005 **15** 3 **War Poet**[48] 3857 5-9-8 **92**.. DanielTudhope 11 63
(David O'Meara) *hld up towards rr: sme hdwy towards inner over 3f out: sn rdn and wknd* **12/1**
-063 **16** 4 **Warlu Way**[27] 4575 5-9-6 **90**.. PhillipMakin 1 55
(John Dunlop) *in tch on inner: rdn along 4f out: sn wknd* **25/1**
0030 **17** 1 ¾ **Tepmokea (IRE)**[41] 4111 6-9-3 **90**.......................... MichaelMetcalfe(3) 7 52
(Mrs K Burke) *led: rdn along over 3f out: drvn and hdd wl over 2f out: sn wknd* **20/1**
0600 **18** shd **Right Step**[24] 4684 5-9-0 **91**..........................(v[1]) MichaelJMMurphy(7) 19 53
(Alan Jarvis) *trckd ldrs: effrt over 3f out: sn rdn along and wknd* **25/1**
0540 **19** 7 **Fennell Bay (IRE)**[13] 5078 3-8-13 **93**........................ SilvestreDeSousa 10 44
(Mark Johnston) *dwlt: a bhd* **16/1**

2m 29.18s (-4.02) **Going Correction** -0.10s/f (Good)
WFA 3 from 4yo+ 10lb **19 Ran SP% 130.4**
Speed ratings (Par 109): **109,108,108,108,107 106,104,103,103,101 101,100,99,94,92 89,88,88,83**
Tote Swingers 1&2 £28.50, 2&3 £73.20, 1&3 £54.00 CSF £112.70 CT £1592.25 TOTE £13.30: £3.60, £3.60, £3.90, £1.80; EX 145.10 Trifecta £1974.80 Part won. Pool £2,668.69 - 0.20 winning units..
Owner Leonidas Marinopoulos **Bred** Giacinto Guglielmi **Trained** Newmarket, Suffolk
■ Stewards' Enquiry : Neil Callan three-day ban: careless riding (7, 9, 10 Sep)

FOCUS
There was 5.8mm of rain the previous day but it was dry overnight and the ground was good (GoingStick 7.4; Home straight: stands' side 7.1, centre 7.3; far side 7.2). After riding in the first Frankie Dettori said: "It is good ground" but Robert Winston said: "It is on the easy side of good," David Allan said: "It is good to soft," Eddie Ahern said: "It is loose" and Silvestre de Sousa said: "There is a lot of give, it's a bit sticky and dead." The rail had been moved in 10m from the 1m1f point to the entrance to the home straight, reducing distances by 27yds in races of 1m plus. This is a race in which 3yos are often favoured in the betting, but only two of the previous nine winners represented the Classic generation, and once again the market leaders were eclipsed by an older horse. Sectional times suggest they went progressively slower through the first five furlongs, but then the pace picked up gradually and the quickest three furlongs (all sub 12sec) were between the half mile point and the furlong pole. Most of those who contested the finish had been ridden with patience. Solid handicap form.

NOTEBOOK
Kirthill(IRE) didn't run well at Goodwood last time but his previous effort at Ascot gave him every chance off a mark of 98, with the prospect of improvement for this longer trip and with his stable in such cracking form. Given the way the race unfolded being held up way off the pace proved an advantage, and he came through strongly in the straight. He's unexposed over this trip and probably has more to offer. (tchd 12-1 in a place)
Martin Chuzzlewit(IRE) ◆ was wearing a visor for the first time, but the stats suggest that's not a negative with horses from his stable. Having his first run since May, he deserves plenty of credit for doing by far the best of those that raced close to the front, and he's fully capable of winning something similar even after a rise in the weights. He did hang left under pressure, but that was surely just as a result of tiredness. (tchd 11-1)
Tropical Beat had the race run to suit, but he's not straightforward and, although he flew down the outside in the closing stages having been held up in last for much of the race, he was all the time hanging left and had his head in the air. (op 20-1)
Willie Wag Tail(USA), who got no luck in running at Goodwood last time, again didn't have everything go his way, as he was coming through to have his chance when hampered by the winner. However, he was the one to blame, in hanging left at the time, and so while he was keeping on again at the finish, he was to a large degree responsible for his own downfall. (tchd 5-1 in places)
Nanton(USA) keeps coming back for more, and again ran a smashing race. This wouldn't normally be his sort of track, but the way the race was run did set up things for the closers, and he showed he's a long way from being a back number. (tchd 33-1 in places)
Bridle Belle, back on her last winning mark, didn't run badly considering she raced a lot closer to the pace than most that finished in front of her. She should remain competitive off this sort of rating. (op 14-1)
Rio's Rosanna(IRE) was keeping on for pressure when she got badly squeezed up between horses inside the final 2f. She deserves rating as having finished closer than the official margin would suggest. (op 14-1)
Late Telegraph(IRE) was caught wider than ideal from his outside draw and also raced closer to the pace than was optimal.
Silver Lime(USA), whose sire's stock tend to need time between their races, was returning to the track just 22 days after winning at Goodwood. He travelled well enough through the race, and made a forward move which looked dangerous, but didn't see his race out, and perhaps he found this trip stretching him a touch (it was a steadily run race he won over 1m3f last time). (op 13-2)

Stand To Reason(IRE) could have probably done with softer ground, but he appeared to fail the stamina test over this longer trip.
John Biscuit(IRE), despite the decent gallop, was keen early, and he raced closer to the leaders than was good for him. (op 11-1)
Silvery Moon(IRE) paid for having too much use made of him.
Expert Fighter(USA), who also raced prominently early, travelled well into the lead but soon hit the wall with over 2f to run. He might need faster ground.

5559 IRISH THOROUGHBRED MARKETING GIMCRACK STKS (GROUP 2) (C&G) 6f

2:30 (2:32) (Class 1) 2-Y-O **£95,741** (£36,210; £18,097; £9,040) **Stalls** Centre

Form				RPR
1	**1**		**Blaine**[41] 4114 2-8-12 0 PhillipMakin 6 (Kevin Ryan) *cl up: led 2f out: rdn and hdd ins fnl f: drvn and rallied to ld again towards fin* **6/1**	108+
2001	**2**	*hd*	**Heavy Metal**[22] 4736 2-9-1 108 JoeFanning 7 (Mark Johnston) *cl up: chal 2f out: rdn and slt ld ins fnl f: sn drvn: hdd and no ex towards fin* **8/1**	110
1163	**3**	*1*	**Cay Verde**[22] 4736 2-8-12 102 WilliamBuick 3 (Mick Channon) *hld up: hdwy 2f out: sn rdn: styd on wl fnl f* **9/1**	104
12	**4**	*nk*	**Odooj (IRE)**[10] 5201 2-8-12 0 PaulHanagan 4 (William Haggas) *chsd ldrs: hdwy 2f out: sn rdn and kpt on u.p fnl f* **11/1**	103
211	**5**	*nse*	**Pearl Acclaim (IRE)**[6] 5371 2-8-12 0 RichardHughes 8 (Richard Hannon) *chsd ldrs: hdwy 2f out: rdn ent fnl f: sn one pce* **9/2**[2]	103
4145	**6**	*1*	**Euxton Hall (IRE)**[22] 4736 2-8-12 98 TonyHamilton 5 (Richard Fahey) *led: rdn along and hdd 2f out: drvn ent fnl f and kpt on same pce* **25/1**	99
232	**7**	*1 1/2*	**Lewisham**[43] 4008 2-8-12 107 JamesDoyle 1 (Noel Quinlan) *dwlt: a in rr* **5/1**[3]	95
1412	**8**	*nk*	**Morawij**[24] 4687 2-8-12 106 NeilCallan 2 (Roger Varian) *t.k.h: chsd ldrs: effrt and hdwy 2f out: sn rdn and wknd appr fnl f* **9/4**[1]	94

1m 11.53s (-0.37) **Going Correction** -0.175s/f (Firm) **8** Ran SP% **113.2**
Speed ratings (Par 106): **95,94,93,93,92 91,89,89**
Tote Swingers 1&2 £4.50, 2&3 £8.40, 1&3 £9.80 CSF £51.41 TOTE £9.00: £3.10, £2.30, £2.70; EX 59.40 Trifecta £301.60 Pool £8,222.74 - 20.17 winning units..
Owner Matt & Lauren Morgan **Bred** Toby Barker **Trained** Hambleton, N Yorks
■ Stewards' Enquiry : Joe Fanning two-day ban: use of whip (7, 9 Sep)

FOCUS
Not a strong edition of this famous juvenile event, and it has been rated at the lower end of the race averages. The race has been rated around the Richmond Stakes form. Recent Gimcrack winners have tended to make sprinters and a number have failed to progress to better things, but last year's scorer Caspar Netscher has gone some way towards bucking those trends. It proved difficult to make ground from off the pace and the first two were always prominent.

NOTEBOOK
Blaine prevailed, sticking his neck out willingly to hold off a much more experienced opponent. Kept for this after winning a maiden over C&D on his debut last month - three former Gimcrack winners also won that event - he travelled nicely and did not hang as he had first time. The Kevin Ryan operation won the Gimcrack with Amadeus Wolf in 2005 and that colt went on to take the Group 1 Middle Park next time. Blaine figures among the entries for the Newmarket race but, while he is a smart colt with further improvement in him, he will have to step up on this bare form. His trainer thinks he'll be more the finished article next year, when sprinting is likely to be his game. (op 8-1)
Heavy Metal is a doughty performer and he ran a fine race under the 3lb penalty for his win in this grade in the Richmond Stakes at Goodwood. He had every chance and is clearly thriving now. He holds Group 1 entries in the Middle Park and the Vincent O'Brien (National) Stakes, the latter over 7f. (tchd 9-1 and 10-1 in places)
Cay Verde again finished behind Heavy Metal, with whom he was 3lb better off after finishing third to him in the Richmond. The colt kept straight this time and, after being briefly held up in his run, was staying on nicely at the end. On this evidence he will stay 7f. (op 10-1)
Odooj(IRE), whose trainer had won two of the last six Gimcracks, ran on from towards the rear. This was the easiest ground he had raced on and judging by his action he will be happiest back on a sound surface. (op 17-2)
Pearl Acclaim(IRE) ran with credit six days after landing a decent conditions race at Ripon, but the rise in grade on this quick reappearance found him out. The Mill Reef Stakes remains a viable target. (op 4-1)
Euxton Hall(IRE)'s limitations have been exposed in stakes races and he could not hold off the challengers after showing bright pace. He's been beaten by Heavy Metal in each of their three meetings now. (tchd 28-1)
Lewisham, supplemented for £13,000, was very slowly away and could never get into the race. Still a maiden, but an arguably unlucky second to Alhebayeb in the July Stakes last time when some way in front of Heavy Metal, he is capable of picking up a decent prize but will need to break better. Official explanation: jockey said that the colt was slow away (tchd 11-2 and 6-1 in a place)
Morawij raced keenly early on and failed to pick up when asked. He had been kept to 5f since making a winning debut over this trip, finishing in the frame in the Norfolk and the Molecomb, and did not appear to get home on this rain-eased ground. (op 5-2)

5560 SKY BET STRENSALL STKS (GROUP 3) 1m 208y

3:05 (3:06) (Class 1) 3-Y-O+ **£42,532** (£16,125; £8,070; £4,020; £2,017; £1,012) **Stalls** Low

Form				RPR
0016	**1**		**Dubai Prince (IRE)**[21] 4759 4-9-5 116 FrankieDettori 2 (Mahmood Al Zarooni) *hld up in rr: smooth hdwy on outer 3f out: led 2f out: sn rdn and edgd lft: styd on wl fnl f* **4/1**[2]	115+
3133	**2**	*1 1/4*	**Side Glance**[27] 4610 5-9-9 114 JimmyFortune 8 (Andrew Balding) *hld up in tch: hdwy 3f out: effrt and n.m.r wl over 1f out: sn swtchd rt and rdn: styd on u.p fnl f: tk 2nd nr line* **5/1**[3]	116
-651	**3**	*nk*	**Tazahum (USA)**[20] 4822 4-9-5 109 PaulHanagan 4 (Sir Michael Stoute) *hld up in rr: hdwy 3f out: rdn to chal 2f out and ev ch tl drvn and one pce fnl f: lost 2nd nr line* **7/1**	111
3461	**4**	*1/2*	**Barefoot Lady (IRE)**[28] 4556 4-9-2 110 TonyHamilton 3 (Richard Fahey) *chsd clr ldr: tk clsr order 3f out: effrt 2f out and ev ch tl rdn and one pce ent fnl f* **7/1**	107
1240	**5**	*2*	**Questioning (IRE)**[34] 4320 4-9-9 114 (p) WilliamBuick 5 (John Gosden) *trckd ldng pair: effrt 3f out: rdn over 2f out: sn one pce* **9/1**	110
4224	**6**	*1/2*	**Stipulate**[21] 4760 3-8-12 108 TomQueally 1 (Sir Henry Cecil) *trckd ldrs: hdwy 3f out: rdn along whn bmpd 2f out: sn drvn and btn* **2/1**[1]	105
3152	**7**	*1 1/2*	**Fury**[42] 4074 4-9-5 107 (p) RichardHughes 7 (William Haggas) *led and sn clr: rdn along 3f out: hdd 2f out and sn wknd* **8/1**	101

1m 47.73s (-4.27) **Going Correction** -0.10s/f (Good)
WFA 3 from 4yo+ 7lb **7** Ran SP% **116.1**
Speed ratings (Par 113): **114,112,112,112,110 109,108**
Tote Swingers 1&2 £2.50, 2&3 £4.80, 1&3 £5.00 CSF £24.83 TOTE £4.20: £2.30, £2.80; EX 22.40 Trifecta £76.00 Pool £2,465.10 - 23.98 winning units..
Owner Godolphin **Bred** Mrs Eithne Hamilton **Trained** Newmarket, Suffolk

FOCUS
Sectional times confirmed what the eye suggested, which it that the early pace was strong, and that set things up for those ridden to challenge late. Solid form, just about up to grade.

NOTEBOOK
Dubai Prince(IRE) has always had the ability but, since being transferred to Godolphin at the end of his juvenile career and getting injured, for different reasons he's not always been able to show it. His best is more than good enough to see him win races like this, though, and with the good gallop setting things up for him back over this more suitable trip, he showed a nice turn of foot to settle matters late on. He idled a little in front, had more in hand than the bare margin, and is now likely to be stepped up in class again, with the Group 2 Prix Dollar the favourite as his most likely engagement. Incidentally, Godolphin have now won five of the last nine runnings of this race. (op 9-2 tchd 7-2)
Side Glance lacked the winner's acceleration but had a 4lb penalty to carry so emerges with plenty of credit. A consistent sort, he's a good guide to the level of the form. (op 9-2)
Tazahum(USA), second in this race last year, travelled as well as anything into contention but didn't find enough for pressure to seriously threaten the winner. The balance of his form suggests he's not quite up to winning at this level. (op 6-1)
Barefoot Lady(IRE), the only filly in the line-up, has good course form and ran her usual honest race. She's probably run close to her best and is another guide to the form. (op 13-2)
Questioning(IRE) faced no easy task under his penalty and things were made tougher for him when Fury went to the front and denied him what had looked likely to be an uncontested lead. Softer ground suits him better as well. (op 8-1)
Stipulate, the only 3yo in the field, did nothing to alter the view that the colts of his generation are below average. He was slightly hampered 2f out, but that was no great excuse. (op 10-3 tchd 7-2)
Fury was lit up by the first-time cheekpieces and went off far too fast in front. Well beaten by Dubai Prince here last time, he simply helped set things up for his old rival. (tchd 17-2)

5561 COOLMORE NUNTHORPE STKS (BRITISH CHAMPIONS SERIES) (GROUP 1) 5f

3:40 (3:43) (Class 1) 2-Y-O+ **£141,775** (£53,750; £26,900; £13,400; £6,725; £3,375) **Stalls** Centre

Form				RPR
1041	**1**		**Ortensia (AUS)**[21] 4762 7-9-8 115 WilliamBuick 8 (Paul Messara, Australia) *sn outpcd and bhd: swtchd lft and rdn along over 2f out: hdwy on far rail over 1f out: styd on strly ins fnl f to ld nr fin* **7/2**[1]	118+
2542	**2**	*nk*	**Spirit Quartz (IRE)**[21] 4762 4-9-11 107 FrankieDettori 10 (Robert Cowell) *in tch: hdwy wl over 1f out: sn rdn: styd on ins fnl f to ld last 100yds: hdd and no ex nr fin* **14/1**	120
3010	**3**	*1 1/4*	**Hamish McGonagall**[21] 4762 7-9-11 110 DavidAllan 1 (Tim Easterby) *qckly away and set str pce: clr 1/2-way: rdn over 1f out: drvn ins fnl f: hdd last 100yds: hld whn n.m.r towards fin* **14/1**	116
0006	**4**	*1 1/4*	**Humidor (IRE)**[21] 4762 5-9-11 105 (t) SilvestreDeSousa 4 (George Baker) *midfield: hdwy 2f out: sn rdn and kpt on fnl f: nrst fin* **50/1**	111
1100	**5**	*nk*	**Beyond Desire**[21] 4762 5-9-8 106 NeilCallan 9 (Roger Varian) *cl up centre: rdn along 2f out: drvn over 1f out: kpt on same pce fnl f* **33/1**	107
0-12	**6**	*shd*	**Bated Breath**[66] 3238 5-9-11 118 JamesDoyle 15 (Roger Charlton) *chsd ldrs towards stands' side: rdn along 2f out: kpt on u.p fnl f* **7/2**[1]	110
2223	**7**	*3/4*	**Sole Power**[66] 3238 5-9-11 115 WayneLordan 18 (Edward Lynam, Ire) *racd nr stands' rail: towards rr: gd hdwy 1/2-way: rdn to chse ldrs wl over 1f out: wknd fnl f* **7/1**[3]	107
032	**8**	*hd*	**Masamah (IRE)**[10] 5204 6-9-11 108 (b) GrahamLee 14 (Kevin Ryan) *prom centre: rdn along 2f out: drvn over 1f out: wknd fnl f* **20/1**	106
-111	**9**	*nk*	**Pearl Secret**[69] 3158 3-9-9 109 JamieSpencer 19 (David Barron) *racd towards stands' rail: hld up: hdwy 2f out: rdn along and n.m.r over 1f out: n.d* **6/1**[2]	105+
-000	**10**	*nk*	**Tangerine Trees**[21] 4762 7-9-11 111 (v) TomEaves 20 (Bryan Smart) *racd towards stands' rail: chsd ldrs: rdn along 2f out: wknd fnl f* **25/1**	104
0010	**11**	*shd*	**Dandy Boy (ITY)**[41] 4100 6-9-11 113 PatDobbs 16 (David Marnane, Ire) *towards rr: rdn along and hdwy wl over 1f out: styd on fnl f: nvr rchd ldrs* **25/1**	104
1362	**12**	*nk*	**Nocturnal Affair (SAF)**[14] 5067 6-9-11 113 (t) RichardHughes 5 (David Marnane, Ire) *midfield: rdn along 2f out: n.d* **20/1**	103
-315	**13**	*1 1/4*	**Angels Will Fall (IRE)**[21] 4762 3-9-6 104 RobertWinston 12 (Charles Hills) *midfield: rdn along and hung lft 2f out: n.d* **25/1**	95
0031	**14**	*1/2*	**Monsieur Joe (IRE)**[21] 4790 5-9-11 110 RichardMullen 17 (Robert Cowell) *racd towards stands' rail: chsd ldrs: rdn along 2f out: sn wknd* **22/1**	96
0204	**15**	*3/4*	**Confessional**[21] 4762 5-9-11 106 (be) EddieAhern 6 (Tim Easterby) *midfield: rdn along 1/2-way: sn wknd* **33/1**	94
4200	**16**	*shd*	**Secret Witness**[6] 5370 6-9-11 106 (b) JimmyFortune 11 (Ronald Harris) *a towards rr* **66/1**	93
0115	**17**	*nk*	**Tiddliwinks**[55] 3650 6-9-11 112 PhillipMakin 13 (Kevin Ryan) *racd towards stands' rail: chsd ldrs: rdn along and hanging lft fr 1/2-way: sn wknd* **16/1**	92
4404	**18**	*1 1/4*	**Bogart**[20] 4794 3-9-9 107 PaulMulrennan 2 (Kevin Ryan) *prom: centre: rdn along 2f out: sn drvn and wknd* **28/1**	88
1004	**19**	*6*	**Invincible Ash (IRE)**[12] 5137 7-9-8 111 (p) KierenFallon 7 (M Halford, Ire) *a bhd* **33/1**	63

57.62s (-1.68) **Going Correction** -0.175s/f (Firm)
WFA 3 from 4yo+ 2lb **19** Ran SP% **131.6**
Speed ratings: **106,105,103,101,101 100,99,99,98,98 98,97,95,94,93 93,93,91,81**
Tote Swingers 1&2 £14.50, 2&3 £25.40, 1&3 CSF £49.80 TOTE £4.50: £2.10, £4.30, £4.60; EX 57.10 Trifecta £1630.60 Pool £6,390.47 - 2.90 winning units..
Owner A D N Fraser, Miss A C N Fraser & Ms E J H Ridley **Bred** L D Rhodes **Trained** Australia

FOCUS
This was the biggest ever field for the Nunthorpe Stakes, which was first run in its modern form in 1922. It was an open renewal, well up to the race's recent level, but it contained just three previous winners in the highest grade. July Cup winner Mayson was not declared, and former dual winner Borderlescott and 2yo Ceiling Kitty were among several to miss the cut as a maximum field lined up, minus former winner Kingsgate Native whose blood was wrong. The third showed blinding pace despite racing on his own towards the far side and the first three home ended up hard under the inside rail. Those racing on the opposite flank were apparently disadvantaged. The winner, third and fourth all went to post early. The time just broke the standard. There are doubts over the form and Ortensia is rated a length off her Goodwood level.

NOTEBOOK

Ortensia(AUS) thundered home from a long way off the pace to snatch the race close home. Australia's first Nunthorpe winner - she has been based in Newmarket since April - she had disappointed in the King's Stand and couldn't cope with the bad ground in the July Cup, but she showed her true mettle in the King George Stakes and confirmed her superiority over no fewer than eight of her rivals from Goodwood, with whom she was 7lb better off. First home in Grade 1 sprints at Ascot (Australia), Randwick (disqualified) and Meydan (beat Sole Power), she has only once met the sprint queen Black Caviar, when third to her in November 2010. She will remain in Britain for a tilt at the Betfred Sprint Cup at Haydock, where the 6f and flat track will suit her fine, and she must have serious claims provided it doesn't get too soft. William Buick believes it's important that she can run straight as she's not as effective if she has to weave through horses. (op 9-2 after early 5-1)

Spirit Quartz(IRE) struck the front it looked like he would prevail, but he could not resist his old rival's strong burst. This Group 3 winner in Italy has run a string of consistent races for his current connections without managing to land a first prize. The Prix de l'Abbaye could be a suitable target and he may be supplemented for Haydock. His trainer believes he'll be better still at five. (op 16-1)

Hamish McGonagall ran another cracker and he obviously keeps his best efforts for this track. He had been down the field in Ortensia's Goodwood race. (op 18-1)

Humidor(IRE), sixth to Ortensia at Goodwood, had the least chance on adjusted BHA figures. He was well drawn as it transpired and ran on for fourth. Connections believe a soft-ground Abbaye would be ideal for him. (op 66-1)

Beyond Desire ran a big race down the centre and just missed out on a frame finish. (op 40-1)

Bated Breath, four times second in top-level sprints but yet to win one, sidestepped the July Cup because of the ground. He was unfavourably berthed in stall 15 as it turned out and the rain was against him, but he still ran a creditable race and it's hard to argue he was greatly below form. Should he get his conditions he will be a major player in the Betfred Sprint Cup, in which he was beaten a pixel by Dream Ahead last year. (op 9-2 after early 5-1)

Sole Power has run a string of good races this season without getting the rewards and this was another sound run. Unfortunately for him he raced nearest to the stands' rail and the action was on the other side of the track. The bit of ease in the ground was not ideal for him either. (op 6-1)

Masamah(IRE), blinkered for the first time since 2009, was always towards the fore near the centre and achieved the best placing of Kevin Ryan's three runners.

Pearl Secret was 2-2 at York and the Sandown Listed event he won last time out in June was won by Margot Did before she took this year. The colt was starting to run on near the stands' side when his rider was forced to snatch up, costing him at least a length. His trainer holds him in high regard and he remains a colt of considerable potential. (op 5-1)

Tangerine Trees has found it a struggle this season, and he could not sustain his early dash here. (op 22-1)

Dandy Boy(ITY) had never run at 5f before and found the trip too sharp. (tchd 28-1)

Nocturnal Affair(SAF) is not quite up to this level.

Bogart showed bags of pace before dropping away on this step down to 5f, albeit after shunning the far side where he was drawn. Paul Mulrennan reported that the colt hung right. Official explanation: jockey said that the colt hung right (op 40-1)

5562 SKY BET MOBILE CONVIVIAL MAIDEN STKS — 7f

4:15 (4:17) (Class 2) 2-Y-O — **£16,172** (£4,812; £2,405; £1,202) **Stalls** Low

Form				RPR
6	**1**		**Wentworth (IRE)**[20] 4803 2-9-3 0 ... RichardHughes 8 (Richard Hannon) *hld up: hdwy whn n.m.r over 2f out: swtchd rt and rdn over 1f out: styd on strly ins fnl f: led nr fin* **6/4**[1]	84+
34	**2**	½	**Lord Of The Garter (IRE)**[12] 5126 2-9-3 0 ... KierenFallon 11 (Brian Meehan) *hld up in tch: hdwy 3f out: chsd ldr 2f out: rdn to chal over 1f out: drvn to ld ins fnl f: hdd and no ex nr fin* **28/1**	83
3	**3**	½	**Bright Strike (USA)**[27] 4595 2-9-3 0 ... WilliamBuick 5 (John Gosden) *trckd ldr: led 2f out: jnd and rdn over 1f out: hdd ins fnl f: one pce last 50yds* **7/2**[2]	82
	4	2 ¼	**Market Town (USA)** 2-9-3 0 ... MichaelHills 3 (Charles Hills) *hld up towards rr: sltly hmpd over 4f out: swtchd to outer and hdwy over 2f out: sn rdn and styd on fnl f* **11/1**	76+
30	**5**	2 ¾	**Greeleys Love (USA)**[13] 5083 2-9-3 0 ... PhillipMakin 9 (Kevin Ryan) *dwlt and hld up in rr: hdwy over 2f out: sn rdn and no imp* **66/1**	69
	6	4 ½	**Tribal Path (IRE)** 2-9-3 0 ... NeilCallan 10 (Mark Johnston) *prom: cl up 1/2-way: rdn along over 2f out: sn wknd* **6/1**	57
2	**7**	2 ½	**Reggae Star**[10] 5184 2-8-12 0 ... SilvestreDeSousa 2 (Mark Johnston) *led: rdn along and hdd 2f out: sn drvn and wknd* **16/1**	46
0	**8**	1 ½	**Substantivo (IRE)**[20] 4792 2-9-3 0 ... TomQueally 7 (Alan Jarvis) *a in rr* **66/1**	49
	9	nk	**Forging The Path (USA)** 2-9-3 0 ... PaulHanagan 1 (Richard Fahey) *chsd ldrs: rdn along 3f out: sn wknd* **25/1**	46
22	**U**		**Brave Command (USA)**[17] 4917 2-9-3 0 ... FrankieDettori 6 (Mahmood Al Zarooni) *hld up in tch whn slipped and uns rdr 1/2-way: fatally injured* **5/1**[3]	

1m 25.14s (-0.16) **Going Correction** -0.10s/f (Good) **10** Ran SP% **117.7**
Speed ratings (Par 100): **96,95,94,92,89 84,81,79,79,**
Tote Swingers 1&2 £8.80, 2&3 £9.90, 1&3 £2.70 CSF £56.65 TOTE £2.50: £1.30, £3.90, £1.70; EX 57.10 Trifecta £189.30 Pool £2,968.90 - 11.60 winning units..

Owner Mrs John Magnier & Michael Tabor & Derrick Smith **Bred** Denis McDonnell **Trained** East Everleigh, Wilts

■ Stewards' Enquiry : Phillip Makin £140 fine: arrived to parade ring late
Tom Queally £140 fine: arrived to parade ring late
Neil Callan £140 fine: arrived to parade ring late

FOCUS

The third time this valuable maiden has been run as a 7f contest, and it featured seven Group-race entries. The early pace wasn't strong but it steadily increased to 2f out before slowing again inside the final couple of furlongs. The form is not as strong as might have been expected, but the winner has more to offer.

NOTEBOOK

Wentworth(IRE) showed plenty of ability on his debut at Goodwood when not getting the best of luck in running and was sent off a short price here to get off the mark. He travelled well through the race but the gaps would not come for him 2f out, so he was switched. He lost a bit of momentum with that manoeuvre but Hughes had just enough time left to get him going again and he finished well to get up close home and win snugly. Although he's by Acclamation, there's stamina on the dam side of his pedigree, and the way he races suggests he could already do with a mile. He won't be rushed this year as he's very much seen as one for next year, but he looks useful. (op 11-8 tchd 7-4)

Lord Of The Garter(IRE) improved on his first two starts and showed that this trip is not beyond him. He could go the nursery route now if connections so choose, but he has the ability to win a maiden first. (op 25-1)

Bright Strike(USA) couldn't get cover early and again raced keenly, so in the circumstances he did well to finish so close. There's better to come and he should be suited by challenging off a stronger gallop. (op 9-2)

Market Town(USA) ◆, one of three newcomers in the field, was taking on rivals who had already shown a fair level of ability. He had to swerve to avoid the stricken Brave Command turning in, and wasn't beaten up as he stayed on nicely for fourth. Out of a half-sister to top-class 1m2f dirt performer Aptitude and Grade 1 winner Sleep Easy, he should come on for this and take a maiden before being stepped up in class (entered in the Royal Lodge, Dewhurst and Racing Post Trophy). (op 10-1)

Greeleys Love(USA) was hampered at Ayr last time so this was probably more like a step up on his debut effort when he ran with promise. He could be an interesting sort for nurseries.

Tribal Path(IRE) ◆ shaped with encouragement on his debut. He ran green once pressure was applied, but this first foal of Navajo Moon, a dual Listed winner over 1m1f, ran well for a long way and should come on plenty for this debut outing. (tchd 13-2)

Reggae Star, the only filly in the field, had the run of things out in front, but she couldn't make it tell against these rivals. She'll find her level in time. (tchd 14-1)

Brave Command(USA) sadly broke down badly on the bend into the straight. (op 6-1 tchd 9-2)

5563 TYREGIANT.COM STKS (NURSERY) — 6f

4:50 (4:52) (Class 2) 2-Y-O — **£16,172** (£4,812; £2,405; £1,202) **Stalls** Centre

Form				RPR
6100	**1**		**Mary's Daughter**[20] 4820 2-8-4 82 ... LauraBarry(7) 18 (Richard Fahey) *chsd ldrs: hdwy and cl up over 2f out: rdn to ld over 1f out and sn edgd lft: kpt on wl u.p fnl f* **33/1**	89
154	**2**	¾	**Normal Equilibrium**[13] 5088 2-9-0 85 ... HarryBentley 2 (Roger Varian) *hld up in tch: hdwy over 2f out: chsd ldrs wl over 1f out: rdn to chal ins fnl f and ev ch tl drvn and no ex last 75yds* **14/1**	90
4345	**3**	hd	**Regal Dan (IRE)**[13] 5088 2-8-7 78 ... KierenFallon 8 (Charles Hills) *hld up: hdwy over 2f out: rdn to chse ldrs over 1f out: styd on wl fnl f* **16/1**	83+
21	**4**	3 ¾	**Majestic Moon (IRE)**[25] 4637 2-8-8 79 ... TonyHamilton 1 (Richard Fahey) *rrd s and s.i.s: bhd: hdwy 3f out: rdn over 2f out: styd on appr fnl f: nrst fin* **7/2**[2]	76+
2201	**5**	nk	**Royal Aspiration (IRE)**[18] 4877 2-9-2 87 ... MichaelHills 7 (William Haggas) *cl up: rdn to ld wl over 2f out: drvn and hdd over 1f out: grad wknd* **18/1**	79
3661	**6**	nk	**Prince Regal**[10] 5213 2-8-6 84 6ex ... MichaelJMMurphy(7) 9 (Alan Jarvis) *t.k.h early: chsd ldrs: rdn along 2f out: kpt on same pce* **16/1**	75
1062	**7**	nk	**The Taj (USA)**[13] 5088 2-9-7 92 ... PaulHanagan 4 (Richard Hannon) *hld up towards rr: hdwy on inner 2f out: sn rdn and no imp fnl f* **7/1**	82
103	**8**	½	**Jubilee Brig**[20] 4804 2-9-0 85 ... TomQueally 5 (Gary Moore) *towards rr: sme hdwy over 2f out: sn rdn and n.d* **25/1**	74
13	**9**	½	**Pure Excellence**[20] 4820 2-8-8 79 ... SilvestreDeSousa 14 (Mark Johnston) *towards rr: hdwy and in tch over 2f out: sn rdn and btn* **6/1**[3]	66
13	**10**	2	**Diggory Delvet**[13] 5109 2-8-6 77 ... PatrickMathers 13 (Richard Fahey) *a towards rr* **25/1**	58
331	**11**	nse	**Indignant**[22] 4742 2-8-13 84 ... RichardHughes 12 (Richard Hannon) *cl up: rdn along wl over 2f out: sn wknd* **12/1**	65
31	**12**	2 ½	**Burning Blaze**[27] 4612 2-9-0 85 ... JamieSpencer 6 (Kevin Ryan) *led: rdn along and hdd wl over 2f out: drvn wl over 1f out and sn wknd* **11/4**[1]	59
4143	**13**	1 ¾	**Mayfield Girl (IRE)**[20] 4827 2-8-10 81 ... DavidAllan 11 (Mel Brittain) *in rr fr 1/2-way* **25/1**	49
31	**14**	1 ¾	**Mitchell**[38] 4178 2-8-4 75 ... MartinLane 15 (David Barron) *towards rr: effrt and sme hdwy on wd outside 3f out: sn rdn along and nvr a factor* **20/1**	38

1m 11.1s (-0.80) **Going Correction** -0.175s/f (Firm) **14** Ran SP% **126.3**
Speed ratings (Par 100): **98,97,96,91,91 90,90,89,89,86 86,83,80,78**
Tote Swingers 1&2 £69.80, 2&3 £36.90, 1&3 £49.90 CSF £436.09 CT £7657.20 TOTE £38.00: £6.60, £5.10, £4.00; EX 724.80 Trifecta £2237.40 Part won. Pool £3,023.53 - 0.50 winning units..

Owner Mr And Mrs J D Cotton **Bred** Floors Farming And Dominic Burke **Trained** Musley Bank, N Yorks

■ Stewards' Enquiry : Michael J M Murphy two-day ban: careless riding (7 and 9 Sept)

FOCUS

A competitive edition of a nursery whose best recent winner was subsequent Group 3 scorer Prince Of Light. The field shunned the stands' side, racing down the centre at first, and the first three, who finished clear, ended up near the far rail, which had been the favoured flank in the Nunthorpe. Some of the lightly raced types failed to fire. There was no fluke about the winner's improved form.

NOTEBOOK

Mary's Daughter had been comfortably held on her nursery debut, albeit racing on the wrong side, and looked badly drawn in 18. After racing prominently down the centre, she edged to her left when in front and ended up not far from the inside rail, keeping on well. She's well at home in yielding ground.

Normal Equilibrium enjoyed a nice tow from his owners' other runner towards the far side and had his chance, but could not get past the filly. His three previous runs had all been over 5f on fast ground and he stepped up for this different test. (op 16-1)

Regal Dan(IRE) ◆ missed the break but was doing some sterling late work after having to wait for the gaps to appear. The only maiden in the field, and behind today's runner-up at Haydock on his nursery bow, he improved for the extra furlong and should be getting off the mark soon. (tchd 18-1)

Majestic Moon(IRE) was very awkward leaving the stalls. The Ayr maiden winner was running on to good effect and, a Mill Reef Stakes entry, he should be respected when he next appears. (op 9-2, tchd 5-1 in places)

Royal Aspiration(IRE) showed plenty of pace before fading inside the last. (op 20-1)

Prince Regal was penalised for his win in a Yarmouth maiden. He caught the eye in behind horses and stayed on when in the clear, but cannot be classed as unlucky.

The Taj(USA), conceding 5lb or more to his rivals, was covered up towards the far side before running on. The return to 6f was fine for him. (op 8-1)

Jubilee Brig, again somewhat keen, was staying on after having to wait for a clear passage.

Pure Excellence, 3lb higher than when a luckless third in a decent nursery at Newmarket, could not build on the promise of that run. (tchd 11-2)

Burning Blaze carried the same colours as the runner-up, but weakened tamely after setting the pace (op 3-1 tchd 5-2)

T/Jkpt: Not won. T/Plt: £3,637.70 to a £1 stake. Pool: £271,336.37 - 54.45 winning tickets
T/Qpdt: £368.40 to a £1 stake. Pool: £17,923.64 - 36.00 winning tickets JR

5564 - 5569a (Foreign Racing) - See Raceform Interactive

[5471] DEAUVILLE (R-H)

Friday, August 24

OFFICIAL GOING: Turf: good; fibresand: standard

5570a PRIX DE LA REBOURSIERE (MAIDEN) (UNRACED 2YO FILLIES) (TURF) 7f 110y

1:20 (12:00) 2-Y-O **£10,000** (£4,000; £3,000; £2,000; £1,000)

RPR

1 **Milena's Dream (IRE)** 2-9-0 0 .... Pierre-CharlesBoudot 11 78
(Y De Nicolay, France) **35/1**

2 ¾ **Apparition (FR)** 2-9-0 0 .... MarcLerner(6) 15 76
(S Wattel, France) **30/1**

3 3 **Summer Cider (IRE)** 2-9-0 0 .... ThierryJarnet 2 69
(D Guillemin, France) **73/10**

4 shd **Joyeuse Marche** 2-9-0 0 .... MaximeGuyon 6 69
(A Fabre, France) **5/2[1]**

5 nse **La Pedrera (IRE)** 2-9-0 0 .... AurelienLemaitre 9 69
(F Head, France) **5/1[2]**

6 1 **Eva Luna (FR)** 2-9-0 0 .... ChristopheSoumillon 12 66
(J-C Rouget, France) **11/2[3]**

7 2 **Lady Ness (FR)** 2-9-0 0 .... ThomasHuet 13 62
(Mlle C Brunaud, France) **36/1**

8 nk **Fair Moon (FR)** 2-9-0 0 ....(p) ThierryThulliez 4 61
(S Wattel, France) **21/1**

9 ½ **Glorious Melody (FR)** 2-9-0 0 .... NadegeOuakli 10 60
(Robert Collet, France) **49/1**

10 ½ **Arbisselle (FR)** 2-9-0 0 .... MorganDelalande 3 59
(Y Barberot, France) **54/1**

0 **Missalavie (FR)** 2-9-0 0 .... JeromeCabre 14
(P Van De Poele, France) **22/1**

0 **Bonne Amie (FR)** 2-9-0 0 .... GeraldMosse 7
(Tom Dascombe) *missed break: a at rr: rdn 1/2-way: nt qckn: nvr a factor* **21/1**

0 **Childa (IRE)** 2-9-0 0 .... TheoBachelot 8
(S Wattel, France) **38/1**

0 **Special Glace (FR)** 2-9-0 0 .... JulienAuge 5
(Y Fouin, France) **43/1**

0 **Silasol (IRE)** 2-9-0 0 .... OlivierPeslier 1
(C Laffon-Parias, France) **63/10**

1m 36.7s (8.30) **15** Ran SP% **117.2**

WIN (incl. 1 euro stake): 36.20. PLACES: 8.90, 8.80, 3.10. DF: 266.20. SF: 399.40.

Owner Patrick Fellous **Bred** M Henochsberg & Mme P Ades-Hazan **Trained** France

[5531] GOODWOOD (R-H)

Saturday, August 25

OFFICIAL GOING: Good to soft (7.4)

Wind: Fresh, half against Weather: Overcast, showers from Race 5 onwards

5571 WHITELEY CLINIC PRESTIGE STKS (GROUP 3) (FILLIES) 7f

2:15 (2:17) (Class 1) 2-Y-O

£22,684 (£8,600; £4,304; £2,144; £1,076; £540) **Stalls** Low

Form RPR

11 1 **Ollie Olga (USA)**[28] 4599 2-9-0 0 .... MartinHarley 3 104
(Mick Channon) *trckd ldrs in 5th: gng strly over 2f out: rdn and prog over 1f out: led jst ins fnl f: hrd pressed last 100yds: battled on wl* **5/1[2]**

112 2 ½ **Sky Lantern (IRE)**[14] 5103 2-9-0 0 .... RichardHughes 4 103
(Richard Hannon) *trckd ldng trio: shkn up over 2f out: prog u.p over 1f out: chsd wnr and chal last 100yds: could nt qckn nr fin* **10/11[1]**

145 3 1 **Amazonas (IRE)**[30] 4514 2-9-0 90 .... HayleyTurner 6 100
(Ed Dunlop) *hld up in 6th: slt stumble 5f out: rdn over 2f out: prog over 1f out: r.o fnl f to take 3rd nr fin* **14/1**

5521 4 nk **Annie's Fortune (IRE)**[23] 4739 2-9-0 85 .... PaulHanagan 2 100
(Alan Jarvis) *trckd ldng pair: clsd over 2f out: rdn to ld over 1f out: hdd and one pce jst ins fnl f* **11/1**

1366 5 3½ **Momalorka**[14] 5103 2-9-0 90 .... PatDobbs 7 91
(William Haggas) *v awkward s and nrly uns rdr: hld up in last: rdn and no prog over 2f out: no ch after: passed wkng rivals fnl f* **16/1**

115 6 shd **Redressthebalance (IRE)**[14] 5103 2-9-0 93 .... RichardKingscote 1 90
(Ralph Beckett) *led to over 1f out: wknd qckly fnl f* **9/1[3]**

2124 7 1¼ **Savanna La Mar (USA)**[14] 5103 2-9-0 95 ....(b[1]) ChrisCatlin 10 87
(Sir Mark Prescott Bt) *trckd ldr: chal fr 3f out: lost 2nd wl over 1f out: wandering and wknd* **12/1**

3 8 2¾ **Arbeel**[23] 4739 2-9-0 0 .... GeorgeBaker 8 80+
(Peter Chapple-Hyam) *uns rdr and bolted coming on to the trck: stdd s: hld up in 7th: pushed along and no prog 2f out: sn btn* **14/1**

1m 28.53s (1.53) **Going Correction** +0.275s/f (Good) **8** Ran SP% **114.3**

Speed ratings (Par 101): **102,101,100,99,95 95,94,91**

toteswingers 1&2 £1.10, 2&3 £6.80, 1&3 £7.60 CSF £9.90 TOTE £7.70: £1.70, £1.10, £4.30; EX 11.30 Trifecta £289.30 Pool: £926.78 - 2.37 winning units..

Owner Nick & Olga Dhandsa & John & Zoe Webster **Bred** Greenwood Lodge Farm Inc **Trained** West Ilsley, Berks

FOCUS

Fresh ground on lower bend and distances as advertised. There had been 14mm of rain since the previous afternoon and the going was changed to good to soft. Fresh ground had been opened up on the lower bend. This didn't look a particularly strong Group 3 but the form is straightforward and fits in with the ten-year race averages.

NOTEBOOK

Ollie Olga(USA), winner of her first two starts over 6f, extended her unbeaten record stepped up in trip, and scored with a bit up her sleeve. She travelled noticeably well in behind the pace and quickened when the gap came, before idling a touch close home, and there's probably more to come from her. Her trainer hinted that she'd take her chance in a Group 1 next. (op 11-2)

Sky Lantern(IRE), runner-up in the Sweet Solera last time out, was sent off a short price, but having been brought to have every chance down the outside she took a while to pick up when the winner went on. A more positive ride might help in future, but she has plenty of size about her and looks the type who will do better next year. (tchd 4-5 tchd evens in a place)

Amazonas(IRE) didn't handle the fast ground at Sandown last time and appreciated this easier surface. However, she stumbled over half a mile from home, which didn't help her cause, and she hung right in the closing stages as she was staying on. Back on a more galloping track on good or easier ground she might yet win a Group race, over this trip or a mile. Official explanation: jockey said that the filly slipped five furlongs out (tchd 16-1)

Annie's Fortune(IRE), who won her maiden over this C&D last time, had every chance and briefly hit the front inside the final 2f, but she wasn't quite good enough to see it out. (op 10-1 tchd 12-1)

Momalorka exited the stalls awkwardly and her rider did well to stay on, but that meant she was at the tail of the field early on and struggled to get competitive. (tchd 20-1)

Redressthebalance(IRE) made the running but dropped out quickly once headed. She doesn't look up to this class. (op 12-1)

Savanna La Mar(USA), blinkered for the first time, was all over the place when asked to pick up, and perhaps this daughter of Curlin was unsuited by the softish ground.

Arbeel, who was a big price when making a promising debut at Newmarket, was taking a significant step up in class. She unseated her rider as she got onto the track, which probably didn't help, so isn't one to write off. (op 12-1)

5572 BETFAIR SUMMER DOUBLE SECOND LEG (HERITAGE H'CAP) 7f

2:45 (2:47) (Class 2) 3-Y-0+

£62,250 (£18,640; £9,320; £4,660; £2,330; £1,170) **Stalls** Low

Form RPR

032 1 **Imperial Guest**[21] 4802 6-9-4 98 .... TomQueally 8 107
(George Margarson) *hld up in midfield: stdy prog fr 2f out: rdn and picked up wl jst over 1f out: r.o to ld last 50yds* **12/1**

0362 2 ½ **Arnold Lane (IRE)**[23] 4740 3-8-12 97 .... MartinHarley 6 103
(Mick Channon) *wl in tch in midfield: prog over 1f out: r.o to chal fnl f: upsides 50yds out: jst outpcd* **6/1[1]**

0061 3 nk **The Confessor**[24] 4703 5-8-10 90 .... CathyGannon 11 97
(Henry Candy) *pressed ldr: rdn over 2f out and looked to be struggling: rallied over 1f out: styd on to chal 100yds out: jst outpcd* **10/1**

4030 4 nk **Bertiewhittle**[7] 5370 4-8-13 93 .... RichardKingscote 3 99
(David Barron) *towards rr: rdn and prog wl over 1f out: styd on wl fnl f: nrst fin* **7/1[2]**

20-6 5 hd **Webbow (IRE)**[21] 4794 10-9-1 95 .... DaneO'Neill 9 100
(Julie Camacho) *led: tk main body of field down centre in st: rdn over 1f out: sn jnd: hdd and no ex last 50yds* **25/1**

2103 6 ¾ **Ducal**[24] 4703 4-8-10 90 .... KieranO'Neill 2 93
(Mike Murphy) *in tch in midfield: rdn and prog fr jst over 2f out: c to chal and upsides 1f out: wknd last 100yds* **12/1**

1304 7 1¾ **Powerful Presence (IRE)**[19] 4880 6-8-4 91 .... DavidBergin(7) 7 90+
(David O'Meara) *pressed ldng pair: styd alone far side in st: wl on terms tl fdd fnl f* **8/1[3]**

0006 7 dht **Redact (IRE)**[14] 5102 3-9-1 100 .... RichardHughes 15 97+
(Richard Hannon) *hld up and sn in last: stl there over 2f out: hrd rdn over 1f out: r.o fnl f: nrst fin* **20/1**

3054 9 ¾ **Citrus Star (USA)**[14] 5102 5-8-13 93 .... ChrisCatlin 5 90
(Chris Wall) *wl in tch on inner: effrt over 2f out: no imp on ldrs over 1f out: fdd* **14/1**

020 10 1 **White Frost (IRE)**[14] 5102 4-8-7 92 .... MatthewLawson(5) 14 86
(Charles Hills) *chsd ldrs on outer: lost pl 2f out: steadily fdd* **25/1**

03-0 11 nse **Johnny Castle**[22] 4761 4-9-0 94 .... PatDobbs 12 88
(Amanda Perrett) *wl in tch in midfield: rdn and no imp on ldrs over 1f out: fdd* **33/1**

5050 12 1 **Rakaan (IRE)**[7] 5356 5-8-10 90 ....(p) LiamJones 16 81
(Jamie Osborne) *dwlt: wl in rr: no real prog fnl 2f* **28/1**

6111 13 1 **Fulbright**[22] 4761 3-9-9 108 .... RobertHavlin 18 94
(Mark Johnston) *stmbld s: in tch on outer: rdn over 2f out: steadily wknd* **7/1[2]**

3002 14 1¼ **Mabait**[22] 4761 6-8-10 97 ....(p) AliceHaynes(7) 20 82
(David Simcock) *dropped in fr wdst draw and hld up in last trio: effrt over 2f out: no prog over 1f out: wknd* **20/1**

0350 15 hd **Gatepost (IRE)**[7] 5334 3-8-11 96 ....[1] PaulHanagan 13 79
(Richard Fahey) *wl in rr: effrt over 2f out: no prog whn short of room briefly over 1f out: wknd* **25/1**

5000 16 shd **Bronze Prince**[7] 5356 5-8-11 94 .... MarkCoumbe(3) 10 78
(Michael Attwater) *prom: rdn over 2f out: sn wknd* **50/1**

-550 17 ¾ **Decent Fella (IRE)**[22] 4761 6-9-0 94 ....(vt) LiamKeniry 17 76
(Andrew Balding) *racd on outer: a towards rr: struggling over 2f out* **20/1**

4010 18 1¾ **Field Of Dream**[22] 4761 5-9-10 104 ....(b) GeorgeBaker 4 82
(Jamie Osborne) *s.s: hld up wl in rr: effrt over 2f out: no prog whn short of room briefly over 1f out: wknd* **9/1**

6000 19 1 **Justonefortheroad**[28] 4609 6-8-7 94 .... LauraBarry(7) 1 69
(Richard Fahey) *in tch on inner: n.m.r after 2f: no prog over 2f out: wknd over 1f out* **25/1**

1m 27.26s (0.26) **Going Correction** +0.275s/f (Good)

WFA 3 from 4yo+ 5lb **19** Ran SP% **129.6**

Speed ratings (Par 109): **109,108,108,107,107 106,104,104,103,102 102,101,100,98,98 98,97,95,94**

toteswingers 1&2 £12.50, 2&3 £10.90, 1&3 £12.50 CSF £74.33 CT £778.84 TOTE £16.10: £3.00, £1.50, £3.50, £2.10; EX 74.00 Trifecta £761.60 Pool: £2,161.31 - 2.10 winning units..

Owner John Guest Racing **Bred** John Guest Racing Ltd **Trained** Newmarket, Suffolk

FOCUS

No winner of this competitive handicap had emerged from a double-figure stall in the previous ten years, and that trend continued (seven of the first nine were actually drawn in single figures) despite the majority of the field coming towards the centre of the track in the straight. It was a well run race and the form looks pretty solid.

NOTEBOOK

Imperial Guest gained deserved compensation for his narrow defeat in the Stewards' Cup, putting in his usual strong finish and defying a 4lb higher mark in the process. Equally effective over 6f and 7f, and on fast and easy ground, the Ayr Gold Cup looks a natural target for him next.

Arnold Lane(IRE) travelled as well as the winner in midfield and also stayed on strongly, but just like at the Glorious meeting he found one too good. The easing of the ground was definitely in his favour as he likes to get his toe in. (op 13-2 tchd 7-1)

The Confessor, a winner in lesser company over the C&D at the Glorious meeting, got out well from stall 11 and was never far from the front. He ran a sound race off a 4lb higher mark and is a good guide to the level of the form. (tchd 8-1)

Bertiewhittle appreciated the return to 7f and was finishing to some purpose. He could well pop up in something similar. (op 11-1 tchd 13-2)

Webbow(IRE), second in this last year, took them along and held off the closing pack well for a long time. This was a big step up on his reappearance effort and there's still life in the 10yo yet. (tchd 28-1)

Ducal, third to The Confessor here last time out, looked a big threat when coming with his challenge a furlong out, but he didn't quite see it through. He's showing he can be just as effective on turf as he is on Polytrack, though.

Powerful Presence(IRE), who is handicapped up to his best, was the only one to stay on the far rail as they came into the straight, and it didn't look a disadvantage at all. (op 10-1)

Redact(IRE) was drawn out in stall 15 and was held up at the back of the field, so he wasn't well placed given the way the race panned out. He was motoring at the finish, however, and might be one to keep in mind back on a stiffer track. (op 10-1)
Citrus Star(USA) wants quicker ground ideally. (op 12-1)
White Frost(IRE) hasn't done much since fitted with a hood.
Fulbright had a tough draw to overcome, and when he stumbled leaving the stalls things just got more difficult for him. Caught wide on the turn, he couldn't mount a serious challenge in the straight. He's had a busy time of it. Official explanation: jockey said that the colt stumbled coming out of the stalls (op 6-1)
Field Of Dream couldn't pick up at all and perhaps the ground wasn't to his liking. (op 11-1)

5573 BETFAIR CELEBRATION MILE (GROUP 2) 1m
3:20 (3:21) (Class 1) 3-Y-O+ **£56,710** (£21,500; £10,760; £5,360; £2,690) **Stalls** Low

Form RPR
1100 **1** **Premio Loco (USA)**[28] 4610 8-9-1 111 GeorgeBaker 6 115
(Chris Wall) *led: set mod pce but untrbld: rdn over 1f out: hdd ent fnl f: edgd lft but rallied to ld last 50yds* **20/1**
5-11 **2** *nk* **Thistle Bird**[29] 4527 4-8-12 108 HayleyTurner 4 111
(Roger Charlton) *trckd ldr: shkn up over 2f out: drvn and r.o to ld ent fnl f: styd on but hdd last 50yds* **8/1**
4133 **3** *hd* **Aljamaaheer (IRE)**[22] 4760 3-8-9 109 PaulHanagan 2 113
(Roger Varian) *t.k.h: hld up in 3rd: rdn 2f out: clsd 1f out: chal and looked likely wnr 100yds out but could n.g.t w an effrt* **7/4**[1]
121 **4** *1 1/4* **Chachamaidee (IRE)**[25] 4686 5-9-1 113 TomQueally 3 111
(Sir Henry Cecil) *dwlt: hld up in last: effrt on outer over 2f out: drvn and tried to chal 1f out: one pce* **3/1**[3]
1401 **5** *3 1/2* **Trumpet Major (IRE)**[22] 4760 3-8-9 114 RichardHughes 5 103
(Richard Hannon) *hld up in 4th: rdn and effrt over 2f out: hanging and nt qckn over 1f out: sn btn* **9/4**[2]

1m 41.21s (1.31) **Going Correction** +0.45s/f (Yiel)
WFA 3 from 4yo+ 6lb **5** Ran SP% **108.0**
Speed ratings (Par 115): **111,110,110,109,105**
CSF £140.83 TOTE £25.90: £4.60, £2.50; EX 89.00.
Owner Bernard Westley **Bred** Kidder, Cole & Griggs **Trained** Newmarket, Suffolk

FOCUS
There were question marks over a few of these beforehand on various counts, and with no confirmed front-runner it always promised to be messy. The pace was ordinary and the form may not be reliable, rated through Premio Loco who matched his best form of the past year.

NOTEBOOK
Premio Loco(USA) dictated a steady early gallop. This ground is not what he wants, but he enjoyed such a tactical advantage that, despite being headed narrowly inside the last and being matched at a barely believable 999-1 for £25 in-running, he rallied to win quite cosily in the end. A grand old servant, this was his fifth win at Group 2 level. (op 14-1)
Thistle Bird, winner of a couple of Listed races in her previous two starts, tracked the leader and edged ahead briefly inside the last, but couldn't hold off the renewed challenge of Premio Loco. She's progressive and should be able to find a fillies' Group 3 before long. (op 15-2 tchd 7-1)
Aljamaaheer(IRE), unlucky in running when behind Trumpet Major here in a Group 3 at the Glorious meeting, was keen early off the steady gallop. He still looked to be coming with a winning run when delivered down the outside inside the last, but his time in front was brief as he edged right towards his rivals as they rallied. He still looks capable of better than he has shown to date. (op 9-4)
Chachamaidee(IRE), carrying a penalty and held up in last off the steady gallop on ground softer than ideal, didn't have much in her favour, especially as most of her wins have come over 7f. She was keeping on at the finish and didn't run badly in the circumstances. (op 11-4)
Trumpet Major(IRE) got a little chopped for room approaching the final furlong, but he was struggling to pick up anyway, and quicker ground suits him better. (op 2-1)

5574 BONHAMS MAIDEN AUCTION STKS 1m
3:55 (3:55) (Class 5) 2-Y-O **£3,234** (£962; £481; £240) **Stalls** Low

Form RPR
2322 **1** **Botanica (IRE)**[9] 5274 2-8-9 82 RichardHughes 9 79+
(Richard Hannon) *mde all: stretched clr wl over 1f out: in n.d after: eased last 50yds* **2/1**[1]
64 **2** *2* **Jontleman (IRE)**[74] 3009 2-8-10 0 MartinHarley 6 73+
(Mick Channon) *trckd ldrs in 5th: plld out and prog over 2f out: tk 2nd wl over 1f out: styd on and sn clr of rest but no imp on wnr* **5/1**[3]
3 *2 1/2* **Beautiful Story (IRE)** 2-8-5 0 ChrisCatlin 2 63+
(Mick Channon) *hld up in last pair: pushed along and stl there wl over 1f out: prog ins fnl f: r.o to take 3rd last 75yds* **7/1**
24 **4** *1/2* **Living The Life (IRE)**[23] 4739 2-8-5 0 PaulHanagan 8 62
(Jamie Osborne) *hld up in 6th: outpcd wl over 1f out: effrt to press for pls whn nt clr run jst ins fnl f: kpt on* **5/2**[2]
4 **5** *3/4* **Rakticate (IRE)**[11] 5207 2-8-5 0 CathyGannon 7 60
(J S Moore) *chsd ldng trio: rdn 2f out: sn outpcd: pressing for a pl 1f out: one pce* **20/1**
6 **6** *shd* **Brick Rising**[11] 5207 2-8-10 0 LiamKeniry 4 65
(Andrew Balding) *chsd wnr: lost 2nd wl over 1f out and easily outpcd: fdd and lost pls last 75yds* **25/1**
0 **7** *1/2* **Forced Family Fun**[21] 4792 2-8-11 0 HayleyTurner 3 64
(Michael Bell) *chsd ldng pair: rdn 2f out: sn outpcd: fdd ins fnl f* **8/1**
5 **8** *1 3/4* **Alpine Jerry (IRE)**[15] 5061 2-7-11 0 NoelGarbutt(7) 5 53
(J S Moore) *dwlt: hld up in last: wd in st and rdn over 2f out: no prog* **40/1**

1m 44.21s (4.31) **Going Correction** +0.45s/f (Yiel) **8** Ran SP% **113.2**
Speed ratings (Par 94): **96,94,91,91,90 90,89,87**
toteswingers 1&2 £2.50, 2&3 £8.60, 1&3 £4.70 CSF £11.97 TOTE £2.60: £1.30, £1.90, £2.00; EX 12.00.
Owner Carmichael Humber **Bred** Millenium Partnership **Trained** East Everleigh, Wilts

FOCUS
A straightforward win from Botanica, who enjoyed a soft lead. She was close to her pre-race figure, while the runner-up improved.

NOTEBOOK
Botanica(IRE) was gifted an uncontested lead. Richard Hughes said thank you very much, bunched them up in behind at the top of the straight and only had to ask his filly to quicken with 2f to run, at which point she bounded clear to win as she pleased. She's a useful type, but this was as easy peasy as it gets. (op 6-4)
Jontleman(IRE), back from a break, had work to do on the ratings, but didn't shape badly given that he had to make his own room approaching the 2f pole and the winner got first run on him. He's now eligible for nurseries. (op 11-2 tchd 6-1)
Beautiful Story(IRE), the only newcomer in the field, cost only 8,000euros, but she's a half-sister to Pippo di Lucilla, a 1m-1m2f winner in Italy, and Aurora Sky, a four-time 1m2f AW winner. She showed definite promise here, staying on from the back late in the day, and can do better next time. (op 10-1)
Living The Life(IRE) got chopped for room a furlong out but rallied late on. The trip suited her and she's another for whom nurseries now become an attractive option. (tchd 11-4)
Rakticate(IRE) was under pressure some way out but she kept on to just about confirm Wolverhampton form with the sixth. (op 25-1)
Brick Rising finished almost seven lengths behind today's fifth on their respective debuts.
Forced Family Fun is out of a Northumberland Plate winner so is bred to come into his own over much further next year. (op 9-1)
Alpine Jerry(IRE) Official explanation: jockey said that the filly hung left

5575 WINDFLOWER MARCH STKS (LISTED RACE) 1m 6f
4:30 (4:30) (Class 1) 3-Y-O+ **£19,848** (£7,525; £3,766; £1,876; £941) **Stalls** High

Form RPR
2401 **1** **Quest For Peace (IRE)**[22] 4759 4-9-12 111 RichardHughes 7 115
(Luca Cumani) *trckd ldr to 6f out and fr over 4f out: shkn up 2f out: clsd 1f out: drvn ahd last 120yds* **2/1**[2]
5504 **2** *1* **Electrolyser (IRE)**[23] 4737 7-9-10 109 AdamKirby 2 111
(Clive Cox) *led: rdn over 2f out: kpt on but hdd and outpcd last 120yds* **9/2**[3]
-340 **3** *1 1/2* **Berling (IRE)**[22] 4759 5-9-7 99 DaneO'Neill 4 106
(John Dunlop) *hld up in last: rdn to take 4th over 3f out: no imp and hanging wl over 1f out: styd on to take 3rd nr fin* **14/1**
-134 **4** *nk* **Harris Tweed**[44] 4010 5-9-12 115 PaulHanagan 3 111
(William Haggas) *hld up in tch: chsd ldng pair over 3f out: sn rdn: tried to cl 2f out: nt qckn over 1f out: one pce and lost 3rd nr fin* **6/4**[1]
511/ **5** *61* **Alandi (IRE)**[357] 7-9-7 0 [1] GeorgeBaker 5
(P J Prendergast, Ire) *cl up: chsd ldr 6f out to over 4f out: sn wknd: t.o and eased* **17/2**

3m 7.99s (4.39) **Going Correction** +0.45s/f (Yiel) **5** Ran SP% **108.7**
Speed ratings (Par 111): **105,104,103,103,68**
CSF £10.78 TOTE £3.10: £1.60, £1.90; EX 11.70.
Owner O T I Racing **Bred** Macquarie **Trained** Newmarket, Suffolk

FOCUS
Both Harris Tweed and Electrolyser like to make the running, but had they taken each other on it would have just set things up for Quest For Peace, so the connections of Harris Tweed decided to take him back this time.

NOTEBOOK
Quest For Peace(IRE) did well to win considering the ground wasn't really to his liking and the leader had an easy time of it in front, but he was always travelling comfortably in behind him and, once switched off the rail, he found a nice turn of foot to settle matters. He did flash his tail under pressure but he responded and won cosily in the end. He'll go into quarantine on September 6th in preparation for the Melbourne Cup, for which he's a 25-1 shot, and it's quite likely that he'll take in the Caulfield Cup first. (op 5-2)
Electrolyser(IRE) got the run of things out in front. Adam Kirby was able to set a pace to suit himself and, having given him a breather at the top of the hill, he took a bit of passing in the straight. The winner was just too good, but it was a sound effort. (op 4-1 tchd 7-2)
Berling(IRE) didn't help his cause by hanging, but he didn't have his ground, so it wasn't a bad effort, especially given the way the race was run. (tchd 12-1)
Harris Tweed, denied his usual front-running role, was keen off the pace and couldn't pick up sufficiently to throw down a challenge in the straight. (op 11-8 tchd 5-4)
Alandi(IRE), who didn't achieve anything when out in Australia, was having his first outing for his new stable and was eased off with over 2f to run, having lost his action. He may be retired to stud now. Official explanation: jockey said that the horse lost its action (op 9-1 tchd 10-1)

5576 BONHAMS EBF FILLIES' STKS (H'CAP) 6f
5:05 (5:07) (Class 3) (0-95,92) 3-Y-O+ **£9,703** (£2,887; £1,443; £721) **Stalls** High

Form RPR
0213 **1** **My Sharona**[23] 4740 3-8-12 83 RichardHughes 2 95+
(Sylvester Kirk) *cl up: trckd ldr 2f out: waited tl nudged into ld last 100yds: comf* **6/4**[1]
1001 **2** *3/4* **Six Wives**[10] 5223 5-8-12 80 MartinHarley 7 87
(Scott Dixon) *mde most: drvn over 1f out: hdd last 100yds: kpt on but no ch w wnr* **14/1**
5006 **3** *1* **Fillionaire**[7] 5365 3-8-8 79 ow2 RobertHavlin 3 83
(Mick Channon) *chsd ldrs: rdn over 2f out: wnt 3rd over 1f out: kpt on but nvr able to chal* **6/1**[3]
5220 **4** *1 1/4* **Tip Top Gorgeous (IRE)**[28] 4588 3-8-9 80 RichardKingscote 4 80
(J S Moore) *in tch in last pair: rdn over 2f out: one pce and no imp over 1f out* **12/1**
23 **5** *1* **Ray Of Joy**[50] 3822 6-8-13 81 CathyGannon 1 78
(J R Jenkins) *s.i.s: in tch in last pair: rdn 1/2-way: one pce and no imp on ldrs over 1f out* **8/1**
3312 **6** *2 1/2* **Ihtifal**[13] 5128 3-9-5 90 (t) ChrisCatlin 6 79
(Saeed Bin Suroor) *ponied to post and reluctant to go down: chsd ldr to 2f out: sn dropped away* **5/1**[2]

1m 12.77s (0.57) **Going Correction** +0.20s/f (Good)
WFA 3 from 4yo+ 3lb **6** Ran SP% **96.4**
Speed ratings (Par 104): **104,103,101,100,98 95**
toteswingers 1&2 £3.50, 2&3 £7.80, 1&3 £2.10 CSF £16.33 CT £49.44 TOTE £2.10: £1.50, £3.20; EX 15.50.
Owner Verano Quartet II **Bred** Seaton Partnership **Trained** Upper Lambourn, Berks

FOCUS
Not a bad little fillies' handicap, run in a reasonable time. The winner continues on the upgrade.

NOTEBOOK
My Sharona ◆ got to race off the same mark as when third in a stronger heat over 7f here at the Glorious meeting, and the drop back in distance on easy ground proved right up her street. She travelled well and Richard Hughes was keen to win as cosily as possible, and it's clear she had a lot more in hand than the winning margin suggests. She could be in for a successful autumn. (op 2-1)
Six Wives has done all her winning over 5f and never on ground as slow as this, so she had a bit to prove, and in the circumstances this was a good run against a well-handicapped rival. (op 9-1)
Fillionaire, whose only win to date came on her debut over this C&D, hadn't run over 6f since. She was keeping on at the finish but probably still needs to drop a pound or two. (op 10-1)
Tip Top Gorgeous(IRE), below par on fast ground last time, returned to form on this easier surface. (op 16-1)
Ray Of Joy, another who likes to get her toe in, was a little disappointing with conditions in her favour. (op 13-2)
Ihtifal had shown improvement for fast ground in her previous two starts and didn't handle these conditions anywhere near as well. (op 4-1 tchd 11-2)

5577 GREENE KING MAIDEN STKS (H'CAP) 2m
5:40 (5:40) (Class 5) (0-70,65) 3-Y-O **£3,234** (£962; £481; £240) **Stalls** High

Form RPR
0362 **1** **Silver Samba**[22] 4776 3-9-7 65 LiamKeniry 5 72+
(Andrew Balding) *dwlt: sn trckd ldng pair: wnt 2nd 6f out: rdn to ld wl over 1f out: styd on wl fnl f* **11/4**[2]
2302 **2** *2* **Looks Like Rain**[33] 4399 3-9-2 60 RichardHughes 2 64
(Brian Ellison) *hld up in detached last pair early: clsd 1/2-way: rdn over 3f out: kpt on same pce fr over 2f out to take 2nd last strides* **2/1**[1]

4305 **3** ½ **Isobella**[17] 4941 3-8-9 **53**..............................(p) RobertHavlin 1 57
(Hughie Morrison) *stdd s: hld up in detached last pair early: stdy prog on outer 3f out: gng wl 2f out: chsd wnr 1f out: could nt qckn and no imp: lost 2nd last strides* **10/1**

4540 **4** ½ **Dalmo**[21] 3621 3-9-1 **59**..............................(b) GeorgeBaker 6 62
(Gary Moore) *led: set decent pce early: drvn and hdd wl over 1f out: no ex ins fnl f* **12/1**

2 **5** *shd* **Filatore (IRE)**[12] 5152 3-9-4 **62**.............................. ChrisCatlin 4 66
(Bernard Llewellyn) *in tch: pushed along over 4f out: keeping on u.p whn trapped against rail over 1f out: plld out and r.o last 100yds: no ch* **7/2**[3]

0044 **6** 1 **Flashy Star**[11] 5219 3-9-2 **60**..............................(v) MartinHarley 8 62
(Mick Channon) *in tch: chsd ldng pair over 5f out: rdn over 2f out: lost 3rd and fdd over 1f out* **8/1**

006 **7** 45 **The Ploughman**[9] 5280 3-8-2 **46** oh1.............................. CathyGannon 3
(John Bridger) *chsd ldr to 6f out: wknd 4f out: t.o* **25/1**

3m 36.0s (7.00) **Going Correction** +0.45s/f (Yiel) **7** Ran SP% **114.0**
Speed ratings (Par 100): **100,99,98,98,98 97,75**
toteswingers 1&2 £1.10, 2&3 £3.70, 1&3 £4.30 CSF £8.63 CT £44.88 TOTE £4.20: £2.00, £1.40; EX 7.90.
Owner BA Racing **Bred** Ptarmigan Bloodstock Ltd **Trained** Kingsclere, Hants

FOCUS
Run in driving rain, most of these 3yos were trying this sort of trip for the first time, and it was run at a good gallop as well, so it was a proper test. The form makes sense too.
T/Plt: £184.20 to a £1 stake. Pool: £98,198.95. 388.98 winning tickets. T/Qpdt: £39.60 to a £1 stake. Pool: £3,608.44. 67.30 winning tickets. JN

5550 NEWMARKET (R-H)

Saturday, August 25

OFFICIAL GOING: Good to firm changing to good to soft after race 5 (4.00)
The meeting featured the historic Newmarket Town Plate over 3m6f, not under Rules. It was won by Raifteiri, ridden by Clare Twemlow for trainer Neil King.
Wind: Light, across Weather: Sunshine giving way to thundery showers

5578 EUROPEAN BREEDERS' FUND MAIDEN STKS 6f
1:45 (1:45) (Class 4) 2-Y-O **£4,528** (£1,347; £673; £168; £168) **Stalls** Low

Form RPR

2 **1** **Mutazamen**[15] 5062 2-9-3 0.............................. MartinDwyer 1 83+
(Richard Hannon) *mde all: set stdy pce tl qcknd over 2f out: shkn up over 1f out: edgd lft ins fnl f: r.o wl: readily* **11/8**[1]

2 1 ¼ **Anna's Pearl** 2-9-3 0.............................. SebSanders 4 79+
(Ralph Beckett) *chsd wnr: rdn over 2f out: styd on same pce ins fnl f* **13/2**

3 *nk* **Homage (IRE)** 2-9-3 0.............................. ShaneKelly 8 78+
(Jeremy Noseda) *s.s: sn chsng ldrs: rdn over 1f out: edgd lft ins fnl f: styd on* **9/2**[3]

2 **4** ½ **Right Touch**[19] 4877 2-9-3 0.............................. FrederikTylicki 5 77
(Richard Fahey) *plld hrd and prom: rdn over 2f out: styd on same pce fnl f* **7/2**[2]

50 **4** *dht* **Sinaadi (IRE)**[7] 5352 2-8-9 0.............................. RyanPowell(3) 6 72
(Clive Brittain) *chsd ldrs: rdn over 2f out: styaed on same pce ins fnl f* **16/1**

6 6 **Valley Of Wings** 2-9-3 0.............................. MickaelBarzalona 3 59
(Robert Cowell) *s.s: sn pushed along in rr: rdn over 1f out: wknd fnl f* **20/1**

7 8 **Kraken (IRE)** 2-9-3 0..............................(v[1]) J-PGuillambert 9 35
(Luca Cumani) *s.i.s: sn pushed along in rr: rdn and wknd over 1f out* **14/1**

1m 14.34s (1.84) **Going Correction** -0.125s/f (Firm) **7** Ran SP% **113.2**
Speed ratings (Par 96): **82,80,79,79,79 71,60**
toteswingers: 1&2 £2.40, 1&3 £2.00, 2&3 £4.30 CSF £10.79 TOTE £2.40: £1.20, £2.80; EX 9.80.

Owner Hamdan Al Maktoum **Bred** Alpha Bloodstock Limited **Trained** East Everleigh, Wilts

FOCUS
Stands' side track used with stalls on stands' side except 1m2f and 1m5f: centre. Not the most competitive of Newmarket maidens, though winners should emerge from it. The order didn't change that much during the contest. The form is worth giving a chance to.

NOTEBOOK
Mutazamen went one better than when a promising second of 14 on his debut here a fortnight earlier. Given a positive ride over this shorter trip, he edged away from the stands' rail over a furlong out, but never really looked like being caught and was well in control at the line. A return to further shouldn't bother him and he should progress further. (op 7-4 tchd 15-8)
Anna's Pearl ♦, an 80,000gns half-brother to seven winners in Germany including their 1,000 Guineas scorer My Emma, ran a promising debut. Always on the shoulder of the winner, he was off the bridle over 2f from home, but stuck at it gamely and it shouldn't be long before he goes one better. (op 15-2)
Homage(IRE), out of a 7f juvenile winner, managed to get across to track the winner against the stands' rail from his high draw. He couldn't take advantage of the favourite edging off the rail and providing him with an inviting gap, but he still stuck on well enough. Entries in the Middle Park and Dewhurst suggest that he is held in some regard and he should step up from this. (op 5-1)
Right Touch ran a promising race when chasing home a 90-rated rival on his Ripon debut earlier this month, but although he didn't appear to improve on that here, he was keen enough early and didn't see a great deal of daylight on occasions. He is worth another chance. (op 12-1)
Sinaadi(IRE) ran better than on her second start having been trapped out wide throughout, but she will remain vulnerable to an improver and may be better off in a nursery. (op 12-1)
Valley Of Wings, out of a five-time winning sprinter, missed the break and ended up well beaten, but his stable aren't renowned for 2yos and the best of him is likely to be in the longer term. (op 22-1 tchd 25-1)
Kraken(IRE), a 42,000gns half-brother to four winners over a variety of trips, one of whom was also successful over hurdles and fences, was visored for this debut and looked clueless. (op 12-1 tchd 9-1)

5579 LETTERGOLD NURSERY 7f
2:20 (2:20) (Class 3) (0-95,92) 2-Y-O **£7,762** (£2,310; £1,154; £577) **Stalls** Low

Form RPR

15 **1** **I'm Back (IRE)**[28] 4599 2-8-11 **82**.............................. MickaelBarzalona 4 85
(Saeed Bin Suroor) *dwlt: racd keenly and sn prom: shkn up over 2f out: rdn whn rdr dropped whip over 1f out: led ins fnl f: pushed out* **5/1**[3]

0051 **2** *nk* **Masarah (IRE)**[17] 4947 2-8-0 **74**.............................. RyanPowell(3) 7 76
(Clive Brittain) *s.i.s: hld up: hdwy over 2f out: rdn and ev ch ins fnl f: r.o* **10/1**

5212 **3** ½ **Hipster**[10] 5232 2-8-10 **81**..............................(b[1]) SebSanders 5 82
(Ralph Beckett) *chsd ldr tl led over 1f out: sn rdn and edgd rt: hdd ins fnl f: styd on* **7/1**

2505 **4** *hd* **Newstead Abbey**[29] 4526 2-8-8 **79**.............................. RichardMullen 6 79
(David Brown) *hld up: swtchd lft over 1f out: running on whn nt clr run and swtchd lft ins fnl f: nt rch ldrs* **13/2**

531 **5** *shd* **Hajam**[15] 5032 2-9-7 **92**.............................. MartinDwyer 1 92
(James Tate) *chsd ldrs: swtchd lft over 1f out: rdn and ev ch ins fnl f: styd on* **9/2**[2]

311 **6** ½ **Shrewd**[42] 4090 2-8-8 **86**.............................. IanBurns(7) 8 84
(Michael Bell) *chsd ldrs: rdn and ev ch whn hung lft ins fnl f: styd on same pce* **4/1**[1]

01 **7** 2 ½ **Meringue Pie**[30] 4502 2-8-11 **82**.............................. ShaneKelly 3 74
(Richard Hannon) *led over 5f: no ex ins fnl f* **11/2**

434 **8** *nk* **Montcliffe**[24] 4710 2-7-12 **69**.............................. JimmyQuinn 2 60
(Richard Fahey) *hld up: rdn over 1f out: nt trble ldrs* **10/1**

1m 25.05s (-0.65) **Going Correction** -0.125s/f (Firm) **8** Ran SP% **114.2**
Speed ratings (Par 98): **98,97,97,96,96 96,93,92**
toteswingers: 1&2 £14.40, 1&3 £5.70, 2&3 £8.70 CSF £52.90 CT £348.84 TOTE £6.60: £2.20, £2.80, £2.00; EX 57.50.
Owner Godolphin **Bred** Darley **Trained** Newmarket, Suffolk

FOCUS
A decent contest of its type with the majority making their nursery debuts, while this was also a new trip for a few. The market suggested a tight race and that was confirmed as there was barely 2l covering the front six. The time was good but the form can't be rated higher any higher.

NOTEBOOK
I'm Back(IRE) had plenty to prove on this nursery debut having run so poorly here on his second start and things didn't look promising for him early, as he was slow to break and then took quite a hold in the middle of the field. However, to his great credit he responded well to pressure and quickened up nicely up the hill to hit the front close to the line. He could develop into a nice sort if he learns to settle. (op 6-1)
Masarah(IRE) was raised 7lb for winning a five-runner Kempton nursery last time which looked harsh, but she justified the rise with a fine effort in defeat especially as she was forced to make her effort wide on the track. (tchd 11-1)
Hipster, up a furlong and with first-time blinkers replacing the cheekpieces, seemed likely to win when leading 2f from home and soon bagged the stands' rail, but he didn't quite get up the hill. He may need an easier 7f. (op 6-1 tchd 11-2)
Newstead Abbey, another up a furlong and gelded since his last outing, is another whose effort can be marked up as he was forced to make his run very wide and ended up close to the far rail. He should break his duck before too long. (op 8-1 tchd 6-1)
Hajam, making his nursery debut over an extra furlong after bolting up in a weak Brighton maiden, was brought through to hold every chance inside the last furlong, but failed to quicken and there seemed few excuses. (tchd 5-1 in a place)
Shrewd, bidding for a hat-trick for today's rider on this nursery debut, was proven over the trip, but had never raced on ground quicker than good to soft before and the way he edged away to his left inside the last furlong, after holding every chance, suggested that conditions may not have suited him. (op 9-2 tchd 5-1)
Meringue Pie's stable had won this race three times in the previous four years and he enjoyed the run of the race out in front, but he was in trouble as soon as he was joined by the eventual third passing the 2f pole. (op 9-2)

5580 RACING UK H'CAP 1m 5f
2:50 (2:51) (Class 2) (0-100,98) 3-Y-O+ **£25,876** (£7,700; £3,848; £1,924) **Stalls** Centre

Form RPR

411- **1** **Caravan Rolls On**[330] 6497 4-9-5 **89**.............................. PatCosgrave 2 98
(Peter Chapple-Hyam) *hld up: hdwy u.p over 1f out: edgd lft and styd on to ld towards fin* **8/1**

0466 **2** *nk* **Qushchi**[20] 4848 4-9-4 **88**.............................. WilliamCarson 5 96
(William Jarvis) *trckd ldrs: racd keenly: rdn to ld and hung lft ins fnl f: hdd towards fin* **16/1**

2322 **3** 2 ¾ **A Boy Named Suzi**[21] 4800 4-10-0 **98**.............................. ShaneKelly 6 102+
(James Eustace) *hld up: hdwy over 1f out: nt clr run ins fnl f: styd on: nt rch ldrs* **13/2**[3]

2-24 **4** ¾ **Repeater**[14] 5078 3-9-0 **95**.............................. StevieDonohoe 3 101+
(Sir Mark Prescott Bt) *hood removed sltly late: s.i.s: hld up: hdwy over 2f out: hmpd and lost pl over 1f out: r.o ins fnl f: nvr trbld ldrs* **7/2**[1]

5- **5** 2 ¼ **Benefit Of Porter (IRE)**[29] 4568 8-8-12 **82**.............................. MartinDwyer 9 82
(Patrick Sinnott, Ire) *a.p: led 2f out: sn rdn and hung rt: hdd and no ex ins fnl f* **16/1**

4120 **6** *nk* **Handsome Man (IRE)**[24] 4700 3-8-7 **88**.............................. MickaelBarzalona 12 93+
(Saeed Bin Suroor) *hld up: hdwy over 2f out: sn edgd rt: rdn and ev ch ins fnl f: styng on whn hmpd sn after: eased* **7/2**[1]

1321 **7** *nk* **Moon Trip**[9] 5256 3-8-5 **86**.............................. FrannyNorton 8 85
(Mark Johnston) *chsd ldr tl rdn to ld over 2f out: sn hdd: hmpd over 1f out: wknd ins fnl f* **4/1**[2]

1401 **8** 4 **Sula Two**[18] 4905 5-8-3 **80**.............................. PhilipPrince(7) 11 73
(Ron Hodges) *s.i.s: sn prom: rdn whn hmpd over 2f out: wknd over 1f out* **28/1**

50-0 **9** 4 **Fulgur**[21] 4795 4-9-10 **94**.............................. J-PGuillambert 1 81
(Luca Cumani) *plld hrd and prom: stdd and lost pl over 8f out: pushed along over 4f out: wknd over 1f out* **7/1**

3000 **10** 1 **The Betchworth Kid**[14] 5076 7-9-5 **89**..............................(p) FergusSweeney 7 74
(Alan King) *led: rdn and hdd over 2f out: wknd over 1f out* **25/1**

2m 43.15s (-0.85) **Going Correction** +0.025s/f (Good)
WFA 3 from 4yo+ 11lb **10** Ran SP% **120.4**
Speed ratings (Par 109): **103,102,101,100,99 99,98,96,93,93**
toteswingers: 1&2 £54.70, 1&3 £6.30, 2&3 £7.50 CSF £131.14 CT £891.09 TOTE £8.80: £2.40, £5.50, £2.30; EX 146.40.
Owner Pearl Bloodstock Ltd **Bred** Miss K Rausing **Trained** Newmarket, Suffolk
■ Stewards' Enquiry : Martin Dwyer two-day ban: careless riding (Sep 9-10)
William Carson four-day ban: careless riding (Sep 9-12)
Mickael Barzalona two-day ban: careless riding (Sep 9-10)
Pat Cosgrave two-day ban: use of whip (10-11 Sept)

FOCUS
It was raining heavily leading up to this race. A decent staying handicap, but a rough race and a few of these can have their performances marked up. The pace seemed ordinary. The winner stepped up on his 3yo efforts.

NOTEBOOK
Caravan Rolls On, winner of four of his last five starts in 2011, is proven fresh so the 330-day absence may not have been so much of an issue. Ridden with plenty of confidence, he was produced with a well-timed effort from off the pace to hit the front around 50yds from the line and, although several of his rivals didn't enjoy the rub of the green, this was still a good effort to win off a 9lb higher mark than when last seen. He didn't race as a 2yo, so his best days are probably still ahead of him. (op 7-1 tchd 13-2)
Qushchi had dropped to a mark 1lb lower than for her last win following some indifferent efforts this season and probably should have won this. Having been produced with her effort against the stands' rail to hold every chance a furlong from home, she then hung violently away to her left and basically threw it away. (op 12-1)

A Boy Named Suzi had never finished worse than third in his 11 previous outings, including winning twice and chasing home Motivado (fourth in the Ebor less than an hour later) at Goodwood last time, but as a result he continues to edge up the weights. Held up in last place, he was still travelling well passing the 2f pole, but just as he was being delivered with his effort inside the last furlong, the door was shut on him and there was no way back. He deserves a change of luck. (tchd 7-1)

Repeater hasn't been helping himself by taking a keen grip lately, but his chance was compromised here through no fault of his own, as he was just starting to make his effort when meeting serious traffic problems over a furlong from home. (op 5-1 tchd 11-2)

Benefit Of Porter(IRE) has been running well under both codes in Ireland this year and had every chance when narrowly hitting the front 2f from home, but she had taken a keen grip in the early stages and that may have counted against her.

Handsome Man(IRE), who had questions to answer following a modest effort at Goodwood, was ridden into contention coming to the last 2f but he looked held by the front pair when badly squeezed out by them inside the last furlong and was then eased right off. (op 5-1)

Moon Trip stays 2m well and was put up 6lb for his easy win over that trip at Beverley nine days earlier, but he seemed to find this C&D too sharp when a well-beaten third three starts back and, although battling for the lead coming to the last 2f, was again made to look one-paced from that point. (op 5-1)

5581 CHRIS BLACKWELL MEMORIAL HOPEFUL STKS (LISTED RACE) 6f

3:25 (3:25) (Class 1) 3-Y-0+

£18,714 (£7,095; £3,550; £1,768; £887; £445) **Stalls** Low

Form				RPR
2443	**1**		**Hitchens (IRE)**[20] 4838 7-9-7 113 ... MartinDwyer 10 (David Barron) *hld up: hdwy over 1f out: shkn up to ld wl ins fnl f: r.o* **7/1**	117
4-41	**2**	*1*	**Markab**[89] 2559 9-9-4 109 ... FergusSweeney 7 (Henry Candy) *led: rdn over 1f out: hdd and unable qck wl ins fnl f* **9/1**	111
0006	**3**	*3*	**Sirius Prospect (USA)**[42] 4100 4-9-4 112 ...(b) ShaneKelly 9 (Dean Ivory) *hld up in tch: rdn over 1f out: styd on same pce ins fnl f* **11/2**[2]	101
0000	**4**	*nk*	**Es Que Love (IRE)**[7] 5370 3-8-11 106 ... FrannyNorton 6 (Mark Johnston) *chsd ldr: rdn and ev ch wl over 1f out: styd on same pce ins fnl f* **6/1**[3]	96
5201	**5**	*hd*	**Scarf (AUS)**[51] 3784 5-9-0 108 ... MickaelBarzalona 4 (Saeed Bin Suroor) *racd alone on stands' side: prom: rdn over 2f out: edgd lft and styd on same pce ins fnl f* **2/1**[1]	96
131-	**6**	*nk*	**Blanche Dubawi (IRE)**[329] 6531 4-8-9 101 ... PatCosgrave 1 (Noel Quinlan) *hld up: hdwy over 1f out: sn rdn: styd on* **9/1**	90+
2001	**7**	*5*	**Desert Law (IRE)**[14] 5077 4-9-0 105 ... SebSanders 5 (Andrew Balding) *prom: rdn over 1f out: wknd ins fnl f* **8/1**	79
5435	**8**	*¾*	**Lui Rei (ITY)**[14] 5077 6-9-0 103 ... RichardMullen 8 (Robert Cowell) *s.i.s: sn in tch: drvn along 1/2-way: wknd wl over 1f out* **9/1**	76

1m 10.88s (-1.62) **Going Correction** +0.025s/f (Good)
WFA 3 from 4yo+ 3lb 8 Ran SP% **116.6**
Speed ratings (Par 111): **111,109,105,105,105 104,97,96**
toteswingers: 1&2 £7.10, 1&3 £7.70, 2&3 £14.90 CSF £68.45 TOTE £5.80: £2.10, £1.80, £1.90; EX 26.60.
Owner Laurence O'Kane & Paul Murphy **Bred** Curragh Bloodstock Agency Ltd **Trained** Maunby, N Yorks

FOCUS
An interesting Listed sprint in which the majority of the field raced down the centre of the track. Good form for the grade with the penalised winner running to last year's July Cup mark.

NOTEBOOK
Hitchens(IRE) may have been unlucky not to win a similar race at Chester last time, but gained ample compensation here. Ridden patiently, he was produced with a well-timed effort towards the far side of the field to hit the front around half a furlong from home. He is proving ultra-consistent and this was a decent effort considering he was carrying a 7lb penalty for his Group 3 success at Meydan at the start of the year. (op 11-2 tchd 5-1)

Markab was returning from three months off, but has won following a much longer absence than that and he had his ideal conditions. He made a bold bid to make every yard of the running up the middle of the track, but the winner just had the legs of him on the run to the line. (op 11-2)

Sirius Prospect(USA) hit top form at this time last year and was far from disgraced in both the Diamond Jubilee and July Cup in his two previous starts, so this was much less daunting. He was doing all his best work late here and it wouldn't be a surprise to see him enjoy another profitable autumn when the ground is more likely to be suitable. (op 9-2 tchd 6-1)

Es Que Love(IRE) showed up for a long way and this was a lot better than when finishing a tailed-off last in the Great St Wilfrid just seven days earlier. (op 7-1)

Scarf(AUS) raced alone against the stands' rail. It didn't do him much good, though, as he was going nowhere off the bridle over 2f out, but he needs a stiffer test and easier ground than this in any case. (op 3-1)

Blanche Dubawi(IRE) ◆, not seen since narrowly winning a Newmarket fillies' Listed event last October, ran a very creditable reappearance and is worth keeping an eye on. (op 11-1 tchd 12-1)

Desert Law(IRE) was back in form having won the Shergar Cup Dash last time, but an effort coming to the last furlong here came to nothing. He has now been well held in four tries in Pattern company. (tchd 17-2)

5582 NEWMARKET EQUINE HOSPITAL H'CAP 6f

4:00 (4:00) (Class 3) (0-90,87) 3-Y-0 **£8,409** (£2,502; £1,250; £625) **Stalls** Low

Form				RPR
1-05	**1**		**Idler (IRE)**[14] 5082 3-8-5 71 ... FrannyNorton 1 (Mark Johnston) *mde all: rdn over 1f out: hung lft ins fnl f: styd on gamely* **4/1**[3]	86
1214	**2**	*1½*	**Minalisa**[13] 5128 3-8-12 78 ... SebSanders 5 (Rae Guest) *hld up in tch: chsd wnr 1/2-way: rdn and ev ch over 1f out: carried lft ins fnl f: no ex towards fin* **5/2**[1]	88
1-50	**3**	*4½*	**Pearl Diva (IRE)**[43] 4070 3-9-7 87 ... PatCosgrave 3 (Peter Chapple-Hyam) *prom: rdn over 2f out: no ex fnl f* **5/1**	83
213	**4**	*½*	**Uprise**[33] 4412 3-8-7 76 ... RyanPowell(3) 4 (George Margarson) *s.i.s: sn prom: rdn over 2f out: no ex fnl f* **10/1**	70
2141	**5**	*nk*	**Represent (IRE)**[9] 5279 3-8-5 71 ... MickaelBarzalona 6 (Mick Channon) *s.i.s: hld up: hdwy u.p over 1f out: no ex ins fnl f* **7/2**[2]	64
6424	**6**	*½*	**Mister Musicmaster**[11] 5195 3-8-12 78 ... JamesMillman 2 (Rod Millman) *chsd wnr to 1/2-way: sn rdn: outpcd fr over 1f out* **11/2**	69

1m 13.43s (0.93) **Going Correction** +0.275s/f (Good) 6 Ran SP% **111.9**
Speed ratings (Par 104): **104,102,96,95,94 94**
toteswingers: 1&2 £2.30, 1&3 £2.50, 2&3 £1.90 CSF £14.32 TOTE £5.80: £2.90, £2.10; EX 18.30.
Owner Sheikh Hamdan Bin Mohammed Al Maktoum **Bred** Darley **Trained** Middleham Moor, N Yorks

FOCUS
There was another thunderstorm before this race. The sextet all raced down the centre of the track in this fair 3yo handicap and the front pair pulled well clear of the others. They have been given a bit of credit for this.

NOTEBOOK
Idler(IRE) had been below his best in two starts earlier this month following a lengthy absence, but the last thing you need to do is allow a Johnston horse the run of the race out in front and his opponents played into his hands. He did edge away to his left inside the last furlong, but wasn't stopping and never really looked like getting caught. The rain wouldn't have been a problem to him and he can probably build on this, as he will be fresher than many heading into the autumn. (op 9-2 tchd 5-1)

Minalisa didn't find the race panning out for her when tried on fast ground for the first time here a fortnight earlier and the rain would have been welcome for her, too. She tried her hardest to get on terms with the winner from over a furlong out, but although intimidated by him as he hung into her in the closing stages, she looked second best on merit. She only made her racecourse debut in June, so still has a bit of scope. (tchd 9-4 and 11-4)

Pearl Diva(IRE) was making her handicap debut having been outclassed in a York Group 3 last time. She still didn't show enough here to prove that she has trained on. (op 6-1)

Uprise didn't run badly on his debut for the yard at Windsor last time and was withdrawn from a race here the previous day on account of the quick ground, so the conditions ought to have come in his favour, but he was comfortably left behind by the front two. (op 15-2)

Represent(IRE), winner of two of her previous three starts, was beaten off this mark in between those two successes and although that was over 1m, this performance suggests that this mark is beyond her.

Mister Musicmaster is more exposed than most and is now on a losing run of 12. (tchd 5-1)

5583 HOME OF RACING H'CAP 1m 2f

4:35 (4:45) (Class 3) (0-95,95) 3-Y-0+ **£8,409** (£2,502; £1,250; £625) **Stalls** Centre

Form				RPR
05-0	**1**		**Specific Gravity (FR)**[25] 4684 4-9-9 90 ... PatCosgrave 3 (Sir Henry Cecil) *chsd ldrs: led over 1f out: rdn clr* **8/1**	103
0603	**2**	*5*	**Licence To Till (USA)**[3] 5492 5-9-11 92 ... FrannyNorton 10 (Mark Johnston) *led: rdn and hdd over 1f out: no ex ins fnl f* **7/2**[1]	95
604	**3**	*1*	**St Ignatius**[17] 4944 5-8-9 76 ...(p) ShaneKelly 2 (Alan Bailey) *chsd ldr tl rdn over 1f out: no ex fnl f* **22/1**	77
310	**4**	*1¼*	**Zamdy Man**[23] 4741 3-8-8 83 ... FrederikTylicki 9 (Venetia Williams) *hld up: outpcd over 2f out: styd on ins fnl f* **4/1**[2]	82
41-0	**5**	*1*	**Jiwen (CAN)**[99] 2248 4-9-6 87 ... MartinDwyer 1 (Roger Varian) *prom: rdn over 1f out: wknd fnl f* **8/1**	84
5-1	**6**	*2½*	**Prince Of Orange (IRE)**[21] 4791 3-8-11 86 ... AhmedAjtebi 7 (Mahmood Al Zarooni) *s.i.s: hld up: hdwy over 3f out: rdn and hung lft 2f out: wknd fnl f* **9/2**[3]	78
2114	**7**	*27*	**Silent Moment (USA)**[38] 4216 3-9-3 92 ... MickaelBarzalona 4 (Saeed Bin Suroor) *hld up: pushed along over 3f out: wknd and eased over 2f out: t.o* **7/2**[1]	30
614/	**8**	*75*	**Oriental Cat**[228] 7100 5-9-1 82 ... SebSanders 6 (Venetia Williams) *s.i.s: a in rr: wknd over 3f out: t.o* **14/1**	

2m 9.3s (3.80) **Going Correction** +0.45s/f (Yiel)
WFA 3 from 4yo+ 8lb 8 Ran SP% **115.9**
Speed ratings (Par 107): **102,98,97,96,95 93,71,11**
CSF £36.66 CT £598.48 TOTE £10.70: £2.70, £1.70, £4.70; EX 40.40.
Owner Niarchos Family **Bred** Suc S Niarchos **Trained** Newmarket, Suffolk

FOCUS
The rain was coming down again before this race and the ground was changed to good to soft from good to firm. There was a ten-minute delay due to a power cut. With a few of the eight remaining runners appearing not to cope with the ground, it remains to be seen how strong this form is, but the winner did it nicely. The second was close to his York mark.

NOTEBOOK
Specific Gravity(FR) ◆ was entitled to need his return from 339 days off at Goodwood last month and was a different proposition this time. A useful performer in the first half of his 3yo season, including finishing fourth in the Hampton Court at Royal Ascot, he won his maiden as a 2yo on soft ground very easily indeed which was significant considering the amount of rain that had fallen. He was still on the bridle when produced with his effort coming to the last 2f and found plenty when asked to quicken. He will go up a fair chunk for this, but still looks set for a good autumn. (tchd 17-2)

Licence To Till(USA), making a quick reappearance after finishing third in a stronger handicap at York three days earlier, tried to make all and ran his race, but came up against a rival with a touch of class who proved much too good for him from over a furlong out. (op 11-4)

St Ignatius likes to go from the front, but couldn't lead this time and had to be content with a stalking role. He had every chance, ran his race, and should be winning again when able to dictate. (op 25-1)

Zamdy Man's proximity may have been partly due to running on past rivals who had already given up, but he remains unexposed and may be worth a try over 1m4f. (op 9-2 tchd 5-1)

Jiwen(CAN), returning from another absence, could probably have done without the rain and also remains unexposed. (tchd 7-1)

Prince Of Orange(IRE), making his handicap debut having defied a 317-day absence since his debut when taking a slowly-run Doncaster maiden earlier this month, was close enough when produced with an effort against the far rail over a furlong out, but then stopped to nothing. (op 4-1)

Silent Moment(USA) has been in fine form on Polytrack this year, but was 6lb higher than when a beaten favourite at Lingfield last time and ran a shocker here. The rain-softened ground is one possible excuse. (op 4-1)

5584 TURFTV H'CAP 5f

5:10 (5:15) (Class 4) (0-85,85) 3-Y-0+ **£5,175** (£1,540; £769; £384) **Stalls** Low

Form				RPR
0132	**1**		**Last Sovereign**[8] 5320 8-9-1 83 ...(b) JacobButterfield(7) 2 (Ollie Pears) *racd centre: a.p: led wl over 1f out: rdn and hung lft ins fnl f: r.o* **5/1**	95
0243	**2**	*2¼*	**Flash City (ITY)**[30] 4501 4-9-5 85 ...(v) JustinNewman(5) 10 (Bryan Smart) *led centre: overall ldr 3f out: hung rt and hdd wl over 1f out: styng on same pce whn hung lft ins fnl f: 2nd of 7 in gp* **4/1**[3]	89
0222	**3**	*1¼*	**Macdillon**[9] 5272 6-8-12 73 ... WilliamCarson 5 (Stuart Kittow) *racd centre: hmpd s: hld up: hdwy 1/2-way: rdn and edgd lft over 1f out: styd on same pce fnl f: 3rd of 7 in gp* **3/1**[1]	72
0301	**4**	*½*	**Whozthecat (IRE)**[5] 5412 5-9-2 82 6ex ...(b) JasonHart(5) 11 (Declan Carroll) *led and racd alone far side: hdd 3f out: sn rdn: styd on same pce fnl f* **7/2**[2]	80
2052	**5**	*½*	**Oldjoesaid**[18] 4924 8-9-4 79 ... FrederikTylicki 3 (Paul Midgley) *racd centre: hmpd s: sn outpcd: r.o ins fnl f: nvr nrr: 4th of 7 in gp* **11/2**	75
-050	**6**	*2*	**Indian Tinker**[96] 2347 3-8-13 76 ... ShaneKelly 7 (Robert Cowell) *racd centre: wnt rt s: chsd ldrs: riddeover 1f out: wknd fnl f: 5th of 7 in gp* **14/1**	65
545	**7**	*nk*	**Nomoreblondes**[9] 5272 8-9-0 75 ...(v) RoystonFfrench 1 (Paul Midgley) *racd centre: prom: pushed along 1/2-way: rdn and wknd over 1f out: 6th of 7 in gp* **16/1**	63

6004 **8** *nse* **Bubbly Ballerina**[77] [2914] 3-9-3 **80**.................................. FrannyNorton 9 67
(Alan Bailey) *racd centre: chsd ldrs: rdn over 1f out: sn wknd: last of 7 in gp* **14/1**

1m 0.68s (1.58) **Going Correction** +0.45s/f (Yiel)
WFA 3 from 4yo+ 2lb **8** Ran SP% **118.5**
Speed ratings (Par 105): **105,101,99,98,97 94,94,94**
toteswingers: 1&2 £3.40, 1&3 £5.00, 2&3 £5.20 CSF £26.32 CT £71.70 TOTE £6.40: £2.00, £1.60, £1.80; EX 40.00.
Owner Richard Walker **Bred** Gestut Hof Ittlingen & Cheveley Park Stud Ltd **Trained** Norton, N Yorks

FOCUS
Fast and furious stuff in the this sprint handicap and they raced all over the track. The rain had affected the ground but the form is taken at face value.
T/Plt: £179.40 to a £1 stake. Pool: £68,531.64. 278.71 winning tickets. T/Qpdt: £31.50 to a £1 stake. Pool: £3,963.80. 92.90 winning tickets. CR

5108 REDCAR (L-H)
Saturday, August 25

OFFICIAL GOING: Good to firm changing to good after race 2 (6.00)
Wind: light against Weather: overcast

5585 CHIC HATS & BAKERS TAILORING FASHION SHOW LADY AMATEUR RIDERS' H'CAP 1m 2f
5:25 (5:29) (Class 5) (0-75,75) 3-Y-O+ **£2,495** (£774; £386; £193) **Stalls** Low

Form RPR
2544 **1** **Tenhoo**[15] [5039] 6-9-12 **65**.. MissCWalton(3) 6 74
(Eric Alston) *midfield: smooth hdwy over 2f out: sn upsides: rdn ins fnl f: kpt on: led towards fin* **8/1**[3]

0-63 **2** *nk* **Major Domo (FR)**[19] [4883] 4-9-7 **62**.................................. MissRSmith(5) 4 70
(Micky Hammond) *midfield: hdwy over 2f out: rdn to ld over 1f out: sn strly pressed: kpt on: hdd nr fin* **18/1**

1520 **3** *2 1/2* **Harare**[11] [5199] 11-9-9 **64**......................................(v) MissPhillipaTutty(5) 15 67
(Karen Tutty) *s.i.s: hld up: pushed along and stl in rr over 2f out: hdwy over 1f out: swtchd rt appr fnl f: kpt on: nrst fin* **33/1**

1300 **4** *3/4* **Moody Tunes**[19] [4864] 9-10-1 **70**........................ MissALMurphy(5) 2 72
(Tom Dascombe) *led: rdn whn hdd over 1f out: plugged on* **14/1**

0212 **5** *nse* **Tidal Run**[8] [5290] 4-10-6 **75**.. MissSMDoolan(5) 3 76
(Mick Channon) *trckd ldrs: rdn over 2f out: kpt on one pce* **7/2**[2]

5213 **6** *1 1/2* **Gold Rules**[16] [5001] 5-10-10 **74**..................................... MissJCoward 14 72
(Michael Easterby) *midfield: rdn over 2f out: sn one pce* **3/1**[1]

2663 **7** *1/2* **Rub Of The Relic (IRE)**[8] [5290] 7-9-10 **65**................(v) MissHDukes(5) 1 62
(Paul Midgley) *trckd ldrs: rdn and outpcd 3f out: plugged on fr over 1f out* **14/1**

4065 **8** *3 1/2* **Tapis Libre**[42] [4080] 4-9-10 **67**....................................... MissAHesketh(7) 8 57
(Michael Easterby) *prom: rdn 3f out: wknd appr fnl f* **16/1**

6011 **9** *3 3/4* **Valantino Oyster (IRE)**[9] [5253] 5-9-9 **62**..........(p) MissJRRichards(3) 12 45
(Tracy Waggott) *prom on outer: rdn 3f out: wknd over 1f out* **9/1**

-540 **10** *5* **Moynahan (USA)**[35] [4317] 7-10-8 **75**........................ MissHCuthbert(3) 13 48
(Thomas Cuthbert) *hld up: rdn over 3f out: nvr threatened* **12/1**

2420 **11** *hd* **Daniel Thomas (IRE)**[100] [2199] 10-9-13 **68**.....(tp) MissKMargarson(5) 10 41
(Richard Guest) *slowly away: hld up: a towards rr: hung rt fr over 1f out* **20/1**

50- **12** *9* **Conjuror's Bluff**[404] [4154] 4-9-10 **67**..................... MissVictoriaCasey(7) 5 22
(Frederick Watson) *hld up in midfield: rdn over 3f out: sn wknd* **150/1**

0212 **13** *2* **Dean Iarracht (IRE)**[9] [5253] 6-9-11 **61**........................(p) MrsCBartley 11 12
(Tracy Waggott) *v.s.a: hld up: rdn over 3f out: sn btn* **9/1**

2m 8.07s (0.97) **Going Correction** -0.075s/f (Good) **13** Ran SP% **118.9**
Speed ratings (Par 103): **93,92,90,90,90 88,88,85,82,78 78,71,69**
toteswingers: 1&2 £27.10, 1&3 £27.90, 2&3 £80.50 CSF £140.26 CT £4444.00 TOTE £10.90: £2.80, £6.10, £7.50; EX 196.10.
Owner Buist, Long, Thompson **Bred** A G Antoniades **Trained** Longton, Lancs

FOCUS
A fair handicap for lady amateur riders. They went an honest gallop on ground officially described as Good to firm but the winning time was over five seconds slower than standard. Straightforward form.
Dean Iarracht(IRE) Official explanation: trainer could offer no explanation for the poor performance shown

5586 EAGLESCLIFFE.TV RAILWAY STATION BARGAIN FARES MEDIAN AUCTION MAIDEN STKS 6f
6:00 (6:00) (Class 5) 2-Y-O **£2,587** (£770; £384; £192) **Stalls** Centre

Form RPR
02 **1** **Seven Of Clubs (IRE)**[15] [5040] 2-9-3 0.......................... PJMcDonald 11 76
(Noel Quinlan) *mde all: rdn over 1f out: kpt on: edgd sltly lft fnl 100yds: jst hld on* **11/10**[1]

0222 **2** *nse* **Bogsnog (IRE)**[10] [5222] 2-9-3 74.. GrahamLee 3 76
(Linda Stubbs) *witb ldr: rdn 2f out: kpt on: received slt bump fr wnr fnl 75yds: jst hld* **9/2**[2]

3 *1 3/4* **Another Claret** 2-9-3 0.. BarryMcHugh 8 70+
(Richard Fahey) *hld up in midfield: pushed along over 2f out: hdwy to chse ldng pair over 1f out: kpt on* **16/1**

0 **4** *1 1/2* **Navajo Nights**[63] [3401] 2-9-3 0.. TomEaves 1 65+
(Bryan Smart) *racd keenly: prom: rdn over 2f out: one pce in 4th fnl f* **16/1**

00 **5** *3 3/4* **Kat Moon**[7] [5339] 2-8-7 0.. AdamCarter(5) 7 48
(Tim Easterby) *chsd ldrs: rdn over 2f out: grad wknd over 1f out* **25/1**

00 **6** *nk* **Lady Niramax**[40] [4132] 2-8-12 0.. AndrewMullen 9 47
(David Nicholls) *chsd ldrs: rdn over 2f out: grad wknd over 1f out* **66/1**

50 **7** *1 1/4* **Reggie Bond**[8] [5311] 2-9-3 0.. PaddyAspell 12 48
(Geoffrey Oldroyd) *dwlt: hld up: pushed along 1/2-way: minor late hdwy: nvr threatened* **40/1**

3006 **8** *1/2* **Strong Conviction**[11] [5213] 2-9-3 75.............................. SamHitchcott 4 47
(Mick Channon) *in tch: rdn over 2f out: wknd over 1f out* **11/1**

0 **9** *2* **Agripin (IRE)**[21] [4825] 2-9-3 0... TedDurcan 10 40
(David Barron) *hld up: pushed along 1/2-way: nvr threatened* **7/1**[3]

10 *1 1/2* **Don Juan** 2-9-3 0.. DanielTudhope 13 36
(Eric Alston) *hld up: pushed along over 2f out: n.d* **33/1**

11 *3/4* **Red Charmer (IRE)** 2-9-3 0.. PaulMulrennan 6 33
(Ann Duffield) *hld up: a towards rr* **12/1**

5 **12** *6* **Darkside**[22] [4778] 2-9-3 0..(b) DavidNolan 2 14
(Michael Easterby) *dwlt: hld up: pushed along over 2f out: btn whn bmpd over 1f out* **66/1**

13 *23* **Highway United (IRE)** 2-8-12 0.................................... MichaelO'Connell 5
(John Weymes) *dwlt: hld up: bhd fr 1/2-way* **100/1**

1m 12.85s (1.05) **Going Correction** +0.175s/f (Good) **13** Ran SP% **119.3**
Speed ratings (Par 94): **100,99,97,95,90 90,88,87,85,83 82,74,43**
toteswingers: 1&2 £3.50, 1&3 £4.80, 2&3 £9.00 CSF £5.44 TOTE £2.10: £1.30, £1.10, £4.60; EX 8.60.
Owner Newtown Anner Stud Farm Ltd **Bred** A F O'Callaghan **Trained** Newmarket, Suffolk
■ Stewards' Enquiry : P J McDonald one-day ban: careless riding (9 Sep)

FOCUS
A fair median auction juvenile maiden. The winning time was over three seconds slower than standard and the ground was changed to Good from good to firm after this contest. The winner did not quite need to match his Haydock form.

NOTEBOOK
Seven Of Clubs(IRE), along with the runner-up, held the strongest form claims coming into this contest and they duly fought this one out between them from fully 2f from home. He got up by a nose in a rousing photo-finish but had to survive a stewards' inquiry after brushing the runner-up about 75 yards from the line. He was a £60,000 purchase in April and looks a fair sprint handicapper in the making. (op Evens tchd 10-11 and 5-4 in a place)
Bogsnog(IRE) lost little caste in defeat and looks capable of winning a similar contest. He is another fair sprint handicapper for the future in any case. (tchd 5-1)
Another Claret produced an encouraging debut display in third. He looks one to note for a similar contest over 6f/7f in the weeks ahead. (op 18-1)
Navajo Nights, returning from a two-month break since a poor 7f debut here on soft ground in June and this was a much better effort. He still looked inexperienced by running away to his left up the centre of the track. He will be of more interest once qualified for nursery handicaps. (op 20-1)
Red Charmer(IRE) gained positive paddock reports on debut and has a taking sprint pedigree. He attracted each-way support but failed to get seriously involved. (op 16-1)

5587 MARKET CROSS JEWELLERS NOVICE MEDIAN AUCTION STKS 7f
6:30 (6:31) (Class 5) 2-Y-O **£2,587** (£770; £384) **Stalls** Centre

Form RPR
01 **1** **No Jet Lag (USA)**[26] [4646] 2-9-1 85.................................... TedDurcan 2 94+
(David Lanigan) *trckd ldr in 2nd: pushed along to ld appr fnl f: sn clr: eased fnl 50yds: impressive* **4/9**[1]

212 **2** *5* **Red Joker (IRE)**[38] [4206] 2-9-1 79.................................. RobertWinston 1 78
(Alan Swinbank) *led: rdn whn hdd appr fnl f: sn no ch w wnr* **3/1**[2]

13 **3** *2 1/2* **Silent Footsteps (IRE)**[38] [4206] 2-9-1 81.......................... TomEaves 3 72
(Michael Dods) *hld up in 3rd: rdn 2f out: sn no imp* **11/2**[3]

1m 29.78s (5.28) **Going Correction** +0.175s/f (Good) **3** Ran SP% **109.6**
Speed ratings (Par 94): **76,70,67**
CSF £2.17 TOTE £1.30; EX 2.10.
Owner Iraj Parvizi **Bred** Greenwood Lodge Farm Inc **Trained** Upper Lambourn, Berks

FOCUS
A decent small-field median auction novice stakes for juveniles, and the useful winner impressed. The gallop was modest until halfway.

NOTEBOOK
No Jet Lag(USA) finished a never-nearer seventh of 18 in a hot Newmarket maiden over 7f on soft ground the previous month and duly won his maiden over 7f at Lingfield on Polytrack about a fortnight later. He arrived with a BHA rating of 85 and looked hard to beat on the book on these favourable terms. He made light work of this opposition, quickening clear from the 1f marker, and is clearly a nice prospect. He is entered in the Group 1 Dewhurst Stakes and Racing Post Trophy in October. He should appreciate a step up to 1m at that stage, so the Racing Post Trophy may be the way to go. (op 1-2 tchd 4-7)
Red Joker(IRE) attempted to dictate off a modest early gallop and upped the tempo about 3f out. He had no response to the winner from 1f out. He may appreciate a return to 6f in nursery handicaps going forward. (tchd 11-4 and 10-3)
Silent Footsteps(IRE) has gone the wrong way since winning over 6f on soft ground at Newcastle on debut in June. He is best watched until regaining some sparkle. (tchd 9-2)

5588 JOHN SMITH'S REDCAR STRAIGHT-MILE CHAMPIONSHIP (QUALIFIER) (H'CAP) 1m
7:00 (7:01) (Class 4) (0-80,79) 3-Y-O+ **£4,398** (£1,309; £654; £327) **Stalls** Centre

Form RPR
2150 **1** **Ingleby Exceed (IRE)**[14] [5111] 4-9-12 **79**.................. DanielTudhope 10 86
(David O'Meara) *trckd ldrs: rdn to ld wl over 1f out: drvn appr fnl f: kpt on* **11/1**

6524 **2** *1/2* **Main Beach**[7] [5338] 5-9-5 **72**...(p) TedDurcan 1 78
(Paul Midgley) *wnt lft s: hld up in rr: rdn over 2f out: hdwy on outer over 1f out: kpt on wl ins fnl f* **12/1**

3320 **3** *shd* **Broctune Papa Gio**[14] [5111] 5-8-11 **67**...................... DeclanCannon(3) 8 73
(Keith Reveley) *in tch: rdn over 2f out: kpt on fnl f* **9/1**

0000 **4** *hd* **Imperator Augustus (IRE)**[15] [5057] 4-9-8 **75**............. DuranFentiman 4 80
(Patrick Holmes) *trckd ldrs: rdn over 2f out: kpt on* **33/1**

3123 **5** *nk* **Hakuna Matata**[14] [5111] 5-9-6 **73**.......................................(p) TomEaves 2 77
(Michael Dods) *hld up in midfield: rdn over 2f out: hdwy over 1f out: kpt on* **4/1**[2]

6000 **6** *1/2* **Dhaular Dhar (IRE)**[11] [5186] 10-9-5 **72**................................ GrahamLee 3 75+
(Jim Goldie) *hld up: pushed along whn n.m.r over 1f out: swtchd to stands' rail appr fnl f: kpt on: nrst fin* **25/1**

3400 **7** *1 1/4* **Dolphin Rock**[19] [4889] 5-9-1 **71**.. PaulPickard(3) 6 71
(Brian Ellison) *led narrowly: rdn whn hdd wl over 1f out: no ex ins fnl f* **7/2**[1]

1232 **8** *1 1/2* **King Pin**[1] [5547] 7-8-11 **64**..(p) BarryMcHugh 11 61
(Tracy Waggott) *hld up in midfield: hdwy to chse ldrs over 1f out: wknd ins fnl f* **15/2**

4000 **9** *1/2* **Aquarian Spirit**[14] [5111] 5-9-4 **71**.. DavidNolan 14 67
(Richard Fahey) *trckd ldrs: pushed along over 3f out: sn outpcd and lost pl: no threat after* **14/1**

2150 **10** *1/2* **Legendary**[28] [4600] 3-9-6 **79**.. LukeMorris 15 74
(Ed Vaughan) *midfield: rdn over 3f out: wknd over 1f out* **13/2**[3]

0000 **11** *1/2* **Little Jimmy Odsox (IRE)**[14] [5110] 4-9-3 **70**..................(p) DavidAllan 5 64
(Tim Easterby) *w ldr: rdn over 2f out: wknd appr fnl f* **16/1**

0000 **12** *1/2* **Music Festival (USA)**[7] [5338] 5-8-7 **60** oh2....................... KellyHarrison 9 52
(Jim Goldie) *midfield: rdn 2f out: sn wknd* **66/1**

0000 **13** *9* **Fighter Boy (IRE)**[14] [5085] 5-9-3 **70**............................... PaulMulrennan 7 42
(Michael Easterby) *slowly away: hld up: a towards rr* **14/1**

1m 38.21s (0.21) **Going Correction** +0.175s/f (Good)
WFA 3 from 4yo+ 6lb **13** Ran SP% **120.8**
Speed ratings (Par 105): **105,104,104,104,103 103,102,100,100,99 99,98,89**
toteswingers 1&2 £14.40, 2&3 £19.80, 1&3 £16.20 CSF £136.06 CT £1295.77 TOTE £15.90: £4.40, £4.50, £4.00; EX 193.10.
Owner Dave Scott **Bred** Dave Scott **Trained** Nawton, N Yorks
■ Stewards' Enquiry : Daniel Tudhope trainer's representative's said regarding the apparen improvement of form that the filly was better suited by the slower ground.

FOCUS
A fair handicap for 3-y-os and up. They went a decent gallop and produced the best comparative winning time on the card. Small personal bests from the first three.

5589 JANICE BAXTER IS 60 TODAY H'CAP — 1m 6f 19y
7:30 (7:30) (Class 6) (0-65,63) 3-Y-O — **£1,940** (£577; £288; £144) **Stalls** Low

Form — RPR
-503 **1** — **Sweet Fairnando**[14] 5115 3-8-11 **53**................................(b[1]) DavidAllan 2 — 64
(Tim Easterby) *midfield: pushed along and hdwy 4f out: led 3f out: sn rdn: kpt on wl* **11/2**[3]
1610 **2** *2 1/4* **Vexillum (IRE)**[9] 5280 3-9-6 **62**.......................... SamHitchcott 1 — 69
(Mick Channon) *t.k.h early: hld up: hdwy 4f out: rdn to chse wnr 2f out: kpt on but a hld* **8/1**
450 **3** *1* **Asteroid Belt (IRE)**[17] 4955 3-8-12 **54**.......................... PJMcDonald 3 — 60
(Chris Grant) *hld up: pushed along and hdwy over 3f out: angled to outer over 2f out: sn rdn: styd on* **8/1**
0-24 **4** *7* **Lady Mandy**[129] 1448 3-8-9 **51** ow1.......................... StevieDonohoe 4 — 47
(Ian Williams) *trckd ldrs: rdn over 3f out: wknd ins fnl f* **11/2**[3]
5006 **5** *6* **Istan Star (USA)**[8] 5330 3-8-3 **45**..........................(v) LukeMorris 5 — 33
(Julie Camacho) *led: hdd 4f out: sn rdn and one pce: wknd fnl f* **16/1**
6064 **6** *4* **Roughlyn**[5] 5408 3-8-3 **45**..........................(p) AndrewMullen 9 — 27
(Lisa Williamson) *hld up in midfield: rdn 4f out: nvr threatened* **14/1**
5405 **7** *1 1/2* **Captain Baldwin**[11] 5187 3-8-3 **45**..........................(v) DuranFentiman 6 — 25
(Jim Goldie) *prom: led narrowly 4f out: rdn whn hdd 3f out: wknd over 1f out* **28/1**
2414 **8** *6* **Scarlet Prince**[14] 5115 3-9-7 **63**.......................... BarryMcHugh 10 — 35
(Tony Coyle) *hld up: pushed along over 5f out: rdn over 3f out: sn btn* **5/1**[2]
6522 **9** *3* **Little Red Minx (IRE)**[14] 5114 3-8-12 **54**.......................... DanielTudhope 8 — 22
(David O'Meara) *in tch: rdn over 3f out: sn wknd* **9/2**[1]
0405 **10** *1* **Baileys Over Ice**[21] 4826 3-8-10 **52**.......................... GrahamLee 11 — 18
(James Given) *trckd ldrs: rdn over 3f out: sn wknd* **15/2**
0600 **11** *46* **Medecis Mountain**[14] 5113 3-8-0 **45**..........................(p) JulieBurke[(3)] 7
(John Wainwright) *midfield: wknd over 4f out: sn bhd* **100/1**
-000 **12** *dist* **Royal Gig**[8] 5330 3-7-12 **45**..........................[1] KatiaScallan[(5)] 12
(Tim Etherington) *trckd ldrs: lost pl 8f out: t.o fnl 6f* **100/1**

3m 4.27s (-0.43) **Going Correction** -0.075s/f (Good) — **12** Ran SP% **117.6**
Speed ratings (Par 98): **98,96,96,92,88 86,85,82,80,79 53,**
toteswingers 1&2 £13.20, 2&3 £5.30, 1&3 £7.40 CSF £48.40 CT £352.67 TOTE £5.50: £2.80, £3.50, £3.20; EX 43.80.
Owner Oakhill Stud **Bred** Oakhill Stud **Trained** Great Habton, N Yorks

FOCUS
A modest staying handicap for 3-y-os. The first three were clear and the form is rated around the runner-up.
Little Red Minx(IRE) Official explanation: trainer could offer no explanation for the poor performance shown
Royal Gig Official explanation: jokcye said that the filly hung left handed throughout

5590 FOLLOW REDCARRACING ON FACEBOOK & TWITTER H'CAP — 6f
8:00 (8:02) (Class 6) (0-55,55) 3-Y-O+ — **£2,045** (£603; £302) **Stalls** Centre

Form — RPR
-020 **1** — **Ingleby Angel (IRE)**[35] 4348 3-8-12 **51**.......................... DanielTudhope 11 — 62
(David O'Meara) *hld up in tch: pushed along over 2f out: gd hdwy over 1f out: drvn appr fnl f: r.o wl: led fnl 100yds* **7/1**[3]
0604 **2** *1 3/4* **Scarlet Rocks (IRE)**[16] 5013 4-9-5 **55**.......................... DavidAllan 8 — 60
(Ron Barr) *chsd ldrs: rdn over 2f out: led jst ins fnl f: hdd fnl 100yds: kpt on* **14/1**
5650 **3** *nk* **John Coffey (IRE)**[35] 4348 3-9-0 **53**.......................... AdrianNicholls 14 — 57+
(David Nicholls) *hld up: hdwy 1/2-way: sn in tch: rdn over 1f out: ev ch jst ins fnl f: kpt on* **20/1**
4304 **4** *3* **Red Shadow**[16] 5014 3-8-11 **53**.......................... DaleSwift[(3)] 20 — 48
(Alan Brown) *midfield: pushed along 1/2-way: hdwy over 1f out: kpt on fnl f* **14/1**
0505 **5** *nk* **Jebel Tara**[11] 5185 7-9-0 **50**..........................(bt) KellyHarrison 16 — 44
(Ian Semple) *prom: rdn over 2f out: wandered u.p over 1f out: no ex ins fnl f* **14/1**
0625 **6** *nk* **Thrust Control (IRE)**[1] 5543 5-9-0 **50**..........................(p) MichaelO'Connell 3 — 43
(Tracy Waggott) *chsd ldr: rdn over 2f out: no ex ins fnl f* **5/1**[2]
1205 **7** *hd* **Piste**[1] 5542 6-9-5 **55**..........................(e) PaulMulrennan 15 — 47
(Tina Jackson) *chsd ldr: rdn to ld over 1f out: hdd jst ins fnl f: wknd* **12/1**
2306 **8** *3 1/2* **Dotty Darroch**[14] 5082 4-9-3 **53**.......................... RobertWinston 9 — 34
(Robin Bastiman) *midfield: pushed along 1/2-way: sn no imp* **12/1**
4004 **9** *3/4* **Maggie Mey (IRE)**[8] 5317 4-9-1 **51**.......................... DuranFentiman 17 — 30
(Lawrence Mullaney) *awkward s: hld up: rdn over 2f out: nvr threatened* **12/1**
4-00 **10** *nk* **Jaldarshaan (IRE)**[162] 927 5-9-3 **53**.......................... BarryMcHugh 7 — 31
(Colin Teague) *s.i.s: hld up: rdn over 2f out: nvr threatened* **40/1**
5034 **11** *3/4* **Arrow Lake (FR)**[11] 5215 3-9-2 **55**.......................... LukeMorris 12 — 30
(Noel Quinlan) *midfield: rdn over 2f out: wknd over 1f out* **7/1**[3]
3136 **12** *7* **Hab Reeh**[67] 3256 4-9-2 **52**..........................(b) PJMcDonald 5
(Ruth Carr) *led: rdn whn hdd over 1f out: wknd* **7/2**[1]
2000 **13** *3/4* **Whiteoak Lady (IRE)**[11] 5203 7-8-10 **53**..........................(p) GemmaTutty[(7)] 4
(Karen Tutty) *hld up: pushed along 1/2-way: a towards rr* **33/1**
5604 **14** *3/4* **Media Jury**[6] 5389 5-8-9 **50**..........................(v) AdamCarter[(5)] 10
(John Wainwright) *midfield: rdn 1/2-way: sn wknd* **20/1**
340 **15** *2* **Green Warrior**[24] 4717 4-8-10 **49**..........................(be) DeclanCannon[(3)] 18
(Richard Guest) *chsd ldr: wknd 2f out* **33/1**
3000 **16** *13* **Cheyenne Red (IRE)**[108] 1987 6-8-13 **49**.......................... TomEaves 1
(Michael Herrington) *wnt lft s: hld up: a in rr* **40/1**

1m 12.64s (0.84) **Going Correction** +0.175s/f (Good)
WFA 3 from 4yo+ 3lb — **16** Ran SP% **127.3**
Speed ratings (Par 101): **101,98,98,94,93 93,93,88,87,87 86,76,75,74,72 54**
toteswingers 1&2 £32.10, 2&3 £120.50, 1&3 £9.90 CSF £97.50 CT £1900.99 TOTE £7.40: £2.40, £4.10, £2.80, £3.50; EX 134.20.
Owner Dave Scott **Bred** Dave Scott **Trained** Nawton, N Yorks

FOCUS
A moderate sprint handicap for 3-y-os and up. The form is not rated too positively, but is arguably worth a bit more at face value.
Maggie Mey(IRE) Official explanation: jockey said that the filly slipped leaving the stalls
Cheyenne Red(IRE) Official explanation: jockey said that the gelding slipped leaving the stalls
T/Plt: £1153.60 to a £1 stake. Pool of £43775.69 -27.70 winning tickets. T/Qpdt: £89.50 to a £1 stake. Pool of £4793.42 - 39.30 winning tickets. AS

[5417]WINDSOR (R-H)
Saturday, August 25

OFFICIAL GOING: Good (good to firm in places) changing to soft after race 1 (5.15)
Wind: Moderate behind Weather: Cloudy, showers

5591 SPORTINGLIFE.COM NOVICE MEDIAN AUCTION STKS — 6f
5:15 (5:17) (Class 5) 2-Y-O — **£2,911** (£866) **Stalls** Low

Form — RPR
2612 **1** — **Ask Dad**[9] 5270 2-9-5 97.......................... PatDobbs 1 — 95
(Richard Hannon) *trckd ldr: chal 2f out: led over 1f out: sn clr: easily* **2/7**[1]
431 **2** *11* **Dance With Dragons (IRE)**[21] 4792 2-9-2 78.......................... TomQueally 2 — 68
(Paul Cole) *led: jnd 2f out: hdd over 1f out: sn no ch w wnr* **11/4**[2]

1m 14.33s (1.33) **Going Correction** 0.0s/f (Good) — **2** Ran SP% **104.4**
Speed ratings (Par 94): **91,76**
TOTE £1.30.
Owner Andrew Tinkler **Bred** Wallace Holmes & Partners **Trained** East Everleigh, Wilts

FOCUS
Inner of straight dolled out 10yds at 6f and 2yds at winning post. Top bend dolled out 2yds from normal configuration adding 11yds to races beyond a mile. This was a foregone conclusion on official figures, and so it proved. The winner is given a token rating to form.

NOTEBOOK
Ask Dad was rated 19lb superior to his rival, and it was predictably no contest. Effective from 5f-7f, he is a smart juvenile. (op 2-5 tchd 1-4)
Dance With Dragons(IRE), successful at 7f, had little chance with the classy winner on these terms, but he gave him a good race for 5f and should win more races. (op 2-1 tchd 3-1)

5592 TOTEPOOL MOBILE TEXT TOTE TO 89660 FILLIES' H'CAP — 1m 67y
5:45 (5:45) (Class 5) (0-75,76) 3-Y-O+ — **£2,911** (£866; £432; £216) **Stalls** Low

Form — RPR
-041 **1** — **Classic Falcon (IRE)**[14] 5095 3-8-10 **65**.......................... LiamJones 8 — 72
(William Haggas) *chsd ldrs: styd stands' side and chal 2f out tl led wl over 1f out: drvn out* **6/1**[3]
2062 **2** *3/4* **Choral Festival**[5] 5417 6-9-12 **75**.......................... KieranO'Neill 9 — 81
(John Bridger) *chsd ldrs: styd stands' side: chal over 2f out tl wl over 1f out: kpt on fnl f: nt gng pce of wnr: fin 2nd in gp* **4/1**[2]
4460 **3** *3/4* **Bold Ring**[19] 4872 6-8-0 **56** oh1.......................... JoeyHaynes[(7)] 7 — 60
(Eric Wheeler) *chsd ldrs: styd stands' side: kpt on fnl f but nt quite gng pce of ldng duo: fin 3rd in gp* **33/1**
446 **4** *1 1/4* **Emmuska**[30] 4505 3-9-1 **70**.......................... PatDobbs 4 — 70
(Richard Hannon) *sn led: styd stands' side: hrd pressed fr over 2f out: hdd wl over 1f out: wknd fnl 120yds: fin 4th in gp* **13/2**
632 **5** *1 1/4* **Feelthedifference**[16] 5019 3-9-1 **70**.......................... TomQueally 2 — 68
(Sir Henry Cecil) *s.i.s: in rr and wnt far side over 3f out: nvr gng pce of stands' side bunch fr over 2f out: styd on to hd far side gp fnl 120yds but nvr any ch* **9/4**[1]
6452 **6** *shd* **Larkrise Star**[15] 5063 5-8-13 **65**.......................... PatrickHills[(3)] 10 — 63
(Dean Ivory) *in tch: hdwy to chse ldrs and wnt far side over 3f out: no ch w stands' side bunch fr over 2f out: styd on to fin wl hld 2nd in gp fnl 120yds* **8/1**
20 **7** *1 3/4* **Berwin (IRE)**[78] 2866 3-9-5 **74**.......................... DarryllHolland 5 — 67
(Sylvester Kirk) *chsd ldrs: wnt to far side 4f out and led that gp but no ch w stands' side bunch over 2f out: dropped to wl hld 3rd in gp fnl 120yds* **20/1**
4235 **8** *1 1/2* **Abigails Angel**[13] 5120 5-9-6 **72**.......................... MarkCoumbe[(3)] 1 — 63
(Brett Johnson) *chsd ldrs: wnt far side over 3f out: no ch w stands' side bunch over 2f out: wknd over 1f out and fin 4th in gp* **11/1**
6602 **9** *3/4* **Push Me (IRE)**[16] 5008 5-9-9 **72**.......................... MartinLane 3 — 61
(Jamie Poulton) *chsd ldrs: racd far side over 3f out: sn rdn: wknd fr 2f out: fin 5th in gp* **10/1**

1m 45.49s (0.79) **Going Correction** 0.0s/f (Good)
WFA 3 from 5yo+ 6lb — **9** Ran SP% **114.6**
Speed ratings (Par 100): **96,95,94,93,92 91,90,88,87**
toteswingers 1&2 £4.40, 2&3 £40.10, 1&3 £22.30 CSF £29.99 CT £728.06 TOTE £5.70: £1.90, £1.80, £7.30; EX 23.50 Trifecta £182.40 Part won. Pool of £246.50 - 0.63 winning units..
Owner Sheikh Hamdan Bin Maktoum Al Maktoum **Bred** Robert Berns **Trained** Newmarket, Suffolk

FOCUS
Prompted by the change in going to soft following a deluge during the first race, the runners split into two groups in the home straight. However, the stands' side quartet, who took the obvious route, filled the first four places, and the other five appeared to have been at a disadvantage. The winner is rated close to her latest Lingfield form.
Larkrise Star Official explanation: jockey said that the mare was unsuited by the soft ground
Berwin(IRE) Official explanation: jockey said that the filly was unsuited by the soft ground

5593 TOTEPOOL AUGUST STKS (LISTED RACE) — 1m 3f 135y
6:15 (6:15) (Class 1) 3-Y-O+ — **£18,714** (£7,095; £3,550; £1,768; £887) **Stalls** Centre

Form — RPR
1321 **1** — **Cameron Highland (IRE)**[23] 4725 3-8-7 106 ow1.......................... NeilCallan 3 — 114
(Roger Varian) *mde all: drvn and styd on strly fr 2f out: clr over 1f out: unchal* **9/4**[2]
1662 **2** *4 1/2* **Goldoni (IRE)**[37] 4261 3-8-6 99.......................... DavidProbert 2 — 105
(Andrew Balding) *disp 2nd to 6f out: styd cl 3rd tl drvn to take 2nd over 1f out: kpt on but nvr any ch w wnr* **3/1**[3]
3024 **3** *3* **Songcraft (IRE)**[22] 4759 4-9-2 110.......................... SilvestreDeSousa 5 — 100
(Saeed Bin Suroor) *disp 2nd tl chsd wnr 6f out: rdn and no imp over 2f out lost 2nd over 1f out and sn btn* **7/4**[1]
2-20 **4** *7* **Roxy Flyer (IRE)**[21] 4800 5-8-11 95.......................... PatDobbs 4 — 83
(Amanda Perrett) *s.i.s towards rr: rdn 3f out: sn wknd* **9/1**
1010 **5** *6* **Vasily**[21] 4800 4-9-2 92.......................... TomQueally 1 — 78
(Robert Eddery) *towards rr but in tch: rdn: hung lft and btn over 3f out* **10/1**

2m 27.53s (-1.97) **Going Correction** 0.0s/f (Good)
WFA 3 from 4yo+ 10lb — **5** Ran SP% **111.2**
Speed ratings (Par 111): **106,103,101,96,92**
CSF £9.44 TOTE £3.10: £1.80, £1.50; EX 8.80.
Owner H R H Sultan Ahmad Shah **Bred** Epona Bloodstock Ltd **Trained** Newmarket, Suffolk

FOCUS
A race worthy of its Listed level despite the small field, but the pace was ordinary. The runner-up set the standard, with the favourite disappointing and the winner up 6lb.

NOTEBOOK
Cameron Highland(IRE), a progressive colt, had no problem with the longer trip. He looks capable of making the step in Group 3 company at any distance from 1m2f to 1m4f. (op 2-1)

Goldoni(IRE) was simply beaten by a slightly better opponent, but he is a decent horse in his own right. Rated 99, and therefore not the easiest to place, he deserves to win more races if connections can find the right opportunities. (op 7-2 tchd 11-4)
Songcraft(IRE) has been at least the equal of the winner at 1m2f, but hasn't been convincing in two attempts beyond 1m3f. (op 15-8)
Roxy Flyer(IRE) has some fine form to her name, but she had a bit to find at the weights against these classy opponents. The challenge for connections will be that she is likely to have a tough task in handicaps too. (op 10-1 tchd 11-1 and 17-2)
Vasily, on difficult terms here, would have a better chance in high-class handicaps. (op 17-2 tchd 11-1)

5594 TOTEPOOL.COM WINTER HILL STKS (GROUP 3) 1m 2f 7y
6:45 (6:45) (Class 1) 3-Y-O+

£31,190 (£11,825; £5,918; £2,948; £1,479; £742) **Stalls** Centre

Form				RPR
5305	**1**		**Lay Time**[21] 4801 4-8-11 109 .... JimmyFortune 1 (Andrew Balding) *chsd ldrs: wnt 2nd over 2f out: sn chalng: slt ld 1f out: sn hrd drvn: hld on all out* **4/1**[2]	110
0-35	**2**	nse	**Primevere (IRE)**[84] 2711 4-8-11 104 .... HayleyTurner 5 (Roger Charlton) *led: rdn and jnd ins fnl 2f: narrowly hdd 1f out: styd chalng u.p and rallied in clsng stages: jst failed* **9/1**	110
1201	**3**	1	**Grandeur (IRE)**[23] 4735 3-8-6 106 .... WilliamBuick 2 (Jeremy Noseda) *in tch: pushed along 2f out: hdwy ins fnl f to take 3rd fnl 120yds but no imp on ldng duo* **11/4**[1]	111+
350	**4**	1 1/4	**Tales Of Grimm (USA)**[22] 4760 3-8-6 99 .... KierenFallon 3 (Sir Michael Stoute) *in rr but in tch: hdwy 3f out: pressed ldrs and rdn in 3rd fr 2f out: wknd into 4th fnl 120yds* **4/1**[2]	108
-000	**5**	7	**Rio De La Plata (USA)**[147] 1148 7-9-0 118 .... SilvestreDeSousa 7 (Saeed Bin Suroor) *sn chsng ldr: rdn 3f out: wknd qckly over 1f out* **4/1**[2]	94
3201	**6**	1/2	**Coupe De Ville (IRE)**[15] 5064 3-8-7 112 ow1 .... PatDobbs 6 (Richard Hannon) *chsd ldrs tl rdn and btn 2f out* **5/1**[3]	94

2m 7.83s (-0.87) **Going Correction** 0.0s/f (Good)
WFA 3 from 4yo+ 8lb **6** Ran SP% **113.3**
Speed ratings (Par 113): **103,102,102,101,95 95**
toteswingers 1&2 £7.20, 2&3 £11.00, 1&3 £1.50 CSF £37.63 TOTE £4.90: £2.40, £4.80; EX 51.40.
Owner R Barnett **Bred** W And R Barnett Ltd **Trained** Kingsclere, Hants

FOCUS
No more than a fair field for a Group 3. It was run at a medium tempo and the first two were always well placed. The winner set the standard.

NOTEBOOK
Lay Time, who has been running well in Group 1 and 2 company, found these opponents more suitable but only just made it on ground that was softer than ideal. Effective from 1m to 1m2f, she may now go in search of valuable international prizes. (op 7-2 tchd 10-3 and 9-2)
Primevere(IRE) stays a bit further than this, and her stamina nearly snatched the race near the finish. She is at home in Group 3 races despite just missing out in three attempts this season (op 8-1)
Grandeur(IRE) was worth a crack at this company following some smart performances in good handicaps, and he wasn't far away. Still improving, he is worth keeping to Pattern company and ran as if likely to stay further. (tchd 3-1)
Tales Of Grimm(USA), good enough to win a Listed race, will need to find more to score at this higher level. However, he did well to get into contention after being slightly left behind turning for home and is worth another try. (op 9-2 tchd 5-1)
Rio De La Plata(USA) normally contests stronger races than this. He was expected to need this race following a break, but after four below-par efforts this year he needs to demonstrate that he is as good as he was.
Coupe De Ville(IRE) had a good chance on official figures, but he has yet to prove that he can cut it in Group 3 company. (op 7-1)

5595 RACING POST FORM WITH TOTEPOOL MOBILE H'CAP 1m 67y
7:15 (7:15) (Class 4) (0-85,85) 3-Y-O+ **£5,175** (£1,540; £769; £384) **Stalls** Low

Form				RPR
1225	**1**		**Fire Ship**[35] 4319 3-9-5 **84** .... NeilCallan 6 (William Knight) *trckd ldrs: disp 2nd 3f out tl led appr fnl 2f: sn drvn: qckd wl clr ins fnl f: easily* **15/8**[1]	100
6006	**2**	8	**Roayh (USA)**[29] 4529 4-9-11 **84** .... (p) SilvestreDeSousa 4 (Saeed Bin Suroor) *chsd ldrs: rdn 3f out: n.m.r and edgd lft 2f out: styd on u.p to take 2nd over 1f out but nvr any ch w easy wnr* **7/2**[3]	83
-000	**3**	1 1/4	**Moon Pearl (USA)**[29] 4557 3-9-6 **85** .... (b) MartinLane 9 (Ralph Beckett) *s.i.s: in rr: rdn and styd on fr 3f out: disp 2nd 2f out but nvr any ch w easy wnr: wknd and wl hld 3rd ins fnl f* **10/1**	80
1252	**4**	2 1/4	**Rocky Reef**[29] 4534 3-8-11 **76** ow1 .... (v) JimmyFortune 2 (Andrew Balding) *led: rdn 3f out and sn jnd: hdd appr fnl 2f: sn no ch w easy wnr: wknd appr fnl f* **10/3**[2]	66
0000	**5**	3 1/2	**Shifting Star (IRE)**[21] 4799 7-9-12 **85** .... (t) KieranO'Neill 7 (John Bridger) *chsd ldrs: rdn over 3f out: sn btn* **25/1**	68
0100	**6**	1 3/4	**Franco Is My Name**[16] 5007 6-9-4 **77** .... (p) DaneO'Neill 5 (Peter Hedger) *s.i.s: rdn 3f out: a in rr* **14/1**	55
1010	**7**	1 1/2	**Nazreef**[126] 1510 5-9-12 **85** .... (vt) DarryllHolland 10 (Hughie Morrison) *chsd ldr tl rdn 3f out: wknd qckly 2f out* **15/2**	60

1m 43.51s (-1.19) **Going Correction** 0.0s/f (Good)
WFA 3 from 4yo+ 6lb **7** Ran SP% **111.5**
Speed ratings (Par 105): **105,97,95,93,90 88,86**
toteswingers 1&2 £2.60, 2&3 £7.70, 1&3 £3.10 CSF £8.10 CT £47.12 TOTE £2.80: £1.80, £2.10; EX 9.70 Trifecta £269.80 Pool: £437.61 - 1.20 winning units..
Owner IGP Partnership & P Winkworth **Bred** Yorton Farm **Trained** Patching, W Sussex

FOCUS
A decent race, run at a good pace in the conditions, and won by the most progressive runner. There wasn't much depth to the race.

5596 CHAIN OF HOPE RACE FOR JAMAICA H'CAP 1m 3f 135y
7:45 (7:45) (Class 5) (0-70,74) 3-Y-O+ **£2,911** (£866; £432; £216) **Stalls** Centre

Form				RPR
031-	**1**		**Bright Abbey**[346] 6052 4-9-10 **69** .... (v) CPGeoghegan(3) 10 (Philip Hobbs) *chsd ldrs: wnt 2nd 6f out: led wl over 2f out: rdn and narrowly hdd 1f out: styd chalng and rallied wl to ld again last stride* **4/1**[3]	80
5520	**2**	nse	**Quixote**[22] 4776 3-9-0 **66** .... (t) TomQueally 4 (Clive Brittain) *in rr: hdwy over 3f out to press ldrs 2f out: led 1f out: styd hrd pressed tl ct last stride* **11/2**	77
54/3	**3**	6	**Presto Volante (IRE)**[10] 5239 4-9-6 **62** .... HayleyTurner 2 (Amanda Perrett) *in rr: rdn and dropped away 4f out: styd on u.p to take wl-hld 3rd fr 2f out* **11/4**[2]	63
6323	**4**	4 1/2	**Barachiel**[39] 4181 4-9-5 **61** .... WilliamBuick 3 (Luke Dace) *chsd ldrs: rdn and outpcd 3f out: no ch after and plugged on for mod 4th fnl f* **9/4**[1]	54
52-0	**5**	nk	**Langley**[10] 5239 5-9-5 **61** .... (t) DavidProbert 6 (Tim Vaughan) *in tch: hdwy 4f out: chsd ldrs u.p over 2f out: sn wknd* **12/1**	54
/063	**6**	20	**Moose Moran (USA)**[13] 5124 5-9-13 **69** .... (v) KirstyMilczarek 1 (Olivia Maylam) *led: hdd & wknd wl over 2f out* **8/1**	28

2m 31.65s (2.15) **Going Correction** 0.0s/f (Good)
WFA 3 from 4yo+ 10lb **6** Ran SP% **111.6**
Speed ratings (Par 103): **92,91,87,84,84 71**
toteswingers 1&2 £5.40, 2&3 £2.40, 1&3 £2.10 CSF £25.14 CT £67.63 TOTE £4.20: £1.50, £3.20; EX 28.30 Trifecta £159.70 Pool: £345.47 - 1.60 winning units..
Owner Mrs Caren Walsh **Bred** Pendley Farm **Trained** Withycombe, Somerset

FOCUS
More standard fare than previous races on the card, but the relatively unexposed winner has some potential, particularly over jumps. The first pair were clear and the form is rated around the runner-up.
T/Plt: £220.30 to a £1 stake. Pool of £39174.61 -129.76 winning tickets. T/Qpdt: £67.20 to a £1 stake. Pool of £5889.44 - 64.83 winning tickets. ST

5558 YORK (L-H)
Saturday, August 25

OFFICIAL GOING: Good to soft (good in places; 7.1)
Wind: Light, half against Weather: Cloudy with sunny periods

5597 BETFRED CITY OF YORK STKS (LISTED RACE) 7f
2:00 (2:00) (Class 1) 3-Y-O+

£28,355 (£10,750; £5,380; £2,680; £1,345; £675) **Stalls** Low

Form				RPR
2032	**1**		**Gordon Lord Byron (IRE)**[13] 5137 4-9-0 109 .... WilliamBuick 8 (T Hogan, Ire) *trckd ldrs: smooth hdwy over 2f out: swtchd lft and effrt to chse ldr over 1f out: rdn to ld ent fnl f: styd on strly* **5/1**[3]	118
4040	**2**	2 3/4	**Bannock (IRE)**[22] 4761 3-8-9 106 .... SilvestreDeSousa 5 (Mark Johnston) *trckd ldr: cl up 1/2-way: led over 2f out: rdn and jnd over 1f out: hdd ent fnl f: sn drvn and kpt on same pce* **5/1**[3]	109
-010	**3**	3	**Dubawi Sound**[24] 4703 4-9-0 96 .... (t) JamieSpencer 11 (David Brown) *hld up in rr: hdwy wl over 2f out: sn rdn: styd on fnl f* **9/2**[2]	102
3410	**4**	4	**Smarty Socks (IRE)**[22] 4761 8-9-0 97 .... DanielTudhope 9 (David O'Meara) *hld up in rr: hdwy on inner 3f out: rdn to chse ldrs 2f out: sn drvn and one pce* **14/1**	92
3204	**5**	hd	**Doncaster Rover (USA)**[42] 4078 6-9-0 105 .... TonyHamilton 4 (Richard Fahey) *trckd ldrs: effrt over 3f out: sn rdn along and wknd 2f out* **5/1**[3]	91
0-60	**6**	3/4	**Royal Blue Star (IRE)**[72] 3092 4-8-9 95 .... (p) GrahamLee 2 (Mrs John Harrington, Ire) *led: rdn along 3f out: sn hdd & wknd fnl 2f* **25/1**	84
5010	**7**	2	**Eton Forever (IRE)**[35] 4321 5-9-0 109 .... NeilCallan 1 (Roger Varian) *trckd ldng pair: hdwy 3f out: effrt and rdn over 2f out: drvn and wknd wl over 1f out* **11/4**[1]	84
5-66	**8**	10	**Beacon Lodge (IRE)**[105] 2075 7-9-0 112 .... (e[1]) AdrianNicholls 13 (David Nicholls) *hld up towards rr: sme hdwy on outer 1/2-way: sn rdn along and btn* **18/1**	57
-100	**9**	9	**Talwar (IRE)**[66] 3265 3-9-0 100 .... (v[1]) JimmyFortune 3 (Jeremy Noseda) *dwlt: hld up towards rr: effrt over 3f out: sn rdn along and wknd over 2f out* **20/1**	35

1m 24.25s (-1.05) **Going Correction** +0.125s/f (Good)
WFA 3 from 4yo+ 5lb **9** Ran SP% **115.4**
Speed ratings (Par 111): **111,107,104,99,99 98,96,85,74**
toteswingers: 1&2 £4.50, 1&3 £5.70, 2&3 £5.40 CSF £30.18 TOTE £5.10: £1.80, £2.00, £2.40; EX 31.40 Trifecta £159.10 Pool: £1,447.75 - 6.73 winning units..
Owner Morgan J Cahalan **Bred** Roland H Alder **Trained** Nenagh, Co Tipperary

FOCUS
Rail realignment between 1m1f and entrance to home straight reduced distances on Round course by about 27yds. After 3mm of rain overnight and more in the morning, the ground was changed to good to soft, good in places. The jockeys reported it was riding on the soft side of good or "dead". A good, competitive Listed race and an up-to-scratch race for the grade, although not many showed their form.

NOTEBOOK
Gordon Lord Byron(IRE), who has been running well over sprint trips in Ireland on heavy ground, had nevertheless proved his stamina for this distance and beyond in the past. He was always travelling well just behind the leaders and found plenty when asked for his effort. The Ayr Gold Cup, for which he was quoted at around 16-1 afterwards, could be on the agenda, although he has other options. (op 4-1 tchd 11-2 in a place)
Bannock(IRE) has run his best recent races in Listed and Group company and did so again, going on around the quarter-mile pole and galloping on well, although no match for the winner. His three wins have all been on flat tracks. (tchd 9-2)
Dubawi Sound, one of the least experienced in the field, was up in class but was the subject of market support. He was held up before running on well late and, although no match for the principals, he deserves extra credit considering the pace bias that has been evident for most of the meeting. (op 10-1)
Smarty Socks(IRE), hampered on his return from a break at Ascot, had a bit to find on the ratings but goes particularly well over C&D. He did his best, having been held up early, but the overnight rain had probably made the ground softer than ideal. (op 12-1 tchd 11-1)
Doncaster Rover(USA) was attempting to win this race for the second successive year. However, he has been below his best in his last couple of starts and that was again the case here, his first start for a new trainer. (op 11-2)
Royal Blue Star(IRE) had a bit to find on official ratings but ran as well as could have been expected after setting the pace. The search for black type with her continues. (op 20-1)
Eton Forever(IRE) was sent off favourite, having been impressive when winning a Royal Ascot handicap off 103. However, after racing just behind the leaders he found little when put under pressure and was eased late on. he had an excuse though as the representative of Roger Varian reported that the gelding had lost both front shoes. Official explanation: trainer's representative said the gelding had lost both front shoes (op 7-2)
Beacon Lodge(IRE) had struggled for new connections since being bought for 75,000gns last autumn and the 15-week break, during which time he was gelded, and the application of an eyeshield failed to re-ignite him. (op 12-1)

Talwar(IRE) had struggled in Group company since his reappearance success at this level in April, and the drop in class plus the addition of a visor following a break failed to produce a more encouraging effort. (op 16-1)

5598 BETFRED MELROSE STKS (H'CAP) 1m 6f

2:30 (2:33) (Class 2) (0-105,98) 3-Y-O

£43,575 (£13,048; £6,524; £3,262; £1,631; £819) **Stalls** Low

Form RPR

211 **1** **Guarantee**[35] 4346 3-9-4 **95**.. PhillipMakin 14 111+
(William Haggas) *hld up in rr: gd hdwy over 2f out: led jst ins fnl f: edgd lft: styd on strly* **9/1**

121 **2** 3 ½ **Biographer**[23] 4732 3-9-4 **95**.. TedDurcan 6 106
(David Lanigan) *hld up in rr: hdwy 6f out: led and edgd lft over 1f out: hdd and no ex jst ins fnl f* **8/1**[3]

3103 **3** 1 **Cardinal Walter (IRE)**[24] 4700 3-8-9 **86**..................... JamieSpencer 11 96
(David Simcock) *hld up in rr: hdwy on outer over 3f out: edgd lft over 1f out: styd on wl to take 3rd clsng stages* **5/1**[1]

-221 **4** 1 ¼ **Mysterious Man (IRE)**[59] 3484 3-8-6 **83**........................ DavidProbert 7 91+
(Andrew Balding) *prom: chsng ldrs whn n.m.r and swtchd rt over 2f out: upsides and edgd lft 1f out: kpt on same pce* **14/1**

5022 **5** 2 ½ **Gabrial's Star**[18] 4925 3-8-8 **85**.. TomEaves 5 89
(Bryan Smart) *mid-div: drvn over 7f out: styd on fnl 2f* **25/1**

1313 **6** 1 ¾ **Flashman**[21] 4796 3-8-0 **77**... LukeMorris 8 79
(Richard Fahey) *mid-div: drvn over 4f out: kpt on one pce fnl 2f* **11/1**

-232 **7** 3 ½ **Beyond Conceit (IRE)**[56] 3614 3-8-11 **88**.................. RobertWinston 9 85+
(Tom Tate) *trckd ldrs: t.k.h: hmpd over 3f out and over 2f out: swtchd rt over 1f out: kpt on* **20/1**

1325 **8** 3 ¼ **Choisan (IRE)**[18] 4925 3-8-1 **78**.................................. DuranFentiman 17 70
(Tim Easterby) *led tl over 8f out: n.m.r over 2f out: wkng whn hmpd appr fnl f* **50/1**

3116 **9** 1 ½ **Cockney Sparrow**[108] 1973 3-8-3 **83** ow2............ AdamBeschizza(3) 15 73
(Peter Chapple-Hyam) *chsd ldrs: drvn over 3f out: wknd over 1f out* **20/1**

3233 **10** 1 ¼ **Daneking**[10] 5228 3-8-3 **80**.. NickyMackay 16 69
(John Gosden) *trckd ldrs: t.k.h: led over 8f out: clr over 6f out: hdd 2f out: sn hmpd: wknd fnl f* **20/1**

2016 **11** 9 **Gabrial The Great (IRE)**[14] 5089 3-9-1 **92**..................... KierenFallon 18 68
(Michael Bell) *swtchd lft after s: in rr: hdwy 8f out: drvn over 3f out: led briefly and edgd lft 2f out: wkng whn hmpd over 1f out* **12/1**

31-1 **12** nk **Future Security (IRE)**[22] 4755 3-8-7 **84**................. SilvestreDeSousa 1 60
(Saeed Bin Suroor) *hld up in rr: hdwy over 3f out: edgd lft over 2f out: wknd over 1f out* **10/1**

1113 **13** 2 ¾ **Sir Graham Wade (IRE)**[14] 5089 3-9-5 **96**.................... JoeFanning 2 68
(Mark Johnston) *in rr: drvn 4f out: nvr a factor* **6/1**[2]

211 **14** nk **Courtesy Call (IRE)**[18] 4930 3-8-0 **82**......................... DarrenEgan(5) 3 53
(Mark Johnston) *mid-div: drvn 7f out: lost pl over 4f out: sn bhd* **20/1**

1100 **15** 60 **Rule Book (IRE)**[14] 5078 3-8-12 **89**............................... JimmyFortune 10
(Richard Hannon) *chsd ldrs: lost pl 5f out: sn bhd: eased whn t.o: virtually p.u* **33/1**

211 **R** **Monshak (IRE)**[42] 4079 3-8-10 **87**.......................................(v[1]) GrahamLee 4
(Sir Michael Stoute) *ref to r: lft at s* **6/1**[2]

2m 57.44s (-2.76) **Going Correction** -0.025s/f (Good) **16** Ran SP% **125.9**

Speed ratings (Par 106): **106,104,103,102,101 100,98,96,95,94 89,89,87,87,53**

toteswingers: 1&2 £12.50, 1&3 £14.50, 2&3 £12.40 CSF £73.90 CT £413.03 TOTE £9.90: £2.60, £2.50, £1.70, £3.40; EX 79.40 Trifecta £220.80 Pool: £2,635.73 - 8.83 winning units..

Owner Highclere Thoroughbred Racing-Authorized **Bred** Highbury Stud Ltd **Trained** Newmarket, Suffolk

■ Stewards' Enquiry : Robert Winston one-day ban: careless riding (9 Sep)

FOCUS

The rails had been moved in 10 metres from the 1m1f point to the entrance to the home straight, reducing distances of races 1m and over by 27 yards. As one would expect for a contest of this nature, virtually all of these could be given some sort of chance if running up to their best. The gallop seemed decent, but quite a few in rear were pulling quite hard. The time was decent and this looked a strong Melrose. The level is set around the fifth and the race averages.

NOTEBOOK

Guarantee ◆ looked a little free at the back of the field, but came with a really well-judged run around rivals, after being second last turning in, to win going away, while giving the impression he mentally still has progress to make. In landing this, he became the highest-rated winner in the last ten years and is surely a Group horse in the making. Connections indicated afterwards they will aim their colt towards the final Classic if he remains in good heart. (op 7-1)

Biographer, who is entered in the Cesarewitch, had been raised 7lb for his Ffos Las success and was another to make his challenge from a rear-field sit. He basically bumped into a smart and equally unexposed performer at the top of his game. (op 7-1)

Cardinal Walter(IRE) was in last place rounding the final bend and Jamie Spencer was forced to take various routes in the final 3f before getting in the clear. The colt tended to hang in behind the first two once out, and may not be the easiest ride. (op 9-2)

Mysterious Man(IRE) ◆, who holds a Group 3 entry, was forced to sit in a pocket for a while over 2f out, but got a gap and responded for pressure. Making his handicap debut, it was a good effort in best class of race he has contested since his racecourse debut and can come on for this. (op 11-1)

Gabrial's Star, another entered in the Cesarewitch, was niggled along quite early and stayed on through runners in the final stages. He'd appear to need further at this level. (op 28-1 tchd 33-1)

Flashman chased the leaders and plugged on off his low weight. (op 14-1)

Beyond Conceit(IRE) ◆ was keeping on when meeting all sorts of trouble in running. He wouldn't have won but may have run a nice trial for a possible tilt at the Cesarewitch otherwise. (op 22-1 tchd 25-1)

Daneking took a decisive lead before halfway but could not sustain it, and Nicky Mackay reported that the colt ran too free. Official explanation: jockey said that the colt ran too free (tchd 25-1)

Gabrial The Great(IRE) took a strong grip on the outside of the field and unsurprisingly failed to last out. He was beaten when hampered.

Future Security(IRE) raced freely in rear, with those who fought out the finish, but weakened tamely after holding a chance and was eased. Official explanation: jockey said that the colt had no more to give (op 14-1)

Sir Graham Wade(IRE) never got involved for some reason and can't be judged on this performance. (op 15-2)

Monshak(IRE), wearing headgear for the first time, didn't jump off with her rivals and clearly has temperament issues to answer now. (op 8-1)

5599 WEATHERBYS INSURANCE LONSDALE CUP (BRITISH CHAMPIONS SERIES) (GROUP 2) 2m 88y

3:05 (3:05) (Class 1) 3-Y-O+

£79,394 (£30,100; £15,064; £7,504; £3,766; £1,890) **Stalls** Low

Form RPR

-440 **1** **Times Up**[23] 4737 6-9-1 108.. WilliamBuick 6 115
(John Dunlop) *hld up towards rr: hdwy on outer over 3f out: chsd ldrs 2f out: rdn to ld jst ins fnl f: styd on strly* **11/1**

-412 **2** 2 ¼ **High Jinx (IRE)**[42] 4111 4-9-1 101.. GrahamLee 7 112
(James Fanshawe) *trckd ldrs: hdwy on inner wl over 2f out: sn cl up: rdn over 1f out: kpt on wl fnl f: tk 2nd towards fin* **10/1**

-420 **3** ½ **Lost In The Moment (IRE)**[23] 4737 5-9-1 108...(p) SilvestreDeSousa 10 112
(Saeed Bin Suroor) *trckd ldrs: hdwy 4f out: cl up 3f out: led 2f out and sn rdn: drvn and hdd jst ins fnl f: kpt on same pce* **14/1**

2011 **4** 3 ¾ **Cavalryman**[49] 3881 6-9-1 115.. FrankieDettori 5 107
(Saeed Bin Suroor) *in tch on inner: swtchd to outer 1/2-way: hdwy over 3f out: cl up 2f out: sn rdn and ev ch tl drvn: edgd lft and one pce ent fnl f* **4/1**[2]

-116 **5** 2 ¼ **Simenon (IRE)**[23] 4737 5-9-1 107.. JamieSpencer 4 105
(W P Mullins, Ire) *hld up towards rr: stdy hdwy 4f out: trckd ldrs 3f out: effrt and nt clr run 2f out: swtchd rt and nt clr run wl over 1f out: sn rdn and no imp* **12/1**

6542 **6** 1 ½ **Askar Tau (FR)**[23] 4737 7-9-1 111..............................(v) TedDurcan 9 103
(Marcus Tregoning) *hld up in rr: hdwy wl over 2f out: swtchd lft and rdn wl over 1f out: sn no imp* **16/1**

2-42 **7** 1 ½ **Ibicenco (GER)**[86] 2639 4-9-1 110.. KierenFallon 3 101
(Luca Cumani) *trckd ldr: cl up 6f out: led 3f out and sn rdn: hdd 2f out and sn drvn: wknd appr fnl f* **7/1**[3]

1355 **8** 13 **Thimaar (USA)**[27] 4634 4-9-1 107.. TadhgO'Shea 11 85
(John Gosden) *chsd ldrs: hdwy and cl up 4f out: disp ld 3f out: sn rdn and wknd fnl 2f* **33/1**

-231 **9** 1 ¾ **Saddler's Rock (IRE)**[23] 4737 4-9-1 115......................(t) NGMcCullagh 2 83
(John M Oxx, Ire) *led: rdn along over 4f out: hdd 3f out and sn outpcd* **13/8**[1]

5246 **10** ½ **Glen's Diamond**[49] 3881 4-9-1 112.. TonyHamilton 8 83
(Richard Fahey) *dwlt: hld up: a in rr* **33/1**

-563 **11** 10 **Solar Sky**[21] 4800 4-9-1 106.. IanMongan 1 71
(Sir Henry Cecil) *chsd ldng pair: pushed along over 5f out: rdn along over 4f out and sn wknd* **25/1**

3m 34.64s (0.14) **Going Correction** +0.325s/f (Good) **11** Ran SP% **118.0**

Speed ratings (Par 115): **112,110,110,108,107 106,106,99,98,98 93**

toteswingers: 1&2 £6.70, 1&3 £17.50, 2&3 £19.40 CSF £114.07 TOTE £12.90: £3.10, £2.80, £4.00; EX 108.60 Trifecta £2124.00 Part won. Pool: £2,870.39 - 0.97 winning units..

Owner Mrs I H Stewart-Brown & M J Meacock **Bred** I Stewart-Brown And M Meacock **Trained** Arundel, W Sussex

FOCUS

A competitive Group two whose recent roll of honour is packed with some of the better stayers of recent times, including Bollin Eric, Millenary, Septimus and Sergeant Cecil. The pace was steady early but the favourite wound it up from halfway and the challengers started to commit very early in the straight, leaving the race open for a strong finisher from off the pace. Ordinary form for the race with Saddler's Rock disappointing, but Times Up is rated back to his best.

NOTEBOOK

Times Up progressed nicely and looked a gelding to follow at the end of 2011, but his stable had been struggling for winners and recent form suggested he would struggle to beat a couple of these. However, the race panned out nicely, with the leaders going hard from early in the straight, and he was able to sweep through to take the lead in side the last furlong and win going away. Presumably the Doncaster Cup and another crack at the Qipco Long Distance Cup will be his targets, with options in France. (tchd 10-1 and 12-1)

High Jinx(IRE) ◆ is lightly raced but progressing well and handled this longer trip and step up in class, keeping on in game fashion, having been close to the pace throughout. He looks sure to make his mark at this level, especially next year. (op 9-1)

Lost In The Moment(IRE), narrowly beaten in the Goodwood Cup before finishing sixth in the Melbourne Cup last season, had finished behind at Goodwood this time around. He came to win his race but was run out of it in the latter stages. The impression is he needs fast ground to be at his best and to truly get home over this far. (op 20-1)

Cavalryman was bidding for a hat-trick having won twice at Listed level since being stepped up in trip. He moved into contention apparently going well but his effort petered out in the closing stages. (op 7-2)

Simenon(IRE), who was impressive when scoring twice at Royal Ascot, had his limitations exposed behind today's favourite in the Goodwood Cup, and that was again the case here, as he looked to be travelling well halfway up the straight but could not pick up. (tchd 14-1)

Askar Tau(FR) took this in 2010 and was back again but could not build on his second in the Goodwood Cup, despite beating the winner of that race here. (tchd 20-1)

Ibicenco(GER), having his first start since Sandown at the end of May, was always in the leading group but his effort flattened out in the last quarter-mile and he was eased. (op 8-1)

Thimaar(USA) stays this trip but was beaten in Listed level on his two previous starts and stepping up to Group 2 class proved beyond him. He came through to challenge early in the straight but was soon under pressure and in trouble. He is not up to this level. (op 40-1)

Saddler's Rock(IRE), who followed up his Gold Cup third by beating Askar Tau in the Goodwood Cup, was made plenty of use of, presumably to ensure a decent gallop. He wound it up from halfway, but came under pressure and was taken on early in the straight, then dropped away. Presumably the tactics did not suit. The representative of the trainer reported that the colt was unsuited by the good/soft, good in places and ran too free. Official explanation: jockey said that the colt was unsuited by the good/soft, good in places and ran too free (tchd 6-4 and 7-4 in places)

5600 BETFRED EBOR (HERITAGE H'CAP) 1m 6f

3:40 (3:43) (Class 2) 3-Y-O+

£140,062 (£41,940; £20,970; £10,485; £5,242; £2,632) **Stalls** Low

Form RPR

42-3 **1** **Willing Foe (USA)**[34] 4363 5-9-2 **101**.............................. FrankieDettori 16 110
(Saeed Bin Suroor) *in tch: hdwy 3f out: effrt over 1f out: rdn to chal ent fnl f: sn drvn and hung lft: styd on to ld nr fin* **12/1**

530- **2** nk **Royal Diamond (IRE)**[63] 3411 6-9-0 **99**......................... NGMcCullagh 2 107
(Thomas Carmody, Ire) *led 2f: cl up: rdn to ld over 2f out: hdd jst over 1f out: drvn and rallied to ld ins fnl f: carried bdly lft last 100yds: hdd and no ex nr fin* **16/1**

3111 **3** 1 ½ **Number Theory**[49] 3857 4-8-12 **97**.............................. RussKennemore 4 103
(John Holt) *hld up in midfield: hdwy 3f out: n.m.r 2f out: sn rdn and styd on wl appr fnl f: nrst fin* **16/1**

-001 **4** nk **Motivado**[21] 4800 4-8-12 **97** 4ex.. LukeMorris 8 103
(Sir Mark Prescott Bt) *hld up on inner: hdwy into midfield 1/2-way: effrt over 2f out: sn swtchd rt and rdn: styd on to chse ldrs ins fnl f: kpt on* **7/2**[1]

0215 **5** 1 **Area Fifty One**[42] 4112 4-9-1 **100**.. DavidNolan 7 104
(Richard Fahey) *in tch: hdwy to chse ldrs after 4f: cl up 3f out: rdn and slt ld over 1f out: drvn and hdd ins fnl f: wkng whn n.m.r last 100yds* **25/1**

30 **6** ½ **Steps To Freedom (IRE)**[16] 5027 6-9-5 **109**............(t) DarrenEgan(5) 13 112+
(Mrs John Harrington, Ire) *hld up and bhd: hdwy on outer 3f out: rdn 2f out: styd on fnl f: nrst fin* **25/1**

0611 **7** 1 **Camborne**[63] 3372 4-9-7 **106**..(p) WilliamBuick 14 108
(John Gosden) *hld up in rr: hdwy on outer 3f out: rdn 2f out: chsd ldrs and edgd lft appr fnl f: sn drvn and one pce* **11/2**[3]

4-00 **8** ½ **Tominator**[84] 2709 5-8-12 **97** .... GrahamGibbons 10 98+
(Reg Hollinshead) *hld up towards rr: hdwy on wd outside 3f out: rdn wl over 1f out: styd on fnl f: nt rch ldrs* **20/1**

6/54 **9** 1 ¼ **Dreamspeed (IRE)**[49] 3857 5-9-0 **99** .... JimmyFortune 11 99
(Andrew Balding) *chsd ldrs: rdn along over 2f out: drvn wl over 1f out: wknd appr fnl f* **25/1**

001 **10** 1 ½ **Hurricane Higgins (IRE)**[24] 4697 4-9-0 **99** 4ex........ JoeFanning 3 97
(Mark Johnston) *prom: rdn along 3f out: grad wknd fnl 2f* **33/1**

3-21 **11** *nk* **Qahriman**[71] 3125 4-8-11 **96** .... KierenFallon 1 93+
(Luca Cumani) *in tch: hdwy to chse ldrs whn n.m.r 2f out: sn rdn and no imp* **5/1**[2]

604 **12** *nk* **Bob Le Beau (IRE)**[13] 5134 5-9-2 **104** ....(b) EmmetMcNamara(3) 6 101
(Mrs John Harrington, Ire) *chsd ldrs: rdn along 3f out: wknd fnl 2f* **66/1**

5604 **13** *nk* **Blue Bajan (IRE)**[42] 4111 10-8-13 **98** .... DanielTudhope 12 94+
(David O'Meara) *in rr: hdwy 3f out: swtchd lft top inner 2f out: sn rdn and no imp* **20/1**

2 **14** *nk* **Hammerfest**[23] 5-9-0 **99** .... JimCrowley 21 95+
(J E Hammond, France) *hld up: a in rr* **10/1**

3040 **15** 2 ¼ **Alkimos (IRE)**[42] 4112 4-9-1 **100** ....(p) SilvestreDeSousa 15 93
(Saeed Bin Suroor) *chsd ldrs: rdn along 3f out: drvn and wknd fnl 2f* **16/1**

62-3 **16** 1 **Icon Dream (IRE)**[56] 3625 5-9-1 **100** .... GrahamLee 19 91
(Jim Goldie) *a in rr* **16/1**

3120 **17** 3 ¼ **Crackentorp**[42] 4111 7-9-2 **101** .... DavidAllan 17 88
(Tim Easterby) *cl up: led after 2f: rdn along 3f out: hdd over 2f out and sn wknd* **25/1**

0-53 **18** 3 ¾ **Harrison's Cave**[57] 3599 4-8-11 **96** .... CO'Donoghue 9 78
(A P O'Brien, Ire) *hld up on inner: a towards rr* **16/1**

0100 **19** 2 ½ **Rock A Doodle Doo (IRE)**[14] 5079 5-8-12 **97** ....(b1) JamieSpencer 18 75
(William Jarvis) *a in rr: bhd fnl 3f* **50/1**

3m 0.75s (0.55) **Going Correction** +0.325s/f (Good) **19** Ran SP% **131.8**
Speed ratings (Par 109): **111,110,109,109,109 108,108,108,107,106 106,106,106,105,104 103,102,99,98**
toteswingers: 1&2 £67.00, 1&3 £28.10, 2&3 £74.00 CSF £179.56 CT £3117.68 TOTE £13.00: £3.00, £3.60, £4.30, £2.00; EX 260.90 Trifecta £6707.60 Pool: £59,824.80 - 6.60 winning units..
Owner Godolphin **Bred** Stoneside Stable **Trained** Newmarket, Suffolk
■ Stewards' Enquiry : N G McCullagh four-day ban: use of whip (9, 10, 11, 12 Sept)
Frankie Dettori two-day ban: use of whip (11-14 Sep)

FOCUS
A really competitive renewal for Europe's most valuable handicap, that had been only won by four, five or 6-y-os since Mediterranean took it in 2001 at the age of three. Purple Moon had been the only successful market leader in that time period, a victory that was sandwiched between four winners that started between 14/1 and 100/1. Surprisingly, there was no early speed and the runners mainly dawdled through the first part of the race, meaning the winning time was almost three seconds slower than the Melrose Stakes earlier on the card. The jockeys on the first and second both got four-day whip bans. The form is slightly limited by the lack of pace but the winner posted a 4lb personal best.

NOTEBOOK
Willing Foe(USA), having his first attempt at 1m6f after a solid return effort at Ascot in late July, was produced with a perfect challenge to get up by a narrow margin. Well positioned but wide as the race took shape, the winning rider waited and waited until as late as possible to get the last burst from his horse, and the pair got to the front despite the gelding hanging left late on - Frankie Dettori got a two-day ban for careless riding. Well bred and lightly raced, he can develop into a Group performer at this distance, and is one of a few Godolphin have in mind for another tilt at the Melbourne Cup.

Royal Diamond(IRE), who is entered in the Irish St Leger, was back up in trip after a couple of starts over 1m4f and looked of real interest here considering his form figures over 1m6f prior to this read 211118. Really well ridden considering the lack of a gallop, he tried oh so hard to hold on once rallying back to the front but was denied in the final strides. (op 20-1)

Number Theory, whose last four starts had been at Haydock, was chasing a four timer after landing the Old Newton Cup on his previous outing (up another 5lb for that success) and did really well up in trip after taking a little while to hit top gear while short of space. The gelding is a credit to his connections. (op 20-1)

Motivado, a Cesarewitch entrant, shot to the top of the ante-post lists for this when winning comfortably at Goodwood, and was 6lb well-in, but one got the impression he suffered for the lack of a strong gallop to chase, as he hit a flat spot when the tempo picked up before staying on. It wouldn't be a surprise to see him up to 2m and further now or ridden more prominently. (op 9-2)

Area Fifty One, fifth in the John Smith's Cup on his last outing, had never run over further that 1m4f previously and one has to conclude that even though he ran up to his best, the trip proved too far considering the leaders didn't go hard early.

Steps To Freedom(IRE), the top-weight and a Grade 2 winning hurdler has shown a mainly smart level of form back on the Flat and emerges with a lot of credit, as his trainer reports the gelding needs decent ground. (op 33-1)

Camborne, previously 2-2 after cheekpieces were fitted, got himself into position to strike but wandered left and right for pressure and clearly isn't the most straightforward of geldings, for all that he is talented. (op 7-1)

Tominator, off since finishing down the field at Haydock in early June, and another entered in the Cesarewitch, ran better than his final position suggests. Keen early, he was denied a clear passage on a couple of occasions in the home straight and would have been closer otherwise. (op 16-1)

Qahriman, unexposed and nicely bred, crept into this off joint-bottom weight, and was of obvious interest for a stable enjoying a good spell. Up 6lb for his C&D victory when last seen in June, he was nicely positioned to get involved but simply never picked up for some reason.

Hammerfest had no change of gear when in with half a chance of getting to the leaders, and made no impression. (tchd 11-1)

5601 JULIA GRAVES ROSES STKS (LISTED RACE) 5f
4:15 (4:16) (Class 1) 2-Y-O
£22,684 (£8,600; £4,304; £2,144; £1,076; £540) **Stalls** Centre

Form RPR

2213 **1** **Hoyam**[28] 4577 2-8-9 98 .... JamieSpencer 3 101
(Michael Bell) *hld up in rr: swtchd lft over 2f out: nt clr run: swtchd rt over 1f out: str run to take 2nd last 100yds: led last 50yds: eased fnl strides: readily* **3/1**[3]

1 **2** 1 ¼ **Fire Eyes**[29] 4545 2-9-0 0 .... HarryBentley 4 101
(David Brown) *trckd ldr travelling strly: led wl over 1f out: qcknd over 2 l clr: hdd and no ex last 50yds* **5/2**[1]

0620 **3** 2 **Lasilia (IRE)**[8] 5307 2-8-9 90 .... PhillipMakin 6 88
(Kevin Ryan) *hld up: effrt 2f out: wnt 2nd 1f out: kpt on same pce* **16/1**

5121 **4** 1 ½ **Lucky Beggar (IRE)**[21] 4827 2-9-0 95 .... MichaelHills 7 88
(Charles Hills) *sn trcking ldrs: effrt and 3rd 1f out: kpt on same pce* **11/2**

101 **5** ¾ **Cosmic Chatter**[15] 5055 2-9-0 100 .... GrahamGibbons 1 85
(David Barron) *gave problems in stalls: led: hdd wl over 1f out: wknd appr fnl f* **11/4**[2]

3210 **6** ¾ **Lady Ibrox**[25] 4687 2-8-9 91 .... DaleSwift 2 78
(Alan Brown) *chsd ldr: wknd over 1f out* **12/1**

1m 0.22s (0.92) **Going Correction** +0.375s/f (Good) **6** Ran SP% **109.2**
Speed ratings (Par 102): **107,105,101,99,98 97**
toteswingers: 1&2 £2.40, 1&3 £5.50, 2&3 £5.20 CSF £10.28 TOTE £3.80: £2.00, £1.90; EX 11.10 Trifecta £55.40 Pool: £1,521.22 - 20.29 winning units..
Owner Ahmad Al Shaikh **Bred** Brook Stud Bloodstock Ltd **Trained** Newmarket, Suffolk

FOCUS
Not the strongest of Listed races and only Howick Falls of recent winners managed to win above this level, taking the Flying Childers on his next outing. The pace looked pretty good and the field ended up on the far-side rail. The form is up to the race averages.

NOTEBOOK
Hoyam ◆ had only won a maiden prior to this but had finished runner-up in the Queen Mary and third in the Princess Margaret, the latter over 6f. Held up at the back, her rider got himself blocked behind the rest of the field entering the last 2f and he had to switch right around them. However, the filly picked up really well to lead inside the last and scored comfortably in the end. She looks a natural for the Flying Childers next, and will take a fair amount of beating on this evidence. (tchd 11-4)

Fire Eyes impressed when winning on his Thirsk debut and when he went to the front inside the last 2f here he looked like following up, but was run down late. He would probably have appreciated faster ground than he got here and could be worth a crack at the Flying Childers, which his dam won, given a sound surface. (op 3-1)

Lasilia(IRE), placed at this level after finishing sixth in the Queen Mary, was held up before keeping on late for the minor placing. She might be worth a try over 6f in something like the Firth Of Clyde at Ayr.

Lucky Beggar(IRE), who took a nursery off 91 on his previous start, is clearly on the upgrade and connections were justified in having a go at this. He showed up throughout but could not sustain his effort under pressure late on. (op 5-1)

Cosmic Chatter had won both his starts in lesser company in the style of a very useful performer but had got unsettled at the start in the Windsor Castle and the same thing happened here, as he appeared to try to get under the gates and as a result probably ran too free. He was headed well over a furlong out and could not respond. He has potential but needs to become more settled if he is going to fulfil it. (op 5-2)

Lady Ibrox is pretty quick but was held in a Group 3 last time after showing plenty of pace and the same thing happened here. The evidence is that she is not up to this class, but will not find it easy in handicaps off her current rating. (op 11-1)

5602 BETFRED THE BONUS KING STKS (NURSERY H'CAP) 7f
4:50 (4:53) (Class 2) 2-Y-O **£16,172** (£4,812; £2,405; £1,202) **Stalls** Low

Form RPR

2520 **1** **Old Man Clegg**[17] 4951 2-7-10 **67** .... DominicFox(3) 13 72
(Michael Easterby) *wnt rt s and towards rr: hdwy on outer over 2f out: sn rdn and hung bdly lft ent fnl f: sn drvn to chal and styd on to ld nr fin* **10/1**

0031 **2** *shd* **Salutation (IRE)**[17] 4951 2-8-8 **76** .... JoeFanning 12 81
(Mark Johnston) *hld up: hdwy on wd outside 3f out: rdn to ld and hung bdly lft over 1f out: drvn ins fnl f: hdd and no ex nr fin* **6/1**[3]

1303 **3** 2 **Top Notch Tonto (IRE)**[54] 3695 2-9-4 **89** .... DaleSwift(3) 9 90
(Ian McInnes) *trckd ldrs: hdwy 2f out: sn nt clr run and swtchd lft: effrt whn bdly hmpd ent fnl f: sn rdn and kpt on wl* **14/1**

2411 **4** ½ **Bonnie Lesley (IRE)**[21] 4806 2-8-9 **77** .... JimCrowley 4 79+
(Keith Dalgleish) *trckd ldrs: hdwy to chal over 2f out: sn rdn and bdly hmpd ent fnl f: kpt on* **7/1**

331 **5** *hd* **Medicoe**[18] 4907 2-8-11 **79** .... LukeMorris 5 77
(Sir Mark Prescott Bt) *cl up: led 3f out: sn rdn and hdd wl over 1f out: drvn and bdly hmpd ent fnl f: one pce after* **5/1**[1]

0362 **6** ¾ **Team Challenge**[14] 5109 2-8-0 **68** .... DuranFentiman 10 64
(Tim Easterby) *towards rr: hdwy on outer 2f out: sn rdn and kpt on fnl f: nrst fin* **28/1**

6612 **7** 2 ¼ **Tussie Mussie**[15] 5041 2-7-9 **68** .... DarrenEgan(5) 6 58
(Mark Johnston) *cl up: rdn along wl over 2f out: wkng whn swtchd rt 1f out* **11/1**

1200 **8** 1 ¼ **Blue Lotus (IRE)**[15] 5041 2-8-9 **77** .... DavidAllan 2 65
(Tim Easterby) *trckd ldrs on inner: hdwy 3f out: rdn and bdly hmpd ent fnl f: wknd after* **28/1**

336 **9** 2 ½ **Titus Titan (IRE)**[17] 4960 2-7-12 **69** .... RaulDaSilva(3) 7 49
(Brian Ellison) *in tch: rdn along wl over 2f out: sn wknd* **11/2**[2]

21 **10** *nse* **Simply Shining (IRE)**[29] 4546 2-8-10 **78** .... TonyHamilton 11 58
(Richard Fahey) *cl up: rdn along over 2f out: sn wknd* **7/1**

3223 **11** 7 **Bold Prediction (IRE)**[24] 4707 2-9-0 **82** .... PhillipMakin 8 44
(Richard Hannon) *cl up: rdn along wl over 2f out: sn wknd* **11/1**

0444 **12** ½ **Party Royal**[22] 4763 2-8-12 **80** .... AdrianNicholls 3 41
(Mark Johnston) *led: rdn along over 3f out: sn hdd & wknd* **9/1**

1m 28.88s (3.58) **Going Correction** +0.325s/f (Good) **12** Ran SP% **120.7**
Speed ratings (Par 100): **98,97,95,95,94 93,91,89,87,87 79,78**
CSF £70.19 CT £849.77 TOTE £11.60: £3.30, £2.70, £4.70; EX 113.30 TRIFECTA Not won..
Owner Irkroy Racing & Steve Hull **Bred** R S Cockerill (farms) Ltd **Trained** Sheriff Hutton, N Yorks
■ Stewards' Enquiry : Dominic Fox six-day ban: careless riding (8 -13 Sept)

FOCUS
With so many of these dipping their toe into handicap company for the first time, this looked a tricky puzzle for punters to unravel. It was quite a rough race but the form is straightforward.

NOTEBOOK
Old Man Clegg was 10l behind Salutation in a Newcastle nursery on their previous outing (when starting a shorter price that the Johnston runner) but reversed that form on better terms despite appearing a difficult ride. It didn't come as a huge surprise to see Dominic Fox given a six-day ban for careless riding considering he hampered plenty of horses as his mount hung violently left from the centre of the track, a couple of which held a chance of getting involved. (op 14-1)

Salutation(IRE), raised 6lb for that success on handicap debut last time, came right across to the far rail as well, also causing a little trouble. Had the colt stayed straight, he may well have won. (op 7-1)

Top Notch Tonto(IRE) finished off nicely after getting his run impeded and was one of a few unlucky not to be closer at the end. (op 16-1)

Bonnie Lesley(IRE), previously unbeaten in nurseries, travelled kindly for much of the race but looked held when forced to snatch up with over 1f to go. A drop to 6f might help in the short-term. (op 13-2 tchd 8-1 in a place)

Medicoe was keeping on after a prominent ride but got taken a bit left by both the first and second as they crossed him. (op 11-2)

Team Challenge, trying 7f for the first time, certainly wasn't completely done with when becoming the first victim of Old Man Clegg's sideways movement. (op 33-1)

Titus Titan(IRE), up in trip for his handicap debut, ran poorly as he didn't get tightened up at any stage and was beaten on merit. Perhaps the ground was too soft for him considering his previous best. (op 5-1)

Simply Shining(IRE), the least exposed of these, did get a little short of room but seemed beaten at the time.

Bold Prediction (IRE) Official explanation: jockey said that the colt ran too free

5603 QIPCO FUTURE STARS APPRENTICE STKS (H'CAP) 5f

5:20 (5:21) (Class 2) (0-100,90) 3-Y-O£16,172 (£4,812; £2,405 ; £1,202 Stalls Centre

Form RPR

6334 1 **Heeraat (IRE)**[14] 5080 3 -9-6**89** ... AdamBeschizza 9 98
(William Haggas) *cl up: led wl over 1f out: drvn ins fnl f: hld on wl* **3/1**[1]

0325 2 *nk* **Profile Star (IRE)**[66] 3288 3 -8-7**79** ... DeanHeslop(3) 10 87
(David Barron) *a.p: rdn over 1f out and ev ch tl drvn and no ex towards fin* **33/1**

3165 3 *1/2* **Waseem Faris (IRE)**[7] 5337 3 -8-11**83** ... CharlesBishop(3) 2 89
(Mick Channon) *trckd ldrs: hdwy wl over 1f out: rdn to chal ins fnl f and ev ch tl drvn and no ex towards fin* **8/1**

4520 4 *1 1/4* **Kool Henry (IRE)**[14] 5080 3 -9-7**90** ... RaulDaSilva 3 92
(David O'Meara) *cl up: rdn wl over 1f out: wknd ins fnl f* **8/1**

1105 5 *shd* **Lupin Pooter**[12] 5167 3 -8-9**78** ... HarryBentley 7 79
(David Barron) *chsd ldrs: rdn along 2f out: drvn and one pce ent fnl f* **11/2**[3]

2600 6 *nk* **Last Bid**[28] 4611 3 -9-2**90** ... DarylByrne(5) 4 90
(Tim Easterby) *hld up towards rr: hdwy 2f out: rdn over 1f out: drvn and kpt on fnl f* **10/1**

2213 7 *2 3/4* **Sir Maximilian (IRE)**[18] 4919 3 -8-10**82** ... AshleyMorgan(3) 8 72
(Ed Dunlop) *hld up: sme hdwy 2f out: sn rdn and no imp* **9/2**[2]

0010 8 *1 1/2* **Bop It**[56] 3613 3 -8-13**82** ... LeeTopliss 12 67
(Bryan Smart) *chsd ldrs: rdn over 2f out: sn wknd* **11/1**

1010 9 *2 3/4* **Towbee**[29] 4558 3 -8-9**83** ... (b) DavidSimmonson(5) 13 58
(Michael Easterby) *in tch on wd outside: effrt 2f out: sn rdn and wknd* **20/1**

0133 10 *1 3/4* **Almond Branches**[29] 4558 3 -8-4**76** ... NeilFarley(3) 11 45
(George Moore) *a in rr* **10/1**

000 11 *2* **Powerful Wind (IRE)**[22] 4765 3 -9-1**87** ... DarrenEgan(3) 6 48
(Ronald Harris) *led: rdn along 2f out: sn hdd & wknd* **20/1**

1m 0.38s (1.08)**Going Correction** +0.375s/f (Good) 11Ran SP% **119.8**

Speed ratings (Par 106): **106,105,104,102,102 102,97,95,90,88 84**

toteswingers: 1&2 £16.60, 1&3 £9.10, 2&3 £28.60 CSF £120.67 CT £757.31 TOTE £3.60 : £1.50 , £9.20, £2.50 ; EX 131.20 Trifecta £872.00 Part won. Pool: £1,178.37 - 0.10 winning units.

Owner Hamdan Al Maktoum **Bred** John McEnery **Trained** Newmarket, Suffolk

FOCUS

A good, competitive-looking 3-y-o apprentices' handicap, although the top weight was rated 10lb below the race ceiling. The rain had been pretty steady in the hour leading up to the race and the time was 0.16secs slower than the earlier juvenile Listed race. The form seems sound enough.

NOTEBOOK

Heeraat(IRE) brought some solid form into this, having been in the frame behind subsequent winners in hot handicaps on his two previous starts, with the winner of the latter (Mince) going on to score in Listed company. He travelled well into contention but had to really battle to get the better of the placed horses in a close finish. He deserved this and might have more to offer. 4-1)

Profile Star (IRE)◆, returning from a couple of months off, ran really well having been prominent from the start, and was only just held. He seemed to handle the ground but would have preferred it faster. He looks one to keep on-side. (op 25-1)

Waseem Faris (IRE)narrowly beat today's fourth here in July and they met on the same terms. He tracked the pace before being produced over a furlong out but could not sustain the effort close home. (op 9-1)

Kool Henry (IRE) closely matched with today's third on recent form and the sixth on a couple of runs last season, put up a decent effort under top weight, being in the mix throughout, and along with Wasim Faris helps set the level of the form. (op 10-1)

Lupin Pooter, a winner of three of his six previous starts, ran with credit but has now looked held by the handicapper on his two most recent starts. (op 8-1)

Last Bid, two of whose three wins last season came over C&D (beating Kool Henry narrowly each time), had not scored since but had run well on two of her three subsequent visits to this track. She came from the rear to briefly look a threat over a furlong out before her run petered out. 14-1)

Sir Maximilian (IRE) whose form suggested he would appreciate the rain-softened ground, was held up early and could not pick up sufficiently to land a blow. (op 11-4)

T/Jkpt: Not won T/Plt: £1,411.10 to a £1 stake. Pool: £276,805.00. 143.19 winning tickets. T/Qpdt: £293.40 to a £1 stake. Pool: £10,508.99. 26.50 winning tickets. JR

5604 - 5605a, 5607a - 5608a (Foreign Racing) - See Raceform Interactive

5133

CURRAGH (R-H)

Saturday, August 25

OFFICIAL GOING: Soft to heavy (heavy in places) changing to heavy after race 3 (3.15)

5606a GAIN HORSE FEEDS IRISH ST LEGER TRIAL STKS (GROUP 3) 1m 6f

3:15 (3:17) 3-Y-O+ £31,145 (£9,104; £4,312 ; £1,437)

RPR

1 **Ursa Major (IRE)**[67] 3599 3 -8-11**106** ... FergalLynch 1 114+
(Thomas Carmody, Ire) *hld up last of 5: travelled wl in 3rd over 2f out: sn pressed ldr: qckng wl to ld fnl 150yds: styd on strly* **4/1**[2]

2 *1 3/4* **Hartani (IRE)**[55] 3678 3 -9-0**110** ... PatSmullen 2 114+
(John M Oxx, Ire) *raced cl 3rd tl led over 2f out: sn pressed by wnr: hdd and outpcd fnl 150yds* **5/6**[1]

3 *23* **David Livingston (IRE)**[107] 1995 3 -8-11**108** ... SeamieHeffernan 3 79
(A P O'Brien, Ire) *hld up cl 4th tl pushed along bef home turn and unable qck w ldrs: kpt on again late to take remote 3rd cl home* **4/1**[2]

4 *nk* **Aklan (IRE)**[37] 4280 3 -8-11**110** ... (t) BenCurtis 4 78
(John M Oxx, Ire) *led tl hdd over 2f out: sn no ex w principals: ct cl home for remote 3rd* **6/1**[3]

5 *7* **Eternal Bounty (IRE)**[20] 4854 3 -8-8**98** ... (b[1]) WayneLordan 5 66
(David Wachman, Ire) *racd cl 2nd: pressed ldr 5f out tl wknd qckly ent fnl 3f* **12/1**

3m 12.72s (3.32)**Going Correction** +0.50s/f (Yiel) 5Ran SP% **116.5**

Speed ratings: **110,109,95,95,91**

CSF £8.38 TOTE £5.10 : £2.00 , £1.02 ; DF 10.40 .

Owner Andrew Tinkler **Bred** Woodcote Stud Ltd **Trained** the Curragh, Co Kildare

FOCUS

Not a great turnout given the entries but still an interesting race. Stamina was always going to be heavily emphasised - the distance from second to third was incredible. The going was changed to heavy after the race. It's been rated cautiously for now, through the runner-up to his previous win.

NOTEBOOK

Ursa Major (IRE)is one of the more likeable horses in training and won this pretty tidily, having been running off 88 two runs back. He showed his lazy tendencies in stages but, given how well he stays, it was notable how confident his rider looked as they met the straight. He had to wait in a little pocket and was keen not to get there too soon but Ursa Major soon ranged up alongside the favourite and did not take too long to establish supremacy. He hit the front and was probably only doing enough. Quite what to make of this run is hard to say but, on the face of it, he must rate one of the best stayers in Ireland at the very least. He seems fine on good ground too and is entered in both Legers. There was some suggestion afterwards that the Doncaster Classic is most likely, although one would imagine the Curragh option must be pretty appealing. (op 4/1 tchd 9/2)

Hartani(IRE) was well backed, even though there must be a slight concern at least about the stable form, a worry augmented by a lifeless run minutes earlier at York by Saddler's Rock. Hartani travelled pretty well and readily pulled clear of the remainder but he was soon brushed aside by the winner. He remains progressive and his next run will be interesting. (op 11/10)

David Livingston (IRE)had his tongue out and was dropped in to get the trip. He was game under pressure but beaten half a mile out and this did not really challenge concerns that he has not trained on. (op 4/1 tchd 9/2)

Aklan(IRE) practically trebled in price on course. He had looked potentially flattered by his mark but this was still a really tame run. He should be given another chance. (op 4/1)

Eternal Bounty (IRE)looked a pretty speculative entry and hardly improved for the step up in distance.

5609a IRISH STALLION FARMS EUROPEAN BREEDERS FUND IRISH CAMBRIDGESHIRE (PREMIER H'CAP) 1m

4:55 (4:57) 3-Y-O+

£47,500 (£15,041; £7,125 ; £2,375 ; £1,583 ; £791)

RPR

1 **Punch Your Weight (IRE)**[20] 4857 3 -8-6**86** ... ChrisHayes 6 96+
(A Oliver, Ire) *racd in mid-div: pushed along 3f out: gd hdwy to press ldrs appr fnl f: led 150yds out: styd on wl* **16/1**

2 *1 1/2* **Bold Thady Quill (IRE)**[5] 5525 5 -8-9**90** ... (p) RossCoakley(7) 2 97
(K J Condon, Ire) *hld up in tch: prog to join ldrs over 2f out: sn ev ch: no ex fnl 100yds w wnr* **12/1**

3 *1 1/2* **Sweet Lightning**[55] 3675 7 -9-12**100** ... (t) BenCurtis 10 104+
(Thomas Carmody, Ire) *hld up in rr: plenty to do over 2f out whn nt clr run: styd on strly once clr ins fnl f to get up cl home for 3rd* **12/1**

4 *1/2* **Northern Rocked (IRE)**[21] 4833 6 -9-0**93** ... (b) LeighRoche(5) 17 96
(D K Weld, Ire) *broke wl: racd in 2nd tl led over 2f out: sn pressed and hdd 150yds out: kpt on same pce: passed late for 3rd* **16/1**

5 *3/4* **Along Came Casey (IRE)**[6] 5025 4 -8-8**82** ... PatSmullen 16 83
(D K Weld, Ire) *trckd ldrs on stands' side: no imp appr fnl f: kpt on same pce* **9/1**

6 *nk* **Spa's Dancer (IRE)**[25] 4692 5 -9-7**95** ... SeamieHeffernan 18 95
(Ed de Giles) *sn led: hdd over 2f out: kpt on again tl clsng stages* **10/1**

7 *1 1/2* **Winning Impact (IRE)**[21] 4833 5 -8-3**80** ow1 ... (t) SamJames(3) 5 77
(J G Coogan, Ire) *trckd ldrs towards centre of trck: nvr quite on terms: kpt on same pce fnl f* **16/1**

8 *shd* **New Magic (IRE)**[23] 4749 5 -8-10**91** ... (t) ColinKeane(7) 8 88
(Dermot Anthony McLoughlin, Ire) *racd in mid-div tl clsd to chse ldrs on outer over 2f out: 4th ent fnl f then fdd* **14/1**

9 *1/2* **Learn (IRE)**[31] 4483 3 -9-5**99** ... JPO'Brien 15 94
(A P O'Brien, Ire) *hld up in rr: swtchd towards outer 2f out: kpt on wout ever threatening* **10/1**

10 *3/4* **Sadler's Mark**[19] 4897 5 -8-8**89** ... (b) MarcMonaghan(7) 9 83
(Dermot Anthony McLoughlin, Ire) *racd towards outer: nvr on terms: kpt on same pce fr over 1f out* **10/1**

11 *3 1/2* **Waydownsouth (IRE)**[23] 4748 5 -8-8**82** ... DannyGrant 1 68
(Patrick J Flynn, Ire) *racd in mid-div on wd outside: no imp fnl 2f* **8/1**[3]

12 *1 1/4* **Barack (IRE)**[20] 4853 6 -9-4**97** ... (bt) RonanWhelan(5) 13 80
(W McCreery, Ire) *racd in 3rd tl pushed along over 2f out: sn one pce* **12/1**

13 *nk* **Jembatt (IRE)**[9] 5281 5 -8-7**84** ... (p) IJBrennan(3) 4 66
(Michael Mulvany, Ire) *t.k.h early: covered up towards rr: nvr a threat* **16/1**

14 *nk* **Vastonea (IRE)**[25] 4692 4 -9-8**96** ... DeclanMcDonogh 7 78
(Kevin Prendergast, Ire) *trckd ldrs: 5th appr fnl 2f: sn wknd* **5/1**[1]

15 *1* **Miracle Cure (IRE)**[7] 5397 3 -8-6**86** ... RoryCleary 11 64
(J S Bolger, Ire) *trckd ldrs stands' side: no threat 2f out* **12/1**

16 *1* **Castle Bar Sling (USA)**[25] 4692 7 -8-10**84** ... (p) WayneLordan 12 61
(T J O'Mara, Ire) *nvr bttr than mid-div* **16/1**

17 *1/2* **Takeitfromalady (IRE)**[8] 5301 3 -8-8**88** ... (b) ShaneFoley 14 64
(Ralph Beckett) *racd towards rr on stands' side: nvr a factor* **7/1**[2]

18 *27* **Ballivor (IRE)**[35] 4356 9 -8-10**84** ... FergalLynch 3
(W T Farrell, Ire) *t.k.h: racd up w ldrs tl qckly dropped away 3f out: eased* **16/1**

1m 46.61s (0.61)**Going Correction** +0.325s/f (Good)

WFA 3 from 4yo+ 6lb 18Ran SP% **150.3**

Speed ratings: **109,107,106,105,104 104,102,102,102,101 98,96,96,96,95 94,93,66**

CSF £236.29 CT £2532.14 TOTE £20.20 : £4.00 , £4.50 , £4.60 , £5.10 ; DF 498.70 .

Owner A Oliver **Bred** Michael O'Dea **Trained** Caledon, Co Tyrone

FOCUS

Typically competitive. Andy Oliver's stock was been going one way this season and this was an exceptional training success. Pitching a green maiden winner just 20 days ago into a handicap as tough as this was a gamble and it paid off in no uncertain ways. The unexposed winner produced a big personal best.

NOTEBOOK

Punch Your Weight (IRE)won at Cork looked ordinary but Oliver insisted afterwards that plenty more was to come. So it proved as he basically ran away with this, despite still appearing a shade raw. He was pulled out into the middle when stuck for a run and was always getting on top thereafter. His sire's progeny can be quirky but he looks tough and should have no problem getting further. (op 14/1)

Bold Thady Quill (IRE)nearly won another premier handicap and has been a credit to his trainer. He was teak-tough under pressure and is very likeable. He certainly owes connections nothing and is relishing his racing. (op 14/1)

Sweet Lightning, the class act of the race, ran a stormer on ground far from ideal. He was powering home, at least relative to the rest, in the closing stages and is clearly in good heart - much like all the Carmody runners. (op 16/1)

Northern Rocked (IRE)just got tired in the closing stages, having made an early bid for home. He is probably better over a shade shorter and has little room for scope off this mark. (op 14/1)

Along Came Casey (IRE)the choice of Pat Smullen, was easy to back and seemed to have every chance, travelling well to a point. (op 7/1)

Spa's Dancer (IRE)brings solid handicap form to this and ran a decent race without ever looking like winning.

Winning Impact (IRE)is probably better over 7f and, given the competitive nature of the race, this was creditable. (op 20/1)

Ballivor(IRE) Official explanation: jockey said gelding may have burst a blood vessel

5610 - 5611a (Foreign Racing) - See Raceform Interactive

2322 BADEN-BADEN (L-H)

Saturday, August 25

OFFICIAL GOING: Turf: good to soft

5612a BBAG AUKTIONSRENNEN IFFEZHEIM (CONDITIONS) (2YO FILLIES) (TURF) 6f

3:10 (3:20) 2-Y-O

£29,166 (£29,166; £10,416; £8,333; £4,166; £2,083)

RPR

1 **Molly Mara (GER)**[26] 2-8-11 0 Jean-BernardEyquem 10
(J-C Rouget, France) **21/10**[1]

1 *dht* **Tosca (GER)** 2-8-11 0 SHellyn 13
(Mrs Ilka Gansera-Leveque) *prom thrght: rdn to chal over 1 1/2f out: sn disputing ld: sustained battle w rival thrght fnl f: locked together post: dead heat* **135/10**

3 *1 ½* **Celia (IRE)** 2-9-2 0 FabriceVeron 6
(H-A Pantall, France) **14/5**[2]

4 *1* **Linngara (FR)** 2-9-2 0 THellier 12
(Mario Hofer, Germany) **44/5**

5 *1 ½* **Reality (GER)** 2-8-11 0 ADeVries 5
(U Stech, Germany) **14/1**

6 *2* **Linarda (DEN)** 2-8-11 0 (b) MircoDemuro 3
(M Rulec, Germany) **97/10**

7 *2 ½* **Shoshana (GER)** 2-8-11 0 EPedroza 9
(Frau J Mayer, Germany) **54/1**

8 *1 ¼* **Gold And White (GER)** 2-9-2 0 AStarke 7
(P Schiergen, Germany) **11/2**[3]

9 *6* **Coya (GER)** 2-8-11 0 FilipMinarik 4
(U Stoltefuss, Germany) **42/1**

10 *2 ½* **Deodora (FR)** 2-8-11 0 FredericSpanu 1
(Mario Hofer, Germany) **39/1**

11 *11* **Irish Imagine**[117] 2-8-11 0 StefanieHofer 11
(Mario Hofer, Germany) **91/10**

12 *8* **Double Trouble (GER)** 2-8-11 0 LennartHammer-Hansen 8
(Boze Majic, Germany) **53/1**

13 *47* **Panesidora (GER)** 2-8-11 0 APietsch 2
(C Von Der Recke, Germany) **219/10**

1m 13.27s (2.98) **13** Ran SP% **129.8**

WIN (incl. 10 euro stake): 15 (Molly Mara), 72 (Tosca); PLACES: 31, 15, 19. SF: 366 (Molly Mara - Tosca), 522 (Tosca - Molly Mara)..

Owner Karl-Dieter Ellerbracke **Bred** Gestut Auenquelle **Trained** Pau, France

Owner Mrs I Gansera-Leveque **Bred** Gestut Harzburg **Trained** Newmarket, Suffolk

NOTEBOOK

Tosca(GER) gave her German-born, Newmarket-based trainer a winner, albeit a dead-heat, with her first ever runner.

5613a PREIS DER SPARKASSEN - FINANZGRUPPE (GROUP 3) (4YO+) (TURF) 1m 2f

4:25 (4:34) 4-Y-O+

£26,666 (£9,166; £4,583; £2,500; £1,666; £1,250)

RPR

1 **Mikhail Glinka (IRE)**[20] 5-9-4 0 MircoDemuro 9 112
(A Savujev, Czech Republic) *midfield: rdn over 2f out: r.o to chal over 1f out: led jst ins fnl f: drvn out* **49/10**

2 *½* **Navarra Queen**[34] 4386 4-8-10 0 MrDennisSchiergen 7 103
(P Schiergen, Germany) *hld up in last: rdn to improve 2 1/2f out: effrt to chal ins fnl f: styd on strly to go 2nd cl home* **123/10**

3 *hd* **Neatico (GER)**[34] 5-9-0 0 AStarke 8 107
(P Schiergen, Germany) *hld up in last pair on outer: rdn to improve over 2f out: r.o to chal over 1f out: kpt on wl u.p ins fnl f: dropped to 3rd cl home* **7/1**

4 *2 ½* **King's Hall**[27] 4636 4-9-2 0 LennartHammer-Hansen 6 104
(A Wohler, Germany) *midfield: rdn over 2f out: r.o to go 4th ins fnl f: nt pce to chal* **249/10**

5 *1 ¾* **Theo Danon (GER)**[20] 4-9-2 0 FilipMinarik 2 100
(P Schiergen, Germany) *prom on inner: rdn 2f out: effrt to chal over 1 1/2f out: outpcd by ldrs ins fnl f: plugged on* **93/10**

6 *1 ¼* **Durban Thunder (GER)**[27] 4636 6-9-0 0 THellier 1 96
(P Harley, Germany) *sn led: rdn over 2f out: strly pressed fr over 1 1/2f out: hdd jst ins fnl f: no ex and fdd* **11/5**[1]

7 *7* **Pont Des Arts (FR)**[188] 630 8-8-11 0 FredericSpanu 10 79
(A Schaerer, Switzerland) *trckd ldr in 2nd on outer: rdn over 2f out: c rt over to nr side rail in st: outpcd and btn over 1f out: eased ins fnl f* **17/1**

8 *2 ½* **Russian Tango (GER)**[20] 5-9-2 0 EPedroza 3 79
(A Wohler, Germany) *prom: rdn over 2 1/2f out: no ex and btn over 1f out: fdd and eased ins fnl f* **22/5**[3]

9 *15* **Green Destiny (IRE)**[20] 5-9-2 0 ADeVries 4 49
(A Savujev, Czech Republic) *hld up towards rr on inner: rdn 2 1/2f out: effrt to chal over 1 1/2f out: sn upt on tl no ex jst ins fnl f: fdd: heavily eased and dropped to last sn after: t.o* **16/5**[2]

2m 6.37s (1.38) **9** Ran SP% **129.7**

WIN (incl. 10 euro stake): 59. PLACES: 30, 35, 23. SF: 703.

Owner Ramzan Kadyrov **Bred** Paulyn Ltd **Trained** Czech Republic

5614 - 5617a (Foreign Racing) - See Raceform Interactive

5253 BEVERLEY (R-H)

Sunday, August 26

OFFICIAL GOING: Good (good to firm in places; 7.9)

Wind: light 1/2 behind Weather: overcast

5618 JOHN JENKINS MEMORIAL CLAIMING STKS 7f 100y

1:50 (1:51) (Class 5) 3-Y-O+ **£2,911** (£866; £432; £216) **Stalls** Low

Form RPR

5160 1 **Fathsta (IRE)**[23] 4775 7-9-5 82 GrahamLee 10 78
(Patrick Morris) *hld up in rr: hdwy on ins over 2f out: nt clr run over 1f out: swtchd lft and r.o wl to ld nr fin* **8/1**

5603 2 *½* **Sunnyside Tom (IRE)**[11] 5220 8-8-11 70 LeeTopliss(3) 13 72
(Richard Fahey) *in rr: hdwy over 2f out: styd on and upsides last 50yds: no ex* **9/2**[1]

1110 3 *1 ¼* **Eeny Mac (IRE)**[26] 4679 5-9-1 64 JulieBurke(3) 6 73
(Neville Bycroft) *chsd ldr: drvn over 2f out: led last 100yds: hdd and no ex nr fin* **13/2**[2]

011 4 *2* **Muftarres (IRE)**[11] 5220 7-9-1 70 (b) RussKennemore 11 65+
(Paul Midgley) *s.i.s: hld up in rr: hdwy on ins over 2f out: nt clr run: swtchd lft ins fnl f: r.o* **9/2**[1]

035 5 *nk* **Tislaam (IRE)**[9] 5298 5-9-2 67 (p) RobertWinston 9 65
(Alan McCabe) *hld up in mid-div: nt clr run 2f out: styd on last 100yds* **10/1**

30-0 6 *nk* **Fremen (USA)**[20] 4864 12-9-3 67 AndrewMullen 4 66
(David Nicholls) *trckd ldrs: drvn over 2f out: upsides 1f out: kpt on one pce* **20/1**

1620 7 *1 ¼* **Violent Velocity (IRE)**[11] 5220 9-9-3 75 MichaelO'Connell 2 62
(John Quinn) *trckd ldrs: upsides 2f out: one pce fnl f* **7/1**[3]

00-0 8 *1 ½* **Above Standard (IRE)**[11] 5225 4-8-7 67 DavidSimmonson(7) 3 56
(Michael Easterby) *led: hdd last 100yds: fdd* **40/1**

0100 9 *1 ¼* **Byronic Hero**[28] 4629 3-9-0 79 (v[1]) TonyHamilton 7 58
(Jedd O'Keeffe) *hood removed last moment: dwlt: in rr: kpt on fnl f: nvr a factor* **14/1**

0000 10 *¾* **West End Lad**[24] 4745 9-9-5 77 (b) RoystonFfrench 5 56
(Roy Bowring) *mid-div: effrt 3f out: wknd over 1f out* **11/1**

0002 11 *2* **Brocklebank (IRE)**[11] 5220 3-9-0 75 (tp) PhillipMakin 14 51
(Kevin Ryan) *mid-div: drvn over 2f out: kpt on fnl f: nvr a factor* **8/1**

400- 12 *7* **Freda's Rose (IRE)**[285] 7424 8-8-3 53 ow1 LeonnaMayor(5) 12 22
(Owen Brennan) *in rr and swtchd rt after s: bhd fnl 4f* **100/1**

06 13 *35* **Lady Oz (IRE)**[7] 5387 5-8-12 0 PaulMulrennan 8
(Michael Easterby) *t.k.h: sn in rr: lost pl over 3f out: sn bhd and eased: hopelessly t.o* **80/1**

1m 33.24s (-0.56) **Going Correction** +0.025s/f (Good)

WFA 3 from 4yo+ 5lb **13** Ran SP% **117.9**

Speed ratings (Par 103): **104,103,102,99,99 99,97,95,94,93 91,83,43**

Tote Swingers 1&2 £9.90, 2&3 £6.40, 1&3 £7.90 CSF £42.37 TOTE £10.80: £3.00, £2.00, £2.20; EX 63.50.Fathsta was the subject of a friendly claim

Owner Dr Marwan Koukash **Bred** Brian Miller **Trained** Tarporley, Cheshire

FOCUS

Rail around bottom bend moved in adding 19yds to all distances except 5f. This was quite a competitive claimer and a race of changing fortunes. One rider described the ground as "a bit loose on top." A fair claimer on the figures but the third would seem to limit the form.

Lady Oz(IRE) Official explanation: jockey said that the mare ran too free

5619 IRISH STALLION FARMS EBF MEDIAN AUCTION MAIDEN STKS 1m 100y

2:20 (2:22) (Class 5) 2-Y-O **£3,169** (£943; £471; £235) **Stalls** Low

Form RPR

62 1 **Grey Blue (IRE)**[13] 5162 2-9-3 0 JoeFanning 6 84+
(Mark Johnston) *w ldr: led over 6f out: increased pce over 3f out: drvn clr over 1f out: eased towards fin* **13/8**[1]

2 2 *6* **Mister Marcasite**[9] 5311 2-9-3 0 DavidAllan 7 70
(Mel Brittain) *chsd ldrs: wnt 2nd 5f out: kpt on same pce fnl 2f: no imp* **9/4**[2]

0 3 *2 ½* **Star Of Broadway**[9] 5319 2-8-12 0 AntiocoMurgia(5) 9 64
(Mahmood Al Zarooni) *wnt lft s: sn trcking ldrs: 3rd over 4f out: drvn and outpcd over 3f out: rallied over 1f out: one pce and eased nr fin* **13/2**[3]

3403 4 *1 ½* **Chant (IRE)**[19] 4907 2-9-3 68 PaulMulrennan 3 61
(Ann Duffield) *s.i.s: in rr: hdwy over 2f out: nt clr run on inner over 1f out: styd on last 100yds* **10/1**

6420 5 *hd* **Notional Demand**[22] 4792 2-9-3 67 GrahamGibbons 1 61
(Tim Easterby) *trckd ldrs: drvn over 3f out: one pce* **14/1**

04 6 *¾* **Attansky (IRE)**[13] 5169 2-9-3 0 DuranFentiman 4 59
(Tim Easterby) *mid-div: drvn over 3f out: nvr nr ldrs* **12/1**

4 7 *5* **Silk Scarf (IRE)**[16] 5061 2-8-12 0 RobertWinston 5 43
(Mark H Tompkins) *in rr: bhd fnl 3f* **20/1**

8 *10* **Sad But True (IRE)** 2-9-3 0 TomEaves 2 26
(Alan McCabe) *led tl over 6f out: lost pl over 3f out: sn bhd* **25/1**

05 9 *½* **Chloe's Image**[18] 4952 2-8-12 0 PhillipMakin 8 20
(Philip Kirby) *in rr: bhd fnl 3f* **50/1**

1m 48.11s (0.51) **Going Correction** +0.025s/f (Good) **9** Ran SP% **116.2**

Speed ratings (Par 94): **98,92,89,88,87 87,82,72,71**

Tote Swingers 1&2 £1.60, 2&3 £4.00, 1&3 £4.00 CSF £5.24 TOTE £2.40: £1.20, £1.30, £2.30; EX 6.90.

Owner A D Spence **Bred** Twelve Oaks Stud **Trained** Middleham Moor, N Yorks

FOCUS

Not a particularly competitive maiden and the order didn't change very much, but the winner trotted up. He showed improved form.

NOTEBOOK

Grey Blue(IRE) improved from his debut to finish runner-up on Polytrack last time and this longer trip saw him progress again. Given a no-nonsense front-running ride, he ran his rivals into the ground and went further and further clear up the hill. He holds an entry in the Weatherbys Insurance £300,000 2-Y-O Stakes at the St Leger meeting, but given the way he saw out this extended 1m dropping 2f in trip there may not be ideal. He is still more than capable of winning something rather better than this, however. (op 7-4 tchd 2-1 and 15-8 early in places)

Mister Marcasite showed plenty of promise when second of 14 on his Newcastle debut nine days earlier and had every chance to go one better, but he could never get on terms with the winner over this longer trip. He probably ran into a fair sort again and should be able to find an ordinary maiden. (op 5-2 tchd 2-1)

Star Of Broadway was beaten a long way on his Newmarket debut nine days earlier despite attracting market support, but this longer trip should have suited being out of a 1m4f winner. This was certainly an improvement, but he was made to look one-paced as he tried to get on terms with the winner over the last 2f. (op 6-1 tchd 7-1)

Chant(IRE) looks exposed, but probably ran to his mark. (op 12-1)

5620 COME RACING AT BEVERLEY NEXT SATURDAY NURSERY 5f

2:55 (2:55) (Class 4) (0-85,76) 2-Y-O **£4,398** (£1,309; £654; £327) **Stalls** Low

Form RPR

402 1 **Star Up In The Sky (USA)**[27] 4651 2-9-4 73 AmyRyan 3 77+
(Kevin Ryan) *trckd ldr: led appr fnl f: hld on towards fin* **7/2**[2]

0031 2 *nk* **Sandsend (IRE)**[9] 5313 2-8-5 60 JimmyQuinn 2 62
(Richard Fahey) *chsd ldrs: drvn over 2f out: styd on wl last 75yds: jst hld* **3/1**[1]

4250 3 *1 ¾* **Gold Beau (FR)**[33] 4433 2-9-1 70 GrahamLee 4 66
(Linda Stubbs) *in rr: sn pushed along: hdwy over 1f out: styd on ins fnl f: tk 3rd line* **22/1**

1505 4 *shd* **Rhagori Aur**[22] 4827 2-9-7 76 TomEaves 1 71
(Bryan Smart) *led: hdd appr fnl f: kpt on same pce* **15/2**

4156 **5** ½ **Lucky Lodge**[15] 5109 2-9-1 **70** .... PaulMulrennan 6 64
(Mel Brittain) *chsd ldrs: drvn over 2f out: one pce* **11/1**

51 **6** 3 ¼ **Shrimper Roo**[22] 4825 2-9-6 **75** .... DuranFentiman 5 57
(Tim Easterby) *hld up: hdwy on ins whn hmpd 3f out: hdwy 2f out: sn drvn: wknd fnl f* **7/2**[2]

460 **U** **Fantasy Invader (IRE)**[18] 4960 2-8-8 **62** ow1 .... MichaelO'Connell 7
(John Quinn) *hood stl on whn leaving stalls: sn swvd bdly lft and uns rdr* **9/2**[3]

1m 3.24s (-0.26) **Going Correction** -0.075s/f (Good) 7 Ran SP% **112.1**
Speed ratings (Par 96): **99,98,95,95,94 89,**
Tote Swingers 1&2 £1.80, 2&3 £6.70, 1&3 £6.40 CSF £13.82 CT £191.95 TOTE £4.20: £2.10, £2.10; EX 12.40.
Owner Matt & Lauren Morgan **Bred** Dixiana Stables Inc **Trained** Hambleton, N Yorks

FOCUS
A fair nursery, and straightforward form.

NOTEBOOK
Star Up In The Sky(USA) showed improved form when runner-up in a Polytrack maiden on her third start (had no chance in the Queen Mary on her second outing) and built on that performance on this nursery debut, quickening to the front more than a furlong from home and establishing enough of an advantage to see her race out. She should be able to find more opportunities and always has the option of a return to the all-weather. (op 4-1)
Sandsend(IRE) has improved since switching to nurseries and was 5lb higher than for his Newcastle win nine days earlier. This was another good effort, but the way he came home suggests he could be interesting returned to 6f. (op 11-4)
Gold Beau(FR) hasn't built on early promise in maidens and was down to the minimum trip for the first time on this nursery debut, but he seemed to find everything happening too quickly for him. (op 20-1)
Rhagori Aur has been disappointing since winning on her Thirsk debut and had the run of the race out front here with few excuses. (op 7-1)
Lucky Lodge was off the bridle at halfway and has found life tough in nurseries since winning his maiden. (tchd 10-1)
Shrimper Roo had a couple of subsequent winners behind when winning a Thirsk maiden earlier this month, but he never got into this and was a major disappointment. The Stewards noted that the trainer could offer no explanation for his performance and they ordered the gelding to be routine tested. Official explanation: trainer could offer no explanation for the poor performance shown (tchd 3-1)
Fantasy Invader(IRE) still had the blindfold on as the stalls opened, seemed to get spooked as a result and swerved exiting the gates, dumping his rider on the ground. (op 6-1 tchd 13-2)

5621 BEVERLEY LIONS H'CAP (DIV I) 5f
3:30 (3:30) (Class 6) (0-60,65) 3-Y-O £2,181 (£644; £322) Stalls Low

Form RPR
4062 **1** **Pavers Star**[9] 5294 3-8-3 **47** .... (p) NeilFarley(5) 2 55
(Noel Wilson) *w ldr: led over 4f out: hdd over 1f out: rallied to ld towards fin* **8/1**

514 **2** ½ **Maltease Ah**[5] 5445 3-8-7 **53** .... DavidBergin(7) 9 59
(Alan McCabe) *chsd ldrs on outer: edgd rt jst ins fnl f: hrd rdn and styd on to take 2nd nr fin* **6/1**

2331 **3** ½ **Ypres**[11] 5247 3-9-12 **65** .... PaddyAspell 4 69
(Jason Ward) *trckd ldrs: led narrowly over 1f out: hdd over 1f out and no ex clsng stages* **9/2**[3]

4633 **4** ¾ **Hadrians Rule (IRE)**[9] 5294 3-9-5 **58** .... (p) DavidAllan 8 60
(Tim Easterby) *sn swtchd rt: sn chsng ldrs: kpt on same pce last 150yds* **4/1**[2]

0025 **5** ¾ **Emily Hall**[18] 4956 3-8-11 **50** .... TomEaves 6 49
(Bryan Smart) *s.i.s: hld up towards rr: kpt on fnl 2f: one pce fnl f* **9/1**

6 ¾ **Clubland (IRE)**[41] 4160 3-8-13 **52** .... AmyRyan 3 48
(Kevin Ryan) *restless in stalls: half-rrd s: hdwy over 2f out: swtchd rt and jnd ldrs over 1f out: fdd towards fin* **3/1**[1]

3-04 **7** 2 **Headstight (IRE)**[18] 4953 3-9-1 **54** .... RoystonFfrench 5 45
(Paul Midgley) *chsd ldrs: hung lft over 1f out: one pce whn hmpd jst ins fnl f* **10/1**

5600 **8** 5 **Majestic Angel (IRE)**[33] 4428 3-8-7 **46** oh1 .... BarryMcHugh 7 17
(Brian Rothwell) *chsd ldrs: wknd over 1f out* **66/1**

0006 **9** 9 **Not Bad For A Boy (IRE)**[19] 4929 3-9-2 **55** .... (b) RussKennemore 1
(Barry Leavy) *led over 1f: lost pl over 1f out: sn bhd* **20/1**

1m 3.39s (-0.11) **Going Correction** -0.075s/f (Good) 9 Ran SP% **113.9**
Speed ratings (Par 98): **97,96,95,94,93 91,88,80,66**
Tote Swingers 1&2 £7.70, 2&3 £6.20, 1&3 £4.30 CSF £54.45 CT £244.21 TOTE £8.30: £2.60, £2.20, £1.40; EX 81.50.
Owner Mrs Michael John Paver **Bred** Mrs C K Paver **Trained** Middleham, N Yorks
■ Stewards' Enquiry : David Bergin two-day ban: used whip above permitted level (9 -10 Sep)

FOCUS
A weak sprint handicap in which those that raced away from the inside rail seemed to be at an advantage. The winning time was slower than the nursery and division II. The winner built on his Catterick form.
Headstight(IRE) Official explanation: jockey said that the filly hung left

5622 BEVERLEY MIDDLE DISTANCE SERIES FINAL H'CAP 1m 4f 16y
4:05 (4:05) (Class 5) (0-75,76) 3-Y-O+ £5,498 (£1,636; £817; £408) Stalls Low

Form RPR
4433 **1** **Party Line**[9] 5312 3-9-4 **75** .... JoeFanning 5 84
(Mark Johnston) *led early: chsd ldrs: drvn over 3f out: led jst ins fnl f: styd on gamely* **9/4**[1]

053 **2** 1 **Granston (IRE)**[11] 5227 11-9-11 **72** .... GrahamLee 6 79
(James Bethell) *hld up in mid-div: hdwy to trck ldrs 8f out: nt clr run on inner over 2f out tl swtchd lft jst ins fnl f: kpt on wl: no real imp* **11/2**[3]

0402 **3** 1 ¼ **Coax**[16] 5054 4-9-1 **62** .... DanielTudhope 8 67
(Patrick Holmes) *hld up in rr: hdwy over 4f out: styd on wl fnl f: tk 3rd nr fin* **12/1**

0623 **4** 1 **Tribal Myth (IRE)**[11] 5225 5-9-3 **64** .... (b[1]) AmyRyan 9 67
(Kevin Ryan) *swtchd rt after s: sn led: drvn 3f out: hdd jst ins fnl f: fdd towards fin* **17/2**

5351 **5** ½ **Carragold**[11] 5227 6-9-12 **76** .... DaleSwift(3) 1 79
(Mel Brittain) *t.k.h: trckd ldrs: upsides 8f out: kpt on same pce appr fnl f* **6/1**

0533 **6** ¾ **Meetings Man (IRE)**[19] 4910 5-9-6 **67** .... PJMcDonald 3 68
(Micky Hammond) *t.k.h: trckd ldrs: one pce appr fnl f* **9/2**[2]

1065 **7** ¾ **Maybeme**[11] 5226 6-8-9 **56** oh1 .... JimmyQuinn 7 56
(Neville Bycroft) *dwlt: in rr: drvn over 4f out: hdwy over 2f out: kpt on one pce: nvr a threat* **12/1**

0434 **8** 9 **Pinotage**[11] 5226 4-9-0 **61** .... (p) PhillipMakin 10 47
(Peter Niven) *hld up in rr: hdwy on outer over 3f out: lost pl over 1f out* **12/1**

0-40 **9** 47 **High Five Society**[24] 4747 8-9-4 **65** .... (b) RoystonFfrench 2
(Roy Bowring) *in rr: shkn up after 3f: lost pl over 5f out: t.o 3f out* **40/1**

2m 38.92s (-0.88) **Going Correction** +0.025s/f (Good)
WFA 3 from 4yo+ 10lb 9 Ran SP% **114.7**
Speed ratings (Par 103): **103,102,101,100,100 100,99,93,62**
Tote Swingers 1&2 £3.20, 2&3 £9.70, 1&3 £7.50 CSF £14.53 TOTE £3.00: £1.20, £1.80, £3.60; EX 12.80.
Owner S R Counsell **Bred** Highclere Stud And Balmerino Bloodstock **Trained** Middleham Moor, N Yorks

FOCUS
The final of this series and a decent prize for a 56-75 handicap. Straightforward form.
High Five Society Official explanation: jockey said that the gelding had a breathing problem

5623 MALTON RACING ASSOCIATION OPEN DAY H'CAP 1m 1f 207y
4:40 (4:41) (Class 6) (0-60,60) 3-Y-O £2,070 (£616; £307; £153) Stalls Low

Form RPR
5006 **1** **Hikma (USA)**[23] 4771 3-9-0 **53** .... (b[1]) JoeFanning 9 67+
(Mark Johnston) *mde all: drvn clr over 1f out: eased towards fin* **12/1**

2250 **2** 3 ¼ **Mexican Wave**[41] 4153 3-8-7 **46** oh1 .... (v) AmyRyan 6 49
(Michael Bell) *t.k.h: trckd ldrs: chsd wnr over 2f out: no imp* **12/1**

0033 **3** 1 ¼ **Kathleensluckylad (IRE)**[23] 4771 3-9-3 **56** .... PhillipMakin 4 57+
(Kevin Ryan) *tk fierce hold in rr: hdwy and hung rt over 2f out: swtchd lft over 1f out: kpt on to take 3rd jst ins fnl f* **11/2**[2]

3200 **4** 4 ½ **Mad For Fun (IRE)**[19] 4913 3-8-11 **50** .... RussKennemore 3 42
(Paul Midgley) *in rr: hdwy on inner 4f out: swtchd lft 2f out: kpt on to take modest 4th last 100yds* **18/1**

-434 **5** ½ **Yojojo (IRE)**[17] 4984 3-9-7 **60** .... GrahamLee 8 51
(Gay Kelleway) *chsd ldrs: effrt over 2f out: one pce whn n.m.r over 1f out* **6/1**[3]

6-00 **6** 4 ½ **Justine Time (IRE)**[30] 4549 3-8-9 **48** .... BarryMcHugh 12 30
(Julie Camacho) *t.k.h: w ldrs: hung rt and wknd over 1f out* **25/1**

0600 **7** 6 **Certainly Elusive (IRE)**[67] 3275 3-8-7 **46** .... (b) AndrewElliott 13 16
(Alan Swinbank) *w ldrs: drvn over 3f out: lost pl whn hmpd 2f out* **14/1**

6064 **8** 4 ½ **Only A Round (IRE)**[37] 4313 3-8-7 **46** oh1 .... PJMcDonald 5
(Micky Hammond) *chsd ldrs: wknd over 2f out* **25/1**

6606 **9** 7 **Bollin Tommy**[72] 3111 3-9-5 **58** .... (p) DavidAllan 11
(Tim Easterby) *trckd ldrs: t.k.h: lost pl and hmpd 2f out* **14/1**

2661 **10** 3 ¾ **Penang Pegasus**[12] 5187 3-8-13 **52** .... RobertWinston 2 43+
(David O'Meara) *gave problems in stalls: half-rrd s: t.k.h: trckd ldrs over 7f out: drvn over 3f out: btn whn hmpd on ins over 1f out: heavily eased ins fnl f* **5/4**[1]

6000 **11** 1 **Medecis Mountain**[1] 5589 3-8-4 **46** oh1 .... (p) JulieBurke(3) 10
(John Wainwright) *mid-div: t.k.h: lost pl over 3f out: sn bhd* **100/1**

0000 **12** 87 **Champagne Valley**[15] 5081 3-8-7 **46** oh1 .... PaulQuinn 1
(Sharon Watt) *t.k.h in rr: bdly hmpd after 2f: sn lost pl and bhd: t.o 3f out: virtually p.u: eventually completed* **28/1**

2m 7.42s (0.42) **Going Correction** +0.025s/f (Good) 12 Ran SP% **120.2**
Speed ratings (Par 98): **99,96,95,91,91 87,83,79,73,70 70,**
Tote Swingers 1&2 £11.90, 2&3 £6.40, 1&3 £9.70 CSF £144.34 CT £893.06 TOTE £15.80: £3.50, £2.90, £2.30; EX 105.40.
Owner Sheikh Hamdan Bin Mohammed Al Maktoum **Bred** Darley **Trained** Middleham Moor, N Yorks

FOCUS
A moderate handicap and not very competitive despite the size of the field, with good recent form very thin on the ground. Several of these didn't look straightforward and the form means little outside of the winner, who provided a treble for her trainer and jockey. This was her first real turf form.
Penang Pegasus Official explanation: jockey said that the gelding suffered interference in running

5624 BEVERLEY LIONS H'CAP (DIV II) 5f
5:10 (5:11) (Class 6) (0-60,60) 3-Y-O £2,181 (£644; £322) Stalls Low

Form RPR
0211 **1** **Aubrietia**[5] 5446 3-8-8 **54** .... (b) DavidBergin(7) 3 65+
(Alan McCabe) *hmpd s: sn w ldr: led appr fnl f: pushed out* **8/11**[1]

5165 **2** ½ **Holy Angel (IRE)**[18] 4965 3-9-7 **60** .... DuranFentiman 8 69
(Tim Easterby) *hmpd s: in rr: hdwy on outside over 1f out: styd on wl ins fnl f: tk 2 l 2nd last 50yds: a hld* **13/2**[2]

0600 **3** 1 ½ **First Fast Now (IRE)**[9] 5318 3-8-10 **49** .... PaulMulrennan 1 53
(Nigel Tinkler) *wnt rt s: chsd ldrs: wnt 3rd 1f out: kpt on same pce* **14/1**

6 **4** 1 ¼ **Koolgreycat (IRE)**[20] 4881 3-9-4 **60** .... GaryBartley(3) 9 59
(Noel Wilson) *wnt rt s: led: hdd appr fnl f: edgd rt and wknd last 100yds* **10/1**

346 **5** 1 ½ **Cataract**[9] 5317 3-8-7 **46** oh1 .... (b) BarryMcHugh 4 40
(John Weymes) *hmpd s: hdwy on inner over 3f out: one pce appr fnl f* **40/1**

4024 **6** ¾ **Dartrix**[9] 5318 3-9-5 **58** .... (p) RoystonFfrench 2 49
(Michael Dods) *hmpd s: in rr and drvn along: hdwy on ins and hung rt over 2f out: nt clr run and swtchd lft jst ins fnl f: kpt on* **7/1**[3]

1300 **7** 1 ¼ **Made In The Shade**[23] 4784 3-8-8 **54** .... DanielleMooney(7) 10 41
(Paul Midgley) *chsd ldrs: one pce over 1f out* **16/1**

0053 **8** 1 ¼ **Essexvale (IRE)**[43] 4084 3-8-0 **46** oh1 .... (p) EvaMoscrop(7) 7 28
(Robert Johnson) *in rr: effrt on outer over 2f out: hung lft: nvr a factor* **33/1**

-000 **9** 1 **Wake Up Sioux (IRE)**[40] 4187 3-8-13 **52** .... RobertWinston 5 30
(David C Griffiths) *hmpd s: in rr: hdwy over 1f out: nvr a factor* **14/1**

26-6 **10** 1 **Stans Deelyte**[18] 4970 3-8-11 **50** .... TomEaves 6 25
(Lisa Williamson) *chsd ldrs: drvn over 2f out: wknd over 1f out* **40/1**

1m 2.9s (-0.60) **Going Correction** -0.075s/f (Good) 10 Ran SP% **119.9**
Speed ratings (Par 98): **101,100,97,95,93 92,90,88,86,85**
Tote Swingers 1&2 £2.40, 2&3 £12.20, 1&3 £4.10 CSF £6.04 CT £39.55 TOTE £1.50: £1.10, £2.00, £3.10; EX 8.00.
Owner Mrs M J McCabe **Bred** C J Murfitt **Trained** Averham Park, Notts

FOCUS
The winning time was about half a second faster than the first division. The winner was well in and did not need to quite match her best.
T/Jkpt: £72,735.50 to a £1 stake. Pool: £102,444.40. 1.00 winning ticket. T/Plt: £63.80 to a £1 stake. Pool: £72,747.84. 831.32 winning tickets. T/Qpdt: £17.20 to a £1 stake. Pool £3,940.06. 168.92 winning tickets. WG

5571 GOODWOOD (R-H)

Sunday, August 26

OFFICIAL GOING: Good to soft (good in places; 7.5)

Wind: Light, against Weather: Fine but cloudy

5625 SAN ROSSORE TURF CLUB STKS (H'CAP) 7f

2:10 (2:14) (Class 5) (0-70,71) 3-Y-0+ £3,234 (£962; £481; £240) Stalls Low

Form				RPR
-115	1		**Scottish Glen**[22] 4814 6-9-8 66 GeorgeBaker 13 (Patrick Chamings) *hld up wl off the pce in rr: prog 2f out: str run on outer fnl f to ld last 75yds* 7/1	77
-465	2	3/4	**Gifted Dancer**[15] 5107 3-9-3 66 DaneO'Neill 7 (Henry Candy) *trckd ldrs in 8th: clsd over 2f out: nt clr run sn after: prog over 1f out: rdn to ld last 150yds: hdd and outpcd last 75yds* 5/1[2]	73
260	3	1 1/2	**Absent Amy (IRE)**[74] 3044 3-9-0 63 FergusSweeney 14 (Willie Musson) *hld up wl off the pce in rr: prog over 2f out: clsd on ldrs 1f out: styd on same pce after* 20/1	66
6606	4	nse	**Shamrocked (IRE)**[15] 5099 3-9-2 70 CharlesBishop(5) 3 (Mick Channon) *ref to go to post tl dismntd and led down: pushed up to go prom: chsd ldr 4f out to 3f out: cl up but hanging and nt qckn over 1f out: styd on* 11/2[3]	73
0021	5	1/2	**Stonecrabstomorrow (IRE)**[5] 5444 9-9-3 64 6ex MarkCoumbe(3) 8 (Michael Attwater) *s.i.s: wl off the pce in rr: prog on inner fr 3f out: drvn 2f out: clsd 1f out: one pce after* 16/1	67
0000	6	3/4	**Alnoomaas (IRE)**[4] 5479 3-8-5 54 DavidProbert 11 (Luke Dace) *led at str pce: rdn over 1f out: hdd & wknd last 150yds* 16/1	53
-401	7	4	**King Vahe (IRE)**[11] 5240 3-9-8 71 NeilCallan 2 (Alan Jarvis) *prom: rdn and lost pl over 2f out: struggling whn hmpd over 1f out: fdd* 9/2[1]	60+
4005	8	1	**Reginald Claude**[8] 5346 4-8-5 54 RachealKneller(5) 4 (Mark Usher) *prom: chsd ldr 3f out: rdn to chal 2f out: upsides over 1f out: wknd qckly fnl f* 20/1	42
0000	9	nk	**Barathea Dancer (IRE)**[17] 5008 4-9-8 66 JohnFahy 10 (Roger Teal) *hld up wl off the pce in rr: effrt on inner 3f out: styng on but nt wl enough whn hmpd 2f out: no ch after* 25/1	53
1000	10	4	**Silvee**[8] 5362 5-9-4 62 KieranO'Neill 6 (John Bridger) *a off the pce towards rr: rdn and no prog over 2f out* 16/1	38
0042	11	1 1/2	**Renoir's Lady**[18] 4942 4-8-7 51 oh1 HarryBentley 5 (Simon Dow) *chsd ldrs: rdn over 2f out: wknd over 1f out* 13/2	23
302	12	1 3/4	**Demoiselle Bond**[19] 4920 4-8-10 54 JamieGoldstein 15 (Lydia Richards) *racd wd: chsd ldr 3f: lost pl fr 3f out: wknd 2f out* 33/1	22
-000	13	20	**Eye For The Girls**[11] 5240 6-8-7 51 oh4 (t) SilvestreDeSousa 12 (William Knight) *chsd ldrs: rdn 1/2-way: wknd over 2f out: t.o and eased: sddle slipped* 40/1	
0100	14	32	**Titan Triumph**[118] 1708 8-9-10 68 (t[1]) RichardHughes 1 (William Knight) *a towards rr: wknd sn after 1/2-way: wl t.o and eased* 10/1	

1m 27.89s (0.89) **Going Correction** +0.20s/f (Good)
WFA 3 from 4yo+ 5lb 14 Ran SP% **121.6**
Speed ratings (Par 103): **102,101,99,99,98 97,93,92,91,87 85,83,60,24**
Tote Swingers 1&2 £8.00, 2&3 £27.80, 1&3 £47.40 CSF £39.36 CT £702.18 TOTE £9.50: £2.80, £2.10, £7.20; EX 52.70 Trifecta £809.70 Part won. Pool £1,094.19 - 0.62 winning units. Rollover of £415.79 to Saturday 1st September..
Owner The Foxford House Partnership **Bred** Mrs Ann Jenkins **Trained** Baughurst, Hants
■ Stewards' Enquiry : Dane O'Neill two-day ban: careless riding (9-10 Sept)

FOCUS
Richard Hughes described the ground after the first as "a little loose, but mainly good". It didn't look to be riding too soft. A modest handicap run at a sound pace, and in a time 3.59sec outside standard. The runners remained on the inner once into the straight. The form looks sound and could be worth a bit more.
Eye For The Girls Official explanation: jockey said that the saddle slipped
Titan Triumph Official explanation: jockey said the gelding was never travelling

5626 GREENE KING H'CAP 1m 1f 192y

2:45 (2:45) (Class 2) (0-100,95) 3-Y-O
£12,450 (£3,728; £1,864; £932; £466; £234) Stalls Low

Form				RPR
2-13	1		**Blue Surf**[24] 4735 3-8-13 87 PatDobbs 7 (Amanda Perrett) *hld up in tch: trckd ldrs gng easily 2f out: produced to chal 1f out: led last 100yds: drvn and jst asserted nr fin* 7/2[3]	97+
2055	2	1/2	**Trader Jack**[25] 4700 3-9-1 89 GeorgeBaker 4 (Roger Charlton) *hld up in last pair: prog to trck ldng pair 3f out: rdn to ld over 1f out: hdd last 100yds: battled on wl but jst hld* 11/4[1]	98+
2212	3	3 1/4	**Commend**[8] 5358 3-8-13 87 RichardHughes 2 (Sir Michael Stoute) *cl up in 3rd: waiting for an opening over 2f out: rdn and styd on one pce over 1f out* 3/1[2]	90+
122-	4	1 1/4	**Harvard N Yale (USA)**[244] 7879 3-9-1 89 JimmyFortune 8 (Jeremy Noseda) *t.k.h: trckd ldr: chal over 2f out: lost 2nd over 1f out: fdd* 5/1	89
0-42	5	shd	**Oxford Charley (USA)**[107] 2026 3-9-7 95 FergusSweeney 1 (Mikael Magnusson) *hld up in last pair: wl in tch 3f out: rdn and nt qckn over 2f out: kpt on same pce after* 16/1	95
5-13	6	1 3/4	**Invisible Hunter (USA)**[15] 5091 3-9-7 95 (t) SilvestreDeSousa 3 (Saeed Bin Suroor) *led: rdn over 2f out: hdd over 1f out: steadily wknd* 7/1	91
00	7	10	**Forest Row**[57] 3630 3-8-11 85 JohnFahy 6 (Clive Cox) *t.k.h: hld up in tch: effrt on inner 3f out: wknd 2f out* 16/1	61

2m 8.42s (0.32) **Going Correction** +0.20s/f (Good) 7 Ran SP% **114.8**
Speed ratings (Par 106): **106,105,103,102,101 100,92**
Tote Swingers 1&2 £2.30, 2&3 £2.30, 1&3 £2.10 CSF £13.70 CT £31.26 TOTE £4.40: £2.40, £1.80; EX 13.20 Trifecta £8.60 Pool £691.38 - 59.08 winning units..
Owner The Green Dot Partnership **Bred** Star Pointe Ltd,Brosnan And Williamson **Trained** Pulborough, W Sussex

FOCUS
A valuable and competitive handicap contested by some useful sorts. The pace was only moderate and the first pair came clear late on. A step up from both the first two.

NOTEBOOK
Blue Surf travelled well before playing his hand and just got the better of the runner-up. There had been a question mark over his attitude when third in a handicap at the big meeting here (a short head behind subsequent winner Switzerland) but he toughed it out well this time. Likely to reappear at Sandown or Ascot early next month, he is in the Cambridgeshire but is unlikely to make the cut. (tchd 4-1)
Trader Jack worked his way to the front down the outside and his measure was only taken close home. This was another solid run following his luckless effort at the big Goodwood meeting, and he won't mind a return to 1m4f. (op 10-3 tchd 7-2)
Commend ◆ was temporarily outpaced when having to wait for a run but was staying on quite nicely at the line. He should continue to give a good account. (tchd 11-4)
Harvard N Yale(USA), who had to be reined back into second after proving keen, lacked the pace to race with the leaders at the business end. This was a satisfactory first start since Boxing Day but it didn't entirely prove his stamina for this trip. (op 8-1)
Oxford Charley(USA) was down in grade after contesting a couple of Classic trials in the spring. He was never quite able to challenge and his head carriage marks him down as one to have concerns over. (op 11-1)
Invisible Hunter(USA) had things his way in front but could not retain his position when the pressure was on. A drop back to a mile may suit. (op 13-2 tchd 6-1)
Forest Row, who had taken time to settle, was the first beaten and has something to prove now. (op 14-1)

5627 GREENE KING SUPREME STKS (GROUP 3) 7f

3:20 (3:20) (Class 1) 3-Y-O+
£31,190 (£11,825; £5,918; £2,948; £1,479; £742) Stalls Low

Form				RPR
3154	1		**Producer**[43] 4095 3-8-9 107 RichardHughes 2 (Richard Hannon) *dwlt: hld up in 5th: plld out and rdn wl over 1f out: gd prog fnl f: r.o to ld nr fin* 7/2[2]	112
2024	2	1/2	**The Cheka (IRE)**[21] 4861 6-9-0 110 (v) NeilCallan 3 (Eve Johnson Houghton) *led: kicked on 2f out: drvn fnl f: hdd last strides* 11/4[1]	113
3-53	3	3/4	**Zumbi (IRE)**[15] 5102 3-8-9 103 PatDobbs 8 (Sir Michael Stoute) *hld up in last pair: plld out and effrt jst over 1f out: running on whn nt clr run 150yds out: nt rcvr but styd on to take 3rd last strides* 9/2[3]	111+
-050	4	nk	**I Love Me**[30] 4527 4-8-11 100[1] DavidProbert 5 (Andrew Balding) *trckd ldr to 3f out: styd prom: rdn 2f out: nt qckn over 1f out: kpt on same pce after* 16/1	107
5022	5	hd	**Royal Rock**[22] 4794 8-9-0 109 GeorgeBaker 6 (Chris Wall) *trckd ldng trio: rdn and nt qckn 2f out: kpt on same pce after: nvr able to chal* 8/1	109
036	6	nse	**Saigon**[23] 4760 3-8-9 105 (p) KirstyMilczarek 7 (James Toller) *hld up in last pair: shkn up over 2f out: no prog tl styd on fnl f: nrst fin* 8/1	107
0-01	7	1 1/2	**Regal Realm**[23] 4764 3-8-10 101 (p) JimmyFortune 1 (Jeremy Noseda) *sltly awkward s: trckd ldng pair: wnt 2nd 3f out: rdn and nt qckn over 1f out: wknd ins fnl f* 11/2	104

1m 27.75s (0.75) **Going Correction** +0.20s/f (Good)
WFA 3 from 4yo+ 5lb 7 Ran SP% **110.6**
Speed ratings (Par 113): **103,102,101,101,101 100,99**
Tote Swingers 1&2 £1.10, 2&3 £3.10, 1&3 £2.30 CSF £12.61 TOTE £4.00: £2.10, £1.90; EX 17.10 Trifecta £101.10 Pool £1,679.75 - 12.28 winning units..
Owner J Palmer-Brown **Bred** Cheveley Park Stud Ltd **Trained** East Everleigh, Wilts

FOCUS
Despite the non-runners this was still a good renewal. However the runner-up set no more than an ordinary pace and they finished in a heap, lending a few doubts to the form. The time was relatively slow. The form has been rated at something like face value.

NOTEBOOK
Producer had ground to make up at the furlong pole, but delivered a strong run to win well. At home on undulating tracks, having won four times at Epsom over this trip, he had run well in the Jersey Stakes when just behind recent Hungerford winner Lethal Force, and had failed to act in heavy ground last time. He's a likeable colt with more to offer, although he may not be easy to place now. (op 9-2)
The Cheka(IRE) had been placed in the Grade 1 July Cup and Prix Maurice de Gheest on his last two starts and was back over 7f for the first time this year. Setting his own pace, he looked in command at the furlong pole but the winner gunned him down. His trainer felt he was there to be shot at in front after nothing else wanted to go on. This was a solid effort but he was also beaten in this last year. He's in the Ayr Gold Cup and the British Champions Sprint at Ascot remains a viable target, particularly if the ground is riding soft by then. (op 9-4, tchd 3-1 in a place)
Zumbi(IRE) was a shade unlucky, as he was blocked in his run when picking up from the back before finishing rapidly. He's a smart colt who will be suited by a step up to a mile. (op 4-1)
I Love Me showed a bit more zip in the first-time hood but has not captured her best this year.
Royal Rock, who was mounted on the course, ran respectably but lacked a change of gear and is best at 6f. (op 6-1)
Saigon, trying cheekpieces instead of blinkers, was running on when it was too late on this drop back to 7f. James Toller reported that the colt was unsuited by the ground. Official explanation: jockey said that the colt was unsuited by the good to soft, good in places going. (op 10-1)
Regal Realm was unbeaten in two previous runs over course and distance, including the Oak Tree Stakes last time. She had her chance after tracking the runner-up but faded when the pressure was on. (op 13-2)

5628 ANGLO-IRISH STKS (AMATEUR RIDERS' H'CAP) (IN MEMORY OF THE LATE GAY KINDERSLEY) 1m 1f

3:55 (3:55) (Class 5) (0-75,64) 3-Y-0+ £4,679 (£1,451; £725; £363) Stalls Low

Form				RPR
0640	1		**Catchanova (IRE)**[8] 5349 5-11-5 62 MrROHarding 5 (Eve Johnson Houghton) *mde all: clr after 2f: 6 l up 3f out: sn rdn: out on his feet fnl f but clung on* 9/2	68
6320	2	1 3/4	**Potentiale (IRE)**[10] 5258 8-11-6 63 (v) MrSWalker 3 (J W Hills) *trckd wnr but let him go clr after 2f: rdn 3f out: clsd grad fr over 1f out but nvr able to chal* 10/3[3]	65
3334	3	1 3/4	**South Cape**[11] 5239 9-11-7 64 MissECSayer 2 (Gary Moore) *hld up in 4th and sn wl off the pce: rdn over 3f out: bmpd over 2f out: kpt on to take 3rd fnl f but nvr able to chal* 11/4[2]	62
4601	4	3/4	**Brown Pete (IRE)**[27] 4662 4-11-7 64 (e) MrDLQueally 4 (Richard Guest) *hld up in last: disp 3rd on inner over 3f out: swtchd lft and bmpd rival over 2f out: one pce u.p and lost 3rd fnl f* 5/2[1]	61
4046	5	8	**Saucy Buck (IRE)**[8] 5349 4-10-12 58 MissJMMangan(3) 1 (Jamie Poulton) *hld up in 3rd: squeezed for room over 3f out: no prog over 2f out: sn wknd* 6/1	37

2m 0.99s (4.69) **Going Correction** +0.20s/f (Good) 5 Ran SP% **110.8**
Speed ratings (Par 103): **87,85,83,83,76**
CSF £19.43 TOTE £5.10: £3.10, £2.10; EX 24.20.
Owner Andrew Wyer Darrell Blake Hugh Arthur **Bred** G J King **Trained** Blewbury, Oxon
■ Richard Harding's first Flat winner.
■ Stewards' Enquiry : Mr D L Queally two-day ban: careless riding (TBA)

FOCUS
Another small field for this event, which in recent years was a Fegentri race for amateurs from across Europe. Weak form, the winner given an easy lead.

5629 ALAN MORCOMBE BIRTHDAY (S) STKS — 1m 3f
4:30 (4:30) (Class 4) 3-Y-O — £5,175 (£1,540; £769; £384) Stalls High

Form				RPR
00-0	1		**Navajo Charm**[29] 4584 3-8-7 55 .... KirstyMilczarek 7 (Alan Jarvis) *trckd ldrs: shkn up 3f out: clsd to ld jst over 2f out and sn rdn clr: in n.d after* **20/1**	65
5055	2	6	**Priestley's Reward (IRE)**[15] 5112 3-9-3 68 ....(v) GeorgeBaker 3 (Mrs K Burke) *a.p: hld up in last: prog 3f out: drvn and outpcd 2f out: kpt on to take modest 2nd ins fnl f* **7/2**[2]	64
206	3	¾	**Daring Damsel (IRE)**[57] 3621 3-8-12 63 ....(b) NeilCallan 4 (Paul Cole) *led: drvn 3f out: hdd jst over 2f out and no ch w wnr after: lost 2nd ins fnl f* **8/1**[3]	58
6231	4	2 ¼	**Geanie Mac (IRE)**[10] 4908 3-8-12 62 ....(v) ShaneKelly 5 (Tim Pitt) *trckd ldr: rdn over 3f out: trying to chal whn wnr swept by jst over 2f out: one pce* **2/1**[1]	54
523-	5	6	**Raspberry Fizz**[261] 7684 3-8-7 51 ....(b) JohnFahy 6 (Eve Johnson Houghton) *chsd ldng pair: rdn 3f out: wknd 2f out* **12/1**	38
6552	6	6	**Netley Marsh**[11] 5240 3-8-12 59 ....(b) SeanLevey 1 (Richard Hannon) *hld up in 6th: drvn and struggling over 3f out: sn bhd* **7/2**[2]	32
4000	7	32	**Sir Lexington (IRE)**[6] 5408 3-8-12 60 ....(b[1]) RichardHughes 2 (Richard Hannon) *sn dropped to 5th: reminders after 5f: wknd u.p over 3f out: t.o* **8/1**[3]	

2m 28.94s (2.44) **Going Correction** +0.20s/f (Good) 7 Ran SP% **112.5**
Speed ratings (Par 102): **99,94,94,92,88 83,60**
.The winner was bought in for £8,000.\n\x\x Geanie Mac was claimed by Mr Ken McGarrity for £7,500.
Owner Geoffrey Bishop **Bred** Eurostrait Ltd **Trained** Twyford, Bucks

FOCUS
They went a reasonable pace in this seller, which was a tight race on the figures. A clear best from the winner but the form has been rated a bit cautiously.

5630 GREENE KING STKS (H'CAP) — 7f
5:00 (5:00) (Class 4) (0-80,80) 3-Y-O+ — £4,980 (£1,491; £745; £372; £186; £93) Stalls Low

Form				RPR
000	1		**Bravo Echo**[22] 4824 6-9-7 75 .... J-PGuillambert 1 (Michael Attwater) *sn led: urged along fr 3f out: at least 2 l clr after: all out fnl f but unchal* **10/1**	85
6513	2	2	**Emkanaat**[23] 4775 4-9-12 80 .... NeilCallan 9 (Roger Varian) *bmpd s: sn chsd wnr: drvn wl over 2f out: hanging and nt qckn 1f out: no imp after* **7/2**[2]	85
121-	3	¾	**Chokidar (IRE)**[267] 7625 4-9-7 75 ....(v) SilvestreDeSousa 3 (Scott Dixon) *chsd ldng pair: sltly awkward bnd 5f out: drvn 3f out: one pce and no imp over 1f out: kpt on* **11/2**	78
0600	4	hd	**Rondeau (GR)**[17] 5004 7-9-7 77 .... GeorgeBaker 7 (Patrick Chamings) *hld up in last trio: tried to make prog and pushed along over 2f out: kpt on one pce fr over 1f out* **9/1**	79
0004	5	3 ¼	**Rulesn'regulations**[3] 5502 6-9-4 72 ....(b) PatCosgrave 11 (Matthew Salaman) *hld up in last trio: struggling in last and detached 3f out: no prog tl styd on fnl f* **5/1**[3]	65
-050	6	½	**Galatian**[4] 5486 5-9-7 75 .... JamesMillman 8 (Rod Millman) *hmpd s: racd on outer in last trio: rdn 3f out and no prog: wl hld after* **8/1**	67
0065	7	¾	**Poetic Lord**[31] 4517 3-9-0 73 ....(b) RichardHughes 10 (Richard Hannon) *swvd rt s: chsd ldng trio: drvn 3f out: no prog 2f out: wl btn after: eased last 100yds* **9/4**[1]	67

1m 28.4s (1.40) **Going Correction** +0.20s/f (Good)
WFA 3 from 4yo+ 5lb 7 Ran SP% **115.2**
Speed ratings (Par 105): **100,97,96,96,92 92,91**
Tote Swingers 1&2 £3.40, 2&3 £4.10, 1&3 £8.40 CSF £45.44 CT £215.68 TOTE £9.70: £3.50, £2.20; EX 38.30 Trifecta £289.30 Pool £754.55 - 1.93 winning units..
Owner Canisbay Bloodstock **Bred** Juddmonte Farms Ltd **Trained** Epsom, Surrey

FOCUS
An ordinary handicap for the grade, run in a time half a second slower than the opening Class 5 handicap. There was trouble at the start and it proved an advantage to race prominently, the first three filling the same positions virtually throughout. The winner's first turf form since July last year.
Poetic Lord Official explanation: jockey said that the colt struck into itself
T/Plt: £523.50 to a £1 stake. Pool £77,853.71 - 108.56 winning units. T/Qpdt: £116.00 to a £1 stake. Pool £4,971.90 - 31.70 winning units. JN

5453 YARMOUTH (L-H)
Sunday, August 26

OFFICIAL GOING: Good to soft (good in places) changing to good after race 1 (2.00)
Wind: Fresh across Weather: Cloudy with sunny spells

5631 BRITISH STALLION STUDS SUPPORTING BRITISH RACING EBF MAIDEN FILLIES' STKS — 6f 3y
2:00 (2:02) (Class 5) 2-Y-O — £3,557 (£1,058; £529; £264) Stalls Centre

Form				RPR
32	1		**Nargys (IRE)**[37] 4297 2-9-0 0 .... KierenFallon 4 (Luca Cumani) *hld up in tch: racd keenly: led over 1f out: r.o wl: readily* **8/11**[1]	80+
	2	2 ½	**Marsh Dragon** 2-9-0 0 .... DarryllHolland 7 (Mark H Tompkins) *a.p: chsd ldr 4f out: shkn up to ld over 2f out: hdd over 1f out: styd on same pce ins fnl f* **33/1**	68
5	3	1 ¾	**Evoke (IRE)**[8] 5352 2-9-0 0 .... TedDurcan 6 (Jeremy Noseda) *chsd ldrs: rdn over 1f out: no ex ins fnl f* **7/2**[2]	62
	4	½	**Midnight Flower (IRE)** 2-9-0 0 .... RichardMullen 2 (David Simcock) *prom: shkn up over 1f out: no ex fnl f* **11/1**	61
	5	2 ½	**Butterfly Dream** 2-9-0 0 .... PaulHanagan 1 (William Haggas) *sn led at stdy pce: shkn up and hdd over 2f out: wknd fnl f* **6/1**[3]	53
06	6	1	**Red Eclipse (IRE)**[13] 5176 2-8-7 0 .... NatashaEaton[(7)] 3 (Alan Bailey) *led early: plld hrd: trckd ldrs: pushed along over 2f out: wknd over 1f out* **33/1**	50
	7	1 ¼	**Brynford** 2-9-0 0 .... SaleemGolam 5 (Chris Dwyer) *hld up: rdn and wknd over 1f out* **100/1**	47

1m 15.5s (1.10) **Going Correction** -0.25s/f (Firm) 7 Ran SP% **109.6**
Speed ratings (Par 91): **82,78,76,75,72 71,69**
Tote Swingers 1&2 £5.50, 2&3 £10.50, 1&3 £1.60 CSF £29.17 TOTE £1.70: £1.10, £6.90; EX 19.50.
Owner Sheikh Mohammed Obaid Al Maktoum **Bred** Ballylinch Stud **Trained** Newmarket, Suffolk

FOCUS
The jockeys differed on the state of the ground after the first. Kieren Fallon said "It's quite fast", Ted Durcan stated "It's good ground", while Paul Hanagan reported "It's on the slow side." This had gone to a newcomer on the three previous occasions it had been run, but not this time. The easy winner stumbled on a weak race and can probably rate a lot higher.

NOTEBOOK
Nargys(IRE), back down in distance, had shown more than enough in two previous starts to take a race of this nature and sauntered home after chasing an ordinary early pace. She probably didn't beat much but looks a useful prospect considering she has some size about her. (op 5-6 tchd 4-6)
Marsh Dragon, whose dam was a 6f juvenile winner, was a little keen in behind for a while but made a pleasing start to her career, running all the way to the line for pressure. (op 25-1)
Evoke(IRE) came through to have her chance but still looked a bit green and wandered a little late on. (tchd 4-1)
Midnight Flower(IRE), whose dam is an unraced half-sister to useful French two-year-old sprinter Ascot Glory, was another for which the experience will bring her on. (op 8-1 tchd 12-1)
Butterfly Dream, out of a half-sister to smart stayer and winning hurdler Elusive Dream, had no change of gear and may need further in time. (op 7-1 tchd 15-2)

5632 CONFERENCE AT GREAT YARMOUTH RACECOURSE H'CAP (DIV I) — 1m 3y
2:30 (2:30) (Class 6) (0-60,60) 3-Y-O+ — £2,070 (£616; £307; £153) Stalls Centre

Form				RPR
2061	1		**Enriching (USA)**[12] 5216 4-9-4 54 .... PaulHanagan 7 (Lydia Pearce) *racd centre: chsd ldrs: overall ldr over 3f out: rdn and hung rt fr over 2f out: styd on u.p* **5/2**[1]	65
0066	2	3	**Monsieur Pontaven**[34] 4389 5-8-10 46 ....(b) DarryllHolland 9 (Robin Bastiman) *racd stands' side: sn pushed along to chse ldr that side: shkn up to ld that pair over 3f out: rdn over 2f out: hung lft over 1f out: styd on same pce ins fnl f: 1st of 2 in gp* **11/2**[3]	50
4006	3	2	**Gay Gallivanter**[33] 4435 4-8-10 46 oh1 .... FrannyNorton 8 (Michael Quinn) *led stands' side pair over 4f: sn rdn: styd on same pce fnl f: last of 2 in gp* **12/1**	45
0003	4	1 ¼	**Stilettoesinthemud (IRE)**[18] 4954 4-9-5 55 .... TedDurcan 6 (James Given) *racd centre: hld up: pushed along 1/2-way: hdwy u.p 2f out: no ex fnl f: 2nd of 7 in gp* **6/1**	52
0260	5	8	**Captainrisk (IRE)**[16] 5050 6-8-12 51 ....(v) DominicFox[(3)] 1 (Christine Dunnett) *racd centre: chsd ldrs: rdn over 2f out: sn edgd rt: wknd over 1f out: 3rd of 7 in gp* **14/1**	29
4234	6	2	**Warden Bond**[16] 5052 4-9-0 50 ....(p) CathyGannon 5 (William Stone) *overall ldr in centre over 4f: sn rdn: wknd 2f out: 4th of 7 in gp* **9/2**[2]	24
4305	7	1 ½	**Aiaam Al Wafa (IRE)**[13] 5152 3-9-0 56 ....(p) KierenFallon 4 (Phil McEntee) *racd centre: hld up: hdwy to join ldrs over 3f out: sn rdn: wknd over 1f out: 5th of 7 in gp* **14/1**	26
0000	8	9	**Roman Around**[20] 4870 3-8-3 48 oh1 ow2 .... AdamBeschizza[(3)] 3 (William Knight) *s.i.s: racd centre: sn pushed along in rr: drvn along 1/2-way: bhd fnl 3f: 6th of 7 in gp* **25/1**	
400	9	2 ¾	**Zaheeb**[29] 4584 4-9-10 60 .... MartinLane 2 (Dave Morris) *racd centre: chsd ldrs: led over 4f out tl hdd 3f out: sn rdn: wkng whn nt clr run wl over 1f out: last of 7 in gp* **7/1**	

1m 38.6s (-2.00) **Going Correction** -0.25s/f (Firm)
WFA 3 from 4yo+ 6lb 9 Ran SP% **113.8**
Speed ratings (Par 101): **100,97,95,93,85 83,82,73,70**
Tote Swingers 1&2 £3.90, 2&3 £11.30, 1&3 £7.60 CSF £15.96 CT £125.89 TOTE £2.80: £1.10, £2.20, £4.20; EX 25.90.
Owner Franconson Partners **Bred** Adena Springs **Trained** Newmarket, Suffolk

FOCUS
Modest stuff and the field spilt shortly after the start. It was slightly slower than division II. It didn't take much winning but Enriching built on her latest C&D win.

5633 CONFERENCE AT GREAT YARMOUTH RACECOURSE H'CAP (DIV II) — 1m 3y
3:05 (3:05) (Class 6) (0-60,61) 3-Y-O+ — £2,070 (£616; £307; £153) Stalls Centre

Form				RPR
-600	1		**Wordismybond**[54] 3732 3-9-4 60 .... PaulHanagan 6 (Peter Makin) *racd centre: chsd ldrs: led over 1f out: drvn out* **10/1**	73
0001	2	2	**Mount Mayday (IRE)**[5] 5458 3-9-1 57 6ex ....(t) SaleemGolam 3 (Stuart Williams) *plld hrd and overall ldr in centre: rdn and hdd over 1f out: styd on same pce ins fnl f* **11/4**[2]	65
2042	3	1	**Collectable**[15] 5095 3-8-9 51 ....(t) TedDurcan 4 (Jonathan Portman) *racd centre: hld up: hdwy over 2f out: rdn over 1f out: styd on same pce ins fnl f* **9/4**[1]	57
0-50	4	1 ¼	**Olney Lass**[17] 4981 5-9-5 58 .... SimonPearce[(3)] 5 (Lydia Pearce) *racd centre: hld up: hdwy 1/2-way: rdn over 1f out: styd on same pce* **11/1**	61
6635	5	6	**Exopuntia**[12] 5216 6-8-12 51 .... AdamBeschizza[(3)] 1 (Julia Feilden) *racd centre: chsd ldrs: rdn over 2f out: wknd fnl f* **15/2**	40
3033	6	16	**Putin (IRE)**[5] 5459 4-8-3 46 ....(bt) SiobhanMiller[(7)] 9 (Phil McEntee) *racd alone on stands' side: up w the pce: hung lft fr over 3f out: rdn and wknd over 2f out* **6/1**[3]	
0020	7	10	**Sanad (IRE)**[5] 5458 3-9-2 61 ....(b) DominicFox[(3)] 8 (Anthony Carson) *racd centre: hld up: wknd over 2f out: eased: t.o* **10/1**	
-000	8	6	**Yanbu (USA)**[17] 4986 7-9-0 50 ....(b[1]) KierenFallon 2 (Michael Murphy) *s.i.s: racd centre: sn prom: pushed along 1/2-way: rdn and wknd 3f out: t.o* **28/1**	

1m 38.29s (-2.31) **Going Correction** -0.25s/f (Firm)
WFA 3 from 4yo+ 6lb 8 Ran SP% **113.4**
Speed ratings (Par 101): **101,99,98,96,90 74,64,58**
Tote Swingers 1&2 £6.00, 2&3 £2.10, 1&3 £4.50 CSF £37.16 CT £84.43 TOTE £11.10: £3.30, £1.70, £1.10; EX 41.80.
Owner T W Wellard & Partners **Bred** Henry And Mrs Rosemary Moszkowicz **Trained** Ogbourne Maisey, Wilts

FOCUS
The second division of this modest handicap was run in a time fractionally quicker than the preceding contest. The first three were clear and the winner is rateed back to his 2yo best.

Sanad(IRE) Official explanation: jockey said that the colt moved poorly

5634 SEAFOOD RESTAURANT GREAT YARMOUTH H'CAP 7f 3y
3:40 (3:40) (Class 4) (0-85,83) 3-Y-O+ **£5,040** (£1,508; £754; £377; £188) **Stalls** Centre

Form RPR

1324 **1** **Green Howard**[16] 5057 4-9-12 **83** DarryllHolland 4 91+
(Robin Bastiman) *chsd ldrs: drvn along over 1f out: r.o u.p to ld wl ins fnl f* **7/4**[1]

5062 **2** ½ **Rough Rock (IRE)**[5] 5457 7-8-10 **70** DominicFox(3) 6 77
(Chris Dwyer) *led: rdn and hdd over 1f out: ev ch ins fnl f: r.o* **4/1**[3]

2150 **3** *hd* **Barwick**[44] 4068 4-9-9 **80** TedDurcan 5 86
(Mark H Tompkins) *hld up: hdwy over 2f out: rdn over 1f out: r.o* **15/8**[2]

4226 **4** ½ **Roedean (IRE)**[15] 5107 3-8-4 **66** (tp) CathyGannon 3 69
(William Stone) *chsd ldr: rdn and ev ch fr over 1f out: r.o* **10/1**

405- **5** 1 ½ **Ceremonial Jade (UAE)**[267] 7628 9-9-10 **81** (t) MartinHarley 1 82
(Marco Botti) *trckd ldrs: led over 1f out: sn rdn: hdd and unable qck wl ins fnl f* **12/1**

1m 27.17s (0.57) **Going Correction** -0.25s/f (Firm)
WFA 3 from 4yo+ 5lb **5** Ran SP% **107.9**
Speed ratings (Par 105): **86,85,85,84,82**
CSF £8.62 TOTE £2.60: £1.20, £1.70; EX 7.30.
Owner Ms M Austerfield **Bred** Miss A J Rawding & P M Crane **Trained** Cowthorpe, N Yorks

FOCUS
The ground was given as good all over from good to soft, good in places before this event. A race decimated by five non-runners, and probably not form to go overboard about considering they were all bunched at the end. The second also limits the form.

5635 TRAFALGAR RESTAURANT AT GREAT YARMOUTH RACECOURSE FILLIES' H'CAP 5f 43y
4:15 (4:15) (Class 5) (0-70,65) 3-Y-O+ **£2,911** (£866; £432; £216) **Stalls** Centre

Form RPR

0332 **1** **Miss Polly Plum**[12] 5217 5-8-13 **54** (p) SaleemGolam 7 68
(Chris Dwyer) *mde all: racd keenly: rdn clr fr over 1f out: edgd lft ins fnl f* **5/2**[1]

2553 **2** 5 **Ocean Myth**[10] 5279 3-9-7 **64** TedDurcan 4 60
(Jonathan Portman) *chsd ldrs: rdn to go 2nd over 1f out: sn outpcd* **11/4**[2]

6612 **3** 1 ¼ **Imaginary Diva**[5] 5445 6-9-1 **59** RyanPowell(3) 3 51
(George Margarson) *hmpd s: hld up: effrt and nt clr run over 1f out: nvr on terms* **5/2**[1]

2150 **4** ¾ **Sannibel**[172] 819 4-9-2 **64** NatashaEaton(7) 5 53
(K F Clutterbuck) *chsd wnr tl rdn over 1f out: no ex* **8/1**

0-40 **5** *nse* **Cincinnati Kit**[23] 4757 3-8-12 **55** (t) PaulHanagan 2 44
(Stuart Williams) *wnt rt s: hld up: rdn over 1f out: sn btn* **7/1**[3]

1m 1.33s (-1.37) **Going Correction** -0.25s/f (Firm)
WFA 3 from 4yo+ 2lb **5** Ran SP% **107.4**
Speed ratings (Par 100): **100,92,90,88,88**
CSF £9.13 TOTE £4.50: £2.80, £1.50; EX 9.10.
Owner Mrs J Hughes & Miss C Hughes **Bred** Brookfield Stud & Partners **Trained** Six Mile Bottom, Cambs

FOCUS
A moderate sprint handicap, but the time was reasonable and the winner has been given some credit.
Imaginary Diva Official explanation: jockey said that the mare suffered interference in running just after the start

5636 SCROBY SANDS H'CAP 1m 2f 21y
4:50 (4:50) (Class 5) (0-75,75) 3-Y-O+ **£2,911** (£866; £432; £216) **Stalls** Low

Form RPR

4243 **1** **Jawhar (IRE)**[22] 4805 4-10-0 **75** PaulHanagan 1 84+
(William Haggas) *hld up: hdwy and nt clr run over 2f out: shkn up to ld over 1f out: sn rdn: r.o: eased nr fin* **15/8**[1]

4553 **2** 1 ½ **Manomine**[8] 5336 3-8-9 **64** TedDurcan 4 69
(Clive Brittain) *chsd ldrs: led over 2f out: rdn and hdd over 1f out: styd on same pce ins fnl f* **15/2**[3]

30 **3** *nk* **Ela Gonda Mou**[22] 4823 5-9-0 **66** RosieJessop(5) 2 70
(Peter Charalambous) *hld up: hdwy over 2f out: styd on: nt rch ldrs* **25/1**

6010 **4** 2 ¼ **Sea Fever (IRE)**[73] 3066 3-9-2 **71** KierenFallon 3 71
(Luca Cumani) *hld up: pushed along 1/2-way: hdwy over 2f out: sn rdn and edgd lft: no ex ins fnl f* **9/4**[2]

05-5 **5** 4 **Spyder**[16] 5063 4-9-9 **70** (p) FrannyNorton 7 62
(Jane Chapple-Hyam) *led: rdn and hdd over 2f out: wknd ins fnl f* **14/1**

0222 **6** 7 **The Ducking Stool**[8] 5359 5-9-6 **70** AdamBeschizza(3) 6 48
(Julia Feilden) *hood removed late: s.i.s: hdwy to chse ldr over 8f out: rdn and ev ch over 2f out: wknd over 1f out* **8/1**

4300 **7** 3 ¼ **Count Ceprano (IRE)**[9] 5323 8-8-12 **62** SimonPearce(3) 8 33
(Lydia Pearce) *chsd ldrs: pushed along over 3f out: wknd over 2f out* **33/1**

4222 **8** 10 **La Pampita (IRE)**[21] 4850 3-8-9 **69** DavidKenny(5) 5 20
(William Knight) *s.i.s: racd keenly and sn prom: rdn and wknd over 2f out* **8/1**

2m 6.99s (-3.51) **Going Correction** -0.25s/f (Firm)
WFA 3 from 4yo+ 8lb **8** Ran SP% **113.0**
Speed ratings (Par 103): **104,102,102,100,97 91,89,81**
Tote Swingers 1&2 £3.60, 2&3 £23.10, 1&3 £11.00 CSF £16.30 CT £258.41 TOTE £3.10: £1.60, £2.40, £5.70; EX 17.50.
Owner Hamdan Al Maktoum **Bred** Shadwell Estate Company Limited **Trained** Newmarket, Suffolk

FOCUS
The pace appeared fair from the outset but the winner was always cruising in behind. Ordinary form, the runner-up setting the standard.
La Pampita(IRE) Official explanation: jockey said that the filly ran flat

5637 HOLIDAY ON THE NORFOLK BROADS H'CAP 1m 6f 17y
5:20 (5:21) (Class 6) (0-60,69) 3-Y-O+ **£2,070** (£616; £307; £153) **Stalls** High

Form RPR

0000 **1** **Scripturist**[18] 4971 3-7-9 **46** oh1 (b[1]) NoelGarbutt(7) 8 61
(William Jarvis) *a.p: pushed along over 3f out: rdn to ld wl over 1f out: styd on wl* **33/1**

6-02 **2** 6 **Akula (IRE)**[17] 5022 5-9-8 **54** TedDurcan 9 61
(Mark H Tompkins) *chsd ldrs: ev ch 2f out: sn rdn: styd on same pce fnl f* **9/4**[1]

1422 **3** 2 **Mollyow (IRE)**[3] 5509 4-9-8 **54** CathyGannon 2 58
(Terry Clement) *led: rdn and hdd wl over 1f out: no ex fnl f* **7/2**[2]

203/ **4** 6 **Iceman George**[67] 6669 8-10-0 **60** KierenFallon 1 56
(Lydia Pearce) *hld up: pushed along over 3f out: styd on ins fnl f: nvr nrr* **13/2**[3]

1041 **5** ½ **Foster's Road**[9] 5330 3-9-11 **69** SamHitchcott 10 64
(Mick Channon) *s.i.s: hld up: hdwy over 3f out: sn rdn: wknd over 1f out* **7/2**[2]

-540 **6** *hd* **Saloon (USA)**[9] 5323 8-9-4 **50** (p) FrannyNorton 3 45
(Jane Chapple-Hyam) *hld up: pushed along over 4f out: kpt on ins fnl f: nvr nrr* **12/1**

0505 **7** ½ **Omega Omega**[9] 5330 3-8-2 **49** ow2 AdamBeschizza(3) 6 43
(Julia Feilden) *chsd ldr: pushed along 5f out: rdn over 2f out: wknd fnl f* **12/1**

4041 **8** 2 ¼ **Corvette**[13] 5173 4-9-8 **61** TimClark(7) 5 52
(Michael Appleby) *hld up: hdwy 10f out: rdn over 2f out: sn wknd* **11/1**

0500 **9** 34 **Flaming Telepath**[17] 5022 4-9-0 **46** oh1 (tp) SaleemGolam 4
(Christine Dunnett) *s.i.s: hdwy 11f out: rdn and wknd over 4f out: t.o* **80/1**

3m 6.4s (-1.20) **Going Correction** -0.25s/f (Firm)
WFA 3 from 4yo+ 12lb **9** Ran SP% **116.4**
Speed ratings (Par 101): **93,89,88,85,84 84,84,83,63**
Tote Swingers 1&2 £37.30, 2&3 £2.90, 1&3 £19.50 CSF £108.01 CT £344.01 TOTE £38.10: £10.10, £1.20, £1.50; EX 141.30.
Owner William Jarvis **Bred** Avington Manor Stud **Trained** Newmarket, Suffolk

FOCUS
A surprise winner to this modest staying handicap. The form is taken at face value.
Scripturist Official explanation: trainer's representative said, regarding the apparent improvement of form, that the gelding benefited from a step up in trip and from having blinkers fitted for the first time
Flaming Telepath Official explanation: vet said the filly had been struck into

5638 WEDDINGS AT GREAT YARMOUTH RACECOURSE APPRENTICE H'CAP 1m 2f 21y
5:50 (5:50) (Class 6) (0-60,60) 4-Y-O+ **£2,070** (£616; £307; £153) **Stalls** Low

Form RPR

000 **1** **Highlife Dancer**[12] 5197 4-9-3 **56** (v[1]) ThomasBrown 1 66
(Mick Channon) *chsd ldr: rdn to ld over 1f out: styd on* **6/1**[3]

053 **2** 1 ¾ **Very Well Red**[10] 5266 9-8-8 **47** NoelGarbutt 9 54
(Peter Hiatt) *led: rdn and hdd over 1f out: no ex towards fin* **16/1**

2-00 **3** 1 ¾ **Phase Shift**[32] 4455 4-8-9 **53** RobertTart(5) 2 56
(Brian Ellison) *hld up: hdwy over 3f out: rdn over 1f out: styd on same pce fnl f* **7/2**[1]

0220 **4** 1 ¾ **Entrance**[21] 4843 4-9-5 **58** NatashaEaton 4 58
(Julia Feilden) *hld up: styd on fr over 1f out: nvr trbld ldrs* **8/1**

4016 **5** 1 ½ **Five Hearts**[52] 3793 4-8-13 **52** JasonHart 8 49
(Mark H Tompkins) *prom: outpcd over 3f out: rallied over 1f out: no ex fnl f* **7/2**[1]

6-06 **6** ½ **Nha Trang (IRE)**[40] 4189 5-8-4 **46** oh1 (b) TimClark(3) 6 42
(Michael Appleby) *hld up in tch: racd keenly: rdn over 2f out: wknd fnl f* **25/1**

001 **7** 1 **Pattern Mark**[18] 4958 6-9-2 **58** JacobButterfield(3) 5 52
(Ollie Pears) *hld up: rdn over 2f out: n.d* **5/1**[2]

0663 **8** 2 ¾ **Zennor**[17] 4987 5-9-2 **60** CharlotteJenner(5) 3 48
(George Margarson) *prom: pushed along over 3f out: wknd 2f out* **6/1**[3]

1000 **9** 3 ½ **Land Hawk (IRE)**[20] 4890 6-9-2 **58** SophieSilvester(3) 7 39
(Lydia Pearce) *prom: rdn over 3f out: wknd 2f out* **22/1**

2m 8.49s (-2.01) **Going Correction** -0.25s/f (Firm) **9** Ran SP% **114.9**
Speed ratings (Par 101): **98,96,95,93,92 92,91,89,86**
Tote Swingers 1&2 £10.90, 2&3 £8.80, 1&3 £5.20 CSF £94.66 CT £386.04 TOTE £6.60: £1.70, £2.70, £2.30; EX 57.10.
Owner The Highlife Racing Club **Bred** Imperial & Mike Channon Bloodstock Ltd **Trained** West Ilsley, Berks

FOCUS
A modest contest in which it paid to race handily. The winner is rated back to his earlier form this year.
T/Plt: £35.20 to a £1 stake. Pool £59,052.18 - 1,221.94 winning units. T/Qpdt: £12.40 to a £1 stake. Pool £4,903.33 - 292.60 winning units. CR

5639 - 5640a (Foreign Racing) - See Raceform Interactive

5604 CURRAGH (R-H)
Sunday, August 26

OFFICIAL GOING: Round course - soft to heavy; straight course - heavy

5641a WWW.BETTOR.COM FLYING FIVE STKS (GROUP 3) 5f
3:10 (3:10) 3-Y-O+ **£32,500** (£9,500; £3,000; £3,000)

RPR

1 **My Girl Anna (IRE)**[16] 5067 5-9-2 100 RoryCleary 1 101+
(Muredach Kelly, Ire) *trckd ldrs in 3rd in centre of trck tl swtchd out appr fnl f: sn led: pushed clr and hld on wl* **10/1**

2 1 ¾ **Fire Lily (IRE)**[14] 5137 3-9-5 110 WayneLordan 8 99+
(David Wachman, Ire) *hld up in 5th: pushed along and plenty to do appr fnl f: swtchd to outer and styd on strly clsng stages to go 2nd cl home* **9/4**[1]

3 ¾ **Judge 'n Jury**[15] 5077 8-9-5 (t) KevinManning 3 93+
(Ronald Harris) *smartly away and disp in centre of trck tl hdd ins fnl f: kpt on same pce* **8/1**

3 *dht* **Inxile (IRE)**[16] 5067 7-9-5 (p) AdrianNicholls 2 93+
(David Nicholls) *smartly away and disp in centre of trck tl hdd ins fnl f: kpt on at same pce and ct late for 2nd* **10/3**[3]

5 2 ¼ **Statue Of Dreams (IRE)**[32] 4480 6-9-5 67 (tp) ChrisHayes 4 85?
(James Bernard McCabe, Ire) *racd on wd outside in centre of trck: nvr on terms: kpt on fnl f* **100/1**

6 ½ **Boastful (IRE)**[3] 5523 4-9-2 CO'Donoghue 5 80+
(Mrs K Burke) *hld up: unable to go pce: kpt on fnl f* **13/2**

7 1 ¾ **Eton Rifles (IRE)**[57] 3623 7-9-5 WilliamCarson 6 77+
(Stuart Williams) *racd alone on stands' side: no imp fr 2f out* **3/1**[2]

8 4 ¾ **Stepper Point**[23] 4762 3-9-3 MartinDwyer 7 60+
(William Muir) *sn crossed fr stands' rails to centre of trck: pushed along after 1/2-way: sn wknd* **14/1**

1m 4.62s (1.72) **Going Correction** +0.625s/f (Yiel)
WFA 3 from 4yo+ 2lb **8** Ran SP% **120.0**
Speed ratings: **111,108,107,107,103 102,99,92**
PL: Inxile 0.70, Judge N Jury 1.50. TRIFECTA: M/F/I 52.55 M/F/J 129.35 CSF £34.62 TOTE £11.80: £1.80, £1.02; DF 38.20.
Owner Owen Murphy & Ms A Clancy **Bred** Trevor Dazell **Trained** Ballinasloe, Co. Galway
■ Stewards' Enquiry : Rory Cleary two-day ban; used whipout giving horse time to respond (10th,13th Sept).

FOCUS
This race had been dominated by British-trained sprinters with no home-trained winner since 2001 and the visitors accounted for five of the eight runners. The time was slower than the later handicap, and the fifth is a big limiter for the level of the form.

NOTEBOOK
My Girl Anna(IRE), a three-time winner who had finished a creditable third behind Inxile in a Listed event over the same trip at Tipperary on her previous start, tracked the front-running pair Inxile and Judge 'N Jury before delivering her challenge over 1f out, and responded for pressure to lead entering the final furlong. She was well on top in the closing stages.
Fire Lily(IRE), all of whose three Group 3 wins were achieved over 6f, was tackling this trip for the first time since last year's Queen Mary Stakes. All her wins have been on soft ground but it was heavy here and that, plus the trip, seemed to be against her, as it was only entering the final furlong that she began to close. She ran on well towards the finish. (op 9/4 tchd 5/2)
Judge 'n Jury, another with plenty of form on soft ground and also seeking a 12th win, vied for the lead with Inxile and edged ahead for pressure over 1f out. Soon headed, he kept on to share third place. (op 7/2)
Inxile(IRE), seeking win number 12 of his career, has proved himself adaptable in terms of ground. He disputed the lead for almost 4f and kept on to dead-heat for third place. (op 7/2)
Statue Of Dreams(IRE) faced a big task in this company and he acquitted himself quite well, staying on from over 1f out without posing any sort of threat.
Stepper Point Official explanation: jockey said colt did not handle the heavy ground

5642a GALILEO EUROPEAN BREEDERS FUND FUTURITY STKS (GROUP 2) 7f
3:45 (3:45) 2-Y-O **£47,625** (£15,041; £7,125; £2,375)

			RPR
1		**First Cornerstone (IRE)**[16] 5069 2-9-3 ... ChrisHayes 5 (A Oliver, Ire) *tk quite t.k.h early: sn settled in 3rd: pushed along to take narrow ld appr fnl f: styd on strly to draw away fnl 100yds* **7/2**[2]	114
2	1 ½	**Flying The Flag (IRE)**[52] 3796 2-9-3 ... JPO'Brien 2 (A P O'Brien, Ire) *racd in 2nd: quite green then tl pushed along to press wnr appr fnl f: no ex fnl 100yds* **7/4**[1]	110
3	½	**Birdman (IRE)**[25] 4698 2-9-3 ... PatSmullen 4 (David Simcock) *hld up in 4th against far rails: swtchd out appr fnl f where unable qck w principals: kpt on wl fnl 100yds* **7/4**[1]	109
4	4 ¼	**Kingston Jamaica (IRE)**[31] 4519 2-9-3 100... CO'Donoghue 1 (A P O'Brien, Ire) *sn led: extended advantage 3f out: hdd appr fnl f: sn wknd* **5/1**[3]	98

1m 32.54s (1.74) **Going Correction** +0.50s/f (Yiel) 4 Ran SP% **111.6**
Speed ratings: **110,108,107,102**
CSF £10.22 TOTE £4.10; DF 10.60.
Owner Team Valor **Bred** L K I Bloodstock Ltd **Trained** Caledon, Co Tyrone

FOCUS
With the testing ground robbing the race of the presence of 2000 Guineas favourite Dawn Approach and Mars, the Derby favourite, this was far from a vintage renewal, with no Group-race winner in the line-up. However, the form makes sense rated through the third and fourth.

NOTEBOOK
First Cornerstone(IRE) fully justified the decision to supplement him for the race and went about his job in good style after closing to lead entering the final furlong. He kept on well in the closing stages, showing, as he had done when landing the El Gran Senor Stakes at Tipperary, that he handles testing ground well. (op 100/30 tchd 3/1)
Flying The Flag(IRE), winner of a maiden over the trip on testing ground at Leopardstown on his only previous start, became the Ballydoyle number one here in the absence of Nevis. He tracked his pacemaker and challenged between horses over 1f out but could only keep on at one pace when the winner went about his business.
Birdman(IRE)'s close second to Olympic Glory in the Superlative Stakes on heavy ground at Newmarket represented the best form, but he'd run below that level on better ground at Goodwood early this month. Held up last of the four runners, he was switched left to begin his challenge on the outside just inside the final furlong. He kept on steadily to the line without ever looking as if he would get there. (op 7/4 tchd 15/8)
Kingston Jamaica(IRE) made the running and was three lengths clear 3f out. He began to weaken over a furlong out and was soon headed and done with.

5643a LANWADES STUD FILLIES STKS (GROUP 3) 1m 1f
4:20 (4:20) 3-Y-0+ **£32,500** (£9,500; £4,500; £1,500)

			RPR
1		**Up (IRE)**[8] 5376 3-9-0 110... JPO'Brien 7 (A P O'Brien, Ire) *hld up: 6th 2f out: qckne wl to ld fnl 150yds: drew clr: comf* **3/1**[2]	114+
2	3 ¾	**Aloof (IRE)**[10] 5286 3-9-0 94... WayneLordan 6 (David Wachman, Ire) *racd in 4th: t.k.h: chsd ldrs appr fnl f: kpt on wl wout gng pce of wnr* **20/1**	107
3	¾	**Ballybacka Lady (IRE)**[10] 5286 4-9-7 105... FranBerry 3 (Mrs John Harrington, Ire) *racd in 3rd: led appr fnl f tl hdd fnl 150yds: kpt on same pce* **7/2**[3]	105
4	½	**La Collina (IRE)**[91] 2527 3-9-0 108... DeclanMcDonogh 2 (Kevin Prendergast, Ire) *hld up: pushed along to cl 2f out: nvr quite on terms: kpt on same pce* **6/1**	104+
5	5 ½	**Manieree (IRE)**[350] 5976 4-9-7 114...(b) NGMcCullagh 4 (John M Oxx, Ire) *led: hdd appr fnl f: sn wknd* **11/4**[1]	92
6	nse	**Soon (IRE)**[5] 5463 3-9-0 99... SeamieHeffernan 1 (A P O'Brien, Ire) *hld up in rr: nvr on terms: no imp fnl 2f* **7/1**	92
7	13	**Devotion (IRE)**[5] 5463 3-9-0 105... CO'Donoghue 5 (A P O'Brien, Ire) *chsd ldr tl qckly dropped away fnl 2f* **12/1**	65

1m 55.63s (0.73) **Going Correction** +0.30s/f (Good)
WFA 3 from 4yo 7lb 7 Ran SP% **113.1**
Speed ratings: **108,104,104,103,98 98,87**
CSF £54.52 TOTE £3.90: £2.60, £8.00; DF 65.80.
Owner Derrick Smith & Mrs John Magnier & Michael Tabor **Bred** Smythson **Trained** Ballydoyle, Co Tipperary

FOCUS
It's been rated around the winner and fourth, with the well-bred runner-up rated as running a big personal best.

NOTEBOOK
Up(IRE) had been quite highly-tried and had run a fine race when second in the Poule d'Essai des Pouliches in May. She turned up having run sixth in the Beverly D. Stakes at Arlington only eight days previously, returning to Ballydoyle on Monday. Held up in rear, she began her bid on the outside over 1f out and went to the front inside the final furlong before stretching clear. Obviously tough as well as talented, she will have plenty of options before the end of the season. (op100/30 tchd 7/2)
Aloof(IRE), the lowest rated in the race on official ratings, had finished fourth in the Desmond Stakes on her previous start and she improved on that, progressing from fourth into the straight to go second under pressure over 1f out. However, she was no match for the winner in the closing stages. (op 16/1)
Ballybacka Lady(IRE), a winner at this level early last season, had run second in Group 3s at Leopardstown on her two previous attempts this season, most recently the Desmond Stakes. She appeared to be travelling best as she went to the front under 2f out but she was unable to raise her game inside the final furlong. (op 4/1)
La Collina(IRE), winner of the Group 1 Phoenix Stakes last season, had not run since finishing sixth in the Irish 1,000 Guineas in May and, while she improved her position 2f out and kept on, she was never going well enough to pose a threat on ground which was probably too testing for her. (op 5/1)
Manieree(IRE), absent since scoring the second of back-to-back wins at this level here almost a year ago, relishes testing conditions. However, the lack of a run told against her and, after making the running until 2f out, she was soon done with. (op 5/2 tchd 3/1)

5644 - 5646a (Foreign Racing) - See Raceform Interactive

5612 BADEN-BADEN (L-H)
Sunday, August 26

OFFICIAL GOING: Turf: good to soft

5647a GOLDENE PEITSCHE - POWERED BY BURDA@TURF.DE (GROUP 2) (3YO+) (TURF) 6f
3:50 (3:53) 3-Y-0+

£33,333 (£12,916; £5,416; £3,333; £2,083; £1,250)

			RPR
1		**Ferro Sensation (GER)**[28] 6-9-4 0... MircoDemuro 7 (J Pubben, Holland) *hld up in last: rdn to improve on outer over 2f out: r.o to chal wl ins fnl f: led cl home: cosily* **35/1**	107
2	1	**Govinda (USA)**[14] 5-9-4 0... AStarke 5 (A Wohler, Germany) *led: rdn 2f out: r.o: strly pressed and hdd wl ins fnl f: no rspnse* **74/10**	104
3	1	**Boomerang Bob (IRE)**[22] 4794 3-9-1 0... SebSanders 4 (J W Hills) *midfield: prog on to heels of ldrs 2 1/2f out: rdn 2f out: kpt on one pce ins fnl 1 1/2f* **43/10**[2]	101
4	½	**Smooth Operator (GER)**[28] 6-9-4 0...(b) StefanieHofer 12 (Mario Hofer, Germany) *prom on inner: rdn 2 1/2f out: plugged on u.p ins fnl 1 1/2f: jst hld on for 4th* **77/10**	99
5	shd	**The Call (FR)**[14] 3-9-1 0... FilipMinarik 1 (Uwe Ostmann, Germany) *hld up towards rr: stdy prog fr over 2f out: rdn over 1 1/2f out: kpt on one pce ins fnl 1 1/2f: jst missed out on 4th* **68/10**[3]	99
6	1 ¼	**Verde-Mar (BRZ)**[14] 5-9-4 0... JoaoMoreira 9 (Fabricio Borges, Sweden) *rousted along in midfield to go early gallop: niggled thrght: drvn and outpcd over 1 1/2f out: plugged on to go 6th cl home* **43/10**[2]	95
7	nk	**Walero (GER)**[28] 6-9-4 0... KClijmans 6 (Uwe Ostmann, Germany) *bobbled s and pushed along towards rr: niggled thrght: plugged on u.p ins fnl 1 1/2f: n.d* **223/10**	94
8	3	**August Rush (SAF)**[23] 4790 6-9-4 0... ADeVries 3 (P Bary, France) *midfield: lost pl and dropped towards rr over 3f out: rdn over 2f out: effrt to improve on outer over 1f out: no ex and btn ins fnl f: fdd* **3/1**[1]	84
9	1	**War Artist (AUS)**[14] 9-9-4 0... RobertHavlin 8 (P Harley, Germany) *midfield on inner: rdn over 1 1/2f out: outpcd ins fnl f: fdd* **186/10**	81
10	shd	**Gracia Directa (GER)**[23] 4764 4-9-1 0... DPorcu 10 (D Moser, Germany) *chsd ldr: rdn over 2 1/2f out: brief effrt to chal on outer over 1 1/2f out: kpt on tl no ex and fdd ins fnl f: eased* **121/10**	78
11	½	**Huma Bird**[65] 3366 3-8-11 0... THellier 11 (H-A Pantall, France) *pressed ldr on inner: rdn over 1 1/2f out: kpt on tl no ex and fdd ins fnl f: eased whn btn* **113/10**	75
12	6	**Josephine Blanche (GER)**[14] 4-9-1 0... PJWerning 2 (D Moser, Germany) *midfield on outer: rdn and outpcd over 3f out: dropped to last over 2f out: sn wl bhd: nvr a factor* **44/1**	57

1m 10.92s (0.63)
WFA 3 from 4yo+ 3lb 12 Ran SP% **129.1**
WIN (incl. 10 euro stake): 358. PLACES: 68, 23, 21. SF: 2,609.
Owner Cornelis Derks Van De Ven **Bred** Cornelis Derks Van De Ven **Trained** Holland

NOTEBOOK
Boomerang Bob(IRE) boxed on well but could never quite get to the leader. He's quite a reliable sort and a fair guide to the level of the form.

5570 DEAUVILLE (R-H)
Sunday, August 26

OFFICIAL GOING: Turf: good: fibresand: standard

5648a PRIX DE MEAUTRY LUCIEN BARRIERE (GROUP 3) (3YO+) (TURF) 6f
1:30 (12:00) 3-Y-0+ **£33,333** (£13,333; £10,000; £6,666; £3,333)

			RPR
1		**Jimmy Styles**[22] 4794 8-9-1 0...(p) GeraldMosse 5 (Clive Cox) *trckd ldr: led or disp ld after 1f: wnt on over 2f out: qcknd clr appr fnl f: r.o wl: comf* **12/1**	111
2	¾	**Gammarth (FR)**[23] 4790 4-9-1 0... ChristopheSoumillon 4 (H-A Pantall, France) *chsd ldrs: 4th and rdn 2f out: r.o to go 2nd ins fnl f: r.o u.p and hld on gamely* **6/1**	109
3	hd	**Mariol (FR)**[7] 9-9-1 0... ThierryJarnet 6 (Robert Collet, France) *hld up towards rr: rdn and hdwy over 1f out: r.o u.p to chal for 2nd ins fnl 100yds: hld cl home* **16/1**	108
4	¾	**Kerasona (FR)**[21] 4861 3-8-8 0... Christophe-PatriceLemaire 2 (J-C Rouget, France) *settled in rr on ins: swtchd outside and hdwy 1 1/2f out: short of room 1f out: rdn and kpt on ins fnl f: nvr able to chal* **6/1**	102
5	¾	**Swiss Spirit**[67] 3265 3-8-11 0... JamieSpencer 1 (David Elsworth) *racd keenly on heels of ldrs: checked at 1/2-way and shuffled bk to one fr last: short of room fr over 1f out: r.o fnl 100yds: nvr able to chal* **10/1**	103
6	2	**Restiadargent (FR)**[21] 4861 3-8-8 0... MaximeGuyon 12 (H-A Pantall, France) *chsd ldrs: 3rd and ev ch under 2 1/2f out: rdn and nt qckn fr 1 1/2f out: one pce fnl f* **9/4**[1]	93
7	1	**Shamalgan (FR)**[57] 3657 5-9-1 0... GregoryBenoist 3 (X Nakkachdji, France) *broke wl and led: led or disp ld after 1f: rdn and lost pl fr 2f out* **5/1**[2]	94

8 *nse* **Le Valentin (FR)**[7] 6-9-1 0 AnthonyCrastus 10 94
(Y De Nicolay, France) *t.k.h early: racd midfield: 5th and chalng for 2nd over 1f out: sn rdn and nt qckn: wknd fnl 150yds* **14/1**

9 *3* **Best Of Order (IRE)**[15] 5-9-1 0 (b) MickaelBarzalona 8 84
(E J O'Neill, France) *racd towards rr: rdn and no imp on outside fnl 2f* **25/1**

10 *snk* **Barbayam**[46] 3987 3-8-8 0 OlivierPeslier 13 80
(F Head, France) *midfield on outside: effrt to chse ldng gp 1/2-way: rdn and nt qckn over 2f out: sn wknd* **11/2**[3]

1m 10.4s (-0.60)
WFA 3 from 4yo+ 3lb **10** Ran SP% **124.6**
WIN (incl. 1 euro stake): 19.40. PLACES: 5.90, 2.80, 5.80. DF: 48.50. SF: 143.20.
Owner Gwyn Powell & Peter Ridgers **Bred** Barry Minty **Trained** Lambourn, Berks

NOTEBOOK
Jimmy Styles appreciated the fast ground and, in a race in which it paid to race handily, he was in the right position, having crossed over and grabbed the rail early on. This was his first win at Group level.
Swiss Spirit was keen early, was short of room and didn't have the race run to suit. He's better than this.

5649a PRIX QUINCEY LUCIEN BARRIERE (GROUP 3) (3YO+) (TURF) 1m (R)
2:40 (12:00) 3-Y-0+ **£33,333** (£13,333; £10,000; £6,666; £3,333)

RPR

1 **Fractional (IRE)**[19] 4935 3-8-10 0 MaximeGuyon 9 109
(A Fabre, France) *settled midfield towards outside: effrt between horses ins fnl 2f: qcknd to ld over 1f out: hrd pressed and r.o gamely fnl f: hld on wl cl home* **4/1**[1]

2 *shd* **Moonwalk In Paris (FR)**[49] 3900 4-9-6 0 ChristopheSoumillon 5 114
(J-C Rouget, France) *midfield: following eventual wnr 2 1/2f out: hdwy on outside to chse ldng gp over 1 1/2f out: r.o and pressed wnr thrght fnl f: a jst hld* **7/1**[2]

3 *hd* **King Air (FR)**[14] 5-9-0 0 Christophe-PatriceLemaire 4 108
(R Pritchard-Gordon, France) *settled towards rr on ins: hdwy on rail over 1 1/2f out: wnt 3rd ins fnl f: r.o wl: jst failed to collar first two* **28/1**

4 *1* **Moonday Sun (USA)**[15] 3-8-8 0 GregoryBenoist 1 104
(D Smaga, France) *chsd ldng gp: prog on ins 2f out: w ldrs and ev ch under 1 1/2f out: sn rdn and kpt on at same pce fnl f* **8/1**[3]

5 *3/4* **Sulle Orme (FR)**[37] 4316 4-9-0 0 GeraldMosse 6 104
(C Ferland, France) *midfield: pushed along to hold position 3f out: chsd ldng gp and rdn 2f out: styd on u.p ins fnl f: nt pce to chal* **20/1**

6 *snk* **Sofast (FR)**[56] 3681 3-9-1 0 OlivierPeslier 8 109
(F Head, France) *trckd ldrs: led appr fnl 1 1/2f: rdn and hdd over 1f out: one pce u.p fnl f* **7/1**[2]

7 *2* **Kalamos (USA)**[19] 4935 3-8-8 0 ThierryThulliez 11 98
(P Bary, France) *settled towards rr: hdwy and swtchd outside 2 1/2f out: chal for pls over 1f out: sn rdn and nt qckn: wknd fnl 150yds* **12/1**

8 *1 1/2* **Tifongo (FR)**[50] 3884 3-8-10 0 MickaelBarzalona 13 96
(H-A Pantall, France) *a towards rr: rdn and no imp fnl 2f* **16/1**

9 *1/2* **Tin Horse (IRE)**[14] 5141 4-9-6 0 ThierryJarnet 14 100
(D Guillemin, France) *sn settled midfield on outside: dropped towards rr by 1/2-way: effrt on outside to chse ldrs over 1 1/2f out: rdn and wknd ins fnl f* **4/1**[1]

10 *4* **Sandy's Charm (FR)**[147] 1163 4-8-13 0 Francois-XavierBertras 3 84
(F Rohaut, France) *trckd ldrs: 3rd and scrubbed along over 2f out: wknd fr 1 1/2f out* **9/1**

0 **Celebrissime (IRE)**[14] 7-9-0 0 FlavienPrat 12
(F Head, France) *pressed ldr: led over 2 1/2f out: rdn 2f out: hdd appr fnl 1 1/2f: sn wknd* **25/1**

0 **Konig Concorde (GER)**[28] 7-9-6 0 (p) UmbertoRispoli 7
(C Sprengel, Germany) *chsd ldrs: prom tl rdn and nt qckn over 1 1/2f out: wknd appr fnl f: sn eased* **33/1**

0 **Shamardanse (IRE)**[21] 4-8-10 0 (p) TheoBachelot 10
(S Wattel, France) *led: hdd over 2 1/2f out: wknd qckly: eased fnl f* **40/1**

0 **Hippolyte (FR)**[19] 4935 3-8-8 0 SebastienMaillot 2
(T Clout, France) *racd among bkmarkers: rdn and no imp fnl 2f* **16/1**

1m 35.5s (-5.30) **Going Correction** -0.325s/f (Firm)
WFA 3 from 4yo+ 6lb **14** Ran SP% **123.0**
Speed ratings: **113,112,112,111,110 110,108,107,106,102 , , ,**
WIN (incl. 1 euro stake): 5.00. PLACES: 2.10, 2.40, 5.50. DF: 14.90. SF: 25.30.
Owner Godolphin SNC **Bred** Darley Stud Management Co, Ltd **Trained** Chantilly, France

NOTEBOOK
Fractional(IRE), a heavy ground Listed winner last time out, just held on following a final furlong duel with the runner-up.
Moonwalk In Paris(FR) lost little in defeat and comes out of the race the best horse at the weights.

5650a LUCIEN BARRIERE GRAND PRIX DE DEAUVILLE (GROUP 2) (3YO+) (TURF) 1m 4f 110y
3:10 (12:00) 3-Y-0+ **£95,000** (£36,666; £17,500; £11,666; £5,833)

RPR

1 **Masterstroke (USA)**[38] 4281 3-8-6 0 MickaelBarzalona 7 112+
(A Fabre, France) *broke fast: settled in midfield on ins: mde gd prog u.p 2f out: swtchd towards centre 1 1/2f out: r.o wl u.p fnl f: str fin to get up cl home* **17/2**

2 *snk* **Gatewood**[23] 4759 4-9-3 0 WilliamBuick 4 112
(John Gosden) *settled in 3rd: chal for ld 2 1/2f out: tk ld 2f out: r.o wl fnl f: ct cl home* **13/2**[3]

3 *3/4* **Ok Coral (FR)**[39] 4229 5-9-3 0 NicolasPerret 2 111
(K Borgel, France) *settled in 2nd: looked short of pce 2f out and dropped to 5th: rallied wl u.p: fin wl fnl f to go 2nd fnl 100yds: r.o wl: lost 2nd fnl 25yds* **24/1**

4 *nk* **Top Trip**[43] 4121 3-8-9 0 ThomasHuet 3 113+
(F Doumen, France) *hld up towards rr: mde gd prog ent fnl 1 1/2f: r.o wl fnl f: nt rch ldrs: clst at fin* **9/2**[2]

5 *1 1/4* **Molly Malone (FR)**[85] 2711 4-9-0 0 UmbertoRispoli 10 106
(M Delzangles, France) *hld up towards rr: r.o wl fnl f on wd outside to go 5th cl home* **13/1**

6 *hd* **Don Bosco (FR)**[15] 5117 5-9-3 0 OlivierPeslier 1 108
(D Smaga, France) *sn led: chal and hdd 2f out: styd on wl u.p fnl f: lost 5th cl home* **11/1**

7 *4* **Tenenbaum**[24] 3-8-6 0 MaximeGuyon 9 102
(A Fabre, France) *racd midfield: rdn but no ex 1 1/2f out: short of room ent fnl f: nt hrd rdn whn ch gone: eased* **23/10**[1]

8 *shd* **Usuelo (FR)**[91] 2534 4-9-3 0 AntoineHamelin 11 102
(J-L Guillochon, France) *hld up at rr: rdn but no ex fnl 2f: styd on one pce* **10/1**

9 *shd* **Miss Lago (IRE)**[43] 4120 4-9-0 0 (p) GregoryBenoist 5 99
(E Lellouche, France) *broke slowly: racd at rr of field: rdn but no ex fr 2f out: eased ins fnl f* **21/1**

10 *1/2* **Allied Powers (IRE)**[50] 3857 7-9-3 0 (b[1]) JamieSpencer 8 101
(Michael Bell) *hld up towards rr: rdn but no ex ent fnl 2f: nvr a factor* **24/1**

11 **Prairie Star (FR)**[91] 2534 4-9-3 0 ChristopheSoumillon 6 101
(J E Hammond, France) *settled midfield: rdn but no ex u.p 2f out: sn wknd* **10/1**

2m 39.1s (-7.30) **Going Correction** -0.175s/f (Firm)
WFA 3 from 4yo+ 10lb **11** Ran SP% **118.5**
Speed ratings: **115,114,114,114,113 113,110,110,110,110 110**
WIN (incl. 1 euro stake): 2.30 (Masterstroke coupled with Tenenbaum). PLACES: 3.30, 2.60, 5.30. DF: 25.80. SF: 51.20.
Owner Godolphin SNC **Bred** Darley Stud Management **Trained** Chantilly, France

NOTEBOOK
Masterstroke(USA), winner of a Listed race at Vichy last time out, was suited by the decent gallop and came with a strong finish to get up close home. His rider suggested the colt will improve further for easier ground in future.
Gatewood looked to have been brought with a well-timed run only for the winner to catch him close home. This was still another step up from him, though, and he remains progressive.
Allied Powers(IRE) needs softer ground than he had here.

4751 OVREVOLL (R-H)
Sunday, August 26

OFFICIAL GOING: Turf: heavy

5651a MARIT SVEAAS MINNELOP (GROUP 3) (3YO+) (TURF) 1m 1f
3:41 (12:00) 3-Y-0+ **£86,114** (£27,987; £12,917; £7,750; £5,166)

RPR

1 **Bank Of Burden (USA)**[21] 4863 5-9-6 0 (b) RafaelSchistl 7 101
(Niels Petersen, Norway) *outpcd in rr adrift of field: scrubbed along and hdwy 1/2-way: one of jst two to stay on ins rail turning for home 3f out: led under 2f out and qcknd clr 1 1/2f out: r.o strly fnl f: won easing down* **87/10**

2 *3* **Weald**[21] 4863 7-9-4 0 OliverWilson 2 93
(Hans-Inge Larsen, Sweden) *midfield: prom in stands' side gp 2 1/2f out: swtchd ins and chsd eventual wnr over 1 1/2f out: kpt on but a wl hld by wnr* **56/1**

3 *6 1/2* **Entangle**[31] 6-9-1 0 JacobJohansen 13 76
(Arnfinn Lund, Norway) *a.p on outside: led after 2f: c wd onto stands' rail turning for home 3f out: hdd under 2f out: kpt on at one pce fnl 1 1/2f* **31/5**[2]

4 *1* **Tertullus (FR)**[43] 9-9-4 0 ElioneChaves 6 77
(Rune Haugen, Norway) *chsd ldng gp: midfield 1/2-way: styd w wnr on ins 3f out: swtchd towards stands' side and plugged on fnl 1 1/2f: wnt 4th cl home* **213/10**

5 *1/2* **Jubilance (IRE)**[73] 3-8-11 0 ManuelMartinez 5 76
(Bent Olsen, Denmark) *w ldng gp: rdn and nt qckn 2f out: plugged on at one pce fnl f: lost 4th cl home* **149/10**

6 *2* **Empire Storm (GER)**[42] 4130 5-9-6 0 EPedroza 10 74
(A Wohler, Germany) *chsd ldrs: rdn and no imp over 2f out: fdd ins fnl f* **87/10**

7 *nse* **Touch Of Hawk (FR)**[21] 4863 6-9-4 0 EspenSki 12 72
(Wido Neuroth, Norway) *settled towards rr: outpcd 3f out: styd on past btn horses fr 2f out: nvr plcd to chal* **109/10**

8 *6 1/2* **Fanunalter**[36] 4320 6-9-8 0 JimCrowley 4 62
(Michael Wigham) *w.w towards rr: effrt to chse ldrs on stands' side over 2f out: sn rdn and no further imp: wl btn whn ins fnl f* **6/5**[1]

9 *6* **Palermo (GER)**[50] 3886 6-9-4 0 CarlosLopez 9 45
(Cathrine Erichsen, Norway) *trckd ldrs: 6th 1/2-way: rdn and brief effrt 2f out: sn wknd u.p* **188/10**

10 *6* **Silver Ocean (USA)**[24] 4751 4-9-6 0 Per-AndersGraberg 11 35
(Niels Petersen, Norway) *settled towards rr: short-lived effrt on outside 3f out: sn rdn and wknd fr 2f out* **83/10**[3]

11 *9* **Verglacial (IRE)**[43] 5-9-4 0 ValmirDeAzeredo 8 14
(Francisco Castro, Sweden) *led: hdd after 2f: 3rd 3f out: sn rdn and grad dropped away* **41/1**

F **Without Fear (FR)**[21] 4863 4-9-4 0 PDaCosta 3
(Arnfinn Lund, Norway) *w ldng gp: 2nd whn stmbld and fell sn after 1/2-way* **116/10**

1m 50.7s (0.80)
WFA 3 from 4yo+ 7lb **12** Ran SP% **127.0**
PARI-MUTUEL (all including 1krone stakes): WIN 9.69; PLACE 2.85, 8.62, 2.26; DF 386.01.
Owner Stall Trick Or Treat **Bred** Bjarne Minde **Trained** Norway

NOTEBOOK
Fanunalter, shock winner of the Group 2 Summer Mile at Ascot last time out, was sent off a short price but disappointed, possibly finding conditions too testing.

5652 - (Foreign Racing) - See Raceform Interactive

5260 CHEPSTOW (L-H)
Monday, August 27

OFFICIAL GOING: Soft (heavy in places) changing to heavy after race 5 (4.25)
Wind: Moderate across Weather: Overcast, showers

5653 CHEPSTOW ANNUAL MEMBERS APPRENTICE (S) STKS 1m 2f 36y
2:05 (2:06) (Class 6) 3-4-Y-0 **£1,617** (£481; £240; £120) **Stalls** Low

Form RPR

2120 **1** **Pandorica**[14] 5151 4-8-13 66 (p) DanielMuscutt[(5)] 1 65
(Bernard Llewellyn) *trckd ldrs: chal 3f out: led over 2f out: drvn clr over 1f out: comf* **10/3**[3]

5603 **2** *2* **Tijori (IRE)**[7] 5419 4-9-3 57 ow2 (p) RobertWilliams[(3)] 6 63
(Bernard Llewellyn) *sn chsng ldr: led appr fnl 3f but sn rdn: hdd over 2f out: styd chsng wnr but no imp fr over 1f out* **20/1**

0531 **3** *2* **Bondi Mist (IRE)**[11] 5266 3-8-10 65 JamesRogers 3 57
(Jonathan Portman) *chsd ldrs: rdn and outpcd over 2f out: styd on again to take one pce 3rd appr fnl f* **9/4**[1]

U522 **4** *7* **Volcanic Jack (IRE)**[11] 5261 4-9-4 56 AmyScott 7 43
(Tony Carroll) *racd in rr: hdwy 4f out: chal ins fnl 3f: wknd fr 2f out* **15/2**
2520 **5** *1 1/4* **Offbeat Safaris (IRE)**[24] 4775 4-9-4 76 DarrenEgan 5 41
(Ronald Harris) *t.k.h: chsd ldrs: chal over 3f out tl over 2f out: wknd over 1f out* **5/2**[2]
0502 **6** *1 1/2* **Hawridge Song**[7] 5419 4-9-1 62 (b) ThomasBrown(3) 2 38
(Rod Millman) *rdn over 3f out: a in rr* **15/2**
30-0 **7** *20* **Concrete Jungle (IRE)**[18] 5021 4-9-4 58 CharlesBishop 4
(Natalie Lloyd-Beavis) *led: hdd & wknd appr fnl 3f: t.o* **50/1**
2m 22.63s (12.03) **Going Correction** +0.95s/f (Soft)
WFA 3 from 4yo 8lb 7 Ran SP% **112.7**
Speed ratings (Par 101): **89,87,85,80,79 78,62**
toteswingers 1&2 £13.20, 1&3 £1.20, 2&3 £19.90 CSF £59.51 TOTE £3.80: £1.80, £6.60; EX 31.20.There was no bid for the winner.
Owner Alex James **Bred** Ambersham Stud **Trained** Fochriw, Caerphilly

FOCUS
There had been a lot of rain in the last few days and the going was soft, heavy in places. They were tightly bunched for a long way in this apprentice selling race but they eventually finished strung out and the first two were both trained by Bernard Llewellyn. An ordinary seller run in a slow time, and dubious form.

5654 PREMIER FOOD COURTS NURSERY 5f 16y
2:40 (2:40) (Class 6) (0-65,65) 2-Y-O **£1,704** (£503; £251) **Stalls** Centre

Form RPR
0132 **1** **Khefyn (IRE)**[13] 5194 2-9-7 65 KierenFox 2 79
(Ronald Harris) *trckd ldrs: chal 2f out: led sn after: qcknd clr fnl f: v easily* **7/2**[2]
660 **2** *6* **Colourist**[23] 4816 2-9-7 65 GeorgeBaker 4 57
(Gary Moore) *in rr: hdwy 2f out: pushed along and kpt on fnl f to take wl-hld 2nd fnl 120yds* **8/1**
0605 **3** *1 1/4* **Plexolini**[18] 5010 2-8-12 56 J-PGuillambert 1 44
(Jo Hughes) *led after 1f: jnd 2f out: hdd sn after: styd disputing 2nd but nvr any ch w wnr: dropped to 3rd fnl 120yds* **9/2**[3]
3341 **4** *1 1/2* **Stripped Bear (IRE)**[7] 5403 2-8-5 56 6ex RyanTate(7) 7 38
(Tom Dascombe) *led 1f: styd chsng ldrs: disp 2nd over 1f out but nvr any ch w wnr: wknd fnl f* **3/1**[1]
0625 **5** *3 1/2* **Frosted Off**[25] 4728 2-9-3 61 [1] CathyGannon 5 31
(John Spearing) *rdn along 1/2-way: a struggling to go pce* **6/1**
0440 **6** *7* **Golac**[10] 5291 2-8-11 60 CharlesBishop(5) 8 4
(Mick Channon) *chsd ldrs: rdn over 3f out: btn 1/2-way* **14/1**
2044 **7** *1/2* **Baltic Gin (IRE)**[7] 5424 2-9-1 59 TomMcLaughlin 9 2
(Malcolm Saunders) *early spd: sn bhd* **7/1**
660 **8** *6* **Star Maid**[28] 4651 2-7-10 45 DarrenEgan(5) 3
(Tony Carroll) *chsd ldrs to 1/2-way: wknd rapidly* **25/1**
1m 4.84s (5.54) **Going Correction** +0.95s/f (Soft) 8 Ran SP% **113.8**
Speed ratings (Par 92): **93,83,81,79,73 62,61,51**
toteswingers 1&2 £13.00, 1&3 £3.30, 2&3 £4.60 CSF £31.03 CT £126.71 TOTE £4.70: £1.40, £2.60, £1.60; EX 25.40.
Owner Robert & Nina Bailey **Bred** Ms Kate Wilson **Trained** Earlswood, Monmouths

FOCUS
This looked a competitive nursery but the winner powered clear to gain compensation for a close call last time. The form appears straightforward.

NOTEBOOK
Khefyn(IRE), placed in both runs since his breakthrough win at Ffos Las last month, travelled smoothly into contention and showed a good turn of foot in the conditions to romp clear and improve his record to 2-7. He had looked consistent rather than progressive before this but a switch to soft ground has inspired a big jolt of improvement from this half-brother to useful prolific 5f-1m winner Invincible Force. He has should take some stopping if turned out quickly under a penalty. (tchd 3-1)
Colourist shaped with some promise, staying on steadily off a stiff-looking mark on his nursery debut. This 45,000gns Dutch Art colt has shown patchy form in four starts but he has several 5f-7f winners in his pedigree and could be capable of better. (op 11-2 tchd 5-1)
Plexolini was generally regressive in four maidens but he showed up well for a long way switched to soft turf on this nursery debut. (op 17-2)
Stripped Bear(IRE) couldn't sustain her effort under a penalty for her decisive Kempton win last week but she shaped like a return to more of a speed test would suit. (op 4-1)
Frosted Off was laboured with a hood tried. (tchd 11-2 and 13-2)

5655 IRISH STALLION FARMS E B F MAIDEN STKS (C&G) 1m 14y
3:15 (3:15) (Class 5) 2-Y-0 **£3,169** (£943; £471; £235) **Stalls** Centre

Form RPR
1 **Jebril (FR)** 2-9-0 0 DarryllHolland 4 71
(Jonathan Portman) *s.i.s: green and sn drvn: chsd ldrs 1/2-way: slt advantage 2f out: narrowly hdd 1f out: styd chalng and hung rt and bmpd fnl 130yds: rallied to ld again last stride* **10/1**
2 *nse* **Jullundar (IRE)** 2-8-9 0 CharlesBishop(5) 5 71
(Mick Channon) *in rr: hdwy 3f out: chsd ldrs 2f out: edgd lft ins fnl f: slt advantage fnl 120yds: hdd last stride* **7/2**[3]
06 **3** *nk* **Ivanhoe**[15] 5126 2-9-0 0 DaneO'Neill 3 71
(Michael Blanshard) *in rr: hdwy 3f out: chal fr 2f out and upsides whn hmpd fnl 130yds: rallied and ev ch clsng stages: no ex last strides* **11/1**
52 **4** *1* **Arctic Admiral (IRE)**[7] 5407 2-9-0 0 KieranO'Neill 1 68
(Richard Hannon) *chsd ldr: slt advantage fr 4f out: narrowly hdd 2f out: styd upsides: slt ld 1f out: edgd lft and hdd fnl 120yds: wknd clsng stages* **9/4**[2]
55 **5** *13* **Constans (IRE)**[18] 5005 2-9-0 0 AdamKirby 2 39
(Clive Cox) *led to 1/2-way: sn btn* **13/8**[1]
6 **6** *7* **Luv U Whatever**[19] 4967 2-9-0 0 J-PGuillambert 6 24
(Jo Hughes) *chsd ldrs to 1/2-way: sn btn* **25/1**
1m 45.28s (9.08) **Going Correction** +1.10s/f (Soft) 6 Ran SP% **112.4**
Speed ratings (Par 94): **98,97,97,96,83 76**
toteswingers 1&2 £3.70, 1&3 £16.10, 2&3 £6.90 CSF £44.35 TOTE £7.30: £6.40, £2.40; EX 58.60.
Owner L Raissi **Bred** Mme Heather Murat **Trained** Compton, Berks

FOCUS
The favourite was disappointing in this maiden. There was an exciting finish and the first four pulled a long way clear. They finished in a heap in a slow time.

NOTEBOOK
Jebril(FR), a half-brother to Barn Dance who won a 1m Southwell claimer as a juvenile for the same trainer in December, was slowly away but he gradually worked his way into it and showed plenty of determination to just prevail on his debut. (op 8-1)
Jullundar(IRE) ran very green and hung left under pressure but he deserves a lot of credit for nearly pulling it off in gruelling conditions on his first run. He should have learned a lot and is a £40,000 Refuse To Bend half-brother to smart multiple 6f-1m4f winner Crosspeace. (op 4-1 tchd 3-1)
Ivanhoe travelled well for a long way and kept battling in a big run on his first try on soft ground. He has been progressive in three runs and is a half-brother to Arctic Mirage who won a maiden here on good to soft for the same yard. (tchd 10-1 and 12-1)
Arctic Admiral(IRE) had strong form claims on his improved 8l second behind a useful Godolphin newcomer in a 1m Kempton maiden last week. Always prominent, he handled the soft ground well but just came up a bit short. (tchd 5-2)
Constans(IRE), fifth in a pair of 7f/1m maidens at Doncaster and Sandown, was a strong favourite but he was the first to crack and may not have handled the taxing ground. Official explanation: trainer said colt was unsuited by the soft (heavy in places) ground (op 2-1 tchd 6-4)

5656 IRISH STALLION FARMS EBF MEDIAN AUCTION MAIDEN FILLIES' STKS 1m 14y
3:50 (3:55) (Class 5) 2-Y-O **£3,160** (£943; £471; £235) **Stalls** Centre

Form RPR
1 **Nice Story (IRE)** 2-8-9 0 CharlesBishop(5) 1 75+
(Mick Channon) *in rr: hdwy fr 3f out: led 2f out: drvn and hung rt fnl f: kpt on strly clsng stages* **11/4**[1]
2 *2* **Reveille** 2-9-0 0 DarryllHolland 3 71+
(Hughie Morrison) *sn in tch: chsd ldrs 3f out: chsd wnr fr 2f out: effrt and carried rt ins fnl f: no ex and hld whn swtchd lft clsng stages* **3/1**[2]
00 **3** *9* **Wild Diamond (IRE)**[10] 5319 2-9-0 0 ChrisCatlin 8 51+
(Sir Mark Prescott Bt) *chsd ldrs: rdn and outpcd over 2f out: styd on to take mod 3rd fnl f* **5/1**
0 **4** *1/2* **Black Eyed Girl (IRE)**[5] 5478 2-9-0 0 KieranO'Neill 5 50
(J S Moore) *stdd s: plld hrd and sn led: hdd ins fnl 3f: sn no ch w ldng duo: pluged on for mod 4th fnl 2f* **9/2**[3]
5 *3* **Valley Dreamer** 2-9-0 0 DavidProbert 7 43
(Michael Blanshard) *nvr gng pce to press ldrs: no ch fnl 3f* **11/2**
0 **6** *7* **Phoebe's Perfect**[19] 4946 2-9-0 0 JamesMillman 4 28
(Rod Millman) *uns rdr and loose bef s: chsd ldrs tl wknd over 3f out* **14/1**
0 **7** *5* **Be Royale**[23] 4813 2-8-9 0 DarrenEgan(5) 2 17
(Bryn Palling) *chsd ldrs: led ins fnl 3f: sn hdd: edgd lft and wknd qckly* **16/1**
1m 47.51s (11.31) **Going Correction** +1.10s/f (Soft) 7 Ran SP% **114.4**
Speed ratings (Par 91): **87,85,76,75,72 65,60**
toteswingers 1&2 £2.50, 1&3 £5.60, 2&3 £11.00 CSF £11.31 TOTE £4.90: £2.70, £2.70; EX 9.90.
Owner Jaber Abdullah **Bred** Storeway Ltd **Trained** West Ilsley, Berks
■ Stewards' Enquiry : Charles Bishop three-day ban: careless riding (Sep 10-12); seven-day ban: used whip above permitted level (Sep 13-18, & one day remedial training)

FOCUS
The runners with experience hadn't achieved much and two newcomers pulled clear in this fillies' maiden. Both are open to improvement.

NOTEBOOK
Nice Story(IRE) who was sent off favourite, travelled well into the lead 3f out and showed a good attitude to prevail in a sustained duel with her main market rival on her debut. She looks a fair type and is a first foal of a US winning half-sister to 1m1f Grade 2-placed performer Princess Tru. (op 3-1 tchd 5-2)
Reveille was prominent in the market on her debut and gave it a good shot in the arduous conditions. She should improve for the run and is a 28,000gns half-sister to 7f British and Grade 2/3 US 1m winner Up In Time and 1m4f soft-ground winner Don't Take Me Alive. (tchd 5-2)
Wild Diamond(IRE), beaten more than 20l in two previous maiden runs, looked a bit more streetwise this time but was left behind by the front two. A Hernando half-sister to four winners at up to 1m4f, she could find her niche in middle-distance handicaps next season. (op 8-1)
Black Eyed Girl(IRE), a big filly who finished last of seven at 20-1 in a 1m Kempton maiden last week, pulled hard out in the lead and had nothing left some way out. (tchd 5-1)
Valley Dreamer, a half-sister to useful 1m2f Flat/hurdle winner Discoteca, travelled well into contention out wide but she couldn't pick up and faded on her debut. (op 6-1)
Phoebe's Perfect unseated her rider in the preliminaries and was under pressure when stumbling 4f out in the race. Official explanation: jockey said filly clipped heels approaching 4f out (op 9-1 tchd 16-1)

5657 BATH MARQUEES H'CAP 1m 14y
4:25 (4:26) (Class 5) (0-70,70) 3-Y-0+ **£2,264** (£673; £336; £168) **Stalls** Centre

Form RPR
5221 **1** **Croeso Mawr**[11] 5262 6-9-1 59 CathyGannon 2 77
(John Spearing) *trckd ldrs: slt ld fr 4f out tl drvn clr wl over 1f out: pushed wl ahd fnl f: easily* **7/2**[1]
-001 **2** *12* **Cyril The Squirrel**[13] 5193 8-9-3 61 DarryllHolland 4 51
(Karen George) *chsd ldrs: chal 4f out: chsd wnr over 2f out and again over 1f out: nvr any ch but wl clr of 3rd* **8/1**
3144 **3** *6* **Derfenna Art (IRE)**[31] 4531 3-9-5 69 (t) GeorgeBaker 5 46
(Seamus Durack) *chsd ldrs: styd towards far side and chsd wnr 2f out: no imp and wknd into 3rd over 1f out* **4/1**[2]
66-0 **4** *1 1/2* **Supa Seeker (USA)**[22] 4844 6-8-5 52 RaulDaSilva(3) 7 25
(Tony Carroll) *in tch: rdn over 3f out: styd on same pce fnl 2f* **12/1**
0003 **5** *nse* **No Larking (IRE)**[18] 4986 4-8-10 59 AmyScott(5) 10 32
(Henry Candy) *slt ld 3f: styd pressing ldrs to 4f out: lost position over 3f out: styd on again fnl f: nvr any ch* **7/1**[3]
2530 **6** *1* **Spinning Ridge (IRE)**[28] 4657 7-9-6 69 (b) DarrenEgan(5) 8 40
(Ronald Harris) *in tch: hdwy to chse ldrs 3f out: wknd 2f out* **16/1**
0421 **7** *1 1/2* **Tanforan**[11] 5261 10-8-11 55 KellyHarrison 14 22
(Brian Baugh) *w ldrs: led 5f out to 4f out: wknd fr 2f out* **16/1**
0360 **8** *2 1/2* **Temuco (IRE)**[4] 5501 3-9-3 67 AdamKirby 13 29
(David Evans) *in rr: sme hdwy 3f out: nvr rchd ldrs and sn no ch* **9/1**
0003 **9** *9* **Bidable**[13] 5193 8-9-1 59 DavidProbert 12
(Bryn Palling) *chsd ldrs 5f* **16/1**
0346 **10** *6* **Tweet Lady**[38] 4289 3-9-0 64 JamesMillman 1
(Rod Millman) *chsd ldrs to 1/2-way* **10/1**
/6-0 **11** *3* **Enchanting Smile (FR)**[22] 4844 5-9-4 62 DaneO'Neill 15
(Mark Gillard) *s.i.s: a bhd* **66/1**
4000 **12** *3 3/4* **Quite A Catch (IRE)**[22] 4844 4-9-5 63 (v) TomMcLaughlin 3
(Jonathan Portman) *s.i.s: sn pressing ldrs: wknd 1/2-way* **33/1**
0500 **13** *nk* **Mr Udagawa**[18] 4988 6-9-0 58 (p) MartinLane 9
(Bernard Llewellyn) *s.i.s: a in rr* **16/1**
-000 **14** *5* **Crystal Sky (IRE)**[23] 4817 4-8-7 51 oh6 ChrisCatlin 6
(Natalie Lloyd-Beavis) *a bhd* **50/1**
1m 44.34s (8.14) **Going Correction** +1.10s/f (Soft)
WFA 3 from 4yo+ 6lb 14 Ran SP% **122.5**
Speed ratings (Par 103): **103,91,85,83,83 82,80,78,69,63 60,56,56,51**
toteswingers 1&2 £2.90, 1&3 £4.30, 2&3 £4.70 CSF £31.92 CT £112.75 TOTE £5.90: £2.20, £3.40, £1.60; EX 23.80.
Owner Mrs Richard Evans **Bred** Richard Evans Bloodstock **Trained** Kinnersley, Worcs

FOCUS
The winner completed a double in great style in this handicap and the remote second was a long way clear of the rest. The winner clearly improved again but it's hard to quite know what she achieved here.

5658 MEDINET UK H'CAP 7f 16y
5:00 (5:02) (Class 6) (0-65,65) 3-Y-0+ **£1,617** (£481; £240; £120) **Stalls** Centre

Form RPR
1530 **1** **Nezami (IRE)**[25] 4747 7-9-11 **64**..(b) AmirQuinn 5 76
(Patrick Clinton) *mde virtually all: rdn fr over 1f out: hung rt fnl f: drvn out* **8/1**
-660 **2** *4 1/2* **Rafella (IRE)**[19] 4950 4-8-11 **50**....................................(v[1]) DavidProbert 2 50
(Michael Scudamore) *chsd ldrs: wnt 2nd ins fnl 3f: rdn over 2f out: no imp on wnr fr over 1f out* **16/1**
3330 **3** *1 1/2* **Rapid Water**[12] 5246 6-9-3 **56**....................................(p) AdamKirby 8 52
(Pat Eddery) *chsd ldrs: rdn and one pce fnl 2f* **6/1**[2]
0002 **4** *3 1/4* **Barista (IRE)**[15] 5127 4-9-7 **65**.................................... CharlesBishop(5) 4 53
(Brian Forsey) *sn chsng ldrs: rdn 3f out: outpcd fnl 2f* **7/1**[3]
0000 **5** *4* **Swift Act**[12] 5229 3-9-2 **65**.. DarrenEgan(5) 6 43
(Ronald Harris) *in tch: rdn and lost pl 3f out: no ch after* **11/1**
444 **6** *7* **Norlander**[14] 5156 3-8-10 **59**.. JamesRogers(5) 9 18
(Ralph Beckett) *chsd ldrs: rdn 3f out: btn sn after* **6/1**[2]
/006 **7** *nse* **Cheers Big Ears (IRE)**[11] 5261 6-8-4 **46** oh1............ RaulDaSilva(3) 10
(Richard Price) *stdd s: in rr: rdn 1/2-way and nvr in contention* **25/1**
-450 **8** *17* **Beauchamp Zorro**[18] 5008 4-9-6 **59**................................ DaneO'Neill 12
(Henry Candy) *plld hrd: chsd ldrs: rdn and btn 3f out* **3/1**[1]
000 **9** *6* **Trio Of Trix**[79] 2941 3-8-2 **46** oh1....................................... CathyGannon 1
(Malcolm Saunders) *a wl bhd: t.o* **16/1**
2500 **10** *21* **Pose (IRE)**[23] 4815 5-8-9 **48**..(t) MartinLane 3
(Roger Ingram) *chsd ldrs to 1/2-way: t.o* **20/1**

1m 32.35s (9.15) **Going Correction** +1.25s/f (Soft)
WFA 3 from 4yo+ 5lb **10** Ran SP% **105.9**
Speed ratings (Par 101): **97,91,90,86,81 73,73,54,47,23**
toteswingers 1&2 £30.80, 1&3 £14.30, 2&3 £23.90 CSF £104.30 CT £618.35 TOTE £9.10: £2.60, £4.60, £1.60; EX 116.90.
Owner In The Clear Racing **Bred** Falah Ithnein **Trained** Doveridge, Derbys
■ Billion Dollar Kid (7/1) was withdrawn on vet's advice. Deduct 10p in the £ under R4.
■ Stewards' Enquiry : Amir Quinn four-day ban: used whip above permitted level (Sep 10-13)

FOCUS
They went a fair pace down the centre of the track in this minor handicap but not many got involved and the winner made all. The form could be rated higher at face value, but there are doubts.

5659 CHEPSTOW ANNUAL MEMBERS H'CAP (DIV I) 6f 16y
5:35 (5:35) (Class 6) (0-55,59) 3-Y-0+ **£1,617** (£481; £240; £120) **Stalls** Centre

Form RPR
6601 **1** **Juarla (IRE)**[4] 5504 4-9-3 **59** 6ex...................................... DarrenEgan(5) 4 67+
(Ronald Harris) *trckd ldrs: led over 1f out: drvn and styd on strly ins fnl f* **1/1**[1]
0320 **2** *1 1/2* **Botanist**[4] 5504 5-8-13 **50**..(be) DaneO'Neill 9 54
(Milton Bradley) *in rr: hdwy 2f out: swtchd rt appr fnl f and racd alone towards stands' side: chsd wnr fnl 120yds but nvr any ch* **4/1**[2]
0004 **3** *1 1/4* **Petrarchan**[11] 5261 4-8-9 **46**...(bt) ChrisCatlin 1 46
(Milton Bradley) *chsd ldrs: drvn to ld over 2 out: hdd over 1f out: sn outpcd by wnr: dropped to 3rd fnl 120yds* **9/1**[3]
045 **4** *4* **Depden (IRE)**[19] 4943 4-8-2 **46** oh1.............................. DannyBrock(7) 10 34
(Richard Price) *sn led: rdn to keep advantage over 3f out: hdd over 2f out: sn one pce* **14/1**
006 **5** *1 1/2* **Barnacle**[33] 4456 3-8-6 **46** oh1.. KierenFox 7 29
(Pat Eddery) *in tch: rdn 3f out: no ch w ldrs fnl 2f* **16/1**
600 **6** *3 1/4* **Fonterutoli (IRE)**[6] 5444 5-9-1 **52**....................................(v) AdamKirby 11 26
(Roger Ingram) *slowly away: in rr: in tch w main gp 3f out: pushed along and no imp fnl 2f* **10/1**
6000 **7** *5* **Lana (IRE)**[18] 4981 3-8-10 **50**.. CathyGannon 2
(David Evans) *chsd ldrs: rdn 1/2-way wknd fr 2f out* **14/1**
0000 **8** *9* **Sienna Blue**[7] 5428 4-8-8 **52**...(p) JakePayne(7) 3
(Simon Hodgson) *early spd: rdn over 3f out: wknd over 2f out* **20/1**

1m 19.34s (7.34) **Going Correction** +1.25s/f (Soft)
WFA 3 from 4yo+ 3lb **8** Ran SP% **113.1**
Speed ratings (Par 101): **101,99,97,92,90 85,79,67**
toteswingers 1&2 £1.80, 1&3 £3.70, 2&3 £2.40 CSF £4.87 CT £21.53 TOTE £1.90: £1.10, £1.60, £2.20; EX 5.90.
Owner Robert & Nina Bailey **Bred** D And Mrs D Veitch **Trained** Earlswood, Monmouths
■ Stewards' Enquiry : Darren Egan mattered referred: used whip above permitted level, 5th suspension in 6mths.
Danny Brock two-day ban: used whip above permitted level (Sep 10-11) triggering 18-day suspension under totting up (Sep 14-Oct 01)

FOCUS
The hot favourite completed a double with something in hand in this weak sprint handicap, which was run in a time similar to division II.

5660 CHEPSTOW ANNUAL MEMBERS H'CAP (DIV II) 6f 16y
6:05 (6:05) (Class 6) (0-55,55) 3-Y-0+ **£1,617** (£481; £240; £120) **Stalls** Centre

Form RPR
6006 **1** **Athaakeel (IRE)**[6] 5447 6-8-8 **50**....................................(b) DarrenEgan(5) 7 61
(Ronald Harris) *racd towards stands' side: rdn 2f out: styd on wl fnl f to ld clsng stages* **10/1**
043 **2** *3/4* **Greyemkay**[18] 4993 4-8-2 **46** oh1................................ DanielMuscutt(7) 2 55
(Richard Price) *racd towards far side: chsd ldr: styd on to ld fnl 120yds: hdd and no ex clsng stages* **11/2**[3]
0010 **3** *3* **Flaxen Lake**[4] 5504 5-9-1 **52**..(p) AdamKirby 6 52
(Milton Bradley) *racd towards far side and led: rdn 2f out: hdd & wknd fnl 120yds* **6/1**
0500 **4** *6* **Compton Target (IRE)**[20] 4932 3-8-10 **50**......................(t) ChrisCatlin 10 32
(Milton Bradley) *chsd ldrs towards stands' side: wknd fr 2f out* **10/1**
6055 **5** *1 3/4* **Portrush Storm**[15] 5131 7-8-9 **46** oh1................................ DavidProbert 9 23
(Ray Peacock) *chsd ldrs towards stands' side: wknd fr 2f out* **25/1**
5300 **6** *1 1/4* **Royal Box**[63] 3456 5-9-0 **51**..(p) DarryllHolland 4 24
(Tony Carroll) *chsd ldrs towards far side tl wknd 2f out* **3/1**[1]
3400 **7** *2 1/2* **Cristaliyev**[21] 4890 4-8-12 **49**..(b) KierenFox 3 14
(John Flint) *chsd ldrs towards far side over 3f* **8/1**
5004 **8** *3 3/4* **Forty Proof (IRE)**[34] 4422 4-8-11 **48**..............................(vt) CathyGannon 5
(David Evans) *chsd ldrs stands' side to 1/2-way* **11/1**
0000 **9** *12* **Grande Illusion**[12] 5240 3-8-1 **46** oh1..............................(p) AmyScott(5) 1
(J W Hills) *racd towards far side and sn bhd* **25/1**
0053 **10** *6* **Ever The Optimist (IRE)**[19] 4943 4-9-4 **55**........................ DaneO'Neill 8
(Tony Newcombe) *sn bhd towards stands' side* **9/2**[2]

1m 19.4s (7.40) **Going Correction** +1.25s/f (Soft)
WFA 3 from 4yo+ 3lb **10** Ran SP% **118.2**
Speed ratings (Par 101): **100,99,95,87,84 83,79,74,58,50**
toteswingers 1&2 £29.40, 1&3 £22.30, 2&3 £7.80 CSF £65.04 CT £369.44 TOTE £13.10: £4.50, £2.80, £3.20; EX 102.70.
Owner Drag Star On Swan **Bred** Shadwell Estate Company Limited **Trained** Earlswood, Monmouths

FOCUS
They split into two groups in the second division of a sprint handicap and a runner who raced on the stands' side just reeled in a rival who was on the far side for most of the way. The time was similar to division I and the winner was close to last year's turf best.
T/Plt: £708.80 to a £1 stake. Pool: £52,045.17 - 53.60 winning tickets T/Qpdt: £87.00 to a £1 stake. Pool: £3,440.92 - 29.00 winning tickets ST

[4722] EPSOM (L-H)
Monday, August 27

OFFICIAL GOING: Sprint course - good to firm (good in places; 8.7); derby course - good (good to firm in places; 8.3)
Wind: Fresh, half behind Weather: Fine but cloudy

5661 EPSOM & EWELL BOROUGH 75TH ANNIVERSARY EBF MEDIAN AUCTION MAIDEN STKS 7f
2:00 (2:00) (Class 5) 2-Y-0 **£3,881** (£1,155; £577; £288) **Stalls** Low

Form RPR
45 **1** **Nile Knight**[80] 2888 2-9-3 0.. TedDurcan 6 76+
(Marcus Tregoning) *trckd ldng trio: prog to take 2nd wl over 2f out: drvn over 1f out: styd on to ld last strides* **11/4**[2]
3245 **2** *nk* **Red Refraction (IRE)**[20] 4934 2-9-3 73........................ RichardHughes 2 74
(Richard Hannon) *led: hrd rdn over 1f out: kpt on: hdd last strides* **4/1**[3]
022 **3** *nk* **Swift Cedar (IRE)**[11] 5275 2-8-10 77.................. MichaelJMMurphy(7) 1 76
(Alan Jarvis) *chsd ldng pair: n.m.r briefly on inner 3f out: plld out 2f out: clsd u.p fnl f: nrst fin* **6/5**[1]
4 *3 3/4* **Gigawatt** 2-9-3 0.. PatCosgrave 3 64
(Jim Boyle) *chsd ldrs: 5th st: wnt 4th 2f out and sn clr of rest: shkn up and no imp fnl f* **33/1**
00 **5** *4 1/2* **Lady Bonanova (IRE)**[66] 3339 2-8-12 0.................... HarryBentley 9 47
(Pat Phelan) *dwlt: racd wd in rr: 7th st: lost tch w ldrs 2f out: nvr on terms after* **25/1**
00 **6** *3/4* **Dawn Rock**[22] 4845 2-8-12 0.. SebSanders 8 45
(Simon Dow) *a in rr: 8th st: lost tch w ldrs 2f out* **66/1**
7 *1/2* **Magic Beat** 2-8-12 0... IanMongan 7 44
(Pat Phelan) *nvr beyond midfield: 6th st: rn green and lost tch w ldrs 2f out* **33/1**
0 **8** *1/2* **Seemenomore**[31] 4539 2-9-3 0.. HayleyTurner 4 47
(Michael Bell) *chsd ldr to wl over 2f out: sn lost pl and btn* **14/1**
00 **9** *5* **Privacy Order**[10] 5300 2-8-7 0.. RosieJessop(5) 5 29
(Sir Mark Prescott Bt) *hld up and sn last: detached fr 1/2-way: reminder over 2f out: appeared to fin less tired than sme* **33/1**

1m 24.89s (1.59) **Going Correction** -0.025s/f (Good) **9** Ran SP% **113.0**
Speed ratings (Par 94): **89,88,88,84,78 78,77,76,71**
Tote Swingers 1&2 £2.00, 2&3 £1.60, 1&3 £1.50 CSF £13.01 TOTE £4.90: £1.10, £1.80, £1.30; EX 13.90 Trifecta £13.30 Pool: £544.41 - 30.28 winning units..
Owner R C C Villers **Bred** Mr & Mrs Pakenham, F Hines & J James **Trained** Lambourn, Berks

FOCUS
Despite weekend rain the going remained Good, good to firm in places on the round course and with the rail dolled out up to 5yds from the 1m point to the winning post, increasing distances by 8yds. The jockeys reported the ground as being "lovely". Just a fair juvenile maiden judged on those with ratings and it produced a close finish. The time was modest compared with standard. the second is the key to the level.

NOTEBOOK
Nile Knight had run promisingly on his debut in May but had not built on that next time on easy ground, albeit behind a subsequent dual Group 2 winner. Returning from a break, he chased the leader for most of the way here and gradually wore him down on the climb to the line. He can expect a mark in the mid-70s after this and there might be more to come. (op 9-4)
Red Refraction(IRE) helped set the level, but he had not progressed greatly from his first two runs. He led from the start and looked likely to hold on a furlong out, but was just reeled in. He is up to winning races, though, and surely connections can find a suitable opportunity before long. The Veterinary Officer reported the colt finished stiff in front. Official explanation: vet said colt finished stiff in front (tchd 7-2)
Swift Cedar(IRE) was sent off favourite having gone close on both of his two previous starts. However, after being short of room in behind the leaders early in the straight, he took a while to get out and, although he finished best of all, could not quite get there. His turn should not be long delayed. (op 5-4 tchd 11-10)
Gigawatt ran well and was a clear fourth, although left behind by the first three in the closing stages. He showed signs of inexperience and hopefully will have learnt a lot from the run.

5662 BFWINES.CO.UK H'CAP 6f
2:30 (2:30) (Class 5) (0-75,75) 3-Y-0 **£3,881** (£1,155; £577; £288) **Stalls** High

Form RPR
5063 **1** **Lunar Deity**[5] 5486 3-9-5 **73**..(p) JimmyFortune 8 84
(Eve Johnson Houghton) *w.w in 7th: prog on outer over 2f out: drvn to ld jst over 1f out: hung lft after: styd on wl* **3/1**[1]
4462 **2** *1 1/2* **Pettochside**[13] 5205 3-8-7 **61**..(t) HayleyTurner 2 67
(Stuart Williams) *hld up in 8th and detached fr main gp: stl same pl 2f out: gd prog on outer 1f out: r.o to take 2nd last stride: no ch to chal* **5/1**[3]
2205 **3** *hd* **Ghost Train (IRE)**[12] 5233 3-8-13 **67**..............................(p) JimCrowley 9 72
(Mark Johnston) *chsd ldrs in 5th: rdn and prog on outer 2f out: cl up but hld whn sltly hmpd 1f out: kpt on* **11/2**
0541 **4** *nse* **Langley Vale**[19] 4943 3-8-12 **66** ow1.................................. SebSanders 6 71
(Roger Teal) *chsd ldrs in 6th: shkn up and wl in tch over 2f out: nt qckn over 1f out: styd on fnl f to press for 2nd nr fin* **15/2**
0005 **5** *1 3/4* **Dishy Guru**[15] 5128 3-9-7 **75**.. LiamKeniry 7 75+
(Michael Blanshard) *trckd ldrs in 4th: prog to go 2nd jst over 2f out gng strly: rdn to chal over 1f out: wnr sn wnt by: hld whn hmpd 150yds out and lost pls after* **14/1**
0P00 **6** *3* **Heyward Girl (IRE)**[10] 5320 3-9-0 **75**.................. MichaelJMMurphy(7) 3 65
(Robert Eddery) *led to jst over 1f out: wkng whn hmpd ins fnl f* **7/2**[2]
0000 **7** *1* **Esprit Danseur**[6] 5440 3-8-9 **63**..(p) JimmyQuinn 1 50
(Jim Boyle) *settled in last: sn wl detached: jst pushed along fnl 2f and passed a couple of stragglers: nvr involved* **12/1**
000 **8** *1 1/4* **Monnoyer**[31] 4558 3-9-2 **70**.. IanMongan 5 53
(Scott Dixon) *chsd ldr to jst over 2f out: sn wknd* **16/1**

0000 **9** *4* **Rooknrasbryripple**[4] 5514 3-8-2 **56** oh1......................(e) HarryBentley 4 26
(Ralph Smith) *chsd ldng pair to over 2f out: sn wknd* **40/1**

1m 9.22s (-0.18) **Going Correction** -0.025s/f (Good) 9 Ran SP% **113.7**
Speed ratings (Par 100): **100,98,97,97,95 91,90,88,83**
Tote Swingers 1&2 £2.70, 2&3 £4.60, 1&3 £3.80 CSF £17.88 CT £77.37 TOTE £4.00: £1.30, £2.20, £1.80; EX 16.90 Trifecta £89.60 Pool: £610.80 - 5.04 winning units..
Owner Eden Racing (III) & P A Deal **Bred** Hermes Services Ltd **Trained** Blewbury, Oxon
■ Stewards' Enquiry : Jimmy Fortune three-day ban: careless riding (Sep 10-12)

FOCUS
A run-of-the-mill 3yo sprint handicap and something of a rough race. The winner did not quite to match her previous best, which came here.

5663 TOTEPOOL MOBILE TEXT "TOTE" TO 89660 H'CAP 5f
3:05 (3:06) (Class 2) (0-100,98) 3-Y-O+

£11,205 (£3,355; £1,677; £838; £419; £210) **Stalls** High

Form RPR

0004 **1** **Long Awaited (IRE)**[27] 4690 4-8-12 **86**.....................(b) RichardHughes 3 96+
(David Barron) *broke wl but sn hld up bhd ldng quartet: plld out and effrt 1f out: r.o to ld nr fin: cleverly* **8/1**[3]

016 **2** *3/4* **Fair Value (IRE)**[23] 4799 4-9-2 **90**...................................... SebSanders 5 96
(Simon Dow) *mde most: def advantage 2f out: drvn fnl f: hdd nr fin* **5/1**[1]

1411 **3** *1/2* **Lady Gibraltar**[24] 4765 3-8-5 **88**........................(v) MichaelJMMurphy(7) 7 92
(Alan Jarvis) *w ldrs: rdn over 1f out: hanging sltly and nt qckn: styd on fnl f* **6/1**[2]

2000 **4** *nk* **Swiss Cross**[17] 5065 5-9-4 **92**..(t) JimmyFortune 6 95+
(Phil McEntee) *towards rr and off the pce: urged along over 1f out: r.o fnl f: nrst fin* **14/1**

1000 **5** *nk* **Stone Of Folca**[16] 5077 4-9-10 **98**...................................... JimCrowley 1 100
(John Best) *nt that wl away but gd spd on outer to chse ldrs: rdn over 1f out: styd on but nvr quite able to chal* **10/1**

00 **6** *nk* **Perfect Blossom**[20] 4924 5-7-13 **80**.................................... IanBurns(7) 8 81
(Ian McInnes) *disp ld to 1/2-way: styd prom: fdd ins fnl f* **50/1**

50 **7** *hd* **Albany Rose (IRE)**[65] 3375 4-8-13 **87**.................................. TedDurcan 11 87+
(Rae Guest) *stmbld sltly s: sn outpcd in last pair: pushed along 2f out: r.o wl fnl f: nrst fin* **10/1**

1653 **8** *3/4* **Waseem Faris (IRE)**[2] 5603 3-8-7 **83**............................. HayleyTurner 9 80
(Mick Channon) *cl up 1f: sn outpcd: pushed along 1/2-way: drvn and kpt on fnl f: n.d* **6/1**[2]

3022 **9** *1/2* **Sandfrankskipsgo**[3] 5536 3-8-3 **79**................................ JimmyQuinn 12 75
(Peter Crate) *stmbld s but w ldrs against rail: stl chalng 1f out: wknd: sddle slipped* **8/1**[3]

0544 **10** *2* **Damika (IRE)**[9] 5368 9-8-12 **86**.................................(v) MichaelStainton 4 74
(David Brown) *nvr on the pce: rdn towards rr 2f out: no prog: b.b.v* **10/1**

0-04 **11** *3/4* **Fathom Five (IRE)**[108] 2040 8-8-5 **79** oh1.................. HarryBentley 10 65
(Gary Moore) *nvr on the pce and a towards rr: no prog over 1f out* **16/1**

0100 **12** *9* **Cadeaux Pearl**[9] 5343 4-8-13 **87**....................................(b) KierenFallon 2 40
(Scott Dixon) *sn outpcd: bhd fr 1/2-way: t.o* **14/1**

54.17s (-1.53) **Going Correction** -0.075s/f (Good)
WFA 3 from 4yo+ 2lb 12 Ran SP% **115.9**
Speed ratings (Par 109): **109,107,107,106,106 105,105,104,103,100 98,84**
Tote Swingers 1&2 £5.10, 2&3 £4.30, 1&3 £4.50 CSF £46.60 CT £259.61 TOTE £9.70: £2.40, £2.50, £2.00; EX 31.30 Trifecta £78.90 Pool: £1,126.73 - 10.56 winning units..
Owner Peter Jones **Bred** Mrs C Regalado-Gonzalez **Trained** Maunby, N Yorks

FOCUS
The ground was Good to firm, good in places on the straight track. The good class 5f sprint handicaps at this track are always competitive affairs and this was no different, with the first nine covered by around 3l. The time was fast and the form makes sense.

NOTEBOOK
Long Awaited(IRE), well behind today's fifth in the "Dash", had put up an improved effort in the blinkers on his previous start at Goodwood and finished strongly to take this. He broke well, but could not hold his position and looked to be struggling at halfway. However, he picked up well meeting the rising ground, got a clear run and stayed on best to catch the long-time leader. He gets further and softer ground should not be a problem, so he might be one to keep on-side this autumn.
Fair Value(IRE) had conditions to suit, having scored over C&D on her only previous run on the track. She broke well and attempted to make all, only getting collared near the line. She stays further, but looks one to always consider here. (op 6-1 tchd 9-2)
Lady Gibraltar, a C&D winner in good form, was sent off favourite and ran her race, but could not find the extra up the hill off a 5lb higher mark. (op 5-1)
Swiss Cross ◆ has run well here before, but all his recent efforts have been over 6f. Down to his last winning mark, he came from well off the pace to finish on the heels of the principals, with his rider looking as if he had his hands full. He was one of several that caught the eye. (tchd 16-1)
Stone Of Folca, who was a surprise winner of the "Dash" here at the Derby meeting on his seasonal reappearance when drawn in stall two, had been held since but a couple of those runs were in Group company. Racing off 5lb higher, he came from stall one this time and did not fare badly, despite missing the break fractionally. (tchd 11-1)
Perfect Blossom back with her original trainer this season, has not had much racing recently and has finally fallen below her last winning rating back in 2010. She showed good speed and only lost out in the last half-furlong. (op 40-1)
Albany Rose(IRE) ◆, returning from a couple of months off, could not go the early pace at all but finished strongly, so much so that she passed all her rivals within 50 yards of the line. She is currently 16lb above her last winning mark, but this effort suggests she has another race in her before long. (op 8-1)
Waseem Faris(IRE), making a quick reappearance having run really well at York two days previously, was backed but could not go the pace until staying on late. (op 8-1)
Sandfrankskipsgo, came into this in fine form, having been narrowly beaten on his two previous outings. He tried to make use of the rails draw and ran pretty well before tiring up the hill, especially considering he stumbled coming out of the stalls. Jimmy Quinn reported that the gelding stumbled and the saddle slipped. Official explanation: jockey said saddle slipped (op 7-1)
Damika(IRE) was reported by the Veterinary Officer as having bled. Official explanation: vet said gelding had bled (tchd 12-1)

5664 BORDEAUX FINE WINES CONDITIONS STKS 1m 2f 18y
3:40 (3:40) (Class 3) 3-Y-O+ **£7,470** (£2,236; £1,118; £559; £279) **Stalls** Low

Form RPR

056 **1** **Lyssio (GER)**[23] 4821 5-8-13 83............................... MarkCoumbe(3) 4 94
(Michael Attwater) *trckd ldr: chal over 4f out: narrow ld ent st: sn rdn: gd battle w runner-up after: jst asserted ins fnl f* **12/1**

406 **2** *3/4* **Rockinante (FR)**[11] 5278 3-8-8 105............................. RichardHughes 1 93
(Richard Hannon) *sn led: jnd over 4f out: narrowly hdd ent st: styd upsides after: drvn over 1f out: no ex ins fnl f* **5/2**[3]

2202 **3** *17* **Troopingthecolour**[45] 4060 6-9-2 94..............................(t) JimCrowley 3 59
(Steve Gollings) *trckd ldng pair: rdn ent st: no imp over 2f out: wknd qckly wl over 1f out* **7/4**[1]

4345 **4** *6* **Mehdi (IRE)**[11] 5278 3-8-8 99..(t) KierenFallon 2 47
(Brian Meehan) *chsd ldng pair: rdn ent st: no imp over 2f out: wknd rapidly wl over 1f out* **9/4**[2]

1040 **5** *11* **Emma's Gift (IRE)**[142] 1213 4-8-11 90.......................(b) JimmyQuinn 5 20
(Julia Feilden) *stdd s: hld up in last: pushed along over 3f out: sn wknd and wl bhd* **14/1**

2m 7.56s (-2.14) **Going Correction** -0.025s/f (Good)
WFA 3 from 4yo+ 8lb 5 Ran SP% **110.1**
Speed ratings (Par 107): **107,106,92,88,79**
CSF £41.44 TOTE £12.80: £4.60, £1.60; EX 59.90.
Owner Bagden Wood Building Services Limited **Bred** Gestut Hof Ittlingen **Trained** Epsom, Surrey

FOCUS
This conditions stakes often features Group or Listed performers and had been dominated by Godolphin in recent seasons, but this year's renewal did not have a runner from that stable and did not look the strongest. It was something of a strange race as only the first two were involved from the turn into the straight, and there was a surprise winner. The form is a bit shaky.

NOTEBOOK
Lyssio(GER), formerly very useful in Germany, had run well off a mark of 99 in Dubai during the winter, but had slipped down the weights since returning here and racing back on turf. Down to a mark of 83, he was never far away and took on the leader around 4f out and proved strongest in a prolonged battle to the line. It is difficult to judge what he achieved here but, if this signals a revival, he could be interesting if turned out in a handicap under a penalty. Official explanation: trainer said, regarding apparent improvement in form, that the gelding was a poor traveller, benefited from the short journey and racing in a small field. (tchd 14-1)
Rockinante(FR), a Group 3 winner last season, had a sound chance judged on official ratings and set off in front. His rider eased the pace at about halfway, but was taken on by the winner running into Tattenham Corner and he came out second-best in the head-to-head that ensued. He did little wrong, but this was an opportunity missed. (op 9-4 tchd 2-1)
Troopingthecolour, who completed a hat-trick last season over C&D, has generally been running well in handicaps of late and was sent off favourite. Held up early, he could not respond when the first two kicked for home and was well beaten. (op 2-1)
Mehdi(IRE), with the blinkers he wore on his previous start left off, has mainly struggled in good company since a rewarding juvenile campaign followed by a period in Dubai. He dropped away tamely and might be ready for a break before another trip to Meydan. Kieren Fallon reported that the colt hung left throughout. Official explanation: jockey said colt hung throughout (op 5-2 tchd 11-4)
Emma's Gift(IRE) returning from a break after a successful AW season, could not go the early pace and was always in the rear. This should help get her straight for a return to Polytrack. Jimmy Quinn reported that the filly was never travelling. Official explanation: jockey said filly never travelled (op 12-1)

5665 BORDEAUX FINE WINES AMATEUR DERBY (H'CAP) (FOR GENTLEMAN AMATEUR RIDERS) 1m 4f 10y
4:15 (4:15) (Class 4) (0-85,81) 4-Y-O+ **£6,239** (£1,935; £967; £484) **Stalls** Centre

Form RPR

1-62 **1** **No Heretic**[23] 4823 4-11-7 **81**.................................. MrPCollington 7 94+
(David Simcock) *hld up in last pair: prog and disp 6th st: hdwy on outer to ld 2f out: in command whn hung lft fnl f: styd on wl* **4/1**[1]

5645 **2** *3 1/2* **Kings Troop**[18] 4983 6-10-3 **66**...............................(v) MrNdeBoinville(3) 5 73
(Alan King) *trckd ldrs: 5th st: prog on outer to ld briefly over 2f out: clr w wnr fnl 2f but one pce fr over 1f out* **10/1**

161 **3** *6* **Jamarjo (IRE)**[14] 5158 5-11-0 **79**................................. JamesCowley(5) 3 76
(Steve Gollings) *trckd ldrs: 3rd st: rdn and outpcd over 2f out: kpt on to take modest 3rd over 1f out* **14/1**

0553 **4** *1* **Iron Condor**[18] 4983 5-11-1 **75**... MrRBirkett 6 71
(James Eustace) *s.s: hld up: 9th st: sn rdn: kpt on fr over 2f out: n.d* **14/1**

1000 **5** *nk* **Megalala (IRE)**[23] 4805 11-11-3 **80**.................................. MrCMartin(3) 8 75
(John Bridger) *led to over 2f out: sn outpcd by ldng pair: lost 3rd over 1f out: one pce* **25/1**

2122 **6** *3 1/4* **Arashi**[12] 5226 6-10-4 **64**..(v) MrSWalker 9 54
(Derek Shaw) *in tch: disp 6th st: effrt 3f out: sn outpcd: fdd fnl 2f* **5/1**[2]

430- **7** *1 1/2* **Alazan (IRE)**[24] 2526 6-10-13 **78**............................... MrTCheesman(5) 10 66
(Philip Hobbs) *racd wd: prom: rdn and effrt to chse ldr st: lost pl u.p 3f out: sn btn* **5/1**[2]

4666 **8** *5* **The Bells O Peover**[18] 5002 4-11-2 **76**.......................(b) MrDHDunsdon 1 56
(Mark Johnston) *settled in midfield: disp 6th st: effrt on inner 3f out: wknd 2f out* **6/1**[3]

0001 **9** *10* **Epsom Salts**[39] 4251 7-10-11 **76**...................................... MrFMitchell(5) 2 40
(Pat Phelan) *nvr gng wl: dropped to last and struggling st: sn bhd* **8/1**

2023 **10** *27* **Landesherr (GER)**[41] 4179 5-10-2 **65**..........................(t) MrMEnnis(3) 4
(Steve Gollings) *mostly chsd ldr tl wknd st: t.o* **8/1**

2m 39.46s (0.56) **Going Correction** -0.025s/f (Good) 10 Ran SP% **116.1**
Speed ratings (Par 105): **97,94,90,90,89 87,86,83,76,58**
Tote Swingers 1&2 £6.00, 2&3 £14.90, 1&3 £7.60 CSF £44.47 CT £510.75 TOTE £4.70: £1.40, £3.00, £3.80; EX 54.20 TRIFECTA Not won..
Owner Mrs Fitri Hay **Bred** Belgrave Bloodstock Ltd **Trained** Newmarket, Suffolk

FOCUS
This long-established male Amateur Riders' Derby looked a competitive affair, but was turned into a procession by the top weight. The runner-up helps with the standard.

5666 INVEST IN FINE WINES H'CAP 1m 2f 18y
4:50 (4:53) (Class 3) (0-90,89) 3-Y-O+ **£7,762** (£2,310; £1,154; £577) **Stalls** Low

Form RPR

0-12 **1** **Universal (IRE)**[13] 5209 3-9-5 **88**..................................... KierenFallon 3 97+
(Mark Johnston) *pressed ldr: upsides over 4f out tl led jst over 2f out: drvn and styd on wl* **5/2**[2]

0220 **2** *2* **First Avenue**[98] 2346 7-9-4 **86**............................... CharlotteJenner(7) 4 91
(Laura Mongan) *hld up in 6th: prog and 4th st: chsd ldng pair over 2f out: hanging sn after: shkn up to go 2nd 1f out: styd on but no imp on wnr* **16/1**

-151 **3** *2 3/4* **Initiator**[18] 5006 3-9-4 **87**... JimmyFortune 6 87
(Jeremy Noseda) *t.k.h: sn led: jnd over 4f out: hdd and nt qckn jst over 2f out: one pce after* **9/4**[1]

4/00 **4** *2 3/4* **Too Much Trouble**[16] 5079 6-9-7 **89**.................... MichaelJMMurphy(7) 7 83
(Ed Vaughan) *racd wd thrght: chsd ldrs: 3rd st: nt qckn over 2f out: steadily lft bhd fnl 2f* **5/1**[3]

5106 **5** *hd* **Ramona Chase**[54] 3766 7-9-8 **86**.............................(t) MarkCoumbe(3) 5 80
(Michael Attwater) *chsd ldng pair tl rdn and dropped to 5th st: struggling after: plugged on over 1f out* **15/2**

1020 **6** *2 1/2* **Fork Handles**[5] 5492 4-9-11 **86**.. PatCosgrave 2 75
(Mick Channon) *dwlt: hld up in last: shkn up over 2f out: limited hdwy and no threat to ldrs* **15/2**

0-06 **7** 3 3/4 **Aquilonius (IRE)**[11] 5268 3-8-12 **81**................................(t) JimCrowley 1 62
(Stuart Williams) *in tch: 6th and cl enough st: pushed along 3f out: steadily dropped away* **14/1**

2m 8.9s (-0.80) **Going Correction** -0.025s/f (Good)
WFA 3 from 4yo+ 8lb **7** Ran SP% **112.1**
Speed ratings (Par 107): **102,100,98,96,95 93,90**
Tote Swingers 1&2 £6.20, 2&3 £6.40, 1&3 £1.80 CSF £37.96 TOTE £3.20: £2.00, £5.70; EX 43.80.
Owner Abdulla Al Mansoori **Bred** Grangecon Stud **Trained** Middleham Moor, N Yorks

FOCUS
A good, competitive handicap that the 3yos dominated. The time was 1.34secs slower than the earlier conditions race. There looks more to come from the winner.

NOTEBOOK
Universal(IRE) has found his feet after a belated start this season in handicaps, and he was helped by getting a good lead from his market rival, who was too keen. Once asked in the straight, he asserted after a brief struggle and was always holding the runner-up in the final furlong. (tchd 2-1 and 11-4)
First Avenue goes well for his apprentice rider and had previous form on the track. Returning from a break, he came through to chase the leaders early in the straight and stuck to his task to keep the winner honest. This should sharpen him up for a return to the AW. (op 12-1)
Initiator, lightly raced but progressive, was very keen and soon led, but did not settle in front and that left him vulnerable in the straight. (op 11-4)
Too Much Trouble has dropped in the weights since joining this yard from Dubai, which enabled him to run in this contest. However, he spoilt his chance by racing four wide for most of the trip and, not surprisingly, had nothing left in the straight. (op 11-2 tchd 6-1)
Ramona Chase, who often goes well on this track, was close enough turning in but could not pick up when asked. (op 6-1)

5667 BF WINES H'CAP 1m 114y

5:25 (5:25) (Class 4) (0-80,80) 3-Y-0+ **£5,175** (£1,540; £769; £384) **Stalls** Low

Form RPR

4002 **1** **Maverik**[15] 5120 4-10-0 **80**.. JimCrowley 9 91
(Ralph Beckett) *racd freely: led after 2f: mde rest: drvn and styd on strly fr 2f out* **7/2**[1]

16-5 **2** 2 1/4 **Young Dottie**[212] 351 6-8-13 **65**... IanMongan 7 71
(Pat Phelan) *chsd ldng trio: clsd over 2f out: drvn to chse wnr jst ins fnl f: styd on but no imp* **14/1**

0135 **3** 1 3/4 **Copperwood**[12] 5243 7-9-8 **74**... KierenFallon 3 76
(Mark Johnston) *trckd ldng pair: drvn to chse wnr wl over 1f out: no imp: one pce and lost 2nd jst ins fnl f* **11/2**[3]

5000 **4** 1 **Ellie In The Pink (IRE)**[13] 5218 4-8-13 **72**......... MichaelJMMurphy(7) 4 72
(Alan Jarvis) *dwlt: last early and nt gng that wl: prog on wd outside and 5th st: sn drvn: kpt on one pce fnl 2f: n.d* **8/1**

1656 **5** 1/2 **Xinbama (IRE)**[19] 4939 3-9-3 **76**.................................... JimmyFortune 8 74
(J W Hills) *settled in rr: 8th st: rdn and struggling 3f out: kpt on one pce fnl 2f* **10/1**

234 **6** nk **Whitby Jet (IRE)**[31] 4541 4-9-6 **72**............................... RichardHughes 6 70
(Ed Vaughan) *hld up: dropped to last after 3f: detached fr rest st: stl last and drvn over 1f out: r.o fnl f* **9/2**[2]

5500 **7** 1 **Bloodsweatandtears**[23] 4805 4-9-4 **70**............................ SebSanders 2 65
(William Knight) *dwlt but pushed up to ld: hdd after 2f: lost 2nd and wknd wl over 1f out* **11/2**[3]

-612 **8** 3 1/4 **May Be Some Time**[15] 5132 4-9-8 **74**..............................(t) LiamKeniry 5 62
(Stuart Kittow) *towards rr: 7th st: sn rdn and no prog: wl btn fnl 2f* **13/2**

02-0 **9** 1 **Mountrath**[19] 4939 5-9-2 **68**...(v) HarryBentley 1 54
(Gary Moore) *chsd ldrs: 6th st: no prog over 2f out: sn wknd* **25/1**

1m 44.62s (-1.48) **Going Correction** -0.025s/f (Good)
WFA 3 from 4yo+ 7lb **9** Ran SP% **115.2**
Speed ratings (Par 105): **105,103,101,100,100 99,98,96,95**
Tote Swingers 1&2 £10.80, 2&3 £9.90, 1&3 £2.50 CSF £53.64 CT £266.79 TOTE £5.20: £1.70, £2.90, £2.00; EX 75.30 Trifecta £403.60 Pool: £707.27 - 1.29 winning units..
Owner Athos, Cooper, Quinn, EPL **Bred** J G Davis & Star Pointe Ltd **Trained** Kimpton, Hants

FOCUS
Another competitive contest, but quite an impressive success for the top weight. The winner is rated in line with his winter AW form.
T/Plt: £62.20 to a £1 stake. Pool £68,069.22 - 797.77 winning units. T/Qpdt: £39.60 to a £1 stake. Pool £2,785.62 - 52.01 winning units. JN

5543 NEWCASTLE (L-H)

Monday, August 27

OFFICIAL GOING: Soft (good to soft in places; 6.0)
Wind: Fresh, half against Weather: Overcast, showers

5668 BRITISH STALLION STUDS SUPPORTING BRITISH RACING E.B.F./F1 GROUP MAIDEN STKS 7f

2:15 (2:16) (Class 4) 2-Y-O **£4,334** (£1,289; £644; £322) **Stalls** Centre

Form RPR

525 **1** **Emperatriz**[16] 5083 2-8-12 67...................................... RussKennemore 7 67
(John Holt) *t.k.h early: cl up: led over 2f out: sn rdn along: hld on wl fnl f* **5/1**[3]

06 **2** 1/2 **Khelac**[16] 5083 2-9-3 0.. AndrewElliott 4 71
(Alan Swinbank) *t.k.h: cl up: ev ch over 2f out: rdn and sltly outpcd over 1f out: kpt on fnl f* **25/1**

3 hd **Bell'Arte (IRE)** 2-8-12 0... SilvestreDeSousa 2 65
(Mark Johnston) *t.k.h early: cl up: rdn and effrt over 2f out: sltly outpcd 2f out: r.o fnl f: hld nr fin* **7/1**

03 **4** 3 **Cash Is King**[31] 4555 2-9-3 0... TonyHamilton 9 63
(Richard Fahey) *plld hrd in tch: drvn along over 2f out: edgd lft and styd on fnl f: nt pce to chal* **7/2**[2]

23 **5** shd **Rocky Two (IRE)**[29] 4618 2-9-3 0...................................... TomEaves 5 63
(Michael Dods) *in tch: effrt and drvn along over 2f out: kpt on same pce fnl f* **9/4**[1]

0500 **6** 2 3/4 **El Molino Blanco**[33] 4448 2-8-12 51....................... GrahamGibbons 10 52
(Michael Easterby) *led: hdd and rdn over 2f out: rallied: wknd ins fnl f* **100/1**

7 1 1/2 **Naru (IRE)** 2-9-3 0.. GrahamLee 6 52
(James Tate) *colty in preliminaries: dwlt: hld up: rdn and rn green over 2f out: hdwy over 1f out: nvr able to chal* **6/1**

0 **8** 2 1/2 **Denton Skyline (IRE)**[30] 4587 2-9-0 0.......................... LeeTopliss(3) 3 46
(Michael Dods) *dwlt: hld up: drvn and outpcd over 2f out: sme late hdwy: nvr on terms* **50/1**

0 **9** 1 1/2 **Tobacco**[23] 4792 2-8-12 0... AdamCarter(5) 12 42
(Tim Easterby) *missed break: hld up: struggling over 2f out: sn n.d* **20/1**

56 **10** 2 **Inovate (IRE)**[30] 4587 2-8-12 0.. DarylByrne(5) 1 37
(Tim Easterby) *t.k.h: cl up on outside: outpcd over 2f out: sn btn* **22/1**

11 2 1/2 **Rex Whistler (IRE)** 2-9-3 0... BarryMcHugh 11 31
(Julie Camacho) *prom: drvn over 2f out: wknd wl over 1f out* **25/1**

1m 31.39s (3.59) **Going Correction** +0.10s/f (Good) **11** Ran SP% **116.2**
Speed ratings (Par 96): **83,82,82,78,78 75,73,70,69,66 64**
Tote Swingers 1&2 £27.00, 2&3 £29.90, 1&3 £5.90 CSF £126.15 TOTE £4.70: £1.90, £5.60, £2.00; EX 138.10.
Owner Eric Boumans **Bred** D R Botterill **Trained** Peckleton, Leics

FOCUS
Rail on Round course the same as on Friday. Soft ground, with the GoingStick reading 5.9 before racing, and the time of this opener was over 5secs above standard. Just ordinary maiden form, but straightforward enough.

NOTEBOOK
Emperatriz is probably a bit better than her mark suggests and her two best runs have both come on soft ground, which looks key to the daughter of Holy Roman Emperor. In a race where it proved hard to make up ground from off the pace, the winner was always close up and she saw out the trip well enough to hold on, although she looked to be idling a touch in the final half furlong. If her mark remains unchanged or only goes up marginally, she ought to be competitive in a handicap, providing conditions are suitable. (op 6-1)
Khelac ran his best race so far on the softest ground he has encountered, and his profile is quietly progressive. He stuck to his task well and should be able to win a maiden before moving into handicaps.
Bell'Arte(IRE) has a pedigree that suggests she might stay middle distances in time and this was a highly encouraging first effort. Even just normal improvement will see her off the mark sooner rather than later. (tchd 8-1)
Cash Is King tracked the pace but just couldn't pick up in the ground and never got in a serious blow. He showed little on soft on debut so it looks like he probably needs better ground. (op 10-3 tchd 3-1)
Rocky Two(IRE) was held up and never in the reckoning. He plugged on but didn't run to anything like the level of his first two starts. (op 2-1)
Inovate(IRE) Official explanation: jockey said saddle slipped

5669 NEWCASTLE FLOORING CLAIMING STKS 1m 3y(S)

2:50 (2:51) (Class 6) 3-Y-0+ **£1,617** (£481; £240; £120) **Stalls** Centre

Form RPR

4620 **1** **Moheebb (IRE)**[12] 5220 8-8-13 69..............................(be) TonyHamilton 5 67
(Ruth Carr) *hld up in tch: rdn and effrt over 2f out: led wl ins fnl f: styd on wl* **9/4**[1]

3220 **2** 1 1/2 **Fishforcompliments**[10] 5305 8-8-10 73.......................(p) LeeTopliss(3) 2 64
(Richard Fahey) *hld up in tch: smooth hdwy to ld over 1f out: sn rdn: hdd and no ex wl ins fnl f* **5/1**[2]

3004 **3** 2 1/4 **Nolecce**[6] 5452 5-9-3 57...(p) RobbieFitzpatrick 9 63
(Richard Guest) *hld up in tch: effrt and rdn over 1f out: edgd lft and kpt on ins fnl f* **12/1**

0-05 **4** 1 1/4 **Desert Creek (IRE)**[21] 4864 6-9-13 69.......................... AndrewMullen 6 70
(David Nicholls) *t.k.h: cl up: led briefly wl over 1f out: edgd lft and no ex ins fnl f* **8/1**

0000 **5** 2 1/4 **Wiseman's Diamond (USA)**[11] 5258 7-8-6 60.....(b) RoystonFfrench 10 44
(Paul Midgley) *t.k.h: led to wl over 1f out: outpcd whn checked appr fnl f* **8/1**

00 **6** 2 3/4 **Tropical Duke (IRE)**[11] 5259 6-9-5 43..............................[1] TomEaves 4 50
(Ron Barr) *hld up: rdn over 2f out: kpt on fnl f: nvr able to chal* **40/1**

6600 **7** hd **Rock Of Deauville (IRE)**[14] 5171 5-9-3 48..................(p[1]) GrahamLee 3 48
(Julie Camacho) *dwlt: hld up: drvn over 2f out: nvr rchd ldrs* **14/1**

0600 **8** 18 **Taro Tywod (IRE)**[31] 4547 3-8-12 60...................(v[1]) SilvestreDeSousa 1
(Ann Duffield) *dwlt: bhd: drvn over 3f out: sn struggling: t.o* **7/1**[3]

300 **9** 9 **Punta Baluarte**[10] 5316 6-8-10 31................................ BarryMcHugh 11
(Julie Camacho) *hld up in tch: rdn over 3f out: wknd over 2f out: t.o* **100/1**

66 **10** shd **Giveherachance**[26] 4705 3-8-8 0................................ GrahamGibbons 7
(Ann Duffield) *t.k.h: w ldr to over 3f out: wknd over 2f out: t.o* **40/1**

1050 **11** 1 1/4 **Miami Gator (IRE)**[29] 4620 5-9-6 78....................(v) ConorHarrison(7) 12
(Mrs K Burke) *racd alone stands' rail: cl up tl wknd over 2f out: t.o* **5/1**[2]

1m 43.41s (0.01) **Going Correction** +0.10s/f (Good)
WFA 3 from 5yo+ 6lb **11** Ran SP% **119.1**
Speed ratings (Par 101): **103,101,99,98,95 93,92,74,65,65 64**
.Moheebb was claimed by Mr Robert Johnson for £3,000.\n\x\x
Owner Reach For The Moon & Mrs R Carr **Bred** Hascombe And Valiant Studs **Trained** Huby, N Yorks

FOCUS
All bar one of the runners stayed down the middle and the lone raider down the stands' rail, Miami Gator, was beaten miles. Modest claiming form.

5670 SENDRIG CONSTRUCTION BLAYDON RACE (NURSERY) 1m 3y(S)

3:25 (3:25) (Class 2) 2-Y-0 **£8,086** (£2,406; £1,202; £601) **Stalls** Centre

Form RPR

600 **1** **Grandorio (IRE)**[12] 5242 2-8-7 **66** ow1........................ GrahamGibbons 2 73+
(David O'Meara) *trckd ldrs: led over 2f out: clr whn hung rt ins fnl f: r.o wl* **6/1**[3]

4133 **2** 2 3/4 **Mad Jazz**[18] 5009 2-7-13 **61** ow1.. JulieBurke(3) 7 61
(Tony Coyle) *in tch: effrt and rdn over 2f out: chsd wnr wl ins fnl f: no imp* **8/1**

2210 **3** 1 1/2 **Secret Destination**[23] 4820 2-9-1 **77**................................ DaleSwift(3) 4 74
(Brian Ellison) *led to over 2f out: sn rdn and rallied: one pce whn lost 2nd wl ins fnl f* **7/1**

1613 **4** 1/2 **Yorkshire Icon**[11] 5254 2-9-2 **75**......................................(p) GrahamLee 3 71
(Ann Duffield) *dwlt: sn pushed along and in tch: hdwy and ev ch over 3f out: effrt and rdn over 2f out: one pce fnl f* **6/1**[3]

4110 **5** 3/4 **Jubilee Games**[44] 4093 2-9-7 **80**................................. TonyHamilton 8 74
(Richard Fahey) *hld up: rdn and hdwy over 2f out: one pce over 1f out* **11/2**[2]

6225 **6** 1 1/4 **Out Of The Blocks**[19] 4951 2-8-7 **66**.............................. BarryMcHugh 1 57
(Ruth Carr) *chsd ldng gp: effrt and drvn over 2f out: btn fnl f* **16/1**

040 **7** 1/2 **Foolbythepool**[16] 5083 2-8-11 **70** ow2.............................. PhillipMakin 9 60
(Keith Dalgleish) *t.k.h: hld up: rdn and edgd lft over 2f out: btn fnl f* **14/1**

31 **8** 6 **Beat The Tide**[30] 4587 2-8-13 **72**..................................... TomEaves 10 49
(Michael Dods) *hld up: rdn along over 2f out: sn btn* **9/2**[1]

322 **9** 12 **Excellent Mariner (IRE)**[20] 4907 2-8-10 **69**............ SilvestreDeSousa 5 20
(Mark Johnston) *cl up tl rdn and wknd wl over 2f out* **9/2**[1]

1m 44.7s (1.30) **Going Correction** +0.10s/f (Good) **9** Ran SP% **116.5**
Speed ratings (Par 100): **97,94,92,92,91 90,89,83,71**
Tote Swingers 1&2 £22.20, 2&3 £33.00, 1&3 £37.90 CSF £53.50 CT £347.42 TOTE £8.50: £3.50, £3.50, £2.40; EX 46.20.
Owner Hambleton Racing Ltd - Three In One **Bred** The Grand Splendour Partnership **Trained** Nawton, N Yorks

FOCUS
A reasonable nursery with those towards the top of the weights having shown decent form for the grade, but a lot depended on who could handle the ground best. Straightforward, solid form, and there is more to come from the winner.

NOTEBOOK
Grandorio(IRE) led them a merry dance through the final furlong to get off the mark in emphatic style. He had run over the minimum trip on Fibresand on his third start but he relished the significant step up in trip off an initial mark of 65 (plus a pound overweight) and proved different class off that rating. He is in the Two-Year-Old Trophy at Redcar next month, suggesting connections always thought he was better than a 65-rated horse, and they might try and get him out under a penalty before being reassessed, in which case he'd be very hard to beat. Official explanation: trainer's rep said, regarding apparent improvement in form, that the gelding was suited by the step up in trip. (op 11-2)

Mad Jazz has form on slow ground and she ran right up to her best off a light weight. She ought to have more races in her off this sort of mark. (op 11-1)

Secret Destination, a soft-ground maiden winner, fared much better than in stronger company at Newmarket last time but she looks vulnerable from a handicapping point of view. (op 17-2 tchd 9-1)

Yorkshire Icon travelled well enough into contention but didn't really find a great deal under pressure and although he has won on slow ground, his best efforts have come on a faster surface and over 7f. He is fairly exposed now but might be seen to better effect back under those sorts of conditions. (tchd 13-2)

Jubilee Games travelled well just off the pace but couldn't make any more progress in the final furlong under his big weight. (op 5-1 tchd 9-2)

Beat The Tide had every chance towards the stands' side but dropped off them in the closing stages and probably found conditions too testing. It's way too early to be giving up on him. (op 5-1 tchd 4-1)

5671 KEVIN LEE MEMORIAL FILLIES' H'CAP — 7f
4:00 (4:00) (Class 5) (0-75,75) 3-Y-O+ — **£2,264** (£673; £336; £168) **Stalls** Centre

Form — RPR

030 **1** — **Ryedale Dancer (IRE)**[9] 5338 4-8-8 **57** ow1 .... RobbieFitzpatrick 8 — 64+
(Richard Guest) *hld up and bhd: rdn and hdwy over 1f out: led wl ins fnl f: r.o* — **18/1**

4554 **2** shd **Clumber Place**[29] 4624 6-8-9 **58** .... GrahamLee 7 — 65
(James Given) *t.k.h: cl up: effrt and rdn over 2f out: ev ch wl ins fnl f: kpt on: jst hld* — **9/2**[1]

6600 **3** ½ **Quick Bite (IRE)**[7] 5426 3-9-7 **75** ....(b[1]) RobertWinston 3 — 78
(Hugo Palmer) *cl up: led over 2f out: rdn and qcknd over 1f out: hdd and no ex wl ins fnl f* — **9/2**[1]

-002 **4** 2 **Carrie's Magic**[16] 5084 5-8-4 **56** oh4 .... JulieBurke(3) 5 — 56
(Alistair Whillans) *plld hrd early: trckd ldrs: effrt and rdn 2f out: one pce ins fnl f* — **12/1**

4063 **5** 2 **Foreign Rhythm (IRE)**[7] 5416 7-8-9 **58** .... AmyRyan 9 — 53
(Ron Barr) *hld up in tch: rdn along and effrt over 2f out: edgd lft and no imp over 1f out* — **9/1**

0403 **6** ½ **Loukoumi**[21] 4865 4-8-11 **60** ....(b) TomEaves 6 — 53
(Tim Easterby) *chsd ldng gp: rdn over 2f out: btn fnl f* — **9/2**[1]

2500 **7** 10 **Sabratha (IRE)**[13] 5185 4-8-13 **62** .... TonyHamilton 4 — 28
(Linda Perratt) *stdd s: hld up: rdn and struggling over 2f out: sn btn* — **14/1**

653 **8** 6 **Waveguide (IRE)**[49] 3918 3-9-1 **69** .... SilvestreDeSousa 2 — 17
(David Simcock) *in tch tl rdn and wknd 2f out* — **11/2**[2]

-042 **9** 2¼ **Alluring Star**[107] 2090 4-8-9 **58** .... GrahamGibbons 1
(Michael Easterby) *led tl rdn and hdd over 2f out: sn wknd* — **6/1**[3]

1m 30.0s (2.20) **Going Correction** +0.10s/f (Good)
WFA 3 from 4yo+ 5lb — **9** Ran SP% **113.8**
Speed ratings (Par 100): **91,90,90,88,85 85,73,66,64**
Tote Swingers 1&2 £15.00, 2&3 £6.00, 1&3 £19.20 CSF £95.77 CT £436.87 TOTE £19.00: £3.80, £2.00, £1.70; EX 134.40.
Owner Future Racing (Notts) Limited **Bred** Max Morris **Trained** Stainforth, S Yorks

FOCUS
A modest handicap in which the pace looked sound and they finished well strung out. Modest fillies' form.
Alluring Star Official explanation: jockey said filly lost its action

5672 STP CONSTRUCTION H'CAP — 1m 4f 93y
4:35 (4:35) (Class 6) (0-65,63) 3-Y-O+ — **£1,617** (£481; £240; £120) **Stalls** Low

Form — RPR

4-00 **1** — **Gosforth Park**[21] 4883 6-9-5 **54** .... SilvestreDeSousa 15 — 66
(Mel Brittain) *sn w ldr: led 1/2-way: clr over 4f out: styd on wl fnl 2f: unchal* — **16/1**

0205 **2** 5 **Lakeman (IRE)**[12] 5241 6-9-2 **54** .... DaleSwift(3) 8 — 58
(Brian Ellison) *hld up in midfield: hdwy 3f out: sn rdn: styd on fnl f to take 2nd cl home: no ch w wnr* — **14/1**

0562 **3** hd **Petrocelli**[21] 4869 5-9-4 **53** ....(t) AmyRyan 3 — 57
(Wilf Storey) *hld up: n.m.r over 4f out: hdwy on outside to chse clr wnr over 2f out: rdn over 1f out: one pce fnl f: lost 2nd cl home* — **15/2**[2]

6066 **4** 13 **Law To Himself (IRE)**[26] 4714 5-10-0 **63** ....(v[1]) RobertWinston 6 — 46
(Alan Swinbank) *t.k.h: stdd s: hld up: hdwy on outside 3f out: no imp fr 2f out* — **9/1**[3]

0006 **5** 2 **Kieron's Rock (IRE)**[12] 5226 3-7-9 **45** .... NeilFarley(5) 4 — 25
(Jedd O'Keeffe) *plld hrd: trckd ldrs tl rdn and wknd 2f out* — **20/1**

0566 **6** ½ **Brook Star (IRE)**[42] 4138 4-8-4 **46** ....(p) ConnorNichol(7) 2 — 25
(Michael Dods) *t.k.h: trckd ldrs tl rdn and wknd over 2f out* — **16/1**

0101 **7** ¾ **Madam Lilibet (IRE)**[11] 5265 3-8-13 **58** .... PaddyAspell 9 — 36
(Sharon Watt) *midfield: rdn and outpcd over 4f out: n.d after* — **9/2**[1]

0604 **8** 3 **Tartan Gunna**[14] 5174 6-9-11 **60** .... GrahamLee 13 — 33
(James Given) *midfield: drvn along and outpcd over 3f out: edgd rt and wknd over 2f out* — **12/1**

5640 **9** 1 **Ferney Boy**[21] 4869 6-8-10 **45** .... TonyHamilton 14 — 16
(Chris Fairhurst) *prom: chsd clr wnr over 5f out to over 2f out: sn wknd* — **16/1**

2605 **10** 15 **Border Bandit (USA)**[9] 5345 4-9-7 **56** .... RoystonFfrench 11
(Tracy Waggott) *hld up: drvn along over 5f out: btn fnl 3f* — **15/2**[2]

4030 **11** 2½ **Kian's Joy**[19] 4958 3-8-1 **46** .... AndrewMullen 5
(Jedd O'Keeffe) *missed break: bhd: struggling over 4f out: sn btn* — **25/1**

3320 **12** 12 **Cadgers Brig**[24] 4766 4-9-13 **62** ....(p) TomEaves 12
(Keith Dalgleish) *in tch tl rdn and wknd over 3f out* — **10/1**

006 **13** 42 **Miss Matiz**[10] 5315 5-8-7 **45** .... PaulPickard(3) 7
(Alan Kirtley) *plld hrd: led to 1/2-way: wknd over 4f out: t.o* — **50/1**

060- **U** **Tiny Temper (IRE)**[283] 7458 4-9-6 **62** .... LauraBarry(7) 10
(Richard Fahey) *t.k.h: hld up: effrt but no imp whn clipped heels: stmbld bdly and uns rdr over 2f out* — **9/2**[1]

2m 50.41s (4.81) **Going Correction** +0.45s/f (Yiel)
WFA 3 from 4yo+ 10lb — **14** Ran SP% **121.6**
Speed ratings (Par 101): **101,97,97,88,87 87,86,84,84,74 72,64,36,**
Tote Swingers 1&2 £35.60, 2&3 £18.70, 1&3 £27.40 CSF £221.26 CT £1833.19 TOTE £17.90: £4.00, £4.10, £2.30; EX 163.20.
Owner Mel Brittain **Bred** C A Cyzer **Trained** Warthill, N Yorks

FOCUS
Most of these had plenty to prove in what was quite a weak handicap despite the numbers. The winner matched his Southwell best.
Gosforth Park Official explanation: trainer's rep said, regarding apparent improvement in form, that the gelding was suited by the softer ground and stronger handling.
Madam Lilibet(IRE) Official explanation: trainer said filly is in season
Border Bandit(USA) Official explanation: jockey said gelding never travelled

5673 ROFLOW H'CAP — 1m 6f 97y
5:10 (5:10) (Class 5) (0-75,74) 4-Y-O+ — **£2,264** (£673; £336; £168) **Stalls** Low

Form — RPR

6350 **1** — **Bollin Felix**[9] 5344 8-9-5 **72** ....(b) GrahamGibbons 9 — 83
(Tim Easterby) *hld up: rdn over 4f out: hdwy 3f out: chsd ldr over 1f out: led ins fnl f: kpt on strly* — **9/2**[2]

4-33 **2** 3¼ **River Dragon (IRE)**[126] 1247 7-8-10 **63** .... BarryMcHugh 2 — 69
(Tony Coyle) *led: shkn up over 2f out: rdn and clr over 1f out: hdd ins fnl f: no ex* — **4/1**[1]

2204 **3** 7 **Tobrata**[18] 5012 6-8-6 **59** .... SilvestreDeSousa 7 — 56
(Mel Brittain) *hld up: drvn and outpcd over 3f out: kpt on fr over 1f out: no ch w first two* — **13/2**

4560 **4** 2 **Royal Trooper (IRE)**[33] 4460 6-9-4 **71** .... GrahamLee 8 — 65
(James Given) *t.k.h: sn pressing ldr: rdn over 3f out: lost 2nd over 1f out: wknd fnl f* — **4/1**[1]

5513 **5** 3½ **Mohawk Ridge**[41] 4176 6-9-3 **73** ....(p) LeeToplis(3) 5 — 62
(Michael Dods) *t.k.h: trckd ldrs: rdn over 3f out: wknd 2f out* — **6/1**[3]

00/0 **6** 1¾ **Maxwil**[18] 5002 7-8-12 **65** .... PhillipMakin 3 — 52
(Mrs K Burke) *in tch: drvn and outpcd over 3f out: n.d after* — **12/1**

10-0 **7** 7 **Miss Ferney**[14] 5172 8-8-7 **62** ow1 .... PaulPickard(3) 6 — 40
(Alan Kirtley) *hld up: rdn over 3f out: nvr on terms* — **25/1**

6000 **8** 1 **Boss's Destination**[41] 4176 5-9-7 **74** ....[1] RobertWinston 4 — 49
(Alan Swinbank) *plld hrd: prom: rdn over 3f out: wknd over 2f out* — **12/1**

0505 **9** 7 **Harvey's Hope**[9] 5344 6-9-0 **67** .... TomEaves 10 — 33
(Keith Reveley) *s.i.s: bhd: drvn over 3f out: sn btn* — **7/1**

3m 19.36s (8.06) **Going Correction** +0.45s/f (Yiel) — **9** Ran SP% **117.5**
Speed ratings (Par 103): **94,92,88,87,85 84,80,79,75**
Tote Swingers 1&2 £6.30, 2&3 £4.20, 1&3 £4.60 CSF £23.34 CT £117.66 TOTE £5.00: £2.10, £2.10, £2.20; EX 26.70.
Owner Mrs Sarah Easterby **Bred** Sir Neil & Exors Of Late Lady Westbrook **Trained** Great Habton, N Yorks

FOCUS
A real stamina test, with a sound gallop. The form is rated round the runner-up.

5674 CGC EVENTS H'CAP — 6f
5:45 (5:46) (Class 4) (0-80,77) 3-Y-O+ — **£4,075** (£1,212; £606; £303) **Stalls** Centre

Form — RPR

1 **1** — **Sovereign Street**[35] 4393 4-9-7 **75** .... GrahamLee 9 — 87+
(Ann Duffield) *plld hrd: prom: effrt over 1f out: led ins fnl f: hld on wl towards fin* — **3/1**[1]

5054 **2** hd **Defence Council (IRE)**[7] 5412 4-9-9 **77** .... SilvestreDeSousa 10 — 88
(Mel Brittain) *hld up: rdn and hdwy 2f out: chsd wnr ins fnl f: kpt on: hld cl home* — **13/2**[3]

3333 **3** 1 **Jack Luey**[18] 4998 5-9-4 **77** ....(p) DarylByrne(5) 5 — 84
(Lawrence Mullaney) *t.k.h: trckd ldrs: effrt and rdn over 1f out: kpt on ins fnl f* — **10/1**

4055 **4** 1½ **Green Park (IRE)**[18] 4999 9-9-4 **77** ....(b) NeilFarley(5) 3 — 80
(Declan Carroll) *dwlt: sn trcking ldrs: effrt and rdn 2f out: kpt on same pce ins fnl f* — **14/1**

0014 **5** 1½ **Bunce (IRE)**[76] 3011 4-9-7 **75** .... GrahamGibbons 4 — 73
(David O'Meara) *led: rdn 2f out: hdd and outpcd ins fnl f* — **8/1**

0000 **6** 1 **Cool Marble (IRE)**[37] 4317 5-9-4 **72** ....(b) PhillipMakin 2 — 67
(Jeremy Gask) *dwlt: hld up: rdn over 2f out: kpt on fnl f: nvr able to chal* — **10/1**

0003 **7** 1½ **Toby Tyler**[8] 5389 6-9-3 **71** ....(v) MickyFenton 1 — 61
(Paul Midgley) *hld up in tch: drvn and outpcd 2f out: n.d after* — **8/1**

-056 **8** ¾ **Kellys Eye (IRE)**[21] 4880 5-9-4 **72** .... RobertWinston 8 — 59
(David Brown) *hld up: rdn over 2f out: edgd lft and no imp over 1f out* — **4/1**[2]

4120 **9** 1¼ **Another Citizen (IRE)**[17] 5035 4-8-9 **70** ....(b) GaryMahon(7) 6 — 53
(Tim Easterby) *pressed ldr: rdn over 2f out: wknd appr fnl f* — **14/1**

0014 **10** ¾ **Nasharra (IRE)**[13] 5189 4-9-7 **75** ....(p) AmyRyan 7 — 56
(Kevin Ryan) *hld up: hdwy 1/2-way: rdn and wknd wl over 1f out* — **16/1**

1m 16.04s (1.44) **Going Correction** +0.10s/f (Good) — **10** Ran SP% **118.0**
Speed ratings (Par 105): **94,93,92,90,88 87,85,84,82,81**
Tote Swingers 1&2 £6.50, 2&3 £15.10, 1&3 £5.70 CSF £22.96 CT £178.86 TOTE £4.30: £1.90, £2.50, £2.20; EX 30.90.
Owner Evelyn Duchess Of Sutherland **Bred** Evelyn Duchess Of Sutherland **Trained** Constable Burton, N Yorks

FOCUS
A reasonable sprint handicap. It's doubtful the winner had to improve on her latest Ayr run.
T/Jkpt: Not won. T/Plt: £701.10 to a £1 stake. Pool £72,137.14 - 75.10 winning units. T/Qpdt: £159.30 to a £1 stake. Pool £5,469.89 - 25.40 winning units. RY

5367 RIPON (R-H)
Monday, August 27

OFFICIAL GOING: Good changing to good to soft after race 1 (2.25)
Wind: Fresh behind Weather: Overcast and raining

5675 RACING AGAIN TOMORROW (S) STKS — 6f
2:25 (2:25) (Class 6) 2-Y-O — **£2,045** (£603; £302) **Stalls** High

Form — RPR

050 **1** — **Ena Sharples**[37] 4344 2-8-11 60 .... AdrianNicholls 3 — 62
(David Nicholls) *prom: cl up 1/2-way: led 2f out: rdn over 1f out: drvn and edgd rt ins fnl f: kpt on* — **5/2**[1]

2065 **2** 2 1/4 **Sojourn**[5] 5484 2 -8-11[57] SamHitchcott 5 55
(Mick Channon) *trckd ldrs: hdwy over 2f out: rdn to chse wnr ent fnl f: sn edgd lft and no imp towards fin* **9/2**[2]

0330 **3** 2 1/2 **Mount Seymour (IRE)**[7] 5411 2 -8-13[65] DeclanCannon(3) 7 53
(Nigel Tinkler) *a.p: rdn wl over 1f out: kpt on same pce* **20/1**

400 **4** 1 **Reinvigorate (IRE)**[7] 5424 2 -8-11[0] SeanLevey 9 45
(Richard Hannon) *trckd ldrs: effrt over 2f out: sn rdn and kpt on one pce appr fnl f* **6/1**[3]

3352 **5** hd **Dil Laney (IRE)**[16] 5108 2 -9-2[58] DanielTudhope 10 51
(David O'Meara) *in tch on inner: swtchd rt and hdwy over 2f out: rdn to chse ldrs over 1f out: sn drvn and one pce* **15/2**

2234 **6** 8 **Throwing Roses**[13] 5210 2 -8-11[63] PatrickMathers 6 20
(Ollie Pears) *sn cl up: led after 1 1/2f: rdn along and hdd 2f out: sn drvn and wknd over 1f out* **7/1**

230 **7** 7 **Vegas Belle**[20] 4907 2 -8-11[60] PaulMulrennan 1
(Ollie Pears) *wnt rt s: a in rr* **9/1**

8 4 1/2 **Hah Hah** 2 -8-11[0] FrederikTylicki 2
(Scott Dixon) *chsd ldrs on outer: rdn along 1/2-way: sn wknd* **16/1**

060 **9** 2 1/2 **Hashegotanymoney**[80] 2880 2 -8-9[48] (b[1]) DavidSimmonson(7) 11
(Michael Easterby) *a in rr: bhd fr 1/2-way* **33/1**

04 **10** 6 **Little Squaw (IRE)**[16] 5108 2 -8-11[0] (b) DavidAllan 8
(Tim Easterby) *led 1 1/2f: cl up: rdn along 1/2-way: sn wknd* **20/1**

000 **11** 1 3/4 **Nifty Nadine (IRE)**[12] 5222 2 -8-11[31] (v[1]) PJMcDonald 4
(Nigel Tinkler) *a in rr: bhd fr 1/2-way* **50/1**

1m 15.82s (2.82) **Going Correction** +0.325s/f (Good) **11**Ran SP% **115.6**
Speed ratings (Par 92): **94,91,87,86,86 75,66,60,56,48 46**
Tote Swingers 1&2 £8.00, 2&3 £36.00, 1&3 £20.10 CSF £12.31 TOTE £2.80 : £1.60 , £1.90 , £5.50; EX 15.60 .The winner was bought in for 9,500gns
Owner Ms Sara Hattersley **Bred** T Holdcroft & T Herbert-Jackson **Trained** Sessay, N Yorks

FOCUS
Rail at inner configuration and all distances as advertised. This was a run-of-the-mill juvenile seller, but fair form for the grade and straightforward enough.

NOTEBOOK
Ena Sharples, who had shown ability in three starts in maiden company here including behind Body And Soul and Rosdhu Queen, came in for plenty of support and kicked clear to score in most decisive fashion. Retained at the auction, a claimer or nursery now beckons. (op 11-4 tchd 3-1 and 9-4)
Sojourn, again fitted with a hood, had started slowly when well beaten in a 7f nursery from a mark of 58, but stayed on to chase the winner home and should find a similar event. (op 5-1 tchd 4-1)
Mount Seymour (IRE) up in trip and down to selling company for the first time, has plenty of speed but will struggle in nurseries from a mark of 65. A 5f seller looks his best chance. (op 25-1 tchd 18-1)
Reinvigorate(IRE), back on turf after a modest effort in an AW claimer, looks limited in the extreme. (tchd 13-2)
Dil Laney (IRE) having his eighth start already, is rated 58 and never threatened. He was doing his best work at the finish and is worth a try over seven. His trainer reported that he was unsuited by the easy going. Official explanation: trainer said gelding was unsuited by the track (op 17-2 tchd 9-1)

5676 BILLY NEVETT MEMORIAL H'CAP 6f
3:00 (3:01) (Class 4) (0-85,85) 3-Y-O **£4,528** (£1,347; £673 ; £336) **Stalls** High

Form RPR

3441 **1** **Love Island**[14] 5167 3 -8-4[68] PaulQuinn 2 81+
(Richard Whitaker) *trckd ldrs: hdwy on outer over 2f out: led appr fnl f: sn rdn and r.o wl* **13/2**[2]

2663 **2** 1 1/4 **Rusty Rocket (IRE)**[21] 4881 3 -8-12[76] PaulMulrennan 7 83
(Paul Green) *qckly away: led: rdn wl over 1f out: hdd and drvn appr fnl f: kpt on same pce* **8/1**

4142 **3** 1 **Colbyor**[35] 4393 3 -8-4[68] PatrickMathers 10 72+
(Richard Fahey) *trckd ldrs on inner: effrt over 2f out and sn n.m.r: rdn and nt clr run over 1f out: swtchd rt and drvn ent fnl f: kpt on* **5/1**[1]

4100 **4** 1/2 **Takealookatmenow (IRE)**[49] 3912 3 -8-8[72] (p) AdrianNicholls 4 74
(David Nicholls) *cl up: rdn along over 2f out: drvn and one pce ent fnl f* **12/1**

1061 **5** 1/2 **Lisiere (IRE)**[47] 3954 3 -8-13[80] (b) MichaelMetcalfe(3) 8 81
(Mrs K Burke) *dwlt and in rr: hdwy over 2f out: nt clr run and swtchd rt over 1f out: sn rdn and kpt on fnl f: nrst fin* **7/1**[3]

6051 **6** 3 1/4 **See Clearly**[7] 5416 3 -8-7[71] 6ex ow1 (b) DavidAllan 1 61
(Tim Easterby) *wnt rt s: sn cl up on outer: rdn along over 2f out and grad wknd* **15/2**

1304 **7** 1/2 **Sujet Bellagio**[19] 4965 3 -8-9[73] (b[1]) RobertHavlin 9 62
(Brian Meehan) *chsd ldrs: rdn along over 2f out: sn wknd* **8/1**

6001 **8** 2 **Taffe**[19] 4965 3 -9-3[81] FrederikTylicki 3 63
(James Given) *cl up: rdn along 2f out and ev ch tl drvn and wkng whn n.m.r ent fnl f* **9/1**

4503 **9** 4 **North Star Boy (IRE)**[5] 5128 3 -9-7[85] SeanLevey 6 54
(Richard Hannon) *trckd ldrs: rdn along wl over 2f out: sn wknd* **13/2**[2]

0456 **10** 7 **Whisky Bravo**[12] 5245 3 -8-8[72] (b[1]) PJMcDonald 5 19
(David Brown) *sn outpcd and a bhd* **14/1**

1m 14.52s (1.52) **Going Correction** +0.325s/f (Good) **10**Ran SP% **114.2**
Speed ratings (Par 102): **102,100,99,98,97 93,92,90,84,75**
Tote Swingers 1&2 £14.80, 2&3 £9.80, 1&3 £6.60 CSF £56.30 CT £287.08 TOTE £7.70 : £3.50 , £4.00, £2.50 ; EX 80.60 .
Owner J Barry Pemberton **Bred** Hellwood Farm And J B Pemberton **Trained** Scarcroft, W Yorks

FOCUS
A competitive 3-y-o sprint handicap. The winner more than confirmed her latest Thirsk running.

5677 RIPON ROWELS H'CAP 1m
3:35 (3:35)(Class 2) (0-100,97)3-Y-O+ **£10,081** (£3,017; £1,508; £755; £376) **Stalls** Low

Form RPR

0000 **1** **Osteopathic Remedy (IRE)**[23] 4828 8 -9-0[85] PJMcDonald 4 95
(Michael Dods) *hld up in tch: swtchd lft and hdwy wl over 3f out: rdn to chal 2f out: led over 1f out: drvn and styd on wl fnl f* **12/1**

6560 **2** 1 1/2 **St Moritz (IRE)**[29] 4628 6 -9-12[97] AdrianNicholls 1 104
(David Nicholls) *dwlt: sn led: rdn along over 2f out: hdd over 1f out: drvn and kpt on fnl f* **16/1**

2503 **3** 3 **Toto Skyllachy**[13] 5186 7 -8-13[84] DanielTudhope 3 84
(David O'Meara) *trckd ldrs: pushed along and outpcd over 2f out: rdn over 1f out: styd on fnl f: tk 3rd nr fin* **7/2**[2]

403 **4** hd **Compton**[18] 4997 3 -9-1[92] RichardKingscote 2 92
(Ralph Beckett) *trckd ldrs: hdwy over 3f out: rdn to chse ldng pair wl over 1f out: drvn and wknd fnl f: lost 3rd nr fin* **9/4**[1]

2246 **5** 1 1/4 **Next Edition (IRE)**[16] 5111 4 -8-2[80] EvaMoscrop(7) 6 77
(Philip Kirby) *cl up: rdn along over 2f out: wknd over 1f out* **11/1**

0310 **6** 4 1/2 **Don't Call Me (IRE)**[7] 4684 5 -9-4[96] ShirleyTeasdale(7) 8 82
(David Nicholls) *hld up: a in rr* **10/1**

0030 **7** 3/4 **Take It To The Max**[13] 5186 5 -9-3[88] FrederikTylicki 7 73
(Richard Fahey) *hld up towards rr: hdwy whn sltly hmpd 1/2-way: rdn along over 2f out: sn wknd* **7/1**

3101 **8** 1 1/4 **Mirrored**[9] 5369 6 -9-9[94] DuranFentiman 5 76
(Tim Easterby) *hld up towards rr: hdwy on inner over 2f out: sn rdn and wknd* **5/1**[3]

1m 41.53s (0.13) **Going Correction** +0.25s/f (Good)
WFA 3 from 4yo+ 6lb **8**Ran SP% **113.2**
Speed ratings (Par 109): **109,107,104,104,103 98,97,96**
Tote Swingers 1&2 £24.60, 2&3 £0.00, 1&3 £9.50 CSF £175.40 CT £813.14 TOTE £10.80 : £2.40, £3.30 , £1.70 ; EX 97.70 .
Owner Kevin Kirkup **Bred** Airlie Stud **Trained** Denton, Co Durham
■ Stewards' Enquiry : P J McDonald one-day ban: careless riding (Sep 10)

FOCUS
A fair handicap, run at a steady early pace. The winner had slipped to a good mark and is rated to this year's form.

NOTEBOOK
Osteopathic Remedy (IRE) appearing in this historic race for the fifth consecutive time having won it in 2008 and again in 2010 (from a mark of 87 both times), completed the treble this time from 85. Putting some mediocre efforts behind him, he made it ten career wins on his 67th start. (op 11-1 tchd 10-1 and 14-1)
St Moritz (IRE)has struggled badly since giving a good account of himself in Dubai and had run badly when tried in cheekpieces on his previous start. He was allowed to set his own pace, but in the end was very much second-best. (op 12-1)
Toto Skyllachy, sometimes a front-runner, is 4lb above his last winning mark. He came with a late rattle and would have preferred a stronger early pace. (op 4-1 tchd 3-1)
Compton, fourth in the Britannia, was a 3-y-o taking on his elders. He was keen early and the lunchtime rain was probably not in his favour. (op 10-3)
Next Edition (IRE)had no excuses after matching strides with the pace-setting St Moritz. (op 9-1)
Don't Call Me (IRE)dropped out last, was never in the contest and his third in the Royal Hunt Cup is starting to look a flash in the pan. (op 17-2)

5678 RIPON CHAMPION TWO YRS OLD TROPHY, 2012 (LISTED RACE) 6f
4:10 (4:10) (Class 1) 2-Y-O **£15,311** (£5,805; £2,905 ; £1,447 ; £726) **Stalls** High

Form RPR

0214 **1** **Deauville Prince (FR)**[15] 5140 2 -9-2[93] RichardKingscote 1 104
(Tom Dascombe) *cl up: rdn wl over 1f out: drvn ent fnl f: led last 100yds: styd on* **3/1**[2]

5111 **2** 1 1/4 **Melody Of Love**[20] 4921 2 -8-11[82] PaulMulrennan 2 95
(Ann Duffield) *dwlt: sn trcking ldrs: swtchd lft to inner 1/2-way and sn cl up: led wl over 1f out: rdn and rn green ent fnl f: hdd and no ex fnl 100yds* **7/2**[3]

130 **3** 4 1/2 **Botanic Garden**[16] 5088 2 -9-2[92] [1] DanielTudhope 3 87
(William Haggas) *cl up: led after 1f: rdn along and hdd over 1f out: sn one pce* **7/1**

1004 **4** 14 **Lyric Ace (IRE)**[27] 4687 2 -9-2[95] SeanLevey 5 45
(Richard Hannon) *dwlt: trckd ldrs: swtchd rt to outer and cl up after 2f: rdn along wl over 2f out: sn wknd* **5/2**[1]

1006 **5** 1 3/4 **Pay Freeze (IRE)**[24] 4763 2 -9-2[91] SamHitchcott 4 39
(Mick Channon) *led 1f: sn hdd and lost pl on rail: bhd fr 1/2-way* **7/2**[3]

1m 14.43s (1.43) **Going Correction** +0.325s/f (Good) **5**Ran SP% **110.5**
Speed ratings (Par 102): **103,101,95,76,74**
CSF £13.63 TOTE £4.00 : £2.00 , £3.80 ; EX 12.60 .
Owner N & S Mather, C Ledigo, L Basran **Bred** Ecurie Haras Du Cadran Et Al **Trained** Malpas, Cheshire

FOCUS
Ripon's only Listed race and on paper a strong renewal. The winner is improving run to run.

NOTEBOOK
Deauville Prince (FR) who accounted for Steeler when taking his maiden at Haydock on his third start, went on to finish a highly creditable fourth in a 7f Listed event at Deauville. After taking charge, he had to see off the determined challenge of the filly, but with his stamina proven he was firmly in command at the line. A laidback individual, he has a very good attitude. (op 10-3)
Melody Of Love, who took a maiden here in fine style on her second start, was switched inside over 2f out. Upsides over a furlong out, she made the winner dig deep and finished clear second-best. She is an admirable type who will improve again. (op 10-3)
Botanic Garden, having his second start for this yard, wore a hood. He hung off the rail, letting the runner-up through, and like the rest was left for dead by the first two in the end. (op 6-1)
Lyric Ace (IRE) who met trouble in running when doing best of the hold-up horses in the Group 3 Molecomb, was trying 6f for the first time. After a tardy start and forced to pull wide, he dropped right away before stamina became an issue. He had shown soft ground holds no terrors for him when a respectable seventh in the Super Sprint, so this must go down as a major disappointment. It was reported that he failed to get the trip on the ground. Official explanation: trainer's rep said colt failed to get the trip on the good to soft ground (op 9-4)
Pay Freeze (IRE) tried over 7f at Goodwood, struggled to go the pace and was another to drop right away in the end. He has not gone on since making a good impression when winning second time out at York in May. He was reported to have been unsuited by the ground. Official explanation: trainer's rep said colt was unsuited by the good to soft ground (op 5-1)

5679 SIS LIVE MAIDEN STKS 1m
4:45 (5:26) (Class 5) 3-4-Y-O **£2,587** (£770; £384 ; £192) **Stalls** Low

Form RPR

1 **Star Lahib (IRE)**3 -8-12[0] FrannyNorton 12 82+
(Mark Johnston) *cl up: led over 5f out: rdn clr 2f out: styd on strly* **9/2**[2]

0 **2** 6 **Kept**[19] 4948 3 -9-3[0] RichardKingscote 2 73
(James Fanshawe) *trckd ldrs: hdwy 1/2-way: rdn to chse wnr 3f out: rdn 2f out and no imp* **9/2**[2]

44 **3** 5 **Quiet Route (IRE)**[10] 5316 3 -9-3[0] SeanLevey 1 62
(Brian Ellison) *trckd ldrs on inner: hdwy over 3f out: rdn to chse ldng pair 2f out: sn drvn and no imp* **4/1**[1]

6 **4** 3 1/4 **Albert Tatlock (IRE)**[24] 4780 3 -9-3[0] AdrianNicholls 4 54
(David Nicholls) *t.k.h: led 2 1/2f: cl up: rdn along over 2f out: grad wknd* **12/1**

5 3 1/2 **Discay** 3 -9-3[0] RobertHavlin 13 46
(Mark Johnston) *in tch whn rn wd bnd after 2f: towards rr: sme hdwy over 2f out: n.d* **12/1**

6 nk **Keep It Dark** 3 -9-3[0] PJMcDonald 9 45
(Tony Coyle) *s.i.s and bhd: sme hdwy on inner 3f out: sn rdn and n.d* **16/1**

60 **7** 3/4 **Leonards Pride (IRE)**[10] 5329 3 -8-10[0] LauraSimpson(7) 6 44
(Daniel Mark Loughnane) *trckd ldrs: hdwy on outer to chse ldng pair over 4f out: rdn along 3f out: wknd fnl 2f* **40/1**

00 **8** 2 1/4 **Under Ambition**[16] 5113 4 -9-4[0] DavidAllan 11 33
(Frederick Watson) *towards rr: sme hdwy over 4f out: rdn along over 3f out: nvr a factor* **66/1**

5 **9** 2 1/4 **Tenacity**[38] 4293 3 -9-3[0] DanielTudhope 8 33
(Kate Walton) *chsd ldrs: rdn along over 3f out: grad wknd* **9/2**[2]

-00 **10** 3¾ **Dancing Paddy (IRE)**[21] 4864 4-9-4 0 .... GarryWhillans(5) 3 25
(Alan Swinbank) *t.k.h: chsd ldrs: n.m.r bnd after 2f: sn lost pl and bhd fnl 4f* **11/1**

11 1¼ **Billy Redpath** 4-9-9 0 .... DuranFentiman 7 22
(Frederick Watson) *s.i.s: a bhd* **100/1**

12 16 **Soviet Dream** 3-9-3 0 .... PaulMulrennan 14
(James Fanshawe) *s.i.s: a in rr: bhd fr 1/2-way* **6/1**[3]

1m 43.75s (2.35) **Going Correction** +0.25s/f (Good)
WFA 3 from 4yo 6lb **12** Ran SP% **123.4**
Speed ratings (Par 103): **98,92,87,83,80 79,79,76,74,70 69,53**
Tote Swingers 1&2 £8.10, 2&3 £6.40, 1&3 £6.60 CSF £26.16 TOTE £4.50: £1.10, £2.00, £2.30; EX 29.70.
Owner Jaber Abdullah **Bred** Piercetown Stud **Trained** Middleham Moor, N Yorks

FOCUS
There was a lengthy delay after Eva Moscrop was hurt when her mount Brenkley Melani, who was withdrawn, unseated her on the way to post. A modest maiden. Form was thin on the ground with five newcomers in the line-up and it went to one of the newcomers. She could be capable of better.

5680 TOTEPOOL A BETTER WAY TO BET H'CAP 1m 1f 170y
5:20 (5:50) (Class 5) (0-75,75) 3-Y-O **£2,911** (£866; £432; £216) **Stalls** Low

Form RPR

634 **1** **Narcissist (IRE)**[19] 4948 3-9-3 **71** .... PaulMulrennan 2 85+
(Ed Dunlop) *trckd ldng pair: hdwy on inner 3f out: swtchd lft and rdn to chse ldr wl over 1f out: drvn to chal ent fnl f: sn led and styd on wl* **11/2**

4433 **2** 1½ **Exning Halt**[19] 4945 3-9-2 **70** .... FrederikTylicki 8 81
(James Fanshawe) *trckd ldrs: smooth hdwy over 3f out: led wl over 2f out: rdn over 1f out: jnd and drvn ent fnl f: sn hdd and kpt on same pce towards fin* **3/1**[1]

2132 **3** 11 **Miss Ella Jade**[24] 4771 3-8-2 **56** oh1 .... PaulQuinn 9 44
(Richard Whitaker) *hld up in rr: stdy hdwy 3f out: chsd ldrs 2f out: sn rdn and one pce appr fnl f* **4/1**[2]

520 **4** 5 **Ukrainian Princess**[40] 4212 3-9-0 **75** .... AmeliaGreen(7) 5 52
(Sir Henry Cecil) *hld up and bhd: hdwy on wd outside 3f out: rdn to chal 2f out and ev ch tl drvn and wknd appr fnl f* **9/1**

4000 **5** 3½ **Alpha Arion (IRE)**[18] 5000 3-8-2 **56** oh4 .... DuranFentiman 7 26
(Tim Easterby) *hld up in rr: hdwy 3f out: rdn along over 2f out: n.d* **40/1**

-166 **6** 1¾ **Forster Street (IRE)**[12] 5225 3-8-11 **65** .... DavidAllan 6 31
(Tim Easterby) *trckd ldr: hdwy to ld over 3f out: rdn and hdd wl over 2f out: sn wknd* **11/2**

4403 **7** 6 **Light Zabeel (USA)**[51] 3846 3-9-5 **73** .... SamHitchcott 4 27
(Mick Channon) *chsd ldrs: cl up over 3f out: rdn and wknd qckly over 2f out* **12/1**

3154 **8** 2 **Voice From Above (IRE)**[18] 4996 3-9-0 **68** .... DanielTudhope 3 18
(Patrick Holmes) *hld up in tch: hdwy on inner to chse ldrs 3f out: sn rdn and wknd over 2f out* **5/1**[3]

1200 **9** 19 **Dansili Dutch (IRE)**[19] 4961 3-8-11 **65** .... FrannyNorton 1
(Andrew Crook) *t.k.h: led: rdn along and hdd over 3f out: sn wknd* **14/1**

2m 9.45s (4.05) **Going Correction** +0.25s/f (Good) **9** Ran SP% **119.2**
Speed ratings (Par 100): **93,91,83,79,76 74,70,68,53**
Tote Swingers 1&2 £17.80, 2&3 £8.80, 1&3 £16.00 CSF £23.18 CT £74.86 TOTE £8.00: £2.80, £1.30, £1.60; EX 25.50.
Owner The Honorable Earle I Mack **Bred** Bernard And Nicholas Ferrand **Trained** Newmarket, Suffolk

FOCUS
A modest 3-y-o handicap, run at just a steady pace until the final half-mile. The first pair finished clear.
Dansili Dutch(IRE) Official explanation: jockey said filly ran too free
T/Plt: £61.00 to a £1 stake. Pool £62,335.94 - 745.23 winning units. T/Qpdt: £11.00 to a £1 stake. Pool £3,681.60 - 247.53 winning units. JR

5446 WARWICK (L-H)
Monday, August 27

OFFICIAL GOING: Good to firm (good in places back straight) changing to good after race 6 (5.05)
Wind: Fresh behind Weather: Overcast, turning to rain after race 5

5681 QUANTUM MANUFACTURING H'CAP 6f
2:10 (2:12) (Class 5) (0-70,69) 3-Y-O+ **£2,264** (£673; £336; £168) **Stalls** Low

Form RPR

1413 **1** **Clear Spring (IRE)**[48] 3941 4-9-5 **64** .... NickyMackay 10 77+
(John Spearing) *s.i.s: in rr: hdwy over 1f out: led ins fnl f: rdn out* **13/2**[2]

0123 **2** 1¾ **Two Turtle Doves (IRE)**[15] 5131 6-9-0 **59** .... SeanQuinlan 9 66
(Michael Mullineaux) *chsd ldrs: led over 1f out: rdn and hdd ins fnl f: styd on same pce* **14/1**

054 **3** nk **Loyal N Trusted**[13] 5203 4-8-12 **57** .... LukeMorris 5 63
(Richard Price) *sn pushed along towards rr: hdwy over 1f out: sn rdn and ev ch: styd on same pce ins fnl f* **6/1**[1]

0051 **4** 1 **Amis Reunis**[13] 5203 3-9-0 **62** .... WilliamCarson 2 65
(Anthony Carson) *mid-div: drvn along 1/2-way: hdwy u.p over 1f out: styd on same pce ins fnl f* **13/2**[2]

2435 **5** ¾ **Art Form**[23] 4793 3-9-0 **69** ....(t) WilliamTwiston-Davies(7) 12 69
(Alan McCabe) *s.i.s: hld up: hdwy u.p over 1f out: r.o: nt rch ldrs* **13/2**[2]

0-00 **6** ¾ **Dark Lane**[15] 5120 6-9-5 **64** ....(p) RichardThomas 6 62
(David Evans) *prom: rdn over 1f out: no ex fnl f* **10/1**

0050 **7** ½ **Oratorian (IRE)**[17] 5036 3-9-3 **65** .... JamesDoyle 13 61
(Sylvester Kirk) *mid-div: sn pushed along: losing pl whn hmpd over 4f out: rdn over 1f out: r.o towards fin* **22/1**

000 **8** 1 **Prigsnov Dancer (IRE)**[86] 2693 7-8-1 **53** oh4 ow3 .... JakePayne(7) 7 46
(Garry Woodward) *led: rdn and hdd over 1f out: wknd ins fnl f* **50/1**

000 **9** hd **Steel City Boy (IRE)**[13] 5203 9-8-2 **50** .... RyanPowell(3) 11 43
(Garry Woodward) *chsd ldrs: rdn over 1f out: wknd ins fnl f* **33/1**

60-3 **10** 3 **Euroquip Boy (IRE)**[26] 4708 5-8-9 **59** .... DavidKenny(5) 4 42
(Michael Scudamore) *hld up: hdwy over 2f out: rdn over 1f out: sn wknd* **15/2**[3]

6024 **11** 1½ **Alpha Delta Whisky**[15] 5123 4-9-9 **68** .... MartinDwyer 3 46
(John Gallagher) *chsd ldrs: rdn over 2f out: wknd fnl f* **10/1**

5611 **12** ¾ **Prince Of Passion (CAN)**[14] 5157 4-9-7 **66** .... NeilCallan 14 42
(Derek Shaw) *mid-div: hdwy 1/2-way: rdn 2f out: wknd fnl f* **10/1**

0563 **13** shd **Divertimenti (IRE)**[13] 5205 8-9-2 **61** ....(b) StephenCraine 1 36
(Roy Bowring) *w ldrs: drvn along 1/2-way: wknd over 1f out* **16/1**

0654 **14** ½ **Jemimaville (IRE)**[19] 4943 5-8-5 **50** oh5 .... LiamJones 15 24
(Giles Bravery) *s.i.s: sn pushed along in rr: wknd 2f out* **50/1**

1m 11.75s (-0.05) **Going Correction** -0.05s/f (Good)
WFA 3 from 4yo+ 3lb **14** Ran SP% **117.1**
Speed ratings (Par 103): **98,95,95,93,92 91,91,89,89,85 83,82,82,81**
Tote Swingers 1&2 £14.20, 2&3 £11.30, 1&3 £6.00 CSF £88.56 CT £573.99 TOTE £6.40: £2.30, £4.50, £2.40; EX 101.20.
Owner H James **Bred** Rocal Bloodstock **Trained** Kinnersley, Worcs

FOCUS
About 7mm of rain had fallen on the course since Friday, but it was decided to apply a further 7mm to the stables bend and the home straight up to the top of the hill. The going was Good to firm, good in places. A wide-open sprint handicap in which very few could be ruled out. They went a sound pace throughout and it paid to be held up. The likes of Divertimenti, Steel City Boy and Prigsnov Dancer, who all raced prominently, finished well beaten. Modest form, rated around the runner-up.

5682 FREE RADIO NURSERY 5f 110y
2:45 (2:47) (Class 5) (0-75,76) 2-Y-O **£2,264** (£673; £336; £168) **Stalls** Low

Form RPR

2001 **1** **Opt Out**[3] 5532 2-9-10 **76** 6ex .... JoeFanning 5 81+
(Mark Johnston) *a.p: shkn up to ld 1f out: rdn out* **11/4**[1]

0532 **2** ¾ **This Is Nice (IRE)**[20] 4934 2-9-7 **73** .... JamieSpencer 6 75
(Tom Dascombe) *s.i.s: hld up: hdwy u.p over 1f out: r.o: nt rch wnr* **7/2**[2]

4304 **3** 1 **Ighraa (IRE)**[13] 5202 2-9-7 **73** .... PaulHanagan 3 71
(Brian Meehan) *s.i.s: sn pushed along in rr: hdwy over 1f out: sn rdn: styd on* **15/2**

2256 **4** nse **Indian Affair**[13] 5202 2-9-5 **71** .... LukeMorris 1 69
(Milton Bradley) *chsd ldrs: rdn over 1f out: styd on* **9/2**[3]

230 **5** 1 **Vestibule**[14] 5146 2-9-5 **71** .... NeilCallan 7 66
(Eve Johnson Houghton) *led over 2 1/2f: w ldr: rdn and ev ch 1f out: no ex wl ins fnl f* **12/1**

231 **6** 1½ **Charlemagne Diva**[7] 5411 2-8-6 **58** 6ex .... MartinDwyer 9 48
(Ann Duffield) *trckd ldr: racd keenly: led 3f out: rdn and hdd 1f out: no ex ins fnl f* **17/2**

4363 **7** 2¼ **Ouzinkie (IRE)**[17] 5061 2-8-13 **65** .... MartinHarley 4 47
(Mick Channon) *s.i.s: hld up: swtchd rt and rdn over 1f out: n.d* **8/1**

065 **8** 9 **Her Royal Empress**[26] 4704 2-7-12 **50** oh2 .... NickyMackay 8 3
(James Unett) *chsd ldrs: pushed along over 3f out: wknd over 1f out* **28/1**

1m 5.86s (-0.04) **Going Correction** -0.05s/f (Good) **8** Ran SP% **111.6**
Speed ratings (Par 94): **98,97,95,95,94 92,89,77**
Tote Swingers 1&2 £1.90, 2&3 £4.30, 1&3 £4.60 CSF £11.75 CT £60.71 TOTE £4.00: £2.20, £1.70, £2.50; EX 10.60.
Owner Sheikh Hamdan Bin Mohammed Al Maktoum **Bred** Darley **Trained** Middleham Moor, N Yorks

FOCUS
A competitive nursery ran at a good clip. The winner confirmed his Goodwood improvement and the second posted a personal best.

NOTEBOOK
Opt Out, an emphatic winner of a similar race at Goodwood last Friday, was always travelling well just behind the leaders and, when asked for an effort on the nearside with over a furlong to run, the response was immediate. He won with slightly more in hand than the winning margin suggests and looks capable of further improvement over this trip on this sort of ground. (op 15-8)
This Is Nice(IRE) was popular in the betting ring and emerged as the only danger to the winner in the final furlong. She had run well over 7f at Wolverhampton on her previous start and looks worth stepping up to that sort of trip on turf now. (op 4-1 tchd 10-3)
Ighraa(IRE) ran on strongly on the nearside in the final furlong, although she still displayed signs of greenness. She looks capable of improvement. (op 8-1)
Indian Affair is fairly exposed, but he ran on willingly in the final 2f and was only just denied third place. (op 6-1 tchd 7-1)
Charlemagne Diva was sent to the front early and probably had too much use made of her. Her jockey was not hard on her once her chance had gone and she is better than her finishing position suggests. That said, she is due to go up 16lb for her win at Thirsk last week so she may struggle to find a winning opportunity in the short term. (op 15-2 tchd 7-1)

5683 EXCELERATE RESOURCES H'CAP 1m 6f 213y
3:20 (3:20) (Class 6) (0-60,60) 3-Y-O+ **£1,617** (£481; £240; £120) **Stalls** Low

Form RPR

30-2 **1** **Hi Note**[11] 4004 4-8-13 **52** .... MartinLeonard(7) 2 64+
(Sheena West) *mid-div: hdwy 9f out: led 4f out: eased for a few strides over 1f out: sn picked up again: styd on* **9/2**[2]

5005 **2** 2¼ **Musically**[6] 5452 3-8-10 **55** .... MartinHarley 8 62
(Mick Channon) *hld up: hdwy over 4f out: chsd wnr 2f out: sn rdn: swtchd rt over 1f out: styd on same pce ins fnl f* **8/1**[3]

0542 **3** 6 **Astonished Harry (GER)**[10] 5330 3-8-8 **53** ....(p) ShaneKelly 5 52
(Reg Hollinshead) *led 5f: chsd ldrs: led again 5f out: hdd 4f out: sn rdn: styd on same pce appr fnl f* **11/4**[1]

0050 **4** 5 **Quiet Appeal (IRE)**[19] 4955 3-9-1 **60** .... JoeFanning 12 53
(Mark Johnston) *chsd ldrs: rdn over 2f out: wknd over 1f out* **9/2**[2]

4405 **5** 11 **Cloudy Start**[28] 4664 6-9-9 **60** .... LeonnaMayor(5) 9 38
(Jamie Osborne) *dwlt: hld up: hdwy over 6f out: wknd over 2f out* **12/1**

3044 **6** 2¾ **Sacco D'Oro**[8] 5173 6-9-1 **47** ....(v) SeanQuinlan 6 22
(Michael Mullineaux) *hld up in tch: rdn over 3f out: sn wknd* **25/1**

0304 **7** 23 **Cookieshake**[11] 5264 4-9-0 **46** oh1 ....(b) WilliamCarson 10
(Peter Hiatt) *sn pushed along to chse ldrs: led 8f out: hdd 5f out: rdn and wknd over 2f out: t.o* **28/1**

5-33 **8** 10 **Arctic Wings (IRE)**[14] 5173 8-9-12 **58** .... MichaelO'Connell 7
(Tony Carroll) *hld up: pushed along 10f out: rdn and bhd fnl 8f: t.o* **12/1**

3000 **9** 1¾ **Native Eight (USA)**[25] 4744 3-8-10 **55** .... LukeMorris 4
(Ian Williams) *chsd ldrs: drvn along 12f out: lost pl 10f out: bhd fnl 8f: t.o* **12/1**

3000 **10** 37 **Gulf Coast**[11] 5253 7-9-1 **47** ....(p) NeilCallan 1
(Tim Walford) *sn pushed along and prom: rdn over 6f out: wknd over 3f out: t.o* **9/1**

0230 **11** 38 **Yas Marina (USA)**[35] 4405 4-8-7 **46** oh1 ....(b) DavidBergin(7) 11
(David O'Meara) *chsd ldr tl led 10f out: hdd 8f out: rdn and wknd over 5f out: t.o* **16/1**

3m 21.0s (2.00) **Going Correction** +0.175s/f (Good)
WFA 3 from 4yo+ 13lb **11** Ran SP% **120.4**
Speed ratings (Par 101): **101,99,96,93,88 86,74,69,68,48 28**
Tote Swingers 1&2 £10.00, 2&3 £6.50, 1&3 £4.10 CSF £41.59 CT £119.20 TOTE £5.20: £1.60, £3.60, £1.60; EX 54.30.
Owner Gerald West **Bred** J A And Mrs Duffy **Trained** Falmer, E Sussex
■ Martin Leonard's first winner.

FOCUS
Nothing more than modest fare, especially considering how many of the field were beaten exiting the back straight. The winner is rated in line with her recent hurdles improvement.

5684 IRISH STALLION FARMS E B F MAIDEN STKS (DIV I) 7f 26y
3:55 (3:59) (Class 5) 2-Y-O **£3,234** (£962; £481; £240) **Stalls** Low

Form RPR
1 **Secretinthepark** 2-9-3 0 RichardMullen 7 75
(Ed McMahon) *s.i.s and edgd lft s: sn prom: rdn to ld over 1f out: r.o* **10/1**
43 2 *nk* **Darkening (IRE)**[20] 4921 2-9-3 0 MickaelBarzalona 8 74
(Mahmood Al Zarooni) *plld hrd: led: hung rt fr over 4f out: sn hdd: rdn over 2f out: ev ch fr over 1f out: swvd rt ins fnl f: r.o* **4/1**[3]
4 3 *1 ½* **Tarbawi (IRE)**[26] 4707 2-9-3 0 FrankieDettori 9 70
(Saeed Bin Suroor) *chsd ldr nrly 3f: remained handy: rdn and ev ch over 1f out: no ex nr fin* **3/1**[2]
32 4 *3* **Lord Of Leitrim (IRE)**[16] 5098 2-9-3 0 ShaneKelly 2 63
(Brian Meehan) *chsd ldrs tl led 4f out: rdn: edgd rt and hdd over 1f out: no ex ins fnl f* **7/4**[1]
5 *nk* **Alerted (USA)** 2-8-12 0 JamesDoyle 11 62+
(Roger Charlton) *stdd sn after s: hld up: pushed along over 2f out: r.o ins fnl f: nvr nrr* **11/1**
00 6 *9* **Winslow Arizona (IRE)**[25] 4724 2-9-3 0 JamieSpencer 10 40
(Michael Bell) *prom tl rdn and wknd over 2f out* **33/1**
0 7 *nk* **Kubera (IRE)**[18] 5005 2-9-3 0 NeilCallan 6 39
(J S Moore) *s.i.s and hmpd s: a in rr* **50/1**
8 *¾* **Chocala (IRE)** 2-9-3 0 FergusSweeney 4 37
(Alan King) *mid-div: rdn and wknd over 2f out* **33/1**
0 9 *¾* **Alfie's Rose**[10] 5325 2-9-3 0 LiamJones 5 35
(William Haggas) *s.i.s: a in rr* **12/1**
10 *hd* **See And Be Seen** 2-9-3 0 PatDobbs 3 35
(Sylvester Kirk) *s.i.s: a in rr* **40/1**

1m 26.1s (1.50) **Going Correction** +0.175s/f (Good) **10** Ran SP% **116.8**
Speed ratings (Par 94): **98,97,95,92,92 81,81,80,79,79**
Tote Swingers 1&2 £6.10, 2&3 £2.70, 1&3 £6.10 CSF £48.75 TOTE £13.60: £3.00, £1.30, £1.40; EX 76.30.
Owner Mia Racing **Bred** Mia Racing **Trained** Lichfield, Staffs

FOCUS
Plenty of potential improvers in the first division of the maiden and the form should work out, although the first four were allowed to open a break on the field. The time was nearly two seconds quicker than the second division. The first two were split by the width of the track at the line in a driving finish.

NOTEBOOK
Secretinthepark, whose trainer is 16% with first-time-out 2yos in the past three seasons, was a slightly fortunate winner as the runner-up threw away his chance, but that should not detract from an impressive debut performance. He settled beautifully in behind the leaders and ran on willingly in the home straight along the far-side rail, where he pulled out plenty when challenged close to the finish. He looks sure to come on from this. (op 9-1 tchd 8-1)
Darkening(IRE) ◆ ran well considering he looked to have lost any chance of winning by about halfway after pulling hard throughout the first 2f. He was headed coming into the home bend, which he took awkwardly, after which he proceeded to wander around in the home straight, eventually drifting into the nearside rail. Nevertheless, he ran on like a talented horse, almost getting up again close home, and if his quirks can be ironed out he can surely find winning opportunities. (op 9-2 tchd 5-1)
Tarbawi(IRE) looked set to win about 2f out, but his effort flattened out as he started to hang near the line. He clearly has ability, but perhaps his attitude can be called into question after this performance. (tchd 7-2)
Lord Of Leitrim(IRE), who was well supported following two encouraging runs on Lingfield's Polytrack, took over from Darkening rounding the home turn, but his effort petered out in the final furlong. This has to rate as disappointing, although he was probably not suited by the way the race was run. (op 15-8 tchd 9-4)
Alerted(USA) ◆ was a big eye-catcher. She was very green on the way to post and she raced awkwardly for the first half of the race, but once she was asked for her effort in the final 2f she ran on best of all. She is related to a couple of winners and is her trainer's second runner by First Defence, the sire who also produced Dundonnell. She will undoubtedly improve massively for this initial experience. (op 14-1)

5685 IRISH STALLION FARMS E B F MAIDEN STKS (DIV II) 7f 26y
4:30 (4:31) (Class 5) 2-Y-O **£3,234** (£962; £481; £240) **Stalls** Low

Form RPR
6 1 **Red Avenger (USA)**[83] 2784 2-9-3 0 JoeFanning 9 81+
(Ed Dunlop) *a.p: hmpd sn after s: chsd ldr over 1f out: shkn up to ld ins fnl f: r.o* **9/2**[2]
4 2 *1 ¼* **Tamarkuz (USA)**[17] 5062 2-9-3 0 FrankieDettori 7 78
(Saeed Bin Suroor) *nt clr run and swtchd rt sn after s: led 6f out: rdn over 1f out: hdd and unable qck ins fnl f* **8/13**[1]
0 3 *6* **Epic Battle (IRE)**[24] 4773 2-9-3 0 LiamJones 6 61
(William Haggas) *led 1f: chsd ldrs: pushed along 1/2-way: outpcd fr over 1f out: wnt 3rd ins fnl f* **12/1**
0 4 *¾* **Echo Brava**[20] 4917 2-9-3 0 NeilCallan 5 59
(John Gallagher) *mid-div: pushed along over 2f out: nvr trbld ldrs* **80/1**
0 5 *¾* **Canadian Red**[13] 5207 2-9-3 0 StephenCraine 10 57
(Tom Dascombe) *chsd ldr: rdn over 2f out: wknd over 1f out* **50/1**
6 *2 ¾* **Saved By The Bell (IRE)** 2-9-3 0 MartinDwyer 8 50
(Brian Meehan) *s.i.s: hld up: nvr on terms* **10/1**
7 *1* **Rockpool** 2-8-12 0 JamesDoyle 4 42+
(Roger Charlton) *rn green in rr: n.d* **8/1**[3]
03 8 *1 ¼* **Hartwright**[15] 5121 2-9-3 0 JamieSpencer 2 44
(Michael Bell) *hld up: plld hrd: nvr nr to chal* **10/1**
0 9 *1 ¾* **Bugsy's Babe**[47] 3959 2-8-12 0 KirstyMilczarek 1 34
(George Baker) *chsd ldrs: pushed along 1/2-way: wknd 2f out* **40/1**

1m 27.94s (3.34) **Going Correction** +0.175s/f (Good) **9** Ran SP% **122.7**
Speed ratings (Par 94): **87,85,78,77,77 73,72,71,69**
Tote Swingers 1&2 £1.80, 2&3 £5.40, 1&3 £11.30 CSF £8.11 TOTE £6.70: £2.10, £1.10, £3.50; EX 12.70.
Owner R J Arculli **Bred** Wedgewood Farm **Trained** Newmarket, Suffolk

FOCUS
This was the weaker division of the maiden, run in a much slower time, although the winner looks a decent prospect. The first two drew well clear and the second at least matched his debut form.

NOTEBOOK
Red Avenger(USA), who had run promisingly on debut over 6f at Leicester in June despite displaying signs of greenness, showed that he had learned plenty from that initial experience and won in a very professional manner. He was settled nicely just off the pace and when the leader skipped a couple of lengths clear with over 2f to run, he was always able to keep tabs on him and eventually went past in the last half-furlong to win going away. There should be plenty more to come, especially over further. (op 6-1)
Tamarkuz(USA) shaped well in a Newmarket maiden on debut earlier this month and was backed as if defeat was out of the question here, but he threw away a winning opportunity by hanging. Having jumped off awkwardly, he soon took a prominent position and his jockey took the bull by the horns by kicking on early in the home straight. However, he started to race awkwardly as the pressure was applied and was eventually well beaten by a rival who showed far better track-craft. However, his talent is not in question and he looks sure to win races. (op 4-9)
Epic Battle(IRE) was under strong driving a long way from home, but he battled on well in the home straight. This was an improvement on his debut run at Newmarket and he could win races once he is stepped up in trip.
Echo Brava ran a pleasing race without ever threatening the principals. This was a massive improvement from his initial run at Kempton 20 days earlier. (op 100-1)
Canadian Red also found improvement on his second start and he too could have a future.
Rockpool's rider was unchipped in the paddock before the race and although he was able to take the ride, he missed a later ride on the card after the doctor decided he should be stood down. (op 10-1)

5686 WRIGHT HASSALL SOLICITORS CONDITIONS STKS 7f 26y
5:05 (5:08) (Class 3) 3-Y-O+ **£6,663** (£1,982; £990; £495) **Stalls** Low

Form RPR
0420 1 **Right To Dream (IRE)**[170] 874 3-8-6 98 JoeFanning 1 104
(Brian Meehan) *chsd ldrs: pushed along 1/2-way: shkn up to ld over 1f out: r.o wl* **5/1**
0005 2 *5* **Atlantic Sport (USA)**[9] 5342 7-8-11 96 MartinHarley 2 93
(Mick Channon) *hld up: hdwy over 1f out: rdn to chse wnr fnl f: styd on same pce* **2/1**[2]
3630 3 *1 ½* **Regal Parade**[9] 5370 8-8-11 100 LukeMorris 6 88
(Milton Bradley) *chsd ldr: pushed along 1/2-way: rdn and ev ch over 1f out: no ex fnl f* **9/2**[3]
0002 4 *2* **Balducci**[23] 4822 5-8-11 100 JamieSpencer 5 83
(David Simcock) *led: rdn and hdd over 1f out: wknd ins fnl f* **15/8**[1]
405- 5 *24* **Red Aggressor (IRE)**[310] 7019 3-8-6 96 (b[1]) MartinDwyer 4 16
(Clive Brittain) *hld up: rdn and wknd over 1f out* **12/1**

1m 24.86s (0.26) **Going Correction** +0.275s/f (Good)
WFA 3 from 4yo+ 5lb **5** Ran SP% **110.7**
Speed ratings (Par 107): **109,103,101,99,71**
CSF £15.48 TOTE £6.90: £2.30, £2.70; EX 19.20.
Owner Right Tack Partnership **Bred** Gigginstown House Stud **Trained** Manton, Wilts
■ Morache Music (11/4) was withdrawn due to unsuitable ground. Deduct 25p in the £ under R4, new market formed.

FOCUS
A trappy-looking conditions race on paper but it was turned into a procession. There was driving rain throughout. Muddling form which has been rated cautiously.

NOTEBOOK
Right To Dream(IRE), who had been gelded since his last run at Meydan in March, travelled cosily throughout the contest and forged clear in the final furlong with his jockey only having to nudge him along with hands and heels to maintain the advantage. This was his first try at 7f in this country and he saw it out well. Clearly the gelding operation has had the desired effect, while the blinkers he wore in Meydan were dispensed with. He has always been held in high regard by his connections and he may be able to go onto better things. (op 6-1 tchd 8-1)
Atlantic Sport(USA) is a solid benchmark for the form, although the rain that fell throughout the race probably came too late for him. He stayed on well in the home straight but had no chance with the winner. He looks set to be kept going in handicap company this autumn. (op 5-2 tchd 11-4)
Regal Parade is not the same horse he once was, but he did finish third in a Group 3 over 6f earlier this season. He still races with plenty of zest but it is now two years since he last won and he will always be vulnerable to an improver in this type of event. Luke Morris reported that he slipped on the bend. Official explanation: jockey said gelding slipped on the bend (op 4-1)
Balducci represented an in-form stable and duly attracted some support, but after making the running into the home straight, he found disappointingly little once the pace was increased. (op 13-8 tchd 11-8, 2-1 in a place)
Red Aggressor(IRE), having his first run for 310 days, was easily beaten off and the first-time blinkers had no effect. (op 10-1 tchd 14-1)

5687 E B F HARPER FIELDS CARE HOME - BALSALL COMMON MAIDEN STKS 7f 26y
5:40 (5:45) (Class 5) 3-Y-O+ **£3,234** (£962; £481; £240) **Stalls** Low

Form RPR
6 1 **Morning Call**[11] 5276 3-9-3 0 FergusSweeney 12 73
(Henry Candy) *a.p: led over 1f out: r.o wl* **5/1**[3]
0- 2 *2 ¼* **Beaumont Cooper**[340] 6274 3-9-3 0 MichaelO'Connell 7 67
(Tony Carroll) *s.i.s: hdwy over 4f out: rdn and ev ch over 1f out: styd on same pce ins fnl f* **40/1**
3 3 *3* **Zenafire**[9] 5335 3-9-3 0 ShaneKelly 8 59
(Reg Hollinshead) *chsd ldr tl led over 2f out: rdn and hdd over 1f out: no ex ins fnl f* **4/1**[2]
0 4 *1 ¾* **Trevose (IRE)**[18] 4992 3-9-3 0 WilliamCarson 14 54
(Roy Brotherton) *prom: rdn over 2f out: wknd fnl f* **50/1**
50 5 *1* **Chuckle**[37] 4341 3-8-12 0 (t) NeilCallan 5 47
(Rae Guest) *chsd ldrs: rdn over 2f out: wknd fnl f* **10/1**
6 *2 ½* **Pink Lips** 4-9-3 0 PatDobbs 2 42
(J R Jenkins) *hld up: n.d* **14/1**
3 7 *1* **Another Squeeze**[18] 4992 4-9-0 0 RyanClark(3) 1 39
(Peter Hiatt) *hld up: pushed along over 2f out: nvr on terms* **11/4**[1]
50 8 *shd* **Audeamus (IRE)**[3] 5555 3-8-12 0 StevieDonohoe 3 37
(Tobias B P Coles) *hld up: a in rr* **14/1**
5 9 *5* **Elusive Pursuit**[21] 4874 4-9-3 0 JohnFahy 6 25
(Clive Cox) *led over 4f: rdn and wknd over 1f out* **14/1**
05 10 *hd* **Sandy Lane (IRE)**[48] 3946 3-9-3 0 DaraghO'Donohoe 4 28
(Amy Weaver) *hld up: pushed along 1/2-way: sn wknd* **16/1**
0 11 *10* **Legal Pursuit**[48] 3946 3-9-0 0 MatthewCosham(3) 9
(Edward Bevan) *s.s: outpcd* **100/1**

1m 27.84s (3.24) **Going Correction** +0.275s/f (Good)
WFA 3 from 4yo 5lb **11** Ran SP% **103.7**
Speed ratings (Par 103): **92,89,86,84,82 80,78,78,73,72 61**
Tote Swingers 1&2 £32.40, 2&3 £20.10, 1&3 £2.80 CSF £157.89 TOTE £5.20: £1.80, £11.30, £1.50; EX 141.40.
Owner Mrs Ian Pilkington **Bred** Grasshopper 2000 Ltd **Trained** Kingston Warren, Oxon

FOCUS
The going was changed to Good before this race. The time was slower than the first division of the 2yo maiden run over this trip earlier on the card, but that was almost certainly down to the conditions as the pace looked fairly sound. Fast Samurai, My Stroppy Poppy and Widow Flower were all withdrawn after refusing to go into the stalls. Deduct 5p in the £ under R4.

5688 LEAMINGTON FOOD AND DRINK FESTIVAL H'CAP (BETFAIR 10 FURLONG FLAT SERIES QUALIFIER) 1m 2f 188y
6:10 (6:10) (Class 4) (0-80,80) 3-Y-0+ **£5,175** (£1,540; £769 ; £384) **Stalls** Low

Form RPR
01-0 **1** **Mazeydd**[18] 5006 3 -9-5**80** ....[1] NeilCallan 12 95+
(Roger Varian) trckd ldr: led 2f out: shkn up over 1f out: rdn and edgd lft ins fnl f: styd on wl **2/1**[1]
5113 **2** 3 ½ **Consider Yourself (USA)**[13] 5218 5 -9-10**76** ....(p) WilliamCarson 7 85
(Anthony Carson) led: rdn and hdd 2f out: styd on same pce ins fnl f **10/1**
3410 **3** 9 **Incendiary (IRE)**[25] 4741 3 -9-2**77** .... MichaelHills 1 70
(Hugo Palmer) chsd ldrs: rdn over 2f out: wknd over 1f out **11/4**[2]
0005 **4** ½ **Toughness Danon**[14] 5151 6 -8-13**70** .... DavidKenny(5) 11 62
(Brendan Powell) hld up: rdn over 2f out: nvr nrr **20/1**
-034 **5** 2 ¾ **Significant Move**[25] 4732 5 -9-9**75** ....(tp) FergusSweeney 9 62
(Stuart Kittow) hld up: racd keenly: hdwy over 5f out: rdn over 2f out: sn wknd **5/1**[3]
4263 **6** 3 ½ **Tilsworth Glenboy**[14] 5159 5 -9-11**77** .... PatDobbs 6 58
(J R Jenkins) s.i.s: hld up: a in rr **7/1**
4501 **7** 6 **Bold Cross (IRE)**[13] 5199 9 -8-10**65** .... MatthewCosham(3) 8 35
(Edward Bevan) prom: rdn over 3f out: wknd over 2f out: hung lft over 1f out **18/1**
0040 **8** 5 **Glass Mountain (IRE)**[7] 5417 4 -9-6**72** .... StevieDonohoe 4 33
(Ian Williams) s.i.s: hld up: rdn over 2f out: sn wknd **20/1**

2m 33.68s (12.58) **Going Correction** +0.275s/f (Good)
WFA 3 from 4yo+ 9lb 8Ran SP% **113.0**
Speed ratings (Par 105): **65,62,55,55,53 51,46,43**
Tote Swingers 1&2 £4.10, 2&3 £4.90, 1&3 £2.20 CSF £22.60 CT £53.99 TOTE £3.60 : £2.10 , £2.20, £1.10 ; EX 17.70 .
Owner Sheikh Ahmed Al Maktoum **Bred** Darley **Trained** Newmarket, Suffolk

FOCUS
Four late non-runners meant the field was reduced to eight for this competitive handicap. The early pace was slow and very few got into it. The winning time was 18 seconds below standard. The winner built on his reappearance promise.
T/Plt: £58.20 to a £1 stake. Pool £34,784.96 - 436.29 winning units. T/Qpdt: £13.80 to a £1 stake. Pool £2,085.06 - 111.35 w. units CR 5689a - 5696a (Foreign Racing) See RI

5648 DEAUVILLE (R-H)
Monday, August 27
OFFICIAL GOING: Turf: good; fibresand: standard

5697a PRIX DE VALSEME (CLAIMER) (2YO FILLIES) (FIBRESAND) 6f 110y
4:40 (12:00) 2-Y-0 **£11,250** (£4,500; £3,375 ; £2,250 ; £1,125)

RPR
1 **Nahima (CAN)**[8] 2 -8-10**0** .... MarcLerner(6) 1
(L A Urbano-Grajales, France) **78/10**
2 ½ **Atora Bere (FR)**[6] 2 -9-0**0** .... GeraldMosse 13 76
(M Boutin, France) **23/10**[1]
3 shd **Tourtour (FR)**[8] 2 -8-10**0** ow1 ....(p) ChristopheSoumillon 14 72
(C Boutin, France) **5/1**[3]
4 ¾ **Mesha Dream (FR)**[6] 2 -8-9**0** ....(p) TheoBachelot 6 69
(S Wattel, France) **21/1**
5 hd **Real Tiara (FR)**[7] 2 -8-13**0** .... SebastienMaillot 3 72
(Robert Collet, France) **16/1**
6 1 ½ **City Chope (FR)**[6] 2 -8-6**0** .... AntoineCoutier(3) 10 64
(Y Durepaire, Spain) **4/1**[2]
7 1 ½ **Black Whip (IRE)**[7] 2 -8-6**0** .... AlexisAchard(3) 9 60
(Mlle M Henry, France) **24/1**
8 1 **My Glitters (FR)**[4] 2 -8-9**0** .... AnthonyCrastus 2 57
(P Demercastel, France) **13/1**
9 1 **Solvanna**[14] 5146 2 -8-9**0** .... MatthieuAutier(4) 7 59
(Heather Main) broke wl: racd in cl 2nd to 1/2-way: relegated to 3rd bef st: rdn 2f out: nt qckn: styd on fnl f: nt hrd rdn fnl 100yds **18/1**
10 10 **Sakina (FR)**[8] 2 -8-6**0** .... EddyHardouin(3) 12 27
(P Demercastel, France) **24/1**
0 **Darat Al Ayam (FR)**[108] 2 -8-9**0** .... RonanThomas 4
(R Pritchard-Gordon, France) **30/1**
0 **Austerity (FR)** 2 -8-9**0** .... WilliamsSaraiva 11
(Mme J Bidgood, France) **30/1**
0 **Swiftsure (FR)** 2 -8-9**0** .... FlavienPrat 5
(J-V Toux, France) **62/1**

1m 20.7s (80.70) 13Ran SP% **117.2**
WIN (incl. 1 euro stake): 8.80. PLACES: 2.30, 1.60, 1.90. DF: 11.40. SF: 28.60 .
Owner Jean-Pierre-Joseph Dubois **Bred** Dream With Me Stable Inc **Trained** Pau, France

5698a PRIX DE VALMONT (CLAIMER) (2YO COLTS & GELDINGS) (FIBRESAND) 6f 110y
5:45 (12:00) 2-Y-0 **£11,250** (£4,500; £3,375 ; £2,250 ; £1,125)

RPR
1 **Kalicamix**[17] 5073 2 -9-6**0** .... OlivierPeslier 4 88
(Paul Cole) broke fast: racd in cl 2nd: qcknd to ld early in st 2 1/2f out: sn wnt clr: drew away ins fnl f: easily **33/10**[2]
2 3 **Gottingen (FR)**[17] 5073 2 -8-4**0** .... MatthieuAutier(5) 2 69
(J-C Rouget, France) **63/10**
3 hd **Freestyler (FR)**[9] 5378 2 -8-13**0** .... MaximeGuyon 3 72
(C Boutin, France) **44/5**
4 2 **The Stomp (FR)**[16] 2 -8-10**0** ow1 .... ChristopheSoumillon 5 64
(D Guillemin, France) **9/2**[3]
5 hd **Pont Marie (FR)**[17] 5073 2 -8-13**0** ....(b) GregoryBenoist 7 66
(F Chappet, France) **11/2**
6 nk **Green Medi (FR)**[16] 2 -8-13**0** ....(b) StephanePasquier 9 65
(Y Durepaire, Spain) **14/5**[1]
7 1 ½ **Secret Taboo (FR)**[9] 5378 2 -8-4**0** .... EddyHardouin(3) 1 57
(Robert Collet, France) **34/1**
8 5 **Litian Rocket (FR)**[17] 5073 2 -8-7**0** .... ThibaultSpeicher(7) 10 48
(M Boutin, France) **24/1**
9 1 **King's Risk (FR)**[36] 2 -9-2**0** .... Christophe-PatriceLemaire 6 48
(T Castanheira, France) **16/1**
10 8 **Prince Eliot (FR)**[9] 5378 2 -8-9**0** ....(b) GeraldMosse 5 19
(M Boutin, France) **31/1**

1m 19.2s (79.20) 10Ran SP% **122.9**
WIN (incl. 1 euro stake): 4.30. PLACES: 2.00, 2.10, 3.00. DF: 15.40. 39.20 .
Owner P F I Cole Ltd **Bred** Whatton Manor Stud **Trained** Whatcombe, Oxon

NOTEBOOK
Kalicamix, who had today's runner-up in third when winning a similar contest earlier in the month, confirmed the form despite being worse off at the weights. He loves the surface and is going the right way.

5699 - 5700a (Foreign Racing) - See Raceform Interactive

LES LANDES
Monday, August 27
OFFICIAL GOING: Good

5701a TOT LE PENNEC MEMORIAL H'CAP 5f 100y
3:05 (3:25) 3-Y-0+ **£1,270** (£460; £270)

RPR
1 **Copper Falls**[13] 5191 3 -8-7 .... JoshBaudains 1 48
(Brendan Powell) **1/5**[1]
2 hd **Spanish Bounty**[15] 7 -10-12 .... MattieBatchelor 7 79
(Mrs A Malzard, Jersey) **15/8**[2]
3 3 ½ **Nordic Light (USA)**[29] 8 -8-5 .... JemmaMarshall 9 32
(Mrs A Malzard, Jersey) **10/1**
4 hd **High Voltage**[15] 11 -8-13 ow3 ....(tp) JamieGoldstein 3 39
(Mrs J L Le Brocq, Jersey) **4/1**
5 3 ½ **Toggle**[29] 8 -8-5 ....(p) SophieDoyle 2 20
(Mrs A Corson, Jersey) **15/2**
6 ½ **Fast Freddie**[15] 8 -9-6 ow3 ....(b) MarkLawson 4 33
(Mrs A Corson, Jersey) **9/4**[3]
7 10 **Top Pursuit**[15] 10 -8-5 ....(v) AshlieRidings 6
(Mrs A Corson, Jersey) **9/1**

1m 8.0s (-1.00)
WFA 3 from 5yo+ 2lb 7Ran SP% **109.7**

Owner Mrs P Banfield **Bred** P Banfield **Trained** Upper Lambourn, Berks

5661 EPSOM (L-H)
Tuesday, August 28
OFFICIAL GOING: Good (8.3)
Wind: fresh, across Weather: dry

5702 JRA NURSERY 7f
2:15 (2:17) (Class 5) (0-75,71) 2-Y-0 **£3,881** (£1,155; £577 ; £288) **Stalls** Low

Form RPR
5220 **1** **New Falcon (IRE)**[15] 5155 2 -9-7**71** ....(p) IanMongan 2 78
(James Tate) chsd ldrs: effrt to chse ldr ent fnl 2f: drvn to chal 1f out: led fnl 100yds: r.o wl **7/1**
0303 **2** 1 ¾ **Wellingrove (IRE)**[15] 5178 2 -9-5**69** .... NeilCallan 4 71
(Mark Johnston) t.k.h: chsd ldr tl led 4f out: rdn ent fnl 2f: clr w wnr ent fnl f: hdd and no ex fnl 100yds **7/2**[2]
305 **3** 3 ¼ **Something Magic**[10] 5357 2 -9-7**71** .... JamesDoyle 1 65
(Sylvester Kirk) led tl 4f out: rdn and unable qck jst over 2f out: 3rd and plugged on same pce fr over 1f out **10/1**
000 **4** 1 ½ **Romanoff (IRE)**[32] 4539 2 -9-0**64** .... KierenFallon 7 54
(Luca Cumani) stdd s: t.k.h: hld up in last pair: swtchd rt 4f out: rdn and effrt 3f out: styd on same pce and no imp fr over 1f out **4/1**[3]
0461 **5** 1 ¾ **Vino Collapso (IRE)**[9] 5009 2 -9-4**68** .... JimmyFortune 5 53
(James Given) wnt rt s: chsd ldrs: rdn and unable qck over 2f out: wl hld and one pce fr over 1f out **5/1**
060 **6** 2 ¼ **Epsom Flyer**[47] 3996 2 -8-1**56** .... JemmaMarshall(5) 3 34
(Pat Phelan) in tch in last trio: rdn and effrt over 3f out: no prog and wknd 2f out **20/1**
042 **D** nk **Lisa's Legacy**[16] 5121 2 -9-5**69** .... RichardHughes 6 53
(Richard Hannon) dwlt and short of room s: in rr: pushed along over 3f out: no imp and wl hld whn edgd lft 1f out: nvr trbld ldrs **3/1**[1]

1m 23.44s (0.14) **Going Correction** -0.15s/f (Firm) 7Ran SP% **110.2**
Speed ratings (Par 94): **93,91,87,85,83 80,83**
Tote Swingers 1&2 £3.50, 2&3 £5.50, 1&3 £7.70 CSF £29.28 TOTE £9.00 : £3.00 , £1.90 ; EX 33.90.
Owner Saeed Manana **Bred** Rabbah Bloodstock Limited **Trained** Newmarket, Suffolk

FOCUS
Rail at inner configuration and all distances as advertised. The first pair came right away in this modest nursery as those off the pace struggled to get involved. The runner-up helps to set the level.

NOTEBOOK
New Falcon (IRE)flopped on her nursery debut at Kempton over 1m last time, but her previous form entitled her to plenty of respect in this company and she bounced back with the aid of first-time cheekpieces. She took time to settle, but was well placed throughout and no doubt the headgear helped her cause when locking horns with the runner-up nearing the final furlong. Life will be tougher once she's reassessed. (tchd 6-1)
Wellingrove(IRE) helped force the pace and he posed another gutsy effort on this return to turf, rating a sound benchmark. He was a clear second-best and deserves to land something similar. (op 10-3 tchd 3-1)
Something Magic, despite stepping back up in trip, was aggressively ridden on this switch to a nursery. She was under pressure at the top of the home straight and looks to have begun life in this sphere weighted near her best, but got the trip fine so it's something she may be able to build on. (op 8-1 tchd 12-1)
Romanoff(IRE) had shown very little in three maidens previously, but is from a shrewd outfit and met support for this nursery debut. He proved keen early, but looked a danger wide of runners after straightening for home. The response under pressure was most limited, however, and perhaps the track wasn't for him. (tchd 7-2)
Vino Collapso (IRE)got off the mark on his AW/nursery debut at Southwell 19 days earlier, making him the only one here to have previously scored, and was up 3lb. He looked all at sea in the home straight on this tricky course and shouldn't be judged too harshly. (op 7-1)

Lisa's Legacy seemed sure to enjoy the extra furlong on this nursery debut and his top yard was bidding for a hat-trick in the race. However, he was again outpaced from the start and, while he looked uneasy in the home straight, this was very disappointing. (tchd 10-3)

5703 JOHN AKEHURST H'CAP 6f

2:50 (2:51) (Class 4) (0-85,84) 3-Y-O+ **£6,469** (£1,925; £962; £481) **Stalls** High

Form	Pos	Dist	Horse / Details	RPR
0060	1		**Sacrosanctus**[10] 5368 4-9-10 **84** ... IanMongan 9 (Scott Dixon) *mde all: wnt clr over 3f out: rdn and styd on wl fnl 2f* **8/1**[3]	96
-261	2	3 ¾	**Signor Sassi**[10] 5340 3-9-1 **78** ... NeilCallan 1 (Roger Varian) *chsd ldng trio: effrt to chse clr wnr and swtchd rt ent fnl 2f: kpt on but no imp* **9/4**[1]	78+
2006	3	½	**Avonmore Star**[18] 5035 4-9-4 **78** ... PatDobbs 12 (Richard Hannon) *hld up off the pce in last quartet: hdwy and swtchd rt over 1f out: styd on strly ins fnl f: snatched 3rd on post: nvr trbld ldrs* **20/1**	76
0010	4	nse	**Perfect Pastime**[24] 4824 4-9-7 **81** ...(p) SebSanders 14 (Jim Boyle) *chsd ldrs: rdn and no imp on wnr ent fnl 2f: kpt on same pce after: lost 3rd on post* **16/1**	79
6201	5	1 ½	**Clear Praise (USA)**[16] 5123 5-9-5 **79** ... JimmyFortune 7 (Simon Dow) *taken down early: hld up in midfield: effrt on inner over 2f out: styd on same pce and no threat to wnr fnl f* **12/1**	72
0404	6	½	**Aldermoor (USA)**[7] 5457 6-8-13 **73** ...(v) WilliamCarson 3 (Stuart Williams) *in tch: rdn and unable qck over 2f out: one pce and no threat to wnr fnl 2f* **17/2**	65
0101	7	2 ½	**Pick A Little**[13] 5245 4-9-0 **77** ... RyanClark(3) 2 (Brian Ellison) *in tch in midfield: pushed along 3f out: sn outpcd and wl hld fnl 2f* **10/1**	61
0000	8	½	**We Have A Dream**[18] 5035 7-9-1 **75** ... JamesDoyle 10 (William Muir) *chsd wnr tl ent fnl 2f: sn outpcd and btn: wknd fnl f* **14/1**	57
0210	9	½	**Orders From Rome (IRE)**[10] 5363 3-8-12 **80** ... AmyScott(5) 6 (Eve Johnson Houghton) *bhd: unbalanced on downhill run over 4f out: sme modest hdwy ins fnl f: n.d* **7/1**[2]	61
10	10	1 ¼	**Impel (IRE)**[36] 4412 3-9-4 **81** ... RichardHughes 11 (Richard Hannon) *stdd after s: pushed along and no real hdwy over 2f out: n.d* **20/1**	58
0501	11	1	**Medici Time**[10] 5362 7-9-10 **84** ...(v) EddieAhern 4 (Tim Easterby) *a towards rr: rdn and no hdwy wl over 2f out: n.d* **8/1**[3]	57
4242	12	1 ¾	**Ryan Style (IRE)**[19] 5020 6-8-11 **71** ...(v) KierenFallon 13 (Lisa Williamson) *t.k.h: hld up in midfield: rdn and struggling 3f out: wknd 2f out* **12/1**	39

1m 8.13s (-1.27) **Going Correction** -0.15s/f (Firm)
WFA 3 from 4yo+ 3lb **12** Ran SP% **122.6**
Speed ratings (Par 105): **102,97,96,96,94 93,90,89,88,87 85,83**
Tote Swingers 1&2 £6.60, 2&3 £14.20, 1&3 £37.30 CSF £27.12 CT £362.62 TOTE £9.40: £2.50, £1.70, £5.40; EX 34.60 TRIFECTA Not won. Rollover of £594.56 to Saturday 1st September..
Owner Paul J Dixon **Bred** Worksop Manor Stud **Trained** Babworth, Notts

FOCUS

This looked competitive, but the winner blew them away from the front and again it paid to race handy. The winner rates a length personal best.
Sacrosanctus Official explanation: trainer said, regarding apparent improvement in form, that the gelding was suited by being able to have an uncontested lead.

5704 BRITISH STALLION STUDS SUPPORTING BRITISH RACING EBF MAIDEN STKS 1m 114y

3:25 (3:27) (Class 5) 2-Y-O **£3,881** (£1,155; £577; £288) **Stalls** Low

Form	Pos	Dist	Horse / Details	RPR
203	1		**Royal Skies (IRE)**[40] 4253 2-9-3 78 ... KierenFallon 7 (Mark Johnston) *t.k.h: mde all: rdn jst over 2f out: clr ent fnl f: tiring fnl 75yds and jst hld on: all out* **7/2**[2]	77
2	2	shd	**Van Percy**[24] 4813 2-9-3 0 ... JimmyFortune 3 (Andrew Balding) *chsd ldrs and clr in ldng quartet 1/2-way: rdn to chse wnr over 1f out: drvn and styd on wl ins fnl f: jst failed* **15/8**[1]	77
65	3	5	**Empowerment (IRE)**[15] 5162 2-9-3 0 ... PatDobbs 8 (Richard Hannon) *chsd wnr: rdn over 2f out: lost 2nd: unable qck and edgd lft over 1f out: wknd ins fnl f* **16/1**	66
00	4	1 ½	**Felix Fabulla**[12] 5274 2-9-3 0 ... NickyMackay 5 (Hughie Morrison) *short of room and hmpd s: hld up in last pair: lost tch w ldrs 1/2-way: pushed along and wnt modest 5th 3f out: styd on steadily after: nvr trbld ldrs* **14/1**	62
04	5	2 ¾	**Roman Order (IRE)**[20] 4938 2-9-3 0 ... ShaneKelly 4 (Brian Meehan) *short of room and hmpd s: hld up in last pair: lost tch w ldrs 1/2-way: pushed along and wnt modest 6th over 2f out: no real imp after and nvr trbld ldrs* **6/1**	56
55	6	1 ¾	**Shamaheart (IRE)**[10] 5360 2-9-3 0 ... RichardHughes 2 (Richard Hannon) *chsd ldng pair: rdn jst over 2f out: stl pressing ldrs but struggling to qckn whn nt clr run and hmpd over 1f out: wknd fnl f* **9/2**[3]	53+
6	7	17	**Cape's Best**[28] 4677 2-9-3 0 ... IanMongan 6 (James Tate) *racd in midfield: outpcd by ldrs 1/2-way: dropped to rr over 3f out: bhd fnl 2f* **11/1**	15
	8	4	**Sunblazer (IRE)** 2-9-3 0 ... JamesDoyle 1 (William Muir) *in tch in midfield tl outpcd by ldrs 1/2-way: lost pl and bhd 3f out* **25/1**	6

1m 45.28s (-0.82) **Going Correction** -0.15s/f (Firm) **8** Ran SP% **114.2**
Speed ratings (Par 94): **97,96,92,91,88 87,72,68**
Tote Swingers 1&2 £2.20, 2&3 £7.50, 1&3 £7.10 CSF £10.44 TOTE £3.80: £1.10, £1.50, £4.40; EX 9.80 Trifecta £52.80 Pool: £1,001.43 - 14.01 winning units..
Owner Sheikh Hamdan Bin Mohammed Al Maktoum **Bred** P Moen **Trained** Middleham Moor, N Yorks

FOCUS

This staying maiden was the third straight race on the card where those racing handy dominated and it threw up a cracking finish. The winner is rated back to form and the third and fourth fit in.

NOTEBOOK

Royal Skies(IRE) just did enough to make all and open his account at the fourth attempt. He looked vulnerable throughout the final furlong, but kept responding and deserves extra credit as he proved somewhat free early on. He obviously stays well (plenty of stamina on dam's side of pedigree) and can be placed to strike in nursery company. (tchd 3-1 and 4-1 and 9-2 in a place)
Van Percy ◆ bumped into subsequent Acomb winner Dundonnell on his Lingfield debut 24 days earlier and was well fancied to go one better up in trip. He failed to handle the track and took time to settle, but still only just failed. He fully deserves to break his duck and should do so on a more conventional track. (op 2-1 tchd 9-4)
Empowerment(IRE) failed to see out the trip like the first pair, but proved best of the two from his yard and he now qualifies for a mark.
Felix Fabulla ◆ was set plenty to do from off the pace and it's fair to say he wasn't given at all a hard time when making up plenty of ground in the home straight. He's a deal better than the bare form and nurseries are now an option. (op 16-1)
Roman Order(IRE) was another not helped by being restrained in rear, but he still ran miles below par. Presumably something was amiss. (op 11-2 tchd 13-2)
Shamaheart(IRE) looked ready for a longer trip at Newmarket last time out, but this was a significantly stiffer test up from 6f. He was moving sweetly on the inside 3f out, but got no run and was eased off when his chance evaporated. A drop back to 7f can do the trick now he's eligible for nurseries. (tchd 4-1)
Sunblazer(IRE) Official explanation: trainer's rep said colt lost a near-fore shoe

5705 TERRY MILLS H'CAP 7f

3:55 (3:57) (Class 4) (0-80,79) 3-Y-O **£6,469** (£1,925; £962; £481) **Stalls** Low

Form	Pos	Dist	Horse / Details	RPR
6015	1		**Verse Of Love**[13] 5237 3-9-5 **77** ... CathyGannon 2 (David Evans) *mde all: rdn and qcknd 2f out: wnt clr over 1f out and in n.d fnl f: comf* **11/2**[2]	90
0315	2	5	**Elegant Flight**[19] 4996 3-8-6 **71** ...(v) MichaelJMMurphy(7) 4 (Alan Jarvis) *in tch in midfield: rdn over 2f out: sn outpcd and no ch w wnr over 1f out: rallied and styd on ins fnl f to go 2nd towards fin* **9/2**[1]	71
0150	3	¾	**Hometown Glory**[66] 3393 3-9-6 **78** ...(t) ShaneKelly 5 (Brian Meehan) *chsd wnr: rdn and outpcd 2f out: wl hld whn edgd lft ins fnl f: lost 2nd towards fin* **8/1**	75
3000	4	nk	**Beau Duke (IRE)**[31] 4607 3-8-6 **64** ... DavidProbert 3 (Andrew Balding) *in tch: effrt u.p to chse ldng pair 2f out: sn outpcd by wnr and btn: styng on same pce whn hmpd and edgd lft ins fnl f* **14/1**	61
2412	5	4	**Jack Of Diamonds (IRE)**[17] 5099 3-9-7 **79** ... JamesDoyle 8 (Roger Teal) *hld up in tch: rdn over 2f out: sn outpcd and btn: wl hld over 1f out* **13/2**	65+
3321	6	1	**Mayo Lad (IRE)**[16] 5132 3-9-7 **79** ... RichardHughes 9 (Richard Hannon) *led to post and taken down early: chsd ldrs: rdn and unable qck over 2f out: 5th and wl btn over 1f out: wknd* **9/2**[1]	62+
4151	7	1	**Lolita Lebron (IRE)**[4] 5545 3-9-2 **79** 6ex ... DarylByrne(5) 7 (Lawrence Mullaney) *sn detached in last pair: clsd and in tch 1/2-way: nt clr run briefly over 2f out: sn outpcd and wl btn over 1f out* **6/1**[3]	59
2531	8	shd	**Keyaadi**[19] 4992 3-9-6 **78** ... NeilCallan 1 (Roger Varian) *t.k.h: chsd ldrs: rdn and outpcd by wnr 2f out: plugging on same pce in 4th whn bdly hmpd and snatched up ins fnl f: eased after* **6/1**[3]	67
6	9	1 ¾	**Sweet Mystery (IRE)**[10] 5350 3-8-9 **67** ... RichardThomas 6 (David Evans) *stdd after s: sn detached in last pair: clsd and in tch 1/2-way: rdn over 2f out: sn struggling and wknd 2f out* **50/1**	42

1m 22.37s (-0.93) **Going Correction** -0.15s/f (Firm) **9** Ran SP% **113.4**
Speed ratings (Par 102): **99,93,92,92,87 86,85,85,83**
Tote Swingers 1&2 £5.70, 2&3 £7.20, 1&3 £9.90 CSF £29.85 CT £195.64 TOTE £8.10: £3.20, £1.80, £3.20; EX 39.80 Trifecta £285.40 Pool: £983.62 - 2.55 winning units..
Owner Wayne Clifford **Bred** Mrs S Clifford **Trained** Pandy, Monmouths

FOCUS

A competitive-looking 3-y-o handicap. The pace bias played its part again, however, and there was yet another winner from the front. The form has been rated a bit cautiously.
Lolita Lebron(IRE) Official explanation: trainer said filly suffered from having a difficult journey to the racecourse previous evening.
Keyaadi Official explanation: jockey said gelding suffered interference and lost its action

5706 HAPPY RETIREMENT HOWARD WRIGHT H'CAP 1m 4f 10y

4:30 (4:32) (Class 5) (0-75,74) 3-Y-O+ **£4,528** (£1,347; £673; £336) **Stalls** Centre

Form	Pos	Dist	Horse / Details	RPR
1453	1		**Enery (IRE)**[14] 5211 3-9-1 **71** ... NeilCallan 8 (Mark Johnston) *chsd ldr for 2f: wnt 2nd again over 5f out tl rdn to ld over 3f out: kpt finding ex u.p: strly pressed fnl 100yds: hld on gamely: all out* **9/2**[3]	81
1-04	2	nk	**Novirak (IRE)**[40] 4249 4-9-12 **72** ... EddieAhern 11 (James Fanshawe) *hld up in tch in midfield: hdwy to trck ldrs 4f out: hanging lft down camber and swtchd rt 2f out: sn drvn and hdwy to chal fnl 100yds: no ex and hld towards fin* **11/2**	81
1044	3	1	**Twelve Strings (IRE)**[42] 4199 3-9-4 **74** ... KierenFallon 5 (Luca Cumani) *stdd s: hld up in rr: pushed along 7f out: hdwy u.p over 1f out: styng on and swtchd lft ins fnl f: gng on fin but nvr gng to rch ldrs* **7/2**[1]	82+
-124	4	½	**Reggie Perrin**[47] 3997 4-9-3 **63** ...(v) IanMongan 6 (Pat Phelan) *in tch in midfield: rdn along briefly 8f out: rdn to chse ldrs over 3f out: drvn 2f out: kpt on same pce ins fnl f* **8/1**	70
0-00	5	1 ¼	**Baan (USA)**[26] 4722 9-8-8 **61** ... RyanTate(7) 3 (James Eustace) *pushed along early: racd in last trio: rdn 3f out: hdwy over 1f out: styng on whn carried lft ins fnl f: kpt on but nvr gng pce to rch ldrs* **25/1**	66
4133	6	4 ½	**Seven Veils (IRE)**[20] 4972 3-9-4 **74** ... JamesDoyle 10 (Sir Mark Prescott Bt) *taken down early: in tch in midfield: rdn and hdwy to chse ldrs 5f out: ev ch 3f out tl over 1f out: lost 2nd 1f out and sn btn: eased towards fin* **4/1**[2]	74+
3125	7	3 ¾	**Jane Lachatte (IRE)**[4] 5533 3-9-4 **74** ... WilliamCarson 2 (Stuart Williams) *dwlt: sn rcvrd to chse ldrs: rdn 3f out: keeping on same pce and hld whn hmpd ins fnl f: eased and swtchd rt after* **10/1**	76+
0-00	8	9	**Jacobs Son**[56] 2863 4-9-10 **70** ...(b[1]) SeanLevey 1 (Robert Mills) *led: clr 9f out tl over 4f out: rdn and hdd over 3f out: sn struggling: wl bhd over 1f out* **25/1**	47
2031	9	4 ½	**Mount Abora (IRE)**[11] 5310 5-8-11 **64** ... CharlotteJenner(7) 4 (Laura Mongan) *chsd ldrs: wnt 2nd after 2f tl over 5f out: lost pl and struggling over 3f out: wl bhd over 1f out* **14/1**	34
6004	10	4	**Chemistry Master**[21] 4915 4-9-3 **63** ... JimmyFortune 7 (Jeremy Gask) *hld up in rr: pushed along 5f out: rdn and no hdwy 3f out: wl bhd over 1f out* **20/1**	27

2m 38.47s (-0.43) **Going Correction** -0.15s/f (Firm)
WFA 3 from 4yo+ 10lb **10** Ran SP% **115.1**
Speed ratings (Par 103): **95,94,94,93,92 89,87,81,78,75**
Tote Swingers 1&2 £4.30, 2&3 £4.60, 1&3 £3.10 CSF £28.21 CT £94.35 TOTE £5.70: £1.80, £1.30, £2.10; EX 31.70 Trifecta £154.70 Pool: £1,264.85 - 6.05 winning units..
Owner Sheikh Hamdan Bin Mohammed Al Maktoum **Bred** Ceka Ireland Limited **Trained** Middleham Moor, N Yorks

■ Stewards' Enquiry : Kieren Fallon three-day ban: careless riding (Sep 11-13)

FOCUS
A modest handicap. It was run at a decent pace and proved an eventful race. The bare form is ordinary but the first two look interesting.

5707 RACING POST WEEKENDER OUT EVERY WEDNESDAY H'CAP (BETFAIR 10 FURLONG FLAT SERIES QUALIFIER) 1m 2f 18y
5:00 (5:08) (Class 5) (0-75,75) 3-Y-0+ **£3,881** (£1,155; £577; £288) **Stalls** Low

Form RPR
2436 **1** **Debating Society (IRE)**[41] 4224 3-9-5 **74** NeilCallan 8 89+
(Sir Michael Stoute) *in tch in midfield: hdwy to chse ldrs over 3f out: clsd smoothly to ld 2f out: rdn over 1f out: u.p but a doing enough ins fnl f: eased cl home* **3/1**[1]
-025 **2** *1* **Looking On**[12] 5268 4-9-12 **73** DaneO'Neill 3 84
(Henry Candy) *hld up in last quartet: effrt u.p and wnt 5th ent fnl 2f: styd on wl ins fnl f: chsd wnr wl ins fnl f: kpt on but nvr looked like getting to wnr* **11/1**
2221 **3** *½* **Miss Cap Estel**[15] 5147 3-9-6 **75** DavidProbert 7 85
(Andrew Balding) *in tch in midfield: rdn to chse ldrs 2f out: kpt on wl u.p ins fnl f but nvr looked like rching wnr* **7/2**[2]
3051 **4** *¾* **If I Were A Boy (IRE)**[8] 5417 5-8-9 **63** (p) JoshBaudains(7) 5 71
(Dominic Ffrench Davis) *pressed ldr after 1f: clr w ldr 7f out: led 5f out tl rdn and hdd 2f out: styd on same pce fr over 1f out: lost 2 pls wl ins fnl f* **6/1**[3]
0250 **5** *5* **Coup De Grace (IRE)**[33] 4504 3-7-13 **58** ow1 JemmaMarshall(5) 12 57
(Pat Phelan) *chsd ldr for 1f: chsd ldng pair tl rdn to chse ldr again over 3f out tl 2f out: wknd over 1f out* **14/1**
-336 **6** *6* **Ice Nelly (IRE)**[26] 4733 4-9-6 **67** JimmyFortune 10 53
(Hughie Morrison) *s.i.s: bhd: rdn and effrt 3f out: no real prog: n.d* **10/1**
-560 **7** *nse* **Operettist**[59] 3643 3-9-3 **72** RichardHughes 4 58
(Richard Hannon) *in tch in midfield: rdn and effrt 3f out: 6th and btn 2f out: wknd* **14/1**
2123 **8** *8* **Welsh Nayber**[7] 5441 3-8-11 **66** (v[1]) PatDobbs 1 36
(Amanda Perrett) *hld up in last quartet: rdn and no hdwy over 3f out: wl bhd fnl 2f* **9/1**
44-P **9** *8* **Misk Khitaam (USA)**[102] 2233 4-9-8 **69** EddieAhern 6 23
(John Dunlop) *a in rr: lost tch over 2f out* **25/1**
6105 **10** *17* **Understory (USA)**[60] 3574 5-9-9 **73** SophieDoyle(3) 9
(Tim McCarthy) *led tl 5f out: lost pl 3f out: t.o fnl f* **25/1**

2m 7.34s (-2.36) **Going Correction** -0.15s/f (Firm)
WFA 3 from 4yo+ 8lb **10** Ran SP% **110.0**
Speed ratings (Par 103): **103,102,101,101,97 92,92,85,79,65**
Tote Swingers 1&2 £7.90, 2&3 £7.40, 1&3 £3.10 CSF £32.97 CT £101.03 TOTE £3.40: £1.80, £3.30, £1.10; EX 42.90 Trifecta £474.30 Pool: £942.28 - 1.47 winning units..
Owner Ballymacoll Stud **Bred** Ballymacoll Stud Farm Ltd **Trained** Newmarket, Suffolk
■ Wise Venture was withdrawn (10/1, reluctant to go to post). Deduct 5p in the £ under R4.
■ Stewards' Enquiry : Josh Baudains two-day ban: used whip above permitted level (Sep 11-12)

FOCUS
Not a bad handicap for the grade. They went a solid pace and the first five dominated. The winner rates a bit better than the bare form.
T/Plt: £75.70 to a £1 stake. Pool: £72,718.13 - 701.12 winning tickets T/Qpdt: £12.20 to a £1 stake. Pool: £5,543.59 - 334.56 winning tickets SP

5675 RIPON (R-H)
Tuesday, August 28

OFFICIAL GOING: Soft (5.9)
Wind: moderate 1/2 behind Weather: fine

5708 RIPON-RACES.CO.UK (S) STKS 1m 1f 170y
2:00 (2:01) (Class 6) 3-4-Y-0 **£2,045** (£603; £302) **Stalls** Low

Form RPR
-414 **1** **Future Wonder (IRE)**[19] 5018 3-8-5 62 ow1 PaulPickard(3) 8 58
(Brian Ellison) *hld up towards rr: smooth hdwy 3f out: led on bit appr fnl f: shkn up and edgd rt: drvn clr clsng stages* **13/8**[1]
60-4 **2** *3 ¼* **Spin A Wish**[51] 3889 4-9-1 47 AmyRyan 9 53
(Richard Whitaker) *swtchd rt after s: led: hdd appr fnl f: 1/2 l down and hld whn hmpd last 50yds* **15/2**
0-05 **3** *½* **Valentine's Gift**[38] 4349 4-9-6 44 DuranFentiman 5 54
(Neville Bycroft) *chsd ldr: drvn over 3f out: styd on same pce over 1f out* **16/1**
3604 **4** *10* **Avison (IRE)**[15] 5175 4-9-6 55 PaulHanagan 1 33
(Richard Fahey) *mid-div: effrt over 4f out: one pce fnl 3f* **3/1**[2]
0504 **5** *1* **Deep Applause**[17] 5114 4-9-5 42 ConnorNichol(7) 10 37
(Michael Dods) *mid-div: t.k.h: hung rt over 2f out: one pce* **12/1**
6000 **6** *11* **Airmyles**[15] 5171 4-9-6 47 PatrickMathers 13
(Tracy Waggott) *t.k.h in rr: sme hdwy over 2f out: sn wknd* **66/1**
00- **7** *8* **Petrol**[305] 7133 3-8-12 0 DanielTudhope 11
(David O'Meara) *s.i.s: in rr: drvn 4f out: nvr a factor: eased fnl f* **11/2**[3]
2305 **8** *4* **Bond Style**[17] 5113 3-8-12 57 (e) TomEaves 4
(Bryan Smart) *s.i.s: in rr and reminders 4f out: sn bhd* **12/1**
6000 **9** *9* **Cathcart Castle**[5] 5054 4-9-5 46 (v) ShirleyTeasdale(7) 14
(Simon West) *chsd ldrs: lost pl over 3f out: sn bhd* **40/1**
0 **10** *20* **Lady Ongar**[11] 5316 4-9-1 0 JamesSullivan 3
(Alan Kirtley) *chsd ldrs: lost pl 4f out: sn bhd: t.o 2f out* **100/1**

2m 9.81s (4.41) **Going Correction** +0.50s/f (Yiel)
WFA 3 from 4yo 8lb **10** Ran SP% **116.4**
Speed ratings (Par 101): **102,99,99,91,90 81,75,71,64,48**
Tote Swingers 1&2 £3.80, 2&3 £16.40, 1&3 £7.10 CSF £14.74 TOTE £2.90: £1.50, £2.30, £4.60; EX 13.30.The winner was bought in for 3,200gns.
Owner L S Keys **Bred** Peter Thome **Trained** Norton, N Yorks

FOCUS
Rail at inner configuration and all distances as advertised. A poor seller, run at a steady pace. The winner only had to run to form.

5709 TOTESWINGER FILLIES' MAIDEN AUCTION STKS 5f
2:30 (2:32) (Class 5) 2-Y-0 **£2,587** (£770; £384; £192) **Stalls** High

Form RPR
0242 **1** **Balinka**[10] 5367 2-8-4 68 SilvestreDeSousa 7 65
(Mel Brittain) *mde all: drvn and edgd rt fnl f: styd on to forge clr last 50yds* **5/6**[1]
2 *2* **Pastureyes** 2-8-4 0 JamesSullivan 6 58
(Scott Dixon) *chsd ldrs: kpt on to take 2nd last 50yds* **33/1**
5252 **3** *1 ¼* **Twilight Pearl**[24] 4806 2-8-7 58 DuranFentiman 1 56
(Tim Easterby) *chsd wnr: drvn 2f out: kpt on same pce* **11/2**[2]
4 *1 ¼* **Next Door (IRE)** 2-8-7 0 GrahamGibbons 3 52+
(David Barron) *s.s: in rr: sme hdwy and edgd rt over 1f out: kpt on fnl f* **8/1**
03 **5** *2* **Storma Norma**[13] 5222 2-8-11 0 DavidAllan 8 49
(Tim Easterby) *outpcd and in rr: nvr a factor* **14/1**
6 *½* **Myanne** 2-8-7 0 PaulMulrennan 2 43
(Ann Duffield) *dwlt: swtchd outside and hdwy over 2f out: chsng ldrs over 1f out: wknd last 150yds: will do bttr* **6/1**[3]
6 **7** *10* **Tartania**[13] 5242 2-8-1 0 DeclanCannon(3) 5 4
(Scott Dixon) *mid-div: lost pl over 2f out: sn bhd* **12/1**

1m 2.42s (1.72) **Going Correction** +0.325s/f (Good) **7** Ran SP% **112.6**
Speed ratings (Par 91): **99,96,93,91,88 87,71**
Tote Swingers 1&2 £8.30, 2&3 £13.30, 1&3 £1.90 CSF £32.16 TOTE £1.80: £1.20, £9.80; EX 22.90.
Owner Northgate Grey **Bred** Overbury Stallions Ltd **Trained** Warthill, N Yorks

FOCUS
A weak maiden auction, run at a fair pace. Straightforward form.

NOTEBOOK
Balinka, who was going one better than over an extra furlong here last time, was heavily supported. She put her experience to good use by claiming the rail and never really looked in any danger, despite racing a shade lazily. Her mind was made up for her as they entered the last 2f and she drew steadily clear to win going away. She probably only needed to repeat her previous form to win this and it's likely she'll have to improve if she's going to be competitive in nurseries. She was looking around in the final furlong and could be the ideal type for headgear. (op Evens)
Pastureyes ran with credit on this debut and should be wiser for the experience. She knuckled down well late on and might be able to pick up a small race before the season is out. (op 20-1)
Twilight Pearl is proving disappointing and looks to be going the wrong way. She was under pressure a long way out and didn't appear to be helping her rider. (op 9-2)
Next Door(IRE) plugged on past beaten horses and there was some encouragement to be gleaned from this. She's entitled to come on from this and may appreciate another furlong. (op 10-1 tchd 11-1)
Myanne weakened quickly but could improve. (op 8-1 tchd 17-2)
Tartania looks to have regressed since running with some promise on her debut at Southwell. (op 14-1 tchd 10-1)

5710 SIS LIVE NURSERY 6f
3:05 (3:05) (Class 4) (0-85,85) 2-Y-0 **£3,881** (£1,155; £577; £288) **Stalls** High

Form RPR
012 **1** **Silver Ridge (IRE)**[60] 3562 2-9-7 **85** RichardKingscote 4 87+
(Ralph Beckett) *chsd ldrs: drvn over 2f out: led appr fnl f: kpt on wl* **6/4**[1]
U334 **2** *1 ½* **Rated**[18] 5060 2-9-0 **78** SamHitchcott 3 77
(Mick Channon) *half-rrd s: t.k.h: trckd ldrs after 2f: effrt and nt clr run over 1f out: swtchd rt: hung lft ins fnl f: styd on wl to take 2nd post* **15/2**
2100 **3** *shd* **Sharaarah (IRE)**[32] 4526 2-9-0 **78** PaulHanagan 2 75
(Ed Dunlop) *chsd ldrs: effrt over 2f out: kpt on same pce last 150yds* **3/1**[3]
4136 **4** *2 ½* **Rat Catcher (IRE)**[24] 4827 2-8-11 **75** (b) DavidAllan 1 65
(Tim Easterby) *swtchd lft after s: led: hdd appr fnl f: sn wknd* **20/1**
5403 **5** *¾* **Tatlisu (IRE)**[31] 4614 2-9-2 **80** (p) TonyHamilton 6 67
(Richard Fahey) *chsd ldrs: effrt over 2f out: wknd fnl f* **11/4**[2]

1m 15.52s (2.52) **Going Correction** +0.325s/f (Good) **5** Ran SP% **108.2**
Speed ratings (Par 96): **96,94,93,90,89**
CSF £12.45 TOTE £3.10: £1.50, £3.20; EX 6.90.
Owner The Pickford Hill Partnership **Bred** Ballykilbride Stud **Trained** Kimpton, Hants

FOCUS
An interesting, if only small-field nursery, run at a decent pace. The bare form is straightforward.

NOTEBOOK
Silver Ridge(IRE) gained a hard-fought success on his return from a two-month break. The grey, who had made all of the running when winning easily on the AW at Wolverhampton in June, could never get to the early lead on this occasion but responded gamely for pressure and was eventually well on top at the line. He may have found the ground just a bit too quick for him when beaten at Doncaster previously and the style in which he stayed on up the hill suggests he'll be even more effective once tackling 7f. He may also be more at home on a flatter track, having changed his legs on a couple of occasions when meeting the rising ground. (tchd 11-8 and 13-8)
Rated ran an eyecatching race and would almost certainly have finished closer had he not been short of room for much of the last 2f. He picked up well once finding daylight and ought to be able to pick up a small race in similar conditions in the coming weeks. (op 6-1)
Sharaarah(IRE) was far from disgraced but looks in the grip of the handicapper. She was dropped 4lb following her lacklustre showing at Ascot but may require a bit more assistance if she's going to add to her earlier Kempton victory. (op 4-1 tchd 11-4)
Rat Catcher(IRE) raced freely and failed to last home, but would be of interest if returning to 5f. (op 12-1)
Tatlisu(IRE) never figured and has questions to answer on the back of this. (tchd 7-2)

5711 SAPPER CONDITIONS STKS 5f
3:40 (3:41) (Class 3) 2-Y-0 **£5,670** (£1,697; £848; £424) **Stalls** High

Form RPR
51 **1** **Girl At The Sands (IRE)**[13] 5242 2-8-13 71 GrahamLee 2 71
(James Given) *chsd ldrs: effrt over 2f out: styd on fnl f: led nr fin* **5/1**[3]
051 **2** *½* **Tumblewind**[13] 5222 2-8-11 67 AmyRyan 3 67
(Richard Whitaker) *w ldr: led wl over 1f out: wknd and hdd towards fin* **4/1**[2]
31 **3** *shd* **Stand Of Glory (USA)**[15] 5168 2-9-4 77 PaulHanagan 4 74
(David Simcock) *led: rdn and hdd wl over 1f out: rdr dropped reign appr fnl f: rallied last 100yds* **4/6**[1]
4 *1 ¾* **A J Cook (IRE)** 2-8-11 0 GrahamGibbons 1 62+
(David Barron) *dwlt and jinked rt s: sn chsng ldrs: effrt over 2f out: kpt on same pce appr fnl f* **6/1**

1m 2.54s (1.84) **Going Correction** +0.325s/f (Good) **4** Ran SP% **110.9**
Speed ratings (Par 98): **98,97,97,94**
CSF £22.72 TOTE £5.60; EX 17.70.
Owner Peter Swann **Bred** Rossenarra Bloodstock Limited **Trained** Willoughton, Lincs

FOCUS
Only a handful of runners in this conditions event but it was run at a strong pace. The winer built on her Fibresand win.

NOTEBOOK
Girl At The Sands(IRE) stayed on best of all to follow up her recent Southwell victory. She looked booked for third spot with a furlong or so to run but responded to everything that was thrown at her and arguably won a shade cosily. There's no doubt a stiff 5f suits but the way in which she toughed this out suggests that she'll be even more of a force once tackling longer trips. This soft ground wouldn't be too dissimilar to Fibresand and she ought to remain competitive under these conditions once reassessed. (op 9-2)
Tumblewind ran an excellent race in defeat but, having got the better of a prolonged duel with the odds-on favourite, finished tired. These were very different conditions to those that she won in at Beverley last time but, like many of her sire's progeny, she appeared to handle them. She looks on the upgrade and would have every chance of turning the tables on her conqueror on an easier track.

Stand Of Glory(USA) was the only horse in this according to the market but he was ultimately well held. He raced against the often favoured rail throughout but looked to get bogged down. Quicker ground may well bring with it a return to form. (op 8-11)

A J Cook(IRE) wasn't beaten far and ought to have no problem finding a race. He wasn't knocked around late on and will have learnt plenty from this. (op 10-1 tchd 11-1)

5712 CITY OF RIPON STKS (H'CAP) 1m 1f 170y

4:15 (4:15) (Class 3) (0-90,90) 3-Y-O **£6,931** (£2,074; £1,037; £519; £258) **Stalls** Low

Form RPR

3-0 **1** **Voodoo Prince**[46] 4068 4-9-9 **85** GrahamLee 13 94+
(Ed Dunlop) *dwlt: hld up towards rr: nt clr run and swtchd lft over 2f out: styd on to ld appr fnl f: hung rt: drvn rt out* **8/1**[3]

006 **2** *1* **Barren Brook**[17] 5091 5-9-5 **81** JamesSullivan 10 88+
(Michael Easterby) *dwlt: t.k.h in rr: drvn 4f out: nt clr run on ins 2f out: sn swtchd outside: styd on strly fnl 150yds: tk 2nd post* **8/1**[3]

1414 **3** *nse* **Kay Gee Be (IRE)**[13] 5243 8-9-5 **81** PaulHanagan 3 88
(Richard Fahey) *trckd ldrs: effrt over 3f out: led briefly over 1f out: styd on same pce last 75yds* **9/2**[1]

033- **4** *1 1/2* **Master Of Arts (USA)**[171] 6335 7-10-0 **90** RobertHavlin 4 94
(Mark Johnston) *hld up in mid-div: hdwy over 3f out: trcking ldrs whn nt clr run over 2f out and over 1f out: keeping on same pce whn n.m.r ins fnl f* **11/2**[2]

4056 **5** *5* **Desert Romance (IRE)**[20] 4964 6-9-1 **77** DanielTudhope 7 70
(David O'Meara) *s.i.s: effrt on ins whn nt clr run over 2f out: rdn and one pce over 1f out* **10/1**

4000 **6** *4 1/2* **Just Fabulous**[19] 4997 3-8-4 **74** AndrewElliott 2 58
(George Moore) *chsd ldrs: drvn over 3f out: wknd over 1f out* **10/1**

0161 **7** *1/2* **Lady Chaparral**[22] 4868 5-9-6 **82** TomEaves 1 65
(Michael Dods) *led over 1f: chsd ldrs: led over 2f out: hdd over 1f out: sn wknd* **9/2**[1]

3544 **8** *2 1/4* **Jonny Lesters Hair (IRE)**[13] 5227 7-8-13 **75** DavidAllan 9 53
(Tim Easterby) *sn trcking ldrs: drvn 4f out: lost pl over 1f out* **9/1**

231- **9** *3/4* **Full Speed (GER)**[395] 4555 7-9-5 **81** MichaelO'Connell 12 57
(Philip Kirby) *in rr: effrt over 2f out: sn btn* **33/1**

612 **10** *2 1/4* **Watts Up Son**[17] 5085 4-8-10 **77** (bt) JasonHart(5) 6 49
(Declan Carroll) *racd wd: drvn to ld over 8f out: hdd over 2f out: lost pl over 1f out: eased ins fnl f* **9/1**

2m 8.65s (3.25) **Going Correction** +0.50s/f (Yiel)
WFA 3 from 4yo+ 8lb 10 Ran SP% **115.1**
Speed ratings (Par 107): **107,106,106,104,100 97,96,95,94,92**
Tote Swingers 1&2 £11.20, 2&3 £8.20, 1&3 £7.60 CSF £69.45 CT £324.39 TOTE £7.20: £2.90, £2.70, £2.00; EX 52.50.
Owner Lord Derby **Bred** Stanley Estate And Stud Co **Trained** Newmarket, Suffolk

FOCUS
A strong renewal of this decent handicap but plenty of hard-luck stories with many of the field getting in each other's way in the home straight. Sound enough form.

NOTEBOOK
Voodoo Prince picked up well once extricating himself from a pocket and was good value for his win. The lightly-raced 4yo hadn't been entirely disgraced on his reappearance on similarly soft ground at Newmarket but he'd clearly progressed from that outing and looks the type who could go on to better things. He did show a tendency to lug right into the rail under pressure but still had enough in hand to repel the late challenge of the runner-up. He's entitled to sharpen up again for this and could be an ideal type for the valuable Dubai Duty Free Handicap for which he holds an entry at Newbury next month. (op 7-1)

Barren Brook rattled home from the rear and is one to keep a close eye on in the coming weeks. He was the first off the bridle but really took off once switched to the outside. This ground would have been plenty soft enough for him and he may be weighted to win once getting his optimum conditions. (tchd 9-1)

Kay Gee Be(IRE) ran yet another solid race. He enjoyed a smoother passage than most but deserves plenty of credit given that this trip would be stretching his stamina. He was in front with 2f remaining and a drop back to a mile may well pay dividends. (op 4-1)

Master Of Arts(USA) travelled powerfully but faded late on and may well have needed this. He was stopped in his run on a couple of occasions and is an interesting prospect for the remainder of the year. (op 11-1)

Desert Romance(IRE) had a nightmare run and should be given another chance. He missed the break, possibly by design, but had a wall of horses in front of him when looking to make a move. He's nicely treated on his best form and a fifth career success may not be far away. (op 11-1 tchd 9-1)

Lady Chaparral could not build on her win at Carlisle over shorter. Official explanation: trainer had no explanation for the poor form shown (op 6-1)

Jonny Lesters Hair(IRE) is at his best when making the running and he failed to fire under these restrained tactics. Official explanation: jockey said gelding hung right-handed (op 8-1)

5713 ATTHERACES.COM H'CAP 1m

4:45 (4:45) (Class 5) (0-75,72) 3-Y-O+ **£2,911** (£866; £432; £216) **Stalls** Low

Form RPR

3212 **1** **Hayek**[10] 5338 5-9-6 **71** (b) AdamCarter(5) 5 83+
(Tim Easterby) *hld up in rr: effrt on outside over 3f out: str run to ld over 1f out: edgd rt: hld on towards fin* **6/1**

3316 **2** *nk* **Satwa Laird**[11] 5310 6-9-7 **72** DavidKenny(5) 4 80
(Conor Dore) *hld up in rr: hdwy over 2f out: wnt 2nd jst ins fnl f: kpt on: jst hld* **13/2**

6054 **3** *2* **I Confess**[29] 4657 7-9-1 **68** (v) JordanNason(7) 9 71
(Geoffrey Harker) *dwlt: in rr: effrt on outer 3f out: kpt on to take 3rd nr fin* **16/1**

2406 **4** *1/2* **River Ardeche**[13] 5220 7-9-1 **61** BarryMcHugh 10 63
(Tracy Waggott) *sn chsng ldrs on outer: hmpd after 1f: led over 5f out: hdd over 3f out: led over 2f out: hdd appr fnl f: kpt on same pce* **20/1**

2330 **5** *1/2* **Save The Bees**[4] 5535 4-9-12 **72** GrahamGibbons 11 73
(Declan Carroll) *w ldrs: swtchd rt after 1f: drvn over 4f out: kpt on same pce appr fnl f* **11/2**[3]

0506 **6** *hd* **Flipping**[39] 4295 5-9-0 **60** (p) DavidAllan 3 61
(Eric Alston) *trckd ldrs: t.k.h: n.m.r and hmpd after 1f: stdd into midfield over 5f out: hdwy to chse ldrs over 2f out: kpt on one pce* **7/1**

1356 **7** *8* **Horatio Carter**[8] 5414 7-9-12 **72** (p) DanielTudhope 1 54
(David O'Meara) *chsd ldrs: drvn 4f out: lost pl over 1f out* **9/2**[1]

-031 **8** *2 3/4* **Rex Romanorum (IRE)**[39] 4313 4-9-9 **69** DuranFentiman 6 45
(Patrick Holmes) *mde most tl over 5f out: led over 3f out: hdd over 2f out: wknd appr fnl f* **5/1**[2]

4305 **9** *1 3/4* **Count Bertoni (IRE)**[13] 5225 5-9-0 **67** (b) DavidBergin(7) 8 39
(David O'Meara) *sn chsng ldrs: hmpd after 1f: drvn 4f out: lost pl over 1f out* **11/1**

1000 **10** *23* **Daunt (IRE)**[17] 5093 3-9-1 **67** MichaelO'Connell 2
(John Quinn) *chsd ldrs: drvn over 4f out: lost pl over 3f out: sn bhd: t.o* **25/1**

1m 44.84s (3.44) **Going Correction** +0.50s/f (Yiel)
WFA 3 from 4yo+ 6lb 10 Ran SP% **113.2**
Speed ratings (Par 103): **102,101,99,99,98 98,90,87,86,63**
Tote Swingers 1&2 £6.00, 2&3 £12.00, 1&3 £8.80 CSF £43.34 CT £588.15 TOTE £4.70: £1.60, £2.40, £4.10; EX 27.00.
Owner Numac Engineering Ltd **Bred** Cranford Stud **Trained** Great Habton, N Yorks

FOCUS
A fair handicap run at an even pace. The first three came from the rear and the winner rates better than ever.
Rex Romanorum(IRE) Official explanation: trainer said gelding was unsuited by the track

5714 WAKEMAN STAYERS H'CAP 2m

5:15 (5:15) (Class 6) (0-65,65) 3-Y-O+ **£2,587** (£770; £384; £192) **Stalls** High

Form RPR

450 **1** **Generous Dream**[11] 5315 4-9-6 **57** SilvestreDeSousa 5 70
(Mel Brittain) *mid-div: reminders after 4f: sn chsng ldrs: wnt 2nd over 4f out: chal over 3f out: led over 2f out: drvn rt out* **11/1**

1404 **2** *3 3/4* **Spruzzo**[18] 5056 6-9-10 **61** DuranFentiman 2 69
(Chris Fairhurst) *led: reminders over 10f out: hdd over 2f out: kpt on same pce over 1f out* **11/4**[1]

331 **3** *9* **Bavarian Nordic (USA)**[22] 4869 7-9-10 **61** PaulMulrennan 11 58
(Richard Whitaker) *hld up in rr: hdwy over 5f out: wnt 3rd 4f out: sn trcking ldng pair: wknd over 1f out* **5/1**[3]

6063 **4** *1 3/4* **Seagoing**[11] 5330 3-8-9 **60** (b[1]) DavidAllan 6 55
(Tim Easterby) *dwlt: lost pl and in rr over 7f out: hdwy over 4f out: modest 4th 3f out: one pce* **4/1**[2]

0006 **5** *18* **Polurrian (IRE)**[18] 5054 5-9-9 **60** DanielTudhope 3 34
(David O'Meara) *trckd ldrs: rdn over 3f out: sn wknd* **13/2**

111/ **6** *10* **Golden Groom**[1183] 2573 9-9-4 **55** PaddyAspell 10 17
(Patrick Holmes) *mid-div: t.k.h: drvn 4f out: sn btn* **13/2**

3060 **7** *3* **Lava Steps (USA)**[15] 5172 6-8-5 **49** oh4 (b) DavidBergin(7) 13
(David O'Meara) *swtchd rt after s: chsd ldr: upsides 8f out: wknd 4f out* **20/1**

0-00 **8** *37* **Leaving Alone (USA)**[22] 4867 5-8-12 **49** oh3 (p) JamesSullivan 8
(Edwin Tuer) *hld up in rr: lost pl over 5f out: sn t.o* **25/1**

0555 **9** *10* **Spiders Star**[9] 5384 9-8-12 **49** oh2 MichaelO'Connell 1
(Simon West) *trckd ldrs: drvn over 9f out: lost pl over 6f out: wl bhd and t.o* **12/1**

6/00 **10** *20* **Masra**[22] 4864 9-8-12 **49** oh4 AndrewElliott 14
(David Thompson) *in rr: drvn 9f out: reluctant and sn detached in last: t.o 6f out* **66/1**

3m 41.84s (10.04) **Going Correction** +0.50s/f (Yiel)
WFA 3 from 4yo+ 14lb 10 Ran SP% **116.1**
Speed ratings (Par 101): **94,92,87,86,77 72,71,52,47,37**
Tote Swingers 1&2 £7.20, 2&3 £4.40, 1&3 £5.40 CSF £40.54 CT £174.99 TOTE £9.20: £2.50, £1.60, £2.30; EX 43.20.
Owner Mel Brittain **Bred** Northgate Lodge Stud Ltd **Trained** Warthill, N Yorks

FOCUS
A fierce pace ensured that there was no hiding place in this modest staying handicap. Behind the front pair they were 7lb+ off their best.
Generous Dream Official explanation: trainer said, regarding apparent improvement in form, that the filly benefited by the step up in trip.
T/Plt: £170.60 to a £1 stake. Pool: £63,527.05 - 271.8 winning tickets T/Qpdt: £47.20 to a £1 stake. Pool: £4,565.22 - 71.53 winning tickets WG

5241 SOUTHWELL (L-H)

Tuesday, August 28

OFFICIAL GOING: Standard
Wind: light across Weather: Cloudy

5715 LADBROKES GAME ON! MAIDEN STKS 6f (F)

4:50 (4:51) (Class 5) 2-Y-O **£2,264** (£673; £336; £168) **Stalls** Low

Form RPR

5 **1** **Double Your Money (IRE)**[11] 5325 2-9-3 0 JoeFanning 6 81+
(Mark Johnston) *cl up: led wl over 2f out: sn clr: easily* **1/1**[1]

0524 **2** *5* **Marhaba Malayeen (IRE)**[20] 4951 2-9-3 71 (b[1]) JamieSpencer 8 62
(Kevin Ryan) *chsd ldrs on outer: hdwy to chse wnr wl over 1f out: sn rdn and no imp* **8/1**

0 **3** *2* **Dumbarton Rock**[10] 5360 2-9-3 0 FrannyNorton 3 56
(William Jarvis) *in rr and outpcd: hdwy on inner 2f out: sn rdn and styd on wl fnl f: nrst fin* **33/1**

0 **4** *2 1/2* **Exzachary**[75] 3067 2-9-3 0 J-PGuillambert 4 49
(Jo Hughes) *cl up: led after 1f: rdn along and hdd wl over 2f out: drvn and wknd wl over 1f out: hung rt and lost 3rd ins fnl f* **33/1**

4 **5** *hd* **Look On By**[13] 5242 2-9-3 0 AdrianNicholls 1 48
(Ed McMahon) *led 1f: cl up: rdn along over 2f out: sn one pce* **17/2**

33 **6** *1* **Lyric Piece**[8] 5425 2-8-12 0 LukeMorris 7 42
(Sir Mark Prescott Bt) *sn rdn along and outpcd in rr: swtchd wd and hdwy over 2f out: styd on fnl f: n.d* **6/1**[3]

0 **7** *12* **Muharrib (IRE)**[27] 4710 2-9-3 0 MickaelBarzalona 2 9
(Saeed Bin Suroor) *dwlt and sn rdn along: hdwy and in tch after 2f: rdn wl over 2f out: wknd and eased wl over 1f out* **9/2**[2]

3 **8** *nk* **Marmot Bay (IRE)**[13] 5230 2-8-12 0 FergusSweeney 5 3
(Jamie Osborne) *dwlt and in rr: sme hdwy 1/2-way: sn rdn along and wknd* **14/1**

1m 14.58s (-1.92) **Going Correction** -0.475s/f (Stan) 8 Ran SP% **116.7**
Speed ratings (Par 94): **93,86,83,80,80 78,62,62**
toteswingers 1&2 £2.90, 2&3 £21.60, 1&3 £5.90 CSF £10.32 TOTE £1.70: £1.40, £2.20, £7.20; EX 9.60 Trifecta £474.80 Part won. Pool: £641.71 - 0.80 winning units..
Owner A D Spence **Bred** Twelve Oaks Stud **Trained** Middleham Moor, N Yorks

FOCUS
An ordinary maiden in behind the winner, who was value for extra.

NOTEBOOK
Double Your Money(IRE) was the market mover earlier in the day, being backed down from 100-30, and lived up to his name for those who joined in late, scoring at evens. He was expected to build considerably on his debut promise and won this in emphatic fashion, taking over early in the straight and drawing right away. He looks a decent prospect if he can transfer this sort of form back to turf. (op 5-4 tchd 11-8)

Marhaba Malayeen(IRE) set a fair standard in this maiden with an official mark of 71. He appeared to run his race in the first-time blinkers, but was no match whatsoever for the winner. (op 9-1)

Dumbarton Rock had finished tailed-off last on his Newmarket debut, and improved on that considerably here, staying on late past beaten rivals. Handicaps next season might be his forte.
Exzachary, gelded since his debut, made the running but was left behind when the winner committed. (op 25-1)
Look On By made his debut over 5f earlier in the month and appeared to run his race, if unable to pick up. He is another for handicaps in due course, possibly on turf. (op 15-2 tchd 7-1 and 9-1)
Lyric Piece was always struggling to go the pace, being ridden from an early stage. (op 13-2 tchd 7-1)
Muharrib(IRE) was in trouble on the home turn and eased late on. (op 5-1 tchd 4-1)
Marmot Bay(IRE) dropped away after tracking the pace early. (op 11-1)

5716 LADBROKES MOBILE NURSERY 7f (F)
5:20 (5:20) (Class 6) (0-65,64) 2-Y-O **£1,840** (£543; £271) **Stalls** Low

Form RPR
006 **1** **Winged Icarus (USA)**[27] 4707 2-8-12 **55**.................(v[1]) RobertWinston 3 82+
(Alan McCabe) *mde all: cruised clr 2f out: unchal* **7/2**[1]
5253 **2** *12* **Poetic Verse**[13] 5236 2-9-0 **57**.. JamesMillman 1 51
(Rod Millman) *hld up: hdwy 1/2-way: rdn to chse ldrs over 2f out: sn drvn and kpt on: no ch w wnr* **5/1**[2]
U305 **3** *1 1/4* **Panama Cat (USA)**[34] 4448 2-9-0 **57**................................ PhillipMakin 6 48
(Kevin Ryan) *cl up: chsd wnr 1/2-way: rdn along wl over 2f out: sn drvn and plugged on same pce* **11/2**[3]
5610 **4** *5* **Poetic Princess**[31] 4574 2-9-7 **64**.................................... FrannyNorton 2 42
(Jo Hughes) *trckd ldrs on inner: rdn along over 2f out: sn drvn and one pce* **7/2**[1]
0006 **5** *1 1/2* **If You Can (IRE)**[12] 5254 2-8-9 **52**.. TedDurcan 5 26
(Tim Easterby) *dwlt and sn rdn along in rr: sme hdwy on wd outside fnl 2f: nvr a factor* **5/1**[2]
000 **6** *2 3/4* **Jomari (IRE)**[34] 4448 2-8-1 **49**.......................................(b[1]) NeilFarley(5) 9 16
(Declan Carroll) *prom on outer: rdn along 3f out: drvn over 2f out and sn outpcd* **16/1**
050 **7** *nse* **Cielo Rojo (IRE)**[38] 4327 2-8-6 **49**..............................(p) PatrickMathers 7 16
(Richard Fahey) *s.i.s: a bhd* **12/1**
2005 **8** *2* **Amelia Jay**[18] 5041 2-9-2 **59**.. LukeMorris 4 21
(Danielle McCormick) *prom: rdn along 1/2-way: drvn and wknd wl over 2f out* **22/1**
045 **9** *4 1/2* **Eyeline**[29] 4654 2-9-3 **60**... RussKennemore 8 10
(Reg Hollinshead) *dwlt: in tch: rdn along 3f out: sn wknd* **12/1**

1m 26.82s (-3.48) **Going Correction** -0.475s/f (Stan) 2y crse rec **9 Ran SP% 118.8**
Speed ratings (Par 92): **100,86,84,79,77 74,74,71,66**
toteswingers 1&2 £7.80, 2&3 £5.10, 1&3 £6.40 CSF £21.75 CT £96.43 TOTE £6.30: £2.60, £2.00, £1.70; EX 22.50 Trifecta £258.40 Pool: £548.41 - 1.57 winning units..
Owner Mrs Z Wentworth **Bred** Ronald Kirk, Greg McDonald & John Bates **Trained** Averham Park, Notts

FOCUS
A moderate nursery on paper but it turned into a procession and the time was fast. The usual concerns about how this form will transfer elsewhere.

NOTEBOOK
Winged Icarus(USA), whose trainer landed this in 2010, repeated the feat with this first-time blinkered colt. A 150,000gns 2yo, he had not shown much in three starts on fast turf but the switch to this surface and the fitting of a visor proved a revelation, as the colt made all and came right away for an easy success. He will be heavily punished by the handicapper for this, so probably needs to turn out under a penalty, although connections are entitled to expect him to go on to better things. Official explanation: trainer said, regarding apparent improvement in form, that the colt appreciated running on the all-weather and the fitting of a visor for the first time. (op 4-1 tchd 5-1)
Poetic Verse had run reasonably at around this trip on both fast and soft turf, but was held up early on this Fibresand debut. She ran on late to beat the rest well enough, but the winner had long gone. (op 9-2)
Panama Cat(USA) chased the pace throughout and kept on but was not in the same league as the winner on the day. (tchd 6-1)
Poetic Princess had won over C&D but that success resulted in her carrying top weight and she is not that big. She chased the pace throughout and then went after the leader early in the straight, but could not sustain the effort. (op 10-3)

5717 MIRROR PUNTERS CLUB MAIDEN STKS 1m (F)
5:50 (5:50) (Class 5) 3-Y-O **£2,264** (£673; £336; £168) **Stalls** Low

Form RPR
0-52 **1** **Dubawi Island (FR)**[20] 4948 3-9-3 79..............................(b) MartinDwyer 2 84
(James Tate) *mde all: rdn clr 2f out: styd on strly fnl f: eased towards fin* **2/1**[1]
0230 **2** *7* **Centrifugal (IRE)**[22] 4889 3-9-3 77.. JoeFanning 8 69
(Mark Johnston) *trckd ldng pair: hdwy to chse wnr over 2f out: sn rdn: drvn and no imp fr over 1f out* **5/2**[2]
00 **3** *4 1/2* **My Manekineko**[84] 2799 3-8-12 0............................... DarrenEgan(5) 3 58
(J R Jenkins) *chsd ldrs: rdn along 3f out: drvn and kpt on same pce fnl 2f* **50/1**
0230 **4** *8* **Feeling Good**[87] 2689 3-9-0 71.. PaulPickard(3) 4 39
(Brian Ellison) *in rr: rdn along and sme hdwy over 2f out: drvn and plugged on to take remote 4th nr fin* **9/2**
0 **5** *1 1/2* **Tabib (IRE)**[8] 5421 3-9-3 0... MickaelBarzalona 6 36
(Saeed Bin Suroor) *dwlt: sn pushed along and cl up after 1f: rdn 3f out: wknd over 2f out* **3/1**[3]
00 **6** *7* **Broughtons Maxim**[11] 5297 3-9-3 0.............................. StevieDonohoe 5 20
(Willie Musson) *a in rr: bhd fnl 3f* **80/1**
3 **7** *11* **Roger Ramjet (IRE)**[11] 5329 3-9-3 0..............................(t) SamHitchcott 7
(Brian Meehan) *chsd ldrs: rdn along over 3f out: sn wknd* **9/1**

1m 40.41s (-3.29) **Going Correction** -0.475s/f (Stan) **7 Ran SP% 118.3**
Speed ratings (Par 100): **97,90,85,77,76 69,58**
toteswingers 1&2 £1.90, 2&3 £5.90, 1&3 £6.60 CSF £7.75 TOTE £3.40: £2.00, £1.10; EX 8.70 Trifecta £118.20 Pool: £425.17 - 2.66 winning units..
Owner Saif Ali **Bred** Darley Stud Management Co Ltd **Trained** Newmarket, Suffolk

FOCUS
A fair maiden of its type with the three runners with official ratings all having marks in the 70s, and the two with the highest figures of those had the race between them in the straight.

5718 RICHARD GIBSON H'CAP 1m 6f (F)
6:20 (6:20) (Class 4) (0-80,76) 3-Y-O+ **£4,204** (£1,251; £625; £312) **Stalls** Low

Form RPR
0025 **1** **Cape Safari (IRE)**[14] 5211 3-9-1 **75**..................................(p) LukeMorris 7 84+
(Alan Bailey) *cl up: led wl over 2f out: rdn clr over 1f out: styd on wl u.p fnl f* **15/2**
6004 **2** *2 1/4* **Sherman McCoy**[14] 5211 6-9-7 **69**.................................... JamesMillman 8 74
(Rod Millman) *trckd ldrs: effrt on outer and rdn along 4f out: styd on u.p to chse wnr wl over 1f out: kpt on fnl f* **8/1**
4305 **3** *3 3/4* **Mediterranean Sea (IRE)**[22] 4884 6-9-6 **73**.................. DarrenEgan(5) 3 73
(J R Jenkins) *hld up in tch: hdwy 4f out: rdn to chse ldrs over 2f out: kpt on u.p fnl f* **13/2**
6031 **4** *5* **Veloso (FR)**[13] 5241 10-9-4 **69**.. GaryBartley(3) 6 62
(Noel Wilson) *trckd ldrs: hdwy 4f out: chsd ldng pair 3f out: rdn 2f out: drvn and one pce appr fnl f* **6/1**[3]
2421 **5** *1 3/4* **Three White Socks (IRE)**[43] 4145 5-9-5 **70**..................... DaleSwift(3) 4 60
(Brian Ellison) *dwlt and bhd: pushed along over 5f out: rdn and hdwy over 3f out: wd st: hung lft wl over 1f out: n.d* **9/2**[2]
5-61 **6** *1 1/2* **No Time To Lose**[31] 4585 3-9-2 **76**............................ FergusSweeney 5 64
(Jamie Osborne) *led: rdn along 3f out: hdd wl over 2f out: sn drvn and grad wknd* **5/2**[1]
5-01 **7** *23* **Shifting Gold (IRE)**[147] 1175 6-9-4 **66**..............................(bt) AmyRyan 2 22
(Kevin Ryan) *cl up: rdn along over 4f out: sn wknd* **15/2**
0254 **8** *25* **Lady of Burgundy**[15] 5158 6-9-1 **63**.. LiamKeniry 1
(Mark Usher) *midfield on inner: pushed along 6f out: sn lost pl and bhd fnl 4f* **20/1**

3m 2.31s (-5.99) **Going Correction** -0.475s/f (Stan)
WFA 3 from 5yo+ 12lb **8 Ran SP% 113.8**
Speed ratings (Par 105): **98,96,94,91,90 89,76,62**
toteswingers 1&2 £16.00, 2&3 £4.10, 1&3 £9.50 CSF £64.43 CT £410.34 TOTE £10.20: £4.90, £4.60, £1.10; EX 91.40 TRIFECTA Not won..
Owner John Stocker **Bred** Rabbah Bloodstock Limited **Trained** Newmarket, Suffolk

FOCUS
A competitive staying handicap featuring several multiple course winners.

5719 FOLLOW US ON TWITTER @ SOUTHWELL_RACES H'CAP 5f (F)
6:50 (6:53) (Class 6) (0-55,55) 3-Y-O+ **£1,772** (£523; £261) **Stalls** High

Form RPR
6 **1** **Clubland (IRE)**[2] 5621 3-8-13 **52**.. AmyRyan 8 66
(Kevin Ryan) *mde virtually all: rdn clr over 1f out: drvn out* **9/4**[1]
0523 **2** *2 3/4* **Dazzlin Bluebell (IRE)**[13] 5247 3-8-10 **49**..................(b) TedDurcan 12 53
(Tim Easterby) *cl up: rdn wl over 1f out and ev ch tl drvn and one pce approachng fnl f* **11/1**[3]
552 **3** *nk* **Invigilator**[21] 4928 4-9-1 **55**..(t) RaulDaSilva(3) 6 58
(Derek Shaw) *in tch: hdwy over 2f out: rdn to chse ldng pair over 1f out: kpt on same pce fnl f* **7/1**[2]
526 **4** *1 1/4* **Spirit Of Coniston**[11] 5294 9-9-3 **54**............................. MickyFenton 7 52
(Paul Midgley) *racd towards far side: chsd ldrs: rdn along wl over 1f out: kpt on one pce fnl f* **7/1**[2]
0050 **5** *1 1/4* **Itum**[11] 5327 5-8-13 **50**.. BrettDoyle 2 44
(Christine Dunnett) *racd towards far rail: in tch: rdn along 2f out: sn one pce* **20/1**
0-60 **6** *1 1/4* **Lucky Mark (IRE)**[110] 2010 3-9-2 **55**............................. RobertWinston 5 44
(Garry Moss) *dwlt and towards rr: hdwy 2f out: sn rdn and no imp appr fnl f* **16/1**
4000 **7** *2 1/4* **Bond Blade**[13] 5246 4-8-10 **50** ow1.................................... DaleSwift(3) 13 31
(Suzzanne France) *towards rr: rdn along and sme hdwy 2f out: nvr a factor* **22/1**
5615 **8** *3 1/4* **Simple Rhythm**[18] 5033 6-8-13 **50**........................(p) DaraghO'Donohoe 4 20
(John Ryan) *towards rr and rdn along after 2f: n.d* **25/1**
64 **9** *1/2* **Pinball (IRE)**[21] 4929 6-8-5 **49**..............................(b) ShirleyTeasdale(7) 10 17
(Lisa Williamson) *racd nr stands' rail: chsd ldrs: rdn along 1/2-way and sn wknd* **20/1**
2000 **10** *3/4* **Little Perisher**[7] 5444 5-8-13 **50**.................................(p) J-PGuillambert 14 15
(Paul Howling) *racd towards stands' rail: in rr fr 1/2-way* **50/1**
0042 **11** *2* **Kara's Vision**[13] 5247 3-8-11 **50**..(p) JoeFanning 1
(Robert Cowell) *racd towards far rail: chsd ldrs: rdn along over 2f out: sn wknd* **7/1**[2]
0055 **12** *3* **Silver Linnet (IRE)**[14] 5217 5-9-1 **52**..............................(b) AdamKirby 11
(John Butler) *cl up: rdn along 1/2-way: sn wknd* **11/1**[3]
6 **13** *5* **Fiona's Spirit (IRE)**[5] 5504 5-8-6 **46** oh1.................(tp) MarkCoumbe(3) 3
(Daniel Mark Loughnane) *awkward s and v s.i.s: a bhd* **40/1**
4040 **14** *9* **Mon Duchess**[42] 4174 4-8-13 **50**.. PhillipMakin 9
(Lawrence Mullaney) *towards rr: rdn along over 2f out: sn outpcd: fin lame and dismntd after line* **12/1**

58.35s (-1.35) **Going Correction** -0.225s/f (Stan)
WFA 3 from 4yo+ 2lb **14 Ran SP% 120.6**
Speed ratings (Par 101): **101,96,96,94,92 90,86,81,80,79 76,71,63,48**
toteswingers 1&2 £6.60, 2&3 £4.40, 1&3 £6.90 CSF £25.17 CT £161.99 TOTE £2.40: £1.10, £4.40, £2.60; EX 31.90 Trifecta £44.50 Pool: £254.97 - 4.24 winning units..
Owner Dominic Cork **Bred** Mrs Sharon Slattery **Trained** Hambleton, N Yorks

FOCUS
A very moderate sprint handicap that appeared competitive on paper, but two of the 3yos had it between them for most of the way. The field spread right across the track but the first three raced up the centre.
Pinball(IRE) Official explanation: jockey said mare was slowly away because the blindfold became stuck in the bridle and couldn't be removed on the first attempt.
Silver Linnet(IRE) Official explanation: trainer said mare did not handle the all-weather surface
Fiona's Spirit(IRE) Official explanation: jockey said mare was slowly away

5720 DOWNLOAD THE LADBROKES MOBILE APP H'CAP 7f (F)
7:20 (7:21) (Class 6) (0-55,55) 3-Y-O+ **£1,840** (£543; £271) **Stalls** Low

Form RPR
0051 **1** **Community (USA)**[19] 4981 4-8-13 **54**............................ LeonnaMayor(5) 5 67
(Jamie Osborne) *hld up: smooth hdwy to trck ldrs over 2f out: rdn to chal over 1f out: styd on wl to ld last 100yds: kpt on* **6/1**[2]
0000 **2** *1 3/4* **Ace Of Spies (IRE)**[15] 5179 7-9-5 **55**.................................. LukeMorris 14 63
(Conor Dore) *trckd ldrs: hdwy 3f out: cl up over 2f out: rdn to ld 1 1/2f out: jnd and drvn appr fnl f: hdd and no ex last 100yds* **8/1**
3544 **3** *1 1/4* **Bridge Valley**[22] 4865 5-8-9 **48**..............................(b) DominicFox(3) 13 53
(Jason Ward) *dwlt: sn outpcd and bhd: wd st: gd hdwy towards stands' rail wl over 1f out: fin strly* **13/2**[3]
155 **4** *2 1/2* **Jackie Love (IRE)**[20] 4942 4-8-8 **49**..............................(v) LauraPike(5) 4 47
(Olivia Maylam) *in rr: hdwy over 2f out: rdn to chse ldrs and edgd lft over 1f out: swtchd lft to inner and rdn ent fnl f: kpt on: nrst fin* **9/1**
000 **5** *3* **Pelican Rock (IRE)**[24] 4830 3-9-0 **55**..............................(tp) FrannyNorton 10 43+
(Andrew Crook) *cl up: led briefly wl over 2f out: sn rdn and hdd 2f out: drvn and wknd over 1f out* **10/1**
5405 **6** *hd* **Basle**[18] 5050 5-9-5 **55**..(t) GrahamLee 7 45
(Gay Kelleway) *hld up: hdwy 3f out: rdn to chal wl over 1f out and ev ch tl drvn and wknd ent fnl f* **7/1**
0-00 **7** *2 1/2* **Style Margi (IRE)**[18] 5050 4-9-5 **55**..............................(b) LiamKeniry 12 38
(Ed de Giles) *cl up: rdn to ld 2f out: drvn and hdd 1 1/2f out: grad wknd* **25/1**

5000 **8** 2 1/4 **Saktoon (USA)**[4] 5543 4 -8-851 (v) ShirleyTeasdale(7) 9 28
(Derek Shaw) *chsd ldrs: rdn along over 2f out: sn wknd* **12/1**
030 **9** 3 1/4 **Kodiac Island**[22] 4888 3 -8-1354 AdrianNicholls 8 20
(Ed McMahon) *led: rdn along and edgd lft 3f out: sn hdd & wknd* **20/1**
0062 **10** 6 **Not My Choice (IRE)**[18] 5050 7 -9-555 (t) J-PGuillambert 6
(Paul Howling) *dwlt and swtchd to outer sn after s: in rr: wd st and hdwy to chse ldrs 2f out: sn rdn and wknd* **3/1**[1]
0-00 **11** 8 **Diamond Sunrise (IRE)**[13] 4158 4 -8-849 NeilFarley(5) 3
(Noel Wilson) *prom: rdn along over 3f out: sn wknd* **25/1**
-000 **12** 8 **Royale Ransom**[17] 5095 3 -9-055 MartinDwyer 1
(Sylvester Kirk) *cl up on inner: rdn along whn n.m.r and hmpd wl over 2f out: sn wknd* **20/1**

1m 28.56s (-1.74)**Going Correction** -0.475s/f (Stan)
WFA 3 from 4yo+ 5lb **12**Ran SP% **120.2**
Speed ratings (Par 101): **90,88,86,83,80 80,77,74,70,64 54,45**
toteswingers 1&2 £9.10, 2&3 £11.30, 1&3 £2.90 CSF £51.02 CT £328.52 TOTE £6.90 : £2.60, £2.70, £2.10 ; EX 60.20 Trifecta £192.00 Pool: £381.44 - 1.47 winning units.
Owner Steve Jakes **Bred** Brereton C Jones **Trained** Upper Lambourn, Berks

FOCUS
Another very moderate handicap but again a big field and not much between the runners on ratings.
Not My Choice (IRE) Official explanation: jockey said gelding was slowly away

5721 LADBROKES BET ON YOUR MOBILE APPRENTICE H'CAP 1m (F)
7:50 (7:51) (Class 5) (0-75,75) 3-Y-O **£2,385** (£704; £352) **Stalls** Low

Form RPR
3060 **1** **Dubai Sunshine (IRE)**[11] 5302 3 -9-775 IanBurns(3) 11 94
(Michael Bell) *cl up: led wl over 2f out: rdn clr wl over 1f out: drvn ins fnl f: hld on wl* **6/1**[2]
0113 **2** 3/4 **Kung Hei Fat Choy (USA)**[27] 4713 3 -9-772 (b) LMcNiff 9 89
(James Given) *trckd ldrs: hdwy over 2f out: chsd wnr wl over 1f out and sn rdn: drvn and kpt on fnl f* **6/4**[1]
2654 **3** 6 **Tight Lipped (IRE)**[20] 4949 3 -9-873 (v[1]) DarrenEgan 8 76
(James Eustace) *cl up: led over 4f out: rdn along and hdd wl over 2f out: grad wknd* **7/1**[3]
0105 **4** 3 1/2 **My Boy Ginger**[16] 5132 3 -8-1064 ThomasBrown(3) 7 59
(Rod Millman) *towards rr: hdwy over 3f out: rdn along over 2f out: kpt on same pce* **12/1**
-143 **5** nk **Malih**[19] 5008 3 -9-873 MatthewLawson 4 67
(Jamie Osborne) *dwlt and in rr: hdwy wl over 2f out: sn rdn and no imp fr over 1f out* **9/1**
0104 **6** 3 1/2 **Foursquare Funtime**[16] 5132 3 -9-169 JackDuern(3) 3 55
(Reg Hollinshead) *in tch: chsd ldrs over 3f out: rdn over 2f out and sn wknd* **25/1**
3010 **7** 1 **Jay Kay**[8] 5415 3 -8-556 NeilFarley 10 40
(Danielle McCormick) *towards rr: hdwy and in tch 1/2-way: rdn wl over 2f out: sn wknd* **16/1**
6620 **8** 6 **Darnathean**[11] 5323 3 -8-765 (e) LouisSteward(7) 1 35
(Paul D'Arcy) *a in rr* **20/1**
0000 **9** 4 1/2 **Loyal Master (IRE)**[8] 5415 3 -9-570 GarryWhillans 2 30
(Garry Moss) *chsd ldrs: rdn along 3f out: sn wknd* **50/1**
0005 **10** 1 1/4 **Stellar Express (IRE)**[18] 5043 3 -9-1075 (p) CharlesBishop 5 32
(Michael Appleby) *led: over 3f: chsd ldng pair: rdn along over 3f out and sn wknd* **9/1**
5501 **11** 10 **Rockgoat (IRE)**[10] 5350 3 -9-469 AshleyMorgan 6
(Ian McInnes) *a outpcd and bhd* **12/1**

1m 39.46s (-4.24)**Going Correction** -0.475s/f (Stan) **11**Ran SP% **118.6**
Speed ratings (Par 100): **102,101,95,91,91 87,86,80,76,75 65**
toteswingers 1&2 £4.00, 2&3 £3.80, 1&3 £1.10 CSF £15.14 CT £66.77 TOTE £3.90 : £1.10, £1.10, £3.00 ; EX 17.80 Trifecta £61.50 £448.03 - 5.38 winning units.
Owner Dr Ali Ridha **Bred** Rabbah Bloodstock Limited **Trained** Newmarket, Suffolk

FOCUS
The majority of the field were closely matched in this apprentice handicap but only three were seriously involved in the straight.
Rockgoat(IRE) Official explanation: jockey said gelding did not face the kickback
T/Jkpt: £10,000.00 to a £1 stake. Pool of £25,000.00 - 2.50 winning tickets. T/Plt: £65.10 to a £1 stake. Pool of £60095.95 - 673.66 winning tickets. T/Qpdt: £17.80 to £1 stake. Pool of £5368.40 - 222.56 winning tickets JR

5722a - 5725a (Foreign Racing) See RI

5697 DEAUVILLE (R-H)
Tuesday, August 28
OFFICIAL GOING: Turf: good; fibresand: standard

5726a PRIX D'AFINEBAULT (CLAIMER) (3YO FILLIES) (FIBRESAND) 1m 1f 110y
3:25 (12:00) 3-Y-O **£9,583** (£3,833; £2,875 ; £1,916 ; £958)

RPR
1 **My Virginia (FR)**[38] 3 -9-00 (b) UmbertoRispoli 3 75
(X Thomas-Demeaulte, France) **87/10**
2 3/4 **Nopanicjim (IRE)**[76] 3 -8-40 MarcLerner(5) 12 69
(Rod Collet, France) **6/1**[3]
3 snk **Psyche (FR)**[23] 3 -9-40 JulienAuge 10 77
(C Boutin, France) **19/5**[1]
4 hd **Miss Bridget (FR)**[21] 3 -8-130 MaximeGuyon 4 72
(H-A Pantall, France) **58/10**[2]
5 snk **Susukino (FR)**[21] 3 -8-90 Christophe-PatriceLemaire 1 68
(S Kobayashi, France) **9/1**
6 3/4 **Chiquitita (IRE)**[25] 3 -8-60 EddyHardouin(3) 11 66
(J Heloury, France) **11/1**
7 1 **Princess Steph (IRE)**[15] 5156 3 -8-130 OlivierPeslier 9 68
(Heather Main) *racd 4th towards outside: pulling freely in early stages: rdn 2 1/2f out: nt pce to go w ldrs: styd on wl fnl f* **58/10**[2]
8 2 1/2 **Inrefusable (IRE)** 3 -9-20 GeraldMosse 5 66
(T Clout, France) **41/1**
9 1 1/2 **Fun Victoire (FR)**[25] 3 -8-90 ThomasHuet 2 56
(B Barbier, France) **36/1**
10 3/4 **Pepsy Chope (FR)**[171] 3 -8-90 (p) JohanVictoire 8 54
(C Boutin, France) **17/1**
0 **Caffea (FR)**[31] 3 -9-20 AlexisBadel 7
(Y-M Porzier, France) **17/2**
0 **Cause You're Mine (FR)** 3 -8-60 AntoineCoutier(3) 6
(C Lerner, France) **56/1**

2m 6.6s (126.60) **12**Ran SP% **116.1**
WIN (incl. 1 euro stake): 9.70. PLACES: 2.70, 1.90, 1.80. DF: 33.70. SF: 56.50
Owner Michel Del Valle **Bred** M & Mme G Forien **Trained** France

4864 CARLISLE (R-H)
Wednesday, August 29
OFFICIAL GOING: Soft (good to soft in places; 7.0)
Wind: Fresh, half against Weather: Cloudy, bright

5727 BRITISH STALLION STUDS SUPPORTING BRITISH RACING E B F MAIDEN STKS 5f 193y
2:30 (2:30) (Class 5) 2-Y-O **£3,234** (£962; £481 ; £240) **Stalls** Low

Form RPR
2254 **1** **Bachotheque (IRE)**[11] 5367 2 -9-377 DavidAllan 3 75
(Tim Easterby) *trckd ldrs: hdwy to ld over 1f out: sn rdn and edgd lft: kpt on strly fnl f* **13/8**[1]
04 **2** 2 1/4 **Star Request**[22] 4907 2 -8-120 JoeFanning 10 65
(Keith Dalgleish) *t.k.h: hld up: hdwy to chal over 1f out: carried hd high: kpt on same pce ins fnl f* **8/1**[3]
04 **3** 1 1/4 **Danehill Flyer (IRE)**[14] 5221 2 -9-30 RoystonFfrench 6 65
(Philip Kirby) *prom: rdn and effrt over 2f out: kpt on same pce fnl f* **25/1**
03 **4** 11 **New Rich**[21] 4960 2 -9-30 PaulMulrennan 1 32+
(Michael Dods) *w ldr: ev ch tl rdn and wknd over 1f out* **9/4**[2]
04 **5** nk **Annalova**[16] 5176 2 -8-50 GeorgeChaloner(7) 5 26
(Richard Fahey) *s.i.s: bhd and pushed along: hdwy over 1f out: kpt on fnl f: nvr able to chal* **33/1**
6 1 1/4 **Clarendale (IRE)** 2 -9-30 AndrewElliott 7 27
(Alan Swinbank) *hld up on ins: drvn over 2f out: sn outpcd* **8/1**[3]
06 **7** 3/4 **Just Paul (IRE)**[9] 5410 2 -9-30 FrederikTylicki 4 25
(Kate Walton) *t.k.h: led tl hdd over 1f out: sn wknd* **12/1**
0 **8** 3 **Indies Gold**[12] 5311 2 -9-30 DavidNolan 9 16
(Ann Duffield) *towards rr: struggling over 2f out: sn btn* **100/1**
40 **9** 6 **Masai King (IRE)**[60] 3937 2 -9-30 ChrisCatlin 8
(Robin Bastiman) *prom on outside tl rdn and wknd over 2f out* **18/1**

1m 17.1s (3.40)**Going Correction** +0.525s/f (Yiel) **9**Ran SP% **111.8**
Speed ratings (Par 94): **98,95,93,78,78 76,75,71,63**
Tote Swingers 1&2 £3.40, 2&3 £8.80, 1&3 £7.00 CSF £14.70 TOTE £3.00 : £1.20 , £1.10 , £6.10 ; EX 13.20 Trifecta £99.90 Pool: £686.29 - 5.08 winning units.
Owner Richard Taylor & Philip Hebdon **Bred** Tally-Ho Stud **Trained** Great Habton, N Yorks

FOCUS
Inside rail moved out from 1m to 3f adding 12yds to distances on Round course. An ordinary contest which looked to be run at reasonable gallop. The winner had bumped into some good horses previously and deserved this. The front three were well clear and the form is fairly straightforward.

NOTEBOOK
Bachotheque(IRE), who had an official mark of 77, chased the early leader, moved through over a furlong out and ground out a tough victory. He has some size about him so should have a bit more to come. (op 7-4 tchd 6-4)
Star Request has now showed ability on all starts but didn't see out the trip as well as Bachotheque here. One would imagine she'll head into nurseries. (op 7-1)
Danehill Flyer (IRE) is now qualified for a handicap mark, and would be of interest in that company if reproducing a similar performance to the one he put up here. (op 20-1)
New Rich seemed one of the more likely candidates for victory in a weak-looking field, so this was disappointing considering he was held so early. The jockey reported that colt stopped quickly. Official explanation: jockey said colt stopped quickly (tchd 5-2)
Annalova hadn't shown anything of great note previously but there was a modicum of promise in this effort, albeit she appears to want further. (op 25-1)

5728 CHRISTMAS PARTIES AT CARLISLE RACECOURSE H'CAP (BETFAIR SPRINT FLAT SERIES QUALIFIER) 5f 193y
3:00 (3:00) (Class 5) (0-70,70) 3-Y-O **£3,234** (£962; £481 ; £240) **Stalls** Low

Form RPR
2022 **1** **Blue Shoes (IRE)**[5] 5538 3 -9-164 DavidAllan 8 75
(Tim Easterby) *mde all: rdn wl over 1f out: kpt on strly fnl f* **11/4**[1]
1002 **2** 2 1/4 **Phoenix Clubs (IRE)**[13] 5257 3 -9-770 BarryMcHugh 10 74
(Paul Midgley) *t.k.h: hld up: swtchd lft and hdwy over 1f out: chsd wnr ins fnl f: r.o* **8/1**
P041 **3** nk **Chester Aristocrat**[20] 5000 3 -9-270 DarylByrne(5) 6 73
(Eric Alston) *t.k.h: trckd ldrs: effrt and rdn wl over 1f out: kpt on same pce fnl f* **5/1**
0360 **4** 1 1/2 **Rock Canyon (IRE)**[5] 5538 3 -8-958 (p) FrederikTylicki 5 56
(Linda Perratt) *hld up: effrt and drvn 2f out: kpt on fnl f: nvr able to chal* **16/1**
3135 **5** 1 1/4 **Star City (IRE)**[8] 5415 3 -9-164 (be) PaulMulrennan 3 58
(Michael Dods) *taken early to post: t.k.h: in tch: nt clr run briefly over 2f out: sn rdn: styd on fnl f: nvr able to chal* **9/2**[3]
5005 **6** 1 1/4 **Brunswick Vale (IRE)**[14] 5247 3 -7-1153 oh1 ow2(b) DanielleMooney(7) 12 43
(Paul Midgley) *s.i.s: bhd and outpcd: hdwy over 1f out: kpt on fnl f: nrst fin* **33/1**
-044 **7** nk **Commanche**[51] 3912 3 -9-366 RoystonFfrench 11 55
(Bryan Smart) *chsd ldrs: drvn along over 2f out: outpcd appr fnl f* **7/2**[2]
0-00 **8** hd **Roll Of Thunder**[75] 3111 3 -7-1351 oh1 JulieBurke(3) 1 39
(John Quinn) *trckd ldrs: rdn wl over 2f out: wknd appr fnl f* **14/1**
026 **9** 8 **Lady Bentinck (IRE)**[11] 5335 3 -7-1252 NeilFarley(5) 4 15
(Alan Berry) *s.i.s: hld up: rdn over 2f out: wknd over 1f out* **28/1**
0-03 **10** 2 1/4 **Jack Barker**[18] 5113 3 -8-1160 ChrisCatlin 9 16
(Robin Bastiman) *chsd wnr: drvn 1/2-way: wknd over 1f out* **25/1**

1m 16.62s (2.92)**Going Correction** +0.525s/f (Yiel) **10**Ran SP% **117.6**
Speed ratings (Par 100): **101,98,97,95,93 92,91,91,80,77**
Tote Swingers 1&2 £3.70, 2&3 £4.30, 1&3 £3.50 CSF £25.30 CT £106.27 TOTE £4.70 : £1.80 , £2.60, £1.80 ; EX 21.30 Trifecta £60.50 Pool: £501.43 - 6.13 winning units.
Owner C H Stevens **Bred** Mountarmstrong Stud **Trained** Great Habton, N Yorks

FOCUS
Modest handicap form.

5729 PES SECURITY H'CAP 1m 6f 32y
3:30 (3:30) (Class 4) (0-85,85) 3-Y-O+ **£4,075** (£1,212; £606 ; £303) **Stalls** Low

Form RPR
14 **1** **Red Orator**[141] 1281 3 -8-271 JoeFanning 4 81+
(Mark Johnston) *pressed ldr: led and c to stands' rail over 3f out: rdn and styd on strly fr 2f out* **9/2**[3]
3133 **2** 2 **Getabuzz**[11] 5344 4 -9-1081 DavidAllan 7 87
(Tim Easterby) *hld up: hdwy to chse wnr 2f out: sn rdn and hung lft: edgd rt and kpt on same pce fnl f* **11/4**[2]

1146 **3** 1 ½ **Luctor Emergo (IRE)**[9] 5430 3-7-13 **68**......................(p) AndrewMullen 1 72
(Keith Dalgleish) *prom: effrt and rdn over 3f out: hung rt over 1f out: kpt on ins fnl f* **8/1**

0524 **4** *hd* **Royal Swain (IRE)**[49] 3953 6-9-5 **76**............................ PaulMulrennan 3 80
(Alan Swinbank) *in tch: effrt against stands' rail over 3f out: rdn and edgd rt 2f out: kpt on same pce fnl f* **6/1**

3-05 **5** *8* **Samarkand (IRE)**[5] 5546 4-9-9 **80**....................................... ChrisCatlin 6 72
(Sir Mark Prescott Bt) *hld up towards rr: rdn over 4f out: effrt over 2f out: hung rt and wknd wl over 1f out* **2/1**[1]

0623 **6** *11* **Hot Rod Mamma (IRE)**[11] 5369 5-9-9 **85**................. GarryWhillans(5) 2 62
(Dianne Sayer) *t.k.h: in tch: stdy hdwy 3f out: rdn and wknd 2f out* **20/1**

-000 **7** *4* **Wells Lyrical (IRE)**[66] 3419 7-9-2 **73**......................... RoystonFfrench 8 44
(Bryan Smart) *led to over 3f out: rdn and wknd over 2f out* **28/1**

3m 15.24s (7.74) **Going Correction** +0.525s/f (Yiel)
WFA 3 from 4yo+ 12lb **7** Ran SP% **111.8**
Speed ratings (Par 105): **98,96,96,95,91 85,82**
Tote Swingers 1&2 £1.90, 2&3 £4.80, 1&3 £8.30 CSF £16.48 CT £92.53 TOTE £7.40: £2.60, £2.40; EX 18.00 Trifecta £193.80 Pool: £455.70 - 1.74 winning units..
Owner Newsells Park Stud **Bred** Newsells Park Stud **Trained** Middleham Moor, N Yorks

FOCUS
The pace looked fair from the outset considering the ground, and the leaders headed for the stands' rail once in line for home.
Samarkand(IRE) Official explanation: trainer had no explanation for the poor form shown
Hot Rod Mamma(IRE) Official explanation: jockey said mare ran too free

5730 EDWARDS & PRINGLE INVESTING FOR INCOME H'CAP 1m 1f 61y
4:00 (4:00) (Class 5) (0-70,70) 3-Y-0+ **£2,264** (£673; £336; £168) **Stalls** Low

Form RPR

0645 **1** **Edas**[43] 4179 10-8-7 **54**.. DeanHeslop(5) 4 65
(Thomas Cuthbert) *midfield: hdwy and styd alone far side: overall ldr wl over 1f out: hld on wl fnl f* **5/1**[3]

5150 **2** ½ **Come Here Yew (IRE)**[15] 5188 4-9-8 **69**.......................... NeilFarley(5) 5 79
(Declan Carroll) *prom: drvn and outpcd over 2f out: styd on strly fnl f: jst hld by far side wnr* **9/2**[2]

-002 **3** 2 ¼ **Dandarrell**[20] 5021 5-8-9 **51** oh4...................................... FrederikTylicki 9 56
(Julie Camacho) *cl up: rdn along over 2f out: led briefly stands' side gp ins fnl f: one pce* **8/1**

1340 **4** ¾ **Hydrant**[11] 5345 6-10-0 **70**... MichaelStainton 11 73
(Peter Salmon) *led: brought main gp towards stands' side ent st: hdd that gp ins fnl f: one pce* **3/1**[1]

4205 **5** 1 ½ **High Resolution**[18] 5085 5-9-5 **61**............................... PaulMulrennan 3 61
(Linda Perratt) *hld up: rdn and hdwy over 3f out: no imp fr 2f out* **10/1**

1645 **6** *nk* **Jordaura**[16] 5174 6-9-7 **66**.. JulieBurke(3) 1 65
(Alan Berry) *t.k.h: hld up: rdn along over 3f out: styd on fnl f: nvr able to chal* **33/1**

2416 **7** 1 ½ **Call Of Duty (IRE)**[12] 5290 7-9-12 **68**............................. DavidNolan 8 64
(Dianne Sayer) *hld up: rdn along over 3f out: nvr able to chal* **9/1**

2 **8** *2* **Goldmadchen (GER)**[16] 5174 4-9-4 **60**........................... JoeFanning 10 52
(Keith Dalgleish) *s.i.s: sn cl up: rdn and wknd fr 2f out* **20/1**

5033 **9** *7* **Naburn**[37] 4402 4-9-1 **62**.. GarryWhillans(5) 6 38
(Alan Swinbank) *in tch: struggling over 2f out: sn btn* **6/1**

10 1 ¼ **Grammar**[64] 3-9-5 **68**... BarryMcHugh 7 42
(Colin Teague) *hld up towards rr: stdy hdwy over 4f out: rdn and wknd over 2f out* **40/1**

2m 1.79s (4.19) **Going Correction** +0.525s/f (Yiel)
WFA 3 from 4yo+ 7lb **10** Ran SP% **114.5**
Speed ratings (Par 103): **102,101,99,98,97 97,95,94,87,86**
Tote Swingers 1&2 £4.40, 2&3 £7.10, 1&3 £9.20 CSF £26.64 CT £176.41 TOTE £7.70: £2.30, £2.70, £2.80; EX 27.80 TRIFECTA Not won..
Owner Mrs Joyce Cuthbert **Bred** Stilvi Compania Financiera Sa **Trained** How, Cumbria

FOCUS
A modest contest, landed by the only horse that stayed towards the inside rail in the home straight.

5731 CFM RADIO FILLIES' H'CAP 7f 200y
4:30 (4:31) (Class 5) (0-75,75) 3-Y-0+ **£2,264** (£673; £336; £168) **Stalls** Low

Form RPR

1340 **1** **First Class Favour (IRE)**[11] 5372 4-9-3 **66**....................... DavidAllan 7 75
(Tim Easterby) *in tch: rdn over 3f out: hdwy and edgd rt over 1f out: led ins fnl f: kpt on wl* **4/1**[3]

6040 **2** 2 ½ **Winter Dress**[34] 4490 3-7-11 **57**... NeilFarley(5) 3 59
(Declan Carroll) *t.k.h: led: rdn and edgd lft 2f out: hdd ins fnl f: kpt on same pce* **11/4**[2]

1221 **3** 2 ½ **Oddysey (IRE)**[20] 4996 3-9-6 **75**................................ PaulMulrennan 2 72
(Michael Dods) *trckd ldrs: wnt 2nd over 3f out: rdn and outpcd over 1f out* **6/4**[1]

5106 **4** *nk* **Painted Tail (IRE)**[10] 5383 5-9-8 **71**................................. JoeFanning 5 68
(Alan Swinbank) *trckd ldr to over 3f out: edgd rt and outpcd 2f out* **4/1**[3]

2020 **5** 2 ¾ **Frosty Berry**[32] 4602 3-9-1 **70**... BarryMcHugh 4 59
(John Wainwright) *hld up in tch: struggling over 3f out: btn fnl 2f* **16/1**

1m 43.65s (3.65) **Going Correction** +0.525s/f (Yiel)
WFA 3 from 4yo+ 6lb **5** Ran SP% **112.5**
Speed ratings (Par 100): **102,99,97,96,93**
Tote Swinger 1&2 £6.60 CSF £15.54 TOTE £4.40: £2.90, £3.40; EX 11.80.
Owner S A Heley **Bred** Oghill House Stud **Trained** Great Habton, N Yorks

FOCUS
The gallop set by the leader seemed strong, and the runners looked legless in the last furlong.
First Class Favour(IRE) Official explanation: trainer's rep said, regarding apparent improvement in form, that the filly was better suited by a return to a mile.

5732 DURDAR H'CAP 7f 200y
5:00 (5:03) (Class 4) (0-85,79) 3-Y-0 **£4,075** (£1,212; £606; £303) **Stalls** Low

Form RPR

2452 **1** **Prophesy (IRE)**[9] 5414 3-9-2 **79**....................................... NeilFarley(5) 3 86
(Declan Carroll) *led 2f: cl up: rdn to ld appr fnl f: kpt on strly* **10/11**[1]

1-05 **2** ¾ **Hurler And Farmer (IRE)**[13] 5273 3-9-3 **75**.................... FrederikTylicki 1 80
(Richard Fahey) *reluctant to enter stalls: in tch: rdn over 3f out: effrt and c stands' side over 2f out: styd on strly fnl f* **8/1**

336 **3** ½ **Boots And Spurs**[8] 5473 3-8-13 **74**......................(v) MichaelMetcalfe(3) 5 78
(Mrs K Burke) *cl up: rdn and drifted lft over 1f out: kpt on fnl f: hld nr fin* **6/1**[3]

1104 **4** *hd* **King Of Paradise (IRE)**[28] 4713 3-8-5 **68**...................... DarylByrne(5) 2 72
(Eric Alston) *plld hrd in tch: hdwy to ld after 2f: hdd appr fnl f: kpt on: hld towards fin* **17/2**

6105 **5** *23* **Raheeba**[11] 5372 3-8-13 **71**.. JoeFanning 4 41
(Mark Johnston) *in tch: rdn and c stands' side over 3f out: wknd over 2f out: eased whn btn fnl f* **10/3**[2]

1m 43.8s (3.80) **Going Correction** +0.525s/f (Yiel) **5** Ran SP% **111.4**
Speed ratings (Par 102): **102,101,100,100,77**
CSF £8.99 TOTE £1.80: £1.10, £4.70; EX 9.60.
Owner M Stewart **Bred** King Bloodstock And R Scarborough **Trained** Sledmere, E Yorks
■ Stewards' Enquiry : Frederik Tylicki two-day ban: used whip above permitted level (Sep 12-13)

FOCUS
Runners fanned out across the course as they entered the home straight.
T/Plt: £112.90 to a £1 stake. Pool: £46,262.50 - 299.12 winning tickets T/Qpdt: £49.60 to a £1 stake. Pool: £3,161.20 - 46.06 winning tickets RY

5290 CATTERICK (L-H)
Wednesday, August 29

OFFICIAL GOING: Soft (7.2)
Wind: Moderate half behind Weather: Heavy cloud

5733 BET TOTEPLACEPOT AT TOTEPOOL.COM MEDIAN AUCTION MAIDEN STKS 5f
2:10 (2:11) (Class 6) 2-Y-0 **£2,045** (£603; £302) **Stalls** Low

Form RPR

4 **1** **Chasing Dreams**[20] 5003 2-8-12 0.................................. PhillipMakin 6 74+
(Kevin Ryan) *qckly away: mde all: clr wl over 1f out: easily* **4/9**[1]

04 **2** *4* **Megaleka**[16] 5168 2-8-12 0... DuranFentiman 5 57
(Chris Fairhurst) *trckd ldrs: hdwy on outer 2f out: rdn over 1f out: kpt on to take 2nd ins fnl f: no ch w wnr* **11/1**[3]

6 **3** 2 ¾ **St Mary De Castro**[13] 5255 2-8-12 0.......................... GrahamGibbons 7 47
(Michael Easterby) *cl up: pushed along 1/2-way: rdn along 2f out: sn one pce and lost 2nd ins fnl f* **33/1**

03 **4** 1 ¾ **Fidget**[16] 5168 2-8-12 0.. RobertWinston 1 40
(David Brown) *trckd ldrs on inner: rdn along 2f out: sn one pce* **7/2**[2]

000 **5** 1 ½ **Shepherds Bow**[9] 5410 2-9-3 0.................................... JamesSullivan 2 40
(Michael Easterby) *sn pushed along: a in rr* **50/1**

0004 **6** 1 ¾ **Betty Boo (IRE)**[12] 5313 2-8-5 **48**........................... ShirleyTeasdale(7) 3 29
(Shaun Harris) *chsd ldrs: rdn along over 2f out: sn wknd* **16/1**

1m 1.11s (1.31) **Going Correction** +0.25s/f (Good) **6** Ran SP% **110.6**
Speed ratings (Par 92): **99,92,88,85,83 80**
Tote Swingers 1&2 £1.90, 2&3 £7.30, 1&3 £3.10 CSF £6.42 TOTE £1.70: £1.10, £3.40; EX 5.60.
Owner Hambleton Racing Ltd XXIV **Bred** Genesis Green Stud Ltd & John Troy **Trained** Hambleton, N Yorks

FOCUS
There had been plenty of rain around and the ground was on the soft side, although the time of this opening contest wasn't too bad. An uncompetitive maiden, but a nice winner and one or two of the beaten runners should be capable of better in due course.

NOTEBOOK
Chasing Dreams shaped nicely on her debut at Sandown (5f, good) and readily confirmed that promise, showing good speed from the off before being eased near the line. She'll obviously be worth her place in better company. (op 4-6)
Megaleka reversed recent fast-ground form with Fidget, and both of those now have the option of nurseries. (tchd 12-1)
St Mary De Castro ◆ showed little on her debut at Beverley, but this was an eyecatching display. She wasn't given anything like a hard ride and should be capable of better. (tchd 28-1)
Fidget now has the option of nurseries. (op 3-1)
Shepherds Bow ◆ shaped as though he had ability on his debut, but had been well beaten on his next two starts. This time, although again well beaten, he went some way to confirming that initial impression, and he'll be one to watch when switching to nurseries/handicaps.

5734 YOUR FAVOURITE POOL BETS AT TOTEPOOL.COM MAIDEN STKS 5f 212y
2:40 (2:40) (Class 5) 3-Y-0+ **£2,264** (£673; £336; £168) **Stalls** Low

Form RPR

-205 **1** **Cone Donkey (IRE)**[113] 1960 3-8-12 **63**............................... TomEaves 1 53
(Bryan Smart) *rrd s: sn led: rdn wl over 1f out: drvn and edgd rt fnl f: hld on gamely* **4/1**[2]

0504 **2** ½ **Karate Queen**[21] 4956 7-8-12 **45**.................................... DaleSwift(3) 6 51
(Ron Barr) *hld up towards rr: hdwy over 2f out: rdn to chse ldng pair over 1f out: drvn to chal ins fnl f: kpt on same pce towards fin* **9/2**[3]

6030 **3** 1 ½ **Desert Red (IRE)**[8] 5458 3-8-12 **46**.......................(b) SilvestreDeSousa 3 46
(Phil McEntee) *trckd ldng pair on inner: hdwy over 2f out: sn swtchd rt and rdn to chal over 1f out: drvn and ev ch ins fnl f: edgd lft and wknd last 100yds* **10/1**

5050 **4** 4 ½ **Niceonemyson**[70] 3272 3-9-3 **55**.................................... PaddyAspell 7 37
(Christopher Wilson) *in tch: hdwy to chse ldrs over 2f out: sn rdn and one pce* **17/2**

5 *4* **Imperial Bond** 3-9-3 0.. TonyHamilton 4 24
(Jedd O'Keeffe) *in rr: sme hdwy 2f out: sn rdn and nvr nr ldrs* **25/1**

2 **6** 3 ¼ **Vanity's Girl (IRE)**[81] 2918 3-8-12 0.......................... MichaelO'Connell 10 9
(John Quinn) *in tch: pushed along 1/2-way: rdn over 2f out and sn btn* **2/1**[1]

0/60 **7** ¾ **Heart Beat Song**[11] 5335 4-9-6 **50**.................................... GrahamLee 8 11
(Alan Berry) *chsd ldrs: rdn along bef 1/2-way and sn wknd* **50/1**

-350 **8** *2* **Zaffy (IRE)**[49] 3952 3-8-12 **56**...................................... DuranFentiman 2
(Tim Easterby) *chsd ldr: pushed along 1/2-way: sn rdn and wknd 2f out* **5/1**

/0-0 **9** *4* **Jamaica Grande**[23] 4880 4-9-6 **43**................................. WilliamCarson 5
(Terry Clement) *sn outpcd and a bhd* **100/1**

1m 17.06s (3.46) **Going Correction** +0.575s/f (Yiel)
WFA 3 from 4yo+ 3lb **9** Ran SP% **114.6**
Speed ratings (Par 103): **99,98,96,90,85 80,79,77,71**
Tote Swingers 1&2 £4.40, 2&3 £8.10, 1&3 £3.50 CSF £21.93 TOTE £9.40: £2.10, £2.10, £4.00; EX 25.40.
Owner Dean O'Brien **Bred** Martyn Barber **Trained** Hambleton, N Yorks

FOCUS
The runner-up and third came into this with official marks in the 40s.

5735 FREE RACING POST FORM AT TOTEPOOL.COM H'CAP 1m 7f 177y
3:10 (3:10) (Class 5) (0-70,63) 3-Y-0+ **£2,385** (£704; £352) **Stalls** Centre

Form RPR

2112 **1** **Solar View (IRE)**[10] 5384 3-9-0 **63**................................... LukeMorris 5 72+
(Sir Mark Prescott Bt) *trckd ldrs: niggled along 6f out: pushed along to chse ldng pair over 3f out: rdn over 2f out: drvn to chal over 1f out: led jst ins fnl f: styd on* **1/1**[1]

-230 **2** 1¾ **Finellas Fortune**[25] 4831 7-9-7 **56**...................... GrahamLee 3 63
(George Moore) *prom: hdwy and cl up 7f out: led over 3f out: rdn over 2f out: jnd and drvn over 1f out: hdd jst ins fnl f: no ex* **8/1**[3]

3222 **3** 5 **Bijou Dan**[16] 5172 11-9-10 **59**...................... PJMcDonald 8 60
(George Moore) *led 3f: cl up: led again over 4f out: sn rdn along and hdd over 3f out: drvn and kpt on same pce fnl 2f* **8/1**[3]

0-23 **4** hd **Sheila's Castle**[18] 5114 8-9-2 **58**...................... JackDuern(7) 6 59
(Sean Regan) *hld up and bhd: hdwy 4f out: rdn to chse ldrs over 2f out: sn drvn and no imp* **14/1**

4303 **5** 11 **Amir Pasha (UAE)**[19] 5039 7-9-4 **53**......................(p) TomEaves 1 41
(Micky Hammond) *t.k.h: in tch: hdwy over 3f out: rdn over 2f out: sn drvn and n.d* **14/1**

0340 **6** 1½ **Dan's Heir**[48] 3988 10-8-13 **48**......................(p) JamesSullivan 4 34
(Wilf Storey) *hld up and bhd: sme hdwy over 3f out: sn rdn along and nvr a factor* **16/1**

4453 **7** 5 **Shy**[13] 5253 7-9-4 **60**......................(b) GemmaTutty(7) 2 40
(Karen Tutty) *a in rr* **14/1**

3336 **8** 4 **Shirls Son Sam**[10] 5384 4-9-1 **50**...................... KellyHarrison 7 25
(Chris Fairhurst) *trckd ldrs: led after 3f: rdn along and hdd over 4f out: sn wknd* **13/2**[2]

050 **P** **Aggravation**[26] 4766 10-9-0 **49**...................... TonyHamilton 9
(Chris Grant) *chsd ldrs: rdn along and lost pl over 5f out: bhd whn lost action and p.u 2f out: dismntd* **33/1**

3m 42.56s (10.56) **Going Correction** +0.575s/f (Yiel)
WFA 3 from 4yo+ 14lb **9** Ran SP% **114.4**
Speed ratings (Par 103): **96,95,92,92,87 86,83,81,**
Tote Swingers 1&2 £3.20, 2&3 £5.00, 1&3 £2.40 CSF £9.45 CT £42.46 TOTE £1.40: £1.10, £2.10, £2.40; EX 10.90.
Owner Neil Greig - Osborne House **Bred** Lady Richard Wellesley **Trained** Newmarket, Suffolk

FOCUS
There was further rain ahead of this modest staying event. The pace looked slow for the first circuit and the time was over 18 seconds above standard.

5736 TOTEPOOL.COM SPORTS GAMES BINGO & MORE H'CAP 7f
3:40 (3:40) (Class 4) (0-80,77) 3-Y-O **£4,528** (£1,347; £673; £336) **Stalls** Low

Form RPR
6632 **1** **Rusty Rocket (IRE)**[2] 5676 3-9-0 **76**...................... JoshBaudains(7) 2 85
(Paul Green) *cl up on inner: rdr lost irons bef 1/2-way: rdn and chal 2f out: styd on to ld jst ins fnl f: kpt on gamely* **6/1**

3101 **2** nk **Mick Slates (IRE)**[9] 5415 3-8-8 **68** 6ex...................... JasonHart(5) 3 75
(Declan Carroll) *hld up towards rr: gd hdwy on inner wl over 1f out: rdn and styd on strly fnl f: jst hld* **5/1**[2]

5342 **3** ¾ **Half A Billion (IRE)**[21] 4965 3-9-3 **75**...................... LeeTopliss(3) 5 80
(Michael Dods) *led: rdn along 2f out: drvn and hdd jst ins fnl f: kpt on same pce* **8/1**

1121 **4** 4½ **Daddy Warbucks (IRE)**[16] 5170 3-9-7 **76**...................... AdrianNicholls 10 69
(David Nicholls) *cl up: rdn along over 2f out: drvn wl over 1f out and grad wknd* **11/2**[3]

2253 **5** 2¼ **Eastlands Lad (IRE)**[22] 4913 3-8-7 **62**......................(p) PJMcDonald 9 49
(Micky Hammond) *hld up towards rr: hdwy on wd outside over 2f out: sn rdn and no imp appr fnl f* **7/1**

5163 **6** ½ **Ferdy (IRE)**[18] 5093 3-8-4 **59**...................... WilliamCarson 8 44
(Paul Green) *chsd ldrs: rdn along wl over 2f out: sn wknd* **11/1**

1300 **7** 6 **On The Hoof**[39] 4329 3-9-2 **71**...................... GrahamGibbons 4 40
(Michael Easterby) *dwlt: a towards rr* **14/1**

-051 **8** 3½ **Idler (IRE)**[4] 5582 3-9-8 **77** 6ex...................... SilvestreDeSousa 6 37
(Mark Johnston) *dwlt: hdwy on outer after 2f: rdn to chse ldrs over 2f out: wknd wl over 1f out* **3/1**[1]

5-50 **9** 1¼ **Viola D'Amour (IRE)**[102] 2272 3-9-6 **75**...................... RobertWinston 1 31
(Tom Dascombe) *a in rr* **18/1**

1m 30.66s (3.66) **Going Correction** +0.575s/f (Yiel) **9** Ran SP% **115.2**
Speed ratings (Par 102): **102,101,100,95,93 92,85,81,80**
Tote Swingers 1&2 £4.00, 2&3 £6.50, 1&3 £8.10 CSF £35.95 CT £241.95 TOTE £6.50: £2.20, £2.50, £1.50; EX 31.10.
Owner Seven Stars Racing **Bred** Mike Hyde **Trained** Lydiate, Merseyside

FOCUS
The rain continued. It proved hard to make up ground.
Idler(IRE) Official explanation: jockey said gelding had no more to give

5737 FOLLOW TOTEPOOL ON FACEBOOK AND TWITTER H'CAP 5f 212y
4:10 (4:11) (Class 5) (0-75,81) 3-Y-O+ **£2,264** (£673; £336; £168) **Stalls** Low

Form RPR
6035 **1** **We'll Deal Again**[18] 5093 5-9-5 **70**......................(b) GrahamGibbons 12 80
(Michael Easterby) *quicly away and sn led: jnd and rdn along 2f out: hdd jst over 1f out: drvn and rallied ins fnl f to ld nr fin* **8/1**

0150 **2** nk **Indego Blues**[18] 5110 3-9-6 **74**...................... AdrianNicholls 2 83
(David Nicholls) *trckd wnr: cl up 1/2-way: chal 2f out: sn rdn and led jst over 1f out: drvn ins fnl f: hdd and no ex nr fin* **10/3**[3]

3100 **3** 2¾ **Restless Bay (IRE)**[11] 5338 4-8-12 **69** ow1...........(p) ConorHarrison(7) 1 70
(Mrs K Burke) *towards rr: swtchd to outer and hdwy 2f out: sn rdn and styd on wl fnl f: nrst fin* **16/1**

U112 **4** hd **Llewellyn**[42] 4207 4-9-0 **72**...................... ShirleyTeasdale(7) 7 72
(David Nicholls) *awkward and dwlt s: in rr: hdwy 1/2-way: rdn 2f out and sn chsng ldrs: drvn and kpt on fnl f: nrst fin* **11/4**[1]

0145 **5** 1¼ **Bunce (IRE)**[2] 5674 4-9-3 **75**...................... DavidBergin(7) 11 71
(David O'Meara) *chsd ldrs: hdwy to chse ldng pair 2f out: sn rdn and wknd fnl f* **3/1**[2]

50 **6** 3 **Beach Candy (IRE)**[16] 5150 3-9-2 **70**......................(b[1]) PJMcDonald 8 56
(Phil McEntee) *chsd ldrs: rdn along wl over 2f out: sn btn* **20/1**

1614 **7** 1½ **Only Ten Per Cent (IRE)**[14] 5245 4-9-10 **75**...................... GrahamLee 9 56
(J R Jenkins) *chsd ldrs on inner: rdn along over 2f out: sn wknd* **10/1**

1300 **8** 1½ **Secret City (IRE)**[26] 4784 6-9-2 **67**......................(b) DanielTudhope 10 43
(Robin Bastiman) *a towards rr* **16/1**

0460 **9** 13 **China Excels**[12] 5314 5-8-12 **63**...................... RussKennemore 4
(Sue Smith) *chsd ldng pair to 1/2-way: sn lost pl and bhd* **50/1**

0050 **10** 2½ **Red Roar (IRE)**[9] 5416 5-9-2 **67**...................... TonyHamilton 5
(Alan Berry) *n.m.r s and sn in rr: outpcd and bhd fr 1/2-way* **25/1**

1m 16.79s (3.19) **Going Correction** +0.575s/f (Yiel)
WFA 3 from 4yo+ 3lb **10** Ran SP% **117.3**
Speed ratings (Par 103): **101,100,96,96,95 91,89,87,69,66**
Tote Swingers 1&2 £6.60, 2&3 £13.70, 1&3 £17.40 CSF £34.39 CT £435.15 TOTE £7.70: £3.00, £1.70, £5.10; EX 38.20.
Owner K Wreglesworth **Bred** K Wreglesworth **Trained** Sheriff Hutton, N Yorks

FOCUS
The front two dominated throughout.

5738 DEAL OR NO DEAL AT TOTEPOOL.COM H'CAP 1m 3f 214y
4:40 (4:41) (Class 6) (0-60,60) 3-Y-O **£2,045** (£603; £302) **Stalls** Centre

Form RPR
0400 **1** **Brasingaman Espee**[18] 5115 3-8-7 **46** oh1................(b[1]) AndrewElliott 5 58
(George Moore) *mde all: rdn clr over 3f out: styd on strly* **7/1**

0650 **2** 3¾ **Pugnacious (IRE)**[16] 5164 3-9-1 **54**......................(b[1]) DanielTudhope 11 60
(Mark Johnston) *trckd ldrs on inner: hdwy 4f out: rdn along 3f out: drvn to chse wnr 2f out: no real imp* **8/1**

-006 **3** 9 **Galletto (IRE)**[19] 5063 3-8-9 **48**...................... WilliamCarson 12 40
(Terry Clement) *towards rr: hdwy over 3f out: rdn wl over 2f out: styd on to take modest 3rd ins fnl f* **18/1**

6603 **4** 2¼ **Millymonkin**[11] 5373 3-9-7 **60**......................(t) JamesSullivan 7 48
(Michael Easterby) *chsd ldng pair: rdn along 3f out: drvn 2f out and sn btn* **5/1**[3]

5226 **5** 5 **Margo Channing**[11] 5373 3-9-2 **55**......................(p) PJMcDonald 2 35
(Micky Hammond) *trckd ldrs: pushed along bef 1/2-way: rdn and outpcd over 4f out: plugged on fnl 2f: n.d* **3/1**[1]

5042 **6** 2½ **My New Angel (IRE)**[14] 5246 3-8-7 **46** oh1.............(be) JamieMackay 10 22
(Paul Green) *towards rr: hdwy and in tch 5f out: rdn along over 3f out: n.d* **10/1**

04U0 **7** 2 **No Dominion (IRE)**[34] 4498 3-9-7 **60**...................... GrahamLee 3 33
(James Given) *chsd wnr: rdn along over 3f out: drvn over 2f out: sn wknd* **4/1**[2]

060 **8** 1¼ **Miss Mohawk (IRE)**[12] 5315 3-8-11 **50**...................... MichaelO'Connell 1 21
(Alan Brown) *rdn along sn after s: a in rr* **66/1**

0000 **9** 10 **Darrow (IRE)**[12] 5295 3-9-2 **55**...................... AmyRyan 8 10
(Wilf Storey) *in rr: sme hdwy 1/2-way: sn rdn along and nvr a factor* **16/1**

0000 **10** 1¾ **July Specialists**[33] 4549 3-8-4 **46** oh1...................... DeclanCannon(3) 6
(Richard Guest) *a in rr* **33/1**

5560 **11** 25 **Landaho**[9] 5427 3-8-9 **48** oh1 ow2...................... GrahamGibbons 4
(Hugh McWilliams) *a towards rr* **25/1**

2m 48.79s (9.89) **Going Correction** +0.575s/f (Yiel) **11** Ran SP% **113.8**
Speed ratings (Par 98): **90,87,81,80,76 75,73,72,66,65 48**
Tote Swingers 1&2 £7.20, 2&3 £14.60, 1&3 £26.10 CSF £58.86 CT £961.12 TOTE £6.50: £2.20, £3.40, £6.90; EX 56.50.
Owner R Morgan **Bred** Mrs Heather Morgan **Trained** Middleham Moor, N Yorks

FOCUS
A moderate contest in which two drew clear.

5739 BET US OPEN TENNIS AT TOTEPOOL.COM H'CAP (DIV I) 5f
5:10 (5:10) (Class 6) (0-65,65) 3-Y-O+ **£2,045** (£603; £302) **Stalls** Low

Form RPR
3031 **1** **Come On Dave (IRE)**[20] 5013 3-9-8 **65**...................... AdrianNicholls 11 78
(David Nicholls) *sn led: rdn clr 2f out: kpt on wl fnl f* **4/1**[1]

4034 **2** 1¾ **Mr Mo Jo**[12] 5294 4-9-3 **58**...................... DanielTudhope 5 65
(Lawrence Mullaney) *cl up: rdn along wl over 1f out: kpt on u.p fnl f* **6/1**[2]

654- **3** ½ **Mission Impossible**[302] 7216 7-9-5 **60**......................(p) PatrickMathers 2 65
(Tracy Waggott) *chsd ldrs: rdn 2f out: kpt on u.p fnl f* **10/1**

0300 **4** nk **Sharp Shoes**[32] 4592 5-8-12 **53**...................... PaddyAspell 6 57
(Christopher Wilson) *chsd ldrs: hdwy 2f out: sn rdn and kpt on fnl f* **25/1**

5515 **5** ½ **Mecca's Team**[15] 5190 4-9-7 **65**......................(p) LeeTopliss(3) 9 67
(Michael Dods) *dwlt and towards rr: hdwy 1/2-way: rdn to chse ldrs wl over 1f out: kpt on one pce fnl f* **10/1**

0-00 **6** 2 **Tongalooma**[23] 4866 6-9-6 **64**...................... LucyAlexander(3) 7 59
(James Moffatt) *sn outpcd and rdn along towards rr: hdwy 1/2-way: sn swtchd rt and rdn: styd on fnl f: nrst fin* **13/2**[3]

2140 **7** 3 **Chosen One (IRE)**[12] 5294 7-9-2 **57**...................... JamesSullivan 8 41
(Ruth Carr) *chsd ldng pair: rdn along 2f out: sn drvn and wknd* **8/1**

6U60 **8** 2¾ **Boga (IRE)**[28] 4717 5-8-5 **46** oh1......................(v[1]) JamieMackay 10 20
(Karen Tutty) *dwlt: a in rr* **40/1**

6-54 **9** nk **See Vermont**[64] 3463 4-8-7 **48**...................... DuranFentiman 4 21
(Robin Bastiman) *prom: rdn along 1/2-way: sn wknd* **8/1**

004 **10** 1 **Triskaidekaphobia**[22] 4911 9-8-5 **46**......................(t) AmyRyan 3 15
(Wilf Storey) *stmbld s and rdr lost iron: a in rr* **25/1**

0460 **11** 7 **Boucher Garcon (IRE)**[41] 4245 4-9-1 **61**...................... JasonHart(5) 1
(Declan Carroll) *sn rdn along in rr: bhd fr 1/2-way* **4/1**[1]

1m 0.9s (1.10) **Going Correction** +0.25s/f (Good)
WFA 3 from 4yo+ 2lb **11** Ran SP% **118.2**
Speed ratings (Par 101): **101,98,97,96,96 92,88,83,83,81 70**
Tote Swingers 1&2 £5.00, 2&3 £13.70, 1&3 £11.60 CSF £27.24 CT £230.69 TOTE £5.80: £2.00, £2.30, £3.90; EX 26.90.
Owner Middleham Park Racing XLIV **Bred** Mrs Eithne Hamilton **Trained** Sessay, N Yorks

FOCUS
The first division of a moderate handicap.
Triskaidekaphobia Official explanation: trainer said gelding was unsuited by the soft ground
Boucher Garcon(IRE) Official explanation: jockey said gelding never travelled

5740 BET US OPEN TENNIS AT TOTEPOOL.COM H'CAP (DIV II) 5f
5:45 (5:46) (Class 6) (0-65,65) 3-Y-O+ **£2,045** (£603; £302) **Stalls** Low

Form RPR
3 **1** **Ingenti**[13] 5257 4-8-11 **52**...................... PaddyAspell 7 62
(Christopher Wilson) *cl up centre: led 2f out: rdn clr appr fnl f: kpt on* **4/1**[2]

1553 **2** 3½ **Tuibama (IRE)**[12] 5318 3-9-5 **62**......................(p) GrahamLee 3 59
(Tracy Waggott) *racd on inner rail: led: rdn along and hdd 2f out: sn drvn: kpt on same pce fnl f* **9/2**[3]

0001 **3** ½ **On The High Tops (IRE)**[12] 5294 4-9-5 **60**...................... PJMcDonald 9 56
(Ruth Carr) *racd centre: chsd ldrs: rdn along 2f out: drvn and kpt on same pce fnl f* **7/2**[1]

4000 **4** ¾ **Ever Roses**[43] 4174 4-8-13 **54**......................(v) RussKennemore 1 47
(Paul Midgley) *chsd ldr on inner: swtchd rt to centre and hdwy 2f out: sn rdn and one pce appr fnl f* **15/2**

556 **5** ¾ **Northern Bolt**[42] 4207 7-9-8 **63**...................... PatrickMathers 6 53
(Ian McInnes) *dwlt and rdn along in rr: hdwy over 1f out: styd on: nrst fin* **11/2**

0620 **6** 3¾ **Cross Of Lorraine (IRE)**[21] 4956 9-9-3 **58**................(b) TonyHamilton 8 35
(Chris Grant) *chsd ldrs centre: rdn along over 2f out: sn wknd* **14/1**

4563 **7** 2½ **Duke Of Rainford**[12] 5327 5-8-6 **47**...................... JamesSullivan 2 15
(Michael Herrington) *s.i.s: a in rr* **7/1**

1m 1.09s (1.29) **Going Correction** +0.25s/f (Good)
WFA 3 from 4yo+ 2lb **7** Ran SP% **106.7**
Speed ratings (Par 101): **99,93,92,91,90 84,80**
Tote Swingers 1&2 £2.10, 2&3 £3.10, 1&3 £3.20 CSF £19.19 CT £56.21 TOTE £4.30: £2.70, £2.00; EX 17.30.
Owner David Bartlett **Bred** Mrs Andrea Bartlett **Trained** Manfield, N Yorks

FOCUS
Again, few got involved.
T/Plt: £172.10 to a £1 stake. Pool: £46,806.82 - 198.47 winning tickets T/Qpdt: £53.00 to a £1 stake. Pool: £4,547.96 - 63.45 winning tickets JR

5474 KEMPTON (A.W) (R-H)
Wednesday, August 29

OFFICIAL GOING: Standard
Wind: Moderate, half behind Weather: Overcast early, bright by Race 3

5741 WIN BIG WITH BETDAQ MULTIPLES APPRENTICE H'CAP 1m (P)
5:50 (5:50) (Class 5) (0-70,70) 4-Y-O+ £2,264 (£673; £336; £168) Stalls Low

Form RPR
200 1 **Perfect Mission**21 4939 4-9-3 70 (v) DanielMuscutt(7) 6 83
(Andrew Balding) *led 1f: trckd ldng pair after and a gng wl: clsd to ld jst over 1f out: shkn up and sn clr* 4/1[2]
500 2 3 1/4 **Pastoral Jet**7 5481 4-8-5 51 oh4 RyanPowell 13 57+
(Richard Rowe) *hld up in last trio: stdy prog over 2f out gng wl: shkn up ins fnl f: r.o wl to take 2nd last stride: hopeless task* 20/1
-056 3 hd **Tenessee**6 5506 5-9-0 65 MichaelJMMurphy(5) 12 70
(Jamie Osborne) *pressed ldr after 1f: rdn over 3f out: stl chalng whn wnr swept by jst over 1f out: lost 2nd last stride* 5/2[1]
0006 4 1 1/2 **Pat's Legacy (USA)**33 4541 6-9-6 69 MatthewLawson(3) 9 71
(Jo Hughes) *mde most after 1f: drvn wl over 2f out: hdd jst over 1f out: wknd ins fnl f* 5/1[3]
0460 5 4 **Katmai River (IRE)**37 4413 5-9-0 65 ThomasBrown(5) 4 57
(Mark Usher) *chsd ldrs: drvn wl over 2f out: outpcd wl over 1f out: no imp after* 20/1
6633 6 3/4 **Silver Alliance**55 3793 4-9-8 68 HarryBentley 11 59
(Julia Feilden) *chsd ldrs: rdn wl over 2f out: outpcd wl over 1f out: n.d after* 13/2
0064 7 1 1/4 **May's Boy**20 5008 4-9-0 65 (p) RachealKneller(5) 1 53
(Mark Usher) *chsd ldrs: rdn and no prog over 2f out: fdd over 1f out* 12/1
0540 8 1 **Big Bay (USA)**62 3544 6-9-7 70 (p) AntiocoMurgia(3) 5 56
(Jane Chapple-Hyam) *wl in rr: rdn and fnd nil over 2f out: wl btn after* 16/1
1410 9 3/4 **Shaunas Spirit (IRE)**21 4950 4-8-9 62 PaulBooth(7) 8 46
(Dean Ivory) *s.i.s: rousted along and making rapid prog on inner whn nowhere to go after 1f: snatched up and dropped to rr again: no prog fnl 2f* 11/1
03 10 hd **West Leake (IRE)**21 4950 6-8-11 60 DavidKenny(3) 14 43
(Paul Burgoyne) *racd wd: in tch to over 2f out: sn btn* 16/1
5-00 11 5 **Scarborough Lily**63 3497 4-8-9 58 (v) TobyAtkinson(3) 10 30
(Ed Vaughan) *a towards rr: rdn and looked unenthusiastic over 2f out: wl btn after* 25/1
06/0 12 9 **Head Down**44 4158 6-8-0 51 oh2 (v) NoelGarbutt(5) 2
(Martin Bosley) *s.s: trying to rcvr whn hmpd after 1f and dropped to last again: bhd rest of way* 50/1

1m 39.14s (-0.66) **Going Correction** -0.025s/f (Stan) 12 Ran SP% 121.7
Speed ratings (Par 103): **102,98,98,97,93 92,91,90,89,89 84,75**
toteswingers: 1&2 £16.00, 1&3 £4.50, 2&3 £21.90. CSF £88.43 CT £247.98 TOTE £6.20: £1.80, £7.10, £1.10; EX 114.30 Trifecta £194.30 Part won. Pool: £262.63 - 0.20 winning units..
Owner Mildmay Racing & D H Caslon **Bred** Mildmay Bloodstock **Trained** Kingsclere, Hants

FOCUS
A fair apprentice handicap, run at an even pace.
Head Down Official explanation: jockey said gelding suffered interference in running

5742 BACK OR LAY AT BETDAQ.COM MAIDEN STKS 1m (P)
6:20 (6:21) (Class 5) 2-Y-O £2,264 (£673; £336; £168) Stalls Low

Form RPR
4 1 **Cat O'Mountain (USA)**12 5321 2-9-3 0 FrankieDettori 8 78+
(Mahmood Al Zarooni) *dwlt: quick rcvry to chse ldr after 1f: chal and carried lft over 2f out: rdn to ld wl over 1f out: in n.d fnl f* 2/1[1]
2 1 1/2 **Swing Easy** 2-9-3 0 StevieDonohoe 3 73
(Robert Mills) *dwlt: towards rr: shkn up over 2f out: gd prog and rdn over 1f out: r.o to take 2nd last 100yds: clsng at fin* 33/1
3 hd **Chief Havoc (USA)** 2-9-3 0 WilliamBuick 10 77+
(Jeremy Noseda) *rn green in last trio: shkn up over 2f out: gd prog on outer jst over 1f out: fin wl: encouraging debut* 4/1[3]
04 4 2 3/4 **Storming (IRE)**13 5275 2-9-3 0 DavidProbert 6 67
(Andrew Balding) *led: hung lft over 2f out: hdd wl over 1f out: sltly checked sn after: one pce and lost 2 pls last 100yds* 9/1
0 5 3 **Camp Floyd (USA)**19 5062 2-9-3 0 MickaelBarzalona 4 60
(Mahmood Al Zarooni) *in tch: shkn up over 2f out: no imp and tending to hang over 1f out: fdd* 3/1[2]
05 6 3/4 **Sioux Chieftain (IRE)**15 5207 2-9-3 0 MartinLane 1 58
(Tim Pitt) *in tch: rdn and tried to cl on ldrs 2f out: no hdwy over 1f out: fdd* 50/1
32 7 3 **Contradict**23 4886 2-8-12 0 KierenFallon 5 46
(Sir Michael Stoute) *t.k.h: hld up bhd ldrs: pushed along and no prog 2f out: wknd* 6/1
03 8 6 **Keep Calm**7 5476 2-9-3 0 RichardHughes 2 37
(Richard Hannon) *prom: pushed along bef 1/2-way: btn 2f out: sltly checked 1f out and eased* 12/1
60 9 1 3/4 **Man From Seville**9 5407 2-9-3 0 JimmyFortune 12 33
(Sir Mark Prescott Bt) *in tch on outer: lost pl sn after 1/2-way: toiling in rr over 2f out* 100/1
0 10 10 **Dancing Chief (IRE)**57 3733 2-8-10 0 MichaelJMMurphy(7) 11 10
(Alan Jarvis) *restrained after s: sn detached in last and stlyd there* 33/1

1m 40.03s (0.23) **Going Correction** -0.025s/f (Stan) 10 Ran SP% 119.1
Speed ratings (Par 94): **97,95,95,92,89 88,85,79,78,68**
toteswingers: 1&2 £21.30, 1&3 £3.80, 2&3 £22.90. CSF £79.94 TOTE £3.50: £1.10, £8.10, £3.00; EX 83.70 TRIFECTA Not won..
Owner Godolphin **Bred** Darley **Trained** Newmarket, Suffolk
■ Stewards' Enquiry : Mickael Barzalona one-day ban: careless riding (Sep 12)

FOCUS
An interesting juvenile maiden, run at fair pace and won convincingly by the favourite. The form is based around the third and fourth.

NOTEBOOK
Cat O'Mountain(USA) built on his encouraging debut run at Newmarket earlier in the month. The 2yo, who finished a never-nearer fourth at Newmarket, was much more alert from the gates on this occasion and, despite becoming slightly outpaced as they turned for home, was soon in command. He was being closed down by two newcomers in the final 100 yards however and he may need to improve on this again if he's going to make his mark in nurseries off an almost certain lofty rating. A Derby entry looks optimistic at this stage but he's sure to appreciate a step up to middle-distances next season. (op 5-2 tchd 15-8)
Swing Easy made a really pleasing start to his career and he ought not have any problem getting off the mark. He was virtually friendless in the ring beforehand and was clearly expected to need this. (op 25-1)
Chief Havoc(USA) ◆ may well prove the best of these. Drawn in stall 10, he was forced to race wider than ideal throughout and then got shuffled back as the pace lifted. However, he was putting in some excellent late work and would have grabbed second in another stride. He holds entries in some of the leading juvenile races later in the season and remains a very interesting prospect. (tchd 9-2)
Storming(IRE) appeared to step up on what he'd achieved in his two previous starts. He had most of these off the bridle when committing for home but got tired in the final 2f. That said, he kept on nicely and will be of interest when tackling nurseries. (op 14-1)
Camp Floyd(USA) was in trouble a long way out and lacked the necessary pace to get involved. It's likely he's capable of better but this would have to go down as a disappointing effort. (op 9-2)
Sioux Chieftain(IRE) Official explanation: jockey said gelding hung badly throughout
Contradict, placed over sprint distances on both previous starts, appeared not to stay and a drop in distances surely beckons. (op 4-1)

5743 BETDAQ MOBILE APPS NURSERY 6f (P)
6:50 (6:51) (Class 4) (0-85,85) 2-Y-O £3,428 (£1,020; £509; £254) Stalls Low

Form RPR
01 1 **Titled Gent**16 5176 2-8-13 77 KierenFallon 7 84+
(Brian Meehan) *t.k.h: hld up in 4th: quick move to ld 2f out: clr and drvn 1f out: r.o wl* 5/2[2]
5106 2 2 1/4 **Tommy's Secret**46 4102 2-9-2 80 BrettDoyle 8 79
(Jane Chapple-Hyam) *hld up in last: prog wl over 1f out: styd on fnl f to take 2nd nr fin* 20/1
14 3 1/2 **Exceptionelle**15 5201 2-9-7 85 [1] NeilCallan 4 83
(Roger Varian) *t.k.h: trckd ldng pair: chal 2f out: chsd wnr after but sn outpcd: lost 2nd nr fin* 5/2[2]
015 4 1/2 **Rafale**19 5060 2-8-11 75 PatDobbs 1 71
(Richard Hannon) *hld up in 5th: effrt on inner 2f out: rdn and styd on same pce fr over 1f out* 12/1[3]
301 5 2 1/2 **Ceelo**24 4846 2-9-1 79 RichardHughes 6 68
(Richard Hannon) *pressed ldr: rdn over 2f out: sn lost pl and btn* 7/4[1]
2015 6 1 1/4 **Must Be Me**13 5254 2-8-9 73 JohnFahy 2 58
(Eve Johnson Houghton) *t.k.h: hld up in 6th: shkn up 2f out: no prog and sn btn* 20/1
2150 7 1 3/4 **Three Crowns**12 5307 2-9-5 83 JamesDoyle 5 63
(Ian Wood) *led to 2f out: wkng whn sltly impeded over 1f out* 33/1

1m 13.08s (-0.02) **Going Correction** -0.025s/f (Stan) 7 Ran SP% 113.7
Speed ratings (Par 96): **99,96,95,94,91 89,87**
toteswingers: 1&2 £9.10, 1&3 £1.50, 2&3 £9.30. CSF £48.47 CT £136.06 TOTE £2.90: £1.10, £25.50; EX 65.40 Trifecta £348.20 Part won. Pool: £470.57 - 0.40 winning units..
Owner Lanesborough **Bred** Whatton Manor Stud **Trained** Manton, Wilts

FOCUS
An informative nursery, run at a fair pace. Straightforward form, and the winner may do better again.

NOTEBOOK
Titled Gent readily followed up his Wolverhampton maiden success. The juvenile was always handily placed and, once asked for his effort, fairly sprinted clear to win with plenty in hand. Sporting a cross noseband, he was keen enough in the early stages and looks some way ahead of the handicapper. This win is sure to have done his confidence no harm and, while a tilt at the Group 2 Champagne Stakes at Doncaster looks adventurous, he's progressing rapidly and lacks nothing in terms of size and scope. (op 2-1)
Tommy's Secret ran on strongly and appeared to benefit for this drop back from 7f. He'd won his maiden over the sharp 5f at Goodwood and clearly failed to last home in testing ground at Newcastle last time. This surface appeared to suit and he may have been a shade unfortunate to come up against such an improving type. (tchd 16-1 and 25-1)
Exceptionelle had already proved her effectiveness around here and she again ran with credit. The fact she was wearing a hood suggests she's not straightforward, but she's definitely got ability and settled better than she had on her turf debut last time. (op 7-2)
Rafale, the less-fancied of Richard Hannon's pair, ran a good race and could yet have more to offer. He showed signs of greenness under pressure but was keeping on. He failed to get 7f last time but may be worth another try over it. (op 11-1)
Ceelo may have gone a bit harder than ideal through the early stages, but was swamped with 2f remaining. He was keeping on again at the finish, but wouldn't be one to take short prices about next time. (tchd 13-8 and 2-1)

5744 BETDAQ CASINO GAMES H'CAP 2m (P)
7:20 (7:20) (Class 5) (0-70,66) 3-Y-O £2,264 (£673; £336; £168) Stalls Low

Form RPR
2452 1 **Wayne Manor (IRE)**32 4585 3-9-7 66 JimCrowley 1 74
(Ralph Beckett) *patiently rdn: in tch: prog on inner jst over 2f out: drvn to ld jst over 1f out: styd on wl* 7/4[1]
000 2 3/4 **Gucci D'Oro (USA)**13 5265 3-8-9 54 WilliamBuick 2 61
(David Simcock) *hld up bhd ldrs: cl up over 2f out: drvn over 1f out: styd on to take 2nd ins fnl f: a hld* 14/1
0006 3 3/4 **Albonny (IRE)**15 5219 3-8-8 60 MichaelJMMurphy(7) 9 66
(Alan Jarvis) *racd wd: in tch: rdn over 4f out: prog u.p to ld briefly over 1f out: kpt on same pce fnl f* 16/1
5420 4 3/4 **Somemothersdohavem**12 5323 3-9-7 66 (p) DaraghO'Donohoe 7 71+
(John Ryan) *hld up and last tl over 4f out: stl only 8th 2f out and looking for room: swtchd ins and drvn fnl f: r.o but no ch to chal* 10/1
5102 5 1 3/4 **Vexillum (IRE)**4 5589 3-9-3 62 SamHitchcott 3 65
(Mick Channon) *hld up in rr: rdn 3f out: kpt on same pce u.p fnl 2f: nvr able to chal* 6/1[3]
-244 6 1/2 **Lady Mandy**4 5589 3-8-5 50 PaulHanagan 8 53
(Ian Williams) *trckd ldr 5f and again fr 1/2-way: rdn to ld wl over 2f out: hdd over 1f out: fdd* 8/1
030 7 1 3/4 **Cape Alex**12 5297 3-8-13 58 (p) KierenFallon 6 58
(Clive Brittain) *t.k.h: hld up in tch: cl enough 2f out: wknd jst over 1f out* 10/1
-001 8 12 **Phantom Ranch**27 4744 3-8-9 54 HayleyTurner 4 47
(Hughie Morrison) *led at modest pce: upped the tempo after 6f: urged along 6f out: hdd wl over 2f out: sn wknd: eased* 4/1[2]
0056 9 76 **Vena Amoris (USA)**7 5483 3-8-7 52 JohnFahy 5
(Richard Rowe) *pushed along in rr after 2f: rousted along and rapid prog to press ldr after 5f: lost 2nd 1/2-way: wknd 6f out: t.o* 50/1

3m 30.8s (0.70) **Going Correction** -0.025s/f (Stan) 9 Ran SP% 114.5
Speed ratings (Par 100): **97,96,96,95,95 94,93,87,49**
toteswingers: 1&2 £6.70, 2&3 £18.60, 2&3 £7.90. CSF £28.96 CT £298.28 TOTE £3.30: £1.50, £4.60, £5.50; EX 37.80 Trifecta £221.30 Part won. Pool: £299.08 - 0.64 winning units..
Owner Tullpark Limited **Bred** Tullpark Ltd **Trained** Kimpton, Hants

FOCUS
A lack of pace always looked like being a problem in this staying handicap and so it proved.

Phantom Ranch Official explanation: trainer rep had no explanation for the poor form shown

5745 RACING PLUS THE BEST WEEKEND ACTION MAIDEN FILLIES' STKS 1m 3f (P)
7:50 (7:50) (Class 5) 3-Y-O+ **£2,264** (£673; £336; £168) **Stalls** Low

Form RPR

2 **1** **Seal Of Approval**[61] 3565 3-8-12 0 HayleyTurner 2 82+
(James Fanshawe) *t.k.h: trckd ldr after 100yds: moved up to chal over 4f out: gng bttr than rival after: shkn up and narrow ld over 1f out: edgd rt and rdn to assert last 100yds* **11/10**[1]

5 **2** *½* **Wannabe Loved**[25] 4791 3-8-12 0 WilliamBuick 1 81
(John Gosden) *led after 100yds but set stdy pce: stepped it up whn jnd over 4f out: drvn 3f out: narrowly hdd over 1f out: battled on but hld last 100yds* **11/4**[3]

2-53 **3** *2 ¾* **Moment Of Time**[22] 4916 4-9-7 85 (t) JimmyFortune 5 76
(Andrew Balding) *trckd ldng pair: rdn to chal over 1f out: no ex ins fnl f* **5/2**[2]

00 **4** *17* **My Espoir**[12] 5297 3-8-12 0 JohnFahy 3 45
(Clive Cox) *led 100yds: trckd ldng pair after: struggling once pce lifted over 4f out: wknd 2f out: wl bhd after* **33/1**

50 **5** *11* **Lea Valley**[23] 4888 3-8-12 0 PaulHanagan 7 26
(Julia Feilden) *t.k.h: hld up in last pair: struggling once pce lifted over 4f out: sn bhd: t.o* **40/1**

6 **6** *2 ¼* **Dei Amore (IRE)**[59] 3663 3-8-12 0 JamesDoyle 4 22
(Jonathan Portman) *hld up in last pair: struggling once pce lifted over 4f out: sn bhd: t.o* **25/1**

2m 23.7s (1.80) **Going Correction** -0.025s/f (Stan)
WFA 3 from 4yo 9lb **6** Ran SP% **112.1**
Speed ratings (Par 100): **92,91,89,77,69 67**
toteswingers: 1&2 £1.70, 1&3 £1.10, 2&3 £1.10. CSF £4.39 TOTE £1.50: £1.10, £3.00; EX 3.80.
Owner T R G Vestey **Bred** T R G Vestey **Trained** Newmarket, Suffolk

FOCUS
Limited numbers for this maiden, but some interesting fillies on show.

5746 LADIES DAY AT KEMPTON 08.09.2012 H'CAP 7f (P)
8:20 (8:20) (Class 3) (0-95,93) 3-Y-O+ **£6,663** (£1,982; £990; £495) **Stalls** Low

Form RPR

0404 **1** **Chapter And Verse (IRE)**[12] 5301 6-9-1 82 PatDobbs 8 93
(Mike Murphy) *hld up in last trio: stdy prog on inner over 2f out: rdn to chse wnr over 1f out: r.o to ld ins fnl f: sn in command* **10/1**[3]

2100 **2** *1 ¼* **Mr David (USA)**[11] 5342 5-9-1 87 (b) LeonnaMayor(5) 7 94
(Jamie Osborne) *pressed ldr: led wl over 2f out: rdn over 1f out: hdd and one pce ins fnl f* **16/1**

0402 **3** *½* **Lutine Bell**[11] 5342 5-9-11 92 RichardHughes 4 98
(Mike Murphy) *trckd ldrs: effrt 2f out: drvn and styd on to take 3rd ins fnl f: nvr able to chal* **9/2**[2]

600 **4** *1 ¼* **Noble Citizen (USA)**[18] 5102 7-9-7 88 (b) PaulHanagan 12 91+
(David Simcock) *hld up and sn last: prog 2f out: shkn up and r.o fnl f: nvr nr to chal* **11/1**

2400 **5** *½* **Esprit De Midas**[25] 4802 6-9-4 85 BrettDoyle 10 86
(Dean Ivory) *t.k.h: hld up towards rr: pushed along 3f out: tried to cl fr 2f out: kpt on one pce* **14/1**

1000 **6** *nk* **Dubai Hills**[25] 4828 6-9-9 90 TomEaves 6 90
(Bryan Smart) *trckd ldrs: drvn over 2f out: kpt on same pce fr over 1f out: n.d* **20/1**

5050 **7** *1* **Albaqaa**[26] 4761 7-9-12 93 DarryllHolland 9 91+
(P J O'Gorman) *hld up in last trio: nt clr run briefly wl over 2f out: plld out wd sn after: no prog tl r.o ins fnl f* **9/2**[2]

3141 **8** *1 ¼* **Mizwaaj (IRE)**[70] 3281 3-9-3 89 FrankieDettori 2 82
(Saeed Bin Suroor) *trckd ldng pair: rdn to go 2nd briefly over 1f out: wknd qckly fnl f* **6/4**[1]

0400 **9** *2 ¾* **Bay Knight (IRE)**[12] 5301 6-9-4 88 SophieDoyle(3) 5 75
(Sean Curran) *chsd ldrs: rdn over 2f out: sn lost pl: wknd fnl f* **33/1**

0005 **10** *nk* **Shifting Star (IRE)**[4] 5595 7-9-4 85 (t) KieranO'Neill 1 71
(John Bridger) *led at gd pce: hdd wl over 2f out: wknd rapidly over 1f out* **33/1**

1m 24.91s (-1.09) **Going Correction** -0.025s/f (Stan)
WFA 3 from 4yo+ 5lb **10** Ran SP% **117.0**
Speed ratings (Par 107): **105,103,103,101,101 100,99,98,94,94**
toteswingers: 1&2 £17.40, 1&3 £10.10, 2&3 £17.00. CSF £152.25 CT £819.51 TOTE £11.20: £3.90, £4.60, £1.70; EX 173.70 TRIFECTA Not won..
Owner D J Ellis **Bred** Stuart Weld **Trained** Westoning, Beds

FOCUS
A hot handicap, run at a good pace.

NOTEBOOK
Chapter And Verse(IRE) came with a strong late burst to record his first success in two years. The 6yo has gradually been working his way down the weights and he confirmed the promise of his latest course fourth under a perfectly-timed challenge. Always travelling well towards the rear, he got a dream run against the far rail and always looked likely to get there. He's clearly well suited by this track but is equally effective on fast ground. (op 11-1 tchd 9-1)
Mr David(USA) had finished behind Lutine Bell at Doncaster last time but turned the tables under an enterprising ride. Having moved smoothly to the front with 2f he run, he looked to have pinched it before getting a bit tired late on. He goes particularly well for this rider and appears best served by a fast-run 7f. (op 20-1)
Lutine Bell was given a typically patient ride by Richard Hughes and lost very little in defeat. He was travelling as well as anything as they turned into the straight before being outpaced by the principals. This was his third good run in his last four starts and it surely won't be long before he ends his lengthy losing run. (op 4-1 tchd 7-2)
Noble Citizen(USA) stayed on from a near impossible position. He has struggled to get competitive of late, but looks to be nearing a return his excellent early season form. Official explanation: jockey said horse hung right in final furlong
Mizwaaj(IRE) was returning after a 70-day break. He was in contention until a late stage, but stopped as if something went amiss. (op 13-8 tchd 7-4 and 15-8 in a place)

5747 SCOTT MILLS & STOOSHE LIVE 07.09.2012 H'CAP (LONDON MILE QUALIFIER) 1m (P)
8:50 (8:50) (Class 4) (0-85,85) 3-Y-O **£4,075** (£1,212; £606; £303) **Stalls** Low

Form RPR

0-41 **1** **Storm King**[14] 5231 3-9-0 78 BrettDoyle 3 92+
(Jane Chapple-Hyam) *wl in tch: prog on outer over 2f out: led over 1f out: rdn clr fnl f: decisively* **5/1**[3]

3000 **2** *2 ¾* **Restaurateur (IRE)**[14] 5237 3-8-8 72 (v) DavidProbert 9 78
(Andrew Balding) *hld up in rr: pushed along 3f out: prog and rdn over 1f out: styd on wl to snatch 2nd last stride* **6/1**

226 **3** *shd* **Gaul Wood (IRE)**[20] 5004 3-9-6 84 RichardKingscote 7 90
(Tom Dascombe) *trckd ldrs: rdn over 2f out: prog over 1f out: chsd wnr jst ins fnl f: no imp: lost 2nd last stride* **9/2**[2]

-165 **4** *1 ½* **Balady (IRE)**[30] 4647 3-8-12 76 PaulHanagan 4 78
(John Dunlop) *led at gd pce: drvn and hdd over 1f out: fdd ins fnl f* **16/1**

0423 **5** *1* **Dixie's Dream (IRE)**[13] 5269 3-9-5 83 RichardHughes 5 83
(Richard Hannon) *chsd ldrs on outer: rdn over 3f out: tried to cl over 1f out and ch of a pl: fdd and eased ins fnl f* **8/1**

2154 **6** *1 ¾* **Negin**[30] 4647 3-8-12 76 WilliamBuick 2 72
(Ed Dunlop) *w.w in 7th: prog over 2f out: chsd ldrs over 1f out: wknd fnl f* **14/1**

100 **7** *1* **Equation Of Time**[67] 3393 3-9-4 82 (t) J-PGuillambert 8 76
(Willie Musson) *broke wl but immediately restrained into last pair: pushed along over 2f out: no prog tl kpt on fnl f: nvr remotely involved* **33/1**

2306 **8** *1* **Sir Mike**[14] 5237 3-9-2 80 IanMongan 1 71
(Amanda Perrett) *chsd ldr 3f: drvn over 2f out: wknd over 1f out* **8/1**

0322 **9** *3 ½* **Four Leaves (IRE)**[18] 5107 3-8-12 76 MickaelBarzalona 10 59+
(Marco Botti) *hld up: prog to trck ldr after 3f: chal on inner and upsides wl over 1f out: wknd qckly fnl f* **7/2**[1]

0025 **10** *73* **Asifa (IRE)**[9] 5429 3-9-7 85 (b[1]) FrankieDettori 6
(Saeed Bin Suroor) *hld up in last pair: shkn up over 2f out: virtually p.u over 1f out* **7/1**

1m 38.4s (-1.40) **Going Correction** -0.025s/f (Stan) **10** Ran SP% **121.6**
Speed ratings (Par 102): **106,103,103,101,100 98,97,96,93,20**
toteswingers: 1&2 £12.60, 1&3 £9.70, 2&3 £6.90. CSF £36.79 CT £151.61 TOTE £7.50: £2.90, £2.30, £1.20; EX 63.60 Trifecta £264.40 Part won. Pool: £357.39 - 0.50 winning units..
Owner Norcroft Park Stud **Bred** Norcroft Park Stud And D Laidlaw **Trained** Dalham, Suffolk

FOCUS
A competitive handicap, run at a blistering pace.
Asifa(IRE) Official explanation: jockey said gelding hung right and held its breath
T/Plt: £260.20 to a £1 stake. Pool: £49,256.57 - 138.18 winning tickets. T/Qpdt: £23.30 to a £1 stake. Pool: £5,993.05 - 190.00 winning tickets. JN

5423 WOLVERHAMPTON (A.W) (L-H)
Wednesday, August 29

OFFICIAL GOING: Standard
Wind: Fresh behind Weather: Fine

5748 32RED.COM MAIDEN AUCTION STKS 5f 20y(P)
5:40 (5:40) (Class 5) 2-Y-O **£2,264** (£673; £336; £168) **Stalls** Low

Form RPR

1 **Foxy Forever (IRE)** 2-8-9 0 SeanLevey 2 78
(Michael Wigham) *s.i.s: sn hld up in tch and racd keenly: rdn to ld and edgd lft ins fnl f: r.o* **2/1**[1]

20 **2** *2* **Annaley My Darling (IRE)**[111] 1997 2-8-6 0 FrannyNorton 5 68
(Jo Hughes) *chsd ldr: pushed along 1/2-way: rdn and ev ch ins fnl f: styd on same pce* **5/2**[3]

4205 **3** *nk* **Mandy Lexi (IRE)**[9] 5425 2-8-8 76 JamieSpencer 7 69
(Patrick Morris) *sn led: rdn and edgd rt over 1f out: hdd and unable qck ins fnl f* **10/1**

432 **4** *3 ¼* **Jet Acclaim (IRE)**[22] 4927 2-8-4 65 NickyMackay 1 53
(Marco Botti) *led early: chsd ldrs: pushed along 1/2-way: rdn over 1f out: no ex fnl f* **9/4**[2]

5 *½* **Tonality (IRE)** 2-7-13 0 DarrenEgan(5) 4 51
(J S Moore) *sn outpcd: nvr nrr* **20/1**

5004 **6** *1 ¾* **Mace The Ace**[9] 5423 2-8-4 51 CathyGannon 6 45
(David C Griffiths) *sn outpcd* **66/1**

5055 **7** *1 ¾* **Sound Affects**[14] 5222 2-8-1 43 DominicFox(3) 3 39
(Alan Brown) *prom: rdn 1/2-way: wknd over 1f out* **50/1**

1m 2.49s (0.19) **Going Correction** -0.175s/f (Stan) **7** Ran SP% **110.0**
Speed ratings (Par 94): **91,87,87,82,81 78,75**
toteswingers: 1&2 £1.80, 1&3 £3.00, 2&3 £4.50. CSF £6.69 TOTE £3.90: £3.30, £1.10; EX 9.60.
Owner D Hassan, J Cullinan **Bred** Tally-Ho Stud **Trained** Newmarket, Suffolk

FOCUS
A weak maiden run at a fair pace, with the well-backed favourite staying on well to win cosily. The form makes sense rated around the second and third.

NOTEBOOK
Foxy Forever(IRE), the only colt in the field, who cost 11,000euros in May and is closely related to modest 5f good-ground winner Pat Will, was not the best away and raced keenly but could be called the winner some way from home, staying on powerfully out wide, against two experienced rivals. The yard had only sent out one previous 2yo winner in the last five seasons and there could be more to come from the winner. (op 7-2 tchd 7-4)
Annaley My Darling(IRE), who was well supported on her debut over C&D when caught late on and found the soft ground against her at Chester last time, was more patiently ridden here but still struggled to see out the trip and looks a short finisher, even over the minimum. (op 2-1 tchd 11-4)
Mandy Lexi(IRE), the highest-rated runner in the field, set the pace but was readily passed by the winner and is beginning to looked exposed. (op 7-1)
Jet Acclaim(IRE), who had run well when short-headed over C&D on her nursery debut last time, was nicely positioned on the rail turning for home but found little for pressure and may do better when returned to low-grade nurseries. (op 2-1 tchd 5-2)
Tonality(IRE), a Redcar Two-Year-Old Trophy entry who cost £10,000 and is out of a modest 6f-winning dam (who stayed 1m), was not best away but made some late progress up the rails over this inadequate trip and should come on for this. (tchd 25-1)

5749 32REDPOKER.COM NURSERY 5f 216y(P)
6:10 (6:11) (Class 6) (0-65,65) 2-Y-O **£1,704** (£503; £251) **Stalls** Low

Form RPR

6562 **1** **Meet Me Halfway**[16] 5160 2-9-6 64 TedDurcan 6 68
(Chris Wall) *chsd ldrs: pushed along 1/2-way: r.o u.p to ld wl ins fnl f* **6/1**[2]

0640 **2** *1* **We Are City**[15] 5202 2-9-4 62 TomQueally 2 63
(Michael Bell) *led: rdn over 1f out: hdd wl ins fnl f* **6/1**[2]

506 **3** *hd* **Salvatore Fury (IRE)**[12] 5311 2-9-5 63 PatCosgrave 7 63
(Keith Dalgleish) *hld up: hdwy and nt clr run over 2f out: rdn and swtchd rt over 1f out: r.o* **8/1**[3]

030 **4** *nk* **Glossy Posse**[11] 5357 2-8-13 57 SeanLevey 4 57
(Richard Hannon) *hld up: nt clr run over 2f out: hdwy over 1f out: nt clr run and swtchd rt ent fnl f: r.o: nvr able to chal* **6/1**[2]

005 **5** *¾* **Melodee Princess (IRE)**[25] 4816 2-9-2 65 DarrenEgan(5) 13 62
(Ronald Harris) *a.p: pushed along to chse ldr over 2f out: rdn over 1f out: styd on same pce ins fnl f* **16/1**

006 **6** *½* **My Sweet Lord**[30] 4654 2-8-11 55 TomMcLaughlin 8 51
(Mark Usher) *s.s: outpcd: r.o u.p ins fnl f: nt rch ldrs* **33/1**

3205 **7** *2* **Millie N Aire**[5] 5544 2-9-7 **65**........ FergusSweeney 9 55
(Danielle McCormick) *hld up: pushed along 1/2-way: styd on fr over 1f out: nvr nrr* **16/1**

2041 **8** *½* **Not Now Blondie**[22] 4927 2-9-1 **62**........ RaulDaSilva(3) 12 50
(Chris Dwyer) *hld up: rdn over 1f out: nvr on terms* **6/1**[2]

0400 **9** *2* **Baltic Prince (IRE)**[9] 5423 2-8-11 **55**........ CathyGannon 11 37
(Paul Green) *mid-div: hdwy u.p 1/2-way: hmpd wl over 1f out: no ex fnl f* **33/1**

306 **10** *3½* **Municipal (IRE)**[19] 5040 2-9-4 **62**........ PhillipMakin 1 34
(Michael Dods) *chsd ldr tl rdn over 2f out: wknd fnl f* **7/2**[1]

520 **11** *10* **Silicon Valley**[105] 2164 2-9-2 **60**........ LiamKeniry 3 2
(Dominic Ffrench Davis) *sn outpcd* **28/1**

0040 **12** *3¾* **I'Ve No Money (IRE)**[9] 5403 2-8-12 **56**........(t[1]) FrannyNorton 5
(David C Griffiths) *prom: rdn over 3f out: wknd over 2f out* **25/1**

1m 15.12s (0.12) **Going Correction** -0.175s/f (Stan) **12** Ran SP% **115.4**
Speed ratings (Par 92): **92,90,90,90,89 88,85,85,82,77 64,59**
toteswingers: 1&2 £7.40, 1&3 £7.80, 2&3 £9.20. CSF £39.00 CT £290.59 TOTE £10.40: £3.00, £3.00, £5.50; EX 32.40.
Owner Des Thurlby **Bred** Stratford Place Stud And Watership Down **Trained** Newmarket, Suffolk

FOCUS
This weak yet competitive nursery was run at a decent pace, with the first six home well grouped. The form looks modest but straightforward, the field finishing rather compressed.

NOTEBOOK
Meet Me Halfway had stayed on well enough over 6f at Lingfield when runner-up on her nursery debut last time and she stepped up on that effort with a game victory here, off a 2lb higher mark. Her rider got a nice run up the rail and she responded willingly, suggesting that this trip is her minimum. (op 11-2 tchd 5-1)
We Are City got away quickly from her inside draw and looked to have stolen it when kicking two lengths clear inside the final furlong but was searching for the line late on, and just failed to get home. (op 5-1)
Salvatore Fury(IRE), who was dropping back in trip on his handicap debut, was doing all his best work late but was never quite getting there. (op 12-1)
Glossy Posse was unable to find a decent position early and seemed to be struggling turning for home but made plenty of ground up on her handicap debut suggesting that a longer trip would suit. (op 11-2)
Melodee Princess(IRE) showed good pace from her wide draw to race prominently but paid for doing a bit much early, and could not quicken when asked. (op 14-1 tchd 20-1)
My Sweet Lord had shown little in three 6f maidens prior to this, but made plenty of progress from the rear on his handicap debut, and is another who looks to want further. (op 66-1)
Municipal(IRE), a Redcar Two-Year-Old Trophy and Doncaster sales race entry, had shown ability at a modest level in three starts in turf maidens and was nicely positioned early from his good draw, but found little for pressure and dropped tamely away. (op 9-2)

5750 32REDBET.COM H'CAP 7f 32y(P)
6:40 (6:41) (Class 6) (0-65,64) 4-Y-0+ **£1,704** (£503; £251) **Stalls** High

Form RPR

0-00 **1** **Roy The Boy (USA)**[21] 4939 4-9-6 **64**........ AdamKirby 6 75
(Alan Bailey) *s.i.s: hld up: pushed along and hdwy over 1f out: rdn: nt clr run and swtchd rt 1f out: r.o u.p to ld wl ins fnl f* **12/1**

001 **2** *¾* **Decimate**[14] 5246 4-8-12 **63**........ WilliamTwiston-Davies(7) 12 72
(Alan McCabe) *chsd ldrs tl led over 2f out: rdn and hdd wl ins fnl f* **6/1**

4040 **3** *3* **Dvinsky (USA)**[23] 4872 11-9-5 **63**........(b) AmirQuinn 10 64
(Paul Howling) *chsd ldrs: rdn over 1f out: styd on same pce fnl f* **22/1**

0013 **4** *shd* **Conry (IRE)**[53] 3843 6-9-5 **63**........ JamieSpencer 2 64+
(Ian Williams) *hld up in tch: swtchd rt over 1f out: sn rdn: styd on* **5/2**[1]

0006 **5** *shd* **Powerful Pierre**[10] 5389 5-9-0 **63**........ LMcNiff(5) 8 63
(Ian McInnes) *hld up: rdn over 2f out: r.o ins fnl f: nvr nrr* **33/1**

6542 **6** *1* **Muhandis (IRE)**[9] 5427 4-9-2 **60**........ TomMcLaughlin 3 58+
(Nick Littmoden) *s.i.s: hld up: hdwy over 1f out: nt rch ldrs* **9/2**[3]

0500 **7** *1* **Fleetwoodsands (IRE)**[16] 5179 5-9-4 **62**........(t) LukeMorris 4 57
(Milton Bradley) *prom: rdn over 1f out: styd on same pce* **14/1**

056 **8** *½* **Tiberius Claudius (IRE)**[8] 5454 4-9-4 **62**........ TomQueally 5 56
(George Margarson) *s.i.s: hld up: hdwy over 1f out: sn rdn: no ex fnl f* **16/1**

1500 **9** *1¼* **Odd Ball (IRE)**[9] 5428 5-8-12 **61**........ DarrenEgan(5) 9 51
(Lisa Williamson) *s.i.s: hld up: nt clr run over 1f out: n.d* **25/1**

1003 **10** *7* **Spirit Of Gondree (IRE)**[23] 4872 4-9-4 **62**........(b) CathyGannon 1 33
(Milton Bradley) *chsd ldrs: rdn over 2f out: wknd and eased fnl f* **4/1**[2]

0002 **11** *3½* **Greek Islands (IRE)**[14] 5244 4-9-6 **64**........(v) LiamKeniry 7 26
(Ed de Giles) *led: pushed along and hdd over 2f out: rdn and wknd over 1f out* **14/1**

1m 28.62s (-0.98) **Going Correction** -0.175s/f (Stan) **11** Ran SP% **119.1**
Speed ratings (Par 101): **98,97,93,93,93 92,91,90,89,81 77**
toteswingers: 1&2 £16.50, 1&3 £35.30, 2&3 £14.30. CSF £81.59 CT £1608.04 TOTE £16.20: £4.90, £3.30, £4.90; EX 108.00.
Owner Cakey Bundles 2 **Bred** Rosebrook Farms & Moreau Bloodstock Int **Trained** Newmarket, Suffolk

FOCUS
Another low-grade handicap with the pace a steady one and the front two pulling clear late on.
Muhandis(IRE) Official explanation: jockey said gelding was slowly away

5751 32REDBINGO.COM (S) STKS 1m 141y(P)
7:10 (7:10) (Class 6) 3-Y-0+ **£1,704** (£503; £251) **Stalls** Low

Form RPR

5006 **1** **Justbookie Dot Com (IRE)**[8] 5440 4-9-5 **70**.....(b) SilvestreDeSousa 11 66
(David Evans) *hld up: hdwy over 2f out: rdn to ld and hung rt ins fnl f: styd on* **12/1**

1030 **2** *1¾* **Hurricane Spirit (IRE)**[7] 5480 8-9-4 **78**........ NicoleNordblad(7) 4 68
(Hans Adielsson) *dwlt: hld up: hdwy over 2f out: led 1f out: sn rdn: edgd lft and hdd: styd on same pce* **8/1**[2]

4406 **3** *hd* **Parque Atlantico**[72] 3233 3-8-12 **44**........ FrannyNorton 10 62
(Ed McMahon) *chsd ldrs: rdn and ev ch whn hmpd ins fnl f: sn wknd* **50/1**

1000 **4** *6* **Emerald Wilderness (IRE)**[158] 1034 8-9-11 **95**........(p) EddieAhern 5 57
(Robert Cowell) *chsd ldr: rdn to ld over 1f out: sn hdd: styng on same pce whn hmpd and eased ins fnl f* **8/13**[1]

5005 **5** *1¼* **Son Vida (IRE)**[23] 4889 4-9-11 **70**........(v[1]) CathyGannon 7 51
(Alan Bailey) *led: clr 6f out: rdn: edgd lft and hdd over 1f out: wknd fnl f* **16/1**

040 **6** *3¾* **Alhaban (IRE)**[23] 4889 6-9-11 **74**........ LukeMorris 2 42
(Ronald Harris) *chsd ldrs: rdn over 2f out: wknd over 1f out* **10/1**[3]

065 **7** *2* **Eastern Hills**[43] 4190 7-8-12 **72**........(p) WilliamTwiston-Davies(7) 8 32
(Alan McCabe) *prom: rdn over 2f out: wknd over 1f out* **20/1**

0000 **8** *8* **Can Do Les (IRE)**[8] 5452 3-8-12 **37**........(b) FergusSweeney 1 13
(Richard Phillips) *s.i.s: hld up: drvn along over 3f out: a in rr* **150/1**

0001 **9** *8* **Mahadee (IRE)**[16] 5171 7-9-11 **78**........(b) LiamKeniry 3
(Ed de Giles) *in rr whn hmpd over 7f out: n.d after* **8/1**[2]

/020 **10** *13* **Encompassing (IRE)**[30] 4657 5-9-5 **67**........(t) TedDurcan 9
(Sophie Leech) *hld up: rdn over 5f out: wknd over 2f out* **16/1**

1m 48.73s (-1.77) **Going Correction** -0.175s/f (Stan)
WFA 3 from 4yo+ 7lb **10** Ran SP% **120.1**
Speed ratings (Par 101): **100,98,98,92,91 88,86,79,72,60**
toteswingers: 1&2 £3.60, 1&3 £20.90, 2&3 £65.00. CSF £105.82 TOTE £10.90: £2.10, £2.20, £7.80; EX 114.90.There was no bid for the winner. Emerald Wilderness was claimed by F J Perry for £6,000.
Owner J A & S Wilcox **Bred** Haydock Park Stud **Trained** Pandy, Monmouths
■ Stewards' Enquiry : Nicole Nordblad two-day ban: careless riding (Sep 12-13)
Ted Durcan four-day ban: careless riding (Sep 12-14,16)

FOCUS
An uncompetitive seller run at a sound pace with the well-backed favourite disappointing and the field well strung out passing the post.

5752 32RED H'CAP 1m 1f 103y(P)
7:40 (7:41) (Class 4) (0-85,85) 3-Y-0+ **£4,528** (£1,347; £673; £336) **Stalls** Low

Form RPR

5522 **1** **Position**[9] 5429 3-9-7 **85**........ LukeMorris 1 95
(Sir Mark Prescott Bt) *hld up: hdwy over 5f out: rdn to ld ins fnl f: r.o* **7/2**[1]

-331 **2** *1* **Al Baidaa**[61] 3556 3-9-1 **82**........(b[1]) DominicFox(3) 3 90
(Roger Varian) *plld hrd and a.p: shkn up over 1f out: r.o* **4/1**[2]

0050 **3** *½* **Final Drive (IRE)**[12] 5301 6-9-9 **80**........(tp) AdamKirby 8 87
(John Butler) *hld up: hdwy over 1f out: sn rdn: styd on* **20/1**

1466 **4** *1½* **Shestheman**[20] 4984 3-9-0 **78**........ TedDurcan 12 82+
(David Lanigan) *hld up: hdwy over 1f out: r.o: nt rch ldrs* **5/1**[3]

/0-0 **5** *1* **Marine Boy (IRE)**[18] 5094 6-10-0 **85**........(t) StephenCraine 11 87
(Tom Dascombe) *chsd ldr tl led over 2f out: rdn over 1f out: hdd and no ex ins fnl f* **33/1**

2626 **6** *½* **Patriotic (IRE)**[30] 4662 4-9-9 **83**........ RaulDaSilva(3) 6 84
(Chris Dwyer) *hld up: hdwy over 1f out: nt rch ldrs* **16/1**

0620 **7** *7* **Spanish Plume**[18] 5091 4-9-8 **79**........ ShaneKelly 13 65
(Reg Hollinshead) *chsd ldrs: rdn over 2f out: wknd fnl f* **20/1**

3305 **8** *3¾* **Shamdarley (IRE)**[15] 5186 4-9-8 **79**........[1] PhillipMakin 7 57
(Michael Dods) *hld up: hdwy over 5f out: wknd wl over 1f out* **11/2**

3100 **9** *2* **Caledonia Prince**[109] 2090 4-8-6 **68**........ JemmaMarshall(5) 2 42
(Jo Hughes) *chsd ldrs: rdn over 3f out: wknd 2f out* **50/1**

3460 **10** *½* **Thunderstruck**[141] 1275 7-9-11 **82**........(p) TomQueally 9 55
(Scott Dixon) *s.s: a in rr: bhd fnl 3f* **50/1**

2063 **11** *1* **Grizzle**[21] 4949 3-9-3 **81**........ SilvestreDeSousa 10 52
(Mahmood Al Zarooni) *s.i.s: hld up: hmpd over 2f out: nvr on terms* **7/2**[1]

0303 **12** *3¼* **Sound Advice**[29] 4674 3-9-0 **78**........ PatCosgrave 5 42
(Keith Dalgleish) *led: rdn and hdd over 2f out: wknd over 1f out* **25/1**

1m 59.39s (-2.31) **Going Correction** -0.175s/f (Stan)
WFA 3 from 4yo+ 7lb **12** Ran SP% **122.6**
Speed ratings (Par 105): **103,102,101,100,99 99,92,89,87,87 86,83**
toteswingers: 1&2 £3.10, 1&3 £8.80, 2&3 £21.80. CSF £16.75 CT £250.34 TOTE £2.50: £2.00, £1.80, £8.30; EX 18.10.
Owner Cheveley Park Stud **Bred** Cheveley Park Stud Ltd **Trained** Newmarket, Suffolk

FOCUS
This decent handicap was run at a steady pace, with plenty in contention at the furlong marker.

5753 32RED CASINO MAIDEN STKS 1m 4f 50y(P)
8:10 (8:11) (Class 5) 3-4-Y-0 **£2,264** (£673; £336; £168) **Stalls** Low

Form RPR

4-2 **1** **Enthusiastic**[18] 5105 4-9-8 0........ DarrenEgan(5) 12 83
(Michael Murphy) *hld up: hdwy over 3f out: hmpd over 1f out: led sn after: edgd lft ins fnl f: r.o* **15/2**

4 **2** *1¾* **Spiritoftomintoul**[18] 5105 3-9-3 0........ TomQueally 1 81
(Sir Henry Cecil) *hld up: hdwy over 2f out: rdn over 1f out: styd on same pce whn n.m.r nr fin* **6/1**

3-6 **3** *1¾* **Shada (IRE)**[61] 3565 3-8-12 0........ RichardMullen 6 72
(Sir Michael Stoute) *hld up: hdwy over 7f out: rdn over 1f out: styd on same pce* **7/2**[2]

3 **4** *shd* **Perfect Heart**[18] 5105 3-9-3 0........ EddieAhern 11 77
(John Gosden) *chsd ldrs: led over 5f out: rdn and hdd over 1f out: no ex ins fnl f* **11/4**[1]

5 *2¾* **Maori Dancer (USA)** 3-9-3 0........(t) JamieSpencer 5 73+
(Jeremy Noseda) *hld up: rdn over 2f out: hdwy u.p over 1f out: hung lft and no ex ins fnl f* **8/1**

00 **6** *5* **Cometography (IRE)**[35] 4464 3-9-3 0........(v[1]) PhillipMakin 3 65
(Ismail Mohammed) *hld up: hdwy over 2f out: rdn over 1f out: wknd fnl f* **150/1**

32 **7** *4½* **New Drama (IRE)**[72] 3232 3-8-12 0........ FrannyNorton 7 52
(Mark Johnston) *led 1f: chsd ldr pushed along over 6f out: rdn over 2f out: wknd over 1f out* **5/1**[3]

8 *11* **Eutropius (IRE)** 3-8-12 0........ GarryWhillans(5) 2 40
(Alan Swinbank) *hld up: rdn over 3f out: wknd over 2f out* **50/1**

4 **9** *11* **Entitlement**[12] 5309 3-8-12 0........ ShaneKelly 10 17
(James Fanshawe) *s.i.s: sn prom: rdn and wknd over 2f out: t.o* **14/1**

00 **10** *9* **Autumnus (IRE)**[33] 4542 3-9-3 0........(p) RoystonFfrench 4
(Ismail Mohammed) *prom: drvn along over 5f out: wknd over 3f out: t.o* **100/1**

0- **11** *77* **Gabrial's Hope (FR)**[263] 7709 3-9-3 0........ SilvestreDeSousa 9
(Patrick Morris) *led after 1f: rdn and hdd over 5f out: n.m.r and wknd sn after: t.o* **25/1**

2m 37.9s (-3.20) **Going Correction** -0.175s/f (Stan)
WFA 3 from 4yo 10lb **11** Ran SP% **116.8**
Speed ratings (Par 103): **103,101,100,100,98 95,92,85,77,71 20**
toteswingers: 1&2 £6.70, 1&3 £6.40, 2&3 £6.10. CSF £51.00 TOTE £12.10: £3.70, £1.90, £1.10; EX 31.60.
Owner The Honorable Earle I Mack **Bred** Earle I Mack **Trained** Newmarket, Suffolk

FOCUS
Some powerful stables were represented in this maiden that was run at a steady pace with the front two home, coming from off the pace.
Gabrial's Hope(FR) Official explanation: vet said colt made a noise

5754 £32 BONUS AT 32RED.COM FILLIES' H'CAP 1m 4f 50y(P)
8:40 (8:40) (Class 5) (0-70,68) 3-Y-0+ **£2,264** (£673; £336; £168) **Stalls** Low

Form RPR

0065 **1** **Raving Monsun**[23] 4875 3-8-10 **60**........ SilvestreDeSousa 6 70
(Marco Botti) *dwlt: hld up: hdwy over 2f out: led ins fnl f: r.o wl* **9/2**[3]

6236 **2** *2½* **Dazzling Valentine**[30] 4641 4-9-4 **65**........ NatashaEaton(7) 4 71
(Alan Bailey) *hld up in tch: led over 2f out: rdn and hdd ins fnl f: styd on same pce* **6/1**

The Form Book Flat, Raceform Ltd, Compton, RG20 6NL

-043 **3** 2 3/4 **Zaahya (IRE)**[17] 5125 3-8-11 **61** .... TadhgO'Shea 2 63
(John Dunlop) *prom: pushed along over 2f out: styd on same pce appr fnl f* **13/2**

0-40 **4** 3 3/4 **Panettone (IRE)**[26] 4776 3-8-7 **60** .... DominicFox(3) 7 56
(Roger Varian) *led: hdd over 10f out: chsd ldrs: rdn over 2f out: wknd over 1f out* **12/1**

6-25 **5** 1/2 **Ironically (IRE)**[49] 3968 3-9-1 **65** .... TedDurcan 1 60
(David Lanigan) *hld up: rdn over 2f out: n.d* **7/2**[1]

2531 **6** 2 1/4 **Top Frock (IRE)**[19] 5052 3-9-4 **68** ....(b) AdamKirby 8 59
(Clive Cox) *chsd ldr: led wl over 2f out: sn hdd: rdn and wknd over 1f out* **4/1**[2]

6504 **7** 89 **Gabrial's Lexi (IRE)**[44] 4153 3-8-9 **59** .... JamieSpencer 3
(Ian Williams) *s.i.s: hdwy to ld over 10f out: rdn over 3f out: hdd wl over 2f out: sn wknd and eased: t.o* **9/2**[3]

2m 38.36s (-2.74) **Going Correction** -0.175s/f (Stan)
WFA 3 from 4yo+ 10lb 7 Ran SP% **113.9**
Speed ratings (Par 100): **102,100,98,96,95 94,34**
toteswingers: 1&2 £6.00, 1&3 £1.40, 2&3 £9.20. CSF £30.85 CT £173.38 TOTE £5.50: £3.20, £4.70; EX 41.00.
Owner Newsells Park Stud **Bred** Newsells Park Stud **Trained** Newmarket, Suffolk

FOCUS
Not the strongest of fillies' handicaps, run at a fair pace.
Raving Monsun Official explanation: trainer's rep said, regarding apparent improvement in form, that the filly ran a good race but had nothing else to offer.
T/Jkpt: Not won. T/Plt: £1,195.20 to a £1 stake. Pool: £71,008.29 - 43.37 winning tickets. T/Qpdt: £251.00 to a £1 stake. Pool: £251.00 - 21.80 winning tickets. CR

5647 BADEN-BADEN (L-H)
Wednesday, August 29
OFFICIAL GOING: Turf: good to soft

5755a BELMONDO ZUKUNFTS-RENNEN (GROUP 3) (2YO) (TURF) 7f
6:00 (12:00) 2-Y-O
£26,666 (£9,166; £4,583; £2,500; £1,666; £1,250)

RPR

1 **Ayaar (IRE)**[11] 5348 2-9-2 0 .... MartinHarley 4 97
(Mick Channon) *midfield: rdn over 2f out: r.o to chal ins fnl f: sn led: drvn clr* **41/10**[2]

2 2 **Penelopa** 2-8-13 0 .... APietsch 1 89
(M G Mintchev, Germany) *prom on inner: rdn 2 1/2f out: styd on to go 2nd cl home: no ch w wnr* **43/5**

3 3/4 **Se Gray (USA)** 2-9-2 0 .... ADeVries 9 90
(Frau E Mader, Germany) *hld up towards rr on outer: rdn over 2f out: wnt 3rd ins fnl f: kpt on* **123/10**

4 nk **Mauriac (GER)** 2-9-2 0 .... EPedroza 3 90
(A Wohler, Germany) *led: rdn over 2f out: strly pressed and hdd ins fnl f: no ex and fdd: dropped to 4th cl home* **99/10**

5 1 3/4 **Ocean Applause**[14] 5232 2-9-2 0 .... JimmyQuinn 8 85
(John Ryan) *dropped in fr wd draw and hld up in last: nudged along 3f out: rdn and outpcd 2f out: plugged on to go 5th cl home: n.d* **119/10**

6 1/2 **Nouvelle Neige (GER)**[38] 2-9-1 0 .... MrDennisSchiergen 7 83
(P Schiergen, Germany) *midfield: rdn 3f out: outpcd in rr over 1 1/2f out: plugged on u.p to go 6th post* **49/10**[3]

7 hd **Mister Big Shuffle (GER)** 2-9-2 0 .... FilipMinarik 2 83
(M Figge, Germany) *s.i.s and pushed along to rcvr: hld up towards rr on inner: short of room and forced to drop bk on run to first turn: prog into midfield 3f out: rdn and outpcd 2f out: plugged on to go 7th last strides* **73/10**

8 1/2 **Global Bang (GER)**[24] 2-9-2 0 .... StefanieHofer 6 82
(Mario Hofer, Germany) *plld hrd early: sn trcking ldr in 2nd on outer: rdn 2f out: kpt on tl no ex and btn ins fnl f: fdd and lost multiple pls cl home* **6/4**[1]

9 8 **Isioma**[38] 2-8-13 0 .... AStarke 5 58
(Mario Hofer, Germany) *prom on outer: rdn over 2f out: keeping on whn short of room and forced to check over 1f out: nt rcvr and dropped to last ins fnl f: eased whn btn* **134/10**

1m 25.88s (1.98) 9 Ran SP% **130.4**
WIN (incl. 10 euro stake): 51. PLACES: 21, 32, 31. SF: 451.
Owner Sheikh Mohammed Bin Khalifa Al Maktoum **Bred** Blue Bloodstock Ltd **Trained** West Ilsley, Berks

NOTEBOOK
Ayaar(IRE) took a while to get off the mark, but has been thriving recently and completed the hat-trick in this Group 3. He looks likely to be aiming higher now, and he holds a number of entries including both the Group 2 Champagne Stakes at Doncaster on St Leger day and the Curragh's Group 1 National Stakes on the same day. The plan is to stick to 7f for the time being.

5537 HAMILTON (R-H)
Thursday, August 30
OFFICIAL GOING: Heavy (7.6)
Wind: Fresh, half against Weather: Cloudy

5756 BRITISH STALLION STUDS E B F DEBUTANTS MAIDEN STKS 6f 5y
2:10 (2:11) (Class 5) 2-Y-O **£3,234** (£962; £481; £240) **Stalls** Centre

Form RPR

1 **Willie The Whipper** 2-9-3 0 .... GrahamLee 2 75+
(Ann Duffield) *dwlt: sn trcking ldr: shkn up to ld over 1f out: rn green: kpt on strly to go clr fnl f* **6/4**[1]

2 8 **Marcus Caesar (IRE)** 2-9-3 0 .... GrahamGibbons 3 57+
(David Barron) *led: rdn over 2f out: hdd over 1f out: one pce and eased last 100yds* **2/1**[2]

3 13 **Indie Banned** 2-9-3 0 .... PhillipMakin 5 24+
(Ben Haslam) *cl up: rdn over 2f out: hung rt and sn wknd: eased whn no ch fnl f* **9/4**[3]

4 28 **Dark Marvel (IRE)** 2-8-12 0 .... PaddyAspell 4
(Alan Berry) *in tch 2f: sn struggling: eased whn no ch fnl 2f* **28/1**

1m 20.33s (8.13) **Going Correction** +1.25s/f (Soft) 4 Ran SP% **107.6**
Speed ratings (Par 94): **95,84,67,29**
CSF £4.76 TOTE £1.60; EX 4.80.
Owner Jimmy Kay **Bred** J S B Anderson **Trained** Constable Burton, N Yorks

FOCUS
Rail realignment around the loop added 25yds to races on Round course. Conditions were very testing, described from "bad" to "atrocious". Just four lined up for this 2yo EBF maiden confined to horses that had not run previously - a ludicrous idea at this stage of the season. Only the winner got home and the second and third were eased once held.

NOTEBOOK
Willie The Whipper, out of a mare that won at up to 1m6f, is a half-brother to three winners abroad. A well-made type, if on the leg at present, he sat on the heels of the leader. Showing his inexperience when asked to go and win his race, he came right away in the end. Presumably he will need another outing before he is given a mark. He was his trainer's ninth juvenile winner this year and he should make a decent handicapper at a mile plus at three. (op 7-4)
Marcus Caesar(IRE), a close-coupled gelding, knew his job and was out of the stalls like a flash. He was about four lengths down when he was heavily eased with about 75 yards left to run. He looks quite speedy and will appreciate much better ground than he encountered here. (op 7-4)
Indie Banned, out of a sprint mare, was in trouble soon after halfway and came home in his own time. (op 5-2)

5757 NEILSLAND AND EARNOCK H'CAP 6f 5y
2:40 (2:41) (Class 6) (0-60,65) 3-Y-O **£2,045** (£603; £302) **Stalls** Centre

Form RPR

6006 **1** **Windygoul Lad**[6] 5538 3-9-1 **53** .... AndrewMullen 8 61
(Keith Dalgleish) *prom chsng gp: rdn and wandered 2f out: styd on wl fnl f to ld nr fin* **12/1**

6400 **2** nk **La Salida**[13] 5317 3-9-2 **54** ....(bt) GrahamGibbons 5 61
(David Barron) *led and clr towards far side: rdn 2f out: kpt on fnl f: hdd nr fin* **6/1**[3]

4601 **3** 3 3/4 **Celestial Dawn**[6] 5538 3-9-8 **65** 6ex .... JasonHart(5) 6 61
(John Weymes) *bhd: rdn after 2f: hdwy u.p over 1f out: edgd rt and styd on fnl f: nvr able to chal* **7/2**[1]

-052 **4** hd **Lollypop Lady**[6] 5542 3-8-7 **45** ....(p) JoeFanning 1 40
(Linda Perratt) *dwlt: hld up in tch far side: hdwy 2f out: ev ch last 150yds: sn outpcd* **6/1**[3]

2132 **5** 3 3/4 **Oakbrook**[22] 4956 3-9-6 **58** .... PaulMulrennan 2 42
(Ann Duffield) *prom chsng gp: effrt and rdn over 2f out: wknd appr fnl f* **4/1**[2]

0530 **6** 1 1/4 **Essexvale (IRE)**[4] 5624 3-8-7 **45** ....(p) JamesSullivan 11 25
(Robert Johnson) *hld up towards nr side of gp: rdn along over 2f out: no imp over 1f out* **33/1**

2620 **7** 1 3/4 **Lord Buffhead**[6] 5543 3-9-2 **57** .... DeclanCannon(3) 4 32
(Richard Guest) *taken early to post: prom chsng gp tl hung rt and wknd wl over 1f out* **6/1**[3]

-460 **8** 1 3/4 **Young Freddie (IRE)**[86] 2795 3-9-5 **57** .... TomEaves 7 27
(Bryan Smart) *cl up in chsng gp: rdn and outpcd over 2f out: hung lft and wknd wl over 1f out* **10/1**

604 **9** 8 **Noble Bounty**[113] 1986 3-9-5 **57** .... PhillipMakin 9
(Kevin Ryan) *hld up in tch nr side of gp: struggling over 2f out: sn btn* **8/1**

-000 **10** 15 **Come To Mind**[23] 4913 3-8-7 **45** .... PatrickMathers 10
(Alan Berry) *dwlt: a bhd and struggling* **100/1**

1m 19.72s (7.52) **Going Correction** +1.25s/f (Soft) 10 Ran SP% **116.9**
Speed ratings (Par 98): **99,98,93,93,88 86,84,82,71,51**
toteswingers 1&2 £18.50, 1&3 £16.90, 2&3 £6.70 CSF £82.50 CT £310.28 TOTE £29.10: £4.00, £2.60, £1.10; EX 103.50 Trifecta £389.90 Part won. Pool: £526.94 - 0.50 winning units..
Owner East-West Partnership **Bred** K A Dasmal **Trained** Carluke, S Lanarks

FOCUS
A very modest sprint handicap and the winner and fourth raced isolated towards the far side. Guessy form given the terrible conditions.
Windygoul Lad Official explanation: trainer's rep said, regarding apparent improvement in form, that the gelding settled better on the slower ground.
Lollypop Lady Official explanation: jockey said, regarding appearing to ease, that the filly hung right final 1 1/2f, lost its action and had a breathing problem.

5758 SCOTTISH RACING CLAIMING STKS 5f 4y
3:10 (3:11) (Class 6) 3-Y-O+ **£2,045** (£603; £302) **Stalls** Centre

Form RPR

2402 **1** **Haajes**[10] 5412 8-9-2 **78** ....(b) MickyFenton 1 84
(Paul Midgley) *t.k.h: hung rt thrght: cl up: led over 1f out: drvn out fnl f* **7/4**[1]

0400 **2** 2 1/4 **Arganil (USA)**[24] 4880 7-9-7 **84** ....(p) AmyRyan 2 81
(Kevin Ryan) *in tch: hdwy and ev ch over 1f out: sn rdn: kpt on same pce fnl f* **9/4**[2]

6325 **3** 3/4 **Wicked Wilma (IRE)**[14] 5257 8-8-8 **65** .... JulieBurke(3) 4 68
(Alan Berry) *t.k.h: cl up: effrt and rdn over 1f out: kpt on same pce fnl f* **6/1**

2446 **4** 3 1/2 **Distant Sun (USA)**[6] 5542 8-8-12 **56** ....(p) AndrewMullen 5 56
(Linda Perratt) *prom: drvn over 2f out: no ex over 1f out* **40/1**

0552 **5** 9 **Fol Hollow (IRE)**[21] 5013 7-8-12 **67** .... AdrianNicholls 3 24
(David Nicholls) *led: rdn and hdd over 1f out: sn btn: eased whn btn ins fnl f* **3/1**[3]

1m 5.24s (5.24) **Going Correction** +1.25s/f (Soft) 5 Ran SP% **108.9**
Speed ratings (Par 101): **108,104,103,97,83**
CSF £5.84 TOTE £2.00: £1.10, £2.20; EX 5.80.
Owner N Lomas, A Taylor Snr, A Taylor Jnr **Bred** Irish National Stud **Trained** Westow, N Yorks

FOCUS
In effect a veterans' claimer with the youngest runner seven. The runner-up sets the standard with the second again below his best.
Fol Hollow(IRE) Official explanation: trainer's rep said gelding finished lame off-fore

5759 SCOTTISH TROPHY H'CAP 1m 1f 36y
3:40 (3:40) (Class 4) (0-80,86) 3-Y-O+ **£5,175** (£1,540; £769; £384) **Stalls** Low

Form RPR

1242 **1** **Another For Joe**[12] 5345 4-9-8 **74** .... GrahamLee 4 80
(Jim Goldie) *t.k.h: pressed ldr: led over 2f out: drvn out fnl f* **11/4**[1]

0144 **2** 3/4 **Le Chat D'Or**[31] 4641 4-9-6 **72** ....(t) TomEaves 7 76
(Michael Dods) *chsd ldrs: drvn and outpcd 3f out: rallied over 1f out: chsd wnr ins fnl f: hung rt and no ex towards fin* **10/3**[2]

0240 **3** 2 3/4 **She's A Character**[29] 4702 5-9-1 **74** .... GeorgeChaloner(7) 8 72
(Richard Fahey) *s.i.s: t.k.h: hld up: rdn along over 2f out: edgd rt: kpt on fnl f: no imp* **15/2**

4011 **4** 1/2 **Henry Clay**[9] 5451 3-9-13 **86** 6ex .... JoeFanning 5 83
(Mark Johnston) *led to over 2f out: sn rdn: wandered and no ex ins fnl f* **11/4**[1]

3560 **5** 3/4 **Joshua The First**[42] 4260 3-8-11 **70** .... PaulMulrennan 6 66
(Keith Dalgleish) *prom: rdn over 2f out: edgd rt and no ex over 1f out* **25/1**

3420 **6** ½ **I'm Super Too (IRE)**[24] 4868 5-9-6 **77**........................ GarryWhillans(5) 1 71
(Alan Swinbank) *hld up: stdy hdwy over 3f out: rdn and hung rt over 2f out: sn outpcd: n.d after* **5/1**[3]

2m 9.75s (10.05) **Going Correction** +1.25s/f (Soft)
WFA 3 from 4yo+ 7lb **6** Ran SP% **108.7**
Speed ratings (Par 105): **105,104,101,101,100 100**
toteswingers 1&2 £2.10, 1&3 £5.10, 2&3 £5.30 CSF £11.33 CT £51.65 TOTE £3.20: £1.10, £1.90; EX 9.40 Trifecta £36.20 Pool: £537.05 - 10.95 winning units..
Owner Andrew Dick **Bred** G Merkel **Trained** Uplawmoor, E Renfrews

FOCUS
A tight handicap run at a sound pace in the testing conditions. The time was over 14 seconds slower than the RP standard and the form is rated negatively.

5760 PRESTIGE SCOTLAND MAIDEN STKS — 6f 5y
4:10 (4:12) (Class 5) 3-Y-O+ **£2,726** (£805; £402) **Stalls** High

Form RPR

2336 **1** **Legal Bond**[29] 4711 3-9-3 62.. TomEaves 3 61
(Bryan Smart) *led 1f: cl up: led 1/2-way: sn hrd pressed: hld on wl fnl f* **4/6**[1]

253 **2** 2 **Script**[9] 5448 3-8-12 46.. PatrickMathers 5 50
(Alan Berry) *prom: hdwy and ev ch over 2f out to over 1f out: kpt on ins fnl f* **20/1**[3]

6225 **3** shd **Sabore**[12] 5335 3-8-12 63.. TonyHamilton 4 50
(Richard Fahey) *trckd ldrs: drvn and outpcd over 2f out: rallied over 1f out: kpt on ins fnl f* **7/4**[2]

0200 **4** 4 ½ **Face East (USA)**[24] 4865 4-9-6 47..................................(p) PaddyAspell 6 41
(Alan Berry) *hld up: drvn and hung rt over 2f out: sn outpcd* **33/1**

0 **5** 32 **Roseisle**[26] 4807 4-9-1 0.. PaulMulrennan 1
(Linda Perratt) *dwlt: bhd and outpcd: no ch fr 1/2-way* **66/1**

6300 **6** 47 **Dragon Spirit (IRE)**[6] 5542 3-8-10 45.............................. RossSmith(7) 2
(Linda Perratt) *plld hrd and sddle sn slipped forward: led after 1f to 1/2-way: hung rt to far rail: sn eased: t.o* **22/1**

1m 20.02s (7.82) **Going Correction** +1.25s/f (Soft)
WFA 3 from 4yo 3lb **6** Ran SP% **109.9**
Speed ratings (Par 103): **97,94,94,88,45**
toteswingers 1&2 £1.90, 1&3 £1.10, 2&3 £2.10 CSF £15.71 TOTE £1.50: £1.10, £6.10; EX 10.10.
Owner Andrew Tinkler **Bred** A C M Spalding **Trained** Hambleton, N Yorks

FOCUS
A poor sprint maiden marked down still further by the proximity of the runner-up. The first four home had run 39 times between them and this form is unconvincing.
Roseisle Official explanation: jockey said filly ran too free
Dragon Spirit(IRE) Official explanation: jockey said saddle slipped

5761 GRIFFITHS & ARMOUR H'CAP — 1m 4f 17y
4:45 (4:45) (Class 5) (0-70,70) 3-Y-O+ **£3,234** (£962; £481; £240) **Stalls** Low

Form RPR

-430 **1** **A Southside Boy (GER)**[27] 4768 4-8-9 **51** oh6................[1] TomEaves 5 56
(Jim Goldie) *plld hrd early: trckd ldrs: shkn up to ld 2f out: rdn and hung rt ins fnl f: kpt on wl towards fin* **12/1**

2530 **2** ¾ **Finity Run (GER)**[9] 5456 3-9-4 **70**...................................... JoeFanning 6 74
(Mark Johnston) *led 1f: cl up: led over 3f out to 2f out: sn rdn and rallied: kpt on fnl f: hld towards fin* **85/40**[1]

6553 **3** 7 **Stanley Rigby**[15] 5226 6-9-0 **56**...................................... BarryMcHugh 2 49
(Richard Fahey) *trckd ldrs: effrt over 2f out: edgd lft and outpcd by first two over 1f out: kpt on fnl f: no imp* **4/1**[3]

3206 **4** 1 ¾ **Terenzium (IRE)**[17] 5172 10-8-9 **51** oh3.......................(p) PJMcDonald 1 41
(Micky Hammond) *dwlt: hld up: drvn along over 3f out: sn outpcd: hdwy over 1f out: nvr able to chal* **3/1**[2]

0/15 **5** 9 **Livvy Inn (USA)**[9] 3904 7-9-2 **58**...................................... PaddyAspell 3 34
(Lucinda Russell) *hld up: rdn and outpcd over 2f out: edgd rt and sn btn* **9/2**

0460 **6** 37 **Laybach (IRE)**[9] 5054 8-8-9 **51** oh5...................................... GrahamLee 4
(Jim Goldie) *led after 1f to over 3f out: rdn and wknd over 2f out: t.o* **12/1**

2m 53.22s (14.62) **Going Correction** +1.25s/f (Soft)
WFA 3 from 4yo+ 10lb **6** Ran SP% **110.6**
Speed ratings (Par 103): **101,100,95,94,88 64**
toteswingers 1&2 £3.70, 1&3 £4.30, 2&3 £1.80 CSF £36.72 CT £116.52 TOTE £10.50: £3.30, £2.10; EX 49.00 Trifecta £212.40 Part won. Pool: £287.12 - 0.20 winning units..
Owner Connor & Dunne **Bred** Gestut Karlshof **Trained** Uplawmoor, E Renfrews
■ Stewards' Enquiry : Tom Eaves caution: careless riding.

FOCUS
A poor handicap and another desperate finish on bad ground. The winner was out of the handicap and this is unconvincing form.

5762 HAMILTON-PARK.CO.UK "HANDS AND HEELS" APPRENTICE SERIES H'CAP (ROUND 4) (R E I) — 1m 65y
5:15 (5:15) (Class 6) (0-55,52) 3-Y-O+ **£2,045** (£603; £302) **Stalls** Low

Form RPR

0440 **1** **Star Kingdom (IRE)**[21] 5000 3-8-12 **52**.................. JacobButterfield(3) 5 58
(Brian Ellison) *t.k.h: cl up: led wl over 1f out: pushed out fnl f* **11/4**[2]

006 **2** ¾ **Goodlukin Lucy**[24] 4869 5-9-0 **45**..................................(t[1]) DavidBergin 4 49
(Dianne Sayer) *cl up: rdn and outpcd over 2f out: rallied appr fnl f: kpt on to take 2nd cl home* **4/1**[3]

5045 **3** hd **Deep Applause**[2] 5708 4-8-7 **45**...................................... ConnorNichol(7) 8 49
(Michael Dods) *led: rdn over 3f out: hdd wl over 1f out: rallied: one pce wl ins fnl f* **4/1**[3]

4000 **4** 2 ¾ **Dynamic Drive (IRE)**[45] 4137 5-8-9 **45**.............................. RossSmith(5) 6 43
(Linda Perratt) *t.k.h: cl up: ev ch 2f out: outpcd fnl f* **13/2**

6543 **5** 1 ¼ **Gadobout Dancer**[14] 5258 5-9-3 **51**...................... DavidSimmonson(3) 3 46
(Tony Coyle) *dwlt: hld up in tch: rdn over 2f out: edgd rt ins fnl f: no imp* **9/4**[1]

0000 **6** 20 **Red All Over (IRE)**[9] 5446 3-8-1 **45**...................................... KevinStott(7) 2
(Alan Berry) *hld up: struggling over 4f out: sn btn: t.o* **100/1**

2m 0.62s (12.22) **Going Correction** +1.25s/f (Soft)
WFA 3 from 4yo+ 6lb **6** Ran SP% **111.8**
Speed ratings (Par 101): **88,87,87,84,83 63**
toteswingers 1&2 £2.60, 1&3 £2.30, 2&3 £2.60 CSF £13.91 CT £41.30 TOTE £3.30: £2.40, £1.10; EX 17.10 Trifecta £76.20 Pool: £387.37 - 3.76 winning units..
Owner Koo's Racing Club **Bred** Camogue Stud Ltd **Trained** Norton, N Yorks

FOCUS
A rock bottom 'hands and heels' apprentice handicap run on terrible ground. The winner is rated to this year's best.
T/Plt: £67.70 to a £1 stake. Pool: £37,817.99 - 407.71 winning tickets T/Qpdt: £20.40 to a £1 stake. Pool: £3,420.13 - 123.80 winning tickets RY

5741 KEMPTON (A.W) (R-H)
Thursday, August 30

OFFICIAL GOING: Standard
Wind: Fresh, across. Weather: dry and breezy

5763 32REDBINGO.COM NURSERY — 1m (P)
6:20 (6:21) (Class 6) (0-60,60) 2-Y-O **£1,617** (£481; £240; £120) **Stalls** Low

Form RPR

654 **1** **Getaway Car**[23] 4934 2-9-6 **59**..(p) NeilCallan 12 62
(Gerard Butler) *in tch in midfield on outer: reminders and hdwy to chse ldrs over 3f out: drvn and ev ch over 2f out: led ent fnl f: kpt on wl u.p* **11/2**[1]

430 **2** ½ **Aseela (IRE)**[35] 4494 2-9-7 **60**.. WilliamBuick 2 62
(Clive Brittain) *sn bhd and pushed along: hdwy u.p over 1f out: str run ins fnl f to go 2nd last strides: nt quite rch wnr* **6/1**[2]

6065 **3** hd **Heliconia**[16] 5206 2-9-5 **58**..(b[1]) LukeMorris 8 60
(Sir Mark Prescott Bt) *in tch: chsd ldrs and swtchd lft over 1f out: drvn and pressing wnr whn struck in the face by winning rdr's whip: faltered briefly: kpt on same pce after* **11/1**

5536 **4** ½ **Eastern Dragon (IRE)**[17] 5155 2-9-7 **60**....................(v[1]) HayleyTurner 9 60
(Michael Scudamore) *chsd ldrs: rdn to chse ldr over 2f out: led narrowly 2f out: hdd ent fnl f: styd on same pce u.p fnl 100yds* **10/1**

400 **5** hd **Rosie Future (IRE)**[14] 5267 2-9-2 **55**.............................. TomQueally 14 55
(Rae Guest) *pushed along early in last quartet: rdn and hdwy over 2f out: kpt on fnl f but nvr quite pce to chal* **11/1**

0062 **6** shd **Alpine Mysteries (IRE)**[16] 5206 2-9-6 **59**.......................... TedDurcan 4 59+
(John Dunlop) *in tch in midfield: swtchd rt and hdwy wl over 1f out: kpt on ins fnl f* **8/1**

0064 **7** 3 ½ **Tomway**[16] 5206 2-9-4 **57**.. RichardKingscote 10 49
(Tom Dascombe) *led: rdn over 2f out: hdd 2f out: no ex u.p over 1f out: wknd ins fnl f* **15/2**[3]

000 **8** ½ **Run It Twice (IRE)**[18] 5126 2-9-7 **60**........................(b[1]) FrankieDettori 3 50
(Brian Meehan) *hld up in tch in midfield: rdn and effrt on inner over 2f out: no imp over 1f out and wl hld fnl f* **8/1**

4004 **9** 3 ¼ **Ana Shababiya (IRE)**[17] 5161 2-9-0 **53**...................... RoystonFfrench 6 36
(Ismail Mohammed) *chsd ldr for 2f: chsd ldrs after: rdn over 2f out wknd over 1f out* **25/1**

4656 **10** 1 **Kryena's Rose**[23] 4899 2-9-3 **56**...................................... SamHitchcott 1 37
(Mick Channon) *awkward leaving stalls: racd in last quartet: effrt u.p jst over 2f out: no imp* **20/1**

5003 **11** nse **Linda's Icon**[17] 5161 2-9-4 **57**.. MartinHarley 7 37
(Mick Channon) *chsd ldrs: rdn and struggling over 2f out: wknd over 1f out* **10/1**

000 **12** 9 **Karr Wa Farr (IRE)**[20] 5032 2-9-1 **54**.............................. ChrisCatlin 11 14
(Ed Vaughan) *chsd ldr after 2f tl over 2f out: sn wknd: bhd fnl f* **6/1**[2]

5146 **13** 4 **Stupenda**[12] 5361 2-9-7 **60**.. TadhgO'Shea 5 11
(Denis Coakley) *s.i.s: a bhd: lost tch wl over 1f out* **14/1**

1m 40.71s (0.91) **Going Correction** -0.05s/f (Stan) **13** Ran SP% **128.1**
Speed ratings (Par 92): **93,92,92,91,91 91,88,87,84,83 83,74,70**
Tote Swingers 1&2 £6.80, 2&3 £21.50, 1&3 £16.60 CSF £40.59 CT £378.59 TOTE £6.70: £2.30, £1.80, £6.20; EX 52.30 Trifecta £167.70 Part won. Pool 226.75 - 0.50 winning units..
Owner A D Spence **Bred** Mascalls Stud **Trained** Newmarket, Suffolk

FOCUS
A wide-open nursery, as the market suggested, but weak-looking form with the principals compressed at the finish.

NOTEBOOK
Getaway Car, upped in trip, won despite going widest of all around the bends. He came under pressure a long way out, but there was no faulting the way he responded and he looks sure to stay further. (op 7-1 tchd 5-1)
Aseela(IRE) was soon well behind and ran in snatches, but she came back on the bridle in the straight before staying on for an unlikely second. It would be dangerous to get carried away considering she was never involved in the heat of the race, and her pedigree points to her requiring a bit further in due course. (tchd 13-2)
Heliconia, in first-time blinkers, took a while to pick up but gradually responded and was in with every chance when taking a serious whack over the head from the winning rider's whip around half-a-furlong out. It's possible she would have won, but she still doesn't appeal as one to be too positive about. (op 12-1)
Eastern Dragon(IRE), in a first-time visor, ran into some stronger stayers.
Rosie Future(IRE), upped a couple of furlongs for her nursery debut, was one-paced after getting behind. (op 10-1 tchd 12-1)
Alpine Mysteries(IRE) took an age to pick up after apparently travelling well, and she had to be switched inside, but she was really going on at the finish. Official explanation: jockey said filly clipped heels (op 7-1 tchd 13-2)

5764 32RED CASINO H'CAP — 1m (P)
6:50 (6:51) (Class 6) (0-60,60) 3-Y-O **£1,617** (£481; £240; £120) **Stalls** Low

Form RPR

05-2 **1** **Twenty One Choice (IRE)**[108] 2131 3-8-13 **52**.............. LiamKeniry 12 67+
(Ed de Giles) *hld up in rr: stl last but travelling strly 3f out: swtchd rt and qcknd ent fnl 2f: led ent fnl f: pushed along and in command fnl f: comf* **8/1**

004 **2** 1 ½ **Arabic**[16] 5216 3-9-6 **59**..(p) TomQueally 8 68
(James Fanshawe) *hld up in tch in midfield: rdn and effrt 2f out: chsd wnr ins fnl f: styd on same pce and no threat to wnr* **6/1**[3]

542 **3** 1 **Dana's Present**[21] 4981 3-9-3 **56**.................................. RichardHughes 10 63+
(George Baker) *stdd after s: hld up in last quartet: hdwy to chse ldrs and nt clr run 1f out tl swtchd rt ins fnl f: styd on same pce ins fnl f: wnt 3rd fnl 75yds* **5/1**[1]

0544 **4** ¾ **Wyndham Wave**[8] 5479 3-9-2 **55**.................................. JamesMillman 6 60
(Rod Millman) *chsd ldrs: rdn to ld 2f out: hdd and nt qckn w wnr ent fnl f: styd on same pce and lost 2 pls fnl f* **10/1**

0012 **5** 5 **Plum Bay**[17] 5157 3-9-7 **60**.. DaneO'Neill 1 54
(David Elsworth) *s.i.s: racd in last quartet: hdwy u.p wl over 1f out: kpt on fnl f: nvr trbld ldrs* **10/1**

5400 **6** ½ **Rogue Reporter (IRE)**[16] 5219 3-9-7 **60**...................... WilliamCarson 13 53
(Stuart Williams) *in tch in midfield on outer: hdwy to chse ldrs 3f out: rdn and unable qck ent fnl 2f: wknd over 1f out* **11/2**[2]

5050 **7** nse **Inniscastle Boy**[17] 5148 3-9-7 **60**..................................(b[1]) MartinDwyer 2 53
(William Muir) *sn rdn along in last quartet: hdwy past btn horses over 1f out: styd on u.p fnl f: nvr trbld ldrs* **5/1**[1]

0300 **8** 1 ¼ **First Voice (IRE)**[16] 5203 3-9-3 **56**.............................. RoystonFfrench 4 46
(James Given) *t.k.h: chsd ldrs: looking to switch lft over 2f out: rdn and outpcd 2f out: wl btn ent fnl f* **33/1**

3-20 **9** *1 ¼* **Bada Bing**[44] 4172 3-9-2 **55** LukeMorris 14 42
(Scott Dixon) *in tch: rdn and effrt to chse ldrs 2f out: unable qck and btn over 1f out: wknd fnl f* **14/1**

3000 **10** *1 ½* **Hill Of Dreams (IRE)**[15] 5229 3-8-13 **55** (p) PatrickHills(3) 11 38
(Dean Ivory) *in tch in midfield: lost pl and rdn 1/2-way: wknd ent fnl 2f* **20/1**

-500 **11** *1* **Rode Two Destiny (IRE)**[50] 3972 3-8-10 **52** MatthewCosham(3) 3 33
(David Evans) *in tch in midfield: rdn and unable qck ent fnl 2f: outpcd and wl btn over 1f out: wknd* **25/1**

0204 **12** *13* **Goodie Goodie**[23] 4900 3-8-13 **52** (t) JamesDoyle 9
(Sylvester Kirk) *chsd ldrs: hdwy to press ldr over 5f out: rdn over 3f out: ev ch tl ent fnl 2f: fdd over 1f out: bhd and eased ins fnl f* **20/1**

2026 **13** *8* **Queen Cassiopeia**[15] 5244 3-9-7 **60** HayleyTurner 5
(J R Jenkins) *led: rdn over 2f out: hdd 2f out: sn btn and fdd: wl bhd and eased ins fnl f: t.o* **20/1**

1m 39.25s (-0.55) **Going Correction** -0.05s/f (Stan) **13** Ran SP% **120.0**
Speed ratings (Par 98): **100,98,97,96,91 91,91,89,88,87 86,73,65**
Tote Swingers 1&2 £15.50, 2&3 £4.70, 1&3 £9.70 CSF £51.08 CT £270.15 TOTE £9.00: £2.30, £2.00, £1.80; EX 85.70 Trifecta £244.50 Part won. Pool 330.40 - 0.73 winning units..
Owner Penna Racing **Bred** P Byrne **Trained** Ledbury, H'fords

FOCUS
An ordinary contest. The early pace looked modest but seemed to increase leaving the back straight. The second and third help with the standard.
First Voice(IRE) Official explanation: jockey said gelding ran too free

5765 32RED.COM MEDIAN AUCTION MAIDEN STKS 7f (P)
7:20 (7:20) (Class 5) 2-Y-O **£2,264** (£673; £336; £168) **Stalls** Low

Form RPR

5 **1** **Baltic Knight (IRE)**[25] 4845 2-9-3 0 RichardHughes 11 80+
(Richard Hannon) *dwlt and pushed along early: hld up in tch: rdn and effrt 2f out: hdwy to chal jst ins fnl f: led fnl 75yds: r.o wl and sn in command* **9/1**

32 **2** *1 ¼* **Intimidate**[13] 5303 2-9-3 0 JimmyFortune 9 77
(Jeremy Noseda) *t.k.h: chsd ldrs: sltly hmpd and swtchd lft over 4f out: rdn to chal over 1f out: led 1f out: hdd and styd on same pce fnl 75yds* **7/4**[1]

0 **3** *1 ¾* **Mumeyez**[26] 4792 2-9-3 0 WilliamBuick 7 72+
(John Gosden) *in tch: rdn and effrt 2f out: chsd ldrs ent fnl f: rn green u.p and outpcd by ldng pair fnl 150yds* **13/2**[3]

4 **4** *½* **Mishaal (IRE)**[17] 5162 2-9-3 0 NeilCallan 14 71
(Roger Varian) *t.k.h: chsd ldrs and grad edging rt after s: chsd ldr over 4f out: rdn and effrt 2f out: ev ch over 1f out: no ex and outpcd fnl 150yds* **16/1**

2 **5** *½* **Grand Denial (IRE)**[25] 4846 2-9-3 0 AdamKirby 5 70+
(Clive Cox) *in tch: rdn and effrt wl over 1f out: carried sltly rt and styd on same pce ins fnl f* **11/4**[2]

42 **6** *2 ¼* **Canadian Run (IRE)**[22] 4938 2-9-3 0 StevieDonohoe 3 64
(Robert Mills) *chsd ldrs: effrt u.p 2f out: no ex and btn 1f out: wknd ins fnl f* **7/1**

7 *1 ½* **Miguel Grau (USA)** 2-9-3 0 PatDobbs 4 60
(Marco Botti) *s.i.s: hld up in tch in last quartet: rdn and hdwy over 2f out: no imp and one pce fr over 1f out* **33/1**

0 **8** *½* **Admirals Walk (IRE)**[33] 4604 2-9-3 0 JamesDoyle 12 59
(Sylvester Kirk) *stdd and hmpd sn after s: t.k.h: hld up in tch in last quartet: rdn and hdwy jst over 2f out: no imp over 1f out* **40/1**

04 **9** *hd* **Forceful Flame**[13] 5319 2-9-3 0 FrankieDettori 8 58
(Robert Eddery) *led: rdn ent fnl 2f: hdd 1f out: sn btn and wknd qckly ins fnl f* **20/1**

10 *5* **Kastini** 2-9-3 0 EddieAhern 13 45
(Denis Coakley) *hld up in rr: rdn and outpcd ent fnl 2f: sme hdwy past btn horses over 1f out: nvr trbld ldrs* **50/1**

04 **11** *hd* **Alcaeus**[8] 5476 2-9-3 0 LukeMorris 10 45
(Sir Mark Prescott Bt) *t.k.h: hld up in tch in last quartet: rdn ent fnl 2f: sn outpcd and wl btn over 1f out* **66/1**

12 *5* **Eliza Snow (IRE)** 2-8-12 0 KirstyMilczarek 6 27
(Amy Weaver) *chsd ldr tl over 4f out: lost pl and wknd 2f out* **100/1**

13 *6* **Misleading Promise (IRE)** 2-8-12 0 TobyAtkinson(5) 1 16
(John Butler) *v.s.a: sn rcvrd and in tch in rr: rdn and wknd over 2f out: bhd fnl f* **100/1**

0 **14** *¾* **Aphrodite's Dream**[8] 5476 2-8-12 0 DaneO'Neill 2 9
(Derek Shaw) *in tch in midfield: rdn over 2f out: sn struggling: bhd over 1f out* **100/1**

1m 26.43s (0.43) **Going Correction** -0.05s/f (Stan) **14** Ran SP% **121.3**
Speed ratings (Par 94): **95,93,91,91,90 87,86,85,85,79 79,73,66,65**
Tote Swingers 1&2 £3.70, 2&3 £3.50, 1&3 £8.80 CSF £24.41 TOTE £16.30: £2.20, £1.40, £2.00; EX 40.30 Trifecta £208.50 Pool 524.24 - 1.86 winning units..
Owner Thurloe Thoroughbreds XXX **Bred** Henry O'Callaghan **Trained** East Everleigh, Wilts

FOCUS
A fair maiden, but the early pace looked pretty slow. The form is rated at the mid-point of the race averages, the winner improving from his debut.

NOTEBOOK
Baltic Knight(IRE), who shaped okay on his debut over 6f at Newbury, had too much end-race speed for his rivals. He should make a useful nursery/handicap type. (op 10-1, tchd 11-1 in a place)
Intimidate, on Polytrack for the first time, was a bit keen early and didn't run to the same level as when a close second at Newbury on his previous start. He can win a race but it remains to be seen whether he's really going to progress. (tchd 13-8 and 15-8)
Mumeyez ran green on his debut at Doncaster but showed ability. He got closer this time, but still looked a bit immature and should do better again. (op 15-2)
Mishaal(IRE), fourth on his debut at Lingfield, was much too keen without cover from the widest draw. (op 14-1)
Grand Denial(IRE) didn't build on the form he showed when runner-up over 6f at Newbury on his debut, but he seemed unsuited by the steady pace and still looked immature. (op 5-2)
Misleading Promise(IRE) Official explanation: jockey said colt was slowly away

5766 32REDBET.COM MEDIAN AUCTION MAIDEN STKS 1m 3f (P)
7:50 (7:50) (Class 5) 3-5-Y-O **£2,264** (£673; £336; £168) **Stalls** Low

Form RPR

2 **1** **Tiger Cliff (IRE)**[19] 5100 3-9-3 0 TomQueally 4 79+
(Sir Henry Cecil) *hld up in last pair: rdn and effrt over 2f out: led wl over 1f out: idling in front and kpt up to work fnl f: styd on* **5/2**[2]

60- **2** *1* **Inqadh (USA)**[339] 6400 3-9-3 0 (p) FrankieDettori 2 77
(Saeed Bin Suroor) *chsd ldrs tl wnt 2nd 8f out: rdn to ld and flashed tail 2f out: sn hdd: kpt on same pce ins fnl f* **15/2**

5-4 **3** *2 ¼* **Openly**[104] 2249 3-8-12 0 HayleyTurner 7 68
(James Fanshawe) *chsd ldr tl 8f out: rdn and ev ch 2f out: unable qck and drvn over 1f out: btn and plugged on same pce fnl f* **13/8**[1]

024 **4** *1 ¼* **Falkland (IRE)**[124] 1655 3-9-3 72 (b[1]) WilliamBuick 5 71
(John Gosden) *squeezed for room and lost pl sn after s: sn rcvrd and in tch in midfield: lost pl and rdn 2f out: sme hdwy u.p over 1f out: plugged on same pce and wl hld fnl f* **13/2**

535 **5** *nk* **Ty Gwr**[113] 1989 3-9-3 70 MartinLane 3 70
(David Simcock) *stdd s: t.k.h: hld up in tch in rr: hdwy and nt clr run jst over 2f out: rdn and hdwy wl over 1f out: no imp fnl f* **33/1**

5 **6** *11* **Shea**[17] 5154 3-8-12 0 JimCrowley 6 45
(Ralph Beckett) *wnt rt sn after s: in tch in midfield: rdn 4f out: wknd 2f out* **12/1**

2353 **7** *7* **Safarjal (IRE)**[92] 2612 3-8-12 77 PaulHanagan 1 33
(Charles Hills) *led: rdn wl over 2f: hdd 2f out: sn btn: bhd 1f out: eased wl ins fnl f* **9/2**[3]

2m 20.81s (-1.09) **Going Correction** -0.05s/f (Stan) **7** Ran SP% **120.6**
Speed ratings (Par 103): **101,100,98,97,97 89,84**
Tote Swingers 1&2 £2.60, 2&3 £4.40, 1&3 £1.50 CSF £23.07 TOTE £4.70: £1.10, £4.20; EX 27.40.
Owner W H Ponsonby **Bred** Mrs Clodagh McStay **Trained** Newmarket, Suffolk

FOCUS
Probably not a race to follow, though it was sound run. Improvement from the first two.

5767 32RED H'CAP (FOR LADY AMATEUR RIDERS) 1m 4f (P)
8:20 (8:20) (Class 4) (0-80,80) 4-Y-O+ **£3,930** (£1,219; £609; £304) **Stalls** Low

Form RPR

6043 **1** **St Ignatius**[5] 5583 5-9-12 **73** (p) MissSMDoolan(5) 2 81
(Alan Bailey) *chsd ldr: rdn to ld wl over 1f out: kpt on and asserted fnl 100yds* **9/2**[2]

4506 **2** *¾* **Sir Boss (IRE)**[24] 4884 7-9-10 **69** MissMMullineaux(3) 3 76
(Michael Mullineaux) *in tch in midfield: pushed along and effrt 2f out: rdn and ev ch 1f out: no ex and one pce fnl 100yds* **8/1**

3004 **3** *nk* **Kames Park (IRE)**[14] 5253 10-9-2 **63** MrsAGuest(5) 7 69
(Richard Guest) *s.i.s: hld up in rr: clsd over 2f out: swtchd lft and hdwy over 1f out: chsd ldng pair ins fnl f: kpt on* **12/1**

212 **4** *1 ½* **Spin Cast**[129] 1562 4-9-8 **67** MissHBethell(3) 10 71
(Brian Ellison) *t.k.h: hld up in midfield: hdwy 2f out: pressing ldrs and drvn ent fnl f: one pce and btn whn edgd lft towards fin* **13/2**

0000 **5** *nk* **Mcbirney (USA)**[13] 5323 5-9-6 **67** MrsRWilson(5) 6 70
(Paul D'Arcy) *hld up in last pair: nudged along and effrt on inner wl over 1f out: styd on same pce fnl f: eased nr fin* **3/1**[1]

3003 **6** *5* **Sail Home**[7] 5509 5-9-7 **68** (p) MissSBirkett(5) 5 63
(Julia Feilden) *chsd ldrs: rdn over 2f out: drvn and unable qck wl over 1f out: wknd fnl f* **10/1**

0005 **7** *1* **Megalala (IRE)**[3] 5665 11-10-10 **80** MissSBrotherton 1 74
(John Bridger) *led: rdn and hdd wl over 1f out: btn ent fnl f: sn wknd* **5/1**[3]

6630 **8** *1 ¾* **Rub Of The Relic (IRE)**[5] 5585 7-9-4 **65** (v) MissHDukes(5) 4 56
(Paul Midgley) *in tch: lost pl over 3f out: rdn and plugged on same pce fnl 2f* **9/1**

41-0 **9** *¾* **Encircled**[42] 4251 8-9-13 **74** MissBAndrews(5) 8 64
(J R Jenkins) *hld up in last trio: hdwy over 4f out: rdn and unable qck 2f out: wknd jst over 1f out* **25/1**

2m 34.48s (-0.02) **Going Correction** -0.05s/f (Stan) **9** Ran SP% **114.9**
Speed ratings (Par 105): **98,97,97,96,96 92,92,90,90**
Tote Swingers 1&2 £11.70, 2&3 £25.10, 1&3 £16.00 CSF £39.98 CT £402.98 TOTE £4.30: £2.00, £3.20, £3.90; EX 46.70 Trifecta £132.20 Part won. Pool 178.7 - 0.63 winning units..
Owner A J H **Bred** Simon And Helen Plumbly **Trained** Newmarket, Suffolk
■ Stewards' Enquiry : Mrs R Wilson two-day ban: failed to ride out for 4th (tbn)

FOCUS
A fair lady amateur riders' handicap. The form seems sound enough.

5768 32RED.COM H'CAP (LONDON MILE QUALIFIER) 1m (P)
8:50 (8:50) (Class 3) (0-90,90) 3-Y-O+ **£6,663** (£1,982; £990; £495) **Stalls** Low

Form RPR

13 **1** **Royal Empire (IRE)**[21] 5006 3-9-6 **90** FrankieDettori 5 102+
(Saeed Bin Suroor) *hld up in tch: rdn and hdwy between horses over 1f out: led jst ins fnl f: r.o wl: eased towards fin* **5/4**[1]

3004 **2** *2 ¼* **Weapon Of Choice (IRE)**[19] 5094 4-9-11 **89** TomQueally 1 94
(Stuart Kittow) *pushed along early: in tch in rr of main gp: rdn and hdwy on inner 2f out: drvn and ev ch over 1f out: outpcd by wnr and one pce fnl f* **12/1**

3021 **3** *½* **Afkar (IRE)**[9] 5457 4-8-12 **76** 6ex (b) RichardHughes 2 80
(Clive Brittain) *chsd ldr: hdwy to join ldrs and rdn 2f out: unable qck w wnr and styd on same pce ins fnl f* **20/1**

30-0 **4** *½* **Atlantis Star**[29] 4703 5-9-10 **88** [1] MartinDwyer 6 91
(James Tate) *led: rdn jst over 2f out: hdd and one pce jst ins fnl f* **33/1**

1050 **5** *½* **Come On Blue Chip (IRE)**[21] 5006 3-8-13 **90**(b) MichaelJMMurphy(7) 3 92
(Paul D'Arcy) *sn pushed along in rr of main gp: rdn and effrt wl over 1f out: kpt on ins fnl f* **7/1**[3]

0405 **6** *1 ¼* **Fantasy Gladiator**[8] 5480 6-8-12 **79** (p) AdamBeschizza(3) 8 78
(Robert Cowell) *s.i.s: sn detached in last and rdn along: clsd and in tch 3f out: drvn and plugged on same pce fnl 2f* **16/1**

-001 **7** *nse* **Little Black Book (IRE)**[8] 5480 4-9-4 **82** 6ex (b) LukeMorris 7 81
(Gerard Butler) *in tch in midfield: rdn and unable qck ent fnl 2f: hrd drvn and styd on same pce fr over 1f out* **7/1**[3]

-113 **8** *3 ½* **Discoverer (IRE)**[15] 5237 3-9-2 **86** WilliamBuick 10 80
(John Gosden) *chsd ldrs: rdn and unable qck ent fnl 2f: no ex and btn 1f out: wknd and eased towards fin* **11/4**[2]

101/ **9** *10* **Everybody Knows**[864] 1430 7-9-4 **82** DaneO'Neill 9 50
(Jo Crowley) *chsd ldr tl over 2f out: sn lost pl: bhd fnl f* **33/1**

1m 37.29s (-2.51) **Going Correction** -0.05s/f (Stan)
WFA 3 from 4yo+ 6lb **9** Ran SP% **120.3**
Speed ratings (Par 107): **110,107,107,106,106 105,104,101,91**
Tote Swingers 1&2 £4.50, 2&3 £1.30, 1&3 £3.20 CSF £19.21 CT £212.03 TOTE £2.30: £1.10, £2.80, £2.70; EX 20.40 Trifecta £272.50 Pool 511.93 - 1.39 winning units..
Owner Godolphin **Bred** Twelve Oaks Stud **Trained** Newmarket, Suffolk

FOCUS
A good handicap won in style and in a relatively good time. The winner is value for a bit extra with the second close to his best.

NOTEBOOK
Royal Empire(IRE) ◆ looks pretty smart. He made a winning debut over 1m on the Lingfield Polytrack in July, before a good run in defeat over 1m2f at Sandown, and he very much continued his progression on a surface that evidently suits. It will be interesting to see whether he has many more races this year, or whether he's held back for next year's Dubai Carnival. He looks just the type for Meydan. (op 11-8, tchd 6-4 in a place)

Weapon Of Choice(IRE) was probably up against it conceding 5lb to this winner. He may yet have a bit more to offer. (op 10-1)
Afkar(IRE) ran well off a mark 10lb higher than when winning over 7f on turf last time. (op 16-1)
Atlantis Star, having just his second start of the season, offered some encouragement in a first-time hood. (op 25-1)
Come On Blue Chip(IRE) simply didn't pick up well enough. (op 8-1)
Discoverer(IRE), who had previously shown a real liking for Polytrack, was disappointing, even allowing for racing wide without cover. (op 9-4)

5769 32 FREE AT 32RED.COM FILLIES' H'CAP — 7f (P)
9:20 (9:21) (Class 4) (0-85,85) 3-Y-O+ — **£4,075** (£1,212; £606; £303) **Stalls** Low

Form — RPR

4305 **1** **Triple Charm**[14] 5269 4-9-12 **85**..........(v) FrankieDettori 7 — 93+
(Jeremy Noseda) *hld up in tch in rr: rdn and effrt jst over 1f out: str run u.p fnl f to ld fnl 50yds: gng away at fin* **2/1**[1]

-002 **2** 3/4 **Al Mayasah (IRE)**[23] 4933 4-9-1 **81**.......... AliceHaynes(7) 5 — 87
(David Simcock) *stdd s: t.k.h: chsd ldrs: rdn and effrt over 1f out: led jst ins fnl f: hdd and no ex fnl 50yds* **7/1**[3]

2263 **3** 1 1/4 **Choral**[27] 4775 4-9-8 **81**.......... PatDobbs 3 — 84
(Richard Hannon) *chsd ldrs: rdn and effrt on inner 2f out: led 1f out: sn hdd and styd on same pce* **6/1**[2]

0620 **4** 1 1/2 **Golden Tempest (IRE)**[14] 5269 4-9-6 **79**.......... JimmyFortune 4 — 78
(Eve Johnson Houghton) *led: rdn over 1f out: hdd and unable qck 1f out: wknd ins fnl f* **8/1**

4245 **5** *hd* **Santarini (IRE)**[14] 5262 3-8-8 **72**.......... RichardHughes 8 — 69
(Richard Hannon) *stdd s: hld up in tch in last trio: rdn and effrt over 1f out: styd on same pce: no imp fnl f* **6/1**[2]

3220 **6** *nk* **Russian Ice**[50] 3963 4-9-5 **78**..........(b) BrettDoyle 2 — 75
(Dean Ivory) *hld up in tch: effrt u.p over 1f out: styd on same pce ins fnl f* **10/1**

6361 **7** 2 3/4 **Bint Alzain (IRE)**[13] 5298 3-8-11 **75**..........(tp) LukeMorris 1 — 64
(Gerard Butler) *dwlt: t.k.h: hld up in tch: effrt u.p over 1f out: no prog 1f out: wknd ins fnl f* **8/1**

0-34 **8** 6 **Soho Rocks**[19] 5107 3-8-4 **68**.......... KirstyMilczarek 6 — 41
(James Toller) *t.k.h: chsd ldr: sddle slipped 1/2-way: lost pl wl over 1f out: wknd 1f out* **10/1**

1m 25.67s (-0.33) **Going Correction** -0.05s/f (Stan)
WFA 3 from 4yo 5lb — **8** Ran SP% **114.8**
Speed ratings (Par 102): **99,98,96,95,94 94,91,84**
Tote Swingers 1&2 £7.00, 2&3 £8.20, 1&3 £3.40 CSF £16.54 CT £72.06 TOTE £1.90: £1.10, £2.60, £2.30; EX 18.60 Trifecta £148.70 Pool 526.54 - 2.62 winning units..
Owner Bluehills Racing Limited **Bred** Hesmonds Stud Ltd **Trained** Newmarket, Suffolk

FOCUS
A fair fillies' handicap but not form to get carried away with.
Soho Rocks Official explanation: jockey said saddle slipped
T/Plt: £210.90 to a 1 stake. Pool £68,095.69. 235.65 winning tickets T/Qpdt: £53.50 to a 1 stake. Pool £5,056.81. 69.84 winning tickets SP

5481 LINGFIELD (L-H)
Thursday, August 30

OFFICIAL GOING: Round course - good to firm (good in places); straight course - good (good to firm in places; 8.4)
Wind: Fresh, half against Weather: Cloudy

5770 TERSUS LAUNDRY EQUIPMENT H'CAP — 1m 2f
2:30 (2:30) (Class 6) (0-60,60) 3-Y-O — **£1,704** (£503; £251) **Stalls** Low

Form — RPR

4636 **1** **Joyful Spirit (IRE)**[35] 4506 3-9-4 **57**..........(b) TedDurcan 10 — 74+
(John Dunlop) *racd wd early: mde all and sn spreadeagled field: nt less than 6 l clr after 2f: stl gng strly 2f out: unchal and eased nr fin* **7/2**[1]

004 **2** 6 **Joy To The World (IRE)**[10] 5406 3-8-8 **47**..........(t) ChrisCatlin 11 — 49
(Paul Cole) *chsd wnr and sn clr of the rest: no imp at any stage but kpt on wl whn pressed for 2nd over 2f out* **25/1**

3506 **3** 3 1/4 **Essell**[7] 5501 3-9-4 **57**.......... MartinHarley 12 — 53
(Mick Channon) *sn chsd clr ldng pair: rdn to dispute 2nd over 2f out to over 1f out but no imp on wnr: one pce* **11/2**[3]

005 **4** 2 1/4 **Suedehead**[23] 4931 3-9-5 **58**.......... StevieDonohoe 4 — 49
(William Muir) *mostly in abt 6th but sn wl off the pce: rdn 3f out: kpt on fnl 2f: no ch* **10/1**

0420 **5** 3/4 **High Five Prince (IRE)**[12] 5349 3-8-4 **48**.......... RachealKneller(5) 2 — 38
(Mark Usher) *wl off the pce towards rr: pushed along 3f out: styd on fnl 2f: no ch* **16/1**

-036 **6** *shd* **Lone Foot Laddie (IRE)**[12] 5351 3-9-7 **60**.......... RichardHughes 13 — 49
(Sylvester Kirk) *hld up wl in rr and sn long way off the pce: shkn up 3f out: styd on fnl 2f: no ch* **4/1**[2]

0-40 **7** 3 1/2 **Sovereign Waters**[27] 4754 3-9-2 **55**.......... JimmyFortune 7 — 37
(Eve Johnson Houghton) *mostly chsd ldrs in 5th but wl off the pce: rdn and no prog 3f out: fdd* **12/1**

0-00 **8** 1 1/2 **There's No Rules**[13] 5316 3-8-8 **47** oh1 ow1..........(e[1]) RobbieFitzpatrick 6 — 26
(Richard Guest) *t.k.h: hld up in rr and wl off the pce: no prog fnl 3f* **20/1**

0030 **9** 3/4 **Wyebridge**[31] 4650 3-8-9 **48**..........(p) FergusSweeney 9 — 26
(Gary Moore) *wl off the pce in midfield: no prog 3f out: wknd over 1f out* **14/1**

000 **10** 1 **Kaypea**[49] 4001 3-8-12 **51**.......... HayleyTurner 1 — 27
(Simon Dow) *hld up in 11th long way off the pce: shkn up and no prog 3f out* **33/1**

4601 **11** 1 **Compton Crofter**[9] 5443 3-8-9 **55** 6ex..........(t) NicoleNordblad(7) 3 — 29
(Hans Adielsson) *stdd s: detached in last as wnr blasted off in front: more or less t.o fr 1/2-way: kpt on over 1f out* **8/1**

500 **12** 1/2 **Rowan Rhapsody**[43] 4213 3-8-8 **47**.......... EddieAhern 5 — 20
(Jim Boyle) *racd in 4th but nowhere nr ldr: rdn 3f out: wknd over 2f out* **12/1**

2m 9.82s (-0.68) **Going Correction** -0.10s/f (Good) — **12** Ran SP% **117.3**
Speed ratings (Par 98): **98,93,90,88,88 88,85,84,83,82 81,81**
toteswingers 1&2 £18.90, 1&3 £4.80, 2&3 £30.50 CSF £96.92 CT £478.55 TOTE £4.00: £1.40, £7.40, £2.40; EX 46.70.
Owner Windflower Overseas Holdings Inc **Bred** Windflower Overseas **Trained** Arundel, W Sussex

FOCUS
A poor contest, with all bar one of 12 runners maidens coming into it, and the result wasn't in much doubt from a long way out. Tricky form to pin down, but it has been taken at something like face value for now. Nothing got involved from the rear.

Compton Crofter Official explanation: trainer said gelding did not handle the track

5771 DORMANS PARK H'CAP — 1m 3f 106y
3:00 (3:02) (Class 6) (0-60,60) 3-Y-O+ — **£1,704** (£503; £251) **Stalls** High

Form — RPR

2601 **1** **Pahente**[8] 5483 4-9-5 **51** 6ex..........(p) MichaelO'Connell 3 — 58
(Tony Carroll) *restless stalls: sn trckd ldr: led over 4f out: idled and rdn over 2f out: a finding enough after* **6/4**[1]

00/2 **2** 2 **Blue Zealot (IRE)**[75] 3143 5-9-1 **47**..........(t) JohnFahy 6 — 51
(Anthony Honeyball) *reluctant to enter stalls: hld up in tch: rdn 3f out: chsd wnr wl over 1f out: no real imp* **9/4**[2]

/065 **3** 2 3/4 **Beggar's Opera (IRE)**[8] 5483 5-10-0 **60**..........(t) StevieDonohoe 7 — 59
(Jim Best) *sn led: hdd over 4f out: lost 2nd wl over 1f out: fdd* **16/1**

3063 **4** 1 1/2 **Celtic Charlie (FR)**[17] 5164 7-9-1 **47**.......... IanMongan 2 — 43
(Pat Phelan) *broke first but sn hld up bhd ldrs: disp 2nd 3f out tl wl over 1f out: wknd* **11/4**[3]

/33- **5** 7 **Red Willow**[552] 687 6-9-8 **57**.......... SimonPearce(3) 1 — 41
(John E Long) *t.k.h: hld up in last: outpcd and lost tch over 4f out: shkn up over 2f out: lost no further grnd* **8/1**

2m 33.3s (1.80) **Going Correction** -0.10s/f (Good)
WFA 3 from 4yo+ 9lb — **5** Ran SP% **114.4**
Speed ratings (Par 101): **89,87,85,84,79**
CSF £5.47 TOTE £2.40: £2.10, £1.10; EX 5.30.
Owner Mayden Stud **Bred** Mayden Stud, J A And D S Dewhurst **Trained** Cropthorne, Worcs
■ Locum was withdrawn (5/2, spread a plate). Deduct 25p in the 3 under R4. New market formed.

FOCUS
An already moderate handicap was rendered even weaker by half the declared ten runners not lining up. The winner seems better than ever but, like the other two round course winners, he raced prominently.

5772 INOX KITCHENS TO DINE FOR H'CAP — 2m
3:30 (3:30) (Class 5) (0-75,75) 4-Y-O+ — **£2,726** (£805; £402) **Stalls** Low

Form — RPR

0200 **1** **Saborido (USA)**[19] 5106 6-9-7 **75**.......... JimCrowley 6 — 83
(Amanda Perrett) *led after 1f: mde rest: rdn over 2f out: clr over 1f out: styd on stoutly* **7/2**[2]

4201 **2** 3 **Sunny Future (IRE)**[27] 4756 6-8-13 **67**.......... TomMcLaughlin 3 — 71+
(Malcolm Saunders) *stdd s: hld up: in last tl prog over 2f out: shkn up and styd on to take 2nd ins fnl f: no ch to chal* **11/1**

2124 **3** 3/4 **Our Folly**[28] 4731 4-8-8 **62**..........(t) LukeMorris 7 — 66
(Stuart Kittow) *settled in rr: prog over 3f out: drvn to chse wnr 2f out: no imp: lost 2nd ins fnl f* **7/1**

30-3 **4** 2 1/4 **Whenever**[27] 4756 8-8-10 **64**..........(v) RobertHavlin 5 — 66
(Richard Phillips) *chsd ldng trio but nvr gng sweetly: lost pl over 2f out: nt clr run sn after: plugged on fr over 1f out* **11/1**

-046 **5** *nse* **Sirius Superstar**[19] 5106 4-9-4 **72**..........(p) WilliamBuick 1 — 73
(Andrew Balding) *led 1f: chsd wnr after: shkn up 5f out: hrd rdn over 2f out: sn lost 2nd: fdd* **5/2**[1]

5-00 **6** *hd* **Hawridge King**[33] 4606 10-9-0 **68**..........(v) RichardHughes 10 — 69
(Stuart Kittow) *t.k.h early: hld up in last pair: prog 5f out and prom 3f out: disp 2nd 2f out: wknd jst over 1f out* **12/1**

-521 **7** 8 **Dr Finley (IRE)**[17] 5172 5-8-10 **67**.......... SimonPearce(3) 2 — 58
(Lydia Pearce) *trckd ldrs in 5th: drvn and no prog 3f out: lost pl and sn btn* **6/1**[3]

3005 **8** 1 1/4 **Almail (USA)**[12] 5359 6-9-7 **75**.......... FergusSweeney 8 — 64
(Jamie Osborne) *settled in rr: rdn 3f out: no real prog 2f out: sn wknd* **20/1**

2200 **9** 1 1/4 **Dubai Glory**[21] 4983 4-9-5 **73**.......... ChrisCatlin 4 — 61
(Sheena West) *chsd ldng pair: rdn over 3f out: wknd wl over 2f out* **10/1**

3m 36.0s (1.20) **Going Correction** -0.10s/f (Good) — **9** Ran SP% **115.8**
Speed ratings (Par 103): **93,91,91,90,89 89,85,85,84**
toteswingers 1&2 £8.00, 1&3 £6.50, 2&3 £6.60 CSF £41.63 TOTE £3.80: £1.60, £3.00, £2.00; EX 50.20.
Owner Tracey, Cotton, James, Slade **Bred** R D Hubbard And R Masterson **Trained** Pulborough, W Sussex

FOCUS
A modest staying handicap, though the pace seemed solid enough. The form is rated around the winner.
Whenever Official explanation: jockey said gelding was denied a clear run
Sirius Superstar Official explanation: jockey said gelding hung left
Dr Finley(IRE) Official explanation: jockey said gelding never travelled

5773 TERSUS HEALTHCARE SUPPLIERS MEDIAN AUCTION MAIDEN FILLIES' STKS — 5f
4:00 (4:01) (Class 6) 2-Y-O — **£1,704** (£503; £251) **Stalls** High

Form — RPR

3 **1** **Melbourne Memories**[21] 5003 2-9-0 0.......... AdamKirby 2 — 72+
(Clive Cox) *trckd ldrs: clsd on outer to ld over 1f out: sn in command: rdn out* **4/6**[1]

533 **2** 1 1/2 **Tregereth (IRE)**[23] 4899 2-9-0 62.......... RichardKingscote 3 — 67
(Jonathan Portman) *pressed ldr: rdn to chal and upsides over 1f out: chsd wnr after: readily hld* **6/1**[3]

3 *nk* **Princess Sheila (IRE)** 2-9-0 0.......... LiamKeniry 1 — 66
(J S Moore) *s.i.s: hld up in last and rn green: taken to outer and prog over 1f out: rdn and pressed for 2nd nr fin* **25/1**

4 **4** 2 1/2 **Tristessa**[24] 4886 2-9-0 0.......... DaneO'Neill 7 — 57
(Derek Haydn Jones) *racd against nr side rail: led to over 1f out: sn wknd* **12/1**

6 **5** 3 3/4 **Jubilini**[31] 4645 2-9-0 0.......... IanMongan 5 — 43
(Brett Johnson) *chsd ldrs: rdn over 2f out: wknd over 1f out* **66/1**

022 **6** 3/4 **Puteri Nur Laila (IRE)**[75] 3150 2-9-0 67.......... RichardHughes 6 — 40
(Paul Cole) *pressed ldr: shkn up and fnd nil jst over 2f out: wknd over 1f out* **3/1**[2]

1m 0.1s (1.90) **Going Correction** +0.225s/f (Good) — **6** Ran SP% **112.3**
Speed ratings (Par 89): **93,90,90,86,80 78**
toteswingers 1&2 £1.40, 1&3 £3.20, 2&3 £6.60 CSF £5.41 TOTE £1.90: £1.10, £3.10; EX 3.80.
Owner M P Coleman & R J Coleman **Bred** M P Coleman & R J Coleman **Trained** Lambourn, Berks

FOCUS
A modest juvenile fillies' sprint maiden. The runner-up looks the key and the winner seemingly only had to reproduce her sound debut figure.

NOTEBOOK
Melbourne Memories finished one place ahead of a subsequent winner when a promising third of nine on her Sandown debut earlier this month and duly built on that. The only worry was that she had to be taken out wide in order to get a run, but she quickened up nicely to seal it and can now find something rather better than this. (op 5-6)

Tregereth(IRE)'s recent efforts suggested that the drop in trip on a sharp track like this wasn't going to be ideal, but she ran well for a long way, if lacking the speed of the winner late on. A nursery back over further could see her off the mark. (op 9-2)

Princess Sheila (IRE)was last early, but showed definite signs of ability when switched to the wide outside and stayed on well. A 30,000gns 2yo, she is a sister to the smart Princess Sinead and a half-sister to a 1m winner and also winners in Japan and the US. On this evidence she won't let the family down. (op 20-1)

Tristessa achieved little when fourth of six on her Wolverhampton debut and couldn't capitalise on being able to gain the early advantage against the favoured stands' rail here. (tchd 10-1 and 14-1)

Puteri Nur Laila (IRE)had already finished runner-up in a couple of 5f maidens here (one on Polytrack) and she was up with the pace early, but she faded tamely from over a furlong from home and passed the line with her rider looking down. Her rider reported that the filly moved poorly. Official explanation: jockey said filly moved poorly (op 7-2 tchd 4-1)

5774 LINGFIELD MARRIOTT HOTEL & COUNTRY CLUB H'CAP (DIV I) 6f

4:35 (4:35) (Class 5) (0-70,69) 3-Y-O+ **£2,385** (£704; £352) **Stalls** High

Form RPR

0006 **1** **The Tichborne (IRE)**[33] 4580 4 -9-8**65**...........................(v) JackMitchell 9 78+
(Roger Teal) *hld up in rr and racd agains rail: looking for room fr over 2f out: gap appeared and squeezed through over 1f out: urged along and r.o to ld last 100yds: won gng away* **2/1**[1]

0046 **2** *2* **Dickie Le Davoir**[21] 4998 8 -9-12**69**........................(b) RobbieFitzpatrick 4 76
(Richard Guest) *pushed along in last after 2f: gd prog on outer over 2f out: led over 1f out: r.o but hdd and outpcd last 100yds* **16/1**

0360 **3** *6* **Danzoe (IRE)**[6] 5557 5 -9-4**61**............................. TomMcLaughlin 8 49+
(Christine Dunnett) *hld up towards rr: nt clr run 2f out to 1f out: styd on to take modest 3rd ins fnl f* **12/1**

5342 **4** *2 3/4* **Imjin River (IRE)**[20] 5047 5 -8-8**54**........................ AdamBeschizza(3) 11 33
(William Stone) *racd against nr side rail: mde most to over 1f out: sn lft bhd* **6/1**[3]

0000 **5** *shd* **Haadeeth**[18] 5120 5 -9-7**64**.. RichardHughes 6 43
(David Evans) *hld up in rr: effrt 2f out: outpcd and btn over 1f out* **6/1**[3]

055 **6** *3/4* **Catflap (IRE)**[24] 4885 3 -9-2**62**.. DaneO'Neill 10 38
(Derek Haydn Jones) *trckd ldrs gng wl: effrt 2f out: sltly brushed as wnr wnt by: fnd nil and btn after* **12/1**

3605 **7** *3 1/2* **Belle Bayardo (IRE)**[7] 5150 4 -9-2**64**........................(v) DarrenEgan(5) 7 29
(Ronald Harris) *prog on outer to trck ldrs 1/2-way: rdn 2f out: wknd over 1f out* **9/2**[2]

0402 **8** *3/4* **Red Mischief (IRE)**[14] 5279 3 -9-6**66**.............................. HayleyTurner 2 29
(Harry Dunlop) *pressed ldrs: rdn over 2f out: wknd over 1f out* **8/1**

4400 **9** *1* **Samba Night (IRE)**[8] 5479 3 -9-0**60**.............................(v) LukeMorris 1 19
(James Eustace) *w ldr to 1/2-way: wknd 2f out* **20/1**

1m 12.1s (0.90)**Going Correction** +0.225s/f (Good)
WFA 3 from 4yo+ 3lb **9**Ran SP% **117.2**
Speed ratings (Par 103): **103,100,92,88,88 87,82,81,80**
toteswingers 1&2 £8.60, 1&3 £7.90, 2&3 £19.00 CSF £38.73 CT £317.23 TOTE £2.70 : £1.30 , £4.60, £4.10 ; EX 47.10 .
Owner Chris Simpson & Mick Waghorn **Bred** Ms Alyson Flower And Chris Simpson **Trained** Ashtead, Surrey

FOCUS
A moderate sprint handicap, but the market got it right. The front pair, who eventually came well clear of the rest, occupied the last two places early. The time was similar to division II. The winner has come down a long way in the weights and is still a stone off his 3yo best.
Belle Bayardo (IRE) Official explanation: jockey said gelding hung left

5775 LINGFIELD MARRIOTT HOTEL & COUNTRY CLUB H'CAP (DIV II) 6f

5:05 (5:05) (Class 5) (0-70,68) 3-Y-O+ **£2,385** (£704; £352) **Stalls** High

Form RPR

0430 **1** **Tiger Cub**[73] 3228 3 -9-5**66**..................................(vt[1]) MickaelBarzalona 11 75
(Mrs Ilka Gansera-Leveque) *trckd ldrs against nr side rail: shkn up over 2f out: wnt 2nd wl over 1f out: rdn to ld jst ins fnl f: styd on* **6/1**[3]

4015 **2** *1* **Balti's Sister (IRE)**[62] 3908 3 -9-0**61** ow1........................... AdamKirby 4 67
(Terry Clement) *hld up in last pair: stdy prog on outer fr 1/2-way: rdn and styd on fnl f to take 2nd last strides* **10/1**

201 **3** *nk* **Golden Compass**[40] 4332 4 -9-10**68**............................ WilliamCarson 6 73
(Giles Bravery) *led and sn crossed to nr side rail: rdn over 1f out: hdd and nt qckn jst ins fnl f* **15/8**[1]

6065 **4** *1* **Diamond Vine (IRE)**[7] 5502 4 -9-8**66**...............................(p) KierenFox 9 68
(Ronald Harris) *hld up in rr against nr side rail: urged along fr 1/2-way: no prog tl styd on jst over 1f out: nrst fin* **9/2**[2]

4600 **5** *1 1/4* **Hatta Stream (IRE)**[29] 4708 6 -9-2**60**.............................. RobertHavlin 8 58
(Lydia Pearce) *trckd ldrs: shkn up sn after 1/2-way and nt qckn: struggling after: kpt on fr over 1f out* **9/1**

0104 **6** *1 3/4* **Speedyfix**[13] 5327 5 -8-12**56**.......................................(t) TomMcLaughlin 1 48
(Christine Dunnett) *wl in tch: effrt towards outer over 2f out: disp 3rd jst over 1f out: wknd* **33/1**

046 **7** *3* **Gracie's Gift (IRE)**[15] 5246 10 -8-9**53** oh1 ow2.....(v) RobbieFitzpatrick 7 35
(Richard Guest) *prom: rdn 1/2-way: wknd wl over 1f out* **22/1**

000 **8** *2 3/4* **White Shift (IRE)**[9] 5444 6 -8-2**51** oh6............................ DarrenEgan(5) 5 25
(Paul Howling) *w ldr to wl over 1f out: sn wknd* **50/1**

-220 **9** *8* **Courtland Avenue (IRE)**[27] 4777 3 -9-7**68**.................... JimCrowley 10 16
(Jonathan Portman) *trckd ldrs: n.m.r early: lost pl sn after 1/2-way: sn wknd and bhd* **10/1**

5134 **10** *1 3/4* **Wiltshire Life (IRE)**[87] 2759 3 -9-3**67**.........................(p) RaulDaSilva(3) 2
(Jeremy Gask) *prom towards outer over 3f: wknd rapidly* **14/1**

1540 **11** *1 1/4* **Justbookies Dotnet**[134] 1445 3 -9-5**66**............................(v) JackMitchell 3
(Louise Best) *rdn in last over 3f out: no prog and sn bhd* **33/1**

1m 12.2s (1.00)**Going Correction** +0.225s/f (Good)
WFA 3 from 4yo+ 3lb **11**Ran SP% **114.3**
Speed ratings (Par 103): **102,100,100,98,97 94,90,87,76,74 72**
toteswingers 1&2 £10.90, 1&3 £4.40, 2&3 £4.70 CSF £59.93 CT £157.12 TOTE £9.60 : £2.30 , £3.40, £1.10 ; EX 68.90 .
Owner Helena Halling Racing Syndicates 1 **Bred** Carwell Equities Ltd **Trained** Newmarket, Suffolk
■ A winner with her first runner in Britain for Ilka Gansera-Leveque.
■ Stewards' Enquiry : William Carson 17-day ban: 3 for careless riding, 14 under totting-up - 4 days deferred (Sep 14-26)

FOCUS
The winning time was 0.1 seconds slower than the first division. The winner is rated to her 2yo best.

5776 LADBROKES GAME ON! MAIDEN STKS 7f

5:35 (5:37) (Class 5) 3-Y-O **£2,385** (£704; £352) **Stalls** High

Form RPR

63 **1** **Enrol**[12] 5340 3 -8-12**0**... RichardHughes 5 80+
(Sir Michael Stoute) *stdd s: hld up in last pair and confidently rdn: prog to chse ldr wl over 1f out: sn shkn up: clsd fnl f: drvn to ld nr fin* **4/5**[1]

64 **2** *3/4* **Finesse**[142] 1274 3 -8-12**0**... JimCrowley 1 78
(Ralph Beckett) *wnt lft s: sn prom: mde most fr 4f out: kicked on over 2f out: styd on but hdd nr fin* **20/1**

625 **3** *4* **Gold Edition**[14] 5276 3 -9-3**80**....................................(v) JimmyFortune 2 73
(Jeremy Noseda) *w ldrs: u.p sn after 1/2-way: one pce fr over 2f out* **5/1**[3]

60 **4** *hd* **Treasured Dream**[39] 4366 3 -8-12**0**................................... EddieAhern 7 67
(Amanda Perrett) *trckd ldrs: effrt over 2f out: shkn up to chse ldng pair over 1f out: no imp: lost 3rd last stride* **20/1**

44 **5** *3 3/4* **Fairest (IRE)**[27] 4782 3 -8-12**0**.. RichardMullen 3 57
(Jeremy Noseda) *dwlt: hld up in last pair: effrt over 2f out: no prog over 1f out: wknd* **25/1**

6222 **6** *1/2* **Pashan Garh**[40] 4341 3 -8-12**74**..................................... DarrenEgan(5) 4 61
(Pat Eddery) *w ldrs: u.p sn after 1/2-way: wknd fnl 2f* **11/4**[2]

7 *12* **Easter Chorus** 3 -8-12**0**... JohnFahy 9 23
(Clive Cox) *t.k.h: mde most tor 3f: sn lost pl: wl btn over 2f out* **16/1**

50 **8** *10* **Sir Palomides (USA)**[40] 4341 3 -9-3**0**................................ AdamKirby 8
(William Haggas) *w ldrs to 1/2-way: sn wknd: t.o* **12/1**

1m 24.55s (1.25)**Going Correction** +0.225s/f (Good) **8**Ran SP% **125.8**
Speed ratings (Par 100): **101,100,95,95,91 90,76,65**
toteswingers 1&2 £5.50, 1&3 £2.30, 2&3 £7.50 CSF £26.78 TOTE £1.80 : £1.10 , £4.10 , £1.60 ; EX 22.50 .
Owner Cheveley Park Stud **Bred** Cheveley Park Stud Ltd **Trained** Newmarket, Suffolk

FOCUS
Some big stables were represented here, but the feeling is that this is modest form, especially as the pace appeared ordinary. The winner showed big improvement at face value.
T/Jkpt: £2,500.00 to a £1 stake. Pool: £15,923.64 - 10.00 winning tickets T/Plt: £53.00 to a £1 stake. Pool: £74,678.62 - 1,027.63 winning tickets T/Qpdt: £36.20 to a £1 stake. Pool: £4,284.74 - 87.40 winning tickets JN

5777a - 5780a (Foreign Racing) See RI

5755 BADEN-BADEN (L-H)

Thursday, August 30

OFFICIAL GOING: Turf: good

5781a KRONIMUS-RENNEN (LISTED RACE) (2YO) (TURF) 6f

4:55 (5:07) 2-Y-O **£10,000** (£4,166; £1,666 ; £833)

RPR

1 **Zazera (FR)**[33] 4615 2 -8-13**0**.. OlivierPeslier 8 96
(Mario Hofer, Germany) **29/10**[3]

2 *1 1/4* **Dream Wedding**[39] 2 -8-13**0**.. AStarke 9 92
(Mario Hofer, Germany) **5/1**

3 *1 1/4* **Tipping Over (IRE)**[14] 4205 2 -8-13**0**.................................. JimmyQuinn 5 89
(Hugo Palmer) *broke wl and led: pressed on both sides thrght: rdn over 1f out: hdd ins fnl f: no ex* **14/5**[2]

4 *3/4* **Talqaa**[12] 5352 2 -8-6**0**... DavidProbert 3 79
(Mick Channon) *pressed ldr: 3rd and ev ch whn rdn 1 1/2f out: nt qckn: one pce fnl f* **17/10**[1]

5 *2* **Mountain View (GER)**[39] 2 -9-0**0**.. ADeVries 4 81
(Frau Nina Bach, Germany) **81/10**

6 *2 1/2* **Salinas Road (FR)**[34] 2 -9-2**0**... EPedroza 2 76
(M Figge, Germany) **104/10**

7 *10* **Estrelja (GER)** 2 -8-6**0**.. NRichter 7 36
(D Moser, Germany) **23/1**

1m 10.55s (0.26) **7**Ran SP% **129.6**
WIN (incl. 10 euro stake): 39. PLACES: 14,15, 16. SF: 191
Owner WH Sport International **Bred** Mark Johnston Racing Ltd **Trained** Germany

NOTEBOOK
Tipping Over (IRE) after disputing the lead a furlong from home with the other British raider, was totally eclipsed in the final stages by Mario Hofer's two runners. The trainer was, however, pleased to get some black type but thinks his filly is possibly better over shorter.
Talqaa appeared to run her race but could not respond late on, although her rider reported that the filly got a bit upset at the start because of a loose horse.

5782a DARLEY OETTINGEN-RENNEN (GROUP 2) (3YO+) (TURF) 1m

6:00 (12:00) 3-Y-O+

£33,333 (£12,916; £5,416 ; £3,333 ; £2,083 ; £1,250)

RPR

1 **Highland Knight (IRE)**[14] 5278 5 -9-10............................ DavidProbert 5 114
(Andrew Balding) *broke wl and trckd ldr: led on outside rail over 2 1/2f out: rdn and wnt into decisive ld 1 1/2f out: drvn clr fnl f* **16/5**[2]

2 *3 1/2* **Dux Scholar**[25] 4 -9-10.. MircoDemuro 3 106
(A Savujev, Czech Republic) *chsd ldrs: shuffled bk on inner bef 1/2-way: hdwy towards ins 2 1/2f out: rdn and wnt 2nd appr fnl f: nvr on terms w wnr* **97/10**

3 *3/4* **Vagabond Shoes (IRE)**[63] 3900 5 -9-10................. StephanePasquier 6 104
(Y Durepaire, Spain) *trckd ldrs: 3rd and travelling wl 3f out: rdn and swtchd ins under 2f out: kpt on wout qckning fnl f* **23/5**[3]

4 *1 3/4* **Amarillo (IRE)**[46] 4130 3 -8-9.. AStarke 9 99+
(P Schiergen, Germany) *settled in midfield: 5th whn rdn 2f out: nt qckn: kpt on at same pce fnl f* **23/5**[3]

5 *nk* **Amaron**[88] 2743 3 -8-9.. DavyBonilla 2 98+
(Andreas Lowe, Germany) *settled towards rr: pushed along 3f out: hrd rdn and no imp 2f out: styd on u.p fnl f: nvr plcd to chal* **23/10**[1]

6 *nk* **Energia Dust (BRZ)**[46] 4130 4 -9-10.. SHellyn 11 99
(Fabricio Borges, Sweden) *rushed up fr outside draw to ld: hdd on outside over 2 1/2f out: rdn 2f out: nt qckn: wknd ins fnl f* **52/1**

7 *3/4* **Nafar (GER)**[39] 4 -9-10.. FilipMinarik 10 97+
(W Hickst, Germany) *chsd ldng gp on outside: rdn 2 1/2f out: sn lost pl: one pce fnl f* **38/1**

8 *1* **Sir Oscar (GER)**[46] 4130 5 -9-4... ADeVries 1 98+
(T Potters, Germany) *settled in rr: sme mod prog past btn horses fnl f: nvr in contention* **151/10**

9 *2 1/2* **Wasimah (GER)**[46] 4129 3 -8-9.. WPanov 8 88+
(H J Groschel, Germany) *hld up towards rr: rdn and no imp over 2f out: sn wl btn* **34/1**

10 *1 1/4* **Kolonel (GER)**[94] 2568 3 -8-9.. StefanieHofer 4 85+
(Mario Hofer, Germany) *racd keenly: chsd ldrs on ins: grad wknd fr over 2f out* **142/10**

11 *3 1/2* **Mano Diao**[60] 3683 3 -8-10**0** ow1.. OlivierPeslier 7 78+
(Mario Hofer, Germany) *plld hrd: restrained in rr of midfield: rdn and no imp 2f out: sn wl btn* **87/10**

1m 38.55s (-0.56)
WFA 3 from 4yo+ 6lb **11**Ran SP% **129.6**
WIN (incl. 10 euro stake): 42. PLACES: 19, 24, 16. SF: 343

Owner J C Smith **Bred** Littleton Stud **Trained** Kingsclere, Hants

NOTEBOOK
Highland Knight(IRE)continued the stable's hot streak by winning this Group 2 to give his rider a first Group race success. Usually a front-runner, he was always close up on the leader's outside and Probert went for home as the field swung into the straight, grabbing the favoured outside rail. He was never in any danger from the distance. His trainer decribed this as the gelding's best performance yet. He added that the winner could go next for the Shadwell Mile in Keeneland and then be aimed at the Godolphin Mile at Meydan in the spring.

5274 SALISBURY (R-H)

Friday, August 31

OFFICIAL GOING: Good to soft (good in places)
Wind: mild breeze against Weather: cloudy with sunny periods

5783 SAVILLS "GALLEGO" LADY RIDERS' H'CAP (FOR LADY AMATEUR RIDERS) 1m
4:30 (4:30) (Class 5) (0-70,70) 3-Y-0+ £2,495 (£774; £386; £193) Stalls Low

Form				RPR
4300	1		**Saint Irene**20 5095 3-8-5 **51** oh2 MissAliceMills(5) 1 (Michael Blanshard) *mid-div: hdwy 3f out: led over 1f out: r.o strly to assert fnl 120yds* 8/1	63
40-0	2	4 ½	**Billion Dollar Kid**21 5035 7-10-2 **65** (vt1) MissEJJones 4 (Jo Davis) *prom: rdn 3f out: led 2f out: hdd over 1f out: kpt pressing wnr tl no ex fnl 120yds* 10/1	68
0243	3	8	**George Thisby**16 5240 6-9-13 **62** (p) MissSBrotherton 6 (Rod Millman) *prom: pushed along over 4f out: rdn 3f out: one pce and hld fr 2f out* 6/1	46
3303	4	1 ½	**Rapid Water**4 5658 6-9-4 **56** MissRachelKing(3) 7 (Pat Eddery) *mid-div: rdn over 2f out: wnt 4th over 1f out: nvr threatened ldrs* 11/2[3]	37
3000	5	1 ½	**Gallego**10 5452 10-9-2 **54** MissBeckyBrisbourne(3) 3 (Richard Price) *taken down early: dwlt bdly: detached in last most of way tl sed to cl 2f out: r.o fnl f: nvr any ch* 10/1	31
-005	6	¾	**One Cool Chick**15 5279 4-8-11 **51** oh1 MissKMargarson(5) 2 (John Bridger) *slowly away: tk str hold: towards rr: styd on fnl f: nvr a factor* 33/1	27
0013	7	hd	**Capitol Gain (IRE)**13 5349 3-9-6 **64** (p) MissHayleyMoore(3) 8 (Brian Meehan) *led after 1f: rdn 3f out: sn hung lft: hdd 2f out: wknd* 4/1[1]	38
3004	8	½	**Benandonner (USA)**13 5359 9-10-1 **69** MissMBryant(5) 11 (Paddy Butler) *rdr slow in removing blindfold: dwlt: pushed along over 4f out: a towards rr* 12/1	43
3004	9	3 ¼	**Moody Tunes**6 5585 9-10-2 **70** (p) MissALMurphy(5) 10 (Tom Dascombe) *led for over 1f: prom: rdn over 3f out: sn wknd* 5/1[2]	37
3054	10	¾	**Marvo**22 4988 8-9-6 **62** (p) MissSLewis(7) 13 (Dai Burchell) *mid-div: rdn 3f out: wknd 2f out* 22/1	27
250-	11	22	**Teide Peak (IRE)**303 7233 3-9-6 **68** MrsRWilson(7) 9 (Paul D'Arcy) *taken down early: s.i.s: a towards rr: wl bhd fnl 2f* 16/1	

1m 47.1s (3.60) **Going Correction** +0.35s/f (Good) 11 Ran SP% 116.5
WFA 3 from 4yo+ 6lb
Speed ratings (Par 103): **96,91,83,82,80 79,79,79,75,75 53**
Tote Swingers: 1&2 £1.80, 1&3 £2.70, 2&3 £3.80 CSF £84.58 CT £517.09 TOTE £11.90: £2.80, £3.00, £2.30; EX 143.00 TRIFECTA Not won..
Owner The Breeze-In Partnership **Bred** Usk Valley Stud **Trained** Upper Lambourn, Berks
■ Stewards' Enquiry : Miss E J Jones eight-day ban: used whip above permitted level when clearly second (tbn)

FOCUS
A fair lady riders' handicap, run at a good pace and won in convincing fashion by the bottom-weight Saint Irene, who justified a strong late plunge. The winner is rated in line with her previous best this year.
Gallego Official explanation: jockey said gelding was slowly away
Benandonner(USA) Official explanation: jockey said as the gelding is edgy in stalls she was slow to remove blindfold

5784 BATHWICK TYRES MAIDEN AUCTION STKS (DIV I) 6f
5:00 (5:00) (Class 5) 2-Y-O £2,587 (£770; £384; £192) Stalls Low

Form				RPR
42	1		**Emell**22 4982 2-9-2 0 PatDobbs 4 (Richard Hannon) *mde all: drew wl clr over 1f out: pushed out* 1/1[1]	92
20	2	9	**Almalekiah (IRE)**18 5146 2-8-4 0 JohnFahy 7 (J S Moore) *hld up in last pair but wl in tch: rdn wl over 2f out: no imp tl r.o ent fnl f: wnt 2nd sn after: no ch w wnr* 7/2[2]	53
	3	½	**Jubilante** 2-8-6 0 NickyMackay 8 (Hughie Morrison) *chsd wnr: rdn over 2f out: outpcd by wnr over 1f out: no ex whn lost 2nd ins fnl f* 10/1	54+
35	4	3 ½	**Clement (IRE)**36 4502 2-8-11 0 JimmyFortune 10 (Eve Johnson Houghton) *chsd ldrs: wnt cl 3rd jst over 2f out: sn rdn: one pce after* 6/1[3]	48
0	5	1 ½	**Lucky Black Star (IRE)**15 5275 2-8-13 0 PatCosgrave 3 (George Baker) *chsd wnr: rdn over 2f out: wknd over 1f out* 25/1	46
0	6	1	**Everreadyneddy**27 4792 2-8-9 0 MarcHalford 5 (J S Moore) *in tch tl outpcd over 3f out: nvr threatened* 33/1	39
	7	½	**Unison (IRE)** 2-8-11 0 SebSanders 6 (Peter Makin) *squeezed up s: in last but wl in tch: sme prog over 3f out: nvr a danger* 9/1	39

1m 16.9s (2.10) **Going Correction** +0.35s/f (Good) 7 Ran SP% 112.4
Speed ratings (Par 94): **100,88,87,82,80 79,78**
Tote Swingers: 1&2 £1.80, 1&3 £2.70, 2&3 £3.80 CSF £4.45 CT £32.70 TOTE £1.70: £1.40, £2.30; EX 4.40 Trifecta £32.70 Pool: £358.68 - 8.11 winning units..
Owner Derek And Jean Clee **Bred** D D & Mrs J P Clee **Trained** East Everleigh, Wilts

FOCUS
A host of non-runners meant this was a lot weaker than it may otherwise have been and it was dominated by the well-backed Emell. He could be rated up yo 10lb higher and may be underestimated.

NOTEBOOK
Emell recouped his recent Brighton losses in impressive style. He had shaped with some promise on his debut on heavy ground at Windsor and it looked likely he would get off the mark next time at the Sussex track before wilting late on. However, returned to sprint trips, he made short work of these and could yet make up into a useful handicapper. He put his experience to good use when grabbing the lead and rail in the first furlong and, in truth, had matters in hand shortly afterwards as he piled on the pressure. He may not have beaten a great deal but it seems as though he's improving with his racing and should be of interest over this trip in nurseries, providing he's not too harshly treated. (op 11-8)
Almalekiah(IRE) had looked a winner in waiting after her Bath debut but she's failed to fire in two subsequent starts and has questions to answer after this. She did make laboured headway into second but was never in contention having been off the bridle at halfway. Her debut second had come on rattling fast ground though, and it's possible that she'll be able to confirm some of that promise once faced with similar conditions. (op 3-1)
Jubilante wasn't entirely disgraced and can be expected to improve for this experience. Her trainer isn't renowned for juvenile success and breeding suggests she'll be more effective over further on better ground. (op 9-1)
Clement(IRE) has now qualified for a nursery mark and is one of the more interesting for the future. He got loose in the preliminaries and may not have had his mind entirely on the race. He wasn't knocked around once his chance had gone. (op 7-1)

5785 BATHWICK TYRES MAIDEN AUCTION STKS (DIV II) 6f
5:30 (5:32) (Class 5) 2-Y-O £2,587 (£770; £384; £192) Stalls Low

Form				RPR
	1		**Breton Rock (IRE)** 2-8-13 0 MartinLane 6 (David Simcock) *hld up: swtchd lft over 2f out: sn rdn: str run fr over 1f out: led jst ins fnl f: r.o wl to assert fnl 100yds* 10/1[2]	77
00	2	1 ¼	**Keene's Pointe**36 4487 2-9-2 0 SebSanders 5 (J W Hills) *mid-div: hdwy wl over 3f out: rdn wl over 1f out: ev ch ent fnl f: kpt on but nt pce of wnr fnl 100yds* 40/1	76
6	3	1 ¾	**Squeeze My Brain (IRE)**29 4739 2-8-11 0 JimmyFortune 7 (Ralph Beckett) *cl up: nt clr run over 2f out: shkn up whn gap appeared over 1f out: nt pce to take advantage: keeping on but looking hld whn nt clr run again ent fnl f* 1/2[1]	68+
3233	4	½	**Marchwood**100 2402 2-8-9 75 JohnFahy 9 (J S Moore) *trckd ldrs: led over 2f out: sn rdn: hdd jst ins fnl f: no ex* 10/1[2]	63
	5	4	**Russian Royale** 2-8-6 0 MickaelBarzalona 8 (Stuart Kittow) *hmpd s: towards rr: effrt over 2f out: fdd fnl f* 20/1	48
00	6	5	**Ottauquechee (IRE)**27 4818 2-8-8 0 PatDobbs 3 (Richard Hannon) *w ldr: led over 3f out tl rdn over 2f out: fdd fnl f* 14/1[3]	35
0	7	4 ½	**Astrum**16 5235 2-9-2 0 (b1) JamesMillman 4 (Rod Millman) *led tl rdn and edgd lft jst over 3f out: sn hld: wknd over 1f out* 40/1	29
	8	3 ¾	**Delwyn** 2-8-6 0 JimmyQuinn 1 (Marcus Tregoning) *s.i.s: sn chsng ldrs: wknd over 2f out* 20/1	

1m 17.55s (2.75) **Going Correction** +0.35s/f (Good) 8 Ran SP% 105.9
Speed ratings (Par 94): **95,93,91,90,85 78,72,67**
Tote Swingers: 1&2 £19.90, 1&3 £1.50, 2&3 £9.90 CSF £265.41 TOTE £14.00: £2.50, £8.30, £1.02; EX 251.80 Trifecta £154.40 Part won. Pool: £205.97 - 0.63 winning units..
Owner John Cook **Bred** George Kent **Trained** Newmarket, Suffolk
■ Lilbourne Eliza was withdrawn (13/2, starter's advice). Deduct 10p in the £ under R4.

FOCUS
This looked a shade more competitive than the first division of this maiden. The runner-up will prove the key to the form long-term.

NOTEBOOK
Breton Rock(IRE) continued the excellent form of his yard with juveniles. He didn't go unsupported and, while taking a while to hit top gear, quickened up well in the final 100 yards to win with a bit more in hand the official margin. He was green towards the rear in the early stages but got the hang of things shortly after halfway and really lengthened once switched to the outside. The drying ground would surely have been a concern to connections given his high knee action, and the fact that he was able to win so convincingly suggests he could be an above-average recruit. This trip looks a bare minimum for him. (op 12-1)
Keene's Pointe turned in a career-best effort and this run will have set him up nicely for a nursery campaign. He was keen enough on leaving the stalls and showed signs of greenness when hitting the front. (op 33-1)
Squeeze My Brain(IRE) failed to build on the promise she'd shown at Goodwood. She had a wall of horses ahead of her as they entered the straight but made only steady headway once in the clear. It's likely she's better than she's shown here but she wouldn't be one to be backing again at short prices. (op 5-6)
Marchwood ran with credit, but again had to settle for a minor role. He was readily left behind the principals inside the final furlong and may be worth a try over 7f. (op 15-2)

5786 BATHWICK TYRES NURSERY 1m
6:05 (6:05) (Class 5) (0-75,77) 2-Y-O £2,587 (£770; £384; £192) Stalls Low

Form				RPR
2261	1		**Ronaldinho (IRE)**9 5475 2-9-9 **77** 6ex RichardHughes 10 (Richard Hannon) *hld up: hdwy ins 3f out: bmpd 2f out: sn shkn up: led jst ins fnl f: r.o strly: pushed out* 4/1[2]	82+
506	2	2 ½	**Rioja Day (IRE)**15 5274 2-8-13 **67** SebSanders 1 (J W Hills) *in tch: rdn jst over 3f out: hdwy over 2f out: led briefly ent fnl f: kpt on but nt pce of wnr: jst hld on for 2nd* 14/1	67
563	3	nse	**Stiff Upper Lip (IRE)**19 5119 2-8-8 **62** PatDobbs 3 (Richard Hannon) *trckd ldrs for 1f: sn lost pl and in last trio: nt clr run over 2f out: rdn whn nt clr run again over 1f out: swtchd lft ent fnl f: r.o wl: jst failed to snatch 2nd* 12/1	65+
004	4	8	**Aeronwyn Bryn (IRE)**24 4921 2-8-7 **61** MartinLane 7 (Michael Dods) *stmbld leaving stalls: sn trcking ldrs: rdn to chal 3f out: edgd lft 2f out: led narrowly over 1f out: hdd ent fnl f: fdd* 13/2	43
6001	5	1 ¾	**Lea Valley Black**17 5207 2-9-0 **68** JimmyFortune 2 (Tom Dascombe) *led for over 1f: trckd ldrs: rdn over 2f out: hld whn sltly hmpd jst over 1f out* 10/1	46
0241	6	shd	**Noble Bull (IRE)**22 4982 2-9-7 **75** DarryllHolland 8 (Charles Hills) *trckd ldr after 1f: rdn to ld over 2f out: hdd over 1f out: wknd fnl f* 11/2[3]	53
430	7	2 ¼	**Specialty (IRE)**43 4246 2-9-2 **70** MickyFenton 9 (Pam Sly) *led after 1f: rdn whn hdd over 2f out: stl ev ch over 1f out: wknd ent fnl f* 7/1	43
0361	8	1 ¼	**Aint Got A Scooby (IRE)**16 5236 2-8-10 **64** JohnFahy 5 (Clive Cox) *mid-div: pushed along 5f out: nvr really travelling after: wknd over 1f out* 10/3[1]	34
000	9	nk	**Just Duchess**15 5275 2-7-12 **55** oh7 ow3 SophieDoyle(3) 6 (Michael Blanshard) *mid-div: pushed along fr over 4f out: rdn over 3f out: wknd over 1f out* 80/1	24
205	10	4 ½	**Bamurru (IRE)**15 5260 2-9-2 **70** PatCosgrave 4 (Peter Makin) *s.i.s: in rr: rdn wl over 2f out: nvr any imp: wknd over 1f out* 33/1	29

1m 46.9s (3.40) **Going Correction** +0.35s/f (Good) 10 Ran SP% 111.9
Speed ratings (Par 94): **97,94,94,86,84 84,82,81,80,76**
Tote Swingers: 1&2 £12.30, 1&3 £7.80, 2&3 £17.00 CSF £55.96 CT £622.08 TOTE £5.70: £2.00, £4.30, £4.00; EX 66.40 Trifecta £360.60 Part won. Pool: £487.33 - 0.63. winning units..
Owner Macdonald,Wright,Creed,Smith & Jiggins **Bred** J Fallon **Trained** East Everleigh, Wilts
■ Stewards' Enquiry : Pat Dobbs caution: careless riding.

FOCUS
An informative nursery, run at a strong pace and won as he liked by the progressive Ronaldinho. The first three were clear.

NOTEBOOK

Ronaldinho(IRE) followed up a recent Kempton victory. He had made short work of his rivals over 6f on the AW nine days earlier and had no problem translating that improved form to turf over this longer trip. Given a patient ride, he arrived on the scene going easily at the furlong marker and, despite hanging right under pressure, was soon in command. He'll find it tougher once reassessed but remains open to improvement and has a good attitude. (op 9-2 tchd 7-2, tchd 5-1 in a place)

Rioja Day(IRE) made a really pleasing start to his nursery career. While no match for the winner late on, this was a big step up on what he'd achieved in three maiden runs. He was unfortunate to meet such a well-treated rival on this occasion and compensation surely awaits.

Stiff Upper Lip(IRE), a stablemate of the winner, was doing all his best work late on and will surely be capable of winning off his current mark. He put clear daylight between himself and the rest and would have grabbed second in another stride.

Aeronwyn Bryn(IRE) looked sure to be involved in the finish but stopped quickly in the final 100 yards. (op 6-1)

Noble Bull(IRE) wasn't disgraced but appeared not to last home after helping force the pace. (op 5-1 tchd 6-1)

Aint Got A Scooby(IRE), a winner over 7f at this course last time, never really travelled and ran as if something was amiss. (op 7-2)

5787 WEATHERBYS BLOODSTOCK INSURANCE STONEHENGE STKS (LISTED RACE) 1m

6:35 (6:37) (Class 1) 2-Y-O **£13,043** (£4,945; £2,474; £1,232) **Stalls** Low

Form				RPR
14	**1**		**Go Angellica (IRE)**[36] 4514 2-8-8 0 .... EddieAhern 4 (David Simcock) *trckd ldr tl squeezed out 3f out: cl 4th travelling wl: nt clr run fr 2f out tl gap kindly appeared ins fnl f: qckn up wl to ld nring fin: readily* **5/2**[2]	100+
3125	**2**	½	**Califante**[13] 5379 2-8-8 99 .... RichardHughes 5 (Richard Hannon) *racd in 3rd tl cruised upsides 3f out: led over 1f out: rdn ent fnl f: hdd nring fin* **85/40**[1]	98
13	**3**	1 ½	**Timoneer (USA)**[15] 5270 2-8-13 0 .... MickaelBarzalona 1 (Mahmood Al Zarooni) *j. awkwardly hitting stall gate and nrly unseating rdr: rcvrd composure after 75yds: trckd ldng trio: rdn to chal 2f out: wandered jst ins fnl f: kpt on same pce* **5/2**[2]	101
106	**4**	nk	**Operation Chariot (IRE)**[30] 4698 2-8-13 100 .... JimmyFortune 3 (Andrew Balding) *led: jnd 3f out: rdn 2f out: sn hdd: kpt on same pce fnl f* **7/2**[3]	99

1m 47.26s (3.76) **Going Correction** +0.35s/f (Good) **4** Ran SP% **111.4**
Speed ratings (Par 102): **95,94,93,92**
CSF £8.30 TOTE £4.60; EX 10.30.

Owner Ahmed Jaber **Bred** Rabbah Bloodstock Limited **Trained** Newmarket, Suffolk

FOCUS

A disappointing turnout for this Listed contest, but the winner impressed and the form has been rated to the avertage for the grade despite the slow time.

NOTEBOOK

Go Angellica(IRE), a winner over 7f at Doncaster on her debut, didn't have much go right when fourth in this grade at Sandown last time and it looked like being another luckless run when she was squeezed out with only a furlong remaining. However, she showed a smart turn of foot once getting a gap and came through to win with plenty in hand. This probably wasn't the strongest of Listed races but she's clearly going the right way and will surely be stepped up to Group company. The Fillies' Mile at Newmarket may be a step too far but she's definitely talented and appears to handle any ground. (op 7-2 tchd 4-1)

Califante was bidding to give Richard Hannon his fourth successive win in the race. She had looked to be crying out for this trip when fifth in a Deauville Group 3 last time but arguably found herself in front too early. She lacked the gears of the winner but shouldn't be written off in future if getting a stronger pace to run at. (op 5-2 tchd 2-1)

Timoneer(USA) had cut out the running at Newmarket last time but was forced into a change of tactics having almost unseated when leaving the stalls. However, he didn't lose a great deal of ground and could not be considered in anyway unlucky. He lugged out to his left under pressure and didn't appear to stay. (tchd 11-4)

Operation Chariot(IRE) was allowed an easy time of things up front but dropped away disappointingly once headed. It may be that he was flattered by his proximity to Olympic Glory at Goodwood last time. He could be hard to place from now on. (op 11-4)

5788 WEATHERBYS PRINTING H'CAP 1m 4f

7:10 (7:10) (Class 4) (0-85,84) 3-Y-O **£4,528** (£1,347; £673; £336) **Stalls** Low

Form				RPR
1220	**1**		**Varnish**[22] 4983 3-9-1 78 .... RichardHughes 4 (Richard Hannon) *mid-div: nudged along to make hdwy over 4f out whn bmpd: rdn to chal over 2f out: led wl over 1f out: sn hung rt: only being pushed along whn pestered by str chalr ins fnl f: styd on: nicely rdn* **13/2**[3]	86
1462	**2**	nk	**Cape Savannah**[24] 4930 3-9-3 80 .... MartinLane 6 (David Simcock) *hld up towards rr: pushed along 4f out: rdn and hdwy over 3f out: swtchd lft 2f out: wnt 3rd ent fnl f: fin strly: snatched 2nd fnl stride* **7/1**	87
6351	**3**	shd	**Little Dutch Girl**[18] 5151 3-9-3 80 .... (b) JohnFahy 9 (Clive Cox) *trckd ldrs: rdn 3f out: squeezed through gap over 1f out: str chal sn after whn short of room on rails: egded lft and tried to bite wnr fnl 100yds: kpt on: lost 2nd fnl stride* **9/1**	87
3610	**4**	3 ¾	**Trend Is My Friend (USA)**[30] 4700 3-9-4 81 .... EddieAhern 10 (Amanda Perrett) *trckd ldrs: rdn and ev ch 3f out tl 2f out: styd on same pce* **3/1**[2]	82
0115	**5**	nk	**Scarlet Whispers**[24] 4923 3-9-3 80 .... (p) MickyFenton 5 (Pam Sly) *led: rdn whn jnd 3f out: hdd wl over 1f out: kpt battling away tl no ex ent fnl f* **14/1**	81+
533	**6**	1 ¾	**Marmas**[179] 805 3-8-6 69 .... JimmyQuinn 7 (Marcus Tregoning) *s.i.s: briefly pushed along in last: outpcd over 3f out: sme late prog: nvr threatened* **14/1**	67
61	**7**	2	**Emerald Invader**[24] 4916 3-9-0 77 .... TedDurcan 1 (David Elsworth) *hld up towards rr: making hdwy whn pushed on rails over 4f out: rdn whn swtchd lft wl over 2f out: wknd ent fnl f: nvr trbld ldrs* **9/1**	72
1102	**8**	8	**Rocktherunway (IRE)**[42] 4294 3-9-7 84 .... JimCrowley 2 (Michael Dods) *trckd ldr: rdn to dispute ld 3f out tl 2f out: wknd tamely over 1f out* **9/4**[1]	66

2m 39.52s (1.52) **Going Correction** +0.225s/f (Good) **8** Ran SP% **114.9**
Speed ratings (Par 102): **103,102,102,100,100 98,97,92**
Tote Swingers: 1&2 £12.40, 1&3 £10.90, 2&3 £12.30 CSF £51.14 CT £410.51 TOTE £7.30: £2.40, £2.30, £4.10; EX 46.20 Trifecta £182.90 Pool: £449.92 - 1.82 winning units..

Owner Highclere Thoroughbred Racing - Eleanor **Bred** Carmel Stud **Trained** East Everleigh, Wilts

FOCUS

A competitive 3yo handicap, run at a strong pace. The winner confirmed she was on a potentially good mark.

5789 WESTOVER GROUP H'CAP 1m 6f 21y

7:40 (7:40) (Class 5) (0-75,75) 3-Y-0+ **£2,587** (£770; £384; £192)

Form				RPR
10	**1**		**Stock Hill Fair**[13] 5344 4-9-12 73 .... PatDobbs 3 (Brendan Powell) *mde all: styd on gamely whn rdn fnl 2f: hld on wl ins fnl f* **14/1**	82
0143	**2**	¾	**Burnham**[41] 4323 3-8-12 71 .... RichardHughes 2 (Hughie Morrison) *trckd ldrs: rdn to chse wnr over 2f out: kpt on but a being hld fnl f* **15/8**[1]	79
2166	**3**	½	**Dovils Date**[21] 5044 3-8-12 71 .... JamesMillman 9 (Rod Millman) *trckd ldrs: rdn whn outpcd over 3f out: styd on again fr over 1f out: regained 3rd fnl f: fin wl* **14/1**	78
2232	**4**	3	**Hidden Justice (IRE)**[7] 5533 3-8-13 72 .... EddieAhern 6 (Amanda Perrett) *mid-div: rdn and hdwy over 2f out: styd on same pce fr over 1f out: nvr gng pce to get on terms* **7/1**[3]	75
1040	**5**	¾	**Maydream**[14] 5306 5-9-7 68 .... KieranO'Neill 8 (Jimmy Fox) *mid-div: rdn whn swtchd lft over 2f out: styd on same pce fnl f* **14/1**	70
0113	**6**	2	**Astra Hall**[18] 5151 3-8-6 65 .... JimCrowley 13 (Ralph Beckett) *mid-div: rdn and hdwy over 3f out: nvr threatened ldrs: fdd fnl f* **5/2**[2]	64
1422	**7**	½	**Abundantly**[15] 5280 3-8-8 67 .... DarryllHolland 4 (Hughie Morrison) *trckd wnr: rdn over 3f out: lost 2nd over 2f out: wknd jst over 1f out* **15/2**	65
0060	**8**	7	**The Ploughman**[6] 5577 3-7-12 57 oh12 .... JamieMackay 5 (John Bridger) *a towards rr* **100/1**	45
00-6	**9**	hd	**Carter**[144] 1258 6-10-0 75 .... StevieDonohoe 7 (Ian Williams) *a towards rr* **33/1**	63
505	**10**	8	**Call Me April**[15] 5280 4-8-10 57 oh6 .... TedDurcan 10 (Karen George) *struggling 4f out: a bhd* **40/1**	34

3m 15.44s (8.04) **Going Correction** +0.225s/f (Good)
WFA 3 from 4yo+ 12lb **10** Ran SP% **114.0**
Speed ratings (Par 103): **86,85,85,83,83 82,81,77,77,73**
Tote Swingers: 1&2 £8.20, 1&3 £18.20, 2&3 £6.80 CSF £39.46 CT £387.09 TOTE £18.60: £4.00, £1.10, £3.70; EX 62.40 Trifecta £308.90 Part won. Pool of £417.48 - 0.63 winning units..

Owner Mrs M Fairbairn, E Gadsden & P Dean **Bred** Mrs M Fairbairn And E Gadsden **Trained** Upper Lambourn, Berks

FOCUS

A fair handicap, run at a steady pace. The winner may not have been too flattered and the form is taken at face value.

Stock Hill Fair Official explanation: trainer said, regarding apparent improvement in form, that the gelding was better suited by the softer ground

T/Plt: £316.90 to a £1 stake. Pool: £34,557.24 - 79.60 winning tickets. T/Qpdt: £82.70 to a £1 stake. Pool: £3,512.03 - 31.42 winning tickets. TM

5003 SANDOWN (R-H)

Friday, August 31

OFFICIAL GOING: Good (good to firm in places)

Wind: Moderate across Weather: Sunny spells

5790 ORLEANS NURSERY 5f 6y

2:20 (2:20) (Class 4) (0-85,82) 2-Y-O **£3,881** (£1,155; £577; £288) **Stalls** Low

Form				RPR
0443	**1**		**Effie B**[7] 5527 2-9-4 79 .... MartinHarley 3 (Mick Channon) *trckd ldrs: squeezed through on ins fnl 120yds whn n.m.r: led fnl 50yds: readily* **5/1**	82
0416	**2**	½	**Equitania**[20] 5088 2-9-7 82 .... RichardHughes 4 (Richard Hannon) *t.k.h: led 1f: trckd ldr: led 1f out: sn drvn: hung rt fnl 120yds: hdd and outpcd fnl 50yds* **10/3**[2]	83
41	**3**	nk	**Vectis**[15] 5260 2-9-3 78 .... CathyGannon 7 (Harry Dunlop) *s.i.s: in rr but wl in tch: swtchd lft to outer and hdwy appr fnl f: styd on to take 3rd and edgd rt fnl 120yds: gng on cl home* **11/4**[1]	78
0335	**4**	2	**Bentleysoysterboy (IRE)**[25] 4873 2-8-9 70 .... (p) PaulHanagan 6 (David Elsworth) *chsd ldrs: rdn and effrt over 1f out: hung rt u.p fnl 120yds: sn btn* **13/2**	63
0124	**5**	1 ¼	**Hot Secret**[13] 5332 2-8-13 74 .... WilliamBuick 2 (Andrew Balding) *hld up in rr but in tch: n.m.r 1f out: styng on whn hmpd fnl 120yds: nt rcvr* **4/1**[3]	66
5340	**6**	2 ¼	**Ishi Honest**[27] 4820 2-9-2 77 .... DavidProbert 1 (Mark Usher) *w ldr: led after 1f: rdn 1/2-way: hdd 1f out: sn btn* **10/1**	57

1m 1.82s (0.22) **Going Correction** +0.05s/f (Good) **6** Ran SP% **108.8**
Speed ratings (Par 96): **100,99,98,95,93 89**
Tote Swingers: 1&2 £2.90, 1&3 £3.40, 2&3 £2.00 CSF £20.44 CT £48.09 TOTE £7.00: £3.00, £1.80; EX 15.60 Trifecta £49.80 Pool £838.38 - 12.68 winning units..

Owner R Bastian **Bred** R Bastian **Trained** West Ilsley, Berks

FOCUS

Sprint track at full width. Round course dolled out up to 4yds from 7f to 2f - drop in at that point - adding about 5yds to distances on Round course. A fair nursery despite the small field and the winning time was 1.82 seconds outside standard. Straightforward form that could be rated a fraction higher.

NOTEBOOK

Effie B, who faced some stiff tasks earlier in the season, had started to look exposed but she showed here that she still has what it takes. She had to wait to get a run, but was left with a lovely gap against the inside rail when the leader Ishi Honest wilted a furlong out and proved very brave in sneaking up the second's inside to score. (tchd 6-1)

Equitania threatened to pull too hard early, so was helped by getting a lead from Ishi Honest after a furlong. She had every chance when leading again a furlong from home, but was mugged close to the line. (op 3-1)

Vectis, making his nursery debut after winning a five-runner Chepstow maiden, still looked green there and this effort can be marked up too. He gave away ground at the start and was forced to make his final effort widest, but despite still not looking the finished article he was gaining on the front pair all the way to the line. (op 3-1 tchd 7-2)

Bentleysoysterboy(IRE) has tended to ruin his chances by racing too freely, but he seemed to settle better here and there were no obvious excuses. (op 17-2 tchd 9-1)

Hot Secret travelled well off the pace, but never saw any daylight and was already struggling to get a run when the weakening Ishi Honest falling back into her lap proved the final straw. A line can be put through this. Official explanation: jockey said filly was denied a clear run (op 10-3 tchd 3-1)

5791 WISECALL CLAIMS ASSISTANCE H'CAP — 5f 6y

2:50 (2:53) (Class 5) (0-75,73) 3-Y-O+ — **£2,587** (£770; £384; £192) **Stalls** Low

Form — RPR

016 **1** — **Tom Sawyer**[15] 5272 4-9-1 **64**.....(b) GrahamLee 2 — 77
(Julie Camacho) *trckd ldr: led 3f out: pushed clr wl over 1f out: easily* **10/3**[2]

2230 **2** *5* **Picansort**[69] 3390 5-8-9 **58**..... JimmyQuinn 9 — 53
(Peter Grale) *bmpd s: s.i.s: in rr and swtchd to far rail: hdwy over 1f out: n.m.r on inner ins fnl f: styd on wl to take 2nd clsng stages but nvr any ch w easy wnr* **16/1**

0342 **3** *nk* **Swendab (IRE)**[8] 5502 4-9-9 **72**.....(v) KierenFallon 8 — 66+
(John O'Shea) *wnt lft s: in rr: drvn 1/2-way: hdwy on outer over 1f: styd on wl to cl on 2nd nr line* **11/4**[1]

0023 **4** *hd* **Irish Boy (IRE)**[8] 5514 4-9-6 **69**..... MickyFenton 3 — 62
(Paul Midgley) *led tl hdd 3f out: styd chsng wnr u.p: sn no ch but kpt on tl outpcd into 4th clsng stages* **7/1**

2204 **5** *½* **Liberal Lady**[14] 5296 4-8-11 **60**.....(e) MartinHarley 6 — 51
(Ralph Smith) *chsd ldrs: rdn 2f out: styd on fnl f but nvr gng pce to get nr wnr* **20/1**

501 **6** *1* **Whiskey Junction**[17] 5217 8-8-6 **55**..... KieranO'Neill 5 — 43
(Michael Quinn) *chsd ldrs: rdn and one pce 2f out: styd on again ins fnl f* **10/1**

2052 **7** *1 ¼* **Amazon Twilight**[19] 5122 4-9-9 **72**..... DavidProbert 7 — 55
(Brett Johnson) *racd towards outside: rdn 1/2-way: styd on same pce fnl f* **6/1**[3]

0000 **8** *2 ¼* **Matsunosuke**[8] 5502 10-9-2 **65**..... NeilCallan 10 — 40
(Alan Coogan) *outpcd most of way* **33/1**

30-1 **9** *½* **Peter Island (FR)**[22] 4980 9-9-10 **73**.....(v) DarryllHolland 4 — 46
(John Gallagher) *s.i.s: outpcd* **6/1**[3]

1m 1.38s (-0.22) **Going Correction** +0.05s/f (Good) — **9** Ran SP% **113.5**
Speed ratings (Par 103): **103,95,94,94,93 91,89,86,85**
Tote Swingers: 1&2 £11.20, 1&3 £3.40, 2&3 £6.60 CSF £53.64 CT £164.61 TOTE £4.20: £1.80, £3.80, £1.40; EX 71.50 Trifecta £239.80 Pool £917.16 - 2.83 winning units..
Owner Bolingbroke J Howard FAO Mersey R & Ptns **Bred** Newsells Park Stud **Trained** Norton, N Yorks

FOCUS
An ordinary sprint handicap, though the winner bolted up. He had the far rail and may be flattered, so this doesn't look a race to be too positive about.
Peter Island(FR) Official explanation: jockey said geldign was slowly away

5792 BRITISH STALLION STUDS SUPPORTING BRITISH RACING E B F MAIDEN STKS (DIV I) — 7f 16y

3:25 (3:27) (Class 5) 2-Y-O — **£3,881** (£1,155; £577; £288) **Stalls** Low

Form — RPR

6 **1** — **Etijaah (USA)**[21] 5062 2-9-3 0..... PaulHanagan 7 — 80
(Brian Meehan) *trckd ldr: slt ld 2f out: narrowly hdd sn after: drvn to ld again 1f out: styd on wl u.p: jst hld on* **7/1**[3]

2 *hd* **Havana Beat (IRE)** 2-9-3 0..... LiamKeniry 9 — 79+
(Andrew Balding) *s.i.s: in rr: hdwy on outside fr 2f out: drvn and str run fnl f: fin wl: jst failed* **33/1**

0 **3** *nk* **Correggio**[28] 4773 2-9-3 0..... RichardHughes 2 — 79
(Richard Hannon) *chsd ldrs: rdn and one pce over 1f out: edgd lft ins fnl f and styd on wl to chal fnl 75yds: no ex last strides* **20/1**

4 *1* **Hillstar** 2-9-3 0..... NeilCallan 10 — 76+
(Sir Michael Stoute) *t.k.h: in rr and green: drvn over 2f out: pushed along and hdwy over 1f out: hmpd and swtchd rt ins fnl f: styng on wl clsng stages* **10/1**

5 **5** *nse* **Rangi**[21] 5062 2-9-3 0..... WilliamBuick 4 — 76
(John Gosden) *chsd ldrs: pushed along and one pce 2f out: drvn and styd on ins fnl f: gng on cl home* **7/4**[1]

2 **6** *1 ¼* **Rock God (IRE)**[27] 4803 2-9-3 0..... GrahamLee 6 — 72
(Eve Johnson Houghton) *chsd ldrs: rdn over 2f out: styd wl there tl one pce ins fnl f* **2/1**[2]

0 **7** *½* **Lancelot Du Lac (ITY)**[21] 5062 2-9-3 0..... BrettDoyle 11 — 71+
(Dean Ivory) *t.k.h: trckd ldrs: chal 2f out: led sn after: hdd 1f out: eased whn hld clsng stages* **20/1**

8 *¾* **Sweet Deal (IRE)** 2-9-3 0..... TomQueally 1 — 69+
(Jeremy Noseda) *s.i.s: in rr: pushed along over 2f out: styd on clsng stages* **25/1**

0 **9** *3 ¼* **Tilstarr (IRE)**[20] 5104 2-8-12 0..... KieranO'Neill 8 — 55
(Richard Hannon) *rdn 3f out: a towards rr* **50/1**

06 **10** *5* **Star Of Missouri**[22] 5005 2-9-3 0..... KierenFallon 3 — 47
(Mark H Tompkins) *led: rdn 3f out: hdd 2f out: wknd wl over 1f out* **33/1**

0 **11** *4 ½* **Depict**[14] 5319 2-9-3 0..... MichaelHills 5 — 35
(Charles Hills) *s.i.s: in rr: sme prog on inner over 2f out: nvr in contention and wknd wl over 1f out* **66/1**

1m 30.71s (1.21) **Going Correction** +0.175s/f (Good) — **11** Ran SP% **114.0**
Speed ratings (Par 94): **100,99,99,98,98 96,96,95,91,85 80**
Tote Swingers: 1&2 £23.60, 1&3 £5.30, 2&3 £34.90 CSF £206.66 TOTE £6.50: £1.70, £8.40, £3.80; EX 197.40 TRIFECTA Not won..
Owner Hamdan Al Maktoum **Bred** Shadwell Farm LLC **Trained** Manton, Wilts
■ Stewards' Enquiry : Richard Hughes two-day ban: used whip above permitted level (Sep 14,16)

FOCUS
This had looked an interesting maiden beforehand, but the principals finished in a heap which means the form cannot be rated any higher at this stage. The race should produce winners even so.

NOTEBOOK
Etijaah(USA) split Rangi and Lancelot Du Lac when sixth on his Newmarket debut three weeks earlier and this performance suggests that he has improved the most of the trio from their debuts, which is hardly unusual for the stable's juveniles. Always handy, he proved very game after edging to the front a furlong out and this half-brother to four winners should have no trouble staying 1m. (op 9-1)
Havana Beat(IRE) ◆, a 65,000gns half-brother to two winners, one of whom scored over 2m on the AW and also over hurdles, did well as he wasn't best away but finished with quite a flourish down the wide outside and would have got there with a little further to go. He will appreciate further and should have little trouble in going one better. (tchd 25-1)
Correggio, a 75,000gns brother to the Group 2 winning sprinter Prime Defender, looked in need of the experience on his Newmarket debut and stepped up quite a bit on that. He had every chance after diving to the inside rail after the cutaway and never stopped trying. (op 16-1 tchd 14-1)
Hillstar ◆, a half-brother to two winners including the stable's high-class Crystal Capella, stayed on nicely from the back of the field and would have finished a bit closer had he not been hampered by the third inside the last furlong. A Derby entry, this was a most pleasing introduction considering he was so weak in the market. (op 7-1 tchd 11-1)
Rangi couldn't confirm Newmarket form with the winner and took an age to pick up off the bridle. This was a bit disappointing in view of his entries for the Derby, Champagne Stakes and Racing Post Trophy. (op 5-2)
Rock God(IRE) had three subsequent winners behind him when runner-up on his Goodwood debut, so it was disappointing that he couldn't pick up better when put under pressure having held a good position from the start. It's too early to be giving up on him, though. (op 13-8)
Lancelot Du Lac(ITY) ◆ again finished behind Rangi and Etijaah as he did on his Newmarket debut, but he took quite a grip early and may have found himself in front too soon. He remains one to keep an eye on.
Sweet Deal(IRE), an 82,000euros 2yo and a half-brother to two winners at up to 1m4f in France, didn't fair too badly considering he lost ground at the start and probably needs more time and a stiffer test. Official explanation: jockey said colt was slowly away

5793 BRITISH STALLION STUDS SUPPORTING BRITISH RACING E B F MAIDEN STKS (DIV II) — 7f 16y

4:00 (4:06) (Class 5) 2-Y-O — **£3,881** (£1,155; £577; £288) **Stalls** Low

Form — RPR

5 **1** — **Sanjuro (IRE)**[14] 5304 2-9-3 0..... MartinHarley 9 — 82
(Mick Channon) *chsd ldrs: wnt 2nd and rdn over 1f out: styd on wl u.p to ld fnl 100yds: kpt on strly* **4/1**[2]

6 **2** *½* **Estifzaaz (IRE)**[62] 3634 2-9-3 0..... PaulHanagan 11 — 81
(Charles Hills) *chsd ldr: led appr fnl 2f: rdn over 1f out: hdd and one pce fnl 100yds* **9/2**[3]

0 **3** *4* **Lionheart**[21] 5062 2-9-3 0.....(t) KierenFallon 8 — 70
(Luca Cumani) *in tch: rdn along and hdwy 2f out: tk 3rd fnl f but nvr any ch w ldng duo* **6/1**

4 *2 ¼* **Space Ship** 2-9-3 0..... WilliamBuick 10 — 69+
(John Gosden) *s.i.s: in rr: shkn up over 2f out: kpt on wl fnl f: gng on clsng stages* **7/2**[1]

5 *nse* **Wrecking Ball (IRE)** 2-9-3 0..... JamieSpencer 6 — 64
(Brian Meehan) *in rr: hdwy over 3f out: rdn over 2f out: styd on same pce fr over 1f out* **25/1**

0 **6** *1 ¾* **East Texas Red (IRE)**[14] 5321 2-9-3 0..... KieranO'Neill 4 — 59
(Richard Hannon) *led: rdn 3f out: hdd appr fnl 2f: lost 2nd over 1f out: sn wknd* **16/1**

6 **7** *¾* **Norphin**[24] 4917 2-9-3 0..... TomQueally 3 — 57
(Denis Coakley) *t.k.h: chsd ldrs: wknd ins fnl 2f* **33/1**

8 *1 ¾* **Prospera (IRE)** 2-8-12 0..... RichardThomas 1 — 47
(Ralph Beckett) *chsd ldrs: rdn and wknd ins fnl 3f* **20/1**

9 *5* **Inaugural** 2-9-3 0..... JamesDoyle 2 — 39
(Roger Charlton) *rdn over 3f out: a in rr* **12/1**

20 **10** *2 ½* **King Oliver**[16] 5235 2-9-3 0..... RichardHughes 7 — 42
(Richard Hannon) *s.i.s: a in rr* **5/1**

1m 30.98s (1.48) **Going Correction** +0.175s/f (Good) — **10** Ran SP% **116.5**
Speed ratings (Par 94): **98,97,92,90,90 88,87,85,79,76**
Tote Swingers: 1&2 £4.50, 1&3 £5.40, 2&3 £5.60 CSF £21.79 TOTE £5.00: £1.50, £1.70, £1.90; EX 27.20 Trifecta £89.70 Pool £1,477.97 - 12.18 winning units..
Owner Jon and Julia Aisbitt **Bred** Fortbarrington Stud **Trained** West Ilsley, Berks

FOCUS
Unlike in the first division, the front pair put daylight between themselves and the rest, but the winning time was 0.27 seconds slower. Good, improved efforts from the front pair.

NOTEBOOK
Sanjuro(IRE) ◆ had very much caught the eye when fifth of 11 on his Newbury debut despite running green, but looked much more the finished article here. He was always travelling well just behind the leaders and showed a good attitude to nail the runner-up half a furlong from home. He is bred to appreciate middle-distances next year and looks a nice prospect. (op 9-2 tchd 5-1)
Estifzaaz(IRE) could manage only sixth of 14 on his Newmarket debut when sent off favourite, but this was more like it. In front passing the 2f pole, he couldn't cope with the winner's turn of foot in the latter stages, but came clear of the rest and this 280,000gns colt can go one better before too long. (op 4-1)
Lionheart finished just behind the three horses who took part in the first division of this race when eighth on his Newmarket debut three weeks earlier and stepped up from that effort with a staying-on third. He seems likely to progress with racing. (op 8-1)
Space Ship ◆ is a beautifully bred colt, being by Galileo out of a dual US Grade 1 winner and entries in the Racing Post Trophy and Derby show that he is highly regarded. Held up early, his rider became more animated approaching the last 2f, but it took a long time for the penny to drop. However, he finished his race off nicely under hands-and-heels riding and seems likely to leave this debut effort well behind. (op 4-1 tchd 10-3)
Wrecking Ball(IRE), a 34,000euros colt related to a couple of winners at up to 7f, showed ability out wide and can be expected to improve for the experience. (op 40-1)
King Oliver showed plenty of promise when runner-up on his Newbury debut, but was looking to bounce back after disappointing on softer ground at Salisbury on his second start. Unfortunately he never got into this at all and now has an awful lot to prove. (op 10-3)

5794 DURALOCK FENCING H'CAP — 1m 14y

4:35 (4:36) (Class 4) (0-85,85) 3-Y-O+ — **£4,528** (£1,347; £673; £336) **Stalls** Low

Form — RPR

3310 **1** — **Postscript (IRE)**[8] 5517 4-9-12 **85**..... JamieSpencer 6 — 97
(Ian Williams) *trckd ldr: led over 2f out: drvn clr over 1f out: styd on strly* **11/4**[1]

3050 **2** *2 ¼* **First Post (IRE)**[20] 5094 5-9-5 **78**.....(b[1]) DaneO'Neill 4 — 85
(Derek Haydn Jones) *chsd ldrs: wnt 2nd ins fnl 2f: kpt on u.p fnl f but a readily hld* **9/1**

-024 **3** *¾* **Devdas (IRE)**[34] 4600 3-9-1 **80**..... AdamKirby 7 — 84
(Clive Cox) *sn in tch: rdn and hung rt over 2f out: styd on u.p fr over 1f out to take 3rd fnl 120yds: nt rch ldng duo* **11/2**[2]

1503 **4** *½* **Barwick**[5] 5634 4-9-7 **80**..... TomQueally 9 — 84
(Mark H Tompkins) *s.i.s: in rr: rdn and hdwy towards outside fr 2f out: kpt on clsng stages* **11/2**[2]

0000 **5** *nse* **Sinfonico (IRE)**[14] 5301 4-9-3 **76**.....(e) KieranO'Neill 13 — 80
(Richard Hannon) *s.i.s: in rr: pushed along over 2f out: hdwy on outer over 1f out: kpt on clsng stages* **25/1**

-000 **6** *½* **Leviathan**[65] 3508 5-9-5 **78**..... NeilCallan 10 — 81
(Tony Newcombe) *in rr: pushed along 3f out: hdwy towards outer over 1f out: styd on clsng stages* **12/1**

16-0 **7** *hd* **Newnton Lodge**[133] 1500 3-9-2 **81**..... JamesDoyle 5 — 82
(Roger Charlton) *in tch: rdn and outpcd over 2f out: styd on again fnl f* **14/1**

0014 **8** *nse* **Yojimbo (IRE)**[7] 5535 4-9-8 **81**..... MartinHarley 12 — 83
(Mick Channon) *chsd ldrs: rdn over 2f out: wknd ins fnl f* **14/1**

0-30 **9** *2 ½* **Star Surprise**[44] 4223 4-9-11 **84**..... WilliamBuick 3 — 80
(Michael Bell) *led tl hdd over 2f out: wknd fnl f* **15/2**[3]

5006 **10** ¾ **Freddy Q (IRE)**[13] 5358 3-8-10 82 .... WilliamTwiston-Davies(7) 2 76
(Richard Hannon) *rdn along 3f out: towards rr most of way* **16/1**

25-0 **11** 1 **Sir Francis Drake**[23] 4948 4-9-2 75 .... GeorgeBaker 1 67
(Robert Eddery) *chsd ldrs: rdn 3f out: wknd 2f out* **22/1**

2163 **12** shd **My Lord**[22] 5007 4-9-2 75 .... IanMongan 8 67
(Luke Dace) *t.k.h: in tch: rdn over 2f out: wknd fnl f* **16/1**

1m 43.67s (0.37) **Going Correction** +0.175s/f (Good)
WFA 3 from 4yo+ 6lb **12** Ran SP% **120.2**
Speed ratings (Par 105): **105,102,102,101,101 100,100,100,98,97 96,96**
Tote Swingers: 1&2 £8.40, 1&3 £4.30, 2&3 £8.00 CSF £28.39 CT £131.74 TOTE £3.00: £1.70, £2.80, £1.70; EX 26.90 Trifecta £71.50 Pool £824.01 - 8.52 winning units..
Owner Dr Marwan Koukash **Bred** Darley **Trained** Portway, Worcs

FOCUS
A competitive handicap run at a solid pace. The winner stepped up slightly on his solid penultimate run.

5795 SURBITON MAIDEN FILLIES' STKS 1m 14y
5:05 (5:05) (Class 5) 3-Y-O **£2,587** (£770; £384; £192) **Stalls** Low

Form RPR

-343 **1** **Fulney**[22] 5019 3-9-0 75 .... DaneO'Neill 2 79
(James Eustace) *mde all: drvn and c clr fr 2f out: unchal* **2/1**[1]

3 **2** 3¾ **Merry Jaunt (USA)**[18] 5166 3-9-0 0 .... WilliamBuick 3 70
(John Gosden) *trckd ldrs: drvn and styd on to take 2nd over 1f out: kpt on but nvr any ch w wnr* **9/2**[3]

33 **3** ¾ **Love Tatoo (IRE)**[15] 5276 3-9-0 0 .... LiamKeniry 5 69
(Andrew Balding) *chsd ldrs: rdn over 2f out: styd on to take 3rd jst ins fnl f: nvr any ch w wnr* **7/2**[2]

53 **4** nk **Any Other Day**[24] 4931 3-8-9 0 .... DavidKenny(5) 6 68+
(William Knight) *s.i.s: sn mid-div: pushed along over 2f out: styd on fnl f: gng on cl home* **22/1**

34 **5** 1¼ **Tonle Sap (IRE)**[11] 5421 3-9-0 0 .... AdamKirby 7 65
(Clive Cox) *chsd ldr: rdn over 2f out: sn no ch: lost 2nd over 1f out* **15/2**

5 **6** 1 **Shawka**[14] 5329 3-9-0 0 .... PaulHanagan 9 63
(Charles Hills) *chsd ldrs: rdn over 2f out: sn one pce* **16/1**

00- **7** 1¼ **Furzanah**[318] 6933 3-9-0 0 .... KierenFallon 12 60
(Luca Cumani) *mid-div: drvn over 2f out: nvr gng pce to get into contention* **16/1**

05 **8** nk **Elsie Bay**[20] 5100 3-9-0 0 .... DavidProbert 14 59
(Mark Usher) *in rr: pushed along 3f out: sme late prog fnl f* **66/1**

6 **9** nk **Mohair**[14] 5329 3-9-0 0 .... GrahamLee 13 59
(James Fanshawe) *in rr: pushed alonge and sme hdwy fr over 1f out* **33/1**

10 nk **Hint Of Promise** 3-9-0 0 .... JamesDoyle 10 58+
(Roger Charlton) *s.i.s: in rr: drvn over 2f out: mod prog ins fnl f* **12/1**

06 **11** 2¾ **Who's That Chick (IRE)**[14] 5299 3-9-0 0 .... MartinHarley 4 52
(Ralph Smith) *mid-div and pushed along over 3f out: no ch fnl 2f* **66/1**

60 **12** 2½ **On Stage**[39] 4410 3-9-0 0 .... IanMongan 11 46
(Stuart Kittow) *s.i.s: rdn over 3f out: a in rr* **25/1**

0 **13** 11 **Cowslip**[14] 5299 3-9-0 0 .... KieranO'Neill 8 20
(Richard Hannon) *in rr: sn rdn: hrd drvn and no rspnse over 3f out* **40/1**

1m 44.17s (0.87) **Going Correction** +0.175s/f (Good) **13** Ran SP% **121.5**
Speed ratings (Par 97): **102,98,97,97,95 94,93,93,93,92 90,87,76**
Tote Swingers: 1&2 £3.80, 1&3 £3.10, 2&3 £4.50 CSF £10.34 TOTE £3.00: £1.10, £2.10, £1.40; EX 14.30 Trifecta £24.40 Pool £1,021.74 - 30.93 winning units..
Owner Major M G Wyatt **Bred** Dunchurch Lodge Stud Company **Trained** Newmarket, Suffolk

FOCUS
Older-horse maidens at this time of year, especially those confined to fillies, aren't usually that strong and this proved no exception. Very few ever got into it. The winner set a decent pre-race standard and is rated to form.

5796 ALAN BOON REMEMBRANCE H'CAP 1m 2f 7y
5:35 (5:36) (Class 4) (0-80,80) 3-Y-O **£4,528** (£1,347; £673; £336) **Stalls** Low

Form RPR

-421 **1** **Rhagori**[28] 4753 3-9-6 79 .... JamesDoyle 2 87+
(Ralph Beckett) *hld up in rr: hdwy on ins and qcknd fr 2f out: str run u.p ins fnl f to ld fnl 100yds: hld on all out* **9/4**[1]

0152 **2** hd **Croquembouche (IRE)**[12] 5386 3-9-4 77 .... LiamKeniry 12 84
(Ed de Giles) *led: rdn and hrd pressed fr over 1f out: narrowly hdd fnl 100yds: kpt on wl: no ex fnl strides* **10/1**

2124 **3** hd **Kaafel (IRE)**[16] 5237 3-9-7 80 .... PaulHanagan 15 87
(Charles Hills) *chsd ldrs: wnt 2nd 3f out: str chal fr over 1f out and styd upsides fnl f: no ex cl home* **15/2**[3]

3303 **4** ½ **Savanna Days (IRE)**[17] 5209 3-9-5 78 .... MartinHarley 3 84+
(Mick Channon) *in rr: rdn over 2f out: hdwy over 1f out: str run ins fnl f: gng on clsng stages* **8/1**

053 **5** 1 **Taglietelle**[25] 4888 3-9-1 74 .... DavidProbert 14 78
(Andrew Balding) *chsd ldrs: rdn over 2f out: kpt on fnl f: one pce clsng stages* **14/1**

2504 **6** ½ **Traveller's Tales**[15] 5277 3-8-12 78 .... WilliamTwiston-Davies(7) 13 81
(Richard Hannon) *chsd ldrs: rdn over 2f out: one pce fnl f* **10/1**

-650 **7** ½ **Jupiter Storm**[29] 4741 3-9-2 75 .... GeorgeBaker 10 77
(Gary Moore) *in rr: hdwy on outer fr 2f out: kpt on clsng stages: nt rch ldrs* **6/1**[2]

1005 **8** 1¼ **Golden Jubilee (USA)**[8] 5501 3-8-6 65 .... KieranO'Neill 9 64
(Richard Hannon) *chsd ldr to 3f out: wknd fnl f* **33/1**

5522 **9** 3¾ **Operation Tracer**[14] 5312 3-8-0 62 .... SimonPearce(3) 11 54
(Michael Bell) *t.k.h: in tch: nt clr run 3f out: effrt fr 2f out: nvr rchd ldrs and wknd fnl f* **8/1**

-450 **10** ½ **Top Billing**[22] 5007 3-9-4 77 ....(b) WilliamBuick 7 68
(John Gosden) *chsd ldrs: rdn and wknd over 2f out* **14/1**

300 **11** 1¼ **Rayvin Black**[34] 4601 3-9-6 79 .... TomQueally 5 67
(Mark H Tompkins) *nvr bttr than mid-div* **20/1**

0 **12** 2¼ **Naael (USA)**[22] 5006 3-8-4 66 .... MarkCoumbe(3) 6 50
(Luke Dace) *nvr beyond mid-div* **50/1**

0300 **13** 10 **Dance With Me (IRE)**[16] 5237 3-9-0 73 .... DaneO'Neill 8 37
(Jonathan Geake) *slowly away: a towards rr* **66/1**

2m 11.49s (0.99) **Going Correction** +0.175s/f (Good) **13** Ran SP% **121.7**
Speed ratings (Par 102): **103,102,102,102,101 101,100,99,96,96 95,93,85**
Tote Swingers: 1&2 £8.10, 1&3 £3.60, 2&3 £12.90 CSF £25.60 CT £152.61 TOTE £3.20: £1.10, £3.30, £2.80; EX 24.30 Trifecta £187.50 Pool £630.97 - 2.49 winning units..
Owner Landmark Racing Limited **Bred** P T Tellwright **Trained** Kimpton, Hants

FOCUS
A fair handicap and a thrilling finish with little covering the first four at the line. The form makes sense amongst the principals.

Dance With Me(IRE) Official explanation: jockey said gelding was slowly away

T/Jkpt: Not won. T/Plt: £216.80 to a £1 stake. Pool: £95,538.37 - 321.61 winning tickets T/Qpdt: £67.20 to a £1 stake. Pool: £5,641.28 - 62.10 winning tickets ST

5410 THIRSK (L-H)
Friday, August 31

OFFICIAL GOING: Soft (good to soft in places; straight course 8.3 round course 8.5)
Wind: Light behind Weather: Cloudy with sunny periods

5797 BRITISH STALLION STUDS SUPPORTING BRITISH RACING E B F MAIDEN STKS 1m
2:10 (2:10) (Class 4) 2-Y-O **£4,528** (£1,347; £673; £336) **Stalls** Low

Form RPR

02 **1** **Master Ming (IRE)**[19] 5119 2-9-3 0 .... JoeFanning 5 78
(Brian Meehan) *prom: cl up 1/2-way: led 1 1/2f out: rdn and styd on strly fnl f* **5/2**[2]

02 **2** 4 **Woody Bay**[49] 4069 2-9-3 0 .... PaulMulrennan 1 69
(James Given) *led: rdn along over 2f out: hdd 1 1/2f out: sn drvn and kpt on same pce fnl f* **5/1**[3]

60 **3** 2 **Funding Deficit (IRE)**[20] 5083 2-9-3 0 .... GrahamGibbons 10 65+
(David Barron) *stdd s and hld up towards rr: t.k.h: hdwy on inner to trck ldrs over 3f out: chsd ldng pair and swtchd rt over 2f out: rdn and no imp appr fnl f* **14/1**

4 3½ **Duke Of Yorkshire** 2-9-3 0 .... TomEaves 11 57+
(Declan Carroll) *towards rr: hdwy on outer 1/2-way: chsd ldrs wl over 2f out: sn rdn and no imp* **9/1**

06 **5** ½ **Red Eight (USA)**[16] 5221 2-9-3 0 .... MichaelO'Connell 7 56+
(John Quinn) *chsd ldrs: rdn along wl over 2f out: sn no imp* **14/1**

6 7 **National Poet (IRE)** 2-9-3 0 .... SilvestreDeSousa 2 41+
(Mahmood Al Zarooni) *dwlt and green in rr: hdwy to trck ldrs after 3f: rdn along on inner 3f out: sn wknd* **15/8**[1]

0 **7** 4 **Marble Silver (IRE)**[13] 5339 2-8-12 0 .... DuranFentiman 4 27
(Tim Easterby) *s.i.s: a in rr* **100/1**

00 **8** 3¾ **Portside Blue**[35] 4545 2-9-3 0 .... BarryMcHugh 6 24
(Tony Coyle) *prom: rdn along 1/2-way: sn wknd* **33/1**

00 **9** 2 **Inherited**[13] 5331 2-9-3 0 .... LukeMorris 9 19
(Sir Mark Prescott Bt) *dwlt: sn outpcd and bhd* **33/1**

0 **10** 4½ **Hurricane John (IRE)**[16] 5221 2-9-3 0 .... AdrianNicholls 8 9
(David Nicholls) *in tch on outer: pushed along bef 1/2-way: sn lost pl and bhd fnl 2f* **22/1**

1m 45.03s (4.93) **Going Correction** +0.625s/f (Yiel) **10** Ran SP% **114.6**
Speed ratings (Par 96): **100,96,94,90,90 83,79,75,73,68**
Tote Swingers: 1&2 £3.10, 1&3 £5.70, 2&3 £6.90 CSF £14.64 TOTE £2.00: £1.10, £2.30, £2.80; EX 10.50.
Owner Michael Wilmshurst & N B Attenborough **Bred** Limestone And Tara Studs **Trained** Manton, Wilts

FOCUS
It had been dry since lunchtime the previous day but the ground was still officially soft, good to soft in places (GoingStick 8.0), and looked even more testing than that. Paul Mulrennan came back after the first and described it as "proper soft ground". The rail on the home-bend was again dolled out 3-4 yards to preserve the inner, adding 12yds to races of 7f plus. The dolling on the away-bend which was in place at the previous meeting had been removed. This maiden went to form, with the first two having the strongest credentials on paper coming into the race. The form is rated around the winner and race averages. The first five were clear.

NOTEBOOK
Master Ming(IRE) had a bit to prove on the ground (perhaps the reason for the market drift) but he coped with it well and his stamina really came to the fore at the finish. He's going to appreciate middle distances next season (dam won over 1m3f) and should make up into a useful handicapper. (op 15-8)
Woody Bay had the run of things out in front from his draw in stall one, and had no excuses. It was a fair effort but he simply didn't see out the trip as strongly as the winner.
Funding Deficit(IRE), who ran better than his finishing position suggested at Ayr last time, didn't settle at all off the fairly steady early gallop and in the circumstances he did well to finish third. He has the potential to do much better off a stronger pace in handicap company. (op 20-1)
Duke Of Yorkshire, who's a half-brother to four winners including French Group 1 winner Voix du Nord, ran with promise on his debut as he was drawn out in stall 11 and caught wide throughout. He ought to come on for this. (op 16-1)
Red Eight(USA) probably wants quicker ground judged by his pedigree. Handicaps are an option for him now. (op 16-1 tchd 18-1)
National Poet(IRE), a half-brother to Irish 1,000 Guineas winner Bethrah, has no big-race entries. He showed signs of greenness and should improve for the outing. (op 2-1 tchd 9-4)

5798 WEATHERBYS BANK H'CAP 2m
2:40 (2:40) (Class 4) (0-80,80) 3-Y-O+ **£4,528** (£1,347; £673; £336) **Stalls** Low

Form RPR

1121 **1** **Solar View (IRE)**[2] 5735 3-8-3 69 6ex .... LukeMorris 10 83+
(Sir Mark Prescott Bt) *hld up in tch: niggled along 6f out: hdwy 4f out: chsd ldrs 3f out: rdn to chal 2f out: styd on to ld over 1f out: edgd lft ins fnl f: kpt on* **7/4**[1]

-030 **2** 1¼ **Gordonsville**[30] 4697 9-10-0 80 .... DanielTudhope 11 87
(Jim Goldie) *prom: trckd ldr after 4f: cl up 5f out: led wl over 2f out: rdn wl over 1f out: hdd appr fnl f: kpt on u.p* **12/1**

523 **3** 8 **Ampleforth**[29] 4731 4-9-4 70 ....(b) SilvestreDeSousa 8 67
(Ian Williams) *dwlt and towards rr: hdwy to ld after 4f: rdn along 3f out: sn hdd: drvn and kpt on same pce fnl 2f* **16/1**

20- **4** 3 **Zakatal**[391] 4806 6-10-0 80 .... BarryMcHugh 3 74
(Julie Camacho) *hld up in rr: hdwy over 5f out: rdn along to chse ldrs 3f out: drvn 2f out and no imp* **80/1**

3021 **5** ½ **Sohcahtoa (IRE)**[21] 5056 6-9-0 71 .... LMcNiff(5) 7 64
(David Barron) *hld up in rr: hdwy on inner 3f out: rdn along 2f out: n.d* **20/1**

6132 **6** 5 **Byron Blue (IRE)**[24] 4918 3-8-7 73 .... JoeFanning 6 60
(Jamie Osborne) *cl up: led after 1f: hdd after 4f: pushed along to chse ldng pair over 4f out: rdn over 3f out: grad wknd* **4/1**[2]

3501 **7** 11 **Bollin Felix**[4] 5673 8-9-12 78 6ex ....(b) GrahamGibbons 2 52
(Tim Easterby) *led 1f: prom: rdn along over 4f out: sn wknd* **11/2**

4405 **8** 10 **Jonny Delta**[22] 5002 5-9-3 72 .... GaryBartley(3) 4 34
(Jim Goldie) *hld up: a in rr* **5/1**[3]

-520 **9** 4½ **Uncut Stone (IRE)**[175] 849 4-8-10 62 .... PaulMulrennan 1 19
(Peter Niven) *hld up: a towards rr: outpcd and bhd fnl 5f* **50/1**

0261 **10** 9 **L Frank Baum (IRE)**[29] 4731 5-9-7 80 .... RobertWilliams(7) 5 26
(Bernard Llewellyn) *trckd ldrs: rdn along over 5f out: sn wknd* **16/1**

3m 37.76s (9.46) **Going Correction** +0.625s/f (Yiel)
WFA 3 from 4yo+ 14lb **10** Ran SP% **115.8**
Speed ratings (Par 105): **101,100,96,94,94 92,86,81,79,74**
Tote Swingers: 1&2 £5.60, 1&3 £4.90, 2&3 £16.50 CSF £24.87 CT £258.14 TOTE £2.40: £1.10, £3.60, £3.80; EX 26.60.

Owner Neil Greig - Osborne House **Bred** Lady Richard Wellesley **Trained** Newmarket, Suffolk
FOCUS
A fair handicap. The winner continues on the up and the form is rated around the second.

5799 THEAKSTON LIGHTFOOT MAIDEN CLAIMING STKS 6f
3:15 (3:17) (Class 4) 2-Y-O £3,881 (£1,155; £577; £288) Stalls High

Form RPR
222 1 **Grievous Angel (IRE)**[11] 5423 2-8-12 71..................(v) PaulMulrennan 8 73+
(Ann Duffield) *trckd ldrs: cl up 1/2-way: led 2f out: sn rdn clr: easily* 7/4[1]
50 2 4 ½ **Darkside**[6] 5586 2-8-6 0..................(b) JamesSullivan 4 54
(Michael Easterby) *dwlt and wnt rt s: bhd: hdwy 1/2-way: rdn 2f out: styd on to chse wnr ins fnl f: sn no imp* 22/1
2445 3 2 **Emperor's Daughter**[11] 5403 2-8-0 58.................. SilvestreDeSousa 2 42
(Tim Pitt) *t.k.h: cl up on outer: led 1/2-way: rdn and hdd 2f out: sn drvn and one pce* 7/2[2]
0050 4 3 **Another Ponty**[37] 4450 2-8-8 55..................(b[1]) GrahamGibbons 1 41
(Tim Easterby) *in tch: hdwy 1/2-way: swtchd lft and rdn to chse ldrs 2f out: sn one pce* 12/1
6400 5 3 ¼ **Tiger Prince (IRE)**[28] 4767 2-8-5 55..................(p) AmyRyan 3 28
(Ann Duffield) *cl up: rdn along and ev ch over 2f out: drvn wl over 1f out and sn wknd* 9/1
3 6 nk **Sylvia's Diamond**[22] 5011 2-8-3 0.................. DeclanCannon(3) 7 28
(Richard Guest) *sltly hmpd s and towards rr: hdwy 1/2-way: rdn and n.m.r over 2f out: sn drvn and n.d* 20/1
2523 7 2 ¼ **Twilight Pearl**[3] 5709 2-8-8 58.................. DuranFentiman 6 23
(Tim Easterby) *led: rdn along and hdd 1/2-way: sn wknd* 4/1[3]
36 8 2 ¾ **Derrochadora (IRE)**[58] 3748 2-8-2 0.................. LukeMorris 9 9
(Robert Cowell) *in tch: rdn along wl over 2f out: sn wknd* 12/1
0000 9 nk **Cromwell Rose (IRE)**[28] 4767 2-7-11 45.................. NoelGarbutt(7) 11 10
(John Weymes) *a in rr* 66/1
040 10 ¾ **Cool Sea (IRE)**[18] 5169 2-8-2 43.................. AndrewMullen 5 6
(Nigel Tinkler) *hmpd s and a bhd* 66/1

1m 14.92s (2.22) **Going Correction** +0.35s/f (Good) 10 Ran SP% 116.1
Speed ratings (Par 96): **99,93,90,86,82 81,78,74,74,73**
.Darkside claimed by Mr David Tate £5,000.\n\x\x
Owner Morecool Racing 1 **Bred** Martin Walsh **Trained** Constable Burton, N Yorks
FOCUS
An ordinary race with little depth but the winner impressed.
NOTEBOOK
Grievous Angel(IRE), who was the pick at the weights, travelled strongly and drew right away in the closing stages once asked to go on. It might not be worth getting carried away, and she isn't straightforward (edgy and unseated Paul Mulrennan leaving the paddock here) but she's worn a visor on her last two starts now, and it appears to be having a positive effect in her races. (op 15-8 tchd 13-8)
Darkside, quietly backed at big prices, showed much improved form on this softer ground. He was still pretty green and might have more to offer. (op 33-1)
Emperor's Daughter was keen through the early part of the race, which didn't help her see out this extra furlong. It looks to suit her better than 5f, but she needs to learn to settle. (tchd 4-1)
Another Ponty had a bit to find with the likes of the winner and third on at these weights.
Tiger Prince(IRE) was another who was up against it at the weights. (op 12-1)
Sylvia's Diamond may not have appreciated the testing ground. (op 28-1 tchd 33-1)
Twilight Pearl was disappointing, even allowing for the fact that the race may have come a bit quick. (op 10-3 tchd 3-1)

5800 WEATHERBYS BLOODSTOCK INSURANCE H'CAP 6f
3:50 (3:50) (Class 4) (0-80,79) 3-Y-O £4,528 (£1,347; £673; £336) Stalls High

Form RPR
3423 1 **Catwalk (IRE)**[25] 4876 3-9-2 74..................(v[1]) SilvestreDeSousa 2 87+
(James Fanshawe) *prom: cl up 1/2-way: rdn to ld over 1f out: clr ins fnl f* 7/4[1]
3252 2 3 ¾ **Profile Star (IRE)**[6] 5603 3-9-7 79.................. GrahamGibbons 6 78
(David Barron) *trckd ldng pair on inner: effrt and n.m.r 2f out: swtchd lft: rdn and hdwy over 1f out: kpt on to take 2nd ins fnl f* 11/4[2]
1444 3 1 ¾ **Gowanharry (IRE)**[18] 5167 3-8-8 66..................(t) PaulMulrennan 3 59
(Michael Dods) *sn led: rdn along and jnd over 2f out: drvn and hdd over 1f out: sn one pce* 9/2[3]
003 4 1 ½ **Tidal's Baby**[35] 4534 3-8-9 67.................. MichaelO'Connell 7 54
(Tony Carroll) *dwlt and in rr: swtchd lft and hdwy on outer over 2f out: sn rdn to chse ldrs: drvn and btn appr fnl f* 5/1
4560 5 5 **Whisky Bravo**[4] 5676 3-9-0 72.................. RobertWinston 5 41
(David Brown) *hld up in rr: pushed along 1/2-way: sn rdn and outpcd fnl 2f* 14/1
4630 6 ¾ **I'll Be Good**[7] 5545 3-9-2 74..................(p) TomEaves 1 41
(Robert Johnson) *trckd ldrs: hdwy over 2f out: sn rdn and wknd wl over 1f out* 9/1

1m 14.27s (1.57) **Going Correction** +0.35s/f (Good) 6 Ran SP% 114.5
Speed ratings (Par 102): **103,98,95,93,87 86**
Tote Swingers: 1&2 £1.70, 1&3 £2.20, 2&3 £1.10 CSF £7.02 TOTE £2.60: £1.40, £1.10; EX 5.30.
Owner Cheveley Park Stud **Bred** Forenaghts,Cantillon&cheveley Park Stud **Trained** Newmarket, Suffolk
FOCUS
Little depth to this but a clear personal best from the winner. The time was relatively ordinary.

5801 RETURNABLE PACKAGING SERVICES CLASSIFIED (S) STKS 6f
4:25 (4:25) (Class 5) 3-Y-O+ £2,587 (£770; £384; £192) Stalls High

Form RPR
1124 1 **Llewellyn**[2] 5737 4-9-5 72.................. AdrianNicholls 2 77
(David Nicholls) *trckd ldrs: niggled along 1/2-way: hdwy wl over 1f out: rdn to ld ent fnl f: sn edgd rt and kpt on* 2/1[1]
5251 2 2 ¼ **Ansells Pride (IRE)**[13] 5347 9-8-12 64..................(p) JakePayne(7) 8 70
(Bill Turner) *led: pushed along 1/2-way: rdn 2f out and sn edgd lft: drvn and hdd ent fnl f: kpt on same pce* 7/2[3]
2623 3 1 ¼ **Select Committee**[16] 5223 7-8-13 74..................(v) MichaelO'Connell 7 60
(John Quinn) *trckd ldrs on inner: effrt and n.m.r wl over 1f out: sn rdn and swtchd lft over 1f out: drvn and kpt on ins fnl f* 5/1
000 4 1 ¾ **Go Go Green (IRE)**[46] 4133 6-9-5 73.................. DanielTudhope 5 60
(Jim Goldie) *hld up in tch: effrt 2f out: sn rdn and btn over 1f out* 5/2[2]
0110 5 1 ¼ **Red Cape (FR)**[31] 4680 9-9-5 73..................(b) JamesSullivan 1 56
(Ruth Carr) *cl up: disp ld and ev ch over 2f out: sn rdn and wknd ent fnl f* 8/1
5-30 6 5 **Diva Donkey (IRE)**[161] 1012 3-8-10 50.................. TomEaves 6 34
(Bryan Smart) *a in rr* 50/1

1m 15.67s (2.97) **Going Correction** +0.35s/f (Good)
WFA 3 from 4yo+ 3lb 6 Ran SP% 113.9
Speed ratings (Par 103): **94,91,89,87,85 78**
Tote Swingers: 1&2 £2.10, 1&3 £2.70, 2&3 £2.80 CSF £9.63 TOTE £3.10: £1.60, £2.50; EX 10.20.No bid for the winner.
Owner Middleham Park Racing XXXVIII **Bred** Elite Racing Club **Trained** Sessay, N Yorks
FOCUS
A fairly competitive little race, run at a decent pace for the conditions. The winner is the most likely guide to the form.

5802 JW 4X4 NORTHALLERTON H'CAP 7f
4:55 (4:56) (Class 4) (0-80,80) 3-Y-O+ £4,528 (£1,347; £673; £336) Stalls Low

Form RPR
6430 1 **Fieldgunner Kirkup (GER)**[14] 5314 4-9-7 75.................. GrahamGibbons 5 84
(David Barron) *chsd ldrs: hdwy wl over 2f out: chal wl over 1f out: rdn to ld 1f out: kpt on* 9/1
6331 2 1 ¼ **Chookie Royale**[13] 5341 4-9-5 73..................(p) TomEaves 7 78
(Keith Dalgleish) *trckd ldrs on inner: hdwy 3f out: swtchd rt and chal 2f out: sn rdn and ev ch tl drvn and one pce ins fnl f* 12/1
0250 3 nse **Karaka Jack**[13] 5356 5-9-12 80.................. AdrianNicholls 3 85
(David Nicholls) *hld up towards rr: stdy hdwy over 2f out: rdn to chse ldrs over 1f out: swtchd lft and drvn ins fnl f: edgd lft and kpt on* 9/4[1]
4230 4 1 **My Single Malt (IRE)**[11] 5414 4-9-6 74.................. BarryMcHugh 9 76
(Julie Camacho) *hld up towards rr: hdwy 3f out: rdn to chse ldrs over 1f out: n.m.r and kpt on u.p fnl f* 6/1[2]
1030 5 1 ½ **Viking Warrior (IRE)**[28] 4783 5-8-13 70.................. LeeTopliss(3) 2 68
(Michael Dods) *cl up: led after 2f: rdn and edgd lft over 2f out: drvn and hdd 1f out: grad wknd* 9/1
3021 6 ¾ **Steel Stockholder**[7] 5543 6-8-7 68.................. RobertDodsworth(7) 6 64
(Mel Brittain) *chsd ldrs on outer: hdwy and cl up 1/2-way: rdn and ev ch 2f out: edgd lft over 1f out and grad wknd* 15/2[3]
01-5 7 2 ½ **Dakota Canyon (IRE)**[49] 4075 3-9-5 78.................. TonyHamilton 10 67
(Richard Fahey) *s.i.s: a in rr* 15/2[3]
0234 8 hd **Rio Cobolo (IRE)**[20] 5093 6-8-6 67..................(v) ShirleyTeasdale(7) 4 56
(David Nicholls) *t.k.h: chsd ldrs: hdwy and cl up over 2f out: sn rdn and wknd over 1f out* 9/1
0440 9 shd **Glenridding**[18] 5179 8-9-2 73.................. DaleSwift(3) 11 62
(James Given) *led 2f: cl up: rdn along wl over 2f out: sn wknd* 9/1
6-05 10 26 **Malcheek (IRE)**[213] 368 10-9-5 73.................. DuranFentiman 1
(Tim Easterby) *dwlt: a in rr: bhd fnl 3f* 28/1

1m 30.58s (3.38) **Going Correction** +0.625s/f (Yiel)
WFA 3 from 4yo+ 5lb 10 Ran SP% 119.7
Speed ratings (Par 105): **105,103,103,102,100 99,96,96,96,66**
Tote Swingers: 1&2 £14.60, 1&3 £5.90, 2&3 £5.50 CSF £114.21 CT £329.60 TOTE £10.80: £4.40, £3.60, £1.10; EX 130.60.
Owner Kevin Kirkup **Bred** I And D Meinke **Trained** Maunby, N Yorks
■ Stewards' Enquiry : Dale Swift one-day ban: careless riding (Sep 14)
FOCUS
They went a solid gallop given the conditions and the form seems sound enough with the winner back to his soft-ground best.

5803 TURFTV H'CAP 1m
5:25 (5:27) (Class 5) (0-70,70) 3-Y-O £2,911 (£866; £432; £216) Stalls Low

Form RPR
0201 1 **Ingleby Angel (IRE)**[6] 5590 3-8-8 57 6ex.................. TomEaves 2 69
(David O'Meara) *hld up in rr: stdy hdwy over 2f out: chsd ldrs wl over 1f out: rdn to ld appr fnl f: kpt on wl towards fin* 13/2
0-62 2 1 **Giorgio's Dragon (IRE)**[17] 5185 3-9-0 63.................. TonyHamilton 8 73
(Richard Fahey) *trckd ldrs: pushed along and sltly outpcd over 3f out: hdwy and n.m.r 2f out: rdn to chse wnr ins fnl f: kpt on* 7/2[1]
0005 3 5 **Alabanda (IRE)**[27] 4830 3-8-4 53..................(b) DuranFentiman 10 52
(Tim Easterby) *in tch: hdwy on outer and cl up 5f out: rdn and ev ch over 2f out: drvn over 1f out and kpt on same pce* 10/1
5005 4 ¾ **Mitchum**[18] 5170 3-9-7 70.................. GrahamGibbons 9 67
(David Barron) *prom: led over 5f out: rdn 2f out: drvn and hdd over 1f out: sn wknd* 11/2[3]
-620 5 1 ¾ **Gulf Storm (IRE)**[73] 3257 3-8-6 55..................[1] JoeFanning 5 48
(Bryan Smart) *chsd ldrs on inner: rdn along wl over 2f out: grad wknd* 12/1
3644 6 nk **Saffa Hill (IRE)**[25] 4883 3-9-4 67.................. DanielTudhope 11 59
(Tim Easterby) *led 2f: cl up: rdn along wl over 2f out: grad wknd* 5/1[2]
0304 7 1 ½ **More Bottle (IRE)**[66] 3460 3-7-13 51 oh1.................. DominicFox(3) 4 40
(Tom Tate) *hld up: hdwy on wd outside 3f out: rdn to chse ldrs over 2f out: sn hung lft and wknd* 10/1
2264 8 1 ½ **Roedean (IRE)**[5] 5634 3-9-3 66..................(tp) SilvestreDeSousa 12 51
(William Stone) *trckd ldrs: effrt wl over 2f out: sn rdn and btn* 7/2[1]
000 9 48 **Roc Fort**[14] 5315 3-8-2 51 oh6..................(b[1]) JamesSullivan 6
(Ruth Carr) *a in rr: bhd fnl f* 80/1

1m 46.09s (5.99) **Going Correction** +0.625s/f (Yiel) 9 Ran SP% 116.9
Speed ratings (Par 100): **95,94,89,88,86 86,84,83,35**
Tote Swingers: 1&2 £4.90, 1&3 £13.70, 2&3 £8.00 CSF £29.92 CT £230.02 TOTE £7.00: £2.70, £1.20, £3.30; EX 19.30.
Owner Dave Scott **Bred** Dave Scott **Trained** Nawton, N Yorks
FOCUS
The early pace wasn't particularly strong. The first two finished clear and seemed to improve.
T/Plt: £15.80 to a £1 stake. Pool: £56,921.07 - 2,618.55 winning tickets T/Qpdt: £4.50 to a £1 stake. Pool: £4,423.10 - 714.88 winning tickets JR

5748 WOLVERHAMPTON (A.W) (L-H)
Friday, August 31

OFFICIAL GOING: Standard
Wind: Light across Weather: Cloudy

5804 LADBROKES GAME ON! APPRENTICE H'CAP 1m 141y(P)
6:20 (6:20) (Class 6) (0-60,59) 3-Y-O+ £1,704 (£503; £251) Stalls Low

Form RPR
60-1 1 **Meglio Ancora**[4] 5258 5-9-4 54.................. AmyScott(3) 7 67
(Alastair Lidderdale) *hld up: hdwy over 1f out: rdn to ld and hung lft ins fnl f: r.o* 13/2[3]
0046 2 1 ¾ **Imperial Wave (IRE)**[18] 5175 3-8-12 52..................(b) AdamBeschizza 12 61
(David Lanigan) *a.p: shkn up to ld over 1f out: rdn: hdd and unable qck ins fnl f* 6/1[2]

0240 **3** 1 3/4 **American Lover (FR)**[18] 5171 5-8-11 **47** .... AdamCarter(3) 10 52
(John Wainwright) *chsd ldrs: led 5f out: rdn and hdd over 1f out: styd on same pce fnl f* **16/1**

000 **4** 2 1/2 **Opus Maximus (IRE)**[34] 4586 7-9-10 **57** .... RyanPowell 8 56
(Conor Dore) *hld up: rdn over 2f out: styd on fr over 1f out: nt trble ldrs* **5/1**[1]

2354 **5** shd **Smart Affair**[23] 4971 3-8-5 **50** .... NatashaEaton(5) 3 49
(Alan Bailey) *dwlt: bhd: r.o ins fnl f: nvr nrr* **15/2**

0005 **6** 1 1/4 **Perfect Outlook**[25] 4890 4-9-5 **52** .... RaulDaSilva 1 48
(Jeremy Gask) *hld up: rdn over 1f out: nvr on terms* **11/1**

3320 **7** nk **Baby Driver**[22] 4981 4-8-12 **50** ....(t) NathanSweeney(5) 9 45
(David Evans) *plld hrd and prom: pushed along 3f out: rdn over 1f out: wknd ins fnl f* **8/1**

6005 **8** 1/2 **Princess Gail**[17] 5212 4-8-8 **46** .... RachealKneller(5) 6 40
(Mark Brisbourne) *prom: pushed along over 2f out: sn outpcd* **10/1**

300 **9** 2 **Calypso Magic (IRE)**[22] 5008 4-9-9 **59** .... RosieJessop(3) 11 49
(Olivia Maylam) *chsd ldr tl led over 7f out: hdd 5f out: rdn over 3f out: wknd fnl f* **8/1**

5060 **10** 7 **Mighty Motive**[15] 5266 3-8-7 **52** .... DavidBergin(5) 13 26
(John Mackie) *led 1f: chsd ldrs: rdn over 2f out: wknd over 1f out* **5/1**[1]

1m 48.67s (-1.83) **Going Correction** -0.25s/f (Stan)
WFA 3 from 4yo+ 7lb **10** Ran SP% **118.2**
Speed ratings (Par 101): **98,96,94,92,92 91,91,90,88,82**
Tote Swingers: 1&2 £10.20, 1&3 £9.20, 2&3 £14.80 CSF £45.96 CT £619.55 TOTE £5.30: £2.40, £2.40, £3.90; EX 54.00.
Owner Trinity TT Racing Partnerships **Bred** Mrs R Pease **Trained** Lambourn, Berks

FOCUS
A moderate apprentice riders' handicap for 3yos and up.

5805 SUSAN BOX MEMORIAL MEDIAN AUCTION MAIDEN STKS 1m 141y(P)
6:50 (6:51) (Class 6) 3-4-Y-0 **£1,704** (£503; £251) **Stalls** Low

Form RPR

202 **1** **Cufflink**[66] 3461 3-8-12 73 .... ChrisCatlin 3 75
(Rae Guest) *chsd ldrs: pushed along over 2f out: shkn up to ld ins fnl f: r.o wl* **9/4**[2]

262 **2** 2 1/2 **Medhyaar**[14] 5299 3-8-12 75 ....(t) TadhgO'Shea 1 69
(William Haggas) *plld hrd and sn trcking ldr: pushed along over 2f out: rdn to ld over 1f out: edgd rt: hdd and unable qck ins fnl f* **10/11**[1]

304 **3** 4 1/2 **Green Mitas (ITY)**[23] 4961 3-9-3 61 .... CathyGannon 5 64
(Frank Sheridan) *led: rdn and hdd over 1f out: no ex fnl f* **7/2**[3]

0U5 **4** 8 **Cluaindubhloch (IRE)**[17] 5208 4-9-10 0 .... StephenCraine 2 46
(Tony Carroll) *s.s: bhd: rdn over 1f out: nvr on terms* **100/1**

6 **5** 5 **Blackamoor Harry**[17] 5208 3-9-3 0 .... FrederikTylicki 6 34
(Richard Ford) *hld up: rdn and wknd over 2f out* **100/1**

0 **6** 2 1/2 **My Honychurch**[18] 5177 3-8-12 0 .... LiamJones 4 23
(Frank Sheridan) *plld hrd and prom: pushed along over 3f out: wknd over 2f out* **40/1**

1m 51.27s (0.77) **Going Correction** -0.25s/f (Stan)
WFA 3 from 4yo 7lb **6** Ran SP% **109.8**
Speed ratings (Par 101): **86,83,79,72,68 66**
Tote Swingers: 1&2 £1.10, 1&3 £1.30, 2&3 £1.20 CSF £4.46 TOTE £3.50: £2.00, £1.10; EX 4.40.

Owner C J Murfitt **Bred** C J Murfitt **Trained** Newmarket, Suffolk

FOCUS
A fair auction maiden.

5806 NANTWICHVENEERS.COM CLAIMING STKS 7f 32y(P)
7:20 (7:21) (Class 5) 2-Y-O **£2,264** (£673; £336; £168) **Stalls** High

Form RPR

6412 **1** **Charlie Em**[23] 4951 2-8-10 70 .... FrederikTylicki 4 61+
(Richard Fahey) *hld up: pushed along over 2f out: rdn and hung lft ins fnl f: str run to ld post* **4/6**[1]

0630 **2** shd **Cymeriad**[11] 5424 2-8-4 55 .... CathyGannon 12 55
(Michael Easterby) *led 6f out: rdn and edgd rt over 1f out: hdd post* **33/1**

4560 **3** hd **Northern Harbour (IRE)**[17] 5207 2-8-7 62 .... RyanPowell(3) 11 60
(J S Moore) *s.i.s: hdwy to chse ldr over 5f out: rdn and nt clr run over 1f out: ev ch ins fnl f: r.o* **28/1**

0034 **4** 2 **Annie Besant**[9] 5485 2-8-4 50 .... HarryBentley 3 49
(David C Griffiths) *prom: rdn over 2f out: styd on* **11/1**[3]

2461 **5** 3/4 **Wordsaplenty (IRE)**[14] 5291 2-8-0 59 .... RachealKneller(5) 1 48
(J S Moore) *hld up: hdwy over 1f out: hmpd ins fnl f: styd on* **13/2**[2]

000 **6** 1/2 **Juhaina (IRE)**[16] 5221 2-8-7 41 .... WilliamCarson 10 49
(Ann Duffield) *chsd ldrs: rdn over 2f out: hung lft ins fnl f: styd on same pce fnl f* **66/1**

0136 **7** 1 **Lucky Suit (IRE)**[22] 4991 2-8-0 57 ....(p) DarrenEgan(5) 7 44
(Ronald Harris) *mid-div: hdwy over 2f out: rdn over 1f out: no ex ins fnl f* **14/1**

034 **8** nk **Age Of Bronze**[9] 5478 2-9-0 0 .... RichardMullen 8 52
(Richard Hannon) *led 1f: chsd ldrs: rdn over 2f out: no ex fnl f* **13/2**[2]

0164 **9** 3/4 **Grace Of Hearts**[21] 5046 2-8-3 58 ....(p) HayleyTurner 5 39
(Robert Eddery) *hld up: rdn over 1f out: n.d* **11/1**[3]

000 **10** 27 **Karl Marx (IRE)**[52] 3937 2-8-9 33 ow1 ....(v[1]) FergusSweeney 2
(Mark Usher) *sn outpcd: t.o* **150/1**

0 **11** 6 **Wicked Tara**[18] 5176 2-8-7 0 .... LiamJones 9
(Frank Sheridan) *s.s and swvd rt: hdwy 5f out: rdn and wknd over 2f out: t.o* **50/1**

1m 29.21s (-0.39) **Going Correction** -0.25s/f (Stan) **11** Ran SP% **120.5**
Speed ratings (Par 94): **92,91,91,89,88 87,86,86,85,54 47**
Tote Swingers: 1&2 £10.60, 1&3 £9.10, 2&3 £39.40 CSF £40.56 TOTE £2.50: £1.02, £6.90, £3.30; EX 31.20.Charlie Em claimed by Mr T. Vaughan £11,000.
Owner Mrs E Armstrong & R Marshall **Bred** Highfield Farm Llp **Trained** Musley Bank, N Yorks

FOCUS
Limited form with the second to fourth setting the level.

NOTEBOOK
Charlie Em progressed to finish runner-up in a 7f Newcastle handicap on good ground this month and was a warm order here dropped in class, but her backers were made to sweat. In fact, they should raise a glass to the persistence of jockey Freddie Tylicki for being able to collect. Charlie Em came home with a wet sail up the home straight and forced a three-way photo-finish from an unlikely position. A step up to 1m will see her in an even better light. She was claimed by trainer Tim Vaughan for £11,000. (op Evens)
Cymeriad looked all over the winner until collared in the final strides. She did well from a poor draw and should find a race at this level.
Northern Harbour(IRE) appreciated the drop back to 7f and looks capable of finding a race in this grade over the trip. (op 25-1)
Annie Besant ran respectably in fourth and should appreciate a step up in trip. (op 10-1)
Wordsaplenty(IRE) came home well into fifth and should remain competitive in this grade at up to 1m. Official explanation: jockey said filly suffered interference in running (op 11-2)
Age Of Bronze raced prominently but found disappointingly little from the furlong marker. (op 15-2 tchd 8-1)
Wicked Tara Official explanation: jockey said filly was slowly away

5807 WOLVERHAMPTON-RACECOURSE.CO.UK FILLIES' (S) STKS 5f 20y(P)
7:50 (7:50) (Class 6) 2-Y-O **£1,704** (£503; £251) **Stalls** Low

Form RPR

5352 **1** **Hardy Blue (IRE)**[11] 5403 2-8-12 53 .... FergusSweeney 13 60
(Jamie Osborne) *chsd ldr: rdn to ld over 1f out: styd on* **9/1**

00 **2** nk **Chloe's Dream (IRE)**[45] 4173 2-8-12 0 ....(p) PaulMulrennan 12 59
(Ann Duffield) *a.p: rdn over 1f out: r.o* **25/1**

40 **3** 3 3/4 **Red Star Lady (IRE)**[24] 4927 2-8-9 60 ....(b[1]) MichaelMetcalfe(3) 5 45
(Mrs K Burke) *led: rdn and hdd over 1f out: no ex ins fnl f* **7/1**

00 **4** 1 **Strange Angel (IRE)**[58] 3747 2-8-7 0 .... NathanSweeney(5) 9 42
(David Evans) *prom: rdn over 2f out: styd on same pce fnl f* **20/1**

5132 **5** 1/2 **Coconut Kisses**[11] 5411 2-8-11 69 .... RyanWhile(7) 3 46
(Bill Turner) *hmpd s: chsd ldrs: nt clr run and hit rails wl over 3f out: rdn over 1f out: styd on same pce* **15/8**[1]

6 nse **Lady Jean** 2-8-12 0 .... ChrisCatlin 7 40+
(Reg Hollinshead) *hld up: rdn over 2f out: r.o wl ins fnl f: nvr nrr* **20/1**

00 **7** 1 1/4 **Lyrical Vibe**[16] 5235 2-8-12 0 .... CathyGannon 8 35
(David Evans) *mid-div: drvn along 1/2-way: styd on same pce fr over 1f out* **25/1**

50 **8** 1/2 **Baltic Sea (IRE)**[14] 5325 2-8-9 0 .... MatthewCosham(3) 11 34
(David Evans) *s.i.s: sn pushed along in rr: styd on ins fnl f: nvr nrr* **33/1**

0025 **9** 3/4 **Kimvara**[11] 5424 2-8-7 57 ....(b) DarrenEgan(5) 4 31
(Joseph Tuite) *edgd lft s: plld hrd and sn mid-div: nt clr run over 3f out: sn rdn: nvr on terms* **6/1**[3]

4004 **10** 1/2 **Reinvigorate (IRE)**[4] 5675 2-8-12 0 ....(b[1]) RichardMullen 2 29
(Richard Hannon) *hmpd s: hld up: hung rt over 3f out: rdn over 1f out: hung lft ins fnl f: n.d* **4/1**[2]

4000 **11** 4 **Shirley's Pride**[11] 5403 2-8-12 52 ....(t) RussKennemore 10 15
(John Holt) *mid-div: rdn 1/2-way: wknd over 1f out* **33/1**

12 3 **Fat Bottom Girl** 2-8-12 0 .... FrederikTylicki 6
(Michael Easterby) *hld up: racd on outer: hung rt 1/2-way: sn wknd* **16/1**

0 **13** 2 **True Ally**[29] 4742 2-8-7 0 .... RachealKneller(5) 1
(John Norton) *mid-div: wknd 1/2-way* **150/1**

1m 1.75s (-0.55) **Going Correction** -0.25s/f (Stan) **13** Ran SP% **121.2**
Speed ratings (Par 89): **94,93,87,85,85 85,83,82,81,80 73,69,65**
Tote Swingers 1&2 £77.60, 2&3 £31.70, 1&3 £6.20 CSF £218.10 TOTE £10.90: £2.70, £7.60, £2.20; EX 238.80.No bid for the winner.
Owner Patrick Gage & Tony Taylor **Bred** Philip O'Dwyer **Trained** Upper Lambourn, Berks

FOCUS
A modest juvenile sprint fillies' seller. Weak form as befits the grade.

NOTEBOOK
Hardy Blue(IRE) was recording trainer Jamie Osborne's sixth success from ten runners in selling company this year. She benefited from a good start and raced prominently before getting on top inside the final furlong. She has been competitive in all her starts, particularly when second over this 5f trip at Kempton off 53 in handicap company this month, and built on that promise on these unfavourable terms. She can continue to pay her way in lowly company over this trip. There was no bid for her at the subsequent auction. (tchd 10-1)
Chloe's Dream(IRE) was returning from a six-week break and swapped a first-time visor for cheekpieces. She produced next to nothing on her first two starts but nearly made all from a poor draw here.
Red Star Lady(IRE) wore first-time cheekpieces here but found precious little inside the final furlong. (op 11-2)
Strange Angel(IRE) was returning from a two-month break on this first start for trainer David Evans, who had three runners in this race. She did well to be the first home from that trio. (op 14-1 tchd 22-1)
Coconut Kisses suffered something of a nightmare passage and Ryan While later reported that she raced too free. Official explanation: jockey said filly ran too free (tchd 2-1)
Kimvara edged left at the start and pulled hard. She didn't get the clearest of runs 3f out and the game was up thereafter. (tchd 11-2 and 13-2)
Reinvigorate(IRE) was wearing first-time blinkers but made little impact after being hampered and held up at the start. Jockey Richard Mullen later reported that the filly failed to handle the bend. Official explanation: jockey said filly failed to handle the bend (op 7-1)
True Ally Official explanation: jockey said filly failed to handle the bend and hung left

5808 LADBROKES MOBILE H'CAP 5f 216y(P)
8:20 (8:20) (Class 6) (0-60,65) 3-Y-O+ **£1,704** (£503; £251) **Stalls** Low

Form RPR

0333 **1** **Theresnoneedfordat (IRE)**[8] 5513 3-9-4 **60** ....[1] WilliamCarson 3 74+
(Stuart Williams) *chsd ldrs: hmpd over 5f out: led ins fnl f: edgd lft: r.o wl* **7/2**[2]

0000 **2** 2 **Indieslad**[16] 5220 4-9-7 **60** ....(p) PaulMulrennan 8 68
(Ann Duffield) *hld up: hdwy over 1f out: swtchd rt ins fnl f: r.o* **13/2**

2111 **3** shd **Aubrietia**[5] 5624 3-8-13 **62** 6ex ....(b) DavidBergin(7) 5 70
(Alan McCabe) *chsd ldr: led over 2f out: rdn: hdd and unable qck ins fnl f* **5/2**[1]

0004 **4** 3 **Secret Queen**[13] 5346 5-9-3 **56** .... FrannyNorton 11 54
(Martin Hill) *led early: chsd ldrs: rdn over 1f out: no ex fnl f* **16/1**

6011 **5** hd **Juarla (IRE)**[4] 5659 4-9-7 **65** 12ex .... DarrenEgan(5) 9 62
(Ronald Harris) *mid-div: hdwy over 1f out: sn rdn: styd on same pce ins fnl f* **9/2**[3]

5006 **6** 2 1/4 **Poseidon Grey (IRE)**[14] 5296 3-9-1 **57** .... LiamJones 10 47
(Ian Williams) *hld up: rdn over 2f out: styd on ins fnl f: n.d* **50/1**

2123 **7** nk **Purley Queen (IRE)**[18] 5156 3-9-3 **59** .... ShaneKelly 4 48
(Sylvester Kirk) *prom: hmpd over 5f out: pushed along over 2f out: rdn and wknd fnl f* **10/1**

0364 **8** 1 **Russian Bullet**[10] 5444 3-9-4 **60** .... FergusSweeney 7 46
(Jamie Osborne) *sn led: hdd over 2f out: rdn over 1f out: wknd ins fnl f* **14/1**

0000 **9** 3/4 **Vhujon (IRE)**[32] 4656 7-9-0 **53** .... RobbieFitzpatrick 2 37
(Peter Grayson) *hld up: a in rr* **40/1**

0044 **10** 3 1/2 **Fantasy Fighter (IRE)**[17] 5217 7-8-11 **53** ....(p) AdamBeschizza(3) 6 25
(John E Long) *sn pushed along in rr: nvr on terms* **16/1**

5035 **11** 2 3/4 **Almaty Express**[17] 5191 10-9-6 **59** ....(b) ChrisCatlin 13 23
(John Weymes) *chsd ldrs: rdn over 2f out: wknd wl over 1f out* **16/1**

1m 13.19s (-1.81) **Going Correction** -0.25s/f (Stan)
WFA 3 from 4yo+ 3lb **11** Ran SP% **120.1**
Speed ratings (Par 101): **102,99,99,95,94 91,91,90,89,84 80**
Tote Swingers: 1&2 £8.00, 1&3 £4.60, 2&3 £10.80 CSF £27.37 CT £68.79 TOTE £3.30: £3.10, £3.40, £1.10; EX 36.60.
Owner R Morris J Russell T O'Brien M Nolan **Bred** Denis McDonnell **Trained** Newmarket, Suffolk
■ Stewards' Enquiry : Fergus Sweeney three-day ban: careless riding (Sep 14, 16-17)

FOCUS
A modest sprint handicap for 3yos and up. The winner clocked significantly the best comparative winning time on the card so far.

5809 LADBROKES BET ON YOUR MOBILE H'CAP — 1m 4f 50y(P)
8:50 (8:51) (Class 5) (0-70,70) 3-Y-0+ — £2,264 (£673; £336; £168) Stalls Low

Form — RPR
-112 **1** **Den Maschine**[154] 1112 7-9-11 **70** .... AdamBeschizza(3) 7 — 83+
(Sean Curran) *a.p: led 3f out: rdn clr fr over 1f out: eased nr fin* **11/1**
4563 **2** *6* **King's Road**[18] 5175 7-9-1 **57** ....(t) SamHitchcott 6 — 60
(Anabel K Murphy) *hld up: hdwy over 4f out: chsd wnr over 2f out: outpcd fr over 1f out* **33/1**
061 **3** *3* **Any Given Dream (IRE)**[17] 5208 3-9-3 **69** .... HayleyTurner 9 — 72+
(David Simcock) *hld up: nt clr run over 2f out: hdwy over 1f out: styd on to go 3rd post: nvr nrr* **7/1**[3]
4 *shd* **De Rigueur**[58] 4-8-13 **60** .... TobyAtkinson(5) 5 — 58
(Marco Botti) *prom: pushed along over 3f out: outpcd over 2f out: styd on u.p fnl f* **11/10**[1]
3363 **5** *¾* **Feisty Champion (IRE)**[43] 4250 3-9-3 **69** ....(p) FrannyNorton 11 — 66
(J W Hills) *hld up in tch: outpcd over 2f out: styd on u.p ins fnl f* **3/1**[2]
2016 **6** *2 ¼* **Ostentation**[22] 4987 5-9-3 **66** ....(b) NatashaEaton(7) 1 — 60
(Gay Kelleway) *hld up: hdwy over 2f out: rdn over 1f out: wknd fnl f* **28/1**
6642 **7** *hd* **Jalors (IRE)**[24] 4915 4-9-4 **65** ....(p) DarrenEgan(5) 3 — 58
(Ronald Harris) *led after 1f: rdn and hdd 3f out: wknd over 1f out* **14/1**
2601 **8** *2 ¾* **A Little Bit Dusty**[23] 4959 4-10-0 **70** .... ShaneKelly 2 — 59
(Reg Hollinshead) *led 1f: chsd ldrs: rdn over 3f out: wknd over 1f out* **25/1**
2033 **9** *1 ¼* **Lyric Poet (USA)**[45] 4200 5-10-0 **70** ....(t) WilliamCarson 10 — 57
(Anthony Carson) *hld up: rdn over 2f out: n.d* **16/1**
0100 **10** *1 ½* **Jeer (IRE)**[104] 2260 8-9-3 **66** ....(t) DavidSimmonson(7) 4 — 51
(Michael Easterby) *chsd ldr over 10f out tl led over 4f out: hdd 3f out: wknd over 1f out* **28/1**
5500 **11** *20* **Baharat (IRE)**[104] 2260 4-8-12 **54** ....(bt) RobbieFitzpatrick 8
(Richard Guest) *hld up: a in rr: bhd fnl 3f: t.o* **66/1**

2m 37.12s (-3.98) **Going Correction** -0.25s/f (Stan)
WFA 3 from 4yo+ 10lb — **11** Ran SP% **121.2**
Speed ratings (Par 103): **103,99,97,96,96 94,94,92,92,91 77**
Tote Swingers 1&2 £58.70, 2&3 £18.80, 1&3 £5.10 CSF £331.91 CT £2720.21 TOTE £9.60: £2.30, £7.60, £2.50; EX 168.10.
Owner Paul Morgan **Bred** York Stut & Stald Rainbow **Trained** Hatford, Oxon

FOCUS
A fair middle-distance handicap for 3yos and up. The winning time compares favourably with most of the rest of the card.
Any Given Dream(IRE) Official explanation: jockey said gelding ran too free

5810 DOWNLOAD THE LADBROKES MOBILE APP H'CAP — 1m 1f 103y(P)
9:20 (9:20) (Class 6) (0-65,65) 3-Y-O — £1,704 (£503; £251) Stalls Low

Form — RPR
6304 **1** **Graylyn Valentino**[16] 5231 3-9-4 **62** .... HarryBentley 1 — 71
(Robin Dickin) *hld up: hdwy over 2f out: rdn to ld and edgd lft ins fnl f: r.o* **9/1**
3206 **2** *1* **Lean On Pete (IRE)**[30] 4716 3-9-5 **63** .... PaulMulrennan 11 — 70
(Ollie Pears) *chsd ldrs: rdn to ld over 1f out: hdd and hung lft ins fnl f: styd on* **7/1**[2]
-050 **3** *¾* **Rhossili Bay**[65] 3484 3-8-5 **54** .... LeonnaMayor(5) 6 — 59
(Alastair Lidderdale) *s.i.s: hld up: nt clr run over 1f out: r.o ins fnl f: nvr nrr* **16/1**
5016 **4** *shd* **Exceedexpectations (IRE)**[17] 5216 3-9-6 **64** .... HayleyTurner 9 — 69+
(Michael Bell) *trckd ldrs: rdn over 1f out: hmpd ins fnl f: styd on same pce* **13/8**[1]
5024 **5** *½* **Source Of Light (IRE)**[30] 4709 3-9-4 **62** .... ShaneKelly 7 — 66
(Daniel Mark Loughnane) *hld up in tch: rdn over 1f out: styd on* **20/1**
0315 **6** *2* **Arte Del Calcio**[24] 4906 3-9-1 **62** .... RaulDaSilva(3) 13 — 62
(Tony Carroll) *hld up: rdn over 1f out: r.o ins fnl f: nvr nrr* **14/1**
5500 **7** *1* **Chelsea Mick**[19] 5129 3-8-13 **64** .... DavidBergin(7) 2 — 62
(John Mackie) *chsd ldr: led over 7f out: rdn and hdd over 1f out: wknd ins fnl f* **7/1**[2]
3300 **8** *½* **Attain**[43] 4256 3-9-4 **65** ....(p) AdamBeschizza(3) 4 — 62
(Julia Feilden) *prom: drvn along over 3f out: wknd over 1f out* **10/1**
4605 **9** *nk* **Siouxies Dream**[16] 5246 3-8-8 **52** ....[1] FrannyNorton 12 — 48
(Michael Appleby) *prom: rdn over 2f out: wknd over 1f out* **22/1**
3046 **10** *4* **Edraaq**[20] 5100 3-9-7 **65** ....(t) TadhgO'Shea 10 — 53
(Brian Meehan) *led: hdd over 7f out: chsd ldr: rdn over 1f out: wknd and eased fnl f* **12/1**
0554 **11** *3* **Zain Glory**[39] 4403 3-9-1 **64** ....(tp) DarrenEgan(5) 3 — 45
(Gerard Butler) *s.i.s: hld up and a in rr: wknd over 3f out* **8/1**[3]

1m 59.14s (-2.56) **Going Correction** -0.25s/f (Stan) — **11** Ran SP% **122.6**
Speed ratings (Par 98): **101,100,99,99,98 97,96,95,95,91 89**
Tote Swingers 1&2 £15.20, 2&3 £44.60, 1&3 £26.00 CSF £73.84 CT £1015.08 TOTE £7.80: £1.80, £2.50, £5.60; EX 68.00.
Owner Graham & Lynn Knight **Bred** M Stewart **Trained** Atherstone on Stour, Warwicks

FOCUS
A modest 3yo handicap with the winning time was very respectable for the grade.
Edraaq Official explanation: jockey said gelding hung left
Zain Glory Official explanation: jockey said colt never travelled
T/Plt: £73.30 to a £1 stake. Pool: £70,847.29 - 705.55 winning tickets. T/Qpdt: £24.00 to a £1 stake. Pool: £7,171.19 - 220.60 winning tickets. CR

5501 BATH (L-H)
Saturday, September 1

OFFICIAL GOING: Good to soft
Wind: Brisk ahead Weather: Sunny spells

5811 TIMBERLAND H'CAP — 2m 1f 34y
4:35 (4:37) (Class 6) (0-60,59) 4-Y-0+ — £2,181 (£644; £322) Stalls Centre

Form — RPR
0-21 **1** **Hi Note**[5] 5683 4-8-13 **58** 6ex .... MartinLeonard(7) 5 — 68
(Sheena West) *trckd ldrs: led 3f out: pushed along over 1f out: narrowly hdd ins fnl f: pushed along and rallied to take slt advantage fnl 50yds: all out* **5/4**[1]
044 **2** *nse* **Gordon Flash**[16] 5280 5-8-13 **58** .... WilliamTwiston-Davies(7) 11 — 68
(Charles Hills) *hld up in rr: stdy hdwy 4f out: trckd wnr traveling wl appr fnl 2f: drvn to take slt ld ins fnl f: styd hrd pressed: narrowly hdd fnl 50yds: no ex last stride* **11/2**[3]
-006 **3** *7* **Party Palace**[25] 4904 8-8-0 **45** .... NatashaEaton(7) 2 — 47
(Stuart Howe) *in rr: hdwy and rdn over 3f out: chsd ldrs in 3rd over 2f out: sn no imp and wl hld over 1f out* **33/1**
-501 **4** *8* **Eastern Magic**[25] 4904 5-9-7 **59** .... ShaneKelly 9 — 53
(Reg Hollinshead) *chsd ldr tl over 3f out: sn rdn: wknd 2f out* **9/2**[2]
0120 **5** *3 ½* **Omid**[17] 5241 4-9-4 **56** ....(vt) DarryllHolland 6 — 46
(Nicky Vaughan) *sn drvn to ld: pushed along 7f out: rdn 4f out: hdd 3f out: wknd 2f out* **8/1**
0-00 **6** *13* **Ray Diamond**[60] 2175 7-8-4 **45** ....(p) RyanPowell(3) 3 — 20
(Michael Madgwick) *a in rr* **10/1**
00-5 **7** *9* **Neighbourhood (USA)**[16] 5265 4-8-8 **46** .... FergusSweeney 4 — 11
(James Evans) *in tch: rdn over 3f out: sn btn* **20/1**
000 **8** *2 ¾* **Tanjung Aqas (IRE)**[13] 5384 4-8-5 **46** ....(v) MarkCoumbe(3) 10
(Christopher Kellett) *chsd ldrs: rdn 5f out: wknd 4f out* **50/1**
3154 **9** *10* **Asterales**[25] 4905 5-9-6 **58** .... KellyHarrison 7
(Jo Hughes) *rdn 5f out: sn lost tch* **10/1**

3m 56.23s (4.33) **Going Correction** +0.40s/f (Good) — **9** Ran SP% **117.0**
Speed ratings (Par 101): **105,104,101,97,96 90,85,84,79**
Tote Swingers 1&2 £3.80, 2&3 £10.70, 1&3 £10.10 CSF £8.37 CT £150.55 TOTE £2.10: £1.10, £1.80, £4.40; EX 7.30 Trifecta £249.30 Pool £424.51 - 1.26 winning tickets..
Owner Gerald West **Bred** J A And Mrs Duffy **Trained** Falmer, E Sussex

FOCUS
Races incorporating bottom bend increased in distance by about 12.5yds. Little depth to this staying handicap and the form is rated as average for the grade.
Ray Diamond Official explanation: jockey said gelding never travelled

5812 KURT GEIGER H'CAP — 5f 161y
5:10 (5:13) (Class 4) (0-85,85) 3-Y-0+ — £5,175 (£1,540; £769; £384) Stalls Centre

Form — RPR
3100 **1** **Barons Spy (IRE)**[23] 4998 11-9-6 **84** .... JamesDoyle 9 — 93
(Richard Price) *chsd ldrs: drvn 2f out: chsd ldr over 1f out: rdn to ld fnl 50yds: styd on strly* **20/1**
2000 **2** *1* **Ertikaan**[57] 3822 5-8-11 **80** ....[1] DarrenEgan(5) 8 — 86
(Ronald Harris) *chsd ldrs: led over 1f out: sn drvn hdd and no ex fnl 50yds* **8/1**
2640 **3** *1 ¼* **Emiratesdotcom**[9] 5502 6-8-9 **73** .... FergusSweeney 6 — 79+
(Milton Bradley) *in rr: hdwy on inner and nt clr run fr over 1f out tl ins fnl f: styd to on take 3rd last strides: nt rcvr* **10/1**
6440 **4** *nse* **Fanrouge (IRE)**[21] 5080 3-9-5 **85** ....(p) TomMcLaughlin 10 — 86
(Malcolm Saunders) *in rr: hdwy over 2f out: drvn and tk 3rd ins fnl f: sn one pce: lost 3rd last strides* **7/1**[3]
2316 **5** *3* **Knocker Knowles (IRE)**[20] 5123 3-8-11 **80** .... MatthewCosham(3) 2 — 72
(David Evans) *chsd ldr: rdn over 2f out: wknd fnl f* **20/1**
4403 **6** *½* **Falasteen (IRE)**[19] 5165 5-9-2 **80** .... ShaneKelly 4 — 70
(Milton Bradley) *chsd ldrs: rdn over 1f out: wknd fnl f* **20/1**
0505 **7** *½* **Button Moon (IRE)**[25] 4920 4-8-11 **75** ....(p) KirstyMilczarek 1 — 63
(Ian Wood) *led tl hdd over 1f out: sn btn* **20/1**
5001 **8** *6* **Prime Exhibit**[15] 5305 7-9-2 **80** ....(t) DarryllHolland 3 — 48
(Milton Bradley) *chsd ldrs: rdn and wknd ins fnl 2f* **8/1**
6204 **9** *3 ¼* **O'Gorman**[12] 5422 3-8-10 **83** .... WilliamTwiston-Davies(7) 11 — 41
(Gary Brown) *rrd s and v.s.a: rcvrd and in tch over 2f out: sn rdn and wknd* **4/1**[1]
3210 **10** *hd* **School Fees**[15] 5326 3-8-7 **78** .... AmyScott(5) 5 — 35
(Henry Candy) *outpcd most of way* **5/1**[2]

1m 13.71s (2.51) **Going Correction** +0.40s/f (Good)
WFA 3 from 4yo+ 2lb — **10** Ran SP% **99.5**
Speed ratings (Par 105): **99,97,96,95,91 91,90,82,78,78**
Tote Swingers 1&2 £16.50, 2&3 £13.90, 1&3 £16.50 CSF £103.36 CT £731.92 TOTE £32.00: £5.50, £2.70, £2.90; EX 115.10 TRIFECTA Not won..
Owner Barry Veasey **Bred** Tally-Ho Stud **Trained** Ullingswick, H'fords
■ Valmina was withdrawn (3/1F, ref to ent stalls). Deduct 25p in the 3 under R4.

FOCUS
A competitive enough heat for the grade and the pace looked sound thanks to Button Moon, who faded in the closing stages. The placed horses help set the level of the form.
Emiratesdotcom ◆ Official explanation: jockey said gelding was denied a clear run
O'Gorman Official explanation: jockey said gelding reared as stalls opened

5813 BRITISH STALLION STUDS E B F NOVICE STKS — 5f 161y
5:40 (5:41) (Class 5) 2-Y-O — £3,881 (£1,155; £577; £288) Stalls Centre

Form — RPR
0124 **1** **Liber**[9] 5515 2-9-7 95 .... JimmyFortune 4 — 94+
(Sir Mark Prescott Bt) *mde all: c easily clr over 1f out: unchal* **1/4**[1]
0 **2** *4 ½* **King Of Kudos (IRE)**[22] 5062 2-9-0 0 .... DaneO'Neill 2 — 72
(Richard Hannon) *disp 2nd tl chsd easy wnr ins fnl 2f but nvr any ch* **6/1**[2]
631 **3** *3 ½* **Kodatish (IRE)**[9] 5503 2-9-2 73 .... KierenFox 1 — 62
(Ronald Harris) *plld hrd: chsd ldrs: rdn over 2f out and nvr any ch w ldng duo* **8/1**[3]
1334 **4** *21* **Windforpower (IRE)**[11] 5450 2-9-2 67 ....(p) JamesDoyle 5
(Ronald Harris) *disp tl rdn 2f out: sn lost action and eased fnl f: t.o* **16/1**

1m 13.36s (2.16) **Going Correction** +0.40s/f (Good) — **4** Ran SP% **111.3**
Speed ratings (Par 95): **101,95,90,62**
CSF £2.45 TOTE £1.20; EX 2.60.
Owner William Charnley & Richard Pegum **Bred** Redmyre Bloodstock Ltd **Trained** Newmarket, Suffolk

FOCUS
An uncompetitive novice event and they finished in market order.

NOTEBOOK
Liber was entitled to win this with something to spare given he had so much in hand on the figures, and it turned into a cakewalk as he cruised clear in second gear to make it 2-2 at this venue. Although he is quite exposed for a juvenile he has some smart form to his name, notably in Listed grade, and he will no doubt be aimed at something much more valuable next. (op 4-11)
King Of Kudos(IRE) stepped up on his modest debut effort, where he didn't seem to see out 7f, and certainly looks good enough to win a maiden. (op 11-2)
Kodatish(IRE) was too keen early and could never really get competitive but he'll be seen to better effect in nurseries. Official explanation: jockey said colt ran too freely (op 7-1)
Windforpower(IRE) is exposed and had little chance on these terms anyway. (op 12-1)

5814 HUGO BOSS SOMERSETSHIRE CONDITIONS STKS — 5f 161y
6:10 (6:10) (Class 3) 3-Y-0+ — £8,409 (£2,502; £1,250; £625) Stalls Centre

Form — RPR
5602 **1** **Night Carnation**[27] 4838 4-8-10 102 .... JimmyFortune 3 — 103
(Andrew Balding) *trckd ldrs: led wl over 1f out: drvn out* **2/1**[1]
6303 **2** *¾* **Regal Parade**[5] 5686 8-9-1 100 ....(t) DarryllHolland 4 — 106
(Milton Bradley) *in rr: n.m.r 2f out: swtchd lft sn after: squeezed through fnl f: tk 2nd fnl 100yds: no imp on wnr* **17/2**

6620 **3** 1 3/4 **Sugar Beet**[27] 4838 4-8-5 92 DarrenEgan(5) 5 95
(Ronald Harris) *in rr: hdwy on outer over 2f out: chsd wnr u.p 1f out: no imp: one pce and lost 2nd fnl 100yds* **28/1**

0-10 **4** 6 **Jonny Mudball**[119] 1857 6-9-4 102 (t) SebSanders 7 83
(Tom Dascombe) *sn chsng ldrs towards outside: rdn 2f out: wknd fnl f* **8/1**

5140 **5** 2 1/2 **Rex Imperator**[10] 5487 3-8-13 104 JamesDoyle 2 72+
(Roger Charlton) *towards rr but in tch whn rdn over 2f out: styng on whn hmpd wl over 1f out: nt rcvr* **9/4**[2]

0113 **6** 1/2 **Ballesteros**[91] 2691 3-8-13 107 EddieAhern 6 71+
(Brian Meehan) *trckd ldrs: nt clr run 2f out: effrt whn hmpd over 1f out: nt rcvr* **5/1**[3]

0000 **7** 17 **Oasis Dancer**[28] 4802 5-9-8 98 JimCrowley 1 21
(Ralph Beckett) *led: rdn over 2f out: hdd wl over 1f out: wkng whn hmpd over 1f out: eased whn no ch* **12/1**

1m 12.37s (1.17) **Going Correction** +0.40s/f (Good)
WFA 3 from 4yo+ 2lb 7 Ran SP% **113.5**
Speed ratings (Par 107): **108,107,104,96,93 92,70**
Tote Swingers 1&2 £2.60, 2&3 £15.90, 1&3 £7.20 CSF £19.30 TOTE £2.90: £1.20, £6.00; EX 21.10.
Owner George Strawbridge **Bred** George Strawbridge **Trained** Kingsclere, Hants

FOCUS
A really good conditions event with five of the seven runners having an official rating of 100+ and the pace looked sound, with the pair that cut out the running both dropping out but causing trouble in behind as they weakened. The form looks messy and the third appears the best guide.

NOTEBOOK
Night Carnation skipped clear, free of traffic, to put her seal on the contest. A quality performer when the ground is on the slow side, she had every chance in receipt of the sex allowance and deserves another crack at a Group race now. (tchd 15-8 and 9-4)
Regal Parade stayed on strongly from off the pace, but he might be a touch flattered by that given the pace was so strong and the winner had raced much closer to it. That said, this was an encouraging effort in the first-time tongue-tie and, although clearly not as good as he used to be, he remains capable of finding a race outside of Group and Listed level. (op 10-1)
Sugar Beet shouldn't have been a factor on these terms but she avoided getting involved in the early battle and benefited from the trouble up the inside. She ran very well but is clearly flattered by this. (tchd 25-1)
Jonny Mudball dropped away having disputed the lead and he probably wants faster ground in any case. (op 10-1 tchd 11-1)
Rex Imperator was struggling a long way from home and never got competitive on ground probably too slow for him. He is much better than this. Official explanation: jockey said gelding struck its head on stalls and suffered interference in running; vet said gelding sustained an in jury to a tooth (op 5-2)
Ballesteros ♦, who relishes slow ground, looked a massive threat when looking for room over a furlong out, but he couldn't get free from the traffic and lost all chance. He can clearly be rated much better than the bare form. Official explanation: jockey said gelding suffered interference in running (op 7-2)

5815 HOBBS FILLIES' H'CAP 5f 11y
6:40 (6:43) (Class 4) (0-80,77) 3-Y-O+ **£5,175** (£1,540; £769; £384) **Stalls** Centre

Form RPR
3363 **1** **Ginzan**[9] 5502 4-9-1 71 TomMcLaughlin 7 79
(Malcolm Saunders) *sn trcking ldr: led over 1f out: drvn out fnl 120yds: hld on wl clsng stages* **4/1**[2]

0231 **2** nk **I See You**[8] 5536 3-8-12 69 (p) JimCrowley 2 76
(Peter Makin) *in rr: drvn and hdwy between horses over 1f out: chsd wnr ins fnl f: clsng nr fin but a jst hld* **4/1**[2]

3144 **3** 1 1/2 **Rebecca Romero**[16] 5272 5-9-4 74 EddieAhern 5 76
(Denis Coakley) *chsd ldrs: rdn 2f out: disp 2nd ins fnl f but no imprssion on wnr: no ex clsng stages* **4/1**[2]

5233 **4** 1/2 **Ring For Baileys**[16] 5272 3-8-8 70 DarrenEgan(5) 8 70
(Chris Dwyer) *chsd ldrs 1/2-way: rdn to chal appr fnl f: styd on same pce* **3/1**[1]

0464 **5** nk **Berberana (IRE)**[9] 5514 4-9-0 70 (p) JamesDoyle 3 69
(Jeremy Gask) *in rr but in tch: rdn along 2f out: styd on clsng stages: nvr gng pce to get into contention* **14/1**

1601 **6** 1/2 **Cats Eyes**[18] 5195 3-9-5 76 ShaneKelly 6 73
(Robert Cowell) *sn led: hdd over 1f out: sn btn* **3/1**[1]

/43- **7** 5 **Lady Prodee**[570] 465 4-8-12 68 KierenFox 1 47
(Bill Turner) *chsd ldrs: rdn 2f out: sn btn* **12/1**[3]

1m 4.18s (1.68) **Going Correction** +0.40s/f (Good)
WFA 3 from 4yo+ 1lb 7 Ran SP% **124.4**
Speed ratings (Par 102): **102,101,99,98,97 97,89**
Tote Swingers 1&2 £6.00, 2&3 £3.70, 1&3 £5.40 CSF £22.61 CT £71.14 TOTE £6.90: £3.30, £2.80; EX 24.70 Trifecta £100.50 Pool £400.72 - 2.95 winning tickets..
Owner Paul Nicholas **Bred** Hedsor Stud **Trained** Green Ore, Somerset

FOCUS
Some consistent fillies contesting a competitive-enough event. A personal best from the winner with the second in good form.

5816 OSPREY LONDON H'CAP 1m 3f 144y
7:10 (7:10) (Class 4) (0-80,80) 3-Y-O+ **£5,175** (£1,540; £769; £384) **Stalls** Low

Form RPR
0-00 **1** **Hanoverian Baron**[77] 3163 7-9-12 80 SebSanders 3 91
(Tony Newcombe) *hld up in rr: hdwy on ins over 2f out and nt clr run: swtchd rt fr 2f out: pushed rt to get run wl over 1f out and qcknd to ld appr fnl f: sn drvn clr* **10/1**

1025 **2** 3 3/4 **April Ciel**[11] 5451 3-7-13 67 DarrenEgan(5) 1 72
(Ronald Harris) *chsd ldr: led 1m out: rdn 2f out: hdd appr fnl f: sn outpcd by wnr but kpt on wl for 2nd* **12/1**

4010 **3** nk **Sula Two**[7] 5580 5-9-4 79 PhilipPrince(7) 4 83
(Ron Hodges) *in tch: hdwy 1/2-way: rdn along 3f out: styd on fnl f to take 3rd clsng stages but nvr nr wnr* **8/1**

3-04 **4** hd **Mossbrae**[15] 5297 3-8-12 75 AndreaAtzeni 10 79
(Roger Varian) *chsd ldrs: drvn along and disp 2nd fr 2f out tl appr fnl f: styd on same pce* **9/2**[3]

2522 **5** 3/4 **Spartan Spirit (IRE)**[19] 5159 4-9-2 70 JimmyFortune 7 73
(Hughie Morrison) *prom: dropped to rr over 6f out: stdy hdwy towards outside whn bmpd and lost momentum wl over 1f out: styd on again ins fnl f* **15/2**

2404 **6** 2 1/4 **Hurricane In Dubai (IRE)**[14] 5366 3-8-11 74 EddieAhern 5 73
(Denis Coakley) *chsd ldrs: rdn over 3f out: wknd over 1f out* **4/1**[2]

1426 **7** 1/2 **Honourable Knight (IRE)**[131] 1566 4-9-1 69 DaneO'Neill 8 67
(Mark Usher) *in rr: rdn along over 3f out: effrt over 2f out: nvr rchd ldrs: wknd fnl f* **40/1**

2152 **8** 1 **Three Bards (IRE)**[11] 5455 3-9-0 77 DarrylHolland 6 74
(Mark Johnston) *led tl hdd 1m out: styd chsng ldrs: wknd fr 2f out: btn whn hmpd over 1f out* **5/2**[1]

0136 **9** 15 **Tingo In The Tale (IRE)**[37] 4513 3-8-11 74 JamesDoyle 9 45
(David Arbuthnot) *in rr: hdwy on outer fr 4f out: in tch and u.p 3f out: wknd 2f out* **10/1**

2m 33.65s (3.05) **Going Correction** +0.40s/f (Good)
WFA 3 from 4yo+ 9lb 9 Ran SP% **117.9**
Speed ratings (Par 105): **105,102,102,102,101 100,99,99,89**
Tote Swingers 1&2 £22.60, 2&3 £19.40, 1&3 £9.10 CSF £124.23 CT £1014.12 TOTE £10.00: £2.70, £4.00, £2.40; EX 72.70 Trifecta £236.40 Part won. Pool £319.56 - 0.30 winning tickets..
Owner Paul Moulton **Bred** S Coughlan **Trained** Yarnscombe, Devon
■ Stewards' Enquiry : Seb Sanders two-day ban: careless riding (Sep 16-17)

FOCUS
A soundly run middle-distance handicap and the form looks solid, rated around the first four.

5817 CREW CLOTHING H'CAP 1m 5f 22y
7:40 (7:41) (Class 6) (0-55,56) 3-Y-O+ **£2,070** (£616; £307; £153) **Stalls** High

Form RPR
/033 **1** **Arch Event**[10] 5483 7-9-1 46 oh1 (p) MartinLane 9 56
(Bernard Llewellyn) *chsd ldrs: wnt 2nd over 2f out: drvn to ld 1f out: styd on wl* **25/1**

5532 **2** 1 1/4 **Josie's Dream (IRE)**[18] 5196 4-8-12 48 JemmaMarshall(5) 2 56
(Jo Hughes) *in tch: hdwy 3f out: styd on to chse wnr jst ins fnl f: kpt on but a hld* **6/1**[3]

4361 **3** 2 **Bengal Tiger**[24] 4941 6-9-9 54 JimCrowley 13 59
(Tony Carroll) *towards rr: hdwy fr 4f out: chsd ldrs over 2f out: styd on fr over 1f out to take 3rd clsng stages but no imp on ldng duo* **3/1**[2]

50-0 **4** 3/4 **Annelko**[18] 5196 5-9-9 54 EddieAhern 8 58
(Michael Blake) *sn led: rdn over 2f out: hdd appr fnl f: wknd fnl 120yds* **8/1**

5004 **5** 2 **David's Folly (IRE)**[16] 5265 3-8-4 48 RaulDaSilva(3) 12 49
(Bryn Palling) *sn chsng ldr: rdn over 2f out: wknd over 1f out* **10/1**

0052 **6** 6 **Musically**[5] 5683 3-8-7 53 CharlesBishop(5) 5 45
(Mick Channon) *in rr: sme hdwy 3f out: nvr rchd ldrs: no ch fnl 2f* **5/2**[1]

0050 **7** 2 3/4 **Fuzzy Logic (IRE)**[26] 4870 3-9-0 55 JamesDoyle 6 43
(William Muir) *in tch: hdwy 6f out: rdn 4f out: wknd ins fnl 3f* **9/1**

0051 **8** nk **Sir Dylan**[9] 5508 3-8-10 56 DarrenEgan(5) 1 43
(Ronald Harris) *in rr: sme hdwy on inner whn hmpd by wkng runner: no ch after* **7/1**

004 **9** 8 **Bold Duke**[68] 3430 4-9-6 54 MatthewCosham(3) 4 29
(Edward Bevan) *in rr: drvn 7f out: sme hdwy over 3f out: nvr rchd ldrs and sn wknd* **25/1**

0500 **10** 14 **Dark Celt (IRE)**[16] 5037 3-8-2 46 oh1 RyanPowell(3) 3
(Michael Madgwick) *in rr: hdwy on outside over 3f out: sn hung bdly rt and no ch* **50/1**

0500 **P** **Moonshine Ruby**[19] 5164 6-9-1 46 oh1 KirstyMilczarek 7
(Peter Hiatt) *chsd ldrs: wknd rapidly 3f out: p.u 2f out* **33/1**

2m 56.03s (4.03) **Going Correction** +0.40s/f (Good)
WFA 3 from 4yo+ 10lb 11 Ran SP% **123.2**
Speed ratings (Par 101): **103,102,101,100,99 95,93,93,88,80**
Tote Swingers 1&2 £17.00, 2&3 £3.90, 1&3 £25.30 CSF £171.56 CT £599.98 TOTE £47.00: £4.90, £1.80, £1.90; EX 115.80 Trifecta £289.40 Part won. Pool £391.14 - 0.30 winning tickets..
Owner David Maddocks **Bred** P And Mrs Wafford **Trained** Fochriw, Caerphilly

FOCUS
Most of these find winning very difficult
Moonshine Ruby Official explanation: jockey said mare lost its action
T/Plt: £442.70 to a £1 stake. Pool: £47,573.55 - 78.44 winning tickets. T/Qpdt: £62.70 to a £1 stake. Pool: £5,391.30 - 63.60 winning tickets. ST

5618 BEVERLEY (R-H)
Saturday, September 1

OFFICIAL GOING: Good (good to soft in places in 5f chute) (7.3)
Wind: Light against Weather: Overcast

5818 MONSIEUR BOND EUROPEAN BREEDERS' FUND MAIDEN FILLIES' STKS 7f 100y
2:05 (2:05) (Class 4) 2-Y-O **£4,463** (£1,328; £663; £331) **Stalls** Low

Form RPR
24 **1** **Laudate Dominum (IRE)**[16] 5274 2-9-0 0 FrederikTylicki 5 79
(Richard Fahey) *hld up towards rr: hdwy on inner 2f out: rdn over 1f out: styd on strly ins fnl f to ld last 75yds* **5/1**

43 **2** 1 **Naalatt (IRE)**[24] 4946 2-9-0 0 HarryBentley 7 77
(Mahmood Al Zarooni) *hld up towards rr: hdwy 2f out: rdn to chse ldrs over 1f out: led briefly ins fnl f: hdd and no ex last 75yds* **9/2**[3]

03 **3** 2 3/4 **Willowing (USA)**[14] 5339 2-9-0 0 PhillipMakin 1 70
(Mahmood Al Zarooni) *led 2f: cl up: swtchd lft 3f out: led again over 2f out: rdn over 1f out: hdd & wknd ins fnl f* **7/2**[1]

303 **4** 4 **Summer Dream (IRE)**[36] 4525 2-9-0 78 NickyMackay 3 61
(Marco Botti) *cl up: disp ld over 2f out: rdn and ev ch wl over 1f out: drvn and wknd ent fnl f* **7/2**[1]

4000 **5** 2 1/4 **Shafaani**[29] 4763 2-9-0 70 (t) RobertWinston 4 55
(Clive Brittain) *chsd ldrs: rdn along on wd outside 2f out: drvn and wknd appr fnl f* **7/1**

5 **6** 1 1/2 **Zero Game (IRE)**[21] 5104 2-9-0 0 JamieSpencer 2 52
(Michael Bell) *plld hrd: trckd ldrs tl rapid hdwy to ld after 2f: edgd lft bnd after 3f: edgd rt 3f out: sn rdn and hdd over 2f out: sn wknd* **4/1**[2]

7 1 **Swaying Grace (IRE)** 2-9-0 0 PaulMulrennan 6 49
(Ann Duffield) *dwlt: hld up: a in rr* **40/1**

1m 37.03s (3.23) **Going Correction** +0.15s/f (Good) 7 Ran SP% **114.2**
Speed ratings (Par 94): **87,85,82,78,75 73,72**
Tote Swingers 1&2 £4.10, 2&3 £3.10, 1&3 £4.10 CSF £27.45 TOTE £6.50: £2.80, £2.50; EX 28.20.
Owner Inner Circle Thoroughbreds - Ab Ovo **Bred** Jim McGrath & Reg Griffin **Trained** Musley Bank, N Yorks

FOCUS
Rail around bottom bend moved, adding 19yds to distances on Round course. There was just 1mm of rain overnight and the ground, officially described as good, good to soft in places on the 5f chute (GoingStick 7.3), was called "loose" by Freddie Tylicki and Phil Makin after the first race. The leader was taken on in front from over half a mile out in this fillies' maiden and they started racing for home too far out, resulting in the race being set up for the closers. The race has been rated at just below face value.

NOTEBOOK

Laudate Dominum(IRE) sat off the leading pack and that was to her benefit in the end as the leaders predictably hit the wall and she came through to just see off her fellow closer Naalatt. She stays well and should be a player in mile nurseries. (op 8-1)

Naalatt(IRE) promised to be suited by the stiffer track and extra yardage, and the way the race was run also helped her, for like the winner she hung back off the early dash for the line. Nurseries are now an option for her as well. (tchd 4-1)

Willowing(USA) ◆ took the field along early but was then overtaken by Zero Game on the turn. She rallied to do best of those that raced prominently and, while she just couldn't hold off the two closers, she was arguably the best filly in the field and will be interesting in nurseries. (tchd 4-1)

Summer Dream(IRE) didn't get the trip after going for home too far out. (tchd 4-1)

Shafaani didn't get the trip after going for home too far out, and got involved in some scrimmaging on the turn in.

Zero Game(IRE) just didn't settle early and, having been allowed to go on and take the lead after 2f, struggled to cope with the bend. She was soon done with on the climb to the finish. (op 7-2)

5819 BETFRED "THE BONUS KING" H'CAP — 7f 100y

2:40 (2:40) (Class 4) (0-85,83) 3-Y-0+ — **£5,175** (£1,540; £769; £384) **Stalls** Low

Form	Pos	Dist	Horse	Jockey	RPR	SP
1423	1		**Hi There (IRE)**[28] 4819 3-8-9 **72** — (Richard Fahey) *hld up towards rr: smooth hdwy on outer 3f out: trckd ldrs 2f out: rdn to ld appr fnl f: sn clr and styd on strly*	FrederikTylicki 11	87	**3/1**[1]
2306	2	3 ½	**Wahylah (IRE)**[37] 4496 3-9-2 **79** — (Clive Brittain) *hld up in midfield: hdwy over 2f out: rdn over 1f out: chsd wnr ins fnl f: sn drvn and no imp*	RobertWinston 7	85	**8/1**[3]
0004	3	2	**Imperator Augustus (IRE)**[7] 5588 4-9-2 **75** — (Patrick Holmes) *in tch: hdwy 3f out: rdn to chse ldrs 2f out: drvn and kpt on fnl f*	PhillipMakin 14	77	**14/1**
6441	4	shd	**Shadowtime**[32] 4679 7-8-12 **71** — (Tracy Waggott) *chsd ldrs: hdwy over 2f out: rdn wl over 1f out: kpt on same pce fnl f*	PaulMulrennan 6	73	**17/2**
332	5	nk	**Majuro (IRE)**[18] 5189 8-9-2 **75** — (Charles Smith) *in tch: hdwy over 2f out: sn rdn and styd on fnl f: nrst fin*	(t) RobbieFitzpatrick 3	76	**10/1**
1353	6	hd	**Copperwood**[5] 5667 7-9-1 **74** — (Mark Johnston) *cl up: effrt 3f out: chal 2f out: sn rdn and ev ch tl drvn and wknd ent fnl f*	AdrianNicholls 4	75	**6/1**[2]
1000	7	2	**Paramour**[47] 4136 5-9-9 **82** — (David O'Meara) *prom: effrt over 2f out: sn rdn and wknd over 1f out*	DanielTudhope 13	78	**8/1**[3]
2500	8	3	**Polish World (USA)**[22] 5057 8-9-9 **82** — (Paul Midgley) *led: rdn along 2f out: drvn over 1f out: hdd appr fnl f and wknd qckly*	MickyFenton 2	70	**9/1**
2030	9	2	**George Benjamin**[28] 4829 5-8-12 **78** — (Christopher Kellett) *nvr bttr than midfield*	DannyBrock(7) 10	61	**40/1**
5000	10	nse	**Orpsie Boy (IRE)**[14] 5369 9-9-9 **82** — (Ruth Carr) *a towards rr*	TomEaves 9	65	**25/1**
00-4	11	1 ¼	**Cornus**[13] 5388 10-8-10 **72** — (Alan McCabe) *dwlt and towards rr: sme hdwy over 3f out: sn rdn along and outpcd fr over 2f out*	(be) DeclanCannon(3) 5	52	**50/1**
0030	12	½	**City Of The Kings (IRE)**[21] 5111 7-8-10 **76** — (Ollie Pears) *dwlt: a towards rr*	(p) JacobButterfield(7) 8	55	**20/1**
3056	13	5	**No Poppy (IRE)**[9] 5520 4-9-5 **83** — (Tim Easterby) *a towards rr*	AdamCarter(5) 12	49	**14/1**
00-0	14	3	**Shotley Mac**[34] 4620 8-8-13 **72** — (Neville Bycroft) *chsd ldrs on inner: rdn along wl over 2f out: sn wknd*	(b) DuranFentiman 1	31	**16/1**

1m 33.86s (0.06) **Going Correction** +0.15s/f (Good)
WFA 3 from 4yo+ 4lb — **14** Ran SP% **123.3**
Speed ratings (Par 105): **105,101,98,98,98 98,95,92,90,89 88,87,82,78**
Tote Swingers 1&2 £5.30, 2&3 £24.60, 1&3 £11.70 CSF £26.15 CT £311.37 TOTE £1.30: £1.30, £2.30, £5.50; EX 33.40.
Owner Market Avenue Racing Club Ltd **Bred** J & J Waldron **Trained** Musley Bank, N Yorks

FOCUS

They went a good gallop up front and once again those ridden with a bit more patience were rewarded. The first two home were the two 3yos in the line-up. Another personal best from the winner.

Shotley Mac Official explanation: jockey said gelding had no more to give

5820 BETFRED MOBILE LOTTO H'CAP — 1m 1f 207y

3:15 (3:16) (Class 2) (0-105,94) 3-Y-0 — **£12,938** (£3,850; £1,924; £962) **Stalls** Low

Form	Pos	Dist	Horse	Jockey	RPR	SP
-121	1		**Universal (IRE)**[5] 5666 3-9-10 **94** 6ex — (Mark Johnston) *mde all: rdn over 2f out: drvn ent fnl f and styd on strly*	AdrianNicholls 4	104	**3/1**[1]
1040	2	1 ½	**Chapter Seven**[30] 4735 3-9-7 **91** — (Richard Fahey) *trckd ldrs: hdwy on inner over 2f out: rdn over 1f out: chsd wnr ins fnl f: kpt on*	FrederikTylicki 5	98	**7/1**[3]
1413	3	1 ¼	**Sheikhzayedroad**[28] 4821 3-9-1 **85** — (David Simcock) *stdd s and hld up in rr: hdwy over 2f out: rdn over 1f out: kpt on fnl f*	JamieSpencer 2	90	**3/1**[1]
-062	4	2	**Daghash**[11] 5451 3-8-7 **77** — (Clive Brittain) *chsd ldrs: rdn along on wd outside 2f out: drvn over 1f out and kpt on same pce*	NickyMackay 6	78	**9/1**
1231	5	nk	**Watheeq (USA)**[19] 5163 3-8-5 **78** — (Roger Varian) *trckd ldrs: hdwy over 2f out: rdn wl over 1f out: sn one pce*	DominicFox(3) 8	78	**5/1**[2]
0214	6	1 ¼	**Spirit Of The Law (IRE)**[38] 4459 3-9-2 **86** — (Ed Dunlop) *hld up in rr: hdwy over 2f out: rdn along wl over 1f out: sn no imp*	PaulMulrennan 7	83	**8/1**
615	7	1	**Glittering Gold**[62] 3668 3-9-1 **85** — (Sir Michael Stoute) *trckd wnr: effrt over 2f out and sn rdn: drvn over 1f out: wknd ent fnl f*	RobertWinston 3	80	**15/2**
0461	8	3	**Nemushka**[18] 5218 3-8-11 **81** — (Richard Fahey) *dwlt: t.k.h and sn chsng ldng pair: rdn along over 2f out: wknd wl over 1f out*	(p) PatrickMathers 1	70	**20/1**

2m 7.85s (0.85) **Going Correction** +0.15s/f (Good) — **8** Ran SP% **116.8**
Speed ratings (Par 107): **102,100,99,98,97 96,96,93**
Tote Swingers 1&2 £5.90, 2&3 £4.90, 1&3 £2.80 CSF £25.33 CT £68.29 TOTE £3.40: £1.10, £2.60, £1.10; EX 30.70.
Owner Abdulla Al Mansoori **Bred** Grangecon Stud **Trained** Middleham Moor, N Yorks

FOCUS

Not as classy a race as the conditions would have one believe, as the top-weight was rated 11lb below the ceiling. The winner made all at a decent pace and recorded another best effort.

NOTEBOOK

Universal(IRE) was rather left alone to do his own thing in front, which is a dangerous thing to do with a Mark Johnston-trained runner, especially one who's in form and progressive. For all that he had the run of the race, it wouldn't be a surprise if there's more to come from him as he's only run four times for the yard. (op 11-4 tchd 5-2)

Chapter Seven, who has been gelded since he last ran, didn't do badly but he could have probably done with the ground being a little easier. (op 8-1)

Sheikhzayedroad was held up in last place off what was far from a hectic gallop, which made things tough when he was asked to make up ground. He can do better in a stronger run race. (op 9-2)

Daghash is another who would have appreciated a better gallop, but he is handicapped up to his best. (tchd 8-1)

Watheeq(USA) might need proper fast ground on turf to be seen to best effect. (tchd 11-2)

Spirit Of The Law(IRE) was reined back to race in the final pair and failed to land a blow. He probably needs softer ground. (tchd 9-1)

Glittering Gold was well positioned on the leader's shoulder to attack, but his brief challenge came to nothing and this was rather disappointing on his return from a couple of months off. (tchd 7-1 and 8-1)

5821 BETFRED MOBILE SPORTS H'CAP — 5f

3:45 (3:45) (Class 5) (0-75,75) 3-Y-0+ — **£2,911** (£866; £432; £216) **Stalls** Low

Form	Pos	Dist	Horse	Jockey	RPR	SP
000	1		**Ingleby Star (IRE)**[17] 5223 7-8-8 **65** — (Ian McInnes) *in tch: hdwy wl over 1f out: rdn ent fnl f: sn swtchd lft and str run to ld last 100yds*	(p) PaulPickard(3) 2	76	**12/1**
1155	2	1 ½	**Fear Nothing**[12] 5412 5-9-4 **72** — (David O'Meara) *led to 1/2-way: cl up: rdn and ev ch appr fnl f: sn drvn and kpt on same pce*	DanielTudhope 5	78	**7/2**[1]
0333	3	½	**Ashpan Sam**[23] 4985 3-9-3 **72** — (John Spearing) *dwlt and towards rr: hdwy wl over 1f out: rdn and styd on fnl f: nrst fin*	CathyGannon 11	76+	**13/2**
0103	4	nk	**Sleepy Blue Ocean**[13] 5388 6-9-2 **70** — (John Balding) *cl up: rdn to ld jst over 1f out: drvn and hdd wl ins fnl f: wknd towards fin*	(p) RobertWinston 3	73	**9/2**[3]
501	5	shd	**Diamond Blue**[16] 5257 4-9-3 **71** — (Richard Whitaker) *in tch: hdwy 2f out: sn rdn to chse ldrs: one pce fnl f*	(p) AmyRyan 6	74	**4/1**[2]
5565	6	¾	**Northern Bolt**[3] 5740 7-8-9 **63** — (Ian McInnes) *s.i.s: a bhd*	PatrickMathers 4	63	**16/1**
1400	7	¾	**Alive And Kicking**[63] 3612 4-9-7 **75** — (James Bethell) *in tch on outer: hdwy to chse ldrs 2f out: sn rdn and wknd over 1f out*	JamieSpencer 7	72	**7/1**
4152	8	¾	**Liberty Island (IRE)**[35] 4591 7-9-7 **75** — (Ian Semple) *cl up on outer: led 1/2-way: rdn: edgd rt and hdd over 1f out: sn wknd*	(p) DuranFentiman 12	69	**15/2**
0000	9	3 ¾	**Choc'A'Moca (IRE)**[17] 5223 5-8-8 **62** — (Paul Midgley) *prom: rdn along 1/2-way: sn wknd*	(v) MickyFenton 10	43	**25/1**
001-	10	13	**Captain Royale (IRE)**[311] 7104 7-9-7 **75** — (Tracy Waggott) *chsd ldrs: rdn along 2f out: sn wknd*	(p) PhillipMakin 8		**20/1**

1m 3.32s (-0.18) **Going Correction** +0.05s/f (Good)
WFA 3 from 4yo+ 1lb — **10** Ran SP% **120.2**
Speed ratings (Par 103): **103,100,99,99,99 97,96,95,89,68**
Tote Swingers 1&2 £18.10, 2&3 £6.10, 1&3 £34.00 CSF £55.54 CT £315.60 TOTE £20.40: £3.70, £1.80, £2.20; EX 101.00.
Owner Stephen Hackney **Bred** Pat Cosgrove **Trained** Catwick, E Yorks

FOCUS

They were spread across the track here but the first two raced closest to the far-side rail. It was sound run and the winner showed his first real form this year.

5822 BETFRED BEVERLEY BULLET SPRINT STKS (LISTED RACE) — 5f

4:15 (4:18) (Class 1) 3-Y-0+ — **£18,944** (£7,164; £3,580; £1,788) **Stalls** Low

Form	Pos	Dist	Horse	Jockey	RPR	SP
4620	1		**Borderlescott**[28] 4802 10-9-0 **102** — (Robin Bastiman) *chsd ldrs: hdwy on inner 2f out: rdn to ld 1f out: styd on strly*	FrederikTylicki 1	111	**8/1**[3]
0320	2	1	**Masamah (IRE)**[8] 5561 6-9-0 **108** — (Kevin Ryan) *cl up towards outer: led 1/2-way: edgd lft towards stands' rail wl over 1f out: sn rdn and hdd appr fnl f: kpt on towards fin*	(b) JamieSpencer 7	107	**7/2**[1]
2040	3	½	**Confessional**[8] 5561 5-9-0 **106** — (Tim Easterby) *towards rr: hdwy wl over 1f out: sn rdn and styd on fnl f: nrst fin*	(be) PaulMulrennan 12	106	**12/1**
2020	4	hd	**Pabusar**[29] 4762 4-9-0 **106** — (Ralph Beckett) *in rr: rdn along 1/2-way: hdwy over 1f out: styd on fnl f: nrst fin*	HarryBentley 10	105	**9/1**
0010	5	¾	**Elusivity (IRE)**[29] 4762 4-9-0 **106** — (Brian Meehan) *trckd ldrs on outer: smooth hdwy 2f out: sn ev ch tl rdn and one pce ent fnl f*	JamieMackay 8	102	**10/1**
1230	6	1 ½	**Free Zone**[22] 5067 3-8-13 **105** — (Bryan Smart) *in rr: rdn along 1/2-way: hdwy wl over 1f out: styd on fnl f: nrst fin*	PhillipMakin 11	97	**12/1**
0531	7	nk	**Dinkum Diamond (IRE)**[18] 5204 4-9-0 **102** — (Henry Candy) *in tch: swtchd rt 2f out: rdn and nt clr run over 1f out: styd on fnl f: nrst fin*	CathyGannon 9	99+	**10/1**
6001	8	nk	**Pepper Lane**[14] 5370 5-8-9 **106** — (David O'Meara) *towards rr: rdn along and hdwy wl over 1f out: n.m.r and no imp fnl f*	DanielTudhope 6	90	**13/2**[2]
0650	9	1 ¼	**Ponty Acclaim (IRE)**[10] 5487 3-8-8 **100** — (Tim Easterby) *in tch: hdwy 2f out: sn rdn and no imp appr fnl f*	DuranFentiman 5	85	**13/2**[2]
3505	10	½	**Noble Storm (USA)**[18] 5204 6-9-0 **103** — (Ed McMahon) *cl up on wd outside: effrt and ev ch 2f out: sn rdn and wknd appr fnl f*	AdrianNicholls 16	88	**33/1**
020-	11	¾	**Moorhouse Lad**[350] 6164 9-9-0 **94** — (Garry Moss) *led on wd outside: hdd 1/2-way: sn rdn along and wknd wl over 1f out*	PatrickMathers 13	86	**100/1**
-004	12	shd	**Move In Time**[18] 5204 4-9-0 **99** — (Bryan Smart) *sn rdn along to chse ldrs and cl up after 1f: rdn and hung rt wl over 1f out: sn wknd*	TomEaves 4	85	**10/1**
0012	13	3	**Six Wives**[7] 5576 5-8-9 **80** — (Scott Dixon) *prom towards inner: rdn along over 2f out: sn wknd*	NickyMackay 2	69	**33/1**
-461	14	1 ½	**Cheviot (USA)**[94] 2602 6-9-0 **100** — (Ian Semple) *midfield: rdn along and hld whn hmpd and edgd rt appr fnl f*	(p) RobertWinston 3	69	**20/1**

1m 2.42s (-1.08) **Going Correction** +0.05s/f (Good)
WFA 3 from 4yo+ 1lb — **14** Ran SP% **124.3**
Speed ratings (Par 111): **110,108,107,107,106 103,103,102,100,99 98,98,93,91**
Tote Swingers 1&2 £7.20, 2&3 £17.30, 1&3 £20.40 CSF £36.18 TOTE £9.80: £3.50, £2.00, £4.60; EX 30.60 Trifecta £840.90 Pool: £43,390.74 - 37.18 winning units..

Owner James Edgar & William Donaldson **Bred** J W P Clark **Trained** Cowthorpe, N Yorks

FOCUS
A really competitive heat but again the draw proved crucial, with Borderlescott drawn in stall one and racing closest to the favoured far-side rail. He posted his best form this year, with Masamah close to his recent Goodwood form.

NOTEBOOK
Borderlescott got a lead into the race from Six Wives before taking over and seeing his race out strongly. Understandably, he's not as good as he was at his peak, but he's clearly still got more than enough ability to be competitive at this level. Whether he can follow in the footsteps of last year's winner, Tangerine Trees, and go on and win the Prix de l'Abbaye is more open to doubt, but either way the French Group 1 is likely to be his target now. Incidentally, he has a surprisingly good record when ridden by a rider for the first time, his form figures now reading 611222131821 under those circumstances. (op 9-1)
Masamah(IRE) showed plenty of speed towards the centre of the track and ended up nearer the stands' rail at the finish. Possibly beaten by the draw, he might get the chance to reverse the form in Paris. (op 5-1)
Confessional was back at a more realistic level and did best of the hold-up horses. (op 10-1)
Pabusar was also dropping in class and put up a better effort, keeping on well at the finish. (tchd 10-1)
Elusivity(IRE) did his usual thing and travelled like a dream but didn't find much for pressure.
Free Zone has won from the front on more than one occasion in the past, but he struggled to go the pace early on here and was in last place at halfway, before staying on all too late. (op 16-1)
Dinkum Diamond(IRE), third in this last year, got the better of Masamah last time out, but he was 8lb worse off with that rival this time and couldn't confirm the form. He was short of room in the closing stages, though, and would have finished closer with a clear run. (op 9-1)
Pepper Lane had the hood on again but she didn't break as well as at Ripon and couldn't get to the front this time. (tchd 6-1 and 7-1)
Ponty Acclaim(IRE) travelled into the race quite well but didn't find under pressure what she'd promised. (op 7-1 tchd 6-1)

5823 BETFRED "BONUS KING BINGO" MAIDEN STKS — 5f
4:50 (4:54) (Class 5) 3-Y-0+ **£2,911** (£866; £432; £216) **Stalls** Low

Form				RPR
4	**1**		**Avon Breeze**[14] 5340 3-8-12 0 ... AmyRyan 4 (Richard Whitaker) *dwlt and in rr: hdwy 1/2-way: rdn to ld appr fnl f: sn clr: comf* **4/6**[1]	70+
0-60	**2**	*5*	**Absolute Fun (IRE)**[15] 5312 3-8-12 50 ... DanielTudhope 5 (Tim Easterby) *led: rdn along 2f out: drvn and hdd appr fnl f: one pce* **8/1**[3]	52
2426	**3**	*3 1/2*	**Elegant Girl (IRE)**[28] 4807 3-8-12 67 ...(p) DuranFentiman 9 (Tim Easterby) *in tch: hdwy 2f out: sn rdn and styd on to take modest 3rd ins fnl f* **5/2**[2]	39
5600	**4**	*nk*	**Queen's Princess**[24] 4957 4-8-13 40 ...(p) PaulMulrennan 7 (John Wainwright) *cl up: rdn along 2f out: grad wknd* **40/1**	38
000	**5**	*1/2*	**Busy Bimbo (IRE)**[8] 5542 3-8-5 43 ... JordanHibberd(7) 1 (Alan Berry) *chsd ldrs on inner: rdn along wl over 1f out: sn one pce* **25/1**	36
4404	**6**	*1 3/4*	**Benidorm**[8] 5549 4-8-13 52 ...(v) AdamCarter(5) 2 (John Wainwright) *a in rr* **12/1**	35
00	**7**	*5*	**Kuraanda**[51] 3990 3-8-12 0 ... PatrickMathers 6 (John Wainwright) *chsd ldrs: rdn along over 2f out: sn wknd* **80/1**	12
	8	*7*	**Poppanella (IRE)** 3-8-7 0 ... DarylByrne(5) 3 (Lawrence Mullaney) *s.i.s: a in rr* **12/1**	
06	**9**	*3/4*	**Pilarcita**[47] 4144 3-8-5 0 ... JacobButterfield(7) 8 (Ollie Pears) *prom: chsd ldr after 2f: rdn along 2f out: sn wknd* **40/1**	

1m 4.2s (0.70) **Going Correction** +0.05s/f (Good)
WFA 3 from 4yo 1lb **9** Ran SP% **125.0**
Speed ratings (Par 103): **96,88,82,81,81 78,70,59,57**
Tote Swingers 1&2 £3.30, 2&3 £3.90, 1&3 £1.40 CSF £8.22 TOTE £1.40: £1.10, £2.10, £1.20; EX 10.30.
Owner Grange Park Racing II & Partner **Bred** Hellwood Stud Farm **Trained** Scarcroft, W Yorks

FOCUS
A weak maiden. The level of the form is a bit fluid, with the favourite disappointing.
Kuraanda Official explanation: jockey said filly ran green

5824 STARS OF THE FUTURE APPRENTICE H'CAP — 1m 1f 207y
5:25 (5:26) (Class 6) (0-65,65) 4-Y-0+ **£2,070** (£616; £307; £153) **Stalls** Low

Form				RPR
5435	**1**		**Gadobout Dancer**[2] 5762 5-8-4 **51** ... KevinLundie(3) 10 (Tony Coyle) *trckd ldrs: hdwy to chse ldr 1/2-way: led wl over 2f out: rdn wl over 1f out: drvn and kpt on gamely fnl f* **10/1**	59
0001	**2**	*1/2*	**Highlife Dancer**[6] 5638 4-9-1 **62** 6ex ...(v) RobertTart(3) 7 (Mick Channon) *chsd ldrs: hdwy over 2f out: rdn wl over 1f out: kpt on u.p fnl f* **9/2**[2]	69
1440	**3**	*3/4*	**Cosmic Moon**[33] 4641 4-8-10 **59** ... EireannCagney(5) 4 (Richard Fahey) *dwlt: hld up towards rr: swtchd to outer and hdwy over 2f out: rdn to chse ldrs over 1f out: ch ent fnl f: kpt on same pce* **13/2**	65
521	**4**	*2 3/4*	**Celtic Step**[42] 4350 8-8-8 **55** ... FrancescaWoliter(3) 3 (Peter Niven) *prom: rdn along wl over 2f out: drvn and kpt on same pce fr over 1f out* **9/2**[2]	55
0032	**5**	*1 3/4*	**Sally Friday (IRE)**[24] 4958 4-8-4 **53** ...(p) KevinStott(5) 1 (Edwin Tuer) *hld up in rr: swtchd to outer and hdwy wl over 1f out: sn rdn and kpt on fnl f: nrst fin* **11/2**[3]	50
0234	**6**	*1 1/4*	**Sangar**[14] 5372 4-9-6 **64** ... JacobButterfield 2 (Ollie Pears) *trckd ldrs on inner: hdwy 3f out: rdn 2f out: no imp* **5/2**[1]	58
5203	**7**	*1 1/4*	**Harare**[7] 5585 11-9-5 **63** ...(v) GemmaTutty 12 (Karen Tutty) *s.i.s: a towards rr* **14/1**	55
1040	**8**	*2 3/4*	**Ptolomeos**[42] 4349 9-8-10 **54** ow2 ...(p) ConorHarrison 5 (Sean Regan) *nvr nr ldrs* **22/1**	40
0-00	**9**	*3 3/4*	**Gumnd (IRE)**[38] 4455 5-8-4 **51** oh6 ... PaulMcGiff(3) 8 (Chris Grant) *led: rdn along over 3f out: hdd wl over 2f out and sn wknd* **50/1**	30
0-6	**10**	*5*	**Cross The Boss (IRE)**[31] 4715 5-8-9 **53** ...(t) DavidSimmonson 6 (Ben Haslam) *t.k.h: chsd ldrs: hdwy 3f out: rdn over 2f out: sn wknd* **16/1**	22

2m 8.77s (1.77) **Going Correction** +0.15s/f (Good) **10** Ran SP% **121.6**
Speed ratings (Par 101): **98,97,97,94,93 92,91,89,86,82**
Tote Swingers 1&2 £6.60, 2&3 £13.40, 1&3 £8.90 CSF £57.07 CT £325.24 TOTE £9.50: £3.10, £2.00, £2.20; EX 49.80.
Owner White Rose & Thistle **Bred** P Cutler **Trained** Norton, N Yorks
■ Stewards' Enquiry : Kevin Lundie two-day ban: used whip above permitted level (Sep 16-17)

FOCUS
An ordinary apprentice handicap. The form makes sense.
Ptolomeos Official explanation: jockey said gelding lost its action
T/Plt: £111.50 to a £1 stake. Pool: £73,300.64 - 479.60 winning tickets. T/Qpdt: £13.20 to a £1 stake. Pool: £4,720.31 - 263.58 winning tickets. JR

5331 CHESTER (L-H)
Saturday, September 1

OFFICIAL GOING: Good (good to soft in places; 6.9)
Wind: Light, half against Weather: Fine

5825 BRITISH STALLION STUDS SUPPORTING BRITISH RACING E B F MAIDEN STKS — 7f 2y
1:55 (1:58) (Class 4) 2-Y-O **£5,175** (£1,540; £769; £384) **Stalls** Low

Form				RPR
563	**1**		**Becky Lou (USA)**[37] 4494 2-8-12 88 ... FrannyNorton 1 (Jeremy Noseda) *sn dropped to midfield: pushed along and hdwy 2f out: swtchd rt over 1f out: r.o to ld 150yds out: pushed out whn in command towards fin* **6/5**[1]	73+
0322	**2**	*1 1/2*	**Madame Elizabeth**[19] 5153 2-8-12 75 ... RussKennemore 4 (Reg Hollinshead) *chsd ldrs: pushed along over 2f out: rdn and nt qckn over 1f out: styd on to take 2nd fnl 110yds: no imp on wnr* **13/2**[3]	69
00	**3**	*1 1/2*	**Mirlo Blanco (IRE)**[14] 5331 2-9-3 0 ... DavidNolan 2 (Richard Fahey) *in tch: rdn and nt qckn over 1f out: checked and swtchd rt 110yds out: styd on towards fin* **50/1**	70
2503	**4**	*hd*	**Red Cobra (IRE)**[26] 4877 2-9-3 72 ... PJMcDonald 9 (Tim Easterby) *w ldr: rdn whn stl chalng over 1f out: styd on same pce fnl 100yds* **14/1**	69
2	**5**	*3/4*	**White Coppice**[14] 5331 2-9-3 0 ... TonyHamilton 5 (Richard Fahey) *towards rr: rdn over 1f out: styd on ins fnl f: nt clr run 110yds out: nt pce to chal* **4/1**[2]	68
5	**6**	*2 3/4*	**Mudaawem (USA)**[17] 5221 2-9-3 0 ... JoeFanning 6 (Mark Johnston) *led: rdn whn pressed over 1f out: hdd fnl 150yds: eased whn btn fnl 75yds* **4/1**[2]	62
06	**7**	*4*	**Big Thunder**[19] 5162 2-9-3 0 ... StevieDonohoe 8 (Sir Mark Prescott Bt) *missed break: pushed along early: sme hdwy over 4f out: pushed along 3f out: wknd over 2f out* **33/1**	49
6	**8**	*21*	**Perfect Pasture**[23] 4995 2-9-3 0 ... GrahamLee 3 (Michael Easterby) *racd keenly: hld up: struggling over 3f out: lft bhd over 2f out* **20/1**	

1m 29.04s (2.54) **Going Correction** +0.425s/f (Yiel) **8** Ran SP% **115.1**
Speed ratings (Par 97): **102,100,98,98,97 94,89,65**
Tote Swingers 1&2 £1.90, 2&3 £28.80, 1&3 £15.50 CSF £9.65 TOTE £2.60: £1.10, £1.90, £8.60; EX 8.00.
Owner C Fox **Bred** Clabes Bloodstock & Ashford Stud **Trained** Newmarket, Suffolk

FOCUS
Rail at innermost position and all distances as advertised. The going was changed to good, good to soft in places, (from good to soft) before the first race took place. Franny Norton said after it had been run that "It's on the easy side", while Patrick McDonald reported "It's a bit tacky and lifeless." The winner did not need to be at her best to score, while the runner-up and fourth set the level.

NOTEBOOK
Becky Lou(USA), by far the best of these on RPRs, got the job done but not in eyecatching style. Slowly into stride from a perfect draw, she chased the leaders until finding a way through to get to the front. One would imagine connections may try and get some black type with her if they can this season. (op 11-8)
Madame Elizabeth, back on grass after going close at Kempton, made the winner work for success and maintained her consistent profile. She surely has a victory of some description in her as a 2-y-o. (op 6-1)
Mirlo Blanco(IRE) had been well beaten on his previous two starts, so this seemed a lot better. Connections will have to hope the handicapper doesn't take the form too literally, however, considering his previous efforts earned him RPRs of 44 and 26.
Red Cobra(IRE), trying 7f for the first time, was the most experienced runner in the field and stayed on after pressing the early leader. (op 16-1)
White Coppice, described by his trainer as a big, tall raw horse, had shaped nicely over C&D recently on his first start, but still ran as though needing the experience here. He did meet a bit of trouble in running but it didn't cost him a lot of ground. (op 7-2 tchd 9-2)
Mudaawem(USA) attracted market support but failed to get home after getting away from his stall sharply and leading (op 11-2 tchd 6-1)

5826 GOLDEN SQUARE SHOPPING CENTRE WARRINGTON H'CAP (LISTED RACE) — 1m 5f 89y
2:30 (2:31) (Class 1) (0-110,106) 3-Y-0+
£19,848 (£7,525; £3,766; £1,876; £941; £472) **Stalls** Low

Form				RPR
-000	**1**		**Tominator**[7] 5600 5-9-0 **96** ... GrahamGibbons 7 (Reg Hollinshead) *stdd s: sn swtchd lft: hld up: hdwy over 3f out: rdn and wnt 2nd over 1f out: rdr sn dropped whip: r.o ins fnl f to ld towards fin* **7/1**[2]	104
4431	**2**	*nk*	**Communicator**[14] 5333 4-8-11 **93** ... RichardMullen 6 (Andrew Balding) *hld up: hdwy on outer over 3f out: led jst over 2f out: rdn over 1f out: hdd towards fin* **9/2**[1]	101
5062	**3**	*3/4*	**Scrapper Smith (IRE)**[8] 5540 6-8-10 **92** oh2 ... PJMcDonald 10 (Alistair Whillans) *hld up: nt clr run fr 2f out tl over 1f out: prog ins fnl f: r.o: gng on at fin* **16/1**	99+
0120	**4**	*1 1/4*	**Quiz Mistress**[30] 4738 4-8-12 **94** ... MartinHarley 2 (Hughie Morrison) *midfield: hdwy 4f out: nt clr run over 1f out: styd on ins fnl f: nt rch ldrs* **8/1**[3]	99+
3505	**5**	*1 1/2*	**Midsummer Sun**[29] 4759 4-9-6 **102** ... TomQueally 9 (Sir Henry Cecil) *upset in stalls: midfield: rdn along over 5f out: hdwy on outer over 3f out: chsd ldrs over 1f out: no ex fnl 100yds* **11/1**	105
2155	**6**	*4*	**Area Fifty One**[7] 5600 4-9-4 **100** ... DavidNolan 11 (Richard Fahey) *midfield: hdwy 4f out: rdn whn chsng ldrs 2f out: one pce ins fnl f* **7/1**[2]	97
-110	**7**	*1 1/4*	**Rosslyn Castle**[21] 5089 3-8-4 **96** ... KieranO'Neill 14 (Roger Charlton) *hld up: rdn over 2f out: hdwy over 1f out: one pce and no imp ins fnl f* **9/1**	91
2-30	**8**	*3*	**Icon Dream (IRE)**[7] 5600 5-9-3 **99** ... GrahamLee 1 (Jim Goldie) *led: rdn and hdd jst over 2f out: wknd fnl f* **7/1**[2]	89
1245	**9**	*3/4*	**Naseem Alyasmeen (IRE)**[27] 4848 3-8-4 **96** ... JoeFanning 12 (Mick Channon) *hld up in midfield: hdwy 4f out: nt clr run over 2f out: sn lost pl: btn over 1f out* **25/1**	85
0030	**10**	*3 1/4*	**Never Can Tell (IRE)**[10] 5491 5-9-3 **99** ... FrannyNorton 4 (Jamie Osborne) *w ldr: rdn over 4f out: wknd fnl f: eased whn wl btn fnl 100yds* **10/1**	83
-040	**11**	*11*	**Mohedian Lady (IRE)**[56] 3856 4-9-7 **103** ... StevieDonohoe 5 (Sir Mark Prescott Bt) *trckd ldrs: rdn over 2f out: sn wknd* **20/1**	71
2	**12**	*22*	**Meganisi (IRE)**[105] 2267 5-9-10 **106** ... StephenCraine 3 (Rebecca Curtis) *trckd ldrs: rdn over 5f out: wknd qckly over 3f out* **20/1**	41

140 **13** *51* **Bolivia (GER)**[30] 4738 6-8-10 **92** oh2..........................(t) AdamBeschizza 8
(Lucy Wadham) *trckd ldrs: pushed along 6f out: rdn and wknd over 4f out: t.o* **40/1**

2m 54.34s (1.64) **Going Correction** +0.425s/f (Yiel)
WFA 3 from 4yo+ 10lb **13** Ran SP% **115.9**
Speed ratings (Par 111): **111,110,110,109,108 106,105,103,103,101 94,80,49**
Tote Swingers 1&2 £6.10, 2&3 £23.50, 1&3 £43.50 CSF £35.26 CT £489.73 TOTE £9.10: £1.90, £2.20, £5.70; EX 33.40 Trifecta £520.20 Pool: £1,610.00 - 2.29 winning units..
Owner Mrs Susy Haslehurst **Bred** Mrs S L Brimble **Trained** Upper Longdon, Staffs

FOCUS
A strong staying contest, with some solid handicap and Group race form represented. The first three home were out the back early but the form seems sound with the runner-up to his latest form, backed up by the fourth.

NOTEBOOK
Tominator got into the clear at the right time here and won by a narrow margin despite his jockey dropping his whip over 1f out. We know all about this tough grey now, and he should always be respected in big handicaps when conditions suit. It was interesting to hear afterwards that the gelding is potentially up for sale. (op 6-1)
Communicator ◆, up 9l for his wide-margin victory here over 1m4f, was one of the first hold-up horses to commit on turning in and looked likely to hold on. However, his stride started to shorten late on and he was mugged close to the line. Clearly in good heart, he remains to a horse to be interested in for the short-term at least. (tchd 4-1)
Scrapper Smith(IRE) looks a bit high in the weights and had an awkward draw here, but he came home strongly towards the inside rail after having to wait for some gaps to open.
Quiz Mistress had struggled in Class 1 events previously, but flew home in this one after being locked in a pocket, like the third, at a crucial stage of the race. Official explanation: jockey said filly was denied a clear run (op 10-1 tchd 11-1)
Midsummer Sun, up 6lb despite being well beaten in what was a hot Group 3 last time, didn't help his cause by rearing in the stalls just before the off, but he was still bang there with a chance a furlong out before not finding any extra. He probably isn't the easiest horse to place to have an obvious winning opportunity. (op 9-1)
Area Fifty One finished in front of Tominator the previous weekend but wasn't able to confirm the form. He did start from stall 11, so has that as a potential excuse. (op 6-1)
Rosslyn Castle, a previous course winner, probably wasn't helped by the draw and appeared to race keen while in rear. He should be given another chance. (op 8-1)
Bolivia(GER) Official explanation: trainer said mare was unsuited by the track

5827 CHESTER STANDARD H'CAP 7f 122y
3:05 (3:06) (Class 2) 3-Y-0+
£28,012 (£8,388; £4,194; £2,097; £1,048; £526) **Stalls** Low

Form RPR
0151 **1** **Verse Of Love**[4] 5705 3-7-8 **83** 6ex.................................. NoelGarbutt(7) 3 92
(David Evans) *mde all: rdn over 2f out: hrd pressed ins fnl f: jst hld on* **11/2[1]**

1-42 **2** *shd* **Strictly Silver (IRE)**[9] 5517 3-8-8 **90**................................ JimmyQuinn 13 98+
(Alan Bailey) *dwlt: sn swtchd lft: hld up: hdwy over 3f out: nt clr run over 2f out: r.o strly ins fnl f: tk 2nd cl home: jst failed* **13/2[2]**

0402 **3** *1/2* **Bannock (IRE)**[7] 5597 3-9-10 **106**.................................... JoeFanning 8 113
(Mark Johnston) *trckd ldrs: rdn 2f out: wnt 2nd and chalng ins fnl f: lost 2nd and no ex cl home* **15/2**

5003 **4** *1 1/4* **Alejandro (IRE)**[14] 5334 3-8-7 **89**..................................... BarryMcHugh 4 93
(Richard Fahey) *trckd ldrs: wnt 2nd 2f out: lost 2nd ins fnl f: styd on same pce fnl 100yds* **10/1**

0356 **5** *3/4* **Kyllachy Star**[14] 5369 6-8-9 **86**.. FrannyNorton 9 88
(Richard Fahey) *midfield: pushed along 2f out: hdwy to chse ldrs over 1f out: styd on same pce fnl 100yds* **9/1**

0000 **6** *4* **Capaill Liath (IRE)**[14] 5368 4-8-11 **88**...........................(b[1]) GrahamLee 14 80+
(Kevin Ryan) *dwlt: sn swtchd lft: hld up: pushed along over 2f out: outpcd: styd on ins fnl f: nt trble ldrs* **20/1**

6130 **7** *nk* **Dr Red Eye**[15] 5314 4-8-3 **81** ow2.........................(p) AdamBeschizza(3) 17 74
(Scott Dixon) *w wnr tl rdn 2f out: outpcd over 1f out: dropped away fnl 100yds* **40/1**

0600 **8** *3/4* **Viva Ronaldo (IRE)**[32] 4689 6-8-1 **84** ow1...................... LauraBarry(7) 6 74
(Richard Fahey) *hld up: rdn whn hmpd over 1f out: kpt on ins fnl f: nt trble ldrs* **16/1**

1000 **9** *2* **Grissom (IRE)**[14] 5370 6-9-1 **92**... AndrewElliott 1 76
(Tim Easterby) *in tch: pushed along 2f out: rdn to chse ldrs over 1f out: no imp: wknd fnl 100yds* **16/1**

5425 **10** *shd* **Galician**[14] 5363 3-8-9 **91**.. LiamJones 10 75
(Mark Johnston) *in tch: pushed along and wknd over 2f out* **7/1[3]**

1130 **11** *1/2* **King Of Eden (IRE)**[14] 5342 6-8-11 **88**......................... GrahamGibbons 11 71
(Eric Alston) *midfield: pushed along 4f out: sn lost pl: rdn into midfield again over 1f out: eased whn no imp fnl 75yds* **33/1**

2550 **12** *1* **Dubai Dynamo**[14] 5342 7-9-0 **94**..................................... DaleSwift(3) 2 74
(Ruth Carr) *missed break: hld up: nt clr run over 2f out: nvr able to get on terms* **16/1**

0300 **13** *1/2* **Imperial Djay (IRE)**[9] 5517 7-9-2 **93**............................... PJMcDonald 7 72
(Ruth Carr) *hld up: rdn 3f out: no imp whn nt clr ins fnl f: sn eased* **14/1**

3040 **14** *12* **Powerful Presence (IRE)**[7] 5572 6-9-0 **91**.................... TomQueally 12 40
(David O'Meara) *prom: rdn over 3f out: wknd over 2f out: eased whn wl btn fnl f* **16/1**

4020 **15** *18* **Brae Hill (IRE)**[42] 4321 6-9-8 **99**.................................... TonyHamilton 5 3
(Richard Fahey) *midfield tl wknd over 2f out: t.o* **9/1**

1m 35.44s (1.64) **Going Correction** +0.425s/f (Yiel)
WFA 3 from 4yo+ 5lb **15** Ran SP% **122.4**
Speed ratings (Par 109): **108,107,107,106,105 101,101,100,98,98 97,96,96,84,66**
Tote Swingers 1&2 £11.80, 2&3 £6.80, 1&3 £8.60 CSF £39.11 CT £282.98 TOTE £5.50: £1.90, £2.90, £2.60; EX 54.30 Trifecta £189.90 Pool: £1,360.52 - 5.30 winning units..
Owner Wayne Clifford **Bred** Mrs S Clifford **Trained** Pandy, Monmouths

FOCUS
Very few seemed to get into this competitive heat despite the early pace looking particularly strong. The form is rated around the principals with the fourth the best guide.

NOTEBOOK
Verse Of Love, raised 6lb for his Epsom success, but ridden by a 7lb claimer to help offset the penalty, was always going to take a lot of stopping if breaking from an advantageous draw, and the gelding did just enough to hang on once gaining the lead. One would suspect that he'll need to improve again to collect the hat-trick considering he had a low weight here from a good draw. (op 6-1)
Strictly Silver(IRE) ◆ posted another solid performance after not finding a lot of room roughly 2f out. He hasn't stopped progressing and was definitely a bit unfortunate not to get up.
Bannock(IRE) has maintained a smart level of form since the end of June, most recently in the Listed City Of York Stakes, and emerges as the best horse in the race considering he was giving so much weight away to the first and second. (op 8-1 tchd 7-1)
Alejandro(IRE) travelled for a long way on the bridle just behind the leaders. His turn doesn't look far away if running to a similar level.
Kyllachy Star, a dual C&D winner, is fairly treated on his victories and showed there is still races to be won with him after this performance. (op 17-2 tchd 8-1)
Capaill Liath(IRE), on a fair mark and with blinkers tried for the first time, was the best of those who ran on all too late.
Galician, who'd run over 6f the last twice, was beaten rounding the final bend. (op 9-1)
Brae Hill(IRE) was basically pulled up before the race got serious. (op 10-1 tchd 11-1)

5828 IRISH STALLION FARMS E B F COMBERMERE FILLIES' CONDITIONS STKS 6f 18y
3:40 (3:42) (Class 2) 2-Y-0 **£11,341** (£3,394; £1,697; £849; £423) **Stalls** Low

Form RPR
1 **1** **Queen Aggie (IRE)**[12] 5424 2-8-12 77.................................. PJMcDonald 3 87+
(David Evans) *midfield: hdwy over 1f out: r.o to ld fnl 110yds: in command cl home* **7/1**

1 **2** *1 1/2* **Hoodna (IRE)**[52] 3959 2-9-1 0... FrannyNorton 5 86
(Saeed Bin Suroor) *trckd ldrs: led jst over 1f out: rdn and hdd fnl 110yds: no ex cl home* **11/8[1]**

2 **3** *3 1/2* **Coincidently**[14] 5360 2-8-12 0.. TomQueally 8 72
(Alan Bailey) *prom: ev ch over 1f out: nt qckn: styd on same pce and no imp ins fnl f* **4/1[3]**

3031 **4** *3/4* **Sylvia Pankhurst (IRE)**[15] 5292 2-8-12 73......................... JoeFanning 6 70
(David C Griffiths) *broke wl: trckd ldrs after: rdn over 1f out: one pce fnl f* **20/1**

0031 **5** *3* **Mandy Layla (IRE)**[14] 5332 2-8-12 82................................ GrahamLee 7 61
(Bryan Smart) *sn led: rdn and hdd jst over 1f out: wknd fnl 150yds* **3/1[2]**

3030 **6** *5* **All On Red (IRE)**[28] 4820 2-9-1 88................................. StevieDonohoe 1 49
(Tobias B P Coles) *towards rr: rdr dropped whip: pushed along and outpcd over 2f out: nvr a threat* **9/1**

00 **7** *4* **Pleasant Moment**[12] 5410 2-8-12 0................................... AndrewElliott 4 34
(Tom Dascombe) *forced wd sn after s: a wl bhd* **100/1**

8 *4 1/2* **Beacon Tarn** 2-8-9 0.. TonyHamilton 2 17
(Eric Alston) *rn green: rn wd sn after s: a bhd: nvr on terms* **25/1**

1m 16.13s (2.33) **Going Correction** +0.425s/f (Yiel) **8** Ran SP% **119.2**
Speed ratings (Par 98): **101,99,94,93,89 82,77,71**
Tote Swingers 1&2 £5.40, 2&3 £1.80, 1&3 £4.40 CSF £17.67 TOTE £12.50: £4.40, £1.10, £1.10; EX 32.80 Trifecta £191.90 Pool: £1,787.03 - 6.89 winning units..
Owner Shropshire Wolves 4 **Bred** Mrs Marion Daly **Trained** Pandy, Monmouths

FOCUS
An interesting contest, which brought together a mixture of form, but it looks straightforward and sound with the fourth the best guide.

NOTEBOOK
Queen Aggie(IRE) comfortably won a claimer at Wolverhampton on her racecourse debut, ironically for owner Dr Marwan Koukash, who loves Chester winners, towards the end of last month, and was subsequently claimed out of Richard Fahey's stable for £10,000. That bit of business by David Evans appears shrewd, as the filly stayed on really strongly to get past and easily hold the market leader. There is a chance she could run at Kempton next week. (op 13-2 tchd 8-1)
Hoodna(IRE), off since winning on debut at Kempton in July, was trying grass for the first time in public and got the better of those that shared the pace early, but couldn't repel the final challenge. (op 6-4, tchd 13-8 in places)
Coincidently showed promise in a Newmarket maiden recently, and probably ran to that sort of level again after emerging from the widest stall. (op 11-2)
Sylvia Pankhurst(IRE) came into this off the back of a nursery victory (rated 68 for that success), but was made to look one paced here once off the bridle. (op 16-1)
Mandy Layla(IRE) didn't get home over this trip. (op 4-1)
All On Red(IRE)'s jockey dropped his whip over 2f out when being pushed along. Official explanation: trainer said rider lost whip 3f out (op 8-1)
Beacon Tarn, who cost 80,000gns as a yearling, is a half-sister to several winners, including smart handicapper Docofthebay, but was too green to do herself justice. (op 20-1)

5829 MANCHESTER AIRPORT H'CAP 5f 110y
4:20 (4:23) (Class 3) (0-95,92) 3-Y-0+ **£8,409** (£2,502; £1,250; £625) **Stalls** Low

Form RPR
3310 **1** **Ballista (IRE)**[14] 5368 4-9-5 **90**... FrannyNorton 14 106
(Tom Dascombe) *mde all: over 2 l clr over 1f out: r.o wl to extend advantage ins fnl f* **14/1**

1001 **2** *4* **Mayoman (IRE)**[54] 3903 7-9-3 **88**.................................(v) DavidNolan 9 91
(David O'Meara) *midfield: hdwy whn nt clr run over 1f out: styd on to take 2nd wl ins fnl f: no imp on wnr* **14/1**

6140 **3** *3/4* **Jedward (IRE)**[28] 4799 5-8-13 **87**.................................... JulieBurke(3) 1 88
(Kevin Ryan) *chsd ldrs: rdn over 1f out: styng on whn edgd lft ins fnl f: one pce fnl strides* **9/2[2]**

0043 **4** *3/4* **Sohraab**[8] 5530 8-9-3 **88**..(b) TomQueally 13 86
(Hughie Morrison) *towards rr: hdwy on outer over 1f out: styd on ins fnl f: nvr able to chal* **12/1**

0210 **5** *nk* **Partner (IRE)**[14] 5343 6-8-12 **86**.................................... GaryBartley(3) 12 83
(Noel Wilson) *midfield: pushed along over 4f out: hdwy over 1f out: kpt on ins fnl f* **33/1**

2010 **6** *shd* **Mappin Time (IRE)**[14] 5368 4-9-2 **87**.............................(p) TonyHamilton 2 84
(Tim Easterby) *hld up: hdwy on inner over 1f out: kpt on ins fnl f: nt trble ldrs* **12/1**

000 **7** *1 1/2* **Bathwick Bear (IRE)**[8] 5530 4-8-11 **82**........................ StevieDonohoe 7 74
(David Evans) *towards rr: pushed along over 2f out: kpt on into midfield ins fnl f: nvr trbld ldrs* **20/1**

000 **8** *1/2* **Excel Bolt**[25] 4924 4-9-3 **88**... RichardMullen 3 79
(Bryan Smart) *prom: rdn 2f out: outpcd by wnr over 1f out: wknd wl ins fnl f* **8/1[3]**

00 **9** *1/2* **Lexi's Hero (IRE)**[14] 5370 4-9-7 **92**............................(b) GrahamLee 4 81
(Kevin Ryan) *prom: rdn and outpcd by wnr over 1f out: wknd wl ins fnl f* **11/4[1]**

0000 **10** *hd* **Marine Commando**[14] 5343 4-8-11 **82**............................. PJMcDonald 6 70
(Ruth Carr) *bmpd s: in rr: u.p over 1f out: tried to keep on ins fnl f: nvr able to get on terms* **12/1**

0600 **11** *3/4* **Head Space (IRE)**[14] 5368 4-9-1 **89**................................ DaleSwift(3) 10 75
(Ruth Carr) *upset in stalls: hld up: rdn over 1f out: nvr able to get on terms* **18/1**

5630 **12** *nk* **Doctor Parkes**[10] 5487 6-9-4 **89**....................................... BarryMcHugh 5 74
(Eric Alston) *prom: pushed along 2f out: outpcd by wnr over 1f out: wknd ins fnl f* **8/1[3]**

5050 **13** *1 1/4* **Foxy Music**[38] 4454 8-9-5 **90**.. GrahamGibbons 8 71
(Eric Alston) *prom: squeezed out over 4f out: chsd ldrs after: rdn and hung rt over 2f out: sn wknd* **16/1**

2100 **14** *3/4* **Noodles Blue Boy**[14] 5343 6-8-12 **86**............................. LeeTopliss(3) 15 65
(Ollie Pears) *midfield: rdn over 2f out: wknd over 1f out* **25/1**

1m 7.76s (1.56) **Going Correction** +0.425s/f (Yiel) **14** Ran SP% **126.2**
Speed ratings (Par 107): **106,100,99,98,98 98,96,95,94,94 93,93,91,90**
Tote Swingers 1&2 £22.90, 2&3 £51.90, 1&3 £51.90 CSF £201.54 CT £1066.04 TOTE £32.90: £9.10, £3.70, £1.40; EX 263.40.
Owner Well Done Top Man Partnership **Bred** Sj Partnership **Trained** Malpas, Cheshire

FOCUS
Some useful sprinters lined up for what should have been a competitive heat, but the winner blitzed his rivals and recorded a personal best in doing so.

NOTEBOOK
Ballista(IRE), who appeared to have an disadvantageous draw to emerge from, flew out of the stalls, soon got to the lead after showing blinding speed and won easily. Unfortunately for connections, their gelding can probably expect a hefty rise in the handicap for this. (op 16-1)
Mayoman(IRE) ◆, off since winning in early July, didn't have the clearest route from his midfield sit, but stayed on when it was all too late. This looked a reasonable performance.
Jedward(IRE), eased slightly in distance after not getting home over 6f at Goodwood, had been sold for £21,000 since that effort and was another to keep on without ever emerging as a serious danger to the winner. (op 8-1)
Sohraab has regained a bit of consistency with blinkers being fitted. (op 10-1)
Partner(IRE), again running with out blinkers, was always being held.
Bathwick Bear(IRE) ◆, whose last victory came when beating none other than Mayson in the Ripon Two Yrs Old Trophy, is really well handicapped and should be striking when the right opportunity presents itself. (op 16-1)
Lexi's Hero(IRE) has been coming down the weights, and was below his last winning mark, but still faded out of the picture late on. (op 7-2)
Doctor Parkes had come back down to his last successful rating but weakened after being up there. (op 15-2)
Foxy Music Official explanation: jockey said gelding hung right

5830 MOCOCO H'CAP — 1m 7f 195y
4:55 (4:57) (Class 4) (0-85,83) 3-Y-O+ — £5,822 (£1,732; £865; £432) Stalls Low

Form				RPR
310	1		**New Youmzain (FR)**[37] 4513 3-8-9 **77**...1 MartinHarley 5 (Mick Channon) *racd keenly: trckd ldrs: wnt 2nd over 3f out: led over 2f out: sn rdn: styd on wl fr over 1f out: wl in command towards fin* **5/1**[3]	86
6033	2	2 ½	**Bradbury (IRE)**[22] 5056 4-8-13 **68**...(v[1]) JimmyQuinn 4 (James Bethell) *in tch: outpcd over 4f out: clsd 2f out: styd on to take 2nd ins fnl f: no imp on wnr* **16/1**	74
3411	3	2 ¼	**Suzi's A Class Act**[16] 5280 4-9-7 **79**...(p) AdamBeschizza[(3)] 3 (James Eustace) *hld up: pushed along and hdwy over 4f out: chsd ldrs over 3f out: wnt 2nd 2f out: lost 2nd ins fnl f: kpt on same pce* **11/4**[1]	82
5-41	4	1 ¼	**Ethics Girl (IRE)**[23] 4983 6-9-11 **80**...(t) FrannyNorton 8 (John Berry) *midfield: effrt on outer to chse ldrs over 2f out: one pce fnl 150yds* **13/2**	82
32-6	5	8	**Valid Reason**[15] 5306 5-10-0 **83**... JoeFanning 10 (Dean Ivory) *led: pushed along and hdd over 2f out: wknd over 1f out* **9/2**[2]	75
0642	6	2	**Shabak Hom (IRE)**[12] 5151 5-8-11 **66**... RichardThomas 7 (David Evans) *hld up: pushed along over 3f out: nvr able to get on terms w ldrs* **25/1**	56
51-2	7	1	**Los Nadis (GER)**[42] 2457 8-9-9 **78**... GrahamLee 2 (Jim Goldie) *midfield: rdn over 4f out: sn wknd* **9/2**[2]	67
4211	8	3 ¾	**Lady Bluesky**[33] 4639 9-9-2 **71**... PJMcDonald 6 (Alistair Whillans) *chsd ldr tl over 3f out: rdn and wknd over 2f out* **15/2**	55
35/P	9	7	**Higgy's Ragazzo (FR)**[23] 4983 5-9-8 **77**... TomQueally 9 (Roger Ingram) *hld up in rr: rdn over 4f out: nvr on terms* **33/1**	53
-005	10	2 ½	**Spirit Of Adjisa (IRE)**[30] 4731 8-9-3 **72**...(p) RichardMullen 11 (Andrew Balding) *racd keenly: prom: rdn over 4f out: wknd over 2f out* **20/1**	45

3m 32.69s (4.69) **Going Correction** +0.425s/f (Yiel)
WFA 3 from 4yo+ 13lb — **10** Ran SP% **122.2**
Speed ratings (Par 105): **105,103,102,102,98 97,96,94,91,89**
Tote Swingers 1&2 £8.90, 2&3 £6.10, 1&3 £8.70 CSF £82.32 CT £269.13 TOTE £7.50: £2.20, £4.20, £1.90; EX 58.40.
Owner Jaber Abdullah **Bred** Sarl Haras De Saint-Faust **Trained** West Ilsley, Berks

FOCUS
A few of these came into this in good heart, so the form ought to be reliable enough in the short-term, with the runner-up setting the level.
Shabak Hom(IRE) Official explanation: trainer said gelding was unsuited by the good (good to soft places) ground

5831 GOLDEN SQUARE SHOPPING CENTRE'S "STYLISH LADY" H'CAP — 5f 110y
5:30 (5:32) (Class 5) (0-70,70) 3-Y-O — £4,075 (£1,212; £606; £303) Stalls Low

Form				RPR
2031	1		**Ambitious Boy**[11] 5454 3-9-2 **65**... TomQueally 10 (Reg Hollinshead) *in rr: pushed along over 4f out: hdwy on outer over 1f out: r.o and edgd lft ins fnl f: led fnl stride* **9/1**	73
1636	2	hd	**Ferdy (IRE)**[3] 5736 3-8-10 **59**... JoeFanning 15 (Paul Green) *in rr: hdwy on outer over 2f out: r.o and hung lft ins fnl f: led briefly towards fin: jst denied* **8/1**	66
2114	3	¾	**Economic Crisis (IRE)**[14] 5337 3-9-4 **67**... PaddyAspell 2 (Alan Berry) *prom: led over 3f out: rdn over 1f out: edgd rt ins fnl f: hdd and no ex towards fin* **13/2**[3]	72
2045	4	¾	**Middleton Flyer (IRE)**[15] 5294 3-8-11 **60**...(b) RussKennemore 6 (Paul Midgley) *chsd ldrs: rdn to take 2nd over 1f out: lost 2nd and checked wl ins fnl f: no ex towards fin* **14/1**	62
5015	5	nse	**Baltic Bomber (IRE)**[24] 4953 3-9-0 **63**... MichaelO'Connell 9 (John Quinn) *midfield: rdn over 3f out: hdwy 2f out: styd on ins fnl f: nt pce of ldrs towards fin* **16/1**	65
1430	6	1 ¼	**Just Like Heaven (IRE)**[19] 5167 3-9-3 **66**... TonyHamilton 11 (Tim Easterby) *chsd ldrs: rdn and nt clr run over 1f out: kpt on ins fnl f: one pce towards fin* **12/1**	64
2120	7	2 ¼	**One Kool Dude**[24] 4953 3-8-13 **67**...(v) LMcNiff[(5)] 4 (Michael Bell) *in rr div: rdn over 1f out: kpt on ins fnl f: unable to trble ldrs* **7/1**	57
11U5	8	nk	**Gin Twist**[117] 1912 3-9-7 **70**...(b) FrannyNorton 1 (Tom Dascombe) *midfield: n.m.r and hmpd over 2f out: nvr able to chal* **9/2**[2]	59
6003	9	2	**First Fast Now (IRE)**[6] 5624 3-8-0 **56** oh7... DanielleMooney[(7)] 13 (Nigel Tinkler) *bhd: kpt on modly ins fnl f: nvr able to rch ldrs* **40/1**	38
2105	10	¾	**Roy's Legacy**[8] 5536 3-8-8 **57**...(t) MartinHarley 5 (Shaun Harris) *prom: rdn over 1f out: wknd fnl f* **20/1**	37
1516	11	½	**Elusive Bonus (IRE)**[19] 5167 3-8-13 **69**... DavidBergin[(7)] 3 (David O'Meara) *led: hdd over 3f out: stl cl up 2f out: rdn and wknd over 1f out* **10/3**[1]	47
64	12	4	**Koolgreycat (IRE)**[6] 5624 3-8-11 **60**... GrahamLee 8 (Noel Wilson) *prom: rdn over 1f out: sn wknd* **20/1**	24
030	13	1	**Red Baron (IRE)**[28] 4807 3-9-0 **63**... JimmyQuinn 7 (Eric Alston) *hld up: rdn over 1f out: nvr on terms* **16/1**	24

1m 9.22s (3.02) **Going Correction** +0.425s/f (Yiel) — **13** Ran SP% **126.3**
Speed ratings (Par 101): **96,95,94,93,93 92,89,88,85,84 84,78,77**
Tote Swingers 1&2 £20.50, 2&3 £6.50, 1&3 £11.20 CSF £81.97 CT £530.24 TOTE £14.20: £3.80, £1.50, £2.50; EX 132.20.

Owner C W Wardle & Mrs J E Wardle **Bred** Cecil W Wardle & Mrs Janet E Wardle **Trained** Upper Longdon, Staffs

FOCUS
Fast and furious stuff to conclude the card with, and it paid to come off of the pace. The fourth and fifth, to recent marks, set the standard.
Roy's Legacy Official explanation: jockey said colt hung right
T/Plt: £41.20 to a £1 stake. Pool: £96,962.86 - 1,717.77 winning tickets. T/Qpdt: £19.10 to a £1 stake. Pool: £5,227.45 - 201.72 winning tickets. DO

5790 SANDOWN (R-H)
Saturday, September 1

OFFICIAL GOING: Good to firm (good in places; round course 8.6 straight course 8.5)
Wind: virtually nil Weather: dry

5832 PIPER HEIDSIECK CHAMPAGNE H'CAP — 5f 6y
2:15 (2:17) (Class 3) (0-95,95) 3-Y-O+
£8,092 (£2,423; £1,211; £605; £302; £152) Stalls Low

Form				RPR
0-53	1		**Edge Closer**[51] 4013 8-8-13 **87**... PatDobbs 1 (Tony Carroll) *hld up in tch in midfield: effrt and hdwy over 1f out: rdn to ld 1f out: clr and in command ins fnl f: pushed out: comf* **5/1**[2]	100
03-1	2	2 ¼	**Face The Problem (IRE)**[14] 5343 4-9-7 **95**... KierenFallon 3 (Jamie Osborne) *hld up towards rr: stuck bhd a wall of horses 2f out: hdwy to chse ldrs and nt clr run jst ins fnl f: swtchd lft fnl 100yds and hdwy to chse wnr wl ins fnl f: r.o* **9/2**[1]	100+
1035	3	¾	**Kyleakin Lass**[29] 4765 3-8-13 **88**... RichardHughes 2 (Ian Wood) *hld up towards rr: hdwy against far rail 2f out: nt enough room fr jst over 1f out tl squeezed through gap wl ins fnl f: kpt on: no threat to wnr* **6/1**[3]	94+
-000	4	1	**Ajjaadd (USA)**[35] 4576 6-9-0 **88**...(p) WilliamBuick 12 (Ted Powell) *chsd ldrs: rdn wl over 1f out: chsd wnr jst ins fnl f: styd on same pce and lost 2 pls wl ins fnl f* **14/1**	87+
4510	5	½	**West Coast Dream**[42] 4337 5-9-2 **90**... IanMongan 4 (Roy Brotherton) *led: rdn wl over 1f out: hdd and no ex 1f out: wknd fnl 75yds* **16/1**	87
2640	6	¾	**Arctic Lynx (IRE)**[28] 4799 5-8-8 **82**... HayleyTurner 8 (John Best) *stdd and swtchd rt after s: bhd: hdwy over 1f out: styng on wl whn nt clr run and swtchd lft ins fnl f: gng on fin but nvr trbld ldrs* **16/1**	76
1100	7	¾	**Silvanus (IRE)**[10] 5487 7-9-1 **89**... PaulHanagan 7 (Paul Midgley) *taken down early: hld up in tch: hdwy to chse ldrs and travelling wl enough whn nt clr run over 1f out tl wl ins fnl f: nvr able to chal* **20/1**	84+
0 00	8	1	**The Thrill Is Gone**[10] 5487 4-8-7 **86**... CharlesBishop[(5)] 6 (Mick Channon) *w ldr: rdn and stl ev ch over 1f out: unable qck and btn 1f out: wkng whn sltly hmpd ins fnl f: fdd towards fin* **8/1**	74
031	9	nse	**Rowe Park**[27] 4849 9-8-11 **85**...(p) SaleemGolam 11 (Linda Jewell) *in tch in midfield: drvn 2f out: no imp and styd on same pce fr over 1f out* **28/1**	73
3600	10	2 ½	**Solemn**[14] 5343 7-8-13 **87**...(b) LukeMorris 13 (Milton Bradley) *in tch in midfield: struggling u.p 1/2-way: lost pl and no threat to ldrs fr over 1f out* **20/1**	66
0006	11	hd	**Diamond Charlie (IRE)**[17] 5233 4-8-4 **81** oh1... SimonPearce[(3)] 10 (Simon Dow) *in tch in midfield: rdn ent fnl 2f: sn outpcd and wknd jst over 1f out* **66/1**	59
26	12	1 ¼	**Soap Wars**[33] 4660 7-8-10 **84**... MichaelHills 14 (Hugo Palmer) *chsd ldrs: rdn over 1f out: sn struggling and btn: wknd ins fnl f* **25/1**	58
3600	13	¾	**Catfish (IRE)**[28] 4799 4-9-1 **89**... MickaelBarzalona 9 (Brian Meehan) *taken down early: in tch: rdn ent fnl 2f: sn struggling and btn over 1f out: wknd fnl f* **6/1**[3]	60
0041	14	½	**Piscean (USA)**[8] 5557 7-8-11 **88**...(b) RyanClark[(3)] 5 (Tom Keddy) *s.i.s: sn detached in last and u.p over 3f out: n.d* **16/1**	57

1m 0.36s (-1.24) **Going Correction** -0.05s/f (Good)
WFA 3 from 4yo+ 1lb — **14** Ran SP% **117.2**
Speed ratings (Par 107): **107,103,102,100,99 98,97,95,95,91 91,89,88,87**
Tote Swingers: 1&2 £4.60, 1&3 £6.30, 2&3 £3.80 CSF £24.87 CT £124.32 TOTE £4.50: £1.80, £2.10, £2.30; EX 29.80 Trifecta £50.90 Pool: £1,110.35 - 16.13 winning units..
Owner Godfrey Wilson **Bred** Caroline Wilson **Trained** Cropthorne, Worcs

FOCUS
Round course rail at innermost position and distances as advertised. A decent sprint handicap, although it was dominated by low-drawn runners. The in-form winner may have been best on the day in any case.

NOTEBOOK
Edge Closer, returning from a 51-day break, enjoyed just about the ideal trip, unlike his two nearest rivals. He won well but is unlikely to find things falling so kindly next time. (op 11-2 tchd 6-1)
Face The Problem(IRE) made a successful reappearance for Patrick Morris just two weeks earlier, but raced here for Jamie Osborne. Up 5lb, he had to wait for a clear run and that allowed the winner to get a jump on him. He carried his head a touch high, but looks like a horse with more to offer. (op 11-2)
Kyleakin Lass ◆ travelled well as usual but never had enough room to challenge. She gave the impression she would have gone close with a clear run, and considering the ground was also quicker than ideal, this was encouraging. (op 7-1)
Ajjaadd(USA) ◆, 9lb higher than when winning this race last year, ran well from an unfavourable draw, keeping on after showing speed. (op 11-1 tchd 10-1)
West Coast Dream faced competition up front from the disappointing The Thrill Is Gone, and the pair of them helped set this up for the closers. (op 20-1)
Arctic Lynx(IRE) wasn't travelling early on but finished well. He didn't get the clearest of runs late on, but didn't look unlucky.
Silvanus(IRE) was another who didn't get a clear run and he could have finished closer. Official explanation: jockey said gelding was denied a clear run (tchd 25-1)
Catfish(IRE) was short of room around a furlong out and her jockey soon gave up. (tchd 15-2 in a place)
Piscean(USA) Official explanation: jockey said gelding never travelled

5833 CANDY KITTENS SOLARIO STKS (GROUP 3) — 7f 16y
2:50 (2:50) (Class 1) 2-Y-O
£20,982 (£7,955; £3,981; £1,983; £995; £499) Stalls Low

Form				RPR
1	1		**Fantastic Moon**[29] 4774 2-9-0 0... WilliamBuick 4 (Jeremy Noseda) *t.k.h: stdd bk after 1f and hld up in rr: swtchd lft and rdn 2f out: stl last but wl in tch 1f out: str run u.p ins fnl f to ld last strides* **3/1**[2]	107+

4114 **2** *hd* **Tha'Ir (IRE)**[31] 4698 2-9-0 103 .... SilvestreDeSousa 2 106
(Saeed Bin Suroor) *hld up in last trio: effrt on far rail 2f out: rdn to chal jst over 1f out: drvn to ld ins fnl f: sn hrd pressed and battled on gamely tl hdd and no ex last strides* **9/4**[1]

1012 **3** *hd* **Master Of War**[30] 4736 2-9-0 108 .... RichardHughes 5 105
(Richard Hannon) *stdd after s: hld up in last trio: rdn and effrt 2f out: swtchd lft and hdwy u.p over 1f out: drvn and ev ch ins fnl f: no ex last strides* **9/4**[1]

21 **4** *1 3/4* **Mocenigo (IRE)**[23] 5011 2-9-0 0 .... RobertHavlin 3 101
(Peter Chapple-Hyam) *chsd ldr tl led after 1f: hdd 4f out: chsd ldr tl rdn to ld again 2f out: drvn jst over 1f out: hdd ins fnl f: no ex and outpcd fnl 100yds* **12/1**[3]

5150 **5** *2* **Chilworth Icon**[31] 4698 2-9-3 103 .... [illegible] [illegible]
(Mick Channon) *t.k.h: chsd ldrs: ev ch 2f out: sn rdn and unable qck: btn ins fnl f: wknd fnl 75yds* **22/1**

6 *nk* **Dont Bother Me (IRE)**[23] 5024 2-9-0 0 .... RoryCleary 1 95
(Niall Moran, Ire) *t.k.h: led for 1f: chsd ldrs after: rdn and effrt ent fnl 2f: unable qck over 1f out: styng on same pce and hld whn edgd rt ins fnl f: wknd towards fin* **16/1**

5211 **7** *3 3/4* **Hasopop (IRE)**[49] 4101 2-9-0 96 .... AndreaAtzeni 7 85
(Marco Botti) *t.k.h: chsd ldr over 5f out tl led 4f out: hdd and rdn 2f out: wknd 1f out* **12/1**[3]

1m 28.18s (-1.32) **Going Correction** -0.20s/f (Firm) 7 Ran SP% 112.2
Speed ratings (Par 105): **99,98,98,96,94 93,89**
Tote Swingers: 1&2 £1.70, 1&3 £2.10, 2&3 £1.80 CSF £9.77 TOTE £3.60: £2.20, £1.80; EX 12.50.
Owner Saeed Suhail **Bred** Hascombe And Valiant Studs **Trained** Newmarket, Suffolk

FOCUS
Not always a particularly strong Group 3, but subsequent Breeders' Cup Classic winner Raven's Pass took the 2007 running. The bare form of this year's race doesn't look anything special, although the winner has the potential to rate higher. The first three came from the last three places, but they were probably just the best horses in the race.

NOTEBOOK
Fantastic Moon, so far the only one of 19 juveniles from this yard to make a winning debut in 2012, having landed a novice event at the July course, was the least experienced member of the line-up. After being waited with in last, he took a while to pick up when first coming under pressure, still looking green, but got going in just enough time. He'll need to improve if going for something like the Racing Post Trophy, but a step up to a 1m ought to suit and there should be more to come. (op 7-2 tchd 4-1 in a place)
Tha'Ir(IRE), winner of the Chesham before finishing fourth in the Vintage Stakes, had to wait for a run towards the inside but had his chance. He doesn't look any better than this level, for now at least, but reportedly may go for the Champagne Stakes. (op 5-2)
Master Of War, up in trip after finishing second in the Richmond Stakes, had every chance but just wasn't quite good enough. It wouldn't surprise if he proves better back over shorter in due course, and both the Sirenia Stakes and the Mill Reef have been mentioned as possible targets. (op 5-2)
Mocenigo(IRE) had only won a Southwell maiden on his previous start, but he showed himself to be pretty decent. He was best of those who raced prominently, although he didn't really knuckle down for pressure and perhaps found the ground quicker than ideal. (op 9-1)
Chilworth Icon didn't help himself by racing keenly early. (op 20-1 tchd 25-1)
Dont Bother Me(IRE), successful in a Leopardstown maiden on his previous outing, failed to pick up well enough. (op 14-1)

5834 THOROUGHBRED BREEDERS' ASSOCIATION ATALANTA STKS (GROUP 3) (F&M) 1m 14y
3:25 (3:26) (Class 1) 3-Y-0+

£31,190 (£11,825; £5,918; £2,948; £1,479; £742) **Stalls** Low

Form RPR

1012 **1** **Dank**[21] 5092 3-8-9 100 .... RichardHughes 13 105+
(Sir Michael Stoute) *hld up in tch in midfield: swtchd lft 2f out: rdn and effrt over 1f out: hdwy and chal ins fnl f: r.o wl to ld towards fin* **7/2**[1]

3261 **2** *nk* **Ladys First**[21] 5092 3-8-9 102 .... PaulHanagan 1 104
(Richard Fahey) *chsd ldrs: rdn to chal between horses jst over 1f out: drvn to ld fnl 100yds: hdd and no ex towards fin* **5/1**[2]

-303 **3** *1* **Gathering (USA)**[36] 4556 3-8-9 99 ....(b) WilliamBuick 3 101
(John Gosden) *led: rdn wl over 1f out: hrd pressed after and battled on wl tl edgd rt and hdd fnl 100yds: one pce after* **14/1**

3111 **4** *1/2* **Sweetnessandlight**[13] 5386 3-8-9 81 .... TedDurcan 14 100
(Jason Ward) *s.i.s: hld up in rr: swtchd lft and rdn along 3f out: hdwy over 1f out: edgd rt and kpt on wl ins fnl f* **50/1**

-100 **5** *nk* **Clinical**[28] 4801 4-9-4 109 .... LukeMorris 8 103
(Sir Mark Prescott Bt) *in tch: rdn and effrt 2f out: chsd ldrs and hrd drvn ent fnl f: styd on same pce ins fnl f* **9/1**

0340 **6** *1 1/2* **Irish History (IRE)**[21] 5092 3-8-9 106 .... MickaelBarzalona 16 96
(Mahmood Al Zarooni) *awkward leaving stalls and s.i.s: hld up in rr: swtchd lft and rdn wl over 2f out: gd hdwy u.p over 1f out: no imp ins fnl f* **8/1**

-131 **7** *shd* **Making Eyes (IRE)**[43] 4316 4-9-0 99 .... MichaelHills 4 98+
(Hugo Palmer) *t.k.h: hld up in tch: rdn and unable qck 2f out: sltly outpcd ent fnl f: no threat to ldrs but kpt on again ins fnl f: n.m.r towards fin* **20/1**

0016 **8** *hd* **Falls Of Lora (IRE)**[35] 4616 3-8-13 107 .... SilvestreDeSousa 2 108+
(Mahmood Al Zarooni) *hld up in tch: trying to cl but nt enough room on far rail over 1f out: hdwy to press ldrs but stl n.m.r ins fnl f: gap clsd and bdly hmpd fnl 100yds: nt rcvr* **7/1**[3]

656 **9** *nse* **Night Lily (IRE)**[29] 4764 6-9-0 89 .... WilliamCarson 5 95
(Paul D'Arcy) *in tch in midfield: rdn and effrt wl over 1f out: no imp over 1f out: kpt on u.p ins fnl f but nvr quite gng pce to chal* **66/1**

0133 **10** *1/2* **Moone's My Name**[21] 5092 4-9-0 97 .... JimCrowley 7 94
(Ralph Beckett) *hld up in tch towards rr: nt clr run and looking for gap ent fnl 2f: rdn and hdwy over 1f out: kpt on u.p ins fnl f but nvr threatened ldrs* **16/1**

421 **11** *1/2* **Dalkova**[41] 4366 3-8-9 81 ....(t) PatDobbs 11 95+
(Richard Hannon) *hld up in tch towards rr: rdn and effrt 2f out: no threat to ldrs but styng on u.p ins fnl f whn nt clr run fnl 75yds: nt pushed after* **33/1**

4625 **12** *shd* **Villeneuve**[21] 5092 3-8-9 94 .... MartinDwyer 15 92
(William Muir) *chsd ldr: ev ch and rdn 2f out: no ex and btn jst ins fnl f: fdd fnl 100yds* **66/1**

5321 **13** *1* **Princess Of Orange**[21] 5107 3-8-9 91 .... SebSanders 12 90
(Rae Guest) *stdd and dropped in bhd after s: rdn and effrt 2f out: no imp tl edgd rt and kpt on ins fnl f: nvr trbld ldrs* **18/1**

2344 **14** *4 1/2* **Epernay**[17] 5238 5-9-0 79 ....(vt) IanMongan 10 79
(Ian Williams) *t.k.h: chsd ldrs tl 2f out: sn struggling and wknd over 1f out* **100/1**

6221 **15** *hd* **Burke's Rock**[12] 5420 3-8-9 91 ....(p) HayleyTurner 6 79
(Jeremy Noseda) *hld up in tch in midfield: nt clr run and swtchd rt 2f out: sn rdn and no imp over 1f out: wknd fnl f* **8/1**

-120 **16** *14* **Captivator**[73] 3266 5-9-0 105 .... KierenFallon 9 45
(James Fanshawe) *in tch: rdn and unable qck 2f out: sn struggling and wknd over 1f out: bhd and eased wl ins fnl f* **12/1**

1m 41.08s (-2.22) **Going Correction** -0.20s/f (Firm)
WFA 3 from 4yo+ 5lb 16 Ran SP% 122.8
Speed ratings (Par 113): **103,102,101,101,100 99,99,99,99,98 98,97,96,92,92 78**
Tote Swingers: 1&2 £4.00, 1&3 £11.90, 2&3 £10.90 CSF £19.06 TOTE £5.00: £1.50, £1.60, £5.30; EX 22.30 Trifecta £362.80 Pool: £2,236.02 - 4.56 winning units..
Owner James Wigan **Bred** London Thoroughbred Services Ltd **Trained** Newmarket, Suffolk
■ Stewards' Enquiry : Michael Hills four-day ban: failed to ride out for 6th (Sep 16-19)

FOCUS
A competitive fillies' Group 3, but not particularly strong form for the grade. The winner reversed Haydock form with the runner-up and the third helps with the standard.

NOTEBOOK
Dank was beaten just under a length into second by Ladys First in a Haydock Listed event last time but continued her progression to reverse the form. A close relation of Hong Kong Cup winner Eagle Mountain, this success will have boosted her value as a broodmare prospect and she may yet have a bit more to offer. (op 4-1 tchd 9-2 and 5-1 in places)
Ladys First couldn't dominate this time but still ran another good race. She's a tough sort who may progress further. (op 7-1)
Gathering(USA) was a bit keen early but still saw her race out quite well. She's reportedly set to be trained in the US before long and she should do well out there in a weak fillies' division. (op 12-1)
Sweetnessandlight had won her last three starts, but her sequence began in a seller off just 63 and her most recent success was gained form a mark of only 76. This was a fine effort upped significantly in class, staying on well from a long way back, and she's blatantly thriving. (op 40-1 tchd 66-1 in a place)
Clinical was back down in class but had a tough task under her 4lb penalty. (op 8-1)
Irish History(IRE) ran a lot better than at Haydock last time, but she didn't look straightforward, missing the break before being taken extremely wide with her challenge.
Making Eyes(IRE) found this tougher than the French Listed race she won last time. The Stewards held an enquiry to consider why Michael Hills had appeared to stop riding shortly before the winning post. They found him guilty of failing to ride out on a horse who would have finished sixth, and suspended him for four days, this being his second offence within 12 months. (op 25-1)
Falls Of Lora(IRE), who defeated today's runner-up in a C&D Listed event in July, spent most of the final 2f trying to squeeze between Gathering and the far rail, and nearly ended over the fence at one stage. She would have gone close to winning granted a clear run. The Stewards held an enquiry to consider why Silvestre De Sousa had appeared to stop riding shortly before the winning post. They found him guilty of failing to take all reasonable and permissible measures to obtain the best possible placing in that he failed to ride out on a horse who could have finished sixth, and they suspended him for one day. (op 8-1)
Night Lily(IRE) Official explanation: vet said mare lost a left-hind shoe

5835 PIPER HEIDSIECK CHAMPAGNE & LEVY BOARD H'CAP 1m 2f 7y
4:00 (4:01) (Class 2) 3-Y-0+

£37,350 (£11,184; £5,592; £2,796; £1,398; £702) **Stalls** Low

Form RPR

0-00 **1** **Labarinto**[108] 2176 4-9-1 95 .... GeorgeBaker 14 106
(Sir Michael Stoute) *chsd ldrs: smooth hdwy to join ldrs over 2f out: led 2f out: rdn and qcknd clr ent fnl f: pressed and drvn fnl 100yds: jst lasted* **16/1**

1266 **2** *hd* **Prussian**[21] 5078 3-8-3 90 .... MartinLane 3 101
(Mark Johnston) *chsd ldrs: swtchd lft and effrt to chse clr ldr over 1f out: styd on wl u.p and pressing wnr fnl 100yds: clsng grad towards fin: jst hld* **10/1**

0630 **3** *3 3/4* **Tinshu (IRE)**[28] 4795 6-8-5 85 ....(p) WilliamCarson 1 88
(Derek Haydn Jones) *t.k.h: hld up in tch: rdn and effrt 2f out: outpcd by wnr and looked wl hld over 1f out: swtchd lft and kpt on ins fnl f: wnt 3rd wl ins fnl f: no threat to ldng pair* **33/1**

0360 **4** *hd* **Colour Guard**[13] 5397 4-8-3 83 .... SamHitchcott 13 86+
(Mark Johnston) *in tch: rdn and unable qck ent fnl 2f: edgd rt and styd on wl ins fnl f: no threat to ldng pair* **20/1**

6032 **5** *3/4* **Licence To Till (USA)**[7] 5583 5-9-0 94 .... RobertHavlin 6 95
(Mark Johnston) *led: rdn over 2f out: hdd 2f out and unable qck w wnr over 1f out: 3rd and btn 1f out: wknd ins fnl f* **20/1**

0305 **6** *1* **Miblish**[29] 4760 3-9-0 101 ....(t) RichardHughes 4 100
(Clive Brittain) *hld up in tch: rdn and unable qck 2f out: plugging on same pce and no threat to ldrs whn n.m.r ins fnl f* **12/1**

0630 **7** *nse* **Start Right**[10] 5492 5-9-6 100 ....(p) SilvestreDeSousa 2 99+
(Saeed Bin Suroor) *t.k.h: hld up towards rr: stl plenty to do and nt clr run ent fnl 2f: hdwy over 1f out: keeping on whn nt clr run and swtchd lft wl ins fnl f: nvr trbld ldrs* **10/1**

0-00 **8** *nse* **Fulgur**[7] 5580 4-8-12 92 .... J-PGuillambert 11 91
(Luca Cumani) *t.k.h: in tch: rdn and effrt to chse ldrs over 2f out: unable qck and struggling 2f out: no threat to ldrs fr over 1f out* **14/1**

6110 **9** *1 1/2* **Chain Of Events**[57] 3826 5-8-3 83 .... HayleyTurner 9 79
(Sarah Humphrey) *taken down early: chsd ldr: rdn and ev ch briefly 2f out: sn outpcd and btn 1f out: wknd ins fnl f* **25/1**

5043 **10** *3/4* **Indian Jack (IRE)**[9] 5517 4-8-8 88 .... KierenFallon 8 83+
(Luca Cumani) *hld up in tch towards rr: rdn and effrt ent fnl 2f: no imp and plugged on same pce fr over 1f out* **4/1**[1]

301/ **11** *2 1/4* **Miss Starlight**[121] 5-9-7 101 .... MartinDwyer 10 91
(Ibrahim Saeed Al Malki, Qatar) *hld up in midfield: rdn and no prog ent fnl 2f: no threat to ldrs and edgd rt ins fnl f* **66/1**

0033 **12** *2 1/4* **Fadhaa (IRE)**[20] 5129 4-8-4 84 .... PaulHanagan 17 70
(Charles Hills) *hld up towards rr: hdwy into midfield over 3f out: drvn and no prog over 1f out: edgd rt and wknd 1f out* **16/1**

0002 **13** *1* **Man Of Action (USA)**[21] 5101 5-9-4 98 .... MickaelBarzalona 16 82
(Saeed Bin Suroor) *s.i.s: pushed along early: hld up in rr: rdn and sme hdwy over 2f out: wknd over 1f out* **15/2**[3]

0200 **14** *1/2* **Late Telegraph (IRE)**[8] 5558 4-8-3 83 ....(b[1]) LukeMorris 5 66
(Sir Henry Cecil) *hld up in midfield: drvn and no rspnse over 2f out: wknd wl over 1f out* **8/1**

115 **15** *2 3/4* **Valiant**[51] 4007 3-8-8 95 .... WilliamBuick 12 72
(William Haggas) *stdd after s: hld up in rr: rdn and no prog ent fnl 2f: wl btn and edgd rt over 1f out* **5/1**[2]

0-00 **16** *2 1/2* **Pekan Star**[35] 4610 5-8-9 89 .... AndreaAtzeni 15 61
(Roger Varian) *stdd after s: hld up in rr: rdn and no rspnse ent fnl 2f: bhd over 1f out* **25/1**

2m 9.38s (-1.12) **Going Correction** -0.20s/f (Firm)
WFA 3 from 4yo+ 7lb 16 Ran SP% 125.5
Speed ratings (Par 109): **96,95,92,92,92 91,91,91,90,89 87,85,85,84,82 80**
Tote Swingers: 1&2 £43.40, 1&3 £165.30, 2&3 £83.70 CSF £158.57 CT £5188.02 TOTE £24.70: £4.30, £3.10, £7.30, £5.30; EX 310.40 TRIFECTA Not won..
Owner K Abdulla **Bred** Juddmonte Farms Ltd **Trained** Newmarket, Suffolk
■ Stewards' Enquiry : Martin Lane two-day ban: used whip above permitted level (Sep 30-Oct 1)

FOCUS
A good handicap, but the time was 2.14 seconds slower than the later strongly run Class 4 contest and it proved hard to make up significant amounts of ground. The winner is rated back to his 3yo best.

NOTEBOOK
Labarinto was well beaten in two starts earlier in the season, but he'd since been gelded and his trainer is in much better form now. He was only 2lb higher than when winning at Glorious Goodwood last year and just did enough. It wouldn't surprise to see him build on this, but he's not in the Cambridgeshire. (op 14-1)
Prussian was found out by a 1m4f under a forward ride last time, but this was a lot better and she's evidently still improving. (op 9-1)
Tinshu(IRE) wasn't at her best at Doncaster last time, but prior to that she'd looked better than the bare form at Ascot, and she showed she's on a competitive mark.
Colour Guard, a stablemate of the second, is difficult to predict but this wasn't a bad effort. 25-1)
Licence To Till (USA)who was third in this race last year off 13lb lower, has been busy lately and didn't see his race out.
Miblish went up in the handicap after a good run at Group 3 level last time and was well held. 14-1)
Start Right didn't get much of a run and crossed the line looking as though he had more to offer, but he's not one to trust. (op 11-1 tchd 9-1)
Fulgur was again too keen. (op 12-1)
Indian Jack (IRE)soon dropped towards the rear of the field and was left with too much to do off the modest pace, but even so it was disappointing he made no impression at all. Perhaps a return to 1m will suit. (op 9-2 tchd 7-2)
Valiant, who won his first two starts before being well beaten when favourite for the Group 3 Bahrain Trophy, was on quick ground for the first time after 51 days off. He ran a poor race and can only be watched for the time being. (tchd 11-2)

5836 SOLARIO RACING TWELFTH SHARE SYNDICATES NURSERY 7f 16y
4:30 (4:34) (Class 4) (0-85,83) 2-Y-O £4,528 (£1,347; £673 ; £336) Stalls Low

Form RPR
211 **1** **Law Enforcement (IRE)**[8] 5552 2 -9-7**83**................... RichardHughes 4 91
(Richard Hannon) *chsd ldng pair: wnt 2nd over 4f out: rdn to ld 1f out: styd on strly to go clr ins fnl f: drvn out* **8/11**[1]
012 **2** *2 3/4* **Dusky Queen (IRE)**[4] 5361 2 -9-3**79**............................. PaulHanagan 1 80+
(Richard Fahey) *led for 2f: chsd ldr after tl over 4f out: hemmed in on rail 3f out tl swtchd lft 1f out: styd on to go 2nd wl ins fnl f: no threat to wnr* **3/1**[2]
01 **3** *1/2* **Entwined (IRE)**[25] 4899 2 -8-10**72**... JohnFahy 3 72
(Clive Cox) *hld up in last pair: nt clr run over 2f out tl wl over 1f out: drvn and hdwy to chse ldrs 1f out: styd on same pce ins fnl f* **16/1**
6414 **4** *nk* **Aussie Reigns (IRE)**[8] 5552 2 -8-12**74**........................... WilliamBuick 5 73
(William Knight) *hld up in tch in last pair: clsd 3f out: rdn and effrt wl over 1f out: styd on same pce and no threat to wnr ins fnl f* **8/1**[3]
333 **5** *3/4* **Elegant In Silk (USA)**[8] 5184 2 -8-10**72**................ SilvestreDeSousa 2 69
(William Haggas) *t.k.h: chsd ldr tl led after 2f: rdn and hanging rt wl over 1f out: hdd 1f out: unable qck w wnr and wknd fnl 100yds* **8/1**[3]

1m 28.88s (-0.62)**Going Correction** -0.20s/f (Firm) **5**Ran SP% **111.0**
Speed ratings (Par 97): **95,91,91,90,90**
CSF £3.20 TOTE £1.40 : £1.10 , £1.80 ; EX 2.70 .
Owner M S Al Shahi **Bred** Mrs E J O'Grady **Trained** East Everleigh, Wilts

FOCUS
The time was just 0.70 seconds slower than the Solario Stakes. Only five runners, but an improving winner. Straightforward form.

NOTEBOOK
Law Enforcement (IRE)was completing a hat-trick off 5lb higher than when successful over 1m at the July course last time. His connections are thinking about pattern races for him, having reportedly entered him in a 1m Listed race at Leopardstown. (op 4-5 tchd 5-6)
Dusky Queen (IRE)was kept in by the winner for much of the straight, but it made no difference to the result. She's open to improvement having only had four starts and, considering her breeding, she would be of serious interest if her connections were interested in sending her to Southwell at some stage. Both her sire and her dam's sire have a 26% strike-rate at that course. (op 7-2)
Entwined(IRE), the winner of a Bath maiden over just short of 6f on her second start, had her chance but wasn't good enough. (op 10-1)
Aussie Reigns (IRE)was held by Law Enforcement on their recent Newmarket meeting. (tchd 7-1)
Elegant In Silk (USA)didn't show herself to be well handicapped. (tchd 15-2 and 9-1)

5837 OTG PRODUCTS H'CAP 1m 14y
5:05 (5:08) (Class 4) (0-80,80) 3-Y-O £5,175 (£1,540; £769 ; £384) Stalls Low

Form RPR
2512 **1** **Juvenal (IRE)**[17] 5237 3 -9-7**80**.................................(p) RichardHughes 5 88
(Richard Hannon) *stdd after s: hld up in rr: stl plenty to do and switching rt over 1f out: gd hdwy ent fnl f: qcknd between horses to ld ins fnl f: r.o wl: eased last strides* **5/1**[3]
0231 **2** *1* **Dynamic Duo (IRE)**[12] 5404 3 -8-13**72**................................ PatDobbs 1 77
(Richard Hannon) *t.k.h: chsd ldrs: nt clr run over 2f out: swtchd lft and effrt to chal over 1f out: rdn to ld 1f out: hdd and styd on same pce ins fnl f* **8/1**
0-41 **3** *nse* **Proximity**[54] 3918 3 -9-4**77**.. GeorgeBaker 9 82
(Sir Michael Stoute) *chsd ldrs: rdn and effrt 2f out: stl chsng ldrs whn nt clr run 1f tl ins fnl f: styd on wl u.p fnl 100yds* **9/2**[2]
21-0 **4** *hd* **Fairyinthewind (IRE)**[96] 2557 3 -8-11**70**........................ LukeMorris 10 74
(Paul D'Arcy) *in tch in midfield: switching rt and hdwy over 1f out: styng on whn nt clr run ins fnl f: swtchd lft and kpt on wl towards fin* **25/1**
3552 **5** *hd* **Sunley Pride**[18] 5214 3 -8-12**71**...................................... SamHitchcott 15 75
(Mick Channon) *t.k.h: chsd ldrs: rdn and ev ch 2f out: edgd rt ent fnl f: styd on same pce after* **14/1**
5004 **6** *1/2* **Compton Prince**[15] 5302 3 -8-8**67**.......................................(b) JohnFahy 6 70
(Clive Cox) *led tl 6f out: chsd ldr tl led again 2f out: hung rt u.p over 1f out: hdd 1f out: one pce ins fnl f* **28/1**
0-60 **7** *1* **Besito (IRE)**[37] 4497 3 -9-2**75**... PaulHanagan 7 75
(William Jarvis) *chsd ldr tl led 6f out: rdn and hdd 2f out: unable qck u.p whn sltly hmpd over 1f out: styd on same pce fnl f* **50/1**
063 **8** *nk* **Attenborough (USA)**[30] 4745 3 -9-4**77**........................(p) WilliamBuick 3 80+
(Jeremy Noseda) *in tch: looking to switch lft fr over 2f out: swtchd lft over 1f out: stuck bhd a wall of horses and one pce fnl f: unable to chal* **6/1**
3455 **9** *1* **Scrupul (IRE)**[24] 4949 3 -8-13**72**..................................... KierenFallon 12 69
(Luca Cumani) *hld up in tch in midfield: swtchd lft and effrt 2f out: hung rt in bhd horses and no prog over 1f out: one pce and no threat to ldrs fnl f* **3/1**[1]
2043 **10** *shd* **The Noble Ord**[25] 4901 3 -8-13**72**...........................(t) AdamKirby 14 69
(Sylvester Kirk) *hld up in tch towards rr: rdn and effrt whn carried rt jst over 1f out: kpt on ins fnl f: nvr trbld ldrs* **10/1**
40-2 **11** *3 1/2* **Amelia May**[15] 5322 3 -9-3**76**.................................... DaraghO'Donohoe 8 65
(Ed Vaughan) *stdd s: hld up in rr: hdwy over 3f out: rdn and effrt ent fnl 2f: no prog 1f out: wknd ins fnl f* **14/1**
030 **12** *2 1/2* **Geordie Boy**[102] 2368 3 -8-6**68**.. RyanClark(3) 13 51
(Sheena West) *hld up in rr: effrt u.p in centre jst over 2f out: no imp over 1f out: wknd fnl f* **25/1**
500 **13** *nse* **Ivor's Princess**[20] 5128 3 -9-5**78**.................................(b) JamesMillman 4 61
(Rod Millman) *slowly away and reminders sn after s: nvr gng wl and sn rdn in rr: nvr trbld ldrs* **50/1**

1m 42.41s (-0.89)**Going Correction** -0.20s/f (Firm) **13**Ran SP% **122.7**
Speed ratings (Par 103): **96,95,94,94,94 94,93,92,91,91 88,85,85**
Tote Swingers: 1&2 £6.70, 1&3 £3.70, 2&3 £10.50 CSF £43.74 CT £203.01 TOTE £7.30 : £2.00 , £3.30, £2.30 ; EX 41.00 Trifecta £267.40 Pool: £1,517.85 - 4.20 winning units.
Owner Noodles Racing **Bred** Gerard Callanan **Trained** East Everleigh, Wilts

FOCUS
It was a bit messy in behind with a few of these finding trouble, but it looked like the best horse won. There are doubts over the form but the time was reasonable. The winner continued his progress.
Attenborough(USA) Official explanation: jockey said gelding was denied a clear run

5838 WESTBEACH GROUP H'CAP 1m 2f 7y
5:35 (5:38) (Class 4) (0-80,80) 3-Y-O+ £5,175 (£1,540; £769 ; £384) Stalls Low

Form RPR
5202 **1** **Quixote**[7] 5596 3 -8-9**70**..(t) KierenFallon 4 79
(Clive Brittain) *hld up in midfield: rdn and hdwy to ld over 1f out: edgd rt fnl f: kpt on wl: rdn out* **20/1**
0650 **2** *1 1/4* **Poetic Lord**[6] 5630 3 -8-12**73**... JohnFahy 5 79
(Richard Hannon) *hld up in midfield: effrt u.p on inner 2f out: drvn and chsd wnr 1f out: kpt on same pce ins fnl f* **16/1**
6551 **3** *3/4* **Brigadoon**[19] 5159 5 -9-9**77**.. PaulHanagan 13 82
(William Jarvis) *hld up off the pce in rr: hdwy and in tch 4f out: rdn and hdwy on outer 2f out: styd on to chse ldng pair ins fnl f: no imp towards fin* **20/1**
0511 **4** *1 1/4* **Cape Explorer**[20] 5129 3 -8-13**74**................................... MartinDwyer 15 76+
(James Tate) *led: hrd pressed and rdn 2f out: hdd over 1f out: 3rd and btn jst ins fnl f: plugged on same pce ins fnl f* **11/4**[1]
6321 **5** *nse* **Hip Hip Hooray**[23] 5008 6 -8-12**66**............................. RichardHughes 11 68
(Luke Dace) *hld up off the pce in rr: clsd and in tch 4f out: hdwy u.p 2f out: kpt on u.p fnl f* **8/1**
0-00 **6** *nk* **Hot Spice**[16] 5268 4 -9-7**75**... TedDurcan 3 76
(John Dunlop) *racd in midfield: rdn and effrt over 2f out: keeping on whn jostled 1f out: kpt on but nvr gng pce to rch ldrs* **16/1**
3033 **7** *hd* **Nelson's Bay**[14] 5365 3 -9-4**79**.................................(t) MickaelBarzalona 9 80
(Brian Meehan) *sn pushed along and dropped to rr: rdn and hdwy 4f out: kpt plugging on u.p: edgd rt 1f out: styd on but nvr trbld ldrs* **7/1**[3]
15-0 **8** *shd* **Icebuster**[21] 5094 4 -9-12**80**.. JamesMillman 10 81
(Rod Millman) *sn bhd: clsd and in tch 4f out: pushed along and sme hdwy on inner 2f out: no real imp and stl pushed along tl styd on wl fnl 100yds: nvr threatened ldrs* **12/1**
3321 **9** *2 1/2* **Highland Duke (IRE)**[8] 5197 3 -8-13**74**............................ AdamKirby 8 70
(Clive Cox) *chsd ldrs: rdn and ev ch ent fnl 2f: unable qck and carried rt over 1f out: wknd ins fnl f* **11/2**[2]
1050 **10** *1 3/4* **Talk Of The North**[26] 4875 3 -8-8**69**...........................(b[1]) RobertHavlin 14 61
(Hugo Palmer) *hld up in midfield: rdn and nt qckn whn n.m.r wl over 1f out: carried rt and no hdwy 1f out* **28/1**
233 **11** *nk* **Mizbah**[25] 4923 3 -9-3**78**...(p) SilvestreDeSousa 12 70
(Saeed Bin Suroor) *chsd ldr: rdn and pressing ldrs ent fnl 2f: struggling wl over 1f out: wknd over 1f out* **7/1**[3]
3216 **12** *2 1/4* **Hurakan (IRE)**[31] 4706 6 -8-13**74**...........................(p) DanielMuscutt(7) 2 61
(Richard Price) *chsd ldrs: rdn and unable qck ent fnl 2f: wknd over 1f out* **16/1**
3315 **13** *10* **Know No Fear**[9] 5506 7 -9-3**71**.......................................(p) WilliamBuick 7 38
(Alastair Lidderdale) *in tch: rdn over 2f out: wknd over 1f out: eased whn wl btn ins fnl f* **12/1**
1255 **14** *29* **Eagle Nebula**[15] 5323 8 -9-1**69**... IanMongan 1
(Brett Johnson) *sn rdn along and nvr gng wl in rr: lost tch ent fnl 2f: eased fr over 1f out: t.o* **25/1**

2m 7.24s (-3.26)**Going Correction** -0.20s/f (Firm)
WFA 3 from 4yo+ 7lb **14**Ran SP% **128.0**
Speed ratings (Par 105): **105,104,103,102,102 102,101,101,99,98 98,96,88,65**
Tote Swingers 1&2 £43.40, 2&3 £70.50, 1&3 £17.20 CSF £313.77 CT £6380.20 TOTE £18.30 : £4.80, £7.40 , £6.70 ; EX 369.60 TRIFECTA Not won. .
Owner C E Brittain **Bred** Mr & Mrs R & P Scott **Trained** Newmarket, Suffolk

FOCUS
The visual impression was of a strong pace and the final time was 2.14 seconds faster than the earlier Class 2 handicap. Those ridden patiently unsurprisingly dominated. Sound form.
Eagle Nebula Official explanation: jockey said gelding never travelled
T/Jkpt: Not won. T/Plt: £222.00 to a £1 stake. Pool: £188,367.08 - 619.17 winning tickets. T/Qpdt: £70.50 to £1. Pool: £8,197.20 - 85.98 w. tckts SP 5839a -5843a (Foreign Racing) See RI

5781 BADEN-BADEN (L-H)
Saturday, September 1

OFFICIAL GOING: Turf: good to soft

5844a BADEN RACING STUTEN-PREIS (GROUP 3) (3YO+ FILLIES & MARES) (TURF) 1m 3f
4:25 (12:00) 3-Y-O+

£26,666 (£9,166; £4,583 ; £2,500 ; £1,666 ; £1,250)

RPR
1 **Pagera (FR)**[41] 4386 4 -9-5**0**.. FabriceVeron 11 111+
(H-A Pantall, France) *dropped in and hld up towards rr on inner: rdn to improve over 2f out: r.o to chal 1 1/2f out: led ent fnl f: styd on wl* **17/1**
2 *3* **Opera Gal (IRE)**[7] 5238 5 -9-5**0**.. LiamKeniry 1 106
(Andrew Balding) *led: strly pressed and rdn 2 1/2f out: responded wl to press to extend advantage again 2f out: hdd ent fnl f: kpt on wout matching wnr* **26/5**[2]
3 *4 1/2* **Imagery (GER)**[27] 4862 3 -8-11**0**.. ADeVries 7 98
(J Hirschberger, Germany) *prom on outer: rdn over 3f out: styd on one pce ins fnl 2f: wnt 3rd ins fnl 100yds* **66/10**[3]

4 *1/2* **Hot Blood (IRE)**[63] 3652 4 -9-50 .... AStarke 4 97
(P Schiergen, Germany) *midfield on inner: swtchd out and rdn to improve over 2 1/2f out: plugged on to go 4th ins fnl 100yds: nt pce to chal* **152/10**

5 *1 1/2* **Shimmering Surf (IRE)**[21] 5116 5 -9-50 .... NeilCallan 2 94
(Roger Varian) *trckd ldr in 2nd on outer: rdn over 3f out: moved up to chal 2 1/2f out: qckly seen off: kpt on tl no ex and fdd ins fnl f: dropped to 5th ins fnl 100yds* **6/4**[1]

6 *1 1/2* **Kasumi (GER)**[60] 3746 5 -9-50 .... RPiechulek 6 92
(R Dzubasz, Germany) *dwlt in stalls and v slow to stride: hld up in rr: rdn to try and improve over 3f out: sn outpcd: plugged on to go 6th post* **47/1**

7 *hd* **Leopardin (GER)**[17] 1 0 60 .... MircoDemuro 10 91
(H J Groschel, Germany) *hld up: rdn and outpcd 3f out: only runner to stay far side and impr position on turn into st: tacked across to join rest of field over 1f out: no ex and btn ins fnl f: fdd and dropped to 7th post* **146/10**

8 *nse* **Caitania (IRE)**[20] 5145 3 -8-110 .... Jean-BernardEyquem 12 91
(U Stoltefuss, Germany) *hld up towards rr: rdn and outpcd in last 3f out: plugged on to go 8th ins fnl f* **116/10**

9 *2* **Next Holy (IRE)**[27] 4 -9-50 .... FilipMinarik 9 88
(P Schiergen, Germany) *midfield: rdn 2 1/2f out: sn outpcd: plugged on: n.d* **40/1**

10 *1* **Night Serenade (IRE)**[71] 3367 5 -9-50 .... ThomasHenderson 13 86
(H-A Pantall, France) *hld up towards rr on outer: rdn over 3f out: kpt on one pce tl no ex and fdd ins fnl f* **246/10**

11 *3* **Adriana (GER)** 4 -9-50 .... THellier 14 80
(M Rulec, Germany) *hld up on outer: hdwy into midfield 2 1/2f out: rdn 2f out: sn outpcd and btn: eased cl home* **217/10**

12 *4 1/2* **Skallet (FR)**[19] 5183 4 -9-50 ....(b) FredericSpanu 8 72
(S Wattel, France) *prom in centre: rdn and outpcd over 2 1/2f out: lost pl rapidly 1 1/2f: sn btn: eased ins fnl f* **101/10**

13 *23* **Sworn Sold (GER)**[27] 4862 3 -8-110 .... APietsch 5 31
(W Hickst, Germany) *prom on inner: rdn to maintain position over 4f out: lost pl rapidly over 2f out: sn dropped to last: wl bhd whn eased: t.o* **74/10**

2m 24.35s (5.08)
WFA 3 from 4yo+ 8lb **13**Ran SP%129.1
WIN (incl. 10 euro stake): 180. PLACES: 45, 19, 23. SF: 1,009
Owner Guy Pariente **Bred** G Pariente **Trained** France

NOTEBOOK
Opera Gal (IRE)made the running before keeping on gamely to secure second. The trainer belives the distance was possibly just too far for her on the easy ground and added that she may well be retired.
Shimmering Surf (IRE) while the other British runner, 6-4 favourite Shimmering Surf, ran out of steam to finish fifth. The jockey was disappointed but was of the opinion that she didn't like the ground and said he was having to squeeze her from a long way out.

5845a - 5847a (Foreign Racing) - See Raceform Interactive

VELIEFENDI

Saturday, September 1

OFFICIAL GOING: Turf: good; polytrack: standard

5848a INTERNATIONAL FRANCE GALOP FRBC ANATOLIA TROPHY (LOCAL GROUP 2) (3YO+) (POLYTRACK) 1m 2f (P)

5:30 (12:00) 3-Y-O+ **£95,833** (£38,333; £19,166 ; £9,583)

RPR

1 **Hunter's Light (IRE)**[21] 5090 4 -9-60 .... FrankieDettori 6 116
(Saeed Bin Suroor) *hld up in last trio: smooth hdwy over 2f out: rdn to chal 1 1/2f out: sn led: stretched clr under hands and heels ins fnl f: easily* **4/5**[1]

2 *5* **Zazou (GER)**[34] 4636 5 -9-60 .... ASuborics 2 106
(W Hickst, Germany) *midfield on inner: hdwy fr over 3f out: rdn to chal 2f out: led briefly over 1 1/2f out: qckly hdd and outpcd by wnr: kpt on* **6/7**[2]

3 *1/2* **Prince Alzain (USA)**[8] 5209 3 -8-110 .... FJohansson 8 103
(Gerard Butler) *hld up in last pair: rdn 2 1/2f out: styd on wl to go 3rd cl home* **4/1**

4 *1* **Belgian Bill**[29] 4761 4 -9-60 ....(t) PatCosgrave 7 103
(George Baker) *sltly s.i.s and rousted along to rcvr: hld up towards rr on inner: hdwy fr over 3f out: rdn and brief effrt 2f out: sn outpcd: plugged on: dropped to 4th cl home* **57/10**

5 *1 1/2* **Rampoldi (TUR)**[23] 3 -8-110 .... MehmetKaya 5 98
(S Keresteci, Turkey) *midfield: rdn 3f out: outpcd ins fnl 2f: plugged on* **23/4**

6 *1/2* **Dervis Aga (TUR)**[24] 7 -9-60 ....(b) HalisKaratas 4 99
(S Mutlu, Turkey) *hld up in last: rdn and outpcd in rr 3f out: plugged on down wd outside to go 6th cl home: n.d* **13/4**[3]

7 *2* **Marcret (ITY)**[35] 4610 5 -9-60 .... RichardKingscote 9 95
(Marco Botti) *prom: prog to press ldr 3f out: led gng wl 2 1/2f out: hdd over 1 1/2f out: no ex and fdd: dropped to 7th cl home* **207/10**

8 *18* **Buenos Aires (TUR)**[24] 5 -9-60 ....(bt) SadettinBoyraz 1 59
(S Karagoz, Turkey) *led: hdd after 4f: rdn 3f out: dropped to rr and btn 2f out: sn eased: t.o* **105/10**

9 *3 1/2* **Doku (TUR)**[19] 6 -9-20 .... GokhanGokce 3 48
(D Ergin, Turkey) *trckd ldr in 2nd on outer: led after 4f: rdn and strly pressed 3f out: hdd 2 1/2f out: sn btn and fdd: eased and dropped to last over 1f out: t.o* **16/1**

2m 3.08s (-1.92)
WFA 3 from 4yo+ 7lb **9**Ran SP%201.9
PARI-MUTUEL (including 1Turkish lira stakes): WIN: 1.80; DF 1.90; SF 3.80
Owner Godolphin **Bred** Darley **Trained** Newmarket, Suffolk

NOTEBOOK
Hunter's Light (IRE) on whom Dettori rode a waiting race, had won the Rose of Lancaster Stakes at Haydock on his most recent appearance. He had only a couple behind him as the local hopes set the early pace, but as soon as Dettori asked Hunter's Light for his effort the race was over, the son of Dubawi taking it up over a furlong out and storming clear. It was Godolphin's second success in the contest in four runnings of this race.
Prince Alzain (USA) the winner of a Wolverhampton handicap last time, ran close to that mark to record this Group 2 placing, staying on late.
Belgian Bill, runner-up in tis race in 2011, missed the break before staying on without threatening.
Marcret(ITY), trying synthetics for the first time, was sent to the front turning for home but could not sustain his effort. Soft turf suits him best.

5849a INTERNATIONAL ISTANBUL TROPHY (LOCAL GROUP 2) (3YO+ FILLIES & MARES) (TURF) 1m

7:00 (12:00) 3-Y-O+ **£95,833** (£38,333; £19,166 ; £9,583)

RPR

1 **Rhythm Of Light**[21] 5092 4 -9-60 .... RichardKingscote 2 106
(Tom Dascombe) *hld up towards rr on inner: swtchd out and rdn to improve 2 1/2f out: r.o to chal 1 1/2f out: led jst ins fnl f: kpt on wl u.p cl home* **8/5**[2]

2 *1/2* **Beatrice Aurore (IRE)**[36] 4527 4 -9-60 .... FrankieDettori 8 105
(John Dunlop) *trapped wd early: sn taken bk and hld up in last on inner: swtchd out and rdn to improve over 2f out: styd on to go 2nd wl ins fnl f: nt quite rch wnr* **19/20**[1]

3 *1/2* **Arsaadi (IRE)**[17] 5249 3 -9-00 ow1 .... PatCosgrave 1 102
(William Haggas) *midfield on inner: rdn 2 1/2f out: r.o to go 3rd cl home* **131/10**

4 *1/2* **Survey (GER)**[29] 4764 3 -8-130 .... ASuborics 6 100
(Mario Hofer, Germany) *trckd ldr in 2nd: rdn to chal 2f out: led over 1 1/2f out: hdd jst ins fnl f: kpt on: dropped to 4th cl home* **48/10**

5 *1/2* **Lady Jacamira (GER)**[20] 3 -8-130 .... NRichter 9 98
(R Dzubasz, Germany) *midfield on outer: rdn over 2f out: kpt on one pce ins fnl 1 1/2f* **11/2**

6 *5 1/2* **Symphonic Rhythm (TUR)**[26] 3 -8-130 ....(b) HalisKaratas 4 86
(O Ozelcanat, Turkey) *prom on inner: rdn over 2f out: outpcd over 1f out: fdd: eased whn btn* **9/4**[3]

7 *3 1/2* **Gokcenil (TUR)**[24] 4 -9-60 .... FuatCakar 3 81
(C Turan, Turkey) *led: rdn to extend advantage over 4f out: stl clr on turn into st: strly pressed and hdd over 1 1/2f out: sn btn and wknd: eased ins fnl f* **758/100**

8 *5* **Mihrimahal (TUR)**[24] 3 -8-130 .... AkinSozen 7 66
(H Guney, Turkey) *midfield on outer: rdn over 3f out: no ex and btn 1 1/2f out: eased ins fnl f* **58/10**

9 *4* **Country Love (FR)**[107] 5240 5 -9-60 ....(t) OzcanYildirim 5 60
(Anar Balahuseynov, Azerbaijan) *a towards rr: rdn in last 3f out: sn btn: eased over 1 1/2f out: nvr a factor* **58/10**

1m 34.03s (-1.30)
WFA 3 from 4yo+ 5lb **9**Ran SP%201.3
PARI-MUTUEL (including 1Turkish lira stakes): WIN: 2.60; DF 2.20; SF 4.25
Owner Lowe Silver Deal **Bred** Hermes Services Ltd **Trained** Malpas, Cheshire

NOTEBOOK
Rhythm Of Light, runner-up in this race last season, went one better to head a clean sweep of the places for the British raiders. She is in good form at present and battled on well for a narrow success.
Beatrice Aurore (IRE)bounced back after a below-par effort on ground too fast last time and finished well to pick up some worthwhile place money.
Arsaadi(IRE) seemed to appreciate the removal of blinkers and return to a sounder surface and stayed on late to grab third place.

5509 FOLKESTONE (R-H)

Sunday, September 2

OFFICIAL GOING: Good to firm (round course: 7.5, straight course: stands' side: 8.0, far side 7.7)
Wind: Light, across Weather: dry

5850 LADBROKES.COM APPRENTICE H'CAP 7f (S)

2:00 (2:03) (Class 6) (0-60,60) 3-Y-O+ **£2,181** (£644; £322) **Stalls** High

Form RPR

0414 **1** **Whitstable Native**[34] 4656 4 -9-255 .... DarrenEgan(3) 14 65
(Joseph Tuite) *hld up in tch: chsng ldrs and travelling strly over 2f out: rdn and effrt over 1f out: led ins fnl f: r.o wl* **5/1**[2]

2 *1 3/4* **Dustland Fairytale (IRE)**[91] 6735 4 -9-454 .... AdamBeschizza 6 59
(Sean Curran) *bustled along leaving stalls: chsd ldrs: ev ch and drvn 2f out: led 1f out: hdd and one pce ins fnl f: 2nd of 9 in gp* **5/1**[2]

305 **3** *1 1/4* **Jonnie Skull (IRE)**[2] 5457 6 -9-757 ....(vt) RyanClark 13 59
(Phil McEntee) *chsd ldr: rdn and ev ch 2f out: styd on same pce ins fnl f: 3rd of 9 in gp* **9/1**

0342 **4** *1 3/4* **King's Future**[15] 5350 3 -8-1252 .... KierenFox 11 48
(Lee Carter) *taken down early: led: rdn 2f out: drvn and hdd 1f out: wknd ins fnl f: 4th of 9 in gp* **11/1**

1202 **5** *1/2* **Ereka (IRE)**[12] 5444 4 -8-847 .... TobyAtkinson(3) 9 43
(John Best) *short of room and hmpd leaving stalls: bhd: hdwy over 2f out: nt clr run over 1f out: kpt on u.p fnl f: 5th of 9 in gp* **8/1**[3]

400- **6** *1* **Present Story**[358] 5912 5 -8-1147 .... SeanLevey 1 40
(Ian Wood) *racd in far side trio: midfield overall: rdn 3f out: hdwy and rdn over 2f out: styd on same pce fr over 1f out: 1st of 3 in gp* **28/1**

446 **7** *1 1/2* **Mulberry Brite**[18] 5240 4 -9-154 .... LeonnaMayor(3) 8 43
(Alastair Lidderdale) *bmpd and stdd s: t.k.h: hld up wl bhd: clsd over 2f out: swtchd rt and hdwy 2f out: no imp u.p ent fnl f: 6th of 9 in gp* **8/1**[3]

3042 **8** *3/4* **Gazboolou**[15] 5349 8 -8-847 .... AmyScott(3) 7 34
(Henry Candy) *hood removed late and wnt lft s: bhd: clsd over 2f out: drvn and chsd ldrs over 1f out: no prog 1f out: wknd ins fnl f: 7th of 9 in gp* **4/1**[1]

0500 **9** *2 1/2* **Pindrop**[29] 4793 3 -8-350 .... RyanTate(7) 10 29
(Clive Cox) *racd off the pce in midfield: clsd 3f out: chsd ldrs but unable qck u.p 2f out: wknd jst over 1f out: 8th of 9 in gp* **25/1**

-300 **10** *1* **Abadejo**[40] 4438 4 -9-055 .... WilliamTwiston-Davies(5) 12 33
(J R Jenkins) *chsd ldrs tl ent fnl 2f: sn struggling and wknd over 1f out: 9th of 9 in gp* **50/1**

0420 **11** *1* **Renoir's Lady**[7] 5625 4 -9-050 .... HarryBentley 4 25
(Simon Dow) *racd far side: chsd far side ldr and midfield overall: rdn and effrt to ld trio over 2f out: wknd over 1f out: 2nd of 3 in gp* **8/1**[3]

4606 **12** *35* **Royal Envoy (IRE)**[26] 4928 9 -8-849 .... DanielMuscutt(5) 2
(Paul Howling) *racd in far side trio: led that gp tl 3f out: sn bhd: t.o over 1f out: 3rd of 3 in gp* **33/1**

1m 25.15s (-2.15)**Going Correction** -0.25s/f (Firm)
WFA 3 from 4yo+ 4lb **12**Ran SP%117.2
Speed ratings (Par 101): **102,100,98,96,96 94,93,92,89,88 87,47**
Tote Swingers 1&2 £7.00, 2&3 £13.40, 1&3 £9.20 CSF £28.76 CT £224.09 TOTE £5.90 : £1.90 , £2.00, £3.20 ; EX 43.60 Trifecta £309.70 Pool: £514.84 - 1.23 winning tickets
Owner Bruce Woodward **Bred** D R Botterill **Trained** Great Shefford, Berks

FOCUS
This was an open-looking apprentice handicap. Once again the stands' rail proved the place to be and the trio who went far side were beaten at halfway.

Royal Envoy(IRE) Official explanation: trainer said gelding was unsuited by the good to firm ground

5851 DAVE KENNETH GISBY MEMORIAL MAIDEN STKS 7f (S)
2:30 (2:31) (Class 5) 2-Y-O £3,557 (£1,058; £529; £264) Stalls High

Form RPR
03 1 **Shebebi (USA)**[21] 5126 2-9-3 0 PaulHanagan 2 79+
(John Dunlop) *chsd ldrs: wnt 2nd wl over 1f out: rdn to ld over 1f out: in command and r.o wl fnl f* **6/1**[3]

0 2 2 **Banovallum**[51] 4056 2-9-3 0 LiamKeniry 7 74
(Sylvester Kirk) *chsd ldr tl led and rdn 2f out: hdd over 1f out: unable qck w wnr 1f out: kpt on same pce after* **16/1**

3 1 **Midnight Warrior** 2-9-3 0 JamesDoyle 9 71+
(James Tate) *in tch: rdn and sltly outpcd 2f out: swtchd rt and rallied over 1f out: kpt on to snatch 3rd on post* **25/1**

44 4 nse **Bartack (IRE)**[16] 5325 2-9-3 0 KirstyMilczarek 4 71+
(Luca Cumani) *in tch: rdn and effrt jst over 2f out: drvn and kpt on same pce fr over 1f out: wnt 3rd fnl 100yds tl post* **17/2**

43 5 1 1/4 **Hazzaat (IRE)**[25] 4938 2-9-3 0 AndreaAtzeni 10 67
(Roger Varian) *restless in stalls: s.i.s: pushed along: hdwy into midfield 5f out: rdn 3f out: plugging on but stl plenty to do and nt clr run over 1f out: swtchd lft and kpt on fnl f: nvr gng pce to trble ldrs* **7/4**[1]

04 6 1/2 **Raging Bear (USA)**[24] 5005 2-9-3 0 RichardHughes 3 66
(Richard Hannon) *led tl ent fnl 2f: sn rdn and no ex: 3rd and btn 1f out: wknd and lost 3 pls ins fnl f* **3/1**[2]

7 2 1/4 **Ormindo (USA)** 2-9-3 0 SilvestreDeSousa 6 60
(Mahmood Al Zarooni) *off the pce in last trio: pushed along and sme hdwy jst over 2f out: rdn and no imp over 1f out* **10/1**

8 nk **Ghost Runner (IRE)** 2-9-3 0 TomQueally 1 59
(Sir Henry Cecil) *in tch in midfield: rdn 1/2-way: no prog over 1f out: wknd fnl f* **9/1**

9 4 1/2 **Darkest Night (IRE)** 2-9-3 0 FergusSweeney 8 47
(Jamie Osborne) *hld up in rr: rdn and effrt 2f out: sn struggling and wknd over 1f out* **40/1**

40 10 4 1/2 **Silk Scarf (IRE)**[7] 5619 2-8-12 0 EddieAhern 5 30
(Mark H Tompkins) *dropped towards rr after 2f: rdn and wknd over 2f out: bhd fnl f* **100/1**

1m 25.12s (-2.18) **Going Correction** -0.25s/f (Firm) **10** Ran SP% **118.4**
Speed ratings (Par 95): **102,99,98,98,97 96,93,93,88,83**
Tote Swingers 1&2 £16.70, 2&3 £49.60, 1&3 £17.30 CSF £95.80 TOTE £6.90: £2.60, £4.80, £7.90; EX 106.50 TRIFECTA Not won..

Owner Hamdan Al Maktoum **Bred** Shadwell Farm LLC **Trained** Arundel, W Sussex

FOCUS
An average juvenile maiden. The form makes sense and the winner's latest run could be rated this high.

NOTEBOOK
Shebebi(USA) got an straightforward passage under a positive ride and saw it out readily to land his first success at the third time of asking. His third at Leicester last time was a big step in the right direction and, with ground again to suit, he confirmed himself a progressive 2yo here. This was his trainer's first juvenile winner of 2012. (op 13-2 tchd 7-1)

Banovallum bagged the favoured stands' side rail and, under a sensibly handy ride, improved a bundle on his Newbury debut 51 days earlier. He evidently stays well and this ground was much more to his liking. (op 33-1)

Midnight Warrior, from an in-form yard, fared best of the newcomers and should improve a great deal for the experience. (op 33-1)

Bartack(IRE) proved one-paced up in trip, but he raced more towards the middle of the track and this was a fair effort. He now has the option of nurseries. Official explanation: trainer's rep said colt was unsuited by the track (op 15-2)

Hazzaat(IRE) was badly positioned from the off, however, and covered a fair amount of ground, so is a little better than this. He too now qualifies for nurseries and should find a race in that sphere granted stronger handling. (op 5-2)

Raging Bear(USA) set out to make all but was a sitting duck at the furlong marker and was below his recent Sandown level. At least he can now enter nurseries. (op 9-4)

5852 KM (S) STKS 7f (S)
3:00 (3:00) (Class 6) 3-Y-O+ £2,181 (£644; £322) Stalls High

Form RPR
0345 1 **Kingswinford (IRE)**[16] 5305 6-9-10 74 RichardHughes 5 76
(David Evans) *chsd clr ldng pair: clsd to press ldrs jst over 2f out: rdn to ld wl over 1f out: hrd drvn ins fnl f: r.o wl* ... no — *ld wl over 1f out: rdn and hung rt u.p but kpt on wl fnl f* **5/1**

0 2 1 1/4 **Zing Wing**[39] 4469 4-9-5 65 (t) SilvestreDeSousa 4 68
(Paul Cole) *chsd clr ldng pair: clsd to press ldrs jst over 2f out: rdn to ld 2f out: sn hdd and drvn: styd on same pce fnl f* **9/1**

0332 3 1 1/2 **Beat The Bell**[15] 5347 7-9-5 74 (b) LeonnaMayor(5) 8 69
(Jamie Osborne) *stdd s: t.k.h: hld up bhd: hdwy 3f out: rdn to chse ldng pair over 1f out: no imp ins fnl f* **3/1**[2]

306 4 8 **Celtic Sultan (IRE)**[22] 5110 8-9-5 79 MickyFenton 3 42
(Paul Midgley) *upsides ldr and sn clr: carried grad rt: rdn to ld over 2f out: hdd 2f out: sn btn and wknd over 1f out* **13/8**[1]

00 5 4 1/2 **Queen Hermione (IRE)**[55] 3918 4-9-0 0 (tp) SaleemGolam 1 25
(Linda Jewell) *dwlt and swtchd lft s: a in rr: rdn and wknd jst over 2f out* **200/1**

/0-1 6 shd **Basilica**[12] 5447 4-9-10 80 EddieAhern 6 35
(Bill Turner) *led and sn clr w rival: kpt edging rt: hdd over 2f out: sn rdn and btn: wl bhd fnl f* **4/1**[3]

7 34 **Solars Sun** 3-9-1 0 SeanLevey 2
(Ian Wood) *s.i.s: a bhd: lost tch 3f out: t.o* **28/1**

1m 24.7s (-2.60) **Going Correction** -0.25s/f (Firm)
WFA 3 from 4yo+ 4lb **7** Ran SP% **113.7**
Speed ratings (Par 101): **104,102,100,91,86 86,47**
.The winner was bought by A J Lidderdale for 7,000gns, Celtic Sultan was claimed by A J Lidderdale for £6,000. Zing Wing was claimed by P D Evans for £6,000.\n\x\x

Owner J E Abbey **Bred** J Costello **Trained** Pandy, Monmouths

FOCUS
The two leaders in this seller Basilica and Celtic Sultan cut each other's throats and went a suicidal early pace, teeing it up for the others.

Basilica Official explanation: jockey said gelding hung right throughout

5853 LEASCLIFFHALL.CO.UK H'CAP 6f
3:30 (3:30) (Class 5) (0-75,77) 3-Y-O+ £2,911 (£866; £432; £216) Stalls High

Form RPR
4000 1 **Drawnfromthepast (IRE)**[10] 5502 7-9-2 70 FergusSweeney 9 79
(Jamie Osborne) *chsd ldr tl rdn to ld wl over 1f out: kpt on wl u.p fnl f* **25/1**

0005 2 1/2 **Haadeeth**[3] 5774 5-8-10 64 SilvestreDeSousa 10 71
(David Evans) *taken down early: t.k.h: chsd ldrs: rdn and chsd wnr over 1f out: pressing wnr fnl f: kpt on but a hld* **6/1**[3]

6322 3 3/4 **Rambo Will**[22] 5097 4-9-6 74 RichardHughes 7 79
(J R Jenkins) *t.k.h: chsd ldrs: rdn and effrt to chse ldng pair 1f out: kpt on same pce ins fnl f* **3/1**[1]

4102 4 1/2 **Bavarian Princess (USA)**[9] 5548 4-9-2 77 ConorHarrison(7) 8 80
(Mrs K Burke) *fly-jmpd leaving stalls and s.i.s: hld up in last trio: hdwy 2f out: swtchd rt ent fnl f: styd on same pce u.p ins fnl f* **14/1**

0653 5 1 3/4 **Desert Strike**[12] 5447 6-9-5 73 (p) HayleyTurner 11 71
(Conor Dore) *led: hdd and rdn wl over 1f out: sn hung rt and no ex: plugged on same pce fnl f* **4/1**[2]

0425 6 1 1/2 **Paradise Spectre**[16] 5320 5-9-4 72 JamesDoyle 3 65
(Mrs K Burke) *s.i.s and rdn along leaving stalls: in tch towards rr: rdn and hdwy 2f out: no imp u.p 1f out: plugged on same pce after* **3/1**[1]

0042 7 nk **Silkee Supreme**[12] 5443 3-8-10 66 (b) SeanLevey 2 58
(Richard Hannon) *in tch: rdn and effrt 2f out: styng on same pce and no imp whn pushed rt ent fnl f* **14/1**

106 8 8 **Isola Verde**[46] 4221 3-9-0 70 TomQueally 4 36
(James Fanshawe) *in tch towards rr: rdn and no rspnse wl over 1f out: sn wknd* **16/1**

2614 9 2 1/4 **Efistorm**[12] 5440 11-8-10 69 DarrenEgan(5) 1 28
(Joseph Tuite) *in tch towards rr: effrt 2f out: sn btn and wknd over 1f out* **14/1**

1m 10.7s (-2.00) **Going Correction** -0.25s/f (Firm)
WFA 3 from 4yo+ 2lb **9** Ran SP% **114.0**
Speed ratings (Par 103): **103,102,101,100,98 96,95,85,82**
Tote Swingers 1&2 £25.40, 2&3 £6.50, 1&3 £14.50 CSF £165.63 CT £590.33 TOTE £36.70: £7.80, £2.50, £1.80; EX 177.70 Trifecta £646.20 Pool: £873.31 - 1.00 winning tickets.

Owner Mark Benton **Bred** D And Mrs D Veitch **Trained** Upper Lambourn, Berks

FOCUS
An ordinary sprint handicap, run at a decent pace.

Drawnfromthepast(IRE) Official explanation: trainer said, regarding apparent improvement in form, that the gelding was suited by the quicker ground and weaker race.

Bavarian Princess(USA) Official explanation: jockey said filly was slowly away

Paradise Spectre Official explanation: jockey said gelding was slowly away

5854 LADBROKESGAMES.COM MEDIAN AUCTION MAIDEN STKS 5f
4:00 (4:00) (Class 6) 2-Y-O £2,181 (£644; £322) Stalls High

Form RPR
0303 1 **Cut No Ice (IRE)**[17] 5267 2-8-12 78 (b[1]) RichardHughes 5 74
(Paul Cole) *mde all: shkn up and readily asserted over 1f out: edgd rt ins fnl f: eased towards fin* **2/5**[1]

0002 2 2 1/2 **Marvelino**[11] 5485 2-9-3 73 LukeMorris 3 67
(Pat Eddery) *wnt rt s: sn rdn along in 3rd: chsd clr wnr u.p jst over 1f out: no imp* **7/2**[2]

3 1 **Outbid** 2-8-12 0 FergusSweeney 1 58
(Jamie Osborne) *s.i.s: rn green in rr: rdn and no imp wl over 2f out: styd on 1f out to go 3rd ins fnl f: no ch w wnr* **7/1**[3]

06 4 5 **Many Elements**[11] 5485 2-9-3 0 KierenFox 4 45
(Brett Johnson) *chsd wnr tl over 1f out: sn btn: wknd fnl f* **33/1**

59.2s (-0.80) **Going Correction** -0.25s/f (Firm) **4** Ran SP% **109.1**
Speed ratings (Par 93): **96,92,90,82**
CSF £2.16 TOTE £1.60; EX 2.10.

Owner Denford Stud **Bred** Swordlestown Stud **Trained** Whatcombe, Oxon

FOCUS
A maiden lacking depth. The second and third set the level.

NOTEBOOK
Cut No Ice(IRE) had been found a golden opportunity and she took full advantage, shedding her maiden tag at the fifth time of asking. She travelled all over her rivals in first-time blinkers and didn't have to be extended to score. This was a weak affair, but she ought to be high on confidence now and a return to 6f should suit in nurseries. (op 4-9)

Marvelino is officially rated 5lb lower than the winner and he gives the form a straightforward look. This was his tenth outing, having kicked off in the Brocklesby back in March, and he's clearly vulnerable to anything useful, but does deserve a change of luck. (op 11-4)

Outbid, bred to stay further, took time to get the hang of things on this racecourse debut. She kept on steadily from the furlong marker and ought to improve a deal for this encouraging introduction. (op 10-1 tchd 11-1)

Many Elements tried to go with the winner yet was found wanting from the two-furlong marker and ultimately dropped right out. He now qualifies for nurseries but looks to need more time before coming good. (op 25-1)

5855 ZIPPY MEMORIAL H'CAP 1m 4f
4:30 (4:30) (Class 6) (0-65,70) 3-Y-O £2,181 (£644; £322) Stalls High

Form RPR
2330 1 **Kittens**[17] 5265 3-9-1 59 WilliamCarson 5 66
(William Muir) *in tch: rdn and effrt to chse ldng pair 2f out: drvn and chalng 1f out: led wl ins fnl f: r.o wl* **7/1**

-021 2 nk **Hesperides**[11] 5477 3-9-12 70 RichardHughes 1 76
(Harry Dunlop) *chsd ldrs: effrt to chse ldr 2f out: sn swtchd lft and drvn to chal over 1f out: led fnl 100yds: sn hdd: kpt on but a jst hld after* **10/3**[2]

035 3 3/4 **Kashgar**[19] 5219 3-9-4 62 (v[1]) LukeMorris 2 67
(Michael Bell) *rdn along leaving stalls: led after 2f: rdn and fnd ex over 2f out: drvn and hrd pressed over 1f out: edging rt u.p and hdd fnl 100yds: no ex* **4/1**[3]

0606 4 12 **Merchants Return**[13] 5408 3-8-7 54 SimonPearce(3) 8 40
(Lydia Pearce) *stdd s: hld up in rr: rdn and effrt ent fnl 2f: sn outpcd and modest 4th fr over 1f out* **20/1**

0063 5 9 **Runway Girl (IRE)**[38] 4510 3-9-1 59 JamesDoyle 7 30
(Roger Charlton) *chsd ldrs tl hdwy to press ldr 9f out: rdn and unable qck over 2f out: btn 2f out: sn wknd and wl bhd 1f out* **9/4**[1]

0033 6 15 **Simply**[12] 5452 3-8-11 55 NeilCallan 3
(Eve Johnson Houghton) *led for 2f: in tch after tl rdn and wknd over 2f out: wl bhd and virtually p.u ins fnl f: t.o* **9/2**

-050 7 2 **Farleaze**[13] 5408 3 -8-10**54**.. FergusSweeney 4
(Martyn Meade) *t.k.h early: hld up in tch: rdn and short lived effrt 4f out: wknd over 2f out: wl bhd fnl f: t.o* **33/1**

2m 37.5s (-3.40)**Going Correction** -0.425s/f (Firm) 7Ran SP%112.2
Speed ratings (Par 99): **94,93,93,85,79 69,67**
Tote Swingers 1&2 £4.80, 2&3 £2.20, 1&3 £3.70 CSF £29.32 CT £105.17 TOTE £8.90 : £3.00, £1.30; EX 24.40 Trifecta £65.50 Pool: £764.42 - 8.63 winning tickets .
Owner Muir Racing Partnership - Chester **Bred** Moyns Park Estate And Stud Ltd **Trained** Lambourn, Berks

FOCUS
A moderate 3yo handicap, run at a fair pace and the principals came well clear.

5856 BRITISH STALLION STUDS SUPPORTING BRITISH RACING E B F FILLIES' H'CAP 1m 1f 149y
5:00 (5:01) (Class 4) (0-85,85) 3-Y-0+ **£5,175** (£1,540; £769 ; £384 **Stalls** Centre

Form RPR
5212 1 **Sound Hearts (USA)**[16] 5328 3 -9-5**85**................................ NeilCallan 7 95+
(Roger Varian) *chsd ldrs: chsd clr ldr over 2f out: rdn and chal over 1f out: led and edgd rt ins fnl f: styd on to assert towards fin* **5/1**[2]

6062 2 1 ½ **Cochabamba (IRE)**[24] 4984 4 -9-8**81**.......................... RichardHughes 9 88
(Roger Teal) *chsd ldr tl led after 1f: clr 6f out: rdn over 2f out: hrd pressed over 1f out: hdd ins fnl f: no ex and btn towards fin* **7/1**[3]

0315 3 ¾ **Candycakes (IRE)**[16] 5328 3 -8-11**77**.......................... HayleyTurner 3 82+
(Michael Bell) *t.k.h: hld up in rr: nt clr run over 3f out: rdn and hdwy into modest 5th over 2f out: chsd clr ldng pair over 1f out: r.o wl: swtchd lft ins fnl f: nvr quite getting to ldrs* **10/1**

3362 4 3 ¼ **Corsetry (USA)**[20] 5163 3 -8-9**75**...................................... TomQueally 4 73
(Sir Henry Cecil) *hld up wl bhd: pushed along briefly 6f out: c wd and effrt in modest 7th 2f out: edgd rt and kpt on fnl f: nvr trbld ldrs* **4/1**[1]

1-32 5 2 ¼ **Albaspina (IRE)**[11] 5480 3 -9-1**81**.................................... LukeMorris 8 75
(Sir Mark Prescott Bt) *racd off the pce in midfield: rdn and effrt over 2f out: no imp and plugged on same pce fr over 1f out* **4/1**[1]

6152 6 2 ¼ **Amoya (GER)**[19] 5218 5 -9-7**83**.................................... RaulDaSilva(3) 5 72
(Philip McBride) *led for 1f: chsd ldr tl over 2f out: sn struggling: wknd wl over 1f out* **12/1**

0200 7 7 **Silken Thoughts**[33] 4684 4 -9-12**85**.......................... SilvestreDeSousa 2 59
(John Berry) *racd off the pce in midfield: rdn and effrt over 2f out: no imp over 1f out: wl btn and eased wl ins fnl f* **8/1**

5331 8 19 **Khazeena**[20] 5166 3 -8-13**79**.. PaulHanagan 6 13
(William Haggas) *hld up wl off the pce in last trio: rdn and no hdwy 3f out: t.o fnl f* **15/2**

3660 9 1 ½ **Estrela**[22] 5094 3 -9-5**85**...(p) JamesDoyle 10 16
(Roger Charlton) *chsd ldrs tl 4f out: lost pl and bhd 3f out: t.o fnl f* **10/1**

1m 59.95s (-4.95)**Going Correction** -0.425s/f (Firm)
WFA 3 from 4yo+ 7lb 9Ran SP%117.9
Speed ratings (Par 102): **102,100,100,97,95 94,88,73,72**
Tote Swingers 1&2 £7.30, 2&3 £12.10, 1&3 £7.30 CSF £40.70 CT £340.77 TOTE £5.70 : £2.10 , £2.70, £2.80 ; EX 40.20 Trifecta £861.90 Pool: £1164.74 - 0.63 winning tickets .
Owner Y Masuda **Bred** M A Co , Ltd **Trained** Newmarket, Suffolk

FOCUS
Not a bad handicap. The field were fairly strung out.
T/Jkpt: Not won. T/Plt: £747.50 to a £1 stake. Pool: £87,653.78 - 85.60 winning tickets T/Qpdt: £30.10 to a £1 stake. Pool: £7,707.23 - 189.27 winning tickets SP

5689 DUNDALK (A.W) (L-H)
Sunday, September 2

OFFICIAL GOING: Standard

5858a IRISH STALLION FARMS EUROPEAN BREEDERS MEDIAN AUCTION MAIDEN 6f (P)
2:50 (2:52) 2-Y-0 **£7,187** (£1,666; £729 ; £416)

RPR
1 **Very Elusive (IRE)**[9] 5690 2 -9-2.......................(t) EmmetMcNamara(3) 9 88
(G M Lyons, Ire) *trckd ldrs in 5th: swtchd out over 1f out: sn led: drew away ins fnl 100yds* **16/1**

2 1 **Leitir Mor (IRE)**[9] 5608 2 -9-5102................................(p) KevinManning 7 85
(J S Bolger, Ire) *racd in 2nd: pressed ldr over 1f out: kpt on wout pce of wnr fnl 100yds* **1/1**[1]

3 ½ **Polish Crown**[14] 5382 2 -9-0.. FranBerry 6 78
(Mark Johnston) *broke smartly: led tl hdd 1f out: one pce fnl 100yds* **2/1**[2]

4 2 ½ **Rockabilly Riot (IRE)**[9] 5690 2 -9-580.........................(b¹) GaryCarroll 4 76
(G M Lyons, Ire) *trckd ldrs in 4th: nt qckn w principals appr fnl f: kpt on same pce* **8/1**[3]

5 3 **In Salutem** 2 -9-5.. ShaneFoley 8 67+
(K J Condon, Ire) *slowly away and in rr: plenty to do 2f out: styd on wl fnl f: nrst fin* **25/1**

6 1 ¾ **Victor's Beach (IRE)**[9] 5690 2 -9-0.......................... ConorHoban(5) 10 61
(M Halford, Ire) *racd mid-div: no imp whn hmpd ent fnl f* **40/1**

7 1 ½ **Red Clasp (IRE)**[9] 5689 2 -9-0.. PatSmullen 14 52
(Ms Joanna Morgan, Ire) *racd in 3rd tl wknd appr fnl f* **12/1**

8 2 **Traps Army (IRE)**[11] 5493 2 -9-5.................................. WayneLordan 13 51
(W McCreery, Ire) *racd in mid-div: no imp wl over 1f out* **66/1**

9 ¾ **Aednat**[49] 4122 2 -8-11.. ShaneGorey(3) 5 44
(S Slevin, Ire) *racd in mid-div: nt qckn over 1f out* **50/1**

10 2 ¾ **Firey Sally (IRE)**2 -9-0.. CO'Donoghue 2 35
(Mrs Gillian Callaghan, Ire) *hld up: nvr a threat: kpt on* **25/1**

11 2 ¼ **Mystery Angel (IRE)**2 -9-0.. BenCurtis 11 29
(John C McConnell, Ire) *a towards rr* **50/1**

12 1 **Las Encinas** 2 -8-11.. IJBrennan(3) 1 26
(Adrian McGuinness, Ire) *racd in rr on inner: nvr a threat: wl adrift appr fnl f* **50/1**

13 6 **Trainspotting** 2 -9-5.. NGMcCullagh 12 13
(Charles O'Brien, Ire) *slowly away: a in rr* **33/1**

1m 12.58s (72.58) 13Ran SP%128.5
CSF £33.59 TOTE £15.60 : £2.40 , £1.20 , £1.02 ; DF 43.80 .
Owner Qatar Racing Limited **Bred** James Waldron **Trained** Dunsany, Co. Meath

FOCUS
This looked an above-average maiden. The standard was set by a horse rated 102, the presence of a British raider added to its intrigue and there were some potential improvers in the line-up too.

NOTEBOOK
Very Elusive (IRE)had made the running here last Monday before folding into fifth, but that was quite a decent effort in a good race, and he benefited from a less aggressive ride here. Settled nicely in mid-division, he made up ground quite easily early in the home straight and showed a nice attitude to get on top close home. He's an improving type that should hold his own in stakes races.
Leitir Mor (IRE)is fast running out of excuses. Having raced on bad ground recently, he got his preferred conditions here and was always perfectly placed. When the time came for him to go and win his race 2f out, he looked very ordinary. (op 5/4 tchd 11/8)
Polish Crown, who was narrowly denied at Pontefract last time, went about her business from the front despite stepping up in trip. She looked in trouble 2f from home but kept on well and just wasn't good enough. (op 7/4)
Rockabilly Riot (IRE) a shorter-priced stable companion of the winner, was always prominent but couldn't land a blow when it mattered most. (op 10/1)
In Salutem made an encouraging debut, staying on nicely through beaten horses in the home straight. He'll appreciate further next time.

5857a, 5859a - 5864a (Foreign Racing) - See Raceform Interactive

5844 BADEN-BADEN (L-H)
Sunday, September 2

OFFICIAL GOING: Turf: good

5865a LONGINES - GROSSER PREIS VON BADEN (GROUP 1) (3YO+) (TURF) 1m 4f
4:00 (4:01) 3-Y-0+ **£125,000** (£50,000; £20,833 ; £12,500)

RPR
1 **Danedream (GER)**[43] 4322 4 -9-30.. AStarke 5 116
(P Schiergen, Germany) *prom: trckd ldr after 2f: led on stands' rail under 1 1/2f out: rdn over 1f out: r.o wl fnl f: a holding runner-up* **7/10**[1]

2 ½ **Ovambo Queen (GER)**[42] 4383 5 -9-30.................................. THellier 1 115
(Dr A Bolte, Germany) *a.p: led 2f out towards stands' side: hdd under 1 1/2f out: 3rd and rdn ins fnl f: rallied gamely u.p to regain 2nd: a hld by wnr* **10/1**

3 ½ **Pastorius (GER)**[35] 4636 3 -8-110.. ADeVries 6 117
(Mario Hofer, Germany) *hld up towards rr but wl in tch: chal ldrs on their ins fr 2f out: 2nd and ev ch ins fnl f: sn rdn and no ex: lost 2nd cl home* **41/10**[3]

4 2 ½ **Novellist (IRE)**[63] 3683 3 -8-110.................................... WilliamBuick 8 113
(A Wohler, Germany) *trckd ldng gp: 5th and shkn up 2f out: 4th whn rdn and swtchd ins over 1f out: no imp fnl f* **14/5**[2]

5 6 **Girolamo (GER)**[33] 4685 3 -8-110.................................. MircoDemuro 3 104
(P Schiergen, Germany) *chsd ldr early: dropped bhd ldng gp after 2f: rdn and nt qckn over 2f out: wknd fnl f* **135/10**

6 ½ **Energia Davos (BRZ)**[105] 4 -9-60.......................................(b) SHellyn 7 103
(Fabricio Borges, Sweden) *hld up in rr: styd alone on ins turning for home jst over 2f out: nvr in contention* **203/10**

7 4 **Next Vision (IRE)**[28] 6 -9-60.. EFrank 2 96
(J Hirschberger, Germany) *led: set stdy gallop: rdn and hdd 2f out: wknd qckly* **237/10**

2m 36.23s (2.77)
WFA 3 from 4yo+ 9lb 7Ran SP%129.5
WIN (incl. 10 euro stake): 17. PLACES: 11, 13, 13. SF: 87 .
Owner Gestut Burg Eberstein & Teruya Yoshida **Bred** Gestut Brummerhof **Trained** Germany

NOTEBOOK
Danedream(GER) waved goodbye to Germany with a decisive victory in the Grosser Preis von Baden to remind potential rivals that she will be a tough nut to crack when she defends her Prix de l'Arc de Triomphe crown next month. Bookmakers, however, issued only a lukewarm response after a gutsy performance to land a second victory in her country's most prestigious race. Although she scored by only a half-length from Group 2 winner Ovambo Queen, her superiority was clear as she also held at bay Germany's best 3-y-os, including the Deutsches Derby 1-2-3. She was settled in third, not far off an unexpectedly tepid gallop set by Next Vision, supposedly taking the role of pacemaker for Derby runner-up Novellist. Starke sent Danedream across to the stands' rail as they turned for home in what was the race-winning move as she kicked a couple of lengths ahead. Though she was challenged hard by both the placed horses, she needed only to be kept up to her work to score. Her next race will be the Arc and the Japan Cup will be her final run before retirement.
Ovambo Queen (GER)is now likely to go on her travels, with either the Breeders' Cup Filly & Mare Turf or Japan's Queen Elizabeth II Cup on the agenda.
Pastorius(GER), the Derby winner, may now take on Frankel in the Qipco Champion Stakes.

5866 - 5867a (Foreign Racing) - See Raceform Interactive

5848 VELIEFENDI
Sunday, September 2

OFFICIAL GOING: Turf: good

5868a INTERNATIONAL BOSPHORUS CUP (LOCAL GROUP 2) (3YO+) (TURF) 1m 4f
1:00 (12:00) 3-Y-0+ **£150,000** (£60,000; £30,000)

RPR
1 **Mitico (TUR)**[23] 4 -9-60.. SelimKaya 2
(Z Guneli, Turkey) *led: jnd 3 1/2f out: hdd 2f out: rallied u.p appr fnl f: regained ld 50yds fr home: all out* **1/20**[1]

2 ½ **Hanbes (TUR)**[23] 4 -9-60.. HalisKaratas 3
(A Sacan, Turkey) *trckd ldr: chal on outside 3 1/2f out: led 2f out: r.o u.p fnl f: hdd 50yds out: no ex* **3/5**[2]

3 3 **Kutbey (TUR)**[114] 4 -9-60.. GokhanYildiz 6
(M T Balyemez, Turkey) *settled 3rd: rdn 3f out: nvr on terms w front two* **5/4**[3]

2m 33.37s (4.57) 3Ran SP%202.2
PARI-MUTUEL (including 1Turkish lira stakes): WIN: 1.05; SF 1.45 .
Owner Necati Demirkol **Bred** Necati Demirkol **Trained** Turkey

5869a INTERNATIONAL TOPKAPI TROPHY (LOCAL GROUP 2) (3YO+) (TURF) 1m
2:30 (12:00) 3-Y-0+ **£225,000** (£90,000; £45,000 ; £22,500)

RPR
1 **Master Of Hounds (USA)**[155] 1150 4 -9-60....... ChristopheSoumillon 6 115
(William Haggas) *trckd ldr on outside: 2nd and travelling wl over 2f out: shkn up and qckd to ld appr fnl f: r.o wl* **21/20**[1]

	2	nk	**Archbishop (USA)**[30] 4760 3-8-13 0 ... FrankieDettori 3 (Brian Meehan) *trckd ldrs: 4th on rail and swtchd outside over 2f out: sn rdn: r.o wl u.p fnl f: nt quite get up* **21/10**[2]	111
	3	2 ½	**Indomito (GER)**[21] 5141 6-9-6 0 ... EPedroza 8 (A Wohler, Germany) *trckd ldrs: 3rd and ev ch 2f out: sn rdn: kpt on wout qckning fnl f* **7/2**	108
	4	1	**Fast Stars Line (TUR)**[21] 3-8-13 0 ... AkinSozen 7 (N Kocken, Turkey) *led: kicked clr over 2 1/2f out: hdd appr fnl f: one pce tl fdd cl home* **17/2**	103
	5	1	**Red Duke (USA)**[30] 4760 3-8-13 0 ... JamieSpencer 11 (David Simcock) *hld up in rr: tk sltly clsr order 3f out: gd hdwy on outside under 2f out: styd on wl fnl f: nrest at fin* **169/10**	101
	6	1	**Dutyfree (TUR)**[21] 4-9-6 0 ...(b) AhmetCelik 5 (S Karagoz, Turkey) *scrubbed along to go prom on rail whn hmpd and dropped bk towards rr after 1f: prog into midfield 2 1/2f out: kpt on wout qckning u.p fnl f* **111/10**	101
	7	2 ½	**Pakal (GER)**[35] 4636 3-8-13 0 ... ASuborics 1 (W Figge, Germany) *wnt lft s: hld up towards rr: last 3f out: sme prog over 1f out: nt pce to chal* **89/10**	93
	8	½	**Van Ellis**[28] 4838 3-8-13 0 ... KierenFallon 10 (Mark Johnston) *settled midfield on outside: pushed along to hold pl over 3f out: rdn and no imp fr 2f out* **33/10**	91
	9	2	**Ergoz (TUR)**[21] 4-9-6 0 ...(b) SelimKaya 4 (T Sit, Turkey) *bmpd s: settled at rr of midfield: rdn and no hdwy fr over 2f out* **108/10**	90
	10	nk	**Lucky Bridle (IRE)**[26] 4935 3-9-0 0 ow1 ...(t) GeraldMosse 9 (C Ferland, France) *dwlt: racd freely towards rr: prog into midfield 2f out: sn wknd u.p* **27/1**	87
	11	2 ½	**Non Stop (TUR)**[21] 4-9-6 0 ... GokhanGokce 2 (Y Bulut, Turkey) *midfield: towards rr fr 2 1/2f out: swtchd outside and hrd rdn 2f out: no imp* **51/20**[3]	83

1m 34.49s (-0.84)
WFA 3 from 4yo+ 5lb **11** Ran SP% **201.2**
PARI-MUTUEL (including 1Turkish lira stakes): WIN: 2.05; PLACE (1-2): 1.10, 1.50; DF 3.85; SF 6.00.
Owner Sheikh Mohammed Bin Khalifa Al Maktoum **Bred** Silk And Scarlet Syndicate **Trained** Newmarket, Suffolk

NOTEBOOK
Master Of Hounds(USA), having his first run for his current trainer following a campaign in Dubai in the spring, was given a positive ride and his kick for home after racing in second proved decisive. His trainer is considering a Group 1 in Italy or the Prix Dollar for the colt before he returns to Mike De Kock for another Dubai campaign.
Archbishop(USA) has progressed steadily with racing and went close here after coming out of the pack in the straight. His trainer has done well at the Breeders' Cup in the past and that could be where he is heading next.
Red Duke(USA) came from well back and finished to good effect, but never got seriously involved.
Van Ellis raced on the outside of the field and was being pushed along to hold his place on the home turn.

5870 - 5871a (Foreign Racing) - See Raceform Interactive

5527 FFOS LAS (L-H)
Monday, September 3

OFFICIAL GOING: Soft (good to soft in places) (6.8) changing to soft after race 2 (2.50)
Another all sprint card due to drainage work in the back straight.
Wind: light across Weather: sunny

5872 LOUGHOR MAIDEN STKS 5f
2:20 (2:21) (Class 5) 2-Y-O **£2,264** (£673; £336) **Stalls** Centre

Form				RPR
252	1		**Vincentti (IRE)**[18] 5260 2-9-3 69 ... KierenFox 5 (Ronald Harris) *trckd ldr: shkn up to ld over 1f out: rdn clr fnl 100yds* **1/2**[1]	82+
	2	2 ¾	**Truly Madly (IRE)**[44] 4352 2-8-12 0 ... JohnFahy 1 (John Joseph Murphy, Ire) *in tch: urged along 2f out: drvn to chse wnr 1f out: edgd lft u.p and btn fnl 100yds* **3/1**[2]	67
	3	3 ¼	**Peranova (IRE)**[102] 2433 2-8-12 0 ... MartinHarley 2 (W McCreery, Ire) *led: urged along and hdd over 1f out: wknd fnl f* **6/1**[3]	55

1m 3.88s (5.58) **Going Correction** +0.975s/f (Soft) **3** Ran SP% **106.0**
Speed ratings (Par 95): **94,89,84**
CSF £2.21 TOTE £1.60; EX 2.00.
Owner Robert & Nina Bailey **Bred** Stephanie Hanly **Trained** Earlswood, Monmouths

FOCUS
A drying day, but the ground was still taxing courtesy of the recent wet spell and the runners kicked up plenty of turf in the opener. This 2yo maiden was weakened by the pair of non-runners and the market got it spot on. Tricky form to pin down.
NOTEBOOK
Vincentti(IRE) disposed of the two Irish challengers to break his duck at the fourth attempt. He proved free early and initially had to dig deep to master the runner-up, but he was well on top at the finish. He handled this ground by far the best, but his trainer believes he wants a quicker surface and is a decent performer in the making. Bar one blip over 6f here two runs back, he has developed a decent profile and should win a nursery. (op 10-11)
Truly Madly(IRE) was found out by testing ground over 6f at the Curragh last time, but her previous form entitled her to respect. She moved up nearing the final furlong, but was ultimately put in her place and she ideally needs a sounder surface. (op 6-4)
Peranova(IRE) finished fourth on her debut at Tipperary in May. She showed decent early pace, but was in trouble on this contrasting surface from 2f out and is another that wants better ground. (op 7-1)

5873 CELTIC HOLIDAY PARKS NURSERY 6f
2:50 (2:51) (Class 5) (0-70,71) 2-Y-O **£2,911** (£866; £432; £216) **Stalls** Centre

Form				RPR
2365	1		**Hardy Red (IRE)**[12] 5475 2-9-7 70 ... FergusSweeney 7 (Jamie Osborne) *hld up: hdwy to chse ldrs 4f out: pushed along ins fnl 2f: rdn to ld 1f out: sn drew clr* **9/2**[2]	75
1321	2	2 ¼	**Khefyn (IRE)**[7] 5654 2-9-8 71 6ex ... KierenFox 5 (Ronald Harris) *stdd s: hdwy to ld 4f out: drvn 2f out: hung lft and hdd 1f out: sn brushed aside: eased and jst hld on for 2nd* **1/2**[1]	69
0002	3	nk	**Michael's Song (IRE)**[10] 5532 2-8-5 59 ow2 ... CharlesBishop(5) 1 (Mick Channon) *cl up: rdn 3f out: drvn and ev ch 2f out: one pce fnl f* **13/2**[3]	56
0505	4	1 ¼	**Katy Spirit (IRE)**[10] 5532 2-8-0 52 ... RaulDaSilva(3) 6 (Michael Blanshard) *led: hdd 4f out: rdn and dropped last 3f out: drvn 2f out: plodded on one pce fnl f* **12/1**	46
433	5	5	**Scoobys Girl (IRE)**[20] 5210 2-8-0 49 ... FrankieMcDonald 4 (Daniel Mark Loughnane) *cl up: pushed along 3f out: drvn and wknd 2f out* **20/1**	28

1m 17.33s (7.33) **Going Correction** +0.975s/f (Soft) **5** Ran SP% **110.6**
Speed ratings (Par 95): **90,87,86,84,78**
Tote Swingers 1&2 £5.00 CSF £7.33 TOTE £3.90: £2.90, £1.02; EX 12.10.
Owner Tony Taylor & Patrick Gage **Bred** David Allan **Trained** Upper Lambourn, Berks

FOCUS
Unsurprisingly the ground was officially changed to soft all over after the first two races. A moderate sprint nursery. Again the field elected to head down the centre of the track. The winner is rated back to his best.
NOTEBOOK
Hardy Red(IRE) arrived with something to prove, but he bounced back to his early season form and readily got off the mark at the sixth attempt. His narrow defeat to subsequent Group 2 winner Alhebayeb looked a flash in the pan, but he probably repeated that form here and it proves he can mix it on different ground. This was just his second outing in handicap company and he looked to want all of this trip, indeed his pedigree suggests a stiffer test is what he will want down the line. (op 7-1)
Khefyn(IRE), penalised for his Chepstow win, proved all the rage to give his connections an opening-race double. He moved into the lead after 2f and held every chance, but that positive move probably cost him late on back over this extra furlong. On such ground, dropping back to the minimum should prove his bag. (op 4-9 tchd 8-15)
Michael's Song(IRE) looked uneasy when the chips were down on this testing surface. She's still capable of better in this sphere. (op 6-1 tchd 7-1)
Katy Spirit(IRE) pulled her way into an early lead, but was soon headed off by the runner-up and found herself at the back. She ran close enough to her last-time-out form with the third. (tchd 16-1)
Scoobys Girl(IRE) was well beaten off on this nursery debut and probably needs further already. (tchd 16-1)

5874 STRADEY PARK H'CAP 6f
3:20 (3:21) (Class 6) (0-60,60) 3-Y-O+ **£1,617** (£481; £240; £120) **Stalls** Centre

Form				RPR
432	1		**Greyemkay**[7] 5660 4-8-4 46 oh1 ... MarkCoumbe(3) 2 (Richard Price) *sn led: hdd 4f out: rdn 3f out: regained ld 2f out: strly pressed and hdd over 1f out: rallied wl to ld fnl 50yds* **11/2**[3]	55
6-15	2	hd	**Running Mate (IRE)**[67] 3546 5-9-7 60 ...(t) IanMongan 4 (Jo Crowley) *midfield: hdwy 3f out: pressed wnr 2f out: drvn to ld over 1f out: hdd fnl 50yds* **8/1**	68
0035	3	2 ½	**Red Avalanche (IRE)**[16] 5362 5-9-4 57 ... KirstyMilczarek 5 (Tony Newcombe) *hld up: pushed along early: drvn 4f out: last 3f out: hdwy to chse ldng pair 2f out: wnt lft u.p 1f out: no ex fnl 75yds* **11/4**[1]	57
0-00	4	1 ½	**Tijuca (IRE)**[63] 3702 3-8-5 46 oh1 ... JohnFahy 8 (Ed de Giles) *in tch: hdwy 3f out: drvn and outpcd whn briefly short of room 2f out: plugged on* **50/1**	42
1456	5	hd	**Medam**[19] 5247 3-8-11 52 ... MartinHarley 3 (Shaun Harris) *in tch: lost pl 3f out: rdn and hdwy 2f out: sn one pce* **20/1**	47
5205	6	3	**The Name Is Frank**[19] 5240 7-9-0 60 ...(p) JakePayne(7) 9 (Mark Gillard) *cl up: pressed ldrs 3f out: rdn 2f out: wknd fnl f* **7/1**	45
0061	7	4 ½	**Athaakeel (IRE)**[7] 5660 6-8-12 56 6ex ...(b) DarrenEgan(5) 10 (Ronald Harris) *broke wl: settled into midfield: pushed along over 2f out: no imp over 1f out* **7/1**	27
2-4	8	4	**Nafa (IRE)**[245] 8 4-9-4 57 ... SeanQuinlan 7 (Daniel Mark Loughnane) *hld up: pushed along 3f out: wknd over 1f out* **20/1**	15
0-30	9	5	**Euroquip Boy (IRE)**[7] 5681 5-9-6 59 ...(v[1]) HayleyTurner 1 (Michael Scudamore) *cl up: led 4f out: rdn and hdd 2f out: sn dropped away* **7/2**[2]	
0-04	10	4 ½	**Your Word**[37] 4605 3-8-13 54 ...(b[1]) FergusSweeney 6 (Daniel Kubler) *slow away: sn rcvrd into midfield: drvn 3f out: sn struggling* **25/1**	

1m 16.08s (6.08) **Going Correction** +0.975s/f (Soft)
WFA 3 from 4yo+ 2lb **10** Ran SP% **115.7**
Speed ratings (Par 101): **98,97,94,92,92 88,82,76,70,64**
Tote Swingers 1&2 £6.50, 2&3 £6.10, 1&3 £3.10 CSF £45.62 CT £146.59 TOTE £2.90: £1.20, £3.00, £1.30; EX 60.50.
Owner Richard Price & Maria Slade **Bred** Shade Oak Stud **Trained** Ullingswick, H'fords

FOCUS
A weak sprint handicap and underfoot conditions found out the majority. Similar form to Chepstow from the winner.

5875 IWEC ELECTRICAL H'CAP 5f
3:50 (3:51) (Class 6) (0-60,57) 3-Y-O **£1,617** (£481; £240; £120) **Stalls** Centre

Form				RPR
4450	1		**Bitter Lemon**[18] 5263 3-8-13 49 ...(p) FergusSweeney 4 (Tony Newcombe) *cl up: rdn 2f out: pressed ldr and drifted lft 1f out: kpt on wl to ld fnl 50yds* **11/2**	56
1050	2	¾	**Roy's Legacy**[2] 5831 3-9-2 57 ...(t) DarrenEgan(5) 1 (Shaun Harris) *led: urged along 2f out: drvn 1f out: hdd fnl 50yds* **3/1**[2]	62
5043	3	hd	**Uncle Timmy**[17] 5296 3-9-2 55 ...(vt) SophieDoyle(3) 6 (David Evans) *cl up: pushed along over 1f out: briefly short of room ins fnl f: kpt on one pce* **4/1**[3]	59
0311	4	2 ¼	**Verus Delicia (IRE)**[32] 4734 3-9-3 56 ... MarkCoumbe(3) 2 (Daniel Mark Loughnane) *missed break: hdwy 3f out: drvn 2f out: no imp fr over 1f out* **13/8**[1]	52+
	5	nk	**Model Behaviour (IRE)**[49] 4160 3-8-12 48 ... TadhgO'Shea 5 (Daniel Mark Loughnane) *hld up: pushed along 2f out: no imp fnl f* **6/1**	43

1m 3.25s (4.95) **Going Correction** +0.975s/f (Soft) **5** Ran SP% **112.8**
Speed ratings (Par 99): **99,97,97,93,93**
CSF £22.36 TOTE £11.50: £2.40, £3.20; EX 25.30.
Owner Joli Racing **Bred** Bearstone Stud **Trained** Yarnscombe, Devon

FOCUS
This was an ordinary 3yo sprint handicap and a tight affair. This time the field explored a route nearer to the stands' side, but it was the one that kept to the middle that prevailed. The form is taken at face value with the winner at her best.
Roy's Legacy Official explanation: jockey said colt hung right-handed; trainer's rep said colt lost near-fore shoe
Verus Delicia(IRE) Official explanation: jockey said filly was slowly away

5876 THREE RIVERS H'CAP 5f
4:20 (4:20) (Class 6) (0-65,65) 3-Y-O+ **£1,704** (£503; £251) **Stalls** Centre

Form				RPR
3043	1		**Spic 'n Span**[21] 5149 7-8-7 51 oh2 ...(b) KierenFox 7 (Ronald Harris) *mde all: urged along over 1f out: strly pressed ins fnl f: jst hld on* **9/1**	59

2212 2 nse **Griffin Point (IRE)**[11] 5504 5-9-2 60 (b) MartinHarley 1 68
(William Muir) *cl up: drvn along 2f out: r.o wl to press wnr ins fnl f: jst failed* **4/1**[3]
5520 3 3 3/4 **Ficelle (IRE)**[13] 5446 3-8-11 61 DarrenEgan(5) 3 55
(Ronald Harris) *outpcd early: drvn and effrt over 1f out: no imp on ldng pair: plugged on to grab modest 3rd cl home* **7/2**[2]
01 4 nk **Havin' A Good Time (IRE)**[21] 5177 3-9-3 62 AndreaAtzeni 6 55
(Roger Varian) *cl up: pushed along over 1f out: effrt 1f out: wknd ins fnl f: lost 3rd cl home* **9/2**
0321 5 3 **My Meteor**[21] 5149 5-9-7 65 JohnFahy 4 47
(Tony Newcombe) *hld up: drvn and unable to cl fnl 2f: nvr on terms* **5/2**[1]
-650 6 1 3/4 **Steel Rain**[38] 4535 4-8-12 56 JamesDoyle 5 32
(Nikki Evans) *cl up: rdn over 2f out: sn dropped away* **7/1**
605 7 1 1/4 **Just For Mary**[25] 5013 8-9-3 61 (bt) StephenCraine 2 33
(Daniel Mark Loughnane) *missed break and nvr on terms after: drvn over 2f out: sn btn* **22/1**

1m 2.78s (4.48) **Going Correction** +0.975s/f (Soft)
WFA 3 from 4yo+ 1lb **7 Ran SP% 115.8**
Speed ratings (Par 101): **103,102,96,96,91 88,86**
Tote Swingers 1&2 £3.30, 2&3 £4.00, 1&3 £4.60 CSF £45.69 TOTE £18.80: £8.30, £2.50; EX 42.20.
Owner P Nurcombe **Bred** C A Cyzer **Trained** Earlswood, Monmouths

FOCUS
Not a bad sprint handicap for the class, run at a strong pace, and it proved hard to make up ground on the taxing surface. Straightforward form.
My Meteor Official explanation: trainer said gelding was unsuited by the soft ground

5877 LONETREE LIMITED MCDONALD'S FILLIES' H'CAP 6f
4:50 (4:50) (Class 4) (0-80,77) 3-Y-0+ **£4,528** (£1,347; £673; £336) **Stalls** Centre

Form RPR
0063 1 **Fillionaire**[9] 5576 3-9-5 77 MartinHarley 9 86
(Mick Channon) *mde virtually all: rdn 2f out: fnd plenty for press: on top fnl 75yds* **11/4**[1]
6-00 2 1 1/4 **Supreme Spirit (IRE)**[35] 4655 5-9-5 75 (b) IanMongan 6 80
(Peter Makin) *hld up: hdwy over 2f out: chal away fr rival over 1f out: drvn 1f out: no ex fnl 75yds* **7/1**
4200 3 2 1/4 **Bouncy Bouncy (IRE)**[35] 4655 5-9-7 77 (t) HayleyTurner 2 75
(Michael Bell) *mounted outside paddock: hld up: rdn 3f out: sme hdwy over 1f out: kpt on to take 3rd ins fnl f* **6/1**[3]
-066 4 3/4 **Iced Opal**[46] 4235 3-8-8 66 FergusSweeney 4 61
(Michael Blanshard) *midfield: rdn 3f out: lost pl over 2f out: swtchd rt 1f out: kpt on to press for 3rd ins fnl f* **20/1**
0144 5 4 **Sparking**[41] 4420 5-8-7 66 RossAtkinson(3) 5 49
(Tom Dascombe) *cl up: rdn 3f out: wknd fnl 2f* **10/1**
6-46 6 nk **Blackdown Fair**[14] 5422 3-9-3 75 JamesMillman 3 57
(Rod Millman) *in tch: rdn over 2f out: wknd ins fnl f* **14/1**
1546 7 4 1/2 **Night Trade (IRE)**[12] 5486 5-9-0 75 (p) DarrenEgan(5) 8 42
(Ronald Harris) *in tch: drvn along 3f out: effrt 2f out: no ex fnl f* **9/2**[2]
2050 8 6 **Bella Ophelia (IRE)**[19] 5233 3-9-4 76 JamesDoyle 7 24
(Hughie Morrison) *cl up: rdn 3f out: wknd over 1f out* **6/1**[3]
4515 9 1 1/2 **Shes Rosie**[25] 4989 4-8-13 72 MarkCoumbe(3) 1 15
(John O'Shea) *mounted outside paddock and uns rdr: v awkward leaving stalls: nvr on terms: drvn and no ch 3f out* **8/1**

1m 15.46s (5.46) **Going Correction** +0.975s/f (Soft)
WFA 3 from 4yo+ 2lb **9 Ran SP% 117.6**
Speed ratings (Par 102): **102,100,97,96,91 90,84,76,74**
Tote Swingers 1&2 £5.60, 2&3 £8.30, 1&3 £4.90 CSF £22.94 CT £108.65 TOTE £3.30: £1.70, £3.10, £1.10; EX 18.40.
Owner Mrs Ann C Black **Bred** Mr & Mrs Kevan Watts **Trained** West Ilsley, Berks

FOCUS
A modest sprint handicap in which the first pair dominated from 2f out. Ordinary fillies form.

5878 GLYN ABBEY MEDIAN AUCTION MAIDEN STKS 6f
5:20 (5:20) (Class 6) 3-5-Y-0 **£1,617** (£481; £240; £120) **Stalls** Centre

Form RPR
1 **Angel Way (IRE)**[18] 5283 3-8-12 70 MartinHarley 2 72
(Denis W Cullen, Ire) *chsd ldr: pushed along to ld wl over 1f out: in command fnl 75yds* **4/1**[2]
222 2 1 3/4 **Stir Trader (IRE)**[16] 5340 3-9-3 72 JamesDoyle 3 71
(Roger Charlton) *in tch: pushed along whn sltly hmpd 2f out: drvn to chse wnr 1f out: no ex fnl 75yds* **4/9**[1]
0- 3 1 1/2 **Gaelic Wizard (IRE)**[389] 4970 4-8-12 0 JoshBaudains(7) 5 67
(Dominic Ffrench Davis) *taken down early: led: urged along and drifted rt 2f out: hdd wl over 1f out: sn no imp* **33/1**
323 4 3 1/4 **Gladiatrix**[13] 5446 3-8-12 65 JamesMillman 6 51
(Rod Millman) *hld up: hdwy whn sltly hmpd 2f out: rdn and one pce fnl f* **5/1**[3]
0-0 5 11 **Make Me Smyle**[25] 4992 3-9-3 0 IanMongan 1 21
(Stuart Kittow) *slow away and nvr on terms: wl btn fnl 3f* **50/1**
00- 6 1 3/4 **Desert Spree**[326] 6820 3-8-12 0 RenatoSouza 4 10
(Jeremy Gask) *last pair: struggling fnl 3f* **50/1**

1m 15.8s (5.80) **Going Correction** +0.975s/f (Soft)
WFA 3 from 4yo 2lb **6 Ran SP% 112.8**
Speed ratings (Par 101): **100,97,95,91,76 74**
Tote Swingers 1&2 £1.30, 2&3 £4.40, 1&3 £4.20 CSF £6.30 TOTE £3.70: £3.10, £1.80; EX 7.00.
Owner Mrs Theresa Burns **Bred** Rathasker Stud **Trained** Newlands, Co Kildare

FOCUS
There was a turn-up in this weak maiden.
T/Plt: £152.30 to a £1 stake. Pool: £57,291.46 - 274.56 winning tickets. T/Qpdt: £73.10 to a £1 stake. Pool: £4,962.00 - 50.20 winning tickets. CS

5756 HAMILTON (R-H)
Monday, September 3
5879 Meeting Abandoned - Unraceable ground

5804 WOLVERHAMPTON (A.W) (L-H)
Monday, September 3
OFFICIAL GOING: Standard
Wind: Light behind Weather: Fine

5886 HOLIDAY INN WOLVERHAMPTON NURSERY 5f 216y(P)
2:30 (2:31) (Class 5) (0-75,75) 2-Y-0 **£2,264** (£673; £336; £168) **Stalls** Low

Form RPR
322 1 **Avec Rose**[18] 5255 2-9-1 72 LeeTopliss(3) 5 76+
(Richard Fahey) *chsd ldrs: rdn to ld ins fnl f: r.o* **9/4**[1]
1606 2 3/4 **Cuisine (IRE)**[19] 5236 2-9-3 71 (b[1]) KierenFallon 8 73
(Andrew Balding) *chsd ldrs: rdn: hung lft and ev ch ins fnl f: styd on same pce towards fin* **15/2**
5002 3 1 **Ryedale Valley**[20] 5202 2-8-0 54 DuranFentiman 6 53
(Tim Easterby) *chsd ldr: pushed along over 2f out: rdn over 1f out: styng on whn hmpd wl ins fnl f* **9/2**[3]
101 4 nk **Somethingboutmary**[21] 5160 2-9-2 70 AmyRyan 1 68
(Kevin Ryan) *sn led: rdn over 1f out: hdd and unable qck ins fnl f* **4/1**[2]
150 5 1 1/2 **Columella**[16] 5361 2-9-5 73 LiamJones 4 67
(William Haggas) *hld up: pushed along over 2f out: rdn over 1f out: styd on: nt rch ldrs* **6/1**
2030 6 nk **Secret Symphony**[12] 5475 2-9-4 72 (t) LiamKeniry 2 65
(Sylvester Kirk) *s.i.s: hld up: rdn over 1f out: nvr nrr* **25/1**
2035 7 1 **Dust Whirl**[24] 5032 2-9-7 75 RichardHughes 3 65
(Richard Hannon) *hld up in tch: rdn over 1f out: no ex ins fnl f* **7/1**
046 8 12 **Believe In Me**[35] 4658 2-7-12 52 oh4 (p) JimmyQuinn 7 6
(Julia Feilden) *s.s: a in rr: rdn and wknd over 2f out* **50/1**

1m 14.79s (-0.21) **Going Correction** -0.075s/f (Stan) **8 Ran SP% 113.3**
Speed ratings (Par 95): **98,97,95,95,93 92,91,75**
Tote Swingers 1&2 £4.10, 2&3 £5.40, 1&3 £2.40 CSF £19.62 CT £69.12 TOTE £3.30: £1.10, £2.60, £1.70; EX 18.20 Trifecta £109.80 Pool: £624.75 - 4.21 winning tickets.
Owner The Mick Sweeney Syndicate **Bred** The Mick Sweeney Syndicate **Trained** Musley Bank, N Yorks
■ Stewards' Enquiry : Kieren Fallon two-day ban: careless riding (Sep 17-18)

FOCUS
A modest nursery run in a time 0.39 seconds slower than the following juvenile maiden. Straightforward form.

NOTEBOOK
Avec Rose, switched to Polytrack and upped in trip on her nursery debut, got a good lead into the race and went the shortest way round, but she was made to work hard enough. Things are likely to be tougher next time. (op 2-1 tchd 15-8)
Cuisine(IRE), with blinkers replacing a visor, was dropped in trip and trying Polytrack for the first time. He had his chance, but was inclined to edge left under pressure and probably isn't totally straightforward. (op 12-1)
Ryedale Valley, up 2lb for finishing runner-up on turf last time, chased what looked a strong enough pace and was always held. (op 6-1 tchd 7-1)
Somethingboutmary had won both her previous starts off the turf, a Fibresand maiden on debut and most recently a Lingfield nursery off 5lb lower, but she was comfortably held this time after appearing to go off quickly, closely pursued by the third. (op 3-1)
Columella just hasn't progressed from her debut win. (op 13-2 tchd 9-2)

5887 LIKE US ON FACEBOOK WOLVERHAMPTON RACECOURSE MAIDEN FILLIES' STKS 5f 216y(P)
3:00 (3:01) (Class 5) 2-Y-0 **£2,264** (£673; £336; £168) **Stalls** Low

Form RPR
543 1 **Woodlandsway**[33] 4701 2-9-0 79 RichardHughes 9 79
(Richard Hannon) *led 1f: chsd ldr tl shkn up to ld 2f out: sn rdn: r.o: eased nr fin* **7/4**[2]
3 2 1 1/4 **Give Way Nelson (IRE)**[102] 2426 2-9-0 0 KierenFallon 7 75
(Brian Meehan) *a.p: shkn up over 2f out: rdn to chse wnr over 1f out: sn hung lft: styd on same pce ins fnl f* **13/8**[1]
4522 3 hd **Royal Steps (IRE)**[21] 5178 2-9-0 76 MartinDwyer 5 76
(James Tate) *chsd ldrs: rdn over 1f out: hung lft ins fnl f: styd on* **7/2**[3]
5 4 4 **Best To Better (IRE)**[32] 4742 2-9-0 0 AdamKirby 12 63
(Marco Botti) *hld up: hdwy over 1f out: sn rdn and hung lft: nt trble ldrs* **20/1**
2033 5 1 1/4 **Annie Gogh**[21] 5169 2-9-0 68 DuranFentiman 4 59
(Tim Easterby) *led 5f out: rdn and hdd 2f out: wknd fnl f* **20/1**
6 1/2 **Rangooned** 2-9-0 0 PaulMulrennan 1 57
(Ann Duffield) *chsd ldrs: rdn over 1f out: wknd fnl f* **25/1**
50 7 3/4 **Uknowwhatushoulddo (IRE)**[32] 4742 2-9-0 0 SilvestreDeSousa 2 55
(J S Moore) *mid-div: effrt and swtchd rt wl over 1f out: sn hung lft: n.d* **16/1**
0 8 2 1/2 **Fat Bottom Girl**[3] 5807 2-8-9 0 ow2 DavidSimmonson(7) 3 50
(Michael Easterby) *hld up: rdn over 2f out: n.d* **100/1**
9 hd **Grace Hull** 2-9-0 0 LiamKeniry 6 47
(J S Moore) *s.s: a in rr* **80/1**
10 nk **Aquila Carina** 2-8-11 0 DaleSwift(3) 11 46
(James Given) *in rr: hdwy on outer over 2f out: sn rdn and wknd* **66/1**
11 1/2 **Underwhelm** 2-9-0 0 GrahamGibbons 8 45
(Alan McCabe) *mid-div: rdn over 2f out: sn wknd* **80/1**
12 3 **Windsor Secret** 2-9-0 0 LukeMorris 10 36
(Keith Dalgleish) *sn pushed along in rr: wknd over 2f out* **66/1**

1m 14.4s (-0.60) **Going Correction** -0.075s/f (Stan) **12 Ran SP% 122.4**
Speed ratings (Par 92): **101,99,99,93,92 91,90,87,86,86 85,81**
Tote Swingers 1&2 £2.40, 2&3 £2.40, 1&3 £1.50 CSF £4.81 TOTE £2.10: £1.30, £1.10, £1.10; EX 7.60 Trifecta £18.90 Pool: £733.39 - 28.68 winning tickets.
Owner The Storm Again Syndicate **Bred** Brook Stud Bloodstock Ltd **Trained** East Everleigh, Wilts

FOCUS
Just a fair fillies' maiden in which the 79-rated Woodlandsway enjoyed a comfortable trip, racing up with an ordinary-looking pace, and won in straightforward fashion. The first three were clear and the winner was basically to form.

NOTEBOOK
Woodlandsway probably has a bit more to offer and it's no major surprise to hear she may bid for black type at some stage. (op 9-4)
Give Way Nelson(IRE), absent since finishing third on her debut in May (5f, good), didn't get the run of things to the outside of the winner and was always held. This was a respectable effort after a break and she really ought to win a race. (op 7-4 tchd 6-4)
Royal Steps(IRE), a close second over 7f here off 76 last time, probably could have done with a stronger pace but finished clear of the others. She can win a similar race. (tchd 3-1)
Best To Better(IRE) still looked green under pressure and may yet be capable of better. (op 25-1)
Annie Gogh, switched to Polytrack, came into this officially rated just 68 and had a bit to find. (op 16-1)

Rangooned, a 20,000GBP purchase out of a 7f-1m winner, fared best of the newcomers. (op 22-1)
Uknowwhatushouldo(IRE) ◆ was always poorly placed and could never get competitive. She had made a promising debut before a disappointing effort at Nottingham and there's more to come, especially in nurseries/handicaps.
Fat Bottom Girl is another one to keep an eye on in handicaps. (op 150-1)
Grace Hull showed ability after starting slowly. (op 100-1)

5888 WOLVERHAMPTON-RACECOURSE.CO.UK H'CAP 1m 1f 103y(P)
3:30 (3:31) (Class 4) (0-85,83) 3-Y-O+ £4,204 (£1,251; £625; £312) Stalls Low

Form RPR
3-41 1 **Star Links (USA)**[14] 5429 6-9-5 78............(b) RobertWinston 9 85
(S Donohoe, Ire) *chsd ldrs: rdn over 1f out: hung lft and r.o to ld wl ins fnl f* 4/1[2]
5540 2 nk **Borug (USA)**[23] 5101 4-9-3 76............ MartinDwyer 8 82+
(James Tate) *hld up: hdwy over 1f out: sn rdn: r.o wl: nt quite rch wnr* 3/1[1]
341- 3 ½ **Ajeeb (USA)**[310] 7179 4-9-6 79............ JamieSpencer 11 84
(David Simcock) *led: rdn over 1f out: hdd wl ins fnl f* 17/2
5404 4 hd **Pilgrims Rest (IRE)**[18] 5273 3-9-4 83............ RichardHughes 4 88
(Richard Hannon) *chsd ldrs: rdn over 2f out: styd on* 6/1[3]
0061 5 1 ¼ **Hikma (USA)**[8] 5623 3-8-8 73 6ex............(b) SilvestreDeSousa 10 75
(Mark Johnston) *chsd ldr: rdn and hung lft over 1f out: no ex ins fnl f* 14/1
0630 6 ½ **Grizzle**[5] 5752 3-9-2 81............ MickaelBarzalona 1 82
(Mahmood Al Zarooni) *hld up: rdn over 3f out: hdwy over 1f out: nt rch ldrs* 11/1
4120 7 1 ¼ **Knowe Head (NZ)**[86] 2911 5-9-3 76............ LiamJones 2 74
(James Unett) *hld up: rdn over 2f out: styd on ins fnl f: nvr nrr* 12/1
3630 8 1 ¼ **Lucky Money**[17] 5302 3-8-5 70............ LukeMorris 6 66
(Sir Mark Prescott Bt) *hld up: rdn over 2f out: styd on ins fnl f: nrst fin* 10/1
3210 9 ½ **Aerodynamic (IRE)**[12] 5492 5-9-7 80............ GrahamGibbons 7 75
(Michael Easterby) *hld up: hdwy over 4f out: rdn over 2f out: styd on same pce fr over 1f out* 13/2
3030 10 2 ¼ **Sound Advice**[5] 5752 3-8-13 78............ RobbieFitzpatrick 3 68
(Keith Dalgleish) *hld up: rdn over 2f out: n.d* 50/1
14-6 11 2 ¾ **Simayill**[235] 131 4-9-9 82............ FrannyNorton 5 66
(John Berry) *prom: rdn over 2f out: wknd over 1f out* 20/1

1m 59.09s (-2.61) **Going Correction** -0.075s/f (Stan)
WFA 3 from 4yo+ 6lb 11 Ran SP% 121.7
Speed ratings (Par 105): **108,107,107,107,106 105,104,103,102,100 98**
Tote Swingers 1&2 £3.60, 2&3 £8.00, 1&3 £5.70 CSF £17.05 CT £100.00 TOTE £7.80: £1.90, £1.70, £3.30; EX 22.00 Trifecta £456.00 Part won. Pool: £616.26 - 0.63 winning tickets..
Owner Gerry Dolan & Mrs Marie E Dolan **Bred** Shell Bloodstock **Trained** Cootehill Road, Co Cavan

FOCUS
A fair handicap in which Star Links just held on from a rival who had raced much further back. Decent form for the grade, the winner back to his old best.
Hikma(USA) Official explanation: jockey said filly ran green and hung both ways

5889 DOWNLOAD OUR IPHONE APP MAIDEN STKS 1m 1f 103y(P)
4:00 (4:02) (Class 5) 3-Y-O+ £2,264 (£673; £336; £168) Stalls Low

Form RPR
3- 1 **Representation (USA)**[367] 5668 3-9-4 0............ MickaelBarzalona 11 86+
(Mahmood Al Zarooni) *hld up: hdwy wl over 1f out: rdn to ld ins fnl f: r.o* 13/2[2]
2 2 **Kota Sas (IRE)** 4-9-10 0............ NeilCallan 6 82+
(Roger Varian) *hld up: racd keenly: shkn up 3f out: hdwy over 1f out: edgd lft ins fnl f: styd on* 12/1
4-2 3 ½ **Ruban (IRE)**[17] 5297 3-9-4 0............ SilvestreDeSousa 3 81
(Mahmood Al Zarooni) *trckd ldrs: plld hrd: swtchd rt over 2f out: clipped heels wl over 1f out: rdn and hung lft ins fnl f: styd on same pce* 8/11[1]
4 ½ **Totalize** 3-9-1 0............[1] PatrickHills(3) 10 80+
(Luca Cumani) *dwlt: hld up: hdwy over 1f out: r.o: nt rch ldrs* 80/1
3 5 nk **Surreal (IRE)**[14] 5421 3-8-13 0............ KierenFallon 4 75
(Sir Michael Stoute) *trckd ldrs: plld hrd: swtchd rt and led over 2f out: rdn and hdd ins fnl f: no ex* 15/2
4-25 6 5 **Isthmus**[87] 2866 3-9-4 74............ RichardHughes 5 69
(Amanda Perrett) *chsd ldrs: rdn over 1f out: wknd ins fnl f* 7/1[3]
05 7 5 **Natural Bloom (IRE)**[64] 3666 3-8-13 0............ TomQueally 8 54+
(Sir Henry Cecil) *hld up: nt clr run over 2f out: nvr on terms* 14/1
8 nk **Strawberry Flavour (GER)** 3-8-13 0............ MartinDwyer 1 53
(James Tate) *s.i.s: rcvrd to ld over 7f out: hdd over 2f out: wknd fnl f* 50/1
30 9 ½ **Lieutenant Dan (IRE)**[31] 4780 5-9-3 0............ DanielMuscutt(7) 7 57
(Michael Appleby) *hld up: hdwy over 4f out: wknd wl over 1f out* 100/1
00- 10 4 **Zavier (FR)**[390] 4898 3-9-4 0............ FrannyNorton 2 48
(Mark Johnston) *sn led: hdd over 7f out: chsd ldrs tl rdn and wknd over 2f out* 28/1
6- 11 2 **Glaisdale**[299] 7329 3-8-13 0............(b) LiamKeniry 9 39
(James Toller) *hld up: pushed along over 3f out: wknd over 2f out* 80/1

2m 0.29s (-1.41) **Going Correction** -0.075s/f (Stan)
WFA 3 from 4yo+ 6lb 11 Ran SP% 118.7
Speed ratings (Par 103): **103,101,100,100,100 95,91,90,90,86 85**
Tote Swingers 1&2 £12.10, 2&3 £4.10, 1&3 £3.10 CSF £79.07 TOTE £7.10: £1.90, £3.00, £1.20; EX 70.10 Trifecta £180.40 Pool: £1085.38 - 4.45 winning tickets.
Owner Godolphin **Bred** Darley **Trained** Newmarket, Suffolk

FOCUS
An interesting maiden, but the pace was modest and it was a messy race. The time was 1.20 seconds slower than the earlier Class 4 handicap. The form is above average for the track and time of year.

5890 NAME A RACE TO ENHANCE YOUR BRAND NURSERY 1m 141y(P)
4:30 (4:30) (Class 4) (0-85,79) 2-Y-O £4,075 (£1,212; £606; £303) Stalls Low

Form RPR
3360 1 **Titus Titan (IRE)**[9] 5602 2-8-9 67............ SilvestreDeSousa 5 73+
(Brian Ellison) *chsd ldr: shkn up over 2f out: rdn to ld and hung lft ins fnl f: r.o* 5/1
6001 2 ½ **Grandorio (IRE)**[7] 5670 2-8-11 69 6ex............ GrahamGibbons 4 74+
(David O'Meara) *set stdy pce tl qcknd over 2f out: rdn and hdd whn carried lft ins fnl f: styd on* 15/8[1]
1 3 ½ **Cheektocheek (IRE)**[35] 4658 2-8-11 74............ TobyAtkinson(5) 3 78
(Marco Botti) *a.p: rdn over 1f out: r.o* 16/1
021 4 hd **Blue Wave (IRE)**[23] 5098 2-9-7 79............ MickaelBarzalona 2 82
(Mahmood Al Zarooni) *chsd ldrs: rdn over 2f out: styd on* 4/1[2]
0241 5 1 ¾ **Pippy**[21] 5178 2-8-11 69............ RichardKingscote 6 69
(Tom Dascombe) *hld up: rdn over 1f out: nt trble ldrs* 9/2[3]
054 6 1 ¾ **Abraq**[27] 4917 2-9-1 73............ RichardHughes 2 69
(Ed Dunlop) *hld up: rdn over 1f out: no ex ins fnl f* 9/2[3]

1m 54.25s (3.75) **Going Correction** -0.075s/f (Stan) 6 Ran SP% 113.7
Speed ratings (Par 97): **80,79,79,78,77 75**
Tote Swingers 1&2 £2.50, 2&3 £5.30, 1&3 £7.40 CSF £15.17 TOTE £16.50: £8.10, £2.80; EX 23.00.
Owner Market Avenue Racing Club Ltd **Bred** Ask For The Moon Syndicate **Trained** Norton, N Yorks

FOCUS
A fair nursery, although the pace was not strong and the likeable winner Titus Titan always had the front-running favourite in his sights. The slow pace limits the form but the winner has more to offer as does the second who more than confirmed his recent improvement.

NOTEBOOK
Titus Titan(IRE) ◆ had very much caught the eye in sprint maidens, before perhaps being unsuited by easy ground in a better nursery than this over 7f at York, and he confirmed that earlier promise despite still being green, wandering under pressure. This further step up in trip suited and he has the scope to make a nice 3yo. (tchd 9-2 and 11-2)
Grandorio(IRE) had a penalty for winning on his nursery debut when upped to 1m on testing ground at Newcastle, yet he was only 3lb higher. He did nothing wrong and is progressing nicely. (op 9-4 tchd 5-2)
Cheektocheek(IRE) had reportedly been gelded since making a winning debut over 7f at Yarmouth. This was tougher, but he ran okay behind a couple of progressive types. (op 12-1 tchd 11-1)
Blue Wave(IRE) didn't progress from his recent Lingfield maiden win over 1m. (op 10-3)
Pippy struggled off just 1lb higher than when successful over 7f here last time, though he was probably not helped by being held up out the back in a steadily run race. (op 5-1 tchd 11-2)

5891 BOOK HOSPITALITY AT WOLVERHAMPTON RACECOURSE H'CAP 2m 119y(P)
5:00 (5:00) (Class 6) (0-65,65) 3-Y-O+ £1,704 (£503; £251) Stalls Low

Form RPR
3022 1 **Looks Like Rain**[9] 5577 3-8-11 61............ SilvestreDeSousa 8 71+
(Brian Ellison) *hld up: hdwy over 2f out: rdn over 1f out: styd on to ld wl ins fnl f* 11/4[2]
3 2 1 ¼ **Jawaab (IRE)**[26] 4955 8-9-9 60............ PhillipMakin 6 66
(Philip Kirby) *chsd ldrs: rdn over 2f out: styd on* 7/1[3]
-103 3 nk **Jacob McCandles**[62] 3734 5-9-13 64............ KierenFallon 5 69
(Shaun Lycett) *chsd ldr tl led over 5f out: rdn over 1f out: hdd and unable qck ins fnl f* 10/1
00-1 4 nk **Green To Gold (IRE)**[40] 4004 7-10-0 65............ JamieSpencer 2 70
(Don Cantillon) *hld up: hdwy over 4f out: rdn over 1f out: styd on same pce ins fnl f* 9/4[1]
0410 5 2 ½ **Corvette**[8] 5637 4-9-12 63............ LukeMorris 7 65
(Michael Appleby) *prom: chsd ldr 4f out: rdn over 2f out: no ex ins fnl f* 28/1
0001 6 1 ¼ **Scripturist**[8] 5637 3-7-8 51 6ex............(b) NoelGarbutt(7) 9 51
(William Jarvis) *hld up: rdn over 2f out: styd on ins fnl f: nvr nrr* 7/1[3]
3602 7 ½ **Plus Fours (USA)**[20] 5208 3-8-13 63............ RobbieFitzpatrick 1 63
(Charles Smith) *hld up: hdwy over 2f out: wknd fnl f* 28/1
4 8 5 **Hootie (IRE)**[14] 5430 4-9-5 56............(bt) RichardHughes 3 50
(S Donohoe, Ire) *racd keenly: hld up and bhd: rdn over 1f out: sn wknd* 8/1
9 79 **Madame Gazelle (IRE)**[368] 5663 4-8-11 48 oh3............[1] RobertWinston 10
(S Donohoe, Ire) *set stdy pce tl hdd over 5f out: wknd over 3f out: t.o* 50/1

3m 42.34s (0.54) **Going Correction** -0.075s/f (Stan)
WFA 3 from 4yo+ 13lb 9 Ran SP% 111.5
Speed ratings (Par 101): **95,94,94,94,92 92,92,89,52**
Tote Swingers 1&2 £5.10, 2&3 £9.60, 1&3 £4.50 CSF £20.96 CT £160.60 TOTE £2.20: £1.02, £3.40, £2.40; EX 19.80 Trifecta £150.60 Pool: £818.62 - 4.02 winning tickets.
Owner P Alderson & D J Burke **Bred** Whitley Stud **Trained** Norton, N Yorks

FOCUS
A modestly run staying handicap. The form is set around the third to fifth.

5892 THE BLACK COUNTRY'S ONLY RACECOURSE H'CAP (DIV I) 7f 32y(P)
5:30 (5:30) (Class 5) (0-70,70) 3-Y-O+ £2,264 (£673; £336; £168) Stalls High

Form RPR
6360 1 **The Happy Hammer (IRE)**[84] 2981 6-9-5 65............ CathyGannon 10 74
(Eugene Stanford) *chsd ldrs: led over 5f out: rdn over 1f out: styd on wl* 9/1
0244 2 hd **Al's Memory (IRE)**[23] 5099 3-9-2 66............ RichardHughes 8 73
(David Evans) *a.p: pushed along to chse wnr over 2f out: rdn over 1f out: r.o* 11/4[1]
0134 3 1 ½ **Conry (IRE)**[5] 5750 6-9-3 63............ JamieSpencer 1 67+
(Ian Williams) *trckd ldrs: nt clr run wl over 1f out: sn rdn: r.o* 11/4[1]
0500 4 ½ **Brimstone Hill (IRE)**[60] 3790 3-9-6 70............ WilliamCarson 7 72
(Anthony Carson) *chsd ldrs: rdn over 2f out: r.o* 11/2[2]
3462 5 hd **Unlimited**[21] 5179 10-9-6 66............ AdamKirby 9 69+
(Tony Carroll) *s.i.s: hld up: rdn over 1f out: r.o ins fnl f: nt rch ldrs* 15/2[3]
0000 6 ¾ **Blue Dune**[13] 5454 3-8-6 56 oh1............ SilvestreDeSousa 5 54
(Mark Johnston) *led: hdd over 5f out: rdn over 1f out: no ex ins fnl f* 9/1
0054 7 6 **Yungaburra (IRE)**[21] 5179 8-8-10 56 oh8............(t) FrannyNorton 6 40
(David C Griffiths) *hld up: plld hrd: rdn over 2f out: n.d* 25/1
2000 8 2 ¼ **Lastkingofscotland (IRE)**[19] 5233 6-9-3 70............(b) NoelGarbutt(7) 3 48
(Conor Dore) *s.i.s: rdn over 2f out: a in rr* 18/1
606 9 1 ¼ **Hinton Admiral**[61] 3761 8-9-8 68............ LiamKeniry 2 43
(Conor Dore) *hld up: rdn over 2f out: a in rr* 20/1

1m 29.46s (-0.14) **Going Correction** -0.075s/f (Stan)
WFA 3 from 4yo+ 4lb 9 Ran SP% 114.4
Speed ratings (Par 103): **97,96,95,94,94 93,86,83,82**
Tote Swingers 1&2 £5.30, 2&3 £2.40, 1&3 £5.60 CSF £33.67 CT £87.57 TOTE £19.00: £3.90, £1.30, £3.20; EX 48.10 Trifecta £174.00 Pool £465.59 - 1.98 winning tickets.
Owner Newmarket Connections Ltd **Bred** Rathbarry Stud **Trained** Newmarket, Suffolk

FOCUS
The pace was modest, meaning it proved hard to make up ground, and the time was 1.57 seconds slower than the following division. The winner is rated to last year's winter best.
Blue Dune Official explanation: jockey said filly had no more to give

5893 THE BLACK COUNTRY'S ONLY RACECOURSE H'CAP (DIV II) 7f 32y(P)
6:00 (6:03) (Class 5) (0-70,70) 3-Y-O+ £2,264 (£673; £336; £168) Stalls High

Form RPR
0520 1 **Amoure Medici**[26] 4954 3-9-6 70............[1] PaulMulrennan 4 80
(Ann Duffield) *led: rdn and hdd ins fnl f: rallied to ld post* 11/4[1]
4500 2 shd **Sir Bruno (FR)**[11] 5506 5-9-2 62............(p) LukeMorris 8 73
(Bryn Palling) *a.p: chsd wnr over 1f out: rdn to ld ins fnl f: hdd post* 6/1
4400 3 6 **Glenridding**[3] 5802 8-9-3 66............(p) DaleSwift(3) 5 61
(James Given) *w ldr tl rdn wl over 1f out: wknd ins fnl f* 9/2[3]
4003 4 ¾ **Hawk Moth (IRE)**[14] 5427 4-9-5 65............ CathyGannon 3 58
(John Spearing) *prom: rdn over 1f out: wknd ins fnl f* 11/2

2016 **5** ¾ **Chambles**[31] 4779 3 -9-6**70**........................ KierenFallon 9 50
(Alan McCabe) *chsd ldrs: pushed along 4f out: rdn over 2f out: wknd ins fnl f* **3/1**[2]

-300 **6** 2 ½ **Great Charm (IRE)**[67] 3541 7 -9-8**68**............(t) MickaelBarzalona 2 52
(Daniel Kubler) *hld up: hdwy u.p over 2f out: wknd fnl f* **20/1**

6016 **7** 2 **Memphis Man**[13] 5444 9 -8-7**56** oh7............ MatthewCosham(3) 7 35
(David Evans) *hld up: rdn over 2f out: a in rr* **33/1**

254 **8** 4 ½ **One For Joules (IRE)**[21] 5151 5 -9-7**67**............ JamieGoldstein 6 33
(John Flint) *s.s: a bhd* **12/1**

1m 27.89s (-1.71) **Going Correction** -0.075s/f (Stan)
WFA 3 from 4yo+ 4lb **8**Ran SP% **114.9**
Speed ratings (Par 103): **106,105,99,98,97 94,92,87**
Tote Swingers 1&2 £5.30, 2&3 £6.70, 1&3 £3.50 CSF £19.86 CT £71.82 TOTE £3.00 : £2.00, £2.80, £1.30 ; EX 24.70 Trifecta £294.80 Pool: £533.99 - 1.34 winning tickets .
Owner Mrs D Jeromson **Bred** Breeding Capital Plc **Trained** Constable Burton, N Yorks

FOCUS
The visual impression was of a really strong pace, with Amoure Medici and Glenridding taking each other on, and the final time was 1.57 seconds faster than the first division, yet the early leaders finished first and third respectively. The runner-up was always handy as well, and those held up could never get in a blow. The winner rates a small personal best.
T/Jkpt: £23,391.50 to a £1 stake. Pool: £131,783.55 - 4.00 winning tickets. T/Plt: £18.00 to a £1 stake. Pool: £86,166.35 - 3,486.69 winning tickets. T/Qpdt: £9.40 to a £1 stake. Pool: £6,207.83 - 486.10 winning tickets. CR

5894a - 5898a, 5900a (Foreign Racing) - See Raceform Interactive

CRAON (R-H)
Monday, September 3

OFFICIAL GOING: Turf: good to soft

5899a PRIX DES FOURRAGES THIERRY DUTERTRE (CRITERIUM DE L'OUEST) (LISTED RACE) (2YO) (TURF) 1m 55y
1:20 (12:00) 2-Y-O **£22,916** (£9,166; £6,875 ; £4,583 ; £2,291)

RPR

1 **Alterite (FR)**[29] 2 -8-13**0**............ ChristopheSoumillon 4 100+
(J-C Rouget, France) **11/5**[1]

2 4 **Oasis Cannes**[24] 5060 2 -9-2**0**............ Jean-BernardEyquem 6 94
(Sir Mark Prescott Bt) *racd in 5th for 3f: proged to go 3rd on outside at 1/2-way: rdn to chal for ld 2f out: led briefly 250yds out: hdd 1f out: r.o fnl f to be clr 2nd* **23/10**[2]

3 3 **Cassiopee (FR)**[6] 2 -8-13**0**............ AntoineHamelin 7 84
(Y Barberot, France) **10/1**

4 4 **San Juan (FR)**[39] 2 -9-2**0**............(b) MarcLerner 2 79
(C Lerner, France) **4/1**[3]

5 1 **Patrona Ciana (FR)**[32] 2 -8-13**0**............(p) OlivierPeslier 3 73
(Y Durepaire, Spain) **14/1**

6 8 **Dawn Salute (FR)**[32] 2 -9-2**0**............ FabriceVeron 5 59
(H-A Pantall, France) **10/1**

7 20 **Special Reward**[22] 2 -8-13**0**............ MaximeGuyon 1 12
(H-A Pantall, France) **44/5**

1m 45.15s (105.15) **7**Ran SP% **116.6**
WIN (incl. 1 euro stake): 3.20. PLACES: 1.90, 1.60. SF: 9.10 .
Owner Ecurie La Vallee Martigny Earl **Bred** Ecurie La Vallee Martigny Earl **Trained** Pau, France

NOTEBOOK
Oasis Cannes, winner of a 7f Newmarket nursery off 82 last time out, was well held on this rise in class, but this was still a sound effort.

5625 GOODWOOD (R-H)
Tuesday, September 4

OFFICIAL GOING: Good (7.8)
Wind: Light, half against Weather: Sunny

5901 GOODWOOD RACEHORSE OWNERS GROUP MAIDEN STKS 1m 1f 192y
2:20 (2:20) (Class 5) 3-Y-O **£2,587** (£770; £384 ; £192) **Stalls** Low

Form RPR

2400 **1** **Uriah Heep (FR)**[24] 5105 3 -9-3**87**............ WilliamBuick 7 81+
(Sir Michael Stoute) *hld up early: prog after 4f: wnt 2nd over 4f out: rdn to ld over 1f out: drvn out* **15/8**[1]

3 **2** ¾ **Claude Monet (BRZ)**[27] 4948 3 -8-5**0** ow2............ MickaelBarzalona 1 67+
(Jeremy Noseda) *t.k.h: trckd ldr 3f: stdd: effrt to chal 2f out: nt qckn over 1f out: chsd wnr ins fnl f: styd on but a hld* **2/1**[2]

05 **3** 3 **Eltiqaa (IRE)**[32] 4782 3 -8-12**0**............ RobertHavlin 4 68
(John Gosden) *wl in tch: 4th and cl up over 3f out: shkn up and outpcd 2f out: kpt on fnl f: tk 3rd last stride* **18/1**[3]

43 **4** nse **Afraah (USA)**[40] 4516 3 -8-12**0**............ PaulHanagan 6 68
(Roger Varian) *trckd ldr after 3f: led over 5f out: kicked on 4f out: hdd and nt qckn over 1f out: wknd fnl f: lost 3rd last stride* **2/1**[2]

06 **5** ½ **Addazero**[25] 5048 3 -9-3**0**............ JohnFahy 3 72
(Alastair Lidderdale) *led at mod pce to over 5f out: steadily lost pl wout coming u.p: 5th over 3f out: outpcd 2f out: styd on steadily fnl f* **50/1**

06 **6** 19 **Noosa Boy**[192] 709 3 -9-3**0**............ FrankieMcDonald 5 34
(Luke Dace) *dwlt: hld up in last: no prog 4f out: sn wknd: t.o* **66/1**

7 10 **Mecox Meadow (USA)** 3 -9-3**0**............ LukeMorris 2 14
(Michael Bell) *rn green and sn pushed along in last pair: wknd over 3f out: t.o* **33/1**

2m 9.18s (1.08) **Going Correction** -0.10s/f (Good) **7**Ran SP% **113.1**
Speed ratings (Par 101): **91,90,88,87,87 72,64**
Tote Swingers: 1&2 £2.20, 1&3 £3.80, 2&3 £5.30 CSF £5.84 TOTE £3.10 : £1.10 , £1.60 ; EX 6.90 .
Owner Sir Robert Ogden,Tabor,Magnier,Smith **Bred** Snig Elevage & Balmerino Bloodstock **Trained** Newmarket, Suffolk

FOCUS
Lower bend dolled out 5yds adding 7yds to distances on that course. This was an uncompetitive 3yo maiden by Goodwood standards, which only looked to involve three of the seven runners, and the trio could barely be split in the market. A dawdling early pace contributed to a slow time and it resulted in a 1-2 for owner Sir Robert Ogden. Trick form to assess with the time slow, not rated too positively.

Afraah(USA) Official explanation: jockey said filly hung left in final furlong

5902 EBF RACING UK MAIDEN FILLIES' STKS (DIV I) 1m
2:55 (2:55) (Class 5) 2-Y-O **£3,234** (£962; £481 ; £240) **Stalls** Low

Form RPR

1 **Liber Nauticus (IRE)** 2 -9-0**0**............ KierenFallon 4 87+
(Sir Michael Stoute) *sn pushed along in midfield and rn green: prog over 2f out: drvn and clsd jst over 1f out: swept into the ld 100yds out: sn clr* **11/4**[1]

302 **2** 1 ¾ **Heading North**[18] 5300 2 -9-0**80**............ RichardHughes 1 82
(Richard Hannon) *trckd ldrs: pushed along 3f out: chsd ldng pair over 2f out: clsd over 1f out: coming to chal whn wnr breezed by 100yds out: styd on* **7/2**[2]

0 **3** 1 **Cushion**[31] 4818 2 -9-0**0**............ WilliamBuick 6 80
(John Gosden) *prom: trckd ldr over 4f out: shkn up to ld over 1f out: hdd and outpcd last 100yds: sddle slipped* **11/4**[1]

4 1 ¼ **Great Timing (USA)** 2 -9-0**0**............ MickaelBarzalona 11 77+
(Mahmood Al Zarooni) *wnt lft s: led: shkn up and hdd over 1f out: one pce and lost 2 pls ins fnl f* **5/1**[3]

5 5 **Auction (IRE)** 2 -9-0**0**............ PaulHanagan 2 66+
(Ed Dunlop) *s.s: wl adrift in last early: stl there over 2f out: pushed along and styd on steadily fr wl over 1f out: shaped wl* **25/1**

0 **6** nk **Three Choirs (IRE)**[54] 4011 2 -9-0**0**............ PatDobbs 3 65
(Richard Hannon) *trckd ldrs: outpcd fr over 2f out: n.d over 1f out: fdd* **11/1**

5 **7** 4 ½ **Atalanta Bay (IRE)**[13] 5476 2 -8-9**0**............ KatiaScallan(5) 5 54
(Marcus Tregoning) *trckd ldr to over 4f out: jst pushed along and steadily lost pl: wknd 2f out* **40/1**

8 hd **Princess Patsky (USA)** 2 -9-0**0**............ JamesDoyle 8 54
(Michael Bell) *in tch in midfield: outpcd over 2f out: steadily wknd* **25/1**

9 nse **Brigh (IRE)** 2 -9-0**0**............ EddieAhern 7 54+
(David Simcock) *hld up in 8th: jst pushed along over 2f out: no prog but nt wout sme promise* **14/1**

0 **10** 2 ¼ **Kiwani Bay**[18] 5300 2 -9-0**0**............ JimmyFortune 10 49
(J W Hills) *hld up fr wd draw: a wl in rr: no prog over 2f out* **80/1**

0 **11** 1 ¾ **Pennyweight**[11] 5550 2 -9-0**0**............ LukeMorris 9 45
(James Eustace) *sn pushed along: a towards rr: wknd over 2f out* **100/1**

1m 37.68s (-2.22) **Going Correction** -0.10s/f (Good) **11**Ran SP% **119.6**
Speed ratings (Par 92): **107,105,104,103,98 97,93,93,92,90 88**
Tote Swingers: 1&2 £3.70, 1&3 £3.60, 2&3 £2.70 CSF £12.29 TOTE £3.20 : £1.10 , £2.10 , £1.40 ; EX 16.90 Trifecta £27.80 Pool: £825.30 - 21.95 winning units.
Owner Ballymacoll Stud **Bred** Ballymacoll Stud Farm Ltd **Trained** Newmarket, Suffolk

FOCUS
This looked a decent fillies' maiden, with the front four pulling well clear of the rest, and the winning time was quick. The winner was impressive and looks sure to go forward. Sound form with the first four clear.

NOTEBOOK
Liber Nauticus (IRE)◆ didn't look the likely winner for much of the way as she ran green from the start and had to be niggled along, but she gradually warmed to this racing game and, having been pulled out for her effort over a furlong out, quickened up nicely for a couple of smacks from Kieren Fallon to sweep to the front well inside the last. Out of an unraced mare from the family of Conduit and Spectrum, when the stable have a juvenile winner here first time out it tends to be a good one and this filly, who should relish middle-distances on breeding, is definitely one to follow. (op 7-2)
Heading North set the benchmark with a rating of 80, having made the frame in two of her first three starts, and was up a furlong here. Always handy, she was off the bridle over 2f from home, but no sooner had she got to the leader inside the last than the winner pounced. She was unfortunate to run into one again here and deserves to break her duck. (op 10-3 tchd 3-1)
Cushion, a staying-on seventh of 15 on last month's Newmarket debut over 7f, took a fair hold in a handy position early and, although she was sent to the front over a furlong out, was eventually run down by two stronger finishers. She should win her maiden before too long, but doesn't quite look up to her Fillies' Mile entry on this evidence. Her rider reported that the saddle slipped. Official explanation: jockey said saddle slipped (op 7-2)
Great Timing (USA)◆, a $370,000 half-sister to six winners in the US, lurched out to her left from the outside stall early but was soon bowling along in front. She had little left when tackled over a furlong out, but showed enough here to suggest she can win races with this experience under her belt. (op 9-2 tchd 4-1)
Auction(IRE) ◆ completely blew the start and lost plenty of ground as a result, but was noted making steady late progress against the inside rail. An 80,000euros filly out of a Group 3 winner at up to 1m4f, she will leave this debut effort well behind. Official explanation: jockey said filly was slowly away
Three Choirs (IRE) beaten a long way in what has turned out to be a hot Newmarket maiden on her debut in July, fared better this time and this half-sister to four winners at up to 1m4f can progress again. (op 10-1 tchd 12-1)

5903 REHEAT NURSERY STKS (H'CAP) 6f
3:30 (3:30) (Class 2) 2-Y-O **£7,762** (£2,310; £1,154 ; £577) **Stalls** High

Form RPR

3653 **1** **Sejalaat (IRE)**[25] 5041 2 -8-8**77**............ PaulHanagan 3 81+
(John Dunlop) *hld up last: clsd on ldrs 2f out gng strly: gap appeared over 1f out: sn pushed along to ld jst ins fnl f: r.o wl* **4/1**[3]

21 **2** 1 **Tobacco Road (IRE)**[15] 4330 2 -8-11**80**............ RichardHughes 2 81
(Richard Hannon) *led and crossed to nr side rail: hrd pressed but hld together tl hdd and shkn up over 1f out: r.o to chal jst ins fnl f: outpcd by wnr after* **9/4**[2]

1542 **3** 1 ¾ **Normal Equilibrium**[11] 5563 2 -9-6**89**............ HarryBentley 6 85
(Roger Varian) *trckd ldrs: effrt 2f out: rdn to ld over 1f out to jst ins fnl f: sn outpcd* **2/1**[1]

3421 **4** 3 ¾ **The Sixties**[27] 4952 2 -8-8**77**............(v) MartinHarley 5 62
(Mick Channon) *sn chsd ldr: chal over 2f out: upsides over 1f out: wknd ins fnl f* **13/2**

01 **5** 5 **Cardmaster (IRE)**[13] 5485 2 -8-9**78**............ NeilCallan 8 48
(Eve Johnson Houghton) *sweating: chsd ldrs: rdn 1/2-way: wknd wl over 1f out* **16/1**

5130 **6** 2 ½ **Blackdown Spirit**[24] 5088 2 -9-6**89**............ JamesMillman 7 51
(Rod Millman) *v awkward s and slowest away: rcvrd to be prom: wknd over 1f out* **14/1**

1064 **7** 1 ½ **Belle Intrigue**[11] 5532 2 -7-13**68** ow1............ FrankieMcDonald 4 26
(Amanda Perrett) *t.k.h: in tch: effrt on outer over 2f out: hanging and wknd over 1f out: eased* **33/1**

1m 11.21s (-0.99) **Going Correction** -0.10s/f (Good) **7**Ran SP% **112.9**
Speed ratings (Par 101): **102,100,98,93,86 83,81**
Tote Swingers: 1&2 £2.10, 2&3 £2.40 CSF £13.09 CT £22.08 TOTE £3.60 : £2.20 , £1.50 ; EX 17.70 Trifecta £35.30 Pool: £802.29 - 16.80 winning units. .
Owner Hamdan Al Maktoum **Bred** Shadwell Estate Company Limited **Trained** Arundel, W Sussex

FOCUS
A decent nursery which fell to the only maiden in the field. Improvement from the first two but the third was a little off his York form.

NOTEBOOK

Sejalaat(IRE) had looked an awkward ride when only third of eight when favourite for his nursery debut at Haydock last month, but has plenty of ability as he showed that here to break his duck. Given a patient ride, he travelled nicely in rear and quickened up well out in the centre of the track to lead inside the last, but again his head-carriage wouldn't have been for the purist. He can win again if putting his best foot forward. (op 5-1)

Tobacco Road(IRE), making his nursery debut, wasn't expected to be suited by dropping a furlong here on pedigree, but he managed to get across to the stands' rail and held every chance until out-speeded by the winner. A return to further should see him winning again. (op 10-3)

Normal Equilibrium, raised 4lb for his narrow defeat in a hot York nursery 11 days earlier, was keen enough early but came through to hold every chance over a furlong out until fading well inside the last. This consistent colt should continue to pay his way. (op 7-4)

The Sixties was dropped 1lb after narrowly beating a 68-rated filly returned to maiden company at Newcastle last month. He showed good speed until folding inside the last, but this was his ninth start so he lacks the scope of a few of these. (op 11-2 tchd 5-1)

Cardmaster(IRE), making his nursery debut, was in trouble just after halfway and wasn't good enough. (op 11-1)

Blackdown Spirit had to do a bit of early running to take a handy position following an awkward start and that may have told against him late on. Official explanation: jockey said gelding was slowly away (op 12-1 tchd 16-1)

Belle Intrigue was up against much better opposition here, but nonetheless looked a horrible ride. (op 28-1)

5904 PETER WILLETT STKS (REGISTERED AS THE STARDOM STAKES) (LISTED RACE) 7f

4:05 (4:05) (Class 1) 2-Y-O £14,177 (£5,375; £2,690; £1,340; £672) Stalls Low

Form				RPR
212	1		**Steeler (IRE)**[13] 5488 2-9-0 104 .... KierenFallon 4 (Mark Johnston) *chsd ldr: pushed along and lost 2nd over 2f out: rallied over 1f out: drvn and r.o fnl f to ld last 75yds: readily* **8/15**[1]	100+
1	2	3/4	**Tamayuz Star (IRE)**[23] 5126 2-9-0 0 .... PatDobbs 3 (Richard Hannon) *hld up in last: swift move on outer to ld 2f out: kicked 2 l clr over 1f out: collared last 75yds* **12/1**	98
3332	3	2 1/4	**Sorella Bella (IRE)**[11] 5551 2-8-9 79 .... SamHitchcott 1 (Mick Channon) *racd freely: led and sn 3 l clr: hdd and nt qckn 2f out: lost 2nd 1f out: kpt on* **33/1**	87
2202	4	1 1/4	**Jillnextdoor (IRE)**[17] 5357 2-8-9 86 .... MartinHarley 6 (Mick Channon) *hld up in last pair: effrt whn squeezed out over 2f out: one pce and no prog after* **8/1**[3]	85
14	5	1 1/4	**Professor**[25] 5042 2-9-0 0 .... RichardHughes 2 (Richard Hannon) *t.k.h: restrained into 3rd: lost pl over 2f out: tried to rally over 1f out: wknd ins fnl f: eased* **7/2**[2]	85

1m 26.1s (-0.90) **Going Correction** -0.10s/f (Good) 5 Ran SP% **109.2**

Speed ratings (Par 103): **101,100,97,96,94**

CSF £7.90 TOTE £1.40: £1.10, £2.80; EX 7.80.

Owner Sheikh Hamdan Bin Mohammed Al Maktoum **Bred** Airlie Stud **Trained** Middleham Moor, N Yorks

FOCUS

Run over 1m until the distance was reduced to 7f three years ago, this Listed event has gone to some decent juveniles in recent years, with the 2008 winner Zafisio going on to win the Group 1 Criterium International and the 2009 winner Vale Of York going on to take the Breeders' Cup Juvenile. This year's renewal wasn't that competitive with the five remaining runners representing just three stables and a long odds-on favourite. Steeler is a bit better than the grade and did not need to be at his best. The second can win at this level.

NOTEBOOK

Steeler(IRE) was definitely the one to beat after running the smart Dundonnell close in the Acomb at York 13 days earlier, but although he got the job done, it was far from straightforward. He held the ideal sit early, leading the main group adrift of the clear leader, but got outpaced and crowded when the runner-up swept to the front over a furlong out. However, that gave him something to aim at and he showed a good attitude to quicken up and pull the race out of the fire. He remains a nice prospect and with his trainer appearing to favour a step up to 1m, the Royal Lodge and Racing Post Trophy are the most likely options. (op 1-2 tchd 4-7 and 8-13 in places)

Tamayuz Star(IRE), narrow winner of a 7f maiden on his Leicester debut last month, looked the stable's second string but did better than his stablemate and ran a blinder. He made a bold move to come around the wide outside from last place to hit the front over a furlong out and it may have paid dividends on a different day, but the winner proved too good for him in the run to the line. He still has scope and should be winning again before long. (op 14-1)

Sorella Bella(IRE), in the frame in all six starts in maidens, was soon racing freely out in front but managed to keep enough in reserve to retain third place after being collared over a furlong out and earn some black type, which isn't bad for a filly rated just 79. (op 25-1)

Jillnextdoor(IRE), up another furlong in trip, might have given her stablemate more of a race for third had she not met trouble passing the 2f pole, but wouldn't have achieved any more than that. (tchd 9-1)

Professor, a stablemate of the runner-up, pulled too hard when last of four in a 7f Haydock novice event on his second start and committed the same offence again here. (op 4-1 tchd 10-3)

5905 ROYAL SUSSEX REGIMENT STKS (H'CAP) 2m

4:40 (4:40) (Class 2) (0-105,101) 3-Y-O+ £10,350 (£3,080; £1,539; £769) Stalls High

Form				RPR
4103	1		**Rumh (GER)**[20] 5238 4-9-3 90 .... MickaelBarzalona 6 (Saeed Bin Suroor) *led after 3f and sn at least 3 l clr: shkn up over 2f out: stretched away over 1f out: in n.d after: eased nr fin* **7/1**[3]	102
2462	2	3 1/4	**Gassin Golf**[17] 5344 3-8-6 92 .... LukeMorris 10 (Sir Mark Prescott Bt) *dwlt: hld up in last trio: pushed along 3f out: prog fr 2f out: chsd wnr ins fnl f: nt qckn and no imp* **6/4**[1]	98+
010	3	shd	**Hurricane Higgins (IRE)**[10] 5600 4-10-0 101 .... NeilCallan 2 (Mark Johnston) *trckd ldng pair: shkn up 3f out: effrt to dispute 2nd 2f out tl ins fnl f: styd on but no ch w wnr* **15/2**	107
1325	4	4	**Ruacana**[24] 5078 3-8-0 89 .... RyanPowell(3) 4 (Michael Bell) *trckd ldng pair: rdn to dispute 2nd 2f out to over 1f out: wknd fnl f* **4/1**[2]	90+
1203	5	1/2	**Trovare (USA)**[24] 5106 5-8-9 82 oh2 .... EddieAhern 8 (Amanda Perrett) *settled in 5th: gng bttr than most 3f out: rdn and no rspnse over 2f out: wl btn after* **25/1**	83
5434	6	4	**Mystery Star (IRE)**[13] 5491 7-9-6 93 .... KierenFallon 9 (Mark H Tompkins) *w.w in 6th: rdn and nt qckn 3f out: no imp after: eased whn no ch ins fnl f* **12/1**	90
5652	7	1	**Woolfall Treasure**[24] 5076 7-9-5 92 .... (v) GeorgeBaker 5 (Gary Moore) *led 3f: chsd wnr: rdn 3f out: lost 2nd 2f out: n.m.r briefly and sn btn* **20/1**	87
643	8	nk	**O Ma Lad (IRE)**[18] 5306 4-8-9 82 oh2 .... JamesDoyle 1 (Sylvester Kirk) *hld up in last trio: effrt on inner 4f out: no prog over 2f out: wl btn after* **20/1**	76
-066	9	8	**Seaside Sizzler**[34] 4697 5-9-0 87 .... (bt) WilliamBuick 7 (Ralph Beckett) *hld up in last trio: reminder over 4f out and no prog: sn wl btn* **9/1**	72

3m 30.66s (1.66) **Going Correction** -0.10s/f (Good)

WFA 3 from 4yo+ 13lb 9 Ran SP% **115.3**

Speed ratings (Par 109): **91,89,89,87,87 85,84,84,80**

Tote Swingers: 1&2 £4.20, 1&3 £6.20, 2&3 £3.80 CSF £17.39 CT £82.56 TOTE £9.50: £2.90, £1.10, £2.60; EX 25.20 Trifecta £145.40 Pool: £1,142.89 - 5.81 winning units..

Owner Godolphin **Bred** Stiftung Gestut Fahrhof **Trained** Newmarket, Suffolk

FOCUS

A decent staying handicap, but everything played into the hands of the winner. The winner is rated in line with her best form.

NOTEBOOK

Rumh(GER) was back off the same mark as when bolting up over this trip at Kempton in July. Just as then, she was sent to the front inside the first half-mile and dictated affairs from thereon in. She kept on finding plenty to keep her rivals at bay and it was obvious from over a furlong out that the prize was hers. She looks very decent when races fall her way like this. (op 8-1 tchd 9-1 in a place)

Gassin Golf, having his first try at 2m, was put up 7lb after pulling clear of the third when narrowly beaten over the extended 1m6f at Doncaster last month. In contrast to the winner given a waiting ride, he weaved his way though the field inside the last half-mile, but was never going to trouble the winner. Stamina wasn't an issue. (op 7-4 tchd 15-8 and 2-1 in a place)

Hurricane Higgins(IRE) never figured in the Ebor last time, but had no stamina worries having won over 2m5f off 6lb lower here the time before. He was always close to the pace and had every chance, but could never summon the pace to threaten the filly. (tchd 7-1)

Ruacana, who only made his racecourse debut in February, has proved consistent and looked a stayer when runner-up over 1m6f at Chester in July, but although he was always in a good position here, he didn't appear to quite get home. (op 7-2)

Trovare(USA), 2lb wrong, ran too badly to be true when tailed-off behind a couple of these over 2m5f here last month, but had run better at Newmarket since even though he hung his chance away there. He travelled particularly well off the pace this time, but found nothing like as much off the bridle as had seemed likely.

Mystery Star(IRE) couldn't make an impact having come off the bridle a fair way out and is just 1-35 on turf. (op 10-1)

5906 LOEWE STKS (H'CAP) 6f

5:15 (5:16) (Class 4) (0-80,81) 3-Y-O+ £4,528 (£1,347; £673; £336) Stalls High

Form				RPR
001	1		**Bravo Echo**[9] 5630 6-9-8 81 6ex .... KierenFallon 6 (Michael Attwater) *prom: lost pl over 2f out into midfield: drvn and rallied over 1f out: led jst ins fnl f: hld on* **7/1**	89
1251	2	nk	**Picture Dealer**[26] 4985 3-9-5 80 .... GeorgeBaker 8 (Gary Moore) *trckd ldrs: produced to chal 1f out: pressed wnr last 150yds: jst hld* **6/1**[3]	87
0010	3	hd	**Time Medicean**[17] 5362 6-9-0 76 .... RaulDaSilva(3) 11 (Tony Carroll) *hld up in last pair: rdn 2f out: stl there over 1f out: prog on outer fnl f: r.o to take 3rd last strides* **15/2**	82
2302	4	nk	**Aye Aye Digby (IRE)**[13] 5486 7-9-2 75 .... NeilCallan 3 (Patrick Chamings) *racd against rail: pressed ldr: led briefly 1f out: kpt on same pce ins fnl f* **11/2**[2]	80
0055	5	1	**Dishy Guru**[8] 5662 3-9-0 75 .... LiamKeniry 12 (Michael Blanshard) *hld up in last trio: prog over 1f out to press ldrs ins fnl f: rdn and effrt petered out last 100yds* **25/1**	77
4240	6	1/2	**Great Shot**[27] 4939 4-9-1 74 .... JamesDoyle 4 (Sylvester Kirk) *trckd ldrs: looking for room over 2f out and inclined to hang: nt qckn whn gap appeared over 1f out: kpt on same pce after* **9/2**[1]	74
463	7	hd	**Camache Queen (IRE)**[36] 4655 4-9-5 78 .... EddieAhern 5 (Denis Coakley) *chsd ldrs: n.m.r over 2f out and lost pl: swtchd lft sn after: no prog tl styd on last 100yds* **11/1**	78+
3204	8	nk	**Apollo D'Negro (IRE)**[31] 4824 4-9-5 78 .... (v) JohnFahy 2 (Clive Cox) *pressed ldr: rdn over 1f out: wknd jst ins fnl f* **9/2**[1]	77
6361	9	1	**Rash Judgement**[24] 5097 7-9-2 75 .... FergusSweeney 10 (Stuart Kittow) *hld up in last trio: stl to be asked for effrt whn hmpd against rail 2f out: n.d after* **16/1**	70+
4020	10	1/2	**Yurituni**[18] 5326 5-9-4 77 .... (v) JimmyFortune 1 (Eve Johnson Houghton) *mde most to 1f out: wknd* **20/1**	71
5001	11	1/2	**Masai Moon**[22] 5150 8-9-3 76 .... (b) JamesMillman 7 (Rod Millman) *in tch on outer: reminder 1/2-way: no prog 2f out: wknd over 1f out* **20/1**	68

1m 10.78s (-1.42) **Going Correction** -0.10s/f (Good)

WFA 3 from 4yo+ 2lb 11 Ran SP% **117.9**

Speed ratings (Par 105): **105,104,104,103,102 101,101,101,99,99 98**

Tote Swingers: 1&2 £8.90, 1&3 £13.80, 2&3 £9.60 CSF £47.32 CT £328.41 TOTE £8.80: £3.20, £2.10, £3.00; EX 46.40 Trifecta £443.60 Pool: £1,127.15 - 1.88 winning units..

Owner Canisbay Bloodstock **Bred** Juddmonte Farms Ltd **Trained** Epsom, Surrey

FOCUS

A fair sprint handicap, but they didn't seem to go a breakneck pace early and a couple took a keen hold. Straightforward form.

Great Shot Official explanation: jockey said gelding hung right

5907 EBF RACING UK MAIDEN FILLIES' STKS (DIV II) 1m

5:50 (5:52) (Class 5) 2-Y-O £3,234 (£962; £481; £240) Stalls Low

Form				RPR
5	1		**Snow Rose (USA)**[18] 5300 2-9-0 0 .... MickaelBarzalona 8 (Mahmood Al Zarooni) *mde all: set mod pce: kicked on over 2f out: wandered sltly 1f out: styd on wl* **11/2**[2]	80+
2	2	2	**Jabhaat (USA)**[24] 5104 2-9-0 0 .... PaulHanagan 6 (Ed Dunlop) *trckd ldng quartet: rdn and effrt 2f out: chsd wnr 1f out: styd on but no imp* **3/1**[1]	75
6	3	1 3/4	**Neamour**[24] 5104 2-9-0 0 .... JimmyFortune 3 (David Simcock) *trckd ldng pair: rdn to chse wnr 2f out to 1f out: one pce* **12/1**	71
04	4	1 1/4	**Fair Comment**[24] 5098 2-9-0 0 .... FergusSweeney 5 (Michael Blanshard) *t.k.h: trckd wnr: shkn up over 2f out: lost 2nd sn after: steadily outpcd* **33/1**	68
4	5	1 1/2	**Solace (USA)**[24] 5104 2-9-0 0 .... WilliamBuick 10 (John Gosden) *hld up in midfield: pushed along wl over 2f out: sn outpcd: kpt on nr fin* **3/1**[1]	65
50	6	nk	**Color Shades**[17] 5339 2-9-0 0 .... JohnFahy 7 (Clive Cox) *wnt lft s: sn chsd ldng trio but stl looked green: outpcd over 2f out: fdd* **16/1**	64+
0	7	1	**North Weald (IRE)**[19] 5275 2-9-0 0 .... EddieAhern 4 (J W Hills) *hld up in midfield: pushed along and outpcd 2f out: fdd* **50/1**	62
3	8	hd	**Beautiful Story (IRE)**[10] 5574 2-9-0 0 .... MartinHarley 2 (Mick Channon) *hld up in last pair: shkn up over 2f out: sn outpcd: no ch over 1f out* **7/1**[3]	61

0 **9** ¾ **Azelle**[11] 5551 2-9-0 0 .... RichardHughes 1 59
(Richard Hannon) *hld up in midfield: pushed along over 2f out: sn outpcd: fdd over 1f out* **9/1**

00 **10** ½ **Olympic Jule**[33] 4739 2-9-0 0 .... JamesDoyle 9 58
(John Dunlop) *hld up in last: pushed along and outpcd over 2f out: no ch after* **8/1**

1m 40.31s (0.41) **Going Correction** -0.10s/f (Good) **10** Ran SP% **117.5**
Speed ratings (Par 92): **93,91,89,88,86 86,85,85,84,83**
Tote Swingers: 1&2 £4.20, 1&3 £16.00, 2&3 £8.80 CSF £22.53 TOTE £6.10: £2.70, £1.10, £5.80; EX 26.90 Trifecta £394.90 Pool: £1,158.28 - 2.17 winning units..
Owner Godolphin **Bred** Darley **Trained** Newmarket, Suffolk

FOCUS
This looked much weaker than the first division, which was backed up by the fact that the winner had finished well behind Heading North (runner-up in the first leg) on her debut. The early pace was moderate and winning time was 2.63 seconds slower than division one. The form has been rated at face value around the second.

NOTEBOOK
Snow Rose(USA) looked green when fifth of ten on last month's Kempton debut, but this sister to the top-class Raven's Pass was much more organised over this extra furlong and responded well to a positive ride, making all and keeping on well despite hanging away to her left inside the last. She should progress again, but doesn't look a world-beater. (op 13-2 tchd 7-1)
Jabhaat(USA) had a couple of these behind when second of 13 on her Newmarket debut over 7f last month and had every chance when pulled out wide for her effort over a furlong out, but couldn't quicken enough to bother the winner. She wouldn't want much further than this on pedigree. (op 11-4 tchd 5-2)
Neamour, behind Jabhaat and Solice at Newmarket, travelled well behind the leaders and kept on once under pressure for a fair third, but being out of a 1m4f winner she may not come into her own until tackling middle-distances next year. (op 20-1)
Fair Comment wasn't beaten far when fourth of six on the Lingfield Polytrack on her second start and didn't run badly here either considering she was keen in a prominent position early. Nurseries now beckon. (tchd 40-1)
Solace(USA) should have done better considering she finished between the second and third fillies on her Newmarket debut when meeting trouble in running, but she was making hard work of this from some way out. She may not have been suited by the modest pace, but perhaps she also needs a more time.
Color Shades ◆ disappointed on her second start at Doncaster last month having shown promise on her Newbury debut, but ran better than it may have appeared here as she missed the break and then covered plenty of ground around the wide outside. She could be interesting for nurseries now.

5908 HALNAKER GENTLEMAN AMATEUR RIDERS' H'CAP 1m 3f
6:20 (6:23) (Class 5) (0-70,68) 4-Y-0+ **£2,495** (£774; £386; £193) **Stalls** High

Form RPR

0-42 **1** **Swift Blade (IRE)**[14] 5441 4-11-5 **66** .... (p) MrSWalker 2 76
(Lady Herries) *hld up in last quartet off str pce: smooth prog 4f out: led wl over 2f out: wandered in front: hrd pressed 1f out: urged along and hld on wl* **4/1**[1]

2450 **2** 1¼ **Filun**[26] 4983 7-11-1 **65** .... MrNdeBoinville(3) 5 72
(Anthony Middleton) *hld up in last quartet off str pce: prog on wd outside over 3f out: c to chal 1f out: nt qckn* **12/1**

3404 **3** 1¼ **Decana**[20] 5241 4-10-5 **57** .... MrRPooles(5) 6 62
(Hughie Morrison) *trckd ldrs at str pce: wnt 2nd on inner over 2f out to 1f out: styd on same pce: did best of those racing cl to pce* **17/2**

2014 **4** 3½ **Before Bruce**[25] 5038 5-11-4 **65** .... (vt) MrAJBerry 10 63
(Brendan Powell) *hld up in midfield off str pce: rdn 3f out: chsd ldng trio 2f out: one pce after* **8/1**

-222 **5** 1¼ **Rowan Ridge**[222] 310 4-11-7 **68** .... MrDHDunsdon 3 64
(William Knight) *hld up in last quartet off str pce: rdn and tried to make prog over 3f out: no real imp 2f out: kpt on* **8/1**

0330 **6** 6 **Lyric Poet (USA)**[4] 5809 5-10-10 **64** .... (tp) MrGrahamCarson(7) 7 49
(Anthony Carson) *sn prom: chsd ldr 1/2-way at str pce: chal over 4f out: wknd wl over 2f out* **7/1**[3]

3234 **7** 1¼ **Barachiel**[10] 5596 4-10-6 **60** .... MrCPShoemark(7) 11 43
(Luke Dace) *sn pushed up to go prom on outer: w ldng pair 4f out: wknd wl over 2f out* **10/1**

5133 **8** ½ **Taroum (IRE)**[39] 4536 5-10-13 **65** .... MrCCarroll(5) 8 47
(Tony Carroll) *hld up in last quartet off str pce: rdn over 3f out: no prog and wl btn 2f out* **5/1**[2]

5402 **9** 4½ **Mustajed**[20] 5241 11-10-3 **55** .... (v) MrPMillman(5) 12 29
(Rod Millman) *hld up in midfield: wknd 3f out* **14/1**

5504 **10** 7 **Rosy Dawn**[12] 5509 7-10-0 **54** oh9 .... MrAJones(7) 9 16
(John Bridger) *chsd ldr at str pce to 1/2-way: wknd over 3f out* **33/1**

4600 **11** ¾ **Avalon Bay**[28] 4914 4-10-2 **54** oh7 .... MatthewStanley(5) 4 14
(Pat Eddery) *led at str pce but pressed: hdd & wknd rapidly wl over 2f out* **66/1**

4-50 **12** 25 **Stentorian (IRE)**[19] 4585 4-10-12 **66** .... (p) MrGGorman(7) 1
(Gary Moore) *prom early: sn lost pl and struggling: t.o* **11/1**

2m 27.93s (1.43) **Going Correction** -0.10s/f (Good) **12** Ran SP% **118.1**
Speed ratings (Par 103): **90,89,88,85,84 80,79,79,75,70 70,52**
Tote Swingers: 1&2 £10.20, 1&3 £10.30, 2&3 £31.20 CSF £52.90 CT £392.09 TOTE £5.70: £1.70, £4.50, £2.70; EX 49.10 Trifecta £412.70 Pool: £1,048.50 - 1.88 winning units..
Owner Angmering Park **Bred** Messrs Mark Hanly & James Hanly **Trained** Patching, W Sussex
■ Stewards' Enquiry : Mr S Walker one-day ban: careless riding (Sep 25)

FOCUS
The leaders went off far too quick in this and paid the penalty, whereas the first two home came from well back. The winner is rated in line with a best view of his 3yo form.
T/Plt: £20.30 to a £1 stake. Pool: £66,448.00 - 2,381.14 winning tickets. T/Qpdt: £10.80 to a £1 stake. Pool: £4,999.00 - 339.97 winning tickets. JN

5126 LEICESTER (R-H)
Tuesday, September 4

OFFICIAL GOING: Good to firm (good in places; 8.1)
Wind: Light across Weather: Cloudy

5909 CLUBROOM FILLIES' NURSERY 5f 218y
2:00 (2:01) (Class 3) (0-95,83) 2-Y-0 **£5,822** (£1,732; £865; £432) **Stalls** High

Form RPR

0610 **1** **Excel Yourself (IRE)**[18] 5307 2-9-6 **79** .... MartinDwyer 3 81
(James Tate) *led 5f out: rdn and hung rt fnl f: all out* **12/1**

6111 **2** hd **Jamesbo's Girl**[31] 4804 2-9-7 **80** .... FrederikTylicki 5 81
(Richard Fahey) *hld up: hdwy u.p over 1f out: r.o* **9/4**[1]

522 **3** hd **Lady Of The House (IRE)**[92] 2747 2-9-4 **77** .... PhillipMakin 4 77+
(Kevin Ryan) *chsd ldrs: rdn over 2f out: edgd rt ins fnl f: r.o* **7/2**[3]

1 **4** 1¼ **Bottle Blonde**[15] 5425 2-9-6 **79** .... FrannyNorton 6 76
(Ed McMahon) *trckd ldrs: racd keenly: nt clr run and lost pl over 4f out: rdn over 1f out: edgd rt and r.o ins fnl f* **8/1**

305 **5** 1 **Vestibule**[8] 5682 2-8-12 **71** .... (p) SilvestreDeSousa 1 65
(Eve Johnson Houghton) *led 1f: chsd wnr: rdn over 1f out: no ex wl ins fnl f* **6/1**

4431 **6** 8 **Effie B**[4] 5790 2-9-5 **83** 6ex .... CharlesBishop(5) 2 53
(Mick Channon) *s.i.s: hdwy over 4f out: rdn over 2f out: wknd over 1f out* **3/1**[2]

1m 11.55s (-1.45) **Going Correction** -0.175s/f (Firm) **6** Ran SP% **111.1**
Speed ratings (Par 96): **102,101,101,99,98 87**
Tote Swingers: 1&2 £7.70, 1&3 £8.40, 2&3 £1.10 CSF £38.44 TOTE £37.90: £16.40, £1.10; EX 47.40.
Owner Saif Ali **Bred** Rabbah Bloodstock Limited **Trained** Newmarket, Suffolk

FOCUS
The top weight was rated 12lb lower ceiling and there was a bunch finish, so straightforward form if ordinary for the class. They raced stands' side.

NOTEBOOK
Excel Yourself(IRE) raced away from the main action when well beaten in a Newbury Listed race on her previous start, but prior to that she'd won a Wolverhampton maiden. Upped in trip, she showed herself on a fair mark, but was clinging on at the line having been challenged on both sides, and she might find it tougher to follow up. (tchd 14-1)
Jamesbo's Girl, on a hat-trick after taking a claimer (picked up by these connections for £10,000) and a Goodwood nursery, continued her progression off a 5lb higher mark, although this probably isn't form to get carried away with. (op 5-2)
Lady Of The House(IRE), who had shaped well in 5f maidens, was just held on this nursery debut after three months off. She ought to find a similar event. (tchd 11-4)
Bottle Blonde, a 25-1 debut winner over 6f on Polytrack, still looked green on this switch to turf. She should have learnt from this, and many of her sire's progeny want soft ground. (op 7-1)
Vestibule had a penalty for her recent Sandown win over 5f, but was only 4lb higher. She was caught wide without cover, which didn't help over this longer trip, and had little left when asked. (op 11-2 tchd 7-1)

5910 WILLOUGHBY H'CAP 7f 9y
2:30 (2:30) (Class 4) (0-80,80) 3-Y-0+ **£4,075** (£1,212; £606; £303) **Stalls** High

Form RPR

4130 **1** **Good Authority (IRE)**[13] 5480 5-9-7 **77** .... TomMcLaughlin 6 90
(Karen George) *hld up: hdwy over 1f out: r.o to ld post* **9/1**

001 **2** hd **Konstantin (IRE)**[23] 5120 4-9-10 **80** .... HayleyTurner 14 92
(Marcus Tregoning) *a.p: rdn and hung rt over 1f out: led ins fnl f: hdd post* **12/1**

1600 **3** 1¼ **Muarrab**[46] 4298 3-9-3 **77** .... TadhgO'Shea 12 85
(Ed Dunlop) *hld up: hdwy 1/2-way: rdn and ev ch fr over 1f out tl no ex wl ins fnl f* **10/1**

030 **4** 1 **Amazing Amoray (IRE)**[97] 2597 4-9-7 **77** .... GrahamGibbons 4 83
(David Barron) *w ldr tl led 4f out: rdn over 1f out: hdd and unmable to qckn ins fnl f* **11/2**[2]

0000 **5** 3 **Mujaadel (USA)**[25] 5059 7-8-3 **66** oh1 .... (p) ShirleyTeasdale(7) 5 64
(David Nicholls) *s.i.s: hld up: hdwy over 2f out: rdn over 1f out: no ex ins fnl f* **33/1**

6300 **6** ¾ **Imaginary World (IRE)**[20] 5243 4-8-10 **66** .... SeanLevey 15 62
(Alan McCabe) *mid-div: rdn over 2f out: styd on ins fnl f: nvr trbld ldrs* **22/1**

246 **7** 2½ **Light From Mars**[15] 5429 7-9-5 **75** .... (p) FrannyNorton 7 64
(Patrick Morris) *led 3f: chsd ldr: rdn over 2f out: wknd fnl f* **10/1**

6010 **8** 1¼ **Rossetti**[27] 4939 4-9-4 **74** .... JamieSpencer 8 60
(Ian Williams) *stdd s: hld up and bhd: swtchd rt and hdwy over 1f out: sn rdn: wknd and eased ins fnl f* **9/2**[1]

2361 **9** 4½ **First Class**[17] 5338 4-8-10 **66** oh3 .... SilvestreDeSousa 16 40
(Rae Guest) *hmpd s: sn prom: rdn over 2f out: wknd over 1f out* **15/2**[3]

0036 **10** 4½ **The Guru Of Gloom (IRE)**[42] 4437 4-9-10 **80** .... MartinDwyer 11 41
(William Muir) *hld up in tch: rdn and wknd over 1f out* **28/1**

5021 **11** ¾ **Frozen Over**[27] 4939 4-8-11 **67** ow1 .... SebSanders 13 26
(Stuart Kittow) *chsd ldrs: rdn 1/2-way: wknd over 1f out* **12/1**

5640 **12** 2½ **Kakapuka**[38] 4580 5-9-6 **76** .... AdamKirby 9 29
(Anabel K Murphy) *prom: rdn 1/2-way: wknd over 1f out* **33/1**

1024 **13** ½ **Supaheart**[19] 5262 3-8-13 **73** .... DarryllHolland 17 23
(Hughie Morrison) *prom: rdn over 2f out: sn wknd* **8/1**

0005 **14** 3 **George Baker (IRE)**[38] 4580 5-9-6 **76** .... PatCosgrave 3 19
(George Baker) *in rr: drvn along over 2f out: wknd wl over 1f out* **16/1**

1m 24.33s (-1.87) **Going Correction** -0.175s/f (Firm)
WFA 3 from 4yo+ 4lb **14** Ran SP% **119.6**
Speed ratings (Par 105): **103,102,101,100,96 95,93,91,86,81 80,77,77,73**
Tote Swingers: 1&2 £11.10, 2&3 £41.60 CSF £107.19 CT £1131.60 TOTE £12.50: £4.40, £3.30, £5.90; EX 150.90.
Owner Miss Karen George **Bred** Mountarmstrong Stud **Trained** Higher Eastington, Devon

FOCUS
A fair handicap run at a good pace. The action unfolded up the middle. Solid form.
First Class Official explanation: jockey said gelding had no more to give
Supaheart Official explanation: vet said filly spread a plate and punctured its foot

5911 NELSON RESTAURANT MAIDEN AUCTION STKS (DIV I) 7f 9y
3:05 (3:06) (Class 6) 2-Y-0 **£1,617** (£481; £240; £120) **Stalls** High

Form RPR

3 **1** **Firstkissoflove**[12] 5511 2-8-5 0 .... SilvestreDeSousa 8 71
(Clive Cox) *chsd ldrs: led over 2f out: rdn and hung lft ins fnl f: hung rt nr fin: styd on* **11/4**[1]

05 **2** nk **Gilded Frame**[19] 5274 2-8-9 0 .... HayleyTurner 1 74
(Marcus Tregoning) *chsd ldrs: rdn over 1f out: edgd lft ins fnl f: styd on* **11/4**[1]

3 2½ **Banreenahreenkah (IRE)** 2-8-4 0 .... TadhgO'Shea 2 62
(Denis Coakley) *s.s: hdwy over 2f out: rn green and no ex ins fnl f* **50/1**

06 **4** ¾ **Benoni**[31] 4792 2-8-11 0 .... DaneO'Neill 12 67
(Henry Candy) *s.i.s: sn prom: rdn over 1f out: nt clr run ins fnl f: styd on same pce* **16/1**

0 **5** 8 **Night's Watch**[12] 5511 2-8-13 0 .... WilliamCarson 7 48
(William Jarvis) *hld up: rdn over 2f out: nvr on terms* **16/1**

6 hd **Aye Aye Skipper (IRE)** 2-8-11 0 .... BrettDoyle 6 45
(Dean Ivory) *hld up: shkn up over 2f out: n.d* **66/1**

4 **7** 8 **Spanish Art**[29] 4873 2-9-1 0 .... SeanLevey 4 27
(Richard Hannon) *in rr and sn pushed along: bhd fr 1/2-way* **7/2**[2]

2 **8** 2½ **Clear Loch**[32] 4752 2-8-10 0 .... LiamJones 9 16
(John Spearing) *plld hrd and prom: rdn over 2f out: wknd wl over 1f out* **6/1**[3]

00 **9** 1¾ **Forced Family Fun**[10] 5574 2-8-12 0 .... JamieSpencer 3 13
(Michael Bell) *prom over 4f* **8/1**

0400 **10** 1 3/4 **Purple Day**15 5403 2-8-12 56 MickyFenton 5 8
(Pam Sly) *led over 4f: wknd over 1f out* 66/1
1m 25.62s (-0.58) **Going Correction** -0.175s/f (Firm) **10** Ran SP% **117.7**
Speed ratings (Par 93): **96,95,92,91,82 82,73,70,68,66**
Tote Swingers: 1&2 £1.90, 2&3 £35.40 CSF £10.35 TOTE £2.90: £1.70, £1.30, £19.20; EX 8.90.
Owner The City & Provincial Partnership **Bred** Mr & Mrs A & D Flannigan **Trained** Lambourn, Berks

FOCUS
Probably no more than a fair maiden, and the time was 0.06 seconds slower than the second division. They raced up the middle. The first four were clear and the form could be rated higher.

NOTEBOOK
Firstkissoflove confirmed the promise of her debut third at Folkestone, keeping well having held a good position throughout. She was getting weight from most of these, but should find her level in nurseries. (op 5-2)
Gilded Frame might have found the ground a bit soft last time, having earlier shaped well on her debut at Goodwood, and this was better. She might win a maiden, but is now qualified for a handicap mark. (op 3-1)
Banreenahreenkah(IRE), getting weight from all of her rivals, ran to a modest level on this debut, keeping on despite having been a bit keen early. (op 33-1)
Benoni travelled well, but seemingly a bit too well for his jockey's liking, who said the colt ran too free. This was an encouraging enough third run and he's now qualified for a mark. (tchd 18-1)
Night's Watch, whose bit slipped when well behind today's winner on his debut at Folkestone, hinted at ability this time. (op 12-1)
Aye Aye Skipper(IRE), an 11,000gns gelded half-brother to some winning sprinters, out of a quite useful 5f-7f winner, ran better than the beaten margin suggests. He showed up well to a point and looked set to finish a reasonable fifth before his jockey gave up with around a furlong to run. (op 50-1)
Clear Loch Official explanation: jockey said gelding ran too free

5912 NELSON RESTAURANT MAIDEN AUCTION STKS (DIV II) 7f 9y
3:40 (3:41) (Class 6) 2-Y-O **£1,617** (£481; £240; £120) **Stalls** High

Form RPR
020 **1** **Dark Emerald (IRE)**77 3240 2-9-1 87 JamieSpencer 3 83
(Brendan Powell) *trckd ldrs: swtchd lft over 2f out: rdn to ld over 1f out: edgd lft ins fnl f: all out* 6/5[1]
63 **2** *shd* **Magical Rose (IRE)**18 5319 2-8-7 0 FrannyNorton 6 75
(Paul D'Arcy) *hld up: hdwy over 2f out: rdn and ev ch fr over 1f out: carried lft ins fnl f: styd on* 11/4[2]
63 **3** *6* **Daisie Cutter**13 5485 2-8-1 0 SimonPearce(3) 2 56
(Lydia Pearce) *w ldr: racd keenly: led wl over 1f out: sn hdd: wknd ins fnl f* 16/1
4 *1 1/2* **Perfect Pose (IRE)** 2-8-10 0 SeanLevey 1 57
(Richard Hannon) *snc chsng ldrs: rdn over 1f out: wknd ins fnl f* 5/1[3]
5 *1 1/4* **Loucal** 2-8-11 0 JimmyQuinn 5 55
(Noel Quinlan) *hld up: styd on fr over 1f out: nvr on terms* 25/1
4 **6** *1* **Paddy's Saltantes (IRE)**12 5511 2-8-10 0 DarryllHolland 11 52+
(J S Moore) *s.i.s: sn pushed along in rr: n.d* 14/1
5 **7** *1 1/4* **Bougaloo**50 4140 2-8-10 0 GrahamGibbons 7 48
(Alan McCabe) *prom: rdn over 2f out: wknd over 1f out* 50/1
8 *3/4* **Senator Sam (IRE)** 2-8-10 0 DaleSwift(3) 9 49
(Ann Duffield) *mid-div: sn pushed along: wknd over 1f out* 25/1
00 **9** *1 1/4* **Fossa**20 5230 2-8-11 0 BrettDoyle 10 44
(Dean Ivory) *led: racd keenly: rdn and hdd wl over 1f out: wknd fnl f* 66/1
10 *13* **Iwilsayzisonlyonce** 2-8-12 0 DaneO'Neill 4 10
(Joseph Tuite) *s.s: outpcd* 40/1
1m 25.56s (-0.64) **Going Correction** -0.175s/f (Firm) **10** Ran SP% **114.9**
Speed ratings (Par 93): **96,95,89,87,85 84,83,82,81,66**
Tote Swingers: 1&2 £1.50, 1&3 £2.30, 2&3 £5.60 CSF £4.12 TOTE £1.60: £1.02, £1.30, £7.30; EX 4.60.
Owner K Rhatigan **Bred** Olive O'Connor **Trained** Upper Lambourn, Berks
■ Stewards' Enquiry : Jamie Spencer caution: careless riding.

FOCUS
The time was fractionally quicker than the first division. Again, they raced up the middle. The first two finished clear and the winner proved that his Coventry run did not flatter him.

NOTEBOOK
Dark Emerald(IRE) shaped well when runner-up behind subsequent dual Group-race winner Olympic Glory on his second start, but had been off since running 12th of 22 in the Coventry. Conceding well all round on this return, he just held on and had to survive a stewards' enquiry after edging left under pressure, taking the runner-up in the same direction. There was no contact between the pair, though, and he was always likely to keep the race. He's entitled to come on for this. (op 6-4 tchd 11-10)
Magical Rose(IRE) was keen early and her rider took a while to get serious. Although she kept on, she still looked green and was always just held. She has a bit of size and may go on progressing. Nurseries are now an option. (op 5-2)
Daisie Cutter was getting weight from all of her rivals. She's going the right way and should be competitive in modest nurseries.
Perfect Pose(IRE), a 28,000euros half-sister to a few winners, travelled okay and showed ability on this racecourse debut. (op 4-1)
Loucal, a 10,000GBP half-brother to, among others, useful 6f winner Celtic Sixpence, kept on nicely from off the pace and this was an encouraging debut. (op 20-1)

5913 CHARNWOOD H'CAP 1m 3f 183y
4:15 (4:16) (Class 5) (0-75,75) 3-Y-O+ **£2,264** (£673; £336; £168) **Stalls** Low

Form RPR
5-22 **1** **Headline News (IRE)**28 4916 3-8-13 71 ChrisCatlin 3 79
(Rae Guest) *s.i.s: hld up: racd keenly: hdwy over 2f out: led over 1f out: rdn out* 6/1[3]
12 **2** *3/4* **Madame St Clair (IRE)**29 4875 3-8-6 71 NedCurtis(7) 10 77
(Roger Curtis) *chsd ldrs: led over 2f out: rdn and hdd over 1f out: styd on* 16/1
0054 **3** *2 3/4* **Toughness Danon**8 5688 6-9-7 70 DaneO'Neill 1 72
(Brendan Powell) *sn pushed along and prom: nt clr run and lost pl over 3f out: nt clr run and swtchd lft over 1f out: r.o ins fnl f: nvr able to chal* 12/1
426 **4** *2 3/4* **Port Charlotte**31 4797 3-9-2 74 DarryllHolland 8 72
(Hughie Morrison) *hld up: pushed along over 3f out: styd on fnl f: nvr nrr* 11/1
-000 **5** *1 1/4* **Singzak**37 4626 4-9-3 66 GrahamGibbons 7 62
(Michael Easterby) *sn led: hdd wl over 2f out: styd on same pce fr over 1f out* 6/1[3]
130 **6** *shd* **Circle Of Angels**22 5151 4-9-1 64 JamieSpencer 6 59
(Ian Williams) *s.i.s: hld up: hdwy over 1f out: sn rdn: wknd ins fnl f* 9/1
6131 **7** *3/4* **Bouggatti**12 5509 4-9-12 75 SebSanders 5 69
(Lady Herries) *hld up: hdwy over 3f out: rdn and ev ch over 2f out: wknd fnl f* 9/2[2]
5531 **8** *3* **Saint Thomas (IRE)**20 5225 5-9-0 66 DaleSwift(3) 9 55
(John Mackie) *prom: rdn over 2f out: wknd over 1f out* 11/1
010 **9** *11* **Mazij**15 5413 4-9-6 69 WilliamCarson 4 41
(Peter Hiatt) *chsd ldrs: led wl over 2f out: sn hdd: wknd over 1f out* 33/1
4513 **10** *29* **Ukrainian (IRE)**14 5442 3-9-3 75 (b) SilvestreDeSousa 2
(Mark Johnston) *chsd ldrs: rdn over 3f out: wknd over 2f out: t.o* 11/4[1]
2m 32.8s (-1.10) **Going Correction** -0.10s/f (Good)
WFA 3 from 4yo+ 9lb **10** Ran SP% **116.6**
Speed ratings (Par 103): **99,98,96,94,94 93,93,91,84,64**
Tote Swingers: 1&2 £16.10, 1&3 £10.30, 2&3 £22.40 CSF £96.62 CT £1117.11 TOTE £9.80: £2.80, £4.70, £3.80; EX 55.10.
Owner Chestnuts **Bred** Airlie Stud **Trained** Newmarket, Suffolk

FOCUS
An ordinary handicap run at what looked a modest pace. Unconvincing form.
Ukrainian(IRE) Official explanation: trainer's rep said gelding finished distressed

5914 SHEPSHED H'CAP 1m 60y
4:50 (4:50) (Class 3) (0-90,89) 3-Y-O+ **£6,663** (£1,982; £990; £495) **Stalls** Low

Form RPR
54 **1** **Sam Sharp (USA)**57 3911 6-9-4 83 JamieSpencer 3 91
(Ian Williams) *hld up: hdwy over 1f out: shkn up ins fnl f: r.o to ld nr fin* 9/2
1124 **2** *3/4* **Chosen Character (IRE)**19 5269 4-9-3 82 (vt) RichardKingscote 5 88
(Tom Dascombe) *chsd ldrs: rdn over 2f out: ev ch ins fnl f: r.o* 8/1
0025 **3** *shd* **Crown Counsel (IRE)**12 5517 4-9-5 84 SilvestreDeSousa 8 90
(Mark Johnston) *chsd ldr: rdn to ld over 1f out: hdd nr fin* 3/1[2]
3404 **4** *1 3/4* **Frog Hollow**31 4819 3-9-5 89 JimCrowley 4 92
(Ralph Beckett) *mid-div: hdwy over 2f out: rdn over 1f out: nt clr run ins fnl f: styd on* 10/3[3]
003 **5** *2 1/4* **Lucky Henry**24 5094 3-9-1 85 AdamKirby 1 82
(Clive Cox) *led: rdn and hdd over 1f out: no ex ins fnl f* 5/2[1]
0030 **6** *3* **Cruiser**35 4689 4-9-0 79 (p) MartinDwyer 6 69
(William Muir) *hld up: hdwy over 3f out: rdn and hung rt fr over 2f out: no ex fnl f* 28/1
0000 **7** *2 1/2* **West End Lad**9 5618 9-8-9 77 (b) MarkCoumbe(3) 2 61
(Roy Bowring) *chsd ldrs: rdn over 2f out: wknd over 1f out* 40/1
0440 **8** *4* **Mullins Way (USA)**123 1820 4-8-12 82 JemmaMarshall(5) 7 57
(Jo Hughes) *hld up: a in rr* 33/1
1m 42.86s (-2.24) **Going Correction** -0.10s/f (Good)
WFA 3 from 4yo+ 5lb **8** Ran SP% **114.8**
Speed ratings (Par 107): **107,106,106,104,102 99,96,92**
Tote Swingers: 1&2 £9.30, 1&3 £2.60, 2&3 £4.90 CSF £38.77 CT £125.11 TOTE £6.10: £1.40, £1.90, £1.10; EX 41.00.
Owner N Martin **Bred** Michael Cahan Thoroughbreds **Trained** Portway, Worcs

FOCUS
A decent handicap run at a good pace. The form is rated around the second and third.

NOTEBOOK
Sam Sharp(USA), who was 1lb higher than when last winning in May 2011, had the race run to suit. He has won on soft, but seems even better on quick ground and conditions were more suitable than on his last two starts. (op 7-1)
Chosen Character(IRE) was back on a career-high mark, and not partnered by a claimer for the first time in six starts, but he continued his fine recent run, only being picked off by a rival who had raced further back.
Crown Counsel(IRE) hasn't won since June 2011, but he didn't do much wrong here. He just paid for racing up with a hot pace and can do better if able to get his own way in similar company. (op 11-4 tchd 10-3)
Frog Hollow didn't get the clearest of runs and gave the impression he can do a bit better. (tchd 11-4)
Lucky Henry was hassled up front by Crown Counsel and had little left when it mattered. Official explanation: vet said colt lost a back shoe (op 3-1)

5915 SIX HILLS H'CAP 5f 218y
5:20 (5:23) (Class 5) (0-70,76) 3-Y-O+ **£2,264** (£673; £336; £168) **Stalls** High

Form RPR
3141 **1** **Meandmyshadow**18 5317 4-9-1 67 DaleSwift(3) 5 79
(Alan Brown) *chsd ldrs: led 1/2-way: rdn over 1f out: r.o* 8/1[3]
5356 **2** *2* **Bajan Bear**17 5341 4-9-4 67 (b[1]) DaneO'Neill 9 73
(Michael Blanshard) *s.s: outpcd: hdwy over 1f out: r.o: no ch w wnr* 12/1
0351 **3** *1* **We'll Deal Again**6 5737 5-9-13 76 6ex (b) GrahamGibbons 8 78
(Michael Easterby) *led to 1/2-way: rdn and edgd rt over 1f out: styd on same pce fnl f* 7/1[2]
4622 **4** *1/2* **Pettochside**8 5662 3-8-10 61 (t) WilliamCarson 4 62
(Stuart Williams) *hld up: hdwy over 1f out: nt rch ldrs* 8/1[3]
-650 **5** *1/2* **Black Douglas**14 5454 3-8-13 64 (b[1]) FrannyNorton 11 63
(William Jarvis) *s.i.s: outpcd: r.o wl ins fnl f: nvr nrr* 25/1
0006 **6** *1 1/4* **Sairaam (IRE)**17 5338 6-8-12 64 MarkCoumbe(3) 12 59
(Charles Smith) *sn pushed along in rr: hdwy over 1f out: nt trble ldrs* 20/1
0433 **7** *1/2* **West Leake Hare (IRE)**40 4489 3-9-3 68 (p) JamieSpencer 17 62
(Charles Hills) *sn outpcd: r.o ins fnl f: nrst fin* 6/1[1]
0620 **8** *1/2* **Not My Choice (IRE)**7 5720 7-8-7 56 oh1 (t) SilvestreDeSousa 13 48
(Paul Howling) *prom: rdn 1/2-way: no ex fnl f* 14/1
243 **9** *1 1/2* **Yankee Storm**42 4438 7-8-8 57 (p) JimmyQuinn 1 44
(Michael Wigham) *mid-div: sn pushed along: nvr on terms* 12/1
0462 **10** *4 1/2* **Dickie Le Davoir**5 5774 8-9-6 69 (b) RobbieFitzpatrick 2 42
(Richard Guest) *dwlt: outpcd* 8/1[3]
03 **11** *1* **Royal Selection (IRE)**39 4533 4-8-9 58 DarryllHolland 7 28
(Karen George) *prom: rdn over 1f out: wknd fnl f* 12/1
215 **12** *1/2* **Amosite**27 4969 6-9-2 65 (v) FrederikTylicki 15 33
(J R Jenkins) *prom: rdn 1/2-way: edgd rt and wknd wl over 1f out* 33/1
0234 **13** *nse* **Irish Boy (IRE)**4 5791 4-9-4 67 (v[1]) MickyFenton 3 35
(Paul Midgley) *chsd ldrs: rdn over 1f out: wknd fnl f* 16/1
500 **14** *1/2* **Errigal Lad**42 4438 7-8-7 56 LiamJones 6 22
(Garry Woodward) *s.i.s: outpcd* 33/1
4160 **15** *1* **Bermondsey Bob (IRE)**24 5093 6-9-1 64 ChrisCatlin 14 27
(John Spearing) *chsd ldrs tl wknd wl over 1f out* 18/1
4006 **16** *1* **Dark Falcon (IRE)**11 5545 3-8-11 62 MartinDwyer 16 22
(James Tate) *w ldr to 1/2-way: rdn and wknd over 1f out* 14/1
0154 **17** *nk* **Proper Charlie**11 5531 4-8-13 62 JimCrowley 10 21
(William Knight) *mid-div: sn pushed along: wknd 2f out* 10/1
1m 11.48s (-1.52) **Going Correction** -0.175s/f (Firm)
WFA 3 from 4yo+ 2lb **17** Ran SP% **131.3**
Speed ratings (Par 103): **103,100,99,98,97 96,95,94,92,86 85,84,84,83,82 81,80**
Tote Swingers: 1&2 £24.80, 1&3 £17.50, 2&3 £18.10 CSF £103.45 CT £727.09 TOTE £9.80: £2.00, £4.70, £2.70, £2.90; EX 175.70.
Owner G Morrill **Bred** M J Dawson **Trained** Yedingham, N Yorks

FOCUS
They raced middle to near side, with the main pace appearing to be towards the stands' side for much of the way. Sound form.
Irish Boy(IRE) Official explanation: vet said gelding bled from the nose

T/Jkpt: Not won. T/Plt: £203.00 to a £1 stake. Pool: £59,069.00 - 212.36 winning tickets. T/Qpdt: £12.80 to a £1 stake. Pool: £5,153.00 - 296.29 winning tickets. CR

5053 MUSSELBURGH (R-H)

Tuesday, September 4

OFFICIAL GOING: Good to firm (8.1)

Wind: Fairly strong, half against Weather: Cloudy, bright

5916 SCOTTISH RACING (S) STKS — 5f

1:40 (1:40) (Class 6) 2-Y-O — **£1,811** (£539; £269; £134) **Stalls** High

Form — RPR

015 **1** **Done Dreaming (IRE)**[15] 5411 2-9-3 74 TonyHamilton 3 — 65
(Richard Fahey) *trckd ldrs: swtchd rt and rdn to ld ins fnl f: kpt on wl* **1/1**[1]

500 **2** 1 1/4 **Lady Calantha**[28] 4899 2-8-7 0 JamesSullivan 2 — 50
(Alan Berry) *led: rdn 2f out: hdd ins fnl f: kpt on same pce towards fin* **80/1**

316 **3** 1 1/4 **Charlemagne Diva**[8] 5682 2-8-12 66 PJMcDonald 1 — 50
(Ann Duffield) *cl up on outside: chal over 1f out to ins fnl f: kpt on same pce* **7/4**[2]

403 **4** 3/4 **Red Star Lady (IRE)**[4] 5807 2-8-4 60 (b) DeclanCannon(3) 5 — 42
(Mrs K Burke) *wnt lft s: t.k.h: drvn and outpcd 2f out: kpt on fnl f: no imp* **4/1**[3]

2460 **5** 4 **Sulky Sheila (IRE)**[18] 5313 2-8-7 45 (b) DuranFentiman 4 — 28
(Tim Easterby) *w ldr: drvn 2f out: wknd ent fnl f* **33/1**

1m 1.78s (1.38) **Going Correction** +0.175s/f (Good) — **5** Ran SP% **110.5**

Speed ratings (Par 93): **95,93,91,89,83**

CSF £44.09 TOTE £3.20: £1.30, £9.30; EX 24.20.There was no bid for the winner.

Owner Middleham Park Racing XXVIII **Bred** Pier House Stud **Trained** Musley Bank, N Yorks

FOCUS

Stands bend moved out 2metres. A moderate 2-y-o seller. The form has been viewed negatively, a little below the standard for the grade.

NOTEBOOK

Done Dreaming(IRE), an Ayr maiden race winner, never fired when fifth behind Charlemagne Diva in a claimer at Thirsk where he raced wide. Given plenty of cover this time, he did more than enough when pulled wide and reversed form. (op 11-8)

Lady Calantha, unplaced in three outings for Richard Hannon, was in a seller for the first time. She made the running and battled back to take second spot. Whether she will build on this remains to be seen. (op 66-1)

Charlemagne Diva's rating went up a stone after showing much improved form to win at Thirsk, when possibly helped by racing against the stands' rail. She took a narrow advantage but ultimately had to settle for third spot. She will struggle in nursery company unless her handicap mark is revised. (op 6-4)

Red Star Lady(IRE), in second-time cheekpieces, was having her second start in four days. She was staying on at the death and is worth a try over 6f. (op 9-2)

5917 TOWERGATE UNDERWRITING H'CAP (DIV I) — 1m

2:10 (2:13) (Class 6) (0-60,60) 3-Y-O+ — **£1,876** (£558; £278; £139) **Stalls** Low

Form — RPR

0543 **1** **Dubai Celebration**[17] 5341 4-9-5 55 PaddyAspell 8 — 63
(Julie Camacho) *trckd ldrs: effrt over 1f out: led ins fnl f: rdn out* **3/1**[1]

5055 **2** 1 **Jebel Tara**[10] 5590 7-8-13 49 (bt) TomEaves 14 — 55
(Ian Semple) *cl up: led and rdn over 2f out: hdd ins fnl f: kpt on: hld nr fin* **16/1**

400 **3** 1 1/2 **Praxios**[22] 5171 4-8-12 51 (b) GaryBartley(3) 5 — 53
(Noel Wilson) *midfield: stdy hdwy 1/2-way: effrt and swtchd lft 2f out: kpt on u.p fnl f* **10/1**

0024 **4** 1/2 **Carrie's Magic**[8] 5671 5-9-2 52 MichaelO'Connell 10 — 53
(Alistair Whillans) *trckd ldrs: effrt and rdn over 2f out: kpt on same pce fnl f* **6/1**[3]

6606 **5** hd **Shunkawakhan (IRE)**[21] 5185 9-8-10 46 oh1 (tp) TonyHamilton 11 — 47
(Linda Perratt) *led at modest gallop: rdn and hdd over 2f out: rallied: kpt on same pce fnl f* **50/1**

0601 **6** 1 3/4 **Glenluji**[24] 5081 7-9-6 56 (p) GrahamLee 9 — 53
(Jim Goldie) *hld up: effrt on ins over 2f out: kpt on fnl f: nvr able to chal* **10/1**

656 **7** hd **Whatsofunny (IRE)**[105] 2367 3-9-2 57 PJMcDonald 1 — 53
(Ruth Carr) *t.k.h: in tch on ins: rdn over 2f out: nt qckn appr fnl f* **7/1**

0340 **8** 3/4 **Stormont Bridge**[29] 4888 4-9-10 60 (t) PaulMulrennan 2 — 54
(Maurice Barnes) *dwlt: hld up: effrt whn nt clr run briefly over 2f out and over 1f out: kpt on fnl f: nvr able to chal* **22/1**

6065 **9** 1/2 **Firefly**[36] 4642 3-8-6 47 [1] DuranFentiman 7 — 40
(John Weymes) *hld up: drvn along over 2f out: sme late hdwy: nvr on terms* **20/1**

0644 **10** 3 1/4 **Keys Of Cyprus**[35] 4683 10-9-9 59 AdrianNicholls 12 — 50+
(David Nicholls) *cl up: rdn over 2f out: hung rt and wknd ins fnl f* **11/2**[2]

0000 **11** 2 1/4 **Crocodile Bay (IRE)**[14] 5459 9-8-7 46 oh1 (b) DeclanCannon(3) 3 — 27
(Richard Guest) *s.i.s: hld up: rdn over 2f out: nvr able to chal* **40/1**

5500 **12** 6 **Tectonic (IRE)**[126] 1725 3-9-0 55 (p) JamesSullivan 13 — 22
(Iain Jardine) *t.k.h: midfield on outside: struggling over 2f out: sn beawten* **40/1**

46-0 **13** 8 **Joyful Sound (IRE)**[68] 3549 4-9-7 57 AmyRyan 4 — 5
(Brian Ellison) *hld up: swtchd to outside after 1f: rdn over 2f out: sn btn* **7/1**

1m 40.68s (-0.52) **Going Correction** -0.025s/f (Good)

WFA 3 from 4yo+ 5lb — **13** Ran SP% **119.7**

Speed ratings (Par 101): **101,100,98,98,97 96,95,95,94,91 89,83,75**

Tote Swingers: 1&2 £11.40, 1&3 £8.30, 2&3 £27.10 CSF £52.75 CT £453.64 TOTE £4.80: £1.90, £4.90, £4.70; EX 53.90.

Owner L Bolingbroke, N Gravett & J Camacho **Bred** Wheelers Land Stud **Trained** Norton, N Yorks

FOCUS

A weak handicap run in a similar time to division II. Low-grade, shaky form.

Glenluji Official explanation: jockey said gelding hung left-handed

Stormont Bridge Official explanation: jockey said gelding missed the break

Keys Of Cyprus Official explanation: jockey said gelding hung right throughout

Joyful Sound(IRE) Official explanation: vet said gelding bled from the nose

5918 TOWERGATE UNDERWRITING H'CAP (DIV II) — 1m

2:40 (2:41) (Class 6) (0-60,60) 3-Y-O+ — **£1,876** (£418; £418; £139) **Stalls** Low

Form — RPR

0434 **1** **Tony Hollis**[38] 4603 4-8-7 50 GemmaTutty(7) 9 — 58
(Karen Tutty) *in tch: stdy hdwy over 2f out: led ins fnl f: edgd rt: pushed out* **7/1**

3550 **2** 1 1/4 **Berbice (IRE)**[17] 5362 7-9-7 60 JulieBurke(3) 11 — 65
(Linda Perratt) *hld up: stdy hdwy over 2f out: swtchd lft: effrt and shkn up ins fnl f: kpt on: hld towards fin* **20/1**

U100 **2** dht **Goninodaethat**[24] 5084 4-9-7 57 GrahamLee 2 — 63
(Jim Goldie) *t.k.h: trckd ldrs: effrt over 2f out: kpt on ins fnl f* **8/1**

4066 **4** shd **Cheers Buddy (IRE)**[15] 5428 4-9-2 52 (e) PJMcDonald 10 — 57
(Ian Semple) *cl up: led over 2f out: rdn and hdd ins fnl f: kpt on: hld cl home* **8/1**

3030 **5** 3 3/4 **Outlaw Torn (IRE)**[18] 5312 3-8-12 56 (e) DeclanCannon(3) 8 — 52
(Richard Guest) *midfield: effrt and swtchd lft wl over 1f out: kpt on fnl f: no imp* **6/1**[3]

4306 **6** 1 1/4 **Let's Face Facts**[35] 4676 5-9-1 51 DanielTudhope 6 — 44
(Jim Goldie) *hld up: effrt over 2f out: no imp fr over 1f out* **10/1**

066 **7** nk **Drive Home (USA)**[32] 4783 5-9-4 57 GaryBartley(3) 1 — 50
(Noel Wilson) *t.k.h: trckd ldrs: rdn whn n.m.r 2f out: wknd appr fnl f* **11/2**[2]

0663 **8** 4 **Cannon Bolt (IRE)**[25] 5059 4-9-5 55 (b) RobertWinston 4 — 39
(Robin Bastiman) *t.k.h: led at decent gallop: hdd over 2f out: wknd over 1f out* **10/3**[1]

-002 **9** 1 **New Romantic**[21] 5215 3-8-10 51 (p) BarryMcHugh 13 — 32
(Julie Camacho) *hld up: pushed along and outpcd over 3f out: hung rt and no imp fnl 2f* **8/1**

4450 **10** 9 **Artistic Dawn (IRE)**[18] 5312 3-9-3 58 (v[1]) PaulMulrennan 5 — 19
(John Weymes) *s.i.s: bhd: struggling after 3f: nvr on terms* **28/1**

-600 **11** 4 1/2 **Lowtherwood**[37] 4619 3-8-8 49 TomEaves 12
(Bryan Smart) *midfield on outside: struggling over 3f out: sn btn* **33/1**

060 **12** 1/2 **Tomasini**[37] 4622 3-8-5 46 oh1 JamesSullivan 3
(John Weymes) *s.i.s: hld on ins: rdn whn hmpd over 3f out: sn btn* **50/1**

1m 40.75s (-0.45) **Going Correction** -0.025s/f (Good)

WFA 3 from 4yo+ 5lb — **12** Ran SP% **120.8**

Speed ratings (Par 101): **101,99,99,99,95 94,94,90,89,80 75,75**PL: Berbice £7.30, Goninodaethat £2.90 Tote Exacta: Tony Hollis, Berbice £48.20, Tony Hollis, Goninodaethat £55.90 CSF: TH, B £72.17, TH, G £30.39 Tricast: TH, B, G £585.41 TH,G,B £549.69. Tote Swingers: 1&B £26.60, 1&G £12.70, 2&2 £20.50 TOTE £8.80: £227, £Owner, £Thoroughbred Homes Ltd, £BredSeasons Holidays Trained Trifecta £Osmotherley, N Yorks.

FOCUS

The second division of the weak 1m handicap. The time was similar to that of division I and so is the form.

5919 VISITEASTLOTHIAN.ORG MAIDEN STKS — 7f 30y

3:15 (3:16) (Class 5) 3-Y-O+ — **£2,264** (£673; £336; £168) **Stalls** Low

Form — RPR

2302 **1** **Centrifugal (IRE)**[7] 5717 3-9-3 77 JoeFanning 7 — 82+
(Mark Johnston) *pressed ldr: led over 2f out: edgd rt: clr over 1f out: styd on strly* **5/4**[1]

2043 **2** 5 **Premier Choice**[26] 5000 3-9-3 63 (p) DanielTudhope 2 — 67
(Tim Easterby) *prom: hdwy to chse (clr) wnr over 1f out: edgd rt: no imp fnl f* **6/1**[2]

0230 **3** 6 **Amno Dancer (IRE)**[24] 5087 5-9-7 47 TomEaves 1 — 51
(Ian Semple) *t.k.h: led to over 2f out: hung rt and no ex over 1f out* **33/1**

2 **4** 2 3/4 **Dubawi Cheetah (IRE)**[239] 107 3-8-12 0 TonyHamilton 8 — 38
(Richard Fahey) *t.k.h early: trckd ldrs: rdn along 2f out: sn one pce: edgd rt and wknd fnl f* **5/4**[1]

6 **5** 1 1/2 **Keep It Dark**[8] 5679 3-9-3 0 BarryMcHugh 3 — 39
(Tony Coyle) *hld up in tch: stdy hdwy whn nt clr run briefly over 2f out: outpcd whn n.m.r wl over 1f out: sn btn* **20/1**[3]

0 **6** 1/2 **Carla Allegra**[11] 5549 3-8-12 0 GrahamLee 5 — 32
(Jim Goldie) *towards rr: rdn and effrt over 2f out: hung rt: no imp* **50/1**

0050 **7** nk **Skiddaw View**[11] 5549 4-9-2 37 (t) PaulMulrennan 6 — 33
(Maurice Barnes) *towards rr: drvn along 1/2-way: no imp fnl 2f* **100/1**

000 **8** 19 **Lochluichart (IRE)**[31] 4826 3-9-3 0 (e[1]) JamesSullivan 4
(Ian Semple) *s.i.s: a bhd and outpcd* **100/1**

05 **9** 26 **Roseisle**[5] 5760 4-9-2 0 PJMcDonald 9
(Linda Perratt) *slowly away and wnt bdly lft s: a wl bhd* **100/1**

1m 28.48s (-0.52) **Going Correction** -0.025s/f (Good)

WFA 3 from 4yo+ 4lb — **9** Ran SP% **115.8**

Speed ratings (Par 103): **101,95,88,85,83 83,82,60,31**

Tote Swingers: 1&2 £1.70, 1&3 £5.50, 2&3 £6.20 CSF £9.81 TOTE £2.90: £1.10, £1.30, £3.50; EX 7.40.

Owner Sheikh Hamdan Bin Mohammed Al Maktoum **Bred** Darley **Trained** Middleham Moor, N Yorks

FOCUS

A weak, uncompetitive maiden. The form makes sense.

Roseisle Official explanation: jockey said filly hung left-handed throughout

5920 TURFTV NURSERY — 7f 30y

3:50 (3:51) (Class 5) (0-75,71) 2-Y-O — **£3,234** (£962; £481; £240) **Stalls** Low

Form — RPR

6120 **1** **Tussie Mussie**[10] 5602 2-9-4 68 JoeFanning 8 — 73+
(Mark Johnston) *cl up: led over 2f out: edgd rt: pushed clr over 1f out: unchal* **7/2**[1]

0050 **2** 3 **Clock On Tom**[19] 5254 2-8-2 52 JamesSullivan 3 — 49
(Michael Easterby) *s.i.s: hld up: hdwy on ins over 2f out: nt clr run and swtchd to wd outside appr fnl f: kpt on strly to take 2nd nr fin: no ch w wnr* **14/1**

0202 **3** shd **Relight My Fire**[26] 5010 2-9-1 65 (b) DuranFentiman 10 — 62
(Tim Easterby) *t.k.h: cl up: effrt and chsd (clr) wnr over 1f out: one pce fnl f: lost 2nd nr fin* **8/1**

400 **4** nk **Ingleby Symphony (IRE)**[20] 5242 2-8-8 58 TonyHamilton 4 — 54
(Richard Fahey) *prom: effrt whn short of room over 2f out to over 1f out: kpt on ins fnl f* **4/1**[2]

0160 **5** 1 1/2 **Lucy Bee**[21] 5206 2-8-7 57 AndrewMullen 11 — 49
(Keith Dalgleish) *hld up in tch on outside: drvn over 2f out: kpt on same pce fnl f* **20/1**

5063 **6** 2 3/4 **Salvatore Fury (IRE)**[6] 5749 2-8-13 63 TomEaves 5 — 47
(Keith Dalgleish) *unruly bef s: t.k.h: chsd ldng gp: effrt over 2f out: wandered and outpcd over 1f out* **5/1**[3]

4034 **7** hd **Chant (IRE)**[9] 5619 2-9-4 68 PaulMulrennan 9 — 52
(Ann Duffield) *hld up: pushed along over 2f out: sme late hdwy: nvr on terms* **6/1**

315 **8** 1/2 **American Impact (USA)**[13] 5488 2-9-5 69 BarryMcHugh 2 — 53
(Tony Coyle) *trckd ldrs: rdn over 2f out: one pce whn hmpd appr fnl f: sn btn* **5/1**[3]

0000 **9** *13* **Stand N Applaude**[24] 5109 2 -9-0**64** AdrianNicholls 7 21
(David Nicholls) *led: rdn along and hdd over 2f out: swtchd lft over 1f out: no ex whn hmpd appr fnl f: eased whn btn* **14/1**

1m 30.22s (1.22) **Going Correction** -0.025s/f (Good) **9**Ran SP% **119.0**
Speed ratings (Par 95): **92,88,88,88,86 83,83,82,67**
Tote Swingers: 1&2 £13.00, 1&3 £5.40, 2&3 £20.20 CSF £54.98 CT £376.00 TOTE £2.70 : £7.80, £3.90 ; EX 69.90 .
Owner Inner Circle Thoroughbreds - Carpe Diem **Bred** Mrs Mary Taylor **Trained** Middleham Moor, N Yorks

FOCUS
An ordinary nursery, and the form is straightforward.

NOTEBOOK
Tussie Mussie ◆, runner-up in a stronger nursery at Haydock, found this much easier than the Class 2 race she contested at York last time. She took this in most decisive fashion and will be hard to beat if turned out under a penalty in the next nine days. (op 3-1)
Clock On Tom, disappointing when ridden much more prominently on his handicap bow from a 3lb higher mark, made ground hand over fist when pulled wide off the running rail. He will be suited by the step up to 1m. (op 22-1 tchd 25-1)
Relight My Fire, beaten half a length by Tussie Mussie on the AW at Southwell, met her on 3lb better terms. The Fibresand seems to suit him better but Southwell does not resume until next month. (tchd 7-1)
Ingleby Symphony (IRE) stepping up in trip on her handicap bow, was quite keen early. She was sticking on at the death and still looks inexperienced. (op 5-1 tchd 7-2)
Salvatore Fury (IRE) who gave problems at the start, ran with the choke out in the early stages and looks somewhat tricky. (op 9-2)
Stand N Applaude Official explanation: jockey said colt had no more to give

5921 NAIRN'S OATCAKES H'CAP 1m 4f 100y
4:25 (4:25) (Class 5) (0-70,70) 3-Y-0+ **£3,234** (£962; £481 ; £240) **Stalls** Low

Form RPR
4103 **1** **La Bacouetteuse (FR)**[21] 5188 7 -9-9**70** (v[1]) GarryWhillans(5) 3 78
(Iain Jardine) *hld up: pushed along over 3f out: hdwy over 1f out: styd on wl to ld cl home* **7/1**
0010 **2** *hd* **Stormy Morning**[24] 5115 6 -9-3**59** (p) MichaelO'Connell 10 66
(Philip Kirby) *s.i.s: sn in tch: rdn and hdwy to ld over 1f out: kpt on wl fnl f: hdd cl home* **16/1**
0420 **3** *3/4* **Hawdyerwheesht**[11] 5546 4 -9-1**57** GrahamLee 1 65+
(Jim Goldie) *trckd ldrs: pushed along whn n.m.r over 2f out to wl over 1f out: kpt on wl fnl f: nrst fin* **4/1**[2]
5062 **4** *1/2* **Tiger Webb**[20] 5225 4 -9-2**58** DavidNolan 2 63
(Michael Easterby) *hld up in midfield: stdy hdwy over 2f out: sn pushed along: effrt and ch over 1f out: one pce fnl f* **5/2**[1]
2332 **5** *3/4* **Schmooze (IRE)**[21] 5188 3 -8-7**58** JamesSullivan 9 62
(Linda Perratt) *hld up: rdn over 3f out: hdwy wl over 1f out: kpt on fnl f: nrst fin* **9/2**[3]
-063 **6** *2 1/2* **Grand Diamond (IRE)**[21] 5187 8 -8-9**51** oh3 (p) AndrewElliott 5 51
(Jim Goldie) *trckd ldrs: drvn over 2f out: outpcd fnl f* **18/1**
3300 **7** *3 1/2* **Chatterati (USA)**[14] 5441 3 -8-3**54** (b[1]) JoeFanning 6 49
(Mark Johnston) *cl up: led over 2f out: edgd rt and hdd over 1f out: wknd ins fnl f* **6/1**
2205 **8** *1/2* **Oddsmaker (IRE)**[28] 4910 11 -9-2**58** (t) PaulMulrennan 4 52
(Maurice Barnes) *led: rdn and hdd over 2f out: wknd over 1f out* **22/1**
20 **9** *4* **Goldmadchen (GER)**[6] 5730 4 -9-4**60** (p) AndrewMullen 8 48
(Keith Dalgleish) *towards rr: struggling wl over 2f out: hung rt and sn btn* **40/1**
6633 **10** *12* **Chookie Hamilton**[22] 5174 8 -9-8**64** (b) TomEaves 7 33
(Ian Semple) *hld up towards rr: struggling over 3f out: sn btn* **11/1**

2m 42.28s (0.28) **Going Correction** -0.025s/f (Good)
WFA 3 from 4yo+ 9lb **10**Ran SP% **119.8**
Speed ratings (Par 103): **98,97,97,97,96 94,92,92,89,81**
Tote Swingers: 1&2 £17.60, 1&3 £7.60, 2&3 £15.90 CSF £114.95 CT £514.52 TOTE £10.50 : £2.50, £3.80 , £1.80 ; EX 125.90 .
Owner Miss S A Booth **Bred** Sarl Classic Breeding & Maria R Mendes **Trained** Bonchester Bridge, Borders

FOCUS
A moderate handicap which was well run. A 3lb best from the winner.

5922 KIER CONSTRUCTION H'CAP 2m
5:00 (5:00) (Class 6) (0-65,63) 3-Y-0+ **£1,876** (£558; £278 ; £139) **Stalls** High

Form RPR
044 **1** **Grand Art (IRE)**[22] 5172 8 -9-0**52** (p) GaryBartley(3) 5 62
(Noel Wilson) *hld up: smooth hdwy over 3f out: rdn to ld over 1f out: sn clr: eased nr fin* **14/1**
2314 **2** *5* **Geanie Mac (IRE)**[7] 5629 3 -9-0**62** (b) TomEaves 3 66
(Linda Perratt) *chsd clr ldr: led 5f out: rdn and hdd over 1f out: no ch w wnr* **7/1**
0-05 **3** *1 3/4* **Erycina (IRE)**[24] 5115 4 -8-5**45** NeilFarley(5) 4 47
(Noel Wilson) *prom: effrt and drvn along 3f out: kpt on same pce appr fnl f* **66/1**
43-0 **4** *1 1/4* **Soprano (GER)**[29] 4867 10 -9-11**60** GrahamLee 8 60
(Jim Goldie) *hld up: stdy hdwy 1/2-way: effrt and pushed along 3f out: outpcd fnl 2f* **7/1**
663 **5** *3 1/4* **Petella**[16] 5384 6 -10-0**63** PJMcDonald 1 60
(George Moore) *chsd ldrs: drvn and lost pl over 6f out: rallied over 1f out: nvr able to chal* **9/4**[1]
0462 **6** *4* **Hoar Frost**[22] 5173 7 -8-5**47** (p) GemmaTutty(7) 7 39
(Karen Tutty) *hld up: rdn along over 3f out: no imp fr 2f out* **20/1**
5031 **7** *3 1/4* **Sweet Fairnando**[10] 5589 3 -8-13**61** (b) DuranFentiman 10 49
(Tim Easterby) *hld up in tch: effrt over 3f out: edgd rt and wknd wl over 1f out* **7/2**[2]
300 **8** *2 1/4* **Strikemaster (IRE)**[38] 4590 6 -9-9**58** (t) BarryMcHugh 11 43
(Lee James) *hld up: stdy hdwy on outside over 6f out: rdn and wknd fr 3f out* **9/2**[3]
53 **9** *1 1/4* **Shisha Threesixty (IRE)**[7] 5086 4 -9-7**56** (b) JoeFanning 9 40
(Lucinda Russell) *dwlt: hld up: hdwy over 4f out: rdn and wknd over 2f out* **18/1**
6040 **10** *33* **Jim Tango (FR)**[7] 5172 8 -9-11**60** (bt) PaulMulrennan 2
(Brian Storey) *led and clr to 1/2-way: hdd 5f out: wknd 4f out: t.o* **50/1**

3m 33.08s (-0.42) **Going Correction** -0.025s/f (Good)
WFA 3 from 4yo+ 13lb **10**Ran SP% **116.3**
Speed ratings (Par 101): **100,97,96,96,94 92,90,89,89,72**
Tote Swingers: 1&2 £12.10, 1&3 £41.40, 2&3 £46.80 CSF £106.50 CT £6144.28 TOTE £14.30 : £2.90, £2.20 , £8.20 ; EX 81.80 .
Owner Peter Tsim **Bred** Mrs Teresa Bergin & Mrs Anne Fitzgerald **Trained** Middleham, N Yorks

FOCUS
A weak staying handicap, and unconvincing form. The market leaders disappointed and the third was 7lb wrong.

5923 RACING UK H'CAP 5f
5:35 (5:37) (Class 6) (0-65,63) 3-Y-0+ **£1,876** (£558; £278 ; £139) **Stalls** High

Form RPR
-511 **1** **Lizzy's Dream**[173] 910 4 -9-3**58** RobertWinston 4 68
(Robin Bastiman) *dwlt: hld up: weaved through fr 2f out: rdn to ld wl ins fnl f: kpt on strly* **9/1**
235 **2** *3/4* **Irish Girls Spirit (IRE)**[8] 5327 3 -9-0**56** RussKennemore 11 63+
(Paul Midgley) *prom: hdwy to ld over 1f out: sn rdn: hdd wl ins fnl f: hld nr fin* **6/1**[3]
4464 **3** *1 1/2* **Distant Sun (USA)**[5] 5758 8 -9-1**56** (p) BarryMcHugh 2 58
(Linda Perratt) *bhd on outside: gd hdwy over 1f out: kpt on same pce wl ins fnl f* **40/1**
2500 **4** *hd* **Saxonette**[21] 5190 4 -8-12**53** (p) PJMcDonald 9 54
(Linda Perratt) *midfield: effrt and hdwy over 1f out: kpt on same pce wl ins fnl f* **50/1**
010 **5** *3/4* **Alnair (IRE)**[31] 4798 3 -9-2**63** NeilFarley(5) 6 61
(Declan Carroll) *bhd and sn drvn along: hdwy whn nt clr run over 1f out: kpt on fnl f: nvr able to chal* **16/1**
5400 **6** *nk* **Rutterkin (USA)**[58] 3888 4 -8-10**54** JulieBurke(3) 7 53+
(Alan Berry) *bhd and sn outpcd: rdn and effrt whn nt clr run over 1f out: kpt on fnl f: nrst fin* **40/1**
0035 **7** *shd* **Code Six (IRE)**[11] 5548 3 -9-6**62** TomEaves 14 59
(Bryan Smart) *taken early to post: dwlt: sn drvn along towards rr: hdwy and edgd rt over 1f out: no imp fnl f* **5/1**[2]
00- **8** *2 1/4* **Bang Tidy (IRE)**[402] 4557 3 -9-7**63** PaulMulrennan 5 52
(Brian Ellison) *prom: drvn along over 2f out: outpcd fnl f* **22/1**
-634 **9** *1* **Arriva La Diva**[25] 5058 6 -9-1**56** GrahamLee 12 41
(Linda Perratt) *cl up tl rdn and wknd ins fnl f* **22/1**
61 **10** *nse* **Clubland (IRE)**[7] 5719 3 -9-2**58** 6ex AmyRyan 8 43
(Kevin Ryan) *cl up: led 1/2-way: sn rdn: hdd over 1f out: sn btn* **13/8**[1]
250 **11** *1/2* **Lees Anthem**[77] 3256 5 -8-11**52** [1] PaddyAspell 1 35
(Colin Teague) *midfield: effrt on outside over 1f out: wknd ins fnl f* **25/1**
4466 **12** *2* **Angelo Poliziano**[21] 5190 6 -9-5**60** (p) DuranFentiman 13 36
(George Foster) *led stands' rail to 1/2-way: rdn and wknd over 1f out* **22/1**
1400 **13** *2 1/2* **Chosen One (IRE)**[6] 5739 7 -9-2**57** JamesSullivan 3 24
(Ruth Carr) *cl up tl rdn and wknd over 1f out* **14/1**
006- **14** *15* **Monte Mayor One**[334] 6646 5 -8-12**56** ow2 GaryBartley(3) 10
(Noel Wilson) *bhd and sn drvn along: lost tch fr 1/2-way* **22/1**

1m 1.1s (0.70) **Going Correction** +0.175s/f (Good)
WFA 3 from 4yo+ 1lb **14**Ran SP% **119.7**
Speed ratings (Par 101): **101,99,97,97,95 95,95,91,90,89 89,85,81,57**
Tote Swingers: 1&2 £5.60, 1&3 £16.20, 2&3 £23.20 CSF £55.12 CT £2135.71 TOTE £10.60 : £3.20, £2.80 , £10.90 ; EX 42.70 .
Owner Mrs P Bastiman **Bred** Sheikh Abdulla Bin Isa Al-Khalifa **Trained** Cowthorpe, N Yorks

FOCUS
A tight sprint handicap which was strong run into a headwind. A progressive winner who could improve again.
Alnair(IRE) Official explanation: jockey said gelding hung right-handed throughout
Rutterkin(USA) Official explanation: jockey said gelding was denied a clear run
Monte Mayor One Official explanation: trainer said mare appeared to be lame on pulling up but later was found to be sound
T/Plt: £367.10 to a £1 stake. Pool: £41,263.00 - 82.05 winning tickets. T/Qpdt: £84.10 to a £1 stake. Pool: £3,714.00 - 32.65 w. tickets RY 5924a - 5930a (Foreign Racing) See RI

5811 BATH (L-H)
Wednesday, September 5

OFFICIAL GOING: Good to firm
Wind: Moderate across Weather: Sunny

5931 SDS 10TH ANNIVERSARY FILLIES' H'CAP 1m 2f 46y
2:20 (2:21) (Class 5) (0-75,75) 3-Y-0+ **£2,264** (£673; £336 ; £168) **Stalls** Low

Form RPR
323- **1** **Sunday Bess (JPN)**[336] 6633 4 -9-11**74** RichardKingscote 6 83
(Tom Dascombe) *trckd ldr: led over 1f out: pushed clr: comf* **6/1**[3]
3244 **2** *2 1/4* **Dutch Diamond**[41] 4505 3 -9-4**74** NickyMackay 3 79
(John Gosden) *chsd ldrs: drvn over 2f out: chsd wnr ins fnl f: kpt on but nvr any ch* **9/2**[1]
00 **3** *1 1/4* **Berwin (IRE)**[11] 5592 3 -9-1**71** JamesDoyle 11 73+
(Sylvester Kirk) *hmpd after 1f and in rr: hdwy on outside over 2f out: sn rdn: styd on to take 3rd fnl 40yds but nvr a threat* **12/1**
4420 **4** *3/4* **Urban Daydream (IRE)**[20] 5277 3 -8-12**68** NeilCallan 12 69
(Roger Varian) *in tch: hdwy towards outer fr 3f out: styd on to take one pce 3rd ins fnl f: dropped to 4th fnl 40yds* **7/1**
3502 **5** *nse* **Junior Diary (USA)**[29] 4931 3 -9-1**71** ShaneKelly 14 71
(Brian Meehan) *chsd ldrs: rdn over 2f out: drvn to dispute one pce 3rd ins fnl f: no ex clsng stages* **16/1**
4531 **6** *2* **Elbow Beach**[12] 5528 3 -9-0**70** JamesMillman 5 66
(Rod Millman) *sn led: rdn over 2f out: hdd over 1f out: wknd ins fnl f* **14/1**
5600 **7** *1 1/2* **Operettist**[8] 5707 3 -9-2**72** SeanLevey 7 65
(Richard Hannon) *chsd ldrs: rdn and lost pl fr 4f out: sme prog u.p fnl f* **20/1**
8 *nk* **Headford Lady (IRE)**[28] 4979 7 -9-12**75** CathyGannon 13 68
(James Halpin, Ire) *towards rr: hdwy on outside over 3f out: chsd ldrs 2f out but nvr on terms: one pce fnl f* **25/1**
2125 **9** *1 1/4* **Tidal Run**[11] 5585 4 -9-12**75** MartinHarley 2 65
(Mick Channon) *in rr: hdwy and rdn fr over 2f out: one pce whn nt much daylight fr over 1f out* **15/2**
-000 **10** *1 3/4* **You've Been Mowed**[18] 5369 6 -9-4**72** MatthewLawson(5) 8 59
(Richard Price) *plld hrd: in rr tl hdwy on outside over 3f out: drvn to dispute 3rd over 2f out: wknd over 1f out* **14/1**
-022 **11** *6* **Monopoli**[21] 5239 3 -8-12**68** JimCrowley 10 43
(Ralph Beckett) *in tch: hdwy to chse ldrs fr 4f out: wknd over 2f out* **5/1**[2]
3000 **12** *2 1/4* **Virginia Gallica (IRE)**[41] 4498 3 -8-11**67** SebSanders 15 37
(J W Hills) *a in rr* **16/1**
650 **13** *1 3/4* **Mariet**[25] 5100 3 -8-7**63** LiamKeniry 1 30
(Andrew Balding) *in tch: rdn 4f out: wknd 3f out* **25/1**

2m 11.29s (0.29) **Going Correction** +0.075s/f (Good)
WFA 3 from 4yo+ 7lb **13**Ran SP% **118.6**
Speed ratings (Par 100): **101,99,98,97,97 95,94,94,93,92 87,85,84**
Tote Swingers 1&2 £8.50, 2&3 £14.70, 1&3 £18.60 CSF £31.93 CT £313.91 TOTE £9.80 : £3.00 , £2.30, £4.00 ; EX 55.40 .

Owner A Black **Bred** Shadai Corporation Inc **Trained** Malpas, Cheshire
FOCUS
Races incorporating bottom bend increased in distance by about 12.5yds. This was an ordinary fillies' handicap in which it paid to race handily.

5932 ENGINEERED WATER SYSTEMS MAIDEN AUCTION STKS 5f 161y
2:50 (2:50) (Class 5) 2-Y-O £2,385 (£704; £352) **Stalls** Centre

Form RPR
2222 **1** **Bogsnog (IRE)**11 5586 2-8-13 75 GrahamLee 7 74
(Linda Stubbs) *trckd ldrs: drvn to chal ins fnl f: led fnl 120yds: hld on all out* **9/2**2
25 **2** *shd* **Jubilant Queen**23 5146 2-8-8 0 JohnFahy 10 69
(Clive Cox) *in tch: hdwy over 2f out: styd on wl fnl f to take 2nd clsng stages: gng on last strides: jst failed* **11/2**3
52 **3** *1 1/4* **Tarara**23 5146 2-8-10 0 JimmyFortune 6 67
(Andrew Balding) *pressed ldr tl led over 2f out: rdn fnl f: hdd and outpcd fnl 120yds: wknd cl home* **8/11**1
3404 **4** *1 3/4* **Jamnean**16 5403 2-8-4 53 ChrisCatlin 1 55
(John Holt) *sn led: hdd over 2f out: styd on same pce u.p fr over 1f out* **50/1**
6 **5** *1 3/4* **Elusive Gold (IRE)**27 5003 2-8-11 0 ow1 SebSanders 8 56
(J W Hills) *sn drvn and in tch: styd on same pce fnl 2f* **9/1**
5 **6** *hd* **Tagalaka (IRE)**13 5503 2-8-13 0 NeilCallan 5 57
(Eve Johnson Houghton) *chsd ldrs: drvn and outpcd 1/2-way: styd on u.p fnl f* **20/1**
0 **7** *1 1/4* **Madame Scarlett (IRE)**39 4604 2-8-6 0 FrankieMcDonald 9 46+
(Jo Crowley) *in rr: stl wl off pce and rdn over 1f out: styd on wl clsng stages* **66/1**
0 **8** *nse* **Brynford**10 5631 2-8-6 0 SaleemGolam 3 46
(Chris Dwyer) *in rr: sme hdwy on inner fr 2f out: nvr rchd ldrs: hung lft and wknd fnl f* **66/1**
00 **9** *1* **Pink Mischief**20 5274 2-8-6 0 CathyGannon 11 43
(Harry Dunlop) *outpcd most of way* **33/1**
36 **10** *22* **Cashel's Missile (IRE)**22 5192 2-8-9 0 1 RobertWinston 4
(John Spearing) *slowly away: a bdly outpcd* **25/1**

1m 12.76s (1.56) **Going Correction** +0.025s/f (Good) **10 Ran SP% 118.0**
Speed ratings (Par 95): **90,89,88,85,83 83,81,81,80,50**
Tote Swingers 1&2 £2.60, 2&3 £2.40, 1&3 £2.20 CSF £27.41 TOTE £6.00: £1.80, £1.10, £1.10; EX 23.70.
Owner Facts & Figures **Bred** J R Weston **Trained** Norton, N Yorks
FOCUS
A moderate 2-y-o maiden. Straightforward form, the winner running to his mark and the fourth giving perspective.
NOTEBOOK
Bogsnog(IRE) set the standard with a mark of 75, having been beaten a length or less in his previous four starts, and finally gained a deserved success under his rider who was having his first ride at the track. Always handy, he proved very game when sent to the front inside the last and his consistency should continue to stand him in good stead. (op 7-2)
Jubilant Queen had 6l to find with Tarara on last month's Ffos Las running, but these conditions were very different and she stayed on well down the wide outside over the last 2f, only just failing to get up. A return to further should suit and nurseries now beckon. (op 5-1)
Tarara seemed to be travelling better than anything when sent to the front over 2f out, but she didn't look that happy on the ground and was run out of it. She is worth another chance back on an easier surface and she too can now run in nurseries. (op 5-6)
Jamnean showed plenty of speed from the inside draw for a long way, but she is rated just 53 so needs a return to modest nurseries.
Elusive Gold(IRE), carrying 1lb overweight, finished behind a pair of subsequent winners when an encouraging sixth of nine on last month's Sandown debut and showed some ability again here, but nurseries will be her bag after one more run. (op 11-1)

5933 GEOLIGHT H'CAP 5f 161y
3:20 (3:20) (Class 5) (0-75,75) 4-Y-O+ £2,264 (£673; £336; £168) **Stalls** Centre

Form RPR
1464 **1** **Ice Trooper**22 5205 4-8-12 66 (p) GrahamLee 6 74
(Linda Stubbs) *chsd ldrs: nt seeing much daylight whn swtchd rt ins fnl f: rdn to ld nr fin* **20/1**
0654 **2** *1/2* **Diamond Vine (IRE)**6 5775 4-8-9 68 (p) DarrenEgan(5) 5 74
(Ronald Harris) *in tch: hdwy towards outer over 1f out: str run u.p fnl f to take 2nd cl home: nt pce of wnr* **11/2**3
0062 **3** *1/2* **Mount Hollow**27 4998 7-9-0 75 (p) JackDuern(7) 8 80
(Reg Hollinshead) *in tch: chsd ldrs and rdn 2f out: led 1f out: hdd and outpcd into 3rd nr fin* **5/1**2
-006 **4** *shd* **Dark Lane**9 5681 6-8-10 64 CathyGannon 7 68
(David Evans) *chsd ldrs: rdn over 2f out: one pce u.p appr fnl f: kpt on again clsng stages* **12/1**
0454 **5** *3/4* **Mambo Spirit (IRE)**23 5150 8-9-0 68 JohnFahy 1 70+
(Tony Newcombe) *sn chsng ldrs: rdn and nt clr run fr 1f out and edging lft: kpt on cl home but no imp on ldrs* **8/1**
2100 **6** *nse* **Wooden King (IRE)**40 4530 7-9-7 75 TomMcLaughlin 4 77
(Malcolm Saunders) *s.i.s: in rr: hdwy on outer appr fnl f: kpt on wl clsng stages* **18/1**
1600 **7** *3/4* **Bermondsey Bob (IRE)**1 5915 6-8-10 64 ChrisCatlin 13 63
(John Spearing) *pressed ldr: chal 2f out led over 1f out: sn hdd: wknd fnl 75yds* **7/1**
0001 **8** *nk* **Divine Call**13 5502 5-9-5 73 ShaneKelly 11 71
(Milton Bradley) *s.i.s: in rr: hdwy towards outside fr 2f out: kpt on fnl f: nvr gng pce to rch ldrs* **7/1**
432 **9** *1/2* **Sole Danser (IRE)**25 5093 4-9-2 70 RichardKingscote 2 67+
(Milton Bradley) *in rr: hld up on ins and nvr seeing much daylight fr over 2f out: pushed along and no prog fr over 1f out* **9/2**1
5005 **10** *nk* **Volcanic Dust (IRE)**19 5296 4-9-2 70 RobertWinston 9 66
(Milton Bradley) *s.i.s: in rr: hdwy and in tch 1/2-way: styd on same pce fnl 2f* **33/1**
0-00 **11** *9* **Indian Shuffle (IRE)**12 5531 4-8-12 65 ow1 NeilCallan 12 32
(Jonathan Portman) *sn led: hdd over 1f out: eased whn btn ins fnl f* **16/1**
0000 **12** *4* **Mr Optimistic**62 3778 4-8-8 67 (t) AshleyMorgan(5) 10 20
(Pat Murphy) *chsd ldrs to 1/2-way* **33/1**

1m 11.4s (0.20) **Going Correction** +0.025s/f (Good) **12 Ran SP% 115.8**
Speed ratings (Par 103): **99,98,97,97,96 96,95,95,94,94 82,76**
Tote Swingers 1&2 £15.20, 2&3 £8.00, 1&3 £16.70 CSF £121.73 CT £642.88 TOTE £38.40: £6.70, £3.90, £1.10; EX 127.20.
Owner J P Hames **Bred** Low Ground Stud **Trained** Norton, N Yorks
FOCUS
A modest sprint handicap.
Mambo Spirit(IRE) Official explanation: jockey said gelding was denied a clear run
Divine Call Official explanation: jockey said gelding missed the break

5934 GEOSYSTEMS H'CAP 5f 11y
3:50 (3:50) (Class 5) (0-70,70) 3-Y-O £2,264 (£673; £336; £168) **Stalls** Centre

Form RPR
321 **1** **Angelito**13 5505 3-9-7 70 SeanLevey 6 78
(Ed McMahon) *trckd ldr: led over 1f out: edgd lft u.p sn after: drvn out* **15/8**2
2312 **2** *1 1/4* **I See You**4 5815 3-9-6 69 (p) JimmyFortune 4 75+
(Peter Makin) *led: rdn and hdd over 1f out: hmpd on rail sn after: rdn and rallied ins fnl f: kpt on but no imp on wnr* **6/4**1
3015 **3** *1* **Trending (IRE)**33 4757 3-8-10 62 (b) RaulDaSilva(3) 2 62
(Jeremy Gask) *stdd s: racd in last pl but in tch: shkn up and hdwy 1f: kpt on to take one pce 3rd clsng stages* **5/1**3
6016 **4** *nse* **Sarah Berry**13 5513 3-8-11 60 SaleemGolam 3 60
(Chris Dwyer) *chsd ldrs: disp 3rd thrght and no ch w ldng duo fr over 1f out: dropped to 3rd clsng stages* **25/1**
5532 **5** *2 1/2* **Ocean Myth**10 5635 3-9-1 64 RichardKingscote 5 55
(Jonathan Portman) *disp cl 3rd tl rdn over 2f out: wknd appr fnl f* **6/1**

1m 2.5s **Going Correction** +0.025s/f (Good) **5 Ran SP% 109.6**
Speed ratings (Par 101): **101,99,97,97,93**
Tote Swingers 1&2 £3.00 CSF £5.03 TOTE £2.80: £1.10, £1.40; EX 5.40.
Owner Least Moved Partners **Bred** Least Moved Partners **Trained** Lichfield, Staffs
FOCUS
Not a bad little sprint handicap.

5935 PLASTIC MEDIA ENGINEERING H'CAP 1m 2f 46y
4:20 (4:20) (Class 6) (0-55,55) 4-Y-O+ £1,617 (£481; £240; £120) **Stalls** Low

Form RPR
0422 **1** **Iguacu**13 5506 8-8-6 52 (p) DanielMuscutt(7) 14 61
(Richard Price) *trckd ldr: led over 2f out: edgd rt wl over 1f out: pushed along and styd on strly ins fnl f* **4/1**1
4226 **2** *2 1/4* **Lisselan Pleasure (USA)**14 5481 5-9-1 54 (t) NeilCallan 12 59
(Bernard Llewellyn) *chsd ldrs: wnt 2nd ins fnl 2f: rdn and pushed rt wl over 1f out: kpt on but nt pce of wnr ins fnl f* **6/1**3
3041 **3** *1 1/4* **The Wonga Coup (IRE)**14 5481 5-8-5 49 JemmaMarshall(5) 10 51+
(Pat Phelan) *s.i.s: in rr: hdwy over 2f out: styd on to take 3rd fnl 120yds: no ch w ldng duo* **8/1**
0402 **4** *3/4* **Corrib (IRE)**20 5266 9-8-4 46 (p) RaulDaSilva(3) 8 47
(Bryn Palling) *chsd ldrs: rdn over 2f out: lost one pce 3rd fnl 120yds* **12/1**
0532 **5** *2 3/4* **Very Well Red**10 5638 9-8-8 47 ShaneKelly 13 42
(Peter Hiatt) *sn led: hdd over 2f out: wknd appr fnl f* **15/2**
3433 **6** *1 3/4* **Kyllachykov (IRE)**44 4390 4-8-8 47 RobertWinston 9 39
(Robin Bastiman) *chsd ldrs: rdn 3f out: wknd over 1f out* **5/1**2
0504 **7** *6* **Duneen Dream (USA)**22 5198 7-8-7 46 oh1 SaleemGolam 11 26
(Nikki Evans) *chsd ldrs: rdn 3f out: wknd fr 2f out* **16/1**
0304 **8** *1/2* **My Sister**20 5266 5-8-2 46 oh1 RachealKneller(5) 3 25
(Mark Usher) *in rr: mod hdwy fr over 1f out* **22/1**
0004 **9** *1/2* **Irons On Fire (USA)**18 5351 4-9-2 55 (p) JimmyFortune 4 33
(Lee Carter) *in rr: rdn and sme hdwy 3f out: nvr gng pce to get rch ldrs* **8/1**
0-50 **10** *1 1/2* **Lord Deevert**18 5349 7-8-2 48 JakePayne(7) 6 23
(Bill Turner) *in tch: rdn 3f out: wknd over 2f out* **40/1**
4006 **11** *4* **Regal Rave (USA)**28 4940 5-8-7 46 (b1) JohnFahy 2 13
(Peter Hedger) *t.k.h in rr: hdwy on outer to chse ldrs over 3f out: wknd u.p over 2f out* **12/1**
000/ **12** *8* **Bet Noir (IRE)**954 295 7-8-2 46 oh1 AmyScott(5) 16
(Tony Carroll) *t.k.h in rr: bhd most of way* **50/1**
200 **13** *23* **Devon Diva**28 4940 6-8-8 47 (p) AdamBeschizza 15
(David Bridgwater) *in tch: rdn and bhd fr 3f out: t.o* **40/1**
0043 **14** *17* **Petrarchan**9 5659 4-8-7 46 (bt) ChrisCatlin 5
(Milton Bradley) *chsd ldrs 6f: t.o* **25/1**

2m 11.36s (0.36) **Going Correction** +0.075s/f (Good) **14 Ran SP% 121.2**
Speed ratings (Par 101): **101,99,98,97,95 94,89,88,88,87 84,77,59,45**
Tote Swingers 1&2 £6.60, 2&3 £10.50, 1&3 £6.70 CSF £26.11 CT £188.52 TOTE £3.20: £2.20, £2.80, £3.30; EX 36.50.
Owner Derek & Cheryl Holder **Bred** Cheveley Park Stud Ltd **Trained** Ullingswick, H'fords
FOCUS
A moderate 46-55 handicap for which the winning time was 0.07 seconds slower than the earlier 61-75 fillies' handicap. Again it was a big advantage to race handily.

5936 JRL SPORTS PROMOTIONS H'CAP 1m 5f 22y
4:50 (4:50) (Class 6) (0-60,60) 4-Y-O+ £1,704 (£503; £251) **Stalls** High

Form RPR
0012 **1** **Highlife Dancer**4 5824 4-8-12 56 (v) CharlesBishop(5) 6 64
(Mick Channon) *chsd ldrs: drvn and hdwy whn edgd lft over 2f out: led wl over 1f out: readily* **2/1**1
0033 **2** *2* **Thundering Home**26 5038 5-8-11 55 DavidKenny(5) 7 60
(Richard Mitchell) *hld up in rr: hdwy on outer over 2f out: styd on u.p to chse wnr fnl 150yds: no imp* **10/1**
6032 **3** *3/4* **Tijori (IRE)**9 5653 4-9-3 56 (p) NeilCallan 9 60
(Bernard Llewellyn) *chsd ldrs: rdn and faltered whn hit over hd by rival's whip over 1f out: hung lft ins fnl f: one pce* **7/1**3
5224 **4** *nk* **Volcanic Jack (IRE)**9 5653 4-8-12 56 AmyScott(5) 1 59
(Tony Carroll) *led after 1f: hrd rdn and hdd wl over 1f out: wknd: one pce fnl f* **10/1**
U1 **5** *4* **Liberty Love (IRE)**71 3479 7-9-2 55 (b) MartinHarley 11 52
(Shaun Harley, Ire) *in rr: hdwy over 2f out: styd on same pce fnl f* **4/1**2
053 **6** *5* **Comedy House**25 5100 4-9-4 57 JamieGoldstein 2 47+
(Michael Madgwick) *in tch: hdwy on ins whn bdly hmpd over 2f out: nt rcvr* **7/1**3
0060 **7** *2 1/4* **Admirable Duque (IRE)**18 5359 6-9-0 60 (be) JoshBaudains(7) 8 47
(Dominic Ffrench Davis) *in rr: rdn and sme hdwy on outside wl over 2f out: nvr rchd ldrs* **25/1**
500P **8** *nk* **Moonshine Ruby**4 5817 6-8-0 46 oh1 NoelGarbutt(7) 4 32
(Peter Hiatt) *t.k.h in rr: swtchd rt to outer over 2f out: nvr rchd ldrs* **50/1**
0-60 **9** *2* **Prince Freddie**113 850 4-9-7 60 (p) ChrisCatlin 5 43
(Roy Brotherton) *plld hrd: chsd ldrs: wknd over 2f out* **33/1**
45/6 **10** *5* **Star Hill**21 5239 5-9-4 57 SebSanders 10 33
(Alan King) *led 1f: chsd ldr: rdn over 4f out: wknd 3f out* **10/1**

2m 53.13s (1.13) **Going Correction** +0.075s/f (Good) **10 Ran SP% 114.4**
Speed ratings (Par 101): **99,97,97,97,94 91,90,90,88,85**
Tote Swingers 1&2 £5.00, 2&3 £4.60, 1&3 £4.00 CSF £22.46 CT £117.61 TOTE £3.20: £1.20, £2.60, £2.40; EX 25.80.
Owner The Highlife Racing Club **Bred** Imperial & Mike Channon Bloodstock Ltd **Trained** West Ilsley, Berks

FOCUS
An ordinary staying handicap.
Tijori(IRE) Official explanation: jockey said gelding hung badly left
Star Hill Official explanation: jockey said mare lost its action

5937 SDS RACING EXCELLENCE APPRENTICE TRAINING SERIES H'CAP 5f 161y
5:20 (5:21) (Class 6) (0-55,52) 4-Y-0+ £1,617 (£481; £240; £120) **Stalls** Centre

Form				RPR
4360	1		**Cheery Cat (USA)**139 1487 8-8-9 **45**...(p) JackDuern 3 (Richard Ford) *chsd ldrs: wnt 2nd 1/2-way: sn rdn: styd on to ld fnl 40yds: drvn out* **9/1**	51
454	2	½	**Depden (IRE)**9 5659 4-8-6 **45**... PhilipPrince(3) 4 (Richard Price) *s.i.s: sn prom: rdn over 2f out: styd on wl fnl 120yds to take 2nd last strides: nt rch wnr* **16/1**	50
	3	shd	**Carmen Tango (IRE)**30 4894 5-8-9 **45**... GeorgeChaloner 13 (James Halpin, Ire) *s.i.s: sn in tch: chsd ldrs 1/2-way: styd on u.p fnl f to press for 2nd clsng stages but no imp on wnr* **5/1**1	49+
50	4	hd	**Brandywell Boy (IRE)**22 5191 9-8-11 **47**...(t) JoshBaudains 2 (Dominic Ffrench Davis) *led: drvn 2f out: kpt slt ld tl hdd and no ex fnl 40yds* **7/1**3	51
3006	5	hd	**Royal Box**9 5660 5-8-12 **51**...(p) DanielMuscutt(3) 1 (Tony Carroll) *chsd ldrs on inner: rdn and one pce over 1f out: rallied and ev ch ins fnl f: no ex fnl 40yds* **5/1**1	54
0-04	6	1 ½	**Loved To Bits**13 5504 4-8-9 **52**... JoeyHaynes(7) 6 (Eric Wheeler) *in rr: hdwy on outside over 1f out: kpt on ins fnl f: nt rch ldrs* **16/1**	50
4665	7	nk	**Ridgeway Sapphire**15 5444 5-8-10 **46**...(v) RachealKneller 5 (Mark Usher) *s.i.s: sn in tch: drvn and hdwy over 1f out: styd on same pce ins fnl f* **11/2**2	43
000	8	3 ½	**White Shift (IRE)**6 5775 6-8-4 **45**...(t) RyanTate(5) 12 (Paul Howling) *in rr: racd on outside and nvr gng pce to get into contention* **12/1**	30
0000	9	nse	**Little Perisher**8 5719 5-8-9 **45**...(p) LauraBarry 11 (Paul Howling) *outpcd most of way* **16/1**	30
0040	10	hd	**Forty Proof (IRE)**9 5660 4-8-12 **48**...(t) NoelGarbutt 7 (David Evans) *racd on outside: outpcd most of way* **10/1**	33
00-0	11	3 ¼	**Gwilym (GER)**22 5191 9-9-2 **52**...(p) DavidBergin 10 (Tony Newcombe) *chsd ldrs: rdn 2f out: wknd over 1f out* **8/1**	26
0000	12	2	**Sienna Blue**9 5659 4-8-13 **49**...(b1) JakePayne 9 (Simon Hodgson) *s.i.s: rdn 1/2-way: a outpcd* **50/1**	16

1m 12.41s (1.21) **Going Correction** +0.025s/f (Good) **12** Ran SP% **118.7**
Speed ratings (Par 101): **92,91,91,90,90 88,88,83,83,83 78,76**
Tote Swingers 1&2 £10.70, 2&3 £15.50, 1&3 £14.60 CSF £144.47 CT £816.27 TOTE £5.70: £1.80, £5.10, £3.80; EX 145.40.
Owner The Cataractonium Racing Syndicate **Bred** K L Ramsay & Sarah K Ramsay **Trained** Garstang, Lancs

FOCUS
A weak apprentice riders' sprint handicap.
T/Jkpt: Not won. T/Plt: £30.50 to a £1 stake. Pool: £69,836.00 - 1,670.70 winning tickets. T/Qpdt: £8.50 to a £1 stake. Pool: £4,680.66 - 403.15 winning tickets. ST

5763 KEMPTON (A.W) (R-H)
Wednesday, September 5

OFFICIAL GOING: Standard
Wind: Moderate, half against Weather: Sunny, warm

5938 WIN BIG WITH BETDAQ MULTIPLES CLASSIFIED STKS (DIV I) 1m 2f (P)
5:30 (5:32) (Class 6) 3-Y-0+ £1,617 (£481; £240; £120) **Stalls** Low

Form				RPR
6333	1		**Neige D'Antan**16 5408 3-8-11 54... LukeMorris 6 (Sir Mark Prescott Bt) *in tch in midfield: rdn and prog over 2f out: nt clr run briefly and swtchd rt over 1f out: led ins fnl f: urged along and kpt on* **7/4**1	60
402	2	¾	**Roman Senate (IRE)**22 5212 3-8-11 51...(tp) MartinLane 2 (Martin Bosley) *chsd ldrs: prog to go 2nd over 2f out: drvn to chal over 1f out: kpt on same pce* **16/1**	58
6054	3	shd	**Princess Willow**25 5100 4-9-1 52... SimonPearce(3) 9 (John E Long) *trckd ldr: led 3f out: drvn 2f out: hdd ins fnl f: kpt on* **12/1**	58
0600	4	4 ½	**Hard Road**51 4153 3-8-11 53... HarryBentley 7 (Chris Wall) *racd wd: hld up in rr: rdn 3f out: prog fr 2f out: styd on to take 4th ins fnl f: no ch* **5/2**2	49
3361	5	2	**Avon Supreme**22 5212 4-8-11 51... NatashaEaton(7) 5 (Gay Kelleway) *hld up wl in rr: gng bttr than many but stl there 3f out: prog over 2f out: chsd clr ldng trio over 1f out: no imp and lost 4th ins fnl f* **20/1**	45
/316	6	1 ¼	**Chapter Nine (IRE)**13 5508 6-9-4 55... LiamKeniry 8 (Seamus Mullins) *awkward s and stdd: hld up in last: stl there as r unfolded 3f out: prog 2f out: clsd on ldrs 1f out: rdn and fnd nil fnl f* **8/1**3	43
6005	7	5	**Red Yarn**18 5349 5-9-4 54...(b) MickaelBarzalona 4 (Daniel Kubler) *towards rr: rdn and no prog 3f out: nvr on terms after* **14/1**	33
4401	8	8	**Star Kingdom (IRE)**6 5762 3-8-11 52... TomEaves 11 (Brian Ellison) *t.k.h: prom tl wknd qckly over 2f out* **8/1**3	17
23-5	9	hd	**Raspberry Fizz**10 5629 3-8-11 51...(b) DaneO'Neill 10 (Eve Johnson Houghton) *chsd ldrs: rdn over 3f out: wknd 2f out* **33/1**	16
-004	10	19	**Fauran (IRE)**21 5244 3-8-11 45... KirstyMilczarek 3 (Clive Brittain) *racd freely: led to 3f out: wknd rapidly: t.o* **20/1**	
3066	11	7	**Hubood**24 5125 4-9-1 48... RyanPowell(3) 1 (Zoe Davison) *prom: rdn sn after 1/2-way: wknd rapidly 3f out: t.o* **66/1**	

2m 7.67s (-0.33) **Going Correction** -0.075s/f (Stan)
WFA 3 from 4yo+ 7lb **11** Ran SP% **121.4**
Speed ratings (Par 101): **98,97,97,93,92 91,87,80,80,65 59**
Tote Swingers 1&2 £9.60, 2&3 £23.50, 1&3 £6.10 CSF £32.52 TOTE £3.70: £1.50, £3.90, £4.60; EX 34.90 Trifecta £268.30 Pool: £823.24 - 2.27 winning tickets..
Owner Miss K Rausing **Bred** Miss K Rausing **Trained** Newmarket, Suffolk

FOCUS
A weak classified stakes run at a steady pace with the front three, who were well positioned throughout, pulling clear up the straight. The going was standard.
Hard Road Official explanation: jockey said gelding hung left
Fauran(IRE) Official explanation: jockey said filly ran too free

5939 WIN BIG WITH BETDAQ MULTIPLES CLASSIFIED STKS (DIV II) 1m 2f (P)
6:00 (6:00) (Class 6) 3-Y-0+ £1,617 (£481; £240; £120) **Stalls** Low

Form				RPR
6346	1		**Thecornishcowboy**26 5037 3-8-11 52...(t) BrettDoyle 6 (John Ryan) *trckd ldrs: wnt 3rd 4f out and 2nd over 2f out: drvn to ld over 1f out: styd on* **7/1**	61
0-01	2	2 ½	**Navajo Charm**10 5629 3-9-3 55... KirstyMilczarek 5 (Alan Jarvis) *led at gd pce: hanging sltly lft bnd over 3f out to 2f out: hdd and one pce over 1f out* **4/1**2	62
-003	3	1 ¾	**Phase Shift**10 5638 4-9-4 55... TomEaves 3 (Brian Ellison) *in tch in midfield: rdn over 3f out: prog over 2f out: styd on to take 3rd ins fnl f: unable to chal* **3/1**1	53
5055	4	2 ¾	**Onertother**10 5408 3-8-11 52... LiamKeniry 1 (Joseph Tuite) *in tch: prog over 3f out: wnt cl 3rd 2f out: fdd over 1f out* **11/2**	47
6040	5	1 ½	**Maccabees**23 5164 3-8-11 54...1 DaneO'Neill 7 (Roger Curtis) *t.k.h: chsd ldr after 2f to over 2f out: wknd* **6/1**	44
-203	6	hd	**Chez Vrony**21 5246 6-9-4 45... WilliamCarson 9 (Dave Morris) *hld up in last trio: prog on outer and drvn 3f out: nvr able to rch ldrs and effrt flattened out fnl f* **14/1**	44
2343	7	15	**Mayan Flight (IRE)**14 5481 4-9-4 53... DavidProbert 10 (Tony Carroll) *in tch: drvn over 3f out: wknd qckly over 2f out: t.o* **9/2**3	14
6330	8	2 ¾	**Lyrical Gangster (IRE)**20 2771 3-8-11 55... SamHitchcott 8 (Chris Gordon) *a in rr: rdn and struggling 4f out: t.o* **33/1**	
00-0	9	nse	**Miss Boops (IRE)**16 5405 4-9-1 49... SimonPearce(3) 2 (Zoe Davison) *s.s: hld up in last: lost tch 4f out: t.o* **100/1**	
0/00	10	36	**Super Smile (IRE)**23 5172 4-9-4 39...(t) LukeMorris 4 (Michael Appleby) *chsd ldr 2f: prom tl wknd rapidly 4f out: wl t.o* **66/1**	

2m 7.77s (-0.23) **Going Correction** -0.075s/f (Stan)
WFA 3 from 4yo+ 7lb **10** Ran SP% **117.4**
Speed ratings (Par 101): **97,95,93,91,90 90,78,75,75,47**
Tote Swingers 1&2 £3.40, 2&3 £2.50, 1&3 £7.80 CSF £35.27 TOTE £7.80: £2.90, £1.10, £1.30; EX 44.20 Trifecta £220.20 Pool: £723.13 - 2.43 winning tickets..
Owner C Letcher & J Ryan **Bred** Hadi Al Tajir **Trained** Newmarket, Suffolk

FOCUS
Division two of this classified stakes was run at a steady pace and once again it paid to race handy.
Mayan Flight(IRE) Official explanation: jockey said gelding ran flat
Miss Boops(IRE) Official explanation: jockey said filly jumped awkwardly from stalls
Super Smile(IRE) Official explanation: jockey said filly had no more to give

5940 BACK OR LAY AT BETDAQ.COM NURSERY 5f (P)
6:30 (6:31) (Class 5) (0-70,70) 2-Y-0 £2,264 (£673; £336; £168) **Stalls** Low

Form				RPR
3521	1		**Hardy Blue (IRE)**5 5807 2-8-10 **59** 6ex... FergusSweeney 4 (Jamie Osborne) *w ldr: led over 1f out: drvn and jst hld on* **6/1**	62
6402	2	hd	**We Are City**7 5749 2-8-6 **62**... IanBurns(7) 3 (Michael Bell) *chsd ldrs: 3rd whn swtchd lft off rail jst over 1f out: drvn and r.o to press wnr nr fin: jst hld* **5/1**3	64
0333	3	2 ½	**Blazing Knight (IRE)**28 4947 2-9-6 **69**...(b1) JimCrowley 8 (Ralph Beckett) *outpcd in last pair by 1/2-way: drvn over 1f out: r.o fnl f: tk 3rd last strides* **6/1**	62
400	4	½	**Confidential Creek**40 4545 2-8-13 **62**... TomEaves 2 (Ollie Pears) *mde most to over 1f out: fdd ins fnl f* **3/1**1	53
0533	5	shd	**Napinda**16 5424 2-8-6 **55**... DavidProbert 1 (Philip McBride) *towards rr: rdn over 2f out: sme prog over 1f out: nt pce to threaten* **7/1**	46
3344	6	1 ¼	**Windforpower (IRE)**4 5813 2-9-4 **67**...(b1) LukeMorris 7 (Ronald Harris) *chsd ldrs: hanging lft bnd over 3f out to 2f out and dropped to rr: kpt on again fnl f* **14/1**	53
3100	7	2 ¼	**Snow Angel (IRE)**29 4927 2-9-4 **70**... PatrickHills(3) 10 (J W Hills) *chsd ldrs: rdn over 2f out: wknd over 1f out* **20/1**	48
332	8	1 ½	**Dawn Catcher**13 5503 2-8-12 **66**... DarrenEgan(5) 6 (Tony Carroll) *tried to match strides w ldng pair but racd wdst of the trio: wknd fr 2f out* **4/1**2	39
100	9	¾	**Harleys Rocket**15 5450 2-9-2 **65**... GrahamLee 11 (Brendan Powell) *awkward s and slowest away: last whn wd bnd over 3f out: nvr able to be involved* **20/1**	35+

1m 0.56s (0.06) **Going Correction** -0.075s/f (Stan) **9** Ran SP% **118.9**
Speed ratings (Par 95): **96,95,91,90,90 88,85,82,81**
Tote Swingers 1&2 £4.30, 2&3 £6.60, 1&3 £7.00 CSF £37.21 CT £188.42 TOTE £6.20: £2.90, £2.40, £2.10; EX 12.30 Trifecta £21.40 Pool: £1,423.70 - 49.13 winning tickets..
Owner Patrick Gage & Tony Taylor **Bred** Philip O'Dwyer **Trained** Upper Lambourn, Berks

FOCUS
A competitive sprint nursery run at a fair pace, with runners finding it hard to come from off the pace. Weakish form, the runner-up helping with the level.

NOTEBOOK
Hardy Blue(IRE), who won at Wolverhampton five days previously, was always well positioned and stayed on well for pressure to overcome a 6lb penalty. She looks a progressive type, although she benefited by how the race unfolded and did not have much in hand at the line. (tchd 7-1)
We Are City, a drifter in the market, had failed to make all under an aggressive ride over 6f at Wolverhampton last time and was just unable to reel in the leader here over the minimum. It may be that a more patient ride, returned to 6f, could suit. (op 9-2)
Blazing Knight(IRE), wearing blinkers for the first time, having run well here on his handicap debut in a first-time visor, ran a promising race dropping back in trip. He was near the rear and driven 2f from home but made excellent progress late on, suggesting a return to 6f is needed. (op 7-1)
Confidential Creek, a handicap debutant who had not built on a promising debut in two subsequent runs, travelled comfortably in front but could not quicken up the straight. He is lightly raced and may be open to a shade more improvement. (op 7-2 tchd 11-4)
Napinda, having her first run for Charlie McBride, was another who made progress from the rear when the race was over and may well need a step back up in trip. (op 15-2)
Windforpower(IRE), wearing blinkers for the first time, enjoyed a luckless passage and was driven out wide turning for home, but showed a game attitude to close well up the straight. (tchd 12-1)
Snow Angel(IRE) Official explanation: jockey said filly never travelled
Dawn Catcher Official explanation: jockey said filly hung left

5941 BETDAQ MOBILE APPS CLASSIFIED CLAIMING STKS 1m (P)
7:00 (7:00) (Class 6) 3-Y-0+ £1,617 (£481; £240; £120) **Stalls** Low

Form				RPR
6055	1		**Pravda Street**21 5227 7-8-8 70... SilvestreDeSousa 1 (Brian Ellison) *trckd ldr 1f: styd cl up: rdn to ld over 2f out: edgd lft after: drvn and kpt on wl* **10/3**1	62

5000 **2** 1 ¼ **Rufus Stone (USA)**[23] 5175 4-8-7 50 ow1 (p) BrettDoyle 14 58
(Jane Chapple-Hyam) *rousted along and prog to press ldr after 1f: t.k.h sn after: chalng whn wnr wnt by over 2f out: chsd after: no imp ins fnl f* **33/1**

2010 **3** hd **Officer In Command (USA)**[31] 4844 6-9-2 69 (b) JamesDoyle 6 67
(Paul Rich) *nt that wl away: hld up in last quartet: prog on inner over 2f out: drvn and styd on fnl f: nrly tk 2nd* **9/2**[2]

005 **4** ½ **Handheld**[47] 4315 5-9-2 69 LiamKeniry 4 65
(Ed de Giles) *t.k.h: hld up in 8th: prog 2f out: drvn and kpt on fnl f: nvr able to chal* **6/1**[3]

5306 **5** 1 ¼ **Spinning Ridge (IRE)**[9] 5657 7-8-12 69 (b) LukeMorris 3 59
(Ronald Harris) *wl in tch in midfield: prog over 2f out: chsd ldng pair over 1f out: fdd ins fnl f* **13/2**

3000 **6** 1 ¾ **Koo And The Gang (IRE)**[12] 5547 5-8-10 67 TomEaves 7 52
(Brian Ellison) *led to over 2f out: sn lost pl: one pce over 1f out* **8/1**

4000 **7** hd **Zaheeb**[10] 5632 4-9-2 65 (b) WilliamCarson 12 58
(Dave Morris) *chsd ldrs: drvn over 2f out: nt qckn over 1f out: fdd fnl f* **20/1**

0465 **8** 2 ¼ **Saucy Buck (IRE)**[10] 5628 4-8-7 58 DarrenEgan(5) 8 49
(Jamie Poulton) *a in rr: drvn over 2f out: no real prog* **14/1**

6040 **9** 1 ¼ **Tartan Gunna**[9] 5672 6-8-12 60 (p) GrahamLee 5 46
(James Given) *s.i.s: a wl in rr: pushed along sn after 1/2-way: no great prog* **11/1**

0600 **10** 2 **D'Urberville**[26] 5052 5-9-0 62 RichardHughes 10 43
(J R Jenkins) *mounted on crse and keen to post: racd wd: prog to chse ldng pair over 4f out: lost pl over 2f out: eased over 1f out* **12/1**

6044 **11** 2 ½ **Zip Lock (IRE)**[99] 2581 6-8-13 68 RyanClark(3) 9 40
(Tom Keddy) *v awkward s and lost many l: hld up in last: pushed along and no prog over 2f out* **25/1**

6100 **12** 7 **Moment In The Sun**[16] 5406 3-8-5 63 (v[1]) MickaelBarzalona 13 18
(David Flood) *in tch on outer: wknd wl over 2f out* **20/1**

1m 38.65s (-1.15) **Going Correction** -0.075s/f (Stan)
WFA 3 from 4yo+ 5lb **12** Ran SP% **119.0**
Speed ratings (Par 101): **102,100,100,100,98 97,96,94,93,91 88,81**
Tote Swingers 1&2 £34.80, 2&3 £107.50, 1&3 £3.50 CSF £131.20 TOTE £3.60: £1.10, £16.90, £2.60; EX 164.80 Trifecta £232.50 Pool: £395.89 - 1.26 winning tickets..Pravda Street & Koo And The Gang were subject to friendly claims.
Owner Ms Z Hatcher **Bred** R A Instone **Trained** Norton, N Yorks

FOCUS
A wide-open claimer run at a moderate pace, with the front two home again racing handily throughout.

5942 BETDAQ CASINO GAMES H'CAP 1m (P)
7:30 (7:30) (Class 5) (0-75,75) 3-Y-O **£2,264** (£673; £336; £168) **Stalls** Low

Form RPR

3332 **1** **Engrossing**[16] 5421 3-9-5 73 RichardHughes 8 82
(Richard Hannon) *hld up in midfield gng wl: prog over 2f out: pushed along to cl over 1f out: rdn to ld jst ins fnl f: sn clr* **5/1**[3]

6513 **2** 3 ¼ **Alkadi (IRE)**[18] 5338 3-9-4 72 JoeFanning 3 74
(Mark Johnston) *sn trckd ldng pair: rdn to ld over 1f out: hdd and outpcd jst ins fnl f* **9/2**[2]

4-56 **3** nse **Rock Song**[13] 5512 3-8-11 65 JimCrowley 10 66
(Amanda Perrett) *hld up in rr: rdn on outer over 2f out: prog over 1f out: styd on to take 3rd last 100yds: nrly snatched 2nd* **20/1**

4140 **4** 1 ¾ **Grey Seal (IRE)**[27] 4996 3-9-4 72 TomQueally 12 69
(James Fanshawe) *hld up towards rr: pushed along over 2f out: rdn and styd on fr over 1f out: nvr able to chal* **15/2**

2-00 **5** hd **Opera Buff**[47] 4288 3-9-4 72 LiamKeniry 5 69
(Sylvester Kirk) *hld up in last pair: plenty to do over 2f out: shkn up over 1f out: styd on steadily after: nvr nr ldrs* **25/1**

0601 **6** ¾ **Dubai Sunshine (IRE)**[8] 5721 3-9-0 75 IanBurns(7) 9 70
(Michael Bell) *sn pressed ldr: stl chalng over 2f out but u.p: lost pl and btn wl over 1f out* **9/2**[2]

1132 **7** ½ **Kung Hei Fat Choy (USA)**[8] 5721 3-9-4 72 (b) GrahamLee 2 66
(James Given) *led at gd pce but sn jnd: hdd & wknd over 1f out* **3/1**[1]

6604 **8** 1 ¾ **Falcon's Reign (FR)**[15] 5451 3-9-1 69 LukeMorris 4 59
(Michael Appleby) *chsd ldng trio: drvn and struggling over 2f out: steadily wknd* **33/1**

53-4 **9** 2 ¼ **Confirmed**[29] 4901 3-9-4 72 AdamKirby 7 57
(Clive Cox) *chsd ldrs and racd wd: lost pl wl over 2f out: sn btn* **12/1**

4410 **10** 10 **Cape Joy (IRE)**[18] 5351 3-9-1 69 PatDobbs 6 31
(Richard Hannon) *t.k.h early: prom to 1/2-way: wknd wl over 2f out: t.o* **20/1**

1-00 **11** ½ **Red Bay**[24] 5120 3-9-5 73 BrettDoyle 11 34
(Jane Chapple-Hyam) *a in rr: struggling 3f out: t.o* **20/1**

1m 38.63s (-1.17) **Going Correction** -0.075s/f (Stan) **11** Ran SP% **118.6**
Speed ratings (Par 101): **102,98,98,96,96 96,95,93,91,81 81**
Tote Swingers 1&2 £3.60, 2&3 £16.40, 1&3 £21.80 CSF £25.56 CT £426.70 TOTE £8.50: £2.40, £2.10, £5.60; EX 26.00 Trifecta £354.00 Part won. Pool: 478.37 - 0.10 winning tickets..
Owner Ben CM Wong **Bred** D R Tucker **Trained** East Everleigh, Wilts

FOCUS
A fair handicap run at a sound pace with the winner pulling clear inside the final furlong.

5943 SPORTINGLIFE.COM E B F MAIDEN FILLIES' STKS 6f (P)
8:00 (8:01) (Class 5) 2-Y-O **£3,169** (£943; £471; £235) **Stalls** Low

Form RPR

1 **Spokeswoman (IRE)** 2-9-0 0 SilvestreDeSousa 5 88+
(Saeed Bin Suroor) *t.k.h: trckd ldrs: sltly impeded 2f out and swtchd lft: rdn and prog over 1f out: swept into ld ins fnl f: sn clr* **11/4**[2]

20 **2** 2 ¾ **Jubilee Diamond (IRE)**[77] 3269 2-9-0 0 RichardHughes 2 79
(Richard Hannon) *trckd ldr 1f: styd cl up: pushed into ld over 1f out: hdd and outpcd ins fnl f* **1/1**[1]

3 1 **Broughtons Charm (IRE)** 2-9-0 0 StevieDonohoe 12 75
(Willie Musson) *settled in 8th: pushed along and prog jst over 2f out: styd on to take 3rd last 100yds* **33/1**

6 **4** 2 **Speed Date**[15] 5449 2-9-0 0 JimCrowley 1 69
(Ralph Beckett) *trckd ldrs: prog on inner over 2f out: wnt 2nd and tried to chal over 1f out: wknd ins fnl f* **16/1**

5 nk **Carina Palace** 2-9-0 0 FergusSweeney 3 68
(Jamie Osborne) *wl in rr: prog on inner wl over 1f out: pushed along and styd on same pce fnl f* **33/1**

6 ¾ **Ishisoba** 2-9-0 0 GrahamLee 11 66
(Alastair Lidderdale) *pushed along in last trio after 2f: rdn and styd on fr over 1f out: nrst fin* **50/1**

0 **7** ½ **Sunny Hollow**[35] 4704 2-9-0 0 KirstyMilczarek 8 64
(James Toller) *racd wd: in tch: outpcd fr 2f out: edgd lft but kpt on same pce* **50/1**

60 **8** shd **Amirah (IRE)**[28] 4960 2-9-0 0 DavidProbert 10 64
(Tony Carroll) *chsd ldrs on outer: outpcd fr 2f out: steadily fdd* **33/1**

9 hd **Eminently** 2-9-0 0 PatDobbs 9 63+
(Richard Hannon) *dwlt: hld up in last: stl there 2f out: prog over 1f out: pushed along and kpt on: nt disgracd* **14/1**

10 2 **Koala Bear** 2-9-0 0 TomQueally 7 57
(James Fanshawe) *dwlt: mostly in last pair: shkn up and no real prog 2f out* **8/1**[3]

6 **11** nk **Wildcrafting**[16] 5425 2-9-0 0 JamieSpencer 6 57
(Michael Bell) *led to over 1f out: wknd* **16/1**

04 **12** 1 ½ **Royal Guinevere**[32] 4816 2-9-0 0 BrettDoyle 4 52
(Dean Ivory) *chsd ldr after 1f to 2f out: wknd* **20/1**

1m 12.5s (-0.60) **Going Correction** -0.075s/f (Stan) **12** Ran SP% **123.7**
Speed ratings (Par 92): **101,97,96,93,92 91,91,91,90,88 87,85**
Tote Swingers 1&2 £1.20, 2&3 £16.00, 1&3 £25.60 CSF £5.71 TOTE £2.20: £1.10, £1.10, £16.70; EX 5.60 Trifecta £203.00 Pool: £842.41 - 3.07 winning tickets..
Owner Godolphin **Bred** Darley **Trained** Newmarket, Suffolk

FOCUS
An interesting if uncompetitive looking fillies maiden, run at a decent pace with a most taking performance from the winner. She looks worth a crack at a better grade. The second is rated to the bare form.

NOTEBOOK
Spokeswoman(IRE), a half-sister to several winners including Group 2 winner Miss Lucifer, seemed to be racing a touch keenly in behind the pace and was briefly short of room at the 2f pole before being switched out wide. It took a while for her to pick up but, when given a couple of slaps at the furlong pole, she picked up in the style of an above average filly. (tchd 5-2 and 3-1)
Jubilee Diamond(IRE), who was last seen in the Group 2 Queen Mary Stakes, enjoyed the run of the race and looked the likely winner before being worn down late on. It was slightly disappointing that she was so well beaten but she looks more than capable of landing her maiden. (op 5-4)
Broughtons Charm(IRE), a 52,000gns 2yo who is a half-sister to four winners, including Listed placed March On Beetroot, made a promising debut for a yard not noted for their 2yos. Drawn widest of all she did not enjoy the best of passages but, travelled well into the straight and kept on well to the line. A maiden should be well within her capabilities.
Speed Date raced green on her debut at Warwick and did not have the pace to take advantage of her inside draw here but, stepped up on her debut effort and looks a handicap type. (op 12-1)
Ishisoba, a £10,000 2yo who is a half-sister to three winners, made a little late progress for a stable who is 0-39 with juveniles in recent seasons and this should give connections hope for the future. (op 66-1)
Eminently, a half-sister to numerous winners, most notably the top-class sprinter Reverence, was left with plenty to do but made some decent late progress and should come on for this.
Wildcrafting helped set the strong early pace but, ultimately looked to pay for doing too much through the first half of the race.

5944 MCARTHURGLEN DESIGNER OUTLETS H'CAP 1m 4f (P)
8:30 (8:31) (Class 4) (0-85,85) 3-Y-O+ **£4,075** (£1,212; £606; £303) **Stalls** Centre

Form RPR

0154 **1** **Refractor (IRE)**[24] 5129 4-9-6 79 MartinLane 11 89+
(James Fanshawe) *hld up in 8th: gd prog on outer over 2f out to chse ldr over 1f out: drvn ahd last 150yds: r.o wl* **12/1**

3013 **2** 1 ½ **Kuda Huraa (IRE)**[20] 5268 4-9-12 85 JamieSpencer 10 93
(Roger Varian) *led after 1f: kicked on over 2f out: styd on wl but hdd and outpcd last 150yds* **10/1**

00-1 **3** 3 **Kiwayu**[42] 4466 3-8-13 81 (t) KierenFallon 9 84+
(Luca Cumani) *hld up in 7th: shkn up and effrt whn hmpd and snatched up 2f out: renewed effrt and r.o to take 3rd ins fnl f: no ch to threaten* **7/4**[1]

3613 **4** 1 **Maastricht (IRE)**[12] 5554 3-9-3 85 JoeFanning 2 87
(Mark Johnston) *led 1f: chsd ldr: rdn and nt qckn 2f out: lost 2nd over 1f out: one pce* **9/2**[3]

1644 **5** ¾ **Art Scholar (IRE)**[18] 5344 5-9-11 84 TomQueally 3 84
(Michael Appleby) *trckd ldrs in 5th: rdn over 2f out: nt qckn wl over 1f out: one pce after* **14/1**

0052 **6** nk **Twice Bitten**[23] 5158 4-9-7 80 GeorgeBaker 8 80
(James Toller) *hld up in last: pushed along over 2f out: sn outpcd: stl last 1f out: r.o last 150yds: no ch* **16/1**

133 **7** 1 ¼ **The Holyman (IRE)**[42] 4475 4-9-5 78 DaneO'Neill 5 76
(Jo Crowley) *trckd ldng trio: rdn and edgd rt 2f out: sn outpcd and btn* **14/1**

1-00 **8** shd **Yasir (USA)**[104] 2419 4-9-12 85 (t) TadhgO'Shea 7 83
(Saeed Bin Suroor) *t.k.h hld up in 9th: shkn up and effrt over 2f out: no prog over 1f out* **4/1**[2]

40-6 **9** 1 ½ **Taaresh (IRE)**[168] 817 7-9-1 79 DarrenEgan(5) 6 74
(Kevin Morgan) *hld up in 6th: rdn over 2f out: nt qckn wl over 1f out: wknd* **40/1**

41-2 **10** 1 ¼ **Albert Bridge**[122] 1890 4-9-9 82 JimCrowley 4 75
(Ralph Beckett) *trckd ldng pair: rdn over 2f out: sn lost pl and wknd* **10/1**

2m 32.53s (-1.97) **Going Correction** -0.075s/f (Stan)
WFA 3 from 4yo+ 9lb **10** Ran SP% **122.1**
Speed ratings (Par 105): **103,102,100,99,98 98,97,97,96,95**
Tote Swingers 1&2 £38.90, 2&3 £5.30, 1&3 £10.00 CSF £131.51 CT £317.46 TOTE £18.30: £3.30, £3.40, £1.10; EX 69.20 TRIFECTA Not won..
Owner Mr & Mrs W J Williams **Bred** B Dolan **Trained** Newmarket, Suffolk
■ Stewards' Enquiry : Dane O'Neill one-day ban: careless riding (Sep 19)

FOCUS
A decent handicap run at a steady pace, with a number of runners hampered inside the final furlong and the winner, coming widest of all, missing the interference.

5945 READ NICK LUCK IN RACING PLUS H'CAP 1m 3f (P)
9:00 (9:01) (Class 6) (0-65,64) 3-Y-O **£1,617** (£481; £240; £120) **Stalls** Low

Form RPR

5000 **1** **Bramshill Lass**[14] 5483 3-9-4 61 (b[1]) JimCrowley 7 68
(Amanda Perrett) *trckd ldr: chal over 2f out: led over 1f out: hrd rdn and asserted ins fnl f* **20/1**

000- **2** 1 **Welsh Bard (IRE)**[284] 7559 3-9-4 61 LukeMorris 4 66
(Sir Mark Prescott Bt) *rn in snatches: trckd ldrs: wnt 3rd 3f out: drvn over 2f out: styd on to take 2nd last 75yds* **9/2**[2]

044 **3** shd **Stag Hill (IRE)**[22] 5212 3-8-7 50 LiamKeniry 9 55
(Sylvester Kirk) *hld up in last trio: gd prog over 2f out: rdn over 1f out: clsd grad fnl f: nrly tk 2nd* **25/1**

063 **4** 1 **Daring Damsel (IRE)**[10] 5629 3-9-6 63 (p) SilvestreDeSousa 3 66
(Paul Cole) *led: rdn over 3f out: hrd pressed over 2f out: hdd over 1f out: no ex and lost 2 pls last 75yds* **10/1**

5220 **5** 3 ¼ **Operation Tracer**[5] 5796 3-9-5 62 JamieSpencer 11 59+
(Michael Bell) *stdd s: hld up in last: prog jst over 2f out: hrd rdn to take 5th fnl f but nvr any hope of threatening ldrs* **3/1**[1]

0600 **6** *nk* **The Ploughman**[5] 5789 3-8-7 **50** oh5 KieranO'Neill 6 47
(John Bridger) *in tch in midfield: rdn 4f out: sn struggling in rr: kpt on again fr over 1f out* **66/1**

342U **7** *nk* **Viola Da Gamba (IRE)**[41] 4504 3-9-2 **64** DavidKenny(5) 8 60
(William Knight) *rrd s: hld up in rr: hrd rdn 2f out: plugged on fr over 1f out: nvr on terms* **12/1**

0300 **8** *¾* **Cape Alex**[7] 5744 3-9-1 **58** (p) KierenFallon 13 53
(Clive Brittain) *hld up and racd wd: effrt over 2f out: limited prog and btn over 1f out* **7/1**

000 **9** *¾* **Al Qatari (USA)**[19] 5329 3-8-10 **53** (b) AdamBeschizza 10 47
(William Haggas) *racd wd: in tch: prog 5f out: rdn over 3f out: wknd 2f out* **8/1**

6605 **10** *1* **The New Black (IRE)**[15] 5443 3-9-5 **62** (v) SebSanders 5 54
(Gay Kelleway) *towards rr: rdn 4f out: struggling and btn over 2f out* **9/1**

6433 **11** *1¼* **Twin Shadow (IRE)**[14] 6479 3-9-2 **60** NeilCallan 2 49
(James Fanshawe) *wl in tch: effrt and looked a threat 2f out: sn wknd qckly* **11/2**[3]

6050 **12** *4½* **Siouxies Dream**[5] 5810 3-8-4 **52** (p) DarrenEgan(5) 1 33
(Michael Appleby) *chsd ldng pair tl wknd 3f out* **33/1**

2m 21.07s (-0.83) **Going Correction** -0.075s/f (Stan) 12 Ran SP% **122.0**
Speed ratings (Par 99): **100,99,99,98,96 95,95,95,94,93 92,89**
Tote Swingers 1&2 £21.40, 2&3 £8.30, 1&3 £39.80 CSF £107.99 CT £2317.24 TOTE £41.80: £9.50, £1.90, £8.60; EX 212.40 TRIFECTA Not won..
Owner Mrs Karen Hancock **Bred** Bloomsbury Stud **Trained** Pulborough, W Sussex

FOCUS
A moderate concluding handicap run at a fair pace with the prominent runners once again seeming to have an advantage.
Operation Tracer Official explanation: jockey said gelding ran flat
Viola Da Gamba(IRE) Official explanation: jockey said filly fly leapt out of stalls
T/Plt: £25.70 to a £1 stake. Pool: £63,131.54 - 1,790.69 winning tickets. T/Qpdt: £10.70 to a £1 stake. Pool: £7,213.50 - 498.22 winning tickets. JN

5770 LINGFIELD (L-H)
Wednesday, September 5

OFFICIAL GOING: Good to firm (firm in places on round course)
Wind: Fresh, against Weather: Sunny and warm

5946 IN MEMORY OF RAPPORTEUR NURSERY 7f
2:00 (2:01) (Class 5) (0-75,75) 2-Y-O **£2,385** (£704; £352) **Stalls High**

Form RPR

303 **1** **Hoarding (USA)**[19] 5325 2-9-7 **75** WilliamBuick 11 81+
(John Gosden) *trckd ldrs: nt clr run over 1f out and rdr waited for gap: qcknd to ld fnl 50yds* **11/4**[1]

255 **2** *1* **French Press (IRE)**[19] 5319 2-9-4 **72** RichardMullen 3 72
(David Brown) *pressed ldr: drvn level ins fnl f: nt qckn fnl 50yds* **6/1**[3]

0113 **3** *nk* **Danz Choice (IRE)**[15] 5450 2-9-4 **72** RichardHughes 7 72
(Richard Hannon) *towards rr: rdn 3f out: hdwy and nt clr run over 1f out: swtchd lft into centre and r.o fnl f: hld nr fin* **10/1**

4352 **4** *½* **Pira Palace (IRE)**[21] 5236 2-9-2 **70** PatDobbs 4 68
(Sir Michael Stoute) *led on stands' rail: rdn over 2f out: hdd and nt qckn fnl 50yds* **14/1**

5005 **5** *½* **Kunzea (IRE)**[23] 5161 2-7-10 **53** oh3 ow1 RyanPowell(3) 9 50
(Mick Channon) *bhd: nt clr run on stands' rail 2f out: styd on wl fr over 1f out* **66/1**

4034 **6** *½* **Frege (USA)**[20] 5267 2-9-5 **73** KierenFallon 6 68
(Brian Meehan) *chsd ldrs towards centre: effrt over 2f out: one pce ins fnl f* **12/1**

4243 **7** *2* **Club House (IRE)**[21] 5242 2-9-7 **75** StevieDonohoe 10 65
(Robert Mills) *mid-div: rdn 3f out: no imp fnl 2f* **12/1**

621 **8** *1* **Labienus**[23] 5162 2-9-7 **75** DaneO'Neill 8 65
(David Lanigan) *t.k.h: chsd ldrs tl no ex ins fnl f: 6th and btn whn squeezed for room and eased 100yds out* **7/2**[2]

6560 **9** *4* **Kryena's Rose**[6] 5763 2-8-2 **56** FrannyNorton 5 32
(Mick Channon) *towards rr: mod effrt 3f out: sn btn* **50/1**

630 **10** *1* **Classic Art**[64] 3733 2-9-3 **71** AmirQuinn 12 45
(Roger Teal) *dwlt: outpcd: sn wl bhd* **25/1**

515 **11** *1¼* **Beau Select (IRE)**[22] 5202 2-8-13 **67** (p) AndreaAtzeni 2 37+
(Robert Eddery) *prom over 3f: sn lost pl* **16/1**

243 **12** *15* **Bornean (IRE)**[26] 5032 2-9-7 **75** MickaelBarzalona 1 32+
(Mahmood Al Zarooni) *racd wd of others towards centre: s.i.s: nvr gng wl: modest effrt 3f out: wknd 2f out: eased whn btn over 1f out* **17/2**

1m 23.84s (0.54) **Going Correction** -0.075s/f (Good) 12 Ran SP% **118.0**
Speed ratings (Par 95): **93,91,91,90,90 89,87,86,81,80 79,62**
Tote Swingers 1&2 £6.10, 2&3 £12.20, 1&3 £4.70 CSF £18.94 CT £147.91 TOTE £4.10: £1.70, £2.40, £3.00; EX 27.00 TRIFECTA Not won..
Owner H R H Princess Haya Of Jordan **Bred** Sc A R Di Paolo Agostini & Darley **Trained** Newmarket, Suffolk

FOCUS
A competitive nursery, run at a fair enough gallop, and there was always likely to be some trouble in running with the favoured stands' rail in hot demand. The winner impressed and the form makes plenty of sense.

NOTEBOOK
Hoarding(USA), making his handicap debut, spent much of the second half of the race stuck with nowhere to go, having tracked the early pace against the rail, and would have been a most unlucky loser, but Buick was able to find a way through and he ultimately won with something to spare. The form of his second run at Goodwood has worked out particularly well and he looks capable of defying a rise in a stronger race. (op 4-1)
French Press(IRE), another having his first run in a nursery, was out fast and obtained a decent position from his low draw, racing just one off the rail. He was third best on the day, with Danz Choice looking unlucky, and can win something similar. (tchd 11-2 and 13-2)
Danz Choice(IRE) received a troubled run and had to switch widest of all when trying to challenge, a manoeuvre that cost him second. He can remain competitive from this sort of mark. (op 7-1)
Pira Palace(IRE) did really well to get the rail from stall four and may even have bettered her Salisbury second despite finishing fourth, this being a stronger race. She is limited, though. (op 16-1)
Kunzea(IRE) was finishing fast, having been denied a run, and showed improved form despite being 4lb wrong. She'll want at least 1m and ought to find easier opportunities.
Frege(USA) briefly looked set to play a part, but she'd been forced to challenge wide and ultimately didn't get home. Official explanation: jockey said filly lost a shoe and hung right (op 14-1 tchd 9-1)
Labienus, due to go up 3lb, held obvious claims on this nursery debut, following his Polytrack win here over the same trip, but he was bumped leaving the stalls and ended up racing keenly three off the rail, already being held when squeezed up late. It's possible he wasn't as effective on the turf, but will be off his revised mark next time. (op 11-4)
Bornean(IRE) was stuck very wide from stall one, never giving him a chance. He was eased off late. Official explanation: jockey said colt lost its action (op 11-1)

5947 BRITISH STALLION STUDS SUPPORTING BRITISH RACING E B F MAIDEN FILLIES' STKS 7f
2:30 (2:30) (Class 5) 2-Y-O **£3,234** (£962; £481; £240) **Stalls High**

Form RPR

02 **1** **Ghanaian (FR)**[18] 5339 2-9-0 MickaelBarzalona 6 77
(Mahmood Al Zarooni) *prom: led over 1f out: hld on gamely* **11/4**[1]

63 **2** *nk* **Trucanini**[32] 4818 2-9-0 HarryBentley 11 76
(Chris Wall) *disp ld tl over 1f out: kpt on wl u.p* **7/2**[2]

0 **3** *nk* **Stresa**[25] 5104 2-9-0 WilliamBuick 8 75+
(John Gosden) *hld up in rr: swtchd lft into centre 3f out: hdwy to chse ldrs 1f out: hung lft: r.o* **16/1**

4 *1* **Omoor (IRE)** 2-9-0 DaneO'Neill 3 72+
(John Dunlop) *mid-div: hdwy 2f out: hrd rdn over 1f out: styd on same pce* **8/1**

3 **5** *¾* **Alnawiyah**[25] 5104 2-9-0 PaulHanagan 2 71+
(John Dunlop) *mid-div: rdn over 2f out: styd on fnl f* **6/1**

5 **6** *1* **Thiqa (IRE)**[28] 4946 2-9-0 SilvestreDeSousa 4 69
(Saeed Bin Suroor) *prom tl hrd rdn and outpcd fnl 2f* **4/1**[3]

7 *1¼* **Just Darcy** 2-9-0 RichardMullen 10 64+
(Sir Michael Stoute) *dwlt: outpcd and bhd: rdn 1/2-way: nrst fin* **12/1**

5 **8** *1¼* **Red Catkin**[21] 5230 2-9-0 TomQueally 12 61+
(George Margarson) *towards rr: shkn up and plenty to do 3f out: styng on at fin* **100/1**

40 **9** *1½* **Poetic Belle**[40] 4525 2-8-7 MichaelJMMurphy(7) 14 57
(Alan Jarvis) *disp ld on stands' rail tl wknd qckly over 1f out* **40/1**

06 **10** *shd* **Sand Grouse**[19] 5300 2-9-0 (b) AndreaAtzeni 7 57
(Marco Botti) *chsd ldrs: drvn along 3f out: wknd 2f out* **66/1**

0 **11** *3¾* **Jazz On The Beach**[20] 5267 2-9-0 KierenFallon 9 47
(Luca Cumani) *in tch tl wknd 2f out* **20/1**

12 *17* **Rosa Burn** 2-9-0 IanMongan 1 1
(John Dunlop) *sn outpcd: t.o fnl 4f* **100/1**

1m 23.95s (0.65) **Going Correction** -0.075s/f (Good) 12 Ran SP% **118.5**
Speed ratings (Par 92): **93,92,92,91,90 89,87,86,84,84 80,60**
Tote Swingers 1&2 £1.30, 2&3 £12.10, 1&3 £14.40 CSF £11.90 TOTE £4.70: £1.10, £1.90, £5.80; EX 13.90 Trifecta £215.10 Pool: £753.02 - 2.59 winning tickets..
Owner Godolphin **Bred** M Daguzan-Garros & Rolling Hills Farm **Trained** Newmarket, Suffolk

FOCUS
Quite a decent fillies' maiden by the turf track standards here, with several of the major yards represented. Not a pericularly easy race to assess, but the front two have been rated close to form.

NOTEBOOK
Ghanaian(FR), down 1f in trip, was soon on the pace and, despite racing a bit off the rail, was good enough to hold the rallying runner-up. She'll have no trouble with the return to 1m and should have more to offer in nurseries. (tchd 9-4)
Trucanini travelled well one off the rail, ultimately ending up against it, but was never getting past the winner. She's crying out for 1m and should have no trouble winning. (op 4-1)
Stresa's performance needs upgrading, having made good late headway widest of all. This was a big step up on her initial effort, reversing form with Alnawiyah, and she can find a maiden, possibly over 1m. (op 20-1)
Omoor(IRE), a 130,000gns yearling bred to need further, was nibbled at in the market earlier in the day and fared better than the owner's supposed first-string Alnawiyah. She can probably win a 1m maiden. (op 6-1)
Alnawiyah really caught the eye at Newmarket on debut, but was weak in the market, with stall two a major negative, and never posed a serious threat having raced in midfield. She's probably worth another chance, but may be best left until handicaps now. (op 5-1)
Thiqa(IRE) was unable to build on her debut fifth, racing well away from the stands' rail. (tchd 9-2)
Just Darcy, whose dam was a 1m4f-1m6f winner, made some late headway having been outpaced and should benefit from 1m. (op 20-1)
Red Catkin again hinted at ability and will be one to watch for in modest nurseries.
Poetic Belle will be one to watch for in modest nurseries (op 50-1)
Jazz On The Beach again offered little, but her dam's related to Izzi Top, and it would be no surprise to see her do better switched to middle-distance handicaps next season.

5948 CYPRIUM BAR @ LINGFIELD MARRIOTT MAIDEN STKS 6f
3:00 (3:02) (Class 5) 2-Y-O **£2,385** (£704; £352) **Stalls High**

Form RPR

02 **1** **African Oil (FR)**[16] 5418 2-9-3 MichaelHills 8 81
(Charles Hills) *mde all on stands' rail: hld on gamely fnl f* **9/4**[1]

03 **2** *hd* **Caramack**[26] 5040 2-9-3 RichardHughes 7 80
(Richard Hannon) *stdd s: t.k.h: sn chsng ldrs: drvn to chal ins fnl f: r.o* **11/2**[3]

033 **3** *3¼* **Digress**[21] 5235 2-9-3 **78** RichardMullen 4 71
(Sir Michael Stoute) *trckd wnr: hrd rdn over 1f out: one pce fnl f* **3/1**[2]

2 **4** *3* **Speedfit Boy (IRE)**[22] 5213 2-9-3 TomQueally 5 62
(George Margarson) *mid-div: effrt and hrd rdn over 2f out: no imp over 1f out* **9/1**

0 **5** *3* **Royal Betty**[27] 5003 2-8-12 KierenFox 10 48+
(Lee Carter) *mid-div: rdn over 2f out: nvr able to chal* **80/1**

00 **6** *½* **Delphica (IRE)**[35] 4701 2-8-12 FergusSweeney 9 46
(Gary Moore) *t.k.h: chsd ldrs: rdn over 2f out: wknd wl over 1f out* **50/1**

0 **7** *1¾* **Derwentwater (IRE)**[29] 4917 2-9-3 WilliamBuick 3 46+
(John Gosden) *sn wl bhd: shkn up 2f out: nvr nr ldrs* **20/1**

0 **8** *½* **Mujadora (IRE)**[18] 5367 2-8-12 PaulHanagan 11 39
(William Haggas) *prom over 3f* **25/1**

0 **9** *1* **Positive Parenting (IRE)**[16] 5407 2-8-12 WilliamCarson 12 36
(Stuart Williams) *sn rdn along: a bhd* **66/1**

10 *2¾* **Gold Nugget (IRE)** 2-9-3 PatDobbs 1 33
(Richard Hannon) *outpcd: sn bhd* **40/1**

1m 11.34s (0.14) **Going Correction** -0.075s/f (Good) 10 Ran SP% **96.9**
Speed ratings (Par 95): **96,95,91,87,83 82,80,79,78,74**
Tote Swingers 1&2 £2.10, 2&3 £2.80, 1&3 £1.70 CSF £9.50 TOTE £2.60: £1.10, £1.20, £1.10; EX 10.70 Trifecta £28.80 Pool: £468.83 - 12.03 winning tickets..
Owner Ron Bauer **Bred** S C A De La Perrigne **Trained** Lambourn, Berks

FOCUS
An ordinary juvenile sprint maiden. Both Gold Hunter, who got upset in the stalls, and Koharu, who refused to enter, were withdrawn at the start. Sound form, with the first pair clear.

NOTEBOOK
African Oil(FR) stepped up on his Windsor second, making near enough all against the favoured stands' rail. He may get 7f, but looks quite happy at this trip and will presumably step into handicaps now. (op 7-2)
Caramack has improved with each start and the winner having the rail was probably the difference between the two horses. He can win a maiden, with the return to 7f likely to suit, but now has the option of handicaps. (op 7-1)

Digress was a little disappointing back on this faster ground, following a promising effort at Salisbury, and it would be no surprise to see him step back up in trip and switched to nurseries now. (op 15-8)
Speedfit Boy (IRE)caught the eye on debut and again showed promise in what was a stronger heat. (tchd 17-2 and 10-1)
Royal Betty offered more on this first start for Lee Carter and should have a future in modest handicaps.
Delphica(IRE) is now eligible for a mark and should fare better in nurseries. (op 40-1)
Derwentwater(IRE) wasn't best away on this drop in trip and never got involved, keeping on steadily under quite gentle handling. He'll qualify for a mark after another run. (op 25-1)

5949 YOURRACINGSECRET.CO.UK MAIDEN FILLIES' STKS 6f
3:30 (3:30) (Class 5) 3 Y O I £2,005 (£704; £352) Stalls High

Form RPR
02 **1** **Sushi**15 5453 3 -8-12 WilliamBuick 2 65+
(Rae Guest) *hld up: hdwy in centre over 2f out: led over 1f out: hung rt: drvn out* 9/23
2 1 **Far East** 3 -8-12 DaneO'Neill 7 61+
(Clive Cox) *w ldr: rdn and sltly outpcd 2f out: kpt on fnl f* 11/42
6400 **3** ¾ **Aarti (IRE)**76 3312 3 -8-1268 RichardHughes 6 61+
(William Haggas) *t.k.h: pressed ldng pair: rdn 2f out: disputing cl 2nd and jst hld whn n.m.r nr fin* 1/11
3006 **4** 5 **Enthrall (IRE)**16 5406 3 -8-940 (be1) RyanClark(3) 5 43
(Phil McEntee) *led tl over 1f out: wknd fnl f* 66/1
0 **5** 6 **User Name (USA)**10 3507 3 -8-12 (v1) KierenFallon 4 43+
(Mikael Magnusson) *hld up: hdwy over 2f out: disputing cl 3rd whn n.m.r and snatched up over 1f out: n.d after* 11/1
-006 **6** 2¼ **Monessa (IRE)**13 5514 3 -8-1252 (tp) TomQueally 1 17
(Linda Jewell) *sn outpcd and bhd* 20/1
4 **7** 2½ **Alderton (IRE)**15 5448 3 -8-12 SilvestreDeSousa 3
(Martyn Meade) *in tch: rdn 3f out: wknd 2f out* 20/1
1m 12.6s (1.40)**Going Correction** -0.075s/f (Good) 7Ran SP%114.2
Speed ratings (Par 100): **87,85,84,78,70 67,63**
Tote Swingers 1&2 £2.30, 2&3 £1.30, 1&3 £1.60 CSF £17.07 TOTE £6.10 : £3.40 , £4.00 ; EX 12.60.
Owner The Hightailers **Bred** Shortgrove Manor Stud **Trained** Newmarket, Suffolk
FOCUS
A typically modest 3yo plus sprint maiden.

5950 LINGFIELD PARK OWNERS GROUP (S) STKS 1m 2f
4:00 (4:00) (Class 6) 3-Y-O+ £1,704 (£503; £251) Stalls Low

Form RPR
0-00 **1** **Silver Bullitt**16 5414 4 -9-467 JoeFanning 5 71
(Mark Johnston) *mde all: hrd rdn over 1f out: hld on wl* 6/1
1241 **2** 1 **King's Masque**16 5419 6 -9-965 MartinLane 3 74
(Bernard Llewellyn) *hld up: hdwy over 2f out: drvn to chal ins fnl f: nt qckn fnl 50yds* 7/23
3535 **3** 2½ **Idyllic Star (IRE)**5 5456 3 -8-664 (p) LukeMorris 2 59
(J S Moore) *prom: wnt cl 2nd 3f out: sn rdn: one pce fnl f* 11/42
6200 **4** 1 **Khazium (IRE)**30 4872 3 -8-1166 (t) RichardHughes 4 62
(Brendan Powell) *hld up towards rr: rdn over 2f out: styd on fnl f* 6/1
205U **5** 1¼ **Urban Space**16 5419 6 -9-473 AndreaAtzeni 6 60
(Tony Carroll) *in tch: hrd rdn 2f out: sn btn* 9/41
1350 **6** 1 **Reaction**16 5417 6 -9-462 (p) HarryPoulton(5) 1 63
(Sheena West) *chsd wnr tl 3f out: sn outpcd* 20/1
0 **7** 18 **Wood Meister**13 5510 4 -9-40 FergusSweeney 7 22
(Kevin Tork) *s.s: a last: no ch fnl 4f* 66/1
2m 9.9s (-0.60)**Going Correction** -0.075s/f (Good)
WFA 3 from 4yo+ 7lb 7Ran SP%114.5
Speed ratings (Par 101): **99,98,96,95,94 93,79**
Tote Swingers 1&2 £5.50, 2&3 £2.30, 1&3 £5.10 CSF £27.25 TOTE £8.70 : £3.00 , £2.00 ; EX 22.80.The winner was bought by G. L. Moore for 6,200gns. Idyllic Star was claimed by B. J. Llewellyn for £6,000.
Owner Antoniades Family **Bred** Overbury Stallions Ltd **Trained** Middleham Moor, N Yorks
FOCUS
This had looked quite a competitive seller, but Joe Fanning dictated the pace aboard the class-dropping winner.

5951 FOLLOW US ON TWITTER @LINGFIELDPARK H'CAP 1m 2f
4:30 (4:30) (Class 4) (0-85,85) 3-Y-O £4,075 (£1,212; £606; £303) Stalls Low

Form RPR
4361 **1** **Debating Society (IRE)**8 5707 3 -9-280 6ex KierenFallon 7 92+
(Sir Michael Stoute) *hld up in 4th: rdn 3f out: led over 1f out: styd on u.p* 11/41
3312 **2** ¾ **Al Baidaa**7 5752 3 -9-482 1 AndreaAtzeni 4 91
(Roger Varian) *chsd ldrs: rdn and swtchd rt over 2f out: styd on wl to take 2nd nr fin* 4/12
0200 **3** 1 **Misdemeanour (IRE)**25 5078 3 -9-785 RichardHughes 5 93
(Richard Hannon) *led tl over 1f out: hrd rdn: one pce* 9/23
0140 **4** 4 **Popular**19 5328 3 -9-280 TomQueally 3 79
(Sir Henry Cecil) *hld up in 5th: rdn over 2f out: nvr rchd ldrs* 10/1
241 **5** 2¾ **Estebsaal (IRE)**19 5329 3 -9-482 PaulHanagan 6 76
(John Dunlop) *hld up towards rr: rdn over 2f out: nvr able to chal* 5/1
-210 **6** hd **Handsome Ransom**77 3280 3 -9-785 (p) WilliamBuick 8 78
(John Gosden) *chsd ldr: rdn 3f out: btn whn n.m.r over 2f out* 11/1
6613 **7** 2¾ **Venetian View (IRE)**16 5406 3 -8-872 (v) FergusSweeney 1 60
(Gary Moore) *sn last: drvn along over 3f out: n.d* 25/1
01 **8** 3 **Mawhub**12 5555 3 -9-381 SilvestreDeSousa 2 63
(Saeed Bin Suroor) *towards rr: hdwy in centre 3f out: wknd 2f out* 13/2
2m 8.97s (-1.53)**Going Correction** -0.075s/f (Good) 8Ran SP%116.1
Speed ratings (Par 103): **103,102,101,98,96 96,93,91**
Tote Swingers 1&2 £3.20, 2&3 £4.70, 1&3 £3.40 CSF £14.07 CT £47.51 TOTE £3.10 : £1.10 , £1.50, £1.50 ; EX 18.20 Trifecta £41.90 Pool: £1278.72 - 22.54 winning tickets.
Owner Ballymacoll Stud **Bred** Ballymacoll Stud Farm Ltd **Trained** Newmarket, Suffolk
■ Stewards' Enquiry : Andrea Atzeni one-day ban: careless riding (Sep 19)
FOCUS
The pace was ordinary but this still looks solid form for the grade.

5952 LINGFIELDPARK.CO.UK MEDIAN AUCTION MAIDEN STKS 1m 2f
5:00 (5:00) (Class 6) 3-4-Y-O £1,704 (£503; £251) Stalls Low

Form RPR
5-32 **1** **Noble Silk**19 5315 3 -9-377 PaulHanagan 4 79+
(Lucy Wadham) *hld up: hdwy over 2f out: led over 1f out: hung lft: pushed out* 6/42
004 **2** 1 **Keeping Time**29 4916 3 -9-370 TomQueally 6 77
(Sir Henry Cecil) *sn led: hrd rdn and hdd over 1f out: nt qckn ins fnl f* 14/1
63 **3** 4½ **Caption**42 4458 3 -8-120 RichardMullen 1 63
(Sir Michael Stoute) *trckd ldr: outpcd 2f out: sn btn* 9/13
2-2 **4** 10 **Revered Citizen (USA)**6 5404 3 -9-30 KierenFallon 5 48
(Sir Michael Stoute) *cl 3rd most of way tl wknd 2f out* 5/61
0/ **5** 99 **Miss Thea**734 5691 4 -9-50 1 IanMongan 2
(Lucy Wadham) *in tch: rdn 5f out: sn bhd and virtually p.u: b.b.v* 66/1
2m 11.27s (0.77)**Going Correction** -0.075s/f (Good)
WFA 3 from 4yo 7lb 5Ran SP%112.7
Speed ratings (Par 101): **93,92,88,80,1**
Tote Swingers 3&4 £9.50 CSF £20.15 TOTE £2.70 : £1.10 , £2.40 ; EX 14.90 .
Owner The FOPS **Bred** Mr & Mrs A E Pakenham **Trained** Newmarket, Suffolk
FOCUS
An ordinary maiden.
Miss Thea Official explanation: vet said filly bled from the nose
T/Plt: £27.00 to a £1 stake. Pool: £56,400.23 - 1,522.56 winning tickets. T/Qpdt: £8.50 to a £1 stake. Pool: £4,715.07 - 409.02 w. tckts LM 5953a - 5961a (Foreign Racing) See RI

5088 HAYDOCK (L-H)
Thursday, September 6
OFFICIAL GOING: Good to firm (good in places; 8.9)
Wind: Light half against Weather: Fine and dry

5962 BETFRED BONUS KING BINGO IRISH STALLION FARMS EBF MAIDEN STKS 1m
2:30 (2:31) (Class 5) 2-Y-O £3,234 (£962; £481; £240) Stalls Low

Form RPR
24 **1** **Romantic Settings**19 5339 2 -8-120 TonyHamilton 6 76
(Richard Fahey) *trckd ldrs: pushed along 3f out: hdwy wl over 1f out: drvn to chal appr fnl f: kpt on gamely to ld nr line* 7/22
00 **2** nse **Elhaame (IRE)**30 4917 2 -9-00 PatrickHills(3) 15 81+
(Luca Cumani) *stmbld bdly s and towards rr: smooth hdwy on outer 3f out: trckd ldrs 2f out: rdn to chal over 1f out: led ins fnl f: hdd nr line* 33/1
0 **3** 1¼ **Another Cocktail**20 5303 2 -9-30 DarryllHolland 9 78+
(Hughie Morrison) *trckd ldrs on inner: hdwy whn n.m.r and swtchd rt over 1f out: sn rdn and kpt on fnl f: nrst fin* 20/1
35 **4** ½ **Arlecchino (IRE)**32 4837 2 -9-30 PaulMulrennan 13 77
(Ed McMahon) *trckd ldng pair: cl up over 3f out: led 2f out and sn rdn: drvn and hdd ins fnl f: no ex* 15/23
3 **5** ¾ **Restraint Of Trade (IRE)**8 5534 2 -9-30 MickaelBarzalona 1 75
(Mahmood Al Zarooni) *t.k.h early: trckd ldrs on inner: niggled along 3f out: hdwy 2f out: rdn to chal and ev ch over 1f out tl drvn and wknd ins fnl f* 6/41
0 **6** 2¼ **Raven's Tower (USA)**17 5407 2 -8-120 AntiocoMurgia(5) 14 70+
(Mahmood Al Zarooni) *t.k.h early: trckd ldrs on outer: pushed along 3f out: rdn over 2f out and grad wknd* 12/1
0 **7** 6 **Noble Bacchus (IRE)**17 5040 2 -9-30 RichardKingscote 10 56
(Tom Dascombe) *in tch: effrt 3f out: sn rdn along and n.d* 20/1
05 **8** 3¼ **Returntobrecongill**20 5311 2 -9-30 MichaelStainton 11 49
(Sally Hall) *a towards rr* 80/1
00 **9** ½ **Good Speech (IRE)**12 4494 2 -8-120 AndrewElliott 5 43
(Tom Tate) *led: rdn along 3f out: hdd 2f out and sn wknd* 50/1
05 **10** hd **Camp Floyd (USA)**8 5742 2 -9-30 AhmedAjtebi 7 47
(Mahmood Al Zarooni) *cl up: rdn along to dispute ld over 2f out: wknd wl over 1f out* 10/1
04 **11** 1 **Moorway (IRE)**19 5331 2 -9-30 GrahamGibbons 3 45
(Reg Hollinshead) *a towards rr* 50/1
12 hd **Gabrial The Duke (IRE)**2 -9-30 JamieSpencer 4 44
(Michael Bell) *dwlt: a in rr* 12/1
6 **13** ½ **Flying Tempo**15 5476 2 -9-30 JackMitchell 8 43
(Ed Dunlop) *a towards rr* 100/1
14 6 **Flying Nellie** 2 -8-120 MickyFenton 2 24
(Tom Tate) *dwlt: t.k.h: a towards rr* 50/1
1m 42.7s (-1.00)**Going Correction** -0.175s/f (Firm) 14Ran SP%119.0
Speed ratings (Par 95): **98,97,96,96,95 93,87,83,83,83 82,82,81,75**
toteswingers 1&2 £22.90, 1&3 £12.50, 2&3 £58.70 CSF £123.56 TOTE £3.70 : £1.10, £12.30 , £6.00; EX 152.20 TRIFECTA Not won.
Owner Mel Roberts & Ms Nicola Meese 1 **Bred** Newsells Park Stud **Trained** Musley Bank, N Yorks
FOCUS
All races on Inner Home straight and races on Round course increased in distance by 1yd. An ordinary juvenile maiden, but one that should produce winners, most likely of middle-distance handicaps next season. They went a fair enough gallop.
NOTEBOOK
Romantic Settings posted an improved effort to get off the mark, although she'd probably have finished second had the runner-up not stumbled badly coming out of the stalls. Regardless, she looks a fair prospect for handicaps up to 1m2f next season. (op 9-2 tchd 10-3)
Elhaame(IRE) failed to build on a mildly promising debut when running poorly on Polytrack at Kempton last month, but he holds a Royal Lodge entry and this appeared a more accurate reflection of his ability. Drawn widest and stumbling badly on leaving the stalls, he made a ton of ground out wide and may well have won had his rider been harder on him close home. He should have no trouble going one better and now has the option of handicaps.
Another Cocktail, whose dam is a sister to Gold Cup winner Fame And Glory, is in the Racing Post Trophy and duly improved on his debut effort, appreciating the extra furlong and running on in a manner to suggest he'll want 1m2f this year. (op 25-1)
Arlecchino(IRE), entered in the Royal Lodge, didn't look happy around Chester last time and, despite getting warm, returned to a similar level of form as on debut. (op 7-1 tchd 9-1)
Restraint Of Trade (IRE)ooked no star when third at Goodwood on debut and, having raced keenly, he found disappointingly little. He'll be of more interest once contesting nurseries after another start. (op Evens tchd 10-11)
Raven's Tower (USA)raced wide from his draw yet still showed considerably more than on debut. He too is a backend nursery type, with a drop to 7f unlikely to inconvenience. (op 25-1)
Noble Bacchus (IRE)looks in need of more time and should do better next year. (op 25-1 tchd 18-1)
Returntobrecongill Official explanation: jockey said gelding got upset at the start.
Camp Floyd (USA)is now qualified for a mark and should fare better in ordinary nurseries. Official explanation: jockey said colt had no more to give. (op 14-1 tchd 16-1)
Gabrial The Duke (IRE)closely related to a dual 7f winner, offered little on debut. (op 20-1)

5963 BETFRED MOBILE IRISH STALLION FARMS EBF MAIDEN STKS (C&G) 6f
3:05 (3:07) (Class 5) 2-Y-O £3,234 (£962; £481; £240) Stalls Centre

Form RPR
5 **1** **Bapak Sayang (USA)**24 5176 2 -9-00 PhillipMakin 7 79+
(Kevin Ryan) *led: pushed along and jnd 2f out: hdd over 1f out: led again ins fnl f: styd on strly* 50/1

20 **2** 2 ¾ **Huntsmans Close**[37] 4688 2-9-0 0 JamieSpencer 8 71
(Michael Bell) *racd nr stands' rail: cl up: effrt to ld over 1f out: sn rdn and hdd ins fnl f: one pce* **11/4**[1]

0 **3** ¾ **Khelman (IRE)**[40] 4612 2-9-0 0 TonyHamilton 11 69
(Richard Fahey) *midfield: hdwy 2f out: sn rdn and styd on fnl f: nrst fin* **33/1**

03 **4** ¾ **Erodium**[20] 5304 2-9-0 0 SeanLevey 6 66
(Richard Hannon) *prom: effrt over 2f out: rdn along wl over 1f out: edgd rt and wknd fnl f* **3/1**[2]

5 ¾ **Swift Bounty** 2-8-7 0 MichaelJMMurphy(7) 2 64
(Alan Jarvis) *midfield: hdwy on outer over 2f out: rdn wl over 1f out: kpt on fnl f* **50/1**

6 ½ **Raven's Rock (IRE)** 2-9-0 0 AndreaAtzeni 14 63
(Roger Varian) *chsd ldrs: rdn along 2f out: grad wknd* **17/2**[3]

7 1 ¾ **Marju's Quest (IRE)** 2-9-0 0 DanielTudhope 3 57+
(David Simcock) *towards rr: hdwy 2f out: swtchd lft and rdn over 1f out: nt rch ldrs* **33/1**

0 **8** ¾ **Don Juan**[12] 5586 2-9-0 0 GrahamGibbons 13 55
(Eric Alston) *nvr bttr than midfield* **100/1**

4 **9** *nk* **David Jack**[112] 2202 2-9-0 0 MartinLane 12 54
(Brian Meehan) *s.i.s and bhd: hdwy 1/2-way: sn chsng ldrs: rdn over 2f out: sn drvn and wknd* **3/1**[2]

50 **10** 1 **Mysterious Wonder**[27] 5040 2-9-0 0 AdamBeschizza 5 51
(Peter Salmon) *a towards rr* **33/1**

11 ¾ **Eric The Grey (IRE)** 2-8-11 0 LeeTopliss(3) 1 49
(Richard Fahey) *dwlt: a in rr* **40/1**

05 **12** 2 ½ **Canadian Red**[10] 5685 2-9-0 0 RichardKingscote 9 41
(Tom Dascombe) *a in rr* **66/1**

13 2 ½ **Rene Mathis (GER)** 2-9-0 0 JackMitchell 10 34
(Ed Dunlop) *prom: rdn along wl over 2f out: sn wknd* **12/1**

14 9 **Scepticism (USA)** 2-9-0 0 JoeFanning 4
(Mark Johnston) *chsd ldrs: rdn along wl over 2f out: sn wknd* **12/1**

1m 14.73s (0.93) **Going Correction** +0.05s/f (Good) **14** Ran SP% **120.2**
Speed ratings (Par 95): **95,91,90,89,88 87,85,84,83,82 81,78,74,62**
toteswingers 1&2 £12.00, 1&3 £48.90, 2&3 £14.20 CSF £180.61 TOTE £74.90: £13.00, £1.20, £12.80; EX 183.60 TRIFECTA Not won..
Owner T A Rahman **Bred** Mike Anderson Thoroughbreds LLC **Trained** Hambleton, N Yorks

FOCUS
The leaders appeared to go off fast enough, but few actually got into what looked no more than a fair juvenile maiden. The market leaders failed to shine and it's likely the form is ordinary.

NOTEBOOK
Bapak Sayang(USA) showed speed before dropping out on his debut over this trip at Wolverhampton and had clearly come on appreciably for that experience, judging by the manner in which he saw this out having disputed it for much of the way. He should find his level in handicaps, with this trip looking ideal at present. (op 40-1)
Huntsmans Close had proved too keen on both previous starts and was allowed to stride on this time, Spencer soon bringing him across to the stands' rail. He was last off the bridle, but didn't find as much as the winner. Nurseries are now an option. (op 10-3)
Khelman(IRE) improved markedly on his debut effort, staying on nicely having been outpaced. The way he travelled early suggests there are races to be won with him. (tchd 50-1 and 40-1 in places)
Erodium failed to match the level of his last-time-out Newbury third (7f) but should do better now eligible for a mark. (op 10-3 tchd 4-1)
Swift Bounty, who cost 17,000euros, briefly made a move on the outer and should find easier opportunities. (op 40-1)
Raven's Rock(IRE), a 150,000gns half-brother to 2007 Cornwallis winner Captain Gerrard, proved weak in the market and presumably needed this debut experience. (op 6-1 tchd 9-1)
Marju's Quest(IRE), a 38,000gns half-brother to 1m-1m2f winner Royal Astronomer, was keeping on late, having run green, and will be of interest up in trip next time. (tchd 25-1)
David Jack, not seen since making a promising debut over 5f 112 days earlier, was awkward leaving the stalls and his effort in closing right up at halfway ultimately took a toll. He's entitled to be sharper next time. (op 11-4 tchd 5-2)

5964 BETFRED "4X THE ODDS ON LUCKY 31'S" CONDITIONS STKS 7f
3:35 (3:35) (Class 3) 3-Y-0+ £6,663 (£1,982; £990; £495) Stalls Low

Form RPR

-634 **1** **Set The Trend**[21] 5278 6-8-12 106 DanielTudhope 2 109
(David O'Meara) *mde all: qcknd clr 2f out: rdn over 1f out: drvn ins fnl f: hld on wl* **3/1**[2]

-343 **2** *nk* **Yaa Wayl (IRE)**[189] 755 5-8-12 101 (p) MickaelBarzalona 3 108
(Saeed Bin Suroor) *chsd ldrs: hdwy 2f out: sn rdn and chsd wnr over 1f out: drvn and kpt on wl fnl f* **13/2**

3020 **3** 2 ¼ **Mac's Power (IRE)**[33] 4802 6-8-12 97 (t) JamieSpencer 5 102
(James Fanshawe) *hld up in rr: smooth hdwy over 2f out: swtchd rt and rdn to chse ldng pair ent fnl f: sn rdn and one pce* **5/1**[3]

4104 **4** *nk* **Navajo Chief**[14] 5517 5-8-5 105 MichaelJMMurphy(7) 4 101
(Alan Jarvis) *trckd wnr: effrt and cl up 3f out: rdn along 2f out: sn drvn and one pce* **5/2**[1]

2045 **5** 2 ¼ **Doncaster Rover (USA)**[12] 5597 6-8-12 103 TonyHamilton 7 95
(Richard Fahey) *trckd ldrs: hdwy over 2f out: sn rdn and no imp* **8/1**

500 **6** *nse* **Ptolemaic**[34] 4760 3-8-11 104 (v) TomEaves 1 98
(Bryan Smart) *chsd ldng pair: rdn along on inner wl over 2f out: sn drvn and wknd* **10/1**

0-20 **7** ½ **Justineo**[78] 3265 3-8-8 102 [1] AndreaAtzeni 8 94
(Roger Varian) *t.k.h in rr: hdwy on outer 4f out: rdn along 3f out and sn wknd* **16/1**

1m 27.05s (-3.65) **Going Correction** -0.175s/f (Firm)
WFA 3 from 4yo+ 4lb **7** Ran SP% **109.7**
Speed ratings (Par 107): **113,112,110,109,107 107,106**
toteswingers 1&2 £3.40, 1&3 £4.00, 2&3 £5.50 CSF £20.58 TOTE £4.60: £2.60, £2.60; EX 13.80 Trifecta £59.60 Pool: £777.40 - 9.65 winning tickets..
Owner Corbett Stud **Bred** Old Suffolk Stud **Trained** Nawton, N Yorks

FOCUS
The pace appeared quite fast, courtesy of the winner, but the time was ordinary. The winner is rated to this year's form.

NOTEBOOK
Set The Trend put in a useful effort to keep going, especially considering those who pushed him early faded. His best efforts have come at 1m and it was that extra stamina that saw him home. He's capable of running well at Group 3/weak Group 2 level, but Listed/conditions races will continue to provide him with his best chance of winning. (op 5-2)
Yaa Wayl(IRE), with cheekpieces back on, was running well at Meydan earlier this year and he performed to something like his best on this return from 189 days off. This trip is on the sharp side for him. (op 6-1)
Mac's Power(IRE) is best over a strongly run 6f, so although the race was run to suit, his stamina looked stretched. He remains winless since October 2010. (op 7-1 tchd 9-2)
Navajo Chief is a smart handicapper at further, but he couldn't match the winner for acceleration when that one kicked. He should find more suitable opportunities. (op 11-4)
Doncaster Rover(USA) ran better than at York, but remains below his best. (op 9-1)
Ptolemaic continues to look flattered by his early season efforts and shall remain hard to place from his current mark. (tchd 12-1)
Justineo could have been expected to show more in a first-time hood. (op 14-1)

5965 BETFRED "STILL TREBLE ODDS ON LUCKY 15'S" (S) STKS 1m 3f 200y
4:10 (4:10) (Class 4) 3-5-Y-0 £4,075 (£1,212; £606; £303) Stalls High

Form RPR

0405 **1** **Calaf**[13] 5540 4-9-7 80 [1] DaleSwift(3) 4 71
(Brian Ellison) *hld up in rr: smooth hdwy on inner and cl up 3f out: led on bit 2f out: shkn up and jnd ent fnl f: sn drvn and edgd lft: jst hld on* **8/13**[1]

0055 **2** *nk* **Humungosaur**[52] 4151 3-9-1 74 SeanLevey 6 71
(Richard Hannon) *hld up: hdwy on outer 3f out: cl up 2f out: rdn to chal and edgd lft ent fnl f: sn drvn and ev ch tl no ex towards fin* **9/2**[2]

0552 **3** 5 **Priestley's Reward (IRE)**[11] 5629 3-9-7 68 (p) RobertWinston 5 69
(Mrs K Burke) *cl up: rdn along over 2f out: drvn and n.m.r ent fnl f: sn wknd* **16/1**

00-0 **4** 7 **Lastofthemohicans (FR)**[57] 3962 5-9-10 76 (t) FrederikTylicki 1 52
(Paul Webber) *chsd ldng pair: rdn along 3f out: wknd 2f out* **10/1**

0450 **5** ½ **Laughing Jack**[28] 5007 4-9-10 72 JamieSpencer 3 51
(Tony Carroll) *sn led: rdn along 3f out: hdd 2f out and sn wknd* **6/1**[3]

2m 30.45s (-3.35) **Going Correction** -0.175s/f (Firm)
WFA 3 from 4yo+ 9lb **5** Ran SP% **109.4**
Speed ratings (Par 105): **104,103,100,95,95**
CSF £3.66 TOTE £1.70: £1.60, £1.40; EX 4.10.The winner was bought in for £12,000.
Owner Prism Bloodstock **Bred** Norcroft Park Stud **Trained** Norton, N Yorks
■ Stewards' Enquiry : Sean Levey two-day ban; used whip above permitted level (20th-21st Sept).

FOCUS
They went a fair pace in this seller and the front pair drew clear. The winner is rated a stone off his best on this big class drop.

5966 BETFRED KING'S REGIMENT CUP H'CAP 1m 3f 200y
4:40 (4:41) (Class 3) (0-95,91) 3-Y-0+ £6,663 (£1,982; £990; £495) Stalls High

Form RPR

2211 **1** **Brockwell**[27] 5044 3-8-9 **83** RichardKingscote 2 95
(Tom Dascombe) *led 1 1/2f: prom: effrt to chse ldr 4f out: rdn to ld wl over 1f out: styd on strly* **3/1**[2]

31 **2** 2 ¾ **Ustura (USA)**[20] 5297 3-8-12 **86** (t) MickaelBarzalona 4 93
(Saeed Bin Suroor) *trckd ldrs: effrt and hdwy over 2f out: rdn to chse wnr ins fnl f: sn no imp* **5/1**

1462 **3** 3 **Watered Silk**[25] 5129 4-9-3 **82** (b) RichardMullen 3 84
(Marcus Tregoning) *dwlt: sn chsng ldr and led after 1 1/2f: rdn along 3f out: hdd wl over 1f out: kpt on same pce fnl f* **10/1**

-021 **4** *hd* **Galleon**[20] 5293 3-8-12 **86** RobertWinston 9 88
(Sir Michael Stoute) *trckd ldrs: hdwy 4f out: cl up 3f out: sn rdn and ev ch tl drvn and wknd appr fnl f* **9/4**[1]

4662 **5** *hd* **Qushchi**[12] 5580 4-9-5 **91** MichaelJMMurphy(7) 7 93
(William Jarvis) *trckd ldrs: hdwy 4f out: rdn along 3f out: drvn and one pce fnl 2f* **4/1**[3]

1503 **6** ½ **Tappanappa (IRE)**[92] 2810 5-9-2 **84** (b[1]) DaleSwift(3) 10 85
(Brian Ellison) *dwlt: towards rr: sme hdwy on inner 3f out: sn rdn and n.d* **14/1**

6453 **7** 6 **Tartan Gigha (IRE)**[22] 5224 7-9-3 **82** (p) DanielTudhope 8 73
(Geoffrey Harker) *a in rr* **16/1**

0-00 **8** 1 ¼ **Waldvogel (IRE)**[83] 3114 8-9-1 **80** PaulMulrennan 1 69
(Nicky Richards) *in tch: rdn along over 4f out: sn outpcd* **20/1**

2m 29.5s (-4.30) **Going Correction** -0.175s/f (Firm)
WFA 3 from 4yo+ 9lb **8** Ran SP% **118.8**
Speed ratings (Par 107): **107,105,103,103,102 102,98,97**
toteswingers 1&2 £3.90, 1&3 £5.50, 2&3 £4.80 CSF £19.33 CT £135.31 TOTE £4.30: £1.50, £2.40, £3.60; EX 17.90 Trifecta £165.90 Pool: £816.16 - 3.64 winning tickets..
Owner South Wind Racing 3 **Bred** South Wind Bloodstock **Trained** Malpas, Cheshire

FOCUS
A decent handicap for the grade, run at a reasonable pace. Unexposed 3yos dominated and the form looks fairly solid.

NOTEBOOK
Brockwell registered a third consecutive course win, defying a 7lb rise for last month's victory in quite good style. He can expect to find himself rated around 90 following this and is worth his place in a stronger race now, with 1m6f likely to be within range. (op 4-1)
Ustura(USA) needed every yard of 1m2f when winning his maiden at Kempton and he again took a long time in getting organised, finding the winner was away and gone. A few lengths on from the third, he remains capable of better and will likely benefit from a more forward ride in future. (tchd 11-2)
Watered Silk, with blinkers back on, fared best of the older horses, doing well considering he had to work to get the lead. (op 8-1)
Galleon beat a subsequent scorer when winning his maiden at Catterick and he proved disappointing from a mark of 86 on this handicap debut. Perhaps he needs slower ground. (op 3-1)
Qushchi, up 3lb for her Newmarket second, couldn't reproduce the form despite this being slightly easier. (op 7-2)
Tappanappa(IRE), wearing both blinkers and a hood for the first time on this debut for Brian Ellison, never got into the race, but it would be a surprise were his new trainer not to get improvement out of him at some stage. (op 12-1 tchd 16-1)

5967 BETFRED "5X THE ODDS ON LUCKY 63'S" H'CAP (FOR GENTLEMAN AMATEUR RIDERS) 1m 3f 200y
5:10 (5:10) (Class 5) (0-70,70) 4-Y-0+ £2,183 (£677; £338; £169) Stalls High

Form RPR

6010 **1** **A Little Bit Dusty**[6] 5809 4-11-2 **70** (p) MrFMitchell(5) 5 83
(Reg Hollinshead) *mde all: set stdy pce: qcknd over 4f out: rdn clr fnl 2f: styd on strly* **6/1**

566 **2** 8 **Artisan**[27] 5056 4-10-6 **60** (t) MrDLevey(5) 1 63
(Brian Ellison) *trckd ldrs on inner: hdwy 3f out: rdn to chse wnr over 1f out: hld whn heavily eased ins fnl f: jst hld on for 2nd* **9/2**[3]

202 **3** *nk* **Iulus**[21] 5259 4-10-4 **60** MrOJPimlott(7) 4 60
(John Quinn) *t.k.h: trckd ldrs: sltly outpcd 5f out: hdwy on wd outside over 2f out: sn rdn along and kpt on same pce* **8/1**

6011 **4** ½ **Pahente**[7] 5771 4-10-3 **57** 6ex (p) MrCCarroll(5) 8 56
(Tony Carroll) *prom: effrt 3f out and sn rdn: drvn wl over 1f out and kpt on same pce* **11/4**[2]

3040 **5** 1 ¾ **Merrjanah**[21] 5258 4-10-0 **56** oh8 MrAFrench(7) 6 52
(John Wainwright) *towards rr: hdwy 3f out: sn rdn along and n.d* **33/1**

5441 **6** *hd* **Tenhoo**[12] 5585 6-11-6 **69** MrSWalker 7 65
(Eric Alston) *hld up in rr: stdy hdwy to trck ldrs 1/2-way: effrt to chse wnr 3f out: rdn 2f out: sn drvn and wknd* **7/4**[1]

0050 7 *31* **Swords**[45] 4402 10-10-2 **56** oh11 .... MrJohnWilley(5) 9
(Ray Peacock) *chsd ldrs on outer: pushed along over 5f out: rn wd bnd over 4f out: sn bhd* **66/1**

2m 32.25s (-1.55) **Going Correction** -0.175s/f (Firm) **7** Ran SP% **111.0**
Speed ratings (Par 103): **98,92,92,92,90 90,70**
toteswingers 1&2 £3.20, 1&3 £4.50, 2&3 £5.20 CSF £30.88 CT £208.06 TOTE £5.60: £2.10, £2.00; EX 31.80 Trifecta £210.90 Pool: £743.87 - 2.61 winning tickets..
Owner John P Evitt **Bred** T O C S Limited **Trained** Upper Longdon, Staffs
■ Stewards' Enquiry : Mr C Carroll seven-day ban; used whip above permitted level (25th Sep, 4,th,5th,8th,9th,12th,15th Oct).

FOCUS
Few got into this, with the early pace being steady, and the winner was allowed an easy lead. He is still allowed a bit of credit for this victory.
T/Jkpt: Not won. T/Plt: £562.40 to a £1 stake. Pool: £65,022.87 - 84.39 winning tickets T/Qpdt: £38.40 to a £1 stake. Pool: £5,502.57 - 105.98 winning tickets JR

5938 KEMPTON (A.W) (R-H)
Thursday, September 6

OFFICIAL GOING: Standard
Wind: Light, across Weather: Fine, warm

5968 32REDBINGO.COM CLAIMING STKS 7f (P)
5:40 (5:40) (Class 6) 2-Y-O £1,617 (£481; £240; £120) Stalls Low

Form RPR
1 **Mick Duggan** 2-9-3 0 .... DavidProbert 8 70+
(Rae Guest) *dwlt: hld up in last pair: shkn up over 2f out: hanging and green over 1f out: picked up fnl f: styd on wl to ld last 50yds* **5/2**[2]

4615 2 *1* **Wordsaplenty (IRE)**[6] 5806 2-8-3 59 .... LukeMorris 2 52
(J S Moore) *trckd ldr: rdn over 2f out: drvn ahd over 1f out: kpt on one pce in front: hdd last 50yds* **4/1**[3]

3060 3 *1 3/4* **Red Adair (IRE)**[13] 5532 2-8-12 70 ....(b1) RichardHughes 4 56
(Richard Hannon) *led: mod pce to 1/2-way: shkn up over 2f out: hdd and nt qckn over 1f out: fdd nr fin* **9/4**[1]

0444 4 *hd* **Moonlit Dancer (IRE)**[15] 5484 2-8-12 60 ....(t) SebSanders 6 56
(J W Hills) *stdd s: hld up bhd ldng pair: rdn over 2f out: tried to cl over 1f out: one pce* **9/2**

50 5 *3 3/4* **Alpine Jerry (IRE)**[12] 5574 2-8-1 0 .... RyanPowell(3) 5 38
(J S Moore) *trckd ldng pair: rdn wl over 2f out: wknd wl over 1f out* **8/1**

0 6 *1/2* **Misleading Promise (IRE)**[7] 5765 2-8-7 0 .... TobyAtkinson(5) 7 44
(John Butler) *stdd s: t.k.h in last pair: rdn over 2f out: no prog and wl btn over 1f out* **33/1**

1m 28.37s (2.37) **Going Correction** -0.025s/f (Stan) **6** Ran SP% **111.6**
Speed ratings (Par 93): **85,83,81,81,77 76**
Tote Swingers 1&2 £2.20, 2&3 £1.40, 1&3 £2.10 CSF £12.66 TOTE £3.50: £1.50, £1.90; EX 11.50 Trifecta £20.60 Pool £448.84 - 16.11 winning units..Mick Duggan was claimed by S. P. Hodgson for £15,000.
Owner E P Duggan **Bred** Pendley Farm **Trained** Newmarket, Suffolk

FOCUS
A modest affair, run at a steady pace. The winner justified good market support.

NOTEBOOK
Mick Duggan, a half-brother to three winners at 7f to 1m4f, was ridden with restraint and when asked to pick up the response wasn't immediate. He got the hang of things in the straight though and stayed on strongly to get on top well inside the final furlong, giving his trainer his first two-year-old winner of the season. He'll get further and has a bit of scope so there should be more to come. (op 7-2)
Wordsaplenty(IRE) raced prominently and hit the front entering the final furlong only to be claimed late on. She's consistent and remains in form. (op 3-1)
Red Adair(IRE) set the standard but hasn't built on his early promise and fared little better here on his AW debut in first-time blinkers. (op 5-2 tchd 11-4)
Moonlit Dancer(IRE) ran okay on her second start over 7f and could win a small handicap against her own sex. (op 7-2)

5969 32RED CASINO NOVICE AUCTION STKS 7f (P)
6:10 (6:11) (Class 5) 2-Y-O £2,264 (£673; £336; £168) Stalls Low

Form RPR
1333 1 **Beedee**[41] 4540 2-8-13 80 .... RichardHughes 2 87+
(Richard Hannon) *trckd ldr 1f: styd cl up: shkn up 3f out: sn wnt 2nd again: rdn to ld over 1f out: drew rt away* **7/4**[1]

15 2 *4 1/2* **Arthurs Secret**[47] 4318 2-8-13 0 .... MichaelO'Connell 3 75
(John Quinn) *dwlt: prog to ld after 2f: rdn over 1f out: hdd and nt qckn over 1f out: one pce* **3/1**[3]

1 3 *2 3/4* **Alcando (IRE)**[23] 5192 2-8-11 77 .... ShaneKelly 1 65
(Denis Coakley) *t.k.h early: led 2f: chsd ldr to over 2f out: tried to mount a chal over 1f out: wknd fnl f* **9/4**[2]

0 4 *1* **Runninglikethewind (IRE)**[75] 3387 2-8-11 0 .... TedDurcan 5 63
(Chris Wall) *dwlt: hld up in last: effrt on inner 2f out: wknd jst over 1f out* **5/1**

1m 26.39s (0.39) **Going Correction** -0.025s/f (Stan) **4** Ran SP% **108.8**
Speed ratings (Par 95): **96,90,87,86**
CSF £7.16 TOTE £2.10; EX 7.10.
Owner Derek And Jean Clee **Bred** D D & Mrs J P Clee **Trained** East Everleigh, Wilts

FOCUS
An open contest in which they went steady early and the race developed into a 3f sprint.

NOTEBOOK
Beedee hadn't progressed as expected since winning first time at Chepstow but travelled sweetly and quickened clear to score emphatically on this AW debut. The form may not be too reliable, given the slow early pace, but this was a step forward and he shaped as though he would get further. (op 15-8 tchd 13-8)
Arthurs Secret, down in grade after well held in a Listed race at Ascot previously, had earlier won a maiden in good style at Beverley but was compromised by the soft early fractions. This was only his third run so he's open to improvement and will appreciate a stiffer test.
Alcando(IRE) looked sure to improve on his debut win with this longer trip expected to suit. He led in the early stages but raced quite keenly and would have been better suited by a stronger gallop. (op 2-1)
Runninglikethewind(IRE) started favourite for his debut at Lingfield (turf) 75 days previously but showed his inexperience (got loose in the paddock) and was well beaten. He shaped with more promise on this second start and is likely to improve for the run. (op 7-1 tchd 8-1)

5970 £32 FREE AT 32RED.COM MEDIAN AUCTION MAIDEN STKS 1m (P)
6:40 (6:41) (Class 5) 3-5-Y-O £2,264 (£673; £336; £168) Stalls Low

Form RPR
322 1 **Alraased (USA)**[18] 5387 3-9-4 75 .... PaulHanagan 2 78+
(John Dunlop) *trckd ldng pair: plld out over 2f out: clsd to ld over 1f out: pushed along and sn clr* **8/13**[1]

60 2 *2 3/4* **Mohair**[6] 5795 3-8-13 0 .... GrahamLee 10 63
(James Fanshawe) *prog to chse ldrs over 3f out: rdn over 2f out: styd on over 1f out to take 2nd ins fnl f* **16/1**

22-4 3 *1 1/4* **Silke Top**[28] 5019 3-8-13 68 .... JimCrowley 14 60
(William Jarvis) *led: drvn and hdd over 1f out: outpcd after: lost 2nd ins fnl f* **7/1**[3]

6353 4 *1 3/4* **Shore Performer (IRE)**[20] 5299 3-8-13 68 ....[1] RichardHughes 6 56
(William Haggas) *chsd ldr: rdn over 2f out: tried to chal wl over 1f out: sn outpcd: fdd fnl f* **17/2**

5 *1 3/4* **Bladewood Girl** 4-8-13 0 .... DarrenEgan(5) 12 52
(J R Jenkins) *hld up and sn last of main gp: urged along bef 1/2-way: stl same pl over 2f out: styd on after to take 5th ins fnl f* **50/1**

5220 6 *1 3/4* **Cooler Climes**[84] 3068 3-9-4 75 .... LukeMorris 9 53
(Pat Eddery) *trckd ldng trio: rdn over 3f out: lost pl over 2f out: struggling after* **9/2**[2]

00 7 *hd* **Maligned (USA)**[21] 5276 3-8-13 0 .... TedDurcan 8 47
(Richard Hannon) *chsd ldrs: pushed along 1/2-way: struggling 3f out: sme modest late prog* **25/1**

-000 8 *1/2* **Hawkino (IRE)**[23] 5219 3-9-4 39 ....(v) MichaelO'Connell 11 51?
(Derek Shaw) *t.k.h: hld up towards rr: shkn up 3f out: no great prog* **100/1**

00 9 *1/2* **Snowy Valley**[57] 3972 3-9-1 0 .... RyanPowell(3) 1 50?
(Simon Earle) *s.i.s: hld up in last pair of main gp: pushed along over 2f out: nvr on terms* **100/1**

0000 10 *5* **Triple Salchow**[29] 4937 3-8-8 47 ....(p) LeonnaMayor(5) 3 33
(Alastair Lidderdale) *a towards rr: no ch over 2f out* **66/1**

11 *1/2* **Ivan The Engine** 4-9-9 0 .... CathyGannon 7 37
(Ian Wood) *s.i.s: t.k.h: racd wd in midfield: struggling 3f out: wknd* **50/1**

12 *89* **Later In Life** 3-8-13 0 .... TomMcLaughlin 13
(Christine Dunnett) *s.s: barely able to raise a gallop and immediately t.o: jnd stable companion over 4f out: ambled home* **100/1**

13 *nk* **Jessica's Gold** 3-8-13 0 .... BrettDoyle 4
(Christine Dunnett) *s.s: wl t.o after 1f: jnd by stable companion over 4f out: ambled home* **100/1**

1m 39.33s (-0.47) **Going Correction** -0.025s/f (Stan)
WFA 3 from 4yo 5lb **13** Ran SP% **122.2**
Speed ratings (Par 103): **101,98,97,95,93 91,91,91,90,85 85, ,**
Tote Swingers 1&2 £4.70, 2&3 £11.70, 1&3 £2.20 CSF £14.09 TOTE £1.80: £1.02, £4.00, £2.10; EX 12.70 Trifecta £158.80 Pool £560.23 - 2.61 winning units..
Owner Hamdan Al Maktoum **Bred** Shadwell Farm LLC **Trained** Arundel, W Sussex

FOCUS
Not much strength in depth to this maiden where it was advantageous to race handy. The pace was not strong. The winner is on a decent mark based on his Pontefract form.

5971 32RED.COM H'CAP (DIV I) 6f (P)
7:10 (7:10) (Class 5) (0-70,70) 3-Y-O+ £2,264 (£673; £336; £168) Stalls Low

Form RPR
4330 1 **Belinsky (IRE)**[22] 5223 5-8-13 **62** .... JimCrowley 6 69
(Julie Camacho) *wl in tch: prog 2f out: rdn over 1f out: urged along and styd on to ld last 75yds* **6/1**[3]

6110 2 *nk* **Prince Of Passion (CAN)**[10] 5681 4-9-3 **66** ....(v) NeilCallan 2 72
(Derek Shaw) *mde most: rdn over 2f out: fought on wl tl hdd and no ex last 75yds* **13/2**

-512 3 *hd* **Kinglami**[22] 5229 3-9-5 **70** .... RichardHughes 10 75+
(Brian Gubby) *forced to r wd in midfield fr worst draw: rdn 2f out: styd on steadily fr over 1f out: nvr quite got there* **13/8**[1]

0064 4 *nk* **Dark Lane**[1] 5933 6-9-1 **64** .... CathyGannon 7 68
(David Evans) *hld up in 8th: prog over 1f out: tried to cl on ldrs fnl f: styd on but a hld* **11/2**[2]

0240 5 *1/2* **Alpha Delta Whisky**[10] 5681 4-9-5 **68** .... GrahamLee 1 71
(John Gallagher) *trckd ldng pair: wnt 2nd wl over 1f out and sn chalng: hld ins fnl f: lost pls nr fin* **14/1**

1030 6 *nk* **Perlachy**[14] 5502 8-9-0 **68** ....(v) DarrenEgan(5) 4 71
(Ronald Harris) *hld up in last pair: shkn up and enough to do over 2f out: r.o jst over 1f out: clsd on ldrs fin but no ch to chal* **12/1**

0250 7 *hd* **Sermons Mount (USA)**[23] 5203 6-8-9 **58** ....(p) TomMcLaughlin 5 59
(Paul Howling) *prom: rdn 2f out: stl cl up 1f out: one pce and lost pls last 150yds* **14/1**

6134 8 *3 1/4* **Flashbang**[22] 5233 4-9-1 **69** ....(tp) AshleyMorgan(5) 3 60
(Paul Cole) *chsd ldrs: clsd 2f out: tried to chal on inner 1f out: wknd last 150yds* **13/2**

0505 9 *6* **Itum**[9] 5719 5-8-7 **56** oh6 .... BrettDoyle 9 28
(Christine Dunnett) *rousted along early: w ldr: drvn over 2f out: wknd wl over 1f out* **66/1**

0000 10 *7* **Matsunosuke**[6] 5791 10-9-7 **70** .... MichaelO'Connell 8 19
(Alan Coogan) *hld up in last pair: showed no zest and lost tch over 2f out* **40/1**

1m 12.71s (-0.39) **Going Correction** -0.025s/f (Stan)
WFA 3 from 4yo+ 2lb **10** Ran SP% **119.4**
Speed ratings (Par 103): **101,100,100,99,99 98,98,94,86,76**
Tote Swingers 1&2 £8.90, 2&3 £4.10, 1&3 £3.40 CSF £45.93 CT £95.17 TOTE £11.90: £2.80, £2.90, £1.10; EX 64.90 Trifecta £74.70 Pool £734.67 - 7.27 winning units..
Owner Wentdale Limited **Bred** Camogue Stud Ltd **Trained** Norton, N Yorks

FOCUS
A fair sprint handicap which was run at a strong pace, and it produced a bunched finish. It was the slower division and the form makes sense.

5972 32RED.COM H'CAP (DIV II) 6f (P)
7:40 (7:41) (Class 5) (0-70,70) 3-Y-O+ £2,264 (£673; £336; £168) Stalls Low

Form RPR
0006 1 **Alnoomaas (IRE)**[11] 5625 3-8-5 **56** oh4 .... DavidProbert 7 65
(Luke Dace) *led after 1f: mde rest: rdn 2 l clr 2f out: styd on wl* **9/2**[2]

0403 2 *1* **Dvinsky (USA)**[8] 5750 11-9-0 **63** ....(b) TomMcLaughlin 9 68
(Paul Howling) *chsd wnr over 4f out: rdn over 2f out: styd on fr over 1f out but a hld* **12/1**

1060 3 *1 1/2* **Isola Verde**[4] 5853 3-9-5 **70** ....(v1) TomQueally 6 70
(James Fanshawe) *awkward to load into stalls: hld up in last pair: prog on inner 2f out: drvn and styd on to take 3rd last 75yds* **7/1**

0303 4 *1* **Baby Dottie**[16] 5444 5-8-4 **58** ....(t) JemmaMarshall(5) 2 55
(Pat Phelan) *ld 1f: sn 3rd: rdn and outpcd fr 2f out: fdd nr fin* **15/2**

1153 5 *nk* **Lady Mango (IRE)**[30] 4920 4-9-4 **67** .... LukeMorris 4 63
(Ronald Harris) *chsd ldng trio: rdn and nt qckn over 2f out: sn outpcd: kpt on fnl f* **7/2**[1]

0226 6 *1 1/2* **Tunnager Grove**[52] 4143 3-9-5 **70** .... RobertHavlin 1 61
(Hughie Morrison) *chsd ldrs: rdn over 2f out: nt qckn wl over 1f out: fdd fnl f* **13/2**[3]

5654 **7** 1 **Chevise (IRE)**[20] 5298 4-9-1 **69** DavidKenny(5) 8 57
(Steve Woodman) *nt that wl away: mostly wd towards rr: rdn over 2f out: no real prog* **10/1**

2305 **8** hd **Homeboy (IRE)**[14] 5505 4-9-2 **65** (b1) GeorgeBaker 3 52
(Marcus Tregoning) *stdd s: hld up in rr: gng bttr than most and looking for room 2f out: shkn up over 1f out: nvr involved* **13/2**[3]

3603 **9** 1 **Danzoe (IRE)**[7] 5774 5-8-12 **61** KierenFox 10 45
(Christine Dunnett) *racd wd: a in rr: struggling sn after 1/2-way* **20/1**

0100 **10** 3 1/4 **Jack Smudge**[20] 5296 4-9-6 **69** (p) GrahamLee 5 43
(James Given) *chsd ldrs: rdn over 2f out: wknd over 1f out* **12/1**

1m 12.22s (-0.88) **Going Correction** -0.025s/f (Stan)
WFA 3 from 4yo+ 2lb **10** Ran SP% **120.6**
Speed ratings (Par 103): **104,102,100,99,98 96,95,95,94,89**
Tote Swingers 1&2 £22.80, 2&3 £11.30, 1&3 £12.60 CSF £59.45 CT £380.91 TOTE £5.90: £1.50, £3.50, £2.80; EX 125.00 TRIFECTA Not won..
Owner Mark Benton **Bred** Old Carhue & Grange Bloodstock **Trained** Five Oaks, W Sussex

FOCUS
A fair sprint handicap with an impressive performance by the winner, who totally dominated his rivals from an early stage. it was the quicker division and the form is rated around the runner-up.
Alnoomaas(IRE) Official explanation: trainer said regarding apparent improvement in form that gelding had benefited from the drop back in trip.
Homeboy(IRE) Official explanation: jockey said gelding ran too free.

5973 32RED H'CAP 1m 4f (P)
8:10 (8:10) (Class 4) (0-85,86) 3-Y-O **£4,075** (£1,212; £606; £303) **Stalls** Centre

Form RPR

4-1 **1** **Pallasator**[43] 4458 3-9-7 **85** LukeMorris 3 96
(Sir Mark Prescott Bt) *sweating and fractious bef gng in the stalls: hld up in 5th: stoked up 3f out: gd prog on inner 2f out: led jst over 1f out: urged along and r.o wl* **7/2**[3]

4-01 **2** 1 3/4 **Nordic Quest (IRE)**[136] 1568 3-8-11 **75** JimCrowley 5 83
(Gerard Butler) *hld up in 4th: effrt on outer 2f out: c to chal over 1f out: chsd wnr after: one pce* **10/1**

-031 **3** 3/4 **Saytara (IRE)**[21] 5277 3-9-3 **81** DaneO'Neill 2 88
(Saeed Bin Suroor) *led: rdn over 2f out: hanging and looked awkward over 1f out: sn hdd and btn* **9/2**

1-01 **4** 2 **Mazeydd**[10] 5688 3-9-8 **86** 6ex NeilCallan 4 90
(Roger Varian) *trckd ldr: rdn wl over 2f out: nt qckn and lost 2nd wl over 1f out: fdd* **5/2**[1]

143 **5** 1/2 **Inthar (USA)**[16] 5455 3-9-5 **83** (p) FrankieDettori 1 86
(Saeed Bin Suroor) *trckd ldng pair: rdn to dispute 2nd wl over 1f out: nt qckn and sn btn* **3/1**[2]

120S **6** 4 1/2 **Cresta Star**[16] 5451 3-9-3 **81** RichardHughes 7 77
(Richard Hannon) *hld up in detached last: clsd 4f out: rdn and no prog 2f out: wknd* **12/1**

2m 33.65s (-0.85) **Going Correction** -0.025s/f (Stan) **6** Ran SP% **110.8**
Speed ratings (Par 103): **101,99,99,98,97 94**
Tote Swingers 1&2 £6.40, 2&3 £8.10, 1&3 £3.00 CSF £34.45 TOTE £4.10: £4.00, £7.60; EX 30.50.
Owner Baxter, Gregson, Jenkins & Warman **Bred** Newsells Park Stud **Trained** Newmarket, Suffolk

FOCUS
A decent 3yo handicap which included four last-time-out-winners and the form looks solid. The winner was on a good mark on his handicap debut.

5974 32REDBET.COM H'CAP 1m 3f (P)
8:40 (8:40) (Class 6) (0-55,55) 3-Y-O+ **£1,617** (£481; £240; £120) **Stalls** Low

Form RPR

3040 **1** **Choral Bee**[19] 5351 3-8-7 **54** AmyScott(5) 6 61
(Henry Candy) *a.p: moved up smoothly to ld over 2f out: urged along and kpt on wl fr over 1f out* **14/1**

0564 **2** 1 **Sweet Liberta (IRE)**[16] 5441 3-8-3 **52** DanielMuscutt(7) 5 57
(Andrew Balding) *trckd ldrs: smooth prog to go 2nd over 2f out: rdn and nt qckn over 1f out: styd on but a hld* **9/2**[2]

0503 **3** 1 **Here Comes Jeanie**[19] 5350 3-7-11 **46** oh1 NatashaEaton(7) 9 49
(Michael Madgwick) *hld up in rr: prog on outer 4f out: lost grnd bnd 3f out: renewed hdwy 2f out: wnt 3rd fnl f: styd on* **40/1**

005 **4** 1/2 **Nowdoro**[20] 5315 3-8-4 **46** oh1 LukeMorris 10 49
(Julie Camacho) *mostly in midfield: pushed along 4f out: struggling to hold pl tl r.o fr over 1f out: nrst fin* **8/1**

0654 **5** 1 **Lytham (IRE)**[40] 4586 11-9-1 **49** FergusSweeney 4 50
(Tony Carroll) *dwlt: hld up in rr: rdn and no prog over 2f out: r.o fr over 1f out: nrst fin* **6/1**

5314 **6** 2 1/2 **Chasin' Rainbows**[15] 5481 4-9-4 **52** RichardHughes 11 48
(Sylvester Kirk) *stdd s: hld up in last pair: darted up inner jst over 2f out and sme prog: nvr able to rch ldrs: eased last 100yds* **4/1**[1]

5000 **7** 2 1/2 **Alexs Rainbow (USA)**[77] 3318 4-9-2 **50** DavidProbert 12 42
(Luke Dace) *settled in rr: rdn and prog fr 3f out: hrd drvn to chse ldrs 2f out: no imp 1f out: wknd and eased* **12/1**

6-05 **8** 2 **Mahayogin (USA)**[45] 4402 4-9-2 **55** BrendanPowell(5) 13 43
(Brendan Powell) *stdd s: hld up in last pair: rdn and struggling over 3f out: passed wkng rivals over 1f out* **14/1**

0160 **9** nk **Minstrel Lad**[20] 5323 4-9-3 **54** SimonPearce(3) 1 42
(Lydia Pearce) *chsd ldrs: rdn wl over 2f out: no prog: wknd over 1f out* **5/1**[3]

340 **10** 4 1/2 **Formidable Guest**[19] 5351 8-9-5 **53** JimCrowley 8 32
(Jamie Poulton) *t.k.h early: hld up in midfield: towards rr 3f out but gng wl enough: wknd 2f out* **14/1**

0105 **11** 6 **Al Karlovyyh (IRE)**[29] 4971 3-8-11 **53** TedDurcan 3 22
(Clive Brittain) *chsd ldr 4f: styd prom: rdn and wknd over 2f out* **12/1**

60-0 **12** 3 3/4 **Rollin 'n Tumblin**[30] 4915 8-9-1 **52** MarkCoumbe(3) 2 14
(Michael Attwater) *led to over 7f out: rdn to ld 3f out: hdd & wknd qckly over 2f out* **25/1**

5060 **13** 2 **Grecian Goddess (IRE)**[174] 924 4-8-6 **47** CarolineKelly(7) 14 5
(John Ryan) *racd wd early: prog fr midfield to ld over 7f out: hdd & wknd qckly 3f out* **33/1**

2m 20.9s (-1.00) **Going Correction** -0.025s/f (Stan)
WFA 3 from 4yo+ 8lb **13** Ran SP% **124.9**
Speed ratings (Par 101): **102,101,100,100,99 97,95,94,94,90 86,83,82**
Tote Swingers 1&2 £14.70, 2&3 £28.80, 1&3 £73.70 CSF £78.25 CT £2532.97 TOTE £22.50: £6.30, £1.80, £13.10; EX 94.40 TRIFECTA Not won..
Owner Henry Candy **Bred** Mrs M Burrell **Trained** Kingston Warren, Oxon

FOCUS
A moderate handicap, the pace was honest. The third was 5lb wrong and limits the form.
Choral Bee Official explanation: trainer said regarding apparent improvement in form that filly was better suited by not being crowded.

5975 32REDPOKER.COM H'CAP 6f (P)
9:10 (9:11) (Class 6) (0-65,65) 3-Y-O **£1,617** (£481; £240; £120) **Stalls** Low

Form RPR

0043 **1** **Raffinn**[22] 5229 3-9-7 **65** LiamKeniry 7 74
(Sylvester Kirk) *chsd ldng trio: rdn 2f out: clsd to take 2nd 1f out: drvn ahd last 100yds: styd on wl* **4/1**[2]

636- **2** 1 1/4 **Compton Rainbow**[301] 7342 3-8-11 **62** (t) NicoleNordblad(7) 3 67
(Hans Adielsson) *led: hld together in front tl shkn up over 1f out: hdd and nt qckn last 100yds* **14/1**

345 **3** 1/2 **If So**[44] 4434 3-9-6 **64** [1] GrahamLee 6 67
(James Fanshawe) *w.w in midfield: rdn over 2f out: styd on fr over 1f out: tk 3rd last strides* **3/1**[1]

500 **4** nse **Atlantis Crossing (IRE)**[42] 4506 3-9-6 **64** [1] PatCosgrave 4 67
(Jim Boyle) *chsd ldrs: rdn over 2f out: clsd u.p to chse ldng pair ins fnl f: one pce and lost 3rd last strides* **4/1**[2]

4122 **5** 3/4 **Indiana Guest (IRE)**[14] 5513 3-8-13 **57** (b) TomQueally 1 58
(George Margarson) *trckd ldng pair: tried to chal wl over 1f out: one pce ins fnl f* **13/2**[3]

0514 **6** 1/2 **Amis Reunis**[10] 5681 3-9-1 **62** DominicFox(3) 8 61
(Anthony Carson) *racd wd: chsd ldrs: rdn and outpcd 2f out: hanging sltly but styd on again fnl f* **10/1**

0565 **7** 1 **Illustrious Lad (IRE)**[17] 5406 3-8-11 **55** (p) JimCrowley 9 51
(Jim Boyle) *chsd ldr: rdn to chal 2f out: lost 2nd and wknd 1f out* **20/1**

0433 **8** 2 1/4 **Uncle Timmy**[3] 5875 3-8-11 **55** (vt) RichardHughes 10 44
(David Evans) *hld up in last trio: pushed along over 2f out: kpt on but no ch of rching ldrs* **7/1**

660 **9** 1 **Glennten**[65] 3732 3-9-0 **63** LeeNewnes(5) 5 49
(Sylvester Kirk) *in tch in midfield: effrt on inner 2f out: sn no prog: wknd over 1f out* **25/1**

005 **10** 3 1/2 **Litmus (USA)**[26] 5096 3-9-1 **59** FergusSweeney 2 33
(Simon Dow) *awkward s: hld up in last trio: rdn and no prog over 2f out* **33/1**

6455 **11** nse **Crown Dependency (IRE)**[19] 5347 3-9-2 **65** NathanSweeney(5) 11 39
(David Evans) *t.k.h early: hld up in last trio: shkn up and no prog over 2f out* **25/1**

6500 **12** 1 1/2 **Give Us A Belle (IRE)**[70] 3547 3-8-10 **54** (vt1) BrettDoyle 12 23
(Christine Dunnett) *nvr bttr than 8th and racd wd: wknd over 1f out* **80/1**

1m 12.72s (-0.38) **Going Correction** -0.025s/f (Stan) **12** Ran SP% **123.2**
Speed ratings (Par 99): **101,99,98,98,97 96,95,92,91,86 86,84**
Tote Swingers 1&2 £10.20, 2&3 £16.50, 1&3 £5.00 CSF £56.95 CT £196.78 TOTE £3.20: £1.10, £4.00, £1.30; EX 69.20 Trifecta £766.70 Part won. Pool £1,036.09 - 0.63 winning units..
Owner Neil Simpson **Bred** Mrs S M Mitchell **Trained** Upper Lambourn, Berks

FOCUS
A modest handicap, the pace was decent and those ridden prominently were favoured.
T/Plt: £372.70 to a £1 stake. Pool £57,423.41. 112.45 winning tickets T/Qpdt: £38.40 to a £1 stake. Pool £7,958.56. 153.3 winning tickets JN

5783 SALISBURY (R-H)
Thursday, September 6

OFFICIAL GOING: Good (8.5)
Wind: virtually nil Weather: sunny

5976 EBF WHITSBURY MANOR STUD NOVICE STKS 1m
1:40 (1:41) (Class 4) 2-Y-O **£4,528** (£1,347; £673) **Stalls** Low

Form RPR

1 **1** **Cap O'Rushes**[17] 5407 2-9-3 0 FrankieDettori 2 92+
(Mahmood Al Zarooni) *mde all: pushed along 2f out: rdn ins fnl f: kpt on wl: a holding runner-up* **5/6**[1]

1 **2** 3/4 **Glean**[20] 5303 2-9-3 0 RichardHughes 1 90+
(Richard Hannon) *racd keenly: trckd wnr: plld out for chal over 1f out: sn rdn: kpt on but nt quite gng pce to mount str chal* **Evs**[2]

3 3 **Da Do Run Run** 2-8-12 0 ShaneKelly 3 78+
(Brian Meehan) *trckd wnr: rdn over 2f out: sn hld by ldng pair: kpt on same pce fnl f* **28/1**[3]

1m 43.6s (0.10) **Going Correction** -0.175s/f (Firm) **3** Ran SP% **108.0**
Speed ratings (Par 97): **92,91,88**
CSF £2.02 TOTE £1.70; EX 1.60.
Owner Godolphin **Bred** Darley **Trained** Newmarket, Suffolk

FOCUS
Rail dolled out up to 20ft off far side rail up the straight. A interesting novice event and solid form.

NOTEBOOK
Cap O'Rushes impressed when winning his maiden over this trip at Kempton by 8l last month and was heavily backed to follow up switched to turf. Looking well in himself, he unsurprisingly set out from the front and was able to boss the race. He looked vulnerable in between the final 2f as the pace got serious, but the further he went the better he was and Frankie Dettori timed it right. His sire won the Derby and his dam took the Italian Oaks, so stepping up to around the 1m4f next year should be the making of him and he possesses the scope to maintain his progression. If he turns out again this season then the Group 2 Royal Lodge at Newmarket or the Group 1 Racing Post Trophy at Doncaster next month look the obvious targets, but he'll need supplementing for either of those. (op 4-5 tchd 4-6)
Glean went in at 18-1 when beating a fair yardstick on his Newbury debut last month and represents a top team with a good record in this race. He raced in the slipstream of the winner and looked dangerous when angling out for his challenge. However, he did take time to settle due to the winner dictating his own pace and ultimately that rival outstayed him over this stiffer test. His dam was a quadruple Listed winner over this trip and he's certainly not one to abandon. (op 5-4 tchd 11-8 in a place)
Da Do Run Run ◆, already gelded, faced a stiff task on his debut despite getting 5lb. He showed plenty, though, and it's not hard to envisage him getting off the mark next time out. (tchd 25-1 and 33-1)

5977 EBF QUIDHAMPTON MAIDEN FILLIES' STKS (DIV I) 6f 212y
2:10 (2:13) (Class 3) 2-Y-O **£5,822** (£1,732; £865; £432) **Stalls** Centre

Form RPR

1 **Lanansaak (IRE)** 2-9-0 0 PaulHanagan 11 79+
(Roger Varian) *s.i.s: steadily progged into mid-div: trckd ldrs 2f out: shkn up to ld ins fnl f: r.o strly to assert fnl 100yds: readily* **5/2**[1]

2 1 1/2 **Intiba (USA)** 2-9-0 0 FrankieDettori 10 75+
(Saeed Bin Suroor) *trckd ldr: led 2f out: sn rdn: hdd ins fnl f: no ex* **9/2**[3]

53 **3** 1 1/4 **Rainbow Beauty**[13] 5550 2-9-0 0 NeilCallan 7 72+
(Gerard Butler) *trckd ldrs: rdn 2f out: nt pce to chal: kpt on to go 3rd towards fin* **3/1**[2]

4 **4** *nk* **Martinas Delight (USA)**[72] 3473 2-9-0 0........................ JimCrowley 4 71
(Alan Jarvis) *prom early: trckd ldrs: rdn 2f out: nt clrest of runs on rails: kpt on ins fnl f* **12/1**

5 *nk* **Cocktail Queen (IRE)** 2-9-0 0.. DaneO'Neill 3 70+
(David Elsworth) *mid-div: nt clr run whn pushed along fr over 2f out: swtchd rt ent fnl f: rdn and r.o: will improve* **40/1**

6 *2 ¾* **Whatever You Do (IRE)** 2-9-0 0.. PatDobbs 8 63
(Richard Hannon) *led tl rdn 2f out: wknd ins fnl f* **20/1**

00 **7** *hd* **Golden Causeway**[13] 5551 2-9-0 0................................ MichaelHills 6 62
(Charles Hills) *s.i.s: towards rr: rdn and sme prog wl over 2f out: no further imp fr over 1f out* **13/2**

0 **8** *¾* **Pivotal Silence**[19] 5352 2-9-0 0.. AdamKirby 9 61
(Amanda Perrett) *in tch tl rdn over 2f out: hld whn squeezed up sltly ent fnl f: wknd* **80/1**

9 *nk* **Crystal Peaks** 2-9-0 0.. GrahamLee 1 60
(James Given) *trckd ldrs tl pushed along over3f out: sn rdn: wknd jst over 1f out* **50/1**

10 *½* **Sweet As Honey** 2-9-0 0.. RichardHughes 5 60+
(Richard Hannon) *a towards rr* **10/1**

0 **11** *hd* **Rockpool**[10] 5685 2-9-0 0.. JamesDoyle 2 58
(Roger Charlton) *a towards rr* **25/1**

1m 29.46s (0.86) **Going Correction** -0.175s/f (Firm) **11** Ran SP% **116.1**
Speed ratings (Par 96): **88,86,84,84,84 81,80,79,79,79 78**
toteswingers 1&2 £3.30, 1&3 £2.70, 2&3 £3.80 CSF £13.02 TOTE £3.40: £1.40, £2.00, £1.70; EX 16.40.
Owner Hamdan Al Maktoum **Bred** Shadwell Estate Company Limited **Trained** Newmarket, Suffolk

FOCUS
Usually an informative fillies' maiden and this lot looked a decent bunch. There was a sound pace on and the form looks strong.

NOTEBOOK
Lanansaak(IRE), representing last year's winning connections, got no cover from her outside stall, but was still nicely placed and responded kindly when asked to win the race nearing the final furlong. She was well on top at the finish and obviously has a decent engine. An extra furlong should pose her few problems this year (dam Group placed over 1m4f), but her trainer later said stepping up so soon to the Fillies' Mile may be unwise. (op 3-1 tchd 9-4)
Intiba(USA) ◆, whose trainer sent out a promising debutante to strike at Kempton the previous evening, made a bold bid on this racecourse debut. She was put in her place late by the winner, but wasn't given a hard time when beaten and finished a clear second-best. This well-bred filly should be winning soon. (op 5-1)
Rainbow Beauty was the best of those with previous form and she posted another solid effort without troubling the first pair. She needs to learn to relax more early in her races, but now qualifies for nurseries and deserves to get off the mark. She rates a solid benchmark. (op 9-2)
Martinas Delight(USA) finished fourth behind the smart Maureen on her Newbury debut and looked well for this return from a 72-day break. She now looks to need all of this extra furlong and can be found a maiden on one of the smaller tracks before long. (op 10-1)
Cocktail Queen(IRE) is from a family her trainer knows all about and she ran with promise on her debut, shaping as though she would come on a deal for the run.
Whatever You Do(IRE), who cost 90,000euros, knew her job and fared best of the pair from her top yard, despite being the second string.
Golden Causeway was found to be in season when flopping at Newmarket last time. She got well backed earlier in the day, but drifted out on course and posted a laboured effort wide of runners. She's in danger of becoming disappointing, but at least nurseries are now an option. (op 9-2 tchd 7-1)

5978 EBF QUIDHAMPTON MAIDEN FILLIES' STKS (DIV II) 6f 212y
2:40 (2:43) (Class 3) 2-Y-O £5,822 (£1,732; £865; £432) **Stalls** Centre

Form RPR

2 **1** **Miss Marjurie (IRE)**[29] 4946 2-9-0 0................................ TomQueally 9 79+
(Denis Coakley) *a.p: led 2f out: shkn up whn edging lft ent fnl f: r.o strly fnl 120yds: pushed out* **11/4**[1]

0 **2** *1 ¼* **Mar Mar (IRE)**[33] 4818 2-9-0 0.. FrankieDettori 2 75
(Saeed Bin Suroor) *jinked rt leaving stalls: trckd ldrs: rdn whn bmpd over 1f out: swtchd rt: wnt 2nd fnl 140yds: kpt on but nt pce of wnr fnl 120yds* **3/1**[2]

0 **3** *1 ¼* **Rashfa**[35] 4739 2-9-0 0.. PaulHanagan 5 71+
(John Dunlop) *mid-div: rdn over 2f out: stdy prog whn swtchd lft over 1f out: kpt on fnl f* **18/1**

4 *½* **Janie Runaway (IRE)** 2-9-0 0................................ TomMcLaughlin 8 70
(Malcolm Saunders) *mid-div: outpcd over 2f out: kpt on ins fnl f: nvr trbld ldrs* **80/1**

5 *¾* **Perfect Venture** 2-9-0 0.. AdamKirby 6 68
(Clive Cox) *trckd ldrs: rdn 2f out: chsng wnr whn edgd rt ent fnl f: lost 2nd and no ex fnl 140yds* **22/1**

6 *1 ¼* **Astonishing (IRE)** 2-9-0 0.. WilliamBuick 11 65+
(Sir Michael Stoute) *hld up towards rr: pushed along over 3f out: nvr gng pce to get involved* **7/2**[3]

46 **7** *½* **Red Four**[36] 4701 2-9-0 0.. PatCosgrave 3 63
(George Baker) *led tl rdn 2f out: wknd ins fnl f* **9/1**

00 **8** *2 ½* **Equitissa (IRE)**[19] 5352 2-9-0 0.. PatDobbs 7 56+
(Richard Hannon) *a towards rr* **50/1**

9 *10* **Edge Of Glory** 2-9-0 0.. RichardHughes 4 29
(Richard Hannon) *s.i.s: towards rr: wknd over 1f out* **9/2**

1m 29.61s (1.01) **Going Correction** -0.175s/f (Firm) **9** Ran SP% **114.9**
Speed ratings (Par 96): **87,85,84,83,82 81,80,77,66**
toteswingers 1&2 £2.80, 1&3 £9.60, 2&3 £9.80 CSF £11.03 TOTE £3.30: £1.10, £1.20, £7.10; EX 15.60.
Owner Chris Van Hoorn **Bred** Coleman Bloodstock Limited **Trained** West Ilsley, Berks

FOCUS
The second division of the fillies' maiden was weaker than the preceding heat and, run at a modest pace, it paid to race handily. The form still looks sound enough, though.

NOTEBOOK
Miss Marjurie(IRE) went close on her Kempton debut 29 days previously and she deservedly went one better on this switch to turf. She was given a no-nonsense ride by Tom Queally and kept finding for pressure nearing the final furlong. Ultimately she got the run of the race and things will be tougher from now on, but she's very useful. (op 10-3 tchd 7-2 and 4-1 in a place)
Mar Mar(IRE), whose trainer had the runner-up in the first division, looked a likely improver and met solid support. She got a nice trip until finding trouble around 2f out and, while staying on when in the clear, she still looked green late on. This scopey filly is probably worth another chance. (op 6-1)
Rashfa, stoutly bred, stepped up markedly on her Goodwood debut last month and did some promising late work. Stepping up in trip should be right up her street. (op 16-1 tchd 22-1)
Janie Runaway(IRE), a half-sister to a US Grade 1 winner, was staying on at the finish and her connections will no doubt be delighted with this debut display. There's every chance she'll go close next time out. (op 50-1)
Perfect Venture hails from a yard enjoying a decent season with juveniles. She showed up nicely and clearly has ability, but dropping back to 6f is probably what she wants (speedily bred). (op 16-1 tchd 14-1)
Astonishing(IRE) has a decent pedigree and attracted plenty of support ahead of her debut. She never threatened from off the pace, but this wasn't a strongly run race and she was noted doing her best work late on. Better can be expected next time. (op 5-2)
Edge Of Glory, a half-sister to her yard's useful middle-distance winner Varnish, made a tardy start and ran a tame race. (op 5-1 tchd 7-2)

5979 COUNTRY GENTLEMEN'S ASSOCIATION EBF DICK POOLE FILLIES' STKS (LISTED RACE) 6f
3:15 (3:17) (Class 1) 2-Y-O
£17,580 (£6,665; £3,335; £1,661; £833; £418) **Stalls** Low

Form RPR

1 **1** **Winning Express (IRE)**[28] 5003 2-8-12 0................ RichardHughes 11 102+
(Ed McMahon) *mid-div: hdwy fr 2f out: swtchd rt over 1f out: shkn up to ld fnl 120yds: r.o wl: comf* **10/3**[2]

1530 **2** *1 ¼* **Jadanna (IRE)**[37] 4687 2-8-12 103........................ GrahamLee 7 98
(James Given) *mid-div: rdn over 2f out: hdwy on rails whn bdly squeezed up on rails over 1f out: r.o gamely to go 2nd towards fin* **6/1**[3]

3110 **3** *nk* **Graphic Guest**[78] 3269 2-8-12 97........................ MartinHarley 13 95
(Mick Channon) *hld up towards rr: rdn over 2f out: hdwy sn after: chal for 3rd ins fnl f: kpt on fnl 120yds* **14/1**

21 **4** *hd* **Diaminda (IRE)**[48] 4282 2-8-12 0........................ JimCrowley 6 94
(Alan Jarvis) *hld up towards rr: stl plenty to do whn rdn and nt clr run over 1f out: swtchd lft: v str run ent fnl f: jst failed to snatch 3rd fnl stride: nt rch ldrs* **17/2**

41 **5** *1* **El Manati (IRE)**[36] 4704 2-8-12 0........................ MartinDwyer 3 91
(James Tate) *set scorching pce: sn clr: rdn ent fnl f: hdd fnl 120yds: no ex* **5/2**[1]

421 **6** *½* **Malilla (IRE)**[19] 5357 2-8-12 87........................ AdamKirby 1 90
(Clive Cox) *chsd ldr: rdn over 2f out: no ex whn lost 2nd jst ins fnl f* **14/1**

000 **7** *½* **Threes Grand**[14] 5516 2-8-12 87........................ TomQueally 9 88
(Scott Dixon) *outpcd towards rr early: beginning to make hdwy whn nt clr run over 1f out: styd on: nvr a danger* **50/1**

1105 **8** *nk* **Dream Maker (IRE)**[14] 5515 2-8-12 85................ JimmyFortune 8 88
(Tom Dascombe) *chsd ldrs: rdn over 2f out: wknd over 1f out* **16/1**

10 **9** *1 ¾* **Rayaheen**[42] 4514 2-8-12 85........................ PaulHanagan 10 82
(Richard Hannon) *mid-div: rdn over 2f out: nvr threatened: fdd ins fnl f* **14/1**

452 **10** *3 ¼* **Supernova Heights (IRE)**[19] 5352 2-8-12 80................ FrankieDettori 4 78
(Brian Meehan) *mid-div: rdn over 2f out: little imp whn nt clr run over 1f out: wknd ins fnl f* **20/1**

11 *3 ¼* **Mists Of Time (IRE)** 2-8-12 0........................ PatDobbs 12 63
(Pat Eddery) *s.i.s: a bhd* **100/1**

1 **12** *5* **Tantshi (IRE)**[19] 5352 2-8-12 0........................ NeilCallan 5 69
(Roger Varian) *chsd ldrs: rdn to dispute 2nd 2f out: 4th and hld whn bdly hmpd jst over 1f out eased* **12/1**

1m 13.34s (-1.46) **Going Correction** -0.175s/f (Firm) **12** Ran SP% **117.7**
Speed ratings (Par 100): **102,100,99,99,98 97,97,96,94,89 85,78**
toteswingers 1&2 £3.30, 1&3 £3.80, 2&3 £2.70. CSF £23.28 TOTE £3.80: £1.30, £2.10, £5.90; EX 22.80.
Owner Milton Express Limited **Bred** Yeomanstown Stud **Trained** Lichfield, Staffs

FOCUS
This long-standing Listed event looked up to scratch this year. It was run at a strong pace.

NOTEBOOK
Winning Express(IRE), aboard whom Richard Hughes was a late substitute, got on top inside the final furlong and ran out a taking winner. She was better than the bare form when scoring on her debut at Sandown and proved popular to follow up, despite this being plenty tougher. Hughes proved cool as her main-market rival scorched into an early lead and guided her through runners late on. There is stamina on her dam's side, but she looks a sprinter and there should be even better to come. (op 7-2 tchd 4-1)
Jadanna(IRE) set the level being officially rated 103. She sweated up beforehand, but that didn't stop her from returning to her best and she deserves plenty of credit as she was hampered by the weakening Tantshi 2f out, who was in turn bumped by the winner. She's a very likeable filly. (op 13-2)
Graphic Guest was last seen flopping when bidding for a hat-trick in the Queen Mary at Royal Ascot. Easy to back up in trip, she came with a strong late challenge from well off the pace and clearly retains all her ability. She too can improve further over this distance. (op 12-1)
Diaminda(IRE) got off the mark on her second outing at Ascot in July. She came widest of all when angled out with her effort and stayed on nicely near the finish. She's clearly improving and looks well worth a try over 7f. (op 10-1 tchd 8-1)
El Manati(IRE) looked very promising when breaking the course record and winning by nine lengths at Leicester last month. She was unsurprisingly popular up in class, but gave herself little chance by going off far too hard out in front and was a sitting duck from the furlong marker. She's better than this, but must learn to relax if she's to realise her full potential. (op 11-4 tchd 3-1)

5980 EBF LOCHSONG FILLIES' STKS (H'CAP) 6f 212y
3:45 (3:47) (Class 2) (0-100,94) 3-Y-O+
£11,827 (£3,541; £1,770; £885; £442; £222) **Stalls** Centre

Form RPR

6111 **1** **Baheeja**[14] 5512 3-8-12 **86**.. NeilCallan 4 97+
(Roger Varian) *mid-div: taking clsr order whn swtchd lft over 1f out: shkn up ent fnl f: led fnl 75yds: drifted lft: r.o* **7/2**[2]

0-00 **2** *1* **Valencha**[76] 3331 5-9-6 **90**.. JimmyFortune 3 101+
(Hughie Morrison) *hld up towards rr: hdwy 2f out: snatched up whn wnr swtchd over 1f out: rdn and r.o ent fnl f: keeping on but looking hld whn short of room and snatched up again nring fin* **16/1**

014 **3** *shd* **Free Verse**[41] 4527 3-8-13 **94**................ WilliamTwiston-Davies(7) 12 102
(Richard Hannon) *mid-div: rdn over 2f out: r.o ent fnl f: chal for 2nd fnl 75yds but hld by wnr* **10/1**

21-0 **4** *1* **Poetic Dancer**[110] 2263 3-9-1 **89**................................ AdamKirby 1 94
(Clive Cox) *trckd ldrs: hrd rdn fr 2f out: chal over 1f out: led briefly fnl 100yds: kpt on but no ex* **11/1**

3200 **5** *½* **Russian Rave**[34] 4764 6-9-4 **88**................................ JamesDoyle 8 93
(Jonathan Portman) *hld up towards rr: pushed along and making prog whn nt clr run over 1f out: sn rdn: kpt on ins fnl f* **20/1**

1221 **6** *½* **Alice's Dancer (IRE)**[20] 5324 3-8-10 **84**................ MartinDwyer 5 86
(William Muir) *dwlt bdly: bhd: rdn 2f out: styd on wl fnl f: nt rch ldrs* **18/1**

2131 **7** *½* **My Sharona**[12] 5576 3-8-13 **87**................................ RichardHughes 2 88
(Sylvester Kirk) *stmbld bdly leaving stalls: mid-div: rdn over 2f out: kpt on but nt pce to get on terms fnl f* **11/4**[1]

3312 **8** *shd* **Elusive Flame**[20] 5324 3-9-0 **88**................................ PatDobbs 10 89
(David Elsworth) *trckd ldr: led narrowly over 2f out: rdn whn jnd over 1f out: hdd fnl 100yds: fdd* **13/2**[3]

4020 **9** *shd* **Askaud (IRE)**[37] 4689 4-9-2 **86**................................(b) IanMongan 11 87
(Scott Dixon) *led: rdn and narrowly hdd over 2f out: rallied gamely to dispute ld over 1f out: hdd fnl 100yds: fdd* **12/1**

0400 **10** 3/4 **Deire Na Sli (IRE)**[7] 4321 4 -8-11**86**..........(b) DarrenEgan(5) 7 85
(Martyn Meade) *a towards rr* **33/1**

0631 **11** 1 **Fillionaire**[3] 5877 3 -8-9**83** 6ex.......... MartinHarley 9 79
(Mick Channon) *trckd ldrs: rdn over 2f out: wknd jst over 1f out* **10/1**

411 **12** nk **Dance Company**[30] 4933 3 -8-12**86**.......... JimCrowley 6 81
(William Knight) *mid-div: rdn over 2f out: hld towards rr whn nt clr run and snatched up over 1f out* **16/1**

1m 26.3s (-2.30)**Going Correction** -0.175s/f (Firm)
WFA 3 from 4yo+ 4lb 12Ran SP%121.2
Speed ratings (Par 96): **106,104,104,103,103 102,101,101,101,100 99,99**
toteswingers 1&2 £2.80, 1&3 £9.80, 2&3 £9.60 CSF £60.37 CT £531.70 TOTE £6.20 : £2.20, £5.80, £3.50 ; EX 92.90 .
Owner Sheikh Ahmed Al Maktoum **Bred** Middle Park Stud Ltd **Trained** Newmarket, Suffolk
■ Stewards' Enquiry : Neil Callan two-day ban; careless riding (20th-21st Sept).

FOCUS
A very competitive fillies' handicap, run at a decent tempo and the main action developed towards the near side late on as it proved a messy race. The winner has the potential to rate higher.

NOTEBOOK
Baheeja registered her fourth win on the bounce and completed the task gamely. The winner was a little free early despite the strong pace on. However, she showed her class when asked for everything and looks smart. She was another 6lb higher here and the handicapper will now again have his say, but further improvement cannot be ruled out. (op 9-2)
Valencha, whose yard won this last year, found all sort of trouble in her run and has to rate as unlucky. This was much her best run since resuming and compensation may be forthcoming in the next few weeks. (op 22-1)
Free Verse ended up nearest the stands' rail and posted a solid effort. She's weighted to her best, but is a tough filly and this ground would have been quick enough for her. (op 11-1)
Poetic Dancer got a trouble-free passage down the centre and showed her true colours again back down in trip. It was her second run back, and return from a 110-day layoff, so she's entitled to come on again. (op 14-1)
Russian Rave returned to something like her best and finished with something up her sleeve after meeting some interference. Official explanation: jockey said mare was denied a clear run.
Alice's Dancer (IRE)is a little better than the bare form so she remains progressive. (op 14-1)
My Sharona was 4lb higher for her Goodwood success 12 days earlier. She was confidently ridden back up in trip, but flattened out under pressure and may be better off back on easier ground at this level. (op 7-2)
Elusive Flame had her chance, yet probably paid for racing on the strong early pace. (op 11-2 tchd 5-1)
Dance Company Official explanation: jockey said filly was denied a clear run.

5981 CGA "PERSIAN PUNCH" CONDITIONS STKS 1m 6f 21y
4:20 (4:21) (Class 2) 3-Y-0+ **£9,960** (£2,982; £1,491)

Form RPR
0243 **1** **Songcraft (IRE)**[12] 5593 4 -9-5**108**.......... FrankieDettori 1 111
(Saeed Bin Suroor) *trckd ldr: chal over 2f out: rdn to take narrow ld wl over 1f out: hdd ent fnl f: rallied to regain nk advantage fnl 140yds: hld on: all out* **2/1**[2]

-335 **2** shd **Chiberta King**[35] 4737 6 -9-2**108**..........(p) JimmyFortune 3 108
(Andrew Balding) *led: rdn whn pressed over 2f out: hdd wl over 1f out: looked hld ent fnl f: rallied gamely fnl 120yds: styng on wl nring fin: jst failed* **10/11**[1]

1511 **3** nk **Lily In Pink**[20] 5306 4 -8-11**92**.......... JamesDoyle 4 102
(Jonathan Portman) *trckd ldng pair: chal over 2f out: led ent fnl f: sn rdn and narrowly hdd: styd on but no ex nring fin* **7/2**[3]

3m 4.15s (-3.25)**Going Correction** -0.175s/f (Firm) 3Ran SP%107.9
Speed ratings (Par 109): **102,101,101**
CSF £4.25 TOTE £2.50 ; EX 3.50 .
Owner Godolphin **Bred** Darley **Trained** Newmarket, Suffolk

FOCUS
A decent little staying event and a cracking finish. Muddling conditions race form.

NOTEBOOK
Songcraft(IRE) dug deep and landed his first success since embarking on a British career. He was below par at Windsor on soft ground last time and stamina to prove, but his previous form entitled him to plenty of respect. He was also conceding upwards of 3lb to his two rivals and it was a gutsy effort. Now his stamina is proven, it opens up more options for him, but this was a case of Frankie Dettori being at his brilliant best. (op 5-2)
Chiberta King ran a sound race in the Group 2 Goodwood Cup last time out and was the one to beat at these weights. He unsurprisingly went from the front, but was comfortably headed when the closers loomed up late on. Looking at the manner in which he came back to just go down at the finish, despite being hit by the winner's whip, his rider clearly didn't make it enough of a test and this was probably a missed opportunity. (op 8-11 tchd 4-6)
Lily In Pink looked to be biting off more than she could chew here. However, she's arrived with a highly progressive profile and it looked as though she may collect when cruising into the lead. She was narrowly outbattled near the finish, but this was another clear personal-best and further improvement still looks on the cards. Her official rating will shoot up, though. (op 9-2)

5982 SYDENHAMS MAIDEN STKS 1m 4f
4:50 (4:51) (Class 4) 3-4-Y-0 **£4,204** (£1,251; £625 ; £312) **Stalls** High

Form RPR
6 **1** **Malekov (IRE)**[26] 5105 3 -9-3**0**.......... TomQueally 5 81
(Sir Henry Cecil) *s.i.s: last of the 5 but wl in tch: struggling for a f fr over 5f out: hdwy whn travelling bttr over 3f out: sn rdn: chal over 1f out: tk narrow ld fnl 150yds: hld on: pushed rt out* **11/4**[2]

0204 **2** hd **Harlestone Wood**[16] 5455 3 -9-3**79**.......... FrankieDettori 4 80
(John Dunlop) *hld up in cl 4th: chal wl over 2f out: rdn to ld wl over 1f out: drifted rt: narrowly hdd fnl 150yds: kpt on gamely* **13/8**[1]

00-3 **3** 3 3/4 **Multilateral (USA)**[14] 5510 3 -9-3**77**.......... PatDobbs 3 74
(Amanda Perrett) *trckd ldr: led wl over 2f out: sn rdn whn pressed: hdd wl over 1f out: hld sn after: kpt on same pce* **5/1**

5 **4** 4 **Maori Dancer (USA)**[8] 5753 3 -9-3**0**..........(t) JimmyFortune 2 68
(Jeremy Noseda) *trckd ldng pair: chal 3f out tl rdn over 2f out: sn edgd lft and hld: fdd fnl f* **3/1**[3]

50 **5** 13 **Variety Show (IRE)**[27] 5048 3 -8-12**0**.......... IanMongan 1 49
(Sir Henry Cecil) *led tl rdn wl over 2f out: sn hld: wknd over 1f out* **25/1**

2m 39.12s (1.12)**Going Correction** -0.175s/f (Firm) 5Ran SP%110.3
Speed ratings (Par 105): **89,88,86,83,75**
CSF £7.68 TOTE £2.90 : £1.90 , £1.90 ; EX 9.00 .
Owner H E Sheikh Sultan Bin Khalifa Al Nahyan **Bred** Sheikh Sultan Bin Khalifa Al Nayhan **Trained** Newmarket, Suffolk

FOCUS
There was a sound enough pace on in this 3-y-o maiden and it saw another cracking finish as the two market leaders came well clear. The runner-up set the standard.

5983 CGA RACING EXCELLENCE APPRENTICE H'CAP (WHIPS SHALL BE CARRIED BUT NOT USED) 1m
5:20 (5:21) (Class 5) (0-70,76) 3-Y-0+ **£2,587** (£770; £384 ; £192) **Stalls** Low

Form RPR
0005 **1** **Alshazah**[22] 5239 4 -8-12**58**..........(tp) IanBurns 10 68
(Rod Millman) *mid-div: hdwy over 2f out: led fnl 120yds: r.o wl: pushed out* **11/1**

-500 **2** 1 3/4 **Grand Piano (IRE)**[22] 5240 5 -8-8**59**..........(v) JonathanWilletts(5) 4 65
(Andrew Balding) *trckd ldrs: led 2f out: no ex whn hdd fnl 120yds* **50/1**

5-34 **3** 2 **Lovage**[95] 2733 3 -9-0**65**.......... WilliamTwiston-Davies 8 66
(Roger Charlton) *s.i.s and hmpd s: towards rr: hdwy 3f out: ev ch over 1f out: kpt on same pce fnl f* **9/2**[2]

123 **4** nk **Siouxperhero (IRE)**[14] 5501 3 -8-11**67**.......... RyanTate(5) 3 68
(William Muir) *mid-div: struggling over 4f out: styd on ent fnl f: wnt 4th fnl strides* **8/1**

5201 **5** hd **Daffydowndilly**[28] 4986 4 -9-0**65**..........(t) JoshCrane(5) 5 65
(Hughie Morrison) *slowly away and wnt rt s: sn mid-div: hdwy 3f out: ev ch over 1f out: no ex fnl f* **8/1**

0030 **6** shd **Poetry Writer**[22] 5229 3 -8-8**59**.......... NatashaEaton 9 59
(Michael Blanshard) *towards rr: pushed along 3f out: no imp tl styd on wl fnl f: nvr threatened ldrs* **40/1**

6401 **7** 1 3/4 **Catchanova (IRE)**[11] 5628 5 -9-8**68** 6ex.......... JoshBaudains 14 64
(Eve Johnson Houghton) *sn prom: pushed along wl over 2f out: wknd over 1f out* **12/1**

2001 **8** 2 1/4 **Perfect Mission**[8] 5741 4 -9-13**76** 6ex..........(v) DanielMuscutt(3) 3 67
(Andrew Balding) *led for 1f: chsd ldrs: effrt over 2f out: wknd ent fnl f* **4/1**[1]

4502 **9** 3 1/2 **Edgewater (IRE)**[20] 5310 5 -9-1**66**.......... AaronChave(5) 7 49
(Lee Carter) *mid-div: rdn 3f out: nvr threatened: wknd fnl f* **7/1**[3]

4464 **10** 1 **Emmuska**[12] 5592 3 -8-13**67**.......... RufusVergette(3) 6 47
(Richard Hannon) *led after 1f tl 2f out: fdd* **8/1**

3202 **11** 3/4 **Potentiale (IRE)**[11] 5628 8 -9-3**63**..........(v) JakePayne 1 42
(J W Hills) *prom early: chsd ldrs after 2f: effrt 3f out: sn btn* **14/1**

0500 **12** nk **Oratorian (IRE)**[10] 5681 3 -9-0**65**.......... ThomasBrown 11 43
(Sylvester Kirk) *chsd ldrs tl wknd over 1f out* **20/1**

5526 **13** shd **Netley Marsh**[11] 5629 3 -8-3**59**.......... MeganWhitehead(5) 12 37
(Richard Hannon) *s.i.s: a towards rr* **20/1**

20010 **14** 1 3/4 **Cha Ching (IRE)**[28] 4986 3 -8-4**60**.......... Leah-AnneAvery(5) 2 34
(J W Hills) *stdd s: sn detached: nvr a factor* **25/1**

1m 42.63s (-0.87)**Going Correction** -0.175s/f (Firm)
WFA 3 from 4yo+ 5lb 14Ran SP%124.5
Speed ratings (Par 103): **97,95,93,92,92 92,90,88,85,84 83,83,83,81**
toteswingers 1&2 £88.30, 1&3 £12.50, 2&3 £63.60 CSF £500.21 CT £2917.43 TOTE £14.10 : £4.00, £14.30 , £2.50 ; EX 548.10 .
Owner The Links Partnership **Bred** Brookside Breeders Club **Trained** Kentisbeare, Devon

FOCUS
A competitive race of its type, run at a sound pace. The form is rated around the third and fourth.
T/Plt: £160.10 to a £1 stake. Pool: £46,852.38 - 213.52 winning tickets. T/Qpdt: £79.90 to a £1 stake. Pool: £3,331.47 - 30.82 w. tckts TM 5984a - 5988a (Foreign Racing) See RI

5439 BRIGHTON (L-H)
Friday, September 7

OFFICIAL GOING: Good to firm (7.5)
Wind: Moderate, against Weather: Sunny and warm

5989 PIPECENTER H'CAP 1m 3f 196y
2:10 (2:10) (Class 6) (0-60,60) 3-Y-0 **£1,617** (£481; £240 ; £120) **Stalls** Centre

Form RPR
-404 **1** **Panettone (IRE)**[9] 5754 3 -9-4**60**..........(b[1]) DominicFox(3) 11 72
(Roger Varian) *prom: led over 4f out: hrd rdn over 1f out: styd on* **11/1**

3461 **2** 3 3/4 **Thecornishcowboy**[2] 5939 3 -9-5**58** 6ex..........(t) BrettDoyle 2 64
(John Ryan) *mid-div: hdwy 4f out: kpt on to take 2nd ent fnl f: a hld* **11/2**[3]

042 **3** 4 **Joy To The World (IRE)**[8] 5770 3 -8-4**48** ow1..........(t) AshleyMorgan(5) 7 48
(Paul Cole) *prom: chsd wnr over 3f out tl wknd 1f out* **9/1**

3016 **4** 12 **Critical Point**[22] 5266 3 -8-13**52**.......... LukeMorris 8 32
(Sir Mark Prescott Bt) *in tch: drvn along over 3f out: nt pce of first 3* **10/3**[2]

0500 **5** 3 1/2 **Fuzzy Logic (IRE)**[9] 5817 3 -9-2**55**..........(b[1]) MartinDwyer 6 30
(William Muir) *mid-div: effrt 3f out: no imp* **18/1**

-306 **6** 1 **Skyblue**[29] 5022 3 -8-0**46** oh1..........(b) NoelGarbutt(7) 1 19
(Tobias B P Coles) *s.s and rdn early: towards rr tl passed btn horses fnl 2f* **50/1**

0446 **7** 11 **Flashy Star**[13] 5577 3 -9-5**58**..........(v) MartinHarley 4 14
(Mick Channon) *towards rr: rdn and struggling 3f out: n.d* **15/2**

0615 **8** nk **Hikma (USA)**[4] 5888 3 -9-3**59** 6ex..........(b) RaulDaSilva(3) 10 14
(Mark Johnston) *chsd ldr: led 7f out tl over 4f out: wknd over 3f out* **11/4**[1]

5404 **9** 17 **Dalmo**[13] 5577 3 -9-5**58**..........(b) GeorgeBaker 9
(Gary Moore) *led tl 7f out: wknd 4f out: eased whn wl btn 2f out* **10/1**

0000 **10** 12 **Trio Of Trix**[11] 5658 3 -8-7**46** oh1.......... WilliamCarson 12
(Malcolm Saunders) *s.s: bhd: rdn 5f out: no ch fnl 3f* **100/1**

0000 **11** 7 **Fleeting Indian (IRE)**[43] 4510 3 -8-7**46** oh1.......... SaleemGolam 3
(Linda Jewell) *in tch: rdn over 5f out: sn wknd* **80/1**

-300 **12** 16 **Pearl Frost**[22] 2850 3 -8-13**52**..........(v[1]) IanMongan 5
(Laura Mongan) *mid-div: rdn 5f out: sn wknd* **50/1**

2m 32.9s (0.20)**Going Correction** +0.075s/f (Good) 12Ran SP%115.7
Speed ratings (Par 99): **102,99,96,88,86 85,78,78,66,58 54,43**
toteswingers:1&2 £10.20, 2&3 £9.30, 1&3 £10.90 CSF £68.38 CT £574.13 TOTE £12.50 : £3.50, £2.10, £3.30 ; EX 85.30 .
Owner Duncan Jones & Dr Sosie Kassab **Bred** Bjorn Nielsen **Trained** Newmarket, Suffolk

FOCUS
Rail dolled out between 6f and 3.5f adding about 10yds to distances. This was a weak race. The pace looked good, but the winner was always prominent and few got involved. The winner rates a personal best, with the runner-up setting the standard.

5990 YOU RAISE ME UP H'CAP 1m 1f 209y
2:40 (2:42) (Class 5) (0-70,70) 3-Y-0+ **£2,264** (£673; £336 ; £168) **Stalls** Centre

Form RPR
2362 **1** **Dazzling Valentine**[9] 5754 4 -9-0**65**.......... NatashaEaton(7) 4 73
(Alan Bailey) *mid-div: hdwy on inner to ld over 2f out: hld on gamely whn jnd ins fnl f: all out* **10/1**

0551 **2** *nse* **Kelpie Blitz (IRE)**[17] 5441 3-9-3 **68**................................(t) GeorgeBaker 10 76
(Seamus Durack) *hld up towards rr: hdwy in centre over 2f out: jnd wnr ins fnl f: r.o* **15/2**

0454 **3** *1 ½* **Almuftarris (USA)**[21] 5312 3-9-5 **70**..............................(b) PaulHanagan 11 75
(Ed Dunlop) *hld up in rr: rdn and hdwy 2f out: styd on wl to take 3rd ins fnl f* **4/1**[3]

0061 **4** *2 ¾* **Semeen**[21] 5323 3-9-4 **69**.. J-PGuillambert 9 69
(Luca Cumani) *in tch: drvn to chse ldrs over 2f out: one pce appr fnl f* **10/3**[1]

0121 **5** *1* **Highlife Dancer**[2] 5936 4-9-4 **62** 6ex...............................(v) MartinHarley 8 60
(Mick Channon) *prom: hrd rdn over 2f out: one pce* **7/2**[2]

0035 **6** *3* **No Larking (IRE)**[11] 5657 4-9-1 **59**.. DaneO'Neill 3 51
(Henry Candy) *led tl over 2f out: wknd wl over 1f out* **16/1**

-264 **7** *½* **Kampai**[31] 4914 4-9-5 **70**.. ShirleyTeasdale(7) 1 61
(Julia Feilden) *in tch: rdn and btn over 2f out* **28/1**

3023 **8** *3 ¼* **Travelling**[23] 5231 3-9-3 **68**.. TomQueally 2 52
(Tony Carroll) *hld up towards rr: hdwy on inner 6f out: nt handle hill and lost pl over 3f out: n.d after* **12/1**

3000 **9** *1 ¼* **Blue Deer (IRE)**[23] 5239 4-9-6 **64**.. WilliamCarson 7 46
(Lee Carter) *chsd ldrs tl wknd 2f out* **50/1**

5000 **10** *9* **Focail Eile**[39] 4662 7-9-7 **65**.. ShaneKelly 12 29
(Tim Pitt) *s.s: a in rr: n.d fnl 2f* **50/1**

-003 **11** *36* **Frosty Secret**[28] 5037 3-8-13 **64**..(p) MartinDwyer 5
(Jane Chapple-Hyam) *hld up in rr: hmpd 4f out: nt rcvr and sn t.o* **20/1**

-035 **12** *¾* **I'm Harry**[31] 4901 3-8-13 **64**... MickaelBarzalona 6
(George Baker) *mid-div on rail: hmpd 4f out: nt rcvr and sn t.o* **16/1**

2m 3.58s (-0.02) **Going Correction** +0.075s/f (Good)
WFA 3 from 4yo+ 7lb **12** Ran SP% **117.7**
Speed ratings (Par 103): **103,102,101,99,98 96,95,93,92,85 56,55**
toteswingers:1&2 £10.70, 2&3 £5.20, 1&3 £7.50 CSF £79.63 CT £352.73 TOTE £10.50: £3.10, £2.40, £1.30; EX 52.60.
Owner The Glenbuccaneers **Bred** Chippenham Lodge Stud Ltd **Trained** Newmarket, Suffolk
■ Stewards' Enquiry : Natasha Eaton two-day ban; used whip above permitted level (21st-22nd Sept).

FOCUS
A modest but competitive handicap.

5991 SAM HARRIS BOOKMAKERS H'CAP 7f 214y
3:15 (3:17) (Class 6) (0-60,60) 3-Y-O **£1,617** (£481; £240; £120) **Stalls** Centre

Form RPR

0-00 **1** **Beacon Lady**[69] 3621 3-8-0 **46** oh1.........................[1] NicoleNordblad(7) 6 54
(William Knight) *detached in last pl tl rapid hdwy in centre 1f out: str run to ld nr fin: uns rdr after post* **16/1**

0054 **2** *¾* **Jay Bee Blue**[22] 5263 3-9-6 **59**...(b[1]) JamesDoyle 9 65
(Sean Curran) *hld up towards rr: smooth hdwy 2f out: led 1f out: hrd rdn: ct nr fin* **16/1**

3001 **3** *2 ¼* **Saint Irene**[7] 5783 3-9-2 **55** 6ex.. DaneO'Neill 5 56
(Michael Blanshard) *towards rr: hrd rdn and gd hdwy over 1f out: styd on to take 3rd ins fnl f* **5/1**[2]

4064 **4** *1 ¼* **Saint Boniface**[7] 5443 3-9-7 **60**... SebSanders 4 58
(Peter Makin) *t.k.h towards rr: gd hdwy on inner to ld over 2f out: hdd & wknd 1f out* **11/1**

065 **5** *2 ¼* **Rocquaine (IRE)**[35] 4754 3-8-1 **47**.................................... NoelGarbutt(7) 8 40
(David Evans) *towards rr: rdn 3f out: styd on fr over 1f out* **10/1**

3545 **6** *hd* **Smart Affair**[7] 5804 3-8-7 **46**.. LukeMorris 7 38
(Alan Bailey) *s.s and rdn early: mid-div after 2f: hdwy to press ldrs over 2f out: wknd 1f out* **11/1**

2004 **7** *3 ¼* **Artful Lady (IRE)**[27] 5095 3-8-5 **47**..................................(b[1]) RyanPowell(3) 1 32
(George Margarson) *mid-div: effrt over 2f out: no imp* **16/1**

5062 **8** *3* **Tigertoo (IRE)**[31] 4932 3-8-7 **46**... WilliamCarson 11 24
(Stuart Williams) *in tch: jnd ldrs over 2f out: wknd over 1f out* **9/2**[1]

0033 **9** *3 ¾* **Whinging Willie (IRE)**[17] 5443 3-9-4 **57**............................. GeorgeBaker 3 26
(Gary Moore) *chsd ldrs: chal and n.m.r over 2f out: wknd wl over 1f out* **13/2**[3]

0551 **10** *1 ½* **Tooley Woods (IRE)**[26] 5127 3-8-13 **52**............................... JimCrowley 2 18+
(Tony Carroll) *trckd ldrs: bdly squeezed and snatched up 2f out: nt rcvr and eased* **16/1**

5043 **11** *hd* **Inffiraaj (IRE)**[27] 5095 3-9-2 **55**... MartinHarley 13 21+
(Mick Channon) *led tl over 2f out: rdn whn short of room and eased sn after* **9/2**[1]

000 **12** *7* **Always Eager**[28] 5052 3-9-1 **57**.......................................(b[1]) RaulDaSilva(3) 10
(Mark Johnston) *pressed ldr tl wknd 3f out: btn whn bmpd over 2f out* **14/1**

6500 **13** *6* **Conowen**[17] 5443 3-9-5 **58**...(b[1]) TomQueally 12
(William Jarvis) *chsd ldrs: n.m.r over 2f out: sn wknd: b.b.v* **33/1**

1m 36.64s (0.64) **Going Correction** +0.075s/f (Good) **13** Ran SP% **125.3**
Speed ratings (Par 99): **99,98,96,94,92 92,89,86,82,80 80,73,67**
toteswingers:1&2 £85.60, 2&3 £21.70, 1&3 £37.50 CSF £261.43 CT £1486.58 TOTE £28.90: £6.50, £5.10, £2.10; EX 467.50.
Owner The Pro-Claimers **Bred** Ashley House Stud **Trained** Patching, W Sussex

FOCUS
A moderate handicap run at a strong pace.
Whinging Willie(IRE) Official explanation: jockey said gelding suffered interference in running.
Tooley Woods(IRE) ◆ Official explanation: jockey said filly was denied a clear run.
Conowen Official explanation: trainer said gelding bled from nose.

5992 IRISH STALLION FARMS EBF MAIDEN STKS 6f 209y
3:45 (3:50) (Class 5) 2-Y-O **£3,169** (£943; £471; £235) **Stalls** Centre

Form RPR

00 **1** **Muharrib (IRE)**[10] 5715 2-9-3 0.. MickaelBarzalona 1 76
(Saeed Bin Suroor) *pressed ldr: rdn to ld over 1f out: jst hld on nr fin: all out* **25/1**

3 **2** *nse* **Altharoos (IRE)**[21] 5303 2-9-3 0... PaulHanagan 3 76
(Sir Michael Stoute) *chsd ldrs: rdn over 2f out: clsd on wnr fnl f: r.o wl nr fin: jst failed* **8/11**[1]

532 **3** *2 ½* **Disclaimer**[29] 4995 2-9-3 75.. TomQueally 2 69
(Sir Henry Cecil) *led: hrd rdn and hdd over 1f out: one pce fnl f* **9/4**[2]

4 **4** *3* **Wayfoong Express (IRE)**[18] 5418 2-9-3 0............................ MartinDwyer 4 61
(William Muir) *towards rr: rdn 3f out: styd on fnl f* **7/1**[3]

0 **5** *nk* **Work Ethic (IRE)**[34] 4803 2-9-3 0... LukeMorris 7 60
(Gerard Butler) *hld up in 5th: rdn over 3f out: hung lft over 1f out: no imp* **40/1**

0 **6** *21* **Hanga Roa (IRE)**[21] 5304 2-9-3 0... GeorgeBaker 5
(Gary Moore) *a last: no ch fnl 3f* **80/1**

00 **7** *2 ½* **Seemenomore**[11] 5661 2-9-3 0... JamesDoyle 6
(Michael Bell) *chsd ldrs: rdn 3f out: sn wknd* **50/1**

1m 23.54s (0.44) **Going Correction** +0.075s/f (Good) **7** Ran SP% **110.7**
Speed ratings (Par 95): **100,99,97,93,93 69,66**
toteswingers:1&2 £2.20, 2&3 £1.40, 1&3 £3.20 CSF £42.04 TOTE £22.40: £4.10, £1.50; EX 39.90.
Owner Godolphin **Bred** Lady Richard Wellesley **Trained** Newmarket, Suffolk

FOCUS
Some good-looking horses representing powerful connections and probably not a bad maiden for the track. The winner and fifth could be the keys to the form. The time was almost identical to the following Class 5 handicap for older horses.

NOTEBOOK
Muharrib(IRE) had shown little on his first two starts, but presumably Fibresand didn't suit last time and he was up in trip from 6f. He had the rail to help and just did enough, appearing to run to a useful level. Things are likely to be tougher next time, however. (op 20-1)
Altharoos(IRE) didn't seem to go on quite as much as might have been expected from his debut third at Newbury, just failing after taking an age to pick up. There might be more to come as he gains further experience. (op Evens)
Disclaimer travelled strongly but found little for pressure. The track might not have been ideal but this effort leaves him with a bit to prove. (op 2-1 tchd 15-8)
Wayfoong Express(IRE) didn't build on his Windsor debut, still looking in need of the experience. (op 9-2 tchd 15-2)
Work Ethic(IRE) reportedly lost his action. This was a respectable effort in the circumstances. Official explanation: jockey said colt lost his action.

5993 BRASSERIE ITALIAN BRIGHTON MARINA H'CAP 6f 209y
4:20 (4:20) (Class 5) (0-75,74) 3-Y-O+ **£2,264** (£673; £336; £168) **Stalls** Centre

Form RPR

3060 **1** **Ghostwing**[71] 3541 5-8-13 **63**..(vt) IanMongan 6 75
(Luke Dace) *mde all: qcknd 5 l clr wl over 1f out: rdn along fnl f: a in control* **10/1**

1101 **2** *3* **Eager To Bow (IRE)**[17] 5440 6-9-7 **71**.................................. JimCrowley 4 75
(Patrick Chamings) *hld up in rr: gd hdwy over 1f out: chsd wnr ins fnl f: r.o: a hld* **7/2**[1]

2000 **3** *¾* **Focail Maith**[29] 5004 4-9-9 **73**..(p) ShaneKelly 1 75
(Tim Pitt) *patiently rdn in rr: nt clr run over 1f out: gd hdwy fnl f: gng on at fin* **13/2**[3]

1232 **4** *hd* **Aciano (IRE)**[17] 5440 4-9-7 **71**..(tp) SebSanders 7 72
(Brendan Powell) *sn pressing wnr: outpcd fnl 2f* **7/2**[1]

3013 **5** *nse* **Annes Rocket (IRE)**[26] 5120 7-8-12 **67**...........................(p) KatiaScallan(5) 3 68
(Jimmy Fox) *prom tl outpcd fnl 2f* **6/1**[2]

6140 **6** *¾* **Efistorm**[5] 5853 11-9-5 **69**.. GeorgeBaker 9 68
(Joseph Tuite) *in tch tl rdn and no hdwy fnl 2f* **14/1**

4106 **7** *2 ¼* **Sandbetweenourtoes (IRE)**[48] 4334 3-8-13 **74**............... NedCurtis(7) 8 69
(Roger Curtis) *a abt same pl: hrd rdn 2f out: unable to chal* **7/1**

0004 **8** *1* **Local Singer (IRE)**[28] 5049 4-8-10 **60** oh1.................. TomMcLaughlin 5 54
(Paul Howling) *plld hrd: sn stdd bk into midfield: hdwy on inner 2f out: wknd ins fnl f: eased whn btn* **25/1**

3053 **9** *¾* **Jonnie Skull (IRE)**[5] 5850 6-8-7 **60** oh3.........................(vt) RyanClark(3) 2 51
(Phil McEntee) *t.k.h: chsd wnr tl wknd ent fnl f* **17/2**

1m 23.52s (0.42) **Going Correction** +0.075s/f (Good)
WFA 3 from 4yo+ 4lb **9** Ran SP% **114.7**
Speed ratings (Par 103): **100,96,95,95,95 94,92,90,90**
toteswingers: 1&2 £8.40, 2&3 £6.10, 1&3 £15.10 CSF £44.69 CT £249.64 TOTE £10.00: £3.00, £1.80, £2.00; EX 83.30.
Owner Mark Benton **Bred** D R Botterill **Trained** Five Oaks, W Sussex

FOCUS
This was a modest handicap.

5994 GBI RACING WELCOMES MARATHONBET.COM H'CAP 5f 213y
4:55 (4:56) (Class 6) (0-55,53) 3-Y-O **£1,617** (£481; £240; £120) **Stalls** Centre

Form RPR

0000 **1** **Lana (IRE)**[11] 5659 3-8-13 **50**... StevieDonohoe 6 56
(David Evans) *towards rr: plenty to do 2f out: hrd rdn and hdwy over 1f out: str run to ld fnl strides* **20/1**

0501 **2** *nk* **Strategic Action (IRE)**[15] 5513 3-9-2 **53**.......................(tp) SaleemGolam 4 58
(Linda Jewell) *chsd ldrs: led over 1f out: hrd rdn fnl f: hdd fnl strides* **5/1**[2]

0036 **3** *1* **Green Mountain (IRE)**[17] 5459 3-8-8 **45**.............................(v[1]) ShaneKelly 1 47
(Philip McBride) *led tl over 1f out: one pce* **15/2**

4005 **4** *½* **Rainbow Riches (IRE)**[29] 4981 3-8-5 **45**........................(b[1]) RyanPowell(3) 3 45
(Roger Curtis) *chsd ldr: c wd into centre and hrd rdn 2f out: kpt on fnl f* **10/1**

0005 **5** *¾* **Johnny Splash (IRE)**[27] 5095 3-8-4 **48**....................(p) MartinLeonard(7) 7 46
(Roger Teal) *prom: rdn 2f out: one pce* **6/1**

55-4 **6** *½* **Lady Heartbeat**[247] 27 3-8-13 **50**... DaneO'Neill 5 46+
(Michael Blanshard) *hld up in tch: effrt and nt clr run 2f out: no imp fnl f* **11/2**[3]

0000 **7** *hd* **Peg Peg**[29] 4981 3-8-1 **45**... NoelGarbutt(7) 10 41
(Nerys Dutfield) *s.i.s: racd wd: bhd: effrt 3f out: nvr able to chal* **50/1**

0303 **8** *2 ½* **Desert Red (IRE)**[9] 5734 3-8-8 **45**.....................................(b) LukeMorris 8 33
(Phil McEntee) *mid-div: rdn over 2f out: sn btn* **5/1**[2]

00 **9** *¾* **Minty Jones**[46] 4397 3-8-13 **50**......................................(v[1]) JimmyQuinn 9 35
(Michael Mullineaux) *s.i.s: outpcd in rr* **9/2**[1]

006 **10** *3 ¼* **Rain Dance**[30] 4937 3-8-13 **50**.......................................(b) WilliamCarson 2 25
(Eve Johnson Houghton) *prom over 4f* **12/1**

1m 12.18s (1.98) **Going Correction** +0.075s/f (Good) **10** Ran SP% **116.5**
Speed ratings (Par 99): **89,88,87,86,85 84,84,81,80,76**
toteswingers:1&2 £10.40, 2&3 £9.70, 1&3 £15.30 CSF £117.06 CT £853.23 TOTE £24.70: £4.90, £1.70, £3.00; EX 123.90.
Owner Will Dawson **Bred** Mrs Brid Cosgrove **Trained** Pandy, Monmouths
■ Stewards' Enquiry : Saleem Golam four-day ban; used whip above permitted level (21st-24th Sept).
Ryan Powell four-day ban; used whip above permitted level (21st-24th Sept).

FOCUS
A poor sprint handicap for 3yos, but competitive enough.
Rainbow Riches(IRE) Official explanation: jockey said filly hung right.
Minty Jones Official explanation: jockey said colt hung right.

5995 ROLLAND GORRINGE FILLIES' H'CAP 5f 213y
5:25 (5:25) (Class 5) (0-75,75) 3-Y-O+ **£2,264** (£673; £336; £168) **Stalls** Centre

Form RPR

5050 **1** **Button Moon (IRE)**[6] 5812 4-9-7 **75**....................................(p) SebSanders 8 84
(Ian Wood) *mde all: easily wnt clr 2f out: rdn along fnl f: hld on nr fin* **8/1**

5442 **2** *nk* **Sarangoo**[14] 5531 4-8-12 **66**.. TomMcLaughlin 1 74
(Malcolm Saunders) *towards rr: hdwy over 1f out: str run fnl f: nt quite catch wnr* **6/1**[2]

5233 **3** *2 ½* **Mother Jones**[20] 5347 4-8-11 **65**.................................... StevieDonohoe 9 65
(David Evans) *towards rr: hdwy and hrd rdn 2f out: styd on* **14/1**
2002 **4** *1* **Interakt**[29] 4980 5-9-7 **75**.................................... GeorgeBaker 4 72
(Joseph Tuite) *mid-div: hdwy over 1f out: styd on* **5/1**[1]
1330 **5** *2 ¾* **Scommettitrice (IRE)**[15] 5502 4-8-1 **62**....................(p) NoelGarbutt(7) 11 50
(David Evans) *bhd tl r.o fr over 1f out: nrest at fin* **12/1**
-516 **6** *nk* **Byton**[21] 5308 3-9-4 **74**.................................... DaneO'Neill 10 61
(Henry Candy) *chsd wnr: hrd rdn 2f out: wknd fnl f* **6/1**[2]
234 **7** *½* **Rum Punch**[15] 5513 3-8-8 **64**.................................... ShaneKelly 3 49
(Eve Johnson Houghton) *prom: hrd rdn over 1f out: wknd fnl f* **15/2**
1415 **8** *1 ½* **Represent (IRE)**[13] 5582 3-9-0 **70**.................................... MartinHarley 12 51
(Mick Channon) *bhd tl sme late hdwy* **7/1**
4016 **9** *3 ½* **Big Wave (IRE)**[14] 5548 4-9-4 **72**.................................... TomQueally 2 41
(Alison Hutchinson) *n.m.r after 1f: a towards rr* **13/2**[3]
06 **10** *3 ¾* **Beach Candy (IRE)**[9] 5737 3-9-0 **70**.................................... BrettDoyle 7 27
(Phil McEntee) *sn prom: wknd 2f out* **16/1**
0034 **11** *1 ¾* **Toms River Tess (IRE)**[20] 5347 4-8-4 **61** oh16............ RyanPowell(3) 5 13
(Zoe Davison) *chsd ldrs 4f* **100/1**
055 **12** *1 ¼* **Bobby's Doll**[31] 4903 5-8-0 **61**....................................(p) IanBurns(7) 6
(Terry Clement) *chsd ldrs 4f* **20/1**

1m 10.61s (0.41) **Going Correction** +0.075s/f (Good)
WFA 3 from 4yo+ 2lb **12** Ran SP% **119.9**
Speed ratings (Par 100): **100,99,96,94,91 90,90,88,83,78 76,74**
toteswingers:1&2 £12.10, 2&3 £12.10, 1&3 £33.40 CSF £56.12 CT £681.00 TOTE £9.70: £3.90, £2.30, £4.30; EX 103.60.
Owner Paddy Barrett **Bred** Ballylinch Stud **Trained** Upper Lambourn, Berks

FOCUS
An ordinary fillies' handicap.
Beach Candy(IRE) Official explanation: jockey said filly hung right.

5996 BEST PRICES FOR FOOTBALL BETTING AT BETVICTOR.COM APPRENTICE H'CAP 7f 214y
5:55 (5:55) (Class 6) (0-60,60) 4-Y-0+ **£1,617** (£481; £240; £120) **Stalls** Centre

Form RPR
0053 **1** **One Way Or Another (AUS)**[17] 5440 9-9-3 **59**...(t) ConorHarrison(3) 11 73
(David Evans) *in tch: led over 2f out: sn clr: easily* **4/1**[2]
6U40 **2** *7* **Inpursuitoffreedom**[21] 5323 5-9-7 **60**.................................... NatashaEaton 7 58
(Philip McBride) *towards rr: hdwy 2f out: kpt on to take 2nd ins fnl f: no ch w wnr* **3/1**[1]
002 **3** *¾* **Pastoral Jet**[9] 5741 4-8-7 **46** oh1.................................... JackDuern 1 42
(Richard Rowe) *mid-div: hdwy and hrd rdn over 1f out: styd on* **7/1**
0000 **4** *1* **Green Earth (IRE)**[20] 5349 5-9-4 **57**.................................... JakePayne 4 51
(Pat Phelan) *chsd ldrs: wnt 2nd 2f out: nt pce of wnr* **5/1**[3]
0336 **5** *1 ½* **Putin (IRE)**[12] 5633 4-8-0 **46**....................................(bt) SiobhanMiller(7) 10 36
(Phil McEntee) *awkward s: towards rr: rdn and sme hdwy 2f out: no imp* **12/1**
5000 **6** *¾* **Phluke**[25] 5148 11-9-0 **58**....................................(v) RyanTate(5) 12 47
(Eve Johnson Houghton) *towards rr: hrd rdn over 2f out: nvr rchd ldrs* **16/1**
206- **7** *3 ¼* **Chicamia**[270] 7740 8-8-2 **46**.................................... RobertTart(5) 9 27
(Michael Mullineaux) *s.i.s: bhd tl passed btn horses fnl 2f* **20/1**
2650 **8** *2* **Mark Anthony (IRE)**[19] 5388 5-8-10 **52**.................................... NedCurtis(3) 8 29
(Shaun Harris) *chsd ldrs over 5f* **8/1**
600 **9** *½* **Divine Rule (IRE)**[34] 4817 4-8-3 **47**....................(v) CharlotteJenner(5) 5 22
(Laura Mongan) *led tl wknd over 2f out* **14/1**
3200 **10** *½* **Baby Driver**[7] 5804 4-9-0 **53**.................................... NoelGarbutt 6 27
(David Evans) *prom on outer tl wknd over 2f out* **12/1**
00 **11** *20* **Wishbone (IRE)**[15] 5504 5-8-6 **48**.................................... RufusVergette(3) 3
(Jo Hughes) *prom 5f: wknd qckly* **25/1**

1m 36.4s (0.40) **Going Correction** +0.075s/f (Good) **11** Ran SP% **121.8**
Speed ratings (Par 101): **101,94,93,92,90 90,86,84,84,83 63**
toteswingers:1&2 £4.30, 2&3 £8.00, 1&3 £4.80 CSF £17.08 CT £85.91 TOTE £4.30: £1.30, £1.60, £2.80; EX 22.10.
Owner Mrs E Evans **Bred** Segenho Stud **Trained** Pandy, Monmouths
■ Stewards' Enquiry : Robert Tart five-day ban; used whip when out of contention (21st-25th Sept).

FOCUS
A moderate apprentices' handicap.
T/Plt: £708.20 to a £1 stake. Pool: £62237.93 - 64.15 winning units. T/Qpdt: £55.90 to a £1 stake. Pool: £5564.25 - 73.62 winning units. LM

5653 CHEPSTOW (L-H)
Friday, September 7

OFFICIAL GOING: Good (good to soft in places) changing to good after race 3 (3.25)
Wind: Moderate ahead Weather: Sunny

5997 BET365 MAIDEN AUCTION STKS 1m 14y
2:20 (2:20) (Class 6) 2-Y-0 **£1,617** (£481; £240; £120) **Stalls** High

Form RPR
00 **1** **Imperial Oak**[18] 5418 2-8-9 0.................................... FergusSweeney 8 71+
(Eve Johnson Houghton) *mde virtually all: pushed along and c readily clr wl over 1f out: unchal* **11/1**
66 **2** *7* **Brick Rising**[13] 5574 2-8-11 0....................................(t) DavidProbert 4 57
(Andrew Balding) *chsd ldrs: rdn and one pce 1/2-way: styd on fr 3f out to chse wnr over 2f out but nvr any ch: one pce fr wl over 1f out* **15/8**[2]
006 **3** *1* **Gowertonian (IRE)**[18] 5424 2-8-4 53.................................... DarrenEgan(5) 9 53
(Ronald Harris) *in rr but in tch: hdwy 3f out: rdn over 2f out: styd on for one pce 3rd over 1f out* **33/1**
3 **4** *¾* **Entrapping**[16] 5478 2-9-2 0.................................... SeanLevey 5 58
(Richard Hannon) *s.i.s: sn in tch: rdn and effrt over 2f out: nvr gng pce to get into contention and styd on same pce* **6/4**[1]
5 *4* **Terpsichore** 2-8-4 0.................................... ChrisCatlin 3 37
(Sylvester Kirk) *s.i.s: in rr: sme hdwy 3f out: mod prog fnl f* **10/1**[3]
00 **6** *nk* **Cerys**[43] 4487 2-8-4 0....................................(p) MartinLane 6 38
(Derek Haydn Jones) *sn drvn to press wnr to 3f out: wknd qckly 2f out* **80/1**
7 *nk* **Rock Diamond (IRE)** 2-8-8 0.................................... LiamKeniry 2 40
(Sylvester Kirk) *outpcd most of way* **14/1**
00 **8** *2 ¾* **Shades Of Light**[25] 5146 2-8-4 0.................................... CathyGannon 7 29
(Peter Makin) *chsd ldrs over 4f* **10/1**[3]

1m 37.58s (1.38) **Going Correction** +0.075s/f (Good) **8** Ran SP% **112.1**
Speed ratings (Par 93): **96,89,88,87,83 82,82,79**
toteswingers:1&2 £4.20, 2&3 £16.20, 1&3 £24.90 CSF £30.84 TOTE £12.70: £2.80, £1.10, £5.70; EX 33.10.
Owner Charles Wyndham **Bred** Summertree Stud **Trained** Blewbury, Oxon

FOCUS
This was a weak, low-grade race. The wide-margin winner showed improved form.

NOTEBOOK
Imperial Oak showed some ability on his first start, and while he'd taken a bit of a step back next time, this extra 2f promised to suit on pedigree. Up there from the start on the stands' rail, he drew right away in the closing stages to win easily. He should have more to offer once going handicapping, as he can't be too harshly rated based on the moderate level of opposition he faced here. (op 12-1 tchd 10-1)
Brick Rising was outpaced at halfway and under strong pressure, and although he got rolling in the final 2f he didn't match the level of his Goodwood run. (op 5-2)
Gowertonian(IRE) travelled kindly behind the leader and improved on his previous efforts on this step up in trip. (op 28-1)
Entrapping was disappointing, racing a touch keenly, carrying his head a bit high and failing to pick up. (op 11-10 tchd 13-8)
Cerys, never far away from the lead, but away from the rail, dropped away inside the final furlong and a half, but this still ranked as improvement on her tailed-off efforts over 6f. (tchd 66-1)

5998 MOBILE AT BET365 H'CAP 1m 14y
2:50 (2:51) (Class 6) (0-65,65) 3-Y-0+ **£1,617** (£481; £240; £120) **Stalls** High

Form RPR
2211 **1** **Croeso Mawr**[11] 5657 6-9-10 **65** 6ex.................................... CathyGannon 11 75
(John Spearing) *trckd ldrs: wnt 2nd ins fnl 2f: drvn to ld ins fnl f: styd on strly clsng stages* **15/8**[1]
6221 **2** *½* **Authoritarian**[35] 4754 3-9-1 **61**.................................... SeanLevey 10 70
(Richard Hannon) *in tch and rdn along 1/2-way: styd on fr 2f out: kpt on fnl f to take 2nd clsng stages but readily hld by wnr* **8/1**[3]
0-02 **3** *1 ½* **Billion Dollar Kid**[7] 5783 7-9-7 **65**....................(vt) MarkCoumbe(3) 6 70
(Jo Davis) *chsd ldrs: led over 3f out: drvn and qcknd 4 l clr fr 2f out: hdd ins fnl f: no ex fnl 75yds and lost 2nd clsng stages* **12/1**
0-11 **4** *½* **Meglio Ancora**[7] 5804 5-8-8 **54**.................................... AmyScott(5) 9 58
(Richard Ford) *in rr: hdwy over 3f out: disp 2nd 2f out: sn hrd drvn: edgd lft and styd on same pce ins fnl f* **8/1**[3]
4641 **5** *5* **Camrock Star (IRE)**[25] 5148 3-8-12 **61**.................. MatthewCosham(3) 7 54
(David Evans) *s.i.s: in rr: hdwy over 2f out: sn drvn: styd on same pce fnl f* **12/1**
43-0 **6** *nk* **Witchry**[20] 5362 10-9-7 **62**.................................... KirstyMilczarek 12 54
(Tony Newcombe) *s.i.s and t.k.h: hdwy 3f out: rdn over 2f out: sn btn* **25/1**
462 **7** *3 ½* **Autumn Fire**[22] 5262 3-9-2 **62**.................................... DavidProbert 2 46
(Andrew Balding) *chsd ldr: led over 4f out: hdd over 3f out: wknd 2f out* **9/2**[2]
006 **8** *1* **Fly On By**[18] 5421 3-8-9 **55**.................................... FergusSweeney 1 36
(Henry Candy) *in tch: rdn to chse ldrs 1/2-way: wknd over 2f out* **14/1**
0043 **9** *1* **Nolecce**[6] 5669 5-9-0 **55**....................................(p) RobbieFitzpatrick 5 34
(Richard Guest) *in tch: rdn 3f out: wknd over 2f out* **16/1**
-604 **10** *1 ½* **Thane Of Cawdor (IRE)**[59] 3950 3-8-12 **58**.................... LiamKeniry 4 34
(Joseph Tuite) *chsd ldrs over 5f* **16/1**
0 **11** *12* **Top Spin (FR)**[22] 5266 5-8-10 **51** oh5.................... FrankieMcDonald 3
(Nikki Evans) *slowly away: a in rr* **80/1**
0430 **12** *½* **Doc Hill**[17] 5443 3-8-3 **52** oh5 ow1.................................... SophieDoyle(3) 8
(Michael Blanshard) *led tl hdd over 4f out: sn btn* **50/1**

1m 36.1s (-0.10) **Going Correction** +0.075s/f (Good)
WFA 3 from 5yo+ 5lb **12** Ran SP% **116.0**
Speed ratings (Par 101): **103,102,101,100,95 95,91,90,89,88 76,75**
toteswingers:1&2 £4.30, 2&3 £10.10, 1&3 £6.70 CSF £16.42 CT £143.94 TOTE £2.50: £1.60, £3.60, £5.10; EX 19.60.
Owner Mrs Richard Evans **Bred** Richard Evans Bloodstock **Trained** Kinnersley, Worcs

FOCUS
A moderate yet interesting handicap with three of the runners officially ahead of the handicapper. It was run at a steady pace with the front four pulling clear inside the final furlong.

5999 POKER AT BET365 H'CAP (DIV I) 7f 16y
3:25 (3:27) (Class 6) (0-60,60) 3-Y-0+ **£1,617** (£481; £240; £120) **Stalls** High

Form RPR
2526 **1** **Marah Music**[22] 5263 3-9-6 **60**....................................(p) MartinLane 7 67
(Peter Makin) *hld up in rr: stdy hdwy over 2f out: chsd ldr over 1f out: pushed along and tk slt ld fnl 120yds: kpt on strly* **8/1**
5542 **2** *1 ¼* **Clumber Place**[11] 5671 6-9-8 **58**.................................... CathyGannon 13 63+
(James Given) *pressed ldr tl led wl over 1f out: sn rdn: hdd fnl 120yds: kpt on same pce* **15/8**[1]
00 **3** *¾* **Smirfys Emerald (IRE)**[20] 5335 4-9-1 **51**.................... SeanQuinlan 12 54
(Michael Mullineaux) *s.i.s: in rr: drvn and hdwy over 2f out: hung lft ins fnl f and tk 3rd: nt pce to rch ldng duo* **33/1**
5060 **4** *2* **Georgebernardshaw (IRE)**[14] 5547 7-9-5 **55**......(p) RobbieFitzpatrick 1 53
(Richard Guest) *mde most towards centre of crse tl hdd wl over 1f out: wknd fnl f* **9/1**
-436 **5** *2 ¼* **Trust Me Boy**[29] 4986 4-8-7 **46** oh1.................................... SimonPearce(3) 3 38
(John E Long) *in rr and rdn over 4f out: styd on u.p fr 2f out: nvr any ch* **16/1**
5546 **6** *12* **Set To Go**[29] 4993 5-8-7 **48**....................................(b) BrendanPowell(5) 10
(Brendan Powell) *disp ld early: wknd 3f out* **5/1**[3]
460 **7** *6* **Mulberry Brite**[5] 5850 4-8-13 **54**.................................... AmyScott(5) 2
(Alastair Lidderdale) *disp ld early: wknd over 3f out* **9/2**[2]
0050 **8** *5* **Blissamore**[16] 5479 3-8-4 **49**.................................... CharlesBishop(5) 4
(Hughie Morrison) *disp ld early: wknd over 3f out* **12/1**
0000 **9** *16* **Regency Art (IRE)**[24] 5203 5-9-5 **55**.................................... FergusSweeney 9
(Milton Bradley) *disp ld early: wknd over 3f out* **66/1**

1m 25.69s (2.49) **Going Correction** +0.075s/f (Good)
WFA 3 from 4yo+ 4lb **9** Ran SP% **108.8**
Speed ratings (Par 101): **88,86,85,83,80 67,60,54,36**
toteswingers:1&2 £2.20, 2&3 £10.20, 1&3 £23.50 CSF £21.09 CT £403.77 TOTE £10.60: £2.90, £1.10, £9.20; EX 14.20.
Owner Mrs E Lee, R P Marchant, D M Ahier **Bred** Ermyn Lodge Stud Limited **Trained** Ogbourne Maisey, Wilts

FOCUS
The going was officially changed to good all over, after the third race. A weak handicap run at a fair pace, and the field was well strung out crossing the line.

6000 POKER AT BET365 H'CAP (DIV II) 7f 16y
3:55 (3:55) (Class 6) (0-60,59) 3-Y-0+ **£1,617** (£481; £240; £120) **Stalls** High

Form RPR
-504 **1** **Olney Lass**[12] 5633 5-9-4 **58**.................................... RosieJessop(5) 9 66
(Lydia Pearce) *in rr: hdwy over 3f out: slt ld over 2f out: drvn and hld on wl fnl f* **7/1**[3]

20 **2** *nk* **Valdaw**[42] 4535 4-9-6 **55** MichaelO'Connell 11 62
(Tony Carroll) *chsd ldrs: chal over 2f out: one pce appr fnl f: rallied and kpt on wl fnl 120yds but a hld by wnr* **9/4**[1]

0353 **3** *1 ¾* **Red Avalanche (IRE)**[4] 5874 5-9-8 **57** (p) KirstyMilczarek 1 59
(Tony Newcombe) *hld up in rr: hdwy over 2f out: rdn and styd on to chse ldng duo fnl f: no ex u.p fnl 150yds* **7/2**[2]

0060 **4** *2 ¼* **Cheers Big Ears (IRE)**[11] 5658 6-8-7 **45** MarkCoumbe(3) 6 41
(Richard Price) *bmpd s: in rr: drvn over 2f out: hdwy over 1f out: styd on fnl f to take one pce 4th* **40/1**

0160 **5** *½* **Memphis Man**[4] 5893 9-9-4 **56** MatthewCosham(3) 2 51
(David Evans) *in rr: pushed along and hdwy 3f out: styd on fnl 2f: nvr gng pce to trble ldrs* **12/1**

0400 **6** *1 ¾* **Sleepy Lucy**[17] 5458 3-8-1 **45** (e[1]) DarrenEgan(5) 5 34
(Richard Guest) *in rr: rdn and sme hdwy over 2f out: no prog over 1f out: wknd fnl f* **33/1**

0652 **7** *½* **Bashama**[29] 4993 4-9-1 **50** (p) DavidProbert 4 39
(Nikki Evans) *in rr: hdwy over 3f out: rdn to chse ldrs over 2f out: wknd fnl f* **9/1**

2433 **8** *nk* **Chandrayaan**[28] 5050 5-8-12 **50** (v) SimonPearce(3) 3 38
(John E Long) *in tch and pushed along 1/2-way: nvr rchd ldrs and wknd over 1f out* **12/1**

5004 **9** *¾* **Compton Target (IRE)**[11] 5660 3-8-11 **50** (t) LiamKeniry 12 35
(Milton Bradley) *chsd ldrs: chal wl over 2f put: wknd sn after* **22/1**

0-00 **10** *1 ¾* **Hertford Street**[16] 5481 4-8-3 **45** JoeyHaynes(7) 7 26
(Eric Wheeler) *bmpd s: outpcd most of way* **40/1**

5060 **11** *8* **Belleau (IRE)**[15] 5508 4-8-12 **52** CharlesBishop(5) 8 12
(Matt Sheppard) *early pce: bhd fr 1/2-way* **7/1**[3]

040- **12** *5* **Dickens Rules (IRE)**[296] 7432 3-9-6 **59** (vt[1]) SeanQuinlan 10
(David Bridgwater) *led tl hdd & wknd qckly over 2f out* **25/1**

1m 23.75s (0.55) **Going Correction** +0.075s/f (Good)
WFA 3 from 4yo+ 4lb 12 Ran SP% **119.4**
Speed ratings (Par 101): **99,98,96,94,93 91,90,90,89,87 78,72**
toteswingers:1&2 £8.30, 2&3 £2.90, 1&3 £5.50 CSF £22.02 CT £66.50 TOTE £7.40: £2.00, £1.60, £1.80; EX 41.70.
Owner P J Stephenson **Bred** T H Rossiter **Trained** Newmarket, Suffolk
■ Stewards' Enquiry : Rosie Jessop two-day ban; used whip above permitted level (21st-22nd Sept).
Joey Haynes two-day ban; used whip above permitted level (21st-22nd Sept).

FOCUS
Division two of this low-grade handicap was run 1.94 seconds quicker than the first division, with those racing near the stands' rail seeming to hold an advantage.

6001 BET365 APPRENTICE (S) STKS 7f 16y
4:30 (4:31) (Class 6) 3-4-Y-O £1,617 (£481; £240; £120) Stalls High

Form RPR

5205 **1** **Offbeat Safaris (IRE)**[11] 5653 4-9-0 76 DarrenEgan(3) 9 62
(Ronald Harris) *in tch: hdwy 2f out: rdn: edgd lft and styd on fnl f to ld fnl 120yds: drvn out* **6/4**[1]

4216 **2** *¾* **Kashmiri Star**[26] 5130 3-8-10 59 BrendanPowell(3) 3 59
(Michael Quinn) *led 1f: styd trcking ldrs: led again over 2f out: rdn over 1f out: hdd and nt qckn fnl 120yds* **3/1**[2]

0024 **3** *nk* **Barista (IRE)**[11] 5658 4-9-0 65 CharlesBishop(3) 2 59
(Brian Forsey) *chsd ldrs: led over 3f out: hdd over 2f out: styd chsng ldr tl ins fnl f: no ex fnl 75yds* **6/1**

0005 **4** *5* **Swift Act**[11] 5658 3-8-8 65 (p) KierenFox 10 40
(Ronald Harris) *in rr: hdwy to chse ldrs wl over 2f out: btn sn after* **11/2**[3]

1000 **5** *½* **Lucifers Shadow (IRE)**[18] 5427 3-8-13 52 ThomasBrown(5) 5 48
(Sylvester Kirk) *early spd: bhd 1/2-way: mod prog u.p fnl f* **14/1**

0 **6** *3 ¾* **Bov La Raconteuse**[29] 4992 3-8-3 0 PhilipPrince(5) 4 28
(Carroll Gray) *chsd ldrs: rdn 3f out: wknd 2f out* **100/1**

3210 **7** *2 ¼* **Emma Jean (IRE)**[109] 2351 3-8-6 56 (bt) DanaZamecnikova(7) 6 27
(Frank Sheridan) *t.k.h: chsd ldrs over 4f* **22/1**

600- **8** *hd* **Almirah**[322] 6993 3-8-8 0 MatthewCosham 7 22
(David Evans) *early pce: bhd fr 1/2-way* **16/1**

65 **9** *¾* **Blackamoor Harry**[7] 5805 3-8-10 0 AmyScott(3) 8 25
(Richard Ford) *s.i.s: sn in tch: chsd ldrs and rdn 1/2-way: wknd over 2f out* **50/1**

10 *25* **Smiley Miley (IRE)**[9] 4-8-9 0 JamesRogers(3) 1
(David Lewis) *slowly away: sn rcvrd to ld after 1f: hdd & wknd over 3f out* **100/1**

1m 24.11s (0.91) **Going Correction** +0.075s/f (Good)
WFA 3 from 4yo 4lb 10 Ran SP% **115.5**
Speed ratings (Par 101): **97,96,95,90,89 85,82,82,81,53**
toteswingers:1&2 £1.90, 2&3 £3.30, 1&3 £2.90 CSF £5.75 TOTE £3.20: £1.30, £1.10, £1.80; EX 6.70.The winner was bought in.
Owner Mrs Jan Adams **Bred** Baywood Partnership **Trained** Earlswood, Monmouths

FOCUS
A poor, uncompetitive seller run at a messy pace with the front three pulling clear late on.

6002 CASINO AT BET365 H'CAP 6f 16y
5:05 (5:05) (Class 6) (0-60,60) 3-Y-O+ £1,617 (£481; £240; £120) Stalls High

Form RPR

0540 **1** **Gypsy Rider**[22] 5263 3-8-11 **52** CathyGannon 12 61
(Bryn Palling) *disp ld: edgd lft fr over 2f out and styd upsides: rdn over 1f out: slt advantage ins fnl f: drvn out* **18/1**

1232 **2** *¾* **Two Turtle Doves (IRE)**[11] 5681 6-9-6 **59** SeanQuinlan 1 66
(Michael Mullineaux) *disp ld tl narrow advantage appr fnl 2f: styd hrd pressed tl narrowly hdd ins fnl f: no ex fnl 50yds* **9/2**[1]

6102 **3** *hd* **George Fenton**[17] 5446 3-8-12 **53** (p) RobbieFitzpatrick 7 59+
(Richard Guest) *in tch drvn and hdwy fr 2f out: styd on wl fnl f to take 3rd clsng stages: nt rch ldng duo* **6/1**[2]

6005 **4** *½* **Hatta Stream (IRE)**[8] 5775 6-9-4 **60** SimonPearce(3) 11 65
(Lydia Pearce) *chsd ldrs: rdn over 2f out: styd on wl fnl f: no imp on ldrs cl home* **7/1**[3]

0400 **5** *hd* **Forty Proof (IRE)**[2] 5937 4-8-6 **48** (t) MatthewCosham(3) 9 52
(David Evans) *in rr: drvn over 2f out: hdwy fnl f: kpt on wl clsng stages* **16/1**

3000 **6** *¾* **Huzzah (IRE)**[29] 4993 7-9-4 **57** MichaelStainton 15 59
(Paul Howling) *in rr: drvn and hdwy over 1f out: kpt on wl clsng stages* **17/2**

4400 **6** *dht* **Olynard (IRE)**[32] 4865 6-8-10 **49** SeanLevey 3 51
(Michael Mullineaux) *chsd ldrs: rdn over 2f out: kpt on same pce fnl f* **8/1**

0044 **8** *1 ¾* **Secret Queen**[7] 5808 5-8-8 **54** JoshBaudains(7) 2 50
(Martin Hill) *chsd ldrs: rdn over 2f out: outpcd ins fnl f* **12/1**

0050 **9** *½* **Reginald Claude**[12] 5625 4-8-8 **54** (v) ThomasBrown(7) 17 49
(Mark Usher) *chsd ldrs: rdn over 2f out: wknd ins fnl f* **14/1**

0103 **10** *½* **Flaxen Lake**[11] 5660 5-8-13 **52** (p) ChrisCatlin 8 45
(Milton Bradley) *disp ld 3f: sn rdn: one pce fnl 2f* **12/1**

3202 **11** *½* **Botanist**[11] 5659 5-8-11 **50** (be) LiamKeniry 6 41
(Milton Bradley) *t.k.h in rr: rdn over 2f out: kpt on fnl f but nvr gng pce to get into contention* **12/1**

1643 **12** *1 ¼* **Maria Montez**[26] 5122 3-9-3 **58** MartinLane 13 45
(J W Hills) *outpcd most of way* **20/1**

0-00 **13** *2* **C'Mon You Irons (IRE)**[225] 312 7-8-11 **50** FergusSweeney 10 31
(Mark Hoad) *disp ld over 3f* **33/1**

0-30 **14** *1 ¾* **Pull The Pin (IRE)**[20] 5335 3-9-0 **55** SamHitchcott 16 30
(William Kinsey) *chsd ldrs 4f* **18/1**

0-60 **15** *18* **Ionwy**[191] 739 3-8-12 **53** (p) DavidProbert 4
(Derek Haydn Jones) *in rr: faltered and wknd rapidly over 2f out* **40/1**

1m 12.07s (0.07) **Going Correction** +0.075s/f (Good)
WFA 3 from 4yo+ 2lb 15 Ran SP% **122.9**
Speed ratings (Par 101): **102,101,100,100,99 98,98,96,95,95 94,92,90,87,63**
toteswingers:1&2 £17.10, 2&3 £4.30, 1&3 £12.50 CSF £96.71 CT £577.08 TOTE £19.00: £4.70, £1.90, £2.10; EX 82.40.
Owner Wayne Devine **Bred** Mr And Mrs L Baker **Trained** Tredodridge, Vale Of Glamorgan
■ Stewards' Enquiry : Simon Pearce four-day ban; used whip above permitted level (21st-24th Sept).

FOCUS
A modest if competitive handicap run at a fair pace. The field split into two groups from the off before converging 3f out. The action took place down the far side with the front two home always up with the pace.
Gypsy Rider Official explanation: jockey said saddle slipped.

6003 BET365.COM H'CAP 5f 16y
5:35 (5:36) (Class 6) (0-55,57) 3-Y-O+ £1,617 (£481; £240; £120) Stalls High

Form RPR

0555 **1** **Portrush Storm**[11] 5660 7-8-5 **46** oh1 CharlesBishop(5) 13 58
(Ray Peacock) *racd alone stands' side: mde all: drvn clr fnl f: unchal* **20/1**

5016 **2** *2 ¾* **Whiskey Junction**[7] 5791 8-9-5 **55** SeanLevey 7 57
(Michael Quinn) *chsd ldrs towards centre of crse: styd on for 2nd fnl f but no ch w wnr* **6/1**[3]

3060 **3** *1 ½* **Dotty Darroch**[13] 5590 4-9-1 **51** (p) MichaelO'Connell 6 48
(Robin Bastiman) *chsd ldrs towards centre crse: styd on same pce for 3rd fnl f* **7/1**

6150 **4** *2 ¾* **Simple Rhythm**[10] 5719 6-9-0 **50** (p) DaraghO'Donohoe 2 37
(John Ryan) *racd towards r side and sn chsng wnr: no imp fr 2f out: wknd fnl f* **25/1**

60 **5** *1* **Fiona's Spirit (IRE)**[10] 5719 5-8-7 **46** oh1 MarkCoumbe(3) 4 29
(Daniel Mark Loughnane) *in rr and racd towards far side: rdn 3f out: styd on fnl f: nvr a threat* **50/1**

2516 **6** *1* **Mucky Molly**[52] 4196 4-9-2 **52** KirstyMilczarek 1 31
(Olivia Maylam) *chsd ldrs towards far side to 2f out* **9/2**[2]

6525 **7** *½* **Loyal Royal (IRE)**[67] 3707 9-8-11 **47** (bt) LiamKeniry 8 25
(Milton Bradley) *sn chsng ldrs in centre crse: wknd ins fnl 2f* **12/1**

0431 **8** *nk* **Spic 'n Span**[4] 5876 7-9-5 **55** 6ex (b) KierenFox 10 32
(Ronald Harris) *plunged s: sn rcvrd and chsd ldrs towards centre: wknd ins fnl 2f* **11/4**[1]

4003 **9** *1 ¼* **Miserere Mei (IRE)**[14] 5542 3-8-9 **46** oh1 (e) RobbieFitzpatrick 5 18
(Richard Guest) *racd towards far side: rdn and sme hdwy 2f out: sn wknd* **25/1**

0301 **10** *8* **Copper Falls**[11] 5701 3-8-13 **57** 6ex JoshBaudains(7) 12
(Brendan Powell) *v.s.a: no ch after* **20/1**

59.67s (0.37) **Going Correction** +0.075s/f (Good)
WFA 3 from 4yo+ 1lb 10 Ran SP% **98.5**
Speed ratings (Par 101): **100,95,93,88,87 85,84,84,82,69**
toteswingers:1&2 £10.10, 2&3 £7.10, 1&3 £13.10 CSF £91.31 CT £598.39 TOTE £20.50: £4.10, £1.60, £1.70; EX 99.70.
Owner John P Evitt **Bred** Northmore Stud **Trained** Kyre Park, Worcs
■ First Rebellion was withdrawn (9/2, unruly in stalls). Deduct 15p in the £ under R4.

FOCUS
Another low quality if competitive sprint. It was run at a decent pace and the winner made all under a well-judged ride.
Copper Falls Official explanation: jockey said filly was slowly away.

6004 BET365 H'CAP 1m 4f 23y
6:05 (6:07) (Class 5) (0-70,70) 3-Y-O+ £2,264 (£673; £336; £168) Stalls Low

Form RPR

3430 **1** **Switched Off**[18] 5430 7-9-12 **70** SeanLevey 6 78
(Ed McMahon) *in tch: drvn along 4f out: hdwy 2f out: pushed along ins fnl f: chal fnl 75yds: led cl home* **13/2**[3]

201 **2** *½* **Pandorica**[11] 5653 4-9-8 **66** (p) MartinLane 1 73
(Bernard Llewellyn) *chsd ldrs: chal 2f out: led over 1f out: hdd and outpcd cl home* **12/1**

4013 **3** *2* **Eightfold**[45] 4440 3-8-8 **61** (t) DaraghO'Donohoe 3 67+
(Seamus Durack) *hld up in rr: hdwy on ins but nt clr run fr 3f out tl swtchd lft ins fnl 2f but plenty to do: str run whn swtchd rt ins fnl f: then swtchd lft: fin wl to take 3rd: unlucky* **8/1**

004- **4** *1* **Swift Chap**[16] 2915 6-9-3 **61** (p) SamHitchcott 13 63
(Philip Hobbs) *chsd ldrs: rdn 3f out: styd on fr over 1f out: one pce fnl f* **18/1**

0252 **5** *¾* **April Ciel**[6] 5816 3-8-9 **67** DarrenEgan(5) 10 68
(Ronald Harris) *led: rdn over 2f out: hdd over 1f out: wknd ins fnl f* **2/1**[1]

5400 **6** *2 ¼* **Shannon Spree**[16] 3443 3-8-7 **65** NathanSweeney(5) 8 63
(Alan King) *chsd ldrs: rdn and lost position 5f out: styd on fr over 2f out: nvr a threat* **20/1**

-150 **7** *½* **Dove Cottage (IRE)**[43] 4491 10-9-4 **62** FergusSweeney 14 59
(Stuart Kittow) *chsd ldr and rdn 4f out: wknd fr 2f out* **16/1**

1453 **8** *2* **Tinkerbell Will**[20] 5351 5-8-12 **56** oh6 RichardThomas 2 50
(John E Long) *in rr: rdn and sme hdwy over 3f out: no prog fnl 2f* **25/1**

9 *¾* **The Lemonpie (GER)**[11] 7-8-11 **60** (t) BrendanPowell(5) 7 52
(Brendan Powell) *in rr: drvn over 4f out: nvr gng pce to rch ldrs* **10/1**

610 **10** *1 ½* **Transfer**[15] 5507 7-9-1 **62** MarkCoumbe(3) 5 52
(Richard Price) *chsd ldrs 9f* **20/1**

5254 **11** *4* **Broadway Babe (IRE)**[25] 5154 3-8-9 **62** (bt[1]) CathyGannon 9 46
(Harry Dunlop) *s.i.s: towards rr most of way* **8/1**

6363 **12** *1 ½* **Korngold**[63] 3814 4-9-5 **63** (b) ChrisCatlin 4 44
(John Dunlop) *chsd ldr early: wknd 5f out* **6/1**[2]

2m 37.35s (-1.65) **Going Correction** -0.05s/f (Good)
WFA 3 from 4yo+ 9lb 12 Ran SP% **124.5**
Speed ratings (Par 103): **103,102,101,100,100 98,98,97,96,95 92,91**
toteswingers:1&2 £12.30, 2&3 £18.80, 1&3 £13.60 CSF £83.80 CT £649.21 TOTE £9.40: £2.70, £3.20, £2.20; EX 103.00.
Owner P Nicholls & D Mead **Bred** Mrs Byron Paterson **Trained** Lichfield, Staffs

FOCUS
An ordinary handicap run at a sound pace with the winner coming through late to win under an excellent ride.
Eightfold Official explanation: jockey said gelding was denied a clear run.
T/Plt: £21.80 to a £1 stake. Pool: £59,179.49 - 1980.38 winning units. T/Qpdt: £3.40 to a £1 stake. Pool: £5,373.64 - 1138.85 winning units. ST

5962 HAYDOCK (L-H)
Friday, September 7

OFFICIAL GOING: Good to firm (9.3)
Wind: Light, half against Weather: Cloudy

6005 BETFRED SHARPLES GROUP H'CAP (DIV I) 5f
2:00 (2:00) (Class 4) (0-85,84) 3-Y-O+ **£4,204** (£1,251; £625; £312) **Stalls** Centre

Form RPR
6000 **1** **Hamoody (USA)**[38] 4690 8-8-13 **76** FrannyNorton 9 85
(David Nicholls) *in tch: rdn 2f out: led over 1f out: sn hung lft: a doing enough cl home: hld on wl* **9/2**[1]
5000 **2** ½ **Another Wise Kid (IRE)**[29] 4998 4-9-2 **79** MickyFenton 10 86
(Paul Midgley) *hld up: rdn and hdwy over 1f out: edgd lft and r.o ins fnl f: clsd on wnr towards fin* **10/1**
0100 **3** ¾ **Bop It**[13] 5603 3-9-2 **80** TomEaves 5 84
(Bryan Smart) *midfield: hdwy whn n.m.r over 1f out: kpt on ins fnl f: nt pce of wnr* **11/1**
5030 **4** 1½ **Courageous (IRE)**[16] 5486 6-9-0 **77** RichardKingscote 2 76
(Milton Bradley) *hld up: rdn and hdwy over 1f out: chsd ldrs ins fnl f: kpt on same pce fnl 100yds* **5/1**[2]
31-1 **5** ½ **Queen Grace (IRE)**[35] 4770 5-9-0 **84** ShaneGray(7) 1 81
(Michael J Browne, Ire) *missed break: hld up: rdn and swtchd rt over 1f out: kpt on and hung lft ins fnl f: nvr able to mount serious chal* **9/2**[1]
4420 **6** 1½ **Jinker Noble**[15] 5502 3-8-11 **75** (b) JohnFahy 4 67
(Clive Cox) *broke wl: gd spd and t.k.h: rdn and chalng over 1f out: wknd ins fnl f* **18/1**
3014 **7** ½ **Whozthecat (IRE)**[13] 5584 5-9-0 **82** (b) NeilFarley(5) 6 72
(Declan Carroll) *prom: rdn over 2f out: wknd over 1f out* **5/1**[2]
00 **8** *hd* **Quality Art (USA)**[20] 5343 4-9-0 **80** (t) DeclanCannon(3) 7 69
(Richard Guest) *dwlt: sn led: rdn and hdd over 1f out: wknd ins fnl f* **25/1**
350 **9** *hd* **Diman Waters (IRE)**[22] 5272 5-8-10 **73** KellyHarrison 3 61
(Eric Alston) *hld up: effrt 2f out: nvr quite able to chal: wknd over 1f out* **13/2**[3]
00-0 **10** 7 **Invincible Force (IRE)**[104] 2488 8-8-12 **75** (b) PaulMulrennan 8 38
(Paul Green) *broke wl: led: sn hdd: remained handy tl lost pl over 3f out: bhd fnl 2f* **50/1**

59.91s (-0.89) **Going Correction** -0.075s/f (Good)
WFA 3 from 4yo+ 1lb **10** Ran SP% **111.5**
Speed ratings (Par 105): **104,103,102,99,98 96,95,95,94,83**
toteswingers:1&2 £10.20, 2&3 £12.30, 1&3 £10.40 CSF £47.36 CT £463.67 TOTE £6.10: £1.90, £3.60, £4.30; EX 56.60 TRIFECTA Not won..
Owner Hart Inn I **Bred** Ragged Mountain Farm **Trained** Sessay, N Yorks

FOCUS
All races on Inner Home straight and races on Round course increased in distance by 1yd. The ground had dried out a little from that advertised and was officially good to firm all over. The inside sprint track was being used and the runners came up the centre. The leaders may have gone off too quick in this fair sprint handicap, as none of the trio that disputed the early lead figured in the finish.

6006 BETFRED SHARPLES GROUP H'CAP (DIV II) 5f
2:30 (2:30) (Class 4) (0-85,83) 3-Y-O+ **£4,204** (£1,251; £625; £312) **Stalls** Centre

Form RPR
1520 **1** **Liberty Island (IRE)**[6] 5821 7-8-13 **75** (p) DuranFentiman 9 84
(Ian Semple) *dipped s: hld up in tch: led wl over 1f out: sn edgd lft: r.o: kpt up to work towards fin* **13/2**[2]
0-00 **2** ½ **Thirteen Shivers**[27] 5110 4-9-4 **80** JamesSullivan 5 87
(Michael Easterby) *s.i.s: hld up: swtchd lft and hdwy under 2f out: tk 2nd wl ins fnl f: r.o but nt quite able to chal wnr* **15/2**[3]
U103 **3** 2 **Beau Mistral (IRE)**[20] 5337 3-9-6 **83** PaulMulrennan 3 83
(Paul Green) *hld up: rdn and hdwy to chse ldrs over 1f out: kpt on same pce fnl 100yds* **8/1**
2416 **4** 1¾ **Rylee Mooch**[20] 5362 4-8-12 **77** (e) DeclanCannon(3) 2 71
(Richard Guest) *prom: led over 2f out: rdn and hdd wl over 1f out: no ex fnl 100yds* **8/1**
006 **5** 2 **Perfect Blossom**[11] 5663 5-9-1 **80** DaleSwift(3) 1 67
(Ian McInnes) *prom: rdn and chalng over 1f out: wknd fnl 150yds* **13/2**[2]
1315 **6** *nk* **Triple Dream**[26] 5123 7-9-0 **76** (tp) HayleyTurner 8 61
(Milton Bradley) *prom: outpcd over 2f out: no imp after* **16/1**
1211 **7** ¾ **Sunny Side Up (IRE)**[22] 5272 3-8-5 **75** LauraBarry(7) 4 58
(Richard Fahey) *prom: rdn 2f out: wkng whn edgd lft over 1f out* **9/4**[1]
1010 **8** 2 **Dispol Grand (IRE)**[18] 5412 6-8-13 **75** RussKennemore 7 51
(Paul Midgley) *towards rr: sn pushed along: wl outpcd fnl 2f* **16/1**
4010 **9** ¾ **Lost In Paris (IRE)**[18] 5412 6-9-3 **79** (p) DanielTudhope 6 52
(Tim Easterby) *led: rdn and hdd over 2f out: wknd over 1f out* **8/1**

1m 0.39s (-0.41) **Going Correction** -0.075s/f (Good)
WFA 3 from 4yo+ 1lb **9** Ran SP% **114.3**
Speed ratings (Par 105): **100,99,96,93,90 89,88,85,83**
toteswingers:1&2 £13.90, 2&3 £15.20, 1&3 £9.50 CSF £53.67 CT £398.09 TOTE £7.80: £3.00, £3.10, £2.80; EX 68.40 Trifecta £397.40 Part won. Pool £537.05 - 0.30 winning units..
Owner Highland Racing 6 & Robert Reid **Bred** Pat Grogan **Trained** Carluke, S Lanarks

FOCUS
There were five in a line across the track disputing the early advantage, but the first three home weren't amongst them. The winning time was nearly half a second slower than the first division.
Beau Mistral(IRE) Official explanation: jockey said gelding hung left-handed.

6007 BETFRED IT MEDICS BRITISH STALLION STUDS EBF MAIDEN FILLIES' STKS 6f
3:05 (3:07) (Class 5) 2-Y-O **£3,234** (£962; £481; £240) **Stalls** Centre

Form RPR
1 **Red Turban** 2-9-0 0 TedDurcan 10 74+
(Jeremy Noseda) *s.s: hld up: hdwy wl over 1f out: r.o ins fnl f: led post* **8/1**
3 **2** *shd* **Sky Garden**[81] 3223 2-9-0 0 AdamBeschizza 9 74
(William Haggas) *led: rdn and edgd lft over 1f out: hrd pressed ins fnl f: hdd post* **5/2**[1]
3 *shd* **Mystery Bet (IRE)** 2-9-0 0 TonyHamilton 8 74+
(Richard Fahey) *chsd ldrs: rdn over 1f out: chalng wl ins fnl f: r.o cl home* **7/1**
6 **4** 2½ **Valais Girl**[20] 5357 2-9-0 0 HayleyTurner 7 66
(Marcus Tregoning) *prom: rdn and nt qckn over 1f out: kpt on same pce ins fnl f* **11/2**[3]
4 **5** *hd* **Layla's Oasis**[28] 5040 2-9-0 0 GrahamLee 6 66
(Kevin Ryan) *a.p: rdn and chalng fr over 1f out: no ex fnl 75yds* **9/2**[2]
0 **6** 1¾ **Jubilee Dancer**[70] 3560 2-9-0 0 TomEaves 5 60
(Geoffrey Oldroyd) *chsd ldrs: rdn and ev ch over 1f out: wknd fnl 100yds* **50/1**
06 **7** 5 **Misty Secret (IRE)**[29] 5016 2-9-0 0 GrahamGibbons 3 45
(Jane Chapple-Hyam) *midfield: rdn and outpcd over 1f out: n.d* **66/1**
8 3½ **Roanne (USA)** 2-9-0 0 AdamKirby 4 35
(Clive Cox) *towards rr: pushed along 1/2-way: wknd over 1f out* **11/1**
0 **9** 3¾ **Shes Ellie**[15] 5503 2-9-0 0 RussKennemore 2 24
(John O'Shea) *a in rr: toiling fnl 2f: nvr on terms* **100/1**
3 **10** *nk* **Bell'Arte (IRE)**[11] 5668 2-9-0 0 FrannyNorton 1 23
(Mark Johnston) *in tch tl pushed along and wknd over 2f out* **11/2**[3]

1m 14.54s (0.74) **Going Correction** -0.075s/f (Good) **10** Ran SP% **113.9**
Speed ratings (Par 92): **92,91,91,88,88 85,79,74,69,69**
toteswingers:1&2 £7.60, 2&3 £8.20, 1&3 £8.00 CSF £27.61 TOTE £12.10: £4.10, £1.60, £3.10; EX 37.20 Trifecta £533.30 Part won. Pool £720.71 - 0.10 winning units..
Owner Cheveley Park Stud **Bred** Cheveley Park Stud Ltd **Trained** Newmarket, Suffolk

FOCUS
A fair fillies' maiden, but this was a race affected by the draw. The bigger group of six raced up the centre, but a group of four came up the stands' rail and they were the first four home. The time was modest and the form is rated slightly negatively.

NOTEBOOK
Red Turban was settled last of the four against the stands' rail early and although she didn't have a lot of room to play with when delivered with her effort over a furlong from home, she proved game and poked her nose in front right on the line. Closely related to three winners at up to 1m including a stakes winner in the US, she looks a filly with a future. (op 14-1)
Sky Garden was a disappointing favourite when only third of five on her Windsor debut in June, but was on faster ground here and she travelled powerfully at the head of the stands' side quartet. However, she started to hang away to her left from over a furlong out, giving her rivals a chance, and she lost the race on the line. She should get off the mark before too long, but this was a chance missed. (op 11-4 tchd 3-1)
Mystery Bet(IRE) tracked the pace towards the nearside and kept on gamely under pressure to go down narrowly in a three-way photo. A 36,000euros half-sister to eight winners including the very useful Firebet, she shouldn't let the family down. (op 8-1)
Valais Girl showed some ability when sixth of ten on last month's Newbury debut and ran on again here after getting outpaced coming to the last furlong, though she was racing on the favoured flank as things turned out. (op 9-2)
Layla's Oasis led the centre-field group and did best of those to take that route. She is bred to need much further than this on the dam's side of her pedigree. (op 4-1)
Jubilee Dancer showed nothing on her Doncaster debut in June and did better here, pulling well clear of the rest. (op 80-1 tchd 100-1)
Roanne(USA) Official explanation: jockey said filly ran green.
Shes Ellie Official explanation: jockey said filly hung left-handed.
Bell'Arte(IRE) showed plenty of promise when third on last month's Newcastle debut over 7f, but this shorter trip wasn't sure to suit which is backed up by the dam's side of her pedigree. However, the way she dropped out here was too bad to be true. (op 5-1 tchd 13-2)

6008 BETFRED BOLTON LADS & GIRLS CLUB H'CAP (DIV I) 6f
3:35 (3:36) (Class 4) (0-85,85) 3-Y-O+ **£4,204** (£1,251; £625; £312) **Stalls** Centre

Form RPR
6003 **1** **Escape To Glory (USA)**[14] 5557 4-9-7 **85** HayleyTurner 8 93
(Mikael Magnusson) *midfield: rdn over 2f out: hdwy over 1f out: r.o ins fnl f: led post* **14/1**
046U **2** *nse* **Pea Shooter**[25] 5167 3-9-1 **81** AmyRyan 11 89
(Kevin Ryan) *led: rdn over 1f out: hrd pressed ins fnl f: hdd post* **10/1**
0022 **3** *hd* **Sound Amigo (IRE)**[27] 5110 4-9-5 **83** BarryMcHugh 7 90
(Ollie Pears) *midfield: rdn and hdwy over 1f out: r.o cl home: jst hld* **14/1**
0505 **4** ¾ **New Leyf (IRE)**[50] 4252 6-9-2 **83** (b) DaleSwift(3) 13 88
(Colin Teague) *in rr: rdn 2f out: hdwy over 1f out: r.o u.p ins fnl f: nt quite get to ldrs* **28/1**
6000 **5** ¾ **Rasaman (IRE)**[20] 5343 8-9-1 **79** GrahamLee 14 81
(Jim Goldie) *hld up: rdn and swtchd rt over 1f out: prog ins fnl f: gng on at fin* **12/1**
311 **6** *nse* **Willbeme**[27] 5093 4-8-11 **75** AdamBeschizza 6 77
(Neville Bycroft) *racd keenly: a.p: rdn over 1f out: no ex fnl 50yds* **9/4**[1]
4246 **7** ½ **Mister Musicmaster**[13] 5582 3-8-11 **77** JamesMillman 16 78
(Rod Millman) *hld up in midfield racing on stands' side: rdn over 1f out: kpt on ins fnl f: nt rch ldrs* **33/1**
2040 **8** 1½ **Apollo D'Negro (IRE)**[3] 5906 4-9-0 **78** (b) AdamKirby 12 74
(Clive Cox) *midfield: pushed along over 2f out: no imp over 1f out: one pce ins fnl f* **8/1**[2]
3410 **9** *hd* **Caranbola**[20] 5368 6-9-5 **83** PaulMulrennan 15 78
(Mel Brittain) *prom: rdn 2f out: kpt on same pce ins fnl f* **12/1**
001 **10** 1 **Forest Edge (IRE)**[26] 5130 3-8-5 **71** (b) AndreaAtzeni 9 63
(David Evans) *dwlt: midfield: pushed along 1/2-way: no imp over 1f out: no ex ins fnl f* **28/1**
1210 **11** *nse* **Dark Castle**[111] 2276 3-9-3 **83** TedDurcan 5 75
(Sylvester Kirk) *midfield: rdn over 1f out: no imp fnl f* **9/1**[3]
4146 **12** *hd* **Julius Geezer (IRE)**[14] 5557 4-9-5 **83** RichardKingscote 4 74
(Tom Dascombe) *prom: rdn over 2f out: wknd over 1f out* **9/1**[3]
3245 **13** ½ **Roker Park (IRE)**[14] 5539 7-9-6 **84** [1] DanielTudhope 10 74
(David O'Meara) *in rr: rdn over 2f out: nvr able to get on terms w ldrs* **12/1**
3015 **14** 4 **Orbit The Moon (IRE)**[14] 5557 4-9-2 **80** (tp) TomEaves 1 57
(Michael Dods) *dwlt: prom: rdn over 1f out: sn wknd* **20/1**
0444 **15** 12 **Coolminx (IRE)**[29] 4998 5-9-3 **81** TonyHamilton 2 19
(Richard Fahey) *a in rr and outpcd: eased whn btn fnl f* **25/1**
0-00 **16** 3¾ **Pelmanism**[14] 5539 5-8-13 **77** GrahamGibbons 3
(Brian Ellison) *a outpcd in rr: nvr on terms: eased whn btn fnl f* **20/1**

1m 12.49s (-1.31) **Going Correction** -0.075s/f (Good)
WFA 3 from 4yo+ 2lb **16** Ran SP% **130.6**
Speed ratings (Par 105): **105,104,104,103,102 102,101,99,99,98 98,98,97,92,76 71**
toteswingers:1&2 £3.20, 2&3 £32.60, 1&3 £65.20 CSF £144.15 CT £2042.44 TOTE £12.40: £3.60, £2.80, £4.20, £7.20; EX 139.80 Trifecta £459.10 Part won. Pool £620.44 - 0.63 winning units..
Owner Eastwind Racing Ltd And Martha Trussell **Bred** Castleton Lyons **Trained** Upper Lambourn, Berks

FOCUS
A competitive sprint handicap run at a decent pace. Despite the evidence of the earlier races, only one horse raced up the stands' rail.

6009 BETFRED BOLTON LADS & GIRLS CLUB H'CAP (DIV II) 6f
4:10 (4:11) (Class 4) (0-85,85) 3-Y-0+ £4,204 (£1,251; £625; £312) Stalls Centre

Form RPR
1010 1 **Trade Secret**[20] 5368 5-9-6 **84** PaulMulrennan 2 92
(Mel Brittain) *a.p: rdn over 1f out: r.o to ld ins fnl f: hld on wl cl home* **25/1**
0554 2 *shd* **Green Park (IRE)**[11] 5674 9-8-6 77 (b) LukeLeadbitter(7) 7 85
(Declan Carroll) *racd keenly: hld up: swtchd lft and hdwy over 1f out: r.o ins fnl f: jst hld* **20/1**
3100 3 *3/4* **Hopes N Dreams (IRE)**[57] 4000 4-9-0 **78** AmyRyan 9 84+
(Kevin Ryan) *s.i.s: in rr: nt clr run whn swtchd lft off rail and hdwy 1f out: r.o cl home* **10/1**
1402 4 *hd* **Piddie's Power**[21] 5326 5-9-0 **83** NeilFarley(5) 1 88
(Ed McMahon) *hld up: hdwy on outer over 2f out: ch 1f out: styd on u.p ins fnl f: one pce towards fin* **16/1**
-010 5 *3/4* **Jade**[15] 5520 4-9-0 **81** LeeTopliss(3) 12 84
(Ollie Pears) *in tch: effrt to chse ldrs over 1f out: styd on same pce fnl 75yds* **15/2**[3]
0002 6 *nk* **Barkston Ash**[14] 5539 4-8-6 **75** DarylByrne(5) 15 77
(Eric Alston) *dwlt: chsd ldrs: pushed along 2f out: nt qckn over 1f out: kpt on ins fnl f: one pce towards fin* **9/1**
0210 7 *1* **Decision By One**[26] 5128 3-9-5 **85** (t) RichardKingscote 8 83
(Tom Dascombe) *led: rdn over 1f out: hdd ins fnl f: fdd fnl 50yds* **6/1**[2]
0503 8 *1 1/4* **Mon Brav**[27] 5110 5-9-0 **78** GrahamGibbons 10 76+
(Brian Ellison) *s.i.s: sn pushed along in rr: hdwy u.p over 1f out: n.m.r and hmpd whn no real imp fnl 100yds: sn eased* **15/2**[3]
2200 9 *1/2* **The Nifty Fox**[14] 5539 8-9-2 **80** (p) JamesSullivan 4 73
(Tim Easterby) *midfield: effrt 2f out: ch 1f out: wknd ins fnl 100yds* **40/1**
-000 10 *1 1/4* **Sunraider (IRE)**[125] 1844 5-9-5 **83** MickyFenton 3 72
(Paul Midgley) *prom tl rdn and wknd over 1f out* **12/1**
6061 11 *3/4* **Lucky Numbers (IRE)**[34] 4829 6-9-3 **81** DanielTudhope 6 67
(David O'Meara) *hld up: midfield 1/2-way: rdn over 1f out: no imp* **8/1**
6501 12 *nk* **Chiswick Bey (IRE)**[29] 4998 4-9-5 **83** AdamBeschizza 14 68
(Peter Salmon) *chsd ldrs: pushed along 1/2-way: lost pl 2f out: btn whn hmpd over 1f out* **7/2**[1]
3400 13 *5* **Rothesay Chancer**[49] 4286 4-8-9 **73** GrahamLee 13 42
(Jim Goldie) *hld up: pushed along over 1f out: lft bhd fnl f* **16/1**

1m 13.2s (-0.60) **Going Correction** -0.075s/f (Good)
WFA 3 from 4yo+ 2lb **13** Ran SP% **120.7**
Speed ratings (Par 105): **101,100,99,99,98 98,96,95,94,92 91,91,84**
toteswingers:1&2 £40.00, 2&3 £75.50, 1&3 £56.60 CSF £447.73 CT £5419.78 TOTE £27.10: £8.20, £5.90, £4.50; EX 576.10 TRIFECTA Not won..
Owner Mel Brittain **Bred** Whitsbury Manor Stud **Trained** Warthill, N Yorks

FOCUS
This time the entire field made for the nearside and a couple didn't enjoy much room as a result. The winning time was 0.71 seconds slower than division one.
Trade Secret Official explanation: trainer said regarding apparent improvement in form that the gelding is a poor mover and required treatment after his last race adding, the better ground today helped.
Mon Brav ◆ Official explanation: jockey said gelding was denied a clear run.
Lucky Numbers(IRE) Official explanation: jockey said gelding ran too freely.

6010 BETFRED BOLTON ATLANTIC ROWING CHALLENGE H'CAP 1m 2f 95y
4:45 (4:45) (Class 3) (0-95,95) 3-Y-0+ £11,320 (£3,368; £1,683; £841) Stalls High

Form RPR
2662 1 **Prussian**[6] 5835 3-9-0 **90** FrannyNorton 2 100+
(Mark Johnston) *prom: rdn whn trying to get out and nt clr run under 2f out: plld out jst over 1f out: r.o to ld ins fnl f: sn in command: readily* **11/8**[1]
6415 2 *2* **Proud Chieftain**[20] 5364 4-9-6 **89** DarryllHolland 1 95
(Clifford Lines) *hld up in midfield: niggled along 5f out: rdn 2f out: effrt whn nt clr run over 1f out: sn styd on: nt clr run and plld off rail fnl 150yds: wnt 2nd cl home: no ch w wnr* **14/1**
5206 3 *nk* **Beaufort Twelve**[22] 5273 3-9-0 **90** HarryBentley 3 95
(William Jarvis) *hld up: rdn and hdwy over 2f out: ev ch ins fnl f: sn outpcd by wnr: lost 2nd cl home* **8/1**[3]
1-30 4 *1 1/4* **War Singer (USA)**[38] 4689 5-9-4 **87** (t) HayleyTurner 4 90
(David Pipe) *hld up in rr: rdn and hdwy over 1f out: styd on ins fnl f: nt rch ldrs* **14/1**
3130 5 *2 1/2* **Madam Macie (IRE)**[35] 4761 5-9-11 **94** DanielTudhope 10 92
(David O'Meara) *led: rdn over 1f out: hdd ins fnl f: fdd fnl 100yds* **28/1**
5324 6 *nk* **Jack Who's He (IRE)**[20] 5365 3-8-11 **87** GrahamGibbons 11 85
(David Evans) *midfield: hdwy over 3f out: rdn to chse ldrs 2f out: one pce fnl 100yds: sn eased* **8/1**[3]
2003 7 *1* **Boogie Shoes**[27] 5075 4-9-12 **95** AndreaAtzeni 13 91
(Roger Varian) *prom: rdn 2f out: ev ch over 1f out: wknd ins fnl 100yds* **6/1**[2]
1310 8 *1 1/4* **Silvery Moon (IRE)**[14] 5558 5-9-8 **91** TedDurcan 12 84
(Tim Easterby) *racd keenly: in tch: lost pl over 3f out: outpcd over 2f out: n.d after* **8/1**[3]
1116 9 *3 1/2* **Gala Casino Star (IRE)**[32] 4879 7-8-13 **89** (v) JordanNason(7) 8 76
(Geoffrey Harker) *hld up: hdwy after 2f: chsd ldrs 7f out: wknd over 2f out* **20/1**
0161 10 *12* **Full Toss**[14] 5546 6-8-13 **82** GrahamLee 7 46
(Jim Goldie) *hld up: pushed along 4f out: struggling over 2f out: wl btn* **16/1**

2m 8.25s (-7.25) **Going Correction** -0.55s/f (Hard) course record
WFA 3 from 4yo+ 7lb **10** Ran SP% **117.2**
Speed ratings (Par 107): **107,105,105,104,102 101,101,100,97,87**
toteswingers:1&2 £5.70, 2&3 £16.00, 1&3 £4.40 CSF £23.47 CT £119.84 TOTE £2.90: £1.10, £4.10, £2.60; EX 24.00 Trifecta £231.20 Pool £899.84 - 2.88 winning units..
Owner Sheikh Hamdan Bin Mohammed Al Maktoum **Bred** Darley **Trained** Middleham Moor, N Yorks
■ Stewards' Enquiry : Andrea Atzeni three-day ban; careless riding (21st-23rd Sept).

FOCUS
A decent handicap.
NOTEBOOK
Prussian would have had another 6lb to carry had her narrow defeat in a hot handicap at Sandown six days earlier been taken into account. Although she was always close to the pace, those that backed her would have been very worried up the home straight as she was travelling well but stuck in a pocket. However, she managed to force her way out over a furlong from home and, once seeing daylight, quickened up impressively. She is obviously brave, but things will be much harder for her off her new mark. (op 6-4 tchd 13-8)
Proud Chieftain, still 5lb higher than when scoring at Newmarket two starts back, also endured traffic problems on the inside at various stages up the home straight and by the time he got out the winner had gone. He was very much second-best here and remains capable off this mark when things go more his way.
Beaufort Twelve launched a dangerous-looking challenge down the wide outside over 2f from home, but his effort eventually flattened out. He had run particularly poorly in his two previous starts, so this was an improvement. (op 9-1)
War Singer(USA) ◆ hadn't set the world alight on the Flat or over hurdles since arriving from France, but this was a good effort, especially as he tried to come from last place and ideally needs softer ground than this. He is worth keeping in mind under more suitable conditions. (op 16-1)
Madam Macie(IRE), still 7lb higher than when winning at Hamilton in June, was trying this trip for the first time but, having set the pace until entering the last furlong, gave the impression she didn't stay. (op 25-1 tchd 33-1 in places)
Jack Who's He(IRE), beaten 15 times since winning his first two starts as a juvenile, ran poorly in his only previous try over this far and again didn't get home after being produced wide over 3f out, though he had raced keenly early. His rider reported that the gelding hung right on the bend. Official explanation: jockey said gelding hung right on bend. (op 10-1 tchd 11-1)
Boogie Shoes, with the hood back on, was up to this trip for the first time in over a year but was always in a good position and didn't see his race out. (op 11-2 tchd 5-1)
Silvery Moon(IRE) Official explanation: trainer said gelding was unsuited by going (good to firm).
Full Toss Official explanation: trainer said gelding was never travelling.

6011 BETFRED CLYDE & CO H'CAP 7f
5:15 (5:17) (Class 3) (0-90,90) 3-Y-0+ £6,792 (£2,021; £1,010; £505) Stalls Low

Form RPR
0012 1 **Zacynthus (IRE)**[22] 5269 4-9-1 **87** PatrickHills(3) 1 96+
(Luca Cumani) *hld up: hdwy 1f out: r.o to ld ins fnl 100yds: a doing enough cl home* **6/1**[2]
3012 2 *nk* **Able Master (IRE)**[21] 5314 6-9-6 **89** DanielTudhope 11 97
(David O'Meara) *led: rdn and hdd over 1f out: continued to chal: regained ld briefly wl ins fnl f: r.o u.p: hld cl home* **7/1**[3]
2100 3 *hd* **Cape Classic (IRE)**[27] 5102 4-9-5 **88** AdamBeschizza 14 95
(William Haggas) *hld up in rr: hdwy on outer over 2f out: rdr dropped rein 1f out: r.o ins fnl f: hld cl home* **15/2**
1002 4 *1* **Mr David (USA)**[9] 5746 5-8-13 **87** (b) LeonnaMayor(5) 6 92
(Jamie Osborne) *chsd ldrs: rdn to ld over 1f out: hdd wl ins fnl f: no ex cl home* **14/1**
2610 5 *1* **Lord Aeryn (IRE)**[15] 5517 5-9-6 **89** TonyHamilton 4 91
(Richard Fahey) *in tch: effrt over 1f out: styd on same pce ins fnl f* **9/1**
402 6 *3 1/2* **Nasri**[20] 5356 6-9-5 **88** RichardKingscote 8 81
(Milton Bradley) *prom: rdn to chal 2f out: wknd over 1f out* **5/1**[1]
4000 7 *2 1/4* **Klynch**[20] 5370 6-9-4 **90** (b) DaleSwift(3) 2 77
(Ruth Carr) *prom: rdn over 2f out: wknd over 1f out* **20/1**
0500 8 *2 3/4* **Rakaan (IRE)**[13] 5572 5-9-5 **88** (p) GrahamLee 5 67
(Jamie Osborne) *hld up in midfield: effrt 2f out: btn over 1f out* **10/1**
3001 9 *hd* **Wannabe King**[24] 5186 6-8-13 **89** (v) JordanNason(7) 12 68
(Geoffrey Harker) *in tch: rdn over 2f out: wknd over 1f out* **9/1**
0020 10 *2* **Victoire De Lyphar (IRE)**[34] 4802 5-9-7 **90** JamesSullivan 13 63
(Ruth Carr) *hld up: rdn 2f out: hung lft over 1f out: nvr on terms* **16/1**
-440 11 *shd* **Yair Hill (IRE)**[41] 4609 4-9-2 **85** TedDurcan 10 58+
(John Dunlop) *hld up in rr: swtchd lft whn nt clr run wl over 1f out: n.m.r whn hmpd jst over 1f out: sn eased* **15/2**
5366 12 *3 1/4* **Beckermet (IRE)**[20] 5368 10-8-12 **86** ShaneBKelly(5) 9 50
(Ruth Carr) *in tch: rdn over 2f out: sn wknd* **25/1**

1m 26.27s (-4.43) **Going Correction** -0.55s/f (Hard) course record **12** Ran SP% **117.2**
Speed ratings (Par 107): **103,102,102,101,100 96,93,90,90,87 87,84**
toteswingers:1&2 £5.00, 2&3 £10.90, 1&3 £11.90 CSF £47.14 CT £326.50 TOTE £7.40: £2.90, £2.30, £2.90; EX 38.90 Trifecta £230.40 Pool £570.01 - 1.83 winning units..
Owner Mrs June Bownes **Bred** Keatly Overseas Ltd **Trained** Newmarket, Suffolk

FOCUS
A decent handicap.
NOTEBOOK
Zacynthus(IRE) has certainly regained his form since joining Luca Cumani and made it two wins and a second for his new yard despite being put up another 2lb following his narrow Newmarket defeat. Given a well-judged ride by Patrick Hills, who dropped him out at the start from the inside draw, he made his ground gradually and forced his head in front close to the line. Another rise in his mark beckons, but in his current mood another success must be a possibility. (op 9-1)
Able Master(IRE), back on a more favourable surface, tried to make every yard and proved game when tackled, but the winner's late challenge proved one too many. (op 11-2 tchd 5-1)
Cape Classic(IRE), twice disappointing since winning off 5lb lower at Windsor in May, ran a fine race here as he had little choice but to be dropped right out from the outside stall and was forced to make his effort on the wide outside in the straight. He did extremely well to finish so close and, although he has gained all three of his wins over 6f, he definitely stays this trip. (op 11-2)
Mr David(USA) is off a 7lb higher mark than when winning at Newmarket last month, but is due another 1lb rise following his decent effort at Kempton nine days earlier. He moved up to hold every chance coming to the last furlong, but was then run out of the places. (tchd 16-1)
Lord Aeryn(IRE), back down in trip, didn't have much room to play with when trying to burrow his way up the rail inside the last furlong, but didn't look unlucky. (op 11-1)
Nasri was only narrowly beaten stepped back up to this trip at Newbury last time and was up 2lb, but he didn't see his race out under pressure this time after racing handily. (op 7-1)
Yair Hill(IRE), lightly raced this season, endured a nightmare passage from over a furlong out and was eventually eased right off. This can be ignored. Official explanation: jockey said gelding was denied a clear run. (op 8-1 tchd 7-1)

6012 BETFRED 20-20 TECHNOLOGIES LTD H'CAP 1m 6f
5:45 (5:45) (Class 4) (0-85,84) 3-Y-0+ £4,204 (£1,251; £625; £312) Stalls Low

Form RPR
6-24 1 **Huff And Puff**[14] 5554 5-9-9 **79** PaulMulrennan 6 88
(Amanda Perrett) *led: hdd after 2f: remained handy: upsides fr 4f out: led ent fnl f: kpt on wl towards fin* **11/2**[3]
1345 2 *1* **Winner's Wish**[27] 5106 3-9-1 **82** GrahamLee 4 90
(Jeremy Noseda) *prom: led after 2f: hdd after 5f: remained handy: regained ld over 4f out: sn pressed: hdd ent fnl f: no ex towards fin* **4/1**[1]
2056 3 *5* **Bridle Belle**[14] 5558 4-9-10 **83** LeeTopliss(3) 11 84
(Richard Fahey) *hld up: hdwy to chse ldrs over 3f out: rdn over 2f out: one pce and no imp fr over 1f out* **9/2**[2]
1341 4 *3 1/4* **Venegazzu (IRE)**[24] 5211 3-8-12 **79** (v) TomEaves 2 75
(Peter Chapple-Hyam) *hld up: hdwy on inner over 3f out: chsd ldrs over 2f out: no ex over 1f out* **13/2**
3544 5 *3 3/4* **Blazing Field**[29] 5002 4-9-9 **79** AdamKirby 10 70
(Clive Cox) *prom: lost pl after 3f: pushed along and outpcd over 4f out: plugged on wout threatening fr over 1f out* **10/1**
545/ 6 *7* **Atlantic Tiger (IRE)**[653] 7553 5-9-4 **77** (t) RachaelGreen(3) 3 58
(Anthony Honeyball) *s.i.s: plld hrd: trckd ldrs: led after 5f: hdd over 4f out: wknd qckly* **11/1**

2216 **7** ½ **Daring Indian**[20] 5344 4-9-6 **76**.................................. RichardKingscote 1 57
(Tom Dascombe) *trckd ldrs: rdn over 2f out: wknd over 1f out* **13/2**
P603 **8** ¾ **Kazbow (IRE)**[24] 5200 6-9-11 **84**............................(p) LucyAlexander(3) 5 64
(Chris Grant) *prom tl wknd qckly over 3f out* **18/1**
2-00 **9** 3 ½ **Downhiller (IRE)**[16] 5491 7-9-10 **80**.................................... TedDurcan 7 55
(John Dunlop) *hld up: rdn over 3f out: no imp: lft bhd over 1f out* **7/1**
2m 55.2s (-6.80) **Going Correction** -0.55s/f (Hard) course record
WFA 3 from 4yo+ 11lb **9** Ran SP% **115.4**
Speed ratings (Par 105): **97,96,93,91,89 85,85,84,82**
toteswingers:1&2 £5.80, 2&3 £3.70, 1&3 £6.40 CSF £27.77 CT £107.39 TOTE £8.10: £2.60, £1.50, £2.40; EX 36.40 Trifecta £286.50 Part won. Pool £387.29 - 0.60 winning units..
Owner A D Spence **Bred** Sir Eric Parker **Trained** Pulborough, W Sussex
FOCUS
A fair staying handicap.
Daring Indian Official explanation: trainer said gelding had no more to give.
Downhiller(IRE) Official explanation: jockey said gelding had no more to give.
T/Jkpt: Not won. T/Plt: £2,525.10 to a £1 stake. Pool: £9,3397.59 - 27.00 winning units. T/Qpdt: £137.60 to a £1 stake. Pool: £7,075.32 - 38.05 winning units. DO

5968 KEMPTON (A.W) (R-H)
Friday, September 7

OFFICIAL GOING: Standard
Wind: Light, across Weather: Very warm early evening

6013 MIDLAND FACILITIES APPRENTICE H'CAP 1m (P)
6:20 (6:20) (Class 4) (0-85,80) 3-Y-O+ **£4,075** (£1,212; £606; £303) **Stalls** Low

Form RPR
1332 **1** **Forgive**[18] 5420 3-8-13 **79**.................................. WilliamTwiston-Davies(5) 7 90
(Richard Hannon) *trckd ldr: led over 2f out: rdn and edgd rt over 1f out: styd on wl* **8/1**
5013 **2** 1 ½ **Angelic Upstart (IRE)**[16] 5480 4-9-5 **80**.................... DanielMuscutt(5) 4 87+
(Andrew Balding) *sn in 5th: rdn and prog 2f out: chsd wnr over 1f out: styd on but no imp* **5/2**[2]
0062 **3** 1 ¾ **Roayh (USA)**[13] 5595 4-9-7 **80**.................................(p) AntiocoMurgia(3) 5 83
(Saeed Bin Suroor) *racd wd: sn chsd ldng trio: rdn and nt qckn 2f out: tk 3rd 1f out: styd on same pce after* **7/4**[1]
0503 **4** 1 ¾ **Final Drive (IRE)**[9] 5752 6-9-7 **80**...........................(tp) TobyAtkinson(3) 1 79+
(John Butler) *s.i.s: hld up in last pair: rdn over 2f out: tried to cl 1f out: one pce after* **10/1**
3016 **5** 2 **Junket**[16] 5480 5-9-3 **78**.. RachealKneller(5) 2 72
(Dr Jon Scargill) *hld up in last pair: effrt on inner 2f out: sn no prog and btn* **12/1**
2100 **6** ¾ **Hamis Al Bin (IRE)**[79] 3274 3-9-3 **78**................................ RaulDaSilva 3 71
(Mark Johnston) *trckd ldng pair: effrt to chal 2f out: lost 2nd and wknd over 1f out* **16/1**
4003 **7** 8 **Snow Bay**[18] 5414 6-9-2 **77**....................................... ShirleyTeasdale(5) 6 51
(David Nicholls) *led to over 2f out: wknd qckly over 1f out* **13/2**[3]
1m 37.82s (-1.98) **Going Correction** -0.075s/f (Stan)
WFA 3 from 4yo+ 5lb **7** Ran SP% **112.0**
Speed ratings (Par 105): **106,104,102,101,99 98,90**
toteswingers:1&2 £4.10, 2&3 £2.60, 1&3 £2.10 CSF £27.19 CT £50.39 TOTE £6.40: £3.00, £1.40; EX 27.80 Trifecta £53.30 Pool £343.01 - 4.76 winning units..
Owner Highclere Thoroughbred Racing-Spearmint **Bred** The Athenians And Cheveley Park Stud Ltd **Trained** East Everleigh, Wilts
FOCUS
This apprentice riders' handicap looked more competitive than the market suggested. It was run at an average pace and the form makes sense, the winner building on his latest turf personal best.

6014 LETCHWORTH COURIERS/BRITISH STALLION STUDS EBF MAIDEN STKS 1m (P)
6:50 (6:51) (Class 5) 2-Y-O **£3,234** (£962; £481; £240) **Stalls** Low

Form RPR
3 **1** **Concise**[25] 5162 2-8-12 0.. WilliamBuick 8 81+
(Ed Dunlop) *chsd ldrs: shkn up to go 2nd 2f out: sn clr of rest: clsd grad 1f out: r.o to ld last 75yds* **3/1**[2]
2 1 **Ostaad (IRE)** 2-9-3 0.. FrankieDettori 12 84+
(Saeed Bin Suroor) *racd v wd 1st 3f: led after 2f: gng easily in front after: shkn up over 1f out: hdd and outpcd last 75yds* **4/1**[3]
3 10 **Omnipresent** 2-9-3 0.. RichardMullen 3 61+
(Sir Michael Stoute) *s.i.s: settled in last trio: pushed along 3f out: sme prog and shkn up 2f out: styd on to take modest 3rd nr fin* **10/1**
00 **4** 1 **The Obvious Choice**[20] 5360 2-9-3 0.......................... WilliamCarson 6 58
(Stuart Williams) *led 2f: mostly chsd ldr to 2f out: sn lft bhd and edgd lft: lost 3rd nr fin* **100/1**
5 ¾ **Cast A Vision (USA)** 2-9-3 0.. JimCrowley 11 57+
(Amanda Perrett) *in tch in midfield: pushed along sn after 1/2-way: sme prog fr 2f out: one pce fnl f* **14/1**
6 ½ **Tally Stick (USA)** 2-9-3 0.. AhmedAjtebi 2 56+
(Mahmood Al Zarooni) *hld up towards rr: gng easily but lost pl jst over 2f out: styd on steadily fnl f wout being knocked abt* **15/2**
7 ½ **Pentagram (USA)** 2-9-3 0.. MickaelBarzalona 9 54
(Mahmood Al Zarooni) *chsd ldrs: pushed along firmly fr 1/2-way: no inroads 2f out: wl hld after* **11/4**[1]
0 **8** 1 **Thomasina**[43] 4507 2-8-12 0.. TadhgO'Shea 13 47
(Denis Coakley) *s.i.s: wl in rr: pushed along over 2f out: modest late prog* **50/1**
000 **9** 1 ½ **Inherited**[7] 5797 2-9-3 0.. LukeMorris 7 52+
(Sir Mark Prescott Bt) *towards rr: shuffled along fr over 2f out: nvr on terms: likely to do bttr in time* **80/1**
10 8 **Zain Heart (IRE)** 2-8-9 0.. DominicFox(3) 10 25
(Gerard Butler) *prom: disp 2nd after 2f tl over 2f out: wknd qckly* **20/1**
11 1 **Mutamaiz (IRE)** 2-9-3 0.. MartinDwyer 5 28
(James Tate) *settled in midfield: pushed along sn after 1/2-way: wknd qckly 2f out* **25/1**
12 8 **Burma Days (USA)** 2-9-3 0... JamesDoyle 1 10
(Sylvester Kirk) *s.i.s: a last: wl bhd fnl 2f: t.o* **33/1**
1m 38.94s (-0.86) **Going Correction** -0.075s/f (Stan) **12** Ran SP% **114.9**
Speed ratings (Par 95): **101,100,90,89,88 87,87,86,84,76 75,67**
toteswingers: 1&2 £3.30, 2&3 £7.60, 1&3 £7.00 CSF £13.93 TOTE £2.70: £1.10, £2.70, £3.40; EX 18.50 Trifecta £32.10 Pool £603.63 - 13.89 winning units..
Owner St Albans Bloodstock LLP & Cliveden Stud **Bred** Cliveden Stud Ltd **Trained** Newmarket, Suffolk
FOCUS
An interesting juvenile maiden. There was a fair pace on and two promising sorts went clear in the home straight. A number are capable of better than the bare form.

NOTEBOOK
Concise was a big eyecatcher on her Lingfield debut last month and she confirmed that promise with a likeable success. Well backed, she got a lovely trip through the race from her decent draw but it looked as if she may have allowed the runner-up too much rope a furlong out. However, she knuckled down professionally and really looked better the further she went over this extra furlong. She has speed in her pedigree, but is clearly going to want a stiffer test as she matures and she's well thought of by connections. A crack at a valuable sales race on turf now looks on the cards. (op 5-2 tchd 10-3)
Ostaad(IRE) ◆ very nearly made a winning debut and deserves credit as he did plenty early on from his poor draw. This Derby entrant looks to have a bright future and shouldn't be long in gaining compensation. (op 5-1 tchd 11-2)
Omnipresent fared best of those coming from off the pace and this was an encouraging introduction considering he ran so green. This half-brother to prolific AW winner Stand Guard looks a stayer in the making and better is expected next time out. (tchd 9-1)
The Obvious Choice, stepping up from 6f, travelled an awful lot better than a 100-1 shot and posted his best effort on this switch to Polytrack. He was well suited by racing handily, but is obviously going the right way and 7f is probably his trip at present.
Cast A Vision(USA) showed ability on his debut, but he too may be best dropping back a furlong in the short term. (op 12-1)
Tally Stick(USA) ◆, Godolphin's third string on jockey bookings, endured a troubled passage and it's fair to say he would have finished a fair bit closer under stronger handling. He should go well on his next assignment. (op 13-2 tchd 6-1)
Pentagram(USA) cost $750,000 and was the shortest of the Godolphin trio in the market. He was off the bridle a long way out, though, and looked very one paced. (op 3-1 tchd 5-2 and 10-3 in a place)

6015 EVENTMASTERS.CO.UK/BRITISH STALLION STUDS E B F MAIDEN STKS 6f (P)
7:20 (7:21) (Class 5) 2-Y-O **£3,234** (£962; £481; £240) **Stalls** Low

Form RPR
04 **1** **Inka Surprise (IRE)**[20] 5360 2-9-3 0................................ JimCrowley 11 80+
(Ralph Beckett) *racd wd: sn prom: led over 2f out: shkn up and clr over 1f out: styd on wl* **9/4**[1]
2 2 **Pedro Serrano (IRE)** 2-9-3 0.. DaneO'Neill 6 76+
(Henry Candy) *hld up in midfield: pushed along and prog 2f out: nt clr run briefly 1f out: styd on wl to take 2nd nr fin* **11/1**
3 ½ **Invincible Warrior (IRE)** 2-9-3 0................................ TadhgO'Shea 9 72+
(Brian Meehan) *in tch in midfield: rdn and prog on outer over 2f out: chsd wnr over 1f out: no real imp: lost 2nd nr fin* **14/1**
3 **4** nk **Noble Deed**[20] 5360 2-9-3 0.. LiamJones 1 71
(William Haggas) *prom: rdn 2f out: kpt on same pce after: nvr able to chal* **11/4**[2]
03 **5** 1 ¼ **Gravitational (IRE)**[25] 5176 2-9-3 0................................ JamesDoyle 3 67
(Ed Dunlop) *towards rr: pushed along over 2f out: styd on steadily fr over 1f out: nrest at fin* **14/1**
0 **6** hd **Desert Command**[23] 5235 2-9-3 0................................ JimmyFortune 4 66
(Andrew Balding) *mde most to over 2f out: chsd wnr to over 1f out: one pce and lost pls nr fin* **12/1**
00 **7** 1 ¼ **Admirals Walk (IRE)**[8] 5765 2-8-12 0......................... LeeNewnes(5) 12 63+
(Sylvester Kirk) *settled in detached last: pushed along over 2f out: styd on quite takingly fr over 1f out* **50/1**
30 **8** 1 **Echo Of Silence (FR)**[42] 4539 2-9-3 0....................... JamieSpencer 10 60
(Marco Botti) *prom: pushed along over 2f out: losing pl whn checked briefly over 1f out: fdd* **9/1**
9 1 **Surge Ahead (IRE)** 2-9-3 0.. WilliamBuick 2 57
(Ed Walker) *rn green in midfield: lost pl sn after 1/2-way: no prog fnl 2f* **8/1**[3]
06 **10** ½ **East Texas Red (IRE)**[7] 5793 2-9-3 0.................................. PatDobbs 7 55
(Richard Hannon) *taken steadily in last pair: pushed along over 2f out: kpt on at one pce and no real prog: nt totally disgracd* **25/1**
0 **11** 9 **Bapak Besar (CAN)**[100] 2594 2-9-3 0.............................. PhillipMakin 5 28
(Kevin Ryan) *w ldr to 1/2-way: wknd rapidly over 2f out: t.o* **16/1**
1m 12.96s (-0.14) **Going Correction** -0.075s/f (Stan) **11** Ran SP% **119.6**
Speed ratings (Par 95): **97,94,93,93,91 91,89,88,87,86 74**
toteswingers:1&2 £8.30, 2&3 £36.30, 1&3 £10.50 CSF £29.09 TOTE £3.10: £1.40, £3.50, £5.80; EX 38.40 TRIFECTA Not won..
Owner McDonagh Murphy And Nixon **Bred** J McGrath **Trained** Kimpton, Hants
FOCUS
There should be numerous winners coming out of this juvenile sprint maiden. The balance of those down the field helps with the level.
NOTEBOOK
Inka Surprise(IRE), on his AW debut, was again well backed and this time completed the task in convincing fashion. He got to the leaders travelling powerfully and soon settled the issue once asked for an effort. His success is made more meritorious as he saw plenty of daylight from his wide draw and he's clearly a nice horse in the making. This looks his trip for now, but he ought to stay a little further next year. (op 7-2 tchd 2-1)
Pedro Serrano(IRE) ◆ attracted support for this racecourse debut and would have given the winner a little more to think about had he enjoyed a clear passage in the home straight. Another furlong should be right up his street and he can go one better next time out. (op 10-1)
Invincible Warrior(IRE) responded to pressure from the 2f marker and turned in a promising debut effort. He's bred to be useful at least and is well up to winning a maiden. (op 20-1)
Noble Deed finished one place ahead of the winner on his Newmarket debut 20 days earlier, but despite having the plum draw on this switch to Polytrack he proved easy to back. He lacked an immediate turn of foot, but again ran encouragingly and did his best work towards the finish. (op 5-2 tchd 3-1)
Gravitational(IRE) had to come wide from off the pace in the home straight and kept on steadily. Nurseries are now an option. (op 12-1)
Desert Command went from the front and wasn't disgraced, but is now looking more of one for nurseries.
Surge Ahead(IRE), whose dam was a 7f Listed winner, proved too green to do himself full justice. (op 5-1)

6016 EVENTMASTERS.CO.UK NURSERY 6f (P)
7:50 (7:50) (Class 5) (0-70,70) 2-Y-O **£2,264** (£673; £252; £252) **Stalls** Low

Form RPR
4P42 **1** **Cappadocia (IRE)**[16] 5484 2-9-5 **68**................................ MartinHarley 11 70
(Mick Channon) *racd wd in midfield: rdn over 2f out and no prog: gd hdwy on outer 1f out: str run to ld nr fin* **8/1**
5621 **2** ½ **Meet Me Halfway**[9] 5749 2-9-7 **70** 6ex.............................. GeorgeBaker 5 70
(Chris Wall) *cl up: wnt 2nd 2f out on inner: rdn to ld 1f out: styd on but hdd nr fin* **7/1**
223 **3** ½ **Deepest Blue**[65] 3748 2-9-7 **70**.. JamesDoyle 8 69
(Jamie Osborne) *led: drvn and hdd 1f out: styd on same pce* **11/2**[2]
0524 **3** dht **Autumn Shadow (IRE)**[18] 5411 2-8-9 **58**....................... FrederikTylicki 9 57
(Richard Fahey) *prom: rdn over 2f out: nt qckn over 1f out: styd on fnl f: nvr quite able to chal* **16/1**

620 **5** *nk* **Zain Spirit (USA)**[33] 4837 2-9-6 **69** LukeMorris 6 67
(Gerard Butler) *trckd ldrs: effrt and cl up 2f out: rdn and nt qckn over 1f out: styd on* **11/1**

3032 **6** *½* **Wellingrove (IRE)**[10] 5702 2-9-3 **69** RaulDaSilva(3) 2 66
(Mark Johnston) *hld up in midfield: rdn and prog on inner wl over 1f out: styd on but nvr pce to chal* **5/2**[1]

0426 **7** *2* **Lisa's Legacy**[10] 5702 2-9-6 **69** PatDobbs 12 59
(Richard Hannon) *racd wd towards rr: pushed along bef 1/2-way: no prog and struggling over 2f out: n.d after* **8/1**

602 **8** *nse* **Palladius**[38] 4681 2-9-2 **65** PhillipMakin 7 55
(Kevin Ryan) *t.k.h: pressed ldr to 2f out: wknd qckly fnl f* **10/1**

355 **9** *2 ¼* **Bay Laurel (IRE)**[44] 4463 2-9-4 **67** JimCrowley 1 50
(Harry Dunlop) *settled in rr: off the pce and reminder 2f out: no prog* **13/2**[3]

005 **10** *1* **Stormy Times (IRE)**[18] 5423 2-7-13 **53** RachealKneller(5) 4 33
(Mark Usher) *taken down early: a in rr: rdn and no prog over 1f out* **50/1**

0406 **11** *4* **Our Golden Girl**[16] 5475 2-8-4 **53** DavidProbert 10 21
(Mark Usher) *mostly in last: struggling bef 1/2-way* **40/1**

506 **12** *½* **Double Jeopardy**[15] 5511 2-7-12 **47** oh2 (b) KieranO'Neill 3 14
(Dr Jon Scargill) *a towards rr: rdn and hanging over 2f out: looked reluctant after* **66/1**

1m 13.48s (0.38) **Going Correction** -0.075s/f (Stan) 12 Ran SP% **121.2**
Speed ratings (Par 95): **94,93,92,92,92 91,88,88,85,84 79,78**
TOTE: PL: £1.00 (Deepest Blue), £2.80 (Autumn Shadow); Tricast: £173.32 (DB), £452.08 (AS) toteswingers:1&2 £12.00, 2&3 £4.70 (DB), 1&3 £4.40 (DB), 2&3 £13.20 (AS), 1&3 £18.00 (AS) CSF £64.14 CT £452.08 TOTE £9.30: £3.50, £2.20, £2.80; EX 92.90 TRIFECTA Not won..
Owner Dark Horse Racing Partnership Slx **Bred** Rathasker Stud **Trained** West Ilsley, Berks

FOCUS
A competitive nursery for the grade. It was run at a fair pace and saw a host of chances. Routine, sound form.

NOTEBOOK
Cappadocia(IRE) made amends for failing to justify favouritism on his previous outing and shed his maiden tag at the eighth attempt. He hit a flat spot after initially being asked for his effort, but responded strongly half a furlong out and won a touch cosily. This was a decent effort from stall 11 and he has scope to rate a little higher. (op 12-1)
Meet Me Halfway made a bold bid to defy her penalty for scoring at Wolverhampton nine days earlier and is clearly an improving 2-y-o. She's really benefitted for a switch to Polytrack since going handicapping, but is bred to make her mark on turf. (op 13-2 tchd 6-1)
Deepest Blue, returning from a 65-day break, hit the front passing 2f out and posted another sound effort in defeat on this switch to the AW. He sets the level. (op 20-1)
Autumn Shadow(IRE) saw out the return to this extra furlong well on her AW debut and should be up to winning a small nursery. (op 20-1)
Zain Spirit(USA) ran better again returned to Polytrack and has begun life in nurseries on a workable mark. (op 12-1 tchd 14-1)
Wellingrove(IRE) just lost out at Epsom ten days earlier and was off the same mark back on Polytrack. He ultimately found the drop back in trip against him, though. (op 11-4 tchd 9-4)

6017 EVENTMASTERS.CO.UK/IRISH STALLION FARMS E B F FILLIES' CONDITIONS STKS 7f (P)

8:20 (8:20) (Class 3) 2-Y-O **£5,602** (£1,677; £838; £419; £209) **Stalls** Low

Form RPR

3 **1** **Talent**[20] 5357 2-8-12 0 JimCrowley 3 82+
(Ralph Beckett) *trckd ldr: led 2f out: sn rdn: hrd pressed fnl f: hung lft and bmpd runner-up nr fin* **6/4**[1]

2 *nk* **Hanzada (USA)** 2-8-12 0 WilliamBuick 4 81+
(Ed Dunlop) *cl up in 4th: effrt 2f out: sustained chal fnl f: stl trying whn bmpd nr fin* **7/1**

11 **3** *1* **Queen Aggie (IRE)**[6] 5828 2-9-7 77 PJMcDonald 6 87
(David Evans) *led: set stdy pce for 4f: shkn up and hdd 2f out: styd pressing tl one pce last 150yds* **13/8**[2]

533 **4** *2 ¼* **Rainbow Beauty**[1] 5977 2-8-12 0 LukeMorris 2 72
(Gerard Butler) *trckd ldng pair: effrt on inner over 2f out: outpcd over 1f out* **5/1**[3]

0 **5** *6* **Afro**[30] 4946 2-8-12 0 DaneO'Neill 5 56
(Peter Hedger) *slowly away: a last: lft bhd over 2f out* **50/1**

1m 28.95s (2.95) **Going Correction** -0.075s/f (Stan) 5 Ran SP% **109.2**
Speed ratings (Par 96): **80,79,78,75,69**
CSF £11.79 TOTE £2.90: £1.20, £4.70; EX 13.20.
Owner J L Rowsell & M H Dixon **Bred** Ashbrittle Stud & M H Dixon **Trained** Kimpton, Hants
■ Stewards' Enquiry : Jim Crowley caution; carless riding.

FOCUS
A decent little 2-y-o conditions event for fillies. The winner progressed from her nice debut.

NOTEBOOK
Talent showed the clear benefit of her debut experience at Newbury 20 days earlier and, very well backed, ran out a gutsy winner on this switch to Polytrack. The extra furlong proved up her street and there was plenty to like about her attitude in fending off the runner-up, although she did bump into that rival near the finish. She's bred to stay middle distances and rates a promising filly. (op 7-4)
Hanzada(USA) ◆, a US-bred 225,000gns purchase, improved to throw down a strong challenge to the winner and wasn't helped when that rival lent into him, especially considering it was her debut outing. This was a very pleasing introduction and she's well up to gaining compensation in the coming weeks. (op 9-1)
Queen Aggie(IRE) posted a solid effort under a positive ride back on Polytrack and is developing into a tough performer. She was conceding 9lb to the first pair, who both look decent, and remains on an upwards curve. (op 6-4)
Rainbow Beauty was placed in an above average fillies' maiden at Salisbury the previous day. She felt the pinch in between the final 2f and really the run looked to come too soon as she ran a little below her previous level. (op 9-2)

6018 D & G CONSULTANCY SERVICES H'CAP 1m 3f (P)

8:50 (8:50) (Class 3) (0-95,95) 3-Y-O+
£6,411 (£1,919; £959; £479; £239; £120) **Stalls** Low

Form RPR

-204 **1** **Roxy Flyer (IRE)**[13] 5593 5-9-12 **95** PatDobbs 8 106
(Amanda Perrett) *trckd ldng trio: produced to dispute ld over 1f out: urged along and fnd enough to ld nr fin* **16/1**

0552 **2** *nk* **Trader Jack**[12] 5626 3-8-13 **90** JamesDoyle 9 100
(Roger Charlton) *trckd ldrs in 6th: clsd 2f out: drvn to dispute ld over 1f out: stl upsides 100yds out: nt qckn nr fin* **11/4**[1]

5221 **3** *1 ¼* **Position**[9] 5752 3-9-0 **91** 6ex LukeMorris 4 99
(Sir Mark Prescott Bt) *trckd ldng quartet: rdn and effrt over 2f out: styd on to take 3rd fnl f: no imp on ldng pair* **8/1**[3]

2230 **4** *1* **Assizes**[14] 5540 3-8-10 **90** RaulDaSilva(3) 11 96
(Mark Johnston) *sn trckd ldr fr wd draw: led over 2f out: hdd over 1f out: nt qckn* **11/1**

-406 **5** *nk* **Sandusky**[90] 2932 4-9-6 **89** MickaelBarzalona 2 95
(Mahmood Al Zarooni) *hld up in 7th: prog 2f out: styd on fnl f: nrest at fin but nvr able to threaten* **16/1**

-406 **6** *1 ¼* **Spensley (IRE)**[26] 5129 6-9-5 **88** GeorgeBaker 7 92+
(James Fanshawe) *hld up in last trio in contest where it paid to be handy: prog 2f out: hanging after but styd on wl fnl f: nrest at fin* **12/1**

6036 **7** *1 ¼* **Mountain Range (IRE)**[55] 4103 4-8-13 **82** JimmyFortune 12 83+
(John Dunlop) *s.s: hld up in last: rdn over 2f out: prog over 1f out: styd on: nt disgracd* **8/1**[3]

1140 **8** *1 ¼* **Silent Moment (USA)**[13] 5583 3-8-12 **89** FrankieDettori 13 88
(Saeed Bin Suroor) *qckly away fr wdst draw: led and crossed over: set mod pce after 3f: rdn and hdd over 2f out: wknd over 1f out* **6/1**[2]

1065 **9** *½* **Ramona Chase**[11] 5666 7-9-0 **86** (t) MarkCoumbe(3) 1 84
(Michael Attwater) *hld up in 9th: rdn over 2f out: no prog* **33/1**

110 **10** *1 ½* **Nicholascopernicus (IRE)**[78] 3296 3-8-9 **86** WilliamBuick 10 82
(Ed Walker) *hld up in last trio: rdn over 2f out: one pce and no imp on ldrs over 1f out: fdd fnl f* **6/1**[2]

1/60 **11** *6* **Starluck (IRE)**[47] 4363 7-9-7 **90** (p) LiamKeniry 3 75
(David Arbuthnot) *trckd ldng pair to over 2f out: sn wknd* **20/1**

110- **12** *16* **Cosmic Sun**[482] 2107 6-9-12 **95** FrederikTylicki 6 51
(Richard Fahey) *racd on outer in midfield: wknd 3f out: t.o* **16/1**

2m 18.34s (-3.56) **Going Correction** -0.075s/f (Stan)
WFA 3 from 4yo+ 8lb 12 Ran SP% **118.8**
Speed ratings (Par 107): **109,108,107,107,106 106,105,104,103,102 98,86**
toteswingers:1&2 £17.20, 2&3 £1.50, 1&3 £25.30 CSF £59.89 CT £395.39 TOTE £17.30: £5.50, £1.40, £2.50; EX 85.30 Trifecta £441.10 Part won. Pool £596.18 - 0.50 winning units..
Owner Mr & Mrs F Cotton Mrs S Conway **Bred** Narvick International **Trained** Pulborough, W Sussex

FOCUS
A good, competitive handicap. It was run at an uneven pace, though, and suited those racing handily. The form makes sense amongst the principals.

NOTEBOOK
Roxy Flyer(IRE) gamely mastered the runner-up inside the final furlong and opened her account for the year at the fourth time of asking. She was well beaten on turf the last twice, but went really well on her seasonal return over C&D in July and is clearly very much at home on this surface. Her yard is in decent form and she's a relatively fresh horse for this stage of the season, but doesn't appeal as one for a follow up. (op 20-1)
Trader Jack, back up in trip, proved popular ahead of this AW debut. He was well placed 2f out and looked as though he would do the business, but ultimately the winner was too resolute. His temperament will now come under some scrutiny, although he looked to meet a stronger stayer on the day here.
Position, under a penalty, had his chance back up in trip and ran respectably in defeat. He helps to set the standard. (op 15-2 tchd 7-1)
Assizes, having his first taste of Polytrack, proved his Hamilton flop on soft ground a fortnight earlier to be all wrong and would have probably enjoyed more of a test. He still has just a debut maiden win to his name and is not the easiest to place off a mark of 90, but probably has it in him to win one of these. (op 12-1)
Sandusky was never going to play a serious part off the moderate pace and is better than the bare form. (op 20-1)
Spensley(IRE) won this last year off a 2lb lower mark and has not scored since. He too was undone by the tactical early pace. (op 11-1)
Silent Moment(USA), warm beforehand, got across from her wide draw and was able to boss the race. She found little for pressure, though.
Nicholascopernicus(IRE) was last seen running up to his mark when fancied for the King George V Handicap at Royal Ascot and this was his first outing against elder horses. He proved laboured from off the pace. (tchd 7-1)

6019 EVENTMASTERS.CO.UK H'CAP 2m (P)

9:20 (9:20) (Class 5) (0-75,81) 4-Y-O+ **£2,264** (£673; £336; £168) **Stalls** Low

Form RPR

2001 **1** **Saborido (USA)**[8] 5772 6-9-13 **81** 6ex PatDobbs 7 87
(Amanda Perrett) *led: kicked on over 3f out: drvn over 2f out: hdd jst over 1f out: rallied fnl f: led post* **4/1**[3]

1121 **2** *shd* **Den Maschine**[7] 5809 7-9-8 **76** 6ex JamesDoyle 2 82
(Sean Curran) *cl up in 3rd: rdn over 3f out: sn chsd wnr: drvn and clsd on inner to ld jst over 1f out: kpt on but hdd post* **3/1**[2]

-342 **3** *¾* **Hawridge Star (IRE)**[55] 4096 10-9-7 **75** IanMongan 1 80
(Stuart Kittow) *hld up in last: prog over 2f out: drvn to chse ldng pair over 1f out: clsd grad: nvr quite got there* **13/2**

0045 **4** *1 ¾* **Sandbanks Sizzler (IRE)**[21] 5306 4-9-7 **75** (t) JimCrowley 3 78
(Ralph Beckett) *hld up in tch: rdn over 3f out: prog to chse ldng pair over 2f out: nt qckn and lost 3rd over 1f out: kpt on* **15/8**[1]

5556 **5** *7* **Handles For Forks (IRE)**[15] 5507 4-9-0 **68** MartinHarley 5 63
(Mick Channon) *hld up in tch: shkn up and no rspnse wl over 2f out: sn btn* **10/1**

4223 **6** *3 ¾* **Mollyow (IRE)**[12] 5637 4-7-9 **56** oh2 ShirleyTeasdale(7) 6 46
(Terry Clement) *racd wd: in tch: rdn over 3f out: wknd over 2f out* **20/1**

0216 **7** *15* **Ponte Di Rosa**[70] 3579 4-8-9 **63** LukeMorris 4 35
(Michael Appleby) *chsd wnr to jst over 3f out: sn wknd: eased over 1f out: t.o* **16/1**

3m 29.12s (-0.98) **Going Correction** -0.075s/f (Stan) 7 Ran SP% **112.9**
Speed ratings (Par 103): **99,98,98,97,94 92,84**
toteswingers:1&2 £2.10, 2&3 £1.10, 1&3 £5.30 CSF £15.96 CT £74.19 TOTE £5.50: £2.90, £1.40; EX 12.80 Trifecta £55.60 Pool £379.07 - 5.03 winning units..
Owner Tracey, Cotton, James, Slade **Bred** R D Hubbard And R Masterson **Trained** Pulborough, W Sussex

FOCUS
A modest staying handicap in which the pace wound up a fair way out and there was a cracking finish. The winner is rated back to his old best.
T/Plt: £121.60 to a £1 stake. Pool: £68245.17 - 409.61 winning units. T/Qpdt: £27.10 to a 31 stake. Pool: £7665.2 - 209.05 winning units. JN

5075 ASCOT (R-H)

Saturday, September 8

OFFICIAL GOING: Good to firm (straight course 10.6, round course 9.6)
Wind: Almost nil Weather: Fine, warm

6020 DOWNLOAD THE FREE ASCOT RACECOURSE APP MAIDEN STKS 7f

1:30 (1:32) (Class 4) 2-Y-O **£5,175** (£1,540; £769; £384) **Stalls** High

Form

1 **Snow King (USA)** 2-9-3 0 RobertHavlin 12 85+
(John Gosden) *hld up in nr side gp: smooth prog over 2f out: chal over 1f out: drvn to ld last 100yds: r.o wl* **14/1**

	2	shd	**Telescope (IRE)** 2-9-3 0 ... RichardMullen 14 (Sir Michael Stoute) *t.k.h: hld up in rr: stdy prog 2f out: rdn to chal 1f out: trying hrd whn rdr dropped whip 50yds out: jst failed* **4/1**[1]	84+
26	3	1 1/4	**Vallarta (IRE)**[23] 5275 2-9-3 0 ... MartinHarley 13 (Mick Channon) *trckd nr side ldrs: led gp jst over 2f out and sn overall ldr: drvn and r.o but hdd and outpcd last 100yds* **8/1**	81
	4	3 1/2	**Elkaayed (USA)** 2-9-3 0 ... AndreaAtzeni 6 (Roger Varian) *mde most in centre gp: outpcd by ldng trio fr over 1f out: kpt on* **10/1**	72+
4405	5	nk	**Millers Wharf (IRE)**[24] 5235 2-9-3 77 ... TedDurcan 16 (Richard Hannon) *w ldr nr side and racd against rail: upsides over 2f out: outpcd over 1f out: kpt on* **20/1**	71
	6	1 1/2	**Number One London (IRE)** 2-9-3 0 ... ShaneKelly 5 (Brian Meehan) *trckd ldrs in centre: shkn up over 2f out: rn green and outpcd over 1f out* **40/1**	67+
	7	nk	**Zamoyski** 2-9-3 0 ... EddieAhern 17 (Jeremy Noseda) *s.s: sn in tch on nr side: outpcd over 2f out: rn green after: styd on fnl f* **20/1**	66+
0	8	hd	**Carlarajah**[22] 5319 2-9-3 0 ... AdamKirby 11 (Michael Bell) *pressed nr side ldrs: upsides jst over 2f out: wknd over 1f out* **20/1**	65
04	9	1 1/2	**Empiricist (IRE)**[22] 5304 2-9-3 0 ... GeorgeBaker 15 (Amanda Perrett) *mde most on nr side gp to jst over 2f out: steadily wknd* **7/1**[3]	64
00	10	1 1/2	**Rutherglen**[22] 5303 2-9-3 0 ... PatCosgrave 8 (George Baker) *w ldrs in centre tl wknd wl over 1f out* **100/1**	57
	11	1	**Tawhid** 2-9-3 0 ... MickaelBarzalona 3 (Saeed Bin Suroor) *w ldr in centre: stl upsides whn rn green and wandered 2f out: wknd over 1f out* **8/1**	55
	12	1/2	**Bursledon (IRE)** 2-9-3 0 ... PatDobbs 2 (Richard Hannon) *dwlt: towards rr in centre: shkn up and no prog 2f out: fdd* **20/1**	53
4	13	hd	**Star Of Mayfair (USA)**[34] 4845 2-8-10 0 ... MichaelJMMurphy(7) 9 (Alan Jarvis) *awkward s: racd in centre: nvr bttr than midfield: fdd fnl 2f* **12/1**	53
	14	nk	**Winter Music (IRE)** 2-9-3 0 ... DavidProbert 10 (Andrew Balding) *racd centre: a in rr of gp: limited prog 2f out: sn wknd* **66/1**	52
5	15	2 3/4	**Pinarius (IRE)**[69] 3662 2-9-3 0 ... MichaelHills 7 (Brian Meehan) *lost prom pl in centre gp after 3f: wl in rr after* **33/1**	44
	16	2 1/2	**Meshardal (GER)** 2-9-3 0 ... PaulHanagan 4 (Richard Hannon) *dwlt: hld up in rr of centre gp: no prog 2f out: wknd* **6/1**[2]	38
	17	shd	**King Muro** 2-9-3 0 ... JimmyFortune 1 (Andrew Balding) *chsd ldrs in centre tl wknd over 2f out* **25/1**	37

1m 27.43s (-0.17) **Going Correction** -0.125s/f (Firm) **17** Ran SP% **123.2**
Speed ratings (Par 97): **95,94,93,89,89 87,87,86,85,83 82,81,81,81,77 75,75**
Tote Swingers: 1&2 £16.10, 1&3 £45.00, 2&3 £7.80 CSF £61.31 TOTE £16.20: £4.30, £1.90, £3.00; EX 79.50 Trifecta £394.70 Part won. Pool: £533.46 - 0.10 winning units..
Owner H R H Princess Haya Of Jordan **Bred** Darley **Trained** Newmarket, Suffolk

FOCUS
Rail realignment on Round course added 20yds to 1m 4f races and 10yds to Old Mile. Stands side rail 6yds inside normal position. There were some promising types on show in this opening juvenile maiden and the market suggested it was wide open. With a 17-strong field they unsurprisingly split into two groups early before merging around 3f out and the main action developed down the centre. The principals forged clear in a tight finish. Good starts from the front pair, and the form makes sense.

NOTEBOOK
Snow King(USA) came out on top for his powerful connections. Despite the market suggesting he wasn't fancied for this debut, he moved sweetly through the race and knew his job when asked to knuckle down. He's the first foal of an unraced half-sister to Raven's Pass, who did so well for this yard a few years back, and improvement seems firmly on the cards. He lacks any fancy entries, but looks very useful at least and clearly enjoys quick ground. (op 16-1)
Telescope(IRE) ◆ came in for solid support earlier in the day, but paddock inspection hinted he would come on for the run and he drifted out on course. He came through with a strong late challenge and only just failed, with his rider losing his whip when getting close to the third late on. This son of Galileo is entered in the Racing Post Trophy and should gain compensation next time out. (op 3-1)
Vallarta(IRE) was having his third outing and returned to the sort of form that saw him go close over 6f in a fair Goodwood maiden in July. The return to a quicker surface was more to his liking and he was nicely clear in third, so should be able to pick up a maiden on one of the smaller tracks granted similar ground.
Elkaayed(USA) ◆ is well entered up, but proved easy to back ahead of this debut outing and he shaped as though he needed it. He still showed plenty, however, faring best of those racing nearer the far side and can go close on his next assignment.
Millers Wharf(IRE) set the standard with an official mark of 77. He raced hard against the stands' rail and ran his race, looking at home on the quicker ground.
Number One London(IRE), a 65,000euros purchase, proved too green. He was keeping on nicely late in the day, though, and ought to improve plenty. (op 50-1)
Zamoyski, whose pedigree suggests a mix of speed and stamina, was very easy to back. He did his best work late on after a slow start and it wouldn't surprise to see plenty improvement from him now he has the experience under his belt.

6021 STRATFORD PLACE STUD HYPERION FILLIES' CONDITIONS STKS — 1m (R)
2:00 (2:05) (Class 2) 2-Y-O — **£9,703** (£2,887; £1,443; £721) Stalls Low

Form				RPR
130	1		**Lovely Pass (IRE)**[57] 4064 2-8-12 85 ... (p) AhmedAjtebi 1 (Mahmood Al Zarooni) *trckd ldr: led over 2f out and kicked on: rdn and styd on wl fr over 1f out* **12/1**	94
1	2	2	**Winsili**[28] 5104 2-8-12 0 ... RobertHavlin 5 (John Gosden) *hld up in last trio: effrt on outer whn nudged by rival over 2f out: shkn up over 1f out: styng on whn sltly impeded ins fnl f: tk 2nd last strides: no ch to chal* **9/4**[1]	89+
1	3	hd	**Desert Blossom (IRE)**[15] 5550 2-8-12 0 ... MickaelBarzalona 2 (Mahmood Al Zarooni) *t.k.h: trckd ldng pair: plld out to chse wnr wl over 1f out: hanging lft after: no imp and lost 2nd last strides* **9/4**[1]	89
1	4	1 3/4	**Music Chart (USA)**[15] 5551 2-8-12 0 ... RichardMullen 7 (Mahmood Al Zarooni) *trckd ldng trio: effrt whn edgd lft over 2f out: wandered and nt qckn wl over 1f out: one pce after* **8/1**[3]	85
4515	5	2 3/4	**Mystical Moment**[36] 4763 2-8-12 86 ... PatDobbs 6 (Richard Hannon) *led: set mod pce to 1/2-way: hdd over 2f out: wknd over 1f out* **10/1**	79
1	6	4	**Nice Story (IRE)**[12] 5656 2-8-12 0 ... MartinHarley 3 (Mick Channon) *t.k.h: hld up in last trio: rdn and no prog over 2f out: no ch after* **25/1**	69
213	7	4 1/2	**Fleeting Smile (USA)**[21] 5361 2-8-12 86 ... PaulHanagan 4 (Richard Hannon) *plld hrd: snatched up after 1f: in rr after: wknd over 2f out* **4/1**[2]	59+

1m 43.1s (2.40) **Going Correction** -0.125s/f (Firm) **7** Ran SP% **113.3**
Speed ratings (Par 98): **83,81,80,79,76 72,67**
Tote Swingers: 1&2 £7.30, 1&3 £6.80, 2&3 £1.80 CSF £38.61 TOTE £14.60: £5.80, £1.80; EX 55.90.
Owner Godolphin **Bred** Stowell Park Stud **Trained** Newmarket, Suffolk

FOCUS
This juvenile fillies' conditions event looked a fascinating affair, with four once-raced maiden winners in attendance. It was a steadily run race, though, and the overall form, though useful, looks worth treating with a degree of caution.

NOTEBOOK
Lovely Pass(IRE) ran out a ready winner and showed her true colours again. She arrived with something to prove after looking less than straightforward the last twice, but this was a marked drop in grade and, crucially, she was back on genuinely quick ground. She also raced in first-time cheekpieces and that, along with the extra distance, also has to go down as having helped her cause. Much depends on the headgear continuing to work out and she's clearly a lot better than her current mark of 85 when in the mood. A trip to Meydan in Dubai early next year will probably figure in her plans. (op 14-1)
Winsili, whose trainer/rider took the preceding maiden, won easily on her Newmarket debut last month over 7f. She was ridden to get this stiffer test, but ultimately got too far back off the steady early fractions and certainly wasn't helped when carried left inside the final furlong. There was something to like about the way she made up her ground turning for home and she looks the one to take from the race. (tchd 2-1 and 5-2)
Desert Blossom(IRE) gamely beat a stablemate when off the mark over 7f at Newmarket last month and was her trainer's first string here. She was well placed on the inside, but had to fight to get a run around 2f out and lacked a real turn of foot. She also drifted left late on, not doing the runner-up any favours, and the trip looked to stretch her at this stage. (tchd 2-1 and 5-2)
Music Chart(USA) won the second division of the same maiden stablemate Desert Blossom landed at Newmarket last month, but in a slower time. She had her chance, but still looked green under pressure and failed to see out the extra furlong like the principals. (op 12-1)
Mystical Moment posted a career-best in a competitive nursery at Goodwood off 84 last time out. She went from the front over this longer trip, though, dictating an uneven tempo, and that found out her stamina. (tchd 9-1 and 12-1)
Nice Story(IRE) showed a liking for easy ground when grinding out a 1m Chepstow maiden on her debut 12 days earlier. She faced a much different surface up to this class and, while well beaten off, would have enjoyed a more truly run race. (op 20-1)
Fleeting Smile(USA) gave herself little chance of lasting it out by taking a strong hold out the back and, while she's better than this, she's looking very expensive at $500,000. (op 9-2 tchd 7-2)

6022 ARGENTO WINE NURSERY — 5f
2:35 (2:36) (Class 2) 2-Y-O — **£11,644** (£3,465; £1,731; £865) Stalls High

Form				RPR
0620	1		**The Taj (USA)**[15] 5563 2-9-7 92 ... PaulHanagan 4 (Richard Hannon) *sweating and coltish bef ent stalls: trckd ldng pair: wnt 2nd over 1f out: tending to hang but shkn up to ld 150yds out: readily asserted* **11/2**[3]	97
5422	2	1/2	**Bispham Green**[21] 5332 2-8-2 73 ... KieranO'Neill 10 (Richard Fahey) *racd against rail: led: rdn over 1f out: hdd 150yds out: styd on but readily hld* **8/1**	76
2166	3	1 3/4	**Dominate**[35] 4804 2-9-3 88 ... PatDobbs 6 (Richard Hannon) *hld up last: stl there over 1f out: rdn and r.o against nr side rail fnl f: tk 3rd nr fin: no ch to threaten* **13/2**	86+
1245	4	1/2	**Hot Secret**[8] 5790 2-8-2 73 ... DavidProbert 8 (Andrew Balding) *taken down early: trckd ldrs towards rail: shkn up and nt qckn over 1f out: styd on same pce fnl f* **20/1**	68
313	5	hd	**Stand Of Glory (USA)**[11] 5711 2-8-0 76 ... DarrenEgan(5) 9 (David Simcock) *pressed ldr to over 1f out: wknd ins fnl f: lost 2 pls nr fin* **5/1**[2]	70
0011	6	1 1/2	**Opt Out**[12] 5682 2-8-10 81 ... FrannyNorton 2 (Mark Johnston) *racd towards outer: chsd ldrs: rdn 2f out: wknd jst over 1f out* **9/2**[1]	70
1263	7	nse	**Forray**[21] 5332 2-8-8 79 ... RichardMullen 7 (Ed McMahon) *t.k.h: hld up in last trio: effrt 2f out: nt qckn over 1f out: wl hld after* **5/1**[2]	68
2015	8	1	**Royal Aspiration (IRE)**[15] 5563 2-9-2 87 ... MichaelHills 1 (William Haggas) *racd wdst of all: in tch: rdn 2f out: wknd over 1f out* **8/1**	72
1	9	1	**Foxy Forever (IRE)**[10] 5748 2-8-8 79 ... MickaelBarzalona 3 (Michael Wigham) *t.k.h: hld up in last trio: swtchd to outer and effrt over 1f out: hanging bdly and sn btn* **8/1**	61

59.25s (-1.25) **Going Correction** -0.125s/f (Firm) **9** Ran SP% **118.3**
Speed ratings (Par 101): **105,104,101,100,100 97,97,96,94**
Tote Swingers: 1&2 £13.80, 1&3 £8.70, 2&3 £37.10 CSF £50.04 CT £297.78 TOTE £6.00: £2.00, £3.10, £2.20; EX 55.30 Trifecta £245.10 Pool: £858.10 - 2.59 winning units..
Owner Hamdan Al Maktoum **Bred** Summer Wind Farm **Trained** East Everleigh, Wilts

FOCUS
The first pair pulled clear in this fair nursery, in which those drawn highly were at an advantage, and the form appeals as sound.

NOTEBOOK
The Taj(USA), despite sweating up and proving coltish at the start, defied top weight and handed his bang in-form stable another winner. He looked to find York too sharp off the same mark over 6f last time, but this stiff 5f back on quick ground proved right up his street and he could have been called the winner from the furlong marker. His attitude is a likeable one and, although his Group 1 Middle Park entry is too fanciful, the Redcar Two-Year-Old Trophy back over another furlong next seems looks a viable target. (op 6-1 tchd 5-1)
Bispham Green, who met support, bagged the stands' rail from his plum draw and turned in a bold effort from the front. He only gave way late in the day and, while he's now found one too good on his last three outings, there appears little wrong with his attitude. The handicapper will raise him a few pounds, but his turn does look to be nearing. (op 9-1)
Dominate finished one place ahead of that rival over 6f at York last time. He was undone by this drop back a furlong, though, as he finished fast all too late in the day. He remains on a workable mark. (op 11-2)
Hot Secret posted a slightly improved effort but looks weighted to her best. (tchd 22-1)
Stand Of Glory(USA) failed to really raise his game back on quicker ground. He wasnt given too hard a time once beaten, though, and looks worth a go over 6f. (op 11-2 tchd 6-1)
Opt Out was up another 6lb in this hat-trick bid. It looked a combination of dropping back in trip and his wide draw that found him out. (tchd 5-1)

Forray probably found this ground lively enough and is another weighted near his best. (op 13-2 tchd 15-2)

6023 RITZ CLUB FILLIES' H'CAP 1m (S)
3:10 (3:11) (Class 3) (0-90,90) 3-Y-0+ **£8,409** (£2,502; £1,250; £625) **Stalls** High

Form RPR

5216 **1** **Chigun**[38] 4702 3-9-4 **89** .... EddieAhern 6 102+
(Sir Henry Cecil) *mde all: racd on outer early but grad crossed to nr side rail: rdn and styd on strly fnl 2f: unchal* **7/1**[2]

0143 **2** *3 ¼* **Mrs Greeley**[18] 5457 4-8-10 **76** oh1 .... TedDurcan 1 82
(Eve Johnson Houghton) *dwlt: hld up wl in rr on outer: stdy prog 3f out: rdn to chse wnr over 1f out: styd on but no imp* **14/1**

6003 **3** *1 ¼* **Way Too Hot**[19] 5409 3-9-0 **85** .... AdamKirby 3 88
(Clive Cox) *racd on outer: trckd ldrs: effrt 3f out: rdn to dispute 2nd briefly over 1f out: one pce* **16/1**

0645 **4** *½* **Diala (IRE)**[23] 5271 3-9-4 **89** ....[1] ShaneKelly 8 92+
(William Haggas) *hld up in midfield: shkn up 2f out: trying to cl whn hmpd jst ins fnl f: swtchd rt and r.o: nt rch ldrs* **7/1**[2]

3062 **5** *1* **Wahylah (IRE)**[7] 5819 3-8-5 **79** .... RyanPowell(3) 7 79
(Clive Brittain) *prom on outer: chsd wnr 3f out: no imp: lost 2nd over 1f out: edgd lft and wknd ins after* **10/1**

3050 **6** *1 ½* **Responsive**[31] 4949 3-8-8 **79** .... MartinHarley 9 75
(Hughie Morrison) *taken down early: hld up in rr: rdn over 2f out: kpt on same pce fr over 1f out: n.d* **16/1**

1011 **7** *½* **Speedi Mouse**[22] 5322 3-8-1 **77** .... DarrenEgan(5) 5 72
(Philip McBride) *dwlt: hld up in rr: rdn over 2f out: kpt on same pce fr over 1f out: n.d* **8/1**

0-20 **8** *2* **Dare To Dream**[24] 5237 3-8-11 **82** .... PatDobbs 12 72+
(Richard Hannon) *hld up in rr nr side: nt clr run over 2f out and swtchd rt: sme hdwy over 1f out: n.d* **16/1**

2033 **9** *½* **The Giving Tree (IRE)**[19] 5420 3-8-5 **76** .... DavidProbert 11 65+
(Sylvester Kirk) *hld up: last whn hmpd against nr side rail over 2f out: swtchd rt and styd on after: no ch at all* **12/1**

0410 **10** *8* **Our Gal**[38] 4702 4-9-0 **80** .... MickaelBarzalona 16 51
(Noel Quinlan) *prom nr side: rdn 1/2-way: wknd 3f out* **12/1**

4465 **11** *2 ¾* **Honeymead (IRE)**[16] 5520 4-9-4 **84** .... PaulHanagan 15 49
(Richard Fahey) *trckd ldrs: rdn over 2f out: wknd over 1f out* **15/2**[3]

5150 **12** *3 ¼* **Lady Macduff (IRE)**[16] 5517 3-9-1 **86** .... FrannyNorton 13 43
(Mark Johnston) *prom: rdn 3f out: wknd rapidly over 2f out* **11/2**[1]

0421 **13** *6* **Majestic Zafeen**[19] 5426 3-8-5 **76** oh4 .... WilliamCarson 17 19
(Alastair Lidderdale) *prom nr side tl wknd qckly 3f out* **25/1**

-516 **14** *2* **Catherine Laboure (IRE)**[22] 5302 3-8-5 **76** oh2 .... CathyGannon 14 15
(Eve Johnson Houghton) *prom tl wknd qckly 3f out* **33/1**

025R **R** **Miss Azeza**[29] 5043 3-9-5 **90** ....(b[1]) RichardMullen 4
(David Simcock) *ref to r: tk no part* **25/1**

1m 38.11s (-2.69) **Going Correction** -0.125s/f (Firm) course record
WFA 3 from 4yo 5lb **15** Ran SP% **122.7**
Speed ratings (Par 104): **108,104,103,103,102 100,100,98,97,89 86,83,77,75,**
Tote Swingers: 1&2 £18.70, 1&3 £30.90, 2&3 £60.40 CSF £100.56 CT £998.07 TOTE £8.30: £2.60, £3.70, £4.30; EX 86.70 TRIFECTA Not won..
Owner V I Araci **Bred** Whatton Manor Stud **Trained** Newmarket, Suffolk

FOCUS
Competitive stuff. The field unsurprisingly raced stands' side and there was a fair pace on, but those held up struggled to land a serious blow. The winner was on the upgrade and the second set the standard.

NOTEBOOK
Chigun ◆ bounced back to winning ways and completed the task in decent fashion. She loves to get on with it and went clear when shaken up 2f out against the stands' rail. The race was in safe keeping shortly after she passed the furlong marker and, with relatively few miles on the clock, she looks a smart filly in the making.
Mrs Greeley ran a big race considering she was drawn widest of all in stall 1 and came from well back. She obviously stays this trip fine and it was a career-best effort in defeat.
Way Too Hot kept on well under pressure and ran very close to her recent level back on turf, thus rating a sound benchmark. She remains winless since resuming at three, though. (op 20-1)
Diala(IRE) was equipped with a first-time hood and stepping back up a furlong. She finished with purpose all too late in the day after meeting some trouble on the inside a furlong out and is talented enough to defy this sort of mark, but evidently has her own ideas. (op 13-2)
Wahylah(IRE) held every chance and ran well, but this was her debut over 1m and the stiff finish stretched her stamina.
The Giving Tree(IRE) Official explanation: jockey said filly was denied a clear run.
Our Gal Official explanation: jockey said filly was denied a clear run.
Lady Macduff(IRE) was fancied to show her true colours again, but she proved laboured under pressure and looks one to avoid at present. (op 13-2 tchd 5-1)

6024 FLY LONDON SOUTHEND AIRPORT H'CAP 7f
3:45 (3:47) (Class 2) 3-Y-0+ **£51,752** (£15,400; £7,696; £3,848) **Stalls** High

Form RPR

3106 **1** **Don't Call Me (IRE)**[12] 5677 5-8-10 **96** ....(t) RichardMullen 2 106
(David Nicholls) *trckd ldrs: prog over 2f out: rdn to ld over 1f out: styd on wl* **25/1**

321 **2** *1 ¼* **Imperial Guest**[14] 5572 6-9-2 **102** .... SebSanders 3 109
(George Margarson) *hld up in midfield: stdy prog on outer over 2f out: rdn to chse wnr ins fnl f: no imp nr fin* **12/1**

0020 **3** *½* **Mabait**[14] 5572 6-8-6 **97** .... LauraPike(5) 15 103
(David Simcock) *hld up in last trio: prog jst over 2f out: rdn over 1f out: r.o fnl f to take 4th nr fin* **25/1**

0100 **4** *½* **Field Of Dream**[14] 5572 5-9-3 **103** ....(b) AdamKirby 16 107
(Jamie Osborne) *dwlt and awkward s: hld up in last trio: prog 2f out: rdn over 1f out: r.o fnl f: nrst fin but no ch to threaten* **12/1**

3622 **5** *¾* **Arnold Lane (IRE)**[14] 5572 3-8-9 **99** .... MartinHarley 5 100
(Mick Channon) *prom: chsd wnr and chal over 1f out: wknd and lost 2nd ins fnl f* **11/1**

110 **6** *1 ½* **Primaeval**[78] 3331 6-9-0 **100** ....(v) GeorgeBaker 17 98
(James Fanshawe) *hld up towards rr: effrt wl over 1f out: drvn and styd on same pce fnl f* **15/2**[3]

0304 **7** *nk* **Bertiewhittle**[14] 5572 4-8-7 **93** .... WilliamCarson 10 90
(David Barron) *trckd ldrs: shoved along and nt qckn 2f out: styd on again fnl f* **9/1**

4104 **8** *hd* **Smarty Socks (IRE)**[14] 5597 8-8-10 **96** ow1 .... DanielTudhope 12 93
(David O'Meara) *dwlt: hld up in last trio: rdn over 2f out: kpt on fr over 1f out: n.d* **8/1**

-500 **9** *½* **Xilerator (IRE)**[36] 4761 5-8-7 **93** .... AndrewMullen 1 89
(David Nicholls) *racd freely: hung lft 2f out: sn hdd & wknd* **33/1**

3454 **10** *1 ¼* **Mehdi (IRE)**[12] 5664 3-8-8 **98** ....(bt) EddieAhern 8 89
(Brian Meehan) *prom: rdn and edgd lft 2f out: wknd over 1f out* **33/1**

050 **11** *1 ¾* **Excellent Guest**[16] 5517 5-8-11 **97** .... ShaneKelly 18 84
(George Margarson) *racd alone against nr side rail: on terms w main gp tl wknd over 1f out* **10/1**

4023 **12** *hd* **Bannock (IRE)**[7] 5827 3-8-10 **107** .... MichaelJMMurphy(7) 9 93
(Mark Johnston) *prom: carried sltly lft 2f out: sn wknd* **13/2**[1]

0052 **13** *2 ¼* **Atlantic Sport (USA)**[12] 5686 7-8-9 **95** .... FrannyNorton 14 76
(Mick Channon) *a towards rr: struggling over 2f out* **20/1**

3144 **14** *5* **Global Village (IRE)**[49] 4321 7-8-6 **95** .... RyanClark(3) 7 62
(Brian Ellison) *settled in midfield: effrt over 2f out: wknd wl over 1f out* **7/1**[2]

0000 **15** *½* **King Of Jazz (IRE)**[28] 5102 4-8-8 **94** ow1 .... StevieDonohoe 11 60
(Michael Bell) *nvr beyond midfield: struggling in rr over 2f out* **40/1**

3100 **16** *1 ½* **Memory Cloth**[36] 4761 5-8-13 **99** .... RobertWinston 6 61
(Brian Ellison) *mostly chsd ldr to over 2f out: wkng qckly whn hmpd over 1f out* **25/1**

0063 **17** *¾* **Sirius Prospect (USA)**[14] 5581 4-9-10 **110** ....[1] BrettDoyle 4 70
(Dean Ivory) *rrd s and lost several l: rcvrd rapidly to chse ldrs after 2f: wknd qckly over 2f out* **14/1**

0005 **18** *2 ¼* **Castles In The Air**[28] 5102 7-8-6 **92** .... PaulHanagan 13 46
(Richard Fahey) *nvr beyond midfield: wknd over 2f out* **12/1**

1m 25.12s (-2.48) **Going Correction** -0.125s/f (Firm)
WFA 3 from 4yo+ 4lb **18** Ran SP% **130.5**
Speed ratings (Par 109): **109,107,107,106,105 103,103,103,102,101 99,99,96,90,90 88,87,85**
Tote Swingers: 1&2 £142.70, 2&3 £41.30 CSF £298.15 CT £7649.08 TOTE £36.70: £7.40, £3.50, £5.60, £3.40; EX 501.90 Trifecta £1724.30 Part won. Pool: £2,330.25 - 0.25 winning units..
Owner Matt & Lauren Morgan **Bred** Darley **Trained** Sessay, N Yorks

FOCUS
Another highly competitive handicap. There was just an average pace on and this time only Excellent Guest wanted to race near the stands' rail. Probably ordinary form, with a length personal best from the winner.

NOTEBOOK
Don't Call Me(IRE) picked up strongly when asked for everything at the furlong marker and came home to land by far his biggest prize to date. He had shown very little the last twice, but won off 3lb lower three runs back and was third in the Royal Hunt Cup over an extra furlong here back in June. He goes on any ground and now has form figures at this venue reading 14331. A likely rise will make his life plenty harder, but no doubt another crack at the Hunt Cup will be in his plans next year. (op 33-1)
Imperial Guest came home nearest the far rail and ran a blinder, but his 4lb rise for scoring at Goodwood a fortnight earlier was enough to stop him from following up. He's obviously at the top of his game and may come back here for a Group 3 over 6f as his owners sponser the race. (op 11-1)
Mabait was buried out the back and finished with a real rattle. His losing run goes on, but surely there is a race for him before the season's end.
Field Of Dream was well beaten by the runner-up at Goodwood last time, but had won a big-field handicap over C&D in July off 4lb lower and the return to this venue sparked a revival.
Arnold Lane(IRE) wasn't able to reverse last-time-out Goodwood form with the runner-up on 3lb better terms, but ran another sterling race in defeat and richly deserves to get his head back in front.
Primaeval was fancied to show his last-time-out flop at the Royal Meeting to be all wrong back on this much quicker surface. He lacked a turn of foot when it mattered, though, and perhaps the handicapper now has his measure. He's entitled to come on for it, however. (op 8-1)
Smarty Socks(IRE) had fallen to the same mark as when winning the race last year, although his rider put up 1lb overweight, and was another here reverting to suitably quicker ground. However, he got too far back to land a serious blow. (tchd 7-1)
Xilerator(IRE) Official explanation: jockey said gelding hung left.
Bannock(IRE) arrived with some strong placed efforts to his name, most recently at York's Ebor meeting. He ran a tame race, however, and may be in need of a break. (op 7-1 tchd 6-1)

6025 LADBROKES MOBILE H'CAP (HERITAGE HANDICAP) 1m 4f
4:15 (4:17) (Class 2) 3-Y-0 **£97,035** (£28,875; £14,430; £7,215) **Stalls** Low

Form RPR

4312 **1** **Ahzeemah (IRE)**[28] 5078 3-9-2 **95** ....(p) MickaelBarzalona 9 106
(Saeed Bin Suroor) *trckd ldng gp: plld out wd and prog to ld wl over 1f out: hung rt but in command after: eased nr fin* **11/1**

4212 **2** *nk* **Stencive**[28] 5089 3-9-0 **93** .... EddieAhern 14 106+
(William Haggas) *t.k.h: hld up in 13th: looking for room over 2f out: swtchd rt and gd prog over 1f out: r.o to chse wnr ins fnl f: clsd at fin but no real ch* **10/1**

-210 **3** *1* **Silver Lime (USA)**[15] 5558 3-8-11 **90** .... MartinHarley 13 99+
(Roger Charlton) *hld up in midfield: 10th 3f out: prog 2f out: r.o to dispute 2nd ins fnl f: no ex* **14/1**

6231 **4** *2 ½* **Modernism**[15] 5533 3-8-5 **84** .... FrannyNorton 5 89
(Mark Johnston) *trckd ldng pair: effrt to chal 2f out: chsd wnr sn after but outpcd: lost 2 pls ins fnl f* **20/1**

22-4 **5** *1* **Harvard N Yale (USA)**[13] 5626 3-8-3 **87** .... DarrenEgan(5) 18 90
(Jeremy Noseda) *trapped out wd in midfield: rdn over 2f out: styd on fr over 1f out: nrst fin* **16/1**

141 **6** *nk* **Angel Gabrial (IRE)**[23] 5273 3-8-7 **86** .... TedDurcan 15 89+
(Ian Williams) *hld up in last quartet fr wd draw: threaded path through fr 2f out: styd on fnl f: nrst fin* **16/1**

111 **7** *½* **Gospel Choir**[28] 5089 3-9-5 **98** .... GeorgeBaker 7 100+
(Sir Michael Stoute) *trckd ldrs: wl plcd 3f out: effrt whn bmpd and sqaueezed jst over 2f out: one pce after* **9/2**[1]

101 **8** *1 ¼* **Ruscello (IRE)**[18] 5455 3-8-5 **84** .... MartinLane 17 84
(Ed Walker) *s.s: t.k.h in last: brought wd over 2f out: styd on fr over 1f out: n.d* **25/1**

5400 **9** *1 ½* **Fennell Bay (IRE)**[15] 5558 3-8-5 **91** .... MichaelJMMurphy(7) 12 89
(Mark Johnston) *prom: rdn and disputing 4th 3f out: bmpd jst over 2f out: steadily wknd* **20/1**

1036 **10** *shd* **Scatter Dice (IRE)**[21] 5333 3-9-0 **93** .... AdamKirby 3 90
(Mark Johnston) *prom on inner: stl cl up 2f out: wknd over 1f out* **25/1**

-131 **11** *shd* **Blue Surf**[13] 5626 3-8-13 **92** .... PatDobbs 4 89+
(Amanda Perrett) *hld up towards rr on inner: effrt and gng wl enough whn n.m.r 2f out: trying to stay on whn hmpd jst over 1f out: nt rcvr and eased* **9/1**

541 **12** *½* **Castilo Del Diablo (IRE)**[28] 5105 3-8-2 **81** .... CathyGannon 2 78+
(David Simcock) *hld up wl in rr: no real room fr over 2f out: limited late prog* **12/1**

2616 **13** *hd* **Hajras (IRE)**[17] 5492 3-9-3 **96** .... PaulHanagan 8 92
(Mark Johnston) *trapped out wd in rr: effrt on outer over 2f out: no real prog* **8/1**[3]

3056 **14** *2 ¼* **Miblish**[7] 5835 3-9-7 **100** ....(t) MichaelHills 11 93
(Clive Brittain) *led to wl over 1f out: wknd* **33/1**

5101 **15** *nk* **Opinion (IRE)**[28] 5091 3-9-2 **95** .... RichardMullen 6 87+
(Sir Michael Stoute) *trckd ldrs: wl enough plcd 3f out: looking for room over 2f out: swtchd lft wl over 1f out and effrt: hmpd sn after: nt rcvr and eased* **25/1**

4110 **16** *3* **Stature (IRE)**[38] 4700 3-9-0 **93** .... JimmyFortune 1 80
(Andrew Balding) *t.k.h early: hld up in midfield: n.m.r after 1f: rdn 3f out: sn btn* **33/1**

4021 **17** *1/2* **Caphira**[26] 5154 3-8-2 **81** .... AndreaAtzeni 10 68
(William Knight) *trapped out wd in midfield: effrt 4f out: wknd over 2f out* **50/1**

-632 **18** *1* **Martin Chuzzlewit (IRE)**[15] 5558 3-8-12 **91** ....(v) RobertWinston 19 76
(Sir Michael Stoute) *dropped in fr wd draw and hld up in last trio: stl there 3f out: rdn and no prog over 2f out* **9/1**

3121 **19** *1 3/4* **Sun Central (IRE)**[28] 5078 3-8-13 **92** .... ShaneKelly 16 74+
(William Haggas) *pushed up fr wd draw to press ldr: edgd lft over 2f out: wkng whn hmpd over 1f out: eased* **6/1**[2]

2m 28.54s (-3.96) **Going Correction** -0.125s/f (Firm) **19** Ran SP% **136.0**
Speed ratings (Par 107): **108,107,107,105,104 104,104,103,102,102 102,101,101,100,100 98,97,97,95**
Tote Swingers: 1&2 £42.90, 1&3 £163.20, 2&3 £53.10 CSF £115.55 CT £1606.06 TOTE £15.00: £3.80, £3.50, £3.80, £5.20; EX 180.60 Trifecta £1808.90 Part won. Pool: £2,44.54 - 0.10 winning units..
Owner Godolphin **Bred** G O'Brien **Trained** Newmarket, Suffolk
■ Stewards' Enquiry : Eddie Ahern four day ban; carless riding (22nd-25th Sept).

FOCUS
An outstanding 3yo middle-distance handicap, run at a strong pace. It got messy and several were better than the bare form, which has ben rated on the positive side.

NOTEBOOK
Ahzeemah(IRE) enjoyed a beautiful passage through the race and was ideally placed when wound up for his effort on the outer after straightening for home. He wandered about in front once clear and it's not hard to see why he wears cheekpieces, but he clearly loves this venue as his form figures at the course of 121 now imply. It was just his second outing over the trip and, so long as his temperament can be controlled, he could well make up into a Pattern performer.
Stencive ◆, on of two from his decent stable, has to rate as somewhat unlucky as he met all sorts of trouble when trying to improve in the home straight. By the time he was in the clear the bird had flown, but this was yet another improved effort and he has a big pot in him. (op 12-1)
Silver Lime(USA), unsuited by the ground at York last time, travelled nicely in mid-field. He allowed the winner first run, but kept on strongly under pressure and he too posted a career-best effort. There should be more to come from this lightly raced colt. (op 16-1)
Modernism, one of four Mark Johnston runners, was whacked up 8lb for winning at Goodwood 15 days earlier, but he held every chance from his decent draw and is clearly an improving 3yo. (op 18-1)
Harvard N Yale(USA) ◆ caught the eye staying on with gusto late in the day and he looks on his way back. (tchd 14-1)
Angel Gabrial(IRE), 3lb higher, was another finishing fast from off the pace. (tchd 18-1)
Gospel Choir proved solid back at the C&D that saw him score on his handicap debut two runs back and he was up 8lb for landing the hat-trick at Haydock last time, when he beat the runner-up. That made him a stone higher than when initially beginning life in this sphere and, after having his chance here, it looks as though the handicapper now has his measure. He rates a solid benchmark. (op 5-1 tchd 11-2 in a place)
Ruscello(IRE)'s run needs upgrading somewhat as he missed the break.
Blue Surf met trouble at a crucial stage. (op 12-1)
Hajras(IRE) got going too late over 1m2f at York last time, but that track can often be deceptive and, while he was keeping on late from well off the pace after meeting some trouble, a stiff 1m2f could well be his optimum. (op 9-1)
Opinion(IRE) Official explanation: jockey said colt suffered interference in running.
Sun Central(IRE), the runner-up's stablemate, was raised 7lb for beating the winner 1l over C&D last month. He dropped right out after turning for home, but really stood little chance of seeing it out due to doing so much getting across from his poor draw. This is well worth forgiving. Official explanation: jockey said colt suffered interference in running. (op 7-1)

6026 ASCOT FESTIVAL OF FOOD AND WINE H'CAP — 5f
4:50 (4:55) (Class 3) (0-90,92) 3-Y-0+ **£8,409** (£2,502; £1,250; £625) **Stalls** High

Form RPR

5402 **1** **Kingsgate Choice (IRE)**[21] 5343 5-9-5 **88** .... EddieAhern 18 97
(Ed de Giles) *trckd ldrs on nr side of gp: prog over 1f out: led ins fnl f: hung lft but r.o* **7/1**

5321 **2** *1 1/2* **Intransigent**[24] 5233 3-9-3 **87** .... JimmyFortune 14 91+
(Andrew Balding) *hld up in tch: prog to chal over 1f out: carried rt after: styd on to take 2nd nr fin but wnr clr on other side of trck* **5/1**[1]

0403 **3** *hd* **Fitz Flyer (IRE)**[17] 5487 6-9-7 **90** ....(v) AndrewMullen 12 93
(David Nicholls) *hld up towards rr: prog and rdn sn after 1/2-way: hanging rt over 1f out: r.o fnl f to take 3rd nr fin* **11/2**[2]

1321 **4** *1/2* **Last Sovereign**[14] 5584 8-8-13 **89** ....(b) JacobButterfield(7) 16 90
(Ollie Pears) *led towards nr side: rdn 2f out: hung rt after and ended towards far rail: hdd and lost pls ins fnl f* **12/1**

4113 **5** *1 3/4* **Lady Gibraltar**[12] 5663 3-8-11 **88** ....(v) MichaelJMMurphy(7) 17 83
(Alan Jarvis) *pressed ldr: rdn to chal 2f out: fdd fnl f* **13/2**[3]

0100 **6** *1/2* **Jarrow (IRE)**[21] 5343 5-9-0 **83** .... CathyGannon 2 76
(Milton Bradley) *racd towards far side: prom: styd on same pce fr over 1f out: did best of those that racd there thrght* **20/1**

-000 **7** *1 1/2* **The Thrill Is Gone**[7] 5832 4-9-1 **84** .... MartinHarley 8 72
(Mick Channon) *w ldrs: u.p fr 1/2-way: steadily wknd over 1f out* **16/1**

0000 **8** *nk* **Elna Bright**[30] 5004 7-8-9 **78** .... ShaneKelly 9 65
(Peter Crate) *hld up in tch: rdn and nt qckn 2f out: swtchd lft over 1f out: one pce after* **10/1**

0310 **9** *nk* **Rowe Park**[7] 5832 9-9-2 **85** ....(p) SaleemGolam 4 70
(Linda Jewell) *racd towards far side: nt on terms 2f out: one pce and n.d after* **33/1**

5-40 **10** *1/2* **Alaskan Bullet (IRE)**[21] 5363 3-9-5 **89** .... AdamKirby 13 73
(Michael Bell) *hld up: effrt 2f out: sn no prog and btn* **28/1**

2040 **11** *shd* **O'Gorman**[7] 5812 3-8-12 **82** .... PatDobbs 5 65
(Gary Brown) *dwlt: detached in last early: r.o wl fnl f: nrst fin* **20/1**

162 **12** *2 1/4* **Fair Value (IRE)**[12] 5663 4-9-9 **92** .... SebSanders 1 67
(Simon Dow) *awkward s: hld up and racd towards far side: nt on terms fr 2f out: wknd fnl f* **12/1**

2002 **13** *6* **Noverre To Go (IRE)**[24] 5233 6-9-2 **85** .... PaulHanagan 7 39
(Ronald Harris) *hld up in rr: appeared gng wl enough 1/2-way: wknd rapidly wl over 1f out* **16/1**

060 **14** *1/2* **Burning Thread (IRE)**[17] 5487 5-9-5 **88** .... GeorgeBaker 3 40
(Tim Etherington) *led gp towards far rail but nt on terms w others fr 2f out: wknd over 1f out* **12/1**

-040 **15** *13* **Fathom Five (IRE)**[12] 5663 8-8-7 **76** oh1 .... WilliamCarson 6
(Gary Moore) *prom 2f: sn lost pl: wknd rapidly wl over 1f out: t.o* **20/1**

59.29s (-1.21) **Going Correction** -0.125s/f (Firm)
WFA 3 from 4yo+ 1lb **15** Ran SP% **122.5**
Speed ratings (Par 107): **104,101,101,100,97 96,94,94,93,92 92,88,79,78,57**
Tote Swingers: 1&2 £11.30, 1&3 £13.00, 2&3 £3.70 CSF £35.63 CT £163.62 TOTE £8.00: £3.30, £2.20, £2.60; EX 47.10 Trifecta £209.50 Pool: £1,016.58 - 3.59 winning units..
Owner T Gould **Bred** Michael Staunton **Trained** Ledbury, H'fords
■ Ajjaadd was withdrawn (9/1, ref to ent stalls). Deduct 10p in the £ under R4.
■ Stewards' Enquiry : Jacob Butterfield four-day ban; careless riding (22nd-25th Sept).

FOCUS
A fair sprint handicap. It was run at a sound pace and the runners fanned across the track, but it was the one nearest the stands' side that prevailed. Straightforward form.

NOTEBOOK
Kingsgate Choice(IRE) got well backed and, despite hanging left under maximum pressure half a furlong from home, landed his first success since winning on his seasonal return. He went close off 2lb lower at Doncaster on his previous outing and pretty much everything went his way here. (op 10-1)
Intransigent was upped 8lb for winning on Polytrack last time, but was able to race off just 2lb higher here and predictably attracted support. He was upsides the winner, but his rider elected to switch him right for his effort and that cost him as the fourth carried him all the way over to the far rail. He would very likely have followed up had he waited longer for his challenge, but the handicapper will probably now hike him up. (op 9-2)
Fitz Flyer(IRE) arrived in decent heart and, hitting top gear late in the day, he posted another solid effort in defeat. He sets the level and does deserve to resume winning ways.
Last Sovereign is another in-form sprinter and was 6lb higher than when scoring at Newmarket a fortnight earlier. He raced positively, but didnt help his cause or the runner-up's by hanging badly right under pressure. Perhaps the round was that bit too lively for him.
Lady Gibraltar has developed into a consistent sprinter this season and she's another that gives this form a good look. (op 7-1 tchd 15-2)
Noverre To Go(IRE) Official explanation: jockey said gelding was unruly in stalls and never travelled.
T/Plt: £2,831.90 to a £1 stake. Pool: £137,718.58 - 35.50 winning tickets. T/Qpdt: £277.50 to a £1 stake. Pool: £7,651.35 - 20.40 winning tickets. JN

6005 HAYDOCK (L-H)
Saturday, September 8

OFFICIAL GOING: Good to firm (firm in places) changing to firm after race 1 (1.45)
Wind: light half behind Weather: fine

6027 BETFRED "STILL TREBLE ODDS ON LUCKY 15'S" STKS (REGISTERED AS THE ASCENDANT STAKES) (LISTED RACE) — 1m
1:45 (1:46) (Class 1) 2-Y-O
£13,043 (£4,945; £2,474; £1,232; £618; £310) **Stalls** Low

Form RPR

11U **1** **Havana Gold (IRE)**[27] 5140 2-9-0 0 .... RichardHughes 1 100+
(Richard Hannon) *trckd ldrs: effrt 3f out: led jst over 2f out: rdn and edgd lft ins fnl f: all out towards fin: jst hld on* **6/4**[1]

11 **2** *hd* **Al Waab (IRE)**[23] 5270 2-9-0 0 .... IanMongan 5 100+
(Sir Henry Cecil) *hld up: pushed along and outpcd over 3f out: hdwy over 1f out: tke 2nd wl ins fnl f: r.o strly: jst failed* **9/4**[2]

51 **3** *2 1/4* **Mirsaale**[18] 5439 2-9-0 **80** .... JoeFanning 3 92
(James Tate) *led: hdd jst over 2f out: rdn and stl ev ch tl ins fnl f: no ex fnl 75yds* **11/1**

1024 **4** *shd* **Miss You Too**[21] 5353 2-8-9 **86** .... SamHitchcott 2 87
(Mick Channon) *s.i.s: in rr: hdwy over 2f out: effrt over 1f out: styd on ins fnl f: unable to mount serious chal* **25/1**

512 **5** *3* **Makafeh**[29] 5060 2-9-0 **82** .... KierenFallon 4 85
(Luca Cumani) *led down to s: shkn up leaving stalls: sn prom: racd on and off the bridle: chalng over 2f out: stl ch over 1f out: wknd fnl 110yds* **5/1**[3]

1 **6** *1 3/4* **Azrur (IRE)**[70] 3611 2-9-0 0 .... JamieSpencer 6 82
(Michael Bell) *prom: pushed along and outpcd over 2f out: no imp after: eased whn wl btn fnl 75yds* **7/1**

1m 43.69s (-0.01) **Going Correction** -0.075s/f (Good) **6** Ran SP% **112.1**
Speed ratings (Par 103): **97,96,94,94,91 89**
Tote Swingers: 1&2 £1.40, 1&3 £4.40, 2&3 £5.00 CSF £5.07 TOTE £2.40: £1.90, £1.60; EX 4.00.

Owner Qatar Racing Limited & CSH **Bred** Sir Eric Parker **Trained** East Everleigh, Wilts

FOCUS
All races on outer Stands side home straight. Due to rail alignments this was run over 1m 57 yards, rather than over the bare mile. Comparisons with standard time are misleading. All six of the runners held Group 1 entries going into this and the form looks reasonable for the grade. The pace appeared only ordinary, and limits the form along with the third. The first two can rate higher.

NOTEBOOK
Havana Gold(IRE) came here unlucky not to be unbeaten in three, a slipping saddle having cost him victory in this grade at Deauville last time. He was carrying different colours here, having been sold since his latest start, but remains with Richard Hannon who has now won twice and had the second twice in the four runnings of this event.\n\x\x Settled in fourth and briefly bustled along before making up his ground smoothly to lead, the colt asserted in the final furlong but his lead was being cut back towards the line. He defied worries over the ground and trip and is clearly smart, but will need to pull out more when he's upped in grade. (op 7-4)
Al Waab(IRE) was slightly outpaced at the back in the straight and needed winding up from the two pole, but he was rolling in the final furlong and would have got there with a little further to run. The longer trip suited and he will probably stay 1m2f next season. His maiden win came in soft ground and today's conditions were probably quicker than ideal for him. He could meet the winner again in the Racing Post Trophy, but both will have to improve on this form to figure there. (op 5-2 tchd 2-1 in places)
Mirsaale battled on well from the front but was weakening inside the last and would have been back in fourth in another stride. Another Racing Post Trophy entry, this half-brother to the classy Meeznah is bred for middle-distances next year. (op 14-1)
Miss You Too had a chance on adjusted official figures. She is less than an easy ride, and while she didn't hang this time she again took a keen tug in rear, having become warm in the preliminaries. She did stay on without landing a blow and is worth another chance at this sort of trip. (op 20-1)
Makafeh got loose before the start and had to be trotted to post. His rider was briefly without an iron leaving the stalls and the colt rather ran in snatches, but he only faded out of things in the final furlong. (op 9-2)

Azrur(IRE)'s Doncaster debut victory back in June has not been working out and he was well held. (op 13-2 tchd 15-2)

6028 BETFRED "THE BONUS KING" BE FRIENDLY H'CAP 5f
2:15 (2:16) (Class 2) (0-100,100) 3-Y-0+ **£12,938** (£3,850; £1,924; £962) **Stalls** Centre

Form				RPR
4610	**1**		**Cheviot (USA)**[7] 5822 6-9-7 **100**....(p) DaneO'Neill 13 (Ian Semple) *mde all: rdn over 1f out: r.o ins fnl f: pushed out towards fin* **28/1**	111
3-12	**2**	*1*	**Face The Problem (IRE)**[7] 5832 4-9-3 **96**.... KierenFallon 15 (Jamie Osborne) *hld up in midfield: hdwy over 2f out: sn chsd wnr and rdn: r.o ins fnl f: a hld* **4/1**[1]	103
0041	**3**	*½*	**Long Awaited (IRE)**[12] 5663 4-8-12 **91**....(b) RichardHughes 9 (David Barron) *hld up: hdwy whn nt clr run over 1f out: r.o ins fnl f: gng on at fin* **5/1**[2]	97
0330	**4**	*nk*	**Doc Hay (USA)**[86] 3078 5-9-4 **97**.... JoeFanning 8 (David O'Meara) *midfield: rdn and hdwy over 1f out: r.o ins fnl f: gng on at fin* **20/1**	102
6300	**5**	*1 ¼*	**Doctor Parkes**[7] 5829 6-8-7 **86**.... LukeMorris 10 (Eric Alston) *chsd ldrs: rdn over 2f out: styd on same pce and no imp fr over 1f out* **14/1**	86
0-05	**6**	*½*	**My Propeller (IRE)**[98] 2713 3-9-0 **94**.... FrankieDettori 7 (Peter Chapple-Hyam) *in rr: rdn and hdwy over 1f out: styd on ins fnl f: nt rch ldrs* **10/1**	92
3021	**7**	*1 ¼*	**Tax Free (IRE)**[17] 5487 10-9-2 **95**.... GeraldMosse 3 (David Nicholls) *midfield: pushed along 1/2-way: kpt on ins fnl f: nt rch ldrs: eased fnl 50yds* **5/1**[2]	89
20-0	**8**	*1 ¼*	**Moorhouse Lad**[7] 5822 9-9-0 **93**.... PatrickMathers 1 (Garry Moss) *prom: rdn over 1f out: sn outpcd: no imp after* **50/1**	82
000	**9**	*1 ¼*	**Lexi's Hero (IRE)**[7] 5829 4-8-11 **90**....(p) GrahamLee 4 (Kevin Ryan) *chsd ldrs tl rdn and wknd over 1f out* **8/1**	75
0023	**10**	*¾*	**Master Rooney (IRE)**[21] 5343 6-8-8 **87**.... RoystonFfrench 6 (Bryan Smart) *prom: rdn 2f out: wknd over 1f out* **16/1**	69
002	**11**	*nse*	**Blue Jack**[18] 5447 7-8-8 **87**....(tp) HayleyTurner 12 (Alan McCabe) *in rr: pushed along and outpcd over 2f out: kpt on ins fnl f: nvr gng pce to get competitive* **20/1**	69
3360	**12**	*1*	**Zero Money (IRE)**[17] 5487 6-9-6 **99**....(b) JamesDoyle 11 (Roger Charlton) *prom: rdn over 2f out: sn wknd* **11/2**[3]	77
1030	**13**	*3 ¾*	**Bosun Breese**[21] 5370 7-9-0 **93**.... GrahamGibbons 14 (David Barron) *prom: pushed along over 2f out: sn wknd* **20/1**	58
3-00	**14**	*13*	**Mister Manannan (IRE)**[17] 5487 5-9-1 **94**.... SamHitchcott 2 (David Nicholls) *missed break: a wl bhd: nvr on terms* **40/1**	12

57.84s (-2.96) **Going Correction** -0.35s/f (Firm)
WFA 3 from 4yo+ 1lb **14 Ran SP% 123.6**
Speed ratings (Par 109): **109,107,106,106,104 103,101,99,97,96 96,94,88,67**
Tote Swingers: 1&2 £22.30, 1&3 £44.10, 2&3 £6.40 CSF £131.95 CT £700.62 TOTE £44.30: £10.10, £1.80, £2.20; EX 221.80 Trifecta £806.20 Part won. Pool: £1,089.56 - 0.40 winning units..
Owner Mrs J Penman, R Reid, W Robinson **Bred** Darley **Trained** Carluke, S Lanarks

FOCUS
A competitive sprint handicap, run at a strong gallop in a good time, and sound form. However those drawn low, towards the far side, were not seen to best effect. There was a surprise winner and this rates a personal best.

NOTEBOOK
Cheviot(USA) made all the running and kept up the gallop in fine style despite edging from the stands' side towards the centre of the course in the latter stages. The lightning-fast ground suited him admirably and he was sharper for last weekend's run following a three-month break. His target is the Ayr Gold Cup but that would represent a different test. (op 25-1)
Face The Problem(IRE) has been in fine form in a light campaign and he ran another good race, chasing the winner for much of the way. His awkward head carriage was again in evidence but he didn't do anything obviously wrong, and he should continue to give a good account. (op 9-2)
Long Awaited(IRE) is another in-form sprinter, and he ran on nicely after being let down without getting to the first two. He was up a further 5lb to a career-high mark but is not necessarily weighted out of things. (op 6-1)
Doc Hay(USA) put in a strong finish on this first run since mid-June. He seems most effective over a stiffer 5f and does not have much to work with from his current mark. Joe Fanning reported that the gelding hung right. Official explanation: jockey said gelding hung right handed. (op 16-1)
Doctor Parkes was drawn on the right side of the track and ran respectably. He's come down to 3lb lower than his last winning mark. (op 12-1)
My Propeller(IRE) did best of those to race more towards the far side of the track, but in truth was never able to get in a blow. This was still a more encouraging effort, following a break. (tchd 9-1)
Tax Free(IRE) performed respectably given he was drawn away from the pace. (tchd 11-2)
Zero Money(IRE) was 5lb higher than when taking this race a year ago, his most recent win. He chased the pace on the 'right' side but was on the retreat a good way from home.
Mister Manannan(IRE) lost all chance with a very slow start. Official explanation: jockey said gelding was slowly away. (tchd 50-1)

6029 CELEBRATING 45 YEARS OF BETFRED SUPERIOR MILE (LISTED RACE) 1m
2:50 (2:51) (Class 1) 3-Y-0+
£18,714 (£7,095; £3,550; £1,768; £887; £445) **Stalls** Low

Form				RPR
-112	**1**		**Thistle Bird**[14] 5573 4-9-0 107.... JamesDoyle 7 (Roger Charlton) *hld up: hdwy to chse ldr over 1f out: r.o to ld narrowly fnl 110yds: a doing enough cl home* **3/1**[1]	112
1110	**2**	*nk*	**Fulbright**[14] 5572 3-8-11 108.... JoeFanning 2 (Mark Johnston) *chsd ldr: led over 2f out: rdn over 1f out: hdd narrowly fnl 110yds: r.o u.p but hld after* **3/1**[1]	113
-041	**3**	*1 ¾*	**Boom And Bust (IRE)**[28] 5075 5-9-2 104.... HayleyTurner 4 (Marcus Tregoning) *chsd ldrs: effrt over 2f out: ev ch over 1f out: nt qckn ins fnl f: styd on same pce ins fnl 100yds* **4/1**[2]	109
-611	**4**	*¾*	**Chil The Kite**[49] 4319 3-8-11 97.... WilliamBuick 6 (Hughie Morrison) *hld up in rr: pushed along over 2f out: styd on and lugged lft ins fnl f: nt quite rch ldrs* **4/1**[2]	107
4201	**5**	*3*	**Right To Dream (IRE)**[12] 5686 3-8-11 103.... KierenFallon 5 (Brian Meehan) *midfield: pushed along 3f out: no imp: one pce fr over 1f out* **10/1**[3]	100
062	**6**	*2*	**Rockinante (FR)**[12] 5664 3-8-11 105.... RichardHughes 3 (Richard Hannon) *led: pushed along and hdd over 2f out: wknd over 1f out* **12/1**	96
1322	**7**	*¾*	**Kingsdesire (IRE)**[29] 5064 3-8-11 102....(t) FrankieDettori 8 (Marco Botti) *hld up: effrt 2f out: no imp: bhd fnl f* **14/1**	94

1m 40.77s (-2.93) **Going Correction** -0.075s/f (Good)
WFA 3 from 4yo+ 5lb **7 Ran SP% 113.4**
Speed ratings (Par 111): **111,110,108,108,105 103,102**
Tote Swingers: 1&2 £2.50, 1&3 £2.90, 2&3 £4.00 CSF £11.89 TOTE £3.40: £1.80, £2.40; EX 9.00 Trifecta £23.70 Pool: £2,322.95 - 72.26 winning units..
Owner Lady Rothschild **Bred** The Rt Hon Lord Rothschild **Trained** Beckhampton, Wilts

FOCUS
This was staged over 57 yards further than the advertised distance. An interesting Listed race, it was run at a solid gallop and in a good time. Straightforward for the grade, the first three pretty much to form.

NOTEBOOK
Thistle Bird won her last two races at this level, and was narrowly denied in the Group 2 Celebration Mile at Goodwood latest. Carrying a 3lb penalty here, but still top rated by 4lb on BHA figures, she came from off the pace to run down the second late on. She gave the Charlton stable its second winner of this race in three years, following Cityscape in 2010. Smart and progressive and with more to offer, she holds an entry in the Group 2 Joel Stakes at Newmarket at the end of the month but may not run again this term. (op 5-2)
Fulbright has enjoyed a fine summer and he ran another admirable race, reaching the front with two to run and sticking to his task with tenacity. He's in the Ayr Gold Cup, but also has a stack of options at Group level. (op 7-2)
Boom And Bust(IRE) had also been behind Fulbright in the Betfred Mile at Goodwood two starts back. Moving out of handicap company, he ran a solid race with no discernible excuses. (op 9-2)
Chil The Kite ◆ took time to pick up from the back of the field and by the time he had engaged full gear the race was effectively over, but he came home well. He did hang slightly, but nothing like as much as he had when winning his last two starts. This rates a pleasing Cambridgeshire trial, although his trainer has warned that the colt is not a confirmed runner at Newmarket. (tchd 5-1 in a place)
Right To Dream(IRE) only won a minor race at Warwick and he was held in this better company. His suitability for this trip was not confirmed ether way. (op 11-1)
Rockinante(FR) got to the front and set a strong gallop, but could not hold on in the final quarter mile. (tchd 11-1)

6030 BETFRED SPRINT CUP (BRITISH CHAMPIONS SERIES) (GROUP 1) 6f
3:25 (3:27) (Class 1) 3-Y-0+
£127,597 (£48,375; £24,210; £12,060; £6,052; £3,037) **Stalls** Centre

Form				RPR
-353	**1**		**Society Rock (IRE)**[56] 4100 5-9-3 117.... KierenFallon 3 (James Fanshawe) *stdd s: midfield: rdn and hdwy on inner over 1f out: rn to ld fnl 75yds: in command cl home* **10/1**	122
0321	**2**	*¾*	**Gordon Lord Byron (IRE)**[14] 5597 4-9-3 112.... RichardKingscote 12 (T Hogan, Ire) *midfield: hdwy 1/2-way: led over 1f out: hdd fnl 75yds: hld cl home* **12/1**	120
-126	**3**	*1 ¼*	**Bated Breath**[15] 5561 5-9-3 118.... JamesDoyle 1 (Roger Charlton) *awkward s: sn trckd ldrs: effrt to chal over 1f out: nt qckn ins fnl f: styd on same pce towards fin* **11/4**[2]	116
0100	**4**	*¾*	**Dandy Boy (ITY)**[15] 5561 6-9-3 113.... JamieSpencer 8 (David Marnane, Ire) *s.s: hld up: rdn and hdwy over 1f out: styd on ins fnl f: nt quite able to rch ldrs* **20/1**	113
0400	**5**	*1 ¾*	**Genki (IRE)**[56] 4100 8-9-3 107....(b) HayleyTurner 14 (Roger Charlton) *dwlt: hld up: rdn and swtchd rt 1f out whn struggling to go pce: styd on ins fnl f: nrst fin* **50/1**	108
5102	**6**	*hd*	**Wizz Kid (IRE)**[34] 4861 4-9-0 110.... GeraldMosse 13 (Robert Collet, France) *in rr: niggled along over 4f out: rdn over 1f out: kpt on ins fnl f: nvr gng pce to get competitive* **9/1**	104
002	**7**	*hd*	**Strong Suit (USA)**[21] 5355 4-9-3 120.... RichardHughes 9 (Richard Hannon) *led: rdn and hdd over 1f out: fdd fnl 100yds* **11/2**[3]	106
3164	**8**	*hd*	**Majestic Myles (IRE)**[21] 5355 4-9-3 110.... FrederikTylicki 11 (Richard Fahey) *prom: rdn to chal over 1f out: kpt on same pce ins fnl f: no ex fnl 75yds* **33/1**	106
4431	**9**	*¾*	**Hitchens (IRE)**[14] 5581 7-9-3 114.... GrahamGibbons 4 (David Barron) *trckd ldrs: lost pl bef 1/2-way: outpcd wl over 1f out: kpt on same pce ins fnl f* **16/1**	103
0105	**10**	*1 ¼*	**Elusivity (IRE)**[7] 5822 4-9-3 105.... DaneO'Neill 7 (Brian Meehan) *midfield: rdn over 1f out: no imp: wknd fnl 100yds: sn eased* **80/1**	99
3501	**11**	*1 ¾*	**Hawkeyethenoo (IRE)**[35] 4802 6-9-3 108.... GrahamLee 10 (Jim Goldie) *hld up in rr: rdn over 2f out: failed to pick-up: nvr on terms* **16/1**	94
0411	**12**	*¾*	**Ortensia (AUS)**[15] 5561 7-9-0 115.... WilliamBuick 15 (Paul Messara, Australia) *hld up: impoved into midfield over 3f out: pushed along 2f out: failed to pick-up over 1f out: wknd ins fnl f: eased whn wl btn fnl 75yds* **5/2**[1]	88
0004	**13**	*3 ¼*	**Es Que Love (IRE)**[14] 5581 3-9-1 105.... JoeFanning 2 (Mark Johnston) *stmbld s: sn w ldr: rdn 2f out: wknd over 1f out: eased whn wl btn fnl 100yds* **40/1**	81

1m 10.2s (-3.60) **Going Correction** -0.35s/f (Firm)
WFA 3 from 4yo+ 2lb **13 Ran SP% 122.5**
Speed ratings (Par 117): **110,109,107,106,104 103,103,103,102,100 98,97,92**
Tote Swingers: 1&2 £14.10, 1&3 £7.60, 2&3 £9.60 CSF £121.79 CT £440.73 TOTE £9.30: £2.30, £3.80, £1.60; EX 161.80 Trifecta £1018.40 Pool: £4,541.56 - 3.30 winning units..
Owner Simon Gibson **Bred** San Gabriel Investments **Trained** Newmarket, Suffolk

FOCUS
An ordinary edition of this top sprint, which has held Group 1 status since 1988. There were some big-name absentees, among them July Cup winner Mayson (unsatisfactory scope), Excelebration and Hoof It. In contrast to the earlier 5f handicap, where they spread across the track and the pace was with those drawn high, this time the field bunched towards the far side. The pace was not especially strong and with the favourite below par this form is a little unsatisfactory. Society Rock rates a length personal best, and Gordon Lord Byron continues on a high. Bated Breath was a few pounds off his best.

NOTEBOOK
Society Rock(IRE) behaved better at the start than he sometimes does and got away on terms. Chasing the pace near the far rail, he took a gap when it came for a tenacious victory. The July Cup third was one of only two previous winners at this level, his Group 1 win coming in the 2011 Golden Jubilee Stakes, and this was his first victory since. Ascot is a happy hunting ground for him, and the British Champions Sprint there next month may be suitable, although he trailed home twelfth behind stablemate Deacon Blues in the race last year. (op 9-1)
Gordon Lord Byron(IRE) went close to giving the Irish their first success in this event for 40 years. Raised considerably in grade after taking the Listed City Of York Stakes over 7f last time, he looked set to win when sweeping to the front but was run down in the last half-furlong. The drop in trip was fine for him and he handled the ground remarkably well given most of his form has been in easy conditions. This was certainly a taking trial for the Ayr Gold Cup, in which he has top weight. (op 14-1)
Bated Breath looked to have a bright chance of finally earning Group 1 honours, with the quick ground in his favour. In the event he ran a solid race but just came up short. Connections offered no excuses, but he did slip a bit leaving the stalls and was momentarily short of room at one point when attempting to challenge. Official explanation: jockey said horse slipped start. (op 3-1)
Dandy Boy(ITY) had solid excuses in his two previous ventures into this company in the July Cup (heavy ground) and Nunthorpe (trip too sharp). He travelled nicely here and ran on for fourth, but would have been seen in an even better light had the gallop been stronger. (tchd 22-1)
Genki(IRE) might have been retired had he not performed with zest here, but that could be deferred following this better effort. He had reached the frame in the previous two editions of this race.

Wizz Kid(IRE), a 5l second to Moonlight Cloud in the Group 1 Prix Maurice de Gheest last month, made late progress on the outside without becoming seriously involved. Easier ground would have suited her. (op 12-1)
Strong Suit(USA)'s connections were confident of a good run from their colt, whose only previous run in a top sprint had come in bog-like conditions in the July Cup. The chestnut showed bright pace to lead these proven sprinters, but was back-pedalling in the final furlong. He has not captured his best this term, his Hungerford Stakes second notwithstanding, but it's too soon to be writing him off. He has a number of options remaining this year. (tchd 5-1)
Majestic Myles(IRE) travelled well just off the pace but was fading inside the last on this first try at Group 1 level. He's most effective at 7f.
Hawkeyethenoo(IRE) was unsuited by the firm going. Official explanation: trainer said gelding was unsuited by going (firm). (op 20-1)
Ortensia(AUS), bidding for a hat-trick after 5f wins at Goodwood and York, went to post early as usual. She found herself trapped wide of the bunch with no cover and although she was close enough with two furlongs left, there was none of the overdrive she had produced in the Nunthorpe. A valid excuse was quickly offered as it emerged she suffered an overreach. She now returns to Australia following a fine summer. Official explanation: trainer said mare suffered an over-reach. (tchd 10-3 in a place)

6031 BETFRED MOBILE LOTTO OLD BOROUGH CUP (H'CAP) 1m 6f
4:00 (4:00) (Class 2) (0-105,100) 3-Y-O+**£32,345** (£9,625; £4,810; £2,405) **Stalls** Low

Form RPR
1130 **1** **Sir Graham Wade (IRE)**[14] 5598 3-8-9 **96** KierenFallon 14 108+
(Mark Johnston) *hld up in rr: hdwy whn nt clr run and swtchd lft over 2f out: swtchd rt over 1f out and nt clr run again: prog ins fnl f: rdr had whip knocked out of hand whn r.o to ld towards fin* **7/2**[1]
1363 **2** *hd* **Tropical Beat**[15] 5558 4-9-4 **94** NickyMackay 9 103
(John Gosden) *hld up in rr: hdwy on outer over 2f out: led over 1f out: edgd lft ins fnl f: hdd towards fin* **5/1**[2]
5035 **3** *3* **Itlaaq**[17] 5491 6-9-1 **91** (t) GrahamGibbons 7 96
(Michael Easterby) *hld up in mdfield: hdwy over 2f out: ev ch fr over 1f out: nt qckn wl ins fnl f: kpt on same pce towards fin* **18/1**
6040 **4** *1 ½* **Blue Bajan (IRE)**[14] 5600 10-9-7 **97** GrahamLee 4 102+
(David O'Meara) *hld up: hdwy whn nt clr run and swtchd lft over 2f out: continually denied a run tl ins fnl f: styd on wl towards fin* **11/1**
4421 **5** *shd* **Gosbeck**[25] 5200 4-8-11 **87** DaneO'Neill 2 90
(Henry Candy) *in tch: led 2f out: rdn and hdd over 1f out: no ex fnl 75yds* **15/2**
034 **6** *1 ¼* **Lyric Street (IRE)**[28] 5076 4-9-4 **94** RichardHughes 1 95
(Ed Dunlop) *trckd ldrs: effrt 2f out: nt qckn over 1f out: one pce wl ins fnl f* **11/2**[3]
6450 **7** *¾* **Becausewecan (USA)**[15] 5540 6-8-2 **78** JoeFanning 10 78
(Mark Johnston) *prom: rdn over 3f out: rdn whn chalng over 2f out: wknd ins fnl 100yds* **18/1**
1200 **8** *nk* **Crackentorp**[14] 5600 7-9-10 **100** PaulMulrennan 3 100
(Tim Easterby) *trckd ldrs: lost pl over 4f out: sn outpcd: kpt on ins fnl f but no imp* **33/1**
3650 **9** *1* **High Office**[17] 5491 6-8-9 **85** FrederikTylicki 11 83
(Richard Fahey) *midfield: lost pl over 4f out: unable to get on terms after* **14/1**
3210 **10** *4 ½* **Moon Trip**[14] 5580 3-7-13 **86** LukeMorris 13 78
(Mark Johnston) *midfield: pushed along over 4f out: wknd over 2f out* **13/2**
2010 **11** *6* **Herostatus**[17] 5491 5-8-11 **87** (v) JamesDoyle 5 71
(David O'Meara) *led: rdn and hdd 2f out: wknd over 1f out: eased whn wl btn ins fnl f* **25/1**
-004 **12** *3 ¾* **Ultimate**[21] 4621 6-8-1 **77** JimmyQuinn 12 55
(Brian Ellison) *hld up: struggling 4f out: nvr on terms* **28/1**
213 **13** *19* **Address Unknown**[21] 5333 5-9-9 **99** (vt) JamieSpencer 8 51
(Ian Williams) *prom: rdn over 4f out: btn whn bmpd over 2f out: sn dropped away* **12/1**

2m 57.65s (-4.35) **Going Correction** -0.075s/f (Good)
WFA 3 from 4yo+ 11lb **13** Ran SP% **122.8**
Speed ratings (Par 109): **109,108,107,106,106 105,105,104,104,101 98,96,85**
Tote Swingers: 1&2 £5.60, 1&3 £10.20, 2&3 £25.80 CSF £20.25 CT £286.82 TOTE £4.40: £1.70, £2.40, £4.70; EX 23.20 Trifecta £725.10 Pool: £35,184.56 - 51.60 winning units..
Owner Paul Dean **Bred** P D Savill **Trained** Middleham Moor, N Yorks

FOCUS
This race was run over 107 yards further than the advertised distance. A competitive field for this valuable handicap, but perhaps not as strong a race as it might have been for the money. The pace was pretty brisk and the first two, who finished clear, both came from the back of the field. The Mark Johnston stable has now won this handicap four times since 2003. Sir Graham Wade is rated a bit better than the bare form, which looks solid.

NOTEBOOK
Sir Graham Wade(IRE), one of just two 3yos in the field, had run poorly at York, but had been progressive before that and he resumed his upward curve here. He would have been a most unlucky loser, as he found his path blocked on the inside then his rider had his whip knocked out of his hand inside the final 100 yards, but he came with a strong run when in the clear to pick up the leader in the last strides. He could run under a penalty in the Mallard Handicap at Doncaster next week. The Stewards considered the apparent improvement in form of the winner, compared with his previous run at York, and noted that the trainer could offer no explanation. Official explanation: trainer had no explination as to apparent improvement in form. (tchd 11-2 in a place)
Tropical Beat picked up from the back to lead in the straight, avoiding the trouble by coming down the outside, but could not hold off the winner who'd had an interrupted passage. He seemed to try hard enough this time and saw the trip out well enough. (op 6-1)
Itlaaq's four previous outings this year had all been at York, the last two of them over an extended 2m. He ran a solid race and had every chance but was outpaced by the principals when it mattered. (op 16-1)
Blue Bajan(IRE) was reunited with Graham Lee, who rode him to victory in the 2008 Swinton Hurdle here. The 10-y-o travelled well but was chopped for room on the rail, which might have cost him third place as he ran on well once pulled out. He's very well handicapped on last year's form. (op 12-1)
Gosbeck got to the front in the straight but was cut down inside the last. A 4lb rise for her Salisbury win had taken her to a career-high mark. (op 7-1)
Lyric Street(IRE), back in trip, ran his race with no obvious excuses. He's yet to win a handicap. (op 6-1 tchd 5-1)

6032 BETFRED "BONUS KING BINGO" NURSERY 6f
4:30 (4:30) (Class 2) 2-Y-O **£9,703** (£2,887; £1,443; £721) **Stalls** Centre

Form RPR
3050 **1** **Baddilini**[16] 5515 2-9-7 **87** RichardHughes 1 90
(Alan Bailey) *wnt rt s: hld up: shkn up 2f out: hdwy 1f out: rdn and edgd lft ins fnl f: r.o to ld towards fin* **12/1**
2000 **2** *1* **Blue Lotus (IRE)**[14] 5602 2-8-9 **75** GrahamGibbons 10 75
(Tim Easterby) *chsd ldrs: led over 1f out: sn rdn: hdd towards fin* **33/1**
3411 **3** *nk* **Capo Rosso (IRE)**[29] 5041 2-9-2 **82** RichardKingscote 6 84
(Tom Dascombe) *prom: effrt and nt clr run over 1f out and again ins fnl f: r.o: nvr able to chal* **11/2**[2]
202 **4** *nk* **Star Of Rohm**[43] 4526 2-9-1 **81** JamieSpencer 11 79
(Michael Bell) *hld up: hdwy over 1f out: rdn and edgd lft ins fnl f: r.o* **13/2**
0512 **5** *½* **Tumblewind**[11] 5711 2-8-3 **69** PaulQuinn 7 65
(Richard Whitaker) *hld up: hdwy over 2f out: rdn over 1f out: styd on same pce ins fnl f* **25/1**
0312 **6** *1 ½* **Salutation (IRE)**[14] 5602 2-9-1 **81** JoeFanning 8 73
(Mark Johnston) *sn led: rdn and hdd over 1f out: edgd lft and no ex ins fnl f* **6/1**[3]
01 **7** *nk* **Grey Street**[21] 5367 2-8-8 **74** FrederikTylicki 4 65
(Richard Fahey) *s.i.s and hmpd s: hdwy over 3f out: outpcd over 1f out: r.o ins fnl f* **11/2**[2]
612 **8** *½* **Derwent (USA)**[15] 5527 2-9-4 **84** JamesDoyle 9 73
(Roger Charlton) *hld up: hdwy over 2f out: sn rdn: no ex ins fnl f* **11/2**[2]
41 **9** *2* **Kamchatka**[31] 4960 2-8-12 **78** JimmyQuinn 3 61
(Alan Swinbank) *hmpd s: chsd ldrs: rdn over 1f out: wknd fnl f* **5/1**[1]
2120 **10** *3 ¼* **Bircham (IRE)**[36] 4763 2-9-5 **85** KierenFallon 5 57
(Mahmood Al Zarooni) *chsd ldrs: rdn over 1f out: wknd ins fnl f* **15/2**

1m 12.27s (-1.53) **Going Correction** -0.35s/f (Firm) **10** Ran SP% **116.7**
Speed ratings (Par 101): **96,94,94,93,93 91,90,90,87,83**
Tote Swingers: 1&2 £22.70, 1&3 £10.50, 2&3 £15.40 CSF £335.82 CT £2463.29 TOTE £15.10: £3.80, £7.40, £2.10; EX 492.40 Trifecta £1138.60 Part won. Pool: £1,538.74 - 0.10 winning units..
Owner Mrs A Shone & Mrs V Hubbard **Bred** Mrs A R Ruggles **Trained** Newmarket, Suffolk

FOCUS
A decent nursery and a very open betting market, but a bit of a rough race. The runners converged towards the far side, as they had in the Sprint Cup. Straightforward form, best viewed around the runner-up.

NOTEBOOK
Baddilini had failed to build on his debut success, but had proved largely consistent other than his one try at 7f. Taken early to post, he was involved in buffeting leaving the stalls and was held up. He had to wait for a run, but came through to win a shade comfortably in the end. (tchd 14-1)
Blue Lotus(IRE) went to post early. He got to the front and battled on, and this represented a return to form after some below-par efforts.
Capo Rosso(IRE), a C&D winner off 4lb lower last time, was arguably unlucky not to complete a hat-trick, as he was short of room a couple of times. He came home well, and remains in good heart. (op 5-1)
Star Of Rohm, the only maiden in the field, ran a fair race off a 3lb higher mark than when runner-up at Ascot. (op 7-1)
Tumblewind had her chance, but the extra furlong was perhaps just stretching her late on. (op 22-1)
Salutation(IRE) ran creditably from the front, but is 11lb higher than for his Newcastle win two starts ago. (tchd 5-1)
Grey Street, whose Ripon maiden has been working out well, was doing her best work at the end.
Kamchatka was involved in a barging match with the winner leaving the stalls and failed to fire. (op 9-2)

6033 PLAY RAINBOW RICHES AT BETFRED H'CAP 1m 6f
5:05 (5:05) (Class 3) (0-90,89) 3-Y-O **£8,409** (£2,502; £1,250; £625) **Stalls** Low

Form RPR
110 **1** **Courtesy Call (IRE)**[14] 5598 3-8-13 **81** JoeFanning 8 91+
(Mark Johnston) *prom: lost pl after 2f: hdwy over 3f out: led over 1f out: sn rdn: edgd lft ins fnl f: styd on* **16/1**
2125 **2** *1* **Muntasir (IRE)**[20] 5383 3-9-7 **89** (p) KierenFallon 9 98
(Saeed Bin Suroor) *chsd ldrs: led over 3f out: rdn and hdd over 1f out: styd on* **11/1**
1441 **3** *½* **Lady Kashaan (IRE)**[20] 5383 3-8-7 **75** JimmyQuinn 3 84+
(Alan Swinbank) *chsd ldrs: rdn and ev ch over 2f out: swtchd lft ins fnl f: styd on u.p* **12/1**
3441 **4** *¾* **Ex Oriente (IRE)**[21] 5366 3-9-5 **87** NickyMackay 2 94
(John Gosden) *chsd ldrs: rdn over 2f out: styd on* **8/1**
3136 **5** *1 ¼* **Flashman**[14] 5598 3-8-9 **77** FrederikTylicki 4 83
(Richard Fahey) *prom: rdn over 2f out: styd on same pce fnl f* **5/1**[2]
4522 **6** *1* **Aazif (IRE)**[29] 5044 3-9-2 **84** RichardHughes 7 88
(John Dunlop) *hld up: hdwy over 3f out: rdn over 1f out: no ex ins fnl f* **9/4**[1]
2320 **7** *7* **Beyond Conceit (IRE)**[14] 5598 3-9-5 **87** JamieSpencer 6 81
(Tom Tate) *chsd ldr: hdwy after 2f: sn led: rdn and hdd over 3f out: wknd over 1f out* **11/2**[3]
0251 **8** *2 ½* **Cape Safari (IRE)**[11] 5718 3-9-0 **82** (p) HayleyTurner 10 73
(Alan Bailey) *mid-div: hdwy over 3f out: rdn and wknd over 1f out* **33/1**
506 **9** *7* **Caphene**[22] 5309 3-8-2 **70** PaulQuinn 5 51
(John Dunlop) *s.i.s: sn pushed along in rr: lost tch fnl 4f* **40/1**
011 **10** *99* **Between Us**[18] 5442 3-8-12 **80** LukeMorris 1
(Sir Mark Prescott Bt) *led: hung rt: rdr lost irons and hdd after 2f: sn bhd: t.o* **11/2**[3]

3m 0.12s (-1.88) **Going Correction** -0.075s/f (Good) **10** Ran SP% **116.6**
Speed ratings (Par 105): **102,101,101,100,100 99,95,94,90,33**
Tote Swingers: 1&2 £18.10, 1&3 £18.10, 2&3 £9.90 CSF £179.57 CT £2188.30 TOTE £20.10: £3.40, £3.20, £3.20; EX 126.30 Trifecta £1179.80 Part won. Pool: £1,594.41 - 0.20 winning units..
Owner A D Spence **Bred** Mrs James Wigan **Trained** Middleham Moor, N Yorks

FOCUS
This fair handicap took place over 107 yards further than advertised and was run in a time 2.47sec slower than the earlier Class 2 event. The runners came over to the stands' side on entering the home straight before fanning across the track in the latter stages. The winner showed he's just as good on turf as on the AW, and the second is still on the up too.

NOTEBOOK
Courtesy Call(IRE) got to the front on the stands' rail and ran on well. Well at home on fast ground, as well as on Polytrack, he was winning his fifth handicap this year, the first of which came off just 58. The Stewards considered his apparent improvement in form, compared with his previous run at York, and noted the trainer's explanation that the gelding appeared to benefit from the firm ground on this occasion. Official explanation: trainer said regarding apparent improvement in form that gelding benefited from better ground (firm). (op 12-1)
Muntasir(IRE), a beaten favourite four times in his short career, travelled up well in the first-time cheekpieces and stuck on for second. (op 9-1)
Lady Kashaan(IRE) has progressed well and she ran another solid race off a 5lb higher mark, staying on after having to be switched away from the rail. She had no problem with the trip. (tchd 14-1)
Ex Oriente(IRE) ran creditably off 6lb higher, appearing to stay the extra quarter mile. (tchd 9-1)
Flashman went up 11lb for his C&D win in July and the handicapper has looked in charge since. (op 7-1)
Aazif(IRE) looked well worth a try at this sort of trip, but after travelling up nicely he could not sustain his effort. (tchd 5-2 in places)

Between Us all but ran out at the paddock bend. Official explanation: jockey said filly tried to run out. (tchd 5-1)
T/Jkpt: Part won. £79,461.10 to a £1 stake. Part won. Pool: £111,917.14 - 0.50 winning tickets. T/Plt: £81.00 to a £1 stake. Pool: £155,569.13 - 1,401.04 winning tickets. T/Qpdt: £37.10 to a £1 stake. Pool: £7,067.64 - 140.96 winning tickets. DO

6013 KEMPTON (A.W) (R-H)

Saturday, September 8

OFFICIAL GOING: Standard
Wind: virtually nil Weather: sunny and warm

6034 BETFRED "BIGGER AND BETTER GOALS GALORE" CONDITIONS STKS 7f (P)

1:55 (1:55) (Class 4) 2-Y-O **£4,398** (£1,309; £654) **Stalls** Low

Form RPR
21 1 **Mutazamen**[14] 5578 2-9-2 83 TadhgO'Shea 4 80+
(Richard Hannon) *mde all: pushed along and qcknd clr jst over 2f out: heavily eased fnl 100yds* **1/7**[1]

2 2 1/2 **Vodnik (IRE)** 2-8-12 0 JimCrowley 1 60+
(Sir Michael Stoute) *in tch: rdn 1/2-way: chsd clr wnr 2f out: one pce and no imp tl clsd on eased wnr fnl 100yds* **11/2**[2]

3 3 1/2 **Didnt I Do Well** 2-8-12 0 AdamBeschizza 3 45
(Julia Feilden) *pushed along leaving stalls: chsd wnr: rdn 3f out: outpcd and dropped to last 2f out: plugged on but wl hld after* **66/1**[3]

1m 31.4s (5.40) **Going Correction** -0.075s/f (Stan) **3** Ran SP% **104.4**
Speed ratings (Par 97): **66,63,59**
CSF £1.18 TOTE £1.10; EX 1.10.
Owner Hamdan Al Maktoum **Bred** Alpha Bloodstock Limited **Trained** East Everleigh, Wilts

FOCUS
The last four winners of this contest had already been successful and the last five favourites had gone in, but it would have been a major shock had those trends not continued in this most uncompetitive of events. Very hard to put a meaningful figure to the form.

NOTEBOOK
Mutazamen already had decent turf form on the board and wasn't hard pressed to dominate the two newcomers. The winning margin doesn't reflect his superiority, but this told us nothing new about him. (op 1-5)
Vodnik(IRE), a half-brother to a dual 1m2f Polytrack winner our of a half-sister to Spectrum and Stream Of Gold and to the dams of both Conduit and Petrushka, ran green throughout and is grossly flattered to finish so close to the long odds-on favourite. He looks to need more time. (op 4-1)
Didnt I Do Well, already gelded and out of a half-sister to three winners including one at Listed level, raced wide of his two rivals and was firmly put in his place, but at least he picked up a bit of prize money. (op 50-1)

6035 BETFRED MOBILE SPORTS SEPTEMBER STKS (GROUP 3) 1m 4f (P)

2:30 (2:30) (Class 1) 3-Y-O+
£31,190 (£11,825; £5,918; £2,948; £1,479; £742) **Stalls** Centre

Form RPR
2202 1 **Dandino**[36] 4759 5-9-4 107 JimCrowley 2 113
(James Fanshawe) *hld up wl in tch: rdn and qcknd to ld over 1f out: r.o wl fnl f: rdn out* **7/2**[3]

0-22 2 1 1/4 **Sagramor**[28] 5117 4-9-4 112 DarryllHolland 8 111
(Hughie Morrison) *stdd and dropped in bhd s: hld up in last pair: swtchd rt and rdn 2f out: hdwy to chse wnr ent fnl f: r.o u.p but no imp fnl 100yds* **5/1**

-463 3 1/2 **Modun (IRE)**[21] 5354 5-9-4 110 HarryBentley 3 110
(Saeed Bin Suroor) *dwlt: sn pushed along and rcvrd to r in tch: rdn and effrt to press ldrs 2f out: carried sltly lft over 1f out: chsd ldng pair 1f out: kpt on but no threat to wnr* **10/3**[2]

-330 4 1 **Mijhaar**[56] 4112 4-9-4 104 NeilCallan 6 109
(Roger Varian) *propped and unbalanced leaving stalls: stdd and racd in last: swtchd lft and effrt ent fnl 2f: hdwy over 1f out: chsd ldng trio ins fnl f: kpt on but no threat to wnr* **3/1**[1]

02-6 5 2 1/4 **Arrigo (GER)**[21] 5354 4-9-4 114 SebSanders 7 105
(Ibrahim Saeed Al Malki, Qatar) *hld up in tch: rdn and sltly outpcd jst over 2f out: rallied and hdwy u.p jst over 1f out: styd on same pce and no imp ins fnl f* **33/1**

-302 6 3/4 **Circumvent**[119] 2081 5-9-4 105 FergusSweeney 4 104
(Paul Cole) *led: rdn and qcknd wl over 2f out: edgd lft u.p and hdd over 1f out: unable qck and struggling ent fnl f: wknd fnl 150yds* **16/1**

-255 7 nk **Haya Landa (FR)**[28] 5116 4-9-1 110 FranckBlondel 1 100
(Mme L Audon, France) *chsd ldrs: rdn and effrt to chal wl over 1f out: no ex and outpcd jst over 1f out: wknd fnl f* **16/1**

-014 8 1 **Incendo**[35] 4795 6-9-4 88 (t) MartinLane 5 102?
(James Fanshawe) *stdd s: hld up in tch: rdn and effrt on inner 2f out: sn drvn and no imp: wknd ent fnl f* **33/1**

36-2 9 1 **Calvados Blues (FR)**[21] 5364 6-9-4 110 SilvestreDeSousa 10 100
(Mahmood Al Zarooni) *chsd ldr: rdn and v awkward hd carriage over 2f out: nt qckn and drvn ent fnl 2f: wknd jst over 1f out* **7/1**

2m 30.7s (-3.80) **Going Correction** -0.075s/f (Stan) **9** Ran SP% **117.1**
Speed ratings (Par 113): **109,108,107,107,105 105,104,104,103**
toteswingers 1&2 £3.10, 1&3 £2.70, 2&3 £8.10 CSF £21.79 TOTE £3.50: £1.50, £1.90, £1.80; EX 18.40 Trifecta £43.50 Pool: £850.98 - 14.45 winning units..
Owner Elite Racing Club **Bred** Elite Racing Club **Trained** Newmarket, Suffolk

FOCUS
The seventh running of the September Stakes on Polytrack and although the early pace didn't seem that strong, the winning time was fair. Ordinary form for the grade, rated around the winner.

NOTEBOOK
Dandino hadn't won since landing the Group 2 Jockey Club Stakes at Newmarket in April of last year, but he had been there or thereabouts for his new yard in Group/Listed company on a sound surface this season. Making his AW debut, his sire boasts a 14% strike-rate here, which offered encouragement, and he seemed to take to the surface with no problem at all. Once the gap appeared for him over a furlong from home as the field fanned out, he quickened smartly to the front and won this with some authority. He deserved this.
Sagramor, runner-up in Group 3 company in both of his previous starts this season, won over 7f here as a 2yo but this trip was a new challenge and he was ridden to get it. He looked a danger when diving to the inside after the cutaway and kept on gamely up the far rail, but the winner was always holding him. Despite this decent effort, he does look best over shorter. (op 11-2)
Modun(IRE), trained by Sir Michael Stoute when winning this race last year, made his effort wide coming to the last 2f and though plugging on to the line, this effort does suggest that he is still operating short of his very best. (tchd 7-2)
Mijhaar, who hasn't enjoyed much luck in his recent outings, tried to come from last place and was forced to make his effort widest in the home straight. He stayed on without ever quite getting there and this took his sire's record with his runners here to 0-29. (op 4-1)
Arrigo(GER) didn't show a lot when tailed off behind Mount Athos (a long way behind Modun) on his British debut in the Geoffrey Freer last month and merely plugged on here after losing his position starting up the straight.
Circumvent, returning from 119 days off, looked a non-stayer in his only previous try over this far and, having made the running, fell in a hole once headed by the winner after passing the intersection.
Haya Landa(FR) was right there with every chance over a furlong from home, but then emptied quickly and has only won one of her 14 starts.
Incendo has a fine record here, but had it all to do in this company and a brief effort on the inside after the cutaway came to nothing. (op 28-1)
Calvados Blues(FR) raced prominently until folding under pressure over 2f from home and was inclined to carry his head like an ostrich. (op 13-2 tchd 6-1)

6036 BETFRED LONDON MILE H'CAP (SERIES FINAL) 1m (P)

3:05 (3:07) (Class 2) 3-Y-O+
£27,265 (£8,164; £4,082; £2,041; £1,020; £512) **Stalls** Low

Form RPR
5520 1 **Shavansky**[27] 5129 8-8-6 85 MircoDemuro 16 96
(Rod Millman) *stdd and dropped in bhd after s: hld up in rr: swtchd lft and hdwy on outer 2f out: str run over 1f out: chal ins fnl f: r.o wl to ld towards fin* **33/1**

0505 2 nk **Come On Blue Chip (IRE)**[9] 5768 3-8-4 88 (b) ChrisCatlin 13 98
(Paul D'Arcy) *hld up towards rr: rdn and effrt towards centre over 2f out: hdwy u.p over 1f out: ev ch ins fnl f: drvn to ld wl ins fnl f: sn hdd and no ex* **33/1**

6452 3 1 **Loving Spirit**[22] 5301 4-8-13 92 PatCosgrave 5 100
(James Toller) *hld up in tch in midfield: swtchd lft and effrt towards centre over 1f out: drvn and chsd ldrs 1f out: led ins fnl f: hdd and one pce wl ins fnl f* **8/1**[2]

6660 4 2 1/4 **George Guru**[21] 5356 5-8-11 93 MarkCoumbe(3) 10 96
(Michael Attwater) *hld up in tch: swtchd rt and effrt u.p on inner 2f out: chsd ldrs 1f out: outpcd and btn fnl 150yds* **16/1**

0306 5 hd **Cruiser**[4] 5914 4-8-6 85 KierenFox 11 87
(William Muir) *in tch: hdwy and edgd rt 2f out: rdn to ld over 1f out: drvn and hrd pressed ent fnl f: hdd ins fnl f: wknd fnl 100yds* **33/1**

131 6 3/4 **Royal Empire (IRE)**[9] 5768 3-8-13 97 SilvestreDeSousa 7 98
(Saeed Bin Suroor) *in tch: chsd ldrs and rdn ent fnl 2f: unable qck u.p wl over 1f out: plugged on but no threat to ldrs fnl f* **13/8**[1]

0430 7 1/2 **Indian Jack (IRE)**[7] 5835 4-8-9 88 KirstyMilczarek 1 88
(Luca Cumani) *rdn along leaving stalls: in tch in midfield: swtchd rt and effrt 2f out: hdwy to press ldrs and drvn over 1f out: outpcd and btn jst ins fnl f: wknd fnl 75yds* **8/1**[2]

00-0 8 1 1/4 **Shamir**[22] 5301 5-8-6 85 FergusSweeney 14 82
(Jo Crowley) *in tch in midfield: rdn and unable qck over 2f out: rallied and hdwy u.p jst over 1f out: styd on same pce ins fnl f* **50/1**

0-04 9 3/4 **Atlantis Star**[9] 5768 5-8-7 86 AndreaAtzeni 9 81
(James Tate) *chsd ldrs tl led over 2f out: drvn 2f out: hdd over 1f out: wknd ins fnl f* **16/1**

0210 10 hd **Switzerland (IRE)**[16] 5517 3-8-10 94 MartinLane 3 88
(Mark Johnston) *hld up towards rr: effrt u.p on outer over 2f out: styd on past btn horses jst over 1f out: kpt on but nvr trbld ldrs* **11/1**

4041 11 3/4 **Chapter And Verse (IRE)**[10] 5746 6-8-7 86 NeilCallan 2 79
(Mike Murphy) *hld up towards rr: swtchd lft and hdwy towards inner over 1f out: drvn and no prog ent fnl f: wknd ins fnl f* **16/1**

3110 12 6 **Lockantanks**[22] 5301 5-8-8 92 CharlesBishop(5) 4 71
(Michael Appleby) *hld up in tch: nt clr run and trying to switch lft wl over 1f out: rdn and no prog over 1f out: sn wknd* **33/1**

0021 13 2 **Maverik**[12] 5667 4-8-6 85 JimCrowley 8 59
(Ralph Beckett) *led: rdn and hdd over 2f out: btn and fdd over 1f out: wl btn and eased wl ins fnl f* **9/1**[3]

0042 14 nse **Weapon Of Choice (IRE)**[9] 5768 4-8-10 89 JohnFahy 6 63
(Stuart Kittow) *in tch in midfield: lost pl and nt clr run on inner wl over 1f out: sn rdn and btn: wknd 1f out* **20/1**

-243 15 1/2 **Double Dealer**[22] 5301 4-9-2 95 HarryBentley 12 68
(Mahmood Al Zarooni) *chsd ldr: rdn and ev ch jst over 2f out: outpcd and losing pl whn hmpd wl over 1f out: sn bhd* **14/1**

0100 16 8 **Nazreef**[14] 5595 5-9-10 103 (vt) DarryllHolland 15 58
(Hughie Morrison) *sn rdn along: racd wd and in tch in midfield: lost pl over 2f out: bhd over 1f out* **25/1**

1m 36.67s (-3.13) **Going Correction** -0.075s/f (Stan)
WFA 3 from 4yo+ 5lb **16** Ran SP% **125.3**
Speed ratings (Par 109): **112,111,110,108,108 107,107,105,105,104 104,98,96,96,95 87**
toteswingers 1&2 £47.90, 1&3 £68.20, 2&3 £55.40 CSF £853.61 TOTE £56.50: £6.60, £8.00, £2.50, £3.40; EX 2415.30 TRIFECTA Not won..
Owner The Links Partnership **Bred** George Strawbridge **Trained** Kentisbeare, Devon
■ Stewards' Enquiry : Kieren Fox caution; careless riding.

FOCUS
This is normally a very open handicap, but they sent one horse of a very warm favourite this time. Several of these had already met each other in the qualifiers, so there were many labyrinthine lines of form, but in many ways this was an extraordinary race. Not only were the first two home huge prices, they were both drawn high and were dropped right out at the start. The pace was decent and none of those that helped force it figured in the finish, suggesting they may have gone off too quick. The winning time was good and the form looks solid.

NOTEBOOK
Shavansky has winning form off higher marks than this, but appeared to have it all to do from the outside stall. Having been dropped out last early, he still had plenty of ground to make up starting up the straight, but came with an irresistible effort down the wide outside to snatch the race close to the line. He has plenty of winning form over further, including twice over hurdles, so his stamina would have been an asset given the way the race was run and this was a decent effort from both horse and rider. (tchd 40-1)
Come On Blue Chip(IRE) ran a very similar race to the winner, coming from well back down the wide outside and he was unfortunate to just be run out of it. He had looked something of a Wolverhampton specialist before now, so even though it's a long way away, next March's Lincoln Trial could an ideal target. (op 40-1)
Loving Spirit was closely matched with several of these after his narrow defeat by Switzerland here last month and he was produced to hold every chance entering the last, but he was cut down by two stronger finishers. He hasn't won since his racecourse debut, but did nothing wrong here.
George Guru ◆ has been running creditably on turf this season and was 5lb higher than when winning on the Lingfield Polytrack in March. He ran a blinder here as he darted for the inside rail after the cutaway, while the front three made their efforts much wider, so he deserves extra credit for that. (tchd 18-1)
Cruiser looked like winning when bursting to the front over a furlong from home, but he couldn't maintain it. He did best of those to race close to the pace and his three runs here this year stand way above his turf efforts. (tchd 40-1)

Royal Empire(IRE) was the only one in this field with pretensions to be anything better than a handicapper, as this was just his third start and he only made his racecourse debut in July. Put up 7lb for winning his qualifier nine days earlier, he was backed almost to the exclusion of everything else, but he wasn't travelling that well in a handy position before halfway and although he stayed in the thick of the action until over a furlong from home, he then had no more to offer. Perhaps the hurly burly of a race like this came soon enough in his career and he is worth another chance. (op 9-4)

Indian Jack(IRE), a three-time winner here and back down to a more suitable trip, ran on towards the inside of the track after the cutaway, away from the main action, and wasn't disgraced. (tchd 15-2)

Shamir, a three-time winner over C&D, didn't show much when well behind a few of these on his return from 295 days off here last month, but he was noted making some late progress without offering a threat and may be worth keeping in mind for a winter campaign, as he will be fresher than many.

6037 BETFRED STILL TREBLE ODDS ON LUCKY 15'S H'CAP — 2m (P)

3:35 (3:39) (Class 4) (0-80,79) 3-Y-O — **£5,175** (£1,540; £769; £384) **Stalls** Low

Form — RPR

4204 **1** **Somemothersdohavem**[10] 5744 3-8-8 **66**..........(p) DaraghO'Donohoe 2 — 76
(John Ryan) *stdd s: hld up wl in rr: gd hdwy to ld 3f out: rdn and qcknd clr over 2f out: stl wl clr 1f out: tiring fnl 100yds but a jst lasting home* **14/1**

1315 **2** *hd* **Arch Villain (IRE)**[21] 5366 3-9-4 **76**.......... JimCrowley 7 — 86
(Amanda Perrett) *in tch in midfield: rdn and effrt on outer over 3f out: edgd rt over 2f out: chsd clr wnr over 1f out: styd on steadily and grad clsng on wnr fnl f: nvr quite getting to wnr* **3/1**[1]

4144 **3** *5* **Cellist**[21] 5373 3-9-2 **74**.......... NeilCallan 6 — 78
(William Haggas) *in tch in midfield: pushed along at times: rdn and effrt over 2f out: drvn and no imp over 1f out: plugged on to go 3rd ins fnl f* **6/1**

-531 **4** *2 1/2* **Awesome Pearl (USA)**[32] 4918 3-9-7 **79**.......... HarryBentley 1 — 80
(Sir Mark Prescott Bt) *chsd ldr tl led after 3f: rdn 5f out: hdd 3f out: sn drvn and outpcd: 3rd and wl btn 1f out* **11/2**[3]

0030 **5** *2 1/2* **Singalat**[38] 4700 3-9-7 **79**.......... ChrisCatlin 3 — 77
(James Given) *led for 3f: chsd ldrs: rdn and edgd rt u.p over 2f out: sn outpcd and btn* **12/1**

-203 **6** *9* **Dora's Gift**[33] 4875 3-9-0 **72**..........(b[1]) DarryllHolland 5 — 59
(Hughie Morrison) *short of room s and s.i.s: bhd: hdwy to chse ldrs 6f out: rdn and struggling whn hmpd wl over 2f out: sn wknd and bhd* **10/1**

141 **7** *2 1/2* **Red Orator**[10] 5729 3-9-6 **78**.......... SilvestreDeSousa 4 — 62
(Mark Johnston) *chsd ldrs: rdn and fnd nil over 2f out: sn wknd* **9/2**[2]

2330 **8** *2 3/4* **Daneking**[14] 5598 3-9-7 **79**.......... RobertHavlin 9 — 60
(John Gosden) *t.k.h: hld up in tch: rdn and btn over 2f out: bhd: eased and rdr looking down fnl f* **7/1**

4504 **9** *25* **Jorum**[32] 4918 3-8-13 **71**.......... PatCosgrave 8 — 22
(Sir Henry Cecil) *chsd ldr tl wnt upsides ldr after 3f tl 3f out: struggling whn swtchd lft and rdn over 2f out: sn hmpd and lost pl: wl bhd after: eased fnl f: t.o* **20/1**

3m 26.88s (-3.22) **Going Correction** -0.075s/f (Stan) — 9 Ran SP% **113.6**
Speed ratings (Par 103): **105,104,102,101,99 95,94,92,80**
toteswingers 1&2 £9.40, 2&3 £4.80, 1&3 £37.10 CSF £55.02 TOTE £21.90: £3.30, £2.10, £1.50; EX 72.80.
Owner John Ryan Racing Partnership **Bred** John And Susan Davis **Trained** Newmarket, Suffolk
■ Stewards' Enquiry : Chris Catlin caution; careless riding.
Daragh O'Donohoe two-day ban; used whip above permitted level (22nd-23rd Sept).

FOCUS
They finished very well spread out in this good staying handicap. The winner's Polytrack record is progressive.
Red Orator Official explanation: jockey said gelding had no more to give.
Daneking Official explanation: jockey said colt hung left.

6038 BETFRED "THE BONUS KING" SIRENIA STKS (GROUP 3) — 6f (P)

4:10 (4:10) (Class 1) 2-Y-O

£20,982 (£7,955; £3,981; £1,983; £995; £499) **Stalls** Low

Form — RPR

1301 **1** **Glass Office**[24] 5232 2-9-0 93.......... JimCrowley 9 — 106+
(David Simcock) *hld up in tch: swtchd lft and effrt 2f out: rdn to ld jst ins fnl f: r.o strly and sn clr: impressive* **12/1**

0201 **2** *3 1/2* **Zanetto**[21] 5360 2-9-0 82.......... LiamKeniry 7 — 96
(Andrew Balding) *t.k.h: w ldr: led 2f out and sn drvn: maintained narrow ld tl hdd and outpcd by wnr ins fnl f: sn btn but kpt on to hold 2nd* **25/1**

3412 **3** *hd* **Well Acquainted (IRE)**[16] 5515 2-9-0 95.......... JohnFahy 4 — 95
(Clive Cox) *chsd ldrs: rdn and effrt 2f out: drvn over 1f out: kpt on u.p and pressing for 2nd towards fin: no threat to wnr* **9/2**[2]

2110 **4** *1/2* **Hasopop (IRE)**[7] 5833 2-9-0 96.......... MircoDemuro 5 — 93
(Marco Botti) *hld up towards rr: stl plenty to do and swtchd lft over 1f out: styd on strly ins fnl f: no threat to wnr* **14/1**

2115 **5** *1 1/4* **Pearl Acclaim (IRE)**[15] 5559 2-9-0 103.......... HarryBentley 3 — 90
(Richard Hannon) *led: rdn over 2f out: hdd 2f out but stl ev ch tl outpcd by wnr jst ins fnl f: wknd fnl 75yds* **4/1**[1]

124 **6** *1 3/4* **Odooj (IRE)**[15] 5559 2-9-0 103.......... AdamBeschizza 11 — 84
(William Haggas) *dwlt and rdn along early: towards rr: edgd rt bnd over 4f out: hdwy u.p over 1f out: styd on steadily fnl f: nvr trbld ldrs* **7/1**

212 **7** *nse* **Ashaadd (IRE)**[21] 5371 2-9-0 93.......... NeilCallan 1 — 84
(Roger Varian) *in tch: rdn and chsd ldrs 2f out: drvn and unable qck over 1f out: wknd ins fnl f* **5/1**[3]

2030 **8** *1 1/2* **Mister Marc (IRE)**[16] 5515 2-9-0 95.......... SeanLevey 8 — 80
(Richard Hannon) *chsd ldrs: rdn and unable qck ent fnl 2f: no ex and btn over 1f out: wknd fnl f* **14/1**

1321 **9** *1 1/4* **Faithfilly (IRE)**[24] 5248 2-8-11 100.......... SilvestreDeSousa 12 — 73
(Ed Walker) *in tch on outer: rdn and unable qck ent fnl 2f: wknd jst over 1f out* **12/1**

011 **10** *2* **Intibaah**[15] 5527 2-9-0 92.......... TadhgO'Shea 6 — 70
(Brian Meehan) *short of room s and s.i.s: hld up towards rr: effrt on inner 2f out: no hdwy u.p over 1f out: sn wknd* **11/2**

312 **11** *8* **Boomshackerlacker (IRE)**[57] 4058 2-9-0 97.......... PatCosgrave 10 — 46
(George Baker) *s.i.s: swtchd rt after s: hld up in rr: hmpd bnd over 4f out: hanging rt and trying to switch lft over 2f out: sn wknd* **12/1**

1m 11.71s (-1.39) **Going Correction** -0.075s/f (Stan) — 11 Ran SP% **123.0**
Speed ratings (Par 105): **106,101,101,100,98 96,96,94,92,90 79**
toteswingers 1&2 £63.50, 2&3 £22.80, 1&3 £14.40 CSF £285.33 TOTE £17.10: £4.80, £9.60, £2.00; EX 338.90.
Owner Mrs Fitri Hay **Bred** Bloomsbury Stud **Trained** Newmarket, Suffolk

FOCUS
A competitive renewal of the Sirenia and the joint-biggest field for the race since it was moved on to the Polytrack. The winner impressed and the form is rated in line with the lesser renewals of this.

NOTEBOOK
Glass Office ran out a most impressive winner. He travelled well behind the leaders before being switched out wide over 2f from home, but the turn of foot he produced to settle this was quite taking. He is now 3-3 over C&D and for his sake it's a shame that this race is as good as it gets for 2yos on Polytrack in this country. (op 10-1)

Zanetto was always pressing the pace and looked a possible winner when taking it up over a furlong from home, but the winner then engaged the afterburner. He had the lowest BHA rating in this field, which may put a question mark against the form, but he may be worth giving the benefit of the doubt as he probably improve for the new surface. (tchd 28-1)

Well Acquainted(IRE) ran a blinder when second of 19 in the DBS Premier Yearling Stakes at the Ebor meeting and was always in about the same place here. He just lacked a turn of foot and may need a stiffer 6f or a return to 7f. (op 5-1)

Hasopop(IRE) didn't get home over 7f when stepped up to this level in the Solario, but was doing all his best work late here having been dropped out early. He may be worth another try over further if ridden this way.

Pearl Acclaim(IRE) tried to make all the running, but had little more to offer when headed by the runner-up over a furlong from home. (op 9-2)

Odooj(IRE) finished just ahead of Pearl Acclaim in the Gimcrack, but didn't get going until it was far too late this time. He looks in need of further now. (op 13-2)

Ashaadd(IRE), beaten just over 2l by Pearl Acclaim at Ripon and 3lb better off, held a good position on the inside for a long way but didn't see his race out. (op 6-1)

6039 BETFRED MOBILE CASINO H'CAP — 1m 3f (P)

4:45 (4:45) (Class 4) (0-85,87) 3-Y-O+ — **£5,175** (£1,540; £769; £384) **Stalls** Low

Form — RPR

4531 **1** **Enery (IRE)**[11] 5706 3-8-12 **79**.......... SilvestreDeSousa 8 — 88
(Mark Johnston) *chsd ldrs: wnt 2nd over 3f out: rdn to ld over 1f out: hld on wl u.p fnl f: rdn out* **9/2**[2]

-025 **2** *3/4* **Rawaki (IRE)**[48] 4363 4-9-12 **85**.......... DavidProbert 2 — 92
(Andrew Balding) *hld up in tch: rdn and effrt ent fnl 2f: drvn to press ldr ent fnl f: styd on same pce and a hld fnl 100yds* **9/4**[1]

0303 **3** *3/4* **Nave (USA)**[29] 5063 5-9-0 **73**.......... AdamBeschizza 9 — 79
(David Simcock) *hld up off the pce towards rr: rdn and hdwy over 1f out: styd on wl u.p ins fnl f* **8/1**[3]

1130 **4** *3/4* **Ultimate Destiny**[21] 5366 3-8-9 **76**.......... JimCrowley 7 — 81
(Ralph Beckett) *hld up in midfield: rdn and edgd rt jst over 2f out: hdwy u.p over 1f out: kpt on ins fnl f* **10/1**

5513 **5** *1 1/2* **Brigadoon**[7] 5838 5-8-13 **79**.......... WilliamTwiston-Davies(7) 3 — 81
(William Jarvis) *hld up in midfield: rdn and effrt whn edgd rt jst over 2f out: drvn and hdwy over 1f out: styd on same pce ins fnl f* **12/1**

5450 **6** *1/2* **Aldwick Bay (IRE)**[35] 4823 4-9-8 **81**.......... SeanLevey 4 — 82
(Richard Hannon) *hld up in tch: rdn and effrt to chse ldrs over 1f out: styd on same pce and no imp ins fnl f* **25/1**

-534 **7** *1 1/4* **Anton Dolin (IRE)**[69] 3661 4-9-6 **79**.......... NeilCallan 10 — 80+
(John Dunlop) *hld up in rr of main gp: rdn and effrt towards inner whn pushed rt and hmpd jst over 2f out: styd on same pce fr over 1f out* **8/1**[3]

0561 **8** *1 3/4* **Lyssio (GER)**[12] 5664 5-9-11 **87**.......... MarkCoumbe(3) 12 — 83
(Michael Attwater) *led after 1f: wnt clr 8f out: rdn and c towards centre over 2f out: hdd over 1f out: wknd ins fnl f* **8/1**[3]

3410 **9** *8* **No Compromise**[22] 5328 3-8-11 **78**.......... RobertHavlin 11 — 59
(Hughie Morrison) *hld up wl off the pce in rr of main gp: rdn and no hdwy jst over 2f out: wl btn fnl f* **12/1**

0 **10** *8* **Spin Of A Coin (IRE)**[39] 4689 4-9-2 **80**.......... AshleyMorgan(5) 5 — 47
(Pat Murphy) *stdd and awkward leaving stalls: a off the pce and towards rr of main gp: rdn and effrt whn pushed rt jst over 2f out: sn wknd* **22/1**

0/3- **11** *35* **Vivre Libre**[114] 5-9-7 **80**.......... PatCosgrave 1
(Tom George) *t.k.h: led for 1f: chsd ldrs after: rdn and struggling to qckn whn pushed rt and hmpd jst over 2f out: sn btn and wknd: eased fnl f: t.o* **33/1**

-060 **12** *3 3/4* **Samsons Son**[15] 5558 8-9-10 **83**.......... ChrisCatlin 6
(Terry Clement) *sn detached in last and nvr gng wl: lost tch and t.o fnl 4f* **25/1**

2m 19.14s (-2.76) **Going Correction** -0.075s/f (Stan)
WFA 3 from 4yo+ 8lb — 12 Ran SP% **121.7**
Speed ratings (Par 105): **107,106,105,105,104 103,103,101,95,90 64,61**
toteswingers 1&2 £3.10, 1&3 £6.40, 2&3 £5.80 CSF £14.70 TOTE £5.80: £2.70, £1.30, £2.50; EX 20.20.
Owner Sheikh Hamdan Bin Mohammed Al Maktoum **Bred** Ceka Ireland Limited **Trained** Middleham Moor, N Yorks
■ Stewards' Enquiry : David Probert 18-day ban (takes into account previous offences): used whip above permitted level (Sep 21 - Oct 9)

FOCUS
A fair handicap and the pace was solid. The winner continues on the up.

6040 BETFRED "THE HOME OF GOALS GALORE" H'CAP (DIV I) — 7f (P)

5:20 (5:20) (Class 4) (0-85,85) 3-Y-O+ — **£5,175** (£1,540; £769; £384) **Stalls** Low

Form — RPR

0510 **1** **Idler (IRE)**[10] 5736 3-8-12 **77**.......... SilvestreDeSousa 4 — 88
(Mark Johnston) *pressed ldr tl led 2f out: sn rdn: styd on strly to go clr fnl f: eased cl home* **17/2**

0000 **2** *2 3/4* **Orpsie Boy (IRE)**[7] 5819 9-9-5 **80**.......... MircoDemuro 9 — 85
(Ruth Carr) *stdd after s: t.k.h: hld up in tch in rr: swtchd rt and hdwy over 1f out: styd on wl ins fnl f: wnt 2nd wl ins fnl f: no threat to wnr* **20/1**

1-32 **3** *1/2* **Cantal**[86] 3085 3-9-0 **79**.......... NeilCallan 8 — 81
(Sir Michael Stoute) *t.k.h: hld up in tch: swtchd lft and effrt towards centre 2f out: rdn u.p and pressing for placings ins fnl f: no threat to wnr* **7/2**[2]

050 **4** *hd* **Usain Colt**[35] 4819 3-9-5 **84**.......... SeanLevey 3 — 86
(Richard Hannon) *t.k.h: hld up wl in tch: rdn ent fnl 2f: chsd wnr but no imp wl over 1f out: styd on same pce and lost 2 pls wl ins fnl f* **4/1**[3]

0050 **5** *nk* **Shifting Star (IRE)**[10] 5746 7-9-0 **82**.......... WilliamTwiston-Davies(7) 5 — 84
(John Bridger) *hld up in tch: swtchd rt and effrt on inner 2f out: styd on same pce fnl f* **25/1**

0005 **6** *nk* **Mississippi**[15] 5556 3-9-5 **84**.......... TadhgO'Shea 6 — 84
(Brian Meehan) *stdd s: sn swtchd lft to outer: t.k.h: hdwy to chse ldrs 5f out: pressing ldrs and rdn over 2f out: unable qck over 1f out: styd on same pce fnl f* **11/4**[1]

2052 **7** *3* **Ocean Legend (IRE)**[25] 5193 7-9-2 **77**.......... JimCrowley 7 — 70
(Tony Carroll) *hld up wl in tch: rdn and effrt 2f out: unable qck and drvn over 1f out: wknd ins fnl f* **8/1**

6204 **8** *1/2* **Golden Tempest (IRE)**[9] 5769 4-9-3 **78**.......... JohnFahy 2 — 70
(Eve Johnson Houghton) *t.k.h: led and set stdy gallop: rdn over 2f out: hdd 2f out: unable qck and sn struggling: wknd 1f out* **10/1**

0400 **9** *1 1/4* **Treadwell (IRE)**[21] 5356 5-9-10 **85**.............................. FergusSweeney 1 73
(Jamie Osborne) *hld up in last pair: rdn and no imp wl over 1f out: wknd 1f out* **8/1**

1m 25.07s (-0.93) **Going Correction** -0.075s/f (Stan)
WFA 3 from 4yo+ 4lb **9** Ran SP% **119.3**
Speed ratings (Par 105): **102,98,98,98,97 97,93,93,91**
toteswingers 1&2 £16.80, 1&3 £3.70, 2&3 £10.90 CSF £164.14 TOTE £9.70: £1.70, £4.30, £2.30; EX 131.30.
Owner Sheikh Hamdan Bin Mohammed Al Maktoum **Bred** Darley **Trained** Middleham Moor, N Yorks

FOCUS
They didn't go much of an early pace in this handicap. The winner was always well placed but the form has been taken at something like face value.

6041 BETFRED "THE HOME OF GOALS GALORE" H'CAP (DIV II) 7f (P)
5:50 (5:50) (Class 4) (0-85,85) 3-Y-O+ **£5,175** (£1,540; £769; £384) **Stalls** Low

Form RPR
4005 **1** **Esprit De Midas**[10] 5746 6-9-9 **84**.................................... JimCrowley 5 92
(Dean Ivory) *t.k.h: hld up in tch: effrt u.p 2f out: swtchd rt and hdwy ins fnl f: led fnl 100yds: r.o wl: rdn out* **9/2**[2]

0213 **2** *1/2* **Afkar (IRE)**[9] 5768 4-9-0 **75**..(b) DarryllHolland 4 82
(Clive Brittain) *led: rdn and hdd 2f out: battled on gamely and led again jst ins fnl f: hdd and one pce fnl 100yds* **4/1**[1]

6423 **3** *1* **Midnight Rider (IRE)**[24] 5233 4-9-5 **80**............................ TedDurcan 9 84
(Chris Wall) *stdd and dropped in bhd s: hld up in rr: nt asked for effrt tl over 1f out: swtchd rt and r.o wl ins fnl f: chsng ldrs and n.m.r towards fin* **7/1**

5132 **4** *3/4* **Emkanaat**[13] 5630 4-8-12 **80**................................ JeanVanOvermeire(7) 6 82
(Roger Varian) *chsd ldrs tl wnt 2nd 1/2-way: rdn to ld narrowly 2f out: hdd jst ins fnl f: wknd towards fin* **11/2**

6010 **5** *1 1/2* **Jungle Bay**[22] 5320 5-9-3 **78**...(p) BrettDoyle 3 76
(Jane Chapple-Hyam) *dwlt: sn chsng ldrs: rdn ent fnl 2f: styd on same pce u.p fnl f* **9/1**

6005 **6** *2 1/4* **Dozy Joe**[24] 5234 4-8-11 **72**.. DavidProbert 8 64
(Ian Wood) *stdd s: hld up in tch in last trio: rdn and effrt over 2f out: styd on same pce and no imp over 1f out* **10/1**

0063 **7** *1 3/4* **Avonmore Star**[11] 5703 4-9-3 **78**.. SeanLevey 1 65
(Richard Hannon) *in tch in midfield: rdn and effrt ent fnl 2f: no imp over 1f out: wl hld fnl f* **5/1**[3]

0363 **8** *7* **Hurricane Lady (IRE)**[36] 4772 4-8-13 **74**.......................... NeilCallan 7 43
(Mike Murphy) *stdd s: hld up in tch: rdn and no hdwy jst over 2f out: wknd over 1f out* **7/1**

1100 **9** *2* **Abi Scarlet (IRE)**[57] 4062 3-9-6 **85**.......................... SilvestreDeSousa 2 47
(Hughie Morrison) *chsd ldr tl 1/2-way: rdn 3f out: wknd u.p ent fnl f: fdd* **18/1**

1m 24.86s (-1.14) **Going Correction** -0.075s/f (Stan)
WFA 3 from 4yo+ 4lb **9** Ran SP% **119.6**
Speed ratings (Par 105): **103,102,101,100,98 96,94,86,83**
toteswingers 1&2 £9.80, 1&3 £16.10, 2&3 £4.90 CSF £23.80 TOTE £5.10: £2.00, £2.40, £2.60; EX 40.80.
Owner Geoff Copp **Bred** Jeremy Green And Sons **Trained** Radlett, Herts

FOCUS
They went a slightly better pace in this and the winning time was 0.21 seconds faster than the first division. Pretty ordinary form.
T/Plt: £242.00 to a £1 stake. Pool: £49,763.38 - 150.08 winning tickets T/Qpdt: £220.50 to a £1 stake. Pool: £3,323.21 - 11.15 winning tickets SP

5797 THIRSK (L-H)
Saturday, September 8
OFFICIAL GOING: Good (good to firm in places; 9.9)
Wind: light 1/2 behind Weather: fine and sunny

6042 THIRSK RACECOURSE PAVILION FOR WEDDING RECEPTIONS MAIDEN AUCTION STKS (DIV I) 6f
2:20 (2:20) (Class 5) 2-Y-O **£3,234** (£962; £481; £240) **Stalls** High

Form RPR
5223 **1** **Lady Of The House (IRE)**[4] 5909 2-8-8 77.......................(p) AmyRyan 2 76
(Kevin Ryan) *w ldrs: led appr fnl f: kpt on wl* **9/4**[2]

3240 **2** *2* **The Black Jacobin**[56] 4093 2-8-2 79.............................. NoelGarbutt(7) 4 71
(J S Moore) *chsd ldrs: styd on fnl f: tk 2nd nr fin* **8/1**[3]

4 **3** *shd* **Next Door (IRE)**[11] 5709 2-8-1 0.. RaulDaSilva(3) 7 66
(David Barron) *led: hdd appr fnl f: kpt on same pce* **11/1**

3 **4** *3/4* **Another Claret**[14] 5586 2-8-13 0.. TonyHamilton 9 72
(Richard Fahey) *chsd ldrs: effrt over 2f out: kpt on ins fnl f* **15/8**[1]

00 **5** *5* **Silkelly**[21] 5367 2-8-4 0.. KellyHarrison 1 48
(David O'Meara) *mid-div: effrt over 2f out: nvr nr ldrs* **50/1**

6 *1/2* **Medici Dancer** 2-8-8 0.. PJMcDonald 5 51+
(Tim Easterby) *s.i.s: hdwy over 2f out: kpt on* **20/1**

0 **6** *dht* **Multifact**[19] 5410 2-8-9 0.. BarryMcHugh 3 52
(Michael Dods) *dwlt: in rr: kpt on fnl 2f: nvr a factor* **18/1**

8 *4* **Shesthecaptain (IRE)** 2-8-4 0.. LiamJones 11 35
(John Weymes) *dwlt: in rr: sme hdwy over 1f out: nvr on terms* **66/1**

0 **9** *2* **Wynyard Boy**[114] 2213 2-8-8 0.. AdamCarter(5) 6 38
(Tim Easterby) *in rr: sme hdwy 2f out: nvr a factor* **11/1**

0 **10** *1/2* **Don't Tell**[41] 4618 2-8-4 0.. AndrewElliott 10 27
(George Moore) *wnt rt s: chsd ldrs: wknd 2f out* **50/1**

05 **11** *4* **Southern Sapphire**[42] 4581 2-8-9 0.. JamesSullivan 12 20
(Linda Stubbs) *chsd ldrs: sddle slipped and heavily eased wl over 1f out* **33/1**

00 **12** *1* **Mash Potato (IRE)**[19] 5410 2-8-13 0.. TomEaves 8 21
(Michael Dods) *mid-div: lost pl over 2f out: sn bhd* **18/1**

36 **13** *2 3/4* **Sylvia's Diamond**[8] 5799 2-8-1 0.. DeclanCannon(3) 13 4
(Richard Guest) *mid-div: lost pl over 2f out* **66/1**

1m 11.39s (-1.31) **Going Correction** -0.225s/f (Firm) **13** Ran SP% **118.5**
Speed ratings (Par 95): **99,96,96,95,88 87,87,82,79,79 73,72,68**
toteswingers 1&2 £4.30, 1&3 £3.90, 2&3 £9.10 CSF £19.41 TOTE £3.20: £1.90, £2.40, £3.10; EX 15.90.
Owner Matt & Lauren Morgan **Bred** Highbank Stud **Trained** Hambleton, N Yorks

FOCUS
Rail at normal inner configuration and distances as advertised. The market leaders drew clear in what was a fairly modest maiden. The winner ran pretty much to her Leicester mark.

NOTEBOOK
Lady Of The House(IRE), runner-up from a mark of 77 faced with similar conditions at Leicester four days earlier, looked to race a little awkwardly, despite the fitting of first-time cheekpieces, but she still proved much too good. She can remain competitive returned to handicaps. (op 7-4)
The Black Jacobin, off since finishing well beaten on heavy ground in the Super Sprint, was happier on this quicker ground and seemed helped by the step up to 6f. He'll likely remain vulnerable, though, with him making little appeal in handicaps from his current mark. (tchd 6-1)
Next Door(IRE) improved on her debut effort, benefiting from the step up to 6f on faster ground. She should find an opening once contesting handicaps after another run. (op 9-1)
Another Claret never looked happy on the ground and should leave this form behind returned to slower conditions. (op 11-4)
Silkelly is now qualified for a mark and should benefit from further.
Medici Dancer is related to a couple of fast juveniles and the way she was keeping on last suggests the experience will do her good.
Southern Sapphire Official explanation: jockey said saddle slipped.

6043 IRISH STALLION FARMS E B F MAIDEN STKS 7f
2:55 (2:56) (Class 4) 2-Y-O **£4,851** (£1,443; £721; £360) **Stalls** Low

Form RPR
03 **1** **Epic Battle (IRE)**[12] 5685 2-9-3 0.. LiamJones 6 77+
(William Haggas) *trckd ldrs: hmpd bnd over 4f out: swtchd rt over 1f out: styd on strly to go 2nd last 50yds: led fnl strides: slipped and fell heavily after line* **10/1**

20 **2** *nk* **Reggae Star**[15] 5562 2-8-9 0.. RaulDaSilva(3) 4 71
(Mark Johnston) *led: edgd lft 1f out: hdd and no ex cl home* **7/2**[2]

4 **3** *1 1/2* **Wyldfire (IRE)**[22] 5311 2-9-3 0.. TonyHamilton 8 72+
(Richard Fahey) *s.i.s: hdwy to chse ldrs over 3f out: wnt 2nd over 1f out: styd on same pce* **10/11**[1]

6 **4** *1 3/4* **Pearl Ransom (IRE)**[109] 2376 2-9-3 0.. PhillipMakin 11 68
(Kevin Ryan) *racd v wd first 2f: jnd ldrs over 4f out: kpt on same pce fnl f* **9/2**[3]

53 **5** *3/4* **Causeway Foot (USA)**[28] 5083 2-9-3 0.. PJMcDonald 10 66
(Jedd O'Keeffe) *chsd ldrs: one pce fnl 2f* **14/1**

0 **6** *5* **Apache Rising**[22] 5311 2-9-3 0.. TomEaves 2 53+
(Bryan Smart) *s.i.s: hdwy to chse ldrs after 2f: rdn over 2f out: wknd over 1f out* **20/1**

0 **7** *7* **Red Charmer (IRE)**[14] 5586 2-9-3 0.. MickyFenton 3 37+
(Ann Duffield) *hld up in rr-div: bdly hmpd bnd over 4f out: nt rcvrd* **33/1**

8 *5* **Thirlestane** 2-8-12 0.. JamesSullivan 9 17
(James Given) *dwlt: a in rr* **66/1**

60 **9** *1 1/4* **Index Waiter**[91] 2934 2-9-3 0.. JamieMackay 7 18
(Brian Meehan) *t.k.h: trckd ldrs: hung rt and wd bnd over 4f out: lost pl over 3f out* **20/1**

10 *3/4* **Three Glasses (IRE)** 2-9-3 0.. DavidNolan 1 16
(Tim Easterby) *s.s: in rr-div whn bdly hmpd bnd over 4f out: nt rcvrd* **25/1**

1m 26.43s (-0.77) **Going Correction** -0.125s/f (Firm) **10** Ran SP% **126.3**
Speed ratings (Par 97): **99,98,96,94,94 88,80,74,73,72**
toteswingers 1&2 £5.50, 2&3 £2.50, 1&3 £2.70 CSF £46.15 TOTE £9.00: £2.40, £1.60, £1.10; EX 34.50.
Owner Saleh Al Homaizi & Imad Al Sagar **Bred** Castlemartin Sky & Skymarc Farm **Trained** Newmarket, Suffolk

FOCUS
The pace was steady, but this still looked a fair maiden that should produce winners. Straightforward form, rated through the runner-up.

NOTEBOOK
Epic Battle(IRE) has improved with each start and did really well to win considering he was knocked wide rounding the bend, taking the favourite with him, and then left with many lengths to make up late. He got there in time, though, and rates a decent handicap prospect, providing his confidence isn't affected having slipped and taken a heavy tumble not long after the line. (op 8-1)
Reggae Star bounced back from a poor showing at York, although considering she had an ideal trip in front around the inner, it was disappointing she couldn't hold on (hit 1.01 in running on Betfair). Handicaps are now an option. (op 3-1)
Wyldfire(IRE) had little go his way, failing to get off to a good start and then being carried notably wide by the winner around the bend. He may not have been good enough anyway, but certainly deserves another chance. (op 5-4 tchd 11-8 in a place)
Pearl Ransom(IRE), off 109 days and gelded, stayed wide early from stall 11, but didn't expend too much energy and simply lacked the pace in the straight. He should have no trouble winning up to 1m. (op 10-1)
Causeway Foot(USA) was again keeping on at the one pace and should be suited by 1m once handicapping. (op 12-1)
Apache Rising enjoyed an ideal trip and showed more than on debut. (op 22-1 tchd 25-1)

6044 BARKERS OF NORTHALLERTON H'CAP 6f
3:30 (3:30) (Class 4) (0-80,80) 4-Y-O+ **£6,469** (£1,925; £962; £481) **Stalls** High

Form RPR
0500 **1** **Bonnie Charlie**[15] 5557 6-8-10 **76**.. ShirleyTeasdale(7) 7 84
(David Nicholls) *racd far side: chsd ldrs: styd on strly ins fnl f: led nr fin: 1st of 7 that gp* **12/1**

040 **2** *1/2* **Commanche Raider (IRE)**[20] 5389 5-8-12 **71**...........(p) TonyHamilton 6 78
(Michael Dods) *racd far side: led that gp over 1f out: no ex nr fin: 2nd of 7 that gp* **50/1**

3664 **3** *hd* **Cocktail Charlie**[24] 5223 4-8-9 **73**..................................(p) DarylByrne(5) 3 79
(Tim Easterby) *racd far side: hdwy over 2f out: chsng ldr that side over 1f out: no ex towards fin: 3rd of 7 that gp* **7/1**[2]

1455 **4** *nk* **Bunce (IRE)**[10] 5737 4-8-7 **73**.......................................(t) DavidBergin(7) 17 78
(David O'Meara) *led 9 others stands' side: edgd lft ins fnl f: hdd and no ex clsng stages: 1st of 10 that gp* **12/1**

0542 **5** *shd* **Defence Council (IRE)**[12] 5674 4-9-4 **80**.......................... DaleSwift(3) 19 85
(Mel Brittain) *racd stands' side: w ldr: kpt on same pce last 50yds: 2nd of 10 that gp* **7/2**[1]

1010 **6** *1/2* **Pick A Little**[11] 5703 4-9-1 **77**.. PaulPickard(3) 13 80
(Brian Ellison) *racd stands' side: chsd ldrs: rdn over 2f out: styd on ins fnl f: 3rd of 10 that gp* **18/1**

015 **7** *hd* **Diamond Blue**[7] 5821 4-8-12 **71**..(p) AmyRyan 20 73+
(Richard Whitaker) *rrd s: racd stands' side: bhd: hdwy over 2f out: styd on wl fnl f: 4th of 10 that gp* **15/2**[3]

620 **8** *1/2* **Dickie Le Davoir**[4] 5915 8-8-11 **70**..(b) KellyHarrison 2 71
(Richard Guest) *racd far side: in rr: hdwy over 1f out: styng on at fin: 4th of 7 that gp* **20/1**

6352 **9** *1/2* **Showboating (IRE)**[15] 5557 4-9-6 **79**..(tp) IPoullis 5 78
(Alan McCabe) *racd far side: in rr: hdwy 2f out: kpt on ins fnl f: 5th of 7 that gp* **10/1**

0500 **10** *shd* **Mandalay King (IRE)**[19] 5412 7-8-12 **71**.......................(p) BarryMcHugh 16 70
(Marjorie Fife) *dwlt: hdwy to chse ldrs stands' side over 2f out: one pce fnl f: 5th of 10 that gp* **16/1**

0140 **11** *3* **Nasharra (IRE)**[12] 5674 4-8-12 **74**..(b) JulieBurke(3) 4 63
(Kevin Ryan) *dwlt: racd far side: hdwy over 2f out: hung rt and wknd over 1f out: 6th of 7 that gp* **33/1**

5001 **12** 1 ½ **Illustrious Prince (IRE)**[15] 5531 5-8-6 **72**................ LukeLeadbitter(7) 9 57
(Declan Carroll) *racd stands' side: chsd ldrs: wknd over 1f out: 6th of 10 that gp* **10/1**

0525 **13** ½ **Oldjoesaid**[14] 5584 8-9-5 **78**.............................. MickyFenton 18 61
(Paul Midgley) *racd stands' side: mid-div: drvn over 2f out: wknd over 1f out: 7th of 10 that gp* **14/1**

-600 **14** ½ **Azzurra Du Caprio (IRE)**[35] 4829 4-9-3 **79**..........[1] DeclanCannon(3) 11 60
(Ben Haslam) *racd stands' side: chsd ldrs: rdn over 2f out: wknd over 1f out: 8th of 10 that gp* **20/1**

0045 **15** 1 **Expose**[17] 5486 4-9-4 **77**....................................(b[1]) LiamJones 8 55
(William Haggas) *led 6 others far side: overall ldr and clr that gp over 3f out: wknd and hdd over 1f out: last of 7 that gp* **14/1**

3525 **16** 1 ¾ **Namwahjobo (IRE)**[25] 5189 4-9-1 **74**..............................(v) TomEaves 12 47
(Jim Goldie) *s.i.s: racd stands' side: sme hdwy over 2f out: wknd over 1f out: 9th of 10 that gp* **22/1**

4000 **17** *nk* **Alive And Kicking**[7] 5821 4-9-0 **73**.................... PhillipMakin 10 45
(James Bethell) *racd stands' side: t.k.h: trckd ldrs: lost pl 2f out: last of 10 that gp* **16/1**

1m 10.54s (-2.16) **Going Correction** -0.225s/f (Firm) **17** Ran SP% **129.2**
Speed ratings (Par 105): **105,104,104,103,103 102,102,101,101,101 97,95,94,93,92 90,89**
toteswingers 1&2 £253.60, 1&3 £11.20, 2&3 £46.30 CSF £549.33 TOTE £14.70: £5.00, £11.80, £2.20, £2.40; EX 647.50.

Owner Ann-Marie McManus & Finola Devaney **Bred** C D S Bryce And Mrs M Bryce **Trained** Sessay, N Yorks

FOCUS
A wide-open sprint handicap that saw those who stayed far side come out marginally on top. The form makes sense with the winner close to last year's form.
Alive And Kicking Official explanation: jockey said gelding ran too free.

6045 HAMBLETON CUP (H'CAP) 1m 4f
4:05 (4:05) (Class 4) (0-85,85) 3-Y-O+ **£8,086** (£2,406; £1,202; £601) **Stalls** Low

Form RPR

4331 **1** **Party Line**[13] 5622 3-8-9 **80**.................................... RaulDaSilva(3) 6 90+
(Mark Johnston) *mid-div: hdwy on outside over 3f out: led wl over 1f out: forged clr fnl f* **7/1**[3]

532 **2** 3 ¾ **Granston (IRE)**[13] 5622 11-9-1 **74**.............................. AmyRyan 11 78
(James Bethell) *chsd ldrs: kpt on same pce appr fnl f* **11/1**

3250 **3** *nse* **Choisan (IRE)**[14] 5598 3-8-9 **77**.............................. JamesSullivan 4 81
(Tim Easterby) *chsd ldrs: hmpd after 1f: drvn over 4f out: led over 2f out: hdd wl over 1f out: styd on same pce* **15/2**

4160 **4** ½ **Nice Rose**[87] 3033 3-8-9 **77**.................................... LiamJones 15 80
(Mark Johnston) *mid-div: drvn 4f out: hdwy over 2f out: kpt on wl fnl f* **16/1**

150 **5** *nk* **Royal Straight**[21] 5366 7-9-0 **76**..............................(t) JulieBurke(3) 7 79
(Linda Perratt) *in rr: hdwy over 2f out: kpt on fnl f* **50/1**

130/ **6** ¾ **Crystal Rock (IRE)**[228] 6784 7-9-2 **75**.................... BarryMcHugh 9 76
(Tony Coyle) *swtchd lft after s: led tl over 8f out: one pce fnl 2f* **20/1**

5036 **7** ½ **Tappanappa (IRE)**[2] 5966 5-9-8 **84**..........................(b) DaleSwift(3) 3 85
(Brian Ellison) *s.i.s: in rr: kpt on fnl f: nt rch ldrs* **8/1**

1122 **8** ½ **Honest Deal**[19] 5430 4-9-0 **73**.............................. AndrewElliott 10 73
(Alan Swinbank) *swtchd lft after s: chsd ldr: led over 8f out: hdd over 2f out: wknd over 1f out* **12/1**

5135 **9** 1 **Mohawk Ridge**[12] 5673 6-8-6 **72**..........................(p) ConnorNichol(7) 1 70
(Michael Dods) *trckd ldrs: t.k.h: effrt over 2f out: wknd over 1f out* **33/1**

-110 **10** ½ **Grandiloquent**[22] 5306 3-9-2 **84**.............................. TomEaves 5 81
(Sir Michael Stoute) *trckd ldrs: effrt 3f out: wknd over 1f out* **3/1**[1]

224 **11** *nk* **Roc De Prince**[33] 4882 3-8-12 **80**.............................. TonyHamilton 12 77
(Richard Fahey) *swtchd lft after s: in rr: nvr a factor* **14/1**

43-2 **12** 4 **Miss Topsy Turvy (IRE)**[107] 2423 4-9-3 **76**.................. PhillipMakin 8 67
(John Dunlop) *hld up in mid-div: effrt over 2f out: wknd over 1f out* **4/1**[2]

31-0 **13** 4 ½ **Full Speed (GER)**[11] 5712 7-9-3 **76**........................ MichaelO'Connell 2 59
(Philip Kirby) *in rr: bhd fnl 2f* **25/1**

2m 33.24s (-2.96) **Going Correction** -0.125s/f (Firm)
WFA 3 from 4yo+ 9lb **13** Ran SP% **122.5**
Speed ratings (Par 105): **104,101,101,101,100 100,100,99,99,98 98,95,92**
toteswingers 1&2 £8.80, 1&3 £8.30, 2&3 £11.40 CSF £80.49 TOTE £8.50: £2.50, £2.70, £3.00; EX 59.80.

Owner S R Counsell **Bred** Highclere Stud And Balmerino Bloodstock **Trained** Middleham Moor, N Yorks

FOCUS
Competitive stuff, although with most of them exposed, it was no surprise to see it go to one of the 3yos. The race set up nicely for the closers. Further improvement from the winner.

6046 PERSONAL TOUCHES DIAMOND H'CAP 1m
4:35 (4:35) (Class 3) (0-95,94) 3-Y-O **£9,703** (£2,887; £1,443; £721) **Stalls** Low

Form RPR

1312 **1** **Trail Blaze (IRE)**[21] 5334 3-9-2 **89**.............................. AmyRyan 8 96
(Kevin Ryan) *w ldr: led over 1f out: edgd rt: hld on gamely* **9/2**[3]

13-0 **2** ½ **Mabaany**[105] 2485 3-9-0 **87**.................................... LiamJones 1 93
(William Haggas) *s.i.s: t.k.h: sn trcking ldrs: drvn 3f out: chal over 1f out: no ex clsng stages* **9/1**

1034 **3** ¾ **Our Boy Jack (IRE)**[21] 5334 3-8-4 **84**.................... LauraBarry(7) 3 91+
(Richard Fahey) *t.k.h in mid-div: hdwy over 2f out: chsng ldrs appr fnl f: sddle slipped ins fnl f: nt rcvrd: heavily eased nr fin* **8/1**

0061 **4** 2 ¼ **Charitable Act (FR)**[16] 5501 3-8-0 **76**.................... RaulDaSilva(3) 9 75
(William Muir) *chsd ldrs: drvn over 3f out: one pce fnl 2f* **14/1**

-022 **5** 1 ¾ **Nawwaar (USA)**[23] 5271 3-9-2 **89**.............................. PhillipMakin 7 84+
(John Dunlop) *hld up in rr: effrt over 3f out: kpt on fnl f* **11/4**[1]

31- **6** ½ **Genius Step (IRE)**[353] 6244 3-8-9 **87**.................... AntiocoMurgia(5) 4 81
(Mahmood Al Zarooni) *trckd ldrs: t.k.h: drvn over 3f out: hung rt: swtchd lft over 1f out: one pce* **7/2**[2]

0405 **7** 2 ¼ **Boris Grigoriev (IRE)**[28] 5110 3-8-6 **79**.................... JamesSullivan 5 68
(Michael Easterby) *led: hdd over 1f out: grad wknd* **18/1**

-136 **8** 2 **Invisible Hunter (USA)**[13] 5626 3-9-7 **94**....................(t) MickyFenton 2 78
(Saeed Bin Suroor) *trckd ldrs: t.k.h: lost pl bnd 4f out: wknd 2f out* **7/1**

3000 **9** 1 ¼ **Roger Sez (IRE)**[29] 5043 3-8-9 **87**..........................(p) DarylByrne(5) 6 68
(Tim Easterby) *s.i.s: a in last and sn drvn along* **33/1**

1m 38.05s (-2.05) **Going Correction** -0.125s/f (Firm) **9** Ran SP% **115.6**
Speed ratings (Par 105): **105,104,103,101,99 99,97,95,93**
toteswingers 1&2 £8.50, 2&3 £11.50, 1&3 £5.90 CSF £44.44 TOTE £5.80: £2.10, £2.70, £3.10; EX 46.90.

Owner Mr & Mrs Julian And Rosie Richer **Bred** Edmond Kent **Trained** Hambleton, N Yorks

FOCUS
No hanging around in this 3yo handicap, but with several of the key players failing to give their running, it's probably form to be wary of. A small personal best from the game winner.

NOTEBOOK
Trail Blaze(IRE) has shown before that he's quite capable of maintaining a fast gallop, but he may have been fortunate to win here with the third looking an unlucky loser. Regardless, this really likeable sort has now finished in the first three on all 11 starts since his debut, proving equally effective from 7f-1m and acting on any ground. He shouldn't go up too much and ought to remain competitive in good handicaps, with a rise in distance possibly on the agenda. (tchd 7-2)
Mabaany turned in a much-improved effort on this return from 105 days off. He's clearly benefited from the break and may prove best back at 7f. (op 15-2)
Our Boy Jack(IRE) looked an unlucky loser, his saddle slipping at a vital stage of the race and his rider ultimately having to yank back on the reins close home in order to keep her balance. He'd surely have won with any sort of assistance and remains quietly progressive. Official explanation: jockey said saddle slipped. (tchd 17-2)
Charitable Act(FR) found a 6lb rise for scraping home at Bath too much. (op 10-1)
Nawwaar(USA) was caught out when second at Newmarket last time, but this was plain disappointing, never featuring having been taken back at the start. (tchd 5-2)
Genius Step(IRE) hadn't run since winning a soft-ground maiden over 7f at Goodwood a year ago, but this opening mark looked potentially lenient and he was well backed late on. However, he never looked happy on the fast ground, refusing to let himself down and hanging both ways. He'll be worth another chance when the wetter weather arrives in the coming weeks. (op 13-2)
Invisible Hunter(USA) was another to disappoint, racing keenly having been unable to lead on this drop in trip. (op 6-1 tchd 8-1)
Roger Sez(IRE) Official explanation: jockey said filly was never travelling.

6047 ADORN HATS H'CAP 1m
5:10 (5:10) (Class 5) (0-75,76) 4-Y-O+ **£3,234** (£962; £481; £240) **Stalls** Low

Form RPR

4000 **1** **Dolphin Rock**[14] 5588 5-8-13 **70**.............................. DaleSwift(3) 9 79
(Brian Ellison) *trckd ldrs: led appr fnl f: pushed out* **11/4**[1]

5244 **2** ¾ **Silver Rime (FR)**[21] 5362 7-9-3 **71**.......................... PhillipMakin 8 78
(Linda Perratt) *in rr: hdwy on outside over 2f out: kpt on to take 2nd last 50yds: a hld* **8/1**

0006 **3** ¾ **Thatcherite (IRE)**[61] 3914 4-8-13 **67**....................(t) BarryMcHugh 10 73
(Tony Coyle) *s.i.s: swtchd lft after s: hdwy over 2f out: styd on wl fnl f: tk 3rd nr fin* **7/1**

0216 **4** ¾ **Steel Stockholder**[8] 5802 6-9-1 **69**.......................... PJMcDonald 1 73
(Mel Brittain) *chsd ldrs: led briefly over 1f out: kpt on same pce* **11/1**

6200 **5** 1 **Spanish Plume**[10] 5752 4-9-5 **73**.......................... J-PGuillambert 3 75
(Reg Hollinshead) *chsd ldrs: drvn 3f out: one pce* **9/1**

2121 **6** ¾ **Hayek**[11] 5713 5-9-3 **76**..........................(b) AdamCarter(5) 4 76
(Tim Easterby) *in rr: hdwy on inner over 2f out: swtchd rt ins fnl f: kpt on* **11/2**[2]

0020 **7** *hd* **Cono Zur (FR)**[19] 5429 5-9-6 **74**..........................(b) JamesSullivan 6 73
(Ruth Carr) *led: hdd over 1f out: sn fdd* **14/1**

5242 **8** 2 ½ **Main Beach**[14] 5588 5-9-4 **72**..........................(p) MickyFenton 5 66
(Paul Midgley) *s.i.s: nt clr run and swtchd lft 1f out: nvr a factor* **13/2**[3]

60 **9** ½ **Pirate Chest (IRE)**[41] 4621 4-9-2 **70**.......................... PaddyAspell 13 62
(Patrick Holmes) *mid-div: hdwy on outer over 3f out: wknd over 1f out* **40/1**

3162 **10** *hd* **Satwa Laird**[11] 5713 6-9-2 **75**.............................. DavidKenny(5) 2 67
(Conor Dore) *mid-div: lost pl over 2f out* **9/1**

-000 **11** 7 **L'Astre De Choisir (IRE)**[21] 5369 4-9-0 **68**.................. DavidNolan 12 44
(Michael Easterby) *chsd ldrs: drvn over 3f out: lost pl over 2f out* **16/1**

1m 38.31s (-1.79) **Going Correction** -0.125s/f (Firm) **11** Ran SP% **122.3**
Speed ratings (Par 103): **103,102,101,100,99 99,98,96,95,95 88**
toteswingers 1&2 £8.70, 2&3 £8.70, 1&3 £5.10 CSF £26.36 TOTE £4.20: £1.40, £2.90, £2.70; EX 38.10.

Owner Mia Racing **Bred** Mia Racing **Trained** Norton, N Yorks

FOCUS
Plenty of pace on in this open-looking handicap, and sound form.

6048 RICHARD ELLIS 40TH BIRTHDAY H'CAP 7f
5:40 (5:40) (Class 5) (0-70,70) 3-Y-O **£3,234** (£962; £481; £240) **Stalls** Low

Form RPR

0020 **1** **Sardanapalus**[15] 5556 3-9-7 **70**..........................(p) PhillipMakin 5 80
(Kevin Ryan) *s.i.s: hdwy over 3f out: led over 1f: hung rt then lft: drvn out* **8/1**

0516 **2** 1 ¼ **See Clearly**[12] 5676 3-9-0 **68**..........................(p) DarylByrne(5) 7 76+
(Tim Easterby) *mid-div: hdwy over 2f out: chsng wnr whn hmpd and swtchd rt 1f out: kpt on* **14/1**

2011 **3** *nk* **Ingleby Angel (IRE)**[8] 5803 3-9-0 **63**.......................... TomEaves 13 69+
(David O'Meara) *swtchd lft after s: in rr: hdwy over 2f out: kpt on fnl f* **11/2**[2]

4461 **4** 1 ¾ **Vital Calling**[15] 5549 3-9-7 **70**.............................. PJMcDonald 1 71
(David Barron) *t.k.h in rr: hdwy over 2f out: kpt on same pce fnl f* **13/2**

1500 **5** 3 ¼ **Bitaphon (IRE)**[35] 4830 3-8-13 **65**.......................... RaulDaSilva(3) 6 58
(John Balding) *trckd ldrs: led over 3f out: rdr lost whip: hdd 1f out: sn wknd* **20/1**

5-40 **6** ¾ **Winter Hill**[109] 2382 3-8-13 **62**.............................. AndrewElliott 8 53+
(Tom Dascombe) *s.i.s: hdwy and hung lft over 2f out: nt clr run over 1f out: nvr a threat* **14/1**

-622 **7** 1 ¾ **Giorgio's Dragon (IRE)**[8] 5803 3-9-4 **67**.................. TonyHamilton 9 53
(Richard Fahey) *mid-div: hdwy to chse ldrs over 2f out: wknd over 1f out* **9/2**[1]

3-00 **8** 3 ¼ **Three Darlings (IRE)**[43] 4551 3-8-3 **59**.............. ShirleyTeasdale(7) 3 36
(David Nicholls) *chsd ldrs: lost pl over 1f out* **11/1**

623 **9** 4 **Ginger Monkey (IRE)**[33] 4874 3-9-4 **67**.................... MickyFenton 4 33
(Peter Chapple-Hyam) *led: hdd over 3f out: wknd over 1f out* **6/1**[3]

60-6 **10** 2 ¼ **Shatter (IRE)**[120] 2042 3-9-3 **66**.............................. LiamJones 11 26
(William Haggas) *swtchd lft s: in rr: drvn over 3f out: nvr on terms* **16/1**

0011 **11** ¾ **Ebony Clarets**[28] 5112 3-8-12 **64**.............................. DaleSwift(3) 2 22
(Linda Perratt) *gave problems bef s: chsd ldrs: lost pl 4f out: sn bhd* **12/1**

6064 **12** 13 **Shamrocked (IRE)**[13] 5625 3-9-7 **70**.......................... SamHitchcott 10
(Mick Channon) *in rr: bhd whn heavily eased ins fnl f* **8/1**

1m 25.25s (-1.95) **Going Correction** -0.125s/f (Firm) **12** Ran SP% **123.4**
Speed ratings (Par 101): **106,104,104,102,98 97,95,91,87,84 83,69**
toteswingers 1&2 £24.90, 2&3 £23.80, 1&3 £10.90 CSF £119.54 TOTE £9.40: £2.30, £5.40, £2.30; EX 167.90.

Owner J Nixon **Bred** Rosyground Stud **Trained** Hambleton, N Yorks

FOCUS
Modest but sound handicap form. The winner is no certainty to repeat this on profile.

Winter Hill Official explanation: jockey said filly was denied a clear run.

6049 THIRSK RACECOURSE PAVILION FOR WEDDING RECEPTIONS MAIDEN AUCTION STKS (DIV II) 6f

6:10 (6:10) (Class 5) 2-Y-O **£3,234** (£962; £481; £120; £120) **Stalls** High

Form RPR

5 **1** **Skidby Mill (IRE)**[76] 3415 2-8-8 0 MichaelO'Connell 6 63
(John Quinn) *trckd ldrs: effrt 2f out: r.o to ld last 50yds: readily* **9/2**[1]

5 **2** *1* **Tonality (IRE)**[10] 5748 2-8-4 0 LiamJones 10 56
(J S Moore) *chsd ldrs: kpt on to take 2nd clsng stages: no imp* **20/1**

3 *½* **Sakhees Romance** 2-8-4 0 KellyHarrison 13 54+
(Noel Wilson) *in rr: hdwy over 2f out: styd wl ins fnl f: snatched 3rd post* **14/1**

6423 **4** *shd* **Cracking Choice (IRE)**[15] 5544 2-8-9 66 (p) TomEaves 4 59
(Michael Dods) *led: hdd over 1f out: kpt on same pce ins fnl f* **5/1**[2]

06 **4** *dht* **Knockamany Bends (IRE)**[24] 5222 2-8-10 0 ow1 PaddyAspell 3 60
(John Wainwright) *chsd ldrs: led over 1f out: edgd lft: hdd and no ex ins fnl f: 3rd whn eased fnl strides* **100/1**

6 *shd* **Steelriver (IRE)** 2-8-13 0 PhillipMakin 12 63+
(James Bethell) *s.i.s: hdwy 2f out: kpt on fnl 2f: nvr a threat* **17/2**

3626 **7** *nk* **Team Challenge**[14] 5602 2-8-9 67 JamesSullivan 1 58
(Tim Easterby) *in rr: hdwy over 2f out: kpt on same pce appr fnl f* **9/2**[1]

36 **8** *1* **Krupskaya (FR)**[39] 4696 2-8-4 0 AndrewElliott 11 50
(Mrs K Burke) *in rr: sme hdwy 2f out: kpt on ins fnl f: nvr a factor* **11/2**[3]

0005 **9** *½* **Only For You**[21] 5331 2-8-1 52 RaulDaSilva(3) 2 48
(Alan Brown) *chsd ldrs: wknd ins fnl f* **50/1**

50 **10** *4½* **Pour La Victoire (IRE)**[19] 5410 2-8-10 0 DaleSwift(3) 8 44
(Nigel Tinkler) *chsd ldrs: wknd 2f out* **10/1**

00 **11** *1* **Pink Cadillac (IRE)**[66] 3747 2-8-1 0 DeclanCannon(3) 7 32
(Ben Haslam) *chsd ldrs: wknd over 1f out* **40/1**

12 *5* **Scarlet Spirit (IRE)** 2-8-8 0 PJMcDonald 5 21
(Ann Duffield) *dwlt: in rr: effrt over 2f out: wknd over 1f out* **11/2**[3]

1m 12.23s (-0.47) **Going Correction** -0.225s/f (Firm) 12 Ran SP% **120.2**
Speed ratings (Par 95): **94,92,92,91,91 91,91,90,89,83 82,75**
toteswingers 1&2 £24.00, 1&3 £31.30, 2&3 £32.50 CSF £98.05 TOTE £5.30: £1.80, £4.70, £6.90; EX 76.00.
Owner Ross Harmon **Bred** Michael O'Mahony **Trained** Settrington, N Yorks
■ Stewards' Enquiry : Paddy Aspell seven-day ban; failing to obtain best possible placing (22th-28th Sept).

FOCUS
A lesser contest than the first division, certainly in terms of depth. They finished compressed and this is form to be against.

NOTEBOOK
Skidby Mill(IRE), off for 76 days having made a mildly promising debut at Pontefract, didn't look particularly happy for the first half of the race, seeming to hang, but she really came strong inside the last furlong and ultimately won going away. On this evidence she could progress into a useful handicapper, with improvement possible as she goes up in trip. (op 6-1, tchd 13-2 in a place)
Tonality(IRE) was another to improve nicely on her debut run, racing close the stands' rail and keeping on well. Her dam's a half-sister to smart sprinter Reverence and she should have more to offer. (op 14-1)
Sakhees Romance, a half-sister to 5f-6f winner Kylladdie, did best of he three newcomers, staying on quite nicely, and is entitled to improve quite a bit for the experience. (op 25-1 tchd 28-1)
Knockamany Bends(IRE) took over with 1f to run, briefly looking the winner, but he hung his chance away. This was an improved effort and one that marks him down as a horse to be interest in for low-grade handicaps. (op 66-1)
Cracking Choice(IRE) had his chance, failing to improve for the step up to 6f. (op 66-1)
Steelriver(IRE), whose dam was placed up to 8.5f in France, wasn't the best away on debut, but did stay on nicely and should leave this bare form behind in time. (op 12-1)
Team Challenge, rated 67, was sixth in what seemed a fair nursery at York last time, but he could never get into this having failed to obtain a prominent early pitch. (tchd 5-1)
Krupskaya(FR) is now qualified for a mark and should fare better in handicaps over further. (op 5-1 tchd 13-2)
Only For You Official explanation: jockey said filly lost her action.
Scarlet Spirit(IRE), related to numerous sprint winners, reportedly failed to impress going to the start and she was never involved following a slow start. (tchd 9-2)
T/Plt: £228.40 to a £1 stake. Pool: £53,263.49 - 170.18 winning tickets. T/Qpdt: £88.10 to a £1 stake. Pool: £2,740.50 - 23.00 winning tickets. WG

5886 WOLVERHAMPTON (A.W) (L-H)

Saturday, September 8

OFFICIAL GOING: Standard changing to standard to fast after race 2 (6:00)
Wind: Light behind Weather: Fine

6050 EXPERIENCE A PARTY AT MECCA BINGO H'CAP (DIV I) 7f 32y(P)

5:30 (5:30) (Class 5) (0-75,75) 3-Y-O **£2,911** (£866; £432; £216) **Stalls** High

Form RPR

3051 **1** **Fast Finian (IRE)**[22] 5302 3-9-7 75 PaulMulrennan 4 87
(Paul D'Arcy) *sn prom: led over 2f out: rdn out* **4/1**[2]

0542 **2** *1¾* **Lady Layla**[19] 5426 3-9-4 72 RussKennemore 8 79
(Bryan Smart) *chsd ldrs: rdn to go 2nd over 1f out: styd on* **3/1**[1]

2660 **3** *1¾* **Levi Draper**[21] 5365 3-9-3 71 [1] JackMitchell 1 73
(James Fanshawe) *hld up: hdwy 2f out: sn rdn: styd on* **6/1**

6005 **4** *1¼* **Sky Crossing**[22] 5318 3-9-4 72 RoystonFfrench 7 71
(James Given) *chsd ldr: rdn and hung rt over 2f out: styd on same pce fr over 1f out* **12/1**

5 *1¾* **Desertcougar (IRE)**[45] 4480 3-8-10 64 SeanQuinlan 2 58
(Daniel Mark Loughnane) *s.i.s: hld up: hdwy 2f out: sn rdn: eased whn hld wl ins fnl f* **28/1**

3423 **6** *2* **Half A Billion (IRE)**[10] 5736 3-9-4 75 LeeTopliss(3) 10 64
(Michael Dods) *led: rdn and hdd over 2f out: wknd fnl f* **9/2**[3]

3005 **7** *nk* **Lord Paget**[18] 5446 3-8-1 62 (p) JackDuern(7) 6 50
(Reg Hollinshead) *s.i.s: rdn over 1f out: nvr nrr* **20/1**

2155 **8** *2¾* **Red Trump (IRE)**[21] 5338 3-8-7 66 MatthewLawson(5) 9 47
(Charles Hills) *hld up: rdn 1/2-way: a in rr* **11/2**

0540 **9** *2½* **Sehnsucht (IRE)**[21] 5341 3-9-0 68 (b[1]) StephenCraine 3 42
(Alan McCabe) *sn drvn along and prom: nt clr run over 2f out: wknd sn after* **16/1**

16-0 **10** *18* **Trumpet Voluntary (IRE)**[22] 5308 3-8-11 72 DanielMuscutt(7) 5
(Nicky Vaughan) *s.i.s: a in rr: rdn and wknd 1/2-way: t.o* **25/1**

1m 27.04s (-2.56) **Going Correction** -0.275s/f (Stan) 10 Ran SP% **118.5**
Speed ratings (Par 101): **103,101,99,97,95 93,92,89,86,66**
toteswingers 1&2 £3.20, 1&3 £7.70, 2&3 £7.50 CSF £16.29 CT £73.38 TOTE £4.40: £1.40, £2.00, £1.80; EX 15.40 Trifecta £51.90 Pool: £271.78 - 3.87 winning units..
Owner John W Kennedy **Bred** N Hartery **Trained** Newmarket, Suffolk

FOCUS
A fair handicap, run at a furious pace.

6051 CLEANEVENT CLAIMING STKS 7f 32y(P)

6:00 (6:00) (Class 5) 3-Y-O+ **£2,070** (£616; £307; £153) **Stalls** High

Form RPR

0010 **1** **Prime Exhibit**[7] 5812 7-8-12 86 (t) MatthewLawson(5) 7 82
(Milton Bradley) *hld up: hdwy over 2f out: rdn to ld ins fnl f: r.o* **7/2**[1]

0602 **2** *¾* **Marford Missile (IRE)**[19] 5406 3-9-2 75 StephenCraine 11 82
(Tom Dascombe) *chsd ldrs: rdn and ev ch ins fnl f: unable qck towards fin* **11/1**

0246 **3** *3* **Kimbali (IRE)**[21] 5337 3-9-8 83 JackMitchell 12 80
(Richard Fahey) *s.i.s: on mid-div: rdn 1/2-way: hdwy over 1f out: styd on: nt trble ldrs* **4/1**[2]

252 **4** *nse* **Adranian (IRE)**[22] 5298 3-8-7 71 (b) NoraLooby(7) 3 72
(David C Griffiths) *chsd ldr: led over 2f out: hdd and no ex ins fnl f* **12/1**

2202 **5** *nk* **Fishforcompliments**[12] 5669 8-8-9 67 ow1 (p) LeeTopliss(3) 8 66
(Richard Fahey) *s.i.s: hld up: hdwy over 1f out: nt trble ldrs* **8/1**

0061 **6** *2¼* **Justbookie Dot Com (IRE)**[10] 5751 4-8-11 70 (b) NathanSweeney(5) 9 64
(David Evans) *mid-div: drvn along 3f out: no imp fnl 2f* **9/1**

0055 **7** *hd* **Son Vida (IRE)**[10] 5751 4-8-9 67 (v) NatashaEaton(7) 4 63
(Alan Bailey) *chsd ldrs: rdn over 2f out: wknd fnl f* **10/1**

4050 **8** *1* **April Fool**[39] 4689 8-8-13 79 (b) DanielMuscutt(7) 1 65
(Ronald Harris) *led over 4f: sn rdn: wknd fnl f* **11/2**[3]

010/ **9** *4* **Youm Jamil (USA)**[18] 6097 5-8-11 68 AidenBlakemore(7) 2 52
(Tony Carroll) *hld up and a in rr* **40/1**

0140 **10** *¾* **Sir Mozart (IRE)**[33] 4866 9-9-1 72 PaulMulrennan 5 47
(Barney Curley) *hld up: shkn up over 2f out: nvr nr to chal* **13/2**

1m 26.42s (-3.18) **Going Correction** -0.275s/f (Stan) course record
WFA 3 from 4yo+ 4lb 10 Ran SP% **119.6**
Speed ratings (Par 103): **107,106,102,102,102 99,99,98,93,92**
toteswingers 1&2 £8.60, 1&3 £3.00, 2&3 £8.30 CSF £44.12 TOTE £4.70: £1.10, £3.20, £2.40; EX 41.20 Trifecta £126.90 Part won. Pool: £171.56 - 0.62 winning units..Prime Exhibit was claimed by Daniel Mark Loughnane for £9,000.
Owner Dab Hand Racing **Bred** Matthews Breeding And Racing Ltd **Trained** Sedbury, Gloucs

FOCUS
There was no let up in pace to this claimer and it played in the hands of the closers.

6052 EXPERIENCE A PARTY AT MECCA BINGO H'CAP (DIV II) 7f 32y(P)

6:30 (6:30) (Class 5) (0-75,75) 3-Y-O **£2,911** (£866; £432; £216) **Stalls** High

Form RPR

6004 **1** **Right Result (IRE)**[27] 5130 3-9-7 75 (v) RichardHughes 7 83
(James Bethell) *hld up: hdwy over 2f out: r.o u.p to ld wl ins fnl f* **5/1**

5305 **2** *¾* **Willies Wonder (IRE)**[22] 5308 3-9-2 75 MatthewLawson(5) 1 81
(Charles Hills) *chsd ldrs: rdn and ev ch ins fnl f: styd on* **4/1**[3]

5122 **3** *½* **Fayr Fall (IRE)**[19] 5415 3-9-3 71 (b) DuranFentiman 8 76
(Tim Easterby) *hld up in tch: chsd ldr 2f out: rdn to ld ins fnl f: sn hdd and unable qck* **10/3**[1]

1355 **4** *½* **Star City (IRE)**[10] 5728 3-8-9 63 (be) PaulMulrennan 2 66
(Michael Dods) *led: rdn over 1f out: hdd and no ex ins fnl f* **7/1**

2442 **5** *2½* **Al's Memory (IRE)**[5] 5892 3-8-7 66 NathanSweeney(5) 6 63
(David Evans) *hld up: rdn over 2f out: styd on fr over 1f out: nvr trbld ldrs* **7/2**[2]

0002 **6** *3¾* **Available (IRE)**[20] 5388 3-9-4 72 StephenCraine 3 58
(John Mackie) *chsd ldr tl pushed along 2f out: wknd ins fnl f* **10/1**

1350 **7** *11* **First Bid**[71] 3555 3-9-1 69 (b) GrahamLee 4 26
(James Given) *chsd ldrs: rdn over 2f out: wknd over 1f out* **11/1**

036 **8** *7* **Aureolin Gulf**[30] 4992 3-8-12 66 RussKennemore 5
(Reg Hollinshead) *stdd s: hld up: rdn and wknd over 2f out* **33/1**

1m 27.52s (-2.08) **Going Correction** -0.275s/f (Stan) 8 Ran SP% **114.8**
Speed ratings (Par 101): **100,99,98,98,95 90,78,70**
toteswingers 1&2 £3.30, 1&3 £4.60, 2&3 £4.80 CSF £25.42 CT £75.93 TOTE £9.10: £3.00, £1.10, £1.90; EX 38.60 Trifecta £182.60 Part won. Pool: £246.87 - 0.92 winning units..
Owner Christopher Wright **Bred** Rathbarry Stud **Trained** Middleham Moor, N Yorks

FOCUS
The going was changed to standard to fast before this race. A competitive handicap, run at a decent pace and it produced a thrilling finish.

6053 CLEANDOMAIN H'CAP 5f 216y(P)

7:00 (7:00) (Class 6) (0-65,65) 3-Y-O+ **£2,070** (£616; £307; £153) **Stalls** Low

Form RPR

0/ **1** **Pre Tax Profit (IRE)**[12] 5691 4-8-12 61 (t) DarrenEgan(5) 1 72
(Reginald Roberts, Ire) *chsd ldrs: led 5f out: rdn over 1f out: styd on* **3/1**[1]

1043 **2** *½* **Strong Man**[15] 5543 4-9-2 60 (b) PaulMulrennan 5 69+
(Michael Easterby) *hld up: hdwy over 1f out: r.o to go 2nd towards fin: nt rch wnr* **4/1**[3]

0644 **3** *1¼* **Dark Lane**[2] 5971 6-8-13 62 NathanSweeney(5) 3 67
(David Evans) *a.p: chsd wnr 3f out: sn rdn: styd on same pce ins fnl f: lost 2nd towards fin* **4/1**[3]

5000 **4** *1¼* **Court Applause (IRE)**[46] 4439 4-9-7 65 FrannyNorton 9 66
(William Muir) *s.i.s: hld up: nt clr run over 1f out: r.o ins fnl f: nrst fin* **25/1**

0-10 **5** *1¼* **Elegant Muse**[22] 5326 4-8-10 61 (t) DanielMuscutt(7) 10 58
(Michael Appleby) *chsd ldrs: rdn and swtchd rt over 1f out: styd on same pce* **14/1**

0065 **6** *1½* **Powerful Pierre**[10] 5750 5-9-4 62 (b) GrahamLee 6 54
(Ian McInnes) *sn pushed along in rr: rdn over 1f out: r.o ins fnl f: nvr nrr* **14/1**

5060 **7** *¾* **Methaaly (IRE)**[19] 5416 9-9-5 63 (be) SeanQuinlan 13 53
(Michael Mullineaux) *hld up: rdn: edgd lft and r.o ins fnl f: nvr nrr* **25/1**

5206 **8** *½* **Chjimes (IRE)**[45] 4468 8-9-7 65 (b) KirstyMilczarek 8 53
(Conor Dore) *hld up: rdn over 1f out: nvr on terms* **25/1**

1-00 **9** *3¾* **Fifteentwo**[75] 3451 3-9-5 65 RichardHughes 4 41
(David Nicholls) *hld up in tch: pushed along whn n.m.r over 2f out: wknd fnl f* **7/2**[2]

1504 **10** *nk* **Sannibel**[13] 5635 4-9-4 62 JackMitchell 11 37
(K F Clutterbuck) *chsd ldrs: rdn over 2f out: wknd over 1f out* **25/1**

5505 **11** *1½* **Punching**[24] 5245 8-8-13 62 LauraPike(5) 7 32
(Conor Dore) *led 1f: chsd wnr tl 3f out: rdn and wknd over 1f out* **25/1**

0600 **12** *1¾* **Roodee Queen**[43] 4533 4-9-2 60 LiamKeniry 12 25
(Milton Bradley) *hld up: hdwy over 2f out: wknd over 1f out* **28/1**

1m 13.33s (-1.67) **Going Correction** -0.275s/f (Stan)
WFA 3 from 4yo+ 2lb 12 Ran SP% **123.2**
Speed ratings (Par 101): **100,99,97,96,94 92,91,90,85,85 83,80**
toteswingers 1&2 £4.40, 1&3 £3.40, 2&3 £3.90 CSF £14.21 CT £50.60 TOTE £5.40: £2.00, £1.70, £1.20; EX 18.90 Trifecta £38.80 Pool: £140.81 - 2.68 winning units..
Owner John James Feane **Bred** Lesley Roche **Trained** Rathangan, Co Kildare

FOCUS
A moderate handicap, run at no more than a steady pace.
Strong Man Official explanation: jockey said gelding was slowly away.

6054 BRITISH STALLION STUDS SUPPORTING BRITISH RACING E B F MAIDEN STKS 5f 20y (P)
7:30 (7:30) (Class 5) 2-Y-O £3,137 (£933; £466 ; £233) Stalls Low

Form				RPR
0425	1		**New Fforest**[22] 5307 2 -8-12[86] LiamKeniry 2 (Andrew Balding) *mde all: pushed clr fr over 1f out: easily* 1/10[1]	73+
0	2	4	**Compton Silver**[73] 3499 2 -9-3[0] PaulMulrennan 5 (Hans Adielsson) *prom: chsd wnr over 3f out: pushed along 1/2-way: outpcd fr over 1f out* 28/1	60
4	3	1 1/4	**Miako (USA)**[75] 3452 2 -8-12[0] TobyAtkinson(5) 4 (Marco Botti) *s.i.s: hld up: hdwy over 1f out: sn outpcd* 10/1[2]	55
5050	4	3	**Borough Boy (IRE)**[5] 5544 2 -9-3[65] JoeFanning 1 (Derek Shaw) *s.i.s: hdwy 1/2-way: wkng whn hung lft over 1f out* 25/1[3]	46
0046	5	17	**Mace The Ace**[10] 5748 2 -8-12[56] (p) FrannyNorton 3 (David C Griffiths) *chsd wnr tl over 3f out: wknd 2f out* 80/1	

1m 1.66s (-0.64) **Going Correction** -0.275s/f (Stan) 5Ran SP% 108.5
Speed ratings (Par 95): **94,87,85,80,53**
CSF £6.05 TOTE £1.10 : £1.10, £6.70 ; EX 6.60 .
Owner Elite Racing Club **Bred** Elite Racing Club **Trained** Kingsclere, Hants

FOCUS
An uncompetitive maiden, won as she liked by the hot odds-on favourite who outclassed a weak field.

NOTEBOOK
New Fforest has been keeping much better company than this of late and the bookmakers' boards suggested that she only needed to turn up in order to get off the mark. There were no shocks and she was allowed to coast much of the final furlong having shown bright speed from the gates. This success, while a boost to her confidence, hasn't told us anything that we didn't already know. That said, she's clearly useful and certainly doesn't look badly handicapped at present given her Listed run and previous narrow defeat by subsequent Listed winner, Winning Express.
Compton Silver plugged on at the one-pace but was readily outclassed. This was probably a step up on what she'd achieved on debut, though is clearly limited and will surely do best when handicapped. (op 33-1 tchd 25-1)
Miako(USA) was disappointing. He looked the type to improve significantly on his introduction but doesn't appear to have gone the right way.

6055 GUEST ALFA ROMEO AND FIAT CLAIMING STKS 1m 4f 50y (P)
8:00 (8:00) (Class 6) 3-Y-O+ £2,181 (£644; £322) Stalls Low

Form				RPR
1153	1		**Just Lille (IRE)**[33] 4864 9 -9-9[79] (p) GrahamLee 9 (Ann Duffield) *mde all: shkn up and bmpd over 1f out: styd on wl* 5/4[1]	71
0043	2	3/4	**Kames Park (IRE)**[9] 5767 10 -9-6[65] RobbieFitzpatrick 8 (Richard Guest) *s.i.s: hld up: hdwy over 2f out: rdn over 1f out: r.o to go 2nd nr fin: nt rch wnr* 10/1	66
0424	3	nk	**Turjuman (USA)**[179] 888 7 -8-13[63] (p) NatashaEaton(7) 2 (Alan Bailey) *a.p: jnd wnr over 2f out: rdn and edgd lft over 1f out: unable qck wl ins fnl f* 12/1	66
60-	4	1 1/4	**Mesariya (IRE)**[30] 5025 4 -8-10[80] (t[1]) DarrenEgan(5) 3 (Reginald Roberts, Ire) *slowly in to stride: hld up: styd on u.p fr over 1f out: nt rch ldrs* 9/2[3]	59
5126	5	1 1/4	**Layla's Boy**[30] 5012 5 -9-5[61] (bt) FrannyNorton 6 (John Mackie) *chsd wnr tl over 7f out: remained handy: wnt 2nd again 3f out: rdn and ev ch whn bmpd over 1f out: no ex ins fnl f* 9/1	61
0200	6	1/2	**Jack Dawkins (USA)**[38] 4712 7 -9-8[68] RichardHughes 4 (David Nicholls) *hld up in tch: rdn over 1f out: no ex ins fnl f* 10/3[2]	63
0	7	14	**Father Shine (IRE)**[33] 5293 9 -9-8[0] PatCosgrave 5 (Shaun Harris) *prom: chsd wnr over 7f out tl rdn 3f out: sn wknd* 50/1	41
00-0	8	6	**Ladies Best**[9] 1154 8 -9-3[63] JoeFanning 1 (Christopher Kellett) *hld up: a in rr: wknd 3f out* 50/1	26

2m 39.11s (-1.99) **Going Correction** -0.275s/f (Stan) 8Ran SP% 116.4
Speed ratings (Par 101): **95,94,94,93,92 92,82,78**
toteswingers 1&2 £7.00, 1&3 £4.00, 2&3 £2.90 CSF £16.06 TOTE £2.30 : £1.10, £1.70, £3.60 ; EX 8.40 Trifecta £36.00 Pool: £350.99 - 7.20 winning units. .Mesariya was claimed by Mr Tony Coyle for £6,000.
Owner MPR Warrender Baines Farrington Kay **Bred** Sweetmans Bloodstock **Trained** Constable Burton, N Yorks

FOCUS
A fair claimer, run at a steady pace.

6056 SPOTLESS FACILITY SERVICES H'CAP 1m 4f 50y (P)
8:30 (8:30) (Class 6) (0-60,60) 3-Y-O+ £2,181 (£644; £322) Stalls Low

Form				RPR
03/4	1		**Iceman George**[13] 5637 8 -9-8[59] (v) SimonPearce(3) 4 (Lydia Pearce) *hld up: hdwy 4f out: led over 2f out: sn rdn: styd on* 12/1	66
0500	2	1 1/4	**Inniscastle Boy**[9] 5764 3 -9-0[57] (b) GrahamLee 12 (William Muir) *hld up: hdwy over 2f out: r.o to go 2nd post: nt rch wnr* 11/2[3]	62
2-05	3	hd	**Langley**[14] 5596 5 -9-5[60] (v[1]) DanielMuscutt(7) 6 (Tim Vaughan) *a.p: led 3f out: hdd over 2f out: styd on same pce ins fnl f: lost 2nd post* 10/1	65
0453	4	1 1/2	**Rano Pano (USA)**[37] 4403 3 -8-6[52] ow2 PaulPickard(3) 5 (Brian Ellison) *hld up: hdwy u.p over 1f out: styd on: nt rch ldrs* 7/1	54
5632	5	nk	**King's Road**[8] 5809 7 -9-10[58] (t) RichardHughes 1 (Anabel K Murphy) *hld up: hdwy over 2f out: rdn over 1f out: no ex ins fnl f* 3/1[2]	60
0040	6	6	**Arizona High**[45] 4455 4 -8-12[46] oh1 FrannyNorton 11 (Andrew Crook) *prom: rdn over 2f out: wknd over 1f out* 25/1	38
006	7	2 1/2	**Spanish Trail**[33] 4888 3 -8-8[54] RyanPowell(3) 9 (Christopher Kellett) *prom: lost pl 4f out: no ch whn hung lft over 1f out* 66/1	42
0446	8	1 1/2	**Sacco D'Oro**[8] 5683 6 -8-12[46] (v) SeanQuinlan 2 (Michael Mullineaux) *chsd ldrs: pushed along whn nt clr run and wknd over 2f out* 33/1	32
2005	9	1/2	**Visions Of Johanna (USA)**[38] 2694 7 -9-6[59] DarrenEgan(5) 10 (John Balding) *s.i.s: hld up: wknd over 2f out* 8/1	44
	10	6	**Dunaskin (IRE)**[16] 2348 12 -9-2[50] (b) RobbieFitzpatrick 8 (Richard Guest) *chsd ldr tl rdn and wknd over 2f out* 25/1	25
0504	11	9	**Quiet Appeal (IRE)**[2] 5683 3 -9-2[59] JoeFanning 7 (Mark Johnston) *led 9f: sn wknd* 5/2[1]	20

2m 37.93s (-3.17) **Going Correction** -0.275s/f (Stan)
WFA 3 from 4yo+ 9lb 11Ran SP% 121.5
Speed ratings (Par 101): **99,98,98,97,96 92,91,90,89,85 79**
toteswingers 1&2 £9.20, 1&3 £10.00, 2&3 £10.60 CSF £76.80 CT £703.30 TOTE £14.10 : £3.10, £2.40, £8.20 ; EX 82.80 Trifecta £205.10 Part won. Pool: £277.19 - 0.60 winning units. .
Owner John Mangan **Bred** T J And J Wells **Trained** Newmarket, Suffolk

FOCUS
A modest handicap, run at an even tempo.
Quiet Appeal (IRE) Official explanation: jockey said filly ran too freely.

6057 EVENT MANAGEMENT CATERING H'CAP 1m 141y (P)
9:00 (9:00) (Class 6) (0-65,65) 3-Y-O+ £2,070 (£616; £307 ; £153) Stalls Low

Form				RPR
6540	1		**Fame Again**[33] 4889 4 -9-9[64] PaulMulrennan 5 (Michael Easterby) *mde all: rdn over 1f out: styd on wl* 4/1[2]	73
043	2	1	**Green Mitas (ITY)**[8] 5805 3 -8-13[60] GrahamLee 3 (Frank Sheridan) *chsd ldrs: rdn over 1f out: styd on* 8/1	67
0031	3	nk	**Refreshestheparts (USA)**[17] 5479 3 -8-12[59] PatCosgrave 9 (George Baker) *hld up: rdn over 1f out: edgd lft and r.o wl ins fnl f: nrst fin* 3/1[1]	65+
1514	4	1 1/2	**Mr Chocolate Drop (IRE)**[8] 5081 8 -9-8[63] (t) RussKennemore 1 (Mandy Rowland) *chsd ldrs: rdn over 1f out: styng on same pce whn hmpd ins fnl f* 14/1	66
0155	5	1 1/2	**Climaxfortackle (IRE)**[15] 5547 4 -9-9[64] (v) FrannyNorton 2 (Derek Shaw) *s.i.s: hld up: hdwy u.p over 1f out: nt clr run wl ins fnl f: nt trble ldrs* 7/1	63
0420	6	1/2	**Alluring Star**[12] 5671 4 -8-10[58] DavidSimmonson(7) 8 (Michael Easterby) *chsd wnr: rdn over 2f out: no ex ins fnl f* 25/1	56
21	7	1/2	**Wind Star**[74] 3469 9 -9-0[60] (tp) DavidKenny(5) 6 (Brendan Powell) *mid-div: hdwy over 2f out: rdn over 1f out: no ex ins fnl f* 8/1	57
6200	8	hd	**Darnathean**[11] 5721 3 -8-11[63] (e) DarrenEgan(5) 11 (Paul D'Arcy) *hld up: rdn over 1f out: n.d* 10/1	59
0004	9	nk	**Opus Maximus (IRE)**[8] 5804 7 -9-0[55] (p) HayleyTurner 4 (Conor Dore) *hld up: n.d* 5/1[3]	51
-040	10	9	**Peadar Miguel**[24] 5225 5 -9-7[65] MarkCoumbe(3) 7 (Daniel Mark Loughnane) *prom: rdn over 2f out: wknd over 1f out* 20/1	40
0-44	11	1/2	**Silken Satinwood (IRE)**[25] 5208 3 -8-13[60] RichardHughes 12 (Peter Chapple-Hyam) *s.i.s: hld up: pushed along over 2f out: a in rr* 14/1	34

1m 48.4s (-2.10) **Going Correction** -0.275s/f (Stan)
WFA 3 from 4yo+ 6lb 11Ran SP% 127.4
Speed ratings (Par 101): **98,97,96,95,94 93,93,93,92,84 84**
toteswingers 1&2 £15.70, 1&3 £6.00, 2&3 £4.50 CSF £39.67 CT £117.00 TOTE £7.10 : £2.30, £4.10, £1.90 ; EX 66.60 TRIFECTA Not won. .
Owner Mrs C E Mason **Bred** R H Mason **Trained** Sheriff Hutton, N Yorks
■ Stewards' Enquiry : Russ Kennemore two-day ban; careless riding (22nd-23rd Sept).

FOCUS
Front-runners had been well served at this meeting and there was another all-the-way success in this modest handicap.
Wind Star Official explanation: vet said gelding finished lame.
T/Plt: £6.90 to a £1 stake. Pool: £58,319.54 - 6,115.47 winning tickets T/Qpdt: £2.70 to a £1 stake. Pool: £6,319.02 - 1,727.4 winning tickets CR

6058a -6059a, 6064a, 6067a- 6069a - (Foreign Racing) - See Raceform Interactive

[5281] LEOPARDSTOWN (L-H)
Saturday, September 8

OFFICIAL GOING: Good (good to firm in places)

6060a ICON BREEDERS' CUP JUVENILE TURF TRIAL STKS (LISTED RACE) 1m
4:10 (4:11) 2-Y-O £21,666 (£6,333; £3,000 ; £1,000)

			RPR
1		**Battle Of Marengo (IRE)**[48] 5460 2 -9-3 JPO'Brien 3 (A P O'Brien, Ire) *mde all: sddle slipped bk in running: pushed along into st and wnt 3 l clr appr fnl f: kpt on wl: eased cl home* 9/10[1]	104+
2	1 3/4	**Trading Leather (IRE)** 2 -9-3 KevinManning 5 (J S Bolger, Ire) *chsd ldrs: cl 4th 3f out: rdn over 2f out to dispute 2nd jst ins fnl f: kpt on wl u.p fnl 100yds: no ch w easy wnr* 14/1	99+
3	1	**Dibayani (IRE)**[29] 5069 2 -9-3 ShaneFoley 2 (M Halford, Ire) *hld up in tch: rn wd into st and rdn in 5th 2f out: clsd down centre of trck to dispute 2nd ins fnl f: no ex fnl 100yds* 6/1	97
4	2	**Canary Row (IRE)**[115] 2184 2 -9-3[90] ChrisHayes 1 (P J Prendergast, Ire) *chsd ldrs: cl 3rd on inner under 3f out: sn pushed along and one pce ent fnl f: kpt on* 14/1	92
5	3/4	**Thunder Mountain (IRE)**[40] 4665 2 -9-3 PatSmullen 6 (D K Weld, Ire) *w.w in rr: stl gng wl tl pushed along 2f out: sn no imp: kpt on* 9/2[2]	91
6	1 1/2	**Orgilgo Bay (IRE)**[29] 5069 2 -9-3 GaryCarroll 4 (John C McConnell, Ire) *racd keenly: trckd wnr in 2nd: cl up on outer 3f out: sn rdn and wknd appr fnl f* 5/1[3]	87

1m 38.68s (-2.52) **Going Correction** -0.25s/f (Firm) 6Ran SP% 115.1
Speed ratings: **102,100,99,97,96 95**
CSF £15.95 TOTE £1.50 : £1.10, £3.00 ; DF 15.00 .
Owner Michael Tabor & Derrick Smith & Mrs John Magnier **Bred** Anna Karenina Syndicate **Trained** Ballydoyle, Co Tipperary

FOCUS
What looked competitive on paper turned into a rout. The winner was arguably value for further and the third, fourth and fifth set the level.

NOTEBOOK
Battle Of Marengo (IRE)◆ jumped a roadway, prompting the saddle to slip backwards, but Joseph O'Brien was remarkably composed and it would be wrong to say the lead he had was a soft one. When they turned into the straight everything else was in trouble and the race was over soon afterwards. Battle Of Marengo, gorgeously bred, stayed on all the way to the line and will surely get middle distances next year. The son of Galileo may still be a little green but has a great deal of ability and plenty of class. He is a 20-1 chance for the Derby. Official explanation: jockey said colt jumped road crossing and saddle slipped (op 10/11 tchd Evens)
Trading Leather (IRE)◆, held in high regard by Jim Bolger, turned in a remarkable debut effort. While no threat to the winner, he is crying out for a trip, which he will get next year, and he looks a lovely prospect.
Dibayani(IRE) looked a good bet to come second at one stage but could not really pick up. At the least he is holding his form. (op 11/2)
Canary Row (IRE) had questions to answer after a break and regarding the trip. He did not entirely convince regarding the distance but is a useful and honest horse.
Thunder Mountain (IRE) was easy to back and the doubts about what he achieved at Galway are greater now. There were no obvious excuses. (op 5/1 tchd 11/2)

Orgilgo Bay(IRE) was a bit keen on ground that may have been against him. He was all at sea late in the race and, considering what he achieved previously on easy going, is certainly not one to give up on. (op 9/2)

6061a COOLMORE FUSAICHI PEGASUS MATRON STKS (GROUP 1) (F&M) 1m

4:40 (4:43) 3-Y-0+ **£102,916** (£30,083; £14,250; £4,750)

RPR

1 *shd* **Chachamaidee (IRE)**14 5573 5-9-5 ....(b1) TomQueally 11 116
(Sir Henry Cecil) *slowly away and racd in rr: stl gng wl and swtchd rt appr fnl 2f: sn rdn and sltly hmpd 1f out: r.o strly on outer ins fnl f: jst hld: fin 2nd: awrdd the r* **11/2**

2 **Duntle (IRE)**23 5286 3-9-0 110.. WayneLordan 1 115
(David Wachman, Ire) *chsd ldrs: 4th under 3f out: lost pl into st and short of room: swtchd rt appr fnl f and r.o wl u.p to ld fnl 25yds: jst hld on: fin 1st disqualified and plcd 2nd* **7/2**2

3 ½ **Emulous**80 3266 5-9-5 114.. PatSmullen 8 115
(D K Weld, Ire) *rrd s and racd towards rr: sn chsd ldrs: disp 4th 1/2-way: strly pressed ldr and rdn to ld ins fnl 150yds: sn hdd and no ex fnl 75yds: kpt on* **11/4**1

4 *nk* **Laugh Out Loud**78 3328 3-9-0 .... JohnnyMurtagh 6 113
(Mick Channon) *cl up: racd keenly: led over 5f out: strly pressed appr fnl f and hdd ins fnl 150yds: one pce after* **8/1**

5 1¼ **La Collina (IRE)**13 5643 3-9-0 104.......................... DeclanMcDonogh 10 110
(Kevin Prendergast, Ire) *towards rr: hrd rdn appr 2f out and r.o wl appr fnl f to go 5th fnl 50yds: nvr nrr* **20/1**

6 1 **Alanza (IRE)**21 5355 4-9-5 108... ShaneFoley 5 109
(John M Oxx, Ire) *hld up in rr of mid-div: pushed along in 7th into st: no ex after 2f out whn sltly ham: kpt on* **8/1**

7 *nk* **Ishvana (IRE)**80 3265 3-9-0 108................................ SeamieHeffernan 7 107
(A P O'Brien, Ire) *mid-div: pushed along under 4f out and clsd into 6th appr fnl f: no ex fnl 100yds* **12/1**

8 7 **Maybe (IRE)**57 4065 3-9-0 107... JPO'Brien 2 91
(A P O'Brien, Ire) *chsd ldrs: wnt 2nd 4f out: pushed along appr 2f out and sn no imp: wknd ins fnl f: eased* **4/1**3

9 1½ **Marvada (IRE)**23 5286 4-9-5 100.................................(t) KevinManning 3 89
(K J Condon, Ire) *mid-div: pushed along over 3f out and dropped to rr: no imp fnl 2f* **50/1**

10 1¾ **Ballybacka Lady (IRE)**13 5643 4-9-5 105........................ ChrisHayes 9 85
(Mrs John Harrington, Ire) *towards rr: sme hdwy fr 1/2-way: no imp in 8th fr bef 2f out* **20/1**

11 6½ **After (IRE)**16 5523 3-9-0 98.. CO'Donoghue 4 69
(A P O'Brien, Ire) *led: hdd over 5f out: pushed along on inner into st and wknd under 2f out: eased* **33/1**

1m 37.58s (-3.62) **Going Correction** -0.25s/f (Firm)
WFA 3 from 4yo+ 5lb 11 Ran SP% **128.6**
Speed ratings: **107,108,107,107,105 104,104,97,96,94 87**
CSF £26.61 TOTE £6.10: £1.60, £2.00, £1.50; DF 32.00.

Owner R A H Evans **Bred** Cheval Court Stud **Trained** Newmarket, Suffolk

■ Stewards' Enquiry : Tom Queally caution: used whip above shoulder height.
Wayne Lordan two-day ban: careless riding (tbc)

FOCUS
An open renewal of this Group 1, which produced a stirring finish. The pace was far from frantic and the stewards reversed the first two. The runner-up and fourth have been rated to their best.

NOTEBOOK
Chachamaidee(IRE) was game to the end. The interference she suffered seemed negligible but it did not help and she was seen to be closing the gap ever so slowly towards the finish. She is thriving at five years of age and, remarkably, is now a Group 1 winner.
Duntle(IRE) was involved in a minor barging match with Alanza, forcing the winner a little wider too, and prompting a stewards' enquiry. Duntle was always holding her in the final furlong and eventually mastered Emulous, doing enough to leave the impression that she was the best filly in the race. The decision to reverse the result was controversial and certainly split opinion at the track. When the margin of victory is the minimum, and Duntle's manoeuvre did upset Chachamaidee's momentum a little, there was always a chance the stewards would change the result. The inquiry lasted the guts of half an hour; it was obviously a close call. She ought to have no problem staying further again and would likely have won this easier if they had gone a better gallop. (op 9/2)
Emulous, who left her foes for dead in this 12 months ago, had underwhelmed at Royal Ascot, a performance her trainer attributed to ground conditions. Perhaps a little ease would suit her better but it was disappointing, given how she travelled here, that she took so long to master the pace-setting Laugh Out Loud. Of course, she was beaten by narrow margins in a Group 1, but the feeling lingers that she was capable of better than this. (op 11/4 tchd 3/1)
Laugh Out Loud had a fairly easy time of it up front and was really game when challenged. She must rate a really progressive sort who bounced back from a moderate run at Royal Ascot. If she stays in training she should come back for this next year.
La Collina(IRE) ran a fine race, particularly as she would not really have been suited by how it was run. This season has been a disappointment for her and so finishing close is an encouraging sign. (op 25/1)
Alanza(IRE), involved in the crucial scrimmaging, was unable to pick up. Her rider rode a canny enough race and she was just not good enough.
Maybe(IRE) was quite solid in the market, particularly so for a filly whose form this year has implied that she basically has not trained on. She came into the race under a cloud and comes out of it under a cloud, struggling to make any impact. (op 5/1 tchd 11/2)

6062a KPMG ENTERPRISE STKS (GROUP 3) (REGISTERED AS THE KILTERNAN STAKES) 1m 2f

5:10 (5:13) 3-Y-0+ **£32,520** (£9,520; £4,520; £1,520)

RPR

1 **Alla Speranza**9 5777 3-9-0 98.....................................(t) KevinManning 2 109
(J S Bolger, Ire) *hld up in tch: pushed along in 4th under 3f out: clsd on outer to ld over 100yds out: kpt on wl* **10/1**

2 ½ **Primevere (IRE)**14 5594 4-9-7 .... JohnnyMurtagh 1 108
(Roger Charlton) *broke wl to ld: sn settled in 2nd: clsd on outer to ld 2f out: sn chal and hdd ent fnl f: rallied on far side to take 2nd fnl 100yds* **11/4**2

3 ¾ **Speaking Of Which (IRE)**104 2524 3-9-6 116.............(bt) PatSmullen 4 113
(D K Weld, Ire) *chsd ldrs: clsr in 3rd gng wl under 3f out: wnt 2nd 2f out and led narrowly ent fnl f: sn hdd and no ex fnl 100yds* **4/5**1

4 2 **Defining Year (IRE)**44 4521 4-9-10 103.........................(p) ShaneFoley 5 106
(M Halford, Ire) *w.w in rr: pushed along appr st: rdn ins fnl f and kpt on into n.d 4th fnl 50yds* **11/1**

5 *nk* **Tenth Star (IRE)**9 5777 3-9-3 101... JPO'Brien 6 105
(A P O'Brien, Ire) *trckd ldr tl led narrowly after 1f: jnd under 3f out and sn pushed along: rdn and outpcd fr 2f out* **6/1**3

2m 2.9s (-5.30) **Going Correction** -0.25s/f (Firm)
WFA 3 from 4yo 7lb 5 Ran SP% **113.9**
Speed ratings: **111,110,110,108,108**
CSF £38.07 TOTE £9.70: £4.10, £1.80; DF 48.00.

Owner Miss K Rausing **Bred** Miss K Rausing **Trained** Coolcullen, Co Carlow

■ Stewards' Enquiry : Johnny Murtagh caution: used whip with excessive frequency

FOCUS
The progressive winner ran a persoanl best and the race is best rated through the front-running fifth.

NOTEBOOK
Alla Speranza looked one of the first beaten but was actually well on top at the finish. Having not looked altogether progressive this season, she was game in defeat at Killarney last time and really relished the trip on the decent ground here. The manner of her success certainly suggests she should have decent prospects of staying a little further and one must remember that she has raced seven times. She may stay in training next year and, assuming she stays sound, looks good enough to win again at pattern level.
Primevere(IRE) kept going to press the winner to the wire. She was niggled as they turned in but found a fair bit, without really looking like getting there. She seemed to run her race and is a good, honest type. She is probably best at this trip. (op 100/30 tchd 7/2)
Speaking Of Which(IRE) looked a shade flattered by his easy success in the Gallinule and, while he travelled well here, he was unable to pick up as seemed likely. This was just his fourth race and time remains on his side, though thoughts of his prospects of getting a mile and a half may be put to bed a bit after this. (op 8/11 tchd 4/6)
Defining Year(IRE) had a bit to do in this company and was under pressure a long way out. He ran on without ever remotely threatening. (op 10/1 tchd 12/1)
Tenth Star(IRE) remains disappointing and will possibly struggle to win again. (op 13/2)

6063a RED MILLS IRISH CHAMPION STKS (GROUP 1) 1m 2f

5:45 (5:45) 3-Y-0+
£362,083 (£118,333; £55,833; £18,333; £12,083; £5,833)

RPR

1 **Snow Fairy (IRE)**20 5399 5-9-4 .... FrankieDettori 3 126
(Ed Dunlop) *hld up in mod 4th: hdwy fr 3f out to go 2nd gng best under 2f out: led ent fnl f: edgd lft 100yds out and kpt on wl* **15/8**2

2 1¼ **Nathaniel (IRE)**49 4322 4-9-7 .... WilliamBuick 1 127
(John Gosden) *trckd clr ldr in 2nd: clsr 3f out and nice hdwy to ld 2f out: sn rdn and strly pressed: hdd ent fnl f: sn no ex: kpt on* **13/8**1

3 ¾ **St Nicholas Abbey (IRE)**17 5490 5-9-7 124........................ JPO'Brien 4 125
(A P O'Brien, Ire) *w.w in 5th: wnt mod 3rd appr fnl f: styd on wl u.p wout ever threatening principals* **3/1**3

4 5½ **Light Heavy (IRE)**30 5027 3-9-0 108..........................(tp) KevinManning 2 114
(J S Bolger, Ire) *settled in 3rd: pushed along appr st to cl: no ex fr 2f out: rdn and kpt on fnl f* **25/1**

5 3½ **Born To Sea (IRE)**27 5134 3-9-0 116.........................(b) JohnnyMurtagh 5 107
(John M Oxx, Ire) *hld up in rr: plenty to do 3f out: hdwy into mod 5th ent fnl f: kpt on* **12/1**

6 13 **Daddy Long Legs (USA)**21 5375 3-9-0 113.........(b) SeamieHeffernan 6 81
(A P O'Brien, Ire) *led: sn clr: over 10 l in front 7f out: reduced advantage appr 3f out: pushed along and hdd 2f out: wknd qckly* **20/1**

2m 0.92s (-7.28) **Going Correction** -0.25s/f (Firm)
WFA 3 from 4yo+ 7lb 6 Ran SP% **114.2**
Speed ratings: **119,118,117,113,110 99**
CSF £5.48 TOTE £2.90: £1.10, £1.50; DF 4.50.

Owner Anamoine Ltd **Bred** Windflower Overseas Holdings Inc **Trained** Newmarket, Suffolk

FOCUS
This renewal turned out to be up there with the best of them in terms of the impression it will leave. The fourth has been rated to his best and the runner-up has been rated to his mark.

NOTEBOOK
Snow Fairy(IRE) was able to sit contentedly towards the rear of midfield. Gorgeously ridden by Frankie Dettori, she was allowed to go a grand pace throughout and, when they turned into the straight, she came there travelling best of all. There was a small doubt, given the injury she has had, about whether Snow Fairy could again go through with her effort and beat a King George winner. Showing the determination that was evident in defeat in this 12 months ago, she found more than enough when hitting the front and can be considered quite a tidy winner. The tendon injury she suffered would have ended many careers. Her connections are worthy of considerable acclaim for getting her back to this level. She will hardly trouble Frankel if they meet but the Arc has to be considered a possibility and, given the form she is in, she deserves great respect. Regardless of what else she achieves, legendary status is assured. (op 15/8 tchd 2/1)
Nathaniel(IRE) looked a shade vulnerable, in light of John Gosden's comments about his main target being the Arc and the fact that this trip on drying ground did not place sufficient emphasis on his stamina. He tracked a really hard pace and ran his heart out but simply did not have the toe to match the mare. This did nothing to dampen his prospects with a view to Paris and, if he gets luck in running, he should be bang there in the Arc. (op 7/4)
St Nicholas Abbey(IRE), like Nathaniel, looks a better horse over a mile and a half. Predictably, the race was set up here to make it as much of a stamina test as possible. He travelled well under a really patient ride and looked a threat turning in but simply did not have the ability to reel in the mare. This is what he is at 1m2f and he deserves a crack at another big target over his optimum distance.
Light Heavy(IRE), a speculative runner, justified Jim Bolger's boldness. There was no shame in finishing a well-held fourth and he is clearly good enough to win middle-distance races when his task is more realistic. He runs particularly well here. (op 33/1)
Born To Sea(IRE)'s trainer was convinced that his tame run behind Famous Name was not reflective of his ability. He ran a long way short of a mark of 116 here over a trip that should have suited. Found to be lame behind after the race, he has now been retired to stud.
Daddy Long Legs(USA) went off hard and is clearly not to be judged deeply on this. (op 22/1 tchd 25/1 and 16/1)

6066a IRISH STALLION FARMS EUROPEAN BREEDERS FUND H'CAP (PREMIER HANDICAP) 1m 6f

7:20 (7:26) 3-Y-0+ **£27,083** (£7,916; £3,750; £1,250)

RPR

1 **I Have A Dream**9 5780 3-9-12 **102**....................................... JPO'Brien 13 109
(A P O'Brien, Ire) *cl up: impr to ld wl after 2f: hdd bef st: rallied on inner to ld again 1f out: kpt on wl: all out* **8/1**3

2 *nk* **Call Me Bubbles (FR)**37 4750 3-8-3 **82**.....................(t) LeighRoche(3) 8 89
(W P Mullins, Ire) *chsd ldrs: pushed along in 6th on inner bef st: swtchd rt appr fnl f and r.o wl u.p to chal fnl 100yds: jst hld* **9/2**1

3 1¼ **Strandfield Lady (IRE)**30 5025 7-9-6 **88**...................(b) SamJames(3) 2 93
(H Rogers, Ire) *hld up in rr of mid-div: hdwy on inner into 5th 1f out: rdn into 3rd fnl 100yds: kpt on* **20/1**

4 ½ **Notable Graduate (IRE)**36 4789 4-9-11 **90**.................(bt1) PatSmullen 6 94
(D K Weld, Ire) *mid-div: clsd into 5th appr st: rdn appr fnl f and kpt on wout ever threatening principals* **12/1**

5 *nse* **Teak (IRE)**42 4606 5-8-11 **76** KevinManning 1 80
(Ian Williams) *chsd ldrs: pushed along in 4th appr st: ev ch appr fnl f: sn no ex* **8/1**3

6 *1* **Certerach (IRE)**20 5397 4-9-11 **90** ShaneFoley 11 93
(M Halford, Ire) *towards rr: clsd gng wl under 2f out: n.m.r and swtchd lft to chse ldrs ins fnl f: kpt on: nvr nrr* **12/1**

7 *nk* **All That Rules**18 5462 3-8-11 **87** NGMcCullagh 14 89
(Thomas Carmody, Ire) *mid-div: pushed along in 7th into st: kpt on same pce ins fnl f* **9/2**1

8 *nk* **Admiral Barry (IRE)**84 3177 7-9-3 **82** DeclanMcDonogh 3 84
(Eoin Griffin, Ire) *chsd ldrs: pushed along in 8th appr st: and sn no ex* **20/1**

9 *hd* **Louisville Lip (IRE)**76 2902 5-9-6 **85** DannyGrant 7 87
(Patrick J Flynn, Ire) *dwlt and hld up towards rr: rdn on outer under 2f out and kpt on ins fnl f: nvr nrr* **10/1**

10 *1 1/4* **Domination**7 5569 5-8-12 **77** CO'Donoghue 5 77
(C Byrnes, Ire) *hld up in tch: pushed fr 3f out and n.m.r under 2f out: kpt on* **6/1**2

11 *nse* **Regal Tramp (USA)**6 5864 4-8-9 **77** AndrewPThornton(3) 9 77
(V C Ward, Ire) *led early: settled in 2nd after wl over 2f: regained advantage into st: hdd again 1f out and sn wknd* **16/1**

12 *3/4* **Cry For The Moon (USA)**40 4666 6-9-7 **86** ChrisHayes 10 85
(J H Culloty, Ire) *dwlt and racd in rr: sme late hdwy: nvr a threat* **10/1**

13 *3 1/4* **Clarach (IRE)**36 4786 7-8-12 **77** WayneLordan 12 71
(Anthony Mullins, Ire) *chsd ldrs: 4th 4f out: cl 3rd appr st: sn rdn and wknd qckn ent fnl f: eased* **12/1**

14 *2* **Shelford (IRE)**18 5462 3-9-1 **91** (p) BenCurtis 4 82
(John M Oxx, Ire) *towards rr: rdn 4f out: no imp* **16/1**

3m 2.75s (1.75) **Going Correction** -0.25s/f (Firm)
WFA 3 from 4yo+ 11lb **14** Ran SP% **135.4**
Speed ratings: **85,84,84,83,83 83,83,82,82,82 82,81,79,78**
Pick Six: Not won. CSF £49.53 TOTE £9.30: £2.70, £2.30, £6.60; DF 28.60.
Owner Mrs John Magnier & Michael Tabor & Derrick Smith **Bred** Barry Walters And Balmerino Bloodstock **Trained** Ballydoyle, Co Tipperary

FOCUS
A bunch finish won by the top-rated runner.

NOTEBOOK
I Have A Dream ◆ had won twice previously, once over this course and trip and off a 10lb lower mark. He had run moderately over the distance at Killarney on his previous start but, having led after 3f until headed before the straight, he rallied well for pressure to regain the lead 1f out and dug deep to win all out. He is his trainer's only entry for the Melbourne Cup, for which Stan James quote him at 66-1, but is far from certain to travel and is not yet qualified to pass the ballot or to make the cut for the race. Official explanation: trainer said, regarding apparent improvement in form, that the colt benefited by coming back up in trip and the better ground. (op 8/1 tchd 7/1)
Call Me Bubbles(FR) was on a hat-trick after handicap wins over 1m4f at Roscommon and Galway. Up 15lb since the second of those victories, he was also encountering much quicker ground. Always handy in a race run at an ordinary enough pace for much of the journey, he had every chance from over 1f out and pressed the winner all the way to the line. (op 9/2 tchd 5/1)
Strandfield Lady(IRE), a course specialist over 1m2f, was stepping into unknown territory in terms of distance. At the back of the field approaching the straight, she made significant headway and was probably unlucky not to have finished closer.
Notable Graduate(IRE) has dropped in the ratings and ran a solid race although possibly found the ground quicker than ideal.
Teak(IRE), a winner over the trip at Salisbury on his previous start in July, was 5lb higher here and had every chance before finding no extra from 1f out.
Certerach(IRE), a maiden winner over 1m4f on similar ground at Wexford before finishing third on his handicap debut over that trip on easy ground at Gowran Park, was fighting a losing battle turning for home. (op 11/1)
T/Jkpt: @5,483.60. Pool of @14,623.00 - 2 winning units. T/Plt: @167.10. Pool of @25,520.36 - 114.54 winning units. BF

5597 YORK (L-H)

Sunday, September 9

OFFICIAL GOING: Good to firm (good in places) changing to good to firm after race 3 (2.55)
Wind: light to moderate 1/2 behind Weather: fine and sunny, very warm

6070 JUDITH MARSHALL MEMORIAL STKS (NURSERY) 7f
1:50 (1:52) (Class 4) (0-85,85) 2-Y-O **£5,239** (£1,559; £779; £389) **Stalls** Low

Form RPR

14 **1** **Waterway Run (USA)**22 5361 2-9-0 **78** JimCrowley 12 94+
(Ralph Beckett) *mde all: drvn clr fnl f: eased towards fin* **10/3**1

1 **2** *3 1/4* **Asgardella (IRE)**26 5184 2-8-9 **73** PaulHanagan 15 81+
(Richard Fahey) *sn trcking ldrs: kpt on to take 2nd last 50yds* **10/1**

151 **3** *2* **I'm Back (IRE)**15 5579 2-9-1 **84** DarrenEgan(5) 3 85
(Saeed Bin Suroor) *wnt lft s: trckd ldrs: t.k.h: effrt over 2f out: kpt on to take 3rd last 50yds* **9/2**2

0222 **4** *nk* **Dr Phibes (IRE)**27 5169 2-8-10 **74** RobertWinston 6 74
(Alan Swinbank) *chsd wnr: kpt on same pce appr fnl f* **10/1**

5054 **5** *4* **Newstead Abbey**15 5579 2-9-1 **79** RichardMullen 8 68
(David Brown) *wnt rt s: mid-div: hdwy 3f out: sn chsng ldrs: wknd fnl 150yds* **9/1**

221 **6** *1/2* **Grievous Angel (IRE)**9 5799 2-8-13 **77** (v) PaulMulrennan 4 65
(Ann Duffield) *in rr: hdwy over 2f out: styd on fnl f* **22/1**

3011 **7** *1/2* **Reconsider Baby (IRE)**29 5108 2-8-6 **70** LukeMorris 7 57
(Mrs K Burke) *chsd ldrs: drvn over 4f out: wknd over 1f out* **25/1**

5201 **8** *1 1/2* **Old Man Clegg**15 5602 2-8-9 **73** GrahamGibbons 14 56
(Michael Easterby) *rr-div: hdwy over 2f out: nvr nr ldrs* **11/1**

14 **9** *5* **Luck (IRE)**22 5371 2-9-7 **85** PhillipMakin 10 54+
(Kevin Ryan) *hmpd s: rr-div: sme hdwy over 2f out: nvr on terms* **10/1**

0325 **10** *3/4* **Surround Sound**22 5331 2-8-2 **66** DuranFentiman 5 33+
(Tim Easterby) *t.k.h in mid-div: lost pl bnd over 5f out: sme hdwy whn nt clr run and swtchd lft 2f out: nvr a threat* **40/1**

2256 **11** *2* **Out Of The Blocks**13 5670 2-7-13 **63** (b1) JamesSullivan 11 25+
(Ruth Carr) *hmpd s: a in rr* **33/1**

024 **12** *1 1/2* **Izzy Boy (USA)**29 5083 2-8-8 **72** KierenFallon 2 30+
(Mark Johnston) *hmpd s: in rr and sn drvn along: sme hdwy and edgd rt over 2f out: sn wknd* **7/1**3

133 **13** *2 1/4* **Silent Footsteps (IRE)**15 5587 2-9-0 **78** TomEaves 9 30+
(Michael Dods) *hmpd s: a in rr* **40/1**

15 **14** *3/4* **Slipstream Angel (IRE)**58 4047 2-8-2 **66** PatrickMathers 1 16
(Richard Fahey) *wnt rt s: sn chsng ldrs: drvn over 4f out: lost pl over 2f out* **25/1**

1m 23.21s (-2.09) **Going Correction** -0.30s/f (Firm) **14** Ran SP% **119.2**
Speed ratings (Par 97): **99,95,93,92,88 87,86,85,79,78 76,74,72,71**
Tote Swingers 1&2 £8.30, 2&3 £5.90, 1&3 £4.20 CSF £33.61 CT £155.94 TOTE £3.80: £1.60, £3.20, £2.10; EX 48.70 Trifecta £175.80 Pool: £646.44 - 2.72 winning tickets..
Owner Thurloe Thoroughbreds XX **Bred** Dorothy Alexander Matz **Trained** Kimpton, Hants

FOCUS
Races of 1m and beyond reduced in distance by about 20yds. A decent nursery and the field made straight for the centre of the track on reaching the straight. It paid to be handy. There was an incident just after the start when Newstead Abbey lurched away to his right exiting the stalls, severely hampering Silent Footsteps, Luck and Out Of The Blocks which did that trio no favours at all. The form looks solid with the front four clear.

NOTEBOOK
Waterway Run(USA) ◆ missed all the trouble at the start and was sent straight to the front, from which point she completely dominated this field and it was hard not to be impressed with the way she stretched clear inside the last furlong. She was a beaten favourite in a Newmarket fillies' nursery on her second start, but may have still been learning the game at that point. She is obviously much better than a 78-rated filly and she can win much better races than this. (op 4-1 tchd 9-2)
Asgardella(IRE) was a complete unknown quantity having scraped home in a five-runner Ayr maiden over a similar trip on her only previous start, but this was a much better indication of her ability. She did really well considering she started from the widest draw and never stopped trying, but she was up against a quality rival. She still has scope and should be winning similar events before too long. (op 9-1 tchd 17-2)
I'm Back(IRE), 2lb higher than when winning over this trip at Newmarket but partnered by a talented claimer, stayed on under pressure towards the inside over the last 3f, but could never get on terms with the winner. This looks as good as he is. (op 4-1 tchd 7-2)
Dr Phibes(IRE) was making his nursery debut after finishing runner-up in three consecutive maidens (twice beaten in photos) and again ran with credit here, but he was probably helped by racing handily. (op 17-2)
Newstead Abbey didn't enjoy the run of the race when a length behind I'm Back at Newmarket and enjoyed a 2lb pull, but quite apart from his antics at the start a mid-race move came to little and he looked to be hanging before weakening from the furlong pole. He may need an easier surface. (tchd 8-1)
Grievous Angel(IRE), trying this trip for the first time on her eighth start, was the only one to make any sort of headway from the back of the field, but she was put up 6lb for easily taking a Thirsk claimer she was fully entitled to win and now looks on a stiff mark. (op 16-1)

6071 MINSTER ALARMS E B F MAIDEN STKS 5f 89y
2:25 (2:27) (Class 3) 2-Y-O **£7,439** (£2,213; £1,106; £553) **Stalls** Low

Form RPR

0 **1** **The Art Of Racing (IRE)**62 3916 2-9-3 0 HarryBentley 2 80
(Richard Hannon) *hld up: smooth hdwy over 2f out: shkn up over 1f out: led jst ins fnl f: drvn out: all out* **3/1**1

0 **2** *1/2* **Heaven's Guest (IRE)**22 5367 2-9-3 0 TonyHamilton 7 78
(Richard Fahey) *stdd s: sn trcking ldrs: effrt over 1f out: styd on to take 2nd towards fin* **14/1**

5 **3** *1* **Cross My Heart**19 5449 2-8-12 0 (t) KierenFallon 5 70
(William Haggas) *chsd ldrs: drvn 2f out: styd on same pce last 150yds* **12/1**3

3032 **4** *1 1/4* **Bapak Bangsawan**25 5242 2-9-3 71 PhillipMakin 6 70
(Kevin Ryan) *led: hdd jst ins fnl f: kpt on same pce* **16/1**

24 **5** *3 1/2* **Right Touch**15 5578 2-9-3 0 PaulHanagan 1 58
(Richard Fahey) *chsd ldrs: drvn over 2f out: wknd over 1f out* **3/1**1

0 **6** *3 3/4* **Ridgeblade**36 4825 2-8-12 0 RussKennemore 4 40
(Noel Wilson) *sn trcking ldrs: lost pl over 1f out* **66/1**

4 **7** *9* **A J Cook (IRE)**12 5711 2-9-3 0 GrahamGibbons 3 14
(David Barron) *chsd ldrs: drvn and outpcd over 3f out: bhd fnl 2f* **9/1**2

1m 3.2s (-0.90) **Going Correction** -0.30s/f (Firm) 2y crse rec **7** Ran SP% **81.7**
Speed ratings (Par 99): **95,94,92,90,85 79,64**
Tote Swingers 1&2 £6.30, 2&3 £9.20, 1&3 £5.50 CSF £21.82 TOTE £3.40: £1.70, £5.20; EX 26.20 Trifecta £242.50 Part won. Pool: £327.78 - 0.70 winning tickets..
Owner Qatar Racing Limited **Bred** Carrigbeg Stud & David Powell **Trained** East Everleigh, Wilts

FOCUS
An ordinary maiden with the favourite Rivellino being withdrawn after refusing to enter the stalls (15/8F, deduct 30p in the £ under R4). The remaining seven runners all raced centre-to-far side.

NOTEBOOK
The Art Of Racing(IRE) was a disappointing favourite when only seventh of 11 in a soft-ground Windsor maiden on his debut in July, but was completely different gear on this faster surface. Although in last place early, he travelled into the race like a dream and although he didn't do much after hitting the front, he had established enough of an advantage to see it out. His pedigree is all about speed and there should be plenty more to come from him, but it seems unlikely he would be risked on soft ground again. (op 7-2 tchd 4-1)
Heaven's Guest(IRE) looked the stable's second string, but ended up performing the better of the Fahey pair. Although it took him a little while to respond to pressure, he stayed on nicely after being switched to his right and was closing in on the winner at the line. This was an improvement from his debut effort and he can win races. (op 18-1 tchd 20-1)
Cross My Heart, green when only fifth of seven on last month's Warwick debut, was tried in a tongue-tie this time and ran better having been handy throughout, but she looks one for ordinary nurseries.
Bapak Bangsawan was much the most experienced in the field and tried to make all, but he had no answer once the winner arrived. His rating of 71 provides the benchmark and he will be better off in nurseries away from unexposed types. (op 12-1)
Right Touch had shown more than enough in his first two starts to suggest he could win a race like this, but he was making hard work of it from some way out. He now qualifies for nurseries and may be worth another chance back on an easier surface. (op 7-2 tchd 11-4)

6072 CELEBRATING 45 YEARS OF BETFRED GARROWBY STKS (LISTED RACE) 6f
2:55 (2:56) (Class 1) 3-Y-O+
£18,714 (£7,095; £3,550; £1,768; £887; £445) **Stalls** Low

Form RPR

0011 **1** **Mince**21 5385 3-8-11 105 JamesDoyle 2 116+
(Roger Charlton) *trckd ldrs: led over 1f out: drvn clr: eased nr fin* **2/1**1

-064 **2** *3 1/2* **Colour Of Love (IRE)**21 5390 4-8-9 91 (b) KieranO'Neill 11 99
(W McCreery, Ire) *in rr: hdwy 2f out: styd on wl ins fnl f: tk 2nd nr fin* **16/1**

2306 **3** *nk* **Free Zone**8 5822 3-8-12 104 TomEaves 8 103
(Bryan Smart) *chsd ldrs: kpt on to take 2nd last 50yds* **16/1**

4413 **4** *1 3/4* **Inxile (IRE)**14 5641 7-9-4 110 (p) DaraghO'Donohoe 4 101
(David Nicholls) *led: hdd over 1f out: kpt on same pce* **10/1**

0635 **5** *2 1/2* **Lady Gorgeous**21 5385 3-8-7 99 SamHitchcott 1 84
(Mick Channon) *mid-div: drvn over 2f out: kpt on: nvr a threat* **12/1**

31-6 **6** *1* **Blanche Dubawi (IRE)**15 5581 4-8-9 101 HayleyTurner 3 81
(Noel Quinlan) *hld up in rr: kpt on fnl 2f: nvr nr ldrs* **4/1**2

0010 **7** *1 ¾* **Pepper Lane**[8] 5822 5-8-10 106 ow1............................ DanielTudhope 5 77
(David O'Meara) *chsd ldrs: outpcd over 2f out: swtchd lft over 1f out: kpt on* **8/1**

2000 **8** *4 ½* **Secret Witness**[16] 5561 6-9-0 104..................................(b) LukeMorris 6 66
(Ronald Harris) *dwlt: in rr: sme hdwy over 2f out: nvr on terms* **6/1**[3]

0350 **9** *2 ¼* **Samminder (IRE)**[43] 4598 3-8-12 100.......................... JimmyFortune 9 59
(Peter Chapple-Hyam) *dwlt: in rr: nvr a factor* **20/1**

6203 **10** *6* **Sugar Beet**[8] 5814 4-8-9 92... DarrenEgan 10 35
(Ronald Harris) *in rr: bhd fnl 2f* **33/1**

5304 **11** *1 ¼* **Fratellino**[18] 5487 5-9-4 91..(t) RobertWinston 7 40
(Alan McCabe) *chsd ldrs: wknd over 1f out: sn eased* **25/1**

1m 8.23s (-3.67) **Going Correction** -0.30s/f (Firm) course record
WFA 3 from 4yo+ 2lb **11** Ran SP% **118.8**
Speed ratings (Par 111): **112,107,106,104,101 99,97,91,88,80 78**
Tote Swingers 1&2 £6.80, 2&3 £42.90, 1&3 £8.60 CSF £37.56 TOTE £3.30: £1.40, £3.40, £4.40; EX 43.70 Trifecta £628.10 Pool: £1290.33 - 1.52 winning tickets..
Owner Lady Rothschild **Bred** The Rt Hon Lord Rothschild **Trained** Beckhampton, Wilts

FOCUS
The inaugural running of this 6f Listed race and as impressive a winner as you are likely to see. The field came up the centre and again those that raced close to the pace dominated.

NOTEBOOK
Mince ◆ has looked a most progressive filly lately, but took another giant step forward with this performance under her penalty. She never looked to be out of second gear and once taking over in front coming to the last furlong, quickly bounded further and further clear. Just as at Ascot two starts back, she shattered the course record, in this case knocking 0.35 seconds off the time set by Cape Of Good Hope in the Golden Jubilee Stakes at Royal Ascot At York in 2005. The indications are that she will be back next season and, if maintaining her progress, she can go right to the top. (op 9-4)

Colour Of Love(IRE) came into this in form, but seemed up against it in this company. However, she ran well especially as she tried to come from off the pace and came up against a rival with real star quality. (tchd 14-1)

Free Zone was another probably helped by racing prominently, but all of his best form has come over shorter and this was by some way his best effort over this trip on his third attempt. (op 14-1)

Inxile(IRE), who was only going to run if the ground was suitable, showed his usual decent early speed, but merely provided a lead for the winner and he was completely swept away by her. He does appear best at the minimum trip. (op 9-1 tchd 8-1)

Lady Gorgeous made some late progress, but finished behind Mince for the third consecutive race and is just 1-13. (tchd 14-1)

Blanche Dubawi(IRE) made a creditable reappearance from 329 days off at Newmarket last month and seemed to travel well enough off the pace here, but she couldn't make much impression once off the bridle. It was hard to make up ground in this race, however, so she is worth another chance. (tchd 9-2)

6073 COOPERS MARQUEES STKS (H'CAP) — 1m 2f 88y
3:30 (3:30) (Class 4) (0-80,80) 3-Y-0+ **£5,239** (£1,559; £779; £389) **Stalls** Low

Form RPR

2431 **1** **Jawhar (IRE)**[14] 5636 4-9-11 79.................................... PaulHanagan 12 95+
(William Haggas) *hld up towards rr: smooth hdwy over 3f out: led on bit over 1f out: pushed clr: v readily* **9/2**[1]

5234 **2** *2 ½* **Christmas Light**[37] 4768 5-8-10 67.................................. DaleSwift(3) 13 78
(Brian Ellison) *hld up in rr: hdwy on inner over 3f out: upsides over 1f out: styd on same pce* **14/1**

3442 **3** *3* **Scottish Star**[31] 5007 4-9-9 77..................................... LukeMorris 19 82
(James Eustace) *in rr: hdwy to join ldrs over 3f out: kpt on same pce over 1f out* **16/1**

4454 **4** *¾* **Robert The Painter (IRE)**[22] 5345 4-9-3 71............ GrahamGibbons 5 75
(David O'Meara) *chsd ldr: led over 3f out: hdd over 1f out: kpt on one pce* **11/1**

-062 **5** *¾* **Pass Muster**[39] 4706 5-9-12 80.................................... FrederikTylicki 1 82
(Ollie Pears) *mid-div: hdwy over 3f out: kpt on same pce fnl 2f* **8/1**[2]

1342 **6** *1 ¾* **Lady Loch**[22] 5372 3-9-3 78...(p) TonyHamilton 9 77
(Richard Fahey) *mid-div: sn drvn along: kpt on fnl 2f: nvr a threat* **8/1**[2]

3050 **7** *1 ¼* **Shamdarley (IRE)**[11] 5752 4-9-10 78......................... PaulMulrennan 20 75
(Michael Dods) *in rr: hdwy over 2f out: nvr rchd ldrs* **8/1**[2]

225- **8** *4* **Vimiero (USA)**[113] 6976 5-9-4 79.............................. DannyBenson(7) 18 68
(Jonjo O'Neill) *dwlt: sme hdwy over 2f out: nvr a factor* **40/1**

3515 **9** *¾* **Carragold**[14] 5622 6-9-8 76.. JimmyFortune 6 64
(Mel Brittain) *chsd ldrs: drvn over 3f out: wknd over 1f out* **20/1**

3630 **10** *2 ¾* **Regal Swain (IRE)**[25] 5243 4-9-3 71............................ RobertWinston 2 54
(Alan Swinbank) *chsd ldrs: upsides over 3f out: wknd over 1f out* **20/1**

0565 **11** *shd* **Desert Romance (IRE)**[12] 5712 6-9-8 76...................... DanielTudhope 7 58
(David O'Meara) *hld up in mid-div: effrt and nt clr run over 2f out: nvr a factor* **14/1**

U214 **12** *1 ¼* **King Of Windsor (IRE)**[20] 5429 5-9-11 79.....................(p) TomEaves 8 59
(Keith Dalgleish) *s.i.s: sme hdwy over 2f out: nvr on terms* **16/1**

131 **13** *nse* **Alfred Hutchinson**[106] 2510 4-9-12 80.......................... PhillipMakin 10 60
(Geoffrey Oldroyd) *hld up towards rr: effrt over 3f out: nvr a factor* **8/1**[2]

6430 **14** *¾* **Euston Square**[16] 5546 6-9-4 72.................................... PJMcDonald 16 50
(Alistair Whillans) *sn chsng ldrs: drvn over 3f out: wknd 2f out* **20/1**

1011 **15** *½* **Double Cee**[37] 4768 3-9-2 77... KierenFallon 14 54
(Richard Fahey) *chsd ldrs: nt clr run 2f out: hung lft and lost pl: eased towards fin* **9/1**[3]

65/0 **16** *4* **El Bravo**[25] 5243 6-9-0 75... ShirleyTeasdale(7) 11 45
(Shaun Harris) *in rr: bhd fnl 2f* **66/1**

3600 **17** *4 ½* **Amazing Blue Sky**[25] 5224 6-9-8 76............................ JamesSullivan 4 37
(Ruth Carr) *stmbld s: led: hdd over 3f out: lost pl over 2f out* **40/1**

5440 **18** *3 ½* **Jonny Lesters Hair (IRE)**[12] 5712 7-9-6 74.................... TedDurcan 17 29
(Tim Easterby) *racd wd: chsd ldrs: lost pl over 2f out: bhd whn eased ins fnl f* **25/1**

2m 7.49s (-5.01) **Going Correction** -0.375s/f (Firm)
WFA 3 from 4yo+ 7lb **18** Ran SP% **130.6**
Speed ratings (Par 105): **105,103,100,100,99 98,97,93,93,91 90,89,89,89,88 85,82,79**
Tote Swingers 1&2 £23.00, 2&3 £51.00, 1&3 £12.60 CSF £67.55 CT £972.69 TOTE £5.20: £1.80, £4.60, £3.20, £3.20; EX 113.00 Trifecta £781.30 Part won. Pool: £1,055.89 - 0.10 winning tickets..
Owner Hamdan Al Maktoum **Bred** Shadwell Estate Company Limited **Trained** Newmarket, Suffolk

FOCUS
A competitive handicap, but run at just a fair race and again they came up the centre.

Double Cee Official explanation: jockey said gelding hung left.

6074 CASTLES UK EDUCATIONAL AND RESIDENTIAL FURNITURE STKS (H'CAP) — 2m 88y
4:00 (4:00) (Class 4) (0-85,85) 3-Y-0+ **£5,239** (£1,559; £779; £389) **Stalls** Low

Form RPR

5451 **1** **Mafeteng**[19] 5456 4-8-9 66.. TedDurcan 4 77+
(John Dunlop) *hld up: smooth hdwy on ins over 3f out: shkn up to ld over 1f out: pushed out* **15/2**

-102 **2** *2* **Up Ten Down Two (IRE)**[38] 4744 3-7-12 68 oh3.......(t) JamesSullivan 2 74
(Michael Easterby) *trckd ldr: led over 3f out: hdd over 1f out: styd on same pce* **6/1**[3]

6200 **3** *2 ¾* **Riptide**[33] 4925 6-9-4 75..(p) JamieGoldstein 1 78
(Michael Scudamore) *chsd ldrs: kpt on one pce to take 3rd jst ins fnl f* **16/1**

0225 **4** *3* **Gabrial's Star**[15] 5598 3-9-1 85..(p) TomEaves 8 84
(Bryan Smart) *dwlt: sn chsng ldrs: drvn 6f out: upsides over 3f out: wknd last 150yds* **15/8**[1]

2400 **5** *1 ¾* **French Hollow**[18] 5491 7-9-7 80...................................... FrederikTylicki 6 77
(Tim Fitzgerald) *hld up in rr: effrt over 3f out: one pce fnl 2f* **11/1**

2021 **6** *½* **Maid Of Meft**[21] 5384 5-8-11 68.. MickyFenton 5 65
(Paul Midgley) *hld up in rr: hdwy 7f out: effrt over 4f out: one pce fnl 2f* **14/1**

0260 **7** *nk* **Odin's Raven (IRE)**[50] 3163 7-8-13 73.....................(t) PaulPickard(3) 10 69
(Brian Ellison) *s.s: hdwy over 3f out: one pce fnl 2f* **9/1**

0020 **8** *1 ¼* **Lexington Bay (IRE)**[16] 5540 4-9-13 84........................ PaulHanagan 3 79
(Richard Fahey) *chsd ldrs: shkn up after 2f: drvn over 4f out: fdd over 1f out* **5/1**[2]

4641 **9** *6* **Forrest Flyer (IRE)**[29] 5086 8-8-9 66 oh1........................... GrahamLee 9 54
(Jim Goldie) *trckd ldrs: t.k.h: lost pl 3f out* **16/1**

4042 **10** *4* **Spruzzo**[12] 5714 6-8-9 66 oh2.. DuranFentiman 7 49
(Chris Fairhurst) *led: drvn 6f out: hdd 3f out: lost pl 2f out* **25/1**

3m 33.27s (-1.23) **Going Correction** -0.375s/f (Firm)
WFA 3 from 4yo+ 13lb **10** Ran SP% **118.1**
Speed ratings (Par 105): **88,87,85,84,83 83,82,82,79,77**
Tote Swingers 1&2 £7.90, 2&3 £16.50, 1&3 £23.50 CSF £52.74 CT £707.71 TOTE £9.00: £2.90, £1.70, £5.20; EX 47.00 Trifecta £810.40 Part won. Pool: £1,095.18 - 0.20 winning tickets..
Owner Mrs Jane Poulter **Bred** Mrs J A M Poulter **Trained** Arundel, W Sussex

FOCUS
A fair staying handicap though the pace didn't look that strong.
Lexington Bay(IRE) Official explanation: jockey said gelding had no more to give.

6075 YORK 800 STKS (H'CAP) — 6f
4:35 (4:37) (Class 2) (0-100,97) 3-Y-0 **£12,938** (£3,850; £1,924; £962) **Stalls** Low

Form RPR

3341 **1** **Heeraat (IRE)**[15] 5603 3-9-4 94.................................... PaulHanagan 14 107
(William Haggas) *w ldrs: led after 1f tl over 2f out: styd on to chal ins fnl f: edgd lft and led clsng stages* **9/2**[1]

1001 **2** *nk* **Hamza (IRE)**[22] 5363 3-9-5 95...(b) AmyRyan 10 107
(Kevin Ryan) *w ldrs: led and wnt 3l clr over 2f out: hdd and no ex clsng stages* **10/1**

1262 **3** *1 ½* **Gabriel's Lad (IRE)**[22] 5363 3-8-12 88........................... KierenFallon 13 95
(Denis Coakley) *s.i.s: hdwy over 2f out: chsng ldng pair over 1f out: kpt on same pce* **5/1**[2]

1530 **4** *1 ½* **Jack Dexter**[49] 4367 3-8-8 84... GrahamLee 6 86+
(Jim Goldie) *in rr: hdwy wd outside over 2f out: tk 4th appr fnl f: kpt on* **12/1**

-450 **5** *3 ¼* **Hurry Up George**[113] 2276 3-9-1 96............................ JamesRogers(5) 3 88
(Ralph Beckett) *chsd ldrs: one pce fnl 2f* **33/1**

1126 **6** *2* **Show Flower**[22] 5363 3-9-3 93...................................... SamHitchcott 16 79
(Mick Channon) *s.i.s: hdwy and swtchd rt to stands' side rail over 1f out: kpt on* **20/1**

2522 **7** *1* **Profile Star (IRE)**[9] 5800 3-8-7 83 oh1...................... GrahamGibbons 18 65
(David Barron) *mid-div: effrt over 2f out: kpt on same pce* **25/1**

-000 **8** *¾* **Diamondhead (IRE)**[17] 5517 3-8-7 83............................(t) JamieMackay 9 63
(Brian Meehan) *chsd ldrs: kpt on one pce fnl 2f* **33/1**

0210 **9** *2 ¼* **Springinmystep (IRE)**[29] 5080 3-9-0 90........................ PaulMulrennan 1 63
(Michael Dods) *chsd ldrs: one pce fnl 2f* **22/1**

5030 **10** *½* **Tioman Legend**[22] 5363 3-8-12 93................................ DarrenEgan(5) 12 64
(Roger Charlton) *hld up towards rr: hdwy over 2f out: nvr nr ldrs* **25/1**

1610 **11** *½* **Pale Orchid (IRE)**[22] 5363 3-9-1 91................................... CathyGannon 5 61
(David Evans) *chsd ldrs: one pce fnl 2f* **40/1**

3153 **12** *1* **Charlotte Rosina**[50] 4336 3-8-12 88................................ HayleyTurner 19 56
(Roger Teal) *mid-div: effrt over 2f out: nvr a factor* **20/1**

221 **13** *2 ¾* **Nassau Storm**[49] 4364 3-8-13 89...................................... JimCrowley 7 48
(William Knight) *s.i.s: nvr on terms* **15/2**[3]

106 **14** *½* **Priceless Jewel**[43] 4597 3-8-12 88.................................... JamesDoyle 17 46
(Roger Charlton) *s.i.s: hdwy over 2f out: wknd over 1f out* **9/2**[1]

0100 **15** *2* **Towbee**[15] 5603 3-8-7 83 oh1.. JamesSullivan 4 34
(Michael Easterby) *mid-div: drvn over 2f out: nvr a factor* **66/1**

5204 **16** *nk* **Kool Henry (IRE)**[15] 5603 3-8-13 89............................. DanielTudhope 15 39
(David O'Meara) *led 1f: chsd ldrs: wknd over 1f out* **20/1**

600 **17** *1 ¾* **Chunky Diamond (IRE)**[18] 5487 3-9-4 94........................ JimmyFortune 2 39
(Peter Chapple-Hyam) *s.i.s: a in rr* **16/1**

1503 **18** *4 ½* **Poole Harbour (IRE)**[22] 5363 3-8-12 88............................ TedDurcan 20 18
(Richard Hannon) *in rr stands' side: effrt over 2f out: no imp whn hmpd over 1f out: eased ins fnl f* **12/1**

5060 **19** *6* **B Fifty Two (IRE)**[29] 5077 3-9-7 97................................ SebSanders 8
(J W Hills) *mid-div: hdwy over 2f out: lost pl over 1f out: eased* **25/1**

6006 **20** *1* **Last Bid**[15] 5603 3-8-12 88... DuranFentiman 11
(Tim Easterby) *mid-div: lost pl over 1f out: eased ins fnl f* **33/1**

1m 8.94s (-2.96) **Going Correction** -0.30s/f (Firm) **20** Ran SP% **138.1**
Speed ratings (Par 107): **107,106,104,102,98 95,94,93,90,89 88,88,84,83,81 80,78,72,64,63**
Tote Swingers 1&2 £7.30, 2&3 £11.90, 1&3 £3.90 CSF £45.92 CT £252.64 TOTE £5.00: £1.70, £2.60, £1.70, £3.50; EX 34.30 Trifecta £81.50 Pool: £1386.08 - 12.57 winning tickets..
Owner Hamdan Al Maktoum **Bred** John McEnery **Trained** Newmarket, Suffolk

FOCUS
Again all the action took place up the centre of the track. Considering this had looked a competitive sprint handicap, they finished well spread out and the form looks strong. The winning time was also decent, just 0.71 seconds slower than Mince's record-breaking time in the earlier Listed contest.

NOTEBOOK
Heeraat(IRE) ◆ was 5lb higher than when just beating Profile Star over 5f here last month, but this extra furlong looked to suit him more, as did the better ground, and having raced on the pace with the runner-up throughout, showed real determination to forge ahead in the run to the line. He looks a progressive colt and there should be more to come. (op 6-1 tchd 4-1)

Hamza(IRE), raised 7lb for last month's Newmarket win when he had five of these behind, disputed the lead from the start and having just put his head in front coming to the last 2f, kept on fighting all the way to the line when challenged by the winner. He lost nothing in defeat and has looked as good as ever since returning to sprinting. (op 12-1)
Gabriel's Lad (IRE) beaten nearly 2l by Hamza at Newmarket and 5lb better off, ran a blinder considering he missed the break while the front pair were always to the fore. He tried his hardest to get on terms with them, staying on all the way to the line, and should be winning again before long, especially as he won't mind if the ground eases. (tchd 9-2 and 11-2)
Jack Dexter ◆, back up to probably his best trip, was another to run a noteworthy race as he attempted to come from well off the pace and finished strongly. This ground would have been quick enough for him and this lightly raced gelding will be winning again when conditions ease. (op 10-1)
Hurry Up George tried to match strides with the front pair from the start, but tired over a furlong from home. However, he was returning from 113 days off so this was a decent effort and he should be sharper for the run.
Show Flower was another to miss the break before making some late progress against the stands' rail, but she looks on a stiff mark now following her golden summer. (op 22-1)
Diamondhead(IRE) ◆ had shown nothing (including in the face of some stiff tasks) since winning on his second start at two, but he showed a bit more here and may be dropping to a mark he can be competitive off. He is worth keeping an eye on.
Priceless Jewel's effort just after halfway amounted to little and her rider reported that the filly lost her action. Official explanation: jockey said filly lost her action. (op 6-1 tchd 7-1)

6076 FUTURE CLEANING SERVICES APPRENTICE STKS (H'CAP) 1m 4f
5:05 (5:05) (Class 4) (0-80,80) 4-Y-0+ **£5,239** (£1,559; £779 ; £389) **Stalls** Centre

Form RPR
-232 **1** **Dancing Primo**[30] 5039 6 -8-1074 JackDuern(5) 9 87
(Mark Brisbourne) *in rr: hdwy 4f out: led over 2f out: drvn clr fnl f* **7/1[2]**
2160 **2** 6 **Hurakan (IRE)**[8] 5838 6 -8-872 (p) DanielMuscutt(5) 3 75
(Richard Price) *trckd ldrs: upsides on bit over 3f out: wnt 2nd over 1f out: kpt on same pce* **14/1**
6410 **3** nk **Sedgwick**[22] 5345 10 -8-468 ShirleyTeasdale(5) 6 71
(Shaun Harris) *in rr: hdwy over 3f out: chsng ldrs 2f out: kpt on same pce* **28/1**
2111 **4** 1 ¾ **Standpoint**[22] 5345 6 -9-480 DavidKenny(3) 11 80
(Conor Dore) *mid-div: hdwy over 3f out: chsng ldrs 2f out: kpt on one pce* **8/1[3]**
5062 **5** ½ **Sir Boss (IRE)**[10] 5767 7 -8-771 RachealKneller(5) 12 70
(Michael Mullineaux) *in rr: hdwy on outer over 5f out: upsides gng wl over 3f out: one pce fnl 2f* **16/1**
0431 **6** 1 **St Ignatius**[10] 5767 5 -8-1377 (p) NatashaEaton(5) 4 74
(Alan Bailey) *led: hdd over 2f out: fdd clsng stages* **9/1**
0202 **7** 1 **Vittachi**[29] 5086 5 -8-266 oh2 LauraBarry(5) 8 62
(Alistair Whillans) *s.i.s: in rr: hdwy over 2f out: edeged lft and kpt on fnl f* **25/1**
2060 **8** 3 ¾ **Bright Applause**[16] 5546 4 -8-769 ShaneBKelly(3) 7 59
(Tracy Waggott) *chsd ldrs: effrt 3f out: wknd over 1f out* **16/1**
0200 **9** 1 ½ **King Kurt (IRE)**[2] 4326 4 -9-477 (p) AmyRyan 13 64
(Kevin Ryan) *chsd ldrs: upsides after 2f: edgd lft over 2f out: wknd over 1f out* **8/1[3]**
3262 **10** 1 **Arizona John (IRE)**[21] 5383 7 -9-275 DeclanCannon 10 61
(John Mackie) *mid-div: hdwy over 3f out: one pce whn hmpd over 2f out: wknd over 1f out* **9/1**
3204 **11** 4 ½ **Golden Future**[33] 4910 9 -8-167 FrancescaWoliter(7) 2 46
(Peter Niven) *mid-div: effrt on inner over 3f out: wknd over 2f out* **33/1**
3006 **12** 2 **Veiled Applause**[16] 5546 9 -8-1278 KevinLundie(7) 17 53
(John Quinn) *in rr and swtchd lft after s: drvn over 4f out: nvr on terms* **16/1**
644 **13** 1 ½ **Madrasa (IRE)**[16] 5546 4 -8-766 (bt) AdamBeschizza 16 39
(Keith Reveley) *hld up in rr: rdn 3f out: nvr on terms* **8/1[3]**
5336 **14** 2 **Meetings Man (IRE)**[4] 5622 5 -8-466 oh1 DarrenEgan(3) 15 36
(Micky Hammond) *mid-div: effrt 3f out: edgd rt and sn lost pl* **13/2[1]**
1100 **15** 25 **William Haigh (IRE)**[42] 4249 4 -9-480 GarryWhillans(3) 1
(Alan Swinbank) *chsd ldrs: hmpd on inner and lost pl over 5f out: bhd fnl 3f: eased and virtually p.u: t.o* **20/1**
0306 **16** 59 **Kinyras (IRE)**[50] 4347 4 -8-872 DavidSimmonson(5) 5
(Michael Easterby) *mid-div: rdn and lost pl over 3f out: sn bhd: heavily eased over 1f out: virtually p.u: hopelessly t.o* **16/1**

2m 30.25s (-2.95) **Going Correction** -0.375s/f (Firm) **16**Ran SP% **124.4**
Speed ratings (Par 105): **94,90,89,88,88 87,86,84,83,82 79,78,77,76,59 20**
Tote Swingers 1&2 £26.60, 2&3 £102.60, 1&3 £56.20 CSF £98.72 CT £2612.58 TOTE £9.00 : £2.30, £3.20 , £9.20 , £2.20 ; EX 134.10 TRIFECTA Not won. Pool: £785.40.
Owner L R Owen **Bred** L R Owen **Trained** Great Ness, Shropshire

FOCUS
A competitive apprentice handicap, but the winner bolted up.
T/Jkpt: £10,452.00 to a £1 stake. Pool: £73,605.71 - 5.00 winning tickets. T/Plt: £463.70 to a £1 stake. Pool: £146,296.78 - 230.30 winning tickets. T/Qpdt: £23.40 to a £1 stake. Pool: £11,030.71 - 348.18 winning tickets. WG

6077a, 6082a - 6084a (Foreign Racing) - See Raceform Interactive

5639 CURRAGH (R-H)
Sunday, September 9
OFFICIAL GOING: Good (good to yielding in places)

6078a GO AND GO ROUND TOWER STKS (GROUP 3) 6f
2:45 (2:48) 2-Y-0 **£28,437** (£8,312; £3,937 ; £1,312)

RPR
1 **Leitir Mor (IRE)**[7] 5858 2 -9-399 (tp) KevinManning 10 101
(J S Bolger, Ire) *chsd ldrs: rdn into 2nd and sn chal ent fnl f: led 150yds out: all out: jst hld on* **11/1**
2 shd **Cougar Ridge (USA)**[119] 2099 2 -9-3 WJLee 13 101+
(David Wachman, Ire) *chsd ldrs: cl up 3rd 3f out: lost pl and short of room appr fnl f: swtchd rt to chal and r.o wl on outer towards fin: jst failed: unlucky* **7/1[2]**
3 2 ½ **Royal Empress (IRE)**[5] 5608 2 -9-0 CO'Donoghue 7 90
(David Wachman, Ire) *cl up: pressed ldr 2f out: led 1 1/2f out tl hdd 150yds out: one pce after* **25/1**
4 nk **Tennessee Wildcat (IRE)**[86] 3130 2 -9-390 NGMcCullagh 12 92
(G M Lyons, Ire) *hld up in tch: short of room appr fnl f and swtchd rt: r.o wl wout ever threatening* **33/1**
5 1 ¼ **Lewisham**[16] 5559 2 -9-3 AdamKirby 4 89
(Noel Quinlan) *in rr of mid-div: swtchd rt ins fnl f and n.m.r: r.o wl wout ever threatening principals* **10/1[3]**
6 hd **George Vancouver (USA)**[21] 5398 2 -9-3113 JPO'Brien 11 88
(A P O'Brien, Ire) *hld up in tch: rdn ins fnl f where sltly hmpd: one pce after* **8/13[1]**
7 2 ¾ **Dylanbaru (IRE)**[40] 4687 2 -9-399 (t) WayneLordan 6 80
(T Stack, Ire) *mid-div: n.d fr 2f out* **10/1[3]**
8 nk **Curly Wee (IRE)**[5] 5608 2 -9-0 SeamieHeffernan 8 76
(David Wachman, Ire) *hld up towards rr: sme hdwy over 1f out: hmpd ins fnl f whn forced wd: no ex after: kpt on* **25/1**
9 1 **Lightnin Hopkins (IRE)**[34] 4893 2 -9-398 GaryCarroll 9 76
(G M Lyons, Ire) *led: strly pressed 2f out: sn hdd: wknd ins fnl f* **10/1[3]**
10 1 **Made In Design (IRE)**[13] 5690 2 -9-078 PatSmullen 1 70
(Paul Hickey, Ire) *dwlt: tacked over to nrside: towards rr: nvr a threat fr 1/2-way* **40/1**
11 ¾ **Seeking Luck (IRE)**[7] 5859 2 -9-0 EmmetMcNamara 2 68
(G M Lyons, Ire) *uns rdr bef s: dwlt and settled towards rr: nvr a threat* **20/1**

1m 12.9s (-2.60) **Going Correction** -0.40s/f (Firm) **11**Ran SP% **127.9**
Speed ratings: **101,100,97,97,95 95,91,91,89,88 87**
CSF £87.30 TOTE £8.30 : £1.90 , £2.30 , £6.40 ; DF 84.90 Trifecta £429.25 .
Owner Mrs J S Bolger **Bred** J S Bolger **Trained** Coolcullen, Co Carlow

FOCUS
A Group 3 win for a horse who came into it a maiden. The winner has been rated 4lb higher than his previous best.

NOTEBOOK
Leitir Mor (IRE)chose a Group 3 to put his head in front and all in all it couldn't be considered that much of a surprise. Able to track the lead, the key was probably Manning sending him to the front over a furlong out and managing to get a couple of lengths on his rivals, enough leeway to be able to hold on this time, although he has shown the same vulnerabilities when in front as when trying to go past horses. He just prevailed to gain a deserved change of luck. Whether he'll do it again is open to question, but seeing that he has saved his best this season for stakes races maybe he will. (op 12/1)
Cougar Ridge (USA)was undoubtedly unlucky. Tucked in behind the pace, he had nowhere to go over a furlong out and had to pull out from behind a couple of horses, but he flew when getting daylight and just failed to get up. He's clearly a colt with lots of ability and whether he'll get an extra furlong will be interesting to see.
Royal Empress (IRE)was another filly to have shown a deal of ability in her three winless maiden starts. She was positively ridden and found a bit when asked from the front but couldn't see it out. It was a very fair effort.
Tennessee Wildcat (IRE)has been quite a highly tried colt and again showed why as he sustained his effort from over a furlong out without being good enough. He had looked a bit of a speed horse early in the season and this showed that a step up to 7f might be feasible.
Lewisham was locked away on the stands' rail and never really got into it, keeping on late. (op 8/1)
George Vancouver (USA)was held up behind horses but never really got into it and ran quite flat, certainly a long way below his rating. (op 4/6 tchd 8/11 and 4/7)

6079a REFUSE TO BEND SOLONAWAY STKS (GROUP 3) 1m
3:20 (3:20) 3-Y-0+ **£33,854** (£9,895; £4,687 ; £1,562)

RPR
1 **Famous Name**[28] 5134 7 -9-12119 PatSmullen 9 118
(D K Weld, Ire) *hld up in tch: rdn in 2nd appr fnl f: led fnl 200yds and drvn clr: kpt on wl* **2/5[1]**
2 2 ¾ **One Spirit (IRE)**[97] 2777 4 -9-4101 NGMcCullagh 6 104
(F Dunne, Ire) *chsd ldr: led over 2f out: chal ent fnl f and hdd fnl 200yds: kpt on* **14/1**
3 ¾ **Aloof (IRE)**[14] 5643 3 -8-13103 WJLee 4 101
(David Wachman, Ire) *chsd ldrs: 3rd on inner appr 3f out: rdn over 2f out and sn no imp: kpt on ins fnl f* **16/1**
4 ½ **Declaration Of War (USA)**[368] 3 -9-2 JPO'Brien 1 103
(A P O'Brien, Ire) *hld up towards rr: 7th appr 3f out: rdn to cl 2f out: swtchd lft and kpt on wl ins fnl f wout ever threatening principals* **5/1[2]**
5 1 ¼ **Banna Boirche (IRE)**[14] 5286 6 -9-7105 ShaneFoley 3 101
(M Halford, Ire) *w.w in rr: swtchd lft over 2f out and r.o wl on outer ins fnl f into nvr threatening 5th* **33/1**
6 ½ **Esentepe (IRE)**[81] 3270 3 -9-298 WayneLordan 7 99
(David Wachman, Ire) *hld up: 5th 3f out: rdn and no imp fr under 2f out: kpt on* **14/1**
7 1 **Lady Wingshot (IRE)**[17] 5523 3 -9-2108 KevinManning 5 97
(J S Bolger, Ire) *hld up towards rr: 6th 3f out: sn pushed along and sltly hmpd ins fnl f: eased nr fin* **8/1[3]**
8 1 ¾ **Piri Wango (IRE)**[24] 5284 3 -9-2103 GaryCarroll 2 93
(G M Lyons, Ire) *led: pushed along and hdd over 2f out: sn no ex* **11/1**

1m 38.09s (-7.91) **Going Correction** -0.65s/f (Hard)
WFA 3 from 4yo+ 5lb **8**Ran SP% **129.7**
Speed ratings: **113,110,109,109,107 107,106,104**
CSF £10.94 TOTE £1.40 : £1.02 , £3.50 , £3.90 ; DF 14.40 Trifecta £53.15 .
Owner K Abdulla **Bred** Juddmonte Farms Ltd **Trained** The Curragh, Co Kildare

FOCUS
The decision to bypass an impossible task in the previous day's Irish Champion Stakes was fully justified as Famous Name claimed a 20th success. The standard is set by the second, fourth and sixth.

NOTEBOOK
Famous Name was fractionally short of his best, he had the worst of the draw and Smullen had to use up a bit of petrol in the early stages to make sure that he was handy and didn't get stuck on the wide outside. Subsequently it took him more than a few strides to pick up in the straight but he gradually did and steadily wore down the opposition, winning going away in the end. It was a fine performance, probably his best this season, and it's unlikely to be his last. (op 4/7)
One Spirit (IRE)hadn't been seen out since beating none other than Gordon Lord Byron at Naas in June, the lack of suitable ground probably the main reason for keeping her on the sidelines, but this had to be very close to a career-best effort for her. She went to the front early in the straight and, while she effectively just gave the winner something to run at, she probably would have been beaten further by him had she sat and waited a bit longer. If the ground remains good there's no reason why a decent race can't be won with her.
Aloof(IRE) raced prominently and, while she didn't have the pace to respond when the runner-up went on, she kept going to decent effect. It's hard to know what her trip is and this was the best ground she's raced on for a while, but overall it was a sound effort.
Declaration Of War (USA)did some decent late work on both his seasonal and stable debut and looks certain to come on a good deal for it. (op 4/1)
Banna Boirche (IRE)came home past mostly beaten horses late on. (op 25/1)

6080a IRRESISTIBLE JEWEL BLANDFORD STKS (GROUP 2) (F&M) 1m 2f
3:50 (3:50) 3-Y-0+ **£54,166** (£15,833; £7,500 ; £2,500)

RPR
1 **Up (IRE)**[14] 5643 3 -9-0110 JPO'Brien 7 113
(A P O'Brien, Ire) *hld up in tch: 6th over 3f out: clsd gng best under 2f out: rdn on outer to chal wl ins fnl f: led fnl strides: all out* **3/1[1]**

2 shd **Caponata (USA)**[49] 4376 3-9-0 110 .... PatSmullen 3 113
(D K Weld, Ire) *reported to be coming in season befhand: hld up in tch: clsd appr fnl f and rdn to ld narrowly over 100yds out: strly pressed and hdd fnl strides* **3/1**[1]

3 1 ½ **Nahrain**[36] 4801 4-9-7 .... NeilCallan 1 110+
(Roger Varian) *hld up: 5th 3f out: clsr appr fnl f and rdn: kpt on wout ever threatening principals* **9/2**[2]

4 ½ **Manieree (IRE)**[14] 5643 4-9-7 112 .... (b) NGMcCullagh 2 109
(John M Oxx, Ire) *led at str pce: rdn appr 2f out: chal ins fnl f and hdd over 100yds out: no ex* **7/1**[3]

5 3 **Sea Of Heartbreak (IRE)**[21] 5399 5-9-7 .... RichardHughes 5 103
(Roger Charlton) *dwlt and racd towards rr: 7th over 2f out: rdn and kpt on ins fnl f: nvr a threat* **9/2**[2]

6 1 ¾ **Chrysanthemum (IRE)**[19] 5463 4-9-7 105 .... (b) WayneLordan 4 100
(David Wachman, Ire) *trckd ldr in 2nd: tk clsr order over 2f out: sn struggling to get on terms and wknd ent fnl f* **10/1**

7 6 ½ **Aaraas**[19] 5463 3-9-0 102 .... (b[1]) DeclanMcDonogh 6 87
(Kevin Prendergast, Ire) *chsd ldrs: 3rd 3f out: sn pushed along and wknd appr fnl 2f* **33/1**

8 26 **Soon (IRE)**[10] 5777 3-9-0 99 .... SeamieHeffernan 8 35
(A P O'Brien, Ire) *s.i.s and racd in rr: nvr a factor: eased fnl f* **14/1**

2m 3.33s (-10.97) **Going Correction** -0.775s/f (Hard)
WFA 3 from 4yo+ 7lb **8** Ran SP% **117.6**
Speed ratings: **112,111,110,110,107 106,101,80**
CSF £12.31 TOTE £3.20: £1.30, £1.40, £1.80; DF 8.90 Trifecta £16.45.
Owner Derrick Smith & Mrs John Magnier & Michael Tabor **Bred** Smythson **Trained** Ballydoyle, Co Tipperary

FOCUS
A strong renewal. As expected, there was a fierce early gallop courtesy of Manieree and there was no hiding place. The form looks solid and the two that fought out the finish are improving. The winner has been rated to her best, while the third and fourth are still below their 2011 peaks.

NOTEBOOK
Up(IRE) swooped late down the outside to land a Group 3 here last time and similar tactics were deployed again. Joseph O'Brien has treated us to many a fine ride in his short, but illustrious, riding career to date but this was up there with the best of them. When Manieree and Chrysanthemum became embroiled in a battle early in the home straight, he didn't panic. He tracked the runner-up through and challenged inside the final furlong. It could have gone either way in the final 100yds but she stuck her neck out to shade the verdict. She's an improving filly that travels well and has a nice attitude so her winning for the year might not be over yet. Official explanation: vet said filly returned lame (op 3/1 tchd 11/4)
Caponata(USA) lost very little in defeat. In fact, she enhanced her reputation. She was encountering good ground for the first time and seemed very much at home on it. She travelled well through the race, improved to lead 1f out but just couldn't fend off the winner close home. She should be even better next year when she strengthens up. She's likely to stay 1m4f, too, which will give her trainer plenty of options.
Nahrain showed more sparkle. Once again, she didn't aid her cause by being keen early, but she saw her race out well and looks to be coming to herself. She could head for the Breeders' Cup Filly and Mares contest. (op 9/2 tchd 5/1)
Manieree(IRE), who needed her first run of the season, performed better and made it into a real test. She was challenged early in the home straight but was only headed inside the final furlong. She's another who has been late to blossom this season and could land a Group contest before the campaign draws to a close.
Sea Of Heartbreak(IRE) has been mixing it with the best fillies in the business but was disappointing with seemingly no excuses. She was beaten with 2f to run. (op 9/2 tchd 5/1)
Chrysanthemum(IRE) probably paid the price for chasing a ferocious pace.

6081a MOYGLARE STUD STKS (GROUP 1) (FILLIES) 7f
4:25 (4:27) 2-Y-0
£108,750 (£35,625; £16,875; £5,625; £3,750; £1,875)

RPR

1 **Sky Lantern (IRE)**[15] 5571 2-9-0 .... RichardHughes 11 111
(Richard Hannon) *hld up in mid-div: clsr appr 2f out and qcknd wl on nrside to ld 1f out: drvn clr: easily* **7/1**

2 2 ½ **Scintillula (IRE)**[15] 5607 2-9-0 .... (t) RonanWhelan 10 105
(J S Bolger, Ire) *hld up in tch: 6th 3f out: hrd rdn over 1f out and kpt on wl to take 2nd fnl strides: nrst fin* **33/1**

3 hd **Harasiya (IRE)**[28] 5135 2-9-0 106 .... PatSmullen 4 104
(John M Oxx, Ire) *chsd ldrs: gng wl 2f out and sn asked to cl: wnt 2nd ins fnl f: sn no ch w wnr: denied 2nd fnl strides* **3/1**[1]

4 ½ **Magical Dream (IRE)**[28] 5135 2-9-0 .... SeamieHeffernan 9 103
(A P O'Brien, Ire) *in rr of mid-div: clsr in 8th 3f out: rdn on outer under 2f out and kpt on wl fnl f* **16/1**

5 1 ¾ **Starbright (IRE)**[28] 5133 2-9-0 .... ChrisHayes 12 98
(Kevin Prendergast, Ire) *hld up towards rr: 10th 3f out: swtchd lft over 2f out and r.o wl nrside ins fnl f wout ever threatening* **14/1**

6 nk **Sendmylovetorose**[58] 4064 2-9-0 107 .... CO'Donoghue 7 97
(A Oliver, Ire) *chsd ldrs: cl 4th appr 3f out: sn pushed along and unable qck: one pce fnl f* **9/2**[2]

7 1 **Karamaya (IRE)**[14] 5639 2-9-0 .... NGMcCullagh 5 95
(John M Oxx, Ire) *led: strly pressed under 2f out: hdd 1f out and sn wknd* **16/1**

8 ½ **Diamond Sky (IRE)**[28] 5135 2-9-0 .... KevinManning 8 93
(J S Bolger, Ire) *upset in stalls befhand: hld up towards rr: pushed along over 2f out: kpt on fnl f: nvr nrr* **20/1**

9 2 ¾ **Orpha**[27] 5146 2-9-0 .... WilliamBuick 1 86
(Mick Channon) *hld up in mid-div: drvn over 2f out and no imp: kpt on same pce ins fnl f* **5/1**[3]

10 nk **Private Alexander (IRE)**[85] 3170 2-9-0 .... GaryCarroll 6 86
(G M Lyons, Ire) *trckd ldr in 2nd: t.k.h: rdn and wknd appr fnl f* **20/1**

11 8 ½ **Nandiga (USA)**[28] 5135 2-9-0 92 .... DeclanMcDonogh 2 63
(P J Prendergast, Ire) *nvr bttr than mid-div: n.d fnl 2f: kpt on* **50/1**

12 1 ½ **Snow Queen (IRE)**[15] 5607 2-9-0 91 .... (p) JPO'Brien 13 60
(A P O'Brien, Ire) *v.s.a and racd in rr: tk clsr order towards rr 4f out: rdn on nrside 2f out: sn no imp: eased* **11/1**

13 nk **My Special J'S (USA)**[28] 5135 2-9-0 106 .... JohnnyMurtagh 3 59
(John Patrick Shanahan, Ire) *chsd ldrs: 3rd on inner under 4f out: pushed along over 2f out and sn no imp: eased fnl f* **9/2**[2]

1m 25.14s (-5.66) **Going Correction** -0.65s/f (Hard) **13** Ran SP% **131.7**
Speed ratings: **106,103,102,102,100 100,98,98,95,94 85,83,83**
CSF £240.87 TOTE £6.70: £1.90, £15.10, £1.40; DF 485.70.
Owner B Keswick **Bred** Tally-Ho Stud **Trained** East Everleigh, Wilts

FOCUS
Richard Hannon Jnr described it afterwards as one of the most open Moyglare of recent years. Perhaps that was down to the soft ground which has prevailed over the summer as much as anything. It's been rated through the third for now.

NOTEBOOK
Sky Lantern(IRE) may not be the best filly in the Hannon yard, let alone the best in Britain, but she made short work of these. It was a race where being towards the front of a muddling pace proved disadvantageous and it ended up playing into the hands of a filly with no shortage of speed. The way she quickened up to go and win her race a furlong or so from the finish was impressive and she may well be a progressive filly. It certainly represented a progression from her winning effort when last seen in this country at Naas in June, but whether she ends up being the best long-term prospect to come from this race is likely to be tested.
Scintillula(IRE), a sister of Cuis Ghaire, was effectively having her first chance to show what ability she has as she had only one run on desperate ground behind her, but she fully justified the decision to run and stayed on really nicely from mid-division. Already one can see that she could be a serious filly for next year, possibly over middle distances. (op 33/1 tchd 50/1)
Harasiya(IRE) wasn't quite good enough. First impressions suggested she might not have got the run of the race but she had every chance from a furlong out. She was left for dead by the winner's turn of foot and outstayed by the runner-up. It was still a worthwhile effort. (op 3/1 tchd 100/30)
Magical Dream(IRE) showed that she should be a filly that will stay well as she did some good late work having come off the bridle not long after halfway. The better ground would have suited her as well. (op 20/1)
Starbright(IRE) wasn't close enough or quick enough to get into a challenging position although she kept on to reasonable effect. She looks as though she'll fall a bit short at this level although more cut in the ground would probably have suited her. (op 16/1 tchd 12/1)
Sendmylovetorose got there with every chance but was quite readily outpaced from over a furlong out. (op 9/2 tchd 5/1)
Private Alexander(IRE) ruined her chance by taking too keen a hold early on.
My Special J'S(USA) ran way below her best and dropped away to finish last. (op 9/2 tchd 5/1)

4129 HANOVER (L-H)
Sunday, September 9
OFFICIAL GOING: Turf: good

6085a GROSSER PREIS DER METALLBAU BURCKHARDT GMBH (LISTED RACE) (3YO+ FILLIES & MARES) (TURF) 1m
3:45 (12:00) 3-Y-0+ **£10,000** (£3,666; £2,000; £1,000)

RPR

1 **Waldtraut (GER)**[35] 4862 3-8-13 0 .... JBojko 5 104
(A Wohler, Germany) **13/10**[1]

2 1 ¾ **Palomita (GER)** 4-9-0 0 .... FabienLefebvre 8 97
(Frau Nina Bach, Germany) **76/10**

3 nse **Singapore Joy (FR)**[28] 4-9-0 0 .... DavyBonilla 6 97
(H-A Pantall, France) **3/1**[2]

4 1 ½ **Molly Filia (GER)**[42] 3-8-9 0 .... WPanov 10 93
(Uwe Ostmann, Germany) **103/10**

5 shd **Love Your Looks**[25] 5238 4-9-0 0 .... MartinSeidl 3 93
(Mike Murphy) *broke towards rr: hdwy on rail to chse ldr after 2f: styd prom: led narrowly and briefly over 1 1/2f out: nt qckn over 1f out: one pce u.p fnl f* **61/10**

6 2 ½ **Wanda's Girl**[105] 2531 3-8-9 0 .... ThomasMessina 2 87
(W Hickst, Germany) **89/10**

7 nk **Wolkenburg (GER)**[42] 4-9-3 0 .... FilipMinarik 9 90
(P Schiergen, Germany) **26/5**[3]

8 3 ½ **Eleona (GER)**[884] 5-9-0 0 .... (b) VSchulepov 1 79
(Frau E Mader, Germany) **36/1**

9 ¾ **Kapitala (FR)**[131] 3-8-9 0 .... DavidSamuelMcCann 7 76
(Markus Klug, Germany) **40/1**

1m 39.23s (99.23)
WFA 3 from 4yo+ 5lb **9** Ran SP% **134.4**
WIN (incl. 10 euro stake): 23. PLACES: 11, 17, 13. SF 283.
Owner Gestut Brummerhof **Bred** Gestut Brummerhof **Trained** Germany

5870 LONGCHAMP (R-H)
Sunday, September 9
OFFICIAL GOING: Turf: good

6086a PRIX LA ROCHETTE (GROUP 3) (2YO) (TURF) 7f
1:00 (12:00) 2-Y-0 **£33,333** (£13,333; £10,000; £6,666; £3,333)

RPR

1 **What A Name (IRE)**[19] 2-8-8 0 .... Christophe-PatriceLemaire 7 109
(M Delzangles, France) *hld up in 4th: qcknd wl on outside 2f out: chal for ld 1 1/2f out: tk ld 1f out: r.o strly to take clr advantage: comf* **13/8**[1]

2 1 ¾ **Avantage (FR)**[28] 5140 2-8-11 0 .... GregoryBenoist 6 107
(Mme Pia Brandt, France) *led fr s: rdn to take clr advantage 2f out: r.o wl: chal and hdd 1f out: r.o wl to hold 2nd fnl 50yds* **11/1**

3 nk **Pearl Flute (IRE)**[21] 5398 2-8-11 0 .... UmbertoRispoli 3 106
(F-H Graffard, France) *settled in 3rd: rdn to go 2nd 2f out: r.o wl under presure fnl f* **7/1**

4 ½ **Soblue (IRE)**[16] 2-8-11 0 .... OlivierPeslier 5 105
(A Fabre, France) *hld up in rr: rdn 2f out on outside: r.o wl fnl f: tk 4th on line* **3/1**[2]

5 nse **Guajaraz (FR)**[38] 2-8-11 0 .... ChristopheSoumillon 1 105
(J-C Rouget, France) *hld up towards rr: rdn 2f out: mde prog on ins rail 1f out to go 4th: r.o fnl 100yds: lost 4th on line* **7/2**[3]

6 10 **Linngaro (FR)**[28] 2-8-11 0 .... MaximeGuyon 4 78
(Mario Hofer, Germany) *settled in 2nd: rdn 2 1/2f out: no ex: wknd* **8/1**

1m 22.07s (1.37) **Going Correction** +0.25s/f (Good) **6** Ran SP% **117.3**
Speed ratings: **102,100,99,99,99 87**
WIN (incl. 1 euro stake): 2.40. PLACES: 1.70, 3.60. SF: 17.90.
Owner H H Sheikh Mohammed Bin Khalifa Al Thani **Bred** Robert B Trussell Jr **Trained** France

FOCUS
The winner is a decent prospect and the form is in line with the race averages.

NOTEBOOK
What A Name(IRE) bolted up in a conditions event at Deauville last time, and took this step up in class in her stride, beating the colts in the process. She's in the Cheveley Park, but is unlikely to drop back in distance, which leaves the Marcel Boussac and the Grand Criterium [Prix Jean-Luc Lagaredere] as the other options, and her trainer currently favours sticking to 7f and taking on the colts again in the latter race. As she's owned by a member of Qatar's ruling family, the Qipco 1,000 Guineas looks sure to be in connections' minds longer term, and she's a best price 16-1 with Ladbrokes for the Newmarket Classic.

6087a PRIX DE LUTECE (GROUP 3) (3YO) (TURF) 1m 7f
1:30 (12:00) 3-Y-O £33,333 (£13,333; £10,000; £6,666; £3,333)

RPR

1 **Verema (FR)**[25] 5251 3-8-6 0 Christophe-PatriceLemaire 1 102+
(A De Royer-Dupre, France) *hld up towards rr: rdn over 1 1/2f out: r.o wl fnl f: chal for ld fnl 100yds: led fnl 50yds: styd on wl* **15/2**[3]

2 *nk* **Canticum**[25] 5251 3-8-9 0 GregoryBenoist 5 105
(D Smaga, France) *settled in 3rd: relegated to 4th over 1 1/2f out: picked up wl ent fnl f: led fnl 100yds out: r.o strly: hdd fnl 50yds* **11/4**[2]

3 *3/4* **Only A Pleasure (IRE)**[25] 5251 3-8-9 0 MaximeGuyon 6 104
(A Fabre, France) *settled in 4th: u.str.p 1 1/2f out: r.o ent fnl f: styd on wl* **13/8**[1]

4 *1* **Amiens**[34] 3-8-9 0 Pierre-CharlesBoudot 7 103
(A Fabre, France) *led on settling: stl in front but chal 1 1/2f out: hdd fnl 100yds out: styd on wl* **8/1**

5 *1 1/2* **Rollex Borget (FR)**[25] 5251 3-8-9 0 GeraldMosse 2 101
(J Bertran De Balanda, France) *settled at rr of field u.str hold: r.o u.p on ins rail 1 1/2f out: no ex ins fnl f* **9/1**

6 *1/2* **Je Parts Seul (FR)**[22] 3-8-9 0 ThierryThulliez 4 100+
(P Sogorb, France) *racd in midfield: rdn over 1 1/2f out: bmpd w eventual wnr 250yds out: no ex ins fnl f: styd on* **16/1**

7 *1 1/4* **Valdo Bere (FR)**[25] 5251 3-8-11 0 ThierryJarnet 8 101
(E Leenders, France) *settled in 2nd: rdn to chal for ld 2f out: r.o u.p tl beginning to fade ins fnl f* **14/1**

8 *3* **Ed De Gas**[40] 4685 3-8-11 0 ChrisCatlin 3 97
(Rae Guest) *settled towards rr of field: u.str hold: rdn 2f out: began to make prog on wd outside tl 1f out: no ex: fdd* **12/1**

3m 20.0s (4.00) **Going Correction** +0.25s/f (Good) **8** Ran SP% **117.9**
Speed ratings: **99,98,98,97,97 96,96,94**
WIN (incl. 1 euro stake): 7.60. PLACES: 1.70, 1.30, 1.30. DF: 13.60. SF: 38.40.
Owner H H Aga Khan **Bred** S A Aga Khan **Trained** Chantilly, France

NOTEBOOK
Verema(FR) appreciated the quicker ground and turned Deauville form around with four of her rivals from that Listed race. A big filly, a galloping track is always likely to see her at her best.

6088a PRIX DU PIN (GROUP 3) (3YO+) (TURF) 7f
2:40 (12:00) 3-Y-O+ £33,333 (£13,333; £10,000; £6,666; £3,333)

RPR

1 **Blue Soave (FR)**[15] 4-9-1 0 ThierryThulliez 1 114
(F Chappet, France) *mde all: over 2 l clr and stl gng wl 2f out: rdn over 1 1/2f out: kpt on wl u.p ins fnl f: reduced advantage cl home but nvr in any danger: unchal* **8/1**

2 *1 1/2* **So Long Malpic (FR)**[29] 5-8-11 0 OlivierPeslier 9 106+
(T Lemer, France) *dwlt: sn rcvrd into midfield: rdn over 1f out: r.o to go 2nd fnl strides: nvr able to chal* **9/1**

3 *3/4* **Kendam (FR)**[35] 4861 3-8-8 0 MaximeGuyon 2 103
(H-A Pantall, France) *awkward s: sn prom on inner: sltly short of room on run to first bnd: rdn in 2nd 2f out: gave vain chse to wnr ins fnl 1 1/2f: dropped to 3rd fnl strides* **12/1**

4 *3/4* **Sommerabend**[315] 7193 5-9-1 0 GeraldMosse 4 106+
(U Stoltefuss, Germany) *stdd s and hld up towards rr: short of room on run to first bnd and relegated to last pair: rdn to improve 2f out: styd on to go 4th post: nvr able to chal* **8/1**

5 *nse* **Eightfold Path (USA)**[28] 5-9-1 0 StephanePasquier 8 106+
(P Bary, France) *midfield on outer: rdn 2 1/2f out: r.o to go 3rd jst ins fnl f: no ex and lost 2 pls cl home* **7/1**[3]

6 *hd* **Lockwood**[35] 4861 3-9-2 0 Pierre-CharlesBoudot 5 108+
(A Fabre, France) *midfield on inner: rdn and outpcd over 2 1/2f out: kpt on ins fnl 1 1/2f* **7/2**[1]

7 *nse* **Zantenda**[98] 2742 3-8-8 0 FlavienPrat 12 100+
(F Head, France) *dropped in fr wd draw and hld up in last: rdn 2 1/2f out: styd on down wd outside ins fnl 1 1/2f: nrst fin* **12/1**

8 *4* **Abu Sidra (FR)**[59] 3-8-11 0 MickaelForest 10 92
(J-F Bernard, France) *qckly across fr wd draw: sn trcking ldr in 2nd on outer: rdn and outpcd by wnr 2f out: kpt on tl no ex and btn 1f out: fdd* **10/1**

9 *3 1/2* **Regatta (FR)**[25] 5249 3-8-8 0 AnthonyCrastus 6 80
(E Lellouche, France) *prom on outer: rdn over 2f out: edgd rt and outpcd over 1f out: sn no ex and btn: eased cl home* **20/1**

10 *2 1/2* **American Devil (FR)**[35] 4861 3-8-11 0 ChristopheSoumillon 11 76
(J Van Handenhove, France) *dwlt: hld up towards rr on outer: rdn to try and improve over 2f out: outpcd and btn over 1f out: eased ins fnl f* **4/1**[2]

0 **Cerveza**[7] 4-8-11 0 LouisBeuzelin 3
(F Poulsen, France) *prom on inner: rdn 3f out: outpcd and btn over 1f out: wknd: eased ins fnl f* **50/1**

0 **Emboss (IRE)**[21] 4-8-11 0 UmbertoRispoli 7
(H-A Pantall, France) *hld up in towards rr on inner: rdn over 2f out: qckly btn: dropped to last and eased over 1f out* **10/1**

1m 20.13s (-0.57) **Going Correction** +0.25s/f (Good)
WFA 3 from 4yo+ 4lb **12** Ran SP% **127.2**
Speed ratings: **113,111,110,109,109 109,109,104,100,97**
WIN (incl. 1 euro stake): 11.70. PLACES: 4.20, 3.40, 4.10. DF: 49.40. SF: 134.80.
Owner Mlle K Belluteau & Mme C Gustave **Bred** Mlle K Belluteau **Trained** France

NOTEBOOK
Blue Soave(FR) had the best of the draw and made full use of it, making every yard to complete a hat-trick.

5252 SAN SEBASTIAN (R-H)
Sunday, September 9

OFFICIAL GOING: Turf: good

6089a GRAN PREMIO DE SAN SEBASTIAN (CONDITIONS) (3YO+) (TURF) 1m 6f
6:40 (12:00) 3-Y-O+ £15,000 (£6,000; £3,000; £1,500)

RPR

1 **Australia Day (IRE)**[25] 5252 9-9-2 0 OOrtizdeUrbina 5 93
(Paul Webber) *broke wl: trckd ldr: led after 3f: mde rest. qcknd clr over 2f out: r.o strly fnl f: won easing down* **4/5**[1]

2 *4 3/4* **Casar (IRE)** 4-9-2 0 VJanacek 9 86
(M Delcher-Sanchez, Spain)

3 *4 3/4* **Achtung (SPA)**[25] 5252 4-9-6 0 JulienGrosjean 8 84
(R Lopez Gallego, Spain)

4 *3 1/2* **Tsarabi (IRE)**[185] 7-9-2 0 MlleGloriaMaderoParayre 4 75
(Mlle A Imaz-Ceca, France)

5 *2 1/4* **Entre Copas**[25] 5252 8-9-6 0 JeremyCrocquevieille 6 76
(J-M Osorio, Spain)

6 *nk* **Vergara** 4-8-13 AGomez 7 68
(J-M Osorio, Spain)

7 *dist* **Fading Sky (FR)**[304] 4-8-13 Jean-BaptisteHamel 3
(Mlle A Imaz-Ceca, France)

8 *1* **Gigolo Star (SPA)** 3-8-5 J-LMartinez 1
(J-C Fernandez-Rodriguez, Spain)

9 *8 1/4* **Dansico**[741] 5-9-2 JoseLuisBorrego 2
(J M Borrego, Spain)

3m 5.82s (185.82)
WFA 3 from 4yo+ 11lb **9** Ran SP% **55.6**
WIN (incl. 1 euro stake): 1.80. PLACES: 1.80, 2.80. SF: 9.20..
Owner Skippy & The Partners **Bred** Kenilworth House Stud **Trained** Mollington, Oxon

3684 SAN SIRO (R-H)
Sunday, September 9

OFFICIAL GOING: Turf: good

6090a PREMIO EUPILI (LISTED RACE) (2YO FILLIES) (TURF) 6f
3:20 (12:00) 2-Y-O £15,833 (£6,966; £3,800; £1,900)

RPR

1 **Sandreamer (IRE)**[17] 5516 2-8-9 0 MartinHarley 4 99
(Mick Channon) *trckd ldrs: 4th and gng wl 1/2-way: nowhere to go 2f out: tk gap between two ldrs and led over 1f out: r.o wl fnl f: rallied whn chal cl home* **1/3**[1]

2 *shd* **Grand Treasure (IRE)** 2-8-9 0 MircoDemuro 3 99
(G Colella, Italy) **37/4**

3 *1 3/4* **Girl Of The Rain (IRE)**[99] 2-8-9 0 FabioBranca 6 93
(S Botti, Italy) **111/10**

4 *3* **Catboss (USA)**[70] 2-8-9 0 LManiezzi 2 84
(R Menichetti, Italy) **142/10**

5 *1 1/2* **Panzerotta (IRE)** 2-8-9 0 MSanna 5 80
(Camilla Trapassi, Italy) **44/1**

6 *1 1/4* **Filona (IRE)**[84] 2-8-9 0 DarioVargiu 8 76
(B Grizzetti, Italy) **11/2**[2]

7 *5* **Key Board (ITY)** 2-8-9 0 SUrru 9 61
(S Sordi, Italy) **86/1**

8 *1* **Petite Silhou (IRE)** 2-8-9 0 PierantonioConvertino 1 58
(A Marcialis, Italy) **15/2**[3]

9 *2* **Samba Do Brazil (IRE)**[99] 2-8-9 0 CColombi 7 52
(A Peraino, Italy) **28/1**

1m 10.3s (-1.50) **9** Ran SP% **133.6**
WIN (incl. 1 euro stake): 1.33. PLACES: 1.18, 1.80, 2.04. DF: 5.83.
Owner Jon and Julia Aisbitt **Bred** Epona Bloodstock Ltd **Trained** West Ilsley, Berks

NOTEBOOK
Sandreamer(IRE), sixth in the Lowther, was sent off a short price to take this Listed prize. She quickened well between horses and rallied when challenged, winning with a bit more in hand than the margin suggests.

2807 TABY (R-H)
Sunday, September 9

OFFICIAL GOING: Dirt: standard; turf: good

6091a STOCKHOLM CUP INTERNATIONAL (GROUP 3) (3YO+) (TURF) 1m 4f
3:47 (12:00) 3-Y-O+ £65,543 (£32,771; £15,730; £10,486; £6,554)

RPR

1 **Bank Of Burden (USA)**[14] 5651 5-9-4 0 Per-AndersGraberg 4 104
(Niels Petersen, Norway) *midfield: stdy hdwy on outer fr over 3f out: rdn 2f out: styd on to ld ins fnl f: pushed out: comf* **4/7**[1]

2 *2* **Court Circle**[818] 3038 5-9-4 0 ValmirDeAzeredo 9 101
(Rune Haugen, Norway) *prom on outer: led over 3f out: rdn over 2f out: hdd ins fnl f: kpt on wout matching wnr cl home* **54/1**

3 *1* **Media Hype**[38] 5-9-4 0 GeorgeBaker 5 99
(Mrs K Burke) *dwlt: pushed along to rcvr and sn in midfield on inner: rapid hdwy to trck ldng pair 4f out: rdn 3f out: effrt to chal 1 1/2f out: sn outpcd by wnr: kpt on wl for 3rd ins fnl f* **98/10**

4 *1* **Berling (IRE)**[15] 5575 5-9-4 0 LennartHammer-Hansen 3 98
(John Dunlop) *led: hdd after 4f: prom on inner: rdn and bdly outpcd over 3f out: sn towards rr: rallied and styd on wl to go 4th cl home* **91/10**[3]

5 *3/4* **Touch Of Hawk (FR)**[14] 5651 6-9-4 0 EspenSki 2 96
(Wido Neuroth, Norway) *midfield on outer: rdn to chal over 2f out: outpcd by ldrs over 1f out: kpt on: dropped to 5th cl home* **158/10**

6 *1 3/4* **Without Fear (FR)**[14] 5651 4-9-4 0 FJohansson 11 94
(Arnfinn Lund, Norway) *hld up in last: prog into rr of midfield 4f out: rdn 3f out: wnt 6th over 1f out: plugged on* **41/10**[2]

7 1 ½ **Moe Green (IRE)**[467] 2601 5-9-4 0 .... RafaelSchistl 1 91
(Francisco Castro, Sweden) *prom on inner: pushed along and lost pl over 6f out: short of room and dropped to rr over 3f out: sn rdn: plugged on to go 7th ins fnl f* **142/10**

8 5 **Palermo (GER)**[14] 5651 6-9-4 0 .... OliverWilson 6 83
(Cathrine Erichsen, Norway) *trckd ldr on outer: led after 4f: hdd over 3f out: sn rdn and outpcd: steadily fdd ins fnl 2f* **59/1**

9 ½ **Inspired Cry (USA)**[35] 4863 4-9-4 0 ....(b) ElioneChaves 10 82
(Lennart Reuterskiold Jr, Sweden) *hld up towards rr: rdn in last 4f out: btn over 1f out: nvr a factor* **32/1**

10 2 **Manchester (FR)**[378] 4-9-4 0 .... CarlosLopez 7 79
(Niels Petersen, Norway) *hld up towards rr: prog into midfield 4f out: rdn and outpcd over 2f out: btn over 1f out: dropped to last ins fnl f* **235/10**

2m 29.4s (0.20) **10** Ran SP% **125.5**
PARI-MUTUEL (all including 1sek stake): WIN 1.57; PLACE 1.21, 3.43, 1.85; SF 51.84.
Owner Stall Trick Or Treat **Bred** Bjarne Minde **Trained** Norway

5931 BATH (L-H)
Monday, September 10

OFFICIAL GOING: Firm
Races incorporating bottom bend increased in distance by about 12.5yds.
Wind: Brisk across Weather: Overcast

6092 PROFAB WINDOWS FILLIES' H'CAP 1m 5y
2:20 (2:21) (Class 5) (0-75,73) 3-Y-0+ **£2,264** (£673; £336; £168) **Stalls** Low

Form RPR

2103 1 **Sputnik Sweetheart**[18] 5512 3-9-5 73 .... RichardHughes 3 83+
(Richard Hannon) *t.k.h: led: qcknd over 2f out: drvn clr over 1f out: readily: eased cl home* **11/4**[1]

2140 2 1 ¾ **Saaboog**[26] 5243 3-8-12 66 ....[1] MartinLane 2 69
(James Tate) *chsd ldrs: drvn ins fnl 3f: styd on u.p to take 2nd jst ins fnl f: nvr a threat but clsd on eased wnr* **8/1**[3]

5221 3 2 ¾ **Gold Show**[17] 5529 3-9-3 71 .... MartinHarley 7 68
(Mick Channon) *chsd wnr: rdn ins fnl 3f: sn outpcd and no ch: lost 2nd and no ex ins fnl f* **11/4**[1]

0-02 4 3 **Pearl War (USA)**[40] 4711 3-8-13 67 .... HarryBentley 5 57
(William Haggas) *t.k.h: chsd ldrs: rdn over 2f out: sn btn* **5/1**[2]

63-0 5 2 ¾ **Brief Chat (USA)**[80] 3340 3-9-0 68 .... JimCrowley 4 51
(Amanda Perrett) *in tch: rdn along 3f out: btn 2f out* **16/1**

0100 6 1 ¾ **Cha Ching (IRE)**[4] 5983 3-8-6 60 .... FrannyNorton 1 39
(J W Hills) *in rr: drvn along fr 3f out: swtchd rt over 1f out: no prog* **14/1**

1m 40.87s (0.07) **Going Correction** -0.15s/f (Firm)
WFA 3 from 6yo 5lb **6** Ran SP% **93.7**
Speed ratings (Par 100): **93,91,88,85,82 81**
Tote Swingers 1&2 £2.80, 2&3 £2.70, 1&3 £1.20 CSF £16.57 CT £31.99 TOTE £2.40: £1.10, £3.20; EX 17.00.
Owner Michael Pescod **Bred** Ecurie I M Fares **Trained** East Everleigh, Wilts
■ You've Been Mowed was withdrawn (9/2, ref to ent stalls). Deduct 15p in the £ under R4.

FOCUS
Distances increased by 12.5 yards for races that include the bottom bend. A fair fillies' handicap for 3yos and up. They went a respectable gallop on officially firm ground. The winner dictated and the form is not rated that positively.

6093 WEATHERBYS BLOODSTOCK INSURANCE MAIDEN AUCTION STKS 5f 11y
2:50 (2:50) (Class 6) 2-Y-0 **£1,617** (£481; £240; £120) **Stalls** Centre

Form RPR

3055 1 **Vestibule**[6] 5909 2-8-5 70 ....(p) CathyGannon 2 75
(Eve Johnson Houghton) *mde all: drvn clr appr fnl f: unchal* **11/10**[1]

2334 2 6 **Marchwood**[10] 5785 2-8-10 71 .... LiamKeniry 4 58
(J S Moore) *chsd wnr thrght: pushed along over 2f out: sn no imp and no ch fr over 1f out* **15/8**[2]

44 3 4 **Tristessa**[11] 5773 2-8-5 0 .... AndreaAtzeni 1 38
(Derek Haydn Jones) *chsd ldrs and disputing 3rd: rdn over 2f out: nvr any ch w wnr: no ex ins fnl f* **12/1**

0 4 ¾ **Iwilsayzisonlyonce**[6] 5912 2-9-0 0 .... LukeMorris 5 44
(Joseph Tuite) *disp 3rd: drvn along fr 3f out: nvr any ch w wnr: wknd wl over 1f out* **20/1**

5 4 ½ **Red Diesel (IRE)** 2-8-8 0 .... FrannyNorton 3 22
(Jo Hughes) *a in last pl and pushed along 3f out: mod prog 2f out: wknd over 1f out* **15/2**[3]

1m 6.64s (4.14) **Going Correction** -0.15s/f (Firm) **5** Ran SP% **106.6**
Speed ratings (Par 93): **60,50,44,42,35**
CSF £3.11 TOTE £2.00: £1.10, £1.50; EX 2.80.
Owner Miss E Johnson Houghton **Bred** Peter Onslow & Whatton Manor Stud **Trained** Blewbury, Oxon

FOCUS
A modest sprint juvenile auction maiden. The easy winner is rated to her best.

NOTEBOOK
Vestibule appeared the one to beat beforehand under these conditions having shown fair peak form for a ten-raced maiden at up to 6f on quick ground. She likes to dominate and this small-field scenario was perfect for such tactics. She routed this opposition and will remain of interest if taking up her extended 5f nursery handicap engagement back here under a penalty on Saturday. (op 6-5 tchd 5-4)
Marchwood ran well for a long way over 1f further on good to soft ground at Salisbury the previous month. He offered less encouragement on this quicker ground on this occasion. (op 6-4)
Tristessa failed to build on the modest level of form shown in her two fourth placings at up to 6f on Polytrack/good ground the previous month. (op 10-1)
Red Diesel(IRE) was making his debut, but raced green and showed very little promise under these conditions. (op 12-1)

6094 WEATHERBYS BANK H'CAP 5f 161y
3:20 (3:22) (Class 5) (0-75,77) 3-Y-0+ **£2,264** (£673; £336; £168) **Stalls** Centre

Form RPR

6050 1 **Belle Bayardo (IRE)**[11] 5774 4-8-8 62 .... KierenFox 1 71
(Ronald Harris) *in tch: drvn over 2f out: str run to chse ldr ins fnl f: kpt on wl to ld last strides* **20/1**

0501 2 nk **Button Moon (IRE)**[3] 5995 4-9-9 77 6ex ....(p) SebSanders 9 85
(Ian Wood) *sn trcking ldr: led over 2f out: drvn 3 l clr over 1f out: kpt on u.p: hdd last strides* **15/2**[3]

6400 3 1 **Comptonspirit**[26] 5223 8-8-11 70 .... JamesRogers(5) 2 75
(Brian Baugh) *chsd ldrs: rdn to go 2nd appr fnl f but no imp: kpt on wl clsng stages* **28/1**

6403 4 ½ **Emiratesdotcom**[9] 5812 6-9-6 74 .... LiamKeniry 6 77
(Milton Bradley) *s.i.s: in rr: drvn and hdwy over 1f out: styd on wl clsng stages: nt rch ldrs* **8/1**

5460 5 nk **Night Trade (IRE)**[7] 5877 5-9-2 75 ....(p) DarrenEgan(5) 3 77
(Ronald Harris) *chsd ldrs: drvn and impr towards outer over 1f out: kpt on clsng stages* **9/1**

4545 6 ¾ **Mambo Spirit (IRE)**[5] 5933 8-9-0 68 .... JohnFahy 10 68
(Tony Newcombe) *in rr: hdwy on outside over 1f out: styd on u.p fnl f: nt rch ldrs* **7/1**[2]

6650 7 hd **Style And Panache (IRE)**[20] 5447 4-8-8 62 ....(p) AndreaAtzeni 8 61
(David Evans) *chsd ldrs: rdn and one pce over 1f out: kpt on ins fnl f: no ex nr fin* **22/1**

5130 8 ½ **Cockney Fire**[18] 5502 3-9-2 72 ....(v) RichardHughes 11 69
(David Evans) *hld up in rr: drvn and hdwy over 1f out: nvr gng pce to get into contention* **15/2**[3]

4165 9 2 ½ **Supreme Quest**[21] 5422 3-9-5 75 .... JamesDoyle 4 64
(Roger Charlton) *led: hdd over 2f out: wknd appr fnl f* **16/1**

6542 10 ¾ **Diamond Vine (IRE)**[5] 5933 4-8-13 67 ....(p) LukeMorris 12 54
(Ronald Harris) *mid-div: rdn 2f out: nvr gng pce to get into contention* **13/2**[1]

6000 11 5 **Bermondsey Bob (IRE)**[5] 5933 6-8-10 64 .... ChrisCatlin 15 34
(John Spearing) *chsd ldrs: rdn 1/2-way: wknd over 2f out* **16/1**

1036 12 1 **Bilash**[27] 5205 5-8-11 65 .... TadhgO'Shea 13 32
(Reg Hollinshead) *in rr: racd on outside and rdn over 2f out: a outpcd* **40/1**

0050 13 nk **Volcanic Dust (IRE)**[5] 5933 4-9-2 70 .... FergusSweeney 16 36
(Milton Bradley) *s.i.s: racd on outer: rdn over 2f out: a outpcd* **50/1**

043 14 ¾ **Whitecrest**[34] 4903 4-9-0 68 .... CathyGannon 14 31
(John Spearing) *in tch on outer: rdn 2f out: sn wknd* **9/1**

3423 15 11 **Swendab (IRE)**[10] 5791 4-9-5 73 ....(v) KierenFallon 5
(John O'Shea) *s.i.s: in rr: drvn into mid-div ins fnl 3f: sn wknd: eased whn no ch fnl f* **13/2**[1]

1m 9.85s (-1.35) **Going Correction** -0.15s/f (Firm)
WFA 3 from 4yo+ 2lb **15** Ran SP% **122.5**
Speed ratings (Par 103): **103,102,101,100,100 99,98,98,94,93 87,85,85,84,69**
Tote Swingers 1&2 £42.80, 2&3 £47.50, 1&3 £134.60 CSF £157.98 CT £4306.00 TOTE £34.80: £8.00, £3.60, £7.50; EX 352.70.
Owner William Jones Lisa Harrington **Bred** L Mulryan **Trained** Earlswood, Monmouths
■ Stewards' Enquiry : Kieren Fox two-day ban: used whip above permitted level (Sep 24-25)

FOCUS
A fair sprint handicap for 3yos and up. Straightforward form, the winner's best figure since he was a 3yo.
Swendab(IRE) Official explanation: jockey said gelding never travelled

6095 WESTERN DAILY PRESS MAIDEN STKS 5f 161y
3:50 (3:51) (Class 5) 3-Y-0+ **£2,264** (£673; £336; £168) **Stalls** Centre

Form RPR

234 1 **Gladiatrix**[7] 5878 3-8-12 65 .... JamesMillman 4 69
(Rod Millman) *in rr: pushed along over 3f out: swtchd rt to outside 2f out: str run over 1f out to take narrow ld ins fnl f: pushed along and a doing enough fnl 100yds* **5/2**[2]

53-4 2 ½ **Crazy Too (IRE)**[48] 4425 3-8-12 64 .... MartinLane 5 67
(David Simcock) *chsd ldrs: led over 1f out: jnd then narrowly hdd ins fnl f: kpt on u.p but nvr quite gng pce of wnr* **1/1**[1]

64 3 7 **Jermatt**[20] 5453 3-8-12 0 .... DarrenEgan(5) 8 49
(J R Jenkins) *chsd ldr: led over 2f out: hdd over 1f out: easily outpcd by ldng duo: hld on all out for wl hld 3rd clsng stages* **20/1**

53 4 hd **Brown Volcano (IRE)**[18] 5505 3-9-0 0 .... MarkCoumbe(3) 3 49
(John O'Shea) *slowly away: in rr: rdn over 3f out: clsd on ldrs 2f out: styd on to press for wl hld 3rd clsng stages* **4/1**[3]

060 5 2 **Rain Dance**[3] 5994 3-8-12 50 .... ChrisCatlin 2 37
(Eve Johnson Houghton) *chsd ldrs: rdn over 3f out: sn btn* **18/1**

6 6 4 **Nic's Rebel**[20] 5448 3-8-12 0 .... CathyGannon 1 24
(James Unett) *sn led: hdd over 2f out: sn wknd* **50/1**

7 31 **Jayzee Dancer** 4-9-5 0 .... FergusSweeney 6
(Mark Gillard) *a in rr: lost tch fr 1/2-way* **50/1**

1m 10.74s (-0.46) **Going Correction** -0.15s/f (Firm)
WFA 3 from 4yo 2lb **7** Ran SP% **112.5**
Speed ratings (Par 103): **97,96,87,86,84 78,37**
Tote Swingers 1&2 £1.50, 2&3 £3.50, 1&3 £4.00 CSF £5.16 TOTE £4.10: £1.30, £1.90; EX 6.00.
Owner Harry Dutfield & Partners **Bred** H G And J R Dutfield **Trained** Kentisbeare, Devon

FOCUS
A weak sprint maiden for 3yos and up. The first two finished clear and are rated pretty much to form.

6096 POST WEEKEND NURSERY 1m 2f 46y
4:20 (4:20) (Class 5) (0-75,70) 2-Y-0 **£2,264** (£673; £336; £168) **Stalls** Low

Form RPR

004 1 **Felix Fabulla**[13] 5704 2-9-4 67 .... NickyMackay 5 73+
(Hughie Morrison) *chsd ldrs: chal appr fnl f: sn drvn and asserted: hld on wl clsng stages* **5/2**[1]

5633 2 ½ **Stiff Upper Lip (IRE)**[10] 5786 2-9-1 64 .... RichardHughes 8 68+
(Richard Hannon) *hld up in rr: hdwy 3f out: drvn and qcknd to chse wnr fnl 120yds: a jst hld* **11/4**[2]

6440 3 2 ½ **Lady Marmelo (IRE)**[17] 5550 2-9-7 70 .... MartinHarley 10 68
(Mick Channon) *in rr: hdwy over 2f out: styd on to take one pce 3rd clsng stages* **7/1**

0653 4 1 ¼ **Heliconia**[11] 5763 2-8-10 59 ....(b) LukeMorris 9 55
(Sir Mark Prescott Bt) *sn chsng ldr: chal fr over 2f out tl over 1f out: styd on same pce* **6/1**[3]

5062 5 hd **Rioja Day (IRE)**[10] 5786 2-9-6 69 .... SebSanders 3 64
(J W Hills) *led: rdn and jnd over 2f out: hdd 1f out: sn btn* **7/1**

50 6 9 **Orla's Rainbow (IRE)**[42] 4658 2-9-1 64 ....(b[1]) DarryllHolland 4 42
(John Berry) *chsd ldrs: rdn over 3f out: wknd over 2f out* **14/1**

5601 7 1 ¼ **Myzamour**[27] 5206 2-8-5 54 ....(b) AndreaAtzeni 6 30
(J S Moore) *a in rr: rdn and lost tch fr 3f out* **28/1**

0030 8 12 **Linda's Icon**[11] 5763 2-8-1 55 .... DarrenEgan(5) 1
(Mick Channon) *rdn 4f out: a towards rr* **16/1**

6015 9 9 **Missing Agent**[48] 4421 2-8-11 60 .... CathyGannon 7
(David Evans) *s.i.s: rdn 4f out: a wl bhd* **40/1**

2m 12.17s (1.17) **Going Correction** -0.15s/f (Firm) **9** Ran SP% **113.0**
Speed ratings (Par 95): **89,88,86,85,85 78,60,77,67**
Tote Swingers 1&2 £2.50, 2&3 £4.40, 1&3 £5.40 CSF £9.24 CT £40.08 TOTE £3.50: £1.40, £2.10, £1.80; EX 11.00.
Owner Mrs I Eavis **Bred** Llety Stud **Trained** East Ilsley, Berks

FOCUS
A fair nursery. Straightforward form, with an improved run from the winner.

NOTEBOOK

Felix Fabulla was entering handicap company in the midst of an upward curve after a peak fourth of eight over 1m at Epsom the previous month, despite a luckless passage through that contest. The step up to 1m2f here on firm ground looked potentially ideal on breeding and he duly justified strong market support. He will remain competitive under similar conditions once reassessed for this first career victory. (op 10-3)

Stiff Upper Lip(IRE) ran well off 2lb lower on his handicap debut over 1m at Salisbury on good to soft ground the previous month. He appreciated this 2f longer trip and acted on this firm ground. (op 9-4)

Lady Marmelo(IRE) held the highest BHA rating of 70 in this field for this handicap debut, and she appreciated this 3f step up in trip after posting some fair peak 7f form on good to firm ground at Doncaster three runs ago. (op 9-1)

Heliconia ran better in first time blinkers over 1m at Kempton the previous month. She failed to build on that display here upped in trip on quick ground. (op 13-2 tchd 7-1 and 5-1)

Rioja Day(IRE) may appreciate a return to 1m on good ground or softer. (op 13-2 tchd 15-2)

6097 WESTERN DAILY PRESS "AGENDA" H'CAP — 1m 3f 144y

4:50 (4:51) (Class 6) (0-60,59) 3-Y-O+ — **£1,617** (£481; £240; £120) **Stalls** Low

Form — RPR

2244 **1** **Volcanic Jack (IRE)**^{5} 5936 4-9-8 **55** — KierenFallon 13 — 68
(Tony Carroll) *in tch: hdwy 4f out: chsd ldr over 2f out: led over 1f out: pushed out* **11/4**^{1}

5006 **2** 2 ¾ **Pelham Crescent (IRE)**^{25} 5265 9-9-8 **55** — LukeMorris 5 — 63
(Bryn Palling) *in rr: hdwy 3f out: sn rdn: styd on to chse wnr fnl f: no imp* **12/1**

0412 **3** 4 ½ **Tawseef (IRE)**^{53} 4244 4-9-12 **59** — GeorgeBaker 6 — 60
(Roy Brotherton) *in rr: hdwy over 2f out: styd on to take wl hld 3rd fnl f* **7/2**^{2}

0-04 **4** 2 **Annelko**^{9} 5817 5-9-7 **54** — MartinLane 7 — 51
(Michael Blake) *chsd ldrs: led ins fnl m: 5 l clr 3f out: rdn 2f out: hdd over 1f out: wknd ins fnl f* **5/1**^{3}

2204 **5** 7 **Entrance**^{15} 5638 4-9-2 **56** — NatashaEaton(7) 12 — 41
(Julia Feilden) *s.i.s: in rr: styd on fr over 2f out: nvr any ch* **16/1**

-506 **6** 1 ¾ **Mabel's Song**^{20} 5452 3-9-1 **57** — FergusSweeney 10 — 39
(Henry Candy) *chsd ldrs: rdn 3f out and sn btn* **12/1**

0510 **7** 12 **Sir Dylan**^{9} 5817 3-8-8 **55** — DarrenEgan(5) 3 — 17
(Ronald Harris) *in rr: sn wl bhd: styd on fr 3f out but nvr any ch* **15/2**

540- **8** 6 **Hector Spectre (IRE)**^{584} 428 6-9-5 **52** — (p) AndreaAtzeni 11
(Nikki Evans) *chsd ldrs: rdn and effrt 3f out: sn wknd* **50/1**

424 **9** 8 **Secret Era**^{28} 5164 5-9-9 **56** — DarryllHolland 2
(William Muir) *led tl hdd ins fnl m: rdn 3f out: sn wknd* **8/1**

0040 **10** ¾ **Bold Duke**^{9} 5817 4-9-3 **50** — (p) CathyGannon 4
(Edward Bevan) *a towards rr* **33/1**

-400 **11** 1 ½ **Snow Ridge**^{62} 3939 4-9-3 **50** — (t) RichardThomas 8
(Simon Hodgson) *s.i.s: a in rr* **50/1**

6-00 **12** 17 **Enchanting Smile (FR)**^{14} 5657 5-9-8 **55** — LiamKeniry 1
(Mark Gillard) *chsd ldrs 7f* **100/1**

2m 28.44s (-2.16) **Going Correction** -0.15s/f (Firm)
WFA 3 from 4yo+ 9lb — **12** Ran SP% **117.6**
Speed ratings (Par 101): **101,99,96,94,90 89,81,77,71,71 70,58**
Tote Swingers 1&2 £10.80, 2&3 £7.70, 1&3 £3.00 CSF £36.63 CT £119.99 TOTE £3.60: £1.50, £6.90, £1.10; EX 35.70.

Owner Fortune Seekers **Bred** Michael Guinan **Trained** Cropthorne, Worcs

FOCUS

A moderate middle-distance handicap. It was strong run and the winner produced a small personal best.

Sir Dylan Official explanation: jockey said gelding hung left

Secret Era Official explanation: jockey said mare ran too freely

6098 SOUTHWESTBUSINESS.CO.UK MAIDEN H'CAP — 1m 5f 22y

5:20 (5:20) (Class 5) (0-70,70) 3-Y-O+ — **£2,264** (£673; £336; £168) **Stalls** High

Form — RPR

1 **No Such Number**^{102} 2644 4-10-0 **70** — RichardHughes 6 — 76+
(Julia Feilden) *trckd ldrs: looking for a run and travelling comf wl over 1f out: swtchd lft and qcknd fnl f: led fnl 120yds: drvn and hld on wl cl home* **9/1**

5602 **2** hd **Aleksandar**^{27} 5219 3-9-3 **69** — KierenFallon 7 — 74+
(Luca Cumani) *trckd ldr: led over 2f out: drvn over 1f out: hdd fnl 120yds: kpt on but nt pce of wnr* **5/4**^{1}

4203 **3** 1 ½ **Petaluma**^{20} 5456 3-9-4 **70** — MartinHarley 4 — 73
(Mick Channon) *chsd ldrs: rdn fr 3f out: styd on to take 3rd ins fnl f: nt pce of ldng duo* **6/1**^{2}

6420 **4** ¾ **Jalors (IRE)**^{10} 5809 4-9-8 **64** — LukeMorris 11 — 66
(Ronald Harris) *hld up in tch: rdn along fr 3f out: styd on to dispute 3rd ins fnl f but no imp on ldng duo: one pce clsng stages* **8/1**^{3}

-560 **5** 1 ¾ **Lily Potts**^{77} 3443 3-8-4 **61** — JemmaMarshall(5) 10 — 60
(Chris Down) *chsd ldrs: rdn over 3f out: chsd ldr over 2f out: no imp over 1f out: wknd fnl 120yds* **25/1**

0336 **6** ¾ **Simply**^{8} 5855 3-8-4 **56** oh1 — (p) ChrisCatlin 3 — 54
(Eve Johnson Houghton) *in rr: rdn over 2f out: swtchd rt to outer over 1f out and kpt on but nvr any ch* **33/1**

5-06 **7** 2 ¼ **Cityar (FR)**^{11} 5419 8-8-11 **56** oh10 — (p) RyanPowell(3) 8 — 51
(John O'Shea) *s.i.s: in rr: sme hdwy u.p on outer fr 3f out: sn wknd* **66/1**

5652 **7** dht **Bohemian Rhapsody (IRE)**^{20} 5456 3-9-4 **70** — (p) MartinLane 9 — 65
(J W Hills) *sn led: rdn and hdd over 2f out: wknd wl over 1f out* **6/1**^{2}

0236 **9** 4 ½ **Reset City**^{19} 5474 6-9-8 **64** — (t) CathyGannon 2 — 52
(Ian Williams) *s.i.s: in rr: rdn and sme hdwy on outer over 3f out: sn wknd* **6/1**^{2}

2m 53.0s (1.00) **Going Correction** -0.15s/f (Firm)
WFA 3 from 4yo+ 10lb — **9** Ran SP% **116.7**
Speed ratings (Par 103): **90,89,88,88,87 86,86,86,84**
Tote Swingers 1&2 £4.10, 2&3 £1.90, 1&3 £7.50 CSF £20.72 CT £76.80 TOTE £4.70: £2.10, £1.50, £2.20; EX 9.20.

Owner Good Company Partnership **Bred** Juddmonte Farms Ltd **Trained** Exning, Suffolk

FOCUS

A fair maiden staying handicap for 3yos and up. The time was slow and there was a relatively bunched finish. Improvement from the winner on his British debut.

T/Plt: £41.40 to a £1 stake. Pool: £61,069.88 - 1,075.33 winning tickets. T/Qpdt: £19.50 to a £1 stake. Pool: £4,683.75 - 176.94 winning tickets. ST

5668 NEWCASTLE (L-H)

Monday, September 10

OFFICIAL GOING: Good (good to firm in places; 7.7)

Wind: Fairly strong, across Weather: Overcast

6099 WEATHERBYS BLOODSTOCK INSURANCE/BRITISH STALLION STUDS EBF MAIDEN STKS — 6f

2:00 (2:03) (Class 5) 2-Y-O — **£3,169** (£943; £471; £235) **Stalls** Centre

Form — RPR

06 **1** **Rich Forever (IRE)**^{23} 5367 2-9-3 0 — JamieSpencer 11 — 75
(James Bethell) *trckd ldrs: led over 2f out: rdn and hung rt over 1f out: drvn out fnl f* **12/1**

2 1 ¼ **Rust (IRE)** 2-9-3 0 — PJMcDonald 16 — 71+
(Ann Duffield) *slowly away: hld up: smooth hdwy to press wnr over 1f out: sn rdn: kpt on fnl f: hld nr fin: bttr for r* **16/1**

3 **3** ¾ **Loch Moy**^{67} 3777 2-9-3 0 — TonyHamilton 2 — 69
(Richard Fahey) *dwlt: hld up: rdn and hdwy wl over 1f out: hung lft: kpt on fnl f: nrst fin* **11/2**^{3}

43 **4** 2 ½ **Bond Club**^{21} 5410 2-9-3 0 — RobertWinston 7 — 61
(Geoffrey Oldroyd) *in tch: drvn along over 3f out: rallied over 1f out: nvr able to chal* **8/1**

04 **5** 1 ¾ **Top Town Boy**^{20} 5449 2-9-3 0 — RussKennemore 5 — 56
(John Holt) *t.k.h early: prom: drvn along over 3f out: rallied over 1f out: one pce fnl f* **25/1**

6 1 **Stagweekend (IRE)** 2-9-3 0 — MichaelO'Connell 9 — 53+
(John Quinn) *sn drvn along bhd ldng gp: outpcd over 3f out: rallied over 1f out: nvr able to chal* **33/1**

7 shd **Antonius** 2-9-3 0 — TomEaves 8 — 53+
(Linda Stubbs) *t.k.h: hld up: effrt whn nt clr run wl over 1f out: no imp fnl f* **40/1**

50 **8** 2 ¼ **Mushaakis (IRE)**^{52} 4290 2-9-3 0 — PaulHanagan 3 — 46
(Mark Johnston) *cl up: rdn over 2f out: wknd fnl f* **10/1**

0 **9** 2 **Star Spun (USA)**^{45} 4545 2-9-3 0 — GrahamGibbons 4 — 40
(David Barron) *dwlt: sn in tch: rdn over 2f out: wknd appr fnl f* **11/4**^{2}

20 **10** 1 ¾ **Intrepid (IRE)**^{23} 5360 2-9-3 0 — GrahamLee 1 — 34
(Jeremy Noseda) *t.k.h: prom: rdn over 2f out: wknd wl over 1f out* **5/2**^{1}

UP **11** shd **Fenwick Gale (IRE)**^{43} 4618 2-8-12 0 — PaulMulrennan 6 — 29
(Kevin Ryan) *uns rdr gng to post: led to over 2f out: wknd over 1f out* **33/1**

12 1 ½ **Erica Starprincess** 2-8-12 0 — AndrewMullen 10 — 25
(George Moore) *in tch: drvn along and outpcd over 3f out: no imp fnl 2f* **150/1**

13 ½ **Witch Way Went** 2-8-12 0 — PatrickMathers 12 — 23
(Ian McInnes) *dwlt: sn drvn in rr: struggling after 2f: sme late hdwy: nvr on terms* **200/1**

50 **14** shd **Big Spender (IRE)**^{24} 5291 2-9-0 0 — LeeTopliss(3) 14 — 28
(Ian McInnes) *chsd ldrs tl rdn and wknd 3f out* **200/1**

06 **15** nk **Passionate Poet**^{37} 4825 2-8-10 0 ... 1 — DavidSimmonson(7) 13 — 27
(Michael Easterby) *bhd: drvn along over 3f out: btn fnl 2f* **40/1**

16 30 **Fishlake Rebel** 2-9-3 0 — JamesSullivan 15
(Ruth Carr) *t.k.h in midfield: hung rt over 3f out: sn btn: eased fr over 1f out* **150/1**

1m 15.96s (1.36) **Going Correction** +0.15s/f (Good) — **16** Ran SP% **121.3**
Speed ratings (Par 95): **96,94,93,90,87 86,86,83,80,78 78,76,75,75,74 34**
Tote Swingers 1&2 £22.20, 2&3 £19.00, 1&3 £9.40 CSF £179.87 TOTE £13.50: £3.90, £4.60, £2.50; EX 207.70 TRIFECTA Not won..

Owner Richard T Vickers **Bred** Guy O'Callaghan **Trained** Middleham Moor, N Yorks

FOCUS

Just a modest maiden. The form is rated around the third and fourth.

NOTEBOOK

Rich Forever(IRE) had run better than the bare result over the same trip at Redcar the time before and showed much-improved form, tanking to the front and seeing it out well. Handicaps are the likely next step and he looks to have a decent future. (op 20-1)

Rust(IRE), a half-brother to winners from 5f-7f, made a promising debut, running on nicely having been given a fair bit to do. He should build on this and can probably win an ordinary maiden. (op 20-1)

Loch Moy confirmed his debut promise, challenging towards the far rail having drifted, but never being quite on terms. He should benefit from 7f and looks capable of winning at the right level. (op 6-1)

Bond Club is now qualified for a mark and should fare better upped to 7f. Official explanation: jockey said colt suffered interference in running (op 7-1)

Top Town Boy needed this for a mark and should do better in low-grade nurseries. (tchd 28-1)

Stagweekend(IRE), a half-brother to numerous winners at up to 7f, including at two, was going on late and should improve. (tchd 28-1)

Antonius, half-brother to a 1m4f winner, would have finished closer but for suffering some late interference and should improve once upped in trip. (op 50-1)

Mushaakis(IRE) is likely to fare better once upped in trip and switched to nurseries, for which he is now qualified. (op 11-1 tchd 12-1)

Star Spun(USA) was strong in the market, but produced a tame finishing effort, failing to build on his debut run. Better was clearly expected and he's the type to come good in nurseries. (op 7-2 tchd 4-1)

Intrepid(IRE) took a further step backwards, receiving no cover from his low draw and fading right out. He's left with a bit to prove, but is yet another who could bounce back in nurseries. (op 2-1)

Fishlake Rebel Official explanation: jockey said gelding hung right-handed

6100 DELOITTE/BRITISH STALLION STUDS EBF MAIDEN STKS — 5f

2:30 (2:31) (Class 5) 3-Y-O+ — **£3,557** (£1,058; £529; £264) **Stalls** Centre

Form — RPR

- **1** **Hello Stranger (IRE)** 3-9-3 0 — DuranFentiman 10 — 68
(Tim Easterby) *mid-div: hdwy over 2f out: r.o to ld last 50yds* **10/1**

0300 **2** 1 ¼ **Red Baron (IRE)**^{9} 5831 3-9-3 59 — GrahamGibbons 9 — 63
(Eric Alston) *dwlt: drvn to ld after 1f: hdd and no ex wl ins fnl f* **20/1**

26 **3** 1 **Vanity's Girl (IRE)**^{12} 5734 3-8-12 0 — MichaelO'Connell 11 — 55
(John Quinn) *swtchd lft after s: chsd ldrs: styd on same pce last 150yds* **6/1**^{3}

5055 **4** 1 ¼ **Gran Canaria Queen**^{30} 5087 3-8-12 51 — BarryMcHugh 1 — 50
(Ian Semple) *chsd ldrs: kpt on same pce fnl f* **14/1**

00-0 **5** nk **Bang Tidy (IRE)**^{6} 5923 3-9-3 63 — PaulMulrennan 8 — 54
(Brian Ellison) *t.k.h: led 1f: chsd ldrs: kpt on same pce fnl f* **4/1**^{2}

465 **6** 1 **Cataract**^{15} 5624 3-8-12 44 — (b) JamesSullivan 6 — 46
(John Weymes) *prom: drvn over 2f out: one pce* **50/1**

0504 **7** ½ **Niceonemyson**^{12} 5734 3-9-3 52 — (p) PaddyAspell 5 — 49
(Christopher Wilson) *in rr: hdwy and hung lft 2f out: nvr a factor* **28/1**

56 **8** *¾* **Never Forever**[17] 5549 3-9-3 0 .... PJMcDonald 7 46+
(George Moore) *dwlt: sn outpcd and in rr: kpt on fnl 2f: nvr a factor* **20/1**

005 **9** *1* **Busy Bimbo (IRE)**[9] 5823 3-8-12 42 .... (p) GrahamLee 3 37
(Alan Berry) *prom: outpcd over 2f out: no threat after* **50/1**

030 **10** *1 ¼* **Myjestic Melody (IRE)**[34] 4911 4-8-13 49 .... DanielTudhope 4 33
(Noel Wilson) *hld up in mid-div: effrt over 2f out: wknd over 1f out* **16/1**

0224 **11** *1 ¼* **Blue Tiger**[30] 5096 3-9-3 73 .... (tp) PaulHanagan 13 33
(Saeed Bin Suroor) *swtchd lft after s to join main body: t.k.h towards rr: nvr a factor* **11/8[1]**

060 **12** *9* **Lady Oz (IRE)**[15] 5618 5-8-8 34 ow2 .... DavidSimmonson(7) 2
(Michael Easterby) *chsd ldrs on outer: hung lft and lost pl over 2f out: sn bhd* **100/1**

2004 **13** *hd* **Face East (USA)**[11] 5760 4-8-11 47 .... JordanHibberd(7) 12
(Alan Berry) *swtchd lft after s to join main body: sn outpcd and wl bhd* **100/1**

1m 1.05s (-0.05) **Going Correction** +0.15s/f (Good)
WFA 3 from 4yo+ 1lb **13** Ran SP% **116.9**
Speed ratings (Par 103): **106,104,102,100,99 98,97,96,94,92 90,76,76**
Tote Swingers 1&2 £21.90, 2&3 £13.20, 1&3 £4.10 CSF £192.04 TOTE £21.10: £3.70, £5.10, £1.80; EX 200.90 Trifecta £122.10 Part won. Pool: £165.11 - 0.20 winning tickets..
Owner Norman Jackson **Bred** Mrs M Kehoe **Trained** Great Habton, N Yorks

FOCUS
A typically weak 3yo-plus sprint maiden. No surprise to see the sole newcomer in the field prove good enough.
Bang Tidy(IRE) Official explanation: jockey said gelding ran too free

6101 FREEBETS.COM H'CAP 2m 19y
3:00 (3:00) (Class 6) (0-65,63) 3-Y-O+ **£2,264** (£673; £336; £168) **Stalls** Low

Form RPR

32 **1** **Jawaab (IRE)**[7] 5891 8-9-11 60 .... (v[1]) PhillipMakin 4 69
(Philip Kirby) *in tch: hdwy to ld over 1f out: drvn and styd on strly fnl f* **4/1[2]**

441 **2** *3* **Grand Art (IRE)**[6] 5922 8-9-5 57 6ex .... (p) GaryBartley(3) 11 62
(Noel Wilson) *hld up: stdy hdwy and prom over 2f out: chsd wnr over 1f out: one pce ins fnl f* **10/1**

4503 **3** *1 ¼* **Asteroid Belt (IRE)**[16] 5589 3-8-7 55 .... (p) AmyRyan 1 59
(Chris Grant) *hld up: rdn and hdwy whn nt clr run over 2f out: styd on fnl f: nvr able to chal* **7/2[1]**

6635 **4** *2 ¾* **Petella**[6] 5922 6-10-0 63 .... PJMcDonald 5 63
(George Moore) *hld up: outpcd over 3f out: hdwy wl over 1f out: no imp fnl f* **6/1[3]**

5034 **5** *½* **Descaro (USA)**[22] 5384 6-9-12 61 .... [1] GrahamLee 10 61
(David O'Meara) *trckd ldrs: effrt and drvn 3f out: no imp fr 2f out* **10/1**

0262 **6** *3 ¼* **Hi Dancer**[30] 5115 9-9-2 54 .... DeclanCannon(3) 3 50
(Ben Haslam) *cl up: led 3f out to over 1f out: wknd ins fnl f* **16/1**

5550 **7** *2 ¼* **Spiders Star**[13] 5714 9-8-4 46 oh1 .... (p) ShirleyTeasdale(7) 2 39
(Simon West) *taken early to post: hld up on ins: drvn and outpcd over 2f out: n.d after* **33/1**

005 **8** *7* **Almost Gemini (IRE)**[108] 2453 3-8-8 56 .... JamieSpencer 8 41
(Roger Varian) *t.k.h early: midfield on outside: drvn over 4f out: effrt and hung lft over 2f out: wknd over 1f out* **4/1[2]**

6502 **9** *18* **Pugnacious (IRE)**[12] 5738 3-8-9 57 .... (b) JoeFanning 6 20
(Mark Johnston) *led: rdn over 4f out: hdd 3f out: wknd 2f out* **15/2**

0/0- **10** *5* **Pegasus Prince (USA)**[128] 1153 8-9-4 53 .... TomEaves 7 10
(Brian Storey) *hld up: drvn and struggling over 5f out: sn btn* **100/1**

-550 **11** *1 ¾* **Manager Mick (IRE)**[35] 4867 4-8-11 46 oh1 .... (v) PaddyAspell 9
(John Norton) *cl up tl rdn and wknd over 3f out* **66/1**

3m 36.1s (-3.30) **Going Correction** -0.25s/f (Firm)
WFA 3 from 4yo+ 13lb **11** Ran SP% **117.8**
Speed ratings (Par 101): **98,96,95,94,94 92,91,88,79,76 75**
Tote Swingers 1&2 £6.90, 2&3 £6.60, 1&3 £5.50 CSF £43.55 CT £154.63 TOTE £6.50: £2.40, £2.00, £1.60; EX 47.00 Trifecta £253.80 Pool: £487.04 - 1.42 winning tickets..
Owner L & D Racing **Bred** Hascombe And Valiant Studs **Trained** Castleton, N Yorks

FOCUS
The pace was even and the in-form runners came to the fore.

6102 WEATHERBYS BANK/BRITISH STALLION STUDS EBF MAIDEN STKS 1m (R)
3:30 (3:31) (Class 5) 3-Y-O+ **£3,557** (£1,058; £529; £264) **Stalls** Low

Form RPR

-212 **1** **Sigurwana (USA)**[29] 5125 3-8-12 71 .... PaulHanagan 9 64
(William Haggas) *mde all: drvn over 2f out: hrd pressed ins fnl f: hld on gamely* **5/2[2]**

52 **2** *1* **A'Juba**[17] 5555 3-9-3 0 .... RobertHavlin 4 67
(Saeed Bin Suroor) *t.k.h early: trckd ldrs: effrt and swtchd rt appr 2f out: effrt and pressed wnr fnl f: kpt on: hld nr fin* **1/1[1]**

0 **3** *1 ¾* **Sword In Hand**[114] 2273 3-9-3 0 .... RobertWinston 2 63+
(Alan Jarvis) *in tch: rdn over 2f out: gd hdwy over 1f out: kpt on fnl f: hld nr fin* **20/1**

6044 **4** *2 ¼* **Avison (IRE)**[13] 5708 4-9-8 52 .... DavidNolan 10 58
(Richard Fahey) *chsd wnr: drvn over 2f out: outpcd fnl f* **25/1**

-406 **5** *5* **Shamo Hill Theatre**[73] 3581 5-9-5 45 .... (p) DeclanCannon(3) 5 46
(Lawrence Mullaney) *midfield: drvn along wl over 2f out: outpcd fnl 2f* **200/1**

3 **6** *½* **Spanish Legacy**[17] 5549 3-8-12 0 .... BarryMcHugh 6 40
(Julie Camacho) *prom: drvn along over 2f out: wknd fnl f* **25/1**

5 **7** *1 ½* **Discay**[14] 5679 3-9-3 0 .... JoeFanning 3 41+
(Mark Johnston) *towards rr: drvn and outpcd over 3f out: n.d after* **16/1**

8 *5* **Royal Sea (IRE)**[142] 1535 3-9-3 0 .... DanielTudhope 7 30
(David O'Meara) *hld up: rdn over 3f out: sn btn* **20/1**

0 **9** *8* **Billy Redpath**[14] 5679 4-9-8 0 .... DuranFentiman 1 12
(Frederick Watson) *slowly away: t.k.h in rr: struggling over 3f out: sn btn* **200/1**

50 **10** *3 ¼* **Tenacity**[14] 5679 3-9-3 0 .... PaddyAspell 12
(Kate Walton) *hld up: rdn and outpcd over 4f out: btn over 2f out* **50/1**

11 *3 ¾* **One Million**[379] 5521 3-9-3 0 .... GrahamLee 8
(Rose Dobbin) *in tch tl rdn and wknd wl over 2f out* **40/1**

0 **12** *72* **Kalily**[21] 5421 3-9-3 0 .... J-PGuillambert 11
(Luca Cumani) *s.i.s: sn pushed along in rr: struggling over 3f out: btn and eased fnl 2f* **8/1[3]**

1m 42.51s (-2.79) **Going Correction** -0.25s/f (Firm)
WFA 3 from 4yo+ 5lb **12** Ran SP% **118.2**
Speed ratings (Par 103): **103,102,100,98,93 92,91,86,78,74 71,**
Tote Swingers 1&2 £1.70, 2&3 £7.50, 1&3 £8.40 CSF £4.82 TOTE £2.60: £1.20, £1.10, £4.80; EX 6.30 Trifecta £142.20 Pool: £628.74 - 3.27 winning tickets..
Owner A E Oppenheimer **Bred** Hascombe Stud **Trained** Newmarket, Suffolk

FOCUS
Few got into this modest maiden.
Spanish Legacy Official explanation: jockey said he dropped reins inside final furlong
Kalily Official explanation: jockey said colt slipped on the bend turning into home straight and lost its action

6103 WEATHERBYS BLOODSTOCK INSURANCE H'CAP 1m 4f 93y
4:00 (4:00) (Class 6) (0-65,63) 3-Y-O+ **£1,617** (£481; £240; £120) **Stalls** Low

Form RPR

4140 **1** **Scarlet Prince**[16] 5589 3-8-10 61 .... ShaneBKelly(5) 1 71
(Tony Coyle) *early reminders in rr: pushed along and hdwy over 2f out: led wl ins fnl f: drvn out* **12/1**

3126 **2** *1 ½* **Mr Snoozy**[33] 4955 3-9-3 63 .... GrahamGibbons 6 71
(Tim Walford) *midfield: pushed along over 4f out: hdwy to ld over 2f out: rdn and edgd lft over 1f out: hdd and no ex wl ins fnl f* **4/1[1]**

01 **3** *1 ¼* **Operateur (IRE)**[68] 3753 4-9-5 56 .... PhillipMakin 16 63
(Ben Haslam) *midfield on outside: hdwy to chal over 2f out to over 1f out: one pce ins fnl f* **12/1**

0242 **4** *1 ½* **Zaplamation (IRE)**[18] 5199 7-9-3 61 .... WilliamTwiston-Davies(7) 4 65
(John Quinn) *hld up: smooth hdwy to trck ldrs over 2f out: rdn over 1f out: nt qckn fnl f* **15/2[3]**

0110 **5** *½* **Valantino Oyster (IRE)**[16] 5585 5-9-10 61 .... (p) PatrickMathers 12 64
(Tracy Waggott) *hld up on outside: rdn and hdwy over 2f out: edgd lft and kpt on fnl f: nrst fin* **20/1**

6034 **6** *nk* **Millymonkin**[12] 5738 3-8-13 59 .... (t) PaulMulrennan 7 61
(Michael Easterby) *led 2f: cl up: effrt and rdn over 2f out: no ex fnl f* **8/1**

2120 **7** *nk* **Dean Iarracht (IRE)**[16] 5585 6-9-9 60 .... (p) FrederikTylicki 11 62
(Tracy Waggott) *dwlt: hld up: rdn and hdwy wl over 1f out: kpt on fnl f: nvr able to chal* **16/1**

6300 **8** *12* **Rub Of The Relic (IRE)**[11] 5767 7-9-5 63 .... (v) NedCurtis(7) 2 46
(Paul Midgley) *prom: drvn and lost pl over 3f out: n.d after* **20/1**

-000 **9** *3 ¾* **Medieval Bishop (IRE)**[21] 5414 3-8-9 62 .... GemmaTutty(7) 10 39
(Tim Walford) *hld up: rdn over 3f out: no imp fr over 2f out* **28/1**

4054 **10** *nk* **Authentication**[20] 5456 3-8-5 51 .... (b[1]) JoeFanning 5 27
(Mark Johnston) *t.k.h: cl up: led 1/2-way: rdn and hdd over 2f out: wknd over 1f out* **9/2[2]**

0040 **11** *2 ¼* **Ailsa Craig (IRE)**[26] 5225 6-9-4 60 .... (p) GarryWhillans(5) 9 33
(Edwin Tuer) *prom tl rdn and wknd over 2f out* **16/1**

0066 **12** *11* **Yorksters Prince (IRE)**[25] 5253 5-9-4 55 .... BarryMcHugh 3
(Tony Coyle) *midfield: effrt whn nt clr run wl over 2f out: sn n.d: btn over 1f out* **16/1**

0 **13** *4* **Grammar**[12] 5730 3-8-12 58 .... (b[1]) DanielTudhope 14
(Colin Teague) *t.k.h: trckd ldrs tl rdn and wknd over 2f out: eased whn no ch* **66/1**

4001 **14** *½* **Brasingaman Espee**[12] 5738 3-8-9 55 .... (b) AndrewElliott 13
(George Moore) *t.k.h: led after 2f to 1/2-way: rdn and wknd over 2f out* **16/1**

0005 **15** *6* **Alpha Arion (IRE)**[14] 5680 3-8-4 50 .... DuranFentiman 8
(Tim Easterby) *bhd: drvn along over 4f out: btn fnl 3f* **50/1**

005 **16** *48* **Italian Lady (USA)**[21] 5421 3-9-0 60 .... RobertWinston 15
(Alan Jarvis) *midfield: struggling over 5f out: btn and eased over 2f out* **12/1**

2m 43.33s (-2.27) **Going Correction** -0.25s/f (Firm)
WFA 3 from 4yo+ 9lb **16** Ran SP% **124.1**
Speed ratings (Par 101): **97,96,95,94,93 93,93,85,82,82 81,73,71,70,66 34**
Tote Swingers 1&2 £14.90, 2&3 £10.00, 1&3 £35.30 CSF £57.15 CT £614.06 TOTE £19.40: £3.30, £1.50, £2.80, £2.00; EX 88.20 TRIFECTA Not won..
Owner Mrs Nicola McGreavy **Bred** Southill Stud **Trained** Norton, N Yorks
■ Stewards' Enquiry : Shane B Kelly two-day ban: used whip above permitted level (Sep 24-25)

FOCUS
They went too hard up front in this and the closers were favoured.
Scarlet Prince Official explanation: trainer said, regarding apparent improvement in form, that the gelding benefited from the drop back in trip.

6104 THREE MILE INN H'CAP 6f
4:30 (4:31) (Class 6) (0-55,55) 3-Y-O+ **£1,617** (£481; £240; £120) **Stalls** Centre

Form RPR

0063 **1** **Xpres Maite**[25] 5259 9-9-0 54 .... (b) RyanClark(3) 8 64
(Roy Bowring) *s.s: reminders after s: outpcd in rr: hdwy stands' rail over 1f out: str run to ld nr fin* **8/1[3]**

5142 **2** *¾* **Maltease Ah**[15] 5621 3-8-9 55 ow1 .... WilliamTwiston-Davies(7) 10 63
(Alan McCabe) *led 2f: w ldrs: led over 1f out: hdd last 75yds: kpt on to regain 2nd nr fin* **9/1**

3044 **3** *½* **Red Shadow**[16] 5590 3-8-13 52 .... (p) PatrickMathers 13 58
(Alan Brown) *chsd ldrs: styd on wl to ld last 75yds: hdd and no ex towards fin* **10/1**

5004 **4** *1 ½* **Saxonette**[6] 5923 4-9-2 53 .... (p) PJMcDonald 4 55
(Linda Perratt) *mid-div: hdwy over 2f out: kpt on ins fnl f: no ex* **25/1**

0500 **5** *¾* **Besty**[21] 5416 5-9-3 54 .... (t) PhillipMakin 1 53
(Paul Midgley) *mid-div: hdwy over 2f out: upsides 1f out: kpt on same pce* **20/1**

-360 **6** *½* **Monel**[27] 5189 4-9-2 53 .... GrahamLee 7 51+
(Jim Goldie) *half-rrd s: hld up towards rr: hdwy over 2f out: nt clr run over 1f out: kpt on last 150yds* **20/1**

5-00 **7** *hd* **Lady Platinum Club**[21] 5416 4-8-10 54 .... NedCurtis(7) 3 51
(Geoffrey Oldroyd) *chsd ldrs: kpt on same pce fnl f* **12/1**

0155 **8** *½* **Majestic Breeze (IRE)**[32] 5014 3-8-13 52 .... (p) TomEaves 2 47
(Brian Ellison) *w ldrs: led after 2f: hdd over 1f out: fdd ins fnl f* **12/1**

6004 **9** *¾* **Weetentherty**[17] 5542 5-8-10 50 .... (p) DeclanCannon(3) 5 43
(Linda Perratt) *dwlt: in rr: kpt on fnl 2f: nvr a threat* **33/1**

5212 **10** *1 ¾* **Ursus**[24] 5295 7-9-4 55 .... (p) PaddyAspell 6 42
(Christopher Wilson) *w ldrs: wknd fnl f* **7/1[2]**

-040 **11** *hd* **Findhornbay**[30] 5087 3-8-13 52 .... [1] JoeFanning 15 39
(Keith Dalgleish) *chsd ldrs: fdd over 1f out* **20/1**

264 **12** *¾* **Spirit Of Coniston**[13] 5719 9-9-2 53 .... MickyFenton 12 37
(Paul Midgley) *trckd ldrs: stdd after 2f: effrt and hung lft over 1f out: no threat* **25/1**

6503 **13** *½* **John Coffey (IRE)**[16] 5590 3-8-8 54 .... ShirleyTeasdale(7) 9 37
(David Nicholls) *hld up: w ldrs: wknd appr fnl f* **9/2[1]**

4006 **14** *4* **Thats Molly (IRE)**[24] 5295 3-8-13 52 .... GrahamGibbons 11 22
(Eric Alston) *chsd ldrs: lost pl over 1f out* **8/1[3]**

6040 **15** *3 ½* **Noble Bounty**[11] 5757 3-9-2 55 .... AmyRyan 14 14
(Kevin Ryan) *dwlt: a in rr* **16/1**

1360 **16** ½ **Hab Reeh**[16] 5590 4 -9-0 51 ....(b) JamesSullivan 16
(Ruth Carr) *chsd ldrs stands' side: lost pl 2f out* **12/1**

1m 15.31s (0.71) **Going Correction** +0.15s/f (Good)
WFA 3 from 4yo+ 2lb **16**Ran SP% 125.9
Speed ratings (Par 101): **101,100,99,97,96 95,95,94,93,91 91,90,89,84,79 78**
Tote Swingers 1&2 £10.20, 2&3 £15.50, 1&3 £18.10 CSF £72.28 CT £748.54 TOTE £10.70 : £2.10, £1.70 , £2.70 , £6.80 ; EX 89.00 TRIFECTA Not won. .
Owner Charterhouse Holdings Plc **Bred** S R Bowring **Trained** Edwinstowe, Notts

FOCUS
Those racing middle-to-stands' side were favoured in this sprint handicap.

6105 SWARLANDFENCE.CO.UK H'CAP (DIV I) 7f
5:00 (5:04) (Class 6) (0-60,60) 3-Y-O+ **£1,617** (£481; £240 ; £120) **Stalls** Centre

Form RPR
6030 **1** **Mango Music**[17] 5543 9 -9-9 59 .... BarryMcHugh 12 70
(David Thompson) *dwlt: hld up: hdwy over 2f out: led appr fnl f: kpt on strly* **40/1**
0040 **2** 2¾ **Maggie Mey (IRE)**[16] 5590 4 -9-0 50 .... DanielTudhope 13 54
(Lawrence Mullaney) *prom: rdn over 2f out: chsd wnr fnl f: one pce* **10/1**
0604 **3** 2 **Georgebernardshaw (IRE)**[3] 5999 7 -9-5 55 ....(p) RobbieFitzpatrick 9 53
(Richard Guest) *led to appr fnl f: kpt on same pce* **12/1**
4064 **4** *hd* **River Ardeche**[13] 5713 7 -9-5 60 .... ShaneBKelly(5) 11 58
(Tracy Waggott) *in tch: rdn and edgd rt over 2f out: sn outpcd: edgd lft and kpt on fnl f* **11/2**[2]
4135 **5** 2¼ **Jupiter Fidius**[52] 4295 5 -9-2 59 ....(p) GemmaTutty(7) 15 51
(Karen Tutty) *bhd: drvn along 1/2-way: hdwy over 1f out: kpt on: nvr rchd ldrs* **13/2**[3]
060- **6** *nk* **Gertmegalush (IRE)**[322] 7055 5 -9-2 55 .... GaryBartley(3) 16 46
(Noel Wilson) *hld up: drvn along and outpcd 3f out: rallied over 1f out: nt pce to chal* **16/1**
0244 **7** 1 **Carrie's Magic**[6] 5917 5 -9-2 52 .... MichaelO'Connell 14 40
(Alistair Whillans) *chsd ldr: drvn over 2f out: wknd fnl f* **3/1**[1]
104 **8** 1¼ **Last Destination (IRE)**[23] 5341 4 -9-7 57 .... GrahamLee 10 42
(Nigel Tinkler) *dwlt: bhd tl hdwy over 1f out: kpt on: nvr able to chal* **10/1**
1325 **9** 3¼ **Oakbrook**[11] 5757 3 -9-4 58 .... PaulMulrennan 2 33
(Ann Duffield) *in tch: drvn over 2f out: wknd fnl f* **12/1**
0030 **10** 2¼ **Brave Battle**[17] 5543 4 -9-2 52 ....(v) AmyRyan 4 22
(Ron Barr) *hld up in tch: outpcd over 2f out: sn btn* **25/1**
000 **11** 3 **Geeaitch**[69] 3735 3 -9-6 60 .... TomEaves 7 21
(Anthony Carson) *stdd s: hld up: struggling 1/2-way: sn btn* **10/1**
5630 **12** 6 **Divertimenti (IRE)**[14] 5681 8 -9-7 60 .... RyanClark(3) 1
(Roy Bowring) *midfield: drvn and outpcd over 2f out: sn btn* **25/1**
300 **13** 8 **Overwhelm**[21] 5416 4 -8-10 53 .... WilliamTwiston-Davies(7) 8
(Alan McCabe) *in tch tl rdn and wknd over 2f out: eased whn no ch fnl f* **18/1**
005 **14** 28 **Pelican Rock (IRE)**[13] 5720 3 -8-13 53 ....(v[1]) DuranFentiman 3
(Andrew Crook) *bhd: struggling after 3f: t.o* **40/1**

1m 28.67s (0.87) **Going Correction** +0.15s/f (Good)
WFA 3 from 4yo+ 4lb **14**Ran SP% 120.1
Speed ratings (Par 101): **101,97,95,95,92 92,91,89,86,83 80,73,64,32**
Tote Swingers 1&2 £104.90, 2&3 £33.70, 1&3 £71.30 CSF £372.08 CT £4382.36 TOTE £63.20 : £15.50, £4.10 , £4.30 ; EX 856.80 TRIFECTA Not won. .
Owner C P M Racing **Bred** A G Antoniades **Trained** Bolam, Co Durham
■ Clapped was withdrawn (12/1, ref to ent stalls). Deduct 5p in the £ under R4.

FOCUS
Division one of a low-grade handicap and those middle-to-stands' side again seemed to benefit. Weak form.
Mango Music Official explanation: trainer said, regarding apparent improvement in form, that the mare benefited from the step up in trip.
Last Destination (IRE) Official explanation: jockey said gelding ran flat

6106 SWARLANDFENCE.CO.UK H'CAP (DIV II) 7f
5:30 (5:36) (Class 6) (0-60,60) 3-Y-O+ **£1,617** (£481; £240 ; £120) **Stalls** Centre

Form RPR
60 **1** **Cross The Boss (IRE)**[8] 5824 5 -9-0 50 ....(t) PhillipMakin 9 59
(Ben Haslam) *hld up: stdy hdwy over 2f out: chal ins fnl f: kpt on wl to ld towards fin* **16/1**
6256 **2** *hd* **Thrust Control (IRE)**[16] 5590 5 -8-13 49 ....(p) FrederikTylicki 12 57
(Tracy Waggott) *led: rdn 3f out: hrd pressed fnl f: kpt on: hdd nr fin* **7/1**[2]
0301 **3** ½ **Ryedale Dancer (IRE)**[14] 5671 4 -9-9 59 .... RobbieFitzpatrick 14 66
(Richard Guest) *hld up: rdn over 2f out: hdwy over 1f out: kpt on fnl f: hld nr fin* **8/1**[3]
02 **4** 2½ **Dolly Diva**[17] 5545 3 -9-6 60 .... MickyFenton 1 59
(Paul Midgley) *missed break: bhd: rdn 3f out: gd hdwy fnl f: nt rch first three* **25/1**
-161 **5** ¾ **Burnwynd Boy**[30] 5084 7 -9-7 57 .... PJMcDonald 16 55
(Ian Semple) *hld up in midfield: smooth hdwy over 2f out: rdn over 1f out: kpt on same pce fnl f* **7/2**[1]
4642 **6** 1¼ **Iceblast**[21] 5428 4 -9-3 60 .... MatthewHopkins(7) 15 55
(Michael Easterby) *t.k.h: midfield: drvn and outpcd over 2f out: kpt on fnl f: nvr able to chal* **7/1**[2]
0061 **7** 1¼ **Windygoul Lad**[11] 5757 3 -9-3 57 .... AndrewMullen 13 47
(Keith Dalgleish) *prom: drvn over 2f out: edgd lft and one pce appr fnl f* **16/1**
0034 **8** 1¼ **Stilettoesinthemud (IRE)**[15] 5632 4 -9-4 54 ....(p[1]) PaulMulrennan 8 42
(James Given) *cl up: rdn 3f out: no ex appr fnl f* **11/1**
0000 **9** *nk* **Music Festival (USA)**[16] 5588 5 -9-5 55 .... GrahamLee 7 42
(Jim Goldie) *in tch: drvn along 3f out: wknd over 1f out* **12/1**
6206 **10** 1 **Cross Of Lorraine (IRE)**[12] 5740 9 -9-6 56 ....(b) TonyHamilton 10 40
(Chris Grant) *bhd: drvn along 1/2-way: kpt on fnl f: nvr able to chal* **40/1**
0600 **11** 1½ **Dancing Maite**[27] 5203 7 -9-5 58 ....(b) RyanClark(3) 11 38
(Roy Bowring) *cl up: rdn over 2f out: wknd over 1f out* **25/1**
4020 **12** *nse* **Tukitinyasok (IRE)**[23] 5341 5 -9-6 56 ....(p) TomEaves 4 36
(Clive Mulhall) *cl up tl rdn and wknd over 2f out* **16/1**
3602 **13** *nk* **Bygones For Coins (IRE)**[7] 5543 4 -8-9 52 ....(p) KevinStott(7) 6 31
(Robert Johnson) *in tch: drvn over 2f out: sn wknd* **10/1**
3500 **14** 10 **Zaffy (IRE)**[12] 5734 3 -9-0 54 .... DuranFentiman 5
(Tim Easterby) *reluctant to enter stalls: bhd: struggling over 2f out: sn btn* **25/1**
6050 **15** 16 **Stylistickhill (IRE)**[24] 5310 4 -9-1 54 ....(tp) DeclanCannon(3) 3
(Scott Dixon) *towards rr: struggling after 3f: sn lost tch: t.o* **8/1**[3]

1m 28.83s (1.03) **Going Correction** +0.15s/f (Good)
WFA 3 from 4yo+ 4lb **15**Ran SP% 126.2
Speed ratings (Par 101): **100,99,99,96,95 94,92,91,90,89 88,87,87,76,57**
Tote Swingers 1&2 £22.50, 2&3 £13.30, 1&3 £38.00 CSF £124.37 CT £992.16 TOTE £27.00 : £7.50, £1.90 , £3.00 ; EX 218.40 TRIFECTA Not won. .
Owner Widdop Wanderers **Bred** Dermot Brennan & Associates Ltd **Trained** Middleham Moor, N Yorks

FOCUS
All the momentum was again with the high-drawn runners challenging centre-field in the second division of this handicap.
Cross The Boss (IRE) Official explanation: trainer said, regarding apparent improvement in form, that the gelding benefited from the drop back in trip.
Dancing Maite Official explanation: jockey said gelding had no more to give
Tukitinyasok(IRE) Official explanation: jockey said gelding hung left throughout
Stylistickhill(IRE) Official explanation: vet said filly finished lame left-fore
T/Jkpt: Not won. T/Plt: £224.80 to a £1 stake. Pool: £72,906.72 - 236.65 winning tickets. T/Qpdt: £11.40 to £1. Pool: £7,665.24 - 494.40 w. tckts RY

6107a - 6113a (Foreign Racing) See RI

5909 LEICESTER (R-H)
Tuesday, September 11

OFFICIAL GOING: Good (good to firm in places; 7.8)
Wind: Fresh across Weather: Cloudy

6114 BETFAIR FUNDS THE PJA DOCTOR E B F MAIDEN STKS 7f 9y
2:20 (2:20) (Class 4) 2-Y-O **£4,528** (£1,347; £673 ; £336) **Stalls** High

Form RPR
5 **1** **Penny Rose**[41] 4707 2 -8-12 0 .... JoeFanning 12 80+
(Mark Johnston) *a.p: pushed along over 2f out: led 1f out: r.o* **12/1**
2 ¾ **Greatwood** 2 -9-0 0 .... PatrickHills(3) 10 83+
(Luca Cumani) *s.i.s: hld up: swtchd lft and hdwy over 1f out: r.o to go 2nd towards fin: could nt rch wnr* **7/1**[3]
322 **3** 1¼ **Intimidate**[12] 5765 2 -9-3 84 .... WilliamBuick 3 80
(Jeremy Noseda) *chsd ldrs: rdn and ev ch over 1f out: styd on same pce ins fnl f* **11/8**[1]
4 1¼ **Half A Person (IRE)** 2 -9-3 0 .... PaulHanagan 11 77
(Peter Chapple-Hyam) *chsd ldr tl led wl over 1f out: hdd 1f out: no ex ins fnl f* **18/1**
2230 **5** 3 **Bold Prediction (IRE)**[17] 5602 2 -9-3 82 .... RichardHughes 8 69
(Richard Hannon) *hld up in tch: rdn over 2f out: no ex fnl f* **9/2**[2]
642 **6** *shd* **Jontleman (IRE)**[17] 5574 2 -9-3 76 .... SamHitchcott 4 68
(Mick Channon) *led: rdn and hdd wl over 1f out: no ex fnl f* **10/1**
04 **7** *nk* **Echo Brava**[15] 5685 2 -9-3 0 .... TomQueally 13 68+
(John Gallagher) *hld up: hdwy u.p over 1f out: hung rt ins fnl f: nvr nrr* **80/1**
8 ½ **Soaring Spirits (IRE)** 2 -9-3 0 .... AndreaAtzeni 2 66
(Roger Varian) *prom: rdn over 1f out: wknd ins fnl f* **20/1**
5 **9** 2½ **Sakhee's Rose**[26] 5275 2 -8-12 0 .... JamesDoyle 6 55
(Roger Charlton) *mid-div: pushed along 1/2-way: nvr trbld ldrs* **25/1**
6 **10** *hd* **Mizyen (IRE)**[25] 5303 2 -9-3 0 .... IanMongan 9 59
(James Tate) *hld up: pushed along over 2f out: nvr on terms* **12/1**
00 **11** 2¼ **Astrum**[11] 5785 2 -9-3 0 .... JamesMillman 5 54
(Rod Millman) *hld up: nvr on terms* **150/1**
12 3½ **Herod The Great** 2 -9-3 0 .... FergusSweeney 14 44
(Alan King) *s.i.s: hld up: hdwy over 2f out: rdn and wknd over 1f out* **100/1**
06 **13** *nk* **Foie Gras**[57] 4149 2 -9-3 0 .... DarryllHolland 1 44
(William Muir) *chsd ldrs: rdn over 2f out: wknd fnl f* **80/1**
00 **14** 1¼ **Downright Dizzie**[60] 4056 2 -8-9 0 .... RyanClark(3) 7 35
(Tom Keddy) *a towards rr: bhd fr 1/2-way* **100/1**
0 **15** 2 **Chocala (IRE)**[15] 5684 2 -9-3 0 .... DaneO'Neill 15 35
(Alan King) *mid-div: rdn over 2f out: sn wknd* **100/1**
0050 **16** *hd* **Royal Caper**[25] 5321 2 -9-3 68 .... DaraghO'Donohoe 16 35
(John Ryan) *chsd ldrs: pushed along 1/2-way: wknd over 1f out* **66/1**

1m 25.38s (-0.82) **Going Correction** -0.075s/f (Good) **16**Ran SP% 118.7
Speed ratings (Par 97): **101,100,98,97,93 93,93,92,89,89 87,83,82,81,79 78**
toteswingers 1&2 £17.20, 2&3 £4.20, 1&3 £6.00 CSF £87.99 TOTE £16.20 : £2.60 , £4.00 , £1.60 ; EX 112.20 .
Owner Greenland Park Stud **Bred** Mr & Mrs G Middlebrook **Trained** Middleham Moor, N Yorks

FOCUS
The field came up the centre of the track and this maiden should produce winners. The race is around the third to his latest form, with some down the field and the time fitting.

NOTEBOOK
Penny Rose ◆ is bred to need middle-distances and found 6f too sharp on last month's debut here. She was different gear this time, though, and picked up well to strike the front well inside the last and give her trainer his fourth victory in this race in the past ten years. She can go on from here. (tchd 11-1)
Greatwood ◆, an 85,000gns half-brother to the winning stayer Bridgehampton, was backed to run a big race on this debut and duly did so. Held up out the back early, he came home in most eyecatching style only to find that one had gone beyond recall. He will get further and will be winning before long. (op 16-1)
Intimidate, rated 84 after placing in his first three starts, had every chance entering the last furlong before getting outpaced by the first two. He can win an ordinary maiden, but may be better off in nurseries when exposed sorts. (op 5-4)
Half A Person (IRE) ◆, a 35,000GBP half-brother to a winning juvenile sprinter, was always up with the pace and ran a fine debut. He will be winning races. (op 25-1)
Bold Prediction (IRE) rated 82 and back in a maiden after finishing well beaten in a York nursery when stepped up to this trip, failed to pick up for pressure and he looks to be going the wrong way. (tchd 4-1)
Jontleman(IRE), progressive in his first three starts and rated 76, made the running until picked off over a furlong from home and is another who would probably be better off in nurseries. (op 8-1 tchd 15-2)
Echo Brava ◆ was given plenty to do but stayed on nicely when switched to the nearside and should do even better in nurseries for which he is now qualified. (op 66-1)
Soaring Spirits (IRE) an already gelded half-brother to three winners at up to 1m1f, showed ability on this debut and should appreciate a bit further with this experience under his belt. (op 28-1)

6115 BETTER PRICES ON BETFAIR MOBILE (S) STKS 7f 9y
2:50 (2:50) (Class 6) 2-Y-O **£1,617** (£481; £240 ; £120) **Stalls** High

Form RPR
1 **Laughing Rock (IRE)** 2 -8-7 0 .... AndreaAtzeni 14 62+
(Robert Eddery) *s.i.s: hld up: hdwy over 2f out: shkn up to ld ins fnl f: sn clr* **8/1**
0000 **2** 4 **Cromwell Rose (IRE)**[11] 5799 2 -8-7 40 ....(b[1]) MartinLane 13 50
(John Weymes) *chsd ldrs: pushed along over 2f out: led over 1f out: rdn and hdd ins fnl f: no ex* **100/1**
00 **3** 3¼ **Kubera (IRE)**[15] 5684 2 -8-12 0 .... LiamKeniry 3 47
(J S Moore) *chsd ldrs: rdn over 2f out: no ex fnl f* **10/1**
0 **4** 3½ **Sad But True (IRE)**[6] 5619 2 -8-12 0 ....(v[1]) SeanLevey 2 37
(Alan McCabe) *led: rdn and hdd over 1f out: wknd ins fnl f* **20/1**

0652 **5** ½ **Sojoum**[15] 5675 2-8-7 57 SamHitchcott 9 31
(Mick Channon) *chsd ldrs: rdn over 2f out: wknd over 1f out* **11/4**[1]

254 **6** 1 **Juana Belen**[25] 5291 2-8-8 53 ow1 GrahamGibbons 12 30
(David Barron) *hld up: hdwy 1/2-way: rdn and wknd over 1f out* **11/2**[3]

0250 **7** 1¼ **Kimvara**[11] 5807 2-8-4 55 RyanPowell(3) 4 25
(Joseph Tuite) *prom: rdn over 2f out: wknd over 1f out* **14/1**

000 **8** 1 **Synphonic Air (IRE)**[27] 5221 2-8-7 50 (p) LiamJones 7 23
(John Weymes) *chsd ldrs: rdn over 3f out: wknd over 1f out* **66/1**

050 **9** nk **Tyson The Byson**[53] 4310 2-8-9 46 MichaelMetcalfe(3) 16 27
(Mrs K Burke) *s.i.s: hld up: rdn over 2f out: n.d* **33/1**

063 **10** ¾ **Gowortonian (IRE)**[4] 5997 2-8-7 53 DarrenEgan(5) 6 25
(Ronald Harris) *s.i.s: hdwy over 5f out: rdn and wknd 2f out* **16/1**

0000 **11** 1¼ **Karl Marx (IRE)**[11] 5806 2-8-12 31 (p) DavidProbert 1 22
(Mark Usher) *sn pushed along towards rr: drvn over 4f out: sn bhd* **150/1**

0340 **12** 1½ **Age Of Bronze**[11] 5806 2-8-12 63 RichardHughes 15 18
(Richard Hannon) *hld up: rdn over 2f out: a in rr* **4/1**[2]

4000 **13** 10 **Rio Cato**[32] 5061 2-8-7 45 (v[1]) ChrisCatlin 11
(Ed Dunlop) *hld up: rdn over 2f out: a in rr* **25/1**

6 **14** 13 **Annabella Milbanke**[25] 5291 2-8-7 0 RichardKingscote 5
(John Holt) *chsd ldrs: rdn over 4f out: wknd over 2f out: t.o* **40/1**

2033 **15** 4 **Strawberry Duck (IRE)**[56] 4195 2-8-0 52 IanBurns(7) 8
(Amy Weaver) *in rr: rdn over 4f out: bhd fr over 2f out: t.o* **14/1**

1m 26.29s (0.09) **Going Correction** -0.075s/f (Good) **15** Ran SP% **118.6**
Speed ratings (Par 93): **96,91,87,83,83 82,80,79,79,78 76,75,63,48,44**
toteswingers 1&2 £110.50, 2&3 £106.10, 1&3 £15.30 CSF £664.11 TOTE £11.70: £4.00, £18.30, £3.10; EX 1598.10.The winner was bought by P McEntee for 13,000gns.
Owner EDS Roofing Supplies Ltd **Bred** Moorpark Stud **Trained** Newmarket, Suffolk

FOCUS
A very poor seller for which the winning time was 0.91 seconds slower than the maiden, but the winner looks much better than a plater.

NOTEBOOK
Laughing Rock(IRE), a 3,000GBP 2yo out of a winning juvenile sprinter, was the only newcomer in the field. Held up early, she travelled into the race beautifully and cruised to the front on the bridle inside the last before scooting clear. She is obviously a lot better than this grade and it was no surprise there was plenty of interest in her at the auction. She was eventually sold to Phil McEntee for 13,000gns. (op 12-1 tchd 7-1)
Cromwell Rose(IRE) was blinkered for the first time having shown nothing in her first five starts and stepped up considerably under a prominent ride. She was unlucky to bump into one here, but her rating of 40 doesn't do much for those in behind and it's far from certain she will reproduce this next time. (tchd 80-1)
Kubera(IRE) was down in grade after finishing well beaten in a couple of maidens and showed up for a long way, but may not have achieved very much. He will do well to find a weaker seller than this. (op 16-1)
Sad But True(IRE), dropped in class after finishing tailed-off on last month's Beverley debut, showed more in the first-time visor here but it remains to be seen if he can build on it. (op 16-1)
Sojoum had finished runner-up in both previous tries in sellers, but was disappointing here, coming off the bridle a long way out and not finding very much. (op 3-1 tchd 10-3)
Juana Belen was racing away from Catterick for the first time after showing a little ability in a couple of sellers there, but didn't match that form on this different track. (op 9-2 tchd 6-1)

6116 BETFAIR COMMITS £40 MILLION TO BRITISH RACING CONDITIONS STKS 5f 2y
3:20 (3:20) (Class 3) 3-Y-0+ **£6,931** (£2,074; £1,037; £519; £258) **Stalls** High

Form RPR

3101 **1** **Ballista (IRE)**[10] 5829 4-8-12 99 RichardKingscote 8 109
(Tom Dascombe) *led stands' side: rdn to ld overall over 1f out: r.o wl* **2/1**[1]

10/0 **2** 2¼ **Temple Meads**[129] 1857 4-8-9 109 RichardHughes 4 98
(Ed McMahon) *s.i.s: racd centre: hld up: hdwy 2f out: rdn to chse wnr and hung lft over 1f out: styd on same pce ins fnl f: 1st of 6 in gp* **5/2**[2]

0004 **3** 1¼ **Swiss Cross**[15] 5663 5-8-9 92 (t) DavidProbert 9 93
(Phil McEntee) *chsd wnr on stands' side: rdn over 1f out: styd on same pce fnl f: last of 2 that side* **10/1**

-400 **4** 3½ **Amour Propre**[39] 4762 6-9-0 107 DaneO'Neill 3 85
(Henry Candy) *racd centre: trckd ldrs: racd keenly: overall ldr 1/2-way: rdn: hung lft and hdd over 1f out: wknd ins fnl f: 2nd of 6 in gp* **4/1**[3]

0104 **5** 5 **La Fortunata**[23] 5385 5-8-12 90 AndreaAtzeni 7 65
(Eve Johnson Houghton) *racd centre: chsd ldrs tl rdn and wknd over 1f out: 3rd of 6 in gp* **11/1**

6 1½ **Ubetterbegood (ARG)**[177] 4-9-1 95 PatDobbs 2 63
(Robert Cowell) *racd centre: hld up: rdn 1/2-way: a in rr: 4th of 6 in gp* **28/1**

-436 **7** ½ **Shoshoni Wind**[104] 2602 4-8-4 95 PaulHanagan 6 50
(Kevin Ryan) *racd centre: chsd ldr to 1/2-way: wknd over 1f out: 5th of 6 in gp* **10/1**

1651 **8** 2¾ **El McGlynn (IRE)**[36] 4881 3-7-13 72 HannahNunn(7) 1 43
(Peter Salmon) *racd centre: overall ldr to 1/2-way: wknd wl over 1f out: last of 6 in gp* **66/1**

58.63s (-1.37) **Going Correction** -0.075s/f (Good)
WFA 3 from 4yo+ 1lb **8** Ran SP% **113.4**
Speed ratings (Par 107): **107,103,101,95,87 85,84,80**
toteswingers 1&2 £1.90, 2&3 £5.70, 1&3 £4.00 CSF £7.00 TOTE £3.90: £2.10, £1.10, £3.50; EX 9.00.
Owner Well Done Top Man Partnership **Bred** Sj Partnership **Trained** Malpas, Cheshire

FOCUS
An interesting conditions sprint in which recent wellbeing counted for much more than BHA ratings. The larger group of six raced more towards the centre of the track, but two came up the stands' rail and they finished first and third. The winner showed his Chester win was no fluke.

NOTEBOOK
Ballista(IRE) was very impressive when making all from a terrible draw in a Chester handicap ten days earlier and was raised 9lb for that. Despite still having a bit to find with a few of these on adjusted official ratings, he proved more than up to the task and pulled right away inside the last furlong. How much racing against the stands' rail affected his performance is hard to say, but he looks a most progressive sprinter and is well worth a try at Pattern level. (op 5-2 tchd 15-8)
Temple Meads had the highest BHA rating in the field having won the Weatherbys Super Sprint and Group 2 Mill Reef Stakes as a 2yo, but his 12th of 16 in the Palace House Stakes at Newmarket in May was his only appearance in the past two years. He had every chance until understandably weakening close home, but even though he had 13lb in hand of the winner at the weights, this still has to be considered a better effort. He may well come on again for it and his next outing should be more informative. (op 10-3)
Swiss Cross, without a win in 15 months, ran creditably but he was the only other to take the stands' rail route apart from the winner. He ideally needs further and seems to reserve his very best for Epsom these days. (op 9-1 tchd 11-1)

Amour Propre was having his first start outside of stakes company since his third outing at two, but the way he weakened inside the last after holding every chance a furlong out was worrying. He is looking a shadow of his former self. (op 3-1 tchd 5-1)

6117 BETFAIR SPONSORS THE STABLE STAFF CANTEEN E B F MAIDEN FILLIES' STKS 1m 60y
3:50 (3:50) (Class 4) 2-Y-0 **£4,528** (£1,347; £673; £336) **Stalls** Low

Form RPR

03 **1** **Kikonga**[18] 5551 2-9-0 0 KirstyMilczarek 12 77
(Luca Cumani) *chsd ldrs: rdn to ld ins fnl f: jst hld on* **9/1**[3]

2 nk **Nasijah** 2-9-0 0 IanMongan 6 76+
(James Tate) *a.p: rdn over 2f out: r.o* **40/1**

3 ½ **Muthmera (USA)** 2-9-0 0 PaulHanagan 13 75+
(Roger Varian) *hld up in tch: pushed along over 3f out: r.o* **8/1**[2]

4 ½ **Chittenden (USA)** 2-9-0 0 MickaelBarzalona 3 74
(Mahmood Al Zarooni) *chsd ldr: rdn to ld over 1f out: hdd and unable qck ins fnl f* **8/1**[2]

6 **5** nk **Divergence (IRE)**[18] 5551 2-9-0 0 HayleyTurner 1 73
(Michael Bell) *sn pushed along to chse ldrs: rdn over 2f out: r.o* **16/1**

3 **6** ½ **Centred (IRE)**[25] 5300 2-9-0 0 WilliamBuick 7 72
(Sir Michael Stoute) *hld up in tch: pushed along over 3f out: r.o: nt gng pce to chal* **10/11**[1]

5 **7** 2¾ **Bountiful Bess**[22] 5407 2-9-0 0 MickyFenton 2 66
(Pam Sly) *led: rdn and hdd over 1f out: no ex ins fnl f* **66/1**

0 **8** 1 **Hermosa Vaquera (IRE)**[40] 4739 2-9-0 0 RobertHavlin 8 64
(Peter Chapple-Hyam) *hld up: rdn over 2f out: nvr trbld ldrs* **66/1**

9 hd **Bowland Princess** 2-9-0 0 JamesDoyle 4 63
(Ed Dunlop) *hld up: pushed along over 2f out: nvr on terms* **50/1**

0 **10** nk **Funky Cold Medina**[18] 5550 2-9-0 0 TomQueally 11 62
(Peter Chapple-Hyam) *hld up: rdn over 2f out: n.d* **16/1**

11 6 **Dalaway (IRE)** 2-9-0 0 SamHitchcott 10 50
(Mick Channon) *s.i.s: hld up: hmpd over 4f out: n.d* **80/1**

4 **12** 23 **Perfect Pose (IRE)**[7] 5912 2-9-0 0 RichardHughes 9
(Richard Hannon) *hld up: rdn over 3f out: wknd wl over 1f out: t.o* **16/1**

13 1¾ **Tessarini (USA)** 2-9-0 0[1] AhmedAjtebi 5
(Mahmood Al Zarooni) *hld up: bhd fnl 3f: t.o* **12/1**

1m 45.8s (0.70) **Going Correction** -0.075s/f (Good) **13** Ran SP% **118.6**
Speed ratings (Par 94): **93,92,92,91,91 90,88,87,86,86 80,57,55**
toteswingers 1&2 £49.60, 2&3 £54.10, 1&3 £7.70 CSF £331.88 TOTE £9.00: £2.00, £7.70, £2.80; EX 463.70.
Owner Fittocks Stud **Bred** Fittocks Stud Ltd **Trained** Newmarket, Suffolk

FOCUS
An interesting maiden, but with only about 3l covering the first six it remains to be seen how strong the form is. A few caught the eye, however.

NOTEBOOK
Kikonga improved plenty from her debut when third at Newmarket last time and took another step forward here, quickening up well from a handy position inside the last and holding on well. Admittedly she was the most experienced in the field, but she is bred to come into her own over middle-distances and should be a nice handicapper for next year. (op 10-1)
Nasijah ◆ ran on very nicely down the outside under pressure and was bearing down on the winner at the line. This 30,000gns half-sister to three winners at up to 1m4f should win races and is another likely to improve for a stiffer test at three. (tchd 33-1)
Muthmera(USA) ◆ was also doing all her best work late and came home strongly down the wide outside. Out of a half-sister to several winners, many of whom stayed really well, she is in the Fillies' Mile and can be expected to come on plenty for this. (tchd 10-1)
Chittenden(USA), a £140,000 half-sister to five winners including a Grade 3 winner in the US, looked the winner when hitting the front over a furlong out, but was soon run right out of the places. This was a fair enough introduction. (tchd 9-1)
Divergence(IRE), just over 2l behind Kikonga when sixth of nine on her Newmarket debut, kept plugging on and ran close to the form of that first run with the winner. She is bred to come into her own over middle-distances and looks one for handicaps next year. (op 14-1)
Centred(IRE) is bred to have appreciated this longer trip following her promising debut when third of ten over 7f at Kempton (fifth has won since), but she was having to be niggled along over 3f from home and merely plugged on. This was disappointing. (op 6-5 tchd 5-6)
Bountiful Bess, a fair fifth of ten on her Kempton debut, ran well out in front for a long way and is another bred to make up into a middle-distance handicapper next term. (tchd 50-1 and 80-1)
Tessarini(USA) Official explanation: jockey said filly ran green

6118 BETFAIR DON'T SETTLE FOR LESS H'CAP 1m 3f 183y
4:20 (4:22) (Class 5) (0-70,70) 3-Y-0+ **£2,587** (£770; £384; £192) **Stalls** Low

Form RPR

-620 **1** **Villa Royale**[56] 4183 3-9-1 **68** JamesDoyle 8 78
(Harry Dunlop) *hld up: hdwy over 2f out: led over 1f out: rdn out* **20/1**

6514 **2** ¾ **Scarlet Belle**[21] 5442 3-9-0 **67** HayleyTurner 3 75
(Marcus Tregoning) *chsd ldrs: led 2f out: rdn and hdd over 1f out: styd on* **9/2**[2]

6634 **3** 6 **Grand Gold**[81] 1568 3-9-3 **70** (t) GeorgeBaker 2 68
(Seamus Durack) *hld up: hdwy over 2f out: sn rdn: styd on same pce fnl f* **6/1**

6153 **4** 1½ **Cosmic Halo**[60] 4046 3-8-12 **65** PaulHanagan 7 61
(Richard Fahey) *chsd ldrs: rdn over 2f out: no ex fnl f* **9/4**[1]

0636 **5** 6 **Moose Moran (USA)**[17] 5596 5-9-10 **68** (v) KirstyMilczarek 9 54
(Olivia Maylam) *sn led: rdn and hdd 2f out: wknd fnl f* **33/1**

0500 **6** 7 **Chapelle du Roi (USA)**[25] 5297 3-9-2 **69** (p) TedDurcan 4 44
(David Lanigan) *chsd ldrs: rdn over 3f out: wknd over 2f out: eased fnl f* **8/1**

003 **7** 13 **Seeking The Buck (USA)**[47] 4511 8-9-12 **70** TomQueally 6 24
(Amy Weaver) *s.i.s: hld up: pushed along 1/2-way: rdn over 2f out: sn wknd and eased: t.o* **11/2**

5302 **8** 17 **Finity Run (GER)**[12] 5761 3-9-3 **70** JoeFanning 1
(Mark Johnston) *prom: rdn over 3f out: wknd over 2f out: eased: t.o* **5/1**[3]

2m 32.34s (-1.56) **Going Correction** -0.075s/f (Good)
WFA 3 from 5yo+ 9lb **8** Ran SP% **114.1**
Speed ratings (Par 103): **102,101,97,96,92 87,79,67**
toteswingers 1&2 £19.90, 2&3 £6.10, 1&3 £11.00 CSF £106.80 CT £617.50 TOTE £26.20: £4.80, £2.20, £2.00; EX 171.50.
Owner J H Richmond-Watson **Bred** Lawn Stud **Trained** Lambourn, Berks

FOCUS
An ordinary middle-distance handicap. It was sound run and the first pair were clear, so they've been given some credit for this.

6119 BETFAIR BOOSTS PRIZE MONEY AT LEICESTER H'CAP 7f 9y
4:50 (4:50) (Class 3) (0-95,92) 3-Y-0+ **£6,663** (£1,982; £990; £495) **Stalls** High

Form RPR

304 **1** **Amazing Amoray (IRE)**[7] 5910 4-8-10 **78** oh1 GrahamGibbons 3 85
(David Barron) *led 2f: chsd ldr: rdn to ld 1f out: r.o* **9/2**[1]

0200 **2** *nk* **White Frost (IRE)**[17] 5572 4-9-9 **91** .... MichaelHills 1 97
(Charles Hills) *chsd ldr tl led 5f out: rdn and hdd 1f out: r.o* **15/2**[3]
3000 **3** *3/4* **Democretes**[31] 5102 3-9-0 **86** .... RichardHughes 5 89
(Richard Hannon) *hld up: rdn over 1f out: r.o ins fnl f: nt rch ldrs* **9/2**[1]
0001 **4** *3/4* **Common Touch (IRE)**[26] 5269 4-9-6 **88** .... (p) PaulHanagan 6 90
(Richard Fahey) *chsd ldrs: rdn over 1f out: styd on same pce ins fnl f* **9/2**[1]
5205 **5** *shd* **Kingscroft (IRE)**[85] 3221 4-9-2 **84** .... JoeFanning 4 86
(Mark Johnston) *prom: rdn over 1f out: styd on same pce ins fnl f* **18/1**
0500 **6** *1 1/2* **Albaqaa**[13] 5746 7-9-9 **91** .... DarryllHolland 7 89
(P J O'Gorman) *s.i.s: hld up: hdwy over 1f out: sn rdn: no ex ins fnl f* **12/1**
1036 **7** *1/2* **Ducal**[17] 5572 4-9-8 **90** .... PatDobbs 8 86
(Mike Murphy) *s.i.s: hld up: rdn over 1f out: nvr trbld ldrs* **11/2**[2]
6/04 **8** *3/4* **Head Of Steam (USA)**[24] 5356 5-9-10 **92** .... EddieAhern 2 86
(Amanda Perrett) *chsd ldrs: rdn over 1f out: no ex fnl f* **17/2**
30-0 **9** *17* **Sea Soldier (IRE)**[134] 1708 4-9-2 **84** .... WilliamBuick 10 32
(Andrew Balding) *prom: rdn over 2f out: wknd over 1f out: eased* **11/1**

1m 24.28s (-1.92) **Going Correction** -0.075s/f (Good)
WFA 3 from 4yo+ 4lb **9** Ran SP% **113.5**
Speed ratings (Par 107): **107,106,105,104,104 103,102,101,82**
toteswingers 1&2 £8.70, 2&3 £6.00, 1&3 £4.00 CSF £37.61 CT £159.92 TOTE £4.70: £1.80, £4.10, £1.10; EX 49.60.
Owner Raymond Miquel **Bred** Marie & Mossy Fahy **Trained** Maunby, N Yorks

FOCUS

A decent handicap, but it was an advantage to be handy and the front pair were at the sharp end throughout. Sound form, the second setting the standard.

NOTEBOOK

Amazing Amoray(IRE) was 1lb wrong, but he ran well over C&D last time after a three-month break and that put him spot-on for this. Always handy, he battled on well to hit the front inside the last furlong and he obviously likes this track as both wins have now come here. (op 13-2)
White Frost(IRE) didn't take to the hood in his first two tries, but this was much better. He may have been at an advantage in racing up with the pace, however, and hasn't proved very consistent since completing a hat-trick off 5lb lower more than a year ago. (op 17-2 tchd 9-1)
Democretes, still 8lb higher than when winning a nursery a year ago, hadn't convinced in three previous tries beyond 6f, but this was an improvement especially as he was ridden much more patiently than the first two. He came home strongly and may not be handicapped out of things after all. (op 5-1 tchd 4-1)
Common Touch(IRE) was 3lb higher than when beating a subsequent winner in first-time cheekpieces at Newmarket last time and had every chance, but proved one paced under pressure inside the last furlong. (op 4-1)
Kingscroft(IRE) could never quite get to the leaders from the middle of the pack and although he won seven times in 2011, is now 0-10 this year. (op 16-1 tchd 14-1)
Albaqaa missed the break, which wasn't ideal given the way this race was run, and although he tried to make an effort towards the far side of the track over a furlong from home, he started to hang and could never make an impression. He needs further than this. (op 9-1)
Sea Soldier(IRE) Official explanation: jockey said gelding was unsuited by the good (good to firm places (watered)) ground

6120 READ RYAN MOORE EXCLUSIVELY ON BETFAIR APPRENTICE H'CAP 1m 1f 218y

5:20 (5:20) (Class 6) (0-65,70) 4-Y-O+ **£1,617** (£481; £240; £120) **Stalls** Low

Form RPR
2412 **1** **King's Masque**[6] 5950 6-9-7 **65** .... RobertWilliams 1 73
(Bernard Llewellyn) *a.p: led over 2f out: pushed out* **7/2**[1]
5320 **2** *1 1/2* **Ishikawa (IRE)**[19] 5506 4-9-5 **63** .... WilliamTwiston-Davies 5 68
(Alan King) *hld up: hdwy over 2f out: rdn over 1f out: styd on* **14/1**
5010 **3** *hd* **Bold Cross (IRE)**[15] 5688 9-9-7 **65** .... ThomasBrown 11 70
(Edward Bevan) *hld up: hdwy: nt clr run and swtchd rt over 2f out: rdn over 1f out: styd on* **18/1**
1253 **4** *4* **Honoured (IRE)**[24] 5345 5-9-2 **63** .... (t) DanielMuscutt[(3)] 6 60
(Michael Appleby) *chsd ldrs: rdn over 2f out: sn ev ch: no ex fnl f* **7/2**[1]
1215 **5** *1/2* **Highlife Dancer**[4] 5990 4-9-7 **70** 6ex .... (v) RobertTart[(5)] 9 66
(Mick Channon) *prom: rdn over 3f out: sn outpcd: styd on fnl f* **9/2**[2]
6065 **6** *3 1/2* **Scamperdale**[22] 5430 10-9-5 **63** .... (p) LauraBarry 10 52
(Brian Baugh) *hld up: hdwy over 3f out: wknd fnl f* **8/1**
5343 **7** *4* **Mighty Clarets (IRE)**[19] 5506 5-9-5 **63** .... GeorgeChaloner 8 44
(Barry Leavy) *chsd ldrs: rdn over 3f out: wknd over 1f out* **6/1**[3]
0166 **8** *1/2* **Ostentation**[11] 5809 5-9-7 **65** .... (b) NatashaEaton 3 45
(Gay Kelleway) *hld up: rdn and hung rt over 1f out: n.d* **20/1**
0005 **9** *1 1/2* **Gallego**[11] 5783 10-8-9 **53** .... JackDuern 2 30
(Richard Price) *hld up: a in rr* **18/1**
0-00 **10** *hd* **Mistress Shy**[29] 5179 5-8-7 **51** oh6 .... (t) NoelGarbutt 4 27
(Michael Appleby) *led: rdn and hdd over 2f out: wknd over 1f out* **100/1**
1040 **11** *1 1/2* **Cane Cat (IRE)**[25] 5310 5-8-12 **63** .... (t) AidenBlakemore[(7)] 7 36
(Tony Carroll) *hld up: rdn over 2f out: sn wknd* **20/1**

2m 7.89s (-0.01) **Going Correction** -0.075s/f (Good) **11** Ran SP% **115.7**
Speed ratings (Par 101): **97,95,95,92,92 89,86,85,84,84 83**
toteswingers 1&2 £6.60, 2&3 £16.00, 1&3 £13.40 CSF £52.60 CT £775.11 TOTE £5.70: £1.30, £3.80, £4.00; EX 53.40.
Owner B J Llewellyn **Bred** Deerfield Farm **Trained** Fochriw, Caerphilly

FOCUS

A moderate apprentice handicap. The winner was rated to last week's Lingfield form (well in on that).
Ostentation Official explanation: jockey said gelding hung right
T/Plt: £6,919.10 to a £1 stake. Pool of £62556.71 - 6.60 winning tickets. T/Qpdt: £80.40 to a £1 stake. Pool of £6351.16 - 58.40 winning tickets. CR

5585 REDCAR (L-H)

Tuesday, September 11

OFFICIAL GOING: Good (8.5)
Wind: fresh 1/2 against Weather: fine but very breezy

6121 WEATHERBYS BLOODSTOCK INSURANCE NURSERY 7f

2:30 (2:32) (Class 5) (0-75,72) 2-Y-O **£2,264** (£673; £336; £168) **Stalls** Centre

Form RPR
5242 **1** **Marhaba Malayeen (IRE)**[14] 5715 2-9-6 **71** .... (b) JamieSpencer 15 75
(Kevin Ryan) *w ldrs: led over 4f out: hld on wl* **9/2**[1]
050 **2** *1* **Loki's Strike**[59] 4114 2-8-12 **63** .... (b[1]) RobertWinston 1 67
(Mrs K Burke) *dwlt: edgd rt and hdwy over 2f out: styd on to take 2nd towards fin* **16/1**
0400 **3** *1/2* **Foolbythepool**[15] 5670 2-9-1 **66** .... GrahamLee 4 66
(Keith Dalgleish) *chsd ldrs: kpt on same pce fnl f* **10/1**[3]
056 **4** *2* **Roland**[99] 2747 2-8-2 **53** .... JimmyQuinn 5 48
(Kevin Ryan) *stmbld s: sn w ldrs: one pce fnl f* **12/1**
3046 **5** *1 3/4* **Inchy Coo**[25] 5292 2-9-0 **65** .... (p) DanielTudhope 12 55
(Tim Easterby) *led over 2f: chsd ldrs: one pce appr fnl f* **25/1**
043 **6** *1* **Danehill Flyer (IRE)**[13] 5727 2-9-1 **66** .... RoystonFfrench 10 54
(Philip Kirby) *chsd ldrs: drvn and outpcd over 2f out: kpt on fnl f* **6/1**[2]
400 **7** *1/2* **Oh Boy Oh Boy**[46] 4545 2-7-9 **51** ow1 .... NeilFarley[(5)] 9 38+
(James Moffatt) *s.s: hdwy over 2f out: kpt on: nt rch ldrs* **40/1**
404 **8** *1* **Miss Perfect**[34] 4952 2-8-9 **60** .... (v[1]) MichaelO'Connell 13 44
(John Quinn) *chsd ldrs: outpcd and lost pl over 3f out: kpt on fnl f* **11/1**
0335 **9** *1/2* **Annie Gogh**[8] 5887 2-9-0 **65** .... DuranFentiman 8 48
(Tim Easterby) *t.k.h towards rr: hdwy over 2f out: wknd over 1f out* **12/1**
4064 **10** *2* **Marabout (IRE)**[33] 5009 2-8-6 **57** .... PJMcDonald 6 34
(Mel Brittain) *chsd ldrs: edgd lft over 1f out: sn wknd* **10/1**[3]
4114 **11** *3/4* **Lord Avonbrook**[25] 5292 2-9-7 **72** .... FrannyNorton 14 48
(Andrew Crook) *chsd ldrs: wknd over 1f out* **14/1**
6430 **12** *3/4* **Bayan Kasirga (IRE)**[26] 5254 2-9-5 **70** .... FrederikTylicki 7 44
(Richard Fahey) *trckd ldrs: effrt over 2f out: lost pl over 1f out* **6/1**[2]
5055 **13** *3* **Red Koko (IRE)**[25] 5291 2-7-12 **49** oh4 .... (b[1]) JamesSullivan 16 15
(George Moore) *dwlt: sn chsng ldrs: wknd 2f out* **50/1**
5412 **14** *1 1/2* **Alexandrakollontai (IRE)**[22] 5424 2-8-6 **57** .... BarryMcHugh 2 19
(Alistair Whillans) *rr-div: hdwy 3f out: hmpd over 1f out: sn wknd* **11/1**
050 **15** *8* **Abraham Monro**[24] 5367 2-8-11 **62** .... TomEaves 11 3
(Kate Walton) *t.k.h: lost pl over 4f out: hung rt and sn bhd* **50/1**
F400 **16** *16* **Silver Fawn (IRE)**[97] 2822 2-8-1 **55** ow3 .... DeclanCannon[(3)] 3
(John Weymes) *w ldrs: hung lft and lost pl 3f out: sn bhd* **25/1**

1m 26.08s (1.58) **Going Correction** +0.10s/f (Good) **16** Ran SP% **123.6**
Speed ratings (Par 95): **94,92,92,90,88 86,86,85,84,82 81,80,77,75,66 48**
toteswingers 1&2 £15.70, 2&3 £2.60, 1&3 £36.00 CSF £76.24 CT £727.89 TOTE £4.80: £1.50, £5.20, £3.10, £3.30; EX 96.50 TRIFECTA Not won..
Owner Ahmad Al Shaikh **Bred** Cecil And Miss Alison Wiggins **Trained** Hambleton, N Yorks

FOCUS

The ground had eased slightly following an unexpected 10mm of rain overnight, with Jamie Spencer feeling it to be "on the easy side of good". Few got into what had looked a competitive nursery, the runner-up being the only to one to make ground from off the pace. Only a modest race, but the form may work out.

NOTEBOOK

Marhaba Malayeen(IRE) bumped into a heavily supported winner at Southwell (wore first-time blinkers) and he improved again returning to handicaps, making a lot of the running and seeing it out well. This looks his trip and he may be able to defy a small rise. (op 5-1)
Loki's Strike duly improved on his maiden form switching to nurseries in first-time blinkers, being the only one to make headway from the rear despite meeting trouble. He was hardly knuckling down under pressure, though, and it remains to be seen if the headgear works as well a second time. (op 22-1)
Foolbythepool, down 4lb, fared better returned to 7f on this less testing going. (op 11-1 tchd 12-1)
Roland looked a potential improver up in trip for this nursery debut, having been gelded since last seen in June, but he didn't have the pace to race on. He's entitled to come on again and can find a small race. (op 14-1)
Inchy Coo, up to 7f for the first time, bounced back from a modest effort at Catterick but is now 0-9.
Danehill Flyer(IRE), making his nursery debut, couldn't quicken and looks to need 1m. (op 4-1)
Oh Boy Oh Boy ran with some promise as he was slowest away but did make ground nearest the stands' rail.
Bayan Kasirga(IRE) was again below form and doesn't look to be progressing. (op 7-1 tchd 11-2)
Abraham Monro Official explanation: jockey said gelding hung right-handed throughout
Silver Fawn(IRE) Official explanation: jockey said gelding never travelled

6122 MARKET CROSS JEWELLERS MAIDEN AUCTION STKS 5f

3:00 (3:02) (Class 6) 2-Y-O **£1,704** (£503; £251) **Stalls** Centre

Form RPR
1 **Angus Og** 2-8-8 0 ow2 .... (e[1]) ConorHarrison[(7)] 7 79+
(Mrs K Burke) *wnt lft s: in rr: gd hdwy to ld over 1f out: drew clr* **5/1**[3]
2050 **2** *3 3/4* **Millie N Aire**[13] 5749 2-8-6 62 .... FrannyNorton 6 56
(Danielle McCormick) *trckd ldrs: kpt on same pce fnl f* **3/1**[1]
5005 **3** *1/2* **Why So Fast (IRE)**[48] 4471 2-8-1 62 .... [1] DavidBergin[(7)] 3 56+
(David O'Meara) *trckd ldrs: outpcd over 2f out: edgd rt over 1f out: styd on ins fnl f* **3/1**[1]
6 **4** *1* **Myanne**[14] 5709 2-8-8 0 .... [1] PaulMulrennan 4 53
(Ann Duffield) *n.m.r sn after s: sn trcking ldrs: effrt 2f out: kpt on same pce* **10/3**[2]
60 **5** *1 1/4* **Tartania**[14] 5709 2-8-4 0 .... MircoDemuro 5 44
(Scott Dixon) *led: edgd lft and hdd over 1f out: grad wknd* **20/1**
6 **6** *1/2* **Midnight Dream (FR)**[162] 1164 2-8-13 0 .... TomEaves 8 51
(Linda Stubbs) *dwlt: sn chsng ldrs: one pce over 1f out* **5/1**[3]
00 **7** *5* **Indies Gold**[13] 5727 2-8-11 0 .... GrahamLee 1 31+
(Ann Duffield) *chsd ldrs: outpcd and lost pl over 3f out: sn in rr* **33/1**
0003 **8** *7* **Elusive Shadow**[26] 5255 2-8-4 42 .... PatrickMathers 2
(Alan Brown) *chsd ldrs: lost pl 2f out* **50/1**

58.96s (0.36) **Going Correction** +0.10s/f (Good) **8** Ran SP% **116.1**
Speed ratings (Par 93): **101,95,94,92,90 89,81,70**
toteswingers 1&2 £3.20, 2&3 £2.90, 1&3 £3.40 CSF £20.38 TOTE £7.00: £1.50, £1.20, £1.30; EX 22.00 Trifecta £49.00 Pool: £741.03 - 11.17 winning units..
Owner D Simpson & Mrs E Burke **Bred** Shane O'Sullivan **Trained** Middleham Moor, N Yorks

FOCUS

A moderate juvenile maiden, with the placed runners both exposed 62-rated performers. The winner produced a decent level on his debut.

NOTEBOOK

Angus Og, a 16,000gns gelding whose pedigree is a blend of speed and stamina, was the only newcomer and proved far too good, this despite his rider putting up 2lb overweight. Wearing an eyeshield, he looks capable of making his mark in nurseries. (op 7-1)
Millie N Aire is now 0-9 and will remain vulnerable in maidens. (tchd 11-4)
Why So Fast(IRE) failed to improve for the first-time hood and it may take a drop to claiming/selling level for her to win. (op 7-2)
Myanne showed more than on debut, the first-time hood helping. She's probably one for low-grade handicaps down the line. (op 3-1 tchd 7-2)
Tartania again showed speed and is now qualified for a mark. (op 16-1)
Midnight Dream(FR), well held on April's C&D debut, failed to show any improvement but should find his level once handicapping. (op 11-2 tchd 6-1)

6123 WEATHERBYS FOREIGN EXCHANGE H'CAP 6f

3:30 (3:31) (Class 5) (0-75,75) 3-Y-O+ **£2,264** (£673; £336; £168) **Stalls** Centre

Form RPR
0531 **1** **Midnight Dynamo**[18] 5548 5-9-1 **69** .... GrahamLee 13 79
(Jim Goldie) *chsd ldrs: styd on to ld last 75yds: hung lft: drvn out* **11/1**
1411 **2** *1 3/4* **Meandmyshadow**[7] 5915 4-9-2 **73** 6ex .... DaleSwift[(3)] 5 77
(Alan Brown) *mde most: rdn and edgd lft over 1f out: hdd ins fnl f: no ex* **3/1**[1]

3500 **3** nse **Diman Waters (IRE)**[4] 6005 5-9-0 **73**........................(p) DarylByrne(5) 11 77
(Eric Alston) *chsd ldrs: kpt on same pce fnl f* **11/1**
0006 **4** ¾ **Wildcat Wizard (USA)**[23] 5388 6-8-11 **65**..................... PJMcDonald 10 67
(Paul Midgley) *s.i.s: in rr: hdwy 2f out: keeping on whn hmpd wl ins fnl f* **40/1**
3011 **5** ¾ **Lady Del Sol**[18] 5542 4-9-2 **70**...................................... DanielTudhope 9 69
(Marjorie Fife) *w ldr: one pce appr fnl f* **9/1**[3]
0000 **6** hd **Little Jimmy Odsox (IRE)**[17] 5588 4-9-0 **68**.............(p) TonyHamilton 1 67
(Tim Easterby) *chsd ldrs: effrt over 2f out: hung rt: kpt on fnl f* **4/1**[2]
0030 **7** ½ **Toby Tyler**[15] 5674 6-9-5 **73**..(p) RoystonFfrench 6 70
(Paul Midgley) *in rr: rdn over 2f out: kpt on over 1f out: nvr a threat* **11/1**
8 1¼ **Romanticize**[713] 6478 6-8-11 **65**.................................... PaddyAspell 3 58
(Jason Ward) *in rr: hdwy 2f out: kpt on fnl f* **33/1**
-000 **9** nk **Mey Blossom**[27] 5223 7-8-7 **61** oh2...................................... PaulQuinn 8 53
(Richard Whitaker) *in rr: kpt on fnl 2f: nvr a factor* **33/1**
1016 **10** 2¼ **Circuitous**[22] 5427 4-8-13 **67**..(b) TomEaves 14 52
(Keith Dalgleish) *chsd ldrs: wknd over 1f out* **16/1**
2060 **11** nk **Indian Trail**[22] 5412 12-8-6 **67**................................(b) ShirleyTeasdale(7) 4 51
(David Nicholls) *trckd ldrs: lost pl over 1f out* **22/1**
6410 **12** 3½ **Gap Princess (IRE)**[18] 5557 8-9-4 **72**.....................(p) RobertWinston 12 45
(Geoffrey Harker) *chsd ldrs: lost pl over 1f out* **16/1**
4036 **13** ½ **Loukoumi**[15] 5671 4-8-7 **61** oh2..................................(b) DuranFentiman 2 32
(Tim Easterby) *s.i.s: sn outpcd and in rr* **12/1**
0022 **14** 2½ **Phoenix Clubs (IRE)**[13] 5728 3-9-0 **70**........................ BarryMcHugh 16 33
(Paul Midgley) *wnt rt s: in rr: eased 1f out: fin lame* **14/1**
3330 **15** ¾ **Tabaret**[42] 4680 9-9-0 **68**... AmyRyan 15 29
(Richard Whitaker) *a in rr* **11/1**

1m 12.12s (0.32) **Going Correction** +0.10s/f (Good)
WFA 3 from 4yo+ 2lb **15** Ran SP% **127.1**
Speed ratings (Par 103): **101,98,98,97,96 96,95,94,93,90 90,85,84,81,80**
toteswingers 1&2 £4.80, 2&3 £6.90, 1&3 £18.50 CSF £44.55 CT £403.67 TOTE £13.60: £4.60, £2.00, £4.20; EX 47.80 Trifecta £330.10 Part won. Pool: £446.18 - 0.62 winning units..
Owner Lorimer Racing **Bred** E W Hyslop **Trained** Uplawmoor, E Renfrews

FOCUS
The form horses came to the fore in this modest sprint handicap. The time was ordinary but the form makes sense.
Little Jimmy Odsox(IRE) Official explanation: jockey said gelding hung right-handed throughout
Phoenix Clubs(IRE) Official explanation: trainer said filly finished lame behind

6124 JOHN SMITH'S REDCAR STRAIGHT-MILE CHAMPIONSHIP (QUALIFIER) (H'CAP) 1m
4:00 (4:01) (Class 4) (0-85,85) 3-Y-0+ **£4,075** (£1,212; £606; £303) **Stalls** Centre

Form RPR
0314 **1** **Jo'Burg (USA)**[24] 5369 8-9-6 **81**.................................... DanielTudhope 2 93+
(David O'Meara) *hld up: stdy hdwy stands' side over 2f out: led centre over 1f out: led overall last 75yds: sn clr: readily* **9/2**[1]
2-10 **2** 2¾ **Rio Grande**[62] 3963 3-9-5 **85**...(p) TonyHamilton 1 91+
(Ann Duffield) *taken to r alone far side: overall ldr: hdd and no ex ins fnl f* **33/1**
1125 **3** ¾ **Sabhan (IRE)**[34] 4961 3-8-10 **76**............................ RobertWinston 14 80
(Geoffrey Harker) *s.i.s: hdwy 3f out: sn chsng ldrs: styd on same pce fnl f* **12/1**
2260 **4** ¾ **Ginger Jack**[38] 4821 5-9-8 **83**.. PJMcDonald 7 86+
(Geoffrey Harker) *chsd ldrs: effrt over 2f out: kpt on same pce fnl f* **10/1**
0000 **5** 1¾ **Aquarian Spirit**[17] 5588 5-8-10 **71** oh2.......................... FrederikTylicki 10 70
(Richard Fahey) *chsd ldrs: one pce fnl 2f* **16/1**
0006 **6** ¾ **Dhaular Dhar (IRE)**[17] 5588 10-8-10 **71**........................ GrahamLee 11 68
(Jim Goldie) *chsd ldrs: hung lft and one pce fnl 2f* **14/1**
2465 **7** nk **Next Edition (IRE)**[15] 5677 4-9-0 **78**............................ DaleSwift(3) 9 74
(Philip Kirby) *led main body in centre: hdd that gp over 1f out: one pce* **12/1**
0100 **8** ½ **Kiwi Bay**[24] 5342 7-9-10 **85**... TomEaves 5 80
(Michael Dods) *hld up towards rr: effrt over 2f out: nvr nr ldrs* **8/1**[3]
066 **9** 8 **Silver Sycamore (USA)**[25] 5328 3-9-1 **81**..................... JamieSpencer 4 58
(David Lanigan) *in rr: hdwy and rdn over 2f out: wknd 1f out: sn eased* **5/1**[2]
0043 **10** 1¼ **Imperator Augustus (IRE)**[10] 5819 4-9-0 **75**............. DuranFentiman 3 49
(Patrick Holmes) *chsd ldrs: rdn 2f out: sn wknd* **12/1**
2100 **11** ½ **Musnad (USA)**[73] 3615 4-8-11 **75**............................ PaulPickard(3) 12 48
(Brian Ellison) *in rr: bhd fnl 2f* **25/1**
0006 **12** 11 **Just Fabulous**[14] 5712 3-8-6 **72**.............................. AndrewElliott 13 19
(George Moore) *chsd ldrs: lost pl over 2f out: bhd and eased fnl f* **14/1**
2503 **13** 38 **Karaka Jack**[11] 5802 5-9-5 **80**.. AdrianNicholls 6
(David Nicholls) *slipped s: in rr: eased 2f out: tailed rt off: virtually p.u* **5/1**[2]

1m 37.65s (-0.35) **Going Correction** +0.10s/f (Good)
WFA 3 from 4yo+ 5lb **13** Ran SP% **120.8**
Speed ratings (Par 105): **105,102,101,100,99 98,97,97,89,88 87,76,38**
toteswingers: 1&2 £13.30, 2&3 £29.50, 1&3 £9.20 CSF £156.52 CT £1746.71 TOTE £7.50: £2.20, £8.00, £4.90; EX 149.80 Trifecta £465.70 Part won. Pool of £629.35 - 0.40 winning units..
Owner Richard Walker **Bred** Tim Cooper **Trained** Nawton, N Yorks

FOCUS
Ordinary form for the level, the winner backing up last month's C&D win.
Karaka Jack Official explanation: jockey said gelding slipped leaving stalls

6125 CONGRATULATIONS DANIELLE AND JONNY MAIDEN STKS 6f
4:30 (4:31) (Class 5) 3-Y-0+ **£2,264** (£673; £336; £168) **Stalls** Centre

Form RPR
64 **1** **Albert Tatlock (IRE)**[15] 5679 3-9-3 0............................ AdrianNicholls 6 73
(David Nicholls) *led: hdd over 2f out: styd on to ld last 50yds* **9/2**[2]
4263 **2** 1¾ **Elegant Girl (IRE)**[10] 5823 3-8-12 64..............................[1] PaulMulrennan 3 62
(Tim Easterby) *w ldr: led over 2f out: 2 l clr 1f out: fnd nthing and hdd in clsng stages* **5/1**[3]
6253 **3** 3½ **Gold Edition**[12] 5776 3-9-3 75...(v) GrahamLee 2 56
(Jeremy Noseda) *s.i.s: in rr and sn drvn along: hdwy over 2f out: kpt on to take 3rd last 100yds* **11/10**[1]
5042 **4** 2¾ **Karate Queen**[13] 5734 7-8-11 47.. DaleSwift(3) 8 42
(Ron Barr) *chsd ldrs: one pce fnl 2f* **7/1**
32 **5** 1 **Script**[12] 5760 3-8-12 48... PatrickMathers 12 39
(Alan Berry) *chsd ldrs: edgd lft over 1f out: one pce* **20/1**
0055 **6** 1¼ **Decadence**[25] 5317 4-8-7 45.................................... DanielleMooney(7) 10 35
(Nigel Tinkler) *s.i.s: hdwy over 2f out: nvr nr ldrs* **25/1**
6060 **7** 2¼ **Bollin Tommy**[16] 5623 3-9-3 55.................................(p) DuranFentiman 11 33
(Tim Easterby) *chsd ldrs: outpcd over 2f out: no threat after* **14/1**
6 **8** 4 **Rosa Lottie**[29] 5166 3-8-12 0.. FrannyNorton 7 15
(David C Griffiths) *chsd ldrs: wknd over 2f out* **50/1**
5 **9** ¾ **Touching History (IRE)**[18] 5549 3-9-3 0......................... AndrewElliott 1 17
(Tim Etherington) *chsd ldrs: wknd over 2f out* **25/1**
000- **10** 9 **Donnywardsbird**[395] 5030 4-9-0 30.................................. DarylByrne(5) 4
(Eric Alston) *mid-div: lost pl over 3f out: sn bhd* **100/1**
0000 **11** 1½ **Libby's Lad**[27] 5247 3-9-3 24... AndrewMullen 5
(David C Griffiths) *s.i.s: lost pl over 3f out: sn bhd* **100/1**
00 **12** 23 **Cara's Delight (AUS)**[25] 5317 5-9-0 30......................... DanielTudhope 13
(Frederick Watson) *racd alone stands' side: sn outpcd and in rr: bhd fnl 3f: t.o whn eased over 1f out* **100/1**

1m 12.14s (0.34) **Going Correction** +0.10s/f (Good)
WFA 3 from 4yo+ 2lb **12** Ran SP% **119.0**
Speed ratings (Par 103): **101,98,94,90,89 87,84,79,78,66 64,33**
toteswingers 1&2 £3.40, 2&3 £2.60, 1&3 £3.00 CSF £25.99 TOTE £4.60: £1.40, £1.80, £1.10; EX 33.10 Trifecta £90.20 Pool: £958.34 - 7.86 winning units..
Owner D Nicholls **Bred** Golden Vale Stud **Trained** Sessay, N Yorks

FOCUS
A typically weak 3yo-plus sprint maiden, with the fourth rated just 47. The time was reasonable and the winner posted a clear personal best.

6126 HOLD YOUR CHRISTMAS PARTY @ REDCAR RACECOURSE H'CAP 1m 6f 19y
5:00 (5:00) (Class 6) (0-65,66) 3-Y-0+ **£1,704** (£503; £251) **Stalls** Low

Form RPR
-632 **1** **Major Domo (FR)**[17] 5585 4-10-0 **65**.............................. PJMcDonald 9 76
(Micky Hammond) *mid-div: hdwy over 3f out: wnt 3rd over 1f out: chsd ldr 1f out: styd on to ld nr fin* **14/1**
4314 **2** nk **Dr Irv**[25] 5330 3-8-11 **59**... PaulMulrennan 11 69
(Kate Walton) *trckd ldr after 1f: led over 3f out: no ex and hdd nr fin* **4/1**[1]
0-00 **3** 8 **Miss Ferney**[15] 5673 8-9-7 **61**.................................... DeclanCannon(3) 1 60
(Alan Kirtley) *hld up in rr: hdwy on outer over 3f out: wnt 2nd over 1f out: one pce* **14/1**
4530 **4** 2¼ **Shy**[13] 5735 7-9-0 **58**...(b) GemmaTutty(7) 5 54
(Karen Tutty) *hld up towards rr: hdwy over 3f out: styd on appr fnl f* **20/1**
6400 **5** 1 **Ferney Boy**[15] 5672 6-8-9 **46** oh1.................................. AndrewElliott 13 40
(Chris Fairhurst) *mid-div: hdwy over 3f out: one pce fnl 2f* **40/1**
00-2 **6** ½ **Maybe I Wont**[34] 4955 7-9-11 **65**............................. LucyAlexander(3) 2 59
(James Moffatt) *hld up in rr: effrt on inner over 3f out: nvr nr ldrs* **6/1**[3]
5220 **7** 1½ **Little Red Minx (IRE)**[17] 5589 3-8-0 **55** ow1............(p) DavidBergin(7) 15 47
(David O'Meara) *mid-div: hdwy 7f out: chsng ldrs 3f out: fdd over 1f out* **11/1**
0406 **8** nk **Arizona High**[3] 6056 4-8-9 **46** oh1............................... FrannyNorton 16 37
(Andrew Crook) *swtchd lft after s: t.k.h: led after 1f: hdd over 3f out: wknd over 1f out* **33/1**
5050 **9** 2½ **Harvey's Hope**[15] 5673 6-9-8 **64**............................ ShaneBKelly(5) 10 52
(Keith Reveley) *s.s: in rr: kpt on fnl 2f: nvr a factor* **11/2**[2]
5005 **10** shd **Al Furat (USA)**[25] 5290 4-9-12 **63**.................................... AmyRyan 3 51
(Ron Barr) *s.s: in rr: plld wd 4f out: nvr on terms* **7/1**
000 **11** 5 **Media Stars**[14] 4955 7-8-10 **47**.................................. JamesSullivan 14 28
(Robert Johnson) *trckd ldrs: t.k.h: drvn 6f out: wknd and eased 2f out* **33/1**
1200 **12** 2¾ **Dean Iarracht (IRE)**[1] 6103 6-9-9 **60**..........................(p) FrederikTylicki 8 37
(Tracy Waggott) *chsd ldrs: wknd 2f out* **10/1**
2302 **13** 6 **Finellas Fortune**[13] 5735 7-9-7 **58**................................ GrahamLee 4 26
(George Moore) *mid-div: hdwy 8f out: drvn 6f out: lost pl over 2f out* **15/2**
0634 **14** 13 **Seagoing**[14] 5714 3-8-11 **59**..(b) DuranFentiman 6
(Tim Easterby) *t.k.h: led 1f: chsd ldrs: drvn 6f out: lost pl 3f out: sn bhd* **18/1**

3m 7.27s (2.57) **Going Correction** +0.225s/f (Good)
WFA 3 from 4yo+ 11lb **14** Ran SP% **123.0**
Speed ratings (Par 101): **101,100,96,94,94 94,93,93,91,91 88,87,83,76**
toteswingers 1&2 £13.00, 2&3 £18.50, 1&3 CSF £68.39 CT £830.33 TOTE £19.60: £4.60, £2.10, £4.50; EX 97.30 Trifecta £424.80 Part won. Pool of £574.17 - 0.80 winning units..
Owner Mrs H E Aitkin **Bred** Langham Hall Stud **Trained** Middleham Moor, N Yorks

FOCUS
The pace appeared honest in this staying handicap and the front pair drew clear. A clear personal best from the winner.

6127 RACING UK ON CHANNEL 432 APPRENTICE H'CAP 7f
5:30 (5:32) (Class 5) (0-70,70) 3-Y-0+ **£2,264** (£673; £336; £168) **Stalls** Centre

Form RPR
3203 **1** **Broctune Papa Gio**[17] 5588 5-9-7 **67**........................... DeclanCannon 17 76
(Keith Reveley) *swtchd lft after 1f: hld up in mid-div: effrt over 2f out: styd on to ld 1f out: drvn out* **5/1**[1]
2562 **2** 1¾ **Thrust Control (IRE)**[1] 6106 5-8-5 **56** oh7........(p) JacobButterfield(5) 15 60
(Tracy Waggott) *reluctant to join others at s: w ldrs: led over 2f out: hdd 1f out: kpt on same pce* **16/1**
-054 **3** ½ **Desert Creek (IRE)**[15] 5669 6-9-1 **66**..................... ShirleyTeasdale(5) 1 71+
(David Nicholls) *mid-div: hdwy and n.m.r 2f out: edgd rt over 1f out: styd on ins fnl f* **8/1**[3]
005 **4** nk **Auto Mac**[29] 5171 4-9-2 **62**..(b) AdamBeschizza 13 64
(Neville Bycroft) *s.i.s: hdwy over 2f out: styd on fnl f* **14/1**
0005 **5** hd **Mujaadel (USA)**[7] 5910 7-9-5 **65**.............................(v[1]) LucyAlexander 11 67
(David Nicholls) *in rr div: reminders and hdwy over 2f out: styd on ins fnl f* **10/1**
2164 **6** 1 **Steel Stockholder**[3] 6047 6-9-2 **69**..................... RobertDodsworth(7) 10 68
(Mel Brittain) *chsd ldrs: one pce over 1f out* **8/1**[3]
0024 **7** ¾ **Ryedane (IRE)**[18] 5543 10-8-7 **60**.........................(b) RachelRichardson(7) 8 57
(Tim Easterby) *chsd ldrs: one pce over 1f out* **25/1**
4-06 **8** ¾ **Who's Shirl**[34] 4954 6-9-7 **70**... LMcNiff(3) 6 65+
(Chris Fairhurst) *mid-div: effrt over 2f out: nt clr run and repeatedly hmpd over 1f out tl swtchd lft jst ins fnl f: kpt on wl* **11/1**
0400 **9** ½ **Just The Tonic**[39] 4769 5-9-7 **67**..................................... PaulPickard 2 60
(Marjorie Fife) *mid-div: hdwy over 2f out: one pce* **40/1**
1103 **10** 1¾ **Eeny Mac (IRE)**[16] 5618 5-9-4 **64**...................................... AmyRyan 12 53
(Neville Bycroft) *led: hdd over 2f out: wkng whn hmpd over 1f out* **15/2**[2]
6306 **11** 1¾ **I'll Be Good**[11] 5800 3-8-13 **70**...................................... KevinStott(7) 16 53
(Robert Johnson) *chsd ldrs: edgd rt and wknd over 1f out* **50/1**
0300 **12** nse **Poppy Golightly**[36] 4890 5-8-7 **56** oh11........................(b[1]) NeilFarley(3) 9 40
(Declan Carroll) *mid-div: drvn over 2f out: nvr a factor* **50/1**
0-15 **13** 1½ **Come Hither**[30] 5130 3-8-10 **65**.................................... DavidBergin(5) 3 44
(David O'Meara) *mid-div: drvn over 2f out: nvr a factor* **8/1**[3]
0400 **14** nse **Whispered Times (USA)**[29] 5171 5-9-1 **61**.................(p) LeeTopliss 5 41
(Tracy Waggott) *t.k.h in rr: nvr on terms: hmpd over 1f out* **16/1**

4006 **15** *shd* **Silly Gilly (IRE)**[26] 5258 8-8-10 **59**............................. GarryWhillans(3) 4 38
(Ron Barr) *chsd ldrs: drvn over 2f out: sn lost pl* **12/1**
0006 **16** *4 ½* **Mubtadi**[43] 4661 4-9-6 **69**...(t) ShaneBKelly(3) 7 36
(Ismail Mohammed) *s.i.s: in rr: no imp whn hmpd over 1f out: eased whn bhd in clsng stages* **12/1**
0066 **17** *25* **Sairaam (IRE)**[7] 5915 6-9-1 **64**..................................... AdamCarter(3) 14
(Charles Smith) *swtchd rt after 1f to r alone stands' side: bhd whn eased over 1f out: t.o* **25/1**

1m 24.89s (0.39) **Going Correction** +0.10s/f (Good)
WFA 3 from 4yo+ 4lb **17** Ran SP% **127.1**
Speed ratings (Par 103): **101,99,98,98,97 96,95,95,94,92 90,90,88,88,88 83,54**
toteswingers 1&2 £27.50, 2&3 £40.60, 1&3 £11.70 CSF £87.02 CT £670.37 TOTE £4.10: £1.10, £4.00, £2.60, £4.50; EX 141.40 TRIFECTA Not won..
Owner Broctune Partners I **Bred** Lesley Winn And Reveley Farms **Trained** Lingdale, Redcar & Cleveland

FOCUS
An open-looking apprentice handicap. A length personal best from the winner.
T/Jkpt: Not won. T/Plt: £36.40 to a £1 stake. Pool of £76203.52 -1524.53 winning tickets. T/Qpdt: £11.70 to a £1 stake. Pool of £5328.02 - 335.62 winning tickets. WG

5961 CHANTILLY (R-H)
Tuesday, September 11
OFFICIAL GOING: Turf: good to soft changing to soft after race 2 (1.20)

6128a PRIX D'ARENBERG (GROUP 3) (2YO) (TURF) 5f 110y
2:20 (12:00) 2-Y-O £33,333 (£13,333; £10,000; £6,666; £3,333)

RPR
1 **Cay Verde**[18] 5559 2-8-11 0.. MartinHarley 6 112+
(Mick Channon) *racd 3rd on outside: qcknd wl to chal for ld 2f out: tk ld 1 1/2f out: sn wnt clr: easily* **9/5**[2]
2 *4 ½* **Baileys Jubilee**[19] 5516 2-8-8 0................................. IoritzMendizabal 4 94
(Mark Johnston) *broke wl to ld: stl in front at 1/2-way: chal 2f out: hdd 1 1/2f out: rdn but no ex fnl f: styd on: clr 2nd* **13/10**[1]
3 *4* **Aksil (FR)**[24] 5379 2-8-8 0.................................... GregoryBenoist 3 81
(M Boutin, France) *racd cl up bhd ldrs: rdn but outpcd fr 1/2-way: nvr a factor fnl 1 1/2f* **13/1**
4 *1 ¾* **Complimentor (IRE)**[40] 2-8-11 0................................ UmbertoRispoli 5 78
(X Thomas-Demeaulte, France) *hld up at rr towards outside: wnt 4th at 1/2-way: rdn but no ex: nvr a factor* **33/10**[3]
5 *15* **Sorry Woman (FR)**[42] 4696 2-8-8 0................................ FabriceVeron 1 26
(H-A Pantall, France) *racd 3rd on ins rail: rdn at 1/2-way: no rspnse: sn wknd* **9/1**

1m 5.22s (0.72) **5** Ran SP% **119.6**
WIN (incl. 1 euro stake): 2.80. PLACES: 1.40, 1.30. SF: 3.70.
Owner Qatar Racing Limited **Bred** Lady Whent **Trained** West Ilsley, Berks

FOCUS
Cay Verde routed them but was the only one to show their form.

NOTEBOOK
Cay Verde appreciated the underfoot conditions and picked up well to win by a wide margin. There's a chance he was the only one able to show his form on this ground and he might be flattered by the bare result, but he'll no doubt get to prove that one way or another in the Middle Park next month.
Baileys Jubilee was a reluctant leader and left behind when the winner quickened by. She doesn't want the ground this soft and connections will be hoping for a sounder surface in the Cheveley Park.

6129a PRIX D'AUMALE (GROUP 3) (2YO FILLIES) (TURF) 1m
2:55 (12:00) 2-Y-O £33,333 (£13,333; £10,000; £6,666; £3,333)

RPR
1 **Peace Burg (FR)**[37] 2-8-9 0.. IoritzMendizabal 2 107+
(J Heloury, France) *settled 3rd on inner: cl up bhd ldrs 1 1/2f out whn unable to find room to chal: swtchd to ins rail 150yds out: r.o strly fnl 100yds: got up on line* **5/2**[1]
2 *hd* **Single (FR)**[32] 2-8-9 0... OlivierPeslier 4 106+
(C Laffon-Parias, France) *setled 4th: rdn to chal ldr 1 1/2f out: qcknd wl to ld 1f out: r.o wl fnl 100yds: ct on line* **7/2**[3]
3 *1 ½* **Indigo Lady**[34] 4967 2-8-10 0 ow1....................... ChristopheSoumillon 6 103
(Peter Chapple-Hyam) *sn led: rdn 1 1/2f out: r.o wl u.p: chal and hdd 1f out: styd on wl* **15/2**
4 *½* **Meri Shika (FR)**[21] 5471 2-8-9 0...................................... ThierryJarnet 9 101
(J Bertran De Balanda, France) *settled 2nd: rdn 1 1/2f out: nt qckn: styd on wl u.p fnl 150yds* **15/1**
5 *¾* **Flotilla (FR)**[43] 2-8-9 0... GregoryBenoist 7 100
(M Delzangles, France) *hld up at rr: swtchd to wd outside in st: r.o wl ent fnl f: nt rch ldrs* **14/5**[2]
6 *1 ¾* **Kensea (FR)**[21] 5471 2-8-9 0... MaximeGuyon 1 96
(H-A Pantall, France) *settled 5th on ins: cl up 1 1/2f out: rdn but no ex 1f out: r.o fnl f: wknd fnl 100yds* **15/2**
7 *1 ½* **Koonunja (IRE)**[24] 5379 2-8-9 0............................... StephanePasquier 3 92
(D Prod'Homme, France) *hld up towards rr: rdn over 1 1/2f out: nt qckn: nvr a factor ins fnl fuurlong* **20/1**
8 *9* **Redressthebalance (IRE)**[17] 5571 2-8-9 0.................... GeraldMosse 5 73
(Ralph Beckett) *racd 6th towards outside: nvr settled: u.p 1 1/2f out: no rspnse: wknd fnl f: eased* **18/1**

1m 41.03s (3.03) **8** Ran SP% **116.9**
WIN (incl. 1 euro stake): 3.50. PLACES: 1.50, 1.60, 2.20. DF: 5.00. SF: 10.70.
Owner Ecurie D Primes **Bred** Ecurie D **Trained** France

FOCUS
The form just about fits with the race averages, although the field finished compressed.

NOTEBOOK
Peace Burg(FR) overcame a troubled passage and quickened well to maintain her unbeaten record, but the bunched finish and proximity of the third means the race cannot be rated too highly. She's likely to head to the Prix Marcel Boussac next.
Indigo Lady, who made all to take a Yarmouth maiden last time out, tried to repeat the trick on this steep rise in class. By Sir Percy out of a mare who won at up to 1m4f, she's bred to stay well, and she ought to make a better 3yo.

5727 CARLISLE (R-H)
Wednesday, September 12
OFFICIAL GOING: Soft changing to heavy after race 1 (1.50)
Wind: Breezy, half against Weather: Overcast

6130 CARLISLE-RACES.CO.UK NURSERY 5f 193y
1:50 (1:52) (Class 5) (0-75,74) 2-Y-O £2,264 (£673; £336; £168) Stalls Low

Form RPR
0045 **1** **Delores Rocket**[43] 4672 2-8-8 **61**...................................(b[1]) AmyRyan 16 73
(Kevin Ryan) *wnt lft s: sn w ldr: led 1/2-way: sn rdn: edgd rt and drew clr fnl f* **20/1**
0453 **2** *5* **Mixed Message (IRE)**[21] 5484 2-8-8 **61**.................... GrahamGibbons 6 58
(Ed McMahon) *prom: rdn and swtchd to stands' rail over 2f out: sn ev ch: kpt on fnl f: no ch w wnr* **9/1**
403 **3** *hd* **Baraboy (IRE)**[26] 5291 2-8-2 **58**.................................. JulieBurke(3) 1 54
(Barry Murtagh) *in tch: effrt and drvn along over 2f out: kpt on fnl f: nt pce to chal* **80/1**
0501 **4** *¾* **Ena Sharples**[16] 5675 2-8-10 **63**................................... AdrianNicholls 9 57
(David Nicholls) *cl up: rdn and effrt whn carried lft and hmpd appr 2f out: kpt on fnl f: no imp* **5/1**[2]
1123 **5** *1 ¾* **Lady Moonlight (IRE)**[19] 5537 2-9-2 **72**.......................... DaleSwift(3) 13 60
(Ann Duffield) *bhd: drvn over 3f out: hdwy over 1f out: kpt on fnl f: nvr able to chal* **5/1**[2]
3635 **6** *nk* **Red Style (IRE)**[44] 4637 2-9-1 **68**................................... BarryMcHugh 5 55
(Paul Midgley) *t.k.h: led to 1/2-way: rdn and no ex fnl f* **9/1**
1 **7** *1* **Poppy Bond**[121] 2123 2-8-13 **66**................................... DuranFentiman 4 50
(Chris Fairhurst) *s.i.s: bhd: effrt and drvn over 2f out: no imp over 1f out* **6/1**[3]
0504 **8** *5* **Cumbrian Craic**[19] 5544 2-9-5 **72**.............................. DanielTudhope 14 41
(Tim Easterby) *bhd: drvn over 3f out: no imp fr 2f out* **9/2**[1]
0523 **9** *2 ¾* **Multisure**[23] 5423 2-9-0 **67**... TonyHamilton 8 27
(Richard Fahey) *prom 2f: sn lost pl and drvn along: n.d after* **20/1**
506 **10** *1* **Baker's Pursuit**[104] 2614 2-8-7 **60**............................ AndrewElliott 10 17
(Jim Goldie) *t.k.h in rr: drvn over 3f out: nvr on terms* **25/1**
0023 **11** *½* **Ryedale Valley**[9] 5886 2-7-12 **54**............................ DeclanCannon(3) 11 9
(Tim Easterby) *towards rr: drvn along 1/2-way: btn over 1f out* **9/1**
3060 **12** *2 ¾* **Municipal (IRE)**[14] 5749 2-8-7 **60**..........................(b[1]) JamesSullivan 2 7
(Michael Dods) *t.k.h: cl up tl rdn and wknd 2f out* **16/1**

1m 17.98s (4.28) **Going Correction** +0.60s/f (Yiel) **12** Ran SP% **116.3**
Speed ratings (Par 95): **95,88,88,87,84 84,83,76,72,71 70,67**
Tote Swingers: 1&2 £29.60, 1&3 £54.10, 2&3 £32.10 CSF £179.87 CT £13469.42 TOTE £18.80: £4.60, £2.80, £9.00; EX 151.30.
Owner J Nixon **Bred** Bearstone Stud **Trained** Hambleton, N Yorks
■ Stewards' Enquiry : Graham Gibbons two-day ban: careless riding (Sep 26-27)

FOCUS
A moderate nursery. The easy winner improved and the form makes sense.

NOTEBOOK
Delores Rocket stayed on strongly down the centre of the track to win in the first-time blinkers. She looked one of the more exposed in the race having already been well beaten in two nurseries, but the combination of softer ground, headgear and a return 6f all worked in her favour and she ran out a convincing winner. While far from ideally drawn on the wide outside, she showed bright early speed and was able to head them all off after a couple of furlongs. There were certainly no prisoners taken at any stage and she deserves plenty of credit for seeing this out so well. This was easily her best effort and a hefty rise in the weights looks on the cards. (op 16-1)
Mixed Message(IRE) came down the stands' side rail, but was ultimately left behind by the winner. She had shown improved form at Lingfield last time and translated that improvement to this much easier surface. She was another that was up there throughout and, despite getting tired late on, did manage her best-ever placing. (op 10-1 tchd 8-1)
Baraboy(IRE) defied his inflated odds on his debut for new connections. Picked up for only £5,000 after his latest selling third, he should give his owner plenty of fun this season and might be able to win a small race off his modest mark. (op 66-1 tchd 100-1)
Ena Sharples, a winner of a Ripon seller last month, turned in a solid effort. She got outpaced with 2f remaining, but was staying on again near the finish. (op 9-2)
Cumbrian Craic struggled to make any impact on this ground. Official explanation: jockey said gelding never travelled (op 11-2)

6131 WATCH RACING UK ON SKY432 H'CAP 1m 1f 61y
2:20 (2:22) (Class 5) (0-70,69) 3-Y-O+ £2,264 (£673; £336; £168) Stalls Low

Form RPR
5605 **1** **Joshua The First**[13] 5759 3-9-3 **68**................................... JoeFanning 9 76
(Keith Dalgleish) *prom: effrt and pushed along 2f out: kpt on fnl f: led nr fin* **14/1**
211 **2** *nk* **Uncle Brit**[44] 4641 6-8-13 **58**... PhillipMakin 15 65
(Malcolm Jefferson) *prom on outside: smooth hdwy to ld over 2f out: rdn over 1f out: edgd rt and pricked ears ins fnl f: hdd nr fin* **9/2**[2]
2055 **3** *1 ¼* **High Resolution**[14] 5730 5-9-0 **59**............................... JamesSullivan 16 64
(Linda Perratt) *hld up: gd hdwy on outside 2f out: chsng ldrs 1f out: edgd rt and kpt on same pce towards fin* **14/1**
6451 **4** *3 ¼* **Edas**[14] 5730 10-8-10 **58**.. DeanHeslop(3) 7 55
(Thomas Cuthbert) *t.k.h: midfield on ins: hdwy whn checked 2f out: rdn and one pce ins fnl f* **7/1**[3]
3665 **5** *1* **Free Art**[41] 4747 4-9-6 **65**... TonyHamilton 8 60
(Geoffrey Harker) *hld up in midfield: effrt and drvn along over 2f out: kpt on same pce appr fnl f* **14/1**
0650 **6** *¾* **Tapis Libre**[18] 5585 4-8-13 **65**............................. DavidSimmonson(7) 14 59
(Michael Easterby) *midfield on outside: drvn along over 2f out: kpt on same pce over 1f out* **22/1**
-520 **7** *2 ¾* **Ravi River (IRE)**[12] 4621 8-9-7 **66**.................................. PaddyAspell 2 54
(Alistair Whillans) *hld up: rdn over 3f out: kpt on fr over 1f out: nvr able to chal* **16/1**
000 **8** *¾* **Desert Vision**[40] 4768 8-9-0 **66**...........................(vt) MatthewHopkins(7) 5 52
(Michael Easterby) *t.k.h: led: rdn and hdd over 2f out: wknd over 1f out* **25/1**
0664 **9** *hd* **Law To Himself (IRE)**[16] 5672 5-9-2 **61**..................(v) RobertWinston 3 46
(Alan Swinbank) *trckd ldrs: effrt and ev ch whn veered bdly rt appr 2f out: rdn and outpcd fnl f* **12/1**
4160 **10** *½* **Call Of Duty (IRE)**[14] 5730 7-9-3 **67**......................... GarryWhillans(5) 11 51
(Dianne Sayer) *hld up: rdn over 3f out: sme late hdwy: nvr on terms* **16/1**
2534 **11** *4* **Honoured (IRE)**[1] 6120 5-8-11 **63**........................(t) DanielMuscutt(7) 1 39
(Michael Appleby) *bhd: drvn over 3f out: nvr on terms* **7/2**[1]
0100 **12** *2* **Osgood**[11] 5310 5-9-10 **69**... MartinHarley 6 40
(Mick Channon) *hld up in midfield: effrt over 2f out: btn over 1f out* **12/1**

0513 **13** *1 3/4* **Indian Giver**[34] 4996 4-9-1 **63** .... PaulPickard(3) 13 30
(Hugh McWilliams) *bhd: drvn along over 3f out: sn btn* **10/1**

0000 **14** *shd* **Loyal Master (IRE)**[15] 5721 3-9-0 **65** .... (p) PatrickMathers 12 32
(Garry Moss) *cl up tl rdn and wknd over 2f out* **50/1**

0 **15** *3 3/4* **Mcmonagle (USA)**[35] 4954 4-9-3 **65** .... (tp) DaleSwift(3) 4 24
(Alan Brown) *trckd ldrs tl rdn and wknd 2f out* **40/1**

2m 5.77s (8.17) **Going Correction** +0.85s/f (Soft)
WFA 3 from 4yo+ 6lb **15** Ran SP% **121.7**
Speed ratings (Par 103): **97,96,95,92,91 91,88,88,87,87 83,82,80,80,77**
Tote Swingers: 1&2 £12.20, 1&3 £30.60, 2&3 £16.40 CSF £73.67 CT £927.08 TOTE £14.60: £4.60, £2.40, £3.50; EX 72.40.
Owner newkeylets **Bred** P Docherty **Trained** Carluke, S Lanarks

FOCUS
A fair handicap, run at a sensible pace. Few got involved, like the card as a whole. The winner is rated back to his best.

6132 ONCE EVERY PRESTON GUILD MAIDEN FILLIES' STKS 6f 192y
2:50 (2:50) (Class 5) 2-Y-O £2,264 (£673; £336; £168) Stalls Low

Form RPR

3323 **1** **Sorella Bella (IRE)**[8] 5904 2-9-0 79 .... MartinHarley 7 75+
(Mick Channon) *t.k.h early: mde all: rdn over 2f out: kpt on strly fnl f: eased nr fin* **1/1**[1]

035 **2** *1 3/4* **Storma Norma**[15] 5709 2-9-0 0 .... DuranFentiman 1 68
(Tim Easterby) *trckd ldrs: effrt and wnt 2nd over 2f out: kpt on fnl f: hld nr fin* **33/1**

4 **3** *4* **Al Thumama**[29] 5184 2-9-0 0 .... AmyRyan 9 58
(Kevin Ryan) *cl up: rdn along over 2f out: kpt on same pce appr fnl f* **11/1**

4 *2* **Ghur (USA)** 2-9-0 0 .... TadhgO'Shea 2 53
(Mark Johnston) *t.k.h: hld up: rdn along over 3f out: hdwy over 1f out: no imp* **15/2**

0 **5** *2 1/2* **Beautifulwildthing**[26] 5311 2-9-0 0 .... GrahamGibbons 3 46
(David Barron) *hld up in tch: drvn over 2f out: sn no imp* **14/1**

2 **6** *4* **Marsh Dragon**[17] 5631 2-9-0 0 .... PhillipMakin 5 36
(Mark H Tompkins) *t.k.h early: trckd ldrs: stdy hdwy over 3f out: rdn and wknd wl over 1f out* **6/1**[3]

7 *8* **Alzavola** 2-9-0 0 .... LukeMorris 8 15
(Sir Mark Prescott Bt) *sn drvn along and rn green in rr: struggling 1/2-way: nvr on terms* **4/1**[2]

0 **8** *20* **Misu Mac**[23] 5410 2-9-0 0 .... MichaelO'Connell 10
(Neville Bycroft) *s.i.s: hld up: stdy hdwy 1/2-way: rdn and wknd over 2f out: t.o* **80/1**

1m 33.09s (5.99) **Going Correction** +0.85s/f (Soft) **8** Ran SP% **115.2**
Speed ratings (Par 92): **99,97,92,90,87 82,73,50**
Tote Swingers: 1&2 £7.80, 1&3 £3.40, 2&3 £9.80 CSF £42.46 TOTE £2.10: £1.50, £5.80, £2.20; EX 19.40.
Owner Mrs Ann C Black **Bred** Rathasker Stud **Trained** West Ilsley, Berks

FOCUS
An ordinary fillies' maiden and all about the winner. The second is the long-term key to the form.

NOTEBOOK
Sorella Bella(IRE) had made the frame on all seven starts prior to this and her latest Listed third behind Steeler at Goodwood set a lofty standard for her rivals to aim at. With ability already proven on soft ground, it was hard to see her getting beaten and, having been sent to the front at an early stage, the result never really looked in doubt. She may be capable of picking up some more valuable black type. (op 10-11)
Storma Norma ran an excellent race, but it remains to be seen what this will do to her handicap mark. This was a big step up on that she'd achieved previously and she appeared to appreciate this step up to 7f.
Al Thumama was well beaten off but did finish clear of the remainder. She was under pressure before halfway and kept on only at the one-pace. She did show signs of greenness but her future surely lies in nurseries. (op 10-1)
Ghur(USA) ought to suited by better ground but she's probably one of the stable's lesser lights. (op 8-1 tchd 9-1)
Marsh Dragon failed to build on an encouraging run at Yarmouth. It's easy to forgive a horse a poor run in these conditions though and it's far too early to give up on her. (op 9-2)
Alzavola ran poorly, despite attracting support. She never travelled at any stage and was allowed to coast home in her own time. (op 13-2 tchd 7-1)

6133 IRISH STALLION FARMS E B F MAIDEN STKS (DIV I) 7f 200y
3:25 (3:26) (Class 5) 2-Y-O £3,408 (£1,006; £503) Stalls Low

Form RPR

22 **1** **Van Percy**[15] 5704 2-9-3 0 .... DavidProbert 6 79+
(Andrew Balding) *t.k.h: cl up: led after 2f: hrd pressed and rdn over 2f out: drew clr fnl f* **7/4**[1]

0 **2** *4* **Ready (IRE)**[24] 5382 2-9-3 0 .... PatrickMathers 4 70
(Garry Moss) *prom: chal over 2f out to over 1f out: nt pce of wnr fnl f* **66/1**

2 **3** *1 3/4* **Jullundar (IRE)**[16] 5655 2-9-3 0 .... MartinHarley 3 66
(Mick Channon) *hld up: rdn and hdwy over 2f out: no imp fnl f* **4/1**[3]

062 **4** *2 1/4* **Khelac**[16] 5668 2-9-3 75 .... RobertWinston 5 61
(Alan Swinbank) *prom: drvn over 2f out: edgd rt and outpcd wl over 1f out* **14/1**

63 **5** *3 1/4* **Corton Lad**[71] 3725 2-9-3 0 .... GrahamGibbons 8 55+
(Keith Dalgleish) *t.k.h: trckd ldrs tl rdn and outpcd over 2f out: n.d after* **33/1**

6 *1 1/2* **Allnecessaryforce (FR)** 2-9-3 0 .... TonyHamilton 9 51
(Richard Fahey) *hld up: drvn and struggling over 3f out: rallied over 1f out: no imp* **14/1**

00 **7** *1 1/2* **Denton Skyline (IRE)**[16] 5668 2-9-3 0 .... BarryMcHugh 1 48
(Michael Dods) *hld up on ins: struggling 3f out: n.d after* **100/1**

060 **8** *nse* **Big Thunder**[11] 5825 2-9-3 0 .... LukeMorris 10 48
(Sir Mark Prescott Bt) *s.i.s: sn drvn and in tch on outside: struggling over 3f out: sn btn* **33/1**

6 **9** *1 1/4* **Tribal Path (IRE)**[19] 5562 2-9-3 0 .... JoeFanning 7 45+
(Mark Johnston) *led 2f: cl up tl edgd rt and wknd 2f out* **15/8**[2]

10 *38* **Mjaal (IRE)** 2-8-12 0 .... PhillipMakin 2
(John Weymes) *s.i.s: sn t.o* **66/1**

1m 47.15s (7.15) **Going Correction** +0.85s/f (Soft) **10** Ran SP% **114.3**
Speed ratings (Par 95): **98,94,92,90,86 85,83,83,82,44**
Tote Swingers: 1&2 £17.20, 1&3 £1.80, 2&3 £35.00 CSF £131.71 TOTE £2.50: £1.10, £6.10, £1.90; EX 90.00.
Owner Mrs L E Ramsden & Richard Morecombe **Bred** Mr & Mrs A E Pakenham **Trained** Kingsclere, Hants

FOCUS
A modest juvenile maiden. The form looks straightforward.

NOTEBOOK
Van Percy showed no ill effects from a hard race at Epsom a fortnight ago. The son of 2006 Derby winner Sir Percy looks to have inherited plenty of stamina and he had no problem seeing this out, despite the testing conditions. He had failed by only short-head at Epsom last time, but appeared more at home on this more conventional track. It's likely we won't see the very best of him until he tackles middle-distances next year, but a strongly run 1m nursery could well bring about further success this season. (tchd 13-8 and 15-8)
Ready(IRE) shaped with promise over 5f on quick ground at Pontefract on his debut and again caught the eye. Stamina was a major concern for him, but there appeared no fluke about his. There's a suspicion that a livelier surface would bring about further improvement.
Jullundar(IRE) helps give some substance to the form. He had just been touched off at Chepstow last month and looked sure to handle conditions. While never seriously threatening, he kept on having been outpaced and is another that will benefit for longer trips. (op 7-2)
Khelac was by no means disgraced. This looked tougher than the Newcastle maiden he was second in and he ought to be competitive in nurseries off his current rating. (op 12-1 tchd 10-1)
Tribal Path(IRE), a tall and rangy type, found this happening a bit too quickly for him. His has some filling out to do and should be seen to better effect with another winter under his belt. (op 2-1)

6134 IRISH STALLION FARMS E B F MAIDEN STKS (DIV II) 7f 200y
4:00 (4:00) (Class 5) 2-Y-O £3,408 (£1,006; £251; £251) Stalls Low

Form RPR

0 **1** **Topamichi**[57] 4194 2-9-3 0 .... (b) PhillipMakin 10 63+
(Mark H Tompkins) *s.i.s: t.k.h in rr: smooth hdwy on outside over 2f out: led 1f out: pushed out fnl f* **4/1**[3]

00 **2** *2* **Tobacco**[16] 5668 2-9-3 0 .... DuranFentiman 1 58+
(Tim Easterby) *trckd ldrs: drvn and outpcd over 3f out: rallied fnl f: kpt on wl to go 2nd nr fin: no ch w wnr* **20/1**

2 **3** *1/2* **Miss Mocca**[29] 5192 2-8-12 0 .... MartinHarley 9 52
(Ian Wood) *led: drvn over 2f out: hdd 1f out: kpt on same pce ins fnl f* **7/2**[2]

3 *dht* **Bravo Ragazzo (IRE)** 2-9-3 0 .... JoeFanning 6 57
(Mark Johnston) *t.k.h early: cl up: effrt and ev ch over 2f out: rdn and edgd rt over 1f out: styd on fnl f* **9/4**[1]

000 **5** *1 3/4* **French Revolution**[26] 5311 2-9-3 47 .... BarryMcHugh 4 53+
(Jedd O'Keeffe) *t.k.h early: hld up bhd ldng gp: drvn and outpcd over 2f out: styd on ins fnl f* **150/1**

5 **6** *nk* **Elusive Thought (IRE)**[36] 4921 2-9-3 0 .... DavidNolan 8 52+
(Tom Tate) *prom: rdn over 3f out: rallied: kpt on same pce fnl f* **8/1**

6 **7** *3 3/4* **Clarendale (IRE)**[14] 5727 2-9-3 0 .... AndrewElliott 3 44
(Alan Swinbank) *cl up tl edgd rt and wknd over 1f out* **15/2**

5 **8** *15* **Alkcama (IRE)**[46] 4587 2-9-3 0 .... LukeMorris 7 11
(John Weymes) *midfield: drvn and outpcd over 4f out: btn fnl 2f* **8/1**

000 **P** **Gambino (IRE)**[33] 5040 2-9-0 45 .... PaulPickard(3) 5
(Hugh McWilliams) *bhd: lost tch and p.u over 3f out* **250/1**

1m 50.14s (10.14) **Going Correction** +0.85s/f (Soft) **9** Ran SP% **112.8**
Speed ratings (Par 95): **83,81,80,80,78 78,74,59,**
Tote: Place: Bravo Ragazzo £0.60, Miss Mocca £0.50. Swingers: 2-8 £3.40, 2-9 £1.60, 8-9 £9.70, 8-10 £3.70, 9-10 £1.50. CSF £72.47 TOTE £4.00: £2.50, £4.70; EX 119.10.
Owner Roalco Limited **Bred** Dullingham Park Stud & M P Bowring **Trained** Newmarket, Suffolk

FOCUS
This was not as strong as the first division, and the time was slow. No reasons to be positive about the form.

NOTEBOOK
Topamichi, a big price and well beaten on his debut at Yarmouth, was hard to fancy on that evidence but he'd been the subject of strong support throughout the day and saw this out best of all. He made ground with ease on the outside and, while taking a while to pick up, showed a willing attitude in the headgear which he also wore on his introduction. Form on ground as soft as this should always be treated with a degree of caution, but he's unlikely to be too harshly dealt with by the handicapper and clearly goes well in this ground. (op 6-1 tchd 13-2)
Tobacco ◆ was the real eyecatcher of the race, picking off a number of rivals in the final furlong. He was one of the first under pressure and looks to have some sort of future when tackling staying trips later in his career.
Miss Mocca appeared not to stay. It was surprising to see her so positively ridden on this notable step up in distance and, having been constantly pestered through the early stages by Clarendale, was running on empty inside the final furlong. (op 5-2)
Bravo Ragazzo(IRE), the only newcomer in the field, ran a pleasing race and should improve on this. As expected, he handled these conditions well. (op 5-2)
French Revolution holds down the level of this form.
Gambino(IRE) Official explanation: jockey said saddle slipped

6135 COMLONGON CASTLE H'CAP 7f 200y
4:30 (4:30) (Class 3) (0-95,94) 3-Y-O+ £6,663 (£1,982; £990; £495) Stalls Low

Form RPR

6122 **1** **Anton Chigurh**[43] 4675 3-8-6 **81** .... RichardKingscote 1 93
(Tom Dascombe) *t.k.h: cl up: led gng wl over 2f out: edgd rt and styd on strly fnl f* **13/8**[1]

33-4 **2** *3 1/4* **Master Of Arts (USA)**[15] 5712 7-9-6 **90** .... JoeFanning 6 95
(Mark Johnston) *cl up: chal over 2f out: sn rdn: kpt on same pce ins fnl f* **3/1**[2]

425 **3** *3 1/2* **Oxford Charley (USA)**[17] 5626 3-9-3 **92** .... DavidProbert 5 88
(Mikael Magnusson) *hld up: hdwy and prom over 2f out: sn rdn: edgd rt over 1f out: sn one pce* **5/1**[3]

0001 **4** *5* **Osteopathic Remedy (IRE)**[16] 5677 8-9-7 **91** .... PhillipMakin 8 76
(Michael Dods) *t.k.h: led to over 2f out: rdn and wknd over 1f out* **9/1**

6236 **5** *10* **Hot Rod Mamma (IRE)**[14] 5729 5-8-9 **84** .... ShaneBKelly(5) 7 46
(Dianne Sayer) *prom: effrt and drvn over 2f out: wknd over 1f out* **17/2**

5500 **6** *5* **Dubai Dynamo**[11] 5827 7-9-8 **92** .... JamesSullivan 4 42
(Ruth Carr) *hld up: rdn over 3f out: wknd fr 2f out* **18/1**

1010 **7** *4 1/2* **Mirrored**[16] 5677 6-9-10 **94** .... DuranFentiman 2 34
(Tim Easterby) *taken early to post: prom tl rdn and wknd over 2f out: collapsed fatally after the line* **16/1**

1m 45.27s (5.27) **Going Correction** +0.85s/f (Soft)
WFA 3 from 5yo+ 5lb **7** Ran SP% **111.4**
Speed ratings (Par 107): **107,103,100,95,85 80,75**
Tote Swingers: 1&2 £1.90, 1&3 £3.10, 2&3 £4.00 CSF £6.19 CT £17.71 TOTE £2.60: £1.40, £2.20; EX 6.70.
Owner Panarea Racing **Bred** Mr & Mrs G Middlebrook **Trained** Malpas, Cheshire

FOCUS
A fair little handicap. The winner was well in and is rated up a length on his latest form.

NOTEBOOK
Anton Chigurh kept on strongly in the final furlong, despite wandering across the track, to win cosily. One of only two 3-y-os in the line-up, he was solid at the head of the market and was able to go one better than he had off a 1lb lower mark at both Southwell and Ayr in July. Having finished strongly over 7f on a couple of previous occasions, it was no surprise to see him take another step forward on this, his first try over 1m. He has a progressive profile and could reappear under a penalty back over 7f at Thirsk next week. (op 15-8)

Master Of Arts(USA) ran well, though remains winless on the Flat since 2008. Hampered when fourth on his return at Ripon last time, he looks in good order at present and might be worth another try over 1m2f. (op 4-1)
Oxford Charley(USA) was tried in Group 3 company on occasions earlier in his career, but this looks much more his level. It's hard to know what he actually achieved here, however, and it may be that he'll need to come down the weights a few more pounds. (op 4-1)
Osteopathic Remedy(IRE) dropped away quickly after being forced to make his own running. Although a winner on heavy in the past, much of his best form has come on better ground. (op 8-1 tchd 10-1)
Mirrored, a six-times winner, collapsed and died after the race. (op 14-1 tchd 12-1)

6136 BUTTERMERE H'CAP 7f 200y
5:05 (5:06) (Class 5) (0-75,74) 3-Y-O **£2,385** (£704; £352) **Stalls** Low

Form RPR
3363 **1** **Boots And Spurs**[14] 5737 3-9-4 **74**........................(v) MichaelMetcalfe(3) 2 82
(Mrs K Burke) *t.k.h early: trckd ldrs: effrt over 2f out: led appr fnl f: kpt on strly: eased nr fin* **11/4**[2]
6040 **2** *3 ¾* **Falcon's Reign (FR)**[7] 5942 3-8-9 **69**.....................(p) DanielMuscutt(7) 1 68
(Michael Appleby) *led: rdn over 2f out: hung lft and hdd appr fnl f: kpt on fnl f: no ch w wnr* **8/1**
0002 **3** *shd* **Restaurateur (IRE)**[14] 5747 3-9-5 **72**...........................(v) DavidProbert 9 71
(Andrew Balding) *hld up in tch: stdy hdwy over 2f out: sn rdn: disp 2nd pl ins fnl f: one pce* **9/4**[1]
0-42 **4** *6* **Dark Ruler (IRE)**[19] 5541 3-9-3 **70**.............................. RobertWinston 8 55
(Alan Swinbank) *t.k.h: cl up tl rdn and wknd appr fnl f* **9/1**
041 **5** *½* **Lanarkshire (IRE)**[169] 1053 3-9-5 **72**.............................. JoeFanning 6 56
(Mark Johnston) *cl up: rdn over 2f out: wknd appr fnl f* **10/3**[3]
01-0 **6** *1 ¾* **Swift Encounter (IRE)**[106] 2589 3-9-5 **72**..................... TonyHamilton 5 52
(Ann Duffield) *hld up on ins: faltered over 4f out: sn rdn and outpcd: n.d after* **16/1**
544 **7** *19* **Artillery Train (IRE)**[19] 5545 3-8-7 **60** oh8.................... JamesSullivan 3
(Tim Etherington) *t.k.h: hld up in tch: struggling over 3f out: sn btn* **40/1**

1m 46.81s (6.81) **Going Correction** +0.85s/f (Soft) 7 Ran SP% **109.9**
Speed ratings (Par 101): **99,95,95,89,88 86,67**
Tote Swingers: 1&2 £4.30, 1&3 £2.00, 2&3 £4.40 CSF £22.56 CT £51.58 TOTE £2.60: £1.20, £5.40; EX 20.90.
Owner Colin Bryce **Bred** Miss G Abbey **Trained** Middleham Moor, N Yorks

FOCUS
A modest handicap which may not have taken much winning. The winner is rated in line with the best view of his latest C&D form.
Swift Encounter(IRE) Official explanation: jockey said gelding became unbalanced and collided with rail 5f out

6137 LLOYD BMW H'CAP 1m 6f 32y
5:35 (5:35) (Class 5) (0-75,76) 3-Y-O+ **£2,264** (£673; £336; £168) **Stalls** Low

Form RPR
5244 **1** **Royal Swain (IRE)**[14] 5729 6-9-11 **75**........................ RachaelGreen(3) 3 83
(Alan Swinbank) *hld up in tch: smooth hdwy 4f out: led over 1f out: hung rt ins fnl f: r.o* **4/1**[3]
/21- **2** *2 ¾* **Bocciani (GER)**[144] 5166 7-9-3 **67**.................................... DaleSwift(3) 5 71
(Brian Ellison) *t.k.h: led 1f: cl up: rdn and outpcd over 3f out: rallied and hung rt over 1f out: styd on fnl f: wnt 2nd nr fin: nt rch wnr* **7/1**
3621 **3** *nse* **Silver Samba**[18] 5577 3-8-11 **69**...................................... DavidProbert 7 73
(Andrew Balding) *cl up: chal 1/2-way: led over 3f out to over 1f out: kpt on same pce ins fnl f: lost 2nd nr fin* **11/10**[1]
-332 **4** *1 ¼* **River Dragon (IRE)**[16] 5673 7-9-4 **65**............................ BarryMcHugh 6 67
(Tony Coyle) *led after 1f to over 3f out: sn drvn along: rallied and hung lft over 1f out: kpt on towards fin* **9/4**[2]
6455 **5** *5* **Stags Leap (IRE)**[22] 4867 5-8-10 **62**............................. ShaneBKelly(5) 2 57
(Dianne Sayer) *hld up in tch: rdn and hdwy over 3f out: wknd over 1f out* **25/1**

3m 26.21s (18.71) **Going Correction** +0.85s/f (Soft)
WFA 3 from 4yo+ 11lb 5 Ran SP% **114.7**
Speed ratings (Par 103): **80,78,78,77,74**
CSF £29.99 TOTE £3.10: £2.00, £2.50; EX 28.10.
Owner Andrew Sparks **Bred** Patrick Cummins **Trained** Melsonby, N Yorks

FOCUS
A moderate staying handicap run in a very slow time. The winner's best form since early last year.
T/Plt: £134.70 to a £1 stake. Pool: £5,5073.38 - 298.44 winning tickets. T/Qpdt: £258.30 to a £1 stake. Pool: £7,837.30 - 22.45 winning tickets. RY

5338 DONCASTER (L-H)
Wednesday, September 12

OFFICIAL GOING: Good to firm changing to good after race 1 (2.00) changing to good (good to soft in places) after race 5 (4.10)
Wind: moderate 1/2 against Weather: overcast, cool, light rain 1st 4

6138 ARENA STRUCTURES NURSERY 7f
2:00 (2:02) (Class 2) 2-Y-O **£9,703** (£2,887; £1,443; £721) **Stalls** High

Form RPR
3453 **1** **Regal Dan (IRE)**[19] 5563 2-9-3 **81**..................................... MichaelHills 4 87+
(Charles Hills) *stdd s: hld up: hdwy 3f out: led over 1f out: hld on gamely* **9/2**[2]
61 **2** *hd* **Red Avenger (USA)**[16] 5685 2-9-4 **82**............................ WilliamBuick 2 87+
(Ed Dunlop) *hld up in rr: hdwy over 2f out: styd on to chal fnl 50yds: jst hld* **5/2**[1]
6616 **3** *½* **Prince Regal**[19] 5563 2-8-7 **78**.............................. MichaelJMMurphy(7) 7 82
(Alan Jarvis) *t.k.h: trckd ldrs: led over 2f out tl over 1f out: kpt on same pce fnl 50yds* **13/2**[3]
3010 **4** *3 ½* **Shahdaroba (IRE)**[20] 5515 2-9-7 **85**............................ JamesMillman 8 80
(Rod Millman) *led: qcknd pce over 2f out: sn hdd: one pce over 1f out* **8/1**
003 **5** *2 ¼* **Mirlo Blanco (IRE)**[11] 5825 2-8-11 **75**......................... PaulHanagan 10 64
(Richard Fahey) *trckd ldrs: drvn over 2f out: hung lft over 1f out: one pce* **14/1**
4115 **6** *¾* **Hunting Rights (USA)**[19] 5552 2-9-4 **82**...................... FrannyNorton 11 69
(Mark Johnston) *w ldr: drvn 3f out: wknd over 1f out* **7/1**
2123 **7** *nk* **Hipster**[18] 5579 2-9-3 **81**...(b) JimCrowley 3 67
(Ralph Beckett) *hld up: hdwy over 2f out: wknd over 1f out* **7/1**
0164 **8** *48* **Claude Greenwood**[28] 5232 2-9-0 **78**.......................... RichardHughes 9
(Sylvester Kirk) *hld up in rr: t.k.h: lost pl over 2f out: bhd and eased over 1f out: virtually p.u: hopelessly t.o* **40/1**

1m 27.01s (0.71) **Going Correction** -0.15s/f (Firm) 8 Ran SP% **105.3**
Speed ratings (Par 101): **89,88,88,84,81 80,80,25**
Tote Swingers: 1&2 £2.80, 1&3 £5.60, 2&3 £3.50 CSF £13.67 CT £52.05 TOTE £4.90: £2.10, £1.40, £1.70; EX 16.40 Trifecta £60.10 Pool: £892.75 - 10.99 winning units..
Owner N N Browne,Paul McNamara,Hon Mrs Napier **Bred** Yeomanstown Stud **Trained** Lambourn, Berks
■ Bonnie Lesley was withdrawn (9/1, ref to ent stalls). Deduct 10p in the £ under R4.

FOCUS
They went a solid gallop here and it paid to be ridden with a bit of patience. Decent nursery form and the winner can rate higher in a better race.

NOTEBOOK
Regal Dan(IRE) got plenty of cover early before coming through to challenge with two and a half furlongs to run. Pulling clear with the placed horses inside the last, he bravely stuck his neck out to hold on, and this longer trip proved a real plus for him, despite his pedigree suggesting it might be a concern. (tchd 4-1 and 5-1)
Red Avenger(USA), a maiden winner over this trip at Warwick last time, was held up in last and steadily came through to challenge, but he could never quite get by the winner. He was in front shortly after the line, though, and a mile should bring about further improvement. (op 11-4 tchd 3-1)
Prince Regal, 6lb lower than when sixth at York, ran a sound race and saw the seventh furlong out perfectly well. A rise in the weights won't make things any easier, though. (op 8-1 tchd 6-1)
Shahdaroba(IRE) deserves some credit as he was taken on in front by Hunting Rights, and while the latter dropped out, Rod Millman's colt held on for fourth. (op 10-1)
Mirlo Blanco(IRE) failed to build on his Chester effort on this handicap debut. (tchd 16-1)
Hipster ddin't benefit from headgear this time. (op 11-2)

6139 NAPOLEONS CASINOS & RESTAURANTS CONDITIONS STKS 6f
2:30 (2:31) (Class 2) 2-Y-O
£9,337 (£2,796; £1,398; £699; £349; £175) **Stalls** High

Form RPR
21 **1** **Cour Valant**[26] 5325 2-8-13 0.. NeilCallan 1 98+
(Noel Quinlan) *led: briefly hdd appr 2f out: pushed along and qcknd clr over 1f out: r.o strly* **7/2**[3]
14 **2** *2* **Upward Spiral**[84] 3269 2-8-8 0.. JamieSpencer 6 87
(Tom Dascombe) *w ldrs on stands' siode: effrt 2f out: styd on to take 2nd last 100yds: no real imp* **5/2**[2]
1 **3** *nk* **Ribaat (IRE)**[33] 5040 2-8-13 0... PaulHanagan 5 91
(Roger Varian) *t.k.h in rr stands' rail: effrt 2f out: hung rt: kpt on to take 3rd nr fin* **6/5**[1]
000 **4** *½* **Threes Grand**[6] 5979 2-8-6 87... MircoDemuro 2 83
(Scott Dixon) *w wnr: led briefly over 2f out: kpt on same pce over 1f out* **22/1**
1062 **5** *½* **Tommy's Secret**[14] 5743 2-8-11 80.................................... BrettDoyle 4 86
(Jane Chapple-Hyam) *trckd ldrs: effrt 2f out: kpt on same pce* **50/1**
0465 **6** *6* **Top Boy**[24] 5382 2-8-11 95... FrannyNorton 3 68
(Derek Shaw) *trckd ldrs: t.k.h: lost pl over 1f out* **14/1**

1m 13.36s (-0.24) **Going Correction** -0.15s/f (Firm) 6 Ran SP% **109.2**
Speed ratings (Par 101): **95,92,91,91,90 82**
Tote Swingers: 1&2 £1.60, 1&3 £1.30, 2&3 £1.20 CSF £11.93 TOTE £4.70: £2.50, £1.30; EX 13.70.
Owner David F O'Rourke **Bred** Plantation Stud **Trained** Newmarket, Suffolk

FOCUS
They didn't go a great pace early and it paid to race handily. Having initially split into two groups, with two racing along the stands' rail, they came together with over 3f to run. Decent form. The winner impressed but the runner-up was below her Ascot form.

NOTEBOOK
Cour Valant was prominent throughout and that was the place to be in a race lacking early pace. Quickening up approaching the final furlong, he won cosily in the end, and now deserves a crack at a Pattern race. He's a top-of-the-ground performer so conditions can't have been too bad here, despite the rain, and his trainer suggested he'll try to go where the ground is suitable in future. (op 9-2)
Upward Spiral, not seen since finishing fourth in the Queen Mary, shaped well following her absence. The sixth furlong was no problem and she's entitled to come on for this. (op 9-4 tchd 11-4)
Ribaat(IRE) was inconvenienced by the steady early pace, pulling hard behind Upward Spiral, who made the running on the stands' side. Still green, he tended to hang right in the closing stages and wouldn't go by the runner-up, so has a bit to prove now, but he deserves another chance. (tchd 11-10 and 5-4)
Threes Grand, who is fairly exposed now, was up with the pace so had things run to suit, and one would have to think that she's run fairly close to her best in defeat. She's a good guide to the level of the form. (op 20-1)
Tommy's Secret faced a stiff task and ran well in the circumstances, although the modest early gallop may mean he's flattered by the bare form. (op 40-1)

6140 SCARBROUGH STKS (LISTED RACE) 5f
3:05 (3:05) (Class 1) 2-Y-O+ **£23,680** (£8,956; £4,476; £2,236) **Stalls** High

Form RPR
2230 **1** **Sole Power**[19] 5561 5-9-9 115.. JohnnyMurtagh 9 113+
(Edward Lynam, Ire) *hld up in rr: t.k.h: nt clr run over 1f out: swtchd rt jst ins fnl f: str run to ld last 30yds: v readily* **5/2**[1]
1-11 **2** *1 ½* **Jwala**[40] 4765 3-9-3 93... ShaneKelly 4 103
(Robert Cowell) *led: hdd and no ex clsng stages* **14/1**
0130 **3** *shd* **Excelette (IRE)**[40] 4762 3-9-6 103...................................... TomEaves 8 106
(Bryan Smart) *led 1f: chsd ldr: kpt on same pce last 50yds* **25/1**
0403 **4** *1 ¼* **Confessional**[11] 5822 5-9-9 106...............................(be) PaulMulrennan 5 104
(Tim Easterby) *chsd ldrs: kpt on same pce fnl f* **12/1**
3202 **5** *½* **Masamah (IRE)**[11] 5822 6-9-9 107............................(p) JamieSpencer 13 102
(Kevin Ryan) *mid-div: hdwy and drvn over 2f out: hung lft and kpt on same pce* **6/1**[3]
110 **6** *nk* **Valbchek (IRE)**[84] 3265 3-9-8 103.................................. WilliamBuick 7 101+
(Jeremy Noseda) *s.i.s: in rr: hdwy on outside over 1f out: kpt on same pce* **5/1**[2]
040- **7** *¾* **Kingsgate Native (IRE)**[375] 5707 7-9-9 113................ RichardHughes 6 98
(Robert Cowell) *hld up in mid-div: effrt over 1f out: kpt on same pce* **11/1**
3620 **8** *hd* **Nocturnal Affair (SAF)**[19] 5561 6-9-9 113........................(t) NeilCallan 2 97
(David Marnane, Ire) *towards rr: kpt on fnl 2f: nvr a factor* **8/1**
0204 **9** *1 ½* **Pabusar**[11] 5822 4-9-9 106.. JimCrowley 10 92
(Ralph Beckett) *mid-div: drvn over 2f out: one pce* **10/1**
13-0 **10** *½* **Roicead (USA)**[87] 3196 5-9-9 104......................(tp) DeclanMcDonogh 12 90
(W McCreery, Ire) *in rr on inner: effrt over 2f out: fdd over 1f out* **20/1**
00- **11** *2* **Timeless Call (IRE)**[10] 5857 4-9-4 90............................ PaulHanagan 11 78
(Reginald Roberts, Ire) *s.i.s: a in rr on inner: nvr on terms* **20/1**

5050 **12** *hd* **Noble Storm (USA)**[11] 5822 6-9-9 102 ... FrannyNorton 1 82
(Ed McMahon) *chsd ldrs on outer: wknd appr fnl f* **50/1**

58.69s (-1.81) **Going Correction** -0.15s/f (Firm)
WFA 3 from 4yo+ 1lb **12** Ran SP% **117.7**
Speed ratings: **108,106,105,103,103 102,101,101,98,97 94,94**
Tote Swingers: 1&2 £8.40, 1&3 £14.60, 2&3 £21.40 CSF £38.12 TOTE £2.80: £1.20, £4.30, £7.70; EX 51.00 Trifecta £1094.30 Pool: £1,863.28 - 1.26 winning units..
Owner Mrs S Power **Bred** G Russell **Trained** Dunshaughlin, Co Meath

FOCUS
Sadly no 2yos took their chance this season, but that didn't detract from a really competitive renewal. A couple of 3yo fillies led the field, ensuring the pace was reasonably sound.

NOTEBOOK
Sole Power was the best of these on official figures and wasn't required to carry a penalty for his previous Group victories, including the 2010 Nunthorpe. Far from disgraced all season, he showed his class here with a quality turn of foot about a furlong out to readily pick off everything in front of him. He's in line to take in as many big sprints as he can, starting with the L'Abbaye then the Hong Kong Sprint, and remains a difficult opponent to beat when things fall right for him. (op 9-4 tchd 2-1 and 11-4)
Jwala had made great strides since starting her winning sequence and this was by far a career-best in defeat. Showing tons of speed from the off, she came home an honourable second but couldn't resist a Group performer late on. (op 20-1)
Excelette(IRE), who had finished behind a few of these in the King George Stakes at Goodwood (trainer subsequently reported that she may not have enjoyed the Sussex track or just had an off day), ran really well and one would imagine that connections will try and get a bit of Group-placed form at least into her if the right opportunity can be found. (op 33-1)
Confessional is not a frequent winner by any means, but often runs well in classy sprints and is a relatively solid marker to rate the race through for those other than Sole Power. (op 11-1 tchd 14-1)
Masamah(IRE), with cheekpieces back on for the first time since the 2011 Prix De L'Abbaye, was in front of Confessional recently at Beverley so the return of the headgear didn't appear to have a beneficial effect. Official explanation: jockey said gelding hung left (op 13-2 tchd 11-2)
Valbchek(IRE), absent since finishing eleventh in the Jersey Stakes, was by far the least experienced of these and hadn't been tested over 5f previously. He wasn't quickly into stride, but shaped like a horse that will be better over further. (op 6-1 tchd 9-2)
Kingsgate Native(IRE), making his debut for Robert Cowell after a 375-day absence, moved strongly for some way before finding the one pace. There is every chance, even though he has gone well fresh previously, that this may have been needed and he can improve from it. (op 10-1 tchd 8-1)
Nocturnal Affair(SAF), who won the Portland on his only previous start here under Neil Callan, failed to land a telling blow. (tchd 9-1)

6141 CLIPPER LOGISTICS LEGER LEGENDS CLASSIFIED STKS 1m (S)
3:40 (3:42) (Class 5) 3-Y-0+ **£6,469** (£1,925; £962; £481) **Stalls** High

Form RPR
6266 **1** **Patriotic (IRE)**[14] 5752 4-11-0 69 ... MickKinane 15 78+
(Chris Dwyer) *racd stands' side: in rr: hdwy over 3f out: led overall over 1f out: jst hld on* **5/1**[1]
226 **2** *nse* **Elijah Pepper (USA)**[37] 4889 7-11-0 70 ... GeorgeDuffield 7 78
(David Barron) *hld up: hdwy over 3f out: chsd wnr over 1f out: hrd rdn and chal last 50yds: jst denied* **12/1**
0054 **3** *4 ½* **Handheld**[7] 5941 5-11-0 69 ... TonyClark 14 68
(Ed de Giles) *racd stands' side: chsd ldrs: led that gp over 3f out: led overall over 2f out: hdd over 1f out: one pce* **16/1**
400 **4** *2* **Masters Blazing**[26] 5322 3-10-9 70 ... WillieRyan 18 63
(John Ryan) *racd stands' side: in rr: hdwy over 2f out: kpt on to take 4th last 50yds* **14/1**
1050 **5** *1 ¼* **Hail Promenader (IRE)**[26] 5322 6-11-0 70 ...(p) LukeHarvey 3 60
(Anthony Carson) *in rr: hdwy over 3f out: one pce over 1f out* **16/1**
2444 **6** *1 ¼* **Hawaana (IRE)**[26] 5323 7-11-0 70 ...(v[1]) GayKelleway 9 57
(Gay Kelleway) *hld up in rr: hdwy over 3f out: hung rt and one pce fnl 2f* **8/1**
3305 **7** *½* **Save The Bees**[15] 5713 4-11-0 70 ...(b[1]) KevinDarley 8 56
(Declan Carroll) *chsd ldrs: one pce fnl 2f* **7/1**[3]
114 **8** *hd* **Muftarres (IRE)**[17] 5618 7-11-0 70 ...(b) TomO'Ryan 1 56
(Paul Midgley) *hld up: hdwy far side over 3f out: sn chsng ldrs: one pce fnl 2f* **14/1**
0241 **9** *2 ¼* **Chookie Avon**[29] 5185 5-11-0 70 ...(p) JohnReid 11 51
(Keith Dalgleish) *swtchd lft after 1f: hld up towards rr: hdwy over 3f out: hung lft: fdd fnl f* **14/1**
5-00 **10** *7* **Sir Francis Drake**[12] 5794 4-11-0 70 ...(p) NickConnorton 2 34
(Robert Eddery) *chsd ldrs: edgd rt over 3f out: upsides over 2f out: wknd over 1f out* **25/1**
2226 **11** *3 ¼* **The Ducking Stool**[17] 5636 5-11-0 69 ... OlliePears 19 27
(Julia Feilden) *s.s: racd stands' side: nvr on terms* **9/1**
600 **12** *½* **Pirate Chest (IRE)**[4] 6047 4-11-0 70 ...[1] GaryBardwell 13 26
(Patrick Holmes) *racd stands' side: chsd ldrs: wknd over 2f out* **33/1**
406 **13** *1* **Alhaban (IRE)**[14] 5751 6-11-0 70 ... DaleGibson 5 23
(Ronald Harris) *chsd ldrs: hmpd over 3f out: edgd rt and wknd 2f out* **28/1**
6032 **14** *2 ½* **Sunnyside Tom (IRE)**[17] 5618 8-11-0 70 ... JulieKrone 6 18
(Richard Fahey) *led centre gp and overall tl over 2f out: sn wknd* **13/2**[2]
00-0 **15** *9* **File And Paint (IRE)**[156] 1249 4-11-0 70 ... AllanMackay 10
(Lawrence Mullaney) *w ldr: t.k.h: lost pl over 2f out: sn bhd: eased fnl f* **25/1**
5324 **16** *6* **Gunner Will (IRE)**[37] 4874 3-10-9 70 ... JamieOsborne 12
(Jamie Osborne) *led stands' side gp tl over 3f out: sn lost pl and bhd: eased* **12/1**

1m 40.9s (1.60) **Going Correction** -0.15s/f (Firm)
WFA 3 from 4yo+ 5lb **16** Ran SP% **124.8**
Speed ratings (Par 103): **86,85,81,79,78 76,76,76,74,67 63,63,62,59,50 44**
Tote Swingers: 1&2 £12.80, 1&3 £22.30, 2&3 £35.90 CSF £63.54 TOTE £6.20: £2.60, £4.10, £4.90; EX 44.00 Trifecta £369.10 Pool: £1,252.15 - 2.51 winning units..
Owner M M Foulger **Bred** Darley **Trained** Six Mile Bottom, Cambs
■ Stewards' Enquiry : George Duffield Fine: £300, used whip above permitted level.

FOCUS
Only an ordinary race in terms of class, but a field full of riding legends obviously heightened public interest. Two came clear at the end, and three of the first four raced stands' side early in a smaller group than those who came towards the centre.

6142 KAT COMMUNICATIONS KNOWLEDGE ABOUT TELECOMS CONDITIONS STKS 1m 2f 60y
4:10 (4:11) (Class 2) 3-5-Y-0 **£12,450** (£3,728; £1,864; £932; £466) **Stalls** Low

Form RPR
4152 **1** **Proud Chieftain**[5] 6010 4-9-2 89 ... DarrylHolland 4 99
(Clifford Lines) *mde all: qcknd pce and chal over 2f out: kpt on wl ins fnl f: gamely* **16/1**
6340 **2** *1 ¼* **Cai Shen (IRE)**[43] 4684 4-9-2 102 ... RichardHughes 2 97
(Richard Hannon) *hld up: effrt over 2f out: tk 2nd last 50yds: no real imp* **9/2**[3]
230- **3** *1 ¼* **Modeyra**[325] 7047 5-8-11 105 ... PaulHanagan 5 89
(Saeed Bin Suroor) *trckd ldrs: effrt and upsides over 2f out: kpt on same pce fnl f* **5/1**
1-65 **4** *1 ¼* **Beaten Up**[102] 2703 4-9-2 117 ... JohnnyMurtagh 3 92
(William Haggas) *dwlt: t.k.h in last: hdwy over 2f out: kpt on same pce: nvr threatened* **13/8**[1]
1- **5** *7* **Swedish Sailor**[323] 7082 3-8-9 0 ... MickaelBarzalona 1 79
(Mahmood Al Zarooni) *t.k.h: trckd wnr: effrt over 2f out: wknd appr fnl f: eased* **5/2**[2]

2m 11.17s (1.77) **Going Correction** -0.025s/f (Good)
WFA 3 from 4yo+ 7lb **5** Ran SP% **107.4**
Speed ratings (Par 109): **91,90,89,88,82**
CSF £76.86 TOTE £16.70: £3.60, £2.00; EX 61.20.
Owner Prima Racing Partnership **Bred** John James **Trained** Exning, Suffolk

FOCUS
Not form to trust as Daryll Holland on the winner was allowed to do his own thing out in front.

NOTEBOOK
Proud Chieftain took full advantage out front, setting a gallop to suit himself and saving enough so that, when challenged 2f out, he had enough left in the tank to repel his rivals. This was a fine ride on a horse who had plenty to find at the weights, but having said that he did arrive here at the top of his game while most of his higher-rated rivals had questions to answer. (op 14-1)
Cai Shen(IRE), who won the race last year from the front, was ridden more patiently this time and settled better than some. That said, given the way the race was run, he was given a bit to do, and his final-furlong challenge was always just being held by the cannily ridden winner. (tchd 4-1 and 5-1)
Modeyra had been absent since last autumn, but she'd won first time up in her first two seasons and finished second in Listed company on her reappearance last term. In the circumstances this was a disappointing effort, and given her profile she wouldn't be a certainty to build on it next time. (op 13-2)
Beaten Up, in search of a confidence booster following his disappointing run in the Coronation Cup back in June, refused to settle in last place, which was far from the ideal position to be in given the way the race was being run. He never got in a blow and, while he needs further and could do with a stronger gallop in future, he now has something to prove. (op 7-4 tchd 15-8)
Swedish Sailor, considered a Derby possible over the winter, missed a couple of engagements in the spring and was making a late return. He didn't really settle behind the leader and dropped out quickly from a furlong and a half out. This wasn't the same horse that beat Noble Mission by 5l on his debut and there have to be questions about how much ability he retains (op 2-1 tchd 15-8)

6143 ELEMENTS MEDISPA H'CAP 7f
4:45 (4:46) (Class 2) (0-100,97) 3-Y-0
£12,450 (£3,728; £1,864; £932; £466; £234) **Stalls** High

Form RPR
0020 **1** **Born To Surprise**[40] 4760 3-9-2 **92** ... JamieSpencer 8 101+
(Michael Bell) *dwlt: hld up in rr: stdy hdwy on outer over 2f out: shkn up to ld jst ins fnl f: edgd rt drvn out* **15/2**[3]
4413 **2** *1 ¼* **Obliteright (IRE)**[26] 5302 3-8-10 **86** ... NeilCallan 13 92
(William Knight) *trckd ldrs: t.k.h: styd on and ev ch jst ins fnl f: no ex* **20/1**
6-00 **3** *¾* **Gold City (IRE)**[25] 5363 3-9-6 **96** ...(t) MickaelBarzalona 7 100
(Saeed Bin Suroor) *hld up: hdwy over 2f out: led over 1f out: hdd jst ins fnl f: kpt on same pce* **16/1**
0034 **4** *hd* **Alejandro (IRE)**[11] 5827 3-8-10 **89** ... LeeTopliss[(3)] 5 92
(Richard Fahey) *sn w ldrs: led over 2f out: hdd over 1f out: kpt on same pce last 100yds* **25/1**
6000 **5** *nk* **Accession (IRE)**[32] 5080 3-8-13 **89** ... JohnFahy 10 92
(Clive Cox) *trckd ldrs: effrt over 2f out: one pce appr fnl f* **20/1**
-422 **6** *¾* **Strictly Silver (IRE)**[11] 5827 3-9-2 **92** ... JimmyQuinn 9 93+
(Alan Bailey) *trckd ldrs: t.k.h: stmbld bdly after 150yds: outpcd over 3f out: n.m.r over 2f out: styd on fnl f* **5/2**[1]
3500 **7** *¾* **Gatepost (IRE)**[18] 5572 3-9-4 **94** ... PaulHanagan 4 93
(Richard Fahey) *chsd ldrs: effrt over 2f out: one pce over 1f out* **25/1**
3500 **8** *½* **Balty Boys (IRE)**[25] 5342 3-9-7 **97** ... JohnnyMurtagh 14 94+
(Charles Hills) *hld up in rr: effrt over 2f out: shkn up and hdwy over 1f out: styng on in promising fashion at fin* **10/1**
-561 **9** *1* **Otto The Great**[19] 5556 3-8-11 **87** ... ShaneKelly 2 82
(Peter Chapple-Hyam) *led tl over 2f out: wknd 1f out* **16/1**
4034 **10** *2 ½* **Compton**[16] 5677 3-9-2 **92** ... JimCrowley 6 80
(Ralph Beckett) *trckd ldrs: hmpd after 150yds: effrt 2f out: wknd fnl f* **12/1**
035- **11** *½* **Magic City (IRE)**[356] 6268 3-8-11 **87** ... RichardHughes 1 73
(Richard Hannon) *s.i.s: sn trcking ldrs: effrt over 2f out: wknd appr fnl f* **9/1**
311 **12** *3* **Discression**[26] 5314 3-8-13 **89** ... GrahamLee 11 67
(Kevin Ryan) *restless in stalls: in rr: drvn 3f out: nvr a factor* **5/1**[2]
-010 **13** *4 ½* **Ewell Place (IRE)**[40] 4760 3-9-6 **96** ... TomEaves 12 62
(Robert Mills) *hld up in rr: effrt over 2f out: lost pl over 1f out* **25/1**
05-5 **14** *3 ¼* **Red Aggressor (IRE)**[16] 5686 3-9-3 **93** ... TomQueally 3 50
(Clive Brittain) *w ldrs: wknd 2f out: sn bhd* **66/1**

1m 26.39s (0.09) **Going Correction** -0.15s/f (Firm) **14** Ran SP% **118.1**
Speed ratings (Par 107): **93,91,90,90,90 89,88,87,86,83 83,79,74,71**
Tote Swingers: 1&2 £26.00, 1&3 £23.60, 2&3 £54.20 CSF £154.96 CT £2394.07 TOTE £8.50: £3.10, £6.50, £5.60; EX 207.10 Trifecta £1511.30 Pool: £2,042.37 - 1.00 winning units..
Owner Dr Ali Ridha **Bred** Rabbah Bloodstock Limited **Trained** Newmarket, Suffolk

FOCUS
The going was changed to good, good to soft after the previous race. Any number of these could be fancied, which suggests this should be solid form, but the leaders didn't seem to set searching fractions early.

NOTEBOOK
Born To Surprise, a previous C&D winner, looked interesting returned to handicap company and produced plenty off the bridle despite needing to come round the field to deliver his challenge. A horse with plenty of size, he seems sure to improve with age and 7f does appear his ideal distance, although a strongly run six might be within scope. (op 8-1 tchd 7-1)
Obliteright(IRE), returned to turf after a couple of good efforts at Kempton, is a really solid performer over this trip and burst out of the pack towards the stands' side to be the best of that group.
Gold City(IRE) shaped like a horse the handicapper has about right, for all that he ran encouragingly.
Alejandro(IRE) hinted at better to come last time at Chester although behind Strictly Silver, and confirmed his wellbeing here, comfortably reversing the form with the Alan Bailey gelding. (op 22-1)
Accession(IRE), without cheekpieces, hadn't been tried over this distance before but showed plenty of promise over it despite wandering. (op 25-1 tchd 28-1)
Strictly Silver(IRE) met a small bit of trouble in running, and did stumble soon after leaving the stalls, but was probably more inconvenienced by the modest early gallop. (tchd 9-4)
Balty Boys(IRE) was along side Born To Surprise in rear for a while, but doesn't possess that same turn of foot. He kept on, but looked anchored by top weight. (op 12-1 tchd 16-1)

Magic City(IRE), absent for almost a year and gelded in the interim, appeared to pull hard in behind the leaders and failed to pick up. He can probably handle a drop in trip. (op 8-1 tchd 15-2)
Discression, chasing a hat-trick after two wins at Newcastle, didn't always have a lot of room in which to manoeuvre and got outpaced over 2f out. (op 9-2)

6144 BJS H'CAP 5f
5:15 (5:20) (Class 4) (0-85,85) 3-Y-O+ **£6,469** (£1,925; £962; £481) **Stalls** High

Form RPR

0036 **1** **Even Stevens**[40] 4770 4-8-12 **76**.....(p) MircoDemuro 9 89
(Scott Dixon) *chsd ldrs on outer: led over 1f out: drvn out* **20/1**

333 **2** 1 3/4 **Jack Luey**[16] 5674 5-8-13 **77**..... NeilCallan 22 84
(Lawrence Mullaney) *in rr stands' side: hdwy 2f out: styd on to take 2nd last 50yds* **12/1**

3145 **3** nk **Cheworee**[33] 5065 3-8-13 **78**..... RichardHughes 10 84
(David Elsworth) *hld up towards rr: smooth hdwy 2f out: styd on to take 3rd last 50yds: no ex* **9/1**[3]

161 **4** 1 1/2 **Tom Sawyer**[12] 5791 4-8-10 **74**.....(b) GrahamLee 7 74
(Julie Camacho) *chsd ldrs towards far side: led over 2f out: hdd over 1f out: kpt on same pce* **12/1**

0120 **5** 2 1/4 **Six Wives**[11] 5822 5-9-2 **80**..... TomQueally 17 72
(Scott Dixon) *chsd ldrs stands' side: effrt over 2f out: kpt on wl fnl f* **14/1**

4021 **6** 1 1/4 **Haajes**[13] 5758 8-9-0 **78**.....(b) MickyFenton 19 69+
(Paul Midgley) *mid-div stands' side: hdwy 2f out: hmpd 1f out: styd on last 75yds* **7/1**[2]

6421 **7** hd **Drift And Dream**[21] 5486 5-8-13 **77**..... HarryBentley 11 64
(Chris Wall) *mid-div: effrt over 2f out: chsng ldrs over 1f out: fdd towards fin* **13/2**[1]

065 **8** hd **Perfect Blossom**[5] 6006 5-9-0 **78**..... PaulHanagan 20 64
(Ian McInnes) *in rr towards stands' side: hdwy over 1f out: styng on at fin* **14/1**

2105 **9** hd **Partner (IRE)**[11] 5829 6-9-3 **84**.....(p) GaryBartley(3) 8 69
(Noel Wilson) *rr-div: hdwy over 2f out: kpt on fnl f: nvr nr ldrs* **12/1**

0000 **10** nk **Marine Commando**[11] 5829 4-9-2 **80**..... PJMcDonald 1 64
(Ruth Carr) *in rr towards far side: hdwy 2f out: kpt on* **10/1**

1000 **11** 1/2 **Noodles Blue Boy**[11] 5829 6-9-0 **85**..... JacobButterfield(7) 18 68
(Ollie Pears) *s.i.s: drvn and sn in tch: one pce fnl 2f* **20/1**

3160 **12** 1/2 **Captain Scooby**[34] 4999 6-8-12 **76**..... RobbieFitzpatrick 6 57
(Richard Guest) *in rr: sme hdwy over 1f out: nvr a factor* **33/1**

000 **13** shd **Excel Bolt**[11] 5829 4-9-7 **85**..... TomEaves 5 65
(Bryan Smart) *trckd ldrs far side: wknd over 1f out* **16/1**

5450 **14** 1 3/4 **Nomoreblondes**[18] 5584 8-8-10 **74**.....(v) JimmyQuinn 15 48
(Paul Midgley) *in rr: nvr a factor* **40/1**

0140 **15** 3/4 **Whozthecat (IRE)**[5] 6005 5-8-13 **82**..... NeilFarley(5) 2 53
(Declan Carroll) *overall ldr towards far side: hdd over 2f out: wknd over 1f out* **16/1**

01-0 **16** 3 **Captain Royale (IRE)**[11] 5821 7-8-8 **72**.....(p) FrannyNorton 21 33
(Tracy Waggott) *a towards rr* **33/1**

400 **17** 4 1/2 **Close To The Edge (IRE)**[45] 4629 4-9-0 **78**..... ShaneKelly 3 22
(Alan McCabe) *s.i.s: in rr towards far side: sme hdwy over 2f out: sn wknd* **20/1**

000 **18** 9 **Powerful Wind (IRE)**[18] 5603 3-9-6 **85**..... JohnFahy 12
(Ronald Harris) *s.i.s: sn chsng ldrs: wknd over 1f out: heavily eased whn bhd* **50/1**

2432 **U** **Flash City (ITY)**[18] 5584 4-9-7 **85**.....(v) JohnnyMurtagh 16
(Bryan Smart) *rrd up in stalls and uns rdr* **9/1**[3]

59.04s (-1.46) **Going Correction** -0.15s/f (Firm)
WFA 3 from 4yo+ 1lb **19** Ran SP% **127.7**
Speed ratings (Par 105): **105,102,101,99,95 93,93,93,92,92 91,90,90,87,86 81,74,60,**
Tote Swingers: 1&2 £11.40, 1&3 £9.90, 2&3 £7.70 CSF £234.91 CT £2396.08 TOTE £28.90: £6.90, £2.80, £2.20, £3.00; EX 420.50 Trifecta £1116.40 Part won. Pool: £1,508.66 - 0.10 winning units..
Owner Paul J Dixon **Bred** Mrs Yvette Dixon **Trained** Babworth, Notts

FOCUS
A wide-open sprint handicap.
Close To The Edge(IRE) Official explanation: jockey said filly reared in stalls; trainer said filly was unsuited by the good (good to soft places) ground
T/Jkpt: Not won. T/Plt: £571.10 to a £1 stake. Pool: £128,550.75 - 164.29 winning tickets.
T/Qpdt: £258.30 to a £1 stake. Pool: £7,837.30 - 22.45 winning tickets. WG

6034 KEMPTON (A.W) (R-H)
Wednesday, September 12

OFFICIAL GOING: Standard
Wind: Moderate, across (away from stands) Weather: Fine but cloudy; heavy rain after race 6

6145 BETDAQ DVINSKY RECORD-EQUALLING 217TH RUN H'CAP 7f (P)
5:45 (5:45) (Class 5) (0-70,70) 3-Y-O+ **£2,264** (£673; £336; £168) **Stalls** Low

Form RPR

02 **1** **Zing Wing**[10] 5852 4-9-7 **67**..... AdamKirby 4 76+
(David Evans) *trckd ldrs: nt clr run and lost pl 2f out: swtchd lft jst over 1f out: str run fnl f to ld post* **7/1**[2]

-3 **2** nk **Sunshine Always (IRE)**[28] 5234 6-9-2 **65**..... MarkCoumbe(3) 10 73
(Michael Attwater) *hld up in midfield: prog over 2f out: swept into ld over 1f out: hung rt but sn 2 l clr: tired nr fin: hdd post* **8/1**[3]

5006 **3** 1 **Saskia's Dream**[31] 5122 4-9-8 **68**..... RobertHavlin 2 73
(Jane Chapple-Hyam) *dwlt: trckd ldrs on inner: tried to chal 2f out: sn outpcd: kpt on to take 3rd nr fin* **7/1**[2]

4032 **4** hd **Dvinsky (USA)**[6] 5972 11-9-3 **63**.....(b) TomMcLaughlin 7 68
(Paul Howling) *pressed ldr: led 3f out: hdd and outpcd over 1f out: kpt on gamely but lost 2 pls nr fin* **10/1**

2053 **5** 2 1/4 **Ghost Train (IRE)**[16] 5662 3-9-1 **70**.....(p) DarrenEgan(5) 8 68
(Mark Johnston) *trckd ldrs: looking for room 2f out: rdn and nt qckn over 1f out: one pce after* **7/2**[1]

0000 **6** nk **Golden Desert (IRE)**[54] 4287 8-9-10 **70**..... SebSanders 1 68+
(Simon Dow) *s.v.s: hld up in last: trying to make prog on inner whn nt clr run 2f out: shoved along and styd on fr over 1f out: nrst fin* **8/1**[3]

0003 **7** nse **Mishrif (USA)**[35] 4966 6-9-7 **67**.....(b) PatDobbs 14 65
(J R Jenkins) *racd wd: pressed ldng pair: upsides gng easily 2f out: nudged by rival over 1f out: folded tamely* **8/1**[3]

0200 **8** 1 **Beautiful Lando (FR)**[63] 3958 4-9-1 **61**.....(v) EddieAhern 11 56
(Heather Main) *hld up in midfield: smooth prog to chal 2f out: sltly intimidated over 1f out: veered rt and gave up* **20/1**

300- **9** 1 1/4 **Spartic**[391] 5213 4-9-6 **66**..... DaneO'Neill 9 58
(Alan McCabe) *racd wd in midfield: pushed along 1/2-way: no prog 2f out: fdd* **33/1**

0006 **10** hd **Bassett Road (IRE)**[37] 4872 4-9-0 **60**..... StevieDonohoe 13 51
(Willie Musson) *hld up in last trio: jst pushed along 2f out: rdn fnl f: no ch* **10/1**

3006 **11** 1/2 **Great Charm (IRE)**[9] 5893 7-9-8 **68**.....(t) GeorgeBaker 12 58
(Daniel Kubler) *awkward s and slowly away: hld up in last trio: taken to outer and shkn up over 1f out: no real prog* **25/1**

0000 **12** 1 **Silvee**[17] 5625 5-9-0 **60**..... KieranO'Neill 5 47
(John Bridger) *nvr bttr than midfield: rdn bef 1/2-way: stl same pl 2f out: wknd fnl f* **25/1**

/40- **13** 15 **Sinchiroka (FR)**[377] 5639 6-9-1 **61**..... JamieGoldstein 6
(Ralph Smith) *mde most to 3f out: wknd rapidly: t.o* **50/1**

1m 25.97s (-0.03) **Going Correction** +0.025s/f (Slow)
WFA 3 from 4yo+ 4lb **13** Ran SP% **116.1**
Speed ratings (Par 103): **101,100,99,99,96 96,96,95,93,93 92,91,74**
Tote Swingers: 1&2 £12.60, 1&3 £5.10, 2&3 £15.40 CSF £56.06 CT £422.97 TOTE £7.50: £2.60, £2.10, £3.60; EX 58.90 Trifecta £444.00 Pool: £2,868.18 - 4.78 winning units..
Owner Exors of the late Mrs Sally Edwards **Bred** Deepwood Farm Stud **Trained** Pandy, Monmouths

■ Stewards' Enquiry : Mark Coumbe three-day ban: careless riding (Sep 26,27,30)

FOCUS
This was just a modest handicap and the pace seemed ordinary. Sound form, with the winner back to her early best.

6146 BACK OR LAY AT BETDAQ.COM H'CAP 1m 4f (P)
6:15 (6:16) (Class 5) (0-75,75) 3-Y-O **£2,264** (£673; £336; £168) **Stalls** Centre

Form RPR

-103 **1** **Livia's Dream (IRE)**[21] 5474 3-9-4 **72**..... GeorgeBaker 13 80
(Ed Walker) *racd on outer: trckd ldng pair: shkn up over 2f out: led over 1f out: rdn and styd on wl* **13/2**[2]

5-43 **2** 3/4 **Openly**[13] 5766 3-9-7 **75**..... HayleyTurner 8 82
(James Fanshawe) *t.k.h: trckd ldng pair: chal and upsides over 1f out: chsd wnr sn after: styd on but a hld* **9/1**

005 **3** shd **Porcini**[40] 4776 3-8-6 **63**..... RaulDaSilva(3) 9 69+
(Philip McBride) *hld up towards rr: rdn over 2f out: prog on outer over 1f out: r.o wl fnl f: nrly snatched 2nd* **11/1**

5233 **4** 1 **Napoleon's Muse (IRE)**[27] 5277 3-9-7 **75**..... SebSanders 6 80
(Ralph Beckett) *hld up in midfield: drvn over 2f out: prog wl over 1f out: tried to chal jst ins fnl f: one pce last 100yds* **11/1**

3-63 **5** 1 3/4 **Shada (IRE)**[14] 5753 3-9-5 **73**..... PatDobbs 14 75
(Sir Michael Stoute) *pressed ldr: rdn over 2f out: lost pl over 1f out but stl cl up: fdd ins fnl f* **8/1**[3]

6003 **6** 3/4 **Just When**[69] 3787 3-8-9 **63**.....(v) LiamKeniry 10 64
(Andrew Balding) *s.s: hld up in last: rdn and prog on inner wl over 1f out: kpt on but nt pce to threaten* **16/1**

0-05 **7** nk **Maria Letizia**[33] 5048 3-9-6 **74**..... WilliamBuick 7 74
(John Gosden) *rousted along to ld: hrd rdn over 2f out: hdd and fdd over 1f out* **13/2**[2]

6211 **8** nk **Attraction Ticket**[30] 5164 3-8-8 **67**..... DarrenEgan(5) 2 67
(David Simcock) *hld up towards rr: prog over 2f out: chsd ldrs u.p over 1f out: wknd ins fnl f* **10/3**[1]

5 **9** 1/2 **Hail Hail (USA)**[21] 5482 3-8-11 **70**..... AshleyMorgan(5) 11 69
(Paul Cole) *wl in tch in midfield: rdn over 2f out: no prog over 1f out: fdd* **66/1**

0204 **10** 2 **Cool Sky**[24] 5387 3-9-5 **73**..... AdamKirby 12 69
(William Knight) *stdd s: t.k.h: hld up in last trio: prog into midfield: over 1f out: wknd fnl f* **20/1**

1360 **11** 1/2 **Tingo In The Tale (IRE)**[11] 5816 3-9-4 **72**..... IanMongan 5 67
(David Arbuthnot) *trckd ldrs in 5th: effrt on inner and cl up 2f out: wknd over 1f out* **20/1**

0464 **12** 1/2 **Whipcrackaway (IRE)**[39] 4224 3-9-4 **72**.....(p) DaneO'Neill 1 66
(Peter Hedger) *wl in tch in midfield: rdn over 2f out: no prog over 1f out: wknd and eased* **16/1**

4234 **13** 2 1/4 **Instrumentalist (IRE)**[30] 5163 3-9-1 **74**..... TobyAtkinson(5) 4 65
(John Best) *hld up in last trio: rdn 3f out: no prog and btn 2f out* **16/1**

0430 **14** 1 1/2 **The Noble Ord**[11] 5837 3-9-3 **71**.....(t) SeanLevey 3 59
(Sylvester Kirk) *a wl in rr: rdn 3f out: sn btn* **28/1**

2m 33.86s (-0.64) **Going Correction** +0.025s/f (Slow) **14** Ran SP% **119.6**
Speed ratings (Par 101): **103,102,102,101,100 100,99,99,99,98 97,97,95,94**
Tote Swingers: 1&2 £12.90, 1&3 £14.20, 2&3 £18.70 CSF £60.63 CT £641.90 TOTE £8.50: £3.00, £2.60, £6.20; EX 64.60 Trifecta £1201.30 Pool: £2,305.35 - 1.42 winning units..
Owner Mrs Olivia Hoare **Bred** Mount Coote Stud And M H Dixon **Trained** Newmarket, Suffolk

FOCUS
It paid to race prominently in this ordinary handicap. The pace wasn't strong and it's hard to rate the form too highly.
Just When Official explanation: jockey said gelding was slowly away

6147 BETDAQ MOBILE APPS NURSERY 7f (P)
6:45 (6:45) (Class 6) (0-65,65) 2-Y-O **£1,617** (£481; £240; £120) **Stalls** Low

Form RPR

000 **1** **Progenitor (IRE)**[30] 5162 2-8-9 **53**..... FrankieMcDonald 9 62+
(David Lanigan) *trckd ldng pair on outer: rdn 2f out: clsd over 1f out: led ins fnl f: r.o wl* **10/1**

056 **2** 1 **Girl Of Cadiz**[27] 5267 2-8-8 **59**..... WilliamTwiston-Davies(7) 11 63
(Richard Hannon) *racd on outer: wl in tch: rdn 2f out: clsd w wnr to chal 1f out: nt qckn last 100yds* **8/1**

0304 **3** 1 1/4 **Glossy Posse**[14] 5749 2-8-13 **57**..... PatDobbs 7 58
(Richard Hannon) *pressed ldr: led 2f out and kicked on: hdd and outpcd ins fnl f* **5/1**[2]

6054 **4** 2 1/2 **Black Dave (IRE)**[20] 5503 2-8-13 **57**..... RichardThomas 5 51
(David Evans) *awkward s and restrained in rr: prog 2f out: one pce and no imp fnl f* **16/1**

656 **5** 1 **Red Dragon (IRE)**[28] 5235 2-9-4 **62**..... WilliamBuick 12 54+
(Charles Hills) *dropped in fr wd draw: hld up in last pair: reminders 2f out: styd on steadily fr over 1f out: nvr nr ldrs* **11/2**[3]

2060 **6** 1/2 **Solvanna**[16] 5697 2-9-1 **59**.....(b[1]) EddieAhern 8 49
(Heather Main) *t.k.h: trckd ldng pair: swtchd to avoid loose horse 2f out: no imp over 1f out: wknd* **12/1**

0466 **7** hd **Tough Lady (IRE)**[36] 4934 2-9-5 **63**..... AdamKirby 3 52
(Mark Johnston) *led to 2f out: wknd over 1f out* **14/1**

0023 **8** 1 1/2 **Michael's Song (IRE)**[9] 5873 2-8-13 **57**..... SamHitchcott 6 42
(Mick Channon) *in tch: no prog wl over 1f out: sn wknd* **20/1**

0001 **9** *4 ½* **Sekumkum (IRE)**[36] 4934 2-9-2 **65**..........................(bt) TobyAtkinson(5) 4 38+
(Marco Botti) *t.k.h: trckd ldrs on inner: repeatedly hmpd fr 4f out to 3f out and dropped to rr: no prog over 1f out* **10/3[1]**

0500 **10** *2 ¼* **Cielo Rojo (IRE)**[15] 5716 2-7-13 **46** ow1......................(p) RaulDaSilva(3) 2 13
(Richard Fahey) *hld up in last pair: rdn and no prog over 2f out* **25/1**

01 **U** **Super Cookie**[33] 5061 2-9-1 **64**.. DarrenEgan(5) 1
(Philip McBride) *uns rdr over 5f out: sddle slipped bdly* **6/1**

1m 27.78s (1.78) **Going Correction** +0.025s/f (Slow) **11** Ran SP% **118.5**
Speed ratings (Par 93): **90,88,87,84,83 82,82,80,75,73**
Tote Swingers: 1&2 £33.70, 1&3 £17.20, 2&3 £7.90 CSF £88.30 CT £454.05 TOTE £17.20: £4.30, £3.70, £1.90; EX 183.80 TRIFECTA Not won..
Owner B E Nielsen **Bred** Rathasker Stud **Trained** Upper Lambourn, Berks

FOCUS
The pace looked slow and this was a really messy race. Super Cookie unseated her rider early on after the saddle slipped and she was then a nuisance when running loose. The winner probably has a good bit more to offer.

NOTEBOOK
Progenitor(IRE) was always handily placed and kept on well after being outpaced early in the straight. This was a step up on the form he showed in three maidens and he'll still be at the right end of the handicap once reassessed. The Stewards held an enquiry to consider the apparent improvement in form of the winner. They interviewed the trainer's representative who stated the colt broke his pelvis early in training and had taken his time to progress. Official explanation: trainer's rep said, regarding apparent improvement in form, that the colt broke its pelvis early in training and had taken its time to progress. (op 25-1)
Girl Of Cadiz did well to go so close considering she was caught wide for most of the way. This was her nursery debut after three runs over 6f and she looks up to winning off this sort of mark. (op 15-2 tchd 7-1)
Glossy Posse, a stablemate of the second, was also up in trip and she just didn't see it out well enough after being forwardly placed. (op 9-2 tchd 11-2)
Black Dave(IRE), up in trip and switched to Polytrack, lost ground when making an awkward start and then took a strong hold. It remains to be seen whether he's straightforward, but he has ability.
Red Dragon(IRE) ◆, making his nursery debut, was another up in trip and switched to Polytrack. He went noticeably wide into the straight and then edged right under pressure, so it's unclear whether or not he's straightforward, but he made late progress without being given a hard time and gave the impression he has more to offer. (op 10-1)
Sekumkum(IRE) lost all chance when badly squeezed against the inside rail on the bend. Official explanation: jockey said colt suffered interference in running (op 11-4 tchd 5-2)

6148 BETDAQ CASINO GAMES MAIDEN FILLIES' STKS 1m 4f (P)
7:15 (7:16) (Class 5) 3-4-Y-0 **£2,264** (£673; £336; £168) **Stalls** Centre

Form RPR

0322 **1** **Bedazzled**[21] 5474 3-8-12 **82**.. HayleyTurner 2 74+
(James Fanshawe) *trckd ldr: led jst over 2f out: pushed along firmly and drew clr over 1f out* **4/5[1]**

0 **2** *2 ¾* **Matured**[39] 4797 3-8-12 0.. MartinLane 6 70
(Ralph Beckett) *dwlt: t.k.h in 4th: shkn up and prog to chse wnr over 1f out: no imp* **12/1**

4 **3** *1 ¼* **Maun Vrat (IRE)**[44] 4648 3-8-12 0................................. PaulMulrennan 5 68+
(Ed Dunlop) *hld up and last tl 5f out: jst pushed along and kpt on steadily fnl 2f: could do bttr* **7/1[3]**

60 **4** *shd* **Sun Seal**[107] 2543 3-8-12 0.. RobertHavlin 7 68+
(Hughie Morrison) *t.k.h: hld up in last trio: jst pushed along on inner and kpt on fnl f: likely improver* **33/1**

5 *5* **Minty Fox** 3-8-12 0.. ChrisCatlin 4 60
(Rae Guest) *in tch: pushed along 1/2-way: dropped to last 5f out and looked like dropping away: urged along and kpt on* **20/1**

3203 **6** *nk* **Red Hand (USA)**[26] 5328 3-8-12 **78**.................................. WilliamBuick 1 61
(John Gosden) *trckd ldng pair: shkn up over 2f out: no rspnse and sn btn: wknd and eased fnl f* **3/1[2]**

06 **7** *hd* **Symfony (IRE)**[20] 5510 3-8-12 0... DaneO'Neill 3 59
(Clive Cox) *led: tried to kick on over 2f out: sn hdd: wknd over 1f out* **33/1**

2m 35.04s (0.54) **Going Correction** +0.025s/f (Slow) **7** Ran SP% **111.4**
Speed ratings (Par 100): **99,97,96,96,92 92,92**
Tote Swingers: 1&2 £2.20, 1&3 £1.80, 2&3 £16.20 CSF £11.11 TOTE £1.90: £1.20, £5.60; EX 14.70.
Owner Cheveley Park Stud **Bred** Cheveley Park Stud Ltd **Trained** Newmarket, Suffolk

FOCUS
A weak fillies' maiden run in a time 1.18 seconds slower than the earlier Class 5 handicap, and Bedazzled probably didn't have to run up to her best to win. The form has been rated cautiously.
Red Hand(USA) Official explanation: jockey said filly stopped quickly

6149 READ RACING PLUS EVERY SATURDAY CONDITIONS STKS 1m (P)
7:45 (7:45) (Class 4) 2-Y-0 **£3,428** (£1,020; £509; £254) **Stalls** Low

Form RPR

2113 **1** **Janoub Nibras (IRE)**[40] 4763 2-9-0 **92**................................ PatDobbs 6 98+
(Richard Hannon) *hld up: stalked ldng pair over 2f out: waited tl pounced jst ins fnl f: qckly drew away* **7/2[2]**

121 **2** *2* **Snowboarder (USA)**[25] 5348 2-9-0 **90**.................... MickaelBarzalona 3 93
(Mahmood Al Zarooni) *led after 2f: rdn over 2f out: hdd jst ins fnl f: easily outpcd* **2/1[1]**

1064 **3** *3* **Operation Chariot (IRE)**[12] 5787 2-9-0 **100**...................... LiamKeniry 1 86
(Andrew Balding) *led at modest pce for 2f: trckd ldr: rdn to chal over 2f out: btn over 1f out: fdd* **7/1[3]**

535 **4** *nk* **Ocean Applause**[14] 5755 2-9-0 **93**....................................... BrettDoyle 5 85
(John Ryan) *cl up bhd ldng pair: drvn over 2f out: wl outpcd over 1f out* **16/1**

1 **5** *dist* **Filfil (USA)**[36] 4917 2-9-0 0... AhmedAjtebi 4
(Mahmood Al Zarooni) *sddle slipped sn after s: styd on terms racing wd for 5f: virtually p.u fnl 2f* **2/1[1]**

1m 40.23s (0.43) **Going Correction** +0.025s/f (Slow) **5** Ran SP% **107.3**
Speed ratings (Par 97): **98,96,93,92,**
CSF £10.32 TOTE £3.30: £2.10, £1.60; EX 10.00.
Owner Saeed H Altayer **Bred** Rathbarry Stud **Trained** East Everleigh, Wilts

FOCUS
This conditions event lost some of its interest almost immediately when Filfil was effectively taken out of the race owing to a slipped saddle. The pace appeared slow and the winner was the only horse to settle, but this was still a pretty useful performance. He's up to Listed class on this evidence.

NOTEBOOK
Janoub Nibras(IRE) cruised along before finding plenty. He is now 3-3 on Polytrack (all here), although he's also effective on turf. It will be interesting to see if he's considered for a campaign in Dubai next year given there are a few options for 3yos out there these days, on both turf and Tapeta. (op 11-4)
Snowboarder(USA), who won his maiden here, was up to 1m for the first time. He didn't seem to do much wrong once in front, but was beaten by a better one on the day. (tchd 7-4)
Operation Chariot(IRE), trying Polytrack for the first time, was too keen and ran well short of his official mark of 100. (op 5-1)
Ocean Applause was keen early and was well held. (tchd 20-1)
Filfil(USA)'s saddle slipped. He had made a winning debut over 7f here. Official explanation: jockey said saddle slipped (op 11-4)

6150 STELJES 25 YEAR CELEBRATION CLASSIFIED CLAIMING STKS 6f (P)
8:15 (8:16) (Class 5) 3-Y-0+ **£2,264** (£673; £336; £168) **Stalls** Low

Form RPR

2114 **1** **Torres Del Paine**[203] 652 5-9-1 75.. PatDobbs 12 76
(Jimmy Fox) *hld up in last: prog 2f out: clsd w many others 1f out: led ins fnl f: styd on wl* **9/1**

3610 **2** *nk* **Bint Alzain (IRE)**[13] 5769 3-8-10 75..........................(tp) RaulDaSilva(3) 8 75
(Gerard Butler) *hld up in last trio: prog towards outer 2f out: c to chal 1f out: pressed wnr last 100yds: jst hld* **7/2[1]**

355 **3** *¾* **Tislaam (IRE)**[17] 5618 5-8-7 71.......................................(p) SeanLevey 1 65
(Alan McCabe) *hld up in rr: prog on inner jst over 2f out: clsd w others on ldng pair 1f out: styd on same pce last 150yds* **11/2[3]**

0052 **4** *shd* **Haadeeth**[10] 5853 5-8-5 62.. RichardThomas 3 62
(David Evans) *chsd ldrs: urged along over 2f out: brought between rivals to chal 1f out: nt qckn* **7/1**

-000 **5** *hd* **Victorian Bounty**[20] 5502 7-8-11 72...................................... DaneO'Neill 2 68
(Tony Newcombe) *mde most: rdn over 2f out: narrowly hdd jst over 1f out: one pce last 150yds* **12/1**

0001 **6** *1* **Drawnfromthepast (IRE)**[10] 5853 7-8-13 70............. FergusSweeney 9 66
(Jamie Osborne) *chsd ldng pair: rdn over 2f out: clsd to chal 1f out: wknd last 150yds* **6/1**

2512 **7** *½* **Ansells Pride (IRE)**[12] 5801 9-8-4 65..........................(p) JakePayne(7) 7 63
(Bill Turner) *w ldr: rdn over 2f out: narrow ld over 1f out: hdd & wknd ins fnl f* **11/1**

3323 **8** *¾* **Beat The Bell**[10] 5852 7-8-1 74...............................(p) LeonnaMayor(5) 10 55
(Jamie Osborne) *fractious bef s: rrd and rel to r initially: ct up on outer after 2f: nt qckn and struggling in last pair 2f out: styd on again fnl f* **5/1[2]**

6540 **9** *¾* **Jemimaville (IRE)**[16] 5681 5-8-5 46................................(v) LiamJones 4 52?
(Giles Bravery) *t.k.h: hld up in midfield: nt qckn 2f out: no prog after* **100/1**

0056 **10** *1 ¼* **One Cool Chick**[12] 5783 4-8-5 54..................................... KieranO'Neill 5 48
(John Bridger) *dwlt: racd on outer towards rr: rdn and no prog 2f out: wl hld after* **40/1**

3040 **11** *½* **Sujet Bellagio**[16] 5676 3-9-0 71................(b) WilliamTwiston-Davies(7) 11 64
(Brian Meehan) *trckd ldrs: rdn over 2f out: sn lost pl and btn* **12/1**

1m 12.61s (-0.49) **Going Correction** +0.025s/f (Slow)
WFA 3 from 4yo+ 2lb **11** Ran SP% **118.2**
Speed ratings (Par 103): **104,103,102,102,102 100,100,99,98,96 95**
Tote Swingers: 1&2 £3.50, 1&3 £13.40, 2&3 £10.60 CSF £40.74 TOTE £11.10: £2.60, £1.50, £2.00; EX 41.70 Trifecta £258.20 Pool: £558.36 - 1.60 winning units..Torres Del Paine claimed by Mr B. R. Johnson £10,000.
Owner Mrs Sarah-Jane Fox **Bred** Deepwood Farm Stud **Trained** Collingbourne Ducis, Wilts

FOCUS
A modest claimer that set up for the closers. Ordinary form for the grade, anchored by the ninth and tenth.

6151 BOOK YOUR CHRISTMAS PARTY AT KEMPTON PARK H'CAP (DIV I) 1m (P)
8:45 (8:45) (Class 6) (0-65,65) 3-Y-0 **£1,617** (£481; £240; £120) **Stalls** Low

Form RPR

2451 **1** **Silver Lace (IRE)**[28] 5229 3-9-4 **62**.................................. GeorgeBaker 2 76
(Chris Wall) *hld up in midfield: prog on inner jst over 2f out: rdn to ld ins fnl f: edgd lft but hld on wl* **11/4[1]**

2062 **2** *nk* **Lean On Pete (IRE)**[12] 5810 3-9-5 **63**........................... PaulMulrennan 5 76
(Ollie Pears) *hld up in midfield: prog fr 2f out: drvn to chal ins fnl f: styd on but a hld* **6/1[2]**

4U00 **3** *1 ¾* **No Dominion (IRE)**[14] 5738 3-8-12 **56**........................ RoystonFfrench 4 65
(James Given) *led 2f: led again over 4f out: drvn over 1f out: hdd ins fnl f: hld whn tightened up sn after* **14/1**

-563 **4** *1 ½* **Rock Song**[7] 5942 3-9-7 **65**.. PatDobbs 6 71
(Amanda Perrett) *racd on outer: wl in tch: shkn up and nt qckn over 2f out: styd on same pce fr over 1f out* **11/4[1]**

0032 **5** *½* **Riviera Romance**[21] 5479 3-8-4 **51** oh1........................ RaulDaSilva(3) 12 56
(J W Hills) *racd on outer: hld up in midfield: rdn and nt qckn over 2f out: styd on same pce fr over 1f out* **10/1**

0320 **6** *hd* **Trusting (IRE)**[21] 5479 3-8-13 **57**.............................. FergusSweeney 14 61
(Eve Johnson Houghton) *trckd ldrs: wnt 3rd over 3f out: rdn to chal jst over 1f out: wknd quite qckly fnl f* **25/1**

003 **7** *1 ¼* **My Manekineko**[15] 5717 3-9-4 **62**... DaneO'Neill 1 63
(J R Jenkins) *t.k.h: hld up in last pair of main gp: rdn and no prog 3f out: sme hdwy over 1f out: n.d* **20/1**

3460 **8** *1 ¼* **Tweet Lady**[16] 5657 3-9-7 **65**.. JamesMillman 9 63
(Rod Millman) *led after 2f to over 4f out: pressed ldr to over 2f out: pushed along and steadily wknd* **20/1**

4006 **9** *hd* **Rogue Reporter (IRE)**[13] 5764 3-8-13 **57**........................ SaleemGolam 8 55
(Stuart Williams) *hld up in midfield: rdn 2f out: no prog and btn over 1f out* **9/1[3]**

6304 **10** *1 ¾* **My Scat Daddy (USA)**[25] 5349 3-8-7 **51**..........................(t) KieranO'Neill 7 45
(Brett Johnson) *chsd ldng pair: drvn 1/2-way: sn lost pl and struggling* **14/1**

0000 **11** *¾* **Luna Rosa (IRE)**[46] 4584 3-8-7 **51** oh3.........................(t[1]) SamHitchcott 3 43
(Clive Cox) *t.k.h: hld up in last pair of main gp: rdn over 3f out: sn struggling* **40/1**

600 **12** *18* **Glennten**[6] 5975 3-9-0 **63**.. LeeNewnes(5) 13
(Sylvester Kirk) *broke on terms but stdd fr wdst draw and sn 5 l bhd rest: no impact after: t.o* **40/1**

1m 38.74s (-1.06) **Going Correction** +0.025s/f (Slow) **12** Ran SP% **118.3**
Speed ratings (Par 99): **106,105,103,102,101 101,100,99,99,97 96,78**
Tote Swingers: 1&2 £5.10, 1&3 £18.10, 2&3 £18.90 CSF £17.78 CT £195.84 TOTE £4.50: £1.60, £2.20, £5.30; EX 22.80 Trifecta £80.60 Pool: £309.53 - 2.84 winning units..
Owner The Equema Partnership **Bred** Liam Queally **Trained** Newmarket, Suffolk

FOCUS
This was sound run and the time was 1.10 seconds quicker than the second division. Solid form, the winner building on her 7f win.

Glennten Official explanation: jockey said gelding was slowly away; trainer's rep said gelding did not face the kickback

6152 BOOK YOUR CHRISTMAS PARTY AT KEMPTON PARK H'CAP (DIV II) 1m (P)

9:15 (9:16) (Class 6) (0-65,65) 3-Y-O **£1,617** (£481; £240; £120) **Stalls** Low

Form RPR

5423 **1** **Dana's Present**[13] 5764 3-8-12 **56** .... WilliamBuick 10 64
(George Baker) *fractious bef ent stalls: w.w in 8th off str pce: gd prog over 2f out: led over 1f out: sn in command: drvn out* **3/1**[1]

5500 **2** *1 ½* **More Than Words (IRE)**[23] 5409 3-9-5 **63** .... PatDobbs 13 68
(Richard Hannon) *hld up in last quartet in strly run r: prog 2f out: styd on wl fnl f to take 2nd last stride* **12/1**

0220 **3** *shd* **Casa Bex**[28] 5229 3-9-2 **63** .... (tp) RaulDaSilva(3) 14 67
(Philip McBride) *racd on outer: chsd ldrs in 5th: rdn 2f out: styd on to chse wnr 1f out: no imp: lost 2nd last stride* **15/2**

0620 **4** *hd* **Tigertoo (IRE)**[5] 5991 3-8-7 **51** oh5 .... SaleemGolam 11 55
(Stuart Williams) *w.w in 6th: effrt over 2f out: clsd over 1f out to dispute 2nd ins fnl f: kpt on* **9/1**

6053 **5** *nse* **Divine Pamina (IRE)**[36] 4914 3-9-7 **65** .... GeorgeBaker 2 69
(Jim Boyle) *hld up in 7th off str pce: pushed along 2f out: clsd 1f out: styd on to press for a pl nr fin* **5/1**[3]

0320 **6** *shd* **Princess Maya**[47] 4531 3-9-3 **61** .... DaneO'Neill 1 65
(Jo Crowley) *chsd ldng trio in strly run r: effrt on inner 2f out: tried to cl 1f out: kpt on same pce* **12/1**

0324 **7** *2 ½* **Admiralty**[23] 5428 3-9-7 **65** .... (b[1]) RoystonFfrench 8 65
(Ismail Mohammed) *chsd ldng pair in strly run event: clsd to ld briefly wl over 1f out: wknd fnl f: short of room nr fin* **7/2**[2]

-350 **8** *¾* **Capriska**[36] 4932 3-8-7 **51** oh1 .... JamieMackay 3 47
(Willie Musson) *pushed along in last early and wl off the pce: struggling 3f out: styd on wl fnl f* **20/1**

050 **9** *2 ¼* **Sandy Lane (IRE)**[16] 5687 3-8-13 **57** .... DaraghO'Donohoe 6 48
(Amy Weaver) *racd freely: mde most at str pce: hdd wl over 1f out: sn wknd* **12/1**

0045 **10** *5* **Flying Kitty**[20] 5513 3-8-7 **51** oh3 .... KieranO'Neill 5 30
(John Bridger) *a in last quartet: struggling fr 3f out* **33/1**

60 **11** *2 ¾* **Sweet Mystery (IRE)**[15] 5705 3-9-4 **62** .... RichardThomas 4 35
(David Evans) *a in last quartet: u.p and struggling 3f out* **40/1**

6060 **12** *2 ¼* **Guava**[72] 3694 3-8-7 **58** .... ShirleyTeasdale(7) 7 26
(Shaun Harris) *w ldr at str pce tl wknd rapidly over 2f out* **33/1**

1m 39.84s (0.04) **Going Correction** +0.025s/f (Slow) **12** Ran SP% **121.8**
Speed ratings (Par 99): **100,98,98,98,98 98,95,94,92,87 84,82**
Tote Swingers: 1&2 £14.30, 1&3 £6.40, 2&3 £26.00 CSF £39.99 CT £219.24 TOTE £4.50: £1.70, £2.90, £3.30; EX 42.20 Trifecta £296.10 Pool: £536.23 - 1.34 winning units..
Owner Whitsbury Racing Club **Bred** Newsells Park Stud **Trained** Whitsbury, Hants

FOCUS
The time was over a second slower than the first division despite a decent pace. It's hard tpo rate the race too positively owing to the overstrong gallop.
Divine Pamina(IRE) Official explanation: jockey said colt was denied a clear run
T/Plt: £156.30 to a £1 stake. Pool: £74,664.00 - 348.53 winning tickets. T/Qpdt: £18.30 to a £1 stake. Pool: £7,542.00 - 303.60 winning tickets. JN

5997 CHEPSTOW (L-H)

Thursday, September 13

OFFICIAL GOING: Good (good to firm in places; 7.3)
Wind: Virtuallynil Weather: Sunny

6153 32RED/BRITISH STALLION STUDS E B F MAIDEN FILLIES' STKS 7f 16y

2:10 (2:11) (Class 5) 2-Y-O **£3,169** (£707; £707; £235) **Stalls** High

Form RPR

3022 **1** **Heading North**[9] 5902 2-9-0 80 .... PatDobbs 12 75+
(Richard Hannon) *in rr: hdwy over 2f out: drvn to ld ins fnl f: pushed along fnl 120yds: easily* **10/11**[1]

2 *2 ¼* **Lilbourne Eliza (IRE)** 2-9-0 0 .... JamesDoyle 14 68
(Richard Hannon) *chsd ldrs: rdn and ev ch 1f out: nt gng pce of wnr ins fnl f: jnd for 2nd on line* **16/1**

2 *dht* **Lady Pimpernel** 2-9-0 0 .... DaneO'Neill 5 68
(Henry Candy) *chsd ldrs: rdn and one pce 2f out: styd on wl fnl 120yds to share 2nd on line but no ch w wnr* **4/1**[2]

4 *½* **Danat Al Atheer** 2-9-0 0 .... LiamJones 1 67
(William Haggas) *led: rdn 2f out: hdd ins fnl f: sn one pce* **10/1**

0 **5** *2 ¼* **Prospera (IRE)**[13] 5793 2-9-0 0 .... JimCrowley 7 61
(Ralph Beckett) *chsd ldrs: rdn over 2f out: wknd ins fnl f* **8/1**[3]

6 *3 ¼* **Uganda Glory (USA)** 2-9-0 0 .... PatCosgrave 15 53
(George Baker) *chsd ldrs: rdn over 2f out: styd wl there tl wknd fnl f* **28/1**

7 *5* **Foxy Dancer (IRE)** 2-9-0 0 .... CathyGannon 13 40
(Richard Hannon) *s.i.s: in rr: rdn over 2f out: mod prog fnl f* **16/1**

5 **8** *1 ½* **Valley Dreamer**[17] 5656 2-8-11 0 .... SophieDoyle(3) 6 36
(Michael Blanshard) *chsd ldrs: rdn 3f out: wknd ins fnl 2f* **66/1**

46 **9** *4* **Chelsea Grey (IRE)**[35] 4990 2-8-9 0 .... DarrenEgan(5) 10 25
(Ronald Harris) *chsd ldrs tl wknd over 2f out* **50/1**

0 **10** *2 ½* **So Lyrical**[26] 5357 2-9-0 0 .... MartinLane 11 19
(Peter Makin) *rdn along 4f out: a in rr* **50/1**

11 *5* **Atilia** 2-9-0 0 .... KirstyMilczarek 3
(George Baker) *chsd ldrs to 1/2-way* **66/1**

11 *dht* **July Waits (USA)** 2-9-0 0 .... ChrisCatlin 9
(Sir Mark Prescott Bt) *s.i.s: a in rr* **33/1**

13 *8* **Boogie De Bispo** 2-9-0 0 .... FergusSweeney 2
(Stuart Kittow) *s.i.s: sn rdn: a in rr* **100/1**

14 *30* **Bella Michelle** 2-9-0 0 .... StevieDonohoe 8
(William Muir) *virtually p.u sn after s: no ch after* **50/1**

1m 23.16s (-0.04) **Going Correction** -0.15s/f (Firm) **14** Ran SP% **120.6**
Speed ratings (Par 92): **94,91,91,90,88 84,78,77,72,69 64,64,54,20**
PL: Lady Pimpernel £1.80 Lilbourne Eliza £3.70 EX: Heading North/Lady Pimpernel £2.90, HN/LE £6.10 CSF: HN/LP £2.04, HN/LE £9.08. toteswingers: 1&LP £1.90, 1&LE £4.20, LP&LE £11.40 TOTE £2.10: £1.10.
Owner P T Tellwright **Bred** P T Tellwright **Trained** East Everleigh, Wilts

FOCUS
An uncompetitive fillies' maiden run at a fair pace with the winner coming widest of all and the front six pulling a long way clear. The winner is rated a bit better than the bare result, with the next few the key to the level.

NOTEBOOK
Heading North, the most experienced runner in the field, set a decent standard and, despite looking in some trouble 2f out, picked up well when switched wide. This trip looks to be her minimum and one can expect her to go on from this. (op 8-11)
Lilbourne Eliza(IRE), a stablemate of the winner, did best of those racing up the stands' rail. A half-sister to 1m 2yo winner Escholido (RPR 77) and German/French 1m and 1m2f winner Terre Neuve, she stayed the trip well and will be better for the experience. (op 20-1)
Lady Pimpernel, an 8,500gns daughter of a dam who's related to a few French middle-distance winners, was well supported at fancy prices and made an encouraging debut for a yard not noted for their 2yos. She did not respond immediately to pressure but picked up late and can be expected to come on plenty. (op 20-1)
Danat Al Atheer, whose dam was well related but wasn't up to much in Ireland, was another who showed promise on her debut. Racing out wide, she was sent for home over 3f out and showed a willing attitude to battle all the way to the line, although was ultimately well beaten. (op 12-1)
Prospera(IRE), a half-sister to a Breeders' Cup Marathon winner, travelled kindly in front but was unable to quicken over this inadequate trip. (op 9-1 tchd 10-1)
Uganda Glory(USA), a half-sister to a couple of winners in the US, cost 80,000gns in May and this run should give connections hope for the future. She showed up for a long way before fading inside the final furlong and can be expected to come on a good deal for this, especially when stepped up in trip. (op 33-1 tchd 25-1)
Bella Michelle Official explanation: jockey said filly apperared to be lame but subsequently returned sound

6154 32RED.COM/BRITISH STALLION STUDS E B F MAIDEN FILLIES' STKS 7f 16y

2:45 (2:47) (Class 5) 3-Y-O **£3,234** (£962; £481; £240) **Stalls** High

Form RPR

4652 **1** **Gifted Dancer**[18] 5625 3-9-0 69 .... DaneO'Neill 4 76
(Henry Candy) *trckd ldr: drvn to ld ins fnl 2f and 1 l clr 1f out: edgd rt u.p ins fnl f: hld on all out* **7/2**[2]

3332 **2** *shd* **Shaleek**[26] 5335 3-8-9 71 .... (b) DarrenEgan(5) 9 75
(Roger Varian) *led tl hdd ins fnl 2f: 1 l down 1f out: rallied and carried rt ins fnl f: gng on last strides: could nt quite get bk up* **9/2**[3]

32 **3** *2* **Ebble**[28] 5276 3-9-0 0 .... NickyMackay 14 70
(John Gosden) *chsd ldrs: rdn and edgd lft over 2f out: styd on for one pce 3rd fnl f* **11/4**[1]

6- **4** *4 ½* **Pomarine (USA)**[320] 7165 3-9-0 0 .... JamesDoyle 1 58
(Amanda Perrett) *chsd ldrs: rdn over 2f out and sn outpcd* **9/2**[3]

4-04 **5** *½* **It's My Time**[51] 4434 3-9-0 67 .... MartinLane 11 57
(David Simcock) *in tch: rdn 3f out: styd on same pce fnl 2f* **12/1**

24 **6** *6* **Prime Run**[192] 805 3-9-0 0 .... JimCrowley 12 40
(David Simcock) *chsd ldrs: rdn over 2f out and sn btn* **15/2**

7 *1 ¾* **Rosa Lockwood** 3-9-0 0 .... KirstyMilczarek 5 36
(Tony Carroll) *s.i.s: in rr: pushed along 3f out: mod hdwy fr 2f out: r.o in clsng stages* **100/1**

8 *7* **La Giaconda** 3-8-7 0 .... RyanTate(7) 8 17
(Clive Cox) *s.i.s: in rr: drvn along 1/2-way: mod prog fnl f* **25/1**

9 *hd* **Fantastic Indian** 3-9-0 0 .... ChrisCatlin 7 16
(Roy Brotherton) *s.i.s: a in rr* **100/1**

10 *22* **Aujourd'Hui** 3-9-0 0 .... PatDobbs 13
(Richard Hannon) *s.i.s: a bhd* **14/1**

11 *1 ¼* **Smirfys Blackcat (IRE)** 3-9-0 0 .... SeanQuinlan 6
(Michael Mullineaux) *s.i.s: a bhd* **100/1**

-06 **12** *6* **Kiss My Heart**[203] 663 3-8-11 0 .... SophieDoyle(3) 2
(Eric Wheeler) *in rr and rdn 1/2-way: sn lost tch* **100/1**

1m 23.16s (-0.04) **Going Correction** -0.15s/f (Firm) **12** Ran SP% **119.2**
Speed ratings (Par 98): **94,93,91,86,85 79,77,69,68,43 42,35**
toteswingers 1&2 £4.00, 2&3 £3.60, 1&3 £3.60 CSF £19.62 TOTE £4.60: £1.90, £1.10, £1.40; EX 18.90.
Owner Dale / Deal / Candy **Bred** Ash Place Stud **Trained** Kingston Warren, Oxon

FOCUS
This 3yo fillies' maiden was run at a sound pace with the field well strung out from an early stage, and few were able to get competitive. The form is rated around the runner-up.
Rosa Lockwood Official explanation: jockey said filly was slowly away
Kiss My Heart Official explanation: trainer's rep said filly was unsuited by the track

6155 WESTERN DAILY PRESS NURSERY 5f 16y

3:20 (3:20) (Class 5) (0-75,74) 2-Y-O **£2,264** (£673; £336; £168) **Stalls** High

Form RPR

0103 **1** **Secret Sign**[22] 5475 2-9-7 **74** .... (v) MartinLane 4 77
(Brian Meehan) *in tch: hdwy 2f out: drvn to ld fnl 120yds: hld on wl* **7/1**[2]

4461 **2** *½* **Spray Tan**[30] 5194 2-8-7 **60** .... KirstyMilczarek 6 61
(Tony Carroll) *pressed ldrs: slt ld 2f out: sn rdn: hung lft over 1f out: hung rt ins fnl f and hdd fnl 120yds: one pce* **16/1**

4022 **3** *½* **We Are City**[8] 5940 2-8-3 **63** .... IanBurns(7) 7 62
(Michael Bell) *chsd ldrs: rdn fr 2f out: hung rt and kpt fnl f: nt qckn in clsng stages* **7/1**[2]

6313 **4** *1 ¼* **Kodatish (IRE)**[12] 5813 2-9-6 **73** .... KierenFox 5 69
(Ronald Harris) *chsd ldrs: rdn 2f out: kpt on ins fnl f: nvr gng pce to chal* **7/1**[2]

6053 **5** *1 ¼* **Plexolini**[17] 5654 2-7-10 **54** .... DarrenEgan(5) 12 44
(Jo Hughes) *in tch: rdn over 1f out: styd on fnl f: could nt rch ldrs* **12/1**

3333 **6** *hd* **Blazing Knight (IRE)**[8] 5940 2-9-2 **69** .... (b) JimCrowley 8 58
(Ralph Beckett) *chsd ldrs: chal 2f out and sn rdn: wknd ins fnl f* **7/1**[2]

5054 **7** *nk* **Katy Spirit (IRE)**[10] 5873 2-7-13 **52** .... NickyMackay 1 40
(Michael Blanshard) *in tch drvn to chse ldrs over 2f out: one pce fnl f* **40/1**

6461 **8** *¾* **Monkey Bar Flies (IRE)**[23] 5450 2-9-3 **73** .... LeeTopliss(3) 10 59
(Richard Fahey) *chsd ldrs: rdn over 2f out: sn one pce* **4/1**[1]

1500 **9** *1 ¾* **Majestic Red (IRE)**[23] 5450 2-9-0 **67** .... TomMcLaughlin 2 46
(Malcolm Saunders) *chsd ldrs rdn 2f out: wknd fnl f* **28/1**

1523 **10** *nk* **Risky Rizkova**[20] 5532 2-9-0 **67** .... MatthewDavies 9 45
(Jonathan Portman) *rdn and outpcd 3f out: kpt on fnl f but nvr any ch* **14/1**

0156 **11** *½* **Must Be Me**[15] 5743 2-9-4 **71** .... FergusSweeney 3 47
(Eve Johnson Houghton) *outpcd most of way* **14/1**

3266 **12** *2 ¾* **Whistling Buddy**[21] 5503 2-9-1 **68** .... (p) CathyGannon 11 34
(Peter Makin) *led 3f: sn btn* **8/1**[3]

1m 0.26s (0.96) **Going Correction** -0.15s/f (Firm) **12** Ran SP% **113.9**
Speed ratings (Par 95): **86,85,84,82,80 80,79,78,75,75 74,69**
toteswingers 1&2 £27.00, 2&3 £24.90, 1&3 £10.50 CSF £108.95 CT £809.56 TOTE £8.20: £2.20, £5.00, £4.00; EX 133.70.
Owner Trelawny II **Bred** Whitsbury Manor Stud **Trained** Manton, Wilts

FOCUS
A fairly competitive sprint nursery run at a decent pace, with the runners spread across the track and the front three home racing up the centre.

NOTEBOOK
Secret Sign, racing over the minimum for the first time and wearing a visor for the second, was held up early but came through strongly at the 2f pole before his stamina kicked in late on. The sound pace played to his strengths and he was always in command inside the final furlong. (op 8-1)

Spray Tan, 3lb higher than when scoring at Bath on her handicap debut last time, was always handily placed but was hanging under pressure inside the final furlong and was just outstayed by the winner. (op 14-1 tchd 12-1)
We Are City, back on the turf after two narrow defeats on the AW, was another who veered left and then right when coming under pressure before keeping on to the line. She seems to find reasons not to win at present. (op 15-2 tchd 13-2)
Kodatish(IRE) was briefly hampered at the furlong pole, but stayed on again late and remains in good heart. Official explanation: jockey said colt was denied a clear run (op 6-1 tchd 11-2)
Plexolini was last for much of the way before running past beaten rivals late on and found this trip, under these quicker conditions, too sharp. (tchd 14-1)
Blazing Knight(IRE) is becoming a frustrating type. He stayed on in eyecatching style having been held up at Kempton last time, but found little off the bridle here having raced handily and does not look the most genuine. (op 6-1)
Whistling Buddy helped set the generous pace racing up the stands' side, but ultimately looked to pay for doing too much through the first half and folded tamely. (op 10-1)

6156 MORGAN COLE LLP SUPPORTS TY HAFAN NURSERY 1m 14y
3:55 (3:56) (Class 6) (0-65,63) 2-Y-O £1,617 (£481; £240; £60; £60) Stalls High

Form RPR
000 **1** **Knight's Parade (IRE)**[24] 5407 2-8-13 **55**....(b[1]) JimCrowley 14 56
(Amanda Perrett) *chsd ldrs: led 2f out: hrd drvn whn jnd ins fnl f and edgd lft: hld on all out* **9/1**
0000 **2** *shd* **Run It Twice (IRE)**[14] 5763 2-9-2 **58**....(b) MartinLane 2 59
(Brian Meehan) *in rr: hdwy fr 3f out: chsd ldrs 1f out: hung rt ins fnl f and sn pressing wnr: no ex last strides* **25/1**
0150 **3** *3/4* **Missing Agent**[3] 6096 2-9-1 **60**....(v[1]) MatthewCosham(3) 4 61
(David Evans) *chsd ldrs: styng on whn bdly hmpd ins fnl f: rallied to take 3rd last strides* **50/1**
060 **4** *hd* **Gabrial The Boss (USA)**[47] 4595 2-9-4 **60**.... GeorgeBaker 15 59
(David Simcock) *in tch hdwy 3f out: chsng ldrs whn edgd lft ins fnl f and bmpd: styd on: nvr quite gng pce to chal* **9/2[1]**
2532 **4** *dht* **Poetic Verse**[16] 5716 2-9-2 **58**.... JamesMillman 1 57
(Rod Millman) *chsd ldrs: drvn and one pce 2f out: styd on again fnl f: kpt on clsng stages* **9/1**
541 **6** *3/4* **Getaway Car**[14] 5763 2-9-6 **62**....(p) JamesDoyle 7 59
(Gerard Butler) *chsd ldrs: drvn and outpcd 3f out: kpt on u.p fnl f: nvr gng pce to chal* **13/2[3]**
4051 **7** *1 1/2* **Warrant Officer**[58] 4195 2-9-7 **63**.... MatthewDavies 12 57
(Mick Channon) *chsd ldrs: led over 3f out: hdd 2f out: wknd fnl f* **20/1**
6152 **8** *nk* **Wordsaplenty (IRE)**[7] 5968 2-9-1 **57**.... FergusSweeney 13 50
(J S Moore) *led tl hdd over 3f out: wknd appr fnl f* **20/1**
602 **9** *1* **Dance Off (IRE)**[31] 5168 2-9-3 **62**.... LeeTopliss(3) 9 53
(Richard Fahey) *t.k.h in tch: rdn and sme hdwy 2f out: nvr gng pce to get into contention* **8/1**
006 **10** *shd* **Ottauquechee (IRE)**[13] 5785 2-9-4 **60**.... PatDobbs 3 50
(Richard Hannon) *in rr: rdn and no prog over 2f out* **16/1**
000 **11** *2* **Icanboogie**[30] 5206 2-8-0 **45**.... RaulDaSilva(3) 8 31
(Karen George) *in tch chsd ldrs and rdn 3f out: wknd 2f out* **20/1**
0055 **12** *1 1/2* **Kunzea (IRE)**[8] 5946 2-8-2 **49**.... DarrenEgan(5) 16 31
(Mick Channon) *outpcd most of way* **5/1[2]**
0000 **13** *8* **Just Duchess**[13] 5786 2-8-0 **45**.... SophieDoyle(3) 5 9
(Michael Blanshard) *bhd fr 1/2-way* **66/1**
343 **14** *2* **Ace Pearl (USA)**[35] 5010 2-9-4 **60**.... CathyGannon 10 19
(David Brown) *in rr and sn drvn along and hung lft: sme prog 1/2-way: sn wknd* **8/1**
0540 **15** *14* **Smooth Handle**[44] 4672 2-8-0 **49**.... RyanTate(7) 11
(Tom Dascombe) *chsd ldrs 3f* **25/1**
6010 **16** *10* **Myzamour**[3] 6096 2-8-9 **54**....(b) RyanPowell(3) 6
(J S Moore) *a in rr* **33/1**

1m 36.76s (0.56) **Going Correction** -0.15s/f (Firm) **16** Ran SP% **124.7**
Speed ratings (Par 93): **91,90,90,89,89 89,87,87,86,86 84,82,74,72,58 48**
CSF £225.06 CT £10654.32 TOTE £9.10: £3.20, £5.90, £14.10, £1.70; EX 353.50.
Owner The Recitation Partnership **Bred** E Heary **Trained** Pulborough, W Sussex
■ Stewards' Enquiry : Martin Lane caution: careless riding.

FOCUS
A modest if competitive handicap, run at a fair pace with the front two fighting out a thrilling finish inside the final furlong.

NOTEBOOK
Knight's Parade(IRE), wearing blinkers for the first time on his handicap debut, was ideally positioned and saw it out gamely inside the final furlong to land a bit of a touch. He had shown little in three maiden runs but this was very much the day, and his effort can be slightly upgraded as he raced up the stands' rail, which had not seemed the place to be through the afternoon. Official explanation: trainer's rep said, regarding apparent improvement, that the gelding had benefited from the first-time blinkers. (tchd 8-1)
Run It Twice(IRE) was well beaten on his nursery debut behind Getaway Car at Kempton last time but showed his best form here, racing over 1m on the turf for the first time. He looks more than capable of scoring off this current mark.
Missing Agent was done no favours by the runner-up when badly hampered at the furlong pole before staying on strongly to the line. The first-time visor obviously helped. (op 40-1)
Poetic Verse, who was noted travelling kindly up the centre of the track, was initially outpaced before closing again late and is another who may prefer a bit more cut. (op 11-2)
Gabrial The Boss(USA), stepping up in trip and running for the first time since being gelded, was another well backed on his handicap debut and looked dangerous when coming with his effort a furlong from home, but he was unable to quicken. The ground may have been quicker than ideal. (op 11-2)
Getaway Car stayed on well when winning a Kempton 0-60 handicap on his first try over this trip last time, but could never get competitive in this slightly better grade. (op 11-2 tchd 5-1)
Warrant Officer was handily pace early, but raced a shade keenly and understandably weakened late on. (op 16-1)
Ace Pearl(USA), running on the turf for the first time and stepping up 2f on his handicap debut, was struggling from an early stage and was never able to get competitive. (op 9-1 tchd 10-1)
Myzamour Official explanation: jockey said filly never travelled

6157 JOAN SHILLAW 90TH BIRTHDAY CELEBRATION H'CAP 1m 14y
4:25 (4:26) (Class 6) (0-60,60) 3-Y-O+ £1,617 (£481; £240; £120) Stalls High

Form RPR
0000 **1** **Menadati (USA)**[27] 5310 4-9-5 **55**.... KirstyMilczarek 3 67
(Peter Hiatt) *chsd ldrs: wnt 2nd 4f out: chal 2f out: led over 1f out: drvn out ins fnl f* **7/1**
0001 **2** *1 1/4* **Belle Park**[21] 5506 5-9-1 **51**.... TomMcLaughlin 13 60
(Karen George) *in rr: hdwy u.p over 2f out: chsd wnr 1f out: kpt on fnl f but no imp* **4/1[2]**
030 **3** *3 3/4* **West Leake (IRE)**[15] 5741 6-9-8 **58**.... GeorgeBaker 6 58
(Paul Burgoyne) *in rr: hdwy 3f out: styd on fr over 1f out to take 3rd fnl 120yds: no ch w ldng duo* **18/1**
0020 **4** *1 1/2* **Greek Islands (IRE)**[15] 5750 4-9-8 **58**....(b[1]) ChrisCatlin 4 55
(Ed de Giles) *t.k.h and led: jnd 2f out: hdd over 1f out: sn btn* **16/1**
4205 **5** *nse* **High Five Prince (IRE)**[14] 5770 3-8-5 **46**.... CathyGannon 2 43
(Mark Usher) *chsd ldrs: drvn along over 3f out: styd on same pce fr over 1f out* **16/1**
0551 **6** *8* **Siberian Belle (IRE)**[23] 5459 3-8-1 **49**....(p) LauraBarry(7) 7 27
(Richard Fahey) *in tch: rdn and no rspnse over 3f out: no ch after* **3/1[1]**
2006 **7** *2* **Midas Moment**[41] 4753 4-9-3 **58**....(p) DarrenEgan(5) 5 32
(William Muir) *s.i.s: in rr: hdwy 1/2-way and chsd ldrs 3f out: sn rdn: wknd over 2f out* **16/1**
0055 **8** *1 1/2* **Boragh Waters (IRE)**[23] 5458 3-8-5 **46** oh1....(t) MartinLane 10 16
(Brian Meehan) *s.i.s: in rr: rdn 3f out: mod prog fnl f* **33/1**
0063 **9** *1/2* **Alfie Joe**[28] 5261 3-7-12 **46**.... PhilipPrince(7) 8 15
(Ron Hodges) *a in rr* **8/1**
0511 **10** *3/4* **Community (USA)**[16] 5720 4-9-5 **60**.... LeonnaMayor(5) 1 27
(Jamie Osborne) *chsd ldr to 4f out: wknd fr 3f out* **9/2[3]**
0000 **11** *15* **Quite A Catch (IRE)**[17] 5657 4-9-9 **59**....(v) MatthewDavies 9
(Jonathan Portman) *slowly away: a in rr* **16/1**
06-0 **12** *1 1/2* **Chicamia**[6] 5996 8-8-10 **46**....(v[1]) SeanQuinlan 14
(Michael Mullineaux) *slowly away: a in rr* **25/1**

1m 34.74s (-1.46) **Going Correction** -0.15s/f (Firm)
WFA 3 from 4yo+ 5lb **12** Ran SP% **122.4**
Speed ratings (Par 101): **101,99,96,94,94 86,84,82,82,81 66,65**
toteswingers 1&2 £8.00, 2&3 £17.60, 1&3 £31.10 CSF £36.28 CT £507.21 TOTE £6.10: £2.10, £1.50, £4.60; EX 61.20.
Owner Carl Demczak **Bred** Stonestreet Thoroughbred Holdings LLC **Trained** Hook Norton, Oxon

FOCUS
A moderate handicap run at a blistering pace with the field well strung out and the front five pulling a long way clear. The winner's first form since the AW during the winter.
Community(USA) Official explanation: trainer's rep said gelding bled from the nose
Quite A Catch(IRE) Official explanation: jockey said gelding reared leaving stalls

6158 32RED CASINO H'CAP 7f 16y
5:00 (5:01) (Class 6) (0-60,58) 3-Y-O+ £1,617 (£481; £240; £120) Stalls High

Form RPR
0065 **1** **Royal Box**[8] 5937 5-9-1 **49**....(p) CathyGannon 2 58
(Tony Carroll) *mde all: rdn over 2f out: styd on wl thrght fnl f* **8/1**
0543 **2** *1 1/4* **Loyal N Trusted**[17] 5681 4-9-9 **57**....(p) JamesDoyle 5 63
(Richard Price) *t.k.h: stdd in rr: stdy hdwy 2f out: drvn and styd on to chse wnr ins fnl f: kpt on but a hld* **11/4[1]**
1502 **3** *3/4* **Percythepinto (IRE)**[23] 5459 3-9-4 **56**....(t) GeorgeBaker 12 59
(George Baker) *s.i.s: hld up in rr: hdwy 2f out: sn rdn: styd on to take 3rd ins fnl f: no imp on ldng duo* **9/2[2]**
0423 **4** *1/2* **Collectable**[18] 5633 3-8-13 **51**....(t) MatthewDavies 4 52
(Jonathan Portman) *prom: chsd wnr over 2f out: outpcd u.p fnl f* **6/1[3]**
1605 **5** *1 1/2* **Memphis Man**[6] 6000 9-9-5 **56**.... MatthewCosham(3) 1 54
(David Evans) *s.i.s: in rr: pushed along and hdwy over 1f out: styd on fnl f: nvr a threat* **20/1**
6000 **6** *1 3/4* **Voodoo (IRE)**[58] 4185 3-8-4 **45**....(t) RyanPowell(3) 3 37
(Ian Williams) *chsd ldrs: rdn over 2f out: wknd fnl f* **25/1**
6000 **7** *2 3/4* **Rio Royale (IRE)**[112] 2413 6-9-4 **52**.... PatDobbs 9 38
(Amanda Perrett) *chsd ldr tl over 2f out: sn btn* **16/1**
2500 **8** *3* **Sermons Mount (USA)**[7] 5971 6-9-10 **58**.... TomMcLaughlin 10 36
(Paul Howling) *in rr: rdn over 2f out: mod prog over 1f out* **12/1**
6520 **9** *1/2* **Bashama**[6] 6000 4-8-9 **50**....(p) DanielMuscutt(7) 6 27
(Nikki Evans) *chsd ldrs: rdn over 3f out: wknd over 2f out* **14/1**
4006 **10** *hd* **Olynard (IRE)**[6] 6002 6-9-1 **49**....[1] SeanQuinlan 13 25
(Michael Mullineaux) *chsd ldrs tl wknd over 2f out* **7/1**
0000 **11** *2 3/4* **Men Don't Cry (IRE)**[36] 4937 3-8-10 **48**....(p) ChrisCatlin 11
(Ed de Giles) *chsd ldrs: rdn and wknd 3f out* **25/1**

1m 24.0s (0.80) **Going Correction** -0.15s/f (Firm)
WFA 3 from 4yo+ 4lb **11** Ran SP% **115.4**
Speed ratings (Par 101): **89,87,86,86,84 82,79,75,75,75 71**
toteswingers 1&2 £5.10, 2&3 £3.70, 1&3 £6.10 CSF £28.84 CT £112.93 TOTE £10.40: £3.10, £1.20, £1.20; EX 29.90.
Owner Jason Tucker **Bred** The Queen **Trained** Cropthorne, Worcs

FOCUS
A weak handicap run at a fair pace, with the runners once again racing off the rails inside the final furlong. Ordinary form for the grade.

6159 RACING POST WEEKENDER OUT EVERY WEDNESDAY H'CAP 1m 4f 23y
5:30 (5:30) (Class 6) (0-65,65) 3-Y-O+ £1,617 (£481; £240; £120) Stalls Low

Form RPR
4/33 **1** **Presto Volante (IRE)**[19] 5596 4-9-8 **61**....(p) JamesDoyle 16 78
(Amanda Perrett) *trckd ldrs: slt ld 3f out: narrowly hdd appr fnl 2f: styd upsides and str chal fnl f: led and edgd rt fnl 120yds: all out* **4/1[1]**
0000 **2** *shd* **English Summer**[24] 5430 5-9-6 **62**....(t) LeeTopliss(3) 11 79
(David Simcock) *in tch: hdwy on outside 4f out: chal 3f out: slt ld over 2f out: styd hrd pressed and jnd fnl f: pushed rt and hdd fnl 120yds: kpt on: jst failed* **8/1[3]**
0323 **3** *6* **Tijori (IRE)**[8] 5936 4-9-6 **59**....(p) MartinLane 3 66
(Bernard Llewellyn) *chsd ldrs: drvn 3f out: styd on for one pce 3rd fnl f* **8/1[3]**
-255 **4** *3* **Ironically (IRE)**[15] 5754 3-9-2 **64**....(b[1]) DaneO'Neill 5 68
(David Lanigan) *in rr: hdwy over 2f out: effrt between horses and n.m.r ins fnl f: styd on same pce* **11/2[2]**
000 **5** *1/2* **Edgware Road**[127] 1984 4-9-6 **62**.... SophieDoyle(3) 13 63
(Sean Curran) *led tl hdd 3f out: styd chsng ldrs tl wknd 2f out* **16/1**
6305 **6** *3 1/2* **Spring Secret**[20] 5528 6-9-0 **56**.... RaulDaSilva(3) 10 52
(Bryn Palling) *in rr: mod prog u.p fnl 2f* **20/1**
-334 **7** *1 1/2* **Neil's Pride**[24] 5413 3-8-9 **57**.... ChrisCatlin 8 50
(Richard Fahey) *chsd ldrs: rdn 3f out: wknd over 2f out* **4/1[1]**
1330 **8** *1/2* **Taroum (IRE)**[9] 5908 5-9-12 **65**.... CathyGannon 9 58
(Tony Carroll) *in tch: rdn 4f out: wknd ins fnl 3f* **9/1**
42U0 **9** *4* **Viola Da Gamba (IRE)**[8] 5945 3-8-11 **64**.... DavidKenny(5) 12 50
(William Knight) *s.i.s: towards rr most of way* **14/1**
0144 **10** *4 1/2* **Before Bruce**[9] 5908 5-9-7 **65**....(vt) BrendanPowell(5) 6 44
(Brendan Powell) *sn chsng ldr: rdn 4f out: wknd 3f out* **10/1**
4000 **11** *15* **Snow Ridge**[3] 6097 4-8-5 **51** oh1....(t) JakePayne(7) 1
(Simon Hodgson) *a in rr* **66/1**
3140 **12** *shd* **Kozmina Bay**[89] 3142 3-8-9 **57**.... NickyMackay 2
(Jonathan Portman) *chsd ldrs: rdn and btn 4f out* **25/1**

2m 37.92s (-1.08) **Going Correction** -0.05s/f (Good)
WFA 3 from 4yo+ 9lb **12** Ran SP% **119.3**
Speed ratings (Par 101): **101,100,96,94,94 92,91,90,88,85 75,75**
toteswingers 1&2 £4.30, 2&3 £15.40, 1&3 £6.50 CSF £35.71 CT £249.01 TOTE £5.00: £1.60, £3.40, £2.40; EX 48.10.

Owner Mrs S Conway Mr & Mrs M Swayne Mr A Brooke Mrs R D **Bred** R A Major **Trained** Pulborough, W Sussex

FOCUS

A competitive handicap run at a fair pace with the front two pulling clear inside the final furlong. The form could be worth more, with the winner unexposed and the second down in the weights.
T/Plt: £95.50 to a £1 stake. Pool of £55101.57 - 421.08 winning tickets. T/Qpdt: £63.40 to a £1 stake. Pool of £3501.96 - 40.83 winning tickets. ST

6138 DONCASTER (L-H)

Thursday, September 13

OFFICIAL GOING: Good (good to soft in places; 8.3)

Wind: light 1/2 against Weather: fine

6160 EUROPEAN BREEDERS' FUND CARRIE RED FILLIES' NURSERY (H'CAP) 6f 110y

1:15 (1:16) (Class 2) 2-Y-O **£19,407** (£5,775; £2,886; £1,443) **Stalls** High

Form				RPR
1112	**1**		**Jamesbo's Girl**[9] 5909 2-9-3 **80** PaulHanagan 17 (Richard Fahey) *towards rr stands' side: hdwy over 2f out: led last 75yds: hld on wl* **8/1**	88
321	**2**	¾	**Nargys (IRE)**[18] 5631 2-9-5 **82** JamieSpencer 1 (Luca Cumani) *hld up in rr: hdwy on outside 3f out: chal jst ins fnl f: sn rdn: no ex towards fin* **7/1**[3]	88
130	**3**	½	**Pure Excellence**[20] 5563 2-9-1 **78** FrannyNorton 14 (Mark Johnston) *w ldrs: led over 2f out: hdd ins fnl f: kpt on same pce* **7/1**[3]	83
421	**4**	1	**Annecdote**[28] 5274 2-8-13 **76** JohnFahy 19 (Jonathan Portman) *in rr: hdwy over 2f out: kpt on fnl f* **6/1**[2]	78
2012	**5**	4	**Steer By The Stars (IRE)**[68] 3858 2-9-1 **78** JoeFanning 11 (Mark Johnston) *w ldrs: led 3f out: sn hdd: wknd fnl f* **14/1**	69
135	**6**	2 ½	**Elle Woods (IRE)**[26] 5361 2-9-4 **81** PaulMulrennan 20 (Michael Dods) *swtchd lft s: hld up towards rr: hdwy over 2f out: kpt on fnl f* **16/1**	65
5322	**7**	¾	**This Is Nice (IRE)**[17] 5682 2-8-12 **75** (p) RichardKingscote 15 (Tom Dascombe) *sn led: hdd 3f out: wknd over 1f out* **16/1**	56
2201	**8**	1 ¼	**New Falcon (IRE)**[16] 5702 2-8-13 **76** (p) NeilCallan 9 (James Tate) *mid-div: effrt over 2f out: nvr trbld ldrs* **20/1**	54
216	**9**	½	**Mollyvator (IRE)**[49] 4514 2-9-1 **78** MartinHarley 6 (Mrs K Burke) *dwlt: mid-div: hdwy over 2f out: one pce whn rdr dropped whip over 1f out* **11/2**[1]	55
16	**10**	nk	**Strange Magic (IRE)**[47] 4577 2-9-1 **78** TonyHamilton 12 (Richard Fahey) *trckd ldrs: t.k.h: pushed along over 2f out: grad wknd* **20/1**	54
4003	**11**	nk	**Dream Vale (IRE)**[24] 5411 2-8-5 **68** JamesSullivan 10 (Tim Easterby) *dwlt: in rr: sme hdwy 2f out: nvr a factor* **50/1**	43
5223	**12**	nk	**Royal Steps (IRE)**[10] 5887 2-9-0 **77** MartinDwyer 4 (James Tate) *w ldrs on wd outside: edgd lft over 1f out: sn wknd* **25/1**	51
1201	**13**	2	**Tussie Mussie**[9] 5920 2-8-11 **74** 6ex SilvestreDeSousa 8 (Mark Johnston) *w ldrs: lost pl over 1f out* **12/1**	42
3053	**14**	4	**Something Magic**[16] 5702 2-8-7 **70** ow2 WilliamBuick 16 (Sylvester Kirk) *broke fast and led early: chsd ldrs: lost pl over 2f out* **25/1**	27
0452	**15**	hd	**Projectisle (IRE)**[20] 5537 2-8-9 **72** AmyRyan 13 (Kevin Ryan) *chsd ldrs: drvn over 2f out: sn wknd* **25/1**	29
2161	**16**	2 ¾	**Penny Garcia**[20] 5537 2-9-0 **77** DuranFentiman 18 (Tim Easterby) *a towards rr* **25/1**	26
3234	**17**	4	**It's Taboo**[20] 5527 2-8-13 **76** JimmyFortune 2 (Mark Usher) *in rr div far side: bhd fnl 2f* **25/1**	14
0226	**18**	4 ½	**Puteri Nur Laila (IRE)**[14] 5773 2-8-4 **67** LukeMorris 7 (Paul Cole) *in rr: bhd fnl 2f* **66/1**	

1m 19.47s (-0.43) **Going Correction** +0.10s/f (Good) **18** Ran SP% **124.1**

Speed ratings (Par 98): **106,105,104,103,98 96,95,93,93,92 92,92,89,85,85 81,77,72**

toteswingers 1&2 £8.20, 2&3 £8.60, 1&3 £13.10 CSF £54.79 CT £434.84 TOTE £9.00: £1.90, £2.20, £1.90, £2.00; EX 56.60 Trifecta £717.10 Part won. Pool: £969.17 - 0.92 winning units..

Owner Hardisty Rolls **Bred** Lady Juliet Tadgell **Trained** Musley Bank, N Yorks

FOCUS

A very competitive heat for the class. The first four were clear and the form should work out. Those drawn high seemed at an advantage.

NOTEBOOK

Jamesbo's Girl has progressed since being purchased out of a claimer by Richard Fahey, and showed an excellent attitude for pressure to gain a fourth success of the year. One would imagine that connections may try and get some black type for her now, with something like the Firth Of Clyde at Ayr a possible target. (op 9-1)

Nargys(IRE) ◆, making her handicap debut, tended to race a bit freely out the back and was one of the last to come off the bridle. She got almost level with the winner inside the final furlong but couldn't quite get to the front. It would be surprising if the Lawman filly doesn't progress further, especially as she did by far the best of those in a single-digit stall. (op 11-2)

Pure Excellence hit the front inside the final couple of furlongs and kept on in fair style. She's another with a bit of scope to make physical improvement. (op 9-1)

Annecdote ◆, running in her first nursery, was never able to get to the leading three after being held up towards the back. That said, she looks capable of winning off this sort of mark. (op 13-2 tchd 7-1)

Steer By The Stars(IRE), back down in distance on her first start since early July, is entitled to come on for the outing and, being by Pivotal, will probably be suited by more ease in the ground.

Mollyvator(IRE), last seen finishing sixth in a 7f Listed event, hit a flat spot at halfway and never really got involved. The fact her jockey lost his whip in the latter stages had little effect on her final position. (op 13-2)

6161 JAPAN RACING ASSOCIATION SCEPTRE STKS (GROUP 3) (F&M) 7f

1:50 (1:50) (Class 1) 3-Y-O+ **£32,560** (£12,314; £6,154; £3,074) **Stalls** High

Form				RPR
-600	**1**		**Sunday Times**[77] 3542 3-8-10 100 JamieSpencer 16 (Peter Chapple-Hyam) *s.i.s: confidently rdn in rr: gd hdwy over 1f out: led ins fnl f: drvn out* **22/1**	104
-110	**2**	1	**Gamilati**[41] 4764 3-8-10 110 MickaelBarzalona 17 (Mahmood Al Zarooni) *racd jst bhd stands' side ldr: rdn and overall ldr over 1f out: sn rdn and edgd lft: hdd ins fnl f: r.o: hld nr fin* **9/1**[3]	101+
-002	**3**	½	**Valencha**[7] 5980 5-9-0 90 RichardHughes 1 (Hughie Morrison) *hld up: effrt and pushed along whn bdly checked and plenty to do over 1f out: gd hdwy fnl f: nrst fin* **14/1**	103+
-043	**4**	nk	**Instance**[21] 5520 4-9-0 90 (p) JimmyFortune 11 (Jeremy Noseda) *awkward s: hld up: rdn and hdwy wl over 1f out: kpt on ins fnl f* **28/1**	100
1120	**5**	2 ¼	**Sentaril**[62] 4070 3-8-10 105 JohnnyMurtagh 18 (William Haggas) *led one other and overall ldr stands' rail: drifted lft and hdd over 1f out: btn ins fnl f* **3/1**[1]	93+
0143	**6**	2	**Appealing (IRE)**[41] 4764 3-8-10 98 WilliamBuick 14 (Marco Botti) *hld up: hdwy nr side of main gp whn hung lft over 1f out: sno chsng ldrs: wknd ins fnl f* **16/1**	88
0165	**7**	¾	**Radio Gaga**[21] 5523 3-8-10 98 GrahamGibbons 15 (Ed McMahon) *hld up in midfield: rdn over 2f out: no imp fnl frlong* **12/1**	86
-010	**8**	1	**Regal Realm**[18] 5627 3-8-13 101 (p) TomQueally 2 (Jeremy Noseda) *s.i.s: hld up: hdwy on outside of main gp over 1f out: kpt on fnl f: nvr able to chal* **14/1**	86
2330	**9**	nk	**Alsindi (IRE)**[137] 1699 3-8-10 98 SilvestreDeSousa 6 (Clive Brittain) *cl up: rdn and ev ch main gp over 2f out: wknd appr fnl f* **33/1**	82
2104	**10**	3	**Libys Dream (IRE)**[124] 2078 4-9-0 95 RichardKingscote 12 (Tom Dascombe) *prom: effrt and drvn over 2f out: edgd lft and wknd over 1f out* **25/1**	75
6250	**11**	2	**Villeneuve**[12] 5834 3-8-10 94 MartinDwyer 10 (William Muir) *towards rr: drvn along over 3f out: btn fnl 2f* **66/1**	69
24	**12**	¾	**Coolnagree (IRE)**[21] 5523 3-8-10 100 DeclanMcDonogh 13 (W McCreery, Ire) *in tch: rdn on nr side of main gp over 2f out: outpcd whn bdly hmpd over 1f out* **14/1**	67
6010	**13**	¾	**Bonnie Brae**[54] 4321 5-9-0 105 EddieAhern 5 (David Elsworth) *hld up in tch: drvn and effrt over 2f out: wknd over 1f out* **6/1**[2]	66
011	**14**	1	**I'm So Glad**[28] 5271 3-8-10 96 MartinHarley 7 (Mick Channon) *led main centre gp to over 1f out: sn rdn and wknd* **16/1**	62
1400	**15**	1	**Inetrobil (IRE)**[41] 4764 3-8-10 100 (p) PhillipMakin 3 (Kevin Ryan) *cl up: drvn over 2f out: wknd over 1f out* **40/1**	59
1506	**16**	16	**Neutrafa (IRE)**[33] 5092 4-9-0 93 MichaelO'Connell 9 (John Mackie) *prom tl rdn and wknd fr over 2f out* **66/1**	
123	**17**	shd	**Perfect Step (IRE)**[49] 4497 3-8-10 90 NeilCallan 8 (Roger Varian) *t.k.h: trckd ldrs tl rdn and wknd over 2f out: eased whn btn over 1f out* **9/1**[3]	
24-6	**18**	34	**Miss Work Of Art**[25] 5385 3-8-10 101 PaulHanagan 4 (Richard Fahey) *prom: drvn and hung lft wl over 2f out: sn wknd: eased whn no ch over 1f out* **16/1**	

1m 25.37s (-0.93) **Going Correction** +0.10s/f (Good)

WFA 3 from 4yo+ 4lb **18** Ran SP% **124.6**

Speed ratings (Par 113): **109,107,107,106,104 102,101,100,99,96 94,93,92,91,90 71,71,32**

toteswingers 1&2 £43.70, 2&3 £27.90, 1&3 £68.10 CSF £201.94 TOTE £30.60: £9.80, £2.60, £6.30; EX 194.60 Trifecta £1218.30 Part won. Pool: £1646.45 - 0.10 winning units..

Owner Allan Belshaw **Bred** Times Of Wigan Ltd **Trained** Newmarket, Suffolk

FOCUS

They went hard from the front in this competitive Group 3, setting it up for the closers, and those drawn low were at a disadvantage. The fourth is the key to the form.

NOTEBOOK

Sunday Times bounced back to something like her best 2yo form and continued the Classic generation's stranglehold on the race. She has struggled to find her feet since resuming at three, but was runner-up in the Group 1 Cheveley Park last year and is a class act on her day. This was on the back of a 77-day break and, judging by the way she put this to bed after scything through the pack under confident handling, she has clearly now come right again. A strongly run 7f seems her optimum and there could be more to come from her this autumn, but she won't be that simple to place from here. (op 16-1)

Gamilati made a bold bid. She showed her true colours again returned to a flatter track, on what was just her second run back in Britain, and this effort bodes well for her future. If kept in training, a return to Meydan next year will surely be on her agenda, and a return to the Tapeta surface should suit. (op 8-1)

Valencha, drawn in stall one, proved best of the older horses. She endured a luckless passage in a handicap at Salisbury a week earlier and again found trouble at a crucial stage here. The manner in which she finished, having raced upsides the winner until 2f out, suggests she would have gone mighty close with a clear run and she richly deserves a change of fortune. Official explanation: jockey said mare suffered interference in running

Instance, stepping up from handicap company, got going late in the day and ran a personal-best up in class aided by first-time cheekpieces. Her official mark will now be raised accordingly and make things tougher, but she might find further improvement for a stiffer test. (op 25-1)

Sentaril was back up in trip, but looked to pay here for doing too much too soon in leading on the near rail. Her best trip remains open to debate and she has something to prove, but she may well be the sort to improve physically as a 4-y-o. Official explanation: jockey said filly hung left (op 10-3)

Appealing(IRE) kept on at the same pace having raced prominently and reversed her last-time-out Goodwood form in this class with Regal Realm. (op 18-1)

Regal Realm, back against her own sex, proved laboured after a sluggish start from her low draw. (op 12-1)

Bonnie Brae Official explanation: jockey said mare ran flat

Perfect Step(IRE) Official explanation: trainer said filly had been struck into

Miss Work Of Art Official explanation: jockey said filly lost a front shoe

6162 WEATHERBYS INSURANCE £300,000 2-Y-O STKS 6f 110y

2:20 (2:23) (Class 2) 2-Y-O

£206,900 (£82,793; £41,396; £20,656; £10,349; £10,349) **Stalls** High

Form				RPR
511	**1**		**The Gold Cheongsam (IRE)**[40] 4820 2-8-1 97 FrannyNorton 10 (Jeremy Noseda) *trckd ldrs: led over 1f out: hld on towards fin* **11/4**[1]	90
5315	**2**	nk	**Hajam**[19] 5579 2-9-2 92 MartinDwyer 7 (James Tate) *in rr: sn pushed along: hdwy over 2f out: swtchd rt over 1f out: styd on wl: jst hld* **66/1**	104
1	**3**	½	**Haafaguinea**[38] 4873 2-8-3 0 JohnFahy 6 (Clive Cox) *dwlt: in rr: hdwy on outside over 3f out: styd on fnl f: no ex last 50yds* **33/1**	90
1106	**4**	½	**Indian Jade**[21] 5515 2-8-3 92 JimmyQuinn 2 (Kevin Ryan) *chsd ldrs: n.m.r over 1f out: styd on same pce last 150yds* **12/1**	89
553	**5**	1	**Parliament Square (IRE)**[25] 5398 2-9-5 0 (p) JPO'Brien 13 (A P O'Brien, Ire) *trckd ldrs: effrt over 2f out: kpt on ins fnl f* **8/1**	102
1631	**6**	½	**Hototo**[21] 5515 2-8-6 101 PaulMulrennan 12 (Kevin Ryan) *led: hdd over 1f out: fdd ins fnl f* **6/1**[2]	87
3013	**7**	1 ¼	**King Dragon (IRE)**[26] 5371 2-8-9 90 ShaneKelly 5 (Brian Meehan) *reminders sn after s: in rr: hdwy over 2f out: nt clr run and hung lft over 1f out: kpt on ins fnl f* **40/1**	89
6310	**8**	nse	**Saint Jerome (IRE)**[21] 5515 2-8-6 83 HayleyTurner 1 (Marcus Tregoning) *in rr: hdwy 3f out: kpt on same pce fnl f* **33/1**	84
1241	**9**	nk	**Liber**[12] 5813 2-8-6 95 LukeMorris 3 (Sir Mark Prescott Bt) *chsd ldrs: one pce over 1f out* **16/1**	83
3126	**10**	¾	**Salutation (IRE)**[5] 6032 2-8-9 81 SilvestreDeSousa 18 (Mark Johnston) *chsd ldrs: one pce over 1f out* **50/1**	84

11 **11** *3/4* **Flyman**[30] 5201 2-8-6 0 PaulHanagan 16 79
(Richard Fahey) *chsd ldrs: outpcd over 2f out: kpt on one pce* **7/1**[3]

0550 **12** *2 1/2* **Polski Max**[21] 5515 2-9-0 82 TonyHamilton 19 80
(Richard Fahey) *in rr: sme hdwy over 1f out: nvr a factor* **100/1**

0065 **13** *1 1/2* **Pay Freeze (IRE)**[17] 5678 2-8-3 91 HarryBentley 14 65
(Mick Channon) *chsd ldrs: effrt over 2f out: wknd over 1f out* **20/1**

242 **14** *1/2* **Letstalkaboutmoney (IRE)**[38] 4873 2-8-3 85 (v) WayneLordan 17 63
(Mrs K Burke) *mid-div: drvn 3f out: nvr a factor* **40/1**

6551 **15** *4 1/2* **Colmar Kid (IRE)**[24] 5418 2-8-6 82 EddieAhern 21 54
(Richard Hannon) *in rr: nvr on terms* **40/1**

410 **16** *1 1/4* **Carlton Blue (IRE)**[21] 5515 2-8-6 81 (t) MartinHarley 8 51
(Paul Cole) *chsd ldrs: lost pl over 2f out* **80/1**

1 **17** *1* **My Boy Bill**[166] 1131 2-9-0 0 GrahamGibbons 15 56
(Michael Easterby) *dwlt: a in rr* **10/1**

010 **18** *4* **Meringue Pie**[19] 5579 2-8-10 80 ow1 RichardHughes 22 41
(Richard Hannon) *in rr: bhd fnl 2f* **33/1**

1 **19** *1 1/2* **Beach Club**[24] 5410 2-8-6 0 MickaelBarzalona 4 33
(David Brown) *chsd ldrs: drvn over 3f out: lost pl over 2f out* **16/1**

621 **20** *8* **Grey Blue (IRE)**[18] 5619 2-8-6 84 JoeFanning 20 11
(Mark Johnston) *dwlt: in rr: bhd fnl 2f: eased in clsng stages* **33/1**

0044 **21** *9* **Lyric Ace (IRE)**[17] 5678 2-8-3 93 KieranO'Neill 11
(Richard Hannon) *trckd ldrs: t.k.h: lost pl over 2f out: bhd whn eased over 1f out* **33/1**

1m 19.7s (-0.20) **Going Correction** +0.10s/f (Good) **21** Ran SP% **125.6**
Speed ratings (Par 101): **105,104,104,103,102 101,100,100,99,99 98,95,93,93,87 86,85,80,79,69 59**
toteswingers 1&2 £102.30, 2&3 £0.00, 1&3 £33.60 CSF £251.90 TOTE £4.00: £2.10, £17.50, £11.10; EX 295.30 TRIFECTA Not won..
Owner Arashan Ali **Bred** Tally-Ho Stud **Trained** Newmarket, Suffolk

FOCUS
A valuable juvenile prize. The last two winners of this either won or were placed in Group 1 company subsequently as a 2yo. The winner's time was slower than the opening nursery and several down the field anchor the form. The winner did not need to produce her best.

NOTEBOOK
The Gold Cheongsam(IRE) was in here off bottom weight, so held an obvious chance of landing the huge prize considering her form and that she holds a Cheveley Park entry. However, it was far from plain sailing as she was locked away in the pack for a long time and only just had enough in hand to hold the runner-up. She'll need to improve again to be a serious contender for the Newmarket Group 1 later this month, but she does have plenty of sales race entries, which might be the right route for her. (op 3-1)

Hajam didn't possess eyecatching form (he was beaten off top weight in a nursery last time but was reported to have not got home over 7f), so this looks a big leap forward, especially as he was giving over a stone away to the filly. (op 50-1)

Haafaguinea ◆, a 25-1 winner on his racecourse debut at Kempton in early August, was on his toes beforehand. He's possibly the one to take from the race if kept to a sensible level. Slowly away, he travelled nicely out the back before making good ground towards the head of affairs. He surely has more to offer but doesn't hold any significant entries. (op 25-1)

Indian Jade, who got a little short on room late on, did best of those who contested the sales race at York last time and looks a game sort. (op 14-1 tchd 16-1 in a place)

Parliament Square(IRE), whose stable won this in 2011, ran really well to be third in the Prix Morny (runner-up, stablemate George Vancouver, has disappointed since at a lower level) but didn't totally convince with attitude here under strong pressure. It's difficult to blame the weight either, as the runner-up had inferior form but carried only 2lb less. (op 7-1)

Hototo was arguably the one to beat if repeating his best form, as he'd finished in front of plenty of these previously. He showed smart speed from the stalls but didn't see the last half a furlong out as well as those around him. Any distance between 5f-6f ought to suit. (op 7-1)

King Dragon(IRE) seemed to be ridden confidently but found his way blocked a few times in the latter stages while keeping on.

Flyman briefly looked dangerous but had no change of gear when required. (op 8-1)

My Boy Bill looked fit enough following his absence. (op 9-1)

6163 DFS PARK HILL STKS (GROUP 2) (F&M) 1m 6f 132y
2:55 (2:55) (Class 1) 3-Y-0+
£45,368 (£17,200; £8,608; £4,288; £2,152; £1,080) **Stalls** Low

Form RPR

50-1 **1** **Wild Coco (GER)**[42] 4738 4-9-4 113 TomQueally 6 108
(Sir Henry Cecil) *hld up in mid-div: hdwy on inner and nt clr run over 2f out: wnt 2nd 1f out: styd on wl to ld last 75yds: readily* **7/4**[1]

2010 **2** *1 1/4* **Hazel Lavery (IRE)**[42] 4738 3-8-6 100 WilliamCarson 8 106
(Charles Hills) *trckd ldrs on outer: dropped in rr after 4f: drvn over 4f out: styd on fnl 2f: tk 2nd post* **16/1**

-113 **3** *shd* **Estimate (IRE)**[42] 4738 3-8-6 110 PaulHanagan 7 106
(Sir Michael Stoute) *trckd ldrs: led over 3f out: 3 l clr over 1f out: hdd ins fnl f: kpt on same pce* **7/2**[2]

3211 **4** *shd* **Gallipot**[22] 5474 3-8-6 91 WilliamBuick 4 106
(John Gosden) *trckd ldrs: pushed along over 3f out: chsd ldr over 2f out: styd on same pce over 1f out* **12/1**

-131 **5** *1* **Ambivalent (IRE)**[39] 4848 3-8-6 101 NeilCallan 2 105
(Roger Varian) *t.k.h in rr: hdwy over 2f out: kpt on same pce* **4/1**[3]

0214 **6** *2 3/4* **Bite Of The Cherry**[21] 5519 3-8-6 97 HayleyTurner 9 101
(Michael Bell) *sn w ldr: drvn over 3f out: sn outpcd* **20/1**

211R **7** *3 1/2* **Monshak (IRE)**[19] 5598 3-8-6 87 FrannyNorton 5 96
(Sir Michael Stoute) *led: qcknd pce over 4f out: hdd over 3f out: wknd over 2f out* **25/1**

44-3 **8** *nk* **Cracking Lass (IRE)**[21] 5519 5-9-4 100 TonyHamilton 3 96
(Richard Fahey) *in rr: drvn over 4f out: nvr a factor* **33/1**

-100 **9** *1 1/2* **Kailani**[84] 3292 3-8-6 105 MickaelBarzalona 1 94
(Mahmood Al Zarooni) *trckd ldrs: t.k.h: drvn over 3f out: lost pl and hung rt over 2f out* **7/1**

3m 5.94s (-1.46) **Going Correction** +0.275s/f (Good)
WFA 3 from 4yo+ 12lb **9** Ran SP% **116.2**
Speed ratings (Par 115): **114,113,113,113,112 111,109,109,108**
toteswingers 1&2 £6.90, 2&3 £11.40, 1&3 £2.60 CSF £32.54 TOTE £3.20: £1.50, £4.10, £1.10; EX 40.70 Trifecta £165.80 Pool: £3828.93 - 17.08 winning units..
Owner Gestut Rottgen **Bred** Gestut Rottgen **Trained** Newmarket, Suffolk

FOCUS
This wasn't all that competitive for a Group 2 and it was run at a steady early pace, but the best horse still prevailed. There are doubts over the form and Wild Coco did not need to match her best.

NOTEBOOK
Wild Coco(GER) had returned with a bang when winning at Glorious Goodwood over just shy of this trip last month. That was her first success in Group company, but if anything this step up a level looked weaker and she was unsurprisingly popular with the slight ease in the ground to her liking. She was nearly undone by the lack of a gallop, but her class came to the fore inside the final furlong and the long straight helped her cause. She must be rated better than the bare form and was conceding 12lb to the trio of 3-y-os that made her work to get on top, so really it was a career-best effort. A crack at the valuable Fillies' And Mares' Stakes on British Champions Day at Ascot next month is likely to be her next port of call and she can go close to making it 3-3 for the year providing the ground is not quick.

Hazel Lavery(IRE) was well beaten by the winner at Goodwood last time out. The muddling pace was probably the reason she managed to close to gap here, but she too didn't enjoy the run of the race and no doubt she is an improving filly over a trip. (tchd 14-1)

Estimate(IRE) finished third behind the winner last time out, on 3lb worse terms. Paul Hanagan, taking over from the injured Ryan Moore, kicked her for home 3f out and she made a bold bid. She was nearing the end of her tether from half a furlong out, but might well have held on for second had Hanagan been more vigorous nearing the business end. Her peak effort came over 2m in the Queen's Vase back in June and it will be very interesting to see if she's kept in training, as she's in the right hands to improve as she matures. (tchd 4-1)

Gallipot had finally shown her worth on Polytrack the last twice and beat two subsequent winners on her previous outing. This was all together tougher, however, so this was a decent effort in defeat and she only just missed out on a place. She got the extra distance without much fuss and remains on an upwards curve.

Ambivalent(IRE) is not the most straightforward, but arrived on the back of a personal-best in Listed company at Newbury last month on quicker ground and her pedigree hinted further improvement may be forthcoming for the longer trip. She improved to have her chance from off the pace and stayed well enough, but may well prefer genuinely quick ground. She was beaten by the runner-up on an easy surface at Newmarket three runs back and so probably rates the most sensible guide for this form. (op 5-1)

6164 CROWNHOTEL-BAWTRY.COM IRISH E B F MAIDEN STKS 1m (S)
3:30 (3:30) (Class 3) 2-Y-0
£7,439 (£2,213; £1,106; £553) **Stalls** High

Form RPR

1 **Glenard** 2-9-3 0 MichaelHills 8 79+
(Charles Hills) *t.k.h in rr: hdwy and edgd rt 2f out: swtchd lft appr fnl f: str run to ld post* **14/1**

3 **2** *shd* **Sicur**[20] 5553 2-9-0 0 PatrickHills[(3)] 11 79
(Luca Cumani) *trckd ldr: led 2f out: edgd rt ins fnl f: hdd post* **14/1**

4 **3** *1/2* **Space Ship**[13] 5793 2-9-3 0 WilliamBuick 13 78
(John Gosden) *hld up in mid-div: hdwy over 2f out: chsng ldrs 1f out: no ex in clsng stages* **5/2**[1]

4 *1* **Winterlude (IRE)** 2-8-12 0 AntiocoMurgia[(5)] 14 76
(Mahmood Al Zarooni) *in rr: rapid hdwy to join ldrs over 2f out: one pce whn sltly hmpd twice last 50yds* **11/1**

5 *1* **Lions Arch (IRE)** 2-9-3 0 JimmyFortune 12 73+
(Richard Hannon) *hld up: hdwy over 1f out: styd on same pce last 100yds* **40/1**

5 **6** *hd* **Ennistown**[27] 5321 2-9-3 0 MickaelBarzalona 9 73
(Mahmood Al Zarooni) *chsd ldrs: continually hung violently lft and cocked jaw: kpt on same pce fnl f* **5/1**[3]

7 *2 1/4* **Flemish School** 2-8-12 0 LukeMorris 2 63
(Gerard Butler) *dwlt: in rr: hdwy over 2f out: kpt on ins fnl f* **25/1**

5 **8** *1/2* **Emulating (IRE)**[47] 4595 2-9-3 0 RichardHughes 1 66
(Richard Hannon) *hld up in mid-div: hdwy to join ldrs 1f out: wknd last 100yds* **6/1**

9 *2 3/4* **Cape Of Hope (IRE)** 2-9-3 0 RobertHavlin 15 60
(Peter Chapple-Hyam) *hld up towards rr: hdwy over 2f out: rdn and wknd over 1f out* **7/2**[2]

10 *nse* **Tuscan Fun** 2-9-3 0 NeilCallan 6 60
(Roger Varian) *s.i.s: in rr: hdwy and nt clr run over 1f out: sn wknd* **33/1**

11 *hd* **Love Marmalade (IRE)** 2-9-3 0 PhillipMakin 5 60
(Kevin Ryan) *trckd ldrs: t.k.h: wknd over 1f out* **33/1**

66 **12** *1 1/4* **Haverstock**[91] 3062 2-9-3 0 JoeFanning 7 57
(Mark Johnston) *led: hdd 2f out: sn wknd* **33/1**

50 **13** *8* **Bougaloo**[9] 5912 2-9-3 0 MartinHarley 4 38
(Alan McCabe) *trckd ldrs: drvn over 2f out: lost pl 2f out* **200/1**

14 *7* **Darakti (IRE)** 2-9-0 0 DeclanCannon[(3)] 10 22
(Alan McCabe) *in rr: reminders over 3f out: lost pl over 2f out: sn bhd* **100/1**

0400 **15** *3/4* **Cool Sea (IRE)**[13] 5799 2-8-5 43 DanielleMooney[(7)] 3 15
(Nigel Tinkler) *s.s: in rr: rdn over 2f out: sn bhd* **150/1**

1m 41.47s (2.17) **Going Correction** +0.10s/f (Good) **15** Ran SP% **120.7**
Speed ratings (Par 99): **93,92,92,91,90 90,87,87,84,84 84,83,75,68,67**
toteswingers 1&2 £12.00, 2&3 £5.30, 1&3 £9.80 CSF £185.51 TOTE £19.80: £4.20, £4.30, £1.40; EX 140.80 Trifecta £462.80 Pool: £1313.51 - 2.10 winning units..
Owner John C Grant **Bred** Denford Stud Ltd **Trained** Lambourn, Berks

FOCUS
A 2yo maiden that has gone to some decent horses in the past, most notably four-time Group winner Kite Wood in 2008, and Nathaniel was just beaten on his second start in this race in 2010. They raced down the middle once more and it looked an advantage to race handily as there was an ordinary tempo set early on. This appeals as good maiden form.

NOTEBOOK
Glenard did really well to get up at the line for a winning debut as he came from well back and found a tricky passage inside the final furlong. An imposing colt, he showed his inexperience early but looked potentially smart when the penny dropped and has to be rated value for a deal further than the narrow winning margin. He's in the Derby (bred to stay 1m4f), but has no fancy entries this term and his trainer later reported he would be taking it steady with him. The Autumn Stakes at Newmarket next month could be next for him, a path stablemate Perennial also took after winning this maiden on his debut last year, and finished runner-up in that. (op 16-1)

Sicur, third of four at Newmarket on his debut 20 days previously, proved keen up front. He was ideally placed as a result, however, and very nearly opened his account over the extra furlong. He has scope and should make up into a decent middle-distance performer next year, but can obviously win his maiden at two en-route. (op 20-1)

Space Ship ◆, representing the same connections as Nathaniel, came from well back when running with promise on his debut at Sandown 13 days earlier and proved popular to shed his maiden tag up to this trip. He again came from an unpromising position off the uneven pace, though, and once again failed to really show his true colours. He could well turn out to be the best of these. (op 3-1)

Winterlude(IRE) ◆, his yard's second string, made eyecatching headway from off the pace nearest the stands' rail from halfway and looked a big player. He flattened out near the finish, but this well-bred colt looks a sure-fire maiden winner and could be one to follow. (op 12-1)

Lions Arch(IRE), another stable second string, was coltish beforehand. He would have enjoyed a stronger pace and did some decent late work. He cost 1000,000euros and should begin to pay off some of that in the coming weeks.

Ennistown, a well-made colt, was Godolphin's number one hope and had his chance, improving on his debut fifth at Newmarket. However, he threw his head around under pressure late on and appeared to be feeling something, but connections later put it down to greenness. (op 7-1)

Flemish School, one of two fillies in the race, was drawn low and made her effort nearest the far rail. She ought to come on nicely and may benefit for a drop to 7f in the short term.
Emulating(IRE) was the choice of Richard Hughes and met support. He travelled nicely, but failed to see out the extra furlong. (op 13-2)
Cape Of Hope(IRE), half-brother to a host of winners, attracted strong support earlier in the day but drifted out on course. He moved sweetly early on, but found little for pressure and looks to need more time. (op 5-2 tchd 4-1)

6165 LADBROKES BINGO H'CAP — 6f

4:05 (4:05) (Class 3) (0-90,90) 3-Y-0+ **£9,703** (£2,887; £1,443; £721) **Stalls** High

Form — RPR

2414 **1** **Amadeus Wolfe Tone (IRE)**[26] 5363 3-9-2 **87**.......(p) JamieSpencer 19 — 99
(Jamie Osborne) *chsd ldng pair stands' side: hdwy to ld ent fnl f: drvn and hld on wl* **9/2**[2]

3200 **2** ¾ **Misplaced Fortune**[21] 5520 7-9-4 **90**..............(v) DaleSwift(3) 7 — 99
(Nigel Tinkler) *prom: rdn and hdwy to ld briefly appr fnl f: kpt on: hld towards fin* **16/1**

1231 **3** *nk* **Goldream**[27] 5320 3-9-2 **87**.............. RichardHughes 17 — 95
(Luca Cumani) *hld up: rdn over 2f out: hdwy over 1f out: edgd lft and kpt on fnl f: hld cl home* **4/1**[1]

6001 **4** *1* **Another Try (IRE)**[35] 4999 7-8-11 **83**.............. MichaelMetcalfe(3) 14 — 88
(Alan Jarvis) *led main centre gp to over 1f out: kpt on same pce u.p fnl f* **14/1**

230 **5** *hd* **My Kingdom (IRE)**[27] 5320 6-9-1 **84**..............(t) WilliamCarson 21 — 88+
(Stuart Williams) *hld up: rdn over 2f out: hdwy over 1f out: kpt on fnl f: nrst fin* **20/1**

3120 **6** *hd* **Elusive Flame**[7] 5980 3-9-3 **88**.............. WilliamBuick 4 — 92
(David Elsworth) *cl up: led main gp briefly over 1f out: kpt on same pce ins fnl f* **7/1**[3]

3136 **7** *shd* **Capone (IRE)**[187] 866 7-9-5 **88**.............. ShaneKelly 18 — 91
(Garry Moss) *hld up: rdn and hdwy over 1f out: kpt on fnl f: nvr able to chal* **20/1**

2503 **8** *1* **Seeking Magic**[40] 4799 4-9-4 **87**..............(t) AdamKirby 2 — 87
(Clive Cox) *plld hrd in tch: effrt and rdn over 2f out: nt qckn ins fnl f* **8/1**

0434 **9** *nse* **Sohraab**[12] 5829 8-9-4 **87**..............(b) MartinHarley 22 — 87
(Hughie Morrison) *chsd stands' side ldr: effrt over 2f out: no ex over 1f out* **10/1**

3000 **10** ½ **Novellen Lad (IRE)**[26] 5342 7-9-2 **85**.............. JamieMackay 9 — 83+
(Willie Musson) *stdd s: hld up: shkn up briefly whn n.m.r ins fnl f: kpt on steadily: nvr nr to chal* **40/1**

2450 **11** ½ **Roker Park (IRE)**[6] 6008 7-9-1 **84**..............(b) DanielTudhope 5 — 81+
(David O'Meara) *hld up: rdn over 2f out: no imp fr over 1f out* **16/1**

0106 **12** *nse* **Mappin Time (IRE)**[12] 5829 4-9-3 **86**..............(p) PaulMulrennan 1 — 83
(Tim Easterby) *prom: drvn along over 2f out: wknd over 1f out* **25/1**

4100 **13** *2* **Carambola**[6] 6008 6-9-0 **83**.............. JimmyFortune 10 — 73
(Mel Brittain) *cl up: ev ch over 2f out: sn rdn: wknd over 1f out* **20/1**

0000 **14** ½ **Dickie's Lad (IRE)**[22] 5487 4-9-2 **85**..............(t) PhillipMakin 20 — 74
(Kevin Ryan) *led stands' side trio to 2f out: sn rdn and btn* **10/1**

0200 **15** 2¾ **Victoire De Lyphar (IRE)**[6] 6011 5-9-7 **90**.............. JamesSullivan 15 — 70
(Ruth Carr) *prom tl rdn and wknd fr 2f out* **14/1**

5010 **16** *1* **Medici Time**[16] 5703 7-9-1 **84**..............(v) EddieAhern 12 — 61
(Tim Easterby) *trckd ldrs: drvn over 2f out: wknd wl over 1f out* **33/1**

1m 13.09s (-0.51) **Going Correction** +0.10s/f (Good)
WFA 3 from 4yo+ 2lb — **16** Ran SP% **128.6**
Speed ratings (Par 107): **107,106,105,104,104 103,103,102,102,101 100,100,98,97,93 92**
toteswingers 1&2 £16.50, 2&3 £9.60, 1&3 £3.50 CSF £71.16 CT £337.11 TOTE £5.70: £1.50, £5.40, £1.30, £4.40; EX 143.60 Trifecta £502.50 Pool: £835.36 - 1.23 winning units..
Owner B T McDonald **Bred** Brian Williamson **Trained** Upper Lambourn, Berks

FOCUS
Despite a few non-runners, this was a cracking sprint for useful types run at a sound gallop. The field split into two groups, one much smaller than the other. The form is rated around the second.

NOTEBOOK
Amadeus Wolfe Tone(IRE) was kept to the stands' side with only a couple of others before picking up nicely to get to the front when the field came together. He fought on bravely enough while challenged and the trainer feels sure that 6f is the gelding's ideal distance. Ayr next week is the plan as long as the going doesn't become soft. (op 5-1 tchd 11-2)
Misplaced Fortune, with a visor back on, didn't look on a winning mark considering her best performances, so this was a good effort. (op 14-1)
Goldream has developed into a consistent sprinter and gained another placing despite taking plenty of pushing to stay involved. (op 9-2)
Another Try(IRE), up 5lb for his Haydock success, had every chance from the front but didn't quite see it out.
My Kingdom(IRE) didn't have a lot of space late on and is a bit better than his final position. That said, he probably isn't the most straightforward of characters.
Elusive Flame, who usually races over 7f, got to the front at what appeared the right stage of the race but couldn't hold on. (op 8-1)
Capone(IRE) ◆, off since running on the AW during the winter/spring, shaped nicely from a rear-field position and will be of interest next time. (op 25-1)
Seeking Magic Official explanation: jockey said gelding ran too free
Novellen Lad(IRE) ◆ Official explanation: jockey said gelding was denied a clear run
Roker Park(IRE) Official explanation: jockey said gelding was denied a clear run

6166 DFS H'CAP — 1m 2f 60y

4:35 (4:35) (Class 2) (0-110,105) 3-Y-0+**£16,172** (£4,812; £2,405; £1,202) **Stalls** Low

Form — RPR

4442 **1** **Black Spirit (USA)**[83] 3329 5-9-10 **103**..............(t) AdamKirby 2 — 111
(Clive Cox) *trckd ldrs: effrt over 2f out: led over 1f out: drvn out* **7/2**[3]

1060 **2** 1½ **Resurge (IRE)**[75] 3635 7-9-0 **93**..............(t) NeilCallan 3 — 98
(Stuart Kittow) *hld up towards rr: effrt over 3f out: chsng ldrs over 1f out: n.m.r ins fnl f: styd on to take 2nd last strides* **14/1**

0021 **3** *nk* **Trade Storm**[21] 5517 4-9-11 **104**.............. JamieSpencer 6 — 109
(David Simcock) *hld up in last: effrt over 3f out: chsng ldrs over 1f out: edgd lft ins fnl f: no ex* **3/1**[1]

5-01 **4** ¾ **Specific Gravity (FR)**[19] 5583 4-9-6 **99**.............. TomQueally 4 — 102
(Sir Henry Cecil) *led tl over 8f out: chsd ldr: kpt on same pce fnl f* **10/3**[2]

4000 **5** *6* **Sandagiyr (FR)**[21] 5517 4-9-12 **105**.............. MickaelBarzalona 5 — 97
(Saeed Bin Suroor) *dwlt: sn trcking ldrs: t.k.h: led over 8f out: clr over 7f out: hdd over 1f out: sn wknd* **9/1**

3004 **6** *7* **Spanish Duke (IRE)**[22] 5492 5-9-2 **95**.............. EddieAhern 1 — 73
(John Dunlop) *trckd ldrs: t.k.h: sme hdwy over 2f out: sn wknd and bhd* **10/3**[2]

2m 9.75s (0.35) **Going Correction** +0.275s/f (Good) — **6** Ran SP% **110.0**
Speed ratings (Par 109): **109,107,107,106,102 96**
toteswingers 1&2 £6.30, 2&3 £7.50, 1&3 £2.10 CSF £43.82 TOTE £4.30: £2.10, £5.00; EX 48.40.
Owner A D Spence **Bred** Arundel Farm Llc **Trained** Lambourn, Berks

FOCUS
A tight little handicap, run at an uneven early pace but it still proved a decent test. Exposed form, the winner to his Royal Ascot mark.

NOTEBOOK
Black Spirit(USA) made light of an 83-day absence to score. He proved easy to back despite being the form choice on his last two outings behind the progressive Gatewood earlier this season and, when coming under pressure 3f out, it seemed he may be in need of the run. However, he dug deep and saw it out strongly inside the final furlong. It was a first success since his 3yo season, the handicapper should not put him up that much and he deserves a shot at the Cambridgeshire later this month. Whether connections allow him to run there under a penalty remains to be seen, however, and perhaps something like a Group 3 abroad may be more suitable. (op 3-1)
Resurge(IRE) went without the blinkers he flopped in when last seen back in June. He appreciated the way the race was run and did his best work towards the finish, returning to near his best.
Trade Storm was up 6lb for winning his first race for his current yard at York 21 days previously. He had something to prove on this debut over 1m2f and didn't help his cause by forfeiting around 5l with a tardy start. He kept on for maximum pressure throughout the home straight, however, and looked to stay well enough. (op 7-2)
Specific Gravity(FR) got back to winning ways in good style at Newmarket last time and was 9lb higher. He needs all of this trip and unsurprisingly went out to lead, but proved free when soon headed for that position. The 4yo kept to his task when under pressure, but now looks held by the handicapper. (op 7-2)
Sandagiyr(FR) faced his easiest task for a while, but again failed to see out his race and is one to avoid at present. (op 10-1 tchd 8-1)
Spanish Duke(IRE) was 2lb lower than when placed in this event two years back and returned to something akin to his best when making the frame at York last month. He proved free when initially reined back by his rider, but looked a player when angling towards the centre after making up ground turning for home. However, he found nil for pressure and his rider later reported that he lost his action. Official explanation: jockey said gelding lost its action (op 3-1 tchd 7-2)
T/Jkpt: Not won. T/Plt: £83.10 to a £1 stake. Pool of £186919.05 - 1641.04 winning tickets.
T/Qpdt: £7.30 to a £1 stake. Pool of £11528.81 - 1167.09 winning tickets. WG

5702 EPSOM (L-H)

Thursday, September 13

OFFICIAL GOING: Good (good to firm in places; 8.3)
Rail dolled out 3yds from 6f to winning post adding about 5yds to advertised distances.
Wind: light, half behind Weather: dry and sunny

6167 DOWNLOAD EPSOM'S ANDROID OR IPHONE APP NOW MAIDEN STKS — 6f

2:00 (2:02) (Class 4) 2-Y-0 **£3,881** (£1,155; £577; £288) **Stalls** High

Form — RPR

452 **1** **Veturia (USA)**[24] 5425 2-8-12 **73**.............. GrahamLee 1 — 72
(Kevin Ryan) *racd keenly: mde virtually all: pushed along and wnt clr wl over 1f out: looked wl in command tl tiring and rdn fnl 75yds: jst lasted* **3/1**[1]

3 **2** *shd* **Jubilante**[13] 5784 2-8-12 0.............. DarryllHolland 3 — 72+
(Hughie Morrison) *dwlt and pushed along leaving stalls: bhd: swtchd rt: rn green and no imp over 2f out: str run on outer 1f out: chsd clr ldr fnl 100yds: clsng qckly towards fin: jst failed* **10/1**

44 **3** 1½ **Mishaal (IRE)**[14] 5765 2-9-3 0..............[1] AndreaAtzeni 7 — 72
(Roger Varian) *in tch: rdn and effrt 2f out: styd on to chse clr ldr ins fnl f tl fnl 100yds: kpt on but nvr gng pce to chal* **3/1**[1]

4 2¼ **You Da One (IRE)** 2-9-3 0.............. DavidProbert 6 — 65
(Andrew Balding) *dwlt and pushed along leaving stalls: in tch: switching rt and rdn wl over 1f out: kpt on same pce fnl f* **11/2**

044 **5** 2½ **Talqaa**[14] 5781 2-8-12 0.............. SamHitchcott 5 — 53
(Mick Channon) *chsd ldrs: rdn to chse clr ldr 2f out: sn outpcd by wnr and no imp: edgd lft and lost 2nd ins fnl f: wknd fnl 100yds* **7/2**[2]

002 **6** *2* **Keene's Pointe**[13] 5785 2-9-3 80.............. SebSanders 2 — 52
(J W Hills) *chsd ldr tl 2f out: sn rdn and unable qck: lost pl and btn whn n.m.r jst over 1f out: wknd ins fnl f* **5/1**[3]

1m 10.83s (1.43) **Going Correction** +0.05s/f (Good) — **6** Ran SP% **113.4**
Speed ratings (Par 97): **92,91,89,86,83 80**
toteswingers 1&2 £4.10, 2&3 £5.10, 1&3 £2.40 CSF £32.19 TOTE £3.80: £2.00, £3.90; EX 34.00.
Owner Mrs R G Hillen & Sean P Graham **Bred** Gulf Coast Farms LLC **Trained** Hambleton, N Yorks

FOCUS
A fair juvenile maiden. They went an honest gallop and the form looks straightforward.

NOTEBOOK
Veturia(USA), officially rated 73 after three respectable displays at up to 7f, just managed to make all the running here on quicker ground. She should remain competitive in fair nursery/handicap company under similar conditions. (op 7-2 tchd 11-4)
Jubilante took a while to adjust to the gradients but stepped up markedly on her modest 6f Salisbury debut, just failing to get up. She is a half-sister to useful 7f-1m winner Justonefortheroad and looks capable of winning a similar contest over 7f. (tchd 9-1 and 12-1)
Mishaal(IRE) was wearing a first-time hood but found only marginal improvement on his two Polytrack efforts. (op 7-2 tchd 4-1)
You Da One(IRE) cost 45,000gns as a yearling and showed a modicum of promise on his debut after a slow start. He has something to build on at up to 7f this term. (op 13-2 tchd 15-2)
Talqaa finished fourth in a Baden-Baden Listed contest over this trip on good ground the previous month but disappointed here. (op 11-4)
Keene's Pointe arrived with a BHA rating of 80 but ran poorly on this return to quick ground. (op 11-2 tchd 13-2)

6168 BRITISH STALLION STUDS SUPPORTING BRITISH RACING E B F MEDIAN AUCTION MAIDEN STKS — 7f

2:30 (2:31) (Class 5) 2-Y-0 **£3,881** (£1,155; £577; £288) **Stalls** Low

Form — RPR

0 **1** **Imperial Glance**[27] 5303 2-9-3 0.............. DavidProbert 3 — 73
(Andrew Balding) *mde virtually all: edgd rt over 3f out: rdn and forged ahd wl over 1f out: kpt on gamely u.p fnl f* **6/1**[3]

0 **2** *shd* **The Scuttler (IRE)**[34] 5062 2-9-3 0.............. SamHitchcott 5 — 73
(Mick Channon) *chsd ldrs: rdn and effrt 2f out: chsd wnr wl over 1f out: ev ch ins fnl f: kpt on wl u.p: jst hld* **8/1**

3 ¾ **Elnadwa (USA)** 2-8-12 0.............. TadhgO'Shea 1 — 66
(Saeed Bin Suroor) *t.k.h: hld up in tch: effrt and swtchd lft over 1f out: pressed ldrs 1f out: rn green ins fnl 75yds* **85/40**[1]

3 **4** 4½ **House Of Orange (IRE)**[23] 5439 2-8-10 0.............. MichaelJMMurphy(7) 6 — 59
(Mark Johnston) *dwlt: sn rdn along in rr and nt handling downhill run tl 1/2-way: swtchd lft and hdwy over 2f out: chsd ldrs u.p over 1f out: no ex and btn 1f out: wknd* **6/1**[3]

60 **5** *1* **Dark Justice (IRE)**[22] 5476 2-8-12 0................................ GrahamLee 2 51
(Tim Pitt) *stdd s: hld up off the pce in last pair: clsd and in tch whn pushed lft over 1f out: no ex and btn 1f out: wknd* **11/1**

2 **6** *1 1/4* **Reveille**[17] 5656 2-8-12 0.................................... DarryllHolland 4 48
(Hughie Morrison) *w ldr: j. path and unbalanced over 3f out: unable qck and lost 2nd wl over 1f out: wknd ent fnl f* **9/4**[2]

1m 25.41s (2.11) **Going Correction** +0.05s/f (Good) **6** Ran SP% **110.8**
Speed ratings (Par 95): **89,88,88,82,81 80**
toteswingers 1&2 £12.40, 2&3 £4.40, 1&3 £5.70 CSF £48.41 TOTE £11.00: £5.60, £4.10; EX 57.80.
Owner Mrs Sandie Newton **Bred** Mrs J S Newton **Trained** Kingsclere, Hants

FOCUS
A modest median auction maiden for juveniles. Not easy to rate with little pre-race form to go on.

NOTEBOOK
Imperial Glance stepped up on the form of his modest debut in a better-class 7f Newbury maiden. He was reminiscent of his sire Passing Glance, a dual winner here, in being quickly away from the gates on his way to a thoroughly game front-running performance. He should continue to improve at up to 1m under similar circumstances. (op 8-1)
The Scuttler(IRE) produced a modest debut over this trip on good to firm ground at Newmarket the previous month. This was a much-better effort and he has a future in modest nursery handicap company. (tchd 7-1)
Elnadwa(USA) is a half-sister to a 6f dirt winner in the US and is out of a Grade 1 winner. She has performed respectably here at a difficult venue for debutantes and should build on this display, perhaps on a more conventional track at up to 1m. (op 11-4 tchd 2-1)
House Of Orange(IRE) ran a strange race in that he started poorly, showed ability in the middle section and then finished tamely. He looks like a heavy-topped individual who will be better judged on a more conventional track. (op 5-1)
Reveille ran well over 1m on soft ground at Chepstow on debut the previous month. She never looked happy at this track on quicker ground. Darryll Holland, her rider, reported that the filly jumped the path approaching 3f out and was unbalanced thereafter. Official explanation: jockey said filly jumped path approaching 3f out and became unbalanced thereafter (op 15-8 tchd 7-4)

6169 ARDENT TIDE FOR CIS PAYMENTS H'CAP 1m 114y
3:05 (3:07) (Class 5) (0-75,75) 3-Y-O **£4,528** (£1,347; £673; £336) **Stalls** Low

Form RPR
1234 **1** **Siouxperhero (IRE)**[7] 5983 3-8-13 **67**.........................(b) DarryllHolland 5 74
(William Muir) *chsd ldrs: wnt 2nd after 2f: rdn and outpcd 3f out: kpt on u.p fr over 1f out: led fnl 50yds: styd on wl* **7/2**[3]

1654 **2** *1/2* **Balady (IRE)**[15] 5747 3-9-7 **75**.. TadhgO'Shea 6 81
(John Dunlop) *dwlt: hdwy to ld after 1f and set stdy gallop: rdn and qcknd clr 3f out: hanging lft down camber after: pressed and stl hanging into rail ins fnl f: hdd and no ex fnl 50yds* **10/3**[2]

5004 **3** *2 3/4* **Brimstone Hill (IRE)**[10] 5892 3-9-2 **70**............................ GrahamLee 3 70
(Anthony Carson) *in tch: rdn and outpcd 3f out: rallied u.p ent fnl f: kpt on but nvr gng pce to chal* **7/1**

0 **4** *1 1/4* **Eternal Gift (FR)**[61] 4082 3-9-7 **75**.................................... SebSanders 4 72
(Rae Guest) *hld up in tch: rdn and hdwy to chse clr ldng pair jst over 2f out: no imp and one pce fr over 1f out* **16/1**

0030 **5** *1* **Titus Star (IRE)**[47] 4603 3-9-0 **68**...................................... LiamKeniry 2 62
(J S Moore) *hld up in tch: t.k.h on downhill run 5f out: short of room and lost pl over 2f out: swtchd lft wl over 1f out: plugged on but no threat to ldrs fnl f* **12/1**

4030 **6** *2 1/4* **Light Zabeel (USA)**[17] 5680 3-9-3 **71**............................. SamHitchcott 1 60
(Mick Channon) *led for 1f: chsd ldr tl over 5f out: rdn and outpcd 3f out: wknd over 1f out* **16/1**

0411 **7** *1 1/2* **Classic Falcon (IRE)**[19] 5592 3-8-13 **67**.................... AdamBeschizza 7 53
(William Haggas) *taken down early: v s.i.s and rdn along early: in tch: hdwy on outer over 4f out: sn rdn: outpcd 3f out: no threat to ldrs fr over 1f out* **15/8**[1]

1m 46.18s (0.08) **Going Correction** +0.05s/f (Good) **7** Ran SP% **112.0**
Speed ratings (Par 101): **101,100,98,97,96 94,92**
toteswingers 1&2 £1.10, 2&3 £4.00, 1&3 £4.20 CSF £14.91 TOTE £6.20: £2.90, £2.70; EX 17.40.
Owner Muir Racing Partnership - Bath **Bred** J & J Waldron **Trained** Lambourn, Berks

FOCUS
A weak 3yo handicap for the grade, with the favourite disappointing. The exposed winner rates a small personal best.
Classic Falcon(IRE) Official explanation: jockey said filly was upset in preliminaries and reared over at start

6170 LIGHTHOUSE CLUB JUMP JOCKEYS DERBY H'CAP (TO BE RIDDEN BY PROFESSIONAL NATIONAL HUNT JOCKEYS) 1m 4f 10y
3:40 (3:42) (Class 4) (0-80,80) 4-Y-O+ **£6,469** (£1,925; £962; £481) **Stalls** Centre

Form RPR
-042 **1** **Novirak (IRE)**[16] 5706 4-11-5 **75**..................................... DenisO'Regan 6 84
(James Fanshawe) *trckd ldrs: chsd clr ldr over 2f out: clsd and upsides over 1f out: nudged into narrow ld 1f out: nudged along and a jst doing enough fnl f* **7/2**[1]

6660 **2** *nk* **The Bells O Peover**[17] 5665 4-11-5 **75**......................(b) JasonMaguire 3 83
(Mark Johnston) *led: clr 3f out: rdn over 2f out: hdd 1f out: kpt on u.p but a hld by wnr after* **8/1**

0103 **3** *3/4* **Sula Two**[12] 5816 5-11-9 **79**.. TimmyMurphy 10 85
(Ron Hodges) *hld up in midfield: hdwy on inner whn nt clr run and hmpd 3f out: swtchd rt and gd hdwy over 2f out: chsd ldng pair over 1f out: kpt on wl ins fnl f* **12/1**

6452 **4** *4 1/2* **Kings Troop**[17] 5665 6-10-10 **66**...............................(v) JimmyMcCarthy 5 65
(Alan King) *in tch: rdn and effrt 3f out: drvn and no imp over 1f out: 4th and one pce fnl f* **5/1**[2]

115 **5** *1 3/4* **Lieutenant Kojak**[53] 4365 4-11-10 **80**.................... DominicElsworth 11 76
(Peter Charalambous) *hld up in rr: hdwy on outer over 1f out: styd on wl fnl f: nvr trbld ldrs* **6/1**[3]

5534 **6** *nk* **Iron Condor**[17] 5665 5-11-4 **74**...................................... PaddyBrennan 12 70
(James Eustace) *hld up towards rr: swtchd lft and hdwy over 2f out: kpt on fnl f: nvr trbld ldrs* **12/1**

5225 **7** *2 1/2* **Spartan Spirit (IRE)**[12] 5816 4-11-0 **70**.................... TomScudamore 13 62
(Hughie Morrison) *hld up in midfield: rdn and effrt 3f out: no imp and btn 2f out: plugged on but wl hld after* **9/1**

0010 **8** *7* **Epsom Salts**[17] 5665 7-11-6 **76**.. ColinBolger 2 57
(Pat Phelan) *s.i.s: hld up towards rr: rdn and struggling 3f out: sn outpcd and wl btn fnl 2f: plugged on past btn horses fnl f* **20/1**

2436 **9** *hd* **Shesha Bear**[28] 5277 7-11-2 **72**...............................(p) HaddenFrost 14 52
(Jonathan Portman) *in tch in midfield: rdn and effrt over 3f out: no imp and sn struggling: wl btn fnl 2f* **10/1**

220- **10** *nk* **Compton Blue**[26] 7228 6-11-3 **73**...........................(p) RobertThornton 9 53
(Alan King) *in tch: rdn and unable qck 3f out: sn outpcd and struggling: bhd over 1f out* **20/1**

1114 **11** *2* **Standpoint**[4] 6076 6-11-10 **80**.. DaveCrosse 1 57
(Conor Dore) *chsd ldrs: wnt 2nd 4f out tl wl over 2f out: sn struggling u.p: wknd 2f out* **14/1**

2032 **12** *21* **Holden Eagle**[49] 4491 7-10-10 **66**.............................. LiamTreadwell 8
(Tony Newcombe) *w ldr tl 4f out: lost pl qckly ent fnl 3f: bhd fnl 2f: t.o* **25/1**

5/P0 **13** *7* **Higgy's Ragazzo (FR)**[12] 5830 5-11-0 **70**..............(p[1]) MattieBatchelor 4
(Roger Ingram) *v.s.a: nvr gng wl in rr: lost tch 5f out: t.o fnl 2f* **66/1**

2m 40.52s (1.62) **Going Correction** +0.05s/f (Good) **13** Ran SP% **120.3**
Speed ratings (Par 105): **96,95,95,92,91 90,89,84,84,84 82,68,64**
toteswingers 1&2 £7.10, 2&3 £53.40, 1&3 £23.10 CSF £30.07 CT £309.91 TOTE £4.60: £2.10, £3.00, £4.60; EX 34.50.
Owner Norman Brunskill **Bred** Loughbrown Stud **Trained** Newmarket, Suffolk

FOCUS
A fair middle-distance handicap for older horses and restricted to professional National Hunt jockeys. The winning time was respectable considering the horses were carrying heavier weights than normal. Straightforward form.

6171 TILLEY & BARRETT DEMOLITION H'CAP (DIV I) 7f
4:15 (4:16) (Class 5) (0-75,75) 3-Y-O+ **£4,528** (£1,347; £673; £336) **Stalls** Low

Form RPR
3325 **1** **Majuro (IRE)**[12] 5819 8-9-3 **75**..................................(t) DavidBergin[(7)] 8 84
(Charles Smith) *hld up in tch: hdwy to chal and sltly hmpd over 1f out: sn led: r.o strly fnl f: readily* **9/2**[2]

2406 **2** *1 1/2* **Great Shot**[9] 5906 4-9-9 **74**.. SeanLevey 7 79
(Sylvester Kirk) *chsd ldr tl led ent fnl 2f: rdn and edgd rt over 1f out: sn hdd: styd on same pce fnl f* **7/2**[1]

0215 **3** *2* **Stonecrabstomorrow (IRE)**[18] 5625 9-8-9 **63**.......... MarkCoumbe[(3)] 5 63+
(Michael Attwater) *awkward leaving stalls and slowly away: bhd: sme hdwy but stl plenty to do over 2f out: styd on strly fr over 1f out: wnt 3rd fnl 75yds: gng on wl towards fin but nvr able to chal* **14/1**

0050 **4** *1 1/2* **Safe House (IRE)**[24] 5415 3-8-7 **69**..................... MichaelJMMurphy[(7)] 6 64
(Mark Johnston) *dwlt: sn in tch in midfield: sltly hmpd 5f out: rdn and effrt over 2f out: chsd clr ldng pair 1f out: one pce and no imp after: lost 3rd fnl 75yds* **8/1**

-023 **5** *3* **Leadenhall Lass (IRE)**[22] 5486 6-8-5 **61**............... JemmaMarshall[(5)] 2 48
(Pat Phelan) *taken down early: chsd ldrs: rdn and effrt to chal over 2f out: sn struggling to qckn and outpcd 2f out: wknd over 1f out* **7/1**

0040 **6** *nk* **Cravat**[40] 4819 3-9-3 **72**... LiamKeniry 10 58
(Ed de Giles) *stdd after s: hld up off the pce in last quartet: sme hdwy over 2f out: kpt on fnl f but n.d* **8/1**

0006 **7** *1* **Space Station**[32] 5120 6-9-8 **73**...................................(b) SebSanders 1 57
(Simon Dow) *in tch in midfield: stmbld on downhill run 5f out: rdn and unable qck over 2f out: sn outpcd and btn: wknd over 1f out* **8/1**

141 **8** *9* **Paphos**[26] 5349 5-8-10 **61** oh2......................................(e) SaleemGolam 9 21
(Stuart Williams) *stdd and swtchd lft after s: a bhd: swtchd rt and no rspnse whn rdn over 2f out: wl bhd fnl f* **13/2**[3]

0000 **9** *3/4* **Esprit Danseur**[17] 5662 3-8-6 **61** oh1..........................(p) MircoDemuro 3 18
(Jim Boyle) *led tl ent fnl 2f: sn struggling and outpcd wknd wl over 1f out* **20/1**

3031 **10** *7* **Rezwaan**[125] 2044 5-9-6 **71**.. FrankieMcDonald 4
(Murty McGrath) *t.k.h: stdd bk into last quartet after 1f: sn wl off the pce: rdn and lost tch over 2f out* **20/1**

1m 24.62s (1.32) **Going Correction** +0.05s/f (Good)
WFA 3 from 4yo+ 4lb **10** Ran SP% **115.8**
Speed ratings (Par 103): **94,92,90,88,84 84,83,73,72,64**
toteswingers 1&2 £6.40, 2&3 £11.40, 1&3 £12.90 CSF £20.47 CT £198.67 TOTE £6.30: £1.70, £2.10, £2.80; EX 26.40.
Owner Willie McKay **Bred** Tally-Ho Stud **Trained** Temple Bruer, Lincs

FOCUS
The first division of a fair 7f handicap for 3yos and up. It was 0.35sec slower than the second division. Few got involved and the form is rated around the runner-up.

6172 TILLEY & BARRETT DEMOLITION H'CAP (DIV II) 7f
4:45 (4:45) (Class 5) (0-75,74) 3-Y-O+ **£4,528** (£1,347; £673; £336) **Stalls** Low

Form RPR
1230 **1** **Purley Queen (IRE)**[13] 5808 3-8-6 **60** oh3.................. SaleemGolam 10 70
(Sylvester Kirk) *racd in midfield: rdn 4f out: hdwy u.p on outer over 1f out: led 1f out: r.o wl and sn clr: rdn out* **25/1**

6-52 **2** *2 1/4* **Young Dottie**[17] 5667 6-9-2 **66**.. IanMongan 9 71
(Pat Phelan) *chsd ldrs: rdn 3f out: kpt on u.p to chse wnr ins fnl f: no imp* **5/1**[2]

4041 **3** *shd* **Lutine Charlie (IRE)**[65] 3949 5-8-10 **60**.......................... TadhgO'Shea 8 65
(Pat Eddery) *sn bhd: plenty to do but sme hdwy over 2f out: str run and swtchd lft ins fnl f: pressing for 2nd cl home: no threat to wnr* **16/1**

2254 **4** *3/4* **Serene Oasis (IRE)**[21] 5512 3-9-6 **74**........................(v) SamHitchcott 7 76
(Mick Channon) *upsides ldr: stl on bit 2f out: shkn up and fnd v little over 1f out: styd on same pce ins fnl f* **5/1**[2]

4046 **5** *1 1/4* **Aldermoor (USA)**[16] 5703 6-9-5 **74**..................(v) TobyAtkinson[(5)] 4 73
(Stuart Williams) *w ldr tl led 5f out: rdn and edgd rt over 1f out: hdd and no ex 1f out: wknd ins fnl f* **8/1**

0004 **6** *shd* **Beau Duke (IRE)**[16] 5705 3-8-8 **62**................................ DavidProbert 5 60
(Andrew Balding) *chsd ldrs: effrt u.p on inner over 2f out: no ex ent fnl f: wknd ins fnl f* **5/1**[2]

0015 **7** *3/4* **Avonrose**[27] 5326 5-9-8 **72**...(v) DarryllHolland 2 69
(Derek Shaw) *t.k.h: hld up in tch: rdn and fnd little over 1f out: wknd ins fnl f* **9/2**[1]

0430 **8** *6* **Indian Art (IRE)**[27] 5305 6-9-10 **74**.................................. SeanLevey 6 55
(Sylvester Kirk) *sn rdn along and dropped to rr: n.d* **10/1**

6-02 **9** *8* **Finlodex**[113] 2387 5-9-1 **65**..................................... FrankieMcDonald 3 24
(Murty McGrath) *sn rdn along: struggling bdly and outpcd in last trio 5f out: wl bhd fnl 3f* **20/1**

0033 **10** *16* **Hoover**[31] 5157 4-8-11 **61**..(tp) MircoDemuro 1
(Jim Boyle) *t.k.h: led tl 5f out: steadily lost pl: bhd 2f out: t.o fnl f* **15/2**[3]

1m 24.27s (0.97) **Going Correction** +0.05s/f (Good)
WFA 3 from 4yo+ 4lb **10** Ran SP% **114.6**
Speed ratings (Par 103): **96,93,93,92,91 90,90,83,74,55**
toteswingers 1&2 £16.70, 2&3 £8.80, 1&3 £26.50 CSF £143.46 CT £1454.44 TOTE £37.50: £7.60, £1.80, £4.30; EX 146.50.
Owner D Boocock & P D Merritt **Bred** Mark & Pippa Hackett **Trained** Upper Lambourn, Berks

The Form Book Flat, Raceform Ltd, Compton, RG20 6NL

FOCUS
The second division of a fair 7f handicap for 3yos and up. They posted a faster time than the first instalment. The winner posted a clear personal best at face value.

6173 TRADE & CONSTRUCTION RACEDAY H'CAP (BETFAIR SPRINT FLAT SERIES QUALIFIER) 6f
5:15 (5:16) (Class 5) (0-75,75) 3-Y-O £4,528 (£1,347; £673; £336) Stalls High

Form RPR
6224 **1** **Pettochside**[9] 5915 3-8-7 **61**............(t) DavidProbert 4 70
(Stuart Williams) *hld up in tch: rdn and effrt 2f out: hdwy to ld jst over 1f out: in command and pushed out fnl f* **7/2**[1]
020 **2** 1 **Brocklebank (IRE)**[18] 5618 3-9-7 **75**............(tp) GrahamLee 9 80
(Kevin Ryan) *chsd ldrs: rdn and effrt to chse wnr ent fnl f: styng on same pce and hld whn swtchd rt ins fnl f* **15/2**[3]
4011 **3** 3 ¼ **Ziefhd**[24] 5406 3-9-3 **74**............(p) MarkCoumbe(3) 7 68
(Tim McCarthy) *led tl rdn and hdd jst over 2f out: unable qck u.p over 1f out: no ch w ldng pair and one pce fnl f* **14/1**
4150 **4** 1 **Represent (IRE)**[6] 5995 3-9-2 **70**............ SamHitchcott 1 61
(Mick Channon) *in tch towards rr: hmpd over 4f out: rdn and effrt 2f out: no ex u.p 1f out: plugged on same pce fnl f* **9/1**
0000 **5** ½ **Marygold**[56] 4235 3-9-1 **69**............(v[1]) AdamBeschizza 5 59
(Lee Carter) *sn rdn along: hdwy to chse ldr over 4f out: led jst over 2f out: sn rdn and edgd lft: hdd jst over 1f out: no ex and btn 1f out: wknd ins fnl f* **20/1**
1113 **6** nse **Aubrietia**[13] 5808 3-8-2 **63**............(v[1]) DavidBergin(7) 3 52+
(Alan McCabe) *taken down early: chsd ldr tl hmpd over 4f out: short of room and lost pl 2f out: swtchd rt over 1f out: kpt on but no ch w ldrs fnl f* **7/2**[1]
2334 **7** 1 ½ **Ring For Baileys**[12] 5815 3-9-2 **70**............ SebSanders 8 55
(Chris Dwyer) *in tch towards rr: rdn and effrt over 2f out: edgd lft and no imp over 1f out: wknd ins fnl f* **10/1**
0225 **8** ¾ **Lupo D'Oro (IRE)**[50] 4477 3-9-2 **75**............ TobyAtkinson(5) 6 57
(John Best) *dwlt: a towards rr: in tch: rdn over 3f out: swtchd rt and no imp 2f out: wknd over 1f out* **10/1**
0555 **9** 5 **Dishy Guru**[9] 5906 3-9-7 **75**............ LiamKeniry 2 41
(Michael Blanshard) *in tch: hmpd and lost pl over 4f out: rdn and no hdwy wl over 1f out: wknd ent fnl f: eased cl home* **9/2**[2]

1m 10.78s (1.38) **Going Correction** +0.05s/f (Good) **9** Ran SP% **114.0**
Speed ratings (Par 101): **92,90,86,85,84 84,82,81,74**
toteswingers 1&2 £4.30, 2&3 £15.40, 1&3 £6.50 CSF £29.73 CT £325.66 TOTE £5.80: £1.20, £2.30, £3.90; EX 26.90.
Owner James Thom **Bred** New Hall Stud **Trained** Newmarket, Suffolk

FOCUS
A fair 3yo sprint handicap run in a modest time. The winner was up a length on his recent C&D run.
Lupo D'Oro(IRE) Official explanation: jockey said gelding was slowly away; trainer said gelding was unsuited by the track
T/Plt: £2,165.60 to a £1 stake. Pool of £52360.55 - 17.65 winning tickets. T/Qpdt: £56.20 to a £1 stake. Pool of £4811.86 - 63.32 winning tickets. SP

6050 WOLVERHAMPTON (A.W) (L-H)
Thursday, September 13

OFFICIAL GOING: Standard changing to standard to fast after race 2 (6.20)
Wind: Fresh, behind Weather: Overcast

6174 VISIT ATTHERACES.COM/LEGER APPRENTICE H'CAP 1m 1f 103y(P)
5:45 (5:45) (Class 6) (0-60,60) 3-Y-O+ £1,704 (£503; £251) Stalls Low

Form RPR
2346 **1** **Warden Bond**[18] 5632 4-9-3 **57**............(p) JoshCrane(5) 5 68
(William Stone) *hld up in tch: nt clr run over 2f out: rdn to ld and edgd lft ins fnl f: r.o wl* **9/1**
0313 **2** 3 ¾ **Refreshestheparts (USA)**[5] 6057 3-9-4 **59**............ JoshBaudains 10 65
(George Baker) *hld up: hdwy over 2f out: led over 1f out: rdn: hung lft and hdd ins fnl f: hit rails and lost action sn after* **11/4**[1]
4612 **3** 2 ¼ **Thecornishcowboy**[6] 5989 3-8-10 **58** 6ex............(t) BradleyBosley(7) 6 56+
(John Ryan) *hld up: nt clr run 3f out: hdwy over 1f out: nt clr run and swtchd rt ins fnl f: r.o to go 3rd post: nvr nrr* **7/2**[2]
1064 **4** hd **Lady Percy (IRE)**[31] 5148 3-9-2 **57**............ RachealKneller 8 55
(Mark Usher) *chsd ldr 2f: remained handy: rdn over 2f out: wknd fnl f* **14/1**
-005 **5** ¾ **Greeley House**[34] 5052 4-9-10 **59**............ ThomasBrown 3 55
(Chris Wall) *trckd ldrs: wnt 2nd over 2f out tl rdn over 1f out: wknd ins fnl f* **6/1**[3]
5040 **6** 2 ½ **Gabrial's Lexi (IRE)**[15] 5754 3-9-1 **56**............(v[1]) GeorgeChaloner 11 47
(Ian Williams) *s.i.s: hdwy over 7f out: rdn over 3f out: wknd over 1f out* **16/1**
2055 **7** hd **Harrys Yer Man**[31] 5175 8-9-0 **49**............ JackDuern 2 40
(Mark Brisbourne) *s.i.s: hld up: rdn over 1f out: nvr on terms* **20/1**
0000 **8** 1 ½ **Goal (IRE)**[45] 4662 4-9-8 **57**............ NoelGarbutt 4 45
(Charles Smith) *led: clr over 3f out: rdn and hdd over 1f out: wknd fnl f* **7/1**
2403 **9** ½ **American Lover (FR)**[13] 5804 5-8-6 **46**............ KevinLundie(5) 7 33
(John Wainwright) *hld up: hmpd over 2f out: n.d* **20/1**
5032 **10** ¾ **Isingy Red (FR)**[34] 5049 4-9-11 **60**............(p) WilliamTwiston-Davies 1 45
(Jim Boyle) *prom: hmpd over 7f out: rdn over 2f out: wknd over 1f out* **14/1**
-000 **11** 15 **Perfect Example (IRE)**[22] 5479 3-9-0 **55**............(b[1]) ShirleyTeasdale 9
(Ismail Mohammed) *prom: chsd ldr over 7f out tl rdn and wknd over 2f out* **50/1**

1m 58.59s (-3.11) **Going Correction** -0.275s/f (Stan)
WFA 3 from 4yo+ 6lb **11** Ran SP% **116.4**
Speed ratings (Par 101): **102,98,96,96,95 93,93,92,91,90 77**
toteswingers: 1&2 £6.70, 1&3 £9.70, 2&3 £3.50 CSF £32.79 CT £105.62 TOTE £10.40: £2.30, £1.70, £1.60; EX 42.80 Trifecta £152.60 Pool: £2,664.87 - 12.92 winning units..
Owner J A Ross & Miss C Scott **Bred** Park Farm Racing **Trained** West Wickham, Cambs

FOCUS
A moderate handicap in which a gallop that increased after about 3f suited those held up. The winner edged towards the far rail the in the straight and posted a personal best.

6175 FOLLOW US ON TWITTER @WOLVESRACES MAIDEN STKS 7f 32y(P)
6:20 (6:21) (Class 5) 2-Y-O £2,264 (£673; £336; £168) Stalls High

Form RPR
42 **1** **Tamarkuz (USA)**[17] 5685 2-9-3 0............ SilvestreDeSousa 4 80+
(Saeed Bin Suroor) *led: hdd over 5f out: chsd ldr tl led over 2f out: clr fnl f: easily* **10/11**[1]
2 2 **Infinite Magic (USA)** 2-9-3 0............ RichardHughes 2 69
(Jeremy Noseda) *a.p: rdn to go 2nd over 1f out: no ch w wnr* **6/1**[2]
3 nk **Hanalei Bay (IRE)** 2-9-3 0............ JoeFanning 5 68
(Keith Dalgleish) *chsd ldrs: rdn over 1f out: styd on* **28/1**
0 **4** 3 ½ **Miguel Grau (USA)**[14] 5765 2-9-3 0............ JimmyQuinn 1 60
(Marco Botti) *chsd ldrs: rdn over 2f out: styd on same pce fr over 1f out* **14/1**
5 1 ¾ **Slip Of The Tongue** 2-9-3 0............ LukeMorris 6 56
(Sir Mark Prescott Bt) *hld up: rdn and hung lft over 1f out: nvr trbld ldrs* **40/1**
6 1 **Avatar Star (IRE)** 2-9-3 0............ AndreaAtzeni 9 53
(Marco Botti) *s.i.s: hld up: styd on ins fnl f: n.d* **20/1**
0 **7** nse **Silvio Dante (USA)**[48] 4555 2-9-3 0............ FrannyNorton 11 53
(Kevin Ryan) *plld hrd and prom: led over 5f out: pushed along and hung rt over 2f out: wknd over 1f out* **25/1**
0 **8** 3 **Thwart**[33] 5104 2-8-12 0............ JimCrowley 12 41
(Ralph Beckett) *s.i.s: hld up: nvr nr to chal* **15/2**[3]
9 hd **Tight Knit (USA)** 2-9-3 0............ HayleyTurner 7 45
(James Tate) *hld up: rdn over 2f out: a in rr* **33/1**
5 **10** ¾ **Pairumani Prince (IRE)**[125] 2039 2-9-3 0............ PaulHanagan 8 43
(Ed Dunlop) *hld up: a in rr* **12/1**
11 5 **Cuban Tash** 2-9-3 0............(t) RichardKingscote 3 31
(Tom Dascombe) *mid-div: pushed along over 4f out: wknd over 1f out* **12/1**

1m 28.4s (-1.20) **Going Correction** -0.275s/f (Stan) **11** Ran SP% **117.9**
Speed ratings (Par 95): **95,92,92,88,86 85,85,81,81,80 74**
toteswingers: 1&2 £1.80, 1&3 £10.40, 2&3 £20.50 CSF £5.82 TOTE £2.00: £1.10, £1.70, £10.00; EX 6.30 Trifecta £155.50 Pool: £5,031.45 - 23.94 winning units..
Owner Godolphin **Bred** John D Gunther **Trained** Newmarket, Suffolk

FOCUS
An uncompetitive maiden run at a reasonable gallop. The ready winner raced centre-to-far side in the straight. He's value for a wider margin.

NOTEBOOK
Tamarkuz(USA), who had shown fair form in maidens, didn't have to improve to win on this AW debut with plenty in hand. Life will be tougher in handicaps but he's only had three races and there's almost certainly better to come. (tchd 5-6)
Infinite Magic(USA), a fairly easy to back first foal of a very useful 7f-1m1f winner in UK/USA, raced with the choke out and was green under pressure but showed enough on this debut run to suggest a small event can be found with this experience behind him. (op 11-2 tchd 5-1)
Hanalei Bay(IRE), a 16,000gns half-brother to multiple 7f-1m2f turf and Polytrack winner (including in Listed company) Indiana Gal, was weak in the market but showed a modest level of form to pull clear of the remainder on this racecourse debut. He's entitled to improve for this. (op 25-1)
Miguel Grau(USA) wasn't disgraced on his debut and probably ran to a similar level this time. Ordinary nurseries are likely to be the way forward in due course.
Slip Of The Tongue, a Derby entry who cost 42,000euros as a yearling and who is a half-brother to 7f soft-ground Listed winner Kinetica and to useful 1m2f fast-ground winner Four Nations, was green but caught the eye without being knocked about on this racecourse debut. A stiffer test of stamina will suit and he'll do better over further once qualified for a handicap mark. (op 33-1)
Silvio Dante(USA) Official explanation: jockey said colt hung right off the bend
Thwart, the only filly in the field, had shown ability on turf on her debut but she failed to match that on this AW debut after being restrained on the outside. It's a fair bet she'll leave these bare facts behind at some point. (op 7-1)

6176 WATCH THE ST LEGER LIVE ON ATR FILLIES' H'CAP 7f 32y(P)
6:50 (6:50) (Class 4) (0-80,80) 3-Y-O+ £4,204 (£1,251; £625; £312) Stalls High

Form RPR
00 **1** **Cockney Dancer**[62] 4068 3-9-1 **75**............ RobertWinston 6 83
(Charles Hills) *chsd ldrs: shkn up over 2f out: led 1f out: rdn out* **18/1**
2121 **2** ½ **Subtle Knife**[24] 5409 3-9-6 **80**............ WilliamCarson 10 87+
(Giles Bravery) *s.i.s: hld up: hdwy over 1f out: rdn and edgd lft ins fnl f: r.o* **3/1**[1]
5132 **3** 2 **Alkadi (IRE)**[8] 5942 3-8-12 **72**............ JoeFanning 2 73
(Mark Johnston) *led: hdd over 4f out: rdn and ev ch 1f out: styd on same pce* **4/1**[2]
1005 **4** ½ **Maz**[24] 5426 4-8-10 **66** oh2............ FrannyNorton 1 67
(Alan Bailey) *prom: pushed along 1/2-way: rdn over 1f out: styd on same pce fnl f* **16/1**
1544 **5** 1 ¾ **Methayel (IRE)**[36] 4939 4-9-4 **74**............ SilvestreDeSousa 7 70
(Clive Brittain) *chsd ldrs: led over 4f out: rdn and hdd 1f out: no ex* **6/1**[3]
-002 **6** nk **Supreme Spirit (IRE)**[10] 5877 5-9-7 **77**............(p) RichardHughes 4 72
(Peter Makin) *hld up: racd keenly: hdwy and hmpd over 1f out: nt trble ldrs* **6/1**[3]
2404 **7** ½ **Fenella Fudge**[20] 5548 4-8-10 **66**............(v) GrahamGibbons 8 60
(Derek Shaw) *hld up: hdwy over 1f out: sn rdn: no imp fnl f* **12/1**
0-06 **8** 2 ½ **Cheers For Thea (IRE)**[26] 5372 7-9-2 **72**............(bt) DuranFentiman 3 59
(Tim Easterby) *prom: rdn over 2f out: wkng whn hmpd 1f out* **7/1**
6544 **9** 4 ½ **Jeannie Galloway (IRE)**[20] 5539 5-9-5 **75**............(v) LukeMorris 9 50
(Keith Dalgleish) *prom: rdn over 2f out: bmpd and wknd over 1f out* **9/1**

1m 27.46s (-2.14) **Going Correction** -0.275s/f (Stan)
WFA 3 from 4yo+ 4lb **9** Ran SP% **114.9**
Speed ratings (Par 102): **101,100,98,97,95 95,94,91,86**
toteswingers: 1&2 £10.60, 1&3 £9.00, 2&3 £1.80 CSF £71.37 CT £268.28 TOTE £36.00: £6.70, £1.10, £1.90; EX 130.20 Trifecta £781.20 Pool: £3,061.75 - 2.90 winning units..
Owner Phil Cunningham **Bred** P M Cunningham **Trained** Lambourn, Berks
■ Stewards' Enquiry : Franny Norton two-day ban: careless riding (Sep 27,30)

FOCUS
A fair fillies' handicap in which the pace increased after 3f. The winner came down the centre and the ground was subsequently changed to "standard to fast". The winner's first real form since early last year.

6177 32RED MAIDEN STKS 5f 216y(P)
7:20 (7:20) (Class 5) 2-Y-O £2,264 (£673; £336; £168) Stalls Low

Form RPR
02 **1** **Excuse To Linger**[31] 5176 2-9-3 0............ RichardHughes 8 80
(Jeremy Noseda) *chsd ldr tl shkn up to ld ins fnl f: rdn out* **8/11**[1]

45 **2** *1 ¾* **Layla's Oasis**[6] 6007 2-8-12 0.. FrannyNorton 10 70
(Kevin Ryan) *led: rdn over 1f out: hdd and unable qck ins fnl f* **9/1**

5 **3** *1 ¼* **Carina Palace**[8] 5943 2-8-12 0...................................... FergusSweeney 4 66
(Jamie Osborne) *hld up: hdwy over 2f out: r.o ins fnl f: nrst fin* **12/1**

0 **4** *1 ¾* **Attenshun (IRE)**[98] 2844 2-9-3 0..........................(v[1]) RichardKingscote 5 66
(Tom Dascombe) *chsd ldrs: rdn over 2f out: styd on same pce fnl f* **16/1**

5 *¾* **Smart Spender (IRE)** 2-9-3 0.. J-PGuillambert 1 64+
(Jo Hughes) *s.i.s: hld up: plld hrd: hdwy over 2f out: nt trble ldrs* **66/1**

60 **6** *shd* **Captain McCaw**[28] 5274 2-9-3 0.. ShaneKelly 7 63
(Brian Meehan) *hld up: rdn over 1f out: nvr on terms* **8/1[3]**

7 *½* **Enzaal (USA)** 2-9-3 0.. PaulHanagan 9 62
(Mark Johnston) *mid-div: pushed along 1/2-way: sn outpcd* **7/1[2]**

45 **8** *1 ¼* **Hit The Lights (IRE)**[24] 5410 2-9-3 0........................[1] GrahamGibbons 3 58
(Ollie Pears) *chsd ldrs: rdn over 2f out: wknd fnl f* **16/1**

9 *12* **Sand Orchid** 2-8-12 0.. JohnFahy 6 17
(Stuart Kittow) *s.i.s: outpcd* **66/1**

4032 **10** *2 ¾* **Fly Fisher (IRE)**[58] 4191 2-9-3 65.. TomEaves 2 14
(Ian Semple) *hld up: rdn over 2f out: wknd over 1f out* **25/1**

1m 13.72s (-1.28) **Going Correction** -0.275s/f (Stan) **10** Ran SP% **117.8**
Speed ratings (Par 95): **97,94,93,90,89 89,88,87,71,67**
toteswingers: 1&2 £2.60, 1&3 £2.60, 2&3 £8.30 CSF £8.20 TOTE £2.10: £1.10, £2.90, £2.60; EX 10.00 Trifecta £62.10 Pool: £3,516.51 - 41.86 winning units..
Owner A Ferguson **Bred** Mrs J Kersey **Trained** Newmarket, Suffolk

FOCUS
Another uncompetitive maiden in which the gallop was soon reasonable. The winner came down the centre. Straightforward form.

NOTEBOOK
Excuse To Linger who showed fair form when chasing home a subsequent winner (pair clear) here last time, didn't have to improve to win this uncompetitive event in workmanlike fashion. He should stay 7f and, although he lacks much in the way of physical scope, he may do better. (op 4-6)
Layla's Oasis had shown modest form on both turf starts and matched that under a positive ride on this AW debut. She now has the option of handicaps and should pick up a small event. (op 12-1)
Carina Palace had shown ability at a modest level on her debut at Kempton and she ran to a similar level. She'll be well suited by the step up to 7f and should improve. (op 8-1)
Attenshun(IRE), tried on AW, wasn't disgraced in the face of a stiffish task with the first-time visor fitted. Run-of-the mill nurseries will be the way forward with him. (op 25-1 tchd 28-1)
Smart Spender(IRE), the first foal of a multiple Polytrack/Fibresand 5f winner, wasn't disgraced under a fairly considerate ride on this racecourse debut. He should do better. (op 80-1)
Captain McCaw, dropping in trip after failing to get home over 7f in soft ground last time, wasn't totally disgraced on this AW debut but shaped as though the return to further would suit. (op 10-1 tchd 12-1)
Enzaal(USA), a half-brother to a fair 7f-1m winner in Qatar. His pedigree coupled by the way he ran suggests strongly that a much stiffer test of stamina will suit in due course. (op 8-1 tchd 9-1)

6178 MIRROR PUNTERS CLUB H'CAP (DIV I) 5f 216y(P)
7:50 (7:50) (Class 6) (0-60,60) 3-Y-O+ **£1,704** (£503; £251) **Stalls** Low

Form RPR
0061 **1** **Alnoomaas (IRE)**[7] 5972 3-9-3 **58** 6ex.............................. RichardHughes 6 72+
(Luke Dace) *chsd ldr tl led over 2f out: shkn up over 1f out: r.o* **10/11[1]**

40-3 **2** *1 ¼* **Forzarzi (IRE)**[80] 3456 8-8-7 **49** oh1 ow3...................... PaulPickard(3) 11 59
(Hugh McWilliams) *hld up: hdwy over 2f out: rdn to chse wnr ins fnl f: r.o* **40/1**

2122 **3** *2* **Griffin Point (IRE)**[10] 5876 5-9-7 **60**..........................(b) StevieDonohoe 4 64
(William Muir) *chsd ldrs: rdn over 1f out: styd on same pce ins fnl f* **13/2[2]**

0000 **4** *2* **Vhujon (IRE)**[13] 5808 7-8-11 **50**.................................... RobbieFitzpatrick 2 47
(Peter Grayson) *s.i.s: hld up: hdwy and nt clr run ins fnl f: r.o: nt rch ldrs* **40/1**

3443 **5** *hd* **Here Now And Why (IRE)**[30] 5190 5-9-4 **57**.................(p) TomEaves 12 54
(Ian Semple) *hld up: hdwy over 1f out: sn rdn: no imp fnl f* **14/1**

00-5 **6** *1* **Ave Sofia**[23] 5447 3-8-9 **50**.. RussKennemore 13 43
(John Holt) *s.i.s: outpcd: rdn and swtchd rt over 1f out: r.o ins fnl f: nvr nrr* **33/1**

0001 **7** *½* **Lana (IRE)**[6] 5994 3-8-13 **54** 6ex.................................... SilvestreDeSousa 3 46
(David Evans) *mid-div: hdwy over 1f out: no ex ins fnl f* **10/1[3]**

0000 **8** *nk* **Wake Up Sioux (IRE)**[18] 5624 3-8-8 **49**.......................... FrannyNorton 5 40
(David C Griffiths) *sn led: rdn and hdd over 2f out: wknd fnl f* **33/1**

0510 **9** *1 ¼* **Jerry Ellen (IRE)**[24] 5428 3-8-9 **50**..........................(b) DuranFentiman 9 37
(Tim Easterby) *chsd ldrs: rdn over 2f out: hung lft and wknd fnl f* **13/2[2]**

0350 **10** *½* **Almaty Express**[13] 5808 10-9-5 **58**.................................(b) LukeMorris 1 43
(John Weymes) *broke wl and led early: chsd ldrs: pushed along and n.m.r over 2f out: wknd fnl f* **12/1**

0500 **11** *nk* **Avoncreek**[38] 4865 8-8-7 **46**..(v) WilliamCarson 8 30
(Brian Baugh) *broke wl: n.m.r and lost pl 4f out: sn pushed along and n.d after* **25/1**

0002 **12** *shd* **Ace Of Spies (IRE)**[16] 5720 7-9-3 **56**.............................. HayleyTurner 10 40
(Conor Dore) *mid-div: rdn over 2f out: wknd over 1f out* **16/1**

1m 13.52s (-1.48) **Going Correction** -0.275s/f (Stan)
WFA 3 from 5yo+ 2lb **12** Ran SP% **123.0**
Speed ratings (Par 101): **98,96,93,91,90 89,88,88,86,86 85,85**
toteswingers: 1&2 £10.80, 1&3 £1.20, 2&3 £13.80 CSF £65.47 CT £184.24 TOTE £2.20: £1.30, £6.70, £1.60; EX 49.70 Trifecta £248.40 Pool: £4,495.96 - 13.39 winning units..
Owner Mark Benton **Bred** Old Carhue & Grange Bloodstock **Trained** Five Oaks, W Sussex

FOCUS
A moderate handicap in which the gallop was sound, and it was the faster division. The winner raced towards the far rail in the straight. The second lends doubts to the form.

6179 MIRROR PUNTERS CLUB H'CAP (DIV II) 5f 216y(P)
8:20 (8:20) (Class 6) (0-60,60) 3-Y-O+ **£1,704** (£503; £251) **Stalls** Low

Form RPR
0540 **1** **Yungaburra (IRE)**[10] 5892 8-8-9 **48**..........................(tp) FrannyNorton 13 55
(David C Griffiths) *hld up: hdwy and nt clr run over 1f out: r.o to ld wl ins fnl f* **14/1**

3424 **2** *¾* **Imjin River (IRE)**[14] 5774 5-9-4 **57**.............................. RichardHughes 9 62
(William Stone) *led early: chsd ldrs: rdn to ld ins fnl f: sn hdd: kpt on* **4/1[1]**

1105 **3** *nk* **Novalist**[25] 5389 4-9-7 **60**..(b) DanielTudhope 1 64
(Robin Bastiman) *s.i.s: hld up: hdwy over 1f out: rdn and ev ch ins fnl f: styd on* **9/2[2]**

0066 **4** *hd* **Poseidon Grey (IRE)**[13] 5808 3-8-13 **54**.............................. LiamJones 4 57
(Ian Williams) *a.p: rdn and ev ch ins fnl f: styd on* **14/1**

2303 **5** *shd* **Amno Dancer (IRE)**[9] 5919 5-8-8 **47**..........................(b) DuranFentiman 7 50
(Ian Semple) *hld up: hdwy over 1f out: sn rdn: r.o* **6/1[3]**

3600 **6** *½* **Ballinargh Girl (IRE)**[20] 5548 4-9-7 **60**..........................(b[1]) JoeFanning 5 61
(Danielle McCormick) *sn led: rdn over 1f out: hdd ins fnl f: styd on same pce* **17/2**

2051 **7** *1* **Cone Donkey (IRE)**[15] 5734 3-9-5 **60**.................................... TomEaves 10 58
(Bryan Smart) *chsd ldr: rdn over 1f out: ev ch ins fnl f: no ex* **6/1[3]**

0002 **8** *shd* **Dingaan (IRE)**[37] 4929 9-8-9 **48**.................................... RobbieFitzpatrick 12 46
(Peter Grayson) *hld up: rdn over 1f out: r.o ins fnl f: nt rch ldrs* **14/1**

-055 **9** *2 ¼* **Colamandis**[98] 2838 5-8-7 **49** oh1 ow3..........................(p) PaulPickard(3) 6 40
(Hugh McWilliams) *s.i.s: hld up: rdn over 1f out: nvr on terms* **80/1**

1050 **10** *nk* **Kai**[29] 5247 3-9-1 **56**..(be) SilvestreDeSousa 8 46
(Alan McCabe) *prom: rdn over 2f out: wknd ins fnl f* **8/1**

0062 **11** *½* **Roundelay**[36] 4970 3-8-5 **46**.. WilliamCarson 2 34
(Anthony Carson) *prom: rdn over 1f out: wknd wl ins fnl f* **9/1**

1m 14.09s (-0.91) **Going Correction** -0.275s/f (Stan)
WFA 3 from 4yo+ 2lb **11** Ran SP% **119.6**
Speed ratings (Par 101): **95,94,93,93,93 92,91,91,88,87 87**
toteswingers: 1&2 £7.10, 1&3 £9.40, 2&3 £4.40 CSF £70.54 CT £307.04 TOTE £30.90: £5.20, £2.10, £1.60; EX 102.90 Trifecta £178.30 Pool: £301.27 - 1.25 winning units..
Owner D W Noble **Bred** Newlands House Stud **Trained** Bawtry, S Yorks

FOCUS
A moderate handicap in which the gallop was sound and several were in a line inside the last furlong. It was the slower division and the form is muddling, rated on the negative side. The winner raced towards the centre in the straight.

6180 ATR ST LEGER MICROSITE NOW LIVE H'CAP 5f 20y(P)
8:50 (8:50) (Class 6) (0-55,55) 3-Y-O+ **£1,704** (£503; £251) **Stalls** Low

Form RPR
0540 **1** **Sally's Swansong**[33] 5093 6-8-11 **50**..........................(b) LukeMorris 4 61
(Eric Alston) *a.p: rdn over 1f out: edgd lft and styd on u.p to ld wl ins fnl f* **11/1**

0246 **2** *1 ¼* **Choice Pearl (USA)**[22] 5479 3-8-13 **53**..........................(bt[1]) HarryBentley 5 60
(Tobias B P Coles) *s.i.s: sn pushed along in rr: hdwy over 1f out: r.o u.p to go 2nd post: nt rch wnr* **9/2[2]**

0554 **3** *hd* **Gran Canaria Queen**[3] 6100 3-8-13 **53**..........................(v) TomEaves 1 59
(Ian Semple) *led: rdn over 1f out: hdd and unable qck wl ins fnl f* **6/1[3]**

523 **4** *nse* **Invigilator**[16] 5719 4-9-2 **55**..(t) GrahamGibbons 3 61+
(Derek Shaw) *chsd ldrs: rdn over 1f out: n.m.r ins fnl f: eased nr fin* **7/2[1]**

3000 **5** *¾* **Nine Before Ten (IRE)**[45] 4653 4-9-2 **55**.................. SilvestreDeSousa 6 58
(Charles Smith) *chsd ldr: rdn over 1f out: no ex ins fnl f* **14/1**

3004 **6** *¾* **Rightcar**[37] 4928 5-9-0 **53**.. RobbieFitzpatrick 2 53
(Peter Grayson) *hld up: r.o ins fnl f: nvr nrr* **9/1**

6040 **7** *½* **Media Jury**[19] 5590 5-8-7 **53**..(p) KevinLundie(7) 9 52
(John Wainwright) *hld up: rdn over 1f out: r.o: nt trble ldrs* **50/1**

265 **8** *½* **Ladydolly**[21] 5504 4-8-11 **55**..(p) DarrenEgan(5) 11 52
(Roy Brotherton) *prom: rdn over 1f out: styd on* **16/1**

000 **9** *2 ¾* **Prigsnov Dancer (IRE)**[17] 5681 7-8-4 **50**............................ JakePayne(7) 8 37
(Garry Woodward) *chsd ldrs: rdn over 1f out: wknd ins fnl f* **20/1**

56-0 **10** *½* **Wood Nymph (IRE)**[26] 5340 3-8-13 **53**.............................. DuranFentiman 7 38
(Tim Easterby) *in rr: drvn along over 3f out: n.d* **8/1**

4330 **11** *½* **Uncle Timmy**[7] 5975 3-9-1 **55**..(vt) RichardHughes 13 38
(David Evans) *stdd s: rdn over 1f out: a in rr* **8/1**

0564 **12** *2* **Chicarito**[21] 5505 3-8-12 **52**..(p) DarryllHolland 10 28
(John Gallagher) *hld up: pushed along 1/2-way: sn wknd* **16/1**

1m 1.03s (-1.27) **Going Correction** -0.275s/f (Stan)
WFA 3 from 4yo+ 1lb **12** Ran SP% **120.4**
Speed ratings (Par 101): **99,97,96,96,95 94,93,92,88,87 86,83**
toteswingers: 1&2 £8.30, 1&3 £12.20, 2&3 £6.30 CSF £60.88 CT £334.87 TOTE £18.00: £4.90, £2.10, £1.60; EX 87.40 Trifecta £215.40 Part won. Pool: £291.17 - 0.10 winning units..
Owner Miss F Fenley **Bred** Southern Seafoods **Trained** Longton, Lancs

FOCUS
A moderate handicap in which the gallop was sound. The winner raced centre-to-far side in the straight. Pretty ordinary form.
Invigilator Official explanation: jockey said he stopped riding shortly before post as he was running on the heels of the winner
Uncle Timmy Official explanation: jockey said gelding moved poorly

6181 WILLIAM BUICK EXCLUSIVE BLOG ON ATTHERACES.COM/LEGER H'CAP 1m 4f 50y(P)
9:20 (9:20) (Class 5) (0-75,74) 3-Y-O+ **£2,264** (£673; £336; £168) **Stalls** Low

Form RPR
0452 **1** **Daliance (IRE)**[43] 4714 3-9-3 **74**.................................... RichardKingscote 6 85
(Tom Dascombe) *chsd ldrs: pushed along over 3f out: styd on u.p to ld wl ins fnl f* **2/1[1]**

2136 **2** *½* **Gold Rules**[19] 5585 5-9-11 **73**.. JamesSullivan 4 83
(Michael Easterby) *hld up: hdwy over 1f out: rdn and ev ch ins fnl f: r.o* **12/1**

6622 **3** *1* **Sky Khan**[24] 5405 3-9-0 **71**.. RichardHughes 1 79
(Ed Dunlop) *a.p: rdn to ld 1f out: hdd wl ins fnl f* **11/4[2]**

3051 **4** *4 ½* **Hyperlink (IRE)**[26] 5373 3-9-1 **72**.................................... JoeFanning 2 73
(Mark Johnston) *led: rdn and hdd over 2f out: edgd lft and no ex fnl f* **9/2[3]**

6032 **5** *¾* **Superciliary**[22] 5482 3-8-7 **64**.. JimCrowley 3 64
(Ralph Beckett) *chsd ldr tl led over 2f out: rdn and hdd ins fnl f: sn hung lft and no ex* **16/1**

006 **6** *2 ¼* **Take The Stage (IRE)**[40] 4791 3-8-9 **71**.......................... DarrenEgan(5) 9 67
(Jeremy Noseda) *hld up: rdn over 2f out: wknd fnl f* **7/1**

14U4 **7** *nk* **Royal Etiquette (IRE)**[24] 5417 5-8-12 **65**.......................... LeonnaMayor(5) 8 61
(Lawney Hill) *s.i.s: hld up: rdn over 1f out: n.d* **25/1**

443 **8** *55* **Iz She**[24] 5404 4-9-3 **65**.. DarryllHolland 7
(William Knight) *hld up: wknd and eased over 2f out: t.o* **20/1**

2m 35.36s (-5.74) **Going Correction** -0.275s/f (Stan)
WFA 3 from 4yo+ 9lb **8** Ran SP% **112.9**
Speed ratings (Par 103): **108,107,107,104,103 102,101,65**
toteswingers: 1&2 £9.00, 1&3 £2.00, 2&3 £10.00 CSF £26.69 CT £65.59 TOTE £4.10: £1.60, £2.70, £1.10; EX 20.50 Trifecta £130.90 Pool: £484.80 - 2.74 winning units..
Owner The Illusionists **Bred** Societa Agricola Gem Srl **Trained** Malpas, Cheshire

FOCUS
A fair handicap run in a good time. The winner came down the centre and the first three pulled clear. The form looks solid.
Iz She Official explanation: jockey said filly moved poorly

T/Plt: £6.40 to a £1 stake. Pool: £70,736.82. 7,945.12 winning tickets. T/Qpdt: £4.20 to a £1 stake. Pool: £8,289.40. 1,437.50 winning tickets. CR

LAYTOWN (L-H)

Thursday, September 13

OFFICIAL GOING: Standard

6184a NEPTUNE CLAIMING RACE 7f

5:40 (5:40) 4-Y-O+ £4,025 (£933; £408 ; £233)

RPR

1 **Jeangeorges (IRE)**[23] 5465 6 -10-362 DannyGrant 70
(Patrick J Flynn, Ire) *chsd ldrs: hdwy to get on terms bef 2f out: rdn to ld over 1 1/2f out and extended advantage towards fin* **8/1**

2 4 1/4 **Romeo's On Fire (IRE)**[7] 5691 8 -10-354 ChrisHayes 59
(Adrian McGuinness, Ire) *hld up in tch: hrd rdn appr fnl 2f whn short of room and kpt on wl into 2nd fnl 150yds: no ch w wnr* **9/2**[2]

3 2 **Fleeting Moment (IRE)**[9] 4165 7 -10-056 AndrewPThornton(3) 54
(Patrick Martin, Ire) *chsd ldrs: pushed along over 2f out and no imp on ldrs: kpt on u.p ins fnl f to go 3rd nr fin* **9/2**[2]

4 nk **Fabbiaano (IRE)**[4] 6084 4 -9-1260 MarkEnright(5) 53
(James Bernard McCabe, Ire) *sn led: strly pressed under 3f out: pushed along and hdd 2f out and kpt on same pce fnl f* **5/1**[3]

5 shd **Raise The Rafters (IRE)**[30] 333 7 -10-354 DJCasey 53
(A L T Moore, Ire) *hld up towards rr: rdn 2f out and sn swtchd rt: styd on late ins fnl f: n.d* **7/1**

6 3/4 **Buaiteoir (FR)**[27] 5322 6 -10-3 GaryCarroll 50
(Amy Weaver) *slowly away and racd in rr: sme hdwy on outer under 3f out: rdn appr fnl f: sn no ex: eased* **10/3**[1]

7 1/2 **Valley Tiger**[59] 4158 4 -10-3 (t) SeamieHeffernan 49
(P J Rothwell, Ire) *cl up on nr side: almost on terms and rdn 2f out: sn no ex* **16/1**

8 1 1/4 **The Educator (IRE)**[18] 4571 5 -10-359 PaulTownend 46
(Cecil Ross, Ire) *cl up: disp early: pushed along over 2f out and sn outpcd appr fnl f: wknd* **16/1**

9 4 1/4 **Alubari**[5] 5929 5 -10-057 IJBrennan(3) 34
(Adrian McGuinness, Ire) *chsd ldrs early: rdn bef 3f out and wknd to rr: nvr a threat* **8/1**

10 9 1/2 **Luzhniki (IRE)**[435] 3750 5 -9-1144 EmmetMcNamara(3) 6
(Patrick Allen, Ire) *hld up towards rr: pushed along over 2f out and sn n.d: wknd* **33/1**

1m 24.1s (84.10) 10Ran SP% **125.5**
CSF £47.48 TOTE £15.10 : £4.30 , £2.30 , £1.40 ; DF 43.10 .
Owner Mrs B Cooney **Bred** Camogue Stud Ltd **Trained** Carrick-On-Suir, Co Waterford

FOCUS
A nothing race in the general scheme of things but the beach was the catalyst for a return to form for Jeangeorges, who won as he liked.

NOTEBOOK
Jeangeorges(IRE)'s three wins prior to this came on fast terrain or the all-weather yet, despite labouring on soft ground this year, the handicapper was slow to drop him in the weights. This proved him correct; whether the horse can cope with the rise now is another matter. Danny Grant, rider: "We were fairly confident coming here and he has been struggling due to ground." (op 7/1)
Romeo's On Fire (IRE)was fancied to run well and did. The problem is Laytown only race once a year; away from here he is nearly four years without success. (op 6/1)
Fleeting Moment (IRE)is generally very hard to win with and found this trip a bit sharp, staying on best of all. He might win another on the AW over a mile. (op 6/1)
Buaiteoir(FR), a notable runner here, never looked like getting involved. (op 11/4)

6182a - 6183a, 6185a- 6187a (Foreign Racing) See RI

5825 CHESTER (L-H)

Friday, September 14

OFFICIAL GOING: Good to soft (good in places; 6.9)

Rail between 6f and 1.5f moved out 3yds adding 13yds to races 1, 2 5, 7 & 8, 14yds to races 3 & 6, and 26yds to race 4.

Wind: Fresh, half against Weather: Overcast

6188 ICELOLLY.COM E B F MAIDEN STKS 7f 122y

1:40 (1:40) (Class 4) 2-Y-O £4,851 (£1,443; £721 ; £360) Stalls Low

Form RPR

0 1 **Daaree (IRE)**[42] 4773 2 -9-00 (t) RobertHavlin 1 72+
(Saeed Bin Suroor) *in rr: shkn up 2f out: hdwy whn nt clr run over 1f out: bmpd rival and led ins fnl f: edgd rt: kpt on wl cl home* **11/8**[1]

2 nk **Gabrial The Master (IRE)** 2 -9-00 TonyHamilton 5 70+
(Richard Fahey) *rn green: in rr: niggled along over 5f out: clsd over 3f out: effrt over 2f out: chalng fr over 1f out: r.o u.p: jst hld* **3/1**[2]

4320 3 3/4 **Bix (IRE)**[32] 5155 2 -9-063 PaddyAspell 4 66
(Alan Berry) *chsd ldr: rdn over 2f out: lost 2nd but stl chalng whn bmpd ins fnl f: hld fnl strides* **9/2**[3]

0 4 1 3/4 **Scepticism (USA)**[8] 5963 2 -9-00 JoeFanning 2 62+
(Mark Johnston) *led: rdn whn hrd pressed over 1f out: hdd ins fnl f: no ex fnl 75yds* **5/1**

0 5 14 **Crafty Wonder (IRE)**[79] 3506 2 -9-00 CathyGannon 3 28
(David Evans) *trckd ldrs: pushed along 5f out: wknd over 2f out: sn lft bhd* **14/1**

1m 38.34s (4.54)**Going Correction** +0.575s/f (Yiel) 5Ran SP% **108.6**
Speed ratings (Par 97): **100,99,98,97,83**
CSF £5.54 TOTE £1.80 : £1.60 , £1.50 ; EX 4.50 .
Owner Godolphin **Bred** Shadwell Estate Company Limited **Trained** Newmarket, Suffolk
■ Stewards' Enquiry : Robert Havlin two-day ban: careless riding (Sep 30-Oct 1)

FOCUS
A fairly modest event by track standards, rated around the third's turf form. The winner hardly needed to improve from his debut.

NOTEBOOK
Daaree(IRE) needed every yard of this trip to open his account. He had failed to get involved when green on his debut at Newmarket and it looked like proving a similar story here as he was pushed along and seemingly in trouble from 3f out. He did nothing very quickly but required a good attitude to extricate himself from a pocket, for which Robert Havlin picked up a two-day suspension. Reportedly a bit edgy and coltish in the preliminaries, there is reason to believe he'll improve for this experience. A mark in the low 70s is likely and it may be that he'll be able to take advantage of that in a nursery on a more galloping track. (op 13-8 tchd 5-4)
Gabrial The Master (IRE)was under pressure a long way out but stuck on well. He was wandering around in the straight and should be a lot wiser for this. He should be able to pick up a small race. (op 9-2)
Bix(IRE) looked fully exposed and his proximity to the front two does temper enthusiasm for the form. A return to handicaps looks his best chance of victory. (op 4-1 tchd 11-2)
Scepticism(USA) enjoyed the run of the race out in front but capitulated quickly in the straight. He is clearly one of his yard's lesser lights and appears to have some strengthening up to do. (op 3-1)

6189 BERKELEY SCOTT NURSERY 7f 2y

2:10 (2:10) (Class 3) (0-95,93) 2-Y-O £7,115 (£2,117; £1,058 ; £529) Stalls Low

Form RPR

064 1 **Sennockian Star**[40] 4837 2 -8-167 FrannyNorton 6 70
(Mark Johnston) *racd keenly: w ldr: led over 4f out: rdn over 1f out: edgd lft ins fnl f: r.o gamely* **4/1**[2]

1105 2 1 1/4 **Jubilee Games**[18] 5670 2 -8-1278 TonyHamilton 1 78
(Richard Fahey) *trckd ldrs: pushed along and outpcd over 2f out: rallied over 1f out: r.o ins fnl f: tk 2nd towards fin: no imp on wnr* **8/1**

3342 3 nk **Rated**[17] 5710 2 -8-1278 SamHitchcott 2 77
(Mick Channon) *led: hdd over 4f out: chsd ldr after: nt qckn over 1f out: kpt on u.p ins fnl f: lost 2nd and hld towards fin* **7/1**[3]

5034 4 5 **Red Cobra (IRE)**[13] 5825 2 -8-975 JamesSullivan 3 62
(Tim Easterby) *broke wl: stdd s: plld hrd: hld up: pushed along over 1f out: no imp* **14/1**

51 5 3/4 **Double Your Money (IRE)**[17] 5715 2 -9-484 JoeFanning 4 69
(Mark Johnston) *trckd ldrs: effrt over 1f out: unable to get to wnr: wknd ins fnl f* **4/6**[1]

1m 29.91s (3.41)**Going Correction** +0.575s/f (Yiel) 5Ran SP% **110.3**
Speed ratings (Par 99): **103,101,101,95,94**
CSF £31.67 TOTE £4.00 : £1.70 , £2.60 ; EX 28.80 .
Owner The Vine Accord **Bred** Cheveley Park Stud Ltd **Trained** Middleham Moor, N Yorks

FOCUS
A modest nursery, run at a fair pace. Straightforward form.

NOTEBOOK
Sennockian Star, who had shown his best piece of form when fourth in a maiden over C&D last time, was not ideally drawn but, with many of his rivals content to sit in behind, he had no problem assuming early control. While setting only an even early tempo, he gradually drew the sting out of his rivals and always looked like holding on off the home turn. He's improved with each outing and should be able to go on again from this. (op 6-1 tchd 13-2)
Jubilee Games was one of the first under pressure but kept on steadily in the straight, without seriously threatening. He has yet to race on anything other than soft, but his action suggests there could be more to come once tackling a firmer surface. (op 6-1 tchd 17-2)
Rated ran another honest race but looks firmly in the grip of the handicapper (op 6-1)
Double Your Money (IRE)an easy winner on the Fibresand at Southwell, he never really looked comfortable and failed to pick up. This was too bad to be true and it would be no surprise to see him bounce back to form when returned on the AW. (op 8-11 tchd 4-5 in places)

6190 ICELOLLY.COM MAIDEN FILLIES' STKS 1m 2f 75y

2:45 (2:45) (Class 5) 3-Y-O+ £4,075 (£1,212; £606 ; £303) Stalls High

Form RPR

-243 1 **Everlong**[106] 2633 3 -8-1285 PaulMulrennan 6 89
(Peter Chapple-Hyam) *mde all: effrtlessly wnt clr over 2f out: shkn up over 1f out: r.o wl: unchal* **13/8**[1]

32 2 14 **Merry Jaunt (USA)**[14] 5795 3 -8-120 RobertHavlin 4 64
(John Gosden) *hld up in tch: pushed along over 3f out: wnt 2nd 2f out: no ch w wnr* **3/1**[2]

0-03 3 4 **Still I'm A Star (IRE)**[8] 5309 3 -8-1274 TomQueally 2 57
(David Simcock) *hld up: pushed along over 3f out: rdn over 2f out: plugged on for 3rd over 1f out: no ch* **9/2**[3]

6622 4 6 **Mama Quilla (USA)**[28] 5316 3 -8-1268 JoeFanning 5 46
(William Haggas) *chsd wnr after 2f: outpcd over 2f out: sn lost 2nd and wknd* **3/1**[2]

4460 5 30 **Sacco D'Oro**[6] 6056 6 -9-546 (v) SeanQuinlan 1
(Michael Mullineaux) *chsd ldr for 2f: remained prom: pushed along over 5f out: sn wknd: toiling 4f out: t.o* **100/1**

4 6 46 **Donatia**[21] 5541 3 -8-120 AdrianNicholls 3
(David Nicholls) *in rr: pushed along 5f out: lost tch over 2f out: t.o* **33/1**

2m 14.64s (3.44)**Going Correction** +0.575s/f (Yiel)
WFA 3 from 6yo 7lb 6Ran SP% **110.2**
Speed ratings (Par 100): **109,97,94,89,65 29**
toteswingers 1&2 £1.80, 1&3 £2.00, 2&3 £2.90 CSF £6.53 TOTE £2.60 : £1.80 , £1.80 ; EX 7.00 .
Owner C G P Wyatt **Bred** Charlie Wyatt **Trained** Newmarket, Suffolk

FOCUS
A weakish maiden, but the time was decent. The winner has been rated roughly to form.

6191 HILL DICKINSON H'CAP 1m 7f 195y

3:20 (3:21) (Class 3) (0-95,89) 3-Y-O+ £7,762 (£2,310; £1,154 ; £577) Stalls Low

Form RPR

341- 1 **Countrywide Flame**[155] 6838 4 -9-984 MichaelO'Connell 7 92+
(John Quinn) *mde all: rdn over 1f out: kpt on gamely ins fnl f: hld on wl fnl strides* **9/4**[1]

40-0 2 3/4 **Ardlui (IRE)**[28] 5306 4 -9-782 TomQueally 9 89
(Alan King) *hld up: niggled along 6f out: hdwy u.p over 4f out: chsd ldrs over 3f out: wnt 2nd over 2f out: styd on ins fnl f: clsd on wnr fnl strides* **10/1**

2 3 2 **Martial Law (IRE)**[66] 4284 6 -9-284 (b) WilliamTwiston-Davies(7) 5 89
(David Pipe) *s.i.s: hld up: pushed along over 5f out: rdn and hdwy 3f out: wnt 3rd u.p jst ins fnl f: styd on: nt rch front two* **13/2**[3]

4406 4 2 1/2 **Swinging Hawk (GER)**[62] 4115 6 -9-277 FrannyNorton 4 79
(Ian Williams) *hld up: hmpd under 5f out: hdwy over 3f out: no imp over 2f out: kpt on one pce fr over 1f out* **5/1**[2]

0504 5 3 3/4 **Mica Mika (IRE)**[27] 5333 4 -9-681 (p) TonyHamilton 2 79
(Richard Fahey) *chsd ldrs: wnt 2nd over 5f out: lost 2nd u.p over 2f out: wknd fnl f* **13/2**[3]

6050 6 20 **Deauville Flyer**[23] 5491 6 -9-1388 TomEaves 1 62
(Tim Easterby) *in tch: n.m.r and hmpd under 5f out: sn rdn and lost pl: bhd after* **10/1**

0530 7 37 **Montaff**[34] 5076 6 -10-089 SamHitchcott 3 18
(Mick Channon) *dwlt: hld up in rr: pushed along over 4f out: hdwy on outer over 3f out: nt rch ldrs: no imp fr over 3f out: wknd wl over 2f out: t.o* **9/1**

2035 8 33 **Trovare (USA)**[10] 5905 5 -9-580 PaulMulrennan 8
(Amanda Perrett) *chsd wnr tl rdn over 5f out: wknd over 4f out: t.o* **16/1**

0-54 9 3 1/2 **Natural High (IRE)**[13] 2411 7 -9-580 PatCosgrave 6
(Sean Curran) *in tch: rdn to chse ldrs over 4f out: wknd over 3f out: t.o* **25/1**

3m 34.38s (6.38)**Going Correction** +0.575s/f (Yiel) 9Ran SP% **112.0**
Speed ratings (Par 107): **107,106,105,104,102 92,74,57,55**
toteswingers 1&2 £6.00, 1&3 £3.00, 2&3 £12.30 CSF £24.88 CT £125.22 TOTE £3.00 : £1.20 , £3.40, £1.70 ; EX 29.70 .
Owner Estio Pinnacle Racing **Bred** Michael Clarke **Trained** Settrington, N Yorks

FOCUS
A good staying handicap. The winner was on a good mark and should do better still.

NOTEBOOK
Countrywide Flame made light of a five-month absence. The 4-y-o, who produced a strong staying display to win the Triumph Hurdle at Cheltenham in March, looks set for another tremendous year and may well head to Newmarket next month for a crack at the Cesarewitch, before returning to hurdles. Off a mark 12lb higher than when making all at Redcar on his previous Flat run in October, he's clearly still improving. He'll pick up a 4lb penalty for this and should make a bold bid to follow in the footsteps of Never Can Tell, who won this same race 12 months ago before going onto success at Newmarket. (op 3-1)
Ardlui(IRE) ♦ lost very little in defeat and he too looks a stayer of some ability. He has yet to win beyond 1m4f on the Flat but saw this out well and ought to be able to gain compensation in the near future. (op 11-1 tchd 12-1)
Martial Law(IRE) ran on from an unpromising position. Slowly away and held up, he rallied strongly without being able to land a blow. He was very easy to back but arguably ran his best race since arriving from France. (op 4-1 tchd 7-2)
Swinging Hawk(GER) ran on having been hampered on the far side and is a little better than the bare form, but is proving hard to win with. (op 9-2 tchd 4-1)
Mica Mika(IRE) ran a solid race. He was the first to give chase to the winner but had stamina issues beforehand and was outstayed in the straight. (op 9-1 tchd 10-1)
Trovare(USA) Official explanation: jockey said gelding hung left and stopped quickly

6192 ICELOLLY.COM HOLIDAYS H'CAP — 7f 2y
3:55 (3:56) (Class 3) (0-95,92) 3-Y-O+ **£7,762** (£2,310; £1,154; £577) **Stalls** Low

Form — RPR

0060 **1** **Clockmaker (IRE)**[27] 5342 6-9-1 **83** PaulMulrennan 3 — 91
(Tim Easterby) *in tch: dropped to midfield over 3f out: clsd over 1f out: r.o ins fnl f to ld towards fin* **17/2**

1300 **2** *nk* **Dr Red Eye**[13] 5827 4-8-13 **81** (p) TomQueally 7 — 88
(Scott Dixon) *led: rdn over 1f out: hdd towards fin* **12/1**

0540 **3** *3/4* **Citrus Star (USA)**[20] 5572 5-9-10 **92** FrannyNorton 13 — 97
(Chris Wall) *midfield: hdwy on inner over 1f out: r.o ins fnl f: nt quite get to front two* **15/2**

1601 **4** *3/4* **Fathsta (IRE)**[19] 5618 7-9-0 **82** TonyHamilton 11 — 85
(Patrick Morris) *hld up: rdn and hdwy over 1f out: styd on ins fnl f: nt quite rch ldrs* **25/1**

1511 **5** *1/2* **Verse Of Love**[13] 5827 3-9-1 **87** CathyGannon 6 — 91+
(David Evans) *a.p: rdn over 1f out: stl ev ch and keeping on for press whn n.m.r and checked fnl 75yds: no ex towards fin* **4/1**[1]

6321 **6** *1/2* **Rusty Rocket (IRE)**[16] 5736 3-8-1 **80** JoshBaudains(7) 5 — 79
(Paul Green) *a.p: sddle slipped over 4f out: rdn and nt qckn ins fnl f: kpt on same pce fnl 100yds* **9/1**

5101 **7** *1 1/4* **Idler (IRE)**[6] 6040 3-8-11 **83** 6ex JoeFanning 2 — 79
(Mark Johnston) *chsd ldrs: outpcd 2f out: keeping on for press whn swtchd rt 1f out: no ex fnl 50yds* **9/2**[2]

040 **8** *3 3/4* **Baby Strange**[41] 4799 8-9-1 **83** BarryMcHugh 8 — 70
(Derek Shaw) *hld up: pushed along 2f out: kpt on but n.d fnl f* **7/1**

006 **9** *1 1/2* **Dubai Hills**[16] 5746 6-9-5 **87** TomEaves 4 — 70
(Bryan Smart) *chsd ldrs: pushed along over 2f out: rdn and wknd over 1f out* **20/1**

0024 **10** *nk* **Mr David (USA)**[7] 6011 5-9-1 **88** (b) LeonnaMayor(5) 1 — 70
(Jamie Osborne) *hld up: nt clr run over 2f out: nvr on terms* **5/1**[3]

0-50 **11** *3* **Dunn'o (IRE)**[105] 2657 7-9-9 **91** (t) AdrianNicholls 9 — 65
(David Nicholls) *hld up in rr: pushed along over 2f out: nvr a factor* **33/1**

1m 29.47s (2.97) **Going Correction** +0.575s/f (Yiel)
WFA 3 from 4yo+ 4lb **11** Ran SP% **118.9**
Speed ratings (Par 107): **106,105,104,103,103 102,101,97,95,95 91**
toteswingers 1&2 £24.10, 1&3 £14.60, 2&3 £18.10 CSF £104.08 CT £822.02 TOTE £10.30: £2.50, £4.40, £2.30; EX 145.00.
Owner Middleham Park Racing XI & Partners **Bred** Lemongrove Stud & Brendan Arthur **Trained** Great Habton, N Yorks
■ Stewards' Enquiry : Tom Queally one-day ban: careless riding (Sep 30)

FOCUS
A competitive handicap, run at a fierce pace, though the time was ordinary. The winner had slipped to a good mark.

NOTEBOOK
Clockmaker(IRE) had dropped 7lb below his last winning mark and he was able to take advantage under a strong ride. He has gone well at this track in the past and relishes a strong pace to aim at. Easy surface is also key and he was much more at home on this ground. He seems to come into his own in the latter part of the year and ought to remain competitive in the coming weeks, with the handicapper unlikely to be too harsh on him. (op 8-1 tchd 9-1)
Dr Red Eye ran a blinder and can be called the moral winner as he led them until the final few strides. Already a winner twice this season, this was a career-best effort as he was 15lb higher than when scoring at Catterick in July. His early pace means he's always going to be best suited to sharp tracks. (op 16-1)
Citrus Star(USA), drawn on the outside, did well to finish as close as he did. He ran on strongly against the inside rail but was never positioned to seriously threaten. His hold-up style is not ideally suited to Chester. (op 8-1)
Fathsta(IRE) was another that relished the brisk pace but he was posted wide throughout. He was finishing as well as anything, though, and his latest claiming win has clearly done his confidence no harm.
Verse Of Love was unable to get his customary lead. He was still in contention for much of the straight, but but weakened quickly in the final 100 yards. (op 5-1)
Idler(IRE) is another that seems most effective when able to dominate. (op 7-2 tchd 5-1)
Mr David(USA) was disappointing. He was shuffled back at an early stage and worryingly appeared to lose interest. (op 6-1)

6193 ICELOLLY.COM H'CAP — 1m 2f 75y
4:25 (4:26) (Class 3) (0-90,90) 3-Y-O **£7,762** (£2,310; £1,154; £577) **Stalls** Low

Form — RPR

-214 **1** **Eastern Destiny**[91] 3124 3-8-8 **77** TonyHamilton 4 — 86
(Richard Fahey) *hld up: hdwy to chse ldrs over 3f out: rdn to ld over 1f out: r.o ins fnl f: gamely prevailed in driving fin* **11/1**

0415 **2** *shd* **Deia Sunrise (IRE)**[36] 5006 3-9-7 **90** RobertHavlin 9 — 99
(John Gosden) *hld up: hdwy 2f out: rdn over 1f out: r.o ins fnl f: str chal towards fin: jst denied* **7/1**[3]

-110 **3** *1* **Clon Brulee (IRE)**[43] 4741 3-8-11 **80** TomEaves 2 — 87
(David Barron) *trckd ldrs: rdn over 3f out: chalng ins fnl f: hld towards fin* **9/2**[2]

2621 **4** *7* **Cottesmore (USA)**[21] 5541 3-8-10 **79** JoeFanning 6 — 73+
(Mark Johnston) *chsd ldr: chalng fr 3f out: rdn over 1f out: no ex fnl 100yds* **11/1**

2123 **5** *2 1/2* **Commend**[19] 5626 3-9-4 **87** PaulMulrennan 1 — 76+
(Sir Michael Stoute) *led: pushed along 2f out: rdn and hdd over 1f out: wknd ins fnl f* **11/4**[1]

4233 **6** *1* **Deepsand (IRE)**[21] 5540 3-8-13 **82** JamesSullivan 7 — 69+
(Tim Easterby) *hld up: hdwy on inner to chse ldrs whn n.m.r and hmpd over 1f out: n.d after* **8/1**

2146 **7** *3 1/2* **Spirit Of The Law (IRE)**[13] 5820 3-9-2 **85** ChrisCatlin 3 — 66
(Ed Dunlop) *plld hrd: chsd ldrs for 2f: sn dropped to midfield: wknd over 4f out: bhd fnl 3f* **9/1**

3130 **8** *1* **Paddyfrommenlo (IRE)**[43] 4745 3-8-10 **79** (p) FrannyNorton 8 — 58
(J W Hills) *in tch: rdn over 5f out: wknd over 2f out* **14/1**

2m 16.09s (4.89) **Going Correction** +0.575s/f (Yiel) **8** Ran SP% **101.8**
Speed ratings (Par 105): **103,102,102,96,94 93,90,90**
toteswingers 1&2 £6.00, 1&3 £3.00, 2&3 £12.30 CSF £66.36 CT £286.01 TOTE £13.10: £2.70, £2.20, £1.70; EX 54.90.
Owner B H Farr **Bred** Worksop Manor Stud **Trained** Musley Bank, N Yorks
■ Swnymor was withdrawn on vey's advice (15/2, deduct 10p in the £ under R4.)

FOCUS
A decent 3-y-o handicap, run to suit the closers. The first two recorded length personal bests.

NOTEBOOK
Eastern Destiny landed the spoils. Off the track since running disappointingly at York in June, she was hard at work a long way out but she was ideally positioned as the aggressively ridden duo hit the wall. Having made the running last time, the decision to ride her with more restraint certainly proved a wise one and she required every ounce of stamina to see off a determined challenge of the runner-up. Despite having won a maiden over 6f as a 2yo, she clearly stays well and may yet have more to offer. (op 16-1)
Deia Sunrise(IRE) didn't enjoy the best of trips (raced wide) but he was another that benefited from the suicidal gallop. He was travelling better than the winner with 3f to remaining but was held-up in his run before renewing his effort. He has no problem coping with this type of surface but his two wins suggests he's most effective on drier ground. (op 13-2 tchd 8-1)
Clon Brulee(IRE) ran a gallant race and arguably comes out this with the most credit. He had spearheaded the chasing group throughout but looked a spent force with fully 4f left. He was nothing if not game though and stayed on strongly up the inside rail to pull a mile clear of the remainder. Much of the action on this card has developed down the centre of the track and there's a suspicion he may have won had he challenged on the same part of the track as the principals. (op 5-1)
Cottesmore(USA) paid for taking on the favourite and is worth another chance. (op 8-1)
Commend did far too much too soon and was cooked nearing the furlong marker. Official explanation: trainer's rep said gelding was unsuited by the track and the good to soft (good in places) ground (op 3-1)

6194 ICELOLLY.COM H'CAP (FOR GENTLEMAN AMATEUR RIDERS) (DIV I) — 6f 18y
5:00 (5:00) (Class 5) (0-70,70) 3-Y-O+ **£3,743** (£1,161; £580; £290) **Stalls** Low

Form — RPR

6362 **1** **Ferdy (IRE)**[13] 5831 3-10-11 **62** MrSWalker 1 — 68
(Paul Green) *handy: effrt 2f out: r.o ins fnl f: led towards fin* **2/1**[1]

5551 **2** *nk* **Portrush Storm**[7] 6003 7-10-2 **56** 6ex MrFMitchell(5) 2 — 61
(Ray Peacock) *midfield: hdwy over 1f out: r.o ins fnl f: clsd to take 2nd towards fin* **9/1**

5162 **3** *nk* **See Clearly**[6] 6048 3-10-12 **68** (p) MrWEasterby(5) 5 — 72
(Tim Easterby) *in rr: sn pushed along: hdwy over 1f out: r.o ins fnl f: gng on fin* **9/4**[2]

2453 **4** *nk* **Wreningham**[59] 4187 7-10-12 **61** MrPCollington 8 — 64
(Pat Eddery) *sn led: rdn over 1f out: hdd and no ex towards fin* **20/1**

4605 **5** *nk* **Hoppy's Flyer (FR)**[28] 5295 4-10-8 **57** (v[1]) MrRBirkett 6 — 59
(Paul Midgley) *in tch: effrt 2f out: chse ldr briefly over 1f out: kpt on same pce fnl 100yds* **10/1**

0524 **6** *1 1/4* **Haadeeth**[2] 6150 5-10-13 **62** MrDHDunsdon 4 — 60
(David Evans) *in tch: outpcd 2f out: kpt on ins fnl f: unable to trble ldrs* **7/1**[3]

1105 **7** *8* **Red Cape (FR)**[14] 5801 9-11-0 **70** (b) MrBHowe(7) 7 — 42
(Ruth Carr) *s.i.s: sddle slipped: bhd: rdr rode wout irons: hdwy over 4f out: chsd ldr 3f out tl over 1f out: sn wknd* **18/1**

0603 **8** *4* **Boudoir (IRE)**[58] 4218 3-11-0 **70** MrJHodson(5) 3 — 30
(Ian Williams) *racd keenly: prom tl rdn and wknd 2f out* **10/1**

0-60 **9** *3 3/4* **Francis Albert**[28] 5294 6-10-2 **56** oh3 MrNSlatter(5) 9
(Michael Mullineaux) *hld up: rdn and outpcd over 2f out: nvr a factor* **40/1**

1m 19.53s (5.73) **Going Correction** +0.575s/f (Yiel)
WFA 3 from 4yo+ 2lb **9** Ran SP% **117.2**
Speed ratings (Par 103): **84,83,83,82,82 80,70,64,59**
CSF £21.45 CT £44.32 TOTE £3.70: £1.20, £2.20, £1.10; EX 28.50.
Owner E Sciarrillo **Bred** David And Elizabeth Kennedy **Trained** Lydiate, Merseyside

FOCUS
A competitive, if moderate amateur riders' handicap and so it proved with little more than 2l covering the first six. It was the slower division.
Red Cape(FR) Official explanation: jockey said saddle slipped

6195 ICELOLLY.COM H'CAP (FOR GENTLEMAN AMATEUR RIDERS) (DIV II) — 6f 18y
5:30 (5:30) (Class 5) (0-70,69) 3-Y-O+ **£3,743** (£1,161; £580; £290) **Stalls** Low

Form — RPR

1246 **1** **Going French (IRE)**[22] 5502 5-11-3 **65** MrFWindsorClive 2 — 72
(Dai Burchell) *mde all: rdn over 1f out: edgd rt ins fnl f: r.o wl: in command towards fin* **9/2**[3]

0600 **2** *2* **Methaaly (IRE)**[6] 6053 9-10-2 **55** oh7 (be) MrDLevey(5) 9 — 56
(Michael Mullineaux) *hld up: hdwy over 3f out: sn prom and 4 wd: rdn 2f out: wnt 2nd ins fnl f: styd on: no imp on wnr towards fin* **11/1**

1200 **3** *1* **Another Citizen (IRE)**[18] 5674 4-11-2 **69** (b) MrWEasterby(5) 6 — 66
(Tim Easterby) *chsd ldr tl over 3f out: ev ch tl rdn and nt qckn over 1f out: styd on same pce fnl 100yds* **10/3**[1]

1102 **4** *nse* **Prince Of Passion (CAN)**[8] 5971 4-11-3 **65** (v) MrSWalker 7 — 62
(Derek Shaw) *hld up: hdwy over 1f out: styd on ins fnl f: nt pce of ldrs* **13/2**

462- **5** *1 1/2* **Interchoice Star**[318] 7216 7-10-3 **56** (p) MrFMitchell(5) 8 — 48
(Ray Peacock) *racd keenly: chsd ldrs: prom 3f out: stl ev ch 2f out: rdn over 1f out: no ex fnl 100yds* **13/2**

2322 **6** *2 3/4* **Two Turtle Doves (IRE)**[7] 6002 6-10-7 **60** MrNSlatter(5) 4 — 44
(Michael Mullineaux) *chsd ldrs tl over 3f out: wl btn over 1f out* **7/2**[2]

0644 **7** *1* **Aquasulis (IRE)**[60] 4154 3-10-11 **61** MrDHDunsdon 3 — 41
(David Evans) *hld up: outpcd over 2f out: nvr a factor* **14/1**

106 **8** *1 1/2* **Catalyze**[46] 4663 4-10-12 **63** (t) MrMPrice(3) 1 — 39
(Charles Smith) *racd keenly in rr: outpcd fnl 2f* **12/1**

1m 19.18s (5.38) **Going Correction** +0.575s/f (Yiel)
WFA 3 from 4yo+ 2lb **8** Ran SP% **112.8**
Speed ratings (Par 103): **87,84,83,82,80 77,75,73**
toteswingers 1&2 £9.10, 1&3 £3.70, 2&3 £4.50 CSF £50.48 CT £185.50 TOTE £5.90: £1.70, £3.40, £1.70; EX 51.10.
Owner Alan Shinton **Bred** Kilnamoragh Stud **Trained** Briery Hill, Blaenau Gwent

FOCUS
The second division of the sprint handicap for amateur riders. The faster division, and rated around the winner.
T/Plt: £513.00 to a £1 stake. Pool: £42,852.09 - 60.97 winning tickets T/Qpdt: £82.90 to a £1 stake. Pool: £4,339.36 - 38.70 winning tickets DO

6160 DONCASTER (L-H)

Friday, September 14

OFFICIAL GOING: Good (overall 8.8; stands' side 8.6; far side 8.8)
Wind: strong 1/2 against Weather: fine but very breezy

6196 POLYPIPE FLYING CHILDERS STKS (GROUP 2) 5f
1:15 (1:15) (Class 1) 2-Y-O

£39,697 (£15,050; £7,532; £3,752; £1,883; £945) **Stalls** High

Form				RPR
1424	1		**Sir Prancealot (IRE)**[26] 5398 2-9-0 111 JohnnyMurtagh 7 (Richard Hannon) *trckd ldrs: effrt appr fnl f: r.o to ld clsng stages* **7/4**[1]	110
4515	2	½	**Bungle Inthejungle**[33] 5136 2-9-0 107 MartinHarley 1 (Mick Channon) *smartly away: led: rdn over 1f out: hdd nr fin* **9/1**	108
612	3	¾	**Sound Of Guns**[28] 5307 2-8-11 99 WilliamBuick 6 (Ed Walker) *dwlt: hld up in rr: hdwy 2f out: kpt on same pce last 75yds* **13/2**[3]	102
4111	4	½	**Ceiling Kitty**[86] 3269 2-9-0 102 RichardKingscote 5 (Tom Dascombe) *chsd ldr: styd on same pce last 100yds* **8/1**	104
2131	5	nk	**Hoyam**[20] 5601 2-8-11 104 JamieSpencer 4 (Michael Bell) *dwlt: hld up towards rr: effrt over 1f out: edgd rt and ended up stands' side rail: kpt on wl fnl 100yds* **11/2**[2]	99
4120	6	½	**Morawij**[21] 5559 2-9-0 106 NeilCallan 8 (Roger Varian) *racd stands' side rail: led one other after 1f: chsd ldrs: edgd rt and kpt on same pce ins fnl f* **8/1**	101
12	7	4	**Fire Eyes**[20] 5601 2-9-0 0 GrahamLee 3 (David Brown) *t.k.h: trckd ldrs: wknd fnl f* **13/2**[3]	86
01	8	6	**Welliesinthewater (IRE)**[25] 5423 2-9-0 77 GrahamGibbons 9 (Derek Shaw) *racd stands' side: led one other 1f: drvn over 2f out: lost pl wl over 1f out* **100/1**	65
511	9	¾	**Girl At The Sands (IRE)**[17] 5711 2-8-11 73 JimCrowley 2 (James Given) *dwlt: sn wl outpcd and bhd* **66/1**	59

59.47s (-1.03) **Going Correction** +0.05s/f (Good) 9 Ran SP% **113.1**
Speed ratings (Par 107): **110,109,108,107,106 105,99,89,88**
toteswingers 1&2 £4.50, 1&3 £3.40, 2&3 £10.30 CSF £18.30 TOTE £2.80: £1.10, £2.70, £2.40; EX 19.50 Trifecta £131.90 Pool: £3,748.61 - 21.03 winning units..
Owner Andrew Tinkler **Bred** Dermot Cantillon And Forenaghts Stud **Trained** East Everleigh, Wilts

FOCUS
The field split into two early with the larger group of seven racing up the centre, while a couple explored a route up the stands' rail. The winning time was 1.47 seconds outside standard and they were running into a headwind. Some great sprinters have won the Flying Childers over the years, but the last to go on and win at a higher level was the subsequent July Cup winner Fleeting Spirit in 2007. This looked a straightforward renewal, with the winner rated to his previous form.

NOTEBOOK
Sir Prancealot(IRE) was back down to the minimum trip for the first time since bolting up in a Sandown Listed event on his second start, having run well over slightly further in the meantime including behind Reckless Abandon in both the Robert Papin and Morny. He was always in a good position behind the leaders in the centre-field group and once asked to go and pick the leader up inside the last, came home strongly to nail him about 50yds from home. There seems no reason why he shouldn't win a big race back over further, but the 7f of the Dewhurst would be a question mark and the Mill Reef might come soon enough, so the Middle Park would seem the logical target. (op 5-2 tchd 11-4 in places)
Bungle Inthejungle ran poorly in the Phoenix Stakes last time after narrowly beating Morawij in the Molecomb, but the extra furlong and soft ground were probably to blame and this was much more like it. He was soon bowling along in front out in the centre after pinging the gates and responded well to pressure when challenged, but the winner proved a shade too classy in the latter stages. He was the most experienced in the field and lacks the scope of a few, but he looks to be all speed and should be up to winning another decent sprint prize. (op 10-1 tchd 11-1)
Sound Of Guns ◆ ran well to finish runner-up in a Newbury Listed event last time and that form has been boosted with the winner going on to take the Lowther and the third, fifth and eighth also winning since. She travelled well at the back of the centre group for a long way, but had to sit and wait for a while in order to get a clear run through and when she did click into gear she had insufficient time to trouble the front pair. She looks more than capable of picking up a Pattern race at some stage. (tchd 7-1)
Ceiling Kitty hadn't been seen since completing a hat-trick when beating Hoyam in the Queen Mary (balloted out of the Nunthorpe) and was the only runner in the field carrying a penalty. She ran really well having held a prominent position in the centre-field group for a long way, but might have just lacked a bit of race-sharpness in the run to the line. This should have put her right if allowed to take her chance in the Cheveley Park. (op 7-1 tchd 13-2)
Hoyam had the beating of Fire Eyes on York running and a 3lb pull for a length gave her a chance of reversing Queen Mary running with Ceiling Kitty, but she ran a rather odd race here. Held up in the centre group after breaking slowly, she looked like playing a part when asked to close over a furlong out, but with Morawij edging left under pressure she found her path blocked and her rider switched her right over to the stands' rail. Even then she didn't appear to have much room to play with and while she wouldn't have won had she been able to run in a straight line, she would have made the frame. (op 4-1 tchd 7-2)
Morawij, back to 5f after pulling his chance away in the Gimcrack, was closely matched with Bungle Inthejungle on previous Molecomb running. His rider decided to bring him over to the stands' rail and he was certainly never far off the leader in the main group, but as was the case at York he didn't see his race out. Whether he was inconvenienced by taking the route he did is hard to say, but he has a few questions to answer now. (op 9-1)
Fire Eyes, whose dam won this race ten years ago, had just over a length to find with Hoyam on York form, but as he was having only his second start there he might have been expected to have done better here. However, despite holding a prominent position the centre group for much of the way, he folded rather tamely inside the last furlong. It's too early to be giving up on him. (tchd 7-1)

6197 LADBROKES MALLARD STKS (H'CAP) 1m 6f 132y
1:50 (1:50) (Class 2) (0-110,102) 3-Y-O+**£25,876** (£7,700; £3,848; £1,924) **Stalls** Low

Form				RPR
1301	1		**Sir Graham Wade (IRE)**[6] 6031 3-9-5 102 6ex KierenFallon 6 (Mark Johnston) *led briefly after 1f: trckd ldrs: effrt over 2f out: styd on wl to ld nr fin* **9/4**[1]	108+
0065	2	nk	**Nanton (USA)**[21] 5558 10-9-2 87 GrahamLee 7 (Jim Goldie) *hld up in mid-div: effrt over 2f out: styd on wl on outside fnl f: tk 2nd post* **9/1**	92
-621	3	nse	**No Heretic**[18] 5665 4-9-4 89 JamieSpencer 10 (David Simcock) *led 13f out: set stdy pce: qcknd pce 4f out: styd on wl: hdd nr fin* **15/2**[3]	94
0001	4	shd	**Tominator**[13] 5826 5-9-13 98 GrahamGibbons 12 (Reg Hollinshead) *dwlt: hld up in rr: hdwy over 2f out: styd on wl ins fnl f* **11/1**	103
11-1	5	hd	**Caravan Rolls On**[20] 5580 4-9-8 93 WilliamBuick 2 (Peter Chapple-Hyam) *hld up towards rr: hdwy on inner whn nt clr run over 2f out: nt clr run and swtchd rt and then lft jst ins fnl f: fin wl* **5/1**[2]	101+
120	6	nse	**Western Prize**[23] 5491 4-9-5 90 JimCrowley 4 (Ralph Beckett) *led 1f: trckd ldrs: edgd lft over 1f out: kpt on same pce clsng stages* **16/1**	95
1113	7	½	**Number Theory**[20] 5600 4-10-0 99 RussKennemore 3 (John Holt) *hld up in rr: effrt over 3f out: hdwy over 2f out: kpt on fnl f* **9/1**	103
6430	8	shd	**O Ma Lad (IRE)**[10] 5905 4-8-10 81 oh1 SilvestreDeSousa 8 (Sylvester Kirk) *sn trcking ldrs: chal over 3f out: hung rt and kpt on same pce fnl 150yds* **40/1**	85
0404	9	2½	**Blue Bajan (IRE)**[6] 6031 10-9-12 97 DanielTudhope 9 (David O'Meara) *trckd ldrs: effrt over 3f out: one pce whn hmpd and eased wl ins fnl f* **10/1**	100+
105/	10	nk	**Martyr**[719] 6388 7-9-12 97 (p) JohnnyMurtagh 11 (George Baker) *sn trcking ldrs: t.k.h: effrt over 2f out: wkng whn edgd rt wl ins fnl f* **50/1**	98
1040	11	¾	**Old Hundred (IRE)**[58] 4216 5-9-8 93 (v) EddieAhern 1 (James Fanshawe) *s.i.s: hld up in rr: nvr on terms* **16/1**	92
001	12	nse	**Hanoverian Baron**[13] 5816 7-9-3 88 DavidProbert 5 (Tony Newcombe) *mid-div: effrt over 3f out: wknd over 1f out* **25/1**	87

3m 8.86s (1.46) **Going Correction** +0.125s/f (Good)
WFA 3 from 4yo+ 12lb 12 Ran SP% **116.6**
Speed ratings (Par 109): **101,100,100,100,100 100,100,100,98,98 98,98**
toteswingers 1&2 £7.30, 1&3 £3.50, 2&3 £7.50 CSF £22.18 CT £132.23 TOTE £3.40: £1.40, £2.40, £2.50; EX 19.30 Trifecta £131.70 Pool: £2,061.53 - 11.57 winning units..
Owner Paul Dean **Bred** P D Savill **Trained** Middleham Moor, N Yorks
■ Stewards' Enquiry : Jim Crowley two-day ban: careless riding (Sep 30-Oct 1)

FOCUS
There was a distinct lack of early pace in this strong-looking handicap, with it only really lifting off the home bend, and predictably the runners finished on top of each other, the first eight being covered by around 1l. There were a couple with claims to being unlucky, so not form to take at face value. The winner is rated only to his Haydock form.

NOTEBOOK
Sir Graham Wade(IRE) again displayed a willing attitude once in front and was always just holding on, despite running into what was thought to be quite a strong headwind. Reappearing under a penalty just six days after a narrow Haydock win (value for considerably more than bare margin having met trouble), he's a horse who ideally would like more a pace to chase himself and, if connections are right in their assessment that he's a future Cup horse, then he's very much one to look forward to next year. One doubts this will be the last of him we see in 2012, though. (op 5-2 tchd 11-4)
Nanton(USA), who got going late from this mark when fourth over 1m4f at York, was some 15lb lower than when narrowly denied in the race a year ago and he suffered the same fate. A stronger pace would have helped, but when considering the run of others, he couldn't be called unlucky. (op 8-1 tchd 10-1)
No Heretic, up 8lb and returning to a longer trip, had the run of the race out in front and no excuses. He can probably win again at a slightly lower level. (op 8-1 tchd 7-1)
Tominator, up 2lb for his narrow Chester win, stays really well, so he would have been one of the worst affected by the lack of pace, finishing strongly from the rear. (op 10-1)
Caravan Rolls On ◆, a winner from 4lb lower on his reappearance at Newmarket, was twice denied a run when trying to come with a challenge from the rear and looked most unlucky. He fairly flashed home, being in front soon after the line, and remains a horse of some potential. (op 11-2 tchd 6-1)
Western Prize ran well without excuse, bouncing back from a disappointing effort at York. (op 14-1)
Number Theory never posed a serious threat and would certainly have appreciated a truer gallop. (tchd 10-1)
O Ma Lad(IRE) was well placed and ran above himself. Official explanation: jockey said gelding hung right
Martyr, wearing first-time cheekpieces, was keen on his return from 719 days off. Official explanation: jockey said gelding ran too freely early stages (tchd 40-1)
Old Hundred(IRE), 7lb higher than when winning this last year, hasn't been in the best of form and the way the race was run didn't suit. (tchd 14-1)

6198 STOBART DONCASTER CUP (BRITISH CHAMPIONS SERIES) (GROUP 2) 2m 2f
2:20 (2:20) (Class 1) 3-Y-O+

£56,710 (£21,500; £10,760; £5,360; £2,690; £1,350) **Stalls** Low

Form				RPR
4401	1		**Times Up**[20] 5599 6-9-1 114 EddieAhern 4 (John Dunlop) *hld up in midfield: stdy hdwy over 2f out: led 1f out: drvn rt out* **5/1**[3]	112
4122	2	nk	**High Jinx (IRE)**[20] 5599 4-9-1 111 GrahamLee 6 (James Fanshawe) *hld up in mid-div: n.m.r over 2f out: edgd rt and hdwy appr fnl f: styd on wl to take 2nd last 50yds: jst hld* **11/2**	111+
103	3	1¼	**Hurricane Higgins (IRE)**[10] 5905 4-9-1 99 NeilCallan 5 (Mark Johnston) *trckd ldrs: chal over 2f out: styd on same pce last 150yds* **25/1**	110
-244	4	½	**Repeater**[20] 5580 3-8-1 94 LukeMorris 7 (Sir Mark Prescott Bt) *s.i.s: hld up in rr: hdwy 4f out: nt clr run 2f out: drvn and hung rt ins fnl f: kpt on towards fin* **11/1**	109
2310	5	½	**Saddler's Rock (IRE)**[20] 5599 4-9-1 115 (t) JohnnyMurtagh 9 (John M Oxx, Ire) *trckd ldrs: t.k.h 1st 6f: settled midfield: effrt and rdn over 3f out: styd on ins fnl f* **11/4**[1]	109
5426	6	nk	**Askar Tau (FR)**[20] 5599 7-9-1 110 (v) GeorgeBaker 1 (Marcus Tregoning) *trckd ldrs on inner: nt clr run over 3f out: rdn over 1f out: one pce* **12/1**	109
-113	7	nse	**Colour Vision (FR)**[43] 4737 4-9-5 117 SilvestreDeSousa 10 (Saeed Bin Suroor) *dwlt: sn trcking ldrs: 2nd after 2f: led over 3f out: hdd 1f out: one pce* **10/3**[2]	113
0304	8	5	**Masked Marvel**[27] 5354 4-9-1 112 (b[1]) WilliamBuick 3 (John Gosden) *hld up towards rr: effrt over 2f out: sn rdn: wknd over 1f out* **9/1**	103
0420	9	1	**Aaim To Prosper (IRE)**[43] 4737 8-9-1 107 LouisBeuzelin 2 (Brian Meehan) *led: hdd over 3f out: lost pl over 1f out* **80/1**	102
0300	P		**Never Can Tell (IRE)**[13] 5826 5-8-12 97 JamieSpencer 8 (Jamie Osborne) *dwlt: hld up in rr: p.u 4f out: fatally injured* **50/1**	

3m 58.11s (3.11) **Going Correction** +0.125s/f (Good)
WFA 3 from 4yo+ 14lb 10 Ran SP% **114.9**
Speed ratings (Par 115): **98,97,97,97,96 96,96,94,94,**
toteswingers 1&2 £6.00, 1&3 £17.30, 2&3 £17.90 CSF £31.75 TOTE £6.50: £2.20, £1.90, £5.40; EX 21.70 Trifecta £346.60 Pool: £3,771.04 - 8.05 winning units..

Owner Mrs I H Stewart-Brown & M J Meacock **Bred** I Stewart-Brown And M Meacock **Trained** Arundel, W Sussex

■ A big-race winner for John Dunlop, a day after announcing he would retire at the end of the season following a 46-year career.

FOCUS

With the winners of the Ascot Gold Cup, Goodwood Cup and Lonsdale Cup in attendance, this year's Doncaster Cup lacked nothing in quality, but unfortunately a race that exists to celebrate the staying power of class horses proved to be anything but with a stop/start gallop and less than 4l covering the front seven. Even so, the race produced a deserving and appropriate winner.

NOTEBOOK

Times Up showed that he was up to this level when winning the Lonsdale Cup at York last time (with three of today's rivals behind) and this victory showed again his liking for a flat, galloping track. With the pace so uneven, his stamina for this extra 2f wasn't severely tested, but he travelled smoothly into contention coming to the final quarter mile and once sent to the front, rather got first run on the runner-up. He was always doing enough to hold on, though, and in his current mood he could well add another top staying event such as the Ascot race on Champions Day in which he was fifth last year, while there are also options in France. (op 9-2)

High Jinx(IRE) ◆ has improved as he has stepped up in trip, chasing home Mount Athos at Newmarket and Times Up at York, and he got closer to his old rival here despite being rather held up in traffic when the winner was making his move. He flew home once out in the clear, but could never quite make up the deficit. This was still a cracking effort in defeat, especially as the drying ground wasn't in his favour, and his best days may still be ahead of him. (op 7-1)

Hurricane Higgins(IRE) had no stamina doubts having won over 3f further at Glorious Goodwood, but he had a bit to find with several of these on BHA ratings. He was probably helped a little by racing close to the pace in a steadily run race, but a speed test wouldn't have been ideal for a horse with an abundance of stamina and he did well to hang in there for so long. He would have to be taken seriously off a mark of 99 in the Cesarewitch.

Repeater was stepping up another 5f in trip and travelled beautifully off the pace, but he didn't have an awful lot of room to play with as the race was taking shape halfway up the home straight. He stayed on well when out in the clear and also holds a Cesarewitch entry (plus an entry at Yarmouth next Thursday), but as a 3yo with a mark of 94 he is going to struggle to get into the big Newmarket handicap. He still has a bright future as a stayer, however, and it may be that next year is when we will be hearing much more of him. (tchd 12-1)

Saddler's Rock(IRE), bidding to become the first horse since Millenary in 2004/5 to win this race in successive years, looked as good as ever when winning the Goodwood Cup last month with four of these behind, but he had questions to answer following his poor effort behind Times Cup at York when he did too much too soon. He was ridden with more restraint this time, albeit it still close to the leaders, but he became outpaced when the tempo increased passing the 3f pole and by the time he ran on again the race was over. (tchd 3-1 and 10-3 in places)

Askar Tau(FR), winner of this race three years ago, was beaten much further by Times Up at York than by Saddlers' Rock at Goodwood, but the easier ground would have had much to do with that. He seemed to hold a good position throughout, but proved one paced when the race began in earnest and it seems that even this ground was nowhere near quick enough for him. (op 14-1)

Colour Vision(FR) was also carrying a 4lb penalty when finishing behind Saddler's Rock and Askar Tau at Goodwood, but he didn't seem to handle the course there and this flatter track and extra 2f ought to have suited him better. He held a good position in a moderately run race and tried to grab the contest by the scruff of the neck when sent past the long-time leader Aaim To Prosper passing the 3f pole, but he could never get clear and wilted tamely after being headed by the winner over a furlong out. This was disappointing. (op 7-2)

Masked Marvel looked as though he would be a force to be reckoned with in Cup races when taking the St Leger a year ago, but has underperformed in the main this year. Connections reached for the blinkers, but they made little difference as he failed to pick up at all when put under pressure. (op 8-1)

Never Can Tell(IRE), last year's Cesarewitch winner, fractured a hind pastern fetlock and had to be put down.

6199 BARRETT STEEL MAY HILL STKS (GROUP 2) (FILLIES) 1m (S)

2:55 (3:01) (Class 1) 2-Y-O

£39,697 (£15,050; £7,532; £3,752; £1,883; £945) **Stalls** High

Form — RPR

11 **1** **Certify (USA)**[34] 5103 2-8-12 0 .... MickaelBarzalona 5 112+
(Mahmood Al Zarooni) *hld up in mid-div: effrt over 1f out and sn chsng ldr: carried rt: styd on to ld nr fin* **4/6**[1]

131 **2** *hd* **Purr Along**[27] 5379 2-8-12 0 .... MartinDwyer 1 111+
(William Muir) *hld up in rr: swtchd lft 2f out: led appr fnl f: edgd rt: no ex and hdd nr fin* **12/1**

101 **3** *8* **Light Up My Life (IRE)**[27] 5361 2-8-12 93 .... EddieAhern 4 93
(Richard Hannon) *led 1f: chsd ldrs: one pce whn sltly hmpd 1f out* **6/1**[2]

13 **4** *¾* **Reyaadah**[34] 5103 2-8-12 0 .... PaulHanagan 6 91
(Charles Hills) *led after 1f: qcknd pce over 2f out: hdd appr fnl f: hung rt and sn wknd* **8/1**[3]

0512 **5** *4* **Masarah (IRE)**[20] 5579 2-8-12 75 .... SilvestreDeSousa 9 82
(Clive Brittain) *trckd ldrs: t.k.h: effrt over 2f out: wknd over 1f out* **66/1**

141 **6** *¾* **Go Angellica (IRE)**[14] 5787 2-8-12 102 .... WilliamBuick 8 80
(David Simcock) *s.s: hld up in rr: drvn over 2f out: wknd over 1f out* **8/1**[3]

7 *½* **Tuttipaesi (IRE)**[75] 2-8-12 0 ....[1] MircoDemuro 10 79
(Marco Botti) *trckd ldrs: effrt over 2f out: wknd over 1f out* **12/1**

1m 38.92s (-0.38) **Going Correction** +0.05s/f (Good) **7** Ran SP% **113.4**
Speed ratings (Par 104): **103,102,94,94,90 89,88**
toteswingers 1&2 £2.70, 1&3 £2.10, 2&3 £5.70 CSF £10.08 TOTE £1.70: £1.30, £3.80; EX 8.20 Trifecta £44.00 Pool: £13,769.09 - 231.48 winning units..
Owner Godolphin **Bred** Hurstland Farm Inc Et Al **Trained** Newmarket, Suffolk

FOCUS

Not much in the way of depth. Although run at something of a steady pace early, the front pair were able to put quite a bit of distance between themselves and the remainder. They have been raced at the top end of the race averages, backed by a fast time.

NOTEBOOK

Certify(USA)'s Sweet Solera victory had been given a major boost when runner-up Sky Lantern won the Group 1 Moyglare at the Curragh on Sunday, but she made surprisingly hard work of this, only asserting in the final strides having been carried right. It's probable she'll benefit from a truer gallop in future, though, and has the Fillies' Mile or Marcel Boussac as her end-of-season aim. Her trainer's post-race comments regarding her lack of size don't bode well with a 3yo campaign in mind, though. (op 8-11)

Purr Along, winner of a Group 3 at Deauville last time (7f, good), is a good-looker and she showed much-improved form for the step up to 1m, readily pulling clear of the third. She's perhaps a better long-term prospect than the winner, given her scope, but she's still some way off being a Group 1 filly. (op 14-1 tchd 11-1)

Light Up My Life(IRE), winner of a 7f Newmarket nursery from a mark of 83 the time before, wasn't up to mixing it at this level. (op 7-1 tchd 15-2)

Reyaadah was beaten more than double the distance she had been by the winner at Newmarket, settling well enough in front but finding little. It's possible racing into a headwind played its part. (tchd 7-1)

Masarah(IRE), rated just 75, travelled well but didn't have the class to race on. (op 40-1)

Go Angellica(IRE) had won an ordinary Listed event at Salisbury the time before, but even so should have fared better. (tchd 15-2 and 9-1)

Tuttipaesi(IRE), a dual Listed winner for a different trainer in Italy, was wearing a hood for this British debut but clearly isn't up to Group level. (tchd 16-1)

6200 ROSSINGTON HALL CONDITIONS STKS 7f

3:30 (3:30) (Class 2) 2-Y-O

£10,893 (£3,262; £1,631; £815; £407; £204) **Stalls** High

Form — RPR

1 **1** **Ashdan**[35] 5062 2-9-2 0 .... WilliamBuick 1 106+
(John Gosden) *led 100yds: trckd ldrs: effrt over 1f out: led last 100yds: styd on wl* **4/5**[1]

011 **2** *1½* **No Jet Lag (USA)**[20] 5507 2-9-0 95 .... JamieSpencer 2 100
(David Lanigan) *t.k.h early: hld up: effrt 2f out: led over 1f out: edgd lft: hdd ins fnl f: styd on same pce* **9/2**[3]

2212 **3** *2¼* **One Word More (IRE)**[33] 5140 2-9-2 100 .... JohnnyMurtagh 3 96
(Charles Hills) *led after 100yds: increased pce over 2f out: hdd over 1f out: kpt on same pce* **4/1**[2]

13 **4** *½* **Ninjago**[27] 5353 2-9-0 0 .... SeanLevey 6 93
(Richard Hannon) *hld up: hdwy over 2f out: hung rt and kpt on same pce over 1f out* **8/1**

1 **5** *1¼* **Georgian Bay (IRE)**[30] 5230 2-9-0 0 .... MartinHarley 4 89
(Mrs K Burke) *trckd ldrs: chal 2f out: kpt on same pce* **20/1**

3033 **6** *¾* **Top Notch Tonto (IRE)**[20] 5602 2-9-2 90 .... PatrickMathers 5 90
(Ian McInnes) *sn w ldr: drvn over 2f out: one pce over 1f out* **28/1**

1m 27.6s (1.30) **Going Correction** +0.05s/f (Good) **6** Ran SP% **113.1**
Speed ratings (Par 101): **94,92,89,89,87 86**
toteswingers 1&2 £3.90, 1&3 £9.80, 2&3 £15.40 CSF £4.92 TOTE £1.80: £1.10, £2.10; EX 4.80.
Owner K Abdulla **Bred** Juddmonte Farms Ltd **Trained** Newmarket, Suffolk

FOCUS

A race Frankel won on his second start in 2010 and the same owner's Ashdan made it 2-2 in quite good style, this despite the race turning into something of a dash following a steady early pace. The winner could be rated 4lb or so better.

NOTEBOOK

Ashdan made it 2-2 in quite good style, this despite the race turning into something of a dash following a steady early pace. The winner, who readily disposed of his field on debut at Newmarket (7f; race produced several winners), had no cover for much of the race and briefly looked in trouble when the runner-up went past on his outside, but Buick hadn't properly asked him at that stage, and he was nicely on top at the line. Entered in the Dewhurst and Racing Post Trophy, he's certainly bred for middle-distances next season and is clearly a smart prospect (20-1 best for next season's Derby). (op 10-11)

No Jet Lag(USA), like the winner, is entered in all the top juvenile races and he made it 2-2 in effortless fashion at Redcar the time before. He looked the likely winner when edging on over 1f out, but as soon as he got to the front he started to hang, making it hard for Spencer to be active aboard him (didn't use whip), and he was always going to come off second best. Although having his fourth run, he still looked a little green and it would be no surprise to see further improvement. He'd be entitled to take his chance in the Dewhurst. (op 5-1 tchd 11-2)

One Word More(IRE), placed in a 7f Listed race at Deauville the time before, looked vulnerable and was duly well held by the two with the most potential. He may have been affected by the headwind. (tchd 7-2)

Ninjago, third in a 7f Listed event at Newbury, had his limitations exposed. Official explanation: jockey said colt hung right (op 15-2 tchd 7-1)

Georgian Bay(IRE), winner of a 7f Kempton maiden on debut, wasn't up to matching these and will end up handicapping, a sphere he should do well in. (op 16-1)

Top Notch Tonto(IRE), placed in a nursery from a mark of 90 the time before, was readily swept aside and probably failed to run to his rating. (op 33-1)

6201 WILLIE MCKAY SPORTS MANAGEMENT H'CAP 6f 110y

4:05 (4:07) (Class 2) (0-105,104) 3-Y-O+ **£12,938** (£3,850; £1,924; £962) **Stalls** High

Form — RPR

1003 **1** **Cape Classic (IRE)**[7] 6011 4-8-10 **90** oh2 .... AdamBeschizza 2 103
(William Haggas) *mid-div: hdwy over 2f out: led last 100yds: edgd lft and r.o wl* **9/1**

1516 **2** *1¾* **Highland Colori (IRE)**[27] 5342 4-8-11 **91** .... DavidProbert 13 98
(Andrew Balding) *chsd ldrs: led 2f out: edgd lft over 1f out: pushed lft by loose horse: hdd and no ex ins fnl f* **6/1**[2]

3-00 **3** *2¼* **Johnny Castle**[20] 5572 4-8-12 **92** .... WilliamBuick 12 92
(Amanda Perrett) *chsd ldrs: styd on fnl f: tk 3rd post* **10/1**

61-0 **4** *shd* **Diescentric (USA)**[27] 5342 5-8-10 **90** oh2 .... MickyFenton 3 90+
(Julie Camacho) *in rr-div: hdwy whn hmpd over 1f out: hmpd ins fnl f: styd on wl towards fin* **66/1**

0-65 **5** *nk* **Webbow (IRE)**[20] 5572 10-9-1 **95** .... JimCrowley 6 94
(Julie Camacho) *chsd ldrs: kpt on same pce fnl f* **16/1**

-012 **6** *hd* **Duke Of Firenze**[48] 4598 3-8-9 **93** .... KierenFallon 10 91+
(Sir Michael Stoute) *trckd ldrs: ev ch whn crowded over 1f out: keeping on same pce whn wnt rt ins fnl f* **15/8**[1]

0460 **7** *hd* **Sir Reginald**[27] 5342 4-8-11 **91** ....[1] FrederikTylicki 5 89
(Richard Fahey) *s.i.s: in rr: effrt on outer over 2f out: chsng ldrs over 1f out: kpt on same pce* **14/1**

-330 **8** *hd* **Ladies Are Forever**[83] 3375 4-9-10 **104** .... RobertWinston 4 101
(Geoffrey Oldroyd) *mid-div: effrt 2f out: kpt on same pce* **33/1**

0210 **9** *¾* **Shropshire (IRE)**[41] 4802 4-9-5 **99** .... JohnnyMurtagh 8 94
(Charles Hills) *t.k.h in mid-div: n.m.r over 2f out: kpt on same pce over 1f out* **10/1**

400 **10** *nk* **Haamaat (IRE)**[26] 5385 4-8-12 **92** .... PaulHanagan 14 86
(William Haggas) *mid-div: effrt over 2f out: one pce over 1f out* **40/1**

0203 **11** *½* **Mac's Power (IRE)**[8] 5964 6-9-3 **97** ....(t) JamieSpencer 7 90
(James Fanshawe) *t.k.h in rr: effrt and swtchd lft over 1f out: nvr a factor* **7/1**[3]

4250 **12** *1½* **Galician**[13] 5827 3-8-6 **90** .... MircoDemuro 11 85+
(Mark Johnston) *mid-div: drvn and lost pl over 3f out: no ch after* **8/1**

0400 **13** *nk* **Powerful Presence (IRE)**[13] 5827 6-8-10 **90** .... DanielTudhope 9 77
(David O'Meara) *led: hdd over 2f out: btn whn hmpd over 1f out* **33/1**

3000 **14** *3* **Imperial Djay (IRE)**[13] 5827 7-8-11 **91** .... PJMcDonald 16 69
(Ruth Carr) *hld up in rr: lost pl over 2f out* **33/1**

1-30 **15** *1* **Rassam (IRE)**[218] 485 3-9-4 **102** .... SilvestreDeSousa 15 77
(Saeed Bin Suroor) *prom: effrt over 2f out: sn wknd* **14/1**

6400 **U** **West Leake Diman (IRE)**[41] 4794 3-9-3 **101** .... GrahamLee 1
(Charles Hills) *rrd s and uns rdr* **66/1**

1m 18.56s (-1.34) **Going Correction** +0.05s/f (Good)
WFA 3 from 4yo+ 2lb **16** Ran SP% **134.3**
Speed ratings (Par 109): **109,107,104,104,103 103,103,103,102,102 101,99,99,96,94**
toteswingers 1&2 £7.70, 1&3 £21.20, 2&3 £18.00 CSF £66.27 CT £605.21 TOTE £12.40: £2.70, £1.90, £2.90, £11.90; EX 83.50 Trifecta £269.90 Pool: £2,260.81 - 6.19 winning units..
Owner Bernard Kantor **Bred** Wentworth Racing **Trained** Newmarket, Suffolk

FOCUS

A decent handicap, but something of a messy race with West Leake Diman unseating his rider after the start and making a nuisance of himself during the race. The form loos solid enough but there was a lack of progressive types.

NOTEBOOK

Cape Classic(IRE) had signalled a return to form when running a blinder from a terrible draw at Haydock seven days earlier and built on that performance here. Although off the bridle over 2f from home, he picked up nicely and although the runner-up was getting into difficulties just as he was being produced to challenge, he won with such authority that he was much the best horse on the day. This intermediate trip was right up his street. (op 8-1)

Highland Colori(IRE) has had a fine season, but seemed to be beaten fair and square off this mark here last time. This slightly shorter trip may not have been ideal, but he had every chance once hitting the front over 2f from home and although done no favours by the loose horse getting in his way and carrying him across the track, he was still blown away by the winner's turn of foot. (op 10-1)

Johnny Castle ◆ showed little in either start for his new yard last month following a 331-day absence, but was beaten less than a length into third off this mark (under today's rider) in a 7f handicap at this meeting last year. Admittedly he enjoyed a clearer run than a few towards the nearside of the track, but this was still a big step forward and he is worth keeping in mind for a nice handicap between now and the end of the season.

Diescentric(USA) ◆, a dual winner for Sir Henry Cecil, ran poorly on his return from 371 days off and debut for the yard here last month, but was another to catch the eye. Given plenty to do, he finished with a rare rattle despite running into trouble half a furlong from home and this was a decent effort from 2lb wrong. He is one to note.

Webbow(IRE) ran very well on just his second start for his new trainer when beaten just over a length into fifth in a similarly hot handicap at Goodwood last time, and he ran well again here having always been handy out in the centre of the track. He seems to retain all his enthusiasm. (op 20-1)

Duke Of Firenze, a progressive colt apart from one flop over 1m in soft ground on his reappearance, split a couple of subsequent winners when just touched off at Newmarket last time and a 4lb rise looked manageable. Always handy, he wasn't done many favours when the loose horse carried the runner-up into him inside the last furlong, but he still finished weakly. Perhaps a dead 6f suits him best and it's too early to be giving up on him. (op 2-1 tchd 9-4)

Sir Reginald ◆ didn't run too well here last time, but he appeared to be running back into form before that and was down another 2lb in a first-time hood. He stayed on well down the wide outside and is wouldn't be a surprise to see him find an opportunity before the season is out.

Mac's Power(IRE) has all the ability in the world, but is a renowned hard ride without a win since scoring off 7lb lower here almost two year ago and he never looked like figuring here. His reported that the gelding ran too free. Official explanation: jockey said gelding ran too free (tchd 13-2)

Galician, whose narrow defeat by Mince off 2lb lower at Ascot last month looks smart form now, didn't see out the extended 7f at Chester last time, but she never looked that happy here. Although she was staying on when hampered half a furlong from home, she was never going to trouble the leaders. (op 10-1)

6202 FRANK WHITTLE PARTNERSHIP CLASSIFIED STKS — 1m 2f 60y

4:35 (4:38) (Class 3) 3-Y-0+

£8,092 (£2,423; £1,211; £605; £302; £152) **Stalls** Low

Form				RPR
-000	**1**		**Dick Doughtywylie**[119] 2248 4-9-4 85 WilliamBuick 2 (John Gosden) *trckd ldrs: lcd 3f out: edgd rt ins fnl f: hld on towards fin* **7/2**[2]	94
4110	**2**	*nk*	**Keene Dancer**[44] 4702 3-8-8 85 KierenFallon 6 (Sir Michael Stoute) *in rr: drvn 4f out: hdwy and swtchd outside over 1f out: chal last 100yds: no ex nr fin* **6/1**[3]	90
0440	**3**	*1 ½*	**Cool Macavity (IRE)**[23] 5492 4-9-4 85 RobertWinston 11 (Charles Hills) *mid-div: hdwy 3f out: chal over 1f out: keeping on same pce whn hmpd towards fin* **10/1**	91
3210	**4**	*nk*	**Maven**[23] 5492 4-9-1 85 DanielTudhope 7 (Tim Easterby) *hld up towards rr: hdwy whn nt clr run over 2f out: chsng ldrs over 1f out: kpt on same pce* **8/1**	87
0650	**5**	*½*	**Ramona Chase**[7] 6018 7-9-1 85 (t) MarkCoumbe(3) 3 (Michael Attwater) *hld up towards rr: t.k.h: swtchd ins over 3f out: kpt on fnl f* **20/1**	89
0506	**6**	*½*	**Classic Punch (IRE)**[21] 5554 9-9-4 81 MartinHarley 9 (David Elsworth) *chsd ldr: upsides 5f out: one pce over 1f out* **20/1**	88
-535	**7**	*1*	**Haylaman (IRE)**[34] 5091 4-9-4 85 PaulHanagan 13 (David Simcock) *hld up in mid-div: hdwy 3f out: one pce over 1f out* **15/2**	86
2235	**8**	*½*	**Sir Quintin (IRE)**[28] 5297 3-8-11 84 DavidProbert 12 (Andrew Balding) *chsd ldrs: fdd ins fnl f* **20/1**	85
0206	**9**	*½*	**Fork Handles**[18] 5666 4-9-1 85 NeilCallan 15 (Mick Channon) *restless in stalls: s.i.s: in rr: hdwy on inner whn n.m.r and lost pl over 3f out: kpt on ins fnl f* **16/1**	81
10	**10**	*1 ½*	**Pink Damsel (IRE)**[85] 3292 3-8-8 82 [1] JamieSpencer 1 (Roger Varian) *mid-div: hdwy to trck ldrs 3f out: drvn over 1f out: eased whn wl hld last 50yds* **5/2**[1]	78
5-00	**11**	*10*	**Tiger Reigns**[27] 5369 6-9-4 84 PJMcDonald 8 (Michael Dods) *chsd ldrs: ev ch tl lost pl over 1f out: eased ins fnl f* **33/1**	62
0-05	**12**	*27*	**Marine Boy (IRE)**[16] 5752 6-9-4 83 (t) RichardKingscote 4 (Tom Dascombe) *led: t.k.h: hdd 3f out: sn lost pl and bhd: eased: t.o* **16/1**	

2m 8.8s (-0.60) **Going Correction** +0.125s/f (Good)
WFA 3 from 4yo+ 7lb **12** Ran SP% **126.0**
Speed ratings (Par 107): **107,106,105,105,104 104,103,103,102,101 93,72**
toteswingers 1&2 £7.90, 1&3 £11.30, 2&3 £11.90 CSF £25.22 TOTE £5.40: £2.10, £1.90, £4.00; EX 35.90 Trifecta £273.50 Pool: £1,685.87 - 4.56 winning units..
Owner Ms Rachel D S Hood **Bred** Ms Rachel Hood **Trained** Newmarket, Suffolk
■ Stewards' Enquiry : William Buick two-day ban: careless riding (Sep 30-Oct 1)

FOCUS

A competitive-looking classified event that was run at a steady early pace. The winner is rated back to his 3yo form.

NOTEBOOK

Dick Doughtywylie had disappointed in three runs earlier this season, but he'd been given a bit of time off and popped up to win a charity race at Newmarket last month. He showed a good attitude to hold the runner-up and looks ready to fulfil the promise he showed at three. (op 4-1 tchd 9-2)

Keene Dancer, 10lb well in with the winner, she was being niggled a fair way out but picked up well and looked to have enough momentum to get there, but her run just flattened out in the final strides. Her efforts needs upgrading, considering she came from off the steady pace, and she is clearly back on track. (tchd 7-1)

Cool Macavity(IRE) went on travelling well but was unable to quite match a pair of less exposed types, being squeezed up close home when already booked for third. (op 11-1 tchd 12-1)

Maven bounced back from a poor effort at York, looking unlucky not to finish closer, and this tough filly may yet be capable of making an impact from this mark returned to handicaps. (op 7-1)

Ramona Chase stayed on again having been short of room and did win from this mark earlier in the season. (op 33-1)

Sir Quintin(IRE) remains a maiden and may be worth a try over 1m4f. (op 25-1)

Fork Handles had little go her way having been dropped in from a wide draw and cane rate better than the bare form. (op 25-1)

Pink Damsel(IRE), a winner of debut before being well beaten in the Ribblesdale, had been off since and disappointed in the first-time hood. She hasn't gone on from that initial effort and looks best left alone at present. (op 11-4)

T/Jkpt: £1,814.40 to a £1 stake. Pool: £96,600.71 - 37.80 winning tickets T/Plt: £109.00 to a £1 stake. Pool: £173,318.52 - 1,159.82 winning tickets T/Qpdt: £25.30 to a £1 stake. Pool: £10,194.47 - 297.96 winning tickets WG

5832 SANDOWN (R-H)

Friday, September 14

OFFICIAL GOING: Good to firm (8.5)

Round course rail dolled out 3-4yds from 9f to winning post, adding about 6yds to distances.

Wind: Fresh, against Weather: Fine but cloudy

6203 BRITISH STALLION STUDS SUPPORTING BRITISH RACING E B F SPRINT MAIDEN STKS — 5f 6y

2:00 (2:02) (Class 5) 2-Y-0

£3,881 (£1,155; £577; £288) **Stalls** Low

Form				RPR
054	**1**		**Shiatsu**[21] 5553 2-9-3 75 PatDobbs 1 (Richard Hannon) *hld up in midfield against rail: prog over 1f out: gap opened and squeezed through to ld last 75yds: jst hld on* **9/2**[2]	75
00	**2**	*nse*	**Extrasolar**[25] 5418 2-9-3 0 (t) AdamKirby 10 (Amanda Perrett) *w.w in midfield: effrt on outer over 1f out: r.o to chal last 75yds: jst failed* **16/1**	75
	3	*¾*	**Pearl Bridge** 2-9-3 0 HarryBentley 9 (Ralph Beckett) *dwlt: sn trckd ldrs and cl up: n.m.r and lost pl over 1f out: r.o again last 150yds: tk 3rd last strides* **3/1**[1]	73+
0	**4**	*hd*	**Global Icon**[25] 5418 2-9-3 0 DaneO'Neill 4 (Richard Hannon) *towards rr: pushed along and stl many in front 1f out: r.o last 150yds: fin best of all* **7/1**[3]	71+
4	**5**	*½*	**Somoud (IRE)**[33] 5121 2-9-3 0 JimmyFortune 12 (J R Jenkins) *gd spd fr wd draw: led and sn crossed to rail: rdn over 1f out: at least a l ahd ins fnl f: swamped last 75yds* **33/1**	70
042	**6**	*½*	**Rock Up (IRE)**[30] 5235 2-9-3 79 LiamKeniry 5 (David Elsworth) *racd against rail: trckd ldrs: looking for room 2f out: rdn to chal for 2nd 1f out: nt qckn after* **9/2**[2]	68
	7	*1 ¼*	**Winnie Perry** 2-9-3 0 AndreaAtzeni 3 (Rod Millman) *dwlt: off the pce in 12th: shkn up 1/2-way: swtchd to far rail 1f out: r.o last 100yds: nrst fin* **66/1**	63+
	8	*nk*	**Blessing Box** 2-8-12 0 SebSanders 2 (Chris Wall) *towards rr: pushed along over 1f out: no imp on ldrs but styd on last 100yds* **8/1**	57+
3	**9**	*½*	**Princess Sheila (IRE)**[15] 5773 2-8-12 0 LiamJones 11 (J S Moore) *prom on outer: rdn over 2f out: chsd ldr u.p jst over 1f out: wknd ins fnl f* **16/1**	55
04	**10**	*1 ¾*	**Dream Ally (IRE)**[26] 5382 2-9-3 0 DarryllHolland 13 (Jedd O'Keeffe) *gd spd fr wd draw to press ldr: rdn 2f out: lost 2nd jst over 1f out: losing pl whn bdly hmpd ins fnl f: eased* **9/1**	64
35	**11**	*½*	**Ladweb**[134] 1767 2-9-3 0 IanMongan 7 (John Gallagher) *sltly impeded after 1f: a towards rr: no prog 1f out* **40/1**	52
56	**12**	*1*	**Tagalaka (IRE)**[9] 5932 2-9-3 0 JohnFahy 8 (Eve Johnson Houghton) *racd on outer: wl in rr: shkn up 2f out: no imp on ldrs* **66/1**	49
	13	*8*	**Provencal** 2-9-3 0 JamesMillman 6 (Rod Millman) *s.s: a detached in last* **33/1**	20

1m 2.96s (1.36) **Going Correction** +0.20s/f (Good) **13** Ran SP% **118.0**
Speed ratings (Par 95): **97,96,95,95,94 93,91,90,87 86,85,72**
toteswingers 1&2 £24.10, 1&3 £7.10, 2&3 £20.10 CSF £70.36 TOTE £6.90: £2.10, £4.20, £1.90; EX 89.00.
Owner Ranjan Mahtani **Bred** Slatch Farm Stud **Trained** East Everleigh, Wilts

FOCUS

A decent maiden. The pace was not very strong and there was a bunch finish.

NOTEBOOK

Shiatsu settled better dropped back from 7f to 5f and finished well against the far rail to narrowly get off the mark on his fourth start. A progressive 75-rated Kyllachy colt, he is a brother to very useful triple 5f winner Befortyfour and has scope for further improvement at this trip. (op 4-1 tchd 5-1)

Extrasolar didn't show a great deal in his first two starts but he finished fast out wide in this much-improved near-miss dropped back to 5f. (op 20-1)

Pearl Bridge, a gelded £28,000 half-brother to smart multiple 5f winner Pearl Secret, ran into traffic problems before staying on strongly in a promising and slightly unlucky debut run. He should improve for the experience and his pedigree is all about speed. (tchd 11-4 and 10-3 in a place)

Global Icon ran green under a hold-up ride before staying on well for a close fourth behind his stablemate on his second run. Out of a 1m2f winning sister to 1m/1m1f Listed scorers In The Limelight and On The Nile, he should continue to progress and shapes like a step up in trip will suit. (op 11-1)

Somoud(IRE) showed plenty of speed from a wide draw before getting swamped in the closing stages on his second run. (op 40-1)

Rock Up(IRE) had leading claims on his 18-1 second in a 6f Salisbury maiden last month but he was a big market drifter and didn't really pick up when he found a gap near the far rail. (op 3-1 tchd 5-1)

Winnie Perry Official explanation: jockey said colt was slowly away

Dream Ally(IRE) showed plenty of improvement when 50-1 fourth in a 5f Pontefract maiden on his second start but he was under pressure and just plugging on here when getting badly hampered in the closing stages. (op 8-1 tchd 13-2)

6204 BRITISH STALLION STUDS SUPPORTING BRITISH RACING E B F MAIDEN STKS — 1m 14y

2:30 (2:33) (Class 5) 2-Y-0

£3,881 (£1,155; £577; £288) **Stalls** Low

Form				RPR
	1		**Flying Officer (USA)** 2-9-3 0 NickyMackay 11 (John Gosden) *trckd ldng trio: prog to go 2nd 2f out: pushed into ld jst over 1f out: pressed and shkn up 100yds out: readily hld rival after* **5/2**[1]	84+
6	**2**	*nk*	**Saved By The Bell (IRE)**[18] 5685 2-9-3 0 MartinLane 4 (Brian Meehan) *trckd ldrs in 5th: drvn and prog 2f out: chsd wnr ins fnl f and sn chalng: styd on but readily hld nr fin* **16/1**	83
	3	*2 ¼*	**Russian Realm** 2-9-3 0 JamesDoyle 9 (Sir Michael Stoute) *settled in 10th and off the pce: pushed along over 2f out: stdy prog after: styd on wl to take 3rd nr fin: fair debut* **6/1**[2]	78+
040	**4**	*½*	**Empiricist (IRE)**[6] 6020 2-9-3 0 IanMongan 3 (Amanda Perrett) *led at mod pce: kicked 2 l clr over 2f out: hdd jst over 1f out: fdd* **6/1**[2]	77
0	**5**	*1 ½*	**Followeveryrainbow**[34] 5104 2-8-12 0 PatDobbs 12 (Richard Hannon) *t.k.h: trckd ldrs in 6th: shkn up over 2f out: kpt on fr over 1f out* **14/1**	69

6 2 1/4 **Mr Fitzroy (IRE)** 2-9-3 0 JimmyFortune 2 68
(Andrew Balding) *trckd ldng pair: disp 2nd 2f out: wknd fnl f* **9/1**

7 1 **Wallenberg** 2-9-3 0 (e[1]) SaleemGolam 10 66
(John Gosden) *t.k.h: hld up in midfield: shkn up and no prog over 2f out: kpt on fnl f* **12/1**

00 8 1/2 **Substantivo (IRE)**[21] 5562 2-9-3 0 DarryllHolland 6 65
(Alan Jarvis) *trckd ldr to 2f out: pushed along and wknd* **40/1**

9 5 **Cyclone** 2-9-3 0 SebSanders 13 53+
(Richard Hannon) *s.v.s: rn green and detached in last trio: nvr a factor but modest late prog* **16/1**

10 2 1/4 **Portmonarch (IRE)** 2-9-3 0 DaneO'Neill 7 48
(David Lanigan) *dwlt: sn in tch in midfield: shkn up and no prog over 2f out: wknd* **20/1**

11 7 **Adeem (USA)** 2-9-3 0 TadhgO'Shea 1 32
(John Dunlop) *s.s: rn green and detached in last trio: drvn 3f out: nvr a factor* **12/1**

12 2 3/4 **Duroble Man** 2-9-3 0 AndreaAtzeni 5 26
(Roger Varian) *t.k.h: in tch in midfield: shkn up and wknd over 2f out* **8/1[3]**

13 2 3/4 **Booktheband (IRE)** 2-9-3 0 KirstyMilczarek 8 19
(Clive Brittain) *sn in detached last trio: a bhd* **50/1**

1m 44.67s (1.37) **Going Correction** +0.05s/f (Good) **13** Ran SP% **121.2**
Speed ratings (Par 95): **95,94,92,91,90 88,87,86,81,79 72,69,66**
toteswingers 1&2 £16.70, 1&3 £3.00, 2&3 £11.60 CSF £47.79 TOTE £3.70: £1.30, £4.40, £2.30; EX 62.00.
Owner George Strawbridge **Bred** George Strawbridge Jr **Trained** Newmarket, Suffolk

FOCUS
A majority of newcomers lined up in this maiden but there were several well-bred types representing top connections and the form could be fairly useful.

NOTEBOOK
Flying Officer(USA), a brother to St Leger hero Lucarno and this year's Great Voltigeur winner Thought Worthy, travelled well into lead out wide and showed determination to hold off a late finisher and land a gamble on his debut. A scopey type with plenty of potential for improvement, he looks another exciting prospect from his family and holds Racing Post Trophy and Derby entries. (op 4-1)
Saved By The Bell(IRE) was never involved at Warwick on his debut but he showed plenty of improvement in this strong finishing close call. He is a 100,000euros Teofilo colt who was entered in the Champagne Stakes and still holds an entry in the Racing Post Trophy.
Russian Realm was prominent in the market on his debut but he was trapped out the back at a crucial stage before flashing home out wide when it was all over. This was an eyecatching debut run from a a Dansili colt who is out of the stable's 1,000 Guineas heroine Russian Rhythm. He could improve significantly next time and holds an entry in the Derby. (op 13-2 tchd 15-2)
Empiricist(IRE) set the standard on his close 80-1 fourth in a decent 7f Newbury maiden two runs back and things looked to be going well for a long way under a trailblazing ride but he couldn't fight off some finishers and faded. This was not a bad effort against some potentially useful rivals and he adds some substance to the form. (op 4-1)
Followeveryrainbow beat only one rival when 9-2 on her debut at Newmarket last month but she showed some promise staying on steadily here.
Mr Fitzroy(IRE) shaped a bit better than his finishing position on his debut. He should improve for the run and is a 72,000euros half-brother to a decent 1m1f winner. (op 12-1 tchd 14-1)
Booktheband(IRE) Official explanation: jockey said colt ran green

6205 SUNGARD H'CAP — 1m 14y
3:05 (3:05) (Class 4) (0-85,85) 3-Y-O — **£4,528** (£1,347; £673; £336) **Stalls** Low

Form RPR

2263 1 **Gaul Wood (IRE)**[16] 5747 3-9-6 **84** LiamKeniry 7 94
(Tom Dascombe) *mostly chsd ldr: led over 2f out: rdn over 1f out: styd on wl* **10/1**

2214 2 1 3/4 **Henry Allingham**[23] 5480 3-9-6 **84** AndreaAtzeni 3 90
(Roger Varian) *trckd ldrs: prog 2f out: rdn to chse wnr over 1f out: styd on but no imp* **7/2[2]**

361 3 1 1/4 **Border Legend**[97] 2941 3-9-4 **82** JamesDoyle 5 85+
(Roger Charlton) *hld up towards rr: prog 2f out: nt clr run briefly jst over 1f out: styd on to take 3rd ins fnl f: no imp on ldng pair* **9/1**

4235 4 3/4 **Dixie's Dream (IRE)**[16] 5747 3-9-4 **82** PatDobbs 2 83
(Richard Hannon) *hld up in last pair: shkn up and same pl 2f out: plld out wd over 1f out: styd on fnl f: nrst fin* **14/1**

001 5 1/2 **Magma**[37] 4948 3-9-2 **80** JimmyFortune 9 80
(Andrew Balding) *led 1f: sn in 3rd: rdn to chse wnr 2f out to over 1f out: fdd* **20/1**

35 6 nk **Lucky Henry**[10] 5914 3-9-7 **85** (p) AdamKirby 11 84
(Clive Cox) *racd wd: in tch in midfield: rdn to press for a pl over 1f out: one pce fnl f* **13/2[3]**

0213 7 nk **Basseterre (IRE)**[83] 3376 3-9-4 **82** MichaelHills 8 81+
(Charles Hills) *slowest away: hld up in last pair: prog on outer 2f out: pressed for a pl jst over 1f out: no ex* **5/2[1]**

2212 8 1/2 **Zaeem**[27] 5365 3-9-5 **83** HarryBentley 1 80
(Mahmood Al Zarooni) *trckd ldrs: shkn up over 2f out: lost pl over 1f out: fdd* **9/1**

-111 9 1/2 **Tigers Tale (IRE)**[92] 3068 3-9-6 **84** (v) DarryllHolland 10 80
(Roger Teal) *prog to ld after 1f: hdd and nt qckn over 2f out: wknd fnl f* **14/1**

233 10 2 **Medici Music**[28] 5315 3-8-8 **72** KirstyMilczarek 4 64
(Luca Cumani) *in tch towards rr: shkn up and no prog over 2f out: fdd over 1f out* **9/1**

1m 43.02s (-0.28) **Going Correction** +0.05s/f (Good) **10** Ran SP% **121.3**
Speed ratings (Par 103): **103,101,100,99,98 98,98,97,97,95**
toteswingers 1&2 £15.80, 1&3 £24.60, 2&3 £11.70 CSF £46.90 CT £339.25 TOTE £15.00: £3.70, £1.40, £3.90; EX 63.40.
Owner Star Sports **Bred** Patrick J Monahan **Trained** Malpas, Cheshire

FOCUS
A competitive handicap involving three last-time-out winners. The pace was fair and the winner scored with something in hand after getting first run. He's been awarded a 5lb personal best.

6206 CHASEMORE CHAMPION CLAIMING STKS — 1m 2f 7y
3:40 (3:41) (Class 4) 3-Y-O — **£6,469** (£1,925; £962; £481) **Stalls** Low

Form RPR

0-23 1 **Ashdown Lad**[232] 308 3-8-7 71 MichaelJMMurphy(7) 5 77+
(William Jarvis) *hld up in last: plld out and prog jst over 2f out: drvn to chse ldr over 1f out: clsd to ld last 100yds: styd on wl* **7/2[2]**

2665 2 1/2 **Presburg (IRE)**[27] 5358 3-9-7 82 LiamKeniry 2 83
(Joseph Tuite) *hld up in 5th: prog to ld over 2f out: drvn over 1f out: hdd and nt qckn last 100yds* **10/3[1]**

2060 3 3 **Island Melody (IRE)**[25] 5405 3-8-4 63 LiamJones 3 60
(J S Moore) *trckd ldng pair: outpcd and lost pl wl over 2f out: styd on again to take 3rd 1f out: no imp* **16/1**

-060 4 2 1/4 **Aquilonius (IRE)**[18] 5666 3-9-2 78 (p) JamesDoyle 1 68
(Stuart Williams) *sn led: hdd over 2f out: sn outpcd: n.d after: plugged on* **9/1**

00 5 2 1/4 **Zaina (IRE)**[23] 5474 3-8-12 78 (tp) AndreaAtzeni 7 59
(Gerard Butler) *mostly pressed ldr: upsides wl over 2f out: sn outpcd: fdd* **7/2[2]**

610 6 2 1/2 **Emerald Invader**[14] 5788 3-9-4 73 DaneO'Neill 6 60
(David Elsworth) *t.k.h: hld up in 6th: prog to chal and w wnr over 2f out: btn over 1f out: wknd bdly fnl f* **13/2**

3563 7 nk **Gold Sceptre (FR)**[35] 5036 3-8-8 67 (b) PatDobbs 4 49
(Richard Hannon) *trckd ldng trio: lost pl and hmpd wl over 2f out: dropped to last and no ch after* **9/2[3]**

2m 10.05s (-0.45) **Going Correction** +0.05s/f (Good) **7** Ran SP% **114.9**
Speed ratings (Par 103): **103,102,100,98,96 94,94**
toteswingers 1&2 £3.90, 1&3 £9.80, 2&3 £15.40 CSF £15.76 TOTE £4.30: £3.30, £2.30; EX 18.50.
Owner The FOPS **Bred** Mr & Mrs A E Pakenham **Trained** Newmarket, Suffolk
■ Stewards' Enquiry : Liam Keniry two-day ban: careless riding (Sep 30-Oct 1)

FOCUS
Five of the seven runners were rated between 71 and 82 in this valuable claimer. The pace was not very strong and the winner can be marked up for landing a gamble from some way back. The form has been rated a little cautiously given the doubts over the grade.

6207 INKERMAN LONDON H'CAP — 1m 2f 7y
4:15 (4:15) (Class 4) (0-80,80) 3-Y-O+ — **£4,075** (£1,212; £606; £303) **Stalls** Low

Form RPR

0252 1 **Looking On**[17] 5707 4-9-6 **74** DaneO'Neill 1 85
(Henry Candy) *mde all at decent pce: kicked on 2f out: styd on wl after: unchal* **5/1[1]**

6343 2 2 1/4 **Grand Gold**[3] 6118 3-8-9 **70** JohnFahy 8 76
(Seamus Durack) *trckd ldng trio: chsd wnr over 2f out: drvn and no imp over 1f out* **7/1**

4020 3 nk **Sakhee's Pearl**[27] 5372 6-9-3 **76** NathanSweeney(5) 4 81
(Jo Crowley) *trckd ldng pair: disp 2nd over 2f out: styd on after: nvr able to chal* **20/1**

0622 4 1 **Choral Festival**[20] 5592 6-9-7 **75** JamesDoyle 6 78
(John Bridger) *trckd ldrs in 6th: effrt over 2f out: wnt 4th over 1f out: no imp after* **12/1**

5-00 5 nk **Icebuster**[13] 5838 4-9-12 **80** JamesMillman 2 83
(Rod Millman) *trckd ldrs in 5th: shkn up and nt qckn over 2f out: kpt on same pce fr over 1f out* **6/1[3]**

/605 6 nse **Scottish Boogie (IRE)**[95] 2988 5-9-4 **72** SebSanders 3 75
(Brendan Powell) *hld up disputing 9th: effrt on inner over 2f out: shoved along and styd on fnl 2f: nvr nr ldrs* **16/1**

5402 7 2 1/4 **Borug (USA)**[11] 5888 4-9-8 **76** IanMongan 13 74+
(James Tate) *hld up in last quartet: rdn over 2f out: sme prog on inner over 1f out: no ch of rching ldrs* **11/2[2]**

6502 8 nk **Poetic Lord**[13] 5838 3-9-1 **76** PatDobbs 14 74
(Richard Hannon) *a abt same pl: rdn and no prog wl over 1f out* **6/1[3]**

445 9 1 **Eponastone (IRE)**[39] 4888 3-8-9 **70** AndreaAtzeni 10 66
(Gerard Butler) *hld up disputing 9th: effrt on outer over 2f out: drvn and no prog over 1f out* **20/1**

U103 10 1 **Edgeworth (IRE)**[25] 5417 6-8-13 **72** BrendanPowell(5) 5 66
(David Bridgwater) *chsd wnr to over 2f out: sn wknd* **22/1**

0005 11 nk **Sinfonico (IRE)**[14] 5794 4-9-8 **76** (e) KieranO'Neill 11 69
(Richard Hannon) *hld up in last pair: shkn up and no prog over 2f out: nvr a factor* **16/1**

220- 12 hd **Dubawi Dancer**[49] 6497 4-9-10 **78** DarryllHolland 12 71
(J S Moore) *hld up in last pair: rdn and no prog over 2f out: nvr a factor* **20/1**

0004 13 10 **Ellie In The Pink (IRE)**[18] 5667 4-8-9 **70** MichaelJMMurphy(7) 7 43
(Alan Jarvis) *hld up disputing 7th: effrt on inner wl over 2f out: wknd wl over 1f out: t.o* **11/1**

004- 14 5 **Zebrano**[239] 7651 6-9-11 **79** (b) AdamKirby 9 42
(Natalie Lloyd-Beavis) *hld up in last quartet: rdn and no prog 3f out: sn wknd: t.o* **50/1**

2m 9.63s (-0.87) **Going Correction** +0.05s/f (Good)
WFA 3 from 4yo+ 7lb **14** Ran SP% **121.5**
Speed ratings (Par 105): **105,103,102,102,101 101,100,99,99,98 98,97,89,85**
toteswingers 1&2 £4.60, 1&3 £24.70, 2&3 £27.80 CSF £36.49 CT £659.06 TOTE £5.50: £2.10, £3.00, £7.20; EX 52.40.
Owner Girsonfield Ltd **Bred** Girsonfield Ltd **Trained** Kingston Warren, Oxon

FOCUS
A fair handicap. The well-backed favourite put in a determined front-running display and not many got involved from off the pace. The form seems sound enough amongst the principals.

6208 HWFA WILLIAMS H'CAP (DIV I) — 1m 14y
4:45 (4:45) (Class 4) (0-80,80) 3-Y-O+ — **£4,075** (£1,212; £606; £303) **Stalls** Low

Form RPR

2040 1 **Golden Tempest (IRE)**[6] 6040 4-9-8 **78** PatDobbs 7 86
(Eve Johnson Houghton) *hld up off str pce: clsd gng easily fr 2f out: shkn up to ld 1f out: rdn out and kpt on* **5/1[3]**

0510 2 3/4 **Saharia (IRE)**[23] 5480 5-9-2 **72** (v) J-PGuillambert 5 78
(Michael Attwater) *restrained into detached last: pushed along and prog over 1f out: str reminders fnl f: r.o to take 2nd post* **16/1**

0140 3 shd **Yojimbo (IRE)**[14] 5794 4-9-10 **80** MatthewDavies 6 86
(Mick Channon) *led at str pce but jnd tl 3f out: u.p and vulnerable over 2f out: battled on wl but hdd 1f out: lost 2nd post* **13/2**

6565 4 1 1/4 **Xinbama (IRE)**[18] 5667 3-8-13 **74** SebSanders 2 77+
(J W Hills) *hld up off str early pce: effrt whn nt clr run wl over 2f out to over 1f out and lost all ch: styd on fnl f* **9/1**

2-51 5 1 **My Body Is A Cage (IRE)**[25] 5421 3-8-12 **73** JimmyFortune 10 74
(Jeremy Noseda) *chsd ldng pair at str pce: wnt 2nd wl over 2f out: chal and upsides over 1f out tl wknd fnl f* **5/2[1]**

6020 6 1 1/2 **Push Me (IRE)**[20] 5592 5-9-1 **71** KierenFox 4 68
(Jamie Poulton) *hld up off str early pce: clsd over 2f out: hung lft and nt qckn fr wl over 1f out* **13/2**

0640 7 3 1/4 **May's Boy**[16] 5741 4-8-10 **66** oh8 (p) HarryBentley 1 56
(Mark Usher) *chsd ldng trio but unable to keep on terms: clsd 2f out: rdn and wknd over 1f out* **20/1**

1151 **8** 3 1/2 **Woolston Ferry (IRE)**[37] 4964 6-9-6 **76**.............................. DaneO'Neill 9 58
(Henry Candy) *matched strides w ldr at str pce tl lost pl qckly wl over 2f out* **7/2**[2]

1m 43.08s (-0.22) **Going Correction** +0.05s/f (Good)
WFA 3 from 4yo+ 5lb 8 Ran SP% **114.8**
Speed ratings (Par 105): **103,102,102,100,99 98,95,91**
toteswingers 1&2 £18.20, 1&3 £5.80, 2&3 £12.60 CSF £78.52 CT £524.35 TOTE £9.50: £2.00, £3.90, £2.30; EX 135.10.
Owner Silver Linings **Bred** Rathasker Stud **Trained** Blewbury, Oxon
■ Stewards' Enquiry : Matthew Davies two-day ban: used whip above permitted level (Sep 30-Oct 1)

FOCUS
They went a strong pace in this handicap and the winner landed a gamble in good style under a waiting ride. The faster division by 1.05sec, but only ordinary form.

6209 HWFA WILLIAMS H'CAP (DIV II) 1m 14y
5:15 (5:15) (Class 4) (0-80,79) 3-Y-O+ **£4,075** (£1,212; £606; £303) **Stalls** Low

Form RPR
1550 **1** **Educate**[36] 5006 3-9-2 **76**.. LiamJones 8 88+
(Ismail Mohammed) *t.k.h: hld up in last pair: stdy prog fr 3f out: rdn to ld 1f out: edgd lft but styd on strly* **10/1**
0502 **2** 1 1/2 **First Post (IRE)**[14] 5794 5-9-10 **79**..................................(b) DaneO'Neill 7 85
(Derek Haydn Jones) *t.k.h: trckd ldng pair: stl gng strly over 2f out: shkn up to ld over 1f out: edgd lft and hdd 1f out: nt qckn and wl hld after* **7/2**[1]
0345 **3** 1 3/4 **Significant Move**[18] 5688 5-9-2 **71**....................................(t) IanMongan 3 73
(Stuart Kittow) *trckd ldng pair: rdn over 2f out: nt qckn and lost pl over 1f out: kpt on to take 3rd again nr fin* **10/1**
333 **4** 3/4 **Love Tatoo (IRE)**[14] 5795 3-8-8 **68**....................................... LiamKeniry 5 69
(Andrew Balding) *pressed ldr: led 2f out to over 1f out: fdd fnl f* **5/1**[3]
0000 **5** 2 **Uncle Fred**[36] 5008 7-9-3 **72**... HarryBentley 2 68
(Patrick Chamings) *dwlt: sn chsd ldrs in 5th: rdn and nt qckn over 2f out: wl hld over 1f out: one pce* **14/1**
-600 **6** hd **Besito (IRE)**[13] 5837 3-8-6 **73**.............................. MichaelJMMurphy[(7)] 9 69
(William Jarvis) *hld up in 7th: sme prog on outer 2f out: chsd ldrs over 1f out: wknd fnl f* **7/1**
0010 **7** 4 **Little Black Book (IRE)**[15] 5768 4-9-9 **78**....................(p) AndreaAtzeni 1 64
(Gerard Butler) *led: drvn and hdd 2f out: sn wknd* **4/1**[2]
3216 **8** nk **Mayo Lad (IRE)**[17] 5705 3-9-5 **79**... PatDobbs 6 65
(Richard Hannon) *t.k.h: hld up in 6th: dropped to last 3f out: pushed along and no prog after* **5/1**[3]
-000 **9** 5 **Sugarformyhoney (IRE)**[25] 5420 3-8-12 **72**................ JimmyFortune 4 46
(Seamus Durack) *hld up in last: effrt on outer over 2f out: no prog over 1f out: wknd qckly fnl f* **33/1**

1m 44.13s (0.83) **Going Correction** +0.05s/f (Good)
WFA 3 from 4yo+ 5lb 9 Ran SP% **115.8**
Speed ratings (Par 105): **97,95,93,93,91 90,86,86,81**
toteswingers 1&2 £6.30, 1&3 £12.70, 2&3 £8.50 CSF £45.16 CT £367.64 TOTE £9.90: £3.40, £1.10, £4.10; EX 49.40.
Owner Sultan Ali **Bred** Lady Legard **Trained** Newmarket, Suffolk

FOCUS
They went a steady pace in the second division of this handicap and the winner did well to score from some way back. The time was 3.83 seconds slower than standard and 1.05sec slower than the first division. The runner-up is the best guide.
T/Plt: £599.00 to a £1 stake. Pool: £58,710.20 - 71.55 winning tickets T/Qpdt: £309.30 to a £1 stake. Pool: £4,264.18 - 10.20 winning tickets JN

6174 WOLVERHAMPTON (A.W) (L-H)
Friday, September 14

OFFICIAL GOING: Standard to fast
Wind: Strong, behind Weather: Overcast

6210 VISIT ATTHERACES.COM/LEGER APPRENTICE H'CAP 1m 4f 50y(P)
5:40 (5:42) (Class 6) (0-55,60) 3-Y-O **£1,704** (£503; £251) **Stalls** Low

Form RPR
0122 **1** **Norfolk Sky**[25] 5408 3-8-11 **54**.................................... ThomasBrown[(5)] 8 64+
(Chris Wall) *hld up in tch: chsd ldr over 2f out: led over 1f out: styd on wl* **9/4**[1]
443 **2** 2 **Stag Hill (IRE)**[9] 5945 3-8-7 **50**................................... DanielMuscutt[(5)] 3 55
(Sylvester Kirk) *a.p: rdn to chse wnr and edgd rt ins fnl f: styd on* **5/1**[3]
0401 **3** 2 1/2 **Choral Bee**[8] 5974 3-9-5 **60** 6ex.. AmyScott[(3)] 4 61
(Henry Candy) *chsd ldr tl led over 3f out: rdn and hdd over 1f out: bmpd and styd on same pce ins fnl f* **9/2**[2]
4534 **4** 6 **Rano Pano (USA)**[6] 6056 3-8-5 **50**.................................... RobertTart[(7)] 2 41
(Brian Ellison) *hld up: hdwy u.p over 1f out: nvr nrr* **8/1**
2446 **5** nk **Lady Mandy**[16] 5744 3-8-10 **48**..(p) RyanPowell 1 39
(Ian Williams) *led over 8f: sn rdn: wknd over 1f out* **10/1**
0050 **6** 1 **Caledonian Lad**[39] 4870 3-8-7 **50**....................................... IanBurns[(5)] 6 39
(Hughie Morrison) *hld up: hdwy over 1f out: nvr on terms* **20/1**
000 **7** 7 **Oh So Charming**[35] 5048 3-8-6 **47** ow1................ MatthewLawson[(3)] 11 25
(Mark Gillard) *s.i.s: hdwy 10f out: rdn over 3f out: sn wknd* **66/1**
0050 **8** 1 1/2 **So Cheeky**[42] 4781 3-8-9 **50**.......................................(p) NeilFarley[(3)] 12 25
(Peter Salmon) *sn pushed along to chse ldrs: rdn and wknd over 2f out* **28/1**
0600 **9** 2 1/2 **Miss Mohawk (IRE)**[16] 5738 3-8-8 **46**............................(p) RaulDaSilva 7 17
(Alan Brown) *hld up: rdn over 7f out: a in rr: wknd over 3f out* **50/1**
5360 **10** 1 1/4 **Corn Maiden**[116] 2341 3-8-11 **49**....................................... RyanClark 9 18
(Phil McEntee) *hld up: rdn over 3f out: sn wknd* **40/1**
500 **11** 5 **Audeamus (IRE)**[18] 5687 3-8-2 **45**................................. NoelGarbutt[(5)] 5 6
(Tobias B P Coles) *hld up: a in rr: bhd fnl 4f* **8/1**
4050 **12** 1/2 **Baileys Over Ice**[20] 5589 3-8-8 **49**................................ ShaneBKelly[(3)] 10 10
(James Given) *prom: rdn over 4f out: wknd over 3f out* **22/1**

2m 37.94s (-3.16) **Going Correction** -0.325s/f (Stan) 12 Ran SP% **115.4**
Speed ratings (Par 99): **97,95,94,90,89 89,84,83,81,80 77,77**
Tote Swingers 1&2 £3.80, 2&3 £3.50, 1&3 £3.30 CSF £11.66 CT £46.31 TOTE £3.10: £1.50, £2.00, £1.90; EX 13.60 Trifecta £51.30 Pool £958.43 - 13.80 winning units..
Owner FarandWide Partners **Bred** Farmers Hill Stud **Trained** Newmarket, Suffolk
■ Thaomas Brown's first winner, on his third ride.

FOCUS
A moderate apprentice handicap in which the gallop was an ordinary one. The winner came down the centre in the straight and the first three finished clear. The winner should continue to progress.

6211 32RED H'CAP 5f 216y(P)
6:15 (6:16) (Class 5) (0-70,69) 3-Y-O **£2,425** (£721; £360; £180) **Stalls** Low

Form RPR
3331 **1** **Theresnoneedfordat (IRE)**[14] 5808 3-9-4 **66**................. PatCosgrave 7 76
(Stuart Williams) *hld up: hdwy over 2f out: rdn to ld wl ins fnl f: r.o* **11/8**[1]
41 **2** 1 1/4 **Avon Breeze**[13] 5823 3-9-3 **65**... AmyRyan 10 71
(Richard Whitaker) *hdwy over 4f out: chsd ldr over 2f out: led over 1f out: rdn: edgd lft and hdd wl ins fnl f* **10/3**[2]
0311 **3** 1/2 **Ambitious Boy**[13] 5831 3-9-7 **69**... ShaneKelly 8 73
(Reg Hollinshead) *s.i.s: hld up: rdn and hdwy over 1f out: r.o* **9/2**[3]
0235 **4** hd **Ooi Long**[24] 5445 3-8-9 **62**.. TobyAtkinson[(5)] 4 66
(Mark Rimmer) *hld up: rdn over 1f out: r.o ins fnl f: nt rch ldrs* **25/1**
0-42 **5** 1 3/4 **Mary Frith**[24] 5448 3-8-8 **56**...(p) LukeMorris 1 54
(William Knight) *chsd ldrs: rdn over 1f out: styd on same pce ins fnl f* **14/1**
1030 **6** 3/4 **Trust Fund Babe (IRE)**[21] 5545 3-8-12 **60**................... DuranFentiman 9 56
(Tim Easterby) *led: rdn and hdd over 1f out: no ex ins fnl f* **25/1**
1U50 **7** 1/2 **Gin Twist**[13] 5831 3-9-3 **68**..(b) RossAtkinson[(3)] 2 62
(Tom Dascombe) *s.i.s: hld up: rdn over 1f out: nvr on terms* **14/1**
4330 **8** 1 1/2 **West Leake Hare (IRE)**[10] 5915 3-9-6 **68**...................(p) HayleyTurner 6 57
(Charles Hills) *chsd ldrs: rdn over 2f out: wknd ins fnl f* **6/1**
0350 **9** 1/2 **Code Six (IRE)**[10] 5923 3-9-3 **65**.................................... RoystonFfrench 5 53
(Bryan Smart) *chsd ldr tl rdn over 2f out: wknd fnl f* **20/1**

1m 13.2s (-1.80) **Going Correction** -0.325s/f (Stan) 9 Ran SP% **123.4**
Speed ratings (Par 101): **99,97,96,96,94 93,92,90,89**
Tote Swingers 1&2 £2.20, 2&3 £4.60, 1&3 £2.70 CSF £6.37 CT £16.69 TOTE £2.50: £1.30, £1.70, £1.30; EX 9.00 Trifecta £17.90 Pool £858.36 - 35.44 winning units..
Owner R Morris J Russell T O'Brien M Nolan **Bred** Denis McDonnell **Trained** Newmarket, Suffolk

FOCUS
A couple of in-form types in a modest handicap. The gallop was sound and the winner came down the centre in the straight. The form seems sound.
Code Six(IRE) Official explanation: jockey said filly hung right

6212 WATCH THE ST LEGER LIVE ON ATR CLAIMING STKS 5f 20y(P)
6:45 (6:45) (Class 6) 2-Y-O **£1,704** (£503; £251) **Stalls** Low

Form RPR
5211 **1** **Hardy Blue (IRE)**[9] 5940 2-8-10 58..................................... CathyGannon 3 64
(Jamie Osborne) *chsd ldrs: pushed along 1/2-way: rdn over 1f out: r.o to ld wl ins fnl f* **2/1**[1]
3414 **2** 1 1/4 **Stripped Bear (IRE)**[18] 5654 2-8-7 60......................... RossAtkinson[(3)] 2 60
(Tom Dascombe) *led 1f: chsd ldr: rdn to ld ins fnl f: sn hdd and unable qck* **7/2**[2]
2053 **3** nk **Mandy Lexi (IRE)**[16] 5748 2-8-11 71..................................... TomQueally 8 59
(Patrick Morris) *led 4f out: rdn and hdd ins fnl f: styd on* **4/1**[3]
3163 **4** 2 1/4 **Charlemagne Diva**[10] 5916 2-8-8 63................................ RoystonFfrench 7 48
(Ann Duffield) *chsd ldrs: hung rt 1/2-way: rdn over 1f out: styd on same pce fnl f* **11/1**
324 **5** 1 1/2 **Jet Acclaim (IRE)**[16] 5748 2-8-9 64............................ SilvestreDeSousa 4 44
(Marco Botti) *hld up: plld hrd: hdwy over 1f out: sn rdn: no ex fnl f* **4/1**[3]
0 **6** 1 1/2 **Hah Hah**[18] 5675 2-8-3 0.. RaulDaSilva[(3)] 6 36
(Scott Dixon) *s.i.s: rdn over 1f out: n.d* **40/1**
004 **7** 1/2 **Strange Angel (IRE)**[14] 5807 2-8-7 49................................. LukeMorris 5 35
(David Evans) *s.i.s: rdn 1/2-way: n.d* **20/1**
4453 **8** 14 **Emperor's Daughter**[14] 5799 2-8-6 55.................................. JimmyQuinn 1
(Tim Pitt) *prom: rdn 1/2-way: wknd over 1f out* **12/1**

1m 1.2s (-1.10) **Going Correction** -0.325s/f (Stan) 8 Ran SP% **118.8**
Speed ratings (Par 93): **95,93,92,88,86 84,83,60**
Tote Swingers 1&2 £3.20, 2&3 £4.00, 1&3 £3.00 CSF £9.61 TOTE £3.60: £1.40, £1.80, £1.30; EX 17.70 Trifecta £39.90 Pool £724.61 - 13.43 winning units..
Owner Patrick Gage & Tony Taylor **Bred** Philip O'Dwyer **Trained** Upper Lambourn, Berks

FOCUS
A modest claimer comprising only fillies and one in which the pace was sound. The principals came down the centre in the straight.

NOTEBOOK
Hardy Blue(IRE) is an in-form sprinter who had a reasonable chance at the weights and showed a good attitude to extend her winning run to three. She should prove just as effective back over 6f and can win again in this grade. (op 11-4)
Stripped Bear(IRE) beat the progressive winner at Kempton last month but couldn't confirm those placings on 3lb worse terms after racing with the choke out. The return to low-grade nurseries may suit. (op 4-1)
Mandy Lexi(IRE), the pick of the weights, was turned over at single-figure odds for the ninth time in her ten starts. She's capable of winning a race in this grade but isn't one to place maximum faith in. (op 9-2 tchd 5-1 and 7-2)
Charlemagne Diva, who had a reasonable chance at the weights on this AW debut, was again below the form she showed when winning a Thirsk claimer last month. She'll have to show a bit more before she's a solid betting proposition again. Official explanation: jockey said filly hung right (op 12-1 tchd 10-1)
Jet Acclaim(IRE) got a good tow into the race but proved disappointing and didn't impress with the way she hung left under pressure. She's in good hands but doesn't seem to be progressing.

6213 ATR ST LEGER MICROSITE NOW LIVE H'CAP 1m 5f 194y(P)
7:15 (7:16) (Class 5) (0-70,72) 3-Y-O **£2,425** (£721; £360; £180) **Stalls** Low

Form RPR
00-2 **1** **Welsh Bard (IRE)**[9] 5945 3-8-13 **61**...................................... LukeMorris 1 70+
(Sir Mark Prescott Bt) *a.p: pushed along 4f out: rdn to ld and edgd rt over 1f out: styd on: readily* **1/1**[1]
2041 **2** 3/4 **Somemothersdohavem**[6] 6037 3-9-10 **72** 6ex...(p) DaraghO'Donohoe 2 79
(John Ryan) *hld up: hdwy over 2f out: rdn: hung rt and ev ch over 1f out: styd on* **4/1**[3]
621 **3** 4 1/2 **Melodrama (IRE)**[25] 5408 3-9-4 **66**..............................(b) JamieSpencer 4 67
(David Lanigan) *chsd ldr: pushed along and hung rt over 2f out: n.m.r wl over 1f out: sn rdn: no ex fnl f* **5/2**[2]
0613 **4** 2 1/2 **Any Given Dream (IRE)**[14] 5809 3-9-7 **69**...................... HayleyTurner 5 66
(David Simcock) *led: rdn and hdd over 1f out: hmpd sn after: wknd ins fnl f* **4/1**[3]

3m 2.58s (-3.42) **Going Correction** -0.325s/f (Stan) 4 Ran SP% **118.6**
Speed ratings (Par 101): **96,95,93,91**
CSF £6.06 TOTE £2.20; EX 6.90.
Owner Eclipse Thoroughbreds - Osborne House **Bred** Whisperview Trading Ltd **Trained** Newmarket, Suffolk

FOCUS
A modest but interesting event with all four runners coming here in decent form. The gallop was an ordinary one and the winner edged towards the centre late on. The form looks muddling but there's more to come from the winner.

Melodrama(IRE) Official explanation: jockey said filly hung right

6214 LIKE US ON FACEBOOK MEDIAN AUCTION MAIDEN STKS 1m 141y (P)

7:45 (7:46) (Class 6) 2-Y-O **£1,704** (£503; £251) **Stalls** Low

Form RPR

3 **1** **Buckstay (IRE)**[31] 5207 2 -9-30 JamieSpencer 12 75
(Peter Chapple-Hyam) *chsd ldrs: rdn over 1f out: styd on u.p to ld post* **7/2**[2]

0 **2** *shd* **Ormindo (USA)**[12] 5851 2 -9-30 SilvestreDeSousa 4 75
(Mahmood Al Zarooni) *chsd ldr tl led over 1f out: rdn and edgd lft ins fnl f: hdd post* **8/1**[3]

6 **3** *3 3/4* **Le Talisman (IRE)**[13] 5478 2 -8-120 AntiocoMurgia(5) 13 67
(Mahmood Al Zarooni) *led: rdn and hdd over 1f out: styd on same pce ins fnl f* **10/1**

0 **4** *2 1/2* **Sweet Deal (IRE)**[14] 5792 2 -9-30 TomQueally 6 61+
(Jeremy Noseda) *s.i.s: hld up: pushed along over 2f out: r.o ins fnl f: nrst fin* **7/4**[1]

5 *2 1/4* **High Troja (IRE)**2 -9-30 TomMcLaughlin 5 56+
(Ed Dunlop) *s.s: outpcd: rdn over 2f out: styd on ins fnl f: nvr nrr* **33/1**

6 *nk* **Sesentum** 2 -9-30 KierenFallon 10 55
(Luca Cumani) *s.i.s: rn green towards rr: hdwy over 2f out: styng on same pce whn edgd lft over 1f out* **14/1**

7 *1/2* **Khotan** 2 -9-30 LukeMorris 1 56+
(Sir Mark Prescott Bt) *hld up: rdn over 2f out: n.d* **40/1**

0 **8** *1* **Rhyolite (IRE)**[35] 5062 2 -8-120 TobyAtkinson(5) 3 52
(Marco Botti) *hld up: hdwy over 3f out: rdn over 2f out: wknd over 1f out* **14/1**

03 **9** *nk* **Star Of Broadway**[19] 5619 2 -9-30 MickaelBarzalona 8 51
(Mahmood Al Zarooni) *chsd ldrs: rdn over 2f out: wknd over 1f out* **8/1**[3]

0 **10** *3/4* **Sunblazer (IRE)**[17] 5704 2 -9-30 MartinDwyer 11 50
(William Muir) *prom: rdn over 3f out: wknd over 2f out* **25/1**

0 **11** *1 3/4* **Darkest Night (IRE)**[12] 5851 2 -9-30 SeanQuinlan 2 46
(Jamie Osborne) *hld up in tch: plld hrd: rdn over 2f out: wknd over 1f out* **50/1**

12 *9* **Prince Rakan (USA)**2 -9-30 HayleyTurner 7 26
(Amy Weaver) *sn pushed along and a in rr* **40/1**

0 **13** *1/2* **Swaying Grace (IRE)**[13] 5818 2 -8-120 RoystonFfrench 9 20
(Ann Duffield) *a towards rr: bhd fnl 4f* **66/1**

1m 49.4s (-1.10)**Going Correction** -0.325s/f (Stan) **13**Ran SP% **118.4**
Speed ratings (Par 93): **91,90,87,85,83 83,82,81,81,80 79,71,70**
Tote Swingers 1&2 £6.00, 2&3 £9.10, 1&3 £8.50 CSF £29.54 TOTE £4.70 : £1.90 , £2.70 , £3. EX 36.70 Trifecta £421.20 Part won. Pool £569.10 - 0.40 winning units.
Owner Mrs Fitri Hay **Bred** M Phelan & Lawman Syndicate **Trained** Newmarket, Suffolk

FOCUS

The market leader disappointed but the first two, who pulled clear late on, showed fair form. The gallop was reasonable and the winner edged towards the far side in the straight.

NOTEBOOK

Buckstay(IRE) ◆ confirmed debut promise and in the process showed a good attitude to hit the front in the closing stages. He'll be even better suited by 1m2f in due course and has the size and scope to make further progress. (tchd 4-1)

Ormindo(USA) stepped up a fair way on the form that he showed over 7f at Folkestone on his debut. He pulled clear of the rest and, although he lacks the physical presence of the winner, he's more than capable of picking up an uncompetitive race in this grade. (op 9-1)

Le Talisman (IRE)was allowed a fairly easy time of it in front and stepped up on the form he showed at Kempton on his debut. He pulled clear of the rest but is likely to remain vulnerable to the more progressive types in this grade. (op 12-1)

Sweet Deal (IRE)again missed the break and was tapped for foot at a crucial stage but he made up a fair amount of ground on the outside in the straight. He'll be suited by the step up to 1m2f (backed up by pedigree) and will be worth another chance granted a stiffer test of stamina. (13-8)

High Troja (IRE)◆, who cost 28,000gns and who is closely related to useful 1m4f-2m winner Kleitomachos, caught the eye on this racecourse debut. He'll be well suited by the step up to 1m2f and beyond and he's sure to win races.

Sesentum, a 34,000gns gelded half-brother to several winners, including smart (at best) turf. dirt and Tapeta winner Sharaayeen, was too green to do himself justice on this racecourse debut but he's in good hands and is open to improvement.

Khotan, a brother to a couple of ordinary maidens, was easy to back and wasn't totally disgraced on this racecourse debut. He'll be seen to much better effect in handicaps over middle distances next year.

6215 ENJOY THE PUNTERS PACKAGE GROUP OFFER MAIDEN STKS 1m 141y (P)

8:15 (8:16) (Class 5) 3-Y-O+ **£2,264** (£673; £336 ; £168) **Stalls** Low

Form RPR

4423 **1** **All Time**[26] 5387 4 -9-466 TomQueally 1 71
(Sir Henry Cecil) *mde all: shkn up over 1f out: rdn out* **5/1**

3 **2** *3/4* **Qanan**[21] 5555 3 -9-30 KierenFallon 7 74+
(Luca Cumani) *s.i.s: hld up: hdwy over 2f out: rdn over 1f out: r.o to go 2nd nr fin: nt rch wnr* **1/1**[1]

3-05 **3** *1/2* **Rawaafed (IRE)**[21] 5555 3 -9-379 ShaneKelly 9 73
(Brian Meehan) *a.p: chsd wnr 3f out: rdn over 1f out: styd on same pce ins fnl f* **4/1**[3]

26 **4** *2 3/4* **Eltifaat (IRE)**[47] 4630 3 -9-30 TadhgO'Shea 6 67
(Sir Michael Stoute) *hld up: hdwy over 2f out: rdn over 1f out: no ex ins fnl f* **9/4**[2]

5 *5* **Desert Berry** 3 -8-120 ChrisCatlin 8 50
(Chris Wall) *hld up: rdn over 1f out: r.o ins fnl f: nvr nrr* **40/1**

6 **6** *1/2* **Narapatisithu (FR)**[38] 4916 5 -9-90 JamieMackay 2 54?
(K F Clutterbuck) *chsd wnr over 5f: sn rdn: wknd over 1f out* **200/1**

7 *1 1/2* **Indie Wonder** 3 -8-50 JackDuern(7) 10 46
(Reg Hollinshead) *outpcd: rdn over 1f out: nvr on terms* **80/1**

- **8** *1 1/2* **Italian Riviera** 3 -9-30 LukeMorris 4 47
(Sir Mark Prescott Bt) *sn pushed along and prom: drvn along over 2f out: wknd over 1f out* **14/1**

5 **9** *1 1/4* **Black Dragon**[182] 833 4 -9-40 TobyAtkinson(5) 12 44
(Mark Rimmer) *s.i.s: plld hrd in rr: rdn over 2f out: n.d* **33/1**

06 **10** *1 3/4* **Alaskan Prince (IRE)**[93] 3024 7 -9-90 AdamBeschizza 3 40
(Peter Salmon) *chsd ldrs: rdn over 2f out: wknd over 1f out* **200/1**

11 *26* **Cape Sky**[15] 5 -9-40 TomEaves 11
(Roy Brotherton) *s.s: a in rr: bhd fnl 3f: t.o* **100/1**

00 **12** *5* **Legal Pursuit**[18] 5687 3 -9-30 SeanQuinlan 5
(Edward Bevan) *chsd ldrs tl rdn and wknd over 2f out: t.o* **100/1**

1m 47.73s (-2.77)**Going Correction** -0.325s/f (Stan)
WFA 3 from 4yo+ 6lb **12**Ran SP% **133.7**
Speed ratings (Par 103): **99,98,97,95,91 90,89,87,86,85 62,57**
Tote Swingers 1&2 £2.90, 2&3 £3.10, 1&3 £4.60 CSF £11.92 TOTE £6.80 : £1.50 , £1.10 , £2.00 ; EX 16.00 Trifecta £34.10 Pool £827.60 - 17.91 winning units.
Owner K Abdulla **Bred** Juddmonte Farms Ltd **Trained** Newmarket, Suffolk

FOCUS

A fair maiden in which the gallop was an ordinary one. The winner raced centre-to-far-side in the straight. The winner made all and there's some doubt over the bare form.

Black Dragon Official explanation: jockey said gelding ran too freely

6216 WILLIAM BUICK EXCLUSIVE BLOG ON ATTHERACES.COM/LEGER H'CAP (DIV I) 7f 32y (P)

8:45 (8:46) (Class 6) (0-65,63) 3-Y-O+ **£1,704** (£503; £251) **Stalls** High

Form RPR

0542 **1** **Jay Bee Blue**[7] 5991 3 -9-259 (b) TomQueally 10 71
(Sean Curran) *hld up: hdwy over 1f out: r.o u.p to ld wl ins fnl f* **11/2**[3]

0152 **2** *1/2* **Balti's Sister (IRE)**[15] 5775 3 -9-262 RossAtkinson(3) 3 73
(Terry Clement) *chsd ldrs: led over 1f out: rdn: edgd lft and hdd wl ins fnl f* **8/1**

0040 **3** *1 3/4* **Tiradito (USA)**[25] 5428 5 -9-1063 SilvestreDeSousa 8 70
(Brian Ellison) *hld up: hdwy wl over 1f out: sn rdn: r.o: wnt 3rd post* **9/4**[2]

5002 **4** *nse* **Sir Bruno (FR)**[11] 5893 5 -9-962 (v1) LukeMorris 2 69
(Bryn Palling) *chsd ldrs: pushed along over 2f out: rdn over 1f out: styd on* **5/4**[1]

-200 **5** *7* **Bada Bing**[15] 5764 3 -8-652 (p) RaulDaSilva(3) 1 39
(Scott Dixon) *led: rdn over 2f out: hdd over 1f out: wknd ins fnl f* **25/1**

3606 **6** *2 3/4* **Untold Melody**[28] 5318 3 -9-663 (p) AmyRyan 7 43
(Kevin Ryan) *chsd ldrs: pushed along and hung rt over 2f out: wknd over 1f out* **11/1**

3030 **7** *nk* **Piccolo Express**[100] 2811 6 -9-760 FrederikTylicki 11 40
(Brian Baugh) *hld up: rdn over 2f out: wknd over 1f out* **20/1**

6200 **8** *3 1/4* **Moody Dancer**[30] 5229 3 -9-360 MartinDwyer 4 30
(William Muir) *chsd ldrs: rdn over 2f out: hmpd wl over 1f out: sn wknd* **20/1**

1m 27.08s (-2.52)**Going Correction** -0.325s/f (Stan)
WFA 3 from 4yo+ 4lb **8**Ran SP% **123.4**
Speed ratings (Par 101): **101,100,98,98,90 87,86,83**
Tote Swingers 1&2 £2.90, 2&3 £5.40, 1&3 £4.40 CSF £50.06 CT £130.91 TOTE £5.90 : £1.50 , £2.70, £1.50 ; EX 23.60 Trifecta £81.90 Pool £459.77 - 4.15 winning units.
Owner Scuderia Vita Bella **Bred** L A C Ashby Newhall Estate Farm **Trained** Hatford, Oxon

FOCUS

A modest handicap run at just a fair pace. The winner edged towards the stands' side in the straight. Sound form.

Untold Melody Official explanation: jockey said filly hung right

6217 WILLIAM BUICK EXCLUSIVE BLOG ON ATTHERACES.COM/LEGER H'CAP (DIV II) 7f 32y (P)

9:15 (9:15) (Class 6) (0-65,65) 3-Y-O+ **£1,704** (£503; £251) **Stalls** High

Form RPR

2026 **1** **Light Burst (USA)**[30] 5229 3 -9-665 RoystonFfrench 5 77
(Ismail Mohammed) *chsd ldrs: led ins fnl f: rdn out* **7/1**

4504 **2** *2* **Amethyst Dawn (IRE)**[21] 5547 6 -8-856 (t) DavidBergin(7) 6 64
(Alan McCabe) *chsd ldr tl led over 2f out: rdn over 1f out: hdd and unable qck ins fnl f* **5/1**[2]

0531 **3** *1 1/2* **One Way Or Another (AUS)** 5996 9 -9-459 (t) RichardThomas 2 63
(David Evans) *hld up: hdwy u.p fr over 1f out: nt rch ldrs* **11/10**[1]

-505 **4** *1 1/2* **Salutary**[30] 5229 3 -8-1358 KierenFallon 3 57
(Jane Chapple-Hyam) *hld up: hdwy over 2f out: rdn over 1f out: styd on* **12/1**

5 **5** *2 1/4* **Desertcougar (IRE)**[6] 6050 3 -9-564 SeanQuinlan 8 56
(Daniel Mark Loughnane) *chsd ldrs: rdn over 1f out: no ex ins fnl f* **16/1**

0002 **6** *1 1/4* **Indieslad**[14] 5808 4 -9-661 (p) TomEaves 7 51
(Ann Duffield) *hld up in tch: rdn over 1f out: no ex fnl f* **10/1**

(tda)621 **7** *1 1/2* **July Days (IRE)**[25] 5428 6 -9-762 FrederikTylicki 9 48
(Brian Baugh) *led over 4f: wknd ins fnl f* **7/1**

4605 **8** *5* **Katmai River (IRE)**[16] 5741 5 -9-863 DavidProbert 1 36
(Mark Usher) *hld up: rdn 1/2-way: a in rr* **6/1**[3]

0100 **9** *5* **Jay Kay**[17] 5721 3 -8-1055 ChrisCatlin 10 13
(Danielle McCormick) *hld up: rdn and wknd over 2f out* **22/1**

5600 **10** *hd* **Prohibition (IRE)**[119] 2237 6 -8-1157 LeonnaMayor(5) 4 15
(John Butler) *s.i.s: hdwy 1/2-way: wknd over 2f out* **33/1**

1m 26.96s (-2.64)**Going Correction** -0.325s/f (Stan)
WFA 3 from 4yo+ 4lb **10**Ran SP% **133.5**
Speed ratings (Par 101): **102,99,98,96,93 92,90,84,79,78**
Tote Swingers 1&2 £7.30, 2&3 £1.10, 1&3 £2.90 CSF £48.44 CT £71.39 TOTE £8.70 : £2.60 , £2.10, £1.60 ; EX 43.50 Trifecta £170.20 Pool £602.82 - 2.62 winning units.
Owner Saeed H Altayer **Bred** C Kidder, N Cole & B Kidder **Trained** Newmarket, Suffolk

FOCUS

Division two of a modest handicap. The gallop was an ordinary one and the winner came down the centre. Those held up struggled to get involved. A 5lb best from the winner.

T/Plt: £9.50 to a £1 stake. Pool £79,168.70. 6036.89 winning tickets T/Qpdt: £8.70 to a £1 stake. Pool £7,423.88. 628.98 w. tckts CR 6218a - 6224a (Foreign Racing) See RI

3178 LYON PARILLY (R-H)

Friday, September 14

OFFICIAL GOING: Turf: soft

6225a CRITERIUM DE LYON (LISTED RACE) (2YO) (TURF) 1m

2:15 (12:00) 2-Y-O **£22,916** (£9,166; £6,875 ; £4,583 ; £2,291)

RPR

1 **Melodique (FR)**[20] 2 -8-100 OlivierPeslier 3 93
(C Laffon-Parias, France) **37/10**[2]

2 *2* **More Than Sotka (FR)**[37] 5379 2 -9-00 ChristopheSoumillon 4 93
(F-H Graffard, France) **19/5**[3]

3 *1/2* **Cassiopee (FR)**[11] 5899 2 -8-100 AntoineHamelin 8 87
(Y Barberot, France) **44/5**

4 *shd* **Le Ring (FR)**2 -9-00 FranckBlondel 6 91
(F Rossi, France) **2/1**[1]

5 *1* **Linguine (FR)**[21] 5552 2 -9-00 IoritzMendizabal 2 89
(Charles Hills) *racd v keenly bhd ldr: settled in 2nd by 1/2-way: rdn 2f out and nt qckn w ldrs: one pce fnl f* **63/10**

6 *1 1/2* **Green Daisy (FR)**[34] 2 -8-100 UmbertoRispoli 5 82
(J Heloury, France) **7/1**

7 *2 1/2* **Vesper (GER)** 2 -8-100 FabriceVeron 7 76
(M Munch, Germany) **34/1**

8 *8* **Tiolache (FR)**[37] 2-8-10 0 GeraldPardon 1 59
(J-M Capitte, France) **27/1**

1m 40.88s (100.88) 8 Ran SP% **118.3**
PARI-MUTUEL (all including 1 euro stakes): WIN 4.70; PLACE 1.90, 1.70, 2.40; DF 8.50; SF 19.30.
Owner Wertheimer & Frere **Bred** Ecurie Des Monceaux **Trained** Chantilly, France

6092 BATH (L-H)

Saturday, September 15

OFFICIAL GOING: Firm (10.4)
Races incorporating bottom bend increased in distance by about 12.5yds.
Wind: Brisk ahead Weather: Cloudy

6226 BATHWICK TYRES TETBURY H'CAP 5f 11y
1:45 (1:47) (Class 4) (0-80,79) 3-Y-O+ **£5,175** (£1,540; £769; £384) **Stalls** Centre

Form RPR
2363 **1** **Demora**[33] 5167 3-8-5 **67** DominicFox(3) 1 75
(Michael Appleby) *mde virtually all but hrd pressed tl rdn and def advantage ins fnl f: hld on all out* **14/1**
0050 **2** *hd* **Beauty Pageant (IRE)**[26] 5412 5-9-2 **74** SeanLevey 15 81
(Ed McMahon) *chsd ldrs: rdn 2f out: styd on wl fnl f to take 2nd clsng stages: nt quite rch wnr* **13/2**[2]
0220 **3** *½* **Sandfrankskipsgo**[19] 5663 3-9-6 **79** SebSanders 7 84
(Peter Crate) *pressed wnr and stl upsides tl ins fnl f: one pce and lost 2nd clsng stages* **10/1**
0634 **4** *nse* **Lujeanie**[22] 5557 6-9-3 **78** (p) PatrickHills(3) 13 83
(Dean Ivory) *in tch: hdwy on outside over 1f out: styd on strly clsng stages: gng on cl home* **10/1**
00- **5** *½* **Big Bad Lily (IRE)**[20] 5646 4-8-9 **67** (b) ShaneKelly 12 70+
(Augustine Leahy, Ire) *in rr: hdwy fr 2f out: nt clr run and swtchd rt 1f out: fin wl* **10/1**
1443 **6** *shd* **Rebecca Romero**[14] 5815 5-9-2 **74** EddieAhern 11 79+
(Denis Coakley) *chsd ldrs: nt clr run appr fnl f: styng on wl whn hmpd last strides* **8/1**[3]
1006 **7** *¾* **Wooden King (IRE)**[10] 5933 7-9-3 **75** TomMcLaughlin 2 75
(Malcolm Saunders) *chsd ldrs: rdn 2f out: kpt on same pce ins fnl f* **14/1**
0304 **8** *1* **Courageous (IRE)**[8] 6005 6-8-11 **76** MichaelJMMurphy(7) 8 72
(Milton Bradley) *in tch: hdwy u.p on inner over 1f out: never seeing much daylight soon after & one pce final 100yds* **6/1**[1]
2431 **9** *½* **Howyadoingnotsobad (IRE)**[29] 5296 4-9-6 **78** HarryBentley 9 73
(Karen George) *chsd ldrs: rdn 2f out: wknd fnl 120yds* **13/2**[2]
100 **10** *1 ¼* **Best Be Careful (IRE)**[30] 5272 4-8-11 **74** RachealKneller(5) 6 64
(Mark Usher) *trckd ldrs: gng on whn nt clr run over 1f out: wknd ins fnl f* **25/1**
0350 **11** *½* **Signifer (IRE)**[26] 5422 3-9-0 **73** SamHitchcott 5 61
(Mick Channon) *chsd ldrs: rdn over 2f out: wknd ins fnl f* **40/1**
4036 **12** *shd* **Falasteen (IRE)**[14] 5812 5-9-5 **77** FergusSweeney 14 65
(Milton Bradley) *s.i.s: in rr: sme hdwy on outer over 1f out: nvr gng pce to get into contention* **20/1**
2200 **13** *¾* **Befortyfour**[47] 4660 7-8-10 **71** (b[1]) MarkCoumbe(3) 10 56
(Charles Smith) *s.i.s: in rr: effrt on outside 2f out: nvr gng pce to get into contention* **33/1**
661 **14** *2* **Blanc De Chine (IRE)**[26] 5422 3-9-5 **78** CathyGannon 4 56
(Peter Makin) *unruly stalls: stmbld bdly s and nrly uns rdr: nt rcvr and a outpcd* **14/1**
1120 **15** *1 ¼* **Crimson Queen**[23] 5502 5-9-2 **74** (b) ChrisCatlin 3 48
(Roy Brotherton) *outpcd* **12/1**

1m 1.12s (-1.38) **Going Correction** -0.15s/f (Firm)
WFA 3 from 4yo+ 1lb 15 Ran SP% **121.0**
Speed ratings (Par 105): **105,104,103,103,103 102,101,100,99,97 96,96,95,91,89**
Tote Swingers 1&2 £40.00, 2&3 £40.00, 1&3 £40.00 CSF £98.14 CT £992.42 TOTE £20.20: £5.70, £2.70, £3.70; EX 250.60.
Owner Dallas Racing **Bred** A M Wragg **Trained** Danethorpe, Notts

FOCUS
Few got into this ordinary handicap. Regulation form.
Lujeanie Official explanation: jockey said gelding hung right
Blanc De Chine(IRE) Official explanation: jockey said filly tried to go under gate

6227 BATHWICK TYRES CHIPPENHAM NURSERY 5f 161y
2:15 (2:17) (Class 4) (0-85,79) 2-Y-O **£4,398** (£1,309; £654; £327) **Stalls** Centre

Form RPR
13 **1** **Alcando (IRE)**[9] 5969 2-9-5 **77** EddieAhern 3 79
(Denis Coakley) *s.i.s: sn chsng ldrs: styd on strly ins fnl f: wnt 2nd fnl 100yds: qcknd to ld last strides* **4/1**[2]
0551 **2** *hd* **Vestibule**[5] 6093 2-8-11 **74** 6ex (p) AmyScott(5) 6 75
(Eve Johnson Houghton) *led: hrd rdn fnl f: kpt on: hdd last strides* **9/2**[3]
3043 **3** *1 ¼* **Ighraa (IRE)**[19] 5682 2-9-1 **73** ShaneKelly 2 70
(Brian Meehan) *chsd ldr: rdn and no imp fnl f: one pce into 3rd fnl 100yds* **9/1**
2401 **4** *¾* **Echion (IRE)**[32] 5202 2-9-4 **76** KieranO'Neill 5 72+
(Richard Hannon) *in rr but in tch: hdwy: nt clr run and swtchd rt appr fnl f: kpt on wl olong otagoo* **6/1**
2312 **5** *½* **Dusty Storm (IRE)**[25] 5450 2-9-6 **78** SeanLevey 1 71
(Ed McMahon) *chsd ldrs: rdn and one pce fnl f* **7/2**[1]
010 **6** *½* **Ishigunnaeatit**[28] 5361 2-9-0 **75** MichaelMetcalfe(3) 8 66
(Mrs K Burke) *chsd ldrs: rdn over 2f out: wknd fnl f* **8/1**
31 **7** *1 ½* **Melbourne Memories**[16] 5773 2-9-6 **78** JohnFahy 9 64
(Clive Cox) *in tch: hdwy on outer over 2f out: sn rdn and nvr gng pce to chal: wknd fnl f* **5/1**
1500 **8** *33* **Three Crowns**[17] 5743 2-9-7 **79** SebSanders 7
(Ian Wood) *slowly away: rdn and btn 3f out: eased* **20/1**

1m 10.96s (-0.24) **Going Correction** -0.15s/f (Firm) 8 Ran SP% **117.2**
Speed ratings (Par 97): **95,94,93,92,91 90,88,44**
Tote Swingers 1&2 £4.60, 2&3 £23.10, 1&3 £12.50 CSF £23.00 CT £153.71 TOTE £8.20: £2.30, £1.70, £2.80; EX 54.20.
Owner The Good Mixers **Bred** E O'Gorman **Trained** West Ilsley, Berks
■ Rated was withdrawn (lame, 12/1). Deduct 5p in the £ under R4. New market formed.

FOCUS
The form of this nursery looks quite solid for the grade, with the second and third good guides.

NOTEBOOK
Alcando(IRE), a C&D maiden winner on debut, didn't last 7f at Kempton next time but he looked on a reasonable mark for this nursery debut and had a lovely tow into the race. A full 6f will probably prove his ideal trip. (new market new market op 6-1)
Vestibule took 11 runs to get off the mark, bolting up in a course maiden over a bare 5f earlier in the week, and she bettered that effort with a narrow defeat under a penalty. (new market new market tchd 4-1)
Ighraa(IRE) was nicely positioned and again looked to run her race, but is now 0-6. A step up to 7f may suit. (new market new market tchd 17-2 and 10-1)
Echion(IRE), up 4lb for his Nottingham victory over 6f, kept on late having been short of room and should have finished closer. (new market new market tchd 11-2)
Dusty Storm(IRE), up 3lb, was trying to stay on when briefly short of room, but she'd have been no closer than third. (new market new market op 4-1 tchd 9-2)
Melbourne Memories challenged wide and ultimately failed to see it out. She could be worth another chance. (new market new market op 6-1 tchd 4-1)

6228 BATHWICK TYRES BATH MAIDEN STKS 1m 3f 144y
2:50 (2:50) (Class 5) 3-Y-O+ **£2,011** (£866; £432; £216) **Stalls** Low

Form RPR
4522 **1** **Dr Yes (FR)**[36] 5048 3-9-3 **84** IanMongan 8 93
(Sir Henry Cecil) *led over 1m out: c easily clr over 3f out: stl 8 l clr 2f out: shkn up sn after and nvr in any danger* **5/6**[1]
4 **2** *4 ½* **Totalize**[12] 5889 3-9-0 0 PatrickHills(3) 10 85
(Luca Cumani) *broke wl: dropped to rr 7f out: drvn 4f out: hdwy fr 3f out: wnt 2nd over 1f out: styd on wl fnl f but no imp on wnr* **7/2**[2]
-333 **3** *6* **Pulverize (USA)**[40] 4882 3-9-3 **80** [1] SebSanders 3 75
(Sir Michael Stoute) *prom: chsd wnr over 3f out but nvr any ch: wknd 2f out and lost 2nd over 1f out* **9/2**[3]
4 **4** *3 ¼* **Smart Ruler (IRE)**[29] 5315 6-9-9 0 JulieBurke(3) 6 70
(James Moffatt) *in tch: hdwy to chse ldrs over 3f out: sn rdn: styd on same pce fnl 2f* **33/1**
5526 **5** *6* **Linkable**[39] 4923 3-9-3 **73** EddieAhern 9 59
(Charles Hills) *in tch: rdn and sme hdwy 4f out: nvr nr ldrs and no ch fnl 3f* **10/1**
-60 **6** *3 ¼* **Straight Shot (IRE)**[131] 1922 3-9-3 0 (t) ShaneKelly 11 54
(Brian Meehan) *led tl hdd over 1m out: lost 2nd over 3f out: sn btn* **16/1**
0 **7** *20* **Refute (IRE)**[26] 5404 3-9-3 0 CathyGannon 2 20
(Harry Dunlop) *chsd ldrs: rdn over 3f out and sn btn* **66/1**
20 **8** *1 ¼* **Maid Of Silk (IRE)**[36] 5048 6-9-4 0 (t) CPGeoghegan(3) 1 13
(Neil Mulholland) *chsd ldrs 7f* **80/1**
66 **9** *½* **Dei Amore (IRE)**[17] 5745 3-8-12 0 JohnFahy 7 12
(Jonathan Portman) *rdn fr stalls: in tch: rdn again and bhd 7f out* **66/1**
10 *2* **Caunay**[104] 5-9-5 0 (t) WilliamTwiston-Davies(7) 5 14
(Neil Mulholland) *s.i.s: a in rr* **50/1**
11 *57* **Late Reg**[119] 13-9-7 0 SeanQuinlan 12
(Liam Grassick) *slowly away: a bhd: t.o* **100/1**
12 *14* **Regency Dreams**[10] 7-9-7 0 RobertWilliams(5) 4
(Nikki Evans) *s.i.s: sn in tch awkward: wd and wknd bnd 5f out* **100/1**

2m 26.38s (-4.22) **Going Correction** -0.225s/f (Firm)
WFA 3 from 5yo+ 9lb 12 Ran SP% **121.0**
Speed ratings (Par 103): **105,102,98,95,91 89,76,75,75,73 35,26**
Tote Swingers 1&2 £1.60, 2&3 £2.90, 1&3 £1.60 CSF £3.92 TOTE £1.70: £1.02, £1.60, £2.20; EX 5.20.
Owner Niarchos Family **Bred** Suc S Niarchos **Trained** Newmarket, Suffolk

FOCUS
Little depth to this maiden. The winner, who stood out on the fugures, set a good pace and is rated to his best.

6229 BATHWICK TYRES MIDSOMER NORTON FILLIES' H'CAP 1m 3f 144y
3:30 (3:30) (Class 5) (0-75,74) 3-Y-O+ **£2,911** (£866; £432; £216) **Stalls** Low

Form RPR
2321 **1** **Dancing Primo**[6] 6076 6-9-5 **74** JackDuern(7) 10 84
(Mark Brisbourne) *in rr but in tch: hdwy: pushed along and n.m.r 3f out: chal 2f out tl led over 1f out and edgd rt: pushed out* **5/4**[1]
422 **2** *3* **Peachez**[23] 5507 4-9-2 **69** (p) AmyScott(5) 4 74
(Alastair Lidderdale) *in rr: hdwy on outer 4f out to chse ldrs 3f out: chal over 2f out tl over 1f out: swtchd lft and styd on fnl f: nt pce of wnr* **8/1**[3]
3301 **3** *nk* **Kittens**[13] 5855 3-8-1 **61** RaulDaSilva(3) 3 66+
(William Muir) *sn towards rr: hdwy on ins over 2f out: styd on to take 3rd fnl 120yds: kpt on cl home* **8/1**[3]
1250 **4** *2 ¼* **Tidal Run**[10] 5931 4-9-12 **74** SamHitchcott 6 75
(Mick Channon) *in rr: hdwy 3f out: styd on fr over 1f out: nt pce to rch ldrs* **20/1**
0534 **5** *nk* **Srinagar Girl**[41] 4850 3-8-12 **69** IanMongan 9 69
(Sir Henry Cecil) *chsd ldrs: led ins fnl 3f: hdd wl over 1f out: wknd ins fnl f* **9/2**[2]
63-1 **6** *¾* **Bollin Dolly**[103] 2034 9-9-8 **73** JulieBurke(3) 5 72
(James Moffatt) *led tl hdd ins fnl 3f: styng on same pce whn n.m.r on inner ins fnl f* **20/1**
5635 **7** *1* **Amistress**[25] 5441 4-9-0 **62** ChrisCatlin 1 59
(Eve Johnson Houghton) *chsd ldr to 7f out: styd chsng ldrs: rdn 3f out: wknd over 1f out* **9/1**
4264 **8** *5* **Port Charlotte**[11] 5913 3-9-1 **72** (b[1]) SebSanders 7 61
(Hughie Morrison) *chsd ldrs: wnt 2nd 7f out: rdn 3f out: wknd 2f out* **14/1**
36-5 **9** *16* **Lady Barastar (IRE)**[204] 689 4-9-3 **65** EddieAhern 2 26
(Amanda Perrett) *in tch: rdn and sme hdwy over 3f out: sn wknd* **33/1**

2m 27.67s (-2.93) **Going Correction** -0.225s/f (Firm)
WFA 3 from 4yo+ 9lb 9 Ran SP% **114.0**
Speed ratings (Par 100): **100,98,97,96,96 95,94,91,80**
Tote Swingers 1&2 £3.20, 2&3 £11.00, 1&3 £5.50 CSF £11.29 CT £56.98 TOTE £2.10: £1.80, £2.80, £1.60; EX 11.00.
Owner L R Owen **Bred** L R Owen **Trained** Great Ness, Shropshire

FOCUS
The form horses dominated this moderate fillies' handicap, which was sound run. The well-in winner did not need to match her York win.

6230 BATHWICK TYRES TROWBRIDGE H'CAP (DIV I) 1m 2f 46y
4:05 (4:05) (Class 6) (0-60,62) 3-Y-O+ **£2,070** (£616; £307; £153) **Stalls** Low

Form RPR
0413 **1** **The Wonga Coup (IRE)**[10] 5935 5-9-2 **49** IanMongan 6 59
(Pat Phelan) *s.i.s: in rr: hdwy on outer over 3f out: chal 2f out: sn slt ld: drvn out fnl f* **7/2**[2]
2441 **2** *2 ¼* **Volcanic Jack (IRE)**[5] 6097 4-9-10 **62** 6ex BrendanPowell(5) 4 68
(Tony Carroll) *hld up in tch: stdy hdwy fr 4f out to chal 2f out: chsd wnr fnl f: no ex and wl hld fnl 100yds* **2/1**[1]
0306 **3** *2 ¼* **Poetry Writer**[9] 5983 3-9-4 **58** FergusSweeney 7 59
(Michael Blanshard) *in tch: hdwy 4f out: drvn and styd on to take one pce 3rd 1f out* **13/2**[3]
00 **4** *2 ½* **El Dececy (USA)**[40] 4872 8-9-3 **53** (p) MarkCoumbe(3) 3 49
(Charles Smith) *led: rdn 3f out: jnd 2f out: sn hdd: wknd fnl f* **20/1**

55 **5** *shd* **Rocquaine (IRE)**[8] 5991 3-8-5 **45** RichardThomas 8 41
(David Evans) *sn in rr: plenty to do 4f out: hdwy over 2f out: styd on fnl f: nvr a threat* **9/1**

/036 **6** *3 ½* **Gavi**[32] 5197 6-9-12 **59** TomMcLaughlin 1 48
(Karen George) *chsd ldrs: rdn 3f out: sn btn* **7/1**

-600 **7** *3 ¼* **Prince Freddie**[10] 5936 4-9-8 **55** (p) ChrisCatlin 5 37
(Roy Brotherton) *chsd ldrs: wnt 2nd over 4f out tl wknd appr fnl 2f* **25/1**

5062 **8** *¾* **Naledi**[17] 5508 8-8-8 **48** DanielMuscutt[(7)] 9 29
(Richard Price) *a towards rr* **10/1**

0000 **9** *8* **Sir Lexington (IRE)**[20] 5629 3-8-12 **52** (b) KieranO'Neill 2 17
(Richard Hannon) *chsd ldr tl rdn and wknd over 4f out* **33/1**

2m 9.09s (-1.91) **Going Correction** -0.225s/f (Firm)
WFA 3 from 4yo+ 7lb 9 Ran SP% **112.0**
Speed ratings (Par 101): **98,96,94,92,92 89,86,86,79**
Tote Swingers 1&2 £1.10, 2&3 £3.80, 1&3 £6.60 CSF £10.23 CT £40.91 TOTE £4.00: £1.30, £2.20, £2.50; EX 5.90.
Owner Celtic Contractors Limited **Bred** Harry Sweeney **Trained** Epsom, Surrey

FOCUS
A pair on in-form runners came to the fore in the first division of this low-grade handicap. It was the faster division by 1.89sec. The winner is rated close to his old best.

6231 BATHWICK TYRES TROWBRIDGE H'CAP (DIV II) 1m 2f 46y
4:40 (4:42) (Class 6) (0-60,59) 3-Y-0+ **£2,070** (£616; £307; £153) **Stalls** Low

Form RPR

0611 **1** **Enriching (USA)**[20] 5632 4-9-12 **59** ShaneKelly 2 65+
(Lydia Pearce) *wnt 2nd after 2f: rdn over 2f out: led wl over 1f out: drvn out fnl f* **7/4**[1]

050 **2** *1 ¼* **Elsie Bay**[15] 5795 3-9-0 **59** RachealKneller[(5)] 4 62
(Mark Usher) *chsd ldr 2f: styd chsng ldrs: rdn and one pce over 2f out: styd on ins fnl f: tk 2nd clsng stages: nt rch wnr* **10/1**

5040 **3** *½* **Duneen Dream (USA)**[10] 5935 7-8-7 **45** DavidKenny[(5)] 5 47
(Nikki Evans) *led: rdn over 2f out: hdd wl over 1f out: one pce u.p fnl f: lost 2nd clsng stages* **16/1**

040/ **4** *1 ¼* **Surprise Us**[13] 7761 5-8-9 **49** DanielMuscutt[(7)] 3 49
(Bernard Llewellyn) *chsd ldrs: rdn and outpcd over 2f out: kpt on again fnl f* **8/1**

4254 **5** *nse* **Zuzu Angel (IRE)**[23] 5506 3-9-3 **57** EddieAhern 6 56
(William Knight) *in tch: pushed along and lost position over 3f out: drvn 2f out: styd on but edgd lft appr fnl f: nt rch ldrs* **2/1**[2]

00 **6** *2 ¾* **Cash Injection**[23] 5508 3-8-4 **47** (t) RaulDaSilva[(3)] 7 41
(Karen George) *rdn in rr over 3f out: nvr gng pce to get into contention* **7/1**[3]

0050 **7** *5* **Gallego**[4] 6120 10-9-1 **53** BrendanPowell[(5)] 8 37
(Richard Price) *slowly away: in rr: hdwy on outer over 3f out: sn rdn: btn 2f out* **14/1**

2m 10.98s (-0.02) **Going Correction** -0.225s/f (Firm)
WFA 3 from 4yo+ 7lb 7 Ran SP% **114.9**
Speed ratings (Par 101): **91,90,89,88,88 86,82**
Tote Swingers 1&2 £4.50, 2&3 £11.30, 1&3 £4.90 CSF £20.25 CT £212.40 TOTE £2.20: £1.60, £4.80; EX 15.30.
Owner Franconson Partners **Bred** Adena Springs **Trained** Newmarket, Suffolk

FOCUS
Little got into this off what was an ordinary gallop. The time was slower than the first division by 1.89sec. The form is a bit shaky and is rated cautiously.

6232 BATHWICK TYRES SWINDON H'CAP 1m 5f 22y
5:10 (5:10) (Class 6) (0-60,68) 3-Y-0+ **£2,181** (£644; £322) **Stalls** High

Form RPR

6246 **1** **Beneath**[17] 5164 5-9-3 **56** (t) WilliamTwiston-Davies[(7)] 6 65
(Neil Mulholland) *hld up in rr: pushed along 5f out: hdwy on outer 3f out: drvn to chal over 1f out: slt ld ins fnl f: drvn out* **20/1**

0062 **2** *1* **Pelham Crescent (IRE)**[5] 6097 9-9-6 **55** RaulDaSilva[(3)] 12 62
(Bryn Palling) *in tch: chsd ldrs fr 6f out: wnt 2nd 3f out: led sn after: jnd over 1f out: hdd u.p ins fnl f: no ex* **7/2**[2]

0332 **3** *2 ½* **Thundering Home**[10] 5936 5-9-6 **57** DavidKenny[(5)] 4 60
(Richard Mitchell) *in rr: pushed along over 3f out: styd on fr over 1f out to take 3rd fnl 75yds* **10/1**

0536 **4** *3* **Comedy House**[10] 5936 4-9-11 **57** JamieGoldstein 9 56
(Michael Madgwick) *led 1f: chsd ldr: chal 2f out tl wknd fr 1f out* **10/1**

-060 **5** *nse* **Cityar (FR)**[5] 6098 8-8-9 **46** (p) BrendanPowell[(5)] 2 45
(John O'Shea) *chsd ldrs: rdn 3f out: one pce fnl 2f* **33/1**

4041 **6** *6* **Panettone (IRE)**[8] 5989 3-9-9 **68** (b) DominicFox[(3)] 11 58
(Roger Varian) *in tch: rdn and hung rt 5f out: hrd drvn over 3f out and no ch after* **11/8**[1]

0405 **7** *3* **Maccabees**[10] 5939 3-8-2 **51** JoshBaudains[(7)] 1 36
(Roger Curtis) *slowly away: plld hrd in rr: c wd and sme prog over 2f out: nvr any ch* **12/1**

-066 **8** *8* **Nha Trang (IRE)**[20] 5638 5-9-0 **46** oh1 (b) KieranO'Neill 5 19
(Michael Appleby) *t.k.h: led after 1f: hdd ins fnl 3f: sn wknd* **40/1**

0331 **9** *2 ¼* **Arch Event**[14] 5817 7-8-12 **51** (p) DanielMuscutt[(7)] 13 21
(Bernard Llewellyn) *chsd ldrs: rdn 4f out and sn btn* **7/1**[3]

4633 **10** *1 ¾* **Bazart**[30] 5265 10-9-7 **58** (tp) RobertWilliams[(5)] 7 25
(Bernard Llewellyn) *in tch: chsd ldrs fr 6f out tl rdn and wknd fr 4f out* **14/1**

2m 50.38s (-1.62) **Going Correction** -0.225s/f (Firm)
WFA 3 from 4yo+ 10lb 10 Ran SP% **119.5**
Speed ratings (Par 101): **95,94,92,91,90 87,85,80,79,78**
Tote Swingers 1&2 £16.60, 2&3 £3.80, 1&3 £23.50 CSF £89.91 CT £770.24 TOTE £25.60: £5.50, £2.40, £2.70; EX 146.60.
Owner Wellcroomed T/A eyewearoutlet.co.uk **Bred** Millsec Limited **Trained** Limpley Stoke, Wilts
■ Stewards' Enquiry : Kieran O'Neill one-day ban: careless riding (Sep 30)

FOCUS
A moderate handicap, but it was sound run. The winner is rated to his AW winter form.

6233 BATHWICK TYRES APPRENTICE H'CAP 5f 161y
5:40 (5:42) (Class 6) (0-60,60) 3-Y-0+ **£2,070** (£616; £307; £153) **Stalls** Centre

Form RPR

2004 **1** **Amber Heights**[30] 5279 4-9-0 **56** AmyScott[(3)] 2 65
(Henry Candy) *s.i.s: sn chsng ldrs: led over 1f out: hrd rdn: styd on wl clsng stages* **7/1**[3]

04 **2** *½* **Brandywell Boy (IRE)**[10] 5937 9-8-3 **47** (t) JoshBaudains[(5)] 10 54
(Dominic Ffrench Davis) *chsd ldrs: rdn over 2f out: styd on to chse wnr fnl f: kpt on but a hld* **14/1**

0000 **3** *4 ½* **Adaeze (IRE)**[23] 5504 4-8-7 **49** (v[1]) MatthewLawson[(3)] 12 41
(Jonathan Portman) *s.i.s: in rr: hdwy 2f out: styd on to take 3rd fnl f: no imp on ldng duo* **20/1**

4005 **4** *1 ¾* **Forty Proof (IRE)**[8] 6002 4-8-4 **48** (t) NathanSweeney[(5)] 5 34
(David Evans) *chsd ldrs: rdn 3f out: one pce fr over 1f out* **12/1**

2056 **5** *1* **The Name Is Frank**[12] 5874 7-9-3 **59** (t) BrendanPowell[(3)] 13 42
(Mark Gillard) *in tch: rdn to chse ldrs 1/2-way: one pce fr over 1f out* **8/1**

0210 **6** *4* **Kyllachy Storm**[23] 5502 8-9-2 **60** PhilipPrince[(5)] 7 30
(Ron Hodges) *slt ld tl hdd 3f out: wknd 2f out* **7/2**[1]

4330 **7** *nk* **Even Bolder**[22] 5531 9-8-12 **58** JoeyHaynes[(7)] 4 27
(Eric Wheeler) *led 3f out: hdd & wknd over 1f out* **14/1**

5-46 **8** *1 ¼* **Lady Heartbeat**[8] 5994 3-8-4 **50** ow2 RyanWhile[(5)] 3 15
(Michael Blanshard) *in rr: drvn 3f out: styd on fnl f: nvr a threat* **16/1**

4500 **9** *nk* **The Jailer**[37] 4993 9-8-4 **48** (p) DanielMuscutt[(5)] 11 12
(John O'Shea) *pressed ldrs over 3f* **16/1**

5430 **10** *nse* **Yanza**[82] 3435 6-8-8 **52** RachealKneller[(5)] 8 16
(Pam Ford) *in rr: sme late hdwy* **33/1**

4542 **11** *1 ¼* **Depden (IRE)**[10] 5937 4-8-2 **46** JackDuern[(5)] 1 5
(Richard Price) *rdn 1/2-way: a in rr* **7/1**[3]

2236 **12** *½* **Alpha Tauri (USA)**[54] 4401 6-8-10 **52** (p) AshleyMorgan[(3)] 6 10
(Charles Smith) *pressed ldrs 3f* **9/2**[2]

0060 **13** *4 ½* **Crabbies Ginger**[51] 4493 4-8-5 **47** oh1 ow1 DavidKenny[(3)] 14
(Lisa Williamson) *s.i.s: in rr: sme hdwy 3f out: sn wknd* **33/1**

5066 **14** *1 ¾* **Tenderly Place**[25] 5458 3-8-5 **46** oh1 (t) RaulDaSilva 9
(William Knight) *s.i.s: outpcd* **28/1**

1m 10.93s (-0.27) **Going Correction** -0.15s/f (Firm)
WFA 3 from 4yo+ 2lb 14 Ran SP% **123.4**
Speed ratings (Par 101): **95,94,88,86,84 79,78,77,76,76 75,74,68,66**
Tote Swingers 1&2 £23.90, 2&3 £74.40, 1&3 £35.40 CSF £99.44 CT £1933.60 TOTE £8.00: £2.50, £3.10, £5.60; EX 108.40.
Owner Ms L Burns **Bred** Howard Barton Stud **Trained** Kingston Warren, Oxon

FOCUS
The front pair drew clear in this low-grade sprint, with the leaders appearing to go off too fast. The first pair were clear and the winner is rated to his AW mark.
Adaeze(IRE) Official explanation: jockey said filly hung left
T/Plt: £67.90 to a £1 stake. Pool: £55,145.61 - 592.54 winning tickets. T/Qpdt: £2.20 to a £1 stake. Pool: £4,218.90 - 1,357.50 winning tickets. ST

6188 CHESTER (L-H)
Saturday, September 15

OFFICIAL GOING: Good (good to soft in places; 7.4)
Rail between 6f and 1.5f moved out further 3yds from Friday making 6yds in total adding 20yd to race 1, 22yd to 5, 26yd to 7, 38yd to 3 and 24yd to rest.
Wind: Light, half behind Weather: Sunny

6234 NEW FASHIONED BANKING H'CAP 5f 16y
1:40 (1:41) (Class 4) (0-85,84) 3-Y-0+ **£5,175** (£1,540; £769; £384) **Stalls** Low

Form RPR

2152 **1** **Cruise Tothelimit (IRE)**[37] 4999 4-8-9 **75** RyanPowell[(3)] 4 84
(Ian Williams) *trckd ldrs: wnt 2nd over 1f out: sn rdn: led wl ins fnl f: r.o* **4/1**[1]

0040 **2** *½* **Bubbly Ballerina**[21] 5584 3-8-8 **77** NatashaEaton[(5)] 3 84
(Alan Bailey) *prom: rdn and sltly outpcd over 1f out: rallied ins fnl f: r.o wl towards fin* **11/1**

1033 **3** *hd* **Beau Mistral (IRE)**[8] 6006 3-9-5 **83** SilvestreDeSousa 1 89
(Paul Green) *w ldr: led 3f out: rdn over 1f out: hdd wl ins fnl f: no ex cl home* **4/1**[1]

3310 **4** *1* **Crimson Knot (IRE)**[22] 5539 4-9-4 **81** RobertWinston 5 83
(Alan Berry) *towards rr: pushed along and hdwy on inner 1/2-way: chsd ldrs and cl up over 1f out: styd on same pce towards fin* **11/1**

260 **5** *1 ¼* **Soap Wars**[14] 5832 7-9-5 **82** MichaelHills 6 80+
(Hugo Palmer) *midfield: hmpd whn n.m.r under 3f out: hdwy to chse ldrs over 1f out: styd on ins fnl f: no imp on ldrs* **20/1**

0001 **6** *¾* **Hamoody (USA)**[8] 6005 8-9-5 **82** PatCosgrave 11 77+
(David Nicholls) *awkward s: bhd: checked whn nt clr run 1/2-way: hdwy over 1f out: r.o ins fnl f: nrst fin* **18/1**

6530 **7** *2 ½* **Waseem Faris (IRE)**[19] 5663 3-9-6 **84** MatthewDavies 7 70
(Mick Channon) *midfield: rdn 2f out: kpt on same pce fnl f: no imp on ldrs* **11/1**

221 **8** *1* **Wild Sauce**[38] 4953 3-9-2 **80** (b) TomEaves 12 63
(Bryan Smart) *hld up: rdn over 1f out: kpt on ins fnl f: nvr able to get on terms* **14/1**

5542 **9** *2* **Green Park (IRE)**[8] 6009 9-8-9 **79** (b) LukeLeadbitter[(7)] 9 54
(Declan Carroll) *in tch: rdn and outpcd over 1f out: dropped away* **10/1**[3]

6034 **10** *nk* **Jamesway (IRE)**[52] 4451 4-9-3 **80** JamesSullivan 2 54
(Ruth Carr) *led to 3f out: remained prom: rdn over 1f out: wknd ins fnl f* **7/1**[2]

0100 **11** *2 ¼* **Dispol Grand (IRE)**[8] 6006 6-8-10 **73** RussKennemore 13 39
(Paul Midgley) *towards rr: outpcd 2f out: nvr a factor* **66/1**

5003 **12** *6* **Diman Waters (IRE)**[4] 6123 5-8-8 **71** TadhgO'Shea 10 16
(Eric Alston) *chsd ldrs on outer: pushed and wknd 1/2-way* **14/1**

2504 **13** *9* **Sonko (IRE)**[40] 4881 3-9-4 **82** (p) FrannyNorton 14
(Tim Pitt) *prom on wd outside: niggled along 3f out: wknd 1/2-way* **28/1**

060 **14** *2 ¼* **Bertoliver**[46] 4690 8-8-8 **71** DavidProbert 8
(Stuart Williams) *in tch: n.m.r and squeezed out 2f out: bhd after* **20/1**

1m 3.12s (2.12) **Going Correction** +0.55s/f (Yiel)
WFA 3 from 4yo+ 1lb 14 Ran SP% **119.7**
Speed ratings (Par 105): **105,104,103,102,100 99,95,93,90,89 86,76,62,58**
Tote Swingers: 1&2 £25.00, 1&3 £4.00, 2&3 £14.80 CSF £46.53 CT £168.77 TOTE £4.00: £1.30, £2.50, £1.90; EX 48.00 Trifecta £301.70 Part won. Pool: £407.82 - 0.60 winning tickets..
Owner Odysian Ltd T/A Cruise Nightspot **Bred** D And Mrs D Veitch **Trained** Portway, Worcs

FOCUS
A decent competitive sprint handicap, run at a fair gallop which suited those racing close up to the pace. The first five home were drawn 4,3,1,5,6. The second and third set the standard.

6235 FREE BET AT CORBETTSPORTS.COM H'CAP 7f 122y
2:10 (2:11) (Class 3) (0-90,90) 3-Y-0+ **£8,409** (£2,502; £1,250; £625) **Stalls** Low

Form RPR

1242 **1** **Chosen Character (IRE)**[11] 5914 4-9-2 **82** (vt) FrannyNorton 10 93
(Tom Dascombe) *mde all: rdn 2f out: hrd pressed and jnd ins fnl f: gamely plld out more towards fin* **8/1**[3]

4021 **2** *hd* **Dream Tune**[30] 5276 3-9-2 **87** SilvestreDeSousa 5 97
(Clive Cox) *chsd wnr: rdn over 1f out: hanging lft whn chalng upsides ins fnl f: jst hld towards fin* **11/4**[1]

3410 **3** 2 **Redvers (IRE)**[28] 5356 4-9-9 **89**.....(b) RobertWinston 12 94
(Ed Vaughan) *hld up: plld out and hdwy over 1f out: edgd lft and r.o ins fnl f: nt rch front pair* **25/1**

-041 **4** ½ **Roninski (IRE)**[35] 5110 4-9-6 **86**..... TomEaves 7 90
(Bryan Smart) *chsd ldrs: rdn and nt qckn over 1f out: styd on same pce and hld ins fnl f* **16/1**

0415 **5** 1¼ **Uppercut**[22] 5535 4-9-3 **83**..... PatCosgrave 3 84+
(Stuart Kittow) *n.m.r s: pushed along early in rr div: rdn and hdwy over 1f out: styd on ins fnl f: nt trble ldrs* **15/2**[2]

1216 **6** nk **Hayek**[7] 6047 5-8-5 **76**.....(b) AdamCarter(5) 17 76+
(Tim Easterby) *hld up in rr: effrt on wd outside 2f out: hdwy over 1f out: styd on ins fnl f: nt rch ldrs* **33/1**

2050 **7** 1 **Al Muheer (IRE)**[23] 5517 7-9-8 **88**.....(b) JamesSullivan 16 85
(Ruth Carr) *hld up in rr: rdn and hdwy over 1f out: styd on ins fnl f: nvr nrr* **33/1**

6124 **8** ½ **Venutius**[42] 4828 5-9-7 **87**..... TadhgO'Shea 15 83
(Ed McMahon) *trckd ldrs: rdn over 2f out: no imp over 1f out: wknd ins fnl f* **12/1**

6000 **9** ½ **Viva Ronaldo (IRE)**[14] 5827 6-9-3 **83**..... TonyHamilton 14 78
(Richard Fahey) *in rr: pushed along 2f out: kpt on fnl f: nvr able to get on terms* **16/1**

614 **10** 1¾ **Rigolleto (IRE)**[22] 5530 4-8-11 **77**..... MatthewDavies 6 68
(Mick Channon) *midfield: pushed along over 2f out: outpcd over 1f out: n.d after* **18/1**

2055 **11** hd **Kingscroft (IRE)**[4] 6119 4-9-4 **84**..... LiamJones 2 74
(Mark Johnston) *midfield: pushed along 3f out: effrt on inner 2f out: no imp on ldrs: wknd wl ins fnl f* **9/1**

011 **12** 5 **Bravo Echo**[11] 5906 6-9-3 **83**..... J-PGuillambert 1 61
(Michael Attwater) *trckd ldrs: pushed along 2f out: wknd over 1f out: eased whn btn ins fnl f* **17/2**

2104 **13** 2¼ **Corporal Maddox**[28] 5342 5-9-10 **90**..... JimCrowley 9 62
(Patrick Morris) *midfield tl pushed along and wknd 2f out* **8/1**[3]

0300 **14** ¾ **George Benjamin**[14] 5819 5-8-5 **76**..... LeonnaMayor(5) 11 46
(Christopher Kellett) *midfield tl wknd over 3f out* **80/1**

5300 **15** 2¼ **Layla's Hero (IRE)**[112] 2489 5-9-7 **87**.....(p) StephenCraine 8 51
(Patrick Morris) *midfield tl rdn and wknd 2f out* **25/1**

1m 36.23s (2.43) **Going Correction** +0.55s/f (Yiel)
WFA 3 from 4yo+ 5lb **15** Ran SP% **120.7**
Speed ratings (Par 107): **109,108,106,106,105 104,103,103,102,101 100,95,93,92,90**
Tote Swingers: 1&2 £3.00, 1&3 £12.30, 2&3 £13.40 CSF £28.49 CT £556.88 TOTE £8.40: £3.10, £1.40, £12.40; EX 33.70 TRIFECTA Not won..
Owner Aykroyd And Sons Ltd **Bred** Moyglare Stud Farm Ltd **Trained** Malpas, Cheshire

FOCUS
A most competitve handicap run at a solid pace where once again it paid to race handy. The winner is rated in line with his recent form.

NOTEBOOK
Chosen Character(IRE), back on a favoured left-handed track, showed bright pace to get away in front from stall 10 and despite setting a sound pace, showed a willing attitude to hold on inside the final furlong, under a fine ride off a mark 6lb higher than when last successful.
Dream Tune was well found in the market off a mark of 87 on his handicap debut, and he looked like picking the winner up late on but, just lost out to a progressive type. He was some way clear of the third. (op 7-2)
Redvers(IRE), who appreciated the return to an easier surface having disappointed on good to firm at Newbury last time, made good late progress, confirming the form that saw him land a competitive ladies' race at Ascot in July. (op 20-1)
Roninski(IRE) landed a Redcar handicap on his second start for connections last time and he ran well here off a 6lb higher mark, but was unable to pick up inside the final furlong, on ground softer then ideal. (op 14-1)
Uppercut, who tends to show his best form going right-handed, could not take advantage of his low draw but was closing well for pressure up the straight over this inadequate trip. (op 9-1)
Hayek was in rear and had to come widest of all round the home turn, but he closed well up the straight and tends to show his best over 1m. (op 25-1)
Kingscroft(IRE) was handicapped to go close but, having missed the kick from his low draw, showed little sparkle and has yet to hit the form of last season. (tchd 17-2 and 10-1)

6236 MINSTRELL RECRUITMENT STAND CUP (LISTED RACE) 1m 4f 66y
2:40 (2:40) (Class 1) 3-Y-O+ **£19,536** (£7,388; £3,692; £1,844) **Stalls** Low

Form RPR

6622 **1** **Goldoni (IRE)**[21] 5593 3-8-6 99..... DavidProbert 3 101
(Andrew Balding) *chsd ldrs: wnt 2nd after 3f: led jst over 2f out: rdn and over 2 l clr over 1f out: a doing enough and hld on wl towards fin* **11/4**[2]

2450 **2** ½ **Naseem Alyasmeen (IRE)**[14] 5826 3-8-1 92..... JamesSullivan 1 96
(Mick Channon) *led for 1f: remained prom: rdn and chsd wnr over 1f out: swtchd lft ins fnl f: styd on wl towards fin but hld* **11/1**

0635 **3** 1 **Good Morning Star (IRE)**[44] 4738 3-8-6 97..... FrannyNorton 2 99
(Mark Johnston) *in tch: pushed along and outpcd over 2f out: effrt to chse ldrs over 1f out: styd on to take 3rd wl ins fnl f: nt trble front two* **17/2**

2460 **4** 1¾ **Glen's Diamond**[21] 5599 4-9-1 109..... TonyHamilton 6 96
(Richard Fahey) *led after 1f: hdd jst over 2f out: rdn over 1f out: kpt on same pce ins fnl f* **7/1**

1556 **5** 6 **Area Fifty One**[14] 5826 4-9-1 99..... JimCrowley 4 87
(Richard Fahey) *hld up: pushed along over 3f out: outpcd over 1f out: wl btn* **4/1**[3]

4633 **6** ¾ **Modun (IRE)**[7] 6035 5-9-1 110..... SilvestreDeSousa 5 85
(Saeed Bin Suroor) *in tch: effrt over 2f out: failed to pick-up over 1f out: sn dropped away* **2/1**[1]

1526 **7** 2 **Amoya (GER)**[13] 5856 5-8-10 82..... RobertWinston 7 77
(Philip McBride) *broke wl: sn stdd: hld up in rr: u.p 2f out: lft bhd over 1f out* **40/1**

2m 42.42s (3.92) **Going Correction** +0.55s/f (Yiel)
WFA 3 from 4yo+ 9lb 7 Ran SP% **113.8**
Speed ratings (Par 111): **108,107,107,105,101 101,100**
Tote Swingers: 1&2 £6.00, 1&3 £2.50, 2&3 £4.30 CSF £31.56 TOTE £3.60: £2.80, £11.90; EX 38.20.
Owner Mick and Janice Mariscotti **Bred** Marston Stud **Trained** Kingsclere, Hants

FOCUS
A modest Listed contest that was run at a steady pace with the field well strung out at the line. The form pair disappointed and the race has been rated cautiously.

NOTEBOOK
Goldoni(IRE) had run well on only his second start over this 1m4f trip when runner-up at Windsor (soft) last time and he was always travelling kindly behind the pace and saw the trip out well, having been sent to the front turning for home. With a number of his market rivals under-performing, this probably took little winning but he looks a progressive type with a game attitude. (op 3-1, tchd 7-2 in places)
Naseem Alyasmeen(IRE) had plenty to do on the figures and was over 8l behind the winner on her penultimate start off these terms, but she stayed on well to get much closer here and she is building up a most progressive profile this season. (tchd 10-1 and 12-1)
Good Morning Star(IRE), returning to the scene of her Cheshire Oaks triumph (11.4f, soft) in May, was under pressure some way out but stayed on strongly to the line. (op 8-1 tchd 9-1)
Glen's Diamond, who has been tried over a variety of trips this season without success, helped set the steady pace but dropped away tamely late on and is becoming disappointing. (op 11-2)
Modun(IRE), the top rated runner in the field, was not helped by the slow pace, but still showed precious little when the gallop quickened, on ground that was softer than he wants. His rider reported that the gelding had no more to give. The Stewards ordered the gelding to be routine tested. Official explanation: jockey said gelding had no more to give (op 9-4)

6237 STELLAR GROUP MAIDEN STKS 7f 2y
3:20 (3:22) (Class 4) 2-Y-O **£5,175** (£1,540; £769; £384) **Stalls** Low

Form RPR

1 **Gabrial's Kaka (IRE)** 2-9-3 0..... TonyHamilton 2 82+
(Richard Fahey) *mde all: drew clr over 1f out: wl in command after* **8/1**[3]

2 3¾ **Gabrial The Thug (FR)** 2-9-3 0..... JimCrowley 1 73+
(Richard Fahey) *in tch: outpcd over 2f out: styd on over 1f out: tk 2nd wl ins fnl f: no ch w wnr* **12/1**

3 ¾ **Gabrial's Wawa** 2-9-3 0..... TomEaves 3 71+
(Richard Fahey) *missed break: towards rr: nt clr run over 2f out: hdwy over 1f out: styd on ins fnl f* **16/1**

62 **4** 2¾ **Estifzaaz (IRE)**[15] 5793 2-9-3 0..... TadhgO'Shea 5 64
(Charles Hills) *w ldr tl faltered on bnd over 2f out: sn outpcd: wknd ins fnl f: sn lost 2nd* **4/9**[1]

56 **5** ½ **Mudaawem (USA)**[14] 5825 2-9-3 0..... FrannyNorton 8 64
(Mark Johnston) *midfield: pushed along 5f out: wl outpcd over 2f out: nvr a danger* **7/1**[2]

0344 **6** 3½ **Annie Besant**[15] 5806 2-8-12 53..... DavidProbert 6 49
(David C Griffiths) *chsd ldrs: rdn and outpcd over 2f out: wknd over 1f out* **50/1**

3 **7** 3¾ **Uncle Bernie (IRE)**[28] 5331 2-9-3 0..... J-PGuillambert 4 50
(Reg Hollinshead) *chsd ldrs: outpcd over 2f out: wknd over 1f out: eased whn wl btn ins fnl f* **7/1**[2]

8 1¼ **Ishi Amy** 2-8-7 0..... LeonnaMayor(5) 9 36
(Alastair Lidderdale) *upset in stalls: s.i.s: a in rr: struggling over 3f out: nvr on terms* **50/1**

9 31 **Cote Reveur** 2-8-12 0..... JimmyQuinn 7
(David C Griffiths) *s.i.s: in rr: outpcd over 3f out: nvr on terms: t.o* **50/1**

1m 31.45s (4.95) **Going Correction** +0.60s/f (Yiel) **9** Ran SP% **124.8**
Speed ratings (Par 97): **95,90,89,86,86 82,77,76,41**
Tote Swingers: 1&2 £3.40, 1&3 £6.40, 2&3 £8.80 CSF £103.71 TOTE £10.70: £2.50, £6.40, £7.40; EX 59.70 Trifecta £133.00 Pool: £1373.71 - 7.64 winning tickets..
Owner Dr Marwan Koukash **Bred** Dave Orme **Trained** Musley Bank, N Yorks

FOCUS
An uncompetitive maiden with two trainers responsible for five of the nine runners and Richard Fahey and Dr Marwan Koukash representatives filling the first three places. The sixth horse gives perspective to the form.

NOTEBOOK
Gabrial's Kaka(IRE), whose dam was a 5f/6f AW winner out of a Listed-placed 6f 2yo winner, was given a good mention prior to racing from his owner, and he ran out a convincing winner. He helped set the early fractions but looked in trouble when the well-backed favourite passed him 2f from home. However, his rider was still confident and he pulled clear again up the straight. This was a taking debut. (op 7-1)
Gabrial The Thug(FR), a half-brother to three French winners, as well as useful British hurdler/chaser Balzaccio, is bred to come into his own over further and he made significant late progress having been outpaced 3f out.
Gabrial's Wawa, whose price increased on all three occasions he went to the sales and is a half-brother to five winners, the best being Shesastar (RPR 93), also stayed on well for pressure and is another who can be expected to come on plenty for this debut. (op 12-1)
Estifzaaz(IRE), whose last run when second at Sandown set a clear standard for the rest of the field, was heavily supported but he dropped away tamely having been sent to the front over 2f out. He raced too freely early on and may have been seen to better effect with a more patient ride but, this was still a disappointing effort. (op 8-11)
Mudaawem(USA), was under pressure some way from home before doing his best work late on and is now qualified for a mark. (op 13-2 tchd 6-1)

6238 HERTZ CAR HIRE NURSERY 5f 110y
3:55 (4:00) (Class 3) (0-95,92) 2-Y-O **£7,246** (£2,168; £1,084; £542; £270) **Stalls** Low

Form RPR

150 **1** **Secret Look**[35] 5088 2-8-10 **81**..... RobertWinston 1 85+
(Ed McMahon) *chsd ldrs: rdn to ld 1f out: pressed wl ins fnl f: r.o and fnd ex towards fin* **9/2**[3]

4316 **2** 1½ **Effie B**[11] 5909 2-8-12 **83**..... MatthewDavies 4 82
(Mick Channon) *in tch: pushed along over 4f out: rdn over 1f out: r.o to take 2nd wl ins fnl f and sn chalng: outpcd by wnr towards fin* **14/1**

4251 **3** 1 **New Fforest**[7] 6054 2-9-1 **86**..... DavidProbert 6 82
(Andrew Balding) *s.i.s: in rr: hdwy to chse ldrs over 3f out: rdn over 1f out: styd on ins fnl f but nt pce to chal front two* **4/1**[2]

1553 **4** 1¾ **Tipping Over (IRE)**[16] 5781 2-9-2 **87**..... MichaelHills 5 77
(Hugo Palmer) *hld up: pushed along wl over 1f out: kpt on ins fnl f: unable to chal* **8/1**

5025 **5** ½ **Storm Moon (USA)**[28] 5332 2-9-7 **92**..... FrannyNorton 8 80
(Mark Johnston) *w ldr: rdn whn chalng over 1f out: wknd ins fnl f* **4/1**[2]

41 **6** ½ **Time And Place**[27] 5382 2-8-3 **74**..... JimmyQuinn 2 61+
(Richard Fahey) *s.i.s: hld up: pushed along 2f out: rdn and hung lft over 1f out: no imp* **9/4**[1]

0315 **7** 2½ **Mandy Layla (IRE)**[14] 5828 2-8-11 **82**..... TomEaves 7 60
(Bryan Smart) *led: rdn over 1f out: sn hdd: wknd ins fnl f* **10/1**

1m 10.04s (3.84) **Going Correction** +0.60s/f (Yiel) **7** Ran SP% **115.8**
Speed ratings (Par 99): **98,96,94,92,91 91,87**
Tote Swingers: 1&2 £14.90, 1&3 £5.00, 2&3 £11.50 CSF £62.74 CT £272.87 TOTE £8.60: £3.80, £7.70; EX 98.80 Trifecta £773.40 Part won. Pool: £1045.20 - 0.72 winning tickets..
Owner S L Edwards **Bred** S L Edwards **Trained** Lichfield, Staffs

FOCUS
A decent nursery run at a strong gallop and unsurprisingly the leaders paid the price up the home straight. The form is rated though the second and third, to their marks.

NOTEBOOK
Secret Look, 1lb lower than when eighth on his nursery debut (5f, good) at Haydock last time, travelled comfortably behind the leaders and picked up again late, when pressed inside the final furlong. He was suited by the strong pace and won with a shade in hand. (tchd 7-2 and 6-1)
Effie B, 4lb higher than when readily scoring at Sandown (5f, good) two starts ago, stayed on well under pressure but could not quicken late on and lacks the scope of the winner. (tchd 16-1)
New Fforest missed the break and had to race wider than ideal on her handicap debut but was staying on well to the line and may be worth a try at 6f. (op 7-2 tchd 9-2)
Tipping Over(IRE) came widest of all into the straight and ran as though finding this too sharp. (op 13-2 tchd 9-1)

Storm Moon(USA) was well supported despite his poor draw but he got into a pace battle with Mandy Layla through the early part of the contest, which compromised the chances of both runners. (op 7-1)
Time And Place was unable to take advantage of his low draw and never looked happy on ground softer than he has encountered before. Official explanation: trainer's rep said colt missed the break (op 5-2 tchd 2-1)

6239 CHESHIRE OAKS H'CAP (DIV I) 7f 122y
4:30 (4:30) (Class 5) (0-75,75) 3-Y-O+ £3,881 (£1,155; £577; £288) Stalls Low

Form RPR
0210 1 **Frozen Over**[11] 5910 4-9-1 66 PatCosgrave 2 75
(Stuart Kittow) *hld up in tch: effrt over 2f out: rdn to ld 1f out: all out towards fin* 10/1
0100 2 nk **Rossetti**[11] 5910 4-9-7 72 TonyHamilton 10 80
(Ian Williams) *hld up: hdwy 2f out: swtchd lft over 1f out: r.o ins fnl f: pressed wnr towards fin* 9/1
6055 3 3/4 **Hoppy's Flyer (FR)**[1] 6194 4-8-10 61 oh4 RussKennemore 8 67
(Paul Midgley) *hld up: hdwy on inner over 1f out and carried lft: styd on ins fnl f: jst hld* 22/1
4003 4 3/4 **Glenridding**[12] 5893 8-9-2 70 (p) DaleSwift(3) 7 75
(James Given) *w ldr: rdn whn chalng over 1f out: stl ev ch ins fnl f: no ex towards fin* 14/1
1215 5 1 **Cyflymder (IRE)**[40] 4868 6-9-9 74 FrannyNorton 3 76
(David C Griffiths) *chsd ldrs: rdn over 1f out: styd on same pce ins fnl f* 5/1[2]
0010 6 3/4 **Illustrious Prince (IRE)**[7] 6044 5-9-0 72 (t) LukeLeadbitter(7) 4 72
(Declan Carroll) *hld up: hdwy 2f out: rdn over 1f out: no imp after* 9/1
6003 7 1/2 **Quick Bite (IRE)**[19] 5671 3-9-5 75 (v[1]) RobertWinston 6 74
(Hugo Palmer) *racd keenly: led: rdn over 1f out: sn hdd: wknd fnl 100yds* 8/1
2304 8 2 1/4 **My Single Malt (IRE)**[15] 5802 4-9-5 73 RyanPowell(3) 5 66
(Julie Camacho) *in tch: rdn 2f out: one pce over 1f out: no imp after* 6/1[3]
3150 9 1 3/4 **Know No Fear**[14] 5838 7-9-1 71 (p) LeonnaMayor(5) 11 60
(Alastair Lidderdale) *hld up: hdwy into midfield over 3f out: rdn and wknd over 2f out* 16/1
422 10 5 **Lady Layla**[7] 6050 3-9-2 72 TomEaves 1 48
(Bryan Smart) *chsd ldrs tl rdn and wknd 2f out* 4/1[1]
6053 11 1 1/2 **Early Applause**[29] 5322 4-9-6 71 MichaelHills 9 44
(Charles Hills) *a bhd: pushed along over 5f out: nvr on terms* 17/2

1m 38.26s (4.46) **Going Correction** +0.65s/f (Yiel)
WFA 3 from 4yo+ 5lb 11 Ran SP% 118.6
Speed ratings (Par 103): **103,102,101,101,100 99,98,96,94,89 88**
Tote Swingers: 1&2 £10.00, 1&3 £28.70, 2&3 £60.00 CSF £97.66 CT £1974.93 TOTE £14.70: £5.30, £3.50, £10.40; EX 182.80 TRIFECTA Not won..
Owner P A & M J Reditt **Bred** Manor Farm Packers Ltd **Trained** Blackborough, Devon

FOCUS
A competitive handicap run at a fair pace, with plenty in with a chance entering the final furlong. Ordinary form.
Frozen Over Official explanation: trainer said, regarding apparent improvement in form, that the gelding ran too keenly on its previous run and was better suited by being held up.
Quick Bite(IRE) Official explanation: jockey said filly lost its action
Early Applause Official explanation: jockey said gelding was outpaced throughout

6240 M&S BANK H'CAP 1m 2f 75y
5:05 (5:05) (Class 5) (0-75,75) 3-Y-O £3,881 (£1,155; £577; £288) Stalls High

Form RPR
2213 1 **Miss Cap Estel**[18] 5707 3-9-7 75 DavidProbert 10 84+
(Andrew Balding) *s.i.s: hld up in rr: hdwy on inner 2f out: nt clr run over 1f out: sn r.o to chal between horses: led ins fnl f: rdn out* 4/1[1]
1214 2 3/4 **Daddy Warbucks (IRE)**[17] 5736 3-9-7 75 PatCosgrave 7 81
(David Nicholls) *led: rdn and hdd jst over 1f out: nt qckn: edgd rt ins fnl f: rallied towards fin but hld* 7/1
56 3 3/4 **Gabrial's King (IRE)**[82] 3448 3-9-1 69 StephenCraine 1 74
(Ian Williams) *chsd ldrs: rdn to ld jst over 1f out: hdd ins fnl f: styd on same pce and hld towards fin* 6/1[3]
6351 4 1 **Buster Brown (IRE)**[29] 5312 3-9-0 71 DaleSwift(3) 5 74+
(James Given) *midfield: pushed along 2f out: effrt whn nt clr run fr over 1f out and again sn after: nt qckn jst ins fnl f: styd on and clsd towards fin* 4/1[1]
5 1/2 **Time Of My Life (IRE)**[50] 4563 3-9-6 74 JamesSullivan 2 76
(Patrick Holmes) *chsd ldrs: effrt 2f out: styd on same pce ins fnl f* 14/1
4451 6 1/2 **Darling Lexi (IRE)**[28] 5336 3-8-8 62 JimCrowley 6 63
(Richard Fahey) *sn chsd ldr tl rdn over 1f out: one pce ins fnl f* 9/2[2]
443 7 3 **Badea**[60] 4188 3-9-1 69 (p) TonyHamilton 3 65
(Richard Fahey) *midfield: pushed along over 4f out: lost pl over 3f out: bhd 2f out: plugged on wout threatening ins fnl f* 10/1
5010 8 1 1/4 **Rockgoat (IRE)**[18] 5721 3-9-1 69 (v[1]) TomEaves 4 62
(Ian McInnes) *hld up: rdn on outer over 2f out: sn outpcd* 28/1
1455 9 hd **Sir Fredlot (IRE)**[23] 5512 3-9-7 75 MichaelHills 8 68
(Charles Hills) *hld up: hdwy on outer 2f out: no imp on ldrs: wknd over 1f out* 9/1
1046 10 17 **Foursquare Funtime**[18] 5721 3-9-0 68 RobertWinston 9 28
(Reg Hollinshead) *hld up: pushed along 2f out: no imp: dropped away over 1f out* 33/1

2m 17.05s (5.85) **Going Correction** +0.65s/f (Yiel) 10 Ran SP% 117.1
Speed ratings (Par 101): **102,101,100,100,99 99,96,95,95,82**
Tote Swingers: 1&2 £5.50, 1&3 £6.20, 2&3 £9.50 CSF £32.42 CT £167.65 TOTE £4.20: £2.00, £3.50, £1.20; EX 25.90 Trifecta £219.20 Pool: £367.42 - 1.24 winning tickets..
Owner J L C Pearce **Bred** J L C Pearce **Trained** Kingsclere, Hants

FOCUS
A wide open handicap run at a fair pace, with an impressive winner bucking the trend of the day, in coming from the rear. Sound enough form, rated around the second and third.

6241 CHESHIRE OAKS H'CAP (DIV II) 7f 122y
5:35 (5:36) (Class 5) (0-75,73) 3-Y-O+ £3,881 (£1,155; £577; £288) Stalls Low

Form RPR
3536 1 **Copperwood**[14] 5819 7-9-9 72 FrannyNorton 7 80
(Mark Johnston) *trckd ldrs: rdn to ld over 1f out: jnd ins fnl f: gamely fnd ex towards fin* 11/2[3]
3451 2 nk **Kingswinford (IRE)**[13] 5852 6-9-5 73 KatiaScallan(5) 8 80
(Alastair Lidderdale) *hld up in midfield: hdwy over 1f out: upsides wnr ins fnl f: hld towards fin* 8/1
1044 3 1 **King Of Paradise (IRE)**[17] 5732 3-9-0 68 TadhgO'Shea 11 73
(Eric Alston) *hld up in rr: rdn and hdwy on outer over 1f out: chsng ldrs whn hung lft ins fnl f: styd on* 8/1
0620 4 1/2 **Striker Torres (IRE)**[31] 5225 6-9-3 66 (v) TomEaves 10 70
(Ian McInnes) *hld up: rdn and hdwy over 1f out: chsd ldrs ins fnl f: one pce towards fin* 14/1
5301 5 hd **Nezami (IRE)**[19] 5658 7-9-7 70 (b) RussKennemore 4 73
(Patrick Clinton) *racd keenly in midfield: nt clr run over 2f out: effrt to chse ldrs over 1f out: swtchd lft ins fnl f: styd on same pce towards fin* 6/1
3401 6 7 **First Class Favour (IRE)**[17] 5731 4-9-8 71 JamesSullivan 1 57
(Tim Easterby) *trckd ldrs: u.p over 1f out: wknd ins fnl f* 9/2[1]
460 7 3 **Light From Mars**[11] 5910 7-9-10 73 JimCrowley 5 51
(Patrick Morris) *chsd ldr tl rdn over 1f out: wknd ins fnl f* 9/2[1]
0045 8 3/4 **Rulesn'regulations**[20] 5630 6-9-9 72 (b) PatCosgrave 9 48
(Matthew Salaman) *hld up: hdwy into midfield over 3f out: rdn and wknd over 2f out* 14/1
0003 9 10 **One Scoop Or Two**[26] 5429 6-9-7 70 (p) J-PGuillambert 3 21
(Reg Hollinshead) *led: rdn and hdd over 1f out: wknd ins fnl f* 5/1[2]

1m 38.51s (4.71) **Going Correction** +0.65s/f (Yiel)
WFA 3 from 4yo+ 5lb 9 Ran SP% 118.3
Speed ratings (Par 103): **102,101,100,100,100 93,90,89,79**
Tote Swingers: 1&2 £9.30, 1&3 £8.80, 2&3 £8.20 CSF £50.01 CT £357.11 TOTE £6.70: £1.60, £3.30, £2.40; EX 59.60 Trifecta £334.70 Part won. Pool: £452.38 - 0.82 winning tickets..
Owner Always Trying Partnership VIII (E) **Bred** Hertford Offset Press **Trained** Middleham Moor, N Yorks

FOCUS
Another wide-open handicap, run at a sound pace with the front two fighting out an exciting finish. It was the slowest of the three C&D times and the form is ordinary.
Nezami(IRE) Official explanation: jockey said gelding was denied a clear run
T/Plt: £10,215.40 to a £1 stake. Pool: £71,368.14 - 5.10 winning tickets. T/Qpdt: Part won. £2,512.90 to a £1 stake. Pool: £3,395.82 - 0.40 winning tickets. £2,037.49 carried forward. DO

6196 DONCASTER (L-H)
Saturday, September 15

OFFICIAL GOING: Good (good to firm in places; 9.0)
Wind: light 1/2 against Weather: fine and sunny

6242 HARRIET POWELL H'CAP 1m (S)
1:50 (1:50) (Class 2) (0-110,104) 3-Y-O+ £12,938 (£3,850; £1,924; £962) Stalls High

Form RPR
0402 1 **Quick Wit**[35] 5102 5-9-10 104 WilliamBuick 3 112
(Saeed Bin Suroor) *wnt rt s: trckd ldrs: drvn over 2f out: styd on to ld last 100yds: hld on nr fin* 6/1[3]
2110 2 3/4 **Anderiego (IRE)**[23] 5517 4-8-12 92 DanielTudhope 1 98
(David O'Meara) *hld up in rr: hdwy over 2f out: led 1f out: hdd last 100yds: no ex* 7/1
5340 3 nk **Invisible Man**[23] 5517 6-9-10 104 (v) FrankieDettori 4 110
(Saeed Bin Suroor) *dwlt and sltly hmpd s: hld up in rr: swtchd rt over 1f out: str run but lft w too much to do* 5/1[2]
-236 4 1 1/2 **Jake's Destiny (IRE)**[44] 4740 3-8-5 90 PaulHanagan 11 92
(George Baker) *swtchd lft after s: chsd ldrs: rdn and hung lft over 1f out: kpt on same pce* 7/2[1]
0203 5 3/4 **Mabait**[7] 6024 6-8-13 98 LauraPike(5) 7 98
(David Simcock) *mid-div: effrt over 2f out: one pce over 1f out* 14/1
0260 6 hd **Bancnuanaheireann (IRE)**[29] 5301 5-8-11 91 RichardHughes 9 91
(Michael Appleby) *chsd ldrs: drvn 3f out: one pce whn slighly hmpd over 1f out* 12/1
0506 7 1 **Norse Blues**[28] 5356 4-8-10 90 oh2 JamesDoyle 5 88
(Sylvester Kirk) *led: qcknd pce 3f out: hdd 1f out: fdd towards fin* 11/1
5602 8 7 **St Moritz (IRE)**[19] 5677 6-9-6 100 AdrianNicholls 10 82
(David Nicholls) *chsd ldrs: drvn 3f out: wkng whn hmpd over 1f out* 9/1
2206 9 hd **Vainglory (USA)**[23] 5517 8-8-11 91 MartinLane 12 72
(David Simcock) *hld up in rr: nvr a factor* 16/1
-030 10 12 **Red Gulch**[212] 586 5-9-8 102 MickaelBarzalona 6 55
(Mahmood Al Zarooni) *in rr: drvn and hung rt over 2f out: sn bhd* 10/1
0303 11 30 **Mia's Boy**[72] 3784 8-8-12 92 AndreaAtzeni 8
(Chris Dwyer) *in rr: drvn 3f out: sn lost pl: bhd whn eased over 1f out: t.o* 12/1

1m 35.72s (-3.58) **Going Correction** -0.20s/f (Firm)
WFA 3 from 4yo+ 5lb 11 Ran SP% 121.0
Speed ratings (Par 109): **109,108,107,106,105 105,104,97,97,85 55**
Tote Swingers 1&2 £6.10, 2&3 £4.30, 1&3 £4.30 CSF £49.21 CT £195.45 TOTE £6.30: £1.70, £3.30, £2.30; EX 63.10 Trifecta £287.60 Pool: £1433.30 - 3.69 winning tickets..
Owner Godolphin **Bred** Ptarmigan Bloodstock Limited **Trained** Newmarket, Suffolk

FOCUS
Winning jockey William Buick called the ground "beautiful, borderline on the fast side". The time was just 0.2sec outside the track record, confirming it was riding quick. Two of the last four winners of this good handicap have gone on to win in the top grade, namely Virtual (Lockinge Stakes) and Capponi (also second in the Dubai World Cup), but this edition was short on progressive types. The top weight was rated 6lb below the race ceiling. The pace was solid and the main action took place down the centre of the track, with the first three coming out of the three lowest-numbered stalls. The first seven home finished in a bunch clear of the rest, but the form looks sound enough with the first two better than ever.

NOTEBOOK
Quick Wit, from the stable which won this last year, was one of the first under a shove, but he knuckled down well to take over inside the final furlong. Runner-up over 7f last time, he was suited by this truly-run mile and won't mind a return to further still. The Cambridgeshire must come into consideration for this tough sort, who picks up a 4lb penalty for Newmarket which will see him near the head of the weights. Man Of Action, the stable's winner of this last year, was a beaten favourite in the big autumn handicap. (tchd 11-2)
Anderiego(IRE) returned to form after being foiled in his bid for a York hat-trick, going on a furlong out and sticking on well. He has risen 16lb since joining his current trainer at the beginning of the campaign. (tchd 13-2)
Invisible Man, the winner's stablemate, should have finished closer. Held up, he was still swinging along in eighth a furlong and a half out, Frankie Dettori seemingly keen to delay his challenge in the anticipation that the leaders were going to start coming back to him. Dettori had to wait a few strides to switch around Mabait approaching the furlong pole and his mount picked up well down the stands' side from there, but the damage had been done. Without a win since the 2010 Royal Hunt Cup, Invisible Man met trouble at York last time and is no easy ride, but this was not Dettori at his best. (tchd 9-2)
Jake's Destiny(IRE), the only 3-y-o in the field, had his chance but seemed to hang under pressure and may have been wary of letting himself down on the ground, the quickest he's raced on so far. He's probably worth another chance. His rider confirmed the gelding had hung. Official explanation: jockey said gelding hung left-handed (op 9-2 tchd 5-1)
Mabait is on a decent mark and this was another respectable effort, but he is without a win for over two years now. (tchd 16-1)

Bancnuanaheireann(IRE) was briefly trapped in a pocket but it didn't make any significant difference to his eventual position. He has not been able to build on his Goodwood second on his debut for the stable. (op 10-1)
Norse Blues, who had his way in front but faded once headed, won the Spring Mile win over C&D off 85, and he has now been beaten all 12 times he has run off higher marks than that. Last year's Spring Mile winner Eton Forever went on to finish second in this. (op 14-1)
St Moritz(IRE) has become well handicapped and ran a better race at Ripon last time, but he could not get to the front and was disappointing. (op 8-1 tchd 7-1)
Mia's Boy Official explanation: jockey said gelding never travelled

6243 ONE CALL INSURANCE CHAMPAGNE STKS (GROUP 2) (C&G) 7f

2:25 (2:25) (Class 1) 2-Y-O **£46,558** (£17,651; £8,833; £4,400; £2,208) **Stalls** High

Form RPR
11 **1** **Toronado (IRE)**[56] 4318 2-8-12 0 RichardHughes 1 113+
(Richard Hannon) *mde all: qcknd pce after 2f: drvn 2f out: hld on gamely* **11/4**[2]

311 **2** ½ **Dundonnell (USA)**[24] 5488 2-8-12 106 JamesDoyle 5 112+
(Roger Charlton) *trckd ldng pair: hdwy 3f out: drvn and 2nd over 1f out: almost upsides ins fnl f: no ex nr fin* **5/6**[1]

1142 **3** 2¼ **Tha'Ir (IRE)**[14] 5833 2-8-12 108 FrankieDettori 3 106
(Saeed Bin Suroor) *trckd wnr: drvn over 2f out: hung rt over 1f out: styd on same pce* **9/2**[3]

1130 **4** ½ **Maxentius (IRE)**[45] 4698 2-8-12 104 WilliamBuick 2 105
(Peter Chapple-Hyam) *hld up in rr: hdwy and drvn over 2f out: kpt on same pce* **14/1**

1203 **5** ¾ **Birdman (IRE)**[20] 5642 2-8-12 108 MartinLane 6 103
(David Simcock) *hld up in rr: hdwy 3f out: sn drvn and chsng ldrs: kpt on same pce* **14/1**

1m 24.88s (-1.42) **Going Correction** -0.20s/f (Firm) **5** Ran SP% **112.7**
Speed ratings (Par 107): **100,99,96,96,95**
Tote Swingers 2&5 £2.60 CSF £5.63 TOTE £3.50: £1.80, £1.20; EX 5.70.
Owner Carmichael Humber **Bred** Paul Nataf **Trained** East Everleigh, Wilts
■ Stewards' Enquiry : William Buick two-day ban: used whip above permitted level (Oct 2-3)

FOCUS
This is usually a decent Group 2, and in 2006 Cockney Rebel was only third before taking the following year's 2000 Guineas. The latest running was an interesting contest, although the bare form looks a bit muddling as Toronado was allowed a totally uncontested lead, setting just an ordinary gallop, and the runner-up was inconvenienced. They raced on the stands' side. The form makes plenty of sense and the winner can probably rate higher again.

NOTEBOOK
Toronado(IRE) had won his first two starts over this trip, most recently an Ascot Listed event in July, but his rider feels 7f is his bare minimum. While he didn't exactly make this a true test, he was at a significant advantage in being allowed to dominate and had saved plenty to see off Dondonnell, who in contrast used plenty of energy when moving into a challenging position. If the front two were to meet again over this trip, then the runner-up could be expected to reverse form, but Toronado should be suited by going up in distance, even if it's unlikely he'll enjoy such a soft time in Group company again any time soon. (op 5-2 tchd 9-4)
Dundonnell(USA) ◆, much like when winning the Acomb Stakes, did not have the race run to suit, having to travel wide without cover to avoid being caught out when the pace lifted. He should be capable of better when finally getting a truly run race and he still looks worth his place in something like the Dewhurst. (op 10-11 tchd Evens)
Tha'Ir(IRE) found this tougher than the Solario Stakes, in which he was a close second, and is short of this level. (op 5-1 tchd 11-2)
Maxentius(IRE) ran better than in the Vintage Stakes last time, but he hasn't really gone on from his third in the Superlative Stakes, which was run on pretty bad ground.
Birdman(IRE) has shown his best form on a heavy surface was nowhere near as effective this time. (op 16-1)

6244 LADBROKES PORTLAND (H'CAP) 5f 140y

3:00 (3:02) (Class 2) 3-Y-O+

£37,350 (£11,184; £5,592; £2,796; £1,398; £702) **Stalls** High

Form RPR
3304 **1** **Doc Hay (USA)**[7] 6028 5-8-11 97 DanielTudhope 21 108
(David O'Meara) *dwlt: swtchd lft after s: hld up in rr: effrt and swtchd stands' side over 1f out: str run to ld nr fin* **20/1**

-122 **2** nk **Face The Problem (IRE)**[7] 6028 4-8-11 97 KierenFallon 18 107
(Jamie Osborne) *dwlt: in rr: gd hdwy over 2f out: led overall 100yds out: hdd fnl strides* **6/1**[2]

0000 **3** 1¼ **Secret Witness**[6] 6072 6-9-4 104 (b) JamesDoyle 12 110
(Ronald Harris) *chsd ldrs: kpt on wl fnl f* **33/1**

0610 **4** nk **Barnet Fair**[28] 5370 4-8-5 91 KierenFox 16 96
(Richard Guest) *trckd ldrs: upsides 1f out: edgd lft: kpt on same pce last 75yds* **16/1**

006 **5** nk **Ancient Cross**[24] 5487 8-8-8 94 (t) WilliamBuick 22 98
(Michael Easterby) *in rr: hdwy over 2f out: styd on fnl f* **12/1**

2122 **6** hd **Prodigality**[22] 5530 4-8-4 90 JoeFanning 8 93+
(Ronald Harris) *racd far side: hld up in mid-div: hdwy to ld that side 2f out: led overall 1f out: hdd last 100yds: no ex: 1st of 7 that gp* **4/1**[1]

5211 **7** nk **Picabo (IRE)**[36] 5065 4-8-7 93 ow1 DaneO'Neill 17 95
(Henry Candy) *in rr: hdwy over 2f out: kpt on fnl f* **9/1**[3]

0605 **8** 1½ **Kaldoun Kingdom (IRE)**[24] 5487 7-8-7 93 PaulHanagan 20 90
(Richard Fahey) *mid-div: hdwy over 2f out: kpt on same pce fnl f* **14/1**

4021 **9** ½ **Kingsgate Choice (IRE)**[7] 6026 5-8-7 93 LiamKeniry 1 88
(Ed de Giles) *racd far side: chsd ldrs: wnt cl 2nd that gp wl over 1f out: fdd last 150yds: 2nd of 7 that gp* **20/1**

5322 **10** ½ **Mass Rally (IRE)**[24] 5487 5-8-8 94 (b) PaulMulrennan 10 88+
(Michael Dods) *hld up in mid-div: hdwy whn hmpd over 1f out: no threat after* **12/1**

5314 **11** nk **Steps (IRE)**[35] 5077 4-8-9 95 (b) NeilCallan 5 88
(Roger Varian) *racd far side: in rr: effrt over 2f out: styd on fnl f: 3rd of 7 that gp* **10/1**

-616 **12** 1½ **Singeur (IRE)**[28] 5370 5-8-9 95 DarryllHolland 15 83
(Robin Bastiman) *mid-div: effrt over 2f out: nvr a threat* **16/1**

3040 **13** nk **Fratellino**[6] 6072 5-8-5 91 (t) MartinLane 19 78
(Alan McCabe) *chsd ldrs: wknd over 1f out* **33/1**

1000 **14** nse **Bajan Tryst (USA)**[42] 4802 6-9-0 100 GrahamLee 11 86
(Kevin Ryan) *in rr div: hdwy over 2f out: kpt on fnl f* **33/1**

-531 **15** nk **Edge Closer**[14] 5832 8-8-8 94 PatDobbs 14 79
(Tony Carroll) *chsd ldrs: wknd appr fnl f* **20/1**

0040 **16** shd **Move In Time**[14] 5822 4-8-8 97 (v[1]) LeeTopliss(3) 13 82
(Bryan Smart) *overall ldr in centre gp: edgd rt and hdd 1f out: wknd* **33/1**

-660 **17** 1 **Beacon Lodge (IRE)**[21] 5597 7-9-3 110 ShirleyTeasdale(7) 6 92
(David Nicholls) *racd far side: in rr: nvr on terms: 4th of 7 that gp* **66/1**

6500 **18** 1 **Captain Dunne (IRE)**[24] 5487 7-8-13 99 TedDurcan 2 77
(Tim Easterby) *led 6 other far side: hdd 2f out: sn edgd rt and wknd: 5th of 7 that gp* **50/1**

0210 **19** 1 **Tax Free (IRE)**[7] 6028 10-8-9 95 AdrianNicholls 4 70+
(David Nicholls) *racd far side: chsd ldrs that side: drvn over 2f out: hmpd and lost pl over 1f out: 6th of 7 that gp* **14/1**

1405 **20** 19 **Rex Imperator**[14] 5814 3-9-2 104 GeorgeBaker 7
(Roger Charlton) *upset in stalls: racd far side: hld up in rr: sme hdwy over 2f out: lost pl over 1f out: sn bhd and eased: t.o: last of 7 that gp* **11/1**

1m 6.01s (-2.79) **Going Correction** -0.20s/f (Firm) course record
WFA 3 from 4yo+ 2lb **20** Ran SP% **131.7**
Speed ratings (Par 109): **110,109,107,107,107 106,106,104,103,103 102,100,100,100,99 99,98,97,95,70**
Tote Swingers 1&2 £26.40, 2&3 £122.40, 1&3 £127.10 CSF £131.69 CT £4105.20 TOTE £24.40: £4.90, £1.70, £7.20, £6.50; EX 131.70 Trifecta £8287.30 Pool: £66,347.46 - 8.10 winning tickets..
Owner S Laffan **Bred** Colts Neck Stables Llc **Trained** Nawton, N Yorks

FOCUS
The course record, dating back to the 2007 edition of this race, was lowered by 0.62 seconds. The runners were spread across the track in the closing stages, but they had split into two groups early on and those who were in the smaller bunch of seven, towards the far side, struggled. Indeed, only two of the first ten finishers came from a single-figure stall. A personal best from the winner and the second is better than ever.

NOTEBOOK
Doc Hay(USA) was a couple of places behind Face The Problem when fourth at Haydock the previous week, but that was his first run after almost three months off and he was able to reverse form, helped by challenging later than the runner-up. This was a career best from a mark 17lb higher than when last successful and there's no telling how much further he could progress in an ordinary division. He may now go for the Ayr Gold Cup.
Face The Problem(IRE) looked the best horse on the day but was in front soon enough and was just caught after edging left. He can do even better if delivered later, and he's a possible for the Ayr Gold Cup. (op 8-1 tchd 11-2)
Secret Witness had been a bit below form in recent starts but he looked to run right up to his best this time. (op 40-1)
Barnet Fair, 3lb higher than when winning at Ascot on his penultimate start, ran just about as well as ever. He's only a 4yo and can make further progress. (op 20-1 tchd 25-1)
Ancient Cross, 6lb lower than when fourth in this last year, has been running quite well without doing enough in similar races this season and it was the same story this time. (op 14-1 tchd 16-1)
Prodigality ◆, representing the same connections as the third-placed finisher, fared best of those from the far-side group. He's holding his form extremely well. (op 5-1 tchd 11-2)
Picabo(IRE), who carried 1lb overweight, couldn't complete a hat-trick off 10lb higher than when successful over 6f at the July course last time. She probably wants more of a test. (op 8-1)
Kingsgate Choice(IRE), up 5lb for winning at Ascot, was second best of those who raced in the far-side group. (op 25-1)
Mass Rally(IRE) needs things to go his way but met trouble when beginning to stay on. (op 10-1)
Rex Imperator Official explanation: jockey said gelding became upset in stalls

6245 LADBROKES ST LEGER STKS (BRITISH CHAMPIONS SERIES) (GROUP 1) (ENTIRE COLTS & FILLIES) 1m 6f 132y

3:40 (3:45) (Class 1) 3-Y-O

£311,905 (£118,250; £59,180; £29,480; £14,795; £7,425) **Stalls** Low

Form RPR
-123 **1** **Encke (USA)**[24] 5489 3-9-0 112 MickaelBarzalona 1 121
(Mahmood Al Zarooni) *hld up in mid-div: hdwy and handy 4th 3f out: led over 1f out: sn drvn 3 l clr: hld on wl* **25/1**

-111 **2** ¾ **Camelot**[77] 3651 3-9-0 124 JPO'Brien 7 120
(A P O'Brien, Ire) *hld up towards rr: hdwy on inner 3f out: nt clr run and swtchd rt over 2f out: shkn up: hung lft and chsd wnr 1f out: styd on but nvr gng to get there* **2/5**[1]

3113 **3** 3 **Michelangelo**[46] 4685 3-9-0 111 FrankieDettori 4 116
(John Gosden) *mid-div: hdwy over 3f out: styd on same pce to take 3rd last 100yds* **10/1**[2]

1 **4** 1½ **Ursa Major (IRE)**[21] 5606 3-9-0 111 JohnnyMurtagh 5 114
(Thomas Carmody, Ire) *chsd ldrs: drvn over 4f out: wnt handy 2nd over 3f out: kpt on same pce fnl 2f* **10/1**[2]

1242 **5** hd **Main Sequence (USA)**[24] 5489 3-9-0 115 TedDurcan 6 113
(David Lanigan) *s.s: hld up in last: effrt over 3f out: styd on fnl f: tk 5th last 100yds* **10/1**[2]

1431 **6** 8 **Thought Worthy (USA)**[24] 5489 3-9-0 115 WilliamBuick 3 102
(John Gosden) *led early: trckd ldr: led over 3f out: hdd over 1f out: wknd last 150yds: eased towards fin* **10/1**[2]

2111 **7** 1¼ **Guarantee**[21] 5598 3-9-0 105 PhillipMakin 9 100
(William Haggas) *hld up in rr: drvn over 3f out: nvr a factor* **12/1**[3]

5115 **8** 1¾ **Thomas Chippendale (IRE)**[24] 5489 3-9-0 111 TomQueally 2 98
(Sir Henry Cecil) *trckd ldrs: t.k.h: wnt handy 3rd over 3f out: wknd fnl f* **14/1**

5305 **9** 16 **Dartford (USA)**[28] 5354 3-9-0 74 RobertHavlin 8 76
(John Gosden) *sn led: qcknd pce over 5f out: lost pl over 2f out: sn bhd* **100/1**

3m 3.81s (-3.59) **Going Correction** -0.275s/f (Firm) **9** Ran SP% **127.0**
Speed ratings (Par 115): **98,97,96,95,95 90,90,89,80**
Tote Swingers 1&2 £6.60, 2&3 £2.90, 1&3 £22.20 CSF £39.44 CT £158.06 TOTE £32.30: £4.70, £1.10, £3.00; EX 65.00 Trifecta £750.90 Pool: £12,177.98 - 12.00 winning tickets..
Owner Godolphin **Bred** Darley **Trained** Newmarket, Suffolk
■ Camelot's defeat denied Aidan O'Brien a place in history as the only trainer to win all five British Classics in the same season.

FOCUS
One of the most keenly anticipated Classics for years, but a slightly unsatisfactory conclusion and a disappointing one for neutral observers. It was a quality edition on paper, with a three-time Classic winner at the head of the market and the form of the major trials well represented too. The John Gosden duo Great Heavens and Shantaram were the most notable absentees. The pace was just steady, only lifting on the approach to the long home straight, and a number were keen to go faster down the back, the favourite among them. With Camelot below par (8lb off his Derby figure) the form has been rated as an average renewal. Encke is rated up 6lb with the third and fourth close to their marks. Only Conduit and Sixties Icon have bettered Encke's figure in the last ten years.

NOTEBOOK
Encke(USA) took time to wind up but then produced a decent turn of pace at a crucial point to go perhaps three lengths to the good, taking first run on Camelot. He's a notably game colt and he stuck his neck out to hold the favourite, who was clawing him back all too late. He turned around form from a falsely run Great Voltigeur with Thought Worthy and Main Sequence, finding improvement for the extra two and a furlongs on only his sixth career start. Prevously he'd been beaten a nose in the Gordon Stakes, a race which has now contained four of the of the last seven St Leger winners. He's clearly a stronger stayer than his brother Genius Beast, who beat just one home in this last year. A sixth St Leger winner for Godolphin, but the first for Mahmood Al Zarooni, he doesn't hold an Arc entry but is likely to stay in training at four, when he will be aimed at the big middle-distance races. The Dubai Sheema Classic in March could be a target. There's more progress in this tough and likeable colt, who won a handicap off 90 little more than two months ago. (tchd 33-1)

Camelot was attempting to become only the 15th colt to win the Triple Crown and the first since Nijinsky in 1970. Unbeaten in five races, four of them in Group 1 company, he had underfoot conditions to suit following his win in bad ground in the Irish Derby, and appeared much the best of a modest crop of 3yos. His stamina was a leap in the dark, but on both RPRs and BHA ratings he had 9lb in hand, and the race looked his to lose. Held up near the back, and taking a bit of a tug, he only had two behind him turning in with Joseph O'Brien looking for an 'out' near the rail. The colt was still cruising when the gap came with a quarter of a mile to run, but at that point Encke was about to make the best of his way home. Camelot's head momentarily went up as his jockey gave him a couple of cracks and there was none of the instant acceleration which had been anticipated. The favourite ran on in the final furlong and was closing at the line, but the winner wasn't stopping. This wasn't a case of Camelot not staying, but the trip perhaps blunted his speed, and the lack of a true gallop meant the race did not unfold tactically as connections would have liked. Indeed Aidan O'Brien said straight afterwards that he should have run a pacemaker or two so that the colt settled better. The trainer later said that the colt clipped heels early, which lit him up. The combination of factors meant the colt was below his best, enough to deny him a place in history. No decision has been made as to whether he will run again this season - although the Arc is stil a possibility and he's in the Champion Stakes too - or if he stays in training at four. His connections deserve great credit for taking up this challenge, but unfortunately his defeat is likely to mean that Triple Crown winners will become even rarer in future. Since Nijinsky only Nashwan and Sea The Stars had won the first two legs, and both ducked the challenge of the St Leger, while Reference Point, successful in both races 25 years ago, and Shergar, only fourth at 4-9 in 1981, are the only other Derby winners since 1970 to have run at Doncaster. (tchd 4-9)
Michelangelo, from a yard that had won three of the last five Legers, was deserted by William Buick. He never really looked like winning but stayed on for third, a creditable effort from a colt of his limited experience. The track suited him better than Goodwood, where he had been a place behind Encke in the Gordon Stakes. (op 11-1)
Ursa Major(IRE) took his chance here rather than in the Irish version at the Curragh, which looked much the easier option, but his connections had the ideal alternative there in Royal Diamond. He ran well, holding a similar placing throughout but lacking a change of gear. This progressive colt's previous runs on turf had all been in soft ground. (op 12-1)
Main Sequence(USA) gave away several lengths leaving the stalls but the steady pace meant he was quickly in touch at the back of the field. He stayed on down the outer and momentarily looked like challenging for third, but his stamina was ebbing away in the dying strides. He finished only slightly further behind Camelot than he had in the Derby. (op 9-1)
Thought Worthy(USA), a brother to the 2007 St Leger winner Lucarno, had Encke back in third when making all in the Great Voltigeur at York last month. Tracking stablemate Dartford, he committed for home in the straight but couldn't hold on. He didn't stay, even in this steadily run race, while the ground was quicker than he'd have liked. (op 11-1 tchd 9-1)
Guarantee, lightly raced and progressive, looked worth his place in the field after his taking win in the Melrose Handicap at the Ebor meeting, but he was always towards the rear. A truer gallop would have suited but in truth he was not good enough. (op 14-1)
Thomas Chippendale(IRE) raced quite keenly in the first part of the race and lacked a change of gear alongside the rail in the straight, weakening badly in the final furlong. His stablemate Noble Mission had beaten both Encke and Michelangelo in the Gordon Stakes. (op 16-1)
Dartford(USA) duly set the pace, but it wasn't the searching gallop a lot of his opponents would have expected.

6246 OLBG PARK STKS (GROUP 2) — 7f

4:15 (4:18) (Class 1) 3-Y-O+

£56,710 (£21,500; £10,760; £5,360; £2,690; £1,350) **Stalls** High

Form — RPR

1120 **1** — **Libranno**[28] 5355 4-9-4 110 .... KierenFallon 3 — 117
(Richard Hannon) *trckd ldrs: t.k.h 1st 2f: drvn 4f out: styd on to ld 1f out: hld on gamely* **16/1**

1025 **2** *½* **Pastoral Player**[28] 5355 5-9-4 113 .... DarryllHolland 6 — 116
(Hughie Morrison) *stdd s: hld up in rr: hdwy and swtchd outer over 1f out: chsd wnr ins fnl f: no ex clsng stages* **8/1**

3421 **3** *4* **Lethal Force (IRE)**[28] 5355 3-9-0 115 .... (b) AdamKirby 2 — 105
(Clive Cox) *led after 1f: qcknd pce 5f out: hdd 1f out: kpt on same pce: struck into* **7/1**[3]

0020 **4** *¾* **Strong Suit (USA)**[7] 6030 4-9-4 117 .... RichardHughes 5 — 103
(Richard Hannon) *hld up in mid-div: effrt and edgd rt over 2f out: swtchd lft 1f out: kpt on same pce* **6/4**[1]

105 **5** *1 ¼* **Penitent**[30] 5286 6-9-4 115 .... DanielTudhope 8 — 99+
(David O'Meara) *prom: pushed along and outpcd over 4f out: short of room on inner over 2f out: swtchd outside over 1f out: styd on* **9/1**

1640 **6** *3 ¼* **Majestic Myles (IRE)**[7] 6030 4-9-4 110 .... PaulHanagan 7 — 91
(Richard Fahey) *t.k.h in rr: drvn and n.m.r over 2f out: wknd over 1f out* **14/1**

-265 **7** *nse* **Foxtrot Romeo (IRE)**[46] 4686 3-9-0 111 .... JohnnyMurtagh 1 — 96
(Bryan Smart) *uns rdr leaving paddock: trckd ldrs: t.k.h: n.m.r appr fnl f: wknd and eased fnl 150yds* **8/1**

6416 **8** *½* **Soul (AUS)**[28] 5355 5-9-4 117 .... FrankieDettori 4 — 94
(Saeed Bin Suroor) *led 1f: trckd ldrs: drvn over 2f out: nt clr run on inner appr fnl f: sn wknd and eased* **9/2**[2]

1m 23.16s (-3.14) **Going Correction** -0.20s/f (Firm)
WFA 3 from 4yo+ 4lb — **8** Ran SP% **115.5**
Speed ratings (Par 115): **109,108,103,103,101 97,97,97**
Tote Swingers 1&2 £9.10, 2&3 £7.00, 1&3 £6.90 CSF £136.73 TOTE £19.50: £3.20, £2.50, £1.90; EX 107.10 Trifecta £501.50 Pool: £3524.26 - 5.20 winning tickets..
Owner Mcdowell Racing **Bred** O McDowell **Trained** East Everleigh, Wilts
■ Stewards' Enquiry : Adam Kirby one-day ban: careless riding (Sep 30)

FOCUS
A messy race. The early pace didn't look strong and a few of these found trouble after the field edged towards the stands' rail in the closing stages. A reowrking of the Hungerford Stakes form, rated around today's front pair who finished clear.

NOTEBOOK
Libranno ran poorly in the Hungerford Stakes on his previous start, but this is up there with his best form. He wasn't ridden as forwardly as is often the case, and despite coming under pressure a fair way out, the different tactics seemingly helped. A race like the Challenge Stakes at Newmarket (won last year by stablemate Strong Suit) could be a suitable target, although he'll have to prove he can repeat this level and anyway that race will probably require even more. (op 12-1)
Pastoral Player looked to run close to his best in pulling well clear of the others. He may yet have a bit more to offer. (tchd 9-1)
Lethal Force(IRE) was allowed too big a lead when winning the Hungerford Stakes on his previous start, but a repeat scenario was unlikely to unfold and he couldn't match that level of form. Adam Kirby reported the colt was struck into. Official explanation: jockey said colt was struck into (op 9-2)
Strong Suit(USA), turned out quickly after being well held under a front-running ride in the Haydock Sprint Cup, was ridden with more restraint this time (more familiar tactics), but he again disappointed. A stronger end-to-end gallop would have helped, but this leaves him with plenty to prove. (op 2-1)
Penitent, racing on ground that might have been faster than ideal, was left with a lot to do when short of room against the stands' rail just as he was looking to challenge. Official explanation: jockey said gelding suffered interference in running (op 12-1 tchd 16-1)
Majestic Myles(IRE) didn't see his race out after being keen. He was outclassed in the Haydock Sprint Cup last time, but will be worth another try over 6f. Official explanation: jockey said gelding suffered interference in running
Foxtrot Romeo(IRE), who got loose in the paddock and slipped over, didn't do anything quickly for pressure but was keeping on when hampered in the closing stages. He was eased once his chance had passed, and all things considered this is easily excused. A return to 1m might help. Official explanation: jockey said colt suffered interference in running and had no more to give (tchd 9-1)
Soul(AUS) was plugging on but not doing enough when short of room against the rail late on. The beaten margin was exaggerated as a result. Frankie Dettori reported the gelding lost his action. Official explanation: jockey said gelding lost its action (tchd 4-1)

6247 AGRIARGO UK TRACTOR CHALLENGE NURSERY — 1m (S)

4:50 (4:51) (Class 2) 2-Y-O — **£9,703** (£2,887; £1,443; £721) **Stalls** High

Form — RPR

3321 **1** — **Rising Legend**[38] 4938 2-8-13 **79** .... RichardHughes 2 — 86
(Richard Hannon) *hld up: stdy hdwy on outer 3f out: w ldrs over 1f out: led and edgd rt 100yds out: hld on gamely* **8/1**[3]

031 **2** *½* **Hoarding (USA)**[10] 5946 2-9-3 **83** .... WilliamBuick 5 — 89
(John Gosden) *hld up in rr: hdwy and swtchd outside over 2f out: chsng ldrs over 1f out: led jst ins fnl f: sn hdd: no ex nr line* **11/4**[1]

0241 **3** *nk* **Ajmany (IRE)**[29] 5319 2-9-1 **81** .... KierenFallon 11 — 86
(Luca Cumani) *dwlt: drvn to chse ldrs over 2f out: ev ch fnl f: kpt on same pce clsng stages* **7/2**[2]

0103 **4** *1* **Glory Awaits (IRE)**[43] 4774 2-9-7 **87** .... GrahamLee 10 — 90
(Kevin Ryan) *led: drvn along 4f out: hdd jst ins fnl f: no ex* **16/1**

451 **5** *4* **Nile Knight**[19] 5661 2-8-10 **76** .... TedDurcan 7 — 70
(Marcus Tregoning) *hld up in rr: hdwy 3f out: chsng ldrs 1f out: kpt on one pce* **12/1**

61 **6** *7* **Red Runaway**[24] 5478 2-8-12 **78** .... HayleyTurner 8 — 56
(Ed Dunlop) *hld up towards rr: effrt and n.m.r over 2f out: wknd over 1f out* **8/1**[3]

1332 **7** *13* **Mad Jazz**[19] 5670 2-7-7 **66** oh1 ow2 .... KevinLundie(7) 3 — 14
(Tony Coyle) *w ldrs: drvn over 4f out: lost pl over 1f out: eased whn bhd* **20/1**

P421 **8** *2 ¾* **Cappadocia (IRE)**[8] 6016 2-8-6 **72** .... AdrianNicholls 6 — 13
(Mick Channon) *t.k.h: w ldrs: drvn over 3f out: lost pl over 1f out: sn bhd and eased* **25/1**

3220 **9** *7* **Excellent Mariner (IRE)**[19] 5670 2-8-2 **68** .... JoeFanning 12
(Mark Johnston) *trckd ldrs: t.k.h: lost pl 2f out: eased whn bhd* **20/1**

61 **10** *19* **Winged Icarus (USA)**[18] 5716 2-8-9 **75** .... (v) NeilCallan 9
(Alan McCabe) *trckd ldrs: lost pl over 1f out: sn eased and bhd* **10/1**

1m 37.3s (-2.00) **Going Correction** -0.20s/f (Firm) 2y crse rec — **10** Ran SP% **107.1**
Speed ratings (Par 101): **102,101,101,100,96 89,76,73,66,47**
Tote Swingers 1&2 £4.00, 2&3 £2.70, 1&3 £5.00 CSF £24.61 CT £70.30 TOTE £9.60: £2.50, £1.60, £1.40; EX 26.30 Trifecta £108.20 Pool: £1567.74 - 10.72 winning tickets..
Owner M S Al Shahi **Bred** Cheveley Park Stud Ltd **Trained** East Everleigh, Wilts

FOCUS
They raced stands' side in this good nursery. Decent form with the front four clear off a sound pace.

NOTEBOOK
Rising Legend clearly wasn't affected when Shebebi, who had to be withdrawn, played up in the adjacent stall. He took five goes to get off the mark, landing a Brighton maiden (7f, good to soft) last time, but he's clearly improving. He was suited by the longer trip and the 1m2f Zetland Stakes at Newmarket was mentioned as a possible target. (op 17-2)
Hoarding(USA), up 8lb for winning on his nursery debut over 7f at Lingfield, had his chance when switched wide and just missed out. This was a useful effort in defeat. (op 5-2 tchd 9-4)
Ajmany(IRE), successful in a 7f maiden at the July course on his fourth start, took an age to respond to pressure and was never quite doing enough. (op 11-2)
Glory Awaits(IRE), upped to 1m for the first time, ran a useful race under top weight. (op 14-1)
Nile Knight found this tougher than the 7f Epsom maiden he won last time.
Red Runaway, a recent Kempton maiden winner, found this a struggle.

6248 MOLLART COX H'CAP — 1m 4f

5:20 (5:20) (Class 2) (0-105,98) 3-Y-O+ **£12,938** (£3,850; £1,924; £962) **Stalls** Low

Form — RPR

1411 **1** — **Viking Storm**[35] 5079 4-9-9 **95** .... PaulHanagan 1 — 106+
(Harry Dunlop) *hld up towards rr: nt clr run fr 3f out tl swtchd rt appr fnl f: styd on wl to ld nr fin* **4/1**[2]

4241 **2** *hd* **Fattsota**[55] 4363 4-9-10 **96** .... AdamKirby 4 — 106
(Marco Botti) *trckd ldrs: hdwy on ins to join ldr over 2f out: hrd rdn to ld last 50yds: hdd last strides* **4/1**[2]

321 **3** *½* **New Hampshire (USA)**[48] 4621 4-8-13 **88** .... LeeTopliss(3) 5 — 97
(Tony Coyle) *led: hdd ins fnl f: no ex* **14/1**

1230 **4** *1 ¾* **Rio's Rosanna (IRE)**[22] 5558 5-9-2 **88** .... HayleyTurner 7 — 94
(Richard Whitaker) *slowly away: hld up towards rr: nt clr run over 3f out: styd on fnl f: tk 4th last 50yds* **9/2**[3]

0360 **5** *1* **Scatter Dice (IRE)**[7] 6025 3-8-11 **92** .... JoeFanning 3 — 97
(Mark Johnston) *trckd ldrs: nt clr run on inner over 3f out: one pce fnl 2f* **12/1**

6320 **6** *hd* **Martin Chuzzlewit (IRE)**[7] 6025 3-8-10 **91** .... (v) KierenFallon 6 — 95
(Sir Michael Stoute) *hld up in rr: hdwy over 7f out: chsng ldrs 4f out: sn drvn: one pce fnl 2f* **11/4**[1]

/540 **7** *9* **Dreamspeed (IRE)**[21] 5600 5-9-12 **98** .... LiamKeniry 2 — 88
(Andrew Balding) *dwlt: sn trcking ldrs: t.k.h: hung lft and wknd over 1f out* **14/1**

0140 **8** *1 ¼* **Incendo**[7] 6035 6-8-13 **85** .... (t) GrahamLee 8 — 73
(James Fanshawe) *hld up in rr: hdwy over 7f out: wknd 2f out* **9/1**

2m 28.7s (-6.20) **Going Correction** -0.275s/f (Firm)
WFA 3 from 4yo+ 9lb — **8** Ran SP% **115.9**
Speed ratings (Par 109): **109,108,108,107,106 106,100,99**
Tote Swingers 1&2 £4.10, 2&3 £7.90, 1&3 £4.70 CSF £20.71 CT £203.02 TOTE £4.10: £1.50, £2.10, £2.90; EX 13.60 Trifecta £103.10 Pool: £2507.42 - 17.98 winning tickets..
Owner Be Hopeful Partnership **Bred** Charlie Wyatt **Trained** Lambourn, Berks
■ Stewards' Enquiry : Adam Kirby two-day ban: used whip above permitted level (Oct 1-2)

FOCUS
This handicap was won in 2010 by Times Up, Friday's Doncaster Cup scorer. The topweight in this year's edition ran off 7lb below the race maximum, but this was still a well contested event, run at a brisk pace, and the form is solid enough. The winner may do a bit better still.

NOTEBOOK
Viking Storm was trapped on the rails towards the back when the race was about to take shape, but once switched out he picked up strongly, getting up on the line. That's four wins from five starts this season, including a leg of the Shergar Cup last time, and he's still progressing. He gets further but a truly run race at this trip seems ideal. (op 3-1)
Fattsota ◆'s Ascot victory received a boost as third home Willing Foe won the Ebor next time, and he came here unexposed at the trip. He made a bold attempt to follow up off this 5lb higher mark, getting past the long-time leader on the rail late on only to be nailed on the line. There's another good race in him. His rider picked up a two-day whip ban. (tchd 7-2 and 9-2)

New Hampshire(USA) fought on with typical tenacity once tackled and only conceded defeat deep inside the last. This was his first run over the full 1m4f and he saw it out well. (op 12-1)
Rio's Rosanna(IRE) is a tough cookie and she stayed on from the back without getting in a blow. She's a pretty consistent mare who acts on most ground. (op 11-2)
Scatter Dice(IRE) ran her race but is still 5lb above her winning mark from Ascot and her improvement seems to have levelled out. (op 10-1)
Martin Chuzzlewit(IRE) wasn't beaten far but could never deliver a telling blow. This was better than his Ascot run, but the effect of the visor looks to be wearing off. (op 7-2 tchd 4-1)
Dreamspeed(IRE), who's well handicapped on his 2010 stakes race form, may have found the ground a little quick for him. (op 8-1)
Incendo travelled well as usual but, not for the first time, failed to deliver.
T/Jkpt: Not won. T/Plt: £54.70 to a £1 stake. Pool: £202,745.99 - 2,704.75 winning tickets.
T/Qpdt: £23.50 to a £1 stake. Pool: £11,041.91 - 347.21 winning tickets. WG

6145 KEMPTON (A.W) (R-H)

Saturday, September 15

OFFICIAL GOING: Standard
Wind: Light, half behind Weather: Fine, warm

6249 BETFAIR. DON'T SETTLE FOR LESS H'CAP 5f (P)
5:50 (5:51) (Class 6) (0-60,60) 3-Y-O £2,070 (£616; £307; £153) Stalls Low

Form RPR
0502 1 **Roy's Legacy**[12] 5875 3-9-0 **60**.....(t) MichaelJMMurphy(7) 9 69
(Shaun Harris) *mde all and sn crossed to rail fr wd draw: rdn clr over 1f out: kpt on: unchal* **11/4[1]**
0030 2 2 3/4 **First Fast Now (IRE)**[14] 5831 3-8-3 **49**..... DanielleMooney(7) 6 48
(Nigel Tinkler) *hld up in last: prog through rivals fr over 1f out: styd on to take 2nd last 75yds: no ch w wnr* **22/1**
10 3 nk **Drinmoy Lad (IRE)**[52] 4480 3-9-5 **58**..... CathyGannon 3 56
(Michael McElhone, Ire) *chsd wnr: rdn fr 1/2-way: no imp over 1f out: lost 2nd last 75yds* **9/2[3]**
2462 4 nse **Choice Pearl (USA)**[2] 6180 3-9-0 **53**.....(bt) HarryBentley 8 51
(Tobias B P Coles) *awkward s: hld up in 5th: effrt on outer wl over 1f out: sn rdn and nt qckn: styd on ins fnl f* **3/1[2]**
405 5 1 **Cincinnati Kit**[20] 5635 3-8-9 **53**.....(t) TobyAtkinson(5) 5 47
(Stuart Williams) *disp 2nd: rdn wl over 1f out: no imp on wnr: wknd last 100yds* **12/1**
3640 6 2 **Russian Bullet**[15] 5808 3-9-5 **58**..... SeanQuinlan 2 45
(Jamie Osborne) *settled in last pair: nt clr run v briefly over 1f out: reminder ent fnl f: nvr involved* **5/1**
0420 7 2 **Kara's Vision**[18] 5719 3-8-4 **50**.....(v[1]) HannahNunn(7) 1 30
(Robert Cowell) *sn in 4th: rdn 2f out: wknd over 1f out* **16/1**
1m 0.38s (-0.12) **Going Correction** -0.05s/f (Stan) 7 Ran SP% 104.4
Speed ratings (Par 99): **98,93,93,93,91 88,85**
toteswingers 1&2 £9.30, 1&3 £3.20, 2&3 £12.60 CSF £47.88 CT £200.63 TOTE £3.60: £1.10, £9.30; EX 48.60 TRIFECTA Not won..
Owner Karl Blackwell Steve Mohammed S A Harris **Bred** A Christou **Trained** Carburton, Notts

FOCUS
A modest sprint featuring inconsistent horses, few of whom had been in top form recently. There's a bit of doubt about the winner repwating this form elsewhere.

6250 BETTER PRICES ON BETFAIR MOBILE H'CAP (BETFAIR 10 FURLONG FLAT SERIES QUALIFIER) (DIV I) 1m 2f (P)
6:20 (6:20) (Class 5) (0-70,69) 3-Y-O+ £3,881 (£1,155; £577; £288) Stalls Low

Form RPR
034 1 **Positively**[29] 5329 3-9-3 **67**..... PatDobbs 6 81
(Sir Michael Stoute) *prom and a gng wl: wnt 2nd 2f out: led over 1f out: shkn up and sn clr* **5/2[1]**
0230 2 3 1/2 **Landesherr (GER)**[19] 5665 5-9-1 **65**..... MichaelJMMurphy(7) 2 72
(Steve Gollings) *hld up in midfield: prog over 2f out: rdn and kpt on to take 2nd ins fnl f: no ch w wnr* **4/1[2]**
004 3 2 1/4 **Hurricane Hymnbook (USA)**[57] 4296 7-9-12 **69**..... JamieMackay 11 72
(Willie Musson) *s.i.s: hld up in last pair: prog 2f out: styd on to take 3rd nr fin: no ch* **10/1**
000 4 1/2 **Calypso Magic (IRE)**[15] 5804 4-9-0 **57**..... StevieDonohoe 3 59
(Olivia Maylam) *trckd ldr: quick move to ld over 4f out: drvn and hdd over 1f out: fdd ins fnl f* **20/1**
0500 5 hd **Talk Of The North**[14] 5838 3-8-9 **66**.....(b) NoelGarbutt(7) 9 67
(Hugo Palmer) *hld up in 9th: prog arnd outer of field fr 3f out: tried to cl on ldrs over 1f out: kpt on same pce* **9/1**
4200 6 2 1/2 **Daniel Thomas (IRE)**[21] 5585 10-9-10 **67**.....(tp) CathyGannon 10 63
(Violet M Jordan) *s.s: hld up in last pair: stl last over 1f out: cajoled along and r.o to take 6th nr fin: nvr involved* **20/1**
0004 7 1 3/4 **Height Of Summer (IRE)**[33] 5159 4-9-12 **69**..... GeorgeBaker 1 62
(Chris Wall) *prom: rdn in cl 3rd whn nt clr run wl over 1f out: wknd fnl f* **7/1[3]**
6000 8 nse **Operettist**[10] 5931 3-9-3 **67**..... SeanLevey 8 60
(Richard Hannon) *nvr bttr than midfield: struggling in rr over 2f out: v modest late hdwy* **12/1**
50-0 9 1 1/2 **Teide Peak (IRE)**[15] 5783 3-9-0 **64**..... SebSanders 4 54
(Paul D'Arcy) *in tch: chsd ldng quartet 1/2-way: no imp over 1f out: wknd and eased fnl f* **40/1**
2540 10 6 **One For Joules (IRE)**[12] 5893 5-9-10 **67**..... SeanQuinlan 7 45
(John Flint) *a towards rr: rdn and no prog 3f out: wknd 2f out* **14/1**
0002 11 shd **Audacious**[29] 5323 4-9-10 **67**..... AndreaAtzeni 5 44
(Michael Quinn) *led at mod pce: surprised and hdd over 4f out: drvn to try to chal 3f out: wknd rapidly 2f out* **8/1**
2m 6.74s (-1.26) **Going Correction** -0.05s/f (Stan)
WFA 3 from 4yo+ 7lb 11 Ran SP% 117.6
Speed ratings (Par 103): **103,100,98,98,97 95,94,94,93,88 88**
toteswingers 1&2 £2.30, 1&3 £5.20, 2&3 £6.90 CSF £11.60 CT £85.52 TOTE £2.70: £1.10, £1.80, £3.90; EX 16.10 Trifecta £118.00 Pool: £682.79 - 4.28 winning tickets..
Owner K Abdulla **Bred** Juddmonte Farms Ltd **Trained** Newmarket, Suffolk

FOCUS
A routine race of its type, run at a stop-go tempo, but won by a runner with some potential at a sensible level. The time was similar to that of division II and the runner-up helps set the standard.

Audacious Official explanation: jockey said gelding stopped quickly

6251 BETTER PRICES ON BETFAIR MOBILE H'CAP (BETFAIR 10 FURLONG FLAT SERIES QUALIFIER) (DIV II) 1m 2f (P)
6:50 (6:50) (Class 5) (0-70,69) 3-Y-O+ £3,881 (£1,155; £577; £288) Stalls Low

Form RPR
2124 1 **Spin Cast**[16] 5767 4-9-10 **67**..... SilvestreDeSousa 10 76
(Brian Ellison) *trckd ldng pair: rdn and prog to chal 2f out: gd battle w runner-up after: drvn to ld last 100yds* **9/2[3]**
5011 2 3/4 **My Mate Jake (IRE)**[26] 5405 4-9-9 **66**.....(b) CathyGannon 8 73
(James Given) *trckd ldr: rdn to ld 2f out: sn jnd: drew clr w wnr after: hdd last 100yds* **4/1[2]**
3041 3 6 **Graylyn Valentino**[15] 5810 3-9-1 **65**..... HarryBentley 3 60
(Robin Dickin) *hld up: rdn 2f out: sme prog over 1f out but easily lft bhd by ldng pair* **11/2**
0005 4 2 **Mcbirney (USA)**[16] 5767 5-9-11 **68**..... SebSanders 4 59
(Paul D'Arcy) *hld up towards rr: pushed along 3f out: outpcd and btn over 1f out: modest late prog* **4/1[2]**
10/0 5 nk **Youm Jamil (USA)**[7] 6051 5-8-12 **62**..... AidenBlakemore(7) 7 52
(Tony Carroll) *hld up in last: lft bhd fr 2f out: nudged along and styd on ins fnl f: no ch* **40/1**
0103 6 1/2 **Officer In Command (USA)**[10] 5941 6-9-12 **69**.....(b) DaneO'Neill 9 58
(Paul Rich) *s.i.s: hld up and racd wd: rdn and prog on wd outside to chal over 2f out: lost grnd bnd sn after: wknd over 1f out* **12/1**
060 7 1 3/4 **Wise Venture (IRE)**[42] 4796 3-8-10 **67**..... MichaelJMMurphy(7) 5 53
(Alan Jarvis) *led: rdn and hdd 2f out: wknd tamely* **10/3[1]**
1400 8 1 3/4 **Bennelong**[33] 5159 6-9-10 **67**..... AmirQuinn 1 49
(Richard Rowe) *trckd ldrs: gng wl over 2f out: rdn and fnd nil wl over 1f out: wknd* **16/1**
2m 6.8s (-1.20) **Going Correction** -0.05s/f (Stan)
WFA 3 from 4yo+ 7lb 8 Ran SP% 112.7
Speed ratings (Par 103): **102,101,96,95,94 94,92,91**
toteswingers 1&2 £1.20, 1&3 £5.10, 2&3 £3.20 CSF £22.12 CT £99.07 TOTE £4.40: £1.10, £2.30, £1.50; EX 13.80 Trifecta £27.40 Pool: £753.46 - 20.33 winning tickets..
Owner W A Bethell **Bred** P W Harris **Trained** Norton, N Yorks

FOCUS
The second division of this race went to a more exposed runner than the first, with the first two clear. A similar time to division I.

6252 DIANA'S 60TH BIRTHDAY H'CAP 1m (P)
7:20 (7:20) (Class 6) (0-55,57) 3-Y-O+ £2,070 (£616; £307; £153) Stalls Low

Form RPR
2050 1 **Ermyntrude**[25] 5441 5-9-0 **50**.....(v) IanMongan 13 59
(Pat Phelan) *settled in midfield: rdn over 2f out: 8th over 1f out: gd prog after: drvn to ld last 100yds but immediately jnd: r.o wl and jst prevailed* **5/1[2]**
3034 2 nse **Rapid Water**[15] 5783 6-9-2 **52**.....(p[1]) CathyGannon 9 61
(Pat Eddery) *hld up wl in rr: stl only 11th and rdn over 1f out: gd prog on outer after: chal and w wnr 100yds out: r.o but jst pipped* **8/1**
02 3 1 1/4 **Valdaw**[8] 6000 4-9-7 **57**..... PatDobbs 10 63
(Tony Carroll) *trckd ldng quartet: prog 2f out: rdn to ld towards inner jst over 1f out: hdd and outpcd last 100yds* **11/4[1]**
0056 4 2 1/2 **Northern Spy (USA)**[58] 4252 8-9-5 **55**..... SebSanders 8 55
(Simon Dow) *trckd ldng pair: rdn over 2f out: cl enough over 1f out: outpcd fnl f* **12/1**
0240 5 nse **Victorian Number (FR)**[29] 5310 4-9-1 **54**..... SophieDoyle(3) 7 54
(Geoffrey Deacon) *disp ld tl led 3f out: drvn and hdd jst over 1f out: fdd* **16/1**
0160 6 hd **Querido (GER)**[66] 3964 8-9-5 **55**.....(tp) SilvestreDeSousa 14 55
(Paddy Butler) *hld up towards rr: effrt on outer over 2f out: sme prog over 1f out: one pce after* **16/1**
1320 7 3/4 **The Bay Bandit**[143] 1608 5-9-3 **53**.....(e) GeorgeBaker 3 51
(Neil Mulholland) *hld up in midfield: prog on inner over 2f out: drvn to chal over 1f out: wknd ins fnl f* **11/1**
-000 8 1 **Style Margi (IRE)**[18] 5720 4-9-2 **52**.....(b) DaneO'Neill 6 48
(Ed de Giles) *chsd ldng pair: rdn over 2f out: cl enough over 1f out: wknd fnl f* **40/1**
0-00 9 2 1/2 **Beat Up**[42] 4817 6-9-1 **51**.....(b[1]) SeanLevey 1 41
(Patrick Chamings) *dwlt: t.k.h: hld up in midfield: effrt on inner over 2f out: no prog over 1f out: fdd* **9/1**
0000 10 3/4 **Gallantry**[38] 4950 10-9-5 **55**..... TomMcLaughlin 12 43
(Paul Howling) *settled in 6th: shkn up over 2f out: nt pce to hold position over 1f out then impeded: no ch after* **16/1**
4600 11 nk **Mulberry Brite**[8] 5999 4-8-7 **50**.....(p) SemiraPashai(7) 11 38
(Alastair Lidderdale) *dwlt: a wl in rr: pushed along and no real prog fnl 2f* **33/1**
0000 12 1 **Ensnare**[75] 3712 7-9-2 **52**.....(t) StevieDonohoe 5 37
(Willie Musson) *dwlt: hld up and sn last: reminder and no prog over 1f out: reminder ins fnl f* **7/1[3]**
0300 13 2 1/2 **Oliver's Gold**[14] 5481 4-9-2 **52**.....(bt) MartinDwyer 4 32
(Shaun Harris) *s.s: sn pushed along and a wl in rr* **16/1**
5000 14 1 1/4 **Guilded Warrior**[37] 4987 9-9-5 **55**.....(e) FergusSweeney 2 32
(Paddy Butler) *disp ld to 3f out: wknd qckly over 2f out* **66/1**
1m 39.7s (-0.10) **Going Correction** -0.05s/f (Stan) 14 Ran SP% 123.4
Speed ratings (Par 101): **98,97,96,94,94 93,93,92,89,88 88,87,85,83**
toteswingers 1&2 £7.40, 1&3 £4.60, 2&3 £5.30 CSF £45.65 CT £135.65 TOTE £7.10: £2.70, £3.60, £1.30; EX 53.50 Trifecta £399.70 Pool: £669.86 - 1.24 winning tickets..
Owner Epsom Racegoers No. 2 **Bred** Ermyn Lodge Stud Limited **Trained** Epsom, Surrey

FOCUS
A low-grade contest that didn't take much winning. Sound if limited form.

6253 BETFAIR BOOSTS PRIZE MONEY AT KEMPTON FILLIES' NURSERY 1m (P)
7:50 (7:50) (Class 5) (0-75,75) 2-Y-O £2,911 (£866; £432; £216) Stalls Low

Form RPR
033 1 **Willowing (USA)**[14] 5818 2-9-5 **73**..... SilvestreDeSousa 4 77
(Mahmood Al Zarooni) *trckd ldr: pushed along 3f out: rdn to ld over 2f out: at least 2 l clr 1f out: drvn rt out w tail flicking* **7/4[1]**
630 2 3/4 **Signature Dish (IRE)**[31] 5221 2-8-13 **67**..... MartinDwyer 3 69
(Andrew Balding) *in tch: chsd ldng pair 3f out: drvn to go 2nd jst over 1f out: tried to cl but no imp last 75yds* **7/2[3]**
0224 3 2 1/2 **Blue Nova**[29] 5300 2-9-7 **75**..... GeorgeBaker 6 72
(Jeremy Noseda) *hld up in tch: outpcd over 2f out: rdn and kpt on same pce to take 3rd ins fnl f* **9/4[2]**

406 **4** *2 ¼* **Glen Ginnie (IRE)**[45] 4704 2-8-13 **67**.................................. DaneO'Neill 8 58
(Charles Hills) *s.s: hld up in last: rdn on outer 2f out: kpt on fnl f: nvr a threat* **11/1**

044 **5** *hd* **Fair Comment**[11] 5907 2-9-5 **73**.................................. FergusSweeney 5 64
(Michael Blanshard) *hld up in 6th: shkn up and no rspnse over 2f out: sme prog over 1f out: n.d* **16/1**

400 **6** *2 ¼* **Poetic Belle**[10] 5947 2-8-1 **62**.................................. MichaelJMMurphy(7) 1 48
(Alan Jarvis) *led to over 2f out: wknd over 1f out* **10/1**

040 **7** *13* **Burlesque Star (IRE)**[24] 5485 2-8-5 **59**.................................. SaleemGolam 2 15
(Harry Dunlop) *chsd ldng pair to 3f out: wknd qckly: t.o* **25/1**

1m 40.08s (0.28) **Going Correction** -0.05s/f (Stan) 7 Ran SP% **116.5**
Speed ratings (Par 92): **96,95,92,90,90 88,75**
toteswingers 1&2 £2.20, 1&3 £1.10, 2&3 £2.90 CSF £8.61 CT £13.75 TOTE £2.70: £1.10, £2.90; EX 9.20 Trifecta £27.50 Pool: £1,053.65 - 28.31 winning tickets..
Owner Godolphin **Bred** Darley **Trained** Newmarket, Suffolk

FOCUS
Juast a fair nursery, but some good stables were represented and several runners were having just their fourth run after qualifying in maidens. The winner may have idled.

NOTEBOOK
Willowing(USA) had done well in three turf maidens and the switch to a Polytrack nursery saw her get off the mark straight away. She didn't win by far but should improve again. (tchd 13-8 and 15-8 and 2-1 in places)
Signature Dish(IRE) showed promise in three turf maidens and appears to have entered nurseries on a handy mark. She should continue to play a major part in similar races, and a return to turf shouldn't be a problem. (op 6-1)
Blue Nova, carrying top-weight in her first nursery, acquitted herself well and deserves to win a race soon. If she is dropped a couple of pounds, she will go that much closer. (op 2-1 tchd 5-2)
Glen Ginnie(IRE) showed enough in maidens, both on turf and sand, to suggest she can win in handicap company, but this opening mark looked a bit tough. (op 12-1 tchd 14-1)
Fair Comment should find a handicap, either on turf or Polytrack, if she is lowered a few pounds on the evidence of this first effort.
Poetic Belle hadn't got home over 7f in her previous two races, and the step up to 1m for her first nursery produced a similar result. She has contested some decent races and will be more at home against lesser opponents. (op 9-1)

6254 BETFAIR COMMITS £40 MILLION TO BRITISH RACING MAIDEN FILLIES' STKS 6f (P)
8:20 (8:21) (Class 5) 3-Y-0+ **£2,911** (£866; £432; £216) **Stalls** Low

Form RPR
3453 **1** **If So**[9] 5975 3-8-12 64.................................. EddieAhern 2 68+
(James Fanshawe) *led 100yds: trckd ldng pair after: prog to ld over 1f out: pushed clr: comf* **11/8[2]**

-5 **2** *2 ¾* **Gull Rock**[138] 1705 3-8-12 0.................................. DaneO'Neill 6 59+
(Henry Candy) *hld up in 4th: prog on outer to go 2nd 1f out: styd on but no ch w wnr* **13/2[3]**

5 **3** *2 ¾* **Transfix**[65] 3990 3-8-12 0.................................. SilvestreDeSousa 1 50
(Ed Vaughan) *racd in 5th: rdn over 2f out: kpt on to take 3rd fnl f: n.d* **6/5[1]**

40 **4** *2* **Alderton (IRE)**[10] 5949 3-8-12 0.................................. SeanLevey 7 44
(Martyn Meade) *led after 100yds to over 1f out: wknd fnl f* **66/1**

0000 **5** *2 ¾* **Bonbon Bonnie**[57] 4296 4-9-0 30..................................(be[1]) TomMcLaughlin 5 35
(Phil McEntee) *chsd ldr after 100yds to 2f out: wknd* **100/1**

6 *7* **Miss Jo B** 3-8-9 0.................................. RyanClark(3) 8 13
(Phil McEntee) *dwlt: nvr on terms in last pair: wknd 2f out* **18/1**

05 **P** **User Name (USA)**[10] 5949 3-8-12 0..................................(v) IanMongan 3
(Mikael Magnusson) *a in last pair: lost action over 2f out: p.u and dismntd* **25/1**

1m 14.06s (0.96) **Going Correction** -0.05s/f (Stan)
WFA 3 from 4yo 2lb 7 Ran SP% **112.5**
Speed ratings (Par 100): **91,87,83,81,77 68,**
toteswingers 1&2 £1.50, 1&3 £1.10, 2&3 £1.90 CSF £10.33 TOTE £2.90: £1.20, £4.50; EX 9.00 Trifecta £9.10 Pool: £974.65 - 78.96 winning tickets..
Owner Hopper, Grundy, Handscombe **Bred** Mr & Mrs K W Grundy, Mr & Mrs P Hopper **Trained** Newmarket, Suffolk

FOCUS
The winner was rated 64, so this was a weakish maiden. The winner did not need to improve much.

6255 BOOK KEMPTON TICKETS ON 0844 579 3008 H'CAP 2m (P)
8:50 (8:50) (Class 6) (0-65,66) 3-Y-0+ **£2,070** (£616; £307; £153) **Stalls** Low

Form RPR
0063 **1** **Albonny (IRE)**[17] 5744 3-8-4 **61**.................................. MichaelJMMurphy(7) 7 72+
(Alan Jarvis) *hld up in midfield: prog 3f out to trck ldr jst over 2f out: rdn to ld jst over 1f out: styd on wl* **9/4[2]**

566 **2** *2 ½* **Benartic (IRE)**[16] 4648 8-9-13 **64**.................................. DaneO'Neill 9 71
(Harry Dunlop) *sn trckd ldrs: prog to go 2nd over 3f out: clsd to ld over 2f out: hdd and one pce jst over 1f out* **33/1**

0221 **3** *1 ¾* **Looks Like Rain**[12] 5891 3-9-2 **66**.................................. SilvestreDeSousa 6 71
(Brian Ellison) *trckd ldrs: n.m.r briefly after 2f: prog to take 3rd jst over 3f out: clsd 2f out: one pce fr over 1f out* **11/8[1]**

2540 **4** *nse* **Lady of Burgundy**[18] 5718 6-9-9 **60**.................................. GeorgeBaker 4 65
(Mark Usher) *stdd s: hld up in last: gd prog to take 5th over 2f out: shkn up and styd on: nrly snatched 3rd but no ch to threaten* **14/1**

-005 **5** *7* **Baan (USA)**[18] 5706 9-9-1 **59**.................................. RyanTate(7) 8 56
(James Eustace) *hld up in last trio: prog and v wd bnd 3f out: sn outpcd: kpt on same pce fnl 2f* **11/1[3]**

0040 **6** *nk* **Irons On Fire (USA)**[10] 5935 4-9-6 **57**.................................. CathyGannon 10 53
(Lee Carter) *wl in rr: drvn over 3f out: outpcd wl over 2f out: kpt on same pce after* **25/1**

-000 **7** *½* **Jacobs Son**[18] 5706 4-10-0 **65**.................................. StevieDonohoe 2 61
(Robert Mills) *hld up in last trio: drvn and outpcd wl over 2f out: kpt on same pce fnl 2f* **25/1**

5025 **8** *3* **Squad**[23] 5509 6-9-12 **63**..................................(v) EddieAhern 3 55
(Simon Dow) *hld up in midfield: prog 3f out: rdn and in tch against rail 2f out: wknd qckly over 1f out* **14/1**

5456 **9** *11* **Barbirolli**[23] 5509 10-8-8 **48** oh3.................................. RyanClark(3) 5 27
(William Stone) *nvr beyond midfield: wknd wl over 2f out* **66/1**

600- **10** *1* **Cossack Prince**[17] 3281 7-8-13 **50**..................................(b[1]) IanMongan 1 28
(Laura Mongan) *led: clr 5f out: wknd and hdd over 2f out: eased over 1f out* **33/1**

6006 **11** *3* **The Ploughman**[10] 5945 3-7-12 **48** oh3.................................. KieranO'Neill 11 22
(John Bridger) *mostly chsd ldr to over 3f out: wknd over 2f out* **25/1**

0-00 **12** *1 ¾* **Rollin 'n Tumblin**[9] 5974 8-8-8 **48** oh2.................................. MarkCoumbe(3) 12 20
(Michael Attwater) *t.k.h: trckd ldrs tl wknd 3f out* **50/1**

/060 **13** *5* **Giant Sequoia (USA)**[37] 5022 8-9-7 **58**..................................(t) DaraghO'Donohoe 13 24
(Barney Curley) *nt that wl away: racd wd: prog to dispute 2nd after 3f: wknd over 3f out: t.o* **25/1**

3m 28.55s (-1.55) **Going Correction** -0.05s/f (Stan)
WFA 3 from 4yo+ 13lb 13 Ran SP% **119.3**
Speed ratings (Par 101): **101,99,98,98,95 95,94,93,87,87 85,85,82**
toteswingers 1&2 £50.60, 1&3 £1.80, 2&3 £25.70 CSF £84.58 CT £139.64 TOTE £3.50: £1.70, £8.40, £1.10; EX 101.60 TRIFECTA Not won..
Owner M&J Partnership **Bred** J Costello **Trained** Twyford, Bucks

FOCUS
The first and third were both in good form over 2m coming into this, so it was more competitive that it might have been. The pace was not strong and few got involved from the rear. The winner built on his latest C&D run.
Cossack Prince Official explanation: jockey said gelding ran too free

6256 BETFAIR SUPPORTS GRASSROOTS RACING AT KEMPTON H'CAP 7f (P)
9:20 (9:21) (Class 4) (0-80,80) 3-Y-0+ **£5,175** (£1,540; £769; £384) **Stalls** Low

Form RPR
0622 **1** **Don Libre**[29] 5302 3-8-11 **76**..................................(t) AshleyMorgan(5) 10 87
(Paul Cole) *trckd ldr: pushed along to cl over 1f out: led ins fnl f: sn in command: readily* **6/1[3]**

3156 **2** *1* **Forks**[25] 5457 5-9-1 **71**.................................. BrettDoyle 12 80
(Jane Chapple-Hyam) *led at decent pce: kicked on over 2f out: hdd ins fnl f: styd on* **9/1**

0056 **3** *1 ¾* **Dozy Joe**[7] 6041 4-8-13 **69**..................................(p) SebSanders 2 73
(Ian Wood) *hld up in midfield on inner: rdn over 2f out: prog wl over 1f out: styd on to take 3rd nr fin* **25/1**

1600 **4** *½* **Flameofthforest (IRE)**[22] 5530 5-9-7 **77**..................................(b[1]) EddieAhern 4 80
(Ed de Giles) *wl plcd: chsd ldng pair 2f out: hld 1f out: lost 3rd nr fin* **8/1**

0506 **5** *¾* **Galatian**[20] 5630 5-9-2 **72**.................................. JamesMillman 14 73+
(Rod Millman) *dropped in fr wd draw: hld up last: taken out wd over 2f out: stormed home fnl f: no ch of chalng* **20/1**

106 **6** *1 ¾* **Jake The Snake (IRE)**[22] 5531 11-9-1 **76**.................................. LauraPike(5) 13 72
(Tony Carroll) *hld up wl in rr: shkn up over 2f out: sme prog over 1f out: nt pce to threaten* **25/1**

430 **7** *nk* **My Son Max**[29] 5320 4-9-10 **80**.................................. SilvestreDeSousa 11 75
(P J O'Gorman) *wl in tch on outer: rdn and nt qckn over 2f out: one pce after* **9/2[2]**

0630 **8** *½* **Avonmore Star**[7] 6041 4-9-7 **77**.................................. SeanLevey 3 71
(Richard Hannon) *wl in tch: rdn over 2f out: brief prog over 1f out: sn no hdwy and btn* **10/1**

0600 **9** *1 ¼* **Point North (IRE)**[60] 4190 5-9-10 **80**.................................. IanMongan 9 71
(John Balding) *dwlt: rousted up to chse ldng pair: drvn over 2f out: sn lost pl and btn* **16/1**

6111 **10** *1* **It's A Mans World**[26] 5414 6-8-13 **72**.................................. PaulPickard(3) 5 60
(Brian Ellison) *racd wd towards rr: drvn and no prog over 2f out: tried to make sme hdwy over 1f out: no ch* **7/2[1]**

0360 **11** *2 ½* **The Guru Of Gloom (IRE)**[11] 5910 4-9-8 **78**.................................. MartinDwyer 6 59
(William Muir) *t.k.h early: hld up in rr: rdn and no prog over 2f out: wl btn over 1f out* **6/1[3]**

410- **12** *1* **Elsie's Orphan**[325] 7097 5-9-3 **73**.................................. GeorgeBaker 7 51
(Patrick Chamings) *prom: rdn over 2f out: wknd over 1f out: eased* **16/1**

3000 **13** *nk* **Legal Legacy**[34] 5120 6-9-3 **73**.................................. AmirQuinn 1 51
(Richard Rowe) *dwlt: nvr bttr than midfield on inner: u.p and struggling over 2f out: wknd* **40/1**

0056 **14** *3 ¼* **Gung Ho Jack**[39] 4919 3-8-10 **75**.................................. TobyAtkinson(5) 8 44
(John Best) *s.s: a wl in rr: wl btn over 2f out* **40/1**

1m 24.45s (-1.55) **Going Correction** -0.05s/f (Stan)
WFA 3 from 4yo+ 4lb 14 Ran SP% **128.3**
Speed ratings (Par 105): **106,104,102,102,101 99,99,98,97,95 93,91,91,87**
toteswingers 1&2 £10.60, 1&3 £15.20, 2&3 £56.80 CSF £59.60 CT £1322.65 TOTE £6.60: £2.60, £2.60, £7.60; EX 72.70 TRIFECTA Not won..
Owner Mrs E A Bass **Bred** Mrs E A Bass **Trained** Whatcombe, Oxon

FOCUS
The best-quality race of the night, though few of them were at the top of their game beforehand. The pace was testing and the first two posted personal bests.
T/Plt: £31.60 to a £1 stake. Pool: £72,830.45 - 1,682.31 winning tickets T/Qpdt: £6.10 to a £1 stake. Pool: £6,630.50 - 791.48 winning tickets JN

6099 NEWCASTLE (L-H)
Saturday, September 15

OFFICIAL GOING: Good (good to firm in places in final 3f; 7.7)
Rail after winning post around back of the course moved to provide the best ground possible.
Wind: Fresh, half against Weather: Sunny, hot

6257 FREEBETTING.CO.UK/BRITISH STALLION STUDS E B F MAIDEN FILLIES' STKS 1m 3y(S)
1:30 (1:31) (Class 5) 2-Y-0 **£3,557** (£1,058; £529; £264) **Stalls** High

Form RPR
1 **Power Of Light (IRE)** 2-9-0 0.................................. FrederikTylicki 8 75+
(Mahmood Al Zarooni) *trckd ldrs gng wl: shkn up to ld over 1f out: qcknd clr fnl f* **10/3[2]**

2 *7* **A Star In My Eye (IRE)** 2-9-0 0.................................. BarryMcHugh 9 59
(Kevin Ryan) *dwlt: sn rn green in rr: swtchd lft and hdwy 3f out: ev ch over 1f out: one pce fnl f: bttr for r* **7/1**

0 **3** *2* **Brigh (IRE)**[11] 5902 2-9-0 0.................................. AdamBeschizza 4 54
(David Simcock) *t.k.h early: cl up: led over 2f out to over 1f out: kpt on same pce* **4/1[3]**

00 **4** *1 ½* **Marble Silver (IRE)**[15] 5797 2-9-0 0.................................. DuranFentiman 12 51
(Tim Easterby) *hld up: stdy hdwy over 2f out: sn pushed along: kpt on fnl f: no imp* **100/1**

5 **5** *1* **Spieta (IRE)**[28] 5339 2-9-0 0.................................. KirstyMilczarek 3 48
(Luca Cumani) *dwlt: sn in tch: stdy hdwy after 3f: rdn along over 2f out: one pce fr over 1f out* **11/8[1]**

00 **6** *8* **Santa Fe Stinger**[28] 5339 2-8-9 0.................................. DarylByrne(5) 1 30
(Tim Easterby) *dwlt: hld up on outside: drvn along over 3f out: no imp fr 2f out* **100/1**

0 **7** *6* **Windsor Secret**[12] 5887 2-9-0 0.................................. AndrewMullen 11 16
(Keith Dalgleish) *led to over 2f out: sn rdn and wknd* **100/1**

0 **8** *20* **Trinket Box (USA)**[50] 4546 2-8-9 0.................................. AntiocoMurgia(5) 7
(Mahmood Al Zarooni) *trckd ldrs tl wknd over 2f out* **9/1**

 The Form Book Flat, Raceform Ltd, Compton, RG20 6NL

9 2 **Icy Reply** 2-9-0 0 .... LukeMorris 6
(Sir Mark Prescott Bt) *hld up in tch: drvn and outpcd over 3f out: btn fnl 2f* **25/1**

1m 44.32s (0.92) **Going Correction** -0.05s/f (Good) **9** Ran SP% **114.5**
Speed ratings (Par 92): **93,86,84,82,81 73,67,47,45**
Tote Swingers: 1&2 £4.20, 1&3 £4.00, 2&3 £3.60 CSF £26.02 TOTE £4.00: £1.80, £2.30, £1.40; EX 18.70.
Owner Godolphin **Bred** Rabbah Bloodstock Limited **Trained** Newmarket, Suffolk
■ Stewards' Enquiry : Kirsty Milczarek two-day ban: failed to ride out for 4th (Sep 30-Oct 1)

FOCUS
A modest field and the time was slow, but a taking debut winner.

NOTEBOOK
Power Of Light(IRE) ◆ landed some decent bets on her debut. The first foal of a useful 6f and 1m winner, she came right away inside the final furlong and looked right at home on the quick surface. Her trainer's juveniles continue in fine form and she could be smart at around 1m2f next term. It will be very interesting to see where she's pitched in next. (op 7-2 tchd 3-1)
A Star In My Eye(IRE), bred to stay well, posted a pleasing debut effort as she ran distinctly green, and already looks to need all of this trip. She can get closer next time granted normal improvement. (op 15-2 tchd 8-1)
Brigh(IRE), ninth behind a promising sort at Goodwood on her debut, paid late on for running with a choke out early doors. She's now looking more like one for nurseries. (tchd 9-2)
Marble Silver(IRE) was having her third outing and turned in her most encouraging effort so far. She now qualifies for nurseries.
Spieta(IRE), an eye-catcher on her Leicester debut 28 days earlier, didn't help her cause with a sluggish start and found just the same pace when put under pressure. This was disappointing, but it's obviously too soon to be writing her off. (op 6-4 tchd 7-4)

6258 DELOITTE H'CAP (DIV I) 1m (R)
2:00 (2:00) (Class 6) (0-65,65) 3-Y-0+ **£2,070** (£616; £307; £153) **Stalls** Low

Form RPR
0023 1 **Dandarrell**[17] 5730 5-8-10 **51** oh1 .... FrederikTylicki 4 59
(Julie Camacho) *trckd ldr: rdn over 2f out: led over 1f out: kpt on wl fnl f* **5/1**[2]
0005 2 1 1/2 **Wiseman's Diamond (USA)**[19] 5669 7-9-3 **58** ....(b) MickyFenton 2 63
(Paul Midgley) *led: rdn over 2f out: hdd over 1f out: rallied: hld last 75yd* **20/1**
054 3 1/2 **Auto Mac**[4] 6127 4-9-7 **62** .... LukeMorris 3 65
(Neville Bycroft) *prom: effrt and rdn over 2f out: kpt on ins fnl f* **7/2**[1]
0553 4 2 **High Resolution**[3] 6131 5-8-13 **59** .... ShaneBKelly(5) 5 58
(Linda Perratt) *hld up on ins: rdn and hdwy over 1f out: kpt on fnl f: nrst fin* **6/1**[3]
5506 5 1/2 **Cottam Donny**[22] 5547 4-9-4 **59** .... GrahamGibbons 6 57
(Mel Brittain) *t.k.h: in tch: effrt and rdn over 2f out: one pce fnl f* **6/1**[3]
4065 6 hd **Shamo Hill Theatre**[5] 6102 5-8-6 **52** oh6 ow1 ....(p) DarylByrne(5) 8 49+
(Lawrence Mullaney) *hld up: rdn over 2f out: styd on fnl f: nvr able to chal* **40/1**
4000 7 3 **Whispered Times (USA)**[4] 6127 5-9-6 **61** ....(p) RoystonFfrench 11 51
(Tracy Waggott) *in tch on outside: rdn over 2f out: wknd fnl f* **16/1**
6016 8 1 **Glenluji**[11] 5917 7-8-8 **56** .... SophieRobertson(7) 1 44
(Jim Goldie) *taken early to post: dwlt: sn midfield on ins: rdn and outpcd 2f out: n.d after* **25/1**
5001 9 3/4 **Monthly Medal**[22] 5547 9-9-3 **58** ....(t) AmyRyan 15 44
(Wilf Storey) *taken early to post: dwlt: hld up and bhd: stdy hdwy on outside 2f out: sn rdn and no imp* **7/1**
0053 10 1 **Alabanda (IRE)**[15] 5803 3-8-5 **51** .... DuranFentiman 12 35
(Tim Easterby) *bhd: drvn over 2f out: nvr able to chal* **14/1**
2530 11 2 1/4 **Madame Blavatsky (FR)**[22] 5547 4-8-9 **57** .... GeorgeChaloner(7) 16 36
(Karen McLintock) *hld up: stdy hdwy over 2f out: wknd over 1f out* **25/1**
0305 12 3/4 **Outlaw Torn (IRE)**[11] 5918 3-8-6 **55** ....(e) DeclanCannon(3) 9 32
(Richard Guest) *hld up: rdn over 2f out: hmpd over 1f out: nvr on terms* **16/1**
0250 13 1 3/4 **The Lodge Road (IRE)**[37] 5001 4-9-10 **65** .... PJMcDonald 7 38
(Martin Todhunter) *midfield: lost pl over 3f out: sn rdn and btn* **20/1**
0266 14 6 **Dolly Royal (IRE)**[74] 3731 7-8-10 **51** oh4 ....(p) PatrickMathers 10 10
(Robert Johnson) *in tch tl rdn and wknd 2f out* **50/1**

1m 42.18s (-3.12) **Going Correction** -0.35s/f (Firm)
WFA 3 from 4yo+ 5lb **14** Ran SP% **120.0**
Speed ratings (Par 101): **101,99,99,97,96 96,93,92,91,90 88,87,85,79**
Tote Swingers: 1&2 £16.30, 1&3 £6.60, 2&3 £29.70 CSF £109.18 CT £336.30 TOTE £4.80: £1.80, £6.30, £2.20; EX 101.10.
Owner Jocelyn Waller **Bred** Peter Onslow **Trained** Norton, N Yorks

FOCUS
An open handicap. They went a fair pace, but it still it paid to race handily. It was the faster division and the winner is rated back to something like his 2010 best.
Monthly Medal Official explanation: trainer had no explanation for the poor form shown

6259 DELOITTE H'CAP (DIV II) 1m (R)
2:35 (2:37) (Class 6) (0-65,65) 3-Y-0+ **£2,070** (£616; £307; £153) **Stalls** Low

Form RPR
344 1 **Talent Scout (IRE)**[26] 5414 6-9-5 **60** ....(p) DuranFentiman 4 74
(Tim Walford) *mde all: rdn and qcknd clr 2f out: hld on wl fnl f: unchal* **9/2**[3]
0113 2 1 1/4 **Ingleby Angel (IRE)**[7] 6048 3-9-3 **63** .... DavidNolan 6 77+
(David O'Meara) *t.k.h: hld up in midfield: hdwy 2f out: chsd (clr) wnr ins fnl f: clsd nr fin but a hld* **6/2**[1]
00-0 3 4 **Burns Night**[143] 1598 6-9-10 **65** .... AdamBeschizza 9 67
(Peter Salmon) *prom: rdn and effrt over 2f out: kpt on same pce fnl f* **3/1**[2]
2000 4 1/2 **Seldom (IRE)**[26] 5414 6-9-6 **61** .... GrahamGibbons 10 62
(Mel Brittain) *chsd wnr: rdn over 2f out: one pce and lost 2nd ins fnl f* **14/1**
1-00 5 1 1/4 **Galilee Chapel (IRE)**[43] 4771 3-9-1 **61** .... AmyRyan 3 59
(Alistair Whillans) *trckd ldrs: rdn and outpcd 2f out: n.d after* **25/1**
5054 6 1 1/4 **Whats For Pudding (IRE)**[32] 5185 4-8-5 **51** oh5 .... NeilFarley(5) 7 46
(Declan Carroll) *cl up: drvn over 2f out: wknd ins fnl f* **20/1**
6300 7 hd **Simpson Millar**[25] 5446 3-8-2 **51** oh6 .... DeclanCannon(3) 5 46
(Noel Wilson) *t.k.h: hld up in midfield: rdn over 2f out: styd on fnl f: nvr able to chal* **50/1**
3013 8 4 1/2 **Ryedale Dancer (IRE)**[5] 6106 4-9-4 **59** .... AndrewMullen 15 43
(Richard Guest) *hld up: rdn over 2f out: sme late hdwy: nvr able to chal* **7/1**
-000 9 1 3/4 **Roll Of Thunder**[17] 5728 3-8-5 **51** oh3 ....[1] BarryMcHugh 16 31
(John Quinn) *hld up towards rr: effrt and pushed along over 2f out: sn btn* **33/1**
6020 10 1 3/4 **Icewan**[22] 5547 3-8-11 **57** .... MickyFenton 8 33
(Paul Midgley) *s.i.s: bhd: drvn wl over 2f out: sn btn* **33/1**
6/00 11 1 **King Of The Moors (USA)**[51] 4511 9-9-1 **56** ....(b) KellyHarrison 11 30
(John Spearing) *s.i.s: hld up: rdn over 2f out: sn wknd* **33/1**
560 12 nk **Whatsofunny (IRE)**[11] 5917 3-8-9 **55** .... PJMcDonald 2 28
(Ruth Carr) *in tch on ins tl rdn and wknd 2f out* **16/1**
06 13 82 **Tropical Duke (IRE)**[19] 5669 6-8-7 **53** oh3 ow2 .... ShaneBKelly(5) 13
(Ron Barr) *upset in stalls: slowly away: sn t.o: eased whn no ch fnl 4f* **28/1**

1m 42.88s (-2.42) **Going Correction** -0.35s/f (Firm)
WFA 3 from 4yo+ 5lb **13** Ran SP% **119.6**
Speed ratings (Par 101): **98,96,92,92,91 89,89,85,83,81 80,80,**
Tote Swingers: 1&2 £1.50, 1&3 £6.90, 2&3 £5.00 CSF £14.83 CT £39.78 TOTE £5.70: £2.00, £1.10, £1.60; EX 12.70.
Owner John Stacey **Bred** Johnston King **Trained** Sheriff Hutton, N Yorks

FOCUS
The second division of the 1m handicap. It was another race where, despite a sound tempo being on, it proved a struggle coming from off the pace. The time was 0.7sec slower than division I. The winner's best form this year.
Ryedale Dancer(IRE) Official explanation: jockey said filly suffered interference in running
Tropical Duke(IRE) Official explanation: jockey said gelding became upset in the stalls

6260 ROYAL MAIL H'CAP 6f
3:10 (3:11) (Class 5) (0-75,75) 4-Y-0+ **£2,911** (£866; £432; £216) **Stalls** High

Form RPR
200 1 **Dickie Le Davoir**[7] 6044 8-9-1 **69** ....(b) RobbieFitzpatrick 9 78
(Richard Guest) *bhd: rdn over 3f out: hdwy and swtchd lft over 1f out: led ins fnl f: kpt on wl* **12/1**
1505 2 nk **Bandstand**[43] 4784 6-8-13 **67** .... RoystonFfrench 2 75
(Bryan Smart) *in tch: effrt over 2f out: chal ins fnl f: kpt on: hld nr fin* **20/1**
14 3 1 1/2 **Zomerlust**[86] 3304 10-9-2 **70** ....(b) MichaelO'Connell 5 73
(John Quinn) *trckd ldrs: smooth hdwy to ld over 1f out: sn rdn: hdd ins fnl f: kpt on same pce* **14/1**
0026 4 1/2 **Barkston Ash**[8] 6009 4-9-2 **75** .... DarylByrne(5) 10 77+
(Eric Alston) *in tch: effrt and hdwy over 1f out: kpt on ins fnl f: no imp last 100yds* **10/3**[1]
-060 5 1/2 **Who's Shirl**[4] 6127 6-9-2 **70** .... KellyHarrison 11 70
(Chris Fairhurst) *dwlt: sn pushed along in rr: hdwy and swtchd lft over 1f out: kpt on fnl f: nvr able to chal* **5/1**[2]
0300 6 1/2 **Toby Tyler**[4] 6123 6-9-5 **73** ....(v) MickyFenton 7 71
(Paul Midgley) *hld up: rdn and hdwy over 1f out: kpt on fnl f: nt pce to chal* **10/1**
2340 7 1 **Rio Cobolo (IRE)**[15] 5802 6-8-11 **65** ....(b) AndrewMullen 12 60
(David Nicholls) *led to over 1f out: outpcd ins fnl f* **8/1**
1-00 8 3 1/2 **Captain Royale (IRE)**[3] 6144 7-8-13 **72** ....(p) ShaneBKelly(5) 4 56
(Tracy Waggott) *cl up: rdn and ev ch over 1f out: sn wknd* **33/1**
0-40 9 hd **Cornus**[14] 5819 10-8-13 **70** ....(be) DeclanCannon(3) 1 53
(Alan McCabe) *in tch: drvn over 2f out: wknd over 1f out* **40/1**
1400 10 3/4 **Nasharra (IRE)**[7] 6044 4-9-5 **73** ....(b) AmyRyan 8 54
(Kevin Ryan) *cl up on outside: ev ch over 2f out to over 1f out: sn btn* **10/1**
6606 11 6 **Hills Of Dakota**[35] 5084 4-8-13 **67** .... GrahamGibbons 14 29
(David Barron) *prom: drvn over 2f out: wknd over 1f out* **6/1**[3]
0064 12 7 **Wildcat Wizard (USA)**[4] 6123 6-8-11 **65** .... PJMcDonald 6
(Paul Midgley) *missed break: bhd on outside: struggling over 2f out: sn btn* **9/1**

1m 15.14s (0.54) **Going Correction** -0.05s/f (Good) **12** Ran SP% **117.8**
Speed ratings (Par 103): **94,93,91,90,90 89,88,83,83,82 74,65**
Tote Swingers: 1&2 £28.50, 1&3 £9.20, 2&3 £13.30 CSF £230.27 CT £3410.29 TOTE £10.50: £3.00, £6.70, £3.30; EX 128.70.
Owner Future Racing (Notts) Limited **Bred** P And Mrs A G Venner **Trained** Stainforth, S Yorks

FOCUS
A modest sprint handicap run at a good pace. They unsurprisingly kept stands' side but the first two raced away from the rail. The form makes sense.

6261 VELOCITY "SPECIALIST IN RECRUITMENT" H'CAP 7f
3:50 (3:51) (Class 5) (0-75,75) 3-Y-0 **£2,911** (£866; £432; £216) **Stalls** High

Form RPR
106 1 **Iffraam (IRE)**[38] 4961 3-9-5 **73** ....(b[1]) PJMcDonald 7 81
(Michael Dods) *cl up: rdn over 1f out: led ins fnl f: kpt on strly* **7/1**[3]
3060 2 1 3/4 **I'll Be Good**[4] 6127 3-8-9 **70** .... KevinStott(7) 2 73
(Robert Johnson) *led: rdn over 1f out: hdd ins fnl f: kpt on: hld towards fin* **14/1**
1223 3 1 3/4 **Fayr Fall (IRE)**[7] 6052 3-9-3 **71** ....(v[1]) DuranFentiman 5 70
(Tim Easterby) *t.k.h early: prom: effrt and hdwy over 1f out: kpt on same pce ins fnl f* **2/1**[1]
-406 4 3/4 **Winter Hill**[7] 6048 3-8-5 **62** .... RossAtkinson(3) 8 59
(Tom Dascombe) *hld up last but in tch: effrt and rdn over 1f out: no imp fnl f* **10/3**[2]
2253 5 2 1/2 **Sabore**[16] 5760 3-8-7 **61** oh1 ....(p) PatrickMathers 4 51
(Richard Fahey) *prom on outside: rdn over 2f out: btn fnl f* **11/1**
0054 6 4 **Mitchum**[15] 5803 3-9-0 **68** .... GrahamGibbons 3 47
(David Barron) *trckd ldrs tl rdn and wknd over 1f out* **10/3**[2]
0000 7 7 **Daunt (IRE)**[18] 5713 3-8-9 **63** .... MichaelO'Connell 9 23
(John Quinn) *t.k.h: hld up in tch: rdn over 2f out: wknd over 1f out* **16/1**

1m 28.94s (1.14) **Going Correction** -0.05s/f (Good) **7** Ran SP% **112.9**
Speed ratings (Par 101): **91,89,87,86,83 78,70**
Tote Swingers: 1&2 £8.70, 1&3 £9.10, 2&3 £2.20 CSF £90.40 CT £265.56 TOTE £7.70: £4.60, £5.30; EX 80.80.
Owner Andrew Tinkler **Bred** Roalso Ltd **Trained** Denton, Co Durham

FOCUS
A tight little handicap and it saw a host of chances late on. The form is not that convincing, but the winner rates a personal best.
Mitchum Official explanation: jockey said colt hung left-handed

6262 SENDRIG CONSTRUCTION H'CAP 1m 2f 32y
4:25 (4:26) (Class 6) (0-60,60) 3-Y-0+ **£2,070** (£616; £307; £153) **Stalls** Low

Form RPR
3200 1 **Cadgers Brig**[19] 5672 4-9-10 **60** ....(p) FrederikTylicki 1 68
(Keith Dalgleish) *cl up: led after 2f: rdn over 2f out: hrd pressed ins fnl f: jst hld on* **10/1**
3406 2 shd **Echo Of Footsteps**[26] 5413 3-9-3 **60** .... GrahamGibbons 10 67
(Michael Herrington) *hld up in midfield: hdwy to chse wnr over 1f out: chal ins fnl f: jst hld* **22/1**
-234 3 2 **Sheila's Castle**[17] 5735 8-9-0 **57** .... ConorHarrison(7) 6 60
(Sean Regan) *s.i.s: hld up: hdwy on outside over 2f out: kpt on fnl f: nt rch first two* **14/1**

0444 **4** *hd* **Avison (IRE)**[5] 6102 4-9-2 **52** DavidNolan 12 55
(Richard Fahey) *midfield: effrt and drvn over 2f out: styd on ins fnl f* **7/1**[3]
0240 **5** *nk* **Graceful Act**[75] 3693 4-9-2 **57** ShaneBKelly(5) 4 59
(Ron Barr) *t.k.h: prom: outpcd over 2f out: rallied over 1f out: no ex ins fnl f* **40/1**
6024 **6** *1 3/4* **Sinatramania**[31] 5225 5-9-5 **55** RoystonFfrench 9 54
(Tracy Waggott) *t.k.h: hld up: rdn and hdwy on outside 2f out: no imp fnl f* **12/1**
5062 **7** *3/4* **Goldenveil (IRE)**[25] 5452 4-8-11 **54** GeorgeChaloner(7) 2 51
(Richard Fahey) *t.k.h: cl up: rdn over 2f out: no ex ins fnl f* **9/2**[1]
400 **8** *1* **Maska Pony (IRE)**[40] 4882 8-9-7 **57** PJMcDonald 5 52
(George Moore) *in tch: drvn and lost pl 1/2-way: rallied over 1f out: nvr rchd ldrs* **6/1**[2]
5/53 **9** *1/2* **Shaker Style (USA)**[108] 2600 6-9-5 **58** LucyAlexander(3) 15 52
(Barry Murtagh) *hld up: rdn along over 3f out: hdwy over 1f out: kpt on: nt pce to chal* **28/1**
232 **10** *2* **Military Call**[36] 5059 5-9-8 **58** PaddyAspell 16 48
(Alistair Whillans) *bhd: drvn over 3f out: sme late hdwy: nvr on terms* **10/1**
0430 **11** *4* **Nolecce**[8] 5998 5-9-8 **58** (p) IPoullis 8 40
(Richard Guest) *hld up: rdn over 2f out: btn over 1f out* **25/1**
-000 **12** *3/4* **Cobbs Quay**[80] 3485 4-9-9 **59** LukeMorris 7 40
(Daniel Kubler) *t.k.h: cl up: rdn and ev ch over 3f out: wknd appr fnl f* **10/1**
3536 **13** *1* **Retreat Content (IRE)**[61] 4137 4-9-6 **56** DuranFentiman 3 35
(Linda Perratt) *led 2f: cl up: outpcd whn n.m.r 2f out: sn btn* **16/1**
0325 **14** *nk* **Sally Friday (IRE)**[14] 5824 4-9-2 **52** (p) AmyRyan 13 30
(Edwin Tuer) *s.i.s: hld up: hdwy on outside and prom 1/2-way: rdn and wknd over 2f out* **10/1**
6050 **15** *3 1/4* **Border Bandit (USA)**[19] 5672 4-9-0 **55** (p) GarryWhillans(5) 11 27
(Tracy Waggott) *prom: rdn over 3f out: outpcd whn n.m.r wl over 1f out: sn btn* **12/1**

2m 11.66s (-0.24) **Going Correction** -0.125s/f (Firm)
WFA 3 from 4yo+ 7lb **15** Ran SP% **123.3**
Speed ratings (Par 101): **95,94,93,93,92 91,90,90,89,88 84,84,83,83,80**
Tote Swingers: 1&2 £37.60 CSF £222.83 CT £3082.46 TOTE £11.80: £3.10, £6.90, £5.70; EX 413.10.
Owner John F Allan **Bred** Jock Allan **Trained** Carluke, S Lanarks
■ Stewards' Enquiry : Conor Harrison three-day ban: careless riding (Sep 30-Oct 1-2)
David Nolan seven-day ban: used whip above permitted level, down shoulder in the forehand without giving gelding time to respond (Sep 30-Oct 1-5)

FOCUS
A wide-open handicap. There was a solid pace on and the winner is rated to his turf best.
Cadgers Brig Official explanation: trainer said, regarding apparent improvemen t in form, that the gelding appreciated the better ground.
Sinatramania Official explanation: jockey said gelding hung left-handed in straight
Sally Friday(IRE) Official explanation: jockey said filly hung left-handed in straight

6263 F1 "PRINT & SPRINT" H'CAP — 1m 4f 93y
4:55 (4:55) (Class 5) (0-75,75) 3-Y-O — £2,911 (£866; £432; £216) Stalls Low

Form RPR
6660 **1** **Rythmic**[66] 3968 3-9-0 **68** FrederikTylicki 2 77
(Mark Johnston) *cl up: led over 3f out: rdn and styd on wl fr 2f out* **11/2**[3]
1336 **2** *1 1/4* **Seven Veils (IRE)**[18] 5706 3-9-4 **72** LukeMorris 7 79
(Sir Mark Prescott Bt) *trckd ldrs: effrt and ev ch over 3f out: edgd lft over 2f out: kpt on same pce fnl f* **7/2**[2]
0443 **3** *nse* **Twelve Strings (IRE)**[18] 5706 3-9-7 **75** KirstyMilczarek 3 82+
(Luca Cumani) *dwlt: t.k.h and sn chsng ldrs: drvn and outpcd 3f out: rallied over 1f out: styd on wl fnl f: nt pce to chal* **5/4**[1]
3112 **4** *2* **Maybeagrey**[28] 5373 3-9-5 **73** DuranFentiman 5 77
(Tim Easterby) *stdd s: hld up: effrt and hdwy over 2f out: kpt on same pce fnl f* **6/1**
4215 **5** *1 1/2* **Arley Hall**[28] 5373 3-9-6 **74** BarryMcHugh 4 75
(Richard Fahey) *prom: effrt and edgd lft over 2f out: one pce over 1f out* **7/1**
-000 **6** *48* **Willy McBay**[35] 5114 3-8-7 **61** oh16 AndrewMullen 1
(George Moore) *led to over 3f out: sn rdn and struggling: t.o* **100/1**
2651 **7** *1 1/2* **Croftamie**[39] 4912 3-9-4 **72** RoystonFfrench 8
(Tracy Waggott) *hld up in tch: struggling 1/2-way: t.o fnl 3f* **22/1**

2m 43.58s (-2.02) **Going Correction** -0.125s/f (Firm) **7** Ran SP% **114.2**
Speed ratings (Par 101): **101,100,100,98,97 65,64**
Tote Swingers: 1&2 £2.60, 1&3 £2.00, 2&3 £1.80 CSF £24.90 CT £38.19 TOTE £6.90: £4.60, £1.10; EX 31.80.
Owner Sheikh Hamdan Bin Mohammed Al Maktoum **Bred** Darley **Trained** Middleham Moor, N Yorks

FOCUS
Sound form for the class despite a modest time. The winner is rated back to something like her 2yo form.
Rythmic Official explanation: trainer's rep had no explanation for the apparent improvement in form.
Croftamie Official explanation: jockey said filly never travelled

6264 S V RUTTER H'CAP — 5f
5:25 (5:26) (Class 6) (0-65,65) 3-Y-O+ — £1,343 (£1,343; £307; £153) Stalls High

Form RPR
0342 **1** **Mr Mo Jo**[17] 5739 4-9-1 **59** FrederikTylicki 14 69
(Lawrence Mullaney) *cl up: rdn 2f out: disp ld ins fnl f: kpt on wl* **3/1**[1]
0454 **1** *dht* **Middleton Flyer (IRE)**[14] 5831 3-8-7 **59** (b) NedCurtis(7) 9 69
(Paul Midgley) *w ldr: led 1f out: sn jnd: kpt on fnl f: kpt on wl* **14/1**
5245 **3** *1* **Ambitious Icarus**[22] 5538 3-9-2 **61** (e) RobbieFitzpatrick 4 67
(Richard Guest) *hld up: rdn over 2f out: hdwy over 1f out: kpt on fnl f: nt rch dead-heaters* **14/1**
4620 **4** *1 1/4* **Ballarina**[29] 5294 6-8-11 **55** LukeMorris 1 57
(Eric Alston) *led at str pce to 1f out: kpt on: no ex last 75yds* **9/1**
3313 **5** *3/4* **Ypres**[20] 5621 3-9-6 **65** PaddyAspell 7 64
(Jason Ward) *in tch: rdn along and hdwy over 1f out: kpt on fnl f: no imp towards fin* **11/2**[2]
0000 **6** *shd* **Choc'A'Moca (IRE)**[14] 5821 5-9-2 **60** (v) MickyFenton 10 58
(Paul Midgley) *midfield: drvn along over 2f out: rallied over 1f out: kpt on fnl f: nt pce to chal* **33/1**
0-02 **7** *1 1/4* **Sir Nod**[26] 5416 10-9-7 **65** BarryMcHugh 11 59
(Julie Camacho) *hld up: rdn 1/2-way: hdwy over 1f out: kpt on: nvr able to chal* **14/1**
105 **8** *1* **Alnair (IRE)**[11] 5923 3-9-3 **62** GrahamGibbons 16 52
(Declan Carroll) *in tch: effrt and rdn over 2f out: one pce fnl f* **10/1**
4660 **9** *hd* **Angelo Poliziano**[11] 5923 6-8-8 **57** (p) LMcNiff(5) 15 47
(George Foster) *hld up: rdn over 2f out: no imp over 1f out* **20/1**

0000 **10** *1 1/4* **Nearly A Gift (IRE)**[30] 5257 3-8-11 **56** (t) KellyHarrison 8 41
(Tim Easterby) *s.i.s: bhd tl hdwy over 1f out: sn rdn and no imp* **50/1**
4643 **11** *3/4* **Distant Sun (USA)**[11] 5923 8-8-12 **56** (p) AmyRyan 12 38
(Linda Perratt) *midfield: drvn and outpcd 2f out: sn n.d* **20/1**
5155 **12** *5* **Mecca's Team**[17] 5739 4-9-1 **64** (p) ShaneBKelly(5) 2 28
(Michael Dods) *in tch: drvn along 1/2-way: no ex whn hmpd over 1f out* **11/1**
1652 **13** *2* **Holy Angel (IRE)**[20] 5624 3-9-5 **64** DuranFentiman 13 21
(Tim Easterby) *bhd: drvn along 1/2-way: sn btn* **8/1**[3]

1m 0.7s (-0.40) **Going Correction** -0.05s/f (Good)
WFA 3 from 4yo+ 1lb **13** Ran SP% **113.3**
Speed ratings (Par 101): **101,101,99,97,96 96,94,92,92,90 88,80,77**Tote: win Mr Mo Jo £2.00, Middleton Flyer £10.00 places MMJ £1.50, MF £5.00, £2.40 Exacta: MMJ, MH £32.60, MF, MMJ £44.60 CSF: MMJ, MFI £19.39, MF, MMJ £23.14 Tricast: MMJ, MF, AI £198.64, MF, MMJ, AI £238.77. TS: 1&2 £10.70, 1&3 £21.60, 2&3 £22.60 CT £27 TOTE £0Owner: £Gap Personnel, £Bred, £Maurice Burns, £TrainedWestow, N Yorks n Trifecta £This dead-heat gave Freddie Tylicki a five-timer from five rides on the card. 1.
Owner Ontoawinner 3 **Bred** D A Flavell **Trained** Great Habton, N Yorks
■ This dead-heat gave Freddie Tylicki a five-timer from five rides on the card.

FOCUS
On The High Tops was withdrawn (9/1, upset in stalls). Deduct 10p in the £ under R4. A moderate sprint handicap in which the first pair, who dead-heated, were always up there. The form appears sound.
Holy Angel(IRE) Official explanation: jockey said gelding stopped quickly
T/Plt: £15,996.90 to a £1 stake. Pool: £52,592.76 - 2.40 winning tickets. T/Qpdt: £833.90 to a £1 stake. Pool: £4,508.09 - 4.00 winning tickets. RY

6265 - (Foreign Racing) - See Raceform Interactive

6077 CURRAGH (R-H)
Saturday, September 15

OFFICIAL GOING: Yielding (good to yielding in places on round course)

6266a FLAME OF TARA EUROPEAN BREEDERS FUND STKS (LISTED RACE) (FILLIES) — 1m
3:30 (3:31) 2-Y-O — £32,500 (£9,500; £4,500; £1,500)

RPR
1 **Spinacre (IRE)**[26] 5431 2-9-0 ChrisHayes 7 99+
(Kevin Prendergast, Ire) *chsd ldrs: wnt 3rd 3f out gng best: led ent fnl f and kpt on wl: comf* **3/1**[2]
2 *2 1/4* **Reglisse (IRE)**[36] 5069 2-9-0 95 JamieSpencer 4 94
(Edward Lynam, Ire) *hld up in tch: pushed along under 2f out into 2nd ent fnl f: sn no ch w wnr: kpt on* **6/1**
3 *3 3/4* **Rasmeyaa (IRE)** 2-9-0 PatSmullen 3 85+
(D K Weld, Ire) *reluctant to load: hld up in tch: pushed along in 5th 3f out: wnt nvr threatening 3rd 1f out and kpt on towards fin* **9/2**
4 *2 3/4* **Madam Mo (IRE)**[6] 6077 2-9-0 DeclanMcDonogh 5 79
(P J Prendergast, Ire) *dwlt: pushed along to sn r in 2nd: prog to dispute 3f out and led 2f out: sn jnd and no ex ent fnl f* **14/1**
5 *2 3/4* **Uleavemebreathless**[12] 5894 2-9-0 ShaneFoley 2 73
(A Oliver, Ire) *chsd ldrs: pushed along in 4th over 3f out and one pce fnl 2f* **5/2**[1]
6 *3 1/4* **Greek Goddess (IRE)**[16] 5778 2-9-0 SeamieHeffernan 1 65
(A P O'Brien, Ire) *led: jnd 3f out: rdn over 2f out and sn wknd* **7/2**[3]
7 *nk* **Burnt Sienna (IRE)**[6] 6077 2-9-0 GaryCarroll 6 65
(John Joseph Murphy, Ire) *in rr thrght: nvr a factor* **40/1**

1m 43.52s (-2.48) **Going Correction** -0.50s/f (Hard) **7** Ran SP% **117.4**
Speed ratings: **92,89,86,83,80 77,76**
CSF £22.11 TOTE £3.80: £2.10, £2.80; DF 25.60.
Owner Ecurie La Boetie **Bred** Mrs Lisa Kelly **Trained** Friarstown, Co Kildare

FOCUS
Spinacre more than backed up her maiden win form, with the second, also by Verglas, helping with the level.

NOTEBOOK
Spinacre(IRE) ◆ showed more star quality here after her wide-margin win at Roscommon had been questioned as to its value. She had an extra when the pace quickened up and, while she did get a shade of first run on the runner-up, she was holding her quite comfortably. It was a classy performance from a filly who hasn't stopped progressing all year, which may augur well for her prospects of continuing to improve over the winter. (op 11/4)
Reglisse(IRE) has been highly tried since winning her maiden in July and she's probably another one that has suffered a bit from the lack of good ground. She couldn't quicken as effectively as one or two others when the tempo increased but she saw out her race well without threatening the winner. She got the mile well, suggesting that a more truly run race would have helped her a good deal more. (op 11/2 tchd 13/2)
Rasmeyaa(IRE) ◆ presumably must have been showing Dermot Weld plenty at home for him to run her in such a race on debut. She travelled well but showed her inexperience inside the last and her effort flattened out. It would be a big surprise, though, if there wasn't significant improvement in her. (op 7/2)
Madam Mo(IRE) travelled close to the pace and was in a good position to take advantage once the pace quickened. In the end she wasn't quite good enough, but it was an effort that was a significant improvement on what she had done previously. (op 14/1 tchd 12/1)
Uleavemebreathless was keen tracking the lead on the inside but she was in trouble once the pace quickened and never got into it after that. It was quite a flat and lifeless effort. Official explanation: vet said filly was found to be coughing (op 7/2)
Greek Goddess(IRE) Official explanation: jockey said filly travelled to 2f out, emptied quickly

6268a NEWBRIDGE 200 RENAISSANCE STKS (GROUP 3) — 6f
4:30 (4:32) 3-Y-O+ — £31,145 (£9,104; £4,312; £1,437)

RPR
1 **Maarek**[63] 4092 5-9-8 109 JamieSpencer 8 116
(David Peter Nagle, Ire) *in rr: niggled along bef 1/2-way: hdwy appr 2f out: swtchd rt 1f out and kpt on wl to ld fnl 100yds: styd on* **4/1**[2]
2 *1/2* **Starspangledbanner (AUS)**[34] 5137 6-9-5 114 SeamieHeffernan 10 111
(A P O'Brien, Ire) *hld up towards rr: 8th 1/2-way: n.m.r and swtchd rt 2f out: rdn ent fnl f and kpt on wl to chal: no ex fnl 100yds* **8/1**
3 *2 1/4* **Fire Lily (IRE)**[20] 5641 3-9-5 110 WayneLordan 6 106
(David Wachman, Ire) *chsd ldrs: 6th 1/2-way: clsd on outer 2f out and ev ch ent fnl f: rdn and no ex fnl 200yds* **2/1**[1]
4 *nk* **Firebeam**[46] 4686 4-9-5 PatSmullen 7 103
(William Haggas) *chsd ldr in 2nd: hdwy to ld 1 1/2f out: sn strly pressed and hdd: no ex cl home: kpt on* **4/1**[2]
5 *1 3/4* **Lady Wingshot (IRE)**[6] 6079 3-9-3 107 KevinManning 11 97
(J S Bolger, Ire) *chsd ldrs: 4th 3f out: sn pushed along and no imp ent fnl f: swtchd rt and kpt on* **11/1**

6 1 1/4 **Experience (IRE)**112 2513 3-9-0 103 ....(p) WJLee 2 90
(David Wachman, Ire) *settled in 3rd: pushed along 2f out: no ex and one pce fnl f* **14/1**

7 2 **Santo Padre (IRE)**36 5067 8-9-5 106 .... FergalLynch 3 87
(David Marnane, Ire) *towards rr: rdn and sme hdwy 1f out: nvr a threat* **20/1**

8 1 1/2 **Swiss Dream**93 3092 4-9-2 .... MartinHarley 4 79
(David Elsworth) *led: strly pressed over 2f out: sn hdd and no ex ins fnl f* **7/1**3

9 5 1/2 **Bulbul (IRE)**66 3983 3-9-0 95 .... DeclanMcDonogh 5 61
(Kevin Prendergast, Ire) *chsd ldrs on outer: pushed along appr fnl 2f and no imp* **25/1**

10 2 3/4 **Croisultan (IRE)**103 2777 6-9-5 104 .... ShaneFoley 9 56
(D K Weld, Ire) *towards rr: pushed along under 3f out: no imp* **25/1**

11 14 **Arctic (IRE)**36 5067 5-9-5 105 ....(bt1) MichaelHussey 12 11
(Tracey Collins, Ire) *chsd ldrs: 5th on inner 1/2-way: no ex fnl 2f* **18/1**

1m 12.33s (-3.17) **Going Correction** -0.25s/f (Firm)
WFA 3 from 4yo+ 2lb **11** Ran SP% **129.7**
Speed ratings: **111,110,107,106,104 102,100,98,90,87 68**
CSF £39.33 TOTE £4.80: £1.40, £2.20, £1.30; DF 44.90.
Owner Lisbunny Syndicate **Bred** New England Stud & P J & P M Vela **Trained** Fethard, Co Tipperary

FOCUS

A rare sprint in Ireland in that it wasn't dominated by cross-Channel raiders. A slight personal best from the winner.

NOTEBOOK

Maarek has been a credit to his trainer as he continues to produce his best after a long season, and giving weight away all round would indicate that he has hardly produced a better performance this season. In addition to that he was outpaced and struggling for much of the way but he gradually both picked up and picked off his opponents, battling hard under pressure and wasn't to be denied. It's been a terrific season for this horse and this shows that he hasn't stopped progressing, either. He's in the Ayr Gold Cup. (op 4/1 tchd 9/2)

Starspangledbanner(AUS) sustained his effort despite a tendency to hang left inside the final furlong and a half but the winner just had a shade more momentum. It will be interesting to see where he goes after this but some bigger targets can certainly be looked at with a bit more confidence. (op 6/1)

Fire Lily(IRE) probably ran a shade below her mark. She was never that far away from the decent clip that was set but she just couldn't match the two in front of her. It does make one wonder whether her best is done for this season. (op 3/1)

Firebeam showed plenty of speed but just couldn't sustain it as speedier types quickened again. He is probably more of a 7f horse in any case. (op 4/1)

Lady Wingshot(IRE) is another who's more at home over an extra furlong at least and just got tapped a bit for speed inside the two-furlong pole. She kept going at one pace. (op 10/1 tchd 12/1)

Experience(IRE) was somewhat one-paced from well over a furlong out.

Arctic(IRE) Official explanation: trainer said gelding made a noise when pulling up

6270a GAIN ELITE 10 H'CAP 5f

5:30 (5:33) 3-Y-O+ **£19,500** (£5,700; £2,700; £900)

RPR

1 **Cape Of Approval (IRE)**41 4852 3-9-5 **87** .... WayneLordan 2 96
(T Stack, Ire) *towards rr: gd hdwy fr over 2f out on far side: clsd to chal 150yds out: kpt on wl to ld nr fin* **4/1**1

2 nk **First In Command (IRE)**22 5530 7-8-11 **78** ....(t) PatSmullen 7 86
(Daniel Mark Loughnane) *chsd ldrs: swtchd lft over 1f out and qcknd to ld 100yds out: hdd nr fin* **8/1**

3 2 1/4 **Battleroftheboyne (IRE)**7 6064 3-9-12 **94** .... GaryCarroll 6 94
(Michael Mulvany, Ire) *mid-div: prog on outer to cl into 3rd fnl 100yds: kpt on: nvr a threat* **11/1**

4 shd **Nini Ok (IRE)**27 5390 3-8-10 **78** ....(b) JamieSpencer 8 78
(John Joseph Murphy, Ire) *slowly away and in rr: n.m.r and swtchd rt over 1f out: kpt on wl wout ever threatening principals* **8/1**

5 nk **Theyturnedmedown (IRE)**40 4894 4-8-2 **72** ....(bt) LeighRoche(3) 1 70
(J G Coogan, Ire) *trckd over to nr side to chse ldrs: 5th 1/2-way: sn pushed along and ev ch 1f out: no ex cl home* **13/2**3

6 1/2 **Statue Of Dreams (IRE)**20 5641 6-8-8 **80** ....(tp) RonanWhelan(5) 9 77
(James Bernard McCabe, Ire) *chsd ldrs: cl 5th 1/2-way: ev ch ent fnl f: sn no ex* **12/1**

7 1 3/4 **Srucahan (IRE)**20 5646 3-8-8 **76** ....(b) ChrisHayes 5 66
(P D Deegan, Ire) *towards rr: n.d fr 2f out: kpt on* **20/1**

8 nk **Amour Fou (IRE)**13 5857 4-7-11 **71** oh4 .... SamanthaBell(7) 3 60
(W T Farrell, Ire) *towards rr: sme hdwy and pushed along under 2f out: no ex on outer ins fnl f* **14/1**

9 hd **Patrickswell (IRE)**2 6185 8-8-4 **71** ....(p) RoryCleary 12 60
(Marcus Callaghan, Ire) *broke wl to r promly early: n.d fr after 1/2-way* **14/1**

10 hd **Copper Dock (IRE)**27 5392 8-8-8 **75** .... BenCurtis 10 63
(T G McCourt, Ire) *prom: 3rd 1/2-way: pushed along appr fnl f and sn outpcd* **12/1**

11 1 1/2 **Faleena (IRE)**20 5646 3-9-1 **83** ....(t) DannyGrant 11 65
(Patrick J Flynn, Ire) *broke wl: led after 1f: strly pressed and hdd 1 1/2f out: wknd fnl f* **6/1**2

12 1 **Ucanchoose (IRE)**20 5646 6-8-1 **73** ....(b) MACleere(5) 13 52
(Andrew Slattery, Ire) *broke wl on nrside to ld: hdd after 1f: pushed along fr 3f out and sn wknd* **10/1**

13 6 **Invincible Ridge (IRE)**27 5392 4-9-5 **86** ....(bt) NGMcCullagh 4 43
(D J Bunyan, Ire) *towards rr: n.d fnl 2f* **8/1**

1m 0.41s (-2.49) **Going Correction** -0.25s/f (Firm)
WFA 3 from 4yo+ 1lb **13** Ran SP% **131.9**
Speed ratings: **109,108,104,104,104 103,100,100,99,99 97,95,85**
CSF £39.81 CT £349.44 TOTE £3.40: £2.00, £3.10, £3.70; DF 20.60.
Owner Mrs Maureen Haughey **Bred** Abbeville And Meadow Court Par **Trained** Golden, Co Tipperary

FOCUS

The progressive Cape of Approval posted another personal best.

NOTEBOOK

Cape Of Approval(IRE) ◆ completed a hat-trick and once again showed the drop back to sprint trips has been the making of him. He came with a sustained effort from just after halfway and might even have got there too soon as he drifted left under pressure. He recovered his stride enough to hold off the runner-up and perhaps the lesson of this is to come with as late a run as possible as he is capable of sustaining a strong effort particularly if he has something to run at. (op 5/1 tchd 11/2)

First In Command(IRE) was patiently ridden and never really left the stands' side rail and, while his run wasn't perfect, he got enough splits at the right time to have every chance. Despite appearances, the winner was always likely to have enough in hand to have beaten him should it have got a bit closer. Still, he's been hugely consistent and maybe deserves to have won one or two more.

Battleroftheboyne(IRE) was waited with to come with one run if at all possible and, while he did have every chance, he's not the biggest horse and his impost probably just wore him down sufficiently. (op 8/1)

Nini Ok(IRE) ◆ missed the break and, while she got back onto the heels of the leaders, she was short of room at vital stages and ended up coming home very strongly. But for all that she would certainly have been placed at least. (op 10/1)

Theyturnedmedown(IRE) showed speed and was travelling well over a furlong out but his effort flattened out. (op 6/1)

Statue Of Dreams(IRE) faded inside the last half-furlong. (op 10/1)

6271a GAIN HORSE FEEDS IRISH ST. LEGER (GROUP 1) 1m 6f

6:05 (6:06) 3-Y-O+

£96,666 (£31,666; £15,000; £5,000; £3,333; £1,666)

RPR

1 **Royal Diamond (IRE)**21 5600 6-9-11 104 .... NGMcCullagh 9 110
(Thomas Carmody, Ire) *chsd ldrs in 4th: t.k.h and impr to take clsr order appr st: rdn over 1f out and styd on wl to ld fnl stride* **16/1**

2 hd **Massiyn (IRE)**37 5027 3-9-0 110 ....(t) ShaneFoley 1 110
(M Halford, Ire) *chsd ldrs: t.k.h: clsd u.p to ld 150yds out: strly pressed and edgd lft nr fin: hdd on line* **13/2**

3 shd **Brown Panther**28 5354 4-9-11 .... RichardKingscote 8 110+
(Tom Dascombe) *hld up in tch: cl 7th 3f out and pushed along on outer: hrd rdn 2f out and clsd ins fnl f: jst hld* **10/3**2

4 nk **Aiken**84 3369 4-9-11 .... JimmyFortune 6 109
(John Gosden) *chsd ldrs: pushed along in 2nd under 3f out: sn hrd rdn and kpt on wl u.p ins fnl f: hld* **9/2**

5 1 3/4 **Simenon (IRE)**21 5599 5-9-11 107 .... PatSmullen 2 107
(W P Mullins, Ire) *w.w towards rr: clsd 3f out: n.m.r 1f out and kpt on wl to take 5th fnl strides* **16/1**

6 nk **Fame And Glory**86 3293 6-9-11 118 .... JamieSpencer 7 107
(A P O'Brien, Ire) *attempted to make all at mod pce: qcknd and over 2 l clr 3f out: rdn appr fnl f and hdd 150yds out: no ex towards fin* **11/4**1

7 2 **Shu Lewis (IRE)**19 5696 6-9-8 .... ShaneGorey 5 101?
(Ms M Dowdall Blake, Ire) *towards rr: rdn under 3f out and kpt on nrside ins fnl f: nvr nrr* **100/1**

8 1/2 **Hartani (IRE)**21 5606 3-9-0 111 .... Christophe-PatriceLemaire 4 103
(John M Oxx, Ire) *trckd ldr in 2nd: drvn 3f out and no ex: eased nr fin* **4/1**3

9 11 **Steps To Freedom (IRE)**21 5600 6-9-11 108 ....(t) KevinManning 3 88
(Mrs John Harrington, Ire) *w.w in rr: pushed along 3f out and sn no imp* **20/1**

3m 8.47s (-0.93) **Going Correction** +0.225s/f (Good)
WFA 3 from 4yo+ 11lb **9** Ran SP% **118.8**
Speed ratings: **111,110,110,110,109 109,108,108,101**
CSF £118.97 TOTE £20.20: £3.60, £2.50, £2.70; DF 174.30.
Owner Andrew Tinkler **Bred** Moyglare Stud Farm Ltd **Trained** the Curragh, Co Kildare

■ Niall McCullagh's first Group 1 winner, and a winner for Tommy Carmody with his first runner in a Classic.

■ Stewards' Enquiry : Richard Kingscote caution: used whip with excessive frequency.

FOCUS

It's hard to say that this race was anything other than sub-standard with the one horse of proven quality running below his best in this contest for the second year, and the winner of a mares' bumper beaten only about four lengths. The form is rated around the winner , second and fifth.

NOTEBOOK

Royal Diamond(IRE), despite how keen he was early on, was suited by the way the race unfolded as he can both quicken and stay. In the end it was a very much a last-gasp effort but he got there. To put it into perspective, however, he had been beaten in three handicaps coming into this and, while one of those was the Ebor Handicap, it does give the best indication of the type of contest this was. (op 14/1)

Massiyn(IRE) has been consistent all season and the indications that he has continued to give as a horse that really stays well was confirmed here. He also raced a little bit keenly and was caught a bit flat-footed turning in, but he did pick up well and ran to the line while suffering the misfortune of his head being down on the wrong stride as they got to the line. He's progressing and there must be every chance that they'll hold onto him for a 4-y-o campaign and maybe a crack at some of the Cup races. (op 8/1)

Brown Panther was inconvenienced by the lack of pace probably more than anything as he was quite short of tactical speed and took some stoking up when the pace increased. And for all that he came home marginally stronger than anything else. Second in the British equivalent last year, he should be a force in Group races at around this trip next year but clearly would appreciate a more strongly run race. (op 7/2)

Aiken was stepping up to this trip for the first time and it might have been expected for a horse best at around 1m4f to have been more able to respond when some pace was injected. He fell a bit short of that but stayed on almost as well as anything else. (op 5/1 tchd 11/2)

Simenon(IRE) had earned his place in this race. He just wasn't good enough, although the gears he had shown at Ascot weren't good enough to get him into contention here over this trip and at this more sedate pace. Ascot's British Champions Long Distance Cup is his aim.

Fame And Glory looked to have quickened it at the right time, but his stride started to shorten over a furlong out and it was disappointing that he couldn't pull out a bit more. This run and his Ascot effort must lead more in the direction of him being retired. (op 11/4 tchd 5/2)

Shu Lewis(IRE) her only being beaten four lengths was testament to how much the slow pace was a great leveller. Her run was a typical one for the race as she lost her place under pressure when the pace quickened but ran on again inside the last furlong or so.

Hartani(IRE) raced a bit keenly while tracking the lead and found little in the straight. (op 4/1 tchd 7/2)

6272a GOFFS VINCENT O'BRIEN STKS (REGISTERED AS THE NATIONAL STAKES) (GROUP 1) (ENTIRE COLTS & FILLIES) 7f

6:40 (6:40) 2-Y-O

£96,666 (£31,666; £15,000; £5,000; £3,333; £1,666)

RPR

1 **Dawn Approach (IRE)**88 3240 2-9-3 115 .... KevinManning 2 123+
(J S Bolger, Ire) *settled in 3rd: pushed along to cl fr 2f out: qcknd wl ent fnl f to sn ld: edgd lft briefly u.p and r.o strly towards fin: easily* **2/5**1

2 4 3/4 **Designs On Rome (IRE)**23 5522 2-9-3 91 .... DannyGrant 7 111
(Patrick J Flynn, Ire) *w.w in rr: pushed along 1/2-way on nrside: r.o wl appr fnl f and wnt 2nd fnl 100yds: nvr nrr* **28/1**

3 4 1/4 **Leitir Mor (IRE)**6 6078 2-9-3 105 ....(tp) RonanWhelan 5 100
(J S Bolger, Ire) *trckd ldr in 2nd down centre of trck: clsr under 2f out: rdn and no ex ins fnl f: kpt on* **12/1**3

4 1 1/2 **Probably (IRE)**34 5136 2-9-3 106 .... WayneLordan 1 96
(David Wachman, Ire) *hld up in tch: pushed along in 4th over 2f out: one pce ent fnl f: kpt on* **12/1**3

5 2 **Ayaar (IRE)**17 5755 2-9-3 .... MartinHarley 4 91
(Mick Channon) *towards rr: pushed along 2f out and one pce fnl f: kpt on* **20/1**

6 1 1/4 **Nevis (IRE)**[58] 4275 2-9-3 ... JPO'Brien 3 88
(A P O'Brien, Ire) *hld up towards rr: niggled along 2f out and sn rdn: kpt on: n.d* **9/2**[2]

7 3/4 **Flying The Flag (IRE)**[20] 5642 2-9-3 ... SeamieHeffernan 6 86
(A P O'Brien, Ire) *led: racd alone on far side: wl clr 1/2-way: rdn and strly pressed appr fnl f: sn hdd & wknd qckly* **12/1**[3]

1m 25.5s (-5.30) **Going Correction** -0.50s/f (Hard) 7 Ran SP% **120.9**
Speed ratings: **110,104,99,98,95 94,93**
Pick Six: Not won. CSF £18.93 TOTE £1.50: £1.02, £14.40; DF 26.40.
Owner Godolphin **Bred** J S Bolger **Trained** Coolcullen, Co Carlow
■ A new title for this historic event, traditionally the National Stakes.

FOCUS
Any doubts about whether Dawn Approach would come back in the same form as he was up to and including Ascot were blown away with a performance of complete authority. This rates the best renewal for some time, Dawn Approach the joint best winner on RPRs with his sire.

NOTEBOOK
Dawn Approach(IRE) ◆ has been sold to Godolphin since his Coventry Stakes win. Any doubts about whether he would come back in the same form as he was up to and including Ascot were blown away with a performance of complete authority. He took a couple of strides to pick up when coming off the bridle but when he did so he really did quicken up and took over the race very quickly, keeping up that gallop all the way to the line. He couldn't have done much more and firmly cements his place as the leading Irish juvenile. (op 4/9)
Designs On Rome(IRE) was happy to sit at the back of the field and be taken along by those in front of him and as most of those began to run out of petrol he was running on. Second place was the best that could possibly have been hoped for and it worked to perfection. It won't get into the At the Races ride-of-the-week highlight reel but it deserves to be in there. (op 25/1 tchd 33/1)
Leitir Mor(IRE) chased the clear leader and did a fine job of giving the winner the perfect tow into the race. It would have been a fine stable coup had they finished first and second but it wasn't to be. (op 12/1 tchd 14/1)
Probably(IRE) could never get into it on this drying ground. It's even arguable whether he really got home over this 7th furlong.
Ayaar(IRE) looked progressive having completed a hat-trick but found this opposition a completely different proposition and he couldn't cope.
Nevis(IRE) could never get into it.
Flying The Flag(IRE) was sacrificed as a trailblazing front-runner.
T/Jkpt: @9,606.30. Pool of @25,616.00 - 2 winning tickets. T/Plt: @463.40. Pool of @23,170.27 - 37.49 winning tickets. BF

6267 - 6273a (Foreign Racing) - See Raceform Interactive

6226 BATH (L-H)
Sunday, September 16

OFFICIAL GOING: Firm (10.6)
Races incorporating bottom bend increased in distance by about 12.5yds.
Wind: Fresh breeze, against Weather: overcast and dry

6274 BATHWICK TYRES BRIDGEND H'CAP (DIV I) 1m 5y
2:10 (2:11) (Class 6) (0-60,60) 3-Y-O **£2,070** (£616; £307; £153) **Stalls** Low

Form RPR

-000 1 **True Prince (USA)**[33] 5198 3-8-7 **46** oh1 ... (b[1]) SeanLevey 2 59
(Amanda Perrett) *trckd ldrs: led over 2f out: sn rdn: clr ent fnl f: kpt on wl* **16/1**

0013 2 3 1/2 **Saint Irene**[9] 5991 3-9-4 **57** ... DaneO'Neill 10 62
(Michael Blanshard) *trckd ldrs: rdn over 2f out: sn chsng wnr: styd on but a being readily hld* **3/1**[1]

5510 3 1 3/4 **Tooley Woods (IRE)**[9] 5991 3-8-13 **52** ... DavidProbert 6 53
(Tony Carroll) *hld up towards rr: stdy prog fr 3f out: sn rdn: wnt 3rd over 1f out: styd on but no further imp on front pair* **7/1**[3]

665 4 3 1/2 **Uncle Roger (IRE)**[38] 4985 3-9-7 **60** ... PatDobbs 7 53
(Eve Johnson Houghton) *in rr and reminders sn after s: nvr travelling: styd on u.p fnl 2f: nvr threatened ldrs* **3/1**[1]

0036 5 1/2 **Trulee Scrumptious**[23] 5556 3-8-11 **55** ... (v[1]) RosieJessop(5) 5 47
(Peter Charalambous) *bmpd leaving stalls: in last pair: rdn jst ins 3f out: styd on fnl 2f: nvr trbld ldrs* **5/1**[2]

0-05 6 3 **Silent Laughter**[33] 5215 3-8-13 **52** ... EddieAhern 1 37
(Jonathan Portman) *t.k.h: hld up towards rr: rdn and hdwy over 2f out: fdd fnl f* **7/1**[3]

3000 7 3 1/2 **Welsh Royale**[25] 5479 3-8-13 **52** ... (b[1]) MartinDwyer 3 29
(William Muir) *wnt rt s: led tl rdn over 2f out: wknd fnl f* **20/1**

0630 8 nse **Alfie Joe**[3] 6157 3-8-0 **46** ... PhilipPrince(7) 8 23
(Ron Hodges) *mid-div tl rdn over 3f out: sn in rr* **10/1**

0-04 9 6 **Silent Mistress**[26] 5458 3-8-7 **46** oh1 ... JamieMackay 4
(J R Jenkins) *carried rt s: mid-div: rdn over 3f out: wknd wl over 1f out* **20/1**

000- 10 5 **Peters Pleasure**[297] 7526 3-8-7 **46** oh1 ... AdamBeschizza 9
(Robert Cowell) *pressed ldr tl pushed along over 4f out: rdn over 3f out: wknd 2f out* **33/1**

1m 40.23s (-0.57) **Going Correction** -0.15s/f (Firm) 10 Ran SP% **119.1**
Speed ratings (Par 99): **96,92,90,87,86 83,80,80,74,69**
toteswingers 1&2 £8.70, 2&3 £3.20, 1&3 £13.80 CSF £63.72 CT £391.54 TOTE £24.40: £5.70, £1.10, £2.70; EX 113.20.
Owner Harwoods Racing Club **Bred** Muirfield Farm **Trained** Pulborough, W Sussex

FOCUS
Races incorporating bottom bend increased in distance by about 12.5yds. After a dry night, the ground was officially firm. A modest handicap, in which the top-weight was rated 60. It was the pick of the three C&D times and the winner is rated back to his nursery form.

6275 BATHWICK TYRES BRISTOL H'CAP 1m 5y
2:40 (2:40) (Class 5) (0-70,70) 3-Y-O+ **£2,911** (£866; £432; £216) **Stalls** Low

Form RPR

0130 1 **Capitol Gain (IRE)**[16] 5783 3-9-0 **64** ... (p) JamieMackay 10 71
(Brian Meehan) *racd keenly: disp ld: rn wd on bnd over 4f out: clr ldr over 2f out: rdn clr: kpt on wl and in command fnl f* **9/1**

0012 2 1 1/4 **Cyril The Squirrel**[20] 5657 8-9-1 **61** ... DarryllHolland 7 66+
(Karen George) *s.i.s: last: rdn and nt clrest of runs but nvr stopped: steadily swtchd rt fr 2f out: r.o ins fnl f: wnt 2nd fnl 40yds* **4/1**[2]

2212 3 1/2 **Authoritarian**[9] 5998 3-9-0 **64** ... SeanLevey 9 67
(Richard Hannon) *mid-div: rdn and hdwy over 2f out: disp 2nd fr over 1f out: kpt on same pce fnl f* **7/2**[1]

3215 4 hd **Hip Hip Hooray**[15] 5838 6-9-6 **66** ... IanMongan 8 68
(Luke Dace) *s.i.s: towards rr: pushed along and stdy prog on outer fr 3f out: styd on fnl f: wnt 4th fnl stride* **4/1**[2]

3-44 5 shd **Typography**[34] 5147 3-9-6 **70** ... MartinDwyer 4 72
(William Muir) *trckd ldrs: rdn over 2f out: disp 2nd wl over 1f out tl no ex fnl strides* **20/1**

345 6 1 3/4 **Tonle Sap (IRE)**[16] 5795 3-9-6 **70** ... (p) AdamKirby 2 68
(Clive Cox) *disp ld tl rdn over 2f out: kpt chsng ldrs tl no ex ins fnl f* **8/1**

6415 7 2 3/4 **Camrock Star (IRE)**[9] 5998 3-8-11 **61** ... SilvestreDeSousa 3 53
(David Evans) *s.i.s: mid-div: outpcd towards rr 3f out: nt clr run over 1f out: sme late prog but nvr a danger* **7/1**[3]

0243 8 1 1/2 **Barista (IRE)**[9] 6001 4-8-13 **59** ... PatCosgrave 6 47
(Brian Forsey) *mid-div: rn wd on bnd over 3f out: rdn and hdwy over 2f out: fdd fnl f* **14/1**

4350 9 shd **Bajan Story**[24] 5501 3-8-13 **63** ... DaneO'Neill 5 51
(Michael Blanshard) *slowly away and sn pushed along to chse ldrs: rdn 3f out: wknd ent fnl f* **16/1**

-015 10 1 **Fire King**[33] 5193 6-9-2 **67** ... (p) BrendanPowell(5) 1 53
(Barry Brennan) *hld up towards rr: rdn wl over 2f out: nvr any imp* **25/1**

1m 41.09s (0.29) **Going Correction** -0.15s/f (Firm)
WFA 3 from 4yo+ 4lb 10 Ran SP% **117.0**
Speed ratings (Par 103): **92,90,90,90,89 88,85,83,83,82**
toteswingers 1&2 £9.00, 2&3 £3.30, 1&3 £7.90 CSF £45.10 CT £142.22 TOTE £10.70: £3.50, £1.90, £1.60; EX 50.40.
Owner N Attenborough,Mrs L Mann,M Wilmshurst **Bred** Pier House Stud **Trained** Manton, Wilts
■ Stewards' Enquiry : Martin Dwyer two-day ban: careless riding (Sep 30-Oct 1)

FOCUS
Just a so-so handicap, with the top-weight after a withdrawal rated 67, but competitive enough on paper. The time was slow and the form is a bit muddling.

6276 BATHWICK TYRES NEWPORT MEDIAN AUCTION MAIDEN FILLIES' STKS 5f 161y
3:10 (3:11) (Class 5) 2-Y-O **£2,911** (£866; £432; £216) **Stalls** Centre

Form RPR

202 1 **Jubilee Diamond (IRE)**[11] 5943 2-9-0 82 ... PatDobbs 4 70+
(Richard Hannon) *trckd ldrs: led over 1f out: kpt up to work and in command fnl f* **2/5**[1]

5055 2 1 1/4 **Kwanto**[38] 4991 2-9-0 39 ... TomMcLaughlin 5 62
(Malcolm Saunders) *pushed along early towards rr: hdwy on inner 3f out: sn rdn: wnt 2nd jst over 1f out: kpt on but a being hld by wnr* **66/1**

3 1 **Small Fury (IRE)** 2-9-0 0 ... J-PGuillambert 9 60+
(Jo Hughes) *s.i.s: in rr: hdwy over 2f out: sn pushed along: r.o nicely to go 3rd ins fnl f* **33/1**

00 4 1 1/4 **Shes Ellie**[9] 6007 2-8-9 0 ... BrendanPowell(5) 6 55
(John O'Shea) *in tch: rdn: hdwy and ev ch 2f out: kpt on same pce fnl f* **66/1**

52 5 shd **Tonality (IRE)**[8] 6049 2-9-0 0 ... DavidProbert 3 55
(J S Moore) *trckd ldrs: rdn to ld 2f out: hdd over 1f out: no ex ins fnl f* **10/1**[3]

0 6 1 1/2 **Koharu**[55] 4408 2-9-0 0 ... EddieAhern 11 50
(Peter Makin) *hld up: hdwy 3f out: sn rdn: wknd ins fnl f* **8/1**[2]

3 7 nk **Outbid**[14] 5854 2-9-0 0 ... AdamKirby 7 49
(Jamie Osborne) *mid-div: pushed along and nt best of runs fr over 2f out: nt gng pce to get involved whn clr passage ent fnl f* **8/1**[2]

5332 8 3 1/4 **Tregereth (IRE)**[17] 5773 2-9-0 67 ... DarryllHolland 2 38
(Jonathan Portman) *led tl rdn 2f out: wknd ent fnl f* **8/1**[2]

00 9 7 **Bugsy's Babe**[20] 5685 2-9-0 0 ... KirstyMilczarek 10
(George Baker) *sn pushed along: a towards rr* **50/1**

65 10 4 1/2 **Jubilini**[17] 5773 2-9-0 0 ... IanMongan 1
(Brett Johnson) *w ldr tl rdn over 2f out: wknd over 1f out* **50/1**

1m 11.83s (0.63) **Going Correction** -0.025s/f (Good) 10 Ran SP% **123.7**
Speed ratings (Par 92): **94,92,91,89,89 87,86,82,73,67**
toteswingers 1&2 £15.30, 2&3 £47.00, 1&3 £6.30 CSF £67.48 TOTE £1.50: £1.10, £10.50, £3.90; EX 42.00.
Owner Mrs J Wood **Bred** Tally-Ho Stud **Trained** East Everleigh, Wilts
■ Stewards' Enquiry : Brendan Powell five-day ban: used whip above permitted level without giving filly time to respond (Sep 30-Oct 1-4)

FOCUS
Little obvious depth to this juvenile fillies' maiden and the winner was the clear pre-race form pick. The second was much improved.

NOTEBOOK
Jubilee Diamond(IRE), twice second previously and with an official rating of 82, outpointed these rivals with the minimum of fuss. She raced keenly early on, but looked happier when easing to the front at the 2f marker and needed only a few nudges to collect. Whether she is up to scoring off her handicap mark is now a matter for conjecture. (op 4-9)
Kwanto, rated just 39 after five earlier runs, is sure to be used as a stick with which to beat the overall form. It is hard to see why she should suddenly have improved, but it appears she has.
Small Fury(IRE), a first-time-out half-sister to a winner at this trip, showed promise. She can win a little race. (op 25-1)
Shes Ellie had achieved little on her two previous runs, but showed up well from the start here. Nurseries are now an option.
Koharu, seventh in a fair Windsor maiden on her only previous outing, was rather disappointing. Fourth early, she failed to hold her place in the closing stages. (op 9-1)
Bugsy's Babe Official explanation: jockey said filly suffered interference at start

6277 BATHWICK TYRES H'CAP 5f 161y
3:40 (3:40) (Class 5) (0-70,70) 4-Y-O+ **£2,911** (£866; £432; £216) **Stalls** Centre

Form RPR

0135 1 **Annes Rocket (IRE)**[9] 5993 7-9-4 **67** ... (p) PatDobbs 7 76
(Jimmy Fox) *confidently rdn: stdd s: in last: cruised through to trck ldrs wl over 1f out: qcknd up wl to ld fnl 75yds: r.o: readily* **10/1**

2333 2 1/2 **Mother Jones**[20] 5995 4-9-2 **65** ... SilvestreDeSousa 4 72
(David Evans) *racd keenly: trckd ldrs: rdn 2f out: led ent fnl f: no ex whn hdd fnl 75yds* **11/2**[3]

4003 3 1 3/4 **Comptonspirit**[6] 6094 8-9-2 **70** ... JamesRogers(5) 6 71
(Brian Baugh) *led for 1f: prom: led over 2f out: sn rdn: hdd ent fnl f: kpt on but no ex* **17/2**

3562 4 shd **Bajan Bear**[12] 5915 4-9-5 **68** ... (b) DaneO'Neill 2 69
(Michael Blanshard) *dwlt: sn in last pair: pushed along over 2f out: hdwy wl over 1f out: sn rdn: kpt on ins fnl f* **5/1**[2]

5456 5 1/2 **Mambo Spirit (IRE)**[6] 6094 8-9-5 **68** ... AdamKirby 9 67
(Tony Newcombe) *stdd s: in last trio: hdwy over 2f out: sn rdn to chse ldrs: one pce fnl f* **9/2**[1]

4422 6 1/2 **Sarangoo**[9] 5995 4-9-7 **70** ... TomMcLaughlin 1 68
(Malcolm Saunders) *trckd ldrs: rdn over 2f out: one pce fnl f* **5/1**[2]

0501 7 2 **Belle Bayardo (IRE)**[6] 6094 4-9-5 **68** 6ex ... KierenFox 3 59
(Ronald Harris) *mid-div: pushed along 3f out: nvr gng pce to get involved* **11/2**[3]

0306 8 7 **Perlachy**[10] 5971 8-9-2 **65** ... (v) KellyHarrison 8 34
(Ronald Harris) *trckd ldrs: rdn over 2f out: nt gng pce to chal: wknd over 1f out* **25/1**

6605 **9** *3* **Dreams Of Glory**[78] 3618 4-8-9 **58** .... DavidProbert 10 17
(Ron Hodges) *led after 1f: rdn and hdd over 2f out: wknd over 1f out* **7/1**

1m 10.5s (-0.70) **Going Correction** -0.025s/f (Good) **9** Ran SP% **118.2**
Speed ratings (Par 103): **103,102,100,99,99 98,95,86,82**
toteswingers 1&2 £6.80, 2&3 £8.60, 1&3 £12.10 CSF £65.55 CT £496.22 TOTE £10.80: £2.50, £2.30, £3.30; EX 56.80.
Owner Claire Underwood, Fay Thomas & S-J Fox **Bred** S Coughlan **Trained** Collingbourne Ducis, Wilts

FOCUS
A wide-open handicap, in which none could be confidently discounted. The winner has been rated in line with his penultimate rfun at Folkestone.

6278 BATHWICK TYRES SUPPORTING BATH RACECOURSE H'CAP 1m 2f 46y
4:10 (4:10) (Class 5) (0-70,69) 3-Y-O+ **£2,011** (£866; £432; £216) **Stalls** Low

Form RPR

4121 **1** **King's Masque**[5] 6120 6-9-5 **69** .... RobertWilliams(5) 7 80
(Bernard Llewellyn) *in last pair but wl in tch: swtchd rt and hdwy fr 3f out: led 2f out: rdn clr: drifted lft: styd on strly: readily* **7/4**[1]

3050 **2** *3 ¾* **Princess Steph (IRE)**[19] 5726 3-9-0 **65** .... DarryllHolland 4 68
(Heather Main) *trckd ldrs: led briefly jst over 2f out: sn rdn: kpt on but a being readily hld by wnr* **10/1**

4533 **3** *2 ½* **Finch Flyer (IRE)**[11] 5508 5-8-10 **55** oh2 ....(p) SilvestreDeSousa 6 53
(Aytach Sadik) *s.i.s: in last: pushed along over 4f out: outpcd 3f out: styd on fr over 1f out but no threat to ldng pair* **6/1**

4221 **4** *1* **Iguacu**[11] 5935 8-8-5 **57** ....(p) DanielMuscutt(7) 5 53
(Richard Price) *trckd ldrs: rdn whn short of room wl over 1f out: hld after: kpt on same pce* **4/1**[2]

0324 **5** *1 ¾* **James Pollard (IRE)**[23] 5528 7-9-4 **68** ....(t) BrendanPowell(5) 3 61
(Bernard Llewellyn) *in tch: rdn to chse ldrs over 2f out: kpt on same pce fr over 1f out* **16/1**

3652 **6** *hd* **Spiritual Art**[20] 5481 6-8-11 **56** ....(v) PatCosgrave 1 48
(Luke Dace) *s.i.s: rcvrd to ld after 1f: rdn and hdd over 2f out: edgd lft wl over 1f out: sn btn* **9/2**[3]

0050 **7** *1 ¾* **Golden Jubilee (USA)**[16] 5796 3-8-12 **63** .... PatDobbs 2 52
(Richard Hannon) *led for 1f: trckd ldr: rdn over 2f out: bmpd wl over 1f out: wknd ent fnl f* **7/1**

2m 9.1s (-1.90) **Going Correction** -0.15s/f (Firm)
WFA 3 from 5yo+ 6lb **7** Ran SP% **116.3**
Speed ratings (Par 103): **101,98,96,95,93 93,92**
toteswingers 1&2 £6.20, 2&3 £10.10, 1&3 £2.40 CSF £21.45 TOTE £2.40: £1.40, £5.00; EX 27.50.
Owner B J Llewellyn **Bred** Deerfield Farm **Trained** Fochriw, Caerphilly

FOCUS
Seemingly a tight handicap on paper, but turned into a one-horse race with King's Masque building on recent efforts. The pace was sound.

6279 BATHWICK TYRES CARDIFF MAIDEN STKS 1m 2f 46y
4:40 (4:43) (Class 5) 3-Y-O **£4,398** (£1,309; £654; £327) **Stalls** Low

Form RPR

-552 **1** **Miracle Maid**[30] 5309 3-8-12 80 .... AdamKirby 7 80+
(Clive Cox) *mde all: pushed clr over 2f out: drifted rt: kpt up to work over 1f out: unchal* **7/4**[1]

-346 **2** *9* **Hunt A Mistress (IRE)**[122] 2204 3-8-12 74 .... SilvestreDeSousa 6 63
(Paul Cole) *trckd ldrs: rdn 3f out: wnt 2nd wl over 2f out: no ch w easy wnr* **13/2**[2]

55- **3** *4* **Wye Valley**[342] 6744 3-8-12 0 .... EddieAhern 1 55
(Amanda Perrett) *trckd ldrs: rdn 3f out: sn outpcd: styd on to go 3rd ins fnl f* **8/1**[3]

0065 **4** *2 ½* **Barnacle**[20] 5659 3-8-12 44 .... DavidKenny(5) 4 56?
(Pat Eddery) *s.i.s: last but in tch: struggling over 3f out: plugged on past btn horses fr over 1f out: nvr a threat* **80/1**

04 **5** *1* **Trevose (IRE)**[20] 5687 3-9-3 0 .... IanMongan 5 54
(Roy Brotherton) *trckd ldrs: rdn 3f out: sn one pce* **100/1**

30 **6** *½* **Roger Ramjet (IRE)**[19] 5717 3-9-3 0 ....(t) MartinDwyer 2 53
(Brian Meehan) *trckd wnr: rdn over 2f out: sn no ch w easy wnr: lost 2nd wl over 1f out: wknd sn after* **18/1**

2m 8.51s (-2.49) **Going Correction** -0.15s/f (Firm) **6** Ran SP% **68.3**
Speed ratings (Par 101): **103,95,92,90,89 89**
toteswingers 1&2 £1.20, 2&3 £2.10, 1&3 £1.70 CSF £3.76 TOTE £1.50: £1.10, £1.80; EX 5.30.
Owner D J Burke **Bred** Whitley Stud **Trained** Lambourn, Berks

FOCUS
With the late withdrawal of the favourite Courage, who refused to go into the stalls, Miracle Maid stood out in this run-of-the-mill maiden. This could represent improved form, though her rivals were not totally convincing.

6280 BATHWICK TYRES GLOUCESTER H'CAP 2m 1f 34y
5:10 (5:10) (Class 6) (0-60,58) 3-Y-O+ **£2,070** (£616; £307; £153) **Stalls** Centre

Form RPR

0224 **1** **Lucky Diva**[33] 5196 5-9-7 **58** ....(p) JakePayne(7) 9 66
(Bill Turner) *hld up bhd: smooth hdwy on inner 3f out: led over 2f out: sn clr: rdn over 1f out: a enough in hand: drvn out* **9/2**[2]

660- **2** *1* **Annaluna (IRE)**[7] 6825 3-8-12 **54** .... StevieDonohoe 8 61
(David Evans) *trckd ldrs: rdn over 2f out: chsd wnr over 1f out: styd on: clsng wl at fin* **7/1**[3]

-300 **3** *5* **Tokyo Brown (USA)**[37] 5074 3-9-2 **58** .... EddieAhern 2 59
(Heather Main) *mid-div: rdn wl over 2f out: styd on to go 3rd over 1f out but a being comf hld by ldng pair* **16/1**

06-4 **4** *1 ½* **On Alert**[20] 3969 4-8-10 **45** ....(t) BrendanPowell(5) 7 44
(Seamus Durack) *s.i.s: mid-div: rdn over 2f out: wnt 4th over 1f out: styd on same pce* **18/1**

002/ **5** *nk* **Sangfroid**[63] 1759 8-9-10 **54** .... DavidProbert 4 53
(Tim Vaughan) *hld up towards rr: rdn wl over 2f out: no imp tl styd on fr over 1f out: nvr threatened ldrs* **7/1**[3]

3053 **6** *1 ½* **Isobella**[22] 5577 3-8-11 **53** ....(b[1]) DarryllHolland 5 50
(Hughie Morrison) *hld up towards rr: hdwy whn nt clr run briefly over 2f out: sn swtchd rt and rdn: chsd ldrs over 1f out: no further imp fnl f* **7/2**[1]

5/00 **7** *2* **Leopard Hills (IRE)**[41] 4884 5-9-8 **52** .... AdamKirby 12 47
(Tony Carroll) *led: rdn and hdd over 2f out: wknd over 1f out* **12/1**

3366 **8** *14* **Simply**[6] 6098 3-8-12 **54** ....(p) PatDobbs 13 32
(Eve Johnson Houghton) *sn prom: rdn 3f out: sn hld: wknd over 1f out* **7/2**[1]

4356 **9** *1 ½* **Dream Catcher (SWE)**[33] 5196 9-9-7 **58** ....(p) DannyBenson(7) 11 34
(Jonjo O'Neill) *trckd ldrs: rdn wl over 2f out: sn btn* **8/1**

0040 **10** *6* **Imperial Elegance**[15] 4510 3-8-3 **45** .... SilvestreDeSousa 1 14
(Mick Channon) *trckd ldrs tl rdn 4f out: btn 3f out: eased fnl f* **20/1**

0-00 **11** *71* **Highland Cadett**[24] 5508 5-8-10 **45** .... DavidKenny(5) 10
(Pam Ford) *mid-div: effrt over 3f out: wknd over 2f out: virtually p.u over 1f out* **100/1**

3m 50.43s (-1.47) **Going Correction** -0.15s/f (Firm)
WFA 3 from 4yo+ 12lb **11** Ran SP% **123.3**
Speed ratings (Par 101): **97,96,94,93,93 92,91,85,84,81 48**
toteswingers 1&2 £8.90, 2&3 £23.20, 1&3 £11.70 CSF £38.14 CT £478.08 TOTE £5.00: £3.00, £2.80, £5.10; EX 39.70.
Owner Darren Coombes **Bred** Gracelands Stud **Trained** Sigwells, Somerset
■ Stewards' Enquiry : Eddie Ahern one-day ban: careless riding (Sep 30)

FOCUS
A modest staying handicap with a top-weight rated 58. The winner has a decent record here and rates a small personal best.
Sangfroid Official explanation: jockey said gelding hung left
Imperial Elegance Official explanation: jockey said filly had no more to give
Highland Cadett Official explanation: trainer said gelding was unsuited by the fast ground

6281 BATHWICK TYRES BRIDGEND H'CAP (DIV II) 1m 5y
5:40 (5:40) (Class 6) (0-60,59) 3-Y-O **£2,070** (£616; £307; £153) **Stalls** Low

Form RPR

6500 **1** **First Glance**[43] 4830 3-8-5 **46** .... DominicFox(3) 5 52
(Michael Appleby) *led tl over 4f out: rdn to regain ld wl over 1f out: sn strly pressed: hld on gamely: all out* **7/1**

2110 **2** *½* **Waspy**[26] 5443 3-9-5 **57** ....(t) PatCosgrave 8 62
(George Baker) *hld up but in tch: hdwy over 2f out: rdn for str chal over 1f out: kpt on but no ex towards fin* **9/2**[3]

0000 **3** *1 ¾* **Pass The Time**[24] 5508 3-8-7 **45** ....(p) SeanLevey 2 46
(Neil Mulholland) *hld up in tch: rdn over 3f out: no imp tl styd on to take 3rd ent fnl f: kpt on* **16/1**

6000 **4** *1 ¼* **Opus (IRE)**[52] 4490 3-9-0 **52** ....(t) PatDobbs 1 50
(Amanda Perrett) *trckd ldrs: rdn wl over 2f out: kpt on same pce* **6/1**

0644 **5** *5* **Saint Boniface**[9] 5991 3-9-7 **59** .... EddieAhern 7 45
(Peter Makin) *racd keenly: hld up in tch: rdn in last pair 3f out: nvr any real imp on ldrs fnl 2f* **7/2**[1]

0430 **6** *4* **Inffiraaj (IRE)**[9] 5991 3-9-1 **53** .... MatthewDavies 4 30
(Mick Channon) *sn trcking ldrs: led over 4f out: rdn and hdd wl over 1f out: sn wknd* **7/2**[1]

400 **7** *22* **Sovereign Waters**[17] 5770 3-9-0 **52** .... SilvestreDeSousa 3
(Eve Johnson Houghton) *trckd ldrs: failed to take bnd wl over 4f out: sn rdn: wknd over 2f out: eased fnl f* **4/1**[2]

1m 40.72s (-0.08) **Going Correction** -0.15s/f (Firm) **7** Ran SP% **115.3**
Speed ratings (Par 99): **94,93,91,90,85 81,59**
toteswingers 1&2 £2.50, 2&3 £8.20, 1&3 £6.80 CSF £38.74 CT £488.49 TOTE £8.60: £2.40, £2.30; EX 53.80.
Owner Sarnian Racing **Bred** Judith Jones **Trained** Danethorpe, Notts
■ Stewards' Enquiry : Dominic Fox nine-day ban: used whip above permitted level (Sep 30-Oct 1-6,8-9)

FOCUS
A poor finale, in which the top-weight was rated just 59. It was slower by half a second than the first division and looks the weaker form.
First Glance Official explanation: trainer's rep said, regarding apparent improvement in form, that the gelding was better suited by the faster ground and drop in class.
Saint Boniface Official explanation: trainer said gelding was unsuited by the firm ground
T/Jkpt: Part won. £25,000.00 to a £1 stake. Pool of £23,024.02 - 0.50 winning tickets. T/Plt: £54.00 to a £1 stake. Pool of £105981.55 -1431.74 winning tickets. T/Qpdt: £29.20 to a £1 stake. Pool of £8819.12 -222.95 winning tickets. TM

5872 FFOS LAS (L-H)
Sunday, September 16

OFFICIAL GOING: Good to soft (good in places; 7.7) changing to good to soft after race 1 (2.30) changing to soft after race 4 (4.00)
Wind: Fresh, across Weather: Light rain

6282 WALTERS UK/BRITISH STALLION STUDS E B F MAIDEN FILLIES' STKS 5f
2:30 (2:30) (Class 4) 2-Y-O **£4,528** (£1,347; £673; £336) **Stalls** Centre

Form RPR

2024 **1** **Jillnextdoor (IRE)**[12] 5904 2-9-0 88 .... SamHitchcott 1 79+
(Mick Channon) *trckd ldrs: smooth hdwy 2f out: rdn to ld 1f out: pushed clr* **5/6**[1]

0444 **2** *3* **Starlight Angel (IRE)**[34] 5146 2-9-0 68 .... LukeMorris 5 68
(Ronald Harris) *trckd ldng pair: hdwy to ld over 1f out: edgd lft and sn hdd: outpcd by wnr fnl f* **16/1**

223 **3** *3 ½* **Polish Crown**[14] 5858 2-9-0 0 .... JoeFanning 2 55
(Mark Johnston) *disp ld 1f: cl up: rdn to ld narrowly over 2f out: hdd over 1f out: sn one pce* **13/8**[2]

0 **4** *2* **Greenery (IRE)**[29] 5357 2-9-0 0 .... CathyGannon 4 48
(Roger Charlton) *racd keenly: led: hdd over 2f out: sn dropped to last: one pce* **8/1**[3]

1m 0.4s (2.10) **Going Correction** +0.50s/f (Yiel) **4** Ran SP% **109.6**
Speed ratings (Par 94): **103,98,92,89**
CSF £12.41 TOTE £2.00; EX 10.90.
Owner Nick & Olga Dhandsa & John & Zoe Webster **Bred** Summerhill B/S & Lynch Bages **Trained** West Ilsley, Berks

FOCUS
Not a bad little 2yo fillies' maiden. They went a sound pace down the centre and finished fairly strung out, suggesting the steady drizzle throughout the day had indeed got into the ground. There was also a strong wind against them. The winner was fully entitled to win as she did.

NOTEBOOK
Jillnextdoor(IRE) deservedly shed her maiden tag at the sixth time of asking and completed the task in decent style, as she was entitled to with her main-market rival flopping. She has been highly tried and was back down from 7f after a fair effort in Listed company on her previous outing. Her connections have always stated she's well thought of, though, and she may now be about to come good on that promise as her confidence will be high after this easy win. (op 8-11 tchd 10-11)
Starlight Angel(IRE), back down in trip, looked a brief threat to the winner nearing 1f out, but was firmly put in her place when that rival asserted. She helps to set the level and deserves to find an opening. (op 12-1)
Polish Crown ran well below her previous level on this return to turf and to the minimum trip. Perhaps the ground was to blame. (op 2-1)

Greenery(IRE), despite showing much more early pace this time, was again well beaten off by the winner and probably needs a quicker surface. She has some scope. (op 9-1)

6283 FELINFOEL CELTIC PRIDE NURSERY 6f
3:00 (3:01) (Class 6) (0-60,60) 2-Y-O **£2,070** (£616; £307; £153) **Stalls** Centre

Form RPR

340 **1** **Angels Calling**[27] 5424 2-8-13 **55**........................... MichaelMetcalfe(3) 9 60+
(Mrs K Burke) *trckd ldrs: let down to ld 2f out: drvn clr fnl f* **4/1**[2]

6255 **2** *2 ¾* **Frosted Off**[20] 5654 2-9-7 **60**........................... CathyGannon 6 57
(John Spearing) *towards rr: swtchd rt and hdwy over 2f out: chsd wnr ent fnl f: sn hung lft and no imp* **7/1**

400 **3** *¾* **Masai King (IRE)**[10] 5727 2-9-5 **58**........................... FrederikTylicki 5 53
(Robin Bastiman) *in tch: n.m.r over 2f out: rdn over 1f out: r.o ins fnl f* **7/2**[1]

0230 **4** *2 ½* **Michael's Song (IRE)**[4] 6147 2-9-4 **57**........................... SamHitchcott 2 44
(Mick Channon) *w ldrs: rdn over 2f out: kpt on same pce* **11/2**[3]

0050 **5** *1* **Amelia Jay**[19] 5716 2-9-2 **55**........................... ChrisCatlin 3 39
(Danielle McCormick) *racd keenly early: hld up in tch: rdn 2f out: unable qck: wknd ins fnl f* **12/1**

4044 **6** *2 ¼* **Jamnean**[11] 5932 2-9-2 **55**........................... RussKennemore 4 33
(John Holt) *racd keenly early: hld up in tch: rdn over 2f out: sn one pce* **8/1**

0046 **7** *shd* **Betty Boo (IRE)**[18] 5733 2-7-13 **45**........................... ShirleyTeasdale(7) 1 22
(Shaun Harris) *s.i.s: racd keenly: sn chsng ldrs: led narrowly over 2f out: sn hdd & wknd* **16/1**

4406 **8** *21* **Golac**[20] 5654 2-9-0 **53**........................... FrannyNorton 8
(Mick Channon) *chsd ldrs: rdn over 2f out: sn wknd: eased fnl f: t.o* **14/1**

054 **9** *4* **Sarahmanda**[33] 5192 2-9-5 **58**........................... LukeMorris 7
(Peter Makin) *led tl hdd over 2f out: wknd qckly: eased fnl f: t.o* **4/1**[2]

1m 14.76s (4.76) **Going Correction** +0.50s/f (Yiel) **9 Ran SP% 121.5**
Speed ratings (Par 93): **88,84,83,80,78 75,75,47,42**
toteswingers: 1&2 £4.40, 1&3 £4.50, 2&3 £5.80 CSF £34.01 CT £110.75 TOTE £7.00: £1.80, £2.20, £1.70; EX 38.80 Trifecta £182.90 Pool: £1,255.84 - 5.08 winning units..
Owner Ontoawinner & Mrs E Burke **Bred** Kb Spigot Ltd **Trained** Middleham Moor, N Yorks

FOCUS
A moderate nursery that looked wide-open. Again the main action developed towards the centre of the track. Straightforward form, the winner confirming earlier promise.

NOTEBOOK
Angels Calling showed her tame effort on her AW last time out to be all wrong and she ran out a clear-cut winner on this nursery debut. Well backed beforehand, she was ideally placed to strike when things got serious and evidently enjoys some cut underfoot. There could well be more to come despite a likely rise in the weights. (tchd 9-2)
Frosted Off, who went to post early, didn't go unbacked and returned to something like his previous best with the hood left off. Official explanation: jockey said gelding hung left (op 8-1)
Masai King(IRE) was very well backed for this switch to a nursery and was partnered by a jockey that arrived in scintillating form. He had to fight for a run in between the final 2f, but it made no difference to the overall result and he ultimately looked in need of a stiffer test. He can build on this. (op 7-1 tchd 15-2)
Michael's Song(IRE) had her chance and turned in a fair effort. (op 4-1)
Sarahmanda dropped right out. Presumably she failed to handle the ground. Official explanation: jockey said filly stopped quickly (tchd 7-2)

6284 CARLSBERG NURSERY 5f
3:30 (3:31) (Class 4) (0-85,85) 2-Y-O **£4,398** (£1,309; £654; £327) **Stalls** Centre

Form RPR

2521 **1** **Vincentti (IRE)**[13] 5872 2-9-0 **78**........................... LukeMorris 5 84+
(Ronald Harris) *chsd ldrs: rdn 2f out: led appr fnl f: r.o: comf* **11/4**[2]

1 **2** *1 ½* **Scatty Cat (IRE)**[38] 4990 2-9-0 **78**........................... MichaelHussey 3 78
(Peter McCreery, Ire) *dwlt: t.k.h bhd ldrs: swtchd lft over 1f out: chsd wnr 1f out: hung lft and a being hld* **9/2**[3]

1031 **3** *1 ¾* **Secret Sign**[3] 6155 2-9-2 **80** 6ex........................... (v) MartinLane 1 73
(Brian Meehan) *in tch: drvn along after 1f: sltly outpcd 2f out: stl last 1f out: styd on to go 3rd nr fin* **11/4**[2]

1000 **4** *¾* **Bridge Night**[30] 5307 2-9-7 **85**........................... ChrisCatlin 2 75
(Eve Johnson Houghton) *w ldrs: stl ev ch over 1f out: sn rdn and one pce* **11/1**

342 **5** *1 ¾* **Clean Blow (USA)**[26] 5449 2-8-6 **70**........................... FrannyNorton 4 54
(David Brown) *led: rdn over 1f out: sn hdd: wknd ins fnl f* **9/4**[1]

1m 0.57s (2.27) **Going Correction** +0.50s/f (Yiel) **5 Ran SP% 110.6**
Speed ratings (Par 97): **101,98,95,94,91**
CSF £14.98 TOTE £3.70: £2.00, £3.00; EX 10.60.
Owner Robert & Nina Bailey **Bred** Stephanie Hanly **Trained** Earlswood, Monmouths

FOCUS
A modest nursery. They went a strong early pace and the form should work out. The winner was value for a bit extra.

NOTEBOOK
Vincentti(IRE) followed up his C&D maiden success 13 days earlier with a ready effort and is evidently a progressive sprinter. He wouldn't have minded the easing ground, despite being thought of by his trainer as a horse that is best on a sound surface, and he came nicely clear near the business end. A bold bid for the hat-trick can be expected. (op 3-1 tchd 7-2)
Scatty Cat(IRE) scraped home when winning a Chepstow maiden on her second outing last month. She kept on well without seriously threatening the winner and has begun life in this sphere on a fair mark. (op 7-2 tchd 3-1)
Secret Sign wore a first-time visor when winning at Chepstow three days earlier and that was retained. Under a penalty, he hit something of a flat spit before keeping on again towards the finish and probably could have done without the ground easing. (op 3-1 tchd 9-4)
Bridge Night ran more encouragingly, but looks held by the handicapper. (op 10-1)
Clean Blow(USA) looked to pay for doing too much from the front. Official explanation: trainer said filly was unsuited by the good to soft ground (op 5-2 tchd 3-1)

6285 DOUBLE DRAGON "NATIONAL ALE OF WALES" H'CAP 6f
4:00 (4:01) (Class 4) (0-85,82) 3-Y-O **£5,175** (£1,540; £769; £384) **Stalls** Centre

Form RPR

010 **1** **Forest Edge (IRE)**[9] 6008 3-8-10 **71**........................... (b) CathyGannon 4 81
(David Evans) *led 1f: styd cl up: rdn over 2f out: led again over 1f out: hld on wl u.p* **14/1**

3333 **2** *nk* **Ashpan Sam**[15] 5821 3-8-11 **72**........................... LukeMorris 1 81
(John Spearing) *towards rr: swtchd lft and hdwy 2f out: chsd wnr appr fnl f: r.o u.p: jst hld* **15/2**

6310 **3** *2 ½* **Fillionaire**[10] 5980 3-9-7 **82**........................... SamHitchcott 7 83
(Mick Channon) *s.i.s: in tch: rdn 1/2-way: sn chsng ldrs: kpt on fnl f tl no ex last 75yds* **5/1**[3]

2460 **4** *1* **Mister Musicmaster**[9] 6008 3-9-1 **76**........................... JamesMillman 3 74
(Rod Millman) *cl up: rdn 2f out: sn ev ch: one pce fnl f* **7/1**

2142 **5** *1* **Minalisa**[22] 5582 3-9-5 **80**........................... ChrisCatlin 2 75
(Rae Guest) *prom: rdn and unable qck over 1f out: wknd fnl f* **9/4**[1]

4211 **6** *hd* **Selfara**[24] 5514 3-9-5 **80**........................... (bt) GeorgeBaker 6 74
(Roger Charlton) *cl up: led after 1f tl over 1f out: steadily wknd* **3/1**[2]

6524 **7** *15* **Duke Of Aricabeau (IRE)**[23] 5536 3-8-8 **72**....... (p) MichaelMetcalfe(3) 5 18
(Mrs K Burke) *in tch tl wknd over 1f out: t.o* **13/2**

1m 13.05s (3.05) **Going Correction** +0.50s/f (Yiel) **7 Ran SP% 116.7**
Speed ratings (Par 103): **99,98,95,93,92 92,72**
toteswingers: 1&2 £9.00, 1&3 £7.30, 2&3 £4.80 CSF £114.30 TOTE £18.80: £6.00, £3.10; EX 87.00.
Owner Peter Swinnerton **Bred** Alberto Panetta **Trained** Pandy, Monmouths

FOCUS
A modest sprint handicap, run at a strong pace and the first pair came well clear. However it's unlikely they improved, more a case of fancied runners disappointing.

6286 OJ WILLIAMS SUPPLIER OF FUEL AND LUBRICANTS H'CAP 5f
4:30 (4:31) (Class 3) (0-95,92) 3-Y-O+ **£8,409** (£2,502; £1,250; £625) **Stalls** Centre

Form RPR

0353 **1** **Kyleakin Lass**[15] 5832 3-9-2 **88**........................... JoeFanning 8 97
(Ian Wood) *hld up in rr: hdwy 2f out: rdn to ld appr fnl f: hld on wl* **3/1**[2]

606 **2** *nk* **Cheveton**[23] 5530 8-8-8 **79**........................... TadhgO'Shea 6 87
(Richard Price) *trckd ldrs: rdn and chal 1f out: r.o u.p fnl f: jst hld* **7/2**[3]

000 **3** *1 ½* **Bathwick Bear (IRE)**[15] 5829 4-8-8 **79**........................... CathyGannon 2 82
(David Evans) *led: rdn over 1f out: sn hdd: kpt on same pce* **7/1**

0024 **4** *3 ¼* **Pearl Blue (IRE)**[29] 5343 4-9-5 **90**........................... GeorgeBaker 9 81
(Chris Wall) *hld up in rr: rdn 2f out: sn swtchd rt: wnt 4th 1f out: no imp on ldrs* **7/4**[1]

005- **5** *1* **Thats A Fret (IRE)**[3] 6182 6-8-0 **78** oh10........... (b) ShirleyTeasdale(7) 3 66
(Liam McAteer, Ire) *racd keenly: trckd ldrs: rdn 2f out: wknd over 1f out* **12/1**

0/0- **6** *8* **Arthur's Edge**[449] 3410 8-9-1 **86**........................... FrankieMcDonald 7 45
(Christopher Mason) *chsd ldrs: rdn 2f out: sn wknd* **22/1**

2030 **7** *2 ¾* **Sugar Beet**[7] 6072 4-9-7 **92**........................... LukeMorris 5 41
(Ronald Harris) *chsd ldrs: sltly hmpd after 1f: rdn 1/2-way: wknd over 1f out: eased fnl f* **12/1**

59.91s (1.61) **Going Correction** +0.50s/f (Yiel)
WFA 3 from 4yo+ 1lb **7 Ran SP% 115.8**
Speed ratings (Par 107): **107,106,104,98,97 84,80**
toteswingers: 1&2 £3.10, 1&3 £3.10, 2&3 £5.20 CSF £14.35 CT £66.87 TOTE £3.70: £2.10, £2.60; EX 13.60 Trifecta £80.20 Pool: £893.75 - 8.24 winning units..
Owner C R Lambourne, M Forbes, D Losse **Bred** West Dereham Abbey Stud **Trained** Upper Lambourn, Berks
■ Stewards' Enquiry : Tadhg O'Shea two-day ban: used whip above permitted level (Sep 30-Oct 1)

FOCUS
The ground was officially eased to soft all over. A good sprint handicap. It was run at a solid pace and the first three dominated from the furlong marker. The form looks sound enough.

NOTEBOOK
Kyleakin Lass deservedly got back to winning ways. She travels like a dream when getting cut in the ground and loomed up going sweetly in between the final 2f. She hit the front entering the last furlong, but had to dig deep from there to hold off the persistent challenge of Cheveton and really this ground was even tough enough for her. Further improvement is hard to rule out from this likeable 3yo. (tchd 11-4)
Cheveton ◆'s last five wins had all come in this month since 2009. He had his ground and made a bold bid. This was a decent effort, confirming him very much back on track, and no doubt a return to Ayr will now be on his agenda. He should make a bold bid for a third successive win at that meeting and connections will be hoping he makes the cut again for the Silver Cup. (tchd 4-1)
Bathwick Bear(IRE) posted a solid effort in defeat, on ground that was soft enough for him, and is well enough handicapped on old form to think he can find another opening before the season's end. (op 6-1 tchd 5-1)
Pearl Blue(IRE), well backed, was faced with a slightly easier task than of late and her last two wins came on testing ground. It was clear from halfway she struggling, however, and she was well beaten off. (op 9-4 tchd 5-2)
Sugar Beet Official explanation: jockey said filly lost its action

6287 SAXTON DRILLING LTD MAIDEN STKS 5f
5:00 (5:01) (Class 4) 3-Y-O+ **£5,175** (£1,540; £769; £384) **Stalls** Centre

Form RPR

642 **1** **Finesse**[17] 5776 3-8-12 73........................... JimCrowley 1 67+
(Ralph Beckett) *cl up: shkn up to ld appr fnl f: pushed out firmly to hold advantage* **1/2**[1]

0-3 **2** *nk* **Gaelic Wizard (IRE)**[13] 5878 4-8-11 0........................... JoshBaudains(7) 4 71
(Dominic Ffrench Davis) *led tl rdn and hdd appr fnl f: kpt on but a being hld* **4/1**[2]

-4 **3** *6* **My Time**[34] 5177 3-9-3 0........................... SeanQuinlan 2 49
(Michael Mullineaux) *s.i.s: in tch in last: pushed along 1/2-way: sn outpcd by ldrs: stuck on to go mod 3rd ins fnl f* **14/1**

534 **4** *½* **Brown Volcano (IRE)**[6] 6095 3-9-3 0........................... LukeMorris 3 48
(John O'Shea) *dwlt: sn chsng ldrs: rdn 1/2-way: outpcd by principals 2f out: lost 3rd ins fnl f* **6/1**[3]

1m 0.48s (2.18) **Going Correction** +0.50s/f (Yiel)
WFA 3 from 4yo 1lb **4 Ran SP% 107.6**
Speed ratings (Par 105): **102,101,91,91**
CSF £2.78 TOTE £1.60; EX 3.10.
Owner P K Gardner **Bred** Springcombe Park Stud **Trained** Kimpton, Hants

FOCUS
The first pair predictably dominated this weak maiden. The time was reasonable in the circumstances.

6288 HOLSTEN VIER H'CAP 5f
5:30 (5:30) (Class 6) (0-60,64) 3-Y-O+ **£2,181** (£644; £322) **Stalls** Centre

Form RPR

6000 **1** **Novabridge**[123] 2165 4-9-4 **60**........................... (b) CPGeoghegan(3) 5 70
(Neil Mulholland) *s.i.s and chsd along towards rr: hdwy 1/2-way: led appr fnl f: drvn out* **25/1**

103 **2** *1 ½* **Drinmoy Lad (IRE)**[1] 6249 3-9-4 **58**........................... JimCrowley 7 63
(Michael McElhone, Ire) *towards rr: hdwy 1/2-way: sn chsng ldrs: r.o ins fnl f: ducked lft 100yds out: sn no imp on wnr* **4/1**[2]

3605 **3** *½* **Cape Royal**[34] 5149 12-9-6 **59**........................... (bt) ChrisCatlin 3 62
(Milton Bradley) *led tl hdd appr fnl f: kpt on u.p* **14/1**

4310 **4** *nk* **Spic 'n Span**[9] 6003 7-9-3 **56**........................... (b) LukeMorris 6 58
(Ronald Harris) *wnt to post early: chsd ldrs: rdn 2f out: sn ev ch: one pce fnl f* **13/2**[3]

6506 **5** *1 ¾* **Steel Rain**[13] 5876 4-9-0 **53**........................... (b[1]) FrankieMcDonald 13 48
(Nikki Evans) *in rr: hdwy 2f out: sn hung rt: edgd lft u.p and no further imp fnl f* **16/1**

3000 **6** *1* **Tenancy (IRE)**[23] 5543 8-8-4 **50**........................... (b) ShirleyTeasdale(7) 9 42
(Shaun Harris) *chsd ldrs: rdn 1/2-way: sn wknd* **16/1**

0120 **7** *3* **Red Rhythm**[34] 5149 5-9-5 **58**....(vt) CathyGannon 11 39
(David Evans) *sed wrongly fr stall 14: in tch: rdn 1/2-way: sn wknd* **8/1**
5111 **8** *½* **Lizzy's Dream**[12] 5923 4-9-11 **64**.... FrederikTylicki 14 43
(Robin Bastiman) *sed wrongly fr stall 11: in tch: rdn 1/2-way: no rspnse and sn in rr: eased whn no ch ins fnl f* **10/11**[1]

1m 1.65s (3.35) **Going Correction** +0.50s/f (Yiel)
WFA 3 from 4yo+ 1lb 8 Ran SP% **119.1**
Speed ratings (Par 101): **93,90,89,89,86 84,80,79**
toteswingers: 1&2 £15.40, 1&3 £15.50, 2&3 £4.00 CSF £127.05 CT £1499.20 TOTE £28.40: £3.50, £1.40, £3.20; EX 211.80 Trifecta £632.00 Part won. Pool: £854.07 - 0.40 winning units..
Owner Dajam Ltd **Bred** Bishopswood Bloodstock & Trickledown Stud **Trained** Limpley Stoke, Wilts
■ Stewards' Enquiry : Cathy Gannon one-day ban: started from wrong stall (Sep 30)
Frederik Tylicki one day ban: started from wrong stall (Sep 30)

FOCUS
They went hard early on in this ordinary sprint handicap and the principals raced nearer the far rail late on. The winner is rated to his winter AW form.
Steel Rain Official explanation: jockey said gelding hung right
Lizzy's Dream Official explanation: trainer said gelding was unsuited by the soft ground
T/Plt: £667.30 to a £1 stake. Pool: £74,405.36. 81.39 winning tickets. T/Qpdt: £72.10 to a £1 stake. Pool: £5,570.62. 57.10 winning tickets. RL

WOODBINE (R-H)
Saturday, September 15
OFFICIAL GOING: Turf: yielding

6289a NATALMA STKS (GRADE 2) (2YO FILLIES) (TURF) 1m (T)
8:45 (12:00) 2-Y-O
£94,936 (£37,974; £15,822; £7,911; £3,164; £1,582)

RPR
1 **Spring Venture (USA)**[28] 2-8-7 0....(b) PHusbands 6 102
(Mark Casse, Canada) **49/20**[1]
2 *1 ¾* **Spring In The Air (CAN)**[42] 2-8-7 0.... GKGomez 7 98
(Mark Casse, Canada) **91/10**
3 *nk* **Nancy O (IRE)**[21] 2-8-7 0.... DJMoran 5 97
(Carolyn M Costigan, U.S.A) **197/10**
4 *nk* **Kitten's Dumplings (USA)**[34] 2-8-7 0.... RosieNapravnik 8 97
(Michael J Maker, U.S.A) **59/10**
5 *nk* **Coconut Shrimp (USA)** 2-8-7 0.... JJCastellano 10 96
(Todd Pletcher, U.S.A) **56/10**[2]
6 *½* **Shenandoah Lady (USA)** 2-8-7 0.... ERosaDaSilva 2 95
(Steve Attard, Canada) **80/1**
7 *1 ½* **Carmel Beauty (USA)** 2-8-7 0....(b) ASolis 13 91
(Barbara J Minshall, Canada) **101/1**
8 *1 ¼* **Tiz Ro (CAN)** 2-8-7 0.... LContreras 11 88
(Gregory De Gannes, Canada) **57/10**[3]
9 *½* **Dancing For Glory (USA)** 2-8-7 0.... EmmaJayneWilson 4 87
(Chad C Brown, U.S.A) **153/10**
10 *1* **Summer Of Fun (USA)**[21] 2-8-7 0.... JesseMCampbell 1 85
(George Weaver, U.S.A) **11/1**
11 *½* **Rutherford Rd (CAN)**[83] 2-8-7 0.... JVBridgmohan 3 84
(Michael J Doyle, Canada) **60/1**
12 *4 ¾* **Fearless Jacq (IRE)**[30] 5267 2-8-7 0.... RMaragh 14 73
(David Simcock) *trapped v wd in midfield early: hdwy on to heels of ldrs 4f out: rdn and brief effrt 2f out: sn no ex and btn: wknd: eased ins fnl f* **98/10**
13 *2 ¼* **Sure Would (CAN)**[28] 2-8-7 0.... JStein 12 68
(Michael Keogh, Canada) **26/1**
14 *12* **Bwana Go Fast (USA)**[35] 2-8-7 0....(b) ERamsammy 9 40
(Nathan Squires, Canada) **95/1**

1m 37.27s (97.27) 14 Ran SP% **120.6**
PARI-MUTUEL (all including $2 stakes): WIN 6.90; PLACE (1-2) 4.60, 8.80; SHOW (1-2-3) 3.80, 6.40, 9.90; SF 66.00.
Owner Gary Barber & Stoneway Farm LLC **Bred** Stoneway Farm **Trained** North America

3206 DORTMUND (R-H)
Sunday, September 16
OFFICIAL GOING: Turf: good

6290a GROSSER PREIS VON DSW21 - DEUTSCHES ST LEGER (GROUP 3) (3YO+) (TURF) 1m 6f
4:00 (12:00) 3-Y-O+
£26,666 (£9,166; £4,583; £2,500; £1,666; £1,250)

RPR
1 **Altano (GER)**[74] 3768 6-9-6 0.... EPedroza 3 110
(A Wohler, Germany) *hld up towards rr: hdwy on outside 1/2-way to trck ldrs: 4th and rdn over 2f out: r.o u.p to ld over 1f out: drvn out* **49/10**
2 *1 ½* **Tidespring (IRE)**[49] 4634 4-9-3 0.... FabriceVeron 7 105
(H-A Pantall, France) *settled in rr: last 2 1/2f out: rdn and hdwy under 2f out: 3rd and ev ch appr 1f out: r.o u.p fnl f* **29/10**[2]
3 *2* **Wilddrossel (GER)**[42] 4862 3-8-7 0.... EFrank 8 102
(Markus Klug, Germany) *trckd ldr on outside: 2nd and rdn over 2f out: edgd lft and then rt over 1f out: kpt on at one pce fnl f* **18/5**[3]
4 *1 ½* **Nymphea (IRE)**[42] 4862 3-8-7 0.... MrDennisSchiergen 6 100
(P Schiergen, Germany) *midfield: rdn and outpcd 2f out: styd on fr 1 1/2f out: nt pce to chal* **5/2**[1]
5 *¾* **Tahini (GER)**[21] 4-9-6 0.... RPiechulek 2 102
(W Giedt, Germany) *trckd ldr on ins: 3rd and ev ch 2 1/2f out: sn rdn and nt qckn fr 2f out: fdd fnl f* **138/10**
6 *1* **Earlsalsa (GER)**[133] 1901 8-9-6 0.... JBojko 1 101
(C Von Der Recke, Germany) *racd freely in midfield on ins: dropped towards rr 1/2-way: rdn and short-lived effrt to chse ldrs under 2f out: sn rdn and nt qckn: plugged on u.p fnl f* **105/10**
7 *2* **Nexius (IRE)**[28] 5402 3-8-10 0.... APietsch 5 98
(W Hickst, Germany) *led: rdn 1 1/2f out: hdd over 1f out: wknd qckly fnl f* **118/10**
8 *6* **Donn Halling (IRE)**[21] 4-9-6 0.... MartinSeidl 9 89
(V Luka Jr, Czech Republic) *racd freely in midfield on outside: rdn and lost pl 2 1/2f out: bhd fnl 1 1/2f* **11/2**

3m 1.14s (-4.36)
WFA 3 from 4yo+ 10lb 8 Ran SP% **131.6**
WIN (incl. 10 euro stake): 59. PLACES: 19, 17, 16. SF: 255.
Owner Frau Dr I Hornig **Bred** Gestut Hof Ittlingen **Trained** Germany

NOTEBOOK
Altano(GER), whose half-brother, the likely favourite Araldo, was withdrawn due to the ground, quickened up to win cosily.

5145 MUNICH (L-H)
Sunday, September 16
OFFICIAL GOING: Turf: good to soft

6291a BAYERISCHE HAUSBAU - GROSSE EUROPA MEILE (GROUP 2) (3YO+) (TURF) 1m
3:45 (12:00) 3-Y-O+
£33,333 (£12,916; £5,416; £3,333; £2,083; £1,250)

RPR
1 **Combat Zone (IRE)**[56] 6-9-1 0.... NRichter 6 104
(Mario Hofer, Germany) *prom thrght: rdn over 2 1/2f out: r.o to chal over 1f out: led ins fnl f: strly pressed cl home: jst hld on all out* **91/10**
2 *hd* **Gereon (GER)**[63] 4130 4-9-1 0.... GHind 4 104
(C Zschache, Germany) *broke wl: trckd ldr in 2nd: rdn over 2 1/2f out: kpt on wl u.p to chal wl ins fnl f: jst failed* **218/10**
3 *1* **Neatico (GER)**[22] 5613 5-9-1 0.... KClijmans 5 102+
(P Schiergen, Germany) *midfield: rdn 3f out: outpcd over 1f out: rallied and styd on strly cl home: wnt 3rd fnl strides* **71/10**[3]
4 *½* **Felician (GER)** 4-9-1 0.... RobertHavlin 8 101
(F J Leve, Germany) *midfield: rdn 2f out: hung lft u.p: styd on to go 3rd ins fnl 100yds: dropped to 4th fnl strides* **94/10**
5 *1* **Alianthus (GER)**[84] 3425 7-9-1 0.... ADeVries 1 98
(W Giedt, Germany) *led: rdn to extend advantage over 2 1/2f out: clsd down and strly pressed over 1f out: hdd ins fnl f: sn no ex and fdd: dropped to 5th cl home* **6/4**[1]
6 *hd* **Sir Oscar (GER)**[17] 5782 5-9-4 0.... AurelienLemaitre 9 101
(T Potters, Germany) *hld up last in main body of field: rdn over 2 1/2f out: kpt on one pce u.p ins fnl 2f: n.d* **44/5**
7 *1* **Pakal (GER)**[14] 5869 3-8-11 0 ow1.... THellier 7 95
(W Figge, Germany) *midfield on outer: rdn over 2f out: outpcd over 1f out: plugged on ins fnl f* **49/10**[2]
8 *4* **Nordic Truce (USA)**[49] 5-9-1 0.... LennartHammer-Hansen 10 86
(P Schiergen, Germany) *hld up towards rr on outer: rdn over 3f out: sn outpcd and btn: nvr a factor* **161/10**
9 *¾* **Theo Danon (GER)**[22] 5613 4-9-1 0....(b) FilipMinarik 3 85
(P Schiergen, Germany) *hld up towards rr on inner: rdn 3f out: sn outpcd and btn: nvr a factor* **41/5**
10 *3* **Mano Diao**[17] 5782 3-8-10 0.... StefanieHofer 2 77
(Mario Hofer, Germany) *hld up in detached last: rdn over 3f out: racd alone on far side rail in st: sn outpcd and btn: nvr a factor* **165/10**

1m 37.03s (97.03)
WFA 3 from 4yo+ 4lb 10 Ran SP% **125.8**
WIN (incl. 10 euro stake): 101. PLACES: 31, 46, 20. SF: 4106.
Owner Guido-Werner Hermann-Schmitt **Bred** Twelve Oaks Stud **Trained** Germany

6086 LONGCHAMP (R-H)
Sunday, September 16
OFFICIAL GOING: Turf: good to soft

6292a QATAR PRIX DU PETIT COUVERT (GROUP 3) (3YO+) (TURF) 5f (S)
12:30 (12:00) 3-Y-O+ **£33,333** (£13,333; £10,000; £6,666; £3,333)

RPR
1 **Monsieur Joe (IRE)**[23] 5561 5-8-13 0.... OlivierPeslier 5 114
(Robert Cowell) *broke wl: racd in 2nd travelling wl: chal for ld 1 1/2f out: tk ld 250yds out: r.o wl: comf* **9/4**[1]
2 *¾* **Inxile (IRE)**[7] 6072 7-8-13 0....(p) AdrianNicholls 3 111
(David Nicholls) *sn led: chal for ld 1 1/2f out: hdd 250yds out: r.o wl: a being hld* **3/1**[2]
3 *4* **Flash Mash (USA)**[44] 4790 4-8-9 0.... GregoryBenoist 6 93
(X Nakkachdji, France) *racd towards rr on outside: outpcd by ldrs: r.o wl ent fnl f: unable to catch ldrs* **13/2**
4 *2* **Sea Trial (FR)**[44] 4790 3-8-11 0....(p) ThierryThulliez 1 89
(Mme C Head-Maarek, France) *broke wl on ins: nt pce to go w ldrs at 1/2-way: r.o wl ent fnl f: styd on wl* **14/1**
5 *¾* **Marchand D'Or (FR)**[42] 4861 9-8-13 0.... DavyBonilla 2 87+
(M Delzangles, France) *outpcd fr s: wl in rr tl running on wl ins fnl 1 1/2f* **4/1**[3]
6 *snk* **August Rush (SAF)**[21] 5647 6-8-13 0.... Christophe-PatriceLemaire 7 86
(P Bary, France) *prom early: rdn but no ex fr over 1 1/2f out: fdd fnl f* **10/1**
7 *7* **Stepper Point**[21] 5641 3-8-11 0....(p) ChristopheSoumillon 8 88+
(William Muir) *broke fast on outside to r 4th: prom tl 2f out whn began to weaken: eased fnl f* **7/1**

56.35s (0.05) **Going Correction** +0.30s/f (Good)
WFA 3 from 4yo+ 1lb 7 Ran SP% **117.4**
Speed ratings: **111,109,103,100,99 98,87**
WIN (incl. 1 euro stake): 4.00. PLACES: 1.40, 1.30, 1.40. DF: 4.10. SF: 7.40.
Owner Mrs Helen Checkley **Bred** Nicola And Eleanor Kent **Trained** Six Mile Bottom, Cambs

FOCUS
The front-running runner-up has been rated just off his recent form, with the winner to a slight personal best.

NOTEBOOK
Monsieur Joe(IRE) was well beaten in the Nunthorpe last time, but prior to that he'd won a Deauville Listed event and here he seemed to produce a career best. He's not sure to take his chance in the Prix de l'Abbaye, with a return to Dubai early next year said to be the main plan.
Inxile(IRE) proved suited by the return to 5f and ran close to his recent best. Connections felt the ground was quicker than ideal and the Abbaye is said to be the target.
Marchand D'Or(FR) kept on after starting slowly.

Stepper Point was below form, although he was heavily eased once held.

6293a QATAR PRIX FOY (GROUP 2) (4YO+ COLTS, FILLIES & MARES) (TURF) 1m 4f

1:30 (12:00) 4-Y-0+ **£61,750** (£23,833; £11,375; £7,583; £3,791)

RPR

1 **Orfevre (JPN)**[84] 3428 4-9-2 0 ChristopheSoumillon 5 119+
(Yasutoshi Ikee, Japan) *hld up towards rr: qcknd wl on ins 2 1/2f out: chal for ld 2f out: led 1 1/2f out: wnt clr: styd on wl fnl f: nvr threatened* **10/11**[1]

2 *1* **Meandre (FR)**[56] 4383 4-9-2 0 MaximeGuyon 2 117+
(A Fabre, France) *racd in 3rd: r.o wl u.p fnl 2f: got up for 2nd 50yds out: nvr threatened wnr* **7/4**[2]

3 *nk* **Joshua Tree (IRE)**[28] 5400 5-9-2 0 FrankieDettori 4 116
(Marco Botti) *settled in 2nd: led briefly 350yds out: hdd 1 1/2f out: styd on wl fnl f: lost 2nd 50yds out* **16/1**

4 *6* **Fiorente (IRE)**[66] 4010 4-9-2 0 KierenFallon 3 107
(Sir Michael Stoute) *hld up towards rr: rdn early in st: nt pce to go w ldrs: styd on fr 1 1/2f out: nt hrd rdn fnl 100yds* **6/1**[3]

5 *3 1/2* **Aventino (JPN)**[182] 8-9-2 0 AnthonyCrastus 1 101
(Yasutoshi Ikee, Japan) *led fr s: set mod pce: qcknd at 1/2-way: r.o wl early in st: hdd 350yds out: no ex u.p: fdd* **150/1**

2m 34.26s (3.86) **Going Correction** +0.30s/f (Good) 5 Ran SP% **109.6**
Speed ratings: **99,98,98,94,91**
WIN (incl. 1 euro stake): 1.70. PLACES: 1.10, 1.20. SF: 2.50.
Owner Sunday Racing Co Ltd **Bred** Shadai Corporation Inc **Trained** Japan

FOCUS
The pacemaker covered the first 1400m 6.84 seconds slower than the leader in the Vermeille. As such, the winner couldn't match his top-class Japanese form, with the third limiting the level.

NOTEBOOK
Orfevre(JPN) was a bit keen under restraint in last place, but he still readily won the sprint to the line once getting a gap between the inside rail and his pacemaker in the straight. He didn't do a great deal in front, his exertions just telling on his first start since June, but was never in any danger. There's good reason to think he can do a lot better now he's had a run, while a stronger pace should help, and his best form is of a similar standard to other Japanese-trained horses who have gone close to winning the Arc. Last year he became his country's first Triple Crown winner since Deep Impact in 2005 (third in this race the following year, but later disqualified), while both El Condor Pasa (1999) and Nakayama Festa (2010) finished runner-up in the race for Japan.
Meandre(FR) had won his last two starts in Group 1 company, but he's not in the same league as Orfevre and was always held. He was only sixth in last year's Arc and it's doubtful he'll do much better this time.
Joshua Tree(IRE) had a race-fitness edge and was well placed.
Fiorente(IRE) looked like belatedly fulfilling his potential when readily defeating Joshua Tree in the Princess of Wales's Stakes at the July course last time, but this was disappointing. He didn't look comfortable under pressure and is left with plenty to prove once again.

6294a QATAR PRIX NIEL (GROUP 2) (3YO COLTS & FILLIES) (TURF) 1m 4f

2:40 (12:00) 3-Y-0 **£61,750** (£23,833; £11,375; £7,583; £3,791)

RPR

1 **Saonois (FR)**[105] 2743 3-9-2 0 AntoineHamelin 2 114+
(J-P Gauvin, France) *hld up towards rr u.str hold: relegated to last 2f out: no room to chal tl 100yds out whn qcknd wl between horses: led 50yds out: r.o strly: comf* **5/1**[3]

2 *1 1/4* **Bayrir (FR)**[29] 5375 3-9-2 0 Christophe-PatriceLemaire 6 112
(A De Royer-Dupre, France) *hld up in rr: r.o wl on outside in st: wnt 2nd 50yds out: nvr rchd ldr* **5/2**[2]

3 *shd* **Last Train**[64] 4121 3-9-2 0 MaximeGuyon 5 112
(A Fabre, France) *settled in 2nd: rdn early in st: relegated to 4th 1 1/2f out: rallied ent fnl f: r.o wl to go 3rd 50yds out* **7/4**[1]

4 *nk* **Remus De La Tour (FR)**[91] 3204 3-9-2 0 DavyBonilla 1 111
(K Borgel, France) *settled in 3rd on ins: r.o u.p fr 1 1/2f out: styd on wl fnl f* **14/1**

5 *hd* **Kesampour (FR)**[105] 2743 3-9-2 0 GregoryBenoist 4 111
(M Delzangles, France) *led fr s: r.o wl in st: stl in front 150yds out: hdd 100yds out: r.o wl: no ex fnl 50yds* **5/1**[3]

6 *snk* **Smoking Sun (USA)**[32] 5250 3-9-2 0 StephanePasquier 3 111
(P Bary, France) *settled in 4th on outer: r.o u.p: qcknd wl to go 2nd 150yds out: led 100yds out: ev ch but no ex ent fnl 75yds: hdd 50yds out: styd on* **16/1**

2m 35.31s (4.91) **Going Correction** +0.30s/f (Good) 6 Ran SP% **110.8**
Speed ratings: **95,94,94,93,93 93**
WIN (incl. 1 euro stake): 4.80 PLACES: 2.70, 2.30 SF: 22.10.
Owner Pascal Treyve **Bred** Earl Haras De Nonant Le Pin **Trained** France

FOCUS
The pace was even slower than in the Prix Foy, with the leader covering the first 1800m in a time 1.97 seconds slower than the pacesetter in the earlier contest. A sprint to the line ensued and the final 600m went by in splits of 11.73, 11.07 and 11.71. The form is rated around the fourth and fifth.

NOTEBOOK
Saonois(FR) had shown good speed to win a slowly run French Derby over 1m2.5f when last seen in June. This was a visually impressive performance, the colt sealing the race in a matter of strides after having to wait until inside the final 200m to deliver his challenge, but can he be as effective off a likely much stronger gallop in the Arc? If you believe so, then prices of around 10-1 are probably fair enough, particularly considering the excellent record of 3yos in the race, but it's hard to be confident, and soft ground would also be a major concern. He'd need to be supplemented for the Arc.
Bayrir(FR) only made his debut in May but he won four of his first five starts, including the Prix Eugene Adam and most recently the Secretariat Stakes in the US. Upped to this trip for the first time, he ran a nice Arc trial, keeping on without being given a hard time but just lacking the speed of the winner. There may be more to come in a truly run race and he'll be of interest if supplemented for the main event.
Last Train didn't really build on the form of his close second to Imperial Monarch in the Grand Prix de Paris, but the steady pace probably didn't help and he was entitled to need the run.
Remus De La Tour(FR), a Group 3 winner last time, had a bit to do in this company and didn't prove himself, for all that he wasn't beaten far.
Kesampour(FR) was responsible for the slow pace, so it was disappointing he failed to beat a rival, but he may have needed the run, his first since finishing fourth to Saonois in the Prix du Jockey Club.

6295a QATAR PRIX VERMEILLE (GROUP 1) (3YO+ FILLIES & MARES) (TURF) 1m 4f

3:10 (12:00) 3-Y-0+ **£166,658** (£66,675; £33,337; £16,654; £8,341)

RPR

1 **Shareta (IRE)**[24] 5518 4-9-2 0 Christophe-PatriceLemaire 9 114+
(A De Royer-Dupre, France) *prom thrght: impr to trck ldr in 2nd after 4f: smooth hdwy to ld over 2f out: rdn clr over 1f out: comf* **7/2**[1]

2 *2* **Pirika (IRE)**[36] 5116 4-9-2 0 Pierre-CharlesBoudot 7 110+
(A Fabre, France) *hld up in last trio: hdwy on outer fr over 2f out: rdn 1 1/2f out: styd on thrght fnl f: wnt 2nd fnl strides: no ch w wnr* **33/1**

3 *hd* **Solemia (IRE)**[36] 5116 4-9-2 0 ChristopheSoumillon 6 110
(C Laffon-Parias, France) *midfield: rdn 2f out: styd on to go 2nd ins fnl 100yds: dropped to 3rd fnl strides* **16/1**

4 *1 1/4* **Yellow And Green**[84] 3423 3-8-8 0 ThierryThulliez 13 108+
(N Clement, France) *dropped in fr wd draw and hld up in last: had to wait for run over 2f out: swtchd to outer and rdn to improve 1 1/2f out: styd on to go 4th fnl strides: nvr able to chal* **20/1**

5 *shd* **Galikova (FR)**[20] 5399 4-9-2 0 OlivierPeslier 1 108+
(F Head, France) *midfield on inner: short of room and shuffled bk 2f out: swtchd out and rdn to improve 1 1/2f out: styd on to go 5th fnl strides: nvr able to chal* **4/1**[2]

6 *1/2* **Sagawara**[49] 4633 3-8-8 0 ThierryJarnet 8 107
(A De Royer-Dupre, France) *midfield on outer: hdwy fr over 2f out: rdn and 2nd 1 1/2f out: kpt on tl no ex wl ins fnl f: fdd and lost multiple pls cl home* **33/1**

7 *1 3/4* **Princess Highway (USA)**[56] 4378 3-8-8 0 PatSmullen 11 104
(D K Weld, Ire) *midfield on outer: rdn 2 1/2f out: brief effrt to chal over 1 1/2f out: sn outpcd and fdd* **9/2**[3]

8 *2 1/2* **Sediciosa (IRE)**[105] 2741 3-8-8 0 GregoryBenoist 10 100
(Y Barberot, France) *disp ld early: sn hdd but remained prom on outer: rdn 2f out: swtchd to rail and outpcd over 1f out: fdd ins fnl f* **16/1**

9 *1/2* **Romantica**[26] 5472 3-8-8 0 MaximeGuyon 3 99
(A Fabre, France) *hld up towards rr on inner: rdn 2 1/2f out: kpt on one pce ins fnl 1 1/2f: n.d* **8/1**

10 *1* **Salomina (GER)**[42] 4862 3-8-8 0 AStarke 2 98
(P Schiergen, Germany) *broke wl to dispute ld early: sn hdd but remained prom on inner: short of room on rail over 2f out: in clr and rdn 1 1/2f out: sn no ex and btn: fdd* **7/1**

11 *3* **La Pomme D'Amour**[36] 5116 4-9-2 0 MickaelBarzalona 5 93
(A Fabre, France) *t.k.h early: hld up towards rr: rdn to try and improve 2 1/2f out: outpcd and btn over 1f out: fdd: eased cl home* **9/1**

12 *8* **Sydarra (FR)**[32] 5249 3-8-8 0 FlavienPrat 12 80
(F Head, France) *crossed over fr wd draw and sn led: rdn and hdd over 2f out: qckly btn and wknd: eased over 1f out* **150/1**

13 *1 1/2* **Sarah Lynx (IRE)**[15] 5845 5-9-2 0 (b) FrankieDettori 4 78
(J E Hammond, France) *slowly away: hld up in last trio on inner: rdn 2f out: outpcd in last over 1f out: sn btn: eased ins fnl f* **25/1**

2m 29.06s (-1.34) **Going Correction** +0.30s/f (Good)
WFA 3 from 4yo+ 8lb 13 Ran SP% **120.9**
Speed ratings: **116,114,114,113,113 113,112,110,110,109 107,102,101**
WIN (incl. 1 euro stake): 3.30 (Shareta coupled with Sagawara). PLACES: 1.70, 9.40, 5.20 DF: 92.20 SF: 80.20.
Owner H H Aga Khan **Bred** His Highness The Aga Khan's Studs S C **Trained** Chantilly, France

FOCUS
The pace was much better than in the Prix Foy and the Prix Niel, but still not overly quick. Weak form rated around the second, third, fourth and sixth.

NOTEBOOK
Shareta(IRE), who was always forwardly placed, comfortably followed up her Yorkshire Oaks success. A 5l second to Danedream in last year's Arc, she could again make the places next month but it's doubtful she has improved enough to take the top prize. She looks short enough at around 10-1.
Pirika(IRE) has yet to win above Listed level and her proximity does little for the form, although this was only her third start of the season.
Solemia(IRE) was a nose too good for Shareta when winning a Group 2 in May, although she was getting 2lb and looks flattered by that form. This was still a solid effort, however.
Yellow And Green still had an awful lot to do when forced to switch wide early in the straight, so she did well to finish so close.
Galikova(FR) didn't get the clearest of runs in the straight but wasn't unlucky. She ran okay but has yet to prove as good as last year.
Princess Highway(USA), who won the Ribblesdale before finding the ground too soft in the Irish Oaks, found disappointingly little for pressure.

6296a QATAR PRIX DU MOULIN DE LONGCHAMP (GROUP 1) (3YO+ COLTS, FILLIES & MARES) (TURF) 1m

3:45 (12:00) 3-Y-0+ **£214,275** (£85,725; £42,862; £21,412)

RPR

1 **Moonlight Cloud**[35] 5141 4-8-13 0 ThierryJarnet 1 123
(F Head, France) *broke awkwardly fr stalls: sn wnt 2nd: relegated to 3rd bef st: qcknd wl to chal for ld 2f out: r.o wl: tk narrow ld 1f out: r.o wl u.p: jst hld on* **10/11**[1]

2 *hd* **Farhh**[25] 5490 4-9-2 0 FrankieDettori 4 126
(Saeed Bin Suroor) *sn led: set gd pce: chal 2f out: r.o wl: hdd 1f out: raillied u.p: r.o strly fnl 100yds: jst failed* **11/8**[2]

3 *6* **Sarkiyla (FR)**[32] 5249 3-8-8 0 Christophe-PatriceLemaire 2 108
(A De Royer-Dupre, France) *settled at rr of field: stl wl in rr 2f out: r.o fnl f but no ch w ldrs* **12/1**[3]

4 *2 1/2* **Caspar Netscher**[35] 5141 3-8-11 0 ShaneKelly 3 106
(Alan McCabe) *settled in 3rd: wnt 2nd bef st: rdn 2f out: r.o but fnd no ex ins fnl f: wknd* **14/1**

1m 36.9s (-1.50) **Going Correction** +0.30s/f (Good)
WFA 3 from 4yo 4lb 4 Ran SP% **108.8**
Speed ratings: **119,118,112,110**
WIN (incl. 1 euro stake): 2.00. PLACES: 1.10, 1.10. SF: 2.70.
Owner George Strawbridge **Bred** George Strawbridge **Trained** France

FOCUS
A really disappointing turnout numerically, but a fascinating tactical battle between Moonlight Cloud and Farhh. Unsurprisingly, Frankie Dettori wanted to dictate on the Godolphin runner, who was dropping in trip and whose main rival still had to conclusively prove her stamina. The fractions looked sensible (first 600m covered in 0.40.28, and 1000m in 1.03.21), and Farhh basically just wasn't quite good enough. The third helps set the level.

NOTEBOOK
Moonlight Cloud, a dual Prix Maurice de Gheest winner, had been hampered at a crucial stage when upped to this trip for only the second time in the Jacques le Marois (well beaten in 1000 Guineas only other try), but she still managed a close fourth that day and here she proved in no uncertain terms she gets 1m. She reportedly now goes for the Breeders' Cup Mile, a race her trainer won three times with Goldikova, and must hold strong claims with her blend of speed and stamina looking ideal.
Farhh will apparently now go to Ascot on British Champions Day for either the QEII or the Champions Stakes. While he continues to run well in Group 1 company, his top-level record now reads 0-5 and things are unlikely to get any easier, although softer ground may help.
Sarkiyla(FR) had only won a Deauville Group 3 last time and this was a lot tougher.

Caspar Netscher was well below his Jacques le Marois form, for all that he was flattered to finish just behind Moonlight Cloud on that occasion.

6297a QATAR PRIX GLADIATEUR (GROUP 3) (4YO+) (TURF) 1m 7f 110y

4:20 (12:00) 4-Y-O+ **£33,333** (£13,333; £10,000; £6,666; £3,333)

RPR

1 **Ivory Land (FR)**[112] [2534] 5-9-4 0 StephanePasquier 8 118+
(A De Royer-Dupre, France) *midfield on inner: rdn over 2f out: swtchd out and r.o to chal over 1f out: led ins fnl f: strly pressed cl home but a doing enough* **9/2**[2]

2 *nk* **Miss Lago (IRE)**[21] [5650] 4-8-10 0 (p) GregoryBenoist 7 110+
(E Lellouche, France) *hld up towards rr: rdn over 2f out: hdwy on outer fr over 1 1/2f out: styd on to chal wl ins fnl f: nvr quite on terms w wnr* **12/1**

3 *2 ½* **Willing Foe (USA)**[22] [5600] 5-8-11 0 FrankieDettori 9 108
(Saeed Bin Suroor) *midfield: swtchd out and rdn to improve over 2f out: effrt to chal over 1f out: styd on to go 3rd ins fnl f: outpcd by front pair cl home* **10/3**[1]

4 *2* **Kasbah Bliss (FR)**[112] [2534] 10-9-6 0 ThierryJarnet 2 114
(F Doumen, France) *hld up: rdn and outpcd over 1 1/2f out: styd on to go 4th fnl strides* **16/1**

5 *¾* **Vadamar (FR)**[28] [5400] 4-9-4 0 (b[1]) Christophe-PatriceLemaire 3 111
(M Delzangles, France) *led: rdn and over 2 l clr 2f out: kpt on tl no ex and hdd ins fnl f: fdd and dropped to 5th fnl strides* **9/2**[2]

6 *2 ½* **Usuelo (FR)**[21] [5650] 4-9-2 0 AntoineHamelin 10 106
(J-L Guillochon, France) *trckd ldr on inner: wnt 2nd 5f out: rdn over 2f out: effrt to chal over 1f out: kpt on tl no ex and fdd ins fnl f* **25/1**

7 *1 ¼* **Telbes**[56] 4-8-11 0 AlexisAchard 1 100
(M Delzangles, France) *hld up in last: rdn 2 1/2f out: awkward u.p and outpcd over 1 1/2f out: plugged on* **8/1**

8 *10* **Lone Ranger (FR)**[49] [4634] 4-8-11 0 ChristopheSoumillon 5 88
(A De Royer-Dupre, France) *midfield on inner: briefly short of room and checked over 4f out: rdn over 2f out: kpt on tl no ex and btn ins fnl f: fdd and eased* **7/1**[3]

9 *nk* **Silver Valny (FR)**[27] 6-8-11 0 ThomasMessina 4 87
(Mlle M-L Mortier, France) *midfield on outer: rdn 2 1/2f out: outpcd over 1f out: sn btn and fdd: eased* **25/1**

10 *2* **Gentoo (FR)**[27] 8-8-11 0 (p) MaximeGuyon 13 85
(A Lyon, France) *hld up towards rr: rdn to improve 3f out: outpcd 1 1/2f out: sn btn: eased ins fnl f* **25/1**

11 *7* **Inside Man (IRE)**[49] [4634] 6-8-11 0 (b) AnthonyCrastus 11 77
(E Lellouche, France) *midfield on outer: hdwy 3f out: rdn and brief effrt over 2f out: no ex and btn 1 1/2f out: wknd rapidly and immediately eased* **16/1**

12 *dist* **Flamingo Fantasy (GER)**[28] [5400] 7-8-11 0 (p) OlivierPeslier 6
(S Smrczek, Germany) *trckd ldr on outer: lost pl rapidly over 3f out: sn last and btn: eased over 2f out: t.o* **12/1**

3m 18.16s (-3.34) **12 Ran SP% 121.7**
WIN (incl. 1 euro stake): 6.60. PLACES: 2.30, 4.30, 1.90. DF: 69.70. SF: 120.50.
Owner Eduardo Fierro **Bred** Suc Z Hakam **Trained** Chantilly, France

FOCUS
The race has been rated around the runner-up and fourth, with the progressive winner running to a personal best.

NOTEBOOK
Ivory Land(FR) followed up his recent C&D Group 2 victory, appearing to produce a career-best. He's likely to run in the Prix du Cadran.
Willing Foe(USA) won the Ebor off 101 last time and that form was given a significant boost when the runner-up, who was getting 2lb, won the Irish St Leger. He ran well, but not up to his best, and connections felt the York race had taken more out of the horse than they'd anticipated.

6289 WOODBINE (R-H)

Sunday, September 16

OFFICIAL GOING: Turf: good changing to firm after northern dancer turf stakes); polytrack: fast

6298a CANADIAN STKS (GRADE 2) (3YO+ FILLIES & MARES) (TURF) 1m 1f

8:05 (8:05) 3-Y-O+ **£113,924** (£45,569; £18,987; £9,493; £4,556; £1,898)

RPR

1 **Barefoot Lady (IRE)**[23] [5560] 4-8-1 0 DJMoran 4 106
(Richard Fahey) *prom on inner: swtchd out and rdn to chal 2f out: led ent fnl f: edgd lft: drvn clr* **36/5**

2 *1 ½* **All Star Heart (CAN)**[34] 5-8-7 0 BBlanc 5 109
(Ronald McAnally, U.S.A) **22/5**[3]

3 *¾* **Stars To Shine (USA)**[29] [5376] 5-8-7 0 ASolis 3 107
(Mark Frostad, Canada) **66/10**

4 *2 ¾* **Kapitale (GER)**[29] [5376] 4-8-5 0 MircoDemuro 9 100
(A Wohler, Germany) **11/4**[1]

5 *nse* **Indian Pond (CAN)**[70] 4-8-3 0 ERosaDaSilva 8 97
(Mark Casse, Canada) **28/1**

6 *1 ¾* **Smart Sting (USA)**[64] 4-8-5 0 (b) JRVelazquez 7 96
(Roger L Attfield, Canada) **7/1**

7 *2 ¼* **Moment Of Majesty (CAN)**[28] 5-8-5 0 ow2 GOlguin 1 91
(Sue Leslie, Canada) **19/2**

8 *1* **Laughing (IRE)**[49] 4-8-7 0 LContreras 2 91
(Alan E Goldberg, U.S.A) **15/4**[2]

9 *2 ¼* **Shimmering Moment (USA)**[49] 5-8-2 0 ow1 SheldonRussell 6 81
(Francis Abbott III, U.S.A) **247/10**

1m 45.89s (105.89) **9 Ran SP% 121.0**
PARI-MUTUEL (all including $2 stakes): WIN 16.40; PLACE (1-2) 8.40, 5.90; SHOW (1-2-3) 5.50, 3.70, 4.60; SF 93.80.
Owner Mrs H Steel **Bred** Arbawny Ventures 2000uc **Trained** Musley Bank, N Yorks

NOTEBOOK
Barefoot Lady(IRE) appreciates genuinely quick ground and won this quite easily despite edging left for pressure late on. She will probably run in the E P Taylor Stakes back here before heading to the Goffs November Breeding Stock Sale later this year.

6299a NORTHERN DANCER TURF STKS PRESENTED BY VTECH (GRADE 1) (3YO+) (TURF) 1m 4f (T)

9:37 (9:37) 3-Y-O+

£189,873 (£63,291; £31,645; £15,822; £7,594; £3,164)

RPR

1 **Wigmore Hall (IRE)**[29] [5377] 5-8-11 0 JamieSpencer 7 114
(Michael Bell) **37/10**[2]

2 *nk* **Al Khali (USA)**[29] [5380] 6-8-7 0 GKGomez 3 110
(William Mott, U.S.A) **61/20**[1]

3 *1* **Forte Dei Marmi**[28] 6-8-11 0 ASolis 5 112
(Roger L Attfield, Canada) **21/4**

4 *2 ¾* **Scalo**[28] 5-8-9 0 UmbertoRispoli 4 106
(A Wohler, Germany) **77/20**[3]

5 *7 ¾* **Irish Mission (CAN)**[42] 3-7-12 0 ow1 (b) JStein 8 91
(Mark Frostad, Canada) **123/20**

6 *4 ½* **Musketier (GER)**[64] 10-8-9 0 JRVelazquez 6 86
(Roger L Attfield, Canada) **41/10**

7 *hd* **Ojibway Signal (CAN)**[42] 4-8-7 0 LContreras 2 84
(David R Bell, Canada) **29/1**

8 *14* **Celtic Conviction (CAN)**[13] 4-8-7 0 JesseMCampbell 1 62
(Michael J Doyle, Canada) **67/1**

2m 28.28s (-1.32)
WFA 3 from 4yo+ 8lb **8 Ran SP% 121.0**
PARI-MUTUEL (all including $2 stakes): WIN 9.40; PLACE (1-2) 4.90, 4.50; SHOW (1-2-3) 3.50, 3.10, 4.00; SF 39.90.
Owner M B Hawtin **Bred** K And Mrs Cullen **Trained** Newmarket, Suffolk

NOTEBOOK
Wigmore Hall(IRE) appreciated the fast ground and dug deep when strongly challenged inside the last. This was his first win since taking this race last year.

6300a RICOH WOODBINE MILE STKS (GRADE 1) (3YO+) (TURF) 1m (T)

10:42 (10:44) 3-Y-O+

£379,746 (£126,582; £63,291; £31,645; £12,658; £6,329)

RPR

1 **Wise Dan (USA)**[36] 5-8-9 0 JRVelazquez 3 128+
(Charles Lopresti, U.S.A) **11/20**[1]

2 *3 ¼* **Hunters Bay (USA)**[43] 5-8-7 0 EmmaJayneWilson 6 118
(Reade Baker, Canada) **14/1**

3 *1* **Cityscape**[35] [5141] 6-8-12 0 JamesDoyle 7 121
(Roger Charlton) **33/10**[2]

4 *2* **Riding The River (USA)**[21] 5-8-9 0 (b) PHusbands 1 113
(David Cotey, U.S.A) **17/1**

5 *1* **Dance And Dance (IRE)**[43] [4822] 6-8-5 0 GKGomez 2 107
(Ed Vaughan) **167/10**

6 *½* **Big Band Sound (USA)**[21] 5-8-9 0 TPizarro 5 110
(Daniel J Vella, Canada) **129/10**[3]

7 *2* **Worthadd (IRE)**[63] [4130] 5-8-7 0 LContreras 9 103
(Sir Mark Prescott Bt) **175/10**

8 *4 ½* **Hollinger (CAN)**[56] 5-8-6 0 ow1 ASolis 8 92
(Roger L Attfield, Canada) **40/1**

9 *22* **Artic Fern (CAN)**[21] 5-8-5 0 JStein 4 40
(Michael Keogh, Canada) **108/1**

1m 34.07s (94.07) **9 Ran SP% 121.6**
PARI-MUTUEL (all including $2 stakes): WIN 3.10; PLACE (1-2) 2.70, 6.30; SHOW (1-2-3) 2.10, 4.40, 2.90; SF 27.30.
Owner Morton Fink **Bred** Mort Fink **Trained** USA

NOTEBOOK
Wise Dan(USA) got a nice tow into the race from the two leaders and quickened up well in the straight before drawing clear. This was an impressive win, even allowing for Cityscape being a little below form, and he's put down a marker for the Breeders' Cup Mile, although the Classic will also be considered as he's has shown a similar level of form on dirt, albeit only at up to 1m1f.
Cityscape didn't travel as well as he did at Meydan or in the Jacques Le Marois according to his rider. The ground wasn't used as an excuse but for one reason or another he wasn't thought to be at his best. RPRs rate him as having run 5lb below his Dubai Duty Free win.

5989 BRIGHTON (L-H)

Monday, September 17

OFFICIAL GOING: Good to firm (firm in places; watered) changing to firm after race 1 (2:20)

Rail dolled out from 6f to 2.5f adding 18yds to distances. The bend at 4f at narrowest configuration.

Wind: Moderate, against Weather: Sunny

6301 RACING POST WEEKENDER OUT EVERY WEDNESDAY/E.B.F. MEDIAN AUCTION MAIDEN STKS 6f 209y

2:20 (2:20) (Class 6) 2-Y-O **£2,522** (£750; £375; £187) **Stalls Low**

Form RPR

6222 1 **Tropical Song**[33] [5230] 2-9-3 83 RobertHavlin 1 74+
(John Gosden) *mde all: rdn and in control fnl 2f* **1/6**[1]

40 2 *2 ¾* **Spanish Art**[13] [5911] 2-9-3 0 RichardHughes 5 67
(Richard Hannon) *chsd wnr: drvn along 3f out: nt qckn appr fnl f* **15/2**[2]

50 3 *hd* **Pinarius (IRE)**[9] [6020] 2-9-3 0 NeilCallan 3 66
(Brian Meehan) *chsd ldng pair: drvn to dispute 2nd ent fnl f: one pce* **12/1**[3]

4 *4 ½* **Amulet** 2-8-12 0 MartinLane 4 49
(David Simcock) *s.i.s: in rr: effrt over 2f out: wknd over 1f out* **14/1**

06 5 *20* **Hanga Roa (IRE)**[10] [5992] 2-9-3 0 TomQueally 2
(Gary Moore) *dwlt: in tch: rdn 4f out: wknd over 2f out* **66/1**

1m 24.11s (1.01) **Going Correction** +0.125s/f (Good) **5 Ran SP% 113.3**
Speed ratings (Par 93): **99,95,95,90,67**
CSF £2.36 TOTE £1.10: £1.02, £2.40; EX 2.60.
Owner Normandie Stud Ltd **Bred** Normandie Stud Ltd **Trained** Newmarket, Suffolk

FOCUS
Rail dolled out from 6f to 2.5f, adding 18 yds; the 4f bend at its narrowest configuration. A fair juvenile maiden rated tentatively through the runner-up. They went a proper gallop on ground officially described as good to firm, firm in places. The ground was officially changed to firm after this contest.

NOTEBOOK
Tropical Song was on something of a retrieval mission after finishing second at similarly prohibitive odds over this 7f trip on his AW debut at Kempton the previous month. He arrived with a BHA rating of 83 having previously finished runner-up in two 7f Sandown maidens on good/good to firm ground in July. He is susceptible to speedier individuals over this 7f trip, as he is likely to need 1m2f next year, but there was nothing in this field with the ability to trouble him. He duly made this a true test from the front and was roused to settle the matter in the final furlong. He may struggle off this mark in nurseries. (tchd 2-11)
Spanish Art failed to build on a modest fourth of seven over 6f at Kempton on debut in August when down the field over 7f on good to firm ground at Leicester this month. This was more like it and he may prove competitive in modest nursery company. (op 9-1)
Pinarius(IRE) finished a respectable last of five on debut in a better-class conditions' contest at Salisbury over 6f on good to firm ground in July, but disappointed in a maiden over 7f at Ascot on similar ground this month. This was more like that debut display and he has a future in modest handicaps.
Amulet made a slow start on debut here but showed ability in the middle part of this contest. She can build on this initial experience and a drop back in trip to 5f/6f may help her.

6302 HARDINGS CATERING SERVICES H'CAP 7f 214y
2:50 (2:50) (Class 6) (0-65,71) 3-Y-0+ **£1,617** (£481; £240; £120) **Stalls** Low

Form RPR
0261 **1** **Light Burst (USA)**[3] 6217 3-9-12 **71** 6ex............ TomQueally 6 85+
(Ismail Mohammed) *hld up: hdwy over 3f out: led on bit over 1f out: sn clr: easily* **13/8**[1]
6446 **2** *8* **Ermyn Flyer**[46] 4726 3-8-6 **56**............ JemmaMarshall(5) 2 52
(Pat Phelan) *chsd ldr: led after 2f tl over 1f out: no ch w wnr* **7/1**
5-05 **3** *1 ½* **Lady Bellatrix**[39] 5019 3-9-3 **62**............ JimCrowley 1 55
(Mark H Tompkins) *sn trcking ldrs on inner: one pce appr fnl f* **20/1**
006 **4** *3* **Fonterutoli (IRE)**[21] 5659 5-8-10 **51** oh1............1 RobertHavlin 8 37
(Roger Ingram) *s.s: in rr: hdwy 3f out: hrd rdn 2f out: sn btn* **20/1**
0006 **5** *1 ¾* **Phluke**[10] 5996 11-9-0 **55**............ CathyGannon 4 37
(Eve Johnson Houghton) *chsd ldrs: hrd rdn over 2f out: wknd wl over 1f out* **14/1**
2015 **6** *6* **Daffydowndilly**[11] 5983 4-9-10 **65**............(t) DarryllHolland 3 33
(Hughie Morrison) *dwlt: sn prom on outer: wknd 2f out* **3/1**[2]
232 **7** *1* **Conducting**[41] 4914 4-9-10 **65**............ NeilCallan 5 31
(Gay Kelleway) *in tch tl wknd over 2f out: eased whn wl btn over 1f out* **9/2**[3]

1m 36.23s (0.23) **Going Correction** +0.125s/f (Good)
WFA 3 from 4yo+ 4lb 7 Ran SP% **110.0**
Speed ratings (Par 101): **103,95,93,90,88 82,81**
toteswingers 1&2 £2.90, 1&3 £5.20, 2&3 £10.80 CSF £12.58 CT £147.24 TOTE £2.60: £1.60, £4.50; EX 13.70.
Owner Saeed H Altayer **Bred** C Kidder, N Cole & B Kidder **Trained** Newmarket, Suffolk
FOCUS
A modest handicap for 3-y-os and up and the form is not taken too literally, although that may underrate the winner. The ground was changed to firm prior to this contest.
Daffydowndilly Official explanation: jockey said filly never travelled

6303 TALK TO VICTOR H'CAP 5f 213y
3:20 (3:20) (Class 4) (0-80,80) 3-Y-0+ **£4,075** (£1,212; £606; £303) **Stalls** Low

Form RPR
4131 **1** **Clear Spring (IRE)**[21] 5681 4-8-11 **70**............ NickyMackay 7 81+
(John Spearing) *hld up in tch: led wl over 1f out: sn in control: rdn out* **3/1**[1]
0631 **2** *1* **Lunar Deity**[21] 5662 3-9-2 **77**............(p) RichardHughes 8 84
(Eve Johnson Houghton) *hld up in 6th: hdwy 2f out: chsd wnr fnl f: r.o* **3/1**[1]
0104 **3** *3* **Perfect Pastime**[20] 5703 4-9-7 **80**............(p) TomQueally 4 77
(Jim Boyle) *sn outpcd and last: hrd rdn 2f out: styd on wl fnl f* **6/1**[3]
3040 **4** *¾* **Courageous (IRE)**[2] 6226 6-8-12 **76**............ MatthewLawson(5) 1 71
(Milton Bradley) *prom tl no ex 1f out* **4/1**[2]
2015 **5** *2 ¼* **Clear Praise (USA)**[20] 5703 5-9-6 **79**............ HayleyTurner 5 67
(Simon Dow) *dwlt: towards rr on outer: rdn over 2f out: nvr able to chal* **10/1**
0024 **6** *2 ¾* **Interakt**[10] 5995 5-9-1 **74**............ HarryBentley 3 53
(Joseph Tuite) *chsd ldrs tl wknd over 1f out* **10/1**
6441 **7** *½* **Commandingpresence (USA)**[30] 5346 6-8-9 **68**............ KieranO'Neill 2 45
(John Bridger) *prom tl wknd over 1f out* **18/1**
0-10 **8** *4* **Peter Island (FR)**[17] 5791 9-8-13 **72**............(v) DarryllHolland 6 37
(John Gallagher) *led at gd pce tl wl over 1f out: wknd qckly* **16/1**

1m 10.15s (-0.05) **Going Correction** +0.125s/f (Good)
WFA 3 from 4yo+ 2lb 8 Ran SP% **113.6**
Speed ratings (Par 105): **105,103,99,98,95 92,91,86**
toteswingers 1&2 £2.10, 1&3 £3.70, 2&3 £3.70 CSF £11.76 CT £49.22 TOTE £4.90: £1.20, £1.40, £1.60; EX 11.70.
Owner H James **Bred** Rocal Bloodstock **Trained** Kinnersley, Worcs
FOCUS
A fair sprint handicap in which the runner-up sets the standard.

6304 IAN CARNABY APPRENTICE (S) H'CAP 1m 1f 209y
3:50 (3:50) (Class 6) (0-65,62) 3-Y-0+ **£1,617** (£481; £240; £120) **Stalls** Centre

Form RPR
2055 **1** **High Five Prince (IRE)**[4] 6157 3-8-6 **48** oh2............ RachealKneller 10 57
(Mark Usher) *hld up in midfield: hdwy in centre 2f out: led over 1f out: pushed clr: easily* **9/2**[2]
0000 **2** *9* **Always Eager**[10] 5991 3-8-10 **52**............ MichaelJMMurphy 2 43
(Mark Johnston) *disp ld: led 5f out tl over 2f out: easily outpcd by wnr 1f out* **9/2**[2]
0050 **3** *1 ¼* **Denton Dancer**[38] 5037 3-8-4 **51**............ RyanTate(5) 9 40
(James Eustace) *hld up towards rr: hdwy to chal over 2f out: one pce appr fnl f* **14/1**
2020 **4** *1 ¼* **Potentiale (IRE)**[11] 5983 8-9-5 **62**............(v) Leah-AnneAvery(7) 3 48
(J W Hills) *dwlt: bhd: gd hdwy to chse ldrs on ins rail over 1f out: n.m.r and no ex ent fnl f* **7/1**[3]
-440 **5** *1 ¼* **Goodwood Starlight (IRE)**[5] 5052 7-9-1 **58**............(vt[1]) AprilKitchener(7) 8 42
(Jim Best) *plld hrd: prom on outer tl outpcd fnl 2f* **16/1**
5000 **6** *5* **Mr Udagawa**[21] 5657 6-9-0 **53**............(p) DanielMuscutt(3) 1 27
(Bernard Llewellyn) *hld up in tch: led over 2f out tl wknd over 1f out* **15/2**
2262 **7** *3* **Lisselan Pleasure (USA)**[12] 5935 5-9-5 **55**............(t) RobertWilliams 5 23
(Bernard Llewellyn) *s.s: towards rr: effrt over 2f out: sn drvn along: wknd wl over 1f out* **9/4**[1]
5040 **8** *1* **Rosy Dawn**[13] 5908 7-8-12 **48** oh3............1 NoelGarbutt 4 14
(John Bridger) *disp ld tl 5f out: wknd 3f out* **14/1**
6000 **9** *7* **Avalon Bay**[13] 5908 4-8-12 **48** oh3............ IanBurns 6
(Pat Eddery) *t.k.h: chsd ldrs tl wknd over 2f out* **33/1**

2m 4.84s (1.24) **Going Correction** +0.125s/f (Good)
WFA 3 from 4yo+ 6lb 9 Ran SP% **113.6**
Speed ratings (Par 101): **100,92,91,90,89 85,83,82,77**
toteswingers 1&2 £5.40, 1&3 £5.80, 2&3 £13.40 CSF £24.61 CT £258.82 TOTE £5.70: £2.40, £1.10, £4.30; EX 24.90.Potentiale was claimed by Mr A. J. D. Lidderdale for £3,000.
Owner Miss D G Kerr **Bred** Sean Madigan **Trained** Upper Lambourn, Berks
FOCUS
A modest apprentice riders' selling handicap with little solid, and the form is rated cautiously.

6305 CHAMPIONS LEAGUE IN-PLAY AT BETVICTOR.COM H'CAP 1m 3f 196y
4:20 (4:21) (Class 6) (0-60,60) 3-Y-0+ **£1,617** (£481; £240; £120) **Stalls** Centre

Form RPR
0164 **1** **Critical Point**[10] 5989 3-8-9 **51**............(b) LukeMorris 3 64
(Sir Mark Prescott Bt) *prom: squeezed for room and rdn over 2f out: rallied and led over 1f out: styd on wl* **5/1**
0006 **2** *2 ¾* **Blue Dune**[14] 5892 3-8-12 **54**............ NeilCallan 5 63
(Mark Johnston) *chsd ldr: chal 3f out: nt qckn fnl f* **5/1**
5642 **3** *2 ¼* **Sweet Liberta (IRE)**[11] 5974 3-8-4 **53**............ DanielMuscutt(7) 7 58
(Andrew Balding) *hld up in tch: wnt cl 3rd 4f out: led over 2f out tl over 1f out: no ex* **11/4**[1]
221 **4** *2* **Locum**[35] 5174 7-9-12 **60**............ JimCrowley 6 62
(Mark H Tompkins) *chsd ldrs: rdn and outpcd fnl 2f* **4/1**[3]
0060 **5** *19* **Fight (IRE)**[45] 4754 3-8-8 **50**............ HayleyTurner 8 21
(John Best) *towards rr: rdn 5f out: n.d whn hung lft fnl 2f* **20/1**
3166 **6** *10* **Chapter Nine (IRE)**[12] 5938 6-9-5 **53**............(p) RichardHughes 2
(Seamus Mullins) *stdd in rr s: hdwy 3f out: 5th and no imp whn eased 1f out: virtually p.u* **7/2**[2]
-106 **7** *hd* **Sommersturm (GER)**[68] 3979 8-9-10 **58**............ TomQueally 4
(Barney Curley) *hld up in 6th: dropped to last 5f out: sn wl bhd* **20/1**
0060 **8** *nse* **Choisirez (IRE)**[12] 3470 3-8-4 **46** oh1............(vt) CathyGannon 1
(David Evans) *sn rdn up to ld: hdd over 2f out: wknd qckly* **33/1**

2m 34.39s (1.69) **Going Correction** +0.125s/f (Good)
WFA 3 from 6yo+ 8lb 8 Ran SP% **114.7**
Speed ratings (Par 101): **99,97,95,94,81 75,74,74**
toteswingers 1&2 £5.30, 1&3 £3.30, 2&3 £3.70 CSF £29.19 CT £81.83 TOTE £5.20: £2.20, £2.40, £1.30; EX 26.20.
Owner G Moore - Osborne House **Bred** Lofts Hall, M Philipson & Cheveley Park **Trained** Newmarket, Suffolk
FOCUS
A modest middle-distance handicap for 3-y-os and up. The form is rated around the first two.

6306 MONEY BACK ON ENGLAND T20, BETVICTOR.COM H'CAP 6f 209y
4:50 (4:50) (Class 6) (0-65,65) 3-Y-0+ **£1,617** (£481; £240; £120) **Stalls** Low

Form RPR
0-04 **1** **Malekat Jamal (IRE)**[28] 5426 3-9-3 **62**............ HayleyTurner 1 71
(David Simcock) *hld up in 6th: rdn and hdwy 2f out: styd on in centre to ld fnl 100yds* **9/2**[2]
2153 **2** *1 ½* **Stonecrabstomorrow (IRE)**[4] 6171 9-9-4 **63**............ MarkCoumbe(3) 5 68+
(Michael Attwater) *dwlt: bhd: gd hdwy in centre to ld 2f out: edgd lft: hdd and no ex fnl 100yds* **7/2**[1]
0145 **3** *6* **Comadoir (IRE)**[27] 5440 6-9-0 **61**............(p) NathanSweeney(5) 4 50
(Jo Crowley) *w ldr tl 2f out: sn outpcd* **7/2**[1]
1225 **4** *2 ½* **Indiana Guest (IRE)**[11] 5975 3-8-12 **57**............(b) TomQueally 2 39
(George Margarson) *chsd ldrs tl wknd over 1f out* **13/2**
1520 **5** *1 ½* **Paperetto**[30] 5346 4-9-1 **64**............ DanielCremin(7) 3 42
(Robert Mills) *slt ld tl 2f out: wknd over 1f out* **5/1**[3]
3015 **6** *1* **One Last Dream**[24] 5531 3-8-7 **59**............ DanielMuscutt(7) 8 34
(Ron Hodges) *chsd ldrs on outer tl wknd over 2f out* **9/2**[2]
5260 **7** *17* **Highland Harvest**[54] 4469 8-8-9 **56** ow2............(b) HarryPoulton(5) 7
(Jamie Poulton) *chsd ldrs: wknd rapidly 3f out: bhd whn hung lft fnl 2f* **25/1**

1m 23.57s (0.47) **Going Correction** +0.125s/f (Good)
WFA 3 from 4yo+ 3lb 7 Ran SP% **114.7**
Speed ratings (Par 101): **102,100,93,90,88 87,68**
toteswingers 1&2 £22.80, 1&3 £36.50, 2&3 £68.90 CSF £20.69 CT £60.68 TOTE £7.00: £2.90, £3.50; EX 13.30.
Owner Saeed Manana **Bred** Adrian Purvis & Luke Barry **Trained** Newmarket, Suffolk
FOCUS
A modest handicap for 3-y-os and up but soundly run. The second is rated a bit off his best.

6307 BETTER PRICES AT BETVICTOR H'CAP 5f 59y
5:20 (5:20) (Class 5) (0-70,68) 3-Y-0+ **£2,264** (£673; £336; £168) **Stalls** Low

Form RPR
3332 **1** **Mother Jones**[1] 6277 4-9-4 **65**............ RichardHughes 2 73
(David Evans) *stdd s: hld up in 5th: hdwy over 1f out: fnd gap and qcknd through to dispute ld ins fnl f: jst got up: cleverly* **11/8**[1]
430 **2** *shd* **Whitecrest**[7] 6094 4-9-7 **68**............ CathyGannon 6 75
(John Spearing) *hld up in 6th: hdwy in centre over 1f out: slt ld ins fnl f: r.o: jst hdd fnl strides* **9/2**[2]
3034 **3** *2 ¾* **Baby Dottie**[11] 5972 5-8-5 **57**............(t) JemmaMarshall(5) 5 55
(Pat Phelan) *chsd ldr: disp ld over 1f out tl ins fnl f: one pce* **7/1**[3]
3305 **4** *½* **Scommettitrice (IRE)**[10] 5995 4-8-13 **60**............(p) LukeMorris 4 56
(David Evans) *led: jnd over 1f out: hdd and no ex ins fnl f* **7/1**[3]
6123 **5** *hd* **Imaginary Diva**[22] 5635 6-8-13 **60**............ TomQueally 7 55
(George Margarson) *t.k.h: trckd ldrs on outer: rdn over 1f out: no ex ins fnl f* **8/1**
0061 **6** *1 ¾* **Pucon**[27] 5445 3-8-12 **63**............ MarkCoumbe(3) 1 52
(Roger Teal) *plld hrd in rr: hdwy 2f out: disp ld over 1f out tl wknd ins fnl f* **15/2**
2660 **7** *2 ½* **Pharoh Jake**[24] 5531 4-8-7 **54** oh7............ KieranO'Neill 3 39
(John Bridger) *prom: rdn over 2f out: cl up whn bdly hmpd on ins rail ent fnl f: nt rcvr* **25/1**

1m 3.5s (1.20) **Going Correction** +0.125s/f (Good)
WFA 3 from 4yo+ 1lb 7 Ran SP% **112.0**
Speed ratings (Par 103): **95,94,90,89,89 86,82**
toteswingers 1&2 £2.20, 1&3 £3.10, 2&3 £6.20 CSF £7.35 TOTE £2.50: £1.40, £2.20; EX 8.00.
Owner Mike Nolan **Bred** New Hall Stud **Trained** Pandy, Monmouths
■ Stewards' Enquiry : Mark Coumbe two-day ban: careless riding (Oct 1-2)

FOCUS
A modest sprint handicap for 3-y-os and up in which the first two set the standard. The seven horses were spread across the track in a straight line 1f from home.
T/Plt: £25.50 to a £1 stake. Pool: £58,689.08 - 1,677.72 winning tickets T/Qpdt: £18.10 to a £1 stake. Pool: £4,883.87 - 198.79 winning tickets LM

5916 MUSSELBURGH (R-H)
Monday, September 17

OFFICIAL GOING: Good to firm (8.1)
Wind: Fairly strong, half against Weather: Cloudy, showers from race 4

6308 ARCHERFIELD, WE PLAY A DIFFERENT GAME H'CAP (DIV I) 7f 30y
2:10 (2:10) (Class 6) (0-65,65) 3-Y-O+ £1,940 (£577; £288; £144) Stalls Low

Form RPR
0-50 **1** **Summer Dancer (IRE)**[30] 5341 8-9-7 **65** MickyFenton 8 74
(Paul Midgley) *hld up: stdy hdwy over 2f out: edgd rt over 1f out: rdn to ld ins fnl f: kpt on wl* **5/1**
0110 **2** 1 ¼ **Ebony Clarets**[9] 6048 3-9-0 **61** FrederikTylicki 1 67
(Linda Perratt) *s.i.s: bhd and sn detached: hdwy on outside over 2f out: chsd wnr ins fnl f: kpt on* **15/2**
660 **3** 3 **Drive Home (USA)**[13] 5918 5-8-11 **55** (p) DanielTudhope 2 53
(Noel Wilson) *in tch on ins: effrt whn no room over 2f out to over 1f out: sn swtchd lft: styd on fnl f: nvr able to chal* **5/2**[1]
0552 **4** 1 ½ **Jebel Tara**[13] 5917 7-8-7 **51** (bt) PJMcDonald 9 45
(Ian Semple) *t.k.h: in tch on outside: hdwy to ld over 1f out: hdd ins fnl f: sn outpcd* **7/1**
000R **5** ½ **Ivestar (IRE)**[28] 5416 7-8-9 **53** (p) GrahamGibbons 3 46
(Michael Easterby) *hld up: effrt and pushed along whn n.m.r briefly over 1f out: no imp fnl f* **40/1**
1002 **6** nk **Goninodaethat**[13] 5918 4-8-13 **57** GrahamLee 5 49
(Jim Goldie) *prom: drvn over 2f out: no imp fnl f* **4/1**[3]
3554 **7** 3 ½ **Star City (IRE)**[9] 6052 3-9-1 **62** (be) TomEaves 7 44
(Michael Dods) *t.k.h: early ldr: prom: effrt and ev ch over 2f out: carried rt over 1f out: sn btn* **7/2**[2]
5004 **8** 1 **Naafetha (IRE)**[55] 4426 4-8-7 **51** oh3 (b[1]) BarryMcHugh 4 31
(George Foster) *t.k.h: cl up on ins: rdn over 2f out: wknd over 1f out* **66/1**
0000 **9** 4 **Crocodile Bay (IRE)**[13] 5917 9-8-4 **51** oh6 (b) DeclanCannon(3) 6 20
(Richard Guest) *t.k.h: sn led: rdn and hdd over 1f out: sn btn* **66/1**

1m 29.32s (0.32) **Going Correction** +0.075s/f (Good)
WFA 3 from 4yo+ 3lb **9** Ran SP% **117.1**
Speed ratings (Par 101): **101,99,96,94,93 93,89,88,83**
toteswingers 1&2 £9.20, 1&3 £6.60, 2&3 £5.00 CSF £42.28 CT £115.58 TOTE £8.40: £2.10, £2.00, £1.30; EX 50.50.
Owner The Howarting's Partnership **Bred** Eddie O'Leary **Trained** Westow, N Yorks
■ Stewards' Enquiry : Micky Fenton two-day ban: careless riding (Oct 1-2)

FOCUS
The stands' bend was out two metres and likewise the bottom bend. A split screen replay of the two divisions showed the pace was quicker than in the second leg, yet the final time was slower, and those held up were favoured. The winner is rated a length off last year's form.

6309 ARCHERFIELD, WE PLAY A DIFFERENT GAME H'CAP (DIV II) 7f 30y
2:40 (2:40) (Class 6) (0-65,60) 3-Y-O+ £1,940 (£577; £288; £144) Stalls Low

Form RPR
5-21 **1** **Twenty One Choice (IRE)**[18] 5764 3-9-3 **59** PhillipMakin 8 74+
(Ed de Giles) *trckd ldrs: smooth hdwy to ld over 1f out: pushed clr ins fnl f: eased last 50yds* **9/4**[1]
3050 **2** 1 ¾ **Outlaw Torn (IRE)**[2] 6258 3-8-10 **55** (e) DeclanCannon(3) 7 64
(Richard Guest) *pressed ldr: led over 2f out to over 1f out: kpt on fnl f: no ch w wnr* **6/1**[3]
5502 **3** 4 **Berbice (IRE)**[13] 5918 7-9-4 **60** JulieBurke(3) 2 58
(Linda Perratt) *s.i.s: t.k.h in rr: smooth hdwy to chse (clr) ldrs over 1f out: rdn and no imp fnl f* **6/1**[3]
6-60 **4** 1 ¾ **Eilean Mor**[34] 5189 4-9-6 **59** AndrewElliott 5 52
(R Mike Smith) *in tch: drvn along over 2f out: no imp over 1f out* **50/1**
6630 **5** ¾ **Cannon Bolt (IRE)**[13] 5918 4-9-1 **54** RobertWinston 3 45
(Robin Bastiman) *stdd s: plld hrd in rr: nt clr run and swtchd lft wl over 1f out: no imp fnl f* **7/2**[2]
-000 **6** ¾ **Gumnd (IRE)**[16] 5824 5-8-7 **46** oh1 PJMcDonald 6 35
(Chris Grant) *hld up: rdn along and effrt over 2f out: edgd rt and no imp over 1f out* **33/1**
6065 **7** 2 ¼ **Shunkawakhan (IRE)**[13] 5917 9-8-7 **46** oh1 (tp) TomEaves 4 29
(Linda Perratt) *prom: drvn over 2f out: wknd over 1f out* **25/1**
0000 **8** 5 **Cara's Request (AUS)**[63] 4134 7-9-4 **57** AdrianNicholls 1 27
(David Nicholls) *led to over 2f out: rdn and wknd over 1f out* **6/1**[3]
3066 **9** 15 **Let's Face Facts**[13] 5918 5-8-10 **49** GrahamLee 9
(Jim Goldie) *bhd: struggling after 3f: nvr on terms* **9/1**

1m 28.81s (-0.19) **Going Correction** +0.075s/f (Good)
WFA 3 from 4yo+ 3lb **9** Ran SP% **114.6**
Speed ratings (Par 101): **104,102,97,95,94 93,91,85,68**
CSF £15.79 CT £70.81 TOTE £2.60: £1.50, £1.90, £2.00; EX 24.10.
Owner Penna Racing **Bred** P Byrne **Trained** Ledbury, H'fords

FOCUS
The time was 0.51 seconds faster than the first division and the runner-up sets the standard to this year's turf best.
Cannon Bolt(IRE) Official explanation: jockey said gelding hung left

6310 LOGANBET - BERT LOGAN YOUR LOCAL BOOKMAKER (S) STKS 7f 30y
3:10 (3:10) (Class 6) 2-Y-O £1,617 (£481; £240; £120) Stalls Low

Form RPR
0015 **1** **Lea Valley Black**[17] 5786 2-9-2 68 RichardKingscote 4 66
(Tom Dascombe) *t.k.h: pressed ldr: led 2f out: sn rdn: edgd rt appr fnl f: drvn out* **15/8**[1]
1605 **2** 2 ¼ **Lucy Bee**[13] 5920 2-8-11 54 AndrewMullen 3 53
(Keith Dalgleish) *dwlt: t.k.h and sn trcking ldrs: effrt and rdn 2f out: styd on to take 2nd cl home: no ch w wnr* **7/1**
0500 **3** ½ **Tyson The Byson**[6] 6115 2-8-11 46 (p) RobertWinston 5 52
(Mrs K Burke) *t.k.h: led at stdy gallop: rdn and hdd 2f out: one pce fnl f: lost 2nd cl home* **25/1**
50 **4** 3 ¾ **Lady Raffa**[147] 1556 2-8-7 0 ow1 TomEaves 2 37
(Michael Dods) *s.i.s: hld up: effrt and rdn over 2f out: no imp over 1f out* **14/1**
3525 **5** 1 ½ **Dil Laney (IRE)**[21] 5675 2-8-11 56 DanielTudhope 6 37
(David O'Meara) *t.k.h: prom: effrt over 2f out: wknd over 1f out* **3/1**[2]
2546 **6** 4 ½ **Juana Belen**[6] 6115 2-8-1 53 NeilFarley(5) 7 20
(David Barron) *in tch on outside tl hung rt and wknd 2f out* **15/2**
302 **7** ¾ **Special Report (IRE)**[31] 5291 2-8-4 61 DanielleMooney(7) 1 23
(Nigel Tinkler) *hld up in tch on ins: struggling over 2f out: sn btn* **5/1**[3]

1m 31.86s (2.86) **Going Correction** +0.075s/f (Good) **7** Ran SP% **111.2**
Speed ratings (Par 93): **86,83,82,78,76 71,70**
toteswingers 1&2 £3.30, 1&3 £6.90, 2&3 £18.30 CSF £14.74 TOTE £2.40: £1.60, £3.60; EX 10.60.There was no bid for the winner.
Owner London Market Racing Club **Bred** A J Coleing **Trained** Malpas, Cheshire

FOCUS
A weak race run in a moderate time and rated accordingly around the placed horses.

NOTEBOOK
Lea Valley Black, a maiden winner on his penultimate start, outclassed his rivals on this drop in trip, despite looking a bit awkward in his hood. He can win again at this sort of level. (op 9-4)
Lucy Bee just wasn't good enough. She would have been 9lb better off with the winner in a handicap. (op 6-1)
Tyson The Byson, who had his chance under a forward ride, had 17lb to find with the winner. (op 28-1)
Dil Laney(IRE), reported to have been unsuited by the track at Ripon on his previous start, was keen this time and offered nothing. (op 11-4 tchd 10-3)

6311 BRIAN & BEVERLEY'S WEDDING DAY CELEBRATION H'CAP 1m 6f
3:40 (3:40) (Class 5) (0-75,75) 3-Y-O+ £2,587 (£770; £384; £192) Stalls Centre

Form RPR
630- **1** **Mason Hindmarsh**[327] 7102 5-9-1 **62** GrahamLee 7 70
(Karen McLintock) *hld up on outside: hdwy over 2f out: effrt and drvn over 1f out: styd on wl to ld cl home* **16/1**
0005 **2** nse **Singzak**[13] 5913 4-9-3 **64** GrahamGibbons 10 72
(Michael Easterby) *cl up: drvn wl over 2f out: styd on fnl f: led briefly nr fin: jst hld* **6/1**[2]
6602 **3** ½ **The Bells O Peover**[4] 6170 4-10-0 **75** (b) JoeFanning 3 82
(Mark Johnston) *led: qcknd clr over 2f out: sn pushed along: kpt on fnl f: hdd nr fin* **11/8**[1]
412 **4** 1 ¾ **Grand Art (IRE)**[7] 6101 8-8-10 **57** (p) DanielTudhope 5 62
(Noel Wilson) *hld up in tch: rdn and effrt 2f out: kpt on same pce fnl f* **7/1**[3]
/400 **5** 1 **Silk Drum (IRE)**[42] 4867 7-8-11 **63** ShaneBKelly(5) 4 67
(Dianne Sayer) *t.k.h: hld up: rdn and hdwy 2f out: kpt on same pce fnl f* **20/1**
0215 **6** nk **Sohcahtoa (IRE)**[17] 5798 6-9-5 **71** LMcNiff(5) 1 74
(David Barron) *hld up: hdwy on outside 2f out: rdn and no imp fnl f* **15/2**
/4-0 **7** 8 **Royal Entourage**[11] 4831 7-9-12 **73** MichaelO'Connell 2 65
(Philip Kirby) *s.i.s: sn pushed into midfield: struggling over 2f out: sn btn* **40/1**
4134 **8** 4 **Nay Secret**[30] 5086 4-8-4 **56** oh6 NeilFarley(5) 6 42
(Jim Goldie) *prom tl rdn and wknd fr 2f out* **25/1**
031 **9** 2 ¾ **La Bacouetteuse (FR)**[13] 5921 7-9-6 **72** (v) GarryWhillans(5) 8 55
(Iain Jardine) *bhd and sn detached: struggling over 3f out: nvr on terms* **7/1**[3]
3142 **10** 16 **Geanie Mac (IRE)**[13] 5922 3-8-7 **64** ow2 (b) TomEaves 9 24
(Linda Perratt) *cl up tl rdn and wknd fr wl over 2f out* **14/1**

3m 5.0s (-0.30) **Going Correction** +0.075s/f (Good)
WFA 3 from 4yo+ 10lb **10** Ran SP% **116.8**
Speed ratings (Par 103): **103,102,102,101,101 100,96,94,92,83**
toteswingers 1&2 £13.30, 1&3 £6.50, 2&3 £3.50 CSF £106.63 CT £221.89 TOTE £24.10: £4.60, £2.40, £1.20; EX 220.00.
Owner Brian Chicken **Bred** Newsells Park Stud **Trained** Ingoe, Northumberland

FOCUS
There was a heavy shower ahead of this fair staying handicap and it was run in gloomy conditions. They looked to go a fair gallop and the form is straightforward ratd around the first four.
La Bacouetteuse(FR) Official explanation: jockey said gelding never travelled

6312 WILLIAM HILL NURSERY 5f
4:10 (4:10) (Class 3) (0-95,80) 2-Y-O £7,762 (£2,310; £1,154; £577) Stalls High

Form RPR
5054 **1** **Rhagori Aur**[22] 5620 2-9-1 **74** TomEaves 6 80
(Bryan Smart) *pressed ldr: led and rdn wl over 1f out: edgd lft: kpt on strly fnl f* **9/1**
4222 **2** 1 ½ **Bispham Green**[9] 6022 2-8-13 **77** ShaneBKelly(5) 3 78
(Richard Fahey) *in tch on outside: drvn and outpcd over 3f out: rallied over 1f out: wnt 2nd ins fnl f: kpt on: nt pce of wnr* **5/2**[1]
5140 **3** ½ **Lady Poppy**[25] 5515 2-9-6 **79** PJMcDonald 4 78
(George Moore) *chsd ldrs: drvn along 1/2-way: wnt 2nd over 1f out to ins fnl f: kpt on same pce* **7/2**[2]
41 **4** 1 ¼ **Chasing Dreams**[19] 5733 2-9-7 **80** PhillipMakin 5 75
(Kevin Ryan) *prom: effrt and rdn whn n.m.r briefly over 1f out: sn swtchd lft: one pce ins fnl f* **7/2**[2]
0151 **5** 1 ¾ **Done Dreaming (IRE)**[13] 5916 2-9-1 **74** TonyHamilton 2 62
(Richard Fahey) *bhd and outpcd: hdwy 1f out: nvr able to chal* **9/1**
1232 **6** 1 ¼ **La Sylphe**[24] 5544 2-9-0 **73** GrahamGibbons 7 57
(David Barron) *led to wl over 1f out: sn rdn: wknd ent fnl f* **4/1**[3]

1m 0.71s (0.31) **Going Correction** +0.075s/f (Good) **6** Ran SP% **113.0**
Speed ratings (Par 99): **100,97,96,94,92 90**
toteswingers 1&2 £3.70, 1&3 £5.00, 2&3 £2.60 CSF £32.14 CT £94.54 TOTE £12.20: £5.20, £1.10; EX 45.90.
Owner Ceffyl Racing **Bred** Usk Valley Stud **Trained** Hambleton, N Yorks

FOCUS
A disappointing nursery the for the class, the top weight being rated 15lb below the race ceiling. The winner is rated to debut form, backed up by the placed horses.

NOTEBOOK
Rhagori Aur belatedly confirmed the promise of her debut win gained back in May, keeping on well having shown good speed from the off. Her trainer thinks there might be more to come. (op 17-2)
Bispham Green, up 4lb for his second-place finish in an Ascot nursery, was never going the required pace and could only plug on to take the runner-up spot for the fourth consecutive race. He's still looking for his first win. (op 11-4)
Lady Poppy couldn't confirm earlier form with the winner and second but still ran with credit.
Chasing Dreams found this a lot tougher than the moderate Catterick maiden she won on her previous start, but may come on for the experience. (tchd 10-3)
Done Dreaming(IRE) was successful on two of his first four starts, the most recent in a C&D seller, but he was never going at any stage this time. (op 11-1)

La Sylphe dropped away most disappointingly as the pace she set was not strong enough to blunt the winner's finishing effort. (tchd 9-2)

6313 ST ANDREWS TIMBER AND BUILDING SUPPLIES CLAIMING STKS — 1m 1f

4:40 (4:40) (Class 6) 3-Y-O+ — **£1,617** (£481; £240; £120) **Stalls** Low

Form — RPR

1531 **1** **Just Lille (IRE)**[9] 6055 9-9-9 79 ....(p) GrahamLee 3 — 77
(Ann Duffield) *cl up: led and rdn over 2f out: styd on gamely fnl f* **3/1**[2]

4143 **2** *3/4* **Kay Gee Be (IRE)**[20] 5712 8-9-4 83 .... TonyHamilton 4 — 71
(Richard Fahey) *prom: effrt and drvn over 2f out: chsd wnr ins fnl f: kpt on towards fin* **11/10**[1]

5650 **3** *hd* **Desert Romance (IRE)**[8] 6073 6-9-8 76 .... DanielTudhope 9 — 74
(David O'Meara) *t.k.h: hld up: gd hdwy on outside wl over 1f out: chsd ldrs ins fnl f: r.o* **5/1**[3]

6200 **4** *1 1/2* **Mangham (IRE)**[24] 5547 7-8-7 57 ....(p) NeilFarley(5) 5 — 61
(George Foster) *s.i.s: t.k.h in rr: hdwy and prom over 1f out: one pce ins fnl f* **66/1**

0066 **5** *2 1/4* **Dhaular Dhar (IRE)**[6] 6124 10-9-1 71 .... GaryBartley(3) 2 — 62
(Jim Goldie) *hld up: rdn over 2f out: effrt on ins over 1f out: no imp fnl f* **12/1**

0600 **6** *shd* **Bold Marc (IRE)**[42] 4864 10-8-8 67 .... PJMcDonald 1 — 52
(Mrs K Burke) *hld up on ins: rdn over 2f out: no imp fr over 1f out* **33/1**

6043 **7** *shd* **Georgebernardshaw (IRE)**[7] 6105 7-8-11 52 ....(p) DeclanCannon(3) 6 — 58?
(Richard Guest) *led to over 2f out: rdn and no ex over 1f out* **40/1**

0313 **8** *6* **Triple Eight (IRE)**[31] 5314 4-9-12 70 ....(b) MichaelO'Connell 7 — 56
(Philip Kirby) *prom: effrt and drvn over 2f out: hung rt wl over 1f out: sn btn* **16/1**

0300 **9** *21* **City Of The Kings (IRE)**[16] 5819 7-9-8 74 ....(p) TomEaves 11
(Ollie Pears) *bhd on outside: drvn over 3f out: sn struggling: t.o* **33/1**

0-06 **10** *7* **Fremen (USA)**[22] 5618 12-8-8 65 .... AdrianNicholls 10
(David Nicholls) *cl up: drvn over 2f out: outpcd whn hmpd wl over 1f out: sn btn* **16/1**

1m 54.3s (0.40) **Going Correction** +0.075s/f (Good) — **10** Ran SP% **118.6**
Speed ratings (Par 101): **101,100,100,98,96 96,96,91,72,66**
toteswingers 1&2 £2.30, 1&3 £4.30, 2&3 £2.20 CSF £6.61 TOTE £5.30: £1.80, £1.10, £1.20; EX 10.20.
Owner MPR Warrender Baines Farrington Kay **Bred** Sweetmans Bloodstock **Trained** Constable Burton, N Yorks
■ Stewards' Enquiry : Adrian Nicholls caution: failed to take all reasonable and permissable measures to obtain best possible placing.
Michael O'Connell one-day ban: careless riding (Oct 1)

FOCUS
It rained ahead of this race and PJ McDonald said: "They are just knocking the top off but it's basically decent ground still." It was a fair claimer but the form is muddling and anchored by the fourth and seventh.

6314 FEARLESS FREDDIE THE PLACE TO BET H'CAP — 5f

5:10 (5:10) (Class 5) (0-70,70) 3-Y-O+ — **£2,587** (£770; £384; £192) **Stalls** High

Form — RPR

0411 **1** **Imperial Legend (IRE)**[34] 5190 3-9-2 **70** ....(p) ShirleyTeasdale(7) 3 — 82+
(David Nicholls) *hld up: hdwy on outside over 1f out: rdn and led ins fnl f: edgd lft: hld on wl nr fin* **4/1**[1]

0621 **2** *hd* **Pavers Star**[22] 5621 3-7-13 **51** oh1 ....(p) NeilFarley(5) 9 — 62
(Noel Wilson) *t.k.h: led: rdn and edgd rt over 1f out: hdd ins fnl f: carried lft: kpt on: jst hld* **5/1**[2]

4435 **3** *2 3/4* **Here Now And Why (IRE)**[4] 6178 5-8-11 **57** ....(p) DuranFentiman 4 — 58
(Ian Semple) *t.k.h: hld up in tch: rdn and outpcd 2f out: rallied fnl f: kpt on: nt pce of first two* **5/1**[2]

0030 **4** *1* **Miserere Mei (IRE)**[10] 6003 3-8-1 **51** oh6 ....(e) DeclanCannon(3) 8 — 49
(Richard Guest) *in tch: hdwy and cl up over 1f out: kpt on same pce ins fnl f* **66/1**

3253 **5** *2 3/4* **Wicked Wilma (IRE)**[18] 5758 8-9-2 **65** .... JulieBurke(3) 1 — 53
(Alan Berry) *cl up on outside: effrt and rdn 2f out: wknd ins fnl f* **8/1**

6055 **6** *2 1/2* **Nickel Silver**[34] 5205 7-9-6 **66** ....(v) TomEaves 6 — 45
(Bryan Smart) *cl up: effrt and ev ch over 1f out: sn rdn and wknd* **12/1**

640 **7** *nse* **Koolgreycat (IRE)**[16] 5831 3-8-11 **58** .... FrederikTylicki 7 — 36
(Noel Wilson) *in tch: effrt and pushed along 2f out: no imp fnl f* **9/1**

1000 **8** *1/2* **Blown It (USA)**[37] 5082 6-9-7 **67** .... JoeFanning 12 — 44
(Keith Dalgleish) *dwlt: bhd: rdn and hdwy over 1f out: nvr able to chal* **6/1**

3006 **9** *1 1/4* **Dragon Spirit (IRE)**[18] 5760 3-8-6 **53** oh6 ow2 .... BarryMcHugh 11 — 25
(Linda Perratt) *hld up in midfield against stands' rail: rdn over 2f out: wknd over 1f out* **66/1**

4000 **10** *2 1/4* **Chosen One (IRE)**[13] 5923 7-8-9 **55** .... JamesSullivan 5 — 19
(Ruth Carr) *cl up tl rdn and wknd over 1f out* **20/1**

4432 **11** *2* **Love You Louis**[25] 5514 6-9-10 **70** ....(v) GrahamLee 10 — 27
(J R Jenkins) *cl up: drvn over 2f out: wknd over 1f out* **11/2**[3]

1m 0.53s (0.13) **Going Correction** +0.075s/f (Good)
WFA 3 from 5yo+ 1lb — **11** Ran SP% **119.6**
Speed ratings (Par 103): **101,100,96,94,90 86,86,85,83,79 76**
toteswingers 1&2 £4.90, 1&3 £5.50, 2&3 £7.20 CSF £23.91 CT £104.47 TOTE £5.60: £1.50, £3.40, £1.60; EX 15.00.
Owner Pinnacle Mujadil Partnership **Bred** Newlands House Stud **Trained** Sessay, N Yorks
■ Stewards' Enquiry : Shirley Teasdale two-day ban: careless riding (Oct 1-2)

FOCUS
A competitive sprint handicap and the form looks sound enough.

6315 BLACK JACK RACING, MUSSELBURGH'S NO. 1 BOOKMAKER H'CAP — 1m 4f 100y

5:40 (5:40) (Class 6) (0-65,64) 3-Y-O+ — **£1,940** (£577; £288; £144) **Stalls** Low

Form — RPR

4203 **1** **Hawdyerwheesht**[13] 5921 4-9-5 **57** .... GrahamLee 13 — 64
(Jim Goldie) *hld up: gd hdwy on outside over 2f out: sn rdn: led wl ins fnl f: styd on strly* **4/1**[2]

0011 **2** *1 1/4* **Pertuis (IRE)**[31] 5290 6-9-11 **63** .... PJMcDonald 10 — 68
(Micky Hammond) *hld up and bhd: gd hdwy over 2f out: styd on to go 2nd towards fin: nt rch wnr* **9/2**[3]

0102 **3** *1/2* **Stormy Morning**[13] 5921 6-9-8 **60** ....(p) MichaelO'Connell 5 — 64
(Philip Kirby) *prom: rdn to ld over 2f out: edgd rt over 1f out: hdd and no ex wl ins fnl f* **6/1**

0004 **4** *1/2* **Dynamic Drive (IRE)**[18] 5762 5-8-12 **50** oh5 .... TomEaves 6 — 53
(Linda Perratt) *in tch: drvn along 3f out: rallied: kpt on same pce ins fnl f* **25/1**

013 **5** *1/2* **Operateur (IRE)**[7] 6103 4-9-4 **56** .... PhillipMakin 9 — 59
(Ben Haslam) *hld up in tch: hdwy and ev ch over 2f out: sn rdn: kpt on same pce fnl f* **7/2**[1]

000 **6** *4 1/2* **There's No Rules**[18] 5770 3-8-1 **50** oh5 ....(e) DeclanCannon(3) 3 — 46
(Richard Guest) *hld up towards rr: drvn along 3f out: hdwy over 1f out: nvr able to chal* **25/1**

0636 **7** *2 3/4* **Grand Diamond (IRE)**[13] 5921 8-8-12 **50** oh2 .... DanielTudhope 12 — 41
(Jim Goldie) *hld up: rdn along over 2f out: no imp wl over 1f out* **14/1**

0130 **8** *3* **Talk Of Saafend (IRE)**[16] 4869 7-9-4 **59** .... LucyAlexander(3) 8 — 46
(Dianne Sayer) *hld up: rdn over 3f out: sme hdwy over 1f out: nvr on terms* **16/1**

04 **9** *7* **Dimashq**[41] 4912 10-8-12 **50** oh3 .... MickyFenton 2 — 26
(Paul Midgley) *hld up: struggling 3f out: btn fnl 2f* **40/1**

/00- **10** *2* **Strobe**[20] 5790 8-8-12 **50** oh1 ....(p) PaddyAspell 11 — 23
(Lucy Normile) *pressed ldr: rdn and ev ch 3f out: wknd 2f out* **66/1**

0065 **11** *1 3/4* **Kieron's Rock (IRE)**[21] 5672 3-8-5 **50** oh5 ow1 .... AndrewElliott 1 — 21
(Jedd O'Keeffe) *plld hrd early: cl up tl rdn and wknd over 2f out* **25/1**

2050 **12** *1 1/2* **Oddsmaker (IRE)**[13] 5921 11-8-11 **54** ....(t) GarryWhillans(5) 7 — 22
(Maurice Barnes) *led at decent gallop to over 2f out: sn rdn and wknd* **16/1**

6150 **U** **Hikma (USA)**[10] 5989 3-9-4 **64** ....(v[1]) JoeFanning 4
(Mark Johnston) *stmbld bdly and uns rdr s* **8/1**

2m 44.98s (2.98) **Going Correction** +0.075s/f (Good)
WFA 3 from 4yo+ 8lb — **13** Ran SP% **119.7**
Speed ratings (Par 101): **93,92,91,91,91 88,86,84,79,78 77,76,**
toteswingers 1&2 £4.60, 1&3 £5.00, 2&3 £2.60 CSF £21.14 CT £109.15 TOTE £5.10: £1.50, £1.60, £2.50; EX 21.00.
Owner J S Morrison **Bred** Baldernock Bloodstock Ltd **Trained** Uplawmoor, E Renfrews

FOCUS
A weak handicap in which the pace looked overly strong and the front two came from well back. The placed horses to recent form help set the level.
T/Plt: £23.40 to a £1 stake. Pool: £56,215.93 - 1749.13 winning tickets T/Qpdt: £8.90 to a £1 stake. Pool: £4,258.68 - 351.99 winning tickets RY

6210 WOLVERHAMPTON (A.W) (L-H)

Monday, September 17

OFFICIAL GOING: Standard
Wind: almost nil Weather: mild

6316 32RED APPRENTICE H'CAP — 1m 141y(P)

2:00 (2:00) (Class 6) (0-55,54) 3-Y-O+ — **£1,704** (£503; £251) **Stalls** Low

Form — RPR

6204 **1** **Tigertoo (IRE)**[5] 6152 3-7-13 **46** .... LouisSteward(7) 11 — 57
(Stuart Williams) *chsd ldr: led 2f out: sn qcknd clr: pushed out: easy* **5/2**[1]

5456 **2** *2 1/4* **Smart Affair**[10] 5991 3-8-3 **48** ....(e[1]) RobertTart(5) 13 — 54
(Alan Bailey) *slowly away: hdwy into midfield 4f out: pushed along to chse wnr 2f out: drvn and no ch w wnr 1f out: jst hld on for 2nd* **8/1**[3]

0604 **3** *3/4* **Fortunate Bid (IRE)**[35] 5171 6-9-5 **54** ....(p) JacobButterfield 4 — 58
(Linda Stubbs) *in tch: rdn 3f out: outpcd 2f out: drvn and plugged on to take 3rd fnl f* **5/1**[2]

0426 **4** *3 1/2* **My New Angel (IRE)**[19] 5738 3-8-7 **47** .... PhilipPrince 2 — 43
(Paul Green) *cl up: rdn over 2f out: one pce and no ex over 1f out* **9/1**

5003 **5** *nk* **Meydan Style (USA)**[39] 5015 6-8-7 **45** .... JordanNason(3) 3 — 41
(Richard Ford) *t.k.h in midfield: urged along 3f out: rdn and one pce fnl 2f* **8/1**[3]

0300 **6** *1 3/4* **Divine Success (IRE)**[45] 4771 3-8-1 **46** .... PaulMcGiff(5) 1 — 38
(Richard Fahey) *led: pushed along and hdd 2f out: wknd over 1f out* **14/1**

6-04 **7** *2 1/2* **Supa Seeker (USA)**[21] 5657 6-8-8 **50** .... AidenBlakemore(7) 10 — 36
(Tony Carroll) *t.k.h in rr: hdwy 3f out: pushed along 2f out: sn no imp* **5/1**[2]

0453 **8** *1* **Deep Applause**[18] 5762 4-8-3 **45** ....(v) ConnorNichol(7) 6 — 28
(Michael Dods) *slow away: hld up: briefly short of room on inner after 1f: drvn along over 2f out: nvr any imp* **12/1**

600 **9** *nk* **Leonards Pride (IRE)**[21] 5679 3-8-5 **45** .... TimClark 5 — 28
(Daniel Mark Loughnane) *dwlt: midfield: urged along 4f out: sn struggling* **28/1**

00 **10** *1* **Clearing House**[33] 5234 7-8-10 **52** .... CarolineKelly(7) 9 — 32
(John Ryan) *hld up: pushed along 3f out: no imp fnl 2f* **50/1**

1m 50.84s (0.34) **Going Correction** -0.15s/f (Stan)
WFA 3 from 4yo+ 5lb — **10** Ran SP% **113.9**
Speed ratings (Par 101): **92,90,89,86,85 84,82,81,81,80**
toteswingers 1&2 £4.70, 1&3 £3.60, 2&3 £7.60 CSF £22.47 CT £94.01 TOTE £3.30: £1.20, £2.20, £2.40; EX 21.10 Trifecta £87.10 Pool: £323.86 - 2.75 winning units..
Owner John Godfrey & Robert Haag **Bred** J Godfrey **Trained** Newmarket, Suffolk
■ Stewards' Enquiry : Aiden Blakemore one-day ban: careless riding (Oct 1)
Louis Steward one-day ban: failed to ride to draw (Oct 1)

FOCUS
A moderate apprentice handicap and few got into it from off the pace. The pace was muddling and there are doubts over the form with the first two the best guides.

6317 DOWNLOAD OUR IPHONE APP (S) STKS — 1m 141y(P)

2:30 (2:30) (Class 6) 3-5-Y-O — **£1,704** (£503; £251) **Stalls** Low

Form — RPR

0616 **1** **Justbookie Dot Com (IRE)**[9] 6051 4-9-9 70 ....(b) SilvestreDeSousa 5 — 75
(David Evans) *in tch: pushed along 3f out: hdwy on outer over 2f out: pushed along to chal for ld over 1f out: drifted rt but styd on to ld fnl f: qcknd rt away fnl 100yds* **13/8**[1]

2203 **2** *3* **Casa Bex**[5] 6152 3-8-9 63 ....(tp) RaulDaSilva(3) 4 — 62
(Philip McBride) *cl up: urged along over 2f out: effrt to press ldr over 1f out: ev ch fnl f: unable to go w wnr fnl 100yds* **2/1**[2]

00 **3** *2 3/4* **Spin Of A Coin (IRE)**[9] 6039 4-9-4 76 ....(b) AshleyMorgan(5) 6 — 62
(Pat Murphy) *cl up: hdwy to press ldr 5f out: led over 2f out: pushed along ins fnl 2f: hdd over 1f out: sn one pce* **5/1**

0550 **4** *6* **Son Vida (IRE)**[9] 6051 4-9-9 65 ....(v) AdamKirby 1 — 48
(Alan Bailey) *led at slow pce: pressed 5f out tl drvn and wknd over 2f out: sn btn* **9/2**[3]

5 *22* **Winnetou** 3-8-12 0 ....(b[1]) AndreaAtzeni 3
(Frank Sheridan) *slowly away and lost grnd s: rcvrd and in tch after 2f: pushed along 4f out: struggling fnl 3f* **28/1**

50-P **P** **Kathindi (IRE)**[61] 4209 5-8-12 30 .... LeonnaMayor(5) 2
(Michael Chapman) *v awkward leaving stalls and sn trailing field: a in last: eased and t.o fnl 3f: p.u fnl f* **150/1**

1m 49.8s (-0.70) **Going Correction** -0.15s/f (Stan)
WFA 3 from 4yo+ 5lb — **6** Ran SP% **110.4**
Speed ratings (Par 101): **97,94,91,86,67**
toteswingers 1&2 £1.40, 1&3 £2.50, 2&3 £2.30 CSF £4.96 TOTE £2.90: £1.60, £1.40; EX 4.50.There was no bid for the winner.
Owner J A & S Wilcox **Bred** Haydock Park Stud **Trained** Pandy, Monmouths

FOCUS
A poor seller in which the winning time was over a second faster than the opening apprentice handicap. The winner is rated to this year's form.
Kathindi(IRE) Official explanation: vet said gelding finished lame

6318 32RED.COM NURSERY 7f 32y(P)
3:00 (3:01) (Class 6) (0-65,65) 2-Y-O £1,704 (£503; £251) **Stalls** High

Form RPR
0044 **1** **Aeronwyn Bryn (IRE)**[17] 5786 2-9-3 **61**......................(t) PaulMulrennan 6 65+
(Michael Dods) *prom: pushed along to ld over 1f out: edgd rt ins fnl f: rdn out* **12/1**
0001 **2** *¾* **Progenitor (IRE)**[5] 6147 2-9-1 **59** 6ex........................ FrankieMcDonald 8 61+
(David Lanigan) *cl up on outer: urged along 3f out: rdn and briefly lost pl over 2f out: hdwy over 1f out: drvn: hanging lft and nt helping rdr fnl f: unable to rch wnr* **10/3**[1]
0544 **3** *¾* **Black Dave (IRE)**[5] 6147 2-8-13 **57**......................... SilvestreDeSousa 11 57
(David Evans) *towards rr on outer: pushed along over 3f out: hdwy on wd outside ent st: drvn and hanging lft wl over 1f out: stdy prog and continued to hang ins fnl f: gng on cl home* **9/1**
0010 **4** *nk* **Sekumkum (IRE)**[5] 6147 2-9-7 **65**....................................(b) AdamKirby 7 65
(Marco Botti) *midfield on outer: hdwy 3f out: pushed along 2f out: drvn over 1f out: swtchd lft fnl f: kpt on* **5/1**[2]
5364 **5** *¾* **Eastern Dragon (IRE)**[18] 5763 2-9-2 **60**......................(v) JimmyQuinn 9 58
(Michael Scudamore) *towards rr: urged along over 2f out: hdwy over 1f out: drvn fnl f: no ex fnl 75yds* **17/2**
600 **6** *1 ¼* **Index Waiter**[9] 6043 2-8-13 **57**...(b[1]) ShaneKelly 4 52
(Brian Meehan) *rousted along and sn led: rdn and hdd over 1f out: drvn and grad wknd ins fnl f* **10/1**
504 **7** *2* **Persian Wave**[39] 4982 2-9-4 **62**... MartinDwyer 5 52
(James Tate) *squeezed out s: in rr: rdn 4f out: drvn and struggling fnl 3f: one pce* **14/1**
030 **8** *½* **Keep Calm**[19] 5742 2-8-12 **63**........................ WilliamTwiston-Davies(7) 3 52
(Richard Hannon) *midfield: urged along 3f out: drvn and wknd fnl 2f* **12/1**
5243 **9** *¾* **Autumn Shadow (IRE)**[10] 6016 2-8-12 **59**...................... LeeTopliss(3) 1 46
(Richard Fahey) *cl up: urged along over 3f out: drvn and wknd fnl 2f* **11/2**[3]
0024 **10** *nk* **Lincolnrose (IRE)**[63] 4139 2-9-2 **60**... IPoullis 12 46
(Alan McCabe) *a in rr: drvn 3f out: no imp fnl 2f* **50/1**
0010 **11** *2* **Whitford (IRE)**[26] 5475 2-9-7 **65**.. AndreaAtzeni 2 46
(Chris Dwyer) *midfield: rdn and lost pl over 2f out: btn fnl f* **11/1**

1m 29.25s (-0.35) **Going Correction** -0.15s/f (Stan) 11 Ran SP% **117.1**
Speed ratings (Par 93): **96,95,94,93,93 91,89,88,87,87 85**
toteswingers 1&2 £13.00, 1&3 £15.60, 2&3 £5.90 CSF £51.61 CT £387.44 TOTE £14.70: £4.90, £1.10, £3.10; EX 89.20 Trifecta £508.90 Part won. Pool: £687.71 - 0.81 winning units..
Owner Andrew Tinkler **Bred** Owenstown Stud **Trained** Denton, Co Durham

FOCUS
A moderate if competitive nursery and the pace was solid. The winner is rated backed to her debut mark but the form is limited.

NOTEBOOK
Aeronwyn Bryn(IRE) had a tongue tie on for this AW debut and appreciated the shorter trip after failing to see out 1m on easy ground at Salisbury. She got a nice tow from the leader and, having been sent to the front over a furlong from home, stayed on well despite hanging right inside the last. She looks worth persevering with on this surface. (op 16-1)
Progenitor(IRE), carrying a 6lb penalty after making a successful nursery debut at Kempton five days earlier, was inclined to hang when in with every chance over a furlong from home and was never quite doing enough. He may prefer going right-handed. (op 3-1 tchd 7-2)
Black Dave(IRE) ◆, nearly 5l behind Progenitor at Kempton five days earlier and 6lb better off, is the one to take from the contest as he was forced to race wide throughout from his high draw and was given plenty to do, yet was finishing better than anything down the wide outside. He can win a similar event granted better luck. (op 12-1)
Sekumkum(IRE)'s last effort behind Progenitor at Kempton could be ignored as he was badly hampered, but he still had it to do off 9lb higher than when winning over C&D the time before. Having slipstreamed the favourite throughout, he had his chance on turning in, but was inclined to hang under pressure and couldn't land a blow. (op 9-2 tchd 4-1)
Eastern Dragon(IRE) went straight from 6f to 1m so this was his first try at this in-between trip. Another given a bit to do, he ran with credit as he made his effort closer to the inside in the straight, away from the other principals. (op 9-1 tchd 10-1)
Index Waiter, making his nursery and AW debuts, proved a springer in the market but appeared to do too much too soon in the first-time blinkers. (op 20-1)
Whitford(IRE) Official explanation: jockey said colt hung left-handed

6319 32RED CASINO H'CAP 7f 32y(P)
3:30 (3:30) (Class 5) (0-75,81) 3-Y-O+ £2,264 (£673; £336; £168) **Stalls** High

Form RPR
3251 **1** **Majuro (IRE)**[4] 6171 8-9-6 **81** 6ex.................................(t) DavidBergin(7) 7 91
(Charles Smith) *t.k.h: cl up: hdwy 3f out: swept through to ld over 2f out: rdn clr over 1f out: drvn and edgd rt ins fnl f: all out* **11/2**[3]
-001 **2** *nk* **Roy The Boy (USA)**[19] 5750 4-9-2 **70**.............................. AdamKirby 12 79+
(Alan Bailey) *in rr: hdwy 3f out: swtchd to wd outside outer 2f out and hdwy: drvn and swtchd bk to inner over 1f out: kpt on strly ins fnl f: jst failed: unlucky* **9/2**[2]
5201 **3** *¾* **Amoure Medici**[14] 5893 3-9-4 **75**.................................. PaulMulrennan 9 82
(Ann Duffield) *in tch on outer: pushed along over 2f out: wd ent st: drvn and plugged on to take 3rd fnl f* **4/1**[1]
4512 **4** *2 ¾* **Kingswinford (IRE)**[2] 6241 6-9-0 **73**............................. KatiaScallan(5) 4 73
(Alastair Lidderdale) *midfield: pushed along over 2f out: swtchd to inner and rdn over 1f out: plugged on one pce ins fnl f* **7/1**
0543 **5** *nk* **I Confess**[20] 5713 7-8-12 **73**......................................(b) JordanNason(7) 11 72+
(Geoffrey Harker) *in rr: urged along over 3f out: swtchd to inner and mod hdwy over 2f out: plugged on one pce fnl f* **16/1**
1006 **6** *½* **Jumeirah Palm Star**[35] 5156 3-9-3 **74**................................ SeanLevey 8 71
(Richard Hannon) *in rr: rdn over 3f out: no ch 2f out: kpt on wl fnl f: nvr nr ldrs* **14/1**
0-11 **7** *nk* **Scottish Lake**[33] 5234 4-9-5 **73**..................................(b) KirstyMilczarek 5 70
(Olivia Maylam) *sn led: pushed along and hdd 2f out: drvn and wknd fr over 1f out* **4/1**[1]
6400 **8** *3 ½* **Kakapuka**[13] 5910 5-9-6 **74**..(p) IanMongan 3 61
(Anabel K Murphy) *prom: rdn 2f out: drvn and wknd fnl f* **14/1**
1500 **9** *1 ½* **Know No Fear**[2] 6239 7-8-12 **71**............................(p) LeonnaMayor(5) 10 54
(Alastair Lidderdale) *stdd s: in rr: no run on inner over 2f out: eventually weaved past btn rivals fnl f but ch had gone* **16/1**
0-30 **10** *6* **Khajaaly (IRE)**[184] 941 5-9-5 **73**.. JimmyQuinn 6 40
(Julia Feilden) *awkward s: in rr: hdwy into midfield over 4f out: pushed along 3f out: drvn and wknd fnl 2f* **28/1**
1420 **11** *10* **Pipers Piping (IRE)**[214] 584 6-9-1 **72**......................... RossAtkinson(3) 1 12
(John Butler) *in rr: drvn along and struggling 3f out: t.o fnl f* **25/1**
0100 **12** *12* **Mazovian (USA)**[31] 5322 4-9-5 **73**.............................. RussKennemore 2
(Michael Chapman) *midfield: rdn and lost pl 4f out: toiling fnl 3f: t.o* **66/1**

1m 27.42s (-2.18) **Going Correction** -0.15s/f (Stan)
WFA 3 from 4yo+ 3lb 12 Ran SP% **120.0**
Speed ratings (Par 103): **106,105,104,101,101 100,100,96,94,87 76,62**
toteswingers 1&2 £8.20, 1&3 £7.20, 2&3 £3.40 CSF £30.37 CT £113.79 TOTE £8.00: £2.50, £2.50, £1.10; EX 46.80 Trifecta £373.50 Pool: £868.33 - 1.72 winning units..
Owner Willie McKay **Bred** Tally-Ho Stud **Trained** Temple Bruer, Lincs

FOCUS
A fair handicap run at a good pace and the form looks sound, rated around the first three.

6320 32RED SUPPORTING BRITISH RACING MAIDEN STKS 5f 20y(P)
4:00 (4:03) (Class 5) 2-Y-O £2,264 (£673; £336; £168) **Stalls** Low

Form RPR
32 **1** **Moviesta (USA)**[41] 4921 2-9-3 0.................................. RoystonFfrench 9 84+
(Bryan Smart) *cl up on outer: rdn along 2f out: led 1f out: kpt on wl* **8/11**[1]
2 *4 ½* **Secret Missile** 2-9-3 0... MartinDwyer 1 68
(William Muir) *in rr and nudged along thrght: hdwy over 2f out: swtchd lft over 1f out: kpt on ins fnl f: wnt 2nd fnl 50yds* **13/2**[3]
0324 **3** *½* **Bapak Bangsawan**[8] 6071 2-9-3 71.. AmyRyan 4 66
(Kevin Ryan) *sn led: pushed along over 1f out: hdd 1f out: wknd and lost 2nd fnl 50yds* **7/2**[2]
6 **4** *1 ¼* **Rangooned**[14] 5887 2-8-12 0... PaulMulrennan 6 57
(Ann Duffield) *midfield: pushed along and hdwy over 2f out: wd ent st and sn chsd ldrs: drvn and no ex fnl f* **12/1**
43 **5** *4* **Miako (USA)**[9] 6054 2-9-3 0.. AdamKirby 5 47
(Marco Botti) *prom: urged along over 2f out: drvn and wknd over 1f out* **14/1**
6 *¾* **Lebresem** 2-9-3 0.. IanMongan 7 44
(James Tate) *midfield: urged along 3f out: lost pl 2f out: btn fnl f* **25/1**
06 **7** *nk* **Misleading Promise (IRE)**[11] 5968 2-8-12 0........... TobyAtkinson(5) 8 43
(John Butler) *slow away: in rr: pushed along 4f out: drvn and no imp fnl 2f* **66/1**
00 **8** *8* **Aphrodite's Dream**[18] 5765 2-8-9 0............................... RaulDaSilva(3) 3 10
(Derek Shaw) *in tch: briefly short of room over 3f out: rdn 2f out: sn wknd* **100/1**

1m 0.96s (-1.34) **Going Correction** -0.15s/f (Stan) 2y crse rec 8 Ran SP% **114.1**
Speed ratings (Par 95): **104,96,96,94,87 86,85,73**
toteswingers 1&2 £2.90, 1&3 £1.60, 2&3 £2.90 CSF £6.10 TOTE £1.80: £1.02, £1.70, £1.50; EX 8.40 Trifecta £24.20 Pool: £1,358.65 - 41.43 winning units..
Owner Harry Redknapp **Bred** John D Gunther **Trained** Hambleton, N Yorks

FOCUS
A modest maiden and they finished well spread out. The winner impressed, scoring in a good time, and the third helps set the level.

NOTEBOOK
Moviesta(USA), placed in maidens at Pontefract and Ripon, covered a fair amount of ground on the outside of the leading group early, but that didn't stop him from shooting clear once in front inside the last. He may not have beaten very much here, but can hold his own in something better. (op 10-11)
Secret Missile, a 45,000GBP half-brother to the winning sprinter Novalist, did well as he was taken off his feet early yet finished in pleasing style to grab second at a respectful distance. He should come on for this and another furlong may suit. (op 6-1 tchd 7-1)
Bapak Bangsawan, rated 71 after making the frame four times from five starts in maidens, tried to burn his rivals off from the start once again but proved no match for the winner once headed. He has had plenty of chances now and is beginning to look a short runner. (op 10-3 tchd 3-1)
Rangooned showed speed before fading over 6f here on her debut and had every chance over a furlong out here before hanging and being done for toe. She looks one for nurseries eventually. (op 10-1)
Miako(USA) has now shown ordinary form in three maidens here, but may improve now that he qualifies for a mark. (op 11-1 tchd 10-1)
Misleading Promise(IRE) Official explanation: jockey said colt ran green

6321 £32 BONUS AT 32RED.COM H'CAP (DIV I) 5f 216y(P)
4:30 (4:31) (Class 6) (0-55,55) 3-Y-O+ £1,704 (£503; £251) **Stalls** Low

Form RPR
5234 **1** **Invigilator**[4] 6180 4-9-2 **55**...(t) MartinDwyer 12 65
(Derek Shaw) *in rr: stl in last 2f out: pushed along and hdwy over 1f out: swtchd rt and chsd ldrs 1f out: styd on wl to ld fnl 75yds* **9/2**[2]
1550 **2** *1* **Majestic Breeze (IRE)**[7] 6104 3-8-11 **52**..............(p) SilvestreDeSousa 3 59
(Brian Ellison) *cl up: urged along 2f out: drvn to ld over 1f out: hdd fnl 75yds* **11/4**[1]
554 **3** *¾* **Jackie Love (IRE)**[20] 5720 4-8-5 **49**................................(v) LauraPike(5) 7 54
(Olivia Maylam) *midfield: urged along over 2f out: short of room 2f out: swtchd lft over 1f out: drvn and ev ch 1f out: no ex fnl 75yds* **14/1**
0503 **4** *3 ½* **Brailsford (IRE)**[39] 5014 3-8-12 **53**............................ RoystonFfrench 11 46
(Ismail Mohammed) *rousted along to chse ldrs on outer: rdn to press ldrs 2f out: drvn and one pce fnl 125yds* **15/2**
0020 **5** *1 ¼* **Dingaan (IRE)**[4] 6179 9-8-9 **48**................................... RobbieFitzpatrick 10 37
(Peter Grayson) *v slow away: urged along 4f out: swtchd to outer over 1f out: kpt on wl ins fnl f* **20/1**
0664 **6** *nk* **Poseidon Grey (IRE)**[4] 6179 3-8-13 **54**.............................. LiamJones 6 42
(Ian Williams) *in tch: pushed along over 2f out: drvn 1f out: one pce and no imp ins fnl f* **7/1**[3]
0005 **7** *1 ¼* **Lucifers Shadow (IRE)**[10] 6001 3-9-0 **55**...................... SaleemGolam 9 45
(Sylvester Kirk) *cl up: rdn 3f out: styng on whn short of room over 1f out: nt rcvr* **8/1**
2020 **8** *¾* **Botanist**[10] 6002 5-8-11 **50**...(be) LiamKeniry 13 32
(Milton Bradley) *in rr: travelling wl 3f out: rdn 2f out: drvn and one pce fnl f* **10/1**
0000 **9** *1 ½* **Little Perisher**[12] 5937 5-8-9 **48**................................(p) MichaelStainton 2 25
(Paul Howling) *pressed ldr: urged along and led over 2f out: drvn and drifted rt ent st: hdd over 1f out: wknd ins fnl f* **40/1**
6300 **10** *3 ½* **Divertimenti (IRE)**[7] 6105 8-8-6 **48** ow1........................(b) RyanClark(3) 5 14
(Roy Bowring) *led: pressed 4f out: pushed along over 2f out and hdd: drvn and wknd over 1f out* **10/1**
6000 **11** *1 ¾* **Mystical Witch**[96] 3050 3-8-9 **50**.. JimmyQuinn 4
(Christine Dunnett) *in rr: rdn over 3f out: no imp fnl 2f* **100/1**
0-00 **12** *3 ½* **Gwilym (GER)**[12] 5937 9-8-11 **50**................................(tp) PaulMulrennan 8
(Tony Newcombe) *midfield: rdn 3f out: lost pl 2f out: sn btn* **22/1**

1m 13.66s (-1.34) **Going Correction** -0.15s/f (Stan)
WFA 3 from 4yo+ 2lb 12 Ran SP% **117.6**
Speed ratings (Par 101): **102,100,99,95,93 92,91,90,88,83 81,76**
toteswingers 1&2 £3.60, 1&3 £8.50, 2&3 £7.70 CSF £16.43 CT £163.82 TOTE £3.60: £1.10, £1.80, £5.10; EX 17.90 Trifecta £114.30 Pool: £908.44 - 5.88 winning units..
Owner The Warren Partnership **Bred** Granham Farm And P Hearson Bloodstock **Trained** Sproxton, Leics

FOCUS
A moderate 47-55 sprint handicap with few solid and the form best rated around the winner and third.

Gwilym(GER) Official explanation: trainer said gelding bled from the nose

6322 £32 BONUS AT £32RED.COM H'CAP (DIV II) 5f 216y(P)
5:00 (5:01) (Class 6) (0-55,55) 3-Y-0+ **£1,704** (£503; £251) **Stalls** Low

Form				RPR
4565	1		**Medam**[14] 5874 3-8-11 **52**...(t) FrannyNorton 3 (Shaun Harris) *midfield: rdn 2f out: swtchd lft and hdwy over 1f out: drvn to ld fnl 125yds: won gng away* **15/2**	64
4410	2	2 1/4	**Avonlini**[119] 2350 6-8-12 **51**... KellyHarrison 10 (Brian Baugh) *cl up on outer: urged along 3f out: drvn over 1f out: kpt on wl to take 2nd fnl 35yds: no ch w wnr* **20/1**	56
00-0	3	hd	**Monumental Man**[80] 3555 3-8-11 **52**... PaulMulrennan 5 (James Unett) *in tch: urged along and hdwy over 2f out: drvn and ev ch 1f out: no ex fnl 75yds* **16/1**	56
1422	4	nk	**Maltease Ah**[7] 6104 3-8-13 **54**... SilvestreDeSousa 4 (Alan McCabe) *prom: rdn to chse ldr 2f out: drvn over 1f out: no ex ins fnl f* **2/1**[1]	57
0054	5	1/2	**Forty Proof (IRE)**[2] 6233 4-8-9 **48**...(t) StevieDonohoe 8 (David Evans) *midfield on outer: lost pl 3f out: drvn and plenty to do 2f out: kpt on ins fnl f: nvr a threat* **11/2**[2]	49
0004	6	1/2	**Vhujon (IRE)**[4] 6178 7-8-11 **50**... RobbieFitzpatrick 9 (Peter Grayson) *in rr: urged along over 2f out: drvn over 1f out: kpt on same pce ins fnl f* **9/1**	50
0005	7	1	**Nine Before Ten (IRE)**[4] 6180 4-8-9 **55**...(t) DavidBergin(7) 1 (Charles Smith) *t.k.h: prom: pushed along 2f out: drvn over 1f out: no ex ins fnl f* **12/1**	52
1504	8	nk	**Simple Rhythm**[10] 6003 6-8-4 **48**...(p) NatashaEaton(5) 2 (John Ryan) *led: pushed along over 1f out: drvn and hdd fnl 125yds and lost several pls rapidly* **25/1**	44
0006	9	1	**Huzzah (IRE)**[10] 6002 7-9-1 **54**... MichaelStainton 11 (Paul Howling) *t.k.h in rr: drvn over 2f out: no imp fnl f* **9/1**	46
3601	10	1/2	**Cheery Cat (USA)**[12] 5937 8-8-3 **49**...(p) JackDuern(7) 7 (Richard Ford) *midfield: pushed along 3f out: struggling fnl 2f* **12/1**	40
1030	11	2	**Flaxen Lake**[10] 6002 5-8-13 **52**...(p) LiamKeniry 6 (Milton Bradley) *midfield: rdn over 2f out: no hdwy fnl f* **7/1**[3]	36
5000	12	3/4	**Give Us A Belle (IRE)**[11] 5975 3-8-9 **50**...(vt) JimmyQuinn 13 (Christine Dunnett) *in rr: struggling fnl 3f* **66/1**	32
0000	13	1 3/4	**Sleights Boy (IRE)**[40] 4956 4-8-7 **46**...(v) RoystonFfrench 12 (Ian McInnes) *a in rr: struggling fnl 3f* **25/1**	22

1m 13.55s (-1.45) **Going Correction** -0.15s/f (Stan)
WFA 3 from 4yo+ 2lb 13 Ran SP% **128.2**
Speed ratings (Par 101): **103,100,99,99,98 98,96,96,94,94 91,90,88**
toteswingers 1&2 £22.80, 1&3 £36.50, 2&3 £68.90 CSF £160.05 CT £2445.43 TOTE £9.80: £2.40, £5.80, £10.80; EX 220.70 Trifecta £651.00 Part won. Pool: £879.77 - 0.40 winning units..
Owner Burton Agnes Bloodstock **Bred** Burton Agnes Stud Co Ltd **Trained** Carburton, Notts

FOCUS
The winning time was 0.11 seconds faster than the first division and a personal-best from the winner, backed up by the second.

6323 32REDBET.COM H'CAP 1m 4f 50y(P)
5:30 (5:30) (Class 6) (0-60,62) 3-Y-0+ **£1,704** (£503; £251) **Stalls** Low

Form				RPR
3	1		**Azrag (USA)**[47] 4712 4-9-11 **58**...(p) PaulMulrennan 4 (Gerard Butler) *cl up: pushed along 3f out: drvn to press ldr over 1f out: forged ahd cl home* **14/1**	65
6064	2	nse	**Merchants Return**[15] 5855 3-8-6 **50**...(v[1]) SimonPearce(3) 10 (Lydia Pearce) *midfield: hdwy 4f out: urged along to ld 3f out: drvn and strly pressed fr 2f out tl hdd fnl strides* **16/1**	57
6423	3	1 1/4	**White Deer (USA)**[49] 4652 8-9-7 **54**...(v) RoystonFfrench 11 (Geoffrey Harker) *in rr: hdwy 4f out: pushed along 3f out: drvn 1f out: wnt 3rd ins fnl f: kpt on* **16/1**	59
4412	4	3/4	**Volcanic Jack (IRE)**[2] 6230 4-10-1 **62** 6ex... IanMongan 1 (Tony Carroll) *midfield: pushed along 3f out: drvn to chse ldrs 2f out: ev ch 1f out: no ex fnl 100yds* **4/1**[2]	66
1330	5	2 1/2	**Astroscarlet**[40] 4971 3-9-4 **59**... TedDurcan 2 (Mark H Tompkins) *led: hdd after 3f: remained prom tl rdn and lost pl whn tempo increased 3f out: plugged on same pce* **9/2**[3]	59
0040	6	2 1/2	**Opus Maximus (IRE)**[9] 6057 7-9-6 **53**... KirstyMilczarek 9 (Conor Dore) *in rr: pushed along 3f out: no imp fnl 2f* **20/1**	49
5002	7	hd	**Inniscastle Boy**[9] 6056 3-9-2 **57**...(b) MartinDwyer 7 (William Muir) *cl up: led 4f out: pushed along and hdd 3f out: drvn and wknd fnl 2f* **10/3**[1]	52
0033	8	hd	**Phase Shift**[12] 5939 4-9-6 **53**... SilvestreDeSousa 6 (Brian Ellison) *slow away: drvn along 4f out: no imp fnl 2f* **11/2**	48
0165	9	9	**Anginola (IRE)**[28] 5419 3-9-4 **59**...(v) SeanLevey 3 (David Evans) *t.k.h: midfield: pushed along 3f out: drvn and no ex over 1f out* **33/1**	40
5644	10	1 1/2	**We Used To Wait (USA)**[26] 5483 3-9-4 **59**... AndreaAtzeni 12 (Peter Chapple-Hyam) *cl up tl led after 3f: urged along and hdd 4f out: drvn and wknd qckly 3f out* **15/2**	37
0	11	12	**Bull Market (IRE)**[32] 5265 9-9-3 **50**... JamieGoldstein 5 (Alan Jones) *in rr: rdn over 4f out: sn struggling* **33/1**	

2m 40.75s (-0.35) **Going Correction** -0.15s/f (Stan)
WFA 3 from 4yo+ 8lb 11 Ran SP% **117.5**
Speed ratings (Par 101): **95,94,94,93,91 90,90,90,84,83 75**
toteswingers 1&2 £22.20, 1&3 £9.10, 2&3 £18.60 CSF £211.88 CT £3572.98 TOTE £14.50: £4.50, £6.80, £3.70; EX 191.20 TRIFECTA Not won..
Owner Fawzi Abdulla Nass **Bred** Aislabie Bloodstock **Trained** Newmarket, Suffolk

■ Stewards' Enquiry : Simon Pearce two-day ban: used whip above permitted level (Oct 1-2)

FOCUS
A moderate middle-distance handicap and a messy race with no pace on early. The runner-up is rated to his maiden form, backed up by the fourth.

T/Jkpt: Not won. T/Plt: £10.40 to a £1 stake. Pool: £59,413.92 - 4,168.58 winning tickets T/Qpdt: £7.60 to a £1 stake. Pool: £4,665.56 - 450.55 winning tickets CS

6324 - 6327a (Foreign Racing) - See Raceform Interactive

5850 FOLKESTONE (R-H)
Tuesday, September 18

OFFICIAL GOING: Good to firm (straight course: far side 7.7, stands' side 8.1, round course 7.2)
One furlong of rail down the bank on the Round course moved out 2m to give fresh ground.
Wind: light behind Weather: breezy and sunny

6328 TONY AND KAREN MARRIED HERE TODAY MAIDEN STKS 7f (S)
2:20 (2:20) (Class 5) 3-Y-0+ **£2,385** (£704; £352) **Stalls** High

Form				RPR
2065	1		**Strada Facendo (USA)**[31] 5365 3-9-2 77... KirstyMilczarek 4 (Luca Cumani) *mde all: urged along 2f out: rdn clr ins fnl f* **5/4**[1]	86
	2	4	**Last Fighter (IRE)** 3-9-2 0... SilvestreDeSousa 1 (Saeed Bin Suroor) *t.k.h in 3rd: pushed along 2f out: drvn and hung rt over 1f out: wnt 2nd 1f out: no ch w wnr* **11/4**[2]	75+
2455	3	4 1/2	**Santarini (IRE)**[19] 5769 3-8-11 70... RichardHughes 2 (Richard Hannon) *chsd ldr: rdn 2f out: drvn and lost 2nd 1f out: no ex* **7/2**[3]	58
2533	4	14	**Gold Edition**[7] 6125 3-9-2 75...(p) JamieSpencer 3 (Jeremy Noseda) *slowly away: in last and reminders early: rdn w little rspnse ins fnl 3f: eased fnl f* **15/2**	25

1m 24.94s (-2.36) **Going Correction** -0.35s/f (Firm) 4 Ran SP% **105.1**
Speed ratings (Par 103): **99,94,89,73**
CSF £4.59 TOTE £2.30; EX 5.20.
Owner Scuderia Archi Romani **Bred** Scuderia Archi Romani Di Paolo Agostini **Trained** Newmarket, Suffolk

FOCUS
An interesting maiden despite the small field size, run at an honest pace with the well-backed favourite making all to win impressively. He is rated to his previous best handicap form.

6329 EASTWELLMANOR.CO.UK CLAIMING STKS 7f (S)
2:50 (2:50) (Class 6) 3-Y-0+ **£1,704** (£503; £251) **Stalls** High

Form				RPR
6022	1		**Marford Missile (IRE)**[10] 6051 3-8-13 78... HayleyTurner 5 (Tom Dascombe) *chsd ldr: rdn over 2f out: kpt on wl to ld 1f out: drvn out: jst hld on* **3/1**[2]	82
5000	2	nse	**Rakaan (IRE)**[11] 6011 5-9-10 85... JamieSpencer 9 (Jamie Osborne) *slowly away: in rr: hdwy 2f out: wnt 3rd and rdn 1f out: kpt on wl: jst failed* **11/10**[1]	90
6004	3	4	**Rondeau (GR)**[23] 5630 7-9-10 76... JimCrowley 6 (Patrick Chamings) *led: urged along ins fnl 2f: hdd 1f out: wknd fnl 100yds* **7/1**[3]	79
0056	4	4	**Soweto Star (IRE)**[87] 3388 4-9-2 70...[1] JamesDoyle 7 (John Best) *in tch: rdn over 2f out: sn one pce: btn fnl f* **8/1**	60
54	5	2 1/2	**Frognal (IRE)**[50] 4661 6-8-13 75...(bt) CathyGannon 4 (Violet M Jordan) *in rr: rdn 2f out: no imp fnl f* **12/1**	51
6000	6	3 1/2	**Divine Rule (IRE)**[11] 5996 4-8-10 45...(v) EddieAhern 8 (Laura Mongan) *hld up: rdn and swtchd rt over 2f out: drvn and no imp fnl f* **100/1**	38
4004	7	9	**Spin Again (IRE)**[41] 4966 7-9-0 61... BrettDoyle 3 (John Ryan) *in rr: pushed along over 2f out: struggling over 1f out: eased ins fnl f* **28/1**	18
0000	8	2 1/4	**Legal Legacy**[3] 6256 6-9-3 73... AmirQuinn 2 (Richard Rowe) *in tch: urged along 3f out: wknd fnl 2f: eased fnl f* **25/1**	15

1m 24.97s (-2.33) **Going Correction** -0.35s/f (Firm)
WFA 3 from 4yo+ 3lb 8 Ran SP% **112.2**
Speed ratings (Par 101): **99,98,94,89,86 82,72,70**
toteswingers 1&2 £2.10, 2&3 £2.60, 1&3 £4.70 CSF £6.35 TOTE £4.40: £1.70, £1.10, £1.30; EX 7.20.
Owner The MHS 4x10 Partnership **Bred** Miss Mary Davidson & Mrs Steffi Von Schilcher **Trained** Malpas, Cheshire

FOCUS
Not a bad contest for the grade, run at a fair pace with the two top rated runners in the field pulling clear and fighting out an exciting finish. The winner is rated to his recent best with the second marginally off his best and the third to this year's form.

6330 OLDPOTEGATESTATION.CO.UK MAIDEN STKS 7f (S)
3:20 (3:21) (Class 5) 2-Y-0 **£2,385** (£704; £352) **Stalls** High

Form				RPR
02	1		**Banovallum**[16] 5851 2-9-3 0... LiamKeniry 10 (Sylvester Kirk) *mde virtually all: urged along 2f out: drvn 1f out: hld on wl* **8/1**	81
	2	1 1/2	**Melvin The Grate (IRE)** 2-9-3 0... JamieSpencer 13 (Andrew Balding) *hld up: hdwy over 2f out: swtchd rt over 1f out: wnt 2nd 1f out: kpt on wl: jst failed* **8/1**	77+
202	3	3/4	**Almalekiah (IRE)**[18] 5784 2-8-12 70... DavidProbert 12 (J S Moore) *in tch: rdn 2f out: pressed ldr over 1f out: no ex fnl 75yds* **9/1**	70
4055	4	3 3/4	**Millers Wharf (IRE)**[10] 6020 2-9-3 77... RichardHughes 9 (Richard Hannon) *in tch: pushed along over 2f out: drvn and kpt on same pce over 1f out: eased fnl 50yds: nvr a threat* **4/1**[1]	67+
43	5	3 1/4	**Tarbawi (IRE)**[22] 5684 2-9-3 0... SilvestreDeSousa 5 (Saeed Bin Suroor) *in tch: rdn over 2f out: drvn and hung rt over 1f out: no imp ins fnl f* **13/2**[3]	56+
30	6	hd	**Country Western**[45] 4803 2-9-3 0... JamesDoyle 3 (Charles Hills) *in rr: rdn over 3f out: plugged on one pce fnl 2f: nvr a realistic threat* **4/1**[1]	55+
	7	2 3/4	**Three Streets (IRE)** 2-9-3 0... MickaelBarzalona 1 (Mahmood Al Zarooni) *in rr: rdn over 2f out: kpt on same pce fnl f: nvr able to chal* **11/2**[2]	48+
3	8	3	**Midnight Warrior**[16] 5851 2-9-3 0... IanMongan 6 (James Tate) *cl up: drvn 2f out: wknd fnl f* **9/1**	40
	9	2 1/4	**Woza Moya (USA)** 2-9-3 0... HayleyTurner 11 (Gay Kelleway) *midfield: rdn and wknd over 1f out* **66/1**	34+
	10	5	**Exclusion (USA)** 2-8-12 0... NeilCallan 4 (Noel Quinlan) *in tch: urged along over 2f out: wknd over 1f out* **66/1**	15
0	11	1/2	**Kraken (IRE)**[24] 5578 2-9-3 0... KirstyMilczarek 7 (Luca Cumani) *midfield: rdn over 2f out: steadily wknd* **40/1**	19
60	12	7	**Flying Tempo**[12] 5962 2-9-3 0... EddieAhern 14 (Ed Dunlop) *struggling fnl 3f: t.o* **150/1**	
05	13	10	**Royal Betty**[13] 5948 2-8-12 0... KierenFox 8 (Lee Carter) *cl up to 1/2-way: drvn and lost pl 3f out: t.o* **66/1**	

00 **14** 2 1/4 **Positive Parenting (IRE)**[13] 5948 2-8-12 0.................. SaleemGolam 2
(Stuart Williams) *a in rr: struggling fnl 2f: t.o* **150/1**

1m 25.14s (-2.16) **Going Correction** -0.35s/f (Firm) 14 Ran SP% **119.2**

Speed ratings (Par 95): **98,96,95,91,87 87,84,80,78,72 71,63,52,49**

toteswingers 1&2 £15.10, 2&3 £16.30, 1&3 £12.30 CSF £69.33 TOTE £9.30: £2.80, £2.90, £3.40; EX 87.00.

Owner Chris Wright & The Hon Mrs J M Corbett **Bred** Whitsbury Manor Stud And Mrs M E Slade **Trained** Upper Lambourn, Berks

FOCUS

This was competitive enough, but the winner was allowed a softish lead and that proved crucial. The first three home were drawn 10,13 and 12, which tempers enthusiasm for the form.

NOTEBOOK

Banovallum had been beaten over C&D here on his last start but he was soon in front, kept on finding for pressure and none of his rivals were good enough to pass him. It was undoubtedly an advantage to grab the rail, but he is improving with racing and handles these conditions well. (op 17-2 tchd 9-1 and 15-2)

Melvin The Grate(IRE), a 200,000gns yearling who is a brother to four winners including Group 3 winner Air Chief Marshall and this year's Irish 2,000 Guineas runner-up Foxtrot Romeo, ran a most encouraging race for a yard whose runners tend to improve for their debut. He had to be switched off the rail for his effort but showed plenty here and can go on from this. (op 10-1 tchd 11-1)

Almalekiah(IRE) appreciated the return to a quicker surface and handled the step up to 7f fine and looks a ready type for nurseries. (op 17-2)

Millers Wharf(IRE), the most experienced runner in the field, raced close to the pace but ran as though finding this too sharp. (op 9-2)

Tarbawi(IRE) raced keenly enough out wide, but he did not really go through with his effort and this was slightly disappointing. (op 6-1)

Country Western ran well on his debut at Newmarket, but has not really built on that in two runs since and is another who could come into his own over further. (tchd 9-2)

Three Streets(IRE), a Derby entrant who is related to six winners including French Derby hero Anabaa Blue and other Listed winners over trips from 7f-1m2f, came widest of all and will probably seen to better effect over further. (op 7-1)

6331 LADBROKES.COM H'CAP — 7f (S)

3:50 (3:50) (Class 4) (0-85,83) 3-Y-O £4,851 (£1,443; £721; £360) Stalls High

Form				RPR
3021	**1**		**Centrifugal (IRE)**[14] 5919 3-9-0 **76**.................................. FrannyNorton 5 (Mark Johnston) *mde all: rdn 2f out: fnd plenty for press and clr ins fnl f: eased cl home* **2/1**[1]	89
0111	**2**	4 1/2	**Take A Note**[32] 5308 3-9-1 **77**.. JimCrowley 2 (Patrick Chamings) *hld up in last: pushed along and hdwy over 1f out: drvn and chsd wnr in vain ins fnl f* **11/4**[2]	78
504	**3**	2	**Usain Colt**[10] 6040 3-9-7 **83**.. RichardHughes 3 (Richard Hannon) *t.k.h: cl up: rdn 2f out: drvn and ev ch over 1f out: wknd ins fnl f* **11/4**[2]	78
0-12	**4**	1	**Diamond Belle**[29] 5409 3-9-2 **78**... NeilCallan 1 (Noel Quinlan) *cl up: drvn over 2f out: ev ch over 1f out: wknd fnl f* **3/1**[3]	71

1m 24.35s (-2.95) **Going Correction** -0.35s/f (Firm) 4 Ran SP% **111.7**

Speed ratings (Par 103): **102,96,94,93**

CSF £7.89 TOTE £2.00; EX 4.10.

Owner Sheikh Hamdan Bin Mohammed Al Maktoum **Bred** Darley **Trained** Middleham Moor, N Yorks

FOCUS

A small yet competitive handicap run at a sound gallop with the winner once again making all up the stands' rail. The winner recorded a personal best but the form is a little fluid.

6332 LADBROKESBINGO.COM NURSERY — 6f

4:20 (4:20) (Class 5) (0-70,74) 2-Y-O £2,385 (£704; £352) Stalls High

Form				RPR
653	**1**		**Empowerment (IRE)**[21] 5704 2-9-7 **70**......................... RichardHughes 6 (Richard Hannon) *chsd ldr: clr w rival over 1f out: rdn to ld fnl 100yds: sn in command* **85/40**[2]	78+
5512	**2**	3	**Vestibule**[3] 6227 2-9-6 **74** 6ex...(p) AmyScott(5) 10 (Eve Johnson Houghton) *led: rdn and clr w wnr over 1f out: drvn and hdd fnl 100yds: sn brushed aside* **7/4**[1]	73
036	**3**	2 3/4	**Grilletto (USA)**[29] 5407 2-9-6 **69**.......................................(b1) NeilCallan 4 (James Tate) *slowly away: rdn to chse ldrs after 1f: rdn over 2f out: unable qck w ldng pair over 1f out: no ex* **13/2**[3]	60
000	**4**	4	**Fossa**[14] 5912 2-8-6 **55**.. HayleyTurner 8 (Dean Ivory) *in rr: drvn over 2f out: plugged on same pce fnl f: nvr a threat* **16/1**	34+
0410	**5**	1/2	**Not Now Blondie**[20] 5749 2-8-12 **61**................................. AndreaAtzeni 5 (Chris Dwyer) *in rr: drvn 4f out: mod hdwy 3f out: no ex fnl f* **12/1**	38
054	**6**	nk	**Silk Fairy (IRE)**[35] 5213 2-8-6 **55**....................................... JimmyQuinn 7 (Noel Quinlan) *in rr: struggling 3f out: kpt on past btn horses fnl f: nvr a threat* **20/1**	31+
550	**7**	1	**Bay Laurel (IRE)**[11] 6016 2-9-2 **65**................................(v1) JamesDoyle 1 (Harry Dunlop) *in rr: drvn and hung rt over 1f out: mod late prog fnl f: nvr a threat* **18/1**	38+
0640	**8**	1 3/4	**Belle Intrigue**[14] 5903 2-9-2 **65**..[1] JimCrowley 2 (Amanda Perrett) *midfield: drvn 3f out: struggling fnl 2f* **14/1**	33
045	**9**	6	**Xerxes (IRE)**[26] 5511 2-7-7 **49**..[1] NoelGarbutt(7) 3 (Hugo Palmer) *midfield: drvn 3f out: sn struggling* **33/1**	+

1m 11.63s (-1.07) **Going Correction** -0.35s/f (Firm) 9 Ran SP% **114.9**

Speed ratings (Par 95): **93,89,85,80,79 78,77,75,67**

toteswingers 1&2 £1.90, 2&3 £3.00, 1&3 £2.90 CSF £6.17 CT £18.98 TOTE £3.30: £1.40, £1.10, £2.20; EX 7.20.

Owner M S Al Shahi **Bred** Pier House Stud **Trained** East Everleigh, Wilts

FOCUS

Not the most competitive nursery, but run at a decent pace, with the front two in the market dominating from a long way out. Again track position was important. The winner did it well, and the second is a good guide.

NOTEBOOK

Empowerment(IRE) had performed with credit in three maidens at trips up to an extended mile and ran out a cosy winner back in trip, on his handicap debut. He was unable to grab the favoured stands' rails but quickened clear impressively although this was not the strongest of contests. (op 11-4 tchd 2-1)

Vestibule, having her 13th start of the season, was able to bag the rail from her high draw but was beaten by a better handicapped rival, and she finished well clear of the third. (tchd 6-4 and 15-8)

Grilletto(USA), wearing blinkers for the first time and dropping in trip for his handicap debut, raced close to the pace but lacked the gears of the front two and may well require further. (op 10-1)

Fossa, who had led on his last two starts over 7f, was outpaced from some way out on his handicap debut and was doing his best work late, although was beaten a long way. (op 25-1)

Silk Fairy(IRE) was unable to get competitive early, but made a touch of progress late on when the race was all over. (op 25-1)

Bay Laurel(IRE) has not been progressing with racing and the first-time visor did not bring much improvement here, although she was not helped by having to race wide throughout from her low draw. (op 12-1)

6333 LADBROKESGAMES.COM H'CAP — 1m 4f

4:50 (4:51) (Class 4) (0-85,85) 3-Y-O+ £4,851 (£1,443; £721; £360) Stalls High

Form				RPR
5311	**1**		**Enery (IRE)**[10] 6039 3-8-13 **80**... FrannyNorton 1 (Mark Johnston) *midfield: urged along 3f out: drvn and hdwy 2f out: str run on inner to ld 1f out: forged ahd* **7/2**[3]	89
5503	**2**	1	**Saint Helena (IRE)**[31] 5359 4-9-1 **74**..............................[1] JamesDoyle 2 (Harry Dunlop) *cl up: rdn 3f out: led 2f out: drvn and hdd 1f out: kpt on: no ex fnl 75yds* **20/1**	81
2000	**3**	3	**Silken Thoughts**[16] 5856 4-9-10 **83**................................. CathyGannon 8 (John Berry) *hld up: drvn 3f out: effrt on inner 2f out: kpt on to take 3rd fnl f* **33/1**	85+
3122	**4**	1 1/4	**Al Baidaa**[13] 5951 3-9-4 **85**.. NeilCallan 6 (Roger Varian) *in tch: drvn along 3f out: effrt over 2f out: wknd fnl f* **5/2**[1]	85
231	**5**	shd	**Infinite Hope (USA)**[26] 5510 3-9-1 **82**.......................... KirstyMilczarek 9 (Luca Cumani) *midfield: dropped to last 4f out: drvn 3f out: swtchd rt and kpt on ins fnl f: nvr a threat* **11/1**	82+
6104	**6**	3/4	**Trend Is My Friend (USA)**[18] 5788 3-9-0 **81**.................... EddieAhern 5 (Amanda Perrett) *sn led: urged along 3f out: drvn and hdd 2f out: sn wknd* **7/1**	80
1-10	**7**	3 1/2	**Future Security (IRE)**[24] 5598 3-9-2 **83**................. SilvestreDeSousa 7 (Saeed Bin Suroor) *cl up: rdn 3f out: drvn and wknd over 1f out* **3/1**[2]	76
0-04	**8**	9	**Tuscan Gold**[32] 5306 5-9-9 **82**.. IanMongan 4 (Laura Mongan) *hld up: rdn 3f out: wknd 2f out: dropped away: eased ins fnl f* **12/1**	61

2m 35.18s (-5.72) **Going Correction** -0.35s/f (Firm)

WFA 3 from 4yo+ 8lb 8 Ran SP% **112.0**

Speed ratings (Par 105): **105,104,102,101,101 100,98,92**

CSF £64.55 CT £1939.64 TOTE £4.90: £1.90, £4.30, £7.20; EX 57.20.

Owner Sheikh Hamdan Bin Mohammed Al Maktoum **Bred** Ceka Ireland Limited **Trained** Middleham Moor, N Yorks

FOCUS

A decent, competitive handicap run at a sound pace with plenty in contention a furlong out. The winner is rated to his latest Aw mark with the runner-up in line with his 3-y-o form.

Future Security(IRE) Official explanation: jockey said colt had no more to give.

6334 LISADESIGN.CO.UK H'CAP — 1m 1f 149y

5:20 (5:22) (Class 6) (0-65,65) 3-Y-O+ £1,704 (£503; £251) Stalls Centre

Form				RPR
0364	**1**		**Caterina**[32] 5305 3-9-3 **64**..(b) RichardHughes 1 (Richard Hannon) *midfield: hdwy 3f out: rdn to ld over 2f out: kpt on wl ins fnl f* **4/1**[2]	76
6123	**2**	1 3/4	**Thecornishcowboy**[5] 6174 3-8-13 **60**...............................(t) BrettDoyle 5 (John Ryan) *midfield: hdwy over 3f out: drvn 2f out: effrt over 1f out: duelling for 2nd ins fnl f* **3/1**[1]	68
3000	**3**	hd	**Chatterati (USA)**[14] 5921 3-8-5 **52**................................(b) FrannyNorton 3 (Mark Johnston) *slowly away: in rr: hdwy over 3f out: drvn 2f out: kpt on and battling for 2nd ins fnl f* **9/2**[3]	60
20-6	**4**	6	**Uncle Dermot (IRE)**[29] 5417 4-9-8 **63**............................... JamesDoyle 4 (Brendan Powell) *towards rr: hdwy into midfield 1/2-way: urged along 3f out: drvn and effrt 2f out: no ex fnl f* **16/1**	58
0300	**5**	1 1/4	**Geordie Boy**[17] 5837 3-9-1 **65**.. RyanClark(3) 11 (Sheena West) *a in rr: struggling fnl 4f: plugged on past btn rivals fnl 2f: nvr any hope of catching ldrs* **22/1**	57
0-03	**6**	2 3/4	**Play The Blues (IRE)**[45] 4812 5-9-0 **62**.........................(t) NedCurtis(7) 9 (Roger Curtis) *towards rr: on wd outside whn rdn 4f out: one pce fnl 2f* **10/1**	49
6014	**7**	3 3/4	**Brown Pete (IRE)**[23] 5628 4-9-9 **64**...............................(e) CathyGannon 2 (Violet M Jordan) *drvn along to ld shortly after s: sn established clr advantage: rdn and reduced ld over 3f out: drvn and hdd over 2f out: sn btn* **7/1**	43
4100	**8**	2 3/4	**Shaunas Spirit (IRE)**[20] 5741 4-9-5 **60**........................... JimCrowley 10 (Dean Ivory) *midfield: dropped to rr after 3f: rdn over 3f out: no imp* **12/1**	33
0050	**9**	4	**Harry Lime**[63] 4196 4-8-10 **51** oh6....................................... JimmyQuinn 8 (Fleur Hawes) *midfield: urged along 5f out: drvn and no ex fnl 2f* **66/1**	16
0000	**10**	10	**Blue Deer (IRE)**[11] 5990 4-9-6 **61**.. KierenFox 7 (Lee Carter) *in tch: drvn 4f out: sn struggling: t.o* **16/1**	
006	**11**	7	**Cometography (IRE)**[20] 5753 3-9-0 **61**.................(b1) RoystonFfrench 6 (Ismail Mohammed) *hld up: rdn 4f out: btn fnl 3f: t.o* **11/1**	

2m 3.25s (-1.65) **Going Correction** -0.35s/f (Firm)

WFA 3 from 4yo+ 6lb 11 Ran SP% **118.4**

Speed ratings (Par 101): **92,90,90,85,84 82,79,77,74,66 60**

toteswingers 1&2 £2.70, 2&3 £3.10, 1&3 £3.90 CSF £16.52 CT £56.67 TOTE £5.80: £2.40, £1.80, £1.90; EX 11.70.

Owner De La Warr Racing & Newsells Park Stud **Bred** Newsells Park Stud & Cheveley Park Stud **Trained** East Everleigh, Wilts

FOCUS

A modest if competitive handicap run at a fierce pace, with the front three clear and the field well strung out crossing the line. A personal-best from the winner backed up by the placed horses.

Cometography(IRE) Official explanation: trainer said colt was unsuited by track.

T/Plt: £143.20 to a £1 stake. Pool of £53413.83 - 272.27 winning tickets. T/Qpdt: £49.20 to a £1 stake. Pool of £4434.77 - 66.63 winning tickets. CS

6042 THIRSK (L-H)

Tuesday, September 18

OFFICIAL GOING: Good to soft (soft in places; 8.3)

Wind: Fresh half behind Weather: Cloudy with sunny periods

6335 BUY THIRSK ANNUAL BADGES FOR CHRISTMAS MAIDEN FILLIES' STKS — 6f

2:10 (2:13) (Class 5) 2-Y-O £2,726 (£805; £402) Stalls High

Form				RPR
005	**1**		**Silkelly**[10] 6042 2-9-0 0.. DanielTudhope 4 (David O'Meara) *sn led and mde virtually all: rdn and edgd lft ins fnl f: kpt on* **25/1**	72
	2	1 1/4	**Vicky Valentine** 2-9-0 0... PhillipMakin 16 (Kevin Ryan) *cl up: pushed along and sltly outpcd 2f out: rdn and styng on whn n.m.r and swtchd rt ins fnl f: kpt on wl towards fin* **4/1**[2]	68+

3 ¾ **Meeting In Paris (IRE)** 2-9-0 0 .... JamieMackay 7 66+
(Brian Meehan) *prom: cl up 1/2-way: rdn to chal wl over 1f out and ev ch tl one pce ins fnl f* **8/1[3]**

24 4 nk **Burning Dawn (USA)**[47] 4742 2-9-0 0 .... GrahamLee 15 65
(David Brown) *trckd ldrs: hdwy over 2f out: rdn wl over 1f out and kpt on same pce* **6/4[1]**

5 2 ¼ **Maid A Million** 2-9-0 0 .... SebSanders 11 58
(David Elsworth) *trckd ldrs on inner: hdwy over 2f out: rdn wl over 1f out: no imp fnl f* **14/1**

4 6 5 **Hit The Note**[33] 5255 2-9-0 0 .... PJMcDonald 9 43
(Ann Duffield) *chsd ldrs: rdn along wl over 2f out: sn one pce* **28/1**

06 7 1 ¼ **Ridgeblade**[9] 6071 2-8-12 0 ow1 .... GaryBartley(3) 8 41
(Noel Wilson) *midfield: pushed along 1/2-way: rdn over 2f out: kpt on: nvr nr ldrs* **66/1**

6 8 1 ½ **Angel Grigio**[113] 2537 2-9-0 0 .... (v[1]) TomEaves 14 35
(Bryan Smart) *chsd ldrs: rdn along wl over 2f out: sn wknd* **10/1**

9 2 ¾ **Dewi Chinta (IRE)** 2-9-0 0 .... AmyRyan 10 27
(Kevin Ryan) *chsd ldrs: rdn along 1/2-way: sn wknd* **12/1**

10 1 **Branston Jubilee** 2-9-0 0 .... JoeFanning 5 24
(Geoffrey Harker) *midfield: rdn along 1/2-way: n.d* **25/1**

045 11 4 ½ **Annalova**[20] 5727 2-9-0 0 .... TonyHamilton 12 10
(Richard Fahey) *dwlt and hmpd s: a in rr* **40/1**

0 12 1 **Highway United (IRE)**[24] 5586 2-9-0 0 .... MichaelO'Connell 6 7
(John Weymes) *wnt lft s: midfield: rdn along and outpcd fr 1/2-way* **200/1**

00 13 1 ½ **Fat Bottom Girl**[15] 5887 2-9-0 0 .... JamesSullivan 1 3
(Michael Easterby) *a in rr* **100/1**

0 14 20 **Erica Starprincess**[8] 6099 2-9-0 0 .... AndrewMullen 13
(George Moore) *wnt lft s: a bhd* **200/1**

0 15 3 **Shesthecaptain (IRE)**[10] 6042 2-9-0 0 .... ChrisCatlin 3
(John Weymes) *a in rr: bhd fr 1/2-way* **100/1**

1m 12.63s (-0.07) **Going Correction** -0.075s/f (Good) **15 Ran SP% 112.6**
Speed ratings (Par 92): **97,95,94,93,90 84,82,80,76,75 69,68,66,39,35**
toteswingers 1&2 £18.00, 2&3 £6.40, 1&3 £26.80 CSF £105.84 TOTE £32.50: £6.10, £2.10, £2.30; EX 167.90.
Owner Middleham Park Racing XLVIII **Bred** Broughton Bloodstock **Trained** Nawton, N Yorks

FOCUS
A modest fillies' maiden in which those that raced up with the pace from the start dominated. Despite the easing ground and the blustery conditions, a winning time wasn't bad, suggesting the ground wasn't too testing on the sprint track. Surprise improvement from the winner, and the next two can do better.

NOTEBOOK
Silkelly had been well held in her first three starts, though she wasn't disgraced from the worst stall over C&D last time and had a low draw again here. However, she showed good speed to get across to the stands' rail in front and kept on pulling out a bit more when challenged. She may have improved for the easier ground, in which case she could find another opportunity in nurseries this autumn. (tchd 28-1)
Vicky Valentine showed good speed from the stands' rail draw and kept on all the way to the line. She was crossed by the winner inside the last furlong, but it made no difference to the result. A half-sister to the winning juvenile sprinter Ralphy Boy, this was a pleasing introduction and she should be able to go one better in a similar event. (op 11-2 tchd 6-1)
Meeting In Paris(IRE) had a low draw to contend with, like the winner, but she also showed enough speed to take a prominent early position and stuck on well. Out of a winning juvenile sprinter, the stable's newcomers usually come on a good deal from their debuts and she should be no exception. (tchd 6-1)
Burning Dawn(USA) had shown enough ability in her first two starts to suggest she could win a race like this and she held every chance, but she could only plug on for pressure. She now qualifies for a nursery mark and can do better in that sphere, but may appreciate another furlong. (op 15-8)
Maid A Million, a 30,000gns filly out of a half-sister to the Group 1 winner Rajeem, was being niggled along before halfway but she was by no means beaten up and pulled well clear of the rest. Improvement can be expected. (op 12-1)
Erica Starprincess Official explanation: trainer said filly finished with sore shins.

6336 THIRSK RACECOURSE PAVILION FOR WEDDING RECEPTIONS (S) STKS 5f
2:40 (2:41) (Class 5) 2-Y-O **£2,587** (£770; £384; £192) **Stalls** High

Form RPR

1325 1 **Coconut Kisses**[18] 5807 2-8-12 61 .... JoeFanning 1 67
(Bill Turner) *sn w ldrs: led over 2f out: edgd rt 1f out: pushed out* **9/2[2]**

0053 2 2 ¾ **Why So Fast (IRE)**[7] 6122 2-8-0 62 .... DavidBergin(7) 9 52
(David O'Meara) *sn outpcd in mid-div: hdwy over 2f out: styd on to take 2nd last 100yds: no imp* **5/2[1]**

4234 3 ¾ **Cracking Choice (IRE)**[10] 6049 2-8-12 66 .... (p) PaulMulrennan 6 54
(Michael Dods) *led: hdd over 2f out: hung lft over 1f out: kpt on same pce* **5/2[1]**

2346 4 4 **Throwing Roses**[22] 5675 2-8-7 59 .... JamesSullivan 7 35
(Ollie Pears) *swvd lft s: sn outpcd and in rr: sme hdwy over 1f out: nvr a factor* **9/1[3]**

005 5 2 **Lady Of Seville (IRE)**[36] 5168 2-8-9 53 ow2 .... GrahamGibbons 3 30
(Tom Tate) *edgd rt after s: chsd ldrs: wknd over 1f out* **22/1**

00 6 6 **Cazza**[38] 5108 2-8-7 0 .... (v[1]) AdrianNicholls 5 9
(David Nicholls) *s.s: hmpd after 1f: sme hdwy over 2f out: wknd over 1f out* **50/1**

4 7 15 **Dark Marvel (IRE)**[19] 5756 2-8-7 0 .... TomEaves 8
(Alan Berry) *sn wl outpcd and bhd: t.o 2f out* **100/1**

64 P **Myanne**[7] 6122 2-8-7 0 .... (p) PJMcDonald 4
(Ann Duffield) *chsd ldrs: wnt lft and p.u after 1f: fatally injured* **9/2[2]**

1m 0.01s (0.41) **Going Correction** -0.075s/f (Good) **8 Ran SP% 110.8**
Speed ratings (Par 95): **93,88,87,81,77 68,44,**
toteswingers 1&2 £3.00, 2&3 £2.00, 1&3 £2.70 CSF £15.09 TOTE £6.50: £1.50, £1.10, £1.60; EX 18.50.There was no bid for the winner.
Owner P Venner **Bred** P And Mrs Venner And Trickledown Stud **Trained** Sigwells, Somerset

FOCUS
One colt against seven fillies in this modest seller and not a race to dwell on, but the winner put in a decent performance for the grade.

NOTEBOOK
Coconut Kisses's latest effort at Wolverhampton could be ignored and she ran perfectly well in a C&D claimer before that, so she had plenty going for her. She was soon travelling well in a disputed lead and, once asked to go and win her race, the response was immediate. She had upwards of 6lb to find with a few on these terms, so it will be interesting to see how the handicapper reacts if connections wish to try her in a nursery. (op 4-1)
Why So Fast(IRE) was dropped in grade having finished third in a Redcar maiden seven days earlier on her debut for the yard when sporting a first-time hood. She plugged on to grab second late on, but never looked like winning and will need to find an even weaker seller. (op 11-4 tchd 10-3)
Cracking Choice(IRE), in the frame in five of his first six starts, was another dropped into a seller for the first time, but having matched strides with the winner for much of the way he was burned off inside the last furlong. He is now looking exposed as modest. (op 11-4 tchd 9-4)
Throwing Roses never got into it and has gradually lost her way after showing early ability. (op 13-2)

6337 THIRSKRACECOURSE.NET NURSERY 7f
3:10 (3:10) (Class 5) (0-75,74) 2-Y-O **£2,726** (£805; £402) **Stalls** High

Form RPR

305 1 **Greeleys Love (USA)**[25] 5562 2-9-5 72 .... PhillipMakin 1 78+
(Kevin Ryan) *in tch on inner: swtchd rt and hdwy wl over 2f out: chsng ldrs whn nt clr run over 1f out: sn swtchd lft and rdn: styd on strly to ld last 50yds* **11/2[3]**

2224 2 ¾ **Dr Phibes (IRE)**[9] 6070 2-9-7 74 .... RobertWinston 7 77
(Alan Swinbank) *in tch: hdwy 1/2-way: swtchd lft and rdn to chal 2f out: led jst over 1f out: rdn and edgd rt ins fnl f: hdd and no ex last 50yds* **7/2[1]**

0322 3 2 ¼ **Brazilian Clown (IRE)**[33] 5254 2-9-0 67 .... RichardKingscote 4 64
(Tom Dascombe) *cl up: led after 2f: pushed along and edgd rt 3f out: rdn and hung persistently rt wl over 1f out: hdd appr fnl f: kpt on same pce* **7/1**

046 4 1 ¼ **Attansky (IRE)**[23] 5619 2-8-6 64 .... DarylByrne(5) 13 59+
(Tim Easterby) *towards rr: swtchd to wd outside and hdwy 3f out: rdn along 2f out: styd on wl fnl f: nrst fin* **20/1**

3053 5 ½ **Panama Cat (USA)**[21] 5716 2-8-4 57 ow1 .... AmyRyan 10 50
(Kevin Ryan) *prom: cl up on outer 3f out: rdn 2f out and ev ch tl drvn and one pce appr fnl f* **14/1**

0505 6 1 ½ **Makinson Lane (IRE)**[32] 5292 2-9-4 71 .... TonyHamilton 12 60
(Richard Fahey) *chsd ldrs: hdwy on outer and cl up 1/2-way: rdn along over 2f out: grad wknd* **28/1**

2023 7 1 ¼ **Relight My Fire**[14] 5920 2-8-12 65 .... (p) DavidAllan 11 50
(Tim Easterby) *towards rr: hdwy on wd outside 3f out: chsd ldrs and rdn over 2f out: sn drvn and one pce* **10/1**

006 8 1 **Rocket Ronnie (IRE)**[90] 3271 2-8-5 58 .... AdrianNicholls 16 41+
(David Nicholls) *t.k.h and racd wd: in rr: hdwy over 2f out: swtchd lft and rdn wl over 1f out: n.d* **25/1**

0502 9 nk **Loki's Strike**[7] 6121 2-8-10 63 .... (b) SeanLevey 3 45
(Mrs K Burke) *dwlt and sn pushed along to stay in tch: hdwy and chsd ldrs 1/2-way: rdn along wl over 2f out and grad wknd* **4/1[2]**

0564 10 1 ¼ **Roland**[7] 6121 2-7-13 55 ow2 .... JulieBurke(3) 2 34
(Kevin Ryan) *led 2f: cl up on inner: pushed along 3f out: rdn over 2f out and grad wknd* **7/1**

500 11 1 ¼ **Uknowwhatushouldoo (IRE)**[15] 5887 2-9-2 69 .... (p) GrahamGibbons 5 45
(J S Moore) *cl up: ev ch over 2f out: sn rdn and wknd* **16/1**

006 12 3 ¼ **Precision Strike**[40] 5010 2-8-0 56 ow1 .... DeclanCannon(3) 9 23
(Richard Guest) *stmbld s and s.i.s: a in rr* **40/1**

050 13 2 **Noosa Sound**[32] 5311 2-8-13 66 .... PJMcDonald 6 28
(John Davies) *chsd ldrs: rdn along wl over 2f out: sn wknd* **40/1**

1m 28.79s (1.59) **Going Correction** +0.20s/f (Good) **13 Ran SP% 121.2**
Speed ratings (Par 95): **98,97,94,93,92 90,89,88,87,86 85,81,79**
toteswingers 1&2 £4.80, 2&3 £4.50, 1&3 £6.90 CSF £23.87 CT £143.44 TOTE £6.60: £1.90, £2.70, £2.00; EX 22.60.
Owner Crone Stud Farms Ltd **Bred** Brushwood Stable **Trained** Hambleton, N Yorks

FOCUS
A competitive nursery in which the runners stayed away from the inside rail after turning in. The winning time suggesting the ground on the round course was riding slower than the straight. The form makes sense and the winner has more to come.

NOTEBOOK
Greeleys Love(USA) ◆ was making his nursery debut after showing ability in three maidens over this trip. Held up early, he was under pressure passing the 2f pole, but responded well and can be considered to have won this with more in hand than the official margin, as he had to be switched left for his effort after the original gap he was aiming for closed. There should be plenty more to come from him. (op 6-1)
Dr Phibes(IRE), off the same mark as when fourth in a stronger nursery at York nine days earlier, was another being ridden along a fair way out. He managed to forge his way to the front entering the last furlong, but then started to hang away to his right and the winner nailed him around 50yds from the line. He has now finished runner-up four times from six starts and deserves to get his head in front. (tchd 4-1)
Brazilian Clown(IRE), runner-up in both previous tries in nurseries and up 2lb, made a bold bid to make every yard and wasn't beaten off until inside the last furlong. He has had more chances than a few, but is running consistently well just now. (op 8-1)
Attansky(IRE) ◆, making his nursery debut, had run his best race in three maidens over this C&D and was noted doing all his best work late down the wide outside. This was a good effort from his high draw and he probably still has some improvement left in him. (op 25-1)
Panama Cat(USA), a well-beaten third of nine on her nursery debut at Southwell, performed better here, racing wide of the leading group and holding every chance until entering the last. (op 16-1)
Makinson Lane(IRE), stepping up a furlong, ran creditably considering he covered plenty of ground around the wide outside, but didn't convince he saw out the longer trip in the ground. (op 25-1)

6338 JAMES HERRIOT HALL CONFERENCE & BANQUETING H'CAP 7f
3:40 (3:41) (Class 4) (0-85,84) 3-Y-O+ **£4,204** (£1,251; £625; £312) **Stalls** High

Form RPR

4301 1 **Fieldgunner Kirkup (GER)**[18] 5802 4-9-1 78 .... GrahamGibbons 10 88
(David Barron) *trckd ldr: led over 1f out: drvn out* **10/1**

5033 2 1 **Toto Skyllachy**[22] 5677 7-9-7 84 .... DanielTudhope 13 91
(David O'Meara) *chsd ldrs: styd on fnl 2f: tk 2nd towards fin* **13/2[2]**

0311 3 ¾ **Comrade Bond**[69] 3977 4-9-0 77 .... PaulMulrennan 5 82
(Mark H Tompkins) *sn trcking ldrs: styd on same pce fnl f* **9/1**

5000 4 1 ¼ **Polish World (USA)**[17] 5819 8-9-3 80 .... MickyFenton 15 82
(Paul Midgley) *racd wd 1st 2f: led: hdd over 1f out: kpt on same pce* **22/1**

2100 5 ½ **Mingun Bell (USA)**[32] 5301 5-9-4 81 .... PhillipMakin 6 82
(Ed de Giles) *chsd ldrs: kpt on same pce fnl 2f* **15/2[3]**

5420 6 nk **Green Park (IRE)**[3] 6234 9-8-9 79 .... (b) LukeLeadbitter(7) 4 79
(Declan Carroll) *s.i.s: hdwy on ins over 2f out: kpt on one pce fnl f* **18/1**

5030 7 nk **Mon Brav**[11] 6009 5-8-12 78 .... PaulPickard(3) 8 77+
(Brian Ellison) *chsd ldrs: hmpd and lost pl bnd over 4f out: kpt on fnl 2f* **9/1**

0000 8 ½ **Paramour**[17] 5819 5-8-10 80 .... DavidBergin(7) 12 78+
(David O'Meara) *in rr: kpt on fnl 2f: nvr a factor* **11/2[1]**

5425 9 hd **Defence Council (IRE)**[10] 6044 4-9-3 80 .... DavidAllan 7 77
(Mel Brittain) *chsd ldrs: hmpd and lost pl bnd over 4f out: hdwy over 2f out: wknd ins fnl f* **17/2**

2050 10 ¾ **Solar Spirit (IRE)**[31] 5368 7-8-13 81 .... ShaneBKelly(5) 3 76
(Tracy Waggott) *s.i.s: t.k.h: kpt on fnl 2f: nvr a factor* **10/1**

1343 11 1 **Conry (IRE)**[15] 5892 6-8-10 73 .... GrahamLee 1 65
(Ian Williams) *hld up towards rr: nvr a factor* **14/1**

3460 **12** *shd* **Mutafaakir (IRE)**[117] 2428 3-8-11 **77** JamesSullivan 16 69
(Ruth Carr) *s.i.s: a in rr* **33/1**

0002 **13** *2 1/2* **Orpsie Boy (IRE)**[10] 6040 9-9-0 **80** DaleSwift(3) 11 65
(Ruth Carr) *t.k.h: trckd ldrs: sltly hmpd and lost pl bnd over 4f out* **12/1**

4420 **14** *6* **Springheel Jake**[25] 5539 3-8-11 **77** PJMcDonald 9 46
(Ann Duffield) *chsd ldrs: lost pl 3f out* **16/1**

01- **15** *67* **Red Eyes**[179] 1024 4-8-13 **76** AdrianNicholls 14
(David Nicholls) *s.i.s: sn bhd: t.o 4f out: virtually p.u* **28/1**

1m 27.89s (0.69) **Going Correction** +0.20s/f (Good)
WFA 3 from 4yo+ 3lb **15** Ran SP% **125.4**
Speed ratings (Par 105): **104,102,102,100,100 99,99,98,98,97 96,96,93,86,10**
toteswingers 1&2 £10.40, 2&3 £4.40, 1&3 £6.90 CSF £74.70 CT £639.41 TOTE £13.00: £3.20, £3.10, £3.50; EX 70.60.

Owner Kevin Kirkup **Bred** I And D Meinke **Trained** Maunby, N Yorks

FOCUS
A competitive handicap run at a true pace and best rated around the winner and third. Again the runners came up the centre of the track.

Red Eyes Official explanation: jockey said gelding moved poorly throughout.

6339 THIRSK RACECOURSE CHRISTMAS PARTY NIGHTS £29.95 H'CAP (DIV I) 1m 4f

4:10 (4:10) (Class 4) (0-85,85) 3-Y-O+ **£4,204** (£1,251; £625; £312) **Stalls** Low

Form RPR

3530 **1** **Noble Alan (GER)**[52] 4613 9-9-12 **85** PaddyAspell 6 93
(Nicky Richards) *hld up in tch: hdwy over 3f out: trckd ldrs 2f out: rdn to ld ent fnl f: hld on wl towards fin* **5/1**[3]

2332 **2** *nk* **Suegioo (FR)**[33] 5273 3-9-1 **82** MircoDemuro 3 89
(Marco Botti) *hld up and bhd: hdwy on wd outside 3f out: rdn to chal over 1f out and ev ch whn drvn and edgd lft ins fnl f and no ex last 50yds* **6/4**[1]

0120 **3** *1 1/4* **Queen's Estate (GER)**[47] 4735 3-8-9 **76** JoeFanning 10 81
(Mark Johnston) *trckd ldrs: hdwy to chse clr ldr 3f out: cl up 2f out: led 1 1/2f out and sn rdn: hdd and drvn ent fnl f: kpt on same pce* **7/2**[2]

120 **4** *nk* **Watts Up Son**[21] 5712 4-8-13 **77** (bt) NeilFarley(5) 5 82
(Declan Carroll) *led and sn clr: rdn along wl over 2f out: drvn and hdd 1 1/2f out: kpt on u.p fnl f* **25/1**

5425 **5** *3/4* **Kathleen Frances**[27] 5474 5-9-4 **77** (b[1]) PhillipMakin 8 82
(Mark H Tompkins) *hld up in rr: hdwy over 3f out: swtchd rt and effrt to chse ldrs 2f out: rdn and ev ch whn n.m.r and hmpd ent fnl f: one pce after* **7/1**

4530 **6** *1 1/2* **Tartan Gigha (IRE)**[12] 5966 7-9-8 **81** DanielTudhope 4 82
(Geoffrey Harker) *trckd ldrs: hdwy 3f out: effrt 2f out: sn rdn to chal and ev ch whn n.m.r and hmpd jst ins fnl f: one pce after* **16/1**

/3-0 **7** *12* **Maneki Neko (IRE)**[32] 5290 10-8-12 **71** oh2 TonyHamilton 2 53
(Edwin Tuer) *chsd ldrs: rdn along 3f out: sn wknd* **33/1**

310 **8** *3/4* **Xclaim**[48] 4714 4-8-12 **71** oh1 PJMcDonald 7 52
(Micky Hammond) *hld up: a towards rr* **22/1**

6305 **9** *1* **Tricksofthetrade (IRE)**[62] 4209 6-8-13 **72** RobertWinston 9 51
(Alan Swinbank) *a towards rr* **25/1**

1-00 **10** *12* **Full Speed (GER)**[10] 6045 7-9-0 **73** MichaelO'Connell 1 33
(Philip Kirby) *chsd clr ldr: rdn along over 3f out and sn wknd* **50/1**

2m 37.01s (0.81) **Going Correction** +0.20s/f (Good)
WFA 3 from 4yo+ 8lb **10** Ran SP% **114.2**
Speed ratings (Par 105): **105,104,103,103,103 102,94,93,93,85**
toteswingers 1&2 £3.50, 2&3 £1.90, 1&3 £3.70 CSF £11.86 CT £29.05 TOTE £7.30: £1.90, £1.30, £1.30; EX 20.00.

Owner Craig Bennett **Bred** Gestut Kussaburg **Trained** Greystoke, Cumbria

■ Stewards' Enquiry : Mirco Demuro seven-day ban: excessive use (Oct 2-6, 8-9)

FOCUS
A good middle-distance handicap, but although the pace was strong thanks to the fourth horse there were six in a line a furlong from home. The form looks pretty sound rated around the placed horses and the fifth.

Tricksofthetrade(IRE) Official explanation: jockey said gelding moved poorly around final bend and straight.

6340 THIRSK RACECOURSE CHRISTMAS PARTY NIGHTS £29.95 H'CAP (DIV II) 1m 4f

4:40 (4:40) (Class 4) (0-85,84) 3-Y-O+ **£4,204** (£1,251; £625; £312) **Stalls** Low

Form RPR

002 **1** **Stormy Weather (FR)**[25] 5546 6-9-9 **84** (b) DaleSwift(3) 5 92+
(Brian Ellison) *hld up and bhd: hdwy on outer 3f out: rdn to chse ldrs wl over 1f out: drvn to chal over 1f out: styd on wl to ld nr line* **6/1**

41 **2** *hd* **White Nile (IRE)**[32] 5315 3-8-12 **78** RobertWinston 10 86+
(David Simcock) *hld up in rr: hdwy 4f out: chsd ldrs 3f out: rdn to chal wl over 1f out: styd on to ld ins fnl f: sn drvn and hdd on line* **11/8**[1]

5322 **3** *1 1/2* **Granston (IRE)**[10] 6045 11-9-2 **74** GrahamLee 1 80
(James Bethell) *hld up in tch: hdwy over 4f out: chsd ldr 3f out: rdn to ld wl over 1f out: drvn and hdd ins fnl f: kpt on same pce* **10/1**

1542 **4** *1* **Bold Cuffs**[25] 5528 3-8-7 **73** ChrisCatlin 6 77+
(Sir Mark Prescott Bt) *rdn along sn after s to chse ldr: led 7f out: clr 4f out: rdn wl over 2f out: hdd wl over 1f out: drvn and one pce fnl f* **11/2**[3]

30/6 **5** *1* **Crystal Rock (IRE)**[10] 6045 7-9-1 **73** BarryMcHugh 2 75
(Tony Coyle) *chsd ldrs: rdn along wl over 2f out: drvn over 1f out: sn one pce* **14/1**

4313 **6** *nk* **Key Gold**[30] 5383 3-8-10 **76** JoeFanning 3 78
(Mark Johnston) *chsd ldng pair: rdn along and n.m.r on inner over 2f out: drvn and one pce fr over 1f out* **9/2**[2]

4/0- **7** *26* **Tamanaco (IRE)**[325] 5686 5-9-3 **75** GrahamGibbons 8 35
(Tim Walford) *chsd ldrs: rdn along 5f out: sn wknd and bhd fnl 3f* **33/1**

2000 **8** *18* **King Kurt (IRE)**[9] 6076 4-9-5 **77** (b[1]) AmyRyan 9
(Kevin Ryan) *led 5f: chsd ldr tl rdn along and wknd over 3f out: sn bhd* **18/1**

2m 37.06s (0.86) **Going Correction** +0.20s/f (Good)
WFA 3 from 4yo+ 8lb **8** Ran SP% **113.9**
Speed ratings (Par 105): **105,104,103,103,102 102,85,73**
toteswingers 1&2 £3.60, 2&3 £3.20, 1&3 £3.50 CSF £14.56 CT £80.75 TOTE £7.90: £2.50, £2.20, £1.60; EX 19.00.

Owner Keith Hanson & Steve Catchpole **Bred** Ecurie Skymarc Farm **Trained** Norton, N Yorks

FOCUS
The early pace again looked strong with a couple going off hard in front and the winning time was just 0.05 seconds slower than the first division. The third helps set the standard, backed up by the fourth and fifth.

6341 THIRSK RACECOURSE CONFERENCE CENTRE MAIDEN STKS 1m

5:10 (5:15) (Class 5) 3-Y-O+ **£2,587** (£770; £384; £192) **Stalls** Low

Form RPR

2-45 **1** **Self Employed**[38] 5090 5-9-7 75 MickyFenton 6 65
(Garry Woodward) *s.i.s: t.k.h: hdwy over 4f out: wnt 3rd 1f out: kpt on to ld nr fin* **2/1**[2]

2 *1/2* **Volcanic Wind (USA)** 3-9-3 0 FrederikTylicki 1 64
(Saeed Bin Suroor) *chsd ldr: drvn over 3f out: led jst ins fnl f: hdd and no ex towards fin* **1/1**[1]

65 **3** *hd* **Keep It Dark**[14] 5919 3-9-3 0 DarryMcHugh 3 63
(Tony Coyle) *led: hdd jst ins fnl f: styd on same pce in clsng stages* **20/1**

05- **4** *3/4* **Kuwait Star**[292] 7590 3-9-3 0 PaddyAspell 8 62
(Jason Ward) *restless in stalls: hld up towards rr: hdwy over 4f out: chsng ldrs over 3f out: 4th 1f out: kpt on same pce* **50/1**

0 **5** *6* **Royal Sea (IRE)**[8] 6102 3-9-3 0 DanielTudhope 2 48
(David O'Meara) *sn chsng ldrs: drvn over 3f out: wknd appr fnl f* **8/1**[3]

36 **6** *10* **Spanish Legacy**[8] 6102 3-8-12 0 GrahamLee 7 20
(Julie Camacho) *in rr: sme hdwy over 2f out: nvr on terms* **8/1**[3]

0 **7** *hd* **Urbonite (IRE)**[53] 4551 3-8-12 0 GarryWhillans(5) 10 24
(Alan Swinbank) *chsd ldrs: outpcd 4f out: sn lost pl* **66/1**

0500 **8** *nk* **Skiddaw View**[14] 5919 4-9-2 39 (t) PaulMulrennan 12 19
(Maurice Barnes) *in tch: drvn over 3f out: lost pl over 2f out* **200/1**

9 *3 1/2* **Bondi Beach Boy** 3-8-10 0 JordanNason(7) 9 16
(James Turner) *dwlt: a in rr: bhd fnl 3f* **40/1**

10 *5* **Dylan George** 3-9-3 0 PJMcDonald 5
(George Moore) *s.i.s: sn drvn along in rr: bhd fnl 3f* **20/1**

0 **11** *26* **Brenkley Melani**[32] 5316 4-9-2 0 TomEaves 4
(Tim Fitzgerald) *in rr: bhd over 4f out: t.o over 3f out* **100/1**

00 **12** *13* **Stars Legacy**[46] 4780 3-8-12 0 AndrewMullen 13
(George Moore) *in rr: bhd over 4f out: t.o over 3f out: virtually p.u* **100/1**

1m 44.12s (4.02) **Going Correction** +0.20s/f (Good)
WFA 3 from 4yo+ 4lb **12** Ran SP% **123.4**
Speed ratings (Par 103): **87,86,86,85,79 69,69,69,65,60 34,21**
toteswingers 1&2 £1.80, 2&3 £7.50, 1&3 £8.40 CSF £4.31 TOTE £3.00: £1.10, £1.20, £3.80; EX 5.80.

Owner Garry Woodward **Bred** R G Percival And Mrs A Lockhart **Trained** Bolham, Notts

FOCUS
Plenty of dead wood in this maiden and, with little covering the front four at the line, the form looks very limited and rather shaky. It took a very long time for the whole field to be installed.

6342 NEXT MEETING - SATURDAY 20TH APRIL 2013 H'CAP 1m

5:40 (5:42) (Class 5) (0-75,75) 3-Y-O+ **£3,234** (£962; £481; £240) **Stalls** Low

Form RPR

0212 **1** **Multi Bene**[26] 5501 3-9-4 **73** GrahamGibbons 1 83
(Ed McMahon) *trckd ldrs: hdwy 3f out: rdn to chse ldr wl over 1f out: styd on wl ins fnl f to ld nr line* **5/1**[3]

4544 **2** *hd* **Robert The Painter (IRE)**[9] 6073 4-9-6 **71** (v[1]) DanielTudhope 6 81
(David O'Meara) *cl up: led 1/2-way: pushed clr over 2f out: rdn over 1f out: drvn ins fnl f: hdd and no ex nr line* **7/2**[2]

0001 **3** *2* **Dolphin Rock**[10] 6047 5-9-5 **73** DaleSwift(3) 3 78
(Brian Ellison) *in tch on inner: hdwy over 3f out: rdn to chse ldrs over 2f out: kpt on fnl f* **10/3**[1]

0543 **4** *2 3/4* **Desert Creek (IRE)**[7] 6127 6-9-1 **66** AdrianNicholls 10 65+
(David Nicholls) *in rr: swtchd outside and hdwy 2f out: sn rdn and styd on wl fnl f: nrst fin* **11/2**

4000 **5** *nk* **Just The Tonic**[7] 6127 5-8-13 **67** PaulPickard(3) 18 65
(Marjorie Fife) *prom: rdn along to chse ldr 3f out: drvn wl over 1f out and kpt on same pce* **40/1**

6201 **6** *3* **Moheebb (IRE)**[22] 5669 8-9-4 **69** (v) RobertWinston 2 60
(Robert Johnson) *dwlt and in rr: hdwy over 3f out: rdn along wl over 2f out: kpt on: n.d* **16/1**

3560 **7** *3* **Horatio Carter**[21] 5713 7-8-12 **70** DavidBergin(7) 7 55
(David O'Meara) *dwlt: a towards rr* **16/1**

4414 **8** *3 3/4* **Shadowtime**[17] 5819 7-9-6 **71** BarryMcHugh 12 47
(Tracy Waggott) *towards rr: effrt and sme hdwy 3f out: rdn over 2f out and n.d* **16/1**

3110 **9** *3/4* **Toymaker**[115] 2491 5-9-10 **75** GrahamLee 5 49
(James Given) *a towards rr* **11/1**

0630 **10** *1/2* **Switchback**[45] 4805 4-9-5 **70** PaulMulrennan 8 43
(Michael Easterby) *chsd ldrs: rdn along over 3f out: sn wknd* **25/1**

1321 **11** *hd* **Availed Speaker (IRE)**[179] 1013 3-8-8 **70** EireannCagney(7) 14 43
(Richard Fahey) *a in rr* **16/1**

1-50 **12** *12* **Ykikamoocow**[92] 3215 6-9-4 **69** JoeFanning 11 14
(Geoffrey Harker) *chsd ldrs: rdn along 3f out: sn wknd* **25/1**

0200 **13** *12* **Cono Zur (FR)**[10] 6047 5-9-7 **72** (b) JamesSullivan 4
(Ruth Carr) *led: rdn along and hdd 1/2-way: wknd 3f out* **33/1**

1m 41.53s (1.43) **Going Correction** +0.20s/f (Good)
WFA 3 from 4yo+ 4lb **13** Ran SP% **122.3**
Speed ratings (Par 103): **100,99,97,95,94 91,88,85,84,83 83,71,59**
toteswingers 1&2 £5.40, 2&3 £3.80, 1&3 £5.80 CSF £22.50 CT £68.90 TOTE £7.50: £2.10, £2.60, £2.20; EX 32.20.

Owner Mrs Richards & Mrs Brazier **Bred** Mickley Stud **Trained** Lichfield, Staffs

FOCUS
Just a fair handicap, but they went a good pace and nothing got into it from off the pace. The winning time was 2.59 seconds quicker than the maiden and the form is rated at face value.
T/Jkpt: Not won. T/Plt: £33.30 to a £1 stake. Pool of £66783.32 - 1463.52 winning tickets. T/Qpdt: £5.40 to a £1 stake. Pool of £5098.06, 686.28 winning tickets. JR

[5631]YARMOUTH (L-H)

Tuesday, September 18

OFFICIAL GOING: Good to firm (7.0)

Wind: medium across Weather: dry

6343 BRITISH STALLION STUDS SUPPORTING BRITISH RACING E B F MAIDEN FILLIES' STKS — 6f 3y

2:30 (2:31) (Class 5) 2-Y-0 — **£3,234** (£962; £481; £240) **Stalls** Centre

Form — RPR

4520 **1** — **Supernova Heights (IRE)**[12] 5979 2-9-0 80 .... MartinLane 4 — 83+
(Brian Meehan) *lw: chsd ldr tl rdn to ld over 1f out: clr and in command fnl f: r.o wl: comf* — **5/2**[1]

32 **2** *3 ¾* **Sky Garden**[11] 6007 2-9-0 0 .... AdamBeschizza 5 — 72
(William Haggas) *lw: led: rdn and hdd over 1f out: no ex and btn whn edgd lft ins fnl f: plugged on same pce* — **5/2**[1]

3 *2 ¼* **Yahilwa (USA)** 2-9-0 0 .... TomQueally 11 — 68+
(James Tate) *leggy: stdd s: t.k.h: hld up in midfield: switching lft 2f out: hdwy and rn green ent fnl f: styd on to go 3rd fnl 75yds: nvr threatened ldrs* — **28/1**

4 *¾* **Ilsa Lund (IRE)** 2-9-0 0 .... LukeMorris 8 — 63
(Peter Chapple-Hyam) *w'like: hld up in midfield: rdn and outpcd by ldng pair wl over 1f out: rallied ent fnl f: kpt on steadily ins fnl f: nvr gng pce to threaten ldrs* — **12/1**

5 *nk* **Primadonna Girl (IRE)** 2-9-0 0 .... RichardMullen 10 — 62
(Sir Michael Stoute) *w'like: str: bit bkwd: stdd s: t.k.h: hld up in midfield: rdn and unable qck ent fnl f: no threat to ldrs but rallied and kpt on steadily ins fnl f* — **10/1**

6 *nk* **Hekaayaat (USA)** 2-9-0 0 .... PaulHanagan 12 — 61
(Roger Varian) *w'like: str: bit bkwd: in tch in midfield: rdn and unable qck wl over 1f out: no threat to ldrs but plugged on again ins fnl f* — **9/2**[2]

00 **7** *1 ¼* **Sunny Hollow**[13] 5943 2-9-0 0 .... MartinHarley 2 — 57
(James Toller) *t.k.h: hld up in tch in midfield: rdn and unable qck wl over 1f out: plugged on same pce and wl hld fnl f* — **50/1**

8 *1* **Bright Glow** 2-9-0 0 .... TedDurcan 1 — 57+
(David Lanigan) *w'like: str: bit bkwd: stdd s: hld up in rr: pushed along and no imp 2f out: sme modest prog ins fnl f: n.d* — **9/1**[3]

00 **9** *hd* **El Mirage (IRE)**[32] 5304 2-9-0 0 .... ShaneKelly 6 — 54
(Dean Ivory) *plld hrd: chsd ldrs: 3rd and outpcd over 1f out: sn btn: wknd ins fnl f* — **33/1**

10 *1 ¾* **Oh So Sassy** 2-9-0 0 .... HarryBentley 3 — 49
(Chris Wall) *w'like: bit bkwd: in tch towards rr: rdn along and rn green wl over 1f out: wknd over 1f out* — **40/1**

11 *7* **Lexi's Beauty (IRE)** 2-9-0 0 .... TomMcLaughlin 7 — 28
(Ed Dunlop) *w'like: bit bkwd: a towards rr: rdn and no imp 2f out: wknd over 1f out* — **66/1**

12 *2 ¾* **Interception (IRE)** 2-9-0 0 .... DaneO'Neill 13 — 19+
(David Lanigan) *w'like: bit bkwd: stdd s: hld up in rr: lost tch over 1f out* — **28/1**

0 **13** *8* **Eliza Snow (IRE)**[19] 5765 2-9-0 0 .... J-PGuillambert 9
(Amy Weaver) *leggy: t.k.h: chsd ldrs tl 1/2-way: sn struggling: bhd and eased ins fnl f: sddle slipped* — **200/1**

1m 13.88s (-0.52) **Going Correction** -0.075s/f (Good) — **13** Ran SP% **118.3**

Speed ratings (Par 92): **100,95,92,91,90 90,88,87,86,84 75,71,60**

toteswingers 1&2 £2.50, 2&3 £11.90, 1&3 £15.80 CSF £7.63 TOTE £3.20: £1.20, £1.90, £7.10; EX 10.00 Trifecta £139.70 Pool: £783.46 - 4.15 winning units..

Owner Ballymacoll Stud **Bred** Ballymacoll Stud Farm Ltd **Trained** Manton, Wilts

FOCUS

Some interesting types lined up for this juvenile fillies' maiden. The form pair dominated and there were several of interest in behind.

NOTEBOOK

Supernova Heights(IRE) stamped her authority on the race from some way out. Closely related to a clutch of decent winners, she was the most experienced filly on show and clearly appreciated this return to maiden company, having been outclassed in a Listed race last time. Unable to get near the lead at Sandown, she was able to share the early workload with her chief market rival and that pair dominated throughout. She strode out impressively once asked for her effort and was value for a deal more than the official margin of success. It's hard to know what the handicapper will do with her after this, but she ought to be competitive in nurseries if left on her current mark of 80. A step back up to 7f could bring about further improvement. (op 3-1)

Sky Garden ran a solid race but was readily outpointed inside the final 2f. She had been collared close home over this trip previously and may benefit for a more conservative ride. A mark in mid-to-high 70s can be expected and it's likely connections will waste no time in pursuing the nursery route. (op 9-4 tchd 11-4)

Yahilwa(USA) ◆ finished strongly on the far side. Running green throughout, she picked up eyecatchingly without being knocked around and should be much more competitive next time. (op 33-1)

Ilsa Lund(IRE) looks to have ability. (op 9-1)

Hekaayaat(USA) was by no means the quickest away, but was staying on pleasingly under only hands-and-heels riding. A step up in trip should pay dividends. (op 5-1 tchd 4-1)

Interception(IRE) was awkwardly away and looked in need of this experience. She was by no means disgraced but could be more of a longer term project. (op 25-1)

6344 RACHAEL KEATLEY MEMORIAL NURSERY (FOR THE JACK LEADER CHALLENGE TROPHY) — 1m 3y

3:00 (3:01) (Class 4) (0-85,81) 2-Y-O — **£3,428** (£1,020; £509; £254) **Stalls** Centre

Form — RPR

600 **1** — **Open Letter (IRE)**[47] 4739 2-8-2 62 .... NickyMackay 2 — 63+
(Mark Johnston) *lw: chsd ldrs: rdn 2f out: ev ch fnl f: led fnl 75yds: styd on wl: rdn out* — **12/1**

032 **2** *½* **Astrosapphire**[25] 5534 2-8-12 72 .... TedDurcan 4 — 72
(Mark H Tompkins) *lw: led: rdn 2f out: hdd 1f out but stl ev ch: 3rd and one pce wl ins fnl f: wnt 2nd last stride* — **11/1**

210 **3** *shd* **A Certain Romance**[46] 4763 2-9-7 81 .... FrankieDettori 1 — 81
(Peter Chapple-Hyam) *stdd s: hld up in tch: rdn and hdwy 2f out: ev ch and edgd rt 1f out: edgd lft and no ex cl to home: lost 2nd last stride* **10/1**

61 **4** *½* **Claim (IRE)**[34] 5221 2-9-3 77 .... RichardMullen 6 — 76
(Sir Michael Stoute) *t.k.h: w ldr: rdn 2f out: drvn to ld 1f out: edgd lft u.p and hdd fnl 75yds: no ex and lost 3 pls after* — **15/8**[1]

3315 **5** *2* **Medicoe**[24] 5602 2-9-6 80 .... LukeMorris 3 — 75
(Sir Mark Prescott Bt) *lw: trckd ldrs: rdn and effrt over 2f out: stl pressing ldrs but struggling to qckn whn short of room and hmpd 1f out: styd on same pce and hld after* — **9/4**[2]

444 **6** *1 ¾* **Bartack (IRE)**[16] 5851 2-8-13 73 .... J-PGuillambert 7 — 63
(Luca Cumani) *in tch: rdn over 2f out: unable qck and styd on same pce fr over 1f out* — **11/2**[3]

565 **7** *hd* **Jathabah (IRE)**[53] 4525 2-8-10 70 .... MartinLane 5 — 60
(Clive Brittain) *hld up in tch: rdn and unable qck ent fnl 2f: styd on same pce fr over 1f out* — **25/1**

1m 40.81s (0.21) **Going Correction** -0.075s/f (Good) — **7** Ran SP% **109.9**

Speed ratings (Par 97): **95,94,94,93,91 90,89**

toteswingers 1&2 £19.20, 2&3 £6.10, 1&3 £8.80 CSF £119.18 TOTE £20.50: £6.90, £3.40; EX 113.30.

Owner Sheikh Hamdan Bin Mohammed Al Maktoum **Bred** Rabbah Bloodstock Limited **Trained** Middleham Moor, N Yorks

FOCUS

A tactically run affair and a bunch finish, so the form can't be rated positively. The winner can improve on the bare form.

NOTEBOOK

Open Letter(IRE) got off the mark on her nursery debut. She had failed to go on from an encouraging debut run when finishing down the field in maidens at Doncaster and Goodwood, but it was a very different story here as she took full advantage of her feather weight. She has a long way to go to repay her 100,000gns price tag, but she clearly has ability and is unlikely to be too heavily penalised given the narrow margin of victory. She, like so many of Mark Johnston's runners, showed bravery in spades as she was the meat in the sandwich for much of the final furlong. It's possible that she would have won even more easily had the race been run at a stronger pace, as she clearly saw the trip out well. Official explanation: trainer said regarding apparent improvement in form that filly was better suited running in a handicap for the first time and appreciated the step up to 1m. (op 14-1 tchd 11-1)

Astrosapphire enjoyed the run of the race out in front but did well to finish second having been swamped with 1f remaining. She has done well since making an inauspicious debut at Newmarket and should be able to find a small race. (op 9-1 tchd 17-2)

A Certain Romance, a winner over 6f earlier in the season, was lugging into the winner under pressure and may have found this trip stretching her stamina. Softer ground may also help. (op 15-2)

Claim(IRE), who was bidding to follow-up her Beverley maiden win, was much too free through the early stages and ran out of petrol as a result. She doesn't looked badly treated but will need to settle better. (op 2-1)

6345 THOMAS PRIOR MEMORIAL MAIDEN STKS — 6f 3y

3:30 (3:31) (Class 5) 3-Y-0+ — **£2,264** (£673; £336; £168) **Stalls** Centre

Form — RPR

6 **1** — **Pink Lips**[22] 5687 4-9-0 0 .... DarryllHolland 3 — 53
(J R Jenkins) *lw: dwlt: in tch: rdn along over 3f out: 4th and looked wl hld over 1f out: reminders and hdwy ins fnl f: str run to ld cl home* — **7/1**[3]

0064 **2** *nk* **Enthrall (IRE)**[13] 5949 3-8-12 47 ....(be) LukeMorris 4 — 52
(Phil McEntee) *led: rdn 2f out: hrd drvn over 1f out: kpt on u.p tl hdd and no ex cl home* — **14/1**

6 **3** *1* **Game All (IRE)**[140] 1736 3-8-12 0 .... TomQueally 5 — 49
(Hugo Palmer) *angular: lw: stdd s: hld up in tch: effrt u.p to chse ldr over 1f out: pressed ldr and drvn ins fnl f: styd on same pce and btn fnl 75yds* — **5/6**[1]

0-3 **4** *4 ½* **Atmanna**[119] 2361 3-8-12 0 .... TedDurcan 2 — 34
(Clive Brittain) *lw: chsd ldr: rdn and unable qck 2f out: lost 2nd and btn over 1f out: wknd fnl f* — **2/1**[2]

0-00 **5** *21* **Jamaica Grande**[20] 5734 4-9-5 41 .... LiamJones 6
(Terry Clement) *sn rdn along and nvr gng wl: in tch tl over 2f out: sn bhd* — **80/1**

1m 13.76s (-0.64) **Going Correction** -0.075s/f (Good)

WFA 3 from 4yo 2lb — **5** Ran SP% **108.3**

Speed ratings (Par 103): **101,100,99,93,65**

CSF £74.22 TOTE £6.00: £2.90, £5.20; EX 37.10.

Owner Mr & Mrs J Sales **Bred** Southill Stud **Trained** Royston, Herts

FOCUS

A weak maiden and the form looks very weak and hard to be positive about.

6346 AT THE RACES CONDITIONS STKS — 6f 3y

4:00 (4:02) (Class 3) 3-Y-0+ — **£6,490** (£1,942; £971; £486; £242) **Stalls** Centre

Form — RPR

4350 **1** — **Lui Rei (ITY)**[24] 5581 6-8-4 102 .... MichaelJMMurphy(5) 4 — 99
(Robert Cowell) *t.k.h: pressed ldr: rdn to ld over 1f out: in command and pushed out fnl 100yds* — **10/3**[3]

2013 **2** *½* **Artistic Jewel (IRE)**[30] 5385 3-8-12 100 .... RichardMullen 2 — 102
(Ed McMahon) *led and set stdy gallop: rdn 2f out: hdd over 1f out and edgd lft u.p 1f out: kpt on but a hld fnl 100yds* — **6/4**[1]

0630 **3** *1 ¼* **Sirius Prospect (USA)**[10] 6024 4-8-9 106 ....(b) ShaneKelly 3 — 93
(Dean Ivory) *lw: rrd as stalls opened and s.i.s: sn rcvrd and hld up in tch: rdn and effrt over 1f out: hdwy u.p to chse ldrs wl ins fnl f: no imp and eased cl home* — **15/8**[2]

000 **4** *¾* **Piazza San Pietro**[45] 4799 6-8-9 89 .... LukeMorris 5 — 91
(Zoe Davison) *t.k.h: w ldrs: swtchd rt to r towards stands' rail after 1f: ev ch and edgd lft u.p wl over 1f out: no ex and btn ins fnl f* — **16/1**

0 **5** *3* **Caratteraccio (IRE)**[100] 2967 4-8-12 97 .... TobyAtkinson(5) 1 — 89
(Marco Botti) *t.k.h: chsd ldrs: rdn 2f out: unable qck and btn 1f out: wknd ins fnl f* — **25/1**

1m 14.8s (0.40) **Going Correction** -0.075s/f (Good)

WFA 3 from 4yo+ 2lb — **5** Ran SP% **107.6**

Speed ratings (Par 107): **94,93,91,90,86**

CSF £8.37 TOTE £3.70: £2.80, £1.10; EX 8.80.

Owner Rei Of Sunshine Partnership **Bred** Az Ag Antezzate Srl **Trained** Six Mile Bottom, Cambs

FOCUS

A disappointing turn out for this conditions event and it led to a tactical affair which played into the hands of the winner. The form looks muddling and shaky.

NOTEBOOK

Lui Rei(ITY) continued the good run of form of Robert Cowell's sprinters. The 6-y-o had missed the break when running a rare poor race in Listed company last time and, although not the quickest away on this occasion, was soon ideally positioned to strike in a slowly run race. He was a winner over the minimum trip at Goodwood earlier in the year and he put that speed to good use in the final 2f. It's debatable as to what he actually achieved here, but he's clearly holding his form well and should remain competitive for the remainder of the campaign. (op 11-4)

Artistic Jewel(IRE) ran well but lacked the gears of the winner. She had a bit on her plate on these terms and would have appreciated a stiffer test. She was forced into making her own running and should be seen in a better light when returning to more patient tactics. (op 7-4 tchd 15-8 and 11-8)

Sirius Prospect(USA) ran a little better than the bare result suggests. Having reared and fly jumped on leaving the stalls, he was soon back on terms thanks to the pedestrian early pace and travelled well before failing to pick up under pressure. He looks some way removed from the progressive gelding we saw at around this time last year. (op 2-1)

Piazza San Pietro ran as well as could have been expected. (op 22-1 tchd 25-1)

Caratteraccio(IRE), making his British debut, was readily left behind and has something to prove off his current mark. (op 12-1 tchd 11-1)

6347 NICHOLSONS OF STALHAM JCB DEALERS H'CAP 5f 43y

4:30 (4:30) (Class 4) (0-85,83) 3-Y-0+ **£4,075** (£1,212; £606; £303) **Stalls** Centre

Form RPR

0650 **1** **Perfect Blossom**[6] 6144 5-9-2 **78**.................................. PaulHanagan 4 92+
(Ian McInnes) *lw: hld up wl in tch: swtchd rt and hdwy over 1f out: pushed along and qcknd to ld fnl 100yds: sn in command and pricking ears: pushed out: readily* **11/2**

0402 **2** *1 ½* **Bubbly Ballerina**[3] 6234 3-8-9 **77**............................ NatashaEaton(5) 7 84
(Alan Bailey) *lw: chsd ldrs: rdn to chse ldr wl over 1f out: led ent fnl f: hdd and outpcd by wnr fnl 100yds: kpt on* **5/2**[1]

0002 **3** *1 ¼* **Another Wise Kid (IRE)**[11] 6005 4-9-7 **83**.......................... TedDurcan 6 85
(Paul Midgley) *dwlt: in tch in rr: rdn and effrt over 1f out: styd on u.p to go 3rd wl ins fnl f: no threat w wnr* **4/1**[3]

0450 **4** *1* **Expose**[10] 6044 4-9-0 **76**...(b) LiamJones 2 74
(William Haggas) *stdd s: hld up in tch in last pair: rdn and effrt over 1f out: styd on same pce ins fnl f* **11/1**

0506 **5** *nk* **Indian Tinker**[24] 5584 3-8-5 **73**............................ MichaelJMMurphy(5) 1 70
(Robert Cowell) *in tch: rdn and effrt to chse ldrs wl over 1f out: unable qck ent fnl f: btn and kpt on same pce fnl 150yds* **9/1**

0000 **6** *½* **The Thrill Is Gone**[10] 6026 4-9-5 **81**................................ MartinHarley 5 77
(Mick Channon) *lw: led: rdn wl over 1f out: hdd ent fnl f: no ex and wknd fnl 100yds* **7/2**[2]

0600 **7** *11* **Bertoliver**[3] 6234 8-8-9 **71**...(p) LukeMorris 3 27
(Stuart Williams) *sn pushed along: chsd ldr tl wl over 1f out: wknd ent fnl f: bhd and eased wl ins fnl f* **16/1**

1m 1.66s (-1.04) **Going Correction** -0.075s/f (Good)
WFA 3 from 4yo+ 1lb **7** Ran SP% **110.4**
Speed ratings (Par 105): **105,102,100,99,98 97,80**
toteswingers 1&2 £3.70, 2&3 £2.20, 1&3 £3.20 CSF £18.26 TOTE £9.00: £4.10, £1.70; EX 23.90.
Owner Mrs Ann Morris **Bred** Mrs A Morris **Trained** Catwick, E Yorks

FOCUS
A decent, if small-field handicap, run at a strong pace and sound form rated around the placed horses.

6348 GREENE KING IPA H'CAP 1m 3f 101y

5:00 (5:07) (Class 2) (0-100,92) 3-Y-0**£9,955** (£2,979; £1,489; £745; £371) **Stalls** Low

Form RPR

0624 **1** **Daghash**[17] 5820 3-8-5 **76**.. MartinLane 3 83
(Clive Brittain) *chsd ldrs: rdn and effrt 3f out: led ent fnl 2f: sustained duel w runner-up after: kpt on wl u.p and a jst holding rival* **14/1**

1100 **2** *½* **Stature (IRE)**[10] 6025 3-9-0 **92**.............................. ThomasBrown(7) 8 98
(Andrew Balding) *lw: taken down early: t.k.h: chsd ldr: rdn to ld 3f out: hdd ent fnl 2f: sustained duel w wnr after: kpt on wl but a jst hld* **16/1**

2104 **3** *2 ¼* **Willie Wag Tail (USA)**[25] 5558 3-9-6 **91**........................ GeorgeBaker 2 93
(Ed Walker) *hld up in last pair: rdn and effrt over 2f out: no imp tl drvn and styd on to chse ldng pair 1f out: kpt on u.p but nvr gng pce to chal: eased nr fin* **10/11**[1]

0210 **4** *4 ½* **Expert Fighter (USA)**[25] 5558 3-9-5 **90**........................ FrankieDettori 4 85
(Saeed Bin Suroor) *lw: stdd s: hld up in rr: hdwy and in tch 4f out: rdn to chse ldrs over 2f out: btn ent fnl f: wknd* **6/1**[3]

2304 **5** *¾* **Assizes**[11] 6018 3-9-4 **89**.. LiamJones 5 82
(Mark Johnston) *led tl 3f out: drvn and unable qck ent fnl 2f: btn jst over 1f out: wknd fnl f* **7/1**

0162 **6** *10* **Maria's Choice (IRE)**[25] 5554 3-8-13 **84**.................... RichardMullen 1 60
(Sir Michael Stoute) *chsd ldrs tl lost pl u.p jst over 3f out: wknd 2f out: bhd fnl f* **9/2**[2]

2m 28.26s (-0.44) **Going Correction** +0.025s/f (Good) **6** Ran SP% **109.9**
Speed ratings (Par 107): **102,101,100,96,96 88**
toteswingers 1&2 £7.00, 2&3 £4.30, 1&3 £4.30 CSF £175.80 CT £382.35 TOTE £18.40: £3.90, £5.20; EX 117.50 Trifecta £256.20 Pool: £1052.86 - 3.04 winning units..
Owner Mohammed Al Nabouda **Bred** Rabbah Bloodstock Limited **Trained** Newmarket, Suffolk

FOCUS
A decent 3-y-o handicap, run at a fair pace and a gritty performance by the winner, who recorded a personal-best, with the second rated back to his Newmarket form.

NOTEBOOK
Daghash got the better of a prolonged duel with the runner-up. The winner had failed to get his head in front since winning a 7f Beverley maiden 12 months ago but he'd shown improved form over middle-distances in recent starts, most notably when beaten only a head at Warwick on his penultimate start. He hasn't always looked the most straightforward but he ran straight and true all the way to the line here and responded gamely to pressure. He holds no imminent entries but should remain competitive once reassessed and could improve again if taking another step up in trip. (tchd 16-1)
Stature(IRE), sporting his now customary hood, lost very little in defeat. He made his challenge upsides the winner but was off the bridle much earlier. A winner on soft and good to firm this season, he's clearly versatile and appears to still be on the upgrade.
Willie Wag Tail(USA) failed to build on his unlucky York run. He again didn't get the smoothest of passages, but was in the clear in plenty of time and simply failed to pick up as well as the principals. It may be that he's high enough in the weights now. (tchd 5-6)
Assizes got into a nice rhythm up front but wilted relatively tamely. (op 13-2 tchd 6-1)
Maria's Choice(IRE)'s jockey reported that the colt was never travelling. Official explanation: jockey said colt was never travelling. (op 5-1 tchd 11-2)

6349 "MOULTON NURSERIES" H'CAP 1m 6f 17y

5:30 (5:30) (Class 4) (0-85,84) 3-Y-0+ **£4,075** (£1,212; £606; £303) **Stalls** High

Form RPR

61 **1** **Malekov (IRE)**[12] 5982 3-9-1 **81**.. TomQueally 11 91+
(Sir Henry Cecil) *tall: lw: v.s.a and rdn along early: hld up in last pair: rdn and hdwy over 3f out: drvn to chse ldrs and edgd lft u.p 1f out: led fnl 100yds: styd on wl* **9/2**[2]

4113 **2** *1* **Suzi's A Class Act**[17] 5830 4-9-9 **79**.........................(p) AdamBeschizza 6 87
(James Eustace) *chsd ldr: rdn wl over 2f out: drvn and ev ch ent fnl f: led ins fnl f: hdd and one pce fnl 100yds* **9/2**[2]

-414 **3** *1* **Ethics Girl (IRE)**[17] 5830 6-9-10 **80**............................(t) DarryllHolland 10 87
(John Berry) *hld up in midfield: effrt and hmpd over 2f out: rallied and hdwy 1f out: swtchd rt and styd on wl u.p fnl 100yds* **16/1**

-055 **4** *nk* **Samarkand (IRE)**[20] 5729 4-9-12 **82**................................ LukeMorris 3 89
(Sir Mark Prescott Bt) *hld up in last quartet: swtchd lft and hdwy ent fnl 2f: drvn and chsd ldrs over 1f out: styd on same pce ins fnl f* **9/1**[3]

1160 **5** *2* **Cockney Sparrow**[24] 5598 3-9-0 **80**................................ FrankieDettori 1 84
(Peter Chapple-Hyam) *chsd ldrs: rdn and effrt 3f out: unable qck u.p 2f out: kpt on same pce fr over 1f out* **10/3**[1]

3-20 **6** *nk* **Miss Topsy Turvy (IRE)**[10] 6045 4-9-5 **75**........................ TedDurcan 9 78
(John Dunlop) *in tch in midfield: rdn and effrt over 2f out: unable qck over 1f out: styd on same pce fnl f* **16/1**

6134 **7** *nk* **Maastricht (IRE)**[13] 5944 3-9-4 **84**.................................... LiamJones 5 87
(Mark Johnston) *lw: led: rdn wl over 2f out: drvn and hdd ins fnl f: wknd fnl 75yds* **9/2**[2]

-050 **8** *3* **Blimey O'Riley (IRE)**[66] 4103 7-9-0 **70**........................ RichardMullen 8 69
(Mark H Tompkins) *hld up in tch in last quartet: rdn and effrt on outer 3f out: sltly hmpd and swtchd rt 2f out: no imp after* **14/1**

0526 **9** *4* **Twice Bitten**[13] 5944 4-8-12 **68**.. RobertHavlin 2 61
(James Toller) *t.k.h: hld up in midfield: rdn and no rspnse over 2f out: wknd wl over 1f out* **14/1**

0543 **10** *1 ¼* **Toughness Danon**[14] 5913 6-8-9 **70**.......................... DavidKenny(5) 12 61
(Brendan Powell) *hld up in last pair: rdn and no rspnse wl over 2f out: sn wknd and bhd over 1f out* **20/1**

0503 **11** *20* **Cappielow Park**[69] 3974 3-7-8 **65** oh1.......................... NatashaEaton(5) 4 28
(Fleur Hawes) *t.k.h: chsd ldrs tl lost pl 3f out: bhd 2f out: t.o and eased ins fnl f* **40/1**

3m 6.03s (-1.57) **Going Correction** +0.025s/f (Good)
WFA 3 from 4yo+ 10lb **11** Ran SP% **119.9**
Speed ratings (Par 105): **105,104,103,103,102 102,102,100,98,97 86**
toteswingers 1&2 £3.80, 2&3 £9.00, 1&3 £10.20 CSF £25.66 CT £303.63 TOTE £6.60: £3.50, £2.40, £3.90; EX 21.20 Trifecta £188.40 Pool: £1303.92 - 5.12 winning units..
Owner H E Sheikh Sultan Bin Khalifa Al Nahyan **Bred** Sheikh Sultan Bin Khalifa Al Nayhan **Trained** Newmarket, Suffolk

FOCUS
A competitive handicap, run at an honest pace and the form looks sound rated around the placed horses.
T/Plt: £3,549.90 to a £1 stake. Pool of £56409.37 -11.60 winning tickets. T/Qpdt: £516.20 to a £1 stake. Pool of £4604.63 - 6.60 winning tickets. SP

6350 - 6351a (Foreign Racing) - See Raceform Interactive

6324 LISTOWEL (L-H)

Tuesday, September 18

OFFICIAL GOING: Heavy (soft to heavy in places on jumps courses)

6352a IRISH STALLION FARMS EUROPEAN BREEDERS FUND FILLIES H'CAP 1m

3:35 (5:07) 3-Y-0+ **£10,833** (£3,166; £1,500; £500)

RPR

1 **Loreto (IRE)**[14] 5927 3-9-0 **79**.. KevinManning 4 85
(J S Bolger, Ire) *mid-div whn checked 1/2-way: sn drvn along and 4th home turn: styd on wl to ld fnl 150yds: pushed clr* **9/2**[1]

2 *2* **Cheval Rouge (IRE)**[9] 6083 5-9-4 **82**.........................(bt) SamJames(3) 7 83
(H Rogers, Ire) *hld up: pushed along in 5th home turn: styd on wl ent fnl f to go 2nd cl home* **8/1**[3]

3 *hd* **Balrath Hope (IRE)**[53] 4562 3-9-5 **84**...................... DeclanMcDonogh 6 85
(Gavin Cromwell, Ire) *racd cl 2nd: pressed ldr 1/2-way: led over 1f out tl hdd fnl 150yds: ct cl home for 2nd* **10/1**

4 *3 ¾* **Mamma Rosa (IRE)**[14] 5927 4-8-7 **68**............................(b) DannyGrant 2 60
(Patrick J Flynn, Ire) *tried to make all: hdd over 1f out: no ex fnl f* **9/2**[1]

5 *3 ½* **Antiquus (IRE)**[8] 6110 3-8-4 **69**...................................... WayneLordan 5 53
(Ms Joanna Morgan, Ire) *racd in 3rd tl no ex over 1f out* **5/1**[2]

6 *3 ¾* **Gra Geal Mo Chroi (IRE)**[26] 5526 7-8-2 **68**.............(b) ConorHoban(5) 3 43
(Augustine Leahy, Ire) *slowly away: bhd for much of way: sme late hdwy* **9/1**

7 *1* **Balladiene (IRE)**[28] 5463 6-9-9 **87**................................ RonanWhelan(3) 8 60
(Jarlath P Fahey, Ire) *hld up towards rr: plenty to do home turn: kpt on: nvr nrr* **12/1**

8 *1 ¾* **Edith Cowan (IRE)**[93] 3200 3-8-11 **76**............................ NGMcCullagh 9 45
(Charles O'Brien, Ire) *hld up: sme hdwy to chse ldrs bef home turn: sn no imp* **9/1**

9 *34* **Ariyfa (IRE)**[39] 5043 4-9-6 **81**...(t) BenCurtis 1
(Noel Quinlan) *trckd ldrs in 4th on inner tl pushed along and wknd qckly 3f out* **5/1**[2]

1m 58.68s (10.58)
WFA 3 from 4yo+ 4lb **9** Ran SP% **117.6**
CSF £41.37 CT £345.17 TOTE £4.10: £1.40, £2.70, £3.60; DF 74.80.
Owner Cathal D Brosnan **Bred** Epona Bloodstock Ltd **Trained** Coolcullen, Co Carlow

FOCUS
A race of changing fortunes. The first two are rated to their marks.

NOTEBOOK
Loreto(IRE) wasn't one that could have been seen to be one of the likelier winners turning into the straight, but she was the one that kept going best in spite of an awkward head carriage and the possible tendency to hang right. It didn't come close to stopping her, though, as she won going away. One wouldn't imagine she's that progressive but she'll remain useful at this level. (op 4/1)
Cheval Rouge(IRE) has had a terrifically consistent summer with the ground coming to her aid on several occasions. It did again here although she could only stay on at one pace from a bit back having been off the bridle quite early. It was a typical sort of effort from her and she doesn't really show any sign of regressing. (op 15/2)
Balrath Hope(IRE) has been disappointing but she might be coming down to a more winnable mark. She was positively ridden and took it up entering the straight before eventually running out of steam. She might have been expected to stay on better having won over 1m2f but she couldn't keep up the gallop.
Mamma Rosa(IRE) looked as though she was out in front on sufferance and she was keen which didn't help her get home despite being close enough to have every chance in the straight. (op 9/2 tchd 4/1)
Antiquus(IRE) had a decent position most of the way but was quite one-paced in the straight. (op 11/2)
Ariyfa(IRE) Official explanation: jockey said filly did not handle the heavy ground

6353 - (Foreign Racing) - See Raceform Interactive

5818 BEVERLEY (R-H)

Wednesday, September 19

OFFICIAL GOING: Firm (9.0)

Rail around bottom bend moved out to give fresh ground and making track wider. All distances as advertised.

Wind: Fresh against Weather: Cloudy with sunny periods

6354 BEVERLEY ANNUAL BADGEHOLDERS (S) NURSERY 5f

2:00 (2:00) (Class 6) (0-65,65) 2-Y-O £1,704 (£503; £251) Stalls Low

Form RPR

002 1 **Chloe's Dream (IRE)**19 5807 2-9-1 59...................(p1) PaulMulrennan 9 65
(Ann Duffield) sn led: rdn clr over 1f out: styd on strly **8/1**

4040 2 3 3/4 **Miss Perfect**8 6121 2-9-2 60...................................(v) MichaelO'Connell 6 52
(John Quinn) chsd ldrs: rdn along 2f out: styd on u.p fnl f **9/2**2

0050 3 1 3/4 **Only For You**11 6049 2-8-9 56... DaleSwift(3) 1 42
(Alan Brown) cl up: rdn along 2f out: kpt on same pce appr fnl f **18/1**

4000 4 shd **Baltic Prince (IRE)**21 5749 2-8-7 51............................... CathyGannon 8 36
(Paul Green) dwlt and in rr: hdwy 2f out: sn rdn and styd on fnl f: nrst fin **16/1**

3446 5 1/2 **Windforpower (IRE)**14 5940 2-9-7 65..............................(p) KierenFox 4 48
(Ronald Harris) s.i.s and bhd: swtchd lft 2f out and sn rdn: styd on fnl f: nrst fin **11/2**3

0532 6 1 1/2 **Why So Fast (IRE)**1 6336 2-8-11 62.................... DavidBergin(7) 10 40
(David O'Meara) cl up: rdn along 2f out: chsd wnr ent fnl f: no imp **4/1**1

6525 7 2 1/4 **Sojoum**8 6115 2-8-13 57... FrannyNorton 11 26
(Mick Channon) dwlt: a in rr **13/2**

4005 8 3 1/2 **Tiger Prince (IRE)**19 5799 2-8-6 50...............................(p) PJMcDonald 5 6
(Ann Duffield) prom: chsd wnr 2f out: sn rdn and wknd appr fnl f **10/1**

3464 9 6 **Throwing Roses**1 6336 2-9-1 59.................................... JamesSullivan 3
(Ollie Pears) chsd ldrs on inner: rdn along 1/2-way: sn wknd **15/2**

4000 10 3 **Purple Day**15 5911 2-8-6 50...(p) JimmyQuinn 7
(Pam Sly) chsd ldrs: rdn along 1/2-way: sn wknd **33/1**

1m 3.17s (-0.33) **Going Correction** -0.225s/f (Firm) 10 Ran SP% **113.0**

Speed ratings (Par 93): **93,87,84,84,83 80,77,71,62,57**

Tote Swingers 1&2 £9.70, 2&3 £13.30, 1&3 £14.70 CSF £42.46 CT £640.94 TOTE £8.00: £2.10, £1.40, £5.10; EX 58.10.There was no bid for winner.

Owner Paddy Bowles **Bred** Maurice Burns **Trained** Constable Burton, N Yorks

FOCUS

After a dry night and a bright and breezy morning the going was changed to Firm. After the opener winning rider Paul Mulrennan reckoned it was "quick but safe". A modest selling nursery, but a clear-cut winner who had this in the bag some way from home. Not a race to be positive about.

NOTEBOOK

Chloe's Dream(IRE), beaten a neck by a horse that has won twice since when fitted with cheekpieces rather than a visor on her third start on the all-weather at Wolverhampton, had a hood added on her handicap bow. She dominated the field from the off and was never in any danger. She is certainly better than a 59-rated filly. (op 7-1)

Miss Perfect, very solid on the morning line, had finished well beaten over 7f on her nursery bow when visored for the first time. She came through late to snatch second spot, but the winner was gone beyond recall. She is due to race from a 3lb lower mark in future and 6f may prove the answer. (op 5-1 tchd 4-1)

Only For You, making her handicap bow on her eighth start, paid the price for trying to keep tabs on the winner. (op 16-1 tchd 20-1)

Baltic Prince(IRE), dropped 4lb after finishing out the back on his handicap bow on the all-weather, ran his best race yet, staying on late after stumbling at the start. Official explanation: jockey said colt stumbled leaving stalls (op 25-1)

Windforpower(IRE), winner of an all-weather nursery at Lingfield in July from a 2lb higher mark, has gone the wrong way since and with the cheekpieces back on, he blew his chance at the start. Official explanation: jockey said gelding missed the break (tchd 6-1)

Why So Fast(IRE), runner-up in a non-handicap seller at Thirsk the previous day, wears a hood for a reason and looks a tricky customer. (op 7-2)

6355 BRITISH STALLION STUDS E B F MAIDEN FILLIES' STKS 7f 100y

2:30 (2:30) (Class 5) 2-Y-O £3,169 (£943; £471; £235) Stalls Low

Form RPR

22 1 **Jabhaat (USA)**15 5907 2-9-0 0... GrahamLee 4 72+
(Ed Dunlop) t.k.h: trckd ldng pair: hdwy and cl up 2f out: led over 1f out: jnd and rdn ins fnl f: kpt on wl **1/1**1

63 2 shd **Squeeze My Brain (IRE)**19 5785 2-9-0 0........................ SebSanders 7 72
(Ralph Beckett) trckd ldng pair: effrt on outer whn carried lft over 2f out: rdn over 1f out and styd on to chal ins fnl f: sn drvn and ev ch tl nt qckn nr fin **6/4**2

00 3 2 3/4 **Barefoot Sandy**33 5300 2-9-0 0...................................... BarryMcHugh 3 65
(Tony Coyle) sltly hmpd s: t.k.h: hld up in rr: hdwy over 2f out: rdn along to chse ldrs over 1f out: kpt on fnl f: nrst fin **125/1**

05 4 2 **Beautifulwildthing**7 6132 2-9-0 0............................... GrahamGibbons 1 60
(David Barron) led: rdn along over 2f out: hdd over 1f out: sn one pce **18/1**

5 9 **Val's Diamond (IRE)** 2-9-0 0.. PJMcDonald 6 39
(Ann Duffield) t.k.h: cl up: rdn along and edgd lft over 2f out: sn wknd **25/1**

60 6 4 1/2 **Bint Youmzain (IRE)**49 4701 2-9-0 0............................. FrannyNorton 2 28
(Mick Channon) sltly hmpd s: in tch on inner: rdn along over 2f out: sn wknd **9/1**3

0 7 hd **Equinox**34 5255 2-9-0 0.. TomEaves 5 27
(Bryan Smart) hld up in tch: rdn along over 2f out: sn wknd **50/1**

1m 33.62s (-0.18) **Going Correction** -0.30s/f (Firm) 7 Ran SP% **111.9**

Speed ratings (Par 92): **89,88,85,83,73 68,67**

Tote Swingers 1&2 £1.30, 2&3 £23.40, 1&3 £14.40 CSF £2.55 TOTE £2.20: £1.20, £1.60; EX 2.70.

Owner Hamdan Al Maktoum **Bred** Shadwell Farm LLC **Trained** Newmarket, Suffolk

FOCUS

A 2yo maiden fillies' race run at just a steady pace. The winner did not need to be at her best to win.

NOTEBOOK

Jabhaat(USA), runner-up at Newmarket and Goodwood on her first two starts, has a best RPR of 78. Quite keen, she looked to be travelling much the best when taking charge. Pushed out with hands and heels, in the end she did just enough. (op 5-4)

Squeeze My Brain(IRE), who recorded a RPR of 71 when sixth on her debut at Goodwood, was sent off at 1-2 when only third over 6f on softish ground at Salisbury next time. Carried wide over 2f out, under a much more forceful ride she was only just denied in the end. She had a much harder race than the winner. (op 13-8 tchd 15-8)

Barefoot Sandy, who showed nothing on her first two starts, was having her first start for this trainer. After taking a knock at the start, she was very free but kept on surprisingly well to claim third spot. This will have blown a possible low nursery mark out of the water. (op 100-1)

Beautifulwildthing, never a factor when fifth on testing ground at Carlisle, set the pace this time but folded in the closing stages. A nursery over 7f could be next. (op 20-1 tchd 16-1)

Val's Diamond(IRE), quite keen on her debut, ducked badly left with over 2f left to run and tired. This should have taught her a fair bit. Official explanation: jockey said filly hung left-handed (op 28-1 tchd 33-1)

Bint Youmzain(IRE), odds-on when well beaten over 5f on her debut at Folkestone, was awkward leaving the stalls and, hard at work turning in, looked paceless. (op 6-1 tchd 11-2)

6356 RACING AGAIN NEXT TUESDAY MAIDEN AUCTION STKS 7f 100y

3:05 (3:06) (Class 5) 2-Y-O £2,264 (£673; £336; £168) Stalls Low

Form RPR

632 1 **Magical Rose (IRE)**15 5912 2-8-8 77............................ FrannyNorton 1 74
(Paul D'Arcy) trckd ldrs: hdwy over 2f out: rdn to chse clr ldr wl over 1f out: drvn and styd on u.p fnl f to ld nr fin **15/8**1

603 2 hd **Funding Deficit (IRE)**19 5797 2-8-9 68.................... GrahamGibbons 11 75
(David Barron) led and sn clr: pushed along wl over 1f out: rdn ent fnl f: drvn and edgd lft last 100yds: hdd and no ex nr fin **8/1**

3222 3 3 1/2 **Madame Elizabeth**18 5825 2-8-6 74.................................... AmyRyan 4 63
(Reg Hollinshead) chsd clr ldr: rdn along over 2f out: drvn over 1f out: kpt on same pce fnl f **5/2**2

00 4 1 3/4 **Red Charmer (IRE)**11 6043 2-9-1 0............................. PaulMulrennan 9 68
(Ann Duffield) in tch: hdwy over 2f out: sn rdn: styd on fnl f: nrst fin **80/1**

0 5 4 **Senator Sam (IRE)**15 5912 2-9-1 0................................ PJMcDonald 13 59+
(Ann Duffield) chsd ldrs: rdn along wl over 2f out: sn one pce **66/1**

4205 6 1/2 **Notional Demand**24 5619 2-8-4 66............................ AdamCarter(5) 8 52
(Tim Easterby) prom: rdn along over 2f out: sn one pce **33/1**

0006 7 7 **Jomari (IRE)**22 5716 2-8-9 45.. JoeFanning 2 35
(Declan Carroll) trckd ldrs on inner: hdwy over 3f out: rdn along over 2f out: sn wknd **100/1**

002 8 7 **Tobacco**7 6134 2-8-13 0... DuranFentiman 5 23
(Tim Easterby) a towards rr **20/1**

6 9 1 3/4 **Medici Dancer**11 6042 2-8-10 0...................................... AndrewElliott 3 16
(Tim Easterby) a towards rr **14/1**

22 10 1 3/4 **Mister Marcasite**24 5619 2-8-11 0..................................... DavidAllan 12 12
(Mel Brittain) chsd ldrs: effrt on outer over 2f out: sn rdn and wknd **4/1**3

00 11 1 1/4 **Haaf'n Haaf**50 4677 2-8-2 0................................ MatthewHopkins(7) 6 8
(Michael Easterby) a towards rr **200/1**

12 shd **Threepence** 2-8-11 0.. PaulQuinn 7 9
(Richard Whitaker) unruly in preliminaries: v.s.a and green: a bhd **33/1**

1m 31.81s (-1.99) **Going Correction** -0.30s/f (Firm) 12 Ran SP% **116.0**

Speed ratings (Par 95): **99,98,94,92,88 87,79,71,69,67 66,66**

Tote Swingers 1&2 £4.70, 2&3 £5.70, 1&3 £3.20 CSF £16.83 TOTE £3.40: £1.60, £2.10, £1.80; EX 16.70.

Owner K Snell **Bred** Patrick A Cluskey **Trained** Newmarket, Suffolk

FOCUS

No hanging about in this 2yo maiden auction. The headstrong leader soon showed in a clear lead and was only worn down near the finish. The winner is rated roughly to form.

NOTEBOOK

Magical Rose(IRE), with an official rating of 77, has improved with each outing and was only just beaten on her previous start over 7f at Leicester. She went in pursuit of the clear leader and, making up about 4l in the final furlong, she showed ahead near the line. She clearly has a very willing attitude and might make an even better 3-y-o. (op 2-1 tchd 9-4)

Funding Deficit(IRE), rated just 68 after three previous starts, soon pulled his way into a long lead. Treading water inside the final furlong, he was worn down near the line. He ran about 10lb above his mark and would have a serious chance if turned out again in the 7f nursery at Catterick on Saturday. (tchd 15-2)

Madame Elizabeth, rated 74, was in receipt of 2lb from the winner. Stepping up slightly in trip and encountering fast ground for the first time, she tried to keep tabs on the leader and had no excuse. (op 11-4 tchd 9-4)

Red Charmer(IRE), put out of the race when badly hampered on his second start, kept on in his own time and will be worth a second look if turned out for a mile nursery. (op 66-1)

Senator Sam(IRE) stepped up on his debut effort, staying on nicely up the home straight. On paddock inspection he will not reach his full powers until next year. (tchd 50-1)

Mister Marcasite, runner-up in his two previous starts, did not fare anywhere as near as well this time and he was reported to have been unsuited by the firm ground. Official explanation: trainer's rep said colt was unsuited by the firm ground (tchd 5-1)

6357 GET MARRIED AT BEVERLEY RACECOURSE H'CAP (DIV I) 5f

3:40 (3:41) (Class 5) (0-75,75) 3-Y-O+ £2,264 (£673; £336; £168) Stalls Low

Form RPR

0623 1 **Mount Hollow**14 5933 7-9-0 75...................................(p) JackDuern(7) 4 85
(Reg Hollinshead) midfield: rdn along over 2f out: hdwy over 1f out: styd on u.p ins fnl f to ld last 30yds **5/1**2

4306 2 1 3/4 **Just Like Heaven (IRE)**18 5831 3-8-9 64.......................... DavidAllan 2 68
(Tim Easterby) led: rdn along wl over 1f out: drvn ins fnl f: hdd and no ex last 30yds **4/1**1

0150 3 nse **Diamond Blue**11 6044 4-9-2 70...1 AmyRyan 7 74+
(Richard Whitaker) rrd s and blind removed late: s.i.s and bhd: rdn and hdwy over 1f out: styd on wl fnl f: nrst fin **4/1**1

1330 4 3/4 **Almond Branches**25 5603 3-9-6 75............................ PJMcDonald 10 76
(George Moore) dwlt and towards rr: hdwy on outer 2f out: rdn over 1f out: kpt on same pce fnl f **10/1**

6233 5 nk **Select Committee**19 5801 7-8-12 73...............(v) DavidSimmonson(7) 5 73
(John Quinn) trckd ldrs: effrt ent fnl f: sn rdn and ev ch tl drvn and one pce fnl 50yds **7/1**3

6000 6 nk **Amadeus Denton (IRE)**37 5167 3-8-10 72............... ConnorNichol(7) 3 71
(Michael Dods) cl up: rdn and ev ch over 1f out: drvn and wknd ins fnl f **22/1**

4641 7 1 1/4 **Ice Trooper**14 5933 4-9-1 69..(p) GrahamLee 6 63
(Linda Stubbs) hld up: hdwy 2f out: sn rdn and no imp appr fnl f **7/1**3

2340 8 1 1/4 **Irish Boy (IRE)**15 5915 4-9-0 68.................................... MickyFenton 8 58
(Paul Midgley) cl up: rdn along 2f out: grad wknd **20/1**

5000 9 nk **Mandalay King (IRE)**11 6044 7-9-2 70......................(p) PaulMulrennan 1 59
(Marjorie Fife) in tch on inner: rdn along wl over 1f out: no imp **8/1**

5160 10 nk **Elusive Bonus (IRE)**18 5831 3-8-6 68........................ DavidBergin(7) 9 56
(David O'Meara) cl up: rdn along 2f out: sn wknd **14/1**

1m 3.37s (-0.13) **Going Correction** -0.225s/f (Firm)

WFA 3 from 4yo+ 1lb 10 Ran SP% **117.6**

Speed ratings (Par 103): **92,89,89,87,87 86,84,82,82,82**

Tote Swingers 1&2 £5.10, 2&3 £4.30, 1&3 £6.50 CSF £25.59 CT £90.61 TOTE £9.40: £4.00, £2.00, £1.10; EX 37.80.

Owner Paul Shaw & Mark Round **Bred** G Robinson **Trained** Upper Longdon, Staffs

The Form Book Flat, Raceform Ltd, Compton, RG20 6NL

FOCUS
There was a heavy shower ahead of part one of this wide-open sprint handicap. It was the slower division. The winner rates a length personal best.
Diamond Blue Official explanation: jockey said filly reared as stalls opened and blindfold became stuck in hood and was slowly away

6358 GET MARRIED AT BEVERLEY RACECOURSE H'CAP (DIV II) 5f
4:10 (4:11) (Class 5) (0-75,75) 3-Y-0+ **£2,264** (£673; £336; £168) **Stalls** Low

Form RPR
0600 **1** **Indian Trail**[8] 6123 12-8-6 **67**.................................(b) ShirleyTeasdale(7) 9 78
(David Nicholls) *hld up towards rr: gd hdwy wl over 1f out: swtchd lft and rdn ent fnl f: qcknd wl to ld last 50yds* **16/1**
6556 **2** *1 1/4* **Bronze Beau**[30] 5412 5-9-7 **75**.......................................(tp) GrahamLee 3 81
(Linda Stubbs) *led: rdn over 1f out: drvn ins fnl f: hdd and no ex last 50yds* **7/1**[3]
1552 **3** *shd* **Fear Nothing**[18] 5821 5-8-11 **72**...................................... DavidBergin(7) 7 78
(David O'Meara) *cl up: chal 2f out: rdn over 1f out and ev ch tl drvn and nt qckn wl ins fnl f* **11/4**[1]
0000 **4** *1/2* **Mey Blossom**[8] 6123 7-8-7 **61** oh2.......................................(p) PaulQuinn 8 65
(Richard Whitaker) *in rr and rdn along 1/2-way: hdwy over 1f out: kpt on ins fnl f: nrst fin* **33/1**
6520 **5** *1* **Holy Angel (IRE)**[4] 6264 3-8-9 **64**.................................. DuranFentiman 2 64
(Tim Easterby) *trckd ldrs on inner: hdwy to chse ldng pair over 1f out: rdn ent fnl f and kpt on same pce* **12/1**
1050 **6** *shd* **Red Cape (FR)**[5] 6194 9-9-2 **70**...................................(b) JamesSullivan 6 70
(Ruth Carr) *towards rr: hdwy wl over 1f out: sn rdn: kpt on fnl f: nrst fin* **40/1**
001 **7** *3/4* **Ingleby Star (IRE)**[18] 5821 7-8-13 **70**..........................(p) PaulPickard(3) 1 67
(Ian McInnes) *towards rr: rdn along 1/2-way: sme late hdwy* **8/1**
3332 **8** *1 1/4* **Ashpan Sam**[3] 6285 3-9-3 **72**....................................... CathyGannon 10 65
(John Spearing) *chsd ldrs: rdn along 2f out: sn btn* **11/4**[1]
3300 **9** *1/2* **Tabaret**[8] 6123 9-9-0 **68**.. AmyRyan 4 59
(Richard Whitaker) *chsd ldrs: rdn along 2f out: sn wknd* **22/1**
362 **10** *10* **Dreaming Of Rubies**[37] 5167 3-9-5 **74**..........................(t) PhillipMakin 5 29
(Ben Haslam) *cl up: rdn 2f out: drvn and wknd over 1f out* **6/1**[2]
1m 1.94s (-1.56) **Going Correction** -0.225s/f (Firm)
WFA 3 from 5yo+ 1lb **10** Ran SP% **114.5**
Speed ratings (Par 103): **103,101,100,100,98 98,97,95,94,78**
Tote Swingers 1&2 £9.80, 2&3 £3.70, 1&3 £19.00 CSF £118.91 CT £414.10 TOTE £29.10: £6.80, £1.50, £1.40; EX 164.30.
Owner Martin Love **Bred** Whitsbury Manor Stud **Trained** Sessay, N Yorks

FOCUS
Division two and the winner's time was over a second quicker than part one. The form makes a fair bit of sense.
Dreaming Of Rubies Official explanation: jockey said filly stopped quickly

6359 SHEILA STAMFORD ALWAYS REMEMBERED BIRTHDAY H'CAP 1m 4f 16y
4:45 (4:45) (Class 4) (0-85,82) 3-Y-0 **£4,528** (£1,347; £673; £336) **Stalls** Low

Form RPR
0305 **1** **Singalat**[11] 6037 3-9-2 **77**.. GrahamLee 2 83
(James Given) *chsd clr ldr: tk clsr order 3f out: chal 2f out: sn niggled along: rdn over 1f out: kpt on gamely u.p to ld last 50yds* **8/1**
5114 **2** *1/2* **Cape Explorer**[18] 5838 3-8-13 **74**.................................. PaulMulrennan 1 79
(James Tate) *led: clr after 3f: pushed along and jnd 2f out: rdn over 1f out: drvn ent fnl f: hdd and no ex last 50yds* **11/4**[2]
4152 **3** *nk* **Spanish Wedding**[32] 5366 3-9-7 **82**..............................(b) SebSanders 5 87
(Marco Botti) *trckd ldng pair: hdwy 2f out: rdn to chal over 1f out: drvn ent fnl f and ev ch tl no ex last 50yds* **9/2**[3]
0-13 **4** *1* **Kiwayu**[14] 5944 3-9-6 **81**..(t) KirstyMilczarek 6 84
(Luca Cumani) *hld up in rr: hdwy on outer over 2f out: rdn to chse ldrs over 1f out: sn drvn and no imp fnl 150yds* **2/1**[1]
2155 **5** *1* **Arley Hall**[4] 6263 3-8-13 **74**... TonyHamilton 3 76
(Richard Fahey) *trckd ldrs on inner: effrt over 2f out: rdn along over 1f out: drvn and one pce ent fnl f* **12/1**
1604 **6** *1/2* **Nice Rose**[11] 6045 3-9-1 **76**.. JoeFanning 4 77
(Mark Johnston) *hld up in tch: effrt and hdwy 3f out: rdn along 2f out: drvn and no imp appr fnl f* **11/2**
2m 35.23s (-4.57) **Going Correction** -0.30s/f (Firm) **6** Ran SP% **112.4**
Speed ratings (Par 103): **103,102,102,101,101 100**
Tote Swingers 1&2 £3.30, 2&3 £2.30, 1&3 £6.70 CSF £30.18 TOTE £9.30: £3.30, £1.50; EX 38.50.
Owner Danethorpe Racing Partnership **Bred** Mrs S Clifford **Trained** Willoughton, Lincs

FOCUS
A strongly run 3yo handicap, yet the first two were one-two throughout. A bunch finish, but the form still seems sound.
Kiwayu Official explanation: jockey said gelding hung right-handed in straight

6360 WATCH RACING UK ON SKY CHANNEL 432 MAIDEN STKS 5f
5:15 (5:28) (Class 5) 2-Y-0 **£2,264** (£673; £336; £168) **Stalls** Low

Form RPR
05 **1** **Pipers Note**[32] 5367 2-9-3 0.. AmyRyan 12 76+
(Richard Whitaker) *wnt bdly lft and lost many l s: bhd: hdwy wl over 1f out: sn rdn and styd on strly ins fnl f to ld last 50yds* **8/1**
3 **2** *2* **Quality Mark (USA)**[114] 2556 2-9-3 0.................................... GrahamLee 5 69+
(Jeremy Noseda) *prom: chsd ldr fr 1/2-way: rdn along and green wl over 1f out: kpt on same pce fnl f* **4/1**[3]
4 **3** *1/2* **Anderton (IRE)**[30] 5410 2-9-3 0.. TonyHamilton 8 67
(Richard Fahey) *led: rdn clr over 1f out: hung violently lft to stands' rail ins fnl f: hdd and no ex last 50yds* **2/1**[1]
4 *3/4* **Gallena** 2-8-12 0.. KellyHarrison 7 59
(William Haggas) *midfield: hdwy wl over 1f out: rdn and kpt on fnl f: nrst fin* **9/2**
63 **5** *5* **St Mary De Castro**[21] 5733 2-8-12 0............................. JamesSullivan 4 41
(Michael Easterby) *chsd ldrs: rdn along 2f out: sn one pce* **33/1**
000 **6** *1* **Royal Jenray**[33] 5313 2-9-3 50.. AndrewElliott 3 42
(Jedd O'Keeffe) *chsd ldr: rdn along wl over 1f out: sn wknd* **100/1**
7 *hd* **Cool And Clear (IRE)** 2-9-3 0... DavidAllan 9 41
(Tim Easterby) *chsd ldrs: rdn along wl over 2f out: grad wknd* **25/1**
8 *hd* **Accelerant (IRE)** 2-9-3 0.. PhillipMakin 2 41+
(Kevin Ryan) *in tch on inner: pushed along 1/2-way: rdn and nt clr run 2f out: sn wknd* **7/2**[2]
04 **9** *4 1/2* **My Claire**[107] 2770 2-8-5 0.. DanielleMooney(7) 1 19
(Nigel Tinkler) *a towards rr* **14/1**
0 **10** *3 1/2* **Fishlake Rebel**[9] 6099 2-9-3 0.. PJMcDonald 10 11
(Ruth Carr) *a towards rr* **100/1**
1m 4.51s (1.01) **Going Correction** -0.225s/f (Firm) **10** Ran SP% **120.3**
Speed ratings (Par 95): **82,78,78,76,68 67,66,66,59,53**
Tote Swingers 1&2 £7.50, 2&3 £3.30, 1&3 £5.70 CSF £40.73 TOTE £9.60: £2.10, £2.50, £1.30; EX 57.50.
Owner Mrs Jill Willows **Bred** Wadacre Stud **Trained** Scarcroft, W Yorks

FOCUS
Drama ahead of this 5f 2yo maiden race. Fancied newcomer Level Best unseated Joe Fanning going to the start and ran loose. His rider looked shaken and the horse was withdrawn. Quality Mark unseated Graham Lee at the start and loose too. It was a dramatic event too and the form is rated negatively.

NOTEBOOK
Pipers Note, on his second start, went violently left leaving the stalls and was well detached in last. He made ground hand over fist in the final 2f and shot past the errant Anderton in the closing stages. It was a race that must be treated with extreme caution, but he clearly has a decent amount of ability. (old market op 8-1 new market)
Quality Mark(USA) was last of three in a novice event on his debut at Windsor in May on his only previous start. He unseated Graham Lee at the start and ran the entire length of the track before being caught and led back to the start. He had to be held in the stalls after his pre-race antics and is clearly worth another chance. (old market tchd 5-2 and 3-1 new market op 3-1)
Anderton(IRE), who showed promise over 6f first time at Thirsk, set the pace and looked to have it in the bag when cocking his jaw and veering badly left inside the final 100yds. It is to be hoped it was just inexperience, but there must be a question mark over his attitude after this display. (old market tchd 4-1 new market op 5-2)
Gallena, the first foal of a Group 3 winner, is not very big. She stuck on late from a mid-field position and will have learnt plenty. (old market op 14-1 new market op 7-1)
Accelerant(IRE), a newcomer, met traffic problems when trying to move into contention soon after halfway. His rider accepted that this was not his day and he can be expected to do a fair bit better next time. (old market op 9-1 new market op 4-1)

6361 STARS OF THE FUTURE RACING EXCELLENCE APPRENTICE TRAINING SERIES CLASSIFIED STKS 1m 100y
5:50 (5:51) (Class 6) 3-Y-0+ **£1,704** (£503; £251) **Stalls** Low

Form RPR
03 **1** **Praxios**[15] 5917 4-8-11 51.......................................(v[1]) ConorHarrison(3) 17 54
(Noel Wilson) *midfield: hdwy 3f out: chsd ldrs 2f out: rdn to ld ent fnl f: sn hung lft: hung rt fnl 100yds: kpt on* **11/1**
0004 **2** *1/2* **Kheskianto (IRE)**[34] 5258 6-9-0 46..................................(t) JakePayne 6 53
(Michael Chapman) *hld up and bhd: gd hdwy 3f out: chsd ldrs wl over 1f out: rdn and ch whn carried sltly lft jst ins fnl f: sn rdn and kpt on* **16/1**
4030 **3** *2 1/4* **American Lover (FR)**[6] 6174 5-8-9 46........................ KevinLundie(5) 13 48
(John Wainwright) *hld up in rr: hdwy wl over 2f out: rdn to chse ldrs over 1f out: kpt on fnl f* **16/1**
0030 **4** *1 1/4* **Politbureau**[35] 5226 5-8-11 52................................ DavidSimmonson(3) 3 45
(Michael Easterby) *chsd ldrs: hdwy over 2f out: sn rdn and no imp appr fnl f* **12/1**
0-00 **5** *2* **Louis Hull**[32] 5338 3-8-7 54..................................(p) JacobButterfield(3) 14 40
(Garry Moss) *chsd ldrs: hdwy to trck ldng pair 3f out: effrt and ev ch over 1f out: sn rdn and wknd fnl f* **25/1**
-053 **6** *2* **Valentine's Gift**[22] 5708 4-9-0 49................................ GeorgeChaloner 12 36
(Neville Bycroft) *hld up and bhd: hdwy over 2f out: rdn over 1f out: styd on fnl f: nrst fin* **14/1**
0340 **7** *1* **Stilettoesinthemud (IRE)**[9] 6106 4-9-0 54........................ DavidBergin 1 33
(James Given) *led: rdn along over 2f out: drvn and hdd ent fnl f: sn wknd* **7/1**[3]
5-00 **8** *1 1/2* **Stadium Of Light (IRE)**[8] 5241 5-9-0 48..................(t) NatashaEaton 15 30
(Shaun Harris) *stmbld bdly s: midfield: effrt over 2f out: sn swtchd to outer and rdn: n.d* **33/1**
5516 **9** *1/2* **Siberian Belle (IRE)**[6] 6157 3-8-10 49..........................(p) LauraBarry 11 29
(Richard Fahey) *chsd ldrs: rdn along wl over 2f out: grad wknd* **15/2**
0543 **10** *3/4* **Blue Top**[37] 5170 3-8-7 52..(tp) GemmaTutty(3) 5 27
(Tim Walford) *midfield: effrt wl over 2f out: sn rdn along and n.d* **3/1**[1]
40 **11** *shd* **Byron Bear (IRE)**[37] 5171 4-9-0 49.. NedCurtis 9 27
(Paul Midgley) *hld up and bhd: hdwy wl over 2f out: swtchd lft and rdn wl over 1f out: n.d* **9/2**[2]
600 **12** *6* **Whatsofunny (IRE)**[4] 6259 3-8-10 55........................... RachealKneller 7 13
(Ruth Carr) *cl up: effrt to dispute ld 2f out: sn rdn and wknd* **14/1**
650 **13** *3 1/2* **Lucky For Some**[123] 2287 5-8-9 40..............................(p) JoshCrane(5) 8
(Marjorie Fife) *a in rr* **33/1**
0-06 **14** *1/2* **Misty Eyes**[54] 4551 3-8-5 45.. JordanNason(5) 10
(Geoffrey Harker) *t.k.h: in tch: rdn along wl over 2f out and sn wknd* **40/1**
0600 **15** *6* **Tomasini**[15] 5918 3-8-10 37.. JackDuern 16
(John Weymes) *midfield: effrt and in tch 3f out: sn rdn and wknd* **66/1**
000 **16** *1 1/2* **Icing Sugar**[29] 5447 4-8-7 41... KevinStott(7) 2
(Mike Sowersby) *a bhd* **125/1**
1m 46.39s (-1.21) **Going Correction** -0.30s/f (Firm)
WFA 3 from 4yo+ 4lb **16** Ran SP% **123.0**
Speed ratings (Par 101): **94,93,91,90,88 86,85,83,83,82 82,76,72,72,66 64**
Tote Swingers 1&2 £33.50, 2&3 £44.70, 1&3 £44.50 CSF £169.03 TOTE £10.30: £2.70, £5.60, £5.10; EX 74.00.
Owner Simon Twiggs Matt Morgan Noel Wilson **Bred** P V And Mrs J P Jackson **Trained** Middleham, N Yorks
■ Stewards' Enquiry : Conor Harrison two-day ban: careless riding (Oct 3-4)

FOCUS
A rock-bottom finale confined to apprentice riders. They were soon well strung out. A weak race, in which the winner only had to run to this year's form.
T/Plt: £70.30 to a £1 stake. Pool: £44,178.90 - 458.66 winning tickets. T/Qpdt: £34.50 to a £1 stake. Pool: £3,927.34 - 84.20 winning tickets. JR

[6249] KEMPTON (A.W) (R-H)
Wednesday, September 19

OFFICIAL GOING: Standard
Wind: Moderate, across Weather: Fine

6362 WIN BIG WITH BETDAQ MULTIPLES MEDIAN AUCTION MAIDEN STKS 5f (P)
5:45 (5:46) (Class 6) 3-4-Y-0 **£1,617** (£481; £240; £120) **Stalls** Low

Form RPR
650 **1** **Illustrious Lad (IRE)**[13] 5975 3-9-3 53..........................(p) PatCosgrave 3 55
(Jim Boyle) *trckd ldr: pushed into ld wl over 1f out: sn 2 l up: drvn fnl f: hld on* **3/1**[2]

0363 **2** *½* **Green Mountain (IRE)**[12] 5994 3-8-12 45........(vt) ShaneKelly 4 48
(Philip McBride) *chsd ldng pair: rdn 2f out: chsd wnr 1f out: clsd gap 100yds out: nt qckn nr fin* **7/1**[3]

3 *1 ¼* **Ella Fitzgerald (IRE)** 3-8-12 0........ ChrisCatlin 5 44
(Rae Guest) *sn pushed along in 5th: rn green and hanging whn rdn over 1f out: styd on fnl f to take 3rd last strides* **5/2**[1]

50 **4** *nk* **Elusive Pursuit**[23] 5687 4-8-13 0........ AdamKirby 1 42
(Clive Cox) *chsd ldng trio: pushed along 1/2-way: effrt u.p to dispute 2nd briefly over 1f out: one pce after* **3/1**[2]

3000 **5** *2* **Abadejo**[17] 5850 4-9-4 52........(v[1]) FergusSweeney 6 40
(J R Jenkins) *racd freely: led to wl over 1f out: fading whn short of room 150yds out* **11/1**

4656 **6** *7* **Cataract**[9] 6100 3-8-12 44........(b) DavidProbert 2 10
(John Weymes) *sn outpcd: a in last pair: bhd fnl 2f* **8/1**

0 **7** *3* **Stoneacre Thirsk (IRE)**[33] 5299 3-8-12 0........ RobbieFitzpatrick 7
(Peter Grayson) *s.i.s: outpcd and a in last: wl bhd fnl 2f* **40/1**

1m 0.36s (-0.14) **Going Correction** -0.125s/f (Stan)
WFA 3 from 4yo 1lb **7** Ran SP% **113.0**
Speed ratings (Par 101): **96,95,93,92,89 78,73**
toteswingers 1&2 £2.00, 2&3 £4.20, 1&3 £1.30 CSF £23.31 TOTE £5.20: £3.40, £1.40; EX 18.90.
Owner Inside Track Racing Club **Bred** Whisperview Trading Ltd **Trained** Epsom, Surrey

FOCUS
A very weak maiden. It was run at a decent pace and the form looks straightforward, rated through the second.
Abadejo Official explanation: jockey said gelding suffered interference in running

6363 BETDAQ MOBILE APPS NURSERY 1m 2f (P)
6:15 (6:15) (Class 5) (0-75,75) 2-Y-O **£2,264** (£673; £336; £168) **Stalls** Low

Form RPR

6332 **1** **Stiff Upper Lip (IRE)**[9] 6096 2-8-10 64........ RichardHughes 7 69+
(Richard Hannon) *trckd ldrs: shkn up 2f out: clsd to ld jst ins fnl f: forged clr* **3/1**[2]

0626 **2** *2 ¾* **Alpine Mysteries (IRE)**[20] 5763 2-8-5 59........ SilvestreDeSousa 3 59
(John Dunlop) *trckd ldrs: rdn 2f out: tried to chal on inner 1f out: sn outpcd: kpt on to take 2nd last strides* **14/1**

401 **3** *hd* **Royal Prize**[28] 5476 2-9-7 75........ JimCrowley 8 74
(Ralph Beckett) *jnd ldr after 1f: rdn to ld wl over 1f out: hdd and outpcd jst ins fnl f: lost 2nd last strides* **2/1**[1]

0546 **4** *nk* **Abraq**[16] 5890 2-9-3 71........ JamesDoyle 4 70
(Ed Dunlop) *hld up disputing 5th: rdn over 2f out: tk 4th jst over 1f out: styd on nr fin* **14/1**

4403 **5** *2 ¾* **Lady Marmelo (IRE)**[9] 6096 2-9-2 70........ PatCosgrave 1 64
(Mick Channon) *hld up in last pair: rdn and effrt over 1f out: sn no imp on ldrs* **20/1**

6534 **6** *1 ¼* **Heliconia**[9] 6096 2-8-5 59........(b) ChrisCatlin 2 50
(Sir Mark Prescott Bt) *rousted along early but stl towards rr: rdn over 2f out: no real prog* **16/1**

003 **7** *hd* **Shooting Jacket (USA)**[30] 5407 2-9-0 68........ MickaelBarzalona 6 59
(Mahmood Al Zarooni) *hld up in last pair: rapid prog on outer to press ldng pair 4f out: rdn over 2f out: wknd over 1f out* **9/2**[3]

4563 **8** *7* **Walter White (IRE)**[37] 5155 2-9-1 69........ JimmyFortune 5 47
(Andrew Balding) *led: jnd after 1f: rdn and hdd wl over 1f out: wknd qckly* **6/1**

2m 7.91s (-0.09) **Going Correction** -0.125s/f (Stan) **8** Ran SP% **114.8**
Speed ratings (Par 95): **95,92,92,90 89,89,83**
toteswingers 1&2 £3.30, 2&3 £4.50, 1&3 £2.30 CSF £43.59 CT £101.92 TOTE £3.00: £1.10, £3.80, £1.20; EX 35.30 Trifecta £251.70 Pool: £8076.52 - 23.74 winning units..
Owner Richard Hitchcock Alan King **Bred** B Kennedy **Trained** East Everleigh, Wilts

FOCUS
A moderate staying nursery, run at an average pace and the form should work out. The winner is on the upgrade.

NOTEBOOK
Stiff Upper Lip(IRE) came right away once hitting top gear and deservedly opened his account at the sixth attempt. He was just held at this trip at Bath nine days earlier when he finished a clear second-best and was off the same mark on this AW debut. The surface was evidently up his street and, ridden more handily, there was a lot to like about the way he went about his business. Much depends on a likely reaction from the handicapper, but he'll be high on confidence and may well go in again. (op 7-2)
Alpine Mysteries(IRE), yet to race on turf, was never far away on the inside and saw out the extra 2f stoutly. She rates the benchmark and deserves to go one better. (op 10-1)
Royal Prize enjoyed switching to this surface when off the mark over 7f here last month. Well backed, he got a positive ride on this marked step up in trip and was ultimately a sitting duck for the winner. He still ran well and is on a workable mark, but perhaps a drop back to 1m will help in the short term. (op 15-8 tchd 9-4 in a place)
Abraq proved one paced when asked for his effort nearing the furlong marker, but saw out the stiffer test well and looks well worth more positive handling over this trip.
Lady Marmelo(IRE) was beaten further here than was the case by the winner at Bath last time, but shaped as though a stronger pace would have helped. (op 16-1)
Shooting Jacket(USA), third over 1m here last time, was rushed up on the far side and had his chance on this nursery debut. He blatantly failed to get home, though. (op 5-1)

6364 BACK OR LAY AT BETDAQ.COM H'CAP 1m 2f (P)
6:45 (6:46) (Class 5) (0-70,70) 3-Y-O **£2,264** (£673; £336; £168) **Stalls** Low

Form RPR

6361 **1** **Joyful Spirit (IRE)**[20] 5770 3-9-4 67........(b) WilliamBuick 1 81
(John Dunlop) *mde all at decent pce: stretched field fr over 3f out: clr over 2f out: hd sltly awkward over 1f out but styd on wl* **9/1**[3]

500 **2** *4* **Bobs Her Uncle**[54] 4542 3-8-13 62........ MircoDemuro 5 68
(James Bethell) *prom: rdn 3f out: chsd clr wnr 2f out: clr of rest over 1f out but no imp* **20/1**

1 **3** *2 ½* **Dr Houseman**[39] 5100 3-9-7 70........ EddieAhern 13 71+
(Amanda Perrett) *hld up in last quartet and racd wd: pushed along 3f out: stl jst pushed along and styd on wl fnl f to take 3rd nr fin: hopeless task* **5/1**[1]

4516 **4** *½* **Darling Lexi (IRE)**[4] 6240 3-8-13 62........ MickaelBarzalona 4 62
(Richard Fahey) *hld up in last quartet: rdn and struggling over 2f out: styd on wl fnl f: nrst fin* **12/1**

0306 **5** *nk* **Alvitude (USA)**[47] 4755 3-9-4 67........ JamesDoyle 12 66+
(Roger Charlton) *w.w in last pair: drvn over 2f out: prog over 1f out: styd on fnl f: given no ch* **14/1**

534 **6** *½* **Any Other Day**[19] 5795 3-9-4 67........ JimCrowley 11 65+
(William Knight) *hld up wl in rr: rdn over 2f out: styd on fr over 1f out: nrst fin but given no ch* **9/1**[3]

5532 **7** *1 ¼* **Harry Buckle**[89] 3345 3-9-7 70........ RichardHughes 14 66
(Philip McBride) *wl in tch on outer: shkn up 3f out: rdn and prog to chse clr ldng pair jst over 1f out: nudged along after: lost several pls last 50yds* **11/2**[2]

053 **8** *1 ¼* **Eltiqaa (IRE)**[15] 5901 3-9-7 70........ PaulHanagan 6 63
(John Gosden) *hld up in midfield: rdn and prog on inner over 2f out: wnt 3rd briefly over 1f out but no ch: wknd fnl f* **9/1**[3]

5443 **9** *1* **District Attorney (IRE)**[56] 4466 3-9-2 65........ DarryllHolland 9 56
(William Haggas) *mostly chsd wnr to 3f out: wknd over 1f out* **11/2**[2]

00-0 **10** *1 ¼* **Furzanah**[19] 5795 3-9-1 67........ PatrickHills(3) 8 56
(Luca Cumani) *mostly in last quartet: no ch 2f out: nvr a factor* **16/1**

604 **11** *1 ½* **Chronic Flame (TUR)**[215] [illegible] 3-8-13 62........ HayleyTurner 3 48
(Marcus Tregoning) *t.k.h: prom: rdn to chse wnr 3f out to 2f out: sn wknd qckly* **20/1**

5316 **12** *3 ¾* **Top Frock (IRE)**[21] 5754 3-9-5 68........(b) AdamKirby 10 46
(Clive Cox) *racd on outer: wnt prom after 3f: drvn 3f out: wknd wl over 1f out* **14/1**

5403 **13** *4* **Valley Queen**[34] 5262 3-9-2 65........ DavidProbert 7 35
(Mark Usher) *prom: pushed along 4f out: wknd 3f out* **33/1**

2m 4.74s (-3.26) **Going Correction** -0.125s/f (Stan) **13** Ran SP% **116.8**
Speed ratings (Par 101): **108,104,102,102,102 101,100,99,98,97 96,93,90**
toteswingers 1&2 £60.40, 2&3 £53.30, 1&3 £4.00 CSF £176.79 CT £1002.22 TOTE £5.90: £2.40, £9.40, £2.20; EX 265.60 TRIFECTA Not won..
Owner Windflower Overseas Holdings Inc **Bred** Windflower Overseas **Trained** Arundel, W Sussex

FOCUS
A wide-open looking 3yo handicap and they went a sound pace. The winner did it well in a good time.

6365 BETDAQ CASINO GAMES H'CAP 1m 4f (P)
7:15 (7:17) (Class 6) (0-65,65) 3-Y-O **£1,617** (£481; £240; £120) **Stalls** Centre

Form RPR

0053 **1** **Porcini**[7] 6146 3-9-5 63........ RichardHughes 3 71
(Philip McBride) *chsd ldrs: shkn up 4f out: clsd u.p 2f out: disp ld jst over 1f out: drvn ahd ins fnl f* **4/1**[2]

0060 **2** *½* **Cape Rainbow**[47] 4776 3-8-11 55........ DavidProbert 9 62
(Mark Usher) *trckd ldr: rdn over 2f out: disp ld jst over 1f out: hdd ins fnl f: styd on but hld* **8/1**

0001 **3** *¾* **Bramshill Lass**[14] 5945 3-9-7 65........(b) JimCrowley 13 71
(Amanda Perrett) *hld up in rr fr wd draw: prog and nt clr run over 3f out: drvn over 2f out: styd on wl fr over 1f out: tk 3rd last 75yds: jst unable to chal* **11/1**

5532 **4** *1 ¼* **Manomine**[24] 5636 3-9-6 64........ SilvestreDeSousa 1 68
(Clive Brittain) *trckd ldrs: rdn to chse ldng pair over 3f out: chal u.p jst over 1f out: nt qckn fnl f: lost 3rd last 75yds* **2/1**[1]

353 **5** *1 ¾* **Kashgar**[17] 5855 3-9-3 61........(b[1]) StevieDonohoe 4 62
(Michael Bell) *led at gd pce: had plenty in trble 3f out: hdd and fdd jst over 1f out* **10/1**

3000 **6** *6* **Attain**[19] 5810 3-9-2 60........(b[1]) LiamKeniry 8 52
(Julia Feilden) *hld up towards rr: hmpd wl over 3f out: prog over 2f out but no ch: tk modest 6th over 1f out* **16/1**

-232 **7** *4* **Better Be Mine (IRE)**[104] 2850 3-8-13 57........ EddieAhern 2 42
(John Dunlop) *hld up in last trio: nt clr run over 3f out: sme prog over 2f out but no ch: tk modest 7th fnl f* **6/1**[3]

1600 **8** *4* **Like Clockwork**[84] 3483 3-9-2 60........ WilliamBuick 11 39
(Mark H Tompkins) *hld up in last: pushed along and stl there 3f out: passed wkng rivals fnl f* **7/1**

623 **9** *¾* **Elegant Ophelia**[81] 3622 3-9-6 64........ DarryllHolland 10 42
(Dean Ivory) *chsd ldng pair to over 3f out: sn wknd* **16/1**

006 **10** *nk* **Zenaad (USA)**[208] 693 3-9-1 59........(t) J-PGuillambert 6 36
(Seamus Durack) *hld up in midfield: rdn to go 6th over 3f out: no imp on ldrs: wknd over 1f out* **33/1**

0065 **11** *3 ½* **Istan Star (USA)**[25] 5589 3-8-4 51 oh6........(v) RyanPowell(3) 12 23
(Julie Camacho) *forced to r on outer fr wd draw: prom tl wknd over 3f out* **40/1**

050 **12** *1 ¼* **Iron Butterfly**[55] 4516 3-9-0 58........ JamesDoyle 5 28
(James Eustace) *nvr bttr than midfield: pushed along 5f out: wknd wl over 3f out* **16/1**

5-00 **13** *44* **Retromania (IRE)**[70] 3965 3-8-7 51 oh1........ HayleyTurner 7
(John Best) *t.k.h: early: hld up in midfield: pushed along 5f out: wknd qckly over 3f out: virtually p.u* **40/1**

2m 32.34s (-2.16) **Going Correction** -0.125s/f (Stan) **13** Ran SP% **134.1**
Speed ratings (Par 99): **102,101,101,100,99 95,92,89,89,89 86,85,56**
toteswingers 1&2 £13.70, 2&3 £31.30, 1&3 £9.60 CSF £40.87 CT £349.22 TOTE £5.00: £2.20, £3.60, £3.80; EX 51.30 Trifecta £1473.90 Part won. Pool: £1991.81 - 0.10 winnning units..
Owner PMRacing **Bred** Cheveley Park Stud Ltd **Trained** Newmarket, Suffolk

FOCUS
A moderate 3-y-o handicap and another open-looking affair. It was run at a fair tempo and the first five came clear. The form makes sense among the principals.
Like Clockwork Official explanation: jockey said gelding hung right
Iron Butterfly Official explanation: jockey said filly stopped quickly

6366 RACING PLUS/BRITISH STALLION STUDS E B F MAIDEN FILLIES' STKS 1m (P)
7:45 (7:49) (Class 5) 2-Y-O **£3,234** (£962; £481; £240) **Stalls** Low

Form RPR

1 **Hot Snap** 2-9-0 0........ EddieAhern 13 79+
(Sir Henry Cecil) *difficult to load into stalls: hld up in midfield: prog 2f out: rdn to ld jst over 1f out: pressed ins fnl f: readily fnd enough* **7/1**[3]

2 *½* **Mango Diva** 2-9-0 0........ JimmyFortune 12 78+
(Sir Michael Stoute) *s.i.s: wl in rr: prog into midfield over 2f out: drvn and clsd on ldrs over 1f out: wnt 2nd last 150yds and chal: hld nr fin* **16/1**

432 **3** *1* **Naalatt (IRE)**[18] 5818 2-9-0 77........ MickaelBarzalona 4 76
(Mahmood Al Zarooni) *trckd ldrs: cl enough and rdn over 1f out: nt qckn but styd on fnl f* **5/4**[1]

5 **4** *¾* **Alerted (USA)**[23] 5684 2-9-0 0........ JamesDoyle 7 74
(Roger Charlton) *reluctant to enter stalls: trckd ldrs: prog to go 2nd 2f out: chal and upsides jst over 1f out: one pce fnl f* **5/1**[2]

0 **5** *2 ¼* **Tessarini (USA)**[8] 6117 2-9-0 0........ AhmedAjtebi 8 69
(Mahmood Al Zarooni) *t.k.h: prom on outer: chsd ldr over 3f out to 2f out: nt qckn but styd cl up tl wknd fnl f* **25/1**

6 *¾* **Charm Cry (USA)** 2-9-0 0........ SilvestreDeSousa 9 67+
(Mark Johnston) *prog to ld after 3f: drvn and hdd jst over 1f out: wknd fnl f* **16/1**

00 **7** *2 ½* **Pivotal Silence**[13] 5977 2-9-0 0........ AdamKirby 1 62
(Amanda Perrett) *s.i.s: sn in tch on inner: prog 3f out: tried to cl on ldrs over 1f out: wknd fnl f* **33/1**

0 **8** *9* **Downhill Dancer (IRE)**[39] 5104 2-9-0 0 .... WilliamBuick 2 41
(Brian Meehan) *led 3f: chsd ldr to over 3f out: styd cl up tl wknd qckly wl over 1f out* **15/2**

0 **9** *3/4* **Sweet As Honey**[13] 5977 2-9-0 0 .... RichardHughes 5 39
(Richard Hannon) *a in rr: shkn up and lft bhd over 2f out* **11/1**

10 *1 1/2* **Lucky Di** 2-9-0 0 .... DaneO'Neill 3 36
(Peter Hedger) *dwlt: hld up in last pair: pushed along over 2f out: nvr a factor* **100/1**

11 *1 3/4* **Tawafeeg (USA)** 2-9-0 0 .... JimCrowley 11 32
(James Tate) *pushed along early: wnt prom on outer after 3f: wknd qckly over 2f out* **33/1**

50 **12** *hd* **Atalanta Bay (IRE)**[15] 5902 2-9-0 0 .... HayleyTurner 10 31
(Marcus Tregoning) *a towards rr: lost tch over 2f out* **40/1**

06 **13** *13* **Be Very Careful**[37] 5153 2-9-0 0 .... KieranO'Neill 8 1
(Richard Hannon) *sn struggling: wl bhd fnl 3f: t.o* **66/1**

1m 39.86s (0.06) **Going Correction** -0.125s/f (Stan) **13** Ran SP% **120.1**
Speed ratings (Par 92): **94,93,92,91,89 88,86,77,76,75 73,73,60**
toteswingers 1&2 £13.80, 2&3 £8.90, 1&3 £3.30 CSF £106.25 TOTE £6.70: £2.70, £5.20, £1.10; EX 114.80 Trifecta £124.70 Pool: £2667.05 - 15.82 winning units..
Owner K Abdulla **Bred** Juddmonte Farms Ltd **Trained** Newmarket, Suffolk

FOCUS
A fair juvenile fillies' maiden but the time was slow. The third helps with the level.

NOTEBOOK
Hot Snap ◆ hit top gear nearing the final furlong and ran out a ready debut winner. This half-sister to her stable's former star Midday proved easy enough to back, which suggests connections believe she would improve nicely for the run, and she does look to have a bright future as she's plenty of size about her. She obviously stays well and could well be Pattern class down the line. (op 13-2)
Mango Diva ◆ came from well back, allowing the winner first run, and posted a pleasing debut effort. Bred for middle-distances on her dam' side, the market also suggested she would need the experience and it's not hard to envisage her going one better. (op 14-1 tchd 12-1)
Naalatt(IRE) had improved with each of her previous three outings and was well backed to open her account. She held every chance stepped up a furlong and rates a solid benchmark. (op 6-4 tchd 13-8 in places)
Alerted(USA), fifth on her debut at Warwick, travelled sweetly and ran an improved race, but failed to see out the extra furlong like the principals. A drop back to 7f may well do the trick. (op 9-2)
Tessarini(USA), Godolphin's second string, was another who failed to see out the distance that convincingly, but this was a big step in the right direction after her turf debut eight days earlier.
Charm Cry(USA) was very easy to back, but knew her job and made her way to the front. It looked a case of her needing the run, though, and perhaps a sharper test would be ideal in the short term

6367 SPORTINGLIFE.COM FILLIES' H'CAP 7f (P)
8:15 (8:15) (Class 4) (0-85,85) 3-Y-O+ **£4,075** (£1,212; £606; £303) **Stalls** Low

Form RPR

0422 **1** **Whimsical (IRE)**[27] 6520 3-9-4 **85** .... RichardHughes 6 90+
(Richard Hannon) *trckd ldr: led 2f out gng easily: sed dash for the fin over 1f out and stole a l: hrd pressed ins fnl f: jst hld* **5/4**[1]

340 **2** *hd* **Colorful Notion (IRE)**[31] 5385 3-9-4 **85** .... AdamKirby 5 89
(Marco Botti) *t.k.h: hld up bhd ldrs: drvn between rivals to chse wnr jst over 1f out: clsd grad fnl f: jst hld* **8/1**

2206 **3** *shd* **Russian Ice**[20] 5769 4-8-12 **76** ....(b) ShaneKelly 3 80
(Dean Ivory) *hld up towards rr: clsd fr 2f out: drvn and one of several to press wnr ins fnl f: styd on but a jst hld* **8/1**

-466 **4** *nk* **Blackdown Fair**[16] 5877 3-8-5 **72** .... MircoDemuro 1 75+
(Rod Millman) *hld up on inner: taken bk to last 2f out then swtchd to outer: lot to do after: r.o wl fnl f: fin best of all* **20/1**

6102 **5** *nk* **Bint Alzain (IRE)**[7] 6150 3-8-8 **75** ....(t[1]) HayleyTurner 4 77
(Gerard Butler) *hld up and sn in last: prog on outer over 1f out: rdn and clsd fnl f: one pce last 75yds* **8/1**

5000 **6** *2 1/2* **Ivor's Princess**[18] 5837 3-8-8 **75** .... DavidProbert 8 70
(Rod Millman) *dwlt: in tch: rdn and nt qckn whn dash sed over 1f out: one pce after* **12/1**

021 **7** *shd* **Zing Wing**[7] 6145 4-8-9 **73** 6ex .... CathyGannon 9 68
(David Evans) *prom: rdn to press wnr 2f out to jst over 1f out: wknd* **7/1**[3]

0022 **8** *nse* **Al Mayasah (IRE)**[20] 5769 4-8-12 **83** .... AliceHaynes(7) 2 78
(David Simcock) *t.k.h: cl up on inner tl wknd jst over 1f out* **5/1**[2]

1000 **9** *6* **Abi Scarlet (IRE)**[11] 6041 3-9-1 **82** .... JimmyFortune 7 61
(Hughie Morrison) *led to 2f out: wkng whn hmpd over 1f out* **40/1**

1m 26.48s (0.48) **Going Correction** -0.125s/f (Stan)
WFA 3 from 4yo 3lb **9** Ran SP% **121.8**
Speed ratings (Par 102): **92,91,91,91,90 88,88,87,81**
toteswingers 1&2 £4.00, 2&3 £6.60, 1&3 £4.80 CSF £13.20 CT £62.97 TOTE £2.60: £1.10, £2.20, £4.20; EX 13.20 Trifecta £52.80 Pool: £577.44 - 8.08 winning units..
Owner Miss Yvonne Jacques **Bred** Churchtown House Stud **Trained** East Everleigh, Wilts

FOCUS
This was a fair fillies' handicap. There was an average pace on and that resulted in a very tight finish. A muddling race run in a modest time.

6368 SPORTINGLIFE.COM RACING H'CAP (DIV I) 6f (P)
8:45 (8:45) (Class 4) (0-85,82) 3-Y-O+ **£4,075** (£1,212; £606; £303) **Stalls** Low

Form RPR

0000 **1** **We Have A Dream**[22] 5703 7-8-11 **72** .... HayleyTurner 3 81
(William Muir) *pressed ldr: led 2f out to jst over 1f out: kpt finding for press fnl f: led last strides* **8/1**

6-12 **2** *shd* **Yeeoow (IRE)**[162] 1271 3-9-4 **81** .... MartinHarley 2 90
(Mrs K Burke) *trckd ldrs: clsd 2f out: rdn to take narrow ld jst over 1f out: hrd pressed fnl f: hdd last strides* **9/4**[1]

2130 **3** *nse* **Sir Maximilian (IRE)**[25] 5603 3-9-5 **82** .... WilliamBuick 6 91
(Ed Dunlop) *hld up in last pair: prog over 2f out: rdn and clsd over 1f out: str chal and upsides nr fin: could nt qckn last strides* **9/2**[2]

4034 **4** *1 1/2* **Emiratesdotcom**[9] 6094 6-9-3 **78** .... ChrisCatlin 7 82
(Milton Bradley) *dwlt: mostly in last to over 1f out: rdn and styd on wl fnl f: nrst fin* **12/1**

6113 **5** *1/2* **Dream Catcher (FR)**[32] 5362 4-8-10 **76** .... AmyScott(5) 9 79
(Henry Candy) *trckd ldrs: urged along to mount a chal jst over 1f out: nt qckn and fdd last 100yds* **8/1**

0505 **6** *1 1/4* **Shifting Star (IRE)**[11] 6040 7-8-12 **80** .... WilliamTwiston-Davies(7) 8 79
(John Bridger) *towards rr: u.p fr 1/2-way and struggling after: styd on fnl f* **16/1**

0315 **7** *1/2* **Where's Reiley (USA)**[221] 525 6-9-7 **82** ....(b) RichardHughes 4 79
(Alastair Lidderdale) *trckd ldrs: cl enough 2f out: nt qckn over 1f out: fdd fnl f* **20/1**

034 **8** *1 1/2* **Kuanyao (IRE)**[57] 4437 6-9-7 **82** .... SebSanders 1 74
(Peter Makin) *pushed up to ld: hdd 2f out: wknd jst over 1f out* **6/1**[3]

306 **9** *3/4* **Sheikh The Reins (IRE)**[38] 5128 3-8-13 **76** .... JimCrowley 5 66
(John Best) *w.w in rr: pushed along and no prog 2f out: reminder over 1f out: nvr in it* **7/1**

1m 11.75s (-1.35) **Going Correction** -0.125s/f (Stan)
WFA 3 from 4yo+ 2lb **9** Ran SP% **116.3**
Speed ratings (Par 105): **104,103,103,101,101 99,98,96,95**
toteswingers 1&2 £2.30, 2&3 £3.20, 1&3 £8.80 CSF £26.56 CT £93.57 TOTE £8.70: £3.20, £1.10, £1.80; EX 33.60 Trifecta £290.50 Pool: £639.91 - 1.63 winning units..
Owner The Dreaming Squires **Bred** Whitsbury Manor Stud **Trained** Lambourn, Berks

FOCUS
A competitive sprint handicap run at a strong pace and it saw the principals fight out a blanket finish. It was the slowr division but the form looks sound enough.

6369 SPORTINGLIFE.COM RACING H'CAP (DIV II) 6f (P)
9:15 (9:15) (Class 4) (0-85,83) 3-Y-O+ **£4,075** (£1,212; £606; £303) **Stalls** Low

Form RPR

1534 **1** **Delft**[33] 5308 3-9-0 **78** .... JimmyFortune 5 86+
(Jeremy Noseda) *w.w disputing 6th: prog over 1f out: drvn to ld last 100yds: sn in command: quite decisively* **7/2**[2]

2100 **2** *3/4* **Dark Castle**[12] 6008 3-9-5 **83** .... LiamKeniry 6 89+
(Sylvester Kirk) *t.k.h: trckd ldr 1f: restrained: prog to ld 1f out: hdd and outpcd last 100yds* **7/4**[1]

100 **3** *hd* **Impel (IRE)**[22] 5703 3-9-3 **81** ....(b[1]) RichardHughes 2 86+
(Richard Hannon) *w.w disputing 6th: prog 2f out: drvn and tried to chal over 1f out: styd on same pce* **11/2**[3]

30-0 **4** *shd* **Judd Street**[231] 378 10-9-1 **77** .... DaneO'Neill 7 82
(Eve Johnson Houghton) *hld up in last: rdn and prog on outer over 1f out: styd on fnl f but jst lacked pce to chal* **33/1**

002 **5** *1/2* **Ertikaan**[18] 5812 5-9-6 **82** .... LukeMorris 1 85
(Ronald Harris) *trckd ldrs: rdn to chal wl over 1f out: one pce ins fnl f* **8/1**

0030 **6** *3/4* **Tagula Night (IRE)**[35] 5233 6-9-4 **80** ....(b) ShaneKelly 8 81
(Dean Ivory) *hld up in last pair: prog on inner 2f out: tried to press ldrs 1f out: one pce* **10/1**

1340 **7** *3* **Flashbang**[13] 5971 4-8-7 **69** oh1 ....(t) SilvestreDeSousa 9 60
(Paul Cole) *sn prom: wnt 2nd over 2f out: rdn to ld over 1f out: hdd & wknd 1f out* **16/1**

4320 **8** *4* **Speightowns Kid (USA)**[32] 5362 4-8-8 **73** .... RaulDaSilva(3) 3 52
(Jeremy Gask) *led: shkn up over 2f out: hdd & wknd qckly over 1f out* **16/1**

6535 **9** *1/2* **Desert Strike**[17] 5853 6-9-4 **80** ....(p) HayleyTurner 4 57
(Conor Dore) *trckd ldr after 1f to over 2f out: sn wknd* **16/1**

1m 11.45s (-1.65) **Going Correction** -0.125s/f (Stan)
WFA 3 from 4yo+ 2lb **9** Ran SP% **114.8**
Speed ratings (Par 105): **106,105,104,104,103 102,98,93,92**
toteswingers 1&2 £1.10, 2&3 £5.00, 1&3 £5.50 CSF £9.93 CT £32.05 TOTE £7.10: £1.40, £2.00, £1.30; EX 12.50 Trifecta £42.20 Pool: £805.26 - 14.09 winning units..
Owner Cheveley Park Stud **Bred** Cheveley Park Stud Ltd **Trained** Newmarket, Suffolk

FOCUS
The second division of the 6f handicap and another competitive race. It was just the faster division. They didn't go that hard early on, but the closers still dominated the finish. Sound form.
T/Jkpt: £13,375.90 to a £1 stake. Pool of £65937.95 - 3.50 winning tickets. T/Plt: £28.70 to a £1 stake. Pool of £59150.59 -1499.88 winning tickets. T/Qpdt: £15.10 to a £1 stake. Pool of £7037.55 - 343.97 winning tickets. JN

6203 SANDOWN (R-H)
Wednesday, September 19

OFFICIAL GOING: Sprint course - good (good to firm in places; 8.2); round course - good to firm (good in places; 8.4)
Bend dolled out 2-3 yards negligible effect on distances.
Wind: Moderate ahead Weather: Sunny intervals

6370 SUPPORT THE RACEHORSE SANCTUARY H'CAP 5f 6y
2:20 (2:20) (Class 5) (0-75,75) 3-Y-O+ **£2,587** (£770; £384; £192) **Stalls** Low

Form RPR

0630 **1** **Rocket Rob (IRE)**[26] 5557 6-9-4 **72** ....(b) WilliamBuick 1 79+
(Willie Musson) *stdd s: hld up in rr: swtchd lft to outer 1f out: drvn and qcknd ins fnl f: str run to ld clsng stages: comf* **5/2**[1]

2223 **2** *1/2* **Macdillon**[25] 5584 6-9-5 **73** .... LiamKeniry 7 78
(Stuart Kittow) *chsd ldrs: n.m.r and rdn ins fnl f: kpt on to take 2nd last strides but nvr gng pce of wnr* **7/1**

4645 **3** *nk* **Berberana (IRE)**[18] 5815 4-9-1 **69** ....(p) JamesDoyle 3 73
(Jeremy Gask) *pressed ldrs: led over 1f out: sn hrd drvn: hdd clsng stages: lost 2nd last strides* **14/1**

3024 **4** *nse* **Aye Aye Digby (IRE)**[15] 5906 7-9-7 **75** .... GeorgeBaker 9 79
(Patrick Chamings) *led briefly early: chsd ldrs: rdn 2f out: styd on thrght fnl f: kpt on clsng stages but nvr gng pce of wnr* **6/1**[3]

2405 **5** *1 1/4* **Alpha Delta Whisky**[13] 5971 4-8-13 **67** .... IanMongan 4 66
(John Gallagher) *sn led: rdn 2f out: hdd over 1f out: wknd clsng stages* **12/1**

4436 **6** *nse* **Rebecca Romero**[4] 6226 5-9-6 **74** .... RichardHughes 2 73+
(Denis Coakley) *hld up in tch: nt clr run thrght fnl f: nt rcvr: fin on bridle* **3/1**[2]

1045 **7** *nk* **The Strig**[27] 5514 5-8-11 **65** ....(v) MartinHarley 8 63
(Stuart Williams) *in tch: rdn and nt clr run fnl f: kpt on clsng stages* **25/1**

3156 **8** *1/2* **Triple Dream**[12] 6006 7-9-7 **75** ....(tp) AdamKirby 11 71
(Milton Bradley) *chsd ldrs: rdn over 2f out: styd on fnl f: nvr gng pce to get involved* **25/1**

2320 **9** *3/4* **Taizong (IRE)**[49] 4708 3-8-10 **65** .... SilvestreDeSousa 5 58+
(Ian Williams) *chsd ldrs: rdn over 1f out: hmpd on inner ins fnl f: sn btn* **7/1**

0000 **10** *2 1/4* **Mr Optimistic**[14] 5933 4-8-9 **63** ....(t[1]) KieranO'Neill 10 48
(Pat Murphy) *outpcd most of way* **66/1**

1m 1.28s (-0.32) **Going Correction** +0.025s/f (Good)
WFA 3 from 4yo+ 1lb **10** Ran SP% **116.4**
Speed ratings (Par 103): **103,102,101,101,99 99,99,98,97,93**
Tote Swingers 1&2 £9.50, 2&3 £19.80, 1&3 £9.40 CSF £20.18 CT £209.72 TOTE £4.20: £2.30, £2.20, £3.60; EX 26.90 Trifecta £156.50 Pool: £812.50 - 3.84 winning tickets..
Owner Bill Hinge & John Searchfield **Bred** Mrs Marita Rogers **Trained** Newmarket, Suffolk

FOCUS
A typically competitive sprint handicap for the course, with racing room at a premium for some of the runners. The winner kept out of trouble and this is still 10lb off his best form of last year.
Rebecca Romero Official explanation: jockey said mare was denied a clear run

The Strig Official explanation: jockey said gelding was denied a clear run

6371 BRITISH STALLION STUDS SUPPORTING BRITISH RACING E B F MAIDEN STKS — 1m 14y

2:50 (2:51) (Class 5) 2-Y-O — **£3,881** (£1,155; £577; £288) **Stalls** Low

Form — RPR

2 **1** **Havana Beat (IRE)**[19] [5792] 2-9-3 0 .... LiamKeniry 6 — 81+
(Andrew Balding) *trckd ldrs: pushed along 2f out: led ins fnl f: styd on strly clsng stages* **9/4**[1]

35 **2** *2 ¾* **Restraint Of Trade (IRE)**[13] [5962] 2-9-3 0 .... MickaelBarzalona 10 — 75
(Mahmood Al Zarooni) *led after 1f: hrd pressed and drvn 2f out: kpt on u.p and hdd ins fnl f: nt pce of wnr and hld on all out for 2nd* **7/1**

2 **3** *shd* **Nichols Canyon**[41] [5005] 2-9-3 0 .... WilliamBuick 1 — 75+
(John Gosden) *s.i.s: in rr: pushed along over 2f out: hdwy over 1f out: styd on ins fnl f to take 3rd last strides and cl on 2nd but no ch w wnr* **11/4**[2]

5 **4** *hd* **Unmoothaj**[38] [5126] 2-9-3 0 .... PaulHanagan 3 — 74+
(Charles Hills) *in tch drvn and hdwy fr 2f out: hung rt and green fnl f: kpt on wl clsng stages to press plcd horses but no ch w wnr* **3/1**[3]

6 **5** *½* **Yul Finegold (IRE)**[60] [4330] 2-9-3 0 .... PatCosgrave 5 — 73
(George Baker) *led 1f: styd chsng ldr: ev ch and rdn 2f out: outpcd into 3rd fnl f: dropped two further pls last strides* **100/1**

6 **6** *7* **Tally Stick (USA)**[12] [6014] 2-9-3 0 .... AhmedAjtebi 4 — 57
(Mahmood Al Zarooni) *in tch: rdn and hung rt ins fnl 2f: sn btn* **10/1**

7 *1 ½* **Great Hall** 2-9-3 0 .... EddieAhern 7 — 54+
(Brian Meehan) *s.i.s: in rr: sme prog fr over 1f out* **33/1**

8 *2 ¼* **Elidor** 2-9-3 0 .... MartinHarley 9 — 48
(Mick Channon) *rdn over 3f out: a towards rr* **16/1**

00 **9** *nk* **Pennyweight**[15] [5902] 2-8-12 0 .... DaneO'Neill 8 — 43
(James Eustace) *bmpd s: sn chsng ldrs: rdn hung rt and wknd fr 2f out* **100/1**

0 **10** *20* **Gold Nugget (IRE)**[14] [5948] 2-9-3 0 .... RichardHughes 2
(Richard Hannon) *in tch tl over 3f out: sn bhd* **50/1**

1m 42.64s (-0.66) **Going Correction** -0.05s/f (Good) — **10** Ran SP% **116.8**
Speed ratings (Par 95): **101,98,98,97,97 90,88,86,86,66**
Tote Swingers 1&2 £3.00, 2&3 £2.90, 1&3 £1.10 CSF £18.79 TOTE £4.20: £1.30, £1.90, £1.90; EX 14.70 Trifecta £29.60 Pool: £1,070.30 - 26.75 winning tickets..
Owner Mick and Janice Mariscotti **Bred** Ms Natalie Cleary **Trained** Kingsclere, Hants

FOCUS
Muddling form, with those who raced prominently dominating. As a result the runs of the third and fourth can be upgraded. The winner is another who was better than the bare form.

NOTEBOOK
Havana Beat(IRE) confirmed the promise of his debut second over 7f here, seeing it out well, though he had been ideally positioned throughout and it's probable there wouldn't be as much between him and the third and fourth horses were they to meet again. Nonetheless he remains capable of better and is very much viewed as a horse for next year. (tchd 2-1)
Restraint Of Trade(IRE) ran his best race to date, attempting to make all but not quite seeing it out as well as the winner. He's now qualified for a mark and should find an opening at some stage. (op 11-2)
Nichols Canyon, runner-up to a Listed-placed stablemate in a C&D maiden on debut, blew the start and was then never in a position to win the race. He finished well, though, and is another who can have his effort upgraded. He should relish 1m2f. (op 5-2)
Unmoothaj, entered in the Dewhurst, improved on his debut effort in a decent Leicester maiden, but was never in with a chance of winning having got too far back. He's better than the bare result and can win a maiden. (op 4-1tchd 9-2 in places)
Yul Finegold(IRE) ran well above market expectations, although he was well positioned the way the race worked out. Still, this was a big step up from his debut.
Tally Stick(USA), better than the bare result at Kempton on debut, lacked the pace to get into this, having been held up, and is probably one for nurseries. (op 12-1)
Great Hall, a half-brother to Group-placed Short Affair as well as Listed-placed Bon Spiel, ran as though the experience was needed, as is often the case with newcomers from this yard.
Elidor, half-brother to Irish Derby winner Treasure Beach, was never in the hunt but should come on a good deal. (tchd 20-1)

6372 RACEHORSE SANCTUARY RESCUE & RE-HOMING CENTRE NOVICE STKS — 7f 16y

3:25 (3:25) (Class 4) 2-Y-O — **£3,881** (£1,155; £577; £288) **Stalls** Low

Form — RPR

1 **1** **Montiridge (IRE)**[68] [4056] 2-9-3 0 .... RichardHughes 4 — 96+
(Richard Hannon) *sn trcking ldrs in 3rd: trckd ldr wl over 1f out: drvn and styd on wl thrght fnl f to ld clsng stages* **30/100**[1]

51 **2** *hd* **Baltic Knight (IRE)**[20] [5765] 2-9-0 0 .... WilliamBuick 2 — 92
(Richard Hannon) *sn led: drvn and qcknd fr 2f out: kpt on wl fnl f: hdd clsng stages* **8/1**[3]

31 **3** *6* **Lazarus Bell**[26] [5553] 2-9-3 0 .... MartinLane 3 — 79
(Brian Meehan) *sn trcking ldrs: drvn to dispute 2nd 2f out: nt pce of wnr and wknd into 3rd ins fnl f* **10/1**

525 **4** *4* **Choral Prince (IRE)**[28] [5478] 2-8-12 75 .... EddieAhern 5 — 63
(Mike Murphy) *rdn over 2f out: a in rr* **50/1**

15 **5** *¾* **Filfil (USA)**[7] [6149] 2-9-3 0 .... AhmedAjtebi 1 — 67
(Mahmood Al Zarooni) *t.k.h: trckd ldr: rdn over 2f out: wknd over 1f out* **7/1**[2]

1m 31.07s (1.57) **Going Correction** -0.05s/f (Good) — **5** Ran SP% **111.6**
Speed ratings (Par 97): **89,88,81,77,76**
CSF £3.59 TOTE £1.30: £1.10, £2.30; EX 4.30.
Owner M Clarke,J Jeffries,R Ambrose,B Reilly **Bred** Century Bloodstock **Trained** East Everleigh, Wilts

FOCUS
The pace was steady in this novice event, yet the Hannon pair still managed to pull clear. The winner did it well and the second helps with the level.

NOTEBOOK
Montiridge(IRE) put up a decent effort to overcome the lack of pace, which he took a long time to settle off, and get the better of his useful front-running stablemate. Impressive winner of a good Newbury maiden on debut, he had no trouble with the faster ground here, and this highly regarded sorts effort can be upgraded when considering he'd apparently missed some work. Entered in the Racing Post Trophy, he's a horse we should be hearing plenty more of, with connections nominating the Royal Lodge as the aim. (op 1-2 tchd 8-15)
Baltic Knight(IRE), ready winner of a 7f Kempton maiden, had the run of the race in front and really did push the winner, drawing nicely on from the remainder. He's clearly useful. (op 7-1 tchd 13-2)
Lazarus Bell, winner of a fair small-field Newmarket maiden, was up a furlong but didn't have the pace, or indeed class, to match the front pair. He'll presumably take the nursery route. (op 9-1 tchd 8-1)
Choral Prince(IRE) was well held and is unlikely to find life easy from his current mark in nurseries. (op 33-1)
Filfil(USA), whose saddled slipped at Kempton last week, ran poorly on this turf debut, taking a big step backward from his debut win. Official explanation: jockey said colt ran too freely and had no more to give (op 11-2 tchd 5-1)

6373 JOHN DUNLOP FORTUNE STKS (LISTED RACE) — 1m 14y

4:00 (4:00) (Class 1) 3-Y-O+ — **£18,714** (£7,095; £3,550; £1,768) **Stalls** Low

Form — RPR

1102 **1** **Fulbright**[11] [6029] 3-9-0 108 .... SilvestreDeSousa 4 — 114
(Mark Johnston) *trckd ldr: chal fr 3f out tl led wl over 1f out: hrd rdn and hung rt fnl 120yds: drvn out* **6/4**[1]

6513 **2** *nk* **Tazahum (USA)**[26] [5560] 4-9-4 110 .... PaulHanagan 2 — 113
(Sir Michael Stoute) *led: jnd 3f out: hdd u.p over 1f out: rallying and ev ch whn bmpd and hit rail fnl 120yds: kpt on wl but nt rcvr* **7/4**[2]

533 **3** *2 ½* **Gabrial (IRE)**[39] [5090] 3-9-0 108 .... RichardHughes 1 — 108
(Richard Fahey) *chsd ldrs in 3rd: rdn ins fnl 3f: no ch w ldng duo fnl 2f* **11/4**[3]

0-00 **4** *11* **Theladyinquestion**[103] [2896] 5-8-13 87 .... WilliamBuick 3 — 77
(Andrew Balding) *a last: shkn up and btn ins fnl 3f: eased ins fnl f* **33/1**

1m 41.78s (-1.52) **Going Correction** -0.05s/f (Good)
WFA 3 from 4yo+ 4lb — **4** Ran SP% **106.0**
Speed ratings (Par 111): **105,104,102,91**
CSF £4.27 TOTE £2.30; EX 3.50.
Owner Sheikh Hamdan Bin Mohammed Al Maktoum **Bred** R F And S D Knipe **Trained** Middleham Moor, N Yorks
■ Stewards' Enquiry : Silvestre De Sousa three-day ban: careless riding (Oct 3-5)

FOCUS
Even with likely pace-setter Set The Trend coming out, this was run at a sound enough gallop, Tazahum going on from Fulbright, and that pair fought out the finish, with the latter just doing enough. He had to survive a stewards' enquiry, though, having slightly bumped the runner-up, causing him to very briefly change stride, which in turn would have cost him some momentum. The form makes sense at face value.

NOTEBOOK
Fulbright has flourished this season, like many a 3-y-o from the yard does, winning four handicaps from 6f-1m on all sorts of ground, and now adding a first Listed success having gone down narrowly in the same grade at Haydock recently. Extremely tough, he'll presumably take his chance in Group company now. (op 11-8 tchd 13-8)
Tazahum(USA) has rediscovered his best form of late, finishing third in a Group 3 at York last time, and he was certainly coming back at the winner when the slight interference took place. One can't say for certain it cost him, but it would have been mightily close. (op 15-8)
Gabrial(IRE), down in class, was surprisingly outpaced by the front two. This was below his recent best and he'll presumably return to 1m2f now. (tchd 5-2 and 3-1)
Theladyinquestion, rated just 87, looked out of her depth and was comprehensively beaten. (tchd 25-1)

6374 RACEHORSE SANCTUARY FLAGSHIP MOORCROFT BOY H'CAP — 1m 14y

4:35 (4:35) (Class 2) (0-100,97) 3-Y-O
£9,835 (£2,945; £1,472; £736; £368; £184) **Stalls** Low

Form — RPR

1205 **1** **Razorbill (USA)**[39] [5094] 3-8-11 87 .... RichardHughes 2 — 96
(Charles Hills) *led: narrowly hdd 4f out: styd pressing ldr and drvn to ld again over 1f out: kpt on wl fnl 120yds* **3/1**[2]

1316 **2** *½* **Royal Empire (IRE)**[11] [6036] 3-9-7 97 .... SilvestreDeSousa 3 — 105
(Saeed Bin Suroor) *trckd wnr: led 4f out but styd hrd-pressed: rdn over 2f out: hdd over 1f out: kpt on but nt pce of wnr fnl 120yds* **9/4**[1]

4210 **3** *1 ¾* **Benzanno (IRE)**[53] [4603] 3-8-3 79 .... DavidProbert 6 — 83
(Andrew Balding) *in tch: hdwy on ins and nt clr run ins fnl 2f: chsd ldng duo fnl f but no imp* **14/1**

-600 **4** *1 ¾* **Unex Michelangelo (IRE)**[33] [5301] 3-9-1 91 .... WilliamBuick 7 — 91
(John Gosden) *chsd ldrs: rdn over 2f out: sn one pce* **6/1**[3]

5052 **5** *½* **Come On Blue Chip (IRE)**[11] [6036] 3-8-8 84 .... (b) ChrisCatlin 5 — 83
(Paul D'Arcy) *s.i.s: in rr: drvn over 2f out: sme late prog* **13/2**

2100 **6** *¾* **Switzerland (IRE)**[11] [6036] 3-8-13 94 .... MichaelJMMurphy(5) 4 — 91
(Mark Johnston) *in rr but in tch: rdn 3f out: styd on same pce fr over 1f out* **6/1**[3]

1460 **7** *2 ¼* **Kahruman (USA)**[27] [5517] 3-9-6 96 .... (b[1]) PaulHanagan 1 — 88
(William Haggas) *chsd ldrs: pushed along over 2f out: wknd sn after* **8/1**

1m 44.03s (0.73) **Going Correction** -0.05s/f (Good) — **7** Ran SP% **115.5**
Speed ratings (Par 107): **94,93,91,90,89 88,86**
Tote Swingers 1&2 £2.00, 2&3 £4.30, 1&3 £5.40 CSF £10.43 TOTE £3.20: £1.30, £2.00; EX 12.00.
Owner K Abdulla **Bred** Juddmonte Farms Inc **Trained** Lambourn, Berks

FOCUS
The market leaders were soon dominating at the head of the race and little else got into it. The pace was steady and the form may not prove reliable, although it makes some sense.

NOTEBOOK
Razorbill(USA) bounced back from a slightly disappointing effort at Haydock, receiving a well-judged ride from Hughes who waited on him in front, allowing the runner-up to head him in the straight, aware that he had plenty left. He'll need to progress to defy a rise. (op 7-2 tchd 4-1)
Royal Empire(IRE) bounced back from a below-par effort at Kempton, taking over from the winner turning in only to give way again. He's worth another try at 1m2f. (op 11-4)
Benzanno(IRE) had little room throughout on the rail, meeting trouble when trying to come with a run, and he should probably have been involved with the front pair. This showed his last-time-out running in a claimer to be all wrong. (op 16-1 tchd 12-1)
Unex Michelangelo(IRE) proved one-paced and may be worth one more chance in a race with more pace to it. (op 13-2 tchd 7-1)
Come On Blue Chip(IRE), 4lb lower than when recording a career-best at Kempton the time before, was held up in a race that suited prominent racers and can be given another chance. (op 11-2)
Switzerland(IRE) was unable to confirm Kempton form with the fourth and this mark looks high enough for now. (tchd 7-1)
Kahruman(USA) was too keen in the first-time blinkers. (op 6-1)

6375 KEN MANLEY MEMORIAL FILLIES' H'CAP — 1m 14y

5:05 (5:05) (Class 4) (0-85,84) 3-Y-O — **£4,075** (£1,212; £606; £303) **Stalls** Low

Form — RPR

3321 **1** **Forgive**[12] [6013] 3-9-7 **84** .... RichardHughes 3 — 93
(Richard Hannon) *trckd ldrs: rdn 2f out: led ins fnl f: kpt on wl* **6/1**[1]

3431 **2** *½* **Fulney**[19] [5795] 3-9-0 **77** .... DaneO'Neill 9 — 85
(James Eustace) *led: rdn over 2f out: hdd ins fnl f: one pce* **8/1**[2]

4153 **3** *1 ¼* **Anya**[32] [5372] 3-8-9 **72** .... HayleyTurner 13 — 77
(Ed Walker) *chsd ldrs: rdn over 2f out: styd on to take 3rd ins fnl f but nt pce of ldng duo* **10/1**[3]

1-04 **4** *2 ¼* **Fairyinthewind (IRE)**[18] [5837] 3-8-7 **70** .... EddieAhern 1 — 70
(Paul D'Arcy) *chsd ldrs: rdn over 2f out: styd on for one pce 4th fnl f* **10/1**[3]

The Form Book Flat, Raceform Ltd, Compton, RG20 6NL

0330 **5** *1* **The Giving Tree (IRE)**[11] 6023 3-8-12 **75**...................... WilliamBuick 14 73+
(Sylvester Kirk) *s.i.s: in rr: pushed along ins fnl 3f: styd on fr over 1f out: kpt on clsng stages: nvr a threat* **6/1**[1]
110 **6** *shd* **Dance Company**[13] 5980 3-9-7 **84**................................... JimCrowley 12 81+
(William Knight) *in rr: pushed along over 2f out: styd on fnl f: nt rch ldrs* **10/1**[3]
1006 **7** *nk* **Amber Silk (IRE)**[30] 5420 3-8-10 **78**........................ MatthewLawson(5) 7 75+
(Charles Hills) *in rr: drvn over 2f out: sme hdwy fnl f* **12/1**
2120 **8** *2* **Roxelana (IRE)**[60] 4335 3-8-12 **75**............................(p) JimmyFortune 10 67
(Jeremy Noseda) *chsd ldr: rdn over 2f out: wknd fnl f* **11/1**
21-4 **9** *shd* **Al Mahmeyah**[105] 2820 3-9-0 **77**.. SeanLevey 2 69
(Richard Hannon) *mid-div: rdn 3f out: no ch fnl 2f* **20/1**
2216 **10** *2* **Alice's Dancer (IRE)**[13] 5980 3-9-7 **84**.................. StevieDonohoe 4 71
(William Muir) *t.k.h in rr: drvn ins fnl 3f: no ch fnl 2f* **16/1**
41 **11** *nk* **Quality Pearl (USA)**[47] 4780 3-8-13 **76**........................... HarryBentley 6 63
(Luca Cumani) *in tch: rdn 3f out: wknd ins fnl 2f* **6/1**[1]
0330 **12** *nk* **Afnoon (USA)**[39] 5107 3-8-7 **70**...................................... PaulHanagan 11 56
(John Dunlop) *mid-div: rdn 3f out: wknd 2f out* **10/1**[3]
0410 **13** *1 1/4* **Silvas Romana (IRE)**[30] 5420 3-8-10 **78**............ MichaelJMMurphy(5) 8 61
(Mark Brisbourne) *rdn 3f out: towards rr most of way* **16/1**

1m 42.84s (-0.46) **Going Correction** -0.05s/f (Good) **13** Ran SP% **122.9**
Speed ratings (Par 100): **100,99,98,96,95 94,94,92,92,90 90,89,88**
Tote Swingers 1&2 £8.90, 2&3 £19.30, 1&3 £15.70 CSF £54.12 CT £499.33 TOTE £6.80: £2.70, £2.50, £3.70; EX 35.10 Trifecta £502.40 Part won. Pool: £678.93 - 0.10 winning tickets..
Owner Highclere Thoroughbred Racing-Spearmint **Bred** The Athenians And Cheveley Park Stud Ltd **Trained** East Everleigh, Wilts

FOCUS
Following the trend, despite this looking an open fillies' handicap, few got involved from off the modest pace. The first two were both improved.
Afnoon(USA) Official explanation: jockey said filly hung right

6376 WILDWOOD GOLF AND COUNTRY CLUB H'CAP (BETFAIR 10 FURLONG FLAT SERIES QUALIFIER) 1m 2f 7y

5:35 (5:36) (Class 4) (0-85,84) 3-Y-O **£5,175** (£1,540; £769; £384) **Stalls** Low

Form RPR
2021 **1** **Quixote**[18] 5838 3-8-13 **76**..(t) RobertWinston 2 87
(Clive Brittain) *in rr: hdwy on ins whn nt clr run 2f out: drvn to chse ldr over 1f out: styd on to ld fnl 120yds: hld on all out* **15/2**[3]
4044 **2** *shd* **Pilgrims Rest (IRE)**[16] 5888 3-9-0 **84**.......... WilliamTwiston-Davies(7) 9 94
(Richard Hannon) *chsd ldrs: drvn to ld over 1f out: hdd fnl 120yds: rallied u.p: jst failed* **8/1**
3034 **3** *5* **Savanna Days (IRE)**[19] 5796 3-9-3 **80**.......................... MartinHarley 11 80
(Mick Channon) *s.i.s: in rr: rdn and hdwy over 2f out: styd on to take wl hld 3rd fnl 120yds* **10/1**
1023 **4** *1/2* **Al Wajba (USA)**[26] 5556 3-9-5 **82**..................................(p) DaneO'Neill 10 81
(William Haggas) *in tch: drvn and hdwy on outer over 2f out: styd on same pce for 4th fnl f* **20/1**
0031 **5** *1/2* **Royal Dutch**[32] 5351 3-8-7 **70**.. EddieAhern 13 68+
(Denis Coakley) *in rr: pushed along towards outer fr 2f out: styd on ins fnl f* **11/1**
0103 **6** *2* **Keepax**[26] 5533 3-9-1 **78**... GeorgeBaker 12 72
(Chris Wall) *in rr: drvn over 2f out: sme hdwy fnl f: nvr a threat* **8/1**
22-1 **6** *dht* **Dulkashe (IRE)**[120] 2379 3-9-2 **82**.................................. PatrickHills(3) 1 76
(Luca Cumani) *chsd ldrs: drvn over 2f out: wknd ins fnl f* **11/2**[2]
1522 **8** *2 1/4* **Croquembouche (IRE)**[19] 5796 3-9-3 **80**......................... LiamKeniry 3 70
(Ed de Giles) *sn led: drvn 3f out: hdd & wknd over 1f out* **9/1**
2106 **9** *3* **Handsome Ransom**[14] 5951 3-9-5 **82**.......................(b[1]) WilliamBuick 5 66
(John Gosden) *in rr: pushed along and no prog 3f out* **16/1**
0614 **10** *1 1/4* **Charitable Act (FR)**[11] 6046 3-8-13 **76**........................... DarryllHolland 4 57
(William Muir) *chsd ldr: rdn 3f out: wknd fr 2f out* **22/1**
2100 **11** *2 3/4* **Hector's Chance**[56] 4466 3-8-9 **72**...................................... JohnFahy 8 48
(Heather Main) *s.i.s: a in rr* **50/1**
1243 **12** *3 1/2* **Kaafel (IRE)**[19] 5796 3-9-6 **83**.. PaulHanagan 7 52
(Charles Hills) *in tch: chsd ldrs and rdn over 2f out btn sn after* **8/1**
2-21 **13** *2 1/4* **Sunnybridge Boy (IRE)**[31] 5387 3-8-11 **77**.......... MichaelMetcalfe(3) 6 41
(Mrs K Burke) *in tch: rdn and btn 3f out* **5/1**[1]

2m 7.84s (-2.66) **Going Correction** -0.05s/f (Good) **13** Ran SP% **121.5**
Speed ratings (Par 103): **108,107,103,103,103 101,101,99,97,96 94,91,89**
Tote Swingers 1&2 £18.30, 2&3 £20.70, 1&3 £7.00 CSF £66.08 CT £615.27 TOTE £9.20: £4.20, £2.30, £4.30; EX 82.00 TRIFECTA Not won..
Owner C E Brittain **Bred** Mr & Mrs R & P Scott **Trained** Newmarket, Suffolk

FOCUS
The pace appeared fair, although the hold-up horses again struggled to get involved. The winner more than confirmed his previous C&D win.
Dulkashe(IRE) Official explanation: trainer's rep said filly would be better suited by faster ground than the good to firm (good in places)
T/Plt: £16.90 to a £1 stake. Pool: £61,640.88 - 2,662.21 winning tickets. T/Qpdt: £9.30 to a £1 stake. Pool: £3,481.03 - 274.38 winning tickets. ST

6343 YARMOUTH (L-H)

Wednesday, September 19

OFFICIAL GOING: Good to firm (watered) (7.1)
Wind: fairly light, across Weather: dry, bright spells

6377 BRITISH STALLION STUDS SUPPORTING BRITISH RACING E B F MAIDEN STKS 7f 3y

2:10 (2:14) (Class 5) 2-Y-O **£3,234** (£962; £481; £240) **Stalls** Centre

Form RPR
342 **1** **Lord Of The Garter (IRE)**[26] 5562 2-9-3 84.................. FrankieDettori 2 83
(Brian Meehan) *lw: chsd ldr: rdn and ev ch whn hung sharply lft over 1f out: looked hld after tl rallied and str run ins fnl f to ld fnl 75yds: sn in command and eased last strides* **8/11**[1]
00 **2** *3/4* **Lancelot Du Lac (ITY)**[19] 5792 2-9-3 0.............................. BrettDoyle 1 80
(Dean Ivory) *t.k.h: hld up in tch: rdn and effrt to chse ldrs 2f out: led over 1f out: edgd rt but looked wnr ins fnl f tl hdd and no ex fnl 75yds* **17/2**
2052 **3** *1 3/4* **Living Desert**[41] 5016 2-9-3 87.. RobertHavlin 5 75
(James Toller) *led: rdn 2f out: hung lft u.p and hdd over 1f out: continued to hang lft and wknd fnl 100yds* **5/1**[3]
4 *nk* **Magique (IRE)** 2-8-12 0.. JamieSpencer 4 69+
(Jeremy Noseda) *leggy: stdd s: hld up in rr: pushed along and sme hdwy over 1f out: wnt modest 4th ins fnl f: stl pushed along but r.o strly and clsng qckly on ldrs at fin* **20/1**
5 *5* **Argaki (IRE)** 2-9-3 0.. RichardMullen 8 61+
(Sir Michael Stoute) *w'like: awkward leaving stalls: t.k.h: hld up in midfield: rdn 1/2-way: outpcd and btn 2f out: wl hld but plugged on fnl f* **28/1**
03 **6** *nk* **Lionheart**[19] 5793 2-9-3 0..(t) KierenFallon 6 60
(Luca Cumani) *lw: t.k.h: chsd ldrs: rdn 2f out: drvn and unable qck over 1f out: wknd fnl f* **4/1**[2]
7 *1* **Gold Burst (IRE)** 2-9-3 0.. PatDobbs 3 57
(Richard Hannon) *w'like: s.i.s: a in rr: rdn and struggling 3f out: wknd 2f out* **20/1**
8 *28* **Shining Cross (IRE)** 2-9-3 0.. TomQueally 9
(George Margarson) *w'like: bit bkwd: chsd ldrs tl 1/2-way: sn lost pl: wl bhd over 1f out: t.o* **80/1**

1m 27.14s (0.54) **Going Correction** -0.15s/f (Firm) **8** Ran SP% **119.3**
Speed ratings (Par 95): **90,89,87,86,81 80,79,47**
Tote Swingers 1&2 £2.60, 2&3 £5.70, 1&3 £1.80 CSF £8.11 TOTE £1.80: £1.10, £2.00, £1.50; EX 8.70.
Owner Bayardo **Bred** Ms Patricia Walsh **Trained** Manton, Wilts

FOCUS
Probably a fair maiden, but it proved to be anything but easy for the well-backed favourite. The form is rated at face value.

NOTEBOOK
Lord Of The Garter(IRE) was made to work really hard to gain his first victory and probably won't be the easiest to place now, although a step up to 1m might help his cause considering how nicely he rallied in the final stages. (op Evens)
Lancelot Du Lac(ITY) ◆, who raced freely early, ran really well again in defeat. He looks to have the physical scope to keep progressing. (op 7-1 tchd 9-1)
Living Desert, trying 7f for the first time, had the highest official mark of the couple who possessed one, but hung left under pressure when needing to keep straight. (op 11-2 tchd 6-1 and 9-2)
Magique(IRE) ◆, who cost 38,000euros as a yearling and is a half-sister to stable's smart handicapper Grandeur, ran here in preference to a conditions-race entry at Newbury later in the week and very much caught the eye with the way she finished after being held up out the back. (op 22-1 tchd 16-1)
Argaki(IRE), a half-brother to middle-distance winners and out of an unraced half-sister to 1m4f Group 1 winner Posidonas, came from a stable with a fair record in this contest, but wasn't seemingly expected to go close judged by the betting and only made an adequate start to his career. (op 25-1)
Lionheart had shown promise previously, but weakened tamely in the final furlong. He is now qualified for a handicap mark. (op 9-2 tchd 5-1)

6378 DANNY WRIGHT MEMORIAL FILLIES' H'CAP (FOR THE CHALLENGE TROPHY) 6f 3y

2:40 (2:41) (Class 5) (0-75,74) 3-Y-O+ **£2,264** (£673; £336; £168) **Stalls** Centre

Form RPR
311 **1** **Links Drive Lady**[38] 5122 4-9-5 **72**.................................. KierenFallon 11 83
(Dean Ivory) *hld up in rr: gd hdwy to ld 1f out: in command and r.o wl fnl f: rdn out* **7/1**
-246 **2** *1* **Oh So Spicy**[39] 5097 5-9-5 **72**... TedDurcan 9 80
(Chris Wall) *t.k.h: hld up in midfield: rdn and hdwy over 1f out: pressed ldrs and hung lft over 1f out: chsd wnr and styd on same pce fnl f* **11/2**[2]
1504 **3** *3/4* **Represent (IRE)**[6] 6173 3-9-0 **69**.................................. SaleemGolam 7 75
(Mick Channon) *stdd s: hld up in rr: rdn over 2f out: hdwy u.p ent fnl f: kpt on wl to go 3rd cl home* **25/1**
2431 **4** *nk* **Palmette**[39] 5096 3-9-4 **73**...(b) RobertHavlin 8 78
(John Gosden) *lw: in tch: rdn and effrt to chal over 1f out: led jst over 1f out tl hdd 1f out: unable qck and styd on same pce fnl f* **6/1**[3]
5166 **5** *1* **Byton**[12] 5995 3-8-12 **72**... AmyScott(5) 12 73
(Henry Candy) *in tch: rdn and effrt to press ldrs over 1f out: unable qck 1f out: plugged on same pce fnl f* **8/1**
0603 **6** *3 1/4* **Isola Verde**[13] 5972 3-9-1 **70**...(v) TomQueally 5 61
(James Fanshawe) *in tch: rdn and unable qck 2f out: outpcd and btn 1f out: swtchd rt and plugged on fnl f* **16/1**
5022 **7** *1* **Millibar (IRE)**[36] 5195 3-9-5 **74**.................................(p) TomMcLaughlin 3 62
(Nick Littmoden) *in tch: rdn and chsd ldrs 2f out: unable qck over 1f out: wknd fnl f* **16/1**
3321 **8** *shd* **Miss Polly Plum**[24] 5635 5-8-10 **63**..............................(p) AndreaAtzeni 1 51
(Chris Dwyer) *led: hdd and hung sharply lft over 1f out: sn btn and wknd 1f out* **20/1**
0160 **9** *1/2* **Big Wave (IRE)**[12] 5995 4-9-4 **71**.......................... AdamBeschizza 2 57
(Alison Hutchinson) *chsd ldr tl 2f out: sn struggling u.p: wknd ent fnl f* **18/1**
0221 **10** *5* **Al Janadeirya**[29] 5448 4-9-6 **73**................................... JamieSpencer 10 43
(Peter Chapple-Hyam) *hood removed late and dwlt: sn rcvrd and in tch in midfield: rdn and unable qck wl over 1f out: wknd 1f out: edgd lft ins fnl f* **11/2**[2]
4301 **11** *5* **Tiger Cub**[20] 5775 3-9-2 **71**..(vt) FrankieDettori 6 25
(Mrs Ilka Gansera-Leveque) *chsd ldrs: rdn and struggling over 2f out: lost pl and bhd over 1f out: wknd fnl f* **4/1**[1]

1m 13.34s (-1.06) **Going Correction** -0.15s/f (Firm)
WFA 3 from 4yo+ 2lb **11** Ran SP% **114.3**
Speed ratings (Par 100): **101,99,98,98,96 92,91,91,90,83 77**
Tote Swingers 1&2 £7.70, 2&3 £34.20, 1&3 £45.60 CSF £43.95 CT £906.98 TOTE £8.70: £2.80, £2.80, £7.60; EX 64.30.
Owner It's Your Lucky Day **Bred** Peter Webb **Trained** Radlett, Herts

FOCUS
It paid to be held up in this handicap, as the first three weren't in the firing line early. Straightforward form.
Al Janadeirya Official explanation: jockey said he failed to hear starter say remove blinds and filly was very slowly away; trainer's rep said filly was unsuited by the good to firm ground
Tiger Cub Official explanation: trainer said filly finished sore

6379 E B F AT THE RACES JOHN MUSKER FILLIES' STKS (FOR THE JOHN MUSKER TROPHY) (LISTED RACE) 1m 2f 21y

3:15 (3:18) (Class 1) 3-Y-O+
£18,552 (£7,062; £3,534; £1,762; £884; £445) **Stalls** Low

Form RPR
0006 **1** **Semayyel (IRE)**[30] 5409 3-8-10 80..............................(b) FrederikTylicki 5 99
(Clive Brittain) *in tch: trcking ldrs and travelling strly whn nt clr run 2f out tl swtchd rt over 1f out: rdn and qcknd to ld 1f out: sn clr and r.o strly: readily* **125/1**
3515 **2** *5* **Aniseed (IRE)**[27] 5519 3-8-10 95................................ JamieSpencer 7 89
(William Haggas) *stdd s: hld up in last pair: rdn and effrt on outer 2f out: hdwy and edgd lft ent fnl f: styd on wl to go 2nd fnl 50yds: no ch w wnr* **20/1**

01/0 **3** ¾ **Miss Starlight**[18] 5835 5 -9-2 95 .... FrankieDettori 2 88
(Ibrahim Saeed Al Malki, Qatar) *hld up in midfield: effrt on inner 3f out: nt clr run 2f out: swtchd rt jst over 1f out: styd on wl fnl f to go 3rd towards fin: no ch w wnr* **66/1**

23-1 **4** ½ **Sunday Bess (JPN)**[4] 5931 4 -9-2 80 .... RichardKingscote 9 87
(Tom Dascombe) *lw: chsd ldr: rdn to ld 2f out: hdd 1f out: sn outpcd by wnr and btn: plugged on tl lost 2 pls fnl 50yds* **25/1**

6120 **5** ½ **Emirates Queen**[35] 5238 3 -8-10 109 .... KierenFallon 8 86+
(Luca Cumani) *lw: taken down early: hld up in tch: effrt and pushed along on inner over 3f out: nt clr run over 2f out and dropped to rr whn swtchd rt wl over 1f out: rallied and styd on wl ins fnl f: no ch w wnr* **9/2**[2]

1-05 **6** ½ **Jiwen (CAN)**[25] 5583 4 -9-2 86 .... (b[1]) TadhgO'Shea 6 85
(Roger Varian) *t.k.h: hld up in tch in midfield: effrt to chse ldrs 3f out: rdn and pressed ldrs 2f out: nt qckn and btn 1f out: wl hld whn flashed tail wl ins fnl f* **28/1**

210 **7** 1 ¼ **Dalkova**[18] 5834 3 -8-10 85 .... (t) PatDobbs 12 82
(Richard Hannon) *in tch: effrt and nt clr run ent fnl 2f: rdn and effrt over 1f out: outpcd and btn 1f out: styd on same pce and wl hld fnl f* **20/1**

1114 **8** *nk* **Sweetnessandlight**[18] 5834 3 -8-10 100 .... TedDurcan 13 81
(Jason Ward) *taken down early: t.k.h: hld up in tch in midfield: rdn and effrt on outer 3f out: no ch w wnr but edgd lft and kpt on fnl f: hmpd and eased towards fin* **14/1**[3]

0415 **9** *nk* **Qaadira (USA)**[35] 5238 3 -8-10 81 .... RobertHavlin 10 81
(John Gosden) *taken down early: hld up in rr: rdn and effrt over 2f out: no imp: no ch w wnr but plugged on fnl f* **40/1**

0405 **10** 1 ¾ **Emma's Gift (IRE)**[23] 5664 4 -9-2 90 .... (b) AdamBeschizza 4 77
(Julia Feilden) *hld up wl in tch: rdn and effrt over 2f out: unable qck and struggling over 1f out: btn 1f out and wknd fnl f* **100/1**

1005 **11** 3 ¼ **Clinical**[18] 5834 4 -9-10 107 .... LukeMorris 11 79
(Sir Mark Prescott Bt) *t.k.h: chsd ldrs: rdn to press ldrs 3f out: hrd drvn and unable qck over 1f out: wknd fnl f: eased wl ins fnl f* **14/1**[3]

4024 **12** 2 ¼ **Timepiece**[31] 5399 5 -9-2 114 .... TomQueally 1 66+
(Sir Henry Cecil) *chsd ldrs: waiting for gap on inner fr 3f out: bdly hmpd wl over 2f out and again 2f out: stl trapped on inner whn hmpd again and shuffled bk over 1f out: swtchd rt fnl 150yds: no hdwy and heavily eased fnl 50yds* **4/6**[1]

-056 **13** 3 **Firdaws (USA)**[27] 5519 3 -8-10 97 .... (b[1]) NeilCallan 3 60
(Roger Varian) *t.k.h: led: rdn over 2f out: wandered rt and lft and hdd 2f out: btn over 1f out: wknd qckly: eased wl ins fnl f* **33/1**

2m 7.86s (-2.64) **Going Correction** -0.075s/f (Good)
WFA 3 from 4yo+ 6lb **13**Ran SP% **117.0**
Speed ratings (Par 108): **107,103,102,102,101 101,100,99,99,98 95,93,91**
Tote Swingers 1&2 £117.60, 2&3 £65.00, 1&3 £151.60 CSF £1685.11 TOTE £109.70 : £18.20, £4.20, £14.10 ; EX 3227.70 .
Owner Saeed Manana **Bred** Rabbah Bloodstock Limited **Trained** Newmarket, Suffolk

FOCUS
As the starting prices of the first three suggest, this was a huge shock, so the form looks really unreliable until proven otherwise. Not strong form for the grade either, and the time was ordinary, but the winner rates a personal best.

NOTEBOOK
Semayyel(IRE), sixth of seven in a handicap on her previous outing, did possess a bit of back class, as her 40-1 second in the Radley Stakes last year proved, but it's fair to say she hadn't scaled anywhere near those heights as a 3-y-o and this was obviously a big a surprise. That said, she travelled strongly for a long time and won in decisive fashion when in the clear. (op 100-1)
Aniseed(IRE) earned some valuable black type with a running-on second. She'd been comfortably held when tried in Pattern company before, although one of those attempts had come in the Musidora. (op 22-1 tchd 25-1)
Miss Starlight posted an encouraging effort. She does at least have a Group 2 under her belt, the Qatar Oaks in December of last year. (tchd 50-1)
Sunday Bess (JPN) who won a 0-75 handicap last time, was nicely positioned 2f out, but didn't get home as well as those in front of her. (op 18-1)
Emirates Queen came into this off a poor run on soft ground, a surface said not to suit, but had form that gave her clear place chances at least. Sent to the start early and loaded without a jockey on her back, she wasn't quickly away, needed shoving along when in the home straight and took an age to pick up. Then when she started to get going, the gaps didn't appear when Kieren Fallon needed them. One got the impression that she's either hard work or wants further. (op 5-1)
Jiwen(CAN) pulled really hard in the first-time blinkers. (op 33-1)
Sweetnessandlight seemed to get worked up before entering the stalls and never got involved. 16-1)
Timepiece, who did appear to be flashing her tail on the way to the start, looked the one to beat if she could reproduce anything close to her last two efforts against these inferior rivals, as there seemed little reason to believe she could get beaten, especially as she didn't carry a penalty for her Group 1 victory in the Falmouth last season. Close up against the inside rail, Tom Queally appeared to be banking on Neil Callan and Firdaws allowing his mount to come inside them, but the Varian filly wandered a couple of times under pressure, denying the favourite any chance of getting past or through in a crowded finish. A line is easily drawn through the performance of the Cecil-trained mare and Tom Queally subsequently reported that the mare hung badly left. Official explanation: jockey said mare hung badly left (tchd 8-13)

6380 VAUXHALL HOLIDAY PARK H'CAP (FOR THE GOLDEN JUBILEE TROPHY) 1m 2f 21y
3:50 (3:50) (Class 3) (0-90,88) 3-Y-O+ **£6,490** (£1,942; £971 ; £486 ; £242) **Stalls** Low

Form RPR

0004 **1** **Emerald Wilderness (IRE)**[21] 5751 8 -9-2 80 .... FrederikTylicki 8 89
(Mark Rimmer) *t.k.h: hld up in tch: hdwy to press ldrs 2f out: rdn and ev ch over 1f out: led ins fnl f: styd on wl* **33/1**

4623 **2** 1 ¼ **Watered Silk**[13] 5966 4 -9-3 81 .... (v[1]) RichardMullen 4 87
(Marcus Tregoning) *dwlt and hmpd s: in tch in midfield: rdn and effrt to chse ldrs on inner 2f out: drvn over 1f out: kpt on same pce ins fnl f: wnt 2nd last stride* **15/2**[3]

1-64 **3** *shd* **Anjaz (USA)**[39] 5089 3 -9-4 88 .... FrankieDettori 6 94
(Saeed Bin Suroor) *chsd ldr tl led and gng strly over 2f out: drvn and hrd pressed over 1f out: hdd ins fnl f: no ex and styd on same pce after: lost 2nd last stride* **7/2**[1]

4103 **4** 1 **Incendiary (IRE)**[23] 5688 3 -8-7 77 .... RobertHavlin 7 81
(Hugo Palmer) *lw: chsd ldrs: effrt u.p over 2f out: drvn and ev ch over 1f out: no ex and btn ins fnl f: plugged on same pce after* **25/1**

3604 **5** 2 ½ **Colour Guard**[18] 5835 4 -9-5 83 .... NeilCallan 2 82
(Mark Johnston) *lw: chsd ldrs: rdn over 2f out: drvn and no imp over 1f out: wl hld and plugged on same pce fnl f* **9/2**[2]

1200 **6** 3 ¼ **Commitment**[90] 3296 3 -9-2 86 .... KierenFallon 5 78
(Luca Cumani) *hld up in last trio: rdn and effrt over 2f out: no imp and no threat to ldrs fnl 2f* **9/2**[2]

1100 **7** *nk* **Chain Of Events**[18] 5835 5 -9-3 81 .... RichardKingscote 3 73
(Sarah Humphrey) *lw: led: drvn and hdd over 2f out: btn over 1f out: wknd 1f out* **16/1**

-005 **8** 6 **Alakhan (IRE)**[39] 5111 6 -9-4 82 .... TomQueally 9 62
(Ian Williams) *t.k.h: hld up in last pair: rdn and effrt wl over 2f out: no imp: wl hld whn edgd lft 1f out* **12/1**

1513 **9** 2 **Initiator**[23] 5666 3 -9-3 87 .... JamieSpencer 1 63
(Jeremy Noseda) *hld up in rr: rdn and no hdwy 3f out: bhd fnl 2f* **7/2**[1]

2m 7.97s (-2.53) **Going Correction** -0.075s/f (Good)
WFA 3 from 4yo+ 6lb **9**Ran SP% **112.9**
Speed ratings (Par 107): **107,106,105,105,103 100,100,95,93**
Tote Swingers 1&2 £31.30, 2&3 £7.20, 1&3 £12.50 CSF £255.89 CT £1097.10 TOTE £57.50 : £7.10, £2.90 , £1.70 ; EX 280.80 .
Owner F J Perry **Bred** Mrs Joan Murphy **Trained** Newmarket, Suffolk

FOCUS
A useful bunch lined up for this contest, but the winner had been disappointing on his most recent outing, and is better known for being a very useful AW performer. However, the time compared favourably to the Listed event that preceded it. The surprise winner is rated back to last year's turf form.

NOTEBOOK
Emerald Wilderness (IRE) returned to turf on his debut for Mark Rimmer, was beaten at 8-13 in a Polytrack seller last time but did enough here to collect a first Flat turf victory since July 2009. A change of scenery and removal of headgear had a beneficial effect, although he was clearly well-treated on his best AW form. (op 28-1 tchd 25-1)
Watered Silk, tried in a visor, won on his only previous start here and clearly likes the place considering this performance. That said, the handicapper seems to have him about right for now. (op 13-2)
Anjaz(USA), down in distance but open to more improvement, appeared the one to beat 3f out but she didn't pick up as looked likely off the bridle. The filly isn't the strongest of finishers for some reason. (op 10-3 tchd 4-1)
Incendiary(IRE) has shown his best turf form in ground with ease in it, so will be of more interest when the rain comes. (op 22-1)
Colour Guard had been running well since the end of July, but was one-paced late on here. (op 4-1)
Commitment, off the track since running in the King George V Stakes at Royal Ascot, has done the majority of his racing on a softer surface, so can be excused this. (op 13-2 tchd 7-1)
Initiator, who was ponied to the start, had appeared to enjoy genuinely quick ground considering both of her successes had come on it, but he made no impression soon after tacking on to the main group in the home straight. (op 4-1 tchd 10-3)

6381 SEA-DEER H'CAP 1m 3y
4:20 (4:22) (Class 4) (0-85,85) 3-Y-O+ **£4,075** (£1,212; £606 ; £303) **Stalls** Centre

Form RPR

1411 **1** **Shena's Dream (IRE)**[11] 5019 3 -8-11 76 .... KierenFallon 7 85
(William Haggas) *mde all: rdn 2f out: hrd pressed and drvn over 1f out: asserted and edgd rt wl ins fnl f: styd on gamely* **11/4**[1]

221 **2** ½ **Alraased (USA)**[13] 5970 3 -9-3 82 .... TadhgO'Shea 6 90
(John Dunlop) *t.k.h: chsd ldrs tl wnt 2nd 5f out: ev ch u.p over 1f out: no ex and btn fnl 75yds* **7/1**

2504 **3** 1 **Bank On Me**[110] 2678 3 -8-11 76 .... RichardMullen 10 82
(Philip McBride) *lw: in tch: chsd ldng pair and drvn over 1f out: no imp tl kpt on fnl 100yds: nvr quite gng pce to chal ldrs* **16/1**

-260 **4** 1 ¼ **Ruby Night (IRE)**[82] 5365 3 -9-3 82 .... JamieSpencer 2 85
(Michael Bell) *stdd s: hld up in last pair: effrt and hdwy u.p over 1f out: edgd lft u.p 1f out: kpt on fnl f* **16/1**

0622 **5** ½ **Rough Rock (IRE)**[24] 5634 7 -8-10 71 .... AndreaAtzeni 4 73
(Chris Dwyer) *dwlt: sn chsng ldrs: rdn ent fnl 2f: unable qck over 1f out: kpt on ins fnl f but nvr gng pce to threaten ldrs* **14/1**

5034 **6** *shd* **Barwick**[19] 5794 4 -9-5 80 .... TedDurcan 8 81
(Mark H Tompkins) *dwlt: in tch in last quartet: rdn and effrt jst over 2f out: drvn over 1f out: kpt on fnl f but nvr gng pce to chal ldrs* **5/1**[2]

0-11 **7** 1 ¼ **Dannios**[36] 5214 6 -8-4 72 .... (t) NoelGarbutt[(7)] 1 70
(Ed Walker) *stdd s: hld up in rr: rdn and effrt over 2f out: styd on ins fnl f: n.d* **6/1**[3]

2661 **8** 1 **Patriotic (IRE)**[7] 6141 4 -8-7 75 6ex .... ThomasBrown[(7)] 5 71
(Chris Dwyer) *lw: in tch in last quartet: effrt u.p ent fnl 2f: kpt on same pce and no threat to ldrs fnl f* **13/2**

150 **9** 25 **Falcon In Flight**[32] 5365 3 -9-1 80 .... (p) FrankieDettori 3 19
(Jeremy Noseda) *in tch in midfield: rdn and unable qck over 2f out: dropped to rr and btn over 1f out: eased ent fnl f* **17/2**

1m 38.32s (-2.28) **Going Correction** -0.15s/f (Firm)
WFA 3 from 4yo+ 4lb **9**Ran SP% **112.4**
Speed ratings (Par 105): **105,104,103,102,101 101,100,99,74**
Tote Swingers 1&2 £3.50, 2&3 £14.10, 1&3 £9.70 CSF £21.41 CT £253.26 TOTE £3.00 : £1.10, £2.10, £4.80 ; EX 15.60 .
Owner Miss Pat O'Kelly **Bred** Kilcarn Stud **Trained** Newmarket, Suffolk

FOCUS
Plenty of these made some sort of appeal, so the form looks reliable for the class. The winner continues on the up.

6382 GREENE KING IPA H'CAP 5f 43y
4:55 (4:56) (Class 2) (0-100,97) 3-Y-O+ **£9,955** (£2,979; £1,489; £745; £371) Stalls Centre

Form RPR

056 **1** **My Propeller (IRE)**[11] 6028 3 -9-1 92 .... FrankieDettori 6 106+
(Peter Chapple-Hyam) *in tch: trckd ldr jst over 2f out: rdn to ld jst ins fnl f: sn clr and r.o strly: easily* **9/4**[1]

0005 **2** 3 ½ **Stone Of Folca**[23] 5663 4 -9-7 97 .... FrederikTylicki 7 98
(John Best) *taken down early: in tch: rdn and edgd lft over 1f out: hdd ins fnl f: no ex and sn btn: hld on for 2nd cl home* **7/2**[3]

5300 **3** *hd* **Waseem Faris (IRE)**[9] 6234 3 -8-7 84 .... SamHitchcott 4 85
(Mick Channon) *in tch: effrt u.p over 1f out: drvn and kpt on ins fnl f to press for 2nd cl home: no ch w wnr* **8/1**

0004 **4** 2 ½ **Piazza San Pietro**[1] 6346 6 -8-13 89 .... NeilCallan 2 81
(Zoe Davison) *stdd after s: hld up in tch: effrt whn nt clr run and swtchd rt over 1f out: kpt on ins fnl f but no ch w wnr* **11/1**

040 **5** *hd* **Whaileyy (IRE)**[46] 4802 4 -9-5 95 .... (b) AndreaAtzeni 8 86
(Marco Botti) *lw: chsd ldr tl jst over 2f out: unable qck u.p over 1f out: lost 3rd and btn 1f out: wknd ins fnl f* **11/4**[2]

0400 **6** 2 ¼ **Dancing Freddy (IRE)**[63] 4576 5 -8-11 87 .... (tp) SaleemGolam 3 70
(Violet M Jordan) *chsd ldrs: rdn and struggling 2f out: no ex and btn ent fnl f: wknd* **8/1**

0410 **7** 2 ¾ **Piscean (USA)**[18] 5832 7 -8-9 88 .... (b) RyanClark[(3)] 1 61
(Tom Keddy) *a bhd: rdn and no hdwy 2f out: n.d* **28/1**

1m 0.74s (-1.96) **Going Correction** -0.15s/f (Firm)
WFA 3 from 4yo+ 1lb **7**Ran SP% **113.7**
Speed ratings (Par 109): **109,103,103,99,98 95,90**
Tote Swingers 1&2 £3.10, 2&3 £4.00, 1&3 £3.50 CSF £10.30 CT £51.23 TOTE £2.60 : £1.40, £3.40; EX 10.70 .
Owner Joseph Barton **Bred** D J & Mrs Brown **Trained** Newmarket, Suffolk

FOCUS
The first two home were arguably the class horses in the race at the trip. The winner built on her latest promise.

NOTEBOOK
My Propeller (IRE)◆ had a good chance of getting back into the winner's enclosure, and she didn't disappoint. Racing without a hood, she hadn't been disgraced on her last two outings and quickened nicely here after tracking the early leader. With her confidence boosted, she should be respected wherever she runs for the remainder of the season. (op 5-2 tchd 15-8)
Stone Of Folca had won both of his races on his seasonal return (he also finished a head second on his racecourse debut), so might be at his peak when really fresh. That said, there was little wrong with this effort, although he was the best of these on official figures and was entitled to take second. (tchd 4-1)
Waseem Faris (IRE)has been busy during 2012, and stayed on respectably to claim third. (op 7-1 tchd 13-2)
Piazza San Pietro, fourth of five here the previous day over 6f, stayed on but never looked dangerous. (op 10-1 tchd 14-1)
Whaileyy(IRE), given a short break since finishing down the field in the Stewards' Cup, didn't do a lot when off the bridle. (op 3-1 tchd 5-2)

6383 LA CONTINENTAL CAFE BAR GREAT YARMOUTH H'CAP — 2m
5:25 (5:30) (Class 4) (0-85,82) 3-Y-O **£4,075** (£1,212; £606 ; £303) **Stalls** High

Form				RPR
2200	**1**		**Bordoni (USA)**[109] 2718 3 -9-7**82** ... NeilCallan 1 (Mark Johnston) *lw: mde all: rdn 3f out: drew clr 2f out: styd on wl: readily* **9/4**[2]	94+
2033	**2**	2 ¾	**Petaluma**[9] 6098 3 -8-9**70** ... SamHitchcott 5 (Mick Channon) *hld up in tch: rdn to chse ldrs 2f out: kpt on to go 2nd wl ins fnl f: no threat to wnr* **8/1**	77
3152	**3**	1	**Arch Villain (IRE)**[11] 6037 3 -9-1**76** ... PatDobbs 6 (Amanda Perrett) *pressed wnr: rdn 4f out: outpcd and struggling whn edgd lft over 1f out: plugged on same pce and btn fnl f: lost 2nd fnl 75yds* **5/4**[1]	82
215	**4**	9	**Adeste**[34] 5277 3 -9-0**75** ...(b[1]) JamieSpencer 2 (Noel Quinlan) *stdd s: t.k.h: chsd ldrs after 2f tl 6f out: rdn and effrt to press ldrs 4f out: btn 2f out: sn wknd* **14/1**	70
5314	**5**	13	**Awesome Pearl (USA)**[11] 6037 3 -9-3**78** ... LukeMorris 3 (Sir Mark Prescott Bt) *lw: in tch in rr: niggled along 7f out: rdn and struggling 4f out: bhd fnl 2f* **5/1**[3]	57

3m 31.52s (-0.88)**Going Correction** -0.075s/f (Good) **5**Ran SP% **109.7**
Speed ratings (Par 103): **99,97,97,92,86**
Tote Swingers 1&6 £6.90 CSF £18.55 TOTE £3.20 : £2.00 , £2.20 ; EX 16.10 .
Owner Sheikh Hamdan Bin Mohammed Al Maktoum **Bred** Darley **Trained** Middleham Moor, N Yorks

FOCUS
Letting a Mark Johnston runner have a relatively easy lead can often prove a mistake, as the winner proved here. He was on a fair mark on turf. This race was not the strongest with the favourite below his latest form.
T/Plt: £1,530.20 to a £1 stake. Pool: £76,629.78 - 36.55 winning tickets. T/Qpdt: £349.80 to a £1 stake. Pool: £5,957.06 - 12.60 w. tckts SP 6384a - 6386a (Foreign Racing) See RI

5184 AYR (L-H)
Thursday, September 20
6387 Meeting Abandoned - Waterlogged

6362 KEMPTON (A.W) (R-H)
Thursday, September 20
OFFICIAL GOING: Standard
Wind: Light, across Weather: Cloudy

6395 32REDBINGO H'CAP (DIV I) — 1m (P)
5:40 (5:40) (Class 6) (0-55,55) 3-Y-0+ **£1,617** (£481; £240 ; £120) **Stalls** Low

Form				RPR
0023	**1**		**Pastoral Jet**[13] 5996 4 -8-11**50** ... RyanPowell(3) 9 (Richard Rowe) *hld up in last trio on inner: prog over 2f out: clsd on ldrs and edgd lft 1f out: styd on to ld last 75yds* **5/1**[2]	58
6355	**2**	hd	**Exopuntia**[25] 5633 6 -8-13**49** ... JamesDoyle 6 (Julia Feilden) *hld up in midfield: smooth prog over 2f out: led wl over 1f out: hdd and nt qckn jst over 1f out: rallied and upsides ins fnl f: no ex last strides* **25/1**	56
0044	**3**	½	**Having A Ball**[34] 5310 8 -9-0**55** ... MatthewLawson(5) 7 (Jonathan Portman) *hld up in last trio: gd prog on outer over 2f out: led jst over 1f out: hdd and no ex last 75yds* **10/1**	61
5010	**4**	2 ¼	**Silly Billy (IRE)**[17] 572 4 -9-5**55** ... LiamKeniry 10 (Sylvester Kirk) *hld up towards rr: prog over 2f out: clsd to chal and upsides jst over 1f out: wknd last 100yds* **25/1**	56
0462	**5**	1	**Imperial Wave (IRE)**[20] 5804 3 -8-13**53** ...(b) TedDurcan 14 (David Lanigan) *hld up in midfield: swtchd lft and rdn over 2f out: clsd on ldrs over 1f out: fdd ins fnl f* **15/2**	52
066	**6**	2 ¼	**Noosa Boy**[16] 5901 3 -8-12**52** ... IanMongan 13 (Luke Dace) *hld up in last trio: prog over 2f out: tried to cl on ldrs over 1f out: fdd ins fnl f* **25/1**	45
0004	**7**	1 ½	**Opus (IRE)**[4] 6281 3 -8-12**52** ...(t) PatDobbs 4 (Amanda Perrett) *hld up in midfield: tried to make prog 2f out: no hdwy jst over 1f out* **7/1**[3]	42
000	**8**	hd	**Clearing House**[3] 6316 7 -9-2**52** ... KirstyMilczarek 5 (John Ryan) *hld up in midfield: prog and cl up over 1f out: steadily wknd after* **33/1**	41
0000	**9**	1	**Invincible Beauty (IRE)**[66] 3466 3 -8-10**50** ...(t) DaneO'Neill 11 (Seamus Durack) *s.v.s and lost many l: ct up on outer after 3f: rdn over 2f out: sn lost pl and btn* **33/1**	37
0400	**10**	2 ¼	**Rosy Dawn**[3] 6304 7 -8-10**46** oh1 ... KieranO'Neill 12 (John Bridger) *led to wl over 1f out: wknd* **50/1**	28
2041	**11**	4	**Tigertoo (IRE)**[3] 6316 3 -7-13**46** ... LouisSteward(7) 8 (Stuart Williams) *prom: disp 2nd over 2f out: wknd over 1f out* **11/8**[1]	19
000	**12**	2 ¼	**Lal Bhai**[176] 1065 4 -8-12**53** ... AmyScott(5) 1 (Chris Down) *pushed up after s to chse ldr: lost 2nd over 3f out: wknd wl over 1f out* **50/1**	21
5500	**13**	2 ¾	**Lightning Spirit**[54] 4586 4 -9-3**53** ...(p) GeorgeBaker 3 (Gary Moore) *prom: chsd ldr over 3f out to over 2f out: wknd qckly* **20/1**	14

1m 39.14s (-0.66)**Going Correction** -0.15s/f (Stan)
WFA 3 from 4yo+ 4lb **13**Ran SP% **118.2**
Speed ratings (Par 101): **97,96,96,94,93 90,89,89,88,85 81,79,76**
toteswingers 1&2 £13.60, 2&3 £28.00, 1&3 £4.70 CSF £126.62 CT £1204.36 TOTE £5.30 : £2.10, £6.70 , £2.60 ; EX 103.50 TRIFECTA Not won. .
Owner Andy Taylor **Bred** Pearl & David Moore **Trained** Sullington, W Sussex

FOCUS
The first division of a moderate handicap for 3yos and up. The pace was strongly contested. The first and third horses home came from the rear entering the home straight. A small personal best from the winner.

6396 32REDBINGO H'CAP (DIV II) — 1m (P)
6:10 (6:10) (Class 6) (0-55,55) 3-Y-0+ **£1,617** (£481; £240 ; £120) **Stalls** Low

Form				RPR
5444	**1**		**Wyndham Wave**[21] 5764 3 -8-13**53** ...(p) JamesMillman 9 (Rod Millman) *hld up in midfield: hd at awkward angle but prog fr 2f out to ld jst ins fnl f: cajoled along and styd on* **3/1**[2]	62
0006	**2**	1	**Divine Rule (IRE)**[8] 6329 4 -9-0**50** ow2 ...(v) AmirQuinn 8 (Laura Mongan) *trckd ldrs: prog 2f out: chal and upsides 1f out: jst outpcd last 150yds* **25/1**	55
2036	**3**	¾	**Chez Vrony**[15] 5939 6 -8-10**46** oh1 ... DavidProbert 12 (Dave Morris) *wl in tch towards outer: prog 2f out: rdn to chal 1f out: styd on same pce* **10/1**[3]	51
603	**4**	1 ¼	**Bold Ring**[26] 5592 6 -8-12**55** ... JoeyHaynes(7) 6 (Eric Wheeler) *trckd ldrs: wnt 2nd 2f out: rdn to chal and upsides 1f out: fdd last 100yds* **11/1**	57
060	**5**	2 ¼	**Coach Montana (IRE)**[37] 5215 3 -8-10**50** ...(b) BrettDoyle 1 (Jane Chapple-Hyam) *led to 1/2-way: led over 2f out: tried to kick on and edgd rt to far rail: hdd & wknd jst ins fnl f* **20/1**	47
100	**6**	hd	**Carpentras**[58] 4436 4 -9-3**53** ...(b[1]) DarryllHolland 3 (Dr Jon Scargill) *wl in tch in midfield: v awkward bnd 4f out to 3f out: rdn and effrt over 2f out: kpt on but no threat* **20/1**	49
5-00	**7**	2 ¼	**Best In Show**[105] 2862 3 -8-13**53** ...(t) AdamKirby 7 (Roger Curtis) *dwlt: hld up wl in rr: sme prog into midfield and reminder over 1f out: rdn ins fnl f: nvr nr ldrs* **20/1**	44
3200	**8**	¾	**The Bay Bandit**[5] 6252 5 -8-10**53** ... WilliamTwiston-Davies(7) 4 (Neil Mulholland) *sn trckd ldr: led 1/2-way: rdn and hdd over 2f out: wknd over 1f out* **10/1**[3]	43
0000	**9**	nk	**Hawkino (IRE)**[14] 5970 3 -8-6**46** oh1 ...(v) MartinDwyer 5 (Derek Shaw) *dwlt: hld up wl in rr: sme prog on inner over 2f out: no hdwy over 1f out: eased* **20/1**	35
0560	**10**	½	**One Cool Chick**[8] 6150 4 -9-4**54** ... KieranO'Neill 10 (John Bridger) *dwlt: a wl in rr: lost tch over 2f out: nvr on terms after* **40/1**	42
0001	**11**	½	**True Prince (USA)**[4] 6274 3 -8-12**52** 7ex ...(b) JimCrowley 11 (Amanda Perrett) *dwlt: sn pressed ldng pair and racd on outer: rdn over 2f out: wknd over 1f out* **11/4**[1]	39
000	**12**	5	**Maligned (USA)**[14] 5970 3 -9-1**55** ... PatDobbs 14 (Richard Hannon) *racd on outer: a towards rr: struggling and lost tch over 2f out* **12/1**	30
0U54	**13**	6	**Cluaindubhloch (IRE)**[20] 5805 4 -8-10**46** oh1 ... KirstyMilczarek 13 (Tony Carroll) *rrd s: plld hrd: hld up in rr: struggling on outer 3f out: sn wknd* **50/1**	7
00-6	**14**	43	**Present Story**[18] 5850 5 -8-11**47** ... SebSanders 2 (Ian Wood) *prom: rdn over 3f out: sn wknd rapidly: virtually p.u fnl 2f* **14/1**	

1m 39.52s (-0.28)**Going Correction** -0.15s/f (Stan)
WFA 3 from 4yo+ 4lb **14**Ran SP% **119.8**
Speed ratings (Par 101): **95,94,93,92,89 89,87,86,86,85 85,80,74,31**
toteswingers 1&2 £18.20, 1&3 £8.60, 2&3 £108.20 CSF £82.85 CT £685.48 TOTE £4.20 : £2.20 , £6.00, £2.40 ; EX 87.70 TRIFECTA Not won. .
Owner Kentisbeare Racing **Bred** Newsells Park Stud **Trained** Kentisbeare, Devon
■ Stewards' Enquiry : Amir Quinn three-day ban: weighed-in 2lb heavy (Oct 4-6)

FOCUS
The second division of a moderate handicap for 3yos and up. The pace was contested and it helped to challenge from the off the gallop. The winning time was comparatively slower than the first instalment. The winner is rated in line with his C&D latest.
Carpentras Official explanation: jockey said filly ran too free
Cluaindubhloch(IRE) Official explanation: jockey said gelding hung right
Present Story Official explanation: trainer's rep said mare had a breathing problem

6397 32RED.COM MAIDEN STKS — 1m (P)
6:40 (6:40) (Class 5) 3-Y-0+ **£2,264** (£673; £336 ; £168) **Stalls** Low

Form				RPR
0-	**1**		**Net Whizz (USA)**[340] 3823 3 -9-3**0** ... WilliamBuick 12 (Jeremy Noseda) *dwlt: rapid prog on outer fr rr to ld over 5f out: mde rest: pushed clr over 2f out: shkn up and stl looked green over 1f out: styd on wl: impressive* **5/2**[2]	82+
	2	3 ½	**Tropics (USA)** 4 -9-7**0** ... BrettDoyle 3 (Dean Ivory) *t.k.h: hld up in midfield: outpcd fr 3f out: gd prog jst over 2f out: styd on wl to take 2nd last 150yds: no ch w wnr* **66/1**	73+
44	**3**	1	**Spring Tonic**[27] 5555 3 -9-3**0** ... J-PGuillambert 13 (Luca Cumani) *prom: chsd wnr over 5f out to over 3f out: styd on to go 2nd again briefly 1f out: kpt on* **10/1**[3]	71+
	4	1 ¾	**Guest Of Honour (IRE)** 3 -9-3**0** ... AdamKirby 9 (Marco Botti) *dwlt: hld up and last to over 3f out gd prog over 2f out but no ch as ldrs already gone: pushed along and styd on: promising debut* **25/1**	67+
0	**5**	1	**Hint Of Promise**[20] 5795 3 -8-12**0** ... JamesDoyle 6 (Roger Charlton) *hld up in midfield: outpcd fr 3f out: shkn up over 2f out: styd on fr over 1f out: nrst fin* **20/1**	59+
	6	½	**Ehtedaam (USA)** 3 -9-3**0** ... FrankieDettori 2 (Saeed Bin Suroor) *disp ld over 2f: styd prom: chsd wnr over 3f out to 1f out: wknd* **10/11**[1]	63
	7	4 ½	**Embankment** 3 -9-3**0** ... PatDobbs 14 (Amanda Perrett) *dwlt sltly: t.k.h in midfield: outpcd fr 3f out: shkn up and no ch after: plugged on* **25/1**	52+
04	**8**	1 ½	**Rokcella**[31] 5404 3 -8-12**0** ... JohnFahy 11 (Clive Cox) *disp ld over 2f: rdn and outpcd wl over 2f out: sn btn* **50/1**	44
6-	**9**	hd	**Black Minstrel (IRE)**[421] 4446 3 -9-3**0** ... JimCrowley 10 (Amanda Perrett) *a towards rr: outpcd fr 3f out and no ch after: plugged on* **14/1**	48
0	**10**	9	**Sambirano**[35] 5276 3 -9-3**0** ... DarryllHolland 4 (William Knight) *disp ld over 2f: chsd ldrs: wl outpcd fr 3f out: sn wknd* **80/1**	27

6- **11** *1* **The Cash Generator (IRE)**[495] 2097 4-9-7 0............ JamieGoldstein 5 24
(Ralph Smith) *dwlt sltly: hld up towards rr: already struggling whn rn wd bnd 3f out: sn bhd* **33/1**

0 **12** *nk* **Ivan The Engine**[14] 5970 4-9-7 0........................ SebSanders 1 24
(Ian Wood) *hld up in rr: lost tch w ldrs and struggling wl over 2f out: sn bhd* **100/1**

0-4 **13** *2 ¾* **Widow Flower (IRE)**[34] 5299 3-8-12 0........................ MartinDwyer 8 12
(Michael Bell) *disp ld over 2f: wknd 3f out* **66/1**

0 **14** *35* **Soviet Dream**[24] 5679 3-9-3 0........................(p) GeorgeBaker 7
(James Fanshawe) *a in rr: struggling whn carried wd bnd 3f out: t.o* **33/1**

1m 37.34s (-2.46) **Going Correction** -0.15s/f (Stan)
WFA 3 from 4yo 4lb **14** Ran SP% **122.2**
Speed ratings (Par 103): **106,102,101,99,98 98,93,92,92,83 82,81,79,44**
toteswingers 1&2 £44.40, 2&3 £144.40, 1&3 £4.30 CSF £175.07 TOTE £2.90: £1.40, £21.90, £3.40; EX 267.00 TRIFECTA Not won..
Owner Mrs Susan Roy & Tom Ludt **Bred** Woodford Thoroughbreds LLC **Trained** Newmarket, Suffolk

FOCUS
A modest maiden for 3yos and up but the winning time appears decent. Not much form to go on and autumn 3-y-o maidens are often not the strongest, but the winner impressed.
The Cash Generator(IRE) Official explanation: jockey said gelding hung left on the bend

6398 32REDPOKER.COM MEDIAN AUCTION MAIDEN STKS 1m 4f (P)
7:10 (7:13) (Class 6) 3-4-Y-O **£1,617** (£481; £240; £120) **Stalls** Centre

Form RPR

0-2 **1** **Tempest Fugit (IRE)**[142] 1724 3-8-12 0........................ WilliamBuick 9 82+
(John Gosden) *led after 1f: set stdy pce tl chal 1/2-way: urged along and drew clr over 2f out: wl ahd fnl f: eased* **10/11**[1]

2240 **2** *8* **Roc De Prince**[12] 6045 3-9-3 77........................ MartinDwyer 4 74
(Richard Fahey) *led briefly early: trckd wnr: tried to chal 1/2-way: lft bhd fr over 2f out: jst prevailed in battle for 2nd* **11/4**[2]

56 **3** *½* **Shea**[21] 5766 3-8-12 0........................ JimCrowley 7 68
(Ralph Beckett) *trckd ldrs: no ch w wnr fr over 2f out but chal for 2nd rest of way* **8/1**

5355 **4** *2 ¼* **Ty Gwr**[21] 5766 3-9-3 70........................ FergusSweeney 5 69
(David Simcock) *s.s: t.k.h and hld up in last: prog 5f out: wnt 4th over 2f out: kpt on but no threat* **6/1**[3]

0- **5** *9* **Sunny Bank**[321] 7258 3-9-3 0........................ LiamKeniry 2 55
(Andrew Balding) *hld up: rdn over 3f out: sn lft bhd and btn* **20/1**

6 **6** *3* **Bridge That Gap**[142] 1724 4-9-11 0........................ DaneO'Neill 10 50
(Roger Ingram) *dwlt: hld up in rr: prog to go 4th 5f out: wknd over 2f out* **100/1**

50 **7** *1 ½* **Black Dragon**[6] 6215 4-9-6 0........................ TobyAtkinson(5) 6 48
(Mark Rimmer) *dwlt: t.k.h and hld up in last pair: effrt over 3f out: wknd over 2f out* **33/1**

0 **8** *17* **Darwinian**[164] 1261 3-8-12 0........................ DavidProbert 8 16
(Dave Morris) *in tch: effrt 1/2-way: drvn 4f out: sn wknd: t.o* **66/1**

00- **9** *17* **Asparella**[293] 7598 3-8-12 0........................ KieranO'Neill 3
(Raymond York) *t.k.h: led briefly early: drvn and dropped to last 5f out: wl t.o* **100/1**

2m 33.22s (-1.28) **Going Correction** -0.15s/f (Stan)
WFA 3 from 4yo 8lb **9** Ran SP% **115.6**
Speed ratings (Par 101): **98,92,92,90,84 82,81,70,59**
toteswingers 1&2 £1.30, 2&3 £3.50, 1&3 £1.80 CSF £3.40 TOTE £1.50: £1.02, £1.80, £2.10; EX 3.70 Trifecta £16.00 Pool: £1310.17 - 60.35 winning tickets..
Owner A E Oppenheimer **Bred** Michael Woodlock And Seamus Kennedy **Trained** Newmarket, Suffolk

FOCUS
A modest middle-distance median auction maiden for 3-4yos with no depth. The winner did it well and the third and fourth set the standard.

6399 £32 FREE AT 32RED.COM H'CAP 2m (P)
7:40 (7:43) (Class 6) (0-60,64) 3-Y-O+ **£1,617** (£481; £240; £120) **Stalls** Low

Form RPR

252/ **1** **Goldan Jess (IRE)**[32] 6558 8-9-0 **45**........................ AdamKirby 11 54
(Philip Kirby) *mde all: kicked on over 3f out: looked vulnerable fr 2f out: kpt on wl: jst hld on* **25/1**

31 **2** *nse* **Azrag (USA)**[3] 6323 4-10-5 **64** 6ex........................(p) LukeMorris 3 73
(Gerard Butler) *t.k.h: hld up in midfield: rdn over 3f out: prog u.p 2f out: tk 2nd ins fnl f: clsd on wnr fin: jst failed* **6/1**[2]

03-2 **3** *2* **Lakota Ghost (USA)**[192] 600 4-10-0 **59**........................ GeorgeBaker 13 66
(Seamus Durack) *hld up in midfield: smooth prog to chse wnr over 2f out: rdn and fnd nil over 1f out: lost 2nd ins fnl f* **15/2**[3]

002 **4** *3 ¼* **Gucci D'Oro (USA)**[22] 5744 3-8-13 **56**........................(p) WilliamBuick 2 59
(David Simcock) *trckd ldng pair: lost pl sltly over 3f out: renewed effrt 2f out: nt qckn and hld fr over 1f out* **13/8**[1]

-050 **5** *3 ¼* **Mahayogin (USA)**[14] 5974 4-9-6 **51**........................(t) RichardHughes 9 50
(Brendan Powell) *hld up in rr: rdn over 3f out: sme prog over 2f out: one pce and no imp over 1f out* **17/2**

050/ **6** *4* **Causeway King (USA)**[21] 5286 6-9-13 **58**........................(t) HayleyTurner 12 52
(Alex Hales) *chsd wnr to over 2f out: steadily wknd* **25/1**

060- **7** *1* **Burnbrake**[351] 6622 7-9-2 **47**........................ PatDobbs 5 40
(Richard Rowe) *hld up in last trio: sme prog over 3f out: no hdwy last 2f: nvr on terms* **40/1**

000- **8** *3 ¾* **Investment World (IRE)**[429] 4190 4-9-10 **55**........................ DavidProbert 10 43
(Tim Vaughan) *trckd ldng pair: chal for 2nd over 3f out: wknd over 2f out* **40/1**

0000 **9** *3 ¼* **Al Qatari (USA)**[15] 5945 3-8-8 **51**........................(b) MircoDemuro 1 35
(William Haggas) *in tch tl rdn and wknd over 3f out* **6/1**[2]

0000 **10** *½* **Alexs Rainbow (USA)**[14] 5974 4-9-1 **46**........................ IanMongan 7 30
(Luke Dace) *t.k.h: hld up in midfield: rdn over 3f out: wknd over 2f out* **25/1**

6325 **11** *41* **Old Boy Ted**[71] 3969 4-9-3 **48**........................ DarryllHolland 6
(Mark H Tompkins) *hld up in last trio: rdn over 3f out: sn wknd rapidly: t.o* **16/1**

010/ **12** *6* **Tusculum (IRE)**[1234] 1767 9-9-3 **48**........................ DaraghO'Donohoe 4
(Barney Curley) *hld up in last trio: gng strly 7f out: wknd rapidly 4f out: sn wl t.o* **11/1**

3m 30.62s (0.52) **Going Correction** -0.15s/f (Stan)
WFA 3 from 4yo+ 12lb **12** Ran SP% **119.6**
Speed ratings (Par 101): **92,91,90,89,87 85,85,83,81,81 60,57**
toteswingers 1&2 £12.00, 2&3 £4.60, 1&3 £17.20 CSF £163.15 CT £1257.70 TOTE £28.40: £6.30, £2.30, £2.20; EX 113.10 TRIFECTA Not won..
Owner The Jessies,Colin Fletcher,Philip Kirby **Bred** Bendis Partnership **Trained** Castleton, N Yorks

FOCUS
A modest staying handicap for 3yos and up. They didn't go a particularly strong gallop for much of the journey with the winner getting an easy lead. He's rated back to his old Flat form.

6400 32RED CONDITIONS STKS 1m (P)
8:10 (8:12) (Class 4) 3-Y-O+ **£4,075** (£1,212; £606; £303) **Stalls** Low

Form RPR

214- **1** **Pearl Mix (IRE)**[439] 3861 3-8-10 98........................ JimCrowley 7 105
(Ralph Beckett) *trckd ldrs: chal 2f out: narrow ld jst over 1f out: asserted last 150yds* **7/1**

-230 **2** *1* **Mastertheroll s (IRE)**[201] 792 4-9-0 104........................ FrankieDettori 9 103
(Saeed Bin Suroor) *trckd ldr: led over 4f out and maintained gd pce: hrd pressed 2f out: hdd jst over 1f out: styd on but hld last 100yds* **5/2**[1]

/3-5 **3** *¾* **Burj Alzain (IRE)**[40] 5118 4-9-0 98........................ LukeMorris 4 101
(Gerard Butler) *hld up in midfield: prog to chal and upsides 2f out: nt qckn over 1f out: styd on after but a hld* **14/1**

-411 **4** *2 ¼* **Storm King**[22] 5747 3-8-10 86........................ BrettDoyle 10 96
(Jane Chapple-Hyam) *hld up in last pair: drvn on outer over 2f out: styd on fr over 1f out: nrst fin* **6/1**[3]

0504 **5** *shd* **I Love Me**[25] 5627 4-8-9 100........................ KirstyMilczarek 8 91
(Andrew Balding) *t.k.h: hld up in midfield: rdn and nt qckn wl over 1f out: kpt on fnl f* **15/2**

1000 **6** *2 ¼* **Nazreef**[12] 6036 5-9-0 103........................(t) DarryllHolland 5 91
(Hughie Morrison) *hld up in rr: rdn over 2f out: no prog and btn over 1f out: kpt on* **20/1**

-200 **7** *1* **Justineo**[14] 5964 3-8-10 100........................ JamesDoyle 3 88
(Roger Varian) *hld up in last pair: sme prog 2f out: no imp on ldrs over 1f out: fdd* **33/1**

1106 **8** *¾* **Primaeval**[12] 6024 6-9-0 99........................(v) HayleyTurner 2 87
(James Fanshawe) *hld up in rr: rdn and no prog over 2f out: wl btn after* **10/3**[2]

1000 **9** *2 ¼* **Talwar (IRE)**[26] 5597 3-9-8 98........................ WilliamBuick 1 93
(Jeremy Noseda) *trckd ldng pair: rdn over 2f out: sn wknd* **33/1**

-134 **10** *1 ¼* **Counterglow (IRE)**[103] 2920 3-9-1 104........................ AhmedAjtebi 6 84
(Mahmood Al Zarooni) *led at gd pce to over 4f out: chsd ldr to 2f out: eased whn btn over 1f out* **16/1**

0300 **U** **Loyalty**[180] 1034 5-9-0 96........................(v) DaneO'Neill 11
(Derek Shaw) *swvd lft leaving stalls and uns rdr* **33/1**

1m 36.44s (-3.36) **Going Correction** -0.15s/f (Stan)
WFA 3 from 4yo+ 4lb **11** Ran SP% **116.3**
Speed ratings (Par 105): **110,109,108,106,105 103,102,101,99,98**
toteswingers 1&2 £3.70, 2&3 £11.60, 1&3 £21.50 CSF £23.56 TOTE £8.70: £3.20, £2.00, £5.90; EX 23.70 TRIFECTA Not won..
Owner Pearl Bloodstock Ltd **Bred** Jean-Etienne Dubois **Trained** Kimpton, Hants

FOCUS
A good class conditions stakes for 3yos and up although the time was not particularly quick. A clear personal best from the winner.
Counterglow(IRE) Official explanation: jockey said, regarding running and riding, that his orders were to ride handy, the gelding was fresh and keen having not run for a long time and in the home straight it appeared to lose its action; vet said gelding returned post-race normal but was breathing heavily.
Loyalty Official explanation: jockey said, on leaving stalls, gelding threw back its head and hit him in the face, causing him to lose his balance.

6401 32RED CASINO H'CAP 1m (P)
8:40 (8:40) (Class 5) (0-75,75) 3-Y-O **£2,264** (£673; £336; £168) **Stalls** Low

Form RPR

0054 **1** **Sky Crossing**[12] 6050 3-9-2 **70**........................ JimCrowley 4 80
(James Given) *trckd ldr: led over 4f out: kicked on over 2f out: hrd pressed nr fin: jst lasted* **14/1**

054 **2** *nse* **Miss Dashwood**[28] 5510 3-9-2 **70**........................ HayleyTurner 12 80
(James Fanshawe) *hld up towards rr: prog wl over 2f out: rdn to chse wnr ins fnl f: str chal nr fin: jst pipped* **11/1**

5525 **3** *1* **Sunley Pride**[19] 5837 3-9-3 **71**........................ SamHitchcott 10 79
(Mick Channon) *hld up towards rr: prog 2f out: tried to cl on ldrs fnl f: styd on to take 3rd last strides* **14/1**

0046 **4** *nk* **Compton Prince**[19] 5837 3-8-12 **66**........................(b) JohnFahy 9 73
(Clive Cox) *trckd ldrs: prog to chse wnr 2f out: rdn over 1f out: nt qckn and hld after: lost 2nd ins fnl f* **20/1**

5123 **5** *shd* **Kinglami**[14] 5971 3-9-3 **71**........................ RichardHughes 8 78+
(Brian Gubby) *hld up in last pair: prog wl over 1f out: tried to cl on ldrs fnl f: styd on but nvr able to chal* **5/1**[2]

6325 **6** *1 ¼* **Feelthedifference**[26] 5592 3-9-2 **70**........................ IanMongan 6 74
(Sir Henry Cecil) *hld up in last pair: rdn over 3f out: prog and swtchd rt towards inner over 2f out: urged along and kpt on: nvr rchd ldrs* **6/1**

234 **7** *2 ¼* **Sir Trevor (IRE)**[40] 5111 3-9-4 **72**........................ RichardKingscote 1 71
(Tom Dascombe) *led to over 4f out: chsd wnr to 2f out: wknd fnl f* **9/2**[1]

4550 **8** *shd* **Scrupul (IRE)**[19] 5837 3-8-13 **70**........................ PatrickHills(3) 5 69
(Luca Cumani) *hld up in rr: prog on outer over 1f out: no imp on ldrs fnl f* **9/1**

604 **9** *3 ¾* **Treasured Dream**[21] 5776 3-8-11 **65**........................ WilliamBuick 2 55
(Amanda Perrett) *dwlt: hld up towards rr: pushed along whn hmpd 2f out and dropped to last: pushed along again and passed a few stragglers fnl f* **14/1**

0462 **10** *shd* **Almaas (USA)**[34] 5329 3-9-4 **72**........................(tp) FrankieDettori 3 62
(Saeed Bin Suroor) *trckd ldrs: rdn wl over 1f out: sn wknd: eased ins fnl f* **11/2**[3]

1435 **11** *1 ½* **Malih**[23] 5721 3-9-4 **72**........................ FergusSweeney 11 59
(Jamie Osborne) *chsd ldrs to over 2f out: sn wknd* **20/1**

1006 **12** *2 ¾* **Hamis Al Bin (IRE)**[13] 6013 3-9-7 **75**........................ AdamKirby 14 55
(Mark Johnston) *chsd ldng pair to over 2f out: sn wknd* **20/1**

-000 **13** *2 ¼* **Red Hot Secret**[35] 5279 3-8-9 **66**........................ RaulDaSilva(3) 7 41
(Jeremy Gask) *nvr bttr than midfield: u.p fr 1/2-way: wknd over 2f out* **100/1**

1m 37.25s (-2.55) **Going Correction** -0.15s/f (Stan) **13** Ran SP% **118.1**
Speed ratings (Par 101): **106,105,104,104,104 103,101,100,97,97 95,92,90**
toteswingers 1&2 £12.30, 2&3 £32.70, 1&3 £37.00 CSF £150.29 CT £2274.12 TOTE £21.50: £6.40, £4.30, £4.50; EX 206.20 TRIFECTA Not won..
Owner Bolton Grange **Bred** Bolton Grange **Trained** Willoughton, Lincs
■ Stewards' Enquiry : Hayley Turner two-day ban: used whip above permitted level (Oct 4-5)

FOCUS
A fair 3yo handicap. The winning time stands up well with the remainder of the card, considering the grade. Solid form, rated on the positive side.

6402 32REDBET.COM H'CAP 6f (P)
9:10 (9:11) (Class 6) (0-65,67) 3-Y-O £1,617 (£481; £240; £120) Stalls Low

Form				RPR
0611	1		**Alnoomaas (IRE)**[7] 6178 3-9-9 67 6ex RichardHughes 9	75+
			(Luke Dace) *mostly trckd ldr tl led 2f out: hld together tl drvn whn pressed over 1f out: in command last 100yds: eased nr fin* **6/4**[1]	
034	2	½	**Tidal's Baby**[20] 5800 3-9-7 65 DavidProbert 3	69
			(Tony Carroll) *hld up in rr: rdn and prog 2f out: chsd wnr and tried to chal jst over 1f out: styd on but hld ins fnl f* **8/1**	
36-2	3	nse	**Compton Rainbow**[14] 5975 3-9-5 63 (t) JamesDoyle 2	67
			(Hans Adielsson) *sn trckd ldng trio: effrt on inner 2f out: hrd rdn to chal jst over 1f out: styd on but hld ins fnl f* **13/2**[3]	
3502	4	1 ½	**Cynthia Calhoun**[39] 5130 3-9-7 65 AdamKirby 4	64
			(Clive Cox) *trckd ldrs: cl enough wl over 1f out: sn rdn and nt qckn: kpt on same pce after* **5/1**[2]	
2000	5	¾	**Darnathean**[12] 6057 3-9-2 60 SebSanders 6	57
			(Paul D'Arcy) *mde most to 2f out: lost 2nd jst over 1f out: fdd grad* **7/1**	
5420	6	5	**Intomist (IRE)**[77] 3790 3-9-6 64 (p) PatCosgrave 1	45
			(Jim Boyle) *hld up in rr: rdn and no prog over 2f out: no ch after* **12/1**	
U224	7	1 ¾	**Mitie Mouse**[39] 5127 3-9-0 58 (p) PatDobbs 7	33
			(Mike Murphy) *w ldng pair on outer: chal 1/2-way: wknd wl over 1f out* **10/1**	
000	8	3 ¾	**Highway Warrior**[89] 3389 3-8-12 56 ow1 JamieGoldstein 5	19
			(Zoe Davison) *a in rr: wknd over 2f out* **50/1**	
3424	9	1 ½	**King's Future**[18] 5850 3-8-7 58 ow1 (v[1]) AaronChave(7) 8	16
			(Lee Carter) *racd wd in rr: wknd over 2f out* **20/1**	

1m 12.02s (-1.08) **Going Correction** -0.15s/f (Stan) 9 Ran SP% 117.1
Speed ratings (Par 99): **101,100,100,98,97 90,88,83,81**
toteswingers 1&2 £1.50, 2&3 £5.80, 1&3 £2.50 CSF £14.66 CT £62.90 TOTE £1.70: £1.10, £2.60, £1.20; EX 15.20 Trifecta £100.00 Pool: £1224.85 - 9.06 winning tickets..
Owner Mark Benton **Bred** Old Carhue & Grange Bloodstock **Trained** Five Oaks, W Sussex

FOCUS
A modest 3yo handicap, rated around the second and third with a cosy winner.
T/Plt: £191.20 to a £1 stake. Pool: £69,050.16 - 263.51 winning tickets. T/Qpdt: £20.90 to a £1 stake. Pool: £7,332.91 - 258.40 winning tickets. JN

5382 PONTEFRACT (L-H)
Thursday, September 20

OFFICIAL GOING: Good to firm (good in places; 8.1)
Wind: Virtually nil Weather: Overcast

6403 WAKEFIELD LOW CARBON COMMUNITIES AND VISCOUNT APPRENTICE H'CAP 6f
2:30 (2:31) (Class 5) (0-70,75) 3-Y-O+ £2,264 (£673; £336; £168) Stalls Low

Form				RPR
0240	1		**Ryedane (IRE)**[9] 6127 10-8-7 60 (b) RachelRichardson(5) 5	68
			(Tim Easterby) *trckd ldrs: hdwy on inner 2f out: swtchd rt and rdn to chal ent fnl f: led last 100yds: hld on wl* **12/1**	
0656	2	hd	**Powerful Pierre**[12] 6053 5-8-12 60 (v) DavidSimmonson 11	67
			(Ian McInnes) *trckd ldrs: hdwy over 2f out: swtchd rt and rdn over 1f out: styd on to chal ins fnl f and ev ch: jst hld* **20/1**	
4560	3	1 ¼	**Boy The Bell**[34] 5295 5-8-9 57 JacobButterfield 14	60
			(Ollie Pears) *in tch: hdwy on outer to chse ldrs wl over 1f out: sn rdn and kpt on fnl f* **16/1**	
1003	4	1 ½	**Restless Bay (IRE)**[22] 5737 4-9-7 69 (p) ConorHarrison 7	67
			(Mrs K Burke) *hld up in midfield: hdwy over 2f out: rdn to chse ldrs over 1f out: kpt on fnl f: nrst fin* **5/1**[2]	
1500	5	hd	**Half A Crown (IRE)**[56] 4495 7-8-9 64 DanielleMooney(7) 12	62
			(Peter Salmon) *trckd ldrs: effrt 2f out: sn rdn and ev ch: hld whn n.m.r and one pce ins fnl f* **25/1**	
300	6	2	**Myjestic Melody (IRE)**[10] 6100 4-8-4 55 oh6 EvaMoscrop(3) 1	46
			(Noel Wilson) *led: rdn along 2f out: drvn ent fnl f: sn hdd & wknd* **28/1**	
3202	7	1 ¼	**Consistant**[32] 5389 4-9-3 65 DanielMuscutt 6	52
			(Brian Baugh) *cl up: chal 2f out: sn rdn and ev ch: drvn and wkng whn n.m.r ins fnl f* **9/2**[1]	
2330	8	2	**Needy McCredie**[27] 5543 6-8-7 58 JordanNason(3) 15	39
			(James Turner) *midfield: hdwy and in tch on outer 1/2-way: rdn to chse ldrs and hung lft over 1f out: sn no imp* **12/1**	
0424	9	1	**Bartley**[27] 5538 3-8-7 62 (v) PeterSword(5) 3	40
			(Bryan Smart) *a towards rr* **10/1**	
5000	10	1	**Errigal Lad**[16] 5915 7-8-7 55 oh1 GemmaTutty 8	29
			(Garry Woodward) *s.i.s: a in rr* **16/1**	
0000	11	1	**Cathcart Castle**[23] 5708 4-8-1 56 oh10 ow1 (e[1]) GemmaNellist(7) 10	27
			(Simon West) *a in rr* **66/1**	
2001	12	nk	**Dickie Le Davoir**[5] 6260 8-9-8 75 6ex (b) LukeLeadbitter(5) 2	45
			(Richard Guest) *dwlt and sn rdn along: a in rr* **11/2**[3]	
2003	13	¾	**Another Citizen (IRE)**[6] 6195 4-9-2 69 (b) GaryMahon(5) 13	37
			(Tim Easterby) *cl up: rdn along 2f out: wknd appr fnl f* **6/1**	
4006	14	5	**Rutterkin (USA)**[16] 5923 4-8-0 55 oh2 JordanHibberd(7) 4	7
			(Alan Berry) *s.i.s: a in rr* **20/1**	

1m 16.57s (-0.33) **Going Correction** -0.075s/f (Good)
WFA 3 from 4yo+ 2lb 14 Ran SP% 119.1
Speed ratings (Par 103): **99,98,97,95,94 92,90,87,86,85 83,83,82,75**
toteswingers 1&2 £23.50, 1&3 £43.90, 2&3 £61.90 CSF £237.63 CT £3917.04 TOTE £16.50: £5.00, £4.80, £7.00; EX 182.80.
Owner Habton Farms **Bred** Tally-Ho Stud **Trained** Great Habton, N Yorks
■ Rachel Richardson's first winner as an apprentice, to go with one she rode as an amateur.
■ Stewards' Enquiry : Jacob Butterfield two-day ban: used whip in incorrect place (Oct 4-5)

FOCUS
The going was slightly altered prior to racing after 1mm of overnight rain. Clerk of the course Norman Gundill reported that there were "probably more good than good to firm places. The last 2f is good to firm but there is a fantastic cover of grass - the track has not been raced on for five weeks." There was over 30lb separating the official marks of the horses at each end of the weights (bottom five out of the handicap) in what was an open race. The first three all stepped up on recent efforts.

6404 SUBSCRIBE ONLINE AT RACINGUK.COM MEDIAN AUCTION MAIDEN STKS 5f
3:00 (3:00) (Class 5) 2-Y-O £2,264 (£673; £336; £168) Stalls Low

Form				RPR
53	1		**Cross My Heart**[11] 6071 2-8-12 0 (t) AdamBeschizza 4	71+
			(William Haggas) *wnt sltly rt s: mde all: rdn and qcknd clr wl over 1f out: rdn out* **5/2**[2]	
46	2	2 ¼	**Teetotal (IRE)**[27] 5544 2-9-3 64 SilvestreDeSousa 6	67
			(Nigel Tinkler) *wnt rt s: a chsng wnr: rdn wl over 1f out: kpt on same pce u.p fnl f* **12/1**	
0	3	4 ½	**Scarlet Spirit (IRE)**[12] 6049 2-8-12 0 TomEaves 3	46+
			(Ann Duffield) *towards rr: pushed along and rn green 1/2-way: rdn and hdwy on inner wl over 1f out: kpt on fnl f: nrst fin* **11/1**	
	4	nk	**Shatin Secret** 2-9-0 0 GaryBartley(3) 1	50
			(Noel Wilson) *chsd ldng pair: rdn along 2f out: wknd over 1f out: lost 3rd towards fin* **10/1**	
34	5	1 ½	**Another Claret**[12] 6042 2-9-3 0 FrederikTylicki 8	44
			(Richard Fahey) *wnt rt s: sn pushed along in rr: rdn 1/2-way: n.d* **9/4**[1]	
55	6	3 ¾	**Bapak Pesta (IRE)**[43] 4960 2-9-3 0 PhillipMakin 7	31
			(Kevin Ryan) *wnt rt s: in rr: pushed along 1/2-way: rdn 2f out: sn wknd and eased ins fnl f* **11/4**[3]	

1m 3.32s (0.02) **Going Correction** -0.075s/f (Good) 6 Ran SP% 111.1
Speed ratings (Par 95): **96,92,85,84,82 76**
toteswingers 1&2 £3.50, 1&3 £4.90, 2&3 £6.90 CSF £29.26 TOTE £2.30: £1.10, £5.40; EX 13.60.
Owner Hot To Trot Racing Club 2 **Bred** Whitsbury Manor Stud **Trained** Newmarket, Suffolk

FOCUS
It was difficult to know what to make of these as a bunch before the off but it was probably a weak race. The winner did not need to improve.

NOTEBOOK
Cross My Heart, Stepper Point's half-sister, potentially appeared the one to beat if reproducing her York effort. She soon took control from the front, rarely looked in any danger and is a useful sprinter in the making. (op 2-1)

Teetotal(IRE), returned to maiden company after contesting nurseries, was the only one to offer any challenge to the winner. He can collect a victory as a juvenile if presented with a similar opportunity. (op 16-1)

Scarlet Spirit(IRE) ◆ ran much better than she did on her debut, and wasn't given an overly hard time to take a promising third. (op 9-1 tchd 17-2)

Shatin Secret, a half-brother to modest hurdler/chaser Rich Lord among others, attracted some market interest at long odds and wasn't disgraced. (op 20-1)

Another Claret didn't seem suited by the drop in trip. (tchd 5-2)

Bapak Pesta(IRE) will need to improve considerably to make any impression in handicaps. (op 10-3)

6405 BOOK YOUR 22ND OCTOBER TOTESPORT PACKAGE H'CAP 1m 4y
3:30 (3:30) (Class 4) (0-80,80) 3-Y-O+ £4,075 (£1,212; £606; £303) Stalls Low

Form				RPR
4140	1		**Shadowtime**[2] 6342 7-8-12 71 DaleSwift(3) 2	82
			(Tracy Waggott) *t.k.h early: trckd ldrs on inner: swtchd rt and hdwy over 1f out: rdn to ld ins fnl f: styd on wl* **15/2**	
0100	2	2 ¼	**Fastnet Storm (IRE)**[43] 4964 6-9-4 74 GrahamGibbons 5	80
			(David Barron) *cl up: rdn to ld 1 1/2f out: hdd ins fnl f: kpt on same pce* **16/1**	
6503	3	hd	**Desert Romance (IRE)**[3] 6313 6-9-6 76 SilvestreDeSousa 3	81
			(David O'Meara) *sn led: rdn along 2f out: hdd 1 1/2f out: drvn and one pce fnl f* **5/2**[1]	
1403	4	1 ½	**Yojimbo (IRE)**[6] 6208 4-9-10 80 MartinHarley 8	82
			(Mick Channon) *trckd ldrs: hdwy over 2f out: rdn wl over 1f out: kpt on fnl f* **5/1**[2]	
3502	5	½	**Merchant Of Medici**[36] 5224 5-9-3 73 PJMcDonald 12	74
			(Micky Hammond) *hld up in rr: hdwy over 2f out and sn pushed along: swtchd rt and rdn over 1f out: styd on fnl f: nrst fin* **16/1**	
310	6	½	**Alfred Hutchinson**[11] 6073 4-9-10 80 RobertWinston 13	80
			(Geoffrey Oldroyd) *trckd ldrs: hdwy and cl up on outer over 2f out: rdn and edgd lft over 1f out: wknd fnl f* **8/1**	
0360	7	1	**Follow The Flag (IRE)**[33] 5345 8-8-10 66 (v) MichaelO'Connell 1	63
			(Alan McCabe) *trckd ldrs on inner: rdn along over 2f out: sn one pce* **20/1**	
5/00	8	hd	**El Bravo**[11] 6073 6-8-12 75 ShirleyTeasdale(7) 6	72
			(Shaun Harris) *trckd ldrs: hdwy over 2f out: rdn along wl over 1f out and sn one pce* **66/1**	
-600	9	½	**Pleasant Day (IRE)**[85] 3493 5-9-8 78 (b) FrederikTylicki 7	74
			(Richard Fahey) *hld up in rr: sme hdwy 2f out: nvr nr ldrs* **7/1**[3]	
5060	10	1 ½	**Majestic Dream (IRE)**[33] 5369 4-9-3 73 JamesSullivan 9	65
			(Michael Easterby) *chsd ldrs: rdn along 2f out: sn wknd* **14/1**	
51-0	11	1 ½	**Eraada**[148] 1612 3-8-12 72 TadhgO'Shea 11	61
			(Mark Johnston) *a in rr: bhd fnl 3f* **14/1**	
1000	12	3 ¾	**Byronic Hero**[25] 5618 3-9-3 77 MickyFenton 10	57
			(Jedd O'Keeffe) *s.i.s: a in rr* **40/1**	
1000	13	10	**Oratory (IRE)**[33] 5369 6-9-9 79 AdamBeschizza 4	36
			(Peter Salmon) *s.i.s: a towards rr* **12/1**	

1m 44.19s (-1.71) **Going Correction** -0.075s/f (Good)
WFA 3 from 4yo+ 4lb 13 Ran SP% 122.1
Speed ratings (Par 105): **105,102,102,101,100 100,99,98,98,96 95,91,81**
toteswingers 1&2 £25.20, 1&3 £5.50, 2&3 £11.80 CSF £122.22 TOTE £9.70: £2.90, £5.80, £2.00; EX 249.60.
Owner H Conlon **Bred** Darley **Trained** Spennymoor, Co Durham

FOCUS
Any number of these had something to prove for one reason or another, so this probably isn't strong form. The first three home were always prominent and the placed horses are rated in line with this year's form.

6406 ARKLE FINANCE FILLIES' H'CAP 6f
4:00 (4:00) (Class 3) (0-90,90) 3-Y-0+

£6,411 (£1,919; £959; £479; £239; £120) **Stalls** Low

Form RPR

2002 **1** **Misplaced Fortune**[7] 6165 7-9-7 **90**................(v) DaleSwift(3) 6 99
(Nigel Tinkler) *hld up in rr: swtchd to outer and gd hdwy wl over 1f out: str run ins fnl f to ld last 75yds* **15/2**[3]

1310 **2** ¾ **My Sharona**[14] 5980 3-9-5 **87**................ PhillipMakin 4 93
(Sylvester Kirk) *in tch: hdwy to trck ldrs over 2f out: rdn wl over 1f out: chal ins fnl f: drvn to ld briefly last 100yds: sn hdd and nt qckn* **3/1**[1]

0105 **3** 1 **Jade**[13] 6009 4-9-0 **80**................(p) MichaelO'Connell 3 83
(Ollie Pears) *prom on inner: hdwy to chse clr ldr over 2f out: rdn to chal over 1f out: led ent fnl f: sn drvn: hdd and one pce last 100yds* **13/2**[2]

4411 **4** ½ **Love Island**[24] 5676 3-8-8 **76**................ PaulQuinn 5 77
(Richard Whitaker) *hld up towards rr: hdwy 2f out: swtchd lft to inner and rdn ent fnl f: kpt on: nrst fin* **8/1**

4112 **5** 1 ¾ **Meandmyshadow**[9] 6123 4-8-7 **73**................ RobertWinston 7 69
(Alan Brown) *prom: rdn along over 2f out: drvn over 1f out and grad wknd* **17/2**

1023 **6** ½ **Dancheur (IRE)**[34] 5326 3-8-10 **78**................ MartinHarley 1 72
(Mrs K Burke) *led and sn clr at str pce: rdn along and jnd over 1f out: hdd ent fnl f: sn wknd* **3/1**[1]

630 **7** 2 **Camache Queen (IRE)**[16] 5906 4-8-11 **77**................ EddieAhern 9 65
(Denis Coakley) *chsd ldrs: rdn along over 2f out: grad wknd* **16/1**

-503 **8** 5 **Pearl Diva (IRE)**[26] 5582 3-9-3 **85**................ SilvestreDeSousa 8 57
(Peter Chapple-Hyam) *a towards rr* **12/1**

0 **9** 4 ½ **Vale Of Clara (IRE)**[39] 5138 4-9-3 **83**................ TomEaves 2 40
(Peter Niven) *a in rr: bhd fnl 2f* **40/1**

00 **10** 1 ¾ **Mortitia**[56] 4497 4-9-2 **82**................ FrederikTylicki 10 34
(Tim Easterby) *chsd ldrs on outer: rdn along over 2f out: sn wknd* **33/1**

1m 15.59s (-1.31) **Going Correction** -0.075s/f (Good)
WFA 3 from 4yo+ 2lb **10** Ran SP% **115.7**
Speed ratings (Par 104): **105,104,102,102,99 99,96,89,83,81**
toteswingers 1&2 £6.50, 1&3 £8.70, 2&3 £3.90 CSF £30.00 TOTE £6.30: £1.80, £2.40, £2.60; EX 16.20.
Owner W F Burton **Bred** Adrian Smith **Trained** Langton, N Yorks

FOCUS
A useful-looking contest run at a generous gallop, featuring some in-form types and the placed horses are rated as having run close to form.

NOTEBOOK
Misplaced Fortune, who took this contest last year off a 9lb lower mark from Jade and also finished second in 2009, came into the race off a cracking effort at York and probably produced a career-best performance to win going away. Out the back early, she was pulled wide for room when making her bid and charged home once asked to quicken. 4lb well-in here, she may now go for the Coral Sprint at York. (op 5-1)
My Sharona, who stays further than 6f, has been in great heart all year and helps to confirm the level as being above average. (op 10-3 tchd 7-2)
Jade was tried in cheekpieces for the first time and didn't do a great deal wrong in defeat. That said, the handicapper has her about right judged on this run. (op 15-2 tchd 8-1)
Love Island, chasing a hat-trick, can be counted a little unlucky not to have been closer at the end because she didn't always have the gaps when required in the home straight. Paul Quinn wasn't overly hard on his mount close to the line when it was obvious she couldn't win.
Meandmyshadow really hit form after the middle of July but does all her winning in a lower class so, in theory, this was a good performance. (op 10-1 tchd 11-1)
Dancheur(IRE), runner-up to Jade when last seen, was left alone out in front but weakened before the furlong marker. (op 4-1 tchd 11-4)
Camache Queen(IRE) was subsequently reported to be lame by her trainer. Official explanation: vet said filly finished lame
Pearl Diva(IRE) didn't run particularly encouragingly but was thrown wide off the final bend, albeit while being pushed along. (op 11-1 tchd 14-1)

6407 ARKLE FINANCE H'CAP (ROUND 6 OF PONTEFRACT STAYERS CHAMPIONSHIP 2012) 2m 1f 22y
4:30 (4:30) (Class 5) (0-75,72) 3-Y-0+ **£2,264** (£673; £336; £168) **Stalls** Low

Form RPR

21 **1** **Jawaab (IRE)**[10] 6101 8-9-9 **67** 6ex................(v) PhillipMakin 8 77
(Philip Kirby) *trckd ldrs: tk clsr order 4f out: hdwy on inner 2f out: swtchd rt and rdn to chal over 1f out: led jst ins fnl f: drvn clr and styd on wl* **7/2**[1]

0420 **2** 4 ½ **Spruzzo**[11] 6074 6-9-6 **64**................ DuranFentiman 14 69
(Chris Fairhurst) *led and sn clr: rdn along over 2f out: jnd and drvn over 1f out: hdad jst ins fnl f: kpt on* **40/1**

1326 **3** 1 ¼ **Byron Blue (IRE)**[20] 5798 3-9-2 **72**................ EddieAhern 7 76
(Jamie Osborne) *chsd ldrs: hdwy 4f out: rdn to chse ldng pair wl over 1f out: sn drvn and no imp* **8/1**[3]

1120 **4** 2 **Waterford Star (IRE)**[40] 5106 4-9-11 **69**................(v) FrederikTylicki 13 71
(Ian Williams) *hld up and bhd: swtchd to outer and rdn along 2f out: styd on wl fnl f: nrst fin* **8/1**[3]

0216 **5** ½ **Maid Of Meft**[11] 6074 5-9-10 **68**................ MickyFenton 12 69
(Paul Midgley) *midfield: hdwy to chse ldrs 4f out: rdn along over 2f out: sn drvn and one pce* **20/1**

6354 **6** ½ **Petella**[10] 6101 6-9-4 **62**................ AndrewElliott 11 63
(George Moore) *in tch: effrt and hdwy 4f out: rdn along wl over 2f out: sn one pce* **12/1**

6104 **7** ½ **Spanish Fork (IRE)**[11] 2818 3-8-9 **65**................ MartinHarley 4 65
(Mick Channon) *in tch: hdwy to chse ldrs 4f out: rdn wl over 2f out: sn drvn and plugged on same pce* **20/1**

5210 **8** *nse* **Dr Finley (IRE)**[21] 5772 5-9-5 **66**................ SimonPearce(3) 10 66
(Lydia Pearce) *trckd ldrs: hdwy over 4f out: rdn to chse ldr over 2f out: sn drvn and wknd over 1f out* **14/1**

0345 **9** ¾ **Descaro (USA)**[10] 6101 6-9-3 **61**................(v) SilvestreDeSousa 2 60
(David O'Meara) *in tch: hdwy 3f out: rdn along 2f out: sn one pce* **8/1**[3]

5336 **10** ½ **Marmas**[20] 5788 3-8-11 **67**................ TadhgO'Shea 6 66+
(Marcus Tregoning) *hld up towards rr: hdwy over 3f out: rdn and n.m.r wl over 1f out and again ent fnl f: n.d* **5/1**[2]

5200 **11** *nk* **Uncut Stone (IRE)**[20] 5798 4-8-13 **60**................(b) DaleSwift(3) 1 58
(Peter Niven) *chsd clr ldr: rdn along over 4f out: sn wknd* **33/1**

5565 **12** ¾ **Handles For Forks (IRE)**[13] 6019 4-9-3 **66**........ CharlesBishop(5) 15 64
(Mick Channon) *hld up towards rr: hdwy 3f out: effrt whn n.m.r 2f out: sn rdn and no imp* **18/1**

1300 **13** 7 **Blackstone Vegas**[32] 5384 6-9-7 **65**................ MichaelO'Connell 9 55
(Derek Shaw) *hld up and bhd: sme hdwy on inner 3f out: sn rdn and nvr a factor* **25/1**

0000 **14** 7 **Wells Lyrical (IRE)**[22] 5729 7-9-10 **68**................(p) TomEaves 17 50
(Bryan Smart) *hld up in rr pulling hrd: effrt over 4f out: sn rdn and nvr a factor* **40/1**

0-00 **15** 82 **Markington**[65] 4176 9-9-7 **65**................(vt) RobertWinston 3
(Peter Bowen) *hld up and bhd: rdn along and sme hdwy 6f out: drvn over 4f out: sn wknd and bhd: eased fnl 2f* **16/1**

3m 51.11s (6.51) **Going Correction** -0.075s/f (Good)
WFA 3 from 4yo+ 12lb **15** Ran SP% **118.9**
Speed ratings (Par 103): **81,78,78,77,77 76,76,76,76,76 75,75,72,68,30**
toteswingers 1&2 £25.20, 1&3 £6.70, 2&3 £83.20 CSF £170.83 TOTE £3.40: £2.00, £15.80, £4.20; EX 166.40.
Owner L & D Racing **Bred** Hascombe And Valiant Studs **Trained** Castleton, N Yorks

FOCUS
A competitive staying handicap run at a messy pace, with few able to close from the rear.
Descaro(USA) Official explanation: jockey said gelding had no more to give

6408 MICHAEL EASTWOOD'S 60 YEAR EPIC MAIDEN STKS (DIV I) 1m 2f 6y
5:00 (5:00) (Class 5) 3-Y-0+ **£2,264** (£673; £336; £168) **Stalls** Low

Form RPR

1 **Estemaala (IRE)** 3-8-13 0................ MartinHarley 1 77+
(Marcus Tregoning) *in rr and green: hdwy 3f out: rdn to chse ldrs over 1f out: swtchd to outer and styd on wl to ld ins fnl f: kpt on wl* **10/1**

0- **2** 1 **Homeric (IRE)**[323] 7232 3-9-4 0................ PhillipMakin 7 80
(Ed Dunlop) *trckd ldrs: smooth hdwy 3f out: cl up on bit wl over 1f out: shkn up and green 1f out: led briefly and edgd lft ent fnl f: sn hdd and one pce* **9/4**[2]

50 **3** 3 ¾ **Discay**[10] 6102 3-9-4 0................ SilvestreDeSousa 3 72
(Mark Johnston) *led: jnd and pushed along 4f out: rdn over 2f out: drvn and hdd ent fnl f: one pce* **8/1**

4 7 **Anqooda (USA)** 3-8-13 0................ TadhgO'Shea 4 53
(Marcus Tregoning) *trckd ldrs: hdwy 4f out: rdn along over 2f out: drvn wl over 1f out and sn wknd* **6/1**[3]

/5-5 **5** 7 **Oakwell (IRE)**[34] 5316 4-9-10 50................ MichaelStainton 5 44
(Sally Hall) *cl up: disp ld 4f out tl rdn and wknd wl over 1f out* **28/1**

0042 **6** 3 **Keeping Time**[15] 5952 3-9-4 74................ EddieAhern 9 38
(Sir Henry Cecil) *trckd ldrs: pushed along 3f out: rdn over 2f out and sn wknd* **11/8**[1]

5 **7** 19 **Speedy Star (IRE)**[27] 5541 3-9-4 0................ JamesSullivan 8
(Tina Jackson) *chsd ldrs: rdn along 1/2-way: sn wknd* **66/1**

00 **8** 99 **Doting**[47] 4791 3-9-4 0................ AdamBeschizza 6
(Peter Salmon) *s.i.s: a bhd: t.o fnl 3f: virtually p.u fnl f* **100/1**

F **Fatty Foulkes** 4-9-5 0................ GarryWhillans(5) 2
(Alan Swinbank) *in tch on inner: whn fell 6f out: fatally injured* **25/1**

2m 14.2s (0.50) **Going Correction** -0.075s/f (Good)
WFA 3 from 4yo 6lb **9** Ran SP% **117.1**
Speed ratings (Par 103): **95,94,91,85,80 77,62, ,**
toteswingers 1&2 £5.40, 1&3 £5.80, 2&3 £3.80 CSF £32.85 TOTE £12.70: £2.50, £1.20, £2.30; EX 47.20.
Owner Hamdan Al Maktoum **Bred** Shadwell Estate Company Limited **Trained** Lambourn, Berks

FOCUS
Not the strongest of maidens despite runners from some powerful stables. It was run at a sound pace but was 10lb slower than division II.
Keeping Time Official explanation: trainer's rep had no explanation for the poor form shown

6409 MICHAEL EASTWOOD'S 60 YEAR EPIC MAIDEN STKS (DIV II) 1m 2f 6y
5:30 (5:30) (Class 5) 3-Y-0+ **£2,264** (£673; £336; £168) **Stalls** Low

Form RPR

1 **Muharrer** 3-9-4 0................ TadhgO'Shea 6 78+
(Marcus Tregoning) *dwlt and in rr: hdwy and in tch 1/2-way: chsd ldrs over 2f out: wd st and sn rdn: str run on outer to ld ins fnl f: kpt on* **6/1**[3]

23 **2** 1 **Fly Solo**[34] 5316 3-9-4 0................ RobertWinston 2 76
(Alan Swinbank) *led: rdn along over 2f out: drvn and edgd rt over 1f out: hdd ins fnl f: kpt on* **7/2**[2]

32 **3** 1 **Claude Monet (BRZ)**[16] 5901 3-8-4 0................ SilvestreDeSousa 3 60
(Jeremy Noseda) *t.k.h early: cl up: effrt over 2f out: rdn and ev ch wl over 1f out: one pce fnl f* **8/13**[1]

3 **4** *nk* **The Tiddly Tadpole**[12] 5293 7-9-10 0................ AndrewElliott 1 73
(Simon West) *trckd ldrs: effrt to chse ldng pair over 2f out: sn rdn and one pce ent fnl f* **10/1**

5 1 **Frank's Folly (IRE)** 3-9-4 0................ DuranFentiman 5 71
(Tim Walford) *dwlt and in rr: hdwy on inner 3f out: rdn to chse ldrs wl over 1f out: kpt on same pce fnl f* **33/1**

0 **6** 29 **Daghashah**[108] 2768 3-8-13 0................ FrederikTylicki 9
(Clive Brittain) *prom: rdn along bef 1/2-way: sn lost pl and bhd fnl 3f* **16/1**

60- **7** 2 ½ **Cherry Tree Hill (IRE)**[344] 6804 4-9-5 0................ GarryWhillans(5) 8
(Alan Swinbank) *chsd ldng pair: rdn along 3f out: wknd over 2f out* **66/1**

0 **8** 11 **Red Seal**[45] 4882 3-9-4 0................ MickyFenton 7
(Tom Tate) *a towards rr: outpcd and bhd fnl 3f* **66/1**

2m 13.76s (0.06) **Going Correction** -0.075s/f (Good)
WFA 3 from 4yo+ 6lb **8** Ran SP% **119.3**
Speed ratings (Par 103): **96,95,94,94,93 70,68,59**
toteswingers 1&2 £2.80, 1&3 £2.30, 2&3 £1.60 CSF £28.37 TOTE £8.70: £1.60, £1.20, £1.10; EX 27.00.
Owner Hamdan Al Maktoum **Bred** Shadwell Estate Company Limited **Trained** Lambourn, Berks

FOCUS
The second division of this maiden was run at a steady pace with the winner coming latest of all, giving connections success in both divisions. The form makes sense rated around the runner-up and fourth.

6410 BOOK YOUR CHRISTMAS PARTY HERE ON 0113 2876387 H'CAP 1m 4y
6:00 (6:00) (Class 5) (0-70,70) 3-Y-0+ **£2,264** (£673; £336; £168) **Stalls** Low

Form RPR

3441 **1** **Talent Scout (IRE)**[5] 6259 6-8-13 **66** 6ex................(p) GemmaTutty(7) 1 76
(Tim Walford) *t.k.h early: mde all: rdn clr over 1f out: styd on wl towards fin* **5/1**[1]

2342 **2** ¾ **Christmas Light**[11] 6073 5-9-4 **67**................ DaleSwift(3) 13 75+
(Brian Ellison) *hld up in rr: swtchd to outer and gd hdwy wl over 1f out: rdn and str run ins fnl f: nrst fin* **6/1**[2]

3050 **3** 1 ½ **Count Bertoni (IRE)**[23] 5713 5-9-6 **66**................(b) DavidNolan 4 71
(David O'Meara) *hld up towards rr: stdy hdwy on inner over 2f out: chsd ldrs over 1f out: drvn and styd on fnl f* **16/1**

0000 **4** *shd* **Finbar**[33] 5373 3-9-4 **68** .... FrederikTylicki 11 72
(James Given) *in tch: hdwy 3f out: rdn to chse ldrs over 1f out: drvn and kpt on same pce ins fnl f* **12/1**

00 **5** *hd* **Mcmonagle (USA)**[8] 6131 4-9-5 **65** .... (tp) RobertWinston 7 69
(Alan Brown) *chsd wnr: rdn along 2f out: drvn over 1f out: one pce ins fnl f* **40/1**

2346 **6** *½* **Sangar**[19] 5824 4-9-2 **62** .... (b[1]) MichaelO'Connell 14 65+
(Ollie Pears) *midfield: pushed along and sltly outpcd over 2f out: gd hdwy on inner 2f out and sn chsng ldrs: nt clr run and swtchd rt over 1f out: styd on u.p fnl f: nrst fin* **25/1**

6-1 **7** *1 ¼* **Layla's King**[36] 5244 4-9-6 **66** .... MartinHarley 2 66
(David C Griffiths) *trckd ldrs on inner: rdn along over 2f out: drvn over 1f out: one pce* **14/1**

2320 **8** *¾* **King Pin**[26] 5588 7-9-6 **66** .... (p) TomEaves 3 04
(Tracy Waggott) *in tch: hdwy to chse ldrs 2f out: effrt and nt clr run over 1f out: sn rdn and no imp* **14/1**

0260 **9** *1* **Amazing Star (IRE)**[61] 4345 7-9-10 **70** .... MichaelStainton 15 66+
(Declan Carroll) *dwlt and hld up in rr: hdwy on inner 2f out: chsd ldrs whn nt clr run jst over 1f out: nt rcvr* **66/1**

1350 **10** *hd* **Eastward Ho**[37] 5186 4-9-9 **69** .... EddieAhern 6 64+
(Jason Ward) *midfield: effrt whn n.m.r on inner 2f out: n.d* **5/1**[1]

0063 **11** *1 ½* **Thatcherite (IRE)**[12] 6047 4-9-7 **67** .... (t) StephenCraine 10 59
(Tony Coyle) *cl up on outer: rdn along 2f out: drvn over 1f out: sn wknd* **16/1**

262 **12** *1 ½* **Elijah Pepper (USA)**[8] 6141 7-9-10 **70** .... GrahamGibbons 12 58
(David Barron) *midfield on outer: effrt over 2f out: sn rdn and n.d* **9/1**[3]

35 **13** *2 ½* **Ted's Brother (IRE)**[33] 5341 4-9-5 **68** .... (t) DeclanCannon(3) 17 51
(Richard Guest) *dwlt: a in rr* **25/1**

0310 **14** *6* **Rex Romanorum (IRE)**[23] 5713 4-9-9 **69** .... DuranFentiman 16 38
(Patrick Holmes) *midfield on outer: rdn along over 3f out: n.d* **25/1**

4352 **15** *7* **Special Mix**[35] 5258 4-9-7 **67** .... JamesSullivan 5 20
(Michael Easterby) *midfield: rdn along over 2f out: sn wknd* **9/1**[3]

6463 **16** *20* **Saslong**[49] 4727 3-9-2 **66** .... SilvestreDeSousa 9
(Mark Johnston) *chsd ldrs: rdn along over 3f out: sn wknd* **10/1**

0-00 **17** *hd* **Lady Sledmere (IRE)**[80] 3694 4-9-7 **67** .... (t) MickyFenton 8
(Paul Midgley) *chsd ldrs: rdn along over 2f out: sn wknd* **50/1**

1m 45.32s (-0.58) **Going Correction** -0.075s/f (Good)
WFA 3 from 4yo+ 4lb **17** Ran SP% **126.9**
Speed ratings (Par 103): **99,98,96,96,96 95,94,93,92,92 91,89,87,81,74 54,54**
toteswingers 1&2 £9.40, 1&3 £29.10, 2&3 £32.40 CSF £32.60 TOTE £7.10: £1.90, £2.30, £3.70, £2.30; EX 51.10.
Owner John Stacey **Bred** Johnston King **Trained** Sheriff Hutton, N Yorks

FOCUS
This handicap was competitive enough, but the winner was allowed a softish lead and that proved crucial.
Amazing Star(IRE) Official explanation: jockey said gelding was denied a clear run
Eastward Ho Official explanation: jockey said gelding was denied a clear run on the bend
Saslong Official explanation: jockey said colt had no more to give
T/Plt: £3,533.70 to a £1 stake. Pool: £69,465.27 - 14.35 winning tickets T/Qpdt: £64.70 to a £1 stake. Pool: £6,406.22 - 73.26 winning tickets JR

6377 YARMOUTH (L-H)

Thursday, September 20

OFFICIAL GOING: Good to firm (watered; 7.1)
Wind: fairly light, half against Weather: dry, bright spells

6411 BRITISH STALLION STUDS SUPPORTING BRITISH RACING E B F SPRINT MAIDEN STKS 6f 3y

2:20 (2:23) (Class 5) 2-Y-O **£3,150** (£943; £471; £236; £117) **Stalls** Centre

Form RPR

1 **Van Der Neer** 2-9-3 0 .... RichardHughes 11 80+
(Richard Hannon) *chsd ldr: effrt to chal and rn green over 1f out: rdn to ld ins fnl f: r.o wl: readily* **7/2**[2]

202 **2** *1 ¾* **Huntsmans Close**[14] 5963 2-9-3 81 .... JamieSpencer 10 75
(Michael Bell) *led: jnd and rdn over 1f out: drvn and hdd ins fnl f: styd on same pce fnl 100yds* **10/3**[1]

3 *1 ¼* **Mundahesh (IRE)** 2-9-3 0 .... PaulHanagan 2 71+
(William Haggas) *hld up in tch in last trio: rdn and hdwy over 2f out: chsd ldng pair over 1f out: styd on same pce ins fnl f* **8/1**

03 **4** *4* **Dumbarton Rock**[23] 5715 2-9-3 0 .... FrannyNorton 9 59
(William Jarvis) *chsd ldrs: rdn and unable qck 2f out: outpcd by ldng trio and btn 1f out: plugged on* **33/1**

5 *½* **Agerzam** 2-9-3 0 .... AndreaAtzeni 1 58+
(Roger Varian) *in tch: rdn and n.m.r briefly 2f out: outpcd u.p jst over 1f out: no threat to ldrs and one pce fnl f* **5/1**[3]

6 *1 ¼* **Jodies Jem** 2-9-3 0 .... HayleyTurner 5 54
(William Jarvis) *in tch in midfield: rdn and outpcd 2f out: plugged on but no threat to ldrs fnl f* **50/1**

7 *nk* **Mukhabarat (IRE)** 2-9-3 0 .... MickaelBarzalona 4 53
(Saeed Bin Suroor) *t.k.h and rn green: hld up in tch in last trio: hdwy and hanging lft over 2f out: chsd ldrs and drvn over 1f out: sn btn: wknd fnl f* **7/1**

00 **8** *hd* **Derwentwater (IRE)**[15] 5948 2-9-3 0 .... NickyMackay 6 53+
(John Gosden) *stdd s: hld up in tch in rr: swtchd lft and pushed along ent fnl 2f: kpt on but no imp* **50/1**

53 **9** *¾* **Evoke (IRE)**[25] 5631 2-8-12 0 .... KierenFallon 3 45
(Jeremy Noseda) *stdd s: t.k.h and sn in tch in midfield: rdn to chse ldrs and hung lft jst over 2f out: btn over 1f out: sn wknd* **8/1**

10 *1 ½* **Mac's Superstar (FR)** 2-9-3 0 .... MartinLane 7 46
(James Fanshawe) *in tch: rdn and lost pl 2f out: bhd fnl f* **40/1**

24 **11** *nk* **Speedfit Boy (IRE)**[15] 5948 2-9-3 0 .... TomQueally 8 45
(George Margarson) *chsd ldrs tl lost pl ent fnl 2f: bhd fnl f* **11/1**

1m 13.37s (-1.03) **Going Correction** -0.125s/f (Firm) **11** Ran SP% **114.3**
Speed ratings (Par 95): **101,98,97,91,91 89,88,88,87,85 85**
toteswingers 1&2 £2.70, 1&3 £7.00, 2&3 £4.20 CSF £17.30 TOTE £3.90: £1.20, £1.60, £3.20; EX 14.73.
Owner Saeed Manana **Bred** Jeremy Green And Sons **Trained** East Everleigh, Wilts

FOCUS
An interesting maiden. They raced stands' side and the first two came from the top two stalls, with the runner-up giving a good lead to the winner. The second is not perhaps one to use as a literal guide.

NOTEBOOK
Van Der Neer ◆ was probably helped by how the race unfolded, but this was a nice performance on his debut and he looks a useful prospect. A 55,000gns half-brother to a 6f-1m2f winner, he was always travelling nicely and found plenty for pressure. The second horse gives the form a solid look and he is one to keep in mind. (op 4-1)
Huntsmans Close had his chance under a forward ride against the stands' rail. He's finished runner-up on three of his four starts and this looks about as good as he is for now, but entries in the Middle Park and Dewhurst suggest he's thought capable of better. (tchd 3-1 and 7-2)
Mundahesh(IRE) ◆ is a half-brother to Jawhar, a progressive winner at up to 1m2f for the same connections. Entered in the Middle Park, he showed plenty of ability on this racecourse debut without being given a hard time and could be tough to beat in similar company on his next start. (op 17-2)
Dumbarton Rock is now eligible for a mark and should find his level in fair handicaps/nurseries. (op 28-1 tchd 25-1)
Agerzam, a half-brother to a 1m winner, out of a 6f winner, started from what turned out to be the least favourable stall and was a bit short of room when trying to challenge. He might come on for this. (op 9-2 tchd 11-2)
Mukhabarat(IRE) was badly in need of the experience. He was stuck wide, well away from the main action, and hung left. (op 9-1)
Derwentwater(IRE) missed the break and may yet do better. He's now qualified for a mark (tchd 40-1)

6412 BRITISH STALLION STUDS SUPPORTING BRITISH RACING E B F MAIDEN STKS 1m 3y

2:50 (2:51) (Class 5) 2-Y-O **£3,150** (£943; £471; £236; £117) **Stalls** Centre

Form RPR

42 **1** **Flow (USA)**[39] 5126 2-9-3 0 .... TomQueally 1 78+
(Sir Henry Cecil) *mde all: gng best 2f out: pushed along hands and heels and a doing enough fnl f* **8/11**[1]

2 **2** *1* **Swing Easy**[22] 5742 2-9-3 0 .... StevieDonohoe 10 74
(Robert Mills) *t.k.h: chsd ldrs tl wnt 2nd and swtchd rt 5f out: rdn over 1f out: kpt on but a hld fnl f* **9/2**[2]

3 *3* **Leitrim Pass (USA)** 2-9-3 0 .... ShaneKelly 2 67+
(William Haggas) *t.k.h: hld up in tch in midfield: hdwy to chse ldrs and pushed along over 1f out: rn green 1f out: no ex ins fnl f and outpcd fnl 100yds* **10/1**

4 *2* **Press Room (USA)** 2-9-3 0 .... MickaelBarzalona 8 62
(Mahmood Al Zarooni) *stdd s: hld up in tch in rr: rdn and hdwy whn edgd lft over 2f out: chsd ldrs and drvn over 1f out: wknd ins fnl f* **13/2**[3]

0 **5** *2 ½* **Pearl Spice (IRE)**[98] 3062 2-9-3 0 .... HarryBentley 3 56
(Sir Mark Prescott Bt) *sn chsng ldrs: rdn and unable qck ent fnl 2f: wknd over 1f out* **66/1**

6 *1 ¼* **Red Pilgrim (IRE)** 2-9-3 0 .... RobertHavlin 6 54
(James Toller) *in tch in midfield: struggling whn sltly hmpd over 2f out: sn outpcd and wl btn over 1f out* **50/1**

5 **7** *½* **Broughton (GER)**[51] 4677 2-8-12 0 .... AntiocoMurgia(5) 4 52
(Mahmood Al Zarooni) *t.k.h: chsd wnr tl 5f out: rdn and lost pl jst over 2f out: wl hld whn hung lft over 1f out* **12/1**

05 **8** *1* **Night's Watch**[16] 5911 2-9-3 0 .... FrannyNorton 7 50
(William Jarvis) *t.k.h: hld up in tch: lost pl and towards rr whn hung lft over 2f out: wl btn after* **66/1**

0 **9** *¾* **Gabrial The Duke (IRE)**[14] 5962 2-9-3 0 .... HayleyTurner 9 48
(Michael Bell) *s.i.s: hld up in last trio: rdn and effrt wl over 2f out: sn edgd lft and wknd 2f out* **40/1**

10 *7* **Frederick Alfred** 2-9-3 0 .... PaulHanagan 5 32
(Mark H Tompkins) *s.i.s: in tch in rr: rdn 3f out: sn struggling and bhd fnl 2f* **50/1**

1m 40.97s (0.37) **Going Correction** -0.125s/f (Firm) **10** Ran SP% **115.5**
Speed ratings (Par 95): **93,92,89,87,84 83,82,81,81,74**
toteswingers 1&2 £1.70, 1&3 £3.40, 2&3 £5.90 CSF £4.01 TOTE £1.70: £1.10, £1.10, £2.80; EX 4.70.
Owner Niarchos Family **Bred** Flaxman Holdings Ltd **Trained** Newmarket, Suffolk

FOCUS
They raced middle to stands' side. The front two had already shown fair form and there were some interesting newcomers among the beaten runners. The fluent winner will rate higher and the second helps with the level. The time was marginally quicker than the following Class 5 nursery.

NOTEBOOK
Flow(USA) was always going well in the lead and didn't require a hard ride. He's probably not good enough to justify his Racing Post Trophy entry, but he still looks quite decent. (op 4-6 tchd 8-13)
Swing Easy shaped well when runner-up on his debut at Kempton and did so again. He looks a useful type in the making. (op 4-1)
Leitrim Pass(USA), a 75,000gns half-brother to a 1m4f winner, out of a 6f Listed winner, made a pleasing enough introduction and can be expected to do better. (op 11-1 tchd 12-1)
Press Room(USA), who is out of a 5f Listed winner in Australia, came under pressure a long way out and just generally looked in need of the experience, but he showed ability. (op 15-2 tchd 8-1 and 6-1)
Pearl Spice(IRE) ◆ had been gelded since showing ability on his debut in June. This was better and he should make a nice type over middle distances next year. (op 50-1 tchd 40-1)
Night's Watch's rider reported the colt ran too freely early on and the saddle slipped. Official explanation: jockey said colt ran too freely early and saddle slipped (op 50-1)

6413 SEAJACKS NURSERY 1m 3y

3:20 (3:20) (Class 5) (0-70,64) 2-Y-O **£2,264** (£673; £336; £168) **Stalls** Centre

Form RPR

4302 **1** **Aseela (IRE)**[21] 5763 2-9-4 **61** .... TomQueally 4 63
(Clive Brittain) *bhd: racd lazily and pushed along at times: swtchd lft and drvn over 1f out: hdwy to chal fnl 100yds: styd on to ld fnl 50yds: in command and idled towards fin* **9/2**[3]

4521 **2** *nk* **Spithead**[29] 5484 2-9-6 **63** .... JamieSpencer 5 64
(William Haggas) *led: looked to be gng best 2f out: rdn and fnd ex over 1f out: drvn and hrd pressed fnl 110yds: hdd fnl 50yds: kpt on* **5/1**

060 **3** *1* **East Texas Red (IRE)**[13] 6015 2-9-6 **63** .... RichardHughes 1 62
(Richard Hannon) *stdd s: t.k.h: hld up in tch: rdn and effrt ent fnl 2f: pressed ldrs but unable qckn jst over 1f out: styng on same pce whn n.m.r ins fnl f* **7/4**[1]

000 **4** *hd* **Likelikelikelikeit**[62] 4310 2-9-0 **57** .... PaulHanagan 2 56
(Mark H Tompkins) *chsd ldr: rdn and pressing wnr over 1f out: unable qck and one pce ins fnl f: lost 2 pls fnl 100yds* **25/1**

0004 **5** *2 ¾* **Romanoff (IRE)**[23] 5702 2-9-5 **62** .... KierenFallon 3 54
(Luca Cumani) *chsd ldrs: rdn and unable qck 2f out: styd on same pce and hld fnl f* **7/2**[2]

500 **6** *55* **Hot Mustard**[46] 4845 2-9-7 **64**.......... HayleyTurner 6
(Michael Bell) *in tch in last pair: rdn and no rspnse 2f out: btn and heavily eased fr over 1f out: t.o* **13/2**

1m 41.04s (0.44) **Going Correction** -0.125s/f (Firm) **6** Ran SP% **110.6**
Speed ratings (Par 95): **92,91,90,90,87 32**
toteswingers 1&2 £1.70, 1&3 £2.30, 2&3 £2.30 CSF £25.70 TOTE £5.60: £2.60, £1.50; EX 13.90.
Owner Saeed Manana **Bred** Gestut Sohrenhof **Trained** Newmarket, Suffolk

FOCUS
A modest nursery.

NOTEBOOK
Aseela(IRE), 1lb higher than when runner-up on her handicap debut over this trip on Polytrack, did well to collar the long-time leader considering she raced in last and came under pressure a fair way out. She's bred to appreciate much further in due course. (op 4-1)
Spithead led the field against the stands' side rail, appearing to go no more than an ordinary pace. This was a solid effort off a mark 3lb higher than when successful over 7f last time. He probably won't mind a drop in trip. (op 7-2)
East Texas Red(IRE) ◆ was well backed on his nursery debut but ruined his chance by racing keenly. He can exploit this mark if settling better. (op 9-4)
Likelikelikelikeit, upped in trip on her nursery debut, ran just okay after a two-month break. (op 33-1)
Romanoff(IRE) didn't have sufficient room when first looking to challenge and the race gradually got away from him. He wasn't given anything like a hard ride, but Kieren Fallon reported the colt hung right throughout. Official explanation: jockey said colt hung right throughout (op 4-1)
Hot Mustard's rider reported that the colt was never travelling. Official explanation: jockey said colt never travelled (tchd 7-1)

6414 AT THE RACES NURSERY — 7f 3y
3:50 (3:50) (Class 4) (0-80,79) 2-Y-O — **£3,428** (£1,020; £509; £254) **Stalls** Centre

Form — RPR

432 **1** **Darkening (IRE)**[24] 5684 2-9-5 **77**.......... MickaelBarzalona 3 — 84+
(Mahmood Al Zarooni) *led: swtchd to r on stands' rail and hdd after 1f: chsd overall ldrs after: rdn to ld overall over 1f out: styd on wl fnl f* **7/2**[2]

4214 **2** *2 ¼* **Black Monk (IRE)**[36] 5236 2-9-5 **77**.......... RichardHughes 2 — 77
(Richard Hannon) *racd in centre: t.k.h: chsd ldr tl led overall after 1f: edgd rt u.p and hdd over 1f out: no ex ins fnl f* **6/1**[3]

2412 **3** *2 ¼* **Jumeirah Moon**[29] 5475 2-9-0 **72**.......... JamieSpencer 6 — 66
(David Simcock) *racd towards centre: hld up wl in rr: rdn and hdwy 2f out: drvn to chse ldng pair and edgd rt ins fnl f: no imp* **6/1**[3]

442 **4** *1 ¼* **Exotic Guest**[27] 5553 2-9-7 **79**.......... TomQueally 4 — 70
(George Margarson) *racd towards centre: t.k.h early: hld up in midfield: sme hdwy u.p over 1f out: no imp 1f out: wknd fnl 100yds* **15/2**

41 **5** *nse* **Al Mukhdam**[34] 5311 2-9-4 **76**.......... PaulHanagan 7 — 66
(Peter Chapple-Hyam) *racd stands' side: hld up towards rr overall: effrt u.p over 1f out: plugged on but no threat to ldrs fnl f* **5/2**[1]

2552 **6** *1 ¼* **French Press (IRE)**[15] 5946 2-9-2 **74**.......... RichardMullen 1 — 61
(David Brown) *racd towards centre: t.k.h early: chsd overall ldr after 1f tl over 1f out: styd on same pce u.p after: btn whn hmpd fnl 100yds* **7/1**

060 **7** *1 ½* **Star Of Missouri**[20] 5792 2-8-10 **68**.......... KierenFallon 5 — 51
(Mark H Tompkins) *racd towards centre: stdd s: a towards rr: rdn and no real hdwy over 2f out: n.d* **20/1**

31 **8** *½* **Reliant Robin (IRE)**[105] 2844 2-9-6 **78**.......... StevieDonohoe 8 — 60
(Robert Mills) *racd stands' side: t.k.h: hld up in rr: rdn and effrt 2f out: no prog: wl btn fnl f* **22/1**

1m 27.17s (0.57) **Going Correction** -0.125s/f (Firm) **8** Ran SP% **112.7**
Speed ratings (Par 97): **91,88,85,84,84 82,81,80**
toteswingers 1&2 £5.10, 1&3 £4.20, 2&3 £4.00 CSF £23.98 TOTE £3.00: £1.10, £2.30, £2.00; EX 18.50.
Owner Godolphin **Bred** Lisieux Stud **Trained** Newmarket, Suffolk

FOCUS
There were two groups early on, but the field merged towards the stands' rail in the closing stages and there was no track bias.

NOTEBOOK
Darkening(IRE) had shown ability in maidens, but he'd also looked awkward, particularly when just beaten at Warwick last time. He'd reportedly been gelded since then, however, and had the rail to race against in the closing stages. His attitude looked fine this time and he could progress.
Black Monk(IRE) ran his race, finishing clear of the others, but the winner was simply better handicapped. (op 9-2 tchd 13-2)
Jumeirah Moon was 3lb well-in following his recent second over 6f on Polytrack, but he was on turf for only the second time. This was a respectable effort but he was well held. (tchd 11-2 and 13-2)
Exotic Guest, who's entered in the Middle Park, ran okay under top weight and may yet do better. (op 8-1 tchd 7-1)
Al Mukhdam didn't go on from his Newcastle maiden win gained on easy ground. (op 7-2)

6415 RACING WELFARE H'CAP — 1m 6f 17y
4:20 (4:20) (Class 2) (0-100,95) 3-Y-O+ **£9,955** (£2,979; £1,489; £745; £371) **Stalls** High

Form — RPR

1206 **1** **Handsome Man (IRE)**[26] 5580 3-8-11 **88**.......... MickaelBarzalona 11 — 98
(Saeed Bin Suroor) *hld up in last trio: hdwy over 3f out: rdn along hands and heels after and styd on relentlessly to ld fnl 100yds: pushed out* **11/2**

411 **2** *¾* **Montaser (IRE)**[55] 4528 3-9-4 **95**.......... FrannyNorton 1 — 104
(David Simcock) *chsd ldrs: rdn to chse ldr 2f out: led over 1f out: drvn and hdd fnl 100yds: styd on same pce after* **3/1**[2]

0360 **3** *1 ¾* **Tappanappa (IRE)**[12] 6045 5-9-2 **83**.......... MartinLane 2 — 90
(Brian Ellison) *hld up off the pce in last trio: rdn 4f out: hdwy u.p over 1f out: styd on wl to go 3rd fnl 75yds* **28/1**

2312 **4** *2 ½* **Mawaqeet (USA)**[50] 4700 3-9-1 **92**..........(v) PaulHanagan 8 — 95
(Sir Michael Stoute) *in tch in midfield: rdn and effrt over 3f out: no imp u.p over 2f out: plugged on ins fnl f but nvr gng pce to chal* **13/2**

0/00 **5** *¾* **Call It On (IRE)**[19] 4284 6-8-13 **80**.......... JimmyQuinn 9 — 82
(Philip Kirby) *sn led: hdd and drvn over 2f out: battled on wl u.p tl 3rd and btn ins fnl f: lost 2 pls fnl 75yds* **50/1**

2444 **6** *3 ¼* **Repeater**[6] 6198 3-9-3 **94**.......... ChrisCatlin 12 — 91
(Sir Mark Prescott Bt) *t.k.h: hld up wl off the pce in last trio: clsd 5f out: rdn and no imp over 2f out: n.d* **5/2**[1]

2314 **7** *½* **Modernism**[12] 6025 3-8-7 **84**.......... KierenFallon 4 — 81
(Mark Johnston) *led briefly leaving stalls: chsd ldr after tl rdn to ld over 2f out: drvn and hdd over 1f out: 4th and btn 1f out: fdd ins fnl f* **7/2**[3]

0000 **8** *2 ½* **The Betchworth Kid**[26] 5580 7-9-5 **86**.......... TomQueally 3 — 79
(Alan King) *in tch: rdn and no hdwy over 3f out: lost pl and bhd 2f out: wknd over 1f out* **33/1**

3m 5.76s (-1.84) **Going Correction** -0.275s/f (Firm)
WFA 3 from 4yo+ 10lb **8** Ran SP% **112.9**
Speed ratings (Par 109): **94,93,92,91,90 88,88,87**
toteswingers 1&2 £4.10, 1&3 £12.40, 2&3 £11.60 CSF £21.69 TOTE £5.40: £1.70, £1.50, £5.30; EX 27.30.
Owner Godolphin **Bred** Bloomsbury Stud **Trained** Newmarket, Suffolk

FOCUS
A decent staying handicap. The visual impression was of a modest pace, but the winner and third came from well back. The first two are both on the upgrade.

NOTEBOOK
Handsome Man(IRE) ◆ was better than the bare form when behind Repeater at the July course last time (met trouble), but he got one clear run this time and produced a sustained effort under mainly hands-and-heels riding. He's an improving young stayer and should get further. (op 15-2)
Montaser(IRE) had won his last two starts, the most recent off 8lb lower when upped to 2m at Ascot, and connections were hoping he'd complete the hat-trick and pick up a penalty for the Cesarewitch. He looked to have been nicely positioned, but just didn't see his race out as well as the winner, who had raced further back. (tchd 11-4 and 7-2)
Tappanappa(IRE) ◆ hasn't been with this yard for long and, with the headgear removed, he offered encouragement, keeping on nicely but much too late. He can win races for these connections. (op 25-1)
Mawaqeet(USA) hadn't been seen since finishing second to the progressive Sir Graham Wade (winner three times since) over 1m4f at Glorious Goodwood from 5lb lower. This was a slightly disappointing return to action, the longer trip perhaps not suiting. (op 9-2)
Call It On(IRE) ran a respectable race from the front, only being run out of the places near the finish. (tchd 66-1)
Repeater, who was 14lb well-in following his fourth in a muddling Doncaster Cup, ruined his chance by refusing to settle. His trainer's representative reported the race came too soon for the gelding. Official explanation: trainer's rep said race came too soon for gelding having run six days ago. (tchd 9-4 and 11-4)
Modernism travelled well in a decent position but didn't see his race out. He was up in trip, but it's unclear whether a lack of stamina was to blame. (op 9-2 tchd 5-1)

6416 BARTHOLOMEWS FILLIES' H'CAP — 1m 3f 101y
4:50 (4:50) (Class 4) (0-80,80) 3-Y-O+ **£4,075** (£1,212; £606; £303) **Stalls** Low

Form — RPR

5224 **1** **Jennifer J**[43] 4972 3-8-6 **67**.......... PaulHanagan 6 — 78
(Mark H Tompkins) *in tch in midfield: rdn and hdwy to chse ldr jst over 2f out: drvn and ev ch ins fnl f: led but hrd pressed fnl 50yds: hld on wl* **8/1**

541 **2** *hd* **Caskelena (IRE)**[34] 5316 3-8-12 **73**.......... RichardHughes 8 — 84
(Sir Michael Stoute) *stdd and dropped in bhd after s: t.k.h: hld up wl off the pce in rr: stdy hdwy fr 4f out: rdn to chse ldng pair over 1f out: ev ch wl ins fnl f: hld towards fin* **5/1**[1]

110 **3** *1 ¾* **Between Us**[12] 6033 3-9-5 **80**.......... ChrisCatlin 5 — 88
(Sir Mark Prescott Bt) *led and set gd gallop: clr 4f out: drvn over 2f out: battled on wl tl hdd and no ex fnl 50yds* **7/1**

5142 **4** *4* **Scarlet Belle**[9] 6118 3-8-6 **67**.......... RichardMullen 12 — 68
(Marcus Tregoning) *hld up in midfield: nt clr run ent fnl 2f: swtchd rt and hdwy over 1f out: styd on u.p fnl f to go 4th towards fin* **7/1**

2510 **5** *¾* **Cape Safari (IRE)**[12] 6033 3-8-12 **78**..........(p) NatashaEaton[(5)] 7 — 78
(Alan Bailey) *chsd ldr: rdn over 3f out: lost 2nd ent fnl 2f but kpt on u.p tl btn 1f out: wknd ins fnl f* **20/1**

0036 **6** *1 ½* **Sail Home**[21] 5767 5-8-13 **67**.......... JimmyQuinn 13 — 66
(Julia Feilden) *hld up in midfield: rdn and effrt whn swtchd rt 2f out: plugged on same pce and no threat to ldrs fr over 1f out* **50/1**

2442 **7** *nk* **Dutch Diamond**[15] 5931 3-9-0 **75**.......... NickyMackay 14 — 72
(John Gosden) *hld up in midfield: rdn and effrt whn edgd lft wl over 2f out: no imp and btn over 1f out: wknd ins fnl f* **9/1**

-432 **8** *1 ¼* **Openly**[8] 6146 3-9-0 **75**.......... MartinLane 10 — 70
(James Fanshawe) *chsd ldrs: edgd lft and struggling over 2f out: wknd wl over 1f out* **6/1**[3]

2260 **9** *¾* **The Ducking Stool**[8] 6141 5-8-8 **69**.......... RyanTate[(7)] 3 — 64
(Julia Feilden) *hld up in midfield: nt clr run on inner and hmpd over 2f out: shuffled bk and swtchd rt wl over 1f out: no imp* **28/1**

3153 **10** *16* **Candycakes (IRE)**[18] 5856 3-9-3 **78**.......... JamieSpencer 2 — 44
(Michael Bell) *t.k.h: chsd ldrs tl rdn and struggling over 2f out: wknd 2f out: eased ent fnl f* **11/2**[2]

5204 **11** *1 ¾* **Ukrainian Princess**[24] 5680 3-8-12 **73**.......... TomQueally 9 — 36
(Sir Henry Cecil) *sn rdn along and off the pce towards rr: sme hdwy 4f out: sn toiling again: bhd and eased fnl f* **20/1**

5200 **12** *6* **Viking Rose (IRE)**[31] 5420 4-8-13 **67**.......... AndreaAtzeni 1 — 20
(James Eustace) *a off the pce in rr: sme hdwy 4f out: sn struggling again: wl bhd and eased fnl f: t.o* **25/1**

4205 **13** *14* **Dawn Gale (IRE)**[44] 4905 4-9-10 **78**..........(t) RobertHavlin 4
(Hughie Morrison) *reluctant to go to post: s.i.s and nvr gng wl in rr: lost tch 5f out: t.o fnl 4f* **20/1**

54-6 **14** *22* **Miss Exhibitionist**[55] 3429 4-9-1 **69**.......... KierenFallon 11
(Alan King) *sn bhd and nvr gng wl: t.o fnl 4f* **33/1**

2m 25.04s (-3.66) **Going Correction** -0.275s/f (Firm)
WFA 3 from 4yo+ 7lb **14** Ran SP% **118.9**
Speed ratings (Par 102): **102,101,100,97,97 96,95,94,94,82 81,77,66,50**
toteswingers 1&2 £8.00, 1&3 £10.90, 2&3 £8.00 CSF £42.55 TOTE £9.90: £3.90, £2.20, £2.90; EX 72.40.
Owner Russell Trew Ltd **Bred** Russell Trew Ltd **Trained** Newmarket, Suffolk

FOCUS
A fair fillies' handicap run at a strong pace. The winner is rated in line with her Pontrfract form with personal bests from the placed horses.
Candycakes(IRE) Official explanation: jockey said filly lost its action
Viking Rose(IRE) Official explanation: jockey said filly never travelled
Dawn Gale(IRE) Official explanation: jockey said filly never travelled
Miss Exhibitionist Official explanation: jockey said filly never travelled

6417 GREENE KING IPA H'CAP — 6f 3y
5:20 (5:20) (Class 4) (0-80,79) 3-Y-O **£4,075** (£1,212; £606; £303) **Stalls** Centre

Form — RPR

2612 **1** **Signor Sassi**[23] 5703 3-9-6 **78**.......... AndreaAtzeni 1 — 91+
(Roger Varian) *hld up in tch: hdwy 2f out: chal 1f out: rdn to ld ins fnl f: pushed out and r.o wl after* **2/1**[2]

311 **2** *¾* **Saloomy**[44] 4919 3-9-5 **77**.......... RichardHughes 2 — 88+
(David Simcock) *racd keenly: led: rdn wl over 1f out: hrd pressed and drvn 1f out: hdd and styd on same pce ins fnl f* **6/4**[1]

3301 **3** *3 ¼* **Salacia (IRE)**[30] 5453 3-9-7 **79**.......... RoystonFfrench 3 — 80
(Ismail Mohammed) *chsd ldrs: wnt 2nd and rdn jst over 2f out: 3rd and unable qck ent fnl f: wknd fnl 100yds* **5/1**[3]

0535 **4** *6* **Ghost Train (IRE)**[8] 6145 3-8-9 **67**..........(p) KierenFallon 4 — 48
(Mark Johnston) *chsd ldr tl ent fnl 2f: sn drvn and unable qck: wknd 1f out* **11/2**

0164 **5** *7* **Sarah Berry**[15] 5934 3-8-0 **65** oh5.......... HannahNunn[(7)] 5 — 24
(Chris Dwyer) *a in rr: rdn and struggling 1/2-way: lost tch 2f out* **28/1**

1m 13.15s (-1.25) **Going Correction** -0.125s/f (Firm) **5** Ran SP% **108.8**
Speed ratings (Par 103): **103,102,97,89,80**
CSF £5.26 TOTE £3.20: £2.40, £1.50; EX 6.50.
Owner P D Smith **Bred** D G Hardisty Bloodstock **Trained** Newmarket, Suffolk

FOCUS
An interesting 3yo sprint handicap.
T/Plt: £58.20 to a £1 stake. Pool: £90,475.97 - 1,133.71 winning tickets T/Qpdt: £31.10 to a £1 stake. Pool: £5,522.36 - 131.05 w. tckts SP

6418a - 6422a (Foreign Racing) See RI

5184 AYR (L-H)

Friday, September 21

OFFICIAL GOING: Heavy (7.9)
Rail at entry to home straight moved out 12m to a drop in at 3f marker, with a false rail from 5f to start.
Wind: Light, half against Weather: Cloudy bright

6423 CITY REFRIGERATION HOLDINGS (UK) LIMITED/E.B.F. MAIDEN STKS 7f 50y
1:50 (1:50) (Class 4) 2-Y-O £5,369 (£1,597; £798 ; £399) Stalls High

Form				RPR
	1		**Hay Dude** 2 -9-0 0 MichaelMetcalfe(3) 2 (Mrs K Burke) *prom: smooth hdwy to ld 2f out: edgd lft over 1f out: shkn up and qcknd clr appr fnl f: readily* **14/1**	87+
2	2	3 1/4	**Anna's Pearl**27 5578 2 -9-3 0 JimCrowley 1 (Ralph Beckett) *chsd ldrs: drvn and outpcd over 2f out: angled rt over 1f out: chsd clr wnr ins fnl f: styd on: no imp* **4/7**1	79
04	3	8	**Scepticism (USA)**7 6188 2 -9-3 0 JoeFanning 5 (Mark Johnston) *pressed ldr: ev ch and rdn over 2f out: edgd lft and wknd fnl f* **15/2**3	59+
3	4	2 1/2	**Bahamamay**37 5221 2 -9-3 0 TonyHamilton 4 (Richard Fahey) *t.k.h: led to 2f out: sn rdn and btn* **3/1**2	53
	5	8	**Hayley** 2 -8-12 0 GrahamLee 6 (Jim Goldie) *hld up last but in tch: rdn over 2f out: sn wknd* **25/1**	29

1m 38.03s (4.63) **Going Correction** +0.45s/f (Yiel) **5** Ran SP% **110.9**
Speed ratings (Par 97): **91,87,78,75,66**
toteswingers 1&4 £4.70 CSF £23.45 TOTE £10.80 : £2.50 , £1.40 ; EX 19.60 .
Owner Ray Bailey **Bred** Ray Bailey **Trained** Middleham Moor, N Yorks

FOCUS
The meeting had to pass a morning inspection. A fair juvenile maiden. The winning time was nearly ten seconds slower than standard and the ground appeared to be riding heavy, as officially described. Not form to take too literally but the winner was impressive.

NOTEBOOK
Hay Dude failed to fetch his asking price of 26,000 guineas as a yearling in November 2010. He is the first foal out of a decent multiple 7f winner, including on good to soft ground. He started a tad slowly here on debut but settled well in fourth, then moved up travelling well approaching the 2f marker, before quickening away in good fashion, and his trainer Elaine Burke now has a 17% strike-rate with her 2yo runners this term. He looks a nice prospective miler for next term. (op 12-1)
Anna's Pearl would have had his odds-on backers worried from fully 4f out, where he had to be rousted along to stay in touch, but he did at least stick to his task to come through for second. He finished second on his debut over 6f at Newmarket on good to firm ground the previous month but ran below that level on this occasion. (op 4-6)
Scepticism(USA), a half-brother to a US Grade 1 winner, progressed to finish a modest fourth over an extended 7f on good to soft ground at Chester on his second start earlier this month, but failed to finish his race with any real purpose on this ground. He is an imposing individual who will do better in handicaps on better ground next term. (op 7-1)
Bahamamay raced keenly and had very little left in the tank after leading to the 2f marker. (op 11-4)
Hayley didn't appreciate these testing conditions on debut. (tchd 33-1)

6424 SHADWELL STUD HARRY ROSEBERY STKS (FOR THE SOUTH AYRSHIRE CUP) (LISTED RACE) 5f
2:20 (2:21) (Class 1) 2-Y-O
£14,177 (£5,375; £2,690 ; £1,340 ; £672 ; £337) Stalls High

Form				RPR
34	1		**Garswood**52 4688 2 -9-3 0 TonyHamilton 8 (Richard Fahey) *sn pushed along in rr: hdwy and swtchd lft over 1f out: styd on wl fnl f to ld towards fin* **5/1**3	100+
	2	3/4	**Zoola (IRE)**59 4442 2 -8-12 0 RobertWinston 1 (Andrew Heffernan, Ire) *t.k.h: prom: hdwy to ld over 1f out: kpt on fnl f: hdd towards fin* **8/1**	92
5	3	2 3/4	**Boston Rocker (IRE)**27 5608 2 -8-12 0 ShaneFoley 6 (Edward Lynam, Ire) *in tch: effrt and rdn over 2f out: chsd ldr over 1f out to ins fnl f: one pce* **7/4**1	82
0220	4	2	**New Pearl (IRE)**29 5515 2 -9-3 90 GrahamLee 9 (David Brown) *bhd: rdn and swtchd lft 2f out: kpt on fnl f: nvr able to chal* **9/1**	80
2106	5	2 3/4	**Lady Ibrox**27 5601 2 -8-12 91 DaleSwift 7 (Alan Brown) *cl up: drvn along 1/2-way: wknd over 1f out* **16/1**	65
3210	6	2 1/4	**Faithfilly (IRE)**13 6038 2 -9-1 100 DanielTudhope 2 (Ed Walker) *trckd ldrs: led over 2f out to over 1f out: sn wknd* **4/1**2	60
3	7	2 3/4	**Rivellino**61 4362 2 -9-3 0 JimCrowley 10 (Mrs K Burke) *hld up: hdwy on outside over 2f out: rdn and wknd over 1f out* **9/1**	52
2100	8	8	**All Fur Coat**29 5516 2 -8-12 85 GrahamGibbons 3 (Jo Hughes) *led to over 2f out: sn rdn: wknd over 1f out* **16/1**	19

1m 2.94s (3.54) **Going Correction** +0.725s/f (Yiel) **8** Ran SP% **115.9**
Speed ratings (Par 103): **100,98,94,91,86 83,78,66**
toteswingers 1&2 £4.80, 2&3 £3.00, 1&3 £2.80 CSF £44.73 TOTE £6.60 : £1.70 , £2.30 , £1.40 ; EX 48.20 Trifecta £104.60 Pool: £1147.03 - 8.11 winning units. .
Owner David W Armstrong **Bred** Cheveley Park Stud Ltd **Trained** Musley Bank, N Yorks

FOCUS
Just average form for the grade, the runner-up helping with the level. The winner probably has more to offer.

NOTEBOOK
Garswood was returning from a seven-week break since his decent fourth in a Glorious Goodwood 6f maiden on his second start in July. He was held up out the back on the rail but was switched inside the 2f marker to the outside of the pack. He did well to pick up the leader and won a shade cosily. He is a strong traveller who appreciated being settled off a decent pace over this shorter trip. He is a very good 3yo sprinting prospect. (op 6-1)
Zoola(IRE) raced keen early on but did best of those that raced prominently, returning from a two-month break since showing decent 5f form in two starts in Ireland, including when about 2l third in a Listed contest on soft to heavy ground at Tipperary in July. She comprehensively reversed form with the reopposing Tipperary second Boston Rocker. (tchd 9-1)
Boston Rocker (IRE)finished a respectable third but could not confirm her Tipperary superiority over Zoola. She goes well in heavy ground. (tchd 2-1 in a place)
New Pearl (IRE)was held up and came through into a fair fourth. He is back on track after a disappointing York display on reportedly unsuitable good to firm ground the previous month. (op 14-1)
Lady Ibrox weakened over 1f out after racing prominently.
Faithfilly(IRE) won a 5f Listed contest at Deauville on her penultimate start on good to soft ground the previous month but weakened out of this disappointingly inside the 2f marker. (op 7-2)
Rivellino failed to make any significant impression on this contest from the rear, returning from a two-month break since an encouraging 6f good ground Ascot debut in July. (op 8-1)

6425 STENA LINE NURSERY 6f
2:50 (2:58) (Class 3) (0-95,85) 2-Y-O £7,762 (£2,310; £1,154 ; £577) Stalls High

Form				RPR
2541	1		**Bachotheque (IRE)**23 5727 2 -8-13 77 DavidAllan 4 (Tim Easterby) *prom: hdwy to ld wl over 1f out: edgd rt: drvn out fnl f* **9/2**2	82+
4201	2	1 3/4	**Rio's Pearl**39 5153 2 -8-13 77 JimCrowley 2 (Ralph Beckett) *cl up: led gng wl over 3f out: hdd wl over 1f out: kpt on same pce fnl f* **9/2**2	77+
414	3	1 3/4	**Yourartisonfire**41 5109 2 -9-1 82 MichaelMetcalfe(3) 8 (Mrs K Burke) *cl up: drvn and outpcd 2f out: rallied fnl f: kpt on fin* **17/2**	77
3110	4	nk	**Scentpastparadise**29 5515 2 -9-2 80 RoystonFfrench 5 (Ann Duffield) *t.k.h: chsd ldng gp: effrt and rdn over 2f out: no imp fnl f* **33/1**	74
1401	5	1	**Tharawal Lady (IRE)**62 4324 2 -8-13 77 MichaelO'Connell 6 (John Quinn) *prom: rdn along over 2f out: kpt on same pce fnl f* **20/1**	68
0050	6	2 3/4	**Woodland Mill (IRE)**29 5515 2 -8-11 78 LeeTopliss(3) 7 (Richard Fahey) *in tch: rdn and outpcd over 2f out: n.d after* **10/1**	60
140	7	2	**Luck (IRE)**12 6070 2 -9-7 85 PhillipMakin 3 (Kevin Ryan) *sn niggled along in last pl: drvn over 2f out: nvr rchd ldrs* **6/1**3	61
214	8	1/2	**Majestic Moon (IRE)**28 5563 2 -9-1 79 TonyHamilton 10 (Richard Fahey) *plld hrd: led to over 3f out: wknd fr 2f out* **7/4**1	54

1m 17.84s (5.44) **Going Correction** +0.725s/f (Yiel) **8** Ran SP% **114.3**
Speed ratings (Par 99): **92,89,87,86,85 81,79,78**
toteswingers 1&2 £3.60, 2&3 £7.50, 1&3 £5.00 CSF £25.01 CT £166.00 TOTE £5.10 : £1.40 , £1.50 , £2.50 ; EX 25.20 Trifecta £132.00 Pool: £1745.68 - 9.78 winning units. .
Owner Richard Taylor & Philip Hebdon **Bred** Tally-Ho Stud **Trained** Great Habton, N Yorks

FOCUS
A decent nursery handicap but the top-weight had a BHA rating 10lb below the ceiling of 95 for this contest. Despite the bad ground the form has a sound feel to it.

NOTEBOOK
Bachotheque(IRE) twice finished second to subsequent Group 2 winners over 5f/6f on good ground in July, and appeared well treated off a BHA rating of 77 on those efforts. He bounced back from a couple of below-par displays to win his maiden over 6f on soft ground at Carlisle the previous month. He is a likeable individual with a real future in good quality sprint handicaps on good ground, or worse, and won this readily after racing prominently throughout. (tchd 4-1 and 5-1)
Rio's Pearl won her maiden over 7f on Polytrack the previous month but had stronger form when second over an extended 6f on good to soft ground at Doncaster in June. She travelled very well for much of the journey but proved no match for the winner from over 1f out. She should remain competitive in similar company. (tchd 5-1)
Yourartisonfire stuck on gamely for third returning from a six-week break, and is a solid hook for the form in third. (op 10-1 tchd 8-1)
Scentpastparadise returned to form in running respectably on the softest ground she has encountered. (op 25-1)
Tharawal Lady (IRE)did well returning from a two-month break. (op 12-1)
Luck(IRE) has gone the wrong way from a very encouraging debut win over this 6f trip on soft ground at Hamilton. (op 9-1 tchd 5-1)
Majestic Moon (IRE)shaped very encouragingly over 6f on good ground at York the previous month. He proved disappointing on this heavy ground. The stewards ordered that the colt be routine tested as no explanation was forthcoming for the poor showing from the trainer's representative. Official explanation: trainer's rep had no explanation for the poor form shown. (op 2-1 tchd 13-8)

6426 WILLIAM HILL SUPPORTING DUMFRIES HOUSE AYRSHIRE H'CAP 1m
3:25 (3:25) (Class 2) (0-105,100) 3-Y-O+
£12,450 (£3,728; £1,864 ; £932 ; £466 ; £234) Stalls Low

Form				RPR
0014	1		**Osteopathic Remedy (IRE)**9 6135 8 -8-8 91 ConnorNichol(7) 6 (Michael Dods) *t.k.h: chsd ldrs: hdwy to ld over 2f out: rdn and hld on wl fnl f* **9/1**	99
4006	2	1/2	**Extraterrestrial**41 5094 8 -8-5 86 oh4 NeilFarley(5) 4 (Richard Fahey) *hld up in tch: effrt and rdn over 2f out: styd on to chse wnr wl ins fnl f: r.o* **9/1**	93
6105	3	1	**Lord Aeryn (IRE)**14 6011 5 -8-13 89 BarryMcHugh 8 (Richard Fahey) *cl up: chal and rdn over 2f out: one pce wl ins fnl f* **5/1**2	94
0500	4	4 1/2	**Al Muheer (IRE)**9 6235 7 -8-7 88 (b) JasonHart(5) 3 (Ruth Carr) *hld up: rdn along over 2f out: styd on fnl f: no ch w first three* **13/2**	82
3121	5	2 3/4	**Trail Blaze (IRE)**13 6046 3 -8-12 92 AmyRyan 7 (Kevin Ryan) *led: brought main gp centre over 3f out: rdn and hdd over 2f out: sn rdn: wknd wl over 1f out* **2/1**1	80
0300	6	2 1/2	**Take It To The Max**25 5677 5 -8-10 86 (p) TonyHamilton 1 (Richard Fahey) *cl up: effrt and styd w one other far side over 3f out: rdn and wknd 2f out* **6/1**3	68
6020	7	nse	**St Moritz (IRE)**9 6242 6 -9-10 100 AdrianNicholls 2 (David Nicholls) *hld up: drvn along over 2f out: nvr able to chal* **12/1**	82
600	8	10	**Titus Mills (IRE)**27 2211 4 -9-5 95 GrahamLee 5 (Brian Meehan) *hld up in tch: effrt and styd w one other far side over 3f out: hung lft and wknd over 2f out* **10/1**	54

1m 45.47s (1.67) **Going Correction** +0.45s/f (Yiel)
WFA 3 from 4yo+ 4lb **8** Ran SP% **114.4**
Speed ratings (Par 109): **109,108,107,103,100 97,97,87**
toteswingers 1&2 £11.40, 2&3 £8.50, 1&3 £7.30 CSF £85.52 CT £454.00 TOTE £10.30 : £2.40 , £2.90, £1.50 ; EX 55.10 Trifecta £490.10 Pool: £1490.36 - 2.25 winning units. .
Owner Kevin Kirkup **Bred** Airlie Stud **Trained** Denton, Co Durham
■ Connor Nichol's first winner.

FOCUS
A good class handicap for 3yos and up. Pretty streightforward form.

NOTEBOOK
Osteopathic Remedy (IRE)won the same 1m Ripon handicap for the third time in the past five seasons the previous month. He was still able to race off a mark 1lb below his peak-winning rating, achieved over this 1m trip on heavy ground at Newcastle in October 2010, and the old warrior saw off his rivals tenaciously to win his tenth handicap under a capable 7lb-claiming jockey in Connor Nichol. He is entered to race under a penalty over 1f shorter here on Saturday. (tchd 8-1 and 10-1)

Extraterrestrial shaped encouragingly over 1m on good to firm ground at Haydock the previous month. He handles these conditions but has three wins to his name on good ground. He remains on an enticing mark. (tchd 10-1)
Lord Aeryn(IRE) wasn't disgraced but is ideally suited by good or good to firm ground. (op 9-2)
Al Muheer(IRE) handles this sort of ground but was unable to get on terms with the first three from a held-up position. (op 15-2)
Trail Blaze(IRE) has been in tremendous form but proved disappointing on this heavy surface. The stewards noted the trainer's explanation that the colt was suffering the effects of a long season. They ordered that the colt be routine tested. Official explanation: trainer said colt was suffering the effects of a long season. (op 9-4 tchd 5-2)
Take It To The Max didn't appreciate these testing conditions.

6427 HUNTSWOOD H'CAP 5f

4:00 (4:03) (Class 4) (0-85,85) 3-Y-0+ **£5,175** (£1,540; £769; £384) **Stalls** High

Form RPR
-310 **1** **Jamaican Bolt (IRE)**[70] 4073 4-9-7 **85** RobertWinston 4 99+
(Geoffrey Oldroyd) *cl up centre gp: rdn over 1f out: led ins fnl f: kpt on strly: 1st of 8 in gp* **8/1**
0360 **2** *1 ¾* **Arctic Feeling (IRE)**[34] 5343 4-9-3 **81** TonyHamilton 9 89
(Richard Fahey) *in tch centre: rdn and outpcd over 2f out: rallied over 1f out: wnt 2nd towards fin: nt rch wnr: 2nd of 8 in gp* **7/1**[2]
0311 **3** *1* **Come On Dave (IRE)**[23] 5739 3-8-6 **71** AdrianNicholls 5 75
(David Nicholls) *overall ldr centre: rdn 2f out: hdd ins fnl f: kpt on same pce: 3rd of 8 in gp* **15/2**[3]
4000 **4** *nk* **Rothesay Chancer**[14] 6009 4-8-7 **71** oh1 BarryMcHugh 15 74
(Jim Goldie) *led after 1f in stands' side gp: rdn and edgd lft over 1f out: kpt on ins fnl f: 1st of 8 in gp* **20/1**
2223 **5** *¾* **Waking Warrior**[32] 5412 4-8-4 **71** (tp) JulieBurke(3) 8 71
(Kevin Ryan) *in tch centre: drvn along over 2f out: kpt on ins fnl f: 4th of 8 in gp* **12/1**
4-61 **6** *¾* **Above The Stars**[33] 5389 4-8-7 **71** oh1 PatrickMathers 1 69
(Richard Fahey) *hld up on outside of centre gp: effrt and rdn over 2f out: no imp fnl f: 5th of 8 in gp* **33/1**
1330 **7** *nk* **Wicked Wench**[90] 3375 3-9-2 **81** GrahamLee 13 78
(Jo Hughes) *hld up in tch stands' side gp: effrt and rdn wl over 1f out: kpt on fnl f: no imp: 2nd of 8 in gp* **22/1**
3513 **8** *1 ¼* **We'll Deal Again**[17] 5915 5-8-11 **75** (b) GrahamGibbons 18 67
(Michael Easterby) *led 1f stands' side gp: w ldr tl hung lft and no ex over 1f out: 3rd of 8 in gp* **10/1**
0361 **9** *¾* **Even Stevens**[9] 6144 4-9-4 **82** 6ex (p) MircoDemuro 3 74
(Scott Dixon) *prom centre gp: drvn along over 2f out: one pce over 1f out: eased whn hld ins fnl f: 6th of 8 in gp* **13/2**[1]
43 **10** *¾* **Quaroma**[59] 4430 7-8-12 **76** PhillipMakin 2 63
(Paul Midgley) *hld up centre: effrt and hdwy 2f out: no imp fnl f: 7th of 8 in gp* **10/1**
2420 **11** *1* **Church Music (IRE)**[61] 4364 3-9-4 **83** (p) PaulMulrennan 16 66
(Michael Scudamore) *chsd stands' side ldrs: rdn 2f out: btn fnl f: 4th of 8 in gp* **20/1**
4164 **12** *4 ½* **Rylee Mooch**[14] 6006 4-8-8 **77** (e) JasonHart(5) 14 44
(Richard Guest) *hld up stands' side: rdn over 2f out: no imp fr over 1f out: 5th of 8 in gp* **16/1**
2000 **13** *1 ½* **The Nifty Fox**[14] 6009 8-9-1 **79** (p) DavidAllan 19 40
(Tim Easterby) *hld up stands' side gp: drvn over 2f out: nvr on terms: 6th of 8 in gp* **11/1**
0016 **14** *nk* **Hamoody (USA)**[6] 6234 8-8-11 **82** ShirleyTeasdale(7) 11 42
(David Nicholls) *bhd centre: struggling over 2f out: sn btn: last of 8 in gp* **16/1**
2100 **15** *1 ¾* **Sir Geoffrey (IRE)**[36] 5272 6-8-5 **72** (p) DeclanCannon(3) 12 26
(Scott Dixon) *bhd on outside of stands' side gp: struggling over 2f out: sn btn: 7th of 8 in gp* **33/1**
1000 **16** *1 ½* **Towbee**[12] 6075 3-8-10 **82** (b) DavidSimmonson(7) 17 31
(Michael Easterby) *unruly in stalls: dwlt: sn w stands' side ldrs: rdn and wknd 2f out: last of 8 in gp* **20/1**

1m 2.35s (2.95) **Going Correction** +0.725s/f (Yiel)
WFA 3 from 4yo+ 1lb **16** Ran SP% **119.2**
Speed ratings (Par 105): **105,102,100,100,98 97,97,95,94,92 91,84,81,81,78 75**
toteswingers 1&2 £10.20, 2&3 £6.90, 1&3 £7.50 CSF £52.26 CT £384.82 TOTE £9.80: £2.70, £2.20, £1.80, £4.20; EX 61.70 Trifecta £285.10 Pool: £1032.62 - 2.68 winning units..
Owner R C Bond **Bred** Swordlestown Stud **Trained** Brawby, N Yorks

FOCUS
A decent sprint handicap for 3yos and up. Few got involved and five of the first six raced in the centre group, where the pace was. The winner's two best runs have come in testing ground.
Even Stevens Official explanation: trainer said gelding was unsuited by the heavy ground
Rylee Mooch Official explanation: jockey said gelding hung left throughout

6428 DUMFRIES HOUSE H'CAP (FOR THE EGLINTON & WINTON CHALLENGE CUP) 2m 1f 105y

4:35 (4:35) (Class 3) (0-95,94) 4-Y-0+ **£8,409** (£2,502; £1,250; £625) **Stalls** High

Form RPR
1-20 **1** **Los Nadis (GER)**[20] 5830 8-7-13 **77** NeilFarley(5) 8 86
(Jim Goldie) *hld up in tch: pushed along over 6f out: hdwy to ld 3f out: rdn clr fnl f* **12/1**
4005 **2** *2 ½* **French Hollow**[12] 6074 7-8-7 **80** PJMcDonald 6 86
(Tim Fitzgerald) *hld up in tch: smooth hdwy over 4f out: chsd wnr and effrt over 2f out: edgd rt appr fnl f: kpt on: nt rch wnr* **6/1**
110 **3** *3 ¼* **Asker (IRE)**[35] 5306 4-8-12 **85** (b) GrahamLee 5 87
(Marcus Tregoning) *sn niggled in rr: hdwy to chse ldrs after 4f: rdn and effrt 3f out: one pce fnl 2f* **7/2**[1]
0-40 **4** *2 ¼* **Cosimo de Medici**[94] 3241 5-8-13 **86** (t) RobertHavlin 7 86
(Hughie Morrison) *missed break: hld up: hdwy over 3f out: sn rdn: no imp fr 2f out* **9/2**[2]
40P3 **5** *6* **Taikoo**[39] 5158 7-8-5 **78** AdrianNicholls 12 71
(Hughie Morrison) *sn drvn along to chse ldrs: wnt 2nd after 6f: effrt and ev ch over 3f out: wknd 2f out* **5/1**[3]
2010 **6** *2* **Pokfulham (IRE)**[28] 5540 6-8-6 **79** (v) BarryMcHugh 10 70
(Jim Goldie) *led to 3f out: sn drvn: wknd 2f out* **16/1**
0660 **7** *6* **Seaside Sizzler**[17] 5905 5-8-12 **85** (tp) JimCrowley 3 70
(Ralph Beckett) *prom: drvn along 1/2-way: rallied: wknd fr 4f out* **15/2**
021- **8** *33* **Sphinx (FR)**[244] 7162 14-8-2 **75** oh3 (b) PatrickMathers 1 23
(Edwin Tuer) *hld up: outpcd and drvn 5f out: lost tch fr 3f out: t.o* **14/1**
400 **9** *9* **Bolivia (GER)**[20] 5826 6-9-1 **88** (t) PaulMulrennan 11 26
(Lucy Wadham) *t.k.h: chsd ldr 6f: cl up tl rdn and wknd 4f out: t.o* **13/2**

4m 7.53s (7.83) **Going Correction** +0.45s/f (Yiel) **9** Ran SP% **116.7**
Speed ratings (Par 107): **99,97,96,95,92 91,88,73,68**
toteswingers 1&2 £7.50, 2&3 £6.20, 1&3 £5.40 CSF £82.86 CT £310.12 TOTE £13.30: £3.10, £1.60, £1.70; EX 121.30 Trifecta £442.80 Pool: £1316.60 - 2.20 winning units..
Owner Ian G M Dalgleish **Bred** Stiftung Gestut Fahrhof **Trained** Uplawmoor, E Renfrews

FOCUS
A good-class staying handicap for older horses in which they finished well strung out. The form is rated through the second.

NOTEBOOK
Los Nadis(GER) is a triple winner over 2m on good/good to firm ground at Musselburgh, and was racing off 5lb higher than for the last of those successes in October 2011. He ran well to finish a head second over an extended 2m4f on soft ground at Perth over hurdles in April, and that abundant supply of stamina helped enormously here under attritional conditions. He sat midfield, took close order entering the home straight and swept clear 2f out. He is entered in the Cesarewitch at Newmarket next month, a contest which would really suit, but is only on the fringes of getting into such a prestigious handicap. Official explanation: trainer said, the gelding was better suited by the return to the track. (op 11-1)
French Hollow enjoys these conditions and ran another decent race, after three lesser efforts on good to firm ground. (op 11-2)
Asker(IRE) won his first two career starts on heavy ground at up to 1m6f, but disappointed on good ground over a extended 1m5f at Newbury the previous month. This was a better display but he ran into a couple of stouter stayers under the prevailing conditions.
Cosimo de Medici missed the break here returning from a three-month absence. He should come on from this very respectable display. He also holds an entry in the Cesarewitch, and with his higher rating has a better chance of making that contest than the winner. He won a Newmarket trial for that contest on good to firm ground in September 2011, before finishing 16th of 33 off 2lb higher than today in the race itself on good ground. (op 5-1 tchd 11-2, 6-1 in a place)
Taikoo, last year's winner and racing off the same mark, was disappointing. (op 7-1 tchd 9-2)

6429 DUNNE GROUP H'CAP 1m

5:10 (5:10) (Class 5) (0-70,74) 3-Y-0 **£2,911** (£866; £432; £216) **Stalls** Low

Form RPR
1132 **1** **Ingleby Angel (IRE)**[6] 6259 3-9-2 **63** DanielTudhope 6 75+
(David O'Meara) *hld up in last pl: stdy hdwy over 2f out: effrt and swtchd rt over 1f out: led and edgd lft ins fnl f: kpt on wl* **15/8**[1]
1012 **2** *½* **Mick Slates (IRE)**[23] 5736 3-9-2 **68** JasonHart(5) 8 78
(Declan Carroll) *hld up in tch: hdwy to ld whn rn wd over 2f out: sn edgd lft: hdd ins fnl f: kpt on but a hld* **5/1**[3]
1102 **3** *2* **Ebony Clarets**[4] 6308 3-9-0 **61** BarryMcHugh 3 66
(Linda Perratt) *hld up: stdy hdwy 1/2-way: effrt and ev ch over 2f out: rdn and edgd lft over 1f out: one pce ins fnl f* **20/1**
1343 **4** *1* **Fine Altomis**[32] 5415 3-9-7 **68** PaulMulrennan 11 71
(Michael Dods) *cl up: chal over 3f out to over 2f out: rdn and one pce fnl f* **6/1**
6051 **5** *1* **Joshua The First**[9] 6131 3-9-13 **74** 6ex PhillipMakin 5 75
(Keith Dalgleish) *t.k.h: hld up: rdn and hdwy 2f out: hung lft and kpt on fnl f: no imp* **7/1**
3000 **6** *4* **Simpson Millar**[6] 6259 3-8-2 **54** oh9 NeilFarley(5) 10 46
(Noel Wilson) *trckd ldrs: rdn 3f out: outpcd whn n.m.r over 1f out* **50/1**
-505 **7** *½* **Holy Roman Warrior (IRE)**[35] 5314 3-9-4 **65** TonyHamilton 7 55
(Richard Fahey) *trckd ldrs: effrt and ev ch over 2f out: wknd over 1f out* **4/1**[2]
0333 **8** *3 ¼* **Kathleensluckylad (IRE)**[26] 5623 3-8-9 **56**[1] GrahamLee 2 39
(Kevin Ryan) *led to over 2f out: sn rdn and wknd* **10/1**
000 **9** *19* **Destiny Awaits (IRE)**[54] 4630 3-8-8 **55** RoystonFfrench 1
(Ian Semple) *sn pushed along in tch: struggling over 4f out: lost tch fnl 3f* **50/1**

1m 48.41s (4.61) **Going Correction** +0.45s/f (Yiel) **9** Ran SP% **116.0**
Speed ratings (Par 101): **94,93,91,90,89 85,85,81,62**
toteswingers 1&2 £3.50, 2&3 £7.20, 1&3 £8.40 CSF £11.34 CT £139.47 TOTE £2.70: £1.50, £1.90, £5.40; EX 11.60 Trifecta £111.70 Pool: £1718.55 - 11.38 winning units..
Owner Dave Scott **Bred** Dave Scott **Trained** Nawton, N Yorks
■ Stewards' Enquiry : Daniel Tudhope one-day ban: careless riding (Oct 5)

FOCUS
A fair handicap for the grade. The winner is on the up and there looks more to come.
Kathleensluckylad(IRE) Official explanation: jockey said gelding hung right throughout
T/Plt: £60.30 to a £1 stake. Pool: £57,022.46 - 689.96 winning tickets. T/Qpdt: £31.10 to a £1 stake. Pool: £4,046.66 - 96.00 winning tickets. RY

6301 BRIGHTON (L-H)

Friday, September 21

OFFICIAL GOING: Firm (good to firm in places; 8.0)
The first 'matinee' meeting in Britain since 2005. Rail dolled 6f to 3.5f adding about 9yds to distances.
Wind: virtually nil Weather: dry, bright spells

6430 CLUB REVENGE BRIGHTON H'CAP 1m 1f 209y

12:00 (12:00) (Class 5) (0-75,72) 3-Y-0+ **£2,264** (£673; £336; £168) **Stalls** Centre

Form RPR
-001 **1** **Silver Bullitt**[16] 5950 4-9-5 67 GeorgeBaker 10 77
(Gary Moore) *chsd ldr tl led 2f out: gng clr whn veered sharply lft u.p 1f out: in command and rdn out hands and heels fnl f* **12/1**
0316 **2** *1 ½* **Renegotiate**[87] 3469 3-8-3 64 DanielMuscutt(7) 5 70
(Andrew Balding) *hld up wl in tch: rdn and effrt over 2f out: chsd wnr 1f out: kpt on but no imp* **9/1**
4446 **3** *3 ¼* **Hawaana (IRE)**[9] 6141 7-9-8 70 LukeMorris 6 70
(Gay Kelleway) *hld up in tch towards rr: rdn and effrt over 2f out: swtchd rt over 1f out: kpt on u.p ins fnl f: no threat to wnr* **6/1**[3]
0514 **4** *hd* **If I Were A Boy (IRE)**[24] 5707 5-9-1 70 (p) JoshBaudains(7) 8 69
(Dominic Ffrench Davis) *racd keenly: led: rdn and hdd 2f out: unable qck and btn 1f out: plugged on same pce after* **8/1**
01-0 **5** *½* **Orthodox Lad**[30] 5480 4-9-10 72 LiamKeniry 1 70
(Ed de Giles) *t.k.h: chsd ldrs: rdn and pressed ldrs ent fnl 2f: no ex and btn 1f out: plugged on same pce after* **7/1**
1402 **6** *shd* **Saaboog**[11] 6092 3-8-12 66 MartinLane 2 64
(James Tate) *t.k.h: hld up wl in tch: rdn and unable qck over 2f out: outpcd and btn over 1f out: plugged on fnl f* **9/1**
4543 **7** *2 ¼* **Almuftarris (USA)**[14] 5990 3-9-2 70 (b) TadhgO'Shea 3 67+
(Ed Dunlop) *wnt rt and hmpd s: t.k.h: hld up in tch in rr: rdn and effrt wl over 2f out: plenty to do whn nt clr run and swtchd rt 2f out: plugging on but no threat to ldrs whn n.m.r ins fnl f: eased* **3/1**[1]
6365 **8** *½* **Moose Moran (USA)**[10] 6118 5-9-6 68 (b) KirstyMilczarek 7 60
(Olivia Maylam) *in tch in last pair: niggled along 7f out: swtchd rt and drvn over 1f out: no imp* **33/1**
-421 **9** *2 ½* **Swift Blade (IRE)**[17] 5908 4-9-8 70 (p) SebSanders 4 57
(Lady Herries) *t.k.h: hld up in tch in midfield: rdn and nt qckn 2f out: wknd over 1f out* **9/2**[2]

1230 **10** *12* **Welsh Nayber**[24] 5707 3-8-11 65......................................(b) EddieAhern 9 28
(Amanda Perrett) *in tch: rdn and unable qck over 2f out: wknd over 1f out: wl btn and eased ins fnl f* **10/1**

2m 1.43s (-2.17) **Going Correction** -0.075s/f (Good)
WFA 3 from 4yo+ 6lb **10** Ran SP% **120.8**
Speed ratings (Par 103): **105,103,101,101,100 100,98,98,96,86**
toteswingers 1&2 £22.60, 2&3 £22.60, 1&3 £0.00 CSF £119.19 CT £724.92 TOTE £11.00: £3.80, £3.40, £2.20; EX 99.40.
Owner Dahab Racing **Bred** Overbury Stallions Ltd **Trained** Lower Beeding, W Sussex

FOCUS
The rail was dolled out 6f to 3.5f adding about 9yds to race distances. An open-looking contest, run at a steady pace with the winner benefiting from the run of the race. The winner built on his Lingfield selling victory.
Welsh Nayber Official explanation: jockey said gelding hung left

6431 DOWNLOAD 888SPORT FROM THE APP STORE NOW MAIDEN AUCTION STKS 6f 209y
12:30 (12:30) (Class 5) 2-Y-O **£2,264** (£673; £336; £168) **Stalls** Centre

Form RPR
4 **1** **Al Emirati (IRE)**[115] 2571 2-9-0 0.. MartinLane 1 72
(David Simcock) *chsd ldr: rdn and ev ch fr over 2f out: drvn and led narrowly ins fnl f: kpt on wl* **6/5**[1]
3 **2** *nse* **Banreenahreenkah (IRE)**[17] 5911 2-8-4 0..................... TadhgO'Shea 3 62
(Denis Coakley) *led: rdn jst over 2f out: edgd lft down camber 1f out: hdd ins fnl f: kpt on gamely: jst hld* **6/5**[1]
3 *2 ¾* **Don Eduardo** 2-8-9 0.. LiamKeniry 4 59+
(J S Moore) *chsd ldrs: rdn and outpcd over 2f out: looked wl hld tl rallied ins fnl f: styd on wl fnl 100yds* **17/2**[2]
4 *50* **Honeymoon Express (IRE)** 2-8-5 0.............................. JimmyQuinn 2
(Julia Feilden) *stdd s: rn green and sn struggling and rdn: lost tch over 2f out: virtually p.u fnl f: t.o* **14/1**[3]

1m 24.37s (1.27) **Going Correction** -0.075s/f (Good) **4** Ran SP% **108.1**
Speed ratings (Par 95): **89,88,85,28**
CSF £2.85 TOTE £1.80; EX 4.10.
Owner Abdulla Ahmad Al Shaikh **Bred** Grange & Old Carhue Bloodstock **Trained** Newmarket, Suffolk
■ Stewards' Enquiry : Tadhg O'Shea two-day ban: used whip above permitted level (Oct 5-6)

FOCUS
A modest, uncompetitive maiden, run at a fair pace with the front two in the market in command throughout, and fighting out a thrilling finish. The time was slow and the form looks ordinary.

NOTEBOOK
Al Emirati(IRE), a £19,000 half-brother to the useful Liszt, could never get competitive over the minimum on his debut at Chepstow, but was heavily supported here stepping up 2f in trip on his first start for 115 days, and ran out a brave winner. He got a lovely tow into the race but was the first of the principals to come under pressure, although he kept responding and can improve again over further. (op 2-1)
Banreenahreenkah(IRE) had run well when sent off 50-1 on her debut at Leicester and connections were positive with her here. There were times inside the final furlong when she looked to be getting on top, but was almost waiting for her rival to come back to her, and may well need to be produced later. (op 4-5)
Don Eduardo, closely related to 6f 2yo winner Song Of Time and Group-placed 7f AW 2yo winner Caprella, ran a shade green early and did not seem entirely happy on this quickish ground but, looked to be getting the hang of things late on and will have learnt plenty from this. (op 7-1 tchd 9-1)

6432 PIPECENTER H'CAP 6f 209y
1:00 (1:00) (Class 3) (0-95,90) 3-Y-O+ **£9,703** (£2,887; £1,443; £721) **Stalls** Centre

Form RPR
0012 **1** **Konstantin (IRE)**[17] 5910 4-9-0 83....................................... ShaneKelly 7 92
(Marcus Tregoning) *hld up in tch: rdn and effrt ent fnl 2f: drvn and styd on to ld fnl 75yds: jst hld on* **13/2**
6004 **2** *shd* **Noble Citizen (USA)**[23] 5746 7-9-4 87..........................(be) MartinLane 9 96
(David Simcock) *in tch in rr: rdn and effrt towards centre over 2f out: str run ins fnl f to chal fnl 50yds: jst hld* **7/1**
0000 **3** *1* **Kakatosi**[34] 5356 5-8-7 83.. DanielMuscutt(7) 8 89
(Andrew Balding) *chsd ldrs: rdn and effrt to press ldrs 1f out: no ex and one pce fnl 75yds* **8/1**
0031 **4** *1 ¾* **Escape To Glory (USA)**[14] 6008 4-9-6 89.............................. IanMongan 4 90+
(Mikael Magnusson) *chsd ldrs: jnd ldr and rdn 2f out: led ent fnl f: hdd and no ex fnl 75yds: wknd towards fin* **9/1**
0005 **5** *½* **Lord Ofthe Shadows (IRE)**[34] 5356 3-9-4 90.................. DaneO'Neill 1 90
(Richard Hannon) *stdd after s: hld up in tch: swtchd rt 2f out: swtchd bk lft and hdwy over 1f out: n.m.r briefly 1f out: styd on same pce and no imp fnl 100yds* **4/1**[2]
5115 **6** *1 ¼* **Verse Of Love**[7] 6192 3-9-1 87.. CathyGannon 2 84
(David Evans) *led: jnd and rdn 2f out: hdd and drvn ent fnl f: wknd fnl 100yds* **11/4**[1]
2512 **7** *3 ½* **Picture Dealer**[17] 5906 3-8-9 81.. LukeMorris 5 68
(Gary Moore) *dwlt: sn rcvrd to chse ldrs: rdn over 2f out: unable qck over 1f out: wknd ins fnl f* **13/2**
1410 **8** *2 ¼* **Mizwaaj (IRE)**[23] 5746 3-9-3 89.......................................(t) HarryBentley 6 70
(Saeed Bin Suroor) *t.k.h: hld up wl in tch: rdn and effrt 2f out: struggling whn n.m.r ent fnl f: wknd qckly jst ins fnl f* **6/1**[3]

1m 21.24s (-1.86) **Going Correction** -0.075s/f (Good)
WFA 3 from 4yo+ 3lb **8** Ran SP% **121.2**
Speed ratings (Par 107): **107,106,105,103,103 101,97,95**
toteswingers 1&2 £22.60, 2&3 £22.60, 1&3 £0.00 CSF £54.05 CT £302.72 TOTE £7.60: £2.30, £4.80, £3.10; EX 40.00.
Owner Lady Tennant **Bred** Miss Annmarie Burke **Trained** Lambourn, Berks

FOCUS
Plenty of pace on for this decent 7f handicap and it was no surprise to see the finishers, who came wide, dominate. The winner is rated to a length personal best.

NOTEBOOK
Konstantin(IRE), in great form and racing under his optimum conditions, looked to be up against it racing off a career high mark but he came with a sweeping run and held on bravely at the line. He is lightly-raced and this was a career best effort. (op 7-1 tchd 6-1)
Noble Citizen(USA) had shown signs of returning to form when staying on from a difficult position at Kempton last time and, back down to his last winning mark here, could not quite catch the winner, who got first run. He is a useful type when able to come late off a decent pace, and likes these quick conditions. (op 13-2)
Kakatosi, has endured a poor summer but he did best of those who raced up with the pace. Without a win in over two years, he has dropped to a handy mark and is worth following once hitting form. (op 12-1 tchd 14-1)
Escape To Glory(USA) raced prominently before fading late on and tends to show his best when more patiently ridden. (tchd 17-2 and 10-1)
Lord Ofthe Shadows(IRE) was held up early and, having been briefly hampered 2f out, kept hanging to his left under pressure, and did not seem to act on the track. (op 5-1 tchd 11-2)
Verse Of Love, who has enjoyed a fine second half of the summer, was heavily supported but found this a bit too competitive. (op 7-2)
Picture Dealer, racing over 7f for the first time since May, was briefly blocked 2f out but found little for pressure and did not truly convince he stayed. (op 9-2)

6433 TALK TO VICTOR MAIDEN FILLIES' STKS 7f 214y
1:30 (1:30) (Class 4) 3-Y-O+ **£4,204** (£1,251; £625; £312) **Stalls** Centre

Form RPR
2-43 **1** **Silke Top**[15] 5970 3-9-0 70.. CathyGannon 2 68
(William Jarvis) *chsd ldr tl led after 1f: mde rest: rdn and edgd rt over 2f out: drvn and asserted ins fnl f: in command fnl 100yds: eased cl home* **11/4**[2]
5025 **2** *1* **Isatis**[38] 5218 3-9-0 70.. TomQueally 1 66
(Sir Henry Cecil) *t.k.h: in tch: hdwy to join ldrs and bmpd over 2f out: shkn up and fnd little ent fnl f: drvn and could nt qckn ins fnl f: btn fnl 100yds* **8/11**[1]
246 **3** *1 ¼* **Prime Run**[8] 6154 3-9-0 0.. MartinLane 4 63
(David Simcock) *stdd s: t.k.h: effrt u.p on inner 2f out: chsd ldng pair and swtchd rt 1f out: one pce after* **6/1**[3]
4320 **4** *5* **Nevaeh**[78] 3785 3-9-0 65..(p) LukeMorris 3 51
(Pat Eddery) *led for 1f: chsd wnr after: rdn 4f out: stl pressing ldr and bmpd over 2f out: wknd ent fnl f* **11/1**
0 **5** *1 ¼* **Aujourd'Hui**[8] 6154 3-8-7 0.. RufusVergette(7) 5 48
(Richard Hannon) *t.k.h: chsd ldrs: rdn jst over 2f out: wknd over 1f out* **33/1**

1m 36.29s (0.29) **Going Correction** -0.075s/f (Good) **5** Ran SP% **110.1**
Speed ratings (Par 102): **95,94,92,87,86**
CSF £5.17 TOTE £3.00: £1.60, £1.30; EX 5.90.
Owner Kevin Hickman **Bred** Kevin Hickman **Trained** Newmarket, Suffolk

FOCUS
A moderate maiden run at a steady pace with the front three pulling clear late on. The form is rated around the winner and third.

6434 DOWNLOAD THE BETVICTOR SPINCAST APP NOW H'CAP 7f 214y
2:05 (2:05) (Class 5) (0-70,70) 3-Y-O+ **£2,264** (£673; £336; £168) **Stalls** Centre

Form RPR
0413 **1** **Lutine Charlie (IRE)**[8] 6172 5-9-0 60............................... CathyGannon 7 69
(Pat Eddery) *t.k.h: hld up in tch: hdwy to join ldrs 3f out: rdn and ev ch over 2f out: drvn and clr w rival ins fnl f: led last stride* **9/2**[3]
2206 **2** *nse* **Good Luck Charm**[42] 5036 3-9-4 68................................... GeorgeBaker 3 77
(Gary Moore) *t.k.h: chsd ldrs: led travelling wl 2f out: rdn over 1f out: clr w wnr and drvn ins fnl f: hdd last stride* **3/1**[1]
5313 **3** *2 ½* **One Way Or Another (AUS)**[7] 6217 9-9-3 70.......(t) ConorHarrison(7) 4 73
(David Evans) *t.k.h: hld up in midfield: rdn and effrt over 1f out: rdr dropped reins 1f out: styd on u.p to go 3rd last stride* **7/2**[2]
3266 **4** *shd* **Patavium Prince (IRE)**[42] 5050 9-9-8 68.......................... DaneO'Neill 5 71
(Jo Crowley) *t.k.h: chsd ldrs: swtchd lft and effrt to chse ldng pair jst over 1f out: drvn and no ex 1f out: one pce fnl f: lost 3rd last stride* **8/1**
3262 **5** *1 ¼* **Lady Sylvia**[43] 4989 3-9-5 69.. LiamKeniry 6 69
(Joseph Tuite) *chsd ldrs: rdn and unable qck 2f out: btn and one pce ent fnl f* **7/1**
6-00 **6** *¾* **Trumpet Voluntary (IRE)**[13] 6050 3-9-1 65....................(t[1]) ShaneKelly 1 63
(Nicky Vaughan) *hld up in tch in last trio: rdn and hdwy on inner over 1f out: keeping on but wl hld whn nt clr run and swtchd rt ins fnl f* **40/1**
0040 **7** *3 ½* **Benandonner (USA)**[21] 5783 9-9-7 67................................. MartinLane 8 57
(Paddy Butler) *chsd ldr tl wl over 2f out: wknd u.p over 1f out* **9/1**
5205 **8** *nk* **Sasheen**[39] 5148 5-9-0 60... PatCosgrave 2 50
(Jeremy Gask) *sn led: rdn and hdd 2f out: btn ent fnl f: wknd fnl 150yds* **12/1**
0000 **9** *2 ¼* **Crystal Sky (IRE)**[25] 5657 4-8-5 56 oh11.................. LeonnaMayor(5) 10 40
(Natalie Lloyd-Beavis) *hld up in tch in rr: rdn and no hdwy 2f out: wknd over 1f out* **33/1**
6540 **10** *½* **Chevise (IRE)**[15] 5972 4-9-2 67..................................... DavidKenny(5) 11 50
(Steve Woodman) *s.i.s: in tch: rdn and effrt over 2f out: wknd over 1f out* **14/1**

1m 35.06s (-0.94) **Going Correction** -0.075s/f (Good)
WFA 3 from 4yo+ 4lb **10** Ran SP% **118.8**
Speed ratings (Par 103): **101,100,98,98,97 96,92,92,90,89**
toteswingers 1&2 £3.60, 2&3 £1.40, 1&3 £2.80 CSF £18.78 CT £53.35 TOTE £4.40: £1.70, £1.90, £2.10; EX 18.40.
Owner Miss Emma L Owen **Bred** Patrice O'Connell **Trained** Nether Winchendon, Bucks

FOCUS
A fair handicap run at an honest pace that suited those coming from just off the gallop. Just about the winner's best form this year.

6435 FAREWELL TO LYNDA BAXTER NURSERY 7f 214y
2:35 (2:35) (Class 6) (0-60,60) 2-Y-O **£2,045** (£603; £302) **Stalls** Centre

Form RPR
000 **1** **Pink Mischief**[16] 5932 2-8-10 49... DaneO'Neill 8 53+
(Harry Dunlop) *stdd s: t.k.h: hld up in last trio: rdn and hdwy in centre to chse ldrs over 1f out: led ins fnl f: r.o wl* **13/2**
1503 **2** *1 ½* **Missing Agent**[8] 6156 2-9-7 60....................................(v) CathyGannon 1 61
(David Evans) *t.k.h: chsd ldrs: rdn and ev ch 2f out: led jst ins fnl f: sn hdd and styd on same pce* **6/1**[3]
505 **3** *2 ¼* **Alpine Jerry (IRE)**[15] 5968 2-9-3 56.............................. SamHitchcott 2 52
(J S Moore) *stdd s: hld up in tch in last trio: swtchd lft and effrt on inner over 2f out: ev ch 1f out: no ex and wknd fnl 100yds* **20/1**
0002 **4** *hd* **Cromwell Rose (IRE)**[10] 6115 2-8-6 45..........................(b) MartinLane 4 40
(John Weymes) *t.k.h: led tl 3f out: stl ev ch whn edgd rt u.p over 2f out: led again and edgd lft over 1f out: hdd ins fnl f: wknd fnl 100yds* **9/2**[2]
0000 **5** *2* **I'm Watching**[60] 4408 2-8-12 51... PatCosgrave 6 42
(George Baker) *t.k.h: chsd ldr tl led 3f out: rdn over 2f out: hdd over 1f and unable qck: wknd ins fnl f* **14/1**
0604 **6** *1 ¾* **Gabrial The Boss (USA)**[8] 6156 2-9-7 60....................... GeorgeBaker 5 47
(David Simcock) *stdd s: hld up in tch in last trio: rdn and hdwy to chse ldrs 2f out: no ex ent fnl f: wknd ins fnl f* **5/4**[1]
0330 **7** *1* **Strawberry Duck (IRE)**[10] 6115 2-8-13 52...................... HarryBentley 7 36
(Amy Weaver) *in tch in midfield: rdn 3f out: lost pl and drvn wl over 1f out: sn wknd* **20/1**
0060 **8** *4* **Ottauquechee (IRE)**[8] 6156 2-9-0 60......(b[1]) WilliamTwiston-Davies(7) 3 35
(Richard Hannon) *chsd ldrs: unable qck u.p and edgd rt 2f out: wknd over 1f out* **8/1**

1m 36.93s (0.93) **Going Correction** -0.075s/f (Good) **8** Ran SP% **117.5**
Speed ratings (Par 93): **92,90,88,88,86 84,83,79**
toteswingers 1&2 £6.20, 2&3 £7.20, 1&3 £11.20 CSF £46.22 TOTE £10.90: £3.30, £2.50, £9.60; EX 83.00.
Owner The Windsor House Stables Partnership **Bred** Earle I Mack **Trained** Lambourn, Berks

FOCUS
This was run at a fair pace with the winner coming widest of all. Low-grade nursery form, not a race to be positive about.
NOTEBOOK
Pink Mischief had shown little in three maidens at up to 7f but, stepped up to 1m on her handicap debut, she showed much-improved form. This race took little winning but she won despite not looking entirely happy on this track, with this looking to be her minimum trip. Official explanation: trainer said, regarding apparent improvement in form, that the filly was better suited by the step up in trip and by the unusual configuration of the track. (op 6-1)
Missing Agent ran well in a first-time visor at Chepstow last time and ran to a similar level here, with the headgear retained, despite racing keenly in the early part of the race. (op 9-2)
Alpine Jerry(IRE), making her handicap debut, was patiently ridden and enjoyed a nice run up the rail but weakened late on. (op 22-1 tchd 18-1)
Cromwell Rose(IRE)'s first-time blinkers had brought about improvement at Leicester last time and she looked well in here, but did not see out the trip on her first try over 7f. (op 4-1 tchd 5-1)
I'm Watching had shown little in four maiden runs at up to 6f and, while briefly outpaced here, was staying on again late and may need even further in time. (op 12-1)
Gabrial The Boss(USA) ran well when fourth on his handicap debut at Chepstow last time and he was heavily supported here but ran no sort of race. He was held up early but looked unbalanced on the track and did not seem to go through with his effort on the quicker ground. (op 9-4)
T/Plt: £313.30 to a £1 stake. Pool of £33789.12 - 78.72 winning tickets. T/Qpdt: £22.30 to a £1 stake. Pool of £4151.96 -137.48 winning tickets. SP

5946 LINGFIELD (L-H)
Friday, September 21

OFFICIAL GOING: Good to firm
Wind: Almost nil Weather: Overcast, becoming brighter

6436 YOUNG EPILEPSY CLAIMING STKS — 7f 140y
2:10 (2:10) (Class 6) 3-Y-O — **£1,704** (£503; £251) **Stalls** Centre

Form — RPR
1060 **1** **Sandbetweenourtoes (IRE)**[14] 5993 3-8-9 72 ow3.....(p) NedCurtis(7) 6 — 76
(Roger Curtis) *racd against rail: disp ld tl led 3f out: hung lft fr 2f out but sn rdn wl clr* **11/8**[1]
2162 **2** *8* **Kashmiri Star**[14] 6001 3-8-6 59 .... TobyAtkinson(5) 4 — 51
(Michael Quinn) *awkward s: hld up bhd ldrs: rdn to chse wnr over 2f out: sn lft bhd* **11/4**[3]
0055 **3** *9* **Johnny Splash (IRE)**[14] 5994 3-8-0 47 ....(p) IanBurns(7) 1 — 25
(Roger Teal) *racd on outer: rdn and struggling to hold pl 5f out: plugged on into 3rd 2f out* **16/1**
0066 **4** *7* **Monessa (IRE)**[16] 5949 3-8-0 50 ....(tp) NickyMackay 3
(Linda Jewell) *disp ld to 1/2-way: lost pl rapidly: sn bhd and eased: pushed into remote 4th nr fin* **14/1**
3500 **5** *hd* **First Bid**[13] 6052 3-8-7 68 ....(b) SilvestreDeSousa 5
(James Given) *t.k.h: disp ld to 3f out: wknd rapidly* **5/2**[2]
1m 30.96s (-1.34) **Going Correction** -0.075s/f (Good) — **5** Ran SP% **109.9**
Speed ratings (Par 99): **103,95,86,79,78**
CSF £5.44 TOTE £2.20: £1.50, £1.90; EX 6.50.
Owner Mrs Florence Dean **Bred** Barouche Stud Ireland Ltd **Trained** Lambourn, Berks
FOCUS
A weak and uncompetitive claimer. The winner probably didn't improve.
First Bid Official explanation: jockey said colt stopped quickly

6437 ZAEEM JAMAL MAIDEN AUCTION FILLIES' STKS — 7f 140y
2:40 (2:41) (Class 6) 2-Y-O — **£1,704** (£503; £251) **Stalls** Centre

Form — RPR
1 **Annina (IRE)** 2-8-12 0 .... IanMongan 9 — 84+
(John Dunlop) *hld up in 7th: rn green but prog fr 1/2-way: led over 1f out and taken across to nr side rail: sn pushed clr: easily* **4/1**[2]
44 **2** *6* **Martinas Delight (USA)**[15] 5977 2-8-3 0 .... MichaelJMMurphy(5) 5 — 64
(Alan Jarvis) *led narrowly but nvr mde it to nr side rail: rdn and hdd over 1f out: easily outpcd* **5/6**[1]
00 **3** *3 1/4* **Paige Flyer**[42] 5061 2-8-4 0 .... SilvestreDeSousa 10 — 52
(Michael Quinn) *hld up bhd ldrs and racd against rail: rdn over 2f out: kpt on one pce to take 3rd ins fnl f* **66/1**
0 **4** *1 3/4* **Spreading**[49] 4752 2-8-4 0 .... NickyMackay 3 — 48
(Michael Blanshard) *racd on outer: trckd ldrs: cl enough in 3rd 2f out: sn shkn up and wknd* **33/1**
06 **5** *1 1/2* **Caramel Sundae**[37] 5230 2-8-8 0 .... JimmyQuinn 2 — 49
(Marco Botti) *dwlt: sn pushed along in 8th: nvr on terms w ldrs: plugged on to take 5th over 1f out* **11/1**
0 **6** *1 1/2* **Planchette**[28] 5550 2-7-13 0 .... NoelGarbutt(7) 7 — 43
(Jane Chapple-Hyam) *w ldng pair to 3f out: wandered and wknd over 2f out* **16/1**
45 **7** *4* **Rakticate (IRE)**[27] 5574 2-8-6 0 .... AndreaAtzeni 4 — 34
(J S Moore) *in tch towards rr: shkn up and no prog 3f out: nvr a threat after* **11/2**[3]
0 **8** *22* **Magic Beat**[25] 5661 2-7-13 0 .... JemmaMarshall(5) 8
(Pat Phelan) *racd against rail: pressed ldr tl over 2f out: wknd v rapidly t.o* **10/1**
0 **9** *20* **Rosa Burn**[16] 5947 2-8-8 0 .... ChrisCatlin 1
(John Dunlop) *sn t.o* **50/1**
1m 31.33s (-0.97) **Going Correction** -0.075s/f (Good) — **9** Ran SP% **119.6**
Speed ratings (Par 90): **101,95,91,90,88 87,83,61,41**
toteswingers 1&2 £1.10, 2&3 £7.00, 1&3 £17.80 CSF £793.00 TOTE £4.50: £1.60, £1.10, £11.60; EX 10.90.
Owner The Earl Cadogan **Bred** Denis McDonnell **Trained** Arundel, W Sussex
FOCUS
The winner may not have beaten much - the odds-on favourite didn't build on earlier promise and the others don't look up to much - but there was a lot to like about her performance. She could easily rate higher.
NOTEBOOK
Annina(IRE) ◆, representing a trainer who was 0-77 with juvenile newcomers over the past three seasons (0-15 this year) and conceding weight all round, was noticeably green early on, but came right back on the bridle at around halfway. She found things easy from then on, despite still showing her inexperience, and drew clear once in the open. Out of a fair 1m-1m2f winner, Annina looks a smart middle-distance prospect. (op 6-1)
Martinas Delight(USA) had shown plenty of ability on her first two starts, but she was never going that well and proved no match at all for the winner. She was clear of the others, but probably didn't achieve a great deal and perhaps the ground, the fastest she's encountered to date, didn't suit. (op 4-6 tchd 10-11)
Paige Flyer, who showed little on her first two starts, is now qualified for a handicap mark.
Caramel Sundae may yet do better. (op 16-1)
Rakticate(IRE) was nowhere near the form of her first two starts and is another who may have been unsuited by the quick ground. (op 9-2)

6438 YOUNG EPILEPSY BRITISH STALLION STUDS E B F MEDIAN AUCTION MAIDEN STKS — 5f
3:15 (3:15) (Class 6) 2-Y-O — **£2,658** (£785; £392) **Stalls** High

Form — RPR
45 **1** **Somoud (IRE)**[7] 6203 2-9-3 0 .... IanMongan 8 — 73
(J R Jenkins) *racd towards nr side rail: mde virtually all: shkn up to assert over 1f out: pushed out fnl f* **15/8**[1]
3336 **2** *2 3/4* **Blazing Knight (IRE)**[8] 6155 2-9-3 68 .... RichardKingscote 7 — 63
(Ralph Beckett) *racd against rail: chsd ldrs in 5th: rdn wl over 1f out: styd on to take 2nd nr fin* **5/2**[2]
3 *1/2* **Mr Paranoia** 2-8-12 0 .... MichaelJMMurphy(5) 6 — 61+
(Conrad Allen) *dwlt: rn green and adrift in last: prog on outer fr 1/2-way: stl green but styd on wl to press for 2nd nr fin* **9/2**[3]
3342 **4** *nk* **Marchwood**[11] 6093 2-9-3 71 ....(b[1]) AndreaAtzeni 2 — 60
(J S Moore) *w wnr after 1f tl 2f out: btn off over 1f out: no ex and lost 2nd nr fin* **8/1**
600 **5** *hd* **Amirah (IRE)**[16] 5943 2-8-12 69 .... SilvestreDeSousa 4 — 55
(Tony Carroll) *prom on outer but sn pushed along: drvn over 2f out: one pce fr over 1f out* **10/1**
460U **6** *5* **Fantasy Invader (IRE)**[26] 5620 2-9-3 61 .... ChrisCatlin 5 — 42
(John Quinn) *w wnr 1f: styd prom tl wknd u.p 2f out* **12/1**
0050 **7** *3* **Stormy Times (IRE)**[14] 6016 2-8-7 50 .... RachealKneller(5) 9 — 26
(Mark Usher) *sn pushed along in rr: no prog 1/2-way* **33/1**
6550 **8** *2* **Sally Bruce**[29] 5511 2-8-5 52 .... JenniferFerguson(7) 3 — 19
(Louise Best) *dwlt: sn pushed along in rr: no prog 1/2-way* **100/1**
9 *5* **Pastoral Symphony** 2-8-12 0 .... JimmyQuinn 1 — 1
(John Best) *a in rr: wknd 2f out* **25/1**
58.82s (0.62) **Going Correction** -0.075s/f (Good) — **9** Ran SP% **117.2**
Speed ratings (Par 93): **92,87,86,86,86 78,73,70,62**
toteswingers 1&2 £1.70, 2&3 £4.00, 1&3 £3.70 CSF £6.69 TOTE £3.10: £1.50, £1.20, £2.10; EX 9.70.
Owner A Al Sabah **Bred** Mrs C Regalado-Gonzalez **Trained** Royston, Herts
FOCUS
A modest juvenile sprint maiden, but a nice enough winner who posted a personal best. The second helps with the level.
NOTEBOOK
Somoud(IRE) ◆ had the stands' rail to help, but was inclined to hang off it for much of the way and did well to take this so readily. He was confirming the promise of his second start, when he showed good speed from an unhelpful draw at Sandown, and could make a fair sprinter. (op 2-1 tchd 9-4)
Blazing Knight(IRE), with the headgear removed, lacked the speed of the winner but raced against the rail for much of the way and kept on. He's not progressing. (op 3-1)
Mr Paranoia ◆, his trainer's first runner in Britain since 2008, was well backed. He was soon behind and ran green, but showed plenty of ability to keep on so well when switched widest of all with his challenge. This 30,000GBP purchase is open to significant improvement. (op 7-1 tchd 15-2)
Marchwood failed to see his race out in first-time blinkers, (op 6-1 tchd 9-1)
Amirah(IRE), a drifter on Betfair, didn't offer much on this drop in trip. (op 8-1)

6439 C BREWER & SONS H'CAP — 5f
3:50 (3:50) (Class 5) (0-70,70) 3-Y-O+ — **£2,385** (£704; £352) **Stalls** High

Form — RPR
014 **1** **Havin' A Good Time (IRE)**[18] 5876 3-8-11 **61** .... AndreaAtzeni 8 — 70+
(Roger Varian) *trckd ldrs: wnt 2nd 2f out: chal 1f out: drvn ahd last 100yds* **5/1**[3]
4410 **2** *1/2* **Commandingpresence (USA)**[4] 6303 6-9-5 **68** .... KieranO'Neill 10 — 75
(John Bridger) *hld up in tch against rail: rdn and plld out jst over 1f out: r.o to take 2nd nr fin: nvr quite got there* **6/1**
2553 **3** *1/2* **Welease Bwian (IRE)**[28] 5536 3-9-0 **64** ....(v) RichardKingscote 11 — 69
(Stuart Williams) *mde most against rail: pushed along over 1f out: rdn and hdd last 100yds: nt qckn* **7/2**[2]
2354 **4** *1/2* **Ooi Long**[7] 6211 3-8-7 **62** .... TobyAtkinson(5) 1 — 65
(Mark Rimmer) *hld up in last pair: stdy prog on wd outside fr 1/2-way: rdn and styd on fnl f: no imp nr fin* **16/1**
6406 **5** *2 1/2* **Magical Speedfit (IRE)**[43] 5020 7-8-10 **66** .... JordanVaughan(7) 9 — 60
(George Margarson) *hld up in last pair against rail: nt clr run 1/2-way to over 1f out: shkn up and kpt on same pce after* **22/1**
0002 **6** *1 3/4* **Calypso Cay**[90] 3388 4-8-10 **59** .... AdamBeschizza 2 — 47
(Peter Salmon) *racd on outer: in tch: rdn 2f out: steadily wknd* **10/1**
302 **7** *1 1/4* **Whitecrest**[4] 6307 4-9-5 **68** .... ChrisCatlin 6 — 52
(John Spearing) *w ldr to 2f out: wknd* **3/1**[1]
4514 **8** *3/4* **Hannibal Hayes (USA)**[39] 5157 3-8-13 **63** .... TomQueally 7 — 44
(Jeremy Noseda) *a towards rr: pushed along and no prog 2f out* **11/1**
6500 **9** *3/4* **Bookiesindexdotnet**[88] 3450 3-9-6 **70** .... IanMongan 5 — 48
(J R Jenkins) *chsd ldng pair to wl over 1f out: wknd qckly fnl f* **20/1**
3266 **10** *6* **Autocracy**[31] 5445 5-8-9 **58** ....(bt) SilvestreDeSousa 3 — 15
(Daniel Kubler) *racd on outer: in tch: rdn 1/2-way: sn lost pl and btn* **20/1**
58.27s (0.07) **Going Correction** -0.075s/f (Good)
WFA 3 from 4yo+ 1lb — **10** Ran SP% **115.4**
Speed ratings (Par 103): **96,95,94,93,89 86,84,83,82,72**
toteswingers 1&2 £9.50, 2&3 £5.70, 1&3 £5.70 CSF £33.47 CT £111.00 TOTE £5.60: £2.30, £3.00, £1.20; EX 44.70.
Owner A D Spence **Bred** Twelve Oaks Stud Establishment **Trained** Newmarket, Suffolk
FOCUS
A modest sprint handicap dominated by high-drawn runners. Straightforward form among the front three.
Autocracy Official explanation: jockey said gelding had no more to give

6440 YOUNG EPILEPSY H'CAP (DIV I) — 1m 3f 106y
4:25 (4:25) (Class 5) (0-75,75) 3-Y-O+ — **£2,385** (£704; £352) **Stalls** High

Form — RPR
3362 **1** **Seven Veils (IRE)**[6] 6263 3-9-2 **72** .... ChrisCatlin 7 — 86+
(Sir Mark Prescott Bt) *mde virtually all: drvn clr wl over 2f out: in n.d after: eased nr fin* **9/4**[1]
4222 **2** *2 3/4* **Peachez**[6] 6229 4-9-1 **69** ....(p) AmyScott(5) 1 — 76+
(Alastair Lidderdale) *stdd s: hld up in detached last: stdy prog fr 3f out: shkn up and tk 2nd ins fnl f: fin wl but hopeless task* **11/4**[2]
0212 **3** *2 3/4* **Hesperides**[19] 5855 3-9-0 **70** .... CathyGannon 5 — 72
(Harry Dunlop) *s.i.s and pushed along early: settled in rr: prog on outer fr 3f out: drvn to chse clr wnr over 1f out: no imp: lost 2nd ins fnl f* **5/1**[3]
2340 **4** *5* **Instrumentalist (IRE)**[9] 6146 3-9-4 **74** .... JimmyQuinn 8 — 68
(John Best) *prom: chsd wnr wl over 3f out: lft bhd over 2f out: lost 2nd and wknd over 1f out* **11/1**

3620 **5** 6 **Drummond**[34] 5358 3-9-3 **73** DaneO'Neill 9 57
(Clive Cox) *trckd ldrs: effrt 3f out: no prog 2f out: sn wknd* **10/1**

/3-0 **6** nse **Vivre Libre**[13] 6039 5-9-5 **75** WilliamTwiston-Davies(7) 2 59
(Tom George) *hld up: sme prog 5f out: rdn and effrt 3f out: n.d: wknd wl over 1f out* **40/1**

4-P0 **7** 2 ½ **Misk Khitaam (USA)**[24] 5707 4-9-3 **66** TomQueally 4 45
(John Dunlop) *in tch: drvn 5f out: dropped to last over 3f out: wl btn after* **25/1**

006 **8** 5 **Mons Calpe (IRE)**[34] 5359 6-8-12 **61** oh1 (p) SilvestreDeSousa 6 32
(Paul Cole) *dwlt: in tch: rdn 5f out: sn struggling: bhd fnl 3f* **8/1**

1050 **9** 1 ¼ **Understory (USA)**[24] 5707 5-9-4 **72** MichaelJMMurphy(5) 3 41
(Tim McCarthy) *tried to ld but forced to chse wnr: lost 2nd wl over 3f out: wknd qckly 2f out* **16/1**

2m 31.64s (0.14) **Going Correction** +0.10s/f (Good)
WFA 3 from 4yo+ 7lb **9** Ran SP% **114.8**
Speed ratings (Par 103): **103,101,99,95,91 90,89,85,84**
toteswingers 1&2 £2.30, 2&3 £2.90, 1&3 £3.10 CSF £8.41 CT £26.75 TOTE £3.10: £1.40, £1.80, £1.10; EX 10.00.
Owner Mrs Olivia Hoare **Bred** Lynch Bages Ltd & Samac Ltd **Trained** Newmarket, Suffolk

FOCUS
A weak race. The winner did it well and this rates a personal best, with the second to form.

6441 YOUNG EPILEPSY H'CAP (DIV II) 1m 3f 106y
5:00 (5:00) (Class 5) (0-75,80) 3-Y-0+ **£2,385** (£704; £352) **Stalls** High

Form RPR
0002 **1** **English Summer**[8] 6159 5-8-13 **62** (t) SilvestreDeSousa 3 70
(David Simcock) *chsd clr ldng pair to 8f out and fr over 4f out: sn clsd: drvn to ld over 2f out: kpt on dourly* **5/2**[2]

-044 **2** 1 **Mossbrae**[20] 5816 3-9-5 **75** AndreaAtzeni 9 81
(Roger Varian) *led at gd pce but hdd 1/2-way: led again 4f out: drvn and hdd over 2f out: styd on but a hld* **13/2**

6500 **3** shd **Jupiter Storm**[21] 5796 3-9-3 **73** GeorgeBaker 4 79
(Gary Moore) *trckd clr ldng pair 8f out to over 4f out: rdn wl over 2f out: cl enough after but hanging lft and wouldn't sustain a proper chal* **9/2**[3]

346 **4** 1 **Whitby Jet (IRE)**[25] 5667 4-9-8 **71** IanMongan 7 75
(Ed Vaughan) *hld up in last pair: plenty to do fr 5f out: rdn 3f out: styd on to take 4th fnl f: nvr able to chal* **16/1**

4521 **5** 3 **Daliance (IRE)**[8] 6181 3-9-10 **80** 6ex RichardKingscote 1 79
(Tom Dascombe) *hld up in 5th: rdn wl over 2f out: no significant prog after* **2/1**[1]

22 **6** 2 **Madame St Clair (IRE)**[17] 5913 3-8-11 **74** NedCurtis(7) 2 70
(Roger Curtis) *pressed ldr: led 1/2-way to 4f out: stl upsides over 2f out: wknd over 1f out* **10/1**

4502 **7** 56 **Filun**[17] 5908 7-9-3 **66** DaneO'Neill 8
(Anthony Middleton) *hld up in last pair: lost tch 5f out: sn t.o and eased* **20/1**

2m 31.73s (0.23) **Going Correction** +0.10s/f (Good)
WFA 3 from 4yo+ 7lb **7** Ran SP% **113.2**
Speed ratings (Par 103): **103,102,102,101,99 97,57**
toteswingers 1&2 £3.90, 2&3 £4.40, 1&3 £2.30 CSF £18.57 CT £67.94 TOTE £2.60: £1.40, £2.70; EX 13.60.
Owner Dr Marwan Koukash **Bred** Juddmonte Farms Ltd **Trained** Newmarket, Suffolk

FOCUS
The time was marginally slower than the first division, but there was more strength in depth to this race. They looked to go a fair pace. The well-in winner did not need to match his Chepstow form.
Filun Official explanation: jockey said gelding never travelled

6442 BREWERS OF REDHILL H'CAP 1m 2f
5:35 (5:36) (Class 6) (0-60,60) 3-Y-0 **£1,704** (£503; £251) **Stalls** Low

Form RPR
0233 **1** **Grand Liaison**[44] 4971 3-9-1 **54** IanMongan 12 75
(John Berry) *racd wd: cl up: quick move to ld 4f out: ct rest napping and clr 3f out: rdn and styd on wl after* **9/2**[2]

0423 **2** 10 **Joy To The World (IRE)**[14] 5989 3-8-3 **47** (t) AshleyMorgan(5) 14 48
(Paul Cole) *hld up wl in rr: outpcd along w the rest 4f out: rdn and prog on outer fr 3f out: wnt 2nd over 1f out: no ch w wnr* **8/1**

4234 **3** 1 **Collectable**[8] 6158 3-8-12 **51** (t) ChrisCatlin 13 50
(Jonathan Portman) *hld up in rr: detached in last over 3f out: plld out and prog over 2f out: styd on wl to take 3rd last strides: no ch* **8/1**

-001 **4** hd **Beacon Lady**[14] 5991 3-8-7 **51** DavidKenny(5) 9 50
(William Knight) *hld up in last pair: outpcd along w the rest fr 4f out: prog over 2f out: styd on but no ch of threatening* **5/1**[3]

4300 **5** 2 **Doc Hill**[14] 5998 3-8-4 **46** SophieDoyle(3) 10 41
(Michael Blanshard) *in tch: outpcd fr 4f out: rdn and prog to chse clr wnr over 2f out: no imp: lost 2nd over 1f out: fdd* **33/1**

0060 **6** 3 ¼ **Regalo Rosado**[32] 5405 3-8-10 **49** (b[1]) NickyMackay 2 37
(Mike Murphy) *prom: outpcd 4f out: rdn and prom in chsng gp over 2f out: fdd over 1f out* **18/1**

056 **7** 1 ½ **Tallevu (IRE)**[43] 5001 3-9-6 **59** RichardKingscote 5 44
(Tom Dascombe) *trckd ldrs: outpcd by wnr fr 4f out: effrt and prom in chsng gp over 2f out: wknd over 1f out* **4/1**[1]

505 **8** 3 **Variety Show (IRE)**[15] 5982 3-9-2 **55** TomQueally 6 34
(Sir Henry Cecil) *w.w in midfield: urged along 1/2-way: outpcd 4f out: struggling and no prog after* **12/1**

6050 **9** 3 **The New Black (IRE)**[16] 5945 3-9-2 **60** (v) MichaelJMMurphy(5) 4 33
(Gay Kelleway) *nvr gng wl: rdn towards rr 1/2-way: brief effrt 3f out: sn wknd* **11/1**

5000 **10** 6 **Audeamus (IRE)**[7] 6210 3-8-9 **48** oh1 ow2 StevieDonohoe 11
(Tobias B P Coles) *pressed ldrs tl wknd qckly 3f out* **25/1**

0000 **11** 9 **Kaypea**[22] 5770 3-8-9 **48** JimmyQuinn 3
(Simon Dow) *wl in tch: outpcd fr 4f out: no prog over 2f out: wknd over 1f out: eased* **20/1**

505 **12** hd **Lea Valley**[23] 5745 3-8-9 **48** CathyGannon 7
(Julia Feilden) *mostly chsd ldr to over 4f out: wknd qckly over 2f out* **33/1**

0500 **13** 29 **Moataz (USA)**[62] 4329 3-9-2 **55** SilvestreDeSousa 1
(Patrick Morris) *fast away: led to 4f out: chsd wnr to over 2f out: wknd rapidly and eased: t.o* **14/1**

2m 11.78s (1.28) **Going Correction** +0.10s/f (Good) **13** Ran SP% **119.5**
Speed ratings (Par 99): **98,90,89,89,87 84,83,81,78,74 66,66,43**
toteswingers 1&2 £4.40, 2&3 £4.50, 1&3 £6.10 CSF £36.95 CT £246.54 TOTE £3.70: £1.10, £2.40, £3.50; EX 28.10.
Owner Barrie Catchpole & Michael Meaney **Bred** Ashbrittle Stud **Trained** Newmarket, Suffolk

FOCUS
A moderate race, but an improved performance from the lightly raced winner. The form is rated lossely around the time and the runner-up.
T/Plt: £11.00 to a £1 stake. Pool of £43615.76- 2874.80 winning tickets. T/Qpdt: £6.10 to a £1 stake. Pool of £3983.62 - 482.70 winning tickets. JN

5352 NEWBURY (L-H)
Friday, September 21

OFFICIAL GOING: Good to firm (7.2)
Rail moved out from 7f to 5f on round course adding 20m to races on rRound course.
Wind: Moderate across Weather: Low cloud

6443 STHREE PLC EBF MAIDEN STKS (DIV I) 6f 8y
1:25 (1:26) (Class 4) 2-Y-0 **£4,398** (£1,309; £654; £327) **Stalls** Centre

Form RPR
263 **1** **Vallarta (IRE)**[13] 0020 2-9-3 0 MartinHarley 5 85
(Mick Channon) *in rr but in tch: hdwy 2f out: led over 1f out: drvn and styd on strly fnl f* **5/2**[1]

3 **2** 1 ¾ **Homage (IRE)**[27] 5578 2-9-3 0 WilliamBuick 8 80+
(Jeremy Noseda) *in tch: pushed along and hdwy 2f out: styd on wl fnl f to take 2nd clsng stages but no imp on wnr* **7/2**[3]

032 **3** ½ **Caramack**[16] 5948 2-9-3 77 RichardHughes 3 78
(Richard Hannon) *chsd ldrs: drvn to chal over 1f out: nt pce of wnr ins fnl f: kpt on same pce and lost 2nd clsng stages* **10/3**[2]

4 1 ¾ **Don Marco** 2-9-3 0[1] JamesDoyle 2 73
(Roger Charlton) *in rr but in tch: drvn and qcknd over 1f out: styd on fnl f but nvr gng pce to rch ldrs* **16/1**

5 2 **Carry On Clapping (IRE)** 2-8-12 0 PatDobbs 1 62+
(Richard Hannon) *towards rr: drvn 2f out: styd on fnl f but nvr gng pce to get into contention* **25/1**

6 1 ¾ **Bluegrass Blues (IRE)** 2-9-3 0 JamieSpencer 12 62+
(Paul Cole) *racd stands' side: edgd lft to join main gp over 2f out and sn pressing ldrs: wknd ins fnl f* **33/1**

7 1 **Correspondent** 2-9-3 0 KierenFallon 11 59
(Brian Meehan) *chsd ldrs: rdn 2f out: wknd fnl f* **8/1**

06 **8** 1 **Desert Command**[14] 6015 2-9-3 0 JimmyFortune 7 56
(Andrew Balding) *chsd ldr: rdn 2f out: wknd ins fnl f* **20/1**

3 **9** hd **Senator Bong**[49] 4773 2-9-3 0 TedDurcan 10 55
(David Elsworth) *racd alone stands' side and pressed ldrs: drvn over 2f out: wknd over 1f out* **10/1**

55 **10** 2 ½ **Newtown Cross (IRE)**[35] 5303 2-9-3 0 KieranO'Neill 4 48
(Jimmy Fox) *pushed along over 2f out: a outpcd* **100/1**

00 **11** ½ **Anna Law (IRE)**[48] 4825 2-8-12 0 MichaelHills 6 41
(Charles Hills) *t.k.h and led tl hdd over 1f out: sn btn* **100/1**

12 2 ½ **Rathnaree** 2-9-3 0 RichardThomas 9 39+
(Ralph Beckett) *in tch: drvn over 2f out: sn outpcd* **40/1**

1m 12.85s (-0.15) **Going Correction** -0.025s/f (Good) **12** Ran SP% **115.9**
Speed ratings (Par 97): **100,97,97,94,92 89,88,87,86,83 82,79**
toteswingers 1&2 £2.30, 2&3 £3.20, 1&3 £1.10 CSF £10.16 TOTE £3.90: £1.30, £1.80, £1.50; EX 12.70.
Owner Tails & Bargate **Bred** Frank O'Meara **Trained** West Ilsley, Berks

FOCUS
The jockeys confirmed after the first that the ground was riding quick, although the time was nearly two seconds outside standard. Paco Boy won a division of this maiden in 2007, and other notable winners include Pastoral Player and Huntdown. The principals here showed decent form, and it looked the stronger division. The third is probably the long-term key. Most of the field came down the centre but two runners raced on the stands' side, isolated from the main body. The principals ended up on the far side of the main group.

NOTEBOOK
Vallarta(IRE) was the one to beat with a BHA rating of 85, promising placed runs at Goodwood and Ascot having sandwiched a poor effort at Salisbury. Running on well after coming from a little way off the pace, he was not unduly concerned by the drop back in trip but would not mind a return to 7f either. He may not be particularly easy to place from now on but he holds an entry in the Listed Two-Year-Old Trophy at Redcar next month. (op 3-1 tchd 10-3 and 7-2 in a place)
Homage(IRE) ◆ came through nicely for second, building on what he showed on his debut and doing more than enough to suggest he will soon be off the mark. (op 3-1)
Caramack, from the Paco Boy stable, burst through in tandem with the winner but was the first of the two to fold. He may be ready to try 7f again. (op 3-1)
Don Marco ◆ proved best of the newcomers. He represented the connections of Mince, who won a division of this last year and has developed into a smart sprinter. A smallish gelding, he was fitted for this debut with a hood, an item of equipment his smart half-sister Thistle Bird wears. He ran on in pleasing fashion from the back after being switched and should make a nice 3-y-o. (op 14-1)
Carry On Clapping(IRE), the Richard Hannon second string, was ready to run back in May but then picked up an injury. She stayed on from the back and will have learned something. (op 33-1)
Bluegrass Blues(IRE) was one of the two who raced in isolation, but moved over to join the main group after halfway. He could not sustain his forward momentum but will come on for the experience.
Correspondent is closely related to the high-class 6f-1m performer Delegator and he holds a Dewhurst entry. He did not show a great deal on this debut, already on the retreat when slightly short of room approaching the final furlong, but he's likely to improve considerably for the run, as a lot of his trainer's juveniles do. (tchd 9-1)
Rathnaree took the eye in the paddock and may do better in time.

6444 STHREE PLC EBF MAIDEN STKS (DIV II) 6f 8y
2:00 (2:00) (Class 4) 2-Y-0 **£4,398** (£1,309; £654; £327) **Stalls** Centre

Form RPR
64 **1** **Valais Girl**[14] 6007 2-8-12 0 (p) HayleyTurner 7 74
(Marcus Tregoning) *mde all: drvn over 1f out: styd on u.p ins fnl f: kpt on wl clsng stages* **9/1**

25 **2** 1 ½ **Grand Denial (IRE)**[22] 5765 2-9-3 0 AdamKirby 2 74
(Clive Cox) *chsd wnr thrght: drvn and kpt on fr over 1f out: no imp ins fnl f* **2/1**[1]

00 **3** nk **Azelle**[17] 5907 2-8-12 0 PatDobbs 11 68
(Richard Hannon) *chsd ldrs: drvn and styd on fnl f to cl on 2nd nr fin but no imp on wnr* **22/1**

4 1 **Secondo (FR)** 2-9-3 0 JamesDoyle 4 71+
(Roger Charlton) *s.i.s: in rr: swtchd rt and hdwy over 1f out: styd on ins fnl f to take 4th in clsng stages: no imp on wnr* **8/1**[3]

5 nse **Exempt** 2-8-12 0 WilliamBuick 6 65
(Jeremy Noseda) *chsd ldrs: drvn over 2f out: styd on same pce ins fnl f: no ex and lost 4th clsng stages* **8/1**[3]

02 **6** 2 ¼ **King Of Kudos (IRE)**[20] 5813 2-9-3 0 RichardHughes 3 65
(Richard Hannon) *chsd ldrs: rdn over 2f out: wknd fnl f* **5/2**[2]

7 1 ¾ **Countryman** 2-9-3 0 DarryllHolland 8 58+
(Hughie Morrison) *sn pushed along and outpcd: styd on fnl f but nvr a threat* **20/1**

00 **8** ½ **Forbidden Fruit (IRE)**[116] 2550 2-9-3 0 KierenFallon 1 56+
(Brian Meehan) *in tch: pushed along 1/2-way: styd on same pce fnl f* **12/1**

04 **9** ¾ **Iwilsayzisonlyonce**[11] 6093 2-9-3 0 FergusSweeney 5 54
(Joseph Tuite) *in rr: sme prog over 1f out: nvr nr ldrs* **100/1**

0 **10** 2½ **Avanzare**[51] 4701 2-8-12 0 MichaelHills 9 42
(Charles Hills) *s.i.s: pushed along and one pce fnl 3f* **25/1**

1m 13.02s (0.02) **Going Correction** -0.025s/f (Good) **10** Ran SP% **115.8**
Speed ratings (Par 97): **98,96,95,94,94 91,88,88,87,83**
toteswingers 1&2 £5.30, 2&3 £18.50, 1&3 £55.90 CSF £26.16 TOTE £14.60: £3.00, £1.10, £7.80; EX 34.40.
Owner Guy Brook **Bred** Lady Richard Wellesley **Trained** Lambourn, Berks

FOCUS
This looked the weaker division, and the time was marginally slower. The winner stepped up but it's hard to rate this form much higher.

NOTEBOOK
Valais Girl showed something on each of her first two starts and the cheekpieces sharpened her up here. Racing a shade keenly, she made all and the challenges never really came in. Maturing now, she is in a couple of valuable sales races next month but may not run. (op 10-1)
Grand Denial(IRE), back at 6f on turf, raced without cover throughout and stuck on for second. He may not be straightforward but is up to winning a maiden. (tchd 7-4)
Azelle, the stable second string, showed much more than she had in her two previous outings, both of which came over further. It could be than 7f is her ideal trip. (op 16-1)
Secondo(FR) ◆, a half-brother to six winners, the best of them Million Percent, is out of a half-sister to high-class sprinter Averti who raced in these colours. Taking the eye in the preliminaries although he needed two handlers in the paddock, he missed the break and then had to be switched as he ran up the backs of rivals. He was green when first asked to go forward but was closing at the end and looks a ready-made maiden winner.
Exempt, a half-sister to a Grade 3 winner in the US, showed understandable signs of inexperience under pressure and will be more clued up next time. (tchd 9-1)
King Of Kudos(IRE) was below the level he reached at Bath but was not knocked about when held and may bounce back. (op 3-1 tchd 7-2)
Countryman will improve fitness wise. (op 16-1 tchd 14-1)
Forbidden Fruit(IRE), who had been gelded since his last appearance in May, was another who should come on for the outing.

6445 DUBAI DUTY FREE FINEST SURPRISE H'CAP 1m 4f 5y
2:30 (2:30) (Class 3) (0-95,95) 3-Y-O+ **£6,663** (£1,982; £990; £495) **Stalls** Low

Form RPR

1000 **1** **Rule Book (IRE)**[27] 5598 3-8-10 **87** RichardHughes 6 97+
(Richard Hannon) *in tch: hdwy over 2f out: led jst ins fnl f: pushed out: comf* **7/1**

-300 **2** ½ **Cavaleiro (IRE)**[92] 3295 3-9-4 **95** RichardMullen 9 104+
(Marcus Tregoning) *in rr: hdwy 3f out: rdden 2f out: styd on u.p fnl f to take 2nd last strides but no imp on comfortable wnr* **5/1**[2]

0252 **3** shd **Rawaki (IRE)**[13] 6039 4-9-5 **88** JimmyFortune 7 97
(Andrew Balding) *chsd ldrs: rdn to ld appr fnl 2f: jnd 1f out and sn hdd: nt pce of wnr ins fnl f: lost 2nd last strides* **7/2**[1]

0421 **4** 2½ **Novirak (IRE)**[8] 6170 4-8-12 **81** 6ex FrankieDettori 1 86
(James Fanshawe) *chsd ldrs: wnt 2nd 6f out: led appr fnl 3f: rdn and hdd appr fnl 2f: wknd ins fnl f* **7/2**[1]

4423 **5** 4 **Scottish Star**[12] 6073 4-8-12 **81** oh4 JamesDoyle 4 79
(James Eustace) *led 1f: styd chsng ldrs: rdn over 2f out: wknd fnl f* **10/1**

0630 **6** hd **Warlu Way**[28] 5558 5-9-6 **89** (t) TedDurcan 2 87
(John Dunlop) *in rr: pushed along and hung rt 2f out: nvr gng pce to get into contention* **12/1**

5100 **7** 6 **Franciscan**[48] 4800 4-9-8 **91** KierenFallon 5 80
(Luca Cumani) *rdn 4f out: a towards rr* **13/2**[3]

4330 **8** 32 **Purification (IRE)**[41] 5106 4-9-1 **84** (b) WilliamBuick 3 21
(John Gosden) *led after 1f: hdd appr fnl 3f: wknd over 2f out: eased whn no ch fnl f* **10/1**

2m 34.65s (-0.85) **Going Correction** -0.025s/f (Good)
WFA 3 from 4yo+ 8lb **8** Ran SP% **112.8**
Speed ratings (Par 107): **101,100,100,98,96 96,92,70**
toteswingers 1&2 £6.30, 2&3 £6.50, 1&3 £6.10 CSF £40.56 CT £142.35 TOTE £9.60: £2.80, £1.80, £1.40; EX 57.20.
Owner Andrew Tinkler **Bred** Joseph Heavey **Trained** East Everleigh, Wilts

FOCUS
An interesting handicap, if not an especially strong race for the grade. However a slightly positive view has been taken of the form. The pace was a little stop-start.

NOTEBOOK
Rule Book(IRE) seemed to appreciate coming from off the gallop down the outside and won comfortably enough. A winner twice in June, he had been dropped 2lb since a poor run at York, when he was well beaten over 1m6f. The Stewards considered his apparent improvement in form. They noted that Richard Hannon was very disappointed with Rule Book's run at York, but could offer no explanation for the colt's improved form. Official explanation: trainer could offer no explanation regarding apparent improvement in form. (op 11-1)
Cavaleiro(IRE) ◆, gelded during his three-month absence from the track, was dropping in grade. He ran into trouble when improving then took a little time to pick up, but was running on strongly at the end. This was a very pleasing run and there's a handicap to be won with him. (tchd 6-1)
Rawaki(IRE) was 3lb higher than when second to subsequent winner Enery on the Kempton Polytrack. He showed in front narrowly, but his head carriage did not convince than he was fighting as hard as he might have done. (op 4-1)
Novirak(IRE), winner of a jump jockeys' race at Epsom recently, ran respectably under the penalty which left him a pound badly in. A stronger gallop might have suited. (op 3-1)
Scottish Star is largely consistent and wasn't disgraced from 4lb out of the handicap.
Warlu Way, tried in a tongue tie, didn't settle in rear and made only modest late progress. Ted Durcan reported that the horse slipped on the bend. Official explanation: jockey said horse slipped on bend (op 10-1)
Franciscan had excuses on his last two starts and was reported by Kieren Fallon to have slipped on the bend here. Official explanation: jockey said gelding slipped on bend (tchd 6-1 and 7-1)

6446 DUBAI DUTY FREE CONDITIONS STKS 1m 1f
3:05 (3:06) (Class 3) 3-Y-O+
£7,158 (£2,143; £1,071; £535; £267; £134) **Stalls** Low

Form RPR

2013 **1** **Grandeur (IRE)**[27] 5594 3-8-6 108 WilliamBuick 6 105+
(Jeremy Noseda) *hld up in rr: hdwy and pushed along 2f out: drvn and qcknd 1f out: hung lft ins fnl f: led fnl 75yds: kpt on wl* **6/4**[1]

0413 **2** ½ **Boom And Bust (IRE)**[13] 6029 5-8-11 104 HayleyTurner 8 104
(Marcus Tregoning) *led: rdn 2f out: kpt on wl fnl f: hdd and outpcd fnl 75yds* **3/1**[2]

5-00 **3** 1 **Prince Siegfried (FR)**[134] 1994 6-8-11 109 TedDurcan 7 102
(Saeed Bin Suroor) *chsd ldrs: rdn over 2f out: ev ch 1f out: one pce and hld whn carried lft ins fnl f* **16/1**

010 **4** 1½ **Burano (IRE)**[174] 1145 3-9-1 106 KierenFallon 4 107?
(Brian Meehan) *bmpd s: in tch: rdn 3f out: styd on fr over 1f out: sn one pce* **33/1**

1520 **5** hd **Fury**[28] 5560 4-8-11 106 PaulHanagan 5 98
(William Haggas) *wnt lft s: chsd ldrs: rdn over 2f out: outpcd fnl f* **7/1**

3402 **6** 2¼ **Cai Shen (IRE)**[9] 6142 4-8-11 102 RichardHughes 3 93
(Richard Hannon) *in rr: rdn over 2f out: nvr gng pce to get into contention* **11/2**[3]

-212 **7** 1½ **Spring Of Fame (USA)**[211] 678 6-8-11 105 FrankieDettori 1 89
(Saeed Bin Suroor) *chsd ldr: rdn over 2f out: wknd over 1f out* **14/1**

8 1 **Be Perfect (USA)**[185] 3-9-1 101 AdamKirby 2 90
(Marco Botti) *chsd ldrs: rdn over 2f out: wknd over 1f out* **28/1**

1m 54.89s (-0.61) **Going Correction** -0.025s/f (Good)
WFA 3 from 4yo+ 5lb **8** Ran SP% **111.8**
Speed ratings (Par 107): **101,100,99,98,98 96,94,93**
toteswingers 1&2 £1.60, 2&3 £21.40, 1&3 £11.80 CSF £5.67 TOTE £2.30: £1.10, £1.10, £5.50; EX 8.90.
Owner Miss Yvonne Jacques **Bred** Mrs Cherry Faeste **Trained** Newmarket, Suffolk
■ Stewards' Enquiry : William Buick three-day ban: careless riding (Oct 5,6,8)

FOCUS
A good conditions race, but the pace was not true and there are one or two doubts over the form, which has been rated cautiously. The winner did ot match his Windsor latest.

NOTEBOOK
Grandeur(IRE), for whom there was strong support, rewarded his backers in good style. Quickening up down the outside to assert, he did well to win the way he did in a race not run at a true gallop, and there is further improvement to come from this progressive 3-y-o who's capable of securing some winning black type. A race in the USA is a possibility for him next month. (op 15-8 tchd 2-1 in places)
Boom And Bust(IRE)'s rider got over from the outside stall to lead and set her own gallop. The gelding stuck on well when let down and is well up to winning in this grade or in Listed company. He's also in the Cambridgeshire. (op 4-1)
Prince Siegfried(FR), off the track since May, was just about the pick on official ratings on this drop in grade. The Bin Suroor second string on riding arrangements, he would have finished a bit nearer to the first pair had the gap between them not closed on him late on. (op 20-1)
Burano(IRE), absent since contesting the UAE Derby back in March, received a bump from Fury leaving the stalls. He made late headway and would have been suited by a stiffer test at the trip. (op 25-1)
Fury, for whom a small field and fairly steady gallop are not ideal, did not prove his stamina for the trip. The cheekpieces he wore at York were discarded. (op 6-1)
Cai Shen(IRE), held up as he had been when second at Doncaster, was another never able to land a telling blow off the moderate gallop. (tchd 6-1)
Spring Of Fame(USA) has been gelded since his last appearance in Meydan in the spring. The choice of Frankie Dettori, he faded after racing prominently. He needs a longer trip and easier ground. (op 7-1)
Be Perfect(USA), sold out of Jean-Claude Rouget's yard, was running for the first time since March. After travelling up well he was soon on the retreat once off the bridle, but he should be capable of leaving this effort behind. His only previous run on turf came on soft ground. (op 20-1)

6447 HAYNES, HANSON & CLARK CONDITIONS STKS (C&G) 1m (S)
3:40 (3:42) (Class 2) 2-Y-O
£9,337 (£2,796; £1,398; £699; £349; £175) **Stalls** Centre

Form RPR

61 **1** **Wentworth (IRE)**[28] 5562 2-9-2 0 RichardHughes 1 90+
(Richard Hannon) *in tch: shkn up over 2f out: qcknd ins fnl f: r.o wl to ld nr fin: readily* **8/11**[1]

3 **2** ¾ **Chief Havoc (USA)**[23] 5742 2-8-12 0 WilliamBuick 5 84+
(Jeremy Noseda) *trckd ldrs: pushed along and edgd lft over 1f out: chal ins fnl f: slt ld fnl 120yds: hdd and outpcd nr fin* **9/2**[2]

03 **3** 1¼ **Another Cocktail**[15] 5962 2-8-12 0 DarryllHolland 4 81
(Hughie Morrison) *chsd ldrs: rdn 2f out: styd on u.p fnl f to take 3rd clsng stages: nt pce of ldng duo* **14/1**

61 **4** 1 **Etijaah (USA)**[21] 5792 2-9-2 83 PaulHanagan 7 83
(Brian Meehan) *sn led: pushed along over 2f out: jnd ins fnl f: hdd fnl 120yds: wknd clsng stages* **12/1**[3]

5 hd **Flashheart (IRE)** 2-8-12 0 HayleyTurner 2 79+
(Marcus Tregoning) *s.i.s: in rr: rdn and hdwy over 1f out: styd on fnl f: edgd rt clsng stages: kpt on wl* **14/1**

0201 **6** 3 **Dark Emerald (IRE)**[17] 5912 2-8-12 85 KierenFallon 3 72
(Brendan Powell) *in tch: rdn over 3f out: styd in tch tl wknd fnl f* **20/1**

7 14 **Sweeping Rock (IRE)** 2-8-12 0 RichardMullen 6 39
(Marcus Tregoning) *in tch: rdn 3f out: sn btn* **50/1**

1m 39.84s (0.14) **Going Correction** -0.025s/f (Good) **7** Ran SP% **103.8**
Speed ratings (Par 101): **98,97,96,95,94 91,77**
toteswingers 1&2 £1.20, 2&3 £5.00, 1&3 £4.20 CSF £3.24 TOTE £1.70: £1.30, £1.60; EX 3.60.
Owner Mrs John Magnier & Michael Tabor & Derrick Smith **Bred** Denis McDonnell **Trained** East Everleigh, Wilts
■ Altruism (13/20 was withdrawn on vet's adviced at the s). Deduct 10p in the 3 under R4.

FOCUS
The roll of honour for this long-established conditions race contains some illustrious names going back to the likes of Henbit, Shergar and Rainbow Quest. More recently Derby winner Authorized finished third in the 2006 race, a place behind Aqaleem who was third in the Epsom Classic, the previous year's winner Winged Cupid was runner-up in the Racing Post Trophy next time out, while 2007 scorer Centennial took the Great Voltigeur the following season. The withdrawal at the start of Altruism weakened this edition somewhat, but there was still plenty of interest. The form is rated at the lower end of the race averages. Wentworth is smart and can do better still, but his form is some way off the class he seems to be regarded in.

NOTEBOOK
Wentworth(IRE) ◆ had impressed when winning the Convivial Maiden at the York Ebor meeting, and the runner-up there, Lord Of The Garter, boosted the form earlier in the week when winning at Yarmouth. The step up to a mile looked sure to suit the colt, who is highly regarded in the Richard Hannon stable. Racing a little lazily according to his jockey, for a few strides he looked in trouble as he came off the bridle, but once he was switched towards the stands' side his turn of foot was evident as he made up the leeway quickly to win readily. The colt holds Royal Lodge and Dewhurst entries but his trainer is inclined to put him away until the spring now. He has physical improvement to make during the winter and is an intriguing prospect. Interestingly Richard Hughes said he felt more of a French Derby colt here than a Guineas type. (op 4-5 tchd 5-6)
Chief Havoc(USA) shaped with bags of promise despite running green on his debut at Kempton and still looked inexperienced here, hanging left a little when under pressure. It was no disgrace being cut down by such a smart colt as the winner and he should get off the mark soon. (op 5-1 tchd 11-2)
Another Cocktail kept trying after coming under pressure earlier than most. Improving with every run, he has a stamina-packed pedigree and is a nice middle-distance type for next season. He's been given a Derby entry, although it's most unlikely he'll reach that level. (op 12-1)
Etijaah(USA) comes from the Lord Of The Garter yard and his Sandown win has been working out quite well. Making the running, but carrying to his head to one side, he fought on when tackled and only faded in the last half furlong. (tchd 10-1)

Flashheart(IRE) ◆, whose trainer has won this race no fewer than five times, the pick of his winners being the top-class Nayef in 2000, is by that sire. Coltish beforehand, he missed the break and raced in rear, but once he got the hang of things he picked up ground in good fashion. He looks sure to step up on this. (op 20-1)
Dark Emerald(IRE) set the standard with a BHA mark of 85 but he had less scope for improvement than most of these and failed to make his presence tell. (op 16-1)

6448 DUBAI DUTY FREE FULL OF SURPRISES EBF FILLIES' CONDITIONS STKS 7f (S)

4:15 (4:17) (Class 2) 2-Y-0 **£9,337** (£2,796; £1,398; £699; £349) **Stalls** Centre

Form RPR
51 **1** **Penny Rose**[10] 6114 2-9-2 0 KierenFallon 1 88
(Mark Johnston) *trckd ldr: led over 1f out: rdn and edgd rt ins fnl f: r.o stly clsng stages* **5/2**[2]
2 *2 ¼* **Desert Image** 2-8-12 0 MichaelHills 3 78+
(Charles Hills) *in tch: pushed along and hdwy to go 2nd appr fnl f: kpt on wl but nt pce of wnr fnl 120yds* **6/1**[3]
3 *2* **Zipp (IRE)** 2-8-12 0 DarryllHolland 4 73+
(Charles Hills) *in rr: pushed along 3f out: drvn and hdwy over 1f out: kpt on fnl f to take 3rd fnl 120yds but no imp on ldng duo* **25/1**
4 *nk* **Syrenka** 2-8-12 0 HayleyTurner 5 72+
(Marcus Tregoning) *chsd ldrs: drvn over 2f out: styd on same pce appr fnl f* **25/1**
1 **5** *2 ¼* **Lanansaak (IRE)**[15] 5977 2-9-2 0 PaulHanagan 2 70
(Roger Varian) *led and racd keenly: pushed along over 2f out: hdd over 1f out: wknd ins fnl f* **8/11**[1]

1m 27.15s (1.45) **Going Correction** -0.025s/f (Good) **5** Ran SP% **108.5**
Speed ratings (Par 98): **90,87,85,84,82**
CSF £16.21 TOTE £3.60: £1.80, £1.50; EX 11.30.
Owner Greenland Park Stud **Bred** Mr & Mrs G Middlebrook **Trained** Middleham Moor, N Yorks

FOCUS
Only two of the runners in this interesting fillies' race had previous experience. The race averages help with the form.

NOTEBOOK
Penny Rose supplemented her Leicester win in taking fashion. She quickened up well when asked and looks a pacey filly, but she should have no problem with a mile. (op 9-4)
Desert Image ◆ took time to settle but came through to bustle up the winner and this rates a very pleasing debut. Out of a sister to Zafonic and Zamindar, she gave the impression that she'll appreciate easier ground and she should get off the mark this autumn. (op 8-1 tchd 9-1)
Zipp(IRE), the runner-up's stablemate, represented the connections of last year's winner and recent Park Hill second Hazel Lavery. Zipp is bred to come into her own over longer trips next year and she stayed on well to claim third after racing at the back of the field for much of the way. (op 16-1)
Syrenka was outpaced by the principals when the race hotted up but she stuck on reasonably well. She will be seen to better effect over further. (op 14-1)
Lanansaak(IRE), the Salisbury winner was the disappointment. She became keyed up in the preliminaries and raced rather keenly in front. Headed by the winner going to the furlong pole, she weakened quite rapidly in the last half furlong. (op 4-5 tchd 10-11)

6449 DUBAI DUTY FREE CUP (LISTED RACE) 7f (S)

4:50 (4:50) (Class 1) 3-Y-0+

£18,714 (£7,095; £3,550; £1,768; £887; £445) **Stalls** Centre

Form RPR
2015 **1** **Scarf (AUS)**[27] 5581 5-9-2 108 FrankieDettori 9 111
(Saeed Bin Suroor) *led over 5f out: drvn and qcknd over 1f out: a doing enough fnl 100yds* **7/1**
1541 **2** *nk* **Producer**[26] 5627 3-9-2 108 RichardHughes 2 113
(Richard Hannon) *trckd ldrs: swtchd lft and qcknd over 1f out: chsd wnr ins fnl f: kpt on wl and clsng nr fin but a hld* **6/1**
366 **3** *1 ½* **Saigon**[26] 5627 3-8-13 105 KirstyMilczarek 1 106
(James Toller) *in rr: swtchd lft and hdwy appr fnl f: styd on u.p to take 3rd clsng stages but no imp on ldng duo* **9/1**
2-52 **4** *hd* **Skilful**[130] 2127 4-9-2 105 WilliamBuick 10 105
(John Gosden) *trckd ldrs: rdn and one pce appr fnl f: no ex and lost 4th clsng stages* **5/1**[3]
-533 **5** *1 ¾* **Zumbi (IRE)**[26] 5627 3-8-13 104 JamesDoyle 4 101
(Sir Michael Stoute) *in rr: drvn and sme hdwy on outside over 1f out: nvr gng pce to get into contention: wknd fnl 150yds* **4/1**[1]
2015 **6** *1 ½* **Right To Dream (IRE)**[13] 6029 3-8-13 103 JamieSpencer 7 97+
(Brian Meehan) *stdd s: in rr: nt clr run on rails 2f out: swtchd lft u.p 1f out: mod prog clsng stages* **16/1**
0110 **7** *½* **Van Ellis**[19] 5869 3-8-13 108 KierenFallon 6 95
(Mark Johnston) *chsd ldrs: rdn 2f out: wknd ins fnl f* **9/2**[2]
2200 **8** *1 ½* **Edinburgh Knight (IRE)**[34] 5355 5-9-2 107 PaulHanagan 5 91+
(Paul D'Arcy) *in rr: hdwy on inner over 2f out: nvr seeing much daylight over 1f out: nvr rchd ldrs and sn btn* **7/1**
6220 **9** *6* **Silverheels (IRE)**[49] 4760 3-8-13 95 (p) HayleyTurner 8 75
(Paul Cole) *racd in centre and led tl over 5f out: wknd over 2f out* **50/1**

1m 25.53s (-0.17) **Going Correction** -0.025s/f (Good)
WFA 3 from 4yo+ 3lb **9** Ran SP% **112.0**
Speed ratings (Par 111): **99,98,96,96,94 93,92,90,83**
toteswingers 1&2 £6.10, 2&3 £9.20, 1&3 £7.60 CSF £46.53 TOTE £6.50: £1.90, £2.00, £3.20; EX 37.30.
Owner Godolphin **Bred** Woodlands Stud NSW **Trained** Newmarket, Suffolk

FOCUS
A competitive Listed event and a tight one on official figures, but something of a muddling race. The field, with one exception, came over to race towards the stands' side and there were traffic problems for some. The winner is rated close to his best.

NOTEBOOK
Scarf(AUS), in front after a couple of furlongs, enjoyed the run of the race alongside the rail and ran on well to hold on. This was his first victory at this level under the Godolphin banner (he won a conditions stakes over C&D in July) but he won in this grade in Australia last year. (op 8-1 tchd 6-1)
Producer carried a 3lb penalty for his win in Goodwood's Group 3 Supreme Stakes. He raced keenly here but ran on in game style at the end and was closing on the winner at the line, confirming his effectiveness on this different type of track. He confirmed the form with a couple he beat in the Goodwood race. (op 7-1)
Saigon, the Goodwood sixth, was one of those caught up in trouble and he ran on well when manoeuvred into the clear. Going without any headgear here, he has a decent record at Newbury but finds this trip on the sharp side. (op 10-1 tchd 11-1)
Skilful had not been seen since May, when runner-up in this grade at Windsor over an extended mile. Keen through the early parts, he had his chance but was held when he was a little short of room on the fence late on. Better can be expected with the run under his belt. Official explanation: jockey said colt was denied a clear run (op 9-2 tchd 4-1)
Zumbi(IRE), an unlucky third to Producer at Goodwood, had no obvious excuse here, a forward move down the outer flattening out in the final furlong. He's probably in need of 1m now. (op 7-2 tchd 9-2)
Right To Dream(IRE) ran better than he had over a mile at Haydock, but although he finished well he was never seen with a chance. (op 20-1)
Van Ellis is effective at this trip but 6f is perhaps his optimum, and he weakened after chasing the pace. (op 6-1)
Edinburgh Knight(IRE), for whom nothing much went right on this drop in grade, can probably be forgiven this. Official explanation: jockey said gelding was denied a clear run (op 5-1)
Silverheels(IRE), reportedly gelded since his last run, had a lot on at these weights and soon found himself racing alone. (op 40-1)

6450 OPUS ENERGY H'CAP 1m 2f 6y

5:20 (5:22) (Class 4) (0-85,85) 3-Y-0+ **£4,528** (£1,347; £673; £336) **Stalls** Low

Form RPR
4311 **1** **Jawhar (IRE)**[12] 6073 4-9-10 **85** 6ex PaulHanagan 6 97
(William Haggas) *in rr: hdwy towards centre crse 3f out: chsd ldr 1f out: slt ld ins fnl f: styd on wl to assert fnl 50yds* **6/5**[1]
0114 **2** *¾* **Henry Clay**[22] 5759 3-9-4 **85** KierenFallon 8 95
(Mark Johnston) *trckd ldr: led 5f out: c to r in centre crse: drvn over 2f out: sn jnd: styd on tl hdd ins fnl f: nt pce of wnr and edgd lft fnl 50yds* **5/1**[2]
-141 **3** *shd* **Sammy Alexander**[42] 5063 4-9-2 **77** JamieSpencer 11 87
(David Simcock) *in rr: hdwy towards centre crse fr 2f out: hrd drvn and qcknd to chse ldng duo ins fnl f: kpt on but no imp clsng stages* **8/1**[3]
3210 **4** *4* **Highland Duke (IRE)**[20] 5838 3-8-0 **74** RyanTate[(7)] 12 76
(Clive Cox) *chsd ldrs: c to r in centre crse and drvn 3f out: chal ins fnl 2f tl appr fnl f: wknd fnl 120yds* **14/1**
4506 **5** *1 ¼* **Aldwick Bay (IRE)**[13] 6039 4-9-4 **79** PatDobbs 9 78
(Richard Hannon) *in tch: styd to r towards far side and sme hdwy u.p 2f out: wknd ins fnl f* **14/1**
5235 **6** *2* **Kenyan Cat**[40] 5129 5-9-6 **81** RichardMullen 7 76
(Ed McMahon) *chsd ldrs: racd far side fr 4f out: drvn and effrt 2f out: wknd fnl f* **8/1**[3]
-006 **7** *3 ¼* **Hot Spice**[20] 5838 4-9-0 **75** TedDurcan 2 64
(John Dunlop) *chsd ldrs: racd far side: rdn 3f out: wknd over 2f out* **12/1**
1-00 **8** *8* **Covert Decree**[79] 3766 4-9-7 **82** AdamKirby 10 55
(Clive Cox) *in tch: rdn 3f out: wknd sn after* **25/1**
63-0 **9** *1 ½* **Berengar (IRE)**[153] 1506 3-8-8 **75** WilliamBuick 4 45
(Brian Meehan) *styd towards far side fr 4f out: rdn 3f out: a bhd* **40/1**
4110 **10** *32* **Play Street**[38] 5218 3-8-10 **77** HayleyTurner 3
(Jonathan Portman) *led tl hdd 5f out: styd to r far side: wknd 2f out: eased fnl f* **25/1**

2m 7.15s (-1.65) **Going Correction** -0.025s/f (Good)
WFA 3 from 4yo+ 6lb **10** Ran SP% **115.5**
Speed ratings (Par 105): **105,104,104,101,100 98,95,89,88,62**
toteswingers 1&2 £2.60, 2&3 £3.30, 1&3 £3.00 CSF £6.79 CT £33.29 TOTE £1.90: £1.20, £2.10, £1.90; EX 8.80.
Owner Hamdan Al Maktoum **Bred** Shadwell Estate Company Limited **Trained** Newmarket, Suffolk

FOCUS
A fair handicap. Four horses came down the centre of the track in the home straight - the remaining runners staying on the inside - and they filled the first four places. A slightly positive view has been taken of the form.
T/Plt: £16.60 to a £1 stake. Pool: £51,694.35 - 2,268.57 winning tickets. T/Qpdt: £7.60 to a £1 stake. Pool £3,833.86 - 368.58 winning tickets. ST

6316 WOLVERHAMPTON (A.W) (L-H)

Friday, September 21

OFFICIAL GOING: Standard changing to standard to fast after race 2 (6.00)
Wind: half across Weather: overcast and cold

6451 32RED NURSERY 7f 32y(P)

5:30 (5:30) (Class 5) (0-70,70) 2-Y-0 **£2,264** (£673; £336; £168) **Stalls** High

Form RPR
6205 **1** **Zain Spirit (USA)**[14] 6016 2-9-6 **69** LukeMorris 9 70+
(Gerard Butler) *did nt appear in paddock: towards rr: rdn 2f out: hdwy between rivals over 1f out: chsd ldr ins fnl f: fin wl: forced ahd on post* **9/2**[2]
050 **2** *nse* **Camp Floyd (USA)**[15] 5962 2-9-4 **67** (p) MickaelBarzalona 10 68
(Mahmood Al Zarooni) *cl up: led 3f out: sn rdn clr: reduced advantage ins fnl f: ct post* **7/2**[1]
0004 **3** *½* **Baltic Prince (IRE)**[2] 6354 2-7-13 **51** RaulDaSilva[(3)] 4 51
(Paul Green) *in tch: rdn over 2f out: wd ent st: rdn and plugged on one pce ins fnl f* **16/1**
354 **4** *1 ¼* **Clement (IRE)**[21] 5784 2-9-5 **68** (t) FergusSweeney 1 65
(Eve Johnson Houghton) *in rr: urged along over 2f out: short of room over 1f out: swtchd lft and kpt on wl ins fnl f: nvr a threat* **9/1**
2415 **5** *½* **Pippy**[18] 5890 2-9-7 **70** StephenCraine 5 66
(Tom Dascombe) *cl up: urged along over 3f out: drvn 2f out: hung lft and wknd ins fnl f* **13/2**[3]
0451 **6** *nk* **Delores Rocket**[9] 6130 2-8-11 **67** 6ex (b) KevinStott[(7)] 11 62+
(Kevin Ryan) *in rr: hdwy on outer 3f out: pushed along and effrt to chse ldrs over 1f out: sn no ex and rdr dropped whip 1f out* **10/1**
0230 **7** *2* **Ryedale Valley**[9] 6130 2-8-5 **54** DuranFentiman 2 44
(Tim Easterby) *in tch: short of room over 2f out: shuffled bk and dropped to rr: no further imp* **9/1**
0450 **8** *1* **Eyeline**[24] 5716 2-8-7 **66** RussKennemore 7 44
(Reg Hollinshead) *in rr: rdn 3f out: effrt over 2f out: wknd fnl f* **33/1**
060 **9** *shd* **Sand Grouse**[16] 5947 2-8-11 **60** SebSanders 3 56
(Marco Botti) *in tch: rdn 3f out: drvn and effrt over 1f out: pressing for pls whn bdly hmpd ins fnl f: unable to rcvr: eased fnl 50yds* **9/1**
4615 **10** *10* **Vino Collapso (IRE)**[24] 5702 2-9-5 **68** JamesSullivan 8 31
(James Given) *led: drvn and hdd 3f out: sn wknd: eased fnl 100yds* **7/1**

1m 29.42s (-0.18) **Going Correction** -0.175s/f (Stan) **10** Ran SP% **114.2**
Speed ratings (Par 95): **94,93,93,91,91 91,88,87,87,76**
toteswingers: 1&2 £4.90, 2&3 £10.60, 1&3 £18.30 CSF £20.14 CT £233.14 TOTE £7.40: £1.50, £1.10, £8.20; EX 22.20 TRIFECTA Not won..
Owner Asaad Al Banwan **Bred** Nesco II Limited **Trained** Newmarket, Suffolk
■ Stewards' Enquiry : Stephen Craine one-day ban: careless riding (Oct 5)

FOCUS
A run-of-the-mill nursery, which resulted in a thrilling finish. Ordinary form but the winner should remain competitive.

NOTEBOOK
Zain Spirit(USA), who had finished a close up fourth in a 6f nursery at Kempton off this mark 14 days previously, benefitted from Camp Floyd curling up in the final 1f to run out the narrowest of winners. He's from a family that's thrived on artificial services and can go on from here. (op 6-1 tchd 4-1)

Camp Floyd(USA), wearing cheekpieces for the first time, looked certain to make a winning nursery debut when opening up a clear lead over 2f out. His energy reserves were running on empty in the closing stages and he just couldn't quite cling on. He has a race in him on this surface, however the handicapper won't have missed this effort. (op 9-2)

Baltic Prince(IRE) is consistent but is yet to win. He only plugged on. (op 10-1 tchd 9-1)

Clement(IRE) trying 7f and Polytrack for the first time, kept on having come under pressure early. He should get further. (op 10-1 tchd 11-1)

Delores Rocket was 4lb well in under her penalty (excluding inexperience jockey's claim) but faced very different circumstances to when winning easily over 6f on soft ground in first time blinkers at Carlisle nine days previously. A big market drifter, she missed the break and couldn't overcome the task from there. (op 8-1)

6452 RINGSIDE CONFERENCE SUITE - 700 THEATRE STYLE CLASSIFIED CLAIMING STKS 7f 32y(P)

6:00 (6:03) (Class 6) 3-Y-O+ **£1,704** (£503; £251) **Stalls** High

Form RPR

0551 **1** **Pravda Street**[16] 5941 7-9-0 70 TomEaves 7 75
(Brian Ellison) *in tch: rdn over 3f out: plenty to do 2f out: styd on wl fnl f: led fnl 75yds* **7/2**[1]

0505 **2** ½ **Hail Promenader (IRE)**[9] 6141 6-8-9 70 (p) RyanClark(3) 12 72
(Anthony Carson) *in rr: rdn 2f out: wd ent st: drvn and styd on wl ins fnl f: unable to rch wnr* **10/1**

1 **3** ½ **Jouster (IRE)**[11] 6108 4-9-2 68 EddieAhern 3 74
(M D O'Callaghan, Ire) *in tch: hdwy over 2f out: swtchd lft and drvn over 1f out: led 1f out: hdd and lost 2 pls fnl 75yds* **9/1**[3]

650 **4** ¾ **Eastern Hills**[23] 5751 7-8-12 69 (p) SebSanders 6 68
(Alan McCabe) *cl up: rdn to chse ldr over 2f out: drvn and ev ch 1f out: no ex fnl 50yds* **25/1**

3000 **5** 1 ¼ **On The Hoof**[23] 5736 3-9-3 69 JamesSullivan 1 73
(Michael Easterby) *cl up: rdn 3f out: drvn and outpcd 2f out: plugged on* **16/1**

0400 **6** hd **Glass Mountain (IRE)**[25] 5688 4-9-4 69 (p) MickaelBarzalona 9 70
(Ian Williams) *towards rr: hdwy over 3f out: drvn 2f out: kpt on same pce fnl f: nvr a threat* **9/1**[3]

2051 **7** 1 ½ **Offbeat Safaris (IRE)**[14] 6001 4-9-4 69 LukeMorris 11 66
(Ronald Harris) *in rr: rdn 3f out: drvn 2f out: swtchd lft whn btn 1f out: plugged on same pce* **14/1**

6306 **8** ¾ **Buaiteoir (FR)**[8] 6184 6-8-3 70 RaulDaSilva(3) 5 52
(Amy Weaver) *led tl hdd after 1f: remained cl up tl led again 3f out: drvn and hdd 1f out: sn wknd* **16/1**

1400 **9** 6 **Sir Mozart (IRE)**[13] 6051 9-8-10 70 DaraghO'Donohoe 2 40
(Barney Curley) *led after 1f: hdd 3f out: drvn and sn wknd* **8/1**[2]

060 **10** 11 **Hinton Admiral**[18] 5892 8-8-7 66 LauraPike(5) 8 12
(Conor Dore) *a in rr: dropped last and rdn 4f out: eased fnl f: t.o* **40/1**

1m 27.59s (-2.01) **Going Correction** -0.175s/f (Stan)
WFA 3 from 4yo+ 3lb **10** Ran SP% **87.1**
Speed ratings (Par 101): **104,103,102,102,100 100,98,97,90,78**
toteswingers:1&2 £3.60, 2&3 £10.60, 1&3 £5.20 CSF £20.17 TOTE £3.30: £1.10, £3.60, £1.70; EX 29.50 Trifecta £259.70 Part won. Pool £351.03 - 0.20 winning units..Buaiteoir was claimed by Mrs Nikki Evans for £3000.
Owner Ms Z Hatcher **Bred** R A Instone **Trained** Norton, N Yorks

FOCUS

The ten runners were rated between 66-70 in this classified claimer. Unsurprisingly there was a bunch finish. Limited form.

6453 DOWNLOAD OUR IPHONE APP MEDIAN AUCTION MAIDEN FILLIES' STKS 5f 216y(P)

6:30 (6:32) (Class 6) 2-Y-O **£1,704** (£503; £251) **Stalls** Low

Form RPR

42 **1** **Nardin**[72] 3959 2-9-0 0 TadhgO'Shea 3 74
(Ed Dunlop) *in tch: rdn over 2f out: kpt on 1f out: r.o wl to ld on post* **4/1**[3]

4 **2** shd **Midnight Flower (IRE)**[26] 5631 2-9-0 0 TomEaves 10 74
(David Simcock) *dwlt: rcvrd to chse ldrs after 1f: drvn and pressed ldrs over 1f out: led ins fnl f: hdd post* **7/1**

2 **3** ½ **Lilbourne Eliza (IRE)**[8] 6153 2-9-0 0 RichardHughes 4 72
(Richard Hannon) *led: pushed along 2f out: sn strly pressed: hdd ins fnl f: no ex fnl 50yds* **6/4**[1]

0 **4** 2 **Grace Hull**[18] 5887 2-9-0 0 LiamKeniry 8 66
(J S Moore) *in tch: rdn 2f out: drvn and one pce ins fnl f* **50/1**

022 **5** ¾ **Spicy (IRE)**[53] 4645 2-9-0 74 SebSanders 6 64
(Marco Botti) *cl up: pressed ldr over 2f out: drvn and ev ch tl wknd fnl 100yds* **11/4**[2]

0606 **6** 1 ¼ **Solvanna**[9] 6147 2-9-0 59 (v[1]) EddieAhern 2 60
(Heather Main) *t.k.h: in tch: rdn 2f out: drvn and fdd ins fnl f* **14/1**

7 9 **Mojo Bear** 2-8-9 0 LeeNewnes(5) 9 33
(Sylvester Kirk) *uns rdr gng to post: in tch: rdn 3f out and lost pl: btn 2f out* **40/1**

8 1 ¾ **Fiance Fiasco** 2-9-0 0 FergusSweeney 1 28
(James Evans) *slow away: nvr on terms: btn fnl 3f* **40/1**

9 4 **Bella Bijou** 2-8-7 0 JackDuern(7) 7 16
(Owen Brennan) *slow away: a in rr: lost tch fnl 3f* **100/1**

1m 14.3s (-0.70) **Going Correction** -0.175s/f (Stan) **9** Ran SP% **113.7**
Speed ratings (Par 90): **97,96,96,93,92 90,78,76,71**
toteswingers:1&2 £3.40, 2&3 £4.20, 1&3 £1.90 CSF £30.54 TOTE £4.50: £1.70, £4.20, £1.10; EX 24.40 Trifecta £92.10 Pool £1,204.67 - 9.67 winning units..
Owner Hamdan Al Maktoum **Bred** P And Mrs A G Venner **Trained** Newmarket, Suffolk

FOCUS

The front four in the market had all run to a fair level of form coming into this median auction maiden for 2yo fillies. The time and the sixth offer perspective to the form.

NOTEBOOK

Nardin hadn't been seen since finishing runner-up at Kempton 72 days previously. She made her move round the outside of the field at the top of the straight and the momentum gained carried her to victory. Her jockey feels she'll get further and casting an eye over her breeding does nothing to doubt that assertion. (op 9-2)

Midnight Flower(IRE) shaped with promise behind the subsequent 86-rated Nargys on her debut at Yarmouth. She travelled best here but the winner had that all important momentum. She'll go one better next time if kept to fillies' company. (op 8-1 tchd 17-2)

Lilbourne Eliza(IRE), turned out quickly after finishing runner-up at Chepstow eight days previously, took a keen hold in front but responded generously to strong pressure. She can win a similar contest. (op 2-1 tchd 11-8)

Grace Hull stepped up on her debut over C&D in what was an above average fillies' maiden for the track and would be of particular interest at Southwell, a track where her sires' progeny have an excellent record. (tchd 40-1)

Spicy(IRE) was the disappointment of the race. She looked to have just run into one on her previous two starts but, after pressing the pace, she weakened inside the final furlong, and will be suited by dropping back to 5f. (op 2-1)

6454 WEATHERBYS BLOODSTOCK INSURANCE H'CAP 7f 32y(P)

7:00 (7:01) (Class 4) (0-85,85) 3-Y-O+ **£4,204** (£1,251; £625; £312) **Stalls** High

Form RPR

1324 **1** **Emkanaat**[13] 6041 4-8-9 80 JeanVanOvermeire(7) 4 91
(Roger Varian) *cl up: hdwy over 2f out: led over 1f out: sn drvn and edgd rt: hld on wl* **7/1**

0511 **2** hd **Fast Finian (IRE)**[13] 6050 3-8-13 80 SebSanders 2 90
(Paul D'Arcy) *midfield: hdwy over 2f out: pressing wnr when slightly hmprd ins fnl f: rallied and r.o. fnl 50yds* **7/2**[2]

0100 **3** ¾ **Little Black Book (IRE)**[7] 6209 4-9-0 78 (b) LukeMorris 9 86
(Gerard Butler) *in tch: rdn over 2f out: drvn and effrt 1f out: no ex fnl 75yds* **11/1**

0012 **4** 1 ½ **Roy The Boy (USA)**[4] 6319 4-8-7 71 oh1 EddieAhern 3 75
(Alan Bailey) *cl up: rdn 2f out: ev ch 1f out: no ex fnl 100yds* **3/1**[1]

3011 **5** 4 **Smalljohn**[95] 3229 6-8-13 77 (v) TomEaves 12 70
(Bryan Smart) *in tch: rdn 2f out: wknd over 1f out* **20/1**

0101 **6** 1 ½ **Prime Exhibit**[13] 6051 7-9-6 84 (t) TadhgO'Shea 6 73
(Daniel Mark Loughnane) *sltly hmpd s: in rr: wd and nt hrd rdn ent st: drvn over 1f out: sn no imp* **12/1**

0010 **7** 1 **Masai Moon**[17] 5906 8-9-7 85 (b) JamesMillman 7 71
(Rod Millman) *dwlt: urged along 3f out: no imp fr over 1f out* **16/1**

0010 **8** nk **Taffe**[25] 5676 3-9-0 81 FrederikTylicki 5 67
(James Given) *sn led: hdd 1f out: fdd ins fnl f* **14/1**

4150 **9** 1 ¼ **Tenbridge**[60] 4413 3-8-1 71 (p) RaulDaSilva(3) 8 53
(Derek Haydn Jones) *taken down early: in tch: drvn and struggling fnl 3f* **25/1**

0041 **10** 1 ¼ **Right Result (IRE)**[13] 6052 3-8-10 77 (v) RichardHughes 1 56
(James Bethell) *midfield: urged along 3f out: drvn 2f out: btn fnl f* **9/2**[3]

0- **11** 1 ½ **Khaos (IRE)**[32] 5432 3-9-0 81 (b) PatCosgrave 11 56
(M D O'Callaghan, Ire) *a in rr: drvn and no hdwy fnl 2f* **25/1**

1m 26.96s (-2.64) **Going Correction** -0.175s/f (Stan)
WFA 3 from 4yo+ 3lb **11** Ran SP% **118.9**
Speed ratings (Par 105): **108,107,106,105,100 98,97,97,96,94 92**
toteswingers:1&2 £3.80, 2&3 £12.50, 1&3 £8.30 CSF £31.25 CT £272.57 TOTE £5.00: £1.90, £1.40, £5.50; EX 39.00 Trifecta £360.60 Pool £828.63 - 1.70 winning units..
Owner Michael Hill **Bred** C J Mills **Trained** Newmarket, Suffolk
■ South African born Jean Van Overmeire's first winner.

FOCUS

A decent race for the grade with several in form, and in a good time. A personal best from the winner.

Right Result(IRE) Official explanation: jockey said gelding lost its action

6455 32RED.COM H'CAP (DIV I) 7f 32y(P)

7:30 (7:31) (Class 6) (0-65,65) 3-Y-O+ **£1,704** (£503; £251) **Stalls** High

Form RPR

004 **1** **Atlantis Crossing (IRE)**[15] 5975 3-9-3 64 PatCosgrave 12 73
(Jim Boyle) *midfield: rdn over 2f out: drvn and swtchd lft over 1f out: led ins fnl f: kpt on wl* **11/2**[3]

5432 **2** ½ **Loyal N Trusted**[8] 6158 4-9-1 62 (p) MarkCoumbe(3) 4 70
(Richard Price) *midfield: lost pl 3f out: swtchd lft over 1f out: r.o wl ins fnl f: nt rch wnr* **4/1**[2]

5426 **3** 1 ¾ **Muhandis (IRE)**[23] 5750 4-9-6 64 (b) SebSanders 6 67
(Nick Littmoden) *in tch: effrt on outer 2f out: drvn over 1f out: carried rt and kpt on ins fnl f: nabbed 3rd cl home* **8/1**

4206 **4** hd **Alluring Star**[13] 6057 4-8-5 56 MatthewHopkins(7) 9 59
(Michael Easterby) *cl up: rdn over 2f out: carried rt and outpcd over 1f out: plugged on same pce ins fnl f* **33/1**

0006 **5** nk **Legal Eagle (IRE)**[70] 4043 7-9-2 60 (p) SeanQuinlan 7 62
(Paul Green) *midfield: rdn over 2f out: outpcd ins fnl 2f* **22/1**

0034 **6** ½ **Glenridding**[6] 6239 8-9-7 65 (p) FrederikTylicki 5 66
(James Given) *led: rdn 2f out: edgd rt over 1f out: hdd ins fnl f: sn fdd* **4/1**[2]

1555 **7** ½ **Climaxfortackle (IRE)**[13] 6057 4-9-5 63 (v) EddieAhern 8 62
(Derek Shaw) *in tch: hdwy and travelling wl over 2f out: rdn and hung rt over 1f out: drvn and no ex fnl f* **20/1**

0300 **8** nse **Irie Ute**[35] 5305 4-9-0 58 LiamKeniry 1 57
(Sylvester Kirk) *midfield: rdn 3f out: drvn and one pce fnl f* **33/1**

-445 **9** 2 **Fairest (IRE)**[22] 5776 3-9-1 62 RichardHughes 2 56
(Jeremy Noseda) *midfield: rdn 3f out: drvn and no hdwy ins fnl 2f: eased cl home* **7/2**[1]

0404 **10** 4 **Bahri Sheen (IRE)**[42] 5047 4-8-12 56 [1] LukeMorris 10 39
(John Best) *in rr: drvn and struggling 3f out* **20/1**

6505 **11** 15 **Black Douglas**[17] 5915 3-9-3 64 (bt) TomEaves 3
(William Jarvis) *stdd s: a in rr: drvn and struggling 3f out: eased w rdr looking down fnl f* **9/1**

1m 28.78s (-0.82) **Going Correction** -0.175s/f (Stan)
WFA 3 from 4yo+ 3lb **11** Ran SP% **118.5**
Speed ratings (Par 101): **97,96,94,94,93 93,92,92,90,85 68**
toteswingers:1&2 £10.90, 2&3 £6.00, 1&3 £15.50 CSF £25.82 CT £178.92 TOTE £8.10: £2.70, £1.60, £1.70; EX 50.10 Trifecta £334.10 Pool £948.13 - 2.10 winning units..
Owner The 'In Recovery' Partnership **Bred** J K Thoroughbreds & P Doyle Bloodstock **Trained** Epsom, Surrey

FOCUS

An ordinary handicap and the slower division by 0.78sec. The winner built on his latest effort.

Black Douglas Official explanation: jockey said gelding hung left-handed.

6456 32RED.COM H'CAP (DIV II) 7f 32y(P)

8:00 (8:02) (Class 6) (0-65,65) 3-Y-O+ **£1,704** (£503; £251) **Stalls** High

Form RPR

1522 **1** **Balti's Sister (IRE)**[7] 6216 3-8-12 62 RossAtkinson(3) 7 73
(Terry Clement) *in tch on outer: rdn and hdwy over 2f out: drvn to ld 1f out: forged ahd* **9/2**[2]

5042 **2** ½ **Amethyst Dawn (IRE)**[7] 6217 6-8-12 56 (t) SebSanders 9 65
(Alan McCabe) *cl up: drvn and hdwy 2f out: ev ch over 1f out: no ex fnl 75yds* **7/2**[1]

0326 **3** ½ **Charlcot**[123] 2354 4-9-4 62 MickaelBarzalona 6 70
(James Bethell) *in rr: swtchd to outer and rdn over 2f out: drvn and hdwy over 1f out: kpt on but no threat to wnr* **6/1**

600 **4** ½ **Dubai Bay (FR)**[49] 4779 4-9-2 60 MickyFenton 11 67
(Paul Midgley) *sn led: rdn 2f out: hdd 1f out: fdd fnl 100yds* **33/1**

3-64 **5** ½ **Let Your Love Flow (IRE)**[249] 194 3-8-13 60 FrederikTylicki 4 65
(Richard Fahey) *in rr: drvn and struggling fnl 3f: mod late prog* **16/1**

2305 **6** ½ **Lindoro**[37] 5220 7-9-2 **60**....(b) TomEaves 2 64+
(Brian Ellison) *t.k.h: hmpd sn after s: midfield: hdwy over 2f out: nt clr run over 1f out: rdn 1f out: kpt on but nvr able to land a blow: do bttr* **9/2**[2]
1312 **7** 1 ¾ **Footstepsofspring (FR)**[67] 4158 5-9-5 **63**.... J-PGuillambert 1 65+
(Willie Musson) *in rr: drvn 3f out: sn btn* **5/1**[3]
321 **8** nk **Greyemkay**[18] 5874 4-8-0 **51**.... DanielMuscutt(7) 8 49
(Richard Price) *prom: rdn over 1f out: wknd ins fnl f* **25/1**
0324 **9** ½ **Dvinsky (USA)**[9] 6145 11-9-7 **65**....(b) TomMcLaughlin 10 62
(Paul Howling) *drvn to chse ldrs: lost pl 3f out: sn same pce* **16/1**
1060 **10** 1 ¾ **Catalyze**[7] 6195 4-8-12 **63**....(t) DavidBergin(7) 5 55
(Charles Smith) *in tch: wd: drvn and brief effrt over 2f out: no ex over 1f out* **12/1**
40-0 **11** 11 **Sinchiroka (FR)**[9] 6145 6-9-3 **61**.... JamieGoldstein 3 24
(Ralph Smith) *midfield: drvn and tdd fnl 3f* **100/1**

1m 28.0s (-1.60) **Going Correction** -0.175s/f (Stan)
WFA 3 from 4yo+ 3lb **11** Ran SP% **116.8**
Speed ratings (Par 101): **102,101,100,100,99 99,97,96,96,94 81**
toteswingers:1&2 £4.70, 2&3 £4.50, 1&3 £9.10 CSF £20.19 CT £95.63 TOTE £3.90: £2.00, £2.10, £3.10; EX 30.10 Trifecta £232.10 Pool £759.09 - 2.42 winning units..
Owner Mrs Michelle Smith **Bred** P Monaghan, J Collins & G Dillon **Trained** Newmarket, Suffolk

FOCUS
The second division of the 7f handicap was equally competitive and also went to a 3yo. It was the quicker division and the form is fair and solid for the grade.

6457 FOLLOW US ON TWITTER @WOLVESRACES MAIDEN FILLIES' STKS 1m 141y(P)
8:30 (8:33) (Class 5) 3-Y-0+ **£2,264** (£673; £336; £168) **Stalls** Low

Form RPR
434 **1** **Afraah (USA)**[17] 5901 3-8-12 78....[1] TadhgO'Shea 6 73
(Roger Varian) *dwlt: sn pressing ldr: led 5f out: rdn 2f out: taken wd into st: drvn and strly pressed whn drifted lft and bmpd rival ins fnl f: in command fnl 50yds* **7/4**[1]
00 **2** 1 **Capacious**[28] 5555 3-8-12 0.... LukeMorris 2 71
(James Fanshawe) *cl up: urged along 3f out: drvn over 1f out: bmpd ins fnl f: nt rch wnr* **12/1**
0- **3** nk **Honour**[368] 6215 3-8-12 0.... RichardHughes 12 70
(Sir Michael Stoute) *led: hdd 5f out: drvn and ev ch over 1f out: bmpd ins fnl f: no ex fnl 75yds* **9/4**[2]
4 6 **Queen Of Skies (IRE)** 3-8-12 0.... JohnFahy 7 56
(Clive Cox) *in tch: rdn and outpcd 2f out: plugged on: n.d* **20/1**
0 **5** nk **Strawberry Flavour (GER)**[18] 5889 3-8-12 0.... EddieAhern 10 56
(James Tate) *in tch: urged along and lost pl 2f out: styd on same pce: n.d* **12/1**
4- **6** 1 **King's Guest (IRE)**[381] 5814 3-8-12 0.... MartinLane 8 53
(David Simcock) *in rr: outpcd and struggling fnl 3f: plugged on past btn rivals ins fnl 2f: nvr posed a threat* **11/1**
6-0 **7** ¾ **Glaisdale**[18] 5889 3-8-12 0.... PatCosgrave 1 52
(James Toller) *in tch: t.k.h: rdn and lost pl 3f out: no imp after* **50/1**
0 **8** 1 ¼ **Maria Vezzera**[45] 4931 3-8-7 0.... TobyAtkinson(5) 3 49
(Marco Botti) *in rr and t.k.h: struggling fnl 3f: stl green* **6/1**[3]
-000 **9** 2 ½ **Mistress Shy**[10] 6120 5-8-10 36....(t) NoelGarbutt(7) 5 43?
(Michael Appleby) *in tch: lost pl over 3f out: sn btn* **200/1**
04 **10** ½ **My Stroppy Poppy**[43] 4992 3-8-9 0....(t) RaulDaSilva(3) 9 42
(Frank Sheridan) *in rr: drvn and struggling fnl 3f* **33/1**
11 33 **Mahal Nadine** 3-8-12 0.... LiamKeniry 4
(Michael Murphy) *dwlt: a in rr: t.o fnl 3f* **66/1**

1m 49.43s (-1.07) **Going Correction** -0.175s/f (Stan)
WFA 3 from 5yo 5lb **11** Ran SP% **116.8**
Speed ratings (Par 100): **97,96,95,90,90 89,88,87,85,84 55**
toteswingers:1&2 £7.30, 2&3 £5.00, 1&3 £1.80 CSF £23.35 TOTE £2.60: £1.10, £3.50, £1.50; EX 27.50 Trifecta £55.80 Pool £415.16 - 5.50 winning units..
Owner Hamdan Al Maktoum **Bred** Shadwell Farm LLC **Trained** Newmarket, Suffolk

FOCUS
An interesting fillies' maiden featuring some well-bred individuals from top stables. The time was slow and there is some doubt over the bare form, which has been rated cautiously.

6458 32RED CASINO H'CAP 1m 1f 103y(P)
9:00 (9:00) (Class 6) (0-65,65) 3-Y-0+ **£1,704** (£503; £251) **Stalls** Low

Form RPR
0622 **1** **Lean On Pete (IRE)**[9] 6151 3-9-3 **63**.... ShaneKelly 2 71+
(Ollie Pears) *in tch: hdwy over 2f out: travelling wl and produced between horses to press ldrs over 1f out: led fnl 100yds: cheekily* **4/1**[1]
0563 **2** nk **Tenessee**[23] 5741 5-9-8 **63**.... PatCosgrave 6 70
(Jamie Osborne) *led: urged along 3f out: strly pressed over 1f out: hdd fnl 100yds: no ex fnl 25yds* **11/2**[3]
0103 **3** ½ **Bold Cross (IRE)**[10] 6120 9-9-3 **65**.... ThomasBrown(7) 10 71
(Edward Bevan) *in rr: drvn over 3f out: wd ent st: hdwy over 2f out: fin strly* **20/1**
042 **4** ¾ **Arabic**[22] 5764 3-9-1 **61**....(p) LukeMorris 12 65+
(James Fanshawe) *in tch: wd ent st and rdn: lost pl over 1f out: styd on one pce* **11/2**[3]
3461 **5** shd **Warden Bond**[8] 6174 4-9-2 **57**....(p) MartinLane 9 61
(William Stone) *cl up: drvn over 1f out: ev ch 1f out: fdd ins fnl f* **5/1**[2]
0130 **6** hd **Kyle Of Bute**[36] 5258 6-9-7 **62**.... FrederikTylicki 5 66
(Brian Baugh) *in rr: pushed along over 1f out and nt clr run: kpt on* **20/1**
0054 **7** shd **Maz**[8] 6176 4-9-9 **64**.... LiamKeniry 3 68
(Alan Bailey) *midfield: rdn over 1f out: drvn and hung lft ins fnl f: one pce fnl 100yds* **18/1**
0-42 **8** hd **Heezararity**[113] 2619 4-9-10 **65**....(t) RichardHughes 13 68
(David Evans) *in tch: hdwy over 2f out: pressed ldrs gng wl over 1f out: ev ch 1f out: no ex fnl 100yds* **8/1**
5420 **9** ½ **Spey Song (IRE)**[35] 5323 4-9-10 **65**....(b) MickaelBarzalona 1 67
(James Bethell) *in rr: pushed along over 1f out: plugged on same pce: nvr a threat* **10/1**
U05 **10** nk **Strike Force**[43] 4987 8-9-10 **65**....(t) TomEaves 7 66
(Alison Hutchinson) *in rr: pushed along over 2f out: one pce fnl f* **28/1**
2000 **11** nse **Beautiful Lando (FR)**[9] 6145 4-9-6 **61**....(v) EddieAhern 11 62
(Heather Main) *in tch: pushed along over 2f out: same pce ins fnl f* **50/1**
2302 **12** ½ **Landesherr (GER)**[6] 6250 5-9-7 **65**.... RaulDaSilva(3) 8 65
(Steve Gollings) *midfield: pushed along over 2f out: effrt over 1f out: no ex fnl f* **8/1**

2640 **13** 1 **Kampai**[14] 5990 4-9-3 **58**.... AdamBeschizza 4 56
(Julia Feilden) *in tch: drvn and lost pl 3f out: btn fnl 2f* **33/1**

2m 0.37s (-1.33) **Going Correction** -0.175s/f (Stan)
WFA 3 from 4yo+ 5lb **13** Ran SP% **121.9**
Speed ratings (Par 101): **98,97,97,96,96 96,96,96,95,95 95,94,94**
toteswingers:1&2 £5.90, 2&3 £52.10, 1&3 £10.90 CSF £24.34 CT £404.22 TOTE £6.20: £1.90, £1.80, £5.30; EX 29.80 Trifecta £340.40 Part won. Pool £460.12 - 0.21 winning units..
Owner Charles Wentworth **Bred** Mrs T Mahon **Trained** Norton, N Yorks

FOCUS
Another handicap to go the way of a 3yo. An ordinary race, with not many arriving in form. The winner was well in.
T/Jkpt: Not won. T/Plt: £54.50 to a £1 stake. Pool: £98,924.16 - 1,324.68 winning units T/Qpdt: £20.10 to a £1 stake. Pool: £10,510.80 - 386.80 winning units CS

6459 - 6462a (Foreign Racing) - See Raceform Interactive

[4384]MAISONS-LAFFITTE (R-H)
Friday, September 21

OFFICIAL GOING: Turf: good

6463a PRIX SARACA (LISTED RACE) (2YO) (TURF) 6f 110y
1:20 (12:00) 2-Y-0 **£22,916** (£9,166; £6,875; £4,583; £2,291)

RPR
1 **Boomshackerlacker (IRE)**[13] 6038 2-9-0 0.... MaximeGuyon 7 98+
(George Baker) *prom fr s towards outside: wnt 3rd at 1/2-way: shkn up 2 1/2f out: chal for ld 2f out: led 1 1/2f out: r.o wl: wnt clr fnl 100yds: comf* **7/1**
2 1 ½ **Chef Oui Chef (FR)**[9] 2-9-0 0.... Pierre-CharlesBoudot 8 94
(Y De Nicolay, France) **12/1**
3 ½ **Gaiete (FR)**[59] 2-8-10 0.... AnthonyCrastus 4 89
(C Laffon-Parias, France) **7/1**
4 1 ¼ **Charming Touch (USA)**[25] 2-8-10 0.... OlivierPeslier 3 85
(F Head, France) **6/4**[1]
5 nk **Atora Bere (FR)**[12] 2-8-10 0.... GeraldMosse 2 84
(M Boutin, France) **30/1**
6 1 ½ **Tricky Week (FR)**[37] 5248 2-8-10 0.... UmbertoRispoli 5 80
(C Baillet, France) **58/10**[3]
7 nse **Bilge Kagan (IRE)**[61] 2-9-0 0.... IoritzMendizabal 6 84
(A Savujev, Czech Republic) **25/1**
8 8 **Molly Mara (GER)**[27] 5612 2-8-10 0.... ChristopheSoumillon 1 58
(J-C Rouget, France) **7/2**[2]

1m 17.6s (77.60) **8** Ran SP% **116.7**
WIN (incl. 1 euro stake): 8.00. PLACES: 2.60, 2.90, 2.20. DF: 40.60. SF: 60.60.
Owner PJL Racing **Bred** Miss Elaine Marie Smith **Trained** Whitsbury, Hants

FOCUS
The form is rated at the mid point of the race averages.

NOTEBOOK
Boomshackerlacker(IRE) bounced back after being badly hampered at Kempton last time. A tough colt who likes ease in the ground, he could come back to France for a Group race next month.

6464a LA COUPE DE MAISONS-LAFFITTE (GROUP 3) (3YO+) (TURF) 1m 2f (S)
2:20 (12:00) 3-Y-0+ **£33,333** (£13,333; £10,000; £6,666; £3,333)

RPR
1 **Maxios**[41] 5117 4-9-0 0.... StephanePasquier 3 118+
(J E Pease, France) *settled in 3rd: wnt 2nd at 1/2-way: rdn to chal for ld 2f out: r.o wl u.p to ld 250yds out: styd on wl: wnt clr 75yds out: comf* **42/10**[2]
2 1 ½ **Reliable Man**[62] 4322 4-9-0 0.... OlivierPeslier 1 115
(A De Royer-Dupre, France) *racd in 3rd following eventual wnr: wnt 2nd on outside 2f out: r.o wl ent fnl f to briefly threaten ldr 150yds out: no ex fnl 100yds: nt rch ldr* **1/2**[1]
3 2 **Saga Dream (FR)**[19] 5871 6-9-0 0.... ThierryJarnet 4 111
(F Lemercier, France) *hld up in rr: wnt 4th at 1/2-way: rdn 2 1/2f out: r.o fnl 1 1/2f: nt rch ldrs: styd on* **68/10**[3]
4 1 **Red Dubawi (IRE)**[19] 5871 4-9-0 0.... AlexandreRoussel 2 109
(A De Royer-Dupre, France) *settled towards rr: relegated to last at 1/2-way: rdn and r.o 2f out: nt qckn fnl f* **8/1**
5 8 **Quinindo (GER)**[19] 4-9-0 0.... ADeVries 5 93
(Elfie Schnakenberg, Germany) *sn led: set stdy pce: rdn and u.p over 2 1/2f out: hdd 250yds out: no ex: wknd: eased fnl 150yds* **14/1**

2m 3.3s (0.90) **5** Ran SP% **116.5**
WIN (incl. 1 euro stake): 5.20. PLACES: 1.30, 1.10. SF: 13.60.
Owner Niarchos Family **Bred** Niarchos Family **Trained** Chantilly, France

NOTEBOOK
Maxios, beaten at odds-on in a Group 3 at Deauville last time, bounced back and turned over last year's French Derby winner here. He apparently needs time between his races and appreciates some cut in the ground. He could go for the Prix Dollar next.
Reliable Man, last years's Prix Du Jockey Club winner, finished fourth in the King George VI and Queen Elizabeth Stakes last time out, but may have needed this following a two-month break. A return to 1m4f ought to suit, and the Arc, the Canadian International and the Champion Stakes at Ascot are all under consideration.

[6423]AYR (L-H)
Saturday, September 22

OFFICIAL GOING: Heavy (soft in places; 8.1; sprint course: far side 7.9; centre 7.8; stands' side 8.0)
Bottom bend out 4m, exit to bend out 6m; distances on round course increased by 12yds. Rail on far side of straight courseout from 5f to join round course.
Wind: Light, half against Weather: Cloudy

6465 WILLIAM HILL AYR BRONZE CUP (H'CAP) 6f
1:45 (1:46) (Class 4) 3-Y-0+
£12,450 (£3,728; £1,864; £932; £466; £234) **Stalls** Centre

Form RPR
5304 **1** **Jack Dexter**[13] 6075 3-9-8 **84**.... GrahamLee 10 100+
(Jim Goldie) *in tch far side: hdwy wl over 1f out: rdn to ld ins fnl f: edgd rt: pushed out: comf: 1st of 12 in gp* **5/1**[1]
062 **2** 2 ¼ **Cheveton**[6] 6286 8-9-5 **79**.... TadhgO'Shea 4 88
(Richard Price) *chsd far side ldrs: led over 2f out to ins fnl f: kpt on: nt gng pce of wnr: 2nd of 12 in gp* **6/1**[2]

0063 **3** *nk* **Best Trip (IRE)**[29] 5539 5-9-3 **77**.. TomEaves 11 85+
(Brian Ellison) *hld up bhd ldng gp far side: drvn over 2f out: hdwy over 1f out: kpt on fnl f: nrst fin: 3rd of 12 in gp* **14/1**

4500 **4** *1 ¼* **Roker Park (IRE)**[9] 6165 7-9-10 **84**..........................(b) DanielTudhope 15 88
(David O'Meara) *hld up on outside of stands' side gp: rdn over 2f out: styd on fnl f: led that gp towards fin: nt rch far side: 1st of 11 in gp* **16/1**

4440 **5** *nk* **Coolminx (IRE)**[15] 6008 5-9-0 **81**..............................(p) LauraBarry[(7)] 8 84
(Richard Fahey) *cl up far side: ev ch over 2f out to over 1f out: one pce fnl f: 4th of 12 in gp* **16/1**

4206 **6** *½* **Green Park (IRE)**[4] 6338 9-8-10 **77**.....................(b) LukeLeadbitter[(7)] 14 78
(Declan Carroll) *prom on outside of stands' side gp: led that bunch over 1f out: one pce and hdd that gp towards fin: 2nd of 11 in gp* **16/1**

5054 **7** *2 ¾* **New Leyf (IRE)**[15] 6008 6-9-6 **83**.................................(b) DaleSwift[(3)] 16 76
(Colin Teague) *hld up stands' side: drvn over 2f out: styd on fnl f: nrst fin: 3rd of 11 in gp* **20/1**

0106 **7** *dht* **Pick A Little**[14] 6044 4-9-3 **77**.. GeorgeBaker 9 70
(Brian Ellison) *cl up far side: drvn over 2f out: no imp fr over 1f out: 5th of 12 in gp* **33/1**

0005 **9** *shd* **Rasaman (IRE)**[15] 6008 8-9-2 **79**................................... GaryBartley[(3)] 2 71
(Jim Goldie) *hld up far side: rdn and hdwy over 1f out: kpt on fnl f: nvr able to chal: 6th of 12 in gp* **25/1**

1241 **10** *½* **Llewellyn**[22] 5801 4-9-3 **77** 5ex.................................. GrahamGibbons 19 68
(David Nicholls) *cl up stands' side: led that gp briefly 2f out: outpcd fnl f: 4th of 11 in gp* **16/1**

3000 **11** *1 ¼* **Baldemar**[57] 4554 7-9-4 **78**... BarryMcHugh 5 65
(Richard Fahey) *led far side to over 2f out: rdn and wknd over 1f out: 7th of 12 in gp* **25/1**

0/0 **12** *1 ¼* **Ucanchoose (IRE)**[4] 6353 6-8-10 **75**...........................(b) MACleere[(5)] 20 58
(Andrew Slattery, Ire) *led stands' side gp to 2f out: sn rdn and wknd: 5th of 11 in gp* **33/1**

0321 **13** *1 ¼* **Frequency**[39] 5189 5-9-4 **78**..(b) RobertWinston 1 57
(Keith Dalgleish) *hld up far side: rdn and effrt over 1f out: sn no imp: 8th of 12 in gp* **20/1**

5001 **14** *½* **Bonnie Charlie**[14] 6044 6-9-0 **81** 5ex..................... ShirleyTeasdale[(7)] 13 58
(David Nicholls) *hld up bhd far side ldrs: drvn over 2f out: btn over 1f out: 9th of 12 in gp* **12/1**

-000 **15** *½* **Pelmanism**[15] 6008 5-9-3 **77**... JamesSullivan 6 53
(Brian Ellison) *bhd and drvn far side 1/2-way: nvr able to chal: 10th of 12 in gp* **50/1**

5030 **16** *nse* **Karaka Jack**[11] 6124 5-9-6 **80**.. KellyHarrison 3 55
(David Nicholls) *hld up on far side: drvn over 2f out: nvr on terms: 11th of 12 in gp* **22/1**

3602 **17** *hd* **Arctic Feeling (IRE)**[1] 6427 4-9-7 **81**........................... TonyHamilton 25 56
(Richard Fahey) *hld up bhd ldng gp stands' side: drvn along over 2f out: nvr able to chal: 6th of 11 in gp* **8/1**[3]

2204 **17** *dht* **Tip Top Gorgeous (IRE)**[28] 5576 3-9-2 **78**.............(p) DarryllHolland 18 53
(J S Moore) *bhd stands' side: drvn over 2f out: nvr on terms: 7th of 11 in gp* **33/1**

1010 **19** *2 ¼* **Tajneed (IRE)**[35] 5368 9-9-9 **83**.................................... AdrianNicholls 23 51
(David Nicholls) *bhd stands' side: drvn along over 2f out: nvr a factor: 8th of 11 in gp* **11/1**

0001 **20** *4* **Amenable (IRE)**[29] 5539 5-9-9 **83**.............................. PaulMulrennan 21 38
(David Nicholls) *cl up stands' side tl edgd lft and wknd 2f out: 9th of 11 in gp* **16/1**

4002 **21** *1 ¼* **Arganil (USA)**[23] 5758 7-9-10 **84**..................................(p) PhillipMakin 24 35
(Kevin Ryan) *bhd stands' side: drvn over 2f out: sn btn: 10th of 11 in gp* **33/1**

010- **22** *shd* **Dorback**[267] 7926 5-9-6 **80**... DavidAllan 17 30
(David Nicholls) *midfield stands' side: drvn along over 2f out: sn wknd: last of 11 in gp* **40/1**

0160 **23** *6* **Hamoody (USA)**[1] 6427 8-9-7 **81** 5ex........................... FrederikTylicki 12 12
(David Nicholls) *prom far side tl wknd 2f out: eased whn btn fnl f: last of 12 in gp* **33/1**

1m 14.55s (2.15) **Going Correction** +0.50s/f (Yiel)
WFA 3 from 4yo+ 2lb **23** Ran SP% **134.8**
Speed ratings (Par 105): **105,102,101,99,99 98,95,95,95,94 92,91,89,88,88 88,87,87,84,79 77,77,69**
toteswingers 1&2 £4.60, 2&3 £21.90, 1&3 £32.90 CSF £29.07 CT £424.51 TOTE £4.80: £2.30, £2.40, £4.80, £4.50; EX 23.70 Trifecta £179.30 Pool: £1117.27 - 4.61 winning units..
Owner Jim Goldie Racing Club **Bred** Jim Goldie **Trained** Uplawmoor, E Renfrews

FOCUS
Bottom bend out 4m, exit to bend out 6m to a drop-in and distances on Round course increased by 12yds. Rail on far side of straight course tapered out from 5f to join Round course. The ground was again described as heavy but the runners appeared to go through it well enough. The first time the Bronze, Silver and Gold Cups have been run on the same day. A competitive renewal on paper of the minor consolation race for the main feature, with all three previous winners of this event, Coolminx, Cheveton and Baldemar taking part again, and all three ran with credit. The field split into two almost equal groups, and those on the far side seemed to have the advantage throughout, with four of the first five racing on that side. However, the finish was dominated by the well-backed favourite, although the time was 0.4secs slower than the following Silver Cup. A clear personal best from Jack Dexter.

6466 WILLIAM HILL AYR SILVER CUP (H'CAP) 6f
2:20 (2:22) (Class 3) 3-Y-0+

£21,787 (£6,524; £3,262; £1,631; £815; £409) **Stalls** Centre

Form RPR

3220 **1** **Mass Rally (IRE)**[7] 6244 5-9-9 **94**............................(b) PaulMulrennan 20 105
(Michael Dods) *racd stands' side: hld up in mid-div: hdwy over 2f out: edgd lft and styd on fnl f: led last stride: 1st of 11 that gp* **16/1**

5162 **2** *shd* **Highland Colori (IRE)**[8] 6201 4-9-6 **91**.......................... SebSanders 13 102+
(Andrew Balding) *racd far side: in rr: hdwy over 2f out: sn chsng ldrs: led overall jst ins fnl f: hdd post: 1st of 12 that gp* **6/1**[1]

113 **3** *1 ¼* **An Saighdiur (IRE)**[43] 5068 5-9-4 **94**........................ MACleere[(5)] 24 101
(Andrew Slattery, Ire) *led stands' side: edgd lft over 1f out: hdd that gp fnl 50yds: no ex: 2nd of 11 that gp* **8/1**[2]

1123 **4** *¾* **Spinatrix**[35] 5368 4-9-6 **91**..(p) TomEaves 22 95
(Michael Dods) *racd stands' side: w ldr: carried lft appr fnl f: kpt on same pce last 75yds: 3rd of 11 that gp* **14/1**

5000 **5** *1* **Gatepost (IRE)**[10] 6143 3-9-7 **94**................................... BarryMcHugh 23 95
(Richard Fahey) *racd stands' side: chsd ldrs: rdn over 2f out: hung lft: styd on ins fnl f: 4th of 11 that gp* **28/1**

0012 **6** *¾* **Hamza (IRE)**[13] 6075 3-9-8 **95**...(b) PatSmullen 6 94
(Kevin Ryan) *led far side gp tl jst ins fnl f: no ex: 2nd of 12 that gp* **9/1**[3]

1050 **7** *½* **Partner (IRE)**[10] 6144 6-8-13 **87** ow1........................(b) GaryBartley[(3)] 27 84
(Noel Wilson) *racd stands' side: in rr: styd on fnl 2f: nrst fin: 5th of 11 that gp* **66/1**

0040 **8** *¾* **Advanced**[49] 4802 9-9-5 **90**.. KellyHarrison 8 85
(Kevin Ryan) *racd far side: chsd ldrs: one pce fnl 2f: 3rd of 12 that gp* **20/1**

6050 **9** *½* **Kaldoun Kingdom (IRE)**[7] 6244 7-9-1 **93**............. GeorgeChaloner[(7)] 2 86
(Richard Fahey) *racd far side: chsd ldrs: kpt on same pce over 1f out: 4th of 12 that gp* **10/1**

065 **10** *¾* **Ancient Cross**[7] 6244 8-9-9 **94**..................................(t) FrederikTylicki 26 85
(Michael Easterby) *racd stands' side: towards rr: hdwy over 2f out: kpt on fnl f: nvr a threat: 6th of 11 that gp* **16/1**

0560 **11** *nk* **Thunderball**[49] 4799 6-9-3 **88**... MircoDemuro 16 78
(Scott Dixon) *racd stands' side: mid-div: effrt over 2f out: kpt on: nvr a threat: 7th of 11 that gp* **28/1**

0000 **12** *¾* **Grissom (IRE)**[21] 5827 6-9-7 **92**................................... GrahamGibbons 19 79
(Tim Easterby) *racd stands' side: chsd ldrs: one pce fnl 2f: 8th of 11 that gp* **16/1**

4141 **13** *½* **Amadeus Wolfe Tone (IRE)**[9] 6165 3-9-5 **92** 5ex....(p) GeorgeBaker 17 78
(Jamie Osborne) *swtchd lft s and racd far side: hld up towards rr: effrt over 2f out: nvr a factor: 5th of 12 that gp* **9/1**[3]

6050 **14** *1 ½* **Fast Shot**[35] 5368 4-9-4 **89**... DavidAllan 3 70
(Tim Easterby) *racd far side: chsd ldrs: rdn over 2f out: fdd appr fnl f: 6th of 12 that gp* **14/1**

-500 **15** *hd* **Lightning Cloud (IRE)**[63] 4321 4-9-8 **93**........................ PhillipMakin 21 73
(Kevin Ryan) *racd stands' side: in rr: rdn over 2f out: nvr a factor: 9th of 11 that gp* **12/1**

6510 **16** *½* **Street Power (USA)**[49] 4824 7-8-10 **84**........................... DaleSwift[(3)] 25 63
(Jeremy Gask) *s.s: racd stands' side: sme hdwy on outer over 2f out: nvr a factor: 10th of 11 that gp* **28/1**

0012 **17** *nse* **Mayoman (IRE)**[21] 5829 7-9-3 **88**...............................(v) DanielTudhope 9 67
(David O'Meara) *racd far side: in rr: sme hdwy 2f out: nvr a factor: 7th of 12 that gp* **16/1**

1403 **18** *¾* **Jedward (IRE)**[21] 5829 5-9-2 **87**... GrahamLee 1 63
(Kevin Ryan) *racd far side: trckd ldrs: lost pl over 1f out: 8th of 12 that gp* **20/1**

3000 **19** *1 ¼* **Layla's Hero (IRE)**[7] 6235 5-9-2 **87**..............................(p) JimCrowley 10 59
(Patrick Morris) *dwlt: racd far side: in rr: nvr a factor: 9th of 12 that gp* **33/1**

5051 **20** *½* **El Viento (FR)**[35] 5368 4-9-7 **92**.................................(b) TonyHamilton 12 63
(Richard Fahey) *racd far side: mid-div: drvn over 2f out: sn btn: 10th of 12 that gp* **22/1**

0000 **21** *2* **Klynch**[15] 6011 6-9-5 **90**..(b) JamesSullivan 14 54
(Ruth Carr) *swtchd lft s and racd towards far side: in rr: lost pl 2f out: sn bhd: 11th of 12 that gp* **25/1**

1000 **22** *3 ¼* **Cadeaux Pearl**[26] 5663 4-9-2 **87**.................................. RobertWinston 15 41
(Scott Dixon) *racd stands' side: chsd ldrs: wknd 2f out: last of 11 that gp* **50/1**

0101 **23** *6* **Trade Secret**[15] 6009 5-9-4 **89** 5ex................................ DarryllHolland 11 24
(Mel Brittain) *racd far side: mid-div: effrt over 2f out: sn btn: eased in clsng stages: last of 12 that gp* **25/1**

1m 14.15s (1.75) **Going Correction** +0.50s/f (Yiel)
WFA 3 from 4yo+ 2lb **23** Ran SP% **137.3**
Speed ratings (Par 107): **108,107,106,105,103 102,102,101,100,99 99,98,97,95,95 94,94,93,91,91 88,84,76**
toteswingers 1&2 £26.50, 2&3 £12.40, 1&3 £51.70 CSF £102.49 CT £880.85 TOTE £19.30: £4.40, £2.10, £2.10, £4.10; EX 192.40 Trifecta £1323.70 Pool: £2325.48 - 1.30 winning units..
Owner Business Development Consultants Limited **Bred** Round Hill Stud **Trained** Denton, Co Durham

■ Stewards' Enquiry : Paul Mulrennan four-day ban: used whip above permitted level (Oct 6,8-10)
M A Cleere one-day ban: careless riding (Oct 6); seven-day ban: used whip above permitted level (Oct 8-14)

FOCUS
Just a 10lb spread covered the field in this 'consolation' race, now 20 years old and a good-class handicap in its own right. The field split into two similarly sized groups and, in contrast to the Bronze Cup, the stands' side came out on top, with five of the first seven home racing on that side. However the narrow runner-up took the opposite flank and in truth there was no concrete advantage to either side. The first four crossed the line in the centre of the track after drifting over. Not many became involved and the time was 0.45sec quicker than the Bronze Cup, but almost the same as that for the Gold Cup. The riders of the winner and third picked up whip bans. The winner is rated back to his best while the second beat the rest of his group convincingly.

NOTEBOOK
Mass Rally(IRE) picked up well from off the pace in the final furlong to thrust his head in front on the line. Remarkably this was his first win in 25 starts dating back to November 2009 and his first ever on turf, but he has been beaten under a length in four warm handicaps this season. He doesn't tend to find much, but didn't have time to get into a sustained tussle here.
Highland Colori(IRE) was drawn in the centre and might have gone to the stands' side, as a couple drawn immediately to his left did. He got to the front inside the last and, after drifting right under pressure, was nailed on the line. Officially 4lb well in, this progressive handicapper, who gets further, was running from a mark 16lb higher than when successful at Windsor in May. He beat the rest on his side easily. (op 8-1)
An Saighdiur(IRE) is very much at home in testing conditions, having won valuable handicaps in ground officially described as soft to heavy at the Curragh and Tipperary this summer. He travelled well and led his side for much of the way, but couldn't hold on. (op 9-1)
Spinatrix, the winner's stablemate, has a good record over C&D and she ran a plucky race, sticking to her guns although the winner carried her to the left. She's a tough and consistent filly.
Gatepost(IRE) did best of the three 3-y-os, running on late. Equally effective at 7f, he's due to be dropped 2lb now. (op 25-1)
Hamza(IRE), another 3-y-o, was 6lb ahead of the handicapper here. Racing on the far side, he led overall but could not hold on entering the last. (op 12-1)
Partner(IRE), with blinkers refitted and tackling 6f for only the second time this year, ran on from the back of the near-side bunch.
Advanced, running in the Gold or Silver Cup for the seventh successive season, won the main event five years ago and made the frame in this in each of the last two years. He ran another respectable race without ever looking like winning.
Kaldoun Kingdom(IRE), the 2009 winner, was not discredited, but his losing run goes back to March 2010 now. (op 9-1)
Amadeus Wolfe Tone(IRE)'s Doncaster win, for which he was penalised, has been boosted since by runner-up Misplaced Fortune. His rider opted to head for the far side and the gelding could never make his presence felt. The ground had gone against him. (op 10-1)

6467 LAUNDRY COTTAGE STUD FIRTH OF CLYDE STKS (GROUP 3) (FILLIES) 6f
2:50 (2:51) (Class 1) 2-Y-0

£22,684 (£8,600; £4,304; £2,144; £1,076; £540) **Stalls** High

Form RPR

512 **1** **Melody Of Love**[26] 5678 2-8-12 90................................ PaulMulrennan 5 101
(Ann Duffield) *hld up in tch: effrt over 2f out: led and edgd lft ins fnl f: kpt on strly* **7/2**[2]

1001 **2** *1 ½* **Mary's Daughter**[29] 5563 2-8-12 88 TonyHamilton 1 97
(Richard Fahey) *t.k.h: cl up: led over 2f out: hdd ins fnl f: drifted lft u.p: one pce* **11/2**

3665 **3** *2 ¼* **Momalorka**[28] 5571 2-8-12 93 (p) KellyHarrison 6 90
(William Haggas) *in tch: outpcd after 2f: hung lft 1/2-way: edgd rt and hdwy appr fnl f: kpt on: could nt rch first two* **9/2**[3]

2214 **4** *4 ½* **City Girl (IRE)**[30] 5516 2-8-12 96 JimCrowley 7 76
(Ralph Beckett) *trckd ldrs: rdn whn n.m.r briefly over 2f out: sn outpcd: sme late hdwy: n.d* **11/2**

12 **5** *nk* **Scatty Cat (IRE)**[6] 6284 2-8-12 78 MichaelHussey 8 75
(Peter McCreery, Ire) *hld up: swtchd lft after 2f: hdwy and ev ch over 2f out to over 1f out: edgd lft and wknd 1f out* **20/1**

2153 **6** *hd* **Royal Rascal**[30] 5516 2-8-12 101 DavidAllan 4 75
(Tim Easterby) *t.k.h: trckd ldrs: drvn and outpcd over 2f out: btn fnl f* **9/4**[1]

6203 **7** *24* **Lasilia (IRE)**[28] 5601 2-8-12 91 PhillipMakin 2
(Kevin Ryan) *led to over 2f out: wknd over 1f out: eased whn no ch fnl f* **12/1**

1m 16.33s (3.93) **Going Correction** +0.50s/f (Yiel) **7** Ran SP% **114.4**
Speed ratings (Par 102): **93,91,88,82,81 81,49**
toteswingers 1&2 £4.20, 2&3 £9.30, 1&3 £7.20 CSF £22.87 TOTE £5.20: £2.80, £2.40; EX 32.70 Trifecta £141.00 Pool: £ 1154.77- 6.06 winning units..
Owner Mrs P Good **Bred** Mrs P Good **Trained** Constable Burton, N Yorks
■ Stewards' Enquiry : Paul Mulrennan four-day ban: used whip above permitted level (Oct 11,12,14,15)

FOCUS
For many of the previous recent winners, success in this Group 3 has proved to be the high point of their careers. However, Airwave went on to with the Cheveley Park and proved to be a top-class sprinter, while Aspen Darlin subsequently finished second in the Cheveley Park. This edition was run in bad ground and looked weak for the grade on pre-race figures. The winner improved by 7lb on her Ripon form.

NOTEBOOK
Melody Of Love, who was giving the trainer a first Group winner with her first runner at this level, won in good style. Beautifully bred, being by a 2000 Guineas winner out of a mare who is related to such good horses at Tomba, Holding Court and Ordnance Row, all of whom won Group races for this filly's owner, she handled the heavy ground well, as might have been expected from her breeding, and proved just too strong for the runner-up in the last furlong. It will be interesting to see how she goes on from this. (op 4-1 tchd 9-2)
Mary's Daughter bounced back to form when winning a nursery off a mark of 82 at York and ran a fine race, only giving best late on. Related to several winners and out of a half-sister to the top-class Attraction, the black type gained here will considerably increase her paddock value, and she might have more to offer.
Momalorka, held twice at this level since finishing a close third in the Super Sprint, was another to earn valuable black type. Wearing cheekpieces for the first time, she looked to be struggling when last and ridden along before halfway, only to pick up under pressure and finish well to close down the principals, although without looking likely to trouble them.
City Girl(IRE), who finished one place behind Royal Rascal in the Lowther, had previously been beaten at long odds-on on heavy ground and, although reversing placings with her old rival, probably failed to handle the ground again. (op 5-1)
Scatty Cat(IRE), the lowest rated of these, made a mid-race move to deliver a challenge but stopped pretty quickly in the last furlong and might not have got the trip in the conditions.
Royal Rascal stood out on official ratings, having earned an official figure of 101 for finishing third in the Group 2 Lowther Stakes at York. However, despite having won her maiden on soft going, she failed to pick up from halfway having been keen early, and ended up well held. (op 11-4 tchd 2-1)
Lasilia(IRE) handles easy ground and made the running but she dropped away pretty quickly when challenged and is another who probably failed to handle the testing ground. (op 10-1)

6468 WILLIAM HILL AYR GOLD CUP (HERITAGE H'CAP) 6f
3:30 (3:31) (Class 2) 3-Y-0+

£74,700 (£22,368; £11,184; £5,592; £2,796; £1,404) **Stalls** Centre

Form RPR

0034 **1** **Captain Ramius (IRE)**[35] 5370 6-9-0 100 PatSmullen 8 114
(Kevin Ryan) *prom centre: rdn 2f out: led ins fnl f: sn clr* **16/1**

3032 **2** *2 ½* **Regal Parade**[21] 5814 8-8-11 100 (t) DaleSwift(3) 19 106
(Milton Bradley) *towards rr centre: rdn and hdwy 2f out: styd on to go 2nd towards fin: no ch w wnr* **25/1**

6131 **3** *1 ¼* **Maarek**[7] 6268 5-9-9 114 5ex MarkEnright(5) 13 116
(David Peter Nagle, Ire) *hld up centre: rdn and hdwy over 2f out: in tch whn edgd lft over 1f out: kpt on ins fnl f* **8/1**[1]

1013 **4** *¾* **Sholaan (IRE)**[84] 3639 3-8-13 101 (b) KellyHarrison 2 100
(William Haggas) *led towards far side: rdn and qcknd clr 2f out: edgd lft and hdd ins fnl f: sn no ex* **16/1**

0150 **5** *hd* **Colonel Mak**[35] 5370 5-8-13 99 GrahamGibbons 22 98
(David Barron) *prom centre: drvn over 2f out: styd on fnl f: nt gng pce to chal* **14/1**

0200 **6** *hd* **Brae Hill (IRE)**[21] 5827 6-8-13 99 BarryMcHugh 14 97
(Richard Fahey) *disp ld centre to 1/2-way: sn drvn along: styd on u.p ins fnl f* **33/1**

3041 **7** *nk* **Doc Hay (USA)**[7] 6244 5-9-2 102 5ex DanielTudhope 5 99
(David O'Meara) *hld up towards far side: rdn and hdwy over 1f out: kpt on fnl f: nvr able to chal* **14/1**

1615 **8** *½* **Johannes (IRE)**[35] 5370 9-8-3 96 GeorgeChaloner(7) 10 91
(Richard Fahey) *chsd ldrs in centre: drvn along over 2f out: kpt on same pce over 1f out* **40/1**

0523 **9** *½* **Louis The Pious**[35] 5370 4-8-11 97 (p) PaulMulrennan 6 91
(Kevin Ryan) *prom towards far side: drvn along over 2f out: no ex appr fnl f* **16/1**

4221 **10** *¾* **Pintura**[49] 4833 5-9-5 105 (p) PhillipMakin 9 96
(Kevin Ryan) *in tch in centre: effrt and rdn over 1f out: wknd ins fnl f* **16/1**

0105 **11** *½* **Tariq Too**[51] 4751 5-8-12 98 MircoDemuro 20 88
(Amy Weaver) *s.i.s: hld up towards nr side of main gp: effrt over 1f out: no imp fnl f* **20/1**

2630 **12** *½* **Our Jonathan**[35] 5370 5-9-6 106 JimCrowley 12 94
(Kevin Ryan) *hld up centre: drvn and effrt over 2f out: btn fnl f* **10/1**[3]

5010 **13** *nk* **Hawkeyethenoo (IRE)**[14] 6030 6-9-8 108 GrahamLee 3 95
(Jim Goldie) *hld up on far side of main gp: rdn over 2f out: nvr rchd ldrs* **12/1**

6201 **14** *hd* **Borderlescott**[21] 5822 10-9-7 107 5ex FrederikTylicki 1 94
(Robin Bastiman) *cl up towards far side: drvn over 2f out: wknd over 1f out* **25/1**

2100 **15** *1 ½* **Pearl Ice**[84] 3641 4-8-11 97 TomEaves 21 79
(David Barron) *hld up centre: rdn whn n.m.r briefly 2f out: sn no imp* **20/1**

0242 **16** *shd* **The Cheka (IRE)**[27] 5627 6-9-10 110 (v) GeorgeBaker 11 91
(Eve Johnson Houghton) *midfield centre: drvn and outpcd over 2f out: n.d after* **9/1**[2]

0150 **17** *1 ¼* **Alben Star (IRE)**[35] 5370 4-8-10 96 TonyHamilton 16 73
(Richard Fahey) *prom on nr side of main centre gp: rdn over 2f out: wknd over 1f out* **10/1**[3]

1160 **18** *½* **Mirza**[70] 4092 5-9-4 104 DarryllHolland 24 80
(Rae Guest) *prom stands' side: drvn and hung lft over 2f out: wknd over 1f out* **25/1**

2100 **19** *1* **Shropshire (IRE)**[8] 6201 4-8-8 99 MatthewLawson(5) 23 72
(Charles Hills) *cl up stands' side: rdn over 2f out: wknd over 1f out* **25/1**

2436 **20** *nse* **Boastful (IRE)**[27] 5641 4-8-12 101 MichaelMetcalfe(3) 25 74
(Mrs K Burke) *spd stands' side to 2f out: edgd lft and sn wknd* **20/1**

0424 **21** *hd* **Waffle (IRE)**[49] 4802 6-9-4 104 ShaneFoley 15 76
(David Barron) *cl up centre tl rdn and wknd over 1f out* **14/1**

5424 **22** *5* **Morache Music**[70] 4092 4-9-5 105 SebSanders 4 61
(Peter Makin) *bhd and drvn along towards far side: struggling over 3f out: nvr on terms* **25/1**

6600 **23** *4 ½* **Beacon Lodge (IRE)**[7] 6244 7-9-3 110 ShirleyTeasdale(7) 7 51
(David Nicholls) *midfield centre: struggling over 2f out: sn btn* **40/1**

4-60 **24** *8* **Miss Work Of Art**[9] 6161 3-8-6 101 LauraBarry(7) 18 17
(Richard Fahey) *bhd and sn outpcd centre: no ch fr 1/2-way* **50/1**

2015 **25** *3 ¼* **Rodrigo De Torres**[100] 3091 5-8-13 99 AdrianNicholls 27
(David Nicholls) *cl up stands' side tl rdn and wknd over 2f out* **33/1**

6101 **26** *4 ½* **Cheviot (USA)**[14] 6028 6-9-5 105 5ex (p) RobertWinston 17
(Ian Semple) *midfield centre tl wknd over 2f out* **25/1**

1m 14.13s (1.73) **Going Correction** +0.50s/f (Yiel)
WFA 3 from 4yo+ 2lb **26** Ran SP% **140.6**
Speed ratings (Par 109): **108,104,103,102,101 101,101,100,99,98 98,97,97,96,94 94,92,92,90,90 90,83,77,67,62 56**
toteswingers 1&2 £126.70, 2&3 £37.70, 1&3 £39.60 CSF £386.90 CT £3503.00 TOTE £19.10: £5.00, £6.00, £3.20, £4.60; EX 417.70 Trifecta £9735.70 Pool: £43416.09 - 3.30 winning units..
Owner Mrs Clodagh McStay **Bred** P G Lyons **Trained** Hambleton, N Yorks
■ Stewards' Enquiry : Mirco Demuro one-day ban: careless riding (Oct 10)

FOCUS
A classy renewal of this historic and valuable handicap, and solid form. The Bronze and Silver Cups had given contrasting messages regarding which side, if either, was favoured, and this time the field divided into three groups, with four runners racing down the stands' side and larger groups racing in the centre and on the far side. The two main groups merged after a couple of furlongs though, the runners spreading across the track. The time was virtually identical to that of the Silver Cup. Not many got involved and the form is rated through the second and third, with the winner not an obvious improver on profile.

NOTEBOOK
Captain Ramius(IRE) chased the pace near the centre before storming clear inside the final furlong for an emphatic win. Fresher than most, he was having just his third run since returning from the Dubai Carnival, this following decent efforts in the Bunbury Cup and the Great St Wilfrid. His six previous wins had all come at 7f, but he has had limited chances at this trip and this is a race which puts the emphasis on stamina, especially in ground like this. He was well handicapped on his best form from last summer and is well worth another try in Listed company; he won in that grade at Dundalk as a juvenile for Mark Wallace. Giving trainer Kevin Ryan his third Ayr Gold Cup in six runnings, he's by the same sire as the Silver Cup winner Mass Rally. (tchd 18-1)
Regal Parade made his run from further off the gallop than the winner and came home in good style. Successful in this race back in 2008 when trained by David Nicholls, he is without a win since taking the 2010 Prix Maurice de Gheest, but had signalled a return to form in a first-time tongue tie at Bath on his latest start.
Maarek, for whom this race came as something of an afterthought, ran very well off 114. The ground was fine for the penalised Irish challenger, successful twice at Group 3 level in testing conditions this term, including a defeat of Regal Parade and July Cup winner Mayson at Newcastle in June. Fourth in last year's Silver Cup from a mark of 89, he has developed into a very smart sprinter. (op 9-1)
Sholaan(IRE) ◆ still held a clear advantage on the approach to the final furlong and it seemed that he was not going to be caught, but he could not maintain his strong gallop. He had been off the track since June with a bout of ringworm, but had impressed when slamming sprinters his own age in a valuable race at York earlier that month, when a stone lower than today. This was only his third run at sprint trips, and he may have more to offer. (op 14-1)
Colonel Mak, the Silver Cup winner in 2010 and fourth in this last year, has edged down the weights and is well suited to the demands of these big-field sprints.
Brae Hill(IRE) led the centre-field group and stayed on well once headed, as befits a horse with sufficient stamina to win a Lincoln. He did best of his trainer's four runners.
Doc Hay(USA) was running on at the end. He was 2lb well in under a penalty for his Portland win, and the Doncaster form had been boosted by Mass Rally in the Silver Cup.
Johannes(IRE) took the Stewards' Sprint at Goodwood and was half a length behind Captain Ramius in the Great St Wilfrid. This was another respectable effort.
Louis The Pious, the winner's stablemate, ran well for a long way. (op 20-1)
Pintura, another from the Ryan yard, likes to lead and could never get into the action in refitted cheekpieces on this drop in trip.
Tariq Too was never a serious factor on his first ever run at 6f.
Our Jonathan, another from the winning stable, was just a pound higher than when taking this 12 months ago and was well backed. He got away from the stalls on terms this time but was under pressure soon after halfway. (tchd 11-1 in places)
Hawkeyethenoo(IRE) has been well held in this event in the past three years now. The gelding needs to pass a stalls test before he can run again. (op 14-1 tchd 16-1 in places)
Borderlescott, runner-up back in 2006, was 3lb ahead of the handicapper under his Beverley penalty but faded after chasing the pace from stall one.
The Cheka(IRE), runner-up in the July Cup this year and back in a handicap for the first time this season, was below par. Ground conditions shouldn't have troubled him. (op 11-1)
Alben Star(IRE), fifth in the Stewards' Cup, faded after chasing the pace. (op 16-1)
Waffle(IRE), in the frame in the Wokingham and the Stewards' Cup, faded after chasing the pace.
Cheviot(USA) was virtually pulled up in the final furlong.

6469 SKED CONSTRUCTION - CONCRETE'S WHAT WE DO NURSERY 1m
4:05 (4:06) (Class 2) 2-Y-0

£9,337 (£2,796; £1,398; £699; £349; £175) **Stalls** High

Form RPR

0336 **1** **Top Notch Tonto (IRE)**[8] 6200 2-9-4 92 DaleSwift(3) 6 97
(Ian McInnes) *hld up towards rr: effrt over 3f out: led over 2f out: wandered fnl f: hld on gamely* **11/1**

21 **2** *1 ½* **Kolonel Kirkup**[40] 5169 2-8-1 72 MircoDemuro 5 74
(Michael Dods) *hld up in rr: drvn over 3f out: chal on ins 1f out: styd on same pce last 50yds* **4/1**[2]

4114 **3** *3 ½* **Bonnie Lesley (IRE)**[28] 5602 2-8-8 79 PaulMulrennan 2 73
(Keith Dalgleish) *dwlt: sn trcking ldrs: kpt on same pce over 1f out* **9/2**[3]

0122 **4** *hd* **Dusky Queen (IRE)**[21] 5836 2-8-10 81 TonyHamilton 3 75
(Richard Fahey) *trckd ldrs: chal travelling smoothly over 2f out: rdn over 1f out: kpt on same pce* **5/1**

2010 **5** *4 ½* **Old Man Clegg**[13] 6070 2-8-2 73 JamesSullivan 8 57
(Michael Easterby) *chsd ldrs: drvn over 4f out: wknd over 1f out* **7/1**

01 **6** *3/4* **Pearl Castle (IRE)**[29] 5534 2-8-10 **81**.............................. GrahamLee 10 63
(Andrew Balding) *hld up towards rr: effrt over 3f out: rdn over 2f out: sn btn* **9/4**[1]

2103 **7** *2 3/4* **Secret Destination**[26] 5670 2-8-5 **76**.............................. BarryMcHugh 1 52
(Brian Ellison) *led 1f: chsd ldrs: drvn over 2f out: wknd over 1f out* **10/1**

01 **8** *9* **Complexity**[41] 5119 2-8-11 **82**.............................. RobertWinston 7 38
(Charles Hills) *t.k.h: led after 1f: hdd over 2f out: sn lost pl: bhd whn eased clsng stages* **14/1**

1m 47.24s (3.44) **Going Correction** +0.325s/f (Good) **8** Ran SP% **122.2**
Speed ratings (Par 101): **95,93,90,89,85 84,81,72**
toteswingers 1&2 £9.70, 2&3 £4.60, 1&3 £17.90 CSF £58.40 CT £236.00 TOTE £18.00: £3.40, £1.80, £2.10; EX 79.40 TRIFECTA Not won. Pool: £927.61.
Owner Keith Brown **Bred** Seamus Finucane **Trained** Catwick, E Yorks

FOCUS
Due to various rail movements, all races on the round course were run over 12yards further than advertised. A fair range of abilities in this nursery and it proved a tough test for these juveniles. The winner has progressed through the year and the first pair were clear.

NOTEBOOK
Top Notch Tonto(IRE), who finished behind today's fifth at York, was 3lb better off here which entitled him to finish upsides. However, he did better than that and handled the testing surface well, hitting the front over 2f out and battling on bravely despite wandering under pressure. (tchd 12-1)
Kolonel Kirkup had built on his debut effort when taking a 7f maiden on fast ground last time. Held up early, he came through to mount a challenge and looked the likely winner over a furlong out, but his effort just flattened out inside the last furlong. (op 9-2)
Bonnie Lesley(IRE), a nursery winner on soft, overcame a tardy start to track the leaders but could only stay on at the one pace in the straight. Racing off 11lb above her last winning mark, she is probably held by the handicapper at present. (op 4-1 tchd 5-1 in a place)
Dusky Queen(IRE)'s trainer was bidding for his third success in eight years in this contest and the filly ran creditably, doing best of those to race close to the pace early on. This was her first try on ground slower than good and she might have not quite got home. (op 9-2 tchd 11-2)
Old Man Clegg, who had shown decent form with cut in the ground, was close enough early but could not respond to pressure on this testing surface. (op 8-1)
Pearl Castle(IRE) had made all when winning his maiden over this trip at Goodwood, but that was on a sound surface and, held up here, he was in trouble well over 2f from home. (op 10-3)
Secret Destination paid for her efforts in the straight and ended up well beaten.
Complexity paid for her efforts in the straight and ended up well beaten. (op 12-1)

6470 WILLIAMHILL.COM DOONSIDE CUP STKS (LISTED RACE) 1m 2f
4:40 (4:40) (Class 1) 3-Y-O+ **£19,848** (£7,525; £3,766; £1,876; £941) **Stalls** Low

Form RPR

4012 **1** **Opera Gal (IRE)**[21] 5844 5-8-13 105.............................. JimCrowley 6 108
(Andrew Balding) *sn trcking ldr: led gng wl 3f out: sn pushed along and drifted towards far rail: clr 2f out: eased ins fnl f* **8/13**[1]

3026 **2** *11* **Circumvent**[14] 6035 5-9-0 98..............................(tp) PhillipMakin 3 87
(Paul Cole) *chsd ldrs: drvn along 3f out: chsd (clr) wnr 1f out: no imp* **5/1**[2]

0200 **3** *nk* **St Moritz (IRE)**[1] 6426 6-9-0 98.............................. AdrianNicholls 4 86
(David Nicholls) *s.i.s: hld up in tch: hdwy on outside to chse wnr over 2f out: one pce fr over 1f out* **9/1**[3]

2-65 **4** *9* **Arrigo (GER)**[14] 6035 4-9-0 110.............................. SebSanders 1 68
(Ibrahim Saeed Al Malki, Qatar) *led: drvn over 4f out: hdd 3f out: sn wknd* **5/1**[2]

3440 **5** *1* **Epernay**[21] 5834 5-8-9 79..............................(tp) GrahamLee 2 61
(Ian Williams) *plld hrd: trckd ldrs to 3f out: sn rdn and wknd* **12/1**

2m 13.94s (1.94) **Going Correction** +0.325s/f (Good)
WFA 3 from 4yo+ 6lb **5** Ran SP% **112.9**
Speed ratings (Par 111): **105,96,95,88,87**
CSF £4.35 TOTE £1.60: £1.10, £2.20; EX 4.40.
Owner J C Smith **Bred** Littleton Stud **Trained** Kingsclere, Hants

FOCUS
A small field for this Listed contest and the Qatari raider stood out on official ratings. It was a weak race for the grade though, and there were doubts over all bar the easy winner. She is rated around her German form.

NOTEBOOK
Opera Gal(IRE) was carrying a penalty for her win in a soft-ground Listed race at Salisbury last month and had since run a good second in a Group 3 in Germany. She was well backed with doubts over her rivals and duly scored in the simplest of fashion, going on over 2f from home and coming right away to score unchallenged. Unless there are opportunities abroad, connections might consider the race that was formerly the St Simon Stakes at Newbury next month for her. (op 5-6 tchd evens in places)
Circumvent has been racing mainly on Polytrack of late but did handle very soft turf in his youth. Fitted with a tongue tie and with cheekpieces re-fitted for the first time in nearly a year, he travelled reasonably well but came under pressure before the winner kicked and could only keep on at the one speed. (op 4-1)
St Moritz(IRE), reappearing after finishing down the field in a handicap the previous day, was held up at the back before coming through to chase the winner, but he is best at around 1m on a sounder surface and his stamina appeared to ebb in the last quarter-mile. (op 8-1)
Arrigo(GER), a Qatari raider, stood out on official ratings, but he had been well beaten on his only try on soft ground and, despite leading, was being ridden along before halfway and had nothing to offer when taken on by the winner. (tchd 11-2)
Epernay handles this ground and had cheekpieces added to the tongue tie instead of the usual visor. She had a lot to find on the ratings though, and never looked like causing an upset. (op 10-1 tchd 16-1)

6471 JOHN SMITH'S H'CAP 7f 50y
5:15 (5:15) (Class 3) (0-95,97) 3-Y-O+
£8,092 (£2,423; £1,211; £605; £302; £152) **Stalls** High

Form RPR

0014 **1** **Common Touch (IRE)**[11] 6119 4-9-2 **89**..................(b[1]) FrederikTylicki 5 99
(Richard Fahey) *hld up: rdn and hdwy over 2f out: led ins fnl f: edgd lft: hld on wl* **9/1**

0560 **2** *2 1/2* **No Poppy (IRE)**[21] 5819 4-8-8 **81**.............................. PaulMulrennan 4 85
(Tim Easterby) *midfield: drvn and outpcd over 2f out: rallied over 1f out: kpt on ins fnl f: fin 3rd: plcd 2nd* **12/1**

5000 **3** *nk* **Xilerator (IRE)**[14] 6024 5-9-4 **91**.............................. AdrianNicholls 8 94
(David Nicholls) *t.k.h: led: rdn and qcknd 3f out: hdd ins fnl f: sn no ex: fin 4th: plcd 3rd* **4/1**[1]

014 **4** *nk* **Fathsta (IRE)**[8] 6192 7-8-9 **82** ow1.............................. JimCrowley 14 85+
(Patrick Morris) *t.k.h: hld up: rdn over 2f out: kpt on fnl f: nvr able to chal: fin 5th: plcd 4th* **10/1**

3660 **5** *1 1/4* **Beckermet (IRE)**[15] 6011 10-8-11 **84**.............................. JamesSullivan 10 83
(Ruth Carr) *hld up: rdn and hdwy over 2f out: no imp fnl f: fin 6th: plcd 5th* **20/1**

0344 **6** *1 1/2* **Alejandro (IRE)**[10] 6143 3-8-13 **89**.............................. TonyHamilton 9 84
(Richard Fahey) *chsd ldr: rdn and hung lft over 2f out: wknd over 1f out: fin 7th: plcd 6th* **12/1**

1040 **7** *1* **Sam Nombulist**[35] 5342 4-8-11 **84**..............................[1] GrahamLee 11 77
(Richard Whitaker) *dwlt and blkd s: hld up: struggling 3f out: sme late hdwy: nvr on terms: fin 8th: plcd 7th* **11/2**[3]

0200 **8** *1 1/4* **Askaud (IRE)**[16] 5980 4-8-12 **85**..............................(b) MircoDemuro 6 74
(Scott Dixon) *t.k.h: chsd ldrs: drvn over 2f out: wknd over 1f out: fin 9th: plcd 8th* **8/1**

2002 **9** *4 1/2* **White Frost (IRE)**[11] 6119 4-9-6 **93**.............................. RobertWinston 2 71
(Charles Hills) *t.k.h: in tch: drvn and outpcd over 2f out: sn btn: fin 10th: plcd 9th* **13/2**

-500 **10** *5* **Dunn'o (IRE)**[8] 6192 7-8-7 **87**..............................(t) ShirleyTeasdale(7) 1 52
(David Nicholls) *plld hrd: in tch: drvn over 2f out: sn wknd: fin 11th: plcd 10th* **20/1**

0000 **11** *6* **Roger Sez (IRE)**[14] 6046 3-8-6 **82**..............................(b) DavidAllan 13 31
(Tim Easterby) *bhd: struggling 1/2-way: nvr on terms: fin 12th: plcd 11th* **7/1**

0006 **D** *shd* **Capaill Liath (IRE)**[21] 5827 4-9-0 **87**..............................(p) PhillipMakin 3 97
(Kevin Ryan) *hld up: rdn and hdwy 2f out: kpt on wl fnl f: jst hld: fin 2nd: disqualified and plcd last - rdr failed to weigh-in* **9/2**[2]

1m 34.43s (1.03) **Going Correction** +0.325s/f (Good)
WFA 3 from 4yo+ 3lb **12** Ran SP% **134.5**
Speed ratings (Par 107): **107,104,103,103,101 100,99,97,92,86 79,106**
toteswingers 1&2 £15.30, 2&3 £19.10, 1&3 £48.50 CSF £127.56 CT £516.87 TOTE £12.30: £3.60, £6.70, £1.90; EX 207.90 TRIFECTA Not won. Pool: £1286.79.
Owner Nicholas Wrigley & Kevin Hart **Bred** Overbury Stallions Ltd And D Boocock **Trained** Musley Bank, N Yorks

FOCUS
A decent handicap, but one with a back-end feel to it and not many arrived in top form. The pace was strong and the principals came from off the gallop. The runners came down the centre of the course in the home straight. The winner is rated back to something like his 3yo best.

NOTEBOOK
Common Touch(IRE) came from out of the pack to cut down the leader, but was being pegged back near the line. He won in first-time cheekpieces at Newmarket two runs back - on fast ground - and the blinkers bucked his ideas up here.
No Poppy(IRE) was shuffled back early and also became a little unbalanced early in the home straight, but she stayed on to grab third, later promoted a place. This ground was in her favour.
Xilerator(IRE), last year's winner, set a strong gallop and looked like taking some catching turning in, but his exertions eventually told. Ground conditions were right for him and this was a bold effort. (tchd 5-1 in a place)
Fathsta(IRE), whose last two wins came in claimers, was doing his best work at the end. (op 9-1)
Beckermet(IRE) had conditions to suit and ran his race again.
Alejandro(IRE), the winner's stablemate, faded after chasing the pace and can be forgiven this given the prevailing ground. (op 11-1)
Sam Nombulist was squeezed out leaving the stalls and never had a chance of getting to the front, but he was running on when it was all over. (op 8-1 tchd 10-1 in places)
Roger Sez(IRE) has tumbled in the weights and came in for support, but she was at the back of the field throughout. Last season's Firth of Clyde Stakes winner has largely failed to find her form this year. (op 10-1)
Capaill Liath(IRE) raced closest to the inside rail in the straight and ran on from the back, but was just held. Refitted with his usual headgear here, he was back on his last winning mark and had shaped well at Chester last time. He was subsequently disqualified after his rider forgot to weigh in. (op 6-1)

6472 ISLE OF SKYE H'CAP 1m 5f 13y
5:45 (5:46) (Class 3) (0-90,82) 3-Y-O+
£8,092 (£2,423; £1,211; £605; £302; £152) **Stalls** Low

Form RPR

1-20 **1** **Albert Bridge**[17] 5944 4-9-12 **80**.............................. JimCrowley 3 94
(Ralph Beckett) *cl up: led after 6f: mde rest: drvn over 3f out: hld on gamely u.p fnl f* **7/1**

4413 **2** *1/2* **Lady Kashaan (IRE)**[14] 6033 3-8-13 **76**.............................. AndrewElliott 5 89
(Alan Swinbank) *hld up bhd ldng gp: effrt and hdwy over 2f out: chsd wnr over 1f out: kpt on fnl f: hld towards fin* **4/1**[1]

6500 **3** *7* **High Office**[14] 6031 6-9-7 **82**.............................. GeorgeChaloner(7) 10 85
(Richard Fahey) *hld up in tch: smooth hdwy to trck ldrs over 3f out: sn rdn: outpcd fr 2f out* **6/1**

332 **4** *8* **Getabuzz**[24] 5729 4-10-0 **82**.............................. DavidAllan 9 73
(Tim Easterby) *hld up: stdy hdwy 3f out: sn rdn: wknd over 1f out* **11/2**[3]

0200 **5** *2 1/2* **Lexington Bay (IRE)**[13] 6074 4-9-13 **81**.............................. TonyHamilton 1 68
(Richard Fahey) *trckd ldrs: drvn over 3f out: wknd wl over 1f out* **8/1**

101 **6** *1* **Stock Hill Fair**[22] 5789 4-9-9 **77**.............................. PatSmullen 7 62
(Brendan Powell) *cl up: rdn over 3f out: edgd lft and wknd 2f out* **6/1**

4500 **7** *12* **Becausewecan (USA)**[14] 6031 6-9-7 **75**.............................. FrederikTylicki 6 42
(Mark Johnston) *in tch: struggling over 3f out: sn wknd* **9/2**[2]

2600 **8** *4* **Odin's Raven (IRE)**[13] 6074 7-9-0 **71**..............................(bt[1]) DaleSwift(3) 8 32
(Brian Ellison) *missed break: bhd and detached: rdn over 4f out: nvr on terms* **20/1**

3322 **9** *44* **Mistress Of Rome**[33] 5413 3-8-9 **72**..............................(p) PaulMulrennan 2
(Michael Dods) *led 6f: sn drvn along: rallied: wknd over 3f out: eased whn no ch fnl 2f* **10/1**

3m 0.41s (6.41) **Going Correction** +0.325s/f (Good)
WFA 3 from 4yo+ 9lb **9** Ran SP% **119.6**
Speed ratings (Par 107): **93,92,88,83,81 81,73,71,44**
toteswingers 1&2 £6.80, 2&3 £3.60, 1&3 £16.30 CSF £36.48 CT £182.48 TOTE £9.90: £2.90, £1.50, £2.30; EX 66.20 Trifecta £589.40 Pool: £1377.97 - 1.73 winning units..
Owner The Cheyne Walkers **Bred** Miss K Rausing **Trained** Kimpton, Hants
■ Stewards' Enquiry : Andrew Elliott two-day ban: used whip above permitted level (Oct 6,8)

FOCUS
By no means a strong race for the grade, with the top weights 8lb lower than the permitted maximum. The pace was strong and again the runners raced down the middle of the track once in line for home. The first two finished clear and the winner can rate higher.

NOTEBOOK
Albert Bridge was up with the pace throughout, racing wide down the back, and stayed on strongly after showing ahead before the home turn. This was a taking performance from the grey, who was on a racecourse for just the seventh time. Still unexposed at staying trips, he's in the Cesarewitch, for which he picks up a penalty, but he might lack the experience for that race. (op 15-2)
Lady Kashaan(IRE) came with a steady run to challenge the winner, but found him a tough nut to crack. She's proven admirably consistent and progressive on contrasting ground conditions this term. (op 5-1)
High Office, whose stable had won the last three runnings of this, momentarily looked like making it four, but after some smooth headway his effort flattened out. He has become well handicapped. (op 11-2 tchd 5-1)
Getabuzz has been pretty consistent this term and he ran respectably again, for all that he was well held at the line. (tchd 5-1 and 6-1 in a place)
Lexington Bay(IRE), another Fahey runner, won this 12 months ago and is back on his most recent winning mark, but he's not quite firing at present. (op 9-1)
Stock Hill Fair, raised 4lb for his Salisbury win, dropped away after tracking the pace. (op 11-2)

Becausewecan(USA) was third in this race two years ago and is currently 17lb lower than at the start of the season, but he was soundly beaten. Freddie Tylicki reported that the gelding was never travelling. Official explanation: jockey said gelding never travelled (tchd 4-1)
Mistress Of Rome won the four-way battle to lead at the first bend, but had to go pretty hard from the stalls to do so and she dropped right away once headed. (tchd 13-1 in a place)
T/Jkpt: Not won. T/Plt: £239.10 to a £1 stake. Pool of £166094.95 - 506.95 winning tickets.
T/Qpdt: £46.30 to a £1 stake. Pool of £7895.72 - 126.0 winning tickets. RY

5733 CATTERICK (L-H)

Saturday, September 22

OFFICIAL GOING: Good to firm (8.2)
Wind: Virtually nil Weather: Bright and dry

6473 BRITISH STALLION STUDS SUPPORTING BRITISH RACING E B F MAIDEN STKS 5f 212y

1:55 (1:55) (Class 5) 2-Y-O **£3,234** (£962; £481; £240) **Stalls** Low

Form RPR

2 **1** **George Rooke (IRE)**[33] 5410 2-9-3 0 AmyRyan 1 78+
(Kevin Ryan) *slt ld: rdn over 1f out: hdd and drvn ins fnl f: edgd lft and kpt on to ld again nr line* **5/6**[1]

03 **2** *hd* **Khelman (IRE)**[16] 5963 2-9-0 0 LeeTopliss(3) 8 77
(Richard Fahey) *trckd ldng pair: hdwy on inner 2f out: sn rdn and styd on to ld ins fnl f: sn drvn: hdd and no ex nr line* **5/1**[3]

2 **3** *5* **Rust (IRE)**[12] 6099 2-9-3 0 PJMcDonald 2 62
(Ann Duffield) *cl up: rdn along and ev ch over 2f out: drvn and wknd over 1f out* **5/2**[2]

3 **4** *2* **Sakhees Romance**[14] 6049 2-8-12 0 RussKennemore 6 50
(Noel Wilson) *in tch: pushed along and outpcd after 2f: styd on fnl 2f: nrst fin* **16/1**

5 *6* **Mr Vendman (IRE)** 2-9-3 0 MichaelO'Connell 4 37
(Ian Williams) *in tch: pushed along bef 1/2-way: sn outpcd* **25/1**

6 *1* **Diddy Eric** 2-8-12 0 GarryWhillans(5) 3 34
(Micky Hammond) *sn outpcd and a bhd* **25/1**

06 **7** *1* **Cosmic Dream**[113] 2667 2-9-0 0 PaulPickard(3) 7 31
(Garry Moss) *chsd ldrs: rdn along 3f out: wknd fnl 2f* **100/1**

1m 14.0s (0.40) **Going Correction** +0.025s/f (Good) **7** Ran SP% **114.4**
Speed ratings (Par 95): **98,97,91,88,80 79,77**
toteswingers 1&2 £2.30, 2&3 £3.40, 1&3 £1.02 CSF £5.60 TOTE £1.50: £1.20, £2.00; EX 6.10.
Owner Kenneth Macpherson **Bred** Rockfield Farm **Trained** Hambleton, N Yorks

FOCUS
Not too many could be seriously fancied for this juvenile maiden. The winner is rated to his debut form.

NOTEBOOK
George Rooke(IRE), the well supported favourite, confirmed the promise of his debut in tenacious fashion. Kevin Ryan's 2-y-os have been in decent form in recent weeks and the colt, who had kept on to finish second in a messy race on his introduction last month, had clearly learnt from that experience as he broke smartly from his stall and was soon in front. He did look in trouble when headed inside the final furlong, but he really knuckled down for pressure and was able to force his head back in front where it mattered most. He and the runner-up pulled a long way clear of the remainder, giving the form a solid look to it. He shouldn't be too harshly dealt with by the handicapper and ought to be competitive in nurseries in the coming weeks. This track was probably sharp enough for him. (op 11-10 tchd 11-8)
Khelman(IRE) ran a solid race. He was able to race more handily than he had at Haydock last time but was ultimately outstayed by the winner. He will now be qualified to run in nurseries and it's likely that his connections will waste no time in pursuing that route as opposed to keeping him to maiden company. (tchd 9-2)
Rust(IRE) had shown bags of promise on his debut on good ground at Newcastle and may have found these faster conditions and sharper track against him. He was readily left behind in the final furlong and looks to have inherited more stamina than speed. (op 9-4 tchd 2-1)
Sakhees Romance was by no means disgraced but she once again found things happening too quickly for her. She had stayed on late to grab third at Thirsk on debut and was again doing all her best work late on. She will definitely be of interest once handicapped and upped in trip. (op 14-1 tchd 12-1)

6474 HAPPY 60TH BIRTHDAY GEORGE LUMLEY H'CAP 1m 5f 175y

2:30 (2:31) (Class 6) (0-65,70) 3-Y-O **£2,181** (£644; £322) **Stalls** Low

Form RPR

0540 **1** **Authentication**[12] 6103 3-8-6 **50** AndrewMullen 2 69+
(Mark Johnston) *led: rn wd bnd after 5f: rdn clr over 2f out: unchal* **5/1**[3]

1022 **2** *13* **Up Ten Down Two (IRE)**[13] 6074 3-9-5 **70** (t) DavidSimmonson(7) 5 71
(Michael Easterby) *a chsng wnr: rdn along 2f out: sn no imp* **10/3**[1]

3142 **3** *6* **Dr Irv**[11] 6126 3-8-12 **63** DavidBergin(7) 15 56
(Kate Walton) *hld up in rr: hdwy 4f out: rdn along over 2f out: kpt on same pce* **9/2**[2]

0051 **4** *1/2* **Ctappers**[37] 5264 3-9-0 **61** JulieBurke(3) 3 53
(Mick Channon) *hld up in rr: hdwy wl over 2f out: swtchd rt and rdn wl over 1f out: kpt on fnl f* **20/1**

3340 **5** *1/2* **Neil's Pride**[9] 6159 3-8-9 **58** ow3 ShaneBKelly(5) 8 49
(Richard Fahey) *in tch: hdwy to chse ldrs over 4f out: rdn along 3f out: sn btn* **10/1**

0000 **6** *1* **Medieval Bishop (IRE)**[12] 6103 3-8-10 **54** DuranFentiman 7 44
(Tim Walford) *prom: rdn along 4f out: drvn wl over 2f out: sn wknd* **22/1**

3325 **7** *1/2* **Schmooze (IRE)**[18] 5921 3-8-13 **57** PJMcDonald 1 46
(Linda Perratt) *in tch: rdn along over 3f out: no hdwy* **13/2**

4465 **8** *1 3/4* **Lady Mandy**[8] 6210 3-8-2 **46** (p) PaulQuinn 14 33
(Ian Williams) *a towards rr* **12/1**

6000 **9** *1/2* **Miss Mohawk (IRE)**[8] 6210 3-8-2 **46** oh1 (p) PatrickMathers 9 32
(Alan Brown) *a towards rr* **100/1**

-550 **10** *10* **Showsinger**[220] 571 3-8-6 **50** AmyRyan 10 22
(Richard Fahey) *hld up: hdwy and in tch 1/2-way: rdn along to chse ldrs over 4f out: sn wknd* **33/1**

260 **11** *nk* **Gangsterbanksters (FR)**[67] 4172 3-8-11 **62** (v) ConorHarrison(7) 4 34
(Mrs K Burke) *prom: rdn along over 3f out: sn drvn and wknd 2f out* **14/1**

2035 **12** *2* **Chankillo**[67] 4200 3-8-11 **60** HarryPoulton(5) 12 29
(Mark H Tompkins) *towards rr: sddle slipped bef 1/2-way: nvr a factor* **16/1**

6020 **13** *52* **Plus Fours (USA)**[19] 5891 3-9-0 **58** MickyFenton 13
(Charles Smith) *hld up in rr: sme hdwy on outer 5f out: rdn along over 3f out: sn wknd* **22/1**

3m 1.76s (-1.84) **Going Correction** +0.025s/f (Good) **13** Ran SP% **118.0**
Speed ratings (Par 99): **106,98,95,94,94 94,93,92,92,86 86,85,55**
toteswingers 1&2 £4.50, 2&3 £2.60, 1&3 £4.50 CSF £20.20 CT £81.41 TOTE £6.30: £2.20, £2.00, £2.00; EX 29.50.
Owner Sheikh Hamdan Bin Mohammed Al Maktoum **Bred** Darley **Trained** Middleham Moor, N Yorks

FOCUS
A competitive, if low-grade handicap on paper but it was turned into a procession. Front-runners did well through the card. The winner clicked and the form is rated through the second and third.

6475 BAPP GROUP 40TH ANNIVERSARY NURSERY 7f

3:00 (3:02) (Class 4) (0-85,79) 2-Y-O **£4,528** (£1,347; £673; £336) **Stalls** Centre

Form RPR

2231 **1** **Lady Of The House (IRE)**[14] 6042 2-9-7 **79** (p) AmyRyan 5 84
(Kevin Ryan) *set stdy pce: qcknd 2f out: sn jnd and rdn over 1f out: drvn and edgd lft ins fnl f: hld on gamely* **4/1**[2]

0125 **2** *shd* **Steer By The Stars (IRE)**[9] 6160 2-9-6 **78** MichaelStainton 8 83
(Mark Johnston) *trckd ldrs: hdwy 1/2-way: cl up 2f out: rdn to chal over 1f out: ev ch whn rdr dropped reins wl ins fnl f: could nt qckn nr fin* **7/2**[1]

060 **3** *7* **Just Paul (IRE)**[24] 5727 2-8-1 **66** ow3 DavidBergin(7) 2 52
(Kate Walton) *prom on inner: pushed along and outpcd after 2f: hdwy 2f out: sn rdn: kpt on u.p fnl f to take 3rd nr fin* **14/1**

6260 **4** *hd* **Team Challenge**[14] 6049 2-8-8 **66** DuranFentiman 4 51
(Tim Easterby) *trckd ldng pair: hdwy 1/2-way: rdn along over 2f out: drvn over 1f out: sn one pce* **10/1**

1235 **5** *3* **Lady Moonlight (IRE)**[10] 6130 2-8-13 **71** PJMcDonald 3 48
(Ann Duffield) *dwlt: t.k.h: in tch on inner: hdwy to chse ldrs 3f out: rdn along over 2f out: sn one pce* **10/1**

3423 **6** *1/2* **Rated**[8] 6189 2-9-3 **78** JulieBurke(3) 6 54
(Mick Channon) *t.k.h: hld up towards rr: effrt 2f out: sn rdn and no imp* **5/1**[3]

216 **7** *hd* **Grievous Angel (IRE)**[13] 6070 2-8-12 **75** (v) ShaneBKelly(5) 7 50
(Ann Duffield) *hld up: hdwy 3f out: rdn along over 2f out: n.d* **9/1**

51 **8** *1 3/4* **Skidby Mill (IRE)**[14] 6049 2-8-13 **71** MichaelO'Connell 10 42
(John Quinn) *t.k.h: hld up: a in rr* **8/1**

0035 **9** *5* **Mirlo Blanco (IRE)**[10] 6138 2-9-1 **73** PatrickMathers 9 30
(Richard Fahey) *chsd ldrs: rdn along wl over 2f out: sn drvn and wknd* **9/1**

1m 27.49s (0.49) **Going Correction** +0.025s/f (Good) **9** Ran SP% **114.8**
Speed ratings (Par 97): **98,97,89,89,86 85,85,83,77**
toteswingers 1&2 £1.20, 2&3 £51.10, 1&3 £20.40 CSF £18.31 CT £177.39 TOTE £3.70: £1.80, £4.60; EX 10.50.
Owner Matt & Lauren Morgan **Bred** Highbank Stud **Trained** Hambleton, N Yorks

FOCUS
A decent nursery, run at a steady pace and the third race on the card to be won from the front. Time will tell if this was quite as good as the extended distances suggest.

NOTEBOOK
Lady Of The House(IRE) followed up her recent Thirsk success. She had opened her account under similar front-running tactics a fortnight previously, was allowed to dictate throughout and kept on gamely to deny the persistent challenge of the runner-up. Both she and the second deserve plenty of credit, as they pulled well clear of the rest and it's likely that she'll be in for a fair rise in the weights once reassessed. It's clear that she was well suited by the lack of early opposition, but she showed a good attitude and should remain a force to be reckoned with in the coming weeks, especially on sharp tracks such as this. (op 7-2)
Steer By The Stars(IRE) ◆, a winner over 6f at Hamilton earlier in the year, can be considered a shade unfortunate with her rider having dropped his reins inside the final furlong. Her previous effort at York looked strong form and she is definitely going the right way. Compensation surely awaits if getting a stronger pace or when returned to 6f. (tchd 4-1)
Just Paul(IRE), racing from 3lb out of the handicap, performed creditably on his nursery debut. He had shown only limited ability in three maiden starts but appeared to take a step up on that here. He was floundering when the pace lifted 2f out before staying on eyecatchingly at the finish. He might be worth a try over longer trips. (op 20-1)
Team Challenge is beginning to look exposed. (op 14-1)
Rated was too keen and was ultimately undone by the slow pace. (op 6-1 tchd 9-2)

6476 PIN POINT RECRUITMENT SEPTEMBER STKS (H'CAP) 1m 3f 214y

3:40 (3:41) (Class 3) (0-95,90) 3-Y-O+ **£9,703** (£2,887; £1,443; £721) **Stalls** Centre

Form RPR

213 **1** **New Hampshire (USA)**[7] 6248 4-9-12 **90** MichaelO'Connell 2 101
(Tony Coyle) *mde all: sn clr: rdn along 2f out: styd on strly* **5/2**[1]

0204 **2** *4 1/2* **Dark Dune (IRE)**[34] 5383 4-9-0 **78** DuranFentiman 1 82
(Tim Easterby) *trckd ldng pair on inner: hdwy to chse wnr over 3f out: rdn along over 2f out: drvn over 1f out and no imp* **18/1**

3311 **3** *1 1/4* **Party Line**[14] 6045 3-9-1 **87** AmyRyan 8 89
(Mark Johnston) *hld up towards rr: gd hdwy on outer over 5f out: chsd ldng pair 3f out: rdn 2f out and kpt on same pce* **11/4**[2]

5504 **4** *hd* **Tres Coronas (IRE)**[38] 5224 5-8-12 **81** LMcNiff(5) 5 82
(David Barron) *chsd ldrs on inner: rdn along 3f out: drvn 2f out and kpt on same pce* **14/1**

2365 **5** *1 3/4* **Hot Rod Mamma (IRE)**[10] 6135 5-9-1 **82** LucyAlexander(3) 3 81
(Dianne Sayer) *hld up in rr: hdwy wl over 2f out: sn rdn and kpt on: nrst fin* **33/1**

6023 **6** *shd* **Northside Prince (IRE)**[45] 4962 6-9-4 **87** GarryWhillans(5) 4 86
(Alan Swinbank) *prom: rdn along 3f out: grad wknd* **8/1**

6445 **7** *nk* **Art Scholar (IRE)**[17] 5944 5-9-5 **83** AndrewMullen 7 81
(Michael Appleby) *hld up in rr: swtchd to outer and sme hdwy over 2f out: swtchd lft over 1f out: sn swtchd rt and n.d* **16/1**

0563 **8** *2 3/4* **Bridle Belle**[15] 6012 4-8-13 **82** ShaneBKelly(5) 11 76
(Richard Fahey) *trckd ldrs: rdn along 3f out: sn wknd* **6/1**[3]

5306 **9** *3* **Tartan Gigha (IRE)**[4] 6339 7-9-3 **81** PJMcDonald 9 70
(Geoffrey Harker) *trckd ldrs: effrt 4f out: sn rdn along and wknd wl over 2f out* **16/1**

1505 **10** *nk* **Royal Straight**[14] 6045 7-8-9 **76** oh1 (t) JulieBurke(3) 10 64
(Linda Perratt) *dwlt and in rr: hdwy into midfield after 3f: rdn along over 4f out and sn wknd* **33/1**

426 **11** *10* **Judicious**[38] 5227 5-9-4 **82** RenatoSouza 6 54
(Peter Salmon) *prom: rdn along 4f out: sn wknd* **16/1**

2m 36.82s (-2.08) **Going Correction** +0.025s/f (Good)
WFA 3 from 4yo+ 8lb **11** Ran SP% **116.1**
Speed ratings (Par 107): **107,104,103,103,101 101,101,99,97,97 90**
toteswingers 1&2 £10.20, 2&3 £10.50, 1&3 £1.30 CSF £48.78 CT £130.62 TOTE £3.30: £1.10, £3.60, £1.50; EX 79.50.
Owner B Dunn **Bred** Everest Stables Inc **Trained** Norton, N Yorks

FOCUS
A hot handicap for the track and a smart performance from the top-weight, another front-running winner. Improved form from New Hampshire, which could be rated a little higher.

NOTEBOOK

New Hampshire(USA) ◆ was the fourth successive winner on the card to make every yard. He has done well since leaving John Gosden in the spring, this his second win in his last three starts having made all to land the Carlisle Bowl at the end of July from the reopposing Northside Prince. However, this was easily his best performance as he left some very useful handicappers in his wake. He took no prisoners through the first couple of the furlongs but, having been allowed to drop anchor out in front, was always holding the aces and stole an unassailable lead as they entered the home straight. Racing off 6lb higher than when previously successful, he is clearly thriving in his new surroundings and looks an exciting prospect for his small yard for the remainder of the campaign. (op 11-4 tchd 9-4 and 3-1 in a place)

Dark Dune(IRE) ran well but lacked the tactical pace to seriously threaten. He was ridden more positively than at Pontefract last time and his followers can have no complaints. (op 16-1)

Party Line ◆, drawn in stall eight, was forced to race wider than ideal and was always well away from the favoured inside rail in the straight when attempting to challenge. In the circumstances there was a lot to like about this effort. (op 10-3 tchd 7-2 in a place)

Tres Coronas(IRE) was another to shape well. He is gradually working his way back down the weights and might be able to take advantage if getting his favoured softer ground.

Hot Rod Mamma(IRE) ran much better than of late and appeared more at home on this sounder surface. Her last three wins have come over 1m and this distance was always going to stretch her.

Art Scholar(IRE), who had beaten New Hampshire over 1m2f at Doncaster earlier in the year, was seen putting in some good late work. Much of his best form has come on more galloping tracks and there's a suggestion he's not too badly treated at present. Official explanation: jockey said, regarding running and riding, that his orders were to settle the gelding in rear and ask for an effort entering straight, the early pace was strong and the gelding settled well, however, when it slowed in the back straight it became trapped on the inside and lost ground, it was unable to handle the undulating ground in the home straight and was slow to pick up when the pace quickened.

Bridle Belle has been a bit in and out this season but arguably prefers flatter tracks. (op 11-2 tchd 13-2)

6477 HAPPY RETIREMENT PAM MAIDEN STKS — 7f
4:15 (4:15) (Class 5) 3-4-Y-0 — **£2,911** (£866; £432; £216) **Stalls** Centre

Form / RPR

3322 **1** **Shaleek**[9] 6154 3-8-12 70 ......(b) MickyFenton 7 — 76
(Roger Varian) *trckd ldr: hdwy to ld 2f out: sn clr: unchal* **5/6**[1]

-424 **2** *12* **Dark Ruler (IRE)**[10] 6136 3-8-12 68 ...... GarryWhillans(5) 5 — 49
(Alan Swinbank) *hld up and bhd: hdwy on inner 2f out: swtchd rt and rdn over 1f out: styd on to take 2nd ins fnl f: no ch w wnr* **7/1**

4046 **3** *3/4* **Benidorm**[21] 5823 4-9-1 50 ......(v) AdamCarter(5) 13 — 47
(John Wainwright) *trckd ldrs: effrt 3f out: sn rdn and one pce* **50/1**

6-23 **4** *1 1/4* **Peak Storm**[29] 5541 3-9-3 73 ...... RussKennemore 11 — 43
(John O'Shea) *chsd ldrs: rdn along 3f out: drvn 2f out: sn one pce* **5/1**[3]

2533 **5** *1 1/2* **Tahnee Mara (IRE)**[38] 5245 3-8-12 64 ......(b) AmyRyan 10 — 34
(Kevin Ryan) *led: rdn along and hdd 2f out: sn drvn and wknd* **4/1**[2]

325 **6** *3 1/2* **Script**[11] 6125 3-8-12 48 ...... PatrickMathers 14 — 25
(Alan Berry) *chsd ldrs: rdn along 2f out: wknd over 1f out* **40/1**

5306 **7** *1 3/4* **Essexvale (IRE)**[23] 5757 3-8-12 43 ......(p) DuranFentiman 6 — 20
(Robert Johnson) *a in rr* **80/1**

5040 **8** *1/2* **Niceonemyson**[12] 6100 3-9-0 52 ...... JulieBurke(3) 12 — 24
(Christopher Wilson) *a in rr* **25/1**

0056 **9** *19* **Brunswick Vale (IRE)**[24] 5728 3-8-5 50 ......(b) DanielleMooney(7) 8
(Paul Midgley) *s.i.s: a bhd* **33/1**

1m 26.23s (-0.77) **Going Correction** +0.025s/f (Good)
WFA 3 from 4yo 3lb — **9** Ran SP% **116.1**
Speed ratings (Par 103): **105,91,90,89,87 83,81,80,59**
toteswingers 1&2 £2.90, 2&3 £33.10, 1&3 £4.00 CSF £7.19 TOTE £1.80: £1.10, £1.80, £5.60; EX 7.70.
Owner Sheikh Ahmed Al Maktoum **Bred** Darley **Trained** Newmarket, Suffolk

FOCUS

Not a great deal of depth to this maiden and weak form behind the winner, who is rated to the bare form.

Tahnee Mara(IRE) Official explanation: trainer's rep said filly had a breathing problem

6478 FOLLOW US ON TWITTER @CATTERICKRACES H'CAP — 1m 5f 175y
4:50 (4:50) (Class 6) (0-65,64) 4-Y-0+ — **£2,181** (£644; £322) **Stalls** Low

Form / RPR

5662 **1** **Artisan**[16] 5967 4-9-1 61 ......(t) PaulPickard(3) 3 — 75
(Brian Ellison) *hld up in rr: stdy hdwy on inner over 3f out: chsd ldrs 2f out: sn rdn and styd on strly to ld jst ins fnl f: sn clr* **10/1**

-022 **2** *6* **Akula (IRE)**[27] 5637 5-9-0 57 ...... PatrickMathers 2 — 63
(Mark H Tompkins) *a trcking ldr: cl up 3f out: rdn to ld wl over 1f out: drvn and hdd jst ins fnl f: kpt on same pce* **6/1**[3]

0052 **3** *1/2* **Singzak**[5] 6311 4-9-0 64 ...... DavidSimmonson(7) 8 — 69
(Michael Easterby) *led: rdn along 3f out: drvn and hdd wl over 1f out: wknd ent fnl f* **11/4**[1]

3-42 **4** *1 1/4* **Royal Bonsai**[28] 5056 4-9-3 60 ...... MichaelO'Connell 12 — 63
(John Quinn) *trckd ldng pair: effrt 3f out: rdn over 2f out: drvn wl over 1f out and sn one pce* **3/1**[2]

0050 **5** *4* **Al Furat (USA)**[11] 6126 4-8-13 61 ...... ShaneBKelly(5) 14 — 59
(Ron Barr) *hld up and bhd: hdwy 3f out: rdn 2f out: kpt on fnl f: could nt rch ldrs* **16/1**

4212 **6** *1/2* **Eijaaz (IRE)**[46] 4912 11-9-2 59 ......(p) PJMcDonald 9 — 56
(Geoffrey Harker) *hld up towards rr: hdwy over 3f out: rdn and in tch 2f out: sn rdn and no imp* **14/1**

1265 **7** *9* **Layla's Boy**[14] 6055 5-9-0 60 ......(bt) RyanClark(3) 1 — 44
(John Mackie) *chsd ldrs on inner: rdn along 3f out: drvn 2f out: sn edgd rt and wknd* **22/1**

2160 **8** *2 1/4* **Ponte Di Rosa**[15] 6019 4-9-4 61 ...... AndrewMullen 13 — 42
(Michael Appleby) *in tch: rdn along over 3f out: sn wknd* **25/1**

2155 **9** *3 1/4* **Highlife Dancer**[11] 6120 4-8-13 63 ......(v) ThomasBrown(7) 15 — 40
(Mick Channon) *trckd ldrs: rdn along wl over 3f out: sn wknd* **9/1**

2144 **10** *11* **Jan Smuts (IRE)**[47] 4867 4-8-13 56 ......(tp) RussKennemore 10 — 17
(Wilf Storey) *midfield: effrt and hdwy on outer 6f out: rdn along over 4f out and sn wknd* **20/1**

-003 **11** *11* **Miss Ferney**[11] 6126 8-9-3 60 ...... DuranFentiman 6
(Alan Kirtley) *a towards rr* **12/1**

0400 **12** *69* **Jim Tango (FR)**[18] 5922 8-8-12 55 ......(bt) MickyFenton 11
(Brian Storey) *a in rr: rdn along over 5f out: sn wl bhd* **66/1**

3m 2.98s (-0.62) **Going Correction** +0.025s/f (Good) — **12** Ran SP% **119.7**
Speed ratings (Par 101): **102,98,98,97,95 95,89,88,86,80 74,34**
toteswingers 1&2 £12.30, 2&3 £4.20, 1&3 £9.10 CSF £66.68 CT £214.57 TOTE £12.80: £4.30, £2.10, £1.60; EX 95.30.
Owner Dan Gilbert & Kristian Strangeway **Bred** Foursome Thoroughbreds **Trained** Norton, N Yorks

FOCUS

A modest staying handicap run at a searching pace, and this time the winner came from the back. The winner is rated back to his best with the next three close to their recent marks.

Ponte Di Rosa Official explanation: jockey said filly moved poorly in home straight

Miss Ferney Official explanation: jockey said mare moved poorly in home straight

Jim Tango(FR) Official explanation: jockey said gelding failed to handle the paddock bend

6479 RACINGUK.COM H'CAP (DIV I) — 7f
5:25 (5:25) (Class 6) (0-65,71) 3-Y-0+ — **£2,181** (£644; £322) **Stalls** Centre

Form / RPR

603 **1** **Drive Home (USA)**[5] 6308 5-8-6 55 ......(p) NeilFarley(5) 2 — 64
(Noel Wilson) *mde all: drvn over 2f out: kpt on: unchal* **5/1**[1]

0335 **2** *1 1/4* **Rasselas (IRE)**[55] 4620 5-8-13 57 ......(v) PaulQuinn 8 — 63
(David Nicholls) *chsd ldrs: kpt on to take 2nd last 50yds: no imp* **6/1**[2]

3443 **3** *1 1/4* **No Quarter (IRE)**[36] 5295 5-9-0 58 ...... MichaelO'Connell 5 — 61
(Tracy Waggott) *chsd wnr: kpt on same pce appr fnl f* **7/1**

5443 **4** *1 1/2* **Bridge Valley**[25] 5720 5-8-7 51 oh3 ......(b) DuranFentiman 4 — 50
(Jason Ward) *mids-div: hdwy over 2f out: kpt on same pce* **16/1**

5540 **5** *1/2* **Star City (IRE)**[5] 6308 3-8-8 62 ...... ConnorNichol(7) 9 — 59
(Michael Dods) *chsd ldrs: edgd rt 2f out: kpt on one pce* **5/1**[1]

5023 **6** *2 1/4* **Berbice (IRE)**[5] 6309 7-8-13 60 ...... JulieBurke(3) 6 — 51
(Linda Perratt) *s.i.s: hdwy over 2f out: kpt on ins fnl f* **9/1**

-150 **7** *hd* **Come Hither**[11] 6127 3-8-10 64 ...... DavidBergin(7) 13 — 55
(David O'Meara) *chsd ldrs: drvn over 2f out: kpt on one pce* **13/2**[3]

-501 **8** *1/2* **Summer Dancer (IRE)**[5] 6308 8-9-13 71 6ex ...... MickyFenton 7 — 60
(Paul Midgley) *hld up towards rr: hdwy on inner over 2f out: kpt on: nvr nr ldrs* **15/2**

6500 **9** *4 1/2* **Lucky For Some**[3] 6361 5-8-7 51 oh6 ......(p) AmyRyan 3 — 28
(Marjorie Fife) *mid-div: lost pl 4f out: sn bhd: kpt on fnl 2f* **33/1**

0443 **10** *2 1/4* **Red Shadow**[12] 6104 3-8-6 53 ......(p) PatrickMathers 15 — 24
(Alan Brown) *chsd ldrs: wknd over 1f out* **12/1**

4600 **11** *10* **China Excels**[24] 5737 5-9-2 60 ...... RussKennemore 12
(Sue Smith) *mid-div: outpcd over 3f out: wknd over 2f out* **40/1**

5P0- **12** *3 1/2* **Weetfromthechaff**[99] 4601 7-8-7 51 oh4 ......(t) AndrewMullen 10
(Maurice Barnes) *in rr: bhd over 2f out* **50/1**

3050 **13** *36* **Monzino (USA)**[36] 5323 4-8-8 57 ......(b) ShaneBKelly(5) 11
(Michael Chapman) *s.i.s: hdwy on outside over 4f out: sn lost pl: bhd whn eased 2f out: t.o* **20/1**

-000 **14** *30* **Stella Marris**[110] 2749 5-8-7 51 oh6 ...... PJMcDonald 14
(Christopher Wilson) *s.s and wnt lft s: detached in last: t.o over 4f out: virtually p.u 3f out* **66/1**

1m 26.46s (-0.54) **Going Correction** +0.025s/f (Good)
WFA 3 from 4yo+ 3lb — **14** Ran SP% **122.4**
Speed ratings (Par 101): **104,102,101,99,98 96,96,95,90,87 76,72,31,**
toteswingers 1&2 £5.80, 2&3 £7.30, 1&3 £5.50 CSF £33.42 CT £222.56 TOTE £6.90: £1.90, £2.20, £3.00; EX 38.20.
Owner Downes Kennedy Tobin Pallister **Bred** Moyglare Stud **Trained** Middleham, N Yorks

FOCUS

A modest 7f handicap and another front-running success. Straightforward form.

Stella Marris Official explanation: jockey said mare jumped awkwardly from stalls

6480 RACINGUK.COM H'CAP (DIV II) — 7f
5:55 (5:55) (Class 6) (0-65,63) 3-Y-0+ — **£2,181** (£644; £322) **Stalls** Centre

Form / RPR

0553 **1** **Hoppy's Flyer (FR)**[7] 6239 4-9-4 60 ......(v) MickyFenton 15 — 71
(Paul Midgley) *trckd ldrs: cl up over 2f out: sn chal on bit: shkn up to ld and edgd lft ent fnl f: rdn clr and styd on* **11/2**[3]

0546 **2** *2 3/4* **Whats For Pudding (IRE)**[7] 6259 4-8-2 49 oh3 ...... NeilFarley(5) 4 — 53
(Declan Carroll) *dwlt and towards rr: hdwy on inner 3f out: swtchd rt and rdn to chse ldrs wl over 1f out: drvn to chse wnr ins fnl f: no imp towards fin* **9/1**

5622 **3** *2 3/4* **Thrust Control (IRE)**[11] 6127 5-9-0 56 ......(p) MichaelO'Connell 9 — 52
(Tracy Waggott) *slt ld 2f: cl up: rdn over 2f out and ev ch tl rdn and hld whn n.m.r and sltly hmpd ent fnl f: kpt on same pce* **3/1**[1]

6440 **4** *hd* **Keys Of Cyprus**[8] 5917 10-9-1 57 ...... PaulQuinn 3 — 59
(David Nicholls) *in tch: hdwy to chse ldrs over 2f out: rdn and styng on inner whn nt clr run ent fnl f: swtchd rt and rdn: kpt on towards fin* **7/1**

25-4 **5** *1 1/4* **Michael's Nook**[253] 153 5-8-11 58 ...... LMcNiff(5) 5 — 50
(David Barron) *cl up: slt ld on inner after 2f: rdn along 2f out: drvn over 1f out: hdd ent fnl f: sn wknd* **4/1**[2]

00-0 **6** *1* **Zavier (FR)**[19] 5889 3-8-10 55 ...... MichaelStainton 11 — 45
(Mark Johnston) *chsd ldrs: rdn along over 2f out: grad wknd* **7/1**

0650 **7** *3/4* **Shunkawakhan (IRE)**[5] 6309 9-8-4 49 oh4 ......(tp) JulieBurke(3) 1 — 37
(Linda Perratt) *sn outpcd and a in rr* **28/1**

2000 **8** *14* **Dansili Dutch (IRE)**[26] 5680 3-9-1 63 ...... RyanClark(3) 14 — 13
(Andrew Crook) *in rr and rn wd bnd 3f out: nvr a factor* **25/1**

0 **9** *3/4* **Romanticize**[11] 6123 6-9-6 62 ...... PatrickMathers 13 — 10
(Jason Ward) *a towards rr* **12/1**

0000 **10** *7* **North Central (USA)**[39] 5185 5-9-1 57 ......(p) AndrewMullen 6
(Keith Dalgleish) *chsd ldng pair: rdn along 3f out: wknd over 2f out* **12/1**

1m 28.08s (1.08) **Going Correction** +0.025s/f (Good)
WFA 3 from 4yo+ 3lb — **10** Ran SP% **118.1**
Speed ratings (Par 101): **94,90,87,87,86 84,84,68,67,59**
toteswingers 1&2 £13.10, 2&3 £1.40, 1&3 £3.40 CSF £54.92 CT £181.86 TOTE £7.40: £2.50, £2.50, £1.20; EX 83.20.
Owner Gap Personnel **Bred** Georges Sandor **Trained** Westow, N Yorks

FOCUS

The second division of this 7f handicap was even more frantically run than the first although the pace collapsed in the straight. It was the slower division. The winner is rated back to something like his best.

Keys Of Cyprus ◆ Official explanation: jockey said gelding was denied a clear run

Dansili Dutch(IRE) Official explanation: jockey said filly hung right-handed throughout

North Central(USA) Official explanation: vet said gelding bled from the nose

T/Plt: £9.50 to a £1 stake. Pool of £50982.56 - 3910.06 winning tickets. T/Qpdt: £5.30 to a £1 stake. Pool of £2720.68 - 378.90 winning tickets JR

6443 NEWBURY (L-H)
Saturday, September 22

OFFICIAL GOING: Good to firm (firm in places; (8.2)

Rail moved in overnight to provide fresh ground.

Wind: Moderate across Weather: Sunny

6481 WEDGEWOOD ESTATES E B F MAIDEN STKS (DIV I) — 7f (S)
1:30 (1:32) (Class 4) 2-Y-0 — **£4,722** (£1,405; £702; £351) **Stalls** Centre

Form / RPR

0 **1** **Code Of Honor**[36] 5303 2-9-3 0 ...... DaneO'Neill 9 — 82
(Henry Candy) *disp ld tl narrow advantage fr 4f out: jnd again wl over 2f out and sn drvn: rdn 1f out sn asserted: styd on strly* **50/1**

2 *1* **Granell (IRE)** 2-9-3 0 KierenFallon 11 80+
(Brian Meehan) *mid-div: pushed along and hdwy over 2f out: styd on wl fnl f to take 2nd fnl 50yds: kpt on but a hld by wnr* **28/1**

4 **3** *nk* **Market Town (USA)**[29] 5562 2-9-3 0 MichaelHills 1 79
(Charles Hills) *chsd ldrs: pressed wnr wl over 2f out and stl upsides 1f out: no ex fnl 120yds: lost 2nd fnl 50yds* **9/4**[1]

0 **4** *3* **Inaugural**[22] 5793 2-9-3 0 HarryBentley 7 71
(Roger Charlton) *chsd ldrs: drvn over 2f out: styd on same pce for 4th fnl f* **50/1**

44 **5** *1/2* **Wayfoong Express (IRE)**[15] 5992 2-9-3 0 LukeMorris 3 70
(William Muir) *chsd ldrs: drvn along fr 3f out: styd on same pce appr fnl f* **28/1**

6 *1/2* **Pivotal Movement** 2-9-3 0 RichardHughes 5 69
(Richard Hannon) *chsd ldrs: drvn 3f out: one pce fr over 1f out* **5/2**[2]

7 *1/2* **Brownsea Brink** 2-9-3 0 RichardKingscote 6 67+
(Richard Hannon) *trckd ldrs: rdn and one pce 2f out: styd on again ins fnl f* **20/1**

43 **8** *1/2* **Monsieur Rieussec**[59] 4472 2-9-3 0 JimmyFortune 8 66
(Jonathan Portman) *chsd ldrs: rdn over 2f out: one pce fr over 1f out* **6/1**[3]

9 *3/4* **Esteaming** 2-9-3 0 MartinHarley 2 64+
(Mick Channon) *s.i.s: in rr: drvn 3f out: hdwy over 1f out: kpt on fnl f: nvr a threat* **33/1**

10 *nk* **Arms (IRE)** 2-9-3 0 WilliamBuick 4 63+
(J W Hills) *in rr: pushed along 2f out: hdwy appr fnl f: kpt on clsng stages* **40/1**

11 *1 1/4* **Harwoods Star (IRE)** 2-9-3 0 AdamKirby 18 60+
(Amanda Perrett) *in rr: pushed along over 2f out: green and sme late prog fnl f* **40/1**

12 *3/4* **Noble Gift** 2-9-3 0 IanMongan 16 58
(John Dunlop) *in tch: rdn 3f out: wknd fr 2f out* **66/1**

13 *hd* **Bit Of A Gift (FR)** 2-9-3 0 NeilCallan 10 58+
(Roger Varian) *in tch: rdn 3f out: wknd 1f out* **8/1**

14 *3/4* **Not Rigg (USA)** 2-9-3 0 (t) JamieSpencer 12 56
(Andrew Balding) *s.i.s: outpcd most of way* **16/1**

15 *3/4* **Short Squeeze (IRE)** 2-9-3 0 WayneLordan 17 54
(Hugo Palmer) *outpcd most of way* **16/1**

0 **16** *3/4* **Adeem (USA)**[8] 6204 2-9-3 0 PaulHanagan 13 52
(John Dunlop) *outpcd most of way* **40/1**

00 **17** *1/2* **Rockpool**[16] 5977 2-8-12 0 JamesDoyle 15 45
(Roger Charlton) *pressed wnr 3f: wknd over 2f out* **66/1**

0 **18** *nse* **Kastini**[23] 5765 2-9-3 0 ShaneKelly 14 50
(Denis Coakley) *chsd ldrs 4f* **150/1**

1m 25.72s (0.02) **Going Correction** -0.20s/f (Firm) **18** Ran SP% **126.0**
Speed ratings (Par 97): **91,89,89,86,85 84,84,83,82,82 81,80,80,79,78 77,76,76**
toteswingers 1&2 £104.50, 1&3 £37.60, 2&3 £11.90 CSF £1085.79 TOTE £48.60: £8.80, £5.30, £1.60; EX 365.80.
Owner D B Clark/ J J Byrne **Bred** J Byrne And Partners **Trained** Kingston Warren, Oxon

FOCUS
The ground had quickened up a touch and was given as good to firm, firm in places (GoingStick 8.2). The rail was out from the 7f point to the 5f pole on the round course, meaning races on the round course were 20m longer than advertised. Very few got into this from off the pace. The third and fifth help with the level, the winner a big improver. Plenty showed promise down the field.

NOTEBOOK
Code Of Honor provided a shock result, but there was no fluke about it, as he was prominent throughout and found extra when challenged. He did have the valuable advantage of previous experience, having finished in midfield here on his debut last month, but this was still a big step up. A half-brother to eight winners, including Listed winner New Deerfield, he's likely to be given a chance to prove himself in better company now.
Granell(IRE) ◆ ran a very promising race on his debut as he hails from a stable whose juveniles tend to need their first runs. He was staying on strongly at the finish and this half-brother to five winners should come on plenty for the experience. A similar maiden should be a formality. (op 25-1)
Market Town(USA) looked to hold sound claims on the back of his debut fourth in the Convivial maiden at York, form that had been franked since, but he drifted in the market beforehand, and, drawn in stall one, raced keenly on the flank without cover. He can do better. (tchd 3-1 in a place)
Inaugural didn't quite see his race out but this was still a big step up from his debut effort at Sandown.
Wayfoong Express(IRE) appreciated getting back on a more conventional track and returned to something like his debut form. He's now eligible for nurseries and might have better opportunities in that company. (op 33-1)
Pivotal Movement, for whom there was plenty of market support, ran well for a long way. He'll be better for the outing and, being bred as he is (by Pivotal out of a Selkirk mare), it wouldn't come as a surprise if he proved happier on an easier surface. (op 9-4 tchd 2-1)
Brownsea Brink ◆ travelled well in behind the pace and, while he didn't find a great deal for pressure, there was plenty of promise in this debut run. A brother to three time 7f-1m winner Secret Hero, he's capable of building on this. (tchd 16-1)
Monsieur Rieussec got warm beforehand and raced a little too keenly for his own good. (op 7-1 tchd 15-2)
Esteaming stayed on from last place to finish in midfield, suggesting there'll be better to come over a mile. (op 40-1)
Arms(IRE) fluffed the start and ran green, so he didn't run badly in the circumstances.
Harwoods Star(IRE) proved coltish beforehand. (op 33-1)
Bit Of A Gift(FR) also showed signs of greenness and hung left when asked to pick up. He should do better in time. (op 10-1)
Not Rigg(USA) didn't get a clear run and wasn't knocked about in a lost cause. Official explanation: jockey said gelding was denied a clear run (op 20-1)

6482 DUBAI DUTY FREE ARC TRIAL (GROUP 3) 1m 3f 5y
2:05 (2:05) (Class 1) 3-Y-O+ **£31,190** (£11,825; £5,918; £2,948) **Stalls** Low

Form RPR

4421 **1** **Black Spirit (USA)**[9] 6166 5-9-3 106 (t) AdamKirby 2 112
(Clive Cox) *trckd ldr: drvn to ld 2f out: hrd pressed sn after tl fnd ex u.p fnl 120yds* **4/1**[3]

3051 **2** *hd* **Lay Time**[28] 5594 4-9-3 109 JimmyFortune 5 111
(Andrew Balding) *racd in 3rd: hdwy 3f out: str chal fr 2f out: stl upsides u.p ins fnl f: nt quite gng pce of wnr fnl 120yds* **7/2**[2]

-166 **3** *3/4* **Coquet**[30] 5518 3-8-7 103 PaulHanagan 4 107
(Hughie Morrison) *t.k.h in 4th: hdwy and pushed along 3f out: drvn to press ldng duo fr 2f out: no ex and one pce ins fnl f* **6/1**

3211 **4** *27* **Cameron Highland (IRE)**[28] 5593 3-8-10 108 NeilCallan 3 61+
(Roger Varian) *led and racd keenly: qcknd pce 4f out: rdn 3f out: hdd 2f out: wknd fnl f and eased whn no ch* **10/11**[1]

2m 21.85s (0.65) **Going Correction** -0.20s/f (Firm)
WFA 3 from 4yo+ 7lb **4** Ran SP% **108.9**
Speed ratings (Par 113): **89,88,88,68**
CSF £16.78 TOTE £4.60; EX 14.60.
Owner A D Spence **Bred** Arundel Farm Llc **Trained** Lambourn, Berks

FOCUS
A modest Group 3, especially with the absence of Arctic Cosmos, and a race that rarely does what it says on the tin with none of the remaining quartet entered for the Arc. Only one 3yo had been successful in the previous nine runnings, but with the classic generation making up 50% of the field, they had a decent chance this time. However, the older horses again held sway, completing a 1-2. The early pace was not at all strong - they raced in Indian file for the first 6f - and with all four runners in a line passing the 2f pole it eventually produced a tight finish between the front three. The first two set the standard.

NOTEBOOK
Black Spirit(USA) finished only fourth in the 2011 running, but came into this fresh from a Doncaster handicap success and he attracted good market support before the off. Having got a nice lead off the pace-setter, he was brought to win his race over a furlong from home, was then headed briefly entering the last before rallying to the front, but still had time to idle and give the runner-up another chance. He was probably helped by the ordinary pace here, as it didn't test his stamina fully, and he did carry his head at a funny angle at times, but he obviously knows how to battle. (op 11-2)
Lay Time showed that she was up to this level when narrowly winning a Group 3 at Windsor last month, but this was her first try beyond 1m2f. Keen enough behind the leaders early, she seemed to have been produced with a race-winning effort entering the last, but she tended to hang about under pressure, losing the advantage, and it was only the winner idling that gave her another bite at the cherry. In view of how close she got, it would be harsh to blame a lack of stamina and it's more likely she found this ground quicker than she cares for. (op 3-1)
Coquet, a dual Listed-race winner, was an unlucky sixth in the Epsom Oaks, but a particularly poor effort in the Yorkshire version in her only subsequent start was harder to forgive. Held up last early, her rider was the first to get lower in the saddle, but by the time the runners reached the 2f pole she was right there on the outside battling for the lead. However, she tended to roll about under pressure and was never quite doing enough to take her to the front. Whilst this was better than at York, she still has a bit to prove and perhaps she also found the ground quick enough. (tchd 13-2)
Cameron Highland(IRE) was bidding for a hat-trick following comfortable wins over four rivals in both an Epsom conditions event and a Windsor Listed contest (second, third and fourth have all won their only starts since). With his stamina not in doubt, it was a bit surprising he didn't set a stronger tempo, but the way he was so easily picked off inside the last 2f before dropping right out suggested that there were other reasons for this dismal effort and the vet duly reported that the colt had bled from the nose. Official explanation: vet said colt had bled from the nose (tchd Evens)

6483 DUBAI DUTY FREE MILL REEF STKS (GROUP 2) 6f 8y
2:35 (2:35) (Class 1) 2-Y-O
£34,026 (£12,900; £6,456; £3,216; £1,614; £810) **Stalls** Centre

Form RPR

15 **1** **Moohaajim (IRE)**[34] 5398 2-9-1 0 AdamKirby 6 114+
(Marco Botti) *trckd ldrs: nt clr run and swtchd sharply lft appr fnl f: qcknd to ld fnl 140yds: comf* **5/2**[1]

0123 **2** *1 3/4* **Master Of War**[21] 5833 2-9-1 108 RichardHughes 7 108
(Richard Hannon) *led: hrd drvn fnl f: hdd and outpcd fnl 140yds* **9/2**[3]

1 **3** *nk* **Taayel (IRE)**[44] 5016 2-9-1 0 PaulHanagan 5 108+
(John Gosden) *hld up towards rr: hdwy fr 2f out: clsng on ldrs whn bmpd and pushed lft appr fnl f: rcvrd and r.o to cl on 2nd nr fin but no ch w wnr* **10/1**

6331 **4** *2 1/4* **Cay Verde**[11] 6128 2-9-1 110 MartinHarley 1 100
(Mick Channon) *chsd ldrs: rdn and ev ch appr fnl f: wknd fnl 120yds* **15/2**

0012 **5** *1 3/4* **Heavy Metal**[29] 5559 2-9-4 110 KierenFallon 3 98
(Mark Johnston) *chsd ldrs: ev ch appr fnl f: wknd: fnl 150yds* **6/1**

2 **6** *1/2* **Cougar Ridge (USA)**[13] 6078 2-9-1 0 WayneLordan 2 94+
(David Wachman, Ire) *s.i.s: sn chsng ldrs: rdn and wl there whn bmpd and pushed lft appr fnl f: wknd qckly* **4/1**[2]

1214 **7** *6* **Lucky Beggar (IRE)**[28] 5601 2-9-1 94 WilliamBuick 8 76
(Charles Hills) *t.k.h: chsd ldr 3f: wknd fr 2f out* **25/1**

10 **8** *1 1/2* **Funk Soul Brother**[95] 3240 2-9-1 0 MichaelHills 4 71
(Charles Hills) *in rr: sme hdwy over 2f out: nvr rchd ldrs and sn wknd* **14/1**

1m 11.19s (-1.81) **Going Correction** -0.20s/f (Firm) **8** Ran SP% **112.4**
Speed ratings (Par 107): **104,101,101,98,95 95,87,85**
toteswingers 1&2 £2.90, 1&3 £5.80, 2&3 £4.60 CSF £13.29 TOTE £3.70: £1.40, £2.00, £2.80; EX 15.10 Trifecta £89.80 Pool: £920.66 - 7.58 winning units..
Owner Sheikh Mohammed Bin Khalifa Al Maktoum **Bred** Castlemartin Sky & Skymarc Farm **Trained** Newmarket, Suffolk
■ Stewards' Enquiry : Adam Kirby three-day ban: careless riding (Oct 6,8,9)

FOCUS
A bit of a messy race. Moohaajim impressed and was value for a little extra. He looks a top prospect. The form is solid and could be worth a little more.

NOTEBOOK
Moohaajim(IRE) ◆ overcame trouble in running to win well. Having stepped up from an Ascot maiden to take fifth in the Prix Morny last time out, he travelled like the best horse throughout here, but for a moment it looked like he might not get a clear run, as he was stuck behind a wall of horses with 2f to run. Switched to take a gap, he gave Cougar Ridge a hefty bump, but he forced his way through and, once in the clear, quickened up smartly and ran right away from his rivals. He has a fast-ground pedigree and clearly underfoot conditions suited him very well. The Middle Park is the obvious next step, but his pedigree suggests 7f, and a mile next year ought to be within his compass. His turn of foot will always be a big asset, and he's a best price 25-1 with Ladbrokes for the 2000 Guineas. (op 3-1 tchd 10-3)
Master Of War, who led the field over to the stands' rail, seems effective on all sorts of ground and had no trouble with the drop back to 6f. He easily reversed Goodwood form with Heavy Metal on 3lb better terms, is a consistent sort and a good guide to the level of the form. (op 4-1)
Taayel(IRE) ◆, the least experienced colt in the line-up, did well considering he was cannoned into a furlong out, just as he was being delivered with his challenge out wide. This was a big step up from a Yarmouth maiden and he did well to shrug off that incident and keep on for third. There ought to be more to come from him. (tchd 8-1)
Cay Verde hacked up in a French Group 3 on soft ground last time but probably found conditions here plenty quick enough. (op 8-1)
Heavy Metal was struggling to go the pace from an early stage. Perhaps his long season is finally beginning to take its toll. (tchd 11-2 and 13-2)
Cougar Ridge(USA), unlucky not to win a Group 3 at the Curragh last time out, was making no significant progress when hampered by the winner. He lost ground quickly after that incident. (tchd 7-2)
Lucky Beggar(IRE), stepping up from 5f, raced too freely early. (op 16-1)
Funk Soul Brother, not seen since finishing down the field in the Coventry but not unbacked, failed to pick up and dropped right out. (tchd 16-1)

6484 DUBAI DUTY FREE H'CAP 1m 2f 6y
3:10 (3:10) (Class 2) (0-105,103) 3-Y-O+
£43,575 (£13,048; £6,524; £3,262; £1,631; £819) **Stalls** Low

Form RPR

6160 **1** **Hajras (IRE)**[14] 6025 3-8-11 96 PaulHanagan 16 109
(Mark Johnston) *stdd s: in rr: hdwy on outer 3f out: drvn and qcknd to ld over 1f out: edgd lft ins fnl f: r.o strly* **13/2**[3]

3210 **2** *1* **Unex El Greco**[42] 5101 4-9-0 **93**.................................... WilliamBuick 17 104
(John Gosden) *stdd s: in rr: hdwy on outer fr 2f out: drvn to chse wnr fnl f and hung lft thrght: kpt on but a hld* **10/1**

1310 **3** *3 ½* **Blue Surf**[14] 6025 3-8-9 **94** 5ex.. JamesDoyle 11 98
(Amanda Perrett) *in rr: hdwy over 2f out: styd on to take 3rd fnl f but nvr gng pce to rch ldng duo* **6/1**[2]

0601 **4** *1 ¼* **Kirthill (IRE)**[29] 5558 4-9-10 **103**.. KierenFallon 5 105+
(Luca Cumani) *towards rr: hdwy fr 3f out: drvn: hung lft and styd on fr over 1f out: one pce ins fnl f* **9/2**[1]

2020 **5** *¾* **Ottoman Empire (FR)**[31] 5492 6-9-5 **98**........................ JamieSpencer 8 99+
(David Simcock) *hld up in rr: hdwy on ins fr 2f out: nt clr run and hmpd ins fnl f: r.o wl clsng stages* **14/1**

0325 **6** *½* **Licence To Till (USA)**[21] 5835 5-9-1 **94**............................ NeilCallan 10 93
(Mark Johnston) *chsd ldr: led 6f out: hdd over 1f out: wknd fnl f* **20/1**

56 **7** *hd* **Lucky Henry**[8] 6205 3-8-0 **85**...(p) LukeMorris 4 84
(Clive Cox) *t.k.h: chsd ldrs: drvn 3f out: styd on fr over 1f out: nvr gng pce to get into contention* **28/1**

0402 **8** *1 ¼* **Chapter Seven**[21] 5820 3-8-6 **91**.. KieranO'Neill 1 87
(Richard Fahey) *chsd ldrs: rdn 3f out: wknd fnl f* **16/1**

1234 **9** *1 ½* **Expense Claim (IRE)**[70] 4094 3-9-1 **100**........................ JimmyFortune 2 93
(Andrew Balding) *chsd ldrs: rdn 3f out: wknd over 1f out* **9/1**

4000 **10** *4 ½* **Fennell Bay (IRE)**[14] 6025 3-8-1 **91**.................. MichaelJMMurphy(5) 12 75
(Mark Johnston) *chsd ldrs: rdn over 2f out: wknd over 1f out* **16/1**

5022 **11** *4 ½* **First Post (IRE)**[8] 6209 5-7-13 **78**.................................(b) CathyGannon 9 53
(Derek Haydn Jones) *in rr: hdwy on outer 5f out: rdn 3f out: wknd 2f out* **25/1**

6303 **12** *4 ½* **Tinshu (IRE)**[21] 5835 6-8-6 **85**.....................................(p) HarryBentley 15 51
(Derek Haydn Jones) *in rr: hdwy fr 4f out: in tch and rdn 3f out: wknd and n.m.r 2f out* **25/1**

2534 **13** *1* **Mister Music**[35] 5364 3-9-1 **100**.................................... RichardHughes 3 64
(Richard Hannon) *in rr: pushed along 3f out: no prog and btn 2f out* **15/2**

5565 **14** *4* **Area Fifty One**[7] 6236 4-9-7 **100**....................................... DavidNolan 14 56
(Richard Fahey) *sn led: hdd 6f out wknd qckly 2f out* **14/1**

-014 **15** *31* **Specific Gravity (FR)**[9] 6166 4-9-6 **99**.............................. IanMongan 6
(Sir Henry Cecil) *chsd ldrs: wknd 3f out: eased whn no ch fnl f* **16/1**

0000 **16** *½* **Pivotman**[53] 4684 4-8-5 **84**.......................................(t) FrankieMcDonald 7
(Amanda Perrett) *chsd ldrs to 3f out: sn wknd: eased whn no ch fnl f* **40/1**

2m 4.31s (-4.49) **Going Correction** -0.20s/f (Firm)
WFA 3 from 4yo+ 6lb **16** Ran SP% **126.0**
Speed ratings (Par 109): **109,108,105,104,103 103,103,102,101,97 93,90,89,86,61 61**
toteswingers 1&2 £16.30, 1&3 £5.80, 2&3 £18.60 CSF £67.70 CT £423.66 TOTE £7.70: £2.00, £2.90, £2.00, £1.90; EX 88.10 Trifecta £397.20 Pool: £1953.98 - 3.64 winning units..
Owner Hamdan Al Maktoum **Bred** Shadwell Estate Company Limited **Trained** Middleham Moor, N Yorks

FOCUS
A hot and competitive handicap, but the early pace wasn't that strong. Even so, none of those that raced close to the lead in the early stages figured in the finish. The front pair, who eventually came clear, started from the two outside stalls, but as a result they were dropped right out and were brought widest with their efforts in the home straight, suggesting they were on the best part of the track. Personal bests from the first two.

NOTEBOOK
Hajras(IRE) came into this less exposed than most having only made his debut in March, but hadn't really had the chance to show his true form in two starts since winning over this trip off 6lb lower at Ascot in July. He showed his true colours here, though, and having been given a patient ride early, produced an explosive turn of foot when delivered down the wide outside entering the last 2f. Despite hanging away to his left once in front, he had established enough of an advantage by then to withhold the runner-up. He still has the potential to improve further and can develop into a Pattern-class performer, if not this season then certainly next. (op 9-1)
Unex El Greco is still 4lb higher than when winning over this trip at Newmarket in July and had questions to answer after running poorly at the same track next time, but he put that effort well behind him here. Given a similar ride to the winner, in that he was dropped right out from his wide draw, he followed Hajras through on the wide outside inside the last quarter-mile and quickened up powerfully, but he tended to hang under pressure and could never quite get on terms with his rival. He pulled nicely clear of the rest and, on this evidence, can win a nice handicap in his own right. (tchd 11-1)
Blue Surf, who finished just ahead of Hajras having met trouble when stepped up to 1m4f at Ascot last time, stayed on from the middle of the field to grab third and deserves credit as he didn't come wide for this effort, unlike the first two, and was 7lb higher than when winning narrowly at Goodwood last month. He still doesn't have many miles on the clock and can find a decent handicap. (op 7-1)
Kirthill(IRE)'s stable had won four of the previous eight runnings of this race, including with the high-class Presvis in 2008, and this colt came into the race in fine form having successfully stepped up to 1m4f at York last month. Now 5lb higher and back down in trip, he ran into traffic when trying to get closer passing the 3f pole and by the time he saw daylight it was too late. His main problem may have been that he lacked the speed to get himself out of trouble and there are still decent prizes to be won with him back over further. (tchd 5-1 in places)
Ottoman Empire(FR) ◆ was a big eye-catcher, as having been given plenty to do he repeatedly ran into trouble when staying on inside the last furlong and, although he wouldn't have troubled the front pair, he would have finished plenty closer. He hasn't really built on his narrow defeat by Gatewood at Epsom in June and is now 0-11 on turf, but he has shown more than enough to suggest he can win races on the grass. (tchd 16-1)
Licence To Till(USA), stablemate of the winner, deserves a lot of credit as he was up with the pace from the off and did much the best of those that were handy early, only being seen off inside the last furlong. He holds his form well given his busy schedule, but is 4lb above his highest winning mark.
Lucky Henry ran well considering he was trying this trip for the first time, but is 0-9 since going handicapping. (op 33-1)
Chapter Seven was 2lb well in compared to his revised mark having finished second in a decent Beverley handicap last time (first start since being gelded), but even though he was never too far off the pace, he didn't get home and this ground would have been quick enough. (op 20-1)
Expense Claim(IRE) was back in a handicap off a 15lb higher mark than when completing a hat-trick over C&D in the spring, but his biggest problem was that he raced too keenly in a handy position early and paid the penalty. (op 15-2)

6485 DUBAI INTERNATIONAL AIRPORT WORLD TROPHY (GROUP 3) 5f 34y
3:45 (3:52) (Class 1) 3-Y-O+
£31,190 (£11,825; £5,918; £2,948; £1,479; £742) **Stalls** Centre

Form RPR

2105 **1** **Swiss Spirit**[27] 5648 3-8-13 103.. WilliamBuick 4 113+
(David Elsworth) *hld up in rr: drvn and hdwy over 1f out: styd on u.p to ld fnl 120yds: edgd rt: hld on wl* **3/1**[1]

40-0 **2** *shd* **Kingsgate Native (IRE)**[10] 6140 7-9-0 110...................... ShaneKelly 10 113+
(Robert Cowell) *trcking ldrs: nt clr run 1f out and ins fnl f: swtchd rt and str run fnl 100yds: jst failed* **7/1**

3122 **3** *1* **Taajub (IRE)**[42] 5077 5-9-0 103.. IanMongan 7 109
(Peter Crate) *trckd ldrs: pushed along but nt seeing much daylight ins fnl f: drvn and qcknd fnl 100yds to take 3rd clsng stages* **6/1**[3]

1303 **4** *hd* **Excelette (IRE)**[10] 6140 3-8-10 105............................. RoystonFfrench 6 105
(Bryan Smart) *pressed ldrs: slt advantage appr 2f out: jnd 1f out: sn narrowly hdd: one pce fnl 120yds: lost 3rd clsng stages* **11/2**[2]

1150 **5** *½* **Tiddliwinks**[29] 5561 6-9-5 112... NeilCallan 5 111
(Kevin Ryan) *chsd ldrs: chal 1f out: slt ld ins fnl f: hdd and outpcd fnl 120yds* **8/1**

0010 **6** *hd* **Desert Law (IRE)**[28] 5581 4-9-0 105.............................. JimmyFortune 3 106
(Andrew Balding) *chsd ldrs: rdn over 1f out: styd on same pce ins fnl f* **7/1**

2531 **7** *1* **My Girl Anna (IRE)**[27] 5641 5-9-0 106................................. RoryCleary 1 102
(Muredach Kelly, Ire) *pressed ldrs: chal fr 2f out: stl disputing ld 1f out: wknd ins fnl f* **8/1**

3150 **8** *nk* **Angels Will Fall (IRE)**[29] 5561 3-8-10 103.................. PaulHanagan 11 105+
(Charles Hills) *in rr: hdwy: swtchd lft and nt clr run ins fnl f: nt rcvr* **7/1**

0003 **9** *2 ¼* **Secret Witness**[7] 6244 6-9-0 106....................................(b) JamesDoyle 9 93
(Ronald Harris) *rdn 1/2-way: a outpcd* **10/1**

0003 **10** *10* **Judge 'n Jury**[27] 5641 8-9-0 103.......................................(t) LukeMorris 8 57
(Ronald Harris) *led tl hdd appr fnl 2f: wknd qckly over 1f out* **16/1**

59.81s (-1.59) **Going Correction** -0.20s/f (Firm)
WFA 3 from 4yo+ 1lb **10** Ran SP% **129.4**
Speed ratings (Par 113): **104,103,102,101,101 100,99,98,95,79**
toteswingers 1&2 £4.10, 1&3 £3.90, 2&3 £8.10 CSF £27.60 TOTE £3.90: £1.70, £2.70, £2.20; EX 27.80 Trifecta £310.30.
Owner Lordship Stud **Bred** Lordship Stud **Trained** Newmarket, Suffolk

FOCUS
A false start was called after Ballista burst his stall, and the gelding was later withdrawn (5/1, deduct 15p in the £ under R4). In the re-run, they congregated on the stands' side and the race played into the hands of those ridden with a bit of patience. The winner posted a 7lb personal best at face value, with Kingsgate Native close to last year's Nunthorpe form.

NOTEBOOK
Swiss Spirit is a strong traveller over 6f and the drop back to the minimum promised to suit. Avoiding any trouble in running by challenging wide, he got a clear passage while his main rivals were waiting for gaps to arrive, and getting first run on them proved crucial. He could take his chance in the Abbaye next, and he wouldn't be without a chance in an open race. (old market op 4-1 new market)
Kingsgate Native(IRE), who ran as though he would benefit from the outing on his reappearance at Doncaster, was officially best in at the weights. Having looked like he might not get a run, a nice gap opened up next to the rail for him inside the last and he finished strongly to almost join the winner on the line. Although winless since May 2010, he clearly retains plenty of ability. (old market op 15-2 new market op 8-1)
Taajub(IRE), a quietly progressive handicapper this summer, finished well but quite not at the speed of the runner-up. Nevertheless, this was arguably another career-best. (old market op 10-1 new market)
Excelette(IRE) had conditions to suit and posted a solid effort, especially as she was up there the whole way, and considering that she apparently lost a shoe during the race. Official explanation: jockey said filly lost a shoe; vet said filly returned sore. (old market tchd 15-2 new market)
Tiddliwinks faced no easy task under his 5lb penalty. (old market op 11-1 new market)
Desert Law(IRE), who got no cover on the outside, tends to be found out at pattern level. (old market op 14-1 new market op 8-1)
My Girl Anna(IRE) has shown her best form in testing conditions, and the ground may have been too quick for her. Official explanation: trainer said mare sat down in stalls and grazed its hocks. (old market op 12-1 new market)
Angels Will Fall(IRE) ◆ travelled better than anything in behind the pace but the gaps didn't come for her and she finished the race having not been asked for maximum effort. She's much better than her finishing position suggests. Official explanation: jockey said filly was denied a clear run (old market op 15-2 new market)
Secret Witness, who seems to prefer the hustle and bustle of big-field handicaps, never got competitive. (old market op 12-1 new market)

6486 WEDGEWOOD ESTATES E B F MAIDEN STKS (DIV II) 7f (S)
4:20 (4:25) (Class 4) 2-Y-O **£4,722** (£1,405; £702; £351) **Stalls** Centre

Form RPR

1 **Race And Status (IRE)** 2-9-3 0.................................. JimmyFortune 10 85+
(Andrew Balding) *trckd ldrs: drvn and qcknd to ld ins fnl f: styd on strly* **7/1**[3]

33 **2** *2 ¼* **Bright Strike (USA)**[29] 5562 2-9-3 0.............................. WilliamBuick 18 79
(John Gosden) *w ld: led after 2f: drvn ins fnl 2f: hdd ins fnl f and sn nt pce of wnr but kpt on wl for 2nd* **5/4**[1]

3 *1 ½* **Dalgig** 2-9-3 0.. DaneO'Neill 1 75+
(Henry Candy) *wnt lft s: sn chsng ldrs: pushed along 2f out: styd on same pce fnl f* **14/1**

2 **4** *shd* **Sublimation (IRE)**[99] 3119 2-9-3 0...................................... ShaneKelly 8 75+
(Richard Hannon) *towards rr: hdwy fr 2f out: styd on wl fnl f to take 4th last strides: nt trble ldng trio* **25/1**

03 **5** *½* **Correggio**[22] 5792 2-9-3 0.. RichardHughes 2 74
(Richard Hannon) *led 2f: styd pressing ldr tl over 2f out whn rdn: one pce fnl f: wknd fnl 100yds: lost 4th last strides* **9/2**[2]

0 **6** *2 ¼* **Shaishee (USA)**[62] 4362 2-9-3 0...................................... PaulHanagan 5 68+
(Charles Hills) *in tch: hdwy over 2f out: sn pushed along: styd on same pce appr fnl f* **11/1**

7 *4* **Epic Charm** 2-8-12 0.. MartinHarley 12 52
(Mick Channon) *in tch: drvn 2f out: styd on same pce* **50/1**

8 *¾* **Patently (IRE)** 2-9-3 0.. KierenFallon 9 55
(Brian Meehan) *in tch: rdn 3f out: one pce fnl 2f* **28/1**

9 *¾* **David's Secret** 2-8-12 0... CharlesBishop(5) 6 53+
(Hughie Morrison) *in rr: hdwy and nt clr run 1f out: kpt on clsng stages* **25/1**

00 **10** *¾* **Noble Bacchus (IRE)**[16] 5962 2-9-3 0................. RichardKingscote 16 51
(Tom Dascombe) *in rr: shkn up over 2f out: styd on same pce fnl f* **50/1**

11 *1 ½* **Rundell** 2-9-3 0... JamieSpencer 7 48
(Richard Hannon) *chsd ldrs: rdn over 2f out: sn btn* **25/1**

12 *½* **Liberty Jack (IRE)** 2-9-3 0.. JamesDoyle 13 46
(Roger Charlton) *s.i.s: outpcd: mod late prog* **16/1**

13 *3 ½* **Ebony Roc (IRE)** 2-9-3 0.................................... FrankieMcDonald 11 37
(Amanda Perrett) *in rr: mod last prog* **40/1**

14 *hd* **Shy Bride (IRE)** 2-8-7 0...................................... MichaelJMMurphy(5) 14 32
(Alan Jarvis) *in rr: drvn and mod prog over 2f out: sn wknd* **33/1**

15 *¾* **Soul Intent (IRE)** 2-9-3 0.. MichaelHills 4 35
(J W Hills) *in tch to 1/2-way* **40/1**

06 **16** *5* **Sovereign Power**[29] 5534 2-9-3 0.. NeilCallan 3 22
(Paul Cole) *chsd ldrs: rdn and btn over 2f out* **100/1**

17 *2 ½* **Mombasa** 2-9-3 0.. IanMongan 17 15
(John Dunlop) *s.i.s: a in rr* **16/1**

18 1 ½ **Paternoster** 2-9-3 0 .... HarryBentley 15 11
(Roger Charlton) *slowly away: a bhd* **25/1**

1m 24.86s (-0.84) **Going Correction** -0.20s/f (Firm) **18** Ran SP% **133.5**
Speed ratings (Par 97): **96,93,91,91,91 88,83,83,82,81 79,79,75,74,73 68,65,63**
toteswingers 1&2 £2.80, 1&3 £16.30, 2&3 £6.60 CSF £15.62 TOTE £9.20: £2.90, £1.10, £4.30; EX 24.00.
Owner Jackie & George Smith **Bred** John Connaughton **Trained** Kingsclere, Hants

FOCUS
The field were soon racing as one group towards the nearside rail and the winning time was 0.26 seconds faster than the first division. The winner impressed and the second ran to his pre-race mark. Several can improve on the bare form.

NOTEBOOK
Race And Status(IRE) ◆, a 240,000gns half-brother to three winners including the dual Group 3 winner Dunboyne Express, is out of a half-sister to the Oaks winner Love Divine. He very much knew his job here, travelling powerfully to tackle the favourite a furlong from home and pulling nicely clear once sent about his business. In seeing off a rival with some very decent maiden form on the board with such authority, he has marked himself down as a colt to follow and his progress will be watched with keen interest. (op 11-1)
Bright Strike(USA) had finished third in maidens at Newmarket and York in his first two starts and the form of both races could hardly have worked out better (winner of the York race won the Haynes, Hanson and Clark here the previous day). He set a very high standard to aim at here and the market certainty believed this would be his day, but having made much of the running he again came up against a rival with real potential and was comfortably brushed aside by him from the furlong pole. It's still only a matter of time before he lands his maiden, but his Dewhurst and Racing Post Trophy entries are now looking optimistic. (op 2-1)
Dalgig ◆, whose stable won the first division with a once-raced colt, ran a fine debut especially as he saw plenty of daylight in a handy position and wasn't dropped until inside the last furlong. A 70,000gns half-brother to four winners including the Listed-winner Nantyglo, he looks a sure-fire future winner and should improve for further. (op 6-1)
Sublimation(IRE), not seen since finishing a well-beaten second of four when favourite for his Sandown debut in June, was deserted by Richard Hughes here but ultimately did best of the Hannon trio and was noted staying on in taking style over the last couple of furlongs. The break since his debut may have done him some good and he can break his duck before too long. (op 16-1)
Correggio finished just behind a subsequent winner when a close third in a Sandown maiden on his second start and he held every chance in a handy position here, but seemed not to get home and his rider reported that the colt ran too free. There is a mix of speed and stamina on the dam's side of his pedigree and this effort suggests this is far as he wants for now. He now qualifies for a nursery mark. Official explanation: jockey said colt ran too free. (tchd 7-2 and 5-1)
Shaishee(USA) was a disappointing second-favourite on his Ascot debut in July and didn't find a great deal off the bridle here after travelling well for a long way. He is going to have to find plenty more improvement to justify his $325,000 price tag. (op 9-1 tchd 12-1)
Epic Charm, a 22,000gns filly out of a 1m winner in France, showed signs of ability on this debut against the boys and can find easier opportunities.
Patently(IRE), out of a dam who is closely related to a winner at up to 1m3f in the US, also showed ability until tiring over a furlong from home and, like many from his stable, is likely to be much sharper next time. (op 25-1 tchd 20-1)

6487 DUBAI DUTY FREE NURSERY 6f 8y
4:55 (4:59) (Class 3) (0-95,90) 2-Y-O
£7,158 (£2,143; £1,071; £535; £267; £134) **Stalls** Centre

Form RPR
145 **1** **Professor**[18] 5904 2-9-7 **90** .... RichardHughes 7 95
(Richard Hannon) *chsd ldrs: rdn to ld 1f out: drvn out* **9/1**[3]
0650 **2** *hd* **Pay Freeze (IRE)**[9] 6162 2-9-7 **90** .... JamieSpencer 16 94
(Mick Channon) *in rr: swtchd lft and rapid hdwy ins fnl 2f: pressed wnr jst ins fnl f: no ex cl home* **16/1**
51 **3** *2 ¼* **Brazen**[41] 5121 2-8-12 **81** .... WilliamBuick 14 79
(David Simcock) *towards rr: hdwy 2f out: drvn to press wnr 1f out: styd on same pce fnl f* **7/2**[1]
021 **4** *¾* **African Oil (FR)**[17] 5948 2-8-9 **78** .... MichaelHills 2 73
(Charles Hills) *chsd ldrs: rdn over 2f out: one pce fnl f* **6/1**[2]
1663 **5** *2 ¼* **Dominate**[14] 6022 2-9-4 **87** .... DaneO'Neill 12 77
(Richard Hannon) *in rr: hdwy over 1f out: styd on wl fnl f: nt rch ldrs* **9/1**[3]
6163 **6** *¾* **Prince Regal**[10] 6138 2-8-6 **80** .... MichaelJMMurphy(5) 3 66
(Alan Jarvis) *chsd ldrs: rdn over 2f out: wknd ins fnl f* **12/1**
5423 **7** *½* **Normal Equilibrium**[18] 5903 2-9-6 **89** ....(b[1]) HarryBentley 9 74
(Roger Varian) *led after 1f: hdd & wknd 1f out* **9/1**[3]
4113 **8** *shd* **Capo Rosso (IRE)**[14] 6032 2-9-1 **84** .... RichardKingscote 1 69
(Tom Dascombe) *led 1f: chsd ldrs: rdn 1/2-way: wknd fnl f* **10/1**
0150 **9** *nk* **Royal Aspiration (IRE)**[14] 6022 2-9-0 **83** .... KierenFallon 5 67+
(William Haggas) *chsd ldrs: drvn 2f out: wknd fnl f* **16/1**
6531 **10** *2* **Sejalaat (IRE)**[18] 5903 2-9-0 **83** .... PaulHanagan 10 61
(John Dunlop) *in rr: drvn and sme hdwy fr 2f out: nvr rchd ldrs: wknd fnl f* **9/1**[3]
6120 **11** *1* **Derwent (USA)**[14] 6032 2-9-1 **84** ....(b[1]) JamesDoyle 4 59
(Roger Charlton) *in tch: rdn over 2f out and sn btn* **20/1**
030 **12** *½* **Jubilee Brig**[29] 5563 2-9-1 **84** .... JimmyFortune 6 57
(Gary Moore) *s.i.s: in tch: rdn over 2f out: styd on same pce* **16/1**
6146 **13** *shd* **Jollification (IRE)**[36] 5307 2-9-1 **89** .... DavidKenny(5) 15 62
(George Baker) *nvr gng pce to rch ldrs* **33/1**
021 **14** *3 ½* **Seven Of Clubs (IRE)**[28] 5586 2-8-7 **76** .... KieranO'Neill 13 38
(Noel Quinlan) *nvr gng pce to get beyond mid-div* **14/1**
2402 **15** *4 ½* **The Black Jacobin**[14] 6042 2-8-5 **77** .... RaulDaSilva(3) 11 26
(J S Moore) *outpcd most of way* **40/1**
6062 **16** *¾* **Cuisine (IRE)**[19] 5886 2-8-5 **74** ....(b) FrankieMcDonald 8 21
(Andrew Balding) *spd over 3f* **50/1**

1m 11.41s (-1.59) **Going Correction** -0.20s/f (Firm) **16** Ran SP% **129.7**
Speed ratings (Par 99): **102,101,98,97,94 93,93,92,92,89 88,87,87,83,77 76**
toteswingers 1&2 £25.90, 1&3 £6.60, 2&3 £23.80 CSF £149.84 CT £640.80 TOTE £7.30: £2.50, £4.20, £1.80, £2.20; EX 122.80.
Owner Mrs P Good **Bred** Exors Of The Late J R Good **Trained** East Everleigh, Wilts

FOCUS
A competitive nursery in which the joint top-weights came to the fore. The winner built on earlier promise and this is solid nursery form.

NOTEBOOK
Professor was dropping back to 6f having raced too keenly and not got home over 7f in small-field races in his previous two starts. Having a good pace to chase in this big field allowed him to settle, and he came through with a strong run inside the last 2f. He's clearly talented and, when conditions are suitable, could yet make his mark in better company down the road. (op 13-2)
Pay Freeze(IRE) had been disappointing in his last two starts, but a return to fast ground, on which he won his maiden back in May, brought about a return to form. He wasn't best away but was suited by the way race was run, and picked up well from off the good pace set by his owner's other runner Normal Equilibrium. He wandered about a little in front, giving the winner the opportunity to run him down, though.
Brazen, who bolted up in a weak Folkestone maiden last time out, was the least experienced runner in the line-up. He ran a sound race in defeat and can only improve. (op 9-2 tchd 5-1)
African Oil(FR), a winner at Lingfield last time, holds a Middle Park entry, which is clearly very optimistic, but he's not short of ability as he kept on well on the far side having been carried left by the runner-up. (op 7-1)
Dominate didn't get the clearest of runs but finished well once switched to the stands' rail. The return to 6f seemed to suit him. (op 10-1)
Prince Regal were never too far away and he helps set a level for the form. (op 14-1)
Capo Rosso(IRE) Official explanation: jockey said colt had no more to give.
Royal Aspiration(IRE) weakened after showing early pace. (tchd 14-1)
Sejalaat(IRE) struggled to pick up after being hampered with over 2f to run. (op 10-1)
Derwent(USA) didn't improve for the fitting of blinkers, and he just hasn't progressed from his maiden win.

6488 HEATHERWOLD STUD H'CAP 7f (S)
5:30 (5:33) (Class 4) (0-80,80) 3-Y-O **£5,175** (£1,540; £769; £384) **Stalls** Centre

Form RPR
6003 **1** **Muarrab**[18] 5910 3-9-4 **77** .... PaulHanagan 12 87+
(Ed Dunlop) *hld up towards rr: stdy hdwy fr 2f out: led 1f out: pushed out fnl f: comf* **5/1**[1]
0640 **2** *1* **Shamrocked (IRE)**[14] 6048 3-8-6 **70** ....[1] CharlesBishop(5) 14 77
(Mick Channon) *led: rdn over 2f out: hdd 1f out: sn nt pce of wnr but hld on wl u.p for 2nd* **20/1**
-200 **3** *nse* **Dare To Dream**[14] 6023 3-9-7 **80** .... RichardHughes 6 87
(Richard Hannon) *towards rr: hdwy and drvn fr 2f out: styd on wl fnl f to cl on 2nd nr fin but nt pce of wnr* **11/2**[2]
4125 **4** *nk* **Jack Of Diamonds (IRE)**[25] 5705 3-9-2 **75** .... JamesDoyle 16 81
(Roger Teal) *in tch: drvn 2f out: styd on fnl f but nvr gng pce to chal* **12/1**
0625 **5** *hd* **Wahylah (IRE)**[14] 6023 3-9-6 **79** .... NeilCallan 18 85
(Clive Brittain) *in tch: rdn 2f out: hdwy fnl f: kpt on clsng stages* **8/1**[3]
1 **6** *½* **An Cat Dubh (IRE)**[35] 5335 3-9-6 **79** ....(p) KierenFallon 4 83
(Ian Williams) *chsd ldrs: rdn over 2f out: styd on same pce ins fnl f* **5/1**[1]
2544 **7** *½* **Serene Oasis (IRE)**[9] 6172 3-9-0 **73** ....(v) MartinHarley 3 76
(Mick Channon) *chsd ldrs: rdn over 2f out: wknd fnl f* **16/1**
001 **8** *¾* **Cockney Dancer**[9] 6176 3-9-7 **80** .... MichaelHills 13 81
(Charles Hills) *chsd ldrs: rdn over 2f out: wknd fnl f* **16/1**
1503 **9** *½* **Hometown Glory**[25] 5705 3-9-4 **77** ....(t) ShaneKelly 8 76
(Brian Meehan) *in tch: pushed along 2f out: styd on ins fnl f: nvr a threat* **14/1**
3113 **10** *½* **Ambitious Boy**[8] 6211 3-8-11 **70** .... HarryBentley 2 68
(Reg Hollinshead) *towards rr: pushed along fr 2f out: sme prog fnl f* **20/1**
4425 **11** *¾* **Al's Memory (IRE)**[14] 6052 3-8-10 **69** .... StevieDonohoe 9 65
(David Evans) *rdn over 3f out: nvr gng pce to rch ldrs* **25/1**
3152 **12** *nk* **Elegant Flight**[25] 5705 3-8-7 **71** ....(v) MichaelJMMurphy(5) 5 66
(Alan Jarvis) *in rr: drvn along 3f out: sme hdwy 2f out: no prog fnl f* **10/1**
61 **13** *¾* **Morning Call**[26] 5687 3-9-0 **73** .... DaneO'Neill 11 66
(Henry Candy) *outpcd fr 1/2-way* **12/1**
3310 **14** *½* **Little Rainbow**[32] 5440 3-8-9 **68** .... WilliamBuick 10 60
(Clive Cox) *sn chsng ldrs: rdn over 2f out: sn btn* **20/1**
0560 **15** *3 ¼* **Gung Ho Jack**[7] 6256 3-8-11 **75** .... TobyAtkinson(5) 17 58
(John Best) *outpcd* **33/1**
134 **16** *2* **Uprise**[28] 5582 3-9-2 **75** .... IanMongan 1 53
(George Margarson) *chsd ldrs over 3f* **33/1**
0400 **17** *3* **O'Gorman**[14] 6026 3-9-2 **80** .... LeeNewnes(5) 7 50
(Gary Brown) *slowly away: a in rr* **33/1**

1m 24.32s (-1.38) **Going Correction** -0.20s/f (Firm) **17** Ran SP% **129.7**
Speed ratings (Par 103): **99,97,97,97,97 96,96,95,94,94 93,92,92,91,87 85,82**
toteswingers 1&2 £77.80, 1&3 £6.30, 2&3 £61.30 CSF £112.59 CT £601.32 TOTE £6.00: £1.80, £6.60, £1.90, £2.20; EX 154.40.
Owner Hamdan Al Maktoum **Bred** Stratford Place Stud **Trained** Newmarket, Suffolk

FOCUS
A competitive handicap, but with not much covering the principals at the line this looks ordinary form for the grade.
O'Gorman Official explanation: jockey said gelding hung right
T/Plt: £169.40 to a £1 stake. Pool: £89,132.26 - 383.90 winning tickets T/Qpdt: £7.70 to a £1 stake. Pool: £6,517.63 - 624.99 winning tickets ST

5578 NEWMARKET (R-H)
Saturday, September 22

OFFICIAL GOING: Good to firm (8.2)
First meeting on Rowley Mile since May.
Wind: light, across Weather: dry, bright spells

6489 BRITISH STALLION STUDS SUPPORTING BRITISH RACING E B F MAIDEN FILLIES' STKS 1m
1:40 (1:42) (Class 4) 2-Y-O **£4,528** (£1,347; £673; £336) **Stalls** Centre

Form RPR
4 **1** **Great Timing (USA)**[18] 5902 2-9-0 0 .... FrankieDettori 8 82
(Mahmood Al Zarooni) *racd far side: led gp and chsd ldrs overall: rdn and ev ch over 1f out: sustained effrt u.p to ld ins fnl f: styd on: 1st of 6 in gp* **9/4**[1]
6 **2** *½* **Vanity Rules**[64] 4297 2-9-0 0 .... RobertHavlin 17 81
(John Gosden) *racd in centre: overall ldr: rdn 2f out: hrd pressed and cdgd rt u.p over 1f out: battled on wl tl hdd and one pce ins fnl f: 1st of 11 in gp* **9/2**[2]
3 *2* **Hold On Tight (IRE)** 2-9-0 0 .... RichardThomas 4 76+
(Ralph Beckett) *racd far side: in tch: rdn and effrt 2f out: swtchd lft over 1f out: chsd ldng pair ins fnl f: kpt on u.p: 2nd of 6 in gp* **9/1**
4 *¾* **Just One Kiss** 2-9-0 0 .... TomQueally 11 74+
(Sir Henry Cecil) *racd in centre: in tch: rdn to chse ldrs over 1f out: unable qck ent fnl f: styd on same pce fnl f: 2nd of 11 in gp* **11/2**[3]
5 *2 ¼* **Fatima's Gift** 2-9-0 0 .... RichardMullen 13 69+
(David Simcock) *racd in centre: rdn over 2f out: outpcd wl over 1f out: rallied and styd on again fnl 100yds: gng on steadily fin but no threat to ldrs: 3rd of 11 in gp* **50/1**
6 *shd* **Beat Of The Drum (IRE)** 2-9-0 0 .... PatDobbs 16 69+
(Richard Hannon) *racd in centre: in tch in midfield: rdn over 2f out: outpcd wl over 1f out: styd on again ins fnl f: gng on steadily fin but no threat to ldrs: 4th of 11 in gp* **16/1**
00 **7** *¾* **Funky Cold Medina**[11] 6117 2-9-0 0 .... AndreaAtzeni 5 67
(Peter Chapple-Hyam) *racd far side: chsd gp ldr and in tch overall: rdn wl over 1f out: wknd 1f out: 3rd of 6 in gp* **50/1**
000 **8** *½* **Olympic Jule**[18] 5907 2-9-0 68 .... J-PGuillambert 15 66
(John Dunlop) *racd in centre: chsd overall ldr tl 2f out: edgd lft u.p and btn over 1f out: wknd fnl f: 5th of 11 in gp* **66/1**

5 **9** ¾ **Poitin**[40] 5153 2-9-0 0 .... HayleyTurner 12 64
(Harry Dunlop) *racd in centre: t.k.h: hld up in tch: rdn and unable qck 2f out: btn over 1f out: wknd fnl f: 6th of 11 in gp* **50/1**

10 *1* **Wadaa (USA)** 2-9-0 0 ....[1] MartinLane 10 62
(James Tate) *racd in centre: v.s.a: t.k.h and sn rcvrd and hld up towards rr: rdn and struggling over 2f out: wknd over 1f out: 7th of 11 in gp* **33/1**

5 **11** ¾ **Cocktail Queen (IRE)**[16] 5977 2-9-0 0 .... LiamKeniry 6 60
(David Elsworth) *racd in centre: rdn and struggling over 2f out: wknd over 1f out: 8th of 11 in gp* **11/1**

12 *nk* **Estiqaama (USA)** 2-9-0 0 .... AdamBeschizza 7 59
(William Haggas) *racd far side: s.i.s: sn rcvrd and in tch in midfield overall: pushed along and struggling 3f out: wknd 2f out: 4th of 6 in gp* **40/1**

13 *3 ¼* **Skating Over (USA)** 2-9-0 0 .... BrettDoyle 9 52
(Jane Chapple-Hyam) *racd in centre: s.i.s: hld up in tch towards rr: rdn and struggling 3f out: wknd over 2f out: 9th of 11 in gp* **66/1**

14 *6* **Golden Leaves (USA)** 2-9-0 0 .... SilvestreDeSousa 2 38
(Mahmood Al Zarooni) *racd in centre: s.i.s: a towards rr and sn pushed along: rdn and wknd 3f out: lost tch 2f out: 10th of 11 in gp* **11/1**

15 *4* **Tumbledown (USA)** 2-9-0 0 .... AhmedAjtebi 14 28
(Mahmood Al Zarooni) *racd in centre: a towards rr: edgd lft towards stands' rail and struggling 3f out: lost tch 2f out: 11th of 11 in gp* **14/1**

0 **16** *4* **Serenata (IRE)**[94] 3282 2-9-0 0 .... FergusSweeney 3 19
(Paul Cole) *racd far side: in tch in midfield overall: rdn and struggling over 2f out: wknd qckly and edgd lft over 1f out: wl bhd ins fnl f: 5th of 6 in gp* **100/1**

17 *5* **Jalasaat (USA)** 2-9-0 0 .... TedDurcan 1 7
(John Dunlop) *racd far side: s.i.s: a bhd: lost tch over 3f out: 6th of 6 in gp: t.o* **40/1**

1m 38.09s (-0.51) **Going Correction** +0.10s/f (Good) **17** Ran SP% **121.2**
Speed ratings (Par 94): **106,105,103,102,100 100,99,99,98,97 96,96,93,87,83 79,74**
toteswingers 1&2 £1.30, 1&3 £17.60, 2&3 £44.90 CSF £10.62 TOTE £2.70: £1.50, £2.00, £4.10; EX 12.80.

Owner Godolphin **Bred** Pin Oak Stud, Llc **Trained** Newmarket, Suffolk

FOCUS

A decent fillies' maiden run at a fair pace. Most of the runners raced down the centre of the track but the winner was in a smaller group on the far side. The time and race averages help with the ratings.

NOTEBOOK

Great Timing(USA) had leading claims on her 4l fourth in a decent 1m Goodwood maiden on debut this month. Always prominent near the far rail, she needed a bit of motivating 3f out but she knuckled down well to justify favouritism. A $370,000 Raven's Pass half-sister to six winners, this late April foal has plenty of scope for further improvement and should stay 1m2f. (tchd 2-1 and 5-2)

Vanity Rules finished just over 4l sixth of ten in a soft-ground 7f maiden on the July course here on her debut. Strong in the market back from two months off, she set the pace down the centre of the track and looked the likely winner 2f out but she put a dent in her chance by drifting to the far side. However, she still deserves credit for going close on this second run and is a scopey filly who is very well-connected on her dam's side. (op 11-2)

Hold On Tight(IRE) ran green on the far side but she kept battling in a promising debut run. She should have learned quite a bit and is out of a 1m3f US stakes winner. (op 11-1 tchd 8-1)

Just One Kiss, a Cape Cross filly out of a winning half-sister to St Leger winner Sixties Icon, tracked the pace down the middle of the track before staying on steadily in an encouraging debut run for a yard which won this with Light Shift in 2006 and Midday in 2008. (op 7-2)

Fatima's Gift, a 60,000gns Dalakhani half-sister to a several winners at 1m-1m2f, got a bit tapped for speed before staying on late on her debut. (op 66-1)

Beat Of The Drum(IRE), a 100,000gns half-sister to 6f winner Passing Stranger out of a 6f US winning half-sister to high-class 2yo Sander Camillo, shaped with promise staying on steadily on her debut. She should improve for the experience and holds a couple of valuable sales race entries here next month. (tchd 20-1)

Funky Cold Medina seems to be quietly progressing and handicaps could be on the horizon after this qualifying run. (op 66-1 tchd 40-1)

Tumbledown(USA) Official explanation: jockey said filly hung left

6490 £100,000 TATTERSALLS MILLIONS FILLIES' MEDIAN AUCTION STKS 6f

2:10 (2:10) (Class 2) 2-Y-0

£55,494 (£25,223; £10,093; £5,036; £3,036; £2,020) **Stalls** Centre

Form RPR

0 **1** **Victrix Ludorum (IRE)**[35] 5352 2-8-11 0 .... PatDobbs 7 81
(Richard Hannon) *chsd ldr for 2f: styd chsng ldrs: rdn to ld over 1f out: styd on strly ins fnl f: rdn out* **14/1**

10 **2** *1 ¼* **Badr Al Badoor (IRE)**[30] 5516 2-9-1 0 .... HayleyTurner 2 81
(James Fanshawe) *hld up in tch in last trio: hdwy to chse ldrs over 2f out: rdn and unable qck on downhill run over 1f out: drvn 1f out: styd on to chse wnr fnl 75yds: no imp* **2/1**[1]

2160 **3** *1* **Mollyvator (IRE)**[9] 6160 2-8-7 76 ....(p) SilvestreDeSousa 6 70
(Mrs K Burke) *racd keenly: chsd ldr tl wnt 2nd after 2f: upsides ldr 1/2-way: rdn and ev ch wl over 1f out: unable qck 1f out: styd on same pce after* **9/2**[3]

0005 **4** *nk* **Shafaani**[21] 5818 2-8-9 69 ....(bt[1]) KirstyMilczarek 3 71
(Clive Brittain) *stdd after s: in tch in last pair: gd hdwy and squeezed between horses to chal wl over 1f out: hrd drvn and unable qck ent fnl f: one pce* **25/1**

12 **5** *nk* **Asgardella (IRE)**[13] 6070 2-8-11 77 .... TomQueally 4 72
(Richard Fahey) *t.k.h: led tl rdn and hdd over 1f out: no ex u.p ent fnl f: btn and plugged on same pce fnl f* **4/1**[2]

0 **6** *6* **Beacon Tarn**[21] 5828 2-8-11 0 .... TedDurcan 5 54
(Eric Alston) *taken down early: chsd ldrs: rdn 2f out: wknd qckly over 1f out* **66/1**

6440 **7** *hd* **Summer Isles**[46] 4927 2-8-11 70 .... ChrisCatlin 1 54
(Ed Dunlop) *stdd s: hld up in last pair: rdn and short-lived effrt ent fnl 2f: wknd over 1f out* **66/1**

1m 12.22s (0.02) **Going Correction** +0.10s/f (Good) **7** Ran SP% **85.0**
Speed ratings (Par 98): **103,101,100,99,99 91,90**
toteswingers 1&2 £1.80, 2&3 £1.20, 1&3 £3.50 CSF £22.84 TOTE £9.80: £2.60, £1.60; EX 21.20.

Owner Mrs J Wood **Bred** Yukiko Hosokawa **Trained** East Everleigh, Wilts

FOCUS

A modest renewal of this valuable fillies' race, and it was significantly weakened by the withdrawal of 99-rated Graphic Guest, who got upset and went down in the stalls (5/2, deduct 25p in the £ under R4). The pace was decent but the third and fourth were rated 76 and 69 and the form does not look strong. Indeed the winner posted just an average maiden figure.

NOTEBOOK

Victrix Ludorum(IRE) finished seventh of ten in a 6f Newbury maiden on her debut last month and had quite a bit to find here, but she travelled well near the pace and produced a good burst to score with something in hand in a much-improved second run. A scopey 75,000gns half-sister to 10.6f AW winner Flying Plover and a 7f 2yo/2m-2m4f hurdle winner Space Telescope, she should continue to progress and is bred to stay much further than this. (op 12-1 tchd 11-1)

Badr Al Badoor(IRE) beat several subsequent winners when making successful debut in a Doncaster maiden in June before finding things tough in the Lowther last time after an interrupted preparation. Well backed for this less competitive race, she cut her way through the pack but couldn't match the finishing speed of the winner. This was a fair effort by this sister to Group-placed 6f 2yo winner Full Mandate but she has not really progressed from her debut win at Doncaster in June. (op 5-2)

Mollyvator(IRE) had been disappointing in two runs since her soft-ground Haydock maiden win but she was a market springer and bounced back with a solid run with cheekpieces applied. (op 7-1)

Shafaani, a 69-rated maiden, had plenty to find but she seemed to excel herself in first-time blinkers. (op 22-1 tchd 28-1)

Asgardella(IRE), runner-up off 73 in a 7f York nursery last time, set a decent pace but she couldn't respond when attacked on both sides entering the final furlong. (op 7-2)

6491 £100,000 TATTERSALLS MILLIONS MEDIAN AUCTION TROPHY 6f

2:45 (2:45) (Class 2) 2-Y-0

£55,494 (£25,223; £10,093; £5,036; £3,036; £2,020) **Stalls** Centre

Form RPR

12 **1** **Tamayuz Star (IRE)**[18] 5904 2-8-11 0 .... PatDobbs 10 94
(Richard Hannon) *hld up towards rr: rdn and hdwy over 1f out: qcknd to chse clr wnr ins fnl f: str run to ld fnl 50yds: r.o* **6/5**[1]

2012 **2** *nk* **Zanetto**[14] 6038 2-8-9 97 .... LiamKeniry 5 91
(Andrew Balding) *led: rdn and qcknd wl over 1f out: drvn and forged clr ins fnl f: hdd fnl 50yds: kpt on same pce after* **7/2**[2]

04 **3** *1 ¼* **Global Icon**[8] 6203 2-8-9 0 .... SeanLevey 6 87
(Richard Hannon) *in tch in midfield: rdn and effrt whn nt clr run and swtchd rt over 1f out: kpt on wl u.p ins fnl f* **25/1**

2120 **4** *1 ½* **Ashaadd (IRE)**[14] 6038 2-9-1 93 ....(b[1]) AndreaAtzeni 8 89
(Roger Varian) *chsd ldrs: rdn and effrt ent fnl 2f: chsd ldr and drvn over 1f out: unable qck ent fnl f: no ex and lost 2 pls ins fnl f* **7/1**[3]

3015 **5** *2* **Ceelo**[24] 5743 2-8-11 79 .... HayleyTurner 4 79
(Richard Hannon) *chsd ldrs: rdn jst over 2f out: unable qck u.p over 1f out and btn 1f out: plugged on same pce fnl f* **14/1**

0 **6** ¾ **A Ladies Man (IRE)**[36] 5303 2-8-7 0 .... RichardMullen 2 73
(Richard Hannon) *chsd ldr tl wl over 1f out: sn drvn and unable qck: btn 1f out and wknd ins fnl f* **7/1**[3]

0326 **7** *2* **Wellingrove (IRE)**[15] 6016 2-8-11 70 .... SilvestreDeSousa 7 71
(Mark Johnston) *chsd ldrs: drvn and unable qck ent fnl 2f: edgd rt u.p and wknd jst over 1f out* **33/1**

25 **8** *5* **White Coppice**[21] 5825 2-8-13 0 .... TomQueally 1 59
(Richard Fahey) *dwlt and stmbld leaving stalls: a towards rr but in tch: drvn and struggling over 2f out: wknd wl over 1f out* **40/1**

6 **9** *1* **Raven's Rock (IRE)**[16] 5963 2-8-13 0 .... TedDurcan 11 55
(Roger Varian) *in tch towards rr: rdn and struggling over 2f out: wknd wl over 1f out* **16/1**

660 **10** *12* **Haverstock**[9] 6164 2-8-13 68 .... FrankieDettori 9 19
(Mark Johnston) *in tch in midfield: rdn and lost pl 3f out: wl bhd over 1f out* **33/1**

1m 11.93s (-0.27) **Going Correction** +0.10s/f (Good) **10** Ran SP% **117.4**
Speed ratings (Par 101): **105,104,102,100,98 97,94,87,86,70**
toteswingers 1&2 £1.60, 1&3 £4.70, 2&3 £15.20 CSF £5.07 TOTE £2.60: £1.10, £1.90, £6.10; EX 6.50.

Owner Abdulla Al Mansoori **Bred** John Malone **Trained** East Everleigh, Wilts

FOCUS

There was not a great deal of strength in depth in this valuable sales race but the strong favourite ran down his main market rival and the form looks solid. The winner is basically rated to form.

NOTEBOOK

Tamayuz Star(IRE) won a 7f Leicester maiden on his debut and had leading form claims on his close second in a Listed event at Goodwood last time. He took a bit of time to get going dropped back to 6f, but produced a surging run to reel in the long-time leader. He doesn't hold any Group entries at this stage but he looks a willing type with a turn of foot and should have a bright future for his top yard. (op 11-10 tchd 10-11)

Zanetto had solid claims on his much-improved second in a Group 3 at Kempton last time and put in a valiant bid under a trailblazing ride but was picked off close home. He has looked headstrong at times but he is a useful sprinter and this run proves that he is equally effective on fast turf as he is on Polytrack. (op 4-1 tchd 5-1)

Global Icon was under pressure some way out but he stayed on well to build on his improved close fourth in a 5f Sandown maiden last time. Out of a 1m2f winning sister to a couple of 1m/1m1f Listed scorers, he should continue to progress and will appreciate another step up in trip.

Ashaadd(IRE) had a bit of work to do conceding weight all round but he ran well in first-time blinkers. This 93-rated runner looks a decent marker for the form but he is starting to look exposed and will probably need to find further improvement to defy his current mark in a nursery. (op 8-1)

Ceelo showed a good attitude to rally for fifth with quite a bit to find at the weights. (op 12-1 tchd 11-1)

A Ladies Man(IRE) was disappointing as 5-4 favourite in a 7f Newbury maiden on his debut last month but some money arrived for him again and he showed some promise behind his stablemate on this second start. (op 9-1 tchd 11-1)

6492 PRESTIGE VEHICLES E B F FILLIES' H'CAP 1m 4f

3:20 (3:22) (Class 3) (0-95,92) 3-Y-0+ **£8,409** (£2,502; £1,250; £625) **Stalls** Centre

Form RPR

11 **1** **Surprise Moment (IRE)**[36] 5328 3-9-6 **92** .... FrankieDettori 10 102
(Saeed Bin Suroor) *stdd s: hld up in tch: hdwy over 2f out: rdn and qcknd to ld but edgd rt jst over 1f out: kpt on wl ins fnl f* **9/4**[1]

2452 **2** *1* **Infinitum**[37] 5277 3-8-7 **79** ....(p) NickyMackay 5 85
(John Gosden) *hld up in tch: n.m.r: swtchd lft and barging match w rival over 1f out: hdwy u.p 1f out: styd on to chse wnr wl ins fnl f: no imp towards fin* **13/2**

4215 **3** ½ **Gosbeck**[14] 6031 4-9-8 **86** .... FergusSweeney 1 91
(Henry Candy) *hld up in tch: nt clr run wl over 1f out tl swtchd lft arnd wkng rival over 1f out: gd hdwy and drvn to chse wnr jst ins fnl f: one pce fnl 100yds* **5/1**[2]

6625 **4** ½ **Qushchi**[16] 5966 4-9-12 **90** ....(b[1]) TomQueally 9 95
(William Jarvis) *stdd s: hld up in last trio: hdwy whn nt clr run and swtchd lft over 1f out: barging match w rival jst over 1f out and swtchd lft: hdwy u.p ins fnl f: kpt on but edgd rt towards fin* **8/1**

-221 **5** ¾ **Headline News (IRE)**[18] 5913 3-8-4 **76** .... ChrisCatlin 2 79
(Rae Guest) *stdd s: t.k.h: hld up in tch in rr: hdwy on outer and rdn to chse ldrs 2f out: no ex and one pce ins fnl f* **8/1**

2104 **6** 1 1/4 **Princess Caetani (IRE)**[36] 5328 3-8-8 **80**........................ HayleyTurner 6 81
(David Simcock) *t.k.h: chsd ldr: rdn and ev ch 2f out: led over 1f out: sn hdd and unable qck: wknd ins fnl f* **6/1**[3]

20S6 **7** 1 1/4 **Cresta Star**[16] 5973 3-8-8 **80**........................ SeanLevey 4 79
(Richard Hannon) *chsd ldrs: rdn and unable qck whn n.m.r over 1f out: wknd fnl 150yds* **25/1**

1400 **8** 2 3/4 **Silent Moment (USA)**[15] 6018 3-9-1 **87**........................ SilvestreDeSousa 8 82
(Saeed Bin Suroor) *chsd ldrs: rdn and ev ch 2f out: struggling to qckn whn hmpd over 1f out: wknd jst ins fnl f: eased towards fin* **12/1**

2130 **9** 1 3/4 **Cape Rising (IRE)**[29] 5540 5-9-1 **79**........................ TedDurcan 7 71
(Alan Swinbank) *led and set stdy gallop: rdn and qcknd ent fnl 2f: wknd 1f out: eased towards fin* **16/1**

2m 32.31s (0.31) **Going Correction** +0.10s/f (Good)
WFA 3 from 4yo+ 8lb **9** Ran SP% **114.7**
Speed ratings (Par 104): **102,101,101,100,100 99,98,96,95**
toteswingers 1&2 £2.00, 2&3 £7.20, 1&3 £3.20 CSF £16.94 CT £65.86 TOTE £2.80: £1.30, £2.50, £2.20; EX 11.80.
Owner Godolphin **Bred** Darley **Trained** Newmarket, Suffolk
■ Stewards' Enquiry : Frankie Dettori two-day ban: careless riding (Oct 6,8)
Nicky Mackay caution: careless riding.

FOCUS
A competitive fillies' handicap. The pace was steady but a lightly raced Godolphin filly improved her unbeaten record to 3-3 and the form looks strong. The second to fifth were close to their marks.

NOTEBOOK
Surprise Moment(IRE) was unfazed by a step up to 1m4f and made a smooth move into contention out wide before quickening well to score with something in hand. She has been highly progressive in three starts and this half-sister to Ribblesdale winner Flying Cloud has plenty of scope for further improvement at this trip and beyond. (op 5-2)
Infinitum ran into some trouble but she stayed on strongly for a creditable second with cheekpieces applied. A six-figure purchase from a good middle-distance family, she has improved since switched to handicaps and should be closing in on a first win. (op 8-1)
Gosbeck had to wait to find a gap against the far rail but she stayed on well in a second good run since her clear-cut win in a 1m6f Nottingham handicap last month. She needs to elevate her form another notch to defy this career-high mark but she is a very consistent filly with a good attitude and a decent cruising speed. (op 11-2)
Qushchi, wearing blinkers for the first time, got squeezed out at a crucial stage before rallying well when switched out wide. This was a promising run in adverse circumstances from a filly who won this race off 1lb lower last year. (op 13-2)
Headline News(IRE) avoided any trouble out widest of all but she couldn't make an impact off 5lb higher than her handicap debut win in a 0-75 event at Leicester last time. (tchd 15-2, tchd 10-1 in a place)
Princess Caetani(IRE) was never dangerous behind Surprise Moment in a 1m2f Nottingham handicap last time. More prominent tactics were tried over this longer trip but she faded and was beaten a bit further than last time. (op 13-2)

6493 BETFRED CESAREWITCH TRIAL (H'CAP) 2m 2f
3:55 (4:00) (Class 2) (0-105,92) 3-Y-O+ **£32,345** (£9,625; £4,810; £2,405) **Stalls** Centre

Form RPR

/0-0 **1** **Domination**[14] 6066 5-8-9 **77**........................ NGMcCullagh 9 89
(C Byrnes, Ire) *hld up in tch in main gp: clsd on clr ldr 7f out: chsd ldr travelling strly 3f out: rdn to ld ent fnl f: styd on strly and sn clr* **13/2**[3]

1101 **2** 4 1/2 **Courtesy Call (IRE)**[14] 6033 3-8-5 **86**........................ SilvestreDeSousa 8 93
(Mark Johnston) *chsd ldrs tl chsd clr ldr 12f out: led over 4f out: rdn over 2f out: clr w wnr whn hdd jst over 1f out: outpcd fnl f but hld on for 2nd* **5/1**[1]

3426 **3** 1 **Eagle Rock (IRE)**[31] 5491 4-8-13 **81**........................ HayleyTurner 1 87
(Tom Tate) *hld up towards rr: clsd on clr ldr 7f out: nt clr run and switching lft over 2f out: hdwy u.p 2f out: swtchd rt over 1f out: styd on wl ins fnl f: no ch w wnr* **6/1**[2]

2206 **4** 1/2 **Dark Ranger**[57] 4528 6-9-2 **84**........................ MartinLane 7 89
(Tim Pitt) *hld up in midfield: clsd on clr ldr 7f out: rdn to chse ldrs over 2f out: outpcd 2f out: no threat to wnr but kpt on ins fnl f* **20/1**

0006 **5** 3/4 **Bernie The Bolt (IRE)**[42] 5076 6-9-5 **87**........................ LiamKeniry 6 92
(Andrew Balding) *hld up in rr: clsd on clr ldr 7f out: hdwy to chse ldng pair over 2f out: rdn and outpcd wl over 1f out: plugged on but no threat to wnr fnl f* **10/1**

0332 **6** 1 1/2 **Bradbury (IRE)**[21] 5830 4-8-2 **70**........................(v) JimmyQuinn 10 73
(James Bethell) *hld up in midfield: clsd on clr ldr 7f out: rdn and no imp 2f out: no threat to wnr but plugged on fnl f* **28/1**

0350 **7** 2 1/2 **Trovare (USA)**[8] 6191 5-8-11 **79**........................ SeanLevey 12 79
(Amanda Perrett) *hld up in rr: clsd on clr ldr 7f out: hdwy 4f out: rdn and no imp 2f out: wl hld but plugged on fnl f* **33/1**

202 **8** 5 **First Avenue**[26] 5666 7-8-11 **86**........................ CharlotteJenner(7) 17 81
(Laura Mongan) *in tch in main gp: clsd on clr ldr 7f out: rdn and effrt over 2f out: no imp 2f out: wknd over 1f out* **33/1**

0652 **9** 5 **Nanton (USA)**[8] 6197 10-9-5 **87**........................ RobertHavlin 4 76
(Jim Goldie) *hld up towards rr: clsd on clr ldr 7f out: rdn and effrt over 2f out: sn no imp: wknd over 1f out* **13/2**[3]

0100 **10** 7 **Epsom Salts**[9] 6170 7-8-2 **75**........................(p) JemmaMarshall(5) 13 56
(Pat Phelan) *t.k.h: hld up towards rr: clsd on clr ldr 7f out: hdwy 4f out: rdn and no prog over 2f out: wknd 2f out* **66/1**

4346 **11** 2 **Mystery Star (IRE)**[10] 5905 7-9-10 **92**........................ TomQueally 19 71
(Mark H Tompkins) *hld up towards rr: clsd on clr ldr 7f out: rdn over 2f out: sn wknd and wl btn whn edgd rt wl over 1f out: wknd* **28/1**

4-15 **12** 1/2 **Secret Tune**[128] 2214 8-8-9 **77**........................(t) SamHitchcott 2 56
(Charlie Longsdon) *in tch in main gp: clsd on clr ldr 7f out: u.p and no prog over 4f out: wknd over 2f out* **16/1**

0011 **13** hd **Saborido (USA)**[15] 6019 6-9-1 **83**........................ PatDobbs 5 61
(Amanda Perrett) *chsd ldr tl 12f out: styd prom in main gp: clsd on clr ldr 7f out: wknd qckly 3f out: bhd fnl 2f* **20/1**

5445 **14** 1 3/4 **Blazing Field**[15] 6012 4-8-9 **77**........................ JohnFahy 20 54
(Clive Cox) *hld up in rr: clsd on clr ldr 7f out: rdn and no hdwy over 3f out: sn wknd and bhd fnl 2f* **20/1**

2003 **15** 7 **Riptide**[13] 6074 6-8-6 **74**........................(p) KierenFox 18 43
(Michael Scudamore) *rdn along thrght: racd in midfield of main gp: clsd on clr ldr 7f out: u.p and dropped to rr 5f out: wl bhd fnl 2f: t.o* **25/1**

0302 **16** 2 1/2 **Gordonsville**[22] 5798 9-9-0 **82**........................ ChrisCatlin 14 48
(Jim Goldie) *hld up towards rr: clsd on clr ldr 7f out: rdn and no hdwy 3f out: sn wknd and bhd: t.o* **14/1**

2043 **17** 2 1/4 **Dazinski**[31] 5491 6-9-7 **89**........................ TedDurcan 15 53
(Mark H Tompkins) *hld up in midfield: clsd on clr ldr 7f out: rdn and lost pl over 4f out: lost tch over 2f out: t.o* **14/1**

5-01 **18** 37 **Body Language (IRE)**[46] 4925 4-8-13 **81**........................(p) FrankieDettori 3
(Ian Williams) *racd keenly: led and sn wl clr: much reduced ld and pressed 7f out: hdd over 4f out: sn dropped out and wl bhd fnl 2f: t.o* **8/1**

3m 50.29s (-1.71) **Going Correction** +0.10s/f (Good)
WFA 3 from 4yo+ 13lb **18** Ran SP% **129.4**
Speed ratings (Par 109): **107,105,104,104,104 103,102,100,97,94 93,93,93,92,89 88,87,71**
toteswingers 1&2 £6.20, 2&3 £5.90, 1&3 £19.10 CSF £35.55 CT £216.87 TOTE £8.40: £2.60, £1.50, £2.20, £3.80; EX 47.70 Trifecta £440.20 Pool: £1850.26 - 3.11 winning units..
Owner Patrick Wilmott/Ms C Cleary **Bred** M Kerr-Dineen **Trained** Ballingarry, Co Limerick
■ The first Flat winner in Britain for Charles Byrnes.

FOCUS
They went a stop-start gallop in this Cesarewitch trial and an Irish raider was a emphatic winner. He's rated back to the form he showed as a 3yo. The third to sixth set the standard.

NOTEBOOK
Domination had been in good form under both codes in Ireland. He was well backed for this step up to 2m2f and travelled smoothly into contention before quickening clear to record a second Flat win. The style of the win was highly impressive from this 5yo who has found further improvement over hurdles and on the Flat in recent weeks. He is not entered in the Cesarewitch but probably wouldn't have made the cut for that race. (tchd 5-1 and 7-1)
Courtesy Call(IRE) couldn't fight off the surging winner but he put in a brave effort in his bid for a sixth win from his last eight starts. His mark has shot up from 58 to 86 since the end of May but his progress may not have levelled out and he could find further improvement in staying handicaps on fast ground. (op 13-2)
Eagle Rock(IRE) got shuffled back against the far rail before staying on well for third. This was another good effort by a 4yo who is a dual Flat/hurdles winner and is still not fully exposed under both codes. (op 11-1 tchd 12-1)
Dark Ranger who was returning from almost two months off, ran well off 14lb higher than when second in this contest last year. (op 16-1)
Bernie The Bolt(IRE) bounced back with a respectable run off the same mark as when a clear-cut winner of this race in 2009. He has been very lightly raced in recent seasons but this run confirms that most of his ability remains and he is effective on fast and slow ground. (op 9-1 tchd 8-1)
Bradbury(IRE), placed in his last three starts, got a bit outpaced at a crucial stage before plugging on in a second-time visor. (op 25-1)
Trovare(USA) moved well for a long way but he didn't really pick up. (tchd 40-1)
Nanton(USA) had strong claims on his fast finishing second off a potentially lenient mark in a hot 1m6f handicap at Doncaster last week but he couldn't find a finishing kick over this longer trip and was well held. (op 15-2 tchd 6-1)
Body Language(IRE), a clear-cut leader early on, dropped out tamely off 9lb higher than for her win at Ripon last time. (op 9-1 tchd 10-1)

6494 NGK SPARK PLUGS H'CAP 1m
4:30 (4:30) (Class 2) (0-100,100) 3-Y-O+ **£12,938** (£3,850; £1,924; £962) **Stalls** Centre

Form RPR

1143 **1** **Jacob Cats**[35] 5356 3-8-12 **92**........................ PatDobbs 11 100
(Richard Hannon) *stdd s: hld up in rr in slowly run r: rdn and hdwy on far rail over 1f out: chsng ldrs whn nt clr run and swtchd lft 1f out: qcknd and r.o strly to ld cl home* **10/3**[2]

253 **2** nk **Oxford Charley (USA)**[10] 6135 3-8-10 **90**........................(v[1]) FergusSweeney 3 97
(Mikael Magnusson) *t.k.h: chsd ldrs: waiting for gap to open on far rail over 1f out: rdn and qcknd to ld ins fnl f: r.o wl tl hdd and no ex cl home* **10/1**

2112 **3** 1 **Ibtahaj**[80] 3767 3-9-2 **96**........................ FrankieDettori 5 101
(Saeed Bin Suroor) *stdd s: t.k.h: hld up in tch: rdn and effrt 2f out: hdwy u.p and chsd ldrs over 1f out: styd on same pce fnl 100yds* **3/1**[1]

0253 **4** 1/2 **Crown Counsel (IRE)**[18] 5914 4-8-10 **86** oh2........................ SilvestreDeSousa 1 90
(Mark Johnston) *led and set stdy gallop: rdn and qcknd 2f out: drvn over 1f out: hdd ins fnl f: styd on same pce after* **9/2**[3]

002 **5** nk **Stevie Thunder**[56] 4589 7-9-0 **90**........................ TedDurcan 7 93
(Ian Williams) *chsd ldr: rdn 2f out: stl ev ch u.p 1f out: no ex and styd on same pce fnl 100yds* **8/1**

2000 **6** 3/4 **Axiom**[113] 2657 8-9-7 **97**........................ HayleyTurner 9 99
(Ed Walker) *t.k.h: hld up wl in tch in last trio: rdn 2f out: hdwy and chsng ldrs whn pushed lft and sltly hmpd 1f out: kpt on same pce ins fnl f* **33/1**

2060 **7** 1 **Vainglory (USA)**[7] 6242 8-8-8 **89**........................ LauraPike(5) 12 88
(David Simcock) *t.k.h: hld up wl in tch: rdn 2f out: unable qck u.p 1f out: styd on same pce: no imp fnl f* **14/1**

5201 **8** 2 **Shavansky**[14] 6036 8-8-13 **89**........................ JamesMillman 10 84
(Rod Millman) *t.k.h: hld up in midfield tl hdwy to chse ldrs over 6f out: rdn 2f out: outpcd and lost pl over 1f out: one pce and btn fnl f* **16/1**

5006 **9** 4 **Albaqaa**[11] 6119 7-8-13 **89**........................ SeanLevey 13 74
(P J O'Gorman) *stdd s: t.k.h: hld up wl in tch in last trio: rdn and no prog 2f out: wknd over 1f out* **8/1**

0024 **10** 21 **Balducci**[26] 5686 5-9-10 **100**........................ MartinLane 6 37
(David Simcock) *plld hrd: hld up wl in tch in midfield: rdn 2f out: lost pl and btn over 1f out: sn eased and virtually p.u ins fnl f* **20/1**

1m 39.36s (0.76) **Going Correction** +0.10s/f (Good)
WFA 3 from 4yo+ 4lb **10** Ran SP% **117.8**
Speed ratings (Par 109): **100,99,98,98,97 97,96,94,90,69**
toteswingers 1&2 £11.80, 2&3 £6.70, 1&3 £1.60 CSF £37.24 CT £113.54 TOTE £4.40: £1.60, £3.30, £2.00; EX 55.30.
Owner Michael Pescod & Justin Dowley **Bred** Highclere Stud **Trained** East Everleigh, Wilts

FOCUS
They went a very steady pace in this decent handicap and the winner can be marked up for scoring from a long way back. They finished well bunched.

NOTEBOOK
Jacob Cats, beaten by just 1l in a pair of 7f/1m handicaps at Goodwood and Newbury on his last two runs, looked in trouble out the back when the pace increased but he produced a surging run through the pack and got up close home. Still not fully exposed, he has won four of his nine starts and should not go up much for this success. (op 7-2 tchd 3-1)
Oxford Charley(USA) stayed on strongly against the far rail but was just denied by a faster finisher. This was a big run in a first-time visor and he could have more to offer in headgear. (op 12-1 tchd 14-1)
Ibtahaj was just held when odds-on in his hat-trick bid in a 1m Kempton handicap when last seen in July, form which was boosted by the winner going in again off 6lb higher next time. Well backed on his return from 80 days off, he travelled smoothly for a long way but couldn't find a decisive finishing burst from off the sedate pace. However, this was another good run by a lightly raced colt who should be able to win another handicap. (op 7-2)
Crown Counsel(IRE) had the run of the race but he couldn't hold off the finishers and is now 0-20 since his last win in June 2011. (op 6-1)
Stevie Thunder has rediscovered some form on his last two starts and he finished runner-up off 2lb higher in the Cambridgeshire last year. (op 7-1)
Albaqaa got warm beforehand and put a big dent in his chance by racing keenly off the steady pace. (op 15-2)

Balducci Official explanation: jockey said gelding ran too free and lost its action in the dip.

6495 RACING UK H'CAP 6f

5:05 (5:06) (Class 4) (0-85,82) 3-Y-O+ £5,175 (£1,540; £769; £384) Stalls Centre

Form				RPR
1010	1		**Idler (IRE)**[8] 6192 3-9-5 82 SilvestreDeSousa 11 (Mark Johnston) *led tl 1/2-way: chsd ldr tl rdn to ld again 2f out: drvn and hdd ins fnl f: battled on gamely to ld again cl home* 9/2[1]	94
1453	2	*hd*	**Cheworee**[10] 6144 3-9-1 78 [1] LiamKeniry 3 (David Elsworth) *hld up in tch in midfield: hdwy to chse ldrs over 1f out: rdn and chal 1f out: led ins fnl f: kpt on u.p tl hdd and no ex cl home* 8/1	90
300	3	*1 1/2*	**My Son Max**[7] 6256 4-9-3 78 PatDobbs 14 (P J O'Gorman) *t.k.h: chsd ldrs: drvn over 1f out: styd in same pce u.p ins fnl f* 8/1	85
5624	4	*1/2*	**Bajan Bear**[6] 6277 4-8-7 68 MartinLane 9 (Michael Blanshard) *dwlt: hld up in tch in rr: rdn and effrt over 1f out: kpt on wl u.p fnl 100yds* 11/1	73
3520	5	*3/4*	**Showboating (IRE)**[14] 6044 4-9-4 79 (tp) SeanLevey 10 (Alan McCabe) *hld up wl in tch in last trio: swtchd lft and effrt ent fnl f: drvn and styd on fnl 150yds: nvr able to chal* 15/2[3]	82
400	6	*2*	**Baby Strange**[8] 6192 8-9-6 81 RichardMullen 2 (Derek Shaw) *dwlt: hld up in tch towards rr: hdwy into midfield 1/2-way: rdn and unable qck over 1f out: one pce and btn fnl f* 10/1	78
6501	7	*hd*	**Perfect Blossom**[4] 6347 5-9-7 82 6ex TomQueally 15 (Ian McInnes) *travelled strly: hld up in tch: rdn and effrt to chse ldrs over 1f out: no ex jst ins fnl f: wknd fnl 100yds* 8/1	78
3-00	8	*1/2*	**Dominium (USA)**[37] 5269 5-8-13 74 (b) FergusSweeney 1 (Jeremy Gask) *stdd s: hld up in tch tl hdwy to chse ldrs over 4f out: led 1/2-way tl 2f out: sn rdn and unable qck: wknd 1f out* 25/1	68
6344	9	*3/4*	**Lujeanie**[7] 6226 6-9-0 78 (p) PatrickHills(3) 8 (Dean Ivory) *t.k.h: hld up in tch: rdn and unable qck over 1f out: no prog and btn 1f out* 16/1	70
4210	10	*3 1/4*	**Drift And Dream**[10] 6144 5-9-2 77 TedDurcan 6 (Chris Wall) *t.k.h: chsd ldrs: lost pl and rdn over 2f out: wknd over 1f out: eased towards fin* 10/1	59
0061	11	*2 1/4*	**The Tichborne (IRE)**[23] 5774 4-8-12 73 (v) HayleyTurner 7 (Roger Teal) *chsd ldrs tl 2f out: wknd u.p over 1f out: fdd ins fnl f* 5/1[2]	47
0000	12	*1/2*	**Crown Choice**[53] 4690 7-9-5 80 JimmyQuinn 13 (Paul Midgley) *stdd after s: t.k.h: hld up in rr: swtchd lft and effrt over 1f out: no prog: wknd fnl f* 20/1	53

1m 11.82s (-0.38) **Going Correction** +0.10s/f (Good)
WFA 3 from 4yo+ 2lb 12 Ran SP% 121.0
Speed ratings (Par 105): **106,105,103,103,102 99,99,98,97,93 90,89**
toteswingers 1&2 £10.60, 1&3 £18.10, 2&3 £26.40 CSF £41.20 CT £290.45 TOTE £5.10: £1.90, £3.10, £3.10; EX 33.60.
Owner Sheikh Hamdan Bin Mohammed Al Maktoum **Bred** Darley **Trained** Middleham Moor, N Yorks

FOCUS
There was a tight finish in this competitive sprint handicap. The winner is generally progressive and this rates another personal best.
Bajan Bear Official explanation: jockey said gelding hung badly right
T/Plt: £9.30 to a £1 stake. Pool: £80,037.79 - 6,219.72 winning tickets T/Qpdt: £4.00 to a £1 stake. Pool: £3750.67 - 692.42 winning tickets SP

6451 WOLVERHAMPTON (A.W) (L-H)

Saturday, September 22

OFFICIAL GOING: Standard to fast
Wind: slight across Weather: sunny

6496 32RED H'CAP 5f 20y(P)

5:50 (5:51) (Class 6) (0-55,55) 3-Y-O+ £2,070 (£616; £307; £153) Stalls Low

Form				RPR
5401	1		**Sally's Swansong**[9] 6180 6-9-2 54 (b) DavidNolan 10 (Eric Alston) *in tch: urged along and swtchd lft over 1f out: chal between horses ins fnl f: led fnl 75yds* 10/3[1]	62+
0050	2	*nk*	**Nine Before Ten (IRE)**[5] 6322 4-9-2 54 (e[1]) StephenCraine 3 (Charles Smith) *in tch: hdwy 2f out and gng wl: drvn over 1f out: led ins fnl f: hdd and no ex fnl 75yds* 9/1	61
0046	3	*1 1/4*	**Rightcar**[9] 6180 5-8-13 51 RobbieFitzpatrick 5 (Peter Grayson) *in rr: drvn 3f out: styd on over 2f out: wnt 3rd ins fnl f but nvr any hope of catching wnr* 6/1[3]	54
3000	4	*1/2*	**Divertimenti (IRE)**[5] 6321 8-8-5 46 (b) MarkCoumbe(3) 1 (Roy Bowring) *in rr: drvn 3f out: hdwy ins fnl 2f: kpt on but nvr trbld ldrs* 15/2	47
0500	5	*1 1/2*	**Replicator**[46] 4929 7-7-8 46 oh1 (e) JamieMackay 9 (Patrick Gilligan) *dwlt: rdn and wd ent st: kpt on same pce: n.d* 25/1	41
0000	6	*3/4*	**Rooknrasbryripple**[26] 5662 3-8-6 50 (e) AmyScott(5) 2 (Ralph Smith) *led: hdd 4f out: remained cl up tl led again 2f out: drvn over 1f out: hdd ins fnl f* 40/1	43
1046	7	*1/2*	**Speedyfix**[23] 5775 5-9-3 55 (t) TomMcLaughlin 7 (Christine Dunnett) *midfield: rdn over 2f out: swtchd lft ins fnl f and hmpd: no ex fnl 100yds* 13/2	54
5	8	*3/4*	**Model Behaviour (IRE)**[19] 5875 3-8-5 47 RossAtkinson(3) 6 (Daniel Mark Loughnane) *midfield: drvn 2f out: no ex fnl f* 14/1	35
605	9	*2 1/2*	**Fiona's Spirit (IRE)**[15] 6003 5-8-6 49 oh1 ow3 JamesRogers(5) 13 (Daniel Mark Loughnane) *awkward stalls: drvn to ld 4f out: hdd 2f out: sn wknd* 50/1	28
0600	10	*1*	**Love Club**[47] 4885 4-8-8 46 oh1 CathyGannon 8 (Brian Baugh) *in tch: rdn 2f out: drvn and plugging on ins fnl f whn bdly hmpd: nt rcvr* 12/1	22
005	11	*2 1/2*	**College Doll**[100] 3082 3-9-2 55 BrettDoyle 12 (Christine Dunnett) *cl up: rdn over 2f out: wknd fnl f* 33/1	22
042	12	*nk*	**Brandywell Boy (IRE)**[7] 6233 9-9-0 52 (t) AdamKirby 4 (Dominic Ffrench Davis) *in rr: drvn 3f out: styng on same pce but btn whn bdly hmpd ins fnl f: eased* 9/2[2]	17

1m 1.89s (-0.41) **Going Correction** -0.20s/f (Stan)
WFA 3 from 4yo+ 1lb 12 Ran SP% 116.2
Speed ratings (Par 101): **95,94,92,91,89 88,87,86,82,80 76,76**
toteswingers: 1&2 £11.00, 1&3 £3.10, 2&3 £6.70. CSF £32.11 CT £176.28 TOTE £4.20: £1.20, £2.70, £2.40; EX 51.70 TRIFECTA Not won. Pool: £446.99.
Owner Miss F Fenley **Bred** Southern Seafoods **Trained** Longton, Lancs
■ Stewards' Enquiry : Amy Scott one-day ban: careless riding (Oct 6)

FOCUS
Not many of these came into this in decent form. The pace was sound, but it was a weak race and rather messy too. The winner built on her C&D latest.

6497 32RED.COM H'CAP (DIV I) 5f 216y(P)

6:20 (6:24) (Class 5) (0-75,74) 3-Y-O+ £2,911 (£866; £432; £216) Stalls Low

Form				RPR
3311	1		**Theresnoneedfordat (IRE)**[8] 6211 3-9-2 71 AdamKirby 9 (Stuart Williams) *midfield: hdwy over 1f out: pushed into ld 1f out: sn in command: eased cl home* 5/4[1]	86+
1401	2	*3*	**Avonvalley**[47] 4885 5-8-12 66 RobbieFitzpatrick 5 (Peter Grayson) *in rr: nt clr run ins fnl 3f: swtchd rt ent st: kpt on wl: wnt 2nd cl home* 16/1	70
1024	3	*1*	**Prince Of Passion (CAN)**[8] 6195 4-9-0 67 (v) TomMcLaughlin 2 (Derek Shaw) *cl up: drvn 2f out: ev ch over 1f out: one pce ins fnl f* 15/2	69
430	4	*hd*	**Yankee Storm**[18] 5915 7-9-3 70 (b) LukeMorris 4 (Michael Wigham) *in tch: rdn over 2f out: drvn and ev ch over 1f out: nt pce of wnr ins fnl f: no ex fnl 75yds* 16/1	71
0016	5	*1/2*	**Drawnfromthepast (IRE)**[10] 6150 7-9-2 74 LeonnaMayor(5) 1 (Jamie Osborne) *led: urged along 2f out: drvn over 1f out: hdd 1f out: wknd ins fnl f* 6/1[2]	74
0003	6	*3/4*	**Seamus Shindig**[29] 5531 10-8-3 61 AmyScott(5) 8 (Henry Candy) *racd wd: rdn over 2f out: styd on same pce but nvr any threat* 13/2[3]	58
3621	7	*1/2*	**Ferdy (IRE)**[8] 6194 3-8-11 66 CathyGannon 7 (Paul Green) *dwlt: in rr: rdn over 2f out: drvn over 1f out: no ex ins fnl f* 8/1	64
0600	8	*nk*	**Prince James**[67] 4174 5-8-10 70 MatthewHopkins(7) 6 (Michael Easterby) *in tch: rdn over 2f out: carried wd and losing pl ent st: btn fnl f* 33/1	65
0026	9	*2 1/4*	**Available (IRE)**[14] 6052 3-9-1 70 StephenCraine 3 (John Mackie) *midfield: stmbld shortly after s: rdn over 2f out: wknd fnl f* 22/1	57

1m 13.7s (-1.30) **Going Correction** -0.20s/f (Stan)
WFA 3 from 4yo+ 2lb 9 Ran SP% 114.0
Speed ratings (Par 103): **100,96,94,94,93 92,92,91,88**
toteswingers: 1&2 £4.60, 1&3 £3.00, 2&3 £13.30. CSF £24.10 CT £111.20 TOTE £2.20: £1.40, £2.60, £1.80; EX 27.90 Trifecta £173.60 Pool: £1,140.73 - 4.86 winning units..
Owner R Morris J Russell T O'Brien M Nolan **Bred** Denis McDonnell **Trained** Newmarket, Suffolk

FOCUS
Mainly exposed performers, with the obvious exception of the winner, who's on a roll. The form is rated at face value.
Ferdy(IRE) Official explanation: jockey said colt was denied a clear run; vet said colt was stiff behind
Available(IRE) Official explanation: jockey said filly suffered interference at the start

6498 32RED.COM H'CAP (DIV II) 5f 216y(P)

6:50 (6:51) (Class 5) (0-75,74) 3-Y-O+ £2,911 (£866; £432; £216) Stalls Low

Form				RPR
6000	1		**Dancing Maite**[12] 6106 7-8-11 67 (b) MarkCoumbe(3) 8 (Roy Bowring) *t.k.h in tch: hdwy to ld over 3f out: drvn over 1f out: kpt on and nvr looked like being ct ins fnl f* 17/2	72
040	2	*1*	**For Shia And Lula (IRE)**[41] 5130 3-9-3 72 StephenCraine 5 (Daniel Mark Loughnane) *cl up: drvn over 2f out: chsd wnr ins fnl f: kpt on but nvr looked like catching wnr* 8/1[3]	74
6136	3	*1*	**My Own Way Home**[36] 5326 4-8-13 66 AdamKirby 7 (David Evans) *in tch: rdn 2f out: drvn and styd on same pce ins fnl f: wnt 3rd cl home* 9/4[2]	65
0034	4	*1 1/2*	**Restless Bay (IRE)**[2] 6403 4-8-9 69 (p) ConorHarrison(7) 1 (Mrs K Burke) *mounted outside paddock and v reluctant to go to s: in tch: lost pl 4f out: rdn and v one pce fnl 2f: btn fnl f* 11/8[1]	63
000	5	*shd*	**Ishetoo**[47] 4887 8-8-11 64 RobbieFitzpatrick 6 (Peter Grayson) *in rr: rdn over 2f out: no real imp after* 8/1[3]	58
00	6	*nse*	**Molly Jones**[110] 2759 3-8-7 62 LukeMorris 3 (Derek Haydn Jones) *sn led: hdd over 3f out: rdn over 2f out: one pce fnl f* 14/1	56

1m 14.17s (-0.83) **Going Correction** -0.20s/f (Stan)
WFA 3 from 4yo+ 2lb 6 Ran SP% 112.3
Speed ratings (Par 103): **97,95,94,92,92 92**
toteswingers: 1&2 £8.40, 1&3 £5.00, 2&3 £2.70. CSF £69.35 CT £203.18 TOTE £12.90: £5.00, £5.50; EX 96.00 Trifecta £576.50 Part won. Pool: £779.14 - 0.90 winning units..
Owner S R Bowring **Bred** S R Bowring **Trained** Edwinstowe, Notts

FOCUS
An uneventful handicap which was slowly run. The form has been rated on the negative side.

6499 DOWNLOAD OUR IPHONE APP (S) STKS 5f 216y(P)

7:20 (7:21) (Class 6) 2-Y-O £2,070 (£616; £307; £153) Stalls Low

Form				RPR
036	1		**Majestic Jess (IRE)**[135] 1997 2-8-11 63 RichardKingscote 4 (Tom Dascombe) *chsd ldr: urged along 2f out: led over 1f out: in command ins fnl f: comfortable* 10/3[2]	67+
3424	2	*2 1/4*	**Marchwood**[1] 6438 2-8-11 67 (p) JamieSpencer 2 (J S Moore) *led at brisk pce: rdn and hdd over 1f out: sn no ch w wnr but hld on for 2nd* 2/1[1]	60
1515	3	*3/4*	**Done Dreaming (IRE)**[5] 6312 2-9-3 74 DavidNolan 1 (Richard Fahey) *midfield: drvn and hdwy over 2f out: plugged on same pce but nvr a threat* 7/2[3]	64
5600	4	*2*	**Kryena's Rose**[17] 5946 2-8-6 51 CathyGannon 3 (Mick Channon) *towards rr: drvn and struggling fnl 3f: mod late prog: nvr any hope* 25/1	47
5250	5	*3*	**Sojoum**[3] 6354 2-8-6 56 SamHitchcott 9 (Mick Channon) *in rr: drvn 3f out: sn struggling* 12/1	38
6	6	*shd*	**Lady Jean**[22] 5807 2-8-6 0 ChrisCatlin 6 (Reg Hollinshead) *a in rr: btn fnl 2f* 12/1	38
000	7	*1/2*	**Lyrical Vibe**[22] 5807 2-8-6 41 JamieMackay 8 (David Evans) *midfield: t.k.h: drvn ins fnl 3f: no hdwy fnl 2f* 50/1	36
525	8	*3*	**Tonality (IRE)**[6] 6276 2-8-6 0 LukeMorris 7 (J S Moore) *drvn and struggling fnl 3f* 15/2	27

1m 14.11s (-0.89) **Going Correction** -0.20s/f (Stan) 8 Ran SP% 111.6
Speed ratings (Par 93): **97,94,93,90,86 86,85,81**
toteswingers: 1&2 £3.00, 1&3 £3.10, 2&3 £2.90. CSF £9.87 TOTE £3.70: £1.70, £1.70, £1.10; EX 14.20 Trifecta £69.30 Pool: £1,477.99 - 15.76 winning units..The winner was bought by Mark Benton for 8,500gns.
Owner The MHS 2012 Olympic Partnership **Bred** Mrs Eileen Comer **Trained** Malpas, Cheshire

FOCUS
A strong gallop to this seller. The winner looks above average for the grade.

NOTEBOOK

Majestic Jess(IRE) ranged upsides early in the straight before going clear to get off the mark. He had only shown modest form in three 5f maidens but this was improved form and he saw out the extra furlong no problem. An opening mark of 63 looks potentially lenient given he beat some higher-rated rivals here, and so he would have to be of strong interest if turning up in a handicap any time soon, especially as he is still open to more improvement. The winner was was sold to Mark Benton for 8,500 guineas in the auction and he could prove a decent buy. (op 7-2 tchd 3-1)

Marchwood did well to keep going for second given how hard he went from the outset. He ought to find a small race soon. (op 11-4)

Done Dreaming(IRE) had never sampled these conditions before and struggled under his penalty. The step up to 6f didn't bring about any improvement and the edge has just gone off his form now. (op 3-1)

Tonality(IRE) dropped away tamely and looks regressive now. (op 13-2)

6500 32RED CASINO H'CAP — 7f 32y(P)

7:50 (7:50) (Class 6) (0-65,65) 3-Y-O — £2,070 (£616; £307; £153) Stalls High

Form				RPR
-211	1		**Twenty One Choice (IRE)**[5] 6309 3-9-8 65 6ex LiamKeniry 1 — (Ed de Giles) *cl up: shuffled bk over 2f out: swtchd ins and effrt over 1f out: shkn up to ld 1f out: sn in command* 1/1[1]	78+
0164	2	1 1/2	**Exceedexpectations (IRE)**[22] 5810 3-9-7 64 HayleyTurner 9 — (Michael Bell) *cl up: led over 2f out: rdn and pressed over 1f out: hdd 1f out: sn no ch w wnr* 11/4[2]	73
4003	3	2 1/2	**Aarti (IRE)**[17] 5949 3-9-7 64 AdamBeschizza 3 — (William Haggas) *midfield: wd thrght: rdn 3f out: drvn and outpcd 2f out: plugged on ins fnl f: wnt 3rd cl home* 9/1	66
-053	4	1/2	**Lady Bellatrix**[5] 6302 3-9-5 62 SilvestreDeSousa 8 — (Mark H Tompkins) *in tch: rdn and effrt over 2f out: drvn one pce fnl f: lost 3rd cl home* 16/1	63
0050	5	2	**Lord Paget**[14] 6050 3-8-9 59 (v[1]) JackDuern(7) 4 — (Reg Hollinshead) *in tch: rdn over 2f out: drvn and wknd ins fnl f* 33/1	55
064	6	nk	**Shahrazad (IRE)**[40] 5166 3-9-1 58 JamieMackay 2 — (Patrick Gilligan) *taken down early: midfield: rdn over 2f out: mod late hdwy but n.d* 66/1	53
446	7	1 1/2	**Norlander**[26] 5658 3-9-0 57 RichardKingscote 7 — (Ralph Beckett) *a in rr: drvn 3f out: btn fnl 2f* 8/1[3]	48
4550	8	1 1/4	**Crown Dependency (IRE)**[16] 5975 3-9-0 60 MatthewCosham(3) 10 — (David Evans) *midfield: lost pl 3f out: drvn and one pce fnl 2f* 28/1	47
0360	9	1 1/2	**Aureolin Gulf**[14] 6052 3-9-5 62 ShaneKelly 11 — (Reg Hollinshead) *a in rr: struggling fnl 3f* 80/1	45
00	10	1/2	**Monty Fay (IRE)**[58] 4489 3-8-12 55 (tp) LukeMorris 5 — (John Flint) *led: hdd over 2f out: sn fdd: dropped rt away fnl f* 33/1	37
100	11	1 1/4	**Emma Jean (IRE)**[15] 6001 3-8-13 56 (bt) CathyGannon 6 — (Frank Sheridan) *a in rr: struggling fnl 3f* 33/1	34

1m 28.11s (-1.49) **Going Correction** -0.20s/f (Stan) 11 Ran SP% 118.7

Speed ratings (Par 99): **100,98,95,94,92 92,90,89,87,86 85**

toteswingers: 1&2 £2.00, 1&3 £3.70, 2&3 £4.50. CSF £3.49 CT £15.57 TOTE £2.10: £1.10, £1.40, £2.30; EX 6.50 Trifecta £18.70 Pool: £1,253.61 - 49.35 winning units..

Owner Penna Racing **Bred** P Byrne **Trained** Ledbury, H'fords

FOCUS

A fair handicap which was well run. The first two are progressive and the form is rated on the positive side.

6501 IRISH STALLION FARMS E B F MAIDEN STKS — 1m 141y(P)

8:20 (8:22) (Class 5) 2-Y-O — £3,784 (£1,126; £562; £281) Stalls Low

Form				RPR
	1		**Wadi Al Hattawi (IRE)** 2-9-3 0 SilvestreDeSousa 1 — (Saeed Bin Suroor) *in tch: rdn over 2f out: hdwy over 1f out: led 1f out: kpt on wl* 2/1[1]	75+
00	2	2 1/4	**Sunblazer (IRE)**[8] 6214 2-9-3 0 LukeMorris 8 — (William Muir) *cl up: pushed along and led over 2f out: drvn and hdd 1f out: sn no ch w wnr* 50/1	71
5354	3	1 1/4	**Ocean Applause**[10] 6149 2-9-3 90 (p) BrettDoyle 6 — (John Ryan) *in tch: urged along over 2f out: drvn and hdwy over 1f out: no ex fnl 100yds* 3/1[2]	68
	4	nk	**Interior Minister** 2-9-3 0 LiamKeniry 4 — (Mikael Magnusson) *midfield: hdwy on outer 2f out: rdn over 1f out: kpt on same pce: could improve* 20/1	67+
	5	hd	**Now Spun (USA)** 2-9-3 0 AhmedAjtebi 13 — (Mahmood Al Zarooni) *slowly away and green early: in rr: rdn and hdwy 3f out: v wd ent st: hanging rt and v unbalanced over 1f out: almost unrideable ins fnl f: v green: should improve* 5/1[3]	67+
02	6	1 3/4	**The Scuttler (IRE)**[9] 6168 2-9-3 0 SamHitchcott 11 — (Mick Channon) *cl up: rdn 3f out: drvn and effrt over 1f out: no ex ins fnl f* 9/1	63
56	7	3/4	**Zero Game (IRE)**[21] 5818 2-8-12 0 HayleyTurner 10 — (Michael Bell) *t.k.h in rr: rdn 3f out: plugged on same pce* 14/1	57
0	8	hd	**Mutamaiz (IRE)**[15] 6014 2-9-3 0 AdamKirby 3 — (James Tate) *in tch: rdn 3f out: drvn and wknd fnl 2f* 40/1	61
0	9	2 1/2	**Teolagi (IRE)**[48] 4846 2-9-3 0 JamieSpencer 7 — (J S Moore) *in rr: rdn over 2f out: kpt on same pce tl eased ins fnl f: do bttr* 33/1	58+
	10	7	**Conversing (USA)** 2-8-12 0 AntiocoMurgia(5) 9 — (Mahmood Al Zarooni) *in rr: rdn over 3f out: btn fnl 2f* 8/1	41
05	11	3/4	**Crafty Wonder (IRE)**[8] 6188 2-9-0 0 MatthewCosham(3) 12 — (David Evans) *in rr: struggling fnl 3f* 125/1	40
00	12	hd	**Darkest Night (IRE)**[8] 6214 2-9-3 0 FergusSweeney 2 — (Jamie Osborne) *led: hdd and rdn over 2f out: sn wknd* 80/1	39
	13	2 1/2	**Good As New** 2-8-12 0 ChrisCatlin 5 — (Chris Wall) *a in rr: struggling fnl 4f* 50/1	29

1m 48.69s (-1.81) **Going Correction** -0.20s/f (Stan) 13 Ran SP% 118.9

Speed ratings (Par 95): **100,98,96,96,96 94,94,94,91,85 84,84,82**

toteswingers: 1&2 £54.60, 1&3 £1.40, 2&3 £77.90. CSF £131.95 TOTE £2.80: £1.10, £13.10, £1.40; EX 201.70 TRIFECTA Not won. Pool: £614.73.

Owner Godolphin **Bred** Darley **Trained** Newmarket, Suffolk

FOCUS

Probably not maiden form to get carried away with, but a nice start from the winner. The runner-up clearly improved.

NOTEBOOK

Wadi Al Hattawi(IRE), the Godolphin first-string according to jockey bookings, looks a nice middle-distance prospect in the making. The son of Dalakhani came under strong driving three out but the further he went the better he looked and he drew clear in the closing stages for an emphatic success. He is bred to thrive over middle-distances next year and he could be anything at this stage. (op 3-1)

Sunblazer(IRE) had shown little in two previous outings but he took a marked step forward this time and clearly has ability. He can go into nurseries now, for which he shouldn't be overburdened, and further progress should see him off the mark soon.

Ocean Applause has been quite highly tried in his first season, but it's disappointing to see a horse rated as high as he beaten in a Wolverhampton maiden. The addition of cheekpieces had no effect and he has a bit to prove now. (op 11-4 tchd 5-2)

Interior Minister shaped with some promise in fourth, keeping on from midfield without every really threatening. He represents connections who do well with juveniles and there should be plenty more to come from this son of Nayef. (op 12-1)

Now Spun(USA) was all over the shop and clearly far too green to do himself justice on his debut. Despite that, he showed enough to suggest he's got races in him when getting the hang of things. (op 15-2)

The Scuttler(IRE) had every chance turning into the straight, but didn't see his race as strongly as others and may need to step back in trip for now. (op 8-1 tchd 10-1)

6502 FOLEY STEELS H'CAP — 1m 141y(P)

8:50 (8:51) (Class 5) (0-70,70) 3-Y-O — £2,911 (£866; £432; £216) Stalls Low

Form				RPR
1055	1		**Raheeba**[24] 5732 3-9-6 69 (b[1]) MartinLane 12 — (Mark Johnston) *sn led: hdd 5f out: pushed along and led again over 2f out: drvn clr over 1f out: a holding on* 8/1	81
3132	2	2 1/4	**Refreshestheparts (USA)**[9] 6174 3-8-13 62 JamieSpencer 2 — (George Baker) *wl in rr: hdwy 3f out: swtchd lft and rdn over 1f out: styd on to go 2nd ins fnl f but nvr looked like catching wnr* 3/1[1]	69+
6603	3	1/2	**Levi Draper**[14] 6050 3-9-7 70 HayleyTurner 4 — (James Fanshawe) *in tch: rdn over 2f out: drvn to chse wnr 1f out: sn no ch w wnr: lost 2nd fnl 75yds* 7/2[2]	76
0305	4	5	**Titus Star (IRE)**[9] 6169 3-9-2 65 LukeMorris 7 — (J S Moore) *midfield: rdn and hdwy over 2f out: drvn and no imp ins fnl f* 16/1	59
6000	5	nk	**Taro Tywod (IRE)**[26] 5669 3-8-9 58 ShaneKelly 3 — (Mark Brisbourne) *midfield: lost pl 3f out: rdn and no ch of catching principals 2f out: kpt on same pce after* 40/1	51+
4-35	6	1	**Breaking The Bank**[38] 5231 3-9-5 68 StevieDonohoe 5 — (William Muir) *in tch: rdn over 2f out: wknd over 1f out* 15/2	59
0460	7	nk	**Foursquare Funtime**[7] 6240 3-9-1 64 AdamKirby 9 — (Reg Hollinshead) *in rr: drvn and no imp fnl 2f* 25/1	54
2304	8	nk	**Feeling Good**[25] 5717 3-9-3 69 PaulPickard(3) 6 — (Brian Ellison) *midfield: rdn over 2f out: drvn and one pce fnl f* 16/1	59
4004	9	1/2	**Masters Blazing**[10] 6141 3-8-12 61 (p) BrettDoyle 8 — (John Ryan) *midfield: drvn and sme hdwy over 2f out: btn fnl f* 7/1[3]	50
3240	10	1 1/4	**Gunner Will (IRE)**[10] 6141 3-9-5 68 (p) FergusSweeney 1 — (Jamie Osborne) *midfield: drvn and lost pl 4f out: sn struggling* 16/1	54
0005	11	3/4	**On The Hoof**[1] 6452 3-9-6 69 SilvestreDeSousa 10 — (Michael Easterby) *v awkward leaving stalls: last and drvn 3f out: nvr any hope* 16/1	53
432	12	1 1/2	**Green Mitas (ITY)**[14] 6057 3-8-13 62 AndreaAtzeni 11 — (Frank Sheridan) *cl up: led 5f out: hdd over 2f out: sn wknd: eased fnl f* 8/1	43

1m 48.04s (-2.46) **Going Correction** -0.20s/f (Stan) 12 Ran SP% 123.5

Speed ratings (Par 101): **102,100,99,95,94 93,93,93,92,91 91,89**

toteswingers: 1&2 £5.60, 1&3 £5.00, 2&3 £4.30. CSF £33.54 CT £105.56 TOTE £10.70: £3.90, £2.10, £1.20; EX 22.40 Trifecta £63.10 Pool: £385.50 - 4.52 winning units..

Owner Sheikh Hamdan Bin Mohammed Al Maktoum **Bred** Mrs C R Philipson & Lofts Hall Stud **Trained** Middleham Moor, N Yorks

FOCUS

A strongly run handicap in which the first three came clear, giving the form a solid feel for the grade. Raheeba is rated in line with her Musselburgh win.

Taro Tywod(IRE) Official explanation: jockey said filly hung left handed

On The Hoof Official explanation: jockey said gelding reared as stalls opened

Green Mitas(ITY) Official explanation: jockey said colt stopped quickly

6503 32RED SUPPORTING BRITISH RACING H'CAP — 1m 4f 50y(P)

9:20 (9:20) (Class 6) (0-65,65) 3-Y-O+ — £2,070 (£616; £307; £153) Stalls Low

Form				RPR
1000	1		**Jeer (IRE)**[22] 5809 8-9-5 65 (t) MatthewHopkins(7) 4 — (Michael Easterby) *cl up: pushed along and hdwy 3f out: drvn and led ins fnl 2f: strly pressed ins fnl f: hld on gamely* 12/1	72
0/05	2	nk	**Youm Jamil (USA)**[7] 6251 5-9-0 58 GeorgeDowning(5) 7 — (Tony Carroll) *hld up: hdwy over 3f out: rdn to press wnr 1f out: ev ch 100yds out: edgd out fnl 50yds* 8/1	64
6216	3	1 1/4	**Laconicos (IRE)**[36] 5323 10-9-3 61 (t) LauraPike(5) 1 — (William Stone) *led after 3f: hdd 6f out: drvn 3f out: plugged on same pce to press for pls* 6/1	65
3/41	4	3/4	**Iceman George**[14] 6056 8-9-8 61 (v) SilvestreDeSousa 8 — (Lydia Pearce) *in tch: drvn 5f out: hdwy on outer 3f out: laboured prog fnl 2f: nvr looked like catching principals* 7/4[1]	64
5020	5	1 3/4	**Pugnacious (IRE)**[12] 6101 3-8-9 56 (b) MartinLane 5 — (Mark Johnston) *in tch: reminders 7f out: nvr really gng w much zest after: drvn 3f out: one pce fnl 2f* 7/2[2]	56
100	6	1 3/4	**Transfer**[15] 6004 7-9-6 62 (p) MarkCoumbe(3) 9 — (Richard Price) *cl up: led 6f out: drvn and hdd ins fnl 2f: sn wknd* 20/1	59
0040	7	8	**Chemistry Master**[25] 5706 4-9-8 61 NickyMackay 6 — (Jeremy Gask) *led: hdd after 3f: drvn 4f out: sn struggling* 11/2[3]	46
	8	53	**Highland Brave (IRE)**[405] 2040 6-8-12 51 oh6 RussKennemore 2 — (Mandy Rowland) *slowly away: a bhd: drvn 6f out: sn btn: t.o* 50/1	

2m 39.0s (-2.10) **Going Correction** -0.20s/f (Stan)

WFA 3 from 4yo+ 8lb 8 Ran SP% 113.8

Speed ratings (Par 101): **99,98,97,97,96 95,89,54**

toteswingers: 1&2 £9.80, 1&3 £9.30, 2&3 £14.40. CSF £101.55 CT £635.80 TOTE £20.70: £3.90, £1.80, £1.90; EX 151.20 TRIFECTA Not won. Pool: £723.50.

Owner Mrs Jean Turpin **Bred** Floors Farming And Side Hill Stud **Trained** Sheriff Hutton, N Yorks

FOCUS

A weak handicap run at a steady pace so not form to place too much faith in. The winner is rated to his February C&D win.

T/Plt: £69.50 to a £1 stake. Pool: £88,330.03 - 926.65 winning tickets T/Qpdt: £42.80 to a £1 stake. Pool: £7,546.46 - 130.32 winning tickets CS

6504 - 6506a (Foreign Racing) - See Raceform Interactive

6292 LONGCHAMP (R-H)

Saturday, September 22

OFFICIAL GOING: Turf: good to soft

6507a PRIX DES CHENES (GROUP 3) (2YO COLTS & GELDINGS) (TURF) 1m

12:30 (12:00) 2-Y-O **£33,333** (£13,333; £10,000; £6,666; £3,333)

RPR

1 **Pearl Flute (IRE)**[13] 6086 2-9-2 0 .... UmbertoRispoli 7 106
(F-H Graffard, France) *settled 6th: qcknd wl u.p ent fnl f: wnt 2nd 50yds out: r.o strly to take ld 20yds out: hld on wl* **7/1**

2 ¾ **Visiyani (FR)**[20] 2-9-2 0 .... Christophe-PatriceLemaire 3 104
(A De Royer-Dupre, France) *hld up in rr: gd prog on outside 1 1/2f out: r.o strly fnl f: wnt 2nd 20yds out: r.o wl* **13/8**[1]

3 shd **Us Law (IRE)**[16] 2-9-2 0 .... ChristopheSoumillon 5 104
(P Bary, France) *settled 4th: r.o u.p to ld 1f out: r.o wl: hdd 20yds out* **5/1**[3]

4 hd **Deauville Prince (FR)**[26] 5678 2-9-2 0 .... MickaelBarzalona 1 104
(Tom Dascombe) *settled 4th: wnt 3rd bef st: r.o wl u.p fnl f: nt qckn fnl 50yds* **8/1**

5 1 ¾ **Local Lover (FR)**[32] 5471 2-9-2 0 .... MaximeGuyon 8 100
(H-A Pantall, France) *racd 2nd: r.o wl u.p ent fnl f: nt qckn fnl 100yds: styd on* **8/1**

6 1 ¼ **Saint Agnan (FR)**[26] 2-9-2 0 .... GregoryBenoist 4 97
(J-C Rouget, France) *settled 5th: u.p 1 1/2f out: nt qckn: styd on fnl f* **4/1**[2]

7 1 ¼ **San Juan (FR)**[19] 5899 2-9-2 0 ....(b) MarcLerner 2 94
(C Lerner, France) *hld up towards rr: rdn early in st: nt qckn u.p: styd on fnl f* **139/10**

8 2 ½ **Saint Crepin (FR)**[13] 2-9-2 0 .... IoritzMendizabal 6 88
(J-C Rouget, France) *sn led: stl in front u.p 1 1/2f out: hdd 1f out: sn fdd: eased fnl 100yds* **16/1**

1m 45.61s (7.21) **Going Correction** +1.05s/f (Soft) 8 Ran SP% **122.1**
Speed ratings: **105,104,104,103,102 100,99,97**
WIN (incl. 1 euro stake): 8.30. PLACES: 1.70, 1.40, 1.40. DF: 11.60. SF: 24.80.
Owner Pearl Bloodstock Ltd **Bred** Petra Bloodstock Agency Ltd **Trained** France

FOCUS

An ordinary renewal in which the winner is perhaps the best guide to the level.

NOTEBOOK

Pearl Flute(IRE) gave the form of the Prix Morny a bit of a boost as he was only seventh in that Group 1 two starts ago, but the truth is he's improved for stepping up in trip. Settled in sixth place early, he quickened well to win with something in hand. He's entered in the Gran Criterium at Milan and could also be entered in the Criterium International at Saint-Cloud, while the Breeders' Cup Juvenile Turf is also a possibility.

Visiyani(FR), a maiden winner over the C&D earlier in the month, finished his race off strongly, and looks the type who'll be suited by further next year, being out of a mare who was third in the French Oaks.

Deauville Prince(FR), winner of a weakish 6f Listed race at Ripon last time, faced a different test here and probably improved for the longer distance.

6508a PRIX DU PRINCE D'ORANGE (GROUP 3) (3YO) (TURF) 1m 2f

1:30 (12:00) 3-Y-O **£33,333** (£13,333; £10,000; £6,666; £3,333)

RPR

1 **Starboard**[38] 5250 3-9-2 0 .... ChristopheSoumillon 7 111
(John Gosden) *sn led on wd outside: in front ent st: qcknd wl u.p 1 1/2f out: wnt clr 1f out: nvr threatened: comf* **3/1**[1]

2 3 **Prince Mag (IRE)**[37] 5289 3-9-2 0 .... AdrienFouassier 4 105
(A Couetil, France) *hld up towards rr: mde gd prog ent fnl f: qcknd wl u.str.p 150yds out: wnt 3rd 100yds out: r.o wl to go 2nd 50yds out* **180/1**

3 hd **Albion**[70] 4121 3-9-2 0 .... MaximeGuyon 5 105
(A Fabre, France) *settled in 3rd: rdn early in st: r.o wl to go 2nd 1f out: styd on wl: lost 2nd 50yds out: styd on wl* **5/1**

4 ¾ **Gris De Reve (FR)**[38] 5250 3-9-2 0 .... AntoineHamelin 6 103
(J-P Gauvin, France) *hld up towards rr: mde gd prog u.p ent fnl f: r.o wl to go 4th 50yds out* **10/1**

5 ¾ **Lucayan (FR)**[95] 3239 3-9-2 0 .... StephanePasquier 1 102
(F Rohaut, France) *settled midfield: r.o u.p 1 1/2f out to go 5th: styd on one pce fnl 100yds* **9/2**[3]

6 ½ **Mandaean**[128] 2210 3-9-2 0 .... MickaelBarzalona 8 101
(Mahmood Al Zarooni) *hld up in rr: sme prog on wd outside 1f out: nt qckn ins fnl f: styd on* **5/1**

7 1 ¼ **Nutello (USA)**[70] 4121 3-9-2 0 ....(p) OlivierPeslier 3 98
(C Laffon-Parias, France) *settled in 2nd: rdn 1 1/2f out: r.o briefly: no ex 1f out: began to fade ent fnl 150yds* **4/1**[2]

8 2 **Lidari (FR)**[70] 4121 3-9-2 0 .... Christophe-PatriceLemaire 2 94
(J-C Rouget, France) *w.w in midfield: rdn 1 1/2f out: nt qckn: wknd ins fnl f* **8/1**

2m 16.7s (12.70) **Going Correction** +1.55s/f (Heav) 8 Ran SP% **117.3**
Speed ratings: **111,108,108,107,107 106,105,104**
WIN (incl. 1 euro stake): 3.80. PLACES: 1.70, 4.40, 2.30. DF: 30.80. SF: 41.70.
Owner K Abdulla **Bred** Juddmonte Farms Ltd **Trained** Newmarket, Suffolk

NOTEBOOK

Starboard, fourth in the Group 2 Prix Guillaume d'Ornano last time, appreciated the drop in class and ran out an easy winner. He's been rated as running to a small personal best and the plan is to keep him in training as a 4yo, when he should improve again.

Mandaean, off since the Dante, in which he ran poorly, was again disappointing. He hasn't grown and the suspicion is that he hasn't trained on.

6509 - 6510a (Foreign Racing) - See Raceform Interactive

5756 HAMILTON (R-H)

Sunday, September 23

OFFICIAL GOING: Heavy (7.3)

Wind: Fresh, half behind Weather: Cloudy, bright

6511 BET TOTEPLACEPOT TEXT TOTE TO 89660 NURSERY 6f 5y

2:20 (2:22) (Class 5) (0-75,74) 2-Y-O **£2,911** (£866; £432; £216) **Stalls** Centre

Form RPR

4120 1 **Alexandrakollontai (IRE)**[12] 6121 2-8-1 57 ....(b) JulieBurke(3) 5 65+
(Alistair Whillans) *prom: hdwy to ld over 1f out: pushed clr fnl f: readily* **20/1**

5230 2 5 **Twilight Pearl**[23] 5799 2-8-7 60 ....(b[1]) DavidAllan 7 53
(Tim Easterby) *cl up: led over 2f out to over 1f out: kpt on same pce ins fnl f* **12/1**

0535 3 2 ½ **Plexolini**[10] 6155 2-8-0 53 .... JamesSullivan 9 39
(Jo Hughes) *led to over 2f out: rallied: outpcd appr fnl f* **12/1**

450 4 ¾ **Megamunch (IRE)**[32] 5475 2-9-7 74 .... GrahamLee 1 57+
(Linda Stubbs) *bhd on outside: drvn over 2f out: kpt on fnl f: nvr able to chal* **5/1**[3]

6052 5 hd **Lucy Bee**[6] 6310 2-8-1 54 .... AndrewMullen 3 37
(Keith Dalgleish) *bhd: swtchd lft after 2f: rdn over 2f out: kpt on fnl f: n.d* **9/2**[2]

0240 6 6 **Izzy Boy (USA)**[14] 6070 2-9-3 70 .... AdrianNicholls 8 35
(Mark Johnston) *plld hrd: in tch: rdn over 2f out: hung rt and wknd over 1f out* **3/1**[1]

204 7 1 ¾ **Lucy Minaj**[39] 5222 2-8-7 60 .... TomEaves 6 19
(Bryan Smart) *t.k.h: hld up in tch: drvn over 2f out: hung rt and wknd over 1f out* **12/1**

2233 8 hd **Deepest Blue**[16] 6016 2-9-4 71 .... WilliamBuick 2 30+
(Jamie Osborne) *in tch on outside: effrt and rdn 2f out: btn and eased ins fnl f* **3/1**[1]

0060 9 1 ½ **Precision Strike**[5] 6337 2-8-1 55 ow2 .... DeclanCannon(3) 4 11+
(Richard Guest) *hld up bhd ldng gp: drvn along over 2f out: wknd wl over 1f out* **33/1**

1m 15.18s (2.98) **Going Correction** +0.375s/f (Good) **9** Ran SP% **115.6**
Speed ratings (Par 95): **95,88,85,84,83 75,73,73,71**
toteswingers 1&2 £25.10, 2&3 £14.80, 1&3 £28.10 CSF £236.13 CT £3000.95 TOTE £26.00: £6.20, £1.90, £4.20; EX 147.80 Trifecta £631.10 Part won. Pool: £852.91 - 0.80 winning tickets..
Owner R Cabrey W Orr C Spark **Bred** Sean O'Sullivan **Trained** Newmill-On-Slitrig, Borders

FOCUS

Despite a dry night the ground was given as heavy (GoingStick 7.3). Julie Burke, who rode the winner of the first, said it was "heavy, but is starting to dry out so is a bit tacky", while Adrian Nicholls said it was "testing but they're going through it okay". A modest nursery in which few handled conditions. A personal best from the winner.

NOTEBOOK

Alexandrakollontai(IRE) was having her second start for her new yard and coped with the ground better than most of her rivals, drawing right away in the closing stages. The reapplication of blinkers was certainly not a negative, and her trainer mentioned that he might have to turn her out quickly under a penalty now, before the handicapper gets a chance to react. Official explanation: trainer said, regarding apparent improvement in form, that the filly benefited from the reapplication of blinkers. (op 25-1)

Twilight Pearl, who was on her toes beforehand, had blinkers on for the first time. She has form in bad ground and this was a solid effort, but she's not progressing. (op 10-1 tchd 14-1)

Plexolini appreciated the return to 6f and plugged on alongside the stands' rail. (op 18-1)

Megamunch(IRE) didn't cope with conditions as well as expected (maiden win came on soft) and was outpaced more or less throughout. (op 9-2 tchd 6-1)

Lucy Bee didn't seem to benefit a whole lot by switching to the stands' rail. (op 5-1)

Izzy Boy(USA) was always going to struggle to see out the trip in this ground after pulling hard early. (op 4-1)

Lucy Minaj also compromised her chance by racing keenly. (tchd 11-1)

Deepest Blue got tired and was eased in the closing stages. Conditions were probably just too bad for him. Official explanation: trainer's rep said colt was unsuited by the heavy ground (op 11-4)

6512 BRITISH STALLION STUDS SUPPORTING BRITISH RACING E B F MAIDEN STKS 1m 65y

2:50 (2:51) (Class 5) 2-Y-O **£3,234** (£962; £481; £240) **Stalls** Low

Form RPR

3203 1 **Bix (IRE)**[9] 6188 2-9-3 66 .... GrahamLee 1 71
(Alan Berry) *trckd ldrs: stdy hdwy 3f out: led over 1f out: drvn out* **12/1**

23 2 2 ½ **Jullundar (IRE)**[11] 6133 2-9-3 0 .... SamHitchcott 5 66
(Mick Channon) *prom: hdwy over 3f out: effrt and chsd wnr over 1f out: edgd rt: one pce fnl f* **9/4**[2]

4 3 2 ½ **Ghur (USA)**[11] 6132 2-8-12 0 .... WilliamBuick 3 55
(Mark Johnston) *led: rdn over 2f out: hdd over 1f out: kpt on same pce fnl f* **4/1**[3]

4 7 **Dolphin Village (IRE)** 2-9-3 0 .... TonyHamilton 4 45
(Richard Fahey) *s.i.s: hld up: rdn over 3f out: edgd rt and no imp fnl 2f* **10/1**

66 5 13 **Luv U Whatever**[27] 5655 2-9-3 0 .... J-PGuillambert 7 16
(Jo Hughes) *bhd: drvn fr 1/2-way: struggling wl over 3f out: n.d after* **50/1**

64 6 3 ½ **Pearl Ransom (IRE)**[15] 6043 2-9-3 0 .... PhillipMakin 6 8
(Kevin Ryan) *in tch: struggling over 3f out: edgd rt and sn wknd* **2/1**[1]

0 7 12 **Bonne Amie (FR)**[30] 5570 2-8-12 0 .... RichardKingscote 8
(Tom Dascombe) *trckd ldr: struggling over 3f out: sn btn: t.o* **7/1**

1m 55.14s (6.74) **Going Correction** +0.775s/f (Yiel) 7 Ran SP% **115.3**
Speed ratings (Par 95): **97,94,92,85,72 68,56**
toteswingers 1&2 £2.40, 2&3 £2.70, 1&3 £3.40 CSF £40.04 TOTE £10.40: £3.50, £2.50; EX 22.90 Trifecta £94.80 Pool: £771.47 - 6.02 winning tickets..
Owner A B Parr **Bred** Longfort Stud **Trained** Cockerham, Lancs

FOCUS

An ordinary maiden run in bad ground. Straightforward form, the winner rated back to his mark.

NOTEBOOK

Bix(IRE), the most experienced runner in the line-up, was having his seventh start, but just his second for Alan Berry having previously been with Brian Meehan. He saw his race out strongly and will get further in time. (op 10-1)

Jullundar(IRE) had run well in soft/heavy ground in his first two starts but wasn't quite as strong as the winner at the finish. It was another sound effort, though, and handicaps are now an option. (op 6-4 tchd 5-2)

Ghur(USA) ◆, whose trainer had sent out the winner in five of the previous eight years, took them along but got tired in the closing stages. He's not bred for these conditions at all but he's now had two starts in heavy ground, and one more will qualify him for a mark, which could prove tasty once he goes handicapping on a quicker surface or the AW.

Dolphin Village(IRE) showed his inexperience at the start with a slow start and began to wander as he tired inside the last 2f, but this was a decent effort on his racecourse debut considering the conditions, and as a son of Cape Cross he ought to do better on a sounder surface. (op 12-1 tchd 14-1)

Luv U Whatever was never a serious threat.

Pearl Ransom(IRE) wasn't at home in the ground at all. He should have more to offer in handicaps. Official explanation: trainer's rep said gelding was unsuited by the heavy ground (op 3-1 tchd 15-8)

Bonne Amie(FR) came in for some support but was floundering some way out. (op 12-1)

6513 BET TOTEQUADPOT TEXT TOTE TO 89660 E B F CONDITIONS STKS 1m 65y

3:20 (3:21) (Class 3) 3-Y-O+ **£9,056** (£2,695; £1,346; £673) **Stalls** Low

Form RPR

0320 **1** **Gregorian (IRE)**[51] 4760 3-9-0 114 WilliamBuick 4 74
(John Gosden) *t.k.h: trckd ldrs: stdy hdwy over 3f out: rdn to ld ins fnl f: drvn out* **1/7**[1]

520 **2** ¾ **Atlantic Sport (USA)**[15] 6024 7-9-4 94 SamHitchcott 2 72
(Mick Channon) *led: rdn over 2f out: hdd ins fnl f: rallied: hld towards fin* **13/2**[2]

561 **3** 7 **Spread Boy (IRE)**[48] 4865 5-8-11 51 JordanHibberd(7) 1 56
(Alan Berry) *trckd ldr to over 3f out: rdn and wknd fr 2f out* **125/1**

2640 **4** ¾ **Blues Jazz**[40] 5186 6-9-4 78 TomEaves 3 54
(Ian Semple) *in tch: rdn and struggling over 3f out: sn btn* **22/1**[3]

1m 53.69s (5.29) **Going Correction** +0.775s/f (Yiel)
WFA 3 from 5yo+ 4lb **4** Ran SP% **106.0**
Speed ratings (Par 107): **104,103,96,95**
CSF £1.39 TOTE £1.20; EX 1.60.
Owner H R H Princess Haya Of Jordan **Bred** Rathasker Stud **Trained** Newmarket, Suffolk

FOCUS
An uncompetitive conditions race run in a relatively slow time. The third limits the form.

NOTEBOOK
Gregorian(IRE) faced a straightforward task on paper as he had plenty in hand of his rivals on ratings, but he made hard work of landing short odds. He's suited by cut in the ground, but these were extreme conditions, and, while he travelled up to challenge the leader looking as though he'd do it easily, he didn't find as much as he promised for pressure. In this ground it was always likely to be difficult to impress, and clearly he was nowhere near his best, but he got the job done.
Atlantic Sport(USA) would have been 20lb better off with the winner in a handicap, so this was a fine effort. Very much at home in testing ground, conditions swung things in his favour, but he was just unable to bridge the difference in class. (op 15-2 tchd 6-1)
Spread Boy(IRE) handled the ground better than the higher-rated Blues Jazz and won the separate battle for third place prize money of £1,346. (op 100-1)

6514 TOTEPOOL MOBILE TEXT TOTE TO 89660 H'CAP 6f 5y

3:50 (3:50) (Class 5) (0-70,70) 3-Y-O **£3,234** (£962; £481; £240) **Stalls** Centre

Form RPR

0 **1** **Heroic Endeavour (IRE)**[6] 6326 3-8-7 56 oh3 (b) RobertWinston 12 64
(Mrs John Harrington, Ire) *hld up in tch: effrt and drvn 2f out: led ins fnl f: kpt on strly* **7/1**

0610 **2** ¾ **Windygoul Lad**[13] 6106 3-8-8 57 AndrewMullen 6 63
(Keith Dalgleish) *prom: effrt and drvn whn n.m.r briefly over 1f out: styd on wl fnl f to take 2nd towards fin* **12/1**

1143 **3** shd **Economic Crisis (IRE)**[22] 5831 3-9-5 68 GrahamLee 7 74
(Alan Berry) *hld up: effrt whn n.m.r briefly over 2f out and over 1f out: kpt on ins fnl f* **7/1**

3361 **4** 1 **Legal Bond**[24] 5760 3-8-13 62 TomEaves 11 64
(Bryan Smart) *t.k.h: cl up: led over 1f out: sn rdn: edgd rt and hdd ins fnl f: lost two pls towards fin* **7/1**

6013 **5** 1 ½ **Celestial Dawn**[24] 5757 3-8-13 62 JamesSullivan 10 60
(John Weymes) *s.i.s: bhd and outpcd: hdwy whn hung lft 2f out: kpt on fnl f: no imp* **18/1**

3604 **6** 7 **Rock Canyon (IRE)**[25] 5728 3-8-8 57 (p) PJMcDonald 9 32
(Linda Perratt) *led tl rdn and hdd over 1f out: sn wknd* **20/1**

0221 **7** 1 ½ **Blue Shoes (IRE)**[25] 5728 3-9-7 70 DavidAllan 5 40
(Tim Easterby) *cl up: drvn over 2f out: wknd over 1f out* **6/1**[3]

4614 **8** 1 ½ **Vital Calling**[15] 6048 3-9-7 70 GrahamGibbons 4 36
(David Barron) *in tch: rdn over 2f out: wknd over 1f out* **9/2**[2]

1423 **9** 4 **Colbyor**[27] 5676 3-9-5 68 TonyHamilton 1 21
(Richard Fahey) *hld up: drvn and struggling over 2f out: sn btn* **4/1**[1]

2220 **10** 2 ½ **Dream Walker (FR)**[50] 4830 3-9-2 65 PatrickMathers 3
(Ian McInnes) *trckd ldrs: drvn over 3f out: wknd wl over 1f out* **10/1**

1m 15.65s (3.45) **Going Correction** +0.55s/f (Yiel) **10** Ran SP% **116.8**
Speed ratings (Par 101): **99,98,97,96,94 85,83,81,75,72**
toteswingers 1&2 £19.90, 2&3 £18.00, 1&3 £12.60 CSF £87.54 CT £626.01 TOTE £8.80: £2.60, £2.00, £2.40; EX 126.40 Trifecta £306.40 Pool: £869.77 - 2.10 winning tickets..
Owner Lady Brookeborough **Bred** Lady Janet Brookeborough **Trained** Moone, Co Kildare

FOCUS
Quite a competitive handicap but ordinary form. The winner is rated to his Naas July form.
Colbyor Official explanation: trainer's rep had no explanation for the poor form shown

6515 TOTEPOOL E B F FLOWER OF SCOTLAND FILLIES' H'CAP 6f 5y

4:20 (4:21) (Class 3) (0-95,91) 3-Y-O+ **£9,056** (£2,695; £1,346; £673) **Stalls** Centre

Form RPR

4405 **1** **Coolminx (IRE)**[1] 6465 5-8-12 79 (p) TonyHamilton 9 88
(Richard Fahey) *prom: effrt and chsd ldr over 1f out: hung rt: led ins fnl f: kpt on wl* **11/2**

1234 **2** 1 ¼ **Spinatrix**[1] 6466 4-9-7 91 (p) LeeTopliss(3) 7 96
(Michael Dods) *cl up: led over 2f out: edgd rt and hdd ins fnl f: kpt on same pce* **9/4**[1]

16 **3** 2 **Breezolini**[30] 5539 4-8-8 75 RobertWinston 6 74
(Geoffrey Harker) *missed break: bhd: hdwy 2f out: kpt on fnl f: nt rch first two* **11/1**

3144 **4** 4 ½ **Shesastar**[31] 5520 4-9-7 88 GrahamGibbons 8 72
(David Barron) *bhd: checked over 3f out: sn rdn: hdwy over 1f out: nvr able to chal* **5/1**[3]

3300 **5** 4 ½ **Wicked Wench**[2] 6427 3-8-12 81 J-PGuillambert 5 51
(Jo Hughes) *led after 2f to over 2f out: rdn and wknd over 1f out* **12/1**

4231 **6** 3 ¼ **Catwalk (IRE)**[23] 5800 3-9-0 83 (v) WilliamBuick 4 42
(James Fanshawe) *prom: effrt and rdn over 2f out: wknd over 1f out* **7/2**[2]

0615 **7** ½ **Lisiere (IRE)**[27] 5676 3-8-8 80 (b) MichaelMetcalfe(3) 2 38
(Mrs K Burke) *led 2f: cl up: drvn 1/2-way: wknd fr 2f out* **10/1**

1604 **8** 2 ¾ **Muaamara**[66] 4258 3-9-6 89 SamHitchcott 1 38
(Mick Channon) *t.k.h: in tch: rdn and hung lft 2f out: sn btn* **12/1**

5100 **9** 5 **Lollina Paulina**[30] 5539 3-8-9 78 (b[1]) AmyRyan 3 11
(Kevin Ryan) *t.k.h: hld up: edgd lft over 3f out: sn drvn along: btn over 1f out* **25/1**

1m 14.81s (2.61) **Going Correction** +0.55s/f (Yiel)
WFA 3 from 4yo+ 2lb **9** Ran SP% **121.7**
Speed ratings (Par 104): **104,102,99,93,87 83,82,79,72**
toteswingers 1&2 £4.00, 2&3 £6.80, 1&3 £12.70 CSF £19.37 CT £137.40 TOTE £6.30: £1.70, £1.40, £1.90; EX 26.60 Trifecta £701.20 Part won. Pool: £947.61 - 0.81 winning tickets..
Owner Mrs H Steel **Bred** D Couper Snr **Trained** Musley Bank, N Yorks

FOCUS
Two of these were making a quick reappearance having run at Ayr the previous day, and they showed their wellbeing by finishing first and second. Straightforward form in an ordinary time.

NOTEBOOK
Coolminx(IRE), fifth in the Bronze Cup the day before, appreciated the weaker competition back against her own sex and travelled like the winner from some way out. She had to dig deep to see off Spinatrix but she was well on top at the finish. (op 9-1)
Spinatrix, who came here on the back of a fourth place in the Silver Cup the previous day, didn't go down without a fight and posted another solid effort in defeat. (op 3-1 tchd 10-3)
Breezolini missed the kick and trailed the field early on. She kept on well to beat the rest handily enough, but the first two, who have shown their form in stronger company, were just too strong for her. (op 12-1)
Shesastar, back in distance, ran alright, but she probably doesn't want the ground this testing. (op 9-2)
Wicked Wench, who ran at Ayr on Friday, is more effective over the minimum trip, and she just didn't get home here. (op 16-1 tchd 18-1)
Catwalk(IRE) proved very effective in soft at Thirsk last time, and came here for the ground, but these conditions proved altogether more demanding, and her rider reported that the filly didn't handle them. Official explanation: trainer's rep said filly was unsuited by the heavy ground (op 5-2 tchd 9-4)

6516 RACING POST FORM WITH TOTEPOOL MOBILE H'CAP 1m 3f 16y

4:50 (4:50) (Class 5) (0-70,71) 3-Y-O **£3,234** (£962; £481; £240) **Stalls** Low

Form RPR

5215 **1** **Red Tyke (IRE)**[22] 4955 3-8-8 57 oh1 ow1 MichaelO'Connell 1 64
(John Quinn) *t.k.h early: mde all: rdn over 2f out: edgd rt: hld on gamely fnl f* **7/2**[3]

1025 **2** 1 ¼ **Vexillum (IRE)**[25] 5744 3-9-1 64 SamHitchcott 6 69
(Mick Channon) *in tch: effrt over 2f out: rdn and chsd wnr over 1f out: kpt on: hld nr fin* **9/2**

1463 **3** hd **Luctor Emergo (IRE)**[25] 5729 3-9-4 67 (p) TomEaves 3 72
(Keith Dalgleish) *cl up: wnt 2nd over 4f out: swtchd lft over 2f out: hung lft and outpcd over 1f out: styd on ins fnl f* **85/40**[1]

4062 **4** 17 **Echo Of Footsteps**[8] 6262 3-9-0 63 GrahamGibbons 4 39
(Michael Herrington) *plld hrd early: chsd ldr after 3f to over 4f out: edgd rt and wknd 2f out* **11/4**[2]

5040 **5** 14 **Quiet Appeal (IRE)**[15] 6056 3-8-7 56 AdrianNicholls 7
(Mark Johnston) *t.k.h: pressed wnr 3f: lost pl 1/2-way: drvn and struggling over 3f out: sn btn* **15/2**

0000 **6** 3 **Lochluichart (IRE)**[19] 5919 3-8-8 57 oh11 ow1 (e) PJMcDonald 5
(Ian Semple) *t.k.h early: bhd: struggling fr 1/2-way: sn btn* **66/1**

2m 33.8s (8.20) **Going Correction** +0.775s/f (Yiel) **6** Ran SP% **112.3**
Speed ratings (Par 101): **101,100,99,87,77 75**
toteswingers 1&2 £2.60, 2&3 £2.80, 1&3 £2.40 CSF £19.29 TOTE £5.40: £2.00, £2.10; EX 19.90.
Owner T G S Wood **Bred** Tally-Ho Stud **Trained** Settrington, N Yorks

FOCUS
An ordinary handicap, rated around the third.

6517 BET TOTEPOOL TEXT TOTE TO 89660 H'CAP 1m 5f 9y

5:20 (5:20) (Class 4) (0-80,80) 3-Y-O+ **£5,175** (£1,540; £769; £384) **Stalls** Low

Form RPR

6104 **1** **Moidore**[30] 5540 3-9-5 80 MichaelO'Connell 11 89
(John Quinn) *prom: stdy hdwy over 3f out: drvn to ld over 1f out: edgd rt: styd on wl fnl f* **7/4**[1]

1410 **2** 1 ½ **Red Orator**[15] 6037 3-9-2 77 AdrianNicholls 13 84
(Mark Johnston) *led: rdn over 2f out: hdd over 1f out: rallied: hld wl ins fnl f* **7/2**[2]

5430 **3** 2 ¼ **Toughness Danon**[5] 6349 6-9-4 70 (t) PJMcDonald 2 73
(Brendan Powell) *t.k.h: prom: stdy hdwy and ev ch over 2f out: sn rdn: kpt on same pce fnl f* **10/1**

600 **4** 10 **Spirit Of A Nation (IRE)**[33] 3114 7-9-6 72 GrahamLee 5 60
(Jim Goldie) *hld up: drvn and outpcd over 3f out: rallied over 1f out: kpt on: nvr able to chal* **9/1**

313 **5** 2 ½ **Bavarian Nordic (USA)**[26] 5714 7-8-9 61 AmyRyan 8 46
(Richard Whitaker) *t.k.h: prom: hdwy to press ldr after 4f: rdn over 3f out: wknd over 2f out* **9/1**

2110 **6** ½ **Lady Bluesky**[22] 5830 9-9-0 71 GarryWhillans(5) 3 55
(Alistair Whillans) *hld up in tch: drvn and outpcd over 3f out: no imp fnl 2f* **5/1**[3]

033- **7** 14 **Tartan Jura**[489] 2360 4-9-4 70 WilliamBuick 1 33
(Mark Johnston) *pressed ldr 4f: cl up: rdn and rn green over 3f out: wknd over 2f out* **7/1**

3m 3.9s (10.00) **Going Correction** +0.775s/f (Yiel)
WFA 3 from 4yo+ 9lb **7** Ran SP% **116.8**
Speed ratings (Par 105): **100,99,97,91,90 89,81**
toteswingers 1&2 £3.00, 2&3 £7.00, 1&3 £8.20 CSF £8.33 CT £46.74 TOTE £2.80: £1.60, £3.30; EX 10.90 Trifecta £104.20 Pool: £315.52 - 2.24 winning tickets..
Owner Estio Pinnacle Racing **Bred** The Queen **Trained** Settrington, N Yorks
■ Stewards' Enquiry : Michael O'Connell four-day ban: used whip above permitted level (Oct 8-11)

FOCUS
Half of the declared runners had been withdrawn and so this wasn't anywhere near as competitive as it had promised to be, but it still produced a good finish between two relatively unexposed three-year-olds. The first three were clear and the winner rates a small personal best.
T/Plt: £461.10 to a £1 stake. Pool: £55,783.74 - 88.31 winning tickets. T/Qpdt: £28.60 to a £1 stake. Pool: £4,752.93 - 122.85 winning tickets. RY

5953 GOWRAN PARK (R-H)

Sunday, September 23

OFFICIAL GOING: Good (good to firm in places on hurdle course)

6518a DENNY CORDELL LAVARACK & LANWADES STUD FILLIES STKS (GROUP 3) 1m 1f 100y

3:45 (3:45) 3-Y-O+ **£37,916** (£11,083; £5,250; £1,750)

RPR

1 **Aloof (IRE)**[14] 6079 3-9-0 103 WJLee 4 107
(David Wachman, Ire) *led tl hdd after 1f: settled in 2nd: clsd gng best to ld over 1 1/2f out: strly pressed ins fnl f: kpt on wl towards fin* **12/1**

2 ¾ **Beatrice Aurore (IRE)**[22] 5849 4-9-5 102 JohnnyMurtagh 2 105
(John Dunlop) *chsd ldrs: 4th 1/2-way: swtchd lft and r.o wl to chal ent fnl f: sn no ex: kpt on* **3/1**[2]

3 2 ½ **Shebella (IRE)**[33] 5463 3-9-0 105 DeclanMcDonogh 6 100+
(John M Oxx, Ire) *chsd ldrs: pushed along in 5th over 3f out: sn rdn and kpt on wout ever threatening principals ins fnl f* **16/1**

4 ½ **Esentepe (IRE)**[14] 6079 3-9-3 102................................. WayneLordan 5 102+
(David Wachman, Ire) *hld up towards rr: hdwy on outer 3f out to go 4th ent fnl f: kpt on same pce u.p towards fin* **20/1**

5 2¾ **Momentary**[58] 4556 3-9-1 106 ow1..................................(b¹) JPO'Brien 8 94
(Michael Bell) *slowly away: sn pushed along to ld after 1f: hdd 1 1/2f out and sn no ex: wknd fnl f* **14/1**

6 nk **Andromeda Galaxy (FR)**[118] 2570 4-9-5 .... TomQueally 3 93+
(Sir Henry Cecil) *cl up: 3rd 4f out: pushed along to cl over 2f out and sn no imp ins fnl f* **6/1³**

7 2 **Soon (IRE)**[14] 6080 3-9-0 99...................................... SeamieHeffernan 1 88+
(A P O'Brien, Ire) *towards rr: sme hdwy into st: rdn under 2f out and edgd lft fnl f: nvr a threat* **16/1**

8 hd **Caponata (USA)**[14] 6080 3-9-0 110.................................. PatSmullen 10 80+
(D K Weld, Ire) *hld up towards rr: sme hdwy on outer appr st: sn pushed along and no imp under 2f out: eased towards fin* **11/8¹**

9 6½ **Devotion (IRE)**[28] 5643 3-9-0 102........................... CO'Donoghue 7 75+
(A P O'Brien, Ire) *towards rr: rdn and swtchd rt ent fnl f: n.d whn sltly hmpd ins fnl f: eased* **33/1**

10 4¼ **Alla Speranza**[15] 6062 3-9-3 107..................................(t) KevinManning 9 69+
(J S Bolger, Ire) *chsd ldrs: wknd under 3f out: eased ins fnl f* **10/1**

2m 0.27s (-6.73)
WFA 3 from 4yo 5lb **10** Ran SP% **124.3**
CSF £51.30 TOTE £19.20: £4.60, £1.70, £6.00; DF 72.80.
Owner Mrs John Magnier & Michael Tabor & Derrick Smith **Bred** Liberty Bloodstock **Trained** Goolds Cross, Co Tipperary

FOCUS
The consistent Aloof gained due reward for several decent placed efforts and the better ground didn't do her any harm. The form fits the recent race averages, pretty low for a Group 3.

NOTEBOOK
Aloof(IRE) was suited by the strong pace and momentum as much as anything carried her to the front well over a furlong out. In the end once getting there she didn't do a huge amount and looked to have a bit left in the tank should she have needed it. It was a pretty classy performance and if the ground remains good there are plenty of late season options for a filly of her ability. (op 14/1)
Beatrice Aurore(IRE) probably ran as good a race as she has this season. She raced handily enough and was the only one to seriously go in pursuit of the winner from over a furlong out. It was a good performance in the sense that she pulled clear of everything else but she was probably flattered a little by her proximity to the winner. (op 4/1)
Shebella(IRE) ran her best race for a while and the ground was probably key to her decent showing as well. Unable to challenge the first two from over a furlong out, she ran on from mid-division to decent enough effect. It was a run of some encouragement.
Esentepe(IRE) was stepping back up in trip here and she ran as though she shouldn't be bothered by stepping back up to 1m 2f. She just lacked the pace to get into a challenging position but she ran on to reasonable effect.
Momentary pulled her way into an early lead but she probably went off too quickly and had little left to offer when challenged and headed in the straight.
Andromeda Galaxy(FR) appeared to get quite warm in the preliminaries and ended fading in the straight having tracked the winner for much of the way. (op 9/2)
Caponata(USA) might have found the ground a shade too quick for her. She wasn't travelling before they turned in and despite being done no favours by being forced to race very wide in the straight she never looked like challenging. Official explanation: jockey said filly ran flat (op 7/4 tchd 5/4)

6519 - 6521a (Foreign Racing) - See Raceform Interactive

2965 COLOGNE (R-H)
Sunday, September 23

OFFICIAL GOING: Turf: good

6522a WINTERKONIGIN-TRIAL (LISTED RACE) (2YO FILLIES) (TURF) 7f 110y
2:35 (12:00) 2-Y-O **£25,000** (£8,333; £4,583; £2,500; £1,250)

RPR

1 **Viletta (GER)** 2-9-2 0.. KClijmans 1 95
(Uwe Ostmann, Germany) **101/10**

2 ¾ **Next Green (GER)**[25] 2-8-11 0................................... AStarke 8 88
(P Schiergen, Germany) **11/5¹**

3 1¼ **Zazera (FR)**[24] 5781 2-9-2 0.................................. OlivierPeslier 7 90
(Mario Hofer, Germany) **13/5²**

4 ½ **Picayune (GER)** 2-9-2 0... ADeVries 3 89
(A Wohler, Germany) **112/10**

5 3 **Oriental Lady (GER)** 2-9-2 0....................................... EFrank 4 82
(Uwe Ostmann, Germany) **9/1**

6 1 **Shamanda (GER)**[25] 2-8-11 0................................... EPedroza 2 74
(A Wohler, Germany) **61/10**

7 ½ **Dream Wedding**[24] 5781 2-9-2 0.............................. FilipMinarik 6 78
(Mario Hofer, Germany) **91/10**

8 4½ **Tosca (GER)**[29] 5612 2-9-2 0................................... SHellyn 5 68
(Mrs Ilka Gansera-Leveque) *racd keenly and trckd ldrs early: restrained in rr after 2f: rdn and no imp fr 2 1/2f out: wl bhd appr fnl f* **39/10³**

1m 31.54s (91.54) **8** Ran SP% **130.6**
WIN (incl. 10 euro): 111. PLACES: 24, 15, 16. SF: 618.
Owner Gestut Auenquelle **Bred** Gestut Auenquelle **Trained** Germany

6523a PREIS VON EUROPA (GROUP 1) (3YO+) (TURF) 1m 4f
4:15 (12:00) 3-Y-0+ **£83,333** (£25,000; £12,500; £5,833; £2,500)

RPR

1 **Girolamo (GER)**[21] 5865 3-8-13 0............................... AStarke 2 115
(P Schiergen, Germany) *prom early: sn settled in midfield: rdn and wnt 3rd over 2f out: briefly outpcd appr fnl f: styd on wl u.p ins fnl f to ld 50yds out* **74/10**

2 ½ **Feuerblitz (GER)**[42] 5145 3-8-13 0............................ ADeVries 1 114
(M Figge, Germany) *led: hdd after 2f: remained prom: chal ldr 1 1/2f out: sn rdn: r.o u.p to ld 100yds out: hdd fnl 50yds: no ex* **69/10**

3 shd **Araldo**[28] 4-9-6 0.. MartinHarley 6 113
(P Harley, Germany) *settled in rr: last over 3f out: hdwy on outside appr fnl 2f: 5th and hrd rdn 1 1/2f out: styd on wl u.p ins fnl f: nrest at fin* **5/1³**

4 2 **Waldpark (GER)**[21] 4-9-6 0... JBojko 4 110
(A Wohler, Germany) *trckd ldr: chal on outside 2 1/2f out: led over 2f out: rdn over 1f out: hdd 100yds out: no ex* **7/1**

5 8 **Earl Of Tinsdal (GER)**[42] 5145 4-9-6 0........................ EPedroza 5 97
(A Wohler, Germany) *prom: led after 2f: rdn 2 1/2f out: hdd over 2f out: sn wknd* **12/5²**

6 5 **Baschar**[63] 4383 5-9-6 0... FilipMinarik 3 89
(M G Mintchev, Germany) *settled towards rr: rdn and no imp fr 2f out: wl bhd fnl f* **107/10**

7 4½ **Ovambo Queen (GER)**[21] 5865 5-9-3 0.......................... THellier 7 79
(Dr A Bolte, Germany) *settled towards rr: last whn rdr looked down and eased her ent appr fnl 1 1/2f* **8/5¹**

2m 26.37s (-6.53)
WFA 3 from 4yo+ 8lb **7** Ran SP% **130.1**
WIN (incl. 10 euro stake): 84. PLACES: 21, 19, 20. SF: 408.
Owner Gestut Ebbesloh **Bred** Gestut Ebbesloh **Trained** Germany

FOCUS
An ordinary race by Group 1 standards, rated around the first two.

NOTEBOOK
Girolamo(GER) didn't handle the track at Goodwood when only fourth in the Gordon Stakes, and was unsuited by the steady early pace in the Grosser Preis Von Baden last time, but he got the strong gallop he needs this time and stayed on well to edge a tight finish. He wants further than this really.

6511 HAMILTON (R-H)
Monday, September 24

OFFICIAL GOING: Heavy (7.0)
Wind: Fairly strong, half against Weather: Overcast, raining

6524 BRITISH STALLION STUDS SUPPORTING BRITISH RACING EBF MAIDEN STKS 6f 5y
1:40 (1:41) (Class 5) 2-Y-O **£3,234** (£962; £481; £240) **Stalls** Centre

Form RPR

04 1 **Exzachary**[27] 5715 2-9-3 0.......................................¹ J-PGuillambert 5 76
(Jo Hughes) *t.k.h: cl up: ev ch over 2f out: rdn and edgd rt over 1f out: led wl ins fnl f: r.o* **8/1²**

320 2 ½ **Fraserburgh (IRE)**[107] 2929 2-9-3 83.......................... JoeFanning 2 74
(Mark Johnston) *led: rdn over 1f out: hdd and no ex wl ins fnl f* **1/3¹**

0505 3 8 **Amelia Jay**[8] 6283 2-8-12 55.................................... GrahamLee 4 45
(Danielle McCormick) *t.k.h: cl up tl rdn and wknd over 1f out* **16/1**

3 4 13 **Indie Banned**[25] 5756 2-9-3 0................................. PJMcDonald 3 11
(Ben Haslam) *checked sn after s: chsd ldrs: outpcd over 3f out: sn n.d* **10/1³**

5 8 **Northside Ace (IRE)** 2-9-3 0................................. PaulMulrennan 1
(Linda Perratt) *dwlt: in tch 2f: sn struggling: nvr on terms* **14/1**

1m 17.13s (4.93) **Going Correction** +0.70s/f (Yiel) **5** Ran SP% **107.8**
Speed ratings (Par 95): **95,94,83,66,55**
CSF £10.96 TOTE £7.00: £4.30, £1.02; EX 11.80.
Owner Joseph Smith **Bred** Allseasons Bloodstock **Trained** Lambourn, Berks

FOCUS
Racing was given the go ahead following two morning inspections. The ground was described as heavy. A modest juvenile maiden, run in near bottomless ground with a strong crosswind, and something of an upset. The form could be 7lb better or worse.

NOTEBOOK
Exzachary took the scalp of the long odds-on favourite. Already a gelding and sporting first-time hood, he had shown only limited ability in his two previous starts, including on the deep Fibresand surface at Southwell, but was always up with the pace and, despite coming under pressure shortly after halfway, ultimately appeared to handle conditions better than the runner-up. It's unlikely this amounts to a great deal and connections will certainly be hoping that the handicapper doesn't take the from too literally. (op 7-1 tchd 6-1)
Fraserburgh(IRE) travelled like the best horse for most of the way but he simply couldn't quicken and was running up and down on the spot late on. He had failed to fire with ease underfoot at Newmarket prior to his three-month break and it travelled like the best horse for most of the way but he simply couldn't quicken and was running up and down on the spot late on. He had failed to fire with ease underfoot at Newmarket prior to his three-month break and it was surprising to see him in action on this much softer ground. His early-season form, on quick ground, reads well and he should be capable of better once back on a more suitable surface. (op 1-2 tchd 8-15)
Amelia Jay performed as well as could have been expected. Rated 55, she's well and truly exposed.

6525 TOTEPOOL MOBILE TEXT TOTE TO 89660 H'CAP 5f 4y
2:10 (2:10) (Class 4) (0-80,85) 3-Y-0+ **£5,175** (£1,540; £769; £384) **Stalls** Centre

Form RPR

332 1 **Jack Luey**[12] 6144 5-9-8 **78**.................................... DanielTudhope 9 89
(Lawrence Mullaney) *prom: effrt and drvn over 2f out: hdwy over 1f out: led ins fnl f: drvn out* **11/4¹**

6510 2 ½ **El McGlynn (IRE)**[13] 6116 3-8-8 **72**......................... HannahNunn(7) 4 81
(Peter Salmon) *t.k.h: led: rdn and edgd lft wl over 1f out: hdd ins fnl f: kpt on: hdd nr fin* **12/1**

1600 3 1¾ **Captain Scooby**[12] 6144 6-9-2 **75**......................... DeclanCannon(3) 10 78
(Richard Guest) *dwlt: hld up: rdn and hdwy over 1f out: edgd rt and styd on fnl f: could nt rch first two* **14/1**

2511 4 1½ **Majuro (IRE)**[7] 6319 8-9-8 **85** 6ex.........................(t) DavidBergin(7) 8 83
(Charles Smith) *cl up: rdn over 2f out: edgd rt over 1f out: wknd ins fnl f* **11/1**

0216 5 3¾ **Haajes**[12] 6144 8-9-7 **77**...(b) MickyFenton 5 61
(Paul Midgley) *in tch: rdn over 2f out: wknd appr fnl f* **9/2²**

1502 6 hd **Indego Blues**[26] 5737 3-9-7 **78**............................ AdrianNicholls 7 61
(David Nicholls) *t.k.h: hld up: rdn and hdwy over 1f out: wknd ins fnl f* **6/1³**

3104 7 1¾ **Crimson Knot (IRE)**[9] 6234 4-9-10 **80**...................... GrahamLee 6 57
(Alan Berry) *prom: drvn along over 2f out: wknd over 1f out* **9/2²**

-200 8 2½ **Master Bond**[42] 5167 3-9-6 **77**................................ TomEaves 2 45
(Bryan Smart) *dwlt: sn trcking ldrs: rdn over 2f out: wknd over 1f out* **8/1**

1m 2.84s (2.84) **Going Correction** +0.70s/f (Yiel)
WFA 3 from 4yo+ 1lb **8** Ran SP% **111.1**
Speed ratings (Par 105): **105,104,101,99,93 92,89,85**
toteswingers 1&2 £6.30, 2&3 £17.90, 1&3 £7.30 CSF £34.89 CT £377.77 TOTE £3.80: £1.10, £2.20, £3.90; EX 42.20.
Owner The Jack Partnership & S Rimmer **Bred** Miss D A Johnson **Trained** Great Habton, N Yorks

FOCUS
A fair sprint handicap, run at a steady pace in the testing conditions. The time wasn't bad and the first two rate personal bests.

6526 BET TOTEQUADPOT TEXT TOTE TO 89660 CLAIMING STKS 1m 1f 36y
2:40 (2:41) (Class 6) 3-5-Y-O **£2,264** (£673; £336; £168) **Stalls** Low

Form RPR

2403 1 **She's A Character**[25] 5759 5-8-9 73........................ TonyHamilton 1 73
(Richard Fahey) *covered up bhd ldrs: effrt and swtchd rt over 1f out: led ins fnl f: drvn out* **2/1²**

1160 2 2 **Act Your Shoe Size**[44] 5110 3-8-9 83....................... JoeFanning 3 73
(Keith Dalgleish) *cl up: ev ch over 2f out: rdn and led over 1f out to ins fnl f: kpt on same pce* **13/8¹**

-502 **3** *nse* **Underwritten**[13] 3543 3-8-9 72 (v) GrahamLee 2 73
(Donald McCain) *trckd ldrs: stdy hdwy over 3f out: effrt and drvn over 2f outf: one pce fnl f* **7/2**[3]

200 **4** *3 ¾* **Goldmadchen (GER)**[20] 5921 4-8-7 53 TomEaves 4 58
(Keith Dalgleish) *in tch: nt clr run over 2f out to over 1f out: sn rdn and no imp* **33/1**

0500 **5** *3 ¾* **Miami Gator (IRE)**[28] 5669 5-8-13 77 (v) PhillipMakin 5 56
(Mrs K Burke) *led: brought gp to stands' rail ent st: drvn over 3f out: hdd over 1f out: sn wknd* **8/1**

2m 7.47s (7.77) **Going Correction** +1.00s/f (Soft)
WFA 3 from 4yo+ 5lb **5** Ran SP% **107.7**
Speed ratings (Par 101): **105,103,103,99,96**
CSF £5.37 TOTE £3.40: £1.60, £1.40; EX 5.60.
Owner Aykroyd And Sons Ltd **Bred** Genesis Green & Deerpark Stud **Trained** Musley Bank, N Yorks
■ Stewards' Enquiry : Tony Hamilton one-day ban: careless riding (Oct 8)

FOCUS
A competitive, if only small-field claimer, run at a steady pace. Muddling form, limited by the fourth.

6527 BET TOTEPOOL TEXT TOTE TO 89660 MAIDEN STKS 1m 1f 36y
3:10 (3:14) (Class 5) 3-4-Y-0 **£2,587** (£770; £384; £192) **Stalls** Low

Form RPR

2- **1** **Danchai**[341] 6953 3-9-3 0 JoeFanning 9 90+
(William Haggas) *led 2f: cl up: led over 3f out: shkn up and drew clr fnl 2f: readily* **8/13**[1]

02 **2** *9* **Kept**[28] 5679 3-9-3 0 GrahamLee 7 65
(James Fanshawe) *trckd ldrs: effrt and rdn over 2f out: kpt on: no ch w wnr* **13/8**[2]

60 **3** *14* **Cruachan (IRE)**[142] 1867 3-9-3 0 TomEaves 1 34
(Ian Semple) *sn chsng ldrs: drvn over 3f out: wknd over 2f out* **25/1**[3]

0 **4** *11* **One Million**[14] 6102 3-9-3 0 TonyHamilton 6 10
(Rose Dobbin) *bhd: effrt and rdn over 3f out: nvr able to chal* **50/1**

5 *8* **Mrsb** 3-8-12 0 AndrewMullen 8
(Noel Wilson) *hld up: effrt and rdn over 3f out: sn wknd* **25/1**[3]

0- **6** *13* **Princeofperfection**[298] 7590 3-8-10 0 VictorSantos(7) 3
(Richard Ford) *hld up: stdy hdwy over 4f out: hung rt and wknd over 3f out* **100/1**

050 **7** *35* **Roseisle**[20] 5919 4-9-3 0 (t) PaulMulrennan 4
(Linda Perratt) *t.k.h: hdwy to ld after 2f: hdd over 3f out: sn struggling* **100/1**

2m 9.18s (9.48) **Going Correction** +1.00s/f (Soft)
WFA 3 from 4yo 5lb **7** Ran SP% **111.6**
Speed ratings (Par 103): **97,89,76,66,59 48,17**
toteswingers 1&2 £1.20, 2&3 £2.30, 1&3 £2.30 CSF £1.70 TOTE £1.50: £1.10, £1.20; EX 1.90.
Owner Saleh Al Homaizi & Imad Al Sagar **Bred** Brook Stud Bloodstock Ltd **Trained** Newmarket, Suffolk

FOCUS
Only a couple could be seriously fancied for this weak maiden and it was turned into a procession by Danchai. The form pair were clear and the winner could be smart.

6528 RACING POST FORM WITH TOTEPOOL H'CAP 1m 1f 36y
3:40 (3:40) (Class 5) (0-70,70) 3-Y-0+ **£2,911** (£866; £432; £216) **Stalls** Low

Form RPR

5534 **1** **High Resolution**[9] 6258 5-8-10 61 GarryWhillans(5) 7 70
(Linda Perratt) *hld up: stdy hdwy over 2f out: rdn and hung rt over 1f out: led wl ins fnl f: r.o* **6/1**[2]

5442 **2** *½* **Robert The Painter (IRE)**[6] 6342 4-9-10 70 (v) DanielTudhope 8 78
(David O'Meara) *led: rdn and qcknd 2f out: hdd wl ins fnl f: kpt on same pce* **11/10**[1]

5300 **3** *1 ½* **Madame Blavatsky (FR)**[9] 6258 4-8-3 56 oh2 GeorgeChaloner(7) 1 61
(Karen McLintock) *trckd ldr: effrt and drvn along 3f out: kpt on same pce ins fnl f* **12/1**

4403 **4** *12* **Cosmic Moon**[23] 5824 4-9-0 60 TonyHamilton 2 39
(Richard Fahey) *in tch: rdn and hung rt 3f out: sn outpcd* **6/1**[2]

0550 **5** *¾* **Collateral Damage (IRE)**[31] 5547 9-9-6 66 [1] JamesSullivan 9 43
(Tim Easterby) *in tch: drvn and outpcd over 3f out: n.d after* **9/1**

000 **6** *1 ¼* **Goal (IRE)**[11] 6174 4-8-3 56 oh2 (p) DavidBergin(7) 5 30
(Charles Smith) *t.k.h: sn trcking ldrs: drvn and ev ch over 3f out: wknd 2f out* **20/1**

000 **7** *8* **Sabratha (IRE)**[28] 5671 4-9-0 60 PaulMulrennan 6 17
(Linda Perratt) *hld up: rdn and effrt over 3f out: wknd over 2f out* **25/1**

0415 **8** *2 ¾* **Lanarkshire (IRE)**[12] 6136 3-9-5 70 JoeFanning 4 21
(Mark Johnston) *cl up tl rdn and wknd over 2f out* **8/1**[3]

0160 **9** *nk* **Glenluji**[9] 6258 7-8-10 56 oh1 GrahamLee 3
(Jim Goldie) *hld up: drvn over 3f out: wknd over 2f out* **28/1**

2m 8.75s (9.05) **Going Correction** +1.00s/f (Soft)
WFA 3 from 4yo+ 5lb **9** Ran SP% **117.1**
Speed ratings (Par 103): **99,98,97,86,85 84,77,75,74**
toteswingers 1&2 £3.30, 2&3 £7.30, 1&3 £38.60 CSF £12.87 CT £79.03 TOTE £7.50: £2.30, £1.10, £4.10; EX 21.70.
Owner Mrs Helen Perratt **Bred** Old Mill Stud Ltd **Trained** East Kilbride, S Lanarks

FOCUS
A weak handicap, run at a steady pace. The form is rated aorund the winner.

6529 TRY TOTEQUICKPICK IF YOU ARE FEELING LUCKY H'CAP (DIV I) 6f 5y
4:10 (4:11) (Class 6) (0-65,65) 3-Y-0+ **£1,940** (£577; £288; £144) **Stalls** Centre

Form RPR

656 **1** **Northern Bolt**[23] 5821 7-9-8 61 PatrickMathers 9 68
(Ian McInnes) *cl up stands' side: overall ldr over 2f out: hld on wl u.p fnl f* **15/2**

2453 **2** *nk* **Ambitious Icarus**[9] 6264 3-9-7 62 (e) RobbieFitzpatrick 10 68
(Richard Guest) *hld up in tch stands' side: effrt and rdn over 1f out: styd on wl to go 2nd wl ins fnl f: hld nr fin* **11/2**[3]

5524 **3** *2 ¾* **Jebel Tara**[7] 6308 7-8-12 51 (bt) TomEaves 5 48
(Ian Semple) *overall ldr centre to over 2f out: sn rdn: ev ch over 1f out: no ex wl ins fnl f* **8/1**

6-00 **4** *3 ¾* **Lady Of Edge**[35] 5428 3-8-5 46 oh1 JoeFanning 6 31
(Keith Dalgleish) *led stands' side to over 2f out: kpt on same pce over 1f out* **25/1**

5040 **5** *1 ½* **Reason To Believe (IRE)**[49] 4865 4-9-3 56 (b) PhillipMakin 4 36
(Ben Haslam) *cl up centre: drvn and outpcd over 2f out: no imp appr fnl f* **5/2**[1]

1445 **6** *3* **Sparking**[21] 5877 5-9-9 65 RossAtkinson(3) 2 36
(Tom Dascombe) *cl up: centre: drvn over 2f out: hung rt and wknd over 1f out* **7/2**[2]

6010 **7** *12* **Cheery Cat (USA)**[7] 6322 8-8-9 48 (p) GrahamLee 3
(Richard Ford) *chsd centre ldrs to over 3f out: sn struggling* **12/1**

6046 **8** *2* **Rock Canyon (IRE)**[1] 6514 3-9-2 57 (p) PJMcDonald 1
(Linda Perratt) *hld up in tch centre: struggling over 2f out: nvr on terms* **8/1**

0-06 **9** *1 ¼* **Illawalla**[116] 2621 4-8-7 46 oh1 (p) JamesSullivan 7
(Hugh McWilliams) *prom: drvn over 3f out: hung rt and wknd over 2f out* **50/1**

1m 17.95s (5.75) **Going Correction** +0.825s/f (Soft)
WFA 3 from 4yo+ 2lb **9** Ran SP% **113.7**
Speed ratings (Par 101): **94,93,89,84,82 78,62,60,58**
toteswingers 1&2 £6.20, 2&3 £6.40, 1&3 £10.30 CSF £47.54 CT £341.16 TOTE £11.10: £3.70, £1.30, £2.00; EX 58.60.
Owner Keith Brown **Bred** Mrs C Regalado-Gonzalez **Trained** Catwick, E Yorks
■ Stewards' Enquiry : Patrick Mathers four day ban: used whip above the permitted level (Oct 8-11)

FOCUS
A modest sprint handicap, run at a strong pace in worsening conditions, and a slow-motion finish. It was the slower division by 0.66sec. Unconvincing form, rated around the runner-up.

6530 TRY TOTEQUICKPICK IF YOU ARE FEELING LUCKY H'CAP (DIV II) 6f 5y
4:40 (4:41) (Class 6) (0-65,65) 3-Y-0+ **£1,940** (£577; £288; £144) **Stalls** Centre

Form RPR

1023 **1** **George Fenton**[17] 6002 3-8-13 54 (p) J-PGuillambert 5 62
(Richard Guest) *prom: pushed along 1/2-way: effrt wl over 1f out: led ins fnl f: rdn out* **9/2**[3]

6102 **2** *hd* **Windygoul Lad**[1] 6514 3-9-2 57 AndrewMullen 7 64
(Keith Dalgleish) *chsd ldrs: led over 2f out: rdn and wandered over 1f out: hdd ins fnl f: rallied: jst hld* **15/8**[1]

0564 **3** *3 ¼* **Bonnie Prince Blue**[63] 4405 9-9-3 56 DaleSwift 8 53
(Ian McInnes) *in tch: drvn and outpcd after 2f: rallied over 1f out: kpt on fnl f: nt gng pce of first two* **10/1**

4115 **4** *1 ¾* **Orwellian**[46] 5000 3-9-10 65 TomEaves 9 56
(Bryan Smart) *hld up: stdy hdwy over 2f out: rdn over 1f out: kpt on same pce fnl f* **11/4**[2]

0000 **5** *9* **Cheyenne Red (IRE)**[30] 5590 6-8-9 48 ow1 TonyHamilton 10 10
(Michael Herrington) *cl up: effrt and ev ch over 2f out: rdn and wknd over 1f out* **10/1**

5000 **6** *2 ¼* **Tectonic (IRE)**[20] 5917 3-8-11 52 (b[1]) PaulMulrennan 2 7
(Iain Jardine) *led to over 2f out: hung rt and sn wknd* **33/1**

0060 **7** *1 ¼* **Andrasta**[78] 3893 7-8-0 46 oh1 JordanHibberd(7) 1
(Alan Berry) *in tch: drvn and outpcd over 3f out: n.d after* **66/1**

0600 **8** *2 ¾* **Catalyze**[3] 6456 4-9-0 60 (t) DavidBergin(7) 6
(Charles Smith) *bhd: drvn along over 3f out: sn struggling* **10/1**

0060 **9** *7* **Dragon Spirit (IRE)**[7] 6314 3-8-5 46 oh1 JamesSullivan 4
(Linda Perratt) *in tch tl rdn and wknd over 2f out* **40/1**

1m 17.29s (5.09) **Going Correction** +0.825s/f (Soft)
WFA 3 from 4yo+ 2lb **9** Ran SP% **113.8**
Speed ratings (Par 101): **99,98,94,92,80 77,75,71,62**
toteswingers 1&2 £4.40, 2&3 £5.00, 1&3 £7.40 CSF £13.00 CT £78.10 TOTE £5.30: £2.10, £1.10, £3.40; EX 13.60.
Owner Maze Rattan Limited **Bred** R P Williams **Trained** Stainforth, S Yorks

FOCUS
The second division of this 6f handicap was run at a similarly strong pace to the first and it served up an equally close finish. The faster division by 0.66sec, but similarly modest form.

6531 FOLLOW TOTEPOOL ON FACEBOOK AND TWITTER H'CAP 5f 4y
5:10 (5:10) (Class 5) (0-70,70) 3-Y-0+ **£2,911** (£866; £432; £216) **Stalls** Centre

Form RPR

6200 **1** **Lord Buffhead**[25] 5757 3-8-6 56 DeclanCannon(3) 7 65
(Richard Guest) *trckd ldrs: rdn to ld over 1f out: hld on wl fnl f* **9/1**

1344 **2** *nk* **Sandwith**[62] 4430 9-9-1 66 (p) LMcNiff(5) 8 74
(George Foster) *prom: effrt and drvn over 2f out: styd on fnl f: hld nr fin* **11/1**

3004 **3** *2 ½* **Sharp Shoes**[26] 5739 5-8-7 53 TomEaves 4 52
(Christopher Wilson) *in tch: effrt and drvn 2f out: kpt on fnl f: nt gng pce of first two* **6/1**

6430 **4** *1 ¾* **Distant Sun (USA)**[9] 6264 8-8-9 55 (p) PJMcDonald 3 48
(Linda Perratt) *cl up: rdn over 2f out: one pce fnl f* **12/1**

0115 **5** *3 ¾* **Lady Del Sol**[13] 6123 4-9-10 70 (p[1]) DanielTudhope 6 49
(Marjorie Fife) *chsd ldrs: rdn 1/2-way: wknd over 1f out* **11/4**[1]

0000 **6** *4* **Ginger Ted (IRE)**[87] 3571 5-9-10 70 (v) J-PGuillambert 1 35
(Stuart Williams) *sn drvn along in rr: sme hdwy 1/2-way: btn over 1f out* **9/2**[3]

2535 **7** *hd* **Wicked Wilma (IRE)**[7] 6314 8-9-2 65 JulieBurke(3) 5 29
(Alan Berry) *led to over 1f out: wknd ins fnl f* **7/2**[2]

0524 **8** *8* **Lollypop Lady**[25] 5757 3-8-4 51 oh6 (p) JamesSullivan 2
(Linda Perratt) *dwlt: bhd and outpcd: nvr on terms* **14/1**

1m 3.73s (3.73) **Going Correction** +0.825s/f (Soft)
WFA 3 from 4yo+ 1lb **8** Ran SP% **114.0**
Speed ratings (Par 103): **103,102,98,95,89 83,83,70**
toteswingers 1&2 £10.30, 2&3 £6.40, 1&3 £6.50 CSF £100.12 CT £647.33 TOTE £12.30: £4.00, £2.00, £1.70; EX 96.40.
Owner Future Racing (Notts) Limited **Bred** T K & Mrs P A Knox **Trained** Stainforth, S Yorks

FOCUS
This 5f took plenty of getting in this ground. Modest form, the second setting the standard.
T/Plt: £14.30 to a £1 stake. Pool of £36594.08 - 1863.01 winning tickets. T/Qpdt: £4.40 to a £1 stake. Pool of £3366.02 - 556.12 winning tickets. RY

6395 KEMPTON (A.W) (R-H)
Monday, September 24

OFFICIAL GOING: Standard
Wind: Strong across Weather: Overcast

6532 32RED.COM/BRITISH STALLION STUDS EBF MAIDEN STKS 1m 2f (P)
2:20 (2:20) (Class 5) 2-Y-0 **£3,234** (£962; £481; £240) **Stalls** Low

Form RPR

5 **1** **Lord Provost (IRE)**[31] 5534 2-9-3 0 FrankieDettori 5 79+
(Mahmood Al Zarooni) *racd in 2nd: jnd ldr 4f out: led jst ins fnl 2f and sn pushed clr: v easily* **9/4**[1]

06 **2** *4* **Raven's Tower (USA)**[18] 5962 2-9-3 0 MickaelBarzalona 2 70
(Mahmood Al Zarooni) *chsd ldrs: 3rd and drvn 2f out: styd on to take 2nd over 1f out: nvr any ch w v easy wnr* **11/4**[2]

0 **3** *5* **Pentagram (USA)**[17] 6014 2-9-3 0 .... AhmedAjtebi 7 60+
(Mahmood Al Zarooni) *in rr: drvn and green over 2f out: styd on fnl f to take wl hld 3rd last strides* **10/3**[3]

4 *shd* **Ravens Nest** 2-9-3 0 .... StevieDonohoe 1 60
(Robert Mills) *racd in 4th: rdn and styd on same pce fnl 2f: disp wl-hld 4th last strides* **25/1**

34 **5** *nk* **Entrapping**[17] 5997 2-9-3 0 .... RichardHughes 4 59
(Richard Hannon) *led: jnd 4f out: hdd ins fnl 2f: sn btn: lost 2nd over 1f out: dropped two wl-btn pls fnl strides* **7/1**

6 *67* **Moaning Butcher** 2-9-3 0 .... KierenFallon 6
(Mark Johnston) *sn pushed along: lost tch after 3f: t.o* **7/1**

2m 8.2s (0.20) **Going Correction** -0.05s/f (Stan) **6** Ran SP% **109.4**
Speed ratings (Par 95): **97,93,89,89,89 35**
toteswingers 1&2 £3.30, 2&3 £1.40, 1&3 £3.10 CSF £8.20 TOTE £4.20: £2.10, £1.30; EX 7.30.
Owner Godolphin **Bred** Darley **Trained** Newmarket, Suffolk

FOCUS
The only race to use the inner loop at the meeting and an ordinary maiden in which Godolphin representatives made up 50% of the field. They filled the first three places, but a few of these didn't look straightforward. The pace was slow and the form is just fair.

NOTEBOOK
Lord Provost(IRE) ran green when fifth of six on last month's Goodwood debut, but with this extra 2f expected to suit on breeding this proved straightforward and the race was in the bag once he was sent for home over a furlong out. This took his sire's record here to 9-35 and he should be able to make his mark in handicap company over similar trips. (op 5-2 tchd 2-1)
Raven's Tower(USA), stepping up 2f in trip after showing a bit more in the second of two starts in 1m maidens, plugged on when sent in pursuit of his stablemate, but is flattered by how close he got. Ordinary handicaps may be where his future lies. (tchd 5-2)
Pentagram(USA) looked green when sent off favourite for his debut over 1m here earlier this month and he again looked as though the experience was needed, never looking like getting anywhere near his two stable companions. (op 4-1)
Ravens Nest, an 18,000GBP gelding out of a French 1m1f winner, tended to race in snatches and looks to need more time. (op 14-1)
Entrapping was a disappointing favourite on his second start, not impressing with his head carriage, and he looked quirky again here, hesitating in front racing into the back straight and putting his head up and looking reluctant after being headed by the winner starting up the home straight. He looks one to swerve. (op 5-1 tchd 15-2)
Moaning Butcher, out of a modest half-sister to two winners at up to 1m, proved clueless almost from the start. (op 6-1)

6533 32RED.COM MEDIAN AUCTION MAIDEN STKS 7f (P)
2:50 (2:51) (Class 5) 2-Y-O **£2,264** (£673; £336; £168) **Stalls** Low

Form RPR
6 **1** **George Cinq**[52] 4773 2-9-3 0 .... HayleyTurner 8 80+
(Michael Bell) *in tch: hdwy over 2f out: qcknd over 1f out to ld ins fnl f: edgd rt: comf* **6/1**[3]

02 **2** *1* **Ormindo (USA)**[10] 6214 2-9-3 0 .... MickaelBarzalona 2 75
(Mahmood Al Zarooni) *trckd ldrs: chal 2f out: sn led: drvn over 1f out: hdd ins fnl f: nt pce of wnr but hld on wl for 2nd* **1/1**[1]

3 *1* **Secret Art (IRE)** 2-9-3 0 .... JimCrowley 13 73
(Ralph Beckett) *chsd ldr: rdn over 2f out: kpt on same pce fnl f* **5/1**[2]

6 **4** *1 ½* **Aye Aye Skipper (IRE)**[20] 5911 2-9-3 0 .... BrettDoyle 9 69
(Dean Ivory) *chsd ldrs: drvn and styd on same pce fnl 2f* **50/1**

0 **5** *hd* **Unison (IRE)**[24] 5784 2-9-3 0 .... JimmyFortune 4 68
(Peter Makin) *chsd ldrs: drven over 2f out: one pce fr over 1f out* **33/1**

6 **6** *3 ¼* **Valley Of Wings**[30] 5578 2-9-3 0 .... ShaneKelly 11 59
(Robert Cowell) *s.i.s: sn rcvrd to chse ldrs: rdn over 2f out and sn outpcd* **20/1**

0 **7** *2 ¼* **Helamis**[47] 4967 2-8-12 0 .... AndreaAtzeni 14 48
(Stuart Williams) *s.i.s: in rr: drvn and hdwy over 2f out: nvr rchd ldrs* **100/1**

0 **8** *nse* **Al Zein**[50] 4846 2-9-3 0 .... RichardHughes 10 53
(Richard Hannon) *sn led: drvn and jnd 2f out: sn hdd wknd qckly fnl f* **15/2**

9 *¾* **Al Manaal** 2-8-12 0 .... [1] HarryBentley 5 46
(Saeed Bin Suroor) *rdn and towards rr 3f out: mod prog fnl f* **8/1**

00 **10** *nk* **Thomasina**[17] 6014 2-8-12 0 .... TadhgO'Shea 7 45
(Denis Coakley) *green and rdn bnd 3f out: mod late prog* **50/1**

060 **11** *5* **Misleading Promise (IRE)**[7] 6320 2-8-12 0 .... TobyAtkinson(5) 12 37
(John Butler) *s.i.s: a in rr* **100/1**

0 **12** *hd* **Atilia**[11] 6153 2-8-12 0 .... DaneO'Neill 6 31
(George Baker) *a in rr* **66/1**

13 *2* **Born To Run** 2-8-5 0 .... NoelGarbutt(7) 3 26
(Hugo Palmer) *a in rr* **33/1**

14 *3 ½* **Cash Rich** 2-9-3 0 .... FergusSweeney 1 21
(Jamie Osborne) *mid-div: rdn and wknd ins fnl 3f* **20/1**

1m 26.75s (0.75) **Going Correction** -0.05s/f (Stan) **14** Ran SP% **126.6**
Speed ratings (Par 95): **93,91,90,89,88 85,82,82,81,81 75,75,73,69**
toteswingers 1&2 £3.20, 2&3 £3.80, 1&3 £5.30 CSF £12.21 TOTE £8.60: £2.80, £1.10, £1.50; EX 16.40 Trifecta £98.70 Pool: £518.71 - 3.88 winning units..
Owner Tamdown Group Limited **Bred** Oakhill Stud **Trained** Newmarket, Suffolk

FOCUS
Just a fair maiden, but a couple of eye-catching performances. The winner improved and probably has more to offer.

NOTEBOOK
George Cinq showed ability on last month's debut when sixth of 12 in a 6f Newmarket maiden that has produced a couple of winners, and his strength in the market here suggested that he was expected to have improved from that. He produced a nice turn of foot to seal it once pulled out wide, despite edging away to his left late on, and can improve again. (op 8-1 tchd 11-2)
Ormindo(USA) was only just touched off over the extended 1m at Wolverhampton on his second start and got the perfect trip here, tracking the leaders against the inside rail and being committed for home after the cutaway. He didn't do much wrong, but couldn't match the winner's turn of foot and may need to go back up in trip. He can now be handicapped. (op 11-10 tchd 5-4 and 11-8 in a place)
Secret Art(IRE), a 16,000gns half-brother to the multiple winning sprinter White Shift, ran a fine debut and was up on the pace throughout. Although he was crossed by the winner half a furlong out, he wasn't unlucky but showed more than enough here to suggest he will win races. (op 6-1 tchd 13-2)
Aye Aye Skipper(IRE) showed ability on his Leicester debut over this trip earlier in the month and did so again here. He will be interesting once handicapped, but may be one for next year. (op 40-1)
Unison(IRE), last of seven in a 6f maiden on his Salisbury debut last month, ran on up the inside rail and this was a step forward. (op 25-1)
Valley Of Wings, green when sixth of seven in a 6f Newmarket maiden on last month's debut, was another to show improved form here, but he still looked as though the experience would do him good.

6534 32RED/BRITISH STALLION STUDS EBF MAIDEN FILLIES' STKS (DIV I) 7f (P)
3:20 (3:21) (Class 5) 2-Y-O **£3,234** (£962; £481; £240) **Stalls** Low

Form RPR
1 **Zurigha (IRE)** 2-9-0 0 .... RichardHughes 11 80+
(Richard Hannon) *w ldrs tl slt ld 4f out: drvn over 1f out: strly chal ins fnl f but a finding enough and r.o strly in clsng stages* **13/2**[3]

02 **2** *nk* **Mar Mar (IRE)**[18] 5978 2-9-0 0 .... FrankieDettori 1 79
(Saeed Bin Suroor) *chsd ldrs: drvn to go 2nd over 1f out: drvn to press wnr ins fnl f but a being hld* **13/8**[1]

3 *6* **A Touch Of Fashion (USA)** 2-9-0 0 .... LukeMorris 8 63+
(Gerard Butler) *chsd ldrs: rdn over 2f out: styd on to take wl-hld 3rd fnl 120yds* **20/1**

4 *1* **Clear Pearl (USA)** 2-9-0 0 .... HarryBentley 3 60+
(Ed Vaughan) *in tch: drvn over 2f out: styd on to take one pce 3rd ins fnl f: dropped to 4th fnl 120yds* **25/1**

5 *1* **Jacobella** 2-9-0 0 .... JohnFahy 6 57+
(Jonathan Portman) *s.i.s: in rr: hdwy and drvn 2f out: kpt on fnl f but nvr a threat* **50/1**

4 **6** *½* **Chittenden (USA)**[13] 6117 2-9-0 0 .... MickaelBarzalona 5 56
(Mahmood Al Zarooni) *sn slt ld: narrowly hdd 4f out: styd chsng wnr tl over 1f out: sn btn* **11/4**[2]

6 **7** *½* **Ishisoba**[19] 5943 2-9-0 0 .... JamesDoyle 10 55
(Alastair Lidderdale) *chsd ldrs: drvn over 2f out: wknd over 1f out* **14/1**

8 *1 ½* **Tight Fit** 2-9-0 0 .... DaneO'Neill 4 51+
(Henry Candy) *in rr: pushed along 3f out: styd on fr over 1f out but nvr a threat* **8/1**

9 *3 ¼* **Sweet Martoni** 2-9-0 0 .... JimCrowley 13 42+
(William Knight) *s.i.s: in rr: pushed along over 2f out: mod prog fnl f* **20/1**

10 *hd* **Aphrodite Spirit (IRE)** 2-8-9 0 .... MichaelJMMurphy(5) 2 41
(Pat Eddery) *chsd ldrs: rdn over 2f out: sn wknd* **50/1**

50 **11** *2 ¾* **Red Catkin**[19] 5947 2-9-0 0 .... IanMongan 9 34
(George Margarson) *in tch: rdn 3f out: sn btn* **33/1**

12 *¾* **Chiltern Secret** 2-9-0 0 .... StevieDonohoe 7 32
(Martin Bosley) *a towards rr* **100/1**

13 *dist* **New Jersey Girl** 2-9-0 0 .... HayleyTurner 12
(Chris Wall) *green and sn pushed along: bhd fr 1/2-way: eased whn no ch: t.o* **66/1**

1m 26.93s (0.93) **Going Correction** -0.05s/f (Stan) **13** Ran SP% **118.6**
Speed ratings (Par 92): **92,91,84,83,82 81,81,79,75,75 72,71,**
toteswingers 1&2 £8.30, 2&3 £9.40, 1&3 £3.90 CSF £16.00 TOTE £6.50: £2.10, £1.02, £8.10; EX 26.10 Trifecta £221.40 Pool: £490.76 - 1.64 winning units..
Owner Saeed H Altayer **Bred** Sir Nicholas & Lady Nugent **Trained** East Everleigh, Wilts

FOCUS
The front pair pulled clear in this fillies' maiden and the winning time was 0.18 seconds slower than the boys half an hour earlier. A nice start from the winner to repel the form choice, the pair clear.

NOTEBOOK
Zurigha(IRE) ◆ was keen enough in a disputed lead early, but she showed a most admirable attitude after gaining the advantage on her own and really stuck her neck out when challenged. A 72,000gns half-sister to the five-time winner at up to 7f (including in Listed company) Lily's Angel, she looks to have a bright future in her own right. (op 6-1 tchd 7-1)
Mar Mar(IRE) improved plenty from her debut when runner-up in a Salisbury maiden over this trip on her second start and, having been handy throughout, had every chance to get past the winner here had she been good enough. She pulled clear of the rest and should find a race, especially as she now qualifies for a mark. (op 7-4 tchd 15-8)
A Touch Of Fashion(USA), a 38,000gns filly out of a 6f Listed juvenile winner, stayed on in pleasing style to grab third and can be expected to come on for this. (op 28-1 tchd 16-1)
Clear Pearl(USA) ◆, an $80,000 half-sister to two winners in the US, was another doing all her best work late and is likely to progress.
Jacobella, out of a half-sister to a useful juvenile sprinter in the US, very much caught the eye with the way she stayed on having given herself plenty to do following a slow start. She was retained for just 500GBP as a yearling, but has a future on this evidence. (op 66-1)
Chittenden(USA), fourth of 13 in a bunch finish over an extended 1m on her Leicester debut 13 days earlier, dropped out after matching strides with the winner for a long way and this was a step backwards. (op 9-4 tchd 2-1)
Tight Fit ◆, out of a half-sister at up to 7f in France, looked green at the back of the field early, but she showed definite signs of ability late on. (op 16-1)
Sweet Martoni walked out of the stalls and made just modest late headway, but although she is a 17,000gns half-sister to six winners, most of them were strong stayers and so was her dam, so the best of her is likely to be seen when presented with a proper test of stamina much further down the line.

6535 32RED/BRITISH STALLION STUDS EBF MAIDEN FILLIES' STKS (DIV II) 7f (P)
3:50 (3:51) (Class 5) 2-Y-O **£3,234** (£962; £481; £240) **Stalls** Low

Form RPR
2 **1** **Intiba (USA)**[18] 5977 2-9-0 0 .... FrankieDettori 8 75+
(Saeed Bin Suroor) *trckd ldr: slt ld ins fnl 2f: pushed along and styd on strly fnl f* **1/1**[1]

06 **2** *1 ¼* **Three Choirs (IRE)**[20] 5902 2-9-0 0 .... RichardHughes 2 72
(Richard Hannon) *led: narrowly hdd ins fnl 2f: styd on to try and press wnr fr over 1f out but outpcd ins fnl f* **13/2**[3]

6 **3** *1* **La Danza**[81] 3776 2-8-9 0 .... NatashaEaton(5) 11 69
(Alan Bailey) *chsd ldrs: pushed along and styd on wl for 3rd pl ins fnl f but nt gng pce of ldng duo* **66/1**

4 *½* **Pearl Street (USA)** 2-9-0 0 .... HarryBentley 7 68+
(Henry Candy) *s.i.s: in rr: nt clr run over 3f out: hdwy on ins over 2f out: styd on to take 4th fnl f: nvr gng pce to trble ldrs* **11/4**[2]

5 *1 ¼* **Rocksilla** 2-9-0 0 .... HayleyTurner 6 64
(Chris Wall) *chsd ldrs: rdn over 2f out: one pce over 1f out* **66/1**

6 *3* **Playbill** 2-9-0 0 .... NeilCallan 12 57+
(Sir Michael Stoute) *s.i.s: in rr hdwy and bmpd on outer bnd 3f out: drvn and sme prog fnl 2f: nvr any ch* **14/1**

7 *2 ¾* **Sharqawiyah** 2-9-0 0 .... KierenFallon 1 49
(Luca Cumani) *s.i.s: in rr: drvn and sme hdwy over 2f out: nvr in contention and wknd fnl f* **16/1**

26 **8** *4* **Reveille**[11] 6168 2-9-0 0 .... JimmyFortune 3 38
(Hughie Morrison) *chsd ldrs: wknd fr 2f out* **25/1**

9 *11* **Sporting Club Girl** 2-9-0 0 .... JimCrowley 9 8
(William Knight) *a in rr* **66/1**

0 **10** *nse* **Breezily (USA)**[74] 4002 2-9-0 0 .... MickaelBarzalona 4 8
(Mahmood Al Zarooni) *towards rr: sme hdwy on outside whn bmpd 3f out: sn wknd* **20/1**

0 **11** *½* **July Waits (USA)**[11] 6153 2-9-0 0 .... LukeMorris 5 7
(Sir Mark Prescott Bt) *slowly away: green and sn rdn: a in rr* **100/1**

02 **12** *1* **Chamtille (IRE)**[46] 5011 2-9-0 0 .... AndreaAtzeni 10 4
(Derek Haydn Jones) *chsd ldrs to 1/2-way* **100/1**

1m 26.92s (0.92) **Going Correction** -0.05s/f (Stan) **12** Ran SP% **117.6**
Speed ratings (Par 92): **92,90,89,88,87 84,80,76,63,63 63,61**
toteswingers 1&2 £2.40, 2&3 £25.70, 1&3 £17.40 CSF £7.77 TOTE £2.10: £1.20, £1.10, £11.90; EX 7.70 Trifecta £294.00 Pool: £770.83 - 1.94 winning units..
Owner Godolphin **Bred** Darley **Trained** Newmarket, Suffolk

FOCUS
The winning time was just 1/100th of a second quicker than the first division. The winner probably didn't need to match her pre-race mark.

NOTEBOOK
Intiba(USA) showed ability when second of 11 on her Salisbury debut over this trip earlier in the month and although the winner did nothing for the form at Newbury on Friday, she still proved good enough to go one better here. She had to work harder to put the race to bed than had appeared likely after being produced to lead over a furlong out, but she got the job done and should go on from here. (op 6-5 tchd 10-11)
Three Choirs(IRE) showed a lot more at Goodwood on her second start in what looked a decent maiden (second and fourth have won since) and made a brave bid to make every yard here. She battled back gamely after being headed by the winner and can go one better before long. She now gets a mark. (op 6-1 tchd 11-2)
La Danza weakened to finish sixth of nine on her debut in a 6f Haydock maiden in July, but improved plenty here having been given an 81-day break since then. She obviously has ability and may be one for nurseries after one more run.
Pearl Street(USA) ♦, a $290,000 half-sister to a winning juvenile over this trip and a winner in the US, did well to finish where she did as she was out the back early having missed the break. She holds an entry in the totepool.com Two-Year-Old Trophy at Redcar a week on Saturday, but on this evidence she needs every bit of this trip and can win races. (op 9-2)
Rocksilla, out of a 1m Polytrack winner, showed up for a long way and is likely to progress with experience.
Playbill made some late progress after a slow start, but her breeding suggests that middle-distances will bring out the best of her in due course. (op 9-1)
Breezily(USA) Official explanation: jockey said filly ran too freely

6536 32RED H'CAP 6f (P)
4:20 (4:20) (Class 3) (0-95,95) 3-Y-O
£6,411 (£1,919; £959; £479; £239; £120) **Stalls** Low

Form RPR

3212 **1** **Intransigent**[16] 6026 3-9-5 **93** .... JimmyFortune 3 104+
(Andrew Balding) *hld up in rr: smooth hdwy fr 2f out to ld jst ins fnl f: pushed out* **5/2**[1]

5030 **2** *1* **Poole Harbour (IRE)**[15] 6075 3-9-0 **88** .... RichardHughes 7 95
(Richard Hannon) *trckd ldrs: rdn over 2f out: styd on fnl f to take 2nd in clsng strides but no ch w wnr* **9/2**[3]

1530 **3** *nk* **Charlotte Rosina**[15] 6075 3-8-13 **87** .... HayleyTurner 4 93
(Roger Teal) *led 1f: drvn over 2f out: slt ld over 1f out: hdd and outpcd fnl f: lost 2nd in clsng strides* **10/1**

1002 **4** *¾* **Dark Castle**[5] 6369 3-8-9 **83** .... LiamKeniry 2 87
(Sylvester Kirk) *in rr: rdn and hdwy fr 2f out: chsd ldrs ins fnl f: styd on same pce* **11/4**[2]

060 **5** *5* **Priceless Jewel**[15] 6075 3-9-2 **90** .... GeorgeBaker 1 78
(Roger Charlton) *chsd ldrs: rdn over 2f out: wkng whn n.m.r on inner appr fnl f* **5/1**

1135 **6** *nse* **Lady Gibraltar**[16] 6026 3-8-9 **88** ....(v) MichaelJMMurphy(5) 5 75
(Alan Jarvis) *led after 1f: t.k.h: hdd over 1f out and sn btn* **14/1**

0100 **7** *¾* **Ewell Place (IRE)**[12] 6143 3-9-7 **95** .... StevieDonohoe 6 80
(Robert Mills) *pushed along and hung rt fr over 2f out: a in rr* **25/1**

1m 11.48s (-1.62) **Going Correction** -0.05s/f (Stan) **7** Ran SP% **109.7**
Speed ratings (Par 105): **108,106,106,105,98 98,97**
toteswingers 1&2 £1.70, 2&3 £4.90, 1&3 £5.50 CSF £12.87 TOTE £2.90: £2.30, £2.80; EX 15.30.
Owner Kingsclere Racing CLub **Bred** Kingsclere Stud **Trained** Kingsclere, Hants

FOCUS
A decent 3yo sprint handicap and run at a searching pace. Sound form, the winner confirming the good impression of his previous C&D win.

NOTEBOOK
Intransigent, up another 6lb after his recent Ascot second, was 8lb higher than when scoring over this C&D the time before, but he is still progressing and made light of his inflated mark. Held up well off the strong pace early, he impressed with the way he travelled into the contest and found plenty when eventually asked for his effort. There is probably still more to come from him. (op 11-4 tchd 9-4)
Poole Harbour(IRE) has been racing over 6f on turf since easily winning a 7f maiden here back in May. Handy early, he seemed likely to drop out once under pressure over a furlong from home, but the way he ran on again suggests that he needs the longer trip on this surface. (op 5-1 tchd 6-1)
Charlotte Rosina is still 7lb higher than when winning at Newmarket in June, but put up a decent effort as she is most effective when able to dominate and was denied that role here. Even so, she hit the front briefly over a furlong out before the winner pounced and emerges with credit. (op 9-1 tchd 8-1)
Dark Castle, a winner twice and runner-up twice from four starts over C&D, didn't find the race run to suit here five days earlier. He found himself in a truly run race this time and had his chance when produced on the wide outside over a furlong out, but just lacked the pace to deliver a telling blow. (tchd 5-2)
Lady Gibraltar went off like a scalded cat at a tempo she was unlikely to maintain. (op 9-1)

6537 £32 FREE AT 32RED.COM H'CAP 1m 4f (P)
4:50 (4:51) (Class 4) (0-85,85) 3-Y-O **£4,075** (£1,212; £606; £303) **Stalls** Centre

Form RPR

010 **1** **Ruscello (IRE)**[16] 6025 3-9-6 **84** .... GeorgeBaker 5 92+
(Ed Walker) *hld up in tch: hdwy on inner over 2f out: led over 1f out: sn drvn: styd on strly fnl f* **9/4**[1]

-012 **2** *½* **Nordic Quest (IRE)**[18] 5973 3-8-12 **76** .... NeilCallan 8 83
(Gerard Butler) *towards rr tl rapid hdwy over 4f out and sn chsng ldrs: drvn to dispute 2nd fr over 2f out: chsd wnr fr over 1f out: edgd rt fnl f: kpt on but a hld* **11/1**

21 **3** *1 ½* **Tiger Cliff (IRE)**[25] 5766 3-9-3 **81** .... TomQueally 1 86+
(Sir Henry Cecil) *in rr: rdn and one pce over 2f out: styd on u.p fnl f to take 3rd in clsng stages: nt rch ldrs* **7/2**[3]

0210 **4** *1* **Caphira**[16] 6025 3-9-2 **80** .... JimCrowley 2 83
(William Knight) *chsd ldr 3f: styd front rnk: rdn over 2f out: kpt on same pce fnl f* **20/1**

4116 **5** *2* **Kaiser Wilhelm (IRE)**[52] 4776 3-8-4 **71** oh5 ....(t) RaulDaSilva(3) 3 71
(Paul Cole) *chsd ldrs: t.k.h: drvn over 3f out: one pce fnl 2f* **33/1**

4120 **6** *5* **Flying Trader (USA)**[94] 3330 3-8-13 **77** .... BrettDoyle 9 69
(Jane Chapple-Hyam) *chsd ldr after 3f: rdn over 3f out: wknd ins fnl 2f* **16/1**

0214 **7** *1 ½* **Galleon**[18] 5966 3-9-7 **85** .... RichardHughes 7 75
(Sir Michael Stoute) *led: rdn over 2f out: hdd over 1f out: sn btn* **11/4**[2]

06-1 **8** *1 ¾* **Dedication**[132] 2148 3-9-0 **78** ....(t) JamesDoyle 4 65
(Roger Charlton) *rdn over 2f out: a towards rr* **20/1**

-306 **9** *14* **Cherry Street**[89] 3509 3-9-6 **84** .... JimmyFortune 10 49
(Andrew Balding) *in rr: rdn and no rspnse 3f out and sn dropped wl bhd* **16/1**

1065 **10** *4 ½* **Yazdi (IRE)**[65] 4346 3-9-6 **84** ....(t) KierenFallon 6 41
(Brian Meehan) *in tch: rdn and wknd over 3f out* **10/1**

2m 31.48s (-3.02) **Going Correction** -0.05s/f (Stan) **10** Ran SP% **121.3**
Speed ratings (Par 103): **108,107,106,106,104 101,100,99,89,86**
toteswingers 1&2 £5.60, 2&3 £4.00, 1&3 £5.00 CSF £29.10 CT £88.74 TOTE £4.00: £1.70, £1.70, £1.60; EX 32.90 Trifecta £265.30 Pool: £ 688.46 - 1.92 winning units..
Owner Laurence A Bellman **Bred** Ballymacoll Stud Farm Ltd **Trained** Newmarket, Suffolk

FOCUS
A decent middle-distance handicap for the grade, run at a sound pace. The winner continues to progress.

6538 32RED CASINO H'CAP (DIV I) 1m (P)
5:20 (5:20) (Class 4) (0-85,85) 3-Y-O+ **£4,075** (£1,212; £606; £303) **Stalls** Low

Form RPR

4000 **1** **Islesman**[89] 3503 4-8-12 **73** ow1 .... RichardHughes 4 81+
(Heather Main) *trckd ldrs: nt clr run and swtchd lft over 1f out: qcknd ins fnl f to ld fnl 120yds: comf* **7/2**[2]

0010 **2** *nk* **Mahadee (IRE)**[26] 5751 7-9-3 **78** ....(b) LiamKeniry 8 85
(Ed de Giles) *trckd ldr: rdn to ld jst ins fnl f: hdd and outpcd by wnr fnl 120yds* **16/1**

0401 **3** *1 ¼* **Golden Tempest (IRE)**[10] 6208 4-9-5 **80** .... JimmyFortune 6 84+
(Eve Johnson Houghton) *s.i.s: in rr: drvn and hdwy over 1f out: styd on to take 3rd in clsng stages* **7/1**

5361 **4** *1* **Copperwood**[9] 6241 7-9-3 **78** .... KierenFallon 7 80
(Mark Johnston) *led: rdn and wnt rt wl over 1f out: hdd jst ins fnl f: sn btn* **4/1**[3]

3065 **5** *1* **Cruiser**[16] 6036 4-9-10 **85** .... GeorgeBaker 2 84+
(William Muir) *chsd ldrs: hdwy on inner whn bdly hmpd wl over 1f out: styd on fnl f but could nt rcvr* **9/4**[1]

213- **6** *6* **Sim Sala Bim**[458] 3340 4-9-2 **77** .... JamesDoyle 3 63
(Stuart Williams) *in tch: pushed along: swtchd lft wl over 1f out and sn wknd* **8/1**

1000 **7** *¾* **Titan Triumph**[29] 5625 8-9-6 **81** ....(t) JimCrowley 5 65
(William Knight) *t.k.h: chsd ldrs 4f out: wknd fr 2f out* **40/1**

5034 **8** *1* **Final Drive (IRE)**[17] 6013 6-9-7 **82** ....(tp) StevieDonohoe 9 64
(John Butler) *s.i.s: rdn over 3f out: a in rr* **12/1**

1m 39.32s (-0.48) **Going Correction** -0.05s/f (Stan)
WFA 3 from 4yo+ 4lb **8** Ran SP% **112.6**
Speed ratings (Par 105): **100,99,98,97,96 90,89,88**
toteswingers 1&2 £9.50, 2&3 £9.10, 1&3 £6.70 CSF £54.23 CT £370.25 TOTE £3.20: £1.10, £5.10, £2.70; EX 118.40 TRIFECTA Not won. Pool: £740.01.
Owner Les Chevaliers **Bred** Barry Walters **Trained** Kingston Lisle, Oxon
■ Stewards' Enquiry : Kieren Fallon three-day ban: careless riding (Oct 8-10)

FOCUS
A good handicap, but a rough race and a horror show for favourite backers. It was the slower division by a second. The winner did not need to match his best.

6539 32RED CASINO H'CAP (DIV II) 1m (P)
5:50 (5:50) (Class 4) (0-85,85) 3-Y-O+ **£4,075** (£1,212; £606; £151; £151) **Stalls** Low

Form RPR

0-00 **1** **Shamir**[16] 6036 5-9-8 **83** .... IanMongan 7 93
(Jo Crowley) *in tch: hdwy on ins over 2f out: led over 1f out: pushed out cl home: comf* **13/2**

1003 **2** *1 ½* **Little Black Book (IRE)**[3] 6454 4-9-3 **78** ....(b) LukeMorris 6 84
(Gerard Butler) *chsd ldrs: drvn to ld over 2f out: hdd over 1f out: edgd rt u.p and nt pce of wnr ins fnl f* **4/1**[2]

-521 **3** *2 ¾* **Dubawi Island (FR)**[27] 5717 3-9-6 **85** ....(b) NeilCallan 4 85
(James Tate) *chsd ldrs: drvn to chal 2f out: outpcd by ldng duo ins fnl f* **9/2**[3]

0130 **4** *3 ¾* **Snow Trooper**[82] 3767 4-9-2 **77** .... ShaneKelly 1 68
(Dean Ivory) *in rr: drvn along over 3f out: styd on fr over 1f out: nvr any ch* **14/1**

340 **4** *dht* **Sir Trevor (IRE)**[4] 6401 3-8-7 **72** .... HayleyTurner 8 63
(Tom Dascombe) *led: narrowly hdd 5f out: styd pressing ldr and chal wl over 2f out: wknd over 1f out* **15/2**

0056 **6** *13* **Mississippi**[16] 6040 3-9-4 **83** .... KierenFallon 9 44
(Brian Meehan) *w ldr: slt advantage after 3f: rdn 3f out: hdd & wknd qckly over 2f out* **7/2**[1]

4-60 **7** *3 ¼* **Simayill**[21] 5888 4-9-5 **80** .... TomQueally 3 34
(John Berry) *rdn over 3f out: a bhd* **25/1**

4062 **8** *¾* **Great Shot**[11] 6171 4-9-0 **75** .... JamesDoyle 2 27
(Sylvester Kirk) *in tch: rdn and wknd wl over 2f out: eased whn no ch* **6/1**

5346 **9** *21* **Nibani (IRE)**[73] 4061 5-9-2 **77** .... FrankieMcDonald 5
(John Butler) *slowly away: rdn 4f out and a wl bhd* **40/1**

1m 38.31s (-1.49) **Going Correction** -0.05s/f (Stan)
WFA 3 from 4yo+ 4lb **9** Ran SP% **112.7**
Speed ratings (Par 105): **105,103,100,97,97 84,80,80,59**
toteswingers 1&2 £7.90, 2&3 £3.70, 1&3 £6.20 CSF £31.78 CT £128.04 TOTE £9.80: £1.90, £1.80, £1.50; EX 33.80 Trifecta £129.50 Pool: £670.65 - 3.83 winning units..
Owner Kilstone Limited **Bred** Plantation Stud **Trained** Whitcombe, Dorset

FOCUS
They went a very strong pace in this division with the field spread out all over Sunbury by halfway. The winning time was about a second faster than the first leg. The winner is rated back to his best.
Great Shot Official explanation: jockey said gelding hung right

T/Plt: £6.40 to a £1 stake. Pool of £43036.78 - 4834.38 winning tickets. T/Qpdt: £3.80 to a £1 stake. Pool of £3202.51- 621.64 winning tickets. ST

6114 LEICESTER (R-H)

Monday, September 24

OFFICIAL GOING: Soft (7.2)

There were 35 non-runners, mainly owing to the ground. Declarations had been made on good to firm.

Wind: Fresh across Weather: Raining

6540 BRITISH STALLION STUDS SUPPORTING BRITISH RACING EBF KEGWORTH NOVICE STKS — 5f 218y

2:30 (2:30) (Class 4) 2-Y-O — **£4,528** (£1,347; £673; £336) **Stalls** High

Form				RPR
100	1		**Tassel**[94] 3326 2-8-12 0 ... PatDobbs 3 (Richard Hannon) *chsd ldr: shkn up over 2f out: led over 1f out: sn rdn and edgd rt: r.o* **3/1**[3]	83
332	2	*nk*	**Bravo Youmzain (IRE)**[38] 5325 2-8-12 85 ... AdamKirby 5 (Marco Botti) *trckd ldrs: nt clr run and swtchd lft over 1f out: sn rdn: r.o* **2/1**[2]	83+
2134	3	2 ¼	**Kimberella**[58] 4599 2-9-0 88 ... JamieSpencer 4 (Michael Bell) *trckd ldrs: rdn over 1f out: styd on same pce ins fnl f* **11/10**[1]	77
3226	4	1	**Shillito**[36] 5382 2-8-12 74 ... BarryMcHugh 2 (Tony Coyle) *led: rdn over 2f out: hdd over 1f out: no ex ins fnl f* **10/1**	72

1m 14.62s (1.62) **Going Correction** +0.15s/f (Good) — **4** Ran SP% **115.0**

Speed ratings (Par 97): **95,94,91,90**

CSF £9.83 TOTE £4.30; EX 11.10.

Owner Highclere Thoroughbred Racing - Herbert Jones **Bred** Mrs Susan Field **Trained** East Everleigh, Wilts

FOCUS

An interesting novice event despite the small field. They started off stands' side but the winner drifted towards the centre of the track late on. The winner is rated back to her debut form.

NOTEBOOK

Tassel hadn't gone on from her debut maiden win, finishing lame on her next start and again failing to beat a rival in the Albany. However, returning from a three-month break, she defied a 5lb penalty against male opposition. It was a bit disconcerting to see her edge right under pressure and she'll have to prove she can go on from this, but she clearly has plenty of ability.

Bravo Youmzain(IRE) travelled well in behind the pace but didn't respond immediately when first asked and couldn't take advantage of the winner's waywardness. He's yet to win a race but is well to up doing so. (op 5-2)

Kimberella has form on testing ground, but he hadn't been seen for two months and didn't run to his best.

Shillito ran about as well as could have been expected.

6541 ASTON FLAMVILLE FILLIES' NURSERY — 5f 218y

3:00 (3:00) (Class 5) (0-75,73) 2-Y-O — **£2,587** (£770; £384; £192) **Stalls** High

Form				RPR
3524	1		**Pira Palace (IRE)**[19] 5946 2-9-4 70 ... RobertWinston 12 (Sir Michael Stoute) *chsd ldr tl led over 2f out: rdn over 1f out: styd on* **3/1**[1]	77
356	2	¾	**Spiritual Girl**[53] 4742 2-9-1 67 ... JamieSpencer 6 (Michael Bell) *stdd s: hdwy over 3f out: shkn up over 1f out: chsd wnr ins fnl f: sn rdn: styd on* **9/1**	72
3043	3	1 ½	**Glossy Posse**[12] 6147 2-8-6 58 ... KieranO'Neill 1 (Richard Hannon) *sn pushed along in rr: hdwy over 1f out: styd on* **11/2**	58
014	4	1 ½	**Ayasha**[31] 5537 2-9-4 70 ... RoystonFfrench 3 (Bryan Smart) *chsd ldrs: rdn over 1f out: styd on same pce ins fnl f* **6/1**	66
066	5	*nk*	**Red Eclipse (IRE)**[29] 5631 2-8-5 57 ... CathyGannon 14 (Alan Bailey) *chsd ldrs: rdn over 2f out: edgd rt over 1f out: styd on same pce ins fnl f* **16/1**	52
6442	6	*nk*	**Alhaarth Beauty (IRE)**[32] 5511 2-9-6 72 ... PatDobbs 10 (Richard Hannon) *trckd ldrs: rdn and ev ch over 1f out: no ex ins fnl f* **10/3**[2]	66
3406	7	4 ½	**Ishi Honest**[24] 5790 2-9-2 73 ... LeeNewnes(5) 4 (Mark Usher) *prom: pushed along and lost pl 4f out: wknd over 1f out* **5/1**[3]	53
6304	8	8	**Cross Pattee (IRE)**[35] 5425 2-9-7 73 ...[1] WilliamBuick 13 (John Gosden) *led: rdn and hdd over 2f out: wknd over 1f out* **7/1**	29

1m 14.58s (1.58) **Going Correction** +0.15s/f (Good) — **8** Ran SP% **122.8**

Speed ratings (Par 92): **95,94,92,90,89 89,83,72**

toteswingers 1&2 £3.00, 2&3 £12.00, 1&3 £2.40 CSF £33.12 CT £148.93 TOTE £3.90: £1.10, £1.50, £3.10; EX 24.80.

Owner Miss T K Walters **Bred** Malm Partnership **Trained** Newmarket, Suffolk

FOCUS

An ordinary nursery for fillies only. They raced middle to stands' side, but away from the rail. The form makes sense.

NOTEBOOK

Pira Palace(IRE) was clearly suited by the drop in trip on testing ground and gained her first win on her sixth start. She showed a good attitude and may yet do better. (tchd 11-4)

Spiritual Girl, making her nursery debut, travelled well but couldn't find extra when challenging the winner. She'd been off for 53 days and might improve for the run. (op 10-1)

Glossy Posse was never really going that well but stuck on. She'll be worth another try over further.

Ayasha might want better ground. Official explanation: jockey said filly hung right closing stages

Alhaarth Beauty(IRE) was a bit free and didn't see it out on the softest ground she's encountered. (tchd 3-1)

6542 GOLDEN HAND (S) STKS — 7f 9y

3:30 (3:31) (Class 6) 3-Y-O — **£1,617** (£481; £240; £120) **Stalls** High

Form				RPR
0221	1		**Marford Missile (IRE)**[6] 6329 3-9-2 78 ... RichardKingscote 6 (Tom Dascombe) *mde all: racd keenly: rdn over 1f out: edgd rt ins fnl f: styd on* **1/1**[1]	78
2266	2	½	**Tunnager Grove**[18] 5972 3-8-11 68 ... RobertHavlin 12 (Hughie Morrison) *chsd wnr: rdn and hung rt over 1f out: styd on* **10/1**	72
0400	3	2 ½	**Sujet Bellagio**[12] 6150 3-9-2 70 ... MartinLane 13 (Brian Meehan) *s.i.s: hld up: hdwy 3f out: rdn over 1f out: styd on same pce* **10/1**	70
220	4	½	**Lady Layla**[9] 6239 3-8-11 72 ... JamieSpencer 3 (Bryan Smart) *chsd ldrs: pushed along over 2f out: rdn over 1f out: styd on same pce* **13/8**[2]	64
2535	5	8	**Sabore**[9] 6261 3-8-6 57 ...(p) BarryMcHugh 5 (Richard Fahey) *hld up: hdwy over 2f out: rdn and wknd over 1f out* **9/1**[3]	38
0060	6	5	**Thats Molly (IRE)**[14] 6104 3-8-6 49 ...(b[1]) CathyGannon 8 (Eric Alston) *plld hrd and prom: rdn over 2f out: sn wknd* **20/1**	25
6305	7	1 ¼	**One For The Girls**[39] 5261 3-8-4 48 ...(t[1]) JackDuern(7) 4 (Nicky Vaughan) *prom: pushed along 1/2-way: wknd over 2f out* **50/1**	27

1m 27.68s (1.48) **Going Correction** +0.30s/f (Good) — **7** Ran SP% **123.0**

Speed ratings (Par 99): **103,102,99,99,89 84,82**

toteswingers 1&2 £2.30, 2&3 £7.30, 1&3 £2.50 CSF £14.36 TOTE £1.60: £1.40, £3.10; EX 12.60.The winner was bought in for 9500 guineas.

Owner The MHS 4x10 Partnership **Bred** Miss Mary Davidson & Mrs Steffi Von Schilcher **Trained** Malpas, Cheshire

FOCUS

A fair seller. They started off stands' side but the main action ended up taking place towards the centre of the track with the front two drifting right. The form is rated a bit cautiously, but the winner was close to his recent form.

6543 SIS LIVE H'CAP — 5f 2y

4:00 (4:01) (Class 3) (0-95,93) 3-Y-O+ — **£7,115** (£2,117; £1,058; £529) **Stalls** High

Form				RPR
0004	1		**Ajjaadd (USA)**[23] 5832 6-9-1 87 ... KieranO'Neill 10 (Ted Powell) *hld up: hdwy to ld over 1f out: sn rdn: r.o* **5/1**[3]	98+
0-60	2	¾	**R Woody**[55] 4690 5-8-10 82 ... WilliamBuick 15 (Robert Cowell) *hld up: nt clr run over 1f out: rdn and r.o wl ins fnl f: hung rt towards fin: could nt rch wnr* **9/2**[2]	90+
0000	3	1 ¼	**Lexi's Hero (IRE)**[16] 6028 4-9-1 87 ...(p) JamieSpencer 1 (Kevin Ryan) *sn pushed along to ld: rdn 1/2-way: hdd over 1f out: styd on same pce ins fnl f* **3/1**[1]	91
0003	4	¾	**Bathwick Bear (IRE)**[8] 6286 4-8-7 79 ... CathyGannon 8 (David Evans) *hld up: hdwy u.p over 1f out: styd on same pce ins fnl f* **6/1**	80
0000	5	¾	**Noodles Blue Boy**[12] 6144 6-8-11 83 ... BarryMcHugh 13 (Ollie Pears) *s.i.s: hdwy 1/2-way: rdn over 1f out: hung rt and styd on ins fnl f* **12/1**	81
0230	6	½	**Master Rooney (IRE)**[16] 6028 6-8-13 85 ... RoystonFfrench 4 (Bryan Smart) *chsd ldr: rdn and ev ch over 1f out: no ex ins fnl f* **16/1**	82
5000	7	1 ¼	**New Planet (IRE)**[72] 4086 4-9-7 93 ... MichaelO'Connell 5 (John Quinn) *mid-div: lost pl 1/2-way: rdn over 1f out: styd on ins fnl f* **9/2**[2]	85
1020	8	2	**Le Toreador**[33] 5487 7-9-4 90 ...(tp) AmyRyan 11 (Kevin Ryan) *chsd ldrs: rdn 1/2-way: wknd ins fnl f* **8/1**	75
1000	9	¾	**Silvanus (IRE)**[23] 5832 7-9-1 87 ... RussKennemore 3 (Paul Midgley) *prom: rdn over 1f out: wknd fnl f* **8/1**	69
1500	10	13	**Taurus Twins**[64] 4367 6-8-13 85 ...(b) RobertWinston 6 (Richard Price) *s.i.s: racd alone towards centre: nvr on terms: wknd and eased over 1f out* **28/1**	20

1m 1.1s (1.10) **Going Correction** +0.30s/f (Good) — **10** Ran SP% **131.6**

Speed ratings (Par 107): **103,101,99,98,97 96,94,91,90,69**

toteswingers 1&2 £5.40, 2&3 £4.70, 1&3 £4.30 CSF £31.80 CT £86.04 TOTE £8.30: £1.90, £1.30, £2.20; EX 36.00.

Owner Katy & Lol Pratt **Bred** Darley **Trained** Reigate, Surrey

FOCUS

They raced stands' side. An ordinary sprint handicap for the class. The winner rates a small personal best.

NOTEBOOK

Ajjaadd(USA) won well but his task was made easier by the runner-up finding trouble. Ajjaadd was 4lb higher than when taking the same race in 2011 and had returned to form with a good effort from an helpful draw at Sandown last time. He had since refused to enter the stalls at Ascot and was without the cheekpieces he had fitted on his previous start, but he was in the mood on this occasion, travelling well before finding plenty. Although a 6yo, he's not overly raced and could remain competitive off higher marks.

R Woody, returning from 55 days off, looked unfortunate not to give the winner a proper race. Not helped by his draw against the rail, he never had a great deal of room and still had a lot to do a furlong out, but he finished strongly once in the clear. Official explanation: jockey said gelding was denied a clear run

Lexi's Hero(IRE) has mainly struggled this season and was well held in third. (op 11-2)

Bathwick Bear(IRE) didn't build on his back-to-form third at Ffos Las and might have found the ground too soft. (op 8-1)

Noodles Blue Boy won this race in 2010 but hasn't been in much form lately.

New Planet(IRE) didn't offer much after 72 days off.

Taurus Twins Official explanation: jockey said gelding lost its action and moved poorly

6544 HENRY ALKEN CLASSIFIED CLAIMING STKS — 1m 1f 218y

4:30 (4:30) (Class 6) 3-4-Y-O — **£1,940** (£577; £288; £144) **Stalls** Low

Form				RPR
0220	1		**Monopoli**[19] 5931 3-9-1 68 ... RichardKingscote 6 (Ralph Beckett) *hld up in tch: shkn up 1/2-way: chsd ldr over 2f out: rdn to ld over 1f out: styd on* **10/3**[2]	78
0430	2	2 ½	**Tasfeya**[80] 3827 4-9-7 74 ... WilliamBuick 4 (Lee Carter) *led 1f: chsd ldrs tl led again over 3f out: rdn and hdd over 1f out: styd on same pce ins fnl f: eased whn hld nr fin* **9/4**[1]	73
1401	3	2	**Scarlet Prince**[14] 6103 3-9-1 65 ... StephenCraine 3 (Tony Coyle) *prom: rdn over 2f out: styd on same pce fr over 1f out* **4/1**[3]	69
6106	4	¾	**Emerald Invader**[10] 6206 3-9-5 69 ...(t) TedDurcan 1 (David Elsworth) *hld up: hdwy u.p over 2f out: rdn and hung rt over 1f out: no ex ins fnl f* **8/1**	72
0051	5	1 ½	**Alshazah**[18] 5983 4-9-7 63 ...(tp) JamesMillman 2 (Rod Millman) *s.i.s: hld up: rdn over 2f out: nvr trbld ldrs* **8/1**	65
530-	6	6	**Kingarrick**[13] 6799 4-9-2 67 ...(p) SamHitchcott 7 (Charlie Longsdon) *chsd ldrs: chal over 3f out: sn rdn: wknd over 1f out* **8/1**	48
60-4	7	26	**Mesariya (IRE)**[16] 6055 4-9-5 75 ... BarryMcHugh 8 (Tony Coyle) *s.i.s: rcvrd to ld after 1f: rdn and hdd over 3f out: wknd over 2f out: t.o* **6/1**	

2m 12.0s (4.10) **Going Correction** +0.45s/f (Yiel)

WFA 3 from 4yo 6lb — **7** Ran SP% **121.5**

Speed ratings (Par 101): **101,99,97,96,95 90,70**

toteswingers 1&2 £2.60, 2&3 £2.20, 1&3 £3.70 CSF £12.30 TOTE £4.60: £4.10, £1.30; EX 12.00.

Owner Mark & Emma Dixon **Bred** M H Dixon **Trained** Kimpton, Hants

FOCUS

An uncompetitive claimer. It appears a personal best from the winner at face value, but there are doubts.

6545 HIGHFIELDS H'CAP — 1m 60y

5:00 (5:00) (Class 5) (0-75,76) 3-Y-O+ — **£2,587** (£770; £384; £192) **Stalls** Low

Form				RPR
3630	1		**Hurricane Lady (IRE)**[16] 6041 4-9-9 74 ... NickyMackay 13 (Mike Murphy) *hld up: hdwy over 3f out: led 1f out: edgd rt: rdn out* **5/1**[3]	84

1-00 **2** *2 ½* **Ancient Greece**[149] 1680 5-9-10 **75**..............................(t) PatCosgrave 5 79
(George Baker) *set stdy pce tl qcknd over 3f out: rdn and hdd 1f out: styd on same pce* **6/1**

0000 **3** *hd* **West End Lad**[20] 5914 9-9-4 **72**..............................(b) MarkCoumbe(3) 6 76
(Roy Bowring) *hld up: stmbld after 1f: hdwy 5f out: rdn over 2f out: sn outpcd: r.o ins fnl f* **6/1**

-022 **4** *nk* **Buckland (IRE)**[60] 4517 4-9-5 **70**.............................. WilliamBuick 10 73
(Hans Adielsson) *chsd ldr: rdn over 2f out: ev ch 1f out: n.m.r sn after: styd on same pce* **9/4**[1]

060 **5** *7* **Daruband**[35] 5414 4-9-10 **75**..............................(v) JamieSpencer 12 62
(Michael Bell) *prom: rdn over 2f out: wknd over 1f out* **3/1**[2]

4300 **6** *½* **Indian Art (IRE)**[11] 6172 6-9-6 **71**.............................. SeanLevey 3 57
(Sylvester Kirk) *chsd ldrs: rdn 4f out: wknd over 2f out* **10/1**

40-0 **7** *hd* **Broxbourne (IRE)**[59] 4544 3-8-12 **67**.............................. SilvestreDeSousa 2 52
(Mark Johnston) *s.i.s: sn pushed along and prom: lost pl 5f out: sn bhd* **8/1**

1m 50.98s (5.88) **Going Correction** +0.45s/f (Yiel)
WFA 3 from 4yo+ 4lb **7 Ran SP% 121.2**
Speed ratings (Par 103): **88,85,85,85,78 77,77**
toteswingers 1&2 £6.80, 2&3 £7.80, 1&3 £6.40 CSF £37.10 CT £188.69 TOTE £8.40: £4.90, £3.40; EX 45.90.
Owner Borgatti & Moir **Bred** Barbara Prendergast **Trained** Westoning, Beds

FOCUS
The pace looked fair with the runner-up taking them along, and the winner coming from last. This was just a modest race. The first two are rated back to their old best.

6546 RACING EXCELLENCE "HANDS AND HEELS" APPRENTICE SERIES H'CAP 7f 9y
5:30 (5:30) (Class 5) (0-70,70) 3-Y-O+ **£2,264** (£673; £336; £168) **Stalls** High

Form RPR

0012 **1** **Mount Mayday (IRE)**[29] 5633 3-8-8 **60**..............................(t) JasonHart 7 68
(Stuart Williams) *s.i.s: sn chsng ldrs: led over 4f out: pushed along fr over 2f out: styd on* **2/1**[2]

0631 **2** *1 ¼* **Xpres Maite**[14] 6104 9-8-10 **59**..............................(b) JoshBaudains 3 64
(Roy Bowring) *pushed along througout: prom: styd on to go 2nd wl ins fnl f: could nt trble wnr* **4/1**[3]

0450 **3** *1* **Rulesn'regulations**[9] 6241 6-9-2 **70**..............................[1] SemiraPashai(5) 1 72
(Matthew Salaman) *a.p: pushed along to chse wnr over 2f out: styd on same pce ins fnl f* **13/2**

0545 **4** *3 ½* **Forty Proof (IRE)**[7] 6322 4-8-7 **56** oh8..............................(t) PhilipPrince 2 49
(David Evans) *prom: lost pl over 4f out: pushed along over 2f out: no imp fnl f* **16/1**

5422 **5** *nk* **Clumber Place**[17] 5999 6-8-10 **59**.............................. NedCurtis 9 51
(James Given) *led: racd keenly: hdd over 4f out: pushed along over 2f out: sn edgd rt: no ex fnl f* **7/4**[1]

/00- **6** *10* **Lordship (IRE)**[355] 6626 8-8-7 **56** oh6.............................. ShirleyTeasdale 8 21
(Tony Carroll) *hld up: pushed along 1/2-way: wknd over 2f out* **25/1**

0000 **7** *1 ½* **Regency Art (IRE)**[17] 5999 5-8-7 **56** oh9.............................. DanielMuscutt 11 17
(Milton Bradley) *racd keenly: w ldr tl 4f out: wknd over 2f out* **66/1**

1m 28.91s (2.71) **Going Correction** +0.45s/f (Yiel)
WFA 3 from 4yo+ 3lb **7 Ran SP% 114.3**
Speed ratings (Par 103): **102,100,99,95,95 83,81**
toteswingers 1&2 £3.10, 2&3 £3.50, 1&3 £2.40 CSF £10.51 CT £42.48 TOTE £3.20: £1.10, £1.80; EX 12.60.
Owner Paul W Stevens **Bred** Tullamaine Castle Stud **Trained** Newmarket, Suffolk

FOCUS
They raced middle to stands' side. A modest apprentices' handicap that went to the least exposed runner.
T/Jkpt: £8,178.60 to a £1 stake. Pool of £57595.91 -5.0 winning tickets. T/Plt: £226.00 to a £1 stake. Pool of £69214.55 - 223.48 winning tickets. T/Qpdt: £25.10 to a £1 stake. Pool of £5842.24 - 172.20 winning tickets. CR

6547 - 6549a (Foreign Racing) - See Raceform Interactive

4122 FAIRYHOUSE (R-H)
Monday, September 24

OFFICIAL GOING: Heavy

6550a TATTERSALLS IRELAND SUPER AUCTION SALE STKS 7f
5:05 (5:35) 2-Y-O
£51,041 (£19,791; £12,850; £5,908; £2,429; £345)

RPR

1 **Three Sea Captains (IRE)**[30] 5608 2-9-6 102.............. WayneLordan 12 101
(David Wachman, Ire) *hld up in tch: clsd on outer 2f out: hrd rdn to cl ent fnl f and led 100yds out: all out: jst* **7/4**[1]

2 *shd* **Tipping Over (IRE)**[9] 6238 2-8-8 .... ChrisHayes 10 89
(Hugo Palmer) *chsd ldrs: t.k.h: rdn over 2f out on nrside to ld 1 1/2f out: strly pressed and hdd 100yds out: kpt on wl towards fin: jst denied* **6/1**[3]

3 *4 ¼* **The Ticket Man**[20] 5924 2-8-13 .... EmmetMcNamara 13 83
(Mrs John Harrington, Ire) *hld up in mid-div: pushed along into st and clsd into 4th ent fnl f: rdn and kpt on wl wout ever threatening principals* **16/1**

4 *3 ½* **Thunder Mountain (IRE)**[16] 6060 2-9-5 100..............(b[1]) PatSmullen 1 81
(D K Weld, Ire) *trckd ldrs in 4th: clsd into 2nd 3f out on inner gng wl: led over 2f out: sn strly pressed and hdd 1 1/2f out: one pce ins fnl f* **7/2**[2]

5 *nk* **Sylvia Pankhurst (IRE)**[23] 5828 2-8-8 .... FergalLynch 9 69
(David C Griffiths) *hld up towards rr: hdwy on over 2f out: sn rdn and kpt on ins fnl f: n.d* **16/1**

6 *1 ¾* **Royal Empress (IRE)**[15] 6078 2-8-12 95.............................. WJLee 8 69
(David Wachman, Ire) *chsd ldrs: 4th 3f out: niggled along into st and sn no ex: wknd* **7/1**

7 *shd* **Lady Gosford (IRE)**[30] 5604 2-8-10 83.............................. ShaneFoley 6 66
(Edward Lynam, Ire) *hld up in tch: pushed along in 6th 3f out: rdn appr fnl f and kpt on same pce* **8/1**

8 *4* **Chips Are Down (IRE)**[32] 5522 2-8-13 78.............................. GaryCarroll 11 59
(Michael Mulvany, Ire) *mid-div: n.d fnl 2f* **12/1**

9 *6* **Granny On Fire (IRE)**[10] 6220 2-8-6 50.............................. ConorHoban 4 37
(Michael Mulvany, Ire) *s.i.s: n.d fr 3f out* **100/1**

10 *1 ¾* **Rock N Rover (IRE)** 2-8-11 .... CO'Donoghue 7 38
(Noel Meade, Ire) *dwlt and racd in rr: sme late hdwy fnl f: nvr a factor* **20/1**

11 *2 ¼* **Spirit Of The Air (IRE)**[19] 5954 2-8-11 61..............(t) KevinManning 2 32
(John Joseph Murphy, Ire) *chsd ldrs: rdn over 2f out and sn wknd* **100/1**

12 *nk* **Lady Medici**[21] 5894 2-8-8 .... DeclanMcDonogh 5 29
(Kevin Prendergast, Ire) *a bhd: nvr a factor* **20/1**

13 *3 ½* **Toberton (IRE)**[19] 5953 2-8-11 .... SeamieHeffernan 14 23
(T M Walsh, Ire) *sn led: 4 l clr after 1/2-way: jnd and hdd over 2f out: wknd qckly* **33/1**

1m 39.84s (9.34) **13 Ran SP% 130.4**
CSF £13.41 TOTE £3.80: £1.02, £3.40, £2.90; DF 27.60.
Owner Ganley Brothers Partnership **Bred** Newtown Stud **Trained** Goolds Cross, Co Tipperary

FOCUS
A terrific battle inside the final furlong despite the desperate conditions. Straightforward form rated around the first two.

NOTEBOOK
Three Sea Captains(IRE) was entitled to be thought of as the best horse in the race, but with a high draw and being kept wide in the straight it turned into a real struggle. Considering he was off the bridle before the turn into the straight he demonstrated his toughness as the runner-up kept battling and wouldn't go away. He looks set to take a step up in class now, but it's really a question of how much this race might have taken out of him. (op 7/4 tchd 2/1)
Tipping Over(IRE) showed what a leveller the ground is as she almost proved good enough. She kept the winner wide in the straight and it looked as though that horse was getting the better of her a furlong out, but the way she battled back was admirable. The prize money earned here alone shows her to have been a bargain purchase and she certainly has the attitude to win more races.
The Ticket Man had shown some ability in a Roscommon maiden the previous month on bad ground and ran well on it again here. He didn't have the pace to be competitive in any real sense but he kept going all the way to the line and a soft-ground maiden should be winnable for him.
Thunder Mountain(IRE) wouldn't have been at home on the ground by any means, but his inside draw gave him a chance and he travelled like the winner for most of the way. He just wasn't able to pick up on it inside the final furlong and a half. Official explanation: jockey said gelding ducked after one and a half furlongs from water lying on the track (op 7/2 tchd 10/3)
Sylvia Pankhurst(IRE) did some reasonable late work.
Royal Empress(IRE) didn't get home on the ground. (op 7/1 tchd 13/2)

6551 - 6553a (Foreign Racing) - See Raceform Interactive

6090 SAN SIRO (R-H)
Sunday, September 23

OFFICIAL GOING: Turf: good

6554a PREMIO FEDERICO TESIO (GROUP 2) (3YO+) (TURF) 1m 3f
4:35 (12:00) 3-Y-O+ **£39,583** (£17,416; £9,500; £4,750)

RPR

1 **Orsino (GER)**[120] 5-8-11 0.............................. MircoDemuro 4 105
(R Rohne, Germany) *a.p: 2nd and hrd rdn 1 1/2f out: r.o wl u.p ins fnl f: led cl home* **59/20**[3]

2 *½* **Branderburgo (IRE)**[84] 5-8-11 0.............................. MEsposito 7 104
(M Grassi, Italy) *trckd ldr: lft in ld after 3f: kicked clr 2f out: r.o u.str.p fnl f: ct cl home* **41/5**

3 *½* **Aquamarine (JPN)**[78] 3856 4-8-8 0.............................. UmbertoRispoli 2 100
(M Delzangles, France) *settled towards rr: hdwy to chse ldrs fr 2 1/2f out: styd on u.p fnl f: nt pce to chal* **5/2**[2]

4 *2 ½* **Frankenstein**[105] 2968 5-8-11 0.............................. CColombi 1 99
(B Grizzetti, Italy) *hld up in tch: dropped towards rr 1/2-way: rdn and hdwy 2f out: styd on at one pce fnl f* **28/1**

5 *4 ½* **Saratoga Black (IRE)**[105] 2968 5-8-11 0.............................. DarioVargiu 3 91
(B Grizzetti, Italy) *hld up towards rr: short-lived effrt to chse ldrs 2 1/2f out: sn rdn and no further imp: wknd over 1f out* **187/10**

6 *2 ½* **Wild Wolf (IRE)**[91] 3-8-5 0.............................. FabioBranca 5 87
(S Botti, Italy) *midfield: trckd ldrs 1/2-way: 2nd and ev ch 3f out: sn rdn and nt qckn: wknd fnl 1 1/2f* **4/1**

7 *dist* **Orpello (IRE)**[91] 3-8-5 0.............................. AFiori 6
(S Botti, Italy) *led: swvd bdly lft and almost uns rdr and virtually stopped after 3f: rushed up to press ldr again after 5f: remained prom tl wknd qckly fr over 2 1/2f out: t.o* **4/5**[1]

2m 13.8s (-4.80)
WFA 3 from 4yo+ 7lb **7 Ran SP% 184.4**
WIN (incl. 1 euro stake): 3.94. PLACES: 2.60, 3.67. DF: 13.32.
Owner Kurt Fekonja **Bred** Gestut Moenchhof **Trained** Germany

NOTEBOOK
Orsino(GER), who came into this after landing a valuable handicap and a runaway win in a C&D conditions event, turned in a gritty display to reel in the front-running second.

6354 BEVERLEY (R-H)
Tuesday, September 25

OFFICIAL GOING: Good (7.9) changing to good to soft after race 1 (2.10) changing to soft after race 3 (3.10)
Wind: Fresh across Weather: Heavy cloud and rain

6555 BEVERLEY ANNUAL BADGEHOLDERS (S) STKS 1m 4f 16y
2:10 (2:10) (Class 5) 3-4-Y-O **£2,264** (£673; £336; £168) **Stalls** Low

Form RPR

3020 **1** **Finity Run (GER)**[14] 6118 3-8-3 70.............................. JoeFanning 3 52
(Mark Johnston) *mde all: rdn along wl over 1f out: drvn ins fnl f and kpt on gamely* **5/2**[2]

0026 **2** *1 ¼* **Reflect (IRE)**[25] 4460 4-8-9 82..............................(t) DanielMuscutt(7) 8 55
(Tim Vaughan) *trckd ldrs: stdy hdwy over 4f out: effrt 2f out: rdn to chal over 1f out and ev ch: kpt on same pce last 100yds* **3/1**[3]

0536 **3** *½* **Valentine's Gift**[6] 6361 4-9-2 49..............................[1] DuranFentiman 2 54
(Neville Bycroft) *hld up in tch: hdwy on inner over 2f out and sn pushed along: rdn wl over 1f out: styd on ins fnl f* **25/1**

4141 **4** *¾* **Future Wonder (IRE)**[28] 5708 3-8-5 60.............................. PaulPickard(3) 6 53
(Brian Ellison) *hld up in rr: stdy hdwy over 4f out: effrt on outer 2f out: sn rdn and chsd ldrs over 1f out: no imp ins fnl f* **9/4**[1]

0100 **5** *1* **Rockgoat (IRE)**[10] 6240 3-8-13 65.............................. GrahamLee 4 56
(Ian McInnes) *trckd wnr: effrt over 3f out: rdn along over 2f out: drvn over 1f out and sn one pce* **12/1**

5523 **6** *5* **Priestley's Reward (IRE)**[19] 5965 3-8-13 67..............(v) RobertWinston 9 48
(Mrs K Burke) *hld up: hdwy 1/2-way: trckd ldrs 3f out: rdn over 2f out: sn drvn and btn* **6/1**

0000 **7** *9* **Sleights Boy (IRE)**[8] 6322 4-9-2 46.............................. DaleSwift 7 29
(Ian McInnes) *in tch: rdn along 1/2-way: outpcd and bhd fnl 4f* **125/1**

0-00 **8** *58* **Upton Crystal**[71] 4157 4-8-11 43.............................. JamesSullivan 1
(Michael Easterby) *chsd ldrs: lost pl over 3f out: sn bhd and eased* **80/1**

0 **9** *dist* **Roman Eglenovich**[89] 3551 3-8-8 0..............................(b[1]) MartinLane 5
(George Margarson) *a in rr: bhd fr 1/2-way: t.o and virtually p.u 2f out* **80/1**
2m 45.37s (5.57) **Going Correction** +0.30s/f (Good)
WFA 3 from 4yo 8lb **9** Ran SP% **113.4**
Speed ratings (Par 103): **93,92,91,91,90 87,81,42,**
toteswingers 1&2 £2.70, 2&3 £9.60, 1&3 £7.30 CSF £10.13 TOTE £2.40: £1.10, £2.10, £5.80; EX 11.40 Trifecta £113.70 Pool: £605.74 - 3.94 winning tickets..There was no bid for the winner. Reflect was claimed by Mr Derek Shaw for £6,000.
Owner Mark Johnston Racing Ltd **Bred** Gestut Hofgut Heymann **Trained** Middleham Moor, N Yorks
FOCUS
This did not look too bad a contest for the grade, which was run at a steady pace with the winner making all under a well-judged ride. The lowly rated third is a key to the form.

6556 THANKS FOR YOUR SUPPORT IN 2012 MAIDEN AUCTION STKS 5f
2:40 (2:41) (Class 4) 2-Y-O £3,428 (£1,020; £509; £254) **Stalls** Low

Form RPR
6020 **1** **Palladius**[18] 6016 2-8-8 65.............................. AmyRyan 9 69
(Kevin Ryan) *chsd ldr: rdn along over 1f out: styd on wl to ld last 50yds* **6/1**[3]
2 *1 1/2* **Free Island** 2-8-7 0.............................. MartinLane 11 63+
(James Tate) *led: rdn clr wl over 1f out: drvn ins fnl f: hdd and no ex last 50yds* **14/1**
60 **3** *3 3/4* **Bernardino**[99] 3208 2-8-9 0.............................. GrahamGibbons 3 51
(David Barron) *chsd ldrs: rdn along 2f out: kpt on u.p fnl f* **10/1**
2 **4** *1/2* **Hoofalong**[132] 2181 2-8-13 0.............................. JamesSullivan 7 53
(Michael Easterby) *dwlt: hdwy 1/2-way: chsd ldrs 2f out: rdn wl over 1f out: sn btn* **4/5**[1]
2503 **5** *1 3/4* **Gold Beau (FR)**[30] 5620 2-8-12 68.............................. GrahamLee 5 46
(Linda Stubbs) *chsd ldrs: rdn along 2f out: drvn and one pce appr fnl f* **9/2**[2]
0 **6** *6* **Cool And Clear (IRE)**[6] 6360 2-8-11 0.............................. DavidAllan 2 23
(Tim Easterby) *in tch: rdn along 1/2-way: sn wknd* **20/1**
4000 **7** *nk* **Cool Sea (IRE)**[12] 6164 2-7-12 43.............................. DanielleMooney(7) 12 16
(Nigel Tinkler) *a towards rr* **80/1**
00 **8** *3 1/4* **Shesnotforturning (IRE)**[41] 5222 2-8-3 0.............................. JulieBurke(3) 4
(Ben Haslam) *a towards rr* **50/1**
9 *2 3/4* **Haarmonic** 2-8-10 0.............................. RobertWinston 6
(Richard Whitaker) *s.i.s: a bhd* **12/1**
1m 5.8s (2.30) **Going Correction** +0.375s/f (Good) **9** Ran SP% **119.4**
Speed ratings (Par 97): **96,93,87,86,84 74,73,68,64**
toteswingers 1&2 £9.00, 2&3 £16.40, 1&3 £5.20 CSF £85.22 TOTE £4.30: £1.60, £3.40, £3.00; EX 96.80 Trifecta £626.60 Pool: £931.44 - 1.10 winning tickets..
Owner Wood Hall Stud Limited **Bred** Wood Hall Stud Limited **Trained** Hambleton, N Yorks
FOCUS
The going was changed to good to soft, from good after the first race and the rain began falling more heavily prior to this contest. An uncompetitive maiden run at a fair pace with the front two pulling clear inside the final furlong. Improvement from the winner but the favourite was below par.
NOTEBOOK
Palladius did not last home over 6f at Kempton when last seen but, dropping back to the minimum and returning to the track where she finished runner-up in July, ran out a convincing winner. She was ideally positioned just behind the pace and saw it out gamely inside the final furlong. With the favourite underperforming, this did not take much winning but she is with the right yard to continue progressing. (op 11-2 tchd 5-1)
Free Island, a half-sister to several winners, notably Group 1-winning Solider Hollow, showed fine pace to get to the front on the far rail from her wide draw but paid for those efforts late on. This was an encouraging debut. (op 25-1)
Bernardino, dropping back to the minimum after two runs over 6f, was well positioned but took his time to pick up before staying on well to the line, suggesting a step back up in trip is required. (tchd 12-1)
Hoofalong had missed the break before staying on well on his debut at York in May and he was slowly away again here. He travelled kindly into the race, but did not look happy on the softer ground when the pace quickened and found little for pressure. (tchd 4-6)
Gold Beau(FR) made a bit of late progress, but is beginning to look exposed and may need further. (op 5-1)

6557 EDDIE AND VIOLET SMITH CONDITIONS STKS 5f
3:10 (3:10) (Class 3) 3-Y-O+
£6,411 (£1,919; £959; £479; £239; £120) **Stalls** Low

Form RPR
2040 **1** **Kool Henry (IRE)**[16] 6075 3-8-1 88..............................(v[1]) DavidBergin(7) 5 99
(David O'Meara) *cl up: led after 1f: pushed clr wl over 1f out: rdn and edgd rt ent fnl f: kpt on* **14/1**
2100 **2** *1 1/4* **Tax Free (IRE)**[10] 6244 10-8-9 94.............................. AdrianNicholls 1 95
(David Nicholls) *led 1f: cl up: rdn along and edgd lft over 1f out: kpt on fnl f* **5/1**
6500 **3** *3/4* **Ponty Acclaim (IRE)**[24] 5822 3-8-3 99..............................[1] DuranFentiman 2 87
(Tim Easterby) *hld up in tch: pushed along 1/2-way: sn rdn: styd on u.p fnl f: nrst fin* **3/1**[2]
600 **4** *1/2* **Burning Thread (IRE)**[17] 6026 5-8-9 85..............................[1] JamesSullivan 6 90
(Tim Etherington) *chsd ldrs: hdwy 2f out: sn rdn and kpt on same pce fnl f* **33/1**
3063 **5** *3 3/4* **Free Zone**[16] 6072 3-9-2 105.............................. TomEaves 3 85
(Bryan Smart) *chsd ldrs: rdn along over 2f out: sn drvn and wknd* **7/2**[3]
0040 **6** *1 1/4* **Es Que Love (IRE)**[17] 6030 3-8-8 105.............................. KierenFallon 4 72
(Mark Johnston) *prom: chsd wnr after 2f: rdn along wl over 1f out: sn drvn and wknd* **7/4**[1]
1m 4.55s (1.05) **Going Correction** +0.45s/f (Yiel)
WFA 3 from 5yo+ 1lb **6** Ran SP% **109.9**
Speed ratings (Par 107): **109,107,105,105,99 97**
toteswingers 1&2 £5.80, 2&3 £3.10, 1&3 £5.70 CSF £76.19 TOTE £17.30: £4.60, £2.60; EX 99.10.
Owner Middleham Park Racing Equality Racing **Bred** Stephanie Hanly **Trained** Nawton, N Yorks
FOCUS
Some decent types contested this conditions stakes which was run at a sound pace and saw something of a surprise. It's hard to take the race at face value and the first three were probably below par.
NOTEBOOK
Kool Henry(IRE) improved for a first-time visor. The 7lb claim of his decent apprentice also helped, as was his ability to handle the going. He had plenty on at the weights, but is a useful type under these conditions if able to lead. (op 16-1)
Tax Free(IRE) did well to stay on into second having raced keenly through the early part of the race. He hung off the far rail at the 2f pole and came with a sustained challenge more up the centre, and this was another fine run on ground softer than ideal. (tchd 11-2)
Ponty Acclaim(IRE), wearing a hood for the first time, was much better off with Tax Free who beat her at York in August, but was never travelling on this ground. (op 11-4)
Burning Thread(IRE), who had plenty on at the weights, travelled wide throughout and finished close up. This was a much better effort than of late in a first-time hood.
Es Que Love(IRE), last seen in the Group 1 Betfred Sprint Cup and Kieren Fallon's only ride of the day, was well backed but came under pressure some way out and found disappointingly little. All three wins have come on good or better. Official explanation: trainer's rep said, regarding running, that the colt was unsuited by the soft ground (op 5-2 tchd 13-8)

6558 BRITISH STALLION STUDS SUPPORTING BRITISH RACING EBF MAIDEN STKS 7f 100y
3:40 (3:41) (Class 5) 2-Y-O £3,340 (£986; £493) **Stalls** Low

Form RPR
32 **1** **Altharoos (IRE)**[18] 5992 2-9-3 0.............................. PaulHanagan 2 76
(Sir Michael Stoute) *cl up: led wl over 2f out: rdn and hdd over 1f out: drvn and rallied ins fnl f: led on line* **4/5**[1]
4 **2** *hd* **He's A Striker (IRE)**[56] 4677 2-9-3 0.............................. BarryMcHugh 3 76
(Tony Coyle) *sltly hmpd s: sn chsng ldrs: hdwy on inner over 2f out: rdn to ld over 1f out: drvn and edgd rt wl ins fnl f: hdd and no ex nr line* **28/1**
3 *6* **Flashlight (IRE)** 2-9-3 0.............................. JoeFanning 4 62+
(Mark Johnston) *green and outpcd in rr: hdwy on inner 3f out: rdn to chse ldrs over 2f out: kpt on fnl f: nrst fin* **10/1**[3]
63 **4** *4* **Le Talisman (IRE)**[11] 6214 2-8-12 0.............................. AntiocoMurgia(5) 1 53
(Mahmood Al Zarooni) *led: rdn along 3f out: sn hdd and grad wknd fnl 2f* **10/1**[3]
43 **5** *3* **Wyldfire (IRE)**[17] 6043 2-9-3 0.............................. TonyHamilton 6 46
(Richard Fahey) *trckd ldrs: hdwy 1/2-way: rdn along 3f out: sn btn* **9/4**[2]
0 **6** *3 1/4* **Love Marmalade (IRE)**[12] 6164 2-9-3 0.............................. PhillipMakin 5 38
(Kevin Ryan) *in tch: rdn along over 3f out: sn outpcd* **12/1**
06 **7** *6* **Apache Rising**[17] 6043 2-9-3 0.............................. TomEaves 8 24
(Bryan Smart) *sn outpcd and a in rr* **66/1**
000 **8** *14* **Haafn Haaf**[6] 6356 2-9-3 0..............................(b[1]) PaulMulrennan 7
(Michael Easterby) *prom: rdn along 1/2-way: sn wknd* **150/1**
1m 39.9s (6.10) **Going Correction** +0.775s/f (Yiel) **8** Ran SP% **117.8**
Speed ratings (Par 95): **96,95,88,84,80 77,70,54**
toteswingers 1&2 £8.20, 2&3 £6.80, 1&3 £3.10 CSF £31.00 TOTE £1.90: £1.10, £3.80, £2.00; EX 20.50 Trifecta £83.30 Pool: £1,852.72 - 16.45 winning tickets..
Owner Hamdan Al Maktoum **Bred** Shadwell Estate Company Limited **Trained** Newmarket, Suffolk
FOCUS
After the continued heavy rain, the going was changed to soft prior to this race. Some powerful stables lined up for this maiden which was run at a sound pace in the conditions, with few able to get competitive. The first two were clear.
NOTEBOOK
Altharoos(IRE) had shown decent form in two maidens and came into this the clear form pick. However, he had to battle all the way to the line to get on top. He was nicely settled behind the strong pace, but looked in trouble when passed inside the final furlong before showing a game attitude to get back on top. These conditions would not have suited and he looks a handy type for middle-distance handicaps. (op 5-6 tchd 4-6)
He's A Striker(IRE) took a keen grip on his debut, but settled much better here and stepped up on that first run, since when he has changed stables. He travelled well on these testing conditions and looked the likeliest winner inside the final furlong, but lost out to a potentially decent type.
Flashlight(IRE), a 135,000euros foal and half-brother to a 1m2f winner, was unable to go the early pace on his debut but was staying on stoutly late on and will have learnt plenty from this.
Le Talisman(IRE) set the strong early fractions, but was made to pay for those exertions late on. He travelled like a nice sort through the early part of the contest and is now handicapped.
Wyldfire(IRE) was quicker away than on her first two starts, but raced a shade keenly before weakening 2f out. (tchd 5-2)

6559 GEORGE KILBURN MEMORIAL H'CAP 7f 100y
4:10 (4:10) (Class 5) (0-75,77) 3-Y-O+ £2,264 (£673; £336; £168) **Stalls** Low

Form RPR
5435 **1** **I Confess**[8] 6319 7-9-0 68..............................(b) PJMcDonald 2 77
(Geoffrey Harker) *chsd ldrs: hdwy over 2f out: rdn to chal over 1f out: led jst ins fnl f: drvn out* **15/2**
5401 **2** *1 3/4* **Fame Again**[17] 6057 4-9-0 68.............................. PaulMulrennan 5 73
(Michael Easterby) *slt ld: c wd home bnd: rdn over 2f out: drvn over 1f out: hdd jst ins fnl f: kpt on same pce* **13/2**
0005 **3** *1 3/4* **Just The Tonic**[7] 6342 5-8-7 64.............................. PaulPickard(3) 7 65
(Marjorie Fife) *dwlt and in rr: hdwy 3f out: rdn to chse ldrs wl over 1f out: drvn and kpt on fnl f: nrst fin* **10/1**
3050 **4** *3/4* **Save The Bees**[13] 6141 4-8-10 69..............................(b) JasonHart(5) 8 68
(Declan Carroll) *cl up: disp ld 1/2-way: c wd home bnd to stands' rail: rdn 2f out: wknd appr fnl f* **6/1**[3]
1030 **5** *4* **Eeny Mac (IRE)**[14] 6127 5-8-6 63.............................. JulieBurke(3) 13 52
(Neville Bycroft) *chsd ldrs: hdwy 3f out: rdn wl over 1f out: sn one pce* **5/1**[2]
1-06 **6** *2 1/4* **Swift Encounter (IRE)**[13] 6136 3-8-10 67.............................. TonyHamilton 3 50
(Ann Duffield) *s.i.s: a towards rr* **20/1**
1401 **7** *1* **Shadowtime**[5] 6405 7-9-9 77 6ex.............................. DaleSwift 9 58
(Tracy Waggott) *in rr: sme hdwy over 2f out: sn rdn and n.d* **6/1**[3]
0030 **8** *1* **Snow Bay**[18] 6013 6-9-6 74..............................(t) AdrianNicholls 16 52
(David Nicholls) *chsd ldng pair: hdwy over 3f out: sn cl up and styd on inner home st: rdn along 2f out and sn wknd* **12/1**
5033 **9** *57* **Desert Romance (IRE)**[5] 6405 6-9-5 73.............................. DanielTudhope 6
(David O'Meara) *chsd ldng pair: rdn along 3f out and wknd qckly: sn bhd and eased* **3/1**[1]
1m 38.68s (4.88) **Going Correction** +0.775s/f (Yiel)
WFA 3 from 4yo+ 3lb **9** Ran SP% **116.9**
Speed ratings (Par 103): **103,101,99,98,93 91,89,88,23**
toteswingers 1&2 £8.40, 2&3 £11.90, 1&3 £11.40 CSF £56.08 CT £497.68 TOTE £9.90: £1.90, £1.90, £3.40; EX 53.40 Trifecta £335.10 Pool: £638.64 - 1.41 winning tickets..
Owner Brian Harker **Bred** Gestut Sohrenhof **Trained** Thirkleby, N Yorks
FOCUS
This handicap was open enough, despite seven non runners, and run at a fair pace with the field spread across the track late on. The winner's best turf form for three years.
Desert Romance(IRE) Official explanation: vet said gelding finished distressed

6560 EMILIE WILL YOU MARRY NIDGE? H'CAP 1m 100y
4:40 (4:40) (Class 5) (0-75,75) 3-Y-O £2,264 (£673; £336; £168) **Stalls** Low

Form RPR
2022 **1** **Only Orsenfoolsies**[84] 3727 3-8-13 67.............................. PJMcDonald 1 76
(Micky Hammond) *mde most: rdn wl over 2f out: drvn over 1f out: clr ent fnl f: styd on strly* **11/4**[3]
6220 **2** *8* **Giorgio's Dragon (IRE)**[17] 6048 3-8-13 67.............................. PaulHanagan 7 58
(Richard Fahey) *cl up: effrt over 2f out: sn rdn and ev ch wl over 1f out: drvn and one pce appr fnl f* **9/4**[2]
0402 **3** *2* **Falcon's Reign (FR)**[13] 6136 3-8-8 69..............................(p) DanielMuscutt(7) 4 55
(Michael Appleby) *trckd ldng pair: effrt over 2f out: swtchd lft and rdn wl over 1f out: sn one pce* **5/1**

1323 **4** *38* **Alkadi (IRE)**[12] 6176 3-9-4 **72** JoeFanning 3
(Mark Johnston) *trckd ldrs: effrt on inner over 3f out and sn cl up: rdn 2f out: sn wknd and eased* **9/5**[1]

1m 53.8s (6.20) **Going Correction** +0.775s/f (Yiel) 4 Ran SP% **109.8**
Speed ratings (Par 101): **100,92,90,52**
toteswingers 6&7 £4.20 CSF £9.22 TOTE £3.70; EX 8.70.
Owner This Time Next Year Partnership **Bred** Redmyre Bloodstock & Newhall Farm Estate **Trained** Middleham Moor, N Yorks

FOCUS
An open looking event despite the small field size, with the winner making all to win cosily. The runners came middle to stands' side in the bad ground. It's doubtful how much the winner had to improve.

6561 BRIAN AND JASON MERRINGTON MEMORIAL AMATEUR RIDERS' H'CAP (DIV I) 1m 1f 207y
5:10 (5:10) (Class 6) (0-60,60) 3-Y-O+ **£1,559** (£483; £241; £121) **Stalls** Low

Form RPR

5065 **1** **Cottam Donny**[10] 6258 4-10-4 **57** (p) MissLWilson(7) 1 71
(Mel Brittain) *dwlt: hdwy on inner to ld after 2f: rdn 2f out: styd on wl* **13/2**[3]

0650 **2** *6* **Maybeme**[30] 5622 6-10-3 **54** (p) MrDLevey(5) 8 56
(Neville Bycroft) *in tch: hdwy 3f out: rdn along 2f out: styd on to chse wnr 1f out: no imp* **9/2**[2]

0042 **3** *½* **Kheskianto (IRE)**[6] 6361 6-9-9 **46** (t) MissAliceMills(5) 5 47
(Michael Chapman) *hld up towards rr: hdwy into midfield 1/2-way: effrt on inner to chse ldrs wl over 2f out: rdn along and kpt on same pce fnl 2f* **11/1**

2405 **4** *6* **Graceful Act**[10] 6262 4-10-5 **56** MissVBarr(5) 3 45
(Ron Barr) *led 2f: prom: rdn along over 2f out: sn one pce* **18/1**

4351 **5** *9* **Gadobout Dancer**[24] 5824 5-10-3 **54** MissHDukes(5) 9 25
(Tony Coyle) *towards rr: hdwy over 3f out: rdn over 2f out: plugged on: nvr a factor* **7/1**

5533 **6** *6* **Stanley Rigby**[26] 5761 6-10-4 **55** (b) MrJHamilton(5) 14 14
(Richard Fahey) *towards rr: hdwy into midfield over 4f out: rdn along wl over 2f out: nvr nr ldrs* **12/1**

0000 **7** *1 ½* **Media Stars**[14] 6126 7-9-12 **47** oh1 ow1 (t) MissCWalton(3) 12
(Robert Johnson) *midfield: rdn along over 4f out: sn wknd* **66/1**

0624 **8** *4* **Tiger Webb**[21] 5921 4-10-12 **58** MissSBrotherton 2
(Michael Easterby) *towards rr: sme hdwy 4f out: sn rdn and n.d* **5/2**[1]

655 **9** *1* **Rapturous Applause**[40] 5253 4-9-9 **46** oh1 (p) MissRSmith(5) 10
(Micky Hammond) *a towards rr* **20/1**

6630 **10** *1* **Zennor**[30] 5638 5-10-6 **57** MissKMargarson(5) 13
(George Margarson) *prom: effrt on outer to chse wnr 4f out: rdn wl over 2f out: sn wknd* **20/1**

0200 **11** *3 ¾* **Penderyn**[66] 4349 5-9-11 **46** oh1 MissJRRichards(3) 6
(Charles Smith) *cl up: rdn along over 3f out: sn wknd* **40/1**

023 **12** *34* **Iulus**[19] 5967 4-10-6 **59** MrOJPimlott(7) 11
(John Quinn) *chsd ldrs: rdn along over 3f out: sn wknd* **17/2**

2m 17.46s (10.46) **Going Correction** +0.775s/f (Yiel)
WFA 3 from 4yo+ 6lb 12 Ran SP% **117.9**
Speed ratings (Par 101): **89,84,83,79,71 67,65,62,61,61 58,30**
toteswingers 1&2 £8.80, 2&3 £9.40, 1&3 £13.70 CSF £34.17 CT £321.21 TOTE £7.20: £2.90, £2.20, £3.40; EX 45.20 Trifecta £402.40 Part won. Pool: £543.80 - 0.40 winning tickets..
Owner Peter Easterby **Bred** P Easterby **Trained** Warthill, N Yorks
■ Stewards' Enquiry : Mr D Levey two-day ban: used whip above permitted level (Oct 9,12)

FOCUS
This weak amateur riders' handicap was run at a sound pace, with the winner once again making all under a fine ride, and the field well strung out at the line. A similar time to division II. The winner is rated back to his best.

6562 BRIAN AND JASON MERRINGTON MEMORIAL AMATEUR RIDERS' H'CAP (DIV II) 1m 1f 207y
5:40 (5:42) (Class 6) (0-60,60) 3-Y-O+ **£1,559** (£483; £241; £121) **Stalls** Low

Form RPR

0060 **1** **Silly Gilly (IRE)**[14] 6127 8-10-7 **57** MissVBarr(5) 1 67
(Ron Barr) *mde all: rdn clr 2f out: styd on wl fnl f* **8/1**

-650 **2** *1* **Hernando Torres**[36] 5416 4-10-7 **59** MissAHesketh(7) 5 67
(Michael Easterby) *trckd ldrs on inner: hdwy over 3f out: swtchd lft and rdn to chse wnr over 1f out: edgd rt ent fnl f: kpt on* **8/1**

2535 **3** *6* **Eastlands Lad (IRE)**[27] 5736 3-10-4 **60** (p) MissRSmith(5) 8 56
(Micky Hammond) *prom: hdwy to chse wnr 2f out: sn rdn along and kpt on same pce appr fnl f* **7/2**[1]

0405 **4** *2* **Merrjanah**[19] 5967 4-9-10 **48** MrAFrench(7) 13 40
(John Wainwright) *prom: chsd wnr fr 1/2-way: rdn along over 2f out: sn drvn and grad wknd* **12/1**

0650 **5** *7* **Kieron's Rock (IRE)**[8] 6315 3-9-1 **45** MissEmmaBedford(7) 14 23
(Jedd O'Keeffe) *chsd ldrs: rdn along wl over 2f out: grad wknd* **16/1**

2000 **6** *2* **Dean Iarracht (IRE)**[14] 6126 6-10-8 **58** (p) MrGRSmith(5) 11 32
(Tracy Waggott) *hld up in rr: swtchd wd into home st and hdwy over 2f out: sn rdn and n.d* **6/1**[3]

2045 **7** *hd* **Entrance**[15] 6097 4-10-5 **55** MissSBirkett(5) 12 29
(Julia Feilden) *hld up towards rr: effrt and sme hdwy over 3f out: sn rdn along and n.d* **10/1**

3060 **8** *3 ¾* **Orpen Wide (IRE)**[40] 5259 10-9-9 **45** (bt) MissAliceMills(5) 6 11
(Michael Chapman) *a towards rr* **33/1**

0246 **9** *nk* **Sinatramania**[10] 6262 5-10-2 **54** MrJWaggott(7) 3 20
(Tracy Waggott) *hld up in rr: effrt and wd st: sn rdn and nvr a factor* **9/2**[2]

505 **10** *7* **Dzesmin (POL)**[99] 3216 10-10-0 **52** (p) MrsAGuest(7) 10
(Richard Guest) *in tch: effrt 3f out: sn rdn along and wknd* **12/1**

0430 **11** *23* **General Tufto**[56] 4683 7-9-11 **45** (b) MissJRRichards(3) 9
(Charles Smith) *a in rr* **8/1**

2m 17.3s (10.30) **Going Correction** +0.775s/f (Yiel)
WFA 3 from 4yo+ 6lb 11 Ran SP% **121.3**
Speed ratings (Par 101): **89,88,83,81,76 74,74,71,71,65 47**
toteswingers 1&2 £14.30, 2&3 £11.40, 1&3 £7.00 CSF £72.91 CT £270.19 TOTE £8.40: £3.10, £3.10, £2.10; EX 73.90 Trifecta £362.70 Pool: £955.90 - 1.95 winning tickets..
Owner D Thomson **Bred** Barronstown Stud **Trained** Seamer, N Yorks

FOCUS
As in the first division, run in a similar time, the winner dictated the pace from the off and kept on well up the far rail. She is rated close to her best. She is rated to race prominently.
T/Plt: £5,676.70 to a £1 stake. Pool: £52,101.87 - 6.70 winning tickets. T/Qpdt: £337.60 to a £1 stake. Pool: £5,201.53 - 11.40 winning tickets. JR

6328 FOLKESTONE (R-H)
Tuesday, September 25

OFFICIAL GOING: Soft (heavy in places) (straight course - stands side: 6.7; far side : 6.1, round course: 5.9) changing to heavy after race 1 (2.00)
No fewer than 38 non-runners. This may have been the last ever Flat meeting at Folkestone, which is due to close at the end of the year.
Wind: fresh, across Weather: short sharp showers and brighter spells

6563 FOLKESTONE-RACECOURSE.CO.UK H'CAP 5f
2:00 (2:00) (Class 6) (0-60,66) 3-Y-O+ **£1,704** (£503; £251) **Stalls** High

Form RPR

6030 **1** **Danzoe (IRE)**[19] 5972 5-9-5 **58** TomMcLaughlin 14 67
(Christine Dunnett) *chsd ldrs: rdn 1/2-way: swtchd rt and chal between horses 1f out: led ins fnl f: r.o strly* **13/2**

3104 **2** *2* **Spic 'n Span**[9] 6288 7-9-3 **56** (b) LukeMorris 6 58
(Ronald Harris) *taken down early: led: clr 1/2-way: rdn wl over 1f out: hdd and no ex ins fnl f* **4/1**[2]

0001 **3** *1 ¼* **Novabridge**[9] 6288 4-9-6 **66** 6ex (b) WilliamTwiston-Davies(7) 5 63
(Neil Mulholland) *chsd ldr: rdn and effrt 2f out: no ex ins fnl f: wknd fnl 100yds* **5/2**[1]

3632 **4** *5* **Green Mountain (IRE)**[6] 6362 3-8-3 **46** oh1 (vt) RaulDaSilva(3) 7 25
(Philip McBride) *chsd ldrs: rdn 1/2-way: wknd u.p over 1f out* **4/1**[2]

2045 **5** *hd* **Liberal Lady**[25] 5791 4-9-6 **59** (e) MartinHarley 2 38
(Ralph Smith) *hld up in rr: rdn and short-lived effrt wl over 1f out: wknd over 1f out* **10/1**

0162 **6** *4 ½* **Whiskey Junction**[18] 6003 8-9-2 **55** SeanLevey 4 17
(Michael Quinn) *dwlt: sn rdn along and nvr gng wl: in tch tl wknd 2f out* **9/2**[3]

1m 2.0s (2.00) **Going Correction** +0.425s/f (Yiel)
WFA 3 from 4yo+ 1lb 6 Ran SP% **109.2**
Speed ratings (Par 101): **101,97,95,87,87 80**
toteswingers 1&2 £3.40, 2&3 £2.40, 1&3 £3.90 CSF £30.27 CT £74.13 TOTE £11.00: £4.00, £2.20; EX 36.40.
Owner One For All **Bred** Miss Anne Ormsby **Trained** Hingham, Norfolk

FOCUS
Further rain had turned the ground heavy all over, although those who rode in the opener said they were getting through it. Plenty of pace on in this moderate sprint. The winner sets the standard.

6564 GERAINT JONES BENEFIT YEAR NURSERY 5f
2:30 (2:30) (Class 5) (0-70,70) 2-Y-O **£2,385** (£704; £352) **Stalls** High

Form RPR

4442 **1** **Starlight Angel (IRE)**[9] 6282 2-9-5 **68** LukeMorris 5 70
(Ronald Harris) *wnt rt s: chsd ldr tl rdn to ld wl over 1f out: sn edgd lft: clr 1f out: styd on wl* **6/4**[1]

602 **2** *2* **Colourist**[29] 5654 2-9-2 **65** GeorgeBaker 4 60
(Gary Moore) *pushed rt and hmpd s: in tch in rr: rdn and effrt over 2f out: styd on to chse clr wnr ins fnl f: r.o but nvr able to chal* **2/1**[2]

0634 **3** *2 ½* **Secretori**[34] 5475 2-9-2 **65** LiamKeniry 3 51
(Matthew Salaman) *led: hdd and rdn wl over 1f out: sltly hmpd over 1f out: sn drvn and one pce: wknd fnl 100yds* **7/2**[3]

2304 **4** *1 ¼* **Michael's Song (IRE)**[9] 6283 2-8-8 **57** (v[1]) MartinHarley 7 38
(Mick Channon) *chsd ldng pair: rdn 2f out: unable qck over 1f out: styng on same pce whn short of room and swtchd rt ins fnl f: wknd fnl 100yds* **11/2**

1m 2.91s (2.91) **Going Correction** +0.525s/f (Yiel) 4 Ran SP% **110.9**
Speed ratings (Par 95): **97,93,89,87**
toteswingers 2&5 £2.30 CSF £4.94 TOTE £2.90; EX 4.80.
Owner Mrs A Mares **Bred** Hugo Merry **Trained** Earlswood, Monmouths

FOCUS
This ended up being fairly uncompetitive following the three non-runners, with the market leaders coming to the fore late on. It was run on bad ground and the form has not been rated too positively.

NOTEBOOK
Starlight Angel(IRE) gained an overdue first success, never looking in any danger once taking over. She looks to have found her level and can continue to give a good account from a slightly higher mark. (op 13-8 tchd 7-4)
Colourist, impeded by the winner on leaving the stalls, didn't look entirely in love with the ground, although in staying on for second probably ran to a similar level as on last month's nursery debut. (op 15-8 tchd 7-4)
Secretori had run okay on heavy ground previously, so could have been expected to do better having got in front early and bagged the rail. (op 4-1 tchd 9-2)
Michael's Song(IRE), wearing a first-time visor, couldn't lead on this drop in trip and she was already struggling when impeded. (op 13-2 tchd 7-1)

6565 EASTWELLMANOR.CO.UK MAIDEN STKS 6f
3:00 (3:00) (Class 5) 3-Y-O+ **£2,385** (£704; £352) **Stalls** High

Form RPR

-52 **1** **Gull Rock**[10] 6254 3-8-12 0 DaneO'Neill 9 63+
(Henry Candy) *racd against stands' rail: dwlt and pushed along leaving stalls: chsd ldr after 1f: rdn to ld overall 2f out: kpt on wl: eased cl home: 1st of 6 in gp* **5/4**[1]

4260 **2** *1 ¼* **Mister Mackenzie**[60] 4218 3-9-3 62 GeorgeBaker 2 64
(John Best) *stmbld as stalls opened: swtchd to r far side: chsd ldrs overall: rdn and chsd wnr wl over 1f out: kpt on same pce ins fnl f: 1st of 2 in gp* **12/1**

-040 **3** *7* **Arctic Stryker**[59] 4583 3-9-3 68 LukeMorris 3 42
(John Best) *swtchd to racd far side: midfield overall: rdn over 2f out: drvn and unable qck wl over 1f out: sn wknd: 2nd of 2 in gp* **11/2**[3]

5050 **4** *2* **Black Douglas**[4] 6455 3-9-3 64 (b) FrannyNorton 6 35
(William Jarvis) *racd stands' side: bhd: rdn and no hdwy over 2f out: no ch but plugged on past btn horses ins fnl f: 2nd of 6 in gp* **5/2**[2]

0642 **5** *1* **Enthrall (IRE)**[7] 6345 3-8-9 47 (be) RyanClark(3) 1 27
(Phil McEntee) *racd stands' side: swtchd lft after s: led after 1f: rdn and hdd 2f out: wknd qckly wl over 1f out: 3rd of 6 in gp* **12/1**

60 **6** *7* **Scary Canary**[32] 5555 4-9-5 0 IanMongan 7 10
(George Margarson) *racd stands' side: broke fast: t.k.h early: led for 1f: chsd ldrs tl rdn and struggling over 2f out: wknd 2f out: eased cl home: 4th of 6 in gp* **40/1**

66 **7** *1* **Tribal I D (IRE)**[36] 5404 3-9-3 0 [1] PatCosgrave 4
(Jim Boyle) *racd stands' side: midfield overall: rdn and struggling 1/2-way: lost tch 2f out: 5th of 6 in gp* **12/1**

00-0 **8** *10* **Grayfriars**[106] 2971 4-9-5 40 .... JimmyQuinn 5
(J R Jenkins) *racd stands' side: a bhd: lost tch 2f: t.o fnl f: 6th of 6 in gp* **66/1**

1m 14.96s (2.26) **Going Correction** +0.525s/f (Yiel)
WFA 3 from 4yo 2lb **8** Ran SP% **115.4**
Speed ratings (Par 103): **105,103,94,91,90 80,79,66**
toteswingers 1&2 £3.10, 2&3 £4.10, 1&3 £2.40 CSF £18.78 TOTE £2.20: £1.10, £3.10, £1.30; EX 11.90.
Owner Henry Candy **Bred** Bishopswood Bloodstock & Trickledown Stud **Trained** Kingston Warren, Oxon

FOCUS
There was a difference of opinion in this maiden, with runner-up Mister Mackenzie trying his luck far side. As it turned out there wasn't much between them, but it was still Gull Rock against the stands' rail who came out best. A weak race and the winner probably didn't need to improve much on his AW form.

6566 HP TECHNOLOGY H'CAP 7f (S)
3:30 (3:30) (Class 4) (0-85,85) 3-Y-O+ **£4,851** (£1,443; £721; £360) **Stalls** High

Form RPR

1403 **1** **Duster**[39] 5305 5-9-5 **83** .... RobertHavlin 8 92
(Hughie Morrison) *chsd ldr: rdn to chal over 1f out: drvn to ld jst over 1f out: styd on wl* **9/2**[3]

3113 **2** *1 1/4* **Myboyalfie (USA)**[41] 5243 5-8-12 **76** ....(v) IanMongan 3 82
(J R Jenkins) *t.k.h: chsd ldng pair: rdn and effrt wl over 1f out: drvn ent fnl f: chsd wnr and styd on same pce ins fnl f* **9/4**[1]

0300 **3** *1/2* **Master Mylo (IRE)**[34] 5480 5-8-11 **80** .... GeorgeDowning(5) 9 85
(Robert Cowell) *taken down early: awkward leaving stalls: t.k.h: hld up in tch: swtchd rt and n.m.r over 1f out: swtchd rt again 1f out: styd on same pce u.p fnl f* **13/2**

0211 **4** *1 1/2* **Centrifugal (IRE)**[7] 6331 3-9-1 **82** 6ex .... FrannyNorton 5 83
(Mark Johnston) *led: rdn wl over 1f out: drvn and hdd jst over 1f out: wknd fnl 75yds* **5/2**[2]

4452 **5** *1 3/4* **Schoolmaster**[53] 4775 4-8-10 **74** .... LiamKeniry 1 70
(Giles Bravery) *t.k.h: hld up in tch in last pair: rdn and effrt whn n.m.r over 1f out: no imp 1f out: wknd ins fnl f* **5/1**

1m 30.07s (2.77) **Going Correction** +0.525s/f (Yiel)
WFA 3 from 4yo+ 3lb **5** Ran SP% **107.5**
Speed ratings (Par 105): **105,103,103,101,99**
toteswingers 2&8 £7.30 CSF £14.23 CT £53.68 TOTE £8.00: £3.10, £1.50; EX 13.70.
Owner M T Bevan **Bred** Paddock Space **Trained** East Ilsley, Berks

FOCUS
This still had the look of being quite competitive, despite the non-runners. Ordinary but straightforward form.

6567 SHEPHERDNEAME.CO.UK H'CAP 1m 7f 92y
4:00 (4:00) (Class 6) (0-60,60) 3-Y-O+ **£1,704** (£503; £251) **Stalls** High

Form RPR

5401 **1** **Authentication**[3] 6474 3-8-13 **56** 6ex .... FrannyNorton 10 67+
(Mark Johnston) *chsd ldrs: wnt 2nd over 8f out tl led 5f out: rdn and readily wnt clr 2f out: pushed along and a in command fnl f* **10/11**[1]

300 **2** *1 1/2* **Stickleback**[69] 4225 3-8-3 **46** oh1 .... JimmyQuinn 9 51
(Harry Dunlop) *in tch in last pair: reminder and hdwy 5f out: chsd ldrs and rdn 4f out: 3rd and looked wl btn over 1f out: chsd clr wnr ins fnl f: kpt on but nvr a threat* **7/1**[3]

134- **3** *5* **Dark And Dangerous (IRE)**[160] 6891 4-9-12 **58** .... GeorgeBaker 13 57
(Brendan Powell) *in tch in midfield: hdwy 6f out: pressed wnr over 4f out: rdn and unable qck over 2f out: sn brushed aside and btn over 1f out: lost 2nd ins fnl f* **11/4**[2]

4050 **4** *12* **Maccabees**[10] 6232 3-8-1 **51** ow3 .... JoshBaudains(7) 2 34
(Roger Curtis) *hld up in midfield: rdn and hdwy on outer to chse ldrs over 3f out: wknd 2f out: wl btn and eased ins fnl f* **14/1**

05-3 **5** *5* **Dazzling Begum**[256] 160 7-8-11 **46** oh1 .... SimonPearce(3) 8 22
(Lydia Pearce) *bhd: clsd 6f out: 5th and wl in tch 3f out: sn rdn and outpcd: sn wknd and bhd* **20/1**

5005 **6** *8* **Fuzzy Logic (IRE)**[18] 5989 3-8-7 **50** .... HayleyTurner 14 16
(William Muir) *racd against stands' rail tl crossed to inner 10f out: chsd ldr tl over 8f out: lost pl 4f out: sn rdn and btn: wl bhd fnl 2f* **16/1**

0605 **7** *34* **Fight (IRE)**[8] 6305 3-8-7 **50** .... ChrisCatlin 6
(John Best) *t.k.h: led tl 5f out: sn lost pl: t.o fnl 2f* **40/1**

3m 39.48s (9.78) **Going Correction** +0.70s/f (Yiel)
WFA 3 from 4yo+ 11lb **7** Ran SP% **111.3**
Speed ratings (Par 101): **101,100,97,91,88 84,66**
toteswingers 1&2 £2.60, 2&3 £3.40, 1&3 £1.60 CSF £7.63 CT £12.41 TOTE £1.50: £1.40, £2.30; EX 7.50.
Owner Sheikh Hamdan Bin Mohammed Al Maktoum **Bred** Darley **Trained** Middleham Moor, N Yorks

FOCUS
A good test in the conditions and the front pair pulled clear. The winner is rated similar to his Catterick form, and was value for extra.

6568 32RED H'CAP (DIV I) 1m 1f 149y
4:30 (4:30) (Class 6) (0-60,60) 3-Y-O+ **£1,704** (£503; £251) **Stalls** Centre

Form RPR

1232 **1** **Thecornishcowboy**[7] 6334 3-9-4 **60** ....(t) BrettDoyle 1 66
(John Ryan) *broke wl: sn stdd bk to chse ldrs: pushed along and effrt to chal over 2f out: led 2f out: a doing enough u.p fnl f: rdn out* **1/1**[1]

0156 **2** *nk* **Titus Bolt (IRE)**[53] 4754 3-9-3 **59** ....(v) PatCosgrave 11 64
(Jim Boyle) *dwlt: t.k.h and sn rcvrd to ld: rdn and hdd 2f out: sn drvn: looked hld ins fnl f: kpt on towards fin* **5/1**[3]

0551 **3** *3 1/2* **High Five Prince (IRE)**[8] 6304 3-7-13 **46** oh1 .... RachealKneller(5) 10 44
(Mark Usher) *stdd s: hld up in tch in last pair: swtchd lft and effrt jst over 2f out: chsd ldng pair jst over 1f out: no imp ins fnl f* **3/1**[2]

0006 **4** *3 1/4* **Voodoo (IRE)**[12] 6158 3-8-1 **46** oh1 ....(t) RyanPowell(3) 6 37
(Ian Williams) *t.k.h: chsd ldr tl over 2f out: sn unable qck u.p: edgd rt and wknd over 1f out* **16/1**

535- **5** *15* **Kavachi (IRE)**[364] 6437 9-9-10 **60** .... GeorgeBaker 3 19
(Gary Moore) *hld up in tch in last pair: rdn and effrt on inner over 2f out: no prog 2f out: wknd over 1f out: eased wl ins fnl f* **8/1**

2m 13.1s (8.20) **Going Correction** +0.80s/f (Soft)
WFA 3 from 4yo+ 6lb **5** Ran SP% **108.7**
Speed ratings (Par 101): **99,98,95,93,81**
toteswingers 3&5 £4.90 CSF £6.21 TOTE £2.20: £2.40, £2.60; EX 5.50.
Owner C Letcher & J Ryan **Bred** Hadi Al Tajir **Trained** Newmarket, Suffolk

FOCUS
More than half the field came out of this low-grade handicap. It was the slowest of the three C&D races, and the form looks pretty weak.

Voodoo(IRE) Official explanation: jockey said gelding hung right

6569 32RED H'CAP (DIV II) 1m 1f 149y
5:00 (5:00) (Class 6) (0-60,59) 3-Y-O+ **£1,704** (£503; £251) **Stalls** Centre

Form RPR

0003 **1** **Pass The Time**[9] 6281 3-8-1 **45** ....(p) AmyBaker(3) 5 53
(Neil Mulholland) *chsd ldrs: hdwy and ev ch 3f out: rdn to ld 2f out: sn hdd and carried rt: stl pressing wnr but looked hld ins fnl f: kpt on gamely u.p to ld again cl home* **20/1**

0003 **2** *hd* **Chatterati (USA)**[7] 6334 3-8-11 **52** ....(b) FrannyNorton 6 60
(Mark Johnston) *s.i.s: in tch in last pair: hdwy to trck ldrs over 2f out: rdn to ld and edgd rt over 1f out: hrd drvn ins fnl f: outbattled and hdd cl home* **5/4**[1]

0300 **3** *9* **Dangerous To Know**[47] 4994 3-8-10 **51** .... AndreaAtzeni 1 40
(Hughie Morrison) *chsd ldrs: rdn over 2f out: unable qck 2f out: sn wknd* **5/1**[3]

0406 **4** *1* **Opus Maximus (IRE)**[8] 6323 7-9-4 **53** .... HayleyTurner 3 40
(Conor Dore) *sn pushed along to ld: rdn and hdd 2f out: sn btn and wknd* **7/1**

500 **5** *9* **Cairanne**[67] 4296 4-9-5 **54** .... TedDurcan 8 22
(Tom Keddy) *jnd ldr over 7f out tl wl over 2f out: sn lost pl and btn: wl bhd over 1f out* **5/1**[3]

0543 **6** *1/2* **Princess Willow**[20] 5938 4-9-0 **52** .... SimonPearce(3) 7 19
(John E Long) *t.k.h: chsd ldrs: grad stdd bk and in last pair 7f out: rdn and effrt 3f out: sn btn: wl bhd over 1f out* **9/2**[2]

2m 12.54s (7.64) **Going Correction** +0.80s/f (Soft)
WFA 3 from 4yo+ 6lb **6** Ran SP% **113.2**
Speed ratings (Par 101): **101,100,93,92,85 85**
toteswingers 1&2 £4.80, 2&3 £2.30, 1&3 £5.60 CSF £46.79 CT £153.49 TOTE £20.70: £4.60, £3.10; EX 70.30.
Owner Dajam Ltd **Bred** M Burbidge **Trained** Limpley Stoke, Wilts

■ A winner for Amy Baker on her first ride following a six-month sabbatical.
■ Stewards' Enquiry : Amy Baker two-day ban: used whip above permitted level (Oct 9-10)

FOCUS
The 3yos dominated in what was probably the weaker of the two divisions. It was the quicker division and the first two were clear, but the form is weak.

6570 INJUREDJOCKEYS.CO.UK MAIDEN STKS 1m 1f 149y
5:30 (5:32) (Class 5) 3-Y-O+ **£2,385** (£704; £352) **Stalls** Centre

Form RPR

050 **1** **Natural Bloom (IRE)**[22] 5889 3-8-12 65 ....[1] IanMongan 2 70
(Sir Henry Cecil) *chsd ldr tl led over 2f out: clr 1f out: sn rdn: kpt up to work and styd on strly fnl f: rdn out* **6/1**[2]

5 **2** *6* **Miss Fortywinks**[39] 5309 3-8-12 0 .... LiamKeniry 1 57
(Paul Henderson) *led: rdn and hdd over 2f out: kpt on tl no ex and btn 1f out: wknd and edgd lft ins fnl f* **20/1**

4-23 **3** *3 3/4* **Ruban (IRE)**[22] 5889 3-9-3 84 .... MickaelBarzalona 8 55
(Mahmood Al Zarooni) *chsd ldrs: rdn and fnd nil over 2f out: 3rd and no prog u.p over 1f out: wl btn fnl f* **2/7**[1]

0 **4** *4* **Icebreaker Two**[33] 5510 3-9-0 0 .... SimonPearce(3) 6 46
(John E Long) *rn green and pushed along at times: in tch tl rdn and outpcd over 2f out: wl btn 2f out: no ch but styd on again ins fnl f* **66/1**

456 **5** *1 3/4* **Beggar's Banquet (IRE)**[39] 5316 3-9-3 73 .... LukeMorris 11 42
(Ed Vaughan) *t.k.h: hld up in tch: rdn and unable qck over 2f out: sn struggling: wknd 2f out* **10/1**[3]

6 *2* **Toogood (IRE)** 3-9-3 0 .... TedDurcan 10 38
(Alastair Lidderdale) *s.i.s: rn green and a in rr: lost tch 3f out* **25/1**

2m 12.37s (7.47) **Going Correction** +0.80s/f (Soft)
WFA 3 from 4yo 6lb **6** Ran SP% **111.2**
Speed ratings (Par 103): **102,97,94,91,89 88**
toteswingers 1&2 £2.90, 2&3 £1.80, 1&3 £1.40 CSF £83.29 TOTE £4.30: £2.10, £6.10; EX 78.40.
Owner Sir Robert Ogden **Bred** Lynch Bages Ltd & Samac Ltd **Trained** Newmarket, Suffolk

FOCUS
Little depth to this maiden and not form to put much faith in, with the red-hot favourite Ruban blowing out, possibly on account of the ground. Pretty weak form but the winner is entitled to rate this high.

Ruban(IRE) Official explanation: trainer's rep said colt was unsuited by the heavy ground

T/Jkpt: £1,543.40 to a £1 stake. Pool: £25,000.00 - 11.50 winning tickets. T/Plt: £73.30 to a £1 stake. Pool: £66,408.60 - 661.15 winning tickets. T/Qpdt: £4.70 to a £1 stake. Pool: £5,351.88 - 828.64 winning tickets. SP

5901 GOODWOOD (R-H)
Wednesday, September 26

OFFICIAL GOING: Soft (6.2)
Top bend dolled out 3yds,
Wind: Moderate, across (away from stands) Weather: Overcast with rain becoming brighter from Race 3 onwards

6571 IRISH STALLION FARMS EBF LOEWE MAIDEN STKS 7f
1:30 (1:30) (Class 5) 2-Y-O **£3,234** (£962; £481; £240) **Stalls** Low

Form RPR

0 **1** **Zamoyski**[18] 6020 2-9-3 0 .... WilliamBuick 1 83+
(Jeremy Noseda) *chsd ldng trio: pushed along bef 1/2-way: wnt 2nd over 2f out: styd on wl u.p to ld ins fnl f* **7/2**[2]

32 **2** *1 1/4* **Pythagorean**[40] 5304 2-9-3 0 ....[1] JamesDoyle 4 80
(Roger Charlton) *led at str pce: c centre in st: rdn over 1f out: worn down ins fnl f* **8/13**[1]

50 **3** *4 1/2* **Emulating (IRE)**[13] 6164 2-9-3 0 .... RichardHughes 7 69
(Richard Hannon) *chsd ldng pair: rdn over 2f out: edgd towards nr side rail and kpt on same pce* **6/1**[3]

0 **4** *1/2* **Provencal**[12] 6203 2-9-3 0 .... JamesMillman 5 68
(Rod Millman) *stdd s: hld up in last pair: pushed along and prog wl over 1f out: styd on fnl f* **100/1**

0 **5** *1 1/4* **Codebreaker**[40] 5304 2-9-3 0 .... JimmyFortune 8 64
(Hughie Morrison) *hld up disputing 5th: shkn up over 2f out: no imp on ldrs but kpt on fnl f* **16/1**

0060 **6** *4 1/2* **Strong Conviction**[32] 5586 2-9-3 70 .... MartinHarley 6 53
(Mick Channon) *a bhd: rdn 3f out: struggling fnl 2f* **25/1**

0 **7** *3/4* **Marju's Quest (IRE)**[20] 5963 2-9-3 0 .... JamieSpencer 2 51+
(David Simcock) *chsd ldr to over 2f out: sn wknd* **14/1**

00 **8** *1 ½* **Be Royale**[30] 5656 2-8-12 0 PatDobbs 3 43
(Bryn Palling) *hld up disputing 5th: rdn wl over 2f out: sn wknd* **66/1**

1m 29.78s (2.78) **Going Correction** +0.375s/f (Good) **8** Ran SP% **117.3**
Speed ratings (Par 95): **99,97,92,91,90 85,84,82**
toteswingers 1&2 £1.20, 1&3 £2.10, 2&3 £2.00 CSF £6.13 TOTE £3.20: £1.50, £1.02, £1.80; EX 7.00 Trifecta £16.20 Pool: £1,537.07 - 70.07 winning tickets..
Owner Mrs Susan Roy **Bred** N C Appleton & Cheveley Park Stud **Trained** Newmarket, Suffolk

FOCUS
After a deluge of rain at the course the ground was changed to soft prior to racing and clerk of the course Seamus Buckley was of the opinion it was the easiest surface so far here this season. This is often a decent juvenile maiden and was won by none other than Workforce in 2009. Underfoot conditions played a big part, as they went a solid pace and rather predictably the field initially went about tacking over stands' side in the home straight. However, the main action developed down the middle and the first pair dominated. The winner was an improver with the third and fourth helping set the level.

NOTEBOOK
Zamoyski proved distinctly green on his debut in what should prove to be a warm maiden at Ascot 18 days earlier, but showed ability and hails from a yard whose juveniles often show dramatic improvement next time out. He had a little to prove on this ground, but his sire's progeny tend to like some cut underfoot and he stretched out nicely once given the office nearing the final furlong. A flashy chestnut, he still looked inexperienced early on and could make up into a smart colt over a trip next year. (op 9-2)
Pythagorean was the clear form pick after two placed efforts at Newbury, was expected to enjoy this return to easier ground and had the calming influence of a first-time hood. Sent off a hot favourite, he didn't really impress to post as he got wound up, and he spoilt his cause by refusing to settle after being sent to the front early. He was a clear second-best and is obviously useful, but his attitude may hamper his progression. (op 4-9)
Emulating(IRE) failed to see out 1m at Doncaster last time, and there were doubts about how he would handle this contrasting surface despite dropping back down a furlong. He ran his race more towards the stands' side, but didn't look so happy on the surface and this good-looking colt is one to keep on-side now he can enter nurseries. (tchd 7-1)
Provencal, stepping up from 5f, is very much still learning his trade but this was more encouraging than his debut and he fared best of those racing out the back. (op 66-1)
Codebreaker improved a touch on his debut behind the runner-up at Newbury last month, but still found this too taxing and may be more of a 3-y-o handicapper in the making. (tchd 20-1)

6572 R H HALL EBF MAIDEN STKS 1m 1f
2:00 (2:04) (Class 4) 2-Y-O **£4,528** (£1,347; £673; £336) **Stalls** Low

Form RPR
04 **1** **Sweet Deal (IRE)**[12] 6214 2-9-3 0 WilliamBuick 8 79
(Jeremy Noseda) *trckd ldrs: wnt 2nd over 2f out and sn upsides ldr: narrow ld fnl f: drvn out* **3/1**[2]
6 **2** *nk* **Mr Fitzroy (IRE)**[12] 6204 2-9-3 0 JimmyFortune 3 78
(Andrew Balding) *trckd ldrs: wnt 2nd 4f out: led wl over 2f out but sn jnd: narrowly hdd fnl f: styd on but jst hld* **7/2**[3]
3 *4 ½* **Backstage Tour** 2-9-3 0 MickaelBarzalona 11 69+
(Mahmood Al Zarooni) *s.i.s: prog on outer fr rr 5f out: hdwy to take 3rd over 2f out and tried to chal: btn over 1f out: fdd* **6/1**
5 **4** *2 ¾* **Cast A Vision (USA)**[19] 6014 2-9-3 0 JimCrowley 10 64
(Amanda Perrett) *chsd ldr to 4f out: pushed along and sn dropped to midfield: kpt on again to take 4th jst over 1f out* **12/1**
05 **5** *1 ¼* **Afro**[19] 6017 2-8-12 0 DaneO'Neill 2 56
(Peter Hedger) *in tch in midfield: shkn up over 2f out: no imp on ldrs after but kpt on fnl f* **100/1**
2430 **6** *3 ¼* **Club House (IRE)**[21] 5946 2-9-3 72 TomQueally 6 55
(Robert Mills) *led at mod pce: tried to kick on 1/2-way: hdd wl over 2f out: wknd over 1f out* **10/1**
7 *6* **Pether's Moon (IRE)** 2-9-3 0 RichardHughes 1 43
(Richard Hannon) *s.i.s: in tch in midfield: pushed along over 2f out: no prog wl over 1f out: wknd fnl f* **11/4**[1]
0 **8** *2 ¾* **Foxy Dancer (IRE)**[13] 6153 2-8-12 0 PatDobbs 4 32
(Richard Hannon) *t.k.h and prom early: pushed along 1/2-way: wknd over 2f out* **20/1**
9 *8* **Couloir Extreme (IRE)** 2-9-3 0 GeorgeBaker 5 28+
(Gary Moore) *hld up in last trio: shkn up briefly 3f out: no prog and btn 2f out: wknd and eased* **40/1**
10 *6* **Town Mouse** 2-9-3 0 RobertHavlin 7 9
(Hughie Morrison) *difficult to load into stalls: s.s: a in rr: wknd over 2f out* **25/1**

2m 0.64s (4.34) **Going Correction** +0.375s/f (Good) **10** Ran SP% **117.0**
Speed ratings (Par 97): **95,94,90,88,87 84,78,76,69,64**
toteswingers 1&2 £2.70, 1&3 £4.90, 2&3 £4.30 CSF £13.52 TOTE £4.50: £1.50, £1.70, £1.70; EX 14.20 Trifecta £50.60 Pool: £1,438.87 - 21.03 winning tickets..
Owner Mrs Susan Roy **Bred** M Henochsberg & Pontchartrain Stud **Trained** Newmarket, Suffolk

FOCUS
A modest juvenile maiden that would have provided a searching test on such ground. They went an ordinary pace and the action was more towards the stands' side as the first pair came clear in a battling finish. The firfst two came clear and both stepped up on their respective debuts.

NOTEBOOK
Sweet Deal(IRE), whose connections took the preceding juvenile maiden, made it third time lucky with a gutsy effort. He was a beaten favourite on Polytrack last time, but had to come from well back in a race where the principals raced handily and he promised to be well suited by this stiffer test. So it proved as he ground it out from the 2f marker and, despite still looking green under maximum pressure, was always just holding the runner-up. The soft ground was no real issue and, out of a mare who won over 1m2f, it's fair to expect him to stay really well next year. (op 11-4 tchd 10-3 and 7-2 in a place)
Mr Fitzroy(IRE) ◆ wasn't disgraced on his debut at Sandown 12 days earlier and he coped well with this totally contrasting surface, only just going down near the finish. He too clearly stays well and should not be too long in going one better.
Backstage Tour ◆ proved distinctly green out of the gates from the outside stall. There was something to like about the manner in which he moved into contention, though, and he should not be long in winning now he has experience under his belt. Dropping to a sharper test may prove wise in the short term. (op 11-2 tchd 5-1)
Cast A Vision(USA), fifth at Kempton on his debut 19 days earlier, came under some pressure 4f out and did not look so happy on this ground. He needs one more run for a mark. (op 20-1)
Pether's Moon(IRE), drawn on the inside, was beaten soon after turning into the home straight. His dam took a Group 3 on heavy ground, but this surface looked all too much for him and he's evidently considered capable of a lot better. (op 7-2 tchd 5-2)

6573 HILDON NATURAL MINERAL WATER STKS (H'CAP) (DIV I) 1m 3f
2:35 (2:36) (Class 4) (0-85,85) 3-Y-O **£4,528** (£1,347; £673; £336) **Stalls** High

Form RPR
41 **1** **Signed Up**[111] 2856 3-9-7 85 PatDobbs 3 98+
(Amanda Perrett) *trckd clr ldr: clsd to ld against nr side rail over 2f out: shkn up over 1f out: styd on wl* **3/1**[1]
-124 **2** *2* **Man Of Plenty**[110] 2889 3-9-1 79 DaneO'Neill 7 88
(John Dunlop) *dwlt: hld up in last: prog over 2f out: rdn to chse wnr jst over 1f out: styd on but readily hld* **9/2**[3]
031 **3** *3 ½* **Zanotti**[50] 4926 3-9-4 82 (t) NeilCallan 4 85
(Roger Varian) *hld up in 4th: prog to chse wnr over 2f out and sn pressing: rdn and fnd nil over 1f out: sn lost 2nd and btn* **5/1**
6652 **4** *11* **Presburg (IRE)**[12] 6206 3-8-12 81 MichaelJMMurphy(5) 5 64
(Joseph Tuite) *dwlt: hld up in 5th: effrt 3f out: wknd wl over 1f out* **8/1**
1304 **5** *37* **Ultimate Destiny**[18] 6039 3-8-12 76 JimCrowley 9
(Ralph Beckett) *chsd ldng pair: pushed along 5f out: wknd u.p over 2f out: virtually p.u over 1f out* **9/2**[3]
0335 **6** *36* **Tamarrud**[55] 4745 3-8-11 75 (b[1]) FrankieDettori 8
(Saeed Bin Suroor) *racd v freely: led and 10 l clr after 4f: tk field to nr side in st: hdd & wknd rapidly over 2f out: walking at fin* **7/2**[2]

2m 29.7s (3.20) **Going Correction** +0.375s/f (Good) **6** Ran SP% **111.4**
Speed ratings (Par 103): **103,101,99,91,64 37**
toteswingers 1&2 £9.10, 1&3 £3.10, 2&3 £16.90 CSF £16.34 CT £61.60 TOTE £4.10: £1.40, £2.50; EX 10.30 Trifecta £37.40 Pool: £1,529.46 - 30.20 winning tickets..
Owner K Abdulla **Bred** Juddmonte Farms Ltd **Trained** Pulborough, W Sussex

FOCUS
A fair 3-y-o handicap. There was a sound pace on thanks to the front-running Tamarud and they were quick to tack over to the stands' rail after straightening for home. They finished well strung out. The winner looks capable of better.

6574 HILDON NATURAL MINERAL WATER STKS (H'CAP) (DIV II) 1m 3f
3:10 (3:12) (Class 4) (0-85,85) 3-Y-O **£4,528** (£1,347; £673; £336) **Stalls** High

Form RPR
0034 **1** **Ghost Protocol (IRE)**[46] 5101 3-9-7 85 JamieSpencer 5 92
(David Simcock) *hld up in last pair: stl there 2f out: plld out wd and prog over 1f out: drvn and r.o wl to ld last 75yds* **7/2**[1]
0060 **2** *¾* **Freddy Q (IRE)**[26] 5794 3-9-2 80 GeorgeBaker 1 85
(Roger Teal) *hld up in last trio: smooth prog to press ldr over 2f out: pushed into ld over 1f out: drvn fnl f: hdd and nt qckn last 75yds* **20/1**
1611 **3** *¾* **The Quarterjack**[39] 5359 3-8-12 76 PaulHanagan 7 80
(Ron Hodges) *led: narrowly hdd 1/2-way: led again wl over 2f out but pressed: hdd over 1f out: kpt on wl* **5/1**[3]
066 **4** *3 ¼* **Aegaeus**[125] 2430 3-8-11 75 FrankieDettori 9 73
(Ed Dunlop) *t.k.h and quick prog to press ldr over 8f out: led 1/2-way: hdd and hd to one side wl over 2f out: nt qckn* **6/1**
-231 **5** *1 ½* **Ashdown Lad**[12] 6206 3-8-6 75 MichaelJMMurphy(5) 4 70
(William Jarvis) *hld up in last pair: prog on outer and cl enough jst over 2f out: hanging u.p and wknd over 1f out* **11/2**
1-60 **6** *4 ½* **Dandy (GER)**[61] 4529 3-8-13 77 JimmyFortune 6 64
(Andrew Balding) *trckd ldrs: rdn over 2f out: wkng whn edgd lft 1f out* **7/1**
2324 **7** *5* **Hidden Justice (IRE)**[26] 5789 3-8-8 72 (b[1]) EddieAhern 3 50
(Amanda Perrett) *s.s and reminder after 150yds: rapid prog to press ldng pair over 6f out: lost pl and n.m.r 3f out: sn btn: no ch whn sltly hmpd 1f out* **8/1**
0341 **8** *3 ¾* **Positively**[11] 6250 3-8-12 76 PatDobbs 2 48
(Sir Michael Stoute) *trckd ldr to over 8f out: styd handy: drvn wl over 2f out: sn wknd* **9/2**[2]

2m 33.84s (7.34) **Going Correction** +0.375s/f (Good) **8** Ran SP% **115.1**
Speed ratings (Par 103): **88,87,86,84,83 80,76,73**
toteswingers 1&2 £9.10, 1&3 £3.10, 2&3 £16.90 CSF £73.08 CT £349.85 TOTE £5.00: £2.10, £5.80, £1.30; EX 93.00 Trifecta £884.20 Pool: £2,150.82 - 1.80 winning tickets..
Owner A & A **Bred** Knockainey Stud **Trained** Newmarket, Suffolk
■ Stewards' Enquiry : Pat Dobbs jockey said that the filly stopped quickly

FOCUS
This second division of the 1m3f handicap was a more open contest. They went an uneven pace.

6575 EVE TRAKWAY FOUNDATION STKS (LISTED RACE) 1m 1f 192y
3:40 (3:44) (Class 1) 3-Y-O+ **£19,848** (£7,525; £3,766; £1,876; £941) **Stalls** Low

Form RPR
3522 **1** **Primevere (IRE)**[18] 6062 4-8-9 107 (v[1]) JamesDoyle 2 104
(Roger Charlton) *led 150yds: trckd ldr: led 2f out gng strly: edgd lft fr over 1f out: hrd rdn and fnd jst enough fnl f* **9/2**[3]
-120 **2** *nk* **Ektihaam (IRE)**[115] 2743 3-8-8 113 (b[1]) PaulHanagan 1 108
(Roger Varian) *led after 150yds and racd quite freely: stretched on 4f out: rdn and hdd 2f out: sltly intimidated ins fnl f: styd on but jst hld* **11/8**[1]
3-01 **3** *3 ¾* **Voodoo Prince**[29] 5712 4-9-0 90 KierenFallon 5 101
(Ed Dunlop) *pushed along in 4th early to stay in tch: drvn to go 3rd 2f out and cl enough: fdd fnl f* **8/1**
2405 **4** *4* **Questioning (IRE)**[33] 5560 4-9-3 112 (p) WilliamBuick 3 96
(John Gosden) *quite keen early: trckd ldng pair: shkn up 3f out: lost 3rd 2f out: wknd over 1f out* **6/1**
-006 **5** *32* **Pisco Sour (USA)**[80] 3900 4-9-0 110 (p) FrankieDettori 6 29
(Saeed Bin Suroor) *hld up in detached last: cl enough over 4f out: wknd rapidly over 2f out: t.o* **3/1**[2]

2m 9.69s (1.59) **Going Correction** +0.375s/f (Good)
WFA 3 from 4yo 6lb **5** Ran SP% **110.7**
Speed ratings (Par 111): **108,107,104,101,75**
CSF £11.29 TOTE £5.20: £2.50, £1.10; EX 10.40.
Owner A E Oppenheimer **Bred** Hascombe And Valiant Studs **Trained** Beckhampton, Wilts

FOCUS
An interesting Listed event and fair for the grade on paper. It was run at a solid early pace. The third is the doubt over the form.

NOTEBOOK
Primevere(IRE) deservedly resumed winning ways. Warm beforehand, she was equipped with a first-time visor and got lit up through the early parts. She still found most when it mattered, however, and was always just holding the runner-up towards the near side at the business end. This consistent filly acts on most ground and is now a dual winner in this grade. Another overseas venture is likely to be on her agenda before she heads off to stud at the end of the season. (op 7-2)
Ektihaam(IRE) got no run in the French Derby when last seen 115 days previously and had finished second in the Dante the time before, so was understandably popular in the betting. However, the application of first-time blinkers was somewhat concerning and he did not look the most straightforward through the race. His engine remains intact and he's well up to winning in this class, but probably needs all to go his way. (tchd 5-4 and 6-4)
Voodoo Prince won a handicap off 85 on his previous outing so was obviously faced with a stiff task. He didn't travel at all well early, but improved as the race progressed and ultimately ran his best race to-date. (op 10-1)
Questioning(IRE), whose trainer has a good record in this race, looked vulnerable under his penalty and rather spoilt his chance by refusing to settle through the early stages. (op 9-2)

Pisco Sour(USA), whose trainer had won this six times since 2003, was well supported to recapture his best 3-y-o form on this return from an 80-day absence. It was his first run since being gelded, but he also sported first-time cheekpieces and ultimately ran a shocker. It's back to the drawing board with him. (op 5-1)

6576 DISCOVERY FOODS STKS (H'CAP) 1m 4f
4:15 (4:16) (Class 2) (0-105,98) 3-Y-O+ **£10,350** (£3,080; £1,539; £769) **Stalls** High

Form RPR

10- **1** **Eagles Peak**[406] 5185 4-9-11 **95** .... RichardHughes 6 104+
(Sir Michael Stoute) *led to 4f out: styd cl up: chal over 2f out: drvn to ld jst ins fnl f: asserted nr fin* **7/2**[2]

1-30 **2** *3/4* **Cubanita**[123] 2522 3-8-12 **90** .... JimCrowley 9 97
(Ralph Beckett) *trckd ldng trio: prog to ld 4f out: hrd pressed and drvn 2f out: hdd and nt qckn jst ins fnl f: kpt on* **11/2**

1033 **3** *hd* **Cardinal Walter (IRE)**[32] 5598 3-8-11 **89** .... JamieSpencer 8 96+
(David Simcock) *hld up and detached in last early: stdy prog fr 3f out: drvn to chal and upsides over 1f out: nt qckn fnl f* **2/1**[1]

0400 **4** *4* **Alkimos (IRE)**[32] 5600 4-10-0 **98** ....(p) FrankieDettori 4 99
(Saeed Bin Suroor) *hld up in last pair: clsd up over 3f out: shkn up and outpcd fr 2f out: plugged on to take 4th ins fnl f* **9/2**[3]

1100 **5** *1 1/4* **Rosslyn Castle**[25] 5826 3-9-3 **95** .... JamesDoyle 2 94
(Roger Charlton) *dwlt: sn wl in tch: cl up bhd ldng trio 2f out: wknd over 1f out* **9/2**[3]

6505 **6** *shd* **Ramona Chase**[12] 6202 7-9-0 **84** ....(t) NickyMackay 10 82
(Michael Attwater) *sltly awkward s: wl in tch: trckd ldrs 4f out: wknd 2f out* **20/1**

-00P **7** *15* **Classic Vintage (USA)**[68] 4284 6-9-9 **93** .... TomQueally 7 67
(Amanda Perrett) *pushed up to trck ldr after 2f: chal over 4f out: wknd wl over 2f out: t.o* **33/1**

1-24 **8** *1* **Right Stuff (FR)**[137] 1214 9-9-4 **88** .... GeorgeBaker 1 61
(Gary Moore) *trckd ldr 2f: styd prom: wknd wl over 2f out: t.o* **33/1**

2m 42.76s (4.36) **Going Correction** +0.375s/f (Good)
WFA 3 from 4yo+ 8lb **8** Ran SP% **117.9**
Speed ratings (Par 109): **100,99,99,96,95 95,85,85**
toteswingers 1&2 £5.80, 1&3 £2.80, 2&3 £3.70 CSF £23.21 CT £47.64 TOTE £5.50: £2.20, £2.60, £1.10; EX 34.90 Trifecta £183.50 Pool: £2,609.19 - 10.52 winning tickets..
Owner K Abdulla **Bred** Juddmonte Farms Ltd **Trained** Newmarket, Suffolk

FOCUS
A decent handicap and the form is strong with three very useful and relatively unexposed performers pulling clear. The winner can do better still.

NOTEBOOK
Eagles Peak ◆, who looked fit enough following his long absence, won with something to spare. He had looked most promising when winning his maiden in 2011, but had gone missing since being well beaten on his handicap debut last August. There was solid support for him earlier in the day, suggesting he was going well at home, and he got a confident ride from Richard Hughes, who got him into a lovely rhythm. Despite being headed in the home straight and allowing challengers either side of him from 2f out, Hughes always looked confident and he was nicely on top at the line. This lightly raced colt has now proved himself versatile regards going and appears very much to be a Pattern-class performer in the making. (op 3-1 tchd 9-2)
Cubanita ◆ was making her handicap debut after having her last two outings in Pattern company, and she had her ground. She raced really enthusiastically and headed the winner on the stands' side in the home straight, but ultimately got outstayed by that rival. This was a fine effort and one has to think she can be found another opening before the season's end, despite a likely rise. (op 8-1)
Cardinal Walter(IRE), very well backed, finished third in the Melrose Handicap at York's Ebor meeting last month and was up 3lb. He was set plenty to do back down in trip, but still came through with every chance and turned in another improved effort in defeat. He should make a lovely 4-y-o next term. (tchd 15-8 in a place, tchd 5-2 and 9-4 in places)
Alkimos(IRE) hit a flat spot at a crucial stage, but this ground was something of an unknown for him and it was a return to near his best. He gives the form a decent look. (op 11-2)
Rosslyn Castle, who goes well on soft ground, failed to see it out despite this being a drop back in trip and has been unable to build on a promising start to his 3-y-o campaign. (op 5-1)

6577 3663 FIRST FOR FOOD SERVICE STKS (H'CAP) 6f
4:50 (4:52) (Class 4) (0-80,80) 3-Y-O+ **£4,528** (£1,347; £673; £336) **Stalls** High

Form RPR

1406 **1** **Efistorm**[19] 5993 11-8-4 **68** .... MichaelJMMurphy(5) 2 79
(Joseph Tuite) *trckd ldrs on outer: clsd fr 2f out: led 1f out: rdn clr* **33/1**

6140 **2** *2* **Rigolleto (IRE)**[11] 6235 4-8-12 **76** .... CharlesBishop(5) 6 81
(Mick Channon) *trckd across fr wd draw towards nr side rail: pressed ldr: narrow ld jst over 2f out to 1f out: kpt on same pce* **7/1**[3]

1160 **3** *1/2* **Cardinal**[76] 4013 7-9-0 **73** .... JimCrowley 3 76
(Robert Cowell) *racd on outer: trckd ldrs: upsides 2f out to 1f out: one pce* **8/1**

1135 **4** *1/2* **Dream Catcher (FR)**[7] 6368 4-8-12 **76** .... AmyScott(5) 5 77
(Henry Candy) *taken down early: racd on outer: pressed ldng pair: upsides 2f out to over 1f out: one pce* **3/1**[1]

0344 **5** *nse* **Emiratesdotcom**[7] 6368 6-9-0 **73** .... RichardKingscote 13 74
(Milton Bradley) *in tch in midfield: rdn and struggling over 2f out: styd on fnl f: nrst fin* **8/1**

5056 **6** *shd* **Shifting Star (IRE)**[7] 6368 7-9-0 **80** .... WilliamTwiston-Davies(7) 8 81
(John Bridger) *trckd ldrs on outer: rdn and nt qckn over 2f out: styd on ins fnl f* **25/1**

3320 **7** *nk* **Ashpan Sam**[7] 6358 3-8-11 **72** .... NeilCallan 17 72
(John Spearing) *towards rr: pushed along 1/2-way: kpt on fnl 2f: nvr gng pce to threaten* **10/1**

5012 **8** *3/4* **Button Moon (IRE)**[16] 6094 4-9-7 **80** ....(p) SebSanders 11 78
(Ian Wood) *led against nr side rail: hdd jst over 2f out: fdd fnl f* **16/1**

3610 **9** *nk* **Rash Judgement**[22] 5906 7-9-2 **75** .... LiamKeniry 12 72
(Stuart Kittow) *taken down early: hld up bhd ldrs gng wl: shkn up and nt qckn wl over 1f out: fdd* **16/1**

1141 **10** *2* **Torres Del Paine**[14] 6150 5-8-13 **72** .... KieranO'Neill 16 62
(Brett Johnson) *restrained s: hld up in last trio: taken out wd 2f out and sme prog over 1f out: fdd fnl f* **25/1**

5050 **11** *1* **Aqua Ardens (GER)**[68] 4300 4-8-9 **68** .... PatCosgrave 10 55
(George Baker) *mostly in last trio: outpcd fr 1/2-way: no ch after* **50/1**

250 **12** *hd* **Magic Secret**[68] 4286 4-9-6 **79** .... SeanLevey 7 65
(Jeremy Gask) *taken down early: racd on outer: hld up in tch: rdn and no prog 2f out: wknd* **7/2**[2]

0306 **13** *1 3/4* **Tagula Night (IRE)**[7] 6369 6-9-7 **80** ....(b) ShaneKelly 14 61
(Dean Ivory) *racd towards nr side: trckd ldrs: shkn up over 2f out: wknd over 1f out* **7/1**[3]

32 **14** *7* **Sunshine Always (IRE)**[14] 6145 6-8-9 **68** .... J-PGuillambert 15 26
(Michael Attwater) *dwlt: a in last trio: bhd fnl 2f: t.o* **20/1**

1m 13.27s (1.07) **Going Correction** +0.075s/f (Good)
WFA 3 from 4yo+ 2lb **14** Ran SP% **132.7**
Speed ratings (Par 105): **95,92,91,91,90 90,90,89,89,86 85,84,82,73**
toteswingers 1&2 £62.00, 1&3 £71.30, 2&3 £19.60 CSF £262.54 CT £1406.02 TOTE £56.60: £14.60, £3.50, £4.50; EX 571.20 TRIFECTA Not won..
Owner Andrew Liddiard **Bred** E Duggan And D Churchman **Trained** Great Shefford, Berks

FOCUS
A modest sprint handicap. The field raced near side through the first half of the race, but the main action developed away from the stands' rail and the places were filled by those drawn in single figures. The shock winner's best form since last summer.

6578 MERBURY CATERING CONSULTANTS APPRENTICE STKS (H'CAP) 5f
5:25 (5:25) (Class 5) (0-75,75) 3-Y-O+ **£2,587** (£770; £384; £192) **Stalls** High

Form RPR

1532 **1** **Stonecrabstomorrow (IRE)**[9] 6306 9-8-6 **63** .... AshleyMorgan(3) 2 70
(Michael Attwater) *racd on outer: in tch towards rr: shkn up 2f out: r.o wl fnl f to ld last strides* **6/1**[3]

3340 **2** *hd* **Ring For Baileys**[13] 6173 3-8-9 **69** .... ThomasBrown(5) 9 75
(Chris Dwyer) *trckd ldrs: prog to ld jst over 1f out: rdn and edgd rt fnl f: hdd last strides* **5/1**[2]

4102 **3** *hd* **Commandingpresence (USA)**[5] 6439 6-8-9 **68** WilliamTwiston-Davies(5) 7 73
(John Bridger) *racd on outer: trckd ldrs gng wl: led over 2f out: hdd and nt qckn jst over 1f out: styd on* **7/1**

1560 **4** *1/2* **Triple Dream**[7] 6370 7-9-4 **75** ....(tp) MatthewLawson(3) 1 78
(Milton Bradley) *racd on outer: wl on terms w ldrs: upsides over 2f out to over 1f out: nt qckn last 100yds* **16/1**

5010 **5** *1/2* **Belle Bayardo (IRE)**[10] 6277 4-8-12 **66** .... KierenFox 10 68
(Ronald Harris) *ra(c)ed against nr side rail: struggling in last pair 1/2-way: plld out and r.o fnl f: nt rch ldrs* **7/1**

0244 **6** *3 1/4* **Aye Aye Digby (IRE)**[7] 6370 7-9-2 **75** .... DanielMuscutt(5) 6 65
(Patrick Chamings) *sn lost prom pl: struggling in rr 1/2-way: no real prog over 1f out* **5/2**[1]

6453 **7** *1/2* **Berberana (IRE)**[7] 6370 4-9-1 **69** ....(p) RaulDaSilva 8 57
(Jeremy Gask) *racd against nr side rail: led 100yds: prom tl lost pl and btn fr 2f out* **13/2**

3500 **8** *3/4* **Signifer (IRE)**[11] 6226 3-8-12 **70** ....(v) CharlesBishop(3) 5 55
(Mick Channon) *led after 100yds towards nr side: hdd over 2f out: hanging and nt qckn over 1f out: wknd* **10/1**

6463 **9** *1 3/4* **Speak The Truth (IRE)**[125] 2413 6-8-4 **65** .... DanielCremin(7) 4 44
(Jim Boyle) *s.s: hld up and jst in tch 1/2-way: no prog over 1f out: wknd* **25/1**

1m 0.16s (-0.04) **Going Correction** +0.075s/f (Good)
WFA 3 from 4yo+ 1lb **9** Ran SP% **116.7**
Speed ratings (Par 103): **103,102,102,101,100 95,94,93,90**
toteswingers 1&2 £5.40, 1&3 £3.90, 2&3 £10.10 CSF £36.45 CT £218.03 TOTE £7.20: £2.80, £2.40, £2.90; EX 47.90 Trifecta £524.70 Pool: £1,354.52 - 1.91 winning tickets..
Owner The Attwater Partnership **Bred** P Dillon **Trained** Epsom, Surrey

FOCUS
An ordinary sprint handicap. Again the field kept stands' side early but the main action once more developed down the middle of the track. The winner is rated to last year's best.
T/Plt: £8.20 to a £1 stake. Pool: £76,524.09 - 6,785.63 winning tickets T/Qpdt: £5.30 to a £1 stake. Pool: £5,787.19 - 797.12 winning tickets JN

6532 KEMPTON (A.W) (R-H)
Wednesday, September 26

OFFICIAL GOING: Standard
Wind: medium, across Weather: dry

6579 WIN BIG WITH BETDAQ MULTIPLES MAIDEN STKS 5f (P)
5:50 (5:52) (Class 5) 2-Y-O **£2,264** (£673; £336; £168) **Stalls** Low

Form RPR

5 **1** **Exotic Isle**[125] 2426 2-8-12 0 .... HarryBentley 7 68+
(Ralph Beckett) *stdd after s: t.k.h: chsd ldrs: rdn and racd awkwardly over 1f out: hdwy u.p ent fnl f: led fnl 100yds: r.o wl* **7/4**[2]

2305 **2** *1/2* **Bold Prediction (IRE)**[15] 6114 2-9-3 79 .... RichardHughes 5 71
(Richard Hannon) *dwlt: in tch in last trio: sltly hmpd over 3f out: rdn over 2f out: hdwy u.p over 1f out: ev ch ins fnl f: styd on same pce fnl 100yds* **1/1**[1]

0430 **3** *1/2* **Pal Of The Cat**[34] 5503 2-9-3 65 .... FrannyNorton 3 69
(Brian Gubby) *led: rdn wl over 1f out: battled on wl u.p tl hdd and one pce fnl 100yds* **25/1**

30 **4** *2 1/2* **Outbid**[10] 6276 2-8-12 0 .... FergusSweeney 1 56
(Jamie Osborne) *hld up in tch in last trio: rdn and swtchd lft over 1f out: styd on ins fnl f: nvr gng pce to chal* **25/1**

0 **5** *1 3/4* **Henrietta Rose (USA)**[113] 2783 2-8-12 0 .... WilliamBuick 6 49
(Jeremy Noseda) *s.i.s: in tch in rr: rdn and effrt over 1f out: styd on ins fnl f: nvr trbld ldrs* **10/1**

0542 **6** *nk* **Max The Machine**[78] 3937 2-9-3 72 .... DaneO'Neill 4 53
(Derek Shaw) *racd keenly: w ldr: rdn and unable qck over 1f out: btn 1f out: wknd fnl f* **8/1**[3]

360 **7** *nk* **Cashel's Missile (IRE)**[21] 5932 2-9-3 55 .... LukeMorris 2 52
(John Spearing) *chsd ldrs: rdn and unable qck over 1f out: wknd fnl f* **66/1**

1m 0.18s (-0.32) **Going Correction** -0.125s/f (Stan) **7** Ran SP% **115.8**
Speed ratings (Par 95): **97,96,95,91,88 88,87**
toteswingers 1&2 £1.10, 2&3 £3.50, 1&3 £7.60 CSF £3.88 TOTE £3.00: £2.50, £1.10; EX 7.40.
Owner Pearl Bloodstock Ltd & N H Wrigley **Bred** T R G Vestey **Trained** Kimpton, Hants

FOCUS
The market leaders came to the fore late, although this still looks ordinary form. It's been rated around the third.

NOTEBOOK
Exotic Isle, disappointing from a wide draw on her Sandown debut back in May, had reportedly been off with a problem, but the money again came for her and she showed quite a pleasing attitude to get off the mark. This seems her trip and she can make her mark in nurseries. (op 5-2)
Bold Prediction(IRE), rated 79, was down from 7f and found himself outpaced having been slightly checked. He had his chance, briefly looking to be getting the better of the winner, but ultimately he lacked that ones finishing pace. (op 5-6)
Pal Of The Cat's two best efforts have now come when having the run of the race out in front. There were no excuses and his best opportunities will come on easy tracks in nurseries. (op 22-1)
Outbid needed this for a mark and will be of interest switching to modest nurseries. Official explanation: jockey said that the filly was denied a clear run (tchd 33-1)

Henrietta Rose(USA), off since finishing well beaten on June's Leicester debut, showed a little more this time, even if she was really never involved, and will be qualified for a mark following one more run. (op 12-1 tchd 14-1)

Max The Machine, second in a Fibresand maiden when last seen, didn't prove as effective on Polytrack but will be of more interest in nurseries. (op 7-1 tchd 9-1)

Cashel's Missile(IRE) will be of more interest in nurseries.

6580 BACK OR LAY AT BETDAQ.COM H'CAP 1m 2f (P)

6:20 (6:20) (Class 3) (0-95,95) 3-Y-O

£6,411 (£1,919; £959; £479; £239; £120) **Stalls** Low

Form RPR

2213 **1** **Position**[19] 6018 3-9-3 **91** LukeMorris 3 98+
(Sir Mark Prescott Bt) *t.k.h: chsd ldrs: swtchd sharply lft and cannoned into rival over 1f out: drvn to ld jst ins fnl f: r.o u.p: jst lasted* **9/2**[2]

435 **2** *hd* **Inthar (USA)**[20] 5973 3-8-7 **81** MickaelBarzalona 2 87+
(Saeed Bin Suroor) *stdd s: t.k.h: hld up in last trio: effrt whn hmpd and swtchd lft over 1f out: rdr dropped whip and hdwy 1f out: r.o strly ins fnl f: jst hld* **12/1**

0525 **3** *¾* **Come On Blue Chip (IRE)**[7] 6374 3-9-3 **91** (b) WilliamBuick 8 96
(Paul D'Arcy) *stdd s: hld up in tch in rr: pushed along over 2f out: c wd and hdwy over 1f out: r.o wl ins fnl f: snatched 3rd on post* **6/1**[3]

1110 **4** *nse* **Tigers Tale (IRE)**[12] 6205 3-8-10 **84** (v) RichardHughes 5 88
(Roger Teal) *hld up in midfield: rdn and hdwy to chse ldrs whn cannoned into and hmpd over 1f out: stl pressing ldrs ins fnl f: kpt on same pce fnl 100yds: lost 3rd on post* **20/1**

-103 **5** *½* **Valiant Girl**[39] 5358 3-8-12 **86** JamesDoyle 1 91+
(Roger Charlton) *hld up in tch in last trio: rdn and hdwy to chse ldrs whn gap clsd and bdly hmpd over 1f out: rallied ins fnl f: r.o wl towards fin* **9/2**[2]

-103 **6** *2 ¼* **Asatir (USA)**[38] 5386 3-9-7 **95** (p) SilvestreDeSousa 7 94
(Saeed Bin Suroor) *chsd ldr: rdn to press ldr 3f out: led 1f out: sn hdd and unable qck: wknd ins fnl f* **6/1**[3]

1142 **7** *3* **Henry Clay**[5] 6450 3-8-11 **85** KierenFallon 4 78
(Mark Johnston) *t.k.h: led: rdn over 1f out: hdd 1f out: sn btn and wknd* **2/1**[1]

0003 **8** *11* **Moon Pearl (USA)**[32] 5595 3-8-7 **81** oh1 (b) HarryBentley 9 52
(Ralph Beckett) *in tch in midfield: rdn and effrt to chse ldrs over 2f out: lost pl whn sltly hmpd over 1f out: sn btn: eased ins fnl f* **20/1**

2m 5.51s (-2.49) **Going Correction** -0.125s/f (Stan) **8** Ran SP% **115.5**

Speed ratings (Par 105): **104,103,103,103,102 101,98,89**

toteswingers 1&2 £5.80, 2&3 £11.50, 1&3 £4.10 CSF £56.41 CT £322.02 TOTE £5.60: £1.80, £1.50, £2.40; EX 47.80 Trifecta £329.30 Pool: £1682.34 - 3.78 winning units..

Owner Cheveley Park Stud **Bred** Cheveley Park Stud Ltd **Trained** Newmarket, Suffolk

■ Stewards' Enquiry : Luke Morris four day ban: careless riding (10 - 12, 14 Oct)

FOCUS

The pace was a steady one in this decent 3yo handicap and they finished in a bit of a heap. Not form to put too much faith in, with a couple of the runners looking unlucky, but the first two still posted personal bests.

NOTEBOOK

Position is proving consistent and had finished a good third over 1m3f here from this mark the time before. He'd probably have been less affected by a steady gallop than some, and certainly improved his own chances by badly hampering Valiant Girl, who was moving through like a potential winner, when switching sharply left inside the final 2f. He continues to progress none the less and is clearly well suited by Polytrack. (tchd 4-1)

Inthar(USA) fared better down in trip minus the cheekpieces this time, finishing well having also been interfered and just failing to get there. His rider losing his whip may have been the difference between victory and defeat, although whether he can reproduce the form from a higher mark next time remains to be seen. (op 10-1)

Come On Blue Chip(IRE) runs this course well and he put up another decent effort returning to 1m2f, running on having challenged wide. (op 11-2 tchd 13-2)

Tigers Tale(IRE), well held in his bid for a four-timer at Sandown the time before, travelled smoothly into the race, but was up in trip and could find no extra inside the final furlong. He too was hampered by the winner's manoeuvre inside the final 2f. (tchd 25-1)

Valiant Girl, luckless from 3lb lower at Newbury the time before, was coming through with a strong-looking challenge when smashed into by the winner, causing her to be knocked left and sandwiched between runners. This cost her any chance and the way she ran on suggests she'd have gone close. (tchd 5-1)

Asatir(USA) found disappointingly little having sat in a prominent early position. (op 7-1)

Henry Clay, just denied from this mark at Newbury five days earlier, was readily swept aside in the final furlong and may have found the race coming too soon. (op 5-2)

6581 BETDAQ MOBILE APPS MAIDEN STKS 6f (P)

6:50 (6:52) (Class 5) 2-Y-O **£2,264** (£673; £336; £168) **Stalls** Low

Form RPR

3 **1** **Invincible Warrior (IRE)**[19] 6015 2-9-3 0 KierenFallon 6 87+
(Brian Meehan) *wnt directly to post fr pre- parade ring: chsd ldr tl pushed into ld 2f out: sn readily qcknd clr: r.o wl: easily* **4/7**[1]

002 **2** *3* **Extrasolar**[12] 6203 2-9-3 75 (t) AdamKirby 3 75
(Amanda Perrett) *chsd ldng trio: rdn and effrt 2f out: chsd clr wnr wl over 1f out: r.o but no threat to wnr* **5/2**[2]

3 *2* **Keep The Dream** 2-9-3 0 (t) JamieSpencer 9 69+
(Paul Cole) *chsd ldrs: rdn and outpcd by wnr 2f out: kpt on same pce after* **20/1**

54 **4** *3 ¼* **Best To Better (IRE)**[23] 5887 2-8-12 0 AndreaAtzeni 4 51
(Marco Botti) *t.k.h early: hld up in tch: rdn over 2f out: outpcd and wl btn over 1f out: plugged on ins fnl f* **8/1**[3]

5 *¾* **Exit Clause** 2-8-12 0 LeonnaMayor(5) 11 57+
(Alastair Lidderdale) *awkward leaving stalls and rn green early: bhd: hdwy into midfield 4f out: rdn and outpcd jst over 2f out: n.d but plugged on fnl f* **80/1**

00 **6** *2 ¼* **Intrigo**[40] 5319 2-9-3 0 RichardHughes 10 50
(Richard Hannon) *led and crossed to inner: rdn and hdd 2f out: sn btn: wknd fnl f* **20/1**

7 *¾* **Ri Na Si** 2-9-3 0 IanMongan 8 48
(Pat Phelan) *in tch in midfield: rdn and outpcd over 2f out: wl hld and styd on same pce fnl 2f* **33/1**

5500 **8** *nk* **Sally Bruce**[5] 6438 2-8-5 52 JenniferFerguson(7) 7 42
(Louise Best) *s.i.s: bhd: rdn and sme hdwy 2f out: n.d* **100/1**

9 *4 ½* **Tom Hall** 2-9-3 0 LukeMorris 1 34
(John Best) *a towards rr: rdn over 2f out: sn wknd* **33/1**

0 **10** *½* **Ishi Amy**[11] 6237 2-8-12 0 [1] FrankieMcDonald 2 27
(Alastair Lidderdale) *a towards rr: rdn over 2f out: sn wknd* **100/1**

0 **11** *¾* **Last Chance Ranch**[35] 5476 2-9-3 0 DaneO'Neill 5 30
(Derek Shaw) *t.k.h: hld up in rr: rdn and wknd over 2f out* **100/1**

1m 13.05s (-0.05) **Going Correction** -0.125s/f (Stan) **11** Ran SP% **122.9**

Speed ratings (Par 95): **95,91,88,84,83 80,79,78,72,71 70**

toteswingers 1&2 £1.40, 2&3 £4.60, 1&3 £2.90 CSF £2.13 TOTE £2.00: £1.10, £1.10, £3.60; EX 2.50 Trifecta £15.00 Pool: £3128.02 - 154.13 winning units..

Owner Car Colston Hall Stud **Bred** Car Colston Hall Stud **Trained** Manton, Wilts

FOCUS

Little depth to this maiden. The winner did it well and is value for extra.

NOTEBOOK

Invincible Warrior(IRE) confirmed the promise of his C&D debut in quite taking fasion. He can expect a mark in the mid-to-high 80s following this, but there should be more to come and there's no reason why he won't prove as effective on turf. The Redcar Two-Year-Old Trophy is apparently an option. (op 8-13 tchd 4-6)

Extrasolar just missed out in a head-bobber at Sandown (5f) last time, but he saw the longer trip out well, simply being beaten by a superior horse. (op 3-1)

Keep The Dream, half-brother to a fair maiden, was wearing a tongue-tie on debut but showed enough to suggest he could win an ordinary maiden with normal improvement. (op 16-1)

Best To Better(IRE) is now qualified for a mark and should fare better in nurseries over a longer trip, providing she settles. (op 7-1)

Exit Clause, out of an AW winner up to 7f, was noted staying on late having run noticeably green and got behind early. (op 66-1 tchd 100-1)

Intrigo set a decent enough pace before fading and should do better in nurseries ridden with more restraint.

6582 BETDAQ CASINO GAMES MEDIAN AUCTION MAIDEN STKS 1m (P)

7:20 (7:24) (Class 5) 3-5-Y-O **£2,264** (£673; £336; £168) **Stalls** Low

Form RPR

03 **1** **Sword In Hand**[16] 6102 3-8-12 0 MichaelJMMurphy(5) 9 76+
(Alan Jarvis) *racd on outer: t.k.h: hld up in tch: hdwy to chse ldrs 3f out: rdn to chal and rn green over 1f out: led jst ins fnl f: r.o wl: eased cl home* **11/2**[3]

2622 **2** *1* **Medhyaar**[26] 5805 3-8-12 71 (tp) PaulHanagan 3 68
(William Haggas) *led: rdn 2f out: hdd jst ins fnl f: styd on same pce fnl 100yds* **7/1**

2062 **3** *nk* **Good Luck Charm**[5] 6434 3-9-3 68 GeorgeBaker 4 72
(Gary Moore) *chsd ldrs: rdn and effrt on inner 2f out: styd on same pce u.p fnl f* **11/4**[2]

0650 **4** *2* **Wildomar**[92] 3475 3-9-3 67 DaraghO'Donohoe 10 67
(John Ryan) *v.s.a: bhd: hdwy into midfield 1/2-way: rdn and unable qck ent fnl 2f: rallied and styd on ins fnl f* **66/1**

0530 **5** *½* **Flavius Victor (IRE)**[62] 4517 3-9-3 67 RichardHughes 2 66
(Richard Hannon) *t.k.h: chsd ldrs: chsd ldr wl over 2f out tl ent fnl 2f: unable qck and sn outpcd: plugged on fnl f* **6/1**

5 **6** *¾* **Bladewood Girl**[20] 5970 4-9-2 0 IanMongan 12 59
(J R Jenkins) *hld up in tch: rdn and unable qck jst over 2f out: styd on same pce fr over 1f out* **16/1**

0060 **7** *2* **Fly On By**[19] 5998 3-9-3 52 (b[1]) DaneO'Neill 8 59?
(Henry Candy) *s.i.s and sn rdn along: bhd: swtchd lft and hdwy past btn horses over 1f out: styd on same pce fnl f* **20/1**

8 *3* **Tajamal (IRE)** 3-9-3 0 SilvestreDeSousa 5 52+
(Saeed Bin Suroor) *s.i.s: bhd and sn rdn along: sme hdwy 2f out: no imp fr over 1f out: n.d* **2/1**[1]

00- **9** *1 ½* **Midnight Bahia (IRE)**[462] 3282 3-8-12 0 ShaneKelly 13 43
(Dean Ivory) *hld up in midfield: rdn and unable qck over 2f out: sn outpcd and wknd 2f out* **66/1**

00 **10** *½* **Ivan The Engine**[6] 6397 4-9-7 0 SebSanders 6 47
(Ian Wood) *hld up in midfield: rdn and struggling over 2f out: wknd 2f out* **100/1**

00 **11** *8* **Wood Meister**[21] 5950 4-9-2 0 (b[1]) NathanSweeney(5) 1 28
(Kevin Tork) *s.i.s: t.k.h and sn rcvrd to r in midfield: rdn and wknd over 2f out* **100/1**

00-0 **12** *3 ½* **Almirah**[19] 6001 3-8-12 30 CathyGannon 7 15
(David Evans) *chsd ldr tl wl over 2f out: sn wknd* **100/1**

00 **13** *shd* **Cowslip**[26] 5795 3-8-12 0 SeanLevey 14 14
(Richard Hannon) *a towards rr: rdn and wknd over 2f out* **66/1**

1m 38.61s (-1.19) **Going Correction** -0.125s/f (Stan)

WFA 3 from 4yo 4lb **13** Ran SP% **120.3**

Speed ratings (Par 103): **100,99,98,96,96 95,93,90,88,88 80,76,76**

toteswingers 1&2 £5.00, 2&3 £3.70, 1&3 £4.30 CSF £43.10 TOTE £7.60: £2.20, £1.40, £1.50; EX 63.60 Trifecta £116.60 Pool: £2097.65 - 13.30 winning units..

Owner Geoffrey Bishop **Bred** Eurostrait Ltd **Trained** Twyford, Bucks

FOCUS

A modest maiden, most of the older horses having had their chances. The form is rated cautiously but the winner can improve.

6583 RACING PLUS OUT EVERY SATURDAY NURSERY 7f (P)

7:50 (7:53) (Class 6) (0-65,65) 2-Y-O **£1,617** (£481; £240; £120) **Stalls** Low

Form RPR

500 **1** **Mushaakis (IRE)**[16] 6099 2-9-1 **59** PaulHanagan 9 66+
(Mark Johnston) *racd off the pce in midfield: rdn and effrt over 2f out: str run fnl f to ld towards fin* **7/2**[2]

6104 **2** *½* **Poetic Princess**[29] 5716 2-9-2 **60** FrannyNorton 13 63
(Jo Hughes) *chsd ldr after 2f: rdn and sltly outpcd 2f out: rallied u.p 1f out: pressed wnr ins fnl f: r.o to snatch 2nd on post* **20/1**

3645 **3** *nse* **Eastern Dragon (IRE)**[9] 6318 2-9-2 **60** (v) HayleyTurner 6 63
(Michael Scudamore) *chsd ldr tl led over 5f out: rdn and fnd ex 2f out: drvn 1f out: hdd and lost 2 pls towards fin* **7/1**[3]

0562 **4** *1* **Girl Of Cadiz**[14] 6147 2-9-5 **63** RichardHughes 2 63
(Richard Hannon) *led for over 1f: chsd ldrs after: rdn and effrt to chse ldr on inner over 1f out tl ins fnl f: one pce fnl 100yds* **3/1**[1]

600 **5** *2 ½* **Flywheel (IRE)**[33] 5550 2-8-10 **54** (t) KierenFallon 3 47
(Brian Meehan) *in tch in midfield: rdn and effrt over 1f out: styd on same pce ins fnl f* **10/1**

633 **6** *nk* **Daisie Cutter**[22] 5912 2-8-13 **60** SimonPearce(3) 5 53
(Lydia Pearce) *t.k.h: chsd ldrs: rdn and unable qck wl over 1f out: wknd ins fnl f* **14/1**

4006 **7** *½* **Poetic Belle**[11] 6253 2-8-12 **61** MichaelJMMurphy(5) 4 52
(Alan Jarvis) *t.k.h: hld up in tch in midfield: rdn and unable qck 2f out: styd on same pce fr over 1f out* **16/1**

2000 **8** *1* **Sutton Sid**[35] 5484 2-9-7 **65** PatCosgrave 14 54
(George Baker) *hld up towards rr of main gp: rdn and effrt 2f out: drvn and no imp over 1f out* **10/1**

600 **9** *3* **Fit For A King (IRE)**[64] 4433 2-9-6 **64** LukeMorris 8 44
(John Best) *hld up in tch in midfield: effrt and unable qck jst over 2f out: drvn and wknd over 1f out* **12/1**

060 **10** *3 ¼* **Misty Secret (IRE)**[19] 6007 2-8-12 **56**.............................. BrettDoyle 10 28
(Jane Chapple-Hyam) *s.i.s: a towards rr: rdn and edging rt over 2f out: wknd 2f out* **25/1**
060 **11** *2* **Foie Gras**[15] 6114 2-8-12 **56**.............................. NeilCallan 7 22
(William Muir) *hmpd s: a towards rr: rdn and wknd over 2f out* **9/1**
350 **12** *10* **Fruity Bun**[56] 4704 2-8-9 **53**.............................. SamHitchcott 11
(Matthew Salaman) *in rr of main gp: rdn 3f out: sn struggling and wknd: bhd and eased ins fnl f* **66/1**
0500 **13** *27* **Royal Caper**[15] 6114 2-9-2 **60**..............................(p) DaraghO'Donohoe 1
(John Ryan) *s.i.s: a detached in last: t.o and eased fnl f* **50/1**

1m 26.43s (0.43) **Going Correction** -0.125s/f (Stan) **13** Ran SP% **120.2**
Speed ratings (Par 93): **92,91,91,90,87 87,86,85,81,78 75,64,33**
toteswingers 1&2 £20.40, 2&3 £15.60, 1&3 £5.30 CSF £78.45 CT £492.40 TOTE £5.10: £2.10, £3.70, £2.80; EX 79.50 Trifecta £895.00 Pool: £2177.25 - 1.80 winning units..
Owner Hamdan Al Maktoum **Bred** Shadwell Estate Company Limited **Trained** Middleham Moor, N Yorks

FOCUS
Few got into this and the form is just modest if straightforward, although the race should still produce the odd winner.

NOTEBOOK
Mushaakis(IRE), who was well backed, looked the type to improve once handicapping and he proved strong late on, coming from furthest back of the front four. The step up in trip had promised to suit and there should be even more to come from him once upped to 1m. Official explanation: trainer's representative said, regarding the apparent improvement of form, that the colt was suited by the step up in trip and the all-weather surface (op 9-2 tchd 3-1)
Poetic Princess, whose win came in a 7f Fibresand maiden, bounced back from a couple of poor efforts and may find a small race from this mark.
Eastern Dragon(IRE) gave it a good go from the front but again couldn't quite see his race out. He's capable of winning a small race from this sort of mark. (tchd 6-1)
Girl Of Cadiz enjoyed a perfect trip and had her chance, the 4lb rise she'd incurred for finishing runner-up over C&D latest appearing to hold her back. (op 9-4)
Flywheel(IRE) offered a bit more on this switch to nurseries and should improve again upped to 1m. (tchd 8-1)
Daisie Cutter was hampered early and may be worth another chance. (op 12-1 tchd 10-1)

6584 MARTIN COLLINS ENTERPRISES H'CAP 1m 4f (P)
8:20 (8:23) (Class 4) (0-85,85) 4-Y-0+ **£4,075** (£1,212; £606; £303) **Stalls** Centre

Form RPR
4-21 **1** **Enthusiastic**[28] 5753 4-9-0 **78**.............................. NeilCallan 9 91+
(Michael Murphy) *hld up in midfield: shuffled bk towards rr ent fnl 2f: swtchd lft and hdwy over 1f out: str run to ld fnl 50yds: gng away at fin* **11/4**[1]
534- **2** *1* **Rowan Tiger**[200] 6976 6-8-11 **75**.............................. HayleyTurner 10 83
(Dr Richard Newland) *hld up in midfield: hdwy u.p to chse ldrs over 1f out: drvn to ld ins fnl f: hdd and no ex fnl 50yds* **11/1**
-005 **3** *1 ½* **Icebuster**[12] 6207 4-9-0 **78**.............................. JamesMillman 12 84
(Rod Millman) *stdd s: hld up in rr: swtchd sharply lft 2f out: hdwy over 1f out: styng on strly whn swtchd lft wl ins fnl f: snatched 3rd on post* **10/1**
1541 **4** *nse* **Refractor (IRE)**[21] 5944 4-9-5 **83**.............................. MartinLane 6 89
(James Fanshawe) *dwlt: hld up towards rr: swtchd lft and hdwy ent fnl 2f: pressed ldrs and drvn jst ins fnl f: no ex fnl 100yds* **9/2**[2]
0132 **5** *nk* **Kuda Huraa (IRE)**[21] 5944 4-9-7 **85**.............................. JamieSpencer 8 90
(Roger Varian) *chsd ldr tl led 9f out: edgd lft u.p fr 2f out: hdd ins fnl f: no ex and lost 3 pls wl ins fnl f* **13/2**[3]
5135 **6** *¾* **Brigadoon**[18] 6039 5-8-9 **78**.............................. MichaelJMMurphy(5) 3 82
(William Jarvis) *in tch in last trio: c wd and effrt jst over 2f out: hdwy over 1f out: styd on ins fnl f: nt rch ldrs* **16/1**
1530 **7** *1 ½* **Rasheed**[109] 2936 4-9-7 **85**.............................. WilliamBuick 7 86
(John Gosden) *chsd ldrs: wnt 2nd 8f out: drvn and unable qck over 1f out: lost 2nd 1f out: wknd fnl 100yds* **16/1**
0360 **8** *1 ¾* **Mountain Range (IRE)**[19] 6018 4-9-1 **79**.............................. EddieAhern 2 78
(John Dunlop) *in tch in midfield: rdn and effrt 2f out: hdwy to chse ldrs and drvn 1f out: no ex and wknd fnl 100yds* **7/1**
5260 **9** *1 ¼* **Twice Bitten**[8] 6349 4-9-1 **79**.............................. LiamKeniry 1 76
(James Toller) *in tch in midfield: n.m.r over 2f out: swtchd ins and effrt ent fnl 2f: no hdwy u.p over 1f out: wknd ins fnl f* **33/1**
5053 **10** *2 ¼* **Achalas (IRE)**[33] 5546 4-8-12 **76**.............................. JamesDoyle 13 69
(Heather Main) *chsd ldrs: lost pl 3f out: wknd u.p 2f out* **25/1**
3330 **11** *1 ½* **Where's Susie**[133] 2174 7-8-13 **77**.............................. DaneO'Neill 5 68
(Michael Madgwick) *hld up towards rr: swtchd ins and effrt ent fnl 2f: no imp and wknd over 1f out* **50/1**
6023 **12** *½* **The Bells O Peover**[9] 6311 4-8-13 **77**..............................(b) KierenFallon 4 67
(Mark Johnston) *t.k.h: led for 2f: chsd ldrs after tl wknd wl over 1f out* **11/1**
110 **13** *4 ½* **The High Man**[33] 5554 4-9-6 **84**.............................. GeorgeBaker 14 67
(Ed Walker) *dwlt: hdwy to chse ldrs after: rdn and unable qck over 2f out: wknd over 1f out: eased ins fnl f* **8/1**
04-0 **14** *7* **Zebrano**[12] 6207 6-9-5 **83**..............................(b) AdamKirby 11 54
(Natalie Lloyd-Beavis) *v.s.a: a bhd: lost tch over 2f out* **100/1**

2m 30.15s (-4.35) **Going Correction** -0.125s/f (Stan) **14** Ran SP% **129.1**
Speed ratings (Par 105): **109,108,107,107,107 106,105,104,103,102 101,100,97,93**
toteswingers 1&2 £8.70, 2&3 £53.20, 1&3 £22.40 CSF £37.04 CT £285.86 TOTE £4.00: £1.80, £5.20, £3.50; EX 53.10 TRIFECTA Not won..
Owner The Honorable Earle I Mack **Bred** Earle I Mack **Trained** Newmarket, Suffolk

FOCUS
The pace was no more than fair in this good-quality Polytrack handicap, yet those challenging wide from off the pace still prevailed late on. The form looks solid, with improvement from the winner.
The High Man Official explanation: jockey said that the gelding stopped quickly
Zebrano Official explanation: jockey said the gelding had no more to give

6585 BOOK YOUR CHRISTMAS PARTY AT KEMPTON H'CAP (DIV I) 6f (P)
8:50 (8:50) (Class 6) (0-60,60) 3-Y-0+ **£1,617** (£481; £240; £120) **Stalls** Low

Form RPR
4030 **1** **Athwaab**[168] 1305 5-9-3 **56**.............................. GeorgeBaker 1 64
(Noel Chance) *chsd ldrs: rdn and effrt to ld over 1f out: drvn and hdd ins fnl f: rallied gamely and led again last stride* **16/1**
0505 **2** *nse* **Lisselton Cross**[93] 3455 4-8-12 **51**..............................(b[1]) MartinLane 8 59
(Martin Bosley) *wnt to post direct fr pre-parade ring: in tch in midfield: swtchd lft and hdwy over 1f out: rdn to chal fnl 150yds: led narrowly ins fnl f: hdd last stride* **20/1**
2025 **3** *½* **Ereka (IRE)**[24] 5850 4-9-2 **55**.............................. LukeMorris 2 61
(John Best) *in tch in midfield: swtchd rt and hdwy u.p over 1f out: pressed wnr 1f out: unable qck fnl 100yds* **8/1**[3]
5012 **4** *3* **Strategic Action (IRE)**[19] 5994 3-9-1 **56**..............................(p) SaleemGolam 6 53
(Linda Jewell) *in tch: effrt u.p 2f out: outpcd by ldng trio 1f out: styd on same pce fnl f* **10/1**
2003 **5** *shd* **Mary's Pet**[47] 5047 5-9-7 **60**..............................(p) KierenFox 10 56
(Lee Carter) *s.i.s: hld up in last trio: swtchd lft and hdwy 2f out: styd on wl ins fnl f: nvr trbld ldrs* **8/1**[3]
0565 **6** *½* **The Name Is Frank**[11] 6233 7-9-4 **57**..............................(t) FergusSweeney 5 52
(Mark Gillard) *t.k.h: hld up in last trio: rdn and hdwy over 1f out: swtchd rt 1f out: swtchd lft ins fnl f: r.o but nvr trbld ldrs* **9/1**
0500 **7** *hd* **Reginald Claude**[19] 6002 4-8-8 **52**..............................(v) LeeNewnes(5) 4 46
(Mark Usher) *in tch: effrt u.p to chse ldrs over 1f out: no ex 1f out: wknd ins fnl f* **8/1**[3]
4242 **8** *hd* **Imjin River (IRE)**[13] 6179 5-9-5 **58**.............................. RichardHughes 11 52
(William Stone) *in tch in midfield: rdn and effrt 2f out: no imp over 1f out: styd on same pce and wl hld fnl f* **4/1**[1]
00-2 **9** *1 ¼* **Bishopbriggs (USA)**[126] 2401 7-9-6 **59**.............................. AdamKirby 7 49
(John Butler) *led tl drvn and hdd over 1f out: wknd fnl f* **11/2**[2]
4102 **10** *½* **Custom House (IRE)**[111] 2847 4-9-4 **57**.............................. DaneO'Neill 12 45
(John E Long) *wnt to post direct fr pre-parade ring: s.i.s: a bhd* **9/1**
6325 **11** *1 ¾* **Blueberry Fizz (IRE)**[63] 4467 4-8-10 **56**.............................. BradleyBosley(7) 9 38
(John Ryan) *chsd ldr tl 2f out: rdn and sn struggling: wandered and wknd over 1f out: eased towards fin* **10/1**
3010 **R** **Copper Falls**[19] 6003 3-8-6 **54**..............................(v[1]) JoshBaudains(7) 3
(Brendan Powell) *ref to r: tk no part* **16/1**

1m 12.54s (-0.56) **Going Correction** -0.125s/f (Stan)
WFA 3 from 4yo+ 2lb **12** Ran SP% **123.4**
Speed ratings (Par 101): **98,97,97,93,93 92,92,91,90,89 87,**
toteswingers 1&2 £35.00, 2&3 £28.70, 1&3 £6.80 CSF £311.50 CT £2791.89 TOTE £23.90: £7.10, £10.10, £3.50; EX 443.00 Trifecta £800.70 Part won. Pool: £1082.15 - 0.80 winning units..
Owner N P Horsfall **Bred** Shadwell Estate Co Ltd **Trained** Lambourn, Berks

FOCUS
Division one of a weak sprint handicap, and slightly the quicker division. Ordinary form, with the third setting the standard.

6586 BOOK YOUR CHRISTMAS PARTY AT KEMPTON H'CAP (DIV II) 6f (P)
9:20 (9:21) (Class 6) (0-60,60) 3-Y-0+ **£1,617** (£481; £240; £120) **Stalls** Low

Form RPR
3020 **1** **Demoiselle Bond**[31] 5625 4-9-1 **54**.............................. RobertHavlin 7 63
(Lydia Richards) *taken down early: mde all: rdn and edgd lft over 1f out: kpt on wl fnl f* **9/4**[1]
044 **2** *1 ¼* **Leelu**[42] 5234 6-9-7 **60**.............................. NeilCallan 8 65
(David Arbuthnot) *chsd wnr thrght: rdn and unable qck over 1f out: styd on same pce fnl f* **7/2**[2]
5000 **3** *1* **Sermons Mount (USA)**[13] 6158 6-9-3 **56**..............................(p) J-PGuillambert 9 58
(Paul Howling) *chsd ldrs: rdn and effrt ent fnl 2f: styd on same pce u.p fr over 1f out* **11/2**
4 *½* **The Kernigal (IRE)**[105] 3056 3-8-8 **54**..............................(t) AshleyMorgan(5) 4 54
(Pat Murphy) *stdd s: hld up off the pce in last pair: clsd and effrt on inner 2f out: styd on to go 4th wl ins fnl f: nt trble ldrs* **9/2**[3]
00 **5** *¾* **Cliffords Reprieve**[39] 5349 4-9-5 **58**..............................(b) LukeMorris 2 56
(Eric Wheeler) *taken down early: chsd ldrs: rdn and unable qck ent fnl 2f: styd on same pce u.p fr over 1f out* **8/1**
0020 **6** *shd* **Ace Of Spies (IRE)**[13] 6178 7-9-3 **56**.............................. HayleyTurner 5 53
(Conor Dore) *in tch in midfield: rdn and effrt 2f out: no imp and styd on same pce fr over 1f out* **10/1**
6000 **7** *¾* **Prohibition (IRE)**[12] 6217 6-9-3 **56**.............................. AdamKirby 11 51
(John Butler) *s.i.s and early reminder: bhd: clsd and in tch over 2f out: rdn and styd on same pce fnl f* **16/1**
00-0 **8** *1 ¼* **Lady On Top (IRE)**[133] 2171 4-8-4 **50**.............................. NoelGarbutt(7) 12 41
(Nerys Dutfield) *racd on outer: in tch: rdn and unable qck over 2f out: wknd over 1f out* **25/1**

1m 12.78s (-0.32) **Going Correction** -0.125s/f (Stan)
WFA 3 from 4yo+ 2lb **8** Ran SP% **116.5**
Speed ratings (Par 101): **97,95,94,93,92 92,91,89**
toteswingers 1&2 £1.80, 2&3 £2.60, 1&3 £3.50 CSF £10.41 CT £38.13 TOTE £3.20: £1.30, £1.10, £2.20; EX 11.30 Trifecta £88.10 Pool: £1561.06 - 13.10 winning units..
Owner The Demoiselle Bond Partnership **Bred** Mrs Lydia Richards **Trained** Funtington, W Sussex

FOCUS
Less competitive and slightly slower than the first division, and the early leaders held their positions throughout. The winner is rated in line with a best view of his previous form.
T/Jkpt: £2,730.70 to a £1 stake. Pool of £25,000.00 - 6.50 winning tickets. T/Plt: £46.10 to a £1 stake. Pool of £71725.39 -1134.95 winning tickets. T/Qpdt: £14.30 to a £1 stake. Pool of £6853.05 - 354.22 winning tickets. SP

6121 REDCAR (L-H)
Wednesday, September 26
6587 Meeting Abandoned - Waterlogged

TOULOUSE
Wednesday, September 26
OFFICIAL GOING: Turf: good to soft

6595a PRIX PANACEE (LISTED RACE) (3YO+ FILLIES & MARES) (TURF) 1m 4f
5:40 (12:00) 3-Y-0+ **£21,666** (£8,666; £6,500; £4,333; £2,166)

RPR
1 **Brasileira**[25] 5845 4-9-5 0.............................. AntoineHamelin 7 104
(J-M Beguigne, France) **26/1**
2 *nse* **Aigue Marine**[32] 5614 3-8-11 0.............................. ThierryThulliez 6 104
(N Clement, France) **48/10**[2]
3 *¾* **Gloomy Sunday (FR)**[46] 5116 3-8-7 0.............................. JohanVictoire 10 99
(C Ferland, France) **58/10**[3]
4 *½* **Bassamba (FR)**[94] 3423 3-8-11 0..............................(b) Francois-XavierBertras 8 102
(F Rohaut, France) **58/10**[3]
5 *2 ½* **Victorinna (FR)**[25] 5845 4-9-1 0.............................. OlivierPeslier 2 94
(C Laffon-Parias, France) **2/1**[1]
6 *1 ½* **Lumiere Rose**[79] 3-8-7 0.............................. Jean-BernardEyquem 5 92
(J-C Rouget, France) **13/2**
7 *½* **Creme Anglaise**[117] 2655 4-9-1 0.............................. StevieDonohoe 9 91
(Michael Bell) *2nd early towards outside: forced four wd on first bnd and relegated to midfield: rdn bef st: styd on u.p fnl f* **24/1**

8	6	**Two Days In Paris (FR)**[42] 5251 3-8-7 0 .... IoritzMendizabal 4 (J-C Rouget, France) **19/1**		81
9	2	**Famous Lilly (USA)**[54] 4-9-1 0 .... GeraldMosse 1 (A De Royer-Dupre, France) **17/1**		78
10	5	**Night Serenade (IRE)**[25] 5844 5-9-1 0 ....(p) FabriceVeron 3 (H-A Pantall, France) **18/1**		70

2m 32.09s (-0.21)
WFA 3 from 4yo+ 8lb **10** Ran SP% **116.8**
WIN (incl. 1 euro stake): 26.70. PLACES: 5.30, 2.10, 2.70. DF: 75.80. SF: 180.40.
Owner Ecurie Serval **Bred** Petra Bloodstock Agency Ltd **Trained** France

NOTEBOOK
Creme Anglaise ran close to her best RPR, but that wasn't good enough to see her get involved.

6489 NEWMARKET (R-H)

Thursday, September 27

OFFICIAL GOING: Good (overall 7.4, stands' side 7.5; centre 7.2; far side 7.3)
Far side of Rowley Mile course used. Stalls on stands' side except 12f &16f: centre.
Wind: fresh, behind Weather: dry

6596 BRITISH STALLION STUDS SUPPORTING BRITISH RACING EBF MAIDEN STKS (C&G) 1m

2:00 (2:00) (Class 4) 2-Y-O **£4,528** (£1,347; £673; £336) **Stalls** High

Form				RPR
2	1		**Telescope (IRE)**[19] 6020 2-9-0 0 .... RichardHughes 9 (Sir Michael Stoute) *t.k.h: chsd ldr tl led on bit over 1f out: rdn out hands and heels and r.o strly fnl f: comf* **8/13**[1]	86+
4	2	2 ¼	**Elkaayed (USA)**[19] 6020 2-9-0 0 .... PaulHanagan 7 (Roger Varian) *in tch: rdn and sltly outpcd wl over 1f out: rallied u.p ins fnl f: styd on wl to go 2nd towards fin: no threat to wnr* **11/2**[2]	79
	3	½	**Excellent Result (IRE)** 2-9-0 0 .... FrankieDettori 4 (Saeed Bin Suroor) *in tch in midfield: hdwy to chse ldrs 1/2-way: rdn and pressing ldrs over 2f out: unable qck over 1f out: kpt on to chse clr wnr fnl 100yds tl towards fin* **16/1**	78
43	4	¾	**Space Ship**[14] 6164 2-9-0 0 .... WilliamBuick 1 (John Gosden) *led: rdn and hdd over 1f out: edgd rt and one pce ins fnl f: lost 2 pls fnl 100yds* **11/2**[2]	76
0	5	1 ¼	**Soviet Rock (IRE)**[49] 5005 2-9-0 0 .... JimmyFortune 8 (Andrew Balding) *in tch in midfield: rdn and outpcd on downhill run wl over 1f out: plugged on same pce and wl hld fnl f* **50/1**	73
	6	nk	**Glorious Protector (IRE)** 2-9-0 0 .... JamieSpencer 5 (Ed Walker) *stdd after s: t.k.h: hld up in last trio: rdn and hdwy over 1f out: no imp fnl f* **33/1**	72+
	7	½	**Personable** 2-9-0 0 .... MickaelBarzalona 2 (Mahmood Al Zarooni) *rn green in rr: rdn and outpcd 2f out: rallied u.p jst over 1f out: no imp ins fnl f* **16/1**	71+
	8	1	**Autun (USA)** 2-9-0 0 .... TomQueally 3 (Sir Henry Cecil) *v awkward leaving stalls and slowly away: rn green: in tch towards rr: rdn and lost pl over 2f out: plugged on same pce fr over 1f out* **9/1**[3]	69+
	9	4	**Seamless** 2-9-0 0 .... MichaelHills 6 (Charles Hills) *in tch towards rr: rdn and struggling 3f out: bhd over 1f out* **50/1**	60

1m 38.48s (-0.12) **Going Correction** -0.125s/f (Firm) **9** Ran SP% **121.3**
Speed ratings (Par 97): **95,92,92,91,90 89,89,88,84**
toteswingers 1&2 £1.30, 1&3 £4.60, 2&3 £7.10 CSF £4.84 TOTE £1.60: £1.10, £1.40, £3.60; EX 4.60 Trifecta £26.80 Pool: £1,770.42 - 48.86 winning tickets..
Owner Highclere Thoroughbred Racing -Wavertree **Bred** Barronstown Stud **Trained** Newmarket, Suffolk

FOCUS
This looks sure to prove an informative contest despite the lack of early pace, and subsequent winners will undoubtedly emerge from it.

NOTEBOOK
Telescope(IRE) ◆ shaped nicely on his debut, when he also started favourite, and had been given quotes of 20-1 generally for the Derby after that effort. He was sensibly kept close to the leader here from the outset and collected a first success in workmanlike rather than spectacular style. His pedigree strongly suggests middle-distances are what he will require and he will surely head for something like the Dante in the early part of next season. Predictably bookies cut him for Epsom next June, but while he is a likely type for that contest, nothing he did in this race entitled his odds to be trimmed. (op 4-6)
Elkaayed(USA) ◆ finished behind Telescope at Ascot and wasn't good enough to reverse form here over a longer trip. That said, it was another promising effort and he'll win any ordinary maiden. (op 7-1 tchd 5-1)
Excellent Result(IRE) didn't have a really interesting pedigree and changed hands for 70,000euros at the sales, but he made a good start to his a career up against some talented colts and did best of the newcomers. (op 14-1)
Space Ship had shown a useful level of ability in two previous maidens, and helps to make the form look above average. He got an easy lead, but didn't get home as strongly as the three in front of him. (op 9-2)
Glorious Protector(IRE) ◆, who holds a Group 1 entry, is a big sort and really caught the eye just in behind. The stewards held an enquiry into the running and riding of the colt, who broke well from the stalls and was then restrained towards the rear before being asked for an effort from approaching the furlong pole to finish sixth, beaten some 5l. They interviewed the rider and the trainer and also received a report from the vet. The rider reported that the colt had run green in the Dip and also stated that his instructions were to drop the colt in and get him relaxed for the first half of the race and once relaxed get the colt to run to the best of his ability to achieve the best possible place. The trainer confirmed these instructions. Having heard their evidence and viewed recordings of the race the stewards noted their explanations. Official explanation: jockey said regarding the running and riding, that the colt had run green in the dip and also stated that his instructions were to drop the colt in and get him relaxed for the first half of the race and once relaxed get the colt to run to the best of his ability to achieve the best possible place. The trainer confirmed these instructions.
Autun(USA), the first son of Sense Of Joy, who won both her races as a juvenile (her only year on the racecourse), including the Group 3 Prestige Stakes, was clueless and in need of the experience. (op 14-1)

6597 CAMBRIDGE NEWS EXCELLENT HORSERACING COVERAGE NURSERY 1m

2:35 (2:36) (Class 2) 2-Y-O **£7,762** (£2,310; £1,154; £577) **Stalls** High

Form				RPR
612	1		**Red Avenger (USA)**[15] 6138 2-9-6 **85** .... PaulHanagan 2 (Ed Dunlop) *racd in centre: led gp and chsd ldrs overall: rdn over 2f out: ev ch over 1f out: led ins fnl f: hld on u.p cl home: all out: 1st of 5 in gp* **13/2**[2]	91
4321	2	hd	**Darkening (IRE)**[7] 6414 2-9-4 **83** 6ex .... MickaelBarzalona 10 (Mahmood Al Zarooni) *racd stands' side: chsd overall ldr: rdn over 2f out: ev ch over 1f out: led jst ins fnl f: sn hdd: rallied gamely towards fin: jst hld: 1st of 10 in gp* **7/1**[3]	89
0312	3	1 ¼	**Hoarding (USA)**[12] 6247 2-9-7 **86** .... WilliamBuick 6 (John Gosden) *racd in centre: in tch in midfield overall: rdn and effrt to chse clr ldng trio wl over 1f out: kpt on u.p ins fnl f: 2nd of 5 in gp* **9/2**[1]	89
2031	4	1 ½	**Royal Skies (IRE)**[30] 5704 2-8-13 **78** .... KierenFallon 15 (Mark Johnston) *racd stands' side: overall ldr: rdn over 2f out: drvn and hdd jst ins fnl f: no ex: wknd towards fin: 2nd of 10 in gp* **7/1**[3]	77
2421	5	2	**Marhaba Malayeen (IRE)**[16] 6121 2-8-10 **75** ....(b) JamieSpencer 7 (Kevin Ryan) *racd stands' side: in tch in midfield: rdn and effrt over 2f out: 5th and no imp over 1f out: kpt on u.p ins fnl f: 3rd of 10 in gp* **20/1**	70
4144	6	½	**Aussie Reigns (IRE)**[26] 5836 2-8-9 **74** .... JimCrowley 1 (William Knight) *racd in centre: in tch: rdn and effrt over 2f out: 6th and outpcd whn edgd lft u.p over 1f out: plugged on but no threat to ldrs fnl f: 3rd of 5 in gp* **25/1**	67
1	7	nse	**Authorship (IRE)**[49] 4995 2-8-12 **77** .... SilvestreDeSousa 13 (Mahmood Al Zarooni) *racd stands' side: t.k.h: hld up towards rr: rdn and sme hdwy 2f out: stl plenty to do but keeping on whn swtchd lft 1f out: styd on but nvr gng pce to chal: 4th of 10 in gp* **8/1**	70+
0554	8	½	**Millers Wharf (IRE)**[9] 6330 2-8-12 **77** .... RichardHughes 3 (Richard Hannon) *taken down early: racd in centre: hld up in rr: rdn and effrt over 2f out: no imp and looked wl hld over 1f out: kpt on steadily ins fnl f: nvr trbld ldrs: 4th of 5 in gp* **9/1**	69+
044	9	½	**Storming (IRE)**[29] 5742 2-8-6 **71** .... LukeMorris 8 (Andrew Balding) *racd stands' side: racd off the pce towards rr: rdn and effrt over 2f out: no imp u.p over 1f out tl kpt on ins fnl f: nvr trbld ldrs: 5th of 10 in gp* **14/1**	62+
0041	10	3 ¼	**Felix Fabulla**[17] 6096 2-8-7 **72** .... NickyMackay 14 (Hughie Morrison) *racd stands' side: chsd ldrs: rdn and struggling whn edgd lft jst over 2f out: wknd over 1f out: 6th of 10 in gp* **8/1**	56
5251	11	3 ¼	**Emperatriz**[31] 5668 2-8-4 **69** .... HayleyTurner 4 (John Holt) *racd in centre: hld up towards rr: rdn and no hdwy over 2f out: wl btn fnl 2f: 5th of 5 in gp* **33/1**	45
354	12	¾	**Arlecchino (IRE)**[21] 5962 2-8-13 **78** ....(t) TomQueally 16 (Ed McMahon) *racd stands' side: in tch in midfield: rdn 1/2-way: no imp u.p whn nt clr run jst over 2f out: wl btn over 1f out: 7th of 10 in gp* **12/1**	53
0154	13	9	**Rafale**[29] 5743 2-8-8 **73** .... PatDobbs 11 (Richard Hannon) *racd stands' side: hld up towards rr: rdn and struggling over 2f out: sn wknd: bhd and eased wl ins fnl f: 8th of 10 in gp* **33/1**	27
31	14	1 ¾	**Firstkissoflove**[23] 5911 2-8-8 **73** .... JohnFahy 9 (Clive Cox) *racd stands' side: s.i.s: a bhd and sn rdn along: lost tch 2f out: eased wl ins fnl f: 9th of 10 in gp* **33/1**	23
001	15	3 ¾	**Imperial Oak**[20] 5997 2-8-12 **77** .... JimmyFortune 12 (Eve Johnson Houghton) *racd stands' side: chsd ldrs tl lost pl qckly over 2f out: bhd and eased wl ins fnl f: 10th of 10 in gp* **50/1**	18

1m 37.17s (-1.43) **Going Correction** -0.125s/f (Firm) **15** Ran SP% **122.5**
Speed ratings (Par 101): **102,101,100,99,97 96,96,96,95,92 89,88,79,77,73**
toteswingers 1&2 £6.20, 1&3 £4.50, 2&3 £5.00 CSF £48.14 CT £236.17 TOTE £6.80: £2.40, £2.60, £1.40; EX 38.60 Trifecta £47.00 Pool: £1,668.18 - 26.21 winning tickets..
Owner R J Arculli **Bred** Wedgewood Farm **Trained** Newmarket, Suffolk

FOCUS
A typically competitive Newmarket nursery and the winning time was 1.31 seconds faster than the earlier maiden. With the top weights filling the first three places, this looked a decent race of its type. The field split into two early with the larger group of ten racing close to the stands' rail, while a group of five (including the winner and third) raced more towards the centre. The first four home were always up with the pace.

NOTEBOOK
Red Avenger(USA) ◆ had shaped as though this extra furlong would suit when just failing to get up on his nursery debut at Doncaster last time, and he confirmed that view here despite a 3lb higher mark. Having seen plenty of daylight at the head of the smaller group towards the middle of the track, despite edging left under pressure he worked his way into the overall lead over a furlong from home and battled on gamely to just hold on. He still gives the impression he has further improvement in him and he should get a bit further in due course. (tchd 7-1)
Darkening(IRE), like the winner up a furlong in trip, was carrying a 6lb penalty for winning a Yarmouth nursery seven days earlier, but was still 1lb lower than his revised mark. Having raced close to the pace in the nearside group, he had every chance once put under pressure and was battling back gamely at the line. He looks to have improved for being gelded and there should be another day for him. (op 6-1)
Hoarding(USA) ◆, up another 3lb following his recent narrow Doncaster defeat, took a while to respond to pressure in the centre group, but eventually clicked into gear and was doing all his best work late. He too should regain winning form before too long. (tchd 5-1)
Royal Skies(IRE) made a bold bid to make every yard against the stands' rail, but was done for speed from over a furlong out. He is already due a 3lb rise after the form of his Epsom maiden success last month worked out extremely well, but you would never write off one from his yard even off a higher mark. (op 8-1 tchd 9-1 and 10-1 in a place)
Marhaba Malayeen(IRE), up 4lb and trying an extra furlong following his recent Redcar success, could only plug on for pressure in the nearside group and lacks the scope for further improvement of a few of these. (tchd 22-1)
Aussie Reigns(IRE) didn't run badly in the centre-field group, but has now been beaten three times off this mark since making a successful nursery debut at Goodwood off 4lb lower.
Authorship(IRE) ◆ is one to take from the race. He looked green when narrowly winning a six-runner Haydock maiden on his debut last month and he was being ridden along towards the back of the field just after halfway here. However, he eventually clicked into gear and may have finished a bit closer had he not been short of room over a furlong out. Further improvement is very likely. (op 15-2 tchd 7-1)
Millers Wharf(IRE), making his nursery debut on his seventh start and trying a longer trip, could never get involved from off the pace out in the centre and although he is already due to drop 3lb, it looks as though more will be needed if he is to be competitive in nurseries. (op 17-2 tchd 10-1)

Storming(IRE), another making his nursery debut after showing improved form in three maidens, was off the bridle a fair way out but he made a little late headway and may just need a bit more time. (op 20-1)

6598 PRINCESS ROYAL RICHARD HAMBRO EBF STKS (LISTED RACE) (F&M) 1m 4f

3:10 (3:11) (Class 1) 3-Y-O+

£18,714 (£7,095; £3,550; £1,768; £887; £445) **Stalls** Centre

Form RPR

2114 **1** **Gallipot**[14] 6163 3-8-9 102 WilliamBuick 2 108+
(John Gosden) *chsd ldrs: swtchd lft and effrt to chse ldr wl over 1f out: rdn to ld over 1f out and sn clr: styd on strly fnl f: rdn out* **7/2**[1]

-334 **2** *2 1/4* **Albamara**[53] 4848 3-8-9 90 LukeMorris 8 104
(Sir Mark Prescott Bt) *led: rdn 2f out: drvn and hdd over 1f out: sn outpcd by wnr: styd on same pce and hld on for 2nd ins fnl f* **14/1**

5113 **3** *1/2* **Lily In Pink**[21] 5981 4-9-3 92 JamesDoyle 3 104+
(Jonathan Portman) *hld up in midfield: rdn and effrt ent fnl 2f: 8th and stl plenty to do over 1f out: styd on wl ins fnl f: wnt 3rd towards fin: no threat to wnr* **20/1**

65-2 **4** *3/4* **Jehannedarc (IRE)**[56] 4738 4-9-3 107 AntoineHamelin 1 102
(A De Royer-Dupre, France) *hld up in tch in midfield: rdn and effrt ent fnl 2f: chsd ldrs over 1f out: no threat to wnr but kpt on ins fnl f* **6/1**[2]

-113 **5** *3/4* **Khione**[53] 4848 3-8-9 90 KierenFallon 9 101
(Luca Cumani) *s.i.s and pushed along early: racd in last quartet: swtchd lft and effrt 4f out: hdwy to chse ldrs 2f out: no imp over 1f out: no threat to wnr but kpt on again fnl 100yds* **12/1**

2112 **6** *1 1/4* **Sequence (IRE)**[35] 5519 3-8-9 100 RichardHughes 13 99
(Sir Michael Stoute) *t.k.h: chsd ldrs: chsd ldr 3f out and sn rdn: no ex u.p over 1f out: lost 3rd and wknd ins fnl f* **6/1**[2]

2132 **7** *1 1/4* **Set To Music (IRE)**[53] 4848 4-9-6 105 JamieSpencer 10 100
(Michael Bell) *stdd after s: hld up in rr: hdwy 4f out: chsd ldrs and rdn 2f out: no ex and btn over 1f out: wknd ins fnl f* **8/1**

-031 **8** *12* **Bana Wu**[41] 5309 3-8-9 100 JimmyFortune 15 78
(Andrew Balding) *in tch in midfield: hdwy to chse ldrs and rdn 3f out: btn and wknd over 1f out: eased ins fnl f* **15/2**[3]

6254 **9** *5* **Qushchi**[5] 6492 4-9-3 90 (b) PaulHanagan 14 70
(William Jarvis) *hld up in midfield on outer: hdwy to chse ldrs 4f out: rdn over 2f out: sn btn: wl bhd fnl f* **20/1**

2 **10** *3* **Sohar**[75] 4103 4-9-3 79 NickyMackay 4 65
(James Toller) *carried rt after s and hmpd after 1f: hld up in rr: rdn over 4f out: wknd u.p 3f out: bhd fnl 2f* **50/1**

041 **11** *3* **Roxy Flyer (IRE)**[20] 6018 5-9-3 98 PatDobbs 7 60
(Amanda Perrett) *hld up in midfield: nt clr run and shuffled bk over 2f out: sn wknd* **20/1**

4321 **12** *21* **Kunegunda**[51] 4923 3-8-9 85 HayleyTurner 6 27
(James Fanshawe) *in tch tl lost pl over 3f out: bhd fnl 2f: eased fnl f: t.o* **20/1**

12/6 **13** *5* **Elas Diamond**[62] 4556 4-9-3 96 FrankieDettori 12 19
(Jeremy Noseda) *chsd ldr tl 3f out: sn dropped out: eased fr over 1f out: t.o* **12/1**

50 **14** *11* **Ahuqd (IRE)**[35] 5510 3-8-9 0 KirstyMilczarek 5
(Clive Brittain) *a in rr: rdn and struggling over 5f out: lost tch 3f out: t.o* **100/1**

2m 28.5s (-3.50) **Going Correction** -0.125s/f (Firm) **14** Ran SP% **117.7**
WFA 3 from 4yo+ 8lb
Speed ratings (Par 111): **106,104,104,103,103 102,101,93,90,88 86,72,68,61**
toteswingers 1&2 £19.10, 1&3 £14.10, 2&3 £57.80 CSF £48.46 TOTE £4.50: £1.80, £5.50, £4.80; EX 89.50 Trifecta £1196.90 Part won. Pool: £1,617.49 - 0.10 winning tickets..
Owner Lady Rothschild **Bred** Kincorth Investments Inc **Trained** Newmarket, Suffolk

FOCUS

The first two home are out of Group 1-winning race mares. The early gallop looked ordinary and the form has an autumnal feel, but it has been taken at face value. The first two contunue to improve.

NOTEBOOK

Gallipot ◆, easing in distance after a big effort in the Park Hill Stakes last time, proved that run wasn't a fluke with a third victory of the season. She is progressing with experience and one would imagine connections will try and get a Group victory with her next, whether that is this season or next year. (op 4-1, tchd 9-2 in places)

Albamara finished behind a couple she met here last time and was sweating, so her chance didn't appear obvious. However, she stayed on really nicely after leading and has a race of this nature within her capabilities if things work out for her. (op 22-1)

Lily In Pink has enjoyed a successful season over middle distances, and came home strongly after being caught one-paced when the tempo increased. (tchd 16-1)

Jehannedarc(IRE) came from a similar position to the third, but didn't have any change of gear when in the clear. She would have wanted a stiffer test. (tchd 5-1)

Khione ◆'s performance can be marked up as she wasn't going as well as others some way out and needed to be pulled wide to make her challenge. If remaining in training, she should only get better.

Sequence(IRE) raced a bit freely towards the head of affairs and didn't get home. (op 13-2)

Set To Music(IRE) was never quite getting on terms from midfield. (op 6-1)

6599 SOMERVILLE TATTERSALL STKS (GROUP 3) (C&G) 7f

3:40 (3:41) (Class 1) 2-Y-O

£22,684 (£8,600; £4,304; £2,144; £1,076; £540) **Stalls** High

Form RPR

11U1 **1** **Havana Gold (IRE)**[19] 6027 2-8-12 105 RichardHughes 5 107+
(Richard Hannon) *stdd and wnt rt s: in tch in last pair: swtchd lft and hdwy over 1f out: rdn and pressed ldrs over 1f out: led u.p ins fnl f: r.o wl and gng away at fin* **6/5**[1]

4123 **2** *1 1/2* **Well Acquainted (IRE)**[19] 6038 2-8-12 96 AdamKirby 3 103
(Clive Cox) *led: rdn 2f out: hrd pressed and battled on wl tl hdd ins fnl f: no ex but kpt on gamely to hold 2nd fnl 100yds* **9/2**[3]

12 **3** *nk* **Glean**[21] 5976 2-8-12 0 PatDobbs 1 102
(Richard Hannon) *hld up in tch in last pair: swtchd rt and effrt 2f out: drvn and ev ch over 1f out: no ex and styd on same pce fnl 100yds* **7/1**

14 **4** *1 1/4* **Ebn Arab (USA)**[36] 5488 2-8-12 0 PaulHanagan 2 99
(Charles Hills) *t.k.h: rdn and ev ch 2f out tl no ex ins fnl f: wknd towards fin* **7/2**[2]

1505 **5** *2 3/4* **Chilworth Icon**[26] 5833 2-9-1 103 MartinHarley 4 95
(Mick Channon) *squeezed for room leaving stalls: in tch: rdn and effrt 2f out: styd on same pce and no imp fnl f* **20/1**

24 **6** *1* **Canary Row (IRE)**[19] 6060 2-8-12 0 WilliamBuick 6 89
(P J Prendergast, Ire) *in tch: lost pl and sltly hmpd jst over 2f out: swtchd rt and rdn 2f out: no hdwy and wl hld after* **14/1**

3543 **7** *7* **Ocean Applause**[5] 6501 2-8-12 90 (b[1]) MichaelO'Connell 7 71
(John Ryan) *chsd ldrs: rdn over 2f out: wknd u.p over 1f out* **66/1**

1m 23.98s (-1.42) **Going Correction** -0.125s/f (Firm) **7** Ran SP% **111.3**
Speed ratings (Par 105): **103,101,100,99,96 95,87**
toteswingers 1&2 £2.20, 1&3 £2.30, 2&3 £3.50 CSF £6.50 TOTE £1.90: £1.60, £2.40; EX 6.90 Trifecta £24.40 Pool: £2,392.32 - 72.54 winning tickets..
Owner Qatar Racing Limited & CSH **Bred** Sir Eric Parker **Trained** East Everleigh, Wilts

FOCUS

The runners raced towards the nearside of the track, but away from the rail, and the pace looked fair without being anything out of the ordinary. The winner continues to progress but it's hard to rate this form any higher.

NOTEBOOK

Havana Gold(IRE), whose stable had won two of the previous three runnings, was unfortunate not to come into this unbeaten in four starts having been likely to win at Deauville two starts back before his saddle slipped. Ridden with plenty of confidence at the back of the field, he took a little time to pick up after being switched towards the stands' side over 2f from home, but the further he went the better he was going and he quickened up smartly to lead well inside the last. He is only one of several smart juveniles in the yard, but it's hard to knock a record like his and there should be further successes in him. He won't mind a return to 1m. (op 5-6 tchd 5-4)

Well Acquainted(IRE), who won his maiden on his only previous try over this trip, was ridden positively but he didn't look at all comfortable on the downhill run into the Dip, so under the circumstances he did very well to keep on for second. He is proving most consistent and a race like the Horris Hill could be a viable option for him. (op 6-1)

Glean ◆ probably didn't have the race run to suit when second of three at Salisbury on his second start and this was a better indication of his ability. Held up early like the winner, he challenged on the opposite flank to his stable companion and had every chance inside the last furlong. He still has scope and can find a nice race in due course. (op 11-1 tchd 6-1)

Ebn Arab(USA) had a few questions to answer having proved a disappointing second-favourite behind Dundonnell in the Acomb, but although he was always handy and had every chance until weakening in the closing stages here, he isn't fulfilling what seemed possible following his impressive York debut success. (op 9-2)

Chilworth Icon didn't pick up for pressure and continues to look held in Pattern company since winning a San Siro Group 3 in July. His penalty for that only makes things harder. (tchd 25-1)

Canary Row(IRE) was entitled to need his recent return from four months off at Leopardstown and a pair of seconds behind Dawn Approach in the spring was smart form, but he folded disappointingly under pressure and maybe this came too soon. (tchd 12-1 and 16-1)

Ocean Applause, beaten in a Wolverhampton maiden last time, was tried in blinkers but was still outclassed and is now 0-10.

6600 JOCKEY CLUB ROSE BOWL (LISTED RACE) 2m

4:15 (4:22) (Class 1) 3-Y-O+

£18,714 (£7,095; £3,550; £1,768; £887; £445) **Stalls** Centre

Form RPR

-300 **1** **Caucus**[98] 3293 5-9-3 104 WilliamBuick 12 108
(John Gosden) *racd in midfield: hdwy to chse ldrs 4f out: swtchd lft and rdn to chal over 1f out: led 1f out: clr and styd on strly fnl f: rdn out* **12/1**

0114 **2** *2 1/4* **Cavalryman**[33] 5599 6-9-6 115 FrankieDettori 9 108
(Saeed Bin Suroor) *hld up off the pce towards rr: stdy hdwy 5f out: swtchd rt and rdn to chse ldrs over 1f out: chsd wnr but no imp ins fnl f: hld on for 2nd cl home* **5/2**[1]

4203 **3** *hd* **Lost In The Moment (IRE)**[33] 5599 5-9-3 110 (p) SilvestreDeSousa 4 105
(Saeed Bin Suroor) *hld up off the pce towards rr: clsd 5f out: drvn 2f out: styd on u.p ins fnl f: no threat to wnr but pressing for 2nd cl home* **11/4**[2]

05/0 **4** *1 3/4* **Martyr**[13] 6197 7-9-3 96 RichardHughes 6 103
(George Baker) *led for 1f: chsd ldr after: jnd ldr on bit 2f out: led over 1f out: hdd and rdn 1f out: fnd little and wknd fnl 100yds* **25/1**

3352 **5** *2 1/4* **Chiberta King**[21] 5981 6-9-3 107 (p) JimmyFortune 11 100
(Andrew Balding) *chsd ldr tl led after 1f: clr 10f out: jnd and rdn 2f out: hdd over 1f out: wknd ins fnl f* **8/1**[3]

4200 **6** *2 1/2* **Aaim To Prosper (IRE)**[13] 6198 8-9-3 107 KierenFallon 13 97
(Brian Meehan) *chsd ldrs: rdn and effrt 3f out: outpcd over 2f out: plugged on same pce and hld fr over 1f out* **14/1**

34/- **7** *1* **Ocean's Minstrel**[712] 6926 6-9-3 86 DaraghO'Donohoe 8 96?
(John Ryan) *chsd ldrs: rdn 3f out: kpt on u.p tl edgd rt and btn over 1f out: plugged on* **100/1**

4034 **8** *2 1/2* **Berling (IRE)**[18] 6091 5-9-3 99 EddieAhern 7 93
(John Dunlop) *hld up off the pce in midfield: rdn and effrt over 2f out: no imp whn short of room and wknd over 1f out* **10/1**

1132 **9** *7* **Suzi's A Class Act**[9] 6349 4-8-12 79 (p) AdamBeschizza 5 80
(James Eustace) *hld up off the pce towards rr: rdn 4f out: wknd u.p 2f out* **33/1**

/00- **10** *20* **Darley Sun (IRE)**[348] 6857 6-9-3 102 MickaelBarzalona 10 61
(Saeed Bin Suroor) *stdd s: hld up off the pce in rr: effrt u.p 3f out: sn wknd: t.o* **10/1**

4-30 **11** *9* **Cracking Lass (IRE)**[14] 6163 5-8-12 99 TonyHamilton 2 45
(Richard Fahey) *hld up off the pce in rr: rdn and effrt over 3f out: sn wknd: t.o* **20/1**

16-1 **12** *25* **Astromagick**[126] 2412 4-8-12 77 DarryllHolland 3 15
(Mark H Tompkins) *racd in midfield: rdn and dropped to rr 4f out: lost tch over 2f out: t.o* **66/1**

215 **R** **Lordofthehouse (IRE)**[104] 3125 4-9-3 88 PaulHanagan 1
(William Haggas) *walked out of stalls and stopped* **14/1**

3m 23.04s (-7.46) **Going Correction** -0.125s/f (Firm) **13** Ran SP% **119.6**
Speed ratings (Par 111): **113,111,111,110,109 108,108,106,103,93 88,76,**
toteswingers 1&2 £8.40, 1&3 £7.60, 2&3 £2.30 CSF £40.47 TOTE £14.20: £4.30, £1.50, £1.80; EX 61.00 Trifecta £227.50 Pool: £2,588.91 - 8.42 winning tickets..
Owner Normandie Stud Ltd **Bred** Normandie Stud Ltd **Trained** Newmarket, Suffolk

FOCUS

A rather muddling race and the seventh limits the form to some extent. Pretty average form for the grade.

NOTEBOOK

Caucus, absent since finishing well beaten in the Ascot Gold Cup, sat in behind going strongly and was patiently ridden to get on terms. William Buick bided his time when at the head of affairs but the race was soon over once the jockey sent his mount on. The gelding has an entry in the Long Distance Cup, but isn't the sort of horse who can be called reliable, so it's not easy to get excited about his chances for that at this stage. (op 11-1 tchd 14-1)

Cavalryman has rediscovered some form in 2012 and he appeared to be going as well as the winner about 1f out, but Frankie Dettori delayed his effort for a bit too long and couldn't get to Caucus. The Godolphin first-string was second best on the day, but almost got mugged for runner's-up spot by Lost In The Moment. He did nothing to harm his chances of heading to Australia now for the Melbourne Cup. (tchd 11-4)

Lost In The Moment(IRE) kept staying on and is also likely to head to Australia. (op 3-1, tchd 10-3 in a place)

Martyr ◆, probably the biggest eyecatcher with a view to the near future, was fifth in this race back in 2010 when under the care of another trainer. Richard Hughes had the gelding well placed behind the early pacesetter and would have gone even closer had the rider pressed on when catching Chilberta King. Possibly the horse was tired and the jockey was trying to hold him together, but this was a good trial for the Cesarewitch and he can prove to be a leading player for that as long as he stays another 2f. (op 22-1 tchd 28-1)

Chiberta King, second in this last season, has held his form quite well and was offered an easy lead from the start here. Jimmy Fortune looked to do quite a lot right while in that position, slowing and quickening the pace at various stages, but the gelding just wasn't good enough on the day and ended up being passed by four rivals in the final stages. (op 13-2)

Aaim To Prosper(IRE) ◆ has a fair record at this course and ran like a horse in need of further, as he was doing his best work at the end. He is also in the Cesarewitch, which he won in 2010, and will appreciate the extra distance. (op 16-1 tchd 18-1)

Ocean's Minstrel, off since finishing fourth to Aaim To Prosper in the 2010 Cesarewitch, ran a blinder but the bounce factor has to come into consideration after that lengthy absence. (op 66-1)

Astromagick Official explanation: jockey said that the filly moved poorly

6601 ARKLE FINANCE H'CAP 1m

4:50 (4:56) (Class 3) (0-95,94) 3-Y-O+

£7,470 (£2,236; £1,118; £559; £279; £140) **Stalls** High

Form				RPR
2130	**1**		**Basseterre (IRE)**[13] 6205 3-8-8 **82** KierenFallon 2 *(Charles Hills) in tch in midfield: rdn and hdwy 2f out: ev ch ent fnl f: led ins fnl f: kpt on wl: rdn out* **4/1**[2]	90
0030	**2**	*nk*	**Boogie Shoes**[20] 6010 4-9-10 **94** (b[1]) NeilCallan 3 *(Roger Varian) t.k.h early: chsd ldrs: clsd on ldr and swtchd lft over 3f out: chsd ldr over 2f out: edgd rt and led over 1f out: hdd ins fnl f: kpt on u.p* **8/1**	101
5260	**3**	*½*	**Directorship**[82] 3878 6-9-8 **92** GeorgeBaker 9 *(Patrick Chamings) stdd s: hld up in rr: rdn and effrt 2f out: hdwy over 1f out: chsd ldng pair and edgd lft ins fnl f: r.o but nt rch ldng pair* **8/1**	98
5060	**4**	*1 ¾*	**Norse Blues**[12] 6242 4-9-4 **88** JamesDoyle 8 *(Sylvester Kirk) chsd ldrs: wnt 2nd over 3f out tl over 2f out: drvn and unable qck over 1f out: swtchd rt and styd on same pce ins fnl f: sltly hmpd wl ins fnl f* **6/1**	90
2534	**5**	*½*	**Crown Counsel (IRE)**[5] 6494 4-9-0 **84** SilvestreDeSousa 4 *(Mark Johnston) chsd clr ldr tl led over 3f out: rdn: edgd rt and hdd over 1f out: no ex ins fnl f: styd on same pce* **7/2**[1]	85
2000	**6**	*1*	**Mawaakef (IRE)**[47] 5075 4-9-7 **91** DarryllHolland 7 *(J R Jenkins) hld up in tch: effrt u.p 2f out: drvn and styd on same pce fr over 1f out* **20/1**	89
0410	**7**	*nse*	**Chapter And Verse (IRE)**[19] 6036 6-8-5 **80** oh1 MichaelJMMurphy[(5)] 5 *(Mike Murphy) hld up in tch: hdwy to chse ldrs 3f out: rdn and unable qck wl over 1f out: carried rt 1f out: one pce fnl f* **10/1**	78
016-	**8**	*3 ½*	**Ocean Bay**[300] 7606 4-9-4 **88** BrettDoyle 11 *(John Ryan) in tch: rdn and effrt over 2f out: wknd u.p over 1f out* **50/1**	78
4400	**9**	*1 ½*	**Mullins Way (USA)**[23] 5914 4-8-10 **80** J-PGuillambert 10 *(Jo Hughes) stdd s: a in rr: rdn and short-lived effrt over 2f out: wknd u.p wl over 1f out* **33/1**	67
3110	**10**	*5*	**Hefner (IRE)**[56] 4735 3-9-1 **89** RichardHughes 6 *(Richard Hannon) in tch in midfield: rdn and struggling over 2f out: wknd wl over 1f out* **5/1**[3]	64
0	**11**	*64*	**Swerve**[35] 5520 3-9-0 **88** (p) MartinHarley 1 *(Alan McCabe) taken down early and v free to post: led and sn clr: hdd over 3f out and immediately dropped out: t.o fnl 2f* **40/1**	

1m 37.14s (-1.46) **Going Correction** -0.125s/f (Firm)
WFA 3 from 4yo+ 4lb **11** Ran SP% **116.6**
Speed ratings (Par 107): **102,101,101,99,98 97,97,94,92,87 23**
toteswingers 1&2 £5.90, 1&3 £9.40, 2&3 £10.10 CSF £34.29 CT £249.98 TOTE £5.20: £1.20, £3.60, £3.50; EX 26.00 Trifecta £242.50 Pool: £2,130.53 - 6.50 winning tickets..

Owner H R Mould **Bred** D G Hardisty Bloodstock **Trained** Lambourn, Berks

FOCUS

A decent handicap run at a furious early pace. The field split into two for the first half of the contest with three racing wide of the others down the centre of the track. They included the errant Swerve, but the other pair were the first two home. The time was only ordinary and the form is rated around the second and third.

NOTEBOOK

Basseterre(IRE) finished unplaced when favourite at Sandown last time, but might just have needed it following a short break and he was back on form here. Having tracked the pace out towards the centre of the track, he was produced with his effort widest and showed an admirable attitude under pressure despite hanging away to his left late on. He didn't race at two, so may still have a bit of scope and he always has the option of going back on to Polytrack. (tchd 7-2)

Boogie Shoes, 2lb higher than when gaining his last success in this race last year, was tried in blinkers having failed to improve for the fitting of a hood and this was much more like it. Always handy out in the centre of the track, he was produced to lead over a furlong out but had been passed by the winner when done few favours by him nearing the line. This trip seems to suit him best, but much depends on whether he continues to respond to the headgear. (op 7-1 tchd 9-1)

Directorship did well to finish where he did considering where he came from, but he was reported to have bled when running poorly on his last start at Sandown 82 days earlier, which always has to be a concern, and remains 6lb above his last winning mark. (op 17-2 tchd 9-1)

Norse Blues, unplaced all seven starts since making a successful reappearance off 3lb lower in the Spring Mile, didn't enjoy much room throughout the last furlong and would have finished a bit closer otherwise. (op 8-1)

Crown Counsel(IRE), ignoring Swerve, effectively tried to make all against the stands' rail, but that was probably not the place to be and he had run his race by the furlong pole. He is now on a losing run of 21.

Chapter And Verse(IRE), 1lb wrong, was off a 7lb lower mark than on the AW and raced close to the pace, but he didn't get home. He is just 2-24 on turf and still doesn't look that well handicapped on the surface. (op 15-2)

Ocean Bay, making his handicap debut, travelled well for a long way against the stands' rail and should come on for this first run in 300 days. (op 66-1)

Hefner(IRE), who ran poorly over 1m2f at Goodwood last time, had won his two previous starts over this trip and was just 2lb higher than for the second of those, but unfortunately he threw in another stinker. The trainer's representative reported that the colt was unsuited by the track. Official explanation: jockey said that the colt was unsuited by the track (op 6-1 tchd 13-2)

Swerve bolted on the way to the start and did the same thing for the first half of the race before falling in a hole. Official explanation: jockey said that the filly bolted to post and ran too freely (op 33-1 tchd 50-1)

6602 BRITISH STALLION STUDS SUPPORTING BRITISH RACING EBF FILLIES' H'CAP 6f

5:25 (5:25) (Class 2) (0-100,98) 3-Y-O+

£9,960 (£2,982; £1,491; £745; £372; £187) **Stalls** High

Form				RPR
2-21	**1**		**Hezmah**[106] 3049 4-9-1 **92** PaulHanagan 1 *(John Gosden) hld up in tch: hdwy towards centre 1/2-way: rdn to ld 1f out: kpt edging lft but styd on wl fnl f* **10/3**[2]	106
3120	**2**	*1*	**Ladyship**[35] 5520 3-8-13 **92** FrankieDettori 6 *(Sir Michael Stoute) t.k.h: hld up in tch: rdn and effrt to press ldrs over 1f out: chsd wnr and carried lft fnl f: styd on same pce* **2/1**[1]	102
2-14	**3**	*2*	**Swan Song**[55] 4765 3-8-6 **85** [1] LiamKeniry 5 *(Andrew Balding) w ldr tl rdn to ld wl over 1f out: hdd 1f out: styng on same pce and btn whn sltly hmpd and swtchd rt ins fnl f: wknd towards fin* **11/2**[3]	89
000	**4**	*½*	**Haamaat (IRE)**[13] 6201 4-8-11 **88** TadhgO'Shea 9 *(William Haggas) stdd s: t.k.h: hld up in rr: rdn and hdwy but edging rt over 1f out: kpt on ins fnl f: nt rch ldrs* **14/1**	90
5400	**5**	*2 ½*	**Duchess Dora (IRE)**[75] 4113 5-9-7 **98** HayleyTurner 4 *(David Simcock) stdd s: hld up in tch in rr: rdn and hdwy over 1f out: edgd rt and no imp 1f out: wknd ins fnl f* **16/1**	92
1045	**6**	*½*	**La Fortunata**[16] 6116 5-8-8 **90** CharlesBishop[(5)] 10 *(Eve Johnson Houghton) led: rdn and hdd wl over 1f out: wknd fnl f* **12/1**	83
3103	**7**	*3*	**Fillionaire**[11] 6285 3-8-2 **84** oh2 RyanPowell[(3)] 7 *(Mick Channon) in tch: rdn and unable qck wl over 1f out: wknd 1f out* **25/1**	67
620	**8**	*13*	**Fair Value (IRE)**[19] 6026 4-9-1 **92** NeilCallan 2 *(Simon Dow) plld hrd: chsd ldrs: rdn and no ex over 1f out: fdd fnl f* **16/1**	34
4220	**9**	*8*	**Place In My Heart**[55] 4765 3-9-0 **93** RichardHughes 8 *(George Baker) in tch in last trio: no hdwy wl over 1f out: sn btn and eased fnl f* **13/2**	

1m 11.17s (-1.03) **Going Correction** -0.125s/f (Firm)
WFA 3 from 4yo+ 2lb **9** Ran SP% **115.1**
Speed ratings (Par 96): **101,99,97,96,93 92,88,71,60**
toteswingers 1&2 £2.10, 1&3 £3.10, 2&3 £3.20 CSF £10.35 CT £34.71 TOTE £4.80: £1.60, £1.10, £1.40; EX 9.50 Trifecta £35.10 Pool: £2,117.34 - 44.54 winning tickets..
Owner Hamdan Al Maktoum **Bred** Andrew Buxton **Trained** Newmarket, Suffolk

FOCUS

A good fillies' sprint where, as had been proved during the card, it was an advantage to race towards the centre of the course early. The form has been rated slightly on the positive side.

NOTEBOOK

Hezmah ◆, absent since winning at Yarmouth in mid-June, was widest of all after the leaving the stalls slowly but picked up in taking style despite edging left when asked to quicken. Although she was no doubt fit enough after a break, she should come on for this and can hold her own at a higher level. There is a 6f Listed race in October at this track that could be ideal for her. (op 7-2 tchd 4-1)

Ladyship ◆ wasn't disgraced over 7f at York, but the drop in distance looked sure to suit and she ran up to her best without being quite good enough. (op 5-2)

Swan Song ◆, up in trip and now racing in a hood, played up a little before going into the stalls and then when in them, but she showed good speed once racing, away from the rail, and wasn't disgraced. A drop back to 5f won't cause her any issues. (op 9-2)

Haamaat(IRE) was in rear towards the stands' side before making good late ground.

Duchess Dora(IRE) ◆, making her debut for David Simcock without the visor she wore on her final start for John Quinn, has done virtually all of her racing over 5f and shaped as though this run can be improved upon. (tchd 20-1)

Place In My Heart had valid excuses for her moderate effort at Goodwood last time and Richard Hughes reported that the filly lost her action this time. Official explanation: jockey said reported that the filly lost her action (op 6-1)

T/Jkpt: £11,833.30 to a £1 stake. Pool: £25,000.0 - 1.50 winning tickets T/Plt: £23.90 to a £1 stake. Pool: £109,898.57 - 3,351.29 winning tickets T/Qpdt: £13.50 to a £1 stake. Pool: £5,704.06 - 310.55 winning tickets SP

6403 PONTEFRACT (L-H)

Thursday, September 27

OFFICIAL GOING: Soft (6.9)

Wind: Light half behind Weather: Cloudy

6603 IRISH STALLION FARMS EBF STRAWBERRY HILL MAIDEN STKS 6f

2:20 (2:24) (Class 4) 2-Y-O **£4,398** (£1,309; £654; £327) **Stalls** Low

Form				RPR
0	**1**		**Surge Ahead (IRE)**[20] 6015 2-9-3 0 DanielTudhope 2 *(Ed Walker) mde all: rdn clr over 1f out: styd on wl* **7/2**[2]	75+
33	**2**	*1 ¾*	**Loch Moy**[17] 6099 2-9-3 0 FrederikTylicki 3 *(Richard Fahey) trckd ldrs: effrt on inner and edgd lft 2f out: sn rdn to chse wnr over 1f out: drvn and no imp fnl f* **7/4**[1]	70
24	**3**	*hd*	**Flawless Beauty**[34] 5551 2-8-12 0 JimmyQuinn 9 *(Hugo Palmer) trckd ldrs: hdwy on outer over 2f out: rdn to chse ldng pair over 1f out: drvn and kpt on same pce fnl f* **4/1**[3]	64
0	**4**	*3 ¾*	**Antonius**[17] 6099 2-9-3 0 TomEaves 5 *(Linda Stubbs) cl up: rdn along over 2f out: wknd appr fnl f* **14/1**	58
60	**5**	*3*	**Mizyen (IRE)**[16] 6114 2-9-3 0 PaulMulrennan 7 *(James Tate) in tch: effrt over 2f out: sn rdn and no hdwy* **14/1**	49
	6	*2 ¼*	**Chocolate Block (IRE)** 2-8-12 0 PhillipMakin 6 *(William Haggas) dwlt and in rr tl sme late hdwy* **6/1**	37
	7	*½*	**Yorkshireman (IRE)** 2-9-3 0 RobertWinston 1 *(David Brown) sn trcking wnr on inner: rdn along whn n.m.r 2f out: sn wknd* **16/1**	47+
06	**8**	*5*	**Multifact**[19] 6042 2-8-10 0 ConnorNichol[(7)] 8 *(Michael Dods) t.k.h: in tch on outer: rdn along wl over 2f out: sn wknd* **50/1**	26
	9	*¾*	**Spats Colombo** 2-9-3 0 PJMcDonald 4 *(Micky Hammond) sn outpcd and a in rr* **33/1**	24

1m 20.11s (3.21) **Going Correction** +0.375s/f (Good) **9** Ran SP% **117.0**
Speed ratings (Par 97): **93,90,90,85,81 78,77,71,70**
toteswingers 1&2 £2.70, 1&3 £3.40, 2&3 £2.00 CSF £10.16 TOTE £5.00: £1.30, £1.20, £1.60; EX 12.50.
Owner Khalifa Dasmal **Bred** Skymarc Farm **Trained** Newmarket, Suffolk

FOCUS

Robert Winston and Jimmy Quinn felt the ground was "soft" and "heavy" respectively. Few got into this from off the pace in what was an average maiden. The standard is set around the runner-up, the time and the race averages.

NOTEBOOK

Surge Ahead(IRE), green but not without promise in a 6f Kempton maiden on his debut, knew much more this time and always looked to be bossing the opposition. The ground was clearly not a bother and he's a promising type with nurseries in mind. (tchd 9-2)

Loch Moy has run to a similar level on each of his three starts, keeping on at the one pace having stuck to the inside throughout. He's very much bred for 7f/1m and may up his game once sent into nurseries. (op 5-2)

Flawless Beauty has still to match her debut form, but she coped well enough with the ground and again showed enough to suggest she'll be winning races at the right level. (op 10-3)

Antoniusstepped up on his debut effort, getting closer to Loch Moy this time, and will be qualified for a mark following another run. (op 11-1)

Mizyen(IRE) was never involved but now has the option of nurseries. (tchd 12-1)

Chocolate Block(IRE), a half-sister to 5f winner Possible, as well as point/hurdle winner Surprise Us, wasn't the best away and showed distinct signs of greenness. She can leave this form behind on faster ground. (op 10-1)

6604 BHEST ST IGNATIUS CATHOLIC PRIMARY SCHOOL FILLIES' NURSERY — 1m 4y

2:55 (2:55) (Class 4) (0-85,76) 2-Y-O — **£3,428** (£1,020; £509; £254) **Stalls** Low

Form				RPR
320	**1**		**Mad Jazz**[12] 6247 2-8-8 **63** ... BarryMcHugh 6	65
			(Tony Coyle) *led 1f: cl up on inner: hdd and pushed along over 2f out: rdn and cl up wl over 1f out: drvn and rallied ins fnl f: styd on to ld nr line* **15/8**[1]	
3335	**2**	*nse*	**Elegant In Silk (USA)**[26] 5836 2-9-2 **71** ... JoeFanning 4	73
			(William Haggas) *led 1f: cl up: led again over 2f out: rdn wl over 1f out: slt ld whn drvn and edgd lft ins fnl f: hdd and no ex nr line* **11/4**[2]	
0465	**3**	*5*	**Inchy Coo**[16] 6121 2-8-6 **61** ... DuranFentiman 5	53
			(Tim Easterby) *trckd ldrs: rdn along and outpcd 3f out: sn swtchd to inner: hdwy wl over 1f out: rdn and ch appr fnl f: sn one pce* **9/1**	
4064	**4**	*3 1/4*	**Glen Ginnie (IRE)**[12] 6253 2-8-8 **63** ... RobertWinston 2	48
			(Charles Hills) *trckd ldng pair: rdn along over 2f out: sn one pce* **11/2**	
2230	**5**	*12*	**Royal Steps (IRE)**[14] 6160 2-9-7 **76** ... (b[1]) FrederikTylicki 1	33
			(James Tate) *t.k.h: hld up in rr: hdwy on outer 3f out: rdn along 2f out: sn wknd* **7/2**[3]	

1m 51.29s (5.39) **Going Correction** +0.375s/f (Good) **5** Ran SP% **109.1**

Speed ratings (Par 94): **88,87,82,79,67**

CSF £7.11 TOTE £2.40: £1.70, £1.70; EX 7.40.

Owner Chris Green & Tony Coyle **Bred** Usk Valley Stud **Trained** Norton, N Yorks

■ Stewards' Enquiry : Joe Fanning two-day ban: use of whip (11-12 Oct)

FOCUS

All bar one came down the middle of the track once in line for home in this modest nursery. The front pair drew clear and both produced minor personal bests.

NOTEBOOK

Mad Jazz just edged it in a head-bobber. Below par at Doncaster the time before, the return to soft ground was a help to this tough filly but she may prove vulnerable if given too much of a rise. Official explanation: trainer's said, regarding the apparent improvement of form, that the filly was better suited by the soft ground (op 11-4)

Elegant In Silk(USA) travelled best and looked the likely winner turning in, but she gave a little flash of the tail under pressure and appeared not to be concentrating in front, ultimately rallying once headed to just miss out. This ground seems to suit her quite well and it would be no surprise to see headgear applied at some stage in order to help her concentrate. (tchd 9-4)

Inchy Coo was the sole runner to stick to the inside, but she wouldn't have been good enough either way. She's now 0-10. (op 15-2 tchd 10-1)

Glen Ginnie(IRE) can be given another chance on better ground. (tchd 5-1 and 6-1)

Royal Steps(IRE) ran poorly in the first-time blinkers on ground that would have been too soft. (op 11-4)

6605 COMEDY CURRY NIGHT ON FRIDAY 5TH OCTOBER H'CAP — 5f

3:30 (3:30) (Class 5) (0-75,75) 3-Y-O+ — **£2,264** (£673; £336; £168) **Stalls** Low

Form				RPR
0560	**1**		**Kellys Eye (IRE)**[31] 5674 5-9-2 **70** ... RobertWinston 3	79
			(David Brown) *trckd ldrs: hdwy and cl up 2f out: rdn to ld over 1f out: drvn ins fnl f: kpt on wl towards fin* **9/4**[1]	
2110	**2**	*nk*	**Sunny Side Up (IRE)**[20] 6006 3-8-13 **75** ... LauraBarry(7) 6	83
			(Richard Fahey) *hld up towards rr: hdwy 2f out: swtchd rt and rdn over 1f out: styd on wl fnl f* **13/2**[3]	
0220	**3**	*hd*	**Phoenix Clubs (IRE)**[16] 6123 3-9-1 **70** ... BarryMcHugh 2	77
			(Paul Midgley) *trckd ldrs on inner: hdwy 2f out: rdn to chal ent fnl f: sn drvn and ev ch tl no ex towards fin* **5/1**[2]	
5532	**4**	*3*	**Tuibama (IRE)**[29] 5740 3-8-7 **62** ... (p) RoystonFfrench 1	58
			(Tracy Waggott) *led: rdn along and jnd wl over 1f out: sn hdd & wknd fnl f* **17/2**	
1056	**5**	*nk*	**Mercers Row**[41] 5298 5-8-13 **74** ... GemmaTutty(7) 4	69
			(Karen Tutty) *chsd ldr: rdn along over 2f out: grad wknd* **8/1**	
500	**6**	*nk*	**Red Roar (IRE)**[29] 5737 5-8-10 **64** ... PaulMulrennan 7	58
			(Alan Berry) *a in rr* **14/1**	
-000	**7**	*3 3/4*	**Captain Royale (IRE)**[12] 6260 7-9-0 **68** ... (p) DaleSwift 5	49
			(Tracy Waggott) *chsd ldng pair: rdn along over 2f out: sn wknd* **13/2**[3]	
5562	**8**	*4*	**Bronze Beau**[8] 6358 5-9-7 **75** ... (tp) JamesSullivan 8	41
			(Linda Stubbs) *chsd ldrs: rdn along 2f out: sn wknd* **8/1**	

1m 5.81s (2.51) **Going Correction** +0.375s/f (Good)

WFA 3 from 5yo+ 1lb **8** Ran SP% **113.5**

Speed ratings (Par 103): **94,93,93,88,87 87,81,75**

toteswingers 1&2 £4.50, 1&3 £4.10, 2&3 £3.40 CSF £16.89 CT £65.61 TOTE £3.10: £1.60, £1.70, £1.90; EX 15.80.

Owner Ron Hull **Bred** Michael Downey & Roalso Ltd **Trained** Averham Park, Notts

FOCUS

Plenty of pace on early in this sprint and the first two again came more down the middle in the straight. The winner was well in on his old form and this was still 10lb off last year's form.

Bronze Beau Official explanation: jockey said that the gelding missed the break

6606 SIMON SCROPE DALBY SCREW-DRIVER H'CAP — 1m 2f 6y

4:05 (4:05) (Class 2) (0-105,96) 3-Y-O+ — **£10,271** (£3,075; £1,537; £768) **Stalls** Low

Form				RPR
2220	**1**		**Las Verglas Star (IRE)**[36] 5492 4-9-3 **88** ... FrederikTylicki 3	97
			(Richard Fahey) *trckd ldr: effrt 2f out: rdn over 1f out: styd on to chal ent fnl f: sn led and edgd lft: kpt on strly* **11/4**[2]	
341	**2**	*2 1/2*	**Little Rocky**[76] 4060 4-9-5 **90** ... PhillipMakin 1	94
			(David Simcock) *led: rdn along 2f out: drvn and jnd ent fnl f: sn hdd and one pce* **13/8**[1]	
0000	**3**	*1*	**Sirvino**[67] 4365 7-9-4 **94** ... LMcNiff(5) 2	96
			(David Barron) *trckd ldng pair: effrt over 2f out: sn rdn along and no imp appr fnl f* **11/4**[2]	
5112	**4**	*14*	**Kalk Bay (IRE)**[36] 5492 5-9-2 **87** ... (t) PaulMulrennan 5	61
			(Michael Easterby) *hld up in rr: hdwy over 2f out: rdn along wl over 1f out: sn wknd* **4/1**[3]	

2m 15.69s (1.99) **Going Correction** +0.375s/f (Good) **4** Ran SP% **111.4**

Speed ratings (Par 109): **107,105,104,93**

CSF £7.83 TOTE £4.40; EX 8.20.

Owner CBWS Partnership **Bred** Brendan Holland And P Connell **Trained** Musley Bank, N Yorks

FOCUS

They appeared to go a fair enough gallop considering the small field, but still not form to put much faith in. The winner posted a small personal best.

NOTEBOOK

Las Verglas Star(IRE) was always well positioned and got nicely on top late on, bouncing back from a modest effort on ground that was too quick at York. He'll be up to a career-high now, but at least conditions have come in his favour. (op 4-1)

Little Rocky, off since making all from 4lb lower at Newbury in July, had everything go smoothly from the front, so it was disappointing to see him so readily swept aside. He's entitled to come on for it, but does need to improve to win from this mark. (op 15-8 tchd 2-1)

Sirvino, who was trotted up beforehand, was unable to reverse recent Ascot form with the winner, perhaps finding the ground too soft. (op 9-4 tchd 3-1)

Kalk Bay(IRE) had more to prove on the ground than most and failed to run to anything like his recent best. (op 7-2 tchd 3-1)

6607 BRITISH STALLION STUDS EBF FRIER WOOD MAIDEN STKS — 1m 4y

4:40 (4:41) (Class 4) 2-Y-O — **£4,398** (£1,309; £654; £327) **Stalls** Low

Form				RPR
0	**1**		**Pearl Reward (USA)**[128] 2376 2-9-3 0 ... HarryBentley 2	89+
			(Stuart Williams) *trckd ldrs: smooth hdwy to ld 2f out: sn qcknd clr: easily* **11/4**[1]	
04	**2**	*8*	**Dali's Lover (IRE)**[34] 5550 2-8-12 0 ... RobertWinston 4	66
			(Charles Hills) *trckd ldrs: effrt over 2f out: sn rdn: tk 2nd ins fnl f: no ch w wnr* **7/2**[2]	
003	**3**	*1/2*	**Barefoot Sandy**[8] 6355 2-8-12 0 ... BarryMcHugh 3	65
			(Tony Coyle) *in tch on inner: hdwy over 3f out: chsd ldrs 2f out: sn rdn to chse wnr over 1f out: kpt on same pce* **12/1**	
	4	*4*	**Mister Impatience** 2-9-3 0 ... FrederikTylicki 9	62+
			(Mark Johnston) *trckd ldrs: pushed along: green and lost pl after 1 1/2f: towards rr: hdwy 2f out: sn rdn and kpt on: nvr nr ldrs* **5/1**[3]	
0	**5**	*4 1/2*	**Flying Nellie**[21] 5962 2-8-12 0 ... AndrewElliott 6	47
			(Tom Tate) *led: rdn along over 3f out: hdd 2f out and grad wknd* **40/1**	
	6	*2 3/4*	**War Lord (IRE)** 2-9-3 0 ... DanielTudhope 5	46
			(David O'Meara) *midfield: hdwy 3f out: chsd ldrs 2f out: sn rdn and no imp* **7/1**	
650	**7**	*4*	**Trymyluck**[63] 4494 2-8-12 61 ... MickyFenton 7	32
			(Pam Sly) *chsd ldrs on outer: rdn along 4f out: sn wknd* **20/1**	
60	**8**	*3 1/4*	**Cape's Best**[30] 5704 2-9-3 0 ... PaulMulrennan 10	30
			(James Tate) *cl up: rdn along 3f out: wknd fnl 2f* **12/1**	
	9	*23*	**Online** 2-9-3 0 ... RoystonFfrench 8	
			(Tracy Waggott) *s.i.s: a in rr: bhd fr 1/2-way* **40/1**	
	10	*12*	**Gabrial The Tyrant (IRE)** 2-9-3 0 ... JoeFanning 1	
			(Mark Johnston) *s.i.s: a in rr* **11/2**	

1m 48.84s (2.94) **Going Correction** +0.375s/f (Good) **10** Ran SP% **118.5**

Speed ratings (Par 97): **100,92,91,87,83 80,76,73,50,38**

toteswingers 1&2 £3.70, 1&3 £9.00, 2&3 £4.80 CSF £12.30 TOTE £3.80: £1.70, £1.10, £5.10; EX 17.30.

Owner Pearl Bloodstock Ltd **Bred** Nina Gardner & Elizabeth Merryman **Trained** Newmarket, Suffolk

FOCUS

Little depth to this maiden. The winner showed massive improvement but it looked no fluke.

NOTEBOOK

Pearl Reward(USA), who was gambled beforehand, put in a taking performance. Well beaten at 40-1 on his 6f Nottingham debut 128 days earlier, the much softer ground here was clearly not a bother and the way he quickly asserted before powering clear was impressive. It will be interesting to see what mark he's given with nurseries in mind and there should be more to come. (op 5-1 tchd 11-2)

Dali's Lover(IRE) has shown enough to suggest she'll win races once switched to nurseries. (op 10-3 tchd 3-1)

Barefoot Sandy has shown distinct promise on contrasting ground the last twice and is another nursery type. (op 8-1)

Mister Impatience, a brother to useful 1m2f/1m3f Flat/hurdles winner Harry Tricker, looked in need of the experience and should improve for better ground. (op 6-1 tchd 9-2)

Flying Nellie showed more than on her debut and is probably a middle-distance prospect for next year.

Gabrial The Tyrant(IRE), a half-brother to Group-placed 1m4f winner Lady's Secret, was soon toiling, looking green, but many from this yard often improve a great deal from runs one to two. (op 7-2 tchd 6-1)

6608 PONTEFRACT PARK APPRENTICE H'CAP — 1m 4f 8y

5:15 (5:15) (Class 5) (0-75,72) 3-Y-O+ — **£2,264** (£673; £336; £168) **Stalls** Low

Form				RPR
001	**1**		**Gosforth Park**[31] 5672 6-8-11 **63** ... KennyCorbett(7) 2	73
			(Mel Brittain) *trckd ldng pair: hdwy and cl up 3f out: chsd ldr 2f out: sn rdn and styd on to chal ent fnl f: led last 100yds* **8/1**	
0112	**2**	*nk*	**Pertuis (IRE)**[10] 6315 6-8-11 **63** ... KatieDowson(7) 5	72
			(Micky Hammond) *hld up in tch stdy hdwy over 4f out: led over 2f out and sn clr: rdn and jnd ent fnl f: sn drvn: hdd last 100yds: no ex towards fin* **6/1**	
4103	**3**	*20*	**Sedgwick**[18] 6076 10-9-9 **68** ... ShirleyTeasdale 3	45
			(Shaun Harris) *hld up in tch: hdwy to chse ldng pair 3f out: rdn along 2f out: sn no imp* **7/1**	
2030	**4**	*1 1/4*	**Harare**[26] 5824 11-9-0 **62** ... (v) GemmaTutty(3) 8	37
			(Karen Tutty) *in rr: outpcd and bhd after 3f: hdwy 3f out: styd on fnl 2f: nrst fin* **25/1**	
0514	**5**	*5*	**Hyperlink (IRE)**[14] 6181 3-9-4 **71** ... GeorgeChaloner 4	38
			(Mark Johnston) *cl up: led over 4f out: hdd wl over 2f out and sn wknd* **7/2**[2]	
1350	**6**	*5*	**Mohawk Ridge**[19] 6045 6-9-6 **70** ... (p) ConnorNichol(5) 6	29
			(Michael Dods) *hld up towards rr: effrt over 3f out: sn rdn along and nvr a factor* **5/1**[3]	
3100	**7**	*22*	**Dispol Diva**[49] 5012 6-9-2 **61** ... (v) NedCurtis 7	
			(Paul Midgley) *chsd ldrs: rdn along 1/2-way: sn wknd* **16/1**	

1220 **8** *91* **Honest Deal**[19] 6045 4-9-13 **72**.. JasonHart 1
(Alan Swinbank) *t.k.h: sn led and set str pce: rdn along and hdd over 4f out: wknd qckly* **5/2**[1]
2m 45.33s (4.53) **Going Correction** +0.375s/f (Good)
WFA 3 from 4yo+ 8lb **8** Ran SP% **115.1**
Speed ratings (Par 103): **99,98,85,84,81 77,63,2**
toteswingers 1&2 £4.20, 1&3 £6.30, 2&3 £5.50 CSF £55.28 CT £354.37 TOTE £9.70: £2.30, £2.00, £2.60; EX 32.30.
Owner Mel Brittain **Bred** C A Cyzer **Trained** Warthill, N Yorks
■ A winner for Kenny Corbett on his first ride.
FOCUS
The pace appeared quite generous given the conditions and the front pair drew well clear. A personal best from the winner.
Honest Deal Official explanation: trainer said that the gelding ran too freely in the early stages.
T/Plt: £96.20 to a £1 stake. Pool: £49,013.12 - 371.87 winning tickets T/Qpdt: £37.70 to a £1 stake. Pool: £3000.40 - 58.80 winning tickets JR

6496 WOLVERHAMPTON (A.W) (L-H)
Thursday, September 27

OFFICIAL GOING: Standard
Wind: Light behind Weather: Cloudy

6609 32RED MEDIAN AUCTION MAIDEN STKS 5f 216y(P)
5:45 (5:48) (Class 5) 2-Y-O **£2,264** (£673; £336; £168) **Stalls** Low

Form RPR
1 **Line Of Reason (IRE)** 2-9-3 0.. GrahamLee 1 73+
(David Simcock) *a.p: chsd ldr over 1f out: sn rdn: r.o to ld wl ins fnl f* **6/1**[3]
2260 **2** *¾* **Puteri Nur Laila (IRE)**[14] 6160 2-8-12 64.....................(b[1]) MartinLane 10 66
(Paul Cole) *led 5f out: rdn over 1f out: hdd wl ins fnl f* **20/1**
2 **3** *hd* **Secret Missile**[10] 6320 2-9-3 0.................................... StevieDonohoe 12 70
(William Muir) *chsd ldrs: rdn over 1f out: edgd lft ins fnl f: r.o* **3/1**[1]
4 *3 ¼* **Al Udeid (IRE)** 2-9-3 0.. AmyRyan 3 61+
(Kevin Ryan) *sn led: hdd 5f out: chsd ldrs: rdn over 1f out: styd on same pce fnl f* **9/2**[2]
02 **5** *hd* **Compton Silver**[19] 6054 2-9-3 0.. JimCrowley 2 60
(Hans Adielsson) *prom: chsd ldr over 3f out: ev ch over 2f out: styd on same pce fnl f* **9/1**
6 *¾* **Opus Cactus (USA)** 2-8-12 0... AndreaAtzeni 5 53
(Marco Botti) *hld up: hdwy over 1f out: styd on same pce fnl f* **7/1**
064 **7** *1 ¼* **Archie Stevens**[89] 3604 2-9-3 73............................... RichardKingscote 4 54+
(Tom Dascombe) *s.s: hdwy over 2f out: rdn over 1f out: no imp* **11/1**
8 *1 ¼* **Hidden Link** 2-9-3 0.. ChrisCatlin 11 50+
(Sir Mark Prescott Bt) *s.i.s: bhd: r.o ins fnl f: nvr nrr* **66/1**
0 **9** *¾* **Woza Moya (USA)**[9] 6330 2-9-3 0.. TomEaves 6 48
(Gay Kelleway) *prom tl wknd 2f out* **66/1**
10 *½* **She's Some Girl (IRE)** 2-8-7 0.................................. ShaneBKelly[(5)] 8 42
(Richard Fahey) *towards rr: pushed along over 3f out: effrt over 2f out: sn wknd* **25/1**
11 *3* **Jonny Wombat** 2-8-10 0... VictorSantos[(7)] 9 38
(Richard Ford) *a in rr: bhd fr 1/2-way* **100/1**
12 *nk* **Vergality Ridge (IRE)** 2-9-3 0.. KierenFox 7 37
(Ronald Harris) *s.s: a in rr* **9/2**[2]
1m 14.97s (-0.03) **Going Correction** -0.125s/f (Stan) **12** Ran SP% **119.1**
Speed ratings (Par 95): **95,94,93,89,89 88,86,84,83,83 79,78**
toteswingers 1&2 £26.40, 1&3 £4.70, 2&3 £13.40 CSF £124.31 TOTE £10.10: £4.30, £7.80, £1.10; EX 163.90 Trifecta £1799.50 Part won. Pool: £2,431.87 - 0.62 winning tickets..
Owner Tick Tock Partnership **Bred** Corduff Stud Ltd, J Corcoran & J Judd **Trained** Newmarket, Suffolk
■ Stewards' Enquiry : Chris Catlin £560 fine: failed to weigh out
FOCUS
Quite an interesting if modest 2yo median auction maiden. Just fair form, limited by the runner-up.
NOTEBOOK
Line Of Reason(IRE), a half-brother to four winners, certainly knew his job. He came home as straight as a die to show ahead near the line. It now all depends on what mark he is given. (op 15-2 tchd 9-2)
Puteri Nur Laila(IRE), tailed off on her nursery debut on her fifth start running from a mark of 67, bounced back in first-time blinkers. After taking charge she was edged out near the line. She is looking fully exposed already. (op 16-1 tchd 12-1)
Secret Missile, runner-up here over 5f on his debut, had the worst of the draw. He was widest of all turning in and is well worth another chance. (op 9-2 tchd 11-4)
Al Udeid(IRE) made a pleasing debut and the way this son of Verglas was sticking on at the finish he will be suited by a step up to seven. (op 11-4)
Compton Silver, having his third start, probably ran somewhere near the mark (RPR 60) he recorded when runner-up here over 5f. (op 7-1 tchd 10-1)
Opus Cactus(USA), out of a mare that won at up to 1m1f in Italy, was well supported but never figured. The experience will not be lost on him. (op 20-1 tchd 13-2)
Archie Stevens, already rated 73, picked up an injury when fourth at Chester on his third start in late-June. Gelded since, he blew his chance completely exiting the stalls. (op 17-2)

6610 32RED.COM H'CAP 5f 216y(P)
6:15 (6:16) (Class 5) (0-75,77) 3-Y-O+ **£2,264** (£673; £336; £168) **Stalls** Low

Form RPR
2013 **1** **Amoure Medici**[10] 6319 3-9-5 **75**.. GrahamLee 13 88+
(Ann Duffield) *mid-div: hdwy over 2f out: led 1f out: drvn out* **10/3**[2]
3111 **2** *hd* **Theresnoneedfordat (IRE)**[5] 6497 3-9-7 **77** 6ex.......... WilliamCarson 2 89+
(Stuart Williams) *mid-div: hdwy over 2f out: swtchd rt over 1f out: rdn to chse wnr ins fnl f: r.o u.p* **1/1**[1]
0404 **3** *3 ½* **Courageous (IRE)**[10] 6303 6-9-7 **75**...............................(t) LukeMorris 1 76
(Milton Bradley) *a.p: led over 1f out: sn rdn and hdd: styd on same pce* **12/1**
0402 **4** *1 ¼* **For Shia And Lula (IRE)**[5] 6498 3-9-2 **72**.................(p) StephenCraine 9 69
(Daniel Mark Loughnane) *chsd ldrs: rdn and ev ch over 1f out: no ex ins fnl f* **20/1**
6004 **5** *½* **Flameoftheforest (IRE)**[12] 6256 5-9-7 **75**..............................(b) ChrisCatlin 8 70
(Ed de Giles) *s.i.s: hld up: rdn over 1f out: r.o ins fnl f: nrst fin* **8/1**[3]
1330 **6** *¾* **Lady Bayside**[38] 5426 4-9-3 **71**.. TomMcLaughlin 11 64
(Malcolm Saunders) *hld up: rdn over 2f out: r.o ins fnl f: nvr nrr* **18/1**
3564 **7** *3 ½* **Waabel**[75] 4085 5-9-1 **69**.. CathyGannon 4 51
(Violet M Jordan) *sn pushed along: led 5f out: rdn and hdd over 1f out: wknd ins fnl f* **40/1**
5000 **8** *2 ¼* **Oratorian (IRE)**[21] 5983 3-8-12 **75**................................ ThomasBrown[(7)] 10 49
(Sylvester Kirk) *hld up: rdn over 2f out: a in rr* **33/1**
-500 **9** *¾* **Viola D'Amour (IRE)**[29] 5736 3-9-2 **72**..................... RichardKingscote 7 44
(Tom Dascombe) *chsd ldrs: rdn over 2f out: wknd over 1f out* **20/1**
1340 **10** *3 ¼* **Wiltshire Life (IRE)**[28] 5775 3-8-13 **69**...........................(p) JimCrowley 5 31
(Jeremy Gask) *mid-div: rdn over 2f out: sn wknd* **50/1**
2620 **11** *1 ¼* **Kyanight (IRE)**[59] 4655 3-9-2 **72**.. DaneO'Neill 6 30
(Clive Cox) *led 1f: chsd ldr tl rdn and wknd wl over 1f out* **33/1**
0440 **12** *2 ¾* **Zip Lock (IRE)**[22] 5941 6-8-11 **68**.................................. RyanClark[(3)] 3 17
(Tom Keddy) *s.s: rdn and rel to r: a bhd* **66/1**
1m 13.52s (-1.48) **Going Correction** -0.125s/f (Stan)
WFA 3 from 4yo+ 2lb **12** Ran SP% **118.4**
Speed ratings (Par 103): **104,103,99,97,96 95,91,88,87,82 81,77**
toteswingers 1&2 £2.30, 1&3 £6.30, 2&3 £2.70 CSF £6.44 CT £35.11 TOTE £4.30: £1.20, £1.10, £2.30; EX 9.00 Trifecta £56.40 Pool: £2,722.75 - 35.67 winning tickets..
Owner Mrs D Jeromson **Bred** Breeding Capital Plc **Trained** Constable Burton, N Yorks
■ Stewards' Enquiry : Ryan Clark four-day ban; excessive use of whip (11th,12th,14th,15th Oct).
FOCUS
Little depth to this but the form pair came clear and both rate personal bests.

6611 32RED CASINO NURSERY 5f 216y(P)
6:45 (6:46) (Class 5) (0-70,70) 2-Y-O **£2,264** (£673; £336; £168) **Stalls** Low

Form RPR
3362 **1** **Blazing Knight (IRE)**[6] 6438 2-9-3 **66**.................................. JimCrowley 8 71+
(Ralph Beckett) *hld up: hdwy over 2f out: hmpd ins fnl f: rdn to ld wl ins fnl f: r.o* **9/2**[1]
606 **2** *1* **Captain McCaw**[14] 6177 2-8-12 **68**...........(b[1]) WilliamTwiston-Davies[(7)] 6 69
(Brian Meehan) *sn pushed along and prom: rdn and hung lft fr over 1f out: ev ch ins fnl f: styd on* **9/1**
2564 **3** *1 ¾* **Indian Affair**[31] 5682 2-9-7 **70**.................................... RichardKingscote 7 67
(Milton Bradley) *a.p: hmpd 5f out: rdn over 1f out: r.o* **9/1**
6416 **4** *hd* **Flighty Clarets (IRE)**[34] 5537 2-9-2 **70**........................ ShaneBKelly[(5)] 11 65
(Richard Fahey) *trckd ldrs: racd keenly: wnt 2nd over 3f out: led over 1f out: sn rdn and hung lft: hdd and no ex wl ins fnl f* **28/1**
0223 **5** *nse* **We Are City**[14] 6155 2-8-9 **65**... IanBurns[(7)] 3 60
(Michael Bell) *chsd ldr over 1f out: styd on* **9/2**[1]
0021 **6** *¾* **Chloe's Dream (IRE)**[8] 6354 2-9-2 **65** 6ex..................(p) PJMcDonald 13 59
(Ann Duffield) *sn led: rdn and hdd over 1f out: nt clr run and swtchd rt ins fnl f: styd on same pce* **10/1**
055 **7** *¾* **Melodee Princess (IRE)**[29] 5749 2-9-1 **64**........................ LukeMorris 5 56
(Ronald Harris) *s.i.s: hld up: rdn over 2f out: hdwy over 1f out: nt clr run ins fnl f: nt trble ldrs* **22/1**
300 **8** *nse* **Echo Of Silence (FR)**[20] 6015 2-9-0 **68**..................... TobyAtkinson[(5)] 2 59
(Marco Botti) *hld up: hdwy over 2f out: rdn whn hmpd ins fnl f: n.d after* **7/1**[2]
2111 **9** *2 ¼* **Hardy Blue (IRE)**[13] 6212 2-9-5 **68**.............................. FergusSweeney 1 52+
(Jamie Osborne) *broke wl: hmpd and lost pl 5f out: hdwy over 1f out: nt clr run sn after: nt trble ldrs* **8/1**[3]
056 **10** *3* **Frans Hals**[62] 4532 2-8-10 **59**.. ChrisCatlin 9 34
(Dominic Ffrench Davis) *hld up: rdn over 2f out: sn wknd* **9/1**
2552 **11** *hd* **Frosted Off**[11] 6283 2-8-11 **60**... CathyGannon 10 34
(John Spearing) *s.s: outpcd* **40/1**
1014 **12** *9* **Somethingboutmary**[24] 5886 2-9-7 **70**................................ AmyRyan 4 17+
(Kevin Ryan) *prom: pushed along 1/2-way: wknd over 2f out* **8/1**[3]
1m 15.3s (0.30) **Going Correction** -0.125s/f (Stan) **12** Ran SP% **120.4**
Speed ratings (Par 95): **93,91,89,89,89 88,87,86,83,79 79,67**
toteswingers 1&2 £9.80, 1&3 £7.70, 2&3 £22.10 CSF £45.27 CT £357.14 TOTE £5.00: £2.20, £3.00, £3.70; EX 58.40 Trifecta £779.20 Part won. Pool: £1,050.03 - winning tickets..
Owner Circuit Racing **Bred** Tally-Ho Stud **Trained** Kimpton, Hants
FOCUS
A modest but wide-open nursery and severe traffic problems in the final furlong. Straightforward but limited form.
NOTEBOOK
Blazing Knight(IRE), seemingly fully exposed on his eighth start and with the blinkers dispensed with, squeezed through between horses to pull the prize out of the fire near the line. (tchd 4-1 and 5-1)
Captain McCaw, who showed ability on his debut, was making his nursery debut on his fourth start and his second try on the AW. He edged in, causing trouble on his inner, but in the end just missed out. (op 14-1)
Indian Affair, a nine-race maiden, was another to have a fully exposed profile. He finished best of all from an unpromising position. (op 12-1)
Flighty Clarets(IRE), well below his best on soft ground on her nursery debut, was having her first taste of the AW. After striking on once in line for home she came up just short in the end. She was reported to have hung left-handed. (op 22-1 tchd 33-1)
We Are City, a maiden after eight previous starts, had finished second twice and third once on her three most recent outings in nursery company. The step back up to six did not bring any improvement. (tchd 11-2)
Chloe's Dream(IRE), a wide-margin winner of a Beverley selling nursery, carried a 6lb penalty. Hoisted 11lb, she did well to lead from the outside draw but having to do so much running so soon left her with nothing in reserve at the business end where she edged right-handed and contributed to the traffic problems. (op 8-1 tchd 11-1)
Echo Of Silence(FR), making his nursery bow on his second start on the AW, was knocked completely out of his stride when attempting to close just inside the final furlong. (tchd 6-1 and 15-2)
Hardy Blue(IRE), a winner three times over 5f, a seller, a low-grade nursery then a claimer, was reported to have suffered interference soon after the start. (op 6-1)

6612 LIKE US ON FACEBOOK WOLVERHAMPTON RACECOURSE CLAIMING STKS 7f 32y(P)
7:15 (7:17) (Class 6) 2-Y-O **£1,704** (£503; £251) **Stalls** High

Form RPR
3223 **1** **Brazilian Clown (IRE)**[9] 6337 2-8-11 67............(b[1]) RichardKingscote 9 80+
(Tom Dascombe) *s.i.s: reminder after s and sn prom: chsd ldr over 5f out: led over 2f out: sn pushed clr* **10/11**[1]
444 **2** *13* **Moonlit Dancer (IRE)**[21] 5968 2-8-2 60.............................(t) MartinLane 3 40
(J W Hills) *hld up: hdwy over 2f out: wnt 2nd 1f out: no ch w wnr* **6/1**[3]
2160 **3** *3* **Grievous Angel (IRE)**[5] 6475 2-9-4 75..............................(p[1]) GrahamLee 1 48
(Ann Duffield) *sn pushed along in mid-div: lost pl over 5f out: drvn along 1/2-way: styd on to go 3rd nr fin* **9/2**[2]
30 **4** *1* **Marmot Bay (IRE)**[30] 5715 2-8-12 0.................................. FergusSweeney 6 39
(Jamie Osborne) *plld hrd: led: rdn and hdd over 2f out: wknd over 1f out* **12/1**
1360 **5** *1 ½* **Lucky Suit (IRE)**[27] 5806 2-8-4 55... KierenFox 2 28
(Ronald Harris) *chsd ldrs: rdn over 2f out: wknd over 1f out* **25/1**
1520 **6** *3* **Wordsaplenty (IRE)**[14] 6156 2-8-6 56................................. AndreaAtzeni 4 22
(J S Moore) *prom: rdn over 2f out: wknd wl over 1f out* **18/1**
630 **7** *1 ¼* **Gowertonian (IRE)**[16] 6115 2-8-5 63..................................... LukeMorris 10 18
(Ronald Harris) *s.i.s: nvr nrr* **40/1**
2500 **8** *1* **Kimvara**[16] 6115 2-8-4 51...(b) CathyGannon 8 15
(Joseph Tuite) *mid-div: hdwy over 4f out: rdn and wknd over 2f out* **28/1**

00 **9** 3/4 **Mujadora (IRE)**[22] 5948 2-8-4 0 ChrisCatlin 11 13
(William Haggas) *s.i.s: a in rr: bhd whn hung rt over 2f out* **12/1**

00 **10** 21 **True Ally**[27] 5807 2-8-1 0 RachealKneller(5) 5
(John Norton) *prom: pushed along 1/2-way: sn wknd: t.o* **200/1**

1m 28.53s (-1.07) **Going Correction** -0.125s/f (Stan) **10** Ran SP% **115.7**
Speed ratings (Par 93): **101,86,82,81,79 76,75,73,73,49**
toteswingers 1&2 £1.70, 1&3 £1.50, 2&3 £3.80 CSF £6.40 TOTE £1.90: £1.10, £1.90, £1.80; EX 7.10 Trifecta £22.50 Pool: £3,901.24 - 128.06 winning tickets..Brazilian Clown was claimed by Mr C. R. Dore for £6,000.
Owner The MHS 2012 Olympic Partnership **Bred** Carrigbeg Stud & David Powell **Trained** Malpas, Cheshire

FOCUS
The easy winner showed useful form for the grade, and could be rated higher still, but the opposition was weak.

NOTEBOOK
Brazilian Clown(IRE), rated 67, had been placed four times in seven previous starts. Dropped to claiming company and fitted with blinkers for the first time, he half-reared leaving the stalls and had to be given a reminders. Soon upsides the leader, he came right away in the end for a wide-margin victory. The opposition was poor. He was claimed by Conor Dore. (op 11-8)
Moonlit Dancer(IRE), rated 60, had 2lb in hand of the winner at the weights. On her second start in claiming company, she kept on to take a distant second. (op 13-2 tchd 5-1)
Grievous Angel(IRE), winner of a maiden claimer at Thirsk, had cut little ice in two starts in nursery company. She gave away ground at the start and soon driven along only took third spot due to her rider's determination. (op 7-2 tchd 5-1)
Marmot Bay(IRE), having her first taste of Polytrack on her third start, took them along, but after being left for dead by the winner lost two more places with a weak finish. (op 8-1)

6613 STAY AT THE HOLIDAY INN WOLVERHAMPTON FILLIES' H'CAP 1m 141y(P)
7:45 (7:46) (Class 5) (0-75,75) 3-Y-0+ **£2,264** (£673; £336; £168) **Stalls** Low

Form RPR
0551 **1** **Raheeba**[5] 6502 3-9-5 **75** 6ex (b) SilvestreDeSousa 1 85
(Mark Johnston) *s.i.s: sn chsng ldrs: nt clr run 2f out: shkn up over 1f out: rdn to ld ins fnl f: r.o wl* **11/4**[1]

1404 **2** 3/4 **Grey Seal (IRE)**[22] 5942 3-9-1 **71** GrahamLee 9 79
(James Fanshawe) *hld up: hdwy over 2f out: rdn and ev ch ins fnl f: r.o* **11/1**

3053 **3** 2 1/4 **Ssafa**[41] 5310 4-9-1 **71** LeonnaMayor(5) 12 74
(J W Hills) *hld up: hdwy 1/2-way: chsd ldr over 3f out: led over 2f out: rdn over 1f out: hdd and no ex ins fnl f* **25/1**

0-20 **4** nk **Amelia May**[26] 5837 3-9-5 **75** LukeMorris 8 77
(Ed Vaughan) *prom: pushed along over 2f out: nt clr run sn after: rdn over 1f out: styd on same pce ins fnl f* **33/1**

03 **5** 3/4 **Berwin (IRE)**[22] 5931 3-9-1 **71** JamesDoyle 5 71
(Sylvester Kirk) *prom: rdn over 1f out: hung lft ins fnl f: styd on same pce* **10/1**

-060 **6** 3/4 **Cheers For Thea (IRE)**[14] 6176 7-9-2 **67** (t) DuranFentiman 13 66
(Tim Easterby) *hld up: rdn over 1f out: styd on ins fnl f: nt trble ldrs* **18/1**

5030 **7** nk **Judas Jo (FR)**[46] 5122 3-8-9 **65** (p) CathyGannon 11 63
(Gay Kelleway) *hld up: hdwy u.p over 1f out: nt trble ldrs* **66/1**

3006 **8** 1 3/4 **Imaginary World (IRE)**[23] 5910 4-9-0 **65** SeanLevey 7 59
(John Balding) *chsd ldrs: rdn over 2f out: wknd ins fnl f* **20/1**

-515 **9** 3/4 **My Body Is A Cage (IRE)**[13] 6208 3-9-3 **73** JamieSpencer 4 65
(Jeremy Noseda) *s.i.s: hld up: rdn and hung lft over 1f out: n.d* **8/1**[3]

322 **10** hd **Merry Jaunt (USA)**[13] 6190 3-8-12 **68** WilliamBuick 6 60
(John Gosden) *chsd ldrs: pushed along 3f out: rdn and wknd fnl f* **3/1**[2]

0240 **11** 3 1/4 **Supaheart**[23] 5910 3-9-1 **71** RobertHavlin 10 55
(Hughie Morrison) *sn led: rdn and hdd over 2f out: wknd fnl f* **16/1**

2154 **12** 1 1/2 **Hip Hip Hooray**[11] 6275 6-9-1 **66** TomMcLaughlin 3 47
(Luke Dace) *s.s: a in rr* **25/1**

-044 **13** 2 **Fairyinthewind (IRE)**[8] 6375 3-9-0 **70** SebSanders 2 46
(Paul D'Arcy) *trckd ldr: racd keenly: rdn over 2f out: wknd over 1f out* **10/1**

1m 48.77s (-1.73) **Going Correction** -0.125s/f (Stan)
WFA 3 from 4yo+ 5lb **13** Ran SP% **117.3**
Speed ratings (Par 100): **102,101,99,99,98 97,97,95,95,95 92,90,89**
toteswingers 1&2 £7.50, 1&3 £26.80, 2&3 £33.40 CSF £30.72 CT £654.26 TOTE £3.80: £1.80, £4.50, £6.30; EX 39.00 Trifecta £885.10 Pool: £2,057.45 - 1.72 winning tickets..
Owner Sheikh Hamdan Bin Mohammed Al Maktoum **Bred** Mrs C R Philipson & Lofts Hall Stud **Trained** Middleham Moor, N Yorks

FOCUS
A sound pace and, after meeting traffic problems, in the end a clear cut winner. She improved on her latest C&D form.

6614 32RED SUPPORTING BRITISH RACING MAIDEN STKS (DIV I) 1m 4f 50y(P)
8:15 (8:15) (Class 5) 3-Y-0+ **£2,264** (£673; £336; £168) **Stalls** Low

Form RPR
54 **1** **Maori Dancer (USA)**[21] 5982 3-9-3 0 (t) JamieSpencer 10 85
(Jeremy Noseda) *mde all: rdn clr fr over 2f out* **7/4**[2]

66- **2** 6 **Epic Storm (IRE)**[433] 4279 4-9-11 0 JamesDoyle 4 75
(Sean Curran) *hld up: pushed along 3f out: hung lft and wnt 2nd over 1f out: no ch w wnr* **25/1**

02 **3** 7 **Matured**[15] 6148 3-8-12 0 JimCrowley 5 59
(Ralph Beckett) *hld up in tch: racd keenly: chsd wnr 3f out tl wknd over 1f out* **5/4**[1]

4 3 **All That Remains (IRE)**[21] 7-9-8 0 PaulPickard(3) 8 59
(Brian Ellison) *s.i.s: hld up: hdwy over 5f out: rdn and wknd over 2f out* **20/1**

3- **5** 5 **Ehkam (USA)**[355] 6697 3-9-3 0 (t) SilvestreDeSousa 9 51
(Saeed Bin Suroor) *prom: chsd wnr over 7f out tl pushed along 3f out: wknd over 2f out* **9/2**[3]

-0 **6** 6 **Italian Riviera**[13] 6215 3-9-3 0 LukeMorris 7 41+
(Sir Mark Prescott Bt) *plld hrd and prom: stdd and lost pl after 2f: wknd 3f out* **16/1**

7 4 1/2 **Ghazwan (IRE)** 3-9-3 0 SebSanders 6 34
(Conrad Allen) *sn prom: pushed along over 7f out: rdn and wknd 3f out: t.o* **20/1**

0-6 **8** 74 **Muzey's Princess**[41] 5293 6-9-6 0 SeanQuinlan 1
(Michael Mullineaux) *chsd wnr over 4f: sn rdn: wknd over 5f out: t.o* **150/1**

2m 38.73s (-2.37) **Going Correction** -0.125s/f (Stan)
WFA 3 from 4yo+ 8lb **8** Ran SP% **118.9**
Speed ratings (Par 103): **102,98,93,91,88 84,81,31**
toteswingers 1&2 £6.60, 1&3 £1.10, 2&3 £4.80 CSF £48.67 TOTE £4.60: £2.40, £9.60, £1.10; EX 66.40 Trifecta £84.40 Pool: £998.58 - 8.66 winning tickets..
Owner Mrs Seamus Burns **Bred** Claiborne Farm **Trained** Newmarket, Suffolk

FOCUS
A modest maiden and a one-horse race in the home straight. The winner rates a pesonal best but there are doubts over the depth of this form.

6615 32RED SUPPORTING BRITISH RACING MAIDEN STKS (DIV II) 1m 4f 50y(P)
8:45 (8:45) (Class 5) 3-Y-0+ **£2,264** (£673; £336; £168) **Stalls** Low

Form RPR
42 **1** **Totalize**[12] 6228 3-9-0 0 PatrickHills(3) 7 88+
(Luca Cumani) *hld up: hdwy over 3f out: led over 1f out: styd on wl* **9/4**[2]

5 **2** 6 **Minority Interest**[126] 2430 3-9-3 0 GeorgeBaker 6 78
(Sir Michael Stoute) *a.p: chsd ldr over 2f out: rdn and ev ch over 1f out: edgd lft and no ex ins fnl f* **11/10**[1]

60-2 **3** 1 1/4 **Inqadh (USA)**[28] 5766 3-9-3 77 (p) SilvestreDeSousa 4 76
(Saeed Bin Suroor) *chsd ldrs: wnt 2nd over 8f out tl rdn over 2f out: hung lft and ev ch over 1f out: no ex fnl f* **4/1**[3]

4 nse **Hail To The Chief (FR)**[75] 4-9-11 83 (t) GrahamLee 5 76
(Ed Dunlop) *hld up in tch: rdn over 2f out: styd on same pce fr over 1f out* **14/1**

5 1 3/4 **Equalizer** 3-9-3 0 RichardKingscote 9 73
(Tom Dascombe) *led: over 1f out: wknd fnl f* **20/1**

065 **6** 1/2 **Addazero**[23] 5901 3-9-3 72 JohnFahy 3 72
(Alastair Lidderdale) *chsd ldr over 3f: remained handy: rdn over 2f out: wknd over 1f out* **20/1**

44 **7** 3/4 **Smart Ruler (IRE)**[12] 6228 6-9-8 0 JulieBurke(3) 1 71
(James Moffatt) *hld up in tch: rdn over 3f out: wknd wl over 1f out* **33/1**

8 21 **Irene Kennet**[60] 5-9-6 0 SeanQuinlan 2 33
(Mark Rimell) *s.i.s: a in rr: bhd fnl 3f: t.o* **50/1**

00/ **9** 34 **Strangelittlegirl**[680] 7478 4-9-6 0 LukeMorris 8
(Patrick Gilligan) *s.i.s: pushed along and lost tch fnl 7f: t.o* **100/1**

2m 37.96s (-3.14) **Going Correction** -0.125s/f (Stan)
WFA 3 from 4yo+ 8lb **9** Ran SP% **120.5**
Speed ratings (Par 103): **105,101,100,100,98 98,88,84,61**
toteswingers 1&2 £1.60, 1&3 £2.00, 2&3 £1.70 CSF £5.09 TOTE £3.50: £1.20, £1.10, £1.10; EX 8.70 Trifecta £14.90 Pool: £731.24 - 36.09 winning tickets..
Owner Castle Down Racing **Bred** Meon Valley Stud **Trained** Newmarket, Suffolk

FOCUS
Part two of the maiden and the faster by 6lb. Again a most convincing winner, and the form looks more solid than division one. There looks more to come from the winner.

6616 £32 BONUS AT 32RED.COM H'CAP 1m 4f 50y(P)
9:15 (9:16) (Class 6) (0-60,64) 3-Y-0+ **£1,704** (£503; £251) **Stalls** Low

Form RPR
312 **1** **Azrag (USA)**[7] 6399 4-10-2 **64** 6ex PaulMulrennan 8 73+
(Gerard Butler) *a.p: chsd clr ldr over 6f out: carried rt wl over 1f out: sn led: rdn and edgd lft ins fnl f: styd on* **2/1**[1]

044 **2** 1 1/2 **Annelko**[17] 6097 5-9-5 **53** GrahamLee 9 59
(Michael Blake) *hld up: hdwy over 2f out: rdn over 1f out: edgd lft ins fnl f: styd on* **11/2**[3]

6325 **3** 3 **King's Road**[19] 6056 7-9-9 **57** (t) GeorgeBaker 1 58
(Anabel K Murphy) *a.p: rdn and ev ch over 1f out: no ex ins fnl f* **17/2**

005 **4** 1 **Edgware Road**[14] 6159 4-9-12 **60** JamesDoyle 3 60
(Sean Curran) *led 1f: chsd ldr tl over 6f out: remained handy: led wl over 1f out: sn rdn and hdd: no ex ins fnl f* **8/1**

2000 **5** 1/2 **El Libertador (USA)**[40] 5351 6-9-10 **58** (b) LukeMorris 2 57
(Eric Wheeler) *hld up: hdwy over 1f out: styd on same pce ins fnl f* **25/1**

0054 **6** nk **Suedehead**[28] 5770 3-9-0 **56** StevieDonohoe 7 54
(William Muir) *hld up: pushed along over 2f out: styd on ins fnl f: nvr nrr* **9/2**[2]

/052 **7** 1 **Youm Jamil (USA)**[5] 6503 5-9-5 **58** GeorgeDowning(5) 4 55
(Tony Carroll) *hld up: rdn over 1f out: n.d* **11/2**[3]

450- **8** 1 1/4 **Chik's Dream**[272] 7930 5-9-2 **50** AndreaAtzeni 6 45
(Derek Haydn Jones) *hld up: hdwy over 2f out: rdn over 1f out: wknd fnl f* **40/1**

060 **9** 3/4 **Symfony (IRE)**[15] 6148 3-9-4 **60** DaneO'Neill 11 54
(Clive Cox) *prom: rdn over 3f out: wknd fnl f* **12/1**

/0-0 **10** 1/2 **Honest Strike (USA)**[147] 1792 5-9-12 **60** (b1) SeanQuinlan 12 53
(Daniel Mark Loughnane) *led after 1f: clr 7f out: rdn: hung rt and hdd wl over 1f out: wknd fnl f* **50/1**

0-0P **P** **Bold Identity (IRE)**[42] 5264 6-9-12 **60** (b) JohnFahy 5
(Richard Phillips) *s.i.s: sn wl bhd: p.u 10f out* **66/1**

2m 40.51s (-0.59) **Going Correction** -0.125s/f (Stan)
WFA 3 from 4yo+ 8lb **11** Ran SP% **121.4**
Speed ratings (Par 101): **96,95,93,92,92 91,91,90,89,89**
toteswingers 1&2 £3.30, 1&3 £3.80, 2&3 £4.30 CSF £13.33 CT £80.40 TOTE £2.90: £1.10, £2.80, £2.80; EX 19.50 Trifecta £149.00 Pool: £835.90 - 4.15 winning tickets..
Owner Fawzi Abdulla Nass **Bred** Aislabie Bloodstock **Trained** Newmarket, Suffolk

FOCUS
A low-grade handicap run at a sound pace. Sound form, and the well-in winner didn't need to improve.
T/Plt: £19.70 to a £1 stake. Pool: £82,440.47 - 3,042.48 winning tickets T/Qpdt: £15.90 to a £1 stake. Pool: £9311.79 - 431.24 winning tickets CR

6617 - 6624a (Foreign Racing) - See Raceform Interactive

6027 HAYDOCK (L-H)
Friday, September 28

OFFICIAL GOING: Heavy (7.9)
All races on stands' side Home straight. Races on round course increased by 13yds except first race which increased by 63yds.
Wind: Moderate, half against Weather: Fine

6625 VALE UK H'CAP 1m 6f
2:00 (2:00) (Class 3) (0-95,91) 3-Y-0 **£6,663** (£1,982; £990; £495) **Stalls** Low

Form RPR
4-11 **1** **Pallasator**[22] 5973 3-9-7 **91** LukeMorris 6 102
(Sir Mark Prescott Bt) *hld up in rr: niggled along 5f out: hdwy over 2f out: sn in 2nd pl and chalng: led ins fnl f: styd on and in command towards fin* **11/4**[1]

1100 **2** 1 1/4 **Nicholascopernicus (IRE)**[21] 6018 3-9-0 **84** DaneO'Neill 5 93
(Ed Walker) *hld up: hdwy 3f out: led over 2f out: rdn and edgd lft over 1f out: hdd ins fnl f: no ex towards fin* **4/1**[3]

3254 **3** 1 1/4 **Ruacana**[24] 5905 3-9-5 **89** StevieDonohoe 1 96
(Michael Bell) *chsd ldr: led briefly under 3f out: sn rdn: styd on same pce fnl f* **11/2**

2201 **4** *1¾* **Varnish**^{28} 5788 3-8-12 **82**.......................... SeanLevey 3 87
(Richard Hannon) *chsd ldrs: chalng 3f out: rdn 2f out: one pce fnl f* **8/1**

2254 **5** *5* **Gabrial's Star**^{19} 6074 3-9-0 **84**..........................(p) TomEaves 2 82
(Bryan Smart) *hld up in tch: lost pl over 3f out: sn bhd and n.d* **13/2**

4622 **6** *¾* **Cape Savannah**^{28} 5788 3-8-11 **81**.......................... AdamBeschizza 4 78
(David Simcock) *led at stdy pce: shkn up 4f out: hdd under 3f out: wknd wl over 1f out* **7/2**^{2}

3m 9.83s (7.83) **Going Correction** +0.375s/f (Good) **6** Ran SP% **108.7**
Speed ratings (Par 105): **92,91,90,89,86 86**
toteswingers 1&2 £1.10, 1&3 £4.10, 2&3 £5.80 CSF £12.96 TOTE £3.40: £2.00, £3.50; EX 9.50.
Owner Baxter, Gregson, Jenkins & Warman **Bred** Newsells Park Stud **Trained** Newmarket, Suffolk

FOCUS
Racing took place on the outer track. The opener was run over 63yds further than the advertised distance. Conditions were very testing, and the winning jockey in the first described the ground as "bottomless". A decent 3-y-o handicap, in which the runners raced wide down the back straight. The pace was steady, only really increasing on the approach to the home turn, but the first two came from the rear. The winner continues to progress, and the next three were pretty much to form.

NOTEBOOK
Pallasator made it 3-3 this season and is unbeaten on turf. Held up in last, he was being niggled along a good way from home, but made up his ground well in the straight and was on top when he idled in the final 50 yards. The longer trip was fine for him and he handled the underfoot conditions well. Like at Kempton, he got himself in a stew beforehand, and he does not look wholly straightforward, but it could be he is immature. There should be more improvement in this tall individual, who looks the sort to make a nice jumper one day. (op 5-2 tchd 2-1)
Nicholascopernicus(IRE) travelled well before putting his head in front and fought on willingly once tackled. He saw out the trip well enough in the circumstances. (op 7-2)
Ruacana gets further and kept staying on. He's 5lb higher than his last winning mark, but may not be entirely weighted out of things at present. (op 13-2 tchd 7-1)
Varnish had every chance, but may not have stayed in the ground. (op 7-1 tchd 9-1)
Gabrial's Star was the first beaten. He won his maiden last autumn in the mud, but is better served by a sound surface. (op 6-1 tchd 11-2)
Cape Savannah dropped away after making the running and could not turn around Salisbury form with Varnish on these 3lb better terms. This was only his third run on turf, and his first on such testing ground. (op 5-1)

6626 SPEEDY SERVICES LONG SERVERS H'CAP 1m 3f 200y
2:30 (2:31) (Class 5) (0-70,70) 3-Y-O+ **£2,264** (£673; £336; £168) **Stalls** High

Form RPR

4 **1** **De Rigueur**^{28} 5809 4-9-3 **59**..........................(t) AndreaAtzeni 4 75+
(Marco Botti) *chsd ldrs: chalng and wnt 2nd 2f out: led over 1f out: drew clr ins fnl f: styd on wl* **4/1**^{1}

4633 **2** *4* **Luctor Emergo (IRE)**^{5} 6516 3-9-3 **67**..........................(v) JoeFanning 12 75
(Keith Dalgleish) *chsd ldrs: wnt 2nd 7f out: led over 4f out: rdn and hdd over 1f out: one pce and no imp on wnr ins fnl f* **9/2**^{2}

1044 **3** *2½* **Tinseltown**^{42} 5290 6-9-13 **69**..........................(p) AmyRyan 8 73
(Brian Rothwell) *t.k.h: in tch: wnt prom 7f out: chsd ldr over 4f out: rdn 3f out: lost 2nd 2f out: hung lft over 1f out: styd on same pce fnl f* **12/1**

5164 **4** *2¼* **Darling Lexi (IRE)**^{9} 6364 3-8-12 **62**.......................... BarryMcHugh 9 62
(Richard Fahey) *hld up: hdwy over 3f out: chsd ldrs and edgd lft over 2f out: no imp over 1f out: kpt on same pce* **10/1**

133 **5** *4½* **Eightfold**^{21} 6004 3-8-12 **62**..........................(t) DaneO'Neill 11 55
(Seamus Durack) *hld up: rdn and hdwy to chse ldrs over 2f out: no imp over 1f out* **5/1**^{3}

5604 **6** *nk* **Royal Trooper (IRE)**^{32} 5673 6-10-0 **70**.......................... FrederikTylicki 10 63
(James Given) *chsd ldrs: rdn over 2f out: wknd over 1f out* **8/1**

0-13 **7** *3* **Authora (IRE)**^{39} 5413 3-8-13 **63**.......................... PaulMulrennan 5 51
(Peter Chapple-Hyam) *midfield: rdn 5f out: effrt 3f out: wknd under 2f out* **8/1**

0051 **8** *½* **Hyde Lea Flyer**^{38} 5452 7-8-9 **51** oh1.......................... RussKennemore 13 38
(Barry Leavy) *chsd ldr after 1f tl over 7f out: remained handy: rdn and wknd over 2f out* **33/1**

2043 **9** *2¾* **Tobrata**^{32} 5673 6-8-9 **58**.......................... RobertDodsworth$^{(7)}$ 7 41
(Mel Brittain) *s.i.s: hld up: racd keenly and hdwy into midfield after 4f: wknd 4f out* **16/1**

1400 **10** *1¾* **Kozmina Bay**^{15} 6159 3-8-5 **55**.......................... JohnFahy 6 35
(Jonathan Portman) *in rr: pushed along 6f out: nvr on terms* **20/1**

0030 **11** *18* **Joyful Motive**^{42} 5330 3-8-1 **51** oh1.......................... FrannyNorton 2
(Tom Tate) *midfield: pushed along 5f out: wknd 4f out: eased whn btn ins fnl f* **50/1**

0564 **12** *19* **Damascus Symphony**^{87} 3728 4-8-12 **54**.......................... AndrewElliott 3
(James Bethell) *towards rr: struggling 2f out: eased whn btn ins fnl f: t.o* **25/1**

0000 **13** *26* **Eye Of The Tiger (GER)**^{42} 5306 7-9-11 **67**.......................... JimmyQuinn 1
(Barney Curley) *led: hdd over 4f out: sn wknd: t.o* **20/1**

2m 37.18s (3.38) **Going Correction** +0.375s/f (Good)
WFA 3 from 4yo+ 8lb **13** Ran SP% **118.0**
Speed ratings (Par 103): **103,100,98,97,94 93,91,91,89,88 76,63,46**
toteswingers 1&2 £5.20, 1&3 £15.90, 2&3 £10.50 CSF £19.63 CT £200.70 TOTE £4.90: £1.90, £1.70, £3.40; EX 23.60 Trifecta £189.30 Pool: £406.93 - 1.59 winning tickets..
Owner K J P Gundlach **Bred** Cheveley Park Stud Ltd **Trained** Newmarket, Suffolk

FOCUS
A modest handicap run at a reasonable pace and in a time ten seconds outside the standard, but it was the pick of the round-course times. The race was run over 18yds more than the official distance. The second and third set the standard and the winner took advantage of a good mark.

6627 EBF VALE UK MAIDEN FILLIES' STKS 6f
3:05 (3:05) (Class 5) 2-Y-O **£3,234** (£962; £481; £240) **Stalls** Centre

Form RPR

0 **1** **Eminently**^{23} 5943 2-9-0 0.......................... SeanLevey 1 73+
(Richard Hannon) *racd far side: a.p: rdn 2f out: led overall and edgd rt over 1f out: r.o wl fnl f: 1st of 5 in gp* **11/4**^{2}

2 **2** *2¾* **Vicky Valentine**^{10} 6335 2-9-0 0.......................... PhillipMakin 6 64
(Kevin Ryan) *racd far side: prom and keen: rdn and nt qckn over 1f out: no imp on wnr ins fnl f: 2nd of 5 in gp* **2/1**^{1}

0502 **3** *¾* **Millie N Aire**^{17} 6122 2-9-0 59.......................... FrannyNorton 3 62
(Danielle McCormick) *racd far side: overall ldr: rdn and hdd over 1f out: kpt on u.p tl no ex towards fin: 3rd of 5 in gp* **11/1**

4 **4** *¾* **Disko Dasko (FR)**^{109} 2977 2-8-11 0.......................... MichaelMetcalfe$^{(3)}$ 7 60
(Mrs K Burke) *racd far side: hld up and keen: hdwy to press ldrs 2f out: rdn over 1f out: styd on same pce ins fnl f: 4th of 5 in gp* **5/1**^{3}

5 *¾* **Golden Secret** 2-8-10 0.......................... JohnFahy 8 54+
(Clive Cox) *racd stands' side: chsd ldr: led gp over 2f out: edgd lft over 1f out: kpt on ins fnl f: nt pce of ldrs: 1st of 4 in gp* **11/1**

6 *3½* **Dilady** 2-8-10 0.......................... AmyRyan 10 43+
(Kevin Ryan) *racd stands' side: hld up: rdn over 1f out: nvr able to chal: 2nd of 4 in gp* **9/1**

0 **7** *5* **Branston Jubilee**^{10} 6335 2-9-0 0.......................... JoeFanning 11 32+
(Geoffrey Harker) *racd stands' side: chsd ldrs: effrt over 2f out: outpcd and edgd lft over 1f out: eased whn wl btn ins fnl f: 3rd of 4 in gp* **33/1**

60 **8** *2½* **Angel Grigio**^{10} 6335 2-9-0 0..........................(v) TomEaves 9 25+
(Bryan Smart) *racd keenly on stands' side: led gp tl over 2f out: wknd over 1f out: 4th of 4 in gp* **20/1**

9 *1* **Hidden Desire** 2-8-10 0.......................... DuranFentiman 5 18
(Tim Easterby) *racd far side: in rr: niggled along over 4f out: lft bhd over 1f out: 5th of 5 in gp* **25/1**

1m 18.19s (4.39) **Going Correction** +0.50s/f (Yiel) **9** Ran SP% **114.9**
Speed ratings (Par 92): **90,86,85,84,83 78,72,60,67**
toteswingers 1&2 £2.20, 1&3 £4.90, 2&3 £2.30 CSF £8.36 TOTE £3.90: £1.20, £1.20, £2.40; EX 9.00.
Owner Mr & Mrs G Middlebrook **Bred** Mr & Mrs G Middlebrook **Trained** East Everleigh, Wilts

FOCUS
Just an ordinary fillies' maiden. They divided into two groups on leaving the stalls and the first four home came from the group of five who raced down the far side.

NOTEBOOK
Eminently came under pressure with more than a quarter of a mile left, but knuckled down well to assert. There had been definite promise on her debut on the Polytrack, when the stable second string, and she built on that here. A half-sister to Haydock Sprint Cup winner Reverence, who was well at home in muddy conditions, she gave the Hannon team its fourth winner of this maiden in the last eight runnings. (op 4-1 tchd 5-2)
Vicky Valentine could not quicken up in the ground, but probably ran to a similar level as when runner-up at Thirsk on her recent debut. She confirmed her superiority over Branston Jubilee and Angel Grigio, who were both well beaten here. (op 6-4)
Millie N Aire, is another who looks a good guide to the quality of this form. A fully exposed 59-rated performer, she ran creditably, but was racing on perhaps the best of the ground next to the inside rail. (op 10-1)
Disko Dasko(FR), fourth to the smart Agent Allison first time out in June in a maiden that's worked out well, could not step up on that following an absence. She edged away from the far side in the latter part of the race. (op 11-2)
Golden Secret ◆, receiving 4lb from those that had run previously in common with the other newcomers, made a pleasing start. Best of the cluster of four positioned on the stands' side, she had nothing to race with in the latter stages and drifted into the centre of the track. A half-sister to her connections' Prix de L'Abbaye winner Gilt Edge Girl as well as to Group-winning sprinter Godfrey Street, she can leave this running behind. (op 9-1)
Dilady, second best on the nearside, was striding out well when it was all over and can do better with the experience to call on. A half-sister to triple winner Bluie, she's reportedly a big, strapping filly. (op 20-1)

6628 EBF VALE UK MAIDEN STKS (C&G) 6f
3:35 (3:36) (Class 5) 2-Y-O **£3,234** (£962; £481; £240) **Stalls** Centre

Form RPR

434 **1** **Bond Club**^{18} 6099 2-9-0 72.......................... TomEaves 4 70
(Geoffrey Oldroyd) *chsd ldr: effrt 2f out: chalng 1f out: led wl ins fnl f: kpt on wl* **15/8**^{1}

0344 **2** *½* **Red Cobra (IRE)**^{14} 6189 2-9-0 73.......................... DuranFentiman 3 69
(Tim Easterby) *racd freely: led: rdn whn pressed over 1f out: hdd wl ins fnl f: hld cl home* **2/1**^{2}

3 *5* **Lexington Place** 2-8-11 0.......................... LeeTopliss$^{(3)}$ 2 54+
(Richard Fahey) *missed break: racd keenly: prom: effrt over 2f out: outpcd over 1f out: no imp after* **9/4**^{3}

500 **4** *3¼* **Pour La Victoire (IRE)**^{20} 6049 2-9-0 58.......................... PhillipMakin 5 44
(Nigel Tinkler) *chsd ldrs: rdn 2f out: outpcd over 1f out: hung lft whn wl btn ins fnl f* **11/1**

00 **5** *5* **Hazard Warning (IRE)**^{49} 5040 2-8-9 0..........................(b^{1}) AdamCarter$^{(5)}$ 1 29
(Tim Easterby) *veered lft and awkward s: bhd: hung lft fr 1/2-way: rdn 2f out: eased whn wl btn fnl f* **40/1**

1m 18.4s (4.60) **Going Correction** +0.50s/f (Yiel) **5** Ran SP% **109.7**
Speed ratings (Par 95): **89,88,81,77,70**
CSF £5.93 TOTE £2.10: £1.10, £1.90; EX 4.50.
Owner R C Bond **Bred** R C Bond **Trained** Brawby, N Yorks

FOCUS
A weak maiden for the track. The runners congregated on the far rail and the finish was contested by the form pair, who came clear.

NOTEBOOK
Bond Club ran to a similar level on his first three starts and had 2lb in hand of the runner-up on BHA figures. He showed a pleasing attitude to prevail and should prove competitive in late-season nurseries. (op 2-1 tchd 13-8)
Red Cobra(IRE) raced rather keenly in front, despite dropping back in trip, and was worried out of it inside the last. He has not progressed and opportunities like this will not come along very often. (op 5-4)
Lexington Place, a half-brother to the useful sprinter Rex Imperator. He was notably green, slow to break and keen, then not really knowing what to do when let down, but was getting the hang of things late and better can be expected. (op 4-1)
Pour La Victoire(IRE) is decidedly limited. (op 12-1 tchd 16-1)
Hazard Warning(IRE), who raced awkwardly in the first-time blinkers, has yet to beat a rival in three tries now. The latter's rider Adam Carter reported that the colt hung left. Official explanation: jockey said colt hung left (op 33-1)

6629 GRIFFITHS & ARMOUR NURSERY 6f
4:10 (4:12) (Class 4) (0-75,76) 2-Y-O **£3,428** (£1,020; £509; £254) **Stalls** Centre

Form RPR

064 **1** **Benoni**^{24} 5911 2-9-0 **68**.......................... DaneO'Neill 4 73
(Henry Candy) *a.p: rdn over 1f out: led narrowly ins fnl f: kpt on gamely* **7/2**^{2}

6531 **2** *½* **Empowerment (IRE)**^{10} 6332 2-9-8 **76** 6ex.......................... SeanLevey 2 80
(Richard Hannon) *led: rdn over 1f out: hdd narrowly ins fnl f: rallied gamely: hld fnl stride* **11/4**^{1}

3651 **3** *3¾* **Hardy Red (IRE)**^{25} 5873 2-9-7 **75**.......................... FergusSweeney 7 67
(Jamie Osborne) *racd keenly: hld up: hdwy 2f out: rdn to chse ldrs over 1f out: no imp fnl f* **15/2**

0030 **4** *5* **Dream Vale (IRE)**^{15} 6160 2-8-11 **65**.......................... PaulMulrennan 3 42
(Tim Easterby) *chsd ldrs: rdn over 1f out: sn wknd* **7/1**

0554 **5** *3* **Santo Prince (USA)**^{63} 4540 2-9-4 **72**.......................... StevieDonohoe 1 40
(Michael Bell) *prom tl rdn and wknd 2f out* **5/1**^{3}

3401 **6** *3¾* **Angels Calling**^{12} 6283 2-8-7 **61** 6ex.......................... PJMcDonald 6 18
(Mrs K Burke) *in tch: pushed along over 2f out: wknd wl over 1f out* **7/1**

042 **7** *9* **Megaleka**[30] 5733 2-8-6 **60** .... DuranFentiman 8
(Chris Fairhurst) *hld up in tch: rdn over 2f out: hung lft and wknd wl over 1f out* **11/1**

1m 17.49s (3.69) **Going Correction** +0.50s/f (Yiel) **7** Ran SP% **110.7**
Speed ratings (Par 97): **95,94,89,82,78 73,61**
toteswingers 1&2 £3.20, 1&3 £3.90, 2&3 £2.50 CSF £12.63 CT £61.70 TOTE £5.40: £3.90, £1.30; EX 14.50.
Owner Clayton, Frost, Kebell & Candy **Bred** New Hall Farms Estate **Trained** Kingston Warren, Oxon
■ Stewards' Enquiry : Sean Levey 17day ban: used whip above permitted level, 5th occasion since 25th May 2012 (Oct 12 - 29)

FOCUS
A fair nursery in which they finished well strung out behind the first pair.

NOTEBOOK
Benoni had shown promise on each of his three maiden auction starts, all at 7f, and it came together on this nursery debut. He had to work for his success, but did not flinch when it came down to a fight. While he's clearly effective at this trip, he won't mind a return to further on this evidence, and he can progress again. (op 9-2)
Empowerment(IRE) was 4lb well-in under the penalty for his Folkestone win, which came on fast ground. Making the running alongside the rail, he stuck on well when tackled and it's hard to argue that he was much below form. (op 5-2 tchd 9-4 and 3-1 in places)
Hardy Red(IRE) travelled nicely behind horses, but could not quicken when pulled out. Raised 5lb for his ready win at Ffos Las, he remains in good heart but perhaps needs a seventh furlong now. (op 11-2)
Dream Vale(IRE), who has dropped 12lb since going into nurseries, didn't get home in the ground. (op 10-1 tchd 13-2)
Santo Prince(USA), who raced a little apart from the others on the far rail. He may benefit from a return to further on a better surface. (op 4-1)
Angels Calling, a Ffos Las winner last time, was disappointing, as she was 2lb ahead of the handicapper under the penalty and could have been expected to act on the ground. However, the trainer's representative reported that she was unsuited by the heavy going. Official explanation: trainer's rep said filly was unsuited by the heavy ground (op 8-1)

6630 FRANK AND TOM FITZGERALD H'CAP 1m
4:45 (4:45) (Class 3) (0-90,89) 3-Y-O+ **£6,663** (£1,982; £990; £495) **Stalls** Low

Form RPR
2421 **1** **Chosen Character (IRE)**[13] 6235 4-9-3 **87** ....(vt) NatashaEaton(5) 4 96
(Tom Dascombe) *mde all: rdn 1f out: edgd rt ins fnl f: kpt on wl* **11/4**[1]
0-10 **2** *½* **Amaze**[93] 3493 4-9-1 **80** .... BarryMcHugh 1 88
(Brian Ellison) *trckd ldrs: rdn over 2f out: styd on u.p whn chalng for 2nd ins fnl f: tk 2nd post* **12/1**
-000 **3** *hd* **Tiger Reigns**[14] 6202 6-9-1 **80** .... PJMcDonald 5 88
(Michael Dods) *chsd wnr: rdn over 1f out: styd on u.p but hld thrght fnl f: lost 2nd post* **15/2**
0006 **4** *2 ¼* **Leviathan**[28] 5794 5-8-12 **77** ....(t) FergusSweeney 3 79
(Tony Newcombe) *hld up: hdwy 2f out: chsd ldrs over 1f out: kpt on but no imp ins fnl f* **6/1**
1100 **5** *2* **Lockantanks**[20] 6036 5-9-5 **89** .... CharlesBishop(5) 8 87
(Michael Appleby) *trckd ldrs: rdn over 2f out: kpt on same pce fnl f* **16/1**
0062 **6** *hd* **Extraterrestrial**[7] 6426 8-8-12 **82** .... ShaneBKelly(5) 10 79
(Richard Fahey) *midfield: rdn over 2f out: edgd lft over 1f out: kpt on ins fnl f: nvr able to chal* **4/1**[2]
2166 **7** *nk* **Hayek**[13] 6235 5-8-6 **76** ....(b) AdamCarter(5) 6 73
(Tim Easterby) *hld up in rr: hdwy on outer 3f out: rdn over 1f out: kpt on ins fnl f: nvr able to chal* **10/1**
062 **8** *5* **Barren Brook**[31] 5712 5-9-4 **83** .... JamesSullivan 2 68
(Michael Easterby) *midfield tl rdn and wknd wl over 1f out* **5/1**[3]
300U **9** *7* **Loyalty**[8] 6400 5-8-13 **78** ....(v) PatrickMathers 9 47
(Derek Shaw) *hld up: rdn 3f out: lft bhd wl over 1f out* **33/1**

1m 47.28s (3.58) **Going Correction** +0.50s/f (Yiel) **9** Ran SP% **115.0**
Speed ratings (Par 107): **102,101,101,99,97 96,96,91,84**
toteswingers 1&2 £4.80, 1&3 £5.80, 2&3 £11.40 CSF £37.29 CT £224.59 TOTE £3.20: £1.50, £3.70, £3.30; EX 37.90.
Owner Aykroyd And Sons Ltd **Bred** Moyglare Stud Farm Ltd **Trained** Malpas, Cheshire

FOCUS
A decent handicap in which nothing became involved from off the gallop. Another personal best from Chosen Character.

NOTEBOOK
Chosen Character(IRE) made every yard, his rider judging the pace perfectly, and held on well after edging away from the inside in the closing stages. Representing a yard in fine form at present, he has had a terrific time of it with five wins since July on ground ranging from firm to heavy. He's risen 17lb during this period and was defying a career-high mark here, while this was his third win from four runs at Haydock. (op 7-2 tchd 4-1 in a place)
Amaze was easily the least experienced member of this field and he ran well, sticking on against the fence. Off the track since a poor run on his handicap debut three months ago, he will appreciate going back to 1m2f. (op 10-1)
Tiger Reigns, for whom this was something of a return to form, was racing from no less than 17lb lower than when last successful two years ago and had no problems with the ground. (op 7-1 tchd 6-1)
Leviathan didn't get the best of runs and, given that it proved hard to come from off the gallop on this card, he remains one to be interested in. Currently 12lb below his last winning mark, he was equipped with a tongue-tie for the first time. (op 7-1after early price 10-1 in a place, tchd 11-2)
Lockantanks, down the field in a couple of starts on Polytrack since his back-to-back wins in July on a sound surface, ran only respectably off top weight. (op 20-1)
Extraterrestrial, a recent Ayr second, was able to race off 4lb lower and was officially 6lb well-in, but could not take advantage. Trapped wide, he put his head in the air when asked for his effort and could never mount a challenge. (op 7-2)
Barren Brook returned to form at Ripon and winner Voodoo Prince has since run well in a Listed race, but he was unable to show his best on this bad ground. (tchd 11-2)

6631 BETDAQ HAYDOCK PARK APPRENTICE TRAINING SERIES H'CAP (PART OF THE RACING EXCELLENCE INITIATIVE) 1m 2f 95y
5:20 (5:20) (Class 5) (0-70,69) 3-Y-O+ **£2,264** (£673; £336; £168) **Stalls** High

Form RPR
2331 **1** **Grand Liaison**[7] 6442 3-8-4 **60** 6ex.............................. HannahNunn(5) 5 69
(John Berry) *racd keenly in midfield: hdwy 5f out: led 1f out: kpt on and pushed out ins fnl f: jst hld on* **15/8**[1]
430 **2** *shd* **Badea**[13] 6240 3-9-1 **66** ....(b[1]) ShaneBKelly 4 74
(Richard Fahey) *s.i.s: impr to ld after 1f: hdd over 4f out: remained prom: pushed along over 3f out: rallied towards fin: jst failed* **20/1**
6502 **3** *2 ¼* **Hernando Torres**[3] 6562 4-8-9 **59** .... MatthewHopkins(5) 3 63
(Michael Easterby) *dwlt: hld up: hdwy to trck ldrs 7f out: rdn to ld over 2f out: hdd over 1f out: ev ch tl no ex fnl 50yds* **7/1**
56 **4** *3 ¼* **Jordaura**[30] 5730 6-8-12 **64** .... JordanHibberd(7) 8 62
(Alan Berry) *towards rr: nt clr run and checked 2f out: sn swtchd rt: kpt on fnl f: nt trble ldrs* **25/1**
1054 **5** *nse* **My Boy Ginger**[31] 5721 3-9-1 **66** .... AshleyMorgan 10 63
(Rod Millman) *hld up: hdwy on outer 2f out: chsd ldrs over 1f out: styd on same pce and no imp fnl f* **6/1**[3]
3300 **6** *3* **Market Puzzle (IRE)**[42] 5310 5-8-7 **55** oh10..........(p) RachealKneller(3) 1 47
(Mark Brisbourne) *prom: lost pl 3f out: rallied 2f out: edgd rt 2f out: edgd lft u.p over 1f out: wl hld after* **25/1**
2424 **7** *5* **Zaplamation (IRE)**[18] 6103 7-8-13 **61** .... WilliamTwiston-Davies(3) 11 43
(John Quinn) *hld up: rdn over 2f out: nvr on terms* **6/1**[3]
4013 **8** *½* **Choral Bee**[14] 6210 3-8-7 **58** .... AmyScott 9 39
(Henry Candy) *led for 1f: prom: led over 4f out: hdd over 2f out: wknd over 1f out* **17/2**
3621 **9** *14* **Dazzling Valentine**[21] 5990 4-9-6 **68** .... NatashaEaton(3) 2 23
(Alan Bailey) *prom: losing pl whn n.m.r over 2f out: sn edgd lft: eased whn wl btn over 1f out* **11/2**[2]
/000 **10** *5* **El Bravo**[8] 6405 6-9-6 **68** .... ShirleyTeasdale(3) 7 13
(Shaun Harris) *midfield: niggled along 4f out: wknd over 3f out* **20/1**

2m 19.52s (4.02) **Going Correction** +0.50s/f (Yiel)
WFA 3 from 4yo+ 6lb **10** Ran SP% **119.0**
Speed ratings (Par 103): **103,102,101,98,98 96,92,91,80,76**
toteswingers 1&2 £8.30, 1&3 £3.20, 2&3 £16.80 CSF £49.38 CT £221.15 TOTE £2.90: £1.80, £4.80, £2.30; EX 41.60.
Owner Barrie Catchpole & Michael Meaney **Bred** Ashbrittle Stud **Trained** Newmarket, Suffolk
■ Stewards' Enquiry : Shane B Kelly seven-day ban: used whip above permitted level (Oct 12-18)

FOCUS
Just a modest apprentice handicap in which the gallop was fairly steady. The race distance was 13 yards further than advertised. The winner was well in and the runner-up was back to form.
Dazzling Valentine Official explanation: trainer's rep said filly was unsuited by the heavy ground; jockey said filly hung left
T/Plt: £13.70 to a £1 stake. Pool: £57,016.76 - 3,016.86 winning tickets T/Qpdt: £5.20 to a £1 stake. Pool: £4,685.45 - 662.15 winning tickets DO

6596 NEWMARKET (R-H)
Friday, September 28

OFFICIAL GOING: Good (overall 7.7, stands' side 7.8; centre 7.7; far side 7.5)
Far side of Rowley Mile course used. Stalls on far side except 12f: centre.
Wind: fresh, half behind Weather: cloudy, dry

6632 SAKHEE OH SO SHARP STKS (GROUP 3) (FILLIES) 7f
1:15 (1:16) (Class 1) 2-Y-O
£22,684 (£8,600; £4,304; £2,144; £1,076; £540) **Stalls** Low

Form RPR
141 **1** **Waterway Run (USA)**[19] 6070 2-8-12 90.............................. JimCrowley 8 101+
(Ralph Beckett) *chsd ldrs: rdn to chse ldr jst over 2f out: led 1f out: kpt on wl fnl f: rdn out* **5/2**[1]
1013 **2** *½* **Light Up My Life (IRE)**[14] 6199 2-8-12 95.............................. PatDobbs 9 100+
(Richard Hannon) *led: rdn 2f out: edgd rt and clr w wnr over 1f out: hdd 1f out: kpt on wl but a hld ins fnl f* **5/1**[3]
5214 **3** *3* **Annie's Fortune (IRE)**[34] 5571 2-8-12 101............ MichaelJMMurphy 6 93
(Alan Jarvis) *squeezed for room s and slowly away: t.k.h: hld up in last pair: rdn and effrt over 2f out: hdwy to chse ldrs over 1f out: kpt on to go 3rd fnl 100yds: no threat to ldng pair* **6/1**
1 **4** *1* **Power Of Light (IRE)**[13] 6257 2-8-12 0.................... MickaelBarzalona 4 89+
(Mahmood Al Zarooni) *stdd s: hld up in rr: swtchd rt and effrt ent fnl 2f: hdwy u.p to chse ldng pair over 1f out: one pce and no imp after: lost 3rd fnl 100yds* **5/1**[3]
504 **5** *3* **Sinaadi (IRE)**[34] 5578 2-8-12 70.............................. TomQueally 1 82
(Clive Brittain) *in tch in midfield: rdn and effrt over 2f out: outpcd and btn over 1f out: plugged on u.p fnl f* **66/1**
1121 **6** *nk* **Jamesbo's Girl**[15] 6160 2-8-12 86.............................. TonyHamilton 3 81
(Richard Fahey) *chsd ldrs: rdn and struggling over 2f out: wknd over 1f out* **8/1**
1252 **7** *½* **Califante**[28] 5787 2-8-12 99.............................. RichardHughes 2 80
(Richard Hannon) *in tch: shuffled bk towards rr and nt clr run over 2f out: swtchd rt 2f out: rdn whn swtchd lft and bmpd over 1f out: no prog and wl hld after* **9/2**[2]
100 **8** *¾* **Rayaheen**[22] 5979 2-8-12 86.............................. PaulHanagan 7 77
(Richard Hannon) *stdd s and wnt rt s: hld up in tch: rdn and no rspnse over 2f out: wknd over 1f out* **16/1**
0306 **9** *32* **All On Red (IRE)**[27] 5828 2-8-12 85..............................(b[1]) HayleyTurner 5
(Tobias B P Coles) *wnt lft s: racd keenly: chsd ldr tl jst over 2f out: sn dropped out: t.o fnl f* **80/1**

1m 23.86s (-1.54) **Going Correction** -0.05s/f (Good) **9** Ran SP% **114.1**
Speed ratings (Par 102): **106,105,102,100,97 97,96,95,59**
toteswingers 1&2 £5.10, 1&3 £4.20, 2&3 £6.60 CSF £14.93 TOTE £3.30: £1.60, £2.20, £1.60; EX 15.20 Trifecta £151.60 Pool: £1,214.85 - 5.93 winning tickets..
Owner Thurloe Thoroughbreds XX **Bred** Dorothy Alexander Matz **Trained** Kimpton, Hants

FOCUS
There was only half a millimetre of rain overnight and the ground remained good (GoingStick overall 7.7; stands' side 7.8, centre 7.7, far side 7.5), which was confirmed by the riders after the first. Not a race that has had much of a bearing on the following year's Classics in recent seasons. This looked a little below the recent standard for the race but in keeping with the ten-year average. The first two are both improving with racing.

NOTEBOOK
Waterway Run(USA), just like Questing, who was runner-up in this race last year and is now a top filly in the US, is bred for the dirt surface, being by Arch out of a Dixieland Band mare. Interestingly, she's already nominated for the Breeders' Cup Juvenile Fillies Turf so will get her chance to showcase her talents that side of the pond, but in theory it's on the main track that she'll be seen to best effect long term. She reversed Newmarket form with the second on 5lb worse terms. (op 7-2)
Light Up My Life(IRE) gave Waterway Run 5lb and a beating in a nursery on the July course last month. Both fillies have clearly progressed since then, especially Waterway Run, but this was still a good effort in defeat by Light Up My Fire, who was building on her third place in the May Hill. (op 7-1)
Annie's Fortune(IRE) didn't have things go in her favour. She was squeezed out at the start and dropped towards the back of the field, where she raced a touch keenly, and she struggled to land a blow in a race in which the first two were prominent throughout. Official explanation: trainer said filly lost left-fore shoe (op 5-1)
Power Of Light(IRE), who bolted up in an ordinary maiden at Newcastle on her debut, made some late progress once edging over towards the far rail (seen as the place to be in later races). The least experienced filly in the line-up, she still showed signs of greenness, and there should be better to come from her. (op 7-2)
Sinaadi(IRE) excelled herself for connections responsible for last year's winner Alsindi. Her dam stayed 1m6f so she should get a good deal further as a 3yo.
Jamesbo's Girl, progressive in nurseries, wasn't at her best here, and perhaps she's had enough for the year. (tchd 9-1)

Califante travelled well enough but found little when let down. She didn't appear happy on the track. (op 4-1)

Rayaheen, keen early, was another who didn't look comfortable on the track. She hasn't progressed from her maiden win. (op 25-1)

6633 MAWATHEEQ ROSEMARY STKS (LISTED RACE) (F&M) 1m
1:45 (1:46) (Class 1) 3-Y-0+

£18,714 (£7,095; £3,550; £1,768; £887; £445) **Stalls** Low

Form RPR

2161 **1** **Chigun**[20] 6023 3-8-10 99 TomQueally 3 107
(Sir Henry Cecil) *chsd ldrs: rdn to chse ldr wl over 1f out: drvn and ev ch whn carried lft ent fnl f: led fnl 75yds: kpt on wl: drvn out* **5/1**[3]

1121 **2** *nk* **Thistle Bird**[20] 6029 4-9-0 107 JamesDoyle 7 106
(Roger Charlton) *in tch: rdn and effrt wl over 1f out: chsd ldrs and carried lft 1f out: swtchd lft ins fnl f: styd on wl to go 2nd cl home* **11/4**[1]

1330 **3** *nk* **Moone's My Name**[27] 5834 4-9-0 97 JimCrowley 1 105
(Ralph Beckett) *racd along towards far side: overall ldr: edging bk and jnd field whn rdn wl over 1f out: edgd lft u.p over 1f out: hdd and no ex fnl 75yds: lost 2nd cl home* **20/1**

2612 **4** *1 3/4* **Ladys First**[27] 5834 3-8-10 103 (p) PaulHanagan 6 101
(Richard Fahey) *chsd ldr tl 2f out: unable qck and sltly outpcd over 1f out: rallied u.p and kpt on ins fnl f* **15/2**

0121 **5** *nse* **Dank**[27] 5834 3-8-13 104 RichardHughes 8 104+
(Sir Michael Stoute) *hld up in tch in last quartet: rdn and effrt over 1f out: kpt on ins fnl f: nvr gng pce to rch ldrs* **4/1**[2]

1040 **6** *nk* **Libys Dream (IRE)**[15] 6161 4-9-0 92 RichardKingscote 10 100
(Tom Dascombe) *hld up in tch: rdn and effrt ent fnl 2f: no imp tl swtchd lft jst ins fnl f: styd on u.p fnl 100yds* **50/1**

0160 **7** *nk* **Falls Of Lora (IRE)**[27] 5834 3-8-10 107 FrankieDettori 2 99
(Mahmood Al Zarooni) *in tch: rdn and effrt wl over 1f out: unable qck and wandered u.p over 1f out: one pce and btn fnl f* **6/1**

3406 **8** *1 3/4* **Irish History (IRE)**[27] 5834 3-8-10 106 MickaelBarzalona 5 95
(Mahmood Al Zarooni) *in tch: swtchd rt and effrt 2f out: unable qck and outpcd over 1f out: wknd jst ins fnl f* **12/1**

0023 **9** *2 1/2* **Valencha**[15] 6161 5-9-0 99 JimmyFortune 4 89
(Hughie Morrison) *stdd s: t.k.h: hld up in tch in last quartet: rdn and effrt over 1f out: no prog and wl hld fnl f* **12/1**

3210 **10** *7* **Princess Of Orange**[27] 5834 3-8-10 91 SebSanders 9 72
(Rae Guest) *v.s.i.s: a in rr: rdn 2f out: sn wknd* **40/1**

1m 36.18s (-2.42) **Going Correction** -0.05s/f (Good)
WFA 3 from 4yo+ 4lb **10** Ran SP% **113.9**
Speed ratings (Par 111): **110,109,109,107,107 107,107,105,102,95**
toteswingers 1&2 £3.10, 1&3 £17.00, 2&3 £12.70 CSF £18.32 TOTE £5.20: £1.40, £1.50, £4.80; EX 14.90 Trifecta £312.80 Pool: £1,978.60 - 4.68 winning tickets..
Owner V I Araci **Bred** Whatton Manor Stud **Trained** Newmarket, Suffolk

FOCUS
This competitive fillies' and mares' Listed prize was run in a heavy shower of rain. Only Moone's My Name explored a route nearer to the far rail, but she came centre 3f out. Those racing on the pace were no doubt at a significant advantage as it was run at a modest tempo and the overall form should be treated with a degree of caution. The winner needed only marginal improvement on her Ascot win with her form rivals not at their best.

NOTEBOOK
Chigun looked a Pattern performer in the making when hacking up from the front off a mark of 89 at Ascot 20 days earlier and confirmed that impression here with a gutsy effort on her debut up in class. She couldn't dominate this time, but battled bravely, after being carried a little left, for one relatively inexperienced so it was a decent effort. It was her third success as a miler and this does appear to be her optimum. With that in mind races such as the Windsor Forest Stakes at the Royal Meeting back at Ascot next year will now surely be her aim. (op 9-2 tchd 11-2)

Thistle Bird has enjoyed a cracking 2012 and very nearly made it 4-5 for the year. She was close enough if good enough when the pace quickened, but lacked the tactical pace of the winner and was coming back at that rival all too late at the finish. This consistent 4yo rates the best guide for the form. (tchd 5-2 and 3-1)

Moone's My Name, whose trainer/rider took the opener, made a bold bid and this was better again from her return to more positive tactics. She was suited by racing on the pace, but is a tough filly and deserves to win something similar. (tchd 18-1)

Ladys First cut out the early running and held every chance. She went in first-time cheekpieces and didn't raise her game for the application, but is another that can be used to base the form around. (op 10-1)

Dank moved sweetly off the pace, but this certainly wasn't run to suit a hold-up horse and she never had a serious chance to land a blow. Don't abandon her yet. (op 5-1)

Libys Dream(IRE), a little free under early restraint, was doing some decent work late on after coming nearer to the stands' side with her effort. Her run needs upgrading somewhat and it confirms her back on track. (tchd 66-1)

Falls Of Lora(IRE) came home one place ahead of stablemate Irish History, the pair producing fairly laboured efforts. (tchd 11-2)

6634 NAYEF JOEL STKS (BRITISH CHAMPIONS SERIES) (GROUP 2) 1m
2:20 (2:21) (Class 1) 3-Y-0+

£56,710 (£21,500; £10,760; £5,360; £2,690; £1,350) **Stalls** Low

Form RPR

1055 **1** **Penitent**[13] 6246 6-9-3 114 DanielTudhope 4 117
(David O'Meara) *racd far side: led gp and chsd ldrs overall: rdn 3f out: led ent fnl f: kpt on wl ins fnl f: hrd pressed and hld on cl home: all out: 1st of 3 in gp* **10/1**

1332 **2** *nk* **Side Glance**[35] 5560 5-9-3 115 JimmyFortune 6 116
(Andrew Balding) *racd in centre: hld up in tch: rdn over 2f out: hdwy u.p over 1f out: hrd drvn and styd on wl fnl f: chsd wnr wl ins fnl f: pressing wnr cl home: nt quite get up: 1st of 7 in gp* **6/1**[3]

1001 **3** *1 1/4* **Premio Loco (USA)**[34] 5573 8-9-3 111 GeorgeBaker 2 113
(Chris Wall) *racd far side: hld up in midfield overall: rdn and effrt wl over 1f out: drvn and kpt on wl ins fnl f: wnt 3rd towards fin: 2nd of 3 in gp* **16/1**

2246 **4** *1/2* **Stipulate**[35] 5560 3-8-13 108 TomQueally 9 112
(Sir Henry Cecil) *racd in centre: chsd ldrs: rdn to ld wl over 1f out: hdd ent fnl f: no ex and lost 2 pls fnl 100yds: 2nd of 7 in gp* **17/2**

2103 **5** *2* **Joviality**[41] 5376 4-9-0 112 WilliamBuick 7 104
(John Gosden) *racd in centre: stmbld s: chsd overall ldr: rdn 2f out: unable qck ent fnl f: wknd wl ins fnl f: 3rd of 7 in gp* **6/1**[3]

3663 **6** *1* **Saigon**[7] 6449 3-8-13 105 KirstyMilczarek 8 105
(James Toller) *racd in centre: stdd s: t.k.h: hld up in rr: rdn and effrt wl over 1f out: no imp tl styd on u.p fnl 100yds: unable to chal: 4th of 7 in gp* **25/1**

-010 **7** *2 1/2* **Most Improved (IRE)**[47] 5141 3-9-3 116 KierenFallon 11 103
(Brian Meehan) *racd in centre: racd keenly: overall ldr and sn clr: rdn over 2f out: hdd wl over 1f out: edgd rt u.p over 1f out: wknd fnl f: 5th of 7 in gp* **7/2**[1]

1012 **8** *9* **Sovereign Debt (IRE)**[43] 5278 3-8-13 111 JamieSpencer 1 77
(Michael Bell) *racd far side: hld up in rr: rdn and edgd lft jst over 2f out: no hdwy and wknd over 1f out: 3rd of 3 in gp* **8/1**

0010 **9** *4* **Fanunalter**[33] 5651 6-9-3 114 SilvestreDeSousa 10 68
(Michael Wigham) *racd in centre: t.k.h: hld up in rr: rdn and no hdwy 2f out: wknd over 1f out: 6th of 7 in gp* **14/1**

4015 **10** *9* **Trumpet Major (IRE)**[34] 5573 3-8-13 114 RichardHughes 5 46
(Richard Hannon) *racd in centre: in tch in midfield: rdn 2f out: sn struggling and wknd over 1f out: bhd and eased fnl f: 7th of 7 in gp* **5/1**[2]

1m 36.32s (-2.28) **Going Correction** -0.05s/f (Good)
WFA 3 from 4yo+ 4lb **10** Ran SP% **114.6**
Speed ratings (Par 115): **109,108,107,106,104 103,101,92,88,79**
toteswingers 1&2 £11.80, 1&3 £26.90, 2&3 £16.00 CSF £67.64 TOTE £20.90: £10.00, £1.40, £6.70; EX 79.50 Trifecta £1580.70 Pool: £3,246.95 - 1.52 winning tickets..
Owner Middleham Park Racing XVII **Bred** Cheveley Park Stud Ltd **Trained** Nawton, N Yorks

FOCUS
The far rail appeared to be an advantage here. Again few got involved. Penintent is rated to his old best, with Side Glance to this year's form and Premio Loco a length off his Goodwood latest.

NOTEBOOK
Penitent, runner-up in this race two years ago, might have been at an advantage in racing on the far rail, but it's possible he simply went a far more even gallop than Most Improved, who led the group up the centre. Enjoying the run of things on his side of the track, he saw his race out well, appreciating the return to a mile having found 7f too short last time. (op 14-1)

Side Glance took advantage of the good gallop set by Most Improved up the centre and came from off the pace to take second, a clear winner from his group. He's a reliable sort, and the form is easily rated through him. (op 5-1)

Premio Loco(USA) also showed the benefit of racing in the group on the far side, keeping on well for a place without really threatening the winner. (op 14-1)

Stipulate did best of the 3yos, who we know are an ordinary bunch this year. He tended to hang under pressure up the hill, which didn't make his rider's task any easier. (op 12-1 tchd 8-1)

Joviality, who chased Most Improved centre-field, could have probably done with being ridden with a bit more patience. The only filly in the line-up, she didn't do badly in the circumstances. (op 5-1)

Saigon, who had a bit to find at this level, didn't settle early despite the good gallop. (op 28-1 tchd 33-1)

Most Improved(IRE) raced far too enthusiastically in front and was burnt out with 2f to run. (op 4-1)

Fanunalter has excelled himself in small-field races when the pace is steady up front. In this race there was a good gallop on and he was simply outclassed. Official explanation: jockey said gelding had no more to give

Trumpet Major(IRE) hasn't beaten a single horse home in three of his last four starts now, which is concerning. Official explanation: trainer's rep said colt scoped dirty (op 11-2)

6635 SHADWELL FILLIES' MILE (GROUP 1) 1m
2:55 (2:56) (Class 1) 2-Y-0

£92,720 (£35,152; £17,592; £8,763; £4,398; £2,207) **Stalls** Low

Form RPR

111 **1** **Certify (USA)**[14] 6199 2-8-12 111 MickaelBarzalona 2 112+
(Mahmood Al Zarooni) *stdd s: hld up in last pair: hdwy towards far side over 2f out: rdn and qcknd to ld wl over 1f out: clr and edgd lft 1f out: r.o strly: readily* **4/6**[1]

011 **2** *4 1/2* **Roz**[64] 4514 2-8-12 101 JimCrowley 5 102
(Harry Dunlop) *wnt lft s: led for 1f: chsd ldr after: rdn and unable qck w wnr wl over 1f out: no ch w wnr but kpt on u.p to hold 2nd* **8/1**[3]

1453 **3** *1* **Amazonas (IRE)**[34] 5571 2-8-12 102 FrankieDettori 7 100
(Ed Dunlop) *stdd s: t.k.h: hld up in last pair: rdn and effrt 2f out: no ch w wnr but kpt on u.p fnl f: wnt 3rd last strides* **10/1**

5125 **4** *hd* **Masarah (IRE)**[14] 6199 2-8-12 80 TomQueally 4 99
(Clive Brittain) *led after 1f and set stdy gallop: rdn 2f out: sn hdd and outpcd by wnr: no ch w wnr but kpt on fnl f* **100/1**

1210 **5** *3/4* **Discernable**[41] 5379 2-8-12 0 SilvestreDeSousa 3 98
(Mark Johnston) *t.k.h early: chsd ldrs: rdn and outpcd by wnr wl over 1f out: no ch w wnr and one pce fnl f* **11/1**

111 **6** *1/2* **Ollie Olga (USA)**[34] 5571 2-8-12 105 MartinHarley 6 96+
(Mick Channon) *bmpd s: hld up in tch: rdn and effrt 2f out: hanging rt and outpcd sn after: no ch w wnr and styd on same pce fnl f* **7/2**[2]

1m 38.19s (-0.41) **Going Correction** -0.05s/f (Good) **6** Ran SP% **111.7**
Speed ratings (Par 106): **100,95,94,94,93 93**
toteswingers 1&2 £1.80, 1&3 £1.80, 2&3 £3.60 CSF £6.89 TOTE £1.60: £1.20, £3.40; EX 6.30.
Owner Godolphin **Bred** Hurstland Farm Inc Et Al **Trained** Newmarket, Suffolk

FOCUS
A typical Fillies' Mile in many respects. Despite the potential lack of pace being a worry the tempo was a respectable one, although the majority did take time to settle. They raced just off the far rail. Certify more than confirmed her May Hill form and the race overall makes sense.

NOTEBOOK
Certify(USA) came through with her challenge nearest to the far rail and the suspicion is that being there was a help. The classy winner still proved far too strong for this lot, however, and would have won wherever she had raced. Trainer Mahmood Al Zarooni won this for the first time with Lyric Of Light last year and this filly arrived with a very similar profile, having done enough to extend her unbeaten run in the May Hill at Doncaster a fortnight earlier. Certify had already achieved more of the two, though, having taken the Sweet Solera the time before and did look the standout performer on this first foray into a Group 1. Her pre-race odds collapsed after the withdrawal of Winsili and, with Ollie Olga flopping, it was a soft race for the class. However, that should not detract from her performance one bit and she displayed an impressive turn of foot when asked to close up. Indeed she still looked somewhat inexperienced when out in front and the best of her has probably still to be seen. She has now proved herself over the C&D of the 1000 Guineas, for which she was promoted into clear favouritsm for next year in most ante-post books. Ladbrokes stood out afterwards, though, going 12-1 and much does depend on how she matures during the winter with the first fillies' classic in mind. No doubt she is the top filly among the current crop of juveniles and she acts on most ground, so it is very much hoped she can continue her progression at three. (tchd 4-7)

Roz made it 2-3 when making all in Listed company at Sandown and had not been out since due to ground easing against her. The easing surface here therefore wasn't ideal for her, but she posted another solid effort in defeat and got the extra furlong without much fuss. The winner was in a different league, but she's evidently still improving and there's every chance she can pick up a Group race next year on a sound surface.

Amazonas(IRE) could be given a chance of reversing Prestige Stakes form with winner Ollie Olga up a furlong in this higher grade, as she didn't look happy on that circuit and still finished strongly. She duly did so and appreciated the stiffer test, but was obviously helped by that rival failing to fire. (op 12-1 tchd 16-1)

Masarah(IRE) set out to make all and ultimately ran close to her last-time-out Doncaster form with the winner, so rates a solid benchmark.

Discernable was progressive during the summer, but despite it being her first outing over the trip this was the second occasion she has failed to see out her race in Group company. (op 14-1 tchd 16-1)

Ollie Olga(USA) looked awkward and was beaten well before stamina became an issue. It could well be the track wasn't for her and her rider was of that opinion, but perhaps some of the blame can be attributed to her being in season a few weeks earlier. (tchd 4-1)

6636 NUNNERY STUD EBF MAIDEN STKS 7f

3:25 (3:31) (Class 4) 2-Y-O **£5,175** (£1,540; £769; £384) **Stalls** Low

Form RPR

1 **Seek Again (USA)** 2-9-3 0 WilliamBuick 7 85+
(John Gosden) *in tch: hdwy to trck ldrs gng wl ent fnl 2f: rdn to ld ent fnl f: clr and in command fnl 150yds: r.o wl: comf* **4/1**[2]

2 *2 ¼* **Regal Silk** 2-8-12 0 SilvestreDeSousa 15 74+
(Jeremy Noseda) *in tch in midfield: hdwy to chse ldrs gng wl 2f out: rdn over 1f out: outpcd by wnr 1f out: styd on to chse clr wnr fnl 100yds: no imp* **20/1**

4 **3** *1 ¼* **You Da One (IRE)**[15] [6167] 2-9-3 0 JimmyFortune 19 76
(Andrew Balding) *t.k.h: chsd ldr: rdn and ev ch 2f out tl unable qck w wnr ent fnl f: kpt on same pce fnl f* **12/1**[3]

3 **4** *½* **Stamford**[115] [2784] 2-9-3 0 FrankieDettori 8 75
(Mahmood Al Zarooni) *taken down early: broke wl and led: rdn 2f out: hdd and outpcd by wnr ent fnl f: styd on same pce ins fnl f* **4/1**[2]

5 *3 ½* **Mujazif (IRE)** 2-9-3 0 MartinLane 4 66
(Brian Meehan) *in tch: rdn and effrt ent fnl 2f: outpcd and btn over 1f out: wknd fnl f* **33/1**

6 *1* **Dare To Achieve** 2-9-3 0 RichardHughes 3 63
(William Haggas) *chsd ldrs: rdn and unable qck on downhill run wl over 1f out: sn outpcd and btn: wknd fnl f* **7/2**[1]

7 *3 ¼* **King's Request (IRE)** 2-9-3 0 RichardMullen 12 54+
(Sir Michael Stoute) *in tch: rdn and unable qckn over 2f out: wknd u.p over 1f out* **25/1**

8 *¾* **Calculated (USA)** 2-9-3 0 MickaelBarzalona 17 53
(Mahmood Al Zarooni) *in tch: rdn and unable qck ent fnl f: sn btn and wknd over 1f out* **12/1**[3]

9 *nk* **Song Light** 2-9-3 0 SebSanders 11 52+
(David Elsworth) *hld up towards rr: rdn and no imp whn edgd rt over 2f out: no ch but kpt on again ins fnl f* **100/1**

10 *nk* **Hornboy** 2-9-3 0 GrahamLee 2 51+
(Jeremy Noseda) *hld up in midfield: rdn: unable qck and rn green over 2f out: sn outpcd and btn 2f out: wl hld but plugged on fr over 1f out* **25/1**

11 *nse* **Pleasure Bent** 2-9-3 0 KierenFallon 16 51+
(Luca Cumani) *hld up in tch: rdn and outpcd over 2f out: wl hld and plugged on same pce fnl 2f* **20/1**

12 *nk* **Vital Evidence (USA)** 2-9-3 0 PatDobbs 10 50
(Sir Michael Stoute) *in tch in midfield: rdn and unable qck 1/2-way: outpcd over 2f out: no ch but plugged on again fnl f* **12/1**[3]

13 *3 ¼* **Aneedh** 2-9-3 0 MichaelHills 18 42+
(William Haggas) *stdd s: hld up in rr: rdn and outpcd over 2f out: wl hld but styd on past btn horses 2f out: n.d* **50/1**

14 *1 ½* **Mandy's Boy (IRE)** 2-9-3 0 JamieSpencer 1 38+
(Ed Dunlop) *stdd s: hld up in rr: rdn and short-lived effrt over 2f out: wknd wl over 1f out* **40/1**

15 *1 ¼* **Nelson Quay (IRE)** 2-9-3 0 PatCosgrave 20 34+
(Jeremy Gask) *t.k.h: hld up in tch in midfield: rdn and no hdwy over 2f out: sn wknd* **100/1**

0 **16** *4* **Savvy Chic (USA)**[48] [5104] 2-8-12 0 TomQueally 9 19
(Jeremy Noseda) *in tch in midfield: rdn and no rspnse 3f out: sn lost pl and bhd wl over 1f out* **14/1**

17 *1* **Plutocracy (IRE)** 2-9-3 0 TedDurcan 6 21+
(David Lanigan) *stdd s: rn green and a in rr: bhd fnl 2f* **33/1**

18 *1 ¼* **Posh Boy (IRE)** 2-9-3 0 GeorgeBaker 13 18+
(Chris Wall) *hld up in rr: rdn and lost tch jst over 2f out* **66/1**

19 *2 ¼* **Giddy Heights** 2-9-3 0 DarryllHolland 14 12+
(Jeremy Noseda) *s.i.s: rn green and sn rdn along: a bhd: lost tch over 2f out* **40/1**

1m 25.37s (-0.03) **Going Correction** -0.05s/f (Good) **19** Ran SP% **125.4**
Speed ratings (Par 97): **98,95,94,93,89 88,84,83,83,83 82,82,78,77,75 71,70,68,66**
toteswingers 1&2 £23.60, 1&3 £12.70, 2&3 £31.20 CSF £89.52 TOTE £5.70: £2.60, £7.30, £4.30; EX 113.70 TRIFECTA Not won..

Owner K Abdulla **Bred** Juddmonte Farms Inc **Trained** Newmarket, Suffolk

FOCUS

A fascinating 2yo maiden and it looked wide open. Few got seriously involved from off the pace as the first four came well clear, but the race should produce plenty of future winners. This often goes to a juvenile with previous experience so there was plenty to like about the debut effort of the winner. The form is rated around the race averages and the fourth.

NOTEBOOK

Seek Again(USA) knuckled down well to get on top from the furlong marker and handed his yard a fourth winner of the meeting. Half-brother to a very useful 2yo winner over this trip, he ran green around 3f out but responded most kindly to some pressure and he was nicely on top at the finish. A stiffer test should be well within his compass next year and he rates a smart prospect. (op 10-3 tchd 9-2)

Regal Silk ◆, one of two fillies in attendance, was also making her debut and highlighted the current form of her yard's 2yos with a promising display. She made up her ground smoothly and, looking sure to benefit from an extra furlong, should soon go one better.

You Da One(IRE) ◆ made the frame despite a sluggish start over 6f at Epsom on his debut and was expected to enjoy the extra furlong here. He ran a big race, doing best of those with previous experience, and is clearly a useful performer. He too should be off the mark before long. (op 14-1)

Stamford posted a promising debut effort over 6f at Leicester when last seen back in June. He tired late on after cutting out a lot of the running down the centre over this extra furlong, and probably just needed it in this better company. He too looks a very useful prospect. (op 9-2)

Mujazif(IRE) kept on after proving green and turned in an encouraging debut effort. He looks sure to stay further and will hold strong claims next time out.

Dare To Achieve, entered in the Racing Post Trophy, was fancied to go close on this racecourse debut and he knew his job from the gates, leading a trio that kept more towards the far side. It was clear around 2f out he was feeling the pinch, though, and he didn't look too happy on this track under maximum pressure. He's another that should enjoy a stiffer test before too long and can win his maiden this year. (op 4-1)

King's Request(IRE) advertised his inexperience in the preliminaries. He ought to come on a bundle and may prefer quicker ground.

Pleasure Bent shaped with some promise. He ran distinctly green and is a horse with scope. This 150,000gns buy could show up a lot better next time. (tchd 25-1)

6637 AQLAAM GODOLPHIN STKS (LISTED RACE) 1m 4f

4:00 (4:02) (Class 1) 3-Y-0+

£18,714 (£7,095; £3,550; £1,768; £887; £445) **Stalls** Centre

Form RPR

3534 **1** **Retrieve (AUS)**[59] [4684] 5-9-4 108 FrankieDettori 5 113
(Saeed Bin Suroor) *stdd s: hld up in rr: rdn over 3f out: hdwy to chsse clr ldng pair 3f out: clsd u.p over 1f out: styd on dourly to ld wl ins fnl f* **5/2**[1]

1344 **2** *1* **Harris Tweed**[34] [5575] 5-9-11 113 RichardHughes 7 118+
(William Haggas) *sn led: wnt clr w rival over 3f out: rdn wl over 1f out: asserted u.p 1f out: hdd wl ins fnl f: no ex* **7/2**[3]

2431 **3** *nk* **Songcraft (IRE)**[22] [5981] 4-9-4 109 SilvestreDeSousa 3 111
(Saeed Bin Suroor) *hld up in last pair: swtchd lft and rdn 4f out: hdwy to chse clr ldng pair 3f out: clsd and swtchd rt 1f out: chsd ldrs and hung rt u.p ins fnl f: styd on* **11/2**

5405 **4** *1 ¾* **Sea Of Heartbreak (IRE)**[19] [6080] 5-8-13 107 JamesDoyle 4 103+
(Roger Charlton) *t.k.h: chsd ldrs: jnd ldr and wnt clr over 3f out: rdn wl over 1f out: no ex and drvn 1f out: wknd ins fnl f* **10/3**[2]

1521 **5** *7* **Proud Chieftain**[16] [6142] 4-9-4 95 DarryllHolland 6 97
(Clifford Lines) *chsd ldr tl over 3f out: rdn and lost pl 3f out: 5th and wl hld fnl 2f* **22/1**

5400 **6** *10* **Dreamspeed (IRE)**[13] [6248] 5-9-4 95 JimmyFortune 1 81
(Andrew Balding) *t.k.h: hld up in midfield: rdn and no rspnse ent fnl 3f: sn btn and bhd fnl 2f* **16/1**

-150 **7** *39* **Arctic Cosmos (USA)**[133] [2254] 5-9-8 110 (p) WilliamBuick 2 23
(John Gosden) *chsd ldrs: rdn and lost pl over 3f out: drvn and wknd 3f out: t.o and virtually p.u ins fnl f* **7/1**

2m 29.82s (-2.18) **Going Correction** -0.05s/f (Good) **7** Ran SP% **112.0**
Speed ratings (Par 111): **105,104,104,102,98 91,65**
toteswingers 1&2 £2.40, 1&3 £2.20, 2&3 £2.70 CSF £10.94 TOTE £3.40: £2.10, £2.50; EX 8.20.

Owner Godolphin **Bred** Darley **Trained** Newmarket, Suffolk

FOCUS

Decent form for the grade off a solid pace from the runner-up. The winner was best in and is rated close to this year's top handicap form.

NOTEBOOK

Retrieve(AUS) had things set up for him as they started racing a long way from the finish here. He'd been ridden to get the trip on this step up in distance and came through strongly as they hit the rising ground, aided by the front two stopping in front, and is probably flattered a little by the bare form. (op 11-4)

Harris Tweed was taken on in front by Sea Of Heartbreak from half a mile out and forced to race earlier than his rider would have liked. While he responded well and saw off the mare with a furlong and a half to go, he was unsurprisingly run down late by the winner, who'd sat off the battle up front. It's worth remembering that he was giving 7lb to the winner so still comes out as the best horse in the race. (op 9-2)

Songcraft(IRE), like the winner, benefited from sitting well off the battle up front. The lesser fancied of the Godolphin pair, he hung right over to the far rail under pressure but put up a sound enough effort in defeat. (op 7-1)

Sea Of Heartbreak(IRE), who was a bit keen early, travelled up strongly to challenge the leader, but was soon outbattled by him and dropped out of contention for a place. She's best delivered late. (op 11-4 tchd 7-2)

Proud Chieftain, who led the main body of the field slightly away from the far rail, where Harris Tweed raced, from 7f out, was easily seen off once headed by Sea Of Heartbreak half a mile out. He had plenty to find at the weights. (op 20-1 tchd 25-1)

Dreamspeed(IRE) was another who was simply outclassed. (op 20-1 tchd 22-1)

Arctic Cosmos(USA) hasn't beaten a rival home in three starts since making all in a Listed race on Polytrack back in March. (op 5-1 tchd 8-1)

6638 STANDING FOR SUCCESS H'CAP (SILVER CAMBRIDGESHIRE) 1m 1f

4:35 (4:38) (Class 2) 3-Y-0+

£18,675 (£5,592; £2,796; £1,398; £699; £351) **Stalls** Low

Form RPR

2142 **1** **Henry Allingham**[14] [6205] 3-8-13 **84** NeilCallan 25 96
(Roger Varian) *racd in centre: in tch: rdn and effrt 2f out: chsd ldrs and carried lft ins fnl f: styd on to ld cl home: 1st of 12 in gp* **15/2**[1]

0060 **2** *nk* **Classic Colori (IRE)**[48] [5079] 5-9-2 **82** RichardHughes 24 93
(David O'Meara) *racd in centre: in tch: swtchd rt and hdwy 2f out: chsd ldrs and swtchd lft over 1f out: edgd lft u.p 1f out led ins fnl f tl hdd and no ex cl home: 2nd of 12 in gp* **8/1**[2]

0500 **3** *2 ¼* **Shamdarley (IRE)**[19] [6073] 4-8-12 **78** JimCrowley 7 84
(Michael Dods) *racd far side: hld up in midfield: rdn to chse ldrs over 1f out hung lft after: no ex fnl 100yds:1st of 14 in gp* **14/1**

3422 **4** *½* **Christmas Light**[8] [6410] 5-8-1 **67** MartinLane 22 73+
(Brian Ellison) *racd in centre: hld up in tch: rdn and hdwy to chse ldrs whn hmpd and swtchd rt jst ins fnl f: styd on fnl 100yds: 3rd of 12 in gp* **8/1**[2]

0604 **5** *hd* **Norse Blues**[1] [6601] 4-9-8 **88** JamesDoyle 20 93
(Sylvester Kirk) *racd in centre: led gp and chsd ldrs overall: led overall over 3f out: rdn 2f out: hdd ent fnl f: no ex fnl 100yds: 4th of 12 in gp* **18/1**

1610 **6** *½* **Full Toss**[21] [6010] 6-8-13 **82** GaryBartley(3) 2 85
(Jim Goldie) *racd far side: a.p: chsd ldrs 3f out: rdn 2f out: led overall ent fnl f: hdd & wknd ins fnl f: 2nd of 14 in gp* **50/1**

0165 **7** *½* **Junket**[21] [6013] 5-8-12 **78** RichardMullen 19 80
(Dr Jon Scargill) *racd in centre: in tch: rdn and chsd ldrs 2f out: edgd lft and no ex ins fnl f: 5th of 12 in gp* **66/1**

1000 **8** *hd* **Musnad (USA)**[17] [6124] 4-8-9 **75** MickaelBarzalona 4 77+
(Brian Ellison) *racd far side: hld up towards rr: effrt u.p wl over 1f out: styd on ins fnl f: nvr able to chal: 3rd of 14 in gp* **40/1**

532 **9** *1 ½* **Oxford Charley (USA)**[6] [6494] 3-9-7 **92** (v) WilliamBuick 6 91
(Mikael Magnusson) *racd far side: hld up in tch in midfield: hdwy over 2f out: rdn over 1f out: styd on same pce and no imp fnl f: 4th of 14 in gp* **9/1**[3]

0006 **10** *1 ½* **Nazreef**[8] [6400] 5-9-3 **83** (t) DarryllHolland 8 78
(Hughie Morrison) *racd far side: in tch in midfield: effrt 2f out: drvn and styd on same pce fr over 1f out: 5th of 14 in gp* **40/1**

5150 **11** *1 ¾* **Carragold**[19] [6073] 6-8-10 **76** PatCosgrave 26 67
(Mel Brittain) *hld up towards rr in centre: rdn and effrt ent fnl 2f: no imp ent fnl f: 6th of 12 in gp* **40/1**

3141 **12** *¾* **Jo'Burg (USA)**[17] [6124] 8-9-5 **85** 4ex DanielTudhope 14 75
(David O'Meara) *taken down early: racd far side: hld up in rr: rdn and hdwy jst over 2f out: styd on same pce and no imp fnl f: 6th of 14 in gp* **11/1**

4505 **13** *nk* **Laughing Jack**[22] 5965 4-8-3 **72** RaulDaSilva(3) 28 61
(Tony Carroll) *swtchd to r in centre after s: hld up towards rr: rdn and hung lft to stands' side over 2f out: styd on but no threat to ldrs fr over 1f out: 7th of 12 in gp* **66/1**

1030 **14** *1 ¼* **Flaxen Flare (IRE)**[48] 5101 3-8-10 **81** ow1 (v) JimmyFortune 18 67
(Andrew Balding) *racd in centre: hld up in midfield: rdn and no prog ent fnl 2f: no threat to ldrs but kpt on u.p fnl f: 8th of 12 in gp* **20/1**

1110 **15** *nk* **It's A Mans World**[13] 6256 6-8-5 **74** ow2 PaulPickard(3) 10 60
(Brian Ellison) *racd far side: in tch: rdn and unable qck jst over 2f out: no imp over 1f out: 7th of 14 in gp* **25/1**

0651 **16** *3 ½* **Cottam Donny**[3] 6561 4-7-12 **64** 4ex (p) NickyMackay 13 42
(Mel Brittain) *racd far side: prom: rdn to ld overall 4f out tl over 3f out: wknd over 1f out: 8th of 14 in gp* **25/1**

2000 **17** *hd* **Askaud (IRE)**[6] 6471 4-9-6 **86** (p) TomQueally 21 64
(Scott Dixon) *racd in centre: in tch: rdn and struggling over 2f out: wknd over 1f out: 9th of 12 in gp* **33/1**

41 **18** *shd* **Sam Sharp (USA)**[24] 5914 6-9-7 **87** 4ex JamieSpencer 12 64
(Ian Williams) *racd in centre: hld up towards rr: swtchd rt and effrt ent fnl 2f: no imp over 1f out: eased ins fnl f: 10th of 12 in gp* **20/1**

0665 **19** *5* **Dhaular Dhar (IRE)**[11] 6313 10-8-5 **71** PaulHanagan 9 37
(Jim Goldie) *racd far side: hld up towards rr: hdwy over 2f out: rdn and no imp wl over 1f out: wl hld and eased ins fnl f: 9th of 14 in gp* **22/1**

0000 **20** *¾* **Brockfield**[41] 5345 6-8-2 **71** NeilFarley(3) 11 36
(Mel Brittain) *racd far side: hld up in rr: rdn and no hdwy over 2f out: wknd over 1f out: 10th of 14 in gp* **100/1**

1-01 **21** *1 ¼* **Knave Of Clubs (IRE)**[44] 5237 3-8-11 **82** SebSanders 15 44
(Peter Makin) *racd far side: in tch: rdn and struggling 3f out: wknd wl over 1f out: 11th of 14 in gp* **28/1**

6045 **22** *½* **Colour Guard**[9] 6380 4-9-3 **83** SilvestreDeSousa 1 44
(Mark Johnston) *racd far side: in tch: rdn 3f out: sn struggling: wknd wl over 1f out: 12th of 14 in gp* **12/1**

2421 **23** *1 ¼* **Another For Joe**[29] 5759 4-8-12 **78** GrahamLee 23 36
(Jim Goldie) *racd in centre: chsd ldrs: rdn and struggling 3f out: wknd 2f out: 11th of 12 in gp* **16/1**

0620 **24** *2 ¼* **Staff Sergeant**[35] 5540 5-8-11 **77** DaleSwift 5 30
(Jim Goldie) *racd far side: led gp and chsd overall ldr tl led overall 4f out: sn hdd and rdn: lost pl over 2f out: bhd fnl f: 13th of 14 in gp* **50/1**

5000 **25** *4* **Know No Fear**[11] 6319 7-8-0 **71** (p) LeonnaMayor(5) 3 15
(Alastair Lidderdale) *racd far side: chsd ldrs tl rdn and struggling over 3f out: lost pl over 2f out: bhd fnl f: 14th of 14 in gp* **100/1**

0140 **26** *½* **Pendragon (USA)**[51] 4964 9-8-6 **79** ow1 DavidSimmonson(7) 27 22
(Brian Ellison) *racd on stands' side: hld up in rr: gd hdwy to chse ldrs and rdn 4f out: wknd over 2f out: 1st of 2 in gp* **25/1**

1006 **27** *35* **Switzerland (IRE)**[9] 6374 3-9-4 **94** (b) MichaelJMMurphy(5) 29
(Mark Johnston) *racd on stands'rail: overall ldr tl 4f out: sn dropped out: t.o over 1f out: 2nd of 2 in gp* **25/1**

5060 **28** *68* **Fair Trade**[76] 4112 5-9-10 **90** GeorgeBaker 17
(Hughie Morrison) *taken down early: racd in centre: hld up in rr: eased and lost tch over 3f out: t.o and virtually p.u after: 12th of 12 in gp* **25/1**

1m 49.54s (-2.16) **Going Correction** -0.05s/f (Good)
WFA 3 from 4yo+ 5lb **28** Ran SP% **133.5**
Speed ratings (Par 109): **107,106,104,104,104 103,103,103,101,100 98,98,97,96,96 93,93,93,88,88 86,86,85,83,79 79,48,E**
toteswingers 1&2 £16.40, 1&3 £55.00, 2&3 £20.60 CSF £52.42 CT £866.94 TOTE £9.30: £2.80, £2.70, £3.30, £2.30; EX 107.50 Trifecta £1230.70 Pool: £1,995.83 - 1.20 winning tickets..
Owner J Collins, N Horsfall & N O'Sullivan **Bred** Red House Stud **Trained** Newmarket, Suffolk

FOCUS
The consolation race for those not getting a run in the Cambridgeshire. It was a fiercely competitive affair and, although those going far side were ahead of the centre group for most of the race, they began to toil from 2f out and the runners that came towards the stands' rail late on filled the first four places. The first two runnings of this handicap had gone to 3yos and the classic generation came out on top again. The form makes a fair bit of sense, with the winner resuming his progress.

NOTEBOOK
Henry Allingham pounced late in the day. The winner has developed into a consistent performer this year and was already proven on most ground. This slightly longer trip unlocked even further improvement and he appeals as one for a big handicap next year as a 4yo. The Royal Hunt Cup at Ascot looks the ideal target. (op 9-1)
Classic Colori(IRE), well backed, finished a head second off 4lb higher in the race last year and so one really has to feel for the runner-up again. He's winless since his 3yo season, but can surely put that right and fully deserves another opening. (tchd 15-2 and 17-2)
Shamdarley(IRE), despite his low draw, ran a big race and improved two places on his running in the race last term. His run must be upgraded as he came right over from the far-side group a furlong out and, although he's still to win in 2012, his last success came on his next outing after this event last year.
Christmas Light tanked her way through the race down the centre, but found just the same pace when asked for maximum effort and is a tricky horse to actually win with. She now faces a rise up the handicap. (tchd 17-2)
Norse Blues was not beaten far when fourth over 1m here the previous day and he turned in a bold effort under a positive ride. He could have done without the rain over this extra furlong and his turn may well be nearing once more. (op 20-1)
Full Toss led home those that raced on the far side and came nicely clear. This was a definite return to form for him and probably a career-best.
Junket was 8lb higher than her previous outing on turf in July, but posted a solid effort and is a useful filly on her day.
Musnad(USA) arrived with a bit to prove, but bounced back to form and is one to note if reverting to one of the smaller tracks in the coming weeks. (op 50-1)
Oxford Charley(USA) was 2lb higher than when just nabbed over 1m here in a first-time visor six days earlier. He ran well on the far side, but the slightly stiffer test on slower ground found him out. (op 8-1)
Fair Trade Official explanation: jockey said gelding moved poorly

6639 NEWMARKET CHALLENGE WHIP (H'CAP) 1m 2f
5:10 (5:11) (Class 6) (0-85,78) 3-Y-0+ **£0**Stalls Low

Form RPR

1522 **1** **Odin (IRE)**[43] 5268 4-9-4 **78** RichardHughes 3 84
(David Elsworth) *hld up in tch: rdn and effrt jst over 2f out: ev ch 1f out: led ins fnl f: r.o wl: rdn out* **11/4**[1]

4332 **2** *nk* **Exning Halt**[32] 5680 3-8-8 **74** MickaelBarzalona 5 80
(James Fanshawe) *hld up in tch: rdn and effrt ent fnl 2f: ev ch fnl f: no ex towards fin* **10/3**[2]

-100 **3** *nk* **Flash Crash**[171] 1288 3-7-13 **65** ow1 SilvestreDeSousa 6 70
(Robert Cowell) *swtchd to r alone on far side: chsd ldrs: rdn and hung lft over 2f out: Ind field and ev ch over 1f out: no ex fnl 100yds* **40/1**

6-10 **4** *1 ¼* **The Tiger**[39] 5429 4-9-3 **77** FrankieDettori 7 80
(Ed Dunlop) *hld up in rr: hdwy over 2f out: rdn and pressed ldrs over 1f out: no ex ins fnl f: wknd towards fin* **10/3**[2]

1034 **5** *shd* **Incendiary (IRE)**[9] 6380 3-8-11 **77** MichaelHills 4 79
(Hugo Palmer) *chsd ldrs: rdn to ld over 1f out: hdd ins fnl f: no ex and wknd towards fin* **8/1**

0500 **6** *6* **Golden Jubilee (USA)**[12] 6278 3-7-12 **64** oh1 (p) KieranO'Neill 1 54
(Richard Hannon) *chsd ldr: rdn and ev ch wl over 1f out: btn 1f out and wknd fnl f* **28/1**

0410 **7** *¾* **Hayaku (USA)**[37] 5474 4-9-4 **78** (bt) JimCrowley 8 67
(Ralph Beckett) *led tl rdn and hdd over 1f out: wknd fnl f* **16/1**

6201 **8** *1 ¼* **Villa Royale**[17] 6118 3-8-10 **76** ow3 JamesDoyle 2 62
(Harry Dunlop) *hld up in rr: rdn and effrt over 2f out: no prog jst over 1f out: wknd fnl f* **6/1**[3]

5500 **9** *40* **Smokey Oakey (IRE)**[93] 3494 8-9-2 **76** DarryllHolland 9
(Mark H Tompkins) *chsd ldrs tl over 3f out: lost pl and bhd fnl 2f: eased and t.o fnl f* **22/1**

2m 4.29s (-1.51) **Going Correction** 0.05s/f (Good)
WFA 3 from 4yo+ 6lb **9** Ran SP% **114.3**
Speed ratings (Par 101): **104,103,103,102,102 97,97,96,64**
toteswingers 1&2 £2.70, 1&3 £15.60, 2&3 £11.30 CSF £11.61 CT £288.34 TOTE £2.50: £1.10, £1.30, £8.00; EX 11.70 Trifecta £131.20 Pool: £2,669.02 - 15.05 winning tickets..
Owner J C Smith **Bred** Littleton Stud **Trained** Newmarket, Suffolk

FOCUS
This can often be an uncompetitive race featuring very few runners, but there was a good line-up this year. It paid to be ridden with a bit of patience. Slightly shaky form, rated around the first two.
T/Jkpt: Not won. T/Plt: £160.50 to a £1 stake. Pool: £119,849.69 - 545.02 winning tickets T/Qpdt: £35.50 to a £1 stake. Pool: £8,536.06 - 177.54 winning tickets SP

6609 WOLVERHAMPTON (A.W) (L-H)
Friday, September 28

OFFICIAL GOING: Standard
Wind: Light behind Weather: Cloudy

6640 32RED H'CAP 5f 216y(P)
5:45 (5:45) (Class 6) (0-55,58) 3-Y-0+ **£1,704** (£503; £251) **Stalls** Low

Form RPR

4430 **1** **Red Shadow**[6] 6479 3-9-1 **53** (p) RobertWinston 13 63
(Alan Brown) *led 1f: chsd ldr tl led and hung lft fr over 1f out: drvn out* **7/1**[3]

0-32 **2** *2 ¼* **Forzarzi (IRE)**[15] 6178 8-9-3 **53** FrederikTylicki 6 56
(Hugh McWilliams) *s.i.s: hdwy over 2f out: rdn over 1f out: r.o to go 2nd wl ins fnl f: no ch w wnr* **8/1**

0400 **3** *¾* **Media Jury**[15] 6180 5-8-8 **51** (p) KevinLundie(7) 7 52
(John Wainwright) *chsd ldrs: rdn over 1f out: styd on same pce fnl f* **33/1**

0500 **4** *hd* **Kai**[15] 6179 3-9-2 **54** (v) RobertHavlin 2 54
(Alan McCabe) *led 5f out: rdn and hdd whn hmpd over 1f out: no ex ins fnl f* **16/1**

5030 **5** *½* **John Coffey (IRE)**[18] 6104 3-9-2 **54** AdrianNicholls 5 52
(David Nicholls) *mid-div: hdwy over 2f out: rdn over 1f out: styd on* **3/1**[2]

5651 **6** *hd* **Medam**[11] 6322 3-9-6 **58** 6ex (t) FrannyNorton 10 56+
(Shaun Harris) *mid-div: lost pl over 3f out: rdn over 2f out: r.o ins fnl f: nvr trbld ldrs* **11/8**[1]

00R5 **7** *1 ¼* **Ivestar (IRE)**[11] 6308 7-9-2 **52** (p) GrahamGibbons 4 46
(Michael Easterby) *s.i.s: hld up: hdwy over 1f out: nt clr run ins fnl f: nvr trbld ldrs* **22/1**

420 **8** *1* **Brandywell Boy (IRE)**[6] 6496 9-9-2 **52** (t[1]) AdamKirby 8 43
(Dominic Ffrench Davis) *chsd ldrs: rdn over 2f out: no ex fnl f* **20/1**

0610 **9** *1 ½* **Athaakeel (IRE)**[25] 5874 6-9-5 **55** (b) LukeMorris 11 41
(Ronald Harris) *hld up: rdn over 1f out: nvr trbld ldrs* **22/1**

405/ **10** *shd* **Burnt Cream**[774] 5152 5-9-4 **54** (t[1]) CathyGannon 3 39
(Martin Bosley) *s.i.s: hld up: plld hrd: n.d* **50/1**

0050 **11** *1 ¼* **Lucifers Shadow (IRE)**[11] 6321 3-9-3 **55** LiamKeniry 1 36
(Sylvester Kirk) *chsd ldrs: hmpd 5f out: rdn over 1f out: wknd and eased ins fnl f* **10/1**

006- **12** *3 ¼* **Schoolboy Champ**[332] 7216 5-9-5 **55** (t) TomEaves 9 26
(Lisa Williamson) *prom: rdn over 2f out: wknd over 1f out* **28/1**

1m 14.97s (-0.03) **Going Correction** -0.125s/f (Stan)
WFA 3 from 5yo+ 2lb **12** Ran SP% **127.5**
Speed ratings (Par 101): **95,92,91,90,90 89,88,86,84,84 83,78**
toteswingers 1&2 £8.40, 2&3 £24.50, 1&3 £44.10 CSF £60.63 CT £1805.75 TOTE £15.20: £2.80, £1.30, £7.30; EX 106.30 TRIFECTA Not won..
Owner S Pedersen **Bred** Mrs P A & M J Reditt **Trained** Yedingham, N Yorks
■ Stewards' Enquiry : Kevin Lundie two-day ban: used whip above permitted level (Oct 12,14)

FOCUS
A fair tailwind was reported down the home straight. A moderate sprint handicap. The winner has been given credit for an improved performance.
Medam Official explanation: jockey said filly was slowly into stride

6641 DOWNLOAD OUR IPHONE APP (S) STKS 5f 216y(P)
6:15 (6:15) (Class 6) 3-4-Y-0 **£1,704** (£503; £251) **Stalls** Low

Form RPR

1000 **1** **Jack Smudge**[22] 5972 4-9-6 67 (v[1]) FrederikTylicki 4 80
(James Given) *chsd ldrs: rdn over 1f out: led and edgd rt ins fnl f: r.o wl* **10/1**

0026 **2** *5* **Indieslad**[14] 6217 4-9-0 60 (p) PaulMulrennan 2 58
(Ann Duffield) *a.p: chsd ldr over 3f out: rdn to ld ins fnl f: sn hdd and no ex* **9/2**[3]

000 **3** *1 ½* **Dissent (IRE)**[107] 3049 3-8-12 75 FrannyNorton 1 53
(David C Griffiths) *led: racd keenly: rdn over 1f out: hdd & wknd ins fnl f* **3/1**[1]

-105 **4** *nse* **Elegant Muse**[20] 6053 4-9-1 60 (t) CathyGannon 5 54
(Michael Appleby) *mid-div: drvn along 1/2-way: hdwy over 2f out: rdn over 1f out: styd on* **12/1**

6030 **5** *2 ¼* **Boudoir (IRE)**[14] 6194 3-8-13 74 TonyHamilton 11 47
(Ian Williams) *prom: rdn over 2f out: sn outpcd* **13/2**

5203 **6** *hd* **Ficelle (IRE)**[25] 5876 3-8-13 60 LukeMorris 12 46
(Ronald Harris) *sn outpcd: r.o ins fnl f: nvr nrr* **20/1**

U500 **7** *nk* **Gin Twist**[14] 6211 3-8-13 65 (b) RichardKingscote 6 45
(Tom Dascombe) *s.s: bhd: r.o ins fnl f: nvr nrr* **7/2**[2]

2000 **8** *1 ¾* **Moody Dancer**[14] 6216 3-8-7 58 (b[1]) KellyHarrison 7 34
(William Muir) *mid-div: drvn along 1/2-way: hung rt over 2f out: wknd fnl f* **33/1**

000 **9** *8* **Wotsitgotodowithu (IRE)**[53] 4882 4-9-0 47 (v[1]) SeanLevey 10 13
(Alan McCabe) *sn outpcd* **33/1**

-000 **10** *9* **Fifteentwo**[20] 6053 3-8-12 62 AdrianNicholls 8
(David Nicholls) *chsd ldr tl rdn over 3f out: wknd 2f out* **8/1**

0 **11** *14* **Smiley Miley (IRE)**[21] 6001 4-8-10 0 ow1................. RussKennemore 3
(David Lewis) *s.i.s: sn drvn along and prom: wknd over 3f out: t.o* **200/1**

0000 **12** *1* **Libby's Lad**[17] 6125 3-8-12 24.......................................(b[1]) AndrewMullen 9
(David C Griffiths) *a in rr: bhd fr 1/2-way: t.o* **200/1**

1m 13.83s (-1.17) **Going Correction** -0.125s/f (Stan)
WFA 3 from 4yo 2lb **12** Ran SP% **119.7**
Speed ratings (Par 101): **102,95,93,93,90 90,89,87,76,64 45,44**
toteswingers 1&2 £9.50, 1&3 £8.30, 2&3 £3.50 CSF £53.20 TOTE £11.80: £3.60, £2.30, £1.30; EX 58.00 Trifecta £175.50 Pool: £1,219.63 - 5.14 winning tickets..There was no bid for the winner.
Owner Danethorpe Racing Partnership **Bred** P And Mrs A G Venner **Trained** Willoughton, Lincs

FOCUS
A fair seller for 3-4yos. The winner was well above the average standard for the grade, with the time relatively good too. The remainder are rated 10lb+ off.
Dissent(IRE) Official explanation: jockey said colt ran keen early
Elegant Muse Official explanation: jockey said filly hung right
Gin Twist Official explanation: jockey said filly was slowly away

6642 HOLIDAY INN WOLVERHAMPTON H'CAP 1m 5f 194y(P)
6:45 (6:46) (Class 4) (0-80,80) 3-Y-O+ **£4,204** (£1,251; £625; £312) **Stalls** Low

Form RPR

4300 **1** **O Ma Lad (IRE)**[14] 6197 4-9-12 **80**................................ RobertWinston 6 90
(Sylvester Kirk) *hld up: hdwy over 4f out: rdn to ld wl ins fnl f: styd on* **14/1**

1212 **2** *nk* **Den Maschine**[21] 6019 7-9-10 **78**...................................... AdamKirby 10 88
(Sean Curran) *hld up: hdwy over 5f out: led over 1f out: rdn and hdd wl ins fnl f* **6/1**[2]

0624 **3** *3 1/2* **Flying Power**[80] 3945 4-9-7 **75**...................................... PaulMulrennan 2 80
(John Norton) *hld up: hdwy 2f out: sn rdn: edgd lft and styd on same pce ins fnl f* **22/1**

6030 **4** *1 3/4* **Kazbow (IRE)**[21] 6012 6-9-11 **79**...................................... TonyHamilton 8 82
(Chris Grant) *hld up: hdwy over 1f out: styd on: nt trble ldrs* **28/1**

3033 **5** *1* **Nave (USA)**[20] 6039 5-9-6 **74**.. AdamBeschizza 5 75
(David Simcock) *hld up: hdwy u.p over 1f out: nt rch ldrs* **7/1**[3]

1520 **6** *1 1/2* **Three Bards (IRE)**[27] 5816 3-9-2 **80**................................ JoeFanning 9 79
(Mark Johnston) *chsd ldrs: ev ch whn hmpd over 1f out: wknd ins fnl f* **9/4**[1]

0060 **7** *nk* **Merchant Of Dubai**[35] 5540 7-9-12 **80**.......................(p) KellyHarrison 12 79
(Jim Goldie) *chsd ldrs: led over 8f out: rdn: hung rt and hdd over 1f out: wknd ins fnl f* **9/1**

1362 **8** *2 1/4* **Gold Rules**[15] 6181 5-9-9 **77**... JamesSullivan 3 72
(Michael Easterby) *s.i.s: hld up: hdwy and nt clr run over 1f out: wknd ins fnl f* **6/1**[2]

0-60 **9** *5* **Carter**[28] 5789 6-9-8 **76**.. GrahamGibbons 4 64
(Ian Williams) *prom: rdn over 3f out: wknd over 1f out* **25/1**

606- **10** *16* **Simonside**[174] 6095 9-9-5 **73**.. TomEaves 13 39
(Brian Ellison) *stdd s: a in rr: rdn and wknd over 3f out: t.o* **50/1**

0454 **11** *2* **Sandbanks Sizzler (IRE)**[21] 6019 4-9-1 **74**..........(t) JamesRogers(5) 11 37
(Ralph Beckett) *s.i.s: hdwy over 10f out: rdn over 2f out: sn wknd: t.o* **9/1**

0/6- **12** *5* **Bothy**[399] 5435 6-9-11 **79**.. AmyRyan 1 35
(Brian Ellison) *chsd ldr: led 11f out: hdd over 8f out: rdn and wknd 3f out: t.o* **20/1**

330 **13** *1/2* **The Holyman (IRE)**[23] 5944 4-9-8 **76**............................ DaneO'Neill 7 32
(Jo Crowley) *led 3f: chsd ldrs: rdn over 2f out: sn wknd: t.o* **14/1**

3m 1.48s (-4.52) **Going Correction** -0.125s/f (Stan)
WFA 3 from 4yo+ 10lb **13** Ran SP% **123.5**
Speed ratings (Par 105): **107,106,104,103,103 102,102,100,98,88 87,84,84**
toteswingers 1&2 £6.70, 2&3 £20.70, 1&3 £42.50 CSF £92.99 CT £1879.68 TOTE £19.10: £3.50, £2.10, £8.60; EX 103.20 Trifecta £947.60 Part won. Pool: £1,280.60 - 0.79 winning tickets..
Owner John Duddy **Bred** Mrs Brid Cosgrove **Trained** Upper Lambourn, Berks
■ Stewards' Enquiry : Kelly Harrison two-day ban: careless riding (Oct 12,14)

FOCUS
A fair staying handicap. It was sound run and the form looks solid. The third sets the standard.
Three Bards(IRE) Official explanation: jockey said colt suffered interference in running

6643 HOTEL & CONFERENCING MEDIAN AUCTION MAIDEN STKS 7f 32y(P)
7:15 (7:18) (Class 6) 3-5-Y-O **£1,704** (£503; £251) **Stalls** High

Form RPR

0046 **1** **Beau Duke (IRE)**[15] 6172 3-8-10 60.......................... ThomasBrown(7) 1 69
(Andrew Balding) *a.p: led over 1f out: rdn and hung lft ins fnl f: jst hld on* **11/2**[3]

0 **2** *hd* **Dick Bos**[160] 1506 3-9-3 0.. RobertHavlin 9 71+
(Peter Chapple-Hyam) *hld up: swtchd rt and hdwy over 1f out: fin wl* **4/6**[1]

-234 **3** *3* **Peak Storm**[6] 6477 3-9-3 73.. LukeMorris 7 60
(John O'Shea) *a.p: rdn over 1f out: styd on same pce fnl f* **9/1**

3534 **4** *1 1/2* **Shore Performer (IRE)**[22] 5970 3-8-12 65......................... ShaneKelly 12 51
(William Haggas) *hld up in tch: rdn over 1f out: no ex ins fnl f* **4/1**[2]

66 **5** *3 1/4* **Narapatisithu (FR)**[14] 6215 5-9-6 0.............................. JamieMackay 4 47
(K F Clutterbuck) *chsd ldr tl led 2f out: rdn and hdd over 1f out: wknd ins fnl f* **100/1**

0463 **6** *nse* **Benidorm**[6] 6477 4-9-1 50...(v) AdamCarter(5) 10 47
(John Wainwright) *chsd ldrs: rdn over 2f out: wknd ins fnl f* **80/1**

5 **7** *2 1/2* **The Kicking Lord**[231] 499 3-9-3 0...........................[1] AdamBeschizza 8 40
(Mark Brisbourne) *s.i.s: in rr tl styd on ins fnl f: nvr nrr* **20/1**

0- **8** *7* **Vermeyen**[300] 7627 3-9-0 0...................................... SophieDoyle(3) 11 21
(Geoffrey Deacon) *s.i.s: a in rr* **50/1**

0-05 **9** *3/4* **Make Me Smyle**[25] 5878 3-9-3 38.................................... FergusSweeney 3 19
(Stuart Kittow) *led: rdn and hdd 2f out: wknd over 1f out* **66/1**

-060 **10** *2* **Illawalla**[4] 6529 4-9-6 40...(p) FrederikTylicki 5 14
(Hugh McWilliams) *hld up: wknd and eased over 1f out* **100/1**

11 *5* **Sassi Sioux** 3-8-12 0.. TedDurcan 2
(Tom Keddy) *s.s: outpcd* **50/1**

1m 29.79s (0.19) **Going Correction** -0.125s/f (Stan)
WFA 3 from 4yo+ 3lb **11** Ran SP% **118.8**
Speed ratings (Par 101): **93,92,89,87,83 83,81,73,72,69 64**
toteswingers 1&2 £1.40, 2&3 £2.80, 1&3 £2.70 CSF £9.48 TOTE £5.30: £1.10, £1.10, £1.60; EX 12.80 Trifecta £71.90 Pool: £953.22 - 9.81 winning tickets..
Owner The Ten Gallon Partnership I **Bred** Olive O'Connor **Trained** Kingsclere, Hants

FOCUS
A modest maiden in which those with form were less than convincing. The winner was back to something like his early form at face value.

6644 LIKE US ON FACEBOOK WOLVERHAMPTON RACECOURSE MAIDEN STKS (DIV I) 7f 32y(P)
7:45 (7:46) (Class 5) 2-Y-O **£2,264** (£673; £336; £168) **Stalls** High

Form RPR

32 **1** **Give Way Nelson (IRE)**[25] 5887 2-8-12 0....................... KierenFallon 10 75
(Brian Meehan) *chsd ldrs: led over 1f out: drvn out* **11/10**[1]

0 **2** *1/2* **Soaring Spirits (IRE)**[17] 6114 2-9-3 0.............................. NeilCallan 6 79
(Roger Varian) *a.p: pushed along 1/2-way: rdn over 1f out: r.o* **3/1**[2]

0 **3** *1/2* **Tight Knit (USA)**[16] 0175 2-9-3 0.................................. PaulMulrennan 7 78
(James Tate) *chsd ldr: rdn over 2f out: led wl over 1f out: sn hdd: hung lft ins fnl f: styd on* **50/1**

6 **4** *2 3/4* **Charm Cry (USA)**[9] 6366 2-8-12 0.................................... JoeFanning 2 66
(Mark Johnston) *chsd ldrs: shkn up over 1f out: no ex ins fnl f* **3/1**[2]

00 **5** *2 1/4* **Gabrial The Duke (IRE)**[8] 6412 2-9-3 0......................... TonyHamilton 3 65+
(Ian Williams) *sn pushed along in rr: r.o ins fnl f: nrst fin* **80/1**

4 **6** *nk* **Janie Runaway (IRE)**[22] 5978 2-8-12 0........................ TomMcLaughlin 8 61
(Malcolm Saunders) *s.i.s: sn pushed along in rr: drvn 1/2-way: hdwy over 1f out: eased ins fnl f* **12/1**[3]

6302 **7** *8* **Cymeriad**[28] 5806 2-8-12 56.. CathyGannon 4 40+
(Michael Easterby) *led: rdn and hdd wl over 1f out: wknd ins fnl f: sddle slipped* **25/1**

00 **8** *2 1/2* **Duchess Of Gazeley (IRE)**[42] 5300 2-8-12 0...................... ShaneKelly 1 34
(Lydia Pearce) *a in rr: bhd fnl 3f* **66/1**

9 *10* **Great Ormond (IRE)** 2-9-3 0.. PhillipMakin 5 14
(David Simcock) *sn outpcd* **25/1**

1m 28.94s (-0.66) **Going Correction** -0.125s/f (Stan) **9** Ran SP% **117.7**
Speed ratings (Par 95): **98,97,96,93,91 90,81,78,67**
toteswingers 1&2 £1.40, 2&3 £2.80, 1&3 £2.70 CSF £4.56 TOTE £1.60: £1.02, £1.10, £14.90; EX 6.50 Trifecta £107.30 Pool: £1,279.78 - 8.82 winning tickets..
Owner Newsells Park Stud **Bred** Lynn Lodge Stud **Trained** Manton, Wilts

FOCUS
The first division of a modest juvenile maiden.

NOTEBOOK
Give Way Nelson(IRE) was a 42,000euros yearling purchase and is a half-sister to Pasar Sibano, who won a 6f Grade 3 in the US. She ran respectably over 5f at Sandown on debut in May and returned from a four-month break with a fair second over 6f here this month. She buckled down well to break her maiden over this extra furlong, and is a fair prospect for next term, who may not want much further than 7f. (tchd Evens and 5-4)
Soaring Spirits(IRE) showed a bit of promise on debut over 7f at Leicester this month and duly built on that display on this occasion. He may be able to go one better at up to 1m this year. (op 9-2 tchd 6-1 and 11-4)
Tight Knit(USA) is probably one for modest to fair handicaps in due course, after progressing markedly on his moderate debut over this C&D this month. (op 40-1)
Charm Cry(USA) produced a fair sixth over 1m at Kempton on debut this month and ran to a similar level over 1f shorter here. (op 9-4 tchd 2-1)
Gabrial The Duke(IRE) tends to start slowly but went the right way in this contest. He should be able to win a modest handicap over this trip if learning to get out of the gates quicker. (op 50-1)
Janie Runaway(IRE) failed to build on her promising Salisbury debut over this 7f trip this month. (op 14-1)
Cymeriad Official explanation: jockey said saddle slipped

6645 LIKE US ON FACEBOOK WOLVERHAMPTON RACECOURSE MAIDEN STKS (DIV II) 7f 32y(P)
8:15 (8:17) (Class 5) 2-Y-O **£2,264** (£673; £336; £168) **Stalls** High

Form RPR

2 **1** **Infinite Magic (USA)**[15] 6175 2-9-3 0............................. GrahamLee 3 81+
(Jeremy Noseda) *trckd ldrs: edgd rt 6f out: shkn up to ld 1f out: r.o wl* **8/11**[1]

2 *3 3/4* **Lilac Tree** 2-8-12 0.. AntiocoMurgia(5) 8 70+
(Mahmood Al Zarooni) *led: rdn and hdd 1f out: styd on same pce* **10/1**[3]

53 **3** *3* **Carina Palace**[15] 6177 2-8-12 0.................................... FergusSweeney 5 57
(Jamie Osborne) *chsd ldrs: rdn over 1f out: styd on same pce* **14/1**

5 **4** *hd* **Butterfly Dream**[33] 5631 2-8-12 0................................... AdamBeschizza 9 57
(William Haggas) *chsd ldr: rdn over 2f out: wknd fnl f* **20/1**

04 **5** *2 1/4* **Runninglikethewind (IRE)**[22] 5969 2-9-3 0................... HarryBentley 10 57
(Chris Wall) *hld up: hmpd 6f out: rdn over 2f out: nvr trbld ldrs* **16/1**

5 **6** *9* **Slip Of The Tongue**[15] 6175 2-9-3 0.................................. LukeMorris 7 36
(Sir Mark Prescott Bt) *prom: hmpd 6f out: rdn over 2f out: sn wknd* **33/1**

5 **7** *3 3/4* **Wrecking Ball (IRE)**[28] 5793 2-9-3 0.............................. KierenFallon 6 27
(Brian Meehan) *s.i.s: hld up: shkn up over 2f out: wknd over 1f out: eased fnl f* **3/1**[2]

00 **8** *nk* **Madame Scarlett (IRE)**[23] 5932 2-8-7 0..................... NathanSweeney(5) 1 19
(Jo Crowley) *hld up: wknd over 2f out* **66/1**

006 **9** *8* **Cerys**[21] 5997 2-8-12 0...(b[1]) DaneO'Neill 4
(Derek Haydn Jones) *sn pushed along in rr: bhd 1/2-way: t.o* **100/1**

1m 29.56s (-0.04) **Going Correction** -0.125s/f (Stan) **9** Ran SP% **114.7**
Speed ratings (Par 95): **95,90,87,87,84 74,69,69,60**
toteswingers 1&2 £2.60, 2&3 £7.50, 1&3 £2.30 CSF £9.04 TOTE £1.70: £1.02, £2.50, £3.20; EX 10.20 Trifecta £35.30 Pool: £917.58 - 19.21 winning tickets..
Owner Tom Ludt **Bred** Grapestock Llc **Trained** Newmarket, Suffolk

FOCUS
The second division of a fair juvenile maiden. The winning time was comparatively slower than the first instalment.

NOTEBOOK
Infinite Magic(USA) made an encouraging start to his career when runner-up over this C&D this month. He duly built on that promise here in putting this field to the sword from fully 1f out. He is the first foal out of a 7f-1m1f winning dam here/in the US, who is out of a 6f 2yo winning grand-daughter of 1,000 Guineas winner Fairy Footsteps. He looks a nice prospect at up to 1m next term. (tchd 4-6 and 4-5)
Lilac Tree cost 70,000 guineas as a foal. He attempted to make all here on debut but was readily outpointed in the home straight. He has something to build on, though. (op 9-1 tchd 8-1)
Carina Palace produced respectable form on her first two starts over 6f at Kempton/here this month. She failed to build on that promise and may be more of a modest to fair sprint handicap prospect in due course. (op 10-1)
Butterfly Dream has found slight progression from her 6f Yarmouth debut fifth on good to soft ground last month.
Runninglikethewind(IRE) ran respectably after being hampered 6f out.
Slip Of The Tongue found little response from 2f out after being hampered 6f out. (op 25-1)

Wrecking Ball(IRE) performed disappointingly after starting slowly. (op 4-1 tchd 11-4)

6646 MIRROR PUNTERS CLUB H'CAP 1m 141y(P)
8:45 (8:45) (Class 6) (0-55,55) 3-Y-0+ £1,704 (£503; £251) Stalls Low

Form				RPR
3352	1		**Rasselas (IRE)**[6] 6479 5-9-2 **52**....(v) AdrianNicholls 2	62
			(David Nicholls) *mde all: rdn over 1f out: styd on* **1/1**[1]	
6043	2	1 ½	**Fortunate Bid (IRE)**[11] 6316 6-9-4 **54**....(p) GrahamLee 7	61
			(Linda Stubbs) *hld up: hdwy over 1f out: rdn ins fnl f: r.o: nt rch wnr* **15/2**[3]	
0664	3	nk	**Cheers Buddy (IRE)**[24] 5918 4-9-2 **52**....(e) TomEaves 8	58
			(Ian Semple) *chsd ldrs: rdn over 1f out: styd on* **6/1**[2]	
615	4	4 ½	**Avon Supreme**[23] 5938 4-8-10 **51**.... NatashaEaton(5) 6	47
			(Gay Kelleway) *chsd wnr tl rdn over 2f out: styd on same pce fr over 1f out: hung lft ins fnl f* **11/1**	
0660	5	2	**Yorksters Prince (IRE)**[18] 6103 5-9-3 **53**....(b) StephenCraine 5	44
			(Tony Coyle) *s.i.s: hld up: rdn over 3f out: styd on ins fnl f: nvr nrr* **10/1**	
0060	6	1 ¾	**Kielty's Folly**[39] 5427 8-9-4 **54**.... KellyHarrison 1	41
			(Brian Baugh) *trckd ldrs: racd keenly: wnt 2nd over 2f out: rdn over 1f out: wknd fnl f* **14/1**	
0130	7	1 ¾	**Ryedale Dancer (IRE)**[13] 6259 4-9-5 **55**.... RobbieFitzpatrick 3	38
			(Richard Guest) *chsd ldrs: rdn over 2f out: wknd over 1f out* **9/1**	
0000	8	1	**Destiny Awaits (IRE)**[7] 6429 3-9-0 **55**.... PaulMulrennan 11	36
			(Ian Semple) *hld up: rdn over 3f out: a in rr* **50/1**	
4003	9	¾	**Bedibyes**[49] 5049 4-8-10 **51**.... DavidKenny(5) 10	30
			(Richard Mitchell) *hld up: a in rr* **20/1**	

1m 50.16s (-0.34) **Going Correction** -0.125s/f (Stan)
WFA 3 from 4yo+ 5lb 9 Ran SP% 116.9
Speed ratings (Par 101): **96,94,94,90,88 87,85,84,83**
toteswingers 1&2 £2.10, 2&3 £2.90, 1&3 £3.00 CSF £9.28 CT £32.27 TOTE £2.40: £1.10, £2.30, £1.40; EX 10.60 Trifecta £24.90 Pool: £856.80 - 25.42 winning tickets..
Owner J P Honeyman **Bred** Lynch Bages Ltd **Trained** Sessay, N Yorks

FOCUS
A weak handicap in which the winner did not need to match his recent turf form.

6647 £32 BONUS AT 32RED.COM H'CAP 1m 1f 103y(P)
9:15 (9:16) (Class 5) (0-70,73) 3-Y-0 £2,264 (£673; £336; £168) Stalls Low

Form				RPR
0043	1		**Brimstone Hill (IRE)**[15] 6169 3-9-6 **69**.... TomEaves 4	76
			(Anthony Carson) *mid-div: hdwy over 3f out: led 1f out: rdn out* **25/1**	
5634	2	1 ½	**Rock Song**[16] 6151 3-9-2 **65**.... SeanLevey 8	69
			(Amanda Perrett) *led 1f: chsd ldr tl led again over 2f out: rdn and hdd 1f out: styd on same pce* **5/1**[2]	
-005	3	1 ¼	**Opera Buff**[23] 5942 3-9-7 **70**.... LiamKeniry 1	71
			(Sylvester Kirk) *mid-div: drvn along over 3f out: hdwy over 1f out: r.o to go 3rd post* **12/1**	
602	4	shd	**Mohair**[22] 5970 3-9-6 **69**.... GrahamLee 9	70
			(James Fanshawe) *hld up: hdwy over 3f out: rdn over 1f out: styd on same pce ins fnl f: lost 3rd post* **6/1**[3]	
3650	5	1	**Thecornishcockney**[44] 5231 3-9-2 **65**....(t) AdamKirby 11	64
			(John Ryan) *s.i.s: hld up: rdn over 3f out: r.o ins fnl f: nrst fin* **40/1**	
004	6	hd	**Rei D'Oro (USA)**[37] 5482 3-9-7 **70**.... MartinLane 5	69
			(David Simcock) *hld up: drvn along over 3f out: r.o ins fnl f: nvr nrr* **14/1**	
2040	7	nk	**Cool Sky**[16] 6146 3-9-2 **70**.... DavidKenny(5) 6	68
			(William Knight) *s.i.s: hld up: rdn over 3f out: r.o ins fnl f: nvr nrr* **20/1**	
5140	8	nk	**Chignon (IRE)**[63] 4538 3-8-13 **62**....[1] TomQueally 13	59
			(Sir Henry Cecil) *hld up: rdn over 2f out: styd on: nt trble ldrs* **9/1**	
-006	9	½	**Trumpet Voluntary (IRE)**[7] 6434 3-9-2 **65**....(t) ShaneKelly 2	61
			(Nicky Vaughan) *chsd ldrs: rdn over 2f out: styd on same pce fr over 1f out* **50/1**	
5000	10	1 ¾	**Chelsea Mick**[28] 5810 3-8-11 **60**.... GrahamGibbons 10	53
			(John Mackie) *chsd ldrs: rdn over 2f out: no ex ins fnl f* **16/1**	
0030	11	2 ¼	**Frosty Secret**[21] 5990 3-9-1 **64**....(p) LukeMorris 3	52
			(Jane Chapple-Hyam) *hld up: rdn over 2f out: n.d* **28/1**	
3611	12	2 ¾	**Joyful Spirit (IRE)**[9] 6364 3-9-10 **73** 6ex....(b) TedDurcan 12	55
			(John Dunlop) *led over 8f out: rdn and hdd over 2f out: wknd fnl f* **11/8**[1]	

1m 59.35s (-2.35) **Going Correction** -0.125s/f (Stan) 12 Ran SP% 119.8
Speed ratings (Par 101): **105,103,102,102,101 101,101,100,100,98 96,94**
toteswingers 1&2 £19.00, 2&3 £13.10, 1&3 £9.40 CSF £141.39 CT £1614.63 TOTE £34.20: £5.90, £2.00, £4.80; EX 85.80 Trifecta £618.00 Pool: £1,327.88 - 1.59 winning tickets..
Owner G Houghton, S Ebanks-Blake & K P Foley **Bred** Oscar Stud **Trained** Newmarket, Suffolk

FOCUS
A fair 3yo handicap. The winning time was very respectable for the grade. Even with the favourite disappoionting the form is pretty solid.
T/Plt: £114.10 to a £1 stake. Pool: £78,437.38 - 501.63 winning tickets. T/Qpdt: £5.80 to a £1 stake. Pool: £10,930.95 - 1,391.92 winning tickets. CR

6648 - 6656a (Foreign Racing) - See Raceform Interactive

6234 CHESTER (L-H)
Saturday, September 29

OFFICIAL GOING: Heavy (5.1)
Rail moved out between 3 and 9yds adding 37yds to races 1, 3 & 7, 33yds to race 2, 39yds to races 4 &5, 67yds to race 6.
Wind: Moderate, half against Weather: Fine

6657 CLWYD BEARINGS & TRANSMISSION MAIDEN FILLIES' STKS 7f 2y
2:20 (2:20) (Class 4) 2-Y-0 £4,528 (£1,347; £673; £336) Stalls Low

Form				RPR
23	1		**Lilbourne Eliza (IRE)**[8] 6453 2-9-0 0.... SeanLevey 5	72
			(Richard Hannon) *hld up trcking ldrs: effrt on outer over 1f out: led ent fnl f: r.o: in command towards fin* **3/1**[2]	
2223	2	1 ¾	**Madame Elizabeth**[10] 6356 2-9-0 68.... RussKennemore 3	68
			(Reg Hollinshead) *w ldr: rdn over 1f out: ev ch ent fnl f: nt qckn: styd on u.p but hld after* **7/2**[3]	
63	3	nse	**Neamour**[25] 5907 2-9-0 0.... PhillipMakin 2	68
			(David Simcock) *led: rdn over 1f out: hdd ent fnl f: styd on u.p after but hld* **9/4**[1]	
0352	4	1 ¼	**Storma Norma**[17] 6132 2-9-0 70.... PaulMulrennan 1	66
			(Tim Easterby) *hld up trcking ldrs: nt clr run over 1f out: sn swtchd rt but failed to pick-up: no imp after* **9/4**[1]	

1m 36.46s (9.96) **Going Correction** +1.15s/f (Soft) 4 Ran SP% 108.8
Speed ratings (Par 94): **89,87,86,85**
CSF £12.84 TOTE £2.70; EX 6.40.
Owner Andrew Russell **Bred** Peter J Doyle Bloodstock Ltd **Trained** East Everleigh, Wilts

FOCUS
It was dry overnight but there had been plenty of rain in the days leading up to the meeting, and the going was heavy (GoingStick 5.1). The running rail had been moved out as far as possible, i.e. 9yds in the back straight and 3yds in the home straight, adding 33yds to 5.5f, 37yds to 6f & 7f, 39yds to 1m2f & 67yds to 1m5f. Just a small field for this fillies' maiden, and it's debatable that any of them really handled the ground. Not form to dwell on.

NOTEBOOK
Lilbourne Eliza(IRE) got through the ground best, appreciated the return to 7f and came from off the pace to win with a bit in hand. She ought to get further next year. (tchd 11-4)
Madame Elizabeth, whose dam Madame Jones won round here in her day, kept the leader company from the start and had her chance, but she was just going up and down on the spot in the closing stages. (op 3-1)
Neamour doesn't have a pedigree that would suggest she'd be in love with this sort of ground. (op 11-4)
Storma Norma had at least shown an ability to cope with testing conditions at Carlisle last time. Her rider didn't seem very hard on her in the closing stages, even though she was making up ground steadily, and perhaps an excuse will emerge. (op 5-2)

6658 EVERSHEDS NURSERY 5f 110y
2:50 (2:51) (Class 2) 2-Y-0 £9,703 (£2,887; £1,443; £721) Stalls Low

Form				RPR
1065	1		**Lady Ibrox**[8] 6424 2-9-7 **87**.... DaleSwift 2	91
			(Alan Brown) *trckd ldrs: led jst over 1f out: edgd lft wl ins fnl f: r.o gamely* **6/1**[2]	
452	2	½	**Layla's Oasis**[16] 6177 2-8-4 **70**.... CathyGannon 5	72
			(Kevin Ryan) *racd freely w ldr: rdn to ld briefly over 1f out: continued to chal ins fnl f: styd on u.p: hld nr fin* **7/1**[3]	
1003	3	½	**Sharaarah (IRE)**[32] 5710 2-8-12 **78**.... PaulMulrennan 9	79
			(Ed Dunlop) *bhd: hdwy over 1f out: r.o ins fnl f: gng on at fin* **7/1**[3]	
414	4	¾	**Chasing Dreams**[12] 6312 2-8-12 **78**.... PhillipMakin 1	76
			(Kevin Ryan) *led: rdn and hdd over 1f out: no ex fnl 100yds* **7/4**[1]	
0313	5	hd	**Secret Sign**[13] 6284 2-8-13 **79**....(v) RichardMullen 3	77
			(Brian Meehan) *chsd ldrs: rdn 2f out: effrt on inner over 1f out: kpt on same pce ins fnl f* **7/1**[3]	
33	6	3	**Mandy Lexi (IRE)**[15] 6212 2-7-12 **67**....[1] RyanPowell(3) 4	55
			(Patrick Morris) *towards rr: pushed along and hdwy 2f out: styd on to chse ldrs over 1f out: no further imp ins fnl f* **9/1**	
3150	7	4 ½	**Mandy Layla (IRE)**[14] 6238 2-9-2 **82**.... TomEaves 7	55
			(Bryan Smart) *upset in stalls: midfield: rdn over 1f out: no imp: wknd fnl 100yds* **16/1**	
1000	8	1 ¾	**All Fur Coat**[8] 6424 2-9-2 **82**....[1] JoeFanning 8	49
			(Jo Hughes) *s.i.s: in rr: nvr able to get on terms* **12/1**	
4610	9	hd	**Monkey Bar Flies (IRE)**[16] 6155 2-8-6 **72**.... PatrickMathers 10	38
			(Richard Fahey) *racd on outer in midfield: lost pl 2f out: bhd over 1f out* **16/1**	

1m 13.1s (6.90) **Going Correction** +1.15s/f (Soft) 9 Ran SP% 117.6
Speed ratings (Par 101): **100,99,98,97,97 93,87,85,84**
toteswingers 1&2 £8.00, 1&3 £5.60, 2&3 £9.80 CSF £48.36 CT £304.97 TOTE £5.00: £1.70, £1.80, £2.50; EX 63.50.
Owner Rangers Racing **Bred** D Simpson **Trained** Yedingham, N Yorks

FOCUS
They appeared to go quite fast considering the testing conditions, but very few got involved from behind. Straightforward form.

NOTEBOOK
Lady Ibrox, a winner in soft ground round here in July, got a nice pitch tracking the leading pair and challenged off the turn. The handicapper had given her a chance by dropping her 4lb, and this was obviously a drop in class from the pattern races she's been contesting. It also helped that this track clearly suits her very well. (tchd 11-2)
Layla's Oasis disputed the lead one off the rail with Chasing Dreams, and while that one dropped out late on, she battled on well to hold on to second place. It was a fine effort on her handicap debut, and given that she's a daughter of Oasis Dream it wouldn't be a surprise if she's suited by better ground in future. (op 15-2 tchd 13-2)
Sharaarah(IRE) was dropped in from her wide draw and detached in last for much of the race, before staying on well up the straight. The shorter trip didn't help, especially from her outside stall, and she's not one to give up on. (op 8-1)
Chasing Dreams, who won her maiden in soft ground, could have done without being harried up front by Layla's Oasis over this slightly longer trip. (op 2-1 tchd 9-4)
Secret Sign was always just struggling to go the pace on this sharp track. Official explanation: jockey said gelding was denied a clear run closing stages (op 8-1)
Mandy Lexi(IRE), who's still a maiden, appears to be going backwards, and the first-time hood didn't seem to have much of a positive effect. (op 8-1)
Mandy Layla(IRE), who got upset beforehand, needs better ground to be seen at her best. (op 12-1)
Monkey Bar Flies(IRE) Official explanation: jockey said gelding hung right-handed

6659 INNOSPEC H'CAP 7f 2y
3:30 (3:33) (Class 3) (0-95,93) 3-Y-0+ £16,172 (£4,812; £2,405; £1,202) Stalls Low

Form				RPR
0645	1		**Big Note (IRE)**[49] 5080 3-9-3 **92**.... RichardMullen 1	102
			(Andrew Balding) *trckd ldrs: wnt 2nd jst over 2f out: led over 1f out: sn edgd lft: hld on wl cl home* **8/1**	
0062	2	½	**Capaill Liath (IRE)**[7] 6471 4-9-1 **87**....(p) PhillipMakin 4	96+
			(Kevin Ryan) *hld up: nt clr run over 2f out: hdwy over 1f out: r.o to take 2nd wl ins fnl f: clsd on wnr at fin* **4/1**[1]	
0004	3	2 ¾	**Xilerator (IRE)**[7] 6471 5-9-4 **90**.... AdrianNicholls 10	92
			(David Nicholls) *chsd ldrs: rdn and sltly outpcd over 2f out: plld off rail 1f out: styd on ins fnl f: nt quite pce to chal* **9/1**	
3002	4	nk	**Dr Red Eye**[15] 6192 4-8-11 **83**....(p) FrederikTylicki 3	84
			(Scott Dixon) *led: rdn and hdd over 1f out: no ex fnl 100yds* **6/1**[3]	
0000	5	3	**Imperial Djay (IRE)**[15] 6201 7-9-3 **89**.... DaleSwift 11	82
			(Ruth Carr) *in rr: niggled along over 4f out: rdn and hdwy over 1f out: styd on ins fnl f: unable to rch ldrs* **25/1**	
0601	6	1	**Clockmaker (IRE)**[15] 6192 6-9-0 **86**.... PaulMulrennan 14	77
			(Tim Easterby) *in tch: slipped sltly over 4f out: rdn over 1f out: kpt on but n.d fnl f* **16/1**	
0400	7	¾	**Advanced**[7] 6466 9-8-13 **88**.... JulieBurke(3) 9	77
			(Kevin Ryan) *chsd ldr tl jst over 2f out: rdn over 1f out: wknd ins fnl f* **20/1**	
1156	8	2 ¼	**Verse Of Love**[8] 6432 3-8-8 **86**.... RyanClark(3) 5	69
			(David Evans) *n.m.r s: u.p over 1f out: plugged on fnl f: nvr a threat* **10/1**	
4026	9	hd	**Nasri**[22] 6011 6-8-11 **88**....(b[1]) MatthewLawson(5) 7	71
			(Milton Bradley) *midfield: rdn and wknd over 1f out* **20/1**	
0613	10	1 ¼	**The Confessor**[35] 5572 5-9-5 **91**.... CathyGannon 13	70
			(Henry Candy) *chsd ldrs: ev ch 3f out: rdn 2f out: wknd over 1f out* **8/1**	
5114	11	hd	**Majuro (IRE)**[5] 6525 8-8-13 **85**....(t) StephenCraine 6	64
			(Charles Smith) *midfield: pushed along 3f out: wknd over 1f out* **33/1**	

3565 **12** *2 ¼* **Kyllachy Star**[28] 5827 6-8-13 **85** ..... JoeFanning 2 58
(Patrick Morris) *midfield: pushed along 3f out: wknd 2f out* **5/1**[2]
1040 **13** *9* **Corporal Maddox**[14] 6235 5-8-12 **89** ..... GeorgeDowning(5) 8 38
(Patrick Morris) *missed break: in rr: hung bdly rt whn gng nowhere wl over 1f out: nvr on terms* **20/1**

1m 34.22s (7.72) **Going Correction** +1.30s/f (Soft)
WFA 3 from 4yo+ 3lb **13** Ran SP% **119.2**
Speed ratings (Par 107): **107,106,103,102,99 98,97,94,94,93 93,90,80**
toteswingers 1&2 £11.20, 1&3 £8.20, 2&3 £13.70 CSF £36.59 CT £309.48 TOTE £11.90: £2.60, £1.80, £3.20; EX 58.70.
Owner N Botica **Bred** Willow Tree Stud Farm **Trained** Kingsclere, Hants

FOCUS
A competitive handicap. The form is rated around the second and third to their Ayr latest.

NOTEBOOK
Big Note(IRE), although a keen-going sort, got a nice lead through the race while hugging the rail, and having hit the front early in the straight he had just about enough energy left to hold off the late challenge of Capaill Liath. He twice ran well here as a 2yo and clearly the sharp track suits his style of running. (op 7-1)
Capaill Liath(IRE) had the rail to race against, but he was back in the pack and had plenty to do as they swung into the straight. He finished strongly, making up a lot of ground on the winner, but the line came just too soon. He looked unlucky and deserves to find compensation. (op 11-2)
Xilerator(IRE) bounced back to form when finishing two places behind Capaill Liath (later disqualified) at Ayr last time, and this was another sound effort in defeat on his favoured surface. (op 8-1)
Dr Red Eye, runner-up to Clockmaker over the C&D last time, reversed that form with his badly drawn rival. He wasn't really hassled up front so can have no excuses bar the ground not being ideal. (op 13-2, tchd 7-1 in a place)
Imperial Djay(IRE), drawn out in stall 11, has been struggling recently but the handicapper has shown some leniency and this was a little more encouraging.
Clockmaker(IRE), unlike last time, had far from a perfect trip, being trapped wide from his draw in stall 14, and he also slipped with over half a mile to run. (op 12-1)
The Confessor is another who was poorly drawn and forced to race much wider than ideal. (op 7-1)
Kyllachy Star, who has switched stables, was never travelling well despite holding a good pitch on the rail. (op 7-1)

6660 HE SIMM & SON MAIDEN STKS 1m 2f 75y
4:05 (4:05) (Class 4) 3-Y-0+ **£5,175** (£1,540; £769; £384) **Stalls** High

Form RPR
3 **1** **Livery (IRE)**[114] 2856 3-9-3 0 ..... JoeFanning 3 77+
(Jeremy Noseda) *dwlt: trckd ldrs: wnt 2nd 2f out: led over 1f out: sn edgd lft: r.o wl to draw clr ins fnl f: eased towards fin* **1/4**[1]
0552 **2** *9* **Humungosaur**[23] 5965 3-9-3 73 ..... FrederikTylicki 1 55
(Richard Ford) *led: rdn 2f out: hdd over 1f out: no ch w wnr after* **5/1**[2]
6205 **3** *3 ¾* **Gulf Storm (IRE)**[29] 5803 3-9-3 53 ..... RoystonFfrench 2 48
(Bryan Smart) *chsd ldr: rdn 5f out: lost 2nd 2f out: btn over 1f out* **12/1**[3]
0-0 **4** *60* **Gabrial's Hope (FR)**[31] 5753 3-9-3 0 ..... StephenCraine 4
(Patrick Morris) *in rr: rdn 4f out: sn lft bhd: t.o* **22/1**

2m 25.64s (14.44) **Going Correction** +1.30s/f (Soft) **4** Ran SP% **108.7**
Speed ratings (Par 105): **94,86,83,35**
CSF £1.92 TOTE £1.20; EX 1.70.
Owner M Tabor, Mrs J Magnier & D Smith **Bred** C O P Hanbury **Trained** Newmarket, Suffolk

FOCUS
This weak maiden proved straightforward for the favourite. There were doubts over what he met and he did not need to match his promising debut.

6661 SPORTINGBET H'CAP 1m 2f 75y
4:40 (4:40) (Class 2) (0-105,99) 3-Y-0
£31,125 (£9,320; £4,660; £2,330; £1,165; £585) **Stalls** High

Form RPR
4152 **1** **Deia Sunrise (IRE)**[15] 6193 3-9-1 **93** ..... NickyMackay 2 102
(John Gosden) *racd keenly: sn led: hdd over 1f out: continued to chal: regained ld wl ins fnl f: r.o gamely: jst prevailed in driving fin* **7/2**[1]
2120 **2** *shd* **Swnymor (IRE)**[59] 4700 3-8-6 **84** ..... CathyGannon 8 93+
(William Haggas) *midfield: n.m.r briefly over 2f out: hdwy sn after: rdn and edgd lft 1f out: chalng strly sn after: r.o: jst hld in driving fin* **7/1**
6621 **3** *½* **Prussian**[22] 6010 3-9-5 **97** ..... JoeFanning 3 105
(Mark Johnston) *chsd ldr: chalng 2f out: led narrowly over 1f out: hdd wl ins fnl f: no ex cl home* **5/1**[2]
1211 **4** *1* **Universal (IRE)**[28] 5820 3-9-7 **99** ..... FrederikTylicki 7 105
(Mark Johnston) *hld up: in midfield wl over 7f out: prom 5f out: rdn whn carried lft bhd ldrs 1f out: styd on ins fnl f: nt pce to chal front trio after* **7/1**
4133 **5** *1 ¼* **Sheikhzayedroad**[28] 5820 3-8-7 **85** ..... FergusSweeney 10 89
(David Simcock) *hld up in rr: hdwy over 3f out: rdn and hung lft fr over 1f out: kpt on ins fnl f: nt pce to chal ldrs* **11/1**
2131 **6** *hd* **Miss Cap Estel**[14] 6240 3-8-3 **81** ow1 ..... ChrisCatlin 1 84
(Andrew Balding) *chsd ldrs: rdn over 1f out: kpt on same pce ins fnl f* **6/1**[3]
0160 **7** *¾* **Gabrial The Great (IRE)**[35] 5598 3-8-13 **91** ..... PaulMulrennan 9 93+
(Michael Bell) *hld up in rr: rdn and hdwy 2f out: swtchd lft to ins rail over 1f out: one pce and no imp ins fnl f* **7/1**
2463 **8** *3 ½* **Kimbali (IRE)**[21] 6051 3-8-2 **80** ..... JamesSullivan 11 75
(Richard Fahey) *racd keenly: chsd ldrs: rdn and lost pl over 2f out: n.d after* **25/1**
2141 **9** *¾* **Eastern Destiny**[15] 6193 3-8-3 **81** ..... PatrickMathers 4 75
(Richard Fahey) *in tch: rdn and wknd over 2f out* **12/1**
0143 **10** *hd* **Clare Island Boy (IRE)**[50] 5064 3-8-10 **88** ..... SeanLevey 5 81
(Richard Hannon) *hld up: pushed along over 4f out: outpcd 3f out: nvr a danger* **25/1**
2336 **11** *shd* **Deepsand (IRE)**[15] 6193 3-8-4 **82** ..... RoystonFfrench 6 75
(Tim Easterby) *s.i.s: midfield: hmpd after 2f and again wl over 7f out: u.p over 4f out: struggling and bhd fr 3f out* **20/1**

2m 23.8s (12.60) **Going Correction** +1.45s/f (Soft) **11** Ran SP% **119.2**
Speed ratings (Par 107): **107,106,106,105,104 104,103,101,100,100 100**
toteswingers 1&2 £6.40, 1&3 £3.70, 2&3 £6.60 CSF £27.65 CT £121.82 TOTE £4.50: £1.80, £2.80, £2.10; EX 53.10.
Owner M Kerr-Dineen M Hughes Ms R Hood **Bred** John O'Connor **Trained** Newmarket, Suffolk
■ Stewards' Enquiry : Nicky Mackay two-day ban: used whip above permitted level (Oct 14-15)

FOCUS
A decent prize for this 0-105 handicap, although the top-weight was rated 6lb below the ceiling. The early gallop wasn't hectic. The form has been rated slightly positively.

NOTEBOOK
Deia Sunrise(IRE) grabbed the lead on the rail from stall two and was able to dominate at a pace to suit himself. This is why, when he was eventually headed in the straight, he had enough in reserve to rally and get his nose back in front on the line. He doesn't need the ground this soft, but does appreciate some give. (op 6-1)
Swnymor(IRE), a little keen in midfield, could have done with a stronger pace, especially as he was dropping back from 1m4f. Briefly denied a clear run on the turn in, he came with what looked like a winning run down the outside, only to come up marginally short. He remains open to further improvement. (op 8-1)
Prussian, up another 7lb, has had a long season. She was on the shoulder of the leader throughout and had her chance in the straight. (op 9-2 tchd 4-1)
Universal(IRE) likes to be up with the pace, but he found himself trapped three wide throughout here, which harmed his cause. (op 6-1)
Sheikhzayedroad, who lost out in a barging match with the runner-up on the turn, struggled to get involved from the back of the field. (op 10-1 tchd 12-1)
Miss Cap Estel, 5lb higher for her C&D win last time, had the best of the draw and grabbed a nice position tracking the leader on the rail. It's hard to make excuses for her. (tchd 13-2)
Gabrial The Great(IRE) would have been suited by a stronger gallop. (op 8-1)
Eastern Destiny narrowly beat Deia Sunrise here last time out but never really looked like confirming the form on this more testing surface. Official explanation: jockey said filly was denied a clear run (op 10-1)

6662 CARLSBERG H'CAP 1m 5f 89y
5:15 (5:16) (Class 4) (0-85,79) 3-Y-0 **£6,469** (£1,925; £962; £481) **Stalls** Low

Form RPR
2353 **1** **Bank Bonus**[50] 5048 3-9-7 **79** ..... RichardMullen 4 89
(Andrew Balding) *hld up: nt clr run and checked over 3f out: pushed along and hdwy over 2f out: led over 1f out: styd on ins fnl f: in command towards fin* **4/1**[2]
3300 **2** *1 ¼* **Daneking**[21] 6037 3-9-5 **77** ..... NickyMackay 7 85
(John Gosden) *hld up in midfield: hdwy over 4f out: sn chsd ldr: chalng 2f out: led briefly over 1f out: kpt on u.p ins fnl f: hld towards fin* **5/1**
5424 **3** *4 ½* **Bold Cuffs**[11] 6340 3-9-1 **73** ..... ChrisCatlin 2 74+
(Sir Mark Prescott Bt) *led: rdn whn pressed 2f out: hdd over 1f out: one pce ins fnl f* **3/1**[1]
63 **4** *4* **Gabrial's King (IRE)**[14] 6240 3-8-11 **69** ..... PaulMulrennan 6 64
(Ian Williams) *hld up in rr: hdwy to chse ldrs over 3f out: rdn whn cl up over 2f out: wknd 1f out* **10/1**
2312 **5** *20* **News Show**[68] 4403 3-9-3 **75** ..... PhillipMakin 1 40
(David Simcock) *s.i.s: chsd ldrs: pushed along over 4f out: wknd 3f out* **3/1**[1]
0-50 **6** *9* **Young Lou**[134] 2232 3-9-0 **72** ..... RoystonFfrench 5 24
(Robin Dickin) *chsd ldrs: niggled along 5f out: wknd over 4f out* **33/1**
6046 **7** *2 ¼* **Nice Rose**[10] 6359 3-9-2 **74** ..... JoeFanning 3 23
(Mark Johnston) *chsd ldr: pushed along over 5f out: wknd 4f out* **9/2**[3]

3m 13.91s (21.21) **Going Correction** +1.45s/f (Soft) **7** Ran SP% **116.9**
Speed ratings (Par 103): **92,91,88,86,73 68,66**
toteswingers: 1&2 £3.50, 1&3 £3.00, 2&3 £3.70 CSF £25.02 TOTE £4.70: £1.90, £3.90; EX 26.00.
Owner The Queen **Bred** The Queen **Trained** Kingsclere, Hants

FOCUS
This was run at a good gallop but the time was very slow in the bad ground. The form is rated around the runner-up.
Young Lou Official explanation: jockey said filly never travelled

6663 ADVANCED INSULATION PLC H'CAP 6f 18y
5:45 (5:45) (Class 4) (0-85,84) 3-Y-0+ **£6,469** (£1,925; £962; £481) **Stalls** Low

Form RPR
1136 **1** **All Or Nothin (IRE)**[63] 4588 3-9-4 **83** ..... 1 MichaelO'Connell 8 92
(John Quinn) *chsd ldrs: rdn to ld 1f out: rdr sn dropped rein and jnd: rallied and fnd ex towards fin* **9/2**[2]
2066 **2** *½* **Green Park (IRE)**[7] 6465 9-9-0 **77** ..... (b) JoeFanning 11 84
(Declan Carroll) *stdd s: hld up: hdwy on outer 2f out: str chal and upsides wnr ins fnl f: hld fnl strides* **11/2**[3]
6606 **3** *1 ½* **Beckermet (IRE)**[7] 6471 10-9-5 **82** ..... JamesSullivan 3 84
(Ruth Carr) *chsd ldrs: rdn over 1f out: ch jst ins fnl f: styd on same pce fnl 75yds* **8/1**
0034 **4** *2 ½* **Bathwick Bear (IRE)**[5] 6543 4-8-13 **79** ..... RyanClark(3) 10 73
(David Evans) *racd 3 wd w ldrs: led over 3f out: rdn over 1f out: sn hdd: no ex fnl 75yds* **9/1**
0000 **5** *3 ½* **Sunraider (IRE)**[22] 6009 5-9-3 **80** ..... PaulMulrennan 9 63
(Paul Midgley) *hld up: hdwy 3f out: chsd ldrs over 2f out: wknd ins fnl f* **14/1**
40-2 **6** *¾* **Key Ambition**[265] 99 3-9-0 **79** ..... RussKennemore 6 60
(Garry Moss) *w ldr: pushed along over 2f out: rdn over 1f out: edgd rt whn wknd ins fnl f* **14/1**
5004 **7** *½* **Roker Park (IRE)**[7] 6465 7-9-0 **84** ..... (v1) DavidBergin(7) 7 63
(David O'Meara) *in tch: rdn and outpcd 2f out: no imp after* **3/1**[1]
1006 **8** *hd* **Jarrow (IRE)**[21] 6026 5-9-0 **82** ..... MatthewLawson(5) 4 60
(Milton Bradley) *hld up: nt clr run 2f out: rdn over 1f out: nvr able to chal* **10/1**
0000 **9** *4 ½* **Layla's Hero (IRE)**[7] 6466 5-9-0 **82** ..... (v) GeorgeDowning(5) 5 46
(Patrick Morris) *bhd: sn pushed along and outpcd: nvr on terms* **16/1**
0600 **10** *11* **Parisian Pyramid (IRE)**[42] 5368 6-9-5 **82** ..... (p) StephenCraine 2 11
(Patrick Morris) *led: hdd over 3f out: rdn and wknd over 2f out* **10/1**

1m 21.95s (8.15) **Going Correction** +1.45s/f (Soft)
WFA 3 from 4yo+ 2lb **10** Ran SP% **117.1**
Speed ratings (Par 105): **103,102,100,97,92 91,90,90,84,69**
toteswingers 1&2 £3.70, 1&3 £4.40, 2&3 £7.50 CSF £29.67 CT £198.60 TOTE £4.10: £1.10, £1.80, £2.60; EX 33.50.
Owner Ross Harmon **Bred** Ballyhane Stud **Trained** Settrington, N Yorks

FOCUS
A race made up mostly of exposed performers went to one of the two 3yos in the line-up. The runner-up sets the standard.
T/Plt: £272.30 to a £1 stake. Pool: £48,381.18. 129.66 winning tickets. T/Qpdt: £27.80 to a £1 stake. Pool: £3,269.96. 86.90 winning tickets DO

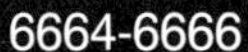

6625 HAYDOCK (L-H)

Saturday, September 29

OFFICIAL GOING: Heavy (8.0)

All races on stands' side Home straight. Races on round course increased by 13yds except fifth race which increased by 63yds.

Wind: Moderate, against Weather: Cloudy

6664 EBF SPORTS360 SUPPORT GEORGECLAXTONTRUST.COM MAIDEN FILLIES' STKS 1m

2:05 (2:06) (Class 5) 2-Y-O **£3,234** (£962; £481; £240) **Stalls** Low

Form RPR

1 **Hollowina** 2-9-0 0 RobertWinston 5 79+
(David Brown) *trckd ldrs: hdwy on outer and cl up over 2f out: rdn to ld over 1f out: styd on strly* **13/2**

40 2 2 1/4 **Northern Star (IRE)**[39] 5471 2-9-0 0 StephenCraine 2 74
(Tom Dascombe) *chsd ldr: tk clsr order 4f out: cl up 3f out: led 2f out: sn rdn: edgd lft and hdd appr fnl f: kpt on same pce* **3/1**[3]

0 3 1 3/4 **Polly's Love (IRE)**[58] 4739 2-9-0 0 AdamKirby 4 70
(Clive Cox) *t.k.h: sn led and clr after 2f: jnd 3f out: rdn and hdd 2f out: kpt on same pce* **11/4**[2]

4 4 1 1/2 **Society Pearl (IRE)**[65] 4494 2-9-0 0 HarryBentley 1 67
(Charles Hills) *trckd ldrs on inner: effrt over 2f out: rdn wl over 1f out: sn no imp* **2/1**[1]

56 5 shd **Dixie Sky (USA)**[72] 4246 2-9-0 0 PJMcDonald 3 66+
(Noel Quinlan) *hld up in tch: effrt 3f out: sn rdn along and no hdwy* **6/1**

00 6 33 **Wicked Tara**[29] 5806 2-9-0 0 LukeMorris 7
(Frank Sheridan) *wnt rt s: a in rr: outpcd and bhd 3f out: sn eased* **100/1**

1m 49.17s (5.47) **Going Correction** +0.475s/f (Yiel) **6** Ran SP% **113.6**

Speed ratings (Par 92): **91,88,87,85,85 52**

toteswingers: 1&2 £7.50, 1&3 £14.90, 2&3 £1.40 CSF £26.63 TOTE £9.10: £3.40, £1.80; EX 46.80.

Owner Peter Onslow **Bred** Peter Onslow **Trained** Averham Park, Notts

FOCUS

Probably nothing more than a fair race of its type on ground that appeared testing enough for juveniles. Adam Kirby said after the first "It's very sticky, and there's a bad patch about three furlongs from home" while Robert Winston, who rode the winner, reported "It's hard work for them out there." The winner did it quite well and the third and fifth help with the level.

NOTEBOOK

Hollowina, the second foal of a mare who developed into a Group class middle-distance performer, looked to have a tough task on debut, but she was well positioned as the race took shape and fought on tenaciously under pressure. Connections have no firm plans for the filly. (op 8-1)

Northern Star(IRE) wasn't beaten far in a Deauville Listed event when last seen on a quicker surface, so does give the contest a decent marker. She shouldn't remain a maiden for long. (op 2-1)

Polly's Love(IRE), a half-sister to Listed class mare Polly's Mark, had a blanket for stalls entry and set off at a good gallop once in front. She did a bit too much when there but gamely plugged on for third. (op 5-1)

Society Pearl(IRE), who was also declared at Chester, hadn't been out since a highly encouraging debut at Doncaster in late July and didn't look obviously suited by the going when off the bridle. (tchd 5-2)

Dixie Sky(USA), off the track since July, was taking another step up in trip on going she hadn't encountered before and was comfortably held. One would presume she'll go into handicaps now. (op 13-2 tchd 7-1)

6665 GORDON SANDERSON'S BIG BIRTHDAY DASH H'CAP 6f

2:35 (2:36) (Class 3) (0-90,88) 3-Y-O+ **£8,409** (£2,502; £1,250; £625) **Stalls** Centre

Form RPR

111- 1 **Take Cover**[312] 7504 5-8-12 **79** RobertWinston 11 89+
(David C Griffiths) *trckd ldrs stands' side: hdwy wl over 1f out: chal ins fnl f: rdn and styd on wl to ld nr line* **13/2**[2]

4250 2 nk **Defence Council (IRE)**[11] 6338 4-8-12 **79** DuranFentiman 16 88
(Mel Brittain) *towards rr stands' side: hdwy 1/2-way: cl up on stands' rail 2f out: rdn to ld ins fnl f: hdd and nt qckn nr fin: 2nd of 7 in gp* **10/1**

3216 3 1 **Rusty Rocket (IRE)**[15] 6192 3-8-4 **80** JoshBaudains(7) 12 86
(Paul Green) *led stands' side gp: cl up: rdn to ld wl over 1f out: sn hung bdly lft: hdd ins fnl f: kpt on: 3rd of 7 in gp* **11/2**[1]

1003 4 2 3/4 **Hopes N Dreams (IRE)**[22] 6009 4-8-12 **79** AmyRyan 14 76
(Kevin Ryan) *in rr stands' side: hdwy 2f out: sn rdn and styd on fnl f: nrst fin: 4th of 7 in gp* **11/2**[1]

0000 5 nk **Klynch**[7] 6466 6-9-6 **87** (b) JamesSullivan 6 83
(Ruth Carr) *chsd ldr far side: rdn along 2f out: sn one pce: 1st of 7 in gp* **12/1**

3013 6 3/4 **Dutch Heritage**[36] 5545 3-8-6 **75** [1] BarryMcHugh 8 69
(Richard Fahey) *s.i.s and bhd far side: rdn along bef 1/2-way: hdwy over 2f out: styd on fnl f: nrst fin: 2nd in gp* **8/1**[3]

0050 7 nse **Rasaman (IRE)**[7] 6465 8-8-11 **78** AndreaAtzeni 1 71
(Jim Goldie) *towards rr far side: rdn and hdwy 2f out: n.d: 3rd of 7 in gp* **14/1**

0004 8 1/2 **Polish World (USA)**[11] 6338 8-8-9 **79** LeeTopliss(3) 13 71
(Paul Midgley) *prom stands' side: cl up 1/2-way: rdn along over 2f out: grad wknd: 5th of 7 in gp* **10/1**

0000 9 4 1/2 **Marine Commando**[17] 6144 4-8-11 **78** PJMcDonald 7 55
(Ruth Carr) *overall ldr far side: rdn along over 2f out: hdd wl over 1f out and grad wknd: 4th of 7 in gp* **12/1**

0000 10 shd **Ralphy Boy (IRE)**[49] 5110 3-8-9 **78** StevieDonohoe 5 55
(Kevin Ryan) *chsd ldr far side: rdn along 2f out: sn wknd: 5th of 7 in gp* **22/1**

0610 11 nk **Lucky Numbers (IRE)**[22] 6009 6-8-7 **81** (e) DavidBergin(7) 2 57
(David O'Meara) *rrd s and dwlt: hdwy to chse ldrs far side 1/2-way: rdn 2f out and sn wknd: 6th of 7 in gp* **10/1**

4100 12 3 **Italian Tom (IRE)**[71] 4286 5-9-5 **86** LukeMorris 10 53
(Ronald Harris) *in tch stands' side: rdn over 2f out: sn wknd: 6th of 7 in gp* **16/1**

0110 13 3 3/4 **Lucky Dan (IRE)**[107] 3065 6-8-1 **75** PhilipPrince(7) 4 30
(Paul Green) *chsd ldrs far side: rdn along 2f out: sn wknd: last of 7 in gp* **25/1**

0030 14 shd **Diman Waters (IRE)**[14] 6234 5-8-7 **74** oh1 (p) JimmyQuinn 17 28
(Eric Alston) *dwlt: sn prom stands' side: rdn along over 2f out and sn wknd: last of 7 in gp* **28/1**

1m 16.54s (2.74) **Going Correction** +0.475s/f (Yiel)

WFA 3 from 4yo+ 2lb **14** Ran SP% **122.1**

Speed ratings (Par 107): **100,99,98,94,94 93,93,92,86,86 85,81,76,76**

toteswingers: 1&2 £13.40, 1&3 £4.40, 2&3 £34.40 CSF £69.46 CT £389.28 TOTE £7.20: £2.60, £4.00, £2.00; EX 95.20.

Owner Norcroft Park Stud **Bred** Norcroft Park Stud **Trained** Bawtry, S Yorks

FOCUS

On official ratings this looked a useful contest, but plenty of these had something to prove and those drawn low had no chance. The winner carried over his progressive AW form and the second and third set the standard.

NOTEBOOK

Take Cover, absent since November 2011, was making his debut for David Griffiths and travelled like a good horse before having to work really hard for success. The move to turf didn't pose any problems for the gelding and he will obviously progress for the outing. (op 7-1)

Defence Council(IRE), down in distance, only had one win in his profile but went really close to doubling his career total. He never shirked the issue down the stands' rail and seems to like this course, as he's now finished second twice here from three runs. (op 11-1 tchd 12-1)

Rusty Rocket(IRE), back to 6f, showed good pace and may well have won had he kept straight from over 1f out considering how far he was beaten. (op 6-1)

Hopes N Dreams(IRE) got away on terms and ran up to her best on what looked the favoured side of the draw. (op 13-2)

Klynch ran badly in the Ayr Silver Cup the previous weekend, but did better this time and did best of those who stayed far side. (op 10-1)

Dutch Heritage, dropped in trip and tried in a hood, was slowly away and gave himself no chance of being involved. However, he caught the eye with the way he finished and can win again if getting away on terms. (op 15-2)

Italian Tom(IRE) Official explanation: jockey said horse hung left

6666 JOSEPH HELER CHEESE LESTER PIGGOTT H'CAP 5f

3:15 (3:17) (Class 2) (0-105,105) 3-Y-O+ **£19,407** (£5,775; £2,886; £1,443) **Stalls** Centre

Form RPR

1222 1 **Face The Problem (IRE)**[14] 6244 4-9-7 **102** AdamKirby 7 111
(Jamie Osborne) *dwlt and towards rr stands' side: hdwy over 2f out: swtchd lft and rdn to chse ldrs over 1f out: styd on ins fnl f to ld nr fin* **10/1**

0413 2 3/4 **Long Awaited (IRE)**[21] 6028 4-8-10 **91** (b) ShaneKelly 16 98
(David Barron) *trckd ldrs stands' side: hdwy on stands' rails 2f out: led ent fnl f: sn rdn and edgd lft: hdd and no ex nr fin: 2nd of 10 in gp* **7/1**[3]

0134 3 1 **Sholaan (IRE)**[7] 6468 3-9-5 **101** (b) LiamJones 8 104
(William Haggas) *dwlt and towards rr stands' side: hdwy 2f out: sn rdn and styd on fnl f: nrst fin: 3rd of 10 in gp* **11/4**[1]

3531 4 1/2 **Kyleakin Lass**[13] 6286 3-8-11 **93** JamesSullivan 9 94
(Ian Wood) *trckd ldrs stands' side: effrt 2f out: sn rdn and kpt on fnl f: 4th of 10 in gp* **14/1**

3140 5 1 1/2 **Steps (IRE)**[14] 6244 4-8-13 **94** (b) AndreaAtzeni 1 90
(Roger Varian) *trckd ldrs far side: hdwy 2f out: rdn to ld that gp over 1f out: kpt on: no ch w stands' side gp fnl f: 1st of 6 in gp* **8/1**

0622 6 1 **Cheveton**[7] 6465 8-8-5 **86** oh3 TadhgO'Shea 11 78
(Richard Price) *dwlt and towards rr stands' side: rdn and hdwy wl over 1f out: kpt on fnl f: nrst fin: 5th of 10 in gp* **13/2**[2]

0333 7 1 1/4 **Beau Mistral (IRE)**[14] 6234 3-8-1 **86** oh1 RaulDaSilva(3) 10 74
(Paul Green) *cl up stands' side: rdn along 2f out: sn one pce: 6th of 10 in gp* **22/1**

4030 8 1 1/4 **Jedward (IRE)**[7] 6466 5-8-5 **86** oh1 AmyRyan 13 69
(Kevin Ryan) *prom stands' side: rdn to ld and overall ldr 2f out: drvn and hdd appr fnl f: wknd qckly: 7th of 10 in gp* **12/1**

1050 9 1/2 **Elusivity (IRE)**[21] 6030 4-9-5 **105** CharlesBishop(5) 2 86
(Brian Meehan) *trckd ldr far side: hdwy to ld that gp 2f out: sn rdn: hdd & wknd over 1f out: 2nd of 6 in gp* **11/1**

5105 10 3 1/2 **West Coast Dream**[28] 5832 5-8-8 **89** ChrisCatlin 12 58
(Roy Brotherton) *sn led stands' side gp: rdn along 2f out and sn wknd: 8th of 10 in gp* **28/1**

0500 11 1 **Foxy Music**[28] 5829 8-8-8 **89** ow1 RobertWinston 14 54
(Eric Alston) *cl up stands' side: rdn along over 2f out: sn wknd: 9th of 10 in gp* **22/1**

4012 12 3/4 **Avonvalley**[7] 6497 5-8-7 **88** oh21 ow2 RobbieFitzpatrick 15 51
(Peter Grayson) *s.i.s and a in rr stands' side: last of 10 in gp* **80/1**

0000 13 shd **Hazelrigg (IRE)**[38] 5487 7-8-8 **89** PJMcDonald 5 51
(Tim Easterby) *in tch far side: rdn along 2f out: sn wknd: 3rd of 6 in gp* **28/1**

5000 14 nk **Captain Dunne (IRE)**[14] 6244 7-9-2 **97** DuranFentiman 3 58
(Tim Easterby) *overall ldr far side: rdn along and hdd 2f out: sn wknd: 4th of 6 in gp* **33/1**

4006 15 1 1/2 **Dancing Freddy (IRE)**[10] 6382 5-8-5 **86** oh1 (tp) HarryBentley 4 42
(Violet M Jordan) *chsd ldrs far side: rdn along over 2f out: sn wknd: 5th of 6 in gp* **25/1**

0030 16 15 **Judge 'n Jury**[7] 6485 8-9-8 **103** (t) LukeMorris 6
(Ronald Harris) *prom far side: rdn along wl over 1f out: sn wknd and eased fnl f: last of 6 in gp* **20/1**

1m 1.96s (1.16) **Going Correction** +0.475s/f (Yiel)

WFA 3 from 4yo+ 1lb **16** Ran SP% **123.8**

Speed ratings (Par 109): **109,107,106,105,103 101,99,97,96,91 89,88,88,87,85 61**

toteswingers: 1&2 £8.60, 1&3 £4.70, 2&3 £8.20 CSF £71.19 CT £262.93 TOTE £8.70: £1.90, £2.50, £1.20, £4.60; EX 69.90 Trifecta £130.20 Pool: £2,007.17 - 11.86 winning tickets..

Owner Dr Marwan Koukash **Bred** J Joyce **Trained** Upper Lambourn, Berks

■ Stewards' Enquiry : Adam Kirby two-day ban: used whip above permitted level (Oct 14-15)

FOCUS

A few smart sprinters took their chance in this, but much like the race that preceded it, you needed to be in the stands'-side group to have a winning chance. A personal best from Face The Problem with the second to form.

NOTEBOOK

Face The Problem(IRE) narrowly failed to land the Portland on his previous start but made no mistake in this after coming with a strong late burst at the right time. He hasn't run badly all season and has again developed into a smart sprinter. (op 9-1)

Long Awaited(IRE) ◆ was just behind Face The Problem over C&D when they last clashed, but was much better off at the weights, so when he travelled up to the head of affairs going well, it seemed very likely he'd be successful. However, he didn't quicken much off the bridle and was worn down by the Jamie Osborne-trained runner. (op 13-2 tchd 6-1)

Sholaan(IRE) was making a quick reappearance after a fine effort in the Ayr Gold Cup, but never really looked like backing up that fine performance up with a victory here. (op 7-2)

Kyleakin Lass ◆, up 5lb for her Ffos Las victory, moved powerfully for a long way before keeping on. She's in good heart and clearly likes ease in the ground.

Steps(IRE), with the hood removed, wasn't far behind Face The Problem in the Portland and ran a cracker here on what was the unfavoured side of the track. (op 13-2)

Cheveton, runner-up in the Ayr Bronze Cup a week previously, has a really good record at Haydock, including when taking this very race in 2010, but looked to find everything happening a stride too quickly this time. (tchd 7-1)

6667 EBF STAINLESS WIRE "REPROCOLOR" FILLIES' H'CAP 1m 2f 95y

3:50 (3:51) (Class 3) (0-90,90) 3-Y-0+ £12,938 (£3,850; £1,924; £962) Stalls High

Form				RPR
3426	1		**Lady Loch**[20] 6073 3-8-6 78 ...1 BarryMcHugh 11 (Richard Fahey) *trckd ldrs: hdwy and cl up 4f out: led wl over 2f out and sn rdn: drvn ent fnl f and styd on gamely* 6/1[3]	87
614	2	1	**Moment In Time (IRE)**[45] 5228 3-8-4 76 oh1 ... LiamJones 4 (David Simcock) *prom: trckd ldr after 2f: effrt 2f out and sn rdn: drvn and ev ch ins fnl f tl no ex last 50yds* 16/1	83
3221	3	hd	**Bedazzled**[17] 6148 3-8-11 83 ... ShaneKelly 9 (James Fanshawe) *trckd ldrs: hdwy and cl up over 3f out: rdn to chal 2f out and ev ch tl drvn and one pce ins fnl f* 4/1[2]	90
2032	4	1	**Oojooba**[45] 5238 3-9-4 90 ... AndreaAtzeni 2 (Roger Varian) *in tch: smooth hdwy to trck ldrs 4f out: effrt and ev ch over 2f out: sn rdn and one pce* 3/1[1]	95
2510	5	3 ¾	**Our Phylli Vera (IRE)**[54] 4875 3-8-4 76 oh7 ... JimmyQuinn 12 (Harry Dunlop) *bhd: hdwy 3f out: rdn over 2f out: styd on fnl f: nrst fin* 33/1	74
2060	6	3 ¼	**Fork Handles**[15] 6202 4-9-3 83 ... PJMcDonald 7 (Mick Channon) *towards rr: hdwy over 3f out: rdn over 2f out: plugged on fnl f: nvr rchd ldrs* 14/1	74
-200	7	1 ½	**Always The Lady**[54] 4879 4-9-1 81 ... AdamKirby 8 (Clive Cox) *bhd: hdwy 3f out: sn rdn and plugged on: nvr nr ldrs* 14/1	70
5105	8	¾	**Cape Safari (IRE)**[9] 6416 3-8-5 77 ... LukeMorris 1 (Alan Bailey) *chsd ldng pair: rdn along 4f out: sn wknd* 9/1	64
3211	9	2 ¾	**Dancing Primo**[14] 6229 6-8-11 84 ... JackDuern(7) 5 (Mark Brisbourne) *in tch: rdn along 4f out: wknd wl over 2f out* 7/1	66
0622	10	3 ¾	**Cochabamba (IRE)**[27] 5856 4-9-3 83 ... MichaelO'Connell 3 (Roger Teal) *led: rdn along 4f out: hdd wl over 2f out: sn drvn and wknd* 10/1	58
-166	11	17	**Morant Bay (IRE)**[90] 3668 3-8-9 81 ... TonyHamilton 10 (Ian Williams) *in rr: sme hdwy over 3f out: sn rdn and wknd* 33/1	23
1530	12	9	**Candycakes (IRE)**[9] 6416 3-8-7 79 ow1 ... StevieDonohoe 6 (Michael Bell) *midfield: rdn along 4f out: sn wknd* 22/1	

2m 17.53s (2.03) **Going Correction** +0.475s/f (Yiel)
WFA 3 from 4yo+ 6lb 12 Ran SP% **120.3**
Speed ratings (Par 104): **110,109,109,108,105 102,101,100,98,95 82,74**
toteswingers: 1&2 £19.30, 1&3 £6.80, 2&3 £8.80 CSF £97.09 CT £432.08 TOTE £8.20: £2.90, £5.90, £2.10; EX 153.90.
Owner David W Armstrong **Bred** Jeremy Green And Sons **Trained** Musley Bank, N Yorks

FOCUS

A decent fillies' handicap in which it paid to be handy. Plenty of these arrived in good heart, so this will probably turn out to be solid form for the going.

NOTEBOOK

Lady Loch swapped cheekpieces for a hood and showed a willing attitude for pressure throughout the final furlong. She's not fully exposed but one would imagine she'll need to find a bit more to win off a mark in the 80s. (op 7-1)

Moment In Time(IRE) ◆, returning to turf and previously unbeaten going left-handed, ran a cracker after always being prominent. A step back up in distance wouldn't be an issue. (tchd 14-1)

Bedazzled, back on turf, ran like a horse not enjoying the ground. That said, she wasn't disgraced if that was the case. (op 9-2 tchd 7-2)

Oojooba has been going up the weights for not getting her head to the front and shaped as though she needs to come down the handicap considering the way she emptied out off the bridle. (op 7-2)

Our Phylli Vera(IRE) has won both of her races on soft, and finished off strongly in this after being in rear off the final bend. Her jockey subsequently reported that they suffered interference. Official explanation: jockey said filly suffered interference in running

Dancing Primo is usually extremely consistent but didn't fire here. The rise in the weights and being a bit keen under restraint was enough to stop her. (op 15-2)

Candycakes(IRE) had an excuse for her last effort and another one here, as she was almost brought down heading into the final bend. (op 20-1)

6668 NATIONWIDE PLATFORMS H'CAP 1m 6f

4:25 (4:25) (Class 2) (0-100,97) 3-Y-0+ £19,407 (£5,775; £2,886; £1,443) Stalls Low

Form				RPR
4132	1		**Lady Kashaan (IRE)**[7] 6472 3-8-1 80 ... JimmyQuinn 9 (Alan Swinbank) *trckd ldng pair: hdwy to ld 3f out: rdn clr over 1f out: styd on wl* 3/1[1]	90+
31S0	2	2 ¼	**Last Shadow**[49] 5078 3-8-6 85 ... LukeMorris 7 (William Muir) *hld up towards rr: hdwy 4f out: rdn to chse ldrs 2f out: kpt on u.p fnl f* 9/2[3]	92
1416	3	½	**Suraj**[77] 4111 3-9-4 97 ... StevieDonohoe 8 (Michael Bell) *hld up in rr: stdy hdwy 3f out: chsd ldrs 2f out: sn rdn and kpt on same pce* 7/2[2]	103
3113	4	¾	**Party Line**[7] 6476 3-8-8 87 ... PJMcDonald 6 (Mark Johnston) *cl up: effrt 3f out: rdn 2f out and ev ch tl drvn and one pce appr fnl f* 9/1	92
155	5	7	**Lieutenant Kojak**[16] 6170 4-8-11 80 ... RobertWinston 3 (Peter Charalambous) *trckd ldrs: pushed along and outpcd over 3f out: sn rdn and plugged on fnl 2f* 11/1	75
6353	6	2 ¾	**Good Morning Star (IRE)**[14] 6236 3-9-4 97 ... LiamJones 2 (Mark Johnston) *led: rdn along and hdd 3f out: sn wknd* 12/1	88
000	7	¾	**Astral Thunder (ARG)**[49] 5076 5-9-11 94 ...(b) AdamKirby 1 (Marco Botti) *chsd ldrs: rdn along 4f out: sn wknd* 33/1	84
0623	8	2 ¼	**Scrapper Smith (IRE)**[28] 5826 6-9-4 92 ... GarryWhillans(5) 4 (Alistair Whillans) *plld hrd: chsd ldrs: prom 6f out: rdn 3f out and sn wknd* 7/2[2]	79
10-0	9	20	**Cosmic Sun**[22] 6018 6-9-10 93 ... TonyHamilton 5 (Richard Fahey) *hld up: a in rr: outpcd and bhd fnl 3f* 33/1	52

3m 11.75s (9.75) **Going Correction** +0.70s/f (Yiel)
WFA 3 from 4yo+ 10lb 9 Ran SP% **119.5**
Speed ratings (Par 109): **100,98,98,98,94 92,92,90,79**
toteswingers: 1&2 £3.40, 1&3 £3.40, 2&3 £4.40 CSF £17.50 CT £48.96 TOTE £4.00: £1.40, £2.00, £1.60; EX 21.70.
Owner G Brogan **Bred** Corduff Stud Ltd & J Corcoran **Trained** Melsonby, N Yorks

FOCUS

The early gallop was predictably modest, and once again being prominent was a positive. The winner continued her progress.

NOTEBOOK

Lady Kashaan(IRE) has developed in to a useful filly and was well ridden here to get back in the winner's enclosure. Jimmy Quinn got his mount to the rail in the home straight before finding her a willing partner for pressure. She can hold her own in these types of races but the low weight she carried probably helped in this. (op 4-1 tchd 9-2 in a place)

Last Shadow, trying this sort of distance for the first time, loves ease in the ground and made a promising return after a short break. Connections will want the rain to keep falling for their gelding. (op 6-1)

Suraj, absent since a modest effort in a Listed contest at York in July, was held up early, which wasn't an advantage considering the way the race developed. He can be given another chance. (op 3-1 tchd 4-1)

Party Line has been kept fairly busy since April and is clearly a tough and hardy type. She possibly didn't see the distance out in this ground. (op 17-2 tchd 15-2)

Scrapper Smith(IRE) came into this off the back of a good run at Chester at the start of September, but pulled too hard just in behind the pacesetter and had nothing left at the end. Official explanation: jockey said gelding ran too free (op 4-1)

6669 EBF GEOFF CROFT 60TH/JUDITH MCKENNA MEMORIAL MAIDEN STKS (C&G) 1m

5:00 (5:01) (Class 5) 2-Y-O £3,234 (£962; £481; £240) Stalls Low

Form				RPR
56	1		**Ennistown**[16] 6164 2-8-9 0 ... AntiocoMurgia(5) 2 (Mahmood Al Zarooni) *hld up in tch: hdwy 3f out: chal 2f out: rdn to ld and edgd lft over 1f out: clr ins fnl f* 11/8[1]	81+
0624	2	4	**Khelac**[17] 6133 2-9-0 72 ... RobertWinston 8 (Alan Swinbank) *prom: hdwy and cl up 1/2-way: led wl over 2f out: sn rdn and hdd over 1f out: drvn and one pce fnl f* 7/1	70
4	3	½	**Duke Of Yorkshire**[29] 5797 2-8-11 0 ... NeilFarley(3) 5 (Declan Carroll) *cl up: rdn along over 2f out: drvn over 1f out and kpt on same pce* 9/2[3]	69
	4	1 ½	**Hawk High (IRE)** 2-9-0 0 ... DuranFentiman 6 (Tim Easterby) *dwlt and in rr: hdwy to chse ldrs 3f out: rdn along 2f out: sn wknd* 9/1	66
2	5	shd	**Gabrial The Master (IRE)**[15] 6188 2-9-0 0 ... TonyHamilton 4 (Richard Fahey) *led: rdn along 3f out: hdd over 2f out and sn drvn: wknd over 1f out* 3/1[2]	65
	6	6	**Prokeel (IRE)** 2-8-9 0 ... DarylByrne(5) 1 (Tim Easterby) *hld up in rr: sme hdwy on outer 3f out: rdn along over 2f out and sn wknd* 20/1	52

1m 48.88s (5.18) **Going Correction** +0.70s/f (Yiel) 6 Ran SP% **112.5**
Speed ratings (Par 95): **102,98,97,96,95 89**
toteswingers 1&2 £2.30, 1&3 £2.20, 2&3 £3.90 CSF £11.81 TOTE £2.20: £1.10, £2.70; EX 12.00.
Owner Godolphin **Bred** Darley **Trained** Newmarket, Suffolk

FOCUS

It's difficult to believe this maiden contained smart types in the making, although the winner did it well. The second limits the form.

NOTEBOOK

Ennistown, who ran in what looked a strong maiden last time at Doncaster, won easily after tracking the leaders. He was pushed out once asserting to collect success and will surely have stiffer tests to come. (op 15-8)

Khelac has an official rating of 72 and ran his race. Whether he up to winning off this BHA mark is open to question. (op 11-2)

Duke Of Yorkshire made a promising debut at the end of August and again displayed ability. He'll make a fair middle-distance handicapper next season if progressing. (op 11-2)

Hawk High(IRE), the fourth foal of an unraced half-sister to a couple of useful handicappers, shaped well after being a bit keen and has something positive to build on. (op 15-2)

Gabrial The Master(IRE), the only remaining runner from three the owner had entered overnight, finished just in front of a subsequent winner on his debut at Chester about two weeks previously but was disappointing here. (op 11-4 tchd 5-2)

6670 SPORTS360.CO.UK H'CAP 1m

5:35 (5:39) (Class 2) (0-105,105) 3-Y-0+ £12,938 (£3,850; £1,924; £962) Stalls Low

Form				RPR
1221	1		**Anton Chigurh**[17] 6135 3-8-5 88 ... LukeMorris 4 (Tom Dascombe) *trckd ldrs: pushed along 4f out: hdwy whn hmpd 2f out: sn rdn and styd on to chse ldng pair ent fnl f: sn drvn and kpt on to chal whn edgd rt last 50yds: sn led and styd on wl* 10/11[1]	94+
1422	2	1	**Vito Volterra (IRE)**[42] 5369 5-8-7 86 oh3 ... AndrewMullen 7 (Michael Smith) *led: rdn 2f out: drvn ins fnl f: jnd and bmpd last 50yds: sn hdd and no ex* 9/1[3]	89
6000	3	2 ¾	**Beacon Lodge (IRE)**[7] 6468 7-9-5 105 ... ShirleyTeasdale(7) 8 (David Nicholls) *t.k.h: chsd ldng pair: swtchd lft and rdn 2f out: drvn over 1f out and kpt on same pce* 25/1	102
5004	4	2 ¾	**Al Muheer (IRE)**[8] 6426 7-8-3 87 ...(b) JasonHart(5) 3 (Ruth Carr) *hld up in rr: hdwy 3f out: rdn to chse ldrs 2f out: sn drvn and one pce* 9/1[3]	78
220	5	6	**Prince Of Sorrento**[69] 4365 5-8-13 92 ... StevieDonohoe 1 (Lee Carter) *chsd ldr: rdn along over 3f out: sn wknd* 11/2[2]	69
5060	6	6	**Neutrafa (IRE)**[16] 6161 4-8-7 91 ... GarryWhillans(5) 5 (John Mackie) *towards rr: effrt and sme hdwy 3f out: sn rdn and wknd over 2f out* 14/1	54

1m 47.46s (3.76) **Going Correction** +0.70s/f (Yiel)
WFA 3 from 4yo+ 4lb 6 Ran SP% **98.3**
Speed ratings (Par 109): **109,108,105,102,96 90**
toteswingers 1&2 £1.20, 1&3 £5.90, 2&3 £6.60 CSF £6.94 CT £56.07 TOTE £1.50: £1.10, £3.00; EX 7.50.
Owner Panarea Racing **Bred** Mr & Mrs G Middlebrook **Trained** Malpas, Cheshire
■ Stewards' Enquiry : Shirley Teasdale three-day ban: careless riding (Oct 14-16)

FOCUS

Not many runners but it looked a contest with a bit of depth. The runner-up was 3lb wrong and the winner did not need to improve much.

NOTEBOOK

Anton Chigurh, the only 3yo in the line-up, made really hard work of landing favouritism. His passage wasn't always clear but he plugged on in relentless style once out of trouble and is value for a little bit more than the winning margin. (op 11-10)

Vito Volterra(IRE) seems to go on most ground and was given a positive ride. He went down narrowly, and did get a small bump late on, but it didn't cause his defeat. (op 10-1 tchd 11-1)

Beacon Lodge(IRE) is on a fair handicap mark considering his best form and likes this course, so his good effort is easy to understand, although it was a little disappointing that he wasn't able to go on when appearing a likely winner. (op 16-1)

Al Muheer(IRE) had his chance but faded. (op 10-1 tchd 12-1)

Prince Of Sorrento ran moderately after a 69-day absence considering he handles ease. (tchd 5-1)

Neutrafa(IRE) looked really dangerous as she moved into contention but dropped right out. (op 11-1)

T/Plt: £100.00 to a £1 stake. Pool: £73,995.24. 540.08 winning tickets. T/Qpdt: £12.70 to a £1 stake. Pool: £5,085.19. 295.05 winning tickets. JR

[6632]NEWMARKET (R-H)

Saturday, September 29

OFFICIAL GOING: Good (overall 7.7, stands' side 7.8; centre 7.7; far side 7.6)
Far side of Rowley Mile course used. Stalls on far side except 12f: centre.
Wind: Fresh, behind Weather: Dry and breezy

6671 JUDDMONTE ROYAL LODGE STKS (GROUP 2) (C&G) 1m
1:55 (1:55) (Class 1) 2-Y-O

£56,710 (£21,500; £10,760; £5,360; £2,690; £1,350) **Stalls** Low

Form RPR

2121 **1** **Steeler (IRE)**[25] 5904 2-8-12 104 KierenFallon 5 113
(Mark Johnston) *lw: w ldrs: pushed along to ld 3f out: drvn and clr w rival over 1f out: asserted ins fnl f: styd on strly* **11/4**[2]

1542 **2** *1* **Artigiano (USA)**[59] 4698 2-8-12 104 FrankieDettori 1 111
(Mahmood Al Zarooni) *chsd ldr: rdn and clr w wnr over 1f out: stl ev ch and drvn ent fnl f: no ex and btn fnl 75yds* **7/1**

112 **3** *3 ½* **Al Waab (IRE)**[21] 6027 2-8-12 102 TomQueally 9 103
(Sir Henry Cecil) *tall: lengthy: hld up wl in tch: rdn and effrt ent fnl 2f: 4th and outpcd over 1f out: no ch w ldng pair but kpt on fnl f to snatch 3rd on post* **4/1**[3]

2035 **4** *nse* **Birdman (IRE)**[14] 6243 2-8-12 105 MartinLane 6 103
(David Simcock) *led: hdd and rdn 3f out: 3rd and outpcd by ldrs over 1f out: styd on same pce fnl f: lost 3rd on post* **22/1**

11 **5** *½* **Fantastic Moon**[28] 5833 2-8-12 0 JohnnyMurtagh 7 102+
(Jeremy Noseda) *lw: stdd and dropped in bhd s: t.k.h: hld up in tch in rr: rdn and effrt whn bmpd and lost pl 2f out: modest 6th and rallied u.p 1f out: styd on wl ins fnl f: no threat to ldrs* **9/4**[1]

2123 **6** *2 ¾* **One Word More (IRE)**[15] 6200 2-8-12 102 WilliamCarson 2 96
(Charles Hills) *lw: t.k.h: hld up in tch: rdn and effrt ent fnl 2f: 5th and outpcd over 1f out: no ch w ldrs but pressing for 3rd fnl f: wknd fnl 75yds* **33/1**

12 **7** *4* **Excess Knowledge**[42] 5353 2-8-12 0 WilliamBuick 4 87
(John Gosden) *t.k.h: hld up wl in tch: rdn and edgd lft 2f out: sn outpcd u.p and wknd over 1f out* **8/1**

214 **8** *2* **Mocenigo (IRE)**[28] 5833 2-8-12 104 RobertHavlin 8 85
(Peter Chapple-Hyam) *stdd and dropped in bhd after s: hld up in tch in rr: rdn and effrt whn hmpd 2f out: nt rcvr and sn bhd* **33/1**

1m 35.67s (-2.93) **Going Correction** -0.15s/f (Firm) 2y crse rec **8 Ran SP% 111.3**
Speed ratings (Par 107): **108,107,103,103,102 100,96,94**
toteswingers: 1&2 £3.70, 1&3 £2.30, 2&3 £5.10 CSF £20.62 TOTE £3.60: £1.40, £1.60, £1.40; EX 19.30 Trifecta £72.80 Pool: £5,928.20 - 60.24 winning tickets..
Owner Sheikh Hamdan Bin Mohammed Al Maktoum **Bred** Airlie Stud **Trained** Middleham Moor, N Yorks

FOCUS
The ground was still officially good but a strong tailwind was assisting the runners up the straight. The jockeys reported it was riding as described. This Group 2 provides an automatic invitation to the winner to run in the Breeders' Cup Juvenile Turf and also earns the winner points for the Kentucky Derby. Inaugurated after the Second World War, several subsequent Derby winners took this in their juvenile season, the latest being Benny The Dip in 1996. However, it has also been won by future 2000 Guineas winners Mister Baileys and, most recently, Frankel. They went a reasonable gallop and the time dipped under standard and in fact broke the juvenile course record, indicating the help the wind was giving, while the first two were in the leading trio throughout. The form is taken at fave value, with a personal best from Steeler.

NOTEBOOK
Steeler(IRE) ♦, second to Dundonnell in the Acomb last month, subsequently beat four next-time-out winners in a a Goodwood Listed race. Never far away here, he showed in front over 2f out before the runner-up regained the advantage, but Fallon always appeared to be saving something and, when he asked for more on meeting the rising ground, the colt responded willingly to assert. A really likeable type, he has plenty of stamina on his dam's side and could well make up into a Derby colt next season, if his progression continues. (tchd 5-2)
Artigiano(USA), an easy maiden winner but beaten on his next three starts, all in Group 2s, has got steadily more competitive, only losing out narrowly to Olympic Glory last time. He made the early running and, given a breather when taken on for the lead, battled back to lead again in the Dip before being unable to hold off the winner up the hill. He is pretty reliable and helps set the standard. (op 8-1)
Al Waab(IRE) had won his first two starts before narrowly losing out to subsequent Group 3 winner Havana Gold at Haydock. He did best of those held up and was staying on well up the hill, suggesting he will appreciate longer distances next year. He also looks to have the scope to do better with another winter behind him. (op 9-2 tchd 5-1 in a place)
Birdman(IRE) had Artigiano behind when narrowly beaten runner-up to the smart Olympic Glory in a Group 2 on heavy going but had been held on three starts since, including in Champagne Stakes on his last start. Ridden positively, he was right there until the principals shook him off running into the Dip, then was caught virtually on the line for third place. He is not quite top class but a return to softer ground should be in his favour. (op 20-1 tchd 25-1)
Fantastic Moon ♦ was the unlucky horse of the race. Having beaten a subsequent winner on his debut in August on fast ground, he followed up from a couple of useful performers in the Group 3 Solario Stakes on his second start. Up in trip and grade, he was hampered when trying to make a forward move over 2f out, just as the first two kicked for home. He stayed on well once in the clear and would have been in the places without the troubled passage. (op 5-2)
One Word More(IRE), second to the smart Toronado on his debut and also runner-up in a Listed race at Deauville, was up in trip and grade. He tracked the pace but was keen early and could not pick up. He goes well on soft ground and may have found the drying surface less than ideal. (op 28-1)
Excess Knowledge, runner-up in a Listed contest on a fast surface last time, tracked the pace but was being pushed along soon after halfway and was left behind when the principals committed for home. (op 15-2)
Mocenigo(IRE), who finished a close fourth behind Fantastic Moon in the Solario on fast ground on his turf debut, was held up at the back and was very keen early, leaving himself nothing in reserve for when the race began in earnest. (op 25-1)

6672 JAGUAR CARS CHEVELEY PARK STKS (GROUP 1) (FILLIES) 6f
2:25 (2:26) (Class 1) 2-Y-O

£92,720 (£35,152; £17,592; £8,763; £4,398; £2,207) **Stalls** Low

Form RPR

111 **1** **Rosdhu Queen (IRE)**[37] 5516 2-8-12 107 JohnnyMurtagh 1 108
(William Haggas) *lw: mde all and racd against far rail: rdn wl over 1f out: hrd pressed 1f out: styd on wl u.p and asserted fnl 100yds: rdn out: 1st of 3 in gp* **4/1**[2]

11 **2** *1* **Winning Express (IRE)**[23] 5979 2-8-12 0 FrannyNorton 2 105
(Ed McMahon) *racd on far side: in tch in midfield overall: effrt and rdn wl over 1f out: hdwy u.p and chsd ldng pair ins fnl f: r.o to go 2nd on post: 2nd of 3 in gp* **13/2**

1222 **3** *nse* **Baileys Jubilee**[18] 6128 2-8-12 103 KierenFallon 12 105
(Mark Johnston) *racd in centre: chsd ldrs: hdwy u.p to chse wnr and edgd rt over 1f out: ev ch 1f out: no ex and btn fnl 100yds: lost 2nd on post: 1st of 8 in gp* **20/1**

142 **4** *1 ¼* **Upward Spiral**[17] 6139 2-8-12 96 WilliamBuick 10 101
(Tom Dascombe) *racd in centre: led gp and chsd wnr tl over 1f out: carried rt and unable qck ent fnl f: styd on same pce ins fnl f: 2nd of 8 in gp* **16/1**

0241 **5** *nse* **Jillnextdoor (IRE)**[13] 6282 2-8-12 88 MartinHarley 3 101
(Mick Channon) *racd far side: hld up towards rr: rdn and effrt 2f out: kpt on u.p ins fnl f: 3rd of 3 in gp* **66/1**

116 **6** *hd* **Sendmylovetorose**[20] 6081 2-8-12 0 CO'Donoghue 11 101
(A Oliver, Ire) *racd in centre: stdd s: hld up in tch in rr: rdn and effrt over 2f out: no imp tl styd on fnl 100yds: 3rd of 8 in gp* **11/1**

1114 **7** *nk* **Ceiling Kitty**[15] 6196 2-8-12 106 RichardKingscote 7 100
(Tom Dascombe) *racd in centre: in tch: rdn and effrt 2f out: drvn and unable qck over 1f out: kpt on same pce ins fnl f: 4th of 8 in gp* **14/1**

5302 **8** *nk* **Jadanna (IRE)**[23] 5979 2-8-12 103 GrahamLee 8 99
(James Given) *racd in centre: rdn ent fnl 2f: unable qck whn squeezed for room and sltly hmpd over 1f out: kpt on same pce fnl f: 5th of 8 in gp* **33/1**

121 **9** *¾* **Maureen (IRE)**[63] 4577 2-8-12 106 RichardHughes 4 96
(Richard Hannon) *racd in centre: hld up wl in tch in midfield: rdn and unable qck whn carried rt and nt clr run over 1f out: swtchd lft 1f out and styd on same pce fnl f: 6th of 8 in gp* **2/1**[1]

1315 **10** *nk* **Hoyam**[15] 6196 2-8-12 102 MickaelBarzalona 9 96
(Michael Bell) *racd in centre: stdd s: t.k.h: hld up in tch in rr: rdn and effrt over 2f out: styd on ins fnl f: nvr gng pce to chal: 7th of 8 in gp* **16/1**

111 **11** *½* **The Gold Cheongsam (IRE)**[16] 6162 2-8-12 97 FrankieDettori 6 98
(Jeremy Noseda) *lw: racd in centre: stdd after s: hld up in tch in rr: rdn and effrt 2f out: stuck bhd horses and switching lft over 1f out: nt clr run and swtchd lft again 1f out: kpt on fnl f: n.d: 8th of 8 in gp* **11/2**[3]

1m 11.1s (-1.10) **Going Correction** -0.15s/f (Firm) **11 Ran SP% 118.0**
Speed ratings (Par 106): **101,99,99,97,97 97,97,96,95,95 94**
toteswingers: 1&2 £5.90, 1&3 £14.10, 2&3 £19.00 CSF £29.85 TOTE £4.40: £1.80, £2.20, £4.00; EX 35.70 Trifecta £721.90 Pool: £3,433.90 - 3.52 winning tickets..
Owner Clipper Logistics **Bred** Old Carhue & Graeng Bloodstock **Trained** Newmarket, Suffolk

FOCUS
An unsatisfactory contest as the runners drawn four and above all shunned the far rail early on, leaving those from the bottom three stalls on their own until the field merged in the latter stages, and the smaller group provided the first two finishers. While it can be argued the front pair were simply the best two horses on the day, the winner was allowed a softer lead than might otherwise have been the case. This was a weak renewal and the form is ordinary for the grade, with a compressed finish.

NOTEBOOK
Rosdhu Queen(IRE) was extending her unbeaten record to four, following up her Lowther success. It had to help that she was allowed to do her own thing and it remains to be seen how effective she'll be next year. She's out of a 1m Group 3 winner and will presumably be trained for the Guineas, but she looks a proper sprinting type. (op 9-2 tchd 5-1)
Winning Express(IRE) ♦, supplemented for this, had come from well off the pace when winning her first two starts, including the Listed Dick Poole at Salisbury, but this time she only had one horse to track and still looked green when first under pressure. There was much to like about how well she ran on, and she has more to offer. (op 11-2 tchd 7-1)
Baileys Jubilee, runner-up on her last three starts in Group company (including behind Rosdhu Queen in the Lowther), fared best of those from the main group. She briefly looked a major threat when produced with her chance, but got tired and lost second on the line. (op 28-1)
Upward Spiral was short of room in the closing stages, but it didn't cost her a place. This was an improvement on the form she showed on her recent return from a break and she should stay further. (op 18-1 tchd 20-1)
Jillnextdoor(IRE) has long been well regarded, but she had to go to Ffos Las to finally win her maiden last time and it's hard to know what she achieved here as she was third best of the far-side trio.
Sendmylovetorose picked up a couple of Group races earlier in the season, including the Cherry Hinton, but she's no longer progressing. (tchd 9-1)
Ceiling Kitty didn't prove as effective over this trip as she is over the minimum. (op 11-1 tchd 10-1)
Jadanna(IRE) was runner-up behind Winning Express last time, but was well held on this occasion.
Maureen(IRE) was drawn low along with the first two but was taken away from two of the main players. However, she was out of sorts anyway, racing a bit keenly without cover and looking in trouble a long way out. She had a setback after winning the Princess Margaret, and while she had reportedly been training well, she couldn't match her earlier form. (tchd 15-8)
Hoyam, whose best effort came at 5f, was much too keen.
The Gold Cheongsam(IRE), successful on her last three starts in lesser company, was under pressure a long way out but was beginning to stay on until her path was continually blocked inside the final couple of furlongs. She would have finished closer with a clear run, although it's hard to say just how much closer. (op 8-1)

6673 KINGDOM OF BAHRAIN SUN CHARIOT STKS (GROUP 1) (F&M) 1m
3:00 (3:02) (Class 1) 3-Y-O+

£90,736 (£34,400; £17,216; £8,576; £4,304; £2,160) **Stalls** Low

Form RPR

335 **1** **Siyouma (IRE)**[41] 5399 4-9-3 114 GeraldMosse 1 119
(F Doumen, France) *lw: chsd clr ldr: rdn 2f out: clsd u.p over 1f out: drvn and led 1f out: edgd lft but kpt on wl fnl f* **12/1**

-213 **2** *¾* **Elusive Kate (USA)**[48] 5141 3-8-13 119 WilliamBuick 3 117
(John Gosden) *stmbld bdly and wnt lft as stalls opened: chsd ldrs: rdn 2f out: edgd lft u.p but styd on fr over 1f out: chsd wnr fnl 100yds: pressing wnr but hld towards fin* **11/4**[2]

1164 **3** *1 ¾* **Laugh Out Loud**[21] 6061 3-8-13 111 MartinHarley 2 113
(Mick Channon) *led and sn clr: stl clr and rdn 2f out: drvn and hdd 1f out: lost 2nd and no ex fnl 100yds* **16/1**

5645 **4** *¾* **La Collina (IRE)**[21] 6061 3-8-13 109 DeclanMcDonogh 6 111
(Kevin Prendergast, Ire) *stdd after s: hld up off the pce in last trio: rdn and effrt on far rail over 2f out: hdwy over 1f out: styd on wl ins fnl f* **33/1**

142 **5** *1* **Chachamaidee (IRE)**[21] 6061 5-9-3 113 TomQueally 5 109
(Sir Henry Cecil) *hmpd and stdd s: t.k.h: hld up off the pce in last pair: rdn and effrt wl over 1f out: hdwy ent fnl f: kpt on but nvr threatened ldrs* **13/2**[3]

3611 **6** *½* **Up (IRE)**[20] 6080 3-8-13 112 JPO'Brien 7 108
(A P O'Brien, Ire) *swtg: hld up off the pce in midfield: rdn over 2f out: drvn and kpt on fr over 1f out: nvr gng pce to chal* **7/1**

112 **7** *4* **Beauty Parlour**[104] 3203 3-8-13 120 ChristopheSoumillon 4 98
(Sir Henry Cecil) *bmpd and hmpd s: hld up off the pce in midfield: rdn and effrt wl over 1f out: no imp* **13/8**[1]

1102 **8** *22* **Gamilati**[16] 6161 3-8-13 **108** FrankieDettori 8 45
(Mahmood Al Zarooni) *lw: t.k.h early: stdd bk to rr after 1f: rdn and no hdwy over 2f out: lost tch and eased over 1f out: t.o* **16/1**

1m 34.66s (-3.94) **Going Correction** -0.15s/f (Firm)
WFA 3 from 4yo+ 4lb **8** Ran SP% **113.0**
Speed ratings (Par 117): **113,112,110,109,108 108,104,82**
toteswingers: 1&2 £4.40, 1&3 £12.10, 2&3 £7.50 CSF £44.11 TOTE £12.40: £2.70, £1.10, £5.80; EX 53.70 Trifecta £611.90 Pool: £12,048.59 - 14.57 winning tickets..
Owner Robert Jeffcock **Bred** Haras De Son Altesse L'Aga Khan Scea **Trained** Bouce, France

FOCUS
Following on from Sahpresa's three consecutive victories in this race, there was a fourth straight French-trained winner. Few were ever involved, with the third taking them along in a clear lead against the far rail. Just an ordinary renewal, rated around the third.

NOTEBOOK
Siyouma(IRE) had a bit to find but was always in the right place and found for pressure up the hill. Doumen has some big plans for the winner, who was building on a couple of okay runs at the top level, having been third in the Falmouth and a close fifth in the Prix Jean Romanet. Evidently the return to 1m and switch to better ground suited and she could be an interesting player on the international scene. (op 11-1)
Elusive Kate(USA)'s shoe reportedly came loose and she was bandaged after the race before returning to the racecourse stables. William Buick thought it might have happened at the start, when the filly stumbled coming out of the stalls, and felt it could have cost her the race. This was a fine effort in the circumstances. Official explanation: jockey said filly stumbled leaving stalls (op 2-1 tchd 3-1)
Laugh Out Loud looked good when the Prix de Sandringham from the front and had returned to form when fourth in the Matron Stakes last time, so it was no surprise to see her go well under a forward ride. She reportedly might return to Newmarket for Challenge stakes, but in the longer term, if she's kept in training, she could find success abroad. The fillies' division in the US is particularly weak, while Meydan has a nice programme for these types.
La Collina(IRE) couldn't reverse Matron Stakes form with Laugh Out Loud but again ran well. (op 40-1)
Chachamaidee(IRE), arguably fortunate to have been awarded the Matron Stakes by the stewards, raced too keenly in a race that didn't set up for the hold-up performers. (tchd 8-1)
Up(IRE) may have been unsuited by the drop to 1m, especially with the pace horses not coming back to her. (op 17-2 tchd 9-1)
Beauty Parlour was bitterly disappointing on her first start for Sir Henry Cecil. Her French form may not be as good as it looked at the time, but clearly this wasn't her true running. She was a bit short of room on leaving the stalls but her jockey wasn't making any excuses. (op 2-1)

6674 BETFRED CAMBRIDGESHIRE (HERITAGE H'CAP) 1m 1f
3:40 (3:40) (Class 2) 3-Y-0+

£99,600 (£29,824; £14,912; £7,456; £3,728; £1,872) **Stalls** Low

Form RPR

1613 **1** **Bronze Angel (IRE)**[100] 3294 3-8-8 **95** (p) WilliamBuick 21 106+
(Marcus Tregoning) *racd in centre: hld up in midfield overall: rdn and hdwy wl over 1f out: hung rt but str run fnl f to ld fnl 50yds: gng away at fin: 1st of 5 in gp* **9/1**[2]

0014 **2** *3/4* **Mull Of Killough (IRE)**[49] 5075 6-9-4 **100** JPO'Brien 7 109
(Jane Chapple-Hyam) *warm: racd far side: chsd ldrs: chsd overall ldr over 2f out: drvn to ld 1f out: kpt on wl tl hdd and outpcd towards fin: 1st of 15 in gp* **33/1**

4132 **3** *3/4* **Boom And Bust (IRE)**[8] 6446 5-9-8 **104** GeorgeBaker 2 111
(Marcus Tregoning) *lw: racd far side: chsd ldr tl led 3f out: rdn ent fnl 2f: hdd 1f out: styd on same pce and edgd lft u.p ins fnl f: 2nd of 15 in gp* **20/1**

2606 **4** *1/2* **Bancnuanaheireann (IRE)**[14] 6242 5-8-9 **91** WilliamCarson 12 97
(Michael Appleby) *racd far side: in tch in midfield overall: rdn and hdwy to chse ldrs over 2f out: kpt on same pce u.p fnl f: 3rd of 15 in gp* **50/1**

2142 **5** *3/4* **Mukhadram**[79] 4012 3-9-0 **101** PaulHanagan 17 106+
(William Haggas) *lw: racd far side: swtchd rt after s: hld up in midfield overall: hdwy gng wl 3f out: rdn and unable qck over 1f out: styd on same pce fnl f: 4th of 15 in gp* **10/1**[3]

6114 **6** *1* **Chil The Kite**[21] 6029 3-8-10 **97** RichardHughes 1 99+
(Hughie Morrison) *racd far side: hld up towards rr: rdn and hdwy 2f out: kpt on ins fnl f: 5th of 15 in gp* **8/1**[1]

6500 **7** *1/2* **Moran Gra (USA)**[21] 6064 5-9-4 **100** (p) DeclanMcDonogh 16 101
(Ms Joanna Morgan, Ire) *lw: racd in centre: chsd gp ldr and in tch overall: rdn to ld gp 3f out: chsd ldrs and styng on same pce whn carried rt ins fnl f: kpt on: 2nd of 5 in gp* **100/1**

2113 **8** *nk* **Jack's Revenge (IRE)**[60] 4689 4-8-8 **90** (bt) GeraldMosse 6 91
(George Baker) *racd far side: hld up in midfield: rdn and effrt to chse ldrs 2f out: no imp over 1f out: styd on same pce fnl f: 6th of 15 in gp* **14/1**

2430 **9** *1 1/2* **Double Dealer**[21] 6036 4-8-13 **95** MickaelBarzalona 34 92
(Mahmood Al Zarooni) *racd nr side: hld up in midfield: led gp 2f out and hdwy to chse overall ldrs over 1f out: hung bdly rt jst ins fnl f: nt rcvr and one pce after: 1st of 13 in gp* **40/1**

5205 **10** *1 3/4* **Fury**[8] 6446 4-9-10 **106** [1] JohnnyMurtagh 33 99+
(William Haggas) *racd nr side: hld up in rr: rdn and hdwy on stands' rail 2f out: nt clr run and swtchd rt over 1f out: styd on fnl f: nvr trbld ldrs: 2nd of 13 in gp* **25/1**

1044 **11** *1/2* **Navajo Chief**[23] 5964 5-9-9 **105** DarryllHolland 15 97
(Alan Jarvis) *racd in centre: led gp and in tch overall: rdn and lost gp ld 3f out: wknd u.p over 1f out: 3rd of 5 in gp* **40/1**

3256 **12** *hd* **Licence To Till (USA)**[7] 6484 5-8-11 **93** FrannyNorton 10 85
(Mark Johnston) *lw: racd far side: chsd ldrs: rdn and unable qck over 2f out: outpcd and btn over 1f out: plugged on: 7th of 15 in gp* **40/1**

/00- **13** *1* **Credit Swap**[248] 6339 7-8-10 **92** JimCrowley 31 82
(Michael Wigham) *racd nr side: hld up in rr: swtchd rt and effrt wl over 1f out: styd onbut no ch: nvr trbld ldrs: 3rd of 13 in gp* **50/1**

1500 **14** *1 1/4* **Prince Of Johanne (IRE)**[37] 5517 6-9-3 **104** (p) BrendanPowell(5) 24 91
(Tom Tate) *racd nr side: prom in gp and chsd ldrs overall: rdn and unable qck over 2f out: wknd over 1f out: 4th of 13 in gp* **25/1**

15 *hd* **Talk About (FR)**[48] 4-8-10 **92** (t) UmbertoRispoli 27 79
(M Delzangles, France) *on toes: racd nr side: hld up in midfield overall: rdn and effrt over 2f out: no imp and plugged on same pce fr over 1f out: 5th of 13 in gp* **18/1**

1102 **16** *nk* **Anderiego (IRE)**[14] 6242 4-8-10 **92** DanielTudhope 9 78
(David O'Meara) *racd far side: hld up in midfield overall: effrt u.p over 2f out: no imp over 1f out: wknd ent fnl f: 8th of 15 in gp* **25/1**

2501 **17** *1 3/4* **King's Warrior (FR)**[77] 4112 5-9-0 **101** MichaelJMMurphy(5) 4 83
(Peter Chapple-Hyam) *racd far side: hld up in rr: rdn and sme hdwy 2f out: no imp over 1f out: wknd fnl f: 9th of 15 in gp* **12/1**

2110 **18** *1/2* **Swiftly Done (IRE)**[57] 4761 5-8-12 **94** JimmyFortune 22 75
(Declan Carroll) *racd far side: swtchd rt after s: hld up in rr: rdn and sme hdwy wl over 2f out: no imp and one pce fr over 1f out: 10th of 15 in gp* **16/1**

2306 **19** *1/2* **Spa's Dancer (IRE)**[35] 5609 5-8-11 **93** LiamKeniry 35 73
(Ed de Giles) *racd nr side: led gp and chsd ldrs overall: lost gp ld and u.p 2f out: wknd over 1f out: 6th of 13 in gp* **40/1**

4523 **20** *1/2* **Loving Spirit**[21] 6036 4-8-10 **92** PatCosgrave 30 71
(James Toller) *racd nr side: hld up in rr: rdn and effrt over 2f out: no prog 2f out and sn wknd: 7th of 13 in gp* **33/1**

104 **21** *2 1/4* **Burano (IRE)**[8] 6446 3-9-5 **106** KierenFallon 13 80
(Brian Meehan) *racd in centre: hld up in midfield overall: rdn and effrt over 2f out: no real prog: wknd over 1f out: 4th of 5 in gp* **40/1**

1310 **22** *1 1/2* **Making Eyes (IRE)**[28] 5834 4-9-3 **99** IanMongan 29 70
(Hugo Palmer) *racd nr side: t.k.h: hld up in midfield: rdn and no hdwy jst over 2f out: wknd over 1f out: 8th of 13 in gp* **50/1**

-100 **23** *1 1/2* **Arabian Star (IRE)**[49] 5075 4-8-2 **91** DanielMuscutt(7) 11 58
(Andrew Balding) *racd far side: overall ldr tl rdn and hdd 3f out: wknd qckly over 1f out: 11th of 15 in gp* **40/1**

6300 **24** *1/2* **Start Right**[28] 5835 5-9-3 **99** (p) SilvestreDeSousa 14 65
(Saeed Bin Suroor) *racd far side: hld up towards rr: rdn and no hdwy wl over 2f out: wknd 2f out and sn bhd12th of 15 in gp* **20/1**

3100 **25** *1 1/4* **Silvery Moon (IRE)**[22] 6010 5-8-9 **91** TedDurcan 3 54
(Tim Easterby) *on toes: racd far side: hld up in midfield overall: rdn and no hdwy over 2f out: wknd wl over 1f out: 13th of 15 in gp* **66/1**

3220 **26** *2 1/4* **Dragonera**[64] 4556 4-9-2 **98** JamesDoyle 8 56
(Ed Dunlop) *racd far side: hld up in midfield overall: rdn and no hdwy wl over 2f out: wknd 2f out: 14th of 15 in gp* **100/1**

1126 **27** *hd* **Levitate**[70] 4339 4-8-9 **91** (v) MartinHarley 5 49
(Alan McCabe) *lw: racd far side: hld up in rr: rdn and no hdwy over 2f out: sn wknd: 15th of 15 in gp* **66/1**

4340 **28** *4* **Rewarded**[45] 5250 3-9-0 **101** KirstyMilczarek 26 50
(James Toller) *racd nr side: prom in gp and chsd ldrs overall: rdn and unable qck over 2f out: wknd wl over 1f out: 9th of 13 in gp* **25/1**

3101 **29** *nk* **Postscript (IRE)**[29] 5794 4-8-10 **92** GrahamLee 28 41
(Ian Williams) *lw: racd nr side: hld up in midfield: rdn and no hdwy over 2f out: sn wknd: 10th of 13 in gp* **20/1**

0046 **30** *3 1/4* **Spanish Duke (IRE)**[16] 6166 5-8-13 **95** EddieAhern 25 36
(John Dunlop) *racd nr side: hld up in midfield overall: rdn and no rspnse over 2f out: sn wknd and bhd: t.o: 11th of 13 in gp* **33/1**

0020 **31** *1* **Man Of Action (USA)**[28] 5835 5-9-1 **97** (v) FrankieDettori 20 36
(Saeed Bin Suroor) *lw: racd in centre: hld up in rr: rdn and no rspnse over 2f out: sn wknd and wl bhd over 1f out: t.o: 5th of 5 in gp* **18/1**

3304 **32** *29* **Mijhaar**[21] 6035 4-9-8 **104** NeilCallan 32
(Roger Varian) *lw: racd nr side: in tch in midfield: rdn and lost pl 4f out: wl bhd 2f out: t.o and eased ins fnl f: 12th of 13 in gp* **12/1**

0500 **33** *5* **Excellent Guest**[21] 6024 5-9-1 **97** TomQueally 19
(George Margarson) *lw: racd nr side: hld up towards rr: rdn 3f out: sn dropped out and bhd: t.o and eased ins fnl f: 13th of 13 in gp* **50/1**

1m 47.73s (-3.97) **Going Correction** -0.15s/f (Firm)
WFA 3 from 4yo+ 5lb **33** Ran SP% **134.6**
Speed ratings (Par 109): **111,110,109,109,108 107,107,106,105,104 103,103,102,101,101 101,99,99,98,98 96,94,93,93,91 89**
toteswingers: 1&2 £68.30, 1&3 £19.10, 2&3 £162.60 CSF £281.84 CT £5788.96 TOTE £9.30: £2.60, £10.80, £5.70, £23.00; EX 379.60 Trifecta £13090.70 Pool: £51,301.59 - 2.90 winning tickets..
Owner Lady Tennant **Bred** Rihana Partnership **Trained** Lambourn, Berks

FOCUS
A massive field and a typically competitive race for the first leg of the autumn double. The field split into three, with the larger group racing far side, another big group raced stands' side, and five in single file up the centre, from where the winner came. However, he did drift across to join those on the far side, who filled the next five places. A decent renewal with three 3yos in the first six. The level is set around the second and fourth and the winner has the potential to rate higher.

NOTEBOOK
Bronze Angel(IRE), progressive over the winter and the spring, had not run since finishing a close third in the Britannia Handicap in June and just crept into the race. Held up in the centre, he was travelling well over 2f out but hung towards the far side under pressure, crossing Moran Gra. However, he found plenty up the hill and in the end scored with something in hand. He looks capable of making up into a Pattern-class performer at around this distance. (op 11-1)
Mull Of Killough(IRE), narrowly beaten in the Lincoln Handicap in March, was 5lb better off with Boom And Bust for a 4l beating at Ascot in August, which enabled him to reverse the form. He looked the winner when hitting the front nearest the far-side rail in the Dip, but could not resist the late surge of the winner. He deserves to win one of these big handicaps.
Boom And Bust(IRE), a progressive front-runner at around 1m who has won a big-field handicap at that trip, had run a close second to the classy Grandeur, who was rated 4lb higher, last time. He showed up throughout down the far side and kept battling away, but could not produce any extra once headed in the Dip. It was still a fine effort. George Baker reported that the gelding hung left. Official explanation: jockey said gelding hung left (op 25-1)
Bancnuanaheireann(IRE), who scored on his belated debut in Ireland last year, had not won since but ran well in decent handicap on his first start for this yard. He seems to like these big-field handicaps and ran well until fading up the hill.
Mukhadram, who won his maiden over 1m of this track, was making his handicap debut off 101 and was well fancied. He made steady progress to mount a challenge over 2f out but could not sustain it on meeting the rising ground. (op 11-1)
Chil The Kite, a progressive performer on good and easy ground, winning handicaps at Doncaster and Ascot, was 6lb higher here but had to be ridden to make ground from the back of the far-side group and never got close enough to mount a challenge, being unable to run to previous form with today's third, despite being 7lb better off.
Moran Gra(USA), a smart Irish miler, had cheekpieces back on instead of the blinkers he wore last time and ran well up the centre of the track, his chance in the closing stages not helped by being done few favours by the winner as that one went past.
Jack's Revenge(IRE) has progressed well this season, scoring over 1m on the July course and ran creditably off a mark 9lb above his last winning rating, despite being up in grade.
Double Dealer, who ran well in good handicap over 1m here last October, had had all four of his outings this year on Polytrack. He ran pretty well, doing best of the stands' side group, despite not looking the most straightforward under pressure.
Fury, a Listed winner over 1m at York in May, had scored on this track as a juvenile and finished third in the Suffolk Stakes over C&D in the spring. Wearing a first-time hood here, he stayed on from the rear down the stands' side to finish second-best in his group.
Navajo Chief, the winner of a 1m1f York handicap in June, had shown much of his best form on flat tracks and was 6lb higher here. He led the centre group and did well to keep going in the latter stages.
Licence To Till(USA), well suited by 1m2f and cut in the ground, usually runs his race and, having his 22nd start of the year, did so again in keeping on towards the far side.
Credit Swap, the 2010 winner, was making only his third appearance on the Flat since that victory, having been racing over hurdles, and his first since rejoining his former trainer.
Prince Of Johanne(IRE) was bidding to take the race for the second successive season, but raced in the stands' side group and failed to pick up under pressure.
King's Warrior(FR), a clear winner of the John Smith's Cup in July when last seen but raised 10lb as a result, was held up on the far side but failed to get involved. (op 14-1)

Mijhaar came back from a long absence to finish third to Fury at York in May (same terms today) and had since run well in Listed and Group 3 company over further. Down in trip, tracked the pace stands' side, he dropped away as if something was amiss. Neil Callan reported that the colt hung left from halfway. Official explanation: jockey said colt hung left from halfway

6675 EBF JERSEY LILY FILLIES' NURSERY 7f
4:15 (4:15) (Class 2) 2-Y-O

£12,450 (£3,728; £1,864; £932; £466; £234) **Stalls** Low

Form RPR
4214 **1** **Annecdote**[16] 6160 2-8-8 **78**........ RichardKingscote 9 84
(Jonathan Portman) *trckd ldrs: rdn 2f out: tk narrow advantage ent fnl f: kpt on wl fnl 75yds: pushed out* **5/1**[2]

2130 **2** *3/4* **Fleeting Smile (USA)**[21] 6021 2-9-2 **86**........ PaulHanagan 1 90
(Richard Hannon) *led for 1f: prom: rdn to ld wl over 1f out: hdd ent fnl f: kpt on w ev ch tl no ex fnl 75yds* **7/1**

021 **3** *nk* **Ghanaian (FR)**[24] 5947 2-8-5 **75**........ MickaelBarzalona 2 78+
(Mahmood Al Zarooni) *lw: mid-div: hdwy over 2f out: rdn and ev ch ent fnl f: kpt on but no ex fnl 75yds* **11/2**[3]

5201 **4** *nk* **Supernova Heights (IRE)**[11] 6343 2-9-3 **87**........ KierenFallon 12 89
(Brian Meehan) *lw: wnt rt leaving stalls: hld up towards rr: hdwy over 3f out: rdn fr 2f out: hung rt but r.o ins fnl f: nt quite rch ldrs: sddle slipped* **17/2**

3221 **5** *3 1/2* **Botanica (IRE)**[35] 5574 2-8-12 **82**........ RichardHughes 11 75
(Richard Hannon) *trckd ldrs: rdn 2f out: kpt on same pce fnl f* **5/1**[2]

41 **6** *3/4* **Need You Now (IRE)**[46] 5210 2-7-12 **68** oh3........(p) KieranO'Neill 4 59+
(Peter Chapple-Hyam) *w'like: stdd s: towards rr: hdwy 3f out: rdn whn swtchd rt 2f out: nt pce to get on terms: styd on ins fnl f* **22/1**

5431 **7** *1 3/4* **Woodlandsway**[26] 5887 2-8-10 **80**........ PatDobbs 6 67
(Richard Hannon) *led after 1f: rdn and hdd wl over 1f out: fdd ins fnl f* **14/1**

2010 **8** *hd* **Tussie Mussie**[16] 6160 2-8-6 **76**........ SilvestreDeSousa 14 62+
(Mark Johnston) *in tch: effrt chsng ldrs over 2f out: wknd fnl f* **14/1**

013 **9** *7* **Entwined (IRE)**[28] 5836 2-8-2 **72**........ JohnFahy 5 40
(Clive Cox) *hmpd whn a little slowly away: towards rr: mid-div after 2f: rdn over 2f out: wknd fnl f* **20/1**

0004 **10** *2 1/4* **Threes Grand**[17] 6139 2-9-7 **91**........ TomQueally 7 53
(Scott Dixon) *mid-div: rdn 2f out: wknd fnl f* **33/1**

1 **11** *1/2* **Red Turban**[22] 6007 2-8-8 **78**........ WilliamBuick 10 39
(Jeremy Noseda) *w'like: hld up towards rr: rdn over 2f out: sn outpcd: nvr threatened: wknd ent fnl f* **9/2**[1]

5334 **12** *9* **Rainbow Beauty**[22] 6017 2-8-4 **74**........ FrannyNorton 8 11
(Gerard Butler) *s.i.s: nvr travelling: a detached* **25/1**

1m 23.38s (-2.02) **Going Correction** -0.15s/f (Firm) **12** Ran SP% **119.2**
Speed ratings (Par 98): **105,104,103,103,99 98,96,96,88,85 85,74**
toteswingers: 1&2 £11.50, 1&3 £8.30, 2&3 £9.40 CSF £38.01 CT £204.93 TOTE £6.20: £2.10, £2.60, £2.30; EX 54.10 Trifecta £117.40 Pool: £1,351.86 - 8.51 winning tickets..
Owner Tom Edwards & Partners **Bred** The Hon Mrs R Pease **Trained** Compton, Berks

FOCUS
A decent fillies' nursery where the action unfolded up the centre of the track. The form appeals as sound.

NOTEBOOK
Annecdote kept on nicely over 6.5f at Doncaster on her previous start and, up 2lb, she found a good deal of improvement for this extra half-furlong. She might not be out again this season and could progress further next term. (op 11-2)
Fleeting Smile(USA) was too keen in a messy conditions race over 1m at Ascot last time and this was better. She has the scope to find further improvement. (op 9-1)
Ghanaian(FR) found this tougher than the Lingfield maiden she won on her previous start and probably showed improved form in defeat. (op 5-1 tchd 6-1)
Supernova Heights(IRE), off the mark in a 6f Yarmouth maiden on her previous start, fared best of those held up and may yet do better. Kieren Fallon reported the filly's saddle slipped. Official explanation: jockey said saddle slipped (op 8-1 tchd 15-2)
Botanica(IRE) might have been unsuited by the drop in trip after making all in a 1m maiden at Goodwood last time. (op 11-2)
Need You Now(IRE) was 3lb out of the weights having run to just a modest level when winning a 6f Polytrack maiden on her second start. It's easy to see why she had cheekpieces on for the first time - she looks a bit lazy - and it wouldn't surprise to see some more severe headgear tried at some point. (op 20-1 tchd 25-1)
Red Turban looked a nice prospect when overcoming greenness to make a winning start in a 6f Haydock maiden, but something may have been amiss this time. (op 4-1 tchd 5-1)
Rainbow Beauty's rider reported the filly was never travelling. Official explanation: jockey said filly never travelled (op 22-1)

6676 RACING UK H'CAP 7f
4:50 (4:51) (Class 2) (0-100,100) 3-Y-O+

£12,450 (£3,728; £1,864; £932; £466; £234) **Stalls** Low

Form RPR
0101 **1** **Idler (IRE)**[7] 6495 3-8-5 **87**........ SilvestreDeSousa 20 103
(Mark Johnston) *lw: mde virtually all on nr side: qcknd clr over 1f out: drifted rt but in n.d after: comf* **10/1**

4103 **2** *4 1/2* **Redvers (IRE)**[14] 6235 4-8-10 **89**........(b) PaulHanagan 14 93+
(Ed Vaughan) *mid-div on nr side: rdn over 2f out: stdy prog sn after: styd on to go 2nd fnl 75yds: no ch w comfortable wnr* **16/1**

-400 **3** *1/2* **Al Aasifh (IRE)**[196] 950 4-9-5 **98**........ FrankieDettori 21 101
(Saeed Bin Suroor) *steadily away: sn in nr side mid-div: hdwy 2f out: sn rdn to dispute 2nd but wnr already kicked clr: kpt on but no ex fnl 75yds* **40/1**

3040 **4** *1/2* **Bertiewhittle**[21] 6024 4-9-0 **93**........ GrahamGibbons 7 94
(David Barron) *mid-div on nr side: hdwy over 2f out: sn rdn: disp 2nd wl over 1f out: kpt on* **9/1**[3]

104 **5** *shd* **Jonny Mudball**[28] 5814 6-9-5 **98**........(t) RichardKingscote 4 99
(Tom Dascombe) *led far side but overall prom: rdn over 2f out: kpt on gamely whn hrd pressed for 2nd over 1f out: no ex nring fin* **40/1**

1040 **6** *shd* **Smarty Socks (IRE)**[21] 6024 8-9-1 **94**........ DanielTudhope 2 95
(David O'Meara) *hld up on far side: hdwy fr 3f out: rdn to dispute 2nd wl over 1f out: kpt on but no ex nring fin* **20/1**

4400 **7** *1* **Yair Hill (IRE)**[22] 6011 4-8-7 **86** oh1........ MircoDemuro 3 84+
(John Dunlop) *hld up on far side: hdwy over 2f out: rdn ent fnl f: kpt on but nt pce to get involved* **16/1**

0060 **8** *nk* **Redact (IRE)**[35] 5572 3-8-11 **100**........ WilliamTwiston-Davies(7) 17 97
(Richard Hannon) *in nr side in mid-div: rdn 3f out: nvr any imp on ldrs: kpt on same pce* **20/1**

0031 **9** *3/4* **Cape Classic (IRE)**[15] 6201 4-9-5 **98**........ AdamBeschizza 16 93
(William Haggas) *lw: mid-div of nr side: hdwy over 3f out: rdn to chse ldrs 2f out: wknd fnl 120yds* **7/2**[1]

-003 **10** *1* **Johnny Castle**[15] 6201 4-8-13 **92**........ WilliamBuick 19 85
(Amanda Perrett) *lw: mid-div on nr side: rdn wl over 1f out: sn edgd lft: nvr any imp* **8/1**[2]

4023 **11** *1 1/4* **Lutine Bell**[31] 5746 5-8-13 **92**........ RichardHughes 12 81
(Mike Murphy) *hld up towards rr on nr side: pushed along and hdwy into midfield wl over 1f out: no further imp fnl f* **16/1**

1-04 **12** *1 1/4* **Diescentric (USA)**[15] 6201 5-8-11 **90**........ MickyFenton 6 76
(Julie Camacho) *lw: trckd ldr on far side: rdn over 2f out: fdd ins fnl f* **20/1**

0051 **13** *1/2* **Esprit De Midas**[21] 6041 6-8-13 **92**........(b) NeilCallan 11 76
(Dean Ivory) *racd nr side: nvr bttr than mid-div* **40/1**

-400 **14** *3/4* **Red Art (IRE)**[58] 4740 3-8-10 **92**........ MichaelHills 1 74
(Charles Hills) *hld up on far side: rdn over 2f out: sme hdwy sn after but nvr a danger: wknd ent fnl f* **00/1**

0005 **15** *3/4* **Accession (IRE)**[17] 6143 3-8-7 **89**........ GeraldMosse 10 69
(Clive Cox) *a towards rr on nr side* **22/1**

1-04 **16** *1* **Poetic Dancer**[23] 5980 3-8-7 **89**........ JohnFahy 18 67
(Clive Cox) *little slowly away: sn w wnr on nr side: rdn over 2f out: wknd ent fnl f* **16/1**

0-0 **17** *2* **Harrison George (IRE)**[50] 5065 7-8-10 **89**........(t) KierenFallon 15 61
(P J O'Gorman) *chsd ldrs on nr side: rdn over 2f out: wknd and eased fnl f* **33/1**

5403 **18** *1/2* **Citrus Star (USA)**[15] 6192 5-9-0 **93**........ FrannyNorton 13 64
(Chris Wall) *racd nr side in tch: rdn over 2f out: wkng whn hmpd ent fnl f* **12/1**

5500 **19** *1/2* **Decent Fella (IRE)**[35] 5572 6-8-13 **92**........(vt) JimmyFortune 9 62
(Andrew Balding) *mid-div on nr side tl lost pl whn rdn 2f out: nt a threat after* **25/1**

5000 **20** *nk* **Balty Boys (IRE)**[17] 6143 3-8-13 **95**........ WilliamCarson 5 64
(Charles Hills) *mid-div on far side: jnd nr side after 2f: rdn over 2f out: wknd over 1f out* **20/1**

-003 **21** *4 1/2* **Gold City (IRE)**[17] 6143 3-9-0 **96**........(t) MickaelBarzalona 8 53
(Saeed Bin Suroor) *hld up towards rr on nr side: sme prog into midfield over 2f out: sn rdn: wknd ent fnl f* **16/1**

1m 23.0s (-2.40) **Going Correction** -0.15s/f (Firm)
WFA 3 from 4yo+ 3lb **21** Ran SP% **128.5**
Speed ratings (Par 109): **107,101,101,100,100 100,99,99,98,97 95,94,93,92,91 90,88,87,87,86 81**
toteswingers: 1&2 £46.30, 1&3 £83.50, 2&3 Not won. CSF £140.28 CT £6177.24 TOTE £10.70: £2.90, £5.20, £8.30, £2.70; EX 237.70 TRIFECTA Not won..
Owner Sheikh Hamdan Bin Mohammed Al Maktoum **Bred** Darley **Trained** Middleham Moor, N Yorks

FOCUS
A strong, competitive handicap in which a number of very useful 3-y-os were taking on seasoned, battle-hardened handicappers, and they would have been encouraged by the fact that three of the previous five winners came from that age group. That record was improved in impressive fashion by Idler, and the form is taken at something like face value.

NOTEBOOK
Idler(IRE), a regular winner who scored off 5lb lower over 6f here the previous weekend, was up in trip and grade off a 5lb higher mark but is clearly improving quickly, gaining his third success here since scoring off 16lb lower just over a month ago. He made most of the running and was in control in the Dip before powering up the hill. There looks to be more to come on this evidence. He is in the Betfred Challenge Cup at Ascot next week but even with a penalty is still not sure to get in. (op 14-1)
Redvers(IRE) got the reward for a string of solid efforts when winning a valuable ladies' race at Ascot but was racing off 5lb higher here. He did well considering he was held up early, staying on for pressure to grab second, although having no chance with the winner. (op 20-1)
Al Aasifh(IRE) has not won since his juvenile days in 2010 and had not been seen since running at Meydan early in the year, where he struggled after a good start there. However, he had useful form off similar marks in this country last season and ran well on this reappearance, coming through to chase the winner before tiring in the latter stages. He should benefit from the outing.
Bertiewhittle ◆, a useful sprinter who had run well since being stepped back up to this trip in recent starts, making the frame in a couple of heritage handicaps, ran another good race. Never far away, he stuck on well for pressure up the hill and deserves to find a similar contest. (op 10-1)
Jonny Mudball ◆ is lightly raced and had been running mainly over 5f of late, contesting Group 3s and conditions races. He had dropped in the handicap recently and was upped in trip, but had won over this far in the past. He led the group on the far side and stayed on well under pressure, losing out in a blanket finish for the places. He could be ready to score again if the ground does not go against him. (op 33-1)
Smarty Socks(IRE), a generally reliable sort in 7f handicaps, had dropped in the weights having been held since winning a conditions race at York in May. He showed up on the far side and made his bid for home over 2f out, but could not sustain his effort. He helps set the level of the form but might prefer a flatter track or a return to Ascot, where he has also gone well. (op 16-1)
Yair Hill(IRE) was progressive last season when winning over C&D in October, but was 5lb higher here. Keen under restraint early on, he stayed on well up the hill towards the far side, and might be one to bear in mind if returning here next month. (op 14-1)
Redact(IRE), a smart juvenile last year, had mainly struggled in Group company this season but had posted better efforts in handicaps the last twice, last time when badly drawn. Held up off the pace, he stayed on quite nicely and gives the impression there is a similar race in him. Whether that is this year or next season off a lower handicap mark remains to be seen. (op 18-1)
Cape Classic(IRE) impressed when winning a good handicap over slightly shorter at Doncaster earlier in the month, but had been raised 8lb for that. Well backed to follow up here, he showed up in the group behind the winner but was under pressure over 2f out and, beaten in the Dip, weakened up the hill. (op 3-1 tchd 4-1)
Johnny Castle, progressive last season, had put up some decent efforts this time and could not reverse Doncaster form with Cape Classic, despite being 8lb better off. That said, he stayed on from well back on a day when it paid to be close to the pace. (op 12-1)
Citrus Star(USA), a close sixth in this last year, showed up well towards the stands' side before backing out of it in the closing stages.

6677 BAILEYS HORSE FEEDS H'CAP 1m 4f
5:25 (5:25) (Class 2) (0-100,95) 3-Y-O **£12,938** (£3,850; £1,924; £962) **Stalls** Centre

Form RPR
0313 **1** **Saytara (IRE)**[23] 5973 3-8-7 **81**........ SilvestreDeSousa 11 97
(Saeed Bin Suroor) *mde all: pushed and readily drew clr ent fnl 2f: in n.d after: pushed out: easily* **14/1**

0535 **2** *7* **Taglietelle**[29] 5796 3-7-13 **76** oh2........ SimonPearce(3) 8 81
(Andrew Balding) *chsd ldrs: rdn and unable qck w wnr ent fnl f: wl hld after but kpt on u.p to go 2nd again ins fnl f* **40/1**

2111 **3** *3/4* **Brockwell**[23] 5966 3-9-3 **91**........ RichardKingscote 15 95+
(Tom Dascombe) *lw: hld up in tch in midfield: rdn and outpcd by wnr ent fnl 2f: no ch w wnr after: swtchd lft and kpt on u.p ins fnl f* **9/1**

6241 **4** *nk* **Daghash**[11] 6348 3-8-6 **80**........ MartinLane 1 83
(Clive Brittain) *chsd wnr tl 2f out: sn edgd rt u.p and outpcd by wnr: no ch w wnr but plugged on fnl f* **16/1**

-636 **5** 3/4 **Perennial**[99] 3330 3-9-7 **95** .... MichaelHills 10 97+
(Charles Hills) *lw: stdd s: t.k.h: hld up in tch in last trio: rdn and effrt jst over 2f out: no ch w wnr but styd on ins fnl f* **14/1**

213 **6** 1 1/4 **Marshgate Lane (USA)**[58] 4741 3-9-6 **94** .... MickaelBarzalona 9 94+
(Mahmood Al Zarooni) *lw: s.i.s: hld up wl in rr: stdy hdwy 4f out: rdn to chse clr wnr 2f out: no imp: lost 2nd and fdd ins fnl f* **9/2**[1]

000 **7** nk **Rayvin Black**[29] 5796 3-8-2 **76** .... MircoDemuro 3 76
(Mark H Tompkins) *t.k.h: hld up in midfield: nt clr run over 2f out: swtchd lft and nt clr run again over 1f out tl 1f out: styd on fnl 100yds: no ch w wnr* **50/1**

3111 **8** hd **Enery (IRE)**[11] 6333 3-8-12 **86** .... FrannyNorton 5 85+
(Mark Johnston) *chsd ldrs: rdn over 4f out: lost pl u.p 3f out: no ch w wnr over 1f out: swtchd rt and kpt on again ins fnl f* **8/1**

1416 **9** 4 **Angel Gabrial (IRE)**[21] 6025 3-8-12 **86** .... KierenFallon 13 79+
(Ian Williams) *t.k.h: hld up towards rr: rdn and effrt over 2f out: outpcd and no ch w wnr whn n.m.r between horses over 1f out: wknd ins fnl f* **6/1**[3]

5522 **10** 5 **Trader Jack**[22] 6018 3-9-4 **92** .... GeorgeBaker 14 77
(Roger Charlton) *stdd s: t.k.h: hld up in rr: swtchd rt and hdwy 1/2-way: trckd ldrs 4f out: rdn and fnd nil ent fnl 2f: wl btn over 1f out: fdd and eased fnl 100yds* **7/1**

30-3 **11** hd **Big Johnny D (IRE)**[78] 4067 3-8-8 **82** .... TedDurcan 4 67
(John Dunlop) *hld up in tch in midfield: rdn and no hdwy over 2f out: wl btn over 1f out: wknd ins fnl and eased towards fin* **9/1**

334 **12** 13 **Goodwood Atlantis (IRE)**[59] 4700 3-8-8 **82** .... PaulHanagan 2 46
(John Dunlop) *lw: hld up in tch in midfield: lost pl and rdn 3f out: bhd and eased 1f out: t.o* **11/2**[2]

3410 **13** 2 1/4 **Amaraja (GER)**[58] 4738 3-9-7 **95** .... TomQueally 7 55
(Sir Henry Cecil) *hld up in midfield: rdn and struggling over 2f out: wknd over 1f out: wl btn and eased ins fnl f: t.o* **25/1**

2063 **14** 2 1/2 **Beaufort Twelve**[22] 6010 3-9-2 **90** .... FrankieDettori 12 46
(William Jarvis) *hld up in last trio: rdn and effrt on outer 4f out: wknd 2f out: wl bhd and eased ins fnl f: t.o* **16/1**

2m 28.17s (-3.83) **Going Correction** -0.15s/f (Firm) **14** Ran SP% **124.8**
Speed ratings (Par 107): **106,101,100,100,100 99,99,98,96,92 92,84,82,81**
toteswingers 1&2 £42.20, 1&3 £21.30, 2&3 £69.50 CSF £503.81 CT £5247.11 TOTE £17.20: £7.10, £9.90, £4.20; EX 641.20 TRIFECTA Not won..
Owner Godolphin **Bred** Peter Savill **Trained** Newmarket, Suffolk

FOCUS
Several of these were unsuited by how the race unfolded and it's doubtful how literally to take the form with the winner seen to good effect from the front. The second to fourth have been rated close to their marks.

NOTEBOOK
Saytara(IRE) made all but this isn't form to take literally. If she's as good as the bare result implies, then she is just about Listed class, but her next run should tell us more. (new market)
Taglietelle was 2lb out of the handicap and still looking for his first win, but he's a half-brother to the stable's smart miler Side Glance and was having only his fifth start. Although a well-beaten second, this was a promising first try at 1m4f. (new market)
Brockwell was on a four-timer after three wins at Haydock and he ran well from an 8lb higher mark. He'll be popular with the jumping brigade if up for sale. (new market)
Daghash was held off 4lb higher than when winning at Yarmouth last time. (old market op 22-1 new market op 20-1)
Perennial ◆ raced further back than those who finished ahead of him and can do better. (new market op 12-1)
Marshgate Lane(USA) ◆ looked at least second best on the day. He was hopelessly placed but was the only runner who made up significant ground in the closing stages, producing a big effort to pass all bar the winner when taken wide, before understandably tiring. Also better than the bare result on his handicap debut at Goodwood, this lightly raced colt remains open to significant improvement. (new market tchd 4-1)
Rayvin Black didn't get a clear run but wasn't unlucky. (old market tchd 66-1 new market)
Enery(IRE), who was looking for a fourth straight success, never had enough room to really get rolling. He might be ready for staying trips and has more to offer. (new market)
Angel Gabrial(IRE) ◆ didn't have the race run to suit, met trouble and was eased. He's another who can be given another chance. (new market tchd 13-2)
Goodwood Atlantis(IRE) Official explanation: jockey said colt never travelled
T/Jkpt: Not won. T/Plt: £660.80 to a £1 stake. Pool: £226,969.17. 250.71 winning tickets. T/Qpdt: £128.30 to a £1 stake. Pool: £11,710.45. 67.50 winning tickets. SP

5708 RIPON (R-H)
Saturday, September 29
6678 Meeting Abandoned - Waterlogged

6640 WOLVERHAMPTON (A.W) (L-H)
Saturday, September 29

OFFICIAL GOING: Standard
Wind: Light, behind Weather: Fine

6685 PHIL ABBISS CELEBRATION CLAIMING STKS — 5f 20y(P)
5:50 (5:50) (Class 6) 3-Y-0+ **£2,070** (£616; £307; £153) **Stalls** Low

Form RPR

3214 **1** **Last Sovereign**[21] 6026 8-8-11 89 ....(b) JacobButterfield(7) 10 98
(Ollie Pears) *chsd ldrs: rdn to ld ins fnl f: r.o* **7/4**[1]

3321 **2** 3 **Mother Jones**[12] 6307 4-8-2 69 .... SophieDoyle(3) 1 74
(David Evans) *s.i.s: hld up: hdwy over 1f out: r.o: no ch w wnr* **12/1**

0000 **3** 1 1/2 **Dickie's Lad (IRE)**[16] 6165 4-9-3 82 ....[1] AmyRyan 2 81
(Kevin Ryan) *broke wl sn lost pl: pushed along over 3f out: rdn over 1f out: r.o ins fnl f* **2/1**[2]

4404 **4** 3/4 **Fanrouge (IRE)**[28] 5812 3-8-5 84 .... RaulDaSilva(3) 5 70
(Malcolm Saunders) *chsd ldrs: rdn 1/2-way: styd on same pce ins fnl f* **7/1**[3]

0000 **5** 3/4 **Powerful Wind (IRE)**[17] 6144 3-8-11 84 .... RobertHavlin 4 70
(Ronald Harris) *sn led: rdn over 1f out: hdd & wknd ins fnl f* **14/1**

2003 **6** 3/4 **Crimea (IRE)**[50] 5058 6-8-6 69 ....(p) PaulQuinn 9 62
(David Nicholls) *sn outpcd: r.o ins fnl f: nvr nrr* **12/1**

0556 **7** 1/2 **Nickel Silver**[12] 6314 7-8-12 69 ....(v) TomEaves 8 66
(Bryan Smart) *chsd ldr tl rdn over 1f out: wknd fnl f* **25/1**

3054 **8** 1 1/2 **Scommettitrice (IRE)**[12] 6307 4-8-2 59 ....(p) JamieMackay 6 50
(David Evans) *s.i.s: in rr whn nt clr run over 3f out: nvr on terms* **50/1**

1200 **9** 2 **Red Rhythm**[13] 6288 5-8-1 58 ....(vt) NatashaEaton(5) 7 47
(David Evans) *hdwy over 3f out: rdn 1/2-way: sn wknd* **50/1**

1m 0.42s (-1.88) **Going Correction** -0.20s/f (Stan)
WFA 3 from 4yo+ 1lb **9** Ran SP% **112.0**
Speed ratings (Par 101): **107,102,99,98,97 96,95,93,89**
toteswingers: 1&2 £5.00, 1&3 £6.30, 2&3 £1.50 CSF £22.66 TOTE £2.80: £1.10, £2.50, £1.10; EX 21.10 Trifecta £42.40 Pool: £406.50 - 7.09 winning units..
Owner Richard Walker **Bred** Gestut Hof Ittlingen & Cheveley Park Stud Ltd **Trained** Norton, N Yorks

FOCUS
With four runners rated in the 80s, this was an above-average claimer. The winner posted a small personal best and the second was pretty much to form.

6686 32RED MEDIAN AUCTION MAIDEN STKS — 5f 216y(P)
6:20 (6:20) (Class 6) 3-Y-0 **£2,181** (£644; £322) **Stalls** Low

Form RPR

2222 **1** **Stir Trader (IRE)**[26] 5878 3-9-3 74 ....(b[1]) JamesDoyle 5 76
(Roger Charlton) *mde all: shkn up over 1f out: r.o up ins fnl f* **1/6**[1]

5543 **2** 3 1/2 **Gran Canaria Queen**[16] 6180 3-8-5 53 ....(v) GeorgeChaloner(7) 6 60
(Ian Semple) *a.p: chsd wnr 1/2-way: ev ch over 1f out: sn rdn: no ex ins fnl f* **8/1**[2]

-43 **3** 5 **My Time**[13] 6287 3-9-3 0 .... SeanQuinlan 2 49
(Michael Mullineaux) *chsd ldrs: rdn over 1f out: styd on same pce* **25/1**

0000 **4** 1 3/4 **Welsh Royale**[13] 6274 3-9-3 47 ....(b) DaneO'Neill 3 43
(William Muir) *chsd ldrs: lost pl 5f out: rdn over 1f out: no imp* **33/1**

3600 **5** 1 **No Plan B (IRE)**[53] 4932 3-8-12 51 .... ShaneKelly 7 35
(Noel Quinlan) *hld up: hdwy over 3f out: rdn over 2f out: wknd over 1f out* **16/1**[3]

00 **6** 3 **Sovereign Waters**[13] 6281 3-8-12 48 ....(b[1]) GrahamLee 1 26
(Eve Johnson Houghton) *chsd wnr to 1/2-way: rdn and wknd wl over 1f out* **33/1**

-000 **7** 8 **Midnite Motivation**[53] 4931 3-8-6 35 ow1 .... GaryHalpin(7) 4
(Derek Shaw) *s.s: plld hrd in rr: wknd over 2f out* **150/1**

1m 13.88s (-1.12) **Going Correction** -0.20s/f (Stan) **7** Ran SP% **113.1**
Speed ratings (Par 99): **99,94,87,85,84 80,69**
toteswingers 1&2 £2.00, 1&3 £2.50, 2&3 £2.50 CSF £1.96 TOTE £1.10: £1.02, £2.50; EX 3.20.
Owner D M Carter **Bred** Newlands House Stud **Trained** Beckhampton, Wilts

FOCUS
A weak maiden which looked a formality on paper, but the 74-rated odds-on favourite had to work to secure victory. The form is rated around the runner-up.

6687 32RED.COM H'CAP — 7f 32y(P)
6:50 (6:52) (Class 5) (0-70,71) 3-Y-0+ **£2,911** (£866; £432; £216) **Stalls** High

Form RPR

600 **1** **Light From Mars**[14] 6241 7-9-4 70 ....(t) GrahamLee 8 79
(Patrick Morris) *hld up: hdwy over 2f out: rdn ins fnl f: r.o to ld nr fin* **13/2**[3]

0563 **2** hd **Dozy Joe**[14] 6256 4-9-2 68 ....(p) JamesDoyle 4 76
(Ian Wood) *chsd ldrs: led over 1f out: rdn and edgd lft ins fnl f: hdd nr fin* **5/1**[1]

0605 **3** 1 1/4 **Who's Shirl**[14] 6260 6-9-3 69 .... KellyHarrison 10 74
(Chris Fairhurst) *hld up: pushed along 1/2-way: hdwy u.p over 1f out: hung rt ins fnl f: r.o* **8/1**

553 **4** 1/2 **Tislaam (IRE)**[17] 6150 5-9-3 69 ....(p) MartinHarley 2 73
(Alan McCabe) *mid-div: nt clr run over 2f out: hdwy and nt clr run over 1f out: styd on u.p* **9/1**

0063 **5** 1 **Saskia's Dream**[17] 6145 4-9-3 69 .... RobertHavlin 3 70
(Jane Chapple-Hyam) *chsd ldrs: rdn and ev ch over 1f out: no ex ins fnl f* **8/1**

0006 **6** 1/2 **Golden Desert (IRE)**[17] 6145 8-9-3 69 .... SebSanders 9 69
(Simon Dow) *s.i.s: hld up: pushed along and hdwy over 2f out: rdn over 1f out: styd on* **11/2**[2]

3502 **7** 1 1/4 **Batgirl**[52] 4966 5-9-3 69 .... DaneO'Neill 5 65
(John Berry) *mid-div: hdwy over 2f out: rdn over 1f out: no ex fnl f* **16/1**

1656 **8** 3/4 **Full Shilling (IRE)**[44] 5279 4-9-2 68 .... AdamKirby 1 62
(John Spearing) *hld up: nt clr run wl over 1f out: nvr on terms* **25/1**

3601 **9** 3/4 **The Happy Hammer (IRE)**[26] 5892 6-9-3 69 .... CathyGannon 11 61
(Eugene Stanford) *s.i.s: hld up: a in rr* **12/1**

0305 **10** shd **Viking Warrior (IRE)**[29] 5802 5-9-3 69 .... TomEaves 6 61
(Michael Dods) *sn led: hdd over 5f out: chsd ldr: rdn and ev ch over 1f out: wknd fnl f* **11/1**

3520 **11** 3 3/4 **Sir George (IRE)**[52] 4964 7-9-2 68 .... ShaneKelly 7 50
(Ollie Pears) *prom: rdn over 2f out: wknd over 1f out* **7/1**

0001 **12** 4 1/2 **Dancing Maite**[7] 6498 7-9-2 71 ....(b) MarkCoumbe(3) 12 41
(Roy Bowring) *plld hrd and prom: led over 5f out: rdn and hdd over 1f out: wknd fnl f* **20/1**

1m 27.96s (-1.64) **Going Correction** -0.20s/f (Stan) **12** Ran SP% **120.6**
Speed ratings (Par 103): **101,100,99,98,97 97,95,94,93,93 89,84**
toteswingers 1&2 £9.80, 1&3 £24.00, 2&3 £10.50 CSF £39.72 CT £273.95 TOTE £8.10: £3.00, £1.90, £2.60; EX 56.10 Trifecta £333.90 Pool: £916.18 - 2.03 winning units..
Owner Dr Marwan Koukash **Bred** Harts Farm And Stud **Trained** Tarporley, Cheshire

FOCUS
Just a routine race of its type in quality, but run at a decent pace, and all the runners were on remarkably similar official ratings. Tricky form to pin down.
The Happy Hammer(IRE) Official explanation: jockey said gelding was denied a clear run

6688 32RED CASINO H'CAP (DIV I) — 5f 20y(P)
7:20 (7:22) (Class 4) (0-85,85) 3-Y-0+ **£5,175** (£1,540; £769; £384) **Stalls** Low

Form RPR

3005 **1** **Doctor Parkes**[21] 6028 6-9-6 84 .... RobertWinston 5 94
(Eric Alston) *chsd ldr 4f out: rdn and hung lft over 1f out: led ins fnl f: r.o* **9/2**[2]

0155 **2** 1 **Clear Praise (USA)**[12] 6303 5-9-4 82 .... SebSanders 11 88
(Simon Dow) *hld up: hdwy over 1f out: edgd lft and r.o ins fnl f: nt rch wnr* **20/1**

5201 **3** 3/4 **Liberty Island (IRE)**[22] 6006 7-9-2 80 ....(p) KellyHarrison 12 84
(Ian Semple) *chsd ldrs: rdn over 1f out: styd on* **14/1**

2116 **4** 1 **Selfara**[13] 6285 3-9-0 79 ....(bt) JamesDoyle 9 79
(Roger Charlton) *s.i.s: hdwy u.p over 1f out: r.o* **11/2**[3]

2210 **5** 1/2 **Wild Sauce**[14] 6234 3-9-0 79 ....(b) TomEaves 1 77
(Bryan Smart) *led 4f out: rdn over 1f out: hdd and no ex ins fnl f* **16/1**

0020 **6** hd **Noverre To Go (IRE)**[21] 6026 6-9-7 85 .... KierenFox 7 83
(Ronald Harris) *s.i.s: sn pushed along in rr: hdwy u.p fr over 1f out: nt rch ldrs* **8/1**

46U2 **7** nk **Pea Shooter**[22] 6008 3-9-5 84 .... AmyRyan 2 81
(Kevin Ryan) *plld hrd and prom: rdn over 1f out: styd on same pce ins fnl f* **3/1**[1]

-002 **8** *nk* **Thirteen Shivers**[22] 6006 4-8-12 **83**..................... DavidSimmonson(7) 4 78
(Michael Easterby) *hld up: hdwy u.p over 1f out: no ex ins fnl f* **12/1**
3165 **9** *3 ½* **Knocker Knowles (IRE)**[28] 5812 3-9-0 **79**.................. CathyGannon 10 62
(David Evans) *s.i.s: outpcd* **28/1**
0060 **10** *hd* **Wooden King (IRE)**[14] 6226 7-8-10 **74**...................... TomMcLaughlin 6 56
(Malcolm Saunders) *chsd ldrs: rdn 1/2-way: wknd fnl f* **20/1**
1110 **11** *2* **Lesley's Choice**[114] 2853 6-9-0 **78** ow1...........................(b) AdamKirby 8 53
(Sean Curran) *led 1f: chsd ldrs: rdn 1/2-way: wknd over 1f out* **8/1**
3200 **12** *2 ¾* **Speightowns Kid (USA)**[10] 6369 4-8-4 **71**.................. RaulDaSilva(3) 3 36
(Jeremy Gask) *sn outpcd* **25/1**

1m 0.55s (-1.75) **Going Correction** -0.20s/f (Stan)
WFA 3 from 4yo+ 1lb **12** Ran SP% **117.8**
Speed ratings (Par 105): **106,104,103,101,100 100,100,99,93,93 90,86**
toteswingers 1&2 £99.10, 1&3 £17.00 2&3 £24.90 CSF £95.99 CT £1191.04 TOTE £4.60: £1.90, £7.20, £4.10; EX 97.50 Trifecta £460.30 Pool: £740.35 - 1.19 winning units.
Owner Joseph Heler **Bred** Joseph Heler **Trained** Longton, Lancs

FOCUS
A well-contested handicap containing some decent sprinters. The time was similar to division II and the form is straightforward.

6689 32RED CASINO H'CAP (DIV II) 5f 20y(P)
7:50 (7:50) (Class 4) (0-85,85) 3-Y-0+ **£5,175** (£1,540; £769; £384) **Stalls** Low

Form RPR
1400 **1** **Whozthecat (IRE)**[17] 6144 5-9-2 **80**..............................(b) JoeFanning 11 93
(Declan Carroll) *mid-div: hdwy over 1f out: rdn to ld wl ins fnl f* **8/1**
212 **2** *1* **Silken Express (IRE)**[40] 5422 3-8-10 **75**........................ JamesDoyle 4 85
(Robert Cowell) *chsd ldrs: rdn to ld ins fnl f: sn hdd and unable qck* **10/3**[2]
3211 **3** *1* **Angelito**[24] 5934 3-8-11 **76**.. SeanLevey 1 82
(Ed McMahon) *chsd ldrs: led over 1f out: hdd and unable qck ins fnl f* **3/1**[1]
1-15 **4** *2 ¼* **Queen Grace (IRE)**[22] 6005 5-9-5 **83**................................ ShaneKelly 9 81
(Michael J Browne, Ire) *a.p: rdn over 1f out: styd on same pce ins fnl f* **5/1**[3]
4022 **5** *1 ¼* **Bubbly Ballerina**[11] 6347 3-8-9 **79**.......................... NatashaEaton(5) 10 72
(Alan Bailey) *chsd ldrs: rdn and ev ch over 1f out: no ex ins fnl f* **12/1**
0020 **6** *½* **Blue Jack**[21] 6028 7-9-6 **84**..(vt) SebSanders 5 76
(Alan McCabe) *sn pushed along in rr: rdn over 1f out: r.o towards fin* **17/2**
432U **7** *nk* **Flash City (ITY)**[17] 6144 4-9-7 **85**..................................(v) TomEaves 6 76
(Bryan Smart) *led: rdn and hdd over 1f out: wknd ins fnl f* **8/1**
5350 **8** *1 ½* **Desert Strike**[10] 6369 6-8-9 **78**.................................(p) DavidKenny(5) 7 63
(Conor Dore) *sn pushed along in rr: nvr on terms* **33/1**
1300 **9** *¾* **Royal Bajan (USA)**[42] 5362 4-9-0 **78**.............................. GrahamLee 3 60
(James Given) *chsd ldrs: rdn over 1f out: wknd ins fnl f* **12/1**
610- **10** *1 ¼* **Secret Millionaire (IRE)**[34] 5646 5-8-13 **82**.......... GeorgeDowning(5) 2 60
(Tony Carroll) *hld up: a in rr* **20/1**
1250 **11** *1 ¾* **Shawkantango**[137] 2140 5-8-7 **71** oh1.......................(v) PatrickMathers 8 43
(Derek Shaw) *s.i.s: outpcd* **33/1**

1m 0.59s (-1.71) **Going Correction** -0.20s/f (Stan)
WFA 3 from 4yo+ 1lb **11** Ran SP% **123.5**
Speed ratings (Par 105): **105,103,101,98,96 95,94,92,91,89 86**
toteswingers 1&2 £16.70, 1&3 £10.70, 2&3 £2.50 CSF £36.00 CT £102.87 TOTE £10.20: £3.30, £1.10, £2.40; EX 60.90 Trifecta £388.60 Pool: £740.61 - 1.41 winning units..
Owner Ninerus **Bred** Liam Queally **Trained** Sledmere, E Yorks

FOCUS
This was run in much the same time as division one. The form has been given a bit of a chance.
Angelito Official explanation: jockey said gelding hung right under pressure

6690 BOOK HORIZONS RESTAURANT AT WOLVERHAMPTON RACECOURSE H'CAP 1m 1f 103y(P)
8:20 (8:20) (Class 6) (0-60,60) 3-Y-0+ **£2,070** (£616; £307; £153) **Stalls** Low

Form RPR
3146 **1** **Chasin' Rainbows**[23] 5974 4-9-1 **51**................................ JamesDoyle 8 59
(Sylvester Kirk) *hld up: hdwy over 1f out: rdn and r.o to ld nr fin* **10/1**
214 **2** *hd* **Celtic Step**[28] 5824 8-9-9 **59**.. DaleSwift 13 66
(Peter Niven) *trckd ldrs: rdn to ld 1f out: hdd nr fin* **15/2**[3]
4231 **3** *½* **Dana's Present**[17] 6152 3-9-5 **60**.................................... LiamKeniry 5 67+
(George Baker) *hld up in tch: nt clr run over 1f out: swtchd lft ins fnl f: r.o wl* **3/1**[1]
245 **4** *¾* **Source Of Light (IRE)**[29] 5810 3-9-5 **60**........................ ShaneKelly 7 65
(Daniel Mark Loughnane) *mid-div: hdwy over 2f out: rdn and ev ch ins fnl f: no ex nr fin* **9/1**
0106 **5** *1 ¼* **Applaude**[44] 5259 7-9-0 **50**.....................................(b) MichaelStainton 10 52
(Chris Bealby) *prom: chsd ldr over 7f out tl led over 2f out: rdn and hdd 1f out: styd on same pce* **33/1**
0002 **6** *2 ½* **Always Eager**[12] 6304 3-9-3 **58**...................................... JoeFanning 3 55
(Mark Johnston) *hld up: hdwy over 2f out: sn rdn: styd on same pce fnl f* **13/2**[2]
0564 **7** *1 ½* **Northern Spy (USA)**[14] 6252 8-9-3 **53**........................... SebSanders 12 47
(Simon Dow) *led: rdn and hdd over 2f out: wknd ins fnl f* **12/1**
3000 **8** *¾* **Count Ceprano (IRE)**[34] 5636 8-9-2 **55**..................... SimonPearce(3) 2 47
(Lydia Pearce) *hld up: racd keenly: nvr on terms* **16/1**
0644 **9** *1* **Lady Percy (IRE)**[16] 6174 3-8-9 **55**........................... RachealKneller(5) 9 45
(Mark Usher) *chsd ldr 2f: remained handy: rdn over 2f out: wknd over 1f out* **11/1**
0004 **10** *1* **Calypso Magic (IRE)**[14] 6250 4-9-6 **56**.....................(t) StevieDonohoe 6 44
(Olivia Maylam) *hld up: rdn over 2f out: n.d* **13/2**[2]
4600 **11** *2 ¾* **Broughton Place**[168] 1379 4-9-1 **51**............................... JamieMackay 4 33
(Willie Musson) *prom: rdn over 3f out: wknd over 2f out* **40/1**
5100 **12** *nk* **Sir Dylan**[19] 6097 3-9-4 **59**... KierenFox 11 40
(Ronald Harris) *hld up: plld hrd: wknd over 2f out* **28/1**
-400 **13** *5* **High Five Society**[34] 5622 8-8-12 **51**......................(b) MarkCoumbe(3) 1 22
(Roy Bowring) *a in rr* **16/1**

2m 0.21s (-1.49) **Going Correction** -0.20s/f (Stan)
WFA 3 from 4yo+ 5lb **13** Ran SP% **119.1**
Speed ratings (Par 101): **98,97,97,96,95 93,92,91,90,89 87,86,82**
toteswingers 1&2 £14.80, 1&3 £5.40, 2&3 £2.30 CSF £81.59 CT £284.69 TOTE £10.10: £3.40, £2.30, £1.80; EX 73.30 Trifecta £480.20 Part won. Pool: £648.92 - 0.73 winning units..
Owner J B J Richards **Bred** J B J Richards **Trained** Upper Lambourn, Berks
■ Stewards' Enquiry : James Doyle three-day ban: used whip without giving filly time to respond (Oct 14-16)

FOCUS
Only a moderate race, but there were some fair performers at this level. The pace was ordinary until it quickened 4f out. The winner posted a personal best, and the second his best run since 2009.
Count Ceprano(IRE) Official explanation: jockey said gelding suffered interference in running
Sir Dylan Official explanation: jockey said gelding hung left

6691 32RED SUPPORTING BRITISH RACING H'CAP 2m 119y(P)
8:50 (8:50) (Class 6) (0-65,72) 3-Y-0+ **£2,070** (£616; £307; £153) **Stalls** Low

Form RPR
0531 **1** **Porcini**[10] 6365 3-9-2 **68**.. RaulDaSilva(3) 5 79+
(Philip McBride) *a.p: rdn over 1f out: r.o to ld wl ins fnl f* **6/1**[3]
0062 **2** *1 ¼* **Blue Dune**[12] 6305 3-8-7 **56**... JoeFanning 4 64+
(Mark Johnston) *chsd ldr tl over 7f out: remained handy: nt clr run over 2f out: rdn over 1f out: r.o* **11/1**
1660 **3** *nk* **Ostentation**[18] 6120 5-9-8 **64**... AmyScott(5) 7 72
(Gay Kelleway) *hld up: hdwy over 2f out: led over 1f out: rdn: edgd lft and hdd wl ins fnl f* **40/1**
3360 **4** *2 ¾* **Shirls Son Sam**[31] 5735 4-8-11 **48**............................... KellyHarrison 10 53
(Chris Fairhurst) *stdd s: hld up and bhd: hdwy over 2f out: rdn over 1f out: styd on same pce fnl f* **28/1**
/414 **5** *5* **Iceman George**[7] 6503 8-9-3 **61**..................................(v) TimClark(7) 9 60
(Lydia Pearce) *hld up: hdwy over 5f out: rdn over 1f out: wknd fnl f* **20/1**
3003 **6** *2 ¼* **Tokyo Brown (USA)**[13] 6280 3-8-8 **57**........................... JamieMackay 2 53
(Heather Main) *plld hrd and prom: lost pl over 7f out: n.d after* **20/1**
3121 **7** *¾* **Azrag (USA)**[2] 6616 4-10-7 **72** 6ex............................... PaulMulrennan 12 67
(Gerard Butler) *hld up in tch: rdn over 1f out: wknd fnl f* **13/8**[1]
0001 **8** *2* **Jeer (IRE)**[7] 6503 8-9-10 **68**.................................(t) MatthewHopkins(7) 3 61
(Michael Easterby) *mid-div: hmpd over 6f out: hdwy over 1f out: wknd fnl f* **25/1**
1033 **9** *5* **Jacob McCandles**[26] 5891 5-9-13 **64**..................... SilvestreDeSousa 13 51
(Shaun Lycett) *sn led: rdn and hdd over 1f out: wknd fnl f* **5/1**[2]
0602 **10** *2 ½* **Cape Rainbow**[10] 6365 3-8-9 **58**.. LiamKeniry 6 42
(Mark Usher) *prom: chsd ldr over 7f out: rdn over 2f out: wknd over 1f out* **13/2**
310/ **11** *¾* **Erdeli (IRE)**[19] 5260 8-9-7 **65**.................................(tp) DanielMuscutt(7) 11 48
(Tim Vaughan) *s.i.s: hld up: rdn over 4f out: wknd over 2f out* **40/1**
12-2 **12** *3 ¼* **Dance For Livvy (IRE)**[165] 521 4-10-0 **65**........................ PJMcDonald 1 44
(Robin Dickin) *hld up: nvr on terms* **16/1**
0 **13** *26* **Parhelion**[37] 5507 5-10-0 **65**.......................................(bt[1]) CathyGannon 8 13
(John Flint) *hld up: hdwy 10f out: rdn over 4f out: wknd 3f out: t.o* **50/1**

3m 38.6s (-3.20) **Going Correction** -0.20s/f (Stan)
WFA 3 from 4yo+ 12lb **13** Ran SP% **120.3**
Speed ratings (Par 101): **99,98,98,96,94 93,93,92,89,88 88,86,74**
toteswingers 1&2 £7.60, 1&3 £39.00, 2&3 £29.70 CSF £64.30 CT £2435.46 TOTE £4.40: £2.90, £2.50, £14.80; EX 74.00 TRIFECTA Not won..
Owner PMRacing **Bred** Cheveley Park Stud Ltd **Trained** Newmarket, Suffolk

FOCUS
The pace was fair enough for the trip. The lack-lustre performance of the short-priced favourite opened the way to a newcomer to 2m, with 3yo fillies filling the first two places. The winner has more to offer.

6692 £32 BONUS AT 32RED.COM H'CAP 1m 141y(P)
9:20 (9:21) (Class 5) (0-75,75) 3-Y-0+ **£2,911** (£866; £432; £216) **Stalls** Low

Form RPR
5102 **1** **Saharia (IRE)**[15] 6208 5-9-6 **72**...(v) ShaneKelly 6 86+
(Michael Attwater) *s.i.s: hld up and bhd: smooth hdwy over 1f out: led on bit wl ins fnl f: easily* **4/1**[1]
3040 **2** *1* **My Single Malt (IRE)**[14] 6239 4-9-6 **72**........................... GrahamLee 11 81
(Julie Camacho) *hld up: hdwy over 2f out: rdn and evry ch ins fnl f: styd on* **11/1**
0030 **3** *½* **One Scoop Or Two**[14] 6241 6-9-3 **69**...................(p) RussKennemore 12 77
(Reg Hollinshead) *chsd ldrs: rdn over 2f out: led over 1f out: edgd lft and hdd wl ins fnl f* **8/1**
5654 **4** *1 ¾* **Xinbama (IRE)**[15] 6208 3-9-2 **73**.. SebSanders 5 77+
(J W Hills) *hld up: hdwy over 2f out: r.o ins fnl f: nt rch ldrs* **5/1**[3]
106 **5** *1 ¼* **Illustrious Prince (IRE)**[14] 6239 5-9-5 **71**........................ JoeFanning 2 72
(Declan Carroll) *s.i.s: hld up: hdwy over 1f out: nt trble ldrs* **14/1**
1301 **6** *1* **Honey Of A Kitten (USA)**[137] 2116 4-9-0 **69**........ MatthewCosham(3) 8 68
(David Evans) *hld up: rdn over 3f out: hdwy over 1f out: wknd ins fnl f* **22/1**
1200 **7** *½* **Knowe Head (NZ)**[26] 5888 5-9-9 **75**............................ PaulMulrennan 1 73
(James Unett) *prom: rdn over 1f out: no ex fnl f* **6/1**
5410 **8** *1 ¼* **Elkhart (IRE)**[43] 5322 3-9-2 **73**............................(b[1]) SilvestreDeSousa 10 68
(Michael Wigham) *led: clr over 5f out: rdn and hdd over 1f out: wknd ins fnl f* **9/2**[2]
1620 **9** *hd* **Satwa Laird**[21] 6047 6-9-4 **75**... DavidKenny(5) 4 69
(Conor Dore) *hld up: hdwy over 2f out: n.m.r and wknd over 1f out* **25/1**
5124 **10** *nk* **Kingswinford (IRE)**[12] 6319 6-9-6 **72**.................................. DaneO'Neill 3 65
(Alastair Lidderdale) *hld up: effrt over 1f out: wknd fnl f* **11/1**
0000 **11** *4 ½* **Lastkingofscotland (IRE)**[26] 5892 6-9-2 **68**..................(b) LiamKeniry 9 51
(Conor Dore) *chsd ldrs: rdn over 2f out: wknd over 1f out* **50/1**
4000 **12** *11* **Kakapuka**[12] 6319 5-9-6 **72**..(p) JamesDoyle 7 30
(Anabel K Murphy) *chsd ldrs: rdn over 2f out: wknd over 1f out* **20/1**

1m 48.6s (-1.90) **Going Correction** -0.20s/f (Stan)
WFA 3 from 4yo+ 5lb **12** Ran SP% **118.5**
Speed ratings (Par 103): **100,99,98,97,96 95,94,93,93,93 89,79**
totewingers 1&2 £16.70, 1&3 £12.40, 2&3 £17.20 CSF £46.12 CT £346.07 TOTE £6.70: £2.10, £3.20, £4.20; EX 60.90 TRIFECTA Not won..
Owner The Attwater Partnership **Bred** Woodcote Stud Ltd **Trained** Epsom, Surrey

FOCUS
A middling sort of race for the track, but run at a good gallop which helped the hold-up runners, including the winner. The runner-up helps set the standard but it's impossible to tell how much the winner had in hand.
Elkhart(IRE) Official explanation: jockey said colt hung left
Kakapuka Official explanation: jockey said gelding ran too freely
T/Plt: £53.50 to a £1 stake. Pool: £80,418.90. 1,095.76 winning tickets. T/Qpdt: £38.50 to a £1 stake. Pool: £8,181.33. 157.00 winning tickets. CR

6693 - 6694a (Foreign Racing) - See Raceform Interactive

4117 BELMONT PARK (L-H)

Saturday, September 29

OFFICIAL GOING: Dirt: standard; turf: yielding

6695a FLOWER BOWL INVITATIONAL STKS (GRADE 1) (3YO+ FILLIES & MARES) (TURF) — 1m 2f (T)

0:38 (12:00) 3-Y-O+

£232,258 (£77,419; £38,709; £19,354; £11,612; £2,300)

Pos	Dist	Horse	Jockey	RPR
1		**Nahrain**[20] 6080 4-8-9 0 (Roger Varian) **5/1**	JRVelazquez 7	114+
2	½	**Zagora (FR)**[35] 5-8-9 0 (Chad C Brown, U.S.A) **69/20**[2]	RADominguez 6	113
3	nse	**Dream Peace (IRE)**[63] 4617 4-8-7 0 (Chad C Brown, U.S.A) **2/1**[1]	JRLeparoux 1	111+
4	½	**I'm A Dreamer (IRE)**[42] 5376 5-8-11 0 (David Simcock) **37/10**[3]	HayleyTurner 4	114+
5	4	**Hessonite (USA)**[20] 4-8-7 0 (David Donk, U.S.A) **143/10**	JLezcano 2	102
6	nse	**Bizzy Caroline (USA)**[26] 4-8-7 0 (Kenneth McPeek, U.S.A) **43/1**	DCohen 5	102
7	13 ½	**Hit It Rich (USA)**[26] 5-8-7 0 (Claude McGaughey III, U.S.A) **17/2**	JJCastellano 3	75
8	2 ¾	**Halo Dolly (USA)**[25] 4-8-9 0 (Jerry Hollendorfer, U.S.A) **141/10**	(b) JRosario 8	71

2m 5.56s (4.27) **8** Ran SP% **119.7**
PARI-MUTUEL (all including $2 stakes): WIN 12.00; PLACE (1-2) 7.90, 4.20; SHOW (1-2-3) 4.30, 3.10, 2.80; SF 63.00.
Owner Sheikh Ahmed Al Maktoum **Bred** Darley **Trained** Newmarket, Suffolk

NOTEBOOK

Nahrain had shaped as though on the way back to form in Ireland on her previous start and built on that effort to land her first success since last year's Prix de l'Opera. She was second in last year's Breeders' Cup Filly & Mare Turf and that race is likely to again be the aim.
I'm A Dreamer(IRE) won the Beverly D at Arlington last time, but she found this a bit tougher.

6696 - 6698a (Foreign Racing) - See Raceform Interactive

6167 EPSOM (L-H)

Sunday, September 30

OFFICIAL GOING: Good (good to soft in places; 7.8)

Rail dolled out up to 8yds from 1m to winning post adding about 12yds to distances.

Wind: fresh, across Weather: cloudy blustery wind

6699 BET TOTEPLACEPOT TEXT TOTE TO 89660 NURSERY — 7f

2:15 (2:15) (Class 4) (0-85,85) 2-Y-O — **£5,175** (£1,540; £769; £384) **Stalls** Low

Form	Pos	Dist	Horse	Jockey	RPR
1230	1		**Hipster**[18] 6138 2-9-2 **80** (Ralph Beckett) *mde most: drvn and clr w rival over 1f out: forged clr 1f out: clr ins fnl f: all out* **7/2**[1]	(v[1]) JamesDoyle 8	84
3331	2	nk	**Beedee**[24] 5969 2-9-7 **85** (Richard Hannon) *chsd ldrs: rdn over 2f out: drvn and outpcd by ldng pair over 1f out: rallied u.p and styd on to chse wnr ins fnl f: clsng towards fin: nt quite get up* **5/1**[2]	RichardHughes 6	88
51	3	2 ¾	**Sanjuro (IRE)**[30] 5793 2-9-5 **83** (Mick Channon) *w ldr: rdn ent fnl 2f: drvn and clr w wnr over 1f out: no ex 1f out: lost 2nd ins fnl f: wknd fnl 100yds* **7/2**[1]	MartinHarley 1	79
443	4	1 ½	**Mishaal (IRE)**[17] 6167 2-8-11 **75** (Roger Varian) *t.k.h: hld up in tch in midfield: rdn and outpcd 2f out: styd on same pce and edgd lft fnl f* **8/1**[3]	NeilCallan 5	67
361	5	2 ¾	**Majestic Jess (IRE)**[8] 6499 2-8-5 **69** (Luke Dace) *broke wl but stdd bk and hld up in last trio: rdn over 3f out: outpcd 2f out: one pce and wl hld after* **20/1**	HarryBentley 4	54
653	6	shd	**Lamusawama**[44] 5311 2-8-7 **71** (Ed Dunlop) *sn pushed along in last trio: rdn and no hdwy over 3f out: no ch w ldrs fnl 2f* **7/2**[1]	PaulHanagan 7	56
1560	7	hd	**Must Be Me**[17] 6155 2-8-5 **69** (Eve Johnson Houghton) *short of room leaving stalls: a bhd: effrt and nt clr run 2f out: no prog over 1f out* **33/1**	CathyGannon 3	53
3155	8	5	**Medicoe**[12] 6344 2-9-1 **79** (Sir Mark Prescott Bt) *t.k.h: chsd ldrs: rdn and unable qck 3f out: wknd and bhd over 1f out* **8/1**[3]	(b[1]) LukeMorris 2	50

1m 25.14s (1.84) **Going Correction** +0.20s/f (Good) **8** Ran SP% **113.3**
Speed ratings (Par 97): **97,96,93,91,88 88,88,82**
Tote Swingers: 1&2 £4.50, 1&3 £3.20, 2&3 £3.40 CSF £20.78 CT £64.44 TOTE £5.30: £2.30, £1.70, £1.10; EX 26.90 Trifecta £53.80 Pool: £523.16 - 7.19 winning tickets..
Owner R Roberts **Bred** Cheveley Park Stud Ltd **Trained** Kimpton, Hants

FOCUS

Rail dolled out up to 8yds from 1m to Winning Post adding about 12yds to distances. It was dry overnight and the ground was given as good, good to soft in places (GoingStick 7.8; home straight - stands' side 8.4, far side 8.1). The early pace wasn't strong and the pace held up. Sound form with the first pair clear.

NOTEBOOK

Hipster, visored for the first time, settled well on the front end and was best placed to quicken off the steady early pace. He handled Tattenham Corner well and is now 2-2 at the track. (op 9-2)
Beedee enjoyed a nice lead into the straight but the winner got first run on him and he was then playing catch-up. By Beat Hollow out of a mare who got 1m2f and is from the family of Sun Princess, he'll stay further. (op 9-2)
Sanjuro(IRE) was keen early, but was up front from the start, which was the place to be given the sedate early gallop, and as a result he was able to hang on for third. (tchd 4-1)
Mishaal(IRE) didn't see his race out, failing to improve for the step up to 7f as anticipated. (op 9-1)
Majestic Jess(IRE) found things tougher back in handicap company. (op 16-1 tchd 22-1)
Lamusawama was struggling from some way out, appearing not to handle the track at all, despite having had previous experience of the place on his second start. (tchd 10-3, tchd 4-1 in a place)
Medicoe just didn't settle off the early gallop and it was no surprise to see him drop right out. (op 7-1)

6700 BET TOTEPOOL TEXT TOTE TO 89660 CONDITIONS STKS — 1m 114y

2:45 (2:46) (Class 3) 2-Y-O — **£7,158** (£2,143; £1,071) **Stalls** Low

Form	Pos	Dist	Horse	Jockey	RPR
1	1		**Gabrial's Kaka (IRE)**[15] 6237 2-9-0 0 (Richard Fahey) *chsd ldr tl rdn to ld over 2f out: edgd lft 1f out: kpt on wl: rdn out* **2/1**[2]	PaulHanagan 2	93+
1131	2	1 ½	**Janoub Nibras (IRE)**[18] 6149 2-9-6 99 (Richard Hannon) *stdd s: hld up in last: rdn and effrt 2f out: drvn to chse wnr 1f out: one pce and no imp fnl 75yds* **8/11**[1]	RichardHughes 4	95
5135	3	hd	**Linguine (FR)**[16] 6225 2-9-0 95 (Charles Hills) *led: rdn and hdd over 2f out: swtchd rt ent fnl f: styd on same pce after and n.m.r wl ins fnl f* **5/1**[3]	WilliamCarson 1	89

1m 50.28s (4.18) **Going Correction** +0.20s/f (Good) **3** Ran SP% **107.9**
Speed ratings (Par 99): **89,87,87**
Tote Swingers: 1&2 £14.10, 1&3 £29.20, 2&3 £5.70 CSF £3.93 TOTE £2.30; EX 3.60.
Owner Dr Marwan Koukash **Bred** Dave Orme **Trained** Musley Bank, N Yorks

FOCUS

Just the three runners but it was a good heat and the scopey winner looks worth keeping onside. The form is rated around the third.

NOTEBOOK

Gabrial's Kaka(IRE) was being niggled along some way out, still looked green and flashed his tail for pressure, but once he got into full stride in the straight he pulled clear to win a shade comfortably. He'll probably appreciate a more galloping track, while he has plenty of size about him and should make up into a nice horse next year. (tchd 15-8 and 9-4)
Janoub Nibras(IRE) comes out of the race as the best horse as he was giving 6lb to the winner, but his rival lacked experience and he'd be no good thing to reverse the form off levels, especially as he seems the type that needs to do everything on the bridle. Nevertheless, this was a sound effort in defeat against a useful rival. (tchd 4-6 and 4-5)
Linguine(FR) didn't seem totally at home on the track but he kept on well after being headed. He's not going to be an easy horse to place off his current mark, though. (op 11-2 tchd 6-1)

6701 BET TOTEQUADPOT TEXT TOTE TO 89660 H'CAP — 1m 114y

3:20 (3:21) (Class 3) (0-90,90) 3-Y-O — **£9,337** (£2,796; £1,398; £699; £349; £175) **Stalls** Low

Form	Pos	Dist	Horse	Jockey	RPR
6016	1		**Dubai Sunshine (IRE)**[25] 5942 3-8-13 **82** (Michael Bell) *chsd ldrs: rdn and effrt over 2f out: ev ch ent fnl f: led fnl 75yds: r.o wl* **25/1**	StevieDonohoe 8	91
2103	2	1 ¼	**Benzanno (IRE)**[11] 6374 3-8-10 **79** (Andrew Balding) *chsd ldrs: switching rt and effrt over 2f out: ev ch ent fnl f: led ins fnl f: sn hdd and one pce* **7/2**[2]	JimmyFortune 3	85
1500	3	2 ½	**Lady Macduff (IRE)**[22] 6023 3-9-1 **84** (Mark Johnston) *led: rdn wl over 2f out: edging rt u.p but battled on wl tl hdd jst over 1f out: no ex ins fnl f: wknd towards fin* **8/1**	SilvestreDeSousa 6	84
024	4	nse	**Swing Alone (IRE)**[37] 5556 3-9-4 **87** (Gay Kelleway) *t.k.h early: hld up in last trio: rdn and outpcd wl over 2f out: styd on to go 5th ins fnl f: swtchd rt and styd on strly to press for 3rd cl home* **10/1**	NeilCallan 2	87+
5253	5	shd	**Sunley Pride**[10] 6401 3-8-2 **76** oh5 (Mick Channon) *chsd ldr: rdn and ev ch ent fnl 2f: led jst over 1f out: hdd ins fnl f: wknd fnl 75yds* **16/1**	KatiaScallan(5) 7	76
0102	6	5	**Campanology**[37] 5556 3-9-7 **90** (Richard Hannon) *hld up in midfield: rdn and no hdwy over 2f out: wknd ent fnl f* **5/1**[3]	RichardHughes 5	78
4106	7	9	**Warfare**[113] 2916 3-8-11 **80** (Kevin Ryan) *t.k.h early: hld up in midfield: rdn and struggling 3f out: wknd wl over 1f out* **9/1**	PhillipMakin 1	48
0110	8	3 ½	**Double Cee**[21] 6073 3-8-8 **77** (Richard Fahey) *in tch towards rr: rdn along and struggling on downhill run 4f out: wknd wl over 1f out* **7/1**	PaulHanagan 9	37
1250	9	7	**Takeitfromalady (IRE)**[36] 5609 3-9-3 **86** (Ralph Beckett) *stmbld s and s.i.s: hld up in tch in rr: rdn and no rspnse over 2f out: wknd wl over 1f out: wl bhd and eased ins fnl f* **10/3**[1]	(b) JamesDoyle 4	30+

1m 46.56s (0.46) **Going Correction** +0.20s/f (Good) **9** Ran SP% **114.4**
Speed ratings (Par 105): **105,103,101,101,101 97,89,85,79**
Tote Swingers: 1&2 £14.10, 1&3 £29.20, 2&3 £5.70 CSF £109.95 CT £789.32 TOTE £27.40: £6.30, £1.60, £3.10; EX 144.00 Trifecta £833.50 Part won. Pool: £1,126.45 - 0.40 winning tickets..
Owner Dr Ali Ridha **Bred** Rabbah Bloodstock Limited **Trained** Newmarket, Suffolk

FOCUS

It paid to race handily here as three of the first four home were in the leading quartet throughout. The form is rated around the runner-up.

NOTEBOOK

Dubai Sunshine(IRE) had only shown ability in one of his previous four starts on turf, but this dual Fibresand winner hadn't run over this sort of trip on grass before, despite his winning form at Southwell coming over a mile. Always well placed, he found plenty down the outside in the straight and was going further clear at the line, so should get 1m2f in time. He's in the horses-in-training sale. (op 22-1)
Benzanno(IRE) has run well here in the past, and did so again, albeit on the back of a nice trip behind the leader. He can have few excuses given the way the race panned out. (op 10-3)
Lady Macduff(IRE) bounced back from a disappointing effort at Ascot, enjoying the run of the race out in front. (tchd 9-1)
Swing Alone(IRE) ◆ was the only one to make up any significant ground from off the pace, and as such he deserves credit. The step up in trip really suited him and he can do better off a stronger gallop. (op 12-1)
Sunley Pride was 5lb wrong at the weights but he was always well placed, towards the front, and that counted for plenty in this race.
Campanology didn't help his cause by racing keenly early. (op 9-2)
Warfare, keen early, hadn't run for 113 days so is entitled to come on for the outing. (op 12-1)
Double Cee wasn't travelling from an early stage. (op 13-2 tchd 15-2)
Takeitfromalady(IRE) didn't pick up at all in the straight and was well below his best. Perhaps something happened when he stumbled leaving the stalls. Official explanation: jockey said gelding slipped leaving stalls and did not handle the track (op 4-1 tchd 3-1)

6702 TOTEPOOL MOBILE TEXT TOTE TO 89660 H'CAP — 1m 2f 18y

3:55 (3:58) (Class 3) (0-95,93) 3-Y-O+ — **£9,337** (£2,796; £1,398; £699; £349; £175) **Stalls** Low

Form	Pos	Dist	Horse	Jockey	RPR
4020	1		**Borug (USA)**[16] 6207 4-8-10 **79** oh1 (James Tate) *hld up in tch in rr: gd hdwy on inner over 2f out: qcknd to ld 2f out and sn rdn clr: edgd rt and styd on wl ins fnl f* **9/2**[3]	NeilCallan 7	91

0602 **2** 2 **Resurge (IRE)**17 6166 7-9-10 **93**......(t) AdamKirby 3 101
(Stuart Kittow) *hld up in midfield: hdwy to chse ldrs whn nt clr run and swtchd rt 2f out: sn rdn to chse ldng pair: kpt on but no real imp on wnr: wnt 2nd last strides* **4/1**2

1230 **3** hd **John Biscuit (IRE)**37 5558 4-9-4 **87**...... JimmyFortune 6 95
(Andrew Balding) *taken down early: t.k.h: chsd ldrs: rdn to chse ldr 2f out: styd on same pce u.p fnl f: lost 2nd last strides* **5/2**1

4/15 **4** 10 **Splendid Light**173 1273 4-9-3 **86**...... MarcHalford 2 74
(John Gosden) *t.k.h: chsd ldr tl 8f out: chsd ldrs after: rdn and high hd carriage over 2f out: wknd over 1f out* **13/2**

5610 **5** 1 3/4 **Lyssio (GER)**22 6039 5-9-4 **87**...... J-PGuillambert 10 71
(Michael Attwater) *chsd ldrs tl wnt 2nd 8f out tl 2f out: sn outpcd and wknd over 1f out* **8/1**

4000 **6** nk **Deire Na Sli (IRE)**24 5980 4-9-0 **83**......(b) JamesDoyle 8 67
(Martyn Meade) *hld up in tch in midfield: rdn and effrt 3f out: no imp and outpcd 2f out: wknd over 1f out* **20/1**

6000 **7** hd **Right Step**37 5558 5-9-6 **89**......(v) DarryllHolland 9 72
(Alan Jarvis) *hld up in last pair: rdn and effrt 3f out: no hdwy and outpcd 2f out: wl btn and edging lft u.p 1f out* **14/1**

0105 **8** 7 **Vasily**36 5593 4-9-9 **92**...... AndreaAtzeni 4 61
(Robert Eddery) *racd keenly: led tl rdn and hdd 2f out: sn outpcd and btn: wl bhd and eased wl ins fnl f* **9/1**

4130 **9** 10 **Brunston**7 1139 6-9-4 **87**...... SebSanders 1 36
(Brendan Powell) *hld up in last pair: rdn and no rspnse 4f out: lost tch 2f out: t.o* **66/1**

2m 9.72s (0.02) **Going Correction** +0.20s/f (Good) 9 Ran SP% **114.1**
Speed ratings (Par 107): **107,105,105,97,95 95,95,89,81**
Tote Swingers: 1&2 £3.90, 1&3 £3.40, 2&3 £2.60 CSF £22.56 CT £53.84 TOTE £5.30: £1.50, £1.80, £1.60; EX 23.80 Trifecta £52.00 Pool: £1,809.34 - 25.70 winning tickets..
Owner Saif Ali **Bred** Rabbah Bloodstock Llc **Trained** Newmarket, Suffolk

FOCUS
This looked fairly competitive on paper. It was well run and in a good time, with the winner rated to something like his best.

NOTEBOOK
Borug(USA), who ran well behind Gatewood here on Oaks day, had slipped 4lb in the weights in the interim, and made the most of the handicapper's leniency, cornering well into the straight and seeing his race out strongly. He's clearly capable around here and will be of interest whenever he returns. (tchd 5-1)
Resurge(IRE)'s rider looked to be caught out slightly by the winner, who got first run on him towards the inside while he was travelling well in behind John Biscuit. In fairness to Kirby, however, once the gelding was switched to challenge he didn't find as much as he'd promised for pressure anyway, and made hard work of securing second. (op 10-3 tchd 3-1)
John Biscuit(IRE), now 11lb higher than when a winner here in July, was always well placed and travelled strongly through the race. He had his chance, but the winner was just better treated at the weights. (op 3-1)
Splendid Light, having his first outing since April, raced keenly early and didn't appeal with his head carriage. He might not be entirely straightforward. (op 6-1 tchd 7-1)
Lyssio(GER) was well held in the end and remains on a stiff enough mark. (tchd 9-1)
Deire Na Sli(IRE) didn't improve for the longer trip.
Right Step, although fairly handicapped on his win here in April, has largely struggled since.
Vasily, who wants quicker ground ideally, raced keenly in front and didn't get home. (op 14-1)

6703 CHANTILLY APPRENTICES' DERBY H'CAP 1m 4f 10y
4:30 (4:30) (Class 4) (0-80,80) 3-Y-0+ **£5,175** (£1,540; £769; £384) **Stalls** Centre

Form RPR

-364 **1** **Moderator**37 5533 3-9-0 **76**...... HarryBentley 6 92+
(Gary Moore) *hld up in tch: hdwy to trck ldrs gng wl 4f out: led 2f out and sn rdn clr: wl clr 1f out: eased fnl 75yds* **16/1**

0530 **2** 3 1/4 **Achalas (IRE)**4 6584 4-9-1 **76**...... RyanTate(7) 15 81
(Heather Main) *in tch in midfield: reminders 6f out: rdn and hdwy 4f out: chsd clr wnr over 1f out: kpt on but no ch w wnr* **25/1**

6601 **3** 1/2 **Rythmic**15 6263 3-8-4 **71**...... MichaelJMMurphy(5) 11 75+
(Mark Johnston) *hld up towards rr: pushed along and n.m.r 6f out: rdn and hdwy on outer over 2f out: hung lft and styd on fr over 1f out: wnt 3rd ins fnl f: no ch w wnr* **5/2**1

4360 **4** 2 **Shesha Bear**17 6170 7-8-13 **70**......(p) MatthewLawson(3) 4 71
(Jonathan Portman) *s.i.s: hld up in rr: rdn and hdwy on outer 4f out: styd on u.p fr over 1f out: no ch w wnr* **20/1**

4316 **5** 3/4 **St Ignatius**21 6076 5-9-3 **76**......(p) NatashaEaton(5) 12 76
(Alan Bailey) *chsd ldrs tl led 4f out: rdn and hdd 2f out: sn outpcd by wnr and btn: wknd ins fnl f* **20/1**

4524 **6** 3/4 **Kings Troop**17 6170 6-8-8 **67** ow1......(v) WilliamTwiston-Davies(5) 9 66
(Alan King) *in tch in midfield: rdn and lost pl over 2f out: rallied and styd on ins fnl f: no ch w wnr* **15/2**3

4255 **7** 1 **Kathleen Frances**12 6339 5-9-9 **77**......(b) AdamBeschizza 7 74
(Mark H Tompkins) *hld up in midfield: clsd to trck ldrs 3f out: rdn and unable qck 2f out: wknd jst over 1f out* **10/1**

102 **8** 2 1/4 **Beat Route**53 4944 5-8-12 **66** oh1...... KierenFox 1 59
(Michael Attwater) *chsd ldrs: rdn and unable qck 3f out: wknd over 1f out* **20/1**

4303 **9** 1 1/2 **Toughness Danon**7 6517 6-8-9 **68**...... GeorgeDowning(5) 14 59
(Brendan Powell) *hld up in rr: rdn and sme hdwy towards inner 2f out: sltly hmpd and no imp over 1f out* **16/1**

03 **10** hd **Ela Gonda Mou**35 5636 5-8-9 **66**...... RosieJessop(3) 13 57
(Peter Charalambous) *mounted on crse and taken down early: mostly chsd ldr tl over 2f out: wknd over 1f out* **28/1**

1244 **11** 2 3/4 **Reggie Perrin**33 5706 4-8-7 **66** oh3......(v) JakePayne(5) 3 52
(Pat Phelan) *in tch in midfield: rdn and lost pl 7f out: rdn and no hdwy on inner 3f out: wknd 2f out* **12/1**

1033 **12** 1 1/2 **Sula Two**17 6170 5-9-7 **80**...... PhilipPrince(5) 5 64
(Ron Hodges) *hld up in last quartet: sme hdwy 4f out: hung lft and wknd wl over 1f out* **10/1**

5320 **13** 27 **Harry Buckle**11 6364 3-8-8 **70**...... RaulDaSilva 8 11
(Philip McBride) *in tch in midfield: rdn and struggling 4f out: wknd over 2f out: t.o* **5/1**2

0050 **14** 2 **Megalala (IRE)**31 5767 11-9-10 **78**...... SeanLevey 10 15
(John Bridger) *led tl 4f out: wknd u.p 3f out: t.o fnl f* **33/1**

5000 **15** 7 **Bloodsweatandtears**34 5667 4-8-11 **68**...... DavidKenny(3) 2
(William Knight) *dwlt: sn in tch in midfield: rdn and wknd 3f out: t.o fnl f* **40/1**

2m 41.25s (2.35) **Going Correction** +0.20s/f (Good)
WFA 3 from 4yo+ 8lb 15 Ran SP% **121.6**
Speed ratings (Par 105): **100,97,97,96,95 95,94,93,92,91 90,89,71,69,65**
Tote Swingers: 1&2 £73.80, 1&3 £11.60, 2&3 £20.00 CSF £371.13 CT £1346.79 TOTE £18.30: £5.10, £8.60, £2.20; EX 643.80 Trifecta £1115.90 Part won. Pool: £1,507.99 - 0.62 winning tickets..
Owner D J Deer **Bred** D J And Mrs Deer **Trained** Lower Beeding, W Sussex

FOCUS
There was a good gallop on and it paid to be ridden with a bit of patience. The winner is rated value for 6l, with the form rated around the runner-up.
Beat Route Official explanation: trainer said gelding did not handle the track
Toughness Danon Official explanation: trainer said gelding hung left and had a breathing problem

6704 TRY TOTEQUICKPICK IF YOU'RE FEELING LUCKY MAIDEN STKS 1m 2f 18y
5:00 (5:01) (Class 5) 3-Y-O **£2,911** (£866; £432; £216) **Stalls** Low

Form RPR

0-23 **1** **Sunpass**158 1606 3-9-3 72...... NickyMackay 9 93+
(John Gosden) *hld up in midfield: hdwy to trck ldr gng wl over 2f out: led 2f out and sn pushed along to go wl clr: r.o wl: v easily* **11/4**1

6 **2** 11 **Elysian**125 2553 3-8-12 0...... RichardHughes 6 67
(Sir Michael Stoute) *chsd ldrs: swtchd rt and drvn to chse ldr briefly over 2f out: 3rd and no ch w wnr over 1f out: wnt modest 2nd 1f out: plugged on* **11/4**1

3 1 1/4 **Break Rank (USA)**121 3-9-3 83...... PhillipMakin 5 70
(Ed de Giles) *hld up in tch: rdn and effrt over 2f out: wnt modest 3rd 1f out: kpt on but no ch w wnr* **20/1**

0 **4** 3 **Omar Khayyam**164 1467 3-9-3 0......(t) JimmyFortune 8 64+
(Andrew Balding) *awkward leaving stalls and v.s.a: bhd: rdn over 3f out: hdwy past btn horses over 1f out: wnt modest 4th ins fnl f: n.d* **10/1**2

66 **5** 4 **Boonga Roogeta**37 5555 3-8-12 0...... LukeMorris 1 51
(Peter Charalambous) *dwlt: sn in tch in midfld: rdn and struggling over 3f out: bhd fnl 2f* **66/1**

0325 **6** 3 **Superciliary**17 6181 3-9-3 64...... JamesDoyle 7 51
(Ralph Beckett) *chsd ldrs tl rdn and unable qck 3f out: sn wknd and bhd* **10/1**2

0442 **7** 3/4 **Mossbrae**9 6441 3-9-3 75...... NeilCallan 2 49+
(Roger Varian) *led for 1f: chsd ldr after tl led again over 3f out: rdn and hdd 2f out: immediately outpcd and btn: lost 2 pls 1f out: rdr looking down ins fnl f: eased* **11/4**1

00 **8** 5 **Peace In Our Time**50 5100 3-9-3 0...... WilliamCarson 4 40
(Anthony Carson) *in tch towards rr: rdn 1/2-way: dropped to last 4f out: lost tch over 3f out* **100/1**

0426 **9** 13 **Keeping Time**10 6408 3-9-3 74...... IanMongan 3 15
(Sir Henry Cecil) *w ldr tl led after 1f: rdn and hdd over 3f out: sn dropped out u.p: t.o* **12/1**3

2m 10.83s (1.13) **Going Correction** +0.20s/f (Good) 9 Ran SP% **113.1**
Speed ratings (Par 101): **103,94,93,90,87 85,84,80,70**
Tote Swingers: 1&2 £2.30, 1&3 £8.70, 2&3 £9.20 CSF £9.59 TOTE £3.60: £1.30, £1.70, £3.20; EX 11.50 Trifecta £110.00 Pool: £1,787.11 - 12.02 winning tickets..
Owner George Strawbridge **Bred** George Strawbridge **Trained** Newmarket, Suffolk

FOCUS
Not a strong maiden, lacking depth, but the winner impressed and has been given credit.
Mossbrae Official explanation: jockey said gelding lost its action

6705 FOLLOW TOTEPOOL ON FACEBOOK AND TWITTER H'CAP 7f
5:30 (5:32) (Class 4) (0-85,85) 3-Y-0+ **£6,469** (£1,925; £962; £481) **Stalls** Low

Form RPR

032 **1** **Fabled City (USA)**38 5512 3-8-5 **72**......(t) LukeMorris 13 84
(Clive Cox) *s.i.s: t.k.h: hld up in last quartet: rdn and hdwy 2f out: chsd ldr over 1f out: sustained chal and edging lft u.p ins fnl f: led last stride* **13/2**

0566 **2** shd **Shifting Star (IRE)**4 6577 7-8-8 **79**...... WilliamTwiston-Davies(7) 8 91
(John Bridger) *hld up in midfield: rdn and hdwy ent fnl 2f: led over 1f out: clr w wnr and carried lft fnl f: hdd last stride* **12/1**

6300 **3** 4 1/2 **Avonmore Star**15 6256 4-8-11 **75**...... RichardHughes 1 75
(Richard Hannon) *hld up in last quartet: rdn and hdwy towards inner 2f out: swtchd rt and chsd clr ldng pair ent fnl f: no imp* **9/1**

0601 **4** 3 1/4 **Ghostwing**23 5993 5-8-7 **71** oh1......(vt) HarryBentley 15 62
(Luke Dace) *sn chsng ldr: rdn to ld 2f out: hdd and outpcd over 1f out: wknd fnl f* **16/1**

5000 **5** 1/2 **Tidentime (USA)**57 4819 3-9-3 **84**...... MartinHarley 14 73
(Mick Channon) *hld up in last pair: rdn and effrt 2f out: hdwy over 1f out: styd on same pce ins fnl f: nvr trbld ldrs* **9/1**

006 **6** nk **Baby Strange**8 6495 8-8-10 **79**...... MichaelJMMurphy(5) 4 68
(Derek Shaw) *s.i.s: hld up bhd: stl last and rdn 2f out: swtchd rt and hdwy over 1f out: no imp fnl f* **9/2**1

-040 **7** 1/2 **Atlantis Star**22 6036 5-9-7 **85**...... NeilCallan 7 72
(James Tate) *t.k.h: hld up in midfield: rdn and unable qck whn edgd lft over 1f out: no imp fr over 1f out* **12/1**

-050 **8** 2 **Dreamwriter (USA)**92 3636 3-9-4 **85**...... PatCosgrave 10 67
(Jim Boyle) *s.i.s: hld up towards rr: hdwy on outer into midfield 4f out: rdn and no hdwy 3f out: wknd wl over 1f out* **40/1**

2132 **9** 1 1/4 **Afkar (IRE)**22 6041 4-8-13 **77**......(v1) TedDurcan 3 56
(Clive Brittain) *chsd ldrs: rdn and ev ch 2f out: sn outpcd and wknd over 1f out: wl btn and eased ins fnl f* **5/1**2

-110 **10** 3/4 **Scottish Lake**13 6319 4-8-11 **75**......(b) JamesDoyle 5 51
(Olivia Maylam) *sn led: rdn and hdd 2f out: sn wknd: wl btn and eased ins fnl f* **16/1**

0000 **11** hd **Baldemar**8 6465 7-8-12 **76**...... PaulHanagan 2 52
(Richard Fahey) *t.k.h: hld up in tch in midfield: rdn and no hdwy over 2f out: wknd over 1f out* **6/1**3

1665 **12** 7 **Byton**11 6378 3-8-4 **71** oh1...... CathyGannon 6 28
(Henry Candy) *chsd ldrs tl 3f out: lost pl u.p 2f out: wl bhd and eased ins fnl f* **12/1**

1m 24.44s (1.14) **Going Correction** +0.20s/f (Good)
WFA 3 from 4yo+ 3lb 12 Ran SP% **119.7**
Speed ratings (Par 105): **101,100,95,92,91 91,90,88,86,85 85,77**
Tote Swingers: 1&2 £23.50, 1&3 £12.10, 2&3 £21.00 CSF £83.05 CT £720.32 TOTE £7.60: £2.20, £3.90, £3.10; EX 110.90 Trifecta £767.40 Part won. Pool: £1,037.14 - 0.60 winning tickets..
Owner The Tenners **Bred** Ben Sangster **Trained** Lambourn, Berks

FOCUS
There was a good pace on here and the closers were favoured. The first pair were clear and the winner improved on his latest form.

T/Plt: £112.90 to a £1 stake. Pool: £80,574.00 - 520.56 winning tickets. T/Qpdt: £16.30 to a £1 stake. Pool: £7,898.00 - 356.67 winning tickets. SP

6308 MUSSELBURGH (R-H)

Sunday, September 30

OFFICIAL GOING: Good to soft (7.2)

Stands' bends out 2m.

Wind: Fresh, half against Weather: Overcast, showers

6706 ROYAL REGIMENT OF SCOTLAND H'CAP (DIV I) — 1m 5f

1:30 (1:30) (Class 4) (0-80,78) 3-Y-O+ **£5,175** (£1,540; £769; £384) **Stalls** Low

Form — RPR

3412 **1** **The Baronet**^{46} 5228 3-9-3 **76** .... ChrisCatlin 8 — 86+
(Sir Mark Prescott Bt) *awkward s: sn pressing ldr: rdn to ld over 2f out: edgd lft over 1f out: edgd rt ins fnl f: drvn out* **7/4**^{1}

2031 **2** *3/4* **Hawdyerwheesht**^{13} 6315 4-8-11 **61** .... GrahamLee 3 — 70
(Jim Goldie) *in tch: hdwy 1/2-way: effrt and disp ld over 2f out: sn rdn: hung lft ins fnl f: kpt on: hld nr fin* **11/2**^{2}

60-U **3** *4* **Tiny Temper (IRE)**^{34} 5672 4-8-12 **62** .... TonyHamilton 5 — 65
(Richard Fahey) *t.k.h: in tch: rdn over 2f out: chsd (clr) ldng pair over 1f out: r.o fnl f* **12/1**

4-00 **4** *nk* **Royal Entourage**^{13} 6311 7-8-10 **67** .... EvaMoscrop(7) 4 — 70
(Philip Kirby) *hld up: hdwy on outside over 2f out: rdn and no imp fr over 1f out* **33/1**

30-1 **5** *1 1/4* **Mason Hindmarsh**^{13} 6311 5-8-9 **66** .... GeorgeChaloner(7) 2 — 67
(Karen McLintock) *hld up: effrt whn nt clr run and swtchd lft over 2f out: styd on fnl f: nrst fin* **8/1**

2156 **6** *3/4* **Sohcahtoa (IRE)**^{13} 6311 6-9-1 **70** .... LMcNiff(5) 1 — 70
(David Barron) *hld up towards rr: stdy hdwy 4f out: rdn over 2f out: sn no imp* **15/2**

33-0 **7** *5* **Tartan Jura**^{7} 6517 4-9-6 **70** .... FrederikTylicki 7 — 62
(Mark Johnston) *trckd ldrs: pushed along fr 1/2-way: rallied: effrt over 2f out: wknd over 1f out* **18/1**

5050 **8** *1 3/4* **Royal Straight**^{8} 6476 7-9-6 **73** .... (t) JulieBurke(3) 9 — 62
(Linda Perratt) *hld up: rdn over 2f out: edgd rt and btn over 1f out* **33/1**

2040 **9** *8* **Golden Future**^{21} 6076 9-9-1 **65** .... (p) TomEaves 11 — 42
(Peter Niven) *led: rdn and hdd over 2f out: wknd over 1f out* **33/1**

2140 **10** *2 1/4* **King Of Windsor (IRE)**^{21} 6073 5-10-0 **78** .... (p) PaulMulrennan 6 — 52
(Keith Dalgleish) *hld up on ins: rdn over 2f out: sn btn* **7/1**^{3}

326 **11** *97* **Raleigh Quay (IRE)**^{47} 5188 5-9-5 **69** .... PJMcDonald 10
(Micky Hammond) *prom: drvn 1/2-way: struggling over 4f out: lost tch fnl 3f* **14/1**

2m 58.27s (6.27) **Going Correction** +0.525s/f (Yiel)
WFA 3 from 4yo+ 9lb — 11 Ran SP% **115.6**
Speed ratings (Par 105): **101,100,98,97,97 96,93,92,87,86 26**
Tote Swingers: 1&2 £2.70, 1&3 £6.70, 2&3 £6.30 CSF £10.50 CT £84.40 TOTE £2.80: £1.40, £2.20, £3.00; EX 10.30.
Owner Charles C Walker - Osborne House **Bred** C C And Mrs D J Buckley **Trained** Newmarket, Suffolk

FOCUS

Stands' bend out 2m. Jockeys who rode in the first had a different opinon about the going compared to the official good to soft. Some riders described the ground as "soft" or "very soft". An ordinary staying contest, in which the gallop didn't look strong for much of the early stages. The time was ordinary but the winner was unexposed and is likely to do better.

Raleigh Quay(IRE) Official explanation: trainer's rep said gelding bled from the nose

6707 ROYAL SCOTS CLUB NURSERY — 5f

2:00 (2:00) (Class 6) (0-65,69) 2-Y-O **£2,264** (£673; £336; £168) **Stalls** High

Form — RPR

5014 **1** **Ena Sharples**^{18} 6130 2-9-4 **62** .... AdrianNicholls 10 — 64
(David Nicholls) *hung rt most of way: chsd ldrs: led over 1f out: drvn out fnl f* **6/1**^{2}

5504 **2** *nk* **Someone's Darling**^{58} 4767 2-9-2 **60** .... GrahamLee 1 — 61
(Jim Goldie) *prom on outside: effrt and edgd lft over 1f out: ev ch ins fnl f: kpt on: hld cl home* **18/1**

0640 **3** *1 1/4* **Marabout (IRE)**^{19} 6121 2-8-11 **55** .... PaulMulrennan 5 — 52
(Mel Brittain) *in tch: drvn along 1/2-way: effrt over 1f out: kpt on fnl f: hld towards fin* **11/1**

042 **4** *hd* **Star Request**^{32} 5727 2-9-4 **62** .... TomEaves 9 — 58
(Keith Dalgleish) *towards rr: drvn 1/2-way: hdwy 1f out: kpt on fnl f: nvr able to chal* **9/4**^{1}

0320 **5** *3 1/4* **Fly Fisher (IRE)**^{17} 6177 2-8-13 **64** .... GeorgeChaloner(7) 6 — 48
(Ian Semple) *dwlt: bhd and drvn along: styd on fnl f: nvr on terms* **28/1**

1634 **6** *shd* **Charlemagne Diva**^{16} 6212 2-9-0 **58** .... (p) PJMcDonald 7 — 42
(Ann Duffield) *cl up: drvn along 2f out: wknd fnl f* **18/1**

060 **7** *1* **Ridgeblade**^{12} 6335 2-8-3 **50** .... NeilFarley(3) 2 — 30
(Noel Wilson) *cl up tl rdn and wknd ent fnl f* **9/1**^{3}

3251 **8** *2 1/2* **Coconut Kisses**^{12} 6336 2-9-4 **69** .... RyanWhile(7) 4 — 40
(Bill Turner) *led to over 1f out: sn rdn and wknd* **9/1**^{3}

0600 **9** *1 1/4* **Municipal (IRE)**^{18} 6130 2-8-12 **56** .... TonyHamilton 8 — 23
(Michael Dods) *s.i.s: sn drvn in rr: hung rt 1/2-way: nvr on terms* **20/1**

1m 3.23s (2.83) **Going Correction** +0.525s/f (Yiel) — 9 Ran SP% **92.1**
Speed ratings (Par 93): **98,97,95,95,90 89,88,84,82**
Tote Swingers: 1&2 £4.40, 1&3 £11.90, 2&3 £23.90 CSF £65.99 TOTE £6.00: £1.50, £2.60, £2.80; EX 56.00.
Owner Ms Sara Hattersley **Bred** T Holdcroft & T Herbert-Jackson **Trained** Sessay, N Yorks
■ Sandsend (7/2) was withdrawn (broke out of stalls and fatally injured). Deduct 20p in the 3 under R4.

FOCUS

A modest contest and straightforward, low-grade form.

NOTEBOOK

Ena Sharples showed a good attitude despite hanging right to hold on. She is developing into a good sort for this level. (op 11-2 tchd 13-2 in a place)

Someone's Darling shaped okay over C&D on her previous start, and did give the winner something to think about in the final stages. She has a small race in her. (op 16-1)

Marabout(IRE), dropping 2f in trip, had never been tried over 5f and didn't appear suited by it. One would imagine he'll go up in distance again. (op 16-1)

Star Request, making her handicap debut, looked far from straightforward and isn't one to trust yet. Tom Eaves reported afterwards that the saddle slipped. Official explanation: jockey said saddle slipped (tchd 5-2)

Fly Fisher(IRE) was slowly away but kept on through runners inside the final furlong.

Coconut Kisses, having her first start in a handicap after landing a seller last time, showed speed but found nothing once challenged. (op 6-1)

6708 IRISH STALLION FARMS EBF MAIDEN STKS — 7f 30y

2:30 (2:31) (Class 5) 2-Y-O **£3,234** (£962; £481; £240) **Stalls** Low

Form — RPR

2242 **1** **Dr Phibes (IRE)**^{12} 6337 2-9-3 78 .... RobertWinston 3 — 77+
(Alan Swinbank) *trckd ldr and clr of rest: hdwy to ld over 1f out: edgd rt: rdn clr fnl f* **1/1**^{1}

3 **2** *3 3/4* **Gabrial's Wawa**^{15} 6237 2-9-3 0 .... TonyHamilton 4 — 68+
(Richard Fahey) *t.k.h: rn green towards rr: nt handle either bnd and plenty to do ent st: gd hdwy 2f out: wnt 2nd nr fin: no ch w wnr* **7/2**^{3}

0 **3** *hd* **Eric The Grey (IRE)**^{24} 5963 2-8-12 0 .... ShaneDKelly(5) 6 — 66
(Richard Fahey) *s.i.s: rn green in rr: hdwy to chse (clr) ldng pair 2f out: wnt 2nd briefly wl ins fnl f: no imp* **20/1**

6032 **4** *3* **Funding Deficit (IRE)**^{11} 6356 2-9-3 77 .... GrahamGibbons 1 — 59
(David Barron) *t.k.h: led to over 1f out: no ex and lost two pls wl ins fnl f* **2/1**^{2}

00 **5** *12* **Fake Or Fortune (IRE)**^{41} 5410 2-9-3 0 .... DuranFentiman 8 — 30
(Tim Walford) *chsd clr ldng pair: drvn over 3f out: wknd 2f out* **50/1**

50 **6** *3/4* **Alkcama (IRE)**^{18} 6134 2-9-3 0 .... PaulMulrennan 2 — 28
(John Weymes) *in tch tl rdn and wknd over 2f out* **28/1**

00 **7** *nk* **Windsor Secret**^{15} 6257 2-8-12 0 .... TomEaves 5 — 22
(Keith Dalgleish) *towards rr: struggling 3f out: nvr on terms* **66/1**

00 **8** *2 1/4* **Swaying Grace (IRE)**^{16} 6214 2-8-12 0 .... PJMcDonald 7 — 16
(Ann Duffield) *towards rr: struggling over 3f out: sn btn* **66/1**

1m 33.69s (4.69) **Going Correction** +0.525s/f (Yiel) — 8 Ran SP% **118.7**
Speed ratings (Par 95): **94,89,89,86,72 71,71,68**
Tote Swingers: 1&2 £5.40, 1&3 £1.50, 2&3 £4.50 CSF £5.05 TOTE £2.10: £1.02, £1.40, £4.60; EX 4.10.
Owner Solway Stayers **Bred** Timothy J Rooney **Trained** Melsonby, N Yorks

FOCUS

A somewhat bizarre race. The early leader went off far too quickly, while the second stayed on after losing lots of ground. The form makes sense.

NOTEBOOK

Dr Phibes(IRE) had shown more than enough to take a contest of this nature, and he finally got off the mark after sitting just behind the leader. The gelding clearly enjoyed tracking the strong gallop but doesn't seem an obvious type to win handicaps off a mark in the high 70s or above when faced with less-exposed rivals. (tchd 11-10)

Gabrial's Wawa completely lost his place on the bend (Tony Hamilton reported that the bit slipped through the colt's mouth) and got behind as a result, but he steadily started to pick off rivals and was finishing fast at the end. Official explanation: jockey said bit slipped through colt's mouth

Eric The Grey(IRE) was slowly into stride but made good progress throughout the home straight and is at least going the right way. (op 22-1)

Funding Deficit(IRE) had progressed with every outing but simply set fractions he couldn't maintain. It didn't come as a surprise to see him fade in the final stages. (op 5-2 tchd 11-4)

6709 GRAPHIC IMPRESSIONS COLOUR PRINTERS H'CAP — 7f 30y

3:00 (3:01) (Class 5) (0-70,70) 3-Y-O+ **£3,234** (£962; £481; £240) **Stalls** Low

Form — RPR

1646 **1** **Steel Stockholder**^{19} 6127 6-9-5 **68** .... PaulMulrennan 8 — 76
(Mel Brittain) *pressed ldr: led 2f out: drvn out fnl f* **5/1**^{2}

0053 **2** *2* **Just The Tonic**^{5} 6559 5-8-12 **64** .... PaulPickard(3) 3 — 67
(Marjorie Fife) *towards rr: effrt on outside over 2f out: styd on fnl f: tk 2nd cl home: nt rch wnr* **4/1**^{1}

2410 **3** *hd* **Chookie Avon**^{18} 6141 5-9-7 **70** .... (p) TomEaves 10 — 72
(Keith Dalgleish) *in tch on outside: effrt and edgd rt over 1f out: kpt on same pce wl ins fnl f* **14/1**

3400 **4** *nk* **Rio Cobolo (IRE)**^{15} 6260 6-9-0 **63** .... (p) AdrianNicholls 6 — 64
(David Nicholls) *led: rdn and hdd 2f out: rallied: kpt on same pce ins fnl f* **6/1**^{3}

100 **5** *1 1/4* **Rex Romanorum (IRE)**^{10} 6410 4-9-4 **67** .... DanielTudhope 9 — 65
(Patrick Holmes) *in tch: effrt and rdn over 2f out: kpt on ins fnl f* **9/1**

0055 **6** *5* **Mujaadel (USA)**^{19} 6127 7-9-1 **64** .... (v) AndrewMullen 1 — 48
(David Nicholls) *hld up on ins: rdn over 2f out: no imp over 1f out* **7/1**

4430 **7** *nk* **Polar Annie**^{37} 5539 7-9-5 **68** .... GrahamLee 2 — 52
(Jim Goldie) *in tch: n.m.r and lost pl bnd ent st: effrt whn n.m.r briefly over 2f out: sme late hdwy: nvr on terms* **8/1**

005 **8** *nk* **Mcmonagle (USA)**^{10} 6410 4-9-2 **65** .... (tp) RobertWinston 5 — 48
(Alan Brown) *trckd ldrs: rdn over 2f out: wknd appr fnl f* **10/1**

5531 **9** *9* **Hoppy's Flyer (FR)**^{8} 6480 4-9-2 **65** .... (v) MickyFenton 12 — 23
(Paul Midgley) *t.k.h: hld up on outside: drvn over 2f out: sn btn* **5/1**^{2}

0-00 **10** *6* **Fairlie Dinkum**^{52} 4996 4-9-2 **68** .... NeilFarley(3) 4
(Andrew Crook) *s.i.s: rdn in rr over 3f out: btn fnl 2f* **28/1**

1m 32.92s (3.92) **Going Correction** +0.525s/f (Yiel)
WFA 3 from 4yo+ 3lb — 10 Ran SP% **120.4**
Speed ratings (Par 103): **98,95,95,95,93 88,87,87,77,70**
Tote Swingers: 1&2 £4.60, 1&3 £5.90, 2&3 £14.60 CSF £26.28 CT £275.13 TOTE £6.30: £2.00, £1.80, £3.90; EX 29.20.
Owner Mel Brittain **Bred** Mrs Joan M Langmead **Trained** Warthill, N Yorks

FOCUS

These were all exposed types, who didn't hold many secrets from the handicapper. Ordinary form, rated around the first three.

Hoppy's Flyer(FR) Official explanation: jockey said filly lost its action final furlong

6710 ROYAL SCOTS EBF FILLIES' H'CAP — 1m

3:35 (3:35) (Class 3) (0-90,84) 3-Y-O+

£8,092 (£2,423; £1,211; £605; £302; £152) **Stalls** Low

Form — RPR

5603 **1** **No Poppy (IRE)**^{8} 6471 4-9-3 **81** .... AdamCarter(5) 9 — 94
(Tim Easterby) *sn pushed along in rr: plenty to do 1/2-way: gd hdwy on outside to ld 2f out: edgd rt: pushed clr fnl f* **8/1**

05 **2** *6* **Zaina (IRE)**^{16} 6206 3-8-9 **72** .... (p) AmyRyan 1 — 71
(Gerard Butler) *towards rr: pushed along 1/2-way: hdwy to chse wnr over 1f out: kpt on fnl f: nt pce to chal* **11/2**^{3}

4100 **3** *nk* **Silvas Romana (IRE)**^{11} 6375 3-9-0 **77** .... PaulMulrennan 7 — 76
(Mark Brisbourne) *hld up: rdn over 3f out: hdwy on outside over 1f out: kpt on fnl f: nrst fin* **22/1**

3655 **4** *2* **Hot Rod Mamma (IRE)**^{8} 6476 5-9-5 **81** .... LucyAlexander(3) 8 — 75
(Dianne Sayer) *swtchd rt s: bhd: stdy hdwy whn n.m.r briefly over 2f out: effrt and rdn over 1f out: edgd rt and one pce fnl f* **10/1**

1602 **5** *2* **Act Your Shoe Size**^{6} 6526 3-9-6 **83** .... GrahamLee 4 — 72
(Keith Dalgleish) *in tch: drvn along over 2f out: outpcd over 1f out* **11/1**

2331 **6** *2 3/4* **Miss Ellany (IRE)**^{43} 5372 3-9-7 **84** .... DanielTudhope 3 — 67
(David O'Meara) *sn w ldr: rdn over 2f out: wknd over 1f out* **2/1**^{1}

1610 **7** *nk* **Lady Chaparral**[33] 5712 5-9-9 **82**................................ TomEaves 6 64
(Michael Dods) *chsd ldrs: drvn 3f out: wknd over 1f out* **13/2**
4650 **8** *1 ½* **Honeymead (IRE)**[22] 6023 4-9-9 **82**.................... TonyHamilton 2 61
(Richard Fahey) *in tch: effrt whn n.m.r briefly and edgd rt 2f out: sn btn* **9/2**[2]
4016 **9** *1 ¼* **First Class Favour (IRE)**[15] 6241 4-8-12 **71**.............. DuranFentiman 5 47
(Tim Easterby) *led at decent gallop: rdn and hdd 2f out: sn btn* **33/1**
1m 44.54s (3.34) **Going Correction** +0.525s/f (Yiel)
WFA 3 from 4yo+ 4lb **9** Ran SP% **116.1**
Speed ratings (Par 104): **104,98,97,95,93 90,90,89,87**
Tote Swingers: 1&2 £12.00, 1&3 £12.70, 2&3 £21.10 CSF £51.74 CT £939.66 TOTE £6.70: £2.60, £1.80, £6.00; EX 58.80.
Owner Exors Of The Late Mrs P M Easterby **Bred** Michael O'Mahony **Trained** Great Habton, N Yorks

FOCUS
The leaders again went off far too quickly and being at the rear in the opening stages was a big advantage. It's hard to take the winner's effort at face value but she has been accorded a small personal best.

NOTEBOOK
No Poppy(IRE), fourth in this last year, found plenty for pressure after getting behind to end up winning comfortably. Racing off 3lb above her previous highest successful mark here, she doesn't look an obvious candidate to follow up even though she loves soft ground. (op 7-1 tchd 6-1)
Zaina(IRE), without a tongue-tie this time, needed plenty of driving a long way out but plugged on for second inside the final furlong. (op 17-2)
Silvas Romana(IRE) had been well beaten on her last two outings, so this looked a step back in the right direction. (op 18-1)
Hot Rod Mamma(IRE) ◆ is edging down to her last winning official rating, and is definitely one to keep an eye on in the coming weeks. (op 9-1 tchd 8-1)
Act Your Shoe Size (op 9-1 tchd 12-1)
Miss Ellany(IRE), up 7lb for her Ripon success back in August, did too much early. Daniel Tudhope later reported that the filly ran flat. Official explanation: jockey said filly ran flat (op 5-2)

6711 ROTECH M&P LTD. H'CAP 1m 1f
4:10 (4:10) (Class 5) (0-70,70) 3-Y-O+ **£3,408** (£1,006; £503) **Stalls** Low

Form RPR
4242 **1** **Dark Ruler (IRE)**[8] 6477 3-9-2 **67**............................ RobertWinston 14 75
(Alan Swinbank) *t.k.h: cl up on outside: ev ch over 2f out: edgd rt and led ins fnl f: drvn and hld on wl* **11/1**
1023 **2** *hd* **Ebony Clarets**[9] 6429 3-8-12 **63**.............................. FrederikTylicki 9 70
(Linda Perratt) *cl up: led and rdn over 2f out: hdd ins fnl f: rallied: hld nr fin* **12/1**
4514 **3** *½* **Edas**[18] 6131 10-8-9 **60** ow2................................ GarryWhillans(5) 10 66
(Thomas Cuthbert) *in tch on outside: smooth hdwy and ev ch 2f out: sn rdn: kpt on fnl f: hld nr fin* **11/1**
5431 **4** *1 ¾* **Dubai Celebration**[26] 5917 4-8-13 **59**.......................... PaddyAspell 1 64
(Julie Camacho) *t.k.h: trckd ldrs: effrt and rdn over 2f out: kpt on ins fnl f* **3/1**[1]
3040 **5** *¾* **Feeling Good**[8] 6502 3-8-8 **59**.................................... DaleSwift 4 63
(Brian Ellison) *midfield on ins: rdn over 2f out: hdwy over 1f out: r.o fnl f* **18/1**
0010 **6** *½* **Monthly Medal**[15] 6258 9-8-12 **58**...............................(t) AmyRyan 2 61+
(Wilf Storey) *hld up: effrt whn n.m.r briefly over 2f out and over 1f out: r.o fnl f: nvr able to chal* **10/1**[3]
2320 **7** *1 ¼* **Military Call**[15] 6262 5-8-11 **57**...............................(v) PJMcDonald 12 57
(Alistair Whillans) *midfield on outside: effrt and rdn over 2f out: edgd rt and one pce over 1f out* **14/1**
2004 **8** *2* **Mangham (IRE)**[13] 6313 7-8-9 **58**..............................(p) NeilFarley(3) 13 53
(George Foster) *hld up: rdn over 2f out: styd on fnl f: nvr able to chal* **20/1**
0236 **9** *3 ¾* **Berbice (IRE)**[8] 6479 7-8-10 **59**.................................... JulieBurke(3) 11 46
(Linda Perratt) *stdd s: hld up: stdy hdwy whn nt clr run over 2f out: rdn: hung rt and no imp over 1f out* **25/1**
6000 **10** *1 ¾* **Pirate Chest (IRE)**[18] 6141 4-9-3 **63**........................(t) DanielTudhope 6 46
(Patrick Holmes) *in tch: drvn and outpcd over 2f out: n.d after* **33/1**
3466 **11** *nk* **Sangar**[10] 6410 4-9-2 **62**......................................(b) MichaelO'Connell 5 45
(Ollie Pears) *t.k.h in midfield: effrt on outside over 2f out: edgd rt: wknd over 1f out* **4/1**[2]
0004 **12** *nk* **Seldom (IRE)**[15] 6259 6-8-13 **59**............................ PaulMulrennan 8 41
(Mel Brittain) *led tl rdn and hdd over 2f out: wknd over 1f out* **16/1**
2001 **13** *4 ½* **Cadgers Brig**[15] 6262 4-9-4 **64**.................................(p) TomEaves 3 36
(Keith Dalgleish) *sn drvn along and early reminders in rr: struggling 3f out: nvr on terms* **10/1**[3]
0000 **14** *1* **Northern Fling**[47] 5186 8-9-10 **70**............................ GrahamLee 7 40
(Jim Goldie) *midfield on outside: lost pl bnd over 4f out: n.d after* **20/1**
1m 58.36s (4.46) **Going Correction** +0.525s/f (Yiel)
WFA 3 from 4yo+ 5lb **14** Ran SP% **121.7**
Speed ratings (Par 103): **101,100,100,100,99 99,97,96,92,91 90,90,86,85**
Tote Swingers: 1&2 £13.30, 1&3 £20.20, 2&3 £13.50 CSF £131.02 CT £1503.02 TOTE £10.00: £3.10, £2.80, £4.70; EX 68.20.
Owner Mrs E Walters **Bred** John Thompson **Trained** Melsonby, N Yorks
■ Stewards' Enquiry : Garry Whillans four-day ban: used whip above permitted level (Oct 14-17)

FOCUS
Modest stuff but it was sound run and produced a good finish. Ordinary form, but sound enough.

6712 ROYAL REGIMENT OF SCOTLAND H'CAP (DIV II) 1m 5f
4:45 (4:45) (Class 4) (0-80,76) 3-Y-O+ **£5,175** (£1,540; £769; £384) **Stalls** Low

Form RPR
5130 **1** **Ukrainian (IRE)**[26] 5913 3-9-4 **75**.............................(v[1]) FrederikTylicki 1 91
(Mark Johnston) *pressed ldr: led in centre 3f out: rdn clr 2f out* **5/1**[2]
501 **2** *8* **Generous Dream**[33] 5714 4-9-2 **64**............................ PaulMulrennan 4 68
(Mel Brittain) *chsd ldng pair: effrt and wnt 2nd over 2f out: rdn and edgd rt over 1f out: kpt on: no imp* **11/1**
4050 **3** *1 ¾* **Jonny Delta**[30] 5798 5-9-8 **70**.................................... GrahamLee 10 71
(Jim Goldie) *hld up: stdy hdwy and in tch over 3f out: drvn and kpt on same pce fr 2f out* **11/2**[3]
-053 **4** *nk* **Beat The Shower**[81] 3953 6-9-8 **70**............................ PJMcDonald 6 71
(Peter Niven) *hld up: rdn and hdwy over 2f out: kpt on fnl f: nvr able to chal* **12/1**
0122 **5** *1* **Nordic Quest (IRE)**[6] 6537 3-9-5 **76**.......................... TonyHamilton 9 75+
(Gerard Butler) *t.k.h: hld up in midfield: n.m.r and shuffled bk bnd over 3f out: effrt and drvn over 2f out: no imp over 1f out* **11/8**[1]
0310 **6** *8* **La Bacouetteuse (FR)**[13] 6311 7-9-5 **72**..............(b[1]) GarryWhillans(5) 7 59
(Iain Jardine) *hld up: rdn over 3f out: nvr able to chal* **20/1**
6000 **7** *1 ¼* **Odin's Raven (IRE)**[8] 6472 7-9-3 **68**........................ PaulPickard(3) 3 54
(Brian Ellison) *s.i.s: bhd: drvn over 5f out: sme late hdwy: nvr on terms* **11/1**
-000 **8** *hd* **Full Speed (GER)**[12] 6339 7-9-3 **65**........................ MichaelO'Connell 8 50
(Philip Kirby) *led to 3f out: sn drvn and wknd 2f out* **40/1**
4005 **9** *14* **Silk Drum (IRE)**[13] 6311 7-8-9 **62**......................(t) ShaneBKelly(5) 5 26
(Dianne Sayer) *in tch: struggling over 3f out: sn btn: t.o* **14/1**
6330 **10** *17* **Chookie Hamilton**[26] 5921 8-8-12 **60**............................ TomEaves 2
(Ian Semple) *in tch to 3f out: sn rdn and btn: t.o* **25/1**
2m 57.12s (5.12) **Going Correction** +0.525s/f (Yiel)
WFA 3 from 4yo+ 9lb **10** Ran SP% **116.2**
Speed ratings (Par 105): **105,100,99,98,98 93,92,92,83,73**
Tote Swingers: 1&2 £6.00, 1&3 £4.50, 2&3 £5.50 CSF £56.74 CT £314.29 TOTE £6.20: £2.20, £2.40, £1.80; EX 41.60.
Owner Sheikh Majid Bin Mohammed al Maktoum **Bred** Mrs Fiona McStay **Trained** Middleham Moor, N Yorks

FOCUS
The faster division but few got involved. The winner impressed and the form has been rated at face value.
Nordic Quest(IRE) Official explanation: jockey said colt was denied a clear run

6713 SCOTTISH RACING H'CAP 5f
5:15 (5:15) (Class 6) (0-60,60) 3-Y-O+ **£2,264** (£673; £336; £168) **Stalls** High

Form RPR
4304 **1** **Distant Sun (USA)**[6] 6531 8-9-2 **55**.............................(p) AmyRyan 9 63
(Linda Perratt) *mde all: rdn 2f out: kpt on strly fnl f* **12/1**[3]
6334 **2** *1 ¾* **Hadrians Rule (IRE)**[35] 5621 3-9-3 **57**..................(p) DanielTudhope 5 59
(Tim Easterby) *in tch: hdwy on outside wl over 1f out: sn rdn: edgd lft and chsd wnr ins fnl f* **4/1**[1]
1050 **3** *nk* **Alnair (IRE)**[15] 6264 3-9-6 **60**..............................(b[1]) GrahamGibbons 3 61
(Declan Carroll) *hld up: rdn and hdwy over 1f out: edgd rt 1f out: kpt on fnl f* **12/1**[3]
6600 **4** *2* **Angelo Poliziano**[15] 6264 6-8-10 **54**..................................[1] LMcNiff(5) 10 47
(George Foster) *blindfold slow to remove: bhd tl hdwy appr fnl f: r.o: nvr able to chal* **18/1**
31 **5** *¾* **Ingenti**[32] 5740 4-9-7 **60**.. PaddyAspell 1 51
(Christopher Wilson) *cl up: rdn and ev ch over 1f out: no ex ins fnl f* **6/1**[2]
4353 **6** *2* **Here Now And Why (IRE)**[13] 6314 5-9-2 **55**.........(p) DuranFentiman 11 39
(Ian Semple) *t.k.h: hld up bhd ldng gp: effrt and rdn 2f out: one pce* **4/1**[1]
0044 **7** *5* **Saxonette**[20] 6104 4-8-13 **52**......................................(p) PJMcDonald 2 18
(Linda Perratt) *bhd on outside: struggling over 2f out: sn btn* **16/1**
5021 **8** *4 ½* **Roy's Legacy**[15] 6249 3-9-6 **60**..................................(t) RobertWinston 6
(Shaun Harris) *cl up: rdn over 2f out: one pce whn checked 1f out* **6/1**[2]
0460 **9** *¾* **Rock Canyon (IRE)**[6] 6529 3-9-3 **57**.......................(p) FrederikTylicki 4
(Linda Perratt) *cl up untl rdn and wknd over 1f out* **20/1**
54-3 **10** *shd* **Mission Impossible**[32] 5739 7-9-7 **60**..................(p) PatrickMathers 13
(Tracy Waggott) *cl up: drvn along 1/2-way: wknd over 1f out* **4/1**[1]
1m 2.76s (2.36) **Going Correction** +0.525s/f (Yiel)
WFA 3 from 4yo+ 1lb **10** Ran SP% **119.9**
Speed ratings (Par 101): **102,99,98,95,94 91,83,75,74,74**
Tote Swingers: 1&2 £12.40, 1&3 £31.30, 2&3 £8.60 CSF £61.32 CT £606.52 TOTE £16.80: £3.50, £1.80, £3.40; EX 103.00.
Owner Jackton Racing Club **Bred** Forging Oaks Llc **Trained** East Kilbride, S Lanarks

FOCUS
A modest if open handicap. It's doubtful if the winner improved and he's rated to his best form in the past year.
Angelo Poliziano Official explanation: jockey said blindfold became stuck on hood making it difficult to remove and gelding was slow away.
Roy's Legacy Official explanation: jockey said colt missed the break and lost its action
T/Jkpt: £8,678.70 to a £1 stake. Pool: £36,671.00 - 3.00 winning tickets. T/Plt: £316.10 to a £1 stake. Pool: £70,359.00 - 162.47 winning tickets. T/Qpdt: £35.70 to a £1 stake. Pool: £6,408.00 - 132.70 winning tickets. RY

6714 - 6715a (Foreign Racing) - See Raceform Interactive

6265 CURRAGH (R-H)
Sunday, September 30

OFFICIAL GOING: Heavy

6716a IRISH STALLION FARMS JOE MCGRATH EUROPEAN BREEDERS FUND H'CAP (PREMIER HANDICAP) 6f
3:10 (3:11) 3-Y-O+ **£24,375** (£7,125; £3,375; £1,125)

RPR
1 **Bubbly Bellini (IRE)**[22] 6064 5-9-0 **85**..........................(p) IJBrennan(3) 4 96
(Adrian McGuinness, Ire) *racd in mid-div: 8th 3f out: clsd under 2f out and pushed along between horses to ld 150yds out: qcknd wl: comf* **11/1**
2 *3 ¼* **Joe Eile (IRE)**[35] 5640 4-9-6 **88**............................ EmmetMcNamara 9 89
(G M Lyons, Ire) *chsd ldrs: 5th 3f out: pushed along to ld narrowly gng wl 1f out: qckly jnd and hdd ins fnl 150yds: no ex* **10/3**[1]
3 *½* **Stones Peak (IRE)**[35] 5640 5-8-9 **80**........................ RonanWhelan(3) 10 79
(Patrick Martin, Ire) *mid-div: short of room appr 1f out: rdn and swtchd to far side and styd on strly into 3rd towards fin: nvr nrr* **10/1**
4 *¾* **Nini Ok (IRE)**[15] 6270 3-8-3 **78**........................ DerekMcCormack(5) 13 75
(John Joseph Murphy, Ire) *chsd ldrs: 7th 3f out: n.m.r and swtchd rt: kpt on far side: nvr nrr* **10/1**
5 *nk* **Allegra Tak (ITY)**[70] 4380 6-8-10 **78**..........................(t) ChrisHayes 14 74
(H Rogers, Ire) *broke wl to ld early: edgd rt appr fnl f and hdd: wknd* **16/1**
6 *shd* **Arbitrageur (IRE)**[20] 6110 3-8-4 **79**............................ ConorHoban(5) 5 75
(Donal Kinsella, Ire) *chsd ldrs: 4th 3f out: sn rdn and no imp ent fnl f* **10/1**
7 *nk* **Invincible Ridge (IRE)**[15] 6270 4-9-0 **85**..................(t) LeighRoche(3) 16 80
(D J Bunyan, Ire) *trckd ldr in 2nd: rdn 1 1/2f out and one pce fnl f* **12/1**
8 *¾* **Hi Emperor (IRE)**[91] 3673 3-8-4 **74**............................ MichaelHussey 11 66
(Sean P Hennessy, Ire) *hld up towards rr: nvr a threat* **14/1**
9 *hd* **Measured Approval (IRE)**[27] 5895 4-8-6 **77**................ SamJames(3) 8 69
(Patrick J Flynn, Ire) *mid-div: rdn under 2f out and kpt on towards fin* **8/1**[3]
10 *nk* **Topadee (IRE)**[17] 6182 5-7-13 **74**............................ ShaneGray(7) 2 65
(Patrick J Flynn, Ire) *hld up in rr: pushed along over 2f out and sme late hdwy far side appr fnl f: n.d* **12/1**
11 *2* **First In Command (IRE)**[15] 6270 7-9-0 **82**..................(t) PatSmullen 12 66
(Daniel Mark Loughnane) *in rr of mid-div: sme hdwy ent fnl f on nrside: n.d* **7/1**[2]
12 *2 ½* **Toufan Express**[3] 6621 10-8-4 **72**............................ NGMcCullagh 15 48
(Adrian McGuinness, Ire) *in rr of mid-div: 9th 3f out: n.d fnl 2f: kpt on* **16/1**
13 *¾* **Core Element (IRE)**[7] 6520 5-9-0 **82**............................ ShaneFoley 3 56
(S Buggy, Ire) *chsd ldrs: 6th 3f out: no ex whn hmpd 1f out: eased* **14/1**
14 *1 ¾* **Possible**[51] 5068 3-8-13 **83**.. WayneLordan 7 51
(Charles O'Brien, Ire) *hld up towards rr: pushed along 2f out and sn n.d: eased* **8/1**[3]

15 *14* **Tornadodancer (IRE)**[254] 237 9-8-4 72..........(b) BenCurtis 1
(T G McCourt, Ire) *towards rr: nvr a factor* **25/1**

16 *23* **Battleroftheboyne (IRE)**[15] 6270 3-9-10 94.......... JPO'Brien 17
(Michael Mulvany, Ire) *prom on nrside: 3rd 1/2-way: sn pushed along and wknd qckly: eased: t.o* **10/1**

1m 17.59s (2.09) **Going Correction** +0.525s/f (Yiel) **16** Ran SP% **146.8**
WFA 3 from 4yo+ 2lb
Speed ratings: **107,102,102,101,100 100,100,99,98,98 95,92,91,89,70 39**
CSF £57.03 CT £423.16 TOTE £22.50: £3.40, £1.20, £3.20, £3.10; DF 92.70.
Owner Gary Devlin **Bred** J P Hand **Trained** Lusk, Co Dublin

FOCUS
The form is rated around the second and sixth, with another personal best from the progressive winner.

NOTEBOOK
Bubbly Bellini(IRE), rated 50 on the first day of June, has made fine progression.confirmed his status as one of the season's most progressive handicappers by winning this off 85. Over a four-month period he has won five of his 11 races, and has been out of the first four only twice, a terrific credit to trainer Ado McGuinness. What made this win particularly meritorious was that his two previous runs had hinted that he might be feeling the effects of his strenuous campaign. Not so it seems, and the more likely explanation is that he thrives at sprint distances, with those two outings having been over 7f. Admittedly, he won twice twice over 7f at Limerick during the summer, but his best displaybefore this was in winning the Rockingham over the minimum trip at today's venue. (op 10-1)
Joe Eile(IRE) was well fancied to defy the 8lb rise in the ratings incurred for a course-and-distance win in August. In common with the winner he has been very dependable, finishing out of the money only twice in 11 runs since January. (op 7-2 tchd 4-1)
Stones Peak(IRE) is holding her form really well.
Nini Ok(IRE) can supplement the single win she has achieved so far, in a Kempton maiden last November.
Allegra Tak(ITY) put a couple of below-par efforts behind her.

6717a C.L. WELD PARK STKS (GROUP 3) (FILLIES) 7f
3:40 (3:41) 2-Y-O **£29,791** (£8,708; £4,125; £1,375)

RPR

1 **Magical Dream (IRE)**[21] 6081 2-9-0 103.......... JPO'Brien 4 103
(A P O'Brien, Ire) *trckd ldr: cl 2nd 3f out: pushed along to ld 1 1/2f out: extended advantage ent fnl f and kpt on wl towards fin* **10/3**[2]

2 *2* **Rawaaq**[73] 4276 2-9-0 .... PatSmullen 1 98
(D K Weld, Ire) *hld up towards rr: hdwy under 2f out to go 2nd jst ins fnl f: kpt on wl u.p wout ever troubling wnr* **11/2**

3 *¾* **Uleavemebreathless**[15] 6266 2-9-0 .... ShaneFoley 7 96
(A Oliver, Ire) *hld up: 5th 3f out: hdwy on nrside over 1f out and styd on wl into n.d 3rd fnl strides* **12/1**

4 *hd* **Spinacre (IRE)**[15] 6266 2-9-0 101.......... ChrisHayes 6 95
(Kevin Prendergast, Ire) *in tch: cl 3rd 3f out: rdn under 2f out and one pce ent fnl f* **7/4**[1]

5 *1 ¾* **Wholelotofrosie (IRE)**[13] 6324 2-9-0 82.......... BenCurtis 3 91
(R Donohoe, Ire) *led: hdd over 1 1/2f out and sn wknd* **16/1**

6 *shd* **Starbright (IRE)**[21] 6081 2-9-0 100.......... DeclanMcDonogh 5 91
(Kevin Prendergast, Ire) *chsd ldrs: cl 4th 3f out: rdn and no ex under 2f out* **4/1**[3]

7 *2 ¼* **Reglisse (IRE)**[15] 6266 2-9-0 95..........(p) JohnnyMurtagh 2 85
(Edward Lynam, Ire) *hld up towards rr: pushed along 2f out and no imp ent fnl f* **10/1**

1m 33.66s (2.86) **Going Correction** +0.525s/f (Yiel) **7** Ran SP% **117.5**
Speed ratings: **104,101,100,100,98 98,95**
CSF £22.82 TOTE £3.40: £2.20, £4.00; DF 18.30.
Owner Mrs John Magnier & Michael Tabor & Derrick Smith **Bred** Roncon, Wynatt & Chelston **Trained** Ballydoyle, Co Tipperary

FOCUS
A first win in this race for Aidan O'Brien since the subsequent dual Classic winner Imagine 12 years previously. The winner is rated to her Moyglare Stakes mark.

NOTEBOOK
Magical Dream(IRE) had already had a run in a Group 1, having finished fourth to Sky Lantern in the Moyglare, and she holds an entry in the Prix Marcel Boussac. Barring a poor run in the Debutante Stakes, she has progressed along the right lines since a debut third behind the impressive Blenheim Stakes winner Viztoria at Naas in June. (op 10-3 tchd 7-2)
Rawaaq, a long-priced maiden winner on her debut, stepped up considerably on the form she showed on her first attempt in Pattern company at Leopardstown in July. She should stay one mile in due course. (op 11-2 tchd 6-1)
Uleavemebreathless did well to reverse previous course form with Spinacre, who failed to run up the level that yielded a Listed win over a furlong farther at the venue earlier in the month
Spinacre(IRE) ran below form and should be given another chance. (op 6-4)
Wholelotofrosie(IRE), whose career began modestly, continues to make progress, though the fact that she was beaten off a mark of 82 in a Listowel nursery puts a bit of a cloud above the form. (op 14-1)

6718a JUDDMONTE BERESFORD STKS (GROUP 2) 1m
4:15 (4:15) 2-Y-O **£51,458** (£15,041; £7,125; £2,375)

RPR

1 **Battle Of Marengo (IRE)**[22] 6060 2-9-3 109.......... JPO'Brien 2 110
(A P O'Brien, Ire) *sweated up befhand: broke wl to trck ldr in 2nd: niggled along appr fnl 3f and on terms 2f out: sn led and drvn clr ent fnl f: kpt on wl: eased nr fin* **4/9**[1]

2 *3 ½* **Orgilgo Bay (IRE)**[13] 6324 2-9-3 101.......... GaryCarroll 1 100
(John C McConnell, Ire) *attempted to make all: pushed along and jnd 2f out: sn no ch w wnr: rdn and kpt on wl ins fnl f to hold 2nd* **8/1**

3 *hd* **Probably (IRE)**[15] 6272 2-9-6 103.......... WayneLordan 4 103
(David Wachman, Ire) *settled in 3rd: pushed along 2f out and sn hung rt: kpt on same pce ins fnl f: jst hld for 2nd* **11/2**[3]

4 *2* **Muaanid**[58] 4785 2-9-3 93.......... PatSmullen 5 95
(D K Weld, Ire) *w.w in rr of quartet: niggled along 3f out: rdn under 2f out and swtchd lft: sn no imp: eased cl home* **4/1**[2]

1m 47.77s (1.77) **Going Correction** +0.425s/f (Yiel) **4** Ran SP% **115.7**
Speed ratings: **108,104,104,102**
CSF £5.32 TOTE £1.10; DF 7.60.
Owner Michael Tabor & Derrick Smith & Mrs John Magnier **Bred** Anna Karenina Syndicate **Trained** Ballydoyle, Co Tipperary

FOCUS
Aidan O'Brien has had a splendid record in this event since Johan Cruyff got the ball rolling in 1996. There is not much depth in this form, with the winner and third helping to set the level.

NOTEBOOK
Battle Of Marengo(IRE) ◆ gave his trainer a success that means he needs only two more to equal the tally of 14 achieved by Vincent O'Brien between 1962 and 1991, a roll of honour that included Nijinsky and Sadler's Wells. Having beaten a subsequent impressive maiden winner despite the inconvenience of a slipped saddle in a Listed race at Leopardstown, the Galileo colt was a worthy odds-on favourite and will be on the Group 1 track for next year. He could get a chance to show his mettle at top level in the Racing Post Trophy, won three years ago by St Nicholas Abbey after landing this prize. (op 2-5 tchd 1-2)
Orgilgo Bay(IRE), third in a Listowel nursery off 102, performed creditably to take the runner-up spot.
Probably(IRE) had been put firmly in his place when fourth to the unbeaten Dawn Approach in the Goffs Vincent O'Brien Stakes. (op 6-1 tchd 5-1)
Muaanid had been mentioned by his trainer as a possible nursery type after winning first time out at Galway. (op 4-1 tchd 5-1)

6719 - 6722a (Foreign Racing) - See Raceform Interactive

6085 HANOVER (L-H)
Sunday, September 30

OFFICIAL GOING: Turf: good to soft

6723a GROSSER PREIS JUNGHEINRICH GABELSTAPLER (GROUP 3) (3YO+ FILLIES & MARES) (TURF) 1m 3f
3:55 (4:00) 3-Y-O+
£26,666 (£9,166; £4,583; £2,500; £1,666; £1,250)

RPR

1 **Calipatria**[56] 5-9-5 0.......... GeraldMosse 11 107+
(H-A Pantall, France) *hld up in last pair: rdn to improve over 2 1/2f out: r.o to chal over 1f out: led ent fnl f: edgd rt u.p once clr: styd on* **13/5**[2]

2 *1 ¾* **Berlin Berlin** 3-8-11 0.......... JohanVictoire 4 103
(Markus Klug, Germany) *midfield: rdn over 2 1/2f out: styd on to go 2nd wl ins fnl f: outpcd by wnr cl home* **119/10**

3 *1 ¼* **Waldtraut (GER)**[21] 6085 3-8-11 0.......... JBojko 5 101
(A Wohler, Germany) *midfield: rdn to chal over 2f out: 2nd and stl ev ch 1f out: no ex and dropped to 3rd wl ins fnl f* **6/4**[1]

4 *nse* **Imagery (GER)**[29] 5844 3-8-11 0.......... ADeVries 6 101
(W Giedt, Germany) *led: rdn and strly pressed fr over 2f out: hdd ent fnl f: no ex and dropped to 4th cl home* **54/10**[3]

5 *1* **Amare**[29] 5845 5-9-5 0..........(b) DaneO'Neill 10 100
(P Harley, Germany) *hld up towards rr on outer: rdn over 2 1/2f out: kpt on one pce u.p ins fnl 1 1/2f: wnt 5th fnl strides* **184/10**

6 *shd* **Lana Jolie (GER)**[46] 4-9-5 0.......... GaetanMasure 8 100
(A Wohler, Germany) *trckd ldr in 2nd: rdn and brief effrt over 2f out: outpcd by ldrs over 1f out: kpt on: dropped to 6th fnl strides* **224/10**

7 *nk* **Global Magic (GER)**[70] 4386 4-9-5 0.......... RJuracek 9 99
(A Wohler, Germany) *hld up in last: rdn to improve 3f out: bdly hmpd and forced to switch lft off rail 2f out: styd on ins fnl f: n.d* **28/1**

8 *4 ½* **Hot Blood (IRE)**[29] 5844 4-9-5 0.......... FilipMinarik 7 91
(P Schiergen, Germany) *midfield on outer: rdn 3f out: hung rt u.p and bdly impeded rival on rail 2f out: sn btn: eased ins fnl f* **134/10**

9 *½* **Kasumi (GER)**[29] 5844 5-9-5 0.......... KieranO'Neill 3 90
(R Dzubasz, Germany) *hld up towards rr on inner: rdn 2 1/2f out: btn over 1f out: steadily fdd ins fnl f* **232/10**

10 *¾* **Malaysia (GER)**[70] 3-8-11 0.......... KClijmans 1 88
(R Dzubasz, Germany) *midfield on inner: rdn over 3f out: outpcd and btn over 1f out: fdd* **138/10**

11 *16* **Sworn Sold (GER)**[29] 5844 3-8-11 0.......... APietsch 2 59
(W Hickst, Germany) *prom on inner: rdn over 3f out: steadily lost pl fr over 2f out: dropped to last over 1f out: sn eased and t.o* **15/2**

2m 22.31s (142.31)
WFA 3 from 4yo+ 7lb **11** Ran SP% **133.6**
WIN (incl. 10 euro stake): 36. PLACES: 14, 19, 13. SF: 338.
Owner Sheikh Mohammed **Bred** Aldridge Racing Partnership **Trained** France

6724 - (Foreign Racing) - See Raceform Interactive

6554 SAN SIRO (R-H)
Sunday, September 30

OFFICIAL GOING: Turf: soft

6725a PREMIO COOLMORE (LISTED RACE) (2YO FILLIES) (TURF) 7f 110y
2:10 (12:00) 2-Y-O **£15,833** (£6,966; £3,800; £1,900)

RPR

1 **Sorella Bella (IRE)**[18] 6132 2-8-9 0.......... SamHitchcott 6 96
(Mick Channon) *mde all: shkn up and qcknd appr fnl 1 1/2f: drew clr fr 1f out: comf* **8/11**[1]

2 *3 ½* **Road Tosky (IRE)**[14] 2-8-9 0.......... MEsposito 1 88
(A Peraino, Italy) **39/1**

3 *1 ½* **Kentra (FR)**[42] 2-8-9 0.......... UmbertoRispoli 3 84
(G Botti, Italy) **73/10**

4 *½* **Gold And White (GER)**[36] 5612 2-8-9 0.......... AStarke 2 83
(P Schiergen, Germany) **48/10**[3]

5 *1 ½* **Deflection (IRE)** 2-8-9 0.......... CristianDemuro 8 79
(S Botti, Italy) **12/5**[2]

6 *4* **Green Nashwan** 2-8-9 0.......... DarioVargiu 4 70
(B Grizzetti, Italy) **177/10**

7 *5* **Unexpectedly (IRE)**[49] 2-8-9 0..........(b) GSanna 5 58
(Camilla Trapassi, Italy) **169/10**

1m 34.4s (-1.10) **7** Ran SP% **130.0**
WIN (incl. 1 euro stake): 1.72. PLACES: 1.24, 4.50, 1.88. DF: 40.45.
Owner Mrs Ann C Black **Bred** Rathasker Stud **Trained** West Ilsley, Berks

NOTEBOOK

Sorella Bella (IRE) third to Saturday's Royal Lodge winner Steeler in the Stardom Stakes at Goodwood this summer, was following up her recent maiden win on heavy ground at Carlisle. The roan filly follows Channon's Chilworth Icon and Sandreamer as winners in Italy this year.

6726a PREMIO SERGIO CUMANI (GROUP 3) (3YO+ FILLIES & MARES) (TURF) 1m

3:20 (12:00) 3-Y-O+ £23,333 (£10,266; £5,600 ; £2,800)

RPR

1 **Nova Hawk**50 4 -9-00 CristianDemuro 6 111
(Rod Collet, France) *settled in midfield wl off pce set by clr ldr: stdy hdwy to ld 1 1/2f out: rdn and edgd rt over 1f out: pushed out: a in control* **13/8**1

2 1 3/4 **Cherry Danon (IRE)**46 5249 3 -8-90 AStarke 7 106
(P Schiergen, Germany) *chsd clr ldr: effrt to chal ldrs 1 1/2f out: rdn and r.o fr over 1f out: a hld by wnr* **11/5**2

3 3 **Samba Brazil (GER)**28 3 -8-90 MircoDemuro 1 99
(A Wohler, Germany) *hld up last wl of pce set by clr ldr: last and rdn over 1f out: styd on wl u.p ins fnl f: got up for 3rd on line: nvr on terms w ldrs* **9/2**

4 shd **Paris To Peking (ITY)**1 4 -9-00 FabioBranca 3 100
(S Botti, Italy) *racd in 4th: rdn and nt qckn over 1 1/2f out: one pce u.p fnl f: lost 3rd on line* **24/1**

5 3/4 **Killachy Loose**21 3 -8-90 DarioVargiu 2 97
(B Grizzetti, Italy) *settled one fr last: styd on u.p fnl f: nvr in contention* **34/1**

6 snk **Sunday Nectar (IRE)**68 4764 4 -9-00 Roberto-CarlosMontenegro 5 98
(X Thomas-Demeaulte, France) *settled in 3rd 10 l bhd ldr: effrt u.p to press ldrs 1 1/2f out: one pce fr 1f out: wknd and lost two pls cl home* **27/10**3

7 5 **Cool Wave**21 3 -8-90 MRossini 4 85
(B Grizzetti, Italy) *sweated up: led: sn clr: hdd 1 1/2f out: wknd qckly: eased fnl 110yds* **19/1**

1m 38.9s (-3.20)
WFA 3 from 4yo 4lb 7Ran SP% 126.4
WIN (incl. 1 euro stake): 2.62. PLACES: 1.69, 2.00. DF: 5.24 .
Owner Teruya Yoshida **Bred** Ermyn Lodge Stud Limited **Trained** France

6727a PREMIO VITTORIO DI CAPUA (GROUP 1) (3YO+) (TURF) 1m

3:55 (12:00) 3-Y-O+ £79,166 (£34,833; £19,000 ; £9,500)

RPR

1 **Amaron**31 5782 3 -8-110 MircoDemuro 2 112
(Andreas Lowe, Germany) *pressed ldr: disp 2nd over 1f out: r.o wl u.p to ld 150yds out: hld on wl* **6/4**1

2 1 **Amarillo (IRE)**31 5782 3 -8-110 AStarke 1 110
(P Schiergen, Germany) *trckd ldrs on ins: swtchd outside st: 3rd and hrd rdn but ev ch 1 1/2f out: sltly outpcd over 1f out: r.o u.p fnl f: a hld* **12/5**2

3 nk **Monami (GER)**56 4862 3 -8-80 CristianDemuro 6 106
(A Wohler, Germany) *chsd ldrs on outside: rdn and nt qckn 3f out: 5th and hrd rdn over 1f out: styd on wl fnl 150yds: tk 3rd cl home* **41/5**

4 nk **Silent Killer (IRE)**112 2969 3 -8-110 FabioBranca 4 108
(S Botti, Italy) *led: wnt 2 l clr over 3f out: pressed and rallied over 1f out: hdd 150yds out: lost 3rd cl home* **71/10**

5 3/4 **King Air (FR)**35 5649 5 -9-20 JamieSpencer 7 108
(R Pritchard-Gordon, France) *chsd ldng gp: rdn and nt qckn fr 2f out: kpt on at same pce fnl f* **31/10**3

6 2 3/4 **Storming Loose**91 5 -9-20 DarioVargiu 5 101
(B Grizzetti, Italy) *in rr: effrt on outside to chse ldrs appr 1/2-way: sn rdn and nt qckn: one pce fr 2f out* **28/1**

7 8 **Malossol (USA)**113 2951 3 -8-110 UmbertoRispoli 3 82
(G Botti, Italy) *a towards rr: bhd whn eased ins fnl f* **96/10**

1m 39.7s (-2.40)
WFA 3 from 5yo 4lb 7Ran SP% 129.9
WIN (incl. 1 euro stake): 2.50. PLACES: 1.43, 1.59. DF: 2.83 .
Owner Gestut Winterhauch **Bred** Genesis Green Stud Ltd **Trained** Germany

NOTEBOOK

Amaron returned to form after a couple of below-par efforts to take this poor Group 1. He had beaten subsequent Royal Ascot winner Energizer at Krefeld in April, before finishing a close fourth in the French 2000 Guineas in May.

6728a - 6731a (Foreign Racing) See RI

6274 BATH (L-H)

Monday, October 1

OFFICIAL GOING: Good (good to firm in places) (8.2) changing to good (good to soft in places) after race 1 (2.20)

Wind: Brisk across Weather: Sunny spells

6732 SEDDON CONSTRUCTION NURSERY 1m 2f 46y

2:20 (2:23) (Class 5) (0-75,73) 2-Y-O £2,264 (£673; £336 ; £168) Stalls Low

Form RPR

0410 1 **Felix Fabulla**4 6597 2 -9-672 NickyMackay 8 77
(Hughie Morrison) *trckd ldrs: drvn to ld over 1f out: drvn out* **9/4**2

056 2 1 **Nine Iron (IRE)**57 4846 2 -8-1062 MartinHarley 2 66
(Mick Channon) *in rr: hdwy fr 3f out: chsd wnr over 1f out: styd on wl u.p fnl f: no ex clsng stages* **7/1**3

3321 3 nk **Stiff Upper Lip (IRE)**12 6363 2 -9-268 RichardHughes 7 71
(Richard Hannon) *in tch: hdwy fr 2f out to chse ldng duo over 1f out: kpt on u.p fnl f: nt qckn nr fin* **7/4**1

0001 4 3 1/4 **Knight's Parade (IRE)**18 6156 2 -8-860 (b) HayleyTurner 1 57
(Amanda Perrett) *sn led: rdn 2f out: hdd over 1f out: one pce fnl f: wknd fnl 100yds* **16/1**

5346 5 3 **Heliconia**12 6363 2 -8-557 (b) LukeMorris 4 48
(Sir Mark Prescott Bt) *s.i.s: sn chsng ldr: rdn over 2f out: wknd over 1f out* **20/1**

1 6 hd **Jebril (FR)**35 5655 2 -9-773 DarryllHolland 5 64
(Jonathan Portman) *s.i.s: in rr: sn drvn and rn in snatches: rdn fr 3f out: in tch w ldrs 2f out: sn btn* **9/1**

5630 7 3 1/4 **Walter White (IRE)**12 6363 2 -8-968 ThomasBrown(7) 3 53
(Andrew Balding) *chsd ldrs: rdn 3f out: wknd 2f out* **16/1**

0002 8 3 **Run It Twice (IRE)**18 6156 2 -8-1062 (b) PaulHanagan 9 41
(Brian Meehan) *in rr: rdn and flashed tail over 3f out: c wd and no rspnse u.p sn after* **18/1**

442 9 11 **Just A Pound (IRE)**18 5207 2 -8-562 JemmaMarshall(5) 6 20
(Jo Hughes) *chsd ldrs tl wknd wl over 2f out* **25/1**

0603 10 8 **Red Adair (IRE)**25 5968 2 -8-1365 (b) SeanLevey 10 8
(Richard Hannon) *t.k.h: stdd in rr: rdn and btn* **33/1**

2m 14.47s (3.47) **Going Correction** +0.325s/f (Good) 10Ran SP% 118.2
Speed ratings (Par 95): **99,98,97,95,92 92,90,87,79,72**
toteswingers 1&2 £5.80, 2&3 £5.60, 1&3 £2.90 CSF £18.42 CT £33.53 TOTE £3.60 : £1.50 , £2.10, £1.10 ; EX 28.30 Trifecta £102.70 Pool: £1,197.36 - 8.62 winning tickets. .
Owner Mrs I Eavis **Bred** Llety Stud **Trained** East Ilsley, Berks

FOCUS

There was 12.5 yards added to race distances that included the bottom bend. The going was inaccurately described as good, good to firm in places at the start of the meeting, and then changed to good, good to soft in places following this opener. Times suggested it was on the soft side. This was just an ordinary nursery, but the form looks reliable with the third setting the level and the first two capable of better.

NOTEBOOK

Felix Fabulla struggled in a much better nursery than this over 1m at Newmarket four days earlier, but prior to that he'd won over C&D and he defied a 5lb higher mark. He's reportedly likely to be gelded at some point and should have more to offer. (op 11-4)

Nine Iron (IRE)◆ had been gelded after hinting at ability in maidens at up to 7f during the summer and he returned from a two-month break with an improved performance. He looks up to winning off a mark in the 60s. (op 8-1)

Stiff Upper Lip (IRE) successful in a Kempton nursery last time, had previously finished runner-up behind Felix Fabulla over C&D. Up 4lb, he ran his race to finish clear of the others. (op 2-1)

Knight's Parade (IRE) was up 5lb for winning on his nursery debut when fitted with first-time blinkers over 1m at Chepstow, but he failed to prove his stamina.

Heliconia is not progressing. (tchd 18-1)

6733 BRITISH STALLION STUDS EBF MAIDEN STKS 1m 2f 46y

2:50 (2:52) (Class 5) 2-Y-O £3,234 (£962; £481 ; £240) Stalls Low

Form RPR

0 1 **Rundell**9 6486 2 -9-30 RichardHughes 9 77+
(Richard Hannon) *in rr: racd wd fr 7f out: hdwy on outer over 3f out: rdn and styd on fr 2f out to ld ins fnl f: r.o strly clsng stages* **11/4**1

0 2 1/2 **Esteaming**9 6481 2 -9-30 MartinHarley 7 76
(Mick Channon) *in rr: rdn and hdwy on inner over 2f out: styd on wl u.p fnl f to take 2nd fnl 50yds but nt quite pce of wnr* **4/1**3

3 3/4 **Newsreader (USA)** 2 -9-30 SilvestreDeSousa 4 75
(Mahmood Al Zarooni) *chsd ldrs: led over 2f out: sn rdn: hdd ins fnl f: one pce and lost 2nd fnl 50yds* **7/2**2

045 4 5 **Roman Order (IRE)**34 5704 2 -9-369 PaulHanagan 5 65
(Brian Meehan) *chsd ldrs: drvn to chal over 2f out: wknd 1f out* **9/2**

0 5 6 **Khotan**17 6214 2 -9-30 LukeMorris 2 56+
(Sir Mark Prescott Bt) *in tch: rdn along fr 5f out: btn ins fnl 3f* **14/1**

665 6 9 **Luv U Whatever**8 6512 2 -9-30 (b1) J-PGuillambert 3 37
(Jo Hughes) *led tl hdd & wknd qckly over 2f out* **100/1**

7 7 **Misteray** 2 -8-100 JakePayne(7) 8 23
(Bill Turner) *chsd ldrs: rdn 4f out: sn btn* **50/1**

8 39 **Sir Frank Morgan (IRE)** 2 -9-30 NeilCallan 6
(Mark Johnston) *green and rdn in rr: nvr travellng: lost tch fnl 4f* **7/1**

2m 14.0s (3.00) **Going Correction** +0.325s/f (Good) 8Ran SP% 109.2
Speed ratings (Par 95): **101,100,100,96,91 84,78,47**
toteswingers 1&2 £3.30, 2&3 £3.50, 1&3 £3.40 CSF £12.61 TOTE £3.40 : £1.90 , £1.10 , £2.10 ; EX 15.60 Trifecta £67.30 Pool: £1,279.63 - 14.06 winning tickets. .
Owner Mrs James Wigan **Bred** Mrs James Wigan **Trained** East Everleigh, Wilts

FOCUS

The time was 0.47 seconds faster than the opening Class 5 nursery and this looks a fair maiden with the first two improving.

NOTEBOOK

Rundell raced widest of all under the champion jockey-elect, probably a shrewd move with the ground on the soft side. It certainly didn't seem to harm the colt's chances and he improved on the form he showed when mid-division in a 7f Newbury maiden first-time up, proving well suited by this much longer trip. His connections anticipate he'll improve again next year and he might not be out again in 2012. (op 7-2 tchd 5-2)

Esteaming made his debut in a different division of the race Rundell had started off in at Newbury, finishing ninth of 18, and like today's winner he was bred to improve for this longer trip. He showed enough to suggest he can win a similar event. (tchd 9-2)

Newsreader(USA) is a half-brother to some really smart types, notably Ancient World, a 1m Group 1 winner in Italy for the same owners (also 1m2f Group 3 winner). He shaped nicely enough, finishing clear of the others. (op 11-4)

Roman Order (IRE) underperformed for the second race in succession. (op 4-1)

6734 BNP PARIBAS "BE HOPEFUL" H'CAP (DIV I) 1m 2f 46y

3:20 (3:21) (Class 5) (0-75,73) 3-Y-O+ £2,264 (£673; £336 ; £168) Stalls Low

Form RPR

2-21 1 **Duke Of Clarence (IRE)**308 816 3 -8-1172 WilliamTwiston-Davies(7) 10 83
(Richard Hannon) *chsd ldrs: racd on outside: hdwy 3f out: led ins fnl 2f: hung bdly rt to stands' rail ins fnl f: hld on all out* **9/1**

6056 2 shd **Scottish Boogie (IRE)**17 6207 5 -9-871 SebSanders 8 82
(Brendan Powell) *s.i.s: in rr: hdwy over 3f out: chal fr 2f out and upsides u.p ins fnl f: jst failed* **4/1**1

0-53 3 2 1/2 **Out Of Nothing**92 3096 9 -9-669 KellyHarrison 3 75
(Dai Burchell) *chsd ldrs: led 6f out: rdn 3f out: edgd rt and hdd 2f out: one pce whn edgd rt ins fnl f* **40/1**

5506 4 1 1/4 **Uphold**81 3997 5 -9-972 (vt) NeilCallan 15 76
(Gay Kelleway) *led tl hdd 6f out: hdd and sltly hmpd 2f out: styd on same pce and edgd rt fnl f* **14/1**

4550 5 2 **Sir Fredlot (IRE)**16 6240 3 -9-573 WilliamCarson 9 73
(Charles Hills) *chsd ldrs: rdn over 2f out: wknd fnl f* **9/1**

2300 6 1 1/2 **Welsh Nayber**10 6430 3 -8-1064 (b) PatDobbs 13 61
(Amanda Perrett) *s.i.s: in rr: racd on outer: hdwy and hung lft fr 2f out: kpt on fnl f: nvr a threat* **16/1**

306 7 shd **Circle Of Angels**27 5913 4 -8-1362 SilvestreDeSousa 11 58
(Ian Williams) *in rr: rdn over 2f out: styd on fnl f: nvr a threat* **8/1**

3245 8 nk **James Pollard (IRE)**9 6278 7 -8-1167 (t) DanielMuscutt(7) 12 63
(Bernard Llewellyn) *chsd ldrs: rdn 3f out: wknd over 1f out* **18/1**

6120 9 1 **May Be Some Time**35 5667 4 -9-1073 (t) FergusSweeney 1 67
(Stuart Kittow) *in rr: drvn and kpt on fnl 2f: nvr rchd ldrs* **14/1**

1030 10 shd **Edgeworth (IRE)**17 6207 6 -9-371 GeorgeDowning(5) 6 65
(David Bridgwater) *rdn 3f out: mod prog fr over 1f out* **12/1**

/20- 11 8 **Bolanderi (USA)**96 5804 7 -9-265 ChrisCatlin 2 43
(Andy Turnell) *chsd ldrs early: bhd fnl 5f* **66/1**

0502 12 6 **Princess Steph (IRE)**15 6278 3 -8-1266 DarryllHolland 5 32
(Heather Main) *chsd ldrs: racd wd and wknd 3f out* **6/1**3

3641 **13** *24* **Caterina**[13] 6334 3-9-1 **69**............................(b) RichardHughes 4
(Richard Hannon) *racd wd and in rr: sme hdwy over 3f out: sn wknd* **9/2**[2]

5506 **14** *5* **King Of Wing (IRE)**[159] 1607 3-9-5 **73**........................(v) PatCosgrave 14
(Jim Boyle) *chsd ldrs: rdn and btn over 3f out* **40/1**

2m 13.48s (2.48) **Going Correction** +0.325s/f (Good)
WFA 3 from 4yo+ 5lb **14** Ran SP% **122.1**
Speed ratings (Par 103): **103,102,100,99,98 97,97,96,96,95 89,84,65,61**
toteswingers 1&2 £11.80, 2&3 £61.40, 1&3 £23.90 CSF £45.10 CT £1410.79 TOTE £9.10: £3.30, £1.80, £12.50; EX 62.10 Trifecta £426.00 Pool: £817.58 - 1.42 winning tickets..
Owner D Dixon, J Stunt, J Fiyaz **Bred** Corduff Stud Ltd & J F Gribomont **Trained** East Everleigh, Wilts

FOCUS
A modest handicap in which the main action unfolded middle to stands' side. The form seems sound enough with the runner-up rated to this year's form.

6735 BNP PARIBAS "BE HOPEFUL" H'CAP (DIV II) 1m 2f 46y
3:50 (3:50) (Class 5) (0-75,75) 3-Y-0+ **£2,264** (£673; £336; £168) **Stalls** Low

Form RPR

0564 **1** **Danube River**[77] 4137 3-8-12 **68**.............................. SilvestreDeSousa 4 80
(Mark Johnston) *mde all: drvn along over 2f out: styd on strly fnl f: unchal* **5/1**[2]

3305 **2** *3* **The Giving Tree (IRE)**[12] 6375 3-9-5 **75**....................... JamesDoyle 13 81
(Sylvester Kirk) *chsd ldrs: rdn over 2f out: styd on fr over 1f out to take 2nd fnl 50yds but no ch w wnr* **9/4**[1]

2525 **3** *1* **April Ciel**[24] 6004 3-8-6 **67**.............................. DarrenEgan(5) 3 71
(Ronald Harris) *chsd wnr: rdn and no imp over 2f out: one pce and lost 2nd fnl 50yds* **7/1**[3]

0003 **4** *4 ½* **Focail Maith**[24] 5993 4-9-8 **73**...................................(p) SeanLevey 5 68
(Tim Pitt) *in rr: drvn and hdwy fr 3f out: nvr gng pce to rch ldrs* **8/1**

0622 **5** *1 ¾* **Pelham Crescent (IRE)**[16] 6232 9-8-10 **61** oh3............ LukeMorris 14 53
(Bryn Palling) *in rr: rdn over 3f out: styd on fr over 1f out: nvr gng pce to rch ldrs* **10/1**

2005 **6** *hd* **Spanish Plume**[23] 6047 4-9-6 **71**.............................. ShaneKelly 8 62
(Reg Hollinshead) *in rr: hdwy 3f out and sn rdn: one pce fnl 2f* **12/1**

2012 **7** *½* **Pandorica**[24] 6004 4-8-11 **69**.....................................(p) DanielMuscutt(7) 6 59
(Bernard Llewellyn) *chsd ldrs: rdn over 3f out: wknd 2f out* **8/1**

4463 **8** *2 ¾* **Hawaana (IRE)**[10] 6430 7-9-3 **68**.............................(v) NeilCallan 7 53
(Gay Kelleway) *in tch: rdn 4f out: wknd 2f out* **9/1**

0310 **9** *2 ¼* **Rezwaan**[18] 6171 5-9-6 **71**.............................. FrankieMcDonald 15 51
(Murty McGrath) *a towards rr* **50/1**

01 **10** *2 ½* **Wordismybond**[36] 5633 3-8-10 **66**.............................. DarryllHolland 2 41
(Peter Makin) *chsd ldrs: rdn and btn 3f out* **14/1**

0540 **11** *16* **Marvo**[31] 5783 8-8-10 **61** oh2.............................. KellyHarrison 1
(Dai Burchell) *chsd ldrs: rdn 4f out: wknd 3f out* **66/1**

2m 13.31s (2.31) **Going Correction** +0.325s/f (Good)
WFA 3 from 4yo+ 5lb **11** Ran SP% **119.1**
Speed ratings (Par 103): **103,100,99,96,94 94,94,92,90,88 75**
toteswingers 1&2 £4.30, 2&3 £5.90, 1&3 £5.70 CSF £16.80 CT £80.69 TOTE £4.80: £2.20, £2.20, £2.80; EX 19.00 Trifecta £79.00 Pool: £785.00 - 7.35 winning tickets..
Owner Sheikh Hamdan Bin Mohammed Al Maktoum **Bred** Darley **Trained** Middleham Moor, N Yorks

FOCUS
It was raining ahead of this contest, but the time was the quickest of fives races at the trip (two of them were juvenile contests), including 0.17 seconds faster than the first division. They raced up the middle of the track in the straight and the runner-up is rated close to his best.

6736 WITHY KING MAIDEN FILLIES' STKS 1m 2f 46y
4:20 (4:20) (Class 5) 3-Y-0+ **£2,264** (£673; £336; £168) **Stalls** Low

Form RPR

2036 **1** **Red Hand (USA)**[19] 6148 3-8-12 79.............................. NickyMackay 2 69+
(John Gosden) *s.i.s: hld up in rr: hdwy 3f out: led over 1f out: sn hrd drvn: hld on all out* **3/1**[2]

604 **2** *hd* **Sun Seal**[19] 6148 3-8-12 75.............................. DarryllHolland 5 68+
(Hughie Morrison) *chsd ldrs: drvn and n.m.r ins fnl 2f: styd on to chse wnr ins fnl f: fin wl: nt quite get up* **7/1**

6 **3** *2 ¼* **Jaja De Jau**[139] 2148 3-8-12 0.....................................(t) JohnFahy 9 63?
(Anthony Honeyball) *chsd ldrs: rdn over 2f out: styd on for one pce 3rd ins fnl f* **16/1**

60- **4** *hd* **Miss Blakeney**[326] 7343 3-8-12 0.............................. HayleyTurner 1 63+
(Marcus Tregoning) *in tch: hdwy fr 3f out: styd on fnl f but nvr gng pce to chal* **10/3**[3]

332 **5** *1* **Christingle**[56] 4888 3-8-12 69.............................. RichardHughes 4 61
(William Haggas) *sn led: rdn and jnd over 2f out: hdd over 1f out: wknd ins fnl f* **5/2**[1]

5 **6** *½* **Minty Fox**[19] 6148 3-8-12 0.............................. PaulHanagan 8 60+
(Rae Guest) *t.k.h: stdd in rr: styd on fr over 1f out: nvr a threat* **12/1**

06 **7** *hd* **Bov La Raconteuse**[24] 6001 3-8-5 0.............................. PhilipPrince(7) 11 59?
(Carroll Gray) *chsd ldrs: rdn 2f out: styd on same pce u.p fnl f* **100/1**

8 *5* **Gwenelda** 3-8-12 0.............................. JimmyFortune 6 49
(Andrew Balding) *in rr: hdwy on ins over 3f out to chal over 2f out: wknd over 1f out* **20/1**

0 **9** *4* **Cape Sky**[17] 6215 5-9-3 0.............................. ChrisCatlin 7 41
(Roy Brotherton) *a in rr* **100/1**

0 **10** *1 ¾* **Indie Wonder**[17] 6215 3-8-12 0.............................. J-PGuillambert 10 38
(Reg Hollinshead) *chsd ldrs: rdn 3f out: wknd over 2f out* **66/1**

05 **11** *40* **Strawberry Flavour (GER)**[10] 6457 3-8-12 0.............................. NeilCallan 3
(James Tate) *chsd ldrs: chal ins fnl 3f: wknd qckly wl over 2f out: eased whn no ch* **20/1**

2m 17.89s (6.89) **Going Correction** +0.325s/f (Good)
WFA 3 from 5yo 5lb **11** Ran SP% **115.7**
Speed ratings (Par 100): **85,84,83,82,82 81,81,77,74,72 40**
toteswingers 1&2 £4.60, 2&3 £19.00, 1&3 £12.00 CSF £22.74 TOTE £3.30: £1.50, £2.80, £5.50; EX 21.20 Trifecta £452.70 Pool: £911.53 - 1.49 winning tickets..
Owner Waratah Thoroughbreds Pty Ltd **Bred** Newsells Park Stud **Trained** Newmarket, Suffolk

FOCUS
A weak fillies' maiden and the form is muddling and not a race to be too positive about. The time was much the slowest of five races at the trip and this wasn't a proper test at the distance. Again, they raced up the middle in the straight.

6737 STONE KING H'CAP 5f 11y
4:50 (4:51) (Class 6) (0-60,60) 3-Y-0+ **£1,617** (£481; £240; £120) **Stalls** Centre

Form RPR

4000 **1** **Cristaliyev**[35] 5660 4-8-8 **47**.....................................(p) JohnFahy 12 56
(John Flint) *in rr: hrd rdn and hdwy appr fnl f: str run fnl f: led cl home* **20/1**

3300 **2** *¾* **Even Bolder**[16] 6233 9-8-10 **56**.............................. JoeyHaynes(7) 7 62
(Eric Wheeler) *in tch: hdwy to chse ldrs over 1f out: chal fnl 50yds: nt pce of wnr cl home* **16/1**

6050 **3** *shd* **Dreams Of Glory**[15] 6277 4-9-3 **56**.............................(b[1]) SilvestreDeSousa 11 62
(Ron Hodges) *chsd ldr: str chal fr 1f out and stl upsides fnl 50yds: one pce cl home* **7/1**

0306 **4** *nk* **Jawim**[38] 5536 3-8-10 **49**.............................. TomMcLaughlin 14 54
(Malcolm Saunders) *chsd ldrs: led 2f out: kpt on u.p fnl f but hrd pressed: hdd cl home* **20/1**

5065 **5** *hd* **Steel Rain**[15] 6288 4-8-11 **50**.............................. FrankieMcDonald 6 54
(Nikki Evans) *s.i.s: towards rr: hdwy fr 2f out: styd on wl fnl f: nt clr run clsng stages and nt rcvr* **14/1**

-000 **6** *¾* **Adventure Story**[16] 6227 5-9-4 **57**.............................. JamesDoyle 2 58
(Tony Carroll) *in rr: hdwy over 1f out: styd on fnl f: nvr gng pce to chal* **11/1**

2240 **7** *¾* **Mitie Mouse**[11] 6402 3-9-2 **55**.............................. PatDobbs 10 53
(Mike Murphy) *in rr: drvn 2f out: styd on fnl f: nt rch ldrs* **14/1**

4064 **8** *¾* **Winter Hill**[16] 6261 3-9-7 **60**.............................. StephenCraine 3 56+
(Tom Dascombe) *in rr: hdwy over 1f out: kpt on fnl f: nt rch ldrs* **9/2**[1]

2000 **9** *6* **Red Rhythm**[2] 6685 5-9-5 **58**.............................(vt) RichardHughes 13 32
(David Evans) *s.i.s: sn chsng ldrs: wknd over 1f out* **6/1**[3]

1235 **10** *nk* **Imaginary Diva**[14] 6307 6-9-3 **59**.............................. RyanPowell(3) 5 32
(George Margarson) *chsd ldrs: wknd wl over 1f out* **12/1**

1042 **11** *1* **Spic 'n Span**[6] 6563 7-9-2 **55**.............................(b) LukeMorris 4 24
(Ronald Harris) *led tl hdd 2f out: sn btn* **5/1**[2]

6050 **12** *2 ½* **Fiona's Spirit (IRE)**[9] 6496 5-8-2 **46** oh1.............................. DarrenEgan(5) 9
(Daniel Mark Loughnane) *chsd ldrs tl wknd 2f out* **50/1**

000 **13** *nk* **Monty Fay (IRE)**[9] 6500 3-8-13 **52**.............................(bt[1]) FergusSweeney 1
(John Flint) *chsd ldrs to 1/2-way* **25/1**

50 **14** *13* **Model Behaviour (IRE)**[9] 6496 3-8-8 **47** oh1 ow1.......... ShaneKelly 15
(Daniel Mark Loughnane) *sddle slipped sn after s: spd to 1/2-way but nt rcvr and eased fnl 2f* **10/1**

1m 4.34s (1.84) **Going Correction** +0.275s/f (Good) **14** Ran SP% **125.5**
Speed ratings (Par 101): **96,94,94,94,93 92,91,90,80,80 78,74,74,53**
toteswingers 1&2 £62.00, 2&3 £33.10, 1&3 £35.00 CSF £309.73 CT £2482.56 TOTE £31.00: £8.60, £5.80, £2.90; EX 453.60 TRIFECTA Not won..
Owner J L Flint **Bred** South Hatch Racing **Trained** Kenfig Hill, Bridgend
■ Stewards' Enquiry : John Fahy caution: careless riding.

FOCUS
A competitive sprint, but really moderate form, with little recent form to go on. They raced middle to stands' side.
Dreams Of Glory Official explanation: jockey said colt hung both ways
Model Behaviour(IRE) Official explanation: jockey said he lost his irons leaving stalls

6738 M J CHURCH H'CAP 2m 1f 34y
5:20 (5:20) (Class 5) (0-75,75) 3-Y-0+ **£2,264** (£673; £336; £168) **Stalls** Centre

Form RPR

25 **1** **Filatore (IRE)**[37] 5577 3-8-4 **62**.............................(p) ChrisCatlin 14 71
(Bernard Llewellyn) *in tch: hdwy to chse ldrs 7f out: rdn and one pce over 2f out: styd on again over 1f out: kpt on wl to ld fnl 100yds: drvn out* **8/1**

-616 **2** *½* **No Time To Lose**[34] 5718 3-9-3 **75**.............................. FergusSweeney 9 83
(Jamie Osborne) *chsd ldrs: led 6f out: rdn and hrd pressed over 2f out: kpt on tl hdd and no ex fnl 100yds* **10/1**

4521 **3** *1 ¼* **Wayne Manor (IRE)**[33] 5744 3-8-12 **70**.............................. JamesDoyle 8 77
(Ralph Beckett) *t.k.h: early: chsd ldrs: rdn and outpcd 3f out: styd on again over 1f out: tk 3rd nr fin but no imp on ldng duo* **7/1**[3]

0514 **4** *hd* **Ctappers**[9] 6474 3-7-11 **60**.............................. DarrenEgan(5) 13 66
(Mick Channon) *in rr: hdwy on outer over 3f out: chsd ldrs fr 2f out: kpt on fnl f but no imp* **20/1**

3521 **5** *1 ½* **Salontyre (GER)**[133] 1905 6-9-7 **68**.............................(p) NeilCallan 7 72
(Bernard Llewellyn) *chsd ldrs: drvn to chal over 2f out: wknd ins fnl f* **16/1**

3360 **6** *½* **Marmas**[11] 6407 3-8-7 **65**.............................. PaulHanagan 5 69
(Marcus Tregoning) *chsd ldrs: rdn over 2f out: styd on same pce* **11/2**[2]

5605 **7** *3 ¼* **Lily Potts**[21] 6098 3-7-13 **62** ow2.............................(p) JemmaMarshall(5) 3 62
(Chris Down) *in tch: hdwy and rdn 3f out: wknd over 1f out* **40/1**

0-21 **8** *nk* **Welsh Bard (IRE)**[17] 6213 3-8-8 **66**.............................. LukeMorris 1 66
(Sir Mark Prescott Bt) *chsd ldrs: lost position 6f out: drvn and hdwy 3f out: wknd u.p 2f out* **15/8**[1]

2241 **9** *6* **Lucky Diva**[15] 6280 5-8-8 **62**.............................(p) JakePayne(7) 10 54
(Bill Turner) *in rr: hdwy 4f out: chsd ldrs 3f out: wknd ins fnl 2f* **25/1**

0442 **10** *¾* **Gordon Flash**[30] 5811 5-8-8 **62** ow2........... WilliamTwiston-Davies(7) 12 54
(Charles Hills) *in tch: chsd ldrs 4f out: rdn 3f out: wknd over 2f out* **15/2**

2012 **11** *17* **Sunny Future (IRE)**[32] 5772 6-9-7 **68**.............................. TomMcLaughlin 2 39
(Malcolm Saunders) *t.k.h: in rr: hdwy 7f out: chsd ldrs 4f out: wknd qckly over 2f out* **16/1**

3136 **12** *13* **Gilded Age**[130] 2412 6-9-10 **71**.............................(tp) SamHitchcott 11 27
(Chris Gordon) *led tl hdd 6f out: wknd qckly 3f out* **33/1**

4m 1.26s (9.36) **Going Correction** +0.325s/f (Good)
WFA 3 from 4yo+ 11lb **12** Ran SP% **120.4**
Speed ratings (Par 103): **90,89,89,89,88 88,86,86,83,83 75,69**
toteswingers 1&2 £16.70, 2&3 £13.40, 1&3 £12.50 CSF £82.98 CT £596.70 TOTE £12.20: £3.60, £3.40, £3.00; EX 88.70 Trifecta £264.00 Pool £745.85 - 2.09 winning tickets..
Owner Bluebirds Racing & Co **Bred** Ballymacoll Stud Farm Ltd **Trained** Fochriw, Caerphilly

FOCUS
The pace was slow and the time was over 21 seconds above standard. Form to treat with caution. Much of the action took place up the centre in the straight. The first three all recorded marginal personal bests, while the next three home set the standard.
Gordon Flash Official explanation: vet said gelding finished lame

6739 RACING EXCELLENCE "HANDS AND HEELS" APPRENTICE SERIES H'CAP 5f 161y
5:50 (5:50) (Class 5) (0-70,68) 3-Y-0 **£2,264** (£673; £336; £168) **Stalls** Centre

Form RPR

341 **1** **Gladiatrix**[21] 6095 3-9-4 **65**.............................. MichaelJMMurphy 6 78
(Rod Millman) *chsd ldrs: chal 2f out: led wl over 1f out: drvn clr fnl f* **9/5**[1]

342 **2** *4* **Tidal's Baby**[11] 6402 3-9-6 **67**.............................. IanBurns 2 67
(Tony Carroll) *in rr but in tch: hdwy over 2f out: styd on to go 2nd fnl f but no ch w wnr* **11/2**[3]

0156 **3** *1 ½* **One Last Dream**[14] 6306 3-8-10 **57**.............................(b) PhilipPrince 3 52
(Ron Hodges) *led: hdd over 2f out: styd chalng tl outpcd appr fnl f* **9/1**

5043 **4** *1* **Represent (IRE)**[12] 6378 3-9-4 **68**.............................. RobertTart(3) 5 60
(Mick Channon) *s.i.s and wl bhd 3f out: hdwy fr 2f out: styd on fnl f: nt rch ldrs* **11/2**[3]

060- **5** *¾* **Rock On Candy**[308] 7569 3-8-12 **59**.............................. ThomasBrown 8 48
(John Spearing) *chsd ldrs: ev ch 2f out: wknd over 1f out* **20/1**

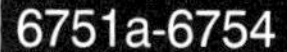

2036 **6** 3 3/4 **Ficelle (IRE)**[3] 6641 3-8-13 **60**.. JoshBaudains 1 37
(Ronald Harris) *s.i.s: in rr: hdwy to chse ldrs over 2f out: wknd over 1f out* **10/1**

021 **7** 1/2 **Sushi**[26] 5949 3-9-4 **65**.. DanielMuscutt 10 40
(Rae Guest) *chsd ldrs: ev ch 2f out: wknd over 1f out* **5/1**[2]

0005 **8** 2 1/2 **Marygold**[18] 6173 3-9-0 **66**..(v) AaronChave(5) 7 33
(Lee Carter) *pressed ldr: slt ld over 2f out: hdd & wknd wl over 1f out* **25/1**

2254 **9** 3/4 **Indiana Guest (IRE)**[14] 6306 3-8-4 **56**................(v[1]) JordanVaughan(5) 4 20
(George Margarson) *in tch: hdwy to chse ldrs over 2f out: wknd qckly wl over 1f out* **10/1**

1m 12.57s (1.37) **Going Correction** +0.275s/f (Good) **9** Ran SP% **119.9**
Speed ratings (Par 101): **101,95,93,92,91 86,85,82,81**
toteswingers 1&2 £16.70, 2&3 £13.40, 1&3 £12.50 CSF £12.45 CT £73.94 TOTE £3.50: £1.10, £2.10, £3.00; EX 13.70 Trifecta £93.80 Pool £738.10 - 5.82 winning tickets..
Owner Harry Dutfield & Partners **Bred** H G And J R Dutfield **Trained** Kentisbeare, Devon

FOCUS
An uncompetitive handicap in which they raced middle to far side. The runner-up looks the best guide to the level.
T/Jkpt: Not won. T/Plt: £100.30 to a £1 stake. Pool: £100,192.53 - 728.96 winning tickets.
T/Qpdt: £87.80 to a £1 stake. Pool: £7,141.98 - 60.14 winning tickets. ST

6524 HAMILTON (R-H)
Monday, October 1
6740 Meeting Abandoned - Waterlogged

6747 - 6750a (Foreign Racing) - See Raceform Interactive

6463 MAISONS-LAFFITTE (R-H)
Monday, October 1
OFFICIAL GOING: Turf: good to soft

6751a PRIX TAHITI (MAIDEN) (UNRACED 2YO FILLIES) (TURF) 7f (S)
11:30 (12:00) 2-Y-0 **£10,000** (£4,000; £3,000; £2,000; £1,000)

RPR

1 **Queen's Daughter (FR)** 2-9-0 0.................................. ThierryThulliez 7 78
(N Clement, France) **53/10**[3]

2 *snk* **White Waves (USA)** 2-8-6 0.............................. MlleAmelieFoulon(8) 5 78
(A Fabre, France) **11/1**

3 1 3/4 **Daivika (USA)** 2-9-0 0... StephanePasquier 14 73
(P Bary, France) **5/2**[1]

4 3/4 **Zoya (FR)** 2-8-10 0... MatthieuAutier(4) 11 71
(J-P Gallorini, France) **22/1**

5 *nk* **Kalevala (FR)** 2-9-0 0... LouisBeuzelin 4 71
(R Pritchard-Gordon, France) **47/1**

6 *shd* **Dear Nofa (IRE)** 2-9-0 0... MaximeGuyon 15 70
(A Fabre, France) **19/5**[2]

7 1 1/4 **Penmaen (IRE)** 2-9-0 0.. FabienLefebvre 16 67
(J E Hammond, France) **15/1**

8 1 1/4 **Bousatet (FR)** 2-9-0 0.. GrahamLee 2 64
(Kevin Ryan) *broke wl: racd in cl 2nd on outside: tk ld early in st 2f out: rdn 1 1/2f out: nt qckn: hdd 1f out: styd on one pce* **11/1**

9 1 **Alice Neney (IRE)** 2-8-10 0.. MarcLerner(4) 17 62
(C Lerner, France) **32/1**

10 1 1/2 **Tora Tora (FR)** 2-8-6 0.. DimitriIbouth(8) 1 58
(M Boutin, France) **76/1**

0 **Sanluquenia (FR)** 2-8-8 0.................................... JimmyTastayre(6) 6
(C Boutin, France) **98/1**

0 **Madrasa (FR)** 2-9-0 0.. BriceRaballand 9
(Mme C Head-Maarek, France) **18/1**

0 **Wizz Up (IRE)** 2-9-0 0.. IoritzMendizabal 13
(Robert Collet, France) **12/1**

0 **Dummy Traou Land (FR)** 2-9-0 0.................................. VincentVion 10
(P Costes, France) **92/1**

0 **Meshaheera (FR)** 2-9-0 0... AllanBonnefoy 8
(F Sanchez, France) **50/1**

1m 32.2s (4.20) **15** Ran SP% **116.0**
WIN (incl. 1 euro stake): 6.30. PLACES: 1.80, 2.90, 1.70. DF: 49.00. SF: 88.60.
Owner Pierre-Paul Richou **Bred** P-P Richou **Trained** Chantilly, France

6752a PRIX DE SAINT-ARNOULT-EN-YVELINES (CLAIMER) (3YO) (TURF) 6f (S)
1:35 (12:00) 3-Y-0 **£9,583** (£3,833; £2,875; £1,916; £958)

RPR

1 **Meniska (FR)**[55] 3-8-13 0.. AnthonyCrastus 4 82
(J-M Capitte, France) **191/10**

2 1/2 **Leffard (IRE)**[62] 3-9-4 0......................................(b) GregoryBenoist 14 85
(F Chappet, France) **83/10**

3 3/4 **Brocklebank (IRE)**[18] 6173 3-8-11 0.............................(p) GrahamLee 13 76
(Kevin Ryan) *broke wl fr outside draw: sn led: hdd 2f out: rallied and r.o wl u.p fnl f* **48/10**[2]

4 3/4 **Noble Fantasy (GER)**[41] 5473 3-8-11 0.................(b) ThierryThulliez 12 73
(Mario Hofer, Germany) **21/1**

5 1 1/2 **Raquette**[143] 3-8-9 0.. AnthonyCaramanolis(6) 9 72
(N Clement, France) **30/1**

6 *hd* **Silent Music (IRE)**[20] 3-9-0 0................................. StevanBourgois(5) 2 76
(Robert Collet, France) **22/1**

7 *shd* **Star Seed (FR)**[15] 3-9-2 0.......................................(p) FranckBlondel 7 72
(M Rolland, France) **16/1**

8 1 **Whip My Heart (IRE)**[20] 3-9-2 0..................................(b) OlivierPeslier 8 69
(U Suter, France) **10/1**

9 1 3/4 **Happy Sun Percy**[15] 3-9-1 0... MaximeGuyon 1 63
(G Doleuze, France) **58/10**[3]

10 2 **Antalia (FR)**[41] 5473 3-8-8 0.. IoritzMendizabal 5 49
(J-C Rouget, France) **4/1**[1]

0 **Chorister Sport (IRE)**[15] 3-8-6 0............ Georges-AntoineAnselin(5) 10
(N Caullery, France) **83/1**

0 **Cruel Summer (FR)**[20] 3-8-13 0.. GeraldMosse 3
(C Boutin, France) **48/10**[2]

0 **Le Maltais (FR)**[41] 5473 3-8-11 0...................................... DavidBreux 6
(P Azzopardi, France) **59/1**

0 **Fresque (FR)** 3-8-11 0..(b) GerardGuillermo 11
(G Guillermo, France) **121/1**

1m 12.2s (-1.20) **14** Ran SP% **115.7**
WIN (incl. 1 euro stake): 20.10. PLACES: 4.90, 3.60, 2.30. DF: 89.60. SF: 167.80.
Owner Johannes Van Der Weide **Bred** 6 C Racing Ltd **Trained** France

6465 AYR (L-H)
Tuesday, October 2
OFFICIAL GOING: Heavy (7.7)
Wind: Fresh, half against Weather: Overcast, showers

6753 CHAMPIONS LEAGUE SPECIALS AT BETVICTOR NURSERY 7f 50y
2:10 (2:41) (Class 6) (0-65,65) 2-Y-0 **£1,704** (£503; £251) **Stalls** High

Form RPR

4004 **1** **Ingleby Symphony (IRE)**[28] 5920 2-8-13 **57**................ TonyHamilton 6 58
(Richard Fahey) *trckd ldrs: led and edgd lft over 2f out: hrd pressed fnl f: hld on wl* **17/2**

000 **2** *shd* **Mash Potato (IRE)**[24] 6042 2-8-10 **54**........................... PaulMulrennan 1 55
(Michael Dods) *t.k.h: cl up: rdn over 2f out: ev ch ins fnl f: kpt on: jst hld* **9/1**

0436 **3** 2 **Danehill Flyer (IRE)**[21] 6121 2-9-5 **63**....................... MichaelO'Connell 7 60
(Philip Kirby) *prom: rdn whn n.m.r over 2f out: rallied and edgd rt over 1f out: kpt on fnl f: nt rch first two* **4/1**[2]

4033 **4** *nk* **Baraboy (IRE)**[20] 6130 2-9-1 **59**.. GrahamLee 5 54
(Barry Murtagh) *in tch: nt clr run over 2f out: effrt and edgd rt over 1f out: kpt on same pce ins fnl f* **16/1**

2560 **5** 1 3/4 **Out Of The Blocks**[23] 6070 2-9-2 **60**.............................(b) PJMcDonald 8 51
(Ruth Carr) *hld up in midfield: stdy hdwy over 2f out: rdn over 1f out: kpt on same pce fnl f* **13/2**

635 **6** 2 1/4 **Corton Lad**[20] 6133 2-9-5 **63**... JoeFanning 3 48
(Keith Dalgleish) *taken early to post: t.k.h: pressed ldr: rdn over 2f out: wknd appr fnl f* **11/1**

3250 **7** 4 1/2 **Surround Sound**[23] 6070 2-9-2 **60**................................. DuranFentiman 9 34
(Tim Easterby) *t.k.h: led: rdn and hdd over 2f out: one pce whn hmpd appr fnl f: sn btn* **20/1**

000P **8** *nse* **Gambino (IRE)**[20] 6134 2-7-12 **45**...................................... NeilFarley(3) 11 19
(Hugh McWilliams) *t.k.h: hld up: effrt whn nt clr run briefly over 2f out: wknd over 1f out* **100/1**

565 **9** 38 **Mudaawem (USA)**[17] 6237 2-9-7 **65**................................. TadhgO'Shea 2
(Mark Johnston) *missed break: hld up on ins: struggling over 3f out: eased whn no ch fnl 2f* **5/1**[3]

1201 **10** 5 **Alexandrakollontai (IRE)**[9] 6511 2-9-2 **63** 6ex..........(b) JulieBurke(3) 10
(Alistair Whillans) *s.i.s: bhd: struggling 4f out: sn btn: eased whn no ch fnl 2f* **3/1**[1]

1m 42.37s (8.97) **Going Correction** +1.075s/f (Soft) **10** Ran SP% **115.5**
Speed ratings (Par 93): **91,90,88,88,86 83,78,78,35,29**
toteswingers 1&2 £7.70, 1&3 £6.30, 2&3 £7.40 CSF £81.65 CT £363.49 TOTE £9.80: £3.40, £2.90, £1.70; EX 93.00 Trifecta £665.90 Part won. Pool: £899.99 - 0.62 winning tickets..
Owner Percy Green Racing 4 & Partner **Bred** Sunderland Holdings Inc **Trained** Musley Bank, N Yorks
■ Stewards' Enquiry : Michael O'Connell two-day ban: careless riding (Oct 16-17)

FOCUS
A modest nursery. They went a sensible gallop on ground officially described as heavy. The winning time was around 14 seconds slower than standard. Limited form, and not a race to dwell on.

NOTEBOOK
Ingleby Symphony(IRE) raced at 5f on her first three starts on good turf at Thirsk and Fibresand at Southwell, appearing ready for a step up in trip. She duly kept on to finish about 3l fourth on her handicap debut over this trip at Musselburgh last month, and she improved again for this stamina test. She will remain of interest if taking up her weekend engagement over an extended 1m under a penalty. (op 8-1)
Mash Potato(IRE) arrived with modest form from three starts at up to 6f, but this ground and longer trip promised to suit on his first start in a nursery off a low rating. He should remain competitive at up to 1m in lowly handicap company on this sort of ground this autumn. (op 15-2 tchd 7-1)
Danehill Flyer(IRE) had to wait for an out up the rail 2f out and ran an honest race in chasing home the front two. He should remain competitive at up to 1m in similar company this autumn. (op 5-1)
Baraboy(IRE) did not really progress on this second start for trainer Barry Murtagh. (op 12-1)
Mudaawem(USA) disappointed under these conditions after starting slowly. The trainer's representative reported that the colt was unsuited by the heavy ground. Official explanation: trainer's rep said colt was unsuited by the heavy ground (op 4-1 tchd 6-1)
Alexandrakollontai(IRE) was soon struggling but the trainer later reported that the filly was in season. Official explanation: trainer said filly was in season (op 10-3 tchd 7-2 and 9-2 in a place)

6754 ARC 4 PLACES AT BETVICTOR MAIDEN AUCTION STKS 6f
2:40 (3:12) (Class 5) 2-Y-0 **£2,264** (£673; £336; £168) **Stalls** Centre

Form RPR

3442 **1** **Red Cobra (IRE)**[4] 6628 2-8-11 70................................ DuranFentiman 4 69
(Tim Easterby) *mde all: rdn over 1f out: kpt on wl fnl f* **1/1**[1]

2 1 1/2 **Brooke's Bounty** 2-9-1 0.. TonyHamilton 3 70+
(Richard Fahey) *trckd wnr: drvn and outpcd over 2f out: rallied over 1f out: kpt on fnl f: nt pce to chal* **9/1**

462 **3** 1 1/2 **Teetotal (IRE)**[12] 6404 2-8-11 68...................................... GrahamLee 5 60
(Nigel Tinkler) *cl up: rdn whn n.m.r briefly over 2f out: one pce fnl f* **4/1**[3]

4 28 **Shagwa (IRE)** 2-8-8 0.. JoeFanning 1
(Mark Johnston) *prom: drvn and outpcd wl over 3f out: sn lost tch: t.o* **11/4**[2]

UP0 **5** 33 **Fenwick Gale (IRE)**[22] 6099 2-8-5 0.................................. JulieBurke(3) 2
(Kevin Ryan) *dwlt: sn extremely rel to r and t.o* **25/1**

1m 21.54s (9.14) **Going Correction** +1.075s/f (Soft) **5** Ran SP% **110.5**
Speed ratings (Par 95): **82,80,78,40,**
CSF £10.79 TOTE £1.90: £1.10, £2.90; EX 9.10.
Owner J & P Baillie & C & G Baillie **Bred** Tally-Ho Stud **Trained** Great Habton, N Yorks

FOCUS
A modest juvenile auction maiden. Straightofrward form, the winner to his recent level.

NOTEBOOK
Red Cobra(IRE) arrived with a BHA rating of 70 after eights starts at up to 7f, and, given the prevailing conditions, it had to be encouraging that he finished a close second over this 6f trip on heavy ground in a similar contest at Haydock the previous week. He was given a confident, no nonsense ride by Duran Fentiman and made all the running in workmanlike fashion. He should find life tougher in modest to fair handicaps from now on but his ability to act such a surface can only help this autumn. (op 11-8)

Brooke's Bounty produced an encouraging debut in splitting the two form horses in second. He is the second foal of a decent winner over 5-7f, who is a half-sister to very smart juvenile sprinter Winker Watson. He looks capable of going one better in the weeks ahead. (op 8-1 tchd 10-1)

Teetotal(IRE) had 2lb to find with the winner on the book. He stays this trip and ran up to form. (op 3-1 tchd 9-2)

Shagwa(IRE) struggled under these conditions on her debut. (op 7-2)

Fenwick Gale(IRE) was particularly recalcitrant in a tailed-off last. (op 14-1)

6755 TALK TO VICTOR H'CAP — 5f

3:40 (3:41) (Class 3) (0-95,94) 3-Y-O+ — **£7,021** (£2,073; £1,037) **Stalls** Centre

Form — RPR

0023 **1** — **Another Wise Kid (IRE)**[14] 6347 4-8-9 **82** .... RussKennemore 1 — 90
(Paul Midgley) *hld up: hdwy on outside over 1f out: ev ch ins fnl f: led cl home* **9/1**

6020 **2** *nse* **Arctic Feeling (IRE)**[10] 6465 4-8-10 **83** .... TonyHamilton 4 — 91
(Richard Fahey) *in tch: hdwy to ld over 1f out: sn rdn: hrd pressed fnl f: hdd cl home* **7/2**[3]

5000 **3** *2½* **Taurus Twins**[8] 6543 6-8-12 **85** .... (b) JoeFanning 2 — 84
(Richard Price) *led tl rdn and hdd over 1f out: kpt on same pce ins fnl f* **25/1**

1 **4** *¾* **Sovereign Street**[36] 5674 4-8-7 **80** oh1 .... PJMcDonald 8 — 76+
(Ann Duffield) *hld up: rdn and hdwy over 1f out: kpt on fnl f: nvr able to chal* **9/4**[1]

6160 **5** *4* **Singeur (IRE)**[17] 6244 5-9-7 **94** .... FrederikTylicki 6 — 76
(Robin Bastiman) *hld up in tch: effrt and rdn over 1f out: btn ins fnl f* **11/4**[2]

4360 **6** *hd* **Shoshoni Wind**[21] 6116 4-9-2 **92** .... JulieBurke(3) 3 — 73
(Kevin Ryan) *trckd ldrs: effrt and rdn over 1f out: wknd ins fnl f* **14/1**

1040 **7** *hd* **Crimson Knot (IRE)**[8] 6525 4-8-7 **80** .... RoystonFfrench 7 — 60
(Alan Berry) *in tch: rdn whn n.m.r over 2f out: wknd over 1f out* **16/1**

0300 **8** *1¼* **Bosun Breese**[24] 6028 7-9-5 **92** .... GrahamGibbons 5 — 68
(David Barron) *cl up: rdn over 2f out: wknd appr fnl f* **12/1**

1m 3.88s (4.48) **Going Correction** +1.075s/f (Soft) — **8** Ran SP% **113.7**
Speed ratings (Par 107): **107,106,102,101,95 95,94,92**
toteswingers 1&2 £5.00, 1&3 £16.50, 2&3 £13.50 CSF £40.12 CT £762.57 TOTE £10.80: £2.90, £1.10, £5.30; EX 46.20 Trifecta £600.40 Pool: £1,257.74 - 1.55 winning tickets..

Owner Michael Ng **Bred** Paul Kavanagh **Trained** Westow, N Yorks

FOCUS

A good-class sprint handicap. The winner recorded significantly the best comparative time on the card so far and the second is rated to this year's form.

NOTEBOOK

Another Wise Kid(IRE) won four races at up to 6f in 2011, including three handicaps over this 5f trip on ground ranging from good to firm to good to soft, and was racing off a mark 1lb higher than for his latest victory at Ripon that September. He handled these conditions particularly well here in running down the well fancied runner-up.

Arctic Feeling(IRE) ran a big race over C&D on heavy ground the previous month, and is best forgiven a disappointing effort the following day. Winner of a Listed juvenile contest over this C&D, he gives this form real substance. He has won over this trip at Wolverhampton, and can be placed to advantage on Polytrack, after narrowly failing to get the job done on this heavy surface. (op 10-3)

Taurus Twins set about making the running but couldn't respond when headed approaching the furlong pole. This was a more encouraging display though, and he has dropped to a competitive mark if getting some better ground over this trip in the weeks ahead. (op 28-1 tchd 20-1)

Sovereign Street was returning from a five-week break since recording a 6f hat-trick on soft ground in July/August, and was held up over this shorter trip, but it proved very difficult for her to make up the ground quickly enough on this surface. She duly finished a never-nearer fourth, but things may pan out differently for her over this trip in the future. (op 2-1)

Singeur(IRE) needs decent ground to be seen to best effect. (op 9-2)

6756 DOWNLOAD THE BETVICTOR SPINCAST APP NOW H'CAP — 7f 50y

4:10 (4:11) (Class 6) (0-60,60) 3-Y-O+ — **£1,704** (£503; £251) **Stalls** High

Form — RPR

0000 **1** — **Sabratha (IRE)**[8] 6528 4-9-2 **60** .... GarryWhillans(5) 8 — 73
(Linda Perratt) *hld up: gd hdwy to ld 2f out: sn rdn and edgd lft: pushed clr fnl f* **16/1**

2143 **2** *5* **Lord Franklin**[39] 5538 3-8-9 **55** .... JasonHart(5) 13 — 55
(Eric Alston) *t.k.h: trckd ldrs: effrt and ev ch 2f out: kpt on: nt pce of wnr* **11/4**[1]

0006 **3** *1½* **Koo And The Gang (IRE)**[27] 5941 5-9-7 **60** .... DaleSwift 4 — 56
(Brian Ellison) *prom: drvn and outpcd over 2f out: styd on fnl f: nvr able to chal* **9/2**[2]

5243 **4** *6* **Jebel Tara**[8] 6529 7-8-11 **50** .... (bt) PaulMulrennan 5 — 31
(Ian Semple) *hld up: hdwy over 2f out: sn rdn: no imp over 1f out* **10/1**

5462 **5** *½* **Whats For Pudding (IRE)**[10] 6480 4-8-6 **48** .... NeilFarley(3) 2 — 27
(Declan Carroll) *s.i.s: bhd: drvn over 2f out: styd on fnl f: nvr able to chal* **15/2**[3]

0660 **6** *1½* **Let's Face Facts**[15] 6309 5-8-7 **46** .... JoeFanning 10 — 21
(Jim Goldie) *in tch: drvn over 2f out: sn outpcd* **16/1**

0026 **7** *nk* **Goninodaethat**[15] 6308 4-9-3 **56** .... GrahamLee 14 — 31
(Jim Goldie) *t.k.h: chsd ldr: racd alone far rail over 2f out: sn ev ch: wknd over 1f out* **9/2**[2]

4600 **8** *10* **Hellbender (IRE)**[39] 5543 6-8-13 **57** .... LMcNiff(5) 9
(George Foster) *towards rr: drvn along over 3f out: btn fnl 2f* **25/1**

6500 **9** *3½* **Mark Anthony (IRE)**[25] 5996 5-8-11 **50** .... (p) GrahamGibbons 1
(Shaun Harris) *led to 2f out: sn rdn and wknd* **9/1**

2400 **10** *9* **Carnival Dream**[49] 5185 7-8-4 **46** oh1 .... JulieBurke(3) 12
(Hugh McWilliams) *s.i.s: bhd and rdn: nvr on terms* **33/1**

6500 **11** *nk* **Shunkawakhan (IRE)**[10] 6480 9-8-7 **46** oh1 .... (tp) BarryMcHugh 3
(Linda Perratt) *hld up: rdn over 3f out: nvr on terms* **40/1**

1m 39.91s (6.51) **Going Correction** +1.075s/f (Soft)
WFA 3 from 4yo+ 2lb — **11** Ran SP% **114.9**
Speed ratings (Par 101): **105,99,97,90,90 88,88,76,72,62 62**
toteswingers 1&2 £10.80, 1&3 £19.10, 2&3 £5.10 CSF £57.62 TOTE £19.40: £4.00, £1.60, £2.10; EX 114.90 Trifecta £361.40 Part won. Pool: £488.41 - 0.20 winning tickets..

Owner Helen Perratt & John Murphy **Bred** Adrian Purvis **Trained** East Kilbride, S Lanarks

FOCUS

A moderate handicap for 3-y-os and up. The early pace was contested and they went a searching gallop and the winner is rated back to her best.

Sabratha(IRE) Official explanation: trainer said, regarding apparent improvement in form, that the filly benefited from the drop in class.

6757 BACK THE BHOYS WITH BETVICTOR H'CAP — 1m 2f

4:40 (4:40) (Class 3) (0-95,92) 3-Y-O+ — **£6,663** (£1,982; £990; £495) **Stalls** Low

Form — RPR

4051 **1** — **Calaf**[26] 5965 4-8-11 **79** .... DaleSwift 4 — 85
(Brian Ellison) *prom: hdwy on outside to ld over 1f out: sn rdn: hung lft ins fnl f: kpt on wl* **7/4**[2]

6025 **2** *1¾* **Act Your Shoe Size**[2] 6710 3-8-10 **83** .... JoeFanning 3 — 85
(Keith Dalgleish) *led: rdn over 2f out: hdd over 1f out: kpt on same pce fnl f* **6/1**[3]

1160 **3** *1¼* **Gala Casino Star (IRE)**[25] 6010 7-8-12 **87** .... (v) JordanNason(7) 2 — 87
(Geoffrey Harker) *cl up: rdn over 2f out: kpt on same pce fnl f* **6/1**[3]

0241 **4** *5* **Muffin McLeay (IRE)**[73] 4347 4-9-10 **92** .... GrahamGibbons 5 — 82
(David Barron) *cl up: rdn and ev ch over 2f out: wknd over 1f out* **6/5**[1]

2m 23.62s (11.62) **Going Correction** +1.075s/f (Soft)
WFA 3 from 4yo+ 5lb — **4** Ran SP% **110.4**
Speed ratings (Par 107): **96,94,93,89**
CSF £11.28 TOTE £3.50; EX 9.30.

Owner Prism Bloodstock **Bred** Norcroft Park Stud **Trained** Norton, N Yorks

FOCUS

A good class handicap for 3yos and up. They went an honest gallop on the testing surface. The runner-up sets the level with the winner to recent form.

NOTEBOOK

Calaf was held up off the pace and came through to land the spoils, after travelling well, in a straightforward manner. He won a seller in a first-time hood, which was retained here, over 2f further at Haydock on good to firm ground the previous month. He obviously handles the ground and his confirmed stamina helped under the conditions. He is entered in a similar contest over this trip and a novice hurdle at the weekend. (op 13-8 tchd 11-8)

Act Your Shoe Size, who reportedly looked well beforehand and made the running, is high enough in the weights at present and probably prefers better ground. (op 13-2)

Gala Casino Star(IRE) is well above his last winning mark, but plugged on gamely enough. (op 5-1)

Muffin McLeay(IRE) proved disappointing compared with his form claims on paper. The representative of the trainer reported that the gelding was unsuited by the heavy ground. Official explanation: trainer's rep said gelding was unsuited by the heavy ground (op 7-4 tchd 15-8)

6758 BEST ODDS GUARANTEED AT BETVICTOR.COM RACING EXCELLENCE APPRENTICE TRAINING SERIES H'CAP — 1m

5:10 (5:11) (Class 6) (0-60,58) 3-Y-O+ — **£1,704** (£503; £251) **Stalls** Low

Form — RPR

2004 **1** — **Goldmadchen (GER)**[8] 6526 4-9-4 **53** .... LauraBarry 2 — 62
(Keith Dalgleish) *hld up: rdn and hdwy 2f out: styd on wl fnl f: led nr fin* **12/1**

5360 **2** *shd* **Retreat Content (IRE)**[17] 6262 4-8-13 **53** .... RossSmith(5) 7 — 62
(Linda Perratt) *in tch: hdwy to ld 2f out: sn rdn: kpt on fnl f: hdd nr fin* **12/1**

613 **3** *3* **Spread Boy (IRE)**[9] 6513 5-8-9 **51** .... JordanHibberd(7) 11 — 53
(Alan Berry) *led and sn clr: hdd 2f out: one pce fnl f* **8/1**

4010 **4** *2½* **Star Kingdom (IRE)**[27] 5938 3-8-13 **54** .... JacobButterfield(3) 10 — 50
(Brian Ellison) *t.k.h: prom: rdn and outpcd over 2f out: rallied over 1f out: one pce fnl f* **11/2**[3]

650 **5** *¾* **Blackamoor Harry**[25] 6001 3-8-7 **45** .... RachealKneller 3 — 40
(Richard Ford) *s.i.s: bhd: rdn over 3f out: hdwy over 1f out: kpt on: nrst fin* **33/1**

62 **6** *hd* **Goodlukin Lucy**[33] 5762 5-8-7 **45** .... (t) DavidSimmonson(3) 9 — 39
(Dianne Sayer) *chsd ldrs: drvn along 3f out: sn outpcd: no imp fnl 2f* **10/1**

5066 **7** *½* **Flipping**[35] 5713 5-9-9 **58** .... (p) JasonHart 8 — 51
(Eric Alston) *t.k.h: hld up on outside: hdwy 3f out: wknd over 1f out* **11/4**[1]

4336 **8** *1* **Kyllachykov (IRE)**[27] 5935 4-8-11 **46** .... JakePayne 4 — 37
(Robin Bastiman) *chsd ldrs: effrt over 2f out: wknd over 1f out* **9/2**[2]

1355 **9** *½* **Jupiter Fidius**[22] 6105 5-9-6 **58** .... (p) GemmaTutty(3) 12 — 48
(Karen Tutty) *broke wl but qckly dropped to rr: rdn over 3f out: sme late hdwy: nvr on terms* **12/1**

0044 **10** *2* **Dynamic Drive (IRE)**[15] 6315 5-9-1 **50** .... GeorgeChaloner 5 — 35
(Linda Perratt) *in tch tl rdn and wknd over 2f out* **12/1**

1600 **11** *10* **Glenluji**[8] 6528 7-8-13 **55** .... SophieRobertson(7) 1 — 17
(Jim Goldie) *hld up on ins: rdn over 2f out: sn btn* **20/1**

1m 52.51s (8.71) **Going Correction** +1.075s/f (Soft)
WFA 3 from 4yo+ 3lb — **11** Ran SP% **118.9**
Speed ratings (Par 101): **99,98,95,93,92 92,91,90,90,88 78**
toteswingers 1&2 £35.30, 1&3 £12.80, 2&3 £28.50 CSF £149.15 TOTE £16.00: £4.10, £4.80, £3.30; EX 286.50 TRIFECTA Not won..

Owner G L S Partnership **Bred** Gestut Gorlsdorf **Trained** Carluke, S Lanarks

FOCUS

A moderate handicap for apprentice riders. The pace once again appeared plenty quick enough on the testing ground, and it helped to ride a more conservative race. The runner-up is rated to this year's form with the third a length off his best.

Spread Boy(IRE) Official explanation: jockey said saddle slipped

T/Plt: £383.60 to a £1 stake. Pool £47,431.65 - 90.25 winning units. T/Qpdt: £79.50 to a £1 stake. Pool £3,521.88 - 32.75 winning units. RY

6563 FOLKESTONE (R-H)

Tuesday, October 2

6759 Meeting Abandoned - Waterlogged

6685 WOLVERHAMPTON (A.W) (L-H)

Tuesday, October 2

OFFICIAL GOING: Standard

Wind: fresh, behind Weather: showers

6765 BET TOTEPLACEPOT TEXT TOTE TO 89660 MAIDEN STKS — 5f 216y(P)

2:00 (2:01) (Class 5) 3-Y-O — **£2,385** (£704; £352) **Stalls** Low

Form — RPR

323 **1** — **Ebble**[19] 6154 3-8-12 70 .... NickyMackay 3 — 61+
(John Gosden) *chsd ldrs: effrt on inner whn pushed lft over 1f out: rdn and qcknd to ld fnl f: edgd rt and r.o wl* **15/8**[1]

2602 **2** *¾* **Mister Mackenzie**[7] 6565 3-9-3 62 .... [1] GeorgeBaker 6 — 64
(John Best) *taken down early: led for 1f: chsd ldr after tl rdn to ld over 1f out: stmbld: edgd lft and hdd fnl 100yds: one pce after* **8/1**

6033 **3** nk **Levi Draper**[10] 6502 3-9-3 69 HayleyTurner 9 63+
(James Fanshawe) *hld up in midfield on outer: hdwy whn nt clr run over 1f out tl swtchd rt ins fnl f: styd on fnl 100yds to snatch 3rd on post* **2/1**[2]

3-42 **4** shd **Crazy Too (IRE)**[22] 6095 3-8-12 63 MartinLane 2 58
(David Simcock) *stdd s: t.k.h: hld up in midfield: hdwy to trck ldrs and swtchd lft over 1f out: sn rdn and ev ch: styng on same pce whn n.m.r fnl 100yds* **6/1**[3]

0420 **5** 1 1/4 **Silkee Supreme**[30] 5853 3-9-3 66 (b) SeanLevey 4 59
(Richard Hannon) *t.k.h: chsd ldrs: effrt to press ldr and drvn ent fnl f: fnd little for press: wknd fnl 100yds* **14/1**

05 **6** 3/4 **Aujourd'Hui**[11] 6433 3-8-12 0 KieranO'Neill 8 51
(Richard Hannon) *dwlt: hld up in last pair: effrt and hdwy u.p on outer over 2f out: unable qck over 1f out: styd on same pce fnl 100yds* **40/1**

3-45 **7** 3 1/2 **Vale Of Lingfield (IRE)**[251] 298 3-9-3 71 [1] LukeMorris 5 45
(John Best) *in tch towards rr: rdn 4f out: sme hdwy u.p on inner over 1f out: btn 1f out and wknd fnl f* **12/1**

8 7 **Spowarticus** 3-9-3 0 MartinHarley 7 23
(Scott Dixon) *a bhd: rdn and struggling 1/2-way: wknd wl over 1f out* **33/1**

60-0 **9** 1 **La Passionata**[42] 5444 3-8-12 43 (t) FergusSweeney 1 15
(Jeremy Gask) *racd keenly: led after 1f tl over 1f out: sn wknd* **100/1**

1m 14.86s (-0.14) **Going Correction** -0.10s/f (Stan) **9** Ran SP% **114.2**
Speed ratings (Par 101): **96,95,94,94,92 91,87,77,76**
toteswingers 1&2 £3.90, 1&3 £1.80, 2&3 £4.20 CSF £17.28 TOTE £2.50: £1.10, £2.40, £1.30; EX 17.40.
Owner James Wigan **Bred** James Wigan **Trained** Newmarket, Suffolk
■ Stewards' Enquiry : Martin Lane two-day ban: careless riding (Oct 16-17)

FOCUS
This meeting replaced the abandoned Folkestone card. A modest 3-y-o maiden and quite a rough race. The winner did not need to match her best.

6766 TOTEPOOL MOBILE TEXT TOTE TO 89660 (S) STKS 5f 216y(P)
2:30 (2:30) (Class 6) 2-Y-O **£1,704** (£503; £251) **Stalls** Low

Form RPR

3630 **1** **Ouzinkie (IRE)**[36] 5682 2-8-11 62 SamHitchcott 2 61
(Mick Channon) *led for 1f: chsd ldrs after: swtchd rt and rdn to chal over 1f out: led ins fnl f: sn in command and r.o wl: comf* **5/2**[2]

3020 **2** 2 1/4 **Special Report (IRE)**[15] 6310 2-8-11 60 SilvestreDeSousa 4 54
(Nigel Tinkler) *chsd ldr over 4f out: rdn and unable qck over 1f out: 3rd and btn 1f out: plugged on to go 2nd again towards fin* **9/1**

4465 **3** nk **Windforpower (IRE)**[13] 6354 2-9-4 65 (p) LukeMorris 6 60
(Ronald Harris) *t.k.h early: stdd and dropped in bhd after s: hld up in rr: rdn over 3f out: nt clr run and swtchd lft over 1f out: styd on wl u.p fnl f: no threat to wnr* **9/2**[3]

5003 **4** 3/4 **Tyson The Byson**[15] 6310 2-8-11 52 (b[1]) MartinHarley 5 51
(Mrs K Burke) *racd freely: led after 1f: rdn over 1f out: clr w wnr 1f out: hdd ins fnl f: sn btn: wknd and lost 2 pls towards fin* **5/1**

0 **5** 1 1/4 **Lexi's Beauty (IRE)**[14] 0343 2-8-6 0 FrannyNorton 3 42
(Patrick Morris) *dwlt: t.k.h: hld up wl in tch: rdn and unable qck over 1f out: edgd rt and wknd fnl f* **25/1**

304 **6** 1 3/4 **Marmot Bay (IRE)**[5] 6612 2-8-7 0 ow1 FergusSweeney 1 38
(Jamie Osborne) *t.k.h: hmpd and dropped to last pair over 3f out: rdn and no hdwy on inner over 1f out: wknd 1f out* **12/1**

06 **7** 4 1/2 **Hah Hah**[18] 6212 2-8-3 0 (p) RaulDaSilva[(3)] 7 23
(Scott Dixon) *dwlt: in tch on outer: rdn and no hdwy wl over 1f out: wknd ent fnl f* **25/1**

1m 15.67s (0.67) **Going Correction** -0.10s/f (Stan) **7** Ran SP% **111.9**
Speed ratings (Par 93): **91,88,87,86,84 82,76**
toteswingers 1&2 £3.60, 1&3 £3.10, 2&3 £3.00 CSF £23.61 TOTE £2.90: £2.50, £3.10; EX 25.80.There was no bid for the winner.
Owner Box 41 **Bred** B Kennedy **Trained** West Ilsley, Berks

FOCUS
Limited form, average for the lowly grade.

NOTEBOOK
Ouzinkie(IRE) had some form on turf which gave him a decent chance in a race like this and he had been gelded since his most recent outing. Always handy, he picked up well enough to cut down the leader inside the last and record his first win at the 13th attempt. The operation may have been the key, but he was also best in on adjusted BHA ratings so he will need to improve again to be competitive outside of this level. (tchd 3-1)
Special Report(IRE), a long way behind Tyson The Byson at Musselburgh last time, had run his best two races to date at Catterick so it may be significant that he performed much better back on a sharp left-handed track. That said, he still proved no match for the winner. (op 8-1 tchd 7-1)
Windforpower(IRE), carrying a 7lb penalty for beating three rivals in a Lingfield Polytrack nursery in July, was off the bridle almost from the start and only consented to stay on when the race was over. (op 11-2)
Tyson The Byson seemed to improve for the fitting of cheekpieces at Musselburgh last time and was tried in blinkers here, but he appeared to do too much in them early. (op 6-1 tchd 7-1)
Marmot Bay(IRE) didn't get home in a 7f claimer here five days earlier, but proved disappointing this time, barely picking up from the back of the field. (tchd 15-8)

6767 BET TOTEQUADPOT TEXT TOTE TO 89660 H'CAP 5f 20y(P)
3:00 (3:00) (Class 4) (0-85,85) 3-Y-O+ **£4,075** (£1,212; £606; £303) **Stalls** Low

Form RPR

610 **1** **Blanc De Chine (IRE)**[17] 6226 3-9-0 78 [1] JimmyFortune 8 86
(Peter Makin) *chsd ldr: rdn over 1f out: styd on u.p to ld wl ins fnl f: hld on wl cl home* **16/1**

2232 **2** nk **Macdillon**[13] 6370 6-8-10 74 LiamKeniry 2 81
(Stuart Kittow) *hld up off the pce in midfield: hdwy u.p 1f out: r.o wl and ev ch wl ins fnl f: r.o* **8/1**[3]

5523 **3** hd **Fear Nothing**[13] 6358 5-8-1 72 DavidBergin[(7)] 10 78
(David O'Meara) *prom in main gp on outer: rdn 2f out: hdwy u.p 1f out: styd on u.p and ev ch towards fin: no ex last strides* **10/1**

0225 **4** 1 **Bubbly Ballerina**[3] 6689 3-8-10 79 NatashaEaton[(5)] 5 81
(Alan Bailey) *hld up off the pce in midfield: rdn and effrt 1f out: styd on wl ins fnl f* **7/1**[2]

5440 **5** nse **Damika (IRE)**[36] 5663 9-9-7 85 MichaelStainton 9 87
(David Brown) *prom in main gp: rdn 2f out: styd on u.p ins fnl f: no imp towards fin* **20/1**

6-05 **6** nk **Little Garcon (USA)**[241] 431 5-9-2 85 MichaelJMMurphy[(5)] 11 86
(Robert Cowell) *taken down early: stdd s: hld up off the pce towards rr: effrt and edging lft ent fnl f: kpt on: nvr trbld ldrs* **8/1**[3]

0005 **7** hd **Powerful Wind (IRE)**[3] 6685 3-9-1 84 DarrenEgan[(5)] 7 84
(Ronald Harris) *racd keenly: led: drew clr after 1f: stl wl and edgd rt whn rdn ent fnl f: drvn and tiring ins fnl f: hdd wl ins fnl f: fdd* **33/1**

1552 **8** 1/2 **Clear Praise (USA)**[3] 6688 5-9-4 82 HayleyTurner 4 81+
(Simon Dow) *taken down early: stdd s: hld up wl off the pce towards rr: pushed along and effrt whn nt clr run and hmpd ent fnl f: swtchd lft: shkn up and styd on towards fin: nvr trbld ldrs* **3/1**[1]

0100 **9** hd **Lost In Paris (IRE)**[25] 6006 6-9-0 78 (p) KierenFallon 3 76
(Tim Easterby) *prom in main gp: rdn 3f out: styd on same pce ins fnl f* **16/1**

-602 **10** 3/4 **R Woody**[8] 6543 5-9-4 82 JimCrowley 6 77
(Robert Cowell) *hld up off the pce towards rr: rdn and effrt over 1f out: kpt on ins fnl f: nvr trbld ldrs* **3/1**[1]

0340 **11** 4 1/2 **Jamesway (IRE)**[17] 6234 4-8-13 77 JamesSullivan 1 56
(Ruth Carr) *taken down early: hld up off the pce towards rr: rdn and effrt over 1f out: wknd and wnt rt fnl f* **16/1**

1m 1.26s (-1.04) **Going Correction** -0.10s/f (Stan) **11** Ran SP% **119.2**
Speed ratings (Par 105): **104,103,103,101,101 101,100,99,99,98 91**
toteswingers 1&2 £3.90, 1&3 £4.70, 2&3 £2.90 CSF £140.14 CT £1388.75 TOTE £32.50: £6.70, £2.90, £3.80; EX 163.70.
Owner R P Marchant & Mrs E Lee **Bred** Newlands House Stud **Trained** Ogbourne Maisey, Wilts

FOCUS
This looked a good sprint handicap, but it developed into an extraordinary race. The third and fourth are rated close to their marks.
Clear Praise(USA) Official explanation: jockey said gelding was denied a clear run

6768 RACING POST FORM WITH TOTEPOOL MOBILE H'CAP 7f 32y(P)
3:30 (3:30) (Class 4) (0-85,85) 3-Y-O **£4,075** (£1,212; £606; £303) **Stalls** High

Form RPR

4506 **1** **Solar Deity (IRE)**[69] 4473 3-9-4 82 MartinHarley 4 95
(Marco Botti) *t.k.h: hld up in tch towards rr: hdwy to chse ldrs and swtchd rt 1f out: pushed along hands and heels and led fnl 100yds: r.o wl: readily* **4/1**[3]

5112 **2** 1 1/4 **Fast Finian (IRE)**[11] 6454 3-9-4 82 SebSanders 7 92
(Paul D'Arcy) *taken down early: chsd ldrs: clsd to join ldrs over 2f out: rdn to ld over 1f out: hrd drvn ent fnl f: hdd and outpcd by wnr fnl 100yds: kpt on* **11/4**[1]

0651 **3** 3/4 **Strada Facendo (USA)**[14] 6328 3-8-13 77 KierenFallon 2 85
(Luca Cumani) *s.i.s: in rr early: stdy hdwy on outer 5f out: rdn to chse ldr over 1f out: drvn and ev ch ent fnl f: no ex and outpcd fnl 100yds* **7/2**[2]

-323 **4** 1 3/4 **Cantal**[24] 6040 3-9-1 79 TomQueally 8 82
(Sir Michael Stoute) *hld up in tch towards rr: hdwy into midfield 5f out: effrt to chse ldrs wl over 1f out: sn rdn and hung lft: wknd ins fnl f* **11/2**

030 **5** 6 **North Star Boy (IRE)**[36] 5676 3-9-5 83 JimmyFortune 5 70
(Richard Hannon) *t.k.h: chsd ldrs: rdn and unable qck whn n.m.r over 1f out: sn wknd* **10/1**

3060 **6** 1 1/2 **Sheikh The Reins (IRE)**[13] 6368 3-8-9 73 LukeMorris 3 56
(John Best) *in tch towards rr: rdn 3f out: wknd u.p over 1f out: wl btn whn swtchd rt 1f out* **20/1**

060 **7** 3 1/4 **Gabrial's Gift (IRE)**[54] 5000 3-9-2 80 SilvestreDeSousa 6 54
(Ian Williams) *led: hdd over 1f out: sn hung lft and wknd: fdd fnl f* **9/1**

210- **8** 2 3/4 **Electrician**[376] 6270 3-9-7 85 ShaneKelly 1 52
(Tim Pitt) *stdd s: hld up in rr: lost tch 2f out: sn eased* **33/1**

0000 **9** 1 3/4 **Diamondhead (IRE)**[23] 6075 3-9-1 79 (t) JamieMackay 9 41
(Brian Meehan) *t.k.h: chsd ldr tl wl over 1f out: sn wknd: fdd fnl f* **16/1**

1m 27.11s (-2.49) **Going Correction** -0.10s/f (Stan) **9** Ran SP% **116.9**
Speed ratings (Par 103): **110,108,107,105,98 97,93,90,88**
toteswingers 1&2 £3.90, 1&3 £4.70, 2&3 £2.90 CSF £15.66 CT £42.27 TOTE £4.00: £1.20, £2.00, £1.40; EX 24.10.
Owner Andrew Tinkler **Bred** Castlemartin Stud And Skymarc Farm **Trained** Newmarket, Suffolk

FOCUS
Another good handicap and the form looks solid and is rated on the positive side, with the third to his turf best.
Gabrial's Gift(IRE) Official explanation: jockey said gelding had no more to give
Electrician Official explanation: jockey said gelding failed to handle the bend

6769 MIRROR PUNTERS CLUB H'CAP 2m 119y(P)
4:00 (4:00) (Class 6) (0-60,60) 3-Y-O+ **£1,704** (£503; £251) **Stalls** Low

Form RPR

4650 **1** **Lady Mandy**[10] 6474 3-8-0 46 oh1 RyanPowell[(3)] 3 57
(Ian Williams) *hmpd after 1f and hld up in last pair after: hdwy 4f out: swtchd rt to outer and hdwy to chse clr wl over 1f out: swtchd lft and clsd ins fnl f: styd on relentessly to ld last strides* **16/1**

0622 **2** hd **Blue Dune**[3] 6691 3-8-13 56 SilvestreDeSousa 4 67+
(Mark Johnston) *led: pushed along and wnt clr over 3f out: stl 5 l clr 1f out: being clsd down and drvn wl ins fnl f: hdd last strides* **11/8**[1]

433 **3** 16 **Zaahya (IRE)**[34] 5754 3-9-3 60 PaulHanagan 6 52
(John Dunlop) *t.k.h: chsd ldrs: shuffled bk into midfield 1/2-way: rdn and hdwy 3f out: 3rd and no imp 2f out: edgd rt and wknd fnl f* **9/4**[2]

0455 **4** 2 1/4 **Nesnaas (USA)**[210] 811 11-9-0 45 FrankieMcDonald 5 35
(Alastair Lidderdale) *s.i.s: bhd and sn pushed along: rdn 7f out: lost tch w ldr over 3f out: styd on past btn horses fr over 1f out: no ch w wnr* **66/1**

-334 **5** 3/4 **Captain Sharpe**[148] 1905 4-9-9 60 (p) RobertWilliams[(5)] 1 48
(Bernard Llewellyn) *hld up in tch: hdwy on outer 6f out: rdn to chse clr ldr over 2f out tl wl over 1f out: sn btn and wknd* **13/2**[3]

200 **6** nk **Maid Of Silk (IRE)**[17] 6228 6-9-6 55 (t) CPGeoghegan[(3)] 10 43
(Neil Mulholland) *t.k.h: chsd ldr tl 10f out: wnt 2nd again over 5f out: outpcd by ldr over 3f out: lost 2nd over 2f out: sn wknd* **16/1**

200- **7** 3/4 **Go Amwell**[164] 5379 9-8-10 47 (p) DarrenEgan[(5)] 8 34
(J R Jenkins) *in tch towards rr: rdn and lost tch over 3f out: wl btn fnl 2f* **20/1**

0000 **8** 2 1/2 **Oh So Charming**[18] 6210 3-8-3 46 oh1 (p) LukeMorris 2 30
(Mark Gillard) *dwlt: in tch towards rr: hdwy to chse ldrs 5f out: hung rt and wknd over 2f out* **66/1**

040 **9** 48 **Imperial Ruby**[40] 5508 3-8-9 52 (b[1]) LiamKeniry 11
(Joseph Tuite) *chsd ldrs early: stdd bk and hld up in midfield after 2f: rdn and btn over 2f out: wl bhd and eased over 1f out: t.o* **33/1**

600 **10** 6 **Grecian Goddess (IRE)**[26] 5974 4-8-7 45 BradleyBosley[(7)] 7
(John Ryan) *in tch: t.k.h after 2f: hdwy to chse ldrs 10f out: lost pl 4f out: sn bhd: t.o and eased fnl f* **100/1**

0505 **11** 23 **Mahayogin (USA)**[12] 6399 4-9-4 50 KierenFallon 9
(Brendan Powell) *dwlt and rdn along early: hdwy to chse ldr 10f out tl over 5f out: sn bhd: t.o and eased fnl 2f* **17/2**

3m 39.0s (-2.80) **Going Correction** -0.10s/f (Stan)
WFA 3 from 4yo+ 11lb **11** Ran SP% **120.2**
Speed ratings (Par 101): **102,101,94,93,92 92,92,91,68,65 55**
toteswingers 1&2 £5.40, 1&3 £6.20, 2&3 £1.60 CSF £38.61 CT £74.95 TOTE £38.30: £5.60, £1.70, £1.02; EX 74.40.
Owner Dr Marwan Koukash **Bred** Floors Farming & Beckhampton Stables Ltd **Trained** Portway, Worcs

FOCUS
A moderate staying handicap and a controversial race. No great depth in this but the first two came clear.
Mahayogin(USA) Official explanation: jockey said gelding never travelled

6770 WOLVERHAMPTON-RACECOURSE.CO.UK MAIDEN STKS 1m 4f 50y(P)
4:30 (4:30) (Class 5) 3-Y-O+ **£2,385** (£704; £352) **Stalls** Low

Form RPR

0-2 **1** **Homeric (IRE)**[12] 6408 3-9-3 0 .... PhillipMakin 1 86
(Ed Dunlop) *chsd ldrs: stl gng wl and nt clr run over 2f out: swtchd rt and effrt over 1f out: swtchd lft and styd on strly to ld wl ins fnl f* **6/1**[3]

2 **2** *nk* **Chancery (USA)**[57] 4882 4-9-10 0 .... DanielTudhope 11 86
(David O'Meara) *hld up in rr: hdwy on outer 3f out: squeezed between rivals and chal wl over 1f out: led narrowly 1f out: drvn and styd on same pce ins fnl f* **5/4**[1]

0- **3** *nse* **Tadmir (USA)**[356] 6805 3-9-3 0 .... SilvestreDeSousa 8 85
(Saeed Bin Suroor) *hmpd and s.i.s: sn in tch in rr: rdn and hdwy on outer to chse ldrs over 2f out: rdn to ld wl over 1f out: hdd 1f out: kpt on same pce u.p after* **8/1**

4522 **4** *1 ½* **Infinitum**[10] 6492 3-8-12 80 .... (p) NickyMackay 9 78
(John Gosden) *in tch in midfield: hdwy 5f out: rdn and ev ch wl over 1f out: no ex and btn ins fnl f* **2/1**[2]

0- **5** *7* **Moonship**[376] 6267 3-9-3 0 .... RichardMullen 6 71
(Sir Michael Stoute) *in tch: rdn to chse ldrs 4f out: struggling and outpcd 2f out: swtchd lft over 1f out: sn wknd* **20/1**

-420 **6** *1 ¼* **Star For Life (USA)**[122] 2708 3-9-3 83 .... (b[1]) GeorgeBaker 10 69
(Mikael Magnusson) *t.k.h: chsd ldr tl led 10f out: hdd 8f out: styd chsng ldrs tl wknd and edgd rt wl over 1f out* **18/1**

3462 **7** *4* **Hunt A Mistress (IRE)**[16] 6279 3-8-12 71 .... MartinHarley 4 58
(Paul Cole) *racd keenly: led for 2f: chsd ldr tl led again 8f out: drvn and hdd wl over 1f out: sn wknd* **33/1**

6-0 **8** *4 ½* **The Cash Generator (IRE)**[12] 6397 4-9-10 0 .... JamieGoldstein 5 56
(Ralph Smith) *chsd ldrs tl 4f out: sn lost pl: bhd over 1f out* **100/1**

66 **9** *4* **Bridge That Gap**[12] 6398 4-9-10 0 .... FergusSweeney 2 49
(Roger Ingram) *t.k.h: hld up in midfield: lost pl and rdn over 3f out: wknd over 2f out* **100/1**

10 *¾* **Tram Express (FR)**[21] 8-9-3 0 .... (t) WilliamTwiston-Davies[(7)] 12 48
(Shaun Lycett) *v.s.a: clsd and in tch 10f out: hdwy on outer 8f out: rdn over 3f out: sn struggling: wknd over 2f out* **100/1**

0 **11** *nk* **Caunay**[17] 6228 5-9-7 0 .... (t) AmyBaker[(3)] 7 48
(Neil Mulholland) *wnt rt s: in tch in rr: rdn and sme hdwy on outer 4f out: sn struggling: wknd over 2f out* **100/1**

2m 38.5s (-2.60) **Going Correction** -0.10s/f (Stan)
WFA 3 from 4yo+ 7lb **11 Ran SP% 120.1**
Speed ratings (Par 103): **104,103,103,102,98 97,94,91,88,88 88**
toteswingers 1&2 £3.40, 1&3 £4.50, 2&3 £3.50 CSF £14.01 TOTE £9.30: £2.50, £1.10, £2.50; EX 23.40.
Owner Highclere Thoroughbred Racing - Jackson **Bred** Lynch Bages Ltd **Trained** Newmarket, Suffolk

FOCUS
This was probably better than most older-horse maidens run at the track and the four market principals pulled clear of the others. The form looks above average with the runner-up to his debut mark.
T/Plt: £54.00 to a £1 stake. Pool £64,907.57 - 876.06 winning units. T/Qpdt: £12.10 to a £1 stake. Pool £6,175.08 - 376.66 winning units. SP

[6579]KEMPTON (A.W) (R-H)
Wednesday, October 3

OFFICIAL GOING: Standard
Wind: Moderate, half behind Weather: Fine but cloudy, heavy shower after race 5

6771 WIN BIG WITH BETDAQ MULTIPLES H'CAP 5f (P)
5:40 (5:40) (Class 7) (0-50,50) 3-Y-O+ **£1,455** (£433; £216; £108) **Stalls** Low

Form RPR

2302 **1** **Perfect Honour (IRE)**[60] 4815 6-8-13 **49** .... (b) WilliamCarson 10 58
(Violet M Jordan) *t.k.h: trckd ldrs and racd on outer: rdn wl over 1f out: styd on to ld jst ins fnl f: sn in command* **6/1**[3]

5050 **2** *2* **Itum**[27] 5971 5-8-13 **49** ow1 .... SebSanders 7 51
(Christine Dunnett) *prom on inner: wnt 2nd 2f out: rdn to ld over 1f out: hdd and one pce jst ins fnl f* **7/1**

0050 **3** *½* **College Doll**[11] 6496 3-9-0 **50** .... BrettDoyle 8 50
(Christine Dunnett) *chsd ldrs in 6th: urged along and prog to take 3rd fnl f: kpt on same pce* **40/1**

6600 **4** *nk* **Pharoh Jake**[16] 6307 4-8-11 **47** .... KieranO'Neill 2 46
(John Bridger) *anticipated stall opening and blew the s: wl off the pce in 9th: prog whn nt clr run and swtchd lft ins fnl f: styd on strly last 100yds* **7/1**

4200 **5** *nk* **Kara's Vision**[18] 6249 3-8-6 **49** .... (p) HannahNunn[(7)] 9 47
(Robert Cowell) *racd wd thrght: prom: lost grnd bnd 2f out: pushed along and kpt on one pce* **20/1**

0302 **6** *1* **First Fast Now (IRE)**[18] 6249 3-8-6 **49** .... DanielleMooney[(7)] 6 43
(Nigel Tinkler) *dwlt: off the pce in 8th: tried to cl fr over 1f out: kpt on same pce* **11/2**[2]

0200 **7** *nse* **Botanist**[16] 6321 5-8-13 **49** .... (be) LukeMorris 11 43
(Milton Bradley) *dwlt: off the pce in 7th: effrt over 1f out: kpt on but n.d* **8/1**

6060 **8** *2 ½* **Royal Envoy (IRE)**[31] 5850 9-8-13 **49** .... (p) MichaelStainton 12 34
(Paul Howling) *chsd ldr to 2f out: sn btn* **16/1**

0005 **9** *3 ¼* **Abadejo**[14] 6362 4-8-13 **49** .... (v) RichardHughes 5 22
(J R Jenkins) *led to over 1f out: wknd qckly* **4/1**[1]

0003 **10** *7* **Adaeze (IRE)**[18] 6233 4-8-8 **49** .... (b[1]) MatthewLawson[(5)] 3
(Jonathan Portman) *v.s.a and then swvd to avoid rival: a t.o* **8/1**

0000 **U** **Triple Salchow**[27] 5970 3-8-6 **47** .... (b[1]) LeonnaMayor[(5)] 4
(Alastair Lidderdale) *rel to r: bucking and threw rdr off shortly after s* **10/1**

1m 0.12s (-0.38) **Going Correction** -0.15s/f (Stan) **11 Ran SP% 119.1**
Speed ratings (Par 97): **97,93,93,92,92 90,90,86,81,69**
toteswingers: 1&2 £11.10, 2&3 £78.30, 1&3 £20.00 CSF £48.35 CT £1555.04 TOTE £4.60: £1.30, £3.70, £8.30; EX 49.10 Trifecta £1335.10 Pool £4,330.10 - 2.40 winning units..
Owner Mrs Jackie Cornwell **Bred** Country Breeders **Trained** Moreton Morrell, Warwicks

FOCUS
This was a weak sprint handicap and it looked wide open. The winner is rated back to her old best.

Adaeze(IRE) Official explanation: jockey said filly suffered interference shortly after start

6772 BETDAQ MOBILE APPS/BRITISH STALLION STUDS EBF MAIDEN STKS 6f (P)
6:10 (6:10) (Class 5) 2-Y-O **£3,234** (£962; £481; £240) **Stalls** Low

Form RPR

5 **1** **Agerzam**[13] 6411 2-9-3 0 .... NeilCallan 4 84+
(Roger Varian) *t.k.h: trckd ldng pair: led on inner 2f out: shkn up and clr 1f out: styd on wl* **13/2**

64 **2** *2 ¾* **Ferjaan**[98] 3505 2-9-3 0 .... TadhgO'Shea 1 75
(John Gosden) *hld up in 6th: shkn up and prog 2f out: rdn to dispute 2nd ins fnl f: no ch w wnr* **5/2**[1]

3 *hd* **Future Reference (IRE)** 2-9-3 0 .... FrankieDettori 11 74
(Saeed Bin Suroor) *trckd ldrs in 4th: pushed along and effrt 2f out: disp 2nd ins fnl f: no ch w wnr* **7/2**[3]

4 **4** *3 ¼* **Isis Blue**[62] 4730 2-9-3 0 .... JamesMillman 3 65+
(Rod Millman) *in tch in 8th: jst pushed along fr over 2f out: kpt on steadily to take 4th nr fin* **14/1**

3 **5** *1 ¼* **Keep The Dream**[7] 6581 2-9-3 0 .... (t) JimCrowley 2 61
(Paul Cole) *led: wandered and hdd 2f out: nt qckn over 1f out: wknd ins fnl f* **6/1**

6 *4 ½* **Great Crested (IRE)** 2-9-3 0 .... ShaneKelly 8 47
(Murty McGrath) *green preliminaries: s.i.s: outpcd in last: pushed along and passed struggling rivals to go 6th over 1f out: no hdwy after* **100/1**

7 *1* **Fort Knox** 2-9-3 0 .... RichardHughes 5 44
(Richard Hannon) *trckd ldr: gng strly over 2f out: shkn up wl over 1f out: sn wknd qckly: eased* **10/3**[2]

8 *hd* **Gold Weight** 2-9-3 0 .... JamieGoldstein 10 44
(Michael Madgwick) *dwlt: a in rr: wd bnd 3f out: bhd after: plugged on* **100/1**

9 *nse* **Malaysian Boleh** 2-9-3 0 .... SebSanders 9 44
(Simon Dow) *a in rr: bhd fr over 2f out: plugged on* **100/1**

10 *shd* **Direct Trade** 2-8-12 0 .... IanMongan 6 38
(Mark Usher) *t.k.h: nvr bttr than midfield: outpcd and bhd fnl 2f* **80/1**

0 **11** *6* **Aphrodite Spirit (IRE)**[9] 6534 2-8-12 0 .... LukeMorris 7 20
(Pat Eddery) *t.k.h: prom over 2f: sn wknd: t.o* **100/1**

1m 12.24s (-0.86) **Going Correction** -0.15s/f (Stan) **11 Ran SP% 113.4**
Speed ratings (Par 95): **99,95,95,90,89 83,81,81,81,81 73**
toteswingers: 1&2 £2.90, 2&3 £4.00, 1&3 £4.60 CSF £22.42 TOTE £7.60: £2.00, £1.50, £1.80; EX 33.60 Trifecta £148.30 Pool £4,275.09 - 21.33 winning units..
Owner Saleh Al Homaizi & Imad Al Sagar **Bred** Saleh Al Homaizi & Imad Al Sagar **Trained** Newmarket, Suffolk

FOCUS
Not a bad juvenile maiden. They went pretty hard up front and previous experience told. The winner impressed and the second and fourth set the level.

NOTEBOOK
Agerzam ◆ showed the clear benefit of his Yarmouth debut 13 days earlier, running out a taking winner. Roger Varian's colt got the run of the race on the inside just off the early leaders, but there was a lot to like about the manner in which he quickened and went about his job from 2f out. He was in control passing the furlong marker and clearly enjoyed this surface. A slightly stiffer test should be within his compass, but it makes sense to race him as a sprinter in the short-term. He could be very useful. (op 8-1)
Ferjaan set the standard on his two encouraging turf efforts and was solid in the market following a 98-day absence. He was rather taken off his feet early, but improved to have his chance 2f out and would have been a little closer with a clearer passage. He might benefit for another furlong and can now enter nurseries. (op 7-2)
Future Reference(IRE) ◆ proved best of the newcomers and deserves credit as he was drawn one from the outside. He's a half-brother to a 1m3f winner, but the dam was a sprinter and he clearly has speed about him. A good-looking colt, he should go very close next time. (tchd 3-1)
Isis Blue again finished fourth on this AW debut, but he was coming back off a 62-day break and kept on promisingly under hands-and-heels riding late in the day. He can win a maiden, but will look more interesting when eligible for nurseries. (op 10-1)
Keep The Dream, third on his debut here last week, took the field along in this better race and was a sitting duck. This was no disgrace, however, and he'll qualify for a mark after his next assignment. (op 9-2)
Fort Knox, Dubawi Gold's brother, was expected to go well on this racecourse debut. However, he refused to settle just off the leader early on and faded 2f out. He's surely capable of better. (op 11-4 tchd 7-2)
Direct Trade Official explanation: jockey said filly hung left in straight

6773 BACK OR LAY AT BETDAQ.COM H'CAP (DIV I) 1m (P)
6:40 (6:42) (Class 6) (0-60,60) 3-Y-O+ **£1,617** (£481; £240; £120) **Stalls** Low

Form RPR

U402 **1** **Inpursuitoffreedom**[26] 5996 5-9-6 **59** .... RichardHughes 2 68+
(Philip McBride) *hld up but rchd midfield by 1/2-way: smooth prog over 2f out: produced to ld last 150yds: shkn up and wl on top nr fin* **8/1**

0000 **2** *¾* **Cobbs Quay**[18] 6262 4-8-13 **55** .... (b[1]) SimonPearce[(3)] 6 61
(Daniel Kubler) *s.i.s and urged along: sn prom and t.k.h: drvn to chal over 1f out: led briefly 1f out: readily hld by wnr after* **14/1**

0004 **3** *½* **Green Earth (IRE)**[26] 5996 5-9-7 **60** .... IanMongan 4 65
(Pat Phelan) *hld up in midfield on inner: rdn and prog fr 2f out: tried to chal 1f out: styd on same pce* **8/1**

0231 **4** *½* **Pastoral Jet**[13] 6395 4-8-12 **54** .... RyanPowell[(3)] 3 58+
(Richard Rowe) *hld up wl in rr: shkn up and prog 2f out: tried to cl on ldrs fnl f: kpt on but nt pce to threaten* **5/1**[2]

0121 **5** *¾* **Mount Mayday (IRE)**[9] 6546 3-9-4 **60** .... (t) WilliamCarson 10 62
(Stuart Williams) *towards rr: rdn on outer over 2f out: styd on u.p fr over 1f out: nvr able to chal* **9/4**[1]

0443 **6** *¾* **Having A Ball**[13] 6395 8-8-13 **57** .... MatthewLawson[(5)] 13 57
(Jonathan Portman) *hld up in last trio: rdn over 2f out: prog over 1f out: kpt on u.p: nvr able to chal* **12/1**

0030 **7** *1* **Spirit Of Gondree (IRE)**[35] 5750 4-9-7 **60** .... (b) LukeMorris 12 58
(Milton Bradley) *pressed ldr: narrow ld over 3f out but sn rdn: battled it out tl hdd & wknd jst ins fnl f* **15/2**[3]

0003 **8** *½* **Sermons Mount (USA)**[7] 6586 6-9-3 **56** .... (p) JimCrowley 11 53
(Paul Howling) *hld up in rr: drvn over 2f out: prog to chse ldrs over 1f out: hanging and wknd fnl f* **20/1**

5000 **9** *nk* **Cativo Cavallino**[102] 3388 9-9-2 **58** .... NataliaGemelova[(3)] 8 54
(John E Long) *t.k.h: prom: rdn over 2f out: steadily fdd over 1f out* **33/1**

0002 **10** *¾* **Rufus Stone (USA)**[28] 5941 4-9-2 **55** .... (p) BrettDoyle 9 50
(Jane Chapple-Hyam) *led: narrowly hdd over 3f out: kpt pressing ldr u.p tl wknd over 1f out* **10/1**

555- **11** *12* **Turn The Tide**[450] 3920 4-9-3 **56** .... JohnFahy 7 23
(Dai Williams) *nvr beyond midfield: wknd over 2f out: t.o* **66/1**

240- **12** 2 1/4 **Big Sur**474 3130 6-9-0 **56** RyanClark(3) 1 18
(Tom Keddy) *dwlt: hld up and sn detached in last: no prog 3f out: sn wknd: t.o* **25/1**

0-00 **13** 3 **Tribouley**78 4196 4-8-11 **57** PaulBooth(7) 14 12
(Dean Ivory) *s.i.s and urged along early: sn prom on wd outside and then t.k.h: wknd 3f out: hung to nr side rail fr over 2f out: t.o* **50/1**

1m 39.62s (-0.18) **Going Correction** -0.15s/f (Stan)
WFA 3 from 4yo+ 3lb **13** Ran SP% **119.9**
Speed ratings: **94,93,92,92,91 90,89,89,88,88 76,73,70**
toteswingers: 1&2 £36.80, 2&3 £30.60, 1&3 £9.60 CSF £108.45 CT £655.68 TOTE £6.00: £2.10, £6.30, £2.50; EX 194.00 Trifecta £1447.20 Pool £2,346.95 - 1.20 winning units..
Owner P J McBride **Bred** Lord Fairhaven **Trained** Newmarket, Suffolk

FOCUS
There were any amount in with a chance 1f out in this moderate handicap. It was the slower division. The winner's best effort since the spring.

6774 BACK OR LAY AT BETDAQ.COM H'CAP (DIV II) 1m (P)
7:10 (7:12) (Class 6) (0-60,60) 3-Y-O+ **£1,617** (£481; £240; £120) **Stalls** Low

Form RPR

2313 **1** **Dana's Present**4 6690 3-9-4 **60** RichardHughes 12 71+
(George Baker) *hld up in last trio: taken wd over 2f out: smooth prog after to ld 1f out: nudged along to assert: easily* **5/4**1

0000 **2** 1 1/4 **Geeaitch**23 6105 3-9-1 **57** WilliamCarson 4 59
(Anthony Carson) *hld up wl in rr: rdn and prog arnd field on wd outside fr 4f out: drvn and c to chal jst over 1f out: kpt on but brushed aside by wnr* **20/1**

5044 **3** 3/4 **Two Sugars**75 4302 4-9-3 **56** KierenFallon 8 56
(Louise Best) *reluctant to enter stalls: chsd ldrs: pushed along 1/2-way: rdn and styd on fr over 1f out to take 3rd wl ins fnl f* **17/2**

064 **4** hd **Fonterutoli (IRE)**16 6302 5-9-3 **56** (e1) FergusSweeney 13 56
(Roger Ingram) *hld up and sn last: prog 2f out: nt clrest of passages fr over 1f out: styd on: nrest at fin* **50/1**

3530 **5** 1/2 **Warbond**99 3470 4-9-6 **59** JamieGoldstein 5 57
(Michael Madgwick) *hld up in midfield: lost pl over 2f out: rdn and prog over 1f out: kpt on same pce fnl f* **16/1**

023 **6** nk **Valdaw**18 6252 4-9-4 **57** NeilCallan 2 55
(Tony Carroll) *trckd ldrs: prog 2f out: drvn and upsides jst over 1f out: fdd fnl f* **11/2**2

0060 **6** dht **Bassett Road (IRE)**21 6145 4-9-7 **60** StevieDonohoe 1 58
(Willie Musson) *fast away but restrained into midfield and t.k.h: rdn and prog 2f out: led for a few strides jst over 1f out: wknd fnl f* **15/2**3

6000 **8** 1 **D'Urberville**28 5941 5-9-7 **60** DarryllHolland 3 55
(J R Jenkins) *taken down early: led: upped pce after 3f: hung lft and drvn 2f out: hdd jst over 1f out: fdd* **25/1**

55 **9** 1 1/4 **Desertcougar (IRE)**19 6217 3-9-4 **60** (b1) SeanQuinlan 11 53
(Daniel Mark Loughnane) *stdd s: tk fierce hold and hld up in rr: crept clsr fr over 2f out: on heels of ldrs jst over 1f out: sn rdn and wknd* **14/1**

6445 **10** 1 1/4 **Saint Boniface**17 6281 3-9-2 **58** SebSanders 9 48
(Peter Makin) *t.k.h: hld up wl in rr: prog on inner jst over 2f out: tried to chal over 1f out: wknd fnl f* **14/1**

2400 **11** 9 **White Flight**111 3083 3-9-4 **60** JimmyFortune 7 29
(Jonathan Portman) *disp 2nd pl to wl over 1f out: wknd rapidly: t.o* **33/1**

2000 **12** 3 1/2 **Arabian Flight**133 2397 3-9-2 **58** KieranO'Neill 6 19
(John Bridger) *taken down early: disp 2nd to jst over 2f out: wknd rapidly: t.o* **66/1**

462- **13** 4 1/2 **Esteem Lord**572 837 6-9-2 **55** IanMongan 14 6
(Zoe Davison) *in tch in midfield tl wknd rapidly 2f out: t.o* **25/1**

1m 39.27s (-0.53) **Going Correction** -0.15s/f (Stan)
WFA 3 from 4yo+ 3lb **13** Ran SP% **120.2**
Speed ratings: **96,94,94,93,93 93,93,92,90,89 80,77,72**
toteswingers: 1&2 £17.80, 2&3 £36.20, 1&3 £4.10 CSF £36.61 CT £171.63 TOTE £2.40: £1.20, £7.80, £1.70; EX 34.50 Trifecta £580.80 Pool £2,543.31 - 3.24 winning units..
Owner Whitsbury Racing Club **Bred** Newsells Park Stud **Trained** Whitsbury, Hants

FOCUS
Richard Hughes was outstanding aboard the winner of the first division of this moderate handicap, but this was an absolute masterclass from him as he doubled up. The faster division, but the form is still weakish. The winner is on the upgrade.
Fonterutoli(IRE) Official explanation: jockey said gelding was denied a clear run
Esteem Lord Official explanation: jockey said gelding became unbalanced in the straight

6775 BETDAQ CASINO GAMES NURSERY 1m (P)
7:40 (7:40) (Class 3) (0-95,86) 2-Y-O **£5,822** (£1,732; £865; £432) **Stalls** Low

Form RPR

1513 **1** **I'm Back (IRE)**24 6070 2-9-4 **83** FrankieDettori 8 91
(Saeed Bin Suroor) *led 100yds: sn restrained into 5th: shkn up and prog over 2f out: led over 1f out: rdn clr: readily* **15/8**1

021 **2** 2 1/4 **Lizzie Tudor**46 5339 2-8-11 **76** JimmyFortune 4 79
(Andrew Balding) *hld up in 6th: rdn and prog over 2f out: styd on to take 2nd jst ins fnl f: no imp on wnr* **7/2**2

155 **3** 2 1/2 **Filfil (USA)**14 6372 2-9-3 **82** MickaelBarzalona 1 79
(Mahmood Al Zarooni) *trckd ldr after 100yds: rdn to ld over 2f out: hdd over 1f out: wl outpcd* **8/1**

5155 **4** 2 3/4 **Mystical Moment**25 6021 2-9-7 **86** SeanLevey 7 77
(Richard Hannon) *chsd ldng pair after 1f: drvn and cl enough 2f out: fdd fnl f* **16/1**

231 **5** 3 **Pompeia**56 4946 2-9-1 **80** JimCrowley 3 64
(Ralph Beckett) *chsd ldng trio after 1f: rdn over 2f out: wknd over 1f out* **9/2**3

2611 **6** 3 **Ronaldinho (IRE)**33 5786 2-9-7 **86** RichardHughes 5 63
(Richard Hannon) *settled in detached last: pushed along 3f out: rdn and no prog 2f out* **6/1**

610 **7** 10 **Winged Icarus (USA)**18 6247 2-8-10 **75** (v) KierenFallon 6 29
(Alan McCabe) *led after 100yds and set str pce: hdd & wknd qckly over 2f out: t.o* **12/1**

1m 37.5s (-2.30) **Going Correction** -0.15s/f (Stan) 2y crse rec **7** Ran SP% **114.2**
Speed ratings (Par 99): **105,102,100,97,94 91,81**
toteswingers: 1&2 £1.60, 2&3 £4.50, 1&3 £3.70 CSF £8.52 CT £40.53 TOTE £3.10: £1.60, £2.40; EX 9.90 Trifecta £58.20 Pool £3,297.54 - 41.89 winning units..
Owner Godolphin **Bred** Darley **Trained** Newmarket, Suffolk

FOCUS
This was a good nursery and, with no hanging about through the early stages, they came home well strung out. The form is possibly worth a shade more, with the time fast.

NOTEBOOK
I'm Back(IRE) was dropped 1lb despite finishing third to a subsequent Group 3 winner at York on his previous outing and took full advantage, breaking the 2-y-o course record on this switch to Polytrack. Confidently ridden wide of runners, he found plenty when asked to go about his business and saw out the extra furlong without fuss. There's probably still more to come from him. (op 5-2)
Lizzie Tudor ◆ beat three subsequent winners in a Doncaster maiden 46 days earlier and there was every chance she'd got in lightly off 76 on this nursery/AW debut. Her rider looked confident enough 2f out, but she lacked anything like the same acceleration of the winner. More positive handling should see her back to winning ways. (op 4-1)
Filfil(USA) showed his true colours again back on Polytrack, but failed to see it out having been more prominently ridden than the front pair. Dropping back to 7f looks on the cards. (op 7-1)
Mystical Moment was well held back down in class. (op 14-1)
Pompeia, a course maiden winner, looked a non-stayer up to this trip. However, she has got plenty of stamina in her pedigree and perhaps something was amiss. (op 7-2)
Ronaldinho(IRE), seeking a hat-trick, was 17lb higher than when initially winning, but he was beaten before the higher mark came into play. (op 5-1)
Winged Icarus(USA) dropped tamely away after setting strong fractions and it will be interesting to see what he can do back on Fibresand. (op 14-1)

6776 RACING PLUS THE BEST WEEKEND ACTION H'CAP 1m 4f (P)
8:10 (8:12) (Class 4) (0-85,85) 3-Y-O+ **£4,075** (£1,212; £606; £303) **Stalls** Centre

Form RPR

-241 **1** **Huff And Puff**26 6012 5-9-11 **84** NeilCallan 10 91
(Amanda Perrett) *trckd ldr after 1f: rdn to ld 2f out: hdd 1f out: rallied wl to ld again fnl 50yds* **9/2**2

1301 **2** hd **Ukrainian (IRE)**3 6712 3-9-1 **81** 6ex (v) KierenFallon 2 88
(Mark Johnston) *led 1f: trckd ldng pair after: drvn to chal 2f out: led 1f out: styd on but worn down last 50yds* **4/1**1

4066 **3** 3/4 **Spensley (IRE)**26 6018 6-9-12 **85** MickaelBarzalona 6 91+
(James Fanshawe) *hld up disputing 4th: rdn over 2f out: wnt 3rd 1f out: clsd gradualy but nvr quite able to chal* **5/1**3

4664 **4** 3/4 **Shesthemar**35 5752 3-8-11 **77** TedDurcan 11 82+
(David Lanigan) *hld up in last pair in modly run event: prog on inner over 2f out: tried to cl on ldrs over 1f out: one pce* **13/2**

4450 **5** 1 1/4 **Art Scholar (IRE)**11 6476 5-9-10 **83** GeorgeBaker 12 86+
(Michael Appleby) *hld up in last in modly run event: sme prog 2f out: rdn over 1f out: styd on: no ch to threaten* **20/1**

0335 **6** 2 **Nave (USA)**5 6642 5-9-1 **74** MartinLane 3 73
(David Simcock) *trckd ldrs disputing 4th: rdn over 2f out: nt qckn and no imp on ldrs over 1f out* **12/1**

3335 **7** 1/2 **Knightly Escapade**40 5554 4-9-5 **78** RichardHughes 5 77
(John Dunlop) *stdd s: hld up in rr in modly run r: tried to cl over 2f out: no imp over 1f out* **9/1**

-000 **8** 1/2 **Yasir (USA)**28 5944 4-9-9 **82** (tp) FrankieDettori 9 80
(Saeed Bin Suroor) *led after 1f: set mod pce: kicked on over 2f out: sn hdd & wknd* **6/1**

0050 **9** 4 1/2 **Four Nations (USA)**46 5344 4-9-1 **74** JimCrowley 7 65
(Amanda Perrett) *hld up in midfield: rdn and wknd over 2f out* **14/1**

-114 **10** 1 1/2 **Rocky Rebel**171 500 4-8-13 **72** DaneO'Neill 4 60
(Chris Bealby) *nvr appeared to be gng wl: towards rr: wknd over 2f out* **33/1**

2m 33.1s (-1.40) **Going Correction** -0.15s/f (Stan)
WFA 3 from 4yo+ 7lb **10** Ran SP% **114.5**
Speed ratings (Par 105): **98,97,97,96,96 94,94,94,91,90**
toteswingers: 1&2 £4.40, 2&3 £4.40, 1&3 £4.20 CSF £22.41 CT £92.51 TOTE £5.40: £1.80, £1.80, £1.40; EX 23.50 Trifecta £179.30 Pool £663.90 - 2.74 winning units..
Owner A D Spence **Bred** Sir Eric Parker **Trained** Pulborough, W Sussex

FOCUS
A fair and competitive handicap. It was run at an uneven pace, though, which meant for a muddling affair. The winner confirmed he's better than ever.

6777 BOOK NOW FOR JUMP SUNDAY 21.10.12 NOVICE STKS 6f (P)
8:40 (8:40) (Class 5) 2-Y-O **£2,264** (£673; £336) **Stalls** Low

Form RPR

134 **1** **Ninjago**19 6200 2-9-2 100 RichardHughes 3 95+
(Richard Hannon) *hld up in 3rd: cruised up to chal over 1f out: led ins fnl f: pushed clr: easily* **5/4**2

1 **2** 1 3/4 **Spokeswoman (IRE)**28 5943 2-9-0 0 FrankieDettori 4 88
(Saeed Bin Suroor) *veered lft s: t.k.h: trckd ldr: led wl over 1f out: sn jnd and rdn: hdd ins fnl f: readily hld after* **8/11**1

100 **3** 3 1/4 **Carlton Blue (IRE)**20 6162 2-9-0 81 (t) AshleyMorgan(5) 2 80
(Paul Cole) *racd freely: led at mod pce: shkn up and hdd wl over 1f out: easily outpcd* **16/1**3

1m 13.36s (0.26) **Going Correction** -0.15s/f (Stan) **3** Ran SP% **108.2**
Speed ratings (Par 95): **92,89,85**
CSF £2.58 TOTE £1.70; EX 2.60.
Owner J Palmer-Brown & Potensis Ltd **Bred** Newsells Park Stud **Trained** East Everleigh, Wilts

FOCUS
An interesting novice event but one run at a fairly slow pace. The winner travelled well and impressed.

NOTEBOOK
Ninjago relished this drop back in trip on his AW debut and ran out an easy winner, handing his rider a treble on the night. His powerful team had won this twice in the past and he set the standard on his Listed third at Newbury. Richard Hughes didn't have to fully extend him to get on top and sprinting is clearly his game at present. He ought to be high on confidence now. (op 11-8)
Spokeswoman(IRE) was a taking debut winner over C&D last month, but it was surprising to see her odds-on in the betting considering Ninjago had achieved more. She had every chance, but always looked to be doing a little too much and was no match at all for the winner. This is probably about as good as she is. (op 4-6)
Carlton Blue(IRE), out the back in sales races on turf the last twice, had pretty much his own way out in front but proved keen. He steadily went backwards in between the final 2f, but faced another stiff task switched to Polytrack and will be better off in a nursery. (tchd 20-1)

6778 BOOK YOUR CHRISTMAS PARTY AT KEMPTON H'CAP 7f (P)
9:10 (9:10) (Class 6) (0-55,55) 3-Y-O+ **£1,617** (£481; £240; £120) **Stalls** Low

Form RPR

3206 **1** **Trusting (IRE)**21 6151 3-9-2 **55** (v1) NeilCallan 2 62
(Eve Johnson Houghton) *hld up in midfield: eased lft jst over 2f out: sustained prog over 1f out: drvn to ld last 100yds: styd on* **13/2**3

0342 **2** nk **Rapid Water**18 6252 6-9-3 **54** (p) DaneO'Neill 7 60+
(Pat Eddery) *dwlt: sn in midfield: nudged rival over 2f out and nt clr run sn after: gd prog on outer jst over 1f out: r.o to take 2nd nr fin* **5/1**1

0000 **3** nse **Men Don't Cry (IRE)**20 6158 3-9-2 **55** (b) LiamKeniry 10 61
(Ed de Giles) *hld up in midfield on outer: prog on outer w wnr over 1f out: nt qckn last 75yds* **40/1**

034 **4** ¾ **Bold Ring**[13] 6396 6-8-10 **54**.......... JoeyHaynes(7) 6 58
(Eric Wheeler) *hld up in midfield: prog over 2f out: led over 1f out: hdd and no ex last 100yds* **12/1**

0062 **5** shd **Divine Rule (IRE)**[13] 6396 4-9-1 **52**..........(v) AmirQuinn 13 56
(Laura Mongan) *slowly away: hld up in last trio: stl there 2f out: gd prog jst over 1f out: fin wl: too much to do* **25/1**

2405 **6** ¾ **Victorian Number (FR)**[18] 6252 4-8-12 **52**..........(p) SophieDoyle(3) 8 54
(Geoffrey Deacon) *trckd ldng pair: cl up 2f out: nt qckn over 1f out and sn lost pl: styd on again last 100yds* **16/1**

-425 **7** hd **Mary Frith**[19] 6211 3-9-1 **54**..........(p) JimCrowley 11 55
(William Knight) *trckd ldrs on outer: rdn to chal 2f out: stl cl enough jst over 1f out: fdd* **10/1**

0104 **8** 1 **Silly Billy (IRE)**[13] 6395 4-9-4 **55**..........(t) RichardHughes 14 55+
(Sylvester Kirk) *hld up in last quintet: nudged by rival over 2f out: tried to make prog over 1f out: nvr clrest of runs and no hdwy fnl f* **13/2**[3]

6340 **9** nk **Do More Business (IRE)**[76] 4241 5-8-13 **53**..........(v) RyanPowell(3) 5 50
(Alison Batchelor) *mde most to over 1f out: fdd fnl f* **25/1**

066 **10** nk **Squirrel Wood (IRE)**[65] 4652 4-9-3 **54**..........(b) GeorgeBaker 9 51+
(Mary Hambro) *dwlt: hld up in last: tried to make prog fr 2f out but nt clr run and nvr able to threaten* **20/1**

4040 **11** ¾ **Bahri Sheen (IRE)**[12] 6455 4-8-12 **54**.......... DarrenEgan(5) 4 49
(John Best) *stdd s: hld up in last trio: tried to make prog fr 2f out: nvr much room and one pce fnl f* **16/1**

1040 **12** ¾ **Takitwo**[43] 5440 9-8-10 **52**.......... MatthewLawson(5) 3 45
(Jonathan Portman) *hld up in last quintet: effrt on inner 2f out: no prog over 1f out* **8/1**

0253 **13** 6 **Ereka (IRE)**[7] 6585 4-9-4 **55**.......... LukeMorris 1 31
(John Best) *trckd ldrs on inner: rdn 2f out: wknd qckly* **6/1**[2]

0651 **14** 1 **Royal Box**[20] 6158 5-9-2 **53**..........(p) WilliamCarson 12 27
(Tony Carroll) *w ldr to over 2f out: wknd qckly u.p* **11/1**

1m 26.04s (0.04) **Going Correction** -0.15s/f (Stan)
WFA 3 from 4yo+ 2lb **14** Ran SP% **120.5**
Speed ratings (Par 101): **93,92,92,91,91 90,90,89,89,88 87,87,80,79**
toteswingers: 1&2 £7.80, 2&3 £92.10, 1&3 £42.60 CSF £37.16 CT £1256.97 TOTE £9.10: £2.20, £1.90, £7.80; EX 47.40 TRIFECTA Not won..
Owner Miss Stephanie Von Schilcher **Bred** Carrigbeg Stud Co Ltd **Trained** Blewbury, Oxon
■ Stewards' Enquiry : Neil Callan one-day ban: careless riding (Oct 17)

FOCUS
A modes, wide-open handicap in which they went a sound pace, and there was a bunch finish. The winner is rated to her best.
Squirrel Wood(IRE) Official explanation: jockey said filly was denied a clear run
Ereka(IRE) Official explanation: jockey said filly ran flat
T/Jkpt: Not won. T/Plt: £126.90 to a £1 stake. Pool £68,432.80 - 393.57 winning units. T/Qpdt: £17.30 to a £1 stake. Pool £9,898.88 - 421.00 winning units. JN

6257 NEWCASTLE (L-H)
Wednesday, October 3

OFFICIAL GOING: Heavy (soft in places; 4.7)
Wind: Fresh, half against Weather: Cloudy

6779 RACING TO SCHOOL ST BENETS PRIMARY SCHOOL E B F MAIDEN STKS — 1m 3y(S)
2:10 (2:10) (Class 4) 2-Y-O **£4,334** (£1,289; £644; £322) **Stalls** Centre

Form RPR

6 **1** **Allnecessaryforce (FR)**[21] 6133 2-9-3 0.......... TonyHamilton 5 71
(Richard Fahey) *trckd ldrs: shkn up and hdwy to ld 2f out: edgd lft ins fnl f: drvn out* **3/1**[2]

6 **2** 1¾ **Stagweekend (IRE)**[23] 6099 2-9-3 0.......... MichaelO'Connell 1 67
(John Quinn) *plld hrd early: chsd ldrs: hdwy and ev ch 2f out: sn rdn: one pce ins fnl f* **9/2**[3]

3 **3** 10 **Bravo Ragazzo (IRE)**[21] 6134 2-9-3 0.......... JoeFanning 4 45
(Mark Johnston) *t.k.h: cl up: led 1/2-way to 2f out: wknd appr fnl f* **8/11**[1]

4 12 **Clouded Vision (IRE)** 2-9-3 0.......... PJMcDonald 2 19
(Noel Quinlan) *hld up in tch: rdn 3f out: wknd fnl 2f* **12/1**

0 **5** 14 **Mjaal (IRE)**[21] 6133 2-8-12 0.......... TomEaves 3
(John Weymes) *led to 1/2-way: rdn and wknd* **100/1**

1m 51.04s (7.64) **Going Correction** +0.775s/f (Yiel) **5** Ran SP% **109.8**
Speed ratings (Par 97): **92,90,80,68,54**
CSF £16.05 TOTE £2.80: £1.50, £2.00; EX 19.20.
Owner Peter O'Callaghan **Bred** G R Bailey Ltd **Trained** Musley Bank, N Yorks

FOCUS
The front pair pulled clear in what was an ordinary maiden. The ground was deep and the form can't be taken too literally.

NOTEBOOK
Allnecessaryforce(FR), very green when sixth on his debut, is by a sire whose progeny can usually handle testing conditions. He still looked inexperienced, but was right on top at the finish. He has a fair bit of size and scope and should make a useful handicapper at three. (op 7-2)
Stagweekend(IRE), sixth in a 6f maiden here that has worked out quite well on his debut, was the only one to go with the winner in the closing stages. He should improve again and go on and do better next year. (op 5-1 tchd 11-2)
Bravo Ragazzo(IRE), who has a top-class pedigree, had finished third in heavy ground first-time at Carlisle. He ran with the choke out and after showing ahead, hung left-handed and fell in a heap. He is surely a lot better than he showed here. (op 4-6 tchd 4-5)
Clouded Vision(IRE) made a tardy start and soon pushed along, dropped right away soon after halfway. (op 10-1)
Mjaal(IRE), tailed-off last behind the winner at Carlisle first time, led on sufferance before being left a long way behind.

6780 BRITISH STALLION STUDS SUPPORTING BRITISH RACING E B F MAIDEN STKS — 7f
2:40 (2:40) (Class 4) 2-Y-O **£4,334** (£1,289; £644; £322) **Stalls** Centre

Form RPR

360 **1** **Krupskaya (FR)**[25] 6049 2-8-12 0.......... MichaelO'Connell 1 66+
(Mrs K Burke) *trckd ldrs: led appr 2f out: sn rdn: hld on wl u.p fnl f* **5/1**[3]

2 ½ **Glacial Age (IRE)** 2-9-3 0.......... DanielTudhope 12 70+
(Jo Hughes) *dwlt: t.k.h in rr: smooth hdwy to chal 2f out: sn rdn and rn green: styd on fnl f: bttr for r* **11/2**

520 **3** ½ **Dark Ocean (IRE)**[47] 5311 2-9-3 75.......... GrahamLee 3 69
(Jedd O'Keeffe) *t.k.h: prom: n.m.r over 2f out: checked and outpcd over 1f out: styd on wl fnl f* **3/1**[2]

0 **4** ½ **Bitusa (USA)**[45] 5382 2-9-3 0.......... RobertWinston 8 67
(Alan Swinbank) *cl up: disp ld briefly appr 2f out: sn rdn: kpt on ins fnl f* **5/1**[3]

235 **5** ½ **Rocky Two (IRE)**[37] 5668 2-9-3 76.......... PaulMulrennan 6 66
(Michael Dods) *cl up: disp ld over 2f out: sn rdn: kpt on same pce ins fnl f* **11/4**[1]

502 **6** 7 **Darkside**[33] 5799 2-9-3 58.......... RoystonFfrench 2 49
(Tracy Waggott) *t.k.h: led to over 2f out: hung bdly rt and wknd wl over 1f out* **22/1**

0 **7** 2 **Troy Boy**[46] 5367 2-9-3 0.......... AdamBeschizza 4 44
(Robin Bastiman) *hld up in tch: pushed along over 3f out: wknd over 2f out* **40/1**

8 3½ **Borodino (IRE)** 2-9-3 0.......... TonyHamilton 10 35
(Richard Fahey) *hld up: stdy hdwy over 3f out: rdn and wknd over 2f out* **11/1**

1m 35.71s (7.91) **Going Correction** +0.775s/f (Yiel) **8** Ran SP% **116.6**
Speed ratings (Par 97): **85,84,83,83,82 74,72,68**
toteswingers 1&2 £5.60, 2&3 £5.20, 1&3 £3.90 CSF £32.85 TOTE £4.20: £3.10, £2.30, £2.50; EX 41.30.
Owner Norton Common Farm & Mrs E Burke **Bred** Peter Webb **Trained** Middleham Moor, N Yorks

FOCUS
Again they raced in one bunch towards the centre, but the final action was close to the stands'-side rail. The form is rated slightly negatively.

NOTEBOOK
Krupskaya(FR), who has taken time to get the grasp of things, broke on terms for the first time on her fourth start. She likes the mud and proved suited by the step up to 7f. After taking a decisive advantage, she seemed to idle and did just enough in the end. She seeks to earn some French premium bonus money later this month. (op 9-2 tchd 11-2)
Glacial Age(IRE), quite a big newcomer, is unfurnished at present. He has a pronounced knee action and was dropped in at the start. He moved up on to the heels of the winner, seemingly travelling much the better, but was beaten to the punch. Hauling her back at the line, he looked much the best horse in the race. He too may seek some French premiums. (op 15-2 tchd 8-1)
Dark Ocean(IRE), rated 75 and absent for six weeks, pulled much too hard. Outpaced when hampered over a furlong out, he finished with quite a rattle. He will need to learn to settle better. (op 10-3 tchd 11-4)
Bitusa(USA), very inexperienced on his debut, showed a fair bit more and is the type to progress further at three. (op 6-1)
Rocky Two(IRE), rated 76 and a beaten favourite over C&D on his third start, is starting to look exposed. (tchd 5-2 and 3-1)
Darkside, claimed after finishing runner-up at Thirsk, had the blinkers left off. He raced much too freely in front then hung violently right as he dropped away. He is clearly not straightforward.
Official explanation: jockey said colt hung right-handed (op 20-1)

6781 BRITISH STALLION STUDS SUPPORTING BRITISH RACING E B F MAIDEN FILLIES' STKS — 6f
3:10 (3:10) (Class 4) 2-Y-O **£4,398** (£1,309; £654; £327) **Stalls** Centre

Form RPR

4 **1** **Danat Al Atheer**[20] 6153 2-9-0 0.......... AdamBeschizza 3 70
(William Haggas) *t.k.h: led tl edgd lft and hdd over 1f out: rallied: styd on to regain ld towards fin* **1/5**[1]

60 **2** nk **Medici Dancer**[14] 6356 2-9-0 0.......... DavidAllan 6 69
(Tim Easterby) *chsd wnr: pushed along over 2f out: hdwy to ld over 1f out: sn drvn: kpt on fnl f: hdd and no ex towards fin* **8/1**[2]

06 **3** 31 **Taxiformissbyron**[125] 2631 2-9-0 0.......... PaulMulrennan 4
(Ollie Pears) *t.k.h: trckd ldrs tl wknd over 2f out* **14/1**

4 6 **Mon Chic** 2-9-0 0.......... MichaelO'Connell 2
(Ollie Pears) *prom: drvn over 3f out: wknd wl over 2f out* **12/1**[3]

1m 19.36s (4.76) **Going Correction** +0.775s/f (Yiel) **4** Ran SP% **108.8**
Speed ratings (Par 94): **99,98,57,49**
CSF £2.44 TOTE £1.20; EX 2.60.
Owner Jaber Abdullah **Bred** Rabbah Bloodstock Limited **Trained** Newmarket, Suffolk

FOCUS
The favourite was sent off long odds-on. She got there in the end, but it was a real struggle. She's rated close to her debut level.

NOTEBOOK
Danat Al Atheer, out of a half-sister to a Breeders' Cup Fillies' and Mares' Turf winner, had finished fourth first-time over 7f on good ground at Chepstow. Her rider had her hard against the stands' side rail after the first furlong. After looking in total charge, she was narrowly headed but showed real battling qualities to get back up near the line. Quite a lightly-made filly, she will surely be seen in much better light on totally different ground at three. (op 1-4)
Medici Dancer, encountering the mud for the first time on her third start, stalked the winner. She worked hard to gain a neck advantage inside the final furlong only to miss out near the line. Her heart is certainly in the right place and she deserves to go one better. (op 11-1)
Taxiformissbyron had shown little in two starts in May. (op 10-1)
Mon Chic showed next to nothing on her debut in very bad ground. (op 11-1 tchd 14-1)

6782 F1 SIGNS & DIGITAL E B F FILLIES' H'CAP (DIV I) — 7f
3:45 (3:45) (Class 5) (0-70,70) 3-Y-O+ **£3,557** (£1,058; £529; £264) **Stalls** Centre

Form RPR

4225 **1** **Clumber Place**[9] 6546 6-8-10 **59**.......... GrahamLee 9 67
(James Given) *plld hrd early: cl up: led over 2f out: drvn out fnl f* **5/2**[1]

2160 **2** 1 **Liliargh (IRE)**[84] 3952 3-9-5 **70**.......... PaulMulrennan 3 75
(Ben Haslam) *midfield: effrt and pushed along 2f out: chsd wnr wl ins fnl f r.o* **16/1**

-000 **3** ¾ **Lady Sledmere (IRE)**[13] 6410 4-8-11 **60**.......... RussKennemore 6 63
(Paul Midgley) *hld up: rdn over 2f out: styd on wl last 150yds: nvr able to chal* **20/1**

1300 **4** nk **Ryedale Dancer (IRE)**[5] 6646 4-8-13 **62**.......... IPoullis 5 64
(Richard Guest) *hld up: hdwy over 2f out: ev ch over 1f out: kpt on same pce last 75yds* **17/2**

6066 **5** hd **Untold Melody**[19] 6216 3-8-3 **61**..........(tp) KevinStott(7) 1 63
(Kevin Ryan) *trckd ldrs: disp ld over 2f out to over 1f out: one pce ins fnl f* **16/1**

0-00 **6** nk **File And Paint (IRE)**[21] 6141 4-9-2 **65**.......... DanielTudhope 4 66
(Lawrence Mullaney) *prom: drvn over 3f out: rallied: kpt on same pce fnl f* **10/1**

1623 **7** 2½ **See Clearly**[19] 6194 3-8-13 **69**..........(p) DarylByrne(5) 8 63
(Tim Easterby) *hld up in tch: rdn over 2f out: btn ins fnl f* **7/2**[2]

0301 **8** hd **Mango Music**[23] 6105 9-9-1 **64**.......... BarryMcHugh 10 58
(David Thompson) *hld up: stdy hdwy 3f out: rdn and wknd over 1f out* **11/2**[3]

2064 **9** 3¾ **Alluring Star**[12] 6455 4-8-1 **57** ow1.......... MatthewHopkins(7) 2 41
(Michael Easterby) *in tch: effrt and pushed along over 2f out: wknd over 1f out* **12/1**

3050 **10** *31* **Sunrise Dance**[67] 4588 3-9-0 **65**.................................. RobertWinston 7
(Robert Johnson) *led to over 2f out: sn rdn: wknd wl over 1f out: t.o* **33/1**

1m 34.12s (6.32) **Going Correction** +0.775s/f (Yiel)
WFA 3 from 4yo+ 2lb **10** Ran SP% **113.0**
Speed ratings (Par 100): **94,92,92,91,91 91,88,88,83,48**
toteswingers 1&2 £7.70, 2&3 £48.20, 1&3 £13.20 CSF £43.56 CT £661.24 TOTE £3.20: £1.30, £2.40, £8.20; EX 36.40.
Owner Catherine Stocks & Julie Walsh **Bred** Worksop Manor Stud **Trained** Willoughton, Lincs

FOCUS
Division one of a competitive fillies' handicap. Again they set off in one group up the centre, but ended up towards the stands' side. Slightly slower than division II, and straightforward, modest form.
Sunrise Dance Official explanation: jockey said filly lost its action

6783 F1 SIGNS & DIGITAL E B F FILLIES' H'CAP (DIV II) 7f
4:20 (4:20) (Class 5) (0-70,69) 3-Y-O+ **£3,557** (£1,058; £529; £264) **Stalls** Centre

Form RPR
243 **1** **Pivotal Prospect**[40] 5548 4-9-1 **63**.............................. RoystonFfrench 4 73
(Tracy Waggott) *mde all: rdn 2f out: styd on strly fnl f* **11/2**[2]
3060 **2** *2* **Gladsome**[46] 5345 4-9-2 **64**.............................. TonyHamilton 8 69
(Jason Ward) *hld up: rdn over 2f out: chsd wnr ins fnl f: kpt on: nt gng pce to chal* **4/1**[1]
1500 **3** *2 ¼* **Come Hither**[11] 6479 3-8-13 **63**.............................. DanielTudhope 2 62
(David O'Meara) *t.k.h: prom: chsd wnr over 2f out to ins fnl f: kpt on same pce* **7/1**
0360 **4** *8* **Loukoumi**[22] 6123 4-8-11 **59**..............................[1] TomEaves 9 37
(Tim Easterby) *bhd: drvn and outpcd over 4f out: sme late hdwy: nvr rchd ldrs* **11/2**[2]
010- **5** *2 ¼* **First Phase**[333] 7294 3-8-13 **63**.............................. DavidAllan 7 36
(Mel Brittain) *in tch: drvn over 3f out: btn wl over 1f out* **11/1**
2000 **6** *4 ½* **Viking Rose (IRE)**[13] 6416 4-9-3 **65**.............................. AdamBeschizza 5 26
(James Eustace) *chsd ldrs: drvn over 3f out: wknd 2f out* **4/1**[1]
6020 **7** *4 ½* **Bygones For Coins (IRE)**[23] 6106 4-8-0 **55** oh4........... KevinStott(7) 1
(Robert Johnson) *prom: drvn over 3f out: wknd over 2f out* **14/1**
2626 **8** *8* **Last Supper**[64] 4675 3-9-5 **69**..............................(b[1]) GrahamLee 6
(James Bethell) *t.k.h: cl up tl rdn and wknd over 2f out* **6/1**[3]

1m 33.9s (6.10) **Going Correction** +0.775s/f (Yiel)
WFA 3 from 4yo 2lb **8** Ran SP% **112.6**
Speed ratings (Par 100): **96,93,91,82,79 74,69,60**
toteswingers 1&2 £5.30, 2&3 £7.30, 1&3 £9.00 CSF £26.83 CT £155.20 TOTE £5.40: £3.40, £2.00, £3.10; EX 23.20.
Owner Christopher James Allan **Bred** Michael E Broughton **Trained** Spennymoor, Co Durham

FOCUS
More of the same, but slightly quicker than division I. It looked even more open than part one, but only the first three home were seriously involved from some way out.
Last Supper Official explanation: jockey said filly did not face the first-time blinkers.

6784 SENDRIG CONSTRUCTION H'CAP 2m 19y
4:50 (4:50) (Class 5) (0-75,75) 3-Y-O+ **£2,264** (£673; £336; £168) **Stalls** Low

Form RPR
3324 **1** **River Dragon (IRE)**[21] 6137 7-9-3 **64**.............................. BarryMcHugh 8 73
(Tony Coyle) *mde all: qcknd 4f out: rdn over 1f out: kpt on strly ins fnl f* **13/2**
5012 **2** *2 ¼* **Generous Dream**[3] 6712 4-9-3 **64**.............................. DavidAllan 9 70
(Mel Brittain) *chsd wnr thrght: rdn over 3f out: effrt 2f out: one pce fnl f* **11/2**[3]
21-0 **3** *1 ¼* **Sphinx (FR)**[12] 6428 14-9-9 **70**..............................(b) PaulMulrennan 1 75
(Edwin Tuer) *hld up in midfield: drvn and outpcd 4f out: rallied 2f out: kpt on fnl f: nvr able to chal* **28/1**
3136 **4** *¾* **Key Gold**[15] 6340 3-9-3 **75**.............................. JoeFanning 3 79
(Mark Johnston) *trckd ldrs: drvn and outpcd over 3f out: rallied over 1f out: kpt on ins fnl f* **7/2**[1]
6332 **5** *nk* **Luctor Emergo (IRE)**[5] 6626 3-8-9 **67**..............................(v) TomEaves 7 71
(Keith Dalgleish) *prom: drvn over 3f out: kpt on same pce fr 2f out* **5/1**[2]
4005 **6** *3 ½* **Ferney Boy**[22] 6126 6-8-9 **56** oh11.............................. AndrewElliott 2 55?
(Chris Fairhurst) *hld up: rdn and outpcd over 3f out: plugged on fnl 2f: no imp* **66/1**
0315 **7** *9* **Bandanaman (IRE)**[53] 5086 6-8-13 **63**.............................. RachaelGreen(3) 4 52
(Alan Swinbank) *hld up: outpcd over 4f out: n.d after* **20/1**
2213 **8** *24* **Looks Like Rain**[18] 6255 3-8-8 **66**.............................. DaleSwift 6 26
(Brian Ellison) *hld up: struggling over 5f out: sn btn* **5/1**[2]
3263 **9** *5* **Byron Blue (IRE)**[13] 6407 3-8-13 **71**.............................. DanielTudhope 10 25
(Jamie Osborne) *hld up in midfield on outside: struggling 4f out: btn over 2f out* **11/2**[3]
-010 **P** **Shifting Gold (IRE)**[36] 5718 6-9-5 **66**..............................(bt) AmyRyan 5
(Kevin Ryan) *hld up: struggling and p.u after 5f: fatally injured* **25/1**
1440 **P** **Jan Smuts (IRE)**[11] 6478 4-8-9 **56** oh1..............................(tp) GrahamLee 11
(Wilf Storey) *t.k.h: hld up: struggling over 3f out: sn btn: t.o whn p.u and dismntd ins fnl f* **25/1**

3m 53.78s (14.38) **Going Correction** +0.975s/f (Soft)
WFA 3 from 4yo+ 11lb **11** Ran SP% **117.1**
Speed ratings (Par 103): **103,101,101,100,100 98,94,82,79,**
toteswingers 1&2 £9.40, 2&3 £18.60, 1&3 £29.10 CSF £39.09 CT £941.59 TOTE £9.40: £2.20, £1.90, £7.80; EX 47.60.
Owner Brian Kerr & Tony Coyle **Bred** Barronstown Stud And Cobra Bloodstock **Trained** Norton, N Yorks

FOCUS
A true test of stamina in the ground and only the first five home were in with a shout in the home straight. The front pair were always 1-2 and the form is rated around them.
Looks Like Rain Official explanation: jockey said filly hung left-handed throughout
Byron Blue(IRE) Official explanation: trainer's rep said colt was unsuited by the heavy (soft in places) ground
Jan Smuts(IRE) Official explanation: jockey said gelding lost its action

6785 S.V. RUTTER H'CAP 1m 3y(S)
5:20 (5:21) (Class 5) (0-70,70) 3-Y-O+ **£2,264** (£673; £336; £168) **Stalls** Centre

Form RPR
2016 **1** **Moheebb (IRE)**[15] 6342 8-9-7 **67**..............................(b) RobertWinston 2 78
(Robert Johnson) *hld up: pushed along over 2f out: gd hdwy to ld appr fnl f: drvn out* **10/1**
0106 **2** *2* **Monthly Medal**[3] 6711 9-8-12 **58**..............................(t) GrahamLee 5 64
(Wilf Storey) *hld up gng wl: smooth hdwy to trck ldrs 2f out: rdn and chsd wnr fnl f: edgd lft: kpt on* **8/1**
1323 **3** *4* **Miss Ella Jade**[37] 5680 3-8-7 **56** oh1.............................. PaulQuinn 6 53
(Richard Whitaker) *hld up: rdn and effrt whn nt clr run briefly over 2f out: styd on fnl f: nt gng pce of first two* **16/1**
6510 **4** *2* **Cottam Donny**[5] 6638 4-9-3 **63** 6ex..............................(p) PaulMulrennan 11 56
(Mel Brittain) *in tch: hdwy over 4f out: led over 2f out to appr fnl f: edgd lft and sn outpcd* **7/2**[1]
3500 **5** *1* **Eastward Ho**[13] 6410 4-9-9 **69**.............................. TonyHamilton 9 59
(Jason Ward) *chsd ldrs: drvn and outpcd 3f out: rallied over 1f out: no imp fnl f* **5/1**[2]
3015 **6** *1 ¼* **Nezami (IRE)**[18] 6241 7-9-10 **70**..............................(b) RussKennemore 8 57
(Patrick Clinton) *dwlt: sn in tch: drvn over 3f out: edgd lft and no imp fr 2f out* **14/1**
3200 **7** *nk* **King Pin**[13] 6410 7-9-5 **65**..............................(p) RoystonFfrench 14 52
(Tracy Waggott) *cl up: effrt and ev ch 2f out: sn rdn and outpcd* **14/1**
4300 **8** *2 ¼* **Nolecce**[18] 6262 5-8-10 **56**..............................(p) IPoullis 7 38
(Richard Guest) *cl up: rdn and outpcd over 3f out: rallied over 1f out: nvr able to chal* **25/1**
000 **9** *1 ¼* **Space War**[44] 5429 5-9-1 **68**.............................. MatthewHopkins(7) 10 47
(Michael Easterby) *t.k.h: w ldr: rdn over 2f out: wknd over 1f out* **14/1**
6050 **10** *4 ½* **Beautiful Day**[116] 2922 4-8-11 **57**.............................. AmyRyan 1 25
(Kevin Ryan) *t.k.h: mde most to over 2f out: sn wknd* **22/1**
1050 **11** *12* **Hawaiian Storm**[101] 3416 3-9-3 **66**.............................. DanielTudhope 4
(Mrs K Burke) *hld up: drvn along 3f out: btn fnl 2f* **20/1**
653 **12** *31* **Keep It Dark**[15] 6341 3-9-2 **65**.............................. BarryMcHugh 16
(Tony Coyle) *hld up: drvn along over 3f out: wknd fr 2f out* **12/1**
0052 **13** *2 ½* **Wiseman's Diamond (USA)**[18] 6258 7-8-10 **59**.......(b) LeeTopliss(3) 15
(Paul Midgley) *in tch: drvn and outpcd over 3f out: btn fnl 2f* **13/2**[3]

1m 48.89s (5.49) **Going Correction** +0.775s/f (Yiel)
WFA 3 from 4yo+ 3lb **13** Ran SP% **119.0**
Speed ratings (Par 103): **103,101,97,95,94 92,92,90,88,84 72,41,38**
toteswingers 1&2 £18.70, 2&3 £22.90, 1&3 £22.80 CSF £84.95 CT £865.08 TOTE £12.30: £4.50, £3.80, £3.20; EX 158.10.
Owner Sterling Racing **Bred** Hascombe And Valiant Studs **Trained** Newburn, Tyne & Wear

FOCUS
They raced in one group towards the centre. The first three home came from off the pace and the overall time was slow. The winner is rated to this year's best.
Keep It Dark Official explanation: trainer said gelding was unsuited by the heavy (soft in places) ground
Wiseman's Diamond(USA) Official explanation: trainer had no explanation for the poor form shown

6786 RACING POST WEEKENDER OUT EVERY WEDNESDAY H'CAP 5f
5:50 (5:50) (Class 6) (0-60,62) 3-Y-O+ **£1,617** (£481; £240; £120) **Stalls** Centre

Form RPR
4-30 **1** **Mission Impossible**[3] 6713 7-9-7 **60**..............................(p) PatrickMathers 4 72
(Tracy Waggott) *in tch: smooth hdwy over 2f out: led wl over 1f out: edgd lft ins fnl f: drvn out* **15/2**[3]
0635 **2** *1 ¼* **Foreign Rhythm (IRE)**[37] 5671 7-8-12 **56**.................. GarryWhillans(5) 5 63
(Ron Barr) *hld up: rdn over 2f out: gd hdwy over 1f out: chsd wnr ins fnl f: r.o* **8/1**
0004 **3** *¾* **Ever Roses**[35] 5740 4-9-0 **53**..............................(v) GrahamLee 10 57
(Paul Midgley) *hld up: rdn and gd hdwy over 1f out: kpt on fnl f: nrst fin* **9/1**
2050 **4** *1 ¼* **Piste**[39] 5590 6-9-1 **54**..............................(e) PaulMulrennan 7 54
(Tina Jackson) *t.k.h: mde most to wl over 1f out: outpcd ins fnl f* **18/1**
2001 **5** *1* **Lord Buffhead**[9] 6531 3-9-6 **62** 6ex.............................. DeclanCannon(3) 3 58
(Richard Guest) *in tch: stdy hdwy over 2f out: effrt wl over 1f out: one pce ins fnl f* **8/1**
0043 **6** *2* **Sharp Shoes**[9] 6531 5-9-0 **53**.............................. PaddyAspell 2 42
(Christopher Wilson) *in tch on outside: rdn and ev ch 2f out: wknd ins fnl f* **12/1**
641- **7** *2* **Melodize**[429] 4607 4-8-12 **58**.............................. DavidBergin(7) 6 40
(David O'Meara) *hld up in tch: stdy hdwy over 2f out: rdn and wknd over 1f out* **12/1**
1022 **8** *1* **Windygoul Lad**[9] 6530 3-9-4 **57**.............................. AndrewMullen 8 35
(Keith Dalgleish) *dwlt: sn drvn along in tch: rdn and wknd over 1f out* **3/1**[1]
120 **9** *3 ¼* **Ursus**[23] 6104 7-9-2 **55**..............................(p) TomEaves 1 22
(Christopher Wilson) *in tch: struggling over 2f out: sn btn* **10/1**
610 **10** *hd* **Clubland (IRE)**[29] 5923 3-9-6 **59**.............................. AmyRyan 9 25
(Kevin Ryan) *t.k.h: cl up tl rdn and wknd over 1f out* **5/1**[2]
2060 **11** *4 ½* **Cross Of Lorraine (IRE)**[23] 6106 9-9-1 **54**..............(b) TonyHamilton 14
(Chris Grant) *t.k.h: cl up tl wknd over 2f out* **16/1**

1m 4.52s (3.42) **Going Correction** +0.775s/f (Yiel) **11** Ran SP% **121.3**
Speed ratings (Par 101): **103,101,99,97,96 93,89,88,83,82 75**
toteswingers 1&2 £13.30, 2&3 £15.00, 1&3 £14.70 CSF £68.47 CT £567.24 TOTE £12.30: £3.40, £1.30, £3.20; EX 92.10.
Owner H Conlon **Bred** Rodney Meredith **Trained** Spennymoor, Co Durham

FOCUS
A low-grade sprint handicap and again they came home well strung out after racing in one group up the centre. It was just about the pick pf the times. The winner was still 8lb off his early 3yo best.
Mission Impossible Official explanation: trainer said, regarding apparent improvement in form, that the gelding benefited from more cover in the race.
Windygoul Lad Official explanation: jockey said gelding never travelled
T/Plt: £168.20 to a £1 stake. Pool of £57174.82 - 248.09 winning tickets. T/Qpdt: £19.50 to a £1 stake. Pool of £6256.56 - 236.77 winning tickets. RY

5325 NOTTINGHAM (L-H)
Wednesday, October 3
OFFICIAL GOING: Good to soft (soft in places in back straight; 6.4)

6787 EBF BETFRED THE BONUS KING MAIDEN STKS 5f 13y
2:20 (2:23) (Class 5) 2-Y-O **£3,234** (£962; £481; £240) **Stalls** High

Form RPR
30 **1** **Senator Bong**[12] 6443 2-9-3 0.............................. DaneO'Neill 13 75
(David Elsworth) *trckd ldrs on wd outside: hdwy wl over 1f out: rdn and styd on ins fnl f: edgd lft and led nr fin* **12/1**
4 **2** *¾* **Gallena**[14] 6360 2-8-12 0.............................. PhillipMakin 2 67
(William Haggas) *trckd ldrs: hdwy 2f out: rdn to ld jst over 1f out: edgd lft ins fnl f: hdd and no ex towards fin* **20/1**
0 **3** *½* **Robot Boy (IRE)**[45] 5382 2-9-3 0.............................. HarryBentley 12 71+
(David Barron) *towards rr: pushed along 1/2-way: hdwy 2f out: sn rdn and styd on fnl f: nrst fin* **7/2**[2]
053 **4** *nk* **Millkwood**[45] 5382 2-9-3 69.............................. GrahamGibbons 10 69
(John Davies) *chsd ldrs: rdn over 1f out: edgd lft ins fnl f: kpt on* **33/1**

06 **5** *1* **Beacon Tarn**[11] 6490 2-8-12 0 .... FrederikTylicki 5 61
(Eric Alston) *led: rdn along wl over 1f out: drvn and hdd appr fnl f: one pce* **66/1**

6 **6** *hd* **Pivotal Movement**[11] 6481 2-9-3 0 .... PatDobbs 9 65
(Richard Hannon) *trckd ldrs: rdn along whn n.m.r over 1f out: kpt on same pce fnl f* **5/2[1]**

04 **7** *½* **Greenery (IRE)**[17] 6282 2-8-12 0 .... MartinHarley 14 58+
(Roger Charlton) *s.i.s and in rr: hdwy over 2f out: swtchd lft wl over 1f out: styd on fnl f: nrst fin* **33/1**

05 **8** *½* **Work Ethic (IRE)**[20] 5992 2-9-3 0 .... SebSanders 3 62
(Gerard Butler) *towards rr: hdwy 2f out: sn rdn and kpt on fnl f: nrst fin* **33/1**

3 **9** *1 ¾* **Mr Paranoia**[12] 6438 2-9-3 0 .... MartinDwyer 4 55
(Conrad Allen) *dwlt: t.k.h: towards rr: styd on appr fnl f* **8/1**

523 **10** *1* **Tarara**[28] 5932 2-8-12 77 .... FrannyNorton 16 47
(Andrew Balding) *towards rr: hdwy 1/2-way: swtchd lft 2f out and sn rdn to chse ldrs: wknd appr fnl f* **4/1[3]**

0 **11** *nk* **Winnie Perry**[19] 6203 2-9-3 0 .... AndreaAtzeni 6 51
(Rod Millman) *chsd ldrs: rdn along 2f out: sn wknd* **20/1**

6066 **12** *1* **Solvanna**[12] 6453 2-8-5 62 .... RyanTate(7) 8 42
(Heather Main) *n.d* **100/1**

13 *4* **Secret Success** 2-9-3 0 .... PaulHanagan 7 33
(Paul Cole) *cl up: rdn along over 2f out: sn wknd* **25/1**

14 *7* **Winter Song (IRE)** 2-8-12 0 .... MichaelHills 11 2
(Charles Hills) *s.i.s: a bhd* **28/1**

15 *4* **Dinas Lane** 2-9-3 0 .... SeanQuinlan 1
(Paul Green) *a in rr* **200/1**

1m 3.4s (2.40) **Going Correction** +0.425s/f (Yiel) **15** Ran SP% **118.2**
Speed ratings (Par 95): **97,95,95,94,92 92,91,91,88,86 86,84,78,66,60**
toteswingers 1&2 £22.70, 2&3 £42.10, 1&3 £12.40 CSF £226.28 TOTE £9.20: £3.00, £8.90, £2.50; EX 240.40 TRIFECTA Not won..
Owner John Dwyer **Bred** Sunley Stud **Trained** Newmarket, Suffolk

FOCUS
An informative juvenile maiden with some big yards represented. A fair standard for the track and time of year.

NOTEBOOK
Senator Bong left a disappointing run at Newbury well behind him, confirming the promise he had shown on his debut at Newmarket. Having travelled smoothly throughout, he came clear to win a shade cosily and should have plenty more to offer. His action suggests he'll be even more effective on slightly better ground. (op 14-1 tchd 16-1)

Gallena stepped up considerably on her Beverley debut run and will surely be capable of winning races. She easily did the best of those to race towards the far side of the track, but was ultimately no match for the winner. This was very different ground to that she had encountered last month and she appears versatile. (op 25-1)

Robot Boy(IRE) was under pressure from halfway, but passed several rivals inside the final furlong and was visibly gaining on the principals. He's clearly held in some regard by connections and will surely gain compensation once tackling 6f. (op 9-2 tchd 6-1)

Millkwood ran arguably his best race and it remains to be seen if his nursery mark will suffer as consequence. Rated just 69 coming into this, you'd have to believe he'd be very competitive if left on that kind of mark. Official explanation: jockey said gelding hung left-handed

Pivotal Movement was far from disgraced. He found things happening too quickly for him, but was staying on pleasingly late on. (op 2-1 tchd 7-4)

Greenery(IRE) was one of the last off the bridle but was never close enough to mount a challenge.

Tarara was something of a disappointment and may not have handled the drop back in distance. (tchd 7-2)

6788 TRACY ISLAND H'CAP — 5f 13y
2:50 (2:53) (Class 5) (0-75,75) 3-Y-0+ **£2,264** (£673; £336; £168) **Stalls** High

Form RPR

4532 **1** **Ambitious Icarus**[9] 6529 3-8-8 62 .... (e) RobbieFitzpatrick 6 74
(Richard Guest) *hld up in rr: hdwy 1/2-way: swtchd lft and effrt over 1f out: rdn to chse ldr jst ins fnl f: led last 100yds and styd on strly* **9/1**

-1 **2** *1 ¼* **Hello Stranger (IRE)**[23] 6100 3-8-12 66 .... DuranFentiman 5 74
(Tim Easterby) *trckd ldrs: smooth hdwy 2f out: led appr fnl f: sn rdn: hdd and no ex last 100yds* **15/2[3]**

2003 **3** *1 ¼* **Bouncy Bouncy (IRE)**[30] 5877 5-9-7 75 .... (t) HayleyTurner 9 78+
(Michael Bell) *hld up in rr: effrt and nt clr run 2f out: swtchd rt and rdn wl over 1f out: styd on strly fnl f: could nt rch front pair* **7/1[2]**

0360 **4** *1 ¼* **Falasteen (IRE)**[18] 6226 5-9-7 75 .... RichardKingscote 11 74
(Milton Bradley) *chsd ldrs: rdn wl over 1f out: styd on fnl f* **16/1**

0041 **5** *hd* **Amber Heights**[18] 6233 4-8-3 62 .... AmyScott(5) 16 60
(Henry Candy) *dwlt and in rr: hdwy on outer over 2f out: rdn to chse ldrs over 1f out: sn edgd lft and one pce* **9/1**

0033 **6** *nk* **Comptonspirit**[17] 6277 8-9-2 70 .... MickyFenton 1 67
(Brian Baugh) *led: rdn 2f out: drvn and hdd appr fnl f: kpt on same pce* **16/1**

6500 **7** *1 ¼* **Style And Panache (IRE)**[23] 6094 4-8-0 61 oh1 .... (p) PhilipPrince(7) 7 53
(David Evans) *midfield: rdn along 2f out: sn one pce* **12/1**

1200 **8** *1 ¼* **One Kool Dude**[32] 5831 3-8-12 66 .... (v) StevieDonohoe 8 54
(Michael Bell) *towards rr: hdwy 2f out: sn rdn and no imp fnl f* **25/1**

0006 **9** *1 ¼* **Ginger Ted (IRE)**[9] 6531 5-9-2 70 .... (p) J-PGuillambert 3 53
(Stuart Williams) *chsd ldrs: rdn along wl over 1f out: grad wknd* **25/1**

020 **10** *½* **Whitecrest**[12] 6439 4-9-2 70 .... FrannyNorton 15 51
(John Spearing) *prom: rdn along 2f out: grad wknd* **8/1**

2500 **11** *1 ¼* **Shawkantango**[4] 6689 5-9-2 70 .... (v) MartinDwyer 2 47
(Derek Shaw) *dwlt: sn prom on outer: rdn along 2f out and sn wknd* **20/1**

1034 **12** *3 ½* **Sleepy Blue Ocean**[32] 5821 6-9-1 69 .... (p) GrahamGibbons 13 33
(John Balding) *chsd ldrs: rdn along 2f out: sn wknd* **10/1**

0-00 **13** *2 ¾* **Invincible Force (IRE)**[26] 6005 8-9-2 70 .... (b) SeanQuinlan 14 24
(Paul Green) *in tch: hdwy to chse ldrs over 2f out: sn rdn and wknd* **50/1**

430 **14** *¾* **Quaroma**[12] 6427 7-9-6 74 .... PhillipMakin 4 26
(Paul Midgley) *in tch: rdn along over 2f out: sn wknd* **9/2[1]**

1m 2.7s (1.70) **Going Correction** +0.425s/f (Yiel) **14** Ran SP% **116.5**
Speed ratings (Par 103): **103,101,99,97,96 96,94,92,90,89 87,81,77,76**
toteswingers 1&2 £11.90, 2&3 £11.00, 1&3 £5.20 CSF £69.21 CT £504.48 TOTE £6.60: £1.50, £3.10, £2.90; EX 80.50 Trifecta £422.20 Part won. Pool: £570.60 - 0.92 winning units..
Owner We Know Partnership & Partner **Bred** L T Roberts **Trained** Stainforth, S Yorks

FOCUS
A competitive, if only fair handicap, run at a solid pace. The winner more than confirmed his recent improvement.

6789 ROSELAND BUSINESS PARK H'CAP — 1m 75y
3:20 (3:27) (Class 4) (0-85,83) 3-Y-0 **£4,140** (£1,232; £615; £307) **Stalls** Centre

Form RPR

21 **1** **Lahaag**[120] 2800 3-9-7 83 .... PaulHanagan 7 95
(John Gosden) *in tch: pushed along over 2f out: r.o strly fnl f: led fnl 50yds* **8/1[3]**

0613 **2** *¾* **Border Legend**[19] 6205 3-9-6 82 .... GeorgeBaker 14 92
(Roger Charlton) *midfield on outer: hdwy 3f out: rdn to ld 2f out: kpt on: hdd fnl 50yds* **7/2[1]**

2213 **3** *1 ¾* **Oddysey (IRE)**[35] 5731 3-8-13 75 .... PhillipMakin 4 82
(Michael Dods) *dwlt: hld up: n.m.r and swtchd rt over 2f out: r.o wl fr over 1f out: wnt 3rd towards fin* **20/1**

2354 **4** *1* **Dixie's Dream (IRE)**[19] 6205 3-9-6 82 .... PatDobbs 10 86
(Richard Hannon) *midfield: rdn over 2f out: hdwy over 1f out: kpt on fnl f* **14/1**

2114 **5** *3 ¼* **Magic Destiny**[54] 5043 3-9-1 80 .... MichaelMetcalfe(3) 6 77
(Mrs K Burke) *in tch: rdn over 2f out: sn one pce and no imp on ldrs* **7/1[2]**

0002 **6** *2* **Emman Bee (IRE)**[46] 5362 3-9-0 76 .... MickaelBarzalona 12 69
(John Gallagher) *trckd ldrs: pushed along over 2f out: sn one pce: wknd ins fnl f* **12/1**

0122 **7** *nse* **Mick Slates (IRE)**[12] 6429 3-8-5 72 .... JasonHart(5) 9 65
(Declan Carroll) *racd keenly: trckd ldrs: rdn over 2f out: one pce and btn whn short of room jst ins fnl f* **12/1**

1-00 **8** *2* **Ellaal**[55] 4997 3-9-6 82 .... MichaelHills 8 70
(Charles Hills) *led for 1f: prom: rdn over 2f out: wknd over 1f out* **20/1**

0341 **9** *1 ¾* **Ascription (IRE)**[74] 4329 3-9-2 78 .... ChrisCatlin 13 62
(Ed Dunlop) *racd keenly: hld up: gd hdwy on outer 3f out: rdn 2f out: wknd ins fnl f* **7/2[1]**

0050 **10** *2* **Stellar Express (IRE)**[36] 5721 3-9-5 81 .... TomQueally 1 61
(Michael Appleby) *led after 1f: rdn 3f out: hdd 2f out: grad wknd* **8/1[3]**

4050 **11** *1 ½* **Boris Grigoriev (IRE)**[25] 6046 3-8-8 77 .... DavidSimmonson(7) 3 54
(Michael Easterby) *hld up: a towards rr* **40/1**

1000 **12** *9* **Equation Of Time**[35] 5747 3-9-4 80 .... (t) J-PGuillambert 11 37
(Willie Musson) *hld up: pushed along whn sltly hmpd over 2f out: nvr threatened* **66/1**

4600 **13** *1 ¾* **Mutafaakir (IRE)**[15] 6338 3-8-11 73 .... JamesSullivan 5 26
(Ruth Carr) *racd keenly: trckd ldrs: rdn 3f out: wknd over 1f out* **50/1**

1m 47.43s (-2.17) **Going Correction** -0.175s/f (Firm) **13** Ran SP% **116.6**
Speed ratings (Par 103): **103,102,100,99,96 94,94,92,90,88 86,77,76**
toteswingers 1&2 £2.80, 2&3 £19.30, 1&3 £13.80 CSF £33.32 CT £565.61 TOTE £9.00: £4.00, £2.00, £7.30; EX 23.60 Trifecta £415.60 Pool: £1190.81 - 2.12 winning units..
Owner Hamdan Al Maktoum **Bred** Shadwell Estate Company Limited **Trained** Newmarket, Suffolk

FOCUS
There was a notable delay to the start of this race due to a stalls handler being kicked by the fractious Emman Bee. An ultra-competitive 3yo handicap and the form is rated on the positive side around the fourth.
Magic Destiny Official explanation: jockey said filly was denied a clear run
Mick Slates(IRE) Official explanation: jockey said gelding was denied a clear run

6790 E B F DOUBLE M CATERING CHALLENGE MAIDEN FILLIES' STKS (DIV I) — 1m 75y
3:55 (3:59) (Class 5) 2-Y-0 **£3,234** (£962; £481; £240) **Stalls** Centre

Form RPR

50 **1** **Cocktail Queen (IRE)**[11] 6489 2-9-0 0 .... DaneO'Neill 6 82+
(David Elsworth) *trckd ldr: cl up 1/2-way: led wl over 2f out: rdn over 1f out: drvn ins fnl f and styd on strly* **9/1**

03 **2** *1 ½* **Cushion**[29] 5902 2-9-0 0 .... RobertHavlin 11 80+
(John Gosden) *t.k.h: trckd ldrs: hdwy over 3f out: rdn to chse wnr wl over 1f out: drvn and no imp ins fnl f* **6/4[1]**

5 **3** *4 ½* **Auction (IRE)**[29] 5902 2-9-0 0 .... PhillipMakin 7 69
(Ed Dunlop) *in tch: hdwy to trck ldrs 1/2-way: effrt over 3f out: rdn to chse ldng pair over 1f out: sn drvn and no imp* **8/1**

4 *1* **The Lark** 2-9-0 0 .... HayleyTurner 2 67+
(Michael Bell) *hld up towards rr: hdwy 1/2-way: n.m.r and swtchd rt over 2f out: sn rdn along: rn green and sltly outpcd: styd on fnl f: nrst fin* **16/1**

5 *shd* **Kalispell (IRE)** 2-9-0 0 .... MickaelBarzalona 13 67
(Mahmood Al Zarooni) *dwlt and in rr: hdwy on wd outside 3f out: rdn along to chse ldrs wl over 1f out: kpt on same pce* **13/2[3]**

6 *1 ¼* **Permeate** 2-9-0 0 .... MichaelHills 8 64+
(Charles Hills) *dwlt and in rr: hdwy on outer 1/2-way: rdn along to chse ldrs 2f out: drvn over 1f out and sn one pce* **33/1**

7 *½* **Elik (IRE)** 2-9-0 0 .... TomQueally 12 63+
(Sir Michael Stoute) *hld up towards rr: hdwy 3f out: pushed along 2f out: styd on fnl f: nvr nr ldrs* **10/1**

35 **8** *2 ¾* **Alnawiyah**[28] 5947 2-9-0 0 .... PaulHanagan 4 57
(John Dunlop) *t.k.h: led: rdn along and hdd wl over 2f out: sn wknd* **4/1[2]**

9 *hd* **Montjess (IRE)** 2-9-0 0 .... RichardKingscote 5 56
(Tom Dascombe) *chsd ldrs: rdn along 3f out: wknd over 2f out* **50/1**

50 **10** *2 ¼* **Bountiful Bess**[22] 6117 2-9-0 0 .... MickyFenton 3 51
(Pam Sly) *trckd ldrs: hdwy on inner 1/2-way: rdn along 3f out: grad wknd* **100/1**

0 **11** *11* **Crystal Peaks**[27] 5977 2-9-0 0 .... FrederikTylicki 9 27
(James Given) *towards rr: effrt whn nt clr run 3f out: sn outpcd and bhd* **66/1**

12 *3* **Al Jasrah (IRE)** 2-9-0 0 .... FrannyNorton 1 21
(Kevin Ryan) *hld up: hdwy on inner to chse ldrs 4f out: sn rdn along and wknd wl over 2f out* **50/1**

00 **13** *2 ¼* **Downhill Dancer (IRE)**[14] 6366 2-9-0 0 .... JamieMackay 14 16
(Brian Meehan) *chsd ldrs: rdn along wl over 3f out: sn wknd* **80/1**

00 **14** *19* **July Waits (USA)**[9] 6535 2-9-0 0 .... ChrisCatlin 15
(Sir Mark Prescott Bt) *a towards rr* **150/1**

1m 49.14s (-0.46) **Going Correction** -0.175s/f (Firm) **14** Ran SP% **120.7**
Speed ratings (Par 92): **95,93,89,88,87 86,86,83,83,80 69,66,64,45**
toteswingers 1&2 £4.50, 2&3 £5.20, 1&3 £15.10 CSF £22.59 TOTE £11.50: £3.20, £1.02, £3.00; EX 31.30 Trifecta £126.60 Pool: £1133.08 - 6.62 winning units..
Owner J C Smith **Bred** Littleton Stud **Trained** Newmarket, Suffolk

FOCUS
Some really well-bred fillies' were on show in this, the first division of the juvenile maiden. The winner looks a decent sort, with the form rated around the second.

The Form Book Flat, Raceform Ltd, Compton, RG20 6NL

NOTEBOOK

Cocktail Queen(IRE) stepped up dramatically on her previous Newmarket effort. She had shaped with real promise at big odds on her introduction over 7f at Salisbury, but was unable to confirm that on quicker ground over this trip at Newmarket just 11 days ago. However, she looked much more at home back on this easier surface and had all bar the favourite well beaten off with fully 2f to run. Kept up to her work late on, her jockey spent most of the final furlong gazing up at the big screen and clearly had plenty of horse left under him. Middle-distances ought to bring about more improvement. (op 7-1 tchd 10-1)

Cushion looked the clear form pick and again ran well, though never looked like getting past the winner. She pulled a long way clear of the remainder and will surely be capable of winning a maiden. That said, she has been made to look a bit one-paced at the end of her races so far and is another that will benefit for longer trips. (op 11-10)

Auction(IRE) had made giant strides late on her debut behind Cushion at Goodwood, but she was beaten even further by that rival on this occasion. She was much closer to the early pace than on her debut and looked sure to play a big part when travelling up strongly. A stronger pace would probably have helped, but she looks raw at this stage and should be seen in a better light as a 3-y-o. (op 12-1 tchd 14-1)

The Lark, from a yard whose youngsters from her yard tend to need their first run, the style in which she was finishing off her race suggests she could be quite useful. (op 50-1)

Kalispell(IRE), bidding to give her trainer back-to-back wins in this race, performed creditably and should have learnt plenty from this. (op 5-1)

Elik(IRE) was another to come home to good effect. She's bred to make a much better 3-y-o and most certainly wasn't knocked about. (op 12-1 tchd 14-1)

6791 E B F DOUBLE M CATERING CHALLENGE MAIDEN FILLIES' STKS (DIV II) — 1m 75y

4:30 (4:31) (Class 5) 2-Y-O — **£3,234** (£962; £481; £240) **Stalls Centre**

Form — RPR

2 **1** **Lady Pimpernel**^{20} 6153 2-9-0 0 DaneO'Neill 7 — 77
(Henry Candy) *trckd ldrs: hdwy 3f out: led over 2f out: rdn wl over 1f out: drvn and kpt on wl fnl f* **9/2^{3}**

3 **2** *3/4* **Muthmera (USA)**^{22} 6117 2-9-0 0 PaulHanagan 1 — 75
(Roger Varian) *trckd ldrs: effrt over 2f out: nt clr run jst over 1f out: sn swtchd rt and rdn: styd on strly fnl f* **7/2^{2}**

3 *nk* **Capella's Song (IRE)** 2-9-0 0 HayleyTurner 15 — 74+
(Michael Bell) *dwlt and in rr: hdwy on inner 1/2-way: swtchd rt to outer and rdn over 2f out: styd on wl fnl f* **25/1**

2 **4** *nk* **Nasijah**^{22} 6117 2-9-0 0 MartinDwyer 13 — 74
(James Tate) *trckd ldrs: hdwy over 3f out: chsd wnr 2f out: sn rdn and kpt on fnl f* **13/2**

0 **5** *nk* **Flemish School**^{20} 6164 2-9-0 0 MickaelBarzalona 10 — 73
(Gerard Butler) *chsd ldrs: swtchd rt and rdn 2f out: kpt on u.p fnl f: nrst fin* **6/1**

6 *2 3/4* **Audacia (IRE)** 2-9-0 0 JimmyQuinn 9 — 67+
(Hugo Palmer) *in rr: hdwy 3f out: swtchd lft and rdn 2f out: kpt on: could nt rch ldrs* **50/1**

7 *1/2* **Waila** 2-9-0 0 TomQueally 12 — 66
(Sir Michael Stoute) *hld up: stdy hdwy on outer 1/2-way: chsd ldrs over 2f out: rdn wl over 1f out: wknd ent fnl f* **12/1**

6 **8** *2* **Beat Of The Drum (IRE)**^{11} 6489 2-9-0 0 PatDobbs 5 — 61
(Richard Hannon) *cl up: led over 3f out: rdn and hdd over 2f out: sn drvn and wknd ent fnl f* **10/3^{1}**

0 **9** *1 1/2* **Bowland Princess**^{22} 6117 2-9-0 0 PhillipMakin 2 — 58
(Ed Dunlop) *nvr bttr than midfield* **50/1**

10 *2 1/4* **Nullarbor Sky (IRE)** 2-9-0 0 FrederikTylicki 14 — 53
(Lucy Wadham) *a towards rr* **25/1**

0 **11** *5* **Dalaway (IRE)**^{22} 6117 2-9-0 0 MartinHarley 8 — 42
(Mick Channon) *in tch: rdn along 3f out: sn drvn and wknd fnl 2f* **50/1**

000 **12** *2 3/4* **Una Bella Cosa**^{76} 4246 2-8-7 48 NoraLooby$^{(7)}$ 4 — 36
(Alan McCabe) *led: rdn along and hdd over 3f out: sn wknd* **200/1**

13 *nk* **Isle Of Beauty** 2-9-0 0 RichardKingscote 11 — 36
(Tom Dascombe) *a towards rr* **33/1**

14 *22* **Lyric Ballad** 2-9-0 0 RobertHavlin 3
(Hughie Morrison) *a towards rr: bhd fnl 3f* **66/1**

0 **15** *27* **Icy Reply**^{18} 6257 2-9-0 0 ChrisCatlin 6
(Sir Mark Prescott Bt) *a in rr: outpcd and bhd fr 1/2-way* **100/1**

1m 49.55s (-0.05) **Going Correction** -0.175s/f (Firm) — **15** Ran SP% **118.3**

Speed ratings (Par 92): **93,92,91,91,91 88,88,86,84,82 77,74,74,52,25**

toteswingers 1&2 £4.10, 2&3 £11.20, 1&3 £16.50 CSF £18.80 TOTE £6.70: £2.20, £1.60, £8.10; EX 23.00 Trifecta £202.30 Pool: £694.57 - 2.54 winning units..

Owner Henry Candy & Partners II **Bred** Harts Farm Stud **Trained** Kingston Warren, Oxon

FOCUS

The second division of this maiden looked as strong, if not stronger than the first on paper. However a bunch finish limits the form.

NOTEBOOK

Lady Pimpernel confirmed the good impression of her 7f Chepstow second. She cost only 8,500gns at the sales in May, but travelled strongly throughout and showed a willing attitude to fend off a host of challengers having committed for home with fully 3f to run. This longer trip was always going to be in her favour and there should be even more to come from her next season when trying middle-distances. The form of her previous run looked good and she appears to have a bright future. (op 4-1)

Muthmera(USA) just got the better of a blanket finish for second and looks a winner waiting to happen. She by no means got the clearest of runs here, but took an age to hit top gear. She looks like being more effective over further. (op 9-2)

Capella's Song(IRE) ran a blinder and shouldn't have to wait long before she opens her account. She was a long way behind the principals as they turned for home and did remarkably well to get as close as she did. Her stable often leaves plenty to work on with its newcomers and this was a most pleasing run. (op 20-1 tchd 18-1)

Nasijah had belied her long odds when second at Leicester previously and again ran a fine race. She was unable to confirm her superiority over Muthmera, but only just got run out of it after a sustained duel with the eventual winner. (op 5-1)

Flemish School stayed on best of the rest. She may be something of a longer term project and requires just one more run to qualify for a handicap mark. (op 5-1 tchd 13-2)

Audacia(IRE) was friendless in the market, but was by no means embarrassed. She was seen keeping on to good effect and should be much more competitive next time.

Una Bella Cosa Official explanation: jockey said filly ran too freely

6792 TOTEPOOL MOBILE TEXT TOTE TO 89660 MAIDEN STKS — 1m 75y

5:00 (5:02) (Class 5) 3-Y-O+ — **£2,264** (£673; £336; £168) **Stalls Centre**

Form — RPR

50 **1** **Viewpoint (IRE)**^{90} 3774 3-9-3 82 PatDobbs 15 — 87+
(Richard Hannon) *hld up in midfield: hdwy to chse ldrs over 2f out: rdn to ld 1f out: edgd lft: kpt on to go clr* **13/2**

22 **2** *3 3/4* **Be My Rock**^{40} 5529 3-8-10 0 ow3 JamieJones$^{(5)}$ 9 — 76
(Rae Guest) *trckd ldrs: rdn 2f out: kpt on: no ch w wnr ins fnl f* **12/1**

5 **3** *2 1/4* **Desert Berry**^{19} 6215 3-8-12 0 GrahamGibbons 14 — 68+
(Chris Wall) *in tch: pushed along over 2f out: kpt on fnl f* **33/1**

4 *3/4* **Bishop's Castle (USA)** 3-9-3 0 FrannyNorton 7 — 71+
(Mark Johnston) *trckd ldrs: rdn over 2f out: led over 1f out: sn hdd and dropped to 4th: plugged on ins fnl f* **11/2^{2}**

32 **5** *1 1/4* **Qanan**^{19} 6215 3-9-3 0 J-PGuillambert 5 — 68+
(Luca Cumani) *in tch: pushed along over 3f out: rdn and ev ch over 1f out: one pce* **6/1^{3}**

0-2 **6** *3 1/4* **Beaumont Cooper**^{37} 5687 3-8-12 0 GeorgeDowning$^{(5)}$ 10 — 61+
(Tony Carroll) *slowly away: hld up in rr: sme hdwy over 3f out: kpt on fr over 1f out: nrst fin* **66/1**

30- **7** *1/2* **Ligurian Sea**^{429} 4614 3-8-12 0 HarryBentley 6 — 55
(Chris Wall) *midfield: pushed along over 3f out: sn one pce and nvr trble ldrs* **25/1**

0 **8** *3 1/4* **La Giaconda**^{20} 6154 3-8-12 0 (t) DaneO'Neill 1 — 47
(Clive Cox) *midfield: pushed along over 3f out: wknd over 1f out* **66/1**

2 **9** *2 1/2* **Starfield**^{60} 4797 3-9-3 0 (e) RobertHavlin 4 — 46
(John Gosden) *led: rdn whn hdd over 1f out: wknd* **11/10^{1}**

0 **10** *3/4* **Asia Minor (IRE)**^{102} 3398 3-8-12 0 MickyFenton 11 — 40
(Dr Jon Scargill) *slowly away: hld up: nvr threatened* **50/1**

45 **11** *1/2* **Balcary Bay**^{44} 5404 3-9-3 0 AndreaAtzeni 17 — 44
(James Eustace) *hld up: nvr threatened* **50/1**

30 **12** *1 1/2* **Another Squeeze**^{37} 5687 4-9-1 0 ChrisCatlin 2 — 35
(Peter Hiatt) *tk str hold: hld up: a towards rr* **66/1**

6-0 **13** *1/2* **Black Minstrel (IRE)**^{13} 6397 3-9-3 0 TomQueally 13 — 39
(Amanda Perrett) *midfield: pushed along over 3f out: wknd over 1f out* **22/1**

0 **14** *31* **Mecox Meadow (USA)**^{29} 5901 3-9-3 0 HayleyTurner 8
(Michael Bell) *hld up: a in rr* **50/1**

0 **15** *36* **Bondi Beach Boy**^{15} 6341 3-9-3 0 FrederikTylicki 12
(James Turner) *w ldr: pushed along and edgd rt over 4f out: sn wknd: t.o fnl 2f* **200/1**

1m 49.73s (0.13) **Going Correction** -0.175s/f (Firm)

WFA 3 from 4yo 3lb — **15** Ran SP% **120.3**

Speed ratings (Par 103): **92,88,86,85,84 80,80,77,74,73 73,71,71,40,4**

toteswingers 1&2 £7.90, 2&3 £39.70, 1&3 £31.70 CSF £75.59 TOTE £8.80: £1.70, £2.70, £12.00; EX 100.90 TRIFECTA Not won..

Owner The Heffer Syndicate **Bred** F Dunne **Trained** East Everleigh, Wilts

FOCUS

There weren't too many that could be seriously fancied for this 3yo maiden. Ordinary form with the favourite disappointing, and the slowest of the C&D times. The winner may do better.

6793 RACING POST FORM WITH TOTEPOOL MOBILE NURSERY — 1m 2f 50y

5:30 (5:31) (Class 5) (0-75,73) 2-Y-O — **£2,264** (£673; £336; £168) **Stalls Low**

Form — RPR

000 **1** **Forced Family Fun**^{29} 5911 2-8-13 **65** HayleyTurner 5 — 68+
(Michael Bell) *prom: chsd ldr fr 1/2-way: led wl over 2f out: rdn and edgd lft over 1f out: drvn out* **17/2**

600 **2** *1 1/2* **Flying Tempo**^{15} 6330 2-7-12 **50** oh1 (b^{1}) JimmyQuinn 12 — 50
(Ed Dunlop) *chsd ldrs: hdwy 3f out: rdn wl over 1f out: styd on fnl f* **33/1**

0142 **3** *1/2* **Magic Channel (USA)**^{51} 5155 2-9-1 **67** PaulHanagan 1 — 66
(Richard Hannon) *chsd ldng pair: hdwy 3f out: rdn wl over 1f out: kpt on* **7/1**

0603 **4** *1/2* **East Texas Red (IRE)**^{13} 6413 2-8-11 **63** PatDobbs 6 — 61
(Richard Hannon) *in tch on inner: hdwy over 3f out: swtchd rt and effrt whn nt clr run over 1f out: sn rdn and one pce fnl f* **9/2^{2}**

000 **5** *4 1/2* **Hi Candy (IRE)**^{91} 3748 2-7-5 **50** oh2 NoelGarbutt$^{(7)}$ 2 — 40+
(Ben Haslam) *towards rr: hdwy 3f out: rdn along over 2f out: kpt on fnl f: nvr nr ldrs* **50/1**

6006 **6** *3/4* **Garmelow Girl**^{51} 5161 2-7-12 **50** oh1 (b^{1}) JamieMackay 8 — 39
(Kevin Ryan) *dwlt: hdwy to chse ldrs after 4f: chsd ldng pair 3f out: rdn 2f out: drvn and one pce ent fnl f* **50/1**

0464 **7** *1 1/2* **Attansky (IRE)**^{15} 6337 2-8-10 **62** DuranFentiman 3 — 48
(Tim Easterby) *in rr: hdwy on outer over 3f out: rdn along over 2f out: sn no imp* **5/1^{3}**

0510 **8** *2 3/4* **Warrant Officer**^{20} 6156 2-8-11 **63** MartinHarley 11 — 44
(Mick Channon) *midfield: effrt 3f out: sn rdn along and no hdwy* **20/1**

022 **9** *3/4* **Woody Bay**^{33} 5797 2-9-7 **73** FrederikTylicki 13 — 53
(James Given) *t.k.h: led and clr: rdn along 3f out: hdd over 2f out and sn wknd* **11/2**

5040 **10** *1* **Persian Wave**^{16} 6318 2-8-7 **59** MartinDwyer 4 — 37
(James Tate) *a towards rr* **25/1**

01 **11** *hd* **Topamichi**^{21} 6134 2-9-1 **67** (b) PhillipMakin 10 — 45
(Mark H Tompkins) *t.k.h early: hld up towards rr: hdwy on wd outside over 3f out: rdn to chse ldrs 2f out: sn btn* **10/3^{1}**

0005 **12** *11* **French Revolution**^{21} 6134 2-8-3 **55** JamesSullivan 7 — 13
(Jedd O'Keeffe) *hld up: a towards rr* **50/1**

060 **13** *62* **Vinifera (USA)**^{63} 4704 2-8-3 **55** KirstyMilczarek 9
(Clive Brittain) *bhd fr 1/2-way* **33/1**

2m 17.92s (3.62) **Going Correction** -0.175s/f (Firm) — **13** Ran SP% **116.7**

Speed ratings (Par 95): **78,76,76,76,72 71,70,68,67,67 66,58,8**

toteswingers 1&2 £32.20, 2&3 £22.10, 1&3 £11.40 CSF £260.99 CT £2044.78 TOTE £16.40: £3.90, £13.20, £2.30; EX 176.70 TRIFECTA Not won..

Owner M B Hawtin **Bred** M B Hawtin **Trained** Newmarket, Suffolk

FOCUS

A competitive, if only modest nursery, run at a steady pace. The form has a limited feel but the winner has more to offer.

NOTEBOOK

Forced Family Fun really hadn't achieved a great deal in three runs in maidens but, trying this trip for the first occasion, did the job well. There's no denying that he was helped by how this race race developed and his sudden injection of pace 2f out left many of his rivals floundering. However, still lightly raced, he remains open to improvement and threatens to be even better when trying 1m4f. Soft ground looks ideal given his high knee action. Official explanation: trainer's rep said, regarding apparent improvement in form, that the gelding was better suited by the good to soft (soft in places) ground (op 5-1)

Flying Tempo was never too far off the pace, but got outpaced before staying on again. Another nursery debutant, he had the blinkers on for the first time and appeared to take well to them. His head carriage wasn't all that encouraging, but he's very lowly rated and can only come on for this.

Magic Channel(USA) ran his usual game race, but is probably high enough in the weights now. He was another to be ridden handily and had no apparent excuses. (op 13-2)

East Texas Red(IRE) ran well and certainly wasn't helped when receiving a hefty bump when mounting his challenge. That said, he had plenty of time to recover and was ultimately well held. It may be that he'll benefit from a return to 1m. (tchd 4-1)

Topamichi ran poorly. He was forced to race wider than ideal and was lit up in the headgear. Heavier ground had brought about significant improvement for him and he may simply have failed to act on this quicker surface. Official explanation: jockey said gelding ran too freely (op 9-2 tchd 3-1)

6794 AJA FEGENTRI GENTLEMEN AMATEUR RIDERS' H'CAP 1m 2f 50y

6:00 (6:01) (Class 5) (0-70,69) 3-Y-0+ **£2,183** (£677; £338; £169) **Stalls** Low

Form RPR

3600 **1** **Follow The Flag (IRE)**[13] 6405 8-11-1 **62**........................(v) MrSWalker 2 73
(Alan McCabe) *in tch on inner: angled towards outer 2f out: sn rdn: styd on wl to ld fnl 50yds* **7/1**[3]

5-55 **2** *1 ¼* **Spyder**[38] 5636 4-11-6 **67**.. MrMEnnis 1 76
(Jane Chapple-Hyam) *led for 1f: trckd ldr: rdn to ld again wl over 2f out: kpt on: hdd fnl 50yds* **6/1**[2]

6502 **3** *5* **Maybeme**[8] 6561 6-10-7 **54**...(p) MrPCollington 4 54
(Neville Bycroft) *hld up: rdn and hdwy on outer over 2f out: kpt on: wnt 3rd ins fnl f: no threat to ldng pair* **9/2**[1]

2600 **4** *½* **The Ducking Stool**[13] 6416 5-11-4 **65**...................... MrFabrizioPerego 7 64
(Julia Feilden) *hld up in rr: hdwy on inner over 2f out: sn rdn: kpt on one pce* **12/1**

3020 **5** *1 ¾* **Landesherr (GER)**[12] 6458 5-11-4 **65**.............................. MrFMitchell 6 60
(Steve Gollings) *midfield on outer: hdwy over 3f out: rdn to chse ldr wl over 1f out: wknd ins fnl f* **7/1**[3]

6336 **6** *2 ½* **Silver Alliance**[35] 5741 4-11-6 **67**.. MrRBirkett 11 57
(Julia Feilden) *midfield: rdn over 2f out: briefly chsd ldrs: wknd ins fnl f* **10/1**

2620 **7** *1 ¼* **Lisselan Pleasure (USA)**[16] 6304 5-10-8 **55**.......(t) MrFWindsorClive 10 43
(Bernard Llewellyn) *slowly away: sn midfield: rdn over 2f out: wknd ins fnl f* **14/1**

6506 **8** *1 ½* **Tapis Libre**[21] 6131 4-11-2 **63**................................ MrDennisSchiergen 9 48
(Michael Easterby) *midfield: pushed along over 3f out: wknd over 1f out* **12/1**

100 **9** *17* **Mazij**[29] 5913 4-11-7 **68**.. MrDHDunsdon 5 21
(Peter Hiatt) *hld up in midfield: rdn over 3f out: sn wknd* **25/1**

10 **10** *6* **Kingaroo (IRE)**[55] 5012 6-10-8 **55**...................................... MrSCrawford 3
(Garry Woodward) *trckd ldrs: rdn over 3f out: sn wknd* **16/1**

5316 **11** *8* **Elbow Beach**[28] 5931 3-11-3 **69**....................................... MrPMillman 12
(Rod Millman) *led after 1f: rdn whn hdd wl over 2f out: wknd* **9/2**[1]

4300 **12** *nse* **General Tufto**[8] 6562 7-10-7 **54** oh9........................(b) MrAngeloGasnier 8
(Charles Smith) *hld up: a bhd* **66/1**

2m 17.62s (3.32) **Going Correction** -0.175s/f (Firm)
WFA 3 from 4yo+ 5lb **12** Ran SP% **118.0**
Speed ratings (Par 103): **79,78,74,73,72 70,69,68,54,49 43,43**
toteswingers 1&2 £10.50, 2&3 £7.20, 1&3 £7.60 CSF £48.44 CT £212.71 TOTE £9.00: £2.10, £3.50, £2.30; EX 52.10 Trifecta £440.70 Pool: £601.63 - 1.01 winning units..
Owner S Gillen **Bred** Martin Francis **Trained** Averham Park, Notts

FOCUS
A modest amateur riders' handicap, run at a sound pace and it required a strong staying performance from the winner. He's rated back to something like his spring turf form.
T/Plt: £648.90 to a £1 stake. Pool of £52893.46 - 59.50 winning tickets. T/Qpdt: £48.30 to a £1 stake. Pool of £4787.58 - 73.35 winning tickets. JR

5976 SALISBURY (R-H)

Wednesday, October 3

OFFICIAL GOING: Last 5f - good to soft; remainder - soft (good to soft in places)
Wind: mild breeze against Weather: cloudy but dry

6795 BRITISH STALLION STUDS E B F BOOKER WHOLESALE MAIDEN STKS (DIV I) 1m

1:30 (1:31) (Class 4) 2-Y-0 **£4,237** (£1,260; £630; £315) **Stalls** Low

Form RPR

4 **1** **So Beloved**[47] 5303 2-9-3 0.. JamesDoyle 8 81+
(Roger Charlton) *mid-div: pushed along and stdy hdwy fr over 2f out: r.o wl to ld fnl 120yds: pushed out* **9/1**

0 **2** *1* **Tawhid**[25] 6020 2-9-3 0.. FrankieDettori 12 78
(Saeed Bin Suroor) *mid-div: hdwy 3f out: rdn to chal 2f out: led and drifted rt ent fnl f: hdd fnl 120yds: kpt on but no ex* **6/1**[3]

2 **3** *1 ¾* **Greatwood**[22] 6114 2-9-0 0.. PatrickHills(3) 15 75
(Luca Cumani) *mid-div: hdwy over 2f out: rdn w ch wl over 1f out: kpt on same pce fnl f* **5/4**[1]

0 **4** *3* **Brownsea Brink**[11] 6481 2-9-3 0.. TedDurcan 16 68
(Richard Hannon) *racd keenly trcking ldrs: rdn to chal over 2f out: led wl over 1f out: drifting rt whn hdd ent fnl f: no ex* **14/1**

5 *1 ¼* **Mujarrad (USA)** 2-9-3 0... TadhgO'Shea 6 65+
(Marcus Tregoning) *slowly away: in rr: nt clr run on rails and swtchd lft over 2f out: sn pushed along: styd on nicely fnl f* **33/1**

5 **6** *1* **Lions Arch (IRE)**[20] 6164 2-9-3 0................................... RichardHughes 5 67+
(Richard Hannon) *sn led: hdd after 1f: trckd ldrs: rdn wl over 1f out: mounting chal whn bdly squeezed up on rails ent fnl f: swtchd lft: no ch after* **9/2**[2]

5 **7** *¾* **Argaki (IRE)**[14] 6377 2-9-3 0... RichardMullen 3 61+
(Sir Michael Stoute) *led for 120yds: chsd ldrs: pushed along over 3f out: rdn over 2f out: wknd ent fnl f* **33/1**

0 **8** *1 ¼* **Mombasa**[11] 6486 2-9-3 0.. EddieAhern 9 59
(John Dunlop) *mid-div: rdn over 2f out: nvr any imp on ldrs* **50/1**

0 **9** *1 ½* **King Muro**[25] 6020 2-9-3 0.. JimmyFortune 11 57+
(Andrew Balding) *led after 1f: rdn whn chal over 2f out: hdd wl over 1f out: styng on at same pce whn bdly hmpd on rails ent fnl f* **40/1**

0 **10** *1* **See And Be Seen**[37] 5684 2-9-3 0..................................... LiamKeniry 1 53
(Sylvester Kirk) *mid-div: rdn over 3f out: wknd fnl f* **150/1**

11 *nk* **Candoluminescence** 2-8-12 0.. IanMongan 2 47
(Roger Charlton) *hld up towards rr: sme prog u.p 2f out: wknd fnl f* **50/1**

12 *1 ¼* **Thorpe (IRE)** 2-9-3 0.. JimCrowley 10 50
(Ralph Beckett) *rdn over 3f out: a towards rr* **14/1**

13 *1 ½* **Guilded Spirit** 2-9-3 0... FergusSweeney 13 46
(Stuart Kittow) *a towards rr* **100/1**

14 *5* **Nandura** 2-8-12 0... LukeMorris 14 30
(Harry Dunlop) *mid-div: rdn 3f out: sn edgd rt: wknd over 1f out* **66/1**

0 **15** *1* **Conversing (USA)**[11] 6501 2-8-12 0.............................. AntiocoMurgia(5) 4 33
(Mahmood Al Zarooni) *trckd ldrs: rdn 3f out: sn lost pl: wknd over 1f out* **40/1**

1m 45.45s (1.95) **Going Correction** +0.30s/f (Good) **15** Ran SP% **118.1**
Speed ratings (Par 97): **102,101,99,96,95 94,93,92,90,89 89,87,86,81,80**
toteswingers 1&2 £5.90, 2&3 £3.60, 1&3 £3.10 CSF £57.71 TOTE £10.70: £2.00, £2.50, £1.20; EX 61.90.
Owner K Abdulla **Bred** Juddmonte Farms Ltd **Trained** Beckhampton, Wilts

FOCUS
This maiden has produced some good performers down the years, including Look Here, who won a division in 2007, and Carlton House among many others. The leader didn't go quick in the early stages, but some of the beaten runners looked tired at the end. A wide track position looked advantageous. There is better to come from the winner.

NOTEBOOK
So Beloved ◆ showed the benefit of his promising Newbury debut with a strong finish here even after racing a bit freely out the back before making his move. There didn't seem any urgency by his trainer for the colt to be seen again this season, so it wouldn't be a surprise if that was it for the son of Dansili this year. (op 8-1)
Tawhid shaped okay in a strong 7f maiden at Ascot last month, but did better with that experience under his belt here. The Godolphin runner appeared to gain the upper hand at the right time, but was worn down by So Beloved in the final half-furlong. (op 7-1 tchd 11-2)
Greatwood showed plenty of promise when runner-up in a large field over 7f at Leicester under this rider last month, faring best of the newcomers, but couldn't go on when holding every chance here. He can win a maiden, but will surely be at his best next season over middle-distances. Luca Cumani reported that the colt was unsuited by the good to soft, soft in places, ground. Official explanation: trainer's rep said colt was unsuited by the good to soft (soft in places) ground (op 11-10)
Brownsea Brink, up in trip, was well placed throughout and ran respectably despite edging right under pressure. (op 20-1)
Mujarrad(USA), whose dam is a Rockfel winner who stayed at least 1m2f and is from the family of US Grade 2 7f winner Kayrawan and high-class Irish sprinter Haatef, was clueless early and held a couple of positions out the back before running on strongly when brought around runners. (op 28-1)
Lions Arch(IRE) was still in with every chance of winning, although being ridden along, when his stablemate Brownsea Brink hampered him towards the inside rail. Richard Hughes reported that the colt hung right. Official explanation: jockey said colt hung right (tchd 5-1)
Argaki(IRE), up in trip after a modest Yarmouth effort, won't come into his own until up in trip next season, or sent to a stiffer track.
Mombasa was making some encouraging late progress when hampered by the wandering Lions Arch.

6796 BRITISH STALLION STUDS E B F BOOKER WHOLESALE MAIDEN STKS (DIV II) 1m

2:00 (2:04) (Class 4) 2-Y-0 **£4,237** (£1,260; £630; £315) **Stalls** Low

Form RPR

1 **Magog** 2-9-3 0.. IanMongan 12 80+
(Roger Charlton) *mid-div: pushed along and prog fr jst over 2f out: led ent fnl f: r.o wl: readily* **16/1**

2 *1 ½* **Ikhtisas (USA)** 2-9-3 0.. FrankieDettori 13 77
(Saeed Bin Suroor) *sn prom: rdn 2f out to chse ldr: kpt on nicely to regain 2nd fnl 120yds whn bmpd: a being readily hld by wnr* **13/2**[3]

0 **3** *2 ¼* **Snoqualmie Chief**[54] 5062 2-9-3 0.. TedDurcan 2 72
(David Elsworth) *t.k.h early: trckd ldrs: rdn over 2f out: kpt on same pce fnl f* **33/1**

4 *hd* **Shababeek (IRE)** 2-9-3 0.. TadhgO'Shea 3 71+
(John Dunlop) *s.i.s: bhd: swtchd lft whn pushed along over 2f out: hdwy over 1f out: styd on wl ins fnl f: snatced 4th fnl stride* **25/1**

5 *hd* **Celebrated Talent (USA)** 2-8-12 0............................ AntiocoMurgia(5) 4 71
(Mahmood Al Zarooni) *led: rdn over 2f out: hdd ent fnl f: edgd lft: no ex fnl 120yds: lost 4th fnl stride* **10/1**

03 **6** *2 ¾* **Mumeyez**[34] 5765 2-9-3 0.. NickyMackay 11 65+
(John Gosden) *mid-div: rdn and hdwy 2f out to chse ldrs: kpt on same pce fnl f* **7/2**[1]

7 *2 ½* **Are You Mine (IRE)** 2-8-12 0.. JimCrowley 1 54+
(Ralph Beckett) *mid-div: rdn over 2f out: sn one pce* **9/1**

8 *½* **Simple Joys** 2-8-12 0.. JimmyFortune 16 53
(Andrew Balding) *s.i.s: towards rr: sme prog into midfield over 1f out: styd on same pce fnl f: nvr trbld ldrs* **33/1**

9 *nse* **Forward March** 2-9-3 0..(e[1]) JamesDoyle 6 58
(Roger Charlton) *racd v keenly: prom tl stdd bk to midfield after 1f: rdn 2f out: no imp: fdd ins fnl f* **14/1**

10 *nk* **Woodstock (IRE)** 2-9-3 0... EddieAhern 9 57+
(Richard Hannon) *hld up towards rr: hdwy into midfield 3f out: sn pushed along w nt best of runs: no further imp fr over 1f out* **6/1**[2]

0 **11** *1 ¾* **Marju Prince**[44] 5418 2-9-3 0.. RichardMullen 15 54
(Sir Michael Stoute) *pushed along over 4f out: a towards rr* **6/1**[2]

0 **12** *¾* **Damian One**[47] 5303 2-9-3 0...................................(v[1]) FergusSweeney 14 52
(Joseph Tuite) *trckd ldrs tl rdn 2f out: sn wknd* **100/1**

0 **13** *1* **Burma Days (USA)**[26] 6014 2-9-3 0....................................... LiamKeniry 7 50
(Sylvester Kirk) *trckd ldrs: rdn over 2f out: sn btn* **100/1**

14 *¾* **Bugsy** 2-9-3 0.. SeanLevey 5 48
(Richard Hannon) *mid-div tl wknd 2f out* **25/1**

15 *½* **Seaside Rock (IRE)** 2-9-3 0.. RichardHughes 10 47+
(Richard Hannon) *mid-div tl lost pl over 5f out: swtchd lft 2f out: sn rdn: no imp* **6/1**[2]

1m 47.49s (3.99) **Going Correction** +0.30s/f (Good) **15** Ran SP% **125.6**
Speed ratings (Par 97): **92,90,88,88,87 85,82,82,82,81 80,79,78,77,77**
toteswingers 1&2 £22.00, 2&3 £39.40, 1&3 £114.60 CSF £115.57 TOTE £26.40: £6.50, £2.10, £15.60; EX 185.20.
Owner Lady Rothschild **Bred** Carwell Equities Ltd **Trained** Beckhampton, Wilts

FOCUS
On previous form this looked like the weaker of the two divisions, but it was encouraging to see two newcomers fight out the finish. There's more to come from the winner and there were some promising runs behind.

NOTEBOOK
Magog, a gelded half-brother to a few middle-distance winners, notably the yard's useful Rosslyn Castle, made a perfect start to his career. Going well in behind, he came with a good run inside the final 2f to get to the front at the right time. It remains to be seen whether ease in the ground is important to him. (op 20-1)
Ikhtisas(USA), a half-brother to useful US mare Distorted Love, was nicely placed just behind his owner's other runner but hit a flat spot before running on again. It would be surprising if he doesn't improve for better ground, considering his pedigree. (tchd 7-1 in a place)
Snoqualmie Chief, who looked warm round the neck, finished last of 14 on his debut 54 days previously, so could be used to hold the form down. On the positive side, he definitely made progress from his initial outing, which was on a much quicker surface.

Shababeek(IRE) ◆, a half-brother to 1m4f-1m6f winner Tactic and the useful Zahoo, ran much like the owner's horse in the first division, out the back before making eye-catching progress from the 2f marker. He was really motoring in the final few strides. (op 20-1)
Celebrated Talent(USA), a $500,000 yearling who is the first foal of a US 1m1f stakes winner, was handed an easy lead and displayed ability. He'll probably be even better on a faster surface. (op 16-1)
Mumeyez, returning to turf, was sent off favourite but never threatened to get to the front. Presumably he'll head into handicaps now. Nicky Mackay reported that the colt lost its action. Official explanation: jockey said colt lost its action (tchd 10-3 and 4-1)
Forward March, who had an eyeshield fitted on debut, looked far from an easy ride and will need to settle much better to have any chance. (tchd 10-1)
Woodstock(IRE), closely related to a few winners, attracted a lot of market interest and travelled strongly for quite a while before fading. He should come on for this first start. (op 33-1)
Marju Prince's jockey was hard at work on his mount a long way from home and the colt may need more time. (op 15-2)
Damian One Official explanation: vet said gelding had an irregular heat beat
Seaside Rock(IRE), a half-brother to five winners, notably Mister Sacha and Mister Charm, was always going to need luck from his position over 4f out as the tempo increased and the gaps never came. He is easily afforded another chance. (op 11-2 tchd 5-1)

6797 IRISH STALLION FARMS E B F MOLSON COORS NOVICE STKS 6f 212y
2:30 (2:30) (Class 4) 2-Y-O **£4,528** (£1,347; £673; £336) **Stalls** Low

Form RPR
512 **1** **Baltic Knight (IRE)**[14] 6372 2-9-0 97 RichardHughes 2 92+
(Richard Hannon) *mde all: pushed along over 1f out: shkn up to assert fnl 120yds: readily* **5/4**[1]
0130 **2** *1 ¾* **King Dragon (IRE)**[20] 6162 2-9-3 90 FrankieDettori 3 89
(Brian Meehan) *trckd ldng pair: rdn for str chal fr 2f out: no ex whn hld fnl 120yds: jst hld on for 2nd* **9/4**[2]
413 **3** *nse* **Vectis**[33] 5790 2-9-3 79 CathyGannon 4 89
(Harry Dunlop) *awkward leaving stalls: racd keenly: hld up in last pair bhd ldrs: tk clsr order over 3f out: rdn 2f out: nt gng pce of front 2 sn after: kpt on fnl 120yds: jst failed to snatch 2nd* **7/1**
0121 **4** *7* **Silver Ridge (IRE)**[36] 5710 2-9-5 90 JimCrowley 5 73
(Ralph Beckett) *prom: rdn to press wnr over 2f out: one pce fr over 1f out* **7/2**[3]
1 **5** *10* **Mick Duggan**[27] 5968 2-9-0 73 EddieAhern 1 42
(Simon Hodgson) *hld up in last pair bhd ldrs tl outpcd over 2f out* **33/1**

1m 30.31s (1.71) **Going Correction** +0.30s/f (Good) **5** Ran SP% **112.9**
Speed ratings (Par 97): **102,100,99,91,80**
CSF £4.51 TOTE £2.40: £1.10, £1.10; EX 5.10.
Owner Thurloe Thoroughbreds XXX **Bred** Henry O'Callaghan **Trained** East Everleigh, Wilts

FOCUS
Three of these had an official mark in the 90s, which suggests this was a very useful race of its type. The form is rated around the balance of the first three's form.

NOTEBOOK
Baltic Knight(IRE) was given a good ride by Richard Hughes, who looked to give his colt a canny ride from the front. The jockey always appeared to have a little bit up his sleeve if something came to him and so it proved in the latter stages. Connections suggested afterwards that there might be a 1m novice race at Kempton their horse could go to. (tchd 13-8 in a place)
King Dragon(IRE) was far from disgraced in a sales race on his previous start under Shane Kelly, and looked a big danger to the winner when he closed up towards the inside rail. However, the gelding didn't pick up once upsides Baltic Knight and was readily beaten off. (op 3-1)
Vectis was last seen running over 5f, but shaped here as though in need of further than this distance considering the way he finished. (op 13-2)
Silver Ridge(IRE), up in trip again, was beaten heading to the 2f marker so can't have run up to his best. (op 3-1)
Mick Duggan, making his debut for Simon Hodgson after being purchased out of the Rae Guest stable when landing a Kempton claimer on his debut, was outclassed and will have easier tasks. (op 25-1)

6798 HIGOS INSURANCE SERVICES SOUTHAMPTON CLAIMING STKS 1m 1f 198y
3:00 (3:00) (Class 5) 3-4-Y-O **£2,264** (£673; £336; £168) **Stalls** Low

Form RPR
021 **1** **Cufflink**[33] 5805 3-8-7 77 NickyMackay 10 68
(Rae Guest) *trckd ldr: rdn 2f out: led over 1f out: kpt on wl: rdn out* **4/1**[3]
-356 **2** *1 ¼* **Breaking The Bank**[11] 6502 3-9-0 66 LukeMorris 3 72
(William Muir) *trckd ldrs: rdn over 2f out: wnt 2nd jst ins fnl f: kpt on but a being hld* **12/1**
4100 **3** *4* **No Compromise**[25] 6039 3-8-8 76 KierenFallon 2 58
(Hughie Morrison) *nvr travelling in last of gp: looked wl btn over 3f out: hdwy over 2f out: chsd ldrs wl over 1f out: kpt on same pce to snatch 3rd wl ins fnl f* **15/8**[1]
0-55 **4** *¾* **Bussa**[64] 4147 4-8-12 60 CathyGannon 9 56
(David Evans) *led: rdn 2f out: hdd over 1f out: sn no ex: lost 2nd towards fin* **25/1**
5630 **5** *1 ¼* **Gold Sceptre (FR)**[19] 6206 3-8-11 66 ow1 (b) RichardHughes 1 57
(Richard Hannon) *hld up: effrt over 2f out: nvr gng pce to get involved* **7/1**
1064 **6** *3 ½* **Emerald Invader**[9] 6544 3-8-8 69 ow1 (t) TedDurcan 5 47
(David Elsworth) *in tch: cl enough travelling wl 2f out: sn rdn: fnd nil: wknd fnl f* **7/1**
3130 **7** *3* **Matavia Bay (IRE)**[47] 5310 4-8-11 66 MichaelJMMurphy(5) 6 44
(Alan Jarvis) *trckd ldrs: rdn 3f out: wknd over 1f out* **7/2**[2]
1000 **8** *98* **Sir Dylan**[4] 6690 3-8-11 54 ow2 EddieAhern 8
(Ronald Harris) *s.i.s: taken wd: sn wl detached: virtually p.u fnl 5f* **33/1**

2m 12.76s (2.86) **Going Correction** +0.20s/f (Good)
WFA 3 from 4yo 5lb **8** Ran SP% **116.5**
Speed ratings (Par 103): **96,95,91,91,90 87,85,6**
.Cufflink was claimed by D McCain Jnr £16000.\n\x\x
Owner C J Murfitt **Bred** C J Murfitt **Trained** Newmarket, Suffolk

FOCUS
An ordinary contest that is unlikely to throw up too many winners in the short-term. The second and fourth are the key to the form and the winner is rated 10lb off his best.
Sir Dylan Official explanation: jockey said gelding hung badly left

6799 HIGOS INSURANCE SERVICES CONDITIONS STKS 6f
3:35 (3:36) (Class 2) 2-Y-O **£7,762** (£2,310; £1,154; £577) **Stalls** Low

Form RPR
1 **1** **Breton Rock (IRE)**[33] 5785 2-8-12 80 MartinLane 5 84
(David Simcock) *hld up in tch: pushed along over 3f out: hdwy 2f out: sn rdn: r.o to ld ins fnl f: rdn out* **9/4**[2]
211 **2** *¾* **Mutazamen**[25] 6034 2-9-4 85 TadhgO'Shea 4 88
(Richard Hannon) *led: rdn wl over 1f out: hdd ins fnl f: kpt on but no ex* **5/2**[3]
3 **3** *2 ¼* **Divine Reward (USA)** 2-8-9 0 JackDuern 1 72
(Reg Hollinshead) *s.i.s: sn pushed along in last but in tch: outpcd over 3f out: hdwy ent fnl f: r.o to go 3rd fnl stride* **100/1**
131 **4** *shd* **Alcando (IRE)**[18] 6227 2-8-12 80 EddieAhern 3 75
(Denis Coakley) *stmbld leaving stalls: t.k.h early: trckd ldrs: rdn wl over 1f out: ev ch ent fnl f: kpt on same pce: lost 3rd fnl stride* **6/1**
3134 **5** *2 ¾* **Kodatish (IRE)**[20] 6155 2-8-12 72 LukeMorris 2 67
(Ronald Harris) *racd keenly: trckd ldr tl rdn 2f out: fdd fnl 120yds* **25/1**
2204 **6** *9* **New Pearl (IRE)**[12] 6424 2-9-1 90 RichardHughes 6 43
(David Brown) *hld up in tch: tk clsr order travelling wl 3f out: rdn wl over 1f out: qckly btn: eased ins fnl f* **2/1**[1]

1m 16.65s (1.85) **Going Correction** +0.30s/f (Good) **6** Ran SP% **111.8**
Speed ratings (Par 101): **99,98,95,94,91 79**
toteswingers 1&2 £1.70, 2&3 £6.90, 1&3 £11.70 CSF £8.24 TOTE £5.20: £3.80, £1.10; EX 10.00.
Owner John Cook **Bred** George Kent **Trained** Newmarket, Suffolk

FOCUS
Three of these had won on their previous start so, while none of these are likely to develop into top-class performers, this looks like fairly strong form. The fourth and fifth are the best guides.

NOTEBOOK
Breton Rock(IRE) won on his debut over C&D in late August and followed that up with another success. Martin Lane was slow to take the hood off his mount leaving the stalls, but that made little difference and David Simcock's colt remains a nice prospect. (op 11-4)
Mutazamen, back on turf and chasing a hat-trick down in distance, would have found the easy ground something new to him so ran respectably, although he did have his own way out in front. He's a solid enough performer, but probably doesn't have much room for manoeuvre off his handicap mark this or next season. (op 9-4 tchd 2-1)
Divine Reward(USA) ◆, who cost $5,500 as a yearling and then £12,000 as a 2-y-o, made an eye-catching start to his career in what was a decent event. Already gelded and ridden by a jockey who couldn't claim his 7lb allowance, he ought to win any ordinary maiden as long as he doesn't regress.
Alcando(IRE) seemed to put up an improved performance even after stumbling at the start. (op 5-1)
Kodatish(IRE) had shown a fair level of ability in the past and ran at least up to his BHA mark. (tchd 28-1)
New Pearl(IRE) looked a decent bet at the weights when considering official ratings, but never picked up when Richard Hughes asked for extra. (op 5-2 tchd 11-4)

6800 HIGOS INSURANCE SERVICES BOURNEMOUTH H'CAP 6f
4:10 (4:12) (Class 4) (0-85,85) 3-Y-O+ **£4,075** (£1,212; £606; £303) **Stalls** Low

Form RPR
2633 **1** **Choral**[34] 5769 4-9-2 **80** SeanLevey 9 90
(Richard Hannon) *chsd ldrs: rdn to ld wl over 1f out: sn edgd lft: r.o wl: rdn out* **11/1**
3111 **2** *1 ¼* **Links Drive Lady**[14] 6378 4-8-13 **77** JimCrowley 8 83+
(Dean Ivory) *chsd ldrs: led briefly 2f out: sn rdn: kpt on but hld by wnr ins fnl f: hld on for 2nd* **8/1**[3]
025 **3** *nse* **Ertikaan**[14] 6369 5-8-13 **82** DarrenEgan(5) 13 88
(Ronald Harris) *trckd ldrs: rdn wl over 2f out: kpt on ins fnl f* **12/1**
3360 **4** *½* **Crew Cut (IRE)**[46] 5362 4-8-11 **78** (p) RaulDaSilva(3) 16 82
(Jeremy Gask) *mid-div: hdwy 2f out: sn rdn: r.o fnl f but nvr getting there* **12/1**
0014 **5** *¾* **Another Try (IRE)**[20] 6165 7-9-0 **83** MichaelJMMurphy(5) 18 85
(Alan Jarvis) *mid-div: hdwy over 2f out: sn rdn: kpt on same pce ins fnl f* **7/1**[2]
2-03 **6** *nk* **Out Do**[151] 1843 3-9-2 **81** KierenFallon 15 82+
(Luca Cumani) *towards rr of mid-div: swtchd rt over 3f out and again whn nt best of runs over 1f out: r.o ent fnl f: nvr threatened ldrs and hld fnl 120yds* **7/1**[2]
6231 **7** *½* **Mount Hollow**[14] 6357 7-8-9 **80** (p) JackDuern(7) 7 79
(Reg Hollinshead) *s.i.s: towards rr: swtchd lft u.p 3f out: styd on ins fnl f: nvr a threat* **20/1**
000 **8** *¾* **Bay Knight (IRE)**[35] 5746 6-9-7 **85** TedDurcan 14 82
(Sean Curran) *s.i.s: towards rr: styd on ent fnl f: nvr a factor* **20/1**
1402 **9** *1 ½* **Rigolleto (IRE)**[7] 6577 4-8-7 **76** CharlesBishop(5) 17 68
(Mick Channon) *in tch: rdn over 2f out: nt gng pce to get on terms* **7/1**[2]
1060 **10** *½* **Pick A Little**[11] 6465 4-8-9 **76** RyanClark(3) 4 66
(Michael Blake) *hmpd s: towards rr: reminders after 1f: hdwy u.p over 1f out: no further imp ins fnl f* **25/1**
1301 **11** *1* **Good Authority (IRE)**[29] 5910 5-9-6 **84** TomMcLaughlin 1 71
(Karen George) *wnt lft s: mid-div: hdwy 3f out: rdn to chse ldrs 2f out: wknd ins fnl f* **6/1**[1]
6000 **12** *½* **Solemn**[32] 5832 7-9-0 **85** (b) DanielMuscutt(7) 6 71
(Milton Bradley) *led: rdn and hdd 2f out: wknd ins fnl f* **20/1**
5120 **13** *4 ½* **Picture Dealer**[12] 6432 3-9-2 **81** JamesDoyle 11 52
(Gary Moore) *mid-div: rdn to chse ldrs 2f out: wknd ent fnl f* **11/1**
0026 **14** *1 ¾* **Supreme Spirit (IRE)**[20] 6176 5-8-13 **77** (v[1]) JimmyFortune 5 43
(Peter Makin) *hmpd s: a towards rr* **16/1**
150 **15** *hd* **Sir Pedro**[60] 4824 3-9-4 **83** DarryllHolland 12 48
(Charles Hills) *t.k.h in midfield: rdn over 2f out: wknd ent fnl f* **25/1**
/0-6 **16** *6* **Arthur's Edge**[7] 6286 8-9-4 **82** FergusSweeney 10 28
(Christopher Mason) *disp ld tl rdn 2f out: sn wknd* **66/1**

1m 15.73s (0.93) **Going Correction** +0.30s/f (Good)
WFA 3 from 4yo+ 1lb **16** Ran SP% **124.3**
Speed ratings (Par 105): **105,103,103,102,101 101,100,99,97,96 95,94,88,86,86 78**
toteswingers 1&2 £13.20, 2&3 £26.30, 1&3 £34.60 CSF £88.84 CT £1099.07 TOTE £19.00: £3.60, £1.10, £4.20, £4.10; EX 119.40.
Owner Longview Stud & Bloodstock Ltd **Bred** Longview Stud & Bloodstock Ltd **Trained** East Everleigh, Wilts

FOCUS
An open-looking contest full of horses that could be given a chance if running up to their best. The leaders appeared to go off quite quickly but not many got involved from off the pace. Sound, straightforward form.

6801 FRANCIS CLARK H'CAP 1m
4:40 (4:41) (Class 6) (0-65,65) 3-Y-O+ **£1,940** (£577; £288; £144) **Stalls** Low

Form RPR
0-64 **1** **Uncle Dermot (IRE)**[15] 6334 4-9-2 **61** KierenFallon 6 74
(Brendan Powell) *t.k.h to s: mid-div tl lost pl 3f out: sn nudged along: hdwy over 2f out: led wl over 1f out: sn in command: r.o strly* **16/1**
0515 **2** *4 ½* **Alshazah**[9] 6544 4-8-11 **63** (p) IanBurns(7) 13 66
(Rod Millman) *towards rr: hdwy fr 3f out: rdn to ld briefly 2f out: kpt on to hold on for 2nd but sn hld by wnr* **7/1**[3]
2123 **3** *¾* **Authoritarian**[17] 6275 3-9-2 **64** SeanLevey 4 65
(Richard Hannon) *chsd ldrs: rdn over 2f out: kpt on ins fnl f but nvr any ch w wnr* **8/1**

0320 **4** *hd* **Isingy Red (FR)**[20] 6174 4 -9-362 ....(p) PatCosgrave 15 62
(Jim Boyle) *mid-div: hdwy 3f out: rdn and ev ch 2f out: kpt on but sn hld by wnr: no ex ins fnl f* **33/1**

0122 **5** *2 1/2* **Cyril The Squirrel**[17] 6275 8 -9-362 .... DarryllHolland 16 57
(Karen George) *mid-div: rdn wl over 2f out: styd on fnl f: nvr threatened ldrs* **15/2**

5036 **6** *3 3/4* **Hereford Boy**[76] 4242 8 -9-665 .... MartinLane 14 51
(Dean Ivory) *hld up towards rr: hdwy over 2f out: sn rdn: nvr rchd ldrs: wknd ins fnl f* **33/1**

3343 **7** *1* **South Cape**[38] 5628 9 -9-362 .... RichardMullen 10 48
(Gary Moore) *mid-div: hdwy over 2f out: sn rdn to chse ldrs: fdd ins fnl f* **12/1**

2-00 **8** *3 1/2* **Mountrath**[37] 5667 5 -8-1365 ....(v) WilliamTwiston-Davies(7) 3 41
(Gary Moore) *prom: led after 2f: rdn over 2f out: hdd sn after: wknd ent fnl f* **50/1**

4010 **9** *6* **Catchanova (IRE)**[27] 5983 5 -9-665 .... FergusSweeney 11 27
(Eve Johnson Houghton) *trckd ldrs: rdn over 2f out: wknd over 1f out* **14/1**

-312 **10** *shd* **For What (USA)**[67] 4584 4 -9-564 .... TedDurcan 2 26
(David Lanigan) *mid-div: hdwy 3f out: rdn to chal whn bmpd 2f out: btn sn after* **5/2**[1]

6-23 **11** *13* **Compton Rainbow**[13] 6402 3 -9-365 ....(t) JamesDoyle 5
(Hans Adielsson) *chsd ldrs tl wknd over 2f out* **25/1**

5640 **12** *9* **Al Aqabah (IRE)**[100] 3443 7 -9-064 ....(b) MichaelJMMurphy(5) 7
(Brian Gubby) *wnt rt s: mid-div tl wknd over 1f out* **12/1**

2005 **13** *1/2* **Shot In The Dark (IRE)**[85] 3475 3 -9-365 .... LiamKeniry 1
(Jonathan Geake) *led for 2f: rdn 3f out: sn wknd* **25/1**

-420 **U** **Heezararity**[12] 6458 4 -9-665 .... CathyGannon 12
(David Evans) *hld up towards rr: bdly hmpd and uns rdr over 5f out* **16/1**

3334 **P** **Love Tatoo (IRE)**[19] 6209 3 -9-365 .... JimmyFortune 9
(Andrew Balding) *mid-div whn lost action over 5f out: immediately p.u: fatally injured* **13/2**[2]

1m 45.93s (2.43) **Going Correction** +0.30s/f (Good)
WFA 3 from 4yo+ 3lb **15**Ran SP%**126.6**
Speed ratings (Par 101): **99,94,93,93,91 87,86,82,76,76 63,54,54, ,**
toteswingers 1&2 £46.80, 2&3 £22.10, 1&3 £18.30 CSF £123.71 CT £1012.70 TOTE £22.10 : £4.80, £2.60 , £2.30 ; EX 249.90 .
Owner K Rhatigan **Bred** Ballyhane Stud **Trained** Upper Lambourn, Berks

FOCUS
There was an unfortunate start to this race when Love Tatoo lost her action and Jimmy Fortune immediately started to pull his mount up - she sadly suffered a fatal injury. Heezararity was in rear when depositing Cathy Gannon to the floor due to being hampered by the injured filly.
Al Aqabah (IRE) Official explanation: jockey said mare lost its action

6802 PICADOR CHEVROLET H'CAP 1m 6f 21y
5:10 (5:12) (Class 5) (0-75,75) 3-Y-0+ **£2,587** (£770; £384 ; £192) **Stalls** Far side

Form RPR

/331 **1** **Presto Volante (IRE)**[20] 6159 4 -9-567 ....(p) JamesDoyle 13 80+
(Amanda Perrett) *in tch: hdwy fr 4f out: led wl over 2f out: styd on strly to draw clr jst over 1f out: comf* **5/1**[2]

26 **2** *3* **Madame St Clair (IRE)**[12] 6441 3 -8-973 .... NedCurtis(7) 9 82
(Roger Curtis) *hld up towards rr: brought wd and hdwy fr over 3f out: w wnr whn rdn and rdr dropped whip 2f out: styd on for clr 2nd but sn hld* **16/1**

-050 **3** *5* **Maria Letizia**[21] 6146 3 -9-273 .... EddieAhern 5 75
(John Gosden) *trckd ldrs: rdn wl over 2f out: styd on for clr 3rd but hld fr wl over 1f out* **11/2**[3]

1443 **4** *6* **Cellist**[25] 6037 3 -9-273 ....(p) LiamJones 10 67
(William Haggas) *mid-div: pushed along on bnd over 6f out: hdwy 5f out: rdn and ev ch 3f out: sn hld: one pce fnl 2f: jst hld on for 4th* **9/2**[1]

4301 **5** *nse* **Switched Off**[26] 6004 7 -9-1274 .... SeanLevey 8 68
(Ed McMahon) *hld up towards rr: hdwy fr 4f out: rdn over 3f out: styd on same pce fnl 2f: nvr trbld ldrs: jst failed to snatch 4th* **13/2**

-006 **6** *1/2* **Hawridge King**[34] 5772 10 -9-466 .... LiamKeniry 7 59
(Stuart Kittow) *hld up towards rr: styd on same pce fnl 2f: nvr trbld ldrs* **12/1**

6030 **7** *2 3/4* **Battleoftrafalgar**[83] 3997 5 -9-567 ....(b) KierenFallon 11 56
(Michael Attwater) *trckd ldr: c wd 5f out: led over 3f out: sn rdn: hdd wl over 2f out: sn hld: wknd fnl f* **20/1**

5650 **8** *3/4* **Handles For Forks (IRE)**[13] 6407 4 -8-1164 .... CharlesBishop(5) 6 52
(Mick Channon) *mid-div: effrt over 3f out: nvr threatened: wl hld whn short of room ent fnl f* **12/1**

3604 **9** *1* **Shesha Bear**[3] 6703 7 -9-870 ....(p) JimmyFortune 2 57
(Jonathan Portman) *hld up towards rr: rdn and prog to chse ldrs 3f out: wknd fnl f* **8/1**

0-05 **10** *11* **Liberate**[45] 4284 9 -9-675 ....(t) WilliamTwiston-Davies(7) 4 46
(Anabel K Murphy) *in tch: hdwy 6f out: effrt 3f out: wknd over 2f out* **33/1**

-206 **11** *2 3/4* **Miss Topsy Turvy (IRE)**[15] 6349 4 -9-1173 .... TedDurcan 12 40
(John Dunlop) *a towards rr* **8/1**

11-0 **12** *17* **Eseej (USA)**[70] 4470 7 -9-370 .... DarrenEgan(5) 14 13
(Geoffrey Deacon) *led tl over 3f out: sn rdn: wknd 2f out* **33/1**

4000 **13** *13* **Steuben (GER)**[40] 5546 6 -9-1375 .... DaraghO'Donohoe 1
(Barney Curley) *chsd ldr tl pushed along 6f out: sn lost pl: wl bhd fnl 3f* **40/1**

3m 8.94s (1.54) **Going Correction** +0.20s/f (Good)
WFA 3 from 4yo+ 9lb **13**Ran SP%**120.1**
Speed ratings (Par 103): **103,101,98,95,94 94,93,92,92,85 84,74,67**
toteswingers 1&2 £11.50, 2&3 £21.20, 1&3 £6.10 CSF £79.29 CT £462.96 TOTE £7.80 : £3.40, £6.90, £2.80 ; EX 77.70 .
Owner Mrs S Conway Mr & Mrs M Swayne Mr A Brooke Mrs R D **Bred** R A Major **Trained** Pulborough, W Sussex

FOCUS
Nothing more than a modest stayers' event, in which plenty either hadn't tried the trip before or had been running over shorter distances recently.
T/Plt: £58.50 to a £1 stake. Pool of £51298.92 - 639.37 winning tickets. T/Qpdt: £9.80 to a £1 stake. Pool of £3985.58 - 298.17 w. tckts TM 6803a (Foreign Racing) See RI

6128 CHANTILLY (R-H)
Wednesday, October 3
OFFICIAL GOING: Turf: good to soft changing to soft after race 5 (1.35): all-weather: standard

6804a PRIX DE CHAUMONT (CLAIMER) (4YO+) (TURF) 1m
2:05 (12:00) 4-Y-0+ **£9,583** (£3,833; £2,875 ; £1,916 ; £958)

RPR

1 **Planet Elder**[53] 5118 4 -8-110 .... StephanePasquier 2 96
(P Bary, France) **48/10**[3]

2 *5* **Polarix**[52] 6 -9-40 .... MaximeGuyon 8 92
(H-A Pantall, France) **7/2**[1]

3 *3 1/2* **Garde Slickly (FR)**[15] 4 -8-110 .... AlexisAchard(4) 11 81
(Mlle Valerie Boussin, France) **25/1**

4 *nse* **Private Jet (FR)**[17] 4 -9-40 ....(b) IoritzMendizabal 5 84
(P Monfort, France) **10/1**

5 *1 3/4* **Primera Vista**[21] 6 -9-10 ....(b) JohanVictoire 7 77
(Mario Hofer, Germany) **9/2**[2]

6 *nk* **Iokastos**[21] 5 -8-110 .... GeraldMosse 9 72
(Mlle C Cardenne, France) **7/1**

7 *1 1/4* **Ohne Tadel (GER)**[275] 18 5 -8-60 .... SoufyaneMoulin(5) 3 69
(S Smrczek, Germany) **41/1**

8 *3/4* **Layer Cake**[59] 6 -9-10 .... OlivierPeslier 10 71
(A Kleinkorres, Germany) **12/1**

9 *11* **New Outlook (USA)**[3] 4 -9-40 .... RonanThomas 1 49
(J E Pease, France) **9/1**

10 *6* **Beautiful Lando (FR)**[12] 6458 4 -8-110 ....(b) DavyBonilla 6 28
(Heather Main) *hld up towards rr on inner: rdn early in st: no rspnse: sn wknd: eased fnl 1 1/2f* **43/1**

0 **El Pib D'Oro (IRE)**[6] 6 -8-110 ....(p) VincentVion 4
(C Schiff, France) **87/1**

0 **Montalban (FR)**[52] 5 -9-10 ....(b) ChristopheSoumillon 13
(D De Waele, France) **13/1**

0 **Islesman**[9] 6538 4 -8-130 .... MatthieuAutier(3) 12
(Heather Main) *broke wl on wd outside: racd midfield: rdn 2f out: nt qckn: sn fdd out of picture: eased fnl f* **34/1**

1m 40.65s (2.65) **13**Ran SP% **116.6**
WIN (incl. 1 euro stake): 5.80. PLACES: 2.30, 2.00, 5.20. DF: 14.20. SF: 24.70 .
Owner Niarchos Family **Bred** Suc S Niarchos **Trained** Chantilly, France

4383 HOPPEGARTEN (R-H)
Wednesday, October 3
OFFICIAL GOING: Turf: good

6805a WESTMINSTER 22 PREIS DER DEUTSCHEN EINHEIT (GROUP 3) (3YO+) (TURF) 1m 2f
3:35 (12:00) 3-Y-0+
£37,500 (£14,166; £6,250 ; £4,166 ; £2,916 ; £1,666)

RPR

1 **Pastorius (GER)**[31] 5865 3 -9-00 .... ADeVries 1 112+
(Mario Hofer, Germany) *prom and tk v t.k.h: sn settled in 3rd: shkn up 2 1/2f out: rdn and hdwy on outside over 1 1/2f out: r.o wl fnl f to ld 75yds out: wl on top at fin* **2/5**[1]

2 *1 1/4* **Durban Thunder (GER)**[39] 5613 6 -9-40 .... SamHitchcott 9 108
(P Harley, Germany) *led: kicked clr 2 1/2f out: rdn over 1 1/2f out: r.o: hdd 75yds out: no ex* **41/5**[3]

3 *nk* **Ostinato (GER)**[80] 4171 4 -9-40 ....(b) KKerekes 6 107+
(Sandor Kovacs, Hungary) *hld up in rr: prog on rail over 2f out: 5th and rdn 1 1/2f out: hrd rdn and styd on strly ins fnl f: nrest at fin* **15/1**

4 *3* **Russian Tango (GER)**[39] 5613 5 -9-40 .... EPedroza 5 101
(A Wohler, Germany) *trckd ldr on outside: rdn and nt qckn 2f out: wknd fnl 150yds* **31/10**[2]

5 *1* **Wasimah (GER)**[34] 5782 3 -8-100 .... WPanov 3 96
(H J Groschel, Germany) *midfield: disp 4th 1/2-way: rdn and nt qckn under 2f out: styd on ins fnl f: nt pce to chal* **172/10**

6 *nk* **Violante (USA)**[31] 4 -9-10 .... FabriceVeron 7 95?
(H-A Pantall, France) *hld up towards rr: disp 4th 1/2-way: briefly outpcd 2f out: kpt on ins fnl f: nt pce to chal* **123/10**

7 *6* **Freemason (GER)** 4 -9-40 .... JBojko 2 86
(R Dzubasz, Germany) *settled next to last: bhd whn hung rt ins fnl f: nvr in contention* **188/10**

2m 2.1s (-4.60)
WFA 3 from 4yo+ 5lb **7**Ran SP%**131.0**
PARI-MUTUEL: WIN (incl. 10 euro stake): 14. PLACES: 11, 16, 18. SF: 53 .
Owner Stall Antanando **Bred** Franz Prinz Von Auersperg & Florian Haffa **Trained** Germany

5715 SOUTHWELL (L-H)
Thursday, October 4
OFFICIAL GOING: Standard
Wind: Light across Weather: Fine and dry

6806 32RED MAIDEN STKS 5f (F)
2:30 (2:32) (Class 5) 3-Y-0 **£2,264** (£673; £336 ; £168) **Stalls** High

Form RPR

00 **1** **Nawarah**[135] 2361 3 -8-120 .... MartinDwyer 2 72
(Conrad Allen) *trckd ldrs: hdwy to ld wl over 1f out: qcknd clr ent fnl f: comf* **28/1**

3-23 **2** *4* **Place That Face**[237] 499 3 -8-1262 .... DarryllHolland 6 58
(Hughie Morrison) *a.p: rdn along 2f out: drvn and kpt on fnl f* **13/2**

3200 **3** *1 1/2* **Taizong (IRE)**[15] 6370 3 -9-363 .... MichaelO'Connell 7 58
(Ian Williams) *chsd ldrs: rdn 2f out: styd on fnl f: nrst fin* **4/1**[2]

0-05 **4** *nk* **Bang Tidy (IRE)**[24] 6100 3 -9-359 .... PaulMulrennan 8 57
(Brian Ellison) *a.p: rdn along 2f out: kpt on same pce fnl f* **8/1**

643 5 *nk* **Jermatt**[24] 6095 3-8-12 54 DarrenEgan(5) 9 55
(J R Jenkins) *in tch: rdn along and hdwy 2f out: kpt on same pce fnl f* **28/1**

6-00 6 *shd* **Wood Nymph (IRE)**[21] 6180 3-8-12 52 DuranFentiman 13 50
(Tim Easterby) *dwlt and in rr: hdwy wl over 1f out: styd on fnl f: nrst fin* **50/1**

2632 7 *½* **Elegant Girl (IRE)**[23] 6125 3-8-12 64 DavidAllan 11 48
(Tim Easterby) *midfield: rdn along 1/2-way: kpt on u.p fnl f: could nt rch ldrs* **6/1**[3]

0-50 8 *½* **Dubai Rythm**[71] 4461 3-9-3 45 (b) LiamKeniry 3 51?
(Michael Appleby) *led: rdn along 2f out: sn hdd & wknd* **25/1**

4624 9 *hd* **Choice Pearl (USA)**[19] 6249 3-8-12 53 (b) HarryBentley 5 46
(Tobias B P Coles) *dwlt: sn chsng ldrs: rdn along wl over 1f out: grad wknd* **14/1**

1355 10 *hd* **Art Form**[30] 5681 3-8-5 68 (t) DavidBergin(7) 4 45
(Alan McCabe) *dwlt: hdwy to chse ldrs over 2f out: rdn and ch wl over 1f out: sn wknd* **2/1**[1]

0246 11 *nk* **Dartrix**[39] 5624 3-8-5 56 (p[1]) ConnorNichol(7) 12 44
(Michael Dods) *a towards rr* **14/1**

60 12 *5* **Rosa Lottie**[23] 6125 3-8-12 0 AndrewMullen 1 26
(David C Griffiths) *a in rr: bhd fr 1/2-way* **100/1**

0-0 13 *5* **Minne Wa Wa**[104] 3356 3-8-12 54 RobertWinston 10 8
(David Brown) *sn outpcd and a bhd* **40/1**

58.25s (-1.45) **Going Correction** -0.225s/f (Stan) **13** Ran SP% **121.5**
Speed ratings (Par 101): **102,95,93,92,92 92,91,90,90,89 89,81,73**
toteswingers 1&2 £39.10, 2&3 £6.80, 1&3 £37.20 CSF £196.80 TOTE £71.00: £10.40, £1.90, £1.40; EX 359.10.
Owner Hassan Al Abdulmalik **Bred** Foursome Thoroughbreds **Trained** Newmarket, Suffolk

FOCUS
A moderate 3yo sprint maiden, but the winner proved different class and provided Conrad Allen with his first winner since resuming training. All the action unfolded centre-to-far side and those drawn high tended to struggle. The winner's first form, but it was no fluke.
Taizong(IRE) Official explanation: jockey said that the colt hung left-handed

6807 32RED.COM H'CAP 1m 4f (F)
3:00 (3:00) (Class 6) (0-60,60) 3-Y-O **£1,704** (£503; £251) **Stalls** Low

Form RPR

4562 1 **Smart Affair**[17] 6316 3-8-9 48 (be[1]) SamHitchcott 1 56
(Alan Bailey) *hld up towards rr: smooth hdwy 5f out: trckd ldrs over 3f out: chal 2f out: sn led and rdn along: styd on fnl f* **12/1**

0006 2 *1 ½* **Medieval Bishop (IRE)**[12] 6474 3-8-12 51 DuranFentiman 9 56
(Tim Walford) *led: rdn along 3f out: hdd 2f out and sn drvn: rallied and kpt on fnl f* **6/1**[3]

4432 3 *nk* **Stag Hill (IRE)**[20] 6210 3-8-13 52 LiamKeniry 7 57
(Sylvester Kirk) *trckd ldrs: smooth hdwy 4f out: led 2f out: sn rdn and hdd over 1f out: drvn and kpt on same pce ins fnl f* **9/2**[1]

3305 4 *½* **Astroscarlet**[17] 6323 3-9-5 58 DarryllHolland 2 62
(Mark H Tompkins) *trckd ldrs on inner: rdn along over 3f out: drvn wl over 1f out: kpt on same pce* **13/2**

006 5 *6* **There's No Rules**[17] 6315 3-8-9 48 oh1 ow2 (e) RobbieFitzpatrick 13 43
(Richard Guest) *in rr: hdwy 3f out: rdn 2f out: kpt on: nrst fin* **16/1**

0000 6 *6* **Miss Mohawk (IRE)**[12] 6474 3-8-7 46 oh1 (p) PatrickMathers 8 31
(Alan Brown) *in rr and sn pushed along: bhd 1/2-way: hdwy on inner over 2f out: sn rdn along and nvr nr ldrs* **80/1**

3000 7 *8* **Cape Alex**[29] 5945 3-9-1 54 [1] RobertWinston 6 26
(Clive Brittain) *in tch: chsd ldrs 5f out: sn rdn along and wknd over 3f out* **13/2**

0205 8 *1* **Pugnacious (IRE)**[12] 6503 3-9-2 55 (v[1]) FrederikTylicki 14 26
(Mark Johnston) *reminders s and sn rdn along to chse ldrs: cl up 1/2-way: rdn along over 3f out: wknd over 2f out* **9/2**[1]

600 9 *4* **Yogic Flyer**[54] 5100 3-8-7 46 oh1 MartinDwyer 12 10
(Gay Kelleway) *chsd ldrs: rdn along over 3f out: sn wknd* **40/1**

5032 10 *1 ¾* **Dewala**[198] 973 3-9-2 55 GrahamLee 10 16
(Michael Appleby) *towards rr: effrt and sme hdwy over 4f out: sn rdn along and n.d* **16/1**

0300 11 *5* **Kian's Joy**[38] 5672 3-8-4 46 oh1 DeclanCannon(3) 3
(Jedd O'Keeffe) *midfield: pushed along and hdwy to chse ldrs over 3f out: rdn whn sddle slipped over 2f out: sn lost pl and bhd* **50/1**

0054 12 *28* **Nowdoro**[28] 5974 3-8-7 46 oh1 JamesSullivan 11
(Julie Camacho) *a in rr: bhd fnl 4f* **5/1**[2]

2m 39.49s (-1.51) **Going Correction** -0.225s/f (Stan) **12** Ran SP% **119.1**
Speed ratings (Par 99): **96,95,94,94,90 86,81,80,77,76 73,54**
toteswingers 1&2 £16.60, 2&3 £7.70, 1&3 £6.40 CSF £82.33 CT £381.18 TOTE £7.10: £4.20, £2.70, £2.20; EX 151.70.
Owner AB Racing Limited **Bred** T E Pocock **Trained** Newmarket, Suffolk

FOCUS
A moderate middle-distance handicap for 3yos, but the pace seemed fair and the front four pulled clear. The third helps with the standard.
Kian's Joy Official explanation: jockey said that he lost his stirrup iron turning in to the home straight
Nowdoro Official explanation: trainer's representive that the gelding was unsuited by the Fibresand surface

6808 IRISH STALLION FARMS EBF MEDIAN AUCTION MAIDEN STKS 5f (F)
3:30 (3:31) (Class 5) 2-Y-O **£3,234** (£962; £481; £240) **Stalls** High

Form RPR

5 1 **Smart Spender (IRE)**[21] 6177 2-9-3 0 ShaneKelly 7 82+
(Jo Hughes) *mde most: rdn and qcknd clr appr fnl f: kpt on strly* **9/2**[3]

465 2 *5* **Oscars Journey**[51] 5213 2-8-12 74 DarrenEgan(5) 6 64
(J R Jenkins) *prom: rdn to chse wnr over 1f out: no imp fnl f* **7/2**[2]

0660 3 *1 ¼* **Solvanna**[1] 6787 2-8-12 62 DarryllHolland 3 55
(Heather Main) *in tch: hdwy 2f out: sn rdn and styd on fnl f: nrst fin* **22/1**

4 *½* **Robyn** 2-8-12 0 NickyMackay 8 53
(Scott Dixon) *chsd ldrs: hdwy and cl up 1/2-way: sn rdn and kpt on same pce appr fnl f* **20/1**

0 5 *1 ¼* **Yorkshireman (IRE)**[7] 6603 2-9-3 0 (v[1]) RobertWinston 1 53
(David Brown) *rdn along and outpcd on outer: in rr 1/2-way: styd on fnl f* **8/1**

5426 6 *nk* **Max The Machine**[8] 6579 2-9-3 72 MartinDwyer 4 52
(Derek Shaw) *prom: rdn along 2f out: drvn and wknd over 1f out* **3/1**[1]

03 7 *2* **Scarlet Spirit (IRE)**[14] 6404 2-8-12 0 PJMcDonald 5 40
(Ann Duffield) *cl up: rdn along 2f out: sn wknd* **25/1**

24 8 *1 ¼* **Hoofalong**[9] 6556 2-9-3 0 JamesSullivan 9 40
(Michael Easterby) *v.s.a: a bhd* **7/2**[2]

6 9 *2 ½* **Con Leche**[132] 2442 2-9-3 0 MichaelO'Connell 2 31
(Scott Dixon) *dwlt: sn cl up: rdn along over 2f out: sn wknd* **50/1**

58.98s (-0.72) **Going Correction** -0.225s/f (Stan) **9** Ran SP% **113.7**
Speed ratings (Par 95): **96,88,86,85,83 82,79,77,73**
toteswingers 1&2 £5.00, 2&3 £17.10, 1&3 £11.10 CSF £19.24 TOTE £4.90: £1.80, £1.90, £4.90; EX 27.50.
Owner Brooklands Racing **Bred** Morgan Ferris **Trained** Lambourn, Berks

FOCUS
A modest 2yo maiden but, as with the opener, a winner who can compete in something better. The form has been rated fairly negatively.

NOTEBOOK
Smart Spender(IRE) could hardly have won more comfortably and confirmed the promise he showed despite pulling hard on last month's Wolverhampton debut. Always handy, he pulled right away in the latter stages and should be able to hold his own in nurseries, especially if returned here. (op 8-1)
Oscars Journey was disappointing last time, but his previous sixth in a hot Newmarket maiden was smart form and his sire's good record here made him of obvious interest. He had every chance and kept trying, but was up against a more progressive rival. His rating of 74 provides the benchmark. (op 10-3)
Solvanna had been very disappointing on turf and Polytrack since narrowly beaten on her Lingfield debut in July, including when only 12th of 15 at Nottingham the previous day. This was better, but she has little in the way of scope. (op 20-1 tchd 25-1)
Robyn, an 8,000GBP half-sister to Je Suis Un Rockstar, who won twice over C&D as a juvenile, by a sire with a 20% strike-rate here, made a fair debut and should come on for it. (op 14-1)
Max The Machine ran his best race so far when runner-up in a similar event over C&D in July, but he was in trouble a fair way out this time. (op 7-2 tchd 5-2)
Hoofalong, who had been taken out of a race at Nottingham the previous day on account of the ground, lost all chance at the start. Official explanation: jockey said that the gelding was slowly away (op 11-4)

6809 32RED CASINO NURSERY 5f (F)
4:00 (4:00) (Class 5) (0-75,75) 2-Y-O **£2,385** (£704; £352) **Stalls** High

Form RPR

2326 1 **La Sylphe**[17] 6312 2-8-13 72 LMcNiff(5) 3 77+
(David Barron) *mde all: rdn along over 1f out: styd on strly* **2/1**[1]

4004 2 *2 ½* **Confidential Creek**[29] 5940 2-8-6 60 JamesSullivan 4 56
(Ollie Pears) *in tch: niggled along after 1f: hdwy 2f out: rdn to chse wnr over 1f out: no imp fnl f* **8/1**

4015 3 *2 ¼* **Tharawal Lady (IRE)**[13] 6425 2-9-7 75 MichaelO'Connell 1 63
(John Quinn) *chsd ldng pair: effrt and cl up 1/2-way: rdn 2f out and sn one pce* **11/2**[3]

5110 4 *½* **Girl At The Sands (IRE)**[20] 6196 2-9-4 72 GrahamLee 5 58
(James Given) *chsd ldrs: hdwy over 2f out: sn rdn and no imp fr over 1f out* **2/1**[1]

0201 5 *shd* **Palladius**[9] 6556 2-9-3 71 6ex AmyRyan 6 57
(Kevin Ryan) *in rr and swtchd lft to wd outside after 1f: hdwy 2f out: sn rdn and n.d* **9/2**[2]

0565 6 *5* **Lothian Countess**[55] 5055 2-9-0 68 PaulMulrennan 7 36
(George Foster) *cl up: rdn over 2f out: wknd wl over 1f out* **50/1**

58.79s (-0.91) **Going Correction** -0.225s/f (Stan) **6** Ran SP% **113.3**
Speed ratings (Par 95): **98,94,90,89,89 81**
toteswingers 1&2 £4.20, 2&3 £3.70, 1&3 £2.90 CSF £19.42 TOTE £2.80: £1.10, £6.00; EX 18.50.
Owner M Dalby **Bred** Denis Barry **Trained** Maunby, N Yorks

FOCUS
Just a fair nursery for which the winning time was 0.19 seconds faster than the preceding maiden. The form could be rated a bit better than this.

NOTEBOOK
La Sylphe's only previous AW start was when winning a five-runner nursery over C&D in July, but some good efforts on turf in the meantime meant she was 9lb higher for this return. It made no difference, though, as she made just about all the running and stretched nicely clear in the run to the line. It remains to be seen if she can find another opportunity to maintain her unbeaten run here following a rise, but she is perfectly capable of winning on turf granted a flat track. (op 5-2 tchd 11-4)
Confidential Creek ran better when fourth on his nursery debut at Kempton last time and was one of his sire's first runners at Southwell (along with Palladius). He ran on well from off the pace without threatening the winner, but still has a bit of scope. (op 7-1)
Tharawal Lady(IRE), making her AW debut, didn't improve for the step up to 6f last time and had every chance back down in trip, but lacked the pace to go with the front pair. Perhaps she needs a bit more time between her races. (tchd 5-1 and 6-1)
Girl At The Sands(IRE), making her nursery debut, was totally out of her depth when last of nine in the Flying Childers last time. She had won her maiden over C&D in August, however, so the surface shouldn't have been a problem, but she found disappointingly little off the bridle. (op 15-8 tchd 7-4)
Palladius, back in a nursery under a 6lb penalty after winning a Beverley maiden nine days earlier, was taken out wide after a furlong and a half and found herself rather isolated, which may not have helped. (op 5-1 tchd 4-1)
Lothian Countess Official explanation: trainer said that the filly finished lame

6810 32RED SUPPORTING BRITISH RACING H'CAP (DIV I) 1m (F)
4:30 (4:31) (Class 6) (0-65,65) 3-Y-O **£1,704** (£503; £251) **Stalls** Low

Form RPR

U003 1 **No Dominion (IRE)**[22] 6151 3-8-12 56 GrahamLee 11 69
(James Given) *hld up: smooth hdwy to trck ldrs over 3f out: chal over 2f out: sn rdn: led appr fnl f: kpt on* **15/8**[1]

5400 2 *½* **Sehnsucht (IRE)**[26] 6050 3-9-0 65 (p) DavidBergin(7) 2 77
(Alan McCabe) *cl up: led 3f out: rdn 2f out: drvn and hdd over 1f out: kpt on wl u.p fnl f* **10/1**

0500 3 *7* **The New Black (IRE)**[13] 6442 3-8-9 58 (e[1]) LeonnaMayor(5) 10 54
(Gay Kelleway) *outpcd and sn rdn along in rr: hdwy over 2f out: sn swtchd to outer and drvn: styd on fnl f: nrst fin* **20/1**

060 4 *2 ¼* **Connishka**[79] 4198 3-8-7 51 oh3 SamHitchcott 5 42
(Alan Bailey) *towards rr: rdn along bef 1/2-way: hdwy over 2f out: rdn to chse ldng pair wl over 1f out: sn one pce: lost 3rd ins fnl f* **20/1**

0534 5 *9* **Lady Bellatrix**[12] 6500 3-9-1 59 PaulMulrennan 3 29
(Mark H Tompkins) *cl up: efftort 3f out: rdn over 2f out: sn drvn and wknd* **13/2**[3]

005 6 *1 ½* **Bada Bing**[20] 6216 3-8-7 51 oh1 NickyMackay 4 17
(Scott Dixon) *prom: rdn along over 3f out: sn wknd* **16/1**

0040 7 *2 ¼* **Fauran (IRE)**[29] 5938 3-8-7 51 oh6 [1] KirstyMilczarek 6 12
(Clive Brittain) *a towards rr* **25/1**

5005 8 *nk* **Bitaphon (IRE)**[26] 6048 3-9-5 63 RobertWinston 8 24
(John Balding) *cl up: rdn along 3f out: sn wknd* **7/2**[2]

0030 9 *11* **My Manekineko**[22] 6151 3-8-11 60 DarrenEgan(5) 1
(J R Jenkins) *t.k.h: led: rdn along and hdd 3f out: sn wknd* **15/2**

0400 **10** *5* **Noble Bounty**[24] 6104 3-8-11 **55** .... AmyRyan 7
(Kevin Ryan) *in tch on outer: rdn along over 3f out: sn wknd* **14/1**

1m 42.19s (-1.51) **Going Correction** -0.225s/f (Stan) **10** Ran SP% **117.1**
Speed ratings (Par 99): **98,97,90,88,79 77,75,75,64,59**
toteswingers 1&2 £4.70, 2&3 £16.30, 1&3 £8.70 CSF £21.40 CT £296.93 TOTE £3.10: £1.90, £3.20, £8.80; EX 21.40.
Owner J Barson **Bred** N Cable & M Smith **Trained** Willoughton, Lincs

FOCUS
A moderate 3yo handicap and the field finished very well spread out. It was 0.89sec faster than division I. The first pair were clear but there was little depth
Bitaphon(IRE) Official explanation: jockey said that the gelding hung both ways

6811 £32 BONUS AT 32RED.COM H'CAP 6f (F)
5:00 (5:01) (Class 5) (0-75,75) 3-Y-O+ **£2,264** (£673; £336; £168) **Stalls** Low

Form RPR

2235 **1** **Waking Warrior**[13] 6427 4-9-2 **70** .... (tp) AmyRyan 9 86
(Kevin Ryan) *trckd ldrs: hdwy 3f out: cl up over 2f out: led 1 1/2f out: styd on strly fnl f* **9/2**[1]

4236 **2** *2* **Half A Billion (IRE)**[26] 6050 3-8-12 **74** .... ConnorNichol(7) 4 84
(Michael Dods) *cl up: led over 2f out: sn rdn and hdd 1 1/2f out: drvn and kpt on fnl f* **11/2**[3]

0005 **3** *2 ¾* **Victorian Bounty**[22] 6150 7-9-2 **70** .... ChrisCatlin 5 71
(Tony Newcombe) *chsd ldrs: rdn along over 2f out: drvn to chse ldng pair appr fnl f: one pce* **12/1**

4554 **4** *½* **Bunce (IRE)**[26] 6044 4-9-5 **73** .... (t) DanielTudhope 7 73
(David O'Meara) *midfield: hdwy over 3f out: chsd ldrs over 2f out: sn rdn and no imp fnl f* **5/1**[2]

6140 **5** *1 ¼* **Only Ten Per Cent (IRE)**[36] 5737 4-9-7 **75** .... DarryllHolland 12 71
(J R Jenkins) *hld up in tch: effrt on outer over 2f out: sn rdn and kpt on same pce appr fnl f* **11/1**

0432 **6** *shd* **Strong Man**[26] 6053 4-8-10 **64** .... (b) PaulMulrennan 3 59
(Michael Easterby) *led: rdn along and hdd over 2f out: sn wknd* **5/1**[2]

1000 **7** *hd* **Mazovian (USA)**[17] 6319 4-9-3 **71** .... RussKennemore 1 66
(Michael Chapman) *chsd ldng pair on inner: rdn along wl over 2f out: grad wknd* **33/1**

0243 **8** *2 ¾* **Prince Of Passion (CAN)**[12] 6497 4-8-13 **67** .... (v) TomMcLaughlin 11 53
(Derek Shaw) *chsd ldrs on inner: rdn along wl over 2f out: sn wknd* **20/1**

0060 **9** *2 ¼* **Great Charm (IRE)**[22] 6145 7-8-8 **62** .... (bt[1]) MartinDwyer 10 41
(Daniel Kubler) *dwlt: a in rr* **20/1**

4206 **10** *2 ¾* **Jinker Noble**[27] 6005 3-9-4 **73** .... LiamKeniry 8 43
(Ed de Giles) *a in rr* **22/1**

5605 **11** *2* **Whisky Bravo**[34] 5800 3-8-13 **68** .... RobertWinston 6 31
(David Brown) *a towards rr* **10/1**

0500 **12** *1 ½* **Bella Ophelia (IRE)**[31] 5877 3-9-5 **74** .... NickyMackay 13 33
(Hughie Morrison) *a towards rr* **7/1**

1m 15.0s (-1.50) **Going Correction** -0.225s/f (Stan)
WFA 3 from 4yo+ 1lb **12** Ran SP% **121.3**
Speed ratings (Par 103): **101,98,94,94,92 92,91,88,85,81 78,76**
toteswingers 1&2 £5.90, 2&3 £12.70, 1&3 £15.30 CSF £28.05 CT £289.64 TOTE £6.10: £1.90, £3.10, £4.90; EX 34.50.
Owner Hambleton Racing Ltd XVII **Bred** Rosyground Stud **Trained** Hambleton, N Yorks

FOCUS
A fair handicap and quite competitive. The first two had both run well here before and the winner stepped up on his recent turf form.
Strong Man Official explanation: jockey said the gelding got its tongue over the bit

6812 PLAY GOLF AT SOUTHWELL GOLF CLUB H'CAP 1m (F)
5:30 (5:31) (Class 5) (0-75,75) 3-Y-O+ **£2,264** (£673; £336; £168) **Stalls** Low

Form RPR

510- **1** **Outpost (IRE)**[385] 6078 4-9-7 **75** .... DarryllHolland 13 88
(Alan Bailey) *hld up towards rr: hdwy on outer and wd st: sn trcking ldrs: rdn over 1f out: styd on to ld ins fnl f: kpt on* **7/1**

0403 **2** *1* **Tiradito (USA)**[20] 6216 5-8-8 **62** .... AmyRyan 6 73
(Brian Ellison) *midfield: hdwy and in tch over 3f out: trckd ldrs wl over 1f out: rdn and ev ch ent fnl f: sn drvn and kpt on same pce* **11/4**[1]

4026 **3** *1 ¼* **Saaboog**[13] 6430 3-8-13 **70** .... PaulMulrennan 10 78
(James Tate) *prom: cl up over 3f out: led 2f out: sn rdn: drvn and hdd ins fnl f: one pce* **6/1**

1000 **4** *nk* **Caledonia Prince**[36] 5752 4-8-13 **67** .... (p) DanielTudhope 12 74
(Jo Hughes) *in tch: hdwy to chse ldrs over 2f out: rdn wl over 1f out: one pce whn n.m.r ent fnl f* **11/2**[3]

4500 **5** *7* **All Right Now**[134] 2405 5-8-12 **66** .... HarryBentley 4 57
(Derek Haydn Jones) *cl up: led over 4f out: rdn over 2f out: sn hdd and grad wknd* **16/1**

0500 **6** *1* **Monzino (USA)**[12] 6479 4-8-9 **63** .... (p) RussKennemore 11 52
(Michael Chapman) *dwlt and in rr: hdwy over 2f out: sn rdn and n.d* **22/1**

046 **7** *¾* **Piceno (IRE)**[150] 1917 4-8-10 **69** .... DarrenEgan(5) 2 56
(Scott Dixon) *chsd ldrs on inner: rdn along wl over 2f out: grad wknd* **16/1**

3210 **8** *2 ¾* **Availed Speaker (IRE)**[16] 6342 3-8-6 **70** .... EireannCagney(7) 1 51
(Richard Fahey) *a towards rr* **20/1**

6-10 **9** *3 ½* **Layla's King**[14] 6410 4-8-11 **65** .... MartinDwyer 7 38
(David C Griffiths) *nvr bttr than midfield* **9/2**[2]

3000 **10** *3 ¼* **George Benjamin**[19] 6235 5-9-5 **73** .... AndrewMullen 5 38
(Christopher Kellett) *chsd ldrs: rdn along over 3f out: sn wknd* **40/1**

6000 **11** *3 ½* **Hellbender (IRE)**[2] 6756 6-9-0 **73** .... LMcNiff(5) 9 30
(George Foster) *a in rr* **50/1**

0325 **12** *9* **Mudhish (IRE)**[71] 4469 7-8-8 **62** ow1 .... (b) RobertWinston 8
(Clive Brittain) *chsd ldrs: rdn along over 2f out: sn wknd* **12/1**

4200 **13** *43* **Pipers Piping (IRE)**[17] 6319 6-9-3 **71** .... LiamKeniry 3
(John Butler) *led: hdd over 4f out: sn wknd: bhd and eased fnl 2f* **33/1**

1m 41.2s (-2.50) **Going Correction** -0.225s/f (Stan)
WFA 3 from 4yo+ 3lb **13** Ran SP% **122.9**
Speed ratings (Par 103): **103,102,100,100,93 92,91,88,85,82 78,69,26**
toteswingers 1&2 £7.10, 2&3 £5.40, 1&3 £10.90 CSF £25.83 CT £133.38 TOTE £9.90: £4.40, £2.80, £1.10; EX 46.80.
Owner Rathordan Partnership **Bred** Martin Dunne **Trained** Newmarket, Suffolk

FOCUS
A fair handicap for the grade, featuring a well-backed winner. The winner, third and fourth have all shown their best previous form at this track.
Pipers Piping(IRE) Official explanation: jockey said that the gelding stopped quickly

6813 32RED SUPPORTING BRITISH RACING H'CAP (DIV II) 1m (F)
6:00 (6:00) (Class 6) (0-65,65) 3-Y-O **£1,704** (£503; £251) **Stalls** Low

Form RPR

4330 **1** **Twin Shadow (IRE)**[29] 5945 3-8-13 **57** .... FrederikTylicki 3 63
(James Fanshawe) *hld up towards rr: hdwy on inner 3f out: rdn to chse clr ldr over 1f out: styd on ins fnl f to ld last 50yds* **3/1**[1]

3240 **2** *1* **Admiralty**[22] 6152 3-9-7 **65** .... (b) RoystonFfrench 10 69
(Ismail Mohammed) *chsd ldng pair: led after 2f and sn clr: rdn wl over 1f out: drvn ins fnl f: hdd and no ex last 75yds* **7/2**[2]

0622 **3** *nk* **Symphony Star (IRE)**[73] 4405 3-8-7 **56** .... DarrenEgan(5) 7 59
(Paul D'Arcy) *chsd ldrs: rdn wl over 2f out: drvn and kpt on fr over 1f out: nrst fin* **9/2**

0540 **4** *shd* **Frederickthegreat**[68] 4602 3-9-2 **60** .... DanielTudhope 4 63
(David O'Meara) *led 2f: prom: rdn along 3f out: drvn 2f out: kpt on appr fnl f* **4/1**[3]

0062 **5** *¾* **Tresabella**[56] 5015 3-8-7 **51** oh4 .... (b) LiamKeniry 2 52
(Michael Appleby) *dwlt and in rr: rdn along over 3f out: styd on wl fnl 2f: nrst fin* **10/1**

0000 **6** *¾* **Hoonose**[51] 5215 3-8-0 **51** oh6 .... DavidBergin(7) 5 50
(Pat Eddery) *chsd ldrs: rdn over 2f out: drvn and kpt on appr fnl f* **14/1**

-005 **7** *3 ¾* **Louis Hull**[15] 6361 3-8-7 **51** oh1 .... (p) AndrewMullen 8 42
(Garry Moss) *prom: chsd clr ldr after 2f: rdn over 2f out: sn drvn and wknd wl over 1f out* **25/1**

1000 **8** *10* **Jay Kay**[20] 6217 3-8-10 **54** .... ChrisCatlin 6 22
(Danielle McCormick) *trckd ldrs on outer: hdwy to chse ldng pair 3f out: rdn over 2f out and sn wknd* **16/1**

0000 **9** *17* **Dansili Dutch (IRE)**[12] 6480 3-9-2 **60** .... ShaneKelly 1
(Andrew Crook) *a in rr: bhd fnl 2f* **33/1**

1m 43.08s (-0.62) **Going Correction** -0.225s/f (Stan) **9** Ran SP% **113.8**
Speed ratings (Par 99): **94,93,92,92,91 91,87,77,60**
CSF £13.33 CT £45.44 TOTE £4.80: £1.90, £1.10, £1.10; EX 16.70.
Owner Clipper Logistics **Bred** Limestone & Tara Studs **Trained** Newmarket, Suffolk

FOCUS
The early gallop was strong in the second division of this moderate handicap and the field were soon well string out, but the pace eventually collapsed and the winning time was 0.89 seconds slower than the first leg. The winner probably didn't need to improve.
T/Plt: £240.10 to a £1 stake. Pool of £69231.54 - 210.42 winning tickets. T/Qpdt: £34.70 to a £1 stake. Pool of £5013.89 - 106.86 winning tickets. JR

5681 WARWICK (L-H)
Thursday, October 4

OFFICIAL GOING: Soft (good to soft in places; 6.2)
Wind: Moderate behind Weather: Sunny spells

6814 BETFAIR FUNDS THE PJA DOCTOR (S) STKS 1m 2f 188y
2:10 (2:11) (Class 5) 3-Y-O **£2,264** (£673; £336; £168) **Stalls** Low

Form RPR

5005 **1** **Lady Romanza (IRE)**[11] 5508 3-8-7 54 .... (p) MatthewLawson(5) 3 61
(Brendan Powell) *in rr but in tch: hdwy 3f out: led wl over 1f out: drvn out fnl f* **33/1**

2554 **2** *1* **Ironically (IRE)**[21] 6159 3-8-12 63 .... (b) TedDurcan 6 59
(David Lanigan) *in rr: hdwy on ins 3f out: rdn to chse wnr fnl f: no imp* **9/2**[2]

1414 **3** *3* **Future Wonder (IRE)**[9] 6555 3-9-1 60 .... PaulPickard(3) 7 62+
(Brian Ellison) *in tch: hdwy 2f out: styng on whn hmpd over 1f out: kpt on again fnl f to take one pce 3rd fnl 50yds* **5/2**[1]

654 **4** *¾* **Uncle Roger (IRE)**[18] 6274 3-9-3 57 .... NeilCallan 12 58
(Eve Johnson Houghton) *chsd ldrs: slt ld 2f out: hdd wl over 1f out: no ex ins fnl f* **12/1**

6-00 **5** *hd* **Glaisdale**[13] 6457 3-8-12 58 .... RobertHavlin 8 53
(James Toller) *in rr but in tch: hdwy over 2f out: styng on whn hmpd over 1f out: kpt on again in clsng stages* **25/1**

0505 **6** *shd* **Altona (IRE)**[114] 2999 3-8-12 63 .... MartinHarley 13 52
(Mick Channon) *chsd ldrs: rdn to press ldrs whn hung bdly rt over 1f out: styd on same pce* **7/1**[3]

4150 **7** *4 ½* **Camrock Star (IRE)**[18] 6275 3-9-4 60 .... AdamKirby 11 51
(David Evans) *in rr: rdn and sme hdwy over 2f sn one pce* **9/1**

5513 **8** *1 ¼* **High Five Prince (IRE)**[9] 6568 3-8-12 55 .... RachealKneller(5) 14 48
(Mark Usher) *t.k.h: led after 2f: sn clr: hdd 2f out: sn btn* **25/1**

3 **9** *nse* **Friendsinlowplaces**[23] 1479 3-9-3 0 .... (t) JamieSpencer 2 48
(Evan Williams) *s.i.s: in rr: sme hdwy u.p 2f out: nvr in contention* **14/1**

0425 **10** *2 ¾* **Supreme Rock**[57] 4945 3-9-3 60 .... (p) StephenCraine 5 43
(Jim Boyle) *chsd ldrs: rdn 3f out: wknd over 2f out* **16/1**

0000 **11** *11* **Loyal Master (IRE)**[22] 6131 3-9-3 58 .... JimmyQuinn 10 24
(Garry Moss) *chsd ldrs: wknd 3f out* **100/1**

634 **12** *2 ¼* **Daring Damsel (IRE)**[29] 5945 3-9-4 58 .... (p) PaulHanagan 9 21
(Paul Cole) *led 2f: chsd ldr to 3f out: sn btn* **15/2**

2m 24.63s (3.53) **Going Correction** +0.325s/f (Good) **12** Ran SP% **112.9**
Speed ratings (Par 101): **100,99,97,96,96 96,93,92,92,90 82,80**
toteswingers 1&2 £25.80, 2&3 £3.40, 1&3 £21.80 CSF £164.93 TOTE £63.90: £8.90, £2.10, £2.80; EX 328.00 TRIFECTA Not won..There was no bid for the winner. Ironically was claimed by N King for £6000.
Owner P Morris **Bred** Neville O'Byrne **Trained** Upper Lambourn, Berks

FOCUS
The pace increased from quite a way out in this seller, with High Five Prince being allowed to stride on having pulled hard early. The race ought to throw up winners at a similar level but the form as it stands is shaky.
Friendsinlowplaces Official explanation: jockey said that the gelding ran too free

6815 BETFAIR. DON'T SETTLE FOR LESS NURSERY 7f 26y
2:40 (2:40) (Class 4) (0-85,83) 2-Y-O **£3,428** (£1,020; £509; £254) **Stalls** Low

Form RPR

1505 **1** **Columella**[31] 5886 2-8-8 **70** .... (p) AdamBeschizza 12 74
(William Haggas) *led 1f: styd chsng ldr: led over 2f out and c to r on stands' rail drvn out fnl f* **20/1**

1133 **2** *1* **Danz Choice (IRE)**[29] 5946 2-8-11 **73** .... RichardHughes 9 75
(Richard Hannon) *in rr: drvn and hdwy fr 2f out: hung rt ins fnl f: tk 2nd in clsng stages: no imp on wnr* **9/1**[3]

4143 **3** *nse* **Yourartisonfire**[13] 6425 2-9-1 **80** .... MichaelMetcalfe(3) 7 81
(Mrs K Burke) *chsd ldrs: drvn fr 3f out: styd on to dispute 2nd ins fnl f but no imp on wnr* **16/1**

220 **4** *hd* **Martial Art (IRE)**61 4803 2-9-3 **79** JimmyFortune 8 80
(Andrew Balding) *t.k.h: chsd ldrs: chsd wnr over 1f out: carried hd high u.p and no imp: lost 2 pls in clsng stages* **10/1**
0214 **5** *1 1/2* **African Oil (FR)**12 6487 2-9-2 **78** MichaelHills 1 75
(Charles Hills) *led after 1f: rdn and hdd over 2f out: styd on same pce fnl f* **7/2**2
1640 **6** *1/2* **Claude Greenwood**22 6138 2-9-2 **78** JamesDoyle 14 74
(Sylvester Kirk) *in rr: rdn over 2f out: styd on u.p fnl f: nt rch ldrs* **100/1**
1030 **7** *1/2* **Secret Destination**12 6469 2-9-0 **76** DaleSwift 4 71
(Brian Ellison) *chsd ldrs: rdn and one pce fnl 2f* **28/1**
5310 **8** *shd* **Haatefina**60 4847 2-8-11 **73** DaneO'Neill 10 67
(Mark Usher) *in rr: rdn over 2f out: styd on u.p fnl f: nvr a threat* **28/1**
026 **9** *1/2* **The Scuttler (IRE)**12 6501 2-8-10 **72** MartinHarley 5 65
(Mick Channon) *in rr: rdn and sme hdwy ins fnl 3f: in tch w ldrs over 1f out: wknd fnl f* **20/1**
1260 **10** *nk* **Salutation (IRE)**21 6162 2-9-6 **82** JoeFanning 6 74
(Mark Johnston) *chsd ldrs: rdn ins fnl 3f: wknd over 1f out* **10/1**
3100 **11** *1/2* **Saint Jerome (IRE)**21 6162 2-9-7 **83** WilliamBuick 2 74
(Marcus Tregoning) *in rr: hrd drvn and little rspnse ins fnl 2f* **2/1**1
3210 **12** *1* **Super Simon (IRE)**61 4804 2-9-2 **78** (v) NeilCallan 3 67
(Paul D'Arcy) *chsd ldrs: rdn 3f out: wknd ins fnl 2f: eased whn no ch* **20/1**
345 **13** *3 1/2* **Another Claret**14 6404 2-8-11 **73** PaulHanagan 13 53
(Richard Fahey) *outpcd most of way* **14/1**

1m 26.15s (1.55) **Going Correction** +0.15s/f (Good) **13 Ran SP% 118.5**
Speed ratings (Par 97): **97,95,95,95,93 93,92,92,92,91 91,89,85**
toteswingers 1&2 £28.70, 2&3 £18.20, 1&3 £38.30 CSF £175.40 CT £2956.13 TOTE £36.90: £4.90, £2.90, £4.10; EX 248.10 TRIFECTA Not won..
Owner St Albans Bloodstock LLP **Bred** Wood Hall Stud Limited **Trained** Newmarket, Suffolk
■ Stewards' Enquiry : Michael Metcalfe one-day ban: careless riding (18 Oct)

FOCUS
The leaders edged over to the stands' side in the straight, with the winner bagging the rail, and those trying to make ground from off the pace were unable to get involved. An ordinary nursery with the second and third setting the level.

NOTEBOOK
Columella, a 5f soft-ground course winner on debut, left her most recent nursery efforts behind returning to this easier surface fitted with first-time cheekpieces, finding plenty under a positive ride. The rail was a help late on but she may be capable of further progress faced with similar conditions. (op 16-1 tchd 14-1)
Danz Choice(IRE) did best of those to challenge more towards the centre of the track, running another solid race having looked a touch unlucky at Lingfield the time before. This versatile sort remains capable of winning again. (op 15-2)
Yourartisonfire had to switch around the winner after losing out in the race to get the stands' rail, but it's doubtful that cost him the race. Having his first try at 7f, he certainly seemed to stay. (op 12-1)
Martial Art(IRE) didn't seem to be knuckling down as hard as some on this nursery debut, not for the first time, and is one to have reservations about. (op 11-1 tchd 9-1)
African Oil(FR), up to 7f for the first time, had a bit to prove on soft ground and ran well enough to suggest he can win from this sort of mark on a faster surface. (op 5-1)
Claude Greenwood was going on late, but this mark still looks a bit beyond him.
Haatefina was never positioned to make a challenge and could be worth another chance.
Salutation(IRE) needs quicker ground. (op 9-1)
Saint Jerome(IRE), although winning his maiden on good to soft, was soon behind having not been the best away and failed to pick up on ground that looked plenty soft enough. He'd run with promise in a pair of sales races and can show this form to be all wrong back on a drier surface. (op 5-2)

6816 BETFAIR SPONSORS THE STABLE STAFF CANTEEN E B F MAIDEN FILLIES' STKS (DIV I) 7f 26y
3:10 (3:12) (Class 5) 2-Y-O **£3,234** (£962; £481; £240) **Stalls** Low

Form RPR
36 **1** **Iberis**47 5339 2-9-0 0 IanMongan 7 73
(Sir Henry Cecil) *chsd ldrs: drvn to go 2nd ins fnl 2f: rdn and edgd lft and rt jst ins fnl f: kpt on wl to ld cl home* **5/1**3
4 **2** *shd* **Magique (IRE)**15 6377 2-9-0 0 WilliamBuick 8 73
(Jeremy Noseda) *t.k.h: disp ld after 1f tl def advantage appr fnl 2f whn edgd rt and c to stands' rail: drvn over 1f out: no ex and hdd cl home* **5/6**1
0 **3** *6* **Tight Fit**10 6534 2-9-0 0 DaneO'Neill 4 59+
(Henry Candy) *slt ld after 1f but a hrd pressed tl hdd appr fnl 2f: sn hrd drvn and no ch w ldng duo but clr 3rd best* **15/2**
0 **4** *4 1/2* **Close Together (IRE)**164 1563 2-9-0 0 StevieDonohoe 6 47
(Robert Mills) *in tch and rdn 3f out: no imp on ldrs and wl hld fnl 2f* **28/1**
5 *5* **Diletta Tommasa (IRE)** 2-9-0 0 AndreaAtzeni 1 35
(Marco Botti) *rdn 3f out: a outpcd towards rr* **16/1**
6 *3 1/4* **Maisie's Moon (USA)** 2-9-0 0 RichardHughes 2 27
(Hughie Morrison) *chsd ldrs: rdn 3f out and sn btn* **11/1**
0 **7** *1* **Fiance Fiasco**13 6453 2-8-9 0 DavidKenny(5) 9 24
(James Evans) *towards rr most of way* **100/1**
0 **8** *1* **Princess Patsky (USA)**30 5902 2-9-1 0 ow1 JamieSpencer 5 23
(Michael Bell) *led 1f: styd chsng ldrs: rdn 3f out: wknd sn after* **4/1**2
0 **9** *23* **Sand Orchid**21 6177 2-9-0 0 AdamKirby 3
(Stuart Kittow) *a in rr: lost tch fnl 3f* **125/1**

1m 25.95s (1.35) **Going Correction** +0.15s/f (Good) **9 Ran SP% 122.4**
Speed ratings (Par 92): **98,97,91,85,80 76,75,74,47**
toteswingers 1&2 £2.10, 2&3 £2.70, 1&3 £4.70 CSF £10.15 TOTE £4.50: £1.10, £1.10, £2.10; EX 14.50 Trifecta £39.70 Pool: £1582.84 - 29.48 winning units..
Owner Dr Catherine Wills **Bred** St Clare Hall Stud **Trained** Newmarket, Suffolk

FOCUS
The front pair drew clear in a maiden lacking depth. The winner is rated back to her debut sort of level.

NOTEBOOK
Iberis had contested quite a decent 1m event at Doncaster the time before and seemed happier returned to this trip. She benefited from the favourite pulling hard early, but is clearly progressing and should do okay in nurseries, given she's now proven on soft ground. (op 4-1)
Magique(IRE) was an eyecatcher on debut, but it took her a while to settle, seeing plenty of daylight also, and it was no surprise to see her worn down late, despite having bagged the stands' rail. Her half-brother Grandeur is best on quicker ground and she can win her maiden on a sounder surface. (op 4-6 tchd Evens)
Tight Fit showed the benefit of her debut run and is another who should be happier on a sounder surface. (op 8-1 tchd 10-1)
Close Together(IRE), very slowly away and well beaten on his Windsor debut (5f) 164 days earlier, offered a little more and will be of interest once switched to nurseries following another run. (op 25-1)
Diletta Tommasa(IRE), whose dam is an unraced half-sister to 7f 2yo Listed winner Protectress, was never going the gallop. (op 18-1)
Maisie's Moon(USA), out of a half-sister to Grade 1 Polytrack winner Square Eddie, made no impact but is entitled to come on for this initial experience. (op 14-1)
Princess Patsky(USA) was well backed to improve on her debut run, which came in a decent Goodwood maiden, but she was quickly brushed aside having made the early running and may not have handled the ground. (op 12-1 tchd 7-2)

6817 BETFAIR SPONSORS THE STABLE STAFF CANTEEN E B F MAIDEN FILLIES' STKS (DIV II) 7f 26y
3:40 (3:41) (Class 5) 2-Y-O **£3,234** (£962; £481; £240) **Stalls** Low

Form RPR
1 **Light Rose (IRE)** 2-9-0 0 JoeFanning 9 79+
(Mark Johnston) *mde all: c readily clr ins fnl 2f: unchal* **13/8**1
00 **2** *3 1/2* **Serenata (IRE)**12 6489 2-9-0 0 NeilCallan 8 66+
(Paul Cole) *chsd ldrs: wnt 2nd over 3f out: sn drvn and no imp on unchal wnr but hld on wl for 2nd* **66/1**
00 **3** *2* **Thwart**21 6175 2-9-0 0 JimCrowley 5 60
(Ralph Beckett) *in tch: drvn and outpcd over 3f out: styd on fr over 1f out to take wl hld 3rd fnl 75yds* **11/4**2
0 **4** *1* **Epic Charm**12 6486 2-9-0 0 MartinHarley 2 58
(Mick Channon) *chsd ldrs: drvn along 3f out: tk wl hld 3rd appr fnl f: one pce into 4th fnl 75yds* **4/1**3
00 **5** *1 1/4* **Jazz On The Beach**29 5947 2-9-0 0 KierenFallon 6 54
(Luca Cumani) *chsd ldrs: rdn and one pce fr over 2f out* **16/1**
00 **6** *1* **North Weald (IRE)**30 5907 2-9-0 0 SebSanders 3 52
(J W Hills) *chsd wnr tl over 3f out: sn one pce* **25/1**
7 *hd* **Mariella** 2-9-0 0 WilliamBuick 7 51+
(Peter Chapple-Hyam) *outpcd in rr: shkn up over 1f out: styd on wl cl home* **8/1**
00 **8** *1 3/4* **Avanzare**13 6444 2-9-0 0 MichaelHills 4 47
(Charles Hills) *in tch: pushed along 3f out: outpcd fnl 2f* **28/1**
9 *11* **Double Star** 2-9-0 0 JohnFahy 1 20
(Jonathan Portman) *a outpcd* **33/1**

1m 27.12s (2.52) **Going Correction** +0.15s/f (Good) **9 Ran SP% 113.5**
Speed ratings (Par 92): **91,87,84,83,82 81,80,78,66**
toteswingers 1&2 £21.60, 2&3 £22.30, 1&3 £2.60 CSF £139.32 TOTE £3.50: £1.20, £12.80, £1.20; EX 79.20 Trifecta £381.80 Pool: £1243.54 - 2.41 winning units..
Owner Jaber Abdullah **Bred** Ceka Ireland Limited **Trained** Middleham Moor, N Yorks

FOCUS
Less depth than in the first division and the time was poor, but the winner did it well.

NOTEBOOK
Light Rose(IRE) ◆ was strong at the head of the market and impressed with the way she readily drew clear, making all. Out of a 7.5f AW winner in France, she's a fine-looker who promises to be better suited by quicker ground and it will be interesting to see how high connections aim next time. (op 6-4 tchd 5-4)
Serenata(IRE) had finished well beaten on both previous starts, and this much-improved effort was hard to predict. Nurseries are now an option and she ought to benefit from 1m. (op 33-1)
Thwart was never in the best position and it would be no surprise to see her raise her game once upped in trip and switching to nurseries. (op 9-2)
Epic Charm travelled well before finding herself badly outpaced off the final bend. She may do better next year. (op 5-1 tchd 11-2)
Jazz On The Beach showed more than on her first two starts and certainly fits the bill as a horse likely to flourish when upped in trip and switching to handicaps next season. (tchd 20-1)
Mariella, a half-sister to 1m2f-1m4f winner Maria Di Scozia, seemed to grasp what was required late on and should benefit from a greater test of stamina. (op 5-1)

6818 BETFAIR COMMITS £40 MILLION TO BRITISH RACING IRISH EBF MAIDEN STKS (C&G) 7f 26y
4:10 (4:11) (Class 5) 2-Y-O **£3,234** (£962; £481; £240) **Stalls** Low

Form RPR
02 **1** **Mission Approved**43 5476 2-9-0 0 RichardHughes 8 76+
(Sir Michael Stoute) *pressed ldr tl led over 2f out: c to stands' rail: drvn and styd on strly fnl f* **9/2**3
0 **2** *2* **Harwoods Star (IRE)**12 6481 2-9-0 0 JimCrowley 12 71
(Amanda Perrett) *chsd ldrs: rdn and styd on wl fnl f to take 2nd last strides but no ch w wnr* **10/1**
02 **3** *nk* **Ready (IRE)**22 6133 2-9-0 0 NeilCallan 13 70
(Garry Moss) *slt ld but hrd pressed tl hdd by wnr over 2f out: styd on but no imp* **16/1**
0 **4** *hd* **Cape Of Hope (IRE)**21 6164 2-9-0 0 WilliamBuick 2 70
(Peter Chapple-Hyam) *chsd ldrs: drvn 2f out: kpt on same pce ins fnl f* **11/4**2
6 **5** *1* **Avatar Star (IRE)**21 6175 2-9-0 0 AdamKirby 11 67
(Marco Botti) *chsd ldrs: pushed along over 2f out: styd on same pce fnl f* **20/1**
6 *1 1/4* **Snowy Dawn** 2-8-7 0 JackDuern(7) 4 64
(Reg Hollinshead) *in rr: drvn over 3f out: styd on ins fnl f: kpt on cl home* **100/1**
52 **7** *3/4* **Herbalist**64 4707 2-9-0 0 DaneO'Neill 1 62
(Henry Candy) *in tch: rdn over 2f out: styd on one pce fnl f* **15/8**1
8 *1* **Lambert Pen (USA)** 2-9-0 0 MartinHarley 5 60
(Mick Channon) *s.i.s: in rr: drvn over 2f out: styd on fnl f* **33/1**
9 *nk* **Veeraya** 2-9-0 0 AdamBeschizza 9 59
(William Haggas) *in tch: pushed along 3f out: styd on fnl f* **25/1**
0 **10** *5* **Ebony Roc (IRE)**12 6486 2-9-0 0 FrankieMcDonald 3 47
(Amanda Perrett) *s.i.s: outpcd* **50/1**
05 **11** *1 1/4* **Gracious George (IRE)**60 4846 2-9-0 0 SeanLevey 6 43
(Jimmy Fox) *outpcd most of way* **12/1**
5 **12** *1 1/2* **Mr Vendman (IRE)**12 6473 2-8-11 0 RyanPowell(3) 14 40
(Ian Williams) *prom 4f* **66/1**

1m 28.04s (3.44) **Going Correction** +0.15s/f (Good) **12 Ran SP% 118.3**
Speed ratings (Par 95): **86,83,83,83,82 80,79,78,78,72 71,69**
toteswingers 1&2 £7.30, 2&3 £10.10, 1&3 £4.60 CSF £45.24 TOTE £3.10: £1.40, £2.30, £2.80; EX 42.50 Trifecta £268.80 Pool: £1438.75 - 3.96 winning units..
Owner K Abdulla **Bred** Juddmonte Farms Ltd **Trained** Newmarket, Suffolk

FOCUS
Those who raced prominently were favoured in this maiden, with little making an impact from the rear. The bare form is only ordinary.

NOTEBOOK
Mission Approved had an ideal sit throughout under Richard Hughes and was always in control having come across to the stands' rail. He's a good-looker who ought to have no trouble staying further, being a half-brother to this year's Supreme Novice winner Cinders And Ashes, and rates a useful prospect for next year. (op 5-1 tchd 7-2)
Harwoods Star(IRE) confirmed the promise of his Newbury debut, again staying on as though he'll relish 1m. (op 8-1)
Ready(IRE) handles the ground and again showed enough to suggest he can win a race this year. (tchd 14-1)
Cape Of Hope(IRE) again failed to meet with market expectations, but the softer ground wouldn't have been ideal and he can yet win a maiden, possibly on AW, stepping back up in trip. (op 9-4 tchd 2-1)

Avatar Star(IRE) improved on his debut effort and is one for handicaps over further next year. (op 16-1)
Snowy Dawn, half-brother to a modest winning hurdler, was one of few to make ground from the rear. He should benefit from 1m.
Herbalist, awarded a race at Leicester by the Stewards prior to losing it on appeal, failed to reproduce the form upped in trip and faced with softer ground. He may bounce back in nurseries. (op 5-2 tchd 11-4)

6819 BETFAIR 10 FURLONG FLAT SERIES FINAL (H'CAP) 1m 2f 188y
4:40 (4:41) (Class 3) 3-Y-O+
£15,562 (£4,660; £2,330; £1,165; £582; £292) **Stalls** Low

Form RPR
1132 **1** **Consider Yourself (USA)**[38] 5688 5-9-3 **76**............(p) WilliamCarson 14 85
(Anthony Carson) *chsd ldrs: rdn over 3f out: led over 2f out and c to stands' rail: drvn out fnl f* **10/1**
204 **2** *1* **Watts Up Son**[16] 6339 4-9-1 **77**..............................(bt) NeilFarley(3) 9 84
(Declan Carroll) *drvn to ld after 1f: rdn over 3f out: hdd over 2f out: styd on fnl 2f: nt pce of wnr fnl f* **16/1**
043 **3** *½* **Hurricane Hymnbook (USA)**[19] 6250 7-8-3 **62**......... JamieMackay 15 68+
(Willie Musson) *in rr: hdwy fr 4f out: kpt on to take 3rd ins fnl f: no imp on wnr* **20/1**
1241 **4** *2¼* **Spin Cast**[19] 6251 4-9-0 **73**.............................. DaleSwift 10 75
(Brian Ellison) *mid-div: hdwy fr 4f out: rdn over 2f out: styd on same pce fnl f* **12/1**
0000 **5** *2¼* **Fennell Bay (IRE)**[12] 6484 3-9-10 **89**....................(b1) JoeFanning 12 88
(Mark Johnston) *chsd ldrs: drvn over 3f out: wknd over 1f out* **7/1**[3]
6224 **6** *1½* **Choral Festival**[20] 6207 6-9-1 **74**.............................. KieranO'Neill 17 70
(John Bridger) *in rr: hdwy over 2f out: styd on fnl f: nvr gng pce to trble ldrs* **16/1**
4660 **7** *1* **Sangar**[4] 6711 4-8-3 **62**.. MartinLane 13 56
(Ollie Pears) *in tch: hdwy 3f out: styd on same pce fnl 2f* **20/1**
0054 **8** *1* **Mcbirney (USA)**[19] 6251 5-8-7 **66**.................. MickaelBarzalona 1 59
(Paul D'Arcy) *in rr: hdwy 3f out: styd on fr over 1f out: nvr rchd ldrs* **6/1**[2]
3366 **9** *¾* **Ice Nelly (IRE)**[37] 5707 4-8-7 **66**.............................. RobertHavlin 3 57
(Hughie Morrison) *slowly away: in rr: rdn 4f out: sme prog fr over 1f out: kpt on nr fin* **28/1**
6111 **10** *½* **Enriching (USA)**[19] 6231 4-8-4 **63**.............................. JimmyQuinn 2 53
(Lydia Pearce) *chsd ldrs: rdn over 3f out: wknd ins fnl 2f* **20/1**
5341 **11** *½* **High Resolution**[10] 6528 5-8-8 **67** 6ex.............................. TomEaves 11 57
(Linda Perratt) *rdn 4f out: a towards rr* **20/1**
2504 **12** *2¾* **Tidal Run**[19] 6229 4-8-9 **73**.............................. CharlesBishop(5) 7 58+
(Mick Channon) *in tch: styng on whn hmpd and stmbld on ins wl over 3f out: no ch after* **16/1**
3611 **13** *½* **Debating Society (IRE)**[29] 5951 3-9-7 **86**.................. KierenFallon 4 70+
(Sir Michael Stoute) *in tch: pushed along and styng on whn hmpd on ins wl over 3f out: nt rcvre and sn btn* **5/2**[1]
5220 **14** *17* **Croquembouche (IRE)**[15] 6376 3-9-0 **79**.................. EddieAhern 5 34
(Ed de Giles) *chsd ldrs 7f* **16/1**
1000 **15** *4* **Chain Of Events**[15] 6380 5-9-6 **79**.............................. JimCrowley 16 27
(Sarah Humphrey) *chsd ldrs: edgd lft and wknd wl over 3f out* **20/1**
0112 **16** *4* **My Mate Jake (IRE)**[19] 6251 4-8-11 **70**..................(b) PaulHanagan 8 12
(James Given) *mid-div: rdn over 4f out: sn wknd* **16/1**
1000 **17** *¾* **Hector's Chance**[15] 6376 3-8-2 **67**.............................. AndreaAtzeni 6 7
(Heather Main) *a in rr* **33/1**

2m 22.71s (1.61) **Going Correction** +0.325s/f (Good)
WFA 3 from 4yo+ 6lb **17** Ran SP% **131.8**
Speed ratings (Par 107): **107,106,105,104,102 101,100,100,99,99 98,96,96,84,81 78,77**
toteswingers 1&2 £43.00, 2&3 £138.80, 1&3 £35.30 CSF £154.63 CT £3182.77 TOTE £11.80: £2.80, £5.30, £5.40, £2.70; EX 289.20 TRIFECTA Not won..
Owner Christopher Wright & Minster Stud **Bred** Liberation Farm & Brandywine Farm **Trained** Newmarket, Suffolk

FOCUS
Few got into what had looked a competitive handicap, with the pace holding up, and the winner again pocketed the stands' rail once in line for home. The winner is rated to his C&D latest.

NOTEBOOK
Consider Yourself(USA) had bumped into an improver over C&D the time before and this race panned out nicely for her. A versatile sort regards trip and ground, she shouldn't go up too much and can continue to give a good account. (tchd 9-1)
Watts Up Son handles soft ground and was always well positioned given the way the race worked out. (tchd 14-1)
Hurricane Hymnbook(USA) fared best of those coming from the rear and obviously needs his effort upgrading.
Spin Cast ran every bit as well as when winning from 6lb lower at Kempton the time before. He's not had many starts for this yard and remains capable of better. (tchd 11-1)
Fennell Bay(IRE) had slipped to a fair mark and received an ideal tow into the race in the first-time blinkers, but he just couldn't quicken. (op 13-2 tchd 6-1)
Choral Festival got too far back, but was going on late and will find easier opportunities. (op 14-1)
Tidal Run met trouble when keeping on.
Debating Society(IRE), who met trouble, wouldn't have won but should have finished a good deal closer. He'd been progressing well previously on quicker ground and is worth another chance. (op 7-2)

6820 BETFAIR SPRINT FLAT SERIES FINAL (H'CAP) 6f
5:10 (5:10) (Class 3) 3-Y-O+
£15,562 (£4,660; £2,330; £1,165; £582; £292) **Stalls** Low

Form RPR
4233 **1** **Midnight Rider (IRE)**[26] 6041 4-9-7 **80**.............................. GeorgeBaker 6 90+
(Chris Wall) *stdd s: hld up in rr: stdy hdwy over 1f out: trckd ldrs on bit ins fnl f: qcknd to ld cl home: cleverly* **5/1**[3]
0633 **2** *¾* **Best Trip (IRE)**[12] 6465 5-9-6 **79**.............................. BarryMcHugh 5 86
(Brian Ellison) *chsd ldrs: drvn to ld 1f out: hdd and outpcd cl home* **7/2**[1]
5205 **3** *1¼* **Showboating (IRE)**[12] 6495 4-9-5 **78**....................(tp) RichardHughes 10 81
(Alan McCabe) *in rr: drvn and hdwy over 1f out: styd on to take 3rd clsng stages: no imp on ldng duo* **12/1**
4000 **4** *nk* **Rafaaf (IRE)**[55] 5065 4-9-2 **75**.............................. AndreaAtzeni 8 78
(Robert Eddery) *in rr: drvn and hdwy over 1f out: kpt on fnl f to press for 3rd but no ch w ldng duo* **25/1**
0105 **5** *½* **Jungle Bay**[26] 6041 5-9-4 **77**..............................(b1) TedDurcan 3 78
(Jane Chapple-Hyam) *chsd ldrs: rdn 2f out: one pce ins fnl f* **28/1**
4024 **6** *shd* **Piddie's Power**[27] 6009 5-9-10 **83**.............................. SeanLevey 12 84
(Ed McMahon) *in tch: rdn over 1f out: kpt on in clsng stages* **25/1**
1043 **7** *½* **Perfect Pastime**[17] 6303 4-9-6 **79**..............................(p) SebSanders 4 78
(Jim Boyle) *pressed ldr: slt ld and c to stands' rail 2f out: hdd 1f out: wknd ins fnl f* **11/1**
0264 **8** *2¼* **Barkston Ash**[19] 6260 4-8-11 **75**..............................(p) JasonHart(5) 7 70
(Eric Alston) *chsd ldrs: rdn 3f out: outpcd fnl 2f* **16/1**
2305 **9** *hd* **My Kingdom (IRE)**[21] 6165 6-9-10 **83**....................(t1) WilliamCarson 14 74
(Stuart Williams) *in rr: pushed along 3f out: a struggling to go pce* **10/1**
1521 **10** *¾* **Cruise Tothelimit (IRE)**[19] 6234 4-9-3 **79**.................. RyanPowell(3) 1 68
(Ian Williams) *slt ld tl hdd 2f out: wknd over 1f out* **15/2**
1211 **11** *¾* **Trojan Rocket (IRE)**[76] 4300 4-9-6 **79**.................. MickaelBarzalona 2 65
(Michael Wigham) *chsd ldrs: rdn over 2f out: sn btn* **9/2**[2]
036 **12** *1¾* **Valmina**[48] 5320 5-8-13 **77**..............................(t) GeorgeDowning(5) 11 58
(Tony Carroll) *outpcd most of way* **28/1**
0000 **13** *3* **Fred Willetts (IRE)**[41] 5557 4-9-6 **79**....................(v) WilliamBuick 9 50
(David C Griffiths) *pressed ldrs 3f* **33/1**
1053 **14** *1½* **Jade**[14] 6406 4-9-7 **80**..............................(b1) PaulHanagan 13 46
(Ollie Pears) *pressed ldrs 3f* **16/1**

1m 11.6s (-0.20) **Going Correction** +0.15s/f (Good) **14** Ran SP% **123.2**
Speed ratings (Par 107): **107,106,104,103,103 103,102,99,99,98 97,94,90,88**
toteswingers 1&2 £5.50, 2&3 £9.00, 1&3 £14.20 CSF £21.88 CT £207.59 TOTE £6.20: £2.30, £2.30, £5.60; EX 30.50 Trifecta £167.80 Pool: £1336.06 - 5.89 winning units..
Owner The Leap Year Partnership **Bred** M Smith & Grennanstown Stud **Trained** Newmarket, Suffolk

FOCUS
No hanging around here and the closers were favoured. It was the standout time and the form makes sense.

NOTEBOOK
Midnight Rider(IRE), narrowly denied by Perfect Pastime over C&D in June, travelled smoothly into the race under a confident George Baker and readily asserted when asked. This was an overdue second career win and she may go on from this now. (op 15-2)
Best Trip(IRE) likes soft ground and has won here over 7f, so it was no surprise to see him put in a big run. (tchd 9-2)
Showboating(IRE) had something to prove on the ground, but he was running on nicely at the end and is capable of winning from this mark. (op 14-1 tchd 16-1)
Rafaaf(IRE) returned to form on this return from a 55-day break. He remains just above his last win mark, however. (op 22-1)
Jungle Bay showed a bit more in the first-time blinkers. (op 33-1)
Perfect Pastime was ridden forward and managed to grab the stands' rail, but he'd probably overdone it early. (op 12-1 tchd 10-1)
Trojan Rocket(IRE) was highly progressive earlier in the year, coming into this having won four of his last five, and he still looked well treated off only 2lb higher, but didn't find much for pressure, ending up centre-field, and may have needed it. (op 6-1)

6821 BETFAIR PRICES ON BETFAIR MOBILE AMATEUR RIDERS' H'CAP 1m 6f 213y
5:45 (5:45) (Class 6) (0-60,60) 3-Y-O+ £1,559 (£483; £241; £121) **Stalls** Low

Form RPR
0614 **1** **Into The Wind**[45] 5419 5-10-9 **60**.............................. MrPMillman(5) 11 70
(Rod Millman) *in rr: hdwy 4f out: led ins fnl 2f: sn drvn: hld on all out* **33/1**
3300 **2** *nk* **Taroum (IRE)**[21] 6159 5-10-11 **60**.............................. MrCMartin(3) 10 69
(Tony Carroll) *hld up in rr: hdwy over 2f out: c to stands' rail and str chal ins fnl f: a jst hld* **12/1**
3310 **3** *2½* **Arch Event**[19] 6232 7-10-5 **51**..............................(p) MrSWalker 14 57
(Bernard Llewellyn) *in tch: hdwy over 2f out: sn rdn styd on to take 3rd fnl f but no imp on ldng duo* **15/2**
3233 **4** *2¼* **Tijori (IRE)**[21] 6159 4-10-12 **58**..............................(p) MrFWindsorClive 8 61
(Bernard Llewellyn) *sn in tch chsd ldrs 4f out: rdn and one pce fnl 2f* **9/1**
443 **5** *nk* **Quiet Route (IRE)**[38] 5679 3-9-13 **60**.............................. MrDLevey(5) 4 63
(Brian Ellison) *in rr but in tch: hdwy to pressed ldrs 5f out: rdn over 2f out: wknd ins fnl f* **2/1**[1]
5014 **6** *nse* **Eastern Magic**[33] 5811 5-10-8 **59**.............................. MrFMitchell(5) 3 62
(Reg Hollinshead) *led after 3f: kpt slt ld but hrd pressed fr 6f out tl hdd ins fnl 2f: wknd fnl f* **7/1**[3]
0055 **7** *1½* **Baan (USA)**[19] 6255 9-10-4 **57**.............................. MrStevieSanders(7) 12 58
(James Eustace) *in rr: hdwy on outside to press ldrs over 5f out: wknd over 1f out* **16/1**
322 **8** *½* **Josie's Dream (IRE)**[33] 5817 4-10-0 **51**.................. MissAliceMills(5) 2 51
(Jo Hughes) *chsd ldrs: rdn 3f out: one pce fnl 2f* **9/2**[2]
224 **9** *nse* **Captain Oats (IRE)**[42] 5508 9-10-2 **55**.................. MissSLBowen(7) 5 55
(Pam Ford) *s.i.s: in rr: hdwy on outside 6f out: sn chsng ldrs: wknd over 3f out* **20/1**
62-0 **10** *2¾* **Princesse Fleur**[43] 2575 4-10-3 **52**.............................. MrNdeBoinville(3) 6 48
(Michael Scudamore) *chsd ldrs: rdn over 3f out: sn btn* **25/1**
0300 **11** *¾* **Inside Knowledge (USA)**[99] 3498 6-10-3 **49**.............. MissSBrotherton 7 44
(Garry Woodward) *in tch: rdn over 3f out: sn wknd* **20/1**
56- **12** *1¼* **Denison Flyer**[399] 5651 5-9-9 **48**....................(p) MissVickiWood(7) 13 42
(Lawrence Mullaney) *in tch: hdwy over 4f out: wknd over 2f out* **40/1**
3350 **13** *6* **Waldsee (GER)**[46] 4904 7-10-4 **57**.............................. MissBHampson(7) 9 43
(Sean Curran) *chsd ldrs: chal over 5f out tl over 3f out: sn wknd* **33/1**
-0PP **14** *39* **Bold Identity (IRE)**[7] 6616 6-11-0 **60**....................(b) MissGAndrews 1
(Richard Phillips) *t.k.h: led 3f: wknd 5f out: t.o* **80/1**

3m 29.32s (10.32) **Going Correction** +0.325s/f (Good)
WFA 3 from 4yo+ 10lb **14** Ran SP% **122.3**
Speed ratings (Par 101): **85,84,83,82,82 82,81,81,81,79 79,78,75,54**
toteswingers 1&2 £42.00, 2&3 £15.60, 1&3 £21.20 CSF £372.73 CT £3292.73 TOTE £37.60: £7.60, £4.60, £4.60; EX 424.50 TRIFECTA Not won..
Owner Eric Gadsden **Bred** Mrs M Fairbairn And E Gadsden **Trained** Kentisbeare, Devon

FOCUS
There was a muddling pace to this amateur riders' handicap and this is not form to put much faith in. The first two came from the rear.
T/Plt: £141.90 to a £1 stake. Pool: £56220.02 - 289.08 winning tickets. T/Qpdt: £18.70 to a £1 stake. Pool of £4071.70 - 160.46 winning tickets. ST

6765 WOLVERHAMPTON (A.W) (L-H)
Thursday, October 4

OFFICIAL GOING: Standard
Wind: Fresh behind Weather: Cloudy

6822 SIS LTD NURSERY 5f 216y(P)
5:40 (5:40) (Class 6) (0-60,60) 2-Y-O £1,704 (£503; £251) **Stalls** Low

Form RPR
030 **1** **Hartwright**[38] 5685 2-9-7 **60**.............................. JamieSpencer 11 69+
(Michael Bell) *hld up: hdwy over 1f out: rdn to ld ins fnl f: edgd rt: drvn clr* **2/1**[1]
040 **2** *3¼* **Iwilsayzisonlyonce**[13] 6444 2-9-1 **59**.................. MichaelJMMurphy(5) 12 59
(Joseph Tuite) *chsd ldrs: rdn and ev ch over 1f out: styd on same pce ins fnl f* **7/1**[3]

5023 **3** ½ **Millie N Aire**[6] 6627 2-9-6 **59** FrannyNorton 13 57
(Danielle McCormick) *led: rdn over 1f out: hdd and no ex ins fnl f* **7/1**[3]
0535 **4** ½ **Panama Cat (USA)**[16] 6337 2-9-2 **55** PhillipMakin 7 52
(Kevin Ryan) *chsd ldrs: rdn over 1f out: styd on same pce ins fnl f* **11/2**[2]
3044 **5** ½ **Michael's Song (IRE)**[9] 6564 2-9-1 **54** MartinHarley 3 49
(Mick Channon) *mid-div: hdwy over 2f out: rdn over 1f out: no ex ins fnl f* **20/1**
006 **6** nk **Blazeofenchantment (USA)**[47] 5371 2-9-4 **57** PatCosgrave 10 51
(Noel Quinlan) *s.i.s: hld up: rdn over 2f out: styd on ins fnl f: nvr trbld ldrs* **33/1**
000 **7** hd **Darkest Night (IRE)**[12] 6501 2-9-2 **55** FergusSweeney 5 49
(Jamie Osborne) *hld up: rdn and hung lft over 1f out: styd on: nvr nrr* **18/1**
500 **8** 1 **Bougaloo**[21] 6164 2-9-1 **54** [1] GrahamGibbons 8 45
(Alan McCabe) *prom: rdn over 2f out: wknd ins fnl f* **22/1**
000 **9** 1 **Astrum**[23] 6114 2-9-6 **59** JamesMillman 1 47
(Rod Millman) *sn pushed along in rr: nvr on terms* **16/1**
0505 **10** 1 **Hats Off**[78] 4220 2-9-3 **56** LukeMorris 4 41
(John Best) *prom: rdn over 2f out: wknd over 1f out* **10/1**
0540 **11** ¾ **Sarahmanda**[18] 6283 2-9-3 **56** (t) StevieDonohoe 9 38
(Peter Makin) *sn pushed along and a in rr* **28/1**
0240 **12** hd **Lincolnrose (IRE)**[17] 6318 2-9-3 **56** IPoullis 2 38
(Alan McCabe) *s.i.s: a in rr* **25/1**
506 **13** 7 **Dashing Storm**[45] 5423 2-8-13 **55** RaulDaSilva(3) 6 16
(Jeremy Gask) *chsd ldrs: rdn over 2f out: wknd over 1f out* **20/1**

1m 16.0s (1.00) **Going Correction** -0.05s/f (Stan) **13** Ran SP% **118.1**
Speed ratings (Par 93): **91,86,86,85,84 84,84,82,81,80 79,78,69**
toteswingers 1&2 £4.80, 2&3 £5.80, 1&3 £5.90 CSF £13.37 CT £82.93 TOTE £3.60: £3.10, £2.20, £2.30; EX 14.60 Trifecta £70.40 Pool: £651.87 - 70.40 winning units..
Owner Mrs L J Garton **Bred** New England Stud And Partners **Trained** Newmarket, Suffolk

FOCUS
The going was Standard. The stalls for the 7f races were on the outside while the remaining races were on the inner. A modest contest with a number of runners making their handicap debuts, run at a fair pace with the well-backed favourite finishing strongly to win well. The next three home all raced prominently. The form can't really be rated any higher.

NOTEBOOK
Hartwright, making his nursery debut, had shown little in three maidens on the turf but had done a good piece of work 10 days before according to his handler, and he was always travelling sweetly in midfield. He had to be asked for an effort 2f from home but got a nice run through the field and was well on top at the line. He can build on this next season. (op 3-1)
Iwilsayzisonlyonce, also well backed on his nursery debut, was ridden prominently and stayed on well to the line but lacked the speed of the winner. (op 6-1)
Millie N Aire helped set the pace and saw the trip out well, but was beaten by two lightly raced, progressive types and remains a maiden after 11 starts. (op 13-2)
Panama Cat(USA)'s latest run when fifth at Thirsk had been franked by the second and third home winning next time but, having travelled strongly behind the gallop, she found little once off the bridle. (op 5-1)
Michael's Song(IRE) kept responding to pressure up the straight but is not progressing with her racing, and might be worth trying over further. (op 14-1)
Astrum raced near the back early and was noted making late progress on his handicap debut, suggesting this trip was on the short side. (op 25-1)
Dashing Storm Official explanation: jockey said that the filly hung left

6823 ELITEDIGITALSYSTEMS.CO.UK H'CAP 5f 216y(P)
6:10 (6:12) (Class 6) (0-60,60) 3-Y-O+ **£2,045** (£603; £302) **Stalls** Low

Form RPR
6426 **1** **Iceblast**[24] 6106 4-8-11 **59** (b) DavidSimmonson(7) 9 71
(Michael Easterby) *hld up: pushed along 1/2-way: hdwy over 1f out: rdn to ld wl ins fnl f: edgd lft and sn clr* **12/1**
4301 **2** 2 ¼ **Red Shadow**[6] 6640 3-9-2 **58** 6ex (p) DavidAllan 2 63
(Alan Brown) *chsd ldrs: rdn to ld over 1f out: hung lft and hdd wl ins fnl f* **17/2**
2341 **3** ¾ **Invigilator**[17] 6321 4-9-4 **59** (t) JoeFanning 10 62
(Derek Shaw) *hld up: rdn over 1f out: r.o ins fnl f: nt rch ldrs* **11/2**[3]
0004 **4** 1 **Mey Blossom**[15] 6358 7-9-5 **60** (p) PaulQuinn 4 59
(Richard Whitaker) *hld up in tch: pushed along 1/2-way: rdn over 1f out: styd on same pce ins fnl f* **18/1**
6516 **5** ¾ **Medam**[6] 6640 3-8-9 **58** (t) ShirleyTeasdale(7) 7 55
(Shaun Harris) *hld up: hdwy over 1f out: styd on same pce fnl f* **14/1**
3056 **6** ½ **Lindoro**[13] 6456 7-9-4 **59** [1] PhillipMakin 13 54
(Brian Ellison) *hld up in tch: racd keenly: rdn over 1f out: styd on same pce fnl f* **5/1**[2]
0125 **7** 1 ¾ **Plum Bay**[35] 5764 3-9-4 **60** JamieSpencer 8 50
(David Elsworth) *hld up: rdn over 1f out: nvr on terms* **9/2**[1]
0262 **8** hd **Indieslad**[6] 6641 4-9-5 **60** (p) PJMcDonald 1 49
(Ann Duffield) *chsd ldrs: rdn over 1f out: wknd fnl f* **9/1**
6004 **9** ¾ **Dubai Bay (FR)**[13] 6456 4-9-5 **60** MickyFenton 3 47
(Paul Midgley) *sn led: rdn and hdd over 1f out: wknd ins fnl f* **12/1**
6002 **10** ¾ **Methaaly (IRE)**[20] 6195 9-9-5 **60** (be) LiamJones 6 44
(Michael Mullineaux) *mid-div: drvn along over 3f out: wknd over 1f out* **20/1**
5-45 **11** ½ **Michael's Nook**[12] 6480 5-9-3 **58** GrahamGibbons 5 41
(David Barron) *chsd ldr: rdn over 1f out: n.m.r and wknd fnl f* **11/2**[3]
0065 **12** ¾ **Legal Eagle (IRE)**[13] 6455 7-9-4 **59** (p) SeanQuinlan 11 39
(Paul Green) *stdd s: a in rr* **28/1**
005 **13** 1 ½ **Cliffords Reprieve**[8] 6586 4-9-3 **58** (b) LukeMorris 12 34
(Eric Wheeler) *led early: chsd ldrs: drvn along 1/2-way: wknd wl over 1f out* **50/1**

1m 14.64s (-0.36) **Going Correction** -0.05s/f (Stan)
WFA 3 from 4yo+ 1lb **13** Ran SP% **123.6**
Speed ratings (Par 101): **100,97,96,94,93 93,90,90,89,88 87,86,84**
toteswingers: 1&2 £31.00, 1&3 £14.30, 2&3 £8.40. CSF £112.14 CT £659.95 TOTE £34.10: £6.50, £1.90, £1.80; EX 191.30 TRIFECTA Not won..
Owner B Padgett **Bred** A C M Spalding **Trained** Sheriff Hutton, N Yorks

FOCUS
This wide-open handicap was run at a sound pace with the winner, who was supported late on, well on top at the line. This was his best form of thr season.
Plum Bay Official explanation: jockey said that the filly didn't face the kick back
Dubai Bay(FR) Official explanation: jockey said that the filly lost action inside the final furlong

6824 BIDS 5 SCREEN SYSTEM FROM MRG H'CAP (DIV I) 5f 216y(P)
6:40 (6:40) (Class 5) (0-75,75) 3-Y-O+ **£2,587** (£770; £384; £192) **Stalls** Low

Form RPR
5065 **1** **Galatian**[19] 6256 5-9-4 **72** JamesMillman 6 83
(Rod Millman) *a.p: rdn to ld ins fnl f: r.o* **4/1**[2]
0120 **2** 1 ¼ **Avonvalley**[5] 6666 5-8-11 **65** RobbieFitzpatrick 8 72
(Peter Grayson) *hld up: hdwy over 1f out: r.o ins fnl f: nt rch wnr* **14/1**
0001 **3** hd **We Have A Dream**[15] 6368 7-9-7 **75** PhillipMakin 4 81
(William Muir) *chsd ldrs: rdn over 2f out: ev ch ins fnl f: styd on same pce* **6/1**
5240 **4** nk **Duke Of Aricabeau (IRE)**[18] 6285 3-9-1 **70** MartinHarley 2 71
(Mrs K Burke) *hld up: rdn over 1f out: r.o ins fnl f: nt rch ldrs: fin 5th: plcd 4th* **20/1**
0260 **5** hd **Available (IRE)**[12] 6497 3-8-12 **67** FrannyNorton 13 67
(John Mackie) *sn led: rdn and hdd 1f out: no ex ins fnl f: fin 6th: plcd 5th* **25/1**
126 **6** ¾ **Cut Across (IRE)**[69] 4530 4-9-3 **71** RobertHavlin 5 68
(Nick Littmoden) *hld up: rdn and hung lft over 1f out: r.o ins fnl f: nvr nrr: fin 7th: plcd 6th* **9/2**[3]
5550 **7** ½ **Climaxfortackle (IRE)**[13] 6455 4-8-8 **62** (v) JoeFanning 7 59
(Derek Shaw) *s.i.s: hld up: nt clr run and r.o ins fnl f: nrst fin: fin 8th: plcd 7th* **20/1**
0006 **8** ½ **Little Jimmy Odsox (IRE)**[23] 6123 4-8-13 **67** (p) DavidAllan 9 62
(Tim Easterby) *chsd ldrs: rdn over 2f out: no ex fnl f: fin 9th: plcd 8th* **7/2**[1]
0640 **9** 1 **Wildcat Wizard (USA)**[19] 6260 6-9-1 **69** MickyFenton 3 61
(Paul Midgley) *hld up: rdn over 1f out: nvr on terms: fin 10th: plcd 9th* **28/1**
3060 **10** 1 ¼ **Perlachy**[18] 6277 8-8-13 **67** (v) LukeMorris 12 55
(Ronald Harris) *mid-div: hdwy over 2f out: rdn over 1f out: wknd fnl f: fin 11th: plcd 10th* **28/1**
4504 **11** 3 ½ **Expose**[16] 6347 4-9-6 **74** (b) LiamJones 11 51
(William Haggas) *plld hrd and prom: rdn over 1f out: wknd fnl f: fin 12th: plcd 11th* **9/1**
0165 **12** 1 ¼ **Drawnfromthepast (IRE)**[12] 6497 7-9-5 **73** FergusSweeney 10 75
(Jamie Osborne) *chsd ldr: rdn to ld 1f out: hdd and no ex ins fnl f: fin 4th: disqualified: rdr failed to weigh in* **17/2**

1m 14.15s (-0.85) **Going Correction** -0.05s/f (Stan)
WFA 3 from 4yo+ 1lb **12** Ran SP% **122.1**
Speed ratings (Par 103): **103,101,101,99,98 97,97,96,95,93 88,99**
toteswingers: 1&2 £7.70, 1&3 £7.30, 2&3 £11.90. CSF £55.11 CT £338.03 TOTE £3.00: £1.10, £4.10, £2.10; EX 82.40 Trifecta £420.20 Part won. Pool: £567.88 - 0.80 winning units.
Owner Tarka Racing **Bred** Mrs B A Matthews **Trained** Kentisbeare, Devon
■ Stewards' Enquiry : Fergus Sweeney three-day ban: failed to weigh in (18, 19 21 Oct)

FOCUS
A fair handicap run at a steady pace with plenty in contention at the furlong pole. It was slightly slower than division II and the winner posted his best figure since last summer.
Expose Official explanation: jockey said that the gelding ran too free

6825 BIDS 5 SCREEN SYSTEM FROM MRG H'CAP (DIV II) 5f 216y(P)
7:10 (7:11) (Class 5) (0-75,75) 3-Y-O+ **£2,587** (£770; £384; £192) **Stalls** Low

Form RPR
5130 **1** **We'll Deal Again**[13] 6427 5-9-7 **75** (h) GrahamGibbons 6 86
(Michael Easterby) *mde all: rdn over 1f out: r.o* **7/1**
0030 **2** 1 ½ **Another Citizen (IRE)**[14] 6403 4-8-13 **67** (b) DavidAllan 4 73
(Tim Easterby) *mid-div: hdwy 1/2-way: rdn to chse wnr ins fnl f: r.o* **4/1**[2]
0120 **3** 2 ¼ **Button Moon (IRE)**[8] 6577 4-9-4 **72** (p) SebSanders 3 71
(Ian Wood) *chsd ldrs: rdn to go 2nd over 1f out tl no ex ins fnl f* **10/1**
0153 **4** 1 ¼ **Trending (IRE)**[29] 5934 3-8-5 **63** (b) RaulDaSilva(3) 7 58
(Jeremy Gask) *prom: rdn over 2f out: styd on same pce fnl f* **12/1**
4605 **5** 2 ¼ **Night Trade (IRE)**[24] 6094 5-9-6 **74** (p) LukeMorris 5 62
(Ronald Harris) *s.i.s: hld up: rdn over 1f out: nvr trbld ldrs* **9/1**
6111 **6** nk **Alnoomaas (IRE)**[14] 6402 3-9-3 **72** TomMcLaughlin 8 59
(Luke Dace) *chsd wnr tl rdn over 1f out: no ex ins fnl f: eased nr fin* **2/1**[1]
5600 **7** 2 **Gung Ho Jack**[12] 6488 3-8-7 **67** TobyAtkinson(5) 11 47
(John Best) *s.s: sn pushed along in rr: nvr nrr* **33/1**
0000 **8** 1 **Hot Sugar (USA)**[70] 4496 3-8-12 **67** FrannyNorton 2 44
(Ed McMahon) *prom: lost pl over 4f out: wknd over 1f out* **16/1**
0005 **9** ½ **Ishetoo**[12] 6498 8-8-8 **62** RobbieFitzpatrick 9 37
(Peter Grayson) *s.s: a in rr* **40/1**
3000 **10** ¾ **Tabaret**[15] 6358 9-8-11 **65** RobertHavlin 10 38
(Richard Whitaker) *prom: rdn over 1f out: wknd fnl f* **28/1**
6410 **11** 2 ¼ **Ice Trooper**[15] 6357 4-9-1 **69** (p) GrahamLee 12 35
(Linda Stubbs) *hld up: a in rr: rdn and wknd over 1f out* **14/1**
5354 **12** 1 ¼ **Ghost Train (IRE)**[14] 6417 3-9-0 **69** (p) JoeFanning 1 31
(Mark Johnston) *mid-div: lost pl over 4f out: bhd whn eased ins fnl f* **5/1**[3]

1m 14.04s (-0.96) **Going Correction** -0.05s/f (Stan)
WFA 3 from 4yo+ 1lb **12** Ran SP% **130.7**
Speed ratings (Par 103): **104,102,99,97,94 93,91,89,89,88 85,83**
toteswingers: 1&2 £8.50, 1&3 £17.10, 2&3 £7.30. CSF £38.45 CT £298.54 TOTE £9.90: £2.70, £2.00, £3.10; EX 42.60 Trifecta £304.70 Pool: £498.31 - 1.21 winning units..
Owner K Wreglesworth **Bred** K Wreglesworth **Trained** Sheriff Hutton, N Yorks

FOCUS
Plenty of out-of-form runners in this contest, run at a fair pace. Slightly faster than division II, but no great depth. The winner confirmed that he's better than ever.
Ishetoo Official explanation: jockey said, regarding the running and riding, tha the gelding had pulled the reins out of his hands as he was reaching for the blinds resulting in slow removal. He added that having missed the break he felt it prudent not to hurry the gelding in the early stages

6826 ABETA, "THANKS-TO-ALL" OUR CUSTOMERS (S) STKS 7f 32y(P)
7:40 (7:40) (Class 6) 2-Y-O **£1,704** (£503; £251) **Stalls** High

Form RPR
0000 **1** **Sutton Sid**[8] 6583 2-8-11 65 PatCosgrave 8 61
(George Baker) *a.p: chsd ldr over 1f out: rdn to ld ins fnl f: styd on* **3/1**[2]
5032 **2** ¾ **Missing Agent**[13] 6435 2-9-2 62 (v) LukeMorris 5 64
(David Evans) *s.i.s: drvn along in rr early: hdwy 1/2-way: rdn over 1f out: r.o* **7/2**[3]
4242 **3** shd **Marchwood**[12] 6499 2-8-11 63 (p) JamieSpencer 10 59
(J S Moore) *led: rdn over 1f out: hdd ins fnl f: styd on* **13/8**[1]
2505 **4** 1 ½ **Sojoum**[12] 6499 2-8-6 53 SamHitchcott 6 50
(Mick Channon) *a.p: rdn and nt clr run over 1f out: swtchd lft: styd on* **25/1**
0202 **5** 2 ¼ **Special Report (IRE)**[2] 6766 2-8-4 60 DanielleMooney(7) 7 50
(Nigel Tinkler) *chsd ldr tl rdn over 1f out: no ex ins fnl f* **10/1**
04 **6** 8 **Sad But True (IRE)**[23] 6115 2-8-11 0 (v) GrahamGibbons 9 30
(Alan McCabe) *chsd ldrs: rdn over 2f out: wknd wl over 1f out* **16/1**
0 **7** ½ **Delwyn**[34] 5785 2-8-1 0 KatiaScallan(5) 3 24
(Marcus Tregoning) *hld up: rdn over 1f out: n.d* **12/1**
60 **8** 7 **Annabella Milbanke**[23] 6115 2-8-6 0 (p) JimmyQuinn 4 7
(John Holt) *hld up: rdn 1/2-way: a in rr* **100/1**
9 nse **Only Dreamin** 2-8-1 0 ow2 JakePayne(7) 1 9
(Bill Turner) *s.s: outpcd* **33/1**

10 *21* **Rustic Rose Dot Uk** 2-8-5 0 ow1 .... RyanWhile[(7)] 2
(Bill Turner) *s.s: outpcd* **40/1**

1m 29.99s (0.39) **Going Correction** -0.05s/f (Stan) **10** Ran SP% **118.2**
Speed ratings (Par 93): **95,94,94,92,89 80,80,72,71,47**
toteswingers: 1&2 £2.10, 1&3 £1.70, 2&3 £2.10. CSF £13.84 TOTE £2.40: £1.10, £1.80, £1.90; EX 14.50 Trifecta £39.10 Pool: £498.31 - 1.21 winning units..There was no bid for the winner. Marchwood was claimed by Miss A Weaver for £6,000.
Owner P Bowden **Bred** Peter Hunt & Mrs Sally Hunt **Trained** Whitsbury, Hants

FOCUS
A low-quality seller run at a decent pace, with the front four well grouped passing the post. The time was decent.

NOTEBOOK
Sutton Sid, dropped to selling class for the first time and best in on official ratings, was well positioned behind the strong pace and came through with a well-timed run up the straight, holding on well at the line. He had proved disappointing in four starts since a promising debut in May but took advantage of this drop in grade. (op 4-1 tchd 9-2)
Missing Agent, who had run well enough in handicaps over 1m on his last two starts, was outpaced turning for home before staying on late. The fitting of the visor, worn on his last three starts, has had a positive effect and his mark of 62 does not look beyond him. (op 11-4 tchd 5-2)
Marchwood showed good pace to get to the front from his wide draw, but he paid for those efforts late on and is becoming a shade frustrating. He was claimed by Amy Weaver. (op 2-1 tchd 9-4)
Sojourn ran slightly better than of late but is beginning to look exposed. (op 16-1)
Special Report(IRE), stepping back up to 7f, helped set the early fractions and was a tired horse late on. (op 9-1 tchd 17-2)

6827 BIDS 5 STUDIO SOFTWARE FROM MRG MEDIAN AUCTION MAIDEN STKS 7f 32y(P)
8:10 (8:17) (Class 5) 3-4-Y-O **£2,587** (£770; £384; £192) **Stalls** High

Form RPR
33- **1** **Yeomanoftheguard**[363] 6662 3-9-0 0 .... LeeTopliss[(3)] 2 71
(Richard Fahey) *got loose prior to the s: led: hdd over 5f out: led again 1/2-way: rdn out* **8/1**
4320 **2** *½* **Green Mitas (ITY)**[12] 6502 3-8-10 62 .... JackDuern[(7)] 10 69
(Frank Sheridan) *hld up: hdwy over 2f out: rdn and ev ch ins fnl f: styd on* **8/1**
3 *¾* **Syncopate** 3-9-3 0 .... KierenFallon 6 67+
(Luca Cumani) *s.i.s: hdwy 4f out: sn pushed along: rdn and edgd lft ins fnl f: styd on* **7/4**[1]
50 **4** *1 ½* **The Kicking Lord**[6] 6643 3-9-3 0 .... AdamBeschizza 5 63
(Mark Brisbourne) *plld hrd and prom: rdn and n.m.r over 1f out: styd on* **33/1**
0403 **5** *1 ¼* **Arctic Stryker**[9] 6565 3-9-3 68 .... LukeMorris 4 60
(John Best) *w ldr tl led over 5f out: hdd 1/2-way: rdn over 2f out: no ex ins fnl f* **13/2**[3]
6-4 **6** *2 ½* **Pomarine (USA)**[21] 6154 3-8-12 0 .... JimCrowley 3 48
(Amanda Perrett) *chsd ldrs: rdn over 2f out: wknd ins fnl f* **9/4**[2]
5 **7** *5* **Winnetou**[17] 6317 3-9-0 0 .... SophieDoyle[(3)] 11 40
(Frank Sheridan) *s.i.s: nvr on terms* **250/1**
4-6 **8** *1* **King's Guest (IRE)**[13] 6457 3-8-12 0 .... MartinLane 7 32
(David Simcock) *chsd ldrs: rdn over 2f out: sn wknd* **12/1**
9 *3 ¾* **Dr Victoria** 3-8-12 0 .... GrahamLee 12 22
(John Norton) *s.i.s: a in rr* **100/1**
0 **10** *¾* **Fantastic Indian**[21] 6154 3-8-12 0 .... WilliamCarson 1 20
(Roy Brotherton) *hld up: rdn 1/2-way: wknd over 2f out* **250/1**
11 *37* **Flow Jo (IRE)** 4-8-7 0 .... JakePayne[(7)] 9
(Karen George) *s.s: outpcd: eased fnl 2f: t.o* **40/1**

1m 29.65s (0.05) **Going Correction** -0.05s/f (Stan)
WFA 3 from 4yo 2lb **11** Ran SP% **117.5**
Speed ratings (Par 103): **97,96,95,93,92 89,83,82,78,77 35**
toteswingers: 1&2 £10.50, 1&3 £4.90, 2&3 £4.60. CSF £69.16 TOTE £11.70: £2.30, £2.20, £1.60; EX 71.10 Trifecta £366.80 Pool: £649.49 - 1.31 winning units..
Owner H J P Farr **Bred** Worksop Manor Stud **Trained** Musley Bank, N Yorks
■ Stewards' Enquiry : Adam Beschizza two-day ban: careless riding (19, 21 Octo)

FOCUS
A modest contest with the second and fourth limiting the form.

6828 WE SPEAK GAMING AT GTECH G2 CLAIMING STKS 1m 4f 50y(P)
8:40 (8:41) (Class 6) 3-Y-O+ **£1,704** (£503; £251) **Stalls** Low

Form RPR
1400 **1** **Incendo**[19] 6248 6-9-10 88 .... (t) EddieAhern 4 79+
(James Fanshawe) *a.p: led on bit over 1f out: easily* **10/11**[1]
5064 **2** *2 ¼* **Uphold**[3] 6734 5-9-7 72 .... (t) MichaelJMMurphy[(5)] 1 72
(Gay Kelleway) *chsd ldrs: shkn up over 2f out: rdn and nt clr run over 1f out: styd on: no ch w wnr* **9/2**[3]
4200 **3** *¾* **Spey Song (IRE)**[13] 6458 4-9-2 64 .... (b) JamieSpencer 6 61
(James Bethell) *hld up: hdwy over 1f out: rdn ins fnl f: styd on same pce* **8/1**
5311 **4** *3* **Just Lille (IRE)**[17] 6313 9-9-7 79 .... (p) GrahamLee 9 61
(Ann Duffield) *led: hdd over 2f out: rdn and ev ch over 1f out: no ex ins fnl f* **5/2**[2]
3050 **5** *6* **One For The Girls**[10] 6542 3-8-11 48 .... (t) LukeMorris 8 49?
(Nicky Vaughan) *sn chsng ldr: pushed along to ld over 2f out: rdn and hdd over 1f out: wknd ins fnl f* **66/1**
0404 **6** *2* **Port Hill**[80] 4156 5-8-10 45 .... JackDuern[(7)] 5 44
(Mark Brisbourne) *hld up: hdwy over 4f out: rdn over 2f out: wknd over 1f out* **66/1**

2m 41.34s (0.24) **Going Correction** -0.05s/f (Stan)
WFA 3 from 4yo+ 7lb **6** Ran SP% **113.2**
Speed ratings (Par 101): **97,95,95,93,89 87**
toteswingers: 1&2 £1.20, 1&3 £2.80, 2&3 £3.10. CSF £5.72 TOTE £2.60: £1.60, £3.60; EX 5.80 Trifecta £32.40 Pool: £570.08 - 12.99 winning units..Incendo was claimed by Ian Williams for £10,000.
Owner Andrew & Julia Turner **Bred** London Thoroughbred Services Ltd **Trained** Newmarket, Suffolk

FOCUS
An uncompetitive claimer, run at a steady pace with the top-rated runner pulling clear on the bit. An easy winner but most of his rivals were not at their best.

6829 SAMVO BETBROKER H'CAP 1m 141y(P)
9:10 (9:10) (Class 6) (0-55,55) 3-Y-O+ **£1,704** (£503; £251) **Stalls** Low

Form RPR
0502 **1** **Outlaw Torn (IRE)**[17] 6309 3-9-1 55 .... (e) RobbieFitzpatrick 9 63
(Richard Guest) *chsd ldr: rdn to ld over 1f out: jst hld on* **11/1**
4063 **2** *hd* **Parque Atlantico**[36] 5751 3-9-1 55 .... FrannyNorton 8 62
(Ed McMahon) *chsd ldrs: rdn over 2f out: r.o* **11/2**
4000 **3** *2 ½* **Aragorn Rouge**[66] 4657 4-8-11 52 .... AdamCarter[(5)] 5 54
(John Wainwright) *a.p: hrd rdn fr over 1f out: styd on same pce ins fnl f* **11/4**[1]
0432 **4** *2* **Fortunate Bid (IRE)**[6] 6646 6-9-3 53 .... (p) GrahamLee 3 50
(Linda Stubbs) *hld up: hdwy over 1f out: styd on same pce ins fnl f* **5/1**[3]
400- **5** *1 ¼* **Geronimo Chief (IRE)**[465] 3460 4-9-5 55 .... (v[1]) ChrisCatlin 7 49
(Ben Haslam) *led: rdn and hdd over 1f out: wknd ins fnl f* **12/1**
154 **6** *hd* **Avon Supreme**[6] 6646 4-8-10 51 .... NatashaEaton[(5)] 6 45
(Gay Kelleway) *mid-div: hdwy u.p over 1f out: no imp fnl f* **20/1**
2050 **7** *¾* **Sasheen**[13] 6434 5-9-5 55 .... (p) EddieAhern 13 47
(Jeremy Gask) *hld up: hdwy 5f out: rdn and wknd fnl f* **16/1**
5054 **8** *6* **Salutary**[20] 6217 3-9-1 55 .... KierenFallon 11 33
(Jane Chapple-Hyam) *chsd ldrs: rdn over 2f out: wknd and eased fnl f* **7/2**[2]
-063 **9** *1 ½* **Dark Orchid**[51] 5215 3-9-1 55 .... JamieSpencer 2 30
(Peter Chapple-Hyam) *hld up: rdn over 1f out: eased ins fnl f* **7/1**
00 **10** *2 ¾* **Mad Ginger Alice**[157] 1717 4-8-11 52 .... LauraPike[(5)] 4 20
(Olivia Maylam) *s.i.s: a in rr* **40/1**
-000 **11** *9* **Tigerbill**[94] 3712 4-9-0 50 .... LukeMorris 10
(Nicky Vaughan) *hld up: hdwy over 2f out: wknd over 1f out* **50/1**
4210 **12** *14* **Tanforan**[38] 5657 10-9-5 55 .... KellyHarrison 1
(Brian Baugh) *a in rr: pushed along 1/2-way: bhd fnl 3f: t.o* **33/1**

1m 49.5s (-1.00) **Going Correction** -0.05s/f (Stan)
WFA 3 from 4yo+ 4lb **12** Ran SP% **127.5**
Speed ratings (Par 101): **102,101,99,97,96 96,95,90,89,86 78,66**
toteswingers: 1&2 £12.40, 1&3 £16.90, 2&3 £6.90. CSF £73.72 CT £222.31 TOTE £17.80: £4.00, £3.00, £2.30; EX 109.00 TRIFECTA Not won..
Owner James S Kennerley **Bred** Derek Veitch & Rory O'Brien **Trained** Stainforth, S Yorks
■ Stewards' Enquiry : Adam Carter seven-day ban: use of whip (18-24 Oct)

FOCUS
A poor-quality handicap run at at steady pace with few able to come from behind. This rates a small personal best from the winner.
Salutary Official explanation: jockey said that the gelding lost action in the home straight
T/Jkpt: Not won. T/Plt: £105.00 to a £1 stake. Pool: £73,993.41 - 514.14 winning tickets. T/Qpdt: £22.50 to a £1 stake. Pool: £8,593.44 - 281.80 winning tickets. CR

6020 ASCOT (R-H)
Friday, October 5

OFFICIAL GOING: Soft (str 8.0, rnd 7.1)
Wind: Moderate, half against Weather: Cloudy, rain from race 4 onwards

6830 ASCOT RACECOURSE H'CAP 7f
2:20 (2:20) (Class 3) (0-95,94) 3-Y-O **£8,409** (£2,502; £1,250; £625) **Stalls** Centre

Form RPR
0340 **1** **Compton**[23] 6143 3-9-3 90 .... JimCrowley 5 100
(Ralph Beckett) *hld up in midfield: prog on outer over 2f out: rdn to ld over 1f out: styd on u.p* **8/1**
1212 **2** *½* **Subtle Knife**[22] 6176 3-8-9 82 .... WilliamCarson 14 90
(Giles Bravery) *settled in last quartet: rdn by 1/2-way: prog u.p whn n.m.r over 1f out: styd on wl to take 2nd last stride* **16/1**
4221 **3** *shd* **Whimsical (IRE)**[16] 6367 3-9-0 87 .... RichardHughes 2 95
(Richard Hannon) *dwlt: hld up in last quartet: rdn and prog on outer 2f out: drvn to chse wnr fnl f: a hld: lost 2nd post* **16/1**
0031 **4** *½* **Muarrab**[13] 6488 3-8-8 81 .... PaulHanagan 10 88+
(Ed Dunlop) *hld up in midfield: prog 2f out: tried to cl on wnr fnl f: styd on same pce* **8/1**
0212 **5** *2* **Dream Tune**[20] 6235 3-9-4 91 .... AdamKirby 12 92
(Clive Cox) *w ldr: led 4f out to 3f out: lost 2nd over 1f out and sn outpcd: kpt on* **4/1**[1]
2100 **6** *¾* **Springinmystep (IRE)**[26] 6075 3-9-2 89 .... PaulMulrennan 7 88
(Michael Dods) *trckd ldrs: poised to chal jst over 2f out: drvn over 1f out: wknd fnl f* **40/1**
0033 **7** *shd* **Way Too Hot**[27] 6023 3-8-12 85 .... DaneO'Neill 17 84
(Clive Cox) *hld up in last quartet: pushed along and no prog over 2f out: shkn up over 1f out: kpt on: nvr nrr* **20/1**
2200 **8** *½* **Silverheels (IRE)**[14] 6449 3-9-6 93 .... ShaneKelly 9 91
(Paul Cole) *dwlt and stdd s: hld up in last quartet: shkn up and no prog 2f out: kpt on fnl f: no ch* **25/1**
4132 **9** *nk* **Obliterieght (IRE)**[23] 6143 3-9-1 88 .... JimmyFortune 16 85
(William Knight) *hld up in midfield gng wl: shkn up 2f out: fdd rather tamely jst over 1f out* **12/1**
1011 **10** *¾* **Idler (IRE)**[6] 6676 3-9-6 93 6ex .... JoeFanning 8 88
(Mark Johnston) *led to 4f out: led again 3f out: drvn and hdd over 1f out: wknd fnl f* **5/1**[2]
100 **11** *1* **Poisson D'Or**[63] 4764 3-8-12 85 .... ChrisCatlin 15 77
(Rae Guest) *prom early: sn in midfield: wknd 2f out* **25/1**
5224 **12** *¾* **Tartiflette**[84] 4062 3-8-11 84 .... GrahamGibbons 11 74
(Ed McMahon) *trckd ldrs: cl up 2f out: rdn and wknd qckly over 1f out* **7/1**
31-6 **13** *8* **Genius Step (IRE)**[27] 6046 3-9-0 87 .... FrankieDettori 13 55
(Mahmood Al Zarooni) *trckd ldrs: pushed along 3f out: wknd wl over 1f out: eased* **6/1**[3]

1m 29.73s (2.13) **Going Correction** +0.35s/f (Good) **13** Ran SP% **120.0**
Speed ratings (Par 105): **101,100,100,99,97 96,96,95,95,94 93,92,83**
toteswingers: 1&2 £51.00, 2&3 £12.70, 1&3 £34.70 CSF £123.18 CT £2079.17 TOTE £10.70: £3.20, £3.80, £2.70; EX 230.00 TRIFECTA Not won. Pool: £822.54.
Owner J H Richmond-Watson **Bred** Lawn Stud **Trained** Kimpton, Hants

FOCUS
The straight course was at its narrowest configuration (6yds off stands' side rail and 8yds off far rail) to preserve ground for Champions Day later in the month. This competitive 3yo handicap was run at an average tempo until nearing halfway but the first four, who pulled clear, came from off the pace and the ground looked easy enough. The winner is rated up a length on his Britannia form.

NOTEBOOK
Compton deservedly landed his first win since his 2yo debut and proved his versatility regards underfoot conditions. He arrived with something of an inconsistent profile, but posted a career-best over 1m here when fourth in the Britannia in June on his seasonal debut, where he finished one place behind last week's Cambridgeshire winner Bronze Angel. That came off a 2lb higher mark and the return to this venue evidently proved up his street. He reportedly now heads to the horses in training sales and should prove popular there. (op 12-1)
Subtle Knife felt the pinch out the back when the pace injected around halfway, but kept responding to her rider's urgings and threw down a strong late challenge. She was tight for room just the winner was winding up with his effort, but it didn't affect the overall result. It was her best effort yet and she's developing into an ultra-consistent handicapper.

Whimsical(IRE), deservedly back to winning ways on Polytrack 16 days earlier, was 2lb higher returned to turf and reverted to more patient tactics. She came under pressure a fair way out nearer the far side, but was willing and posted another solid effort in defeat. This effort suggests returning to 1m may suit. (op 14-1)

Muarrab scored off 4lb lower at Newbury last time out on quicker ground. Buried away in midfield, he came through with every chance and turned in another improved effort on ground likely easy enough for his liking. He may well have another race in him this term. (op 11-1)

Dream Tune went up 4lb for finishing a clear second-best at Chester on his handicap debut last month. He faded from the furlong marker, but fared best racing positively and is not one to abandon yet. (op 9-2)

Idler(IRE) was bidding for a fourth success from his last five outings and lined up 4lb ahead of the handicapper despite the penalty. He has won on soft, but not in this sort of company and was cooked before the final furlong having raced near the pace. (op 4-1 tchd 7-2)

Genius Step(IRE) was expected to improve on his Thirsk comeback over 1m last month, but he was beaten from halfway and now has it to prove. (tchd 13-2)

6831 E B F REDSTONE CLASSIFIED STKS — 1m (S)

2:55 (2:55) (Class 3) 3-Y-O+

£9,337 (£2,796; £1,398; £699; £349; £175) **Stalls** Centre

Form RPR

2364 **1** **Jake's Destiny (IRE)**[20] 6242 3-8-13 90........................(t) PatCosgrave 8 98
(George Baker) *led: brought to nr side rail and narrowly hdd 1/2-way: rdn to ld again 1f out: styd on wl* **7/2**[2]

5-31 **2** *1* **Captain Cat (IRE)**[139] 2279 3-8-13 87.................... JamesDoyle 10 96
(Roger Charlton) *prom early but sn trckd ldrs: gng best whn brought to chal 2f out: rdn and nt qckn over 1f out: styd on to take 2nd ins fnl f: a hld* **5/1**[3]

2631 **3** *1 1/4* **Gaul Wood (IRE)**[21] 6205 3-8-13 89........................ RichardKingscote 1 93
(Tom Dascombe) *racd wdst of all: pushed along in midfield 3f out: drvn and styd on fnl 2f: tk 3rd post* **9/4**[1]

000 **4** *shd* **Titus Mills (IRE)**[14] 6426 4-9-2 90................................(v[1]) KierenFallon 5 93
(Brian Meehan) *pressed wnr after 2f: narrow ld fr 1/2-way: drvn 2f out: hdd 1f out: wknd last 100yds* **22/1**

0200 **5** *shd* **Apostle (IRE)**[50] 5271 3-8-8 90.. LauraPike(5) 7 92
(Michael Bell) *prom towards outer: rdn and nt qckn 2f out: kpt on fnl f: nvr able to chal* **9/1**

14-2 **6** *6* **Gifted Girl (IRE)**[156] 1748 3-8-10 90................................ FrankieDettori 3 76
(Paul Cole) *prom tl wknd fr 2f out* **7/1**

5060 **7** *1/2* **Starwatch**[42] 5535 5-8-9 86............................ WilliamTwiston-Davies(7) 6 77
(John Bridger) *settled in rr: rdn and struggling over 3f out: bhd and no ch 2f out: plugged on* **16/1**

3030 **8** *5* **Mia's Boy**[20] 6242 8-9-2 89.. SaleemGolam 9 66
(Chris Dwyer) *hld up in rr: rdn and no prog over 3f out: wknd and bhd fnl 2f* **33/1**

0055 **9** *2* **Lord Ofthe Shadows (IRE)**[14] 6432 3-8-13 89.......... RichardHughes 2 61
(Richard Hannon) *awkward s and stdd: rdn in rr over 3f out: no prog: eased over 1f out* **8/1**

1m 43.61s (2.81) **Going Correction** +0.35s/f (Good)
WFA 3 from 4yo+ 3lb **9** Ran SP% **116.4**
Speed ratings (Par 107): **99,98,96,96,96 90,90,85,83**
toteswingers:1&2 £5.30, 2&3 £3.80, 1&3 £3.20 CSF £21.64 TOTE £5.10: £1.70, £1.90, £1.20; EX 17.60 Trifecta £80.30 Pool: £1,976.13 - 18.19 winning tickets..
Owner Delancey **Bred** Canice M Farrell Jnr **Trained** Whitsbury, Hants

FOCUS

This fair classified event was another race run at an average pace and there was unsurprisingly a tight finish. Four of the runners broke into the group on the near side after 2f or so, before all bar Gaul Wood merged with them. The winner got back on track with a length personal best.

NOTEBOOK

Jake's Destiny(IRE) due deep against the stands' rail and ran out a gutsy winner, landing his first success since scoring on the AW last year. The only time he had failed to make the frame in four previous outings this season was when finding 7f too sharp in a decent handicap at Glorious Goodwood in August, so this was obviously deserved. A first-time tongue-tie evidently helped his cause and he had little trouble with the softer surface. Surely connections will now be eyeing a big handicap at the Royal Meeting next year, and he is expected to want further as he matures. (tchd 3-1)

Captain Cat(IRE) ◆, an imposing 3yo, was last seen making it third time lucky with a taking success at Newmarket back in May, when he beat a dual subsequent winner. He cruised into contention 2f out, but appeared to blow up somewhat when push came to shove. He was coming back again near the finish and, with improvement on the cards for the run, ought to to prove hard to beat next time out, especially if getting back on some better ground. (op 9-2 tchd 11-2)

Gaul Wood(IRE) beat subsequent Newmarket winner Henry Allingham off 84 at Sandown 21 days earlier and was well backed to follow up. It's hard to gauge whether he was disadvantaged by staying solo down the centre of the track, but this was still another decent effort and he seems versatile regards underfoot conditions. (op 3-1)

Titus Mills(IRE) was never far away towards the stands' side and this was much more encouraging again from him with a first-time visor replacing blinkers. He made a winning debut at this track at two, on his only previous visit, so clearly likes the place. (op 16-1)

Apostle(IRE), who acts well with cut, got a positive ride and returned to the sort of form that saw him just lose out in a lady riders' race over 7f here in July. (op 14-1)

Gifted Girl(IRE) looked interesting on her last-time-out Polytrack form in May and with Frankie Dettori aboard. She sustained an injury after that, however, and looked badly in need of this return. (tchd 6-1)

6832 WEAR IT PINK H'CAP — 1m 4f

3:30 (3:30) (Class 2) (0-105,99) 3-Y-O+ **£12,938** (£3,850; £1,924; £962) **Stalls** Low

Form RPR

2412 **1** **Fattsota**[20] 6248 4-10-0 **99**.. AdamKirby 8 111+
(Marco Botti) *trckd ldng trio: prog to ld 2f out: edgd rt but sn rdn clr: 5 l up ins fnl f: eased nr fin* **9/2**[2]

1134 **2** *2* **Party Line**[6] 6668 3-8-9 **87**.. JoeFanning 1 93
(Mark Johnston) *trckd ldng pair to 3f out: nt qckn and sltly outpcd: styd on to take 2nd over 1f out: no ch w wnr: flattered by proximity* **8/1**

-140 **3** *1 1/4* **Mulaqen**[104] 3372 4-9-10 **95**.. PaulHanagan 2 99
(Marcus Tregoning) *hld up disputing 5th: rdn and nt qckn wl over 2f out: styd on fr over 1f out to take 3rd last 100yds* **4/1**[1]

013 **4** *nk* **Voodoo Prince**[9] 6575 4-9-5 **90**.. KierenFallon 9 94
(Ed Dunlop) *settled in last pair: pushed along 4f out: no prog over 2f out: styd on fnl f to press for 3rd nr fin* **4/1**[1]

010 **5** *1 1/4* **Hanoverian Baron**[21] 6197 7-9-2 **87**................................... JimCrowley 5 89
(Tony Newcombe) *hld up disputing 5th: rdn and sme prog over 2f out: pressed for 2nd over 1f out: wknd fnl f* **16/1**

1420 **6** *1 1/2* **Henry Clay**[9] 6580 3-8-9 **87**... FrankieDettori 7 86
(Mark Johnston) *chsd ldr: led briefly over 2f out: wknd over 1f out* **11/2**[3]

-303 **7** *1/2* **Royal Peculiar**[132] 2504 4-9-5 **90**..................................... TomQueally 10 88
(Sir Henry Cecil) *hld up in last pair: effrt on outer 4f out: rdn and no prog over 2f out: sn btn* **10/1**

3206 **8** *1* **Martin Chuzzlewit (IRE)**[20] 6248 3-8-12 **90**...........(b[1]) RichardHughes 4 87
(Sir Michael Stoute) *reminder to ld and set gd pce: hdd over 2f out: nudged along and wknd: eased fnl f* **6/1**

2m 38.68s (6.18) **Going Correction** +0.75s/f (Yiel)
WFA 3 from 4yo+ 7lb **8** Ran SP% **113.9**
Speed ratings (Par 109): **109,107,106,106,105 104,104,103**
toteswingers: 1&2 £5.80, 2&3 £6.40, 1&3 £4.20 CSF £39.53 CT £154.45 TOTE £5.40: £2.00, £2.90, £1.30; EX 41.40 Trifecta £149.50 Pool: £1,846.11 - 9.13 winning tickets..
Owner Scuderia Rencati Srl **Bred** Azienda Agricola Francesca **Trained** Newmarket, Suffolk
■ Silver Lime was withdrawn (4/1, unsuitable ground). Deduct 20p in the £ under R4. New market formed.

FOCUS

This was weakened by the two non-runners, but still a good-quality handicap. It was the first race of the meeting on the round course and the ground was softer on the far side than the straight track. They went a sound enough pace. The smart winner was value for 4l and the form is sound in behind.

NOTEBOOK

Fattsota finished runner-up at Doncaster 20 days earlier and was therefore 8lb higher than when landing a first domestic success over C&D in July. Despite his big weight, he unsurprisingly proved popular and, under a well-judged ride, scooted clear of rivals inside the final furlong. Some juice underfoot clearly suits and this could spell an end to his handicap days as a hike in the weights looks inevitable. A trip to Dubai's Carnival could well be on his agenda and he looks up to making his mark in Pattern-company. (op 7-2)

Party Line, one of two from her stable, proved a little keen early on just off the pace. She kept to her task gamely under maximum pressure in the home straight and has developed into a tough filly. It was probably another career-best in defeat, but she never stood any chance with the winner.

Mulaqen was returning from a 104-day break with his yard in top form and returned to something like his best. He's entitled to come on for it, but is probably handicapped about right. (op 9-2)

Voodoo Prince, who was a stone ahead of the handicapper after a personal-best effort in Listed company at Goodwood last week, ran a race that is hard to assess. Ridden to get the longer trip, he again went in snatches early on and was well back turning for home. He kept on for pressure, but rather flattened out late in the day and perhaps he needs quicker ground over this far. His rider later blamed a "stop-start" pace, but life will obviously be tougher now from a mark of 104. (op 7-2)

Hanoverian Baron, a previous course winner, loomed up 2f out but was done with passing the furlong marker. This trip on such ground probably found out his stamina.

Henry Clay, stablemate of the runner-up, was not at his best on Polytrack last week and was 2lb higher up in trip. Very well backed, he faded after racing handily and rates a non-stayer on the ground. (op 10-1 tchd 5-1)

Royal Peculiar ◆ caught the eye turning for home but it was his first outing since May and his best form has come on much quicker ground. Look out for this lightly raced 4yo back on a sounder surface before the season is out. (op 17-2 tchd 11-1)

Martin Chuzzlewit(IRE) went from the front in first-time blinkers and paid from 2f out. He looks one to avoid. (op 11-2 tchd 7-1)

6833 KELTBRAY NOEL MURLESS STKS (LISTED RACE) — 1m 6f

4:05 (4:05) (Class 1) 3-Y-O

£19,848 (£7,525; £3,766; £1,876; £941; £472) **Stalls** Low

Form RPR

1212 **1** **Biographer**[41] 5598 3-9-0 99.. TedDurcan 8 103
(David Lanigan) *hld up in last trio: rdn and gd prog 2f out: led jst ins fnl f and edgd rt briefly: styd on strly* **3/1**[1]

3011 **2** *1 3/4* **Sir Graham Wade (IRE)**[21] 6197 3-9-0 104...................... KierenFallon 5 101
(Mark Johnston) *t.k.h in 5th: rdn to cl on ldrs 2f out: keeping on but hld whn squeezed out 1f out: rallied to take 2nd last stride* **7/2**[2]

3002 **3** *nse* **Cavaleiro (IRE)**[14] 6445 3-9-0 95.................................. FrankieDettori 3 100
(Marcus Tregoning) *trckd ldng pair: drvn to chse ldr 2f out: edgd lft over 1f out: clsng to chal whn wnr swept by jst ins fnl f: kpt on but lost 2nd last stride* **9/2**[3]

3536 **4** *3/4* **Good Morning Star (IRE)**[6] 6668 3-8-12 97..................... JoeFanning 4 97
(Mark Johnston) *trckd ldr: led and kicked on over 2f out: edgd lft over 1f out: hdd and one pce jst ins fnl f* **20/1**

0-21 **5** *3/4* **Tempest Fugit (IRE)**[15] 6398 3-8-9 81............................ RobertHavlin 2 93
(John Gosden) *hld up in last trio: prog fr last jst over 2f out: swtchd rt and tried to cl on ldrs over 1f out: one pce fnl f* **25/1**

4440 **6** *nk* **Salford Art (IRE)**[90] 3856 3-8-9 107................................ PaulHanagan 6 92
(David Elsworth) *hld up in last trio: rdn 3f out: struggling 2f out: styd on fnl f: n.d* **6/1**

1S02 **7** *1* **Last Shadow**[6] 6668 3-9-0 85... JamesDoyle 7 96
(William Muir) *chsd ldng trio: rdn 4f out: dropped to last pair and struggling 2f out: plugged on fnl f* **25/1**

11R0 **8** *1 3/4* **Monshak (IRE)**[22] 6163 3-8-9 88.................................. RichardHughes 1 89
(Sir Michael Stoute) *hld up in midfield: drifted bk to rr 6f out: shkn up and no rspnse over 2f out: wknd fnl f* **10/1**

411 **9** *5* **Signed Up**[9] 6573 3-9-0 85... PatDobbs 9 87
(Amanda Perrett) *pushed up to ld fr wd draw: rdn and hdd over 2f out: wknd rapidly over 1f out* **11/2**

3m 9.26s (189.26) **9** Ran SP% **116.6**
toteswingers: 1&2 £3.00, 2&3 £4.20, 1&3 £3.20 CSF £13.36 TOTE £3.80: £1.70, £1.70, £1.30; EX 10.80 Trifecta £25.50 Pool: £2,406.49 - 69.69 winning tickets..
Owner B E Nielsen **Bred** Bjorn E Nielsen **Trained** Upper Lambourn, Berks

FOCUS

A very interesting 3yo Listed event for stayers. It was run at a fair pace considering the ground and there were a number in with a chance 1f out, but the progressive Biographer stamped his authority thereafter. The form is only ordinary gor the grade and the winner did not need to improve in the circumstances.

NOTEBOOK

Biographer turned in a career-best when second in the Melrose at York's Ebor meeting in August and was well backed to go one better on this debut in Listed company. Confidently ridden, he made a promising move after straightening for home and saw it out strongly once hitting full stride, taking his career record to 3-6. His ability to handle such ground was a big plus, but it was still considered testing enough for him and there was a lot to like about the way he went about his business. He looks certain to make his mark in Group races over a trip next year. (tchd 11-4)

Sir Graham Wade(IRE) finished a long way behind the winner at York in August, but was much better judged on his two wins since and lined up rated 5lb higher than his old rival. The ground was a worry beforehand, though, and he did prove easy to back. Keen through the early parts, he improved to have every chance but was beaten prior to being tightened up inside the final furlong. It was still another cracking effort considering he ideally wants a sounder surface and he too rates a Group-class stayer in the making. (op 4-1)

Cavaleiro(IRE) returned to form on quicker ground at Newbury a fortnight earlier and had Frankie Dettori taking over, who was 2-4 for the yard since 2007. His pedigree gave hope for him appreciating the extra 2f and he saw it out well, but he is another that should benefit from a sounder surface as a stayer. (op 4-1 tchd 5-1)

Good Morning Star(IRE) has been somewhat in-and-out since her surprise win in the Cheshire Oaks back in May. She ran a blinder here, though, and deserves extra credit as she helped force the pace. (op 11-1 tchd 10-1)

Tempest Fugit(IRE) was aggressively ridden when winning her maiden back from a break at Kempton 15 days earlier, but was understandably waited with up markedly in class over this longer trip back on turf. She ran well, making up her ground 2f out, and is evidently on an upwards curve. (tchd 20-1)
Salford Art(IRE) reportedly coughed after flopping in the Lancashire Oaks when last seen in July and her yard is now in much better form. The longer trip looked well worth a try and she was best in at the weights down in class, but she didn't impress with how she travelled. Perhaps the run was needed, but she has become hard to catch right. (op 7-1 tchd 15-2 and 8-1)
Last Shadow was in trouble before 2f out but had plenty to find with the principals.
Signed Up probably found this more demanding test coming too soon after his Goodwood handicap success last week. (op 6-1)

6834 WESSEX YOUTH TRUST GORDON CARTER STKS (H'CAP) 2m
4:40 (4:40) (Class 3) (0-95,90) 3-Y-0+ **£7,439** (£2,213; £1,106; £553) **Stalls** Low

Form				RPR
4102	**1**		**Red Orator**[12] 6517 3-8-4 **77** JoeFanning 10 (Mark Johnston) *mde all at gd pce: had most of rivals flat out fr 4f out: clr over 2f out: drvn and kpt on: nvr really threatened* **9/2**[3]	88+
0-02	**2**	*1*	**Ardlui (IRE)**[21] 6191 4-9-9 **85** TomQueally 12 (Alan King) *sn hld up in midfield: prog over 3f out: rdn to chse clr wnr jst over 2f out: clsd grad after: nvr quite able to chal* **7/2**[1]	94
020	**3**	*7*	**First Avenue**[13] 6493 7-9-9 **85** IanMongan 7 (Laura Mongan) *hld up towards rr: prog over 3f out: drvn to go 3rd over 1f out but no ch: one pce* **18/1**	86
0412	**4**	*2*	**Somemothersdohavem**[21] 6213 3-8-0 **73**(p) KirstyMilczarek 11 (John Ryan) *stdd s: hld up in last: lost tch 1/2-way but gng wl enough: prog over 3f out: rchd 6th 2f out: kpt on fnl f: no ch* **25/1**	71
6520	**5**	*nse*	**Woolfall Treasure**[31] 5905 7-10-0 **90**(v) RichardHughes 5 (Gary Moore) *trckd ldng quartet: rdn and lost pl qckly over 6f out: renewed effrt over 3f out: chal for 3rd 1f out: nt qckn: eased and lost 4th last strides* **20/1**	88
2-65	**6**	*½*	**Valid Reason**[34] 5830 5-9-5 **81** ShaneKelly 2 (Dean Ivory) *chsd ldng trio: rdn 5f out: drvn to dispute 2nd briefly over 2f out: sn fdd* **9/1**	79
1365	**7**	*10*	**Flashman**[27] 6033 3-8-4 **77** PaulHanagan 6 (Richard Fahey) *mostly chsd wnr to over 2f out: wknd qckly: eased fnl f* **4/1**[2]	63
2140	**8**	*29*	**Orsippus (USA)**[65] 4697 6-9-6 **82** KierenFallon 1 (Michael Smith) *sltly awkward s: hld up in rr: detached fr main gp 1/2-way and nt gng wl: brief effrt over 4f out: sn wknd: eased 2f out: t.o* **7/1**	33
2	**9**	*3*	**Hawkeshead**[57] 5002 5-9-0 **76** MichaelO'Connell 8 (Ian Williams) *chsd ldng pair: drvn 5f out: wknd over 3f out: t.o* **16/1**	23
0353	**10**	*58*	**Itlaaq**[27] 6031 6-10-0 **90**(t) GrahamGibbons 3 (Michael Easterby) *hld up in rr: prog into midfield 1/2-way: wknd rapidly over 3f out: eased over 2f out: wl t.o* **20/1**	
4/-0	**11**	*10*	**Ocean's Minstrel**[8] 6600 6-9-10 **86** AdamKirby 9 (John Ryan) *hld up in last trio: detached fr 1/2-way: no prog 4f out: eased 2f out: wl t.o* **8/1**	

3m 38.34s (9.34) **Going Correction** +0.75s/f (Yiel)
WFA 3 from 4yo+ 11lb **11** Ran SP% **118.5**
Speed ratings (Par 107): **106,105,102,101,100 100,95,81,79,50 45**
toteswingers:1&2 £4.70, 2&3 £21.30, 1&3 £22.40 CSF £20.16 CT £262.16 TOTE £4.80: £1.90, £2.00, £5.70; EX 17.90 Trifecta £331.50 Pool: £1,989.30 - 4.44 winning tickets..
Owner Newsells Park Stud **Bred** Newsells Park Stud **Trained** Middleham Moor, N Yorks

FOCUS
This looked a competitive staying handicap, but underfoot conditions played a big part and the first pair came well clear as most toiled on the surface. The form is not taken too literally given the ground and could well underestimate the winner.

NOTEBOOK
Red Orator bumped into a progressive winner at Hamilton when back to form 12 days earlier and, off the same mark, deservedly went one better on ground that suits. His two below-par efforts this year have come on AW (albeit he is a Polytrack winner) and this dour stayer still should be capable of further improvement when faced with a real test, as all he does is gallop. He looks one for marathon handicaps next season, in particular the Ascot Stakes over 2m4f at the Royal Meeting. (tchd 5-1)
Ardlui(IRE) ◆ sprung back to life when second at Chester 21 days earlier to Countrywide Flame, the current ante-post favourite for the Cesarewich next week. Off a 3lb higher mark, he proved the only possible danger to the winner off the home turn, despite looking all at sea on the ground and this was another rock-solid display. Another rise is now forthcoming, but he can surely be found an opening before reverting to hurdles later on. Indeed, there could well be a decent handicap to be won with him in that sphere at around 2m4f. (op 9-2 tchd 5-1)
First Avenue was keen early and taken back. He was finished all too late in the home straight and, while this was better again, his losing run continues. (tchd 16-1 and 20-1)
Somemothersdohavem, up in class, was immediately dropped in from his wide draw and ultimately got too far back to land a serious blow. He may have more to offer back on Polytrack. (op 20-1)
Woolfall Treasure goes well at this course. His best form is on better ground, but he is another that's hard to win with. Official explanation: jockey said, regarding appearing to have stopped riding final 1/2f, that he had become very tired and had suffered cramp in his legs; medical officer confirmed his condition.
Flashman raced handily, but dropped out under pressure and couldn't handle the ground. He can do better yet when reverting to a kinder surface and it will be interesting to see if he's sent over hurdles later on. (op 5-1)
Orsippus(USA) Official explanation: jockey said gelding suffered interference in running

6835 PWC H'CAP 6f
5:15 (5:18) (Class 2) (0-105,101) 3-Y-0
£12,450 (£3,728; £1,864; £932; £466; £234) **Stalls** Centre

Form				RPR
2623	**1**		**Gabriel's Lad (IRE)**[26] 6075 3-8-10 **90** KierenFallon 4 (Denis Coakley) *pressed overall ldr in centre: rdn to ld 2f out: at least 2 l clr 1f out: drvn out* **9/2**[1]	100+
1131	**2**	*¾*	**Khubala (IRE)**[42] 5530 3-8-9 **89**(b) FrankieDettori 14 (Ed Dunlop) *hld up in last pair in centre: gd prog over 1f out: r.o to take 2nd ins fnl f: clsd on wnr fin* **5/1**[2]	97
4505	**3**	*1 ¼*	**Hurry Up George**[26] 6075 3-9-1 **95** JimCrowley 7 (Ralph Beckett) *trckd ldrs in centre: rdn 2f out: prog whn n.m.r over 1f out: styd on fnl f: nvr able to chal* **10/1**	99
6121	**4**	*¾*	**Signor Sassi**[15] 6417 3-8-3 **83** AndreaAtzeni 15 (Roger Varian) *trckd ldr nr side but nt on terms: moved over to main gp over 2f out: drvn to dispute 2nd briefly 1f out: one pce* **17/2**	85+
0126	**5**	*1*	**Duke Of Firenze**[21] 6201 3-8-13 **93** RyanMoore 13 (Sir Michael Stoute) *hld up in midfield in centre: rdn and prog 2f out: disp 2nd briefly 1f out: one pce* **11/2**[3]	91
35-0	**6**	*½*	**Magic City (IRE)**[23] 6143 3-8-4 **84** KieranO'Neill 2 (Richard Hannon) *swvd rt s: sn prom in centre: rdn and nt qckn over 1f out: one pce* **16/1**	81
4540	**7**	*¾*	**Mehdi (IRE)**[27] 6024 3-8-13 **93**(t) JimmyFortune 18 (Brian Meehan) *chsd ldng pair nr side: lft in ld of only other rival over 2f out: nvr on terms: kpt on* **12/1**	87
5303	**8**	*nk*	**Charlotte Rosina**[11] 6536 3-8-7 **87** PaulHanagan 9 (Roger Teal) *overall ldr in centre to 2f out: wknd fnl f* **16/1**	80
400U	**9**	*2 ½*	**West Leake Diman (IRE)**[21] 6201 3-9-7 **101** DaneO'Neill 16 (Charles Hills) *racd nr side: a last of gp and nvr on terms: no ch fnl 2f* **66/1**	86
00	**10**	*4 ½*	**Vocational (USA)**[97] 3641 3-9-0 **94** JoeFanning 12 (Mark Johnston) *hld up in last trio of centre gp: rdn and modest prog over 1f out: sn wknd* **40/1**	65
0201	**11**	*½*	**Born To Surprise**[23] 6143 3-9-3 **97** JamieSpencer 10 (Michael Bell) *s.s: hld up in last of main gp in centre: shkn up 2f out: no real prog over 1f out: sn wknd* **5/1**[2]	66
0046	**12**	*nk*	**Eastern Sun (IRE)**[50] 5271 3-9-2 **96**(b[1]) RobertHavlin 11 (John Gosden) *a towards rr of main gp in centre: wknd over 2f out* **25/1**	64
1000	**13**	*2*	**Ewell Place (IRE)**[11] 6536 3-9-1 **95**(b[1]) TomQueally 8 (Robert Mills) *prom in centre gp: wknd rapidly jst over 2f out* **40/1**	57
0302	**14**	*1 ¾*	**Poole Harbour (IRE)**[11] 6536 3-8-8 **88** KirstyMilczarek 17 (Richard Hannon) *led nr side quartet but nt on terms: drifted across to centre over 2f out: sn wknd qckly* **12/1**	44

1m 15.15s (0.65) **Going Correction** +0.35s/f (Good) **14** Ran SP% **123.9**
Speed ratings (Par 107): **109,108,106,105,104 103,102,101,98,92 91,91,88,86**
toteswingers:1&2 £6.00, 2&3 £12.40, 1&3 £12.10 CSF £26.60 CT £228.07 TOTE £5.70: £2.10, £2.00, £3.50; EX 28.70 Trifecta £295.10 Pool: £3,178.84 - 7.97 winning tickets..
Owner Killoran Ennis Conway **Bred** Yeomanstown Stud **Trained** West Ilsley, Berks

FOCUS
A decent 3yo sprint handicap, but it developed into something of a messy race with four keeping stands' side early on and the field covering plenty of the track inside the final 2f. The winner posted a 5lb personal best and this could underestimate him.

NOTEBOOK
Gabriel's Lad(IRE) deservedly resumed winning ways under a positive ride and landed some decent bets in the process. He was always well placed down the centre and saw it out strongly once asked to seal the race. He had placed three times in four outings since a comeback win on the AW and this has to rate a career-best effort. With scope to progress physically, he could land a decent pot as a 4yo next year as he's versatile regards ground. (op 5-1 tchd 11-2)
Khubala(IRE) arrived having won four of his six outings since resuming at three and was fancied to go in again. Up 5lb for winning on soft at Ffos Las in August, he did best of those coming from off the pace and stayed on strongly once switched near side for his challenge. He remains progressive. (op 9-2)
Hurry Up George ran an honest race and ran close to his previous level, rating a solid benchmark for the form. He deserves to win again, but looks held by the handicapper. (op 12-1)
Signor Sassi ◆ still looked well treated despite a 5lb rise for his Yarmouth success 15 days earlier. He moved sweetly into contention, but found himself all alone when coming clear of the stands' side group and is really better than the bare form. The ground was also softer than he cares for and he remains one to follow. (op 8-1 tchd 9-1)
Duke Of Firenze, giving Ryan Moore a first ride back from injury, had his chance yet probably got found out by the ground late on. (op 5-1)
Magic City(IRE) was keeping on too late towards the far side, but this was a step back in the right direction and he's on a workable mark. (op 14-1)
Born To Surprise proved easy to back off a 5lb higher mark and didn't look nearly so effective dropped to a sprint trip. He probably needs all to fall just right, though. (tchd 9-2 and 11-2)
Poole Harbour(IRE) Official explanation: trainer's rep said clolt was unsuited by the soft ground
T/Jkpt: Not won. T/Plt: £72.60 to a £1 stake. Pool: £134,804.14 - 1,353.61 winning tickets.
T/Qpdt: £5.30 to a £1 stake. Pool: £10,650.91 - 1,479.32 winning tickets. JN

6822 WOLVERHAMPTON (A.W) (L-H)
Friday, October 5

OFFICIAL GOING: Standard
Wind: Light half-behind Weather: Cloudy

6836 32RED H'CAP 5f 20y(P)
5:45 (5:45) (Class 6) (0-60,60) 3-Y-0+ **£1,704** (£503; £251) **Stalls** Low

Form				RPR
5432	**1**		**Gran Canaria Queen**[6] 6686 3-8-7 **53**(v) GeorgeChaloner(7) 13 (Ian Semple) *a.p: led over 1f out: styd on* **8/1**	64
0460	**2**	*¾*	**Speedyfix**[13] 6496 5-9-0 **53**(t) TomMcLaughlin 3 (Christine Dunnett) *hld up: hdwy over 1f out: r.o: nt rch wnr* **9/1**	61
6006	**3**	*2 ¼*	**Ballinargh Girl (IRE)**[22] 6179 4-9-6 **59**(b) JamesSullivan 8 (Danielle McCormick) *a.p: chsd ldr over 3f out: rdn over 1f out: styd on same pce ins fnl f* **14/1**	59
5250	**4**	*hd*	**Loyal Royal (IRE)**[28] 6003 9-9-4 **57**(bt) GrahamLee 5 (Milton Bradley) *hld up: hdwy over 1f out: r.o: nt rch ldrs* **20/1**	56
0000	**5**	*½*	**Mr Optimistic**[16] 6370 4-9-2 **60**(t) AshleyMorgan(5) 9 (Pat Murphy) *chsd ldrs: rdn over 1f out: styd on same pce fnl f* **12/1**	58
0455	**6**	*½*	**Liberal Lady**[10] 6563 4-9-1 **59**(e) MichaelJMMurphy(5) 2 (Ralph Smith) *hld up: hdwy over 1f out: sn rdn: no ex ins fnl f* **6/1**[2]	55
6204	**7**	*¾*	**Ballarina**[20] 6264 6-9-1 **54** KellyHarrison 6 (Eric Alston) *led: rdn and hdd over 1f out: no ex ins fnl f: n.m.r towards fin* **7/1**[3]	47
3500	**8**	*½*	**Almaty Express**[22] 6178 10-8-12 **56**(b) DarrenEgan(5) 4 (John Weymes) *prom: pushed along 1/2-way: wknd ins fnl f* **8/1**	47
200	**9**	*nk*	**Ghazeer (IRE)**[51] 5247 3-9-6 **59**(v) MartinDwyer 11 (Derek Shaw) *outpcd: drvn along 1/2-way: r.o ins fnl f: nvr nrr* **12/1**	49
4011	**10**	*nk*	**Sally's Swansong**[13] 6496 6-9-5 **58**(b) DavidAllan 7 (Eric Alston) *hld up: rdn over 1f out: nvr on terms* **5/1**[1]	47
1000	**11**	*2*	**Emma Jean (IRE)**[13] 6500 3-8-12 **54** SophieDoyle(3) 10 (Frank Sheridan) *s.i.s: outpcd* **40/1**	36
6220	**12**	*½*	**Funcheon Vale (IRE)**[45] 5445 3-9-7 **60** NickyMackay 1 (Hughie Morrison) *chsd ldrs: rdn 2f out: wknd and eased fnl f* **8/1**	40

1m 1.33s (-0.97) **Going Correction** -0.175s/f (Stan) **12** Ran SP% **116.0**
Speed ratings (Par 101): **100,98,95,94,94 93,92,91,90,90 87,86**
toteswingers 1&2 £11.50, 2&3 £19.50, 1&3 £20.50 CSF £76.43 CT £1008.37 TOTE £8.60: £2.00, £4.00, £4.60; EX 101.60 Trifecta £367.00 Part won. Pool: £495.97 - 0.62 winning tickets..
Owner M Gillies **Bred** H Moszkowicz And Whitsbury Manor Stud **Trained** Carluke, S Lanarks

FOCUS
A moderate sprint handicap. The pace was on from the outset. Improvement again from the winner back at 5f.

Sally's Swansong Official explanation: jockey said mare suffered interference in running

6837 RINGSIDE CONFERENCE SUITE - 700 THEATRE STYLE CLAIMING STKS 5f 216y(P)

6:15 (6:15) (Class 6) 3-Y-0+ **£1,704** (£503; £251) **Stalls** Low

Form RPR

0506 **1** **Red Cape (FR)**16 6358 9-8-9 68..............................(b) JamesSullivan 11 74
(Ruth Carr) *w ldr tl led wl over 1f out: rdn and hung lft ins fnl f: jst hld on* **25/1**

0206 **2** *nk* **Noverre To Go (IRE)**6 6688 6-9-4 85.......................... DarrenEgan(5) 6 87+
(Ronald Harris) *hld up: hdwy over 1f out: rdn and r.o wl ins fnl f: nt quite rch wnr: too much to do* **5/2**1

3230 **3** *shd* **Beat The Bell**23 6150 7-8-5 71..................................(p) MartinDwyer 12 69
(Jamie Osborne) *dwlt: hdwy over 3f out: rdn over 1f out: edgd lft ins fnl f: r.o* **17/2**3

-400 **4** *1 1/2* **Alaskan Bullet (IRE)**27 6026 3-9-4 86.............................. MartinLane 8 78
(Michael Bell) *hld up in tch: plld hrd: rdn over 1f out: styd on* **4/1**2

4604 **5** *shd* **Mister Musicmaster**19 6285 3-9-4 74.......................... JamesMillman 9 78
(Rod Millman) *hld up: rdn and r.o wl ins fnl f: nt rch ldrs* **10/1**

4061 **6** *1 3/4* **Efistorm**9 6577 11-8-10 63.................................. MichaelJMMurphy(5) 10 68
(Joseph Tuite) *prom: rdn over 2f out: styd on* **12/1**

4043 **7** *1/2* **Courageous (IRE)**8 6610 6-8-13 74..........................(tp) GrahamLee 13 64
(Milton Bradley) *hld up: plld hrd: rdn over 1f out: nvr on terms* **4/1**2

4503 **8** *3/4* **Rulesn'regulations**11 6546 6-9-9 83.............................. PatCosgrave 1 72
(Matthew Salaman) *chsd ldrs: rdn over 2f out: styd on same pce fr over 1f out* **20/1**

5120 **9** *1* **Ansells Pride (IRE)**23 6150 9-8-2 65..........................(p) JakePayne(7) 3 55
(Bill Turner) *led: rdn and hdd wl over 1f out: wknd ins fnl f* **16/1**

460 **10** *1 3/4* **Katy's Secret**81 4143 5-8-3 66................................ ShirleyTeasdale(7) 5 50
(William Jarvis) *s.i.s: outpcd* **25/1**

00 **11** *1* **Vale Of Clara (IRE)**15 6406 4-9-0 80................................ TomEaves 4 51
(Peter Niven) *hld up: rdn over 1f out: n.d* **40/1**

3400 **12** *2 3/4* **Irish Boy (IRE)**16 6357 4-8-12 62.................................(v) NedCurtis(7) 2 47
(Paul Midgley) *mid-div: rdn over 2f out: wknd over 1f out* **40/1**

2000 **13** *1/2* **Speightowns Kid (USA)**6 6688 4-8-12 71.. WilliamTwiston-Davies(7) 7 46
(Jeremy Gask) *chsd ldrs: rdn over 2f out: wknd over 1f out* **50/1**

1m 13.69s (-1.31) **Going Correction** -0.175s/f (Stan)
WFA 3 from 4yo+ 1lb **13** Ran SP% **121.1**
Speed ratings (Par 101): **101,100,100,98,98 96,95,94,93,90 89,85,85**
toteswingers 1&2 £25.90, 2&3 £4.00, 1&3 £24.80 CSF £83.92 TOTE £35.70: £8.00, £2.90, £3.30; EX 110.40 Trifecta £460.60 Part won. Pool: £622.46 - 0.10 winning tickets..There were no claims.
Owner Middleham Park Racing LVI **Bred** Gilles And Mrs Forien **Trained** Huby, N Yorks

FOCUS
A decent claimer. The winner bounced back from some lesser turf efforts.

6838 32RED.COM H'CAP 1m 5f 194y(P)

6:45 (6:45) (Class 6) (0-65,65) 3-Y-0+ **£1,704** (£503; £251) **Stalls** Low

Form RPR

0252 **1** **Vexillum (IRE)**12 6516 3-9-4 **64**...................................... SamHitchcott 13 73
(Mick Channon) *hld up: hdwy over 1f out: styd on u.p to ld post* **9/2**2

4204 **2** *nk* **Jalors (IRE)**25 6098 4-9-7 **63**.. DarrenEgan(5) 3 72
(Ronald Harris) *chsd ldrs: led over 1f out: rdn ins fnl f: hdd post* **7/1**

4233 **3** *2 1/4* **White Deer (USA)**18 6323 8-9-3 **54**..........................(v) RoystonFfrench 12 60
(Geoffrey Harker) *hld up: hdwy over 3f out: rdn over 1f out: styd on same pce ins fnl f* **10/1**

0005 **4** *1 3/4* **El Libertador (USA)**8 6616 6-9-7 **58**..............................(b) GrahamLee 5 61
(Eric Wheeler) *hld up: rdn and r.o ins fnl f: nt rch ldrs* **20/1**

0642 **5** *3/4* **Merchants Return**18 6323 3-8-3 **52**..........................(v) SimonPearce(3) 8 54
(Lydia Pearce) *hld up: hdwy over 1f out: sn rdn: styd on same pce fnl f* **6/1**

6255 **6** *1 1/4* **Brouhaha**67 4639 8-10-0 **65**...................................... RichardKingscote 11 66
(Tom Dascombe) *led: rdn and hdd over 1f out: no ex fnl f* **5/1**3

03-0 **7** *1 1/4* **Alubari**22 6184 5-9-5 **56**.. PaulMulrennan 10 55
(Adrian McGuinness, Ire) *prom: racd keenly: chsd ldr over 2f out: sn rdn: wknd ins fnl f* **14/1**

0366 **8** *2 1/4* **Gavi**20 6230 6-9-5 **56**.. TomMcLaughlin 4 52
(Karen George) *s.i.s: hld up: rdn over 1f out: nvr on terms* **20/1**

4554 **9** *2 1/4* **Nesnaas (USA)**3 6769 11-8-9 **46** oh1.................... FrankieMcDonald 7 39
(Alastair Lidderdale) *hld up: rdn over 3f out: n.d* **40/1**

4046 **10** *nk* **Eanans Bay (IRE)**74 4399 3-8-7 **53**................................... TomEaves 9 45
(Mark H Tompkins) *chsd ldr 10f: sn rdn: wknd over 1f out* **7/2**1

4105 **11** *3/4* **Corvette**32 5891 4-9-10 **61**.. LiamKeniry 6 52
(Michael Appleby) *chsd ldrs: wnt 2nd 4f out tl rdn over 2f out: wknd fnl f* **14/1**

3m 3.06s (-2.94) **Going Correction** -0.175s/f (Stan)
WFA 3 from 4yo+ 9lb **11** Ran SP% **118.2**
Speed ratings (Par 101): **101,100,99,98,98 97,96,95,94,93 93**
toteswingers 1&2 £8.80, 2&3 £11.50, 1&3 £4.90 CSF £35.33 CT £302.94 TOTE £5.70: £2.40, £2.80, £2.30; EX 45.20 Trifecta £421.40 Pool: £694.80 - 1.22 winning tickets..
Owner Insignia Racing (Roundel) **Bred** Rathasker Stud **Trained** West Ilsley, Berks

FOCUS
A modest staying handicap in which they went off at a decent gallop. Sound form.

6839 32RED CASINO MAIDEN STKS 1m 5f 194y(P)

7:15 (7:16) (Class 5) 3-Y-0+ **£2,264** (£673; £336; £168) **Stalls** Low

Form RPR

4320 **1** **Openly**15 6416 3-8-12 77.. EddieAhern 3 85
(James Fanshawe) *chsd ldrs: led over 1f out: sn rdn: styd on wl* **9/2**3

4564 **2** *2* **Sash Of Honour (IRE)**71 4515 3-9-3 82..........................(b1) TomEaves 5 87
(Sir Michael Stoute) *hld up in tch: chsd wnr over 1f out: sn rdn and ev ch: hung rt 1f out: styd on same pce* **4/1**2

43 **3** *nk* **Maun Vrat (IRE)**23 6148 3-8-12 0................................ PhillipMakin 8 82
(Ed Dunlop) *hld up: hdwy over 2f out: rdn over 1f out: styd on* **10/1**

-345 **4** *4 1/2* **Toptempo**55 5105 3-8-12 80.. TedDurcan 6 74
(Mark H Tompkins) *prom: rdn over 3f out: styd on same pce fr over 1f out* **8/1**

222 **5** *2* **Altaria**44 5477 3-8-12 79.. PaulMulrennan 10 71
(Amanda Perrett) *led: rdn and hdd over 1f out: wknd ins fnl f* **8/1**

34 **6** *7* **Perfect Heart**37 5753 3-9-3 0.. NickyMackay 9 65
(John Gosden) *hld up: rdn over 3f out: sme hdwy over 1f out: eased ins fnl f* **9/4**1

4 **7** *8* **All That Remains (IRE)**8 6614 7-9-9 0...................... PaulPickard(3) 13 52
(Brian Ellison) *prom: rdn over 3f out: wknd over 1f out* **50/1**

4 **8** *4* **Hail To The Chief (FR)**8 6615 4-9-12 83......................(t) GrahamLee 1 46
(Ed Dunlop) *chsd ldrs: wnt 2nd over 3f out tl rdn over 2f out: wknd over 1f out* **10/1**

9 *7* **Oscar Prairie (IRE)**12 7-9-12 0...................................... MartinLane 11 35
(Warren Greatrex) *chsd ldr tl rdn over 3f out: sn wknd: t.o* **20/1**

10 *16* **No Diamond**61 5-9-12 0.. LiamKeniry 12
(Michael Appleby) *s.i.s: hdwy over 7f out: rdn and wknd over 3f out: t.o* **250/1**

0 **11** *17* **Ghazwan (IRE)**8 6614 3-9-3 0.. SebSanders 2
(Conrad Allen) *hld up: a in rr: rdn over 5f out: bhd fnl 3f: t.o* **66/1**

3m 1.06s (-4.94) **Going Correction** -0.175s/f (Stan)
WFA 3 from 4yo+ 9lb **11** Ran SP% **118.0**
Speed ratings (Par 103): **107,105,105,103,101 97,93,91,87,77 68**
toteswingers 1&2 £3.80, 2&3 £5.40, 1&3 £11.10 CSF £22.55 TOTE £3.80: £1.20, £1.90, £2.70; EX 22.90 Trifecta £148.70 Pool: £721.84 - 3.59 winning tickets..
Owner J H Richmond-Watson **Bred** Lawn Stud **Trained** Newmarket, Suffolk

FOCUS
A decent staying maiden which was sound run in a reasonable time. The winner seems better on Polytrack on turf.
Perfect Heart Official explanation: jockey said colt would not face the kick-back

6840 32RED SUPPORTING BRITISH RACING H'CAP 7f 32y(P)

7:45 (7:45) (Class 5) (0-75,75) 3-Y-0 **£2,264** (£673; £336; £168) **Stalls** High

Form RPR

0023 **1** **Restaurateur (IRE)**23 6136 3-9-2 **72**..........................(b1) FrannyNorton 3 86
(Andrew Balding) *a.p: shkn up over 1f out: rdn to ld wl ins fnl f: r.o wl* **4/1**1

5030 **2** *2 1/2* **Hometown Glory**13 6488 3-9-5 **75**.................................(t) MartinLane 2 82
(Brian Meehan) *chsd ldr: rdn over 1f out: led ins fnl f: sn hdd and unable qck* **5/1**3

3052 **3** *nk* **Willies Wonder (IRE)**27 6052 3-9-0 **75**................. MatthewLawson(5) 7 81
(Charles Hills) *hld up: hdwy over 1f out: rdn ins fnl f: r.o to go 3rd post* **9/2**2

0541 **4** *shd* **Sky Crossing**15 6401 3-9-3 **73**.. GrahamLee 4 79
(James Given) *led: rdn and hdd ins fnl f: styd on same pce* **4/1**1

4664 **5** *1 1/2* **Blackdown Fair**16 6367 3-9-3 **73**................................ JamesMillman 10 75
(Rod Millman) *chsd ldrs: rdn over 1f out: no ex ins fnl f* **8/1**

1025 **6** *shd* **Bint Alzain (IRE)**16 6367 3-9-0 **75**..........................(t) DarrenEgan(5) 8 76
(Gerard Butler) *s.i.s: hld up: r.o ins fnl f: nvr nrr* **16/1**

4-64 **7** *1 3/4* **Relentless Harry (IRE)**136 2375 3-9-2 **72**...................(t) PatCosgrave 1 69
(George Baker) *s.i.s: in rr: styd on fnl f: nvr trbld ldrs* **10/1**

04 **8** *nse* **Eternal Gift (FR)**22 6169 3-9-2 **72**..............................(b1) SebSanders 12 69
(Rae Guest) *mid-div: rdn over 3f out: styd on same pce fr over 1f out* **33/1**

040 **9** *4 1/2* **Spykes Bay (USA)**60 4876 3-8-13 **72**.................... MichaelMetcalfe(3) 5 56
(Mrs K Burke) *chsd ldrs: rdn over 2f out: wknd ins fnl f* **12/1**

0600 **10** *2 1/2* **Imelda Mayhem**45 5457 3-9-0 **75**.......................... RachealKneller(5) 11 53
(J S Moore) *s.i.s: a in rr* **50/1**

1-0 **11** *3* **Slewtoo**110 1985 3-9-2 **72**.. JamesSullivan 9 42
(Michael Easterby) *s.i.s: a in rr* **33/1**

1m 27.56s (-2.04) **Going Correction** -0.175s/f (Stan) **11** Ran SP% **116.5**
Speed ratings (Par 101): **104,101,100,100,98 98,96,96,91,88 85**
toteswingers 1&2 £4.40, 2&3 £6.20, 1&3 £3.80 CSF £23.35 CT £93.61 TOTE £5.00: £2.00, £1.60, £2.40; EX 23.90 Trifecta £146.10 Pool: £440.48 - 2.23 winning tickets..
Owner Brook Farm Bloodstock **Bred** Glashare House Stud **Trained** Kingsclere, Hants

FOCUS
A fair 3yo handicap and the winning time looks good for the grade. Solid form, with a clear personal best from the winner.

6841 DOWNLOAD OUR IPHONE APP MAIDEN AUCTION STKS 1m 141y(P)

8:15 (8:16) (Class 5) 2-Y-0 **£2,264** (£673; £336; £168) **Stalls** Low

Form RPR

503 **1** **Pinarius (IRE)**18 6301 2-9-0 70..................................(v1) MartinLane 10 75
(Brian Meehan) *mde virtually all: rdn over 1f out: r.o wl* **13/2**2

002 **2** *2 1/4* **Sunblazer (IRE)**13 6501 2-8-13 79.............................. MartinDwyer 7 69
(William Muir) *a.p: chsd wnr over 5f out: rdn over 1f out: r.o* **2/1**1

05 **3** *2 1/4* **Lucky Black Star (IRE)**35 5784 2-8-13 0...................... PatCosgrave 9 64
(George Baker) *chsd wnr tl over 5f out: remained handy: rdn over 1f out: styd on same pce ins fnl f* **33/1**

0560 **4** *1 1/4* **Sakhee's Ichigou**44 5484 2-8-4 52............................... NickyMackay 4 53
(Michael Blanshard) *chsd ldrs: rdn over 1f out: styd on same pce* **50/1**

05 **5** *1 1/4* **Unison (IRE)**11 6533 2-8-12 0 ow1.............................. SebSanders 12 58
(Peter Makin) *hld up: racd keenly: hdwy over 3f out: rdn over 2f out: styd on same pce fr over 1f out* **8/1**3

50 **6** *nk* **Pairumani Prince (IRE)**22 6175 2-8-9 0........................ GrahamLee 11 54
(Ed Dunlop) *hld up: rdn over 3f out: styd on ins fnl f: nvr nrr* **9/1**

42 **7** *1/2* **Poor Duke (IRE)**58 4967 2-8-11 0............................ FergusSweeney 1 55
(Jamie Osborne) *mid-div: rdn over 2f out: no imp fnl f* **2/1**1

8 *hd* **Inessa Armand (IRE)** 2-8-6 0...................................... LiamJones 5 50
(J S Moore) *mid-div: rdn over 3f out: outpcd fr over 2f out* **20/1**

5 **9** *2 1/2* **Terpsichore**28 5997 2-8-1 0.. RyanPowell(3) 3 43
(Sylvester Kirk) *s.i.s: a in rr* **33/1**

0 **10** *nk* **Rock Diamond (IRE)**28 5997 2-8-6 0............................ FrannyNorton 8 44
(Sylvester Kirk) *chsd ldrs: rdn over 2f out: wknd over 1f out* **40/1**

05 **11** *3/4* **Senator Sam (IRE)**16 6356 2-8-12 0............................ PJMcDonald 6 48
(Ann Duffield) *hld up: rdn over 3f out: a in rr* **18/1**

000 **12** *13* **Indies Gold**24 6122 2-8-10 36..................................(v1) PaulMulrennan 2 19
(Ann Duffield) *hld up: rdn over 3f out: wknd over 2f out* **100/1**

1m 51.09s (0.59) **Going Correction** -0.175s/f (Stan) **12** Ran SP% **122.4**
Speed ratings (Par 95): **90,88,86,84,83 83,83,82,80,80 79,68**
toteswingers 1&2 £2.50, 2&3 £27.00, 1&3 £28.60 CSF £19.61 TOTE £13.20: £2.10, £1.10, £14.90; EX 21.00 Trifecta £190.90 Pool: £415.42 - 1.61 winning tickets..
Owner KSB Bloodstock & Sam Sangster **Bred** W P Iceton **Trained** Manton, Wilts
■ Stewards' Enquiry : Nicky Mackay two-day ban: careless riding (Oct 19,21)

FOCUS
Just a fair juvenile auction maiden. The fourth highlights the limitations of the form.

NOTEBOOK
Pinarius(IRE) was racing in a first-time visor and benefited from a tactically astute, and strong-in-the-finish, front-running ride from Martin Lane, who kicked on at just the right time rounding the bend for home. He arrived with a BHA rating of 70, after a peak 3l third of five over 7f on good to firm ground at Brighton the previous month. He appreciated this extended 1m trip on Polytrack and looks a fair handicapper under these conditions, and no more. (op 15-2 tchd 8-1 and 6-1)
Sunblazer(IRE), in second, gives the form fair substance. He finished runner-up over this C&D in a similar contest the previous month and has reproduced a similar level of form. A BHA rating of 79 appears slightly flattering, though. (tchd 15-8 and 9-4)
Lucky Black Star(IRE) recorded his best form here, stepping up in trip on his third start.
Sakhee's Ichigou holds down the level of form in fourth but may prove competitive in modest handicap company after this peak display. (op 40-1)

Pairumani Prince(IRE), who looked well, may appreciate further. (tchd 12-1)
Poor Duke(IRE) failed to get into this contest in a meaningful manner. (op 5-2)

6842 £32 BONUS AT 32RED.COM H'CAP (DIV I) 1m 1f 103y(P)
8:45 (8:46) (Class 5) (0-75,75) 3-Y-0+ **£2,264** (£673; £336; £168) **Stalls** Low

Form RPR

0542 **1** **Miss Dashwood**[15] 6401 3-9-3 **72** .... EddieAhern 7 80+
(James Fanshawe) *trckd ldrs: led over 1f out: rdn out* **15/8**[1]

6140 **2** *1* **Charitable Act (FR)**[16] 6376 3-9-6 **75** .... PhillipMakin 4 81
(William Muir) *led: hdd over 7f out: chsd ldrs: rdn over 1f out: r.o* **10/1**

053 **3** *nk* **Rawaafed (IRE)**[21] 6215 3-9-4 **73** .... MartinLane 10 78
(Brian Meehan) *chsd ldr tl led over 5f out: rdn and hdd over 1f out: styd on* **13/2**[3]

1033 **4** *nk* **Bold Cross (IRE)**[14] 6458 9-8-7 **65** .... ThomasBrown(7) 2 69
(Edward Bevan) *hld up: hdwy over 2f out: rdn over 1f out: styd on* **12/1**

4450 **5** *1 ¾* **Eponastone (IRE)**[21] 6207 3-8-8 **68** .... DarrenEgan(5) 5 69
(Gerard Butler) *hld up in tch: shkn up over 1f out: styd on* **16/1**

302 **6** *2* **Badea**[7] 6631 3-8-11 **66** ....(v) GrahamLee 8 62
(Richard Fahey) *led over 7f out: hdd over 5f out: chsd ldr: rdn over 2f out: wknd ins fnl f* **10/3**[2]

1031 **7** *4* **Resplendent Alpha**[136] 2364 8-9-0 **65** .... FergusSweeney 9 53
(Jamie Osborne) *s.i.s: hld up: rdn over 2f out: n.d* **25/1**

-256 **8** *3* **Isthmus**[32] 5889 3-9-3 **72** .... PaulMulrennan 3 54
(Amanda Perrett) *chsd ldrs: rdn over 3f out: wknd over 1f out* **13/2**[3]

0006 **9** *¾* **Ivor's Princess**[16] 6367 3-9-5 **74** .... JamesMillman 1 54
(Rod Millman) *hld up: a in rr: wknd over 2f out* **40/1**

1m 59.61s (-2.09) **Going Correction** -0.175s/f (Stan)
WFA 3 from 8yo+ 4lb 9 Ran SP% **113.5**
Speed ratings (Par 103): **102,101,100,100,99 97,93,91,90**
toteswingers 1&2 £5.50, 2&3 £14.80, 1&3 £4.20 CSF £21.63 CT £100.86 TOTE £2.00: £1.02, £4.80, £2.50; EX 29.50 Trifecta £32.60 Pool: £382.02 - 8.65 winning tickets..
Owner Helena Springfield Ltd **Bred** Meon Valley Stud **Trained** Newmarket, Suffolk

FOCUS
The first division of a fair handicap. The winning time compared favourably with the second instalment and the form looks sound. There's more to come from the winner.
Isthmus Official explanation: jockey said colt stopped quickly

6843 £32 BONUS AT 32RED.COM H'CAP (DIV II) 1m 1f 103y(P)
9:15 (9:15) (Class 5) (0-75,75) 3-Y-0+ **£2,264** (£673; £336; £168) **Stalls** Low

Form RPR

1312 **1** **Tis Rock 'N' Roll (USA)**[72] 4466 3-9-6 **75** .... TedDurcan 1 84+
(David Lanigan) *chsd ldrs: rdn to ld over 1f out: jst hld on* **15/8**[1]

6300 **2** *hd* **Switchback**[17] 6342 4-9-3 **68** .... PaulMulrennan 10 76
(Michael Easterby) *led 1f: chsd ldrs: rdn over 1f out: r.o* **10/1**

3202 **3** *1 ½* **Ishikawa (IRE)**[24] 6120 4-9-0 **65** .... FergusSweeney 6 70
(Alan King) *hld up: rdn over 2f out: edgd lft and r.o ins fnl f: nt rch ldrs* **5/1**[2]

20 **4** *½* **Sarmatian Knight (IRE)**[71] 4498 3-9-1 **70** .... TonyHamilton 9 74+
(Ian Williams) *hld up: rdn and r.o ins fnl f: nrst fin* **6/1**[3]

4236 **5** *½* **Cyrus Sod**[78] 4254 3-9-4 **73** .... GrahamLee 4 76
(Ed Dunlop) *a.p: rdn over 2f out: styd on* **7/1**

2341 **6** *2 ½* **Siouxperhero (IRE)**[22] 6169 3-9-2 **71** ....(b) MartinDwyer 8 69
(William Muir) *chsd ldrs: rdn over 2f out: styng on same pce whn hmpd ins fnl f* **9/1**

433/ **7** *1 ¾* **Murfreesboro**[74] 171 9-9-0 **65** .... SebSanders 2 59
(Alan Jones) *prom: rdn over 1f out: wknd ins fnl f* **25/1**

150U **8** *½* **Hikma (USA)**[18] 6315 3-9-2 **71** ....(v) FrannyNorton 7 64
(Mark Johnston) *s.i.s: hld up: rdn over 2f out: wknd ins fnl f* **10/1**

0000 **9** *½* **Mistress Shy**[14] 6457 5-8-3 **61** oh16 ....(t) NoelGarbutt(7) 5 53?
(Michael Appleby) *hld up: rdn over 2f out: wknd fnl f* **100/1**

6060 **10** *7* **Whitechapel**[46] 5427 5-8-4 **62** .... DanielMuscutt(7) 3 39
(Keith Goldsworthy) *led over 8f out: rdn and hdd over 1f out: wknd fnl f* **25/1**

2m 0.58s (-1.12) **Going Correction** -0.175s/f (Stan)
WFA 3 from 4yo+ 4lb 10 Ran SP% **115.1**
Speed ratings (Par 103): **97,96,95,95,94 92,90,90,89,83**
toteswingers 1&2 £7.00, 2&3 £8.80, 1&3 £3.20 CSF £21.44 CT £81.92 TOTE £2.30: £1.10, £6.20, £2.10; EX 23.90 Trifecta £124.40 Pool: £321.26 - 1.91 winning tickets..
Owner Catesby W Clay **Bred** Runnymede Farm Inc **Trained** Upper Lambourn, Berks
■ Stewards' Enquiry : Graham Lee caution: careless riding.

FOCUS
The second division of a fair handicap. The winning time was around a second slower than the first instalment. The form makes a fair bit of sense on paper.
T/Plt: £258.70 to a £1 stake. Pool: £75,113.80 - 211.90 winning tickets. T/Qpdt: £20.10 to a £1 stake. Pool: £10,194.24 - 375.10 winning tickets. CR

6411 YARMOUTH (L-H)
Friday, October 5

OFFICIAL GOING: Heavy (5.6)
Wind: fresh,across Weather: dry and breezy

6844 GREAT YARMOUTH TOURIST AUTHORITY MAIDEN AUCTION STKS 1m 3y
12:00 (12:00) (Class 6) 2-Y-0 **£2,045** (£603; £302) **Stalls** Centre

Form RPR

0 **1** **Mandy's Boy (IRE)**[7] 6636 2-8-13 0 .... TomMcLaughlin 4 77+
(Ed Dunlop) *dwlt: in tch in last pair: hdwy to chse ldr 2f out: rdn and ev ch 1f out: led ins fnl f: styd on wl* **9/2**

2 *2 ¼* **Too Difficult (IRE)** 2-8-8 0 ....[1] JamieSpencer 6 67
(Andrew Balding) *s.i.s: sn chsng ldrs: hdwy to ld ent fnl 2f: edgd lft u.p over 1f out: hdd and one pce ins fnl f* **11/4**[2]

3 *2 ¾* **Dude Alert (IRE)** 2-8-11 0 .... RichardMullen 9 64
(Peter Chapple-Hyam) *dwlt: in tch in rr: rdn over 3f out: edging lft and hdwy 2f out: chsd ldng pair jst over 1f out: no imp fnl f* **7/2**[3]

0 **4** *½* **Divine Angel (IRE)**[73] 4433 2-8-8 0 .... LukeMorris 2 60
(Phil McEntee) *chsd ldr: rdn 1/2-way: 4th and outpcd over 1f out: flashed tail u.p but plugged on ins fnl f* **50/1**

0 **5** *2 ½* **Vandross (IRE)**[136] 2376 2-9-0 0 ....(b[1]) FrannyNorton 5 60
(Chris Wall) *chsd ldrs: rdn over 3f out: lost pl and bhd 2f out: n.d but plugged on again ins fnl f* **12/1**

5 **6** *3* **Loucal**[31] 5912 2-8-11 0 .... JimmyQuinn 8 51
(Noel Quinlan) *t.k.h: hld up wl in tch: rdn and no hdwy over 2f out: 5th and btn over 1f out: wknd fnl f* **5/2**[1]

55 **7** *3 ½* **Belle Voir**[111] 3150 2-8-6 0 .... NickyMackay 3 38
(Gay Kelleway) *t.k.h: led tl ent fnl 2f: sn struggling and lost pl: bhd fnl f* **22/1**

1m 46.55s (5.95) **Going Correction** +0.70s/f (Yiel) 7 Ran SP% **109.6**
Speed ratings (Par 93): **98,95,93,92,90 87,83**
toteswingers: 1&2 £2.80, 2&3 £2.10, 1&3 £3.80 CSF £15.80 TOTE £6.40: £2.60, £1.70; EX 19.20.
Owner Dr Marwan Koukash **Bred** John Doyle **Trained** Newmarket, Suffolk

FOCUS
This would have been quite a test for these juveniles in the conditions and, probably with that in mind, they went no pace early.

NOTEBOOK
Mandy's Boy(IRE) had been beaten a long way on his Newmarket debut over 7f seven days earlier, but had obviously learnt from that and this was an easier task by comparison. He picked up well from off the pace and, despite being carried left by the runner-up, saw his race out nicely. He should continue to improve, but his pedigree doesn't shout stamina so this may be as far as he will want to go in a truly run race. (op 6-1 tchd 13-2 and 4-1)
Too Difficult(IRE), a 20,000euros half-sister to the useful 1m winner Royal Blue Star, had a hood on for this debut. She blew the start, but the pace was so slow that she was soon up with the leaders and she was committed for home over 2f out. However, once there she started to hang left and couldn't cope with the winner. She should improve enough to land a routine maiden. (tchd 3-1)
Dude Alert(IRE), a 9,500euros half-brother to a winning juvenile sprinter in Italy, showed signs of greenness at the back early so did well to keep on into third under difficult conditions. (op 3-1 tchd 4-1)
Divine Angel(IRE), last of 13 on her debut over 6f here in July when trained by Rae Guest, helped force the early pace but despite coming off the bridle at halfway, she didn't completely fall apart as might have been anticipated. (op 33-1)
Loucal, a staying-on fifth of ten over 7f on last month's Leicester debut, had every chance passing the 2f but emptied quickly inside the last furlong. This was disappointing and perhaps these conditions weren't for him. (op 11-4 tchd 9-4)

6845 HOLIDAY ON THE NORFOLK BROADS MAIDEN STKS (DIV I) 7f 3y
12:30 (12:32) (Class 5) 2-Y-0 **£3,234** (£962; £481; £240) **Stalls** Centre

Form RPR

223 **1** **Intimidate**[24] 6114 2-9-3 81 .... FrederikTylicki 7 79+
(Jeremy Noseda) *mde all: travelling best 2f out: sn rdn and readily drew clr: easily* **5/4**[1]

5 **2** *5* **High Troja (IRE)**[21] 6214 2-9-3 0 .... TomMcLaughlin 6 66+
(Ed Dunlop) *in tch in midfield: rdn and unable qck over 2f out: kpt on to chse clr wnr jst ins fnl f: no ch w wnr but styd on for clr 2nd* **12/1**

0 **3** *3 ½* **Duroble Man**[21] 6204 2-9-3 0 .... NeilCallan 1 57+
(Roger Varian) *chsd wnr: rdn ent fnl 2f: outpcd by wnr and btn over 1f out: lost 2nd ins fnl f: wknd but hld on for 3rd fnl 100yds* **10/1**

4 *¾* **Mazaaher** 2-9-3 0 .... GeorgeBaker 8 55+
(Marcus Tregoning) *stdd s: hld up in rr: rdn and effrt jst over 2f out: no ch w wnr and plugged on same pce fnl f* **15/2**[3]

5 *nk* **Persepolis (IRE)** 2-9-3 0 .... RichardMullen 2 54+
(Sir Michael Stoute) *t.k.h: hld up in last trio: rdn and effrt over 2f out: styd on same pce and no ch w wnr fr over 1f out* **5/1**[2]

6 *½* **Tenor (IRE)** 2-9-3 0 .... AndreaAtzeni 9 53+
(Roger Varian) *wnt rt s: chsd ldrs: rdn and unable qck over 2f out: no ch w wnr and plugged on same pce fr over 1f out* **12/1**

6 **7** *nk* **Red Pilgrim (IRE)**[15] 6412 2-9-3 0 .... JamieSpencer 5 52
(James Toller) *chsd ldrs: rdn and unable qck over 2f out: wl btn and one pce u.p fr over 1f out: eased towards fin* **10/1**

00 **8** *¾* **Alfie's Rose**[39] 5684 2-9-3 0 .... LiamJones 4 50
(William Haggas) *stdd s: hld up in last trio: no prog u.p ent fnl 2f: n.d* **50/1**

9 *10* **Red Valerian (IRE)** 2-9-3 0 .... MichaelHills 3 25
(Charles Hills) *stdd s: t.k.h: hld up in tch: hdwy 1/2-way: rdn and wknd 2f out: bhd and eased ins fnl f* **20/1**

1m 31.99s (5.39) **Going Correction** +0.70s/f (Yiel) 9 Ran SP% **113.2**
Speed ratings (Par 95): **97,91,87,86,86 85,85,84,72**
toteswingers: 1&2 £4.50, 2&3 £15.60, 1&3 £3.40 CSF £17.60 TOTE £2.10: £1.02, £3.70, £2.10; EX 13.70.
Owner Miss Yvonne Jacques **Bred** D J And Mrs Deer **Trained** Newmarket, Suffolk

FOCUS
Previous experience proved the key in this ordinary maiden. Again the early pace didn't look that strong.

NOTEBOOK
Intimidate, placed in his first four starts and officially rated 81, had never raced on soft ground before, but it proved no obstacle to him as he made every yard and bolted up. Whether he ran to his mark is hard to say, as he was the only horse in the race with a rating, but he does look well worth a try in a nursery with testing conditions obviously not a concern. (op 11-10)
High Troja(IRE) finished a staying-on fifth of 13 on his debut over the extended 1m at Wolverhampton three weeks earlier, but this drop in trip didn't seem to help even in these conditions, and he didn't click into gear until it was too late. He is one to be interested in back over further. (tchd 14-1)
Duroble Man was beaten a very long way on his Sandown debut three weeks earlier, but was still the stable's first string here on jockey bookings. He was close enough early, but found it hard to keep tabs on the winner inside the last 2f and was made to look very one-paced. (tchd 9-1 and 11-1)
Mazaaher, a half-brother to two winners over 1m to 1m2f, missed the break and sat last until making some late progress after being switched to the far side over 2f from home. He can be expected to come on a good deal for the experience. (op 8-1 tchd 6-1)
Persepolis(IRE), a 55,000gns half-brother to the useful Qushchi, a winner at up to 1m4f, made little impact from off the pace but should do better granted a stiffer test in due course. (tchd 11-2)

6846 HOLIDAY ON THE NORFOLK BROADS MAIDEN STKS (DIV II) 7f 3y
1:00 (1:02) (Class 5) 2-Y-0 **£3,234** (£962; £481; £240) **Stalls** Centre

Form RPR

4 **1** **Half A Person (IRE)**[24] 6114 2-9-3 0 .... JamieSpencer 2 83
(Peter Chapple-Hyam) *stdd s: hld up in tch in rr: hdwy 1/2-way: swtchd lft and effrt wl over 1f out: rdn to chal 1f out: hung rt but led fnl 150yds: styd on strly* **13/8**[1]

3 **2** *2 ½* **Flashlight (IRE)**[10] 6558 2-9-3 0 .... FrannyNorton 9 77
(Mark Johnston) *a.p: led over 2f out: rdn wl over 1f out: hdd and no ex fnl 150yds: kpt on* **4/1**[3]

6 **3** *2 ¼* **Jodies Jem**[15] 6411 2-9-3 0 .... AdamBeschizza 6 71
(William Jarvis) *pressed ldr: rdn and ev ch wl over 1f out: drvn and no ex 1f out: wknd fnl 100yds* **16/1**

036 **4** *6* **Lionheart**[16] 6377 2-9-0 72 .... PatrickHills(3) 8 56+
(Luca Cumani) *in tch in midfield: rdn and effrt to press ldrs wl over 1f out: edgd lft and btn 1f out: wknd fnl f* **8/1**

40 **5** *3 ¼* **Tahaf (IRE)**[126] 2662 2-9-3 0 ....(t) RobertWinston 3 48
(Clive Brittain) *t.k.h: led tl over 2f out: rdn and struggling whn squeezed for room over 1f out: sn edgd lft and wknd* **33/1**

00 **6** *1 ½* **Helamis**[11] 6533 2-8-7 0 NannaHansen(5) 7 41+
(Stuart Williams) *t.k.h: hld up in tch: rdn and struggling over 2f out: wknd 2f out* **66/1**

0 **7** *½* **Sweeping Rock (IRE)**[14] 6447 2-9-3 0 GeorgeBaker 5 43
(Marcus Tregoning) *stdd s: hld up in rr: rdn and short-lived effrt 3f out: wknd and wl btn over 1f out: eased wl ins fnl f* **25/1**

0 **8** *5* **Prince Rakan (USA)**[21] 6214 2-9-3 0 LukeMorris 4 31
(Amy Weaver) *in tch: rdn and lost pl 2f out: wl bhd over 1f out* **100/1**

9 *hd* **Putra Eton (IRE)** 2-9-3 0 NeilCallan 1 30
(Roger Varian) *chsd ldrs tl over 2f out: sn rdn and wknd: wl bhd fnl f* **11/4**[2]

1m 31.38s (4.78) **Going Correction** +0.70s/f (Yiel) **9** Ran SP% **111.0**
Speed ratings (Par 95): **100,97,94,87,84 82,81,76,75**
toteswingers: 1&2 £1.80, 2&3 £10.80, 1&3 £4.60 CSF £7.73 TOTE £2.60: £1.10, £1.50, £5.10; EX 7.40.
Owner Joseph Barton **Bred** Garry Chong **Trained** Newmarket, Suffolk

FOCUS
The winning time was 0.61 seconds faster than the first division.

NOTEBOOK
Half A Person(IRE) very much caught the eye when fourth of 16 on his Leicester debut last month and that form has since been boosted, with the winner taking a Newbury conditions event and the third horse Intimidate landing division one of this race. He was always travelling well behind the leaders and, although veering sharply right under pressure when brought with his effort a furlong out, produced a telling turn of foot. He looked as though this experience would bring him on again. (op 2-1)
Flashlight(IRE), a staying-on third of eight over the extended 7f at Beverley on his debut ten days earlier, was one of three sharing the early advantage and was just about in front over a furlong out, but he was blown away by the winner's change of gear. He should benefit from a return to a stiffer test. (op 9-2)
Jodies Jem, a staying-on sixth of 11 on his debut over 6f here 15 days earlier, was another to dispute the early advantage and hung in there for longer than might have been expected. This was a step forward. (tchd 14-1 and 20-1)
Lionheart had an official rating of 72 after showing ability in two of his three previous starts. Minus the tongue-tie here, he was close enough passing the 2f pole, but was then completely left behind by the leading trio. He is not progressing and now may be the time to try him in a nursery. (op 6-1 tchd 5-1)
Putra Eton(IRE), a 400,000gns half-brother to the Listed winning juvenile Pimpernel, was handy early but came off the bridle at halfway and dropped right out. He may be worth another chance on better ground. (op 5-2 tchd 9-4 and 3-1)

6847 GRANGE HOTEL ORMESBY ST MARGARET FILLIES' H'CAP 1m 2f 21y
1:30 (1:30) (Class 4) (0-80,80) 3-Y-0+ **£5,175** (£1,540; £769; £384) **Stalls** Low

Form RPR
4100 **1** **Our Gal**[27] 6023 4-9-9 79 JimmyQuinn 10 87
(Noel Quinlan) *hld up in midfield: rdn and hdwy to join ldr jst over 2f out: sustained dual u.p tl led fnl 100yds: hld on gamely towards fin* **12/1**

1250 **2** *½* **Jane Lachatte (IRE)**[30] 5706 3-8-12 73 JamieSpencer 6 80
(Stuart Williams) *stdd s: hld up in last: rdn and hdwy over 2f out: chsd ldng pair and swtchd rt over 1f out: drvn and pressed wnr wl ins fnl f: kpt on but hld towards fin* **7/2**[2]

3500 **3** *1* **Miss Aix**[50] 5277 4-9-8 78 StevieDonohoe 7 83
(Michael Bell) *hld up in midfield: hdwy to ld jst over 2f out: drvn over 1f out: hdd fnl 100yds: styd on same pce after* **16/1**

-431 **4** *10* **Silke Top**[14] 6433 3-8-9 70 AdamBeschizza 5 55
(William Jarvis) *t.k.h: chsd ldrs: rdn and struggling 3f out: wknd 2f out: no ch w ldrs but kpt on again ins fnl f* **14/1**

1546 **5** *hd* **Negin**[37] 5747 3-9-0 75 TomMcLaughlin 2 60
(Ed Dunlop) *stdd s: hld up in rr: swtchd rt and hdwy u.p to chse ldng trio wl over 1f out: btn 1f out and wknd fnl f* **8/1**

-413 **6** *1 ¾* **Proximity**[34] 5837 3-9-2 77 RichardMullen 8 58
(Sir Michael Stoute) *chsd ldng trio: rdn and unable qck 3f out: lost pl and btn: wknd over 1f out* **3/1**[1]

-420 **7** *5* **Destiny Of Dreams**[71] 4515 4-9-10 80 RobertWinston 1 51
(Jo Crowley) *chsd ldr tl lost pl qckly ent fnl 2f: bhd over 1f out* **6/1**[3]

0-34 **8** *2* **Fearless Dream**[129] 2584 3-9-2 77 NickyMackay 3 44
(John Gosden) *led tl rdn and hdd jst over 2f out: sn dropped out and bhd over 1f out* **7/2**[2]

2m 16.81s (6.31) **Going Correction** +0.70s/f (Yiel)
WFA 3 from 4yo 5lb **8** Ran SP% **115.1**
Speed ratings (Par 102): **102,101,100,92,92 91,87,85**
toteswingers: 1&2 £7.30, 2&3 £16.00, 1&3 £21.60 CSF £54.16 CT £684.93 TOTE £18.60: £4.40, £1.50, £3.30; EX 65.50.
Owner G Wilding **Bred** G Wilding **Trained** Newmarket, Suffolk

FOCUS
Not a bad fillies' handicap, but they didn't go a great early pace in the conditions and the first three pulled a long way clear. The form is rated around the first two.
Proximity Official explanation: trainer's rep said filly was unsuited by the heavy ground
Fearless Dream Official explanation: jockey said filly hung right

6848 INJURED JOCKEYS FUND H'CAP 1m 3f 101y
2:00 (2:01) (Class 3) (0-90,90) 3-Y-0+ **£7,762** (£2,310; £1,154; £577) **Stalls** Low

Form RPR
2523 **1** **Rawaki (IRE)**[14] 6445 4-9-1 88 ThomasBrown(7) 3 96+
(Andrew Balding) *chsd ldrs tl rdn to ld 2f out: hld hd high and racing lazily but a in command after: rdn out* **11/4**[1]

0554 **2** *1 ¼* **Samarkand (IRE)**[17] 6349 4-9-2 82 LukeMorris 8 88
(Sir Mark Prescott Bt) *chsd ldr tl rdn to ld over 2f out: sn drvn and hdd: kpt on u.p but a hld fnl f* **15/2**

-000 **3** *¾* **Fulgur**[34] 5835 4-9-7 90 [1] PatrickHills(3) 7 95
(Luca Cumani) *stdd s: hld up in rr: rdn and effrt on outer 3f out: hdwy over 1f out: kpt on ins fnl f: no threat to wnr* **4/1**[2]

0040 **4** *2 ½* **Layline (IRE)**[57] 4983 5-8-10 76 oh11 [1] NeilCallan 2 76
(Gay Kelleway) *stdd s: t.k.h: hld up in last pair: hdwy u.p over 1f out: one pce and no imp fnl f* **33/1**

0211 **5** *nse* **Quixote**[16] 6376 3-8-11 83 (t) RobertWinston 9 83
(Clive Brittain) *hld up in tch: rdn and hdwy over 2f out: chsd ldng pair but no imp over 1f out: wknd ins fnl f* **9/2**[3]

450- **6** *4* **All Annalena (IRE)**[225] 7580 6-9-3 83 (t) AdamBeschizza 1 77
(Lucy Wadham) *t.k.h: led tl hdd and rdn over 2f out: wknd u.p over 1f out* **10/1**

4001 **7** *1* **Uriah Heep (FR)**[31] 5901 3-9-1 87 RichardMullen 5 79
(Sir Michael Stoute) *hld up in midfield: rdn and no hdwy wl over 2f out: wknd over 1f out* **13/2**

0041 **8** *27* **Emerald Wilderness (IRE)**[16] 6380 8-9-4 84 FrederikTylicki 4 30
(Mark Rimmer) *t.k.h: hld up in tch: rdn and effrt 3f out: wknd over 1f out: wll btn and eased fnl f: t.o* **10/1**

2m 37.58s (8.88) **Going Correction** +0.70s/f (Yiel)
WFA 3 from 4yo+ 6lb **8** Ran SP% **111.1**
Speed ratings (Par 107): **95,94,93,91,91 88,88,68**
toteswingers: 1&2 £6.00, 2&3 £7.40, 1&3 £3.30 CSF £22.46 CT £77.23 TOTE £3.20: £1.10, £3.40, £2.00; EX 20.50.
Owner Kingsclere Racing CLub **Bred** Kingsclere Stud **Trained** Kingsclere, Hants

FOCUS
A decent handicap, but again they went a sensible pace in the conditions.

NOTEBOOK
Rawaki(IRE) had been beaten less than a length the last twice, but was on softer ground than he had encountered before. It proved no bother to him, though, and having taken over in front over a furlong out was always doing enough despite carrying his head a little high. He is still lightly raced for his age, so may still have a bit more improvement left. (op 3-1 tchd 5-2)
Samarkand(IRE), back down in trip, was always in a good position considering stamina wasn't going to be an issue, but having worked his way to the front over 2f out he couldn't quite match the winner for speed, despite staying on. He had a question mark against him on the ground, so this was a good effort but the handicapper does seem to have him where he wants him. (tchd 8-1)
Fulgur had been below form all three starts since his belated reappearance in August, mainly due to pulling too hard, so was tried in a first-time hood here. He was ridden much more patiently than the first two and, although threatening to make an impact when brought widest with his effort over 2f out, tended to hang about inside the last furlong and could make no further impression on the front pair. (op 7-2 tchd 9-2)
Layline(IRE), also tried in a hood, is rated 24lb lower on turf than on the AW which meant he was 11lb wrong here. Doing all his best work late, this was a good effort at the weights and if able to reproduce it he would be of obvious interest from his proper mark on the grass. (tchd 40-1)
Quixote was up another 7lb in his bid for a hat-trick following two successes over 1m2f on fast ground at Sandown, but he didn't find much off the bridle and didn't seem to get home in the conditions. (tchd 4-1 and 5-1)
All Annalena(IRE) made much of the running and should come on for this first start in 225 days. She also has the option of going back over hurdles. (tchd 8-1 and 11-1)
Uriah Heep(FR), back in a handicap after getting off the mark in a Goodwood maiden, never figured and looks to have two ways of running. (op 7-1)
Emerald Wilderness(IRE), 4lb higher than when causing a shock on his debut for the yard over 1m2f here 16 days earlier, couldn't repeat it under these very different conditions. His trainer reported that the gelding was unsuited by the heavy ground. Official explanation: trainer said gelding was unsuited by the heavy ground (op 8-1)

6849 BBC RADIO NORFOLK NURSERY 6f 3y
2:35 (2:37) (Class 5) (0-75,74) 2-Y-0 **£2,587** (£770; £384; £192) **Stalls** Centre

Form RPR
530 **1** **Evoke (IRE)**[15] 6411 2-9-4 71 FrederikTylicki 7 74
(Jeremy Noseda) *trckd ldrs: rdn and effrt to ld over 1f out: r.o wl ins fnl f* **3/1**[2]

034 **2** *½* **Dumbarton Rock**[15] 6411 2-9-0 67 RobertWinston 5 69
(William Jarvis) *chsd ldrs: wnt 2nd over 3f out: rdn and ev ch whn edgd rt over 1f out: kpt on wl u.p but a hld ins fnl f* **15/8**[1]

0600 **3** *4 ½* **Precision Strike**[12] 6511 2-7-13 52 JimmyQuinn 1 40
(Richard Guest) *stdd s: hld up in tch in rr: rdn and effrt over 2f out: 4th and outpcd by ldng pair 1f out: plugged on to go 3rd ins fnl f* **22/1**

4660 **4** *¾* **Tough Lady (IRE)**[23] 6147 2-8-8 61 FrannyNorton 8 48
(Mark Johnston) *chsd ldr tl led after 1f: rdn and hdd over 1f out: sn hmpd and btn 1f out: wknd ins fnl f* **7/2**[3]

0100 **5** *1 ¾* **Whitford (IRE)**[18] 6318 2-8-9 65 RyanClark(3) 6 46
(Chris Dwyer) *led for 1f: chsd ldr tl over 3f out: rdn and unable qck wl over 1f out: btn 1f out and wknd fnl f* **13/2**

030 **6** *¾* **Our Sweet Art**[71] 4494 2-8-13 66 LukeMorris 3 44
(John Best) *plld hrd: hld up in tch: rdn and no hdwy wl over 1f out: wknd u.p 1f out* **11/2**

1m 18.82s (4.42) **Going Correction** +0.70s/f (Yiel) **6** Ran SP% **115.1**
Speed ratings (Par 95): **98,97,91,90,88 87**
toteswingers: 1&2 £2.10, 2&3 £5.20, 1&3 £6.80 CSF £9.41 CT £99.45 TOTE £4.40: £1.70, £5.00; EX 8.80.
Owner Miss Yvonne Jacques **Bred** Yeomanstown Stud **Trained** Newmarket, Suffolk

FOCUS
This looked a weak nursery and the first two pulled right away.

NOTEBOOK
Evoke(IRE) had finished well behind Dumbarton Rock in a C&D maiden 15 days earlier and appeared to have no chance of reversing that form on this nursery debut, but this ground was very different and she out-battled her old rival in gritty style to break her duck. This wasn't a great race, but testing ground seems to bring out the best in her and her sire has done well with his runners on the AW, so she shouldn't be short of opportunities in the coming weeks. (tchd 7-2)
Dumbarton Rock had every chance to confirm recent form with the winner and went down fighting, pulling well clear of the others. He has already run a fair race on the Southwell Fibresand, so he too has options. (op 9-4)
Precision Strike has gone the wrong way since showing promise in his first two starts and may not have achieved much in finishing a remote and never-dangerous third here. (op 25-1)
Tough Lady(IRE) dropped out after making much of the running and has now run moderately in six starts since showing promise on her Hamilton debut. Even her master trainer will do very well to get a win out of her. (op 6-1)
Whitford(IRE), back on turf for the first time since finishing well beaten in his first three starts, folded tamely and remains 9lb higher than when winning a 7f nursery on the Lingfield Polytrack three starts back. (op 9-2)
Our Sweet Art could have done without taking such a keen hold early. (op 5-1 tchd 7-1)

6850 NORFOLK CHAMBER OF COMMERCE NURSERY 5f 43y
3:10 (3:11) (Class 6) (0-65,65) 2-Y-0 **£1,940** (£577; £288; £144) **Stalls** Centre

Form RPR
0065 **1** **Harrogate Fair**[58] 4947 2-8-11 55 LiamJones 2 55
(Michael Squance) *chsd ldrs: rdn and ev ch 2f out: drvn to ld over 1f out: kpt on wl ins fnl f: drvn out* **14/1**

350 **2** *¾* **Ladweb**[21] 6203 2-9-4 62 NeilCallan 4 59
(John Gallagher) *chsd ldr: rdn to ld 2f out: wandered u.p and hdd over 1f out: kpt on same pce ins fnl f* **4/1**[3]

4105 **3** *½* **Not Now Blondie**[17] 6332 2-8-13 60 RyanClark(3) 7 55
(Chris Dwyer) *in tch: hdwy u.p to chse ldrs and edgd lft over 1f out: kpt on same pce ins fnl f* **7/1**

022 **4** *5* **Colourist**[10] 6564 2-9-7 65 GeorgeBaker 3 42
(Gary Moore) *chsd ldrs: outpcd and rdn ent fnl 2f: edgd lft and wknd over 1f out* **11/4**[1]

526 **5** *nse* **Otto The First**[128] 2609 2-8-12 56 LukeMorris 6 33
(John Best) *racd towards nr side: midfield overall: rdn and effrt 2f out: edgd lft and no imp over 1f out* **4/1**[3]

000 **6** ¾ **Cos I Can**[45] 5449 2-8-1 45.. JimmyQuinn 5 19
(Derek Shaw) *sn bhd and pushed along: modest hdwy u.p 1f out: n.d*
33/1

000 **7** *8* **Anna Law (IRE)**[14] 6443 2-8-1 45.................................... FrannyNorton 1
(Charles Hills) *taken down early: sn led: hdd and rdn 2f out: sn wknd: bhd and eased ins fnl f*
3/1[2]

1m 7.59s (4.89) **Going Correction** +0.70s/f (Yiel) 7 Ran SP% **113.8**
Speed ratings (Par 93): **88,86,86,78,77 76,63**
toteswingers: 1&2 £8.80, 2&3 £5.30, 1&3 £12.00 CSF £67.91 TOTE £35.20: £7.60, £3.20; EX 113.10.
Owner Kevin Daniel Crabb **Bred** Kevin Daniel Crabb **Trained** Newmarket, Suffolk

FOCUS
This was an even weaker nursery than the preceding race. There was a difference of opinion early, with a group of five racing up the centre while a couple raced closer to the stands' rail.

NOTEBOOK
Harrogate Fair, back to the minimum trip for the first time since his debut, had shown some ability in the third of his first four starts at Kempton and his subsequent heavy defeat in a nursery at the same track came in a much stronger contest than this. However, it may have been the gelding operation since his last start that contributed to this improved effort and there was no doubting his resolution, as there was never much between him and the runner-up throughout the race until he asserted in the last few strides. Official explanation: trainer said, regarding apparent improvement in form, that since its last run, the horse had been gelded. (tchd 16-1)
Ladweb, making his nursery debut after hinting at ability in three maidens, seems to prefer this sort of ground and battled all the way to the line. (op 5-1)
Not Now Blondie, off the same mark as when winning a Wolverhampton nursery three starts back, kept on to the line and fared much the best of the pair who raced away from the others towards the near side. (op 15-2 tchd 8-1)
Colourist had finished runner-up in nurseries in testing conditions the last twice, but he was beaten 6l by the winner in the first and there were only four runners in the second, so hay may be flattered. He started to hang when put under pressure over 2f from home and never managed to get involved. His rider reported that the colt ran flat. Official explanation: jockey said colt ran flat (op 2-1 tchd 7-4 and 3-1)
Otto The First was returning from 128 days off and, like the winner, had been gelded since last seen. Another to race closer to the stands' rail, he never looked like taking a hand and his stable continues to struggle for winners. (op 9-2)
Anna Law(IRE) was making her nursery debut after beating just two rivals in her first three starts, but they were Class 4 maidens so she should have found this much easier. However, after making much of the early running she folded very disappointingly. (op 9-2)
T/Plt: £51.20 to a £1 stake. Pool £38,577.44 - 549.85 winning units. T/Qpdt: £26.60 to a £1 stake. Pool £3,896.59 - 108.20 winning units. SP

6851 - 6852a (Foreign Racing) - See Raceform Interactive

[6648]DUNDALK (A.W) (L-H)
Friday, October 5

OFFICIAL GOING: Standard

6853a IRISH STALLION FARMS EUROPEAN BREEDERS FUND MEDIAN AUCTION FILLIES MAIDEN — 7f (P)
7:00 (7:01) 2-Y-O **£7,187** (£1,666; £729; £416)

RPR

1 **Majestic Queen (IRE)** 2-9-0 .... MichaelHussey 8 74+
(Tracey Collins, Ire) *w.w: travelled wl to chse ldrs 2f out: nt clr run appr fnl f then qcknd wl between horses to ld ins fnl 50yds* **33/1**

2 *hd* **Almalekiah (IRE)**[17] 6330 2-9-0 .... SeamieHeffernan 12 73
(J S Moore) *w.w: prog into 4th 3f out: led ent fnl f: hdd ins fnl 50yds* **8/1**[3]

3 ½ **Queen Of The Sand (IRE)**[27] 6059 2-9-0 74..................... GaryCarroll 6 72
(G M Lyons, Ire) *hld up: c wd in st: chsd ldrs fnl 2f: kpt on wl* **14/1**

4 *nk* **Love And Cherish (IRE)** 2-9-0 .... WayneLordan 7 71
(David Wachman, Ire) *trckd ldrs: prog into 5th 3f out: nt qckn 2f out: kpt on wl ins fnl f* **4/1**[2]

5 ¾ **Morga (IRE)** 2-9-0 .... KevinManning 9 69
(J S Bolger, Ire) *racd in 3rd: clsd to press ldr 2f out: no ex fnl 100yds* **8/1**[3]

6 ¾ **Windsor Queen (IRE)** 2-9-0 .... BenCurtis 10 67
(Mrs Prunella Dobbs, Ire) *hld up: prog to chse ldrs whn swtchd towards outer 2f out: sltly short of room ent fnl f: no ex* **40/1**

7 1 ¼ **Cocktail Hour (IRE)**[25] 6109 2-9-0 81................................ PatSmullen 3 65
(D K Weld, Ire) *racd in 2nd: led over 2f out: hdd ent fnl f: sn wknd* **8/11**[1]

8 4 ¼ **Melanippe (IRE)**[5] 6714 2-9-0 .... ChrisHayes 2 53
(P D Deegan, Ire) *slowly away: a towards rr* **25/1**

9 5 ½ **Paper Petal (IRE)**[21] 6219 2-8-11 .... SamJames(3) 1 39
(J T Gorman, Ire) *chsd ldrs tl wknd appr home turn* **33/1**

10 *nk* **Las Encinas**[21] 6219 2-8-11 .... IJBrennan(3) 11 38
(Adrian McGuinness, Ire) *a in rr: wl adrift ent fnl 2f* **50/1**

11 *7* **Lady Medici**[11] 6550 2-9-0 .... DeclanMcDonogh 5 30+
(Kevin Prendergast, Ire) *racd in 4th tl pushed along over 2f out: wkng whn hmpd and snatched up sn afterwards: eased* **22/1**

12 1 ½ **Griselda (IRE)**[21] 6219 2-9-0 .... CODonoghue 4 26+
(P F McEnery, Ire) *t.k.h and led tl hdd over 2f out: wknd qckly: eased* **50/1**

1m 24.4s (84.40) **12** Ran SP% **127.2**
CSF £281.97 TOTE £69.00: £23.30, £1.80, £7.00; DF 347.30.
Owner Majestic Queen Partnership **Bred** Sunderland Holdings Ltd **Trained** The Curragh, Co Kildare

FOCUS
Majestic Queen had to overcome missing the break and trouble in running to make a winning debut. The favourite ran poorly and the second and third govern the level of the form.

NOTEBOOK
Majestic Queen(IRE) finished with a flourish when a gap appeared inside the final furlong to hit the front close home.
Almalekiah(IRE) closed on the outside before the straight and looked set for victory when going to front over 1f out. She kept on quite well but was unable to hold of the winner. (op 6/1)
Queen Of The Sand(IRE) ran her best race to date. She made headway in the centre of the track well over 1f out and kept on well inside the final furlong. (tchd 18/1)
Love And Cherish(IRE) making her debut, was soon tracking the leaders and stuck to her task quite well over the final furlong. (op 11/2 tchd 6/1)
Morga(IRE) was always close up and had every chance in the straight before finding no extra in the closing stages.
Cocktail Hour(IRE) was soon disputing the lead. She went on early in the straight but was soon under pressure and dropped away once headed over 1f out. This was disappointing and she has questions to answer now. (op 4/6)
Lady Medici Official explanation: jockey said filly was found to be bleeding from both nostrils

6854a CROWNE PLAZA RACE & STAY RACE — 6f (P)
7:30 (7:32) 3-Y-O+ **£8,625** (£2,000; £875; £500)

RPR

1 **Balmont Mast (IRE)**[47] 5392 4-9-6 100......................... JohnnyMurtagh 1 105
(Edward Lynam, Ire) *reluctant to load: trckd ldrs in 4th: travelled best fr 2f out: swtchd out to ld fnl 150yds and sn qcknd clr* **7/4**[1]

2 2 ½ **Nocturnal Affair (SAF)**[23] 6140 6-9-12 110.................(t) FergalLynch 12 103+
(David Marnane, Ire) *w.w: prog 2f out: styd on wl to take 2nd cl home: nvr trbld wnr* **4/1**[2]

3 ½ **Elusive Ridge (IRE)**[27] 6064 6-9-5 94..........................(p) ColinKeane(7) 4 101
(H Rogers, Ire) *pressed ldrs: led over 2f out tl hdd by wnr fnl 150yds: ct cl home for 2nd* **16/1**

4 ½ **Burj Alzain (IRE)**[15] 6400 4-9-6 .... DeclanMcDonogh 14 94+
(Gerard Butler) *hld up in rr: swtchd to outer early in st: styd on wl ent fnl f: nvr nrr* **6/1**

5 ½ **Experience (IRE)**[20] 6268 3-9-0 101..........................(p) WayneLordan 13 87
(David Wachman, Ire) *restrained and sn trckd over to inner: prog to chse ldrs over 1f out: nvr on terms: kpt on* **5/1**[3]

6 ¾ **Rock Jock (IRE)**[209] 875 5-9-3 99.............................. RonanWhelan(3) 9 90
(John Patrick Shanahan, Ire) *slowly away and towards rr: prog on inner fr 2f out: kpt on wl fnl f* **20/1**

7 ¾ **Norville (IRE)**[27] 6064 5-9-6 89..(p) ChrisHayes 3 87
(Lee Smyth, Ire) *led tl hdd over 2f out: wknd fnl f* **20/1**

8 1 ½ **Invincible Ridge (IRE)**[5] 6716 4-9-3 84.......................(t) LeighRoche(3) 7 83
(D J Bunyan, Ire) *racd in mid-div thrght: no imp fnl 2f* **20/1**

9 ½ **Six Of Hearts**[16] 6385 8-9-3 92..................................(bt[1]) SamJames(3) 6 81
(Cecil Ross, Ire) *chsd ldrs: no imp fnl 2f* **20/1**

10 1 ½ **Pencil Hill (IRE)**[85] 4020 7-9-5 83........................ MeganCarberry(7) 5 82
(Tracey Collins, Ire) *trckd ldrs in 3rd: pushed along 2f out: wknd ent fnl f* **20/1**

11 2 ¼ **Bajan Tryst (USA)**[20] 6244 6-9-12 .... PatSmullen 10 75
(Kevin Ryan) *nvr bttr than mid-div: no threat over 2f out* **7/1**

12 *nse* **Core Element (IRE)**[5] 6716 5-9-7 81........................ EmmetMcNamara 8 70
(S Buggy, Ire) *pressed ldrs towards outer tl wknd 2f out* **25/1**

13 *shd* **Jembatt (IRE)**[7] 6653 5-9-12 80..(p) GaryCarroll 11 75
(Michael Mulvany, Ire) *hld up: c wd in st: nvr a threat* **33/1**

1m 10.31s (70.31)
WFA 3 from 4yo+ 1lb **13** Ran SP% **136.3**
CSF £8.84 TOTE £3.20: £1.02, £1.80, £3.50; DF 12.30.
Owner Derek Iceton **Bred** Limestone & Tara Studs **Trained** Dunshaughlin, Co Meath

FOCUS
Sound form.

NOTEBOOK
Balmont Mast(IRE) gained his previous victories over 5f. He hadn't won since scoring in a handicap here a year ago but he had finished second on his two starts before this race and he ran out an easy winner after being sent to the front early in the final furlong. Rated 100, he was quite well treated by the race conditions and will return here for a 5f Listed event on October 26. (op 3/1)
Norville(IRE) Official explanation: trainer said gelding was found to be lame

6855a DIAMOND STKS (GROUP 3) — 1m 2f 150y(P)
8:00 (8:01) 3-Y-O+ **£31,145** (£9,104; £4,312; £1,437)

RPR

1 **Declaration Of War (USA)**[5] 6721 3-9-3 105......................... JPO'Brien 1 105+
(A P O'Brien, Ire) *restrained on inner in mid-div: travelled wl to trck ldrs whn short of room 2f out: swtchd out appr fnl f: styd on wl to ld cl home* **11/10**[1]

2 ½ **Along Came Casey (IRE)**[30] 5957 4-9-5 98..................... PatSmullen 2 100
(D K Weld, Ire) *racd in 3rd: drvn to ld ent fnl f: ct cl home* **20/1**

3 *2* **Aloof (IRE)**[12] 6518 3-9-0 107... WayneLordan 10 97
(David Wachman, Ire) *sn led: hdd ent fnl f: no ex* **8/1**

4 1 ¼ **Brendan Brackan (IRE)**[20] 6267 3-9-3 108............ EmmetMcNamara 5 98
(G M Lyons, Ire) *hld up in rr: pushed along to chse ldrs on inner fnl 2f: kpt on: nvr on terms* **9/1**

5 *shd* **Light Heavy (IRE)**[27] 6063 3-9-6 112...................(tp) KevinManning 11 100
(J S Bolger, Ire) *racd in 2nd tl pushed along 2f out: no ex ins fnl f* **4/1**[2]

6 *hd* **Banna Boirche (IRE)**[26] 6079 6-9-8 105.............................. ShaneFoley 8 96
(M Halford, Ire) *hld up towards rr: prog whn sltly hmpd appr fnl f: kpt on: nvr nrr* **16/1**

7 *1* **Prince Alzain (USA)**[34] 5848 3-9-3 .... DeclanMcDonogh 6 95
(Gerard Butler) *hld up towards rr: swtchd to outer fnl 2f: kpt on: nvr nrr* **18/1**

8 1 ½ **Black Spirit (USA)**[13] 6482 5-9-8 ....(t) CO'Donoghue 12 91
(Clive Cox) *racd in mid-div: no imp fr over 1f out* **13/2**[3]

9 ¾ **Barack (IRE)**[14] 6462 6-9-8 97...(bt) BenCurtis 3 90
(W McCreery, Ire) *hld up in rr: nvr a threat: kpt on one pce fnl f* **33/1**

10 *hd* **Salam Alaykum (IRE)**[57] 5029 4-9-8 79.................................... JFEgan 4 89?
(Reginald Roberts, Ire) *trckd ldrs: pushed along 2f out: no ex appr fnl f* **66/1**

11 *nk* **Muck 'N' Brass (IRE)**[47] 5397 3-9-3 98.............................. FergalLynch 13 90
(Edward Lynam, Ire) *trckd ldrs in 4th: pushed along 2f out: wknd qckly fnl f* **33/1**

12 *2* **Honourable Emperor (IRE)**[66] 4692 3-9-3 95.................. ChrisHayes 9 86
(Noel Meade, Ire) *a in rr* **33/1**

2m 11.66s (131.66)
WFA 3 from 4yo+ 6lb **12** Ran SP% **128.3**
CSF £35.20 TOTE £1.90: £1.40, £4.20, £2.00; DF 31.80.
Owner Mrs John Magnier, M Tabor, D Smith & Joseph Allen **Bred** Joseph Allen **Trained** Ballydoyle, Co Tipperary
■ Stewards' Enquiry : J P O'Brien one-day ban; careless riding (19th Oct)

FOCUS
The 105 rated Declaration of War, twice successful on all-weather surfaces in France last year, joined Aidan O'Brien early in the summer and is likely to be stepped up considerably in class after this victory. The form matches the race averages.

NOTEBOOK
Declaration Of War(USA) was clearly going best early in the straight. He had to be pulled out from behind horses to get a run and once he found space he went about his business in good style, leading inside the final furlong. Despite drifting left towards the runner-up he was value for more than the half length winning margin. His trainer is considering Ascot later in the month and he could go for either the QE II Stakes or the Qipco Champion Stakes. (op 11/10 tchd evs)
Along Came Casey(IRE), had been raised 16lb to 98 for her easy handicap win at Gowran Park last month. She produced a good effort here, racing prominently and edging ahead entering the final furlong before being grabbed by the winner.
Aloof(IRE) made the running until 1f out from where she could raise no extra.

Brendan Brackan(IRE) was supplemented to this race having been given a rating of 108 after a handicap win over 1m at the Curragh last month. He made headway from behind early in the straight and ran on quite well. It was a effort good enough to justify further attempts at this level next year.
Light Heavy(IRE) had run his best race when fourth in the Irish Champion Stakes, a performance which saw his official rating go up 4lb to 112. This was his first run on this surface and he had every chance before failing to raise his effort from over 1f out. (op 5/1)
Black Spirit(USA), bidding for a hat-trick on just his second try on the surface, failed to run up to form. (op 5/1)

6856 - 6863a (Foreign Racing) - See Raceform Interactive

6656 SAINT-CLOUD (L-H)

Friday, October 5

OFFICIAL GOING: Turf: very soft

6864a PRIX SCARAMOUCHE (LISTED RACE) (3YO+) (TURF) 1m 6f

3:25 (12:00) 3-Y-0+ **£21,666** (£8,666; £6,500; £4,333; £2,166)

RPR

1 **Quiz Mistress**34 5826 4-8-13 0 .... IoritzMendizabal 8 100
(Hughie Morrison) *hld up at rr on settling: mde prog on wd outside fnl turn: qcknd wl u.p over 1 1/2f out: r.o strly fnl f to get up on line in four-way fin* **97/10**

2 *shd* **Aviator (GER)**75 4-9-2 0 ....(b) ThierryThulliez 9 103
(P Harley, Germany) **14/1**

3 *shd* **Hesione (IRE)**84 3-8-4 0 .... AlexisBadel 7 100
(Mme M Bollack-Badel, France) **17/2**

4 *nse* **I'm Your Man (FR)** 3-8-7 0 .... AntoineHamelin 2 103
(A De Royer-Dupre, France) **17/2**

5 *2* **Silver Valny (FR)**7 6-9-2 0 .... ThomasMessina 3 100
(Mlle M-L Mortier, France) **68/10**

6 *hd* **Telbes**19 6297 4-9-2 0 ....(b1) AlexisAchard 5 100
(M Delzangles, France) **5/13**

7 *3/4* **Inside Man (IRE)**19 6297 6-9-4 0 ....(b) OlivierPeslier 1 101
(E Lellouche, France) **9/22**

8 *dist* **King Of Arnor**199 980 4-9-2 0 .... MaximeGuyon 4
(A Fabre, France) **2/11**

3m 19.8s (7.60)
WFA 3 from 4yo+ 9lb **8** Ran SP% **118.1**
WIN (incl. 1 euro stake): 10.70. PLACES: 3.10, 4.00, 2.80. DF: 44.50. SF: 102.10.
Owner The Fairy Story Partnership **Bred** Deepwood Farm Stud **Trained** East Ilsley, Berks

NOTEBOOK
Quiz Mistress has progressed really well since winning a Windsor handicap on her reappearance in May off 76 and gained coveted black type when getting the better of a desperate finish. Soft ground is the key to her.

6830 ASCOT (R-H)

Saturday, October 6

OFFICIAL GOING: Soft (heavy in places on round course)
Wind: Almost nil Weather: Fine

6865 BMW CORNWALLIS STKS (GROUP 3) 5f

2:00 (2:00) (Class 1) 2-Y-O

£20,982 (£7,955; £3,981; £1,983; £995; £499) **Stalls** Centre

Form RPR

5152 **1** **Bungle Inthejungle**22 6196 2-9-3 109 .... MartinHarley 8 107
(Mick Channon) *taken down early: fast away: mde all: hrd pressed and drvn fnl f: hld on gamely* **9/2**

341 **2** *hd* **Garswood**15 6424 2-9-0 106 .... TonyHamilton 6 103
(Richard Fahey) *dwlt and pushed along early: sn trckd ldrs: rdn to go 2nd jst over 1f out: str chal fnl f: could nt qckn nr fin* **7/41**

415 **3** *nk* **El Manati (IRE)**30 5979 2-8-11 96 .... JohnnyMurtagh 7 99
(James Tate) *trckd ldrs: shkn up 2f out: n.m.r as tried to cl 1f out: squeezed between ldng pair nr fin w hd high: r.o* **3/12**

2140 **4** *1 3/4* **Lucky Beggar (IRE)**14 6483 2-9-0 94 .... WilliamCarson 4 96
(Charles Hills) *chsd wnr: rdn over 1f out: sn lost 2nd: fdd ins fnl f* **14/1**

6201 **5** *1 1/2* **The Taj (USA)**28 6022 2-9-0 98 .... DaneO'Neill 5 91
(Richard Hannon) *cl up: rdn and nt qckn over 1f out: wknd fnl f* **4/13**

5211 **6** *6* **Vincentti (IRE)**20 6284 2-9-0 86 .... JamesDoyle 3 69
(Ronald Harris) *racd wd: on terms w ldrs: rdn over 2f out: wknd wl over 1f out* **18/1**

1m 1.73s (1.23) **Going Correction** +0.475s/f (Yiel) **6** Ran SP% **111.5**
Speed ratings (Par 105): **109,108,108,105,103 93**
toteswingers 1&2 £1.80, 2&3 £2.80, 1&3 £2.30 CSF £12.66 TOTE £4.50: £2.10, £1.90; EX 9.20 Trifecta £30.90 Pool: £1452.76 - 34.72 winning units..
Owner Christopher Wright & Miss Emily Asprey **Bred** Stratford Place Stud **Trained** West Ilsley, Berks

FOCUS
The field raced stands' side in this depleted Group 3 2yo sprint, which the right horses dominated. The winner is tough and consistent and this is straightforward form.

NOTEBOOK
Bungle Inthejungle, already a winner at this level and runner-up in a Group 2 the time before, is an out-and-out 5f horse and he got away with the soft ground as opposed to enjoying it. It's doubtful he's capable of winning at a higher level. (op 4-1 tchd 5-1)
Garswood improved on his Ayr Listed win at the trip, this despite getting off to an awkward start. He's now fulfilling his potential and is undoubtedly the one to take from the race with next year in mind. (op 15-8)
El Manati(IRE) is all about speed and riding her with more restraint this time didn't work out, being short of room and then staying on all too late. Space was at a premium for her close home and, ridden from the front as she had been previously, it's possible she'd have won. (op 4-1)
Lucky Beggar(IRE) isn't up to this level and will ultimately be a handicapper. (op 12-1)
The Taj(USA), although making a winning debut on good to soft, had shown his best form on a firmer surface and he never looked happy. (tchd 9-2)
Vincentti(IRE) had won a pair of easy-ground 5f races at Ffos Las, most recently a nursery off 78, and this sharp rise in grade proved beyond him. Official explanation: jockey said colt lost its action (tchd 16-1 and 20-1)

6866 GROSVENOR CASINOS CUMBERLAND LODGE STKS (GROUP 3) 1m 4f

2:30 (2:30) (Class 1) 3-Y-O+

£31,190 (£11,825; £5,918; £2,948; £1,479; £742) **Stalls** Low

Form RPR

1-14 **1** **Hawaafez**65 4738 4-8-11 106 .... JohnnyMurtagh 3 114+
(Marcus Tregoning) *mde all: kicked on over 3f out: rdn clr over 2f out: styd on wl: unchal* **9/41**

6110 **2** *2 1/2* **Camborne**42 5600 4-9-0 106 ....(p) RobertHavlin 8 111
(John Gosden) *stdd s: hld up in last: prog into 4th whn veered bdly lft over 2f out: wnt 2nd and hung rt over 1f out: wouldn't r in st line after: styd on* **3/12**

-313 **3** *3 1/2* **Willing Foe (USA)**20 6297 5-9-0 107 .... SilvestreDeSousa 7 105
(Saeed Bin Suroor) *trckd wnr: rdn and no imp over 2f out: wl hld whn impeded over 1f out: fdd* **9/41**

4313 **4** *nse* **Songcraft (IRE)**8 6637 4-9-0 108 .... RichardMullen 6 105
(Saeed Bin Suroor) *trckd wnr: rdn and no imp over 2f out: fdd over 1f out* **7/13**

5000 **5** *15* **Allied Powers (IRE)**41 5650 7-9-3 104 .... JamieSpencer 1 84
(Michael Bell) *chsd ldng trio: rdn over 3f out: sn wknd: t.o* **12/1**

-654 **6** *3 1/4* **Arrigo (GER)**14 6470 4-9-0 106 ....(b1) SebSanders 2 76
(Ibrahim Saeed Al Malki, Qatar) *hld up in 5th: rdn over 3f out: wknd over 2f out: t.o* **40/1**

2m 37.67s (5.17) **Going Correction** +0.775s/f (Yiel)
WFA 3 from 4yo+ 7lb **6** Ran SP% **109.2**
Speed ratings (Par 113): **113,111,109,108,98 96**
toteswingers 1&2 £2.20, 2&3 £2.10, 1&3 £1.50 CSF £8.73 TOTE £3.00: £1.90, £1.80; EX 7.00 Trifecta £18.00 Pool: £1558.54 - 63.75 winning units..
Owner Hamdan Al Maktoum **Bred** Shadwell Estate Co Ltd **Trained** Lambourn, Berks

FOCUS
No great depth to this and it turned into a solo performance Hawaafez, who got a pretty easy lead. The form is taken at something like face value.

NOTEBOOK
Hawaafez made every yard to provide her in-form trainer with his sixth win in the last 11 runnings of the race. Disappointing at Goodwood the time before, when apparently unsuited by the undulations, Johnny Murtagh made the most of her stamina in the conditions, kicking clear in a race-winning move rounding the final bend. This big, long-striding filly is only just beginning to fulfil her potential and, with her being versatile with regards to both trip and ground, she remains a horse to keep on side. The Long Distance Cup back here on Champions Day will likely be next. (op 2-1 tchd 5-2 and 11-4 in a place)
Camborne, a C&D winner in the Duke of Edinburgh, wasn't seen at his best in the Ebor, but he spoiled any chance he had of catching the winner here by refusing to run straight under pressure, snaking his way up it. He's talented but also has his fare share of quirks and is probably best suited to larger fields. (op 7-2)
Willing Foe(USA), third in a 1m7f Group 3 at Longchamp the time before, proved laboured and would have prefered drier ground. (op 11-4)
Songcraft(IRE) nearly got the better of his supposedly better-fancied stablemate for third, running well considering he dislikes soft ground. (tchd 13-2)
Allied Powers(IRE) is no longer capable of being competitive in Group events in this country. (op 10-1 tchd 9-1)
Arrigo(GER) fared no better in the first-time blinkers and is a horse to leave alone at present. (op 25-1)

6867 JOHN GUEST BENGOUGH STKS (GROUP 3) 6f

3:05 (3:07) (Class 1) 3-Y-O+

£39,697 (£15,050; £7,532; £3,752; £1,883; £945) **Stalls** Centre

Form RPR

0111 **1** **Mince**27 6072 3-8-11 113 .... JamesDoyle 12 110
(Roger Charlton) *led to sn after 1/2-way: pressed ldr after: sustained chal fr over 1f out: led nr fin* **9/41**

4160 **2** *hd* **Soul (AUS)**21 6246 5-9-5 117 .... SilvestreDeSousa 8 116
(Saeed Bin Suroor) *racd w one other in centre to 1/2-way: led sn after: hrd pressed fr over 1f out: hdd nr fin* **4/12**

4440 **3** *3/4* **Eton Rifles (IRE)**41 5641 7-9-1 108 .... WilliamCarson 1 110
(Stuart Williams) *trckd rival in centre to 1/2-way: cl 3rd after: rdn over 1f out: styd on but unable to chal* **9/1**

4034 **4** *1* **Confessional**24 6140 5-9-1 106 ....(be) EddieAhern 9 107
(Tim Easterby) *t.k.h: hld up bhd ldrs: rdn and could nt qckn 2f out: styd on but nvr able to chal* **20/1**

0402 **5** *hd* **Joe Packet**57 5065 5-9-1 95 .... RichardKingscote 5 106?
(Jonathan Portman) *settled towards rr: prog wl over 1f out: drvn and styd on fnl f: nvr able to chal* **33/1**

0225 **6** *3* **Royal Rock**41 5627 8-9-1 109 .... GeorgeBaker 4 97
(Chris Wall) *dwlt: hld up in last pair: prog 2f out: no imp on ldrs 1f out: wl hld after* **10/1**

4005 **7** *1 1/4* **Genki (IRE)**28 6030 8-9-1 107 ....(b) MartinHarley 3 93
(Roger Charlton) *hld up in rr: coaxed along 2f out: sme prog over 1f out: sn no hdwy and btn* **16/1**

4400 **8** *1/2* **Iver Bridge Lad**189 1147 5-9-1 107 ....(b) MichaelO'Connell 11 91
(John Ryan) *chsd ldrs: rdn over 2f out: wknd over 1f out* **25/1**

4240 **9** *10* **Waffle (IRE)**14 6468 6-9-1 103 .... JamieSpencer 10 59
(David Barron) *dwlt: a wl in rr: struggling over 2f out: t.o* **5/13**

0030 **10** *6* **Secret Witness**14 6485 6-9-1 106 ....(b) JoeFanning 2 40
(Ronald Harris) *t.k.h: trckd ldrs: wknd qckly 2f out: t.o* **40/1**

1106 **11** *3* **Valbchek (IRE)**24 6140 3-9-0 103 .... JohnnyMurtagh 13 30
(Jeremy Noseda) *racd alone against nr side rail: on terms to over 2f out: wknd qckly: t.o* **13/2**

1m 14.81s (0.31) **Going Correction** +0.475s/f (Yiel)
WFA 3 from 4yo+ 1lb **11** Ran SP% **119.7**
Speed ratings (Par 113): **116,115,114,113,113 109,107,106,93,85 81**
toteswingers 1&2 £3.20, 2&3 £7.30, 1&3 £7.20 CSF £10.63 TOTE £3.00: £1.40, £1.80, £3.00; EX 9.90 Trifecta £68.00 Pool: £3007.52 - 32.72 winning units..
Owner Lady Rothschild **Bred** The Rt Hon Lord Rothschild **Trained** Beckhampton, Wilts

FOCUS
The two class acts who headed the market fought out the finish in a race that few got into. There was a difference of opinion early, with two groups forming, one down the middle and one stands' side, but they ended up merging. The form is up to scratch for the grade.

NOTEBOOK
Mince took another step up the ladder with this hard-fought win, showing an excellent attitude to get the better of an older, more experienced gelding. A C&D winner at the Shergar Cup, she'd looked a Group performer in the making with a pair of ready Listed wins and it's reasonable to expect even better from her returned to faster ground, which she may have to wait until next season. If continuing to progress, she could make it at the top level in 2013. (op 11-4)

Soul(AUS) had his conditions and bounced right back to form, taking them along centre-field and pushing the winner, to whom he was conceding 8lb, right to the line. He remains smart while there is cut in the ground. (op 7-2 tchd 10-3)
Eton Rifles(IRE) travelled well in behind the speed and returned to something like his best following a couple of subdued efforts. (op 10-1)
Confessional likes soft ground and wasn't far off this season's best, but he continues to come up a bit short at Group level. (op 16-1 tchd 25-1)
Joe Packet, rated 95, ran above himself, but that can often happen in these end-of-season sprints. This won't do his handicap mark any good. (op 28-1 tchd 40-1)
Royal Rock found himself faced with a stronger line-up this time and he never reached a challenging position. (op 8-1 tchd 11-1)
Waffle(IRE) failed to run his race and remains winless since his juvenile days. (op 8-1)

6868 BETFRED CHALLENGE CUP (HERITAGE H'CAP) 7f
3:35 (3:38) (Class 2) 3-Y-0+

£93,375 (£27,960; £13,980; £6,990; £3,495; £1,755) **Stalls** Centre

Form RPR
-524 **1** **Skilful**15 6449 4-9-8 **105** RobertHavlin 4 116+
(John Gosden) *racd towards far side: mde all: clr 3f out: hrd rdn and edgd lft fr over 1f out: hld on* **6/1**2
1061 **2** 1 ½ **Don't Call Me (IRE)**28 6024 5-9-5 **102** (t) RichardMullen 3 109
(David Nicholls) *hld up in last of quartet towards far side: prog to chse wnr over 2f out: clsd grad fnl f: a hld* **16/1**
6225 **3** 2 ¾ **Arnold Lane (IRE)**28 6024 3-9-0 **99** MartinHarley 11 99
(Mick Channon) *hld up in midfield: stdy prog over 2f out: wnt 3rd and rdn over 1f out: could nt qckn and no imp after* **12/1**
0341 **4** 1 ¾ **Captain Ramius (IRE)**14 6468 6-9-9 **106** 6ex PatCosgrave 12 101
(Kevin Ryan) *led gp in centre: chsd clr wnr 3f out to over 2f out: outpcd after: kpt on nr fin* **5/1**1
0020 **5** hd **Captain Bertie (IRE)**64 4761 4-8-12 **95** WilliamCarson 2 89
(Charles Hills) *chsd wnr towards far side: rdn 3f out: lost pl and struggling over 2f out: kpt on nr fin* **12/1**
0310 **6** shd **Cape Classic (IRE)**7 6676 4-9-1 **98** AdamBeschizza 18 92
(William Haggas) *in tch in centre gp: rdn and prog 3f out: chsd ldng trio over 1f out: no imp: fdd last 150yds* **9/1**
1440 **7** ½ **Global Village (IRE)**28 6024 7-8-9 **95** RyanClark(3) 14 88
(Brian Ellison) *in tch in midfield in centre gp: shkn up over 2f out: nt clr run briefly over 1f out: one pce and n.d* **10/1**
1004 **8** 1 ¼ **Field Of Dream**28 6024 5-9-6 **103** (b) JamesDoyle 15 92
(Jamie Osborne) *awkward to post: hld up in last pair: nt clr run briefly over 2f out: n.d after: styd on fnl f* **12/1**
3212 **9** shd **Imperial Guest**28 6024 6-9-7 **104** JamieSpencer 10 93
(George Margarson) *hld up in last: stdy prog over 2f out: rchd 5th 1f out but no ch: wknd qckly last 100yds* **14/1**
0322 **10** 1 ½ **Regal Parade**14 6468 8-9-3 **100** (t) RichardKingscote 8 85
(Milton Bradley) *prom in main gp: rdn 3f out: sn lost pl and btn* **10/1**
0266 **11** 4 **Jamesie (IRE)**28 6064 4-8-12 **95** SilvestreDeSousa 5 69
(David Marnane, Ire) *t.k.h: cl up towards far side: rdn 3f out: wknd over 2f out* **8/1**3
0230 **12** nk **Bannock (IRE)**28 6024 3-9-8 **107** JoeFanning 16 80
(Mark Johnston) *chsd ldrs in centre: rdn over 2f out and pressing for a pl: wknd qckly over 1f out* **16/1**
2006 **13** ½ **Brae Hill (IRE)**14 6468 6-9-1 **98** TonyHamilton 6 70
(Richard Fahey) *dwlt: wl in rr: rdn and no real prog 3f out* **20/1**
6341 **14** 10 **Set The Trend**30 5964 6-9-9 **106** DanielTudhope 13 51
(David O'Meara) *prom in main gp: rdn 1/2-way: sn wknd: t.o* **20/1**

1m 29.21s (1.61) **Going Correction** +0.475s/f (Yiel)
WFA 3 from 4yo+ 2lb **14** Ran SP% **121.3**
Speed ratings (Par 109): **109,107,104,102,101 101,101,99,99,97 93,93,92,81**
toteswingers 1&2 £15.40, 2&3 £43.60, 1&3 £22.20 CSF £99.41 CT £1146.39 TOTE £7.00: £2.70, £3.60, £4.30; EX 95.10 Trifecta £2234.20 Pool: £73158.01 - 24.23 winning units..
Owner Mark Dixon & J L Rowsell **Bred** Ashbrittle Stud & M H Dixon **Trained** Newmarket, Suffolk

FOCUS
This didn't turn out to be as competitive as it had promised, with the pace again holding up and the first two racing in the best place. The winner impressed all the same.

NOTEBOOK
Skilful held on well despite having appeared to idle. He had been contesting better races since landing a 1m handicap from 12lb lower at Haydock last September, but the return to 7f on soft ground proved ideal for the son of Selkirk, who'll be entitled to take his chance up in grade once again having defied a mark of 105 here. (tchd 11-2 and 13-2)
Don't Call Me(IRE), winner of another valuable 7f handicap at the course last time, was up 6lb and faced with softer conditions, but he proved just as effective and may have improved again in defeat. He could be the type to take to Dubai next year.
Arnold Lane(IRE) emerged from the pace with a promising challenge, but he couldn't race on with the front pair. He appreciated the return to softer ground but looks in the control of the handicapper. (op 14-1)
Captain Ramius(IRE), winner of the previous week's Ayr Gold Cup, ran well under a 6lb penalty stepping back up in trip, but unsurprisingly he couldn't see it out as well as some. (op 6-1)
Captain Bertie(IRE) was finishing well towards the far side having been outpaced and remains capable from this sort of mark. (op 14-1)
Cape Classic(IRE) wouldn't have wanted this ground. (op 12-1)
Global Village(IRE) likes this C&D but the race didn't work out for him. He can rate better than the bare result. (op 16-1)
Field Of Dream was another who didn't get the breaks, but he couldn't be considered unlucky. (op 10-1)
Jamesie(IRE) refused to settle and clearly failed to give his running. (tchd 7-1)

6869 MACQUARIE GROUP ROUS STKS (LISTED RACE) 5f
4:10 (4:10) (Class 1) 3-Y-0+

£19,848 (£7,525; £3,766; £1,876; £941; £472) **Stalls** Centre

Form RPR
0410 **1** **Doc Hay (USA)**14 6468 5-8-12 104 DanielTudhope 5 111
(David O'Meara) *stdd s: hld up in tch: prog fr 1/2-way: taken to far rail fnl 2f: chsd ldr 1f out: drvn to ld last 75yds* **6/1**3
0635 **2** nk **Free Zone**11 6557 3-8-12 105 TomEaves 3 110
(Bryan Smart) *led: drvn over 1f out: hdd last 75yds: styd on* **25/1**
5003 **3** 1 ½ **Ponty Acclaim (IRE)**11 6557 3-8-7 97 EddieAhern 8 100
(Tim Easterby) *prom: waiting for a gap over 1f out: sn rdn to try to chal: one pce fnl f* **16/1**
1600 **4** 1 ½ **Mirza**14 6468 5-9-1 102 JohnnyMurtagh 11 102
(Rae Guest) *towards rr: dropped to last 1/2-way and struggling: taken to nr side rail over 1f out: styd on to take 4th last strides* **9/1**
2221 **5** nk **Face The Problem (IRE)**7 6666 4-8-12 108 JamesDoyle 13 98+
(Jamie Osborne) *dwlt: hld up in tch: prog 2f out: chsd ldng trio fnl f: no imp* **2/1**1
5310 **6** nse **My Girl Anna (IRE)**14 6485 5-8-13 106 RoryCleary 10 99
(Muredach Kelly, Ire) *hld up in tch: vigorously drvn fr 2f out: hanging rt but kpt on fr over 1f out: n.d* **6/1**3
2040 **7** 1 **Pabusar**24 6140 4-8-12 106 RichardKingscote 12 94
(Ralph Beckett) *pressed ldr to over 1f out: wknd fnl f* **12/1**
051- **8** 5 **Monsieur Chevalier (IRE)**392 5935 5-8-12 115 PatCosgrave 7 76
(P J O'Gorman) *in tch: n.m.r over 2f out: sn rdn and wknd* **14/1**
0-02 **9** 2 ¼ **Kingsgate Native (IRE)**14 6485 7-8-12 110 ShaneKelly 1 68
(Robert Cowell) *prom: rdn and lost pl 2f out: sn wknd: bled fr the nose* **4/1**2

1m 1.59s (1.09) **Going Correction** +0.475s/f (Yiel) **9** Ran SP% **116.0**
Speed ratings (Par 111): **110,109,107,104,104 104,102,94,90**
toteswingers 1&2 £15.80, 2&3 £21.50, 1&3 £19.50 CSF £138.46 TOTE £6.60: £2.40, £4.70, £4.60; EX 181.50 Trifecta £1295.90 Pool: £2626.86 - 1.50 winning units..
Owner S Laffan **Bred** Colts Neck Stables Llc **Trained** Nawton, N Yorks

FOCUS
Those who ended up nearest the far rail came out on top in this sprint and it's questionable what the form is worth. The race is rated around the runner-up.

NOTEBOOK
Doc Hay(USA) had beaten the favourite Face The Problem in the Portland and, following another creditable run in the Ayr Gold Cup, he posted a career-best to take this Listed prize with his extra stamina really counting late on. It may have been that racing on the far rail late on was an advantage, but he's clearly progressing. (op 15-2 tchd 11-2)
Free Zone made much of the running and briefly looked like being another winner on the day to have set the pace, but her stamina didn't last well enough to hold on. This was a big improvement on recent efforts. (op 20-1)
Ponty Acclaim(IRE) took the Group 3 juvenile sprint on the card a year ago and she returned to something like her best, even if being another perhaps favoured by where she raced. (tchd 20-1)
Mirza had it all to do conceding weight all round and he ended up racing solo against the stands' rail, which probably saw him at a disadvantage. Those factors considered, this was a really good run. (op 14-1)
Face The Problem(IRE) had gained a deserved win the week before but he saw plenty of daylight racing near side of the main group and failed to pick up. He's better than this. (op 11-4, tchd 3-1 in a place)
My Girl Anna(IRE) was never in a position to challenge, not helping her rider by hanging. (op 11-2)
Kingsgate Native(IRE) looked unlucky in a Group 3 at Newbury the time before, but that had come on faster ground and he proved laboured for pressure on this surface. Official explanation: vet said gelding bled from the nose (op 10-3 tchd 3-1)

6870 MILES & MORRISON E B F OCTOBER STKS (LISTED RACE) (F&M) 7f
4:45 (4:45) (Class 1) 3-Y-0+

£19,848 (£7,525; £3,766; £1,876; £941; £472) **Stalls** Centre

Form RPR
1000 **1** **Intense Pink**100 3542 3-8-11 90 SebSanders 2 102
(Chris Wall) *trckd ldr over 5f out: rdn to ld 2f out: styd on strly fnl f* **16/1**
0200 **2** 1 ¼ **Switcher (IRE)**48 5385 3-8-11 95 (v) RichardKingscote 4 99
(Tom Dascombe) *led after 1f: rdn and hdd 2f out: styd on but no imp on wnr fnl f* **14/1**
1205 **3** 1 ¼ **Sentaril**23 6161 3-8-11 105 JohnnyMurtagh 6 96+
(William Haggas) *t.k.h: sn restrained in midfield: rdn and prog 2f out: styd on wl to take 3rd last 75yds* **7/2**1
1432 **4** ¾ **Mrs Greeley**28 6023 4-8-13 79 JohnFahy 5 94?
(Eve Johnson Houghton) *hld up in rr: prog 3f out: taken to far rail and clsd on ldrs 2f out: tried to chal over 1f out: one pce after* **50/1**
1650 **5** ½ **Radio Gaga**23 6161 3-9-0 98 RichardMullen 13 95+
(Ed McMahon) *chsd ldrs but nt on terms: u.p fr 1/2-way: kpt on same pce: n.d* **14/1**
2005 **6** nk **Russian Rave**30 5980 6-8-13 88 DanielTudhope 1 91
(Jonathan Portman) *chsd ldrs: rdn and no imp 2f out: kpt on same pce after: n.d* **25/1**
110 **7** 1 ½ **I'm So Glad**23 6161 3-8-11 96 MartinHarley 16 87
(Mick Channon) *hld up wl in rr towards nr side: stdy prog over 2f out: rdn over 1f out: kpt on but no ch* **20/1**
1-1 **8** shd **Punita (USA)**105 3395 3-8-11 86 SilvestreDeSousa 7 87
(Mahmood Al Zarooni) *t.k.h: hld up in rr: sme prog whn nt clrest of runs 2f out to over 1f out: hanging and no hdwy after* **9/2**2
0100 **9** 1 ½ **Bonnie Brae**23 6161 5-8-13 104 (p) DaneO'Neill 10 83
(David Elsworth) *hld up in rr: nt clr run briefly 3f out: drvn 2f out: one pce and no imp on ldrs* **5/1**3
0230 **10** 1 ¾ **Valencha**8 6633 5-8-13 99 RobertHavlin 3 78
(Hughie Morrison) *trckd ldrs: outpcd over 2f out: wknd over 1f out* **12/1**
0143 **11** 9 **Free Verse**30 5980 3-8-11 96 JamieSpencer 14 54
(Richard Hannon) *racd towards nr side: nvr on terms: no prog and wl btn 2f out: sn bhd* **8/1**
2160 **12** hd **Alice's Dancer (IRE)**17 6375 3-8-11 83 WilliamCarson 12 54
(William Muir) *dwlt: a in rr: struggling sn after 1/2-way: bhd fnl 2f* **50/1**
0434 **13** 2 ¼ **Instance**23 6161 4-8-13 98 JamesDoyle 9 47
(Jeremy Noseda) *trckd ldrs: lost pl over 2f out: wknd qckly over 1f out* **10/1**
3201 **14** 1 **My Queenie (IRE)**66 4702 3-8-11 95 JoeFanning 17 45
(Richard Hannon) *dwlt: towards nr side and a wl in rr: bhd fnl 2f* **20/1**
0506 **15** 1 ¾ **Responsive**28 6023 3-8-11 77 1 EddieAhern 8 40
(Hughie Morrison) *led 1f: lost pl 1/2-way: wknd and eased fnl 2f* **66/1**

1m 29.51s (1.91) **Going Correction** +0.475s/f (Yiel)
WFA 3 from 4yo+ 2lb **15** Ran SP% **123.0**
Speed ratings (Par 111): **108,106,105,104,103 103,101,101,99,97 87,87,84,83,81**
toteswingers 1&2 £75.50, 2&3 £12.90, 1&3 £26.30 CSF £210.86 TOTE £30.50: £6.90, £5.40, £1.70; EX 509.90 TRIFECTA Not won..
Owner D S Lee **Bred** Jeremy Green & Sons & Cheveley Park Stud **Trained** Newmarket, Suffolk
■ Stewards' Enquiry : Seb Sanders two-day ban: used whip above permitted level (Oct 21-22)

FOCUS
Late-season fillies' Listed form and muddling once again, with far side the place to be and not many getting into it from off the pace. A 10lb personal best from the winner.

NOTEBOOK
Intense Pink had looked good earlier in the season when bolting up in soft ground and she rediscovered her form back from a 100-day break. Unlike some, Seb Sanders had clearly been watching the previous race and noted far side was the place to be, steering his filly on to the rail, and the pair were always doing enough. She'd had excuses for her most recent runs and will stay in training next year.
Switcher(IRE) was soon prominent towards the far side from her low draw, but she tended to edge more towards the centre and was always being held. (op 16-1)
Sentaril came from much further back than the front pair and never stood a chance. It says a lot for her that she managed to get as close as she did. (tchd 4-1)
Mrs Greeley, rated just 79, was favoured by where she raced and clearly ran above herself.
Radio Gaga ran about as well as could have been expected under the penalty. (op 16-1)

I'm So Glad can have her effort upgraded, being the only one of those to race nearer the stands' side to really make a move. Racing against the bias ultimately took its toll.
Punita(USA) ◆, off for 105 days having made a successful handicap debut from a mark of 78, was short of room when trying to keep on from the rear and crossed the line with something left. She'll be of interest returned to a handicap. (op 6-1)
Bonnie Brae was briefly denied a clear run but was coming from an unpromising position anyway. (tchd 9-2)
Instance Official explanation: trainer's rep said filly was unsuited by the soft ground

6871 BRIGHTWELLS ASCOT SALES (CONDITIONS STKS) 6f
5:20 (5:21) (Class 2) 2-Y-O **£16,172** (£4,812; £2,405; £1,202) **Stalls** Centre

Form RPR
310 **1** **Melbourne Memories**[21] 6227 2-8-12 75 JamesDoyle 8 90+
(Clive Cox) *trckd ldrs: pushed up to chal 2f out: drvn to ld 1f out: r.o wl and jst hld on* **7/1**
6 **2** *hd* **Birdlover**[17] 5418 2-8-12 0 RichardKingscote 4 89+
(Ralph Beckett) *pressed ldr: led over 2f out: drvn and hdd 1f out: wl clr of rest and battled on wl: jst hld* **5/1**[2]
1306 **3** *8* **Blackdown Spirit**[32] 5903 2-9-3 84 JamesMillman 13 70
(Rod Millman) *hld up in rr: rdn and prog 2f out: kpt on to take 3rd jst ins fnl f: no ch w clr ldng pair* **13/2**[3]
5 **4** *nk* **Jacobella**[12] 6534 2-8-12 0 JohnFahy 10 65+
(Jonathan Portman) *hld up in 12th and wl off the pce: prog in centre 2f out: styd on fnl f: nrly snatched 3rd: no ch* **25/1**
0625 **5** *hd* **Tommy's Secret**[24] 6139 2-9-3 88 BrettDoyle 3 69
(Jane Chapple-Hyam) *prom bhd ldrs: wl outpcd fnl 2f* **4/1**[1]
61 **6** *2* **Ovett**[70] 4581 2-9-3 75 GeorgeBaker 15 63
(Gary Moore) *taken steadily to post: racd freely: led to over 2f out: sn lft bhd by ldng pair: wknd fnl f* **10/1**
4020 **7** *hd* **The Black Jacobin**[14] 6487 2-9-3 74 (b[1]) JamieSpencer 2 62
(J S Moore) *t.k.h: hld up in rr: trying to make prog 2f out but hanging: sharp reminders 1f out: kpt on* **16/1**
1015 **8** *3 ¼* **Pasaka Boy**[49] 5353 2-9-3 89 MartinHarley 11 53
(Jonathan Portman) *chsd ldrs: rdn 2f out: wknd over 1f out* **4/1**[1]
033 **9** *½* **Muskat Link**[51] 5275 2-9-3 67 DaneO'Neill 9 51
(Henry Candy) *chsd ldrs: rdn and hanging 2f out: wknd over 1f out* **12/1**
00 **10** *¾* **Ropehanger**[68] 4646 2-8-12 0 SilvestreDeSousa 7 44
(Lee Carter) *wl in tch in midfield: wknd over 1f out* **40/1**
4000 **11** *1 ¼* **Lobelia**[53] 5192 2-8-12 51 JoeFanning 6 40
(Brian Meehan) *chsd ldrs: rdn and wknd wl over 1f out* **50/1**
3 **12** *4 ½* **Don Eduardo**[15] 6431 2-9-3 0 JohnnyMurtagh 14 32
(J S Moore) *in tch: rdn over 2f out: wknd wl over 1f out* **16/1**
13 *4* **Ava Schmetterling** 2-8-9 0 RobertHavlin 5 12
(Dr Jon Scargill) *sn last: bhd fr 1/2-way* **66/1**

1m 16.14s (1.64) **Going Correction** +0.475s/f (Yiel) 13 Ran SP% 120.8
Speed ratings (Par 101): **108,107,97,96,96 93,93,89,88,87 85,79,74**
toteswingers 1&2 £6.40, 2&3 £8.30, 1&3 £9.40 CSF £41.48 TOTE £9.00: £2.30, £1.90, £2.40; EX 42.90 Trifecta £699.20 Pool: £2702.60 - 2.86 winning units..
Owner M P Coleman & R J Coleman **Bred** M P Coleman & R J Coleman **Trained** Lambourn, Berks
■ Stewards' Enquiry : Brett Doyle two-day ban: used whip above permitted level (Oct 21-22)

FOCUS
With all the jockeys finally cottoning on, the field were fairly well bunched far side and once again it was a couple of prominent racers who dominated. Sound form, with useful efforts from the front two who came clear.

NOTEBOOK
Melbourne Memories, coming across from stall eight, bounced back from a disappointing effort on her nursery debut (ground reportedly too fast), coping fine with the soft ground and just holding on from the rallying second. Further progress will be required if she's to follow up returning to handicaps, however. (tchd 11-2)
Birdlover was well backed and duly improved on her initial effort, racing closest to the far rail but not quite being good enough. She was back in front a couple of strides past the line and looks in need of 7f. She can probably win a modest maiden. (op 7-1 tchd 4-1)
Blackdown Spirit bounced back from a couple of lesser efforts but was still well held by the front pair and isn't easy to place. (op 8-1 tchd 9-1)
Jacobella was a bit of an eyecatcher, finishing late from an unpromising position. She'll be one for handicaps over further following another run.
Tommy's Secret wasn't at his best, this despite having the far rail to race against. The ground was probably too soft but he's another who is going to be hard to place. (tchd 5-1)
Ovett, representing last year's winning trainer/jockey combination, was too keen in front on ground that probably wouldn't have suited. He's worth another chance. (op 8-1)
The Black Jacobin Official explanation: jockey said gelding hung right
Pasaka Boy, dropping in trip, had made a winning debut on soft ground so it was disappointing he could fare no better than eighth. This clearly wasn't his form. (tchd 9-2)
T/Jkpt: Not won. T/Plt: £393.30 to a £1 stake. Pool of £174209.40 - 323.31 winning tickets.
T/Qpdt: £215.60 to a £1 stake. Pool of £8565.89 - 29.40 winning tickets. JN

6671 NEWMARKET (R-H)
Saturday, October 6

OFFICIAL GOING: Soft (6.6)
Wind: Light, half behind Weather: dry and bright

6872 E B F FEDERATION OF BLOODSTOCK AGENTS MAIDEN STKS (DIV I) 1m
1:40 (1:40) (Class 4) 2-Y-O **£5,175** (£1,540; £769; £384) **Stalls** High

Form RPR
2 **1** **Tarikhi (USA)**[50] 5321 2-9-3 0 MickaelBarzalona 13 87+
(Saeed Bin Suroor) *mde all: rdn and readily wnt clr wl over 1f out: styd on strly fnl f: readily* **2/1**[1]
2 *2 ¾* **Jadesnumberone (IRE)** 2-8-12 0 StevieDonohoe 12 75+
(Michael Bell) *in tch: swtchd rt and hdwy ent fnl 2f: chsd wnr and edgd rt over 1f out: no imp on wnr but styd on wl for clr 2nd* **50/1**
3 *4 ½* **Kelvingrove (IRE)** 2-9-3 0 IanMongan 8 70
(Sir Henry Cecil) *rn green: chsd ldrs: reminders after 2f: rdn 1/2-way: outpcd by ldng pair and btn over 1f out: styd on same pce after* **9/1**
0 **4** *¾* **Portmonarch (IRE)**[22] 6204 2-9-3 0 TedDurcan 9 68
(David Lanigan) *stdd s: t.k.h: hld up towards rr: hdwy into midfield 1/2-way: rdn and outpcd 2f out: rallied 1f out and styd on fnl f: no threat to ldng pair* **50/1**
5 *1 ¼* **Duke Of Perth** 2-9-3 0 KierenFallon 4 66+
(Luca Cumani) *in tch in midfield: rdn: rn green and outpcd on downhill run wl over 1f out: wl hld but kpt on again ins fnl f* **16/1**
0 **6** *nk* **Gold Burst (IRE)**[17] 6377 2-9-3 0 RichardHughes 5 65
(Richard Hannon) *racd towards centre: in tch: rdn and unable qck jst over 2f out: outpcd and btn over 1f out: wl hld and one pce fnl f* **33/1**
7 *1 ¾* **Crop Report (USA)** 2-9-3 0 MichaelHills 10 61
(William Haggas) *hld up in tch in rr: rdn along and nt clr run over 2f out: sme hdwy into midfield 2f out: no imp and plugged on same pce fnl f* **25/1**
8 *2 ¼* **Lavender Bay** 2-8-12 0 LukeMorris 11 51
(Tim Pitt) *chsd wnr tl over 1f out: sn outpcd and btn: wknd ins fnl f* **150/1**
5 **9** *nk* **Flashheart (IRE)**[15] 6447 2-9-3 0 HayleyTurner 3 56
(Marcus Tregoning) *racd towards centre for 3f: hld up towards rr: rdn and no hdwy over 2f out: edgd lft and wl hld over 1f out* **3/1**[2]
4 **10** *3 ¼* **Winterlude (IRE)**[23] 6164 2-8-12 0 AntiocoMurgia[(5)] 6 48
(Mahmood Al Zarooni) *hld up in tch in midfield: swtchd rt and effrt over 2f out: no prog wl over 1f out: sn btn and wknd ent fnl f* **7/2**[3]
11 *nk* **Tajheez (IRE)** 2-9-3 0 PaulHanagan 2 48
(Roger Varian) *s.i.s: racd towards centre 3f out: a towards rr: rdn along and struggling over 2f out: sn wknd* **16/1**
12 *2 ½* **Halperion** 2-9-3 0 LiamKeniry 1 42+
(David Elsworth) *racd towards centre for 3f: rn green and a towards rr: rdn and struggling 1/2-way: n.d after* **66/1**
3 **13** *½* **Da Do Run Run**[30] 5976 2-9-3 0 MartinLane 7 41
(Brian Meehan) *v free to post: stdd s: t.k.h: chsd ldrs tl over 2f out: sn wknd: fdd fr over 1f out* **20/1**

1m 41.65s (3.05) **Going Correction** +0.20s/f (Good) 13 Ran SP% 119.9
Speed ratings (Par 97): **92,89,84,84,82 82,80,78,78,74 74,72,71**
toteswingers 1&2 £32.60, 2&3 £46.90, 1&3 £9.80 CSF £134.53 TOTE £2.90: £1.10, £18.30, £2.50; EX 144.50 TRIFECTA Not won..
Owner Godolphin **Bred** Darley **Trained** Newmarket, Suffolk

FOCUS
Following 13.5mm of overnight rain the going was officially soft. Paul Hanagan described the ground as "sticky" after the first. The time for the opener was six seconds slower than standard. Division one of a warm maiden that was won last year by the St Leger winner Encke, it was fairly steadily run and a number of the runners were green, but winners should come out of it. The first two home came out of the two highest stalls and finished clear. The winner could rate a good bit better.

NOTEBOOK
Tarikhi(USA) was second to a fellow Godolphin runner on his debut on fast ground on the July course, and the fourth and fifth, also running in the royal blue, have both won since. He put his experience to good use, grabbed the rail from the inside draw and lengthened nicely for a comfortable win. A Derby entry, he looks a useful prospect but it's hard to know where he stands in the Godolphin pecking order. (op 15-8 tchd 9-4)
Jadesnumberone(IRE), one of two fillies in the race, shaped really well, showing signs of greenness when first required to quicken but running on well. With improvement almost guaranteed, she should win a maiden at least. (op 40-1)
Kelvingrove(IRE), a 180,000gns yearling and a Derby entry, is a half-brother to the high-class Cavalryman. He was noticeably green and needed some sharp early reminders, so did well to finish third, albeit well held by the front two. He will be suited by 1m4f next year. (op 11-1 tchd 8-1)
Portmonarch(IRE), an expensive yearling, travelled quite well. Although unable to race on with the first two, this was still an improvement on his debut effort. (op 40-1)
Duke Of Perth ◆ showed abundant promise, keeping on steadily after missing the break. Luca Cumani has had considerable success with the family, bred at his Fittocks Stud, and this colt is a half-brother to the stakes winners Forte Dei Marmi and Savarain. He will come into his own over further next season. (op 14-1)
Gold Burst(IRE) broke better than he had at Yarmouth and showed ability, but more is needed.
Crop Report(USA), a half-brother to three winners in the USA, looked a nice type in the paddock. He was green in the race and should step up markedly on this. (tchd 28-1)
Lavender Bay ran well for a long way and may have prospects in a maiden confined to her own sex.
Flashheart(IRE) was disappointing and could not confirm the promise of his debut in a decent conditions race at Newbury, although the ground that day had been much quicker. (op 7-2)
Winterlude(IRE), representing the Encke stable, ran a tame race, with the soft ground a plausible excuse for the son of Street Cry. He had two handlers in the paddock. (op 5-1)
Tajheez(IRE) was on his toes, got warm and was very green in the preliminaries. (tchd 14-1)

6873 £300,000 TATTERSALLS MILLIONS 2YO FILLIES' TROPHY 7f
2:15 (2:18) (Class 2) 2-Y-O
£166,513 (£68,131; £30,311; £15,109; £7,570; £3,015) **Stalls** High

Form RPR
01 **1** **Victrix Ludorum (IRE)**[14] 6490 2-9-0 85 RichardHughes 18 95+
(Richard Hannon) *chsd ldr tl led ent fnl 2f: rdn and wnt clr over 1f out: styd on wl fnl f: rdn out* **9/1**
0244 **2** *1 ¼* **Miss You Too**[28] 6027 2-9-0 90 IanMongan 2 92
(David Simcock) *t.k.h: hld up in midfield: rdn and effrt 2f out: hdwy u.p over 1f out: chsd clr wnr ins fnl f: kpt on but no imp fnl 100yds* **20/1**
1110 **3** *hd* **The Gold Cheongsam (IRE)**[7] 6672 2-9-0 98 RyanMoore 12 91+
(Jeremy Noseda) *hld up towards rr: pushed along 3f out: nt clr run ent fnl 2f: rdn and gd hdwy over 1f out: chsd ldng pair ins fnl f: r.o wl to press for 2nd cl home: could nt rch wnr* **7/2**[1]
511 **4** *3* **Penny Rose**[15] 6448 2-9-0 81 KierenFallon 13 84+
(Mark Johnston) *hld up in tch in midfield: nt clr run and shuffled bk ent fnl 2f: swtchd lft and hdwy over 1f out: styd on wl ins fnl f to go 4th cl home: unable to chal* **9/2**[2]
102 **5** *½* **Badr Al Badoor (IRE)**[14] 6490 2-9-0 85 HayleyTurner 3 83
(James Fanshawe) *chsd ldrs: rdn and effrt 2f out: drvn and unable qck over 1f out: plugged on same pce and wl hld fnl f* **12/1**
641 **6** *1* **Valais Girl**[15] 6444 2-9-0 75 (p) TedDurcan 4 80
(Marcus Tregoning) *led: rdn and hdd ent fnl f: drvn and outpcd by wnr over 1f out: lost 2nd ins fnl f: wknd fnl 150yds* **33/1**
7 *1 ½* **Reqaaba** 2-9-0 0 PaulHanagan 9 76+
(John Gosden) *stdd s: hld up towards rr: nt clr run and swtchd lft wl over 1f out: hdwy over 1f out: no threat to ldrs but kpt on fnl f* **14/1**
31 **8** *¾* **Concise**[29] 6014 2-9-0 84 JimmyFortune 19 75
(Ed Dunlop) *in tch: rdn and effrt ent fnl 2f: drvn and wknd over 1f out* **9/1**
125 **9** *½* **Asgardella (IRE)**[14] 6490 2-9-0 77 FrederikTylicki 7 73
(Richard Fahey) *w ldrs tl struggling u.p ent fnl 2f: sn outpcd and wknd over 1f out* **25/1**
1356 **10** *hd* **Elle Woods (IRE)**[23] 6160 2-9-0 78 FergusSweeney 16 73
(Michael Dods) *t.k.h: hld up in midfield: rdn and hdwy to chse ldrs ent fnl 2f: drvn and wknd over 1f out* **33/1**
3021 **11** *nk* **Aseela (IRE)**[16] 6413 2-9-0 64 RobertWinston 14 72
(Clive Brittain) *chsd ldrs but sn rdn along: lost pl ent fnl 2f: wknd u.p over 1f out* **100/1**
1103 **12** *shd* **Graphic Guest**[30] 5979 2-9-0 99 SamHitchcott 6 72
(Mick Channon) *in tch in midfield: effrt and hdwy u.p 2f out: drvn and no hdwy over 1f out: wknd ent fnl f* **17/2**[3]

13 1 ½ **Broadway Duchess (IRE)** 2-9-0 0 .... PatDobbs 11 68
(Richard Hannon) *s.i.s: hld up in rr: swtchd rt 3f out and sme hdwy over 2f out: no hdwy 2f out and sn wknd* **18/1**

14 ½ **Crystal Mist** 2-9-0 0 .... LukeMorris 8 67
(Harry Dunlop) *in tch: rdn after 2f and steadily lost pl: bhd and u.p whn wnt rt 3f out: no ch w ldrs but styd on again past btn horses fnl f* **100/1**

1603 15 nk **Mollyvator (IRE)**[14] 6490 2-9-0 74 .... (p) JimCrowley 1 66
(Mrs K Burke) *racd along on far rail: prom: u.p and struggling wl over 1f out: btn 1f out: fdd fnl f* **28/1**

16 1 **Musikhani** 2-9-0 0 .... LiamKeniry 10 64
(Andrew Balding) *hld up in rr: rdn and struggling wl over 2f out: wknd 2f out* **50/1**

4 17 nk **Of Course Darling**[78] 4297 2-9-0 0 .... MickaelBarzalona 17 63
(Ed Dunlop) *hld up towards rr: rdn and no hdwy over 2f out: wknd 2f out* **16/1**

50 18 2 **Fantacise**[56] 5103 2-9-0 88 .... (b) MartinLane 15 58
(Brian Meehan) *in tch in midfield: rdn and no hdwy over 2f out: sn lost pl and bhd fnl f* **22/1**

0054 19 2 ½ **Shafaani**[14] 6490 2-9-0 75 .... (bt) KirstyMilczarek 5 52
(Clive Brittain) *racd in midfield: rdn and short-lived effrt over 2f out: wknd 2f out and bhd fnl f* **66/1**

1m 25.87s (0.47) **Going Correction** +0.20s/f (Good) **19** Ran SP% **124.2**
Speed ratings (Par 98): **105,103,103,99,99 98,96,95,95,94 94,94,92,92,91 90,90,87,85**
toteswingers 1&2 £34.20, 2&3 £19.40, 1&3 £7.30 CSF £183.84 TOTE £10.00: £2.80, £5.50, £1.70; EX 259.00 Trifecta £749.90 Part won. Pool: £1010.37 - 0.36 winning units..
Owner Mrs J Wood **Bred** Yukiko Hosokawa **Trained** East Everleigh, Wilts

FOCUS
Easily the most valuable race of the year for juvenile fillies, worth £74,000 more to the winner than the Cheveley Park and the Fillies' Mile and four times as much as the Queen Mary at Royal Ascot. Two of the race's four previous winners went on to score at the top level, namely Lillie Langtry (Coronation and Matron Stakes) and Samitar (Irish 1,000 Guineas and Garden City Stakes). This looked a good-quality renewal and it was slightly quicker than the following colts' equivalent. With the exception of Mollyvator, who raced alone on the fair rail, the field formed one group down the centre. The time was excellent but the form can't be rated any higher than this. The winner progresed again.

NOTEBOOK
Victrix Ludorum(IRE) added to the £55,000 she picked up when taking another sales race here last time, confirming the form with the next four home that day. Always towards the fore and travelling strongly, she quickened up nicely to assume control and was never in much danger, although the placed fillies were cutting her back a little towards the line. Clearly a very useful filly, she was suited by the extra furlong and belied any concerns about the soft ground. She can make her mark in Group company. (op 8-1 tchd 10-1)
Miss You Too was on her toes and edgy beforehand. Formerly with Mick Channon but still with the same owner, she ran on well from out of the pack but the winner was in control. She's something of a madam, but she is a useful filly who's capable of picking up some black type. She was twice fourth in Listed races for her previous yard. (op 22-1 tchd 25-1)
The Gold Cheongsam(IRE) landed another valuable sales race at Doncaster before meeting trouble when last of 11 to Rosdhu Queen in the Cheveley Park. Having her first outing over 7f, she ran on well in the latter stages to pick up another hefty chunk of prize-money. (op 4-1)
Penny Rose ◆ was short of room on the approach to the two pole and was shuffled back, but came home in nice style and remains a very interesting prospect. A mile will suit her at this stage. (op 4-1)
Badr Al Badoor(IRE) could not reverse course form with Victrix Ludorum despite being 4lb better off with that filly. She may prove most effective back at 6f. (op 11-1)
Valais Girl, winner of a modest Newbury maiden last time, stepped up on that form with a prominent effort. She was fading in the latter stages as the seventh furlong started to find her out.
Reqaaba ◆, a leggy filly, made pleasing late progress from the rear and was best of the four newcomers. She's related to a stack of winners and won't let the family down. (tchd 16-1)
Concise was not discredited on this turf debut, but the drop back in trip may not have been ideal. (op 11-1 tchd 14-1)
Graphic Guest, withdrawn at the start prior to Victrix Ludorum's win here last month, has since passed a stalls test. Representing the Samitar stable, and a pound best in on BHA figures, she travelled quite well but didn't produce a great deal. She might not have stayed. (op 8-1)
Shafaani Official explanation: trainer said filly failed to stay 7f

6874 £500,000 TATTERSALLS MILLIONS 2YO TROPHY 7f
2:50 (2:52) (Class 2) 2-Y-0

£277,521 (£113,552; £50,519; £25,182; £12,616; £5,026) **Stalls High**

Form RPR

15 1 **Ghurair (USA)**[66] 4698 2-9-3 0 .... PaulHanagan 9 108+
(John Gosden) *travelled strly: chsd ldrs tl led wl over 1f out: sn rdn: hrd pressed and drvn ent fnl f: r.o gamely u.p* **7/4**[1]

1U11 2 hd **Havana Gold (IRE)**[9] 6599 2-9-3 107 .... RichardHughes 3 107+
(Richard Hannon) *stdd s: hld up in tch in last trio: hdwy over 2f out: rdn to chal over 1f out: ev ch fnl f: r.o wl but a jst hld* **2/1**[2]

1 3 3 ½ **Race And Status (IRE)**[14] 6486 2-9-3 0 .... JimmyFortune 4 98+
(Andrew Balding) *mde most tl wl over 1f out: sn drvn and stl ev ch 1f out: no ex and outpcd by ldng pair ins fnl f* **4/1**[3]

22 4 2 ¼ **Anna's Pearl**[15] 6423 2-9-3 0 .... JimCrowley 8 92
(Ralph Beckett) *chsd ldrs: rdn and lost pl 2f out and edgd lft over 1f out: rallied u.p and styd on again ins fnl f: no ch w ldrs* **33/1**

121 5 shd **Tamayuz Star (IRE)**[14] 6491 2-9-3 101 .... PatDobbs 12 92
(Richard Hannon) *stdd s: hld up in tch in rr: rdn and hdwy over 1f out: edgd rt and no imp ins fnl f* **10/1**

6 1 ¾ **Clancy Avenue (USA)**[22] 6220 2-9-3 0 .... WayneLordan 10 87
(T Stack, Ire) *hld up in tch: hdwy to chse ldrs 2f out: sn rdn and outpcd by ldng trio over 1f out: wknd ins fnl f* **40/1**

513 7 1 ½ **Mirsaale**[28] 6027 2-9-3 95 .... IanMongan 13 84
(James Tate) *hld up in tch in rr: swtchd lft and hdwy 2f out: drvn and no prog over 1f out: wknd fnl f* **28/1**

250 8 2 ½ **White Coppice**[14] 6491 2-9-3 72 .... FrederikTylicki 5 77?
(Richard Fahey) *squeezed for room s: hld up in tch in rr: effrt and nt clr run jst over 2f out: rdn and no hdwy wl over 1f out: nvr trbld ldrs* **100/1**

2105 9 hd **Discernable**[8] 6635 2-8-12 99 .... KierenFallon 11 71
(Mark Johnston) *pressed ldrs: rdn and ev ch over 2f out: wknd over 1f out: fdd ins fnl f* **16/1**

021 10 ¾ **Banovallum**[18] 6330 2-9-3 82 .... LiamKeniry 1 75
(Sylvester Kirk) *wnt rt s: hld up in tch in rr: rdn and effrt 2f out: no imp u.p over 1f out: wknd fnl f* **100/1**

043 11 11 **Global Icon**[14] 6491 2-9-3 88 .... TedDurcan 6 46
(Richard Hannon) *hld up in tch towards rr: rdn and effrt over 2f out: no prog whn bmpd wl over 1f out: sn wknd* **50/1**

0523 12 13 **Living Desert**[17] 6377 2-9-3 82 .... MickaelBarzalona 2 12
(James Toller) *in tch: rdn 4f out: losing pl whn bmpd wl over 1f out: sn wknd and wl bhd fnl f* **80/1**

1m 26.18s (0.78) **Going Correction** +0.20s/f (Good) **12** Ran SP% **118.7**
Speed ratings (Par 101): **103,102,98,96,96 94,92,89,89,88 75,61**
toteswingers 1&2 £1.70, 2&3 £2.50, 1&3 £3.00 CSF £5.21 TOTE £2.70: £1.30, £1.20, £1.50; EX 6.90 Trifecta £22.00 Pool: £2335.59 - 78.29 winning units..
Owner Hamdan Al Maktoum **Bred** Kirsten Rausing **Trained** Newmarket, Suffolk

FOCUS
Europe's richest 2yo race and Newmarket's most valuable event, this offered more prize-money than either Guineas, the Oaks, the Sussex Stakes or the Eclipse, among other Group 1s. The best of the four previous winners was Donativum, who went on to take the Breeders' Cup Juvenile Turf after beating future Racing Post Trophy winner Crowded House in this. There was plenty of depth to this edition and the first two, who pulled clear, showed solid, high-class juvenile form. Ghurair can rate higher still and Havana Gold ran to his mark. However, the time was a little slower than that for the earlier fillies' race.

NOTEBOOK
Ghurair(USA) won a hot maiden on his debut (Dundonnell third) before finishing a close fifth behind the Richard Hannon-trained Olympic Glory in the Group 2 Vintage Stakes at Glorious Goodwood. Given a break since, and reported to have grown, he stamped himself as a very smart colt with a battling victory. After striking the front he was strongly challenged by Havana Gold, but he showed the right attitude to prevail despite being less battle-hardened than his rival. He is well up to winning a Group race and holds entries in both the Dewhurst Stakes and the Racing Post Trophy later this month. There's further improvement in him and it would come as no surprise to see him aimed at the 2,000 Guineas back here next spring. (op 9-4)
Havana Gold(IRE) was on his toes beforehand. He was previously unbeaten in four completed starts, most recently the Group 3 Somerville Tattersall Stakes over C&D, and his powerful yard had the 1-2 in this last season. The colt did not get as clear a run as the winner, but was out in ample time and looked to be going the better when ranging alongside, only to be just outpointed. He has had a fine season and this was his best effort yet. Like the winner he is in the Dewhurst and the Racing Post Trophy. (op 7-4 tchd 9-4)
Race And Status(IRE) ◆ did not buckle straight away when tackled by the big two and deserves ample credit for this effort. He was the least experienced member of the field, having won a Newbury maiden (on fast ground) on his sole start. (op 6-1)
Anna's Pearl represented the stable of Oasis Dancer, who won this in 2009. The colt ran a similar sort of race as when a beaten odds-on chance at Ayr, staying on again after hitting a flat spot, and seems to act on most ground. This was a sizeable step up on the form he showed at Ayr, however. (op 25-1)
Tamayuz Star(IRE), the runner-up's stablemate, won a less competitive sales race over 6f here latest. He made late progress nearest the stands' rail without threatening the principals and is capable of picking up more black type. (op 9-1)
Clancy Avenue(USA), an Irish raider, is still a maiden after five starts but showed useful form when runner-up in a Down Royal nursery and travelled strongly for a long way here. He's yet to encounter a sound surface on turf. (op 28-1)
Mirsaale, who had made the running when third to Havana Gold at Haydock, was ridden differently here and was unable to land a blow. (op 25-1 tchd 33-1)
Banovallum Official explanation: jockey said colt hung left

6875 PIPER-HEIDSIECK "RARE" H'CAP 1m 2f
3:20 (3:27) (Class 2) (0-100,99) 3-Y-O

£12,450 (£3,728; £1,864; £932; £466; £234) **Stalls High**

Form RPR

0-41 1 **Blazing Speed**[63] 4797 3-9-3 95 .... JimCrowley 12 105
(James Fanshawe) *t.k.h early: hld up in tch in midfield: hdwy to chse ldrs 4f out: rdn 2f out: styd on to chal ent fnl f: led fnl 100yds: styd on wl and drew clr: rdn out* **10/1**

6213 2 2 **Prussian**[7] 6661 3-9-7 99 .... KierenFallon 15 105
(Mark Johnston) *chsd ldr: rdn to ld ent fnl 2f: drvn over 1f out: clr w wnr 1f out: hdd fnl 100yds: wknd towards fin* **5/1**[1]

6004 3 ½ **Unex Michelangelo (IRE)**[17] 6374 3-8-11 89 .... MichaelHills 9 94
(John Gosden) *hld up towards rr: hdwy and wandered arnd u.p over 1f out: drvn and kpt on wl ins fnl f: pressing for 2nd cl home* **20/1**

1104 4 nk **Tigers Tale (IRE)**[10] 6580 3-8-6 84 .... (v) AndreaAtzeni 4 88
(Roger Teal) *t.k.h: led tl ent fnl 2f: outpcd u.p over 1f out: kpt on same pce ins fnl f* **16/1**

4261 5 nk **Lady Loch**[7] 6667 3-8-4 82 .... MartinLane 10 86
(Richard Fahey) *in tch in midfield: rdn over 4f out: kpt on u.p and chsng ldrs over 1f out: styd on same pce ins fnl f* **6/1**[2]

1332 6 1 ½ **Clayton**[126] 2718 3-9-3 95 .... PaulHanagan 2 96
(Kevin Ryan) *t.k.h: chsd ldrs: rdn and outpcd over 2f out: kpt on same pce over 1f out: wknd ins fnl f* **5/1**[1]

1002 7 2 **Stature (IRE)**[18] 6348 3-8-10 95 .... ThomasBrown(7) 11 92
(Andrew Balding) *hld up in tch in last quartet: rdn and effrt ent fnl 2f: kpt on but no real imp fr over 1f out* **9/1**

1600 8 ¾ **Gabrial The Great (IRE)**[7] 6661 3-8-11 89 .... StevieDonohoe 3 84
(Michael Bell) *stdd s: t.k.h: hld up in rr: stl plenty to do whn swtchd rt and effrt wl over 1f out: plugged on same pce ins fnl f: nvr trbld ldrs* **7/1**[3]

3045 9 hd **Assizes**[18] 6348 3-8-5 88 .... MichaelJMMurphy(5) 1 83
(Mark Johnston) *in tch: rdn and unable qck over 1f out: edgd lft u.p and wknd ent fnl f* **9/1**

2210 10 5 **Burke's Rock**[35] 5834 3-8-13 91 .... (p) RyanMoore 8 76
(Jeremy Noseda) *t.k.h: hld up wl in tch: drvn and unable qck over 1f out: btn 1f out: sn fdd and eased wl ins fnl f* **16/1**

1005 11 3 ½ **Rosslyn Castle**[10] 6576 3-9-1 93 .... (b[1]) JimmyFortune 7 71
(Roger Charlton) *hld up in rr: rdn and no hdwy 2f out: sn wknd: bhd fnl f* **14/1**

5340 12 11 **Mister Music**[14] 6484 3-9-7 99 .... RichardHughes 14 55
(Richard Hannon) *hld up in rr: hdwy into midfield 5f out: rdn and no hdwy 2f out: wknd over 1f out and eased ins fnl f* **16/1**

2m 5.47s (-0.33) **Going Correction** +0.20s/f (Good) **12** Ran SP% **118.3**
Speed ratings (Par 107): **109,107,107,106,106 105,103,103,102,98 96,87**
toteswingers 1&2 £5.50, 2&3 £33.80, 1&3 £11.70 CSF £59.24 CT £996.49 TOTE £11.30: £3.30, £1.40, £8.30; EX 37.00 TRIFECTA Not won..
Owner Dragon Gate **Bred** J Sankey **Trained** Newmarket, Suffolk

FOCUS
A good, open handicap, but probably ordinary form for the grade. A clear best from the unexposed winner with the next few close to their marks. They raced in the centre of the track and it proved difficult to make ground from the rear.

NOTEBOOK
Blazing Speed, the least exposed member of the field, showed useful form when winning a fast-ground Doncaster maiden on his last start two months ago. He was keen again, but knuckled down well to get on top in the final furlong and could have more to offer if given the chance to tackle 1m4f. He'll be on a lofty mark after this. (op 9-1 tchd 8-1)
Prussian, on her toes beforehand, is an admirably tough and consistent filly and at one time it looked as if she was about to add to her five victories this season, but she was worn down inside the last. She was running off a career-high mark here. (op 11-2 tchd 13-2)

Unex Michelangelo(IRE) didn't get the best of runs and lost his pitch before staying on. Dropped 6lb since entering handicaps despite some respectable efforts, he was suited by the return to 1m2f and he handled the easy conditions well. (op 18-1 tchd 25-1)
Tigers Tale(IRE) ran a decent race and stuck on well enough to merit another try at this trip. (tchd 14-1)
Lady Loch ran creditably off a 4lb higher mark in this stronger race, plugging on down the outer after coming under pressure at halfway. (op 8-1 tchd 11-2)
Clayton was very fresh on his first start since finishing second in a valuable Musselburgh handicap at the beginning of June. To his credit he did not drop right away after losing his prominent position, and he won't mind a return to further. Paul Hanagan reported that the gelding hung left throughout. Official explanation: jockey said gelding hung left throughout (op 11-2, tchd 13-2 in a place)
Gabrial The Great(IRE) finds this trip is on the short side and never got into it from the back of the field. He isn't wholly straightforward. (op 8-1 tchd 13-2)
Burke's Rock ran better than her eventual placing suggests. (op 12-1)

6876 E B F FEDERATION OF BLOODSTOCK AGENTS MAIDEN STKS (DIV II) 1m

3:55 (3:57) (Class 4) 2-Y-O £5,175 (£1,540; £769; £384) **Stalls** High

Form RPR
6 **1** **Our Obsession (IRE)**[63] 4818 2-8-12 0 MichaelHills 3 84+
(William Haggas) *chsd ldr tl over 2f out: sn rdn: 3rd and looked hld 1f out: rallied to ld fnl 100yds: edgd lft but sn drew clr: rdn out* **13/2**
2 **2** *3* **Ostaad (IRE)**[29] 6014 2-9-3 0 FrederikTylicki 6 80
(Saeed Bin Suroor) *led and crossed to r against stands' rail: jnd ent fnl 2f: drvn over 1f out: battled on u.p tl hdd & wknd fnl 100yds* **2/1**[1]
6 **3** *1 ½* **Number One London (IRE)**[28] 6020 2-9-3 0 KierenFallon 8 77+
(Brian Meehan) *t.k.h: hld up in tch: 5th and no imp over 1f out tl styd on strly whn met rising grnd ins fnl f: swtchd rt and wnt 3rd cl home* **5/1**[3]
4 *nk* **Layl (USA)** 2-9-3 0 MickaelBarzalona 12 76
(Mahmood Al Zarooni) *chsd ldrs tl hdwy to join ldr on bit ent fnl 2f: racing awkwardkly and hanging rt over 1f out: rdn and fnd nil 1f out: btn fnl 75yds and fdd towards fin* **10/1**
24 **5** *nk* **Sublimation (IRE)**[14] 6486 2-9-3 0 RichardHughes 10 75
(Richard Hannon) *in tch: chsd ldng trio and rdn 2f out: drvn and no imp over 1f out: wknd ins fnl f* **3/1**[2]
6 *7* **Nateeja (IRE)** 2-8-12 0 PaulHanagan 11 55+
(Marcus Tregoning) *bhd in last quartet: rdn and struggling 1/2-way: lost tch w ldrs 2f out: sme modest hdwy ins fnl f* **22/1**
7 *½* **Deficit (IRE)** 2-9-3 0 JimmyFortune 1 59+
(Michael Bell) *s.i.s: a towards rr: swtchd rt and no imp u.p over 2f out: nvr trbld ldrs* **20/1**
8 *½* **Grendisar (IRE)** 2-9-3 0 AndreaAtzeni 2 58
(Marco Botti) *hld up in tch in midfield: rdn and struggling 3f out: btn 2f out and sn wknd* **66/1**
9 *3 ¼* **Relentless (IRE)** 2-9-3 0 NickyMackay 4 51
(John Gosden) *s.i.s: towards rr tl hdwy into midfield 1/2-way: rdn and outpcd over 2f out: wknd wl over 1f out* **14/1**
10 *1 ¼* **Dashing Star** 2-9-3 0[1] TedDurcan 5 48
(David Elsworth) *taken down early: s.i.s: t.k.h: a bhd: lost tch over 2f out* **50/1**
11 *hd* **Bold And Free** 2-9-3 0 LiamKeniry 9 47
(David Elsworth) *s.i.s: a bhd: lost tch over 2f out* **66/1**
0 **12** *6* **Thirlestane**[28] 6043 2-8-9 0 PatrickHills[(3)] 7 29
(James Given) *in tch in midfield: rdn and lost pl 1/2-way: bhd fnl 2f* **125/1**

1m 40.62s (2.02) **Going Correction** +0.20s/f (Good) **12** Ran SP% **118.9**
Speed ratings (Par 97): **97,94,92,92,91 84,84,83,80,79 79,73**
toteswingers 1&2 £4.60, 2&3 £4.30, 1&3 £9.10 CSF £19.10 TOTE £7.60: £3.30, £1.60, £2.50; EX 29.30 Trifecta £318.30 Pool: £1771.02 - 4.11 winning units..
Owner A E Oppenheimer **Bred** Hascombe And Valiant Studs **Trained** Newmarket, Suffolk

FOCUS
Division two of this good maiden was a second quicker than the first. The second and fifth set the standard and the winner is a nice prospect.

NOTEBOOK
Our Obsession(IRE) had caught the eye on her debut on the July course and, like a lot of her juvenile stablemates, showed considerable improvement second time out. Always prominent, she took a while to engage full stride but picked up strongly when meeting the rising ground to win going away. Likely to stay 1m2f plus, she looks a nice prospect for next season. It's early days, but she has an Irish Oaks entry. (tchd 7-1)
Ostaad(IRE) was never far away against the rail and kept on without being able to quicken up. Tackling turf for the first time here, he had also been runner-up on his debut at Kempton, when beaten by Concise, who finished eighth in the big sales race on this card. His turn will come. (op 5-2)
Number One London(IRE) ◆, third on his debut over 7f, was outpaced by the leaders before picking up and flashing home for third. He looks a surefire winner of a maiden and should make a nice handicapper next term. (op 10-1 tchd 11-1)
Layl(USA), representing the stable of Encke, who won this maiden 12 months ago, is out of a Listed winner. Reportedly not the most robust, he travelled well into contention but hung off the bridle and didn't find anything for pressure. He may need time. (op 6-1)
Sublimation(IRE) ran a promising race second time out at Newbury when fourth to Race And Status, who was third in the earlier sales race on this card. The Richard Hannon colt could not build on that, lacking the pace to peg back the leaders. (op 5-2)
Nateeja(IRE) a half-sister to 1m4f Group 3 winner Hawaafez, was well held by the principals but will come into her own when tackling middle distances. (tchd 20-1 and 25-1)
Deficit(IRE), a Racing Post Trophy entry out of a Group 3 winner, missed the break and was not disgraced. (tchd 16-1)

6877 TRM SEVERALS STKS (LISTED RACE) (F&M) 1m 2f

4:25 (4:30) (Class 1) 3-Y-O+ £18,714 (£7,095; £3,550; £1,768; £887; £445) **Stalls** High

Form RPR
-001 **1** **Polygon (USA)**[98] 3632 4-9-5 103 (b) MichaelHills 17 106
(John Gosden) *in tch: chsd ldr over 2f out: rdn and ev ch over 1f out: led ins fnl f: edgd lft and kpt on wl u.p cl home: all out* **20/1**
0-62 **2** *hd* **Dorcas Lane**[77] 4338 4-9-2 99 TedDurcan 16 103
(David Lanigan) *stdd s: hld up in tch in rr: hdwy over 2f out: rdn and ev ch over 1f out: led ins fnl f: sn hdd but stl ev ch: no ex cl home* **12/1**
2121 **3** *1 ¼* **Sound Hearts (USA)**[34] 5856 3-8-11 90 AndreaAtzeni 15 101
(Roger Varian) *led: rdn wl over 1f out: kpt on wl u.p tl hdd and one pce ins fnl f* **14/1**
5152 **4** *2* **Aniseed (IRE)**[17] 6379 3-8-11 94 RichardHughes 20 97+
(William Haggas) *hld up in tch: rdn and effrt to chse ldrs over 1f out: hung rt and styd on same pce ins fnl f: wnt 4th cl home* **20/1**
-610 **5** *½* **Dinvar Diva**[107] 3292 3-8-11 83 NickyMackay 7 96+
(John Gosden) *stdd s: hld up in tch in rr: gd hdwy to chse ldrs 2f out: rdn and ev ch over 1f out tl ins fnl f: wknd fnl 100yds* **50/1**
1146 **6** *1 ¾* **Vow**[107] 3292 3-9-0 109 RyanMoore 8 95
(William Haggas) *in tch: rdn and effrt to chse ldrs wl over 2f out: no ex u.p over 1f out: styd on same pce after* **9/4**[1]
1000 **7** *nk* **Kailani**[23] 6163 3-9-0 103 MickaelBarzalona 18 94
(Mahmood Al Zarooni) *stdd s: hld up in rr: swtchd sharply rt over 2f out: hdwy 2f out: drvn and no imp ent fnl f: wknd fnl 100yds* **11/4**[2]
1/03 **8** *2 ¼* **Miss Starlight**[17] 6379 5-9-2 92 MartinLane 19 87
(Ibrahim Saeed Al Malki, Qatar) *in tch in midfield: rdn 4f out: drvn and outpcd 2f out: kpt on but no threat to ldrs fr over 1f out* **80/1**
212 **9** *nse* **Hippy Hippy Shake**[70] 4608 3-8-11 88 KierenFallon 1 87
(Luca Cumani) *stdd s: hld up in rr: rdn and effrt over 2f out: chsd ldrs but no ex u.p over 1f out: edgd lft 1f out and wknd ins fnl f* **11/1**
2200 **10** *2* **Dragonera**[7] 6674 4-9-2 95 TomMcLaughlin 9 83
(Ed Dunlop) *hld up in tch in rr: sme hdwy u.p over 2f out: no imp and styd on same pce fr over 1f out* **50/1**
1320 **11** *3 ¼* **Set To Music (IRE)**[9] 6598 4-9-5 105 HayleyTurner 10 79
(Michael Bell) *chsd ldrs: rdn and unable qck over 2f out: wknd u.p over 1f out* **7/1**[3]
4-00 **12** *¾* **Crystal Gal (IRE)**[195] 1041 5-9-2 100 IanMongan 12 75
(Lucy Wadham) *chsd ldrs tl 2f out: sn rdn and lost pl: bhd fnl f* **50/1**
2431 **13** *11* **Everlong**[22] 6190 3-8-11 90 JimmyFortune 13 53
(Peter Chapple-Hyam) *racd keenly: chsd ldr tl over 2f out: sn lost pl u.p: bhd fnl f* **9/1**
4150 **14** *5* **Qaadira (USA)**[17] 6379 3-8-11 81 PaulHanagan 11 43
(John Gosden) *in tch in midfield: rdn and struggling over 2f out: wl bhd and eased ins fnl f* **66/1**

2m 5.27s (-0.53) **Going Correction** +0.20s/f (Good)
WFA 3 from 4yo+ 5lb **14** Ran SP% **120.8**
Speed ratings (Par 111): **110,109,108,107,106 105,105,103,103,101 99,98,89,85**
toteswingers 1&2 £11.60, 2&3 £65.40, 1&3 £22.30 CSF £233.65 TOTE £10.80: £2.40, £3.00, £3.60; EX 74.00 Trifecta £1012.10 Pool: £1641.35 - 1.20 winning units..
Owner Lady Rothschild **Bred** Carwell Equities Ltd **Trained** Newmarket, Suffolk

FOCUS
There were half a dozen non-runners in this distaff Listed race, but it was still a competitive affair. The initial pace was not strong and the runners raced down the centre of the track. They were stretched across the course with two to run and the first four home, all drawn high, finished on the stands' side of the pack. There have to be doubts over the solidity of the form, which is ordinary for the grade.

NOTEBOOK
Polygon(USA) beat male opposition when landing the Listed Fred Archer Stakes on the July course and followed up back in trip following a break. The ground was very different here but she is an improved filly in blinkers and showed a good attitude to prevail. This may not be the limit of her improvement, for all that she was helped by a high draw here. (op 14-1)
Dorcas Lane has not matched her 3yo form for Lucy Wadham this term but has been running respectably all the same. Fresher than most at this stage of the campaign, she improved from the back and was carried to her left by the winner when challenging, but it didn't cost her the race. She is just as effective at 1m4f. (tchd 14-1)
Sound Hearts(USA), on her toes beforehand, set the pace and stuck on well to pick up some valuable black type at the first attempt. She has progressed rapidly in recent weeks and handled this softer ground well. Roger Varian's representative reported afterwards that the filly bled from the nose. Official explanation: trainer's rep said filly bled from the nose (op 12-1)
Aniseed(IRE) was runner-up in this grade at Yarmouth latest, albeit in an unsatisfactory affair. Again held up here, she was running on at the end and might appreciate another try at 1m4f. (op 16-1)
Dinvar Diva, who had not been since since finishing last in the Ribblesdale at Royal Ascot in June, looked set to cause a shock when taking it up going well, but was racing wide of the principals down the centre of the track and could not hold on in the final furlong. This was a taking run in the circumstances.
Vow had 4lb in hand on official figures on this return from a summer break and this looked an attractive opportunity for her. The Oaks fourth had her chance but was unable to quicken up. Not given a hard time when held, she may come on for the run with a return to 1m4f likely to suit. It will be interesting to see if she takes her chance in the British Champions Fillies' And Mares' Stakes at Ascot, although if she does she will need to step up considerably on what she showed here. (op 11-4)
Kailani, dropped in trip and grade, made ground smoothly once switched to the outside - away from the favoured flank - and did not find much when required. She had her ground here but has become frustrating. (op 9-2)
Hippy Hippy Shake had her chance on this rise in grade but couldn't find a change of gear. This was her first run in soft ground. (op 9-1 tchd 8-1)
Set To Music(IRE) has been below her best on her last two starts, both here. Hayley Turner reported that the filly had no more to give. Official explanation: jockey said filly had no more to give (op 6-1)

6878 E B F NATIONAL STUD BOADICEA FILLIES' STKS (LISTED RACE) 6f

5:00 (5:03) (Class 1) 3-Y-O+ £18,714 (£7,095; £3,550; £1,768; £887; £445) **Stalls** High

Form RPR
050 **1** **Swiss Dream**[21] 6268 4-9-2 100 LiamKeniry 8 107
(David Elsworth) *mde all and set stdy gallop: stl travelling wl over 1f out: rdn ent fnl f: edgd rt u.p but styd on wl: hld on cl home* **12/1**
3412 **2** *nk* **Ultrasonic (USA)**[48] 5385 3-8-12 102 RyanMoore 3 103+
(Sir Michael Stoute) *stdd s: t.k.h: hld up in tch towards rr: hdwy and swtchd rt over 1f out: racing wd of rivals but r.o wl ins fnl f: str chal fnl 50yds: r.o* **9/2**[2]
1500 **3** *1 ¼* **Angels Will Fall (IRE)**[14] 6485 3-9-1 103 RobertWinston 11 102
(Charles Hills) *stdd s: t.k.h: hld up in midfield: swtchd rt and hdwy 2f out: rdn to chse ldrs over 1f out: pressing wnr but styng on same pce whn carried rt and sltly hmpd ins fnl f* **9/1**
1111 **4** *½* **Baheeja**[30] 5980 3-8-12 91 AndreaAtzeni 7 97+
(Roger Varian) *chsd ldr tl edgd rt wl over 1f out: sltly outpcd u.p 1f out: rallied and styd on again towards fin* **8/1**
-600 **5** *shd* **Miss Work Of Art**[14] 6468 3-8-12 95 FrederikTylicki 1 97
(Richard Fahey) *in tch: effrt u.p to chse ldrs over 1f out: hrd drvn and styd on same pce ins fnl f* **40/1**
-211 **6** *½* **Hezmah**[9] 6602 4-8-13 99 PaulHanagan 9 95
(John Gosden) *t.k.h: hld up in tch: hdwy and rdn to chse ldr over 1f out tl ins fnl f: no ex and btn fnl 100yds: wknd towards fin* **11/4**[1]
2200 **7** *1* **Place In My Heart**[9] 6602 3-8-12 93 JimmyFortune 2 92
(George Baker) *chsd ldrs: rdn and effrt wl over 1f: unable qck and short of room over 1f out: btn and one pce fnl f* **40/1**
13 **8** *1 ½* **Hallelujah**[85] 4070 4-8-13 97 HayleyTurner 5 87
(James Fanshawe) *hld up in midfield: rdn and no imp ent fnl 2f: styd on same pce fnl f* **5/1**[3]
3102 **9** *¾* **My Sharona**[16] 6406 3-8-12 89 TedDurcan 4 85
(Sylvester Kirk) *stdd s: t.k.h: hld up in rr: rdn over 2f out: styd on past btn horses ins fnl f: nvr gng pce to trble ldrs* **16/1**

3300 **10** 1/2 **Ladies Are Forever**[22] 6201 4-8-13 102.......................... KierenFallon 10 83
(Geoffrey Oldroyd) *hld up in tch in last quartet: rdn and effrt wl over 1f out: kpt on but nvr gng pce to chal* **8/1**

2316 **11** 2 1/4 **Catwalk (IRE)**[13] 6515 3-8-12 83...................................(v) JimCrowley 12 76
(James Fanshawe) *in tch: rdn and struggling ent fnl 2f: wknd ent fnl f* **28/1**

6040 **12** 1 3/4 **Muaamara**[13] 6515 3-8-12 87.. SamHitchcott 13 71
(Mick Channon) *chsd ldrs tl over 2f out: sn lost pl and u.p: wknd over 1f out* **66/1**

0220 **13** 1 1/4 **Millibar (IRE)**[17] 6378 3-8-12 73..............................(b[1]) TomMcLaughlin 14 67
(Nick Littmoden) *stdd s: t.k.h: hld up in tch in rr: rdn and effrt ent 2f out: no imp and wknd ent fnl f* **100/1**

1m 13.6s (1.40) **Going Correction** +0.20s/f (Good)
WFA 3 from 4yo 1lb **13** Ran SP% **118.1**
Speed ratings (Par 108): **98,97,95,95,95 94,93,91,90,89 86,84,82**
toteswingers 1&2 £10.80, 2&3 £9.40, 1&3 £15.60 CSF £63.04 TOTE £15.50: £4.20, £1.80, £2.80; EX 79.30 TRIFECTA Not won..

Owner Lordship Stud **Bred** Lordship Stud **Trained** Newmarket, Suffolk

FOCUS
The field packed towards the stands' side in this fillies' Listed race. The form is ordinary for the grade with the winner posting a small personal best.

NOTEBOOK
Swiss Dream was able to claim the rail and, although she edged away from it under pressure, held on well to her advantage. Carrying a penalty for her win in this grade at Nottingham in May, and conceding weight all round here, she was back in class after contesting Group races since. She has a good record on the Rowley Mile, with three wins and a second from four starts. (op 14-1)

Ultrasonic(USA)'s second to Mince at Pontefract looked decent form at this level. She ran another big race from her low draw, which saw her come with her run widest out on the course and just fail to peg back the winner. She's capable of winning in this grade if things go her way. (op 7-2)

Angels Will Fall(IRE) got no run at all in a Newbury Group 3 but had no obvious excuse this time and ran her race, already held when slightly hampered. She remains in good heart. (op 7-1)

Baheeja was up in grade after landing four consecutive races at 7f, three of them handicaps. Given the way she was running on at the end, a return to that trip will suit her. (op 10-1)

Miss Work Of Art, last year's Cheveley Park fourth, ran creditably from what proved to be an unfavourable draw that saw her trapped wide. This was a big improvement on her last two runs. (op 100-1)

Hezmah was tackling her first Listed race. She was soon well placed, but had taken something of a hold and her effort fizzled out in the latter stages. (op 10-3)

Place In My Heart had excuses on her last two starts and this was more like it. (op 50-1)

Hallelujah has gone well fresh and better could have been expected on her first start since July. The ground should have been fine for her. (op 11-2)

6879 PIPER-HEIDSIECK H'CAP 1m
5:35 (5:41) (Class 2) (0-105,105) 3-Y-O+ **£12,938** (£3,850; £1,924; £962) **Stalls** High

Form RPR

3303 **1** **Moone's My Name**[8] 6633 4-9-7 **105**.................................. JimCrowley 2 110
(Ralph Beckett) *chsd ldrs tl rdn to ld over 1f out: edgd rt but styd on gamely fnl f: rdn out* **3/1[1]**

0003 **2** 3/4 **Beacon Lodge (IRE)**[7] 6670 7-8-12 **103**............... ShirleyTeasdale(7) 10 106
(David Nicholls) *taken down early: t.k.h: chsd ldrs: rdn and effrt to chal jst over 1f out: ev ch and carried rt fnl f: no ex towards fin* **9/1**

2302 **3** 2 **Masteroftherolls (IRE)**[16] 6400 4-9-4 **102**.............. MickaelBarzalona 9 100+
(Saeed Bin Suroor) *broke wl: t.k.h: w ldr tl grad stdd bk to rr after 2f: rdn and effrt jst over 1f out: drvn and wnt between rivals to chse ldng pair ins fnl f: r.o but nvr threatened ldng pair* **3/1[1]**

0006 **4** 1 **Axiom**[14] 6494 8-8-10 **94**.. HayleyTurner 6 90
(Ed Walker) *t.k.h: hld up in tch in last trio: rdn and effrt to chse ldrs over 1f out: no imp and one pce ins fnl f* **11/2[2]**

/004 **5** 1/2 **Too Much Trouble**[40] 5666 6-8-2 **91** oh4.........(p) MichaelJMMurphy(5) 7 86
(Ed Vaughan) *t.k.h: hld up in tch in last trio: swtchd rt and hdwy 2f out: rdn and no imp ent fnl f: wknd ins fnl f* **8/1[3]**

0 **6** 1/2 **Be Perfect (USA)**[15] 6446 3-8-13 **100**.............................. AndreaAtzeni 5 94
(Marco Botti) *led tl over 4f out: rdn and unable qck wl over 1f out: wknd ins fnl f* **11/1**

202 **7** 1/2 **Atlantic Sport (USA)**[13] 6513 7-8-10 **94**........................ SamHitchcott 4 87
(Mick Channon) *chsd ldrs tl led 5f out: rdn and hdd over 1f out: wknd 1f out* **8/1[3]**

1m 41.15s (2.55) **Going Correction** +0.20s/f (Good)
WFA 3 from 4yo+ 3lb **7** Ran SP% **105.9**
Speed ratings (Par 109): **95,94,92,91,90 90,89**
toteswingers 1&2 £4.90, 2&3 £5.20, 1&3 £2.70 CSF £25.97 CT £63.97 TOTE £3.20: £1.80, £4.00; EX 18.90 Trifecta £35.60 Pool: £1253.74 - 26.05 winning units..

Owner McDonagh Murphy And Nixon **Bred** Baroness Bloodstock & Tweenhills Stud **Trained** Kimpton, Hants

■ Rassam (7/1) was withdrawn on vet's advice at the s. Deduct 10p in the £ under R4.

FOCUS
A good handicap, although it was weakened by five non-runners and the form is fairly weak for the grade. It was a muddling race, run at only a steady pace on the worst of the ground before turning into a bit of a sprint. There are doubts over the form.

NOTEBOOK
Moone's My Name raced a little way apart from the others in the early stages before edging across to take over in front. She took first run heading down to the final furlong and found enough to hold off the runner-up. Third in a trio of Listed races this season, she has risen 26lb since the start of the campaign. This win proved that she acts on soft ground. (op 4-1 tchd 9-2)

Beacon Lodge(IRE) was one of several who pulled for their heads during the steadily run part of the race. He came through to issue a sustained challenge to the winner, but was always just being held. He was racing off a career-low mark, although he'd never run in a handicap until last month's Portland. (op 7-1 tchd 10-1)

Masteroftherolls(IRE) was back on turf for the first time since Meydan in the spring. Refusing to settle, he was switched away from the rail and lost his pitch before running on at the end. He was not seen to best effect here but is capable of better in a truly run race. (op 5-2 tchd 10-3)

Axiom has become well handicapped, currently on his lowest mark since 2009, but was unable to step up on a fair run here last time which followed a summer break. (tchd 4-1)

Too Much Trouble, racing from 4lb out of the weights, wore first-time cheekpieces. After proving very keen he could not quicken up once pulled to the outside and really needs further. (op 11-1 tchd 12-1)

Be Perfect(USA), who played up at the start, only ran on when it was too late. He's yet to click since coming to Britain, but the best hasn't been seen of him yet. (op 8-1)

Atlantic Sport(USA), making a rare appearance in a mile handicap, faded after making the running. (op 10-1)

T/Plt: £58.20 to a £1 stake. Pool of £88546.6 - 1110.10 winning tickets. T/Qpdt: £14.90 to a £1 stake. Pool of £5204.27 - 257.62 winning tickets. SP

6121 REDCAR (L-H)
Saturday, October 6

OFFICIAL GOING: Soft (good to soft in places; 7.3)
Wind: Light across Weather: Fine & dry

6880 BRITISH STALLION STUDS SUPPORTING BRITISH RACING E B F MAIDEN STKS 7f
2:05 (2:05) (Class 5) 2-Y-O **£2,975** (£885; £442; £221) **Stalls** Centre

Form RPR

0 **1** **Bit Of A Gift (FR)**[14] 6481 2-9-3 0.. NeilCallan 17 76+
(Roger Varian) *bmpd s: hld up: hdwy over 3f out: hung lft and led wl over 1f out: kpt on wl* **4/1[2]**

5323 **2** 1 1/4 **Disclaimer**[29] 5992 2-9-3 75... TomQueally 7 73
(Sir Henry Cecil) *trckd ldrs: drvn over 2f out: styd on same pce last 100yds* **3/1[1]**

42 **3** hd **He's A Striker (IRE)**[11] 6558 2-9-3 0............................ BarryMcHugh 16 73
(Tony Coyle) *wnt rt s: trckd ldrs: t.k.h: hmpd 2f out: kpt on wl towards fin* **4/1[2]**

4 1 1/2 **Lilac Lace (IRE)** 2-8-12 0.. DavidAllan 11 64+
(Tim Easterby) *s.i.s: hdwy 3f out: chsng ldrs over 1f out: kpt on towards fin* **25/1**

5526 **5** 1 **French Press (IRE)**[16] 6414 2-9-3 74....................... GrahamGibbons 15 66
(David Brown) *led: hdd wl over 1f out: wknd last 75yds* **8/1**

032 **6** hd **Khelman (IRE)**[14] 6473 2-9-0 79........................... LeeTopliss(3) 10 66
(Richard Fahey) *chsd ldrs: rdn 2f out: hung rt and kpt on one pce* **9/2[3]**

6 **7** 7 **War Lord (IRE)**[9] 6607 2-8-10 0.................................... DavidBergin(7) 18 48
(David O'Meara) *w ldrs: drvn over 2f out: lost pl over 1f out* **16/1**

8 shd **Dutch Gal** 2-8-12 0.. FrannyNorton 8 43+
(John Holt) *in rr: green and wnt rt over 2f out: kpt on fnl f* **25/1**

00 **9** 3/4 **Artful Prince**[50] 5325 2-9-3 0... JamesSullivan 6 46
(James Given) *chsd ldrs: sn drvn along: reminders over 3f out: sn lost pl* **150/1**

10 7 **High Flame (IRE)** 2-8-7 0.. DarylByrne(5) 14 24
(Tim Easterby) *s.i.s: nvr on terms* **40/1**

11 3/4 **The Mighty Peg** 2-9-3 0.. DuranFentiman 13 27
(Tim Walford) *in rr: bhd fnl 3f* **50/1**

12 nse **Halfwaytocootehill (IRE)** 2-9-3 0.................................. PaddyAspell 5 27
(Ollie Pears) *mid-div: lost pl over 3f out* **33/1**

0005 **13** nk **Shepherds Bow**[38] 5733 2-9-3 0.................................. RoystonFfrench 2 26
(Michael Easterby) *w ldrs: lost pl over 3f out: sn bhd* **200/1**

5 **14** 7 **Val's Diamond (IRE)**[17] 6355 2-8-12 0.............................. PJMcDonald 1 3
(Ann Duffield) *mid-div: lost pl over 3f out: bhd fnl 2f* **50/1**

1m 27.34s (2.84) **Going Correction** +0.425s/f (Yiel) **14** Ran SP% **118.3**
Speed ratings (Par 95): **100,98,98,96,95 95,87,87,86,78 77,77,77,69**
toteswingers 1&2 £4.70, 2&3 £2.90, 1&3 £8.70 CSF £15.17 TOTE £5.00: £1.70, £1.60, £2.10; EX 20.60.

Owner Saeed Suhail **Bred** Stratford Place Stud **Trained** Newmarket, Suffolk

FOCUS
Routine form in this maiden, the winner an improver. As is often the case in a race of this nature, the race didn't really begin in earnest until past halfway.

NOTEBOOK
Bit Of A Gift(FR) had shaped better than the result on last month's debut at Newbury and proved a totally different proposition at the second time of asking, edging left under pressure but soon in command after hitting the front over 1f out. He'll probably get a mark of around 80 on the back of this and appeals as the type to keep on improving with racing. (op 9-2)

Disclaimer is more than good enough to win a race at some point but is starting to look a little exposed, having every chance here. (op 10-3 tchd 7-2)

He's A Striker(IRE) confirmed the form he showed at Beverley and probably would have got second had he not been slightly impeded by the winner around 2f out. He's another who'll be winning before long. (op 7-2)

Lilac Lace(IRE) was a cheap purchase but looks a bargain after this encouraging debut, impressing with the way she made her ground up smoothly from off the pace (missed break). She looks sure to improve and should be something to back in a northern maiden next time, particularly a fillies' only event. (op 33-1 tchd 40-1)

French Press(IRE) wasn't discredited, leaving the impression his stamina may have been just stretched under these conditions. He's well worth a try over 6f at some stage.

Khelman(IRE) had shaped as if he'd be suited by 7f so this was a shade disappointing, edging right under pressure. There's a chance the softer ground was against him (raced only on good to firm previously) and it's still early days. (op 4-1)

Dutch Gal hinted at ability as she passed a few late on. (tchd 20-1)

6881 JOHN SMITH'S REDCAR STRAIGHT-MILE CHAMPIONSHIP FINAL (H'CAP) 1m
2:40 (2:40) (Class 2) 3-Y-O+
£12,450 (£3,728; £1,864; £932; £466; £234) **Stalls** Centre

Form RPR

2604 **1** **Ginger Jack**[25] 6124 5-9-3 **82**... PJMcDonald 1 93
(Geoffrey Harker) *trckd ldrs: hdwy 2f out: rdn to ld 1f out: styd on wl u.p towards fin* **10/1**

0013 **2** 1 1/2 **Dolphin Rock**[18] 6342 5-8-8 **73**... DaleSwift 13 81
(Brian Ellison) *a.p: led wl over 2f out: rdn along over 1f out: hdd and drvn ent fnl f: no ex last 100yds* **11/2[2]**

1410 **3** nk **Jo'Burg (USA)**[8] 6638 8-9-3 **89**.................................... DavidBergin(7) 4 96
(David O'Meara) *dwlt and in rr: smooth hdwy into midfield 3f out: trckd ldrs 2f out: effrt and ev ch over 1f out: sn rdn and one pce* **9/1[3]**

1000 **4** 3/4 **Kiwi Bay**[25] 6124 7-9-5 **84**.. GrahamLee 6 89
(Michael Dods) *hld up in midfield: hdwy 3f out: rdn to chse ldrs over 1f out: kpt on same pce fnl f* **5/1[1]**

1235 **5** 3/4 **Hakuna Matata**[42] 5588 5-8-8 **73**....................................(b) SeanLevey 16 76
(Michael Dods) *hld up towards rr: stdy hdwy over 2f out: n.m.r and swtchd lft over 1f out: sn rdn and kpt on same pce fnl f* **9/1[3]**

620 **6** nk **Elijah Pepper (USA)**[16] 6410 7-8-5 **70**............................ MartinDwyer 10 73
(David Barron) *hld up and bhd: hdwy over 2f out: rdn over 1f out: styd on wl fnl f: nrst fin* **25/1**

5505 **7** 1 **Collateral Damage (IRE)**[12] 6528 9-7-13 **64**.............(t) KellyHarrison 14 64
(Tim Easterby) *hld up towards rr: stdy hdwy on wd outside over 2f out: rdn to chse ldrs over 1f out: kpt on same pce fnl f* **25/1**

0044 **8** nk **Nameitwhatyoulike**[48] 5386 3-8-12 **80**........................... JamesSullivan 17 80
(Michael Easterby) *t.k.h early: hld up in tch on wd outside: hdwy over 2f out: rdn to chse ldrs over 1f out: wknd ins fnl f* **9/1[3]**

6404 **9** 1 **Blues Jazz**[13] 6513 6-8-6 **78**..................................... GeorgeChaloner(7) 12 75
(Ian Semple) *prom: rdn along 3f out: sn wknd* **16/1**

6650 **10** ¾ **Dhaular Dhar (IRE)**[8] 6638 10-8-2 **67**..........................(v[1]) KieranO'Neill 2 63
(Jim Goldie) *slty hmpd s: t.k.h and hld up towards rr: hdwy on wd outside over 2f out: rdn to chse ldrs over 1f out: sn drvn and wknd fnl f* **16/1**

0005 **11** 2¼ **Aquarian Spirit**[25] 6124 5-8-4 **69**................................ PatrickMathers 11 60
(Richard Fahey) *a towards rr: rdn along over 2f out: nvr a factor* **28/1**

0443 **12** *shd* **King Of Paradise (IRE)**[21] 6241 3-8-0 **68**.................. FrannyNorton 15 58
(Eric Alston) *t.k.h: chsd ldrs: rdn along wl over 2f out: sn wknd* **10/1**

1501 **13** *nk* **Ingleby Exceed (IRE)**[42] 5588 4-9-2 **81**.................... GrahamGibbons 9 71
(David O'Meara) *in tch: effrt over 2f out: sn rdn along and wknd wl over 1f out* **9/1[3]**

-006 **14** *shd* **File And Paint (IRE)**[3] 6782 4-8-0 **65**........................ DuranFentiman 3 54
(Lawrence Mullaney) *wnt lft s: led: rdn along over 3f out: hdd wl over 2f out and sn wknd* **40/1**

2031 **15** 2½ **Broctune Papa Gio**[25] 6127 5-8-3 **71**........................ DeclanCannon(3) 7 55
(Keith Reveley) *chsd ldrs: rdn along wl over 2f out: sn wknd* **11/1**

1m 40.26s (2.26) **Going Correction** +0.425s/f (Yiel)
WFA 3 from 4yo+ 3lb **15** Ran SP% **123.9**
Speed ratings (Par 109): **105,103,103,102,101 101,100,100,99,98 96,96,95,95,93**
toteswingers 1&2 £15.60, 2&3 £10.50, 1&3 £21.80 CSF £63.09 CT £540.34 TOTE £11.70: £3.30, £2.60, £2.70; EX 102.10.
Owner C H McGhie **Bred** Darley **Trained** Thirkleby, N Yorks

FOCUS
The final of this series is invariably a competitive affair and this year's renewal looks no exception. The pace was sound.

NOTEBOOK
Ginger Jack had done his winning on quicker ground previously but is evidently just as effective in the mud. He's won off higher marks earlier in his career so won't necessarily look handicapped out of things once reassessed. (tchd 12-1)
Dolphin Rock has quickly refound his form since joining Brian Ellison, running two solid races in defeat since last month's Thirsk success. There's no reason he won't continue to give a good account. (op 7-1)
Jo'Burg(USA) was 8lb higher than when winning over C&D last month and performed at least as well in defeat here, making his ground up smoothly before one-paced under pressure. (op 10-1)
Kiwi Bay was off the same mark as when winning this a year ago but had no real excuses on his follow-up bid, though it's still another creditable effort. (op 11-2)
Hakuna Matata travelled strongly in refitted blinkers and is capable of going close off this mark when things go his way, particularly as he's eligible for weaker races than this. Official explanation: jockey said gelding was denied a clear run (op 17-2)
Elijah Pepper(USA) needs things to drop right and left the impression he's still in form as he kept on from off the pace. (op 22-1)
Collateral Damage(IRE) left the impression he's still in form as he kept on from off the pace.
King Of Paradise(IRE) came into the race in good form and might have been expected to do better. (op 8-1 tchd 15-2)
Ingleby Exceed(IRE) has been inconsistent lately, and was clearly well below the form she showed when winning over C&D in August. Official explanation: jockey said filly had no more to give (tchd 8-1)

6882 TOTEPOOL GUISBOROUGH STKS (LISTED RACE) 7f
3:10 (3:11) (Class 1) 3-Y-O+

£18,714 (£7,095; £3,550; £1,768; £887; £445) **Stalls** Centre

Form RPR

0100 **1** **Eton Forever (IRE)**[42] 5597 5-9-0 **109**.................................. NeilCallan 3 115
(Roger Varian) *chsd ldrs: drvn over 2f out: hung rt and led over 1f out: kpt on wl* **3/1[3]**

244 **2** 2¼ **Firebeam**[21] 6268 4-9-0 **108**.. GrahamLee 10 109
(William Haggas) *w ldrs: led over 2f out: hdd over 1f out: kpt on same pce* **11/4[2]**

0100 **3** 2¼ **Pepper Lane**[27] 6072 5-8-9 **105**.................................. GrahamGibbons 6 98
(David O'Meara) *chsd ldrs: drvn over 3f out: kpt on to take 3rd fnl f* **22/1**

3135 **4** 1 **Dance And Dance (IRE)**[20] 6300 6-9-0 **110**.................... TomQueally 4 101
(Ed Vaughan) *dwlt: hld up in rr: effrt over 2f out: styd on one pce over 1f out* **17/2**

-655 **5** 1¾ **Webbow (IRE)**[22] 6201 10-9-0 **95**..................................... MartinDwyer 9 96
(Julie Camacho) *in rr: effrt over 2f out: kpt on one pce over 1f out* **28/1**

1021 **6** *hd* **Fulbright**[17] 6373 3-9-1 **110**... FrannyNorton 2 99
(Mark Johnston) *w ldrs: effrt over 2f out: hung lft over 1f out: sn wknd* **9/4[1]**

045 **7** 2 **Jonny Mudball**[7] 6676 6-9-0 **98**..(t) DavidAllan 1 90
(Tom Dascombe) *led: hdd over 2f out: wknd over 1f out* **12/1**

5-00 **8** 1½ **Colonial (IRE)**[233] 588 5-9-0 **105**.................................... MickyFenton 8 87
(Saeed Bin Suroor) *hld up in mid-div: t.k.h: effrt over 2f out: lost pl over 1f out* **16/1**

060 **9** 4½ **Dubai Hills**[22] 6192 6-9-0 **85**.. RoystonFfrench 5 75
(Bryan Smart) *mid-div: drvn and outpcd over 2f out: sn wknd* **66/1**

1m 25.69s (1.19) **Going Correction** +0.425s/f (Yiel)
WFA 3 from 4yo+ 2lb **9** Ran SP% **115.8**
Speed ratings (Par 111): **110,107,104,103,101 101,99,97,92**
toteswingers 1&2 £2.90, 2&3 £23.10, 1&3 £26.40 CSF £11.53 TOTE £3.60: £1.30, £1.50, £3.70; EX 14.40.
Owner H R H Sultan Ahmad Shah **Bred** Mrs Brid Cosgrove **Trained** Newmarket, Suffolk

FOCUS
Smart form from the leading pair in an up-to-scatch renewal of this Listed prize. The gallop appeared sound enough for the conditions, the principals all edging over towards the stands' rail in the final 2f.

NOTEBOOK
Eton Forever(IRE) seems to struggle to string good efforts together, but he's undoubtedly smart on his day and added to his Buckingham Palace success at the Royal meeting, drawing nicely clear in the end. He goes well in the mud, which should hold him in good stead in the closing weeks of the season. (op 9-2)
Firebeam is hard to knock for consistency but is clearly vulnerable at Listed/minor pattern level, and had no answer to the winner late on after travelling with all his usual purpose.
Pepper Lane performed a bit better than of late, the longer trip not appearing a problem, but it's still a little below her Great St Wilfrid form, which she was clearly primed for. (op 18-1)
Dance And Dance(IRE), who'd been fifth in a Canadian Grade 1 since last seen over here, has shown his best form under quicker conditions than these and this goes down as just a respectable effort at best. (op 15-2 tchd 7-1)
Webbow(IRE) isn't quite up to this level and wasn't discredited without ever threatening a serious blow. (tchd 33-1)
Fulbright was disappointing as he arrived here on the back of a success at this level at Sandown and was proven in the mud. He's not the type to stay down for long, though. (tchd 5-2)
Colonial(IRE) had been well below his best at Meydan earlier in the year and doesn't appear to have returned from a break in any better form. (tchd 18-1)

6883 TOTEPOOL.COM TWO-YEAR-OLD TROPHY (LISTED RACE) 6f
3:45 (3:45) (Class 1) 2-Y-O

£125,385 (£47,536; £23,790; £11,850; £5,947; £2,984) **Stalls** Centre

Form RPR

1113 **1** **Body And Soul (IRE)**[44] 5515 2-8-1 **95**...................... DuranFentiman 17 94+
(Tim Easterby) *trckd ldrs: smooth hdwy to trck ldr over 2f out: led over 1f out: rdn clr jst ins fnl f: kpt on strly* **4/1[1]**

6316 **2** 2¾ **Hototo**[23] 6162 2-8-12 **102**.. AmyRyan 16 96+
(Kevin Ryan) *led: rdn along 2f out: hdd and drvn over 1f out: kpt on u.p fnl f* **9/2[2]**

1010 **3** ½ **Annunciation**[44] 5515 2-8-3 **98**.. KieranO'Neill 10 86
(Richard Hannon) *trckd ldrs: hdwy over 2f out: rdn and edgd lft ent fnl f: kpt on same pce* **16/1**

501 **4** ½ **Baddilini**[28] 6032 2-8-9 **92**.. GrahamLee 13 90
(Alan Bailey) *dwlt and in rr: hdwy wl over 2f out: rdn and styd on wl fnl f: nrst fin* **20/1**

2012 **5** *nk* **Rio's Pearl**[15] 6425 2-8-1 **78**..(b[1]) HarryBentley 11 81
(Ralph Beckett) *cl up: effrt over 2f out and sn ev ch: rdn and edgd lft over 1f out: wknd fnl f* **9/1**

1303 **6** ¾ **Pure Excellence**[23] 6160 2-8-11 **81**................................ FrannyNorton 15 89
(Mark Johnston) *midfield: rdn along and outpcd wl over 2f out: kpt on fnl f: nrst fin* **16/1**

2415 **7** 1¼ **Jillnextdoor (IRE)**[7] 6672 2-8-11 **103**.............................. TomQueally 8 85
(Mick Channon) *s.i.s and bhd: hdwy and in tch 1/2-way: rdn 2f out: wknd over 1f out* **6/1[3]**

3221 **8** 1½ **Avec Rose**[33] 5886 2-8-7 **75**.. PJMcDonald 1 77
(Richard Fahey) *hld up towards far side: hdwy over 2f out: sn rdn and ch tl drvn and wknd appr fnl f* **28/1**

0506 **9** ½ **Woodland Mill (IRE)**[15] 6425 2-8-4 **76**.......................... PatrickMathers 14 72
(Richard Fahey) *outpcd and in rr: hdwy 2f out: sn rdn and kpt on fnl f: nt rch ldrs* **100/1**

0255 **10** 1¾ **Storm Moon (USA)**[21] 6238 2-9-2 **90**............................ AdrianNicholls 21 79
(Mark Johnston) *in rr: rdn along and hdwy 2f out: nvr nr ldrs* **50/1**

0002 **11** ¾ **Blue Lotus (IRE)**[28] 6032 2-8-12 **76**................................ DavidAllan 4 73
(Tim Easterby) *chsd ldrs: rdn along over 2f out: grad wknd* **50/1**

1 **12** *hd* **Joey's Destiny (IRE)**[117] 2970 2-8-12 **0**............................ SeanLevey 20 72
(George Baker) *nvr nr ldrs* **10/1**

160 **13** *nse* **Strange Magic (IRE)**[23] 6160 2-8-4 **75**.......................... BarryMcHugh 2 64
(Richard Fahey) *racd towards far side: chsd ldrs: rdn along over 2f out: sn wknd* **50/1**

0300 **14** *nk* **Secret Destination**[2] 6815 2-8-1 **76**..........................(p) SimonPearce 18 60
(Brian Ellison) *racd towards stands' side: in tch: rdn along wl over 2f out: sn wknd* **80/1**

061 **15** 1¼ **Rich Forever (IRE)**[26] 6099 2-8-6 **77**............................ JimmyQuinn 22 61
(James Bethell) *racd nr stands' rail: midfield: effrt over 2f out: sn rdn and no hdwy* **40/1**

310 **16** *nk* **Reliant Robin (IRE)**[16] 6414 2-8-6 **75**.......................(b[1]) AndrewMullen 5 60
(Robert Mills) *chsd ldrs towards far side: rdn along wl over 2f out: sn wknd* **66/1**

3152 **17** ¾ **Hajam**[23] 6162 2-9-2 **105**.. MartinDwyer 3 68
(James Tate) *in tch towards far side: pushed along 1/2-way: sn wknd* **8/1**

1430 **18** 2¾ **Mayfield Girl (IRE)**[43] 5563 2-8-1 **80**................................ NeilFarley 7 45
(Mel Brittain) *cl up: rdn along 1/2-way: sn wknd* **66/1**

1204 **19** 6 **Ashaadd (IRE)**[14] 6491 2-9-2 **90**......................................(b) NeilCallan 23 42
(Roger Varian) *a towards rr* **16/1**

0116 **20** ½ **Opt Out**[28] 6022 2-9-2 **81**.. MichaelStainton 9 40
(Mark Johnston) *chsd ldrs: rdn along 1/2-way: sn wknd* **33/1**

516 **21** ½ **Shrimper Roo**[41] 5620 2-8-3 **75**...................................... KellyHarrison 6 26
(Tim Easterby) *cl up: rdn along 1/2-way: sn wknd* **66/1**

1m 13.17s (1.37) **Going Correction** +0.425s/f (Yiel) **21** Ran SP% **126.5**
Speed ratings (Par 103): **107,103,102,102,101 100,98,96,96,93 92,92,92,92,90 90,89,85,77,76 76**
toteswingers 1&2 £2.20, 2&3 £15.50, 1&3 £21.20 CSF £19.45 TOTE £5.00: £1.90, £1.90, £8.30; EX 17.20 Trifecta £189.30 Pool: £1,028.65 - 4.02 winning tickets..
Owner C H Stevens **Bred** Michael Downey & Roalso Ltd **Trained** Great Habton, N Yorks

FOCUS
The usual big field for this valuable Listed prize but not that many could actually be given a serious chance and it ended up being dominated by a couple who'd already enjoyed success in similar contests this term. Straightforward form, with the winner not needing to improve.

NOTEBOOK
Body And Soul(IRE) was 6lb better off with Hototo for York and turned that form around in no uncertain terms, adding to her Super Sprint success in July in good style, soon going strongly just behind her old rival, the result never in doubt once she'd hit the front just over 1f out. Things will obviously be tougher in Listed/Group sprints next term, but she's still getting better on this evidence, while it's worth bearing in mind the yard's two previous winners of this race went on to Group 1 success later in their careers.
Hototo is another who has enjoyed an excellent first season and ran another fine race here, just no match for the winner (who he was conceding 11lb to) after cutting out the running until over 1f out. He may prove tricky to place next term, but has been a real moneyspinner whatever happens from now on. (op 5-1)
Annunciation had been well behind the leading pair at York but confirmed himself a useful colt here, albeit having no excuses. (op 14-1)
Baddilini was another who hadn't done himself justice in the York sales race but ran right up to his best this time, staying on from the pace after a slowish start. He's well worth another try over 7f at some point. (op 16-1)
Rio's Pearl got in off a low weight but this still represents a slight improvement in first-time blinkers, bang there from the off and sticking on despite edging left under pressure. (op 12-1)
Pure Excellence had a bit on at the weights and ran well, leaving the impression 7f could suit her, outpaced in midfield before staying on late.
Jillnextdoor(IRE) hadn't been beaten that far in the Cheveley Park last weekend but didn't help her cause here with a very slow start, the effort of making up the lost ground probably just telling on her in the end. She's still in good form. (op 7-1 tchd 15-2)
Joey's Destiny(IRE) found this too much at this stage of his career and is worth another chance to show himself capable of better. (op 11-1 tchd 12-1)
Hajam had run a blinder when just in front of Hototo at Doncaster but was never travelling here, the softer ground a possible excuse. Official explanation: jockey said colt never travelled (tchd 15-2)

Ashaadd(IRE) ran a stinker in the second-time blinkers and is in danger of going the wrong way.

6884 MARKET CROSS JEWELLERS H'CAP 1m 2f
4:15 (4:16) (Class 4) (0-85,85) 3-Y-O+ £4,075 (£1,212; £606; £303) Stalls Low

Form RPR
1/ 1 **First Mohican**[711] 7150 4-9-5 **80** TomQueally 15 95+
(Sir Henry Cecil) *t.k.h: sn hld up in mid-div on outer: stdy hdwy over 3f out: chalng 2f out: led jst ins fnl f: drvn to win gng away in the end* **7/4**[1]
1-20 2 1 ¼ **Docs Legacy (IRE)**[49] 5358 3-8-6 **72** BarryMcHugh 14 84
(Richard Fahey) *chsd ldrs: led wl over 1f out: hdd jst ins fnl f: no ex* **8/1**[3]
2550 3 3 ½ **Kathleen Frances**[6] 6703 5-9-2 **77** (p) MartinDwyer 10 82
(Mark H Tompkins) *s.i.s: hdwy and edgd rt over 3f out: chsng ldrs 2f out: kpt on same pce* **12/1**
1502 4 ½ **Come Here Yew (IRE)**[38] 5730 4-8-8 **72** NeilFarley(3) 2 76
(Declan Carroll) *s.i.s: in rr: hdwy over 3f out: sn chsng ldrs: kpt on same pce fnl 2f* **12/1**
1500 5 nk **Carragold**[8] 6638 6-8-13 **74** DavidAllan 12 77
(Mel Brittain) *mid-div: drvn 6f out: hdwy over 3f out: kpt on one pce fnl 2f* **16/1**
/0-4 6 5 **King Fingal (IRE)**[114] 2348 7-8-11 **72** JimmyQuinn 5 65
(John Quinn) *mid-div: effrt on inner over 2f out: nt clr run: nvr a factor* **66/1**
0620 7 nk **Barren Brook**[8] 6630 5-9-7 **82** AmyRyan 11 75
(Michael Easterby) *s.v.s: t.k.h in rr: sme hdwy over 2f out: nvr a factor* **8/1**[3]
0300 8 ½ **Karaka Jack**[14] 6465 5-9-3 **78** AdrianNicholls 7 70
(David Nicholls) *hld up in rr: sme hdwy on inner 3f out: nt clr run: n.m.r and swtchd rt jst ins fnl f: nvr a threat* **22/1**
4400 9 ¾ **Jonny Lesters Hair (IRE)**[27] 6073 7-8-11 **72** DuranFentiman 9 62
(Tim Easterby) *trckd ldrs: led over 2f out: hdd wl over 1f out: sn wknd* **28/1**
1442 10 1 **Le Chat D'Or**[37] 5759 4-8-13 **74** (bt[1]) GrahamLee 1 62
(Michael Dods) *trckd ldrs: t.k.h: swtchd rt over 2f out: wknd over 1f out* **5/1**[2]
1020 11 5 **Rocktherunway (IRE)**[36] 5788 3-9-1 **84** LeeTopliss(3) 6 62
(Michael Dods) *trckd ldrs: chal over 2f out: wknd over 1f out* **12/1**
6000 12 6 **Amazing Blue Sky**[27] 6073 6-9-0 **75** PJMcDonald 3 41
(Ruth Carr) *led: hdd over 2f out: sn wknd* **40/1**
4100 13 2 ¾ **Oneofapear (IRE)**[61] 4864 6-9-0 **80** (v[1]) GarryWhillans(5) 4 41
(Alan Swinbank) *chsd ldrs: lost pl over 2f out: sn bhd* **25/1**
1253 14 1 ¼ **Sabhan (IRE)**[25] 6124 3-8-10 **76** RoystonFrench 13 34
(Geoffrey Harker) *in rr: drvn 4f out: bhd fnl 2f* **14/1**

2m 10.31s (3.21) **Going Correction** +0.425s/f (Yiel)
WFA 3 from 4yo+ 5lb **14 Ran SP% 126.5**
Speed ratings (Par 105): **104,103,100,99,99 95,95,94,94,93 89,84,82,81**
toteswingers 1&2 £12.00, 2&3 £25.10, 1&3 £10.00 CSF £15.94 CT £143.09 TOTE £1.60: £1.10, £3.60, £4.20; EX 33.20.
Owner W H Ponsonby **Bred** Bottisham Heath Stud **Trained** Newmarket, Suffolk

FOCUS
Form to view positively from the leading pair who came well clear of the remainder.
King Fingal(IRE) Official explanation: jockey said gelding was denied a clear run
Barren Brook Official explanation: jockey said gelding missed the break

6885 THANKS FOR 53 YEARS DEREK BROWN (S) STKS 1m 2f
4:50 (4:51) (Class 5) 3-5-Y-O £2,328 (£693; £346; £173) Stalls Low

Form RPR
5062 1 **Zenarinda**[49] 5351 5-8-9 59 MartinDwyer 15 71
(Mark H Tompkins) *hld up in rr: smooth hdwy over 4f out: trckd ldrs over 2f out: led wl over 1f out: sn pushed clr: easily* **7/1**
6510 2 11 **Croftamie**[21] 6263 3-8-10 65 (p) PatrickMathers 3 55
(Tracy Waggott) *cl up: led after 3f: rdn along over 2f out: hdd wl over 1f out: kpt on u.p: no ch w wnr* **14/1**
0-40 3 nk **Mesariya (IRE)**[12] 6544 4-8-9 68 BarryMcHugh 6 48
(Tony Coyle) *hld up: hdwy on inner to trck ldrs 1/2-way: effrt 3f out: rdn along 2f out: sn drvn and kpt on same pce* **10/1**
0304 4 3 **Politbureau**[4] 6361 5-8-13 50 MatthewHopkins(7) 5 53
(Michael Easterby) *hld up towards rr: hdwy over 3f out: rdn along over 2f out: drvn and no imp fr wl over 1f out* **20/1**
6640 5 1 ½ **Law To Himself (IRE)**[24] 6131 5-9-0 58 (v) NeilCallan 14 44
(Alan Swinbank) *trckd ldrs: hdwy on outer over 3f out: rdn along over 2f out: plugged on same pce* **5/1**[2]
6655 6 nse **Free Art**[24] 6131 4-9-0 63 PJMcDonald 8 44
(Geoffrey Harker) *hld up towards rr: hdwy on outer over 3f out: swtchd to inner over 2f out: sn rdn along and one pce* **4/1**[1]
2460 7 nk **Sinatramania**[11] 6562 5-9-0 53 RoystonFfrench 4 44
(Tracy Waggott) *trckd ldrs: rdn along over 3f out: drvn over 2f out and sn wknd* **17/2**
0000 8 1 ¾ **Byronic Hero**[16] 6405 3-9-1 73 (t) GrahamLee 7 46
(Jedd O'Keeffe) *hld up: hdwy 3f out: rdn along over 2f out: n.d* **15/2**
4444 9 2 ¼ **Avison (IRE)**[21] 6262 4-9-0 52 JimmyQuinn 2 36
(Richard Fahey) *trckd ldrs: hdwy to chse ldr over 4f out: rdn along wl over 2f out: sn wknd* **11/2**[3]
1/40 10 12 **City Ground (USA)**[30] 1133 5-8-7 77 DavidSimmonson(7) 10 12
(Michael Easterby) *a in rr* **12/1**
5305 11 ½ **Lady Gargoyle**[47] 5413 4-8-2 44 (p) SophieRobertson(7) 11
(Jim Goldie) *plld hrd: led 3f: prom tl wknd wl over 3f out: sn bhd* **25/1**
0000 12 49 **Sir Lexington (IRE)**[21] 6230 3-8-9 46 (b) SeanLevey 9
(Richard Hannon) *towards rr: rdn along 1/2-way: sn bhd and t.o fnl 3f* **33/1**
13 47 **Call It Out**[370] 5-8-11 0 PaulPickard(3) 13
(Alan Kirtley) *s.i.s: a bhd: t.o fnl 3f* **150/1**

2m 11.64s (4.54) **Going Correction** +0.425s/f (Yiel)
WFA 3 from 4yo+ 5lb **13 Ran SP% 122.5**
Speed ratings (Par 103): **98,89,88,86,85 85,85,83,81,72 71,32,**
toteswingers 1&2 £21.40, 2&3 £29.30, 1&3 £17.20 CSF £99.89 TOTE £8.60: £3.10, £5.60, £5.10; EX 122.80.The winner was bought in for £6,200. There were no claims.
Owner Judi Dench & Partners **Bred** Dullingham Park **Trained** Newmarket, Suffolk

6886 WIN A VIP DAY OUT @ REDCARRACING.CO.UK H'CAP (DIV I) 5f
5:25 (5:26) (Class 5) (0-75,75) 3-Y-O+ £2,328 (£693; £346; £173) Stalls Centre

Form RPR
3113 1 **Come On Dave (IRE)**[15] 6427 3-9-3 **71** AdrianNicholls 1 84
(David Nicholls) *mde all: drvn over 2f out: edgd lft: kpt on wl: unchal* **15/8**[1]
1550 2 2 ¼ **Mecca's Team**[21] 6264 4-8-8 **62** (p) SeanLevey 2 67
(Michael Dods) *chsd wnr: kpt on same pce fnl f: no imp* **14/1**
301 3 shd **Mission Impossible**[3] 6786 7-8-12 **66** 6ex (p) PatrickMathers 9 71
(Tracy Waggott) *in rr: hdwy 2f out: styd on fnl f* **5/1**[2]
5620 4 1 **Bronze Beau**[9] 6605 5-9-7 **75** (tp) GrahamLee 4 76
(Linda Stubbs) *trckd ldrs: effrt 2f out: kpt on same pce* **11/1**
-616 5 nse **Above The Stars**[15] 6427 4-8-10 **69** ShaneBKelly(5) 10 70
(Richard Fahey) *outpcd and in rr: hdwy 2f out: kpt on same pce fnl f* **8/1**
1614 6 ½ **Tom Sawyer**[24] 6144 4-9-5 **73** BarryMcHugh 6 72
(Julie Camacho) *hld up in mid-div: effrt 2f out: nvr a threat* **11/2**[3]
0000 7 nk **Pelmanism**[14] 6465 5-9-1 **72** PaulPickard(3) 5 70
(Brian Ellison) *s.s: outpcd and rdn over 2f out: kpt on fnl f* **14/1**
1000 8 2 ¼ **Dispol Grand (IRE)**[21] 6234 6-9-3 **71** PJMcDonald 3 61
(Paul Midgley) *chsd ldrs: wknd 2f out* **16/1**
4443 9 ½ **Gowanharry (IRE)**[36] 5800 3-8-4 **65** (t) ConnorNichol(7) 8 53
(Michael Dods) *trckd ldrs: hung lft and wknd over 1f out* **8/1**

1m 0.16s (1.56) **Going Correction** +0.425s/f (Yiel) **9 Ran SP% 116.6**
Speed ratings (Par 103): **104,100,100,98,98 97,97,93,92**
toteswingers 1&2 £3.60, 2&3 £10.10, 1&3 £3.00 CSF £31.69 CT £117.52 TOTE £2.70: £1.20, £3.80, £1.70; EX 33.80.
Owner Middleham Park Racing XLIV **Bred** Mrs Eithne Hamilton **Trained** Sessay, N Yorks

FOCUS
A race which very few ever threatened to get into.

6887 WIN A VIP DAY OUT @ REDCARRACING.CO.UK H'CAP (DIV II) 5f
5:55 (5:55) (Class 5) (0-75,74) 3-Y-O+ £2,328 (£693; £346; £173) Stalls Centre

Form RPR
0602 1 **I'll Be Good**[21] 6261 3-8-9 **69** KevinStott(7) 1 78
(Robert Johnson) *prom: cl up 1/2-way: rdn to ld ent fnl f: kpt on* **13/2**
1600 2 ½ **Elusive Bonus (IRE)**[17] 6357 3-8-6 **66** DavidBergin(7) 6 73
(David O'Meara) *in tch: hdwy to chse ldng pair 2f out: sn rdn: styd on fnl f* **11/2**[3]
0402 3 nk **Commanche Raider (IRE)**[28] 6044 5-9-5 **72** (p) GrahamLee 2 78
(Michael Dods) *towards rr: hdwy 2f out: sn rdn and styd on fnl f: nrst fin* **4/1**[2]
5102 4 hd **El McGlynn (IRE)**[12] 6525 3-9-0 **74** HannahNunn(7) 9 79
(Peter Salmon) *slt ld: rdn along wl over 1f out: hdd ent fnl f: kpt on same pce* **7/2**[1]
0000 5 ½ **Mandalay King (IRE)**[17] 6357 7-9-1 **68** (p) AmyRyan 5 71
(Marjorie Fife) *sn pushed along and outpcd in rr: rdn and hdwy on wd outside over 1f out: kpt on ins fnl f: nrst fin* **7/1**
4500 6 3 ¼ **Nomoreblondes**[24] 6144 8-9-5 **72** (v) BarryMcHugh 3 64
(Paul Midgley) *in tch: rdn along over 2f out: no imp* **15/2**
0000 7 7 **Captain Royale (IRE)**[9] 6605 7-8-8 **66** ow3 (p) ShaneBKelly(5) 7 33
(Tracy Waggott) *chsd ldrs: rdn along over 2f out: grad wknd* **12/1**
0500 8 4 **Glenlini**[53] 5190 6-8-7 **60** oh13 KieranO'Neill 8 12
(Jim Goldie) *a in rr* **50/1**
3315 9 3 ¾ **Majestic Manannan (IRE)**[61] 4881 3-9-0 **67** AdrianNicholls 4
(David Nicholls) *prom: rdn along 1/2-way: sn wknd* **7/1**

1m 0.75s (2.15) **Going Correction** +0.425s/f (Yiel) **9 Ran SP% 117.4**
Speed ratings (Par 103): **99,98,97,97,96 91,80,73,67**
toteswingers 1&2 £10.10, 2&3 £4.20, 1&3 £5.10 CSF £42.79 CT £164.05 TOTE £7.40: £3.00, £2.30, £2.00; EX 42.40.
Owner Do Well Racing **Bred** Cobhall Court Stud **Trained** Newburn, Tyne & Wear
■ Stewards' Enquiry : David Bergin two-day ban: used whip above permitted level (Oct 21-22)

FOCUS
Similar to the first division in that not many ever threatened to get in a serious blow. The winner, who was one of two who helped force the pace, was always holding the late closers.
Majestic Manannan(IRE) Official explanation: jockey said gelding had no more to give
T/Plt: £119.10 to a £1 stakes. Pool: £61,908.29 - 379.37 winning tickets. T/Qpdt: £34.00 to a £1 stake. Pool: £3,507.31 - 76.30 winning tickets. JR

6836 WOLVERHAMPTON (A.W) (L-H)
Saturday, October 6

OFFICIAL GOING: Standard
Wind: Light half-against Weather: Cloudy

6888 32RED CLAIMING STKS 7f 32y(P)
5:50 (5:50) (Class 6) 3-Y-O+ £2,181 (£644; £322) Stalls High

Form RPR
1005 1 **Lockantanks**[8] 6630 5-9-5 89 DarrenEgan(5) 8 94
(Michael Appleby) *a.p: rdn to ld ins fnl f: r.o* **3/1**[2]
0002 2 ¾ **Rakaan (IRE)**[18] 6329 5-9-10 95 FergusSweeney 2 92
(Jamie Osborne) *a.p: rdn over 1f out: ev ch ins fnl f: styd on* **11/4**[1]
6063 3 1 ½ **Beckermet (IRE)**[7] 6663 10-9-0 82 JamesSullivan 11 78
(Ruth Carr) *trckd ldr: rdn to ld over 1f out: hdd and unable qck ins fnl f* **8/1**
2025 4 ½ **Fishforcompliments**[28] 6051 8-8-8 65 FrankieMcDonald 5 71
(Richard Fahey) *hld up: rdn over 2f out: r.o ins fnl f: nrst fin* **16/1**
145 5 nse **Fathsta (IRE)**[14] 6471 7-9-2 81 RyanPowell(3) 7 81
(Patrick Morris) *chsd ldrs: rdn and ev ch over 1f out: styd on same pce ins fnl f* **11/2**
1016 6 ¾ **Prime Exhibit**[15] 6454 7-8-12 82 (t) MatthewLawson(5) 4 77
(Daniel Mark Loughnane) *hld up: rdn over 1f out: r.o ins fnl; f: nvr nrr* **9/2**[3]
140 7 ½ **Muftarres (IRE)**[24] 6141 7-8-9 68 (b) RussKennemore 12 68
(Paul Midgley) *hld up: rdn over 2f out: nvr on terms* **10/1**
5005 8 1 ¾ **First Bid**[15] 6436 3-8-8 65 [1] LiamJones 10 64
(James Given) *led: rdn and hdd over 1f out: wknd wl ins fnl f* **33/1**

1m 28.3s (-1.30) **Going Correction** -0.15s/f (Stan)
WFA 3 from 5yo+ 2lb **8 Ran SP% 114.3**
Speed ratings (Par 101): **101,100,98,97,97 96,96,94**
Tote Swingers: 1&2 £2.90, 1&3 £4.30, 2&3 £3.80 CSF £11.69 TOTE £3.80: £1.20, £1.70, £3.00; EX 15.50 Trifecta £45.40 Pool: £331.24 - 5.39 winning units..
Owner Dallas Racing **Bred** Jeremy Green And Sons **Trained** Danethorpe, Notts

FOCUS
A useful claimer in which the gallop was fair. The winner came down the centre.
Fishforcompliments Official explanation: vet said gelding sustained a cut eyelid
Fathsta(IRE) Official explanation: jockey said gelding ran too freely

6889 32RED.COM MEDIAN AUCTION MAIDEN STKS 5f 216y(P)
6:20 (6:21) (Class 6) 2-Y-O £2,181 (£644; £322) Stalls Low

Form RPR
04 1 **Grace Hull**[15] 6453 2-8-12 0 FergusSweeney 7 68
(J S Moore) *chsd ldrs: wnt 2nd over 2f out: rdn to ld ins fnl f: r.o* **8/1**

04 **2** *hd* **Attenshun (IRE)**23 6177 2-9-3 0....................(v) ChrisCatlin 1 73
(Tom Dascombe) *led: rdn over 1f out: hdd ins fnl f: r.o* **10/3**2

2602 **3** *½* **Puteri Nur Laila (IRE)**9 6609 2-8-12 68....................(b) JamesSullivan 5 66
(Paul Cole) *s.i.s: sn prom: rdn and swtchd rt over 1f out: r.o wl* **4/1**3

4 *1 ½* **North Pole** 2-9-3 0.................... LukeMorris 11 67
(Sir Mark Prescott Bt) *chsd ldrs: rdn over 2f out: r.o* **11/4**1

5 *nk* **Nelina** 2-8-7 0.................... DarrenEgan(5) 2 61+
(Robert Cowell) *s.i.s: hld up: hdwy over 1f out: r.o: nt rch ldrs* **14/1**

0 **6** *4 ½* **She's Some Girl (IRE)**9 6609 2-8-5 0.................... LauraBarry(7) 13 47
(Richard Fahey) *prom: pushed along 1/2-way: wknd fnl f* **25/1**

060 **7** *1 ¾* **Joeluke**61 4877 2-9-0 0.................... RyanPowell(3) 9 47
(Noel Quinlan) *s.i.s: rdn over 2f out: nvr on terms* **33/1**

00 **8** *1 ½* **Last Chance Ranch**10 6581 2-9-3 0.................... RussKennemore 8 42
(Derek Shaw) *s.i.s: a in rr* **100/1**

9 *9* **Superoo (IRE)** 2-9-3 0.................... JamieMackay 3 15
(Mark Johnston) *chsd ldr tl rdn over 2f out: wknd over 1f out* **11/2**

0 **10** *3* **Tonkalili**138 2349 2-8-12 0.................... LiamJones 10
(James Unett) *mid-div: pushed along 1/2-way: wknd over 2f out* **66/1**

1m 15.24s (0.24) **Going Correction** -0.15s/f (Stan) **10** Ran SP% **112.2**
Speed ratings (Par 93): **92,91,91,89,88 82,80,78,66,62**
Tote Swingers: 1&2 £4.80, 1&3 £4.30, 2&3 £3.70 CSF £32.83 TOTE £12.40: £2.40, £1.90, £1.10; EX 34.70 Trifecta £139.40 Pool: £663.16 - 3.52 winning units..
Owner Ron Hull **Bred** Whitsbury Manor Stud & Pigeon House Stud **Trained** Upper Lambourn, Berks

FOCUS
Little strength in depth in this ordinary maiden and the first five finished in a bit of a heap. The gallop was a reasonable one and the winner raced centre to far side in the straight. Straightforward form.

NOTEBOOK
Grace Hull has improved with every start over C&D and turned in her best effort to get off the mark at the third attempt. There may be a bit more to come in ordinary nurseries. (op 7-1)
Attenshun(IRE) has also improved with every run and he posted his best effort, despite racing with the choke out. While likely to remain vulnerable to the better types in this grade, he's up to winning a minor event. (tchd 4-1)
Puteri Nur Laila(IRE) has had a few chances and doesn't look the most straightforward (tended to edge right under pressure) but he's probably a reasonable yardstick and he wasn't far off his best. He's capable of winning a race but isn't one for maximum faith. (op 7-2 tchd 9-2)
North Pole, a half-brother to several winners, notably this year's Group 1 Golden Shaheen winner Krypton Factor, attracted plenty of support and ran creditably on this racecourse debut. While the bare form of this run is only modest, he's sure to be better for this experience and win races. (op 4-1 tchd 5-2)
Nelina ◆, the first foal of a middle-distance winner in France, was easy to back but caught the eye on this racecourse debut. She'll be suited by a much stiffer test of stamina in due course and is one to keep an eye on, especially when qualified for a mark. (op 16-1 tchd 18-1)
Superoo(IRE), a 40,000gns yearling and half-brother to Group 1-placed juvenile Gallagher (as well as several other winners including smart 7f-1m2f winner Quick Wit), started at single-figure odds but ran as though the race was needed on this racecourse debut. He's in good hands and is entitled to improve. (op 9-2)

6890 PHIL AND SANDRA BADDELEY 40TH WEDDING ANNIVERSARY (S) STKS 5f 20y(P)
6:50 (6:50) (Class 6) 2-Y-O £2,181 (£644; £322) Stalls Low

Form RPR

1500 **1** **Mandy Layla (IRE)**7 6658 2-8-11 78.................... TomEaves 1 63
(Bryan Smart) *led: rdn and hdd over 1f out: looked hld whn nt clr run and lft in ld ins fnl f: jst hld on* **11/10**1

3046 **2** *nk* **Marmot Bay (IRE)**4 6766 2-8-3 63.................... RyanPowell(3) 7 57
(Jamie Osborne) *chsd ldrs: hung rt over 1f out: nt clr run ins fnl f: r.o* **11/1**

4653 **3** *½* **Windforpower (IRE)**4 6766 2-9-2 65....................(p) LukeMorris 5 65
(Ronald Harris) *chsd ldrs: led over 1f out: sn rdn: incommand whn swvd rt ins fnl f: sn hdd: styd on* **9/1**3

142 **4** *1 ¼* **Stripped Bear (IRE)**22 6212 2-8-4 64.................... RyanTate(7) 6 56
(Tom Dascombe) *chsd ldrs: rdn over 1f out: no ex ins fnl f* **15/8**2

0446 **5** *3 ¼* **Jamnean**20 6283 2-8-1 55.................... DarrenEgan(5) 4 39
(John Holt) *sn outpcd: kpt on ins fnl f* **25/1**

66 **6** *1 ½* **Lady Jean**14 6499 2-8-6 0.................... ChrisCatlin 3 34
(Reg Hollinshead) *s.i.s: outpcd* **25/1**

34 **7** *2 ¾* **Red Star Lady (IRE)**32 5916 2-8-6 51....................(b) LiamJones 8 24
(Mrs K Burke) *w ldr tl rdn 1/2-way: wknd over 1f out* **20/1**

8 *8* **Bryter Layter** 2-8-6 0 ow2.................... JackDuern(7) 2
(Christopher Kellett) *s.s: outpcd* **200/1**

1m 1.99s (-0.31) **Going Correction** -0.15s/f (Stan) **8** Ran SP% **113.7**
Speed ratings (Par 93): **96,95,94,92,87 85,80,67**
Tote Swingers: 1&2 £2.90, 1&3 £3.40, 2&3 £5.20 CSF £13.71 TOTE £2.40: £1.20, £2.40, £1.70; EX 11.50 Trifecta £53.90 Pool: £650.40 - 8.92 winning units..No bid for the winner.
Owner Dr Marwan Koukash **Bred** Mrs E J O'Grady **Trained** Hambleton, N Yorks

FOCUS
A modest and uncompetitive seller but a race with a dramatic conclusion as the third threw away a winning chance in the closing stages. The gallop was sound and the winner came down the centre in the straight. This form is best viewed negatively.

NOTEBOOK
Mandy Layla(IRE), the clear pick of the weights, wasn't at her very best but ran out a fortunate winner (benefited from wayward antics of the third) on this AW debut and first run in selling company. She wouldn't be an obvious one to follow up. (op 6-4)
Marmot Bay(IRE), who had a fair chance at the weights judged on her debut form, ran her best race since then but, while the return to 6f should suit, she wouldn't be certain to build on this next time. (op 12-1)
Windforpower(IRE) was in the process of running his best race and looked sure to register his second win when taking up the running early in the straight but threw his chance away by swerving badly right in the closing stages. He has ability but is one to tread very carefully with. (op 8-1 tchd 15-2)
Stripped Bear(IRE), a 5f nursery winner at Kempton in August, had a decent chance at the weights dropped to selling company and wasn't totally disgraced, albeit in a race where there are very few positives to take from any of the runners. (op 7-4 tchd 2-1)

6891 MIRROR PUNTERS CLUB H'CAP 1m 4f 50y(P)
7:20 (7:20) (Class 5) (0-70,70) 3-Y-O+ £3,067 (£905; £453) Stalls Low

Form RPR

2222 **1** **Peachez**15 6440 4-9-5 70....................(p) AmyScott(5) 9 79
(Alastair Lidderdale) *hld up: hdwy over 2f out: led over 1f out: sn rdn and hung lft: jst hld on* **5/1**2

0021 **2** *nk* **English Summer**15 6441 5-9-2 67....................(t) DarrenEgan(5) 2 76
(David Simcock) *hld up: pushed along over 2f out: hdwy over 1f out: rdn and edgd lft ins fnl f: r.o wl: jst failed* **11/8**1

4114 **3** *1* **Laser Blazer**44 5507 4-9-5 65....................(p) FergusSweeney 10 72
(Jeremy Gask) *trckd ldr tl led over 3f out: rdn and hdd over 1f out: styd on* **12/1**

5340 **4** *1 ¼* **Honoured (IRE)**24 6131 5-9-2 62....................(t) TomEaves 12 67
(Michael Appleby) *a.p: rdn over 1f out: styd on* **16/1**

3030 **5** *nse* **Toughness Danon**6 6703 6-9-5 68.................... RyanPowell(3) 6 73
(Brendan Powell) *hld up: hung lft fr over 1f out: r.o ins fnl f: nvr nr to chal* **12/1**

2640 **6** *1 ¼* **Port Charlotte**21 6229 3-9-2 69.................... ChrisCatlin 11 72
(Hughie Morrison) *hld up: hdwy over 2f out: rdn over 1f out: styd on same pce fnl f* **9/1**3

150- **7** *nk* **Evergreen Forest (IRE)**347 7076 4-9-4 67.................... RyanClark(3) 5 69
(Tom Keddy) *chsd ldrs: rdn over 2f out: no ex fnl f* **25/1**

1033 **8** *hd* **Sedgwick**9 6608 10-9-0 67.................... WilliamTwiston-Davies(7) 8 69
(Shaun Harris) *hld up: nt clr run over 1f out: n.d* **14/1**

2165 **9** *1 ¼* **Maid Of Meft**16 6407 5-9-6 66.................... MickyFenton 4 66
(Paul Midgley) *mid-div: hdwy over 5f out: rdn over 2f out: styd on same pce fr over 1f out* **16/1**

0201 **10** *6* **Finity Run (GER)**11 6555 3-9-3 70.................... FrannyNorton 3 61
(Mark Johnston) *led: rdn and hdd over 3f out: wknd over 1f out* **10/1**

4560 **11** *2 ½* **Action Front (USA)**87 3961 4-9-5 65.................... RussKennemore 1 52
(Derek Shaw) *chsd ldrs: rdn over 2f out: wknd over 1f out* **22/1**

2m 41.24s (0.14) **Going Correction** -0.15s/f (Stan)
WFA 3 from 4yo+ 7lb **11** Ran SP% **119.9**
Speed ratings (Par 103): **93,92,92,91,91 90,90,90,89,85 83**
Tote Swingers: 1&2 £1.90, 1&3 £3.40, 2&3 £2.70 CSF £12.42 CT £81.28 TOTE £6.70: £1.80, £1.20, £2.20; EX 17.60 Trifecta £31.80 Pool: £598.50 - 13.89 winning units..
Owner Sally Doyle & Chris Beek **Bred** Mrs Sally Doyle **Trained** Lambourn, Berks

FOCUS
A modest handicap run at an ordinary gallop. The winner drifted to the far rail in the straight.
Toughness Danon Official explanation: jockey said gelding hung left; trainer's rep said gelding had a breathing problem

6892 32RED CASINO H'CAP 1m 1f 103y(P)
7:50 (7:51) (Class 6) (0-55,55) 3-Y-O £2,181 (£644; £322) Stalls Low

Form RPR

3330 **1** **Kathleensluckylad (IRE)**15 6429 3-9-2 55..........(t1) GrahamGibbons 4 66+
(Kevin Ryan) *chsd ldr: rdn to ld 2f out: all out* **5/1**2

0-04 **2** *nse* **Langham Lily (USA)**123 2799 3-8-13 52.................... SebSanders 13 62+
(Chris Wall) *hld up: hdwy 3f out: rdn to chse wnr over 1f out: r.o* **9/1**

0503 **3** *4 ½* **Rhossili Bay**36 5810 3-9-1 54.................... FergusSweeney 12 55
(Alastair Lidderdale) *hld up: hdwy over 1f out: r.o: nt rch ldrs* **6/1**3

0005 **4** *hd* **Taro Tywod (IRE)**14 6502 3-9-2 55.................... ShaneKelly 3 56
(Mark Brisbourne) *chsd ldrs: rdn over 3f out: styd on* **14/1**

6040 **5** *2 ¼* **Thane Of Cawdor (IRE)**29 5998 3-9-1 54.................... MickyFenton 2 50
(Joseph Tuite) *s.i.s: hld up: hdwy over 2f out: styd on: nt trble ldrs* **16/1**

0654 **6** *shd* **Barnacle**20 6279 3-9-2 55.................... RussKennemore 5 51
(Pat Eddery) *s.i.s: hld up: hdwy over 1f out: sn rdn: no ex ins fnl f* **40/1**

040 **7** *2 ¼* **Rokcella**16 6397 3-9-0 53.................... LukeMorris 10 44
(Clive Cox) *hld up: hdwy over 3f out: rdn and wknd over 1f out* **8/1**

2545 **8** *½* **Zuzu Angel (IRE)**21 6231 3-8-11 55.................... DavidKenny(5) 7 45
(William Knight) *hld up: a in rr* **9/1**

0406 **9** *2 ½* **Gabrial's Lexi (IRE)**23 6174 3-9-0 53....................(b1) FrannyNorton 1 38
(Ian Williams) *led: rdn and hdd 2f out: wknd fnl f* **13/2**

4022 **10** *6* **Roman Senate (IRE)**31 5938 3-8-13 52....................(tp) ChrisCatlin 6 24
(Martin Bosley) *mid-div: lost pl 4f out: n.d after* **10/3**1

0054 **11** *3* **Swift Act**29 6001 3-8-11 55....................(p) DarrenEgan(5) 8 21
(Ronald Harris) *hld up: hdwy over 5f out: rdn over 2f out: sn wknd* **28/1**

030- **12** *7* **Doyouknowwhoiam**282 7915 3-9-1 54.................... TomEaves 9
(Geoffrey Oldroyd) *chsd ldrs: rdn over 3f out: wknd 2f out* **40/1**

2m 0.2s (-1.50) **Going Correction** -0.15s/f (Stan) **12** Ran SP% **119.4**
Speed ratings (Par 99): **100,99,95,95,93 93,91,91,89,83 81,74**
Tote Swingers: 1&2 £8.90, 1&3 £5.80, 2&3 £6.10 CSF £49.22 CT £277.69 TOTE £7.30: £2.30, £3.90, £1.10; EX 59.10 Trifecta £280.50 Part won. Pool: £379.09 - 0.50 winning units..
Owner Mrs Kathleen Flynn & Miss R A Galligan **Bred** Brendan Lavery **Trained** Hambleton, N Yorks

FOCUS
A moderate handicap run at a reasonable gallop. The first two deserve credit for pulling clear and the winner raced down the centre in the straight.

6893 JESSUP BUILD DEVELOP NURSERY 1m 141y(P)
8:20 (8:20) (Class 6) (0-60,60) 2-Y-O £2,181 (£644; £322) Stalls Low

Form RPR

0012 **1** **Progenitor (IRE)**19 6318 2-9-7 60.................... TedDurcan 6 68+
(David Lanigan) *chsd ldrs: rdn to ld over 1f out: hung rt ins fnl f: r.o* **13/8**1

6046 **2** *1 ½* **Gabrial The Boss (USA)**15 6435 2-9-1 59.................... DarrenEgan(5) 10 64+
(David Simcock) *hld up: hdwy over 2f out: rdn to chse wnr fnl f: r.o* **11/1**

0525 **3** *2 ¾* **Lucy Bee**13 6511 2-9-0 53.................... JoeFanning 11 52
(Keith Dalgleish) *chsd ldrs: led over 2f out: rdn and hdd over 1f out: no ex ins fnl f* **12/1**

040 **4** *nk* **Moorway (IRE)**30 5962 2-9-7 60.................... GrahamGibbons 3 58
(Reg Hollinshead) *s.i.s: hld up: hdwy over 1f out: styd on same pce ins fnl f* **14/1**

500 **5** *2* **Reggie Bond**42 5586 2-9-1 54.................... TomEaves 7 48
(Geoffrey Oldroyd) *mid-div: hdwy over 2f out: rdn over 1f out: no ex fnl f* **14/1**

5053 **6** *½* **Alpine Jerry (IRE)**15 6435 2-8-12 54.................... RyanPowell(3) 4 47
(J S Moore) *mid-div: hdwy over 2f out: sn rdn: no ex fnl f* **33/1**

460 **7** *½* **Chelsea Grey (IRE)**23 6153 2-8-13 52.................... LukeMorris 12 44
(Ronald Harris) *hld up: swtchd lft sn after s: drvn along 5f out: nvr nrr* **40/1**

0502 **8** *½* **Clock On Tom**32 5920 2-9-1 54.................... JamesSullivan 2 45
(Michael Easterby) *hld up: hmpd over 6f out: nt clr run over 2f out: r.o ins fnl f: nvr trbld ldrs* **10/1**3

005 **9** *2 ½* **Ceekay's Girl**61 4886 2-8-10 52.................... MichaelMetcalfe(3) 9 37
(Mrs K Burke) *prom: chsd ldr over 3f out: led over 2f out: sn rdn and hdd: wknd over 1f out* **25/1**

050 **10** *7* **Day In Day Out**51 5274 2-9-7 60.................... JimCrowley 5 30
(Ralph Beckett) *chsd ldrs: nt clr run over 2f out: sn rdn and wknd* **3/1**2

0640 **11** *5* **Tomway**37 5763 2-9-0 56.................... RossAtkinson(3) 1 15
(Tom Dascombe) *led: hdd 7f out: chsd ldr tl rdn over 3f out: nt clr run over 2f out: sn wknd* **20/1**

4514 **12** ¾ **Windsor Rose (IRE)**[58] 4991 2-9-5 **58**............................ FrannyNorton 8 15
(Mark Brisbourne) *w ldr tl hung rt and led 7f out: hdd over 2f out: wknd wl over 1f out* **33/1**

1m 50.19s (-0.31) **Going Correction** -0.15s/f (Stan) **12** Ran SP% **118.5**
Speed ratings (Par 93): **95,93,91,90,89 88,88,87,85,79 74,74**
Tote Swingers: 1&2 £6.50, 1&3 £2.80, 2&3 £24.00 CSF £19.58 CT £172.10 TOTE £3.30: £1.20, £4.20, £3.90; EX 23.60 Trifecta £38.10 Pool: £358.42 - 6.96 winning units..

Owner B E Nielsen **Bred** Rathasker Stud **Trained** Upper Lambourn, Berks

FOCUS
A moderate handicap run at an ordinary gallop. The first two, who pulled clear, came down the centre in the straight. The form has a fairly solid feel to it.

NOTEBOOK
Progenitor(IRE), from an in-form yard, is a progressive sort who attracted plenty of support and turned in his best effort to notch his second Polytrack win on his first run over 1m. He'll be up in the weights for this but there may well be more to come. (op 9-4)

Gabrial The Boss(USA), returned to Polytrack, ran as well as he ever has done to bustle up a progressive rival. He pulled clear of the remainder and should be able to pick up a similar event. (op 10-1)

Lucy Bee, back on Polytrack, wasn't disgraced in chasing home a couple of less exposed types and she won't mind the return to 7f on this evidence. (op 10-1)

Moorway(IRE) was far from disgraced on this AW and handicap debut, in the process shaping as though a stiffer test of stamina would have suited. He's worth keeping an eye on in similar company this winter. (op 16-1)

Reggie Bond ran as well as he ever has done on this AW and nursery debut but he'll have to show a bit more before he's a solid betting proposition. (op 16-1 tchd 25-1 and 12-1)

Day In Day Out, an unexposed sort who had been gelded since his previous start, proved disappointing. He's in good hands but will be one to watch next time. (op 11-4 tchd 10-3)

Windsor Rose(IRE) Official explanation: jockey said filly hung right-handed

6894 32RED SUPPORTING BRITISH RACING H'CAP (DIV I) 1m 141y(P)
8:50 (8:50) (Class 5) (0-75,75) 3-Y-O+ £2,911 (£866; £432; £216) Stalls Low

Form RPR

4012 **1** **Fame Again**[11] 6559 4-9-4 **69**.......................... JamesSullivan 8 75
(Michael Easterby) *mde all: rdn over 1f out: styd on gamely* **11/4**[1]

060 **2** ¾ **Silverware (USA)**[56] 5111 4-9-10 **75**.......................... TomEaves 5 79
(Linda Stubbs) *s.i.s: hdwy 6f out: rdn over 1f out: styd on* **16/1**

4006 **3** *hd* **Glass Mountain (IRE)**[15] 6452 4-9-3 **68**..................(v) FrannyNorton 3 72
(Ian Williams) *a.p: rdn over 1f out: edgd rt ins fnl f: styd on u.p* **8/1**

6161 **4** *1* **Justbookie Dot Com (IRE)**[19] 6317 4-9-8 **73**............(v) LukeMorris 10 75
(David Evans) *in rr: pushed along early: nt clr run over 2f out: hdwy u.p over 1f out: r.o: nt rch ldrs* **8/1**

0515 **5** ½ **Joshua The First**[15] 6429 3-9-4 **73**.......................... JoeFanning 1 74
(Keith Dalgleish) *chsd wnr tl 7f out: remained handy: wnt 2nd again over 2f out: rdn over 1f out: no ex ins fnl f* **4/1**[2]

6200 **6** ¾ **Satwa Laird**[7] 6692 6-9-7 **72**.......................... HayleyTurner 9 71
(Conor Dore) *hld up: rdn over 1f out: r.o ins fnl f: nt rch ldrs* **11/1**

2324 **7** 3½ **Aciano (IRE)**[29] 5993 4-9-6 **71**..........................(t) SebSanders 4 62
(Brendan Powell) *prom: rdn over 1f out: wknd ins fnl f* **9/2**[3]

5000 **8** 3½ **Moataz (USA)**[15] 6442 3-8-3 **63**.......................... DarrenEgan(5) 2 46
(David Simcock) *hld up: rdn over 1f out: wknd fnl f* **11/1**

0400 **9** *7* **Peadar Miguel**[28] 6057 5-8-12 **63**.......................... ShaneKelly 6 30
(Daniel Mark Loughnane) *trckd wnr 7f out tl rdn over 2f out: wknd over 1f out: eased* **33/1**

1m 48.7s (-1.80) **Going Correction** -0.15s/f (Stan)
WFA 3 from 4yo+ 4lb **9** Ran SP% **112.6**
Speed ratings (Par 103): **102,101,101,100,99 99,96,92,86**
Tote Swingers: 1&2 £4.90, 1&3 £6.20, 2&3 £18.70 CSF £47.56 CT £312.34 TOTE £3.50: £1.50, £4.90, £2.90; EX 54.20 Trifecta £206.40 Part won. Pool: £278.97 - 0.70 winning units..

Owner Mrs C E Mason **Bred** R H Mason **Trained** Sheriff Hutton, N Yorks

FOCUS
Mainly exposed performers in a fair handicap. The gallop was an ordinary one and the winner came down the centre.

Peadar Miguel Official explanation: vet said gelding bled from the nose

6895 32RED SUPPORTING BRITISH RACING H'CAP (DIV II) 1m 141y(P)
9:20 (9:21) (Class 5) (0-75,74) 3-Y-O+ £2,911 (£866; £432; £216) Stalls Low

Form RPR

4032 **1** **Tiradito (USA)**[2] 6812 5-8-12 **62**.......................... TomEaves 10 73+
(Brian Ellison) *a.p: led 1f out: pushed out* **6/4**[1]

2040 **2** 2¼ **Ukrainian Princess**[16] 6416 3-8-8 **69**.......................... AmeliaGreen(7) 8 75+
(Sir Henry Cecil) *hld up: hdwy over 1f out: r.o: nt rch wnr* **16/1**

4322 **3** ½ **Loyal N Trusted**[15] 6455 4-9-1 **65**..........................(p) LukeMorris 2 70
(Richard Price) *s.s: hld up: hdwy over 2f out: rdn over 1f out: styd on fnl f* **13/2**

002 **4** ¾ **Fastnet Storm (IRE)**[16] 6405 6-9-10 **74**.......................... GrahamGibbons 1 77
(David Barron) *led: rdn and hdd 1f out: styd on same pce* **7/2**[2]

0060 **5** *1* **Midas Moment**[23] 6157 4-9-6 **70**.......................... HayleyTurner 9 71
(William Muir) *hld up: hdwy over 1f out: nt rch ldrs* **20/1**

0600 **6** *1* **Majestic Dream (IRE)**[16] 6405 4-9-5 **69**..................(b) JamesSullivan 5 68
(Michael Easterby) *chsd ldr: rdn over 1f out: no ex ins fnl f* **5/1**[3]

3016 **7** *4* **Honey Of A Kitten (USA)**[7] 6692 4-9-1 **68**.......... MatthewCosham(3) 7 57
(David Evans) *chsd ldrs: rdn over 2f out: wknd fnl f* **14/1**

05-0 **8** *6* **Adorable Choice (IRE)**[131] 2539 4-9-8 **72**.......................... JimCrowley 4 48
(Tom Dascombe) *hld up: rdn over 3f out: wknd 2f out* **10/1**

0/0- **9** 1¾ **Lucky Dance (BRZ)**[13] 1098 10-9-8 **72**.......................... SeanQuinlan 3 44
(Graeme McPherson) *prom: rdn over 2f out: sn wknd* **40/1**

1m 48.85s (-1.65) **Going Correction** -0.15s/f (Stan)
WFA 3 from 4yo+ 4lb **9** Ran SP% **121.1**
Speed ratings (Par 103): **101,99,98,97,97 96,92,87,85**
Tote Swingers: 1&2 £4.90, 1&3 £2.40, 2&3 £19.20 CSF £31.65 CT £133.05 TOTE £2.30: £1.10, £4.50, £2.60; EX 26.20 Trifecta £637.10 Part won. Pool: £861.07 - 0.71 winning units..

Owner Bagden Wood Building Services Limited **Bred** F J F M Llc **Trained** Norton, N Yorks

FOCUS
The second division of a fair handicap. The gallop was fair and the winner came down the centre in the straight.

T/Plt: £24.40 to a £1 stake. Pool: £73,933.25 - 2,211.89 winning tickets. T/Qpdt: £7.30 to a £1 stake. Pool: £7,504.74 - 754.50 winning tickets. CR

6507 LONGCHAMP (R-H)
Saturday, October 6

OFFICIAL GOING: Turf: very soft changing to heavy after race 2 (11.55)

6896a QATAR PRIX CHAUDENAY (GROUP 2) (3YO) (TURF) 1m 7f
11:55 (12:00) 3-Y-O £95,000 (£36,666; £17,500; £11,666; £5,833)

RPR

1 **Canticum**[27] 6087 3-9-2 0.......................... GregoryBenoist 10 111
(D Smaga, France) *a.p in gp chsng clr ldr: 2nd and rdn over 2f out: styng on but 4 l down 1f out: r.o u.p to ld cl home* **11/1**

2 *nk* **Les Beaufs (FR)**[42] 5614 3-9-2 0.......................... JulienGuillochon 11 110
(Mme V Seignoux, France) *midfield: moved up on outside to ld on bnd into bk st: sn clr: qcknd again 2 1/2f out to go 7 l clr: 4 l clr and hrd rdn ent fnl f: hdd cl home* **50/1**

3 2½ **Tenenbaum**[41] 5650 3-9-2 0.......................... MaximeGuyon 7 107
(A Fabre, France) *trckd ldrs of main gp: 4th and rdn over 2f out: kpt on fr 1 1/2f out: nt pce to chal* **5/1**

4 *2* **Verema (FR)**[27] 6087 3-8-13 0.......................... Christophe-PatriceLemaire 5 102
(A De Royer-Dupre, France) *midfield: dropped towards rr early in bk st: 9th and swtchd outside under 2 1/2f out: hdwy ins fnl 2f: styd on at same pce fnl f: nvr on terms* **13/2**

5 1¼ **Pale Mimosa (IRE)**[44] 5519 3-8-13 0.......................... PatSmullen 2 101
(D K Weld, Ire) *prom in main gp bhd clr ldr: 3rd and rdn 2 1/2f out: one pce fr 1 1/2f out: fdd fnl 100yds* **9/2**[3]

6 1¾ **Top Trip**[41] 5650 3-9-2 0.......................... ThomasHuet 6 101
(F Doumen, France) *midfield: pushed along to hold pl 1/2-way: 8th and scrubbed along 3f out: shortlived effrt u.p 1 1/2f out: nvr able to chal* **10/3**[1]

7 *4* **Smoky Hill (IRE)**[36] 3-9-2 0.......................... UmbertoRispoli 4 97
(M Delzangles, France) *midfield: rdn and no imp fr over 2f out* **25/1**

8 *18* **Shantaram**[86] 4007 3-9-2 0.......................... ChristopheSoumillon 1 75
(John Gosden) *midfield: rdn and nt qckn over 2f out: sn wknd* **4/1**[2]

9 *1* **Only A Pleasure (IRE)**[27] 6087 3-9-2 0.......... Pierre-CharlesBoudot 8 74
(A Fabre, France) *hld up towards rr: nvr in contention: wl bhd fr 2f out* **14/1**

10 *8* **Valdo Bere (FR)**[27] 6087 3-9-2 0.......................... ThierryJarnet 9 64
(E Leenders, France) *in rr: nvr figured: wl bhd fr 2f out* **40/1**

11 *4* **Mysterious Man (IRE)**[42] 5598 3-9-2 0.......................... DarryllHolland 3 59
(Andrew Balding) *led: hdd on bnd into bk st: chsd clr ldr: rdn 2 1/2f out: no imp: wknd fnl 2f and sn wl bhd* **25/1**

3m 22.82s (6.82) **Going Correction** +0.90s/f (Soft) **11** Ran SP% **118.4**
Speed ratings: **117,116,115,114,113 112,110,101,100,96 94**
WIN (incl. 1 euro stake): 13.60. PLACES: 3.40, 12.50, 2.40. DF: 290.70. SF: 361.20.

Owner K Abdulla **Bred** Juddmonte Farms **Trained** Lamorlaye, France

FOCUS
This looked an ordinary running of the Prix Chaudenay and it proved difficult to make up significant ground, meaning potentially unreliable form.

NOTEBOOK
Canticum was just behind Verema in a C&D Group 3 on his previous start, but this time he was better placed than Alain de Royer-Dupre's filly and did well to peg back the runner-up. This isn't a performance to get carried away with, however.

Les Beaufs(FR) had something to find at this level (well held in a Listed race on previous start), but he's suited by testing ground and nearly pulled off an upset after being allowed to open up a clear and still holding a good five-length advantage entering the straight. He'd had to work to get to the front, having started just about slowest of all before being caught wide early, and it didn't help that his rider kept looking round for dangers late on, but even so he's probably a bit flattered.

Tenenbaum was asked to come from further back than the front two and could make no real impression. He may yet be capable of better.

Verema(FR) was poorly placed - she had only two behind her at the top of the straight - and can be given another chance.

Pale Mimosa(IRE) won her maiden on heavy, but the ground was good when she followed up in a York Listed event and her connections feel she's best suited by a decent surface. Upped in distance from 1m4f, she was well enough placed but couldn't pick up sufficiently and was probably found out by the conditions. This big filly can yet rate higher.

Top Trip had been running well in decent company at around 1m4f and looked set to appreciate this longer distance, but he was never really going

Shantaram was forced to miss the St Leger after failing to recover in time from mucus in his lungs, and testing ground was a concern, for all that he won a weak edition of the Bahrain Trophy on soft when last seen. For one reason or another, he failed to give his true running.

6897a QATAR PRIX DANIEL WILDENSTEIN (GROUP 2) (3YO+) (TURF) 1m
12:30 (12:00) 3-Y-O+ £95,000 (£36,666; £17,500; £11,666; £5,833)

RPR

1 **Zinabaa (FR)**[111] 3205 7-9-3 0.......................... GeraldMosse 2 119
(M Mace, France) *trckd ldrs: short of room and swtchd outside 2f out: 3rd and styng on 1 1/2f out: rdn 1f out: r.o under hands and heels to ld 50yds out: a gng bttr than runner-up* **7/1**

2 ¾ **Dux Scholar**[37] 5782 4-9-1 0.......................... AStarke 3 115
(A Savujev, Czech Republic) *midfield: moved into 3rd over 3f out: qcknd to ld under 2f out: sn jst over 2 l clr: hrd rdn over 1f out: hdd 50yds out: no ex* **14/1**

3 2½ **Evaporation (FR)**[111] 3205 5-8-11 0.......................... OlivierPeslier 8 105
(C Laffon-Parias, France) *dwlt and edgd lft s: w.w in rr: hdwy on outside 1 1/2f out: wnt 3rd ins fnl f: run flattened out and no further imp fnl 100yds* **6/1**[3]

4 ¾ **Sarkiyla (FR)**[20] 6296 3-8-8 0.......................... Christophe-PatriceLemaire 5 104
(A De Royer-Dupre, France) *hld up towards rr: short of room 2f out: 6th and hrd rdn 1 1/2f out: kpt on u.p ins fnl f: nvr on terms* **7/2**[1]

5 ¾ **Highland Knight (IRE)**[37] 5782 5-9-3 0.......................... DarryllHolland 4 108
(Andrew Balding) *led: hdd under 2f out: rdn and one pce fnl f: lost 4th cl home* **9/2**[2]

6 4½ **Tifongo (FR)**[41] 5649 3-8-13 0 ow2.......................... ChristopheSoumillon 7 96
(H-A Pantall, France) *pressed ldr: prom tl wknd fr 1 1/2f out* **16/1**

7 *shd* **Mainsail**[98] 3656 3-8-11 0.......................... MaximeGuyon 6 94
(P Bary, France) *half-rrd as gates opened: 5th on outside: rdn and no imp fr 2f out* **7/2**[1]

8 *10* **Lucayan (FR)**[14] 6508 3-9-2 0..........................(p) StephanePasquier 1 76
(F Rohaut, France) *racd keenly towards rr: moved bhd ldrs fr 3f out: rdn and nt qckn ins fnl 2f: wknd fr 1 1/2f out: wl bhd fnl f* **7/1**

1m 44.49s (6.09) **Going Correction** +0.90s/f (Soft)
WFA 3 from 4yo+ 3lb **8** Ran SP% **114.5**
Speed ratings: **105,104,101,101,100 95,95,85**
WIN (incl. 1 euro stake): 7.10. PLACES: 2.50, 5.10, 2.60. DF: 51.10. SF: 111.50.

Owner Ecurie Victoria Dreams **Bred** Mlle V Dubois, J Dubois & E Dubois **Trained** France

FOCUS

A rank ordinary edition of this Group 2 event, but the pace was honest enough.

NOTEBOOK

Zinabaa(FR) was only fifth in this last year, but he's lightly raced for his age and had since shown improved form. He had to bounce back from a disappointing run when last seen in June, but he's fully effective on demanding ground and did well to win this after losing his place entering the straight and allowing the runner-up to get first run. His effort is particularly creditable considering he had a 2lb penalty.

Dux Scholar ran better than when well held behind Highland Knight last time and clearly didn't mind the ground, although he was helped by a really good ride, so may prove a bit flattered by this form.

Evaporation(FR) ran well on her return from 111 days off, keeping on from further back than the front two, but she's now 0-13 in Group company.

Sarkiyla(FR) was third behind Moonlight Cloud and Farhh in the Prix du Moulin on her previous start, but that was just a four-runner race and she may be flattered by the bare result. This time, she just didn't pick up sufficiently.

Highland Knight (IRE) who had today's runner-up behind when taking a Group 2 in Germany last time, was supplemented for this contest, but he was unproven on the ground and it evidently didn't suit.

Mainsail raced too keenly on his return from a 98-day break.

Lucayan(FR) was another who didn't settle and he was caught on heels before the straight. He had a tough task under a 5lb penalty, but is looking increasingly flattered by his French Guineas success.

6898a QATAR PRIX DOLLAR (GROUP 2) (3YO+) (TURF) 1m 1f 165y

1:00 (12:00) 3-Y-O+ **£95,000** (£36,666; £17,500 ; £11,666 ; £5,833)

RPR

1 **Cirrus Des Aigles (FR)**[32] 2533 6 -9-60 .... OlivierPeslier 7 132+
(Mme C Barande-Barbe, France) *midfield on outer: hdwy into 2nd over 4f out: cruised up to chal 3f out: sn led: rdn 2f out and sn clr: extended advantage ins fnl f: v easily* **4/5**[1]

2 *9* **Hunter's Light (IRE)**[35] 5848 4 -9-40 .... MaximeGuyon 6 112
(Saeed Bin Suroor) *midfield on inner: rdn over 2 1/2f out: swtchd out and styd on to go 2nd cl home: no ch w v easy wnr* **8/1**

3 *snk* **Saga Dream (FR)**[15] 6464 6 -9-00 .... ThierryJarnet 9 107
(F Lemercier, France) *hld up in last pair: rdn over 3f out: styd on one pce ins fnl 2f: wnt 3rd post* **33/1**

4 *hd* **Colombian (IRE)**[49] 5377 4 -9-00 .... ChristopheSoumillon 8 107
(John Gosden) *prom on inner: rdn to try and chal 2f out: sn outpcd by wnr: wnt 2nd over 1f out: styd on ins fnl f but lost 2 pls cl home* **6/1**[3]

5 *1 3/4* **Don Bosco (FR)**[41] 5650 5 -9-00 .... GregoryBenoist 5 103
(D Smaga, France) *led: jnd 3f out: rdn and hdd over 2f out: qckly outpcd by wnr: sn no ex and btn: fdd and dropped to 5th ins fnl f* **14/1**

6 *shd* **Maxios**[15] 6464 4 -9-00 .... StephanePasquier 1 103
(J E Pease, France) *hld up towards rr on inner: rdn over 2 1/2f out: sn outpcd: plugged on to go 6th ins fnl f* **4/1**[2]

7 *3/4* **Red Dubawi (IRE)**[15] 6464 4 -9-00 .... Christophe-PatriceLemaire 3 102
(A De Royer-Dupre, France) *midfield on outer: rdn over 2f out: sn outpcd and btn: fdd and dropped to 7th ins fnl f* **40/1**

8 *15* **Green Destiny (IRE)**[42] 5613 5 -9-00 .... AStarke 2 71
(A Savujev, Czech Republic) *hld up in detached last: rdn to try and improve over 3f out: no prog and sn btn: eased ins fnl f: nvr a factor* **33/1**

2m 7.95s (5.05) **Going Correction** +0.90s/f (Soft) **8**Ran SP% **115.9**

Speed ratings: **115,107,107,107,106 106,105,93**

WIN (incl. 1 euro stake): 2.10. PLACES: 1.30, 1.90, 2.80. DF: 6.30. SF: 8.50 .

Owner Jean-Claude-Alain Dupouy **Bred** M Yvon Lelimouzin & M Benoit Deschamps **Trained** France

FOCUS

Not a strong race, but still a top-class performance from Cirrus Des Aigles, who thrashed his rivals despite carrying a 6lb penalty on his return from an enforced 132-day absence, and on this form he'll be a worthy opponent for Frankel if the ground is soft at Ascot on October 20. The winner is not rated far off his best while the third is rated to the best of this year's form.

NOTEBOOK

Cirrus Des Aigles (FR)successful in this a couple of years previously and runner-up last season, was using this latest running as a prep for the Champion Stakes, a race he won in 2011. His Ascot victory was gained on ground officially described as good, but few are as effective as Cirrus Des Aigles when it comes to ploughing through the mud, and under his optimum conditions he did not require a hard ride. Whether or not he can inflict a first defeat on the mighty Frankel remains to be seen, but testing ground would give him a fighting chance and he's now a 5-1 shot for the showpiece event of British Champions Day.

Hunter's Light (IRE)had really come good on his last couple of starts, taking Group 3 at Haydock and a Polytrack Group 2 in Turkey, and this was another solid effort. It's questionable exactly what the form is worth, with there being a bunch finish for second, but nevertheless there was a lot to like about his performance under a 4lb penalty on ground that might have been softer than ideal.

Saga Dream (FR)ran respectably but is now 0-9 in Group company.

Colombian(IRE) had conditions to suit but didn't see his race out well enough after being a bit keen early.

Maxios, who had today's third behind him when taking a Group 3 last time, might have found conditions too testing.

6899a QATAR PRIX DE ROYALLIEU (GROUP 2) (3YO+ FILLIES & MARES) (TURF) 1m 4f 110y

1:30 (12:00) 3-Y-O+ **£118,750** (£45,833; £21,875 ; £14,583 ; £7,291)

RPR

1 **Dalkala (USA)**[56] 5116 3 -8-70 .... Christophe-PatriceLemaire 2 112
(A De Royer-Dupre, France) *mde all: set stdy pce: rdn over 1 1/2f out: strly pressed ins fnl f: fnd more and a doing enough cl home: clever ride* **3/1**[2]

2 *snk* **Shirocco Star**[44] 5518 3 -8-70 ....(b[1]) DarryllHolland 1 112+
(Hughie Morrison) *prom on inner: rdn in 2nd over 1f out: styd on to chal ins fnl f: kpt on but a being hld by wnr cl home* **5/2**[1]

3 *1 1/2* **La Conquerante**[55] 5142 3 -8-70 .... IoritzMendizabal 3 109
(J-C Rouget, France) *midfield on outer: rdn in 3rd over 1f out: styd on wout matching front pair ins fnl f* **13/2**

4 *nk* **Forces Of Darkness (IRE)**[55] 5142 3 -8-70 .... GregoryBenoist 8 109+
(F Vermeulen, France) *hld up in tch: rdn 2f out: styd on to go 4th ent fnl f: nt pce to chal* **6/1**[3]

5 *5* **Myrtlewood (IRE)**[19] 6327 3 -8-70 .... MaximeGuyon 5 101+
(A Fabre, France) *midfield on inner: rdn over 2f out: outpcd over 1f out: styd on* **12/1**

6 *2 1/2* **Preferential**[35] 5845 3 -8-70 .... StephanePasquier 4 97+
(Mme C Head-Maarek, France) *hld up in last on inner: rdn to improve 1 1/2f out: styd on to go 6th ins fnl f: n.d* **7/1**

7 *6* **Grace Of Dubai (FR)**[19] 6327 3 -8-70 .... UmbertoRispoli 6 87
(M Delzangles, France) *trckd ldr in 2nd: rdn over 2f out: sn outpcd and btn: wknd: eased ins fnl f* **20/1**

8 *3* **Coquet**[14] 6482 3 -8-70 .... GeraldMosse 7 82+
(Hughie Morrison) *hld up in last pair on outer: rdn in last over 2f out: sn wl bhd and btn: eased ins fnl f* **11/1**

2m 57.04s (17.14)**Going Correction** +0.90s/f (Soft) **8**Ran SP% **114.5**

Speed ratings: **83,82,81,81,78 77,73,71**

WIN (incl. 1 euro stake): 4.00. PLACES: 1.50, 1.40, 1.70. DF: 4.60. SF: 10.80 .

Owner H H Aga Khan **Bred** His Highness The Aga Khan Studs Sc **Trained** Chantilly, France

FOCUS

The form horses finished one-two, but this is a result to treat with caution as Dalkala was allowed to set a slow pace in an uncontested lead and just held on from a first-time blinkered filly who has yet to add to her maiden win. The form is rated around the first two and the fourth.

NOTEBOOK

Dalkala(USA)'s form had dipped since a Group 3 success at Saint-Cloud in May and this victory doesn't necessarily mean she's now resumed her progression. She made the running at her own pace and her rider deserves full marks.

Shirocco Star raced enthusiastically in the headgear, directly behind the winner, and was always held when pulled out with her challenge near the line. This was her third defeat by a neck or less since she won her maiden and her attitude has to be questioned.

La Conquerante had a bit to find at this level, but ran well, especially considering she raced further back than the front two.

Forces Of Darkness (IRE)who finished one place ahead of Dalkala in the Prix de Diane, couldn't follow up her recent Group 3 victory.

6900a (Foreign Racing) See RI

[6693]BELMONT PARK (L-H)

Saturday, October 6

OFFICIAL GOING: Dirt: fast; turf: good

6901a FOXWOODS CHAMPAGNE STKS (GRADE 1) (2YO) (DIRT) 1m

9:34 (9:48) 2-Y-O

£154,838 (£51,612; £25,806 ; £12,903 ; £7,741 ; £5,161)

RPR

1 **Shanghai Bobby (USA)**[33] 2 -8-100 ....(b) RosieNapravnik 2 118+
(Todd Pletcher, U.S.A) **33/20**[1]

2 *5* **Goldencents (USA)**[34] 2 -8-100 .... KKrigger 1 107
(Doug O'Neill, U.S.A) **37/10**[3]

3 *1* **Fortify (USA)**[33] 2 -8-100 .... RADominguez 5 104
(Kiaran McLaughlin, U.S.A) **31/5**

4 *1 1/4* **Archwarrior (USA)**[37] 2 -8-100 .... JRVelazquez 4 101
(Todd Pletcher, U.S.A) **69/20**[2]

5 *2 3/4* **Micromanage (USA)**[35] 2 -8-100 .... JRosario 6 95
(Todd Pletcher, U.S.A) **77/20**

6 *1 3/4* **Chief Havoc (USA)**[15] 6447 2 -8-100 .... CVelasquez 3 91
(Jeremy Noseda) **27/1**

1m 35.55s (95.55) **6**Ran SP% **119.6**

PARI-MUTUEL (all including $2 stakes): WIN 5.30; PLACE (1-2) 2.90, 5.40; SHOW (1-2-3) 2.10, 3.20, 3.20; SF 26.00 .

Owner Starlight Racing **Bred** Stonehaven Steadings **Trained** USA

NOTEBOOK

Shanghai Bobby (USA)gained an impressive five-length victory over a strong-looking field. He has now completed a four-timer after stopping the clock in a time significantly faster than Dreaming Of Julia in the Frizette.

Chief Havoc (USA)finished last of six, fading in the straight after travelling well on the far turn.

6902a JAMAICA H'CAP (GRADE 1) (3YO) (TURF) 1m 1f (T)

10:06 (10:19) 3-Y-O

£154,838 (£51,612; £25,806 ; £12,903 ; £7,741 ; £2,580)

RPR

1 **King David (USA)**[23] 3 -8-30 ow3 .... RosieNapravnik 1 103
(Michael J Maker, U.S.A) **28/1**

2 *1/2* **King Kreesa (USA)**[34] 3 -8-40 ....(b) ECastro 7 103
(Jeremiah C Englehart, U.S.A) **239/10**

3 *3/4* **Summer Front (USA)**[49] 5375 3 -8-90 .... RADominguez 4 110+
(Christophe Clement, U.S.A) **5/2**[2]

4 *2 3/4* **Cogito (USA)**[76] 4385 3 -8-60 ....(b[1]) FrankieDettori 3 97
(Brian Meehan) **59/20**[3]

5 *1/2* **Dullahan (USA)**[40] 5699 3 -8-110 .... JRosario 2 101
(Dale Romans, U.S.A) **17/10**[1]

6 *1* **Shkspeare Shaliyah (USA)**[34] 3 -8-20 .... IOrtizJr 5 90
(Doodnauth Shivmangal, U.S.A) **76/1**

7 *nk* **Howe Great (USA)**[33] 3 -8-90 .... JRVelazquez 6 96
(H Graham Motion, U.S.A) **79/20**

1m 52.91s (112.91) **7**Ran SP% **119.9**

PARI-MUTUEL (all including $2 stakes): WIN 58.00; PLACE (1-2) 18.80, 21.20; SHOW (1-2-3) 6.70, 8.00, 3.30; SF 370.00 .

Owner Scarlet Stable **Bred** Ben Lengacher **Trained** USA

FOCUS

The form is limited by the fact the pace was slow and the third was unlucky.

NOTEBOOK

King David (USA) whose rider had earlier won the Champagne Stakes on the unbeaten Shanghai Bobby, was sent off a 28-1 shot, which was hardly surprising as he was claimed just three weeks ago for $35,000. He caught fellow longshot King Kreesa inside the final furlong before scoring by a half-length. He, has now won six of his seven starts this term.

Summer Front (USA)must be regarded an unlucky loser after his jockey Ramon Dominguez tried for an ambitious run up the rail.

Cogito(USA) missed the break and then raced six lengths off a slow pace towards the rear of the field. He was hard driven turning for home and could then only stay on without ever threatening the principals.

5402 DUSSELDORF (R-H)

Sunday, October 7

OFFICIAL GOING: Turf: very soft

6906a GROSSER PREIS DER LANDESHAUPTSTADT DUSSELDORF (GROUP 3) (3YO+) (TURF) 1m 110y

3:10 (12:00) 3-Y-0+

£26,666 (£9,166; £4,583 ; £2,500 ; £1,666 ; £1,250)

RPR

1 **King's Hall**[43] 5613 4 -9-20 AStarke 5 105
(A Wohler, Germany) *trckd ldr on outside: 3 l down and rdn under 2f out: r.o u.p fnl f to chal ldr: led cl home: all out* **27/10**[3]

2 *hd* **Alianthus (GER)**[21] 6291 7 -9-40 SHellyn 3 107
(W Giedt, Germany) *led: 3 l clr over 2f out: rdn over 1f out: r.o: ct cl home* **11/10**[1]

3 *1/2* **Point Blank (GER)**[9] 4 -9-20 StefanieHofer 2 103
(Mario Hofer, Germany) *trckd ldr on ins: 3rd: rdn and no imp ins fnl 2f: styd on u.p fnl f: nt rch ldrs* **73/10**

4 *1/2* **Combat Zone (IRE)**[21] 6291 6 -9-60 NRichter 4 106
(Mario Hofer, Germany) *4th: rdn 3f out: no imp tl styd on ins fnl f: nvr able to chal* **5/2**[2]

5 *3/4* **Felician (GER)**[21] 6291 4 -9-20 RobertHavlin 1 101
(F J Leve, Germany) *settled in last: styd on u.p fr 1f out: nt pce to chal* **48/10**

1m 48.86s (1.28) **5**Ran SP% **132.5**

WIN (incl. 10 euro stake): 37. PLACES: 14, 14. SF: 78

Owner Stall Route 66 **Bred** Gestut Elsetal **Trained** Germany

6903a-6905a,6907a See RI

6896 LONGCHAMP (R-H)

Sunday, October 7

OFFICIAL GOING: Turf: heavy

6908a QATAR PRIX DE L'ABBAYE DE LONGCHAMP (GROUP 1) (2YO+) (TURF) 5f (S)

12:55 (12:00) 2-Y-0+ **£166,658** (£66,675; £33,337 ; £16,654 ; £8,341)

RPR

1 **Wizz Kid (IRE)**[29] 6030 4 -9-70 (p) GeraldMosse 6 116+
(Robert Collet, France) *towards rr early and pushed along: hdwy into midfield over 2f out: rdn in 3rd ent fnl f: r.o to ld last strides: won gng away* **7/1**[3]

2 *nk* **Mayson**[85] 4100 4 -9-110 PaulHanagan 1 119+
(Richard Fahey) *sltly slow to stride: midfield on inner: hdwy to be prom in centre over 2f out: rdn to ld 1 1/2f out: jnd over 1f out: edgd ahd wl ins fnl f: hdd fnl strides* **3/1**[1]

3 *1/2* **Hamish McGonagall**[44] 5561 7 -9-110 DavidAllan 2 117
(Tim Easterby) *prom on inner: rdn to dispute ld over 1f out: stl ev ch tl hdd wl ins fnl f: dropped to 3rd fnl strides* **14/1**

4 *2 1/2* **Ballesteros**[36] 5814 3 -9-110 EddieAhern 13 108
(Brian Meehan) *hld up towards rr on outer: rdn to improve over 2f out: r.o to go 4th ins fnl f: no ch w ldng trio* **25/1**

5 *1 1/2* **Sole Power**[25] 6140 5 -9-110 JohnnyMurtagh 15 103
(Edward Lynam, Ire) *midfield: rdn over 1 1/2f out: outpcd by ldrs ins fnl f: kpt on* **9/1**

6 *1 1/2* **Inxile (IRE)**[21] 6292 7 -9-110 (p) AdrianNicholls 4 97
(David Nicholls) *sn led: rdn over 2 1/2f out: strly pressed and hdd 1 1/2f out: sn no ex and fdd* **16/1**

7 *1/2* **Humidor (IRE)**[44] 5561 5 -9-110 RichardHughes 14 96
(George Baker) *stdd and hld up in last trio on outer: rdn to improve 1 1/2f out: r.o to go 7th ins fnl f: nvr a threat* **25/1**

8 *1* **Monsieur Joe (IRE)**[21] 6292 5 -9-110 OlivierPeslier 5 92
(Robert Cowell) *sn prom: rdn and outpcd 2f out: fdd* **10/1**

9 *nk* **Borderlescott**[15] 6468 10 -9-110 FrederikTylicki 7 91
(Robin Bastiman) *midfield: rdn to maintain position fr over 3f out: outpcd and lost pl over 1 1/2f out: kpt on wout threatening after* **33/1**

10 *snk* **Govinda (USA)**[42] 5647 5 -9-110 EPedroza 8 90
(A Wohler, Germany) *midfield: rdn over 2f out: kpt on ins fnl f* **40/1**

11 *snk* **Spirit Quartz (IRE)**[44] 5561 4 -9-110 FrankieDettori 9 90
(Robert Cowell) *prom in centre: rdn to try and chal 2f out: outpcd and btn over 1f out: fdd* **13/2**[2]

12 *1/2* **Tangerine Trees**[44] 5561 7 -9-110 (b) TomEaves 19 88
(Bryan Smart) *prom on wd outside: rdn and outpcd over 2 1/2f out: fdd* **25/1**

13 *1 1/2* **Tiddliwinks**[15] 6485 6 -9-110 (p) JamieSpencer 10 83
(Kevin Ryan) *sltly s.i.s: hld up in last trio on inner: no room on rail and forced to wait for gap over 1 1/2f out: rdn and kpt on whn in the clr: nvr a factor* **25/1**

14 *nk* **Beyond Desire**[44] 5561 5 -9-70 NeilCallan 17 78
(Roger Varian) *broke wl and sn prom in centre: rdn 2f out: no ex and btn 1 1/2f out: steadily fdd* **25/1**

15 *shd* **Definightly**[56] 5137 6 -9-110 (b) ThierryThulliez 11 81
(Roger Charlton) *prom early: sn relegated to midfield: rdn 3f out: outpcd and btn over 1f out: fdd* **20/1**

16 *1 1/2* **Secret Asset (IRE)**[65] 4762 7 -9-110 GeorgeBaker 18 76
(Jane Chapple-Hyam) *midfield on outer: rdn over 2 1/2f out: outpcd and btn over 1f out: fdd* **33/1**

17 *4 1/2* **Taajub (IRE)**[15] 6485 5 -9-110 IanMongan 12 60
(Peter Crate) *unable to go early gallop and sn rdn in last: sn detached and btn: nvr a factor* **40/1**

18 *10* **Swiss Spirit**[15] 6485 3 -9-110 WilliamBuick 3 24
(David Elsworth) *midfield: rdn and outpcd over 2 1/2f out: sn no ex and fdd: eased whn btn and dropped to last* **9/1**

1m 1.17s (4.87) **Going Correction** +1.40s/f (Soft) **18**Ran SP% **127.2**

Speed ratings: **117,116,115,111,109 106,106,104,104,103 103,102,100,99,99 97,90,74**

WIN (incl. 1 euro stake): 9.30. PLACES: 2.70, 1.80, 5.00. DF: 16.50. SF: 41.80

Owner Mme Maeve Mahony **Bred** Ballylinch Stud **Trained** Chantilly, France

FOCUS

This is usually an ordinary race for the level, like so many of the big European sprints, and the latest running proved no exception. A low draw was again an advantage with the first three drawn in the bottom six stalls. There had been only one French-trained winner in the last ten years (Marchand D'Or in 2008) and the home team had just a single representative this time, but she was able to deny the foreign contingent. While the form isn't particularly strong, this was a good effort from the winner. The third sets the level with the second not far off his July Cup effort.

NOTEBOOK

Wizz Kid (IRE)made an awkward start and raced further back than the front two before making up significant ground late on, winning more comfortably than the margin suggests. A close fifth in last year's running on much quicker ground, she's at her best on a softish surface and left behind a below-par run in the Haydock Sprint Cup. She may now go for the Champions Sprint at Ascot, a race in which she ran second in 2011.

Mayson hadn't been seen since winning a weak July Cup by 5l on heavy ground. He had similar conditions for his follow-up bid, but this shorter trip was always going to make it difficult for him to repeat such a dominant performance, and a sluggish start didn't help his chance. While he did well to see off the third after having to challenge around that rival, he was probably only second best on the day. He may go to Ascot.

Hamish McGonagall was favourably drawn, especially for one who likes to get on with it, and he showed his customary early dash. He probably ran to a similar level as when third in the Nunthorpe on his previous start.

Ballesteros is ideally suited by a demanding surface and he ran well to fare best of those from a double-figure draw. It's doubtful he'll confirm this form back on quick ground, however.

Sole Power, last year's third, was unhelpfully drawn and ideally wants better ground, so this was a good effort in the circumstances.

Inxile(IRE) unsurprisingly found it tough to dominate this field, even from a good draw, but he kept on admirably once headed.

Humidor(IRE), fourth in the Nunthorpe on his previous start, was left with too much to do after being dropped in his from double-figure draw and needed the race to fall apart up front if he was to have any chance.

Monsieur Joe (IRE) who had Inxile behind when winning a C&D Group 3 last time, was soon in trouble and has to be considered disappointing.

Borderlescott was already under pressure when a bit squeezed for room at around halfway.

Govinda(USA) was another who was already under pressure when a bit squeezed for room at around halfway.

Spirit Quartz (IRE)had a number of these behind him when runner-up in the Nunthorpe, but after showing good early speed, he was beaten as soon as he came under pressure and presumably didn't like the ground.

Tangerine Trees has struggled since winning this race last year on decent ground from stall nine. He was out in gate 19 this time, on much worse going than 12 months ago, and was well held.

Tiddliwinks was hopelessly placed and got no sort of run through.

Beyond Desire probably wasn't helped by a combination of the testing ground and a wide draw.

Definightly had conditions to suit but wasn't good enough.

Swiss Spirit, previously progressive and a Group 3 winner last time, found this all too much. He's probably still on the weak side and had never raced on such bad ground. It later emerged that he had sustained a minor muscular pull.

6909a TOTAL PRIX MARCEL BOUSSAC - CRITERIUM DES POULICHES (GROUP 1) (2YO FILLIES) (TURF) 1m

1:30 (12:00) 2-Y-0 **£142,850** (£57,150; £28,575 ; £14,275 ; £7,150)

RPR

1 **Silasol (IRE)**[28] 2 -8-110 OlivierPeslier 4 107
(C Laffon-Parias, France) *mde all: qcknd 2f out: rdn appr 1f out: r.o wl fnl f: gamely hld off chalrs cl home* **10/1**

2 *hd* **Topaze Blanche (IRE)**[20] 2 -8-110 FrankieDettori 8 107
(C Laffon-Parias, France) *towards rr: tk clsr order 3f out: 6th and sltly short of room over 2f out: swtchd outside and styd on wl u.p fr over 1f out: no ex cl home as wnr rallied* **12/1**

3 *hd* **Alterite (FR)**[34] 5899 2 -8-110 ChristopheSoumillon 7 106
(J-C Rouget, France) *t.k.h early: restrained in rr: hdwy on outside over 1 1/2f out: 4th and rdn ent fnl f: r.o u.p but nvr quite getting there* **7/1**

4 *1 1/4* **Flotilla (FR)**[26] 6129 2 -8-110 GregoryBenoist 1 104+
(M Delzangles, France) *midfield on rail: towards rr over 3f out: blocked on ins bhd ldrs fr 2f out tl gap appeared 1f out: rdn and styd on wl fnl 100yds: nt rch ldrs* **25/1**

5 *snk* **Peace Burg (FR)**[26] 6129 2 -8-110 IoritzMendizabal 3 103
(J Heloury, France) *trckd ldr on rail: short of room 1 1/2f out: swtchd outside ldr and styd on u.p ins fnl f: run flattened out fnl 75yds* **9/4**[1]

6 *3/4* **Meri Shika (FR)**[26] 6129 2 -8-110 ThierryJarnet 5 102+
(J Bertran De Balanda, France) *midfield: hemmed in 1 1/2f out: lost pls and swtchd ins 150yds out: styd on u.p fnl 100yds: nvr able to chal* **25/1**

7 *2* **Agent Allison**[107] 3326 2 -8-110 JamieSpencer 9 97
(Peter Chapple-Hyam) *trckd ldr: rdn and nt qckn 1 1/2f out: wknd u.p fnl f* **11/2**[3]

8 *1 3/4* **Purr Along**[23] 6199 2 -8-110 MartinDwyer 2 95
(William Muir) *dwlt: hld up towards rr: in rr and nowhere to go 1 1/2f out: in clr appr fnl f: sn rdn and no imp* **3/1**[2]

9 *nk* **My Special J'S (USA)**[38] 6081 2 -8-110 TadhgO'Shea 10 92
(John Patrick Shanahan, Ire) *prom on outside: rdn and nt qckn ins fnl 2f: wknd fnl f* **10/1**

1m 44.62s (6.22) **Going Correction** +1.00s/f (Soft) **9**Ran SP% **117.2**

Speed ratings: **108,107,107,106,106 105,103,101,101**

WIN (incl. 1 euro stake): 14.30. PLACES: 3.70, 3.00, 2.30. DF: 36.70. SF: 109.10

Owner Wertheimer & Frere **Bred** Wertheimer & Frere **Trained** Chantilly, France

FOCUS

A race with a mixed recent record and it's doubtful any of these are set for stardom at three. The early pace was a steady one, but this still turned into a good test at the distance in the conditions. The front-runners were favoured in the races run here the previous day and the winner again made all the running. Suspect form and below par for the race.

NOTEBOOK

Silasol(IRE) was allowed an easy time in front and, having made all in a C&D conditions race the previous month, she just pulled out enough to hold off the closers. She was able to conserve more energy than the placed runners and would be far from certain to confirm form were they to meet again. It's likely she'll want 1m2f next season.

Topaze Blanche (IRE) a stablemate of the winner, had readily won a conditions race over this trip at Saint-Cloud the time before and she picked up well once switched, but just found it too tough making the ground in the conditions. She's a pacier type than the winner and would be the better French 1000 Guineas prospect of the pair.

Alterite(FR) ◆, a previous Listed winner, needs her effort upgrading considering she was last turning in and covered plenty of ground just to reach a challenging position. Like the runner-up, she was clawing the winner back all the time without being able to get up and this progressive filly is capable of winning at Group level.

Flotilla(FR) was unlucky not to be bang there with the first three, finding herself stuck on the rail with little room before staying on well once in the clear. She hadn't received the best of trips at Chantilly the time before either and may improve for 1m2f next year.

Peace Burg(FR), previously unbeaten, having finished ahead of both the third and fourth previously, was close up on the rail, but had to wait for a run and she then found disappointingly little once in the clear. She'd already won on very soft ground, so conditions can't be put forward as an excuse.
Agent Allison, off since chasing home Newfangled in the Albany, was up 2f in trip and looked a non-stayer in the ground.
Purr Along, denied by subsequent Fillies' Mile winner Certify at Doncaster, was soon poorly positioned having been a bit slow to break and then met trouble when trying to stay on down the straight. Looking at the way she faded late it's possible the ground was too soft for her. It later emerged she'd come into season the day before and had pulled a shoe off during the race.
My Special J'S(USA) has now failed to beat a rival in two starts at Group 1 level.

6910a PRIX JEAN-LUC LAGARDERE (GRAND CRITERIUM) (GROUP 1) (2YO COLTS & FILLIES) (TURF) (SPONSORS AL EMADI) 7f

2:05 (12:00) 2-Y-O **£166,658** (£66,675; £33,337; £16,654; £8,341)

RPR

1 **Olympic Glory (IRE)**[67] 4698 2-9-0 0 RichardHughes 6 117
(Richard Hannon) *midfield on inner: gng wl but locked in pocket 2 1/2f out: swtchd out and rdn 1 1/2f out: r.o to chal ins fnl f: led cl home: pushed out* **6/4**[1]

2 *1 1/4* **What A Name (IRE)**[28] 6086 2-8-10 0 Christophe-PatriceLemaire 7 110
(M Delzangles, France) *hld up in last trio: rdn to improve 1 1/2f out: r.o to go 2nd fnl strides: nt pce of wnr* **3/1**[2]

3 *nk* **Indian Jade**[24] 6162 2-9-0 0 JamieSpencer 5 113
(Kevin Ryan) *racd in 3rd: rdn to chal 2f out: disp ld fr 1 1/2f out: led over 1f out: strly pressed ins fnl f: hdd cl home: no ex and dropped to 3rd last strides* **33/1**

4 *5* **Snowday (FR)**[49] 5398 2-9-0 0 OlivierPeslier 1 101
(C Laffon-Parias, France) *sn trcking ldr in 2nd: rdn to chal 2f out: disp ld fr 1 1/2f out: hdd over 1f out: sn no ex and fdd* **20/1**

5 *1/2* **Pedro The Great (USA)**[56] 5136 2-9-0 0 JPO'Brien 2 100
(A P O'Brien, Ire) *hld up in last trio on inner: hdwy into midfield 2 1/2f out: rdn and outpcd 1 1/2f out: kpt on wout threatening ins fnl f* **9/2**[3]

6 *2 1/2* **Maxentius (IRE)**[22] 6243 2-9-0 0 WilliamBuick 4 93
(Peter Chapple-Hyam) *hld up in last: rdn to try and improve on outer 2f out: kpt on one pce ins fnl 1 1/2f: n.d* **16/1**

7 *1 1/2* **Avantage (FR)**[28] 6086 2-9-0 0 GregoryBenoist 9 90
(Mme Pia Brandt, France) *got across fr wd draw and sn led: rdn and hdd 1 1/2f out: sn no ex and btn: fdd and dropped to last over 1f out: rallied and wnt 7th cl home* **14/1**

8 *1/2* **Tha'Ir (IRE)**[22] 6243 2-9-0 0 FrankieDettori 8 88
(Saeed Bin Suroor) *midfield on outer: rdn 2f out: outpcd and btn over 1f out: dropped to last cl home* **10/1**

1m 25.73s (5.03) **Going Correction** +1.00s/f (Soft) **8 Ran** SP% **112.5**
Speed ratings: **111,109,109,103,102 100,98,97**
WIN (incl. 1 euro stake): 2.20. PLACES: 1.40, 1.60, 4.80. DF: 3.90. SF: 6.80.
Owner Sheikh Joaan Bin Hamad Al Thani **Bred** Denis McDonnell **Trained** East Everleigh, Wilts

FOCUS
Since the millennium the likes of Rock Of Gibraltar, American Post and Oratorio have won this en route to Group 1 success as 3-y-os, but more recent runnings have been less inspiring. Indeed, the last four winners have all so far failed to win again. This latest running didn't look anything special. It's hard to believe Coolmore and Godolphin don't have better youngsters than their chosen representatives, and the third had yet to come close to recording a three-figure RPR in five previous starts. The second is rated to previous form and sets the level.

NOTEBOOK
Olympic Glory(IRE) might have won in spite of the demanding ground. He didn't travel all that strongly and, when asked for his effort, looked vulnerable to the runner-up, who was stalking him going well, but he showed a fine attitude and was always holding that rival once in front. This was his third straight Group-race success, adding to victories in the Superlative Stakes (also gained on testing ground) and the Vintage Stakes (impressive late burst after finding trouble), and his only defeat in five starts came when runner-up to the top-class Dawn Approach in the Coventry. It remains to be seen whether he can make a top-class miler next year, and his breeding isn't exactly loaded with stamina, so quotes of around 16-1 for the 2000 Guineas at Newmarket don't appeal at this stage, especially with connections suggesting he may instead return to France for the Poule d'Essai des Poulains.
What A Name(IRE), the only filly in the line-up, was delivered late, but if anything she was losing ground on the winner at the line. She had won her last two starts on better ground, notably a C&D Group 3 from male opposition, and has a US pedigree, so she deserves extra credit for finishing so close on such testing going, although the winner may also have preferred a faster surface. Whether she's good enough for the 1000 Guineas is questionable.
Indian Jade, fourth in a Doncaster sales race on his previous start, had loads to find but was seemingly helped by the step up from 6.5f and the demanding ground, and racing closer to the pace than the front two may also have been an advantage. He had earlier been considered good enough to contest the Coventry, finishing a respectable eighth of 22, and proved here he's capable of smart form when the ground is on the soft side, but it's doubtful he'll prove as effective back on a decent surface.
Snowday(FR) probably wasn't helped by being taken on up front and soon losing the lead. He had stamina to prove and finished up a fair way behind the first three.
Pedro The Great(USA) hadn't been seen since winning the Phoenix Stakes (6f, soft) in August and proved disappointing, looking beaten as soon as he came off the bridle. Perhaps the ground was too testing.
Maxentius(IRE) was only 2l behind Olympic Glory when third in the Superlative Stakes on heavy, but he was never involved this time.
Avantage(FR), runner-up behind What A Name on his previous start, faded after doing a lot of early running.
Tha'Ir(IRE) found this company a bit hot on ground that probably didn't suit.

6911a PRIX DE L'OPERA LONGINES (GROUP 1) (3YO+ FILLIES & MARES) (TURF) 1m 2f

2:40 (12:00) 3-Y-O+ **£190,466** (£76,200; £38,100; £19,033; £9,533)

RPR

1 **Ridasiyna (FR)**[47] 5472 3-8-11 0 Christophe-PatriceLemaire 6 121+
(M Delzangles, France) *towards rr on ins: hdwy to go 5th turning for home: gd prog 2f out to ld nring 1f out: pushed clr fnl f* **12/1**

2 *3 1/2* **Izzi Top**[49] 5399 4-9-2 0 WilliamBuick 5 114
(John Gosden) *prom in main gp bhd clr front-runner: reeled in ldr and led ins fnl 2f: rdn 1 1/2f out: hdd nring 1f out: one pce fnl f* **2/1**[1]

3 *snk* **Giofra**[49] 5399 4-9-2 0 ChristopheSoumillon 14 114+
(A De Royer-Dupre, France) *towards rr on outside: hdwy over 2f out: styd on u.p fnl 1 1/2f: nvr on terms* **9/2**[2]

4 *2* **Pirika (IRE)**[21] 6295 4-9-2 0 Pierre-CharlesBoudot 8 110
(A Fabre, France) *w.w towards rr: moved into midfield 3f out: styd on u.p ins fnl 1 1/2f to go 3rd 1f out: one pce fnl f* **15/2**[3]

5 *1 3/4* **Rjwa (IRE)**[29] 6068 3-8-11 0 ThierryJarnet 7 106
(F Rohaut, France) *prom in main gp bhd clr ldr: 3rd over 3f out: rdn 2 1/2f out: plugged on at same pce* **16/1**

6 *4* **Galikova (FR)**[21] 6295 4-9-2 0 OlivierPeslier 10 98+
(F Head, France) *hld up towards rr: kpt on fnl 2f: nvr in contention* **9/2**[2]

7 *1 1/2* **Manieree (IRE)**[28] 6080 4-9-2 0 (b) NGMcCullagh 1 95
(John M Oxx, Ire) *led: sn clr: 6 l advantage and rdn 3f out: hdd ins fnl 2f: plugged on at same pce: wknd ins fnl f* **12/1**

8 *1/2* **Quiza Quiza Quiza**[28] 6-9-2 0 CristianDemuro 13 94+
(L Riccardi, Italy) *hld up towards rr: sme mod: late prog: nvr threatened* **25/1**

9 *shd* **Gulsary (IRE)**[78] 4361 3-8-11 0 BegenchmuratAgamuradow 9 94+
(C Aubert, France) *midfield: rdn and no imp fr over 2f out* **100/1**

10 *7* **Sagawara**[21] 6295 3-8-11 0 GeraldMosse 11 80
(A De Royer-Dupre, France) *midfield: styd on into 4th over 3f out: rdn and wknd 2f out: bhd and eased fnl f* **16/1**

11 *5* **Caitania (IRE)**[36] 5844 3-8-11 0 ADeVries 2 70
(U Stoltefuss, Germany) *midfield: rdn and wknd over 2f out* **66/1**

12 *dist* **Ambivalent (IRE)**[24] 6163 3-8-11 0 NeilCallan 3
(Roger Varian) *prom in main gp bhd clr ldr: rdn and wknd over 4f out: bhd whn ins fr 2f out: t.o* **33/1**

13 *2 1/2* **Sydarra (FR)**[21] 6295 3-8-11 0 FlavienPrat 12
(F Head, France) *rdn to chse ldr: bhd fr 1/2-way: t.o* **150/1**

2m 11.13s (7.13) **Going Correction** +1.00s/f (Soft)
WFA 3 from 4yo+ 5lb **13 Ran** SP% **118.5**
Speed ratings: **111,108,108,106,105 101,100,100,100,94 90, ,**
WIN (incl. 1 euro stake): 8.20 (Ridasiyna coupled with Sagawara). PLACES: 3.20, 1.60, 2.10. DF: 20.00. SF: 66.10.
Owner H H Aga Khan **Bred** Hh The Aga Khans Studs Sc **Trained** France

FOCUS
No hanging around in what looked a competitive edition of this prestigious contest. Manieree stormed into a clear lead, and for the first time over the two days the race set up nicely for the closers. It was won by a 3-y-o for the eighth time in the last 11 years.

NOTEBOOK
Ridasiyna(FR), under a well-judged ride, got her career back on track with a first win at the top level, bouncing back from a disappointing effort when losing her unbeaten record in a Group 2 over the trip at Deauville. This race had been spoken of as her target after July's Chantilly victory and a good test at the distance on heavy ground suited the daughter of Motivator ideally. Bred to stay 1m4f, she remains capable of better, this being just her fifth start, and it would be no surprise to see her back next year for the Arc.
Izzi Top might have won had William Buick not gone in pursuit of the tearaway leader, committing early, but it's understandable why he did, with it previously having proven difficult to make ground in the conditions. Runner-up to Snow Fairy in the Prix Jean Romanet, the ground didn't look a problem and she travelled strongly into the lead, but in going on so soon she was left vulnerable at the end and had no answer as the 3-y-o swept past. She ran a huge race in defeat though and may have one last race before being retired.
Giofra, for whom the ground would have been plenty soft enough, bounced back from a slightly below-par effort in the Jean Romanet, finishing well without being able to pick up sufficiently.
Pirika(IRE), a surprise second in the Vermeille, confirmed that was no fluke with another sound effort, keeping on late in the manner of a horse likely to benefit from the return to 1m4f.
Rjwa(IRE), the Diane third, went in pursuit of Izzi Top not long after turning in, but her stamina wasn't up to it in the ground.
Galikova(FR) had her favoured soft ground and a decent pace to aim at, but was again found wanting for pace at the top level. She's been disappointing since last year's Vermeille win.
Ambivalent(IRE) didn't look up to this level and duly struggled.

6912a QATAR PRIX DE L'ARC DE TRIOMPHE (GROUP 1) (3YO+ COLTS, FILLIES & MARES) (TURF) 1m 4f

3:25 (12:00) 3-Y-O **£1,904,666** (£762,000; £381,000; £190,333; £95,333)

RPR

1 **Solemia (IRE)**[21] 6295 4-9-2 0 OlivierPeslier 6 124
(C Laffon-Parias, France) *prom on inner: wnt 2nd 3f out: led gng wl 2 1/2f out: rdn and strly pressed 2f out: sn hdd: rallied u.p and styd on to re-press ldr cl home: led last strides* **33/1**

2 *nk* **Orfevre (JPN)**[21] 6293 4-9-5 0 ChristopheSoumillon 18 126+
(Yasutoshi Ikee, Japan) *hld up in last trio: smooth hdwy on outer over 2f out: rdn to ld 1 1/2f out: hung rt and qcknd clr ins fnl f: looked in full control but began to idle and rapidly diminishing advantage cl home: hdd last strides* **5/1**[2]

3 *7* **Masterstroke (USA)**[42] 5650 3-8-11 0 MickaelBarzalona 17 114+
(A Fabre, France) *midfield on outer: rdn 3f out: r.o to chal 2f out: dropped to 3rd over 1f out: outpcd by front pair ins fnl f: kpt on* **11/1**

4 *1* **Haya Landa (FR)**[29] 6035 4-9-2 0 FranckBlondel 1 111
(Mme L Audon, France) *sn settled in midfield on inner: rdn and gd hdwy over 2f out: stl ev ch 1 1/2f out: sn outpcd by ldrs: styd on to go 4th cl home* **150/1**

5 *1/2* **Yellow And Green**[21] 6295 3-8-8 0 ThierryThulliez 3 109
(N Clement, France) *hld up towards rr on inner: angled out and looking for room 4f out: rdn 3f out: swtchd bk to rail and styd on to go 4th ins fnl f: dropped to 5th cl home* **14/1**

6 *2 1/2* **Great Heavens**[77] 4378 3-8-8 0 WilliamBuick 7 105
(John Gosden) *prom: rdn to chal over 2f out: outpcd over 1f out: no ex and fdd ins fnl f* **6/1**[3]

7 *1* **Camelot**[22] 6245 3-8-11 0 FrankieDettori 5 107
(A P O'Brien, Ire) *midfield on inner: swtchd off rail and hdwy over 3f out: rdn over 2f out: sn outpcd: plugged on to go 7th post* **2/1**[1]

8 *nse* **Sea Moon**[78] 4322 4-9-5 0 RyanMoore 16 107
(Sir Michael Stoute) *dropped in fr wd draw and hld up in last trio on inner: rdn to improve 3f out: styd on one pce ins fnl 2f: wnt 8th post* **9/1**

9 *hd* **Shareta (IRE)**[21] 6295 4-9-2 0 Christophe-PatriceLemaire 11 104
(A De Royer-Dupre, France) *midfield on outer: rdn 3f out: outpcd over 1 1/2f out: plugged on ins fnl f: lost 2 pls last strides* **14/1**

10 *2 1/2* **Bayrir (FR)**[21] 6294 3-8-11 0 GeraldMosse 14 102
(A De Royer-Dupre, France) *hld up towards rr: rdn 3f out: styd on wout threatening ins fnl 2f: wnt 10th ins fnl 75yds* **22/1**

11 *nk* **St Nicholas Abbey (IRE)**[29] 6063 5-9-5 0 JPO'Brien 10 103
(A P O'Brien, Ire) *midfield: rdn 2 1/2f out: outpcd over 1 1/2f out: plugged on: dropped to 11th ins fnl 75yds* **14/1**

12 *2 1/2* **Meandre (FR)**[21] 6293 4-9-5 0 MaximeGuyon 13 99
(A Fabre, France) *hld up towards rr on outer: rdn 3f out: sn outpcd: plugged on* **20/1**

13 *2* **Kesampour (FR)**[21] 6294 3-8-11 0 GregoryBenoist 15 95
(M Delzangles, France) *hld up in last: rdn 3f out: plugged on: nvr a factor* **28/1**

14 *dist* **Mikhail Glinka (IRE)**[43] 5613 5-9-5 0 MircoDemuro 9
(A Savujev, Czech Republic) *prom: rdn and brief effrt 2 1/2f out: sn no ex and btn: steadily wknd and eased over 1f out: t.o* **100/1**

15 *7* **Saonois (FR)**[21] 6294 3-8-11 0.................................... AntoineHamelin 2
(J-P Gauvin, France) *restrained and sn in midfield: rdn and lost pl 3f out: no ex and btn over 1 1/2f out: sn eased and t.o* **9/1**

16 *4* **Ernest Hemingway (IRE)**[143] 2210 3-8-11 0................ CO'Donoghue 4
(A P O'Brien, Ire) *led: wnt clr over 5f out: rdn 4f out: hdd 2 1/2f out: qckly btn and wknd: eased and t.o* **150/1**

17 *dist* **Aventino (JPN)**[21] 6293 8-9-5 0.................................. AnthonyCrastus 8
(Yasutoshi Ikee, Japan) *midfield: swtchd to outer over 6f out: rdn over 3f out: sn btn and eased: t.o* **250/1**

18 *12* **Robin Hood (IRE)**[46] 5490 4-9-5 0......................(b) SeamieHeffernan 12
(A P O'Brien, Ire) *sn trcking ldr in 2nd: rdn over 4f out: sn no ex and lost pl rapidly: last and eased over 2 1/2f out: t.o* **500/1**

2m 37.68s (7.28) **Going Correction** +1.00s/f (Soft)
WFA 3 from 4yo+ 7lb **18** Ran SP% **131.0**
Speed ratings: **115,114,110,109,109 107,106,106,106,104 104,103,101, , , ,**
WIN (incl. 1 euro stake): 41.50. PLACES: 7.00, 2.90, 4.40. DF: 90.90. SF: 293.20.
Owner Wertheimer & Frere **Bred** Wertheimer Et Frere **Trained** Chantilly, France

FOCUS
The build-up to this year's Prix de l'Arc de Triomphe was full of drama and intrigue, and the race itself certainly didn't disappoint from a neutral perspective. However, the form does not look at all reliable. While last season's winner Danedream (stable placed into quarantine) and Nathaniel (high temperature) were unexpectedly ruled out, joining Frankel and Snow Fairy as notable absentees, triple Classic winner Camelot, the subject of an interesting jockey booking, was somewhat surprisingly committed to the race. There were also three supplementary entries in the form of Bayrir, Saonois and Great Heavens. All of that made for a truly fascinating edition of Europe's premier weight-for-age contest, but there was an unheralded winner and there can be little doubt the best horse on the day finished second. It rates the worst edition of the Arc so far this century, Solemia's mark 4lb shy of Danedream's last year. With her fillies' allowance, she rates similar in winning to Marienbard and Dylan Thomas. Orfevre was 3lb off his best and Camelot was well below par.

NOTEBOOK
Solemia(IRE) had some smart form to her name, notably a Group 2 triumph in May when she narrowly defeated Shareta, with subsequent Sun Chariot winner Siyouma back in third, and she clearly needed her prep when only third in the Vermeille, but she still looks a sub-standard Arc winner. While she showed a tremendous attitude to take advantage of the runner-up's waywardness, she enjoyed just about the ideal trip and handled the testing ground better than most. It's doubtful she can repeat this level back on decent ground, but we could find out at the Breeders' Cup.
Orfevre(JPN) was held up well off what seemed no more than an ordinary pace from his wide draw. The top-class Japanese contender looked sure to win when hitting the front up the centre of the course around a furlong and a half out (almost £20,000 traded at 1.01 on the exchanges), but he's a quirky sort and threw away a clear advantage by hanging over the far rail. Whether or not Christophe Soumillon should take some of the blame is debatable, but there can be no question the jockey wouldn't be in such a rush were he able to ride the race again, especially considering his mount had covered plenty of ground from stall 18. The connections had left little to chance, employing a top European rider, bringing their challenger over for a local prep (won the Prix Foy under Soumillon) and fitting the horse with a hood to help him deal with the large crowds. However, the race still got away from Orfevre, who was bidding to become Japan's first winner of the Arc but instead became the third from his country to fill the runner-up's spot.
Masterstroke(USA), successful in the Group 2 Grand Prix de Deauville on his previous start, fared best of a below-par bunch of 3-y-os. He has a round action and seemed happy enough on the ground, but just couldn't go with the front two.
Haya Landa(FR) beat only two rivals when a 16-1 shot for the Group 3 September Stakes on the Kempton Polytrack last time. Evidently these conditions were more suitable, and she enjoyed a ground-saving trip, but her proximity shows how few of her rivals ran to form.
Yellow And Green very much caught the eye when one place behind Solemia in the Vermeille, but she couldn't build on that effort under very different conditions.
Great Heavens, a last-minute substitute for stablemate Nathaniel, had the ground to suit, but she hadn't run since winning the Irish Oaks in July and this race was very much an afterthought. She was well short of her best.
Camelot, another for whom this race hadn't been the number one priority, just didn't pick up sufficiently, adding to his trainer's poor record with 3-y-os at this meeting. The race may have come too soon after his second-place finish in the St Leger, while the ground is another possible excuse, and he also reportedly lost three shoes. However, while he apparently stays in training, he has a surprising amount to prove for a Guineas and dual Derby winner, the form of his wins having not worked out.
Sea Moon hadn't been seen since a closing fifth in the King George and reportedly didn't appreciate the demanding ground.
Shareta(IRE), for whom the heavy turf was no use, had defeated today's winner and fifth in the Prix Vermeille, but is a long-striding filly who needs a decent surface.
Bayrir(FR) was another who probably didn't appreciate the conditions.
St Nicholas Abbey(IRE), another unsuited by the ground, could now try to follow up last year's Breeders' Cup Turf success and reportedly may stay in training.
Meandre(FR) looked ill at ease when asked to challenge.
Kesampour(FR) was disappointing considering these conditions promised to suit.
Saonois(FR) had shown terrific end-race speed to win a couple of slowly run races on decent ground on his last couple of starts, the Prix du Jockey Club and the Prix Niel, but this was a different ball game and he struggled.

6913a QATAR PRIX DE LA FORET (GROUP 1) (3YO+) (TURF) 7f
4:55 (12:00) 3-Y-0+ £142,850 (£57,150; £28,575; £14,275; £7,150)

RPR

1 **Gordon Lord Byron (IRE)**[29] 6030 4-9-2 0.................. WilliamBuick 7 121
(T Hogan, Ire) *trckd ldng gp: disp 4th and gng wl 3f out: qcknd between horses and rdn to chse ldrs over 1f out: r.o strly to ld nring fnl 100yds: drvn out* **5/2**[1]

2 *1 1/2* **Penitent**[9] 6634 6-9-2 0.. DanielTudhope 10 117
(David O'Meara) *trckd ldr: chal on outside to ld 2f out: sn rdn and wnt 2 l clr: hdd 100yds out: no ex* **6/1**[3]

3 *nk* **Kendam (FR)**[28] 6088 3-8-10 0.................................... MaximeGuyon 11 112
(H-A Pantall, France) *racd keenly in rr: last 2f out: rdn and hdwy over 1 1/2f out: styd on strly fnl f: nrest at fin* **33/1**

4 *3* **Pintura**[15] 6468 5-9-2 0.. JamieSpencer 6 108
(Kevin Ryan) *trckd ldrs: 4th and briefly short of room over 2f out: rdn and wnt 2nd over 1f out: rdn and one pce fnl f* **33/1**

5 *1* **Mashoora (IRE)**[70] 4633 3-8-10 0........................ ChristopheSoumillon 5 101
(J-C Rouget, France) *towards rr: 10th and rdn 1 1/2f out: styd on u.p fnl f: nvr nrr* **9/2**[2]

6 *snk* **Blue Soave (FR)**[28] 6088 4-9-2 0.................................. ThierryThulliez 4 105
(F Chappet, France) *led briefly: sn hdd and racd in midfield: 6th and scrubbed along 2 1/2f out: kpt on at same pce fnl f* **7/1**

7 *hd* **Nice Association (FR)**[21] 4-8-13 0........................ StephanePasquier 9 101
(Mme C Head-Maarek, France) *reluctant to enter stalls: racd in midfield: moved into 3rd over 3f out: ev ch whn rdn and nt qckn fnl 2f: one pce fnl f* **50/1**

8 *1 3/4* **Zantenda**[28] 6088 3-8-10 0.. OlivierPeslier 1 96
(F Head, France) *hld up towards rr: rdn and no real imp fr 2f out* **20/1**

9 *1* **Sommerabend**[28] 6088 5-9-2 0.. GeraldMosse 2 97
(U Stoltefuss, Germany) *racd in fnl 3rd: swtchd outside and rdn 2 1/2f out to make mod prog: no further imp fr over 1f out* **9/1**

10 *12* **Lethal Force (IRE)**[22] 6246 3-9-0 0................................(b) AdamKirby 12 65
(Clive Cox) *sn led: hdd 2f out: wknd qckly* **14/1**

11 *3/4* **Starspangledbanner (AUS)**[22] 6268 6-9-2 0...................... JPO'Brien 3 63
(A P O'Brien, Ire) *plld hrd in midfield: settled by 1/2-way: 7th and rdn over 2f out: no imp and wl btn whn eased fnl f* **7/1**

1m 25.17s (4.47) **Going Correction** +1.00s/f (Soft)
WFA 3 from 4yo+ 2lb **11** Ran SP% **115.3**
Speed ratings: **114,112,111,108,107 107,106,104,103,90 89**
WIN (incl. 1 euro stake): 4.40. PLACES: 2.40, 4.00, 4.90. DF: 27.30. SF: 33.40.
Owner Morgan J Cahalan & Adolf Schneider **Bred** Roland H Alder **Trained** Nenagh, Co Tipperary

FOCUS
A rough race, run at a strong gallop, with plenty of early scrimmaging. The ground looked pretty chewed up by this stage of the day. Weak form for the level.

NOTEBOOK
Gordon Lord Byron(IRE) has improved of late, recording a career best when chasing home Society Rock in the Sprint Cup at Haydock, and he justified the decision to supplement him for this, picking up strongly to get nicely on top. Equally effective at 6f-7f and versatile ground-wise, this tough sort may struggle to find a Group 1 as winnable as this. He may now head for the Hong Kong Mile.
Penitent was also supplemented. A dual Group 2 winner this year, including once on heavy, he raced right on the pace and did well to last as long as he did having kicked over 1f out. This probably goes down as a career best from the admirable 6-y-o and he could return to France for a Group 2 at Saint-Cloud in November.
Kendam(FR), held up in last following an awkward start, has looked no better than a Group 3 horse prior to this but she produced a prolonged burst down the straight to just miss second. Her effort needs upgrading considering where she came from, despite there being a strong early pace, but you wouldn't bank on her to repeat this form.
Pintura is a good-quality handicapper and the fact he managed to run so well in fourth underlines the level of the form.
Mashoora(IRE), off for 70 days, ran on late having been nearly last 1f out.
Lethal Force(IRE) was given no chance of getting home having gone off at such a fast gallop.
Starspangledbanner(AUS) was too keen and failed to pick up out of the ground, taking a backward step after his Curragh second.

6914a QATAR PRIX DU CADRAN (GROUP 1) (4YO+) (TURF) 2m 4f
5:25 (12:00) 4-Y-0+ £142,850 (£57,150; £28,575; £14,275; £7,150)

RPR

1 **Molly Malone (FR)**[42] 5650 4-8-13 0............................ UmbertoRispoli 4 112
(M Delzangles, France) *prom thrght: wnt 2nd over 1m out and sn chsng clr ldr: rdn 3f out: hdwy to chal 1 1/2f out: led ent fnl f and sn clr: pushed out* **14/1**

2 *2 1/2* **High Jinx (IRE)**[23] 6198 4-9-2 0.. GrahamLee 9 112+
(James Fanshawe) *midfield on outer: rdn over 3f out: carried hd to one side u.p: styd on thrght fnl 2f: wnt 2nd ins fnl 50yds: nt pce to chal* **10/3**[1]

3 *1/2* **Colour Vision (FR)**[23] 6198 4-9-2 0................................ FrankieDettori 6 112
(Saeed Bin Suroor) *sn trcking ldr in 2nd: dropped to 3rd over 1m out: swtchd to centre of trck and rdn over 2 1/2f out: edgd rt and styd on to to go 2nd 100yds out: dropped to 3rd ins fnl 50yds* **7/2**[2]

4 *1 1/2* **Saddler's Rock (IRE)**[23] 6198 4-9-2 0...................... JohnnyMurtagh 10 110+
(John M Oxx, Ire) *hld up in last: rdn to improve 3f out: edgd rt and carried hd awkwardly u.p: styd on to go 4th ins fnl 50yds: n.d* **6/1**

5 *2* **Nikita Du Berlais (FR)**[24] 5-8-13 0................................ OlivierPeslier 1 105+
(Robert Collet, France) *midfield on outer: rdn over 3f out: styd on wout threatening ins fnl 2f: fin wl and wnt 5th post: nt pce to chal* **4/1**[3]

6 *shd* **Goldtara (FR)**[47] 4-8-13 0.................................. IoritzMendizabal 3 105+
(A Lyon, France) *midfield on inner: rdn 2 1/2f out: plugged on ins fnl 2f: wnt 5th fnl strides: immediately jnd and dropped to 6th post* **33/1**

7 *snk* **Vadamar (FR)**[21] 6297 4-9-2 0....................................(b) JamieSpencer 5 108
(M Delzangles, France) *led and sn over 2 l clr: rdn 2 1/2f out: diminishing advantage and strly pressed 1 1/2f out: hdd ent fnl f: sn no ex and fdd: dropped to 7th fnl strides* **11/1**

8 *8* **Miss Lago (IRE)**[21] 6297 4-8-13 0..........................(p) GregoryBenoist 11 97
(E Lellouche, France) *hld up in last pair on inner: rdn 2 1/2f out: kpt on tl no ex and btn 1f out: coasted home ins fnl f* **8/1**

9 *dist* **Gentoo (FR)**[21] 6297 8-9-2 0..(p) MaximeGuyon 7
(A Lyon, France) *midfield on inner: rdn over 3f out: no ex and btn 1 1/2f out: sn eased and t.o* **25/1**

P **Lone Ranger (FR)**[21] 6297 4-9-2 0..................(p) ChristopheSoumillon 8
(A De Royer-Dupre, France) *hld up in last trio on outer: dropped to last 3f out: sn wl bhd and eased w jockey looking down as if smething amiss: p.u* **25/1**

4m 43.6s (25.60) **Going Correction** +1.00s/f (Soft) **10** Ran SP% **116.3**
Speed ratings: **88,87,86,86,85 85,85,82, ,**
WIN (incl. 1 euro stake): 13.50. PLACES: 3.10, 1.80, 1.90. DF: 34.10. SF: 83.30. JACKPOT: Not won. PLACEPOT: £296.60 to a £1 stake. Pool of £24,525.85 - 60.35 winning tickets..
Owner Dieter Burkle **Bred** D Burkle **Trained** France

FOCUS
Hard to have much faith in the form, with a number of these having had long seasons and needing better ground. That said those in the frame behind the winner are rated close to their latest form.

NOTEBOOK
Molly Malone(FR) has been shaping as though the step up to marathon distances would bring considerable improvement. Both her previous wins had come on similarly testing ground and, having travelled strongly at the head of the chasing pack, she always looked to have the momentum to run down stablemate Vadamar, receiving a good ride. Having just her ninth start, she remains capable of better still and is likely to be a major player in the Prix Royal-Oak over 4f shorter back here in a few weeks' time.
High Jinx(IRE) has readily made the jump from handicapper this season, following his second to Times Up in both the Lonsdale and Doncaster Cups with another really good run in defeat. This ground would have been plenty soft enough and he may yet develop into an Ascot Gold Cup horse next year.
Colour Vision(FR), this year's Gold Cup winner, has now failed to match that form in three subsequent starts, but he ran well considering ground conditions would have been against him.
Saddler's Rock(IRE) stays well but he prefers a sounder surface and proved one-paced. He's been disappointing since the Goodwood Cup.
Nikita Du Berlais(FR), a very smart hurdler, was introduced at the top level for this Flat debut and ran a satisfactory race without having the necessary pace.
Vadamar(FR) again didn't see his race out, although he was ridden positively on ground that wouldn't have suited.

5521 **TIPPERARY** (L-H)

Sunday, October 7

OFFICIAL GOING: Heavy

6917a **COOLMORE STUD HOME OF CHAMPIONS CONCORDE STKS (GROUP 3)** 7f 100y
2:35 (2:35) 3-Y-0+ £35,208 (£10,291; £4,875 ; £1,625)

RPR

1 **Yellow Rosebud (IRE)**[45] 5523 3 -9-3107 (b) PatSmullen 7 110
(D K Weld, Ire) *trckd ldr in 2nd: clsd and brought to stands' side into st: lod 1 1/2f out and kpt on wl ins fnl f* 1/1[1]

2 3 **Lady Wingshot (IRE)**[22] 6268 3 -9-3105 KevinManning 5 103
(J S Bolger, Ire) *w.w in 5th: clsd into 3rd appr st: brought to stands' side and wnt 2nd appr fnl f: sn no ex: kpt on same pce* 15/8[2]

3 1 **Coolnagree (IRE)**[24] 6161 3 -9-098 DeclanMcDonogh 1 97
(W McCreery, Ire) *dwlt and racd in rr: hdwy appr st to chse ldrs under 2f out: sn hrd rdn and kpt on into 3rd ins fnl f: kpt on wl: n.d* 8/1[3]

4 3 1/2 **Among Equals**[49] 5392 3 -9-389 WJLee 6 91
(A P O'Brien, Ire) *hld up in tch: 4th 5f out: pushed along under 3f out and one pce on nrside fnl 2f* 20/1

5 1/2 **Custom Cut (IRE)**[18] 5777 3 -9-3106 RonanWhelan 3 90
(George J Kent, Ire) *attempted to make all: 1 l clr and niggled along over 3f out: jnd into st and hdd 1 1/2f out: no ex ent fnl f* 8/1[3]

6 8 1/2 **Marvada (IRE)**[29] 6061 4 -9-599 ShaneFoley 2 69
(K J Condon, Ire) *chsd ldrs: pushed along in 3rd on inner over 3f out and no imp bef st: wknd* 16/1

1m 46.4s (106.40)
WFA 3 from 4yo 2lb 6Ran SP% 117.6
CSF £3.35 TOTE £1.70 : £1.10 , £2.50 ; DF 3.90 .
Owner Dr R Lambe **Bred** Irish National Stud **Trained** The Curragh, Co Kildare

FOCUS
Not much depth to this Group 3, run on ground few of them would have relished.

NOTEBOOK
Yellow Rosebud (IRE)likes these conditions and was not winning out of turn, getting belated revenge on Lady Wingshot. She travelled well, just off the generous pace and was brought over to the stands' side for what was seemingly the best of the ground in the straight. Her old foe looked a big threat around 2f out but, with the rail to aid her, she pulled quite readily clear in the closing stages. Classy and consistent on this type of ground, she is likely to bid to emulate Emulous, who won this en route to victory in Naas' Garnet Stakes. (op 5-4)
Lady Wingshot (IRE)travelled with her usual zest but was unable to make any real impression on a filly she has beaten twice this season. She is holding her form quite well, having only begun the campaign in July, and it would be no surprise to see her at Naas as well. (op 7-4 tchd 2-1)
Coolnagree(IRE) has been a credit to Willie McCreery. She might have preferred better ground and, while no threat at any stage here, she kept on willingly and is now Group-placed as well as Listed-placed.
Among Equals looked very much up against it on this season's form and he performed about as well as seemed plausible. (op 16-1)
Custom Cut (IRE)has not seemed at his best of late and he was never able to establish a lead of much substance. He has had an excellent campaign and should win more races next year. (op 7-1)

6915a - 6916a & 6918a (Foreign Racing) See RI

6603 **PONTEFRACT** (L-H)

Monday, October 8

OFFICIAL GOING: Good to soft (7.2)
Wind: Light across Weather: Overcast

6919 **BRITISH STALLION STUDS SUPPORTING BRITISH RACING E B F MAIDEN STKS** 1m 2f 6y
2:10 (2:11) (Class 4) 2-Y-0 £4,398 (£1,309; £654 ; £327) Stalls Low

Form RPR

352 1 **Restraint Of Trade (IRE)**[19] 6371 2 -9-377 MickaelBarzalona 4 82+
(Mahmood Al Zarooni) *stdd s and hld up in rr: swtchd wd 6f out and hdwy to join ldrs 1/2-way: led 4f out: rdn clr fnl 2f: easily* 4/9[1]

00 2 9 **Mutamaiz (IRE)**[16] 6501 2 -9-30 MartinDwyer 6 66
(James Tate) *hld up: hdwy 3f out: rdn along 2f out: styd on u.p to take 2nd ins fnl f: no ch w wnr* 14/1[3]

232 3 2 **Jullundar (IRE)**[15] 6512 2 -9-372 MartinHarley 7 61
(Mick Channon) *trckd ldng pair: effrt 3f out and sn rdn along: chsd wnr 2f out: sn drvn and one pce: lost 2nd ins fnl f* 11/4[2]

6 4 3/4 **Moaning Butcher**[14] 6532 2 -9-30 JoeFanning 5 60
(Mark Johnston) *sn led: pushed along 1/2-way: rdn and hdd 3f out: drvn 2f out and sn one pce* 25/1

00 5 3 1/4 **Hurricane John (IRE)**[38] 5797 2 -9-30 AdrianNicholls 2 54
(David Nicholls) *prom: pushed along 1/2-way: rdn over 3f out and sn wknd* 40/1

0 6 52 **Online**[11] 6607 2 -9-30 BarryMcHugh 1
(Tracy Waggott) *a in rr: outpcd and bhd fnl 3f* 100/1

2m 19.44s (5.74) **Going Correction** +0.325s/f (Good) 6Ran SP% 109.9
Speed ratings (Par 97): **90,82,81,80,78 36**
toteswingers 1&2 £2.00, 1&3 £1.10, 2&3 £2.20 CSF £7.75 TOTE £1.50 : £1.10 , £3.60 ; EX 7.60 .
Owner Godolphin **Bred** Kildaragh Stud **Trained** Newmarket, Suffolk

FOCUS
Little depth to this 1m2f juvenile maiden and, although the pace was steady, it still proved a thorough test in the conditions. The runners came centre-field in the straight.

NOTEBOOK
Restraint Of Trade (IRE)had shown enough to win a race such as this and, having made rapid headway to take it up down the back, he never looked in any danger from the home bend. Staying looks his game and he'll probably want at least 1m4f next year, but he may yet be capable of winning again at two, with soft conditions clearly no bother. (tchd 2-5)
Mutamaiz(IRE) came through late for second and continues to progress, albeit slowly. The switch to turf was clearly no inconvenience and he's now qualified for a mark. (op 16-1)
Jullundar(IRE) was disappointing considering he'd been running well on similar ground, the step up to 1m2f not suiting as expected. He may be better switching to nurseries. (op 3-1)
Moaning Butcher showed more than on his debut, when very green, and may win a maiden if he can come on again. 1m4f-plus handicaps next year will likely be his thing.
Hurricane John (IRE)is bred to stay well and is another likely to do better at three. (tchd 33-1)

6920 **JEFF AND MARGARET SMITH MEMORIAL NURSERY** 6f
2:40 (2:40) (Class 4) (0-85,83) 2-Y-0 £3,428 (£1,020; £509 ; £254) Stalls Low

Form RPR

4516 1 **Delores Rocket**[17] 6451 2 -8-873 (b) JulieBurke(3) 9 80+
(Kevin Ryan) *in rr and pushed along 1/2-way: swtchd lft 2f out and gd hdwy on inner: rdn appr fnl f: styd on strly to ld last 75yds* 28/1

1610 2 1 1/2 **Penny Garcia**[25] 6160 2 -9-177 DuranFentiman 1 79
(Tim Easterby) *trckd ldrs on inner: smooth hdwy 2f out: sn chal: rdn to ld jst ins fnl f: drvn and hdd last 75yds* 20/1

0141 3 1 **Ena Sharples**[8] 6707 2 -8-668 6ex AdrianNicholls 5 67
(David Nicholls) *led: rdn along 2f out: drvn over 1f out: hdd jst ins fnl f: kpt on* 12/1

0545 4 1 1/4 **Newstead Abbey**[29] 6070 2 -9-278 GrahamGibbons 13 73
(David Brown) *cl up: rdn wl over 1f out and ev ch tl drvn and one pce ins fnl f* 8/1[3]

051 5 nk **Pipers Note**[19] 6360 2 -9-379 AmyRyan 8 74
(Richard Whitaker) *t.k.h early: hld up: hdwy to chse ldrs 2f out: effrt and n.m.r wl over 1f out: sn swtchd rt and rdn: one pce ins fnl f* 9/1

130 6 nk **Diggory Delvet**[45] 5563 2 -9-076 TonyHamilton 15 69
(Richard Fahey) *s.i.s and in rr: hdwy 2f out: sn rdn and kpt on fnl f: nrst fin* 14/1

14 7 hd **Bottle Blonde**[34] 5909 2 -9-278 TomQueally 12 70
(Ed McMahon) *towards rr: swtchd to outer and hdwy wl over 1f out: sn rdn and kpt on fnl f: nt rch ldrs* 9/1

1252 8 nk **Steer By The Stars (IRE)**[16] 6475 2 -9-783 JoeFanning 11 74
(Mark Johnston) *trckd ldrs: rdn wl over 1f out: wknd ent fnl f* 6/1[2]

010 9 6 **Grey Street**[30] 6032 2 -8-1173 PaulHanagan 10 48
(Richard Fahey) *t.k.h: hld up in midfield: effrt 2f out: sn rdn and btn* 8/1[3]

2264 10 3 3/4 **Shillito**[14] 6540 2 -8-1375 BarryMcHugh 2 35
(Tony Coyle) *cl up: rdn along 2f out: sn drvn and wknd over 1f out* 12/1

410 11 3 1/2 **Kamchatka**[30] 6032 2 -9-177 RobertWinston 6 30
(Alan Swinbank) *prom: effrt 2f out: rdn and wknd appr fnl f* 5/1[1]

1400 12 3/4 **Luck (IRE)**[17] 6425 2 -9-682 (b[1]) EddieAhern 4 29
(Kevin Ryan) *v.s.a and a in rr* 14/1

1364 13 shd **Rat Catcher (IRE)**[11] 5710 2 -8-971 (p) DavidAllan 7 17
(Tim Easterby) *chsd ldrs: rdn along 1/2-way: sn wknd* 25/1

226 14 1/2 **Back In The Frame**[124] 2812 2 -8-1072 SilvestreDeSousa 14 17
(Tom Dascombe) *in tch on wd outside: rdn along wl over 2f out: sn wknd* 20/1

1m 19.53s (2.63) **Going Correction** +0.325s/f (Good) 14Ran SP% 118.7
Speed ratings (Par 97): **95,93,91,90,89 89,88,88,80,75 70,69,69,69**
toteswingers 1&2 £84.80, 1&3 £84.80, 2&3 £34.40 CSF £482.94 CT £7070.15 TOTE £56.80 : £10.70, £6.80 , £4.00 ; EX 792.50 .
Owner J Nixon **Bred** Bearstone Stud **Trained** Hambleton, N Yorks

FOCUS
A highly competitive nursery, run at a fair enough gallop, and the field again came more towards the middle in the straight. However, it was those racing nearer the inside who came out on top. The runner-up and third ran credible, to-form races and the standard looks sensible.

NOTEBOOK
Delores Rocket, who was out the back and under pressure rounding the final bend, produced a strong run to ultimately win with a bit in hand. This was a useful effort when considering she was 6lb higher than for her recent defeat on the AW, but she clearly excels on soft ground and is effective in blinkers. (op 33-1)
Penny Garcia, like the winner, has already shown a real liking for soft ground, both her wins having come on it, and she ran a fine race off a mark 8lb above her last winning one. She too did most of her running around the inner. (op 25-1)
Ena Sharples has done well since winning a seller, scoring in a nursery at Musselburgh last week and bettering that form in defeat here under a penalty. She was on the pace throughout, whereas the first two came from behind, and this clearly progressive filly can go in again. (op 9-1)
Newstead Abbey was another up there for much of the way, but he's well exposed and once again found a few too good. (op 10-1)
Pipers Note was a bit keen and didn't get the best of runs, so may have finished a little closer. He won his maiden on firm ground and will be of more interest returned to a sounder surface. (op 11-1)
Diggory Delvet wasn't best away and could never get close enough to challenge. (op 18-1)
Bottle Blonde made some late headway having got too far back. (op 7-1)
Steer By The Stars (IRE)was a little disappointing, failing to match the form of her last-time-out Catterick second when she should probably have won. (op 5-1)
Grey Street was keen and probably didn't like the ground. (op 7-1)
Kamchatka was again disappointing and is left with something to prove. Official explanation: trainer's rep said colt was unsuited by the good to soft ground (op 13-2 tchd 9-2)
Luck(IRE), wearing first-time blinkers, blew the start and was always toiling. Official explanation: jockey said colt missed the break (op 20-1)
Back In The Frame Official explanation: jockey said filly had no more to give

6921 **£40 TOTEPOOL PACKAGE H'CAP** 1m 4y
3:10 (3:10) (Class 3) (0-95,94) 3-Y-0
£6,411 (£1,919; £959 ; £479 ; £239 ; £120) Stalls Low

Form RPR

2251 1 **Fire Ship**[44] 5595 3 -9-592 EddieAhern 2 101+
(William Knight) *trckd ldrs: hdwy over 2f out: rdn to chse ldr whn sltly hmpd ent fnl f: styd on wl u.p on outer to ld last 50yds* 2/1[1]

1500 2 3/4 **Ardmay (IRE)**[50] 5386 3 -8-1285 (p) AmyRyan 4 92
(Kevin Ryan) *t.k.h: cl up: led 2f out: rdn and edgd rt ent fnl f: sn drvn and hung lft and rt: hdd and no ex last 50yds* 14/1

5003 3 1 1/4 **Lady Macduff (IRE)**[8] 6701 3 -8-1184 JoeFanning 6 88
(Mark Johnston) *trckd ldrs: effrt 2f out: sn rdn and ev ch ins fnl f: sn sltly hmpd and kpt on same pce* 10/1

4231 4 nk **Hi There (IRE)**[37] 5819 3 -8-780 BarryMcHugh 5 83+
(Richard Fahey) *dwlt and hld up in rr: hdwy 2f out: sn rdn and styd on fnl f: nrst fin* 4/1[2]

2166 5 3/4 **Satanic Beat (IRE)**[50] 5386 3 -8-1386 PJMcDonald 8 88
(Jedd O'Keeffe) *trckd ldrs: effrt over 2f out: rdn along wl over 1f out: drvn ent fnl f and kpt on same pce* 16/1

3631 6 shd **Boots And Spurs**[26] 6136 3 -8-780 (v) DuranFentiman 3 81
(Mrs K Burke) *hld up: hdwy on inner over 1f out: sn rdn and no imp ins fnl f* 9/1

3-02 7 1/2 **Mabaany**[30] 6046 3 -9-289 PaulHanagan 7 89
(William Haggas) *hld up: hdwy to chse ldrs 3f out: rdn over 2f out: sn one pce* 6/1[3]

5213 8 1/2 **Dubawi Island (FR)**[14] 6539 3 -8-1285 (b) MartinDwyer 1 84
(James Tate) *led: rdn along 3f out: hdd 2f out and grad wknd* 18/1

1036 **9** *17* **Asatir (USA)**[12] [6580] 3-9-7 **94**..............................(p) SilvestreDeSousa 10 54
(Saeed Bin Suroor) *in tch: hdwy on outer to chse ldrs over 4f out: rdn along 3f out: sn wknd and bhd whn eased over 1f out* **9/1**

1m 47.04s (1.14) **Going Correction** +0.325s/f (Good) **9** Ran SP% **114.5**
Speed ratings (Par 105): **107,106,105,104,103 103,103,102,85**
toteswingers 1&2 £8.30, 1&3 £7.40, 2&3 £18.30 CSF £32.39 CT £229.46 TOTE £3.00: £1.40, £3.80, £2.70; EX 29.60.
Owner IGP Partnership & P Winkworth **Bred** Yorton Farm **Trained** Patching, W Sussex

FOCUS
No more than an even pace to this handicap and it didn't pay to come from too far back. The field kept more towards the inside this time, but the main action unfolded down the centre of the track

NOTEBOOK
Fire Ship, up 8lb for his Windsor success on similar ground, took a while to get there but always gave the impression he would, probably winning with more in hand than the bare margin implies. His rating will be nudging 100 following this, so he'll need to make further progress if he's to follow up. (tchd 7-4 and 9-4 in places)
Ardmay(IRE) was keen in being taken on for the lead and then failed to run straight under pressure. These factors contributed towards him being run down late by the winner, but there should be more opportunities for him, with this ground not a problem. (op 16-1 tchd 18-1)
Lady Macduff(IRE) travelled quite well around the inner, but ultimately failed to pick up on ground that would have been plenty soft enough. (tchd 11-1)
Hi There(IRE) was soon in last place and could never get close enough to throw down a serious challenge. He can be rated better than the bare form. (op 9-2 tchd 5-1)
Satanic Beat(IRE) failed to build on his Thirsk second, the much softer ground probably playing its part. (op 14-1)
Dubawi Island(FR) looks on too high a mark. (op 16-1)
Asatir(USA), who had been a non-runner due to testing ground in the past, ran no sort of race. (tchd 17-2 and 10-1)

6922 PHIL BULL TROPHY CONDITIONS STKS 2m 1f 216y
3:40 (3:40) (Class 3) 3-Y-O+
£6,411 (£1,919; £959; £479; £239; £120) **Stalls** Low

Form RPR
1 **Lieutenant Miller**[46] 6-9-3 0... TomQueally 6 85+
(Nicky Henderson) *hld up in tch: hdwy 4f out: cl up 2f out: rdn to chal over 1f out: drvn ins fnl f: styd on wl to ld nr fin* **11/1**[3]

2443 **2** *shd* **Zuider Zee (GER)**[51] [5374] 5-9-3 108.......................... RobertHavlin 2 85+
(John Gosden) *trckd ldr: hdwy and cl up 2f out: sn rdn: drvn and slt ld ins fnl f: hdd and no ex nr fin* **4/11**[1]

0332 **3** *1 1/4* **Petaluma**[19] [6383] 3-8-0 70.. AndreaAtzeni 4 79
(Mick Channon) *trckd ldrs: hdwy to ld 7f out: jnd and rdn 3f out: drvn over 1f out: hdd ins fnl f: kpt on* **14/1**

00-0 **4** *nk* **Darley Sun (IRE)**[11] [6600] 6-9-3 100......................... MickaelBarzalona 5 84
(Saeed Bin Suroor) *trckd ldrs: pushed along and sltly outpcd over 2f out: rdn over 1f out and sn edgd lft: styd on fnl f* **9/2**[2]

2236 **5** *21* **Mollyow (IRE)**[31] [6019] 4-8-12 53................................ RobertWinston 1 56
(Terry Clement) *hld up in rr: rapid hdwy on outer 6f out: cl up over 4f out: disp ld 3f out: rdn along over 2f out: sn wknd* **66/1**

/0-5 **6** *52* **Feeling Peckish (USA)**[32] [5173] 8-9-3 34..............(t) RussKennemore 3
(Michael Chapman) *led: hdd 7f out: sn lost pl and bhd fnl 3f* **100/1**

4m 8.62s (12.42) **Going Correction** +0.325s/f (Good)
WFA 3 from 4yo+ 12lb **6** Ran SP% **109.0**
Speed ratings (Par 107): **85,84,84,84,74 51**
toteswingers 1&2 £1.60, 1&3 £2.70, 2&3 £1.90 CSF £14.84 TOTE £8.10: £2.80, £1.10; EX 19.70.
Owner W H Ponsonby **Bred** M J Langdell **Trained** Upper Lambourn, Berks
■ Stewards' Enquiry : Robert Havlin four-day ban: used whip above permitted level (Oct 22-25)

FOCUS
They went a steady gallop in the conditions for this marathon contest and there was something of a turn up. Muddling form.

NOTEBOOK
Lieutenant Miller, rated 115 over hurdles and making a belated Flat debut, coped really well with the ground and just out-lasted the hot favourite. Tom Queally did his best to disrupt the runner-up, trying to keep him in from the end of the back straight to the home straight, and on this evidence he'll be capable of developing into a useful Flat performer, with either the Ascot Stakes or Queen Alexandra possible long-term aims, depending on how the handicapper assesses the performance. As for the short-term, he could go back over hurdles. (op 10-1)
Zuider Zee(GER) stood out on recent form and likes soft ground, so it was disappointing he failed to justify short odds. For all that he wouldn't have been suited by the steady pace, he won the November Handicap over 1m4f last year, so should have been able to pick up better than he did. (op 4-9)
Petaluma came into this in fair form, but at a much lower level. She took over a long way out and had the run of things more so than others, so her good placing perhaps shouldn't be that big a shock. Her future lies with the handicapper now. (op 12-1)
Darley Sun(IRE) offered more than when running a poor race his recent Newmarket return, as he was entitled to dropping in grade, but this remains a long way below the best of his form for David Simcock a few years back. (op 4-1)

6923 BOOK YOUR CHRISTMAS PARTY ON 0113 287 6387 CLAIMING STKS 1m 4y
4:10 (4:11) (Class 5) 3-Y-O
£2,264 (£673; £336; £168) **Stalls** Low

Form RPR
2211 **1** **Marford Missile (IRE)**[14] [6542] 3-8-7 78..................... GrahamGibbons 5 86
(Tom Dascombe) *mde all: rdn clr over 1f out: drvn out* **11/4**[3]

6150 **2** *1* **Lisiere (IRE)**[15] [6515] 3-8-9 79.................................(p) SilvestreDeSousa 4 86
(Mrs K Burke) *t.k.h: trckd ldrs: hdwy on inner to chse wnr 3f out: rdn wl over 1f out: drvn and kpt on fnl f* **6/1**

0343 **3** *7* **Our Boy Jack (IRE)**[30] [6046] 3-8-10 85........................... LauraBarry(7) 2 78
(Richard Fahey) *t.k.h: hld up early: hdwy to chse wnr after 2f: rdn along over 2f out: edgd lft over 1f out: sn wknd* **6/4**[1]

4630 **4** *34* **Kimbali (IRE)**[9] [6661] 3-8-9 78.. PaulHanagan 6
(Richard Fahey) *prom: rdn along over 3f out: outpcd over 2f out: bhd and heavily eased fnl f* **5/2**[2]

1m 47.66s (1.76) **Going Correction** +0.325s/f (Good) **4** Ran SP% **109.5**
Speed ratings (Par 101): **104,103,96,62**
CSF £16.54 TOTE £3.60; EX 13.80.
Owner The MHS 4x10 Partnership **Bred** Miss Mary Davidson & Mrs Steffi Von Schilcher **Trained** Malpas, Cheshire
■ Stewards' Enquiry : Graham Gibbons two-day ban: used whip above permitted level (Oct 22-23)

FOCUS
Modest form for the grade.
Kimbali(IRE) Official explanation: trainer's rep had no explanation for the poor form shown

6924 LAURIE BAKER 60TH BIRTHDAY H'CAP 1m 4f 8y
4:40 (4:40) (Class 5) (0-70,69) 3-Y-O
£2,264 (£673; £336; £168) **Stalls** Low

Form RPR
4220 **1** **Abundantly**[38] [5789] 3-9-5 **67**.. TomQueally 6 79
(Hughie Morrison) *hld up in rr: hdwy in to midfield 1/2-way: gd hdwy on inner to join ldrs 2f out: led ent fnl f: sn rdn clr and styd on* **10/1**

003 **2** *2 1/4* **Stunning View (USA)**[75] [4465] 3-9-7 **69**........................... RobertHavlin 5 77
(John Gosden) *trckd ldrs: rdn along and sltly outpcd over 2f out: drvn and edgd rt over 1f out: styd on ins fnl f* **11/2**[3]

3010 **3** *3/4* **Kittens**[23] [6229] 3-8-13 **61**.. MartinDwyer 9 68
(William Muir) *hld up in rr: smooth hdwy on inner 4f out: cl up 3f out: led 2f out: sn rdn: hdd ent fnl f and kpt on same pce* **14/1**

3405 **4** *1 3/4* **Neil's Pride**[16] [6474] 3-8-7 **55**.. PaulHanagan 4 59
(Richard Fahey) *led: rdn along over 2f out: drvn and hdd wl over 1f out: kpt on same pce fnl f* **4/1**[2]

4013 **5** *3 1/4* **Scarlet Prince**[14] [6544] 3-8-12 **65**.................................. ShaneBKelly(5) 7 64
(Tony Coyle) *reminders s: in rr: hdwy over 4f out: rdn along on inner to chse ldrs 2f out: sn drvn and no imp* **6/1**

3635 **6** *2 1/4* **Feisty Champion (IRE)**[38] [5809] 3-9-6 **68**......................... EddieAhern 10 63
(J W Hills) *hld up towards rr: hdwy on outer and in tch 4f out: rdn along 3f out and sn one pce* **9/1**

0016 **7** *3* **Scripturist**[35] [5891] 3-8-9 **57**.. SilvestreDeSousa 12 48
(William Jarvis) *nvr bttr than midfield* **16/1**

2265 **8** *1 1/4* **Margo Channing**[40] [5738] 3-8-7 **55** oh1............................ PJMcDonald 8 44
(Micky Hammond) *in rr: sme hdwy and in tch 1/2-way: rdn along and wknd over 3f out* **25/1**

50 **9** *6* **Hail Hail (USA)**[26] [6146] 3-9-0 **67**................................. AshleyMorgan(5) 1 46
(Paul Cole) *trckd ldrs: hdwy 3f out and sn cl up: rdn 2f out and sn wknd* **28/1**

503 **10** *20* **Discay**[18] [6408] 3-9-4 **66**.. JoeFanning 11 13
(Mark Johnston) *prom: rdn along 4f out: sn wknd: bhd and eased fnl 2f* **9/1**

1262 **11** *shd* **Mr Snoozy**[28] [6103] 3-9-3 **65**.......................................(p) DuranFentiman 3 12
(Tim Walford) *cl up on inner: rdn along 4f out: wknd over 2f out: sn eased and bhd* **7/2**[1]

000 **12** *62* **Isolde's Return**[49] [5413] 3-8-7 **55** oh10.......................... AndrewMullen 2
(George Moore) *in tch: pushed along 1/2-way: sn lost pl and bhd* **125/1**

2m 44.24s (3.44) **Going Correction** +0.325s/f (Good) **12** Ran SP% **121.6**
Speed ratings (Par 101): **101,99,99,97,95 94,92,91,87,74 73,32**
toteswingers 1&2 £11.60, 1&3 £20.10, 2&3 £20.10 CSF £65.09 CT £789.80 TOTE £10.80: £4.00, £2.20, £4.90; EX 64.10.
Owner J Repard and S Dibb **Bred** J Repard & S Dibb **Trained** East Ilsley, Berks

FOCUS
Not bad form for the grade.
Mr Snoozy Official explanation: trainer had no explanation for the poor form shown

6925 BUY YOUR 2013 ANNUAL BADGE TODAY MAIDEN STKS 1m 4y
5:10 (5:10) (Class 5) 3-Y-O
£2,264 (£673; £336; £168) **Stalls** Low

Form RPR
522 **1** **A'Juba**[28] [6102] 3-9-3 77.. SilvestreDeSousa 1 84
(Saeed Bin Suroor) *trckd ldrs: hdwy on inner and cl up 2f out: led wl over 1f out: sn rdn: rn geen and edgd rt: drvn and hung rt ins fnl f: kpt on* **6/5**[1]

4 **2** *1* **Bishop's Castle (USA)**[5] [6792] 3-9-3 0............................. JoeFanning 5 82
(Mark Johnston) *led: rdn along and jnd 2f out: hdd over 1f out: rallied ins fnl f: kpt on* **7/2**[2]

60 **3** *11* **Quan (IRE)**[110] [3289] 3-8-12 0.. GarryWhillans(5) 6 57
(Alan Swinbank) *plld hrd early: towards rr: hdwy into midfield 1/2-way: effrt on inner 2f out and sn chsng ldrs: rdn along wl over 1f out: kpt on: no ch w ldng pair* **80/1**

6 **4** *2 1/2* **Mutaaleq (IRE)**[52] [5297] 3-9-3 0.. TadhgO'Shea 8 51
(Roger Varian) *chsd ldr: rdn along over 2f out: drvn wl over 1f out and sn wknd* **12/1**

4 **5** *1/2* **Guest Of Honour (IRE)**[18] [6397] 3-9-3 0........................ AndreaAtzeni 12 50
(Marco Botti) *cl up on outer: rdn along over 2f out: grad wknd* **11/2**[3]

3-00 **6** *6* **Crossley**[128] [2689] 3-9-3 63.. TonyHamilton 2 36
(Geoffrey Oldroyd) *in tch: effrt to chse ldrs over 4f out: rdn along 3f out: wknd over 2f out* **66/1**

46 **7** *13* **Donatia**[24] [6190] 3-8-12 0.. AndrewMullen 7
(David Nicholls) *a in rr* **100/1**

022 **8** *2 1/2* **Kept**[14] [6527] 3-9-3 70.. EddieAhern 3
(James Fanshawe) *in tch: hdwy to chse ldrs 3f out: rdn along over 2f out: sn wknd* **7/1**

50 **9** *9* **Touching History (IRE)**[27] [6125] 3-9-3 0................ RussKennemore 11
(Tim Etherington) *a in rr: outpcd and bhd fnl 3f* **100/1**

00 **10** *52* **Urbonite (IRE)**[20] [6341] 3-9-3 0.. RobertWinston 9
(Alan Swinbank) *a in rr: outpcd and wl bhd fnl 3f* **100/1**

4 **11** *1 1/4* **Anqooda (USA)**[18] [6408] 3-8-12 0.................................... PaulHanagan 4
(Marcus Tregoning) *hld up towards rr: effrt over 3f out: sn rdn along and outpcd: sn wl bhd and eased* **14/1**

1m 47.91s (2.01) **Going Correction** +0.325s/f (Good) **11** Ran SP% **115.6**
Speed ratings (Par 101): **102,101,90,87,87 81,68,65,56,4 3**
toteswingers 1&2 £2.30, 1&3 £15.60, 2&3 £52.70 CSF £5.22 TOTE £2.30: £1.40, £1.50, £16.20; EX 7.50.
Owner Godolphin **Bred** Darley **Trained** Newmarket, Suffolk

FOCUS
The front pair drew clear in a maiden lacking depth.
Kept Official explanation: trainer's rep said colt was unsuited by the good to soft ground
Urbonite(IRE) Official explanation: trainer said gelding was unsuited by the good to soft ground
T/Plt: £305.20 to a £1 stake. Pool: £55,992.90 - 133.91 winning tickets T/Qpdt: £34.40 to a £1 stake. Pool: £4,607.02 - 98.91 winning tickets JR

[5591]WINDSOR (R-H)

Monday, October 8

OFFICIAL GOING: Soft (6.3)

Wind: Almost nil Weather: Very Overcast, drizzle from race 5 onwards

6926 DAVISBAKERYCARIBBEAN.COM GENTLEMAN AMATEUR RIDERS' H'CAP 5f 10y

2:20 (2:20) (Class 6) (0-65,65) 3-Y-0+ **£1,559** (£483; £241; £121) **Stalls** Low

Form RPR

3411 **1** **Gladiatrix**[7] 6739 3-11-7 **65**........ MrSWalker 4 83
(Rod Millman) *dwlt: off the pce early towards far side: stdy prog fr 1/2-way: rdn to ld 1f out: sn clr* **11/8**[1]

1223 **2** 3 ¾ **Griffin Point (IRE)**[25] 6178 5-11-0 **63**........(b) MrFMitchell(5) 10 68
(William Muir) *w ldr towards far side: hanging but narrow ld 2f out: hdd and outpcd 1f out* **4/1**[2]

4534 **3** 1 ¼ **Wreningham**[24] 6194 7-10-12 **61**........ MrJSherwood(5) 11 61
(Pat Eddery) *mde most towards far side to 2f out: one pce fnl f* **13/2**[3]

0001 **4** 1 ½ **Cristaliyev**[7] 6737 4-10-5 **54** 7ex........(p) MrMatthewBarber(5) 2 49
(John Flint) *racd towards far side: off the pce: rdn 1/2-way: kpt on to take 4th fnl f: n.d* **7/1**

0000 **5** 1 ¼ **Invincible Dream (IRE)**[59] 5036 3-10-7 **51** oh1.....(v) MrFWindsorClive 1 41
(Pat Phelan) *dwlt and s.i.s: wl off the pce towards far side: kpt on u.p over 1f out: no ch* **25/1**

05-0 **6** 2 **Mr Hendrix**[133] 2547 3-10-5 **56**........ MrSShaw(7) 6 39
(Mark Hoad) *led pair that racd nr side: nt on terms fnl 2f* **66/1**

5500 **7** 1 ¾ **Welsh Inlet (IRE)**[84] 4146 4-11-0 **65**........ MrAJones(7) 5 42
(John Bridger) *chsd rival on nr side: nt on terms fr 2f out* **20/1**

0300 **8** nse **Choice Words (USA)**[52] 5298 4-10-11 **60**........(t) MrFTett(5) 12 36
(Natalie Lloyd-Beavis) *trckd ldng trio towards far side: wknd wl over 1f out* **33/1**

-000 **9** ¾ **Dashwood**[52] 5320 5-11-0 **65**........ MrGrahamCarson(7) 9 39
(Anthony Carson) *dwlt: racd far side: t.o after 2f: plugged on over 1f out: nvr in it* **8/1**

0000 **10** 2 ¾ **White Shift (IRE)**[33] 5937 6-10-0 **51** oh6........ MrJBromley(7) 8 15
(Paul Howling) *w ldng pair towards far side to 2f out: wknd qckly* **50/1**

1m 4.12s (3.82) **Going Correction** +0.375s/f (Good) **10** Ran SP% **114.1**
Speed ratings (Par 101): **84,78,76,73,71 68,65,65,64,59**
toteswingers 1&2 £1.10, 1&3 £2.90, 2&3 £5.10 CSF £6.12 CT £26.01 TOTE £2.10: £1.20, £1.40, £1.70; EX 5.00 Trifecta £11.50 Pool: £789.59 - 50.51 winning units..
Owner Harry Dutfield & Partners **Bred** H G And J R Dutfield **Trained** Kentisbeare, Devon
■ Stewards' Enquiry : Mr S Shaw four-day ban: used whip above permitted level (Oct 29,Nov 7,21,27)

FOCUS
This moderate sprint handicap for gentleman amateur riders was run at a solid pace and unsurprisingly the main action came on the far side from 2f out. Sound form.

6927 DAVISBAKERYCARIBBEAN.COM CLAIMING STKS 1m 2f 7y

2:50 (2:50) (Class 5) 3-4-Y-0 **£2,264** (£673; £336; £168) **Stalls** Centre

Form RPR

0210 **1** **Bernisdale**[28] 4411 4-8-10 69........ JohnFahy 8 67
(John Flint) *mde all: set mod pce tl kicked clr 3f out: in n.d fnl 2f: styd on wl* **2/1**[1]

5260 **2** 5 **Netley Marsh**[32] 5983 3-8-10 57........(b) RichardHughes 3 52
(Richard Hannon) *prom: rdn to chse wnr 4f out to over 1f out: kpt on to take modest 2nd again last strides* **13/2**[3]

545 **3** shd **My Boy Ginger**[10] 6631 3-9-2 64........(b[1]) JamesMillman 4 68
(Rod Millman) *hld up in last pair: prog 3f out: drvn to chse clr wnr over 1f out: no imp: lost 2nd last strides* **3/1**[2]

0510 **4** 10 **Offbeat Safaris (IRE)**[17] 6452 4-8-9 66........ DarrenEgan(5) 5 41
(Ronald Harris) *trckd ldrs: prog to dispute 2nd over 3f out to over 2f out: sn wknd* **2/1**[1]

0/0 **5** 1 ¼ **Gladstone (IRE)**[53] 5276 4-8-9 0........ DavidKenny(5) 1 38
(John Panvert) *awkward to post and had to be dismntd and led: s.s: hld up in last: shkn up 4f out: plugged on past wkng rivals fnl 2f* **50/1**

0553 **6** 1 **Johnny Splash (IRE)**[17] 6436 3-7-13 46........(p) IanBurns(7) 2 33
(Roger Teal) *t.k.h early: hld up in tch: effrt 4f out: no prog 3f out* **25/1**

U540 **7** 17 **Cluaindubhloch (IRE)**[18] 6396 4-8-12 43........ ShaneKelly 7
(Tony Carroll) *free to post: t.k.h: prom: disp 2nd 4f out to 3f out: wknd qckly: t.o* **100/1**

8 4 ½ **Neeka**[64] 4-8-13 0........(p) JamieGoldstein 6
(Zoe Davison) *chsd wnr to 4f out: wknd rapidly: t.o* **100/1**

2m 12.26s (3.56) **Going Correction** +0.45s/f (Yiel)
WFA 3 from 4yo 5lb **8** Ran SP% **112.8**
Speed ratings (Par 103): **103,99,98,90,89 89,75,71**
toteswingers 1&2 £3.50, 1&3 £1.10, 2&3 £4.40 CSF £15.31 TOTE £3.30: £1.50, £1.70, £1.30; EX 12.00 Trifecta £33.10 Pool: £1,123.61 - 25.11 winning units..
Owner Roderick James & Geraint Anstee **Bred** Evelyn Duchess Of Sutherland **Trained** Kenfig Hill, Bridgend

FOCUS
There was an uneven pace in this weak claimer and the field began to move to the far side in the home straight nearing the 3f marker. The ground looked hard work for the majority.

6928 E B F SKYBET.COM MAIDEN STKS 1m 67y

3:20 (3:21) (Class 5) 2-Y-0 **£3,299** (£981; £490; £245) **Stalls** Low

Form RPR

04 **1** **Divine Angel (IRE)**[3] 6844 2-8-12 0........ LukeMorris 2 67
(Phil McEntee) *mde all: drvn 2f out: hrd pressed fnl f: hld on wl* **33/1**

063 **2** nk **Ivanhoe**[42] 5655 2-9-3 72........ DaneO'Neill 7 71
(Michael Blanshard) *hld up: prog 3f out: drvn to chse wnr jst over 1f out: str chal after: jst hld* **4/1**[2]

00 **3** ¾ **Eton Rambler (USA)**[75] 4472 2-9-3 0........ PatCosgrave 11 69
(George Baker) *sn chsd wnr: drvn 2f out: looked hld whn lost 2nd and squeezed out jst over 1f out: styd on* **7/2**[1]

4 2 ¼ **Sizzler** 2-9-3 0........ JimCrowley 8 64+
(Ralph Beckett) *s.i.s: t.k.h and hld up in rr: sme prog over 2f out: kpt on quite takingly fr over 1f out* **4/1**[2]

5 ¾ **Prairie Ranger** 2-9-3 0........ JimmyFortune 3 64+
(Andrew Balding) *hld up: sltly impeded 6f out: pushed along over 3f out: prog over 2f out: no imp on ldrs over 1f out* **7/2**[1]

0 **6** 1 **Plutocracy (IRE)**[10] 6636 2-9-3 0........ TedDurcan 4 64+
(David Lanigan) *restrained s and detached in last early: jst pushed along and kpt on steadily fnl 2f* **9/1**[3]

0000 **7** 1 ½ **Karl Marx (IRE)**[27] 6115 2-9-3 31........ LiamKeniry 9 57
(Mark Usher) *prom: shkn up over 3f out: outpcd 2f out: kpt on one pce after* **100/1**

4 **8** ¾ **Ravens Nest**[14] 6532 2-9-3 0........ JimmyQuinn 10 56
(Robert Mills) *s.i.s: wl in tch: shkn up over 3f out: no hdwy 2f out: fdd* **16/1**

0 **9** 14 **Shining Cross (IRE)**[19] 6377 2-9-3 0........ IanMongan 1 25
(George Margarson) *chsd ldrs: awkward bnd 6f out: wknd over 2f out: t.o* **100/1**

10 1 **Hello Sailor** 2-9-3 0........ SebSanders 6 23
(Ralph Beckett) *prom tl wknd 3f out: t.o* **9/1**[3]

1m 49.31s (4.61) **Going Correction** +0.45s/f (Yiel) **10** Ran SP% **115.2**
Speed ratings (Par 95): **94,93,92,90,89 88,87,86,72,71**
toteswingers 1&2 £13.70, 1&3 £26.50, 2&3 £3.60 CSF £159.31 TOTE £37.50: £8.40, £1.40, £2.10; EX 76.00 Trifecta £745.30 Part won. Pool: £1,007.26 - 0.40 winning units..
Owner Steve Jakes **Bred** Yeomanstown Stud **Trained** Newmarket, Suffolk

FOCUS
This modest juvenile maiden saw the field predictably head far side and it paid to race handily as making up ground proved tricky on the soft surface. The runner-up helps set modest level for the track.

NOTEBOOK
Divine Angel(IRE) got her own way out in front after a couple of furlongs and made all in brave fashion. She came under pressure a fair way out, but kept responding and refused to give way near the finish. This was something of a turn up, but she's improved since joining this yard and obviously handles plenty of give. She can make her mark in handicaps around 1m2f next year, despite her pedigree suggesting plenty of speed, and this was a welcome winner for the yard. (op 20-1)
Ivanhoe went close over this trip on similar ground at Chepstow on his third outing last time and so rates a sound guide for this form. It was another solid effort. (op 3-1)
Eton Rambler(USA), up in trip after a 75-day break, was never far away and was in with a chance prior to finding the door shut on him as he attempted to split the first pair a furlong from home. It's hard to say whether it cost him, but on this ground it certainly didn't help, and he could well make amends next time out. (op 5-1)
Sizzler ◆, the first string from his good yard, is a brother to Group 1 winner Gitano Hernando. He ran distinctly green from the off, but showed plenty under considerate handling late on and ought to improve a bundle for the experience. (op 9-2)
Prairie Ranger, who advertised his inexperience in the preliminaries, was fancied to go close on his debut and ran an encouraging race. Like the fourth, his effort can be upgraded somewhat and he ought to go closer next time. (op 4-1)
Plutocracy(IRE) met support at long odds stepping up a furlong. He got well back early on and, despite this being his second outing, still proved too green for his own good. He may prefer a sounder surface, though, and this was a step in the right direction. (op 14-1)

6929 IVOR LAWS MEMORIAL NURSERY 5f 10y

3:50 (3:53) (Class 4) (0-85,85) 2-Y-0 **£3,557** (£1,058; £529; £264) **Stalls** Low

Form RPR

10 **1** **Dutch Masterpiece**[65] 4804 2-9-2 **80**........ GeorgeBaker 3 90+
(Gary Moore) *taken to post steadily after rest had already arrived there: led after 1f: mde rest: shkn up over 1f out: drew clr fnl f: readily* **11/8**[1]

0004 **2** 3 ¼ **Bridge Night**[22] 6284 2-9-2 **80**........(p) JimmyFortune 2 78
(Eve Johnson Houghton) *prom: rdn to chse wnr over 1f out: no imp fnl f* **22/1**

31 **3** nse **Just Charlie**[65] 4816 2-9-7 **85**........ DaneO'Neill 5 83
(Henry Candy) *dwlt: hld up in last pair: prog 2f out: rdn over 1f out: disp 2nd fnl f: no threat to wnr* **9/1**

3212 **4** 1 **Khefyn (IRE)**[35] 5873 2-8-12 **76**........ LukeMorris 7 71+
(Ronald Harris) *dwlt: pushed along in last: rdn and styd on fnl 2f to take 4th nr fin* **11/1**

4162 **5** shd **Equitania**[38] 5790 2-9-6 **84**........ RichardHughes 6 78
(Richard Hannon) *led 1f: pressed wnr to 2f out: lost 2nd over 1f out: one pce* **4/1**[2]

2130 **6** 7 **Dansili Dual (IRE)**[65] 4804 2-9-0 **78**........ PatDobbs 4 47
(Richard Hannon) *cl up to 1/2-way: wknd qckly 2f out* **6/1**[3]

4612 **7** shd **Spray Tan**[25] 6155 2-7-8 **63**........ DarrenEgan(5) 8 31
(Tony Carroll) *in tch to 2f out: wknd qckly over 1f out* **12/1**

400 **8** 12 **Mossgo (IRE)**[111] 3242 2-8-13 **77**........ JimCrowley 1
(John Best) *cl up on outer to 1/2-way: wknd qckly 2f out: t.o* **20/1**

1m 2.45s (2.15) **Going Correction** +0.375s/f (Good) **8** Ran SP% **111.5**
Speed ratings (Par 97): **97,91,91,90,89 78,78,59**
toteswingers 1&2 £8.90, 1&3 £3.10, 2&3 £12.40 CSF £34.41 CT £195.78 TOTE £2.40: £1.20, £5.30, £2.60; EX 38.30 TRIFECTA Not won..
Owner R A Green **Bred** Bumble Bloodstock Ltd **Trained** Lower Beeding, W Sussex

FOCUS
It was a case of gamble landed in this nursery. The runner-up and third help set the opening level.

NOTEBOOK
Dutch Masterpiece, well supported, stamped his authority at the furlong marker and powered to success on his first outing since being gelded. He looked most uneasy at Goodwood in August, but had won well on his debut on Southwell's Fibresand the time before and was heavily backed on this return to a flatter track. The soft ground was also expected to suit and he handled it best of all. A rise will most probably see him back up in class, but he's unexposed and looks very useful. (op 5-2)
Bridge Night was down 5lb and equipped with first-time cheekpieces. She did her best to pressure the winner nearing the final furlong and, while well held by that rival, kept on well thereafter. This ground was probably easy enough for her liking. (op 20-1 tchd 25-1)
Just Charlie was making his nursery debut and conceding weight all round. He travelled well enough on this contrasting surface and has begun life in handicaps on a workable mark. (op 15-2 tchd 7-1)
Khefyn(IRE) looked found out by testing ground over 6f when a beaten odds-on shot at Ffos Las on his previous outing, but here he shaped as though the drop back in trip went against him. (op 8-1 tchd 12-1)
Equitania bagged the far rail, but it was clear soon she was in trouble and one has to think the ground was against her. (op 3-1 tchd 11-4)

6930 2013 ANNUAL MEMBERSHIP £249 ON SALE TODAY MAIDEN STKS 6f

4:20 (4:24) (Class 5) 3-Y-0+ **£2,264** (£673; £336; £168) **Stalls** Low

Form RPR

02 **1** **Dick Bos**[10] 6643 3-9-3 0........ JimmyFortune 6 83+
(Peter Chapple-Hyam) *trckd ldrs: prog to ld 2f out: rdn over 1f out: drew clr fnl f: readily* **2/1**[1]

2250 **2** 4 ½ **Lupo D'Oro (IRE)**[25] 6173 3-9-3 74........ JimCrowley 3 69
(John Best) *sn wl in tch: prog to chse wnr over 1f out and cl enough: outpcd fnl f* **9/2**[3]

3 **3** 1 **Ella Fitzgerald (IRE)**[19] 6362 3-8-12 0........ ChrisCatlin 10 61
(Rae Guest) *trckd ldrs: rdn and cl up over 2f out: one pce over 1f out* **12/1**

6543 **4** *1 ½* **Tight Lipped (IRE)**[41] 5721 3-9-3 72.................................. LukeMorris 8 61
(James Eustace) *chsd ldrs on outer: rdn 1/2-way: kpt on one pce fnl 2f* **5/2**[2]

3050 **5** *½* **Homeboy (IRE)**[32] 5972 4-9-4 61.................................. RichardHughes 2 59
(Marcus Tregoning) *hld up in rr: prog over 3f out: chsd ldrs 2f out: no imp over 1f out* **8/1**

6 *5* **High Net Worth** 3-9-3 0.. DaneO'Neill 4 43+
(Ed Walker) *dwlt: hld up in rr: prog into midfield over 2f out: no hdwy after: fdd fnl f* **18/1**

600 **7** *hd* **Summer Sun**[67] 4746 3-8-12 55.................................... JimmyQuinn 12 38
(Phil McEntee) *racd freely: led to 2f out: wknd over 1f out* **50/1**

000 **8** *1* **Cowslip**[12] 6582 3-8-12 25.. KieranO'Neill 1 35
(Richard Hannon) *nvr on terms w ldrs: modest late prog: nvr a factor* **66/1**

000 **9** *shd* **Highway Warrior**[18] 6402 3-8-13 52 ow1.................... JamieGoldstein 9 35
(Zoe Davison) *prom to 1/2-way: steadily wknd* **80/1**

10 *½* **Living Leader** 3-9-3 0... TomMcLaughlin 13 38
(Nick Littmoden) *s.v.s: wl in rr: pushed along and limited prog 2f out: sn wknd* **40/1**

11 *¾* **Gaelic Ice** 3-8-12 0... JamesMillman 15 30
(Rod Millman) *reluctant to enter stalls: broke on terms: qckly dropped to last after 2f: nvr a factor after* **25/1**

12 *shd* **Resonare** 3-9-3 0... WilliamCarson 11 35
(Stuart Williams) *s.v.s: a wl in rr* **40/1**

000 **13** *nk* **Captain Cavallo**[129] 2665 5-9-4 0.................................(v[1]) ShaneKelly 16 34
(Nicky Vaughan) *chsd ldr to over 2f out: wknd qckly* **66/1**

\- **14** *¾* **Batchworth Firefly** 4-8-13 0 ow3.......................... PatrickHills[(3)] 7 30
(Dean Ivory) *dwlt: a wl in rr: no prog 2f out* **50/1**

-060 **15** *11* **Kiss My Heart**[25] 6154 3-8-5 24.. JoeyHaynes[(7)] 5
(Eric Wheeler) *dwlt: a wl in rr: t.o* **200/1**

16 *shd* **Kerfuffle (IRE)** 3-8-12 0... NickyMackay 14
(Simon Dow) *prom over 2f: sn wknd qckly: t.o* **50/1**

1m 15.82s (2.82) **Going Correction** +0.375s/f (Good)
WFA 3 from 4yo+ 1lb **16** Ran SP% **123.5**
Speed ratings (Par 103): **96,90,88,86,86 79,79,77,77,76 75,75,75,74,59 59**
toteswingers 1&2 £3.60, 1&3 £5.40, 2&3 £7.20 CSF £10.84 TOTE £3.60: £2.10, £1.90, £3.00; EX 13.90 Trifecta £85.20 Pool: £1,729.04 - 15.00 winning units..
Owner The Comic Strip Heroes **Bred** Gracelands Stud **Trained** Newmarket, Suffolk

FOCUS
This weak sprint maiden was run at a solid pace with plenty mindful of the prominent pace bias and underfoot conditions played a big part. Straightforward enough form.

6931 STEVE KEEN CELEBRATION H'CAP (DIV I) 1m 67y
4:50 (4:51) (Class 4) (0-80,80) 3-Y-0+ **£4,204** (£1,251; £625; £312) **Stalls** Low

Form RPR

1301 **1** **Capitol Gain (IRE)**[22] 6275 3-8-6 68..............................(p) JamieMackay 6 76
(Brian Meehan) *racd freely: mde all: rdn at least 2 l clr 2f out: kpt on wl and a in charge* **12/1**

3030 **2** *1* **Mr Spiggott (IRE)**[72] 4600 3-9-4 80.................................. TedDurcan 2 86
(Joseph Tuite) *hld up towards rr: rdn and prog over 2f out: styd on fr over 1f out to take 2nd last 100yds: clsd on wnr but nvr able to chal* **13/2**[3]

6301 **3** *1* **Hurricane Lady (IRE)**[14] 6545 4-9-7 80........................ NickyMackay 5 84
(Mike Murphy) *dwlt: t.k.h in midfield: prog over 2f out: drvn to chse wnr jst over 1f out to last 100yds: kpt on* **12/1**

0050 **4** *½* **Sinfonico (IRE)**[24] 6207 4-9-1 74..............................(e) RichardHughes 9 77
(Richard Hannon) *hld up in last pair: prog on wd outside fr 2f out: styd on to take 4th nr fin* **5/1**[2]

5164 **5** *1 ¼* **Andalieb**[60] 4997 3-9-2 78... GeorgeBaker 3 78
(David Simcock) *t.k.h: trckd ldrs: rdn and tried to cl over 2f out: one pce over 1f out* **10/3**[1]

-002 **6** *1 ½* **Ancient Greece**[14] 6545 5-9-2 75..............................(t) PatCosgrave 7 71
(George Baker) *trckd ldrs: shkn up in 4th over 3f out: trying to chal for a pl whn rdr dropped whip over 1f out: fdd* **11/1**

1005 **7** *2 ½* **Mingun Bell (USA)**[20] 6338 5-9-6 79................................ LiamKeniry 12 69
(Ed de Giles) *prom: chsd wnr 1/2-way to jst over 1f out: wknd qckly* **7/1**

1510 **8** *2* **Woolston Ferry (IRE)**[24] 6208 6-9-3 76..................... FergusSweeney 11 62
(Henry Candy) *hld up towards rr: rdn and no real prog over 2f out* **10/1**

0564 **9** *hd* **Soweto Star (IRE)**[20] 6329 4-8-10 69 ow1........................ JimCrowley 10 54
(John Best) *hld up in last pair: drvn over 3f out: no prog and sn btn* **10/1**

4000 **10** *1 ¾* **Mullins Way (USA)**[11] 6601 4-9-3 76......................... J-PGuillambert 8 57
(Jo Hughes) *a in rr: u.p and struggling sn after 1/2-way: no prog* **20/1**

01 **11** *16* **Fever Few**[52] 5299 3-8-11 73.. BrettDoyle 4 18
(Jane Chapple-Hyam) *fractious stalls: t.k.h: chsd wnr to 1/2-way: wknd rapidly 3f out: t.o* **22/1**

1m 48.05s (3.35) **Going Correction** +0.45s/f (Yiel)
WFA 3 from 4yo+ 3lb **11** Ran SP% **116.6**
Speed ratings (Par 105): **101,100,99,98,97 95,93,91,91,89 73**
toteswingers 1&2 £15.80, 1&3 £14.80, 2&3 £5.40 CSF £87.22 CT £966.25 TOTE £19.30: £3.60, £1.90, £2.40; EX 161.60 TRIFECTA Not won..
Owner N Attenborough,Mrs L Mann,M Wilmshurst **Bred** Pier House Stud **Trained** Manton, Wilts

FOCUS
A moderate handicap. Once again it proved hard to land a serious blow from off the pace.

6932 STEVE KEEN CELEBRATION H'CAP (DIV II) 1m 67y
5:20 (5:20) (Class 4) (0-80,80) 3-Y-0+ **£4,204** (£1,251; £625; £312) **Stalls** Low

Form RPR

1132 **1** **Myboyalfie (USA)**[13] 6566 5-9-3 76................................(v) IanMongan 1 88
(J R Jenkins) *mde all at gd pce: drvn clr fr 2f out: styd on wl: unchal* **11/2**[2]

1304 **2** *3 ¾* **Snow Trooper**[14] 6539 4-9-3 76.. ShaneKelly 7 79
(Dean Ivory) *wl in tch: prog to dispute 2nd 4f out: drvn over 2f out: kpt on but no imp* **4/1**[1]

3614 **3** *shd* **Copperwood**[14] 6538 7-9-2 75.. NickyMackay 9 78
(Mark Johnston) *chsd wnr: drvn and no imp over 2f out: kpt on same pce after* **14/1**

3453 **4** *nk* **Significant Move**[24] 6209 5-8-11 70..............................(t) FergusSweeney 3 72
(Stuart Kittow) *chsd ldrs: rdn over 3f out: struggling over 2f out: styd on u.p fr over 1f out* **8/1**

4131 **5** *½* **Lutine Charlie (IRE)**[17] 6434 5-8-7 66 oh3......................... LukeMorris 11 67
(Pat Eddery) *hld up in rr: rdn over 3f out: kpt on to take 4th over 1f out: one pce after* **14/1**

4602 **6** *½* **Main Line**[63] 4889 3-9-2 78.. TedDurcan 12 78+
(David Lanigan) *sweating: trapped out wd first 2f towards rr: rdn 3f out: kpt on same pce fnl 2f: n.d* **4/1**[1]

1443 **7** *3* **Derfenna Art (IRE)**[42] 5657 3-8-6 68...............................(tp) JohnFahy 10 61
(Seamus Durack) *chsd ldrs: u.p fr 1/2-way: steadily wknd fnl 2f* **11/1**

1630 **8** *1 ½* **My Lord**[38] 5794 4-9-2 75... RichardHughes 4 64
(Luke Dace) *stdd s: hld up in last pair: pushed along and no prog 1/2-way: struggling fnl 3f* **6/1**[3]

460 **9** *2 ¾* **Cocohatchee**[45] 5531 4-8-3 67.................................(p) JemmaMarshall[(5)] 8 50
(Pat Phelan) *hld up towards rr: rdn and no prog 3f out: wl btn whn nt clr run 1f out* **33/1**

5125 **10** *1* **Halling Dancer**[56] 5163 3-9-0 76.. KierenFox 5 57
(Lee Carter) *t.k.h early: trckd ldng pair: rdn and hanging over 3f out: wknd over 2f out: eased* **14/1**

00/ **11** *66* **Aeroplane**[776] 5388 9-9-1 79.. DarrenEgan[(5)] 6
(Richard Price) *a in last pair: wknd bef 1/2-way: sn wl t.o* **50/1**

1m 47.2s (2.50) **Going Correction** +0.45s/f (Yiel)
WFA 3 from 4yo+ 3lb **11** Ran SP% **114.0**
Speed ratings (Par 105): **105,101,101,100,100 99,96,95,92,91 25**
toteswingers 1&2 £4.60, 1&3 £9.90, 2&3 £10.30 CSF £26.82 CT £295.31 TOTE £7.50: £2.00, £2.00, £2.80; EX 32.00 Trifecta £129.30 Pool: £1,150.19 - 6.58 winning units..
Owner D Badham **Bred** Robert Pierz & Robert Brooks **Trained** Royston, Herts

FOCUS
The second division of the moderate 1m handicap and, despite being run at a sound pace, it threw up another winner from the front.
Aeroplane Official explanation: jockey said horse lost its action

6933 SKYBET.COM H'CAP 1m 3f 135y
5:50 (5:51) (Class 4) (0-80,81) 3-Y-0+ **£4,204** (£1,251; £625; £312) **Stalls** Centre

Form RPR

0562 **1** **Scottish Boogie (IRE)**[7] 6734 5-9-4 71............................ SebSanders 4 82
(Brendan Powell) *hld up wl in rr: prog on outer over 3f out: drvn and r.o to take narrow ld last 100yds: styd on* **10/1**

5065 **2** *nk* **Aldwick Bay (IRE)**[17] 6450 4-9-11 78................................ PatDobbs 16 88
(Richard Hannon) *wl in tch: prog 4f out and sn trckd ldrs: rdn to ld wl over 1f out: narrowly hdd last 100yds: styd on but jst hld* **10/1**

1136 **3** *2 ¼* **Astra Hall**[38] 5789 3-8-5 65.. NickyMackay 3 71
(Ralph Beckett) *hld up wl in rr: prog on outer wl over 2f out: drvn and r.o to take 3rd fnl f: one pce after* **9/2**[1]

0560 **4** *¾* **Cresta Star**[16] 6492 3-9-4 78.. RichardHughes 1 83
(Richard Hannon) *hld up wl in rr: prog on outer over 2f out: hanging lft but styd on fnl f: nrst fin* **12/1**

215 **5** *½* **Palus San Marco (IRE)**[70] 4649 3-9-2 76......................... LukeMorris 13 80
(Peter Chapple-Hyam) *prom: drvn over 2f out: kpt on same pce fnl 2f: nvr able to chal* **20/1**

1031 **6** *2* **Livia's Dream (IRE)**[26] 6146 3-9-2 76............................ GeorgeBaker 5 77+
(Ed Walker) *wl in tch: prog over 3f out: sn chsng ldrs: no hdwy wl over 1f out* **11/2**[3]

5302 **7** *nk* **Achalas (IRE)**[8] 6703 4-9-2 76.................................... RyanTate[(7)] 12 76
(Heather Main) *a in midfield: shkn up over 3f out: no imp on ldrs 2f out: one pce after* **14/1**

3012 **8** *nk* **Ukrainian (IRE)**[5] 6776 3-9-2 81 6ex.........................(v) DarrenEgan[(5)] 15 81
(Mark Johnston) *nt that wl away: urged along and sn prom: led over 3f out: drvn and hdd wl over 1f out: wknd* **5/1**[2]

0060 **9** *1 ¼* **Hot Spice**[17] 6450 4-9-6 73.. TedDurcan 2 71
(John Dunlop) *hld up in last: pushed along 4f out: reminders over 2f out: styd on fr over 1f out: nvr involved* **25/1**

31-1 **10** *5* **Bright Abbey**[44] 5596 4-9-7 77..............................(v) CPGeoghegan[(3)] 7 66
(Philip Hobbs) *prom: rdn over 3f out: wknd over 2f out* **8/1**

1300 **11** *½* **Paddyfrommenlo (IRE)**[24] 6193 3-9-3 77......................... JimCrowley 11 65
(J W Hills) *chsd ldrs: struggling to hold pl whn short of room 3f out: sn wknd* **16/1**

1043 **12** *2 ¼* **Paloma's Prince (IRE)**[84] 4151 3-9-2 76.....................(p) PatCosgrave 8 60
(Jim Boyle) *mde most to over 3f out: wknd over 2f out* **20/1**

0053 **13** *1 ¼* **Opera Buff**[10] 6647 3-8-10 70.. LiamKeniry 9 52
(Sylvester Kirk) *hld up wl in rr: rdn 3f out: no prog* **16/1**

4U40 **14** *1 ¾* **Royal Etiquette (IRE)**[25] 6181 5-8-12 65 oh2..................... DaneO'Neill 6 44
(Lawney Hill) *nvr bttr than midfield: short of room 3f out: sn wknd* **40/1**

13-6 **15** *14* **Sim Sala Bim**[14] 6538 4-9-8 75....................................... WilliamCarson 10 30
(Stuart Williams) *hld up wl in rr: rdn and effrt 4f out: wknd qckly over 2f out: t.o* **25/1**

1/00 **16** *23* **Ascalon**[96] 3766 8-9-12 79.. ShaneKelly 14
(Pat Eddery) *w ldr to over 4f out: wknd rapidly: wl t.o* **40/1**

2m 35.86s (6.36) **Going Correction** +0.45s/f (Yiel)
WFA 3 from 4yo+ 7lb **16** Ran SP% **127.7**
Speed ratings (Par 105): **96,95,94,93,93 92,91,91,90,87 87,85,84,83,74 59**
toteswingers 1&2 £22.40, 1&3 £13.70, 2&3 £13.70 CSF £102.04 CT £526.42 TOTE £16.50: £3.60, £3.10, £1.70, £2.80; EX 178.60 Trifecta £1024.20 Part won. Pool: £1,384.08 - 0.40 winning units..
Owner A A Byrne **Bred** Littleton Stud **Trained** Upper Lambourn, Berks
■ Stewards' Enquiry : Richard Hughes four-day ban: used whip above permitted level (Oct 22-25)

FOCUS
A modest handicap, run at a fair pace.
T/Plt: £26.80 to a £1 stake. Pool: £66,703.45 - 1,811.01 winning tickets T/Qpdt: £18.10 to a £1 stake. Pool: £5,091.80 - 207.60 winning tickets JN

6888 WOLVERHAMPTON (A.W) (L-H)
Monday, October 8

OFFICIAL GOING: Standard
Wind: Light against Weather: Raining

6934 32RED H'CAP 7f 32y(P)
2:00 (2:01) (Class 5) (0-75,75) 3-Y-0+ **£2,264** (£673; £336; £168) **Stalls** High

Form RPR

4103 **1** **Chookie Avon**[8] 6709 5-9-2 70...(p) TomEaves 2 80
(Keith Dalgleish) *chsd ldrs: rdn to ld 1f out: jst hld on* **12/1**

001 **2** *hd* **Light From Mars**[9] 6687 7-9-6 74..............................(t) GrahamLee 3 83
(Ian Williams) *mid-div: hdwy over 2f out: rdn over 1f out: r.o* **2/1**[1]

1600 **3** *2 ¼* **Big Wave (IRE)**[19] 6378 4-9-2 70................................ AdamBeschizza 8 73
(Alison Hutchinson) *s.i.s: hld up: rdn: hung lft and r.o ins fnl f: nt rch ldrs* **40/1**

21-3 **4** *nk* **Chokidar (IRE)**[43] 5630 4-9-2 75.........................(v) MichaelJMMurphy[(5)] 1 77
(Scott Dixon) *chsd ldrs: rdn and ev ch over 1f out: styd on same pce* **5/1**[3]

5010 **5** *1 ¾* **Summer Dancer (IRE)**[16] 6479 8-9-2 70............................ MickyFenton 11 67
(Paul Midgley) *s.i.s: hld up: nt clr run over 1f out: r.o ins fnl f: nrst fin* **33/1**

0050 **6** *½* **Mcmonagle (USA)**[8] 6709 4-9-4 72...............................(tp) DaleSwift 12 68
(Alan Brown) *sn led: rdn and hdd 1f out: no ex* **28/1**

2155 **7** *1* **Cyflymder (IRE)**[23] 6239 6-9-5 73...................................... FrannyNorton 6 66
(David C Griffiths) *hld up: hdwy over 1f out: no imp ins fnl f* **7/1**

4100 **8** *1* **Gap Princess (IRE)**[27] 6123 8-9-3 **71**..................(v[1]) RoystonFfrench 10 62
(Geoffrey Harker) *hld up in tch: rdn over 2f out: hung lft and wknd ins fnl f* **33/1**

0224 **9** *nse* **Buckland (IRE)**[14] 6545 4-9-2 **75**............................ MatthewLawson(5) 5 66
(Hans Adielsson) *sn pushed along in rr: nt clr run over 1f out: nvr on terms* **14/1**

10-0 **10** *3/4* **Elsie's Orphan**[23] 6256 5-9-5 **73**...................................... HarryBentley 4 61
(Patrick Chamings) *mid-div: pushed along over 2f out: hdwy over 1f out: wknd fnl f* **28/1**

0520 **11** *5* **Amazon Twilight**[38] 5791 4-9-4 **72**....................................... NeilCallan 7 47
(Brett Johnson) *plld hrd and prom: rdn over 2f out: wknd over 1f out* **20/1**

2221 **12** *9* **Stir Trader (IRE)**[9] 6686 3-9-4 **74**.................................(b) JamesDoyle 9 25
(Roger Charlton) *prom: hmpd 6f out: chsd ldr over 5f out tl rdn over 2f out: wknd over 1f out* **11/4**[2]

1m 28.28s (-1.32) **Going Correction** -0.10s/f (Stan)
WFA 3 from 4yo+ 2lb **12** Ran SP% **123.5**
Speed ratings (Par 103): **103,102,100,99,97 97,96,95,94,94 88,78**
toteswingers 1&2 £6.40, 1&3 £74.20, 2&3 £24.80 CSF £35.44 CT £1007.87 TOTE £10.20: £3.10, £1.30, £11.10; EX 45.70.
Owner Keith Dalgleish Racing Club **Bred** D And J Raeburn **Trained** Carluke, S Lanarks

FOCUS
A competitive feel to this handicap, run at a strong pace.
Gap Princess(IRE) Official explanation: jockey said mare suffered interference shortly after start
Amazon Twilight Official explanation: jockey said filly hung right-handed
Stir Trader(IRE) Official explanation: trainer had no explanation for the poor form shown

6935 HOTEL & CONFERENCING AT WOLVERHAMPTON (S) STKS 5f 20y(P)
2:30 (2:31) (Class 6) 3-4-Y-0 **£1,704** (£503; £251) **Stalls** Low

Form RPR

6100 **1** **Clubland (IRE)**[5] 6786 3-9-4 61.. TomEaves 8 71
(Kevin Ryan) *chsd ldr: rdn to ld ins fnl f: edgd lft: r.o* **3/1**[3]

5040 **2** *1 1/4* **Sonko (IRE)**[23] 6234 3-8-13 79...(p) GrahamLee 5 62
(Tim Pitt) *led: rdn and hdd ins fnl f: styd on same pce* **6/4**[1]

0606 **3** *6* **Airborne Again (IRE)**[54] 5234 3-8-12 68.....................(b[1]) JamesDoyle 4 39
(Harry Dunlop) *pushed along in rr early: hdwy 3f out: rdn over 1f out: styd on same pce* **15/8**[2]

3026 **4** *3* **First Fast Now (IRE)**[5] 6771 3-8-0 49..................... DanielleMooney(7) 1 23
(Nigel Tinkler) *sn outpcd: hdwy 1/2-way: rdn and wknd over 1f out* **16/1**

0054 **5** *2* **Rainbow Riches (IRE)**[31] 5994 3-8-4 44..................(b) RyanPowell(3) 2 16
(Roger Curtis) *chsd ldrs: pushed along 3f out: wknd 1/2-way* **25/1**

00 **6** *6* **Smiley Miley (IRE)**[10] 6641 4-8-7 0.....................(v[1]) FrankieMcDonald 3
(David Lewis) *s.i.s: plld hrd: hdwy over 3f out: rdn and wknd 2f out* **150/1**

1m 1.51s (-0.79) **Going Correction** -0.10s/f (Stan) **6** Ran SP% **110.2**
Speed ratings (Par 101): **102,100,90,85,82 72**
toteswingers 1&2 £1.70, 1&3 £1.60, 2&3 £1.20 CSF £7.61 TOTE £3.60: £1.60, £1.50; EX 9.00.There was no bid for the winner. Sonko was subject to a friendly claim.
Owner Dominic Cork **Bred** Mrs Sharon Slattery **Trained** Hambleton, N Yorks

FOCUS
A modest seller run at a sound pace.

6936 32RED.COM MAIDEN FILLIES' STKS 5f 216y(P)
3:00 (3:02) (Class 5) 2-Y-0 **£3,234** (£962; £481; £240) **Stalls** Low

Form RPR

3 **1** **Broughtons Charm (IRE)**[33] 5943 2-9-0 0................ StevieDonohoe 10 75
(Willie Musson) *trckd ldrs: shkn up to ld over 1f out: hdd ins fnl f: rallied to ld post* **7/2**[2]

2 *shd* **Rebelde (IRE)** 2-9-0 0.. RoystonFfrench 7 75
(Conrad Allen) *trckd ldr: rdn to ld ins fnl f: hdd post* **33/1**

3 *1 1/4* **My Trust (IRE)** 2-9-0 0.. TomEaves 5 74+
(Saeed Bin Suroor) *s.i.s: hld up: nt clr run over 1f out: swtchd lft and r.o wl ins fnl f: nt rch ldrs* **8/1**

50 **4** *2 1/4* **Sakhee's Rose**[27] 6114 2-9-0 0.. JamesDoyle 4 64
(Roger Charlton) *mid-div: hdwy 1/2-way: rdn over 1f out: styd on same pce fnl f* **16/1**

5 *1/2* **Red Tulip** 2-9-0 0.. HayleyTurner 9 66+
(James Fanshawe) *hld up: nt clr run ent fnl f: r.o: nt rchd ldrs* **33/1**

3 **6** *3/4* **Yahilwa (USA)**[20] 6343 2-9-0 0.. NeilCallan 13 60
(James Tate) *plld hrd and prom: rdn over 1f out: no ex ins fnl f* **7/1**[3]

4 **7** *hd* **Ilsa Lund (IRE)**[20] 6343 2-9-0 0.................................... JamieSpencer 12 60
(Peter Chapple-Hyam) *led: rdn and hdd over 1f out: hung lft and wknd ins fnl f* **7/1**[3]

04 **8** *1/2* **Black Eyed Girl (IRE)**[42] 5656 2-8-11 0..................... RyanPowell(3) 11 58
(J S Moore) *hld up: hdwy over 2f out: sn rdn: no ex fnl f* **66/1**

30 **9** *nk* **Princess Sheila (IRE)**[24] 6203 2-9-0 0.............................. LiamJones 3 58
(J S Moore) *mid-div: hdwy 1/2-way: rdn over 1f out: hld whn hmpd ins fnl f* **16/1**

10 *1/2* **Zarla** 2-9-0 0.. GrahamLee 8 56+
(Tom Dascombe) *sn outpcd* **20/1**

3 **11** *1/2* **Meeting In Paris (IRE)**[20] 6335 2-9-0 0............................ MartinLane 2 54
(Brian Meehan) *hld up: rdn over 2f out: n.d* **7/4**[1]

50 **12** *4* **Valley Dreamer**[25] 6153 2-9-0 0....................................... FrannyNorton 6 42
(Michael Blanshard) *broke wl: sn pushed along and lost pl: n.d after* **80/1**

1m 15.33s (0.33) **Going Correction** -0.10s/f (Stan) **12** Ran SP% **119.8**
Speed ratings (Par 92): **93,92,91,88,87 86,86,85,85,84 83,78**
toteswingers 1&2 £38.10, 1&3 £7.00, 2&3 £55.00 CSF £125.26 TOTE £4.90: £1.60, £11.10, £2.90; EX 183.40.
Owner Broughton Thermal Insulation **Bred** West Dereham Abbey Stud **Trained** Newmarket, Suffolk
■ Stewards' Enquiry : Tom Eaves three-day ban: careless riding (Oct 22-24)

FOCUS
An interesting, if modest juvenile fillies' maiden. It was a messy race off a steady pace. The winner has been rated to her debut mark for starters, and the third looked a bit unlucky, with the fifth also better than the facts from rear.

NOTEBOOK
Broughtons Charm(IRE) confirmed the promise of the previous month's Kempton effort. This was by no means an impressive win for the 52,000gns purchase but her attitude couldn't be faulted as she wrestled back a decisive advantage in the final couple of strides. Drawn out wide, she was probably keener than ideal in the early stages, though she would not be sure to confirm form with either the runner-up or the third on these terms in future. The handicapper can't be too hard on her for this, however, and she does remain open to some improvement, especially once stepping up to 7f. (op 4-1)
Rebelde(IRE) looked like causing an upset before visibly tying up in the closing stages. This was a really promising start to her career and there should to be races to be won with her this winter. (tchd 50-1)
My Trust(IRE) would probably have won had the gaps come in time. Slowly away and still with plenty to do as they turned for home, she did well to finish so close. A race of this nature should be easily within her capabilities. (tchd 15-2)
Sakhee's Rose certainly wasn't disgraced and could be one to keep tabs on now she's qualified for a mark. Staying on near to the finish, you'd expect her to return to longer trips next time. (op 14-1)
Red Tulip didn't get the clearest of runs at a vital stage and will have learnt plenty from this.
Ilsa Lund(IRE) enjoyed an easy time of things up front but dropped away disappointingly. She looks to lack pace at this stage of her career and should do better once upped in trip and handicapped. (tchd 13-2)
Meeting In Paris(IRE) ran poorly and may not have acted on this surface. (op 6-4 tchd 2-1)

6937 FOLLOW US ON TWITTER @WOLVESRACES H'CAP 5f 216y(P)
3:30 (3:30) (Class 6) (0-55,55) 3-Y-0+ **£1,704** (£503; £251) **Stalls** Low

Form RPR

3536 **1** **Here Now And Why (IRE)**[8] 6713 5-9-2 **55**............(p) DanielTudhope 11 64
(Ian Semple) *hld up in tch: rdn over 1f out: r.o to ld post* **13/2**[3]

6240 **2** *hd* **Choice Pearl (USA)**[4] 6806 3-8-13 **53**........................(vt[1]) HarryBentley 7 61
(Tobias B P Coles) *chsd ldrs: rdn to ld 1f out: hdd post* **9/1**

-606 **3** *1 1/4* **Lucky Mark (IRE)**[41] 5719 3-8-12 **52**............................ StevieDonohoe 4 56
(Garry Moss) *hld up: hdwy over 1f out: sn rdn: styd on* **20/1**

4224 **4** *1/2* **Maltease Ah**[21] 6322 3-8-7 **54**.. DavidBergin(7) 8 57
(Alan McCabe) *led: rdn: edgd rt and hdd 1f out: no ex wl ins fnl f* **15/2**

5004 **5** *1 3/4* **Kai**[10] 6640 3-8-13 **53**...(b) SeanLevey 2 50
(Alan McCabe) *hld up: hdwy over 1f out: rdn and hung lft ins fnl f: nt rch ldrs* **16/1**

5502 **6** *nk* **Majestic Breeze (IRE)**[21] 6321 3-8-13 **53**............................ DaleSwift 9 49
(Brian Ellison) *hld up: pushed along over 3f out: hdwy u.p over 1f out: no imp fnl f* **11/4**[1]

4102 **7** *1 3/4* **Avonlini**[21] 6322 6-8-12 **51**... KellyHarrison 10 42
(Brian Baugh) *chsd ldr: rdn over 2f out: no ex ins fnl f* **10/1**

0206 **8** *3/4* **Ace Of Spies (IRE)**[12] 6586 7-9-2 **55**................................ HayleyTurner 6 43
(Conor Dore) *chsd ldrs: rdn over 2f out: edgd rt over 1f out: wknd ins fnl f* **25/1**

0-03 **9** *1* **Monumental Man**[21] 6322 3-8-12 **52**.................................... NeilCallan 1 41
(James Unett) *hld up in tch: rdn whn hmpd over 1f out: wknd ins fnl f* **12/1**

0160 **10** *1 1/2* **Circuitous**[27] 6123 4-9-0 **53**... GrahamLee 3 33
(Keith Dalgleish) *hld up: rdn over 1f out: n.d* **6/1**[2]

0505 **11** *1* **Lord Paget**[16] 6500 3-8-8 **55**...(v) JackDuern(7) 5 32
(Reg Hollinshead) *s.s: sn drvn along and a in rr* **14/1**

-300 **12** *2 3/4* **Pull The Pin (IRE)**[31] 6002 3-8-12 **52**........................ AdamBeschizza 12 20
(William Kinsey) *prom: rdn over 2f out: wknd over 1f out* **10/1**

1m 14.36s (-0.64) **Going Correction** -0.10s/f (Stan)
WFA 3 from 4yo+ 1lb **12** Ran SP% **123.1**
Speed ratings (Par 101): **100,99,98,97,95 94,92,91,90,88 86,83**
toteswingers 1&2 £14.10, 1&3 £34.50, 2&3 £36.70 CSF £66.56 CT £1145.17 TOTE £8.40: £2.30, £3.20, £8.20; EX 79.70.
Owner The Jolly Beggars & James Cringan **Bred** Mrs Sandra McCarthy **Trained** Carluke, S Lanarks

FOCUS
A modest handicap, run at a strong pace.
Monumental Man Official explanation: jockey said gelding suffered interference in running

6938 32RED CASINO H'CAP (DIV I) 5f 216y(P)
4:00 (4:01) (Class 4) (0-85,85) 3-Y-0+ **£4,204** (£1,251; £625; £312) **Stalls** Low

Form RPR

0500 **1** **Solar Spirit (IRE)**[20] 6338 7-8-13 **77**.............................. FrannyNorton 8 90
(Tracy Waggott) *hld up: hdwy over 1f out: r.o to ld wl ins fnl f* **10/1**

0350 **2** *1 1/2* **Sutton Veny (IRE)**[51] 5362 6-9-4 **82**............................. JamieSpencer 6 90
(Jeremy Gask) *a.p: shkn up to ld over 1f out: hdd and unable qck wl ins fnl f* **7/1**[3]

6406 **3** *3/4* **Arctic Lynx (IRE)**[37] 5832 5-8-11 **80**................. MichaelJMMurphy(5) 10 86
(Robert Cowell) *hld up: hdwy over 1f out: r.o: nt rch ldrs* **7/2**[1]

0340 **4** *1* **Sleepy Blue Ocean**[5] 6788 6-8-13 **77**......................(p) DanielTudhope 4 79
(John Balding) *a.p: rdn over 1f out: styd on same pce ins fnl f* **12/1**

2165 **5** *1/2* **Haajes**[14] 6525 8-8-12 **76**...(v) MickyFenton 2 77
(Paul Midgley) *prom: rdn over 2f out: styd on same pce fnl f* **16/1**

0-26 **6** *shd* **Key Ambition**[9] 6663 3-8-12 **77**...(t) NeilCallan 7 77
(Garry Moss) *chsd ldrs: rdn over 1f out: styd on same pce ins fnl f* **20/1**

2600 **7** *1/2* **Summerinthecity (IRE)**[113] 3183 5-9-5 **83**...................... JamesDoyle 3 82
(Ed de Giles) *prom: rdn over 1f out: no ex ins fnl f* **5/1**[2]

0000 **8** *nse* **Novellen Lad (IRE)**[25] 6165 7-9-7 **85**......................... StevieDonohoe 11 84
(Willie Musson) *s.i.s: hld up: rdn over 1f out: r.o ins fnl f: nrst fin* **5/1**[2]

3150 **9** *nk* **Where's Reiley (USA)**[19] 6368 6-9-2 **80**.............(b) FrankieMcDonald 13 78
(Alastair Lidderdale) *chsd ldr tl led over 2f out: rdn and hdd over 1f out: no ex ins fnl f* **25/1**

000 **10** *1 1/4* **Khawatim**[51] 5368 4-9-7 **85**.. MartinLane 9 79
(Noel Quinlan) *hld up: rdn over 1f out: n.d* **25/1**

0100 **11** *hd* **Taffe**[17] 6454 3-9-1 **80**... GrahamLee 5 73
(James Given) *trckd ldrs: racd keenly: rdn over 2f out: wknd fnl f* **17/2**

3013 **12** *1/2* **Salacia (IRE)**[18] 6417 3-8-13 **78**...................................... RoystonFfrench 1 70
(Ismail Mohammed) *s.i.s: sn rcvrd to ld: hdd over 2f out: wknd fnl f* **11/1**

1m 13.2s (-1.80) **Going Correction** -0.10s/f (Stan)
WFA 3 from 4yo+ 1lb **12** Ran SP% **122.0**
Speed ratings (Par 105): **108,106,105,103,103 102,102,102,101,100 99,99**
toteswingers 1&2 £15.60, 1&3 £8.80, 2&3 £6.50 CSF £78.69 CT £298.43 TOTE £13.60: £4.70, £2.60, £1.40; EX 114.00.
Owner Christopher James Allan **Bred** Paul Hensey **Trained** Spennymoor, Co Durham

FOCUS
A decent sprint handicap run at a strong pace.

6939 32RED CASINO H'CAP (DIV II) 5f 216y(P)
4:30 (4:33) (Class 4) (0-85,85) 3-Y-0+ **£4,204** (£1,251; £625; £312) **Stalls** Low

Form RPR

3003 **1** **My Son Max**[16] 6495 4-9-0 **78**.. FrannyNorton 2 88
(P J O'Gorman) *chsd ldr: rdn to ld ins fnl f: r.o* **9/1**

0500 **2** *1 3/4* **Partner (IRE)**[16] 6466 6-9-4 **82**..................................(b) DanielTudhope 7 86
(Noel Wilson) *a.p: rdn over 1f out: r.o* **7/1**[3]

5341 **3** *nk* **Delft**[19] 6369 3-9-3 **82**.. JamieSpencer 8 85
(Jeremy Noseda) *chsd ldrs: rdn over 2f out: r.o* **15/8**[1]

2100 **4** *hd* **Decision By One**[31] 6009 3-9-5 **84**................................(t) HayleyTurner 4 87
(Tom Dascombe) *led: rdn and hdd ins fnl f: styd on same pce* **5/1**[2]

-100 **5** *1/2* **Shahzan (IRE)**[113] 3183 4-9-7 **85**..[1] NeilCallan 9 86
(Roger Varian) *s.i.s: hdwy 1/2-way: shkn up over 1f out: edgd lft ins fnl f: r.o* **7/1**[3]

300 **6** *1 1/2* **Camache Queen (IRE)**[18] 6406 4-8-11 **75**............................ GrahamLee 1 71
(Denis Coakley) *chsd ldrs: pushed along over 2f out: no ex fnl f* **14/1**

066 **7** *1/2* **Baby Strange**[8] 6705 8-8-8 **77**..........................(v) MichaelJMMurphy(5) 5 72
(Derek Shaw) *s.i.s: hld up: r.o ins fnl f: nvr nrr* **12/1**

1101 **8** *2* **Johnny Cavagin**[50] 5388 3 -8-12**77**......................(t) RobbieFitzpatrick 13 65
(Richard Guest) *plld hrd and prom: rdn over 1f out: wknd ins fnl f* **9/1**
0 **9** *1 ¼* **Golconde (IRE)**[176] 1409 3 -8-13**78**.................................. JamesDoyle 6 62
(Robert Cowell) *s.i.s: rdn over 1f out: nvr on terms* **50/1**
0000 **10** *1 ¼* **Crown Choice**[16] 6495 7 -8-13**77**.............................. RoystonFfrench 3 57
(Paul Midgley) *hld up: plld hrd: rdn over 2f out: n.d* **20/1**
-000 **11** *16* **Swilly Ferry (USA)**[28] 2707 5 -8-8**79**.................. ShirleyTeasdale(7) 10
(David Nicholls) *mid-div: wknd over 2f out* **25/1**

1m 13.35s (-1.65)**Going Correction** -0.10s/f (Stan)
WFA 3 from 4yo+ 1lb **11**Ran SP%**121.4**
Speed ratings (Par 105): **107,104,104,104,103 101,100,98,96,94 73**
toteswingers 1&2 £11.90, 1&3 £5.70, 2&3 £5.70 CSF £71.51 CT £174.26 TOTE £10.20 : £2.30, £3.10, £1.40 ; EX 119.00 .
Owner Racing To The Max **Bred** Mrs Fiona Denniff **Trained** Newmarket, Suffolk

FOCUS
There weren't too many who could be seriously fancied for the second division of this handicap.
Delft Official explanation: jockey said filly never travelled

6940 DOWNLOAD OUR IPHONE APP H'CAP 1m 4f 50y (P)
5:00 (5:00) (Class 6) (0-60,60) 3-Y-0+ **£1,704** (£503; £251) **Stalls** Low

Form RPR
3250 **1** **Schmooze (IRE)**[16] 6474 3 -9-0**55**... DaleSwift 1 63
(Linda Perratt) *hld up: hdwy over 1f out: rdn to ld and hung rt ins fnl f: styd on wl* **7/1**[3]
0041 **2** *1 ¾* **Goldmadchen (GER)**[6] 6758 4 -9-5**53**................................ TomEaves 8 58
(Keith Dalgleish) *chsd ldrs: rdn over 1f out: styd on same pce ins fnl f* **6/1**[2]
0405 **3** *hd* **Quiet Appeal (IRE)**[5] 6516 3 -8-13**54**........................... FrannyNorton 3 59
(Mark Johnston) *led: rdn over 1f out: hdd and unable qck ins fnl f* **17/2**
2650 **4** *hd* **Layla's Boy**[16] 6478 5 -9-7**58**.......................................(bt) RyanClark(3) 12 63
(John Mackie) *pushed along in rr early: hdwy over 2f out: rdn over 1f out: styd on same pce ins fnl f* **14/1**
0-00 **5** *1* **Teide Peak (IRE)**[23] 6250 3 -9-3**58**.................................(e[1]) NeilCallan 2 62
(Paul D'Arcy) *hld up: hdwy over 4f out: rdn over 2f out: styng on same pce whn n.m.r towards fin* **14/1**
3250 **6** *1 ¼* **Sally Friday (IRE)**[23] 6262 4 -9-2**50**................................(p) GrahamLee 6 51
(Edwin Tuer) *chsd ldr over 7f: wnt 2nd again 4f out: rdn over 1f out: no ex ins fnl f* **16/1**
3253 **7** *¾* **King's Road**[11] 6616 7 -9-9**57**..(t) JamieSpencer 7 57
(Anabel K Murphy) *prom: lost pl over 7f out: hdwy over 2f out: rdn over 1f out: no ex fnl f* **11/4**[1]
1006 **8** *¾* **Transfer**[16] 6503 7 -9-12**60**..(p) JamesDoyle 4 59
(Richard Price) *hld up: rdn over 1f out: n.d* **16/1**
0346 **9** *1 ¾* **Millymonkin**[28] 6103 3 -9-3**58**...(t) JamesSullivan 11 54
(Michael Easterby) *hld up: hdwy 8f out: rdn over 3f out: wknd over 1f out* **8/1**
0-00 **10** *1 ¼* **Honest Strike (USA)**[11] 6616 5 -9-7**55**..........................(b) SeanQuinlan 9 49
(Daniel Mark Loughnane) *mid-div: rdn over 3f out: hung rt over 2f out: wknd wl over 1f out* **40/1**
0050 **11** *nk* **Visions Of Johanna (USA)**[30] 6056 7 -9-2**57**............. DavidBergin(7) 5 50
(John Balding) *prom: rdn over 2f out: wknd over 1f out* **16/1**
12 *68* **Flash Fox (GER)**[159] 5 -8-12**49**.......................................(t) PaulPickard(3) 10
(Brian Ellison) *hld up: plld hrd: hung rt and hdwy over 8f out: chsd ldr over 6f out tl 4f out: wknd over 2f out: eased: virtually p.u ins fnl f: t.o* **8/1**

2m 40.26s (-0.84)**Going Correction** -0.10s/f (Stan)
WFA 3 from 4yo+ 7lb **12**Ran SP%**119.6**
Speed ratings (Par 101): **98,96,96,96,95 95,94,94,92,92 91,46**
toteswingers 1&2 £8.40, 1&3 £7.80, 2&3 £9.10 CSF £49.15 CT £369.17 TOTE £9.70 : £2.30, £2.60, £2.90 ; EX 31.50 .
Owner Jackton Racing Club **Bred** Chris McHale And Oghill House Stud **Trained** East Kilbride, S Lanarks

FOCUS
There was plenty of early pace on in this moderate handicap.
Teide Peak (IRE) Official explanation: vet said gelding lost left fore-shoe
Flash Fox (GER) Official explanation: jockey said gelding hung right-handed

6941 32RED SUPPORTING BRITISH RACING H'CAP 1m 141y (P)
5:30 (5:30) (Class 6) (0-60,60) 3-Y-0+ **£1,704** (£503; £251) **Stalls** Low

Form RPR
5405 **1** **Star City (IRE)**[6] 6479 3 -9-6**60**... TomEaves 9 69
(Michael Dods) *chsd ldrs: led wl over 1f out: drvn out* **10/1**
06 **2** *½* **Goal (IRE)**[14] 6528 4 -9-0**53**...(t) MarkCoumbe(3) 3 61
(Charles Smith) *s.i.s: hld up: hdwy over 4f out: rdn and ev ch over 1f out: hung lft ins fnl f: styd on* **16/1**
6240 **3** *¾* **Tiger Webb**[13] 6561 4 -9-7**57**.. JamesSullivan 8 64+
(Michael Easterby) *mid-div: sn pushed along: hdwy over 2f out: rdn and nt clr run ins fnl f: swtchd rt: r.o* **10/3**[2]
454 **4** *¾* **Source Of Light (IRE)**[3] 6690 3 -9-5**59**.......................... HayleyTurner 5 63
(Daniel Mark Loughnane) *mid-div: hdwy over 2f out: rdn over 1f out: styd on same pce ins fnl f* **6/1**
601 **5** *½* **Cross The Boss (IRE)**[28] 6106 5 -9-10**60**..................(t) JamieSpencer 2 63+
(Ben Haslam) *s.i.s: hld up: hdwy over 1f out: nt clr run ins fnl f: r.o: nt rch ldrs* **9/2**[3]
515 **6** *3 ½* **Archina (IRE)**[48] 5459 3 -9-4**58**.. HarryBentley 7 53
(Chris Wall) *prom: rdn over 2f out: styd on same pce fr over 1f out* **9/1**
0-36 **7** *nse* **Pastures New**[72] 4582 4 -9-7**57**.. SeanLevey 1 52
(Violet M Jordan) *chsd ldrs: rdn over 2f out: wknd ins fnl f* **40/1**
-604 **8** *1 ½* **Eilean Mor**[21] 6309 4 -8-13**54**.................................. MatthewLawson(5) 11 46
(R Mike Smith) *hld up: rdn over 3f out: hdwy over 2f out: nvr trbld ldrs* **33/1**
6223 **9** *½* **Thrust Control (IRE)**[16] 6480 5 -8-13**56**.............(p) JacobButterfield(7) 4 46
(Tracy Waggott) *led: rdn and hdd wl over 1f out: wknd fnl f* **12/1**
0600 **10** *2* **Rock Of Monet**[54] 5247 3 -9-0**54**.................................... StevieDonohoe 6 40
(Ian Williams) *hld up: rdn over 2f out: a in rr* **40/1**
00 **11** *8* **Ellies Image**[51] 5338 5 -9-3**53**...................................... DanielTudhope 13 20
(Brian Baugh) *s.i.s: rdn over 2f out: a in rr* **33/1**
3521 **12** *2* **Rasselas (IRE)**[10] 6646 5 -9-6**56**..................................(v) AdrianNicholls 10 19
(David Nicholls) *sn pushed along to chse ldr: rdn and ev ch over 2f out: wknd over 1f out* **5/2**[1]

1m 49.44s (-1.06)**Going Correction** -0.10s/f (Stan)
WFA 3 from 4yo+ 4lb **12**Ran SP%**127.5**
Speed ratings (Par 101): **100,99,98,98,97 94,94,93,92,91 83,82**
toteswingers 1&2 £32.00, 1&3 £8.10, 2&3 £11.70 CSF £164.96 CT £668.72 TOTE £10.80 : £1.80, £6.50 , £1.90 ; EX 204.00 .
Owner Appleton Davison Dods **Bred** Michael Munnelly **Trained** Denton, Co Durham
■ Stewards' Enquiry : Mark Coumbe three-day ban: careless riding (Oct 22-24)

FOCUS
Another weak race.
Cross The Boss (IRE) Official explanation: jockey said gelding was denied a clear run
T/Jkpt: Not won. T/Plt: £390.90 to a £1 stake. Pool: £68,306.69 - 127.54 winning tickets T/Qpdt: £97.60 to a £1 stake. Pool: £5,645.26 - 42.80 winning tickets CR

6803 CHANTILLY (R-H)
Monday, October 8
OFFICIAL GOING: Turf: very soft changing to heavy after race 6 (2.05)

6942a PRIX HEROD (LISTED RACE) (2YO) (TURF) 7f
12:30 (12:00) 2-Y-O **£22,916** (£9,166; £6,875 ; £4,583 ; £2,291)

RPR
1 **Kensea (FR)**[27] 6129 2 -8-13**0**.. FabriceVeron 8 100
(H-A Pantall, France) **8/1**
2 *1 ¾* **Linngaro (FR)**[29] 6086 2 -9-2**0**...................................... UmbertoRispoli 6 99
(Mario Hofer, Germany) **11/1**
3 *hd* **Holy Dazzle**[41] 2 -8-13**0**.. RonanThomas 7 95
(J E Pease, France) **17/1**
4 *1 ¾* **Gengis (FR)**[26] 2 -9-2**0**... StephanePasquier 1 94
(G Doleuze, France) **23/10**[1]
5 *¾* **Mister Big Shuffle (GER)**[40] 5755 2 -9-2**0** Christophe-PatriceLemaire 2 92
(M Figge, Germany) **19/1**
6 *½* **Paiza (IRE)**[37] 2 -9-2**0**.. MaximeGuyon 3 91
(H-A Pantall, France) **19/5**[2]
7 *hd* **Dibajj (FR)**[26] 2 -8-13**0**... OlivierPeslier 9 87
(C Ferland, France) **9/1**
8 *3* **Whipper Snapper (FR)**[73] 2 -9-2**0**............................ IoritzMendizabal 4 83
(E J O'Neill, France) **15/2**
9 *½* **Tipping Over (IRE)**[14] 6550 2 -8-13**0**............................. GeraldMosse 5 78
(Hugo Palmer) *broke wl: sn prom: led after 2f: rdn 2f out: hdd 1 1/2f out: no ex: fdd fnl f* **63/10**[3]

1m 31.8s (5.70) **9**Ran SP%**116.6**
WIN (incl. 1 euro stake): 9.00. PLACES: 3.10, 4.60, 5.90. DF: 46.30. SF: 95.50 .
Owner Guy Pariente **Bred** G Pariente **Trained** France

NOTEBOOK
Tipping Over (IRE) went close in an Irish sales race on testing ground on her previous start, but she was nowhere near her best this time.

6943a PRIX DE BONNEVAL (LISTED RACE) (3YO+) (TURF) 5f 110y
1:35 (12:00) 3-Y-0+ **£21,666** (£8,666; £6,500 ; £4,333 ; £2,166)

RPR
1 **Sabratah**[66] 4790 4 -9-0**0**... FabriceVeron 4 113
(H-A Pantall, France) **21/1**
2 *1 ¾* **Myasun (FR)**[50] 5 -8-13**0**.. MaximeGuyon 7 106
(C Baillet, France) **19/5**[2]
3 *½* **Lui Rei (ITY)**[20] 6346 6 -8-13**0**... GeraldMosse 2 104
(Robert Cowell) *broke wl: prom on ins rail: wnt 2nd and chal for ld 1 1/2f out: r.o wl u.p fnl f: lost 2nd fnl strides* **11/1**
4 *2* **Flash Mash (USA)**[22] 6292 4 -9-0**0**.........................(b[1]) GregoryBenoist 9 99
(X Nakkachdji, France) **15/2**[3]
5 *snk* **Gammarth (FR)**[43] 5648 4 -9-3**0**......................... ChristopheSoumillon 8 101
(H-A Pantall, France) **5/2**[1]
6 *2 ½* **Mariol (FR)**[22] 9 -9-3**0**.. IoritzMendizabal 13 93
(Robert Collet, France) **11/1**
7 *2 ½* **Pandar**[120] 2967 3 -9-3**0**... OlivierPeslier 6 86
(Robert Cowell) *prom early in centre of trck: rdn but no ex fr 1/2-way: styd fnl f* **10/1**
8 *¾* **Namera (GER)**[22] 3 -8-9**0**.. FilipMinarik 14 75
(P Vovcenko, Germany) **23/1**
9 *1* **Fred Lalloupet**[92] 3901 5 -9-3**0**... FlavienPrat 11 79
(D Smaga, France) **11/1**
10 *2 ½* **Nadeaud (FR)**[109] 3365 3 -9-0**0**...................................... ThierryJarnet 3 69
(D Guillemin, France) **20/1**
0 **Chopouest (FR)**[29] 5 -8-13**0**...................................(b) FredericSpanu 12
(T Castanheira, France) **27/1**
0 **Flavio Forte (GER)** 3 -8-13**0**... ADeVries 10
(U Stoltefuss, Germany) **19/1**

1m 6.02s (1.52) **12**Ran SP%**117.3**
WIN (incl. 1 euro stake): 22.00. PLACES: 6.00, 2.20, 4.50. DF: 60.40. SF: 97.10 .
Owner Guy Heald **Bred** Shutford Stud **Trained** France

NOTEBOOK
Lui Rei (ITY) seemed to better the form of his recent Yarmouth win, despite the ground possibly being softer than ideal.
Pandar couldn't match his decent Italian form on his debut for Robert Cowell, but he may yet do better.

6944a (Foreign Racing) See RI

6430 BRIGHTON (L-H)
Tuesday, October 9
OFFICIAL GOING: Soft changing to heavy after race 1 (2.20)
Wind: medium, behind Weather: rain

6945 BLAKES BUTCHERS MEDIAN AUCTION MAIDEN STKS 6f 209y
2:20 (2:20) (Class 5) 2-Y-O **£2,264** (£673; £336 ; £168) **Stalls** Low

Form RPR
4 **1** **Gigawatt**[43] 5661 2 -9-3**0**... FergusSweeney 5 76
(Jim Boyle) *racd keenly: w ldr: rdn and drew clr w ldr over 2f out: led ins fnl f: styd on wl* **16/1**
520 **2** *¾* **Nenge Mboko**[70] 4688 2 -9-3**76**.. PatCosgrave 7 74
(George Baker) *led: rdn and drew wnr over 2f out: hdd ins fnl f: styd on same pce after* **1/1**[1]
0 **3** *9* **David's Secret**[17] 6486 2 -9-3**0**.. DarryllHolland 6 50
(Hughie Morrison) *dwlt: rcvrd to chse ldrs after 1f: rdn and outpcd by ldrs over 2f out: plugged on but wl btn after* **5/2**[2]
0 **4** *hd* **Vergality Ridge (IRE)**[12] 6609 2 -8-12**0**............................ DarrenEgan(5) 2 49
(Ronald Harris) *broke wl: t.k.h and grad stdd bk to rr: edgd lft and wnt modest 4th 2f out: plugged on but no imp after* **16/1**

402 **5** *2* **Spanish Art**[22] 6301 2-8-10 70 WilliamTwiston-Davies(7) 4 44
(Richard Hannon) *in tch: rdn and struggling 4f out: dropped to rr and lost tch w ldrs over 2f out: plugged on but wl btn after* **13/2**[3]

00 **6** *3 1/4* **Kraken (IRE)**[21] 6330 2-9-0 0 (v) PatrickHills(3) 1 35
(Luca Cumani) *chsd ldrs: rdn and outpcd over 2f out: sn wknd and wl bhd over 1f out* **40/1**

66 **7** *2 1/4* **Valley Of Wings**[15] 6533 2-9-3 0 HayleyTurner 3 29
(Robert Cowell) *dwlt: t.k.h: hld up in tch: rdn 4f out: dropped to rr 3f out: wl bhd over 1f out* **20/1**

1m 26.55s (3.45) **Going Correction** +0.55s/f (Yiel) **7** Ran SP% **110.9**
Speed ratings (Par 95): **102,101,90,90,88 84,82**
toteswingers 1&2 £2.70, 2&3 £1.20, 1&3 £4.40 CSF £30.83 TOTE £16.90: £4.10, £1.60; EX 43.00.
Owner Epsom Equine Spa Partnership **Bred** Paddock Space **Trained** Epsom, Surrey

FOCUS
A fair juvenile auction maiden in which they went a decent gallop. The winning time was just under six seconds slower than standard, and the ground was changed to heavy after the race. The first two dominated from the turn in and finished clear. The form could be worth 3lb more.

NOTEBOOK
Gigawatt, out of a half-sister to smart 6f-7f 2yo winner Manston, was returning from a six-week break since finishing fourth of nine on his debut over this trip at Epsom on good ground, and found marked improvement on this softer going. He came over to the near rail with the runner-up entering the home straight, about 3f out, and crucially wouldn't give up the rail to the favourite in an engaging tussle before going on. He may have more to offer in nurseries under similar conditions this autumn. (op 14-1 tchd 18-1)
Nenge Mboko was returning from a ten-week break since a modest effort in a decent 6f Glorious Goodwood maiden. He set a fair form standard based on his penultimate neck second over 1f shorter on soft ground at Epsom in July. He appeared to get this trip fine but wasn't back to that level after the break. He is a half-brother to the useful 5f-6f, including Group 3, winner Ringmoor Down, and a drop back to 6f on soft ground wouldn't do any harm in the weeks ahead. (op 10-11)
David's Secret may be worth stepping up to 1m on this showing. (op 10-3)
Vergality Ridge(IRE) certainly promised to appreciate these conditions on breeding, and improved on a moderate Wolverhampton debut the previous month. (tchd 20-1)
Spanish Art was entitled to be there or thereabouts on form but was struggling fully 4f from home on this ground. (tchd 5-1)

6946 HARDINGSCATERING.CO.UK NURSERY 6f 209y
2:50 (2:50) (Class 5) (0-75,72) 2-Y-O **£2,264** (£673; £336; £168) **Stalls** Low

Form RPR
5545 **1** **Santo Prince (USA)**[11] 6629 2-9-7 **72** HayleyTurner 8 75
(Michael Bell) *chsd ldrs: rdn 3f out: chsd clr ldr ent fnl f: swtchd lft and styd on u.p to chal ins fnl f: led fnl 50yds: rdn out* **8/1**

5535 **2** *1/2* **Mowhoob**[57] 5155 2-9-7 **72** NickyMackay 4 74
(John Gosden) *chsd ldrs tl led and racd against stands' rail 3f out: rdn over 2f out: clr over 1f out: drvn and hrd pressed ins fnl f: hdd and no ex fnl 50yds* **9/2**[3]

043 **3** *5* **Scepticism (USA)**[18] 6423 2-8-12 **63** FrannyNorton 3 52
(Mark Johnston) *sn led: rdn and hdd 3f out: drvn and btn over 1f out: wl hld 3rd and plugged on same pce fnl f* **4/1**[2]

000 **4** *1* **Perseverent Pete (USA)**[77] 4433 2-7-12 **54** DarrenEgan(5) 1 40
(Christine Dunnett) *chsd ldr tl 3f out: rdn 3f out: outpcd and btn over 1f out: wl hld and plugged on same pce fnl f* **9/1**

0445 **5** *1 1/2* **Fair Comment**[24] 6253 2-9-5 **70** FergusSweeney 2 53
(Michael Blanshard) *in tch in midfield: rdn and outpcd whn hung rt over 2f out: no imp and wl hld fnl 2f* **16/1**

1460 **6** *1 1/2* **Stupenda**[40] 5763 2-8-7 **58** TadhgO'Shea 6 37
(Denis Coakley) *dropped to rr and rdn after 2f: a struggling after: no ch w ldrs fnl 2f: plugged on past btn horses ins fnl f* **25/1**

5600 **7** *1* **Must Be Me**[9] 6699 2-9-4 **69** (p) DarryllHolland 9 45
(Eve Johnson Houghton) *in tch: rdn ent fnl 4f: outpcd and btn wl over 2f out: n.d after* **7/1**

000 **8** *1 1/2* **Pivotal Silence**[20] 6366 2-9-0 **65** IanMongan 7 37
(Amanda Perrett) *dropped to rr and rdn over 4f out: n.d after and wl hld whn edgd lft u.p over 1f out* **12/1**

524 **9** *9* **Arctic Admiral (IRE)**[43] 5655 2-9-5 **70** SeanLevey 5 23
(Richard Hannon) *in tch: rdn and struggling 3f out: wkng whn hmpd over 2f out: wl bhd and eased ins fnl f* **3/1**[1]

1m 27.7s (4.60) **Going Correction** +0.55s/f (Yiel) **9** Ran SP% **114.2**
Speed ratings (Par 95): **95,94,88,87,85 84,83,81,71**
toteswingers 1&2 £4.20, 2&3 £3.80, 1&3 £5.70 CSF £43.37 CT £167.22 TOTE £10.30: £2.80, £1.30, £1.80; EX 37.10.
Owner Leon Caine **Bred** Mogeely Stud **Trained** Newmarket, Suffolk

FOCUS
A fair nursery handicap in which they went a respectable gallop. The first two raced near the rail and this isn't form to take too literally.

NOTEBOOK
Santo Prince(USA) weakened 2f out on heavy ground returning from a two-month break over 1f shorter at Haydock the previous month, and his chance depended on reproducing the level of form shown when 2l fourth of eight in a better-class 7f Newmarket nursery on good to firm ground on his penultimate start in July. He duly did just that, relishing these conditions and following through the runner-up on the near rail, before going on about 100 yards from the line, to post a cosy first success. He should remain competitive once reassessed.
Mowhoob was returning from a two-month break since a fair fifth over 1m at Kempton off this mark and had run well over this trip at Kempton in a good maiden on his penultimate start. He has reproduced a similar level of form on this occasion.
Scepticism(USA) finished a modest fourth in a fair extended 7f Chester maiden on good to soft ground on his penultimate start, and has reproduced a similar level of form.
Perseverent Pete(USA) was returning from an 11-week break and was beaten over 1f out before keeping on at one pace. (op 12-1 tchd 14-1)
Fair Comment didn't offer much.
Arctic Admiral(IRE) proved disappointing under these conditions.

6947 SIS MAIDEN STKS 7f 214y
3:20 (3:21) (Class 4) 2-Y-O **£3,428** (£1,020; £509; £254) **Stalls** Low

Form RPR
6 **1** **Sesentum**[25] 6214 2-9-0 0 PatrickHills(3) 1 78
(Luca Cumani) *chsd ldrs: rdn over 2f out: drvn and ev ch ent fnl f: led ins fnl f: styd on wl* **10/1**[3]

245 **2** *1 1/4* **Sublimation (IRE)**[3] 6876 2-8-10 0 WilliamTwiston-Davies(7) 3 75
(Richard Hannon) *dwlt: hld up in tch: hdwy to chal over 2f out: sn rdn: led and edgd lft over 1f out: hdd and no ex ins fnl f* **1/1**[1]

3 **3** *4 1/2* **Backstage Tour**[13] 6572 2-8-12 0 AntiocoMurgia(5) 4 65
(Mahmood Al Zarooni) *racd keenly: led tl 4f out: styd upsides ldrs: rdn over 2f out: no ex and btn over 1f out: wknd ins fnl f* **11/8**[2]

0 **4** *3 1/4* **Couloir Extreme (IRE)**[13] 6572 2-9-3 0 GeorgeBaker 2 58
(Gary Moore) *t.k.h: w ldr tl led 4f out: hdd over 1f out: sn btn and fdd ins fnl frlong* **40/1**

34 **5** *22* **House Of Orange (IRE)**[26] 6168 2-9-3 0 FrannyNorton 5 18+
(Mark Johnston) *v.s.a: nvr gng wl and a in last: lost tch over 1f out: eased ins fnl f: t.o* **18/1**

1m 41.16s (5.16) **Going Correction** +0.55s/f (Yiel) **5** Ran SP% **108.9**
Speed ratings (Par 97): **96,94,90,87,65**
CSF £20.45 TOTE £14.60: £4.20, £2.50; EX 24.30.
Owner Scuderia Rencati Srl **Bred** D D & Mrs J P Clee **Trained** Newmarket, Suffolk
■ Stewards' Enquiry : William Twiston-Davies two-day ban: used whip above permitted level (Oct 23-24)

FOCUS
A fair juvenile maiden in which they went a sensible gallop on the heavy ground. The winner built on his debut form.

NOTEBOOK
Sesentum was a 34,000gns purchase as a yearling who ran green when a modest sixth on his debut at Wolverhampton the previous month. He progressed markedly under these conditions, where his stamina won the day, after travelling well. He looks a decent 1m2f handicapper in the making. (op 12-1 tchd 9-1)
Sublimation(IRE) set the form standard after a fair 5l fifth in a 1m soft-ground Newmarket maiden three days previously, and a good fourth in a decent 7f Newbury maiden on good to firm ground the previous month. He wasn't at his best here after such a short break between races on very testing ground. He should be able to win something similar, and is a fairly decent middle-distance handicapper of the future in any case. (tchd 10-11 and 11-10)
Backstage Tour raced keenly on the testing ground, and was beaten over 1f out, which was disappointing after a fair debut on soft ground at Goodwood the previous month. (op 6-4 tchd 5-4)

6948 HARDINGS CATERING SERVICES APPRENTICE H'CAP 1m 3f 196y
3:50 (3:50) (Class 6) (0-55,60) 3-Y-O+ **£1,617** (£481; £240; £120) **Stalls** High

Form RPR
0504 **1** **Maccabees**[14] 6567 3-8-8 **49** ow1 NedCurtis 8 59
(Roger Curtis) *hld up wl off the pce in last pair: stdy hdwy 3f out: rdn and styd on wl fr over 1f out to ld ins fnl f: sn clr: being clsd on towards fin but a gng to hold on* **12/1**

0014 **2** *3/4* **Beacon Lady**[18] 6442 3-8-10 **51** RachealKneller 11 60
(William Knight) *stdd s: hld up wl off the pce in rr: c nrest to stands' rail and hdwy 3f out: str run and edging lft over 1f out: chsd clr wnr ins fnl f: r.o wl but nvr quite getting to wnr* **5/1**[2]

0051 **3** *8* **Lady Romanza (IRE)**[5] 6814 3-9-5 **60** 6ex (p) NathanSweeney 12 57
(Brendan Powell) *in tch: rdn to chse ldr 3f out: no ex ent fnl 2f: outpcd by wnr and wknd ins fnl f* **6/1**[3]

5033 **4** *2 3/4* **Here Comes Jeanie**[33] 5974 3-8-5 **46** oh1 NatashaEaton 3 39
(Michael Madgwick) *in tch: rdn to chse ldrs over 2f out: outpcd and btn jst ins fnl f: wknd fnl 150yds* **12/1**

5063 **5** *4 1/2* **Essell**[40] 5770 3-9-0 **55** WilliamTwiston-Davies 7 41
(Mick Channon) *chsd ldrs tl wnt 2nd over 6f out: led over 4f out: drew clr over 2f out: drvn over 1f out: hdd ins fnl f: sn btn and fdd fnl 150yds* **13/2**

0500 **6** *1 3/4* **Iron Butterfly**[20] 6365 3-8-9 **55** RyanTate(5) 13 38
(James Eustace) *in tch in midfield: rdn 5f out: no imp u.p 2f out: wl btn ent fnl f* **8/1**

3600 **7** *1 1/2* **Corn Maiden**[25] 6210 3-8-3 **49** ow2 LewisWalsh(5) 2 30
(Phil McEntee) *chsd ldr tl over 6f out: rdn and lost pl over 4f out: plugged on but n.d fnl 2f* **20/1**

1461 **8** *1 1/2* **Chasin' Rainbows**[10] 6690 4-9-5 **53** ThomasBrown 5 32
(Sylvester Kirk) *hld up in tch towards rr of main gp: hdwy over 2f out: rdn and no prog over 1f out: wknd fnl f* **9/2**[1]

5-35 **9** *2 1/2* **Dazzling Begum**[14] 6567 7-8-9 **46** oh1 (p) TimClark(3) 6 21
(Lydia Pearce) *hld up in tch: hdwy on inner over 4f out: rdn and wknd over 2f out* **28/1**

5034 **10** *6* **Satwa Ballerina**[61] 5022 4-8-13 **52** (b) RobertTart(5) 14 18
(Mark Rimmer) *hld up in tch towards rr of main gp: c towards centre and effrt 3f out: no real prog and wknd 2f out* **20/1**

6265 **11** *1* **Royal Defence (IRE)**[82] 4244 6-9-5 **53** IanBurns 10 18
(Michael Quinn) *in tch: rdn 1/2-way: hdwy to chse ldr 4f out tl 3f out: wknd 2f out: wl btn and eased fnl f* **12/1**

0505 **12** *6* **One For The Girls**[5] 6828 3-8-2 **46** (t) HannahNunn(3) 9
(Nicky Vaughan) *racd keenly: led tl hdd over 4f out: sn dropped out: wl bhd fnl 2f: t.o* **25/1**

003 **13** *2 1/2* **Turbulent Priest**[159] 1770 4-8-10 **47** (b) GemmaTutty(3) 1
(Zoe Davison) *s.i.s: t.k.h: hld up in tch: rdn and struggling 3f out: wknd 2f out: t.o* **20/1**

260 **14** *26* **Femme Royale**[14] 5198 4-8-12 **46** (p) NoelGarbutt 4
(Richard Price) *chsd ldrs tl 5f out: lost pl and bhd 3f out: t.o fnl 2f* **33/1**

2m 43.16s (10.46) **Going Correction** +0.775s/f (Yiel)
WFA 3 from 4yo+ 7lb **14** Ran SP% **121.2**
Speed ratings (Par 101): **96,95,90,88,85 84,83,82,80,76 75,71,70,52**
toteswingers 1&2 £19.80, 2&3 £6.70, 1&3 £22.00 CSF £64.27 CT £407.86 TOTE £13.50: £3.90, £1.80, £2.30; EX 114.80.
Owner Mrs Florence Dean **Bred** Mrs J A Cornwell **Trained** Lambourn, Berks
■ Stewards' Enquiry : Ned Curtis four-day ban: used whip above permitted level (Oct 23-26)

FOCUS
A moderate middle-distance handicap for apprentice riders in which they went a fair gallop in the testing conditions. Unlike most other races on the card, the runners did not come across to the stands' rail in the straight. The winner, on a good mark on 2yo form, had not shown much this year was and rated up slightly 3yo form. Could be worth bit more with third 4lb off latest selling win.

6949 SMITH AND WESTERN RESTAURANTS' H'CAP 1m 1f 209y
4:20 (4:20) (Class 6) (0-65,65) 3-Y-O+ **£1,617** (£481; £240; £120) **Stalls** High

Form RPR
4123 **1** **Tawseef (IRE)**[29] 6097 4-9-4 **59** IanMongan 9 73+
(Roy Brotherton) *in tch: c to r against stands' rail and led wl over 2f out: drew readily clr over 1f out: easily* **2/1**[1]

6400 **2** *4* **Kampai**[18] 6458 4-9-7 **62** AdamBeschizza 3 66
(Julia Feilden) *hld up in tch towards rr: rdn and hdwy in centre to chse clr wnr over 1f out: no imp on wnr but kpt on for clr 2nd* **16/1**

1550 **3** *2 3/4* **Highlife Dancer**[17] 6478 4-9-2 **62** (v) CharlesBishop(5) 2 61
(Mick Channon) *chsd ldrs: rdn over 3f out: 3rd and wl hld fr over 1f out: plugged on* **9/1**

6040 **4** *3/4* **Chronic Flame (TUR)**[20] 6364 3-8-13 **59** (t) HayleyTurner 1 56
(Marcus Tregoning) *t.k.h: chsd ldr tl over 2f out: sn drvn and no ex: 4th and plugged on same pce fnl f* **7/1**[3]

-020 **5** *3 3/4* **Finlodex**[26] 6172 5-9-8 **63** FrankieMcDonald 8 53
(Murty McGrath) *chsd ldrs: rdn and unable qck over 2f out: wknd over 1f out* **50/1**

4000 **6** ¾ **Bennelong**[24] 6251 6-9-5 **65**....(p) DarrenEgan(5) 12 53
(Richard Rowe) *hld up in tch in rr: swtchd lft and sme hdwy 2f out: no imp fr over 1f out: nvr trbld ldrs* **10/1**

3050 **7** 5 **Chrissycross (IRE)**[67] 4776 3-8-6 **55**....(b) MarkCoumbe(3) 4 33
(Roger Teal) *in tch: rdn and no prog over 2f out: wknd over 1f out* **16/1**

030- **8** 8 **Jodawes (USA)**[267] 6789 5-9-3 **58**.... GeorgeBaker 14 20
(Gary Moore) *led tl wl over 2f out: wknd u.p over 1f out: eased ins fnl f* **11/2**[2]

4534 **9** 19 **Final Delivery**[68] 4727 3-9-1 **61**....(b[1]) PatCosgrave 13
(Jim Boyle) *stdd s: plld hrd: hld up in rr: lost tch over 2f out: t.o and eased ins fnl f* **12/1**

4243 **10** 3 **Turjuman (USA)**[31] 6055 7-9-3 **63**....(p) NatashaEaton(5) 7
(Alan Bailey) *in tch towards rr: rdn 4f out: lost tch 2f out: t.o and eased ins fnl f* **14/1**

1240 **11** 2 **Fire In Babylon (IRE)**[194] 1092 4-9-2 **57**.... SebSanders 6
(Michael Wigham) *hld up in tch: rdn and effrt 4f out: wknd u.p 2f out: t.o and eased ins fnl f* **11/1**

2m 11.12s (7.52) **Going Correction** +0.775s/f (Yiel)
WFA 3 from 4yo+ 5lb **11** Ran SP% **116.7**
Speed ratings (Par 101): **100,96,94,94,91 90,86,80,64,62 60**
toteswingers 1&2 £12.90, 2&3 £28.20, 1&3 £7.20 CSF £37.94 CT £241.75 TOTE £2.60: £2.10, £4.30, £1.50; EX 40.20.
Owner Millend Racing Club **Bred** Shadwell Estate Company Limited **Trained** Elmley Castle, Worcs

FOCUS
A modest handicap in which the early gallop appeared slow. The winner again raced closest to the stands' rail in the straight, and he has been rated as returning the form of his C&D win in July.

6950 ITALIAN BRASSERIE BRIGHTON MARINA H'CAP 7f 214y
4:50 (4:50) (Class 6) (0-65,67) 3-Y-0+ **£1,617** (£481; £240; £120) **Stalls** Low

Form RPR

0132 **1** **Saint Irene**[23] 6274 3-8-10 **57**.... HayleyTurner 15 69
(Michael Blanshard) *in tch: c to r against stands' rail and hdwy to press ldrs 3f out: ev ch and rdn 2f out: led over 1f out: styd on wl and clr ins fnl f* **11/4**[1]

0400 **2** 3 ¼ **Byrd In Hand (IRE)**[99] 3705 5-8-8 **59** ow1. WilliamTwiston-Davies(7) 12 64
(John Bridger) *chsd ldr: rdn and ev ch over 2f out: wnt 2nd but outpcd by wnr 1f out: plugged on* **17/2**[3]

-641 **3** ¾ **Uncle Dermot (IRE)**[6] 6801 4-9-4 **67** 6ex.... BrendanPowell(5) 3 70
(Brendan Powell) *s.i.s: bhd: hdwy over 3f out: chsd ldrs and drvn over 1f out: edgd lft and plugged on same pce ins fnl f* **3/1**[2]

0156 **4** ¾ **Daffydowndilly**[22] 6302 4-9-6 **64**....(bt) DarryllHolland 14 65
(Hughie Morrison) *t.k.h: hld up in midfield: hdwy u.p 2f out: styd on same pce and hung lft ins fnl f* **9/1**

4505 **5** ¾ **Salient**[68] 4727 8-9-1 **59**.... KierenFox 4 58
(Michael Attwater) *led: rdn over 2f out: hdd and no ex over 1f out: plugged on same pce and lost 3 pls fnl f* **16/1**

0366 **6** 5 **Hereford Boy**[6] 6801 8-9-4 **65**....(v) PatrickHills(3) 1 53
(Dean Ivory) *hld up in tch: effrt u.p 2f out: 6th and no hdwy over 1f out: wknd fnl f* **10/1**

0330 **7** 7 **Whinging Willie (IRE)**[32] 5991 3-8-10 **57**.... AdamBeschizza 11 29
(Gary Moore) *chsd ldrs: lost pl u.p over 1f out: wl btn over 1f out* **18/1**

0063 **8** nk **Gay Gallivanter**[44] 5632 4-8-0 **51** oh6.... IanBurns(7) 8 22
(Michael Quinn) *in tch in midfield: drvn and no rspnse over 4f out: lost pl 3f out: n.d fnl 2f* **40/1**

-300 **9** 18 **Khajaaly (IRE)**[22] 6319 5-9-0 **63**.... DarrenEgan(5) 5
(Julia Feilden) *t.k.h: chsd ldrs tl rdn and no ex jst over 2f out: wl btn and eased fnl f: t.o* **33/1**

4040 **10** hd **Signora Frasi (IRE)**[74] 4531 7-8-13 **57**.... FergusSweeney 6
(Tony Newcombe) *in tch towards rr: rdn and no hdwy jst over 2f out: wl bhd 1f out: t.o* **10/1**

6526 **11** 3 ¾ **Spiritual Art**[23] 6278 6-8-9 **56**....(v) MarkCoumbe(3) 10
(Luke Dace) *in tch in midfield: rdn and no rspnse over 2f out: sn wknd: t.o* **14/1**

35-5 **12** 27 **Kavachi (IRE)**[14] 6568 9-9-0 **58**.... SebSanders 9
(Gary Moore) *sn pushed along towards rr: bhd and lost tch 3f out: t.o* **33/1**

1m 42.01s (6.01) **Going Correction** +0.775s/f (Yiel)
WFA 3 from 4yo+ 3lb **12** Ran SP% **116.5**
Speed ratings (Par 101): **100,96,96,95,94 89,82,82,64,64 60,33**
toteswingers 1&2 £5.40, 2&3 £6.20, 1&3 £3.30 CSF £25.72 CT £75.60 TOTE £3.80: £1.70, £2.30, £1.40; EX 26.20.
Owner The Breeze-In Partnership **Bred** Usk Valley Stud **Trained** Upper Lambourn, Berks
■ Stewards' Enquiry : Kieren Fox three month ban; used whip above permitted level (4th offence of 7 days or more since May 12) (Oct 26 - Jan 25).

FOCUS
A modest handicap in which the early lead was contested. This was a personal best from the winner on ratings, but she had the stands' rail to help late on.

6951 HARDINGS CATERING, BRIGHTON H'CAP 5f 213y
5:20 (5:20) (Class 6) (0-60,60) 3-Y-0+ **£1,617** (£481; £240; £120) **Stalls** Low

Form RPR

5166 **1** **Mucky Molly**[32] 6003 4-8-13 **52**.... SebSanders 15 60
(Olivia Maylam) *styd wd thrght: chsd ldrs: chsd ldr and drvn 2f out: racing on stands' rail and swtchd lft over 1f out: led ins fnl f: kpt on* **6/1**[3]

5640 **2** ½ **See The Storm**[62] 4966 4-8-7 **46** oh1.... NickyMackay 16 52
(Ian Williams) *styd wd thrght: chsd ldrs: rdn and ev ch over 1f out: led ent fnl f: hdd and one pce ins fnl f* **11/2**[2]

4365 **3** nk **Trust Me Boy**[32] 5999 4-8-7 **46** oh1.... FrankieMcDonald 10 51
(John E Long) *sn rdn along and reminder after 1f: towards rr: c against stands' rail 3f out: stl plenty to do over 1f out: str run 1f out: swtchd lft and chsd ldrs fnl 100yds: could nt quite rch ldrs* **16/1**

5000 **4** 2 ¾ **Pose (IRE)**[43] 5658 5-8-7 **46**....(t[1]) AdamBeschizza 6 43
(Roger Ingram) *hld up in rr: styd on inner 3f out: rdn and hdwy to ld gp and chse ldrs ent fnl f: one pce after* **33/1**

0-33 **5** 2 ½ **Nordic Light (USA)**[43] 5701 8-8-2 **46** oh1....(t) JemmaMarshall(5) 3 35
(Mrs A Malzard, Jersey) *led: rdn and hdd over 2f out: btn over 1f out: wknd ins fnl f* **40/1**

6100 **6** nk **Athaakeel (IRE)**[11] 6640 6-8-10 **54**....(b) DarrenEgan(5) 2 42
(Ronald Harris) *chsd ldrs: styd on inner 3f out: drvn and struggling 2f out: wknd 1f out* **10/1**

6040 **7** 2 ¾ **Microlight**[77] 4438 4-8-7 **46**....(b) RichardThomas 9 25
(John E Long) *chsd ldr tl led over 2f out: c to r against stands' rail over 1f out: sn hdd & wknd ins fnl f* **18/1**

2420 **8** 2 **Imjin River (IRE)**[13] 6585 5-8-9 **53**.... NatashaEaton(5) 11 25
(William Stone) *chsd ldrs: rdn and struggling over 2f out: wknd over 1f out: fdd fnl f* **9/1**

0-00 **9** ¾ **Lady On Top (IRE)**[13] 6586 4-8-2 **48**.... NoelGarbutt(7) 14 18
(Nerys Dutfield) *styd wd: in tch: rdn and no imp over 2f out: wknd over 1f out* **40/1**

3-06 **10** hd **Witchry**[32] 5998 10-9-7 **60**.... FergusSweeney 1 29
(Tony Newcombe) *hld up towards rr: styd on inner 3f out: rdn and effrt 2f out: no imp over 1f out: wl hld and eased ins fnl f* **7/1**

0442 **11** ¾ **Leelu**[13] 6586 6-9-2 **55**.... DarryllHolland 12 22
(David Arbuthnot) *taken down early: sn bustled along in midfield: struggling u.p over 2f out: wknd wl over 1f out* **3/1**[1]

0000 **12** 2 ¼ **Litotes**[105] 3467 4-8-5 **47** oh1 ow1....(v) MarkCoumbe(3) 7
(Michael Attwater) *in tch: rdn and no hdwy jst over 2f out: wknd over 1f out: fdd ins fnl f* **66/1**

00-0 **13** 1 **Peters Pleasure**[23] 6274 3-7-13 **46** oh1....(p) HannahNunn(7) 8
(Robert Cowell) *a bhd: losing tch whn hung bdly lft 2f out: n.d* **50/1**

00 **14** ¾ **Gracie's Games**[46] 5548 6-8-12 **58**....(v) WilliamTwiston-Davies(7) 13
(Richard Price) *a towards rr: c to r against stands' rail 3f out: sn rdn and no hdwy: n.d* **7/1**

1m 14.7s (4.50) **Going Correction** +0.775s/f (Yiel)
WFA 3 from 4yo+ 1lb **14** Ran SP% **121.2**
Speed ratings (Par 101): **101,100,99,96,92 92,88,86,85,84 83,80,79,78**
toteswingers 1&2 £4.90, 2&3 £19.20, 1&3 £21.70 CSF £38.12 CT £525.79 TOTE £7.40: £2.20, £1.90, £7.00; EX 37.80.
Owner P Sweeting **Bred** Paul Sweeting **Trained** Epsom, Surrey

FOCUS
A moderate sprint handicap, and the winner is rated up slightly on her C&D win in July.
T/Plt: £26.20 to a £1 take. Pool of £56312.68 -1564.30 winning tickets. T/Qpdt: £13.50 to a £1 stake. Pool of £4454.12 - 243.46 winning tickets SP

6473 CATTERICK (L-H)
Tuesday, October 9

OFFICIAL GOING: Soft (good to soft in places; 71)
Wind: light 1/2 behind Weather: fine and sunny

6952 YORKSHIRE-OUTDOORS.CO.UK ADVENTURE ACTIVITIES NURSERY (DIV I) 5f 212y
2:00 (2:01) (Class 6) (0-65,64) 2-Y-0 **£2,045** (£603; £302) **Stalls** Low

Form RPR

4532 **1** **Mixed Message (IRE)**[27] 6130 2-9-5 **62**.... RichardMullen 5 66
(Ed McMahon) *trckd ldrs: effrt and swtchd rt over 1f out: styd on ins fnl f to ld towards fin* **10/3**[1]

0304 **2** ½ **Dream Vale (IRE)**[11] 6629 2-8-13 **61**.... DarylByrne(5) 9 63+
(Tim Easterby) *mid-div: hdwy over 2f out: led over 1f out: shkn up and no ex whn hdd nr fin* **6/1**[3]

5042 **3** 1 **Someone's Darling**[9] 6707 2-9-3 **60**.... GrahamLee 6 59
(Jim Goldie) *chsd ldrs: swtchd ins over 1f out: kpt on same pce ins fnl f* **7/2**[2]

5053 **4** ½ **Amelia Jay**[15] 6524 2-8-10 **53**.... JamesSullivan 7 51
(Danielle McCormick) *s.i.s: hld up in rr: hmpd 4f out: hdwy over 2f out: styng on whn hung lft ins fnl f* **25/1**

0603 **5** 2 ¼ **Just Paul (IRE)**[17] 6475 2-8-13 **63**.... DavidBergin(7) 10 54
(Kate Walton) *trckd ldrs: led over 2f out: hdd over 1f out: sn wknd* **6/1**[3]

6003 **6** 1 ¾ **Precision Strike**[4] 6849 2-8-9 **52**.... RobbieFitzpatrick 2 40
(Richard Guest) *in rr: hmpd 4f out: hdwy on inner over 2f out: keeping on whn nt clr run and eased last 50yds* **25/1**

604 **7** nk **Al Khisa (IRE)**[104] 3490 2-9-7 **64**.... AmyRyan 8 49
(Kevin Ryan) *mid-div: drvn over 2f out: nvr a factor* **10/1**

0046 **8** 6 **Kendal Princess (IRE)**[85] 4139 2-8-2 **45**.... DuranFentiman 1 12
(David O'Meara) *led: hdd over 2f out: lost pl over 1f out* **22/1**

635 **9** 3 ½ **St Mary De Castro**[20] 6360 2-9-1 **58**.... GrahamGibbons 12 14
(Michael Easterby) *dwlt: in rr: bhd and rdn 3f out* **14/1**

0603 **U** **Grand Jipeck (IRE)**[53] 5313 2-8-8 **54**....(t) DeclanCannon(3) 4
(Ian McInnes) *dwlt: mid-div: clipped heels and uns rdr 4f out* **15/2**

1m 16.73s (3.13) **Going Correction** +0.425s/f (Yiel) **10** Ran SP% **113.4**
Speed ratings (Par 93): **96,95,94,93,90 88,87,79,74,**
toteswingers 1&2 £6.40, 2&3 £6.70, 1&3 £2.10 CSF £22.17 CT £72.21 TOTE £4.60: £1.80, £2.50, £1.10; EX 26.40 Trifecta £67.10 Pool: £1176.89 - 12.96 winning units..
Owner J C Fretwell **Bred** J Costello **Trained** Lichfield, Staffs

FOCUS
Nine of the ten the runners were still maidens in this low-grade nursery but the pace was strong and the winner finished fast to justify favouritism. There was early drama when Grand Jipeck stumbled and unseated his rider. Straightforward but limited form.

NOTEBOOK
Mixed Message(IRE) was niggled along turning in and then ran into some traffic problems but she found a surging run when switched back towards the far rail and got off the mark with a bit in hand on her seventh start. A willing type who is versatile regarding ground, she could have more to offer in handicaps and shapes like a return to 7f will suit. (tchd 3-1)
Dream Vale(IRE) produced a sweeping run out wide but was just reeled in by a faster finisher. A drop in grade and return to the scene of her maiden win seemed to help spark this revival. (op 8-1)
Someone's Darling went close in a 5f Musselburgh nursery last time and she backed that up with a solid effort returned to 6f. (tchd 10-3)
Amelia Jay didn't get the best of runs before staying on steadily when it was all over. She rates a bit better than her finishing position but is a ten-race maiden with an inconsistent profile. (op 22-1)
Just Paul(IRE) seemed to pay the price for doing too much too soon dropped in trip on his second nursery run.

6953 YORKSHIRE-OUTDOORS.CO.UK ADVENTURE ACTIVITIES NURSERY (DIV II) 5f 212y
2:30 (2:30) (Class 6) (0-65,64) 2-Y-0 **£2,045** (£603; £302) **Stalls** Low

Form RPR

0402 **1** **Iwilsayzisonlyonce**[5] 6822 2-8-13 **59**.... MichaelMetcalfe(3) 2 60
(Joseph Tuite) *prom: effrt 2f out: rdn to chal over 1f out: kpt on wl to ld last 50yds* **17/2**

2425 **2** ½ **Perfect Words (IRE)**[46] 5537 2-9-3 **63**.... PaulPickard(3) 1 63
(Marjorie Fife) *led: rdn along 2f out: jnd and drvn over 1f out: hdd and no ex last 50yds* **20/1**

2302 **3** ¾ **Twilight Pearl**[16] 6511 2-9-3 **60**....(b) DavidAllan 11 57
(Tim Easterby) *chsd ldrs: hdwy 2f out: sn rdn and kpt on fnl f: nrst fin* **7/1**[3]

5354 **4** nk **Panama Cat (USA)**[5] 6822 2-8-12 **55**.... AmyRyan 9 51+
(Kevin Ryan) *bhd: hdwy on wd outside 2f out: sn rdn and styd on fnl f: nrst fin* **6/1**[2]

0000 **5** 3 **Stand N Applaude**[35] 5920 2-9-7 **64**.... AndrewMullen 7 51
(David Nicholls) *prom: rdn along 2f out and ev ch tl drvn: edgd lft and wknd over 1f out* **33/1**

0424 **6** ¾ **Star Request**[9] 6707 2-9-5 **62** .... JoeFanning 5 48
(Keith Dalgleish) *trckd ldrs on inner: n.m.r bnd after 2f: hdwy whn nt clr run on inner over 1f out: kpt on same pce after* **13/8**[1]

0503 **7** 1½ **Only For You**[20] 6354 2-8-10 **53** .... RobertWinston 12 34
(Alan Brown) *towards rr: rdn along 2f out: styd on appr fnl f: nrst fin* **33/1**

003 **8** 1 **Masai King (IRE)**[23] 6283 2-9-0 **57** .... DanielTudhope 4 35
(Robin Bastiman) *dwlt: a towards rr* **12/1**

0402 **9** 3 **Miss Perfect**[20] 6354 2-9-3 **60** ....(v) BarryMcHugh 10 29
(John Quinn) *a towards rr* **8/1**

5353 **10** 8 **Plexolini**[16] 6511 2-8-8 **51** ....[1] J-PGuillambert 8
(Jo Hughes) *chsd ldrs: rdn along over 2f out: sn wknd* **17/2**

0465 **11** 2½ **Mace The Ace**[31] 6054 2-8-9 **52** .... DuranFentiman 3
(Lawrence Mullaney) *a in rr: bhd fnl 2f* **100/1**

360 **12** 1½ **Sylvia's Diamond**[31] 6042 2-8-1 **47** ow2........ DeclanCannon(3) 6
(Richard Guest) *a in rr: bhd fnl 2f* **66/1**

1m 16.7s (3.10) **Going Correction** +0.425s/f (Yiel) **12** Ran SP% **117.9**
Speed ratings (Par 93): **96,95,94,93,89 88,86,85,81,70 67,65**
toteswingers 1&2 £18.10, 2&3 £9.00, 1&3 £7.10 CSF £169.12 CT £1277.86 TOTE £9.90: £2.90, £5.70, £2.10; EX 183.00 Trifecta £718.00 Part won. Pool: £970.38 - 0.20 winning units..

Owner Joseph Tuite **Bred** Brook Stud Bloodstock Ltd **Trained** Great Shefford, Berks

FOCUS
The pace looked decent in the second division of a minor nursery but not many got involved and the first two were always prominent. Again, the form is straightforward enough to rate, but limited.

NOTEBOOK
Iwilsayzisonlyonce, second behind a heavily backed rival in a 6f nursery at Wolverhampton last week, was unfazed by a switch to soft turf and showed a good attitude to get off the mark on his fifth run. He is a gelded half-brother to quite useful dual sprint winner Nosedive and should be able to win more races. (op 13-2)

Perfect Words(IRE) had a bit to prove on testing ground but he made a bold bid from a good draw and was just denied.

Twilight Pearl stayed on well from just off the pace and recorded her third placed effort from three starts in nurseries. She is fairly exposed but blinkers still seem to be working and this was arguably a personal best on her ninth start. (op 13-2)

Panama Cat(USA) struggled for speed early on and was second last turning in, but she finished fast and can be marked up for coming from a long way back against a possible pace bias. (op 15-2)

Stand N Applaude showed a bit more dropped back to 6f but he was still ultimately well held and has an unconvincing six-race profile.

Star Request seemed to find 5f on the sharp side when never dangerous as favourite on her nursery debut last time. She was strongly supported again on this step back up in trip but she looked a bit unbalanced on this tight track and couldn't get involved. (op 15-8)

Masai King(IRE) Official explanation: jockey said colt missed the break

6954 BRITISH STALLION STUDS SUPPORTING BRITISH RACING E B F MAIDEN STKS 5f

3:00 (3:00) (Class 5) 2-Y-O **£3,169** (£943; £471; £235) **Stalls** Low

Form RPR

02 **1** **Heaven's Guest (IRE)**[30] 6071 2-9-3 0........ TonyHamilton 2 80
(Richard Fahey) *chsd ldr: led appr fnl f: drvn out* **15/8**[2]

64 **2** 2½ **Rangooned**[22] 6320 2-8-12 0........ GrahamLee 1 66
(Ann Duffield) *chsd ldrs: kpt on to take 2nd last 100yds: no imp* **9/1**

4522 **3** 1 **Layla's Oasis**[10] 6658 2-8-12 71........ AmyRyan 12 62
(Kevin Ryan) *led: edgd lft after 1f: hung lft and hdd appr fnl f: fdd last 75yds* **5/4**[1]

0 **4** 2¾ **Hollydanfaye**[130] 2663 2-8-9 0........ MichaelMetcalfe(3) 3 52
(Paul Green) *led to post: chsd ldrs: one pce fnl 2f* **66/1**

0420 **5** 2½ **Megaleka**[11] 6629 2-8-12 58........ DuranFentiman 4 43
(Chris Fairhurst) *chsd ldrs: one pce fnl 2f* **25/1**

3 **6** hd **Lexington Place**[11] 6628 2-8-10 0........ LauraBarry(7) 7 49+
(Richard Fahey) *chsd ldrs: one pce fnl 2f* **15/2**[3]

0 **7** 4 **Jonny Wombat**[12] 6609 2-8-10 0........ VictorSantos(7) 8 33
(Richard Ford) *in rr div whn hmpd over 2f out: nvr a factor* **100/1**

0 **8** 1 **Threepence**[20] 6356 2-9-3 0........[1] PaulQuinn 5 29
(Richard Whitaker) *s.i.s: edgd lft over 2f out: nvr a factor* **100/1**

6 **9** nk **Diddy Eric**[17] 6473 2-9-3 0........ PJMcDonald 10 28
(Micky Hammond) *a outpcd and in rr* **66/1**

05 **10** shd **Moss The Boss (IRE)**[159] 1795 2-9-0 0........ LeeTopliss(3) 9 28
(Paul Midgley) *dwlt: sn mid-div: lost pl over 2f out* **66/1**

00 **11** 2¾ **Highway United (IRE)**[21] 6335 2-8-12 0........ ChrisCatlin 6 13
(John Weymes) *mid-div: lost pl over 2f out* **100/1**

12 1¾ **Posh Secret** 2-8-12 0........ BarryMcHugh 11 7
(John Quinn) *dwlt: in rr: lost pl over 2f out* **16/1**

1m 1.85s (2.05) **Going Correction** +0.425s/f (Yiel) **12** Ran SP% **118.2**
Speed ratings (Par 95): **100,96,94,90,86 85,79,77,77,77 72,69**
toteswingers 1&2 £3.50, 2&3 £3.00, 1&3 £1.30 CSF £18.86 TOTE £3.20: £1.10, £1.40, £1.60; EX 19.00 Trifecta £48.30 Pool: £1437.42 - 22.02 winning units..

Owner J K Shannon & M A Scaife **Bred** Yeomanstown Stud **Trained** Musley Bank, N Yorks

FOCUS
There was little strength in depth in this maiden but the second-favourite scored in decent style and they finished fairly strung out. The runner-up is the key to the level, and this looked an improved effort from the winner.

NOTEBOOK
Heaven's Guest(IRE) had leading claims on his much-improved close second in a Class 3 maiden at York last time. A switch to soft ground was an unknown factor but he travelled well just behind the pace and forged clear to get off the mark on his third attempt. A brother to a 5f handicap winner, he should continue to progress and could prove best at sprint trips. (op 7-4 tchd 2-1)

Rangooned was always prominent and kept on well in a solid run on her third start. This was the most fluent display so far from this quietly progressive filly and she could be interesting when switched to nurseries. (op 14-1)

Layla's Oasis had a solid chance on her close second off a mark of 70 on her nursery debut at Chester last time. This free-going filly set the pace on this drop back to 5f and things looked to be going well for a long way but she had no answer when the winner attacked. (op 6-4 tchd 11-10)

Hollydanfaye showed a bit of promise staying on late on her return from 130 days off. (op 80-1)

Megaleka ran poorly on her nursery debut last time but this 58-rated filly bounced back with a respectable effort in race where she had quite a bit to find. (op 20-1)

Lexington Place, third behind a couple of rivals rated in the low 70s in a 6f heavy-ground Haydock maiden on his debut last month, couldn't make an impression behind his better-fancied stablemate on this drop back to 5f. Official explanation: jockey said, regarding running and riding, that his orders were to keep the colt balanced and ride it as she found; trainer confirmed instructions and thought colt had become unbalanced and may have been unsuited by the track: vet said colt was found to be coughing. (op 11-2)

6955 RACINGUK.COM NURSERY 7f

3:30 (3:30) (Class 3) (0-95,80) 2-Y-O **£5,822** (£1,732; £865; £432) **Stalls** Centre

Form RPR

21 **1** **George Rooke (IRE)**[17] 6473 2-9-7 **80**........ AmyRyan 4 82+
(Kevin Ryan) *hung rt and chsd ldrs: led over 1f out: kpt on wl* **2/1**[1]

1052 **2** 1½ **Jubilee Games**[25] 6189 2-9-6 **79**........ TonyHamilton 2 77
(Richard Fahey) *in tch: hdwy over 2f out: chsd wnr jst ins fnl f: styd on same pce* **7/2**[2]

3524 **3** hd **Storma Norma**[10] 6657 2-8-11 **70**........ DuranFentiman 5 68
(Tim Easterby) *in tch: effrt over 2f out: kpt on same pce to take 3rd last 100yds* **16/1**

3260 **4** 1¾ **Wellingrove (IRE)**[17] 6491 2-8-11 **70**........ JoeFanning 3 63
(Mark Johnston) *led: edgd rt and hdd over 1f out: one pce* **11/2**

3145 **5** 1¾ **Sylvia Pankhurst (IRE)**[15] 6550 2-9-0 **73**........ RobertWinston 1 61
(David C Griffiths) *in tch: effrt over 2f out: chsng ldrs over 1f out: fdd fnl 150yds* **6/1**

212 **6** 12 **Kolonel Kirkup**[17] 6469 2-9-4 **77**........ PJMcDonald 6 34
(Michael Dods) *w ldrs: drvn over 3f out: outpcd over 2f out: lost pl over 1f out: sn bhd* **4/1**[3]

1m 29.9s (2.90) **Going Correction** +0.425s/f (Yiel) **6** Ran SP% **111.1**
Speed ratings (Par 99): **100,98,98,96,94 80**
toteswingers 1&2 £2.00, 2&3 £6.30, 1&3 £5.90 CSF £8.98 TOTE £3.70: £1.70, £2.10; EX 10.90.

Owner Kenneth Macpherson **Bred** Rockfield Farm **Trained** Hambleton, N Yorks

FOCUS
A decent nursery. They were tightly bunched for a long way but the progressive winner battled well to score with something in hand. Straightforward form viewed through the runner-up and third.

NOTEBOOK
George Rooke(IRE) showed a good attitude when an odds-on winner of a 6f maiden here last month on his second start. Well backed again, he was not inconvenienced by a switch to 7f on soft ground and toughed it out to make a winning handicap debut. This Rock Of Gibraltar colt has quite a bit of potential for further improvement and should stay at least 1m. (op 9-4)

Jubilee Games got a bit tapped for speed when the pace increased but he rallied well and deserves credit for fighting his way into second. This dual sprint-winning colt is fairly exposed and has raced exclusively on slow turf but he has a good attitude and his running style suggests he is worth another try at 1m. (op 10-3 tchd 3-1)

Storma Norma was also caught out when things got serious but she stayed on strongly in the closing stages on her nursery debut. She could be more potent off a stronger pace next time. (op 12-1)

Wellingrove(IRE) had the run of things out in front but he had no answer when the winner asserted. (op 8-1)

Sylvia Pankhurst(IRE) couldn't make an impact back in a nursery on her 12th run of the season. She looks handicapped near her best off 5lb higher than her 6f win here in August. (tchd 13-2)

Kolonel Kirkup was forced wide for most of the way but it was disappointing how quickly he folded. He didn't have an obvious excuse regarding ground or trip and something may have been amiss.The Stewards considered the running of the gelding and noted the trainer's explanation that the gelding was over the top and probably would not run for the remainder of the season. They ordered that the gelding be routine tested. Official explanation: trainer said, regarding running, that the gelding was over the top and probably would not run for the remainder of the season. (op 7-2)

6956 SKYRAM H'CAP 1m 7f 177y

4:00 (4:00) (Class 6) (0-60,57) 3-Y-O+ **£2,045** (£603; £302) **Stalls** Centre

Form RPR

6222 **1** **Blue Dune**[7] 6769 3-9-2 **57**........ JoeFanning 15 69+
(Mark Johnston) *trckd ldrs: smooth hdwy to ld 1/2-way: rdn clr wl over 2f out: styd on strly* **11/8**[1]

220 **2** 3 **Josie's Dream (IRE)**[5] 6821 4-9-7 **51**........ J-PGuillambert 5 57
(Jo Hughes) *a.p: rdn along to chse wnr 3f out: drvn over 1f out: no imp* **11/2**[2]

3406 **3** nk **Dan's Heir**[41] 5735 10-9-2 **46**........(p) AmyRyan 11 51
(Wilf Storey) *towards rr: hdwy 4f out: rdn along over 2f out: styd on wl appr fnl f: nrst fin* **33/1**

3450 **4** 6 **Descaro (USA)**[19] 6407 6-9-6 **57**........(v) DavidBergin(7) 8 55
(David O'Meara) *trckd ldrs: hdwy over 4f out: rdn to chse ldng pair 2f out: sn drvn and kpt on one pce* **10/1**[3]

000 **5** 2¼ **Strikemaster (IRE)**[35] 5922 6-9-11 **55**........(t) DuranFentiman 14 50
(Lee James) *hld up towards rr: stdy hdwy over 4f out: rdn along 3f out: kpt on fnl 2f: nt rch ldrs* **25/1**

040 **6** 2¾ **Dimashq**[22] 6315 10-9-2 **46**........ BarryMcHugh 10 38
(Paul Midgley) *in tch on inner: hdwy over 4f out: rdn along to chse ldrs 3f out: sn drvn and plugged on one pce* **66/1**

1010 **7** 5 **Madam Lilibet (IRE)**[43] 5672 3-9-2 **57**........ PaulQuinn 12 43
(Sharon Watt) *towards rr: sme hdwy 4f out: rdn along 3f out: nvr nr ldrs* **12/1**

3604 **8** hd **Shirls Son Sam**[10] 6691 4-9-4 **48**........ KellyHarrison 4 34
(Chris Fairhurst) *hld up in rr: sme hdwy 3f out: rdn over 2f out: nvr a factor* **14/1**

3020 **9** 4½ **Finellas Fortune**[28] 6126 7-9-13 **57**........ AndrewMullen 2 37
(George Moore) *hld up: hdwy and in tch 4f out: rdn along 3f out: sn wknd* **14/1**

3035 **10** ¾ **Amir Pasha (UAE)**[41] 5735 7-9-2 **51**........(p) GarryWhillans(5) 9 30
(Micky Hammond) *nvr bttr than midfield* **22/1**

5623 **11** nk **Petrocelli**[43] 5672 5-9-10 **54**........(t) GrahamLee 6 33
(Wilf Storey) *hld up towards rr: stdy hdwy 6f out: rdn along and in tch 3f out: sn wknd* **14/1**

4301 **12** 2½ **A Southside Boy (GER)**[40] 5761 4-9-9 **53**........ DanielTudhope 1 29
(Jim Goldie) *prom: effrt 3f out: sn rdn along and wknd 2f out* **14/1**

2223 **13** 10 **Bijou Dan**[41] 5735 11-9-13 **57**........ PJMcDonald 13 21
(George Moore) *a in rr: rdn along after 4f: bhd fr 1/2-way* **16/1**

0 **14** 1¾ **Dunaskin (IRE)**[31] 6056 12-9-3 **47**........(b) RobbieFitzpatrick 7 9
(Richard Guest) *led: pushed along and hdd 1/2-way: sn lost pl and bhd fnl 4f* **50/1**

0603 **15** 59 **Bocamix (FR)**[55] 5241 6-9-11 **55**........(vt[1]) RobertWinston 3
(Andrew Crook) *prom: rdn along and lost pl over 5f out: sn bhd: eased and t.o fnl 2f* **25/1**

3m 38.33s (6.33) **Going Correction** +0.425s/f (Yiel)
WFA 3 from 4yo+ 11lb **15** Ran SP% **125.3**
Speed ratings (Par 101): **101,99,99,96,95 93,91,91,89,88 88,87,82,81,51**
toteswingers 1&2 £2.70, 2&3 £32.50, 1&3 £20.80 CSF £7.85 CT £188.40 TOTE £2.50: £1.20, £2.30, £9.20; EX 10.50 Trifecta £621.10 Part won. Pool: £839.33 - 0.10 winning units..

Owner Sheikh Hamdan Bin Mohammed Al Maktoum **Bred** Darley **Trained** Middleham Moor, N Yorks

FOCUS

They went a fair pace in this staying handicap and the strong favourite scored in emphatic style. The third has been rated close to this year's form and looks a solid enough guide.

6957 GO RACING IN YORKSHIRE H'CAP — 1m 3f 214y

4:30 (4:30) (Class 5) (0-75,73) 3-Y-O+ — £2,264 (£673; £336; £168) Stalls Centre

Form — RPR

4243 **1** **Bold Cuffs**[10] 6662 3-9-5 **73** .... ChrisCatlin 11 — 87
(Sir Mark Prescott Bt) *trckd ldr: chal 4f out: led over 2f out: edgd lft: drvn clr over 1f out: styd on* **3/1**[2]

4011 **2** *7* **Authentication**[14] 6567 3-8-12 **66** .... JoeFanning 10 — 70
(Mark Johnston) *led: hdd over 2f out: kpt on same pce* **11/4**[1]

1555 **3** *1/2* **Arley Hall**[20] 6359 3-9-3 **71** .... TonyHamilton 8 — 74
(Richard Fahey) *mid-div: hdwy 5f out: wnt 4th 3f out: 3rd 1f out: kpt on one pce* **12/1**

0312 **4** *3/4* **Hawdyerwheesht**[9] 6706 4-9-1 **62** .... GrahamLee 14 — 64
(Jim Goldie) *hld up in mid-div: hdwy 7f out: chsng ldrs 5f out: 3rd 3f out: kpt on one pce* **7/1**[3]

0-26 **5** *1/2* **Maybe I Wont**[28] 6126 7-9-1 **65** .... JulieBurke(3) 7 — 66
(James Moffatt) *s.i.s: in rr: effrt over 3f out: kpt on fnl 2f: nvr a factor* **20/1**

-642 **6** *4* **Aegean Destiny**[110] 3307 5-8-11 **61** .... DeclanCannon(3) 12 — 56
(John Mackie) *in rr div: sme hdwy 3f out: nvr a factor* **14/1**

3360 **7** *6* **Meetings Man (IRE)**[30] 6076 5-8-12 **64** .... GarryWhillans(5) 3 — 50
(Micky Hammond) *mid-div: effrt over 3f out: hung rt: nvr a factor* **14/1**

135 **8** *3 3/4* **Bavarian Nordic (USA)**[16] 6517 7-8-13 **60** .... (v) AmyRyan 6 — 40
(Richard Whitaker) *in rr: nvr on terms* **25/1**

3506 **9** *9* **Mohawk Ridge**[12] 6608 6-9-5 **69** .... (p) LeeTopliss(3) 4 — 36
(Michael Dods) *chsd ldrs: outpcd and rdn over 3f out: sn btn: bhd whn eased fnl f* **22/1**

10 *2* **Slide Show**[445] 4309 4-9-1 **62** .... BarryMcHugh 5 — 26
(Colin Teague) *chsd ldrs: rdn and outpcd over 3f out: sn lost pl* **50/1**

3-00 **11** *6* **Maneki Neko (IRE)**[21] 6339 10-9-4 **65** .... PaddyAspell 9 — 20
(Edwin Tuer) *dwlt: in rr: bhd fnl 4f* **40/1**

6042 **12** *2 3/4* **Sun Seal**[8] 6736 3-9-5 **73** .... RobertHavlin 13 — 24
(Hughie Morrison) *chsd ldrs: rdn 4f out: sn btn: bhd whn eased over 1f out* **15/2**

1510 **13** *24* **Silver Tigress**[50] 5413 4-9-1 **62** .... PJMcDonald 2
(George Moore) *mid-div: lost pl over 4f out: bhd 3f out: eased over 1f out: virtually p.u: t.o* **33/1**

2m 42.86s (3.96) **Going Correction** +0.425s/f (Yiel)
WFA 3 from 4yo+ 7lb — 13 Ran SP% **117.3**
Speed ratings (Par 103): **103,98,98,97,97 94,90,88,82,80 76,74,58**
toteswingers 1&2 £2.60, 2&3 £6.10, 1&3 £8.00 CSF £10.29 CT £85.80 TOTE £3.30: £1.80, £1.50, £4.00; EX 11.70 Trifecta £69.00 Pool: £931.70 - 9.98 winning units..
Owner Fawzi Abdulla Nass **Bred** Aislabie Bloodstock Ltd **Trained** Newmarket, Suffolk

FOCUS

A pair of 3yos were clear some way out in this middle-distance handicap and the winner landed a gamble in style. This was a clear personal best from the winner on ratings and the runner-up ran as well as ever.

Meetings Man(IRE) Official explanation: jockey said gelding hung right
Sun Seal Official explanation: jockey said filly lost its action

6958 CATTERICKBRIDGE.CO.UK AMATEUR RIDERS' H'CAP (DIV I) — 5f

5:00 (5:00) (Class 6) (0-55,55) 3-Y-O+ — £1,975 (£607; £303) Stalls Low

Form — RPR

2206 **1** **Fama Mac**[80] 4348 5-10-9 **55** .... MrAaronJames(5) 6 — 65
(Neville Bycroft) *a cl up: rdn over 1f out: kpt on ins fnl f to ld nr fin* **10/3**[1]

6004 **2** *1/2* **Angelo Poliziano**[9] 6713 6-10-10 **54** .... MrMEnnis(3) 12 — 62
(George Foster) *dwlt and towards rr: gd hdwy 1/2-way: led 1 1/2f out: sn rdn: edgd lft ins fnl f: hdd and no ex towards fin* **14/1**

6330 **3** *1 1/2* **Baybshambles (IRE)**[50] 5416 8-10-9 **55** .... MissVBarr(5) 11 — 58
(Ron Barr) *towards rr: hdwy over 2f out: swtchd rt wl over 1f out: styd on fnl f: nrst fin* **12/1**

040 **4** *shd* **Headstight (IRE)**[44] 5621 3-10-11 **52** .... MrSWalker 3 — 54
(Paul Midgley) *trckd ldrs: hdwy 2f out: rdn and ev ch over 1f out: kpt on same pce fnl f* **11/2**[3]

5232 **5** *2* **Dazzlin Bluebell (IRE)**[42] 5719 3-10-3 **49** .... (b) MrWEasterby(5) 10 — 44
(Tim Easterby) *led: rdn along and hdd 1 1/2f out: grad wknd* **5/1**[2]

0603 **6** *3/4* **Dotty Darroch**[32] 6003 4-10-4 **50** .... (b) MrFMitchell(5) 15 — 43
(Robin Bastiman) *chsd ldrs: hdwy and cl up 1/2-way: sn rdn and wknd over 1f out* **8/1**

3600 **7** *1/2* **Hab Reeh**[29] 6104 4-10-9 **50** .... (bt) MissSBrotherton 9 — 41
(Ruth Carr) *chsd ldrs: rdn 2f out: sn one pce* **9/1**

5000 **8** *1 1/4* **Blue Noodles**[46] 5543 6-9-12 **46** oh1 .... (b[1]) MrAFrench(7) 7 — 32
(John Wainwright) *towards rr: rdn along over 2f out: sme late hdwy* **40/1**

000- **9** *hd* **Micky Mac (IRE)**[384] 6261 8-10-0 **46** .... MissPhillipaTutty(5) 8 — 32
(Colin Teague) *chsd ldrs: rdn along 2f out: sn wknd* **50/1**

000 **10** *1* **Morermaloke**[105] 3463 4-10-2 **46** .... MissHBethell(3) 5 — 28
(Ian McInnes) *a towards rr* **50/1**

0160 **11** *hd* **Military Green (FR)**[61] 5014 3-10-10 **51** .... MissJCoward 2 — 32
(Tim Easterby) *a in rr* **8/1**

3060 **12** *1/2* **Essexvale (IRE)**[17] 6477 3-10-2 **46** oh1 .... (p) MissCWalton(3) 14 — 25
(Robert Johnson) *a in rr* **40/1**

0100 **13** *1* **Cheery Cat (USA)**[15] 6529 8-10-7 **48** .... (p) MissECSayer 1 — 24
(Richard Ford) *a towards rr* **28/1**

-360 **14** *3* **Toffee Nose**[80] 4348 5-10-0 **46** .... MissRSmith(5) 13 — 11
(Ron Barr) *a in rr* **16/1**

0600 **15** *6* **Andrasta**[15] 6530 7-10-2 **46** oh1 .... MissJRRichards(3) 4
(Alan Berry) *a in rr* **80/1**

1m 2.44s (2.64) **Going Correction** +0.425s/f (Yiel) — 15 Ran SP% **121.1**
Speed ratings (Par 101): **95,94,91,91,88 87,86,84,84,82 82,81,79,75,65**
toteswingers 1&2 £12.10, 2&3 £31.70, 1&3 £10.90 CSF £50.66 CT £526.73 TOTE £3.80: £1.90, £4.80, £3.60; EX 58.70 Trifecta £682.60 Part won. Pool: £922.47 - 0.50 winning units..
Owner Mrs C M Whatley **Bred** N Bycroft **Trained** Brandsby, N Yorks

FOCUS

They were spread across the track in this ordinary sprint handicap for amateur riders and the favourite just prevailed. Slightly the faster division.

6959 CATTERICKBRIDGE.CO.UK AMATEUR RIDERS' H'CAP (DIV II) — 5f

5:35 (5:36) (Class 6) (0-55,55) 3-Y-O+ — £1,975 (£607; £303) Stalls Low

Form — RPR

0R50 **1** **Ivestar (IRE)**[11] 6640 7-10-10 **50** .... (v) MissJCoward 15 — 63
(Michael Easterby) *w ldrs: led over 2f out: edgd lft fnl f: styd on wl* **20/1**

000- **2** *2 3/4* **Rio Sands**[375] 6501 7-10-0 **45** .... MrJSherwood(5) 1 — 48
(Richard Whitaker) *mid-div: hdwy 2f out: styd on to take 2nd ins fnl f: no imp* **50/1**

6566 **3** *1 1/2* **Cataract**[20] 6362 3-10-5 **45** .... MrSWalker 11 — 43
(John Weymes) *in rr: hdwy 2f out: styd on ins fnl f* **16/1**

-602 **4** *nse* **Absolute Fun (IRE)**[38] 5823 3-10-5 **50** .... MissJoannaMason(5) 14 — 48
(Tim Easterby) *in rr div: hdwy 2f out: styng on at fin* **11/1**

0325 **5** *hd* **Isle Of Ellis (IRE)**[64] 4865 5-10-2 **47** .... (v) MissRSmith(5) 7 — 44
(Ron Barr) *in rr: hdwy 2f out: swtchd lft and styd on ins fnl f* **12/1**

000 **6** *3/4* **Made In The Shade**[44] 5624 3-10-7 **52** .... (p) MissHDukes(5) 12 — 46
(Paul Midgley) *chsd ldrs: one pce over 1f out* **20/1**

0021 **7** *1/2* **Perfect Honour (IRE)**[6] 6771 6-10-10 **55** 6ex .... (b) MissKMargarson(5) 8 — 47
(Violet M Jordan) *chsd ldrs: one pce over 1f out* **4/1**[1]

133 **8** *nk* **Spread Boy (IRE)**[7] 6758 5-10-8 **51** .... MissJRRichards(3) 9 — 42
(Alan Berry) *in rr: sme hdwy over 1f out: no imp whn hmpd wl ins fnl f* **5/1**[2]

5100 **9** *nk* **Jerry Ellen (IRE)**[26] 6178 3-10-4 **49** .... (b) MrWEasterby(5) 6 — 39
(Tim Easterby) *chsd ldr: led after 1f: hdd over 2f out: wknd over 1f out* **7/1**

2660 **10** *nse* **Dolly Royal (IRE)**[24] 6258 7-10-3 **46** .... (p) MissCWalton(3) 4 — 36
(Robert Johnson) *in rr: sme hdwy far side over 1f out: nvr a factor* **12/1**

-000 **11** *1 3/4* **Three Darlings (IRE)**[31] 6048 3-10-9 **54** .... MissPhillipaTutty(5) 2 — 38
(David Nicholls) *chsd ldrs: lost pl over 1f out* **6/1**[3]

0424 **12** *2 3/4* **Karate Queen**[28] 6125 7-10-4 **49** .... MissVBarr(5) 3 — 23
(Ron Barr) *dwlt: sn chsng ldrs far side: wknd 2f out* **7/1**

040 **13** *2 1/2* **Triskaidekaphobia**[41] 5739 9-10-0 **45** .... (t) MissSMDoolan(5) 10 — 10
(Wilf Storey) *led 1f: lost pl over 2f out* **16/1**

1m 2.77s (2.97) **Going Correction** +0.425s/f (Yiel) — 13 Ran SP% **122.9**
Speed ratings (Par 101): **93,88,86,86,85 84,83,83,82,82 79,75,71**
toteswingers 1&2 £106.20, 2&3 £54.10, 1&3 £47.80 CSF £786.82 CT £15702.02 TOTE £27.90: £5.60, £15.90, £7.30; EX 1326.30 TRIFECTA Not won. Pool: £693.60.
Owner Mrs Krista Brown **Bred** Grenane House Stud & Hatta International Bloodstoc **Trained** Sheriff Hutton, N Yorks

FOCUS

They went a decent pace in the second division of this sprint handicap and there was a surprise result as a 20-1 shot surged clear. It was the slower division and the form does not look solid.
T/Jkpt: £2,927.20 to a £1 stake. Pool of £187594.16 - 45.50 winning tickets T/Plt: £17.60 to a £1 stake. Pool of £62151.14 - 2569.51 winning tickets. T/Qpdt: £4.70 to a £1 stake. Pool of £4260.45 - 663.06 winning tickets. WG

6540 LEICESTER (R-H)

Tuesday, October 9

OFFICIAL GOING: Good to soft (soft in places; 7.7)

Wind: Light across Weather: Cloudy with sunny spells

6960 BRITISH STALLION STUDS SUPPORTING BRITISH RACING E B F MAIDEN FILLIES' STKS (DIV I) — 7f 9y

2:10 (2:10) (Class 4) 2-Y-O — £4,334 (£1,289; £644; £322) Stalls High

Form — RPR

1 **Alta Lilea (IRE)** 2-9-0 0 .... SilvestreDeSousa 9 — 84+
(Mark Johnston) *chsd ldr tl led 1/2-way: rdn over 1f out: r.o wl: wnt rt nr fin* **9/2**[2]

2 *3 1/4* **Thakana** 2-9-0 0 .... PaulHanagan 7 — 75+
(Marcus Tregoning) *s.s: hdwy 5f out: chsd wnr over 1f out: edgd rt ins fnl f: styd on same pce* **5/1**[3]

3 *hd* **Nickels And Dimes (IRE)** 2-9-0 0 .... WilliamBuick 8 — 75+
(John Gosden) *s.s: hld up: hdwy over 1f out: styd on: nrst fin* **3/1**[1]

0 **4** *2 1/4* **Roanne (USA)**[32] 6007 2-9-0 0 .... DaneO'Neill 2 — 69+
(Clive Cox) *mid-div: hdwy over 2f out: rdn over 1f out: styd on same pce fnl f* **13/2**

5 *4* **Puligny (IRE)** 2-9-0 0 .... MichaelHills 3 — 59+
(Charles Hills) *chsd ldrs: rdn over 1f out: wknd ins fnl f* **16/1**

05 **6** *2* **Prospera (IRE)**[26] 6153 2-9-0 0 .... JimCrowley 10 — 54+
(Ralph Beckett) *chsd ldrs: rdn over 2f out: wknd fnl f* **9/2**[2]

7 *shd* **Impertinent** 2-9-0 0 .... MartinHarley 11 — 54
(Jonathan Portman) *hld up: hdwy 1/2-way: rdn over 2f out: wknd over 1f out* **28/1**

8 *3/4* **Just Wondering (IRE)** 2-8-9 0 .... AshleyMorgan(5) 12 — 52
(Ed Dunlop) *s.s: hld up: hdwy over 1f out: wknd ins fnl f* **28/1**

9 *1 1/2* **Miss Tiger Lily** 2-9-0 0 .... LukeMorris 4 — 48
(Harry Dunlop) *s.i.s: sn pushed along in rr: nvr on terms* **25/1**

0 **10** *1 3/4* **Skating Over (USA)**[17] 6489 2-9-0 0 .... BrettDoyle 5 — 44
(Jane Chapple-Hyam) *prom: rdn over 2f out: wknd over 1f out* **33/1**

0 **11** *8* **Bella Bijou**[18] 6453 2-8-7 0 .... JackDuern(7) 6 — 24
(Owen Brennan) *led to 1/2-way: rdn over 2f out: wknd wl over 1f out* **200/1**

12 *3 1/2* **Soubrette** 2-9-0 0 .... EddieAhern 1 — 15
(George Margarson) *s.i.s: hld up: plld hrd: rdn and wknd over 2f out* **40/1**

1m 28.33s (2.13) **Going Correction** +0.075s/f (Good) — 12 Ran SP% **113.9**
Speed ratings (Par 94): **90,86,86,83,78 76,76,75,73,71 62,58**
toteswingers 1&2 £5.30, 2&3 £4.00, 1&3 £3.80 CSF £24.28 TOTE £5.80: £2.00, £2.00, £1.40; EX 23.40.
Owner Mrs S Bianco & Ms J Bianco **Bred** Rockhart Trading Ltd **Trained** Middleham Moor, N Yorks

FOCUS

This was probably a decent fillies' maiden that should produce winners. The form could be worth more.

NOTEBOOK

Alta Lilea(IRE), closely related to the yard's 1m3f-1m5f winner Jeu De Vivre, knew her job and galloped on strongly to provide Mark Johnston with his third win in the last four years in the race. She ought to stay at least 1m and looks a useful prospect. (op 7-2)

Thakana, a half-sister to 8.5f 2yo winner Shaayeq, was strong in the market and travelled best of all, but was unable to race on with the winner. Faster ground is likely to suit and she can go one better, with the step up to 1m not expected to prove a problem. (op 7-1 tchd 15-2)

Nickels And Dimes(IRE), a half-sister to four winners, including 7f Listed scorer Kalahari Gold, lost any chance with a noticeably slow start but she made good ground to challenge widest of all, only for those efforts to take a toll. This was a most promising start and she too looks a ready-made maiden winner. (op 4-1)

Roanne(USA) was backed to improve on her debut effort and she duly did so, but the likelihood is she bumped into a few decent types. (op 10-1 tchd 11-2)

Puligny(IRE), closely related to 6f 2yo winner Barzan, is reportedly the type to do better next year, so this has to go down as a promising start. (op 12-1 tchd 11-1)

Prospera(IRE) looked vulnerable to the newcomers and was duly well held. She'll be of more interest upped to 1m in nurseries. (op 3-1)

6961 RED DEER FILLIES' H'CAP 5f 218y
2:40 (2:40) (Class 5) (0-70,70) 3-Y-0+ **£2,587** (£770; £384; £192) **Stalls** High

Form RPR
-521 **1** **Gull Rock**[14] 6565 3-8-11 **61** DaneO'Neill 6 71+
(Henry Candy) *chsd ldr: led over 1f out: sn rdn: jst hld on* **7/2**[1]
0434 **2** *hd* **Represent (IRE)**[8] 6739 3-9-4 **68** MartinHarley 9 77
(Mick Channon) *s.i.s: hld up: rdn and r.o wl ins fnl f: jst failed* **14/1**
4531 **3** *1 ½* **If So**[24] 6254 3-9-3 **67** EddieAhern 5 71
(James Fanshawe) *hld up: hdwy over 1f out: sn rdn: r.o to go 3rd nr fin: could nt rch ldrs* **8/1**
3306 **4** *½* **Lady Bayside**[12] 6610 4-9-6 **69** TomMcLaughlin 2 72
(Malcolm Saunders) *mid-div: hdwy over 2f out: rdn and hung lft fr over 1f out: styd on same pce ins fnl f* **8/1**
100 **5** *2* **Caramelita**[81] 4300 5-9-4 **67** (v) PaulHanagan 10 63+
(J R Jenkins) *hld up: hdwy over 2f out: rdn over 1f out: hmpd and no ex wl ins fnl f* **25/1**
1136 **6** *½* **Aubrietia**[26] 6173 3-8-13 **63** (b) TomQueally 18 58+
(Alan McCabe) *sn chsng ldrs: rdn over 1f out: hmpd and no ex wl ins fnl f* **16/1**
5500 **7** *2 ¾* **Climaxfortackle (IRE)**[5] 6824 4-8-13 **62** (v) SilvestreDeSousa 17 48+
(Derek Shaw) *s.i.s: hld up: hdwy and nt clr run over 1f out: hmpd ins fnl f: nvr able to chal* **20/1**
5041 **8** *shd* **Olney Lass**[32] 6000 5-8-9 **61** SimonPearce(3) 1 46
(Lydia Pearce) *hld up: rdn over 2f out: styd on ins fnl f: nvr nrr* **20/1**
6560 **9** *2 ¾* **Full Shilling (IRE)**[10] 6687 4-9-4 **67** (p) LukeMorris 7 44
(John Spearing) *hld up: rdn over 2f out: n.d* **25/1**
5324 **10** *1 ¼* **Tamara Bay**[53] 5295 4-8-11 **60** KirstyMilczarek 3 33
(John Davies) *chsd ldrs: rdn over 2f out: wknd ins fnl f* **15/2**[3]
4020 **11** *nk* **Red Mischief (IRE)**[40] 5774 3-9-1 **65** JamesDoyle 4 37+
(Harry Dunlop) *chsd ldr tl led 4f out: rdn and hdd over 1f out: cl up whn hmpd and eased wl ins fnl f* **28/1**
060 **12** *½* **Beach Candy (IRE)**[32] 5995 3-8-12 **65**[1] RyanClark(3) 8 35
(Phil McEntee) *s.i.s: in rr and rdn 1/2-way: nvr on terms* **33/1**
0-00 **13** *nk* **Passionada**[80] 4329 3-9-3 **67** TedDurcan 16 36
(Ed McMahon) *hld up: pushed along 1/2-way: wknd over 1f out* **28/1**
6421 **14** *½* **Finesse**[23] 6287 3-9-6 **70** JimCrowley 14 38
(Ralph Beckett) *prom: rdn over 2f out: hmpd over 1f out: sn wknd* **11/2**[2]
0044 **15** *½* **Mey Blossom**[5] 6823 7-8-11 **60** (p) RussKennemore 11 26
(Richard Whitaker) *hld up: effrt over 2f out: wknd over 1f out* **25/1**
226 **16** *1* **Two Turtle Doves (IRE)**[25] 6195 6-8-11 **60** SeanQuinlan 13 23
(Michael Mullineaux) *chsd ldrs: rdn over 2f out: wknd over 1f out* **20/1**
2050 **17** *nk* **Cut The Cackle (IRE)**[78] 4407 6-8-13 **62** (bt) WilliamCarson 15 24
(Violet M Jordan) *hld up: rdn 1/2-way: a in rr* **40/1**
06 **18** *11* **Molly Jones**[17] 6498 3-8-9 **59** LiamKeniry 12
(Derek Haydn Jones) *led 2f: rdn over 2f out: wknd over 1f out* **66/1**

1m 13.4s (0.40) **Going Correction** +0.075s/f (Good)
WFA 3 from 4yo+ 1lb **18** Ran SP% **123.7**
Speed ratings (Par 100): **100,99,97,97,94 93,90,89,86,84 84,83,83,82,81 80,80,65**
toteswingers 1&2 £13.20, 2&3 £17.20, 1&3 £4.00 CSF £44.81 CT £381.43 TOTE £4.50: £1.50, £3.40, £2.10, £2.10; EX 56.60.
Owner Henry Candy **Bred** Bishopswood Bloodstock & Trickledown Stud **Trained** Kingston Warren, Oxon
■ Stewards' Enquiry : Paul Hanagan two-day ban: careless riding (Oct 23-24)

FOCUS
An open-looking sprint handicap. The front pair came through late towards the stands' rail. The runner-up earned a small personal-best rating in line with best view of previous form.
Climaxfortackle(IRE) Official explanation: jockey said filly was denied a clear run
Mey Blossom Official explanation: jockey said mare was denied a clear run

6962 STOAT (S) STKS 1m 1f 218y
3:10 (3:14) (Class 6) 3-Y-0 **£1,617** (£481; £240; £120) **Stalls** Low

Form RPR
665 **1** **Boonga Roogeta**[9] 6704 3-8-6 0 LukeMorris 1 56
(Peter Charalambous) *mde all: rdn over 2f out: styd on* **9/1**
6054 **2** *2* **Arctic Galaxy (CAN)**[91] 3946 3-8-11 62 WilliamBuick 5 57
(John Gosden) *hld up: hdwy 6f out: rdn over 2f out: styd on to go 2nd ins fnl f: could nt trble wnr* **3/1**[3]
4232 **3** *nk* **Joy To The World (IRE)**[18] 6442 3-8-3 47 (t) RaulDaSilva(3) 7 51
(Paul Cole) *plld hrd and prom: outpcd over 2f out: rallied over 1f out: styd on* **8/1**
5236 **4** *¾* **Priestley's Reward (IRE)**[14] 6555 3-9-2 65 (p) MartinHarley 6 60
(Mrs K Burke) *chsd wnr: rdn over 3f out: styd on same pce ins fnl f* **11/4**[2]
5450 **5** *1 ¾* **Zuzu Angel (IRE)**[3] 6892 3-8-6 55 SilvestreDeSousa 3 46
(William Knight) *hld up: racd keenly: rdn over 2f out: styd on: could nvr trbld ldrs* **5/2**[1]
0064 **6** *7* **Voodoo (IRE)**[14] 6568 3-8-8 38 (t) RyanPowell(3) 2 37
(Ian Williams) *hld up: a in rr* **40/1**
060 **7** *4* **Bov La Raconteuse**[8] 6736 3-7-13 0 PhilipPrince(7) 4 24
(Carroll Gray) *plld hrd and prom: hung lft fr over 4f out: wknd over 3f out* **33/1**

2m 12.63s (4.73) **Going Correction** +0.25s/f (Good) **7** Ran SP% **106.7**
Speed ratings (Par 99): **91,89,89,88,87 81,78**
CSF £31.00 TOTE £10.70: £2.80, £2.50; EX 40.00.There was no bid for the winner.
Owner P Charalambous **Bred** Peter Charles **Trained** Newmarket, Suffolk
■ Arte Del Calcio was withdrawn (7/1, bolted bef r). Deduct 10p in the 3 under R4.

FOCUS
A weak seller. The winner showed down-field maiden form didn't flatter, but only to form with the third up slightly on recent poor handicap form.

6963 SQUIRREL CONDITIONS STKS 1m 1f 218y
3:40 (3:40) (Class 3) 2-Y-0 **£5,822** (£1,732) **Stalls** Low

Form RPR
1353 **1** **Linguine (FR)**[9] 6700 2-8-13 95 WilliamCarson 3 90
(Charles Hills) *mde all: pushed along over 3f out: rdn and hung lft fr over 1f out: styd on wl* **15/8**[2]
561 **2** *1 ¼* **Ennistown**[10] 6669 2-8-13 83 SilvestreDeSousa 4 88
(Mahmood Al Zarooni) *trckd wnr: rdn and ev ch 1f out: sn hung lft and could nt qckn* **2/5**[1]

2m 11.73s (3.83) **Going Correction** +0.25s/f (Good) **2** Ran SP% **106.2**
Speed ratings (Par 99): **94,93**
TOTE £2.60.
Owner Decadent Racing **Bred** Rupert Plersch **Trained** Lambourn, Berks

FOCUS
Just the two runners and a bit of a surprise result, although the winner is the higher rated of the pair.

NOTEBOOK
Linguine(FR) dug in tenaciously to deny the favourite.The form isn't worth much, however, and the winner won't be easy to place, with races such as this likely to continue to provide his best chance of success. (op 6-4 tchd 2-1)
Ennistown, winner of a 1m Haydock maiden on heavy, is a good-looker and he seemed to be travelling best, but still appeared green under pressure and could find no extra. Although disappointing, he looks the type to do much better next year when faced with 1m4f-plus. (op 4-7)

6964 QUORN H'CAP 1m 3f 183y
4:10 (4:11) (Class 4) (0-85,85) 3-Y-0 **£4,528** (£1,347; £673; £336) **Stalls** Low

Form RPR
3120 **1** **Require**[53] 5306 3-9-7 **85** KirstyMilczarek 1 94
(Luca Cumani) *chsd ldrs: rdn to ld over 1f out: jst hld on* **11/2**[1]
1432 **2** *hd* **Burnham**[39] 5789 3-8-10 **74** TomQueally 12 83
(Hughie Morrison) *a.p: rdn and ev ch fr over 1f out: hung rt ins fnl f: styd on* **11/2**[1]
1605 **3** *¾* **Cockney Sparrow**[21] 6349 3-9-0 **78** WilliamBuick 6 86
(Peter Chapple-Hyam) *hld up in tch: rdn over 2f out: edgd rt ins fnl f: r.o* **11/2**[1]
2315 **4** *2* **Ashdown Lad**[13] 6574 3-8-5 **74** MichaelJMMurphy(5) 4 79
(William Jarvis) *hld up: hdwy over 3f out: rdn over 1f out: styd on* **12/1**
513 **5** *nk* **Little Dutch Girl**[39] 5788 3-9-3 **81** (b) JohnFahy 7 85
(Clive Cox) *sn chsng ldr: hmpd 6f out: led 3f out: rdn and hdd over 1f out: no ex ins fnl f* **6/1**[2]
1050 **6** *2* **Cape Safari (IRE)**[10] 6667 3-8-10 **74** (p) LukeMorris 8 75
(Alan Bailey) *hld up: rdn over 2f out: styd on: could nt trble ldrs* **10/1**
1242 **7** *nk* **Man Of Plenty**[13] 6573 3-9-4 **82** DaneO'Neill 9 82
(John Dunlop) *hld up: rdn over 2f out: no imp fnl f* **13/2**[3]
3240 **8** *½* **Hidden Justice (IRE)**[13] 6574 3-8-4 **71** (p) RyanPowell(3) 3 71
(Amanda Perrett) *s.i.s and sn pushed along in rr: rdn over 3f out: nvr on terms* **25/1**
1046 **9** *2* **Trend Is My Friend (USA)**[21] 6333 3-9-2 **80** EddieAhern 2 76
(Amanda Perrett) *prom: racd keenly: rdn over 2f out: wknd and eased ins fnl f* **9/1**
1155 **10** *3 ¾* **Scarlet Whispers**[39] 5788 3-9-1 **79** MickyFenton 13 69
(Pam Sly) *sn led: pushed along and hdd 3f out: wknd fnl f* **25/1**
1 **11** *4* **Canary Wharf (IRE)**[267] 195 3-9-1 **79** (b) MartinHarley 10 63
(Marco Botti) *hld up: hdwy over 3f out: sn rdn: wknd over 2f out* **20/1**

2m 35.93s (2.03) **Going Correction** +0.25s/f (Good) **11** Ran SP% **113.0**
Speed ratings (Par 103): **103,102,102,101,100 99,99,98,97,95 92**
toteswingers 1&2 £6.50, 2&3 £5.70, 1&3 £8.40 CSF £32.70 CT £171.72 TOTE £8.40: £3.40, £2.10, £1.70; EX 30.20.
Owner Duke Of Devonshire **Bred** The Duke Of Devonshire **Trained** Newmarket, Suffolk

FOCUS
Fair form for the grade, with the right horses involved in the finish. The winner and third recorded personal bests, but the form looks sound.
Hidden Justice(IRE) Official explanation: jockey said gelding was slowly away

6965 DORMOUSE MAIDEN STKS 7f 9y
4:40 (4:41) (Class 5) 3-Y-0 **£2,264** (£673; £336; £168) **Stalls** High

Form RPR
5- **1** **Panzanella**[339] 7293 3-8-12 0[1] WilliamBuick 13 90+
(John Gosden) *hld up: hdwy over 2f out: shkn up to ld over 1f out: r.o strly: eased nr fin* **3/1**[2]
2 **2** *6* **Last Fighter (IRE)**[21] 6328 3-9-3 0 SilvestreDeSousa 7 75
(Saeed Bin Suroor) *s.i.s: plld hrd and sn prom: led over 2f out: rdn and hdd over 1f out: sn outpcd* **5/2**[1]
0 **3** *2 ¾* **Basingstoke (IRE)**[143] 2273 3-8-10 0 DanielMuscutt(7) 8 68
(Andrew Balding) *s.i.s: hld up: hdwy 1/2-way: rdn over 1f out: styd on same pce* **8/1**
4565 **4** *2 ¼* **Beggar's Banquet (IRE)**[14] 6570 3-9-3 67 PaulHanagan 3 62+
(Ed Vaughan) *hld up: hdwy over 1f out: nvr trbld ldrs* **33/1**
2226 **5** *¾* **Pashan Garh**[40] 5776 3-9-3 73 LukeMorris 12 59
(Pat Eddery) *led: rdn and hdd over 2f out: wknd over 1f out* **7/1**
00- **6** *5* **Teth**[107] 3-8-12 65[1] WilliamCarson 14 41
(Anthony Carson) *chsd ldrs: rdn over 2f out: wknd over 1f out* **50/1**
7 *2 ½* **Amantius** 3-9-3 0 SamHitchcott 5 39
(John Spearing) *chsd ldrs: drvn along 1/2-way: wknd wl over 1f out* **100/1**
0360 **8** *1 ¾* **Confluence**[49] 5454 3-8-12 54 DaneO'Neill 6 30
(Clifford Lines) *chsd ldrs tl rdn and wknd over 1f out* **66/1**
5 **9** *8* **Newington**[179] 1357 3-8-9 0 SimonPearce(3) 1
(Lydia Pearce) *s.s and wnt rt s: a in rr* **20/1**
43 **10** *2 ¼* **Bull Bay**[49] 5453 3-9-3 0 BrettDoyle 10
(Jane Chapple-Hyam) *trckd ldrs: plld hrd: rdn and wknd over 2f out* **40/1**
0 **11** *1* **Spowarticus**[7] 6765 3-9-3 0 MartinHarley 11
(Scott Dixon) *sn pushed along in rr: bhd fr 1/2-way* **150/1**
0252 **12** *shd* **Isatis**[18] 6433 3-8-12 68 TomQueally 2
(Sir Henry Cecil) *prom tl rdn and wknd over 2f out* **6/1**[3]
5340 **13** *1* **Register (IRE)**[62] 4948 3-9-3 80 MartinDwyer 9
(William Muir) *prom over 4f* **12/1**
14 *18* **Clear Wonder** 3-8-12 0 LiamKeniry 4
(Giles Bravery) *a in rr: bhd fr 1/2-way: t.o* **100/1**

1m 26.22s (0.02) **Going Correction** +0.075s/f (Good) **14** Ran SP% **115.4**
Speed ratings (Par 101): **102,95,92,89,88 82,80,78,68,66 65,65,63,43**
toteswingers 1&2 £2.80, 2&3 £6.20, 1&3 £8.20 CSF £9.83 TOTE £4.10: £1.60, £1.60, £2.30; EX 13.50.
Owner K Abdulla **Bred** Juddmonte Farms Ltd **Trained** Newmarket, Suffolk

FOCUS
No great depth to this maiden, with doubts over the form horses, but the winner looks pretty useful.

6966 BRITISH STALLION STUDS SUPPORTING BRITISH RACING E B F MAIDEN FILLIES' STKS (DIV II) 7f 9y
5:10 (5:10) (Class 4) 2-Y-0 **£4,334** (£1,289; £644; £322) **Stalls** High

Form RPR
1 **Lady Nouf** 2-9-0 0 WilliamBuick 2 77+
(William Haggas) *hld up: hdwy 1/2-way: shkn up to ld wl ins fnl f: edgd rt: r.o* **9/1**
2 *1* **Secret Gesture** 2-9-0 0 JimCrowley 7 75+
(Ralph Beckett) *chsd ldr: rdn over 1f out: r.o* **2/1**[2]
2 **3** *1* **Desert Image**[18] 6448 2-9-0 0 MichaelHills 11 72
(Charles Hills) *led: rdn over 1f out: hdd and unable qck wl ins fnl f* **11/8**[1]
4 *1 ¾* **Perfect Calm (USA)** 2-9-0 0 EddieAhern 4 68+
(Richard Hannon) *chsd ldrs: rdn over 1f out: styd on* **14/1**

5 2¾ **Jillywinks** 2-9-0 0 MartinHarley 9 61+
(Scott Dixon) *s.i.s: sn pushed along in rr: hdwy over 1f out: nt trble ldrs* **50/1**

6 nse **Callmeakhab (IRE)** 2-9-0 0 DaneO'Neill 10 61+
(Charles Hills) *hld up: styd on ins fnl f: nvr nrr* **40/1**

7 3½ **Conserve (IRE)** 2-9-0 0 TomQueally 8 52
(Sir Henry Cecil) *hld up: pushed along over 2f out: nvr on terms* **6/1[3]**

8 6 **Silvala Dance** 2-9-0 0 HarryBentley 5 37
(Chris Wall) *chsd ldrs tl rdn and wknd over 1f out* **66/1**

9 3¼ **Made It (IRE)** 2-9-0 0 WilliamCarson 6 29
(Anthony Carson) *mid-div: pushed along over 4f out: wknd over 2f out* **66/1**

10 2¼ **Loch Fyne Lady** 2-9-0 0 RussKennemore 3 23
(John Holt) *hld up: wknd over 2f out* **100/1**

0 11 3 **Jalasaat (USA)**[17] 6489 2-9-0 0 PaulHanagan 1 16
(John Dunlop) *prom tl wknd over 2f out* **25/1**

1m 27.7s (1.50) **Going Correction** +0.075s/f (Good) **11 Ran SP% 118.6**
Speed ratings (Par 94): **94,92,91,89,86 86,82,75,71,69 65**
toteswingers 1&2 £4.40, 2&3 £1.90, 1&3 £2.80 CSF £27.11 TOTE £16.30: £3.60, £1.10, £1.10; EX 49.00.
Owner Saleh Al Homaizi & Imad Al Sagar **Bred** Saleh Al Homaizi & Imad Al Sagar **Trained** Newmarket, Suffolk

FOCUS
Little between this and division one and again a race that should produce winners.

NOTEBOOK
Lady Nouf, a half-sister to 1m2f Listed winner Nouriya, is entered in next year's Irish Oaks and she saw her race out strongly having come through to challenge. She's going to be suited by 1m and looks well worth her place up in grade. (op 10-1 tchd 12-1)
Secret Gesture, whose dam is a half-sister to Arc winner Sagamix, was well backed and had her chance, just lacking the pace of the winner. She shouldn't have much trouble going one better upped to 1m. (op 4-1)
Desert Image, runner-up to a useful sort on her debut, wasn't quite so effective on the slower ground but still ran to a similar level. She too will benefit from 1m. (op Evens tchd 10-11)
Perfect Calm(USA), a half-sister to two winners in the US, showed ability and should benefit from a sounder surface. She's the type to win a Polytrack maiden. (op 16-1)
Jillywinks, a half-sister to multiple 7f-1m winner Thunderball, was keeping on late and normal progress should see her able to win a minor maiden.
Callmeakhab(IRE), a half-sister to six winners, including 1m Listed winner St Andrews, looked in need of the experience but was going on late and ought to benefit from a stiffer test. (op 33-1)
Conserve(IRE), whose dam is a half-sister to Group 1 winner Proportional, was never involved but should benefit from the experience, as well as a step up in trip. (op 5-1)

6967 LEVERET APPRENTICE H'CAP 7f 9y
5:40 (5:41) (Class 6) (0-60,60) 3-Y-0+ £1,617 (£481; £240; £120) Stalls High

Form RPR

1540 1 **Les Verguettes (IRE)**[103] 3546 4-9-5 **58** AshleyMorgan 12 68
(Chris Wall) *hld up: hdwy 1/2-way: led over 1f out: sn rdn and edgd rt: styd on* **11/1**

6312 2 2¼ **Xpres Maite**[15] 6546 9-9-4 **60** (b) JoshBaudains(3) 6 64
(Roy Bowring) *sn drvn along in rr: hdwy over 4f out: rdn over 2f out: ev ch over 1f out: styd on same pce ins fnl f* **7/1**

4400 3 nk **Athletic**[57] 5175 3-8-8 **52** NoraLooby(3) 10 55
(Alan McCabe) *hld up: hdwy 2f out: rdn over 1f out: styd on* **22/1**

61 4 1½ **Pink Lips**[21] 6345 4-9-1 **54** MichaelJMMurphy 1 53+
(J R Jenkins) *sn pushed along in rr: hdwy u.p over 1f out: swtchd lft: styd on ins fnl f: nrst fin* **8/1**

3640 5 1 **Ace Master**[151] 2046 4-8-12 **56** PhilipPrince(5) 17 52
(Roy Bowring) *chsd ldrs: rdn over 2f out: hung rt fr over 1f out: styd on same pce fnl f* **25/1**

0356 6 nk **No Larking (IRE)**[32] 5990 4-9-3 **56** AmyScott 13 52
(Henry Candy) *led: hdd over 4f out: led again over 2f out: rdn and hdd over 1f out: no ex ins fnl f* **9/2[1]**

0060 7 1¼ **Huzzah (IRE)**[22] 6322 7-8-13 **55** JasonHart(3) 9 47
(Paul Howling) *s.i.s: hld up: hdwy over 2f out: rdn over 1f out: no ex ins fnl f* **13/2[3]**

5002 8 4½ **Grand Piano (IRE)**[33] 5983 5-9-0 **60** (v) AdamMcLean(7) 11 40
(Andrew Balding) *s.i.s: rdn 1/2-way: n.d* **14/1**

210 9 ¾ **Greyemkay**[18] 6456 4-8-7 **51** DanielMuscutt(5) 15 29
(Richard Price) *prom: rdn over 2f out: wknd over 1f out* **10/1**

5603 10 nk **Boy The Bell**[19] 6403 5-9-1 **57** JacobButterfield(3) 16 34
(Ollie Pears) *mid-div: rdn over 2f out: wknd over 1f out* **11/2[2]**

00-6 11 3 **Lordship (IRE)**[15] 6546 8-8-8 **50** JakePayne(3) 3 19
(Tony Carroll) *chsd ldrs: rdn over 2f out: wknd fnl f* **50/1**

2540 12 7 **Indiana Guest (IRE)**[8] 6739 3-8-8 **56** (b) JordanVaughan(7) 14
(George Margarson) *chsd ldrs: rdn and n.m.r over 2f out: sn wknd* **33/1**

0026 13 5 **Calypso Cay**[18] 6439 4-9-1 **59** LukeLeadbitter(5) 5
(Peter Salmon) *prom: led over 4f out tl over 2f out: wknd over 1f out* **18/1**

040 14 1¾ **My Stroppy Poppy**[18] 6457 3-8-8 **52** (t) JackDuern(3) 7
(Frank Sheridan) *prom: rdn over 2f out: sn wknd* **28/1**

602 R **Rafella (IRE)**[43] 5658 4-8-9 **48** (v) DavidKenny 4
(Michael Scudamore) *ref to r* **20/1**

1m 28.26s (2.06) **Going Correction** +0.075s/f (Good)
WFA 3 from 4yo+ 2lb **15 Ran SP% 121.2**
Speed ratings (Par 101): **91,88,88,86,85 84,83,78,77,77 73,65,59,57,**
toteswingers 1&2 £20.20, 2&3 £49.60, 1&3 £88.40 CSF £78.75 CT £1688.83 TOTE £10.90: £3.70, £2.70, £8.90; EX 121.40.
Owner David Gilbert **Bred** Camogue Stud Ltd **Trained** Newmarket, Suffolk

FOCUS
Moderate handicap form that has been rated around the runner-up for now. The closers were favoured.
T/Plt: £61.00 to a £1 stake. Pool of £55793.38 - 667.58 winning tickets. T/Qpdt: £20.00 to a £1 stake. Pool of £3731.38 - 137.50 winning tickets. CR

6934 WOLVERHAMPTON (A.W) (L-H)
Tuesday, October 9

OFFICIAL GOING: Standard
Wind: Virtually nil Weather: Fine

6968 £32 BONUS AT 32RED.COM H'CAP 1m 141y(P)
5:30 (5:30) (Class 6) (0-65,66) 3-Y-0 £1,617 (£481; £240; £120) Stalls Low

Form RPR

3131 1 **Dana's Present**[6] 6774 3-9-10 66 6ex JamieSpencer 3 77+
(George Baker) *hld up: pushed along and hdwy 2f out: rdn to ld ins fnl f: edgd lft: kpt on* **1/1[1]**

0424 2 nk **Arabic**[18] 6458 3-9-5 61 (p) ShaneKelly 6 70
(James Fanshawe) *midfield: rdn to chse ldr over 1f out: kpt on fnl f: wnt 2nd nr fin* **5/1[3]**

645 3 hd **Eamaadd**[51] 5387 3-9-7 63 AndreaAtzeni 9 72
(Roger Varian) *sn led: rdn 2f out: hdd ins fnl f: one pce: lost 2nd nr fin* **7/2[2]**

5421 4 ¾ **Jay Bee Blue**[25] 6216 3-9-7 63 (b) JamesDoyle 5 70
(Sean Curran) *dwlt: hld up in rr: pushed along and hdwy on outer over 1f out: rdn and kpt on fnl f: nrst fin* **5/1[3]**

544 5 3 **Source Of Light (IRE)**[1] 6941 3-8-12 59 (p) ShaneBKelly(5) 8 59
(Daniel Mark Loughnane) *trckd ldrs: rdn over 2f out: no ex ins fnl f* **16/1**

0-00 6 7 **Broxbourne (IRE)**[15] 6545 3-9-7 63 RichardKingscote 7 47
(Mark Johnston) *hld up: pushed along over 3f out: nvr threatened* **33/1**

2235 7 1¼ **Auntie Kathryn (IRE)**[116] 3098 3-8-7 49 oh4 KieranO'Neill 1 30
(Peter Chapple-Hyam) *w ldr: rdn over 2f out: wknd appr fnl f* **33/1**

6440 8 1¾ **We Used To Wait (USA)**[22] 6323 3-9-1 57 LiamJones 2 34
(Peter Chapple-Hyam) *trckd ldrs: rdn over 2f out: sn wknd* **25/1**

0325 9 1 **Riviera Romance**[27] 6151 3-8-8 50 MartinLane 4 25
(J W Hills) *midfield: rdn over 2f out: sn btn* **16/1**

1m 47.94s (-2.56) **Going Correction** -0.275s/f (Stan) **9 Ran SP% 127.0**
Speed ratings (Par 99): **100,99,99,98,96 90,88,87,86**
toteswingers 1&2 £2.50, 2&3 £7.20, 1&3 £2.10 CSF £7.41 CT £14.99 TOTE £1.70: £1.10, £2.30, £1.90; EX 7.40 Trifecta £55.60 Pool: £1269.17 - 16.89 winning units..
Owner Whitsbury Racing Club **Bred** Newsells Park Stud **Trained** Whitsbury, Hants

FOCUS
The ordinary early tempo, which quickened 4f out, wasn't ideal for the hold-up horses. The runner-up helps set the standard.

6969 32REDBET.COM CLAIMING STKS 1m 141y(P)
6:00 (6:00) (Class 6) 3-Y-0+ £1,704 (£503; £251) Stalls Low

Form RPR

000 1 **Desert Vision**[27] 6131 8-8-12 75 (vt) JamesSullivan 6 75
(Michael Easterby) *led: hdd over 5f out: trckd ldr: rdn to ld again appr fnl f: kpt on* **16/1**

1432 2 ¾ **Kay Gee Be (IRE)**[22] 6313 8-8-9 82 ShaneBKelly(5) 9 76
(Richard Fahey) *prom: rdn to chal 2f out: kpt on but a jst hld ins fnl f* **6/4[1]**

3006 3 1¾ **Indian Art (IRE)**[15] 6545 6-8-12 74 JamesDoyle 3 70
(Sylvester Kirk) *midfield: rdn over 2f out: hdwy to chse ldrs over 1f out: kpt on* **12/1**

2420 4 nse **Main Beach**[31] 6047 5-9-0 82 (p) TedDurcan 8 72
(Paul Midgley) *hld up: pushed along over 2f out: hdwy on outer over 1f out: kpt on fnl f: nrst fin* **11/2[3]**

0533 5 1¾ **Ssafa**[12] 6613 4-9-0 71 MartinLane 11 68
(J W Hills) *hld up in rr: rdn over 2f out: kpt on fnl f: nvr threatened ldrs* **16/1**

3000 6 2 **Poppy Golightly**[28] 6127 5-8-1 45 NeilFarley(3) 7 53?
(Declan Carroll) *s.i.s: hld up: rdn 2f out: nvr threatened* **100/1**

455 7 2¾ **Fathsta (IRE)**[3] 6888 7-9-7 81 [1] JamieSpencer 2 64
(Patrick Morris) *t.k.h: hld up: rapid hdwy to ld over 5f out: rdn whn hdd appr fnl f: wknd and eased* **4/1[2]**

1001 8 2 **Munsarim (IRE)**[80] 4334 5-9-7 86 (b) TobyAtkinson(5) 4 64
(Richard Rowe) *midfield: pushed along and hdwy to chse ldrs 2f out: wknd over 1f out* **6/1**

0000 9 6 **Cathcart Castle**[19] 6403 4-8-2 42 (e) GemmaNellist(7) 10 33
(Simon West) *racd keenly: trckd ldrs: wknd 2f out* **150/1**

1m 49.08s (-1.42) **Going Correction** -0.275s/f (Stan)
WFA 3 from 4yo+ 4lb **9 Ran SP% 110.8**
Speed ratings (Par 101): **95,94,92,92,91 89,86,85,79**
toteswingers 1&2 £5.90, 2&3 £4.90, 1&3 £10. CSF £38.05 TOTE £31.60: £4.40, £1.50, £2.80; EX 71.80 Trifecta £1110.40 Part won. Pool: £1500.64 - 0.62 winning units..
Owner A Black,R Edmonds,J Holdroyd,J Quickfall **Bred** Gainsborough Stud Management Ltd **Trained** Sheriff Hutton, N Yorks

FOCUS
An above-average claimer in which they were soon going a decent pace. The form is limited by the sixth-placed horse.

6970 32RED SUPPORTING BRITISH RACING MAIDEN STKS 5f 20y(P)
6:30 (6:30) (Class 5) 2-Y-0 £2,587 (£770; £384; £192) Stalls Low

Form RPR

22 1 **Smart Daisy K**[61] 4990 2-8-12 0 ShaneKelly 6 72+
(Reg Hollinshead) *trckd ldng pair: pushed along appr fnl f: kpt on to ld towards fin: shade cosily* **11/8[1]**

2 2 ½ **Free Island**[14] 6556 2-8-12 0 JamesDoyle 4 68
(James Tate) *w ldr: led over 1f out: sn rdn: kpt on: hdd towards fin* **11/4[3]**

0 3 1½ **Skytrain**[145] 2213 2-9-3 0 SilvestreDeSousa 3 68
(Mark Johnston) *led narrowly: rdn whn hdd over 1f out: edgd lft and no ex ins fnl f* **7/4[2]**

05 4 3¼ **Lexi's Beauty (IRE)**[7] 6766 2-8-12 0 TedDurcan 2 51
(Patrick Morris) *hld up: rdn 2f out: nvr threatened* **33/1**

00 5 3½ **Armada Bay (IRE)**[72] 4618 2-9-3 0 [1] TomEaves 1 44
(Bryan Smart) *trckd ldng pair: rdn 2f out: sn wknd* **40/1**

1m 2.06s (-0.24) **Going Correction** -0.275s/f (Stan) **5 Ran SP% 110.5**
Speed ratings (Par 95): **90,89,86,81,76**
CSF £5.59 TOTE £2.70: £1.50, £1.10; EX 6.20.
Owner Mr & Mrs D J Smart **Bred** D J And Mrs K D Smart **Trained** Upper Longdon, Staffs

FOCUS
Just a routine juvenile maiden, and the winner didn't need to be at her best.

NOTEBOOK
Smart Daisy K, speedy runner-up in two turf maidens, made a successful switch to AW racing. Ridden with a little more restraint this time, she won more comfortably the margin suggests and will be interesting in handicaps under similar tactics. (op 6-5)
Free Island has now finished second in two maidens, the other one on turf. Though no match for the winner, she ran well enough and has every chance of breaking her duck in a similar event. (op 15-8 tchd 7-4)
Skytrain, down the field on his debut (on turf), got much closer in this easier company. He handled the surface well and should be placed to good effect. (op 4-1)
Lexi's Beauty(IRE) looks unlikely to win a maiden but now has a handicap mark. However, she has already been beaten in a seller so connections will need to be realistic. (op 20-1)

The Form Book Flat, Raceform Ltd, Compton, RG20 6NL

Armada Bay(IRE), wearing a first-time hood for this AW debut, now has a handicap mark but he will need to improve on what he has done so far. (op 28-1)

6971 32RED H'CAP 1m 5f 194y(P)
7:00 (7:02) (Class 4) (0-80,77) 3-Y-O **£4,528** (£1,347; £673; £336) **Stalls** Low

Form RPR

3404 **1** **Instrumentalist (IRE)**[18] 6440 3-9-2 72 JamesDoyle 10 81
(John Best) *hld up: rdn and hdwy towards outer over 2f out: drvn to ld narrowly jst ins fnl f: kpt on* **40/1**

3641 **2** *hd* **Moderator**[9] 6703 3-9-6 76 HarryBentley 2 85
(Gary Moore) *in tch on inner: briefly short of room 2f out: rdn over 1f out: ev ch jst ins fnl f: kpt on: jst failed* **7/4**[1]

0222 **3** *shd* **Up Ten Down Two (IRE)**[17] 6474 3-9-0 70 (t) JamesSullivan 1 79
(Michael Easterby) *trckd ldrs: rdn to ld narrowly 2f out: hdd jst ins fnl f: kpt on: jst hld* **8/1**

6505 **4** *shd* **Thecornishcockney**[11] 6647 3-8-7 63 KieranO'Neill 9 71
(John Ryan) *s.i.s: hld up in rr: rdn over 2f out: sn gd hdwy on outer: ev ch appr fnl f: kpt on* **40/1**

6022 **5** *5* **Aleksandar**[29] 6098 3-9-1 71 KirstyMilczarek 8 72
(Luca Cumani) *in tch: rdn and hdwy over 2f out: upsides over 1f out: wknd ins fnl f* **9/2**[2]

6213 **6** *nk* **Silver Samba**[27] 6137 3-8-13 69 LiamKeniry 5 70
(Andrew Balding) *midfield: rdn 2f out: kpt on fnl f: nvr threatened* **8/1**

0000 **7** *4 ½* **Rayvin Black**[10] 6677 3-9-3 73 TomEaves 11 68
(Mark H Tompkins) *hld up: rdn over 2f out: nvr threatened* **14/1**

1644 **8** *2 ¾* **Darling Lexi (IRE)**[11] 6626 3-8-4 60 FrannyNorton 3 51
(Richard Fahey) *trckd ldrs: rdn over 2f out: sn wknd* **10/1**

6520 **9** *nk* **Bohemian Rhapsody (IRE)**[29] 6098 3-8-13 69 (p) MartinLane 6 59
(J W Hills) *prom: rdn over 2f out: sn wknd* **20/1**

1206 **10** *½* **Flying Trader (USA)**[15] 6537 3-9-7 77 BrettDoyle 7 67
(Jane Chapple-Hyam) *hld up: rdn over 2f out: sn btn* **10/1**

3621 **11** *hd* **Seven Veils (IRE)**[18] 6440 3-9-7 77 LukeMorris 4 66
(Sir Mark Prescott Bt) *led: rdn whn hdd 2f out: wknd* **6/1**[3]

2m 58.68s (-7.32) **Going Correction** -0.275s/f (Stan) course record **11** Ran SP% **125.5**
Speed ratings (Par 103): **109,108,108,108,105 105,103,101,101,101 101**
toteswingers 1&2 £40.10, 2&3 £5.40, 1&3 £23.90 CSF £115.93 CT £679.43 TOTE £67.40: £12.40, £1.10, £1.50; EX 198.90 Trifecta £1008.80 Part won. Pool: £1363.25 - 0.40 winning units..
Owner Kingsgate Racing 4 **Bred** Pheroze Sorabjee **Trained** Hucking, Kent
■ Stewards' Enquiry : Kieran O'Neill seven-day ban: used whip above permitted level (Oct 23-27, 29-30)

FOCUS
The pace was inconsistent early on, but the last 1m2f provided a decent test, allowing the winner and fourth to make their moves from the rear. The time was quick and the winner is rated back to his Doncaster form.

6972 32RED.COM NURSERY 1m 141y(P)
7:30 (7:30) (Class 4) (0-80,80) 2-Y-O **£3,557** (£1,058; £529; £264) **Stalls** Low

Form RPR

01 **1** **Daaree (IRE)**[25] 6188 2-8-10 69 (t) SilvestreDeSousa 9 77+
(Saeed Bin Suroor) *trckd ldr: led over 2f out: in command appr fnl f: pushed out: comf* **11/8**[1]

426 **2** *1 ¾* **Glory City (IRE)**[53] 5321 2-9-2 75 (t) AndreaAtzeni 4 77
(Marco Botti) *midfield: rdn and hdwy over 2f out: wandered arnd u.p ent fnl f: kpt on: wnt 2nd fnl 50yds: no ch w wnr* **5/1**[2]

022 **3** *1 ¾* **Ormindo (USA)**[15] 6533 2-8-12 76 AntiocoMurgia(5) 2 75
(Mahmood Al Zarooni) *in tch: hdwy over 2f out: rdn and ev ch over 1f out: edgd lft ins fnl f: no ex and lost 2nd fnl 50yds* **7/1**

4013 **4** *¾* **Royal Prize**[20] 6363 2-9-2 75 JimCrowley 7 72+
(Ralph Beckett) *hld up: rdn and hdwy over 1f out: kpt on fnl f: nrst fin* **5/1**[2]

2051 **5** *6* **Zain Spirit (USA)**[18] 6451 2-8-13 72 LukeMorris 1 56
(Gerard Butler) *trckd ldr: rdn over 2f out: wknd over 1f out* **20/1**

5056 **6** *hd* **Makinson Lane (IRE)**[21] 6337 2-8-7 71 ow2 ShaneBKelly(5) 6 55+
(Richard Fahey) *slowly away: hld up: rdn over 2f out: nvr threatened* **50/1**

0322 **7** *6* **Astrosapphire**[21] 6344 2-9-0 73 TomEaves 3 44
(Mark H Tompkins) *midfield: pushed along over 3f out: wknd over 2f out* **25/1**

6210 **8** *9* **Grey Blue (IRE)**[26] 6162 2-9-5 78 MartinLane 8 31
(Mark Johnston) *led: rdn whn hdd over 2f out: wknd* **6/1**[3]

1m 48.59s (-1.91) **Going Correction** -0.275s/f (Stan) **8** Ran SP% **112.8**
Speed ratings (Par 97): **97,95,93,93,87 87,82,74**
toteswingers 1&2 £2.30, 2&3 £6.70, 1&3 £3.60 CSF £8.11 CT £34.50 TOTE £3.10: £1.30, £2.40, £2.50; EX 11.70 Trifecta £50.70 Pool: £806.02 - 11.76 winning units..
Owner Godolphin **Bred** Shadwell Estate Company Limited **Trained** Newmarket, Suffolk

FOCUS
A decent nursery, run at a solid pace. The runner-up and third were roughly to their marks.

NOTEBOOK
Daaree(IRE), given a chance with an opening mark of 69, stays this trip well and made no mistake. He looks progressive and should leave this form behind as he matures. (op 6-5 tchd 6-4)
Glory City(IRE), tongue-tied for the first time, didn't appear to get home over 1m at Newmarket last time, but this was a different test and he showed that 1m-plus is likely to be his territory. This was a creditable run behind a well-handicapped winner, and he looks sure to improve with experience. (op 7-1)
Ormindo(USA)'s maiden form showed he is capable of winning races, but on this evidence his opening handicap mark will test him. Switching back to maidens shouldn't be a problem. (op 17-2)
Royal Prize has done reasonably well since switching to nurseries, but both runs suggest he has a few pounds too much. (op 9-2)
Zain Spirit(USA) ought to stay 1m on the evidence of his previous race, but the stronger company stretched him. (op 16-1)
Makinson Lane(IRE) may do better in lesser company when the handicapper gives him a chance.
Grey Blue(IRE) found it too much doing the donkey work for these decent juveniles. (op 8-1)

6973 32RED CASINO H'CAP 1m 1f 103y(P)
8:00 (8:01) (Class 5) (0-75,81) 3-Y-O **£2,264** (£673; £336; £168) **Stalls** Low

Form RPR

3121 **1** **Tis Rock 'N' Roll (USA)**[4] 6843 3-9-13 81 6ex TedDurcan 2 91+
(David Lanigan) *sltly awkward s: sn trckd ldrs: pushed along to ld over 1f out: drvn and hung rt jst ins fnl f: stened out fnl 75yds: jst hld on* **4/1**[1]

6-00 **2** *shd* **Layali Dubai (USA)**[109] 3340 3-8-11 65 SilvestreDeSousa 5 74
(Saeed Bin Suroor) *hld up: rdn and gd hdwy over 1f out: r.o wl ins fnl f: jst failed* **10/1**

6544 **3** *shd* **Xinbama (IRE)**[10] 6692 3-9-4 72 MartinLane 11 81
(J W Hills) *hld up: rdn and gd hdwy on wd outside 2f out: r.o wl fnl f* **14/1**

04 **4** *1* **Sarmatian Knight (IRE)**[4] 6843 3-9-2 70 StevieDonohoe 1 77
(Ian Williams) *trckd ldrs: rdn over 2f out: kpt on* **11/2**[3]

404 **5** *1* **Sir Trevor (IRE)**[15] 6539 3-9-2 70 RichardKingscote 9 75
(Tom Dascombe) *swtchd lft to inner at s: midfield: rdn over 1f out: kpt on* **10/1**

3-00 **6** *nk* **Berengar (IRE)**[18] 6450 3-9-4 72 HarryBentley 8 76
(Brian Meehan) *midfield: rdn over 2f out: kpt on one pce* **16/1**

0431 **7** *½* **Brimstone Hill (IRE)**[11] 6647 3-9-4 72 WilliamCarson 3 75
(Anthony Carson) *w ldr: rdn to ld narrowly over 2f out: hdd over 1f out: wknd ins fnl f* **8/1**

002 **8** *2 ¼* **Capacious**[18] 6457 3-9-5 73 EddieAhern 10 71+
(James Fanshawe) *dwlt: hld up: pushed along over 2f out: nvr threatened* **7/1**

2321 **9** *4* **Thecornishcowboy**[14] 6568 3-8-9 63 (t) BrettDoyle 4 53
(John Ryan) *led narrowly: rdn whn hdd over 2f out: wknd over 1f out* **12/1**

006 **10** *2 ¼* **Resito (IRE)**[25] 6209 3-8-11 70 MichaelJMMurphy(5) 6 55
(William Jarvis) *trckd ldrs: rdn over 2f out: wknd over 1f out* **33/1**

6342 **11** *4* **Rock Song**[11] 6647 3-8-11 65 JimCrowley 13 42+
(Amanda Perrett) *in tch on outer: rdn over 2f out: wknd over 1f out* **5/1**[2]

0606 **12** *4* **Sheikh The Reins (IRE)**[7] 6768 3-9-5 73 JamesDoyle 7 42
(John Best) *hld up: pushed along over 2f out: nvr threatened* **33/1**

3234 **13** *2* **Alkadi (IRE)**[14] 6560 3-9-4 72 JoeFanning 12 36
(Mark Johnston) *midfield: rdn over 3f out: wknd over 2f out* **14/1**

1m 59.22s (-2.48) **Going Correction** -0.275s/f (Stan) **13** Ran SP% **126.6**
Speed ratings (Par 101): **100,99,99,98,98 97,97,95,91,89 86,82,80**
toteswingers 1&2 £10.50, 2&3 £43.60, 1&3 £24.50 CSF £47.59 CT £527.72 TOTE £3.40: £2.00, £4.90, £3.90; EX 66.80 Trifecta £580.10 Pool: £964.23 - 1.23 winning units..
Owner Catesby W Clay **Bred** Runnymede Farm Inc **Trained** Upper Lambourn, Berks

FOCUS
A race of some merit. Another personal best from the winner, with the third a reliable guide.
Sarmatian Knight(IRE) Official explanation: jockey said gelding hung left
T/Plt: £12.00 to a £1 stake. Pool £73,439.51- 4,443.04 winning units. T/Qpdt: £10.80 to a £1 stake. Pool £532.45- 7802.02 winning units. AS

6974 - (Foreign Racing) - See Raceform Interactive

6771 KEMPTON (A.W) (R-H)
Wednesday, October 10

OFFICIAL GOING: Standard
Wind: virtual nil Weather: dry

6975 WIN BIG WITH BETDAQ MULTIPLES CLAIMING STKS 6f (P)
5:30 (5:31) (Class 6) 2-Y-O **£1,617** (£481; £240; £120) **Stalls** Low

Form RPR

1110 **1** **Hardy Blue (IRE)**[13] 6611 2-8-5 68 MartinDwyer 7 57
(Jamie Osborne) *chsd ldr: rdn to chal 2f out: led over 1f out: forged clr jst ins fnl f: hrd pressed towards fin: jst hld on* **9/4**[2]

0106 **2** *nse* **Ishigunnaeatit**[25] 6227 2-8-8 71 MartinHarley 4 60
(Mrs K Burke) *t.k.h: hld up in tch: rdn and effrt wl over 1f out: hdwy to chse wnr fnl 100yds: r.o strly: rdr dropped reins cl home: jst failed* **1/1**[1]

4303 **3** *2* **Pal Of The Cat**[14] 6579 2-9-5 75 FrannyNorton 6 65
(Brian Gubby) *wnt rt s: led: rdn 2f out: hdd over 1f out: styd on same pce ins fnl f* **12/1**

4500 **4** *shd* **Eyeline**[19] 6451 2-8-10 52 RussKennemore 8 56
(Reg Hollinshead) *in tch in last trio: rdn 1/2-way: no imp and looked wl hld 2f out: rallied and styd on strly ins fnl f* **40/1**

6030 **5** *hd* **Red Adair (IRE)**[9] 6732 2-8-9 65 SeanLevey 1 54
(Richard Hannon) *racd in last trio: rdn and dropped to last 3f out: no prog tl styd on wl ins fnl f: nvr trbld ldrs* **10/1**[3]

6 *1* **Princess Cammie (IRE)** 2-8-6 0 AndreaAtzeni 5 48
(Mike Murphy) *wnt rt s: rn green: t.k.h and sn in tch in rr: hdwy on outer 3f out: rdn ent fnl 2f: hung lft and btn over 1f out: one pce fnl f* **16/1**

0450 **7** *1 ¾* **Xerxes (IRE)**[22] 6332 2-7-7 45 (b[1]) NoelGarbutt(7) 3 37
(Hugo Palmer) *chsd ldrs: rdn and effrt to chal 2f out: no ex over 1f out: wknd fnl f* **50/1**

1m 13.27s (0.17) **Going Correction** -0.20s/f (Stan) **7** Ran SP% **107.8**
Speed ratings (Par 93): **90,89,87,87,86 85,83**
toteswingers 1&2 £1.30, 2&3 £3.10, 1&3 £1.90 CSF £4.21 TOTE £3.80: £1.50, £1.50; EX 6.80 Trifecta £19.70 Pool: £534.02 - 19.99 winning units..
Owner Patrick Gage & Tony Taylor **Bred** Philip O'Dwyer **Trained** Upper Lambourn, Berks
■ Stewards' Enquiry : Martin Dwyer two-day ban: excessive use (Oct 24-25)

FOCUS
Typically muddling claiming form, with the proximity of Eyeline, officially rated just 52, limiting the level.

NOTEBOOK
Hardy Blue(IRE) met trouble in a better race than this at Wolverhampton on her previous start, but she enjoyed a kind trip this time, managing to get a handy position without conceding much ground from stall seven, and just held on. She had the same chance as Ishigunnaeatit at the weights and doesn't look any better than this level. (op 7-4 tchd 13-8)
Ishigunnaeatit seemed to travel well enough, but she took an age to get going once under pressure, and after changing her lead leg around half-a-furlong out, just failed to reel in the winner. Her rider dropped his reins near the line but didn't stop pushing. (op 7-4)
Pal Of The Cat ran respectably considering he had 7lb to find with the front two, although being allowed to dominate probably helped his cause. (op 6-1)
Eyeline probably ran a bit above his mark, perhaps helped by the drop in trip, but this isn't a race to get carried away with. (op 33-1)
Red Adair(IRE), well beaten over 1m2f last time, seemed to find this an insufficient test. He's now 0-9 and has much to prove. (op 6-1)
Princess Cammie(IRE), a 5,500euros purchase who is rated to winners in Italy, made an awkward start and hung over to the stands' rail in the straight, but she showed some ability on this racecourse debut. Official explanation: jockey said filly was slowly away. (tchd 20-1)

6976 BACK OR LAY AT BETDAQ.COM CLAIMING STKS 1m 3f (P)
6:00 (6:00) (Class 6) 3-4-Y-O **£1,617** (£481; £240; £120) **Stalls** Low

Form RPR

2250 **1** **Spartan Spirit (IRE)**[27] 6170 4-9-2 69 (t) WilliamTwiston-Davies(7) 4 70
(Hughie Morrison) *hld up in last trio: rdn along briefly after 2f: rdn and gd hdwy on inner 2f out: hld hd high but led ins fnl f: jst hld on* **4/1**[2]

6340 **2** *shd* **Daring Damsel (IRE)**[6] 6814 3-8-0 63 (b) RaulDaSilva(3) 1 56
(Paul Cole) *led: rdn and wnt lft 2f out: continued to hang lft and hdd ins fnl f: rallied towards fin: jst hld* **5/1**[3]

3162 **3** *¾* **Renegotiate**[19] 6430 3-8-13 65 DanielMuscutt(7) 6 72
(Andrew Balding) *hld up in tch: rdn and effrt 2f out: kpt on u.p ins fnl f* **10/1**

2340 **4** *½* **Barachiel**[36] 5908 4-9-4 58 JimCrowley 5 63
(Luke Dace) *t.k.h: chsd ldr for 2f: stdd and hld up in tch after: rdn and effrt to chse ldrs wl over 1f out: styd on same pce fnl f* **20/1**

1504 **5** *3* **Ballyheigue (IRE)**[5] 3962 3-9-3 76...............................(b) GeorgeBaker 7 62
(Gary Moore) *chsd ldr after 2f tl 2f out: wknd ins fnl f* **6/1**

0056 **6** *½* **Spanish Plume**[9] 6735 4-9-12 77............................... ShaneKelly 2 64
(Reg Hollinshead) *chsd ldrs: rdn to chse ldr 2f out tl ins fnl f: wknd ins fnl f* **7/1**

5152 **7** *nk* **Alshazah**[7] 6801 4-9-6 73...............................(p) JamesMillman 10 58
(Rod Millman) *stdd and dropped in bhd after s: hld up in last trio: rdn and effrt over 2f out: no hdwy and hung rt over 1f out* **9/4**[1]

503 **8** *2* **Denton Dancer**[23] 6304 3-7-13 49............................... RyanTate(7) 8 46
(James Eustace) *hld up in tch in last trio: rdn and no hdwy over 2f out: plugged on same pce and wl hld fr over 1f out* **66/1**

2600 **9** *15* **Gangsterbanksters (FR)**[18] 6474 3-9-0 58...............(b¹) MartinHarley 3 27
(Mrs K Burke) *in tch in midfield: rdn 3f out: wknd over 2f out and wl bhd fnl f* **16/1**

000 **10** *3¾* **Grecian Goddess (IRE)**[8] 6769 4-8-7 43.................. KirstyMilczarek 9
(John Ryan) *taken down early: chsd ldrs tl 3f out: sn dropped out: bhd fnl 2f* **250/1**

2m 19.42s (-2.48) **Going Correction** -0.20s/f (Stan)
WFA 3 from 4yo 6lb **10** Ran SP% **115.8**
Speed ratings (Par 101): **101,100,100,100,97 97,97,95,84,82**
toteswingers 1&2 £2.80, 2&3 £9.60, 1&3 £5.90 CSF £23.95 TOTE £4.40: £1.20, £1.90, £4.30; EX 20.90 Trifecta £116.50 Pool: £568.69 - 3.61 winning units..
Owner Thurloe Thoroughbred XXVIII **Bred** Swordlestown Stud **Trained** East Ilsley, Berks

FOCUS
Not form to dwell on. The third ran well at the weights and earned a personal-best rating.
Daring Damsel(IRE) Official explanation: jockey said filly hung left away from whip.

6977 BETDAQ MOBILE APPS MAIDEN AUCTION STKS (DIV I) 7f (P)
6:30 (6:30) (Class 5) 2-Y-O **£2,264** (£673; £336; £168) **Stalls** Low

Form RPR

244 **1** **Living The Life (IRE)**[46] 5574 2-8-6 78...................... FergusSweeney 8 70
(Jamie Osborne) *chsd ldrs: rdn and ev ch 2f out: hung lft after: led over 1f out: racing against stands' rail and styd on wl ins fnl f: rdn out* **2/1**[2]

64 **2** *1* **Aye Aye Skipper (IRE)**[16] 6533 2-8-11 0............................ BrettDoyle 4 72
(Dean Ivory) *t.k.h: chsd ldr for 2f: styd in tch: rdn and sltly outpcd 2f out: rallied ins fnl f: styd on wl to go 2nd last strides* **12/1**

3 **3** *nk* **Secret Art (IRE)**[16] 6533 2-8-13 0.................................... JimCrowley 9 73
(Ralph Beckett) *s.i.s: t.k.h: hdwy on outer to press ldr after 2f: rdn and led 2f out: hdd over 1f out: styd on same pce ins fnl f* **5/4**[1]

0 **4** *1* **Countryman**[19] 6444 2-9-0 0.................................... DarryllHolland 11 72+
(Hughie Morrison) *hld up in tch: rdn and outpcd over 2f out: rallied u.p and styd on wl fnl f* **8/1**[3]

23 **5** *¾* **Miss Mocca**[28] 6134 2-8-4 0.. RaulDaSilva(3) 3 63
(Ian Wood) *t.k.h: chsd ldrs: rdn ent fnl 2f: styd on same pce fnl f* **12/1**

66 **6** *nk* **Midnight Dream (FR)**[29] 6122 2-8-11 0............................ TomEaves 2 66
(Linda Stubbs) *led and set stdy gallop: rdn and qcknd over 2f out: hdd 2f out: no ex and btn ins fnl f* **25/1**

000 **7** *2½* **Sunny Hollow**[22] 6343 2-8-5 65.................................. KirstyMilczarek 5 53
(James Toller) *hld up in tch in last pair: rdn 2f out: sme hdwy ent fnl f: nvr trbld ldrs* **20/1**

8 *3* **Show More Faith** 2-9-0 0.. LiamKeniry 7 54
(Sylvester Kirk) *s.i.s: sn in tch in midfield: rdn and outpcd over 2f out: wknd jst over 1f out* **40/1**

000 **9** *nk* **Shades Of Light**[33] 5997 2-8-4 50.................................. FrannyNorton 6 43
(Peter Makin) *taken down early: in tch: rdn and unable qck over 2f out: wknd ent fnl f* **66/1**

10 *2¼* **Rapid Rabbit Foot** 2-8-4 0... ChrisCatlin 1 37
(John Holt) *s.i.s: hld up in tch in rr: rdn and effrt ent fnl 2f: no imp: wknd over 1f out* **50/1**

1m 26.21s (0.21) **Going Correction** -0.20s/f (Stan) **10** Ran SP% **118.8**
Speed ratings (Par 95): **90,88,88,87,86 86,83,79,79,76**
toteswingers 1&2 £6.60, 2&3 £3.10, 1&3 £1.70 CSF £24.83 TOTE £2.70: £1.20, £3.50, £1.10; EX 35.50 Trifecta £44.40 Pool: £839.00 - 13.96 winning units..
Owner Michael Buckley **Bred** Michael Begley **Trained** Upper Lambourn, Berks

FOCUS
Just an ordinary maiden. The pace looked steady and the time was 1.04 seconds slower than the second division. The winner has been rated as 11lb below her best.

NOTEBOOK
Living The Life(IRE) didn't have to improve to get off the mark on her fourth start, although she won despite hanging over to the stands' rail under pressure. It remains to be seen if she's going to progress, but she's reportedly unlikely to run again this season. (op 9-4 tchd 15-8)
Aye Aye Skipper(IRE), one place behind Secret Art over C&D on his previous start, was outpaced when first under pressure but kept on well to reverse form. The runner-up is now qualified for an official mark and could improve again in a stronger-run race. (tchd 16-1)
Secret Art(IRE) was able to get a handy position without taking much out of himself, cutting across from his wide draw just before the bend, but he still failed to build on his debut promise. He's not one to give up on yet, however, as he gives the impression he can still sharpen up plenty. (op 11-8)
Countryman hinted at ability when green on his debut over 6f at Newbury, and he did so again. There should be better to come. (op 9-1)
Miss Mocca was found out by a testing 1m last time, but here she seemed to run to the same sort of level as when second on her debut, and the way she kept on after being a bit keen suggests she may yet do a bit better. She's now qualified for a mark. (op 11-1)
Midnight Dream(FR) ran better on this step up in trip, but setting a modest gallop helped.

6978 BETDAQ MOBILE APPS MAIDEN AUCTION STKS (DIV II) 7f (P)
7:00 (7:02) (Class 5) 2-Y-O **£2,264** (£673; £336; £168) **Stalls** Low

Form RPR

6 **1** **Steelriver (IRE)**[32] 6049 2-9-0 0.................................... TedDurcan 10 86+
(James Bethell) *mde all: rdn and wnt clr wl over 1f out: styd on strly: readily* **8/1**

2 *3¾* **Intermix (IRE)** 2-8-8 0.. RaulDaSilva(3) 5 73
(Paul Cole) *t.k.h: hld up in tch: rdn and effrt to chse clr ldr wl over 1f out: no imp on wnr but kpt on for clr 2nd* **8/1**

4 **3** *3¼* **Syrenka**[19] 6448 2-8-4 0.. HayleyTurner 11 57
(Marcus Tregoning) *t.k.h: chsd wnr after 1f: ev ch and rdn 2f out: unable qck and sn outpcd by wnr: wl hld but plugged on to hold 3rd fnl f* **11/8**[1]

0332 **4** *½* **Branson (IRE)**[50] 5439 2-9-0 72...................................... SeanLevey 4 66
(Richard Hannon) *in tch in midfield: rdn and effrt ent fnl 2f: outpcd and no ch w wnr over 1f out: plugged on and pressing for 3rd fnl f:* **15/2**[3]

4 **5** *½* **Amulet**[23] 6301 2-8-7 0.. MartinLane 3 57
(David Simcock) *hld up in tch: swtchd rt and effrt u.p ent fnl 2f: outpcd and no ch w wnr over 1f out: pressing for 3rd and one pce fnl f* **11/2**[2]

6 *½* **Gigli (IRE)** 2-8-6 0.. AdamBeschizza 2 55+
(William Haggas) *awkward leaving stalls and pushed along early: in tch: rdn and effrt on inner ent fnl 2f: no ch w wnr but plugged on fnl f* **11/1**

5 **7** *nk* **Exit Clause**[14] 6581 2-8-9 0.. MartinHarley 7 57
(Alastair Lidderdale) *t.k.h: chsd ldrs: rdn and outpcd by wnr wl over 1f out: wl btn and plugged on same pce fnl f* **16/1**

400 **8** *3½* **Lilly May (IRE)**[58] 5146 2-8-5 46.................................. AndreaAtzeni 6 44
(Phil McEntee) *chsd wnr for 1f: in tch after tl drvn and unable qck over 2f out: wknd over 1f out* **50/1**

9 *nk* **Dividend Dan (IRE)** 2-8-10 0.. MartinDwyer 8 50+
(Mike Murphy) *s.i.s: in tch in rr: rdn and outpcd ent fnl 2f: n.d after* **25/1**

00 **10** *½* **Kastini**[18] 6481 2-8-11 0.. EddieAhern 1 48
(Denis Coakley) *hld up in tch in rr: pushed along and no prog jst over 2f out: n.d fnl 2f* **28/1**

00 **11** *5* **Magic Beat**[19] 6437 2-7-13 0...................................... JemmaMarshall(5) 9 27
(Pat Phelan) *sn pushed along: in tch towards rr: wknd 2f out* **66/1**

1m 25.17s (-0.83) **Going Correction** -0.20s/f (Stan) **11** Ran SP% **116.4**
Speed ratings (Par 95): **96,91,88,87,86 86,85,81,81,81 75**
toteswingers 1&2 £9.90, 2&3 £4.10, 1&3 £2.90 CSF £67.54 TOTE £10.10: £3.30, £2.30, £1.10; EX 92.90 Trifecta £696.70 Part won. Pool: £941.49 - 0.20 winning units..
Owner B N T Racing **Bred** Kildaragh Stud **Trained** Middleham Moor, N Yorks

FOCUS
The winner impressed and the standard is set around the fourth and eighth.

NOTEBOOK
Steelriver(IRE) ◆ made all of the running in a time just over a second quicker than the first division. He was building on an encouraging debut over 6f at Thirsk and looks a useful type in the making, with his jockey predicting there will be more to come next year. (op 13-2 tchd 6-1)
Intermix(IRE), an already gelded half-brother to a couple of moderate sprint maidens, out of a 1m5.5f Group 2 winner in France, was keen early but plugged on to fare best of the newcomers. (op 12-1)
Syrenka failed to progress from her Newbury debut (fourth in a 7f conditions event), but she's very much bred for stamina and just didn't have the speed. (op 6-4 tchd 15-8)
Branson(IRE) didn't run to his official mark of 72 after 50 days off. (op 6-1 tchd 9-2)
Amulet failed to build sufficiently on her Brighton debut. (op 13-2 tchd 5-1)
Gigli(IRE), a 12,000euros half-sister to a couple of 1m4f winners, ran green but was keeping on at the finish and should improve. (op 14-1)

6979 BETDAQ CASINO GAMES H'CAP 7f (P)
7:30 (7:30) (Class 4) (0-85,85) 3-Y-O+ **£4,075** (£1,212; £606; £303) **Stalls** Low

Form RPR

212 **1** **Alraased (USA)**[21] 6381 3-9-4 **84**.................................. PaulHanagan 6 94+
(John Dunlop) *hld up in midfield: rdn and str run over 1f out: ev ch ins fnl f: r.o wl to ld cl home* **9/4**[1]

00 **2** *shd* **Harrison George (IRE)**[11] 6676 7-9-7 **85**...................(t) DarryllHolland 4 95
(P J O'Gorman) *in tch: rdn and qcknd on inner to chal 2f out: led ent fnl f: r.o wl u.p tl hdd and no ex cl home* **20/1**

3201 **3** *hd* **Rustic Deacon**[62] 5004 5-9-2 **83**.................................. RaulDaSilva(3) 12 92
(Willie Musson) *hld up in tch in midfield: swtchd lft and effrt 2f out: styd on wl and ev ch ins fnl f: r.o wl* **10/1**

4013 **4** *2¾* **Golden Tempest (IRE)**[16] 6538 4-9-2 **80**.......................... TedDurcan 2 82
(Eve Johnson Houghton) *hld up in midfield: rdn and hdwy wl over 1f out: edgd lft over 1f out: kpt on wl ins fnl f: wnt 4th cl home: nvr trbld ldrs* **16/1**

0032 **5** *½* **Little Black Book (IRE)**[16] 6539 4-9-2 **80**......................(b) JimCrowley 1 80
(Gerard Butler) *chsd ldr: swtchd out lft and effrt over 2f out: unable qck 1f out: wknd fnl 100yds* **13/2**[2]

3241 **6** *1¾* **Emkanaat**[19] 6454 4-8-12 **83**.............................. JeanVanOvermeire(7) 11 79
(Roger Varian) *led: rdn wl over 1f out: hdd ent fnl f: wknd ins fnl f* **15/2**[3]

0100 **7** *nk* **Masai Moon**[19] 6454 8-9-5 **83**.................................(b) JamesMillman 8 78
(Rod Millman) *racd off the pce in last trio: swtchd rt and hdwy 2f out: kpt on ins fnl f: nvr trbld ldrs* **50/1**

-445 **8** *3¾* **Numeral (IRE)**[221] 785 4-9-7 **85**.................................. SeanLevey 9 70
(Richard Hannon) *t.k.h: in tch: rdn and unable qck jst over 2f out: wknd over 1f out* **8/1**

5100 **9** *½* **Street Power (USA)**[18] 6466 7-9-4 **82**............................ GeorgeBaker 3 65
(Jeremy Gask) *stdd s: hld up in rr: effrt u.p in centre 2f out: no imp fr over 1f out: nvr trbld ldrs* **12/1**

4000 **10** *1* **Treadwell (IRE)**[32] 6040 5-9-3 **81**.............................. FergusSweeney 10 62
(Jamie Osborne) *hld up in midfield: shuffled bk towards rr and n.m.r ent fnl 2f: one pce and wl hld after* **20/1**

0-00 **11** *½* **Sea Soldier (IRE)**[29] 6119 4-9-4 **82**.............................. JimmyFortune 7 61
(Andrew Balding) *stdd s: hld up in rr: effrt on inner 2f out: no real hdwy: nvr trbld ldrs* **16/1**

1140 **12** *3½* **Majuro (IRE)**[11] 6659 8-9-4 **85**.........................(t) MarkCoumbe(3) 13 55
(Charles Smith) *chsd ldrs: rdn over 2f out: wknd over 1f out* **33/1**

2114 **13** *7* **Centrifugal (IRE)**[15] 6566 3-9-5 **85**............................ SilvestreDeSousa 5 36
(Mark Johnston) *chsd ldrs: rdn and lost pl qckly jst over 2f out: wl bhd and eased fnl 100yds* **12/1**

1m 23.45s (-2.55) **Going Correction** -0.20s/f (Stan)
WFA 3 from 4yo+ 2lb **13** Ran SP% **117.6**
Speed ratings (Par 105): **106,105,105,102,101 99,99,95,94,93 93,89,81**
toteswingers 1&2 £12.00, 2&3 £45.20, 1&3 £7.90 CSF £56.31 CT £400.15 TOTE £4.40: £1.50, £7.60, £4.40; EX 46.50 Trifecta £469.40 Part won. Pool: £634.45 - 0.70 winning units..
Owner Hamdan Al Maktoum **Bred** Shadwell Farm LLC **Trained** Arundel, W Sussex
■ Stewards' Enquiry : Darryll Holland two-day ban; used whip above permitted level (24th-25th Oct).

FOCUS
The first three all looked potentially well treated beforehand and they finished clear of a solid yardstick in Golden Tempest. The time, on a quick track, was the second fastest of 738 races to have been run over this C&D. Strong form.

6980 SPORTINGLIFE.COM NURSERY 7f (P)
8:00 (8:00) (Class 2) 2-Y-O **£7,633** (£2,271; £1,135; £567) **Stalls** Low

Form RPR

421 **1** **Tamarkuz (USA)**[27] 6175 2-8-10 **82**.......................... SilvestreDeSousa 12 98+
(Saeed Bin Suroor) *t.k.h: hld up in midfield on outer: rdn and hdwy 2f out: qcknd to ld ent fnl f: stormed clr: impressive* **11/8**[1]

61 **2** *6* **George Cinq**[16] 6533 2-8-7 **79**.................................. HayleyTurner 9 80+
(Michael Bell) *stdd s: t.k.h: hld up in tch towards rr: effrt 2f out: nt clr run and swtchd lft over 1f out: r.o wl to snatch 2nd on post: no ch w wnr* **9/2**[2]

200 **3** *nse* **King Oliver**[40] 5793 2-8-0 **72**.................................. KieranO'Neill 2 72
(Richard Hannon) *led tl over 4f out: rdn and pressed ldrs over 1f out: 2nd and no ch w wnr fnl f: lost 2nd on post* **33/1**

5410 **4** *nk* **Everleigh**[53] 5361 2-8-5 **77**.................................. PaulHanagan 8 76+
(Richard Hannon) *bhd and n.m.r after 1f: pushed along 5f out: stl plenty to do but hdwy over 1f out: styd on wl fnl f: no ch w wnr* **25/1**

1560 **5** *hd* **Redressthebalance (IRE)**[29] 6129 2-9-7 **93**.................. JimCrowley 6 92
(Ralph Beckett) *hld up in tch: hmpd and lost pl after 1f: hdwy wl over 2f out: no ch w wnr but kpt on u.p fnl f* **20/1**

515 **6** 1 3/4 **Double Your Money (IRE)**[26] 6189 2-8-12 **84**............ FrannyNorton 13 78
(Mark Johnston) *bhd: swtchd sharply rt 5f out: effrt and switching rt 2f out: styd on fnl f: n.d* **15/2**[3]
2206 **7** 1 1/2 **Pearl Noir**[89] 4047 2-7-13 **71**........................ NickyMackay 10 61
(Scott Dixon) *chsd ldrs: wnt 2nd 4f out: rdn and ev ch over 2f out: led over 2f out tl ent fnl f: sn btn: wknd ins fnl f* **40/1**
2311 **8** 1/2 **Lady Of The House (IRE)**[18] 6475 2-8-13 **85**..................(p) AmyRyan 3 73
(Kevin Ryan) *chsd ldrs tl led over 4f out: rdn and hdd over 1f out: wknd ins fnl f* **14/1**
2420 **9** 1 **Letstalkaboutmoney (IRE)**[27] 6162 2-8-13 **85**.............. MartinHarley 5 71
(Mrs K Burke) *hld up towards rr: rdn and effrt over 2f out: plugged on same pce fr over 1f out: nvr trbld ldrs* **14/1**
21 **10** 2 **Miss Marjurie (IRE)**[34] 5978 2-8-9 **81**.......................... EddieAhern 4 61
(Denis Coakley) *awkward leaving stalls: t.k.h: chsd ldrs tl rdn and unable qck jst over 2f out: wknd over 1f out* **10/1**
313 **11** 2 3/4 **Lazarus Bell**[21] 6372 2-9-1 **87**.................................. MartinLane 1 60
(Brian Meehan) *in tch in midfield: rdn and unable qck over 2f out: wknd over 1f out* **16/1**
1003 **12** 3 **Carlton Blue (IRE)**[7] 6777 2-8-9 **81**..........................(t) ChrisCatlin 11 46
(Paul Cole) *nvr gng wl and a bhd* **40/1**
1554 **13** 11 **Mystical Moment**[7] 6775 2-9-0 **86**............................ SeanLevey 7 21
(Richard Hannon) *in tch: rdn and unable qck over 2f out: wknd over 1f out: eased fnl f* **20/1**

1m 23.95s (-2.05) **Going Correction** -0.20s/f (Stan) 2y crse rec **13** Ran SP% **121.5**
Speed ratings (Par 101): **103,96,96,95,95 93,91,91,90,87 84,81,68**
toteswingers 1&2 £2.80, 2&3 £65.90, 1&3 £22.90 CSF £6.35 CT £145.69 TOTE £2.20: £1.20, £1.50, £10.40; EX 9.00 Trifecta £352.10 Part won. Pool: £475.82- 0.63 winning units..
Owner Godolphin **Bred** John D Gunther **Trained** Newmarket, Suffolk

FOCUS
This nursery saw a mightily impressive performance from Tamarkuz, who broke the juvenile track record by 0.78 seconds and was only half a second off the time recorded by the progressive 3yo Alraased (carried 8lb more) in the preceding Class 4 handicap. The third and fourth, as well as the good time, help set the level.

NOTEBOOK
Tamarkuz(USA) ◆ won in some style despite being stuck widest of all throughout (drawn 12), and the way he picked up, having looked up against it early in the straight, was really quite taking. He was following up a Wolverhampton maiden success (runner-up won next time) on his third start, having earlier shaped nicely in a Warwick maiden that worked out well, and he looks pattern class on this surface. He'll surely head to Dubai, with the UAE 2000 Guineas the obvious target if he continues to progress, and he should get 1m. (op 2-1)
George Cinq, a C&D maiden winner on his previous start, didn't get the clearest of runs but was only second best. He won't always bump into such a smart type off his current sort of mark. (op 7-2)
King Oliver hadn't progressed from a promising debut in two subsequent starts, but this was better on his nursery/Polytrack debut. (op 28-1)
Everleigh didn't get the best of trips on her return from almost two months off and could do better. (tchd 28-1)
Redressthebalance(IRE) had to prove she was up to a mark in the 90s, but she ran creditably, especially as she was shuffled back early on. (op 18-1)
Double Your Money(IRE) ◆ didn't look all that comfortably after being switched sharply from a wide-out position and gave the distinct impression he can do better when more helpfully drawn. (op 12-1)
Mystical Moment Official explanation: jockey said filly hung right.

6981 SPORTINGLIFE.COM RACING H'CAP 1m 3f (P)
8:30 (8:32) (Class 5) (0-70,70) 3-Y-O+ £2,264 (£673; £336; £168) Stalls Low

Form RPR
020 **1** **Beat Route**[10] 6703 5-9-9 **70**.................................. J-PGuillambert 12 78
(Michael Attwater) *in tch: rdn and effrt to chal 2f out: led jst ins fnl f: battled on wl: rdn out* **10/1**
006 **2** hd **Sweet Lavender (IRE)**[112] 3283 4-9-2 **63**...................... GeorgeBaker 9 71
(Michael Wigham) *in tch: rdn and effrt over 2f out: ev ch fr over 1f out: no ex cl home* **16/1**
0315 **3** 1/2 **Royal Dutch**[21] 6376 3-9-3 **70**.................................. EddieAhern 14 77+
(Denis Coakley) *hld up in midfield: rdn and hdwy over 1f out: styd on wl to go 3rd wl ins fnl f* **5/2**[1]
3464 **4** nk **Whitby Jet (IRE)**[19] 6441 4-9-4 **70**...................... MichaelJMMurphy(5) 1 76
(Ed Vaughan) *chsd ldrs: rdn and effrt to chal on inner 2f out: led over 1f out tl ins fnl f: no ex towards fin* **4/1**[2]
0625 **5** hd **Sir Boss (IRE)**[31] 6076 7-9-9 **70**.................................. TomEaves 4 76
(Michael Mullineaux) *hld up in rr: gd hdwy on inner wl over 1f out: pressed ldrs 1f out: no ex fnl 75yds* **12/1**
035 **6** 1 1/2 **Berwin (IRE)**[13] 6613 3-9-3 **70**................................ JamesDoyle 11 73
(Sylvester Kirk) *t.k.h: hld up wl bhd: hdwy on outer 2f out: chsd ldrs and drvn 1f out: no imp ins fnl f: eased towards fin* **7/1**
5144 **7** 3 **If I Were A Boy (IRE)**[19] 6430 5-9-0 **68**.................(p) JoshBaudains(7) 8 66
(Dominic Ffrench Davis) *chsd ldr after 1f tl led 3f out: drvn and hdd over 1f out: wknd ins fnl f* **25/1**
1540 **8** 1 **Hip Hip Hooray**[13] 6613 6-9-4 **65**............................ IanMongan 13 61
(Luke Dace) *stdd and dropped in bhd after s: hld up in rr: hdwy on inner wl over 1f out: kpt on fnl f: nvr trbld ldrs* **33/1**
1-00 **9** 1/2 **Eraada**[20] 6405 3-9-2 **69**.. PaulHanagan 3 64
(Mark Johnston) *in tch in midfield: rdn 6f out: drvn and plugged on same pce fr over 2f out: nvr gng pce to threaten ldrs* **12/1**
0656 **10** 3 1/4 **Scamperdale**[29] 6120 10-9-2 **63**................................(p) KierenFox 6 52
(Brian Baugh) *hld up towards rr: hdwy on outer 4f out: chsd ldrs and rdn over 1f out: no ex and wknd ins fnl f* **25/1**
1440 **11** 3/4 **Before Bruce**[27] 6159 5-9-2 **63**..............................(tp) SebSanders 5 51
(Brendan Powell) *in tch in midfield: rdn and unable qck over 2f out: wknd over 1f out* **33/1**
3060 **12** 2 1/4 **Kinyras (IRE)**[31] 6076 4-9-6 **67**.............................. JimmyFortune 7 51
(Michael Easterby) *t.k.h: chsd ldr for 1f: styd chsng ldrs: rdn and pressed ldrs 2f out: sn struggling: fdd 1f out* **6/1**[3]
5400 **13** 2 1/4 **One For Joules (IRE)**[25] 6250 5-9-4 **65**.................. JamieGoldstein 10 45
(John Flint) *s.i.s: a towards rr: rdn and no prog over 2f out: n.d* **40/1**
0-10 **14** 17 **Maoi Chinn Tire (IRE)**[29] 3400 5-9-5 **66**......................(p) SeanQuinlan 2 15
(Jennie Candlish) *racd keenly: led tl 3f out: lost pl qckly and bhd fnl 2f* **50/1**

2m 18.81s (-3.09) **Going Correction** -0.20s/f (Stan)
WFA 3 from 4yo+ 6lb **14** Ran SP% **123.7**
Speed ratings (Par 103): **103,102,102,102,102 101,98,98,97,95 94,93,91,79**
toteswingers 1&2 £82.20, 2&3 £15.00, 1&3 £7.70 CSF £152.06 CT £531.85 TOTE £20.60: £4.30, £6.80, £1.40; EX 240.70 TRIFECTA Not won. Pool: £302.77..
Owner Canisbay Bloodstock **Bred** Canisbay Bloodstock Ltd **Trained** Epsom, Surrey

FOCUS
The first five finished in a bunch and this probably isn't strong form.

6982 DOWNLOAD THE FREE RACING PLUS APP H'CAP 7f (P)
9:00 (9:00) (Class 6) (0-58,58) 3-Y-O+ £1,617 (£481; £240; £120) Stalls Low

Form RPR
0000 **1** **Blue Deer (IRE)**[22] 6334 4-9-5 **58**..........................(p) JimCrowley 13 69
(Lee Carter) *hld up in rr: weaving through and gd hdwy over 1f out: chsd wnr ins fnl f: styd on strly u.p to ld on post* **12/1**
0005 **2** nse **Darnathean**[20] 6402 3-9-3 **58**................................ SebSanders 1 69
(Paul D'Arcy) *taken down early: chsd ldrs: rdn and ev ch 2f out: drvn ahd ent fnl f: kpt on wl tl hdd on post* **11/2**[2]
4441 **3** 2 3/4 **Wyndham Wave**[20] 6396 3-9-2 **57**........................(p) JamesMillman 6 60
(Rod Millman) *chsd ldrs: rdn to ld 2f out: hdd ent fnl f: no ex and wknd fnl 75yds* **15/8**[1]
3000 **4** nk **Irie Ute**[19] 6455 4-9-3 **56**.. LiamKeniry 7 59
(Sylvester Kirk) *hld up in tch towards rr: rdn and effrt 2f out: styd on wl u.p fnl f: could nt rch ldrs* **22/1**
0030 **5** 1/2 **Sermons Mount (USA)**[7] 6773 6-9-2 **55**..................(p) J-PGuillambert 2 56
(Paul Howling) *chsd ldr: carried wd bnd 3f out: drvn and ev ch 2f tl jst over 1f out: wknd fnl 100yds* **20/1**
000 **6** shd **Snowy Valley**[34] 5970 3-9-0 **58**.............................. RyanPowell(3) 10 59
(Simon Earle) *hld up in rr: hdwy u.p over 1f out: styd on fnl f: nvr trbld ldrs* **33/1**
1040 **7** 1/2 **Silly Billy (IRE)**[7] 6778 4-9-2 **55**..............................(t) JamesDoyle 9 55
(Sylvester Kirk) *hld up towards rr: drvn and effrt 2f out: hdwy u.p over 1f out: styng on but no threat to ldrs whn nt clr run and eased towards fin* **6/1**[3]
660 **8** nk **Tribal I D (IRE)**[15] 6565 3-9-2 **57**......................(be[1]) GeorgeBaker 14 56
(Jim Boyle) *t.k.h: hld up in tch in rr: effrt 2f out: kpt on same pce u.p ins fnl f* **16/1**
-000 **9** nk **Sweet Ophelia**[50] 5458 3-9-2 **57**..........................(v[1]) PatCosgrave 4 55
(George Baker) *in tch: effrt ent fnl 2f: drvn to chse ldrs over 1f out: no ex and wknd ins fnl f* **16/1**
50 **10** 3/4 **Bobby's Doll**[33] 5995 5-9-0 **58**...................... MichaelJMMurphy(5) 3 54
(Terry Clement) *in tch in midfield: styd on same pce u.p fnl 2f: nvr trbld ldrs* **40/1**
6000 **11** 3/4 **Catalyze**[16] 6530 4-8-13 **55**................................(t[1]) MarkCoumbe(3) 5 49
(Charles Smith) *stdd and dropped in bhd after s: t.k.h: hld up in tch towards rr: rdn and effrt 2f out but no imp fnl f* **28/1**
0201 **12** hd **Demoiselle Bond**[14] 6586 4-9-5 **58**.......................... RobertHavlin 11 51
(Lydia Richards) *taken down early: led: hung lft bnd 3f out: hdd 2f out: wknd ent fnl f* **11/1**
1020 **13** 1/2 **Custom House (IRE)**[14] 6585 4-9-4 **57**........................ JohnFahy 8 49
(John E Long) *in tch: rdn and no rspnse ent fnl 2f: wknd over 1f out* **16/1**
0530 **14** hd **Jonnie Skull (IRE)**[33] 5993 6-8-11 **57**...................(t) ClaireMurray(7) 12 49
(Phil McEntee) *chsd ldrs on outer: carried wd and lost pl bnd 3f out: bhd after and n.d fnl 2f* **28/1**

1m 25.12s (-0.88) **Going Correction** -0.20s/f (Stan)
WFA 3 from 4yo+ 2lb **14** Ran SP% **119.5**
Speed ratings (Par 101): **97,96,93,93,92 92,92,91,91,90 89,89,89,88**
toteswingers 1&2 £13.00, 2&3 £5.70, 1&3 £7.90 CSF £69.75 CT £189.01 TOTE £15.40: £4.20, £2.50, £1.30; EX 82.60 TRIFECTA Not won. Pool: £307.18..
Owner Mrs I Marshall **Bred** Pier House Stud **Trained** Epsom, Surrey

FOCUS
The winner has been rated as back to last winter's best with the runner-up best form of this year, and the third and fourth close to their recent marks.
Demoiselle Bond Official explanation: jockey said filly hung left.
T/Plt: £14.80 to a £1 stake. Pool of £66722.25 - 3275.10 winning tickets. T/Qpdt: £3.60 to a £1 stake. Pool of £7625.83 -1558.50 winning tickets. SP

6787 NOTTINGHAM (L-H)
Wednesday, October 10

OFFICIAL GOING: Good to soft (soft in places; 6.7)
Wind: Virtually nil Weather: Cloudy but dry

6983 BDN CIVIL ENGINEERING E B F MAIDEN STKS 5f 13y
2:30 (2:32) (Class 5) 2-Y-O £3,234 (£962; £481; £240) Stalls High

Form RPR
04 **1** **Fils Anges (IRE)**[102] 3637 2-9-3 0.......................... JamieSpencer 4 85+
(Michael Bell) *hld up in rr: smooth hdwy 1/2-way: cl up 2f out: shkn up to ld over 1f out: qcknd clr: comf* **10/11**[1]
3354 **2** 4 1/2 **Bentleysoysterboy (IRE)**[40] 5790 2-9-3 67..................(p) DaneO'Neill 6 63
(David Elsworth) *sn led: rdn along and jnd wl over 1f out: hdd appr fnl f: sn drvn and edgd lft: kpt on: no ch w wnr* **6/1**[3]
32 **3** 7 **Quality Mark (USA)**[21] 6360 2-9-3 0........................ WilliamBuick 5 38
(Jeremy Noseda) *cl up: rdn along over 2f out: sn drvn and one pce* **5/2**[2]
4 3/4 **Captain Cruz (IRE)** 2-9-3 0.................................. JamesDoyle 1 35
(Ronald Harris) *dwlt and green in rr: gd hdwy on outer 1/2-way: chsd ldng pair 2f out: sn rdn and one pce* **25/1**
5 3 **Cara Gina** 2-8-12 0.. LiamJones 3 19
(William Haggas) *trckd ldrs: rdn along over 2f out: sn wknd* **17/2**
6600 **6** 10 **Star Maid**[44] 5654 2-8-12 36.................................. DavidProbert 2
(Tony Carroll) *prom: rdn along bef 1/2-way: sn wknd* **150/1**

1m 1.5s **Going Correction** +0.05s/f (Good) **6** Ran SP% **110.3**
Speed ratings (Par 95): **98,90,79,78,73 57**
CSF £6.82 TOTE £2.40: £1.60, £3.40; EX 6.50.
Owner Dermot Hanafin **Bred** Yeomanstown Stud **Trained** Newmarket, Suffolk

FOCUS
The runners came home spread out in this ordinary maiden and the winner did this easily. With the third disappointing, he beat little.

NOTEBOOK
Fils Anges(IRE), off since finishing fourth over 6f at Windsor in June, was well backed, travelled powerfully and quickly stamped his authority, clearly having no trouble with the ground. Nurseries are now an option and he could develop into quite a useful sprint handicapper next season. (op 13-8)
Bentleysoysterboy(IRE) is exposed as modest, but had the possible advantage of the stands' rail and kept on to pull clear of the remainder. He may find a small opening returned to nurseries. (op 7-1 tchd 8-1)
Quality Mark(USA) had shown enough to win a race such as this, but he was unproven on this softer ground and looked laboured. Nurseries are now an option. (op 13-8)
Captain Cruz(IRE), half-brother to a sprinting 2yo winner, had reportedly been pleasing at home and he looked in need of the experience. (op 18-1)

Cara Gina, whose dam was a 5f winner at two, was keen early and then failed to pick up for pressure in the final 2f. She's entitled to improve and may prefer slightly better ground. (op 8-1 tchd 15-2)

6984 BDN CONSTRUCTION NURSERY 5f 13y

3:00 (3:01) (Class 4) (0-80,86) 2-Y-O **£3,428** (£1,020; £509; £254) **Stalls** High

Form RPR

431 **1** **March**[55] 5255 2-9-3 **76** .... AdamKirby 11 85+
(Marco Botti) *hld up towards rr: smooth hdwy wl over 1f out: rdn to ld jst ins fnl f: kpt on* **7/2**[1]

534 **2** 1 ¾ **Millkwood**[7] 6787 2-8-10 **69** .... PJMcDonald 14 71
(John Davies) *hld up towards rr: hdwy on outer wl over 1f out: rdn and ev ch whn hung bedly lft ins fnl f: kpt on* **9/1**

2421 **3** nse **Balinka**[43] 5709 2-8-9 **68** .... SilvestreDeSousa 1 70
(Mel Brittain) *racd wd: prom: hdwy and cl up 2f out: rdn over 1f out and ev ch tl drvn and kpt on same pce ins fnl f* **9/1**

0210 **4** ½ **Seven Of Clubs (IRE)**[18] 6487 2-9-3 **76** ....(b[1]) NeilCallan 4 76
(Noel Quinlan) *led: rdn wl over 1f out: drvn and edgd lft ent fnl f: sn hdd and one pce* **12/1**

1 **5** 2 **Angus Og**[29] 6122 2-8-13 **79** ....(e) ConorHarrison(7) 10 72
(Mrs K Burke) *chsd ldrs: rdn along wl over 1f out: sn drvn and one pce* **4/1**[2]

2630 **6** shd **Forray**[32] 6022 2-9-5 **78** .... RichardMullen 6 70
(Ed McMahon) *in tch: hdwy to chse ldrs wl over 1f out: rdn appr fnl f and one pce* **11/2**[3]

6100 **7** 1 **Monkey Bar Flies (IRE)**[11] 6658 2-8-10 **72** .... LeeTopliss(3) 7 61
(Richard Fahey) *in tch: rdn along and sltly outpcd 2f out: kpt on fnl f* **18/1**

4421 **8** 1 **Starlight Angel (IRE)**[15] 6564 2-9-1 **74** .... JamesDoyle 9 59
(Ronald Harris) *cl up: rdn 2f out and ev ch tl drvn and wknd appr fnl f* **25/1**

5230 **9** ½ **Risky Rizkova**[27] 6155 2-8-8 **67** ....(p) RichardKingscote 8 50
(Jonathan Portman) *chsd ldrs: rdn along over 2f out: sn wknd* **33/1**

136 **10** ½ **Uncomplicated**[53] 5332 2-9-4 **77** .... PatCosgrave 2 59
(Jim Boyle) *wnt lft s: a in rr* **25/1**

104 **11** hd **Scentpastparadise**[19] 6425 2-9-6 **79** .... GrahamLee 3 60
(Ann Duffield) *in tch: rdn along bef half way: sn wknd* **18/1**

451 **12** 1 ¾ **Somoud (IRE)**[19] 6438 2-9-1 **74** .... IanMongan 12 49
(J R Jenkins) *racd nr stands' rail: cl up: rdn along over 2f out: sn edgd lft and wknd* **9/1**

1m 1.56s (0.06) **Going Correction** +0.05s/f (Good) **12** Ran SP% **116.5**
Speed ratings (Par 97): **97,94,94,93,90 89,88,86,85,85 84,82**
toteswingers 1&2 £5.90, 2&3 £8.20, 1&3 £5.90 CSF £33.83 CT £266.26 TOTE £3.80: £1.50, £3.00, £2.30; EX 38.00 Trifecta £131.80 Pool: £431.02 - 242 winning units..
Owner H E Sheikh Sultan Bin Khalifa Al Nahyan **Bred** T K & Mrs P A Knox **Trained** Newmarket, Suffolk

FOCUS
Runners were spread across the track in this nursery, with the main action unfolding more middle to far side late on. The second, third and fourth contribute to a solid level in fair a nursery for the time of year.

NOTEBOOK
March, who accounted for a subsequent scorer when winning her maiden at Beverley, is by a sire whose progeny are beginning to show a real liking for soft ground and she produced a sustained run to get nicely on top. She has plenty of speed and looks capable of mixing it in a better quality of nursery. (op 3-1)
Millkwood, a close-up fourth in a C&D maiden last week, probably bettered that form on this nursery debut, staying on well in the manner of a horse likely to get 6f. (op 10-1 tchd 11-1)
Balinka showed plenty of speed from her low draw and stepped up on the form of her last-time-out maiden win. (op 10-1 tchd 11-1)
Seven Of Clubs(IRE), wearing first-time blinkers for the drop in trip, showed plenty of pace early but proved unable to quicken on with the principals. He'll be happier returned to 6f. Official explanation: jockey said colt hung left-handed. (tchd 10-1)
Angus Og, a ready winner in a first-time eyeshield on his debut, fared okay considering he was the least experienced, although winning from his current mark won't be easy. (op 5-1)
Scentpastparadise Official explanation: trainers representative said filly had breathing a problem.
Somoud(IRE) again displayed plenty of pace nearer the stands' rail on this nursery debut, but looking at how he dropped away, it's likely the ground was against him. (op 17-2 tchd 10-1)

6985 BDN CONSTRUCTION E B F MAIDEN STKS 1m 75y

3:30 (3:31) (Class 5) 2-Y-O **£3,234** (£962; £481; £240) **Stalls** Centre

Form RPR

0 **1** **Autun (USA)**[13] 6596 2-9-3 0 .... TomQueally 7 80+
(Sir Henry Cecil) *trckd ldr: cl up 3f out: led 2f out: jnd and rdn whn edgd rt ent fnl f: hdd briefly ins fnl f: sn led again and styd on strly* **15/8**[1]

32 **2** nk **Sicur**[27] 6164 2-9-0 0 .... PatrickHills(3) 4 79+
(Luca Cumani) *dwlt: sn in tch: hdwy 3f out: effrt to chal over 1f out: rdn and sltly hmpd ent fnl f: led briefly ins fnl f: sn hdd and no ex* **5/2**[2]

3 8 **Berkeley Street (USA)** 2-9-3 0 .... RyanMoore 5 61+
(Sir Michael Stoute) *trckd ldrs: hdwy to chse ldng pair 3f out: rdn along 2f out: kpt on same pce appr fnl f* **6/1**

4 hd **Sadiq** 2-9-3 0 .... SilvestreDeSousa 6 61+
(Saeed Bin Suroor) *dwlt and in rr: hdwy over 3f out: rdn along over 2f out: kpt on u.p fnl f* **4/1**[3]

5 nse **Train Hard** 2-9-3 0 .... JoeFanning 3 61
(Mark Johnston) *led: rdn along 3f out: hdd 2f out: grad wknd* **16/1**

0 **6** 2 ½ **Posh Boy (IRE)**[12] 6636 2-9-3 0 .... HarryBentley 2 55
(Chris Wall) *chsd ldng pair: rdn along over 3f out: grad wknd* **66/1**

7 6 **Belatorio (IRE)** 2-8-12 0 .... GrahamLee 8 37
(James Given) *a towards rr* **50/1**

8 3 **Tallaay (IRE)** 2-9-3 0 .... TadhgO'Shea 1 36
(Mark Johnston) *a in rr* **20/1**

9 4 ½ **Distant Sunrise** 2-8-12 0 .... PJMcDonald 9 21
(Ann Duffield) *in tch: rdn along 4f out: sn wknd* **66/1**

1m 50.49s (1.49) **Going Correction** +0.175s/f (Good) **9** Ran SP% **113.2**
Speed ratings (Par 95): **102,101,93,93,93 90,84,81,77**
toteswingers 1&2 £1.80, 2&3 £3.10, 1&3 £3.20 CSF £6.36 TOTE £2.60: £1.30, £1.50, £1.50; EX 9.20 Trifecta £24.80 Pool: £750.49 - 22.34 winning units..
Owner K Abdulla **Bred** Juddmonte Farms Inc **Trained** Newmarket, Suffolk

FOCUS
This was probably a fair maiden, with the two experienced market leaders drawing clear from a trio of promising newcomers. The runner-up sets a good level.

NOTEBOOK
Autun(USA), very green when beating just one home (albeit beaten little over 6l) behind a useful winner at Newmarket on his debut, showed the benefit of that experience and was always ideally placed to pounce. He showed a likeable attitude when strongly pressed late on and certainly has the size to make a useful 3yo over middle distances. (op 9-4 tchd 7-4)
Sicur set the standard, but he proved a little keen early on and, having come to win his race, proved unable to get past. Clear of the third, he should have no trouble winning an ordinary back-end maiden before going up in trip next season. He also now qualifies for a handicap mark. (op 13-8)
Berkeley Street(USA), closely related to US Grade 3 winner Magic Mission, was nibbled at in the market and made a promising start without being given a hard ride. A sounder surface ought to suit and he can probably win a maiden this year. (op 9-1)
Sadiq, half-brother to 1m-1m1f winner Staff Sergeant, has plenty of stamina on the distaff side of his pedigree and it was no surprise to see him keeping on late, having proved particularly green through the early stages. He too looks a likely improver who should be capable of winning a maiden. Official explanation: jockey said colt ran green. (tchd 5-1)
Train Hard, whose dam won up to 1m6f for the same connections, knew his job and simply ran into a few classier types. He'll be one for middle-distance handicaps next season, but may still be capable of winning an ordinary maiden at two. (op 20-1)
Posh Boy(IRE) will be of more interest once handicapping.
Tallaay(IRE), whose dam is a half-sister to Breeders' Cup Classic winner Drosselmeyer, was too green to make an impact and will likely want faster ground also. (op 22-1 tchd 25-1)

6986 BDN CIVIL ENGINEERING H'CAP 1m 1f

4:00 (4:00) (Class 4) (0-85,83) 3-Y-O **£4,075** (£1,212; £606; £303) **Stalls** Low

Form RPR

0300 **1** **Flaxen Flare (IRE)**[12] 6638 3-9-2 78 ....(v) DavidProbert 2 91
(Andrew Balding) *trckd ldng pair on inner: hdwy 3f out: rdn to chse ldr over 1f out: swtchd rt ent fnl f: styd on wl to ld last 75yds* **9/2**[3]

2133 **2** 1 ¼ **Oddysey (IRE)**[7] 6789 3-8-10 75 .... LeeTopliss(3) 4 85
(Michael Dods) *trckd ldrs: hdwy over 3f out: cl up over 2f out: led wl over 1f out: rdn and edgd lft ent fnl f: sn drvn: hdd and no ex last 75yds* **7/2**[2]

6542 **3** 5 **Balady (IRE)**[27] 6169 3-9-1 77 .... TadhgO'Shea 7 76
(John Dunlop) *led: rdn along 3f out: jnd 2f out: drvn and hdd wl over 1f out: kpt on same pce fnl f* **12/1**

-100 **4** ¾ **Future Security (IRE)**[22] 6333 3-9-5 81 .... SilvestreDeSousa 6 78
(Saeed Bin Suroor) *trckd ldrs: pushed along over 3f out: sn rdn and plugged on same pce fnl 2f* **3/1**[1]

0500 **5** 5 **Stellar Express (IRE)**[7] 6789 3-9-5 81 ....(b[1]) TomQueally 3 67
(Michael Appleby) *hld up in tch: hdwy on outer over 3f out: rdn to chal 2f out: sn drvn and wknd* **16/1**

1460 **6** 7 **Spirit Of The Law (IRE)**[26] 6193 3-9-7 83 .... WilliamBuick 5 54
(Ed Dunlop) *hld up: a in rr* **9/2**[3]

0040 **7** 3 ½ **Masters Blazing**[18] 6502 3-8-4 69 oh1 .... RyanPowell(3) 1 32
(John Ryan) *hld up: a in rr* **16/1**

-641 **8** 5 **Supreme Luxury (IRE)**[104] 3521 3-8-13 75 .... AmyRyan 8 27
(Kevin Ryan) *dwlt: sn chsng ldr: rdn along over 3f out: sn wknd* **9/1**

1m 57.63s (117.63) **8** Ran SP% **113.0**
toteswingers 1&2 £4.90, 2&3 £3.00, 1&3 £5.20 CSF £20.13 CT £175.16 TOTE £6.80: £1.90, £2.60, £2.60; EX 26.10 Trifecta £188.80 Pool: £1510.85 - 5.92 winning units..
Owner Kennet Valley Thoroughbreds VIII **Bred** Denis And Mrs Teresa Bergin **Trained** Kingsclere, Hants

FOCUS
They appeared to go a decent gallop early and the front pair drew a little way clear. The winner was not an obvious improver, but earned a personal-best rating, with the runner-up a fair guide.
Spirit Of The Law(IRE) Official explanation: jockey said colt was unsuited by ground (good to soft - good in places).

6987 BDN CONSTRUCTION H'CAP 1m 2f 50y

4:30 (4:31) (Class 4) (0-85,83) 3-Y-O+ **£4,398** (£1,309; £654; £327) **Stalls** Low

Form RPR

4505 **1** **Art Scholar (IRE)**[7] 6776 5-9-10 **83** .... TomQueally 13 94
(Michael Appleby) *hld up in midfield: smooth hdwy on outer over 3f out: trckd ldrs 2f out: rdn to ld appr fnl f: styd on strly* **25/1**

4313 **2** 1 ½ **Cactus Valley (IRE)**[50] 5451 3-9-4 **82** .... JamesDoyle 3 90
(Roger Charlton) *trckd ldrs: hdwy over 3f out: led 2f out: rdn over 1f out: drvn and hdd appr fnl f* **8/1**[2]

2-16 **3** 3 **Dulkashe (IRE)**[21] 6376 3-9-1 **82** .... PatrickHills(3) 15 84
(Luca Cumani) *hld up and bhd: hdwy on outer 3f out: rdn 2f out: kpt on fnl f: nrst fin* **12/1**[3]

-231 **4** 1 **Sunpass**[10] 6704 3-9-0 **78** 6ex .... WilliamBuick 1 78
(John Gosden) *trckd ldrs: hdwy and cl up 3f out: effrt over 2f out: sn rdn and ev ch tl drvn and wknd over 1f out* **4/6**[1]

0313 **5** 2 ¾ **Zanotti**[14] 6573 3-9-4 **82** ....(t) NeilCallan 7 77
(Roger Varian) *dwlt: sn in tch: trckd ldrs after 3f: effrt on inner 3f out: rdn along over 2f out: sn drvn and one pce* **8/1**[2]

0000 **6** 1 **Pivotman**[18] 6484 4-9-6 **79** ....(t) IanMongan 10 72
(Amanda Perrett) *led: rdn along 3f out: hdd 2f out and grad wknd* **14/1**

2356 **7** hd **Kenyan Cat**[19] 6450 5-9-6 **79** .... RichardMullen 9 72
(Ed McMahon) *chsd ldrs: rdn along over 3f out: sn wknd* **16/1**

0600 **8** 1 **Fair Trade**[12] 6638 5-9-10 **83** .... GrahamLee 11 74
(Hughie Morrison) *in rr: rdn along over 3f out: sme late hdwy* **40/1**

-000 **9** hd **Covert Decree**[19] 6450 4-9-6 **79** .... AdamKirby 4 69
(Clive Cox) *plld hrd early: prom: chsd ldr after 3f: rdn along 3f out: wknd over 2f out* **40/1**

3600 **10** ½ **Mountain Range (IRE)**[14] 6584 4-9-4 **77** .... RyanMoore 12 66
(John Dunlop) *hld up: a towards rr* **12/1**[3]

-600 **11** 3 **Simayill**[16] 6539 4-9-4 **77** .... DaneO'Neill 14 61
(John Berry) *a towards rr* **66/1**

1140 **12** 14 **Standpoint**[27] 6170 6-9-1 **79** .... DavidKenny(5) 8 36
(Conor Dore) *a towards rr: bhd fnl 3f* **40/1**

2m 14.59s (0.29) **Going Correction** +0.175s/f (Good)
WFA 3 from 4yo+ 5lb **12** Ran SP% **122.8**
Speed ratings (Par 105): **105,103,101,100,98 97,97,96,96,96 93,82**
toteswingers 1&2 £15.10, 2&3 £10.00, 1&3 £18.60 CSF £214.43 CT £2554.74 TOTE £28.70: £4.90, £1.70, £3.00; EX 194.50 Trifecta £884.30 Part won. Pool: £1195.12 - 0.20 winning units..
Owner Mrs J Scrivens **Bred** John Ramsbottom **Trained** Danethorpe, Notts

FOCUS
The pace gradually increased in what the betting implied was an uncompetitive handicap, but it didn't work out that way. Sound form.
Sunpass Official explanation: jockey said colt was unsuited by ground (good to soft - good in places)
Covert Decree Official explanation: jockey said filly ran too freely.

6988 BDN CONSTRUCTION APPRENTICE H'CAP 1m 2f 50y

5:00 (5:00) (Class 5) (0-70,74) 3-Y-O+ **£2,264** (£673; £336; £168) **Stalls** Low

Form RPR

5430 **1** **Almuftarris (USA)**[19] 6430 3-9-2 **70** ....(b) AshleyMorgan(3) 10 79
(Ed Dunlop) *hld up towards rr: smooth hdwy on wd outside 3f out: chsd ldrs 2f out: rdn over 1f out: led ins fnl f: styd on strly* **9/1**

6001 **2** *1 ¾* **Follow The Flag (IRE)**[7] 6794 8-9-3 **68** 6ex...............(v) DavidBergin(5) 9 74
(Alan McCabe) *trckd ldrs: hdwy 4f out: cl up over 2f out: rdn and ev ch over 1f out: kpt on same pce ins fnl f* **20/1**

6210 **3** *nk* **Dazzling Valentine**[12] 6631 4-9-3 **68**.......................... NatashaEaton(5) 4 73
(Alan Bailey) *hld up: hdwy 4f out: rdn to chse ldrs 2f out: styd on to ld ent 1f out: hdd and one pce ins fnl f* **18/1**

030 **4** *1 ½* **Ela Gonda Mou**[10] 6703 5-9-3 **66**................................. RosieJessop(3) 3 69
(Peter Charalambous) *a.p: hdwy on inner to ld 3f out: rdn 2f out: drvn and hdd 1f out: kpt on same pce* **7/1**[3]

5050 **5** *nse* **Laughing Jack**[12] 6638 4-9-2 **67**.............................. GeorgeDowning(5) 2 69
(Tony Carroll) *s.i.s and bhd: hdwy over 3f out: rdn 2f out: styd on appr fnl f: nrst fin* **20/1**

5023 **6** *2 ½* **Maybeme**[7] 6794 6-8-5 **56** oh2.............................(p) ShirleyTeasdale(5) 12 54
(Neville Bycroft) *chsd ldrs: hdwy and cl up 3f out: rdn along 2f out: sn drvn and wknd appr fnl f* **16/1**

3434 **7** *1* **Fine Altomis**[19] 6429 3-8-10 **68**.................................... ConnorNichol(7) 8 64
(Michael Dods) *chsd ldrs: rdn along wl over 2f out: grad wknd* **12/1**

443 **8** *hd* **Spring Tonic**[20] 6397 3-9-5 **70**.. PatrickHills 6 65
(Luca Cumani) *hld up in rr: stmbld after 2f: effrt and rdn 3f out: nvr a factor* **7/2**[2]

5641 **9** *1 ¼* **Danube River**[9] 6735 3-9-6 **74** 6ex..................... MichaelJMMurphy(3) 11 67
(Mark Johnston) *trckd ldrs: hdwy 1/2-way: led 4f out: hdd 3f out and sn rdn along: wknd over 2f out* **5/2**[1]

1562 **10** *10* **Titus Bolt (IRE)**[15] 6568 3-8-9 **60**.......................................(v) KierenFox 7 34
(Jim Boyle) *led: rdn along and hdd 4f out: sn wknd* **20/1**

4256 **11** *4* **Mr Fickle (IRE)**[51] 5405 3-9-2 **67**..................................(p) HarryBentley 5 33
(Gary Moore) *a towards rr: bhd fnl 3f* **11/1**

060 **12** *15* **Spanish Trail**[32] 6056 3-8-3 **59** oh5 ow3.......................... JackDuern(5) 1
(Christopher Kellett) *in tch on inner: rdn along and lost pl bef 1/2-way: wl bhd fnl 3f* **150/1**

2m 16.06s (1.76) **Going Correction** +0.175s/f (Good)
WFA 3 from 4yo+ 5lb **12** Ran SP% **115.4**
Speed ratings (Par 103): **99,97,97,96,96 94,93,93,92,84 80,68**
toteswingers 1&2 £21.80, 2&3 £52.30, 1&3 £20.40 CSF £177.05 CT £3130.71 TOTE £9.30: £4.70, £6.20, £6.90; EX 167.40.
Owner Hamdan Al Maktoum **Bred** Shadwell Farm LLC **Trained** Newmarket, Suffolk

FOCUS
A race that set up for the closers. The runner-up and third set the standard.
Spring Tonic Official explanation: jockey said colt stumbled.
Spanish Trail Official explanation: vet said lost its off-fore shoe.
T/Plt: £233.00 to a £1 stake. Pool of £48884.80 - 153.15 winning tickets. T/Qpdt: £41.30 to a £1 stake. Pool of £4244.33, 75.90 winning tickets. JR

6989 - 6996a (Foreign Racing) - See Raceform Interactive

6753 AYR (L-H)
Thursday, October 11

OFFICIAL GOING: Heavy (soft in places; 8.4) changing to heavy after race 5 (4.10)
Wind: Almost nil Weather: Overcast, raining

6997 GILES INSURANCE/E.B.F. MAIDEN STKS — 1m
2:10 (2:11) (Class 4) 2-Y-O — **£4,398** (£1,309; £654; £327) **Stalls** Low

Form RPR

220 **1** **Mister Marcasite**[22] 6356 2-9-3 68....................................... DavidAllan 1 72
(Mel Brittain) *mde all: rdn over 2f out: edgd rt ins fnl f: jst hld on* **11/4**[2]

43 **2** *shd* **Duke Of Yorkshire**[12] 6669 2-9-0 0.................................... NeilFarley(3) 2 72
(Declan Carroll) *trckd ldrs: effrt and swtchd rt over 2f out: drifted rt and styd on wl fnl f: jst hld* **5/2**[1]

30 **3** *6* **Bell'Arte (IRE)**[34] 6007 2-8-12 0.................................. RobertWinston 4 54
(Mark Johnston) *pressed wnr: drvn 3f out: wknd ins fnl f* **5/2**[1]

43 **4** *11* **Al Thumama**[29] 6132 2-8-12 0.. AmyRyan 3 29+
(Kevin Ryan) *swvd bdly rt s and sn wl bhd: hdwy and in tch over 3f out: rdn and wknd 2f out* **5/1**[3]

0 **5** *9* **Sir Frank Morgan (IRE)**[10] 6733 2-9-3 0.......................... GrahamLee 5 15
(Mark Johnston) *prom: pushed along after 3f: rdn and wknd over 3f out* **9/1**

1m 55.7s (11.90) **Going Correction** +1.375s/f (Soft) **5** Ran SP% **110.5**
Speed ratings (Par 97): **95,94,88,77,68**
CSF £10.02 TOTE £4.00: £1.80, £2.00; EX 11.20.
Owner Steven J Box **Bred** Aiden Murphy **Trained** Warthill, N Yorks

FOCUS
This was run in very wet conditions with rain still falling. The jockeys confirmed that the ground was testing, but reported that the horses were getting through the ground. The time for this modest maiden was 17sec outside the standard, and this isn't form to treat too seriously. The winner sets the initial standard. The first two raced on opposite sides of the narrowed track in the latter stages.

NOTEBOOK
Mister Marcasite made all and ran on grimly after sticking to the inner up the straight. Having run well on his first two starts he flopped on a sound surface at Beverley, and the return to testing conditions was in his favour. (op 7-2)
Duke Of Yorkshire was under pressure before the turn but stuck on after switching to the near rail and was just denied. He'll get further and should win a race. (tchd 11-4)
Bell'Arte(IRE) didn't handle the firm ground at Haydock and these conditions weren't ideal either, but she did run respectably. The best hasn't been seen of her, and it could be that 7f on good or easy ground is what she wants. (op 11-4)
Al Thumama basically lost this at the start, as she exited the stalls very slowly while veering out to her right. To her credit she got back on terms in the home straight, but her exertions inevitably told. Amy Ryan reported that the filly was unruly in the stalls and missed the break. Official explanation: jockey said filly was unruly in the stalls and missed the break (op 11-2 tchd 9-2)
Sir Frank Morgan(IRE) is a half-brother to Coventry Stakes winner CD Europe, amongst others, but he has finished a long last in two runs now. He's still green, but is yet to show he has any ability. (op 7-1)

6998 GILES INSURANCE NURSERY — 6f
2:40 (2:43) (Class 5) (0-75,79) 2-Y-O — **£2,264** (£673; £336; £168) **Stalls** High

Form RPR

5161 **1** **Delores Rocket**[3] 6920 2-9-13 **79** 6ex...............................(b) AmyRyan 2 87
(Kevin Ryan) *mde all: rdn over 1f out: edgd rt ins fnl f: kpt on strly* **15/8**[2]

150 **2** *3 ¼* **Slipstream Angel (IRE)**[32] 6070 2-8-11 **63**.............(b[1]) TonyHamilton 3 61
(Richard Fahey) *cl up: rdn and outpcd over 2f out: rallied 1f out: nt pce of wnr* **7/4**[1]

6356 **3** *4 ½* **Corton Lad**[9] 6753 2-8-11 **63**.. TomEaves 6 49
(Keith Dalgleish) *chsd ldrs: sn rdn along: outpcd whn n.m.r over 3f out: styd on fnl f: no imp* **8/1**

2233 **4** *30* **Polish Crown**[25] 6282 2-9-2 **68**....................................... RobertWinston 4
(Mark Johnston) *prom: effrt over 3f out: rdn over 2f out: sn wknd: btn and eased fnl f* **7/2**[3]

1m 20.67s (8.27) **Going Correction** +1.00s/f (Soft) **4** Ran SP% **104.5**
Speed ratings (Par 95): **84,79,73,33**
toteswingers 1&5 £2.70 CSF £5.13 TOTE £2.70; EX 5.10.
Owner J Nixon **Bred** Bearstone Stud **Trained** Hambleton, N Yorks

FOCUS
A very modest nursery where only the first two gave their running in the conditions. The winner is thriving but is not form to take too literally.

NOTEBOOK
Delores Rocket made all out widest on the track to add to Monday's Pontefract victory. She will have no problem with another furlong and has now won her last three on turf. (op 11-8 tchd 5-4)
Slipstream Angel(IRE) won in heavy ground on her debut. Down in trip, she kept trying in the first-time headgear but had to give best inside the last furlong. (op 7-2)
Corton Lad was being chased along from an early stage and merely plugged on for a well beaten third. He's due to be dropped a pound. (op 9-1 tchd 12-1)
Polish Crown dropped away tamely on this nursery bow with the ground an obvious excuse. It may be worth switching her back to Polytrack. The Stewards considered her running, and noted that the trainer's representative could offer no explanation for the filly's performance. They ordered Polish Crown to be routine tested. Official explanation: trainer's rep had no explanation for the poor form shown (op 11-4)

6999 GILES INSURANCE H'CAP (DIV I) — 6f
3:10 (3:10) (Class 4) (0-85,84) 3-Y-O+ — **£4,294** (£1,268; £634) **Stalls** High

Form RPR

2640 **1** **Barkston Ash**[7] 6820 4-8-7 **75**...(p) JasonHart(5) 5 86
(Eric Alston) *pressed ldr: led over 2f out: drvn clr fnl f* **11/2**

2000 **2** *3 ¾* **Victoire De Lyphar (IRE)**[28] 6165 5-9-7 **84**............(e[1]) JamesSullivan 2 84
(Ruth Carr) *fly-jmpd s: sn led: hdd over 2f out: rallied over 1f out: one pce ins fnl f* **10/1**

4000 **3** *6* **Nasharra (IRE)**[26] 6260 4-8-8 **71**..(p) AmyRyan 1 53
(Kevin Ryan) *in tch on outside: effrt over 2f out: outpcd fnl f* **14/1**

0400 **4** *3* **Sam Nombulist**[19] 6471 4-9-5 **82**..............................(v) RobertHavlin 10 55
(Richard Whitaker) *prom: drvn and outpcd over 2f out: sme late hdwy: no ch w first three* **11/4**[1]

2502 **5** *5* **Defence Council (IRE)**[12] 6665 4-9-5 **82**.................... DuranFentiman 9 40
(Mel Brittain) *hld up in tch: effrt and drvn over 2f out: wknd over 1f out* **7/2**[2]

0662 **6** *1 ¼* **Green Park (IRE)**[12] 6663 9-8-9 **79**.........................(b) LukeLeadbitter(7) 4 33
(Declan Carroll) *missed break: bhd: rdn over 2f out: sn btn* **5/1**[3]

250 **7** *1 ½* **Namwahjobo (IRE)**[33] 6044 4-8-10 **73**............................(v) GrahamLee 6 23
(Jim Goldie) *bhd: drvn over 3f out: btn fnl 2f* **12/1**

0005 **8** *2* **Sunraider (IRE)**[12] 6663 5-9-0 **77**..............................(b[1]) MickyFenton 7 21
(Paul Midgley) *chsd ldrs to 1/2-way: sn rdn and wknd* **14/1**

1m 17.51s (5.11) **Going Correction** +1.00s/f (Soft) **8** Ran SP% **111.1**
Speed ratings (Par 105): **105,100,92,88,81 79,77,75**
toteswingers 1&2 £10.00, 2&3 £15.20, 1&3 £15.20 CSF £54.68 CT £700.28 TOTE £5.40: £1.30, £3.10, £5.10; EX 64.50 TRIFECTA Not won. Pool: £1,161.13..
Owner The Selebians **Bred** Jonathan Shack **Trained** Longton, Lancs

FOCUS
A modest handicap run in a time 1.8sec quicker than the second division. Nothing got involved from the rear and the first three home raced widest on the track in the early parts, before the winner edged across. They finished at wide intervals for a sprint handicap. The winner rates a small personal best.
Green Park(IRE) Official explanation: jockey said gelding missed the break

7000 GILES INSURANCE H'CAP (DIV II) — 6f
3:40 (3:41) (Class 4) (0-85,83) 3-Y-O+ — **£4,294** (£1,268; £634) **Stalls** High

Form RPR

1020 **1** **Bond Fastrac**[74] 4629 5-9-5 **81**... TonyHamilton 2 90
(Geoffrey Oldroyd) *prom: rdn to ld over 1f out: edgd rt ins fnl f: drvn out* **18/1**

63 **2** *2* **Breezolini**[18] 6515 4-8-13 **75**.. RobertWinston 8 78
(Geoffrey Harker) *hld up: hdwy to chse ldrs 2f out: sn rdn and edgd lft: kpt on fnl f: nt pce of wnr* **7/2**[1]

0000 **3** *nk* **The Nifty Fox**[20] 6427 8-9-1 **77**..(p) DavidAllan 4 79
(Tim Easterby) *hld up in tch: rdn and effrt 2f out: kpt on ins fnl f* **20/1**

0003 **4** *½* **Dickie's Lad (IRE)**[12] 6685 4-9-4 **80**.....................................(t) AmyRyan 5 81
(Kevin Ryan) *cl up: rdn and ev ch over 2f out: one pce fnl f* **10/1**

3006 **5** *½* **Toby Tyler**[26] 6260 6-8-9 **71**..(v) MickyFenton 9 70
(Paul Midgley) *dwlt: bhd: drvn and hung lft over 2f out: kpt on fnl f: nrst fin* **20/1**

0633 **6** *1 ¾* **Beckermet (IRE)**[5] 6888 10-9-6 **82**................................ JamesSullivan 1 76
(Ruth Carr) *led to over 2f out: rdn and wknd ins fnl f* **9/2**[2]

3011 **7** *1 ¾* **Fieldgunner Kirkup (GER)**[23] 6338 4-9-7 **83**........... GrahamGibbons 6 72
(David Barron) *cl up: led over 2f out to over 1f out: wknd ins fnl f* **5/1**[3]

6200 **8** *1* **Staff Sergeant**[13] 6638 5-8-12 **74**.. GrahamLee 7 60
(Jim Goldie) *t.k.h: in tch: drvn and outpcd over 2f out: sn n.d* **5/1**[3]

0004 **9** *8* **Rothesay Chancer**[20] 6427 4-8-8 **70**............................ BarryMcHugh 10 32
(Jim Goldie) *t.k.h: cl up towards stands' side: rdn and hung lft over 1f out: sn btn* **6/1**

3210 **10** *4 ½* **Frequency**[19] 6465 5-9-2 **78**...(b) TomEaves 3 26
(Keith Dalgleish) *trckd ldr: rdn over 2f out: sn wknd* **14/1**

1m 19.31s (6.91) **Going Correction** +1.20s/f (Soft) **10** Ran SP% **118.6**
Speed ratings (Par 105): **101,98,97,97,96 94,91,90,79,73**
toteswingers 1&2 £16.80, 2&3 £18.40, 1&3 £39.40 CSF £81.67 CT £1321.34 TOTE £27.00: £6.20, £1.60, £5.30; EX 141.20 TRIFECTA Not won. Pool of £979.97..
Owner R C Bond **Bred** Bond Thoroughbred Corporation **Trained** Brawby, N Yorks

FOCUS
Another race short on progressive types, and the slower division by 1.8sec, although the ground was worsening. The winner's best form since he was a 2yo.
Fieldgunner Kirkup(GER) Official explanation: jockey said gelding had no more to give

7001 BUD & JOE PIERONI MEMORIAL H'CAP — 5f
4:10 (4:11) (Class 5) (0-70,70) 3-Y-O — **£2,264** (£673; £336; £168) **Stalls** High

Form RPR

6002 **1** **Elusive Bonus (IRE)**[5] 6887 3-8-10 **66**........................ DavidBergin(7) 6 79
(David O'Meara) *cl up: led over 2f out: clr whn edgd rt ins fnl f: kpt on strly: eased cl home* **9/2**[3]

1433 **2** *7* **Economic Crisis (IRE)**[18] 6514 3-9-7 **70**......................... PaddyAspell 5 59
(Alan Berry) *prom: effrt and chsd (clr) wnr over 1f out: kpt on same pce fnl f* **12/1**

-12 **3** *2* **Hello Stranger (IRE)**[8] 6788 3-9-3 **66**.......................... DuranFentiman 4 48
(Tim Easterby) *in tch: effrt and rdn over 2f out: hdwy over 1f out: no imp fnl f* **9/4**[1]

4230 **4** ½ **Colbyor**[18] 6514 3-9-0 **68** ShaneBKelly(5) 1 49
(Richard Fahey) *bhd and drvn along: hdwy far side over 1f out: no imp fnl f* **6/1**
-043 **5** *hd* **Travis County (IRE)**[156] 1960 3-9-4 **67** DaleSwift 2 47
(Brian Ellison) *slowly away: bhd and rdn: hdwy over 1f out: nvr able to chal* **18/1**
4541 **6** *6* **Middleton Flyer (IRE)**[26] 6264 3-8-9 **63** (b) LMcNiff(5) 8 23
(Paul Midgley) *slt ld to over 2f out: rdn and wknd wl over 1f out* **18/1**
0503 **7** *3¾* **Alnair (IRE)**[11] 6713 3-8-6 **60** (b) JasonHart(5) 7
(Declan Carroll) *stdd in tch: drvn over 2f out: sn wknd* **16/1**
01 **8** *2½* **Heroic Endeavour (IRE)**[18] 6514 3-8-11 **60** (b) GrahamGibbons 3
(David Barron) *t.k.h: cl up tl rdn and wknd over 2f out* **4/1**[2]
0440 **9** *6* **Commanche**[43] 5728 3-9-0 **63** (v[1]) TomEaves 10
(Bryan Smart) *bhd: drvn along 1/2-way: btn fnl 2f* **12/1**
3002 **10** *20* **Red Baron (IRE)**[31] 6100 3-8-13 **62** RobertWinston 9
(Eric Alston) *cl up tl hung lft and wknd 2f out: eased whn no ch ins fnl f* **22/1**

1m 4.97s (5.57) **Going Correction** +1.20s/f (Soft) **10** Ran SP% **119.4**
Speed ratings (Par 101): **103,91,88,87,87 77,71,67,58,26**
toteswingers 1&2 £7.80, 2&3 £5.40, 1&3 £3.00 CSF £58.80 CT £154.21 TOTE £6.80: £1.90, £3.50, £1.10; EX 39.70 Trifecta £219.50 Pool: £1,061.97 - 3.58 winning tickets..
Owner The Three County Partnership **Bred** T Jones **Trained** Nawton, N Yorks

FOCUS
A decent race for the grade on paper. The ground was a big factor in the winner's wide-margin win, and she's been afforded a 6lb personal best.
Red Baron(IRE) Official explanation: jockey said colt hung left

7002 INTECHNOLOGY SERVICES H'CAP — 1m 2f
4:40 (4:40) (Class 3) (0-90,88) 3-Y-0+ **£6,663** (£1,982; £990; £495) **Stalls** Low

Form RPR
-102 **1** **Amaze**[13] 6630 4-9-4 **82** BarryMcHugh 7 86
(Brian Ellison) *hld up: hdwy over 3f out: led appr fnl f: sn drvn: edgd rt ins fnl f: hld on wl* **9/2**
3006 **2** *1* **Hillview Boy (IRE)**[48] 5540 8-9-10 **88** DanielTudhope 6 90
(Jim Goldie) *in tch: rdn along and outpcd over 2f out: rallied over 1f out: styd on fnl f: nt rch wnr* **9/4**[1]
1603 **3** ½ **Gala Casino Star (IRE)**[9] 6757 7-9-2 **87** (p) JordanNason(7) 1 88
(Geoffrey Harker) *cl up: led over 3f out: rdn over 2f out: hdd appr fnl f: edgd lft: one pce last 100yds* **12/1**
0252 **4** *14* **Act Your Shoe Size**[9] 6757 3-8-11 **80** TomEaves 3 53
(Keith Dalgleish) *led 1f: cl up tl rdn and wknd fr 2f out* **11/1**
2042 **5** *10* **Watts Up Son**[7] 6819 4-8-10 **77** (vt) NeilFarley(3) 4 30
(Declan Carroll) *led after 1f to over 3f out: rdn and wknd 2f out* **4/1**[3]
1203 **6** *dist* **Queen's Estate (GER)**[23] 6339 3-8-7 **76** RobertWinston 2
(Mark Johnston) *in tch: outpcd after 4f: lost tch fnl 4f: eased* **11/4**[2]

2m 32.69s (20.69) **Going Correction** +1.875s/f (Heav)
WFA 3 from 4yo+ 5lb **6** Ran SP% **111.6**
Speed ratings (Par 107): **92,91,90,79,71**
toteswingers 1&2 £3.20, 2&3 £5.90, 1&3 £6.90 CSF £14.88 TOTE £4.10: £1.50, £4.00; EX 16.50.
Owner A Farrell, A Williamson, H Lynn **Bred** Cheveley Park Stud Ltd **Trained** Norton, N Yorks

FOCUS
Officially heavy ground now. They went off surprisingly quickly given the desperate conditions and there was a slow-motion finish.

NOTEBOOK
Amaze fought his way to a narrow victory which might have been more emphatic had he not idled markedly. The return to this trip suited the lightly raced gelding, who handled the ground rather than liked it. He's a decent type and he can step up considerably on this in time. (tchd 5-1)
Hillview Boy(IRE), who stays further, held every chance but was going up and down on the spot late on. He has not clicked this season and is currently 6lb lower than when second in a Listed handicap back in May. (op 5-2 tchd 2-1)
Gala Casino Star(IRE), who had cheekpieces on instead of a visor, came through to lead in the straight and battled on grimly when tackled, but had nothing left late on. He's due to be dropped 2lb now. (op 11-1 tchd 10-1)
Act Your Shoe Size paid for pushing the pace. (tchd 12-1)
Watts Up Son was 3lb well in but needed to work hard early to get to the front. (tchd 7-2 and 9-2)
Queen's Estate(GER) was struggling before halfway and was beaten miles. The Stewards considered his running and noted that the trainer's representative could offer no explanation for the colt's performance. Official explanation: trainer's rep had no explanation for the poor form shown (op 3-1)

7003 BEAZLEY MARINE INSURANCE H'CAP — 1m 1f 20y
5:10 (5:10) (Class 5) (0-70,73) 3-Y-0+ **£2,264** (£673; £336; £168) **Stalls** Low

Form RPR
3410 **1** **High Resolution**[7] 6819 5-9-0 **65** GarryWhillans(5) 7 78
(Linda Perratt) *hld up: stdy hdwy over 3f out: led over 1f out: pushed clr fnl f* **17/2**
0000 **2** *4½* **Brockfield**[13] 6638 6-9-7 **67** DavidAllan 9 70
(Mel Brittain) *pressed ldr: led over 3f out: sn rdn: hdd over 1f out: kpt on same pce fnl f* **14/1**
64 **3** *4* **Jordaura**[13] 6631 6-9-3 **63** DanielTudhope 11 57
(Alan Berry) *in tch on outside: rdn and hung rt 3f out: rallied over 1f out: nt pce of first two* **22/1**
0161 **4** *2½* **Moheebb (IRE)**[8] 6785 8-9-13 **73** 6ex (b) RobertWinston 8 62
(Robert Johnson) *in tch: drvn and outpcd over 2f out: no imp over 1f out* **11/2**[1]
4300 **5** *4½* **Euston Square**[32] 6073 6-9-10 **70** DaleSwift 10 49
(Alistair Whillans) *s.i.s: bhd tl hdwy over 2f out: no imp fnl f* **18/1**
0412 **6** *5* **Goldmachen (GER)**[3] 6940 4-8-10 **56** oh3 TomEaves 6 24
(Keith Dalgleish) *trckd ldrs: effrt and rdn over 2f out: wknd over 1f out* **7/1**[2]
2600 **7** *16* **Amazing Star (IRE)**[21] 6410 7-9-10 **70** MichaelStainton 2
(Declan Carroll) *s.i.s: bhd: drvn over 3f out: nvr on terms* **10/1**
0010 **8** *4* **Cadgers Brig**[11] 6711 4-9-4 **64** (p) GrahamLee 5
(Keith Dalgleish) *led to over 3f out: rdn and wknd 2f out* **22/1**
3060 **9** *3* **Icy Blue**[52] 5414 4-9-2 **62** AmyRyan 3
(Richard Whitaker) *t.k.h: midfield: struggling 3f out: sn btn* **11/1**
5005 **10** *6* **Talk Of The North**[26] 6250 3-9-1 **65** (b) RobertHavlin 1
(Hugo Palmer) *prom tl rdn and wknd fr 3f out* **11/1**
0232 **11** *4½* **Ebony Clarets**[11] 6711 3-8-13 **63** FrederikTylicki 12
(Linda Perratt) *trckd ldrs: rdn over 3f out: wknd over 2f out* **11/2**[1]
4034 **12** *6* **Cosmic Moon**[17] 6528 4-8-13 **59** TonyHamilton 13
(Richard Fahey) *hld up on outside: struggling over 3f out: sn btn* **18/1**
6606 **13** ½ **Let's Face Facts**[9] 6756 5-8-7 **56** oh10 NeilFarley(3) 14
(Jim Goldie) *t.k.h: hld up towards rr: struggling over 3f out: sn btn* **80/1**
0032 **14** *3½* **Chatterati (USA)**[16] 6569 3-8-6 **56** oh1 (b) PJMcDonald 4
(Mark Johnston) *midfield on ins: struggling over 3f out: sn wknd* **8/1**[3]

2m 15.03s (17.53) **Going Correction** +1.875s/f (Heav)
WFA 3 from 4yo+ 4lb **14** Ran SP% **117.8**
Speed ratings (Par 103): **97,93,89,87,83 78,64,61,58,53 49,43,43,40**
toteswingers 1&2 £33.30, 2&3 £17.80, 1&3 £25.50 CSF £117.02 TOTE £8.40: £2.40, £7.00, £6.20; EX 142.60 TRIFECTA Not won. Pool: £899.78..
Owner Mrs Helen Perratt **Bred** Old Mill Stud Ltd **Trained** East Kilbride, S Lanarks

FOCUS
The biggest field of the day for this very modest handicap. With the underfoot terrain as it was the form is less than solid. The winner's best figure since last summer.
Ebony Clarets Official explanation: jockey said filly was unsuited by the heavy ground

7004 GILES INSURANCE CORPORATE H'CAP — 7f 50y
5:40 (5:40) (Class 5) (0-75,76) 3-Y-0+ **£2,264** (£673; £336; £168) **Stalls** High

Form RPR
1100 **1** **It's A Mans World**[13] 6638 6-9-0 **71** PaulPickard(3) 14 87
(Brian Ellison) *hld up: hdwy on outside over 2f out: led appr fnl f: pushed clr* **5/1**[2]
4422 **2** *5* **Robert The Painter (IRE)**[17] 6528 4-9-6 **74** (v) DanielTudhope 10 77
(David O'Meara) *led 1f: cl up: led over 3f out: sn rdn: hdd appr fnl f: edgd rt: no ch w wnr* **13/8**[1]
5155 **3** *4* **Joshua The First**[5] 6894 3-9-3 **73** (p) FrederikTylicki 8 66
(Keith Dalgleish) *prom: drvn and outpcd 3f out: edgd lft and rallied over 1f out: no ch w first two* **8/1**[3]
1602 **4** *2¼* **Liliargh (IRE)**[8] 6782 3-9-0 **70** BarryMcHugh 1 57
(Ben Haslam) *hld up: stdy hdwy over 3f out: sn pushed along: kpt on fnl 2f: no imp* **9/1**
4351 **5** *2¾* **I Confess**[16] 6559 7-9-4 **72** (b) PJMcDonald 9 52
(Geoffrey Harker) *hld up bhd ldng gp: drvn and outpcd wl over 2f out: n.d after* **10/1**
0030 **6** *1½* **Quick Bite (IRE)**[26] 6239 3-9-5 **75** RobertWinston 13 51
(Hugo Palmer) *cl up: ev ch over 3f out: drvn over 2f out: wknd over 1f out* **8/1**[3]
0043 **7** *2* **Jinky**[58] 5189 4-8-11 **70** GarryWhillans(5) 2 41
(Linda Perratt) *chsd ldrs tl drvn and wknd 2f out* **8/1**[3]
0000 **8** *3½* **Ralphy Boy (IRE)**[12] 6665 3-9-5 **75** AmyRyan 11 36
(Kevin Ryan) *bhd: struggling over 3f out: nvr on terms* **25/1**
-030 **9** *13* **Ventura Sands (IRE)**[133] 2619 4-9-3 **71** TonyHamilton 5
(Richard Fahey) *t.k.h: led after 1f to over 3f out: sn wknd* **25/1**

1m 45.94s (12.54) **Going Correction** +1.875s/f (Heav)
WFA 3 from 4yo+ 2lb **9** Ran SP% **114.9**
Speed ratings (Par 103): **103,97,92,90,87 85,83,79,64**
toteswingers 1&2 £3.10, 2&3 £3.60, 1&3 £10.20 CSF £13.42 TOTE £6.80: £1.70, £1.20, £2.90; EX 17.50 Trifecta £167.40 Pool: £937.06 - 4.14 winning tickets..
Owner Brian Ellison **Bred** Cheveley Park Stud Ltd **Trained** Norton, N Yorks

FOCUS
A modest handicap, weakened by non-runners and run at a steady pace on the worst of the ground. The time was very slow and it's hard to rate the form too literally. The winner resumed his progress.
T/Plt: £801.10 to a £1 stake. Pool: £54,762.76 - 49.90 winning tickets. T/Qpdt: £68.50 to a £1 stake. Pool: £5,125.51 - 55.30 winning tickets. RY

6975 KEMPTON (A.W) (R-H)
Thursday, October 11

OFFICIAL GOING: Standard
Wind: light to medium, half behind Weather: rain

7005 32RED.COM MAIDEN STKS — 7f (P)
5:20 (5:21) (Class 5) 3-4-Y-0 **£2,264** (£673; £336; £168) **Stalls** Low

Form RPR
2 **1** **Volcanic Wind (USA)**[23] 6341 3-9-3 0 SilvestreDeSousa 7 94+
(Saeed Bin Suroor) *mde all: clr fr 4f out: rdn and r.o strly fr over 1f out: impressive* **5/2**[2]
2 **2** *3¾* **Tropics (USA)**[21] 6397 4-9-5 0 BrettDoyle 10 83+
(Dean Ivory) *rrd as stalls opened: sn rcvrd and chsd ldrs: effrt to chse clr wnr over 2f out: no imp but r.o for clr 2nd: eased fnl 75yds* **5/4**[1]
0 **3** *6* **Spark Of Genius**[128] 2799 3-8-12 0 KirstyMilczarek 14 60
(James Toller) *hld up off the pce in rr of main gp: hdwy into midfield: no ch w ldrs but kpt on fnl f to go 3rd nr fin* **66/1**
2 **4** ½ **Far East**[36] 5949 3-8-12 0 DaneO'Neill 2 58
(Clive Cox) *chsd ldrs: rdn and outpcd over 2f out: 3rd and wl hld over 1f out: plugged on: lost 3rd nr fin* **7/1**
450 **5** *2* **Stormbound (IRE)**[145] 2280 3-9-3 80 NeilCallan 1 58
(Paul Cole) *t.k.h: hld up in tch: rdn and outpcd jst over 2f out: wl hld over 1f out* **5/1**[3]
00 **6** *3¾* **Maria Vezzera**[20] 6457 3-8-9 0 NataliaGemelova(3) 6 43+
(Marco Botti) *hld up wl off the pce in rr: styd on past btn horses over 1f out: nvr trbld ldrs* **25/1**
0-0 **7** *3¾* **Vermeyen**[13] 6643 3-9-0 0 SophieDoyle(3) 9 38
(Geoffrey Deacon) *t.k.h: chsd ldr tl over 2f out: sn wknd* **66/1**
000- **8** *1½* **Tymismoni (IRE)**[364] 6813 4-8-11 49 MarkCoumbe(3) 5 29
(Michael Attwater) *a towards rr of main gp: rdn and no hdwy over 2f out: n.d* **50/1**
03- **9** *hd* **Boris The Bold**[285] 7938 3-9-3 0 JamesDoyle 11 33
(John Best) *in tch tl lost pl and rdn wl over 2f out: sn wknd and no ch fnl 2f* **25/1**
40- **10** *1¾* **Master Jack**[373] 6608 4-9-5 0 MartinDwyer 3 28
(Paul Burgoyne) *in tch in midfield: wd and lost pl bnd 3f out: sn rdn and no hdwy: bhd fnl 2f* **33/1**
00 **11** ½ **Sambirano**[21] 6397 3-8-12 0 DavidKenny(5) 12 27
(William Knight) *a towards rr of main gp: rdn 4f out: wknd and bhd over 2f out* **33/1**
12 *59* **Parsons Green** 3-8-12 0 ShaneKelly 13
(Michael Attwater) *v.s.a: t.o thrght* **50/1**

1m 23.62s (-2.38) **Going Correction** -0.125s/f (Stan)
WFA 3 from 4yo 2lb **12** Ran SP% **122.7**
Speed ratings (Par 103): **108,103,96,96,94 89,85,83,83,81 80,13**
toteswingers: 1&2 £2.60, 1&3 £39.30, 2&3 £59.40. CSF £5.82 TOTE £3.50: £1.20, £1.70, £19.40; EX 7.20 Trifecta £264.00 Pool: £3,560.72 - 9.98 winning units..
Owner Godolphin **Bred** Darley **Trained** Newmarket, Suffolk

FOCUS
Very little in the way of strength in depth to this maiden and the finish was played out by the market principals with Volcanic Wind coming home a ready winner. The time was quick and he looks very useful.

Spark Of Genius Official explanation: jockey said filly did not face the kickback

Parsons Green Official explanation: jockey said, regarding running and riding, that his orders were if the filly jumped well from stalls to ride a normal race, it was nervous in the stalls, froze as the gates opened and was slowly away, it then became detached and did not face the kickback.

7006 32RED/BRITISH STALLION STUDS E B F MAIDEN STKS (DIV I) 6f (P)
5:50 (5:51) (Class 5) 2-Y-O **£3,234** (£962; £481; £240) **Stalls** Low

Form				RPR
642	1		**Ferjaan**[8] 6772 2-9-3 0 PaulHanagan 7 (John Gosden) *mde all: rdn jst over 2f out: styd on wl u.p fnl f: rdn out* **10/11**[1]	71+
0	2	3/4	**Not Rigg (USA)**[19] 6481 2-9-3 0 (t) JamieSpencer 3 (Andrew Balding) *t.k.h: chsd ldrs: swtchd lft and effrt 2f out: drvn to chse wnr over 1f out: r.o wl but a hld fnl f* **3/1**[2]	69+
	3	4 1/2	**Watcheroftheskies** 2-9-3 0 SebSanders 10 (J W Hills) *wnt lft s: hld up in last trio: rdn wl over 2f out: rn green and no hdwy: stl last over 1f out: hdwy and styd on strly ins fnl f: snatched 3rd last stride* **33/1**	55
26	4	shd	**Marsh Dragon**[29] 6132 2-8-12 0 DarryllHolland 9 (Mark H Tompkins) *sn chsng wnr: rdn and unable qck 2f out: 3rd and outpcd 1f out: plugged on tl lost 3rd last stride* **14/1**	50
	5	shd	**Aglaophonos** 2-9-3 0 NeilCallan 8 (Roger Varian) *s.i.s: rdn over 2f out: hdwy and edgd rt over 1f out: no threat to ldrs but styd on wl ins fnl f* **16/1**	55+
0540	6	1/2	**Katy Spirit (IRE)**[28] 6155 2-8-12 48 NickyMackay 2 (Michael Blanshard) *chsd ldrs: rdn and unable qck 2f out: outpcd and btn 1f out: plugged on same pce after* **66/1**	48
006	7	3/4	**Intrigo**[15] 6581 2-9-3 57 RyanMoore 11 (Richard Hannon) *pushed lft s: t.k.h: rn green and hld up in rr: racing awkwardly bnd 4f out: rdn over 2f out: hdwy over 1f out: styd on fnl f: nvr trbld ldrs* **25/1**	51
	8	1/2	**Silca's Dream** 2-9-3 0 MartinHarley 5 (Mick Channon) *t.k.h: hld up in midfield: rdn and unable qck jst over 2f out: outpcd and btn over 1f out: plugged on fnl f* **6/1**[3]	49
	9	9	**Green Monkey** 2-9-3 0 EddieAhern 4 (James Fanshawe) *in tch in midfield: rdn and lost pl ent fnl 2f: bhd fnl f* **14/1**	22

1m 12.57s (-0.53) **Going Correction** -0.125s/f (Stan) **9** Ran SP% **119.2**
Speed ratings (Par 95): **98,97,91,90,90 90,89,88,76**
toteswingers: 1&2 £1.80, 1&3 £11.70, 2&3 £21.80. CSF £3.79 TOTE £2.50: £1.10, £1.60, £6.50; EX 5.40 Trifecta £78.10 Pool: £5,001.57 - 47.36 winning units..

Owner Hamdan Al Maktoum **Bred** Shadwell Estate Company Limited **Trained** Newmarket, Suffolk

FOCUS

This had looked a good opportunity for the well-supported Ferjaan on paper and he duly go the job done, albeit in workmanlike fashion. The front pair were clear and could be rated higher, but the sixth and seventh offer perspective.

NOTEBOOK

Ferjaan had shown a fair level form in three starts over this trip, including over C&D last week, and having put that experience to use when breaking smartly from the gates, always looked likely to break his duck. He was keen enough through the early stages but with many of his rivals floundering with 2f to run, it was only the runner-up who posed any kind of threat. He did require a few stern reminders to put the race to bed but was well in control at the finish. He's clearly no world beater but should be competitive if kept going in nurseries this winter. (op 4-5)

Not Rigg(USA), like many from his yard, improved significantly from his first outing. He pulled well clear of the remainder and should be hard to beat in similar company next time. (op 9-2)

Watcheroftheskies was out with the washing early on and may have found these conditions quick enough. A slower surface and a step up to 7f should bring about considerable improvement.

Marsh Dragon was unsuited by desperate ground at Carlisle last time but found this more to her liking and is now qualified for nurseries. (op 12-1)

Aglaophonos was another newcomer to run with credit. He didn't have the early pace to lay handy but kept on nicely under mainly hands and heels riding.

Silca's Dream wasn't entirely disgraced. She appeared to get tired from 2f out and is probably capable of a bit better. (op 5-1)

7007 32RED/BRITISH STALLION STUDS E B F MAIDEN STKS (DIV II) 6f (P)
6:20 (6:21) (Class 5) 2-Y-O **£3,234** (£962; £481; £240) **Stalls** Low

Form				RPR
2	1		**Exactement (IRE)**[133] 2630 2-8-12 0 JimCrowley 8 (Mrs K Burke) *chsd ldrs: swtchd lft and effrt 2f out: rdn to ld wl over 1f out: c clr w runner-up fnl f: r.o wl: rdn out* **7/2**[2]	76+
3	2	1/2	**Mundahesh (IRE)**[21] 6411 2-9-3 0 PaulHanagan 4 (William Haggas) *t.k.h: chsd ldrs: rdn and effrt on inner 2f out: pressed wnr and c clr of field fnl f: r.o wl but a hld* **11/10**[1]	80+
3202	3	3 3/4	**Fraserburgh (IRE)**[17] 6524 2-9-3 78 SilvestreDeSousa 5 (Mark Johnston) *chsd ldr: rdn and ev ch 2f out: outpcd by ldng pair ent fnl f: one pce and btn fnl f: hld on for 3rd cl home* **9/2**[3]	68
0	4	nk	**Lucky Di**[22] 6366 2-8-12 0 DaneO'Neill 9 (Peter Hedger) *s.i.s: hld up in last pair: rdn 2f out: hdwy ent fnl f: styd on wl and pressing for 3rd cl home* **100/1**	62
000	5	nse	**El Mirage (IRE)**[23] 6343 2-8-12 63 ShaneKelly 7 (Dean Ivory) *hld up in midfield: rdn and effrt 2f out: no threat to ldrs but styd on wl u.p ins fnl f: pressing for 3rd cl home* **33/1**	62
	6	1	**Tartary (IRE)** 2-9-3 0 JamesDoyle 3 (Roger Charlton) *in tch in last pair: rdn: rn green and hung rt over 1f out: no threat to ldrs but styd on ins fnl f* **8/1**	64
0	7	1/2	**Blessing Box**[27] 6203 2-8-12 0 TedDurcan 6 (Chris Wall) *dwlt: t.k.h: hld up in midfield: rdn and unable qck wl over 1f out: btn 1f out: wknd ins fnl f* **20/1**	58
	8	1/2	**Top Trail (USA)** 2-8-12 0 FergusSweeney 1 (Roger Charlton) *in tch in last trio: rdn and no imp ent fnl 2f: n.d but kpt on steadily fnl f* **20/1**	56
0	9	2 3/4	**Tom Hall**[15] 6581 2-8-12 0 DarrenEgan(5) 2 (John Best) *t.k.h: led tl wl over 1f out: btn over 1f out: wknd fnl f* **66/1**	53

1m 13.18s (0.08) **Going Correction** -0.125s/f (Stan) **9** Ran SP% **114.1**
Speed ratings (Par 95): **94,93,88,87,87 86,85,85,81**
toteswingers: 1&2 £1.60, 1&3 £2.60, 2&3 £1.40. CSF £7.27 TOTE £3.90: £1.40, £1.10, £1.20; EX 11.00 Trifecta £25.00 Pool: £5,156.47 - 152.49 winning units..

Owner Mrs Elaine M Burke **Bred** Mogeely Stud **Trained** Middleham Moor, N Yorks

FOCUS

The second division of this juvenile maiden was arguably stronger than the first and it was a taking performance from Exactement, who kept on powerfully to defy her 133-day absence. The first two's efforts could perhaps be upgraded.

NOTEBOOK

Exactement(IRE), who ran well against four previous winners in a novice event on her debut at Newcastle in May, was relatively easy to back here, presumably on account of her four-month break. However, she proved those negative market vibes all wrong, showing a smart turn of foot when striking the front, and had more than enough in hand to see off the persistent runner-up. It's hard to know exactly what she achieved but with a significant gap back to the 78-rated third, the form at this stage looks solid. (tchd 10-3)

Mundahesh(IRE) ran a sound race and it's likely he bumped into an above-average sort. While ridden more prominently than on his debut, he was forced to sit and wait for the cutaway before making his challenge. It's hard to consider him unlucky but he was closer at the finish than at any other stage. (tchd Evens)

Fraserburgh(IRE) is beginning to look exposed at this level and may have to wait for handicaps before winning. This surface was better for him than the heavy ground he faced last time but he was made to look one-paced by the principals and only just hold on for third. (op 4-1)

Lucky Di kept on well but lacked the pace to get involved.

Tartary(IRE) was perhaps the biggest eyecatcher. He was all at sea early on but was getting the hang of it late on. (tchd 9-1)

Blessing Box ran better than her finishing position suggests. She travelled well for much of this and can be found a small race. (op 16-1)

7008 32REDPOKER.COM CLAIMING STKS 1m (P)
6:50 (6:50) (Class 6) 2-Y-O **£1,617** (£481; £240; £120) **Stalls** Low

Form				RPR
0151	1		**Lea Valley Black**[24] 6310 2-9-0 68 RichardKingscote 7 (Tom Dascombe) *mde all: rdn and forged ahd 2f out: 4 l clr 1f out: rdn out hands and heels fnl f: a jst lasting home* **6/4**[1]	61
3400	2	1/2	**Age Of Bronze**[30] 6115 2-9-2 58 RyanMoore 5 (Richard Hannon) *chsd ldrs: allowed ldng trio to go clr 1/2-way: rdn and chsd clr wnr over 1f out: clsd u.p fnl f: nvr quite gng to rch wnr* **10/1**	62
000	3	nk	**Shearian**[106] 3499 2-8-11 0 KierenFallon 6 (Brian Meehan) *pushed along in rr: swtchd rt and gd hdwy over 1f out: wnt 3rd 1f out: styd on wl u.p: nvr quite getting to wnr* **20/1**	56
0460	4	4 1/2	**Believe In Me**[38] 5886 2-8-7 46 (p) AdamBeschizza 3 (Julia Feilden) *t.k.h: hld up towards rr: rdn and effrt ent fnl 2f: wnt 4th 1f out: no real imp fnl f* **50/1**	42
5100	5	1/2	**Warrant Officer**[8] 6793 2-8-11 63 MartinHarley 2 (Mick Channon) *in tch in midfield: hung lft bnd 3f out: no imp u.p fnl 2f* **9/1**	45
00	6	1 1/2	**Dancing Chief (IRE)**[43] 5742 2-8-7 0 MichaelJMMurphy(5) 10 (Alan Jarvis) *s.i.s and pushed along in detached last: sme hdwy on inner 2f out: no imp fr over 1f out* **33/1**	43
5050	7	2 1/2	**Unidexter (IRE)**[59] 5155 2-8-6 63 CharlesBishop(5) 1 (Mick Channon) *hld up in midfield: rdn and no hdwy over 2f out: wl btn over 1f out* **8/1**	36
3	8	1 1/2	**Didnt I Do Well**[33] 6034 2-8-9 0 DarrenEgan(5) 8 (Julia Feilden) *hld up in rr: rdn and no hdwy over 2f out: n.d* **20/1**	36
0005	9	3/4	**I'm Watching**[20] 6435 2-7-13 49 AaronJones(7) 9 (George Baker) *pressed ldrs on outer tl unable qck 2f out: wknd over 1f out: fdd fnl f* **33/1**	26
4442	10	13	**Moonlit Dancer (IRE)**[14] 6612 2-8-5 60 (t) MartinLane 4 (J W Hills) *pressed wnr tl 2f out: sn wknd: wl bhd fnl f* **7/1**[3]	
0010	11	4 1/2	**Imperial Oak**[14] 6597 2-9-2 75 (t) JimmyFortune 11 (Eve Johnson Houghton) *chsd ldrs tl rdn and lost pl qckly wl over 2f out: wl bhd fnl f* **4/1**[2]	

1m 40.22s (0.42) **Going Correction** -0.125s/f (Stan) **11** Ran SP% **120.1**
Speed ratings (Par 93): **92,91,91,86,86 84,82,80,79,66 62**
toteswingers: 1&2 £4.70, 1&3 £5.70, 2&3 £33.60. CSF £17.19 TOTE £3.00: £1.50, £2.60, £7.70; EX 15.00 Trifecta £150.90 Pool: £3,278.68 - 16.07 winning units..Shearian was claimed by Tony Carroll for £5,000.

Owner London Market Racing Club **Bred** A J Coleing **Trained** Malpas, Cheshire

FOCUS

A weak claimer, run at a fair pace but much to like about the performance of Lea Valley Black, who kept on gamely to record a third win in his last four starts.The lesser horses govern the merit of the form.

NOTEBOOK

Lea Valley Black, successful in this grade over 7f at Musselburgh last time, was keener than ideal through the early stages and, having committed for home with fully 3f remaining, deserves considerable credit for this. There to be shot at all the way down the long home straight, he responded gallantly to his jockey's urgings and has to be considered value for a deal more than the eventual margin of victory. The fitting of a hood appears to have been the making of him and, while he beat very little, the style of the win suggests he'd at least be competitive in handicaps off his current mark.

Age Of Bronze was never closer than at the finish and ran well on these unfavourable terms. The step up to 1m clearly suited and the result may well have been different had he been closer at halfway. (op 9-1)

Shearian had failed to beat a single rival in three maiden runs at up to 7f and this has to be considered an improvement. He came from a long way back and, on this evidence, should get even further. (tchd 16-1)

Believe In Me ran up to his mark.

Warrant Officer, a winner on soft ground in July, was left behind 1f out and probably found this surface on the fast side. (op 10-1 tchd 12-1)

7009 32RED CONDITIONS STKS 1m (P)
7:20 (7:20) (Class 4) 2-Y-O **£3,428** (£1,020; £509; £254) **Stalls** Low

Form				RPR
1212	1		**Snowboarder (USA)**[29] 6149 2-9-0 94 MickaelBarzalona 3 (Mahmood Al Zarooni) *t.k.h: chsd ldr tl over 6f out: hld up in tch: swtchd lft and effrt over 1f out: drvn and chal ins fnl f: led wl ins fnl f: jst hld on* **7/4**[1]	91
445	2	nse	**Wayfoong Express (IRE)**[19] 6481 2-9-0 75 MartinDwyer 5 (William Muir) *s.i.s: sn pushed along in last: drvn and no imp 2f out tl str run ins fnl f: jst failed* **20/1**	91+
1034	3	nk	**Luhaif**[56] 5270 2-9-0 105 MartinHarley 2 (Mick Channon) *led: rdn and hrd pressed ent fnl 2f: hdd over 1f out: ev ch thrght fnl f: no ex cl home* **3/1**[3]	90
13	4	hd	**Dashing David (IRE)**[104] 3562 2-9-0 0 SeanLevey 1 (Richard Hannon) *chsd ldrs: effrt on inner and drvn 2f out: ev ch fnl f: unable qck cl home* **6/1**	90
3312	5	1 1/4	**Beedee**[11] 6699 2-9-0 92 RyanMoore 4 (Richard Hannon) *chsd ldr over 6f out: drvn and ev ch 2f out: led over 1f out tl hdd wl ins fnl f: wknd towards fin* **2/1**[2]	87

1m 38.77s (-1.03) **Going Correction** -0.125s/f (Stan) **5** Ran SP% **113.7**
Speed ratings (Par 97): **100,99,99,99,98**
toteswinger: 1&2 £7.40. CSF £30.28 TOTE £1.90: £1.10, £7.70; EX 27.70.

Owner Godolphin **Bred** Fares Farm Llc **Trained** Newmarket, Suffolk

■ Stewards' Enquiry : Mickael Barzalona two-day ban: used whip above permitted level (Oct 25-26)

FOCUS
A strong look to this conditions event, despite the small field, and it served up a thrilling finish with Snowboarder just getting the verdict by the narrowest of margins. It's not form to take at face value.

NOTEBOOK
Snowboarder(USA), yet to be out of the first two, travelled well but took forever to pick up and once eventually getting to the front, was forced to pull out all the stops. Tactics had looked sure to play a big part in the result and, despite a relatively steady pace, it was surprisingly the two hold-up runners in the race who were first past the post. There's little doubt that the winner moved easily the best and he's clearly well suited to this Polytrack surface. However, with so little covering the five runners, it will be wise to treat the form with a degree of caution. (tchd 2-1)
Wayfoong Express(IRE) had a mountain to climb on ratings and it's likely that this has ruined what must have been a lenient handicap mark. Outpaced in rear, he fairly flew home in the final furlong. (tchd 16-1)
Luhaif was allowed to dictate the pace but, headed 2f out, rallied bravely. (op 7-2)
Dashing David(IRE) fared best of the Richard Hannon pair. A winner of a 5f maiden on debut, his stamina appeared to run out late on. (tchd 7-1)
Beedee held every chance but was run out of it in the final furlong. He might be better over 7f. (tchd 9-4)

7010 32RED H'CAP 7f (P)
7:50 (7:51) (Class 2) (0-105,104) 3-Y-O+ **£10,221** (£3,041; £1,519; £759) **Stalls** Low

Form RPR
0004 **1** **Belgian Bill**[40] 5848 4-9-7 101 (t) PatCosgrave 11 110
(George Baker) *chsd ldr: rdn and ev ch over 1f out: drvn to ld ent fnl f: r.o wl and hld on cl home* **11/2[2]**
210 **2** *nk* **Nassau Storm**[32] 6075 3-8-2 89 DarrenEgan(5) 8 97+
(William Knight) *hld up in midfield: rdn and effrt on outer 2f out: hdwy ent fnl f: r.o wl and pressing wnr cl home* **10/1**
3432 **3** *1* **Yaa Wayl (IRE)**[35] 5964 5-9-8 102 (v) SilvestreDeSousa 14 107
(Saeed Bin Suroor) *led and crossed to inner: hrd pressed and drvn wl over 1f out: hdd ent fnl f: kpt on same pce ins fnl f* **10/1**
-534 **4** *nse* **Burj Alzain (IRE)**[6] 6854 4-9-4 98 NeilCallan 5 103
(Gerard Butler) *short of room s: hld up in midfield: effrt u.p to chal over 1f out: no ex and one pce fnl 100yds* **9/2[1]**
2030 **5** *nse* **Mac's Power (IRE)**[27] 6201 6-9-3 97 (t) KierenFallon 6 102
(James Fanshawe) *t.k.h: hld up in midfield: swtchd rt and effrt on inner over 1f out: chsd ldrs and drvn ins fnl f: kpt on same pce fnl 100yds* **7/1[3]**
3051 **6** *hd* **Triple Charm**[42] 5769 4-8-10 90 (v) RyanMoore 13 94+
(Jeremy Noseda) *hld up in last pair: rdn and effrt over 2f out: hdwy ent fnl f: styd on wl: nt rch ldrs* **12/1**
2000 **7** *1 1/4* **Silverheels (IRE)**[6] 6830 3-8-11 93 ShaneKelly 2 94
(Paul Cole) *in tch: rdn and effrt to chse ldrs wl over 1f out: no ex and one pce ins fnl f* **33/1**
0000 **8** *1 1/4* **Oasis Dancer**[40] 5814 5-9-10 104 JimCrowley 7 101
(Ralph Beckett) *t.k.h: hld up in midfield: effrt u.p 2f out: unable qck over 1f out: wknd ins fnl f* **10/1**
0230 **9** *1/2* **Lutine Bell**[12] 6676 5-8-10 90 EddieAhern 9 86
(Mike Murphy) *hld up in rr: nt asked for effrt tl drvn and hdwy ent fnl f: one pce and no imp fnl 100yds* **8/1**
2035 **10** *1/2* **Mabait**[26] 6242 6-8-13 98 LauraPike(5) 4 93
(David Simcock) *hld up in tch in last quartet: rdn and hdwy on inner wl over 1f out: no imp u.p ent fnl f* **14/1**
0300 **11** *1/2* **Docofthebay (IRE)**[89] 4086 8-9-1 95 (b) IanMongan 10 88
(Scott Dixon) *hld up in midfield: effrt u.p ent fnl 2f: sme hdwy over 1f out: no imp fnl f* **33/1**
3560 **12** *3/4* **Graphic (IRE)**[112] 3294 3-8-8 90 SeanLevey 3 81
(Richard Hannon) *chsd ldrs: rdn and unable qck ent fnl 2f: wknd jst ins fnl f* **16/1**
0042 **13** *1/2* **Noble Citizen (USA)**[20] 6432 7-8-9 89 (be) PaulHanagan 12 79
(David Simcock) *hld up in last quartet: rdn and no prog over 2f out: nvr trbld ldrs* **16/1**
4100 **14** *8* **Palace Moon**[68] 4802 7-9-9 103 (t) TomQueally 1 71
(William Knight) *chsd ldrs: rdn and unable qck over 2f out: wknd over 1f out: bhd and eased fnl 100yds* **14/1**

1m 24.48s (-1.52) **Going Correction** -0.125s/f (Stan)
WFA 3 from 4yo+ 2lb **14** Ran SP% **123.1**
Speed ratings (Par 109): **103,102,101,101,101 101,99,98,97,97 96,95,95,86**
toteswingers: 1&2 £21.00, 1&3 £10.90, 2&3 £16.20. CSF £61.25 CT £559.26 TOTE £7.60: £2.60, £3.70, £2.50; EX 84.80 TRIFECTA Not won. Pool: £465.63..
Owner PJL, Cooper & Baker **Bred** Wickfield Stud And Hartshill Stud **Trained** Whitsbury, Hants

FOCUS
A fiercely competitive handicap, run at a steady pace and a smart effort from Belgian Bill, who appreciated this drop in grade. This rates a 4lb personal best.

NOTEBOOK
Belgian Bill was never far away and, having travelled powerfully upsides the leader in the straight, picked up well to record a first AW success. Having been outclassed and failed to stay 1m2f in Group 2 company in Turkey last time, he was still 9lb higher than for his last win, which had come on his seasonal reappearance last year. Far from disgraced in the valuable Betfred Mile at Goodwood on his penultimate start, he saw this out well and clearly retains plenty of enthusiasm. Handicap opportunities will be limited for him from now on and it's likely he'll be aimed, once again, at Dubai. (op 7-1 tchd 9-1)
Nassau Storm stayed on well from off the pace but was never quite able to land a blow. Posted wide throughout, he used valuable energy when making rapid headway between the 2f and 1f markers and can be considered a shade unlucky. (op 11-1)
Yaa Wayl(IRE), drawn in stall 14, he did well to cross to the rail and clearly remains in good heart. (op 6-1)
Burj Alzain(IRE) ran to form in defeat. (op 11-2 tchd 6-1)
Triple Charm rattled home from an unpromising position. (op 10-1 tchd 9-1)
Lutine Bell was another undone by the lack of early pace. He looked menacing when moving up on the inside 3f out but was outpaced when the race finally developed. (op 9-1 tchd 10-1)
Palace Moon dropped out quickly and will surely appreciate a return to 6f. (op 12-1 tchd 10-1)

7011 32REDBET.COM MEDIAN AUCTION MAIDEN STKS 1m 4f (P)
8:20 (8:21) (Class 5) 3-5-Y-O **£2,264** (£673; £336; £168) **Stalls** Centre

Form RPR
6504 **1** **Wildomar**[15] 6582 3-9-3 67 BrettDoyle 4 74
(John Ryan) *s.i.s and rdn along early: in tch: rdn and edgd lft over 1f out: led jst ins fnl f: styd on wl* **25/1**
6024 **2** *2* **Mohair**[13] 6647 3-8-12 69 HayleyTurner 10 66
(James Fanshawe) *t.k.h: hld up in rr: rdn and effrt over 2f out: hdwy u.p over 1f out: kpt on ins fnl f* **4/1[3]**
3-5 **3** *hd* **Ehkam (USA)**[14] 6614 3-9-3 0 (tp) SilvestreDeSousa 8 70
(Saeed Bin Suroor) *t.k.h: hld up in midfield: rdn and effrt over 2f out: hdwy to chse ldrs over 1f out: styd on same pce ins fnl f* **10/1**
0-33 **4** *1/2* **Multilateral (USA)**[35] 5982 3-9-3 77 EddieAhern 7 70
(Amanda Perrett) *hld up in midfield: rdn and effrt over 2f out: no imp u.p over 1f out: styd on fnl 100yds* **7/2[2]**
3200 **5** *1/2* **Harry Buckle**[11] 6703 3-8-12 68 DarrenEgan(5) 6 69
(Philip McBride) *chsd ldrs: wnt 2nd 3f out: rdn to ld over 2f out: edgd lft u.p 2f out: wknd towards fin* **5/1**
6 *1* **Ginger Fizz**[181] 5-9-5 0 ShaneKelly 9 62
(Ben Case) *s.i.s: hld up in last pair: rdn and struggling over 3f out: hdwy and hung rt over 1f out: styd on ins fnl f* **33/1**
2402 **7** *8* **Roc De Prince**[21] 6398 3-9-3 75 PaulHanagan 3 54
(Richard Fahey) *led for 1f: chsd ldr tl led again 7f out: drvn and hdd over 2f out: wknd 1f out: fdd and eased ins fnl f* **3/1[1]**
00 **8** *12* **Let's Confer**[149] 2148 3-8-9 0 MarkCoumbe(3) 5 30
(Michael Attwater) *s.i.s: hld up in rr: rdn and struggling 4f out: bhd fnl 2f* **66/1**
35 **9** *2* **Anychanceofabirdie (USA)**[65] 4916 3-9-3 0 NeilCallan 2 32
(David Simcock) *chsd ldrs: rdn and unable qck over 2f out: wknd and eased over 1f out: virtually p.u towards fin* **16/1**
5265 **10** *hd* **Linkable**[26] 6228 3-9-3 70 JamesDoyle 1 32
(Charles Hills) *rdn along to ld after 1f: hdd 7f out: chsd ldr after tl 3f out: wknd wl over 1f out: wl bhd and eased wl ins fnl f* **7/1**

2m 32.4s (-2.10) **Going Correction** -0.125s/f (Stan)
WFA 3 from 5yo 7lb **10** Ran SP% **119.6**
Speed ratings (Par 103): **102,100,100,100,99 99,93,85,84,84**
toteswingers: 1&2 £29.20, 1&3 £38.70, 2&3 £5.20. CSF £124.59 TOTE £39.90: £6.20, £1.10, £2.50; EX 195.00 TRIFECTA Not won. Pool: £660.14..
Owner W McLuskey **Bred** Wood Hall Stud Limited **Trained** Newmarket, Suffolk

FOCUS
A modest maiden, run at a steady pace and something of an upset with the 67-rated Wildomar defying a massive slide in the market to win fairly convincingly. The form is rated around the winner and fifth.

7012 32REDBINGO.COM H'CAP 2m (P)
8:50 (8:50) (Class 6) (0-65,65) 4-Y-O+ **£1,617** (£481; £240; £120) **Stalls** Low

Form RPR
0250 **1** **Squad**[26] 6255 6-9-3 **61** (v) NeilCallan 4 70
(Simon Dow) *hld up in last pair: rdn and hdwy 2f out: led ent fnl f: edgd rt but sn clr: r.o wl* **14/1**
2440 **2** *2 1/4* **Reggie Perrin**[11] 6703 4-9-5 **63** (v) IanMongan 9 69
(Pat Phelan) *hld up in tch: rdn and effrt to press ldrs 2f out: chsd wnr ins fnl f: styd on* **5/2[1]**
0634 **3** *2 3/4* **Celtic Charlie (FR)**[18] 5771 7-8-3 **52** JemmaMarshall(5) 7 55
(Pat Phelan) *hld up in tch in rr: hdwy 7f out: jnd ldr over 2f out: rdn and led briefly over 1f out: sn hdd and outpcd: 3rd and one pce ins fnl f* **8/1**
1052 **4** *3* **Rodrigo De Freitas (IRE)**[50] 5483 5-9-1 **59** (v) PatCosgrave 5 58
(Jim Boyle) *t.k.h: hld up in tch towards rr: clsng but nt clr run on inner over 2f out: rdn and effrt wl over 1f out: no imp u.p over 1f out* **7/1**
6603 **5** *nk* **Ostentation**[12] 6691 5-9-2 **65** AmyScott(5) 2 64
(Gay Kelleway) *t.k.h: hld up in midfield: swtchd lft and hdwy to chse ldr 11f out: rdn to ld over 2f out: hdd over 1f out: wknd fnl f* **11/4[2]**
000 **6** *shd* **Rollin 'n Tumblin**[26] 6255 8-8-2 **46** oh1 JimmyQuinn 8 45?
(Michael Attwater) *t.k.h: hld up in tch: drvn and effrt to chse ldrs 2f out: outpcd and btn 1f out: plugged on same pce fnl f* **33/1**
0050 **7** *8* **Blue Cossack (IRE)**[45] 5241 4-8-6 **55** DavidKenny(5) 6 44
(Neil King) *dwlt: sn rcvrd to chse ldrs: rdn and struggling ent fnl 3f: wknd 2f out* **14/1**
2316 **8** *1 1/4* **Oneiric**[103] 3620 4-9-2 **60** ShaneKelly 10 48
(Brett Johnson) *t.k.h: hld up in tch in last quartet: rdn and effrt over 2f out: no prog and wknd wl over 1f out* **20/1**
600 **9** *1/2* **Ice Apple**[62] 5048 4-7-13 **46** oh1 NataliaGemelova(3) 1 33
(John E Long) *chsd ldr tl 11f out: chsd ldrs tl lost pl: dropped to rr and rdn over 4f out: wknd over 2f out* **50/1**
4124 **10** *14* **Volcanic Jack (IRE)**[24] 6323 4-9-5 **63** KierenFallon 3 33
(Tony Carroll) *led and set stop s gallop: rdn and hdd over 1f out: fdd qckly over 1f out: t.o* **5/1[3]**

3m 34.69s (4.59) **Going Correction** -0.125s/f (Stan) **10** Ran SP% **118.5**
Speed ratings (Par 101): **83,81,80,79,78 78,74,74,73,66**
toteswingers: 1&2 £6.60, 1&3 £14.80, 2&3 £6.90. CSF £49.24 CT £312.98 TOTE £18.80: £4.30, £1.10, £4.30; EX 73.50 TRIFECTA Not won. Pool: £449.11..
Owner Sarah Snell & Anne Devine **Bred** Juddmonte Farms Ltd **Trained** Epsom, Surrey

FOCUS
A moderate staying handicap, run at a pedestrian gallop. The winner was close to his form from Wolverhampton last November.
Ice Apple Official explanation: jockey said filly was denied a clear run on the bend
Volcanic Jack(IRE) Official explanation: jockey said gelding was keen early and had no more to give
T/Plt: £12.80 to a £1 stake. Pool: £59,432.87 - 3,367.45 winning tickets. T/Qpdt: £9.80 to a £1 stake. Pool: £7,450.70 - 559.80 winning tickets. SP

6864 SAINT-CLOUD (L-H)
Thursday, October 11

OFFICIAL GOING: Turf: heavy

7013a PRIX THOMAS BRYON (GROUP 3) (2YO) (TURF) 1m
1:50 (12:00) 2-Y-O **£33,333** (£13,333; £10,000; £6,666; £3,333)

RPR
1 **Us Law (IRE)**[19] 6507 2-8-11 0 ChristopheSoumillon 3 109
(P Bary, France) *sn led: in front ent st: shkn up 1 1/2f out: wnt clr ent fnl f: nvr threatened: comf* **5/1**
2 *2* **Kenhope (FR)**[20] 2-8-8 0 ThierryJarnet 5 102
(H-A Pantall, France) *racd in 2nd on outside of ldr: rdn 1 1/2f out: chsd eventual wnr through fnl f wout threatening: styd on wl* **4/1[2]**
3 *1* **Visiyani (FR)**[19] 6507 2-8-11 0 Christophe-PatriceLemaire 6 102
(A De Royer-Dupre, France) *hld up towards rr on outside: shkn up 2f out: r.o wl fnl f wout threatening ldrs* **13/10[1]**
4 *1 1/4* **Zenji (USA)**[53] 5398 2-8-11 0 MaximeGuyon 1 100
(A Fabre, France) *slowly away and hld up at rr: mde prog on wd outside ent fnl f: styd on wout threatening ldrs* **6/1**
5 *1/2* **Local Lover (FR)**[19] 6507 2-8-11 0 FabriceVeron 4 99
(H-A Pantall, France) *racd in 3rd on ins: pulling hrd: r.o wl in st: no ex u.p ent fnl f: grad wknd* **19/1**

6 2 1/2 **Melodique (FR)**[27] 6225 2-8-8 0 .... OlivierPeslier 2 90
(C Laffon-Parias, France) *hld up towards rr: rdn but no ex fr 2f out: styd on at one pce fnl f* **43/10**[3]
1m 52.5s (5.00) **6** Ran SP% **118.3**
WIN (incl. 1 euro stake): 6.00. PLACES: 2.90, 2.50. SF: 35.90.
Owner Ecurie Jean-Louis Bouchard **Bred** Ballylinch Stud Ltd **Trained** Chantilly, France

NOTEBOOK
Us Law(IRE)'s rider rode a cunning race to set up a shot at the Group 1 Criterium International. The Irish-bred son of Lawman was asked to make all the running which he did at a leisurely gallop until the straight where pace was injected. His rider was compimentary, saying that the colt relaxed in front and that the rider let him do it himself.

6732 BATH (L-H)
Friday, October 12

OFFICIAL GOING: Soft (6.0)
Wind: Moderate across Weather: Sunny spells

7014 32RED MAIDEN STKS 5f 161y
12:00 (12:00) (Class 5) 2-Y-0 **£2,264** (£673; £336; £168) **Stalls** Centre

Form RPR
42 **1** **Gallena**[9] 6787 2-8-12 0 .... RyanMoore 7 70+
(William Haggas) *trckd ldr: led over 2f out: drvn and styd on strly fnl f* **5/4**[1]
5643 **2** 3 **Indian Affair**[15] 6611 2-9-3 68 .... RichardKingscote 3 65
(Milton Bradley) *led: rdn and hdd over 2f out: no imp on wnr fnl f but styd on wl to hold 2nd* **11/2**
00 **3** nk **Winnie Perry**[9] 6787 2-8-12 0 .... MichaelJMMurphy(5) 4 64
(Rod Millman) *chsd ldrs: drvn to dispute 2nd fnl f: no imp on wnr and dropped to 3rd clsng stages* **10/1**
6 **4** 2 1/4 **Uganda Glory (USA)**[29] 6153 2-8-12 0 .... RichardHughes 8 53
(George Baker) *chsd ldrs: drvn and qcknd to cl on wnr 2f out: no ex ins fnl f* **5/1**[3]
0552 **5** 4 **Kwanto**[26] 6276 2-8-12 65 .... TomMcLaughlin 1 39
(Malcolm Saunders) *pressed ldrs: rdn 2f out: wknd fnl f* **25/1**
5 **6** 3 1/4 **Lady Of The Vine (USA)**[57] 5267 2-8-12 0 .... DavidProbert 5 28
(Andrew Balding) *chsd ldrs: rdn 2f out: wknd over 1f out* **7/2**[2]
1m 15.52s (4.32) **Going Correction** +0.50s/f (Yiel) **6** Ran SP% **111.7**
Speed ratings (Par 95): **91,87,86,83,78 73**
Tote Swingers: 1&2 £1.10, 1&3 £9.00 CSF £8.54 TOTE £1.70: £1.30, £2.30; EX 4.40.
Owner Mr & Mrs R Scott **Bred** Mr & Mrs R & P Scott **Trained** Newmarket, Suffolk

FOCUS
There was 12.5 yards added to race distances that included the bottom bend. Times showed the ground was testing. A weak juvenile maiden in which they raced stands' side. The form is rated on the negative side.

NOTEBOOK
Gallena was the clear form pick after finishing runner-up in a big-field Nottingham maiden (5f, good to soft) on her second start and found this straightforward, drawing away after racing closest to the stands' rail in the straight. She should make a fair handicapper. (op Evens)
Indian Affair, officially rated 68, was simply beaten by a better rival. He's now 0-11. (tchd 5-1 and 6-1)
Winnie Perry didn't build on an encouraging debut at Sandown when well behind Gallena at Nottingham next time, but this was a respectable performance, albeit in a less competitive race, and he's now qualified for a handicap mark. (tchd 11-1)
Uganda Glory(USA) showed ability on her debut over 7f at Chepstow and did so again. (op 8-1)
Lady Of The Vine(USA) didn't build on her Newmarket debut after 57 days off, probably not appreciating the soft ground. (op 4-1 tchd 3-1)

7015 32RED.COM H'CAP 1m 5y
12:30 (12:30) (Class 6) (0-65,65) 3-Y-0+ **£1,617** (£481; £240; £120) **Stalls** Low

Form RPR
1233 **1** **Authoritarian**[9] 6801 3-9-3 64 .... RichardHughes 3 74
(Richard Hannon) *trckd ldrs in 3rd: drvn to ld wl over 1f out: pushed clr fnl 150yds* **3/1**[1]
4306 **2** 2 3/4 **Inffiraaj (IRE)**[26] 6281 3-7-13 51 .... DarrenEgan(5) 13 55
(Mick Channon) *in rr: hdwy 3f out: drvn 2f out: styd on fnl f to take 2nd fnl 75yds: no ch w wnr* **14/1**
-343 **3** 3/4 **Lovage**[36] 5983 3-9-4 65 .... JamesDoyle 14 67
(Roger Charlton) *sn led: drvn and jnd over 2f out: hdd wl over 1f out: one pce ins fnl f: lost 2nd fnl 75yds* **3/1**[1]
0012 **4** 1 **Belle Park**[29] 6157 5-8-11 55 ow1 .... TomMcLaughlin 6 55
(Karen George) *broke wl: sn mid-div: drvn and hdwy over 2f out: styd on fnl f* **7/1**[2]
4030 **5** shd **Valley Queen**[23] 6364 3-9-2 63 .... LiamKeniry 7 62
(Mark Usher) *chsd ldrs: drvn and styd on same pce fnl 2f* **16/1**
4024 **6** 6 **Corrib (IRE)**[37] 5935 9-8-4 51 oh6 ....(p) RaulDaSilva(3) 2 37
(Bryn Palling) *chsd ldr: chal over 2f out: wknd over 1f out* **14/1**
5006 **7** 1 3/4 **Golden Jubilee (USA)**[14] 6639 3-8-12 59 ....(b[1]) RyanMoore 5 41
(Richard Hannon) *in tch: rdn 3f out: wknd over 2f out* **8/1**[3]
0006 **8** 1 **Mr Udagawa**[25] 6304 6-8-7 51 oh2 ....(p) MartinLane 12 30
(Bernard Llewellyn) *in rr: drvn 4f out: mod prog u.p fnl 2f* **20/1**
-554 **9** 2 1/4 **Bussa**[9] 6798 4-9-2 60 ....(vt[1]) StevieDonohoe 8 34
(David Evans) *a towards rr* **20/1**
-000 **10** shd **Vergrigio (IRE)**[57] 5266 3-8-2 52 .... SimonPearce(3) 10 26
(David Pipe) *a towards rr* **40/1**
6500 **11** hd **Darsan (IRE)**[81] 4402 4-8-6 57 .... ClaireMurray(7) 4 30
(Phil McEntee) *s.i.s: in rr: mod hdwy u.p ins fnl 3f: sn wknd* **16/1**
5500 **12** 1 **Crown Dependency (IRE)**[20] 6500 3-8-8 55 .... RichardThomas 11 26
(David Evans) *in tch to 1/2-way* **33/1**
3600 **13** 3 1/2 **Temuco (IRE)**[19] 5657 3-8-13 65 ....(v[1]) NathanSweeney(5) 1 28
(David Evans) *chsd ldrs 5f out: wknd sn after* **25/1**
1m 48.17s (7.37) **Going Correction** +0.90s/f (Soft)
WFA 3 from 4yo+ 3lb **13** Ran SP% **117.5**
Speed ratings (Par 101): **99,96,95,94,94 88,86,85,83,83 83,82,78**
Tote Swingers: 1&2 £16.80, 1&3 £1.10, 2&3 £14.30 CSF £45.64 TOTE £3.40: £1.60, £3.80, £1.10; EX 40.70.
Owner Longview Stud & Bloodstock Ltd **Bred** Longview Stud & Bloodstock Ltd **Trained** East Everleigh, Wilts

FOCUS
A weak handicap. Again, they raced stands' side in the straight. A 4lb personal best from the winner.

7016 32RED CASINO MAIDEN STKS 1m 2f 46y
1:00 (1:00) (Class 5) 3-Y-0+ **£2,264** (£673; £336; £168) **Stalls** Low

Form RPR
52 **1** **Wannabe Loved**[44] 5745 3-8-12 0 .... WilliamBuick 9 92+
(John Gosden) *mde virtually all: drvn clr over 2f out: kpt up to work fnl f: eased cl home* **7/2**[3]
6226 **2** 6 **Courage (IRE)**[64] 5006 3-9-3 82 ....(v[1]) RyanMoore 8 85
(Sir Michael Stoute) *in tch: hdwy 3f out: drvn and styd on to chse wnr wl over 1f out but nvr any ch* **9/4**[1]
2350 **3** 4 1/2 **Sir Quintin (IRE)**[28] 6202 3-9-3 81 .... DavidProbert 6 77
(Andrew Balding) *chsd ldrs: rdn 3f out: one pce over 2f out* **7/2**[3]
2-4 **4** 2 **Pacific Heights (IRE)**[165] 1704 3-9-3 80 .... ShaneKelly 4 73
(Tim Pitt) *stdd towards rr: drvn and styd on fnl 2f: nvr gng pce to rch ldrs* **8/1**
25 **5** shd **Awake My Soul (IRE)**[91] 4067 3-9-3 0 .... RichardHughes 1 73
(Luca Cumani) *chsd wnr 5f out: rdn and no imp 3f out: lost 2nd wl over 1f out: wknd fnl f* **10/3**[2]
00 **6** 7 **Caunay**[10] 6770 5-9-5 0 ....(t) AmyBaker(3) 7 60
(Neil Mulholland) *s.i.s: in rr: hdwy 4f out: wknd fr 3f out* **100/1**
0-5 **7** shd **Sunny Bank**[22] 6398 3-8-10 0 .... ThomasBrown(7) 5 59
(Andrew Balding) *rdn 4f out: a in rr* **50/1**
0 **8** 6 **Irene Kennet**[15] 6615 5-9-3 0 .... SeanQuinlan 3 43
(Mark Rimell) *chsd ldrs: rdn 3f out: sn btn* **100/1**
00 **9** 9 **Refute (IRE)**[27] 6228 3-9-3 0 .... JamesDoyle 2 31
(Harry Dunlop) *pressed wnr 7f out to 6f out: wknd ins fnl 3f* **80/1**
2m 17.83s (6.83) **Going Correction** +0.90s/f (Soft)
WFA 3 from 5yo 5lb **9** Ran SP% **114.6**
Speed ratings (Par 103): **108,103,99,98,97 92,92,87,80**
Tote Swingers: 1&2 £2.80, 1&3 £4.00, 2&3 £3.90 CSF £11.74 TOTE £4.70: £1.70, £1.10, £1.30; EX 13.00.
Owner Normandie Stud Ltd **Bred** Normandie Stud Ltd **Trained** Newmarket, Suffolk

FOCUS
A fair maiden on paper, although the second and third have both had a few chances. The time was relatively good.
Awake My Soul(IRE) Official explanation: jockey said gelding had no more to give

7017 32RED H'CAP 1m 2f 46y
1:30 (1:30) (Class 2) (0-100,90) 3-Y-0+ **£10,221** (£3,041; £1,519; £759) **Stalls** Low

Form RPR
412 **1** **Little Rocky**[15] 6606 4-9-10 90 .... DaneO'Neill 7 101+
(David Simcock) *mde virtually all: pushed along over 2f out: drvn wl clr over 1f out and styd on strly: eased clsng stages* **2/1**[1]
4403 **2** 3 1/2 **Cool Macavity (IRE)**[28] 6202 4-9-7 87 .... WilliamCarson 6 89
(Charles Hills) *in rr but in tch: pushed along 3f out: hdwy over 2f out to take 2nd wl over 1f out but nvr any ch w wnr* **8/1**
2010 **3** 3/4 **Shavansky**[20] 6494 8-9-9 89 .... JamesMillman 3 90
(Rod Millman) *s.i.s: in rr: drvn and hdwy 2f out: styd on to take 3rd fnl 150yds: kpt on cl home but nvr any ch w wnr* **20/1**
1430 **4** 4 1/2 **Clare Island Boy (IRE)**[13] 6661 3-9-2 87 .... RichardHughes 5 79
(Richard Hannon) *pressed wnr 5f: rdn 3f out: styd disputing 2nd tl wl over 1f out: wknd fnl f* **9/1**
/154 **5** 2 1/2 **Splendid Light**[12] 6702 4-9-6 86 .... WilliamBuick 4 73
(John Gosden) *in tch: pushed along and hdwy 3f out: rdn 2f out: no imp: sn wknd* **11/2**[3]
1235 **6** 6 **Commend**[28] 6193 3-9-1 86 .... RyanMoore 2 61
(Sir Michael Stoute) *chsd ldrs: drvn to dsputed 2nd over 2f out but no imp on wnr: wknd rapidly wl over 1f out* **9/4**[2]
1211 **7** 7 **King's Masque**[26] 6278 6-8-12 78 .... MartinLane 8 39
(Bernard Llewellyn) *chsd ldrs: rdn over 2f out: sn btn* **14/1**
2m 18.83s (7.83) **Going Correction** +0.90s/f (Soft)
WFA 3 from 4yo+ 5lb **7** Ran SP% **112.0**
Speed ratings (Par 109): **104,101,100,97,95 90,84**
toteswingers 1&2 £11.20, 2&3 £23.30, 1&3 £7.40 CSF £17.74 TOTE £3.30: £2.00, £2.50; EX 16.80.
Owner C J Murfitt **Bred** C J Murfitt **Trained** Newmarket, Suffolk

FOCUS
A decent handicap, but the top weight (the winner) was rated 10lb below the race ceiling and the time was slow compared with the previous maiden. The runner-up helps with the standard.

NOTEBOOK
Little Rocky, much like the winner of the preceding C&D maiden, was allowed to dominate and stuck to the stands' rail in the straight, but he stopped the clock a second slower than the earlier race. This scenario could hardly have set up better for him, being a confirmed front-runner, and things are likely to be tougher next time. (tchd 9-4)
Cool Macavity(IRE) didn't race as close to the stands' rail as the winner and was always held. He was off a career-high mark. (op 7-1)
Shavansky, for whom this race didn't really set up, stayed on against the stands' rail to post a respectable effort.
Clare Island Boy(IRE) has winning form on easy ground, but maybe these conditions were too testing. (op 11-1 tchd 12-1)
Splendid Light, due to be eased 2lb, again failed to build on earlier promise, but this ground may have been unsuitable. (tchd 6-1)
Commend is another who was probably unsuited by the conditions. (op 5-2 tchd 11-4)

7018 32RED SUPPORTING BRITISH RACING H'CAP 1m 3f 144y
2:05 (2:05) (Class 5) (0-70,70) 3-Y-0+ **£2,264** (£673; £336; £168) **Stalls** Low

Form RPR
0036 **1** **Just When**[30] 6146 3-8-11 62 ....(v) DavidProbert 12 81
(Andrew Balding) *chsd ldrs: led wl over 1f out: drvn wl clr* **4/1**[3]
0120 **2** 13 **Sunny Future (IRE)**[11] 6738 6-9-10 68 .... TomMcLaughlin 13 65
(Malcolm Saunders) *chsd ldr: led over 2f out: hdd wl over 1f out and sn no ch w wnr but styd on wl for 2nd* **16/1**
6426 **3** 1 **Aegean Destiny**[3] 6957 5-9-3 61 .... RobertHavlin 10 56
(John Mackie) *pushed along after s: sn chsng ldrs: drvn over 2f out: no ch w wnr fr over 1f out and styd on for one pce 3rd* **10/3**[2]
3056 **4** 2 **Spring Secret**[29] 6159 6-8-9 56 oh2 .... RaulDaSilva(3) 8 48
(Bryn Palling) *in rr: rdn 7f out and sn chsng ldrs: styd on stands' rail and rdn over 2f out: one pce* **33/1**
5253 **5** 1 3/4 **April Ciel**[11] 6735 3-8-11 67 .... DarrenEgan(5) 14 56
(Ronald Harris) *led tl rdn and hdd over 2f out: sn btn* **3/1**[1]
-006 **6** 4 1/2 **Wily Fox**[101] 3734 5-9-4 62 .... WilliamCarson 7 43
(James Eustace) *towards rr: rdn and sme hdwy 3f out: sn hrd drvn and btn* **20/1**

05U5 **7** *nk* **Urban Space**[37] 5950 6-9-12 70 .... AndreaAtzeni 2 51
(Tony Carroll) *chsd ldrs: rdn 3f out: wknd fr 2f out* **16/1**

40/4 **8** *1 ¼* **Surprise Us**[27] 6231 5-8-12 56 oh8 .... MartinLane 6 35
(Bernard Llewellyn) *chsd ldrs: rdn and btn 3f out* **22/1**

3630 **9** *52* **Korngold**[35] 6004 4-9-4 62 .... (b) DaneO'Neill 3
(John Dunlop) *in tch tl dropped to rr 6f out: t.o fnl 4f* **12/1**

6-50 **10** *2* **Lady Barastar (IRE)**[27] 6229 4-9-4 62 .... JamesDoyle 4
(Amanda Perrett) *in tch: rdn 5f out: wknd 4f out: t.o* **25/1**

0366 **11** *4* **Lone Foot Laddie (IRE)**[43] 5770 3-8-7 58 .... LiamKeniry 5
(Sylvester Kirk) *a in rr: t.o fnl 3f* **20/1**

303/ **12** *8* **Miss Kingwood**[704] 7381 5-9-1 64 .... JemmaMarshall(5) 11
(Jo Hughes) *early spd bhd fr 1/2-way: sn t.o* **50/1**

005- **13** *6* **Malanos (IRE)**[167] 6589 4-9-4 62 .... PatDobbs 9
(Tony Carroll) *rdn 6f out: t.o* **8/1**

2m 39.93s (9.33) **Going Correction** +0.90s/f (Soft)
WFA 3 from 4yo+ 7lb **13** Ran SP% **121.3**
Speed ratings (Par 103): **104,95,94,93,92 89,88,88,53,52 49,44,40**
Tote Swingers: 1&2 £12.50, 1&3 £5.40, 2&3 £15.00 CSF £59.56 CT £241.72 TOTE £5.70: £1.90, £5.10, £1.10; EX 86.40.
Owner Miss E J Lambourne **Bred** George Strawbridge Stables **Trained** Kingsclere, Hants

FOCUS
Unlike in the earlier races, only the fourth horse raced against the stands' rail in the closing stages. The wide-margin winner showed big improvement, but the ground was a likely factor.

7019 32RED ONLINE CASINO H'CAP 5f 11y
2:40 (2:40) (Class 4) (0-85,85) 3-Y-O+ **£4,075** (£1,212; £606; £303) **Stalls** Centre

Form RPR

4111 **1** **Gladiatrix**[4] 6926 3-8-2 71 6ex .... MichaelJMMurphy(5) 12 87
(Rod Millman) *towards rr: stdy hdwy over 2f out: drvn to ld over 1f out: clr ins fnl f: easily* **6/4**[1]

0103 **2** *3* **Time Medicean**[38] 5906 6-8-10 77 .... RaulDaSilva(3) 9 82
(Tony Carroll) *in rr: hdwy 2f out: styd on to take 2nd fnl 120yds but no ch w wnr* **10/1**

2322 **3** *½* **Macdillon**[10] 6767 6-8-10 74 .... LiamKeniry 14 77
(Stuart Kittow) *chsd ldrs: rdn and ev ch 2f out: styd on for 3rd fnl f but nvr any ch w wnr* **9/1**[3]

0253 **4** *1* **Ertikaan**[9] 6800 5-8-13 82 .... DarrenEgan(5) 4 82
(Ronald Harris) *in rr: hdwy over 1f out: styd on fnl f but nvr a threat to wnr* **8/1**[2]

3003 **5** *nk* **Waseem Faris (IRE)**[23] 6382 3-9-0 83 .... CharlesBishop(5) 3 82
(Mick Channon) *chsd ldrs: rdn and ev ch 2f out: one pce whn n.m.r ins fnl f* **16/1**

0060 **6** *½* **Jarrow (IRE)**[13] 6663 5-9-2 80 .... RichardKingscote 8 77
(Milton Bradley) *chsd ldrs: rdn over 2f out: one pce fnl f* **14/1**

205 **7** *hd* **Six Wives**[30] 6144 5-8-9 80 ow1 .... WilliamTwiston-Davies(7) 15 76
(Scott Dixon) *led tl hdd over 1f out: wknd fnl f* **16/1**

0000 **8** *½* **Solemn**[9] 6800 7-9-7 85 .... (b) DaneO'Neill 13 79
(Milton Bradley) *in tch: hdwy 2f out: one pce fnl f* **20/1**

3631 **9** *nk* **Ginzan**[41] 5815 4-8-12 76 .... TomMcLaughlin 2 69
(Malcolm Saunders) *chsd ldrs: ev ch 2f out: wknd fnl f* **16/1**

3610 **10** *½* **Even Stevens**[21] 6427 4-9-4 82 .... (p) IanMongan 11 74
(Scott Dixon) *chsd ldrs on stands' rail: ev ch 2f out: wknd ins fnl f* **12/1**

10-0 **11** *nk* **Secret Millionaire (IRE)**[13] 6689 5-9-2 80 .... PatDobbs 5 70
(Tony Carroll) *n.m.r s: in rr: rdn 1/2-way: nvr gng pce to rch ldrs* **50/1**

0003 **12** *3* **Taurus Twins**[10] 6755 6-9-6 84 .... (b) JamesDoyle 7 64
(Richard Price) *in rr: hdwy to chse ldrs on far side 3f out: wknd over 1f out* **20/1**

3005 **13** *1 ¼* **Wicked Wench**[19] 6515 3-8-10 79 .... JemmaMarshall(5) 6 54
(Jo Hughes) *spd to 1/2-way* **20/1**

0000 **14** *1 ½* **Cadeaux Pearl**[20] 6466 4-9-6 84 .... (b) RichardHughes 10 54
(Scott Dixon) *outpcd most of way* **16/1**

3513 **15** *5* **Charming (IRE)**[80] 4423 3-8-7 71 oh2 .... DavidProbert 1 23
(Olivia Maylam) *spd to 1/2-way* **25/1**

1m 4.32s (1.82) **Going Correction** +0.50s/f (Yiel) **15** Ran SP% **128.2**
Speed ratings (Par 105): **105,100,99,97,97 96,96,95,94,94 93,88,86,84,76**
Tote Swingers: 1&2 £4.90, 1&3 £2.90, 2&3 £28.60 CSF £16.37 CT £116.68 TOTE £2.50: £1.60, £2.90, £2.00; EX 18.90.
Owner Harry Dutfield & Partners **Bred** H G And J R Dutfield **Trained** Kentisbeare, Devon

FOCUS
They were spread out across the track and the main action was middle to stands' side. The winner was well in but this was another step forward. The second sets the standard.
T/Plt: £13.40 to a £1 stake. Pool: £44,924.00 - 2,443.03 winning tickets. T/Qpdt: £12.50 to a £1 stake. Pool: £4,040.00 - 238.62 winning tickets. ST

6968 WOLVERHAMPTON (A.W) (L-H)
Friday, October 12

OFFICIAL GOING: Standard
Wind: Fresh behind Weather: Cloudy

7020 32RED MEDIAN AUCTION MAIDEN STKS (DIV I) 7f 32y(P)
5:40 (5:41) (Class 6) 2-Y-O **£1,704** (£503; £251) **Stalls** High

Form RPR

3 **1** **Elnadwa (USA)**[29] 6168 2-8-12 0 .... SilvestreDeSousa 7 75+
(Saeed Bin Suroor) *chsd ldr: rdn to ld ins fnl f: r.o* **13/8**[1]

036 **2** *2 ¼* **Mumeyez**[7] 6796 2-9-3 0 .... RobertHavlin 6 74
(John Gosden) *led: hung rt and reminder 5f out: rdn over 1f out: hdd and unable qck ins fnl f* **7/2**[2]

32 **3** *1 ¾* **Gabrial's Wawa**[12] 6708 2-9-3 0 .... DaneO'Neill 2 70
(Richard Fahey) *plld hrd and prom: rdn and ev ch over 1f out: styd on same pce fnl f* **7/2**[2]

4 *1 ½* **Ihtikar (USA)** 2-9-3 0 .... TadhgO'Shea 4 67+
(Ed Dunlop) *prom: pushed along 1/2-way: styd on same pce fr over 1f out* **25/1**

00 **5** *1 ½* **Carlarajah**[34] 6020 2-9-3 0 .... HayleyTurner 11 63
(Michael Bell) *hld up: hdwy over 2f out: styd on same pce appr fnl f* **5/1**[3]

4 **6** *¾* **Shagwa (IRE)**[10] 6754 2-8-12 0 .... RyanMoore 8 56
(Mark Johnston) *chsd ldrs: rdn over 2f out: no ex fr over 1f out* **28/1**

04 **7** *1 ½* **Miguel Grau (USA)**[29] 6175 2-9-3 0 .... AdamKirby 9 57+
(Marco Botti) *s.i.s: hld up: shkn up over 1f out: nvr nr to chal* **20/1**

0 **8** *1 ¼* **Hidden Link**[15] 6609 2-9-3 0 .... ChrisCatlin 10 54+
(Sir Mark Prescott Bt) *s.s: pushed along 1/2-way: nvr on terms* **50/1**

9 *4 ½* **Tracks Of My Tears** 2-8-12 0 .... WilliamCarson 3 38
(Giles Bravery) *a in rr: wknd over 2f out* **80/1**

00 **10** *28* **Don Juan**[36] 5963 2-9-3 0 .... SebSanders 5
(Eric Alston) *hld up: hdwy over 2f out: rdn and wknd over 1f out* **66/1**

1m 29.88s (0.28) **Going Correction** -0.125s/f (Stan) **10** Ran SP% **116.0**
Speed ratings (Par 93): **93,90,88,86,85 84,82,81,75,43**
Tote Swingers: 1&2 £2.50, 1&3 £2.20, 2&3 £5.00 CSF £6.89 TOTE £2.40: £1.30, £1.40, £1.60; EX 8.00 Trifecta £33.10 Pool: £1,036.87 - 23.14 winning units..
Owner Godolphin **Bred** Shadwell Farm LLC **Trained** Newmarket, Suffolk

FOCUS
They went an even gallop in the first division of this auction maiden. There was a fair tailwind up the home straight.

NOTEBOOK
Elnadwa(USA), whose dam was top-class from 7f-1m1f as a 3yo in the US, reportedly looked well here beforehand, and improved to run out a decent winner of this contest from an always prominent position, getting well on top inside the final furlong. She should continue to progress at up to 1m next term. (op 11-8 tchd 6-5)
Mumeyez attempted to make all on this occasion but had to give best from 1f out. He appeared to reproduce his Kempton form but may prove hard to place for the remainder of the year. (op 11-2)
Gabrial's Wawa produced fair form over this 7f trip on his first two starts on good/good to soft turf the previous month but ran slightly below peak form on this Polytrack debut. (op 5-2)
Ihtikar(USA), who is a half-brother to the quite smart Anmar, reportedly looked the part prior to this debut. He settled in mid-division and came through quite pleasingly into a never-nearer fourth. He should show the benefit from this decent introduction next time. (op 28-1)
Carlarajah ran respectably in a decent 7f Ascot maiden the previous month on his second start but failed to build on that display on this Polytrack debut. (op 7-1 tchd 15-2)
Shagwa(IRE) finished tailed off over 6f on heavy ground on debut at Ayr ten days before this contest, and has some modest form to build on now. (op 25-1)

7021 32RED MEDIAN AUCTION MAIDEN STKS (DIV II) 7f 32y(P)
6:15 (6:18) (Class 6) 2-Y-O **£1,704** (£503; £251) **Stalls** High

Form RPR

1 **How's Life** 2-8-12 0 .... SilvestreDeSousa 7 71+
(Rae Guest) *chsd ldr: edgd rt over 1f out: sn rdn: led ins fnl f: edgd lft: r.o* **10/3**[2]

0 **2** *1 ½* **Enzaal (USA)**[29] 6177 2-9-3 0 .... DaneO'Neill 2 72+
(Mark Johnston) *led: rdn over 1f out: hdd ins fnl f: styd on same pce* **11/4**[1]

3 *2* **Manazel (USA)** 2-9-3 0 .... (b[1]) TadhgO'Shea 11 67
(John Gosden) *s.i.s: hdwy 1/2-way: rdn over 1f out: styd on same pce* **4/1**[3]

0 **4** *¾* **Borodino (IRE)**[9] 6780 2-9-3 0 .... FrederikTylicki 8 65
(Richard Fahey) *mid-div: sn pushed along: styd on fnl f: nvr trbld ldrs* **10/1**

5 *2 ¼* **Vulcan (IRE)** 2-9-3 0 .... GrahamLee 4 62+
(David Simcock) *hld up: styd on fnl f: nvr trbld ldrs* **4/1**[3]

000 **6** *2 ¾* **Pleasant Moment**[41] 5828 2-8-12 50 .... RichardKingscote 1 48
(Tom Dascombe) *chsd ldrs: rdn over 2f out: wknd over 1f out* **16/1**

00 **7** *18* **Tonkalili**[6] 6889 2-8-12 0 .... (b[1]) LiamJones 6
(James Unett) *s.i.s: sn pushed along in rr: rdn over 2f out: sn wknd* **100/1**

8 *9* **Greenfordgirl (IRE)** 2-8-12 0 .... ChrisCatlin 10
(John Weymes) *sn outpcd: t.o* **66/1**

00 **9** *1 ¼* **Sol Diva**[71] 4739 2-8-12 0 .... SamHitchcott 3 +
(Mick Channon) *plld hrd and prom: sddle slipped sn after s: wknd and eased over 2f out: t.o* **16/1**

1m 30.15s (0.55) **Going Correction** -0.125s/f (Stan) **9** Ran SP% **113.1**
Speed ratings (Par 93): **91,89,87,86,83 80,59,49,48**
Tote Swingers: 1&2 £2.80, 1&3 £1.70, 2&3 £2.10 CSF £12.61 TOTE £3.30: £1.90, £1.70, £1.30; EX 13.10 Trifecta £68.20 Pool: £815.60 - 8.84 winning units..
Owner J H Metzger **Bred** John-Henry Metzger **Trained** Newmarket, Suffolk

FOCUS
They went a fair gallop in the second division. The form could be rated higher, but the proximity of the sixth holds it down.

NOTEBOOK
How's Life, who is a sister to French 7f winner Eternal Gift out of an unraced sister to smart US/French 1m-1m2f winner Live Life, found market support on this debut. She raced prominently behind the second horse home, before cutting him down quite takingly about 1f from home. (op 5-1 tchd 11-4)
Enzaal(USA), who is a half-brother to Abeer, attempted to make all on this occasion, and found some improvement, but he was no match for the winner halfway up the home straight. He probably has a future in handicaps at up to 1m. Official explanation: vet said colt lost a shoe (op 9-4 tchd 3-1)
Manazel(USA), wearing blinkers on this debut, started slowly but to his credit made headway halfway. He finished one-paced in third and should learn plenty from the experience. (op 3-1 tchd 5-1)
Borodino(IRE) found marked improvement on Polytrack here. He stayed on well into fourth from mid-division and is already looking for further. (op 16-1)
Vulcan(IRE), who reportedly looked well beforehand, was held up on debut and stayed on quite well into a respectable fifth up the home straight. There is more to come from him. (op 13-2)
Sol Diva Official explanation: jockey said saddle slipped

7022 THOMPSON GROUP TECHNOLOGY DAY H'CAP 7f 32y(P)
6:45 (6:46) (Class 6) (0-65,65) 3-Y-O+ **£1,704** (£503; £251) **Stalls** High

Form RPR

2402 **1** **Admiralty**[8] 6813 3-8-10 **65** .... ThomasBrown(7) 8 77
(Ismail Mohammed) *mde all: rdn over 1f out: r.o* **9/2**[1]

0600 **2** *2 ¼* **Fortrose Academy (IRE)**[120] 3071 3-9-2 **64** .... DavidProbert 10 70
(Andrew Balding) *chsd wnr: rdn over 1f out: styd on same pce ins fnl f* **11/2**[3]

0060 **3** *nse* **Imaginary World (IRE)**[15] 6613 4-9-3 **63** .... (p) IanMongan 2 69
(John Balding) *mid-div: hdwy u.p over 1f out: r.o* **14/1**

0254 **4** *shd* **Fishforcompliments**[6] 6888 8-9-5 **65** .... FrederikTylicki 12 71
(Richard Fahey) *s.i.s: hld up: rdn over 1f out: r.o ins fnl f: nt rch ldrs* **8/1**

6562 **5** *shd* **Powerful Pierre**[22] 6403 5-9-0 **63** .... (v) DeclanCannon(3) 5 68
(Ian McInnes) *chsd ldrs: rdn over 2f out: styd on* **16/1**

4261 **6** *hd* **Iceblast**[8] 6823 4-8-12 **65** 6ex .... (b) DavidSimmonson(7) 1 70
(Michael Easterby) *hld up: hdwy over 1f out: sn rdn: styd on u.p* **5/1**[2]

4263 **7** *¾* **Muhandis (IRE)**[21] 6455 4-9-4 **64** .... (b) SebSanders 3 67
(Nick Littmoden) *dwlt: hld up: rdn over 1f out: r.o ins fnl f: nvr nrr* **14/1**

4021 **8** *½* **Inpursuitoffreedom**[9] 6773 5-9-5 **65** 6ex .... ShaneKelly 7 66
(Philip McBride) *hld up: shkn up ins fnl f: edgd lft: nt trble ldrs* **14/1**

0024 **9** *nk* **Sir Bruno (FR)**[28] 6216 5-9-0 **65** .... (p) DarrenEgan(5) 9 66
(Bryn Palling) *prom: rdn over 2f out: no ex ins fnl f* **13/2**

6204 **10** *½* **Striker Torres (IRE)**[27] 6241 6-9-5 **65** .... GrahamLee 4 64
(Ian McInnes) *chsd ldrs: rdn over 2f out: no ex ins fnl f* **5/1**[2]

0000 **11** 1 ¼ **Lastkingofscotland (IRE)**[13] 6692 6-9-5 **65**............(b) HayleyTurner 11 61
(Conor Dore) *mid-div: rdn over 2f out: styd on same pce* **33/1**

1m 29.11s (-0.49) **Going Correction** -0.125s/f (Stan)
WFA 3 from 4yo+ 2lb **11** Ran SP% **120.2**
Speed ratings (Par 101): **97,94,94,94,94 93,93,92,92,91 90**
Tote Swingers: 1&2 £13.40, 1&3 £9.00, 2&3 £35.10 CSF £29.73 CT £332.92 TOTE £5.20: £1.50, £2.90, £5.90; EX 34.50 TRIFECTA Not won..
Owner Ahmad Al Shaikh **Bred** Mrs Fiona Denniff **Trained** Newmarket, Suffolk

FOCUS
A modest handicap in which they went a respectable gallop. The form has been taken at face value and could work out quite well.

7023 32RED.COM H'CAP 5f 216y(P)
7:15 (7:20) (Class 5) (0-75,81) 3-Y-0+ **£2,587** (£770; £384; £192) **Stalls** Low

Form RPR

631 **1** **Enrol**[43] 5776 3-9-2 **73**.. RyanMoore 3 89+
(Sir Michael Stoute) *hld up: hdwy over 1f out: r.o to ld wl ins fnl f: rdn out* **1/1**[1]

1301 **2** 3 ¼ **We'll Deal Again**[8] 6825 5-9-4 **81** 6ex...............(b) DavidSimmonson(7) 9 87+
(Michael Easterby) *led: rdn over 1f out: hdd and unable qck wl ins fnl f* **5/1**[2]

0600 **3** nse **Mac Gille Eoin**[63] 5035 8-9-4 **74**.............................. IanMongan 7 80
(Luke Dace) *hld up: hdwy over 2f out: rdn over 1f out: r.o* **20/1**

0001 **4** 3 ¼ **Jack Smudge**[14] 6641 4-9-5 **75**..........................(v) GrahamLee 10 70
(James Given) *chsd ldrs: rdn over 1f out: wknd ins fnl f* **20/1**

4230 **5** nse **Swendab (IRE)**[32] 6094 4-8-11 **72**......................... DarrenEgan(5) 6 67
(John O'Shea) *mid-div: drvn along 1/2-way: styd on u.p ins fnl f: nvr nrr* **33/1**

2000 **6** ½ **Master Bond**[18] 6525 3-9-4 **75**............................(t) SilvestreDeSousa 4 69
(Bryan Smart) *s.i.s: rdn over 1f out: r.o ins fnl f: nrst fin* **14/1**

0013 **7** hd **We Have A Dream**[8] 6824 7-9-5 **75**.......................... JamesDoyle 2 68
(William Muir) *chsd ldrs: pushed along 1/2-way: rdn over 1f out: wknd ins fnl f* **8/1**[3]

-416 **8** 1 **Burnhope**[205] 982 3-9-4 **75**....................................... JimCrowley 13 65
(Scott Dixon) *sn chsng ldr: rdn and ev ch over 1f out: wknd ins fnl f* **20/1**

3604 **9** 1 ¼ **Falasteen (IRE)**[9] 6788 5-9-5 **75**.......................... RichardKingscote 12 61
(Milton Bradley) *prom: rdn over 2f out: wknd over 1f out* **25/1**

215 **10** ½ **Tahlia Ree (IRE)**[56] 5324 3-9-2 **73**......................... HayleyTurner 5 57
(Michael Bell) *s.i.s: a in rr* **11/1**

4023 **11** ½ **Commanche Raider (IRE)**[6] 6887 5-9-2 **72**...............(p) TomEaves 1 55
(Michael Dods) *mid-div: sn pushed along: rdn 1/2-way: sn bhd* **20/1**

0252 **12** 2 **Song Of Parkes**[78] 4495 5-9-4 **74**.............................. ShaneKelly 8 50
(Eric Alston) *chsd ldrs: hung lft over 3f out: rdn and wknd over 1f out* **20/1**

3500 **13** ½ **Desert Strike**[13] 6689 6-9-5 **75**.........................(p) KirstyMilczarek 11 50
(Conor Dore) *sn pushed along in rr: nvr on terms* **50/1**

1m 13.31s (-1.69) **Going Correction** -0.125s/f (Stan)
WFA 3 from 4yo+ 1lb **13** Ran SP% **125.3**
Speed ratings (Par 103): **106,101,101,97,97 96,96,94,93,92 91,89,88**
Tote Swingers: 1&2 £3.50, 1&3 £9.90, 2&3 £18.10 CSF £5.05 CT £72.82 TOTE £2.00: £1.10, £1.80, £5.90; EX 7.90 Trifecta £256.50 Pool: £592.83 - 1.71 winning units..
Owner Cheveley Park Stud **Bred** Cheveley Park Stud Ltd **Trained** Newmarket, Suffolk

FOCUS
A fair sprint handicap in which the pace was contested. The winner could do better still and the second probably improved again.

7024 32RED CASINO H'CAP 1m 5f 194y(P)
7:45 (7:45) (Class 5) (0-75,74) 3-Y-0+ **£2,264** (£673; £336; £168) **Stalls** Low

Form RPR

5311 **1** **Porcini**[13] 6691 3-9-0 **72**.. RaulDaSilva(3) 9 82+
(Philip McBride) *a.p: chsd ldr 10f out: rdn over 1f out: styd on to ld wl ins fnl f* **11/4**[1]

0212 **2** ½ **English Summer**[6] 6891 5-9-7 **67**...........................(t) GrahamLee 12 76+
(David Simcock) *hld up: hdwy over 2f out: rdn over 1f out: ev ch wl ins fnl f: styd on* **4/1**[2]

0523 **3** ½ **Singzak**[20] 6478 4-9-7 **67**.. TomEaves 13 75
(Michael Easterby) *led: rdn over 1f out: hdd and unable qck wl ins fnl f* **5/1**

3356 **4** 2 ¼ **Nave (USA)**[9] 6776 5-9-13 **73**.................................. MartinLane 8 78
(David Simcock) *hld up: hdwy over 2f out: sn rdn: styd on: nt rch ldrs* **6/1**

0330 **5** ½ **Jacob McCandles**[13] 6691 5-9-4 **64**.......................... HayleyTurner 5 68
(Shaun Lycett) *a.p: rdn over 1f out: styd on* **16/1**

0465 **6** 3 **Sirius Superstar**[43] 5772 4-9-11 **71**.......................(v[1]) DavidProbert 2 71
(Andrew Balding) *prom: rdn over 3f out: styd on same pce fnl 2f* **11/1**

432 **7** 4 ½ **Kames Park (IRE)**[34] 6055 10-9-4 **64**..................... RobbieFitzpatrick 10 58
(Richard Guest) *s.i.s: hld up: rdn over 1f out: nvr on terms* **22/1**

3050 **8** 1 ¼ **Dartford (USA)**[27] 6245 3-9-5 **74**.............................. RobertHavlin 6 66
(John Gosden) *chsd ldr 4f: remained handy: rdn over 2f out: wknd fnl f* **9/2**[3]

154 **9** 5 **Adeste**[23] 6383 3-9-3 **72**......................................(b) SilvestreDeSousa 3 57
(Noel Quinlan) *s.i.s: hld up: a in rr* **25/1**

1140 **10** shd **Rocky Rebel**[9] 6776 4-9-12 **72**...............................(b) DaneO'Neill 11 57
(Chris Bealby) *s.i.s: hld up: rdn over 2f out: a in rr* **28/1**

0004 **11** 4 **Sea Change (IRE)**[16] 5188 5-9-1 **61**......................... FrederikTylicki 7 40
(Jim Goldie) *hld up: drvn along 5f out: wknd over 2f out* **33/1**

3m 2.56s (-3.44) **Going Correction** -0.125s/f (Stan)
WFA 3 from 4yo+ 9lb **11** Ran SP% **124.6**
Speed ratings (Par 103): **104,103,103,102,101 100,97,96,94,93 91**
Tote Swingers: 1&2 £3.50, 1&3 £9.90, 2&3 £18.10 CSF £13.93 CT £55.30 TOTE £4.90: £1.50, £1.80, £1.20; EX 16.30 Trifecta £60.90 Pool: £316.18 - 3.84 winning units..
Owner PMRacing **Bred** Cheveley Park Stud Ltd **Trained** Newmarket, Suffolk

FOCUS
A fair staying handicap in which they went an even gallop. Straightforward form, the winner continuing on the upgrade.

7025 STEPHEN AND MANDY ROBINSON SILVER WEDDING MEDIAN AUCTION MAIDEN STKS 1m 141y(P)
8:15 (8:15) (Class 6) 3-5-Y-0 **£1,704** (£503; £251) **Stalls** Low

Form RPR

3325 **1** **Christingle**[11] 6736 3-8-11 69.. LiamJones 8 69+
(William Haggas) *hld up: hdwy over 2f out: rdn over 1f out: r.o to ld wl ins fnl f: edgd lft and sn clr* **4/1**[3]

05 **2** 2 ¼ **Hint Of Promise**[22] 6397 3-8-11 0.............................. JamesDoyle 7 63+
(Roger Charlton) *trckd ldrs: plld hrd: pushed along to go 2nd over 3f out: rdn over 1f out: styd on same pce ins fnl f* **2/1**[2]

2220 **3** 1 ¼ **La Pampita (IRE)**[47] 5636 3-8-11 74.............................. JimCrowley 11 61
(William Knight) *a.p: chsd ldr over 6f out: led 5f out: rdn over 1f out: hdd and no ex wl ins fnl f* **7/4**[1]

0000 **4** 2 **Destiny Awaits (IRE)**[14] 6646 3-9-2 47.......................(p) TomEaves 10 61
(Ian Semple) *hld up: rdn over 1f out: r.o u.p ins fnl f: nrst fin* **50/1**

2343 **5** ½ **Peak Storm**[14] 6643 3-8-11 65.................................... DarrenEgan(5) 9 60
(John O'Shea) *mid-div: hdwy over 2f out: rdn over 1f out: no ex fnl f* **13/2**

6 8 **Thecornishwren (IRE)** 3-8-11 0................................. KirstyMilczarek 3 36
(John Ryan) *led: hdd 5f out: rdn and wknd over 2f out* **25/1**

-050 **7** 1 ¼ **Make Me Smyle**[14] 6643 3-9-2 38.............................(b[1]) IanMongan 6 39
(Stuart Kittow) *sn pushed along in rr: nvr on terms* **33/1**

0000 **8** 14 **Spoken Words**[77] 4547 3-8-8 46..............................(v[1]) PaulPickard(3) 5
(Hugh McWilliams) *mid-div: rdn over 2f out: sn wknd* **66/1**

00-0 **9** 1 ½ **Donnywardsbird**[31] 6125 4-9-6 30.............................. SebSanders 12
(Eric Alston) *sn pushed along in rr: bhd fnl 3f* **100/1**

0-6 **10** ½ **Princeofperfection**[18] 6527 3-8-9 0.......................... VictorSantos(7) 2
(Richard Ford) *mid-div: drvn along 1/2-way: nt clr run over 3f out: sn wknd* **200/1**

0 **11** 3 **Midnami**[62] 5113 3-9-2 0.. PatrickMathers 4
(Linda Stubbs) *plld hrd and prom: rdn over 3f out: sn wknd* **50/1**

1m 49.93s (-0.57) **Going Correction** -0.125s/f (Stan)
WFA 3 from 4yo 4lb **11** Ran SP% **116.7**
Speed ratings (Par 101): **97,95,93,92,91 84,83,71,69,69 66**
Tote Swingers: 1&2 £2.40, 1&3 £2.70, 2&3 £1.10 CSF £12.01 TOTE £6.50: £1.30, £1.10, £1.10; EX 19.90 Trifecta £11.00 Pool: £386.05 - 25.92 winning units..
Owner Cheveley Park Stud **Bred** Cheveley Park Stud Ltd **Trained** Newmarket, Suffolk

FOCUS
A fair auction maiden for 3-5yos in which the gallop was quite steady early on with a couple of horses pulling hard for their heads. Unconvincing form, with the winner not needing to improve.

7026 32RED SUPPORTING BRITISH RACING NURSERY 1m 141y(P)
8:45 (8:46) (Class 6) (0-65,65) 2-Y-0 **£1,704** (£503; £251) **Stalls** Low

Form RPR

0562 **1** **Nine Iron (IRE)**[11] 6732 2-9-4 **62**.............................. MartinHarley 11 66
(Mick Channon) *chsd ldrs: rdn to ld and hung lft over 1f out: jst hld on* **10/3**[2]

6001 **2** nk **Open Letter (IRE)**[24] 6344 2-9-7 **65**..................... SilvestreDeSousa 5 68
(Mark Johnston) *hld up: hdwy over 2f out: rdn over 1f out: r.o wl* **6/1**

01U **3** 1 **Super Cookie**[30] 6147 2-9-1 **64**.............................. DarrenEgan(5) 3 65
(Philip McBride) *hld up in tch: nt clr run over 1f out: rdn ins fnl f: r.o* **10/1**

0104 **4** shd **Sekumkum (IRE)**[25] 6318 2-9-7 **65**.......................(t) AndreaAtzeni 9 66
(Marco Botti) *hld up: hdwy and nt clr run over 1f out: r.o: nt rch ldrs* **4/1**[3]

0665 **5** nk **Red Eclipse (IRE)**[18] 6541 2-8-13 **57**..................... SamHitchcott 13 57+
(Alan Bailey) *s.s: hld up: hdwy over 1f out: r.o* **33/1**

4653 **6** ½ **Inchy Coo**[15] 6604 2-9-1 **59**.. TomEaves 7 58
(Tim Easterby) *led 1f: chsd ldr: rdn over 1f out: styd on same pce ins fnl f* **25/1**

0322 **7** 4 **Missing Agent**[8] 6826 2-9-4 **62**...........................(v) StevieDonohoe 6 53
(David Evans) *chsd ldrs: rdn over 2f out: styd on same pce fr over 1f out* **16/1**

0462 **8** 1 ½ **Gabrial The Boss (USA)**[6] 6893 2-9-1 **59**.................. GrahamLee 2 49+
(David Simcock) *hld up: hmpd over 3f out: nvr nrr* **3/1**[1]

5212 **9** ¾ **Spithead**[22] 6413 2-9-7 **65**.. LiamJones 12 51
(William Haggas) *racd keenly: led over 7f out: rdn and hdd over 1f out: wknd ins fnl f* **9/1**

0000 **10** 15 **Astrum**[8] 6822 2-9-1 **59**.. JamesMillman 1 14
(Rod Millman) *hld up: rdn and edgd lft over 3f out: sn wknd* **25/1**

030 **11** 3 **Star Of Broadway**[28] 6214 2-9-2 **65**..................... AntiocoMurgia(5) 4 13
(Mahmood Al Zarooni) *prom: rdn over 2f out: wknd wl over 1f out* **20/1**

1m 50.95s (0.45) **Going Correction** -0.125s/f (Stan) **11** Ran SP% **122.7**
Speed ratings (Par 93): **93,92,91,91,91 91,87,86,85,72 69**
Tote Swingers: 1&2 £9.50, 1&3 £5.70, 2&3 £7.10 CSF £23.70 CT £190.99 TOTE £5.40: £1.90, £2.20, £5.00; EX 26.40 Trifecta £505.20 Part won. Pool: £682.72 - 0.20 winning tickets..
Owner The Hon Mrs J M Corbett & C Wright **Bred** Patrick F Kelly **Trained** West Ilsley, Berks

FOCUS
A modest nursery handicap, and the form makes sense.

NOTEBOOK
Nine Iron(IRE), racing off the same mark as when second at Bath, obviously possesses a handy level of versatility as regards trip. This was his first run on Polytrack. (op 4-1 tchd 9-2)
Open Letter(IRE) broke her maiden status over 1m at Yarmouth on good to firm ground the previous month off a 3lb lower rating in a better-class contest. She came through from well off the pace, and only narrowly failed to follow up here. (op 9-2 tchd 4-1 and 13-2)
Super Cookie performed respectably once more and a current mark of 64 looks about right for her. (op 9-1)
Sekumkum(IRE) suffered a troubled passage here in a refitted tongue-tie, and looks likely to remain competitive under these conditions. (op 8-1 tchd 9-1)
Red Eclipse(IRE) showed a bit more here after a slow start. (op 40-1)
Inchy Coo is proving difficult to place but would have benefited from a more even trip. (op 28-1)
Gabrial The Boss(USA) was hampered 3f out and proved disappointing thereafter. (op 11-4 tchd 5-2)

7027 £32 BONUS AT 32RED.COM H'CAP 1m 1f 103y(P)
9:15 (9:16) (Class 5) (0-70,70) 3-Y-0+ **£2,264** (£673; £336; £168) **Stalls** Low

Form RPR

0303 **1** **One Scoop Or Two**[13] 6692 6-8-11 **68**......................(p) JackDuern(7) 8 77
(Reg Hollinshead) *hld up: hdwy over 1f out: r.o to ld wl ins fnl f* **8/1**[3]

0104 **2** nse **Sea Fever (IRE)**[47] 5636 3-9-2 **70**.............................. KierenFallon 7 79+
(Luca Cumani) *a.p: nt clr run over 1f out: rdn and ev ch ins fnl f: r.o* **5/2**[1]

2103 **3** ½ **Dazzling Valentine**[2] 6988 4-8-13 **68**..................... NatashaEaton(5) 13 76
(Alan Bailey) *hld up: hdwy over 2f out: led 1f out: sn rdn and edgd lft: hdd and unable qck wl ins fnl f* **10/1**

3002 **4** ¾ **Switchback**[7] 6843 4-8-11 **68**.............................. DavidSimmonson(7) 2 74
(Michael Easterby) *chsd ldrs: rdn over 1f out: ev ch ins fnl f: styd on same pce* **11/1**

0321 **5** 1 **Tiradito (USA)**[6] 6895 5-9-4 **68** 6ex.............................. TomEaves 9 72+
(Brian Ellison) *hld up in tch: rdn over 1f out: styd on* **3/1**[2]

1440 **6** ½ **If I Were A Boy (IRE)**[2] 6981 5-9-4 **68**.....................(p) JamesDoyle 11 71
(Dominic Ffrench Davis) *chsd ldr tl led over 2f out: rdn and hdd 1f out: styd on same pce* **14/1**

3133 **7** ½ **One Way Or Another (AUS)**[21] 6434 9-9-6 **70**..............(t) JimCrowley 6 72
(David Evans) *s.i.s: hld up: hdwy over 1f out: rdn and swtchd lft ins fnl f: styd on same pce* **25/1**

0063 **8** 1 **Glass Mountain (IRE)**[6] 6894 4-9-4 **68**....................(v) FrannyNorton 12 68
(Ian Williams) *chsd ldrs: rdn and ev ch ins fnl f: no ex* **12/1**

3000 **9** 2 ¼ **City Of The Kings (IRE)**[25] 6313 7-8-13 **70**......... JacobButterfield(7) 10 65
(Ollie Pears) *hld up: rdn over 1f out: nvr on terms* **50/1**

1120 **10** *1* **My Mate Jake (IRE)**[8] 6819 4-9-6 **70**........(b) GrahamLee 4 63
(James Given) *hld up: hdwy over 2f out: hmpd over 1f out: no ex whn nt clr run ins fnl f* **9/1**
3-06 **11** *6* **Vivre Libre**[21] 6440 5-8-13 **70**........ WilliamTwiston-Davies(7) 5 51
(Tom George) *hld up: pushed along over 2f out: n.d* **80/1**
0630 **12** *1 1/4* **Thatcherite (IRE)**[22] 6410 4-9-6 **70**........(t) StephenCraine 1 48
(Tony Coyle) *s.i.s: hld up: n.d* **20/1**
0060 **13** *2 3/4* **Hamis Al Bin (IRE)**[22] 6401 3-9-2 **70**........ SilvestreDeSousa 3 42
(Mark Johnston) *led: rdn and hdd over 2f out: hung lft and wknd over 1f out: eased* **14/1**

1m 59.56s (-2.14) **Going Correction** -0.125s/f (Stan)
WFA 3 from 4yo+ 4lb **13** Ran SP% **124.9**
Speed ratings (Par 103): **104,103,103,102,101 101,101,100,98,97 91,90,88**
Tote Swingers: 1&2 £3.50, 1&3 £8.20, 2&3 £3.20 CSF £28.72 CT £215.24 TOTE £11.90: £2.60, £1.50, £3.70; EX 44.70 TRIFECTA Not won..
Owner Showtime Ice Cream Concessionaire **Bred** S And R Ewart **Trained** Upper Longdon, Staffs

FOCUS
A fair handicap in which they went a decent gallop and were well bunched turning in. The winner is rated in line with his latest run.
T/Plt: £8.90 to a £1 stake. Pool: £80,512.00 - 6,573.33 winning tickets. T/Qpdt: £6.80 to a £1 stake. Pool: £7,021.00 - 759.40 winning tickets. CR

6070 YORK (L-H)
Friday, October 12

OFFICIAL GOING: Heavy (soft in places; 6.7)
Wind: fresh 1/2 against Weather: changeable, very breezy

7028 TSG NURSERY 6f
2:00 (2:00) (Class 2) 2-Y-O **£7,633** (£2,271; £1,135; £567) **Stalls** Centre

Form RPR
5500 **1** **Polski Max**[29] 6162 2-8-8 **82**........ PaulHanagan 19 87
(Richard Fahey) *chsd ldrs: led jst ins fnl f: edgd lft: hld on towards fin* **11/2**[2]
0104 **2** *nk* **Shahdaroba (IRE)**[30] 6138 2-8-10 **84**........ TomQueally 5 88
(Rod Millman) *chsd ldrs: chal ins fnl f: no ex nr fin* **13/2**
310 **3** *2 1/2* **Burning Blaze**[49] 5563 2-9-0 **88**........ JamieSpencer 18 85+
(Kevin Ryan) *hld up in rr: hdwy stands' side over 2f out: upsides 1f out: kpt on same pce* **7/1**
3162 **4** *1/2* **Effie B**[27] 6238 2-8-10 **84**........ MartinHarley 10 79
(Mick Channon) *hld up in rr: hdwy over 2f out: kpt on fnl f* **20/1**
4144 **5** *1 1/2* **Chasing Dreams**[13] 6658 2-8-2 **76**........ AmyRyan 1 67
(Kevin Ryan) *w ldr: led over 3f out: hdd jst ins fnl f: sn wknd* **12/1**
1603 **6** *1/2* **Grievous Angel (IRE)**[15] 6612 2-7-12 **72** oh4........(b[1]) JimmyQuinn 3 61
(Ann Duffield) *in rr: hdwy 2f out: kpt on ins fnl f* **25/1**
1200 **7** *nk* **Bircham (IRE)**[34] 6032 2-8-8 **82**........ MickaelBarzalona 9 70
(Mahmood Al Zarooni) *in rr: effrt over 2f out: nvr nr ldrs* **12/1**
4341 **8** *2* **Bond Club**[14] 6628 2-7-12 **72**........ JamesSullivan 17 54
(Geoffrey Oldroyd) *chsd ldrs: drvn over 2f out: wknd over 1f out* **12/1**
5411 **9** *1/2* **Bachotheque (IRE)**[21] 6425 2-8-9 **83**........ DavidAllan 12 64
(Tim Easterby) *trckd ldrs: rdn 2f out: wknd fnl f* **4/1**[1]
106 **10** *1 1/4* **Smoothtalkinrascal (IRE)**[92] 4008 2-9-7 **95**........(v[1]) KierenFallon 8 72
(Brian Meehan) *s.i.s: in rr: effrt over 2f out: nvr a factor* **6/1**[3]
1403 **11** *1 3/4* **Lady Poppy**[25] 6312 2-8-4 **78**........ AndrewMullen 13 50
(George Moore) *led: hdd over 3f out: wknd 2f out* **20/1**
10 **12** *8* **My Boy Bill**[29] 6162 2-8-11 **85**........ GrahamGibbons 7 33
(Michael Easterby) *t.k.h in rr: bhd fnl 2f* **11/1**

1m 15.03s (3.13) **Going Correction** +0.50s/f (Yiel) **12** Ran SP% **120.3**
Speed ratings (Par 101): **99,98,95,94,92 91,91,88,88,86 84,73**
Tote Swingers: 1&2 £10.50, 1&3 £7.80, 2&3 £10.90 CSF £40.58 CT £262.40 TOTE £6.70: £2.70, £2.90, £2.80; EX 59.70 Trifecta £721.40 Part won. Pool: £974.67 - 0.80 winning units..
Owner Market Avenue Racing & Tremousser **Bred** Mike J Beadle **Trained** Musley Bank, N Yorks

FOCUS
There was 34mm of rain on Thursday night and the ground, given as heavy, soft in places (GoingStick 6.9; Home straight: Far side 6.5; Centre 6.7; Stands' side 6.4), was predictably very testing, with Andrew Mullen describing it as "Very heavy ground", Tom Queally reporting that: "It is nearly heavy but they are getting through it" and David Allan saying: "It is not as bad as Ayr yesterday but it is very, very wet." A pretty open nursery. Straightforward form, the front pair to their marks in a good time.

NOTEBOOK
Polski Max, whose improvement had plateaued somewhat since switching back to turf and racing on good ground or faster, appreciated these testing conditions and won with a bit more in hand than the margin would suggest, as he idled a little in front. He's the sort who could do with being out early next term to make the best of any rain in the spring. (op 8-1)
Shahdaroba(IRE), who showed he handles this sort of ground when recording his best previous RPR in the Super Sprint at Newbury, had Tom Queally riding him for the first time, and he pushed the winner all the way to the line. (op 8-1)
Burning Blaze, a disappointing favourite here on his handicap debut last time, showed that form to be all wrong. He picked up well to lead but just didn't see his race out, the ground possibly just that bit too testing for him. (tchd 13-2)
Effie B kept on from off the pace to post a solid effort. More exposed than most, she's likely to remain vulnerable. (tchd 16-1)
Chasing Dreams was up there from the start but didn't see out her race, and a drop back to the minimum ought to suit her. (op 10-1)
Grievous Angel(IRE), blinkered for the first time, ran as well as could be expected from 4lb out of the weights. (op 33-1)
Bircham(IRE) struggled to get involved having raced a bit keenly early. (op 11-1)
Bachotheque(IRE) was disappointing in his hat-trick bid considering he was 2lb well in. (op 7-2 tchd 9-2)
Smoothtalkinrascal(IRE), running in a first-time visor and for the first time since being gelded, never got involved on his return from a three-month break. (op 13-2 tchd 7-1)

7029 GARBUTT & ELLIOTT CONDITIONS STKS 1m 2f 88y
2:30 (2:31) (Class 3) 3-Y-O+ **£9,703** (£2,887; £1,443; £721) **Stalls** Low

Form RPR
-003 **1** **Prince Siegfried (FR)**[21] 6446 6-9-2 **107**........ MickaelBarzalona 5 107
(Saeed Bin Suroor) *hld up in last: pushed along 5f out: hdwy 3f out: led over 1f out: hung lft: rdn out* **5/2**[1]
3040 **2** *1 1/4* **Mijhaar**[13] 6674 4-9-2 **104**........ NeilCallan 9 104
(Roger Varian) *trckd ldng pair: effrt 3f out: n.m.r on stands' side rail and swtchd lft appr fnl f: sn chsng wnr: kpt on same pce* **5/2**[1]
-654 **3** *3 3/4* **Beaten Up**[30] 6142 4-9-2 **114**........[1] GrahamLee 8 97
(William Haggas) *led: increased pce 5f out: hdd over 2f out: rallied over 1f out: kpt on same pce: tk 3rd last 100yds* **11/4**[2]
2340 **4** *1/2* **Expense Claim (IRE)**[20] 6484 3-8-11 **100**........ JimmyFortune 7 96
(Andrew Balding) *trckd ldr: led over 2f out: hdd over 1f out: one pce* **3/1**[3]

2m 17.75s (5.25) **Going Correction** +0.725s/f (Yiel)
WFA 3 from 4yo+ 5lb **4** Ran SP% **108.8**
Speed ratings (Par 107): **108,107,104,103**
CSF £8.87 TOTE £3.00; EX 7.50 TRIFECTA Trifecta cancelled..
Owner Godolphin **Bred** Haras Saint Pair Du Mont **Trained** Newmarket, Suffolk

FOCUS
They finished tired in this conditions race and the form is rated negatively.

NOTEBOOK
Prince Siegfried(FR) came through from off the pace to score. He's not very easy to predict, but this distance on ground with ease in it is what he needs, and a recent outing at Newbury had blown away the cobwebs. He's likely to spend the winter in Dubai. (tchd 9-4)
Mijhaar, who didn't have an excuse on the ground, continues to let his supporters down and just doesn't look like a horse who wants to win. (op 15-8)
Beaten Up, who wore a hood for the first time, really has gone the wrong way since being dropped in at the deep end in the Sheema Classic back in March. This ground is probably a long way from what he really wants, but connections will be hoping he can get back on track as a 5yo. (op 7-2)
Expense Claim(IRE), a progressive sort this year, was going up and down on the one spot in the closing stages and presumably found conditions too testing. (op 4-1)

7030 ACORN WEB OFFSET H'CAP 1m
3:05 (3:05) (Class 2) (0-100,94) 3-Y-O+ **£11,644** (£3,465; £1,731; £865) **Stalls** Low

Form RPR
6031 **1** **No Poppy (IRE)**[12] 6710 4-8-10 **88** 6ex........ AdamCarter(5) 8 97
(Tim Easterby) *hld up towards rr: hdwy on outer over 3f out: chsd ldr 2f out: led ins fnl f: styd on* **11/1**
00-0 **2** *1 1/4* **Credit Swap**[13] 6674 7-9-2 **89**........ RobertWinston 2 95
(Michael Wigham) *s.i.s: in rr: rdn over3 f out: hdwy on outer 2f out: styd on to take 2nd nr fin* **7/1**[2]
1053 **3** *hd* **Lord Aeryn (IRE)**[21] 6426 5-9-2 **89**........ PaulHanagan 10 95
(Richard Fahey) *mid-div: hdwy over 2f out: styd on fnl f: tk 3rd nr fin* **12/1**
0600 **4** *shd* **Vainglory (USA)**[20] 6494 8-8-9 **87**........ LauraPike(5) 4 93
(David Simcock) *mid-div: hdwy on outer over 3f out: hung rt and led over 2f out: hdd ins fnl f: surrendered 2 pls nr fin* **7/1**[2]
4222 **5** *5* **Vito Volterra (IRE)**[13] 6670 5-8-13 **86**........ AndrewMullen 3 80
(Michael Smith) *trckd ldrs: led over 2f out: hdd over 1f out: sn wknd* **14/1**
0122 **6** *3/4* **Able Master (IRE)**[35] 6011 6-9-4 **91**........ DanielTudhope 9 84
(David O'Meara) *led early: trckd ldrs: hmpd 2f out: kpt on same pce* **12/1**
1020 **7** *1* **Anderiego (IRE)**[13] 6674 4-9-7 **94**........ KierenFallon 5 84
(David O'Meara) *mid-div: effrt and nt clr run over 2f out: kpt on one pce* **7/1**[2]
0141 **8** *shd* **Osteopathic Remedy (IRE)**[21] 6426 8-9-0 **94**........ ConnorNichol(7) 14 84
(Michael Dods) *in rr: effrt and nt clr run 3f out: swtchd lft: kpt on fnl f* **10/1**[3]
0033 **9** *7* **Mont Ras (IRE)**[55] 5342 5-8-13 **86**........ TomEaves 15 60
(David O'Meara) *t.k.h in rr: nt clr run over 2f out: n.m.r over 1f out: sn lost pl* **7/1**[2]
6064 **10** *4 1/2* **Bancnuanaheireann (IRE)**[13] 6674 5-9-5 **92**........ TomQueally 13 56
(Michael Appleby) *in rr: rdn 4f out: nvr on terms* **13/2**[1]
0010 **11** *5* **Wannabe King**[35] 6011 6-9-2 **89**........(v) PJMcDonald 11 41
(Geoffrey Harker) *chsd ldrs: hung lft and wknd 2f out* **33/1**
6035 **12** *11* **Suits Me**[51] 5492 9-9-2 **89**........ JamieSpencer 1 16
(David Barron) *drvn to ld: hdd over 2f out: lost pl and eased over 1f out* **12/1**
1240 **13** *6* **Venutius**[27] 6235 5-8-13 **86**........ GrahamGibbons 12
(Ed McMahon) *mid-div: lost pl over 2f out: sn bhd* **14/1**

1m 44.01s (5.01) **Going Correction** +0.725s/f (Yiel) **13** Ran SP% **120.1**
Speed ratings (Par 109): **103,101,101,101,96 95,94,94,87,83 78,67,61**
Tote Swingers: 1&2 £22.10, 1&3 £29.80, 2&3 £32.20 CSF £86.49 CT £984.86 TOTE £9.20: £2.50, £3.50, £4.20; EX 104.40 TRIFECTA Not won..
Owner Exors Of The Late Mrs P M Easterby **Bred** Michael O'Mahony **Trained** Great Habton, N Yorks

FOCUS
They went a fair pace in the conditions thanks to Suits Me, and that set things up for those ridden with a bit more patience. They came stands' side in the straight. Decent form, with the third a fair guide.

NOTEBOOK
No Poppy(IRE) challenged on the wide outside and gradually wore down Vainglory to win a shade cosily. She was 2lb well in under her penalty, relishes testing conditions and is clearly at the top of her game at the moment. Her trainer said she could be a Lincoln type next year. (op 10-1)
Credit Swap, all the better for his run in the Cambridgeshire, had the ground to suit and was putting his best work in at the finish. Although lightly raced on the level over the past two years, he retains plenty of ability. (op 8-1 tchd 17-2)
Lord Aeryn(IRE), consistent as they come, ran another sound race, but he gives himself no chance with the handicapper. (op 11-1)
Vainglory(USA), who won this race last year, probably got to the front a bit too soon, but this was a good effort in defeat. (op 15-2 tchd 13-2)
Vito Volterra(IRE) is at his best when left alone in front, but he had competition for the lead here.
Able Master(IRE) was beginning to weaken when hampered approaching the 2f marker. This trip on this ground looked to stretch his stamina. (op 10-1)
Anderiego(IRE) probably doesn't want the ground this soft. (op 9-1)
Bancnuanaheireann(IRE) was well below his Newmarket form on this more testing surface. Official explanation: trainer said gelding was unsuited by the heavy (soft in places) ground (op 15-2 tchd 6-1)
Suits Me Official explanation: trainer's rep said gelding was unsuited by the heavy (soft in places) ground

7031 BRITTAINS E B F MAIDEN STKS 5f 89y
3:40 (3:41) (Class 4) 2-Y-O **£6,469** (£1,925; £962; £481) **Stalls** Centre

Form RPR
4334 **1** **Shrimpton**[90] 4114 2-8-12 **78**........ MartinHarley 11 74
(Mick Channon) *hld up in rr: hdwy 2f out: r.o to ld last 100yds* **7/2**[3]
43 **2** *1 1/4* **Anderton (IRE)**[23] 6360 2-9-3 **0**........ PaulHanagan 1 75
(Richard Fahey) *led: drvn and hung rt over 1f out: hdd ins fnl f: no ex* **5/2**[2]
6 **3** *1 1/2* **Bluegrass Blues (IRE)**[21] 6443 2-9-3 **0**........ JamieSpencer 3 70
(Paul Cole) *chsd ldrs: drvn over 2f out: chsng ldrs over 1f out: kpt on same pce ins fnl f* **9/4**[1]
4 *3 3/4* **Faffa** 2-8-12 **0**........ AdamCarter(5) 12 57+
(Tim Easterby) *hld up towards rr: hdwy 2f out: kpt on: nvr trbld ldrs* **16/1**
0 **5** *1* **Accelerant (IRE)**[23] 6360 2-9-3 **0**........ NeilCallan 4 54
(Kevin Ryan) *dwlt: t.k.h: sn trcking ldrs: wkng whn sltly hmpd appr fnl f* **8/1**
623 **6** *1* **Teetotal (IRE)**[10] 6754 2-9-3 **68**........ DaleSwift 2 50
(Nigel Tinkler) *chsd ldrs: drvn over 2f out: wknd over 1f out* **17/2**

00 7 1 **Troy Boy**[9] 6780 2-9-3 0 .... DanielTudhope 7 47
(Robin Bastiman) *chsd ldrs: lost pl wl over 1f out* **40/1**

1m 8.59s (4.49) **Going Correction** +0.50s/f (Yiel) **7** Ran SP% **111.5**
Speed ratings (Par 97): **84,82,79,73,72 70,68**
Tote Swingers: 1&2 £2.60, 1&3 £2.90, 2&3 £2.20 CSF £12.02 TOTE £4.20: £2.40, £2.00; EX 8.70 Trifecta £28.90 Pool: £1,393.65 - 39.57 winning units..
Owner Billy Parish **Bred** Jeremy Gompertz **Trained** West Ilsley, Berks

FOCUS
No more than a fair maiden, and with the ground bad and several non-runners it's not hard to be sceptical over the form. The race could be rated up to 4lb higher.

NOTEBOOK
Shrimpton had been given some time off since finishing a seven-length fourth to subsequent Gimcrack winner Blaine here in July, and she returned to break her maiden in good style. She coped well with this very different ground and has the scope to make up into a better 3yo. (op 4-1)
Anderton(IRE) ran a sound race from the front on this much softer ground and now has the option of going the handicapping route.
Bluegrass Blues(IRE) improved on his debut effort but lost out to a couple of rivals with more experience. (op 5-2 tchd 11-4)
Faffa, an already gelded half-brother to seven winners, shaped with some promise on his debut, while \bAccelerant\p still looked green and ought to do better as a handicapper in time. (tchd 12-1)
Accelerant(IRE) still looked green and ought to do better as a handicapper in time. (op 6-1)
Teetotal(IRE) is pretty exposed now. (op 9-1 tchd 8-1)

7032 PARSONAGE HOTEL AND SPA H'CAP 1m 2f 88y
4:15 (4:16) (Class 4) (0-80,80) 3-Y-O **£6,469** (£1,925; £962; £481) **Stalls** Low

Form RPR
5501 1 **Educate**[28] 6209 3-9-7 **80** .... JamieSpencer 9 93+
(Ismail Mohammed) *s.s: hld up in rr: hdwy and swtchd rt over 2f out: led last 100yds: edgd lft: drvn out* **16/1**
3360 2 1 1/2 **Deepsand (IRE)**[13] 6661 3-9-6 **79** .... DavidAllan 14 89
(Tim Easterby) *in rr: hdwy 4f out: led over 2f out: hdd and no ex ins fnl f* **15/2**
-202 3 3/4 **Docs Legacy (IRE)**[6] 6884 3-8-13 **72** .... BarryMcHugh 1 81
(Richard Fahey) *prom: chal over 2f out: keeping on same pce whn sltly hmpd ins fnl f* **7/2**[1]
0221 4 7 **Only Orsenfoolsies**[17] 6560 3-9-2 **75** .... PJMcDonald 3 70
(Micky Hammond) *chsd ldrs: one pce over 1f out* **16/1**
2142 5 1 **Daddy Warbucks (IRE)**[27] 6240 3-9-3 **76** .... AdrianNicholls 19 69
(David Nicholls) *drvn: edgd lft after s to ld: hdd over 2f out: wknd over 1f out* **16/1**
1100 6 nse **Double Cee**[12] 6701 3-9-1 **77** .... LeeTopliss(3) 15 70
(Richard Fahey) *chsd ldrs: drvn over 4f out: hung lft and one pce fnl 2f* **28/1**
0440 7 3 **Nameitwhatyoulike**[6] 6881 3-9-7 **80** .... NeilCallan 7 68+
(Michael Easterby) *hmpd sn after s: hld up in mid-div: effrt over 2f out: kpt on fnl f* **14/1**
0650 8 1 3/4 **Yazdi (IRE)**[18] 6537 3-9-7 **80** ....(t) KierenFallon 20 64
(Brian Meehan) *sn chsng ldrs: wknd over 1f out* **20/1**
5441 9 3 3/4 **Dorry K (IRE)**[53] 5413 3-8-11 **70** .... GrahamGibbons 17 47
(David Barron) *s.s: in rr: sme hdwy over 2f out: nvr on terms* **25/1**
210 10 1/2 **Sunnybridge Boy (IRE)**[23] 6376 3-9-1 **77** .... MichaelMetcalfe(3) 5 53
(Mrs K Burke) *chsd ldrs: wknd 2f out* **25/1**
0501 11 1 1/4 **Natural Bloom (IRE)**[17] 6570 3-8-13 **72** .... TomQueally 4 46
(Sir Henry Cecil) *trckd ldrs: t.k.h: lost pl over 1f out* **7/1**[3]
1321 12 1 3/4 **Ingleby Angel (IRE)**[21] 6429 3-8-10 **69** .... DanielTudhope 11 39
(David O'Meara) *hld up in rr: drvn over 3f out: no imp whn swtchd lft over 1f out* **11/2**[2]
2315 13 1 3/4 **Warcrown (IRE)**[54] 5386 3-9-4 **77** .... TonyHamilton 2 44
(Richard Fahey) *edgd rt sn after s: mid-div: rdn 3f out: sn wknd* **20/1**
1124 14 1 **Maybeagrey**[27] 6263 3-8-13 **72** .... DuranFentiman 10 37
(Tim Easterby) *hld up in rr: drvn 4f out: nvr on terms* **20/1**
3514 15 4 1/2 **Buster Brown (IRE)**[27] 6240 3-8-12 **71** .... DaleSwift 6 28
(James Given) *t.k.h: trckd ldrs: swtchd rt 3f out: lost pl: sn bhd* **10/1**
2121 16 10 **Multi Bene**[24] 6342 3-9-5 **78** .... FrannyNorton 8 16
(Ed McMahon) *hmpd sn after s: t.k.h in mid-div: effrt 3f out: sn hmpd and lost pl: bhd whn eased* **12/1**

2m 18.48s (5.98) **Going Correction** +0.725s/f (Yiel) **16** Ran SP% **128.4**
Speed ratings (Par 103): **105,103,103,97,96 96,94,92,89,89 88,87,85,84,81 73**
Tote Swingers: 1&2 £20.10, 1&3 £15.20, 2&3 £6.60 CSF £124.65 CT £533.92 TOTE £17.90: £3.00, £2.40, £1.70, £3.80; EX 165.80 TRIFECTA Not won..
Owner Sultan Ali **Bred** Lady Legard **Trained** Newmarket, Suffolk
■ Stewards' Enquiry : Dale Swift one-day ban: careless riding (Oct 26)
Jamie Spencer caution: careless riding.

FOCUS
This looked competitive but it was won nicely by the top-weight, who impressed and looks capable of better. The pace was sound.
Double Cee Official explanation: jockey said gelding hung left throughout
Ingleby Angel(IRE) Official explanation: jockey said gelding ran too free

7033 DOWNLOAD THE FREE RACING PLUS APP MEDIAN AUCTION MAIDEN STKS 1m
4:50 (4:50) (Class 4) 2-Y-O **£6,469** (£1,925; £962; £481) **Stalls** Low

Form RPR
05 1 **Soviet Rock (IRE)**[15] 6596 2-9-3 0 .... JimmyFortune 3 79
(Andrew Balding) *sn led: hung rt over 2f out: narrowly hdd ins fnl f: styd on to regain ld nr fin* **9/2**[2]
02 2 1 1/4 **Esteaming**[11] 6733 2-9-3 0 .... MartinHarley 2 76
(Mick Channon) *sn trcking ldrs: upsides over 1f out: led narrowly last 75yds: no ex and hdd nr fin* **3/1**[1]
3 hd **Heroine Required (FR)** 2-8-12 0 .... KierenFallon 1 71+
(William Haggas) *dwlt: in rr: hdwy over 2f out: upsides over 1f out: no ex towards fin* **6/1**
4 5 **Kuantan One (IRE)** 2-9-3 0 .... JamieSpencer 8 68+
(Paul Cole) *led early: chsd ldrs: wknd over 1f out* **10/1**
4 5 2 1/4 **Hawk High (IRE)**[13] 6669 2-9-3 0 .... DuranFentiman 4 60
(Tim Easterby) *t.k.h in rr: hdwy over 3f out: wknd over 1f out* **14/1**
2 6 8 **Gabrial The Thug (FR)**[27] 6237 2-9-3 0 .... PaulHanagan 5 42
(Richard Fahey) *chsd ldrs: drvn over 3f out: lost pl over 1f out* **3/1**[1]
0 7 17 **Tuscan Fun**[29] 6164 2-9-3 0 .... NeilCallan 9
(Roger Varian) *mid-div: drvn over 3f out: sn outpcd: lost pl 2f out: sn bhd* **11/2**[3]

1m 45.5s (6.50) **Going Correction** +0.725s/f (Yiel) **7** Ran SP% **113.6**
Speed ratings (Par 97): **96,94,94,89,87 79,62**
Tote Swingers: 1&2 £3.10, 1&3 £4.50, 2&3 £3.60 CSF £18.14 TOTE £5.30: £2.70, £2.30; EX 18.10 Trifecta £110.80 Pool: £1,393.65 - 9.30 winning units..
Owner Jackie & George Smith **Bred** Grangecon Stud **Trained** Kingsclere, Hants

FOCUS
A bit of a boost for fans of Sir Michael Stoute's Racing Post Trophy entry Telescope. It proved a tough test in the ground and the first two had the edge on experience.

NOTEBOOK
Soviet Rock(IRE), who was fifth to the bright prospect Telescope at Newmarket last month, got off the mark in determined fashion, rallying after being headed inside the last. He appreciated the softer ground and, based on his three runs to-date, he shouldn't be too harshly treated with handicaps in mind. (tchd 11-2)
Esteaming, runner-up over 1m2f last time out, ran another sound race in defeat, and he should make up into a nice middle-distance handicapper next year. (op 7-2)
Heroine Required(FR), who is out of a half-sister to French 10.7f winner Empreinte Celebre and Italian 1m2f winner Avanzino, made an encouraging debut. She was just outstayed by a couple of rivals with more experience, but showed plenty of promise and ought to build on it. (op 8-1)
Kuantan One(IRE), who's a brother to Phoenix Stakes winner La Collina, showed up well for a long way and is the type who should make a better 3yo. (op 17-2 tchd 8-1)
Hawk High(IRE), who was fourth on his first outing at Haydock, didn't help his cause by racing keenly. (op 11-1)
Gabrial The Thug(FR), who got warm beforehand, was another who failed to build on his promising debut. Official explanation: trainer's rep had no explanation for the poor form shown (op 2-1)
Tuscan Fun was well supported but ran poorly and perhaps conditions were too extreme for him. (op 10-1)

7034 FUTURE CLEANING SERVICES GENTLEMAN AMATEUR RIDERS' H'CAP 1m 4f
5:20 (5:20) (Class 4) (0-85,85) 4-Y-O+ **£5,053** (£1,567; £783; £392) **Stalls** Centre

Form RPR
2005 1 **Lexington Bay (IRE)**[20] 6472 4-10-9 **78** ....(p) MrNSlatter(5) 9 84
(Richard Fahey) *chsd ldrs: drvn over 4f out: styd on over 2f out: edgd lft and kpt on to ld towards fin* **5/1**[3]
50-6 2 3/4 **All Annalena (IRE)**[7] 6848 6-10-12 **83** .... MrSamDavis(7) 10 88
(Lucy Wadham) *hld up: hdwy to ld after 2f: hdd and no ex towards fin* **6/1**
2104 3 1 3/4 **Maven**[28] 6202 4-11-1 **84** .... MrWEasterby(5) 6 86
(Tim Easterby) *t.k.h in rr: smooth hdwy 4f out: upsides over 2f out: rdn over 1f out: kpt on same pce ins fnl f* **7/2**[2]
06-0 4 14 **Simonside**[14] 6642 9-10-7 **71** oh1 .... MrFWindsorClive 4 52
(Brian Ellison) *chsd ldrs: drvn 4f out: wknd 2f out* **20/1**
5221 5 74 **Odin (IRE)**[14] 6639 4-10-11 **80** .... MrFMitchell(5) 7
(David Elsworth) *hld up: hdwy 6f out: sn chsng ldrs: hung rt and lost pl over 2f out: bhd whn eased over 1f out: virtually p.u: hopelessly t.o* **5/2**[1]
3100 6 63 **Xclaim**[24] 6339 4-10-2 **71** oh3 .... MrGRSmith(5) 2
(Micky Hammond) *led 2f: drvn 6f out: sn lost pl: t.o over 3f out: virtually p.u: eventually completed* **20/1**
U **Allied Answer**[392] 6142 4-11-7 **85** .... MrSWalker 3
(Steve Gollings) *rrd bdly s: swvd bdly rt and uns rdr* **7/2**[2]

2m 45.75s (12.55) **Going Correction** +0.725s/f (Yiel) **7** Ran SP% **113.5**
Speed ratings (Par 105): **87,86,85,76,26 ,**
Tote Swingers: 1&2 £4.40, 1&3 £4.50, 2&3 £4.50 CSF £33.88 CT £116.38 TOTE £6.80: £3.00, £3.30; EX 42.70 Trifecta £312.80 Pool: £1,500.64 - 3.55 winning units..
Owner Keith Denham & Tony Denham **Bred** Mrs Vanessa Hutch **Trained** Musley Bank, N Yorks

FOCUS
There was drama at the start when the second-favourite Allied Answer unseated his rider, which reduced the competitiveness of the field, but there was still a good three-way battle in the closing stages. Modest form, the winner not needing to match his best.
Lexington Bay(IRE) Official explanation: trainer's rep said, regarding apparent improvement in form, that the gelding was better suited by the application of the first-time cheek pieces.
Odin(IRE) Official explanation: jockey said gelding hung right in straight
T/Jkpt: Not won. T/Plt: £445.60 to a £1 stake. Pool: £106,718.24 - 174.81 winning tickets.
T/Qpdt: £26.60 to a £1 stake. Pool: £8,952.12 - 248.49 winning tickets. WG

7035 - 7037a (Foreign Racing) - See Raceform Interactive

6851 DUNDALK (A.W) (L-H)
Friday, October 12

OFFICIAL GOING: Standard

7038a IRISH STALLION FARMS EUROPEAN BREEDERS FUND STAR APPEAL STKS (LISTED RACE) 7f (P)
7:30 (7:30) 2-Y-O **£31,145** (£9,104; £4,312; £1,437)

RPR
1 **Lines Of Battle (USA)**[78] 4519 2-9-3 101 ....(p) JPO'Brien 2 103+
(A P O'Brien, Ire) *racd in 3rd: pressed ldr ins fnl 2f: led appr fnl f and pushed clr: comf* **9/4**[2]
2 2 1/2 **Tennessee Wildcat (IRE)**[12] 6715 2-9-3 97 .... GaryCarroll 5 95
(G M Lyons, Ire) *hld up in rr: prog on inner 2f out: chsd wnr ins fnl f wout ever getting on terms* **16/1**
3 hd **Hudson's Bay (IRE)** 2-9-3 .... KevinManning 6 94+
(J S Bolger, Ire) *slowly away and in rr: last 2f out then swtchd out rt appr fnl f where green and bmpd rival: styd on strly clsng stages to go 3rd* **12/1**
4 1 **Infanta Branca (USA)**[139] 2512 2-9-0 95 .... SeamieHeffernan 8 89
(A P O'Brien, Ire) *trckd ldrs in 4th: pushed along 2f out: kpt on same pce fnl f* **8/1**
5 1 1/2 **Cougar Ridge (USA)**[20] 6483 2-9-3 104 .... WayneLordan 1 88
(David Wachman, Ire) *chsd ldrs in 5th: pushed along 2f out where nt qckn: kpt on same pce fnl f* **9/2**[3]
6 shd **Horizon Sky (IRE)**[37] 5954 2-9-3 91 .... WJLee 4 88
(David Wachman, Ire) *racd in 2nd: nt qckn w wnr over 1f out: wknd ins fnl f* **20/1**
7 1 **No Jet Lag (USA)**[28] 6200 2-9-3 .... TedDurcan 7 85
(David Lanigan) *w.w: prog whn swtchd rt over 1f out: sn no ex* **7/4**[1]
8 2 **Dark Pulse (USA)**[7] 6852 2-9-3 .... FergalLynch 10 80+
(M D O'Callaghan, Ire) *racd in mid-div: pushed along 2f out: no imp whn bmpd by rival ent fnl f* **33/1**
9 1 **Blue Bullet (IRE)**[14] 6648 2-9-3 89 .... PatSmullen 3 77
(W P Mullins, Ire) *led tl hdd by wnr over 1f out: sn dropped away* **25/1**
10 2 3/4 **Roseraie (IRE)**[61] 5135 2-9-0 96 .... ChrisHayes 9 67
(Kevin Prendergast, Ire) *a in rr: reminders bef home turn: no threat fnl 2f: eased* **16/1**

1m 24.36s (84.36) **10** Ran SP% **127.4**
CSF £41.40 TOTE £3.10: £1.90, £4.10, £1.40; DF 41.40.
Owner J Allen/Mrs J Magnier/M Tabor/D Smith **Bred** Joseph Allen **Trained** Ballydoyle, Co Tipperary

FOCUS
A smart contest for the level. The winner is rated to his mark.

NOTEBOOK

Lines Of Battle(USA) had solid credentials having won over 6f on debut before finishing sixth in the Coventry Stakes and a close second when upped to this trip in a Group 3 event at Leopardstown in July. With cheekpieces fitted for the first time, he raced prominently and went to the front over 1f out from where he stretched away from his rivals. (op 13-8)

Tennessee Wildcat(IRE) has been kept busy since scoring over 5f on his debut here in May. In the frame on all but one of his six subsequent starts, he ran another solid race here although no match for the winner from 1f out.

Hudson's Bay(IRE), making his debut, was the eyecatcher. Last out of the stalls, he was last into the straight before being switched right - he bumped Dark Pulse, who appeared beaten at the time, under 1f out - before running on well to just miss out on second place. (op 16-1)

Infanta Branca(USA), a stablemate of the winner, was having her first run over further than 5f, the trip over which she won her maiden and was also Listed placed. She made a forward move early in the straight but she could make little impression from over 1f out. (op 10-1)

Cougar Ridge(USA), beaten when hampered in the Mill Reef Stakes on his previous start, was the joint-highest rated on official figures. He found little when asked to raise his effort and may need to be dropped back in trip. (op 9/2 tchd 7/2)

No Jet Lag(USA), a dual winner over the trip before running second to Dewhurst Stakes candidate Ashdan at Doncaster last month, was joint-highest rated here. He proved disappointing, failing to pick up when things opened up for him over 1f out.

7039 - 7047a (Foreign Racing) - See Raceform Interactive

6872

NEWMARKET (R-H)

Saturday, October 13

OFFICIAL GOING: Good to soft (7.1)

Wind: light, half behind Weather: dry

7048 DUBAI CHALLENGE STKS (GROUP 2) 7f

1:50 (1:51) (Class 1) 3-Y-0+

£45,368 (£17,200; £8,608; £4,288; £2,152; £1,080) **Stalls** High

Form RPR

0216 **1** **Fulbright**[7] 6882 3-9-1 110 .... JoeFanning 4 115
(Mark Johnston) *in tch: swtchd rt and effrt u.p over 1f out: chsd wnr ent fnl f: chal and clr w ldr ins fnl f: styd on wl u.p to ld fnl 50yds: drvn out* **15/2**[3]

4000 **2** *nk* **Red Jazz (USA)**[56] 5355 5-9-3 109 .... MichaelHills 11 114
(Charles Hills) *led: rdn and fnd ex ent 2f out: drvn and clr w wnr ins fnl f: hdd and no ex fnl 50yds* **12/1**

2253 **3** *3 ¼* **Arnold Lane (IRE)**[7] 6868 3-9-1 99 .... MartinHarley 7 105
(Mick Channon) *stdd after s: hld up in tch in last trio: hdwy u.p ent fnl f: styd on to go 3rd wl ins fnl f: no threat to ldng pair* **14/1**

-630 **4** *1* **Fencing (USA)**[116] 3239 3-9-1 108 .... WilliamBuick 2 103+
(John Gosden) *hld up towards rr: stl travelling wl whn nt clr run 2f out: swtchd rt and effrt u.p over 1f out: kpt on u.p fnl f to go 4th towards fin: no threat to ldng pair* **4/1**[1]

0151 **5** *½* **Scarf (AUS)**[22] 6449 5-9-3 108 .... FrankieDettori 6 101
(Saeed Bin Suroor) *taken down early: chsd ldr tl 1/2-way: styd chsng ldrs: rdn and unable qck over 1f out: 3rd and btn fnl 150yds: wknd and lost 2 pls wl ins fnl f* **4/1**[1]

-300 **6** *hd* **Reply (IRE)**[91] 4100 3-9-1 110 .... JPO'Brien 8 101
(A P O'Brien, Ire) *hld up in tch towards rr: effrt u.p over 1f out: plugged on u.p ins fnl f: nvr gng pce to threaten ldrs* **11/1**

201 **7** *1 ¼* **Libranno**[28] 6246 4-9-7 114 .... RichardHughes 1 101
(Richard Hannon) *chsd ldrs: rdn and unable qck 2f out: wknd ent fnl f* **7/1**[2]

2000 **8** *1 ¾* **Edinburgh Knight (IRE)**[22] 6449 5-9-3 107 ....(v¹) SebSanders 10 93
(Paul D'Arcy) *taken down early: chsd ldrs: wnt 2nd 1/2-way tl over 1f out: wknd ins fnl f* **12/1**

-100 **9** *1 ½* **Telwaar**[115] 3265 3-9-1 98 .... JamesDoyle 9 88
(Peter Chapple-Hyam) *in tch in last trio: rdn wl over 2f out: no prog and wknd 1f out* **40/1**

6001 **10** *½* **Sunday Times**[30] 6161 3-8-12 102 .... JamieSpencer 5 84
(Peter Chapple-Hyam) *s.i.s: a towards rr: effrt and sme hdwy wl over 1f out: wknd ent fnl f: wl btn and eased cl home* **12/1**

14-1 **11** *nk* **Pearl Mix (IRE)**[23] 6400 3-9-1 103 .... JimCrowley 3 86
(Ralph Beckett) *in tch: rdn and unable qck ent fnl 2f: wknd over 1f out* **8/1**

1m 24.03s (-1.37) **Going Correction** +0.10s/f (Good) **11** Ran SP% **115.9**
WFA 3 from 4yo+ 2lb
Speed ratings (Par 115): **111,110,106,105,105 105,103,101,99,99 98**
toteswingers 1&2 £17.80, 2&3 £26.80, 1&3 £17.70 CSF £92.53 TOTE £11.50: £3.50, £3.90, £5.50; EX 111.80 Trifecta £1547.20 Part won. Pool: 2,090.90 - 0.83 winning tickets..
Owner Sheikh Hamdan Bin Mohammed Al Maktoum **Bred** R F And S D Knipe **Trained** Middleham Moor, N Yorks

■ Stewards' Enquiry : Michael Hills two-day ban: used whip above permitted level (Oct 29-30)

FOCUS

It was dry overnight and the going was good to soft (GoingStick: stands' side 7.0; centre 7.0; far side 7.2), confirmed by the jockeys after the first. The stands' side 20metres of the Rowley Mile was being used for the first time since May. With only 7lb separating nine of the 11 runners on adjusted official ratings this looked a pretty tight affair, something which was reflected in the betting, and it didn't look a particularly strong Group 2. A narrow personal best from Fulbright.

NOTEBOOK

Fulbright was disappointing at Redcar the previous week but he's bounced back from similarly poor efforts to win on more than one occasion already this year, and he did so again, putting his stamina to good use to run down the leader inside the last. He's as tough as they come (this was his 12th outing of the campaign), is versatile with regard to ground and distance, and has done nothing but improve all season. He'll no doubt be in Godolphin blue next season, and it remains to be seen if he heads out to Dubai over the winter. (op 8-1 tchd 7-1)

Red Jazz(USA) ran the best race of his career when taking this race two years ago and, although disappointing in his last four starts, he'd been given a break, and he returned to form in no uncertain manner back on a track that suits him well. He set a decent gallop alongside the stands' rail but kept it up well and was only run down inside the last. (op 10-1)

Arnold Lane(IRE) was one of the two with most to prove at this level. No doubt he ran a personal best, but whether he has improved that much is open to debate, as a few of his rivals looked to run below form. (op 16-1)

Fencing(USA), off the track since being hampered and finishing down the field in the St James's Palace Stakes, travelled well to 2f out but couldn't pick up for pressure out wide, where the ground was perhaps softer there than on the rail. He wants a quicker surface really. (op 6-1)

Scarf(AUS) won nicely in Listed company at Newbury last time and, while this demanded a bit more and the ground was softer, he was still a little disappointing. (op 9-2)

Reply(IRE) was third in the Middle Park this time last year and kicked off this season with a third place in the Irish 2000 Guineas, but he's gone backwards since then. This trip might be on the short side for him nowadays. (op 9-1)

Libranno wasn't knocked about inside the last when his chance had gone. He faced no easy task under his penalty and the ground may have been softer than he ideally cares for. (op 11-2)

Edinburgh Knight(IRE), who got no luck in running behind Scarf last time, was visored for the first time. He looked to have a good trail into the race behind the leader Red Jazz, but he found little for pressure. (op 10-1)

Sunday Times walked out of the stalls and could never get close enough to lay down a serious challenge. Her best form is on faster ground. (tchd 14-1)

Pearl Mix(IRE), whose wins have come on Polytrack, had plenty on his plate back on turf, trying easy ground for the first time and taking on tougher opposition. (op 9-1 tchd 10-1)

7049 VISION.AE MIDDLE PARK STKS (GROUP 1) (ENTIRE COLTS) 6f

2:20 (2:22) (Class 1) 2-Y-O

£85,065 (£32,250; £16,140; £8,040; £4,035; £2,025) **Stalls** High

Form RPR

1111 **1** **Reckless Abandon**[55] 5398 2-8-12 0 .... GeraldMosse 2 118
(Clive Cox) *chsd ldr tl led after 1f and edgd lft to r against stands' rail: rdn wl over 1f out: drvn and hrd pressed ins fnl f: hdd wl ins fnl f: battled bk v gamely u.p to ld again last strides* **9/4**[1]

151 **2** *nk* **Moohaajim (IRE)**[21] 6483 2-8-12 0 .... AdamKirby 7 118
(Marco Botti) *hld up in midfield: hdwy jst over 2f out: rdn and chsd wnr over 1f out: drvn and ev ch ins fnl f: styd on to ld wl ins fnl f: no ex and hdd last strides* **9/4**[1]

124 **3** *nk* **Gale Force Ten**[49] 5608 2-8-12 0 ....(p) CO'Donoghue 6 117
(A P O'Brien, Ire) *in tch: effrt u.p wl over 1f out: drvn and chsd ldng pair jst over 1f out: kpt on wl u.p towards fin* **33/1**

32S **4** *1 ¾* **Cristoforo Colombo (USA)**[62] 5136 2-8-12 0 .... RyanMoore 9 111
(A P O'Brien, Ire) *bhd and rdn after 2f: hdwy u.p over 1f out: styd on wl u.p ins fnl f: nvr gng pce to chal* **9/2**[2]

5535 **5** *2 ¾* **Parliament Square (IRE)**[30] 6162 2-8-12 0 ....(p) SeamieHeffernan 4 103
(A P O'Brien, Ire) *towards rr: effrt u.p ent fnl 2f: kpt on fnl f: nvr gng pce to threaten ldrs* **18/1**

3162 **6** *nse* **Hototo**[7] 6883 2-8-12 102 .... FrankieDettori 8 103
(Kevin Ryan) *led for 1f: chsd wnr after tl over 1f out: 4th and btn 1f out: wknd ins fnl f* **16/1**

1232 **7** *¾* **Master Of War**[21] 6483 2-8-12 110 .... RichardHughes 3 101
(Richard Hannon) *stdd s: hld up in rr: clsd and wl in tch 2f out: rdn and no hdwy over 1f out: edgd rt and btn 1f out: wknd ins fnl f* **12/1**

8 *1 ½* **Wexford Opera (IRE)**[15] 6648 2-8-12 0 ....(t) KevinManning 1 96
(J S Bolger, Ire) *in tch in midfield: rdn and effrt over 2f out: no prog u.p over 1f out: wknd fnl f* **50/1**

11 **9** *9* **Blaine**[50] 5559 2-8-12 0 .... JamieSpencer 5 69
(Kevin Ryan) *in tch in midfield: rdn and no imp over 2f out: sn struggling and btn: edgd rt and wknd over 1f out: eased ins fnl f* **11/1**[3]

0125 **10** *3 ¼* **Heavy Metal**[21] 6483 2-8-12 110 .... JoeFanning 10 60
(Mark Johnston) *chsd ldrs tl rdn and no ex ent fnl 2f: wknd over 1f out: bhd fnl f* **25/1**

1m 11.06s (-1.14) **Going Correction** +0.10s/f (Good) **10** Ran SP% **115.6**
Speed ratings (Par 109): **111,110,110,107,104 104,103,101,89,84**
toteswingers 1&2 £2.10, 2&3 £26.10, 1&3 £31.40 CSF £6.65 TOTE £2.60: £1.30, £1.50, £10.00; EX 7.30 Trifecta £295.90 Pool: £105,327.81 - 263.40 winning tickets..
Owner Miss J Deadman & S Barrow **Bred** Car Colston Hall Stud **Trained** Lambourn, Berks

FOCUS

One of the major races for juvenile colts, the best recent winners being subsequent champion sprinters Oasis Dream and Dream Ahead; while Dutch Art and Dark Angel have subsequently made up into promising sires. Although Crusade was a surprise winner of this in 2011, it is often won by an established juvenile from near the head of the market and that was the case again, with the market leaders battling it out up the hill. a solid renewal with the fourth and sixth giving the form a sound appearance.

NOTEBOOK

Reckless Abandon, unbeaten in four previous starts, including the Norfolk Stakes, the Prix Robert Papin and the Prix Morny in emphatic style, jumped out well and won the early battle for the lead. However, they went pretty quick early and he looked a sitting duck for his market rival as they ran into the Dip. He was very keen to post but has matured into a really tough, genuine individual now, having shown wayward tendencies, presumably due to greenness, in his early races and he kept finding for pressure to just prevail. His breeding and his demeanour suggests he is a sprinter pure and simple, and whatever he does from now on he is sure to be popular at stud, as a potential sire of fast juveniles. His trainer deserves plenty of credit for his management of this high-mettled individual, who has been bought by Godolphin but will stay with Cox next season. Time will tell if he is prepared for the Guineas, for which he was priced at between 14-1 and 20-1 after this, or held back for races such as the Diamond Jubilee and July Cup in the summer, especially as his new owners also have Dewhurst winner Dawn Approach for the first Classic. (op 5-2 tchd 10-3 tchd 7-2)

Moohaajim(IRE) ◆ was having just his second start in finishing fifth behind Reckless Abandon in the Prix Morny when looking green, but since then had impressed when beating Master Of War in the Mill Reef on his next start. The apparent choice of jockey Adam Kirby, he was settled early before ranging alongside the winner running into the Dip, looking the most likely winner. However, when asked to win his race up the hill, he could find nothing extra and was just held. He has a low, fast-ground action and the easy surface here might just have found him out. He is bred to be a miler though and will surely be aimed at the 2000 Guineas. (op 5-2)

Gale Force Ten had finished second to Reckless Abandon in the Norfolk Stakes, but was a little below par in the July Stakes next time and then a disappointing favourite in Listed company on his most recent start, both of those races on soft ground. Back on better going, he was in the leading group throughout and finished slightly closer to the winner than at Ascot, doing best of his trainer's trio. He could figure in the 2000 Guineas as well, for although his sire was a sprinter, his dam stayed middle-distances. (tchd 40-1)

Cristoforo Colombo(USA), a debut winner before finishing third in the Coventry at Royal Ascot to Dawn Approach, had fallen when short of room in the Phoenix Stakes on his latest start. Held up at the back, he was being ridden to close the gap over 2f out and never got close enough to land a blow. He is another who might be ideally suited by a sound surface, like his sire. (tchd 4-1)

Parliament Square(IRE), a dual winner on soft ground, later finished third behind Reckless Abandon in the Prix Morny. Held up early, he stayed on past beaten rivals without ever threatening. (op 14-1)

Hototo, the winner of the Windsor Castle at Ascot and a valuable sales race at York, has had a busy season and, after losing out in the early battle for the lead, gradually faded. (op 25-1)

Master Of War, placed in Group races on his last three starts, finishing runner-up to Heavy Metal and Moohaajim in two of them, was held up early and merely stayed on up the hill. (op 16-1 tchd 10-1)

Wexford Opera(IRE), rated 85 when beaten in a nursery last time, had a fair amount to find on that form but ran with credit, having raced on the outside of the field throughout. (tchd 40-1)

Blaine, a half-brother to the stable's smart juvenile winner Bogart, narrowly defeated Heavy Metal in the Gimcrack but, after tracking the pace, came under the pump over 2f out and then appeared not to handle the downhill run. He probably found the ground unsuitable as well and can be given another chance, although he is likely to be contesting sprints next season, and that is notoriously difficult for 3-y-os, especially in the first half of the year. Jamie Spencer reported that the colt stumbled 2f out. Official explanation: jockey said colt stumbled 2f out (tchd 12-1)

Heavy Metal, having his tenth start of the season, had taken on a number of his rivals before, including beating Master Of War in the Richmond Stakes. However, he was well beaten by Moohaajim in the Mill Reef and dropped away rather tamely here, suggesting he was over the top. (op 20-1 tchd 18-1)

7050 DUBAI DEWHURST STKS (GROUP 1) (ENTIRE COLTS & FILLIES) 7f

2:55 (2:57) (Class 1) 2-Y-O

£170,130 (£64,500; £32,280; £16,080; £8,070; £4,050) **Stalls** High

Form RPR

1111 **1** **Dawn Approach (IRE)**[28] 6272 2-9-1 0........................ KevinManning 3 122+
(J S Bolger, Ire) *chsd ldng pair tl rdn to chse ldr ent fnl 2f: swtchd rt and drvn to chal 1f out: led u.p fnl 150yds: styd on wl: eased cl home* **30/100**[1]

2213 **2** *2 ¾* **Leitir Mor (IRE)**[28] 6272 2-9-1 0.................................(tp) RonanWhelan 1 115
(J S Bolger, Ire) *sn pushed along to ld: rdn over 1f out: hdd fnl 150yds: no ex and sn outpcd: plugged on to hold 2nd* **33/1**

26 **3** *¾* **George Vancouver (USA)**[34] 6078 2-9-1 0........................ JPO'Brien 4 113
(A P O'Brien, Ire) *stdd s: hld up in rr: hdwy jst over 2f out: drvn to chse ldng pair over 1f out: plugged on same pce ins fnl f* **16/1**

11 **4** *4* **Ashdan**[29] 6200 2-9-1 0.. WilliamBuick 2 103
(John Gosden) *stdd s: hld up in last pair: rdn over 2f out: hdwy u.p over 1f out: no imp 1f out: wknd ins fnl f* **9/2**[2]

2 **5** *2 ½* **The Ferryman (IRE)**[81] 4445 2-9-1 0................................ RyanMoore 6 96
(A P O'Brien, Ire) *chsd ldr: rdn and lost 2nd ent fnl 2f: sn struggling u.p: wknd over 1f out* **14/1**[3]

100 **6** *4* **Funk Soul Brother**[21] 6483 2-9-1 85................................ MichaelHills 5 86
(Charles Hills) *t.k.h: in tch: rdn and struggling 2f out: edgd rt and wknd over 1f out* **100/1**

1m 24.0s (-1.40) **Going Correction** +0.10s/f (Good) **6** Ran SP% **111.6**
Speed ratings (Par 109): **112,108,108,103,100 96**
toteswingers 1&2 £3.40, 2&3 £12.20, 1&3 £2.20 CSF £14.50 TOTE £1.60: £1.10, £7.10; EX 16.70.

Owner Godolphin **Bred** J S Bolger **Trained** Coolcullen, Co Carlow

FOCUS

A bit of a disappointing turnout for the premier 2yo race of the season, but not altogether surprising, considering that the Middle Park is now run on the same day, the Prix Jean-Luc Lagardere only took place six days earlier, all but preventing any follow-up attempts, and the outstanding 2yo of the year was in the line-up, scaring opposition away. The race taught us little we did not already know, but it cemented the winner's position as favourite for next year's 2000 Guineas, albeit his price for the first colts' Classic was only gently clipped by most firms. They went a good, solid gallop and the winning time compared favourably with that of the Challenge Stakes earlier on the card, being very marginally faster. The winner is rated to his National Stakes form but could rate higher, with the third to his Prix Morny mark.

NOTEBOOK

Dawn Approach(IRE) was, as he always has been throughout his career, strongest at the finish. He wasn't as visually impressive as he was in the Vincent O'Brien National Stakes last time, and the proximity of his stablemate/pacemaker could be used against him, but the evidence of the previous races on the card suggested that making the running on the rail was an advantage, so it would be harsh to be too critical of the winner given his pacemaker was always in the prime spot. In addition to being favourite for the Guineas, Dawn Approach also tops the Derby market with most bookmakers, but his pedigree isn't as convincing for 1m4f. He'll have no trouble getting a mile, and 1m2f ought to be within his compass in time, but his dam is by a sprinter and the Derby trip is likely to stretch him. Jim Bolger was winning this race for an incredible fifth time in the last seven years, and it'll no doubt come as a relief to Dawn Approach's ante-post backers that the colt is to remain with him over the winter in preparation for the Guineas. (op 1-3 tchd 4-11 in a place)

Leitir Mor(IRE) had been 9l behind Dawn Approach in the National Stakes. Although in this race predominantly to provide a good gallop, he is a decent horse in his own right and has improved since being re-fitted with a tongue-tie. He did appear to benefit from where he raced, though.

George Vancouver(USA), a beaten favourite behind Leitir Mor in a 6f Group 3 at the Curragh last time out, is by Henrythenavigator, and like his sire he needs decent ground to show his best. Conditions were not ideal but he ran a sound race and he has the pedigree to get a mile. Perhaps the Breeders' Cup Juvenile Turf will come into consideration. (tchd 14-1)

Ashdan had shown plenty of ability in winning his first two starts but he was taking a big step up in class here. Lack of experience looked to find him out, but he has the pedigree to make a better 3-y-o. (tchd 5-1)

The Ferryman(IRE) showed up well to halfway but was soon struggling to maintain his position. He found this class of opposition too much to deal with at this stage of his career. (op 12-1)

Funk Soul Brother didn't show a great deal in the Mill Reef last time, and again he was well beaten. He could do with a drop in class.

7051 BETFRED CESAREWITCH (HERITAGE H'CAP) 2m 2f

3:35 (3:38) (Class 2) 3-Y-O+

£99,600 (£29,824; £14,912; £7,456; £3,728; £1,872) **Stalls** Low

Form RPR

2006 **1** **Aaim To Prosper (IRE)**[16] 6600 8-9-10 107.................... KierenFallon 1 116
(Brian Meehan) *mid-div: hdwy over 5f out: led 4f out: rdn whn hrd pressed fr 3f out: styd on wl and holding runner-up fnl 120yds: v game* **66/1**

41-1 **2** *½* **Countrywide Flame**[29] 6191 4-8-5 88 4ex........................ JimmyQuinn 7 96
(John Quinn) *in tch: tk clsr order 4f out: chal 3f out: sn rdn: ev ch ent fnl f: carried sltly lft: styd on gamely but no ex fnl 120yds* **7/1**[1]

0014 **3** *2 ¼* **Tominator**[29] 6197 5-9-1 98.. JamieSpencer 3 104
(Jonjo O'Neill) *mid-div on inner: steadily crept clsr fr 4f out: swtchd out to chal 2f out: ch ent fnl f: styd on but no ex* **9/1**[3]

0014 **4** *6* **Motivado**[49] 5600 4-9-6 103... LukeMorris 13 102
(Sir Mark Prescott Bt) *towards rr of mid-div: stdy hdwy fr 4f out: rdn to chse ldrs over 2f out: styd on but hld fnl f* **14/1**

1 **5** *1 ½* **I Have A Dream**[35] 6066 3-8-11 106 4ex.......................... RyanMoore 36 104
(A P O'Brien, Ire) *s.i.s: in rr: swtchd to centre over 4f out: sn rdn and stdy prog: styd on fnl 2f: nvr rchd ldrs* **16/1**

4040 **6** *3 ¾* **Blue Bajan (IRE)**[29] 6197 10-9-0 97.................................. MichaelHills 5 91
(David O'Meara) *towards rr of midfield: stdy prog fr over 3f out: rdn wl over 2f out: styd on but nvr getting to ldrs* **33/1**

-201 **7** *½* **Albert Bridge**[21] 6472 4-8-3 86 4ex................................ HarryBentley 25 79
(Ralph Beckett) *trckd ldrs: rdn on heels of ldrs 3f out: kpt on same pce tl no ex ins fnl f* **20/1**

2064 **8** *1 ½* **Dark Ranger**[21] 6493 6-8-1 84...................................... JamesSullivan 28 75
(Tim Pitt) *towards rr of midfield: hdwy over 4f out: sn rdn to chse ldrs: styd on tl no ex ent fnl f* **66/1**

23 **9** *3* **Martial Law (IRE)**[29] 6191 6-8-1 84.............................(b) KieranO'Neill 23 72
(David Pipe) *mid-div: rdn and hdwy fr over 4f out: chsd ldrs 3f out: wknd over 1f out* **33/1**

5/04 **10** *5* **Martyr**[16] 6600 7-9-0 97.. RichardHughes 15 80
(George Baker) *mid-div: smooth hdwy to trck ldrs travelling wl 4f out: asked for effrt 3f out: wknd qckly* **16/1**

/530 **11** *1 ½* **Nafaath (IRE)**[15] 4697 6-8-5 88................................ MickaelBarzalona 6 69
(Neil King) *trckd ldrs: rdn to chse wnr briefly over 3f out: wknd over 2f out* **40/1**

6-00 **12** *nk* **Sentry Duty (FR)**[73] 4697 10-8-4 87.............................. MartinDwyer 29 68
(Nicky Henderson) *towards rr: hdwy into midfield whn nt clr run on rails 5f out: swtchd lft and rdn over 3f out: nvr threatened ldrs* **40/1**

0102 **13** *1 ½* **Very Good Day (FR)**[52] 5491 5-8-10 93........................ MartinHarley 22 72
(Mick Channon) *towards rr: sme hdwy u.p into midfield over 3f out: wknd over 2f out* **20/1**

1206 **14** *7* **Western Prize**[29] 6197 4-8-7 90.. JimCrowley 17 61
(Ralph Beckett) *mid-div: effrt to chse ldrs 4f out: wknd over 2f out* **25/1**

22-0 **15** *2 ¼* **Cry For The Moon (USA)**[35] 6066 6-8-3 86.................... ChrisHayes 26 55
(J H Culloty, Ire) *hld up towards rr: struggling 5f out: nvr a threat* **40/1**

3001 **16** *8* **O Ma Lad (IRE)**[15] 6642 4-7-12 84 4ex.......................... RaulDaSilva[(3)] 9 44
(Sylvester Kirk) *trckd ldrs: led 5f out tl rdn 3f out: wknd qckly* **66/1**

021 **17** *19* **Stormy Weather (FR)**[25] 6340 6-8-5 88 4ex.................(b) MartinLane 16 27
(Brian Ellison) *hld up towards rr: hdwy in centre fr 6f out: rdn 4f out: wknd over 2f out: eased: t.o* **33/1**

-404 **18** *2* **Cosimo de Medici**[22] 6428 5-8-3 86............................(t) NickyMackay 21 23
(Hughie Morrison) *hld up bhd: swtchd to centre over 5f out: sn rdn: little imp: nvr a factor: eased fr over 1f out: t.o* **25/1**

10-4 **19** *1* **Beyond (IRE)**[73] 4697 5-7-12 86................................ ConorHoban[(5)] 10 22
(David Pipe) *trckd ldrs: rdn to chse ldr over 5f out: wknd over 4f out: eased: t.o* **16/1**

1033 **20** *nse* **Hurricane Higgins (IRE)**[29] 6198 4-9-2 99.................... JoeFanning 19 35
(Mark Johnston) *mid-div: rdn over 3f out: wknd over 2f out: eased: t.o* **16/1**

1 **21** *2 ½* **Olympiad (IRE)**[52] 5491 4-8-13 96................................ PatSmullen 33 29
(D K Weld, Ire) *towards rr of midfield: rdn over 4f out: sn btn: eased: t.o* **8/1**[2]

22 *2 ¼* **Alhellal (IRE)**[112] 3411 6-8-3 86.................................... WayneLordan 30 17
(M Phelan, Ire) *mid-div: pushed along over 6f out: wknd 4f out: eased: t.o* **25/1**

0065 **23** *hd* **Bernie The Bolt (IRE)**[21] 6493 6-8-4 87........................ DavidProbert 11 17
(Andrew Balding) *taken down early: mid-div tl wknd 4f out: eased: t.o* **16/1**

0-00 **24** *3 ¾* **Ashbrittle**[41] 5491 5-8-0 86....................................(b) DeclanCannon[(3)] 34 12
(David Pipe) *mid-div: rdn 4f out: sn btn: eased: t.o* **66/1**

25 *nse* **Decoy (FR)**[41] 6-8-1 84..(b) HayleyTurner 24 10
(David Pipe) *mid-div: struggling fr 1/2-way: wknd 4f out: eased: t.o* **66/1**

5300 **26** *15* **Montaff**[29] 6191 6-8-6 89.. AndreaAtzeni 31
(Mick Channon) *towards rr: making prog whn nt clr run on rails over 4f out tl wl over 3f out: sn rdn: wknd over 2f out* **100/1**

112 **27** *2* **Montaser (IRE)**[23] 6415 3-8-0 95.................................... FrannyNorton 20
(David Simcock) *mid-div tl over 4f out whn rdn: wknd tamely: eased: t.o* **10/1**

-240 **28** *16* **Right Stuff (FR)**[17] 6576 9-8-5 88.................................... JohnFahy 12
(Gary Moore) *quite keen: prom: led after 7f: rdn and hdd 5f out: wknd qckly: eased fnl 2f: t.o* **100/1**

000 **29** *hd* **Astral Thunder (ARG)**[14] 6668 5-8-11 94..................(b) JamesDoyle 32
(Marco Botti) *mid-div: rdn over 5f out: wknd over 4f out: eased: t.o* **100/1**

-300 **30** *10* **Icon Dream (IRE)**[42] 5826 5-9-1 98................................ WilliamBuick 14
(Jim Goldie) *a towards rr: t.o and virtually p.u fnl 3f* **40/1**

0346 **31** *27* **Lyric Street (IRE)**[35] 6031 4-8-6 94............................(b[1]) DarrenEgan[(5)] 35
(Ed Dunlop) *trckd ldrs: rdn over 6f out: sn lost pl: t.o fnl 6f* **50/1**

2-00 **32** *10* **Ermyn Lodge**[63] 5076 6-8-10 93....................................(v) IanMongan 18
(Pat Phelan) *towards rr of mid-div on outer tl 6f out: sn bhd: eased: t.o* **40/1**

115- **P** **Kepler's Law**[390] 6218 4-8-2 85.. ChrisCatlin 2
(Sir Mark Prescott Bt) *led for 7f: rdn over 6f out: towards rr whn lost action and immediately p.u 5f out: fatally injured* **33/1**

215R **R** **Lordofthehouse (IRE)**[16] 6600 4-8-5 88.................. AdamBeschizza 27
(William Haggas) *taken down early: ref to r: tk no part* **50/1**

3m 51.51s (-0.49) **Going Correction** +0.10s/f (Good)
WFA 3 from 4yo+ 12lb **34** Ran SP% **138.2**
Speed ratings (Par 109): **105,104,103,101,100 98,98,97,96,94 93,93,92,89,88 85,76,75,75,75 74,73,73,71,71 64,63,56,56,5**
toteswingers 1&2 £111.00, 2&3 £10.20, 1&3 £152.60 CSF £432.16 CT £4632.93 TOTE £77.10: £14.80, £3.10, £2.60, £4.20; EX 627.90 Trifecta £9181.90 Part won. Pool: £12,408.06 - 0.70 winning tickets..

Owner CGA Racing Partnership 2 **Bred** Stephanie Hanly **Trained** Manton, Wilts

■ Aaim To Prosper became the first dual winner of this race in its long history (it was first run in 1839).

■ Stewards' Enquiry : Kieren Fallon caution: careless riding.
Adam Beschizza five-day ban: struck gelding at start (Oct 27,29-31,Nov 1)

FOCUS

This long-established second leg of the autumn double attracted another massive field but a history-making feat from the winner. The first three were all drawn low and raced in a group in midfield near the rail through the early stages. The winner showed shock improvement and is clearly suited by the C&D.

NOTEBOOK

Aaim To Prosper(IRE), the 2010 scorer, is now unique in becoming the first horse in the race's long history to win it twice. He took this two years ago on similar ground but had not scored since, having been raced exclusively in Group and Listed company (placed at the latter level). Returning to handicapping off a 20lb higher mark, he was always travelling well and, going on around half a mile from home with the runner-up, he stayed on tenaciously, if drifting into his rival in the closing stages, to outstay the rest. This C&D clearly brings out the best of him and presumably connections will plan next year's campaign with an unprecedented hat-trick in this race in mind.

Countrywide Flame, a leading juvenile hurdler last season, winning the Triumph Hurdle, impressed when scoring on his return to the Flat at Chester last month and was only 4lb higher. He raced with the winner for much of the way and they came through together. He battled on bravely but could not get the better of a bigger and older rival up the hill. He lost nothing in defeat and presumably will be given a break after this hard race before returning to hurdles. (op 8-1)

Tominator, the winner of 2011 Northumberland Plate and a Listed scorer this season, had recently joined new connections and, another to race in the group nearest the rail in the middle of the pack, came through to have his chance but could find no more up the hill. He will now be prepared for a hurdling campaign. (op 11-1 tchd 17-2)

Motivado had always looked capable of winning a big handicap and went close when fourth in the Ebor last time. Racing off 6lb higher, he had to be ridden to follow the principals though and could not find any more in the last 2f. He appeared to get the trip but might have preferred a sounder surface.

I Have A Dream ◆, a smart 3-y-o who won a good handicap last time off 4lb lower, ran really well and deserves extra credit as he was drawn widest of all. He could well make up into a Group-class stayer next season. (op 20-1)

Blue Bajan(IRE) had not won since May 2011 but goes on easy ground and, helped by a falling mark, travelled well onto the heels of the leaders, but did not quite get home.

Albert Bridge ◆ had developed into a decent performer at 1m4f-1m6f given soft ground this season and, although 6lb higher, ran creditably considering he was one of the few that remained in the leading group throughout. There is a good staying handicap to be won with him next season given his favoured surface.
Dark Ranger is a generally reliable stayer who finished second in the trial for this in 2011 and fourth in the same race this season. He had struggled off higher marks since finishing a good second at York in May but ran well here, only fading in the latter stages. He is best on good or faster ground.
Martial Law(IRE) has done well returned to the Flat, was 4lb better off with today's runner-up for 2 3/4l compared with Chester running, but was under the pump some way from home. In the circumstances he did well to finish as close as he did.
Martyr, a winner at up to 2m and best on fast ground, travelled noticeably well for a long way but, once ridden to chase the principals over 2f out, there was nothing in the tank. The trip and ground seemed to find him out.
Nafaath(IRE), who ran third in the Ascot Stakes in June, showed up for a good way from his low draw before tiring.
Sentry Duty(FR), a former smart hurdler who had finished sixth in this in each of the last two seasons, had dropped 10lb since the 2011 running and performed with credit once again. However, at the age of ten he is not quite the horse he was.
Olympiad(IRE), a lightly raced Irish-trained colt, had won a York handicap off 7lb lower but had a high draw to overcome. The subject of heavy support leading up to the race, he tracked the pace from the outset but lost his place over half a mile from home and was beaten a long way. (op 11-1 tchd 15-2)
Montaser(IRE), a lightly raced 3-y-o who stays 2m and acts on fast ground, was another fancied runner but he got quite warm beforehand, was drawn quite high and, having been held up, failed to pick up under pressure and finished some way back. Franny Norton reported that the colt ran flat. Official explanation: jockey said colt ran flat (op 11-1)
Astral Thunder(ARG)'s rider reported that the horse lost a shoe. Official explanation: jockey said horse lost a shoe

7052 VISION.AE ROCKFEL STKS (GROUP 2) (FILLIES) 7f
4:05 (4:12) (Class 1) 2-Y-O

£34,026 (£12,900; £6,456; £3,216; £1,614; £810) **Stalls** High

Form RPR
11 **1** **Just The Judge (IRE)**[56] 5353 2-8-12 0 MichaelHills 3 108+
(Charles Hills) *hld up in tch: rdn and effrt wl over 1f out: qckn to ld and edgd lft over 1f out: in command and r.o wl fnl f: rdn out* **6/1**[3]
3212 **2** *1 3/4* **Nargys (IRE)**[30] 6160 2-8-12 86 KierenFallon 9 105+
(Luca Cumani) *t.k.h: hld up in tch: nt clr run wl over 1f out tl ent fnl f: hdwy and edgd rt 1f out: styd on wl to go 2nd fnl 50yds: no threat to wnr* **5/1**[2]
13 **3** *1* **Desert Blossom (IRE)**[35] 6021 2-8-12 0 MickaelBarzalona 4 101
(Mahmood Al Zarooni) *stdd and swtchd lft after s: hld up in rr: swtchd sharply rt and effrt 2f out: hdwy u.p over 1f out: styd on to chse wnr ins fnl f: no imp and lost 2nd fnl 50yds* **12/1**
5121 **4** *3/4* **Melody Of Love**[21] 6467 2-8-12 99 FrankieDettori 1 99
(Ann Duffield) *hld up in tch: rdn and effrt ent fnl 2f: drvn over 1f out: styd on same pce fnl f* **15/2**
6653 **5** *hd* **Momalorka**[21] 6467 2-8-12 93 (p) KellyHarrison 2 98
(William Haggas) *stdd s and sn swtchd lft: hld up in tch: rdn and hdwy ent fnl 2f: drvn over 1f out: kpt on same pce ins fnl f* **50/1**
1 **6** *1* **Zurigha (IRE)**[19] 6534 2-8-12 0 RichardHughes 6 96
(Richard Hannon) *w ldr: rdn and ev ch 2f out: chsd wnr but unable qck over 1f out: lost 2nd ins fnl f: wknd towards fin* **14/1**
2 **7** *1/2* **Scintillula (IRE)**[34] 6081 2-8-12 0 (t) KevinManning 5 95
(J S Bolger, Ire) *in tch: rdn and effrt ent fnl 2f: unable qck u.p and btn whn carried rt 1f out: wknd fnl 100yds* **5/1**[2]
8 *nk* **Gift From Heaven (IRE)**[19] 6547 2-8-12 0 WayneLordan 11 94+
(David Wachman, Ire) *stdd s: hld up in tch in rr: rdn and hdwy over 1f out: drvn and no imp 1f out: wknd ins fnl f* **11/4**[1]
1416 **9** *2 1/4* **Go Angellica (IRE)**[29] 6199 2-8-12 101 WilliamBuick 8 88
(David Simcock) *stdd s: hld up in tch in rr: rdn and no hdwy over 1f out: nvr trbld ldrs* **25/1**
2143 **10** *1 1/2* **Annie's Fortune (IRE)**[15] 6632 2-8-12 100 JimCrowley 10 84
(Alan Jarvis) *led: rdn 2f out: drvn and hdd over 1f out: btn 1f out: wknd fnl f* **11/1**
1254 **11** *1/2* **Masarah (IRE)**[15] 6635 2-8-12 100 TomQueally 7 83
(Clive Brittain) *chsd ldrs: n.m.r and shuffled bk 2f out: rdn and no hdwy wl over 1f out: wknd ent fnl f* **28/1**

1m 25.15s (-0.25) **Going Correction** +0.10s/f (Good) **11** Ran SP% **118.0**
Speed ratings (Par 104): **105,103,101,101,100 99,99,98,96,94 93**
toteswingers 1&2 £8.00, 2&3 £14.50, 1&3 £8.10 CSF £35.60 TOTE £5.90: £1.90, £2.10, £4.30; EX 48.40 Trifecta £145.20 Pool: £1,613.88 - 8.22 winning tickets..
Owner Qatar Racing Limited & Sangster Family **Bred** Mrs J Dempsey **Trained** Lambourn, Berks

FOCUS
The winning time was 1.15sec slower than the Dewhurst. This race hasn't been a bad pointer to the 1000 Guineas in recent years, with winners such as Speciosa and Finsceal Beo taking the Classic, and the likes of Maids Causeway and Music Show going on to run well in defeat. The winner can do better while the fourth and fifth help set the level.

NOTEBOOK
Just The Judge(IRE) ◆ could well prove to be a player in what is looking a pretty open first fillies' Classic. She picked up well when asked to go and win her race, just as she had at Newbury, and with her proven versatility to handle easy and fast ground she has plenty going for her. She'll have no problem with a mile, and Michael Hills was happy to put her up alongside his previous winners of this race, Negligent (third in Guineas), Hula Angel (won Irish Guineas), and Maids Causeway (runner-up in Guineas). Ladbrokes go a best price 20-1 for next year's 1000 Guineas. (op 11-2 tchd 13-2)
Nargys(IRE), who was a little keen early, was stuck behind a wall of horses as the winner was being sent for home and had ground to make up from the bottom of the Dip. She did gradually close the gap, but it would be wrong to suggest she might have won with a clear run. Although beaten in a handicap off 82 last time, little went right for her that day, and clearly those that backed her all the way into 5-1 didn't consider her to be out of her depth here. She should make up into a nice 3-y-o. (op 6-1 tchd 13-2)
Desert Blossom(IRE) ◆, dropped back a furlong in distance, was forced to challenge widest of all, which probably wasn't the place to be. This was an encouraging effort and she should have more to offer next year. (op 11-1)
Melody Of Love, who coped well with extreme conditions to win the Firth of Clyde Stakes last time, had more to do in this company and wasn't at all disgraced. The extra furlong wasn't a problem. (op 8-1 tchd 7-1)
Momalorka was stuck on the outside of the pack for most of the race, which was probably a disadvantage. She's a pretty consistent type, and helps set the level of the form.
Zurigha(IRE) didn't run at all badly considering she'd only won a Kempton maiden previously. She was given no peace up front but did best of the pace-setters and should appreciate better ground in future. (op 16-1)
Scintillula(IRE), runner-up in the Moyglare last time on just her second start, is a sister to Cuis Ghaire (runner-up in 1000 Guineas), Gile Na Greine (third in 1000 Guineas) and Claiomh Solais (fourth in Irish Guineas). She's certainly bred for the job, but she was weak in the betting here and, after racing prominently early, she got unbalanced as she weakened and dropped out, along with the other pace-setters, from the bottom of the Dip. (op 4-1 tchd 6-1)
Gift From Heaven(IRE), who lacked experience, got unbalanced running into the Dip. She could leave this form behind in time. (op 4-1 tchd 9-2)
Annie's Fortune(IRE) couldn't take advantage of having the rail to run against, but she was taken on for the lead, so did not have an easy time of it in front. (op 9-1 tchd 12-1 in places)

7053 AUTUMN STKS (GROUP 3) 1m
4:40 (4:40) (Class 1) 2-Y-O

£22,684 (£8,600; £4,304; £2,144; £1,076; £540) **Stalls** High

Form RPR
2 **1** **Trading Leather (IRE)**[20] 6519 2-9-0 0 KevinManning 4 107+
(J S Bolger, Ire) *chsd ldr: rdn and ev ch over 1f out: drvn to ld ent fnl f: hrd pressed and r.o gamely fnl f: asserted towards fin* **5/2**[1]
11 **2** *3/4* **Montiridge (IRE)**[24] 6372 2-9-0 0 RichardHughes 8 105+
(Richard Hannon) *stdd s: t.k.h: hld up in rr: hdwy into midfield 5f out: sltly hmpd but squeezed through to chse ldrs over 1f out: rdn to chal 1f out: drvn ins fnl f: no ex and btn towards fin* **5/2**[1]
3 *3* **Eye Of The Storm (IRE)**[33] 6107 2-9-0 0 JPO'Brien 2 99+
(A P O'Brien, Ire) *stdd s: t.k.h: hld up in rr: hdwy and nt clr run 2f out: swtchd rt and plenty to do over 1f out: styd on wl fnl f: no threat to ldng pair* **7/1**[3]
1034 **4** *1 1/4* **Glory Awaits (IRE)**[28] 6247 2-9-0 87 JamieSpencer 10 96
(Kevin Ryan) *led: rdn ent fnl 2f: drvn and hdd ent fnl f: wknd ins fnl f* **40/1**
5 *nk* **Galileo Rock (IRE)**[58] 5285 2-9-0 0 WayneLordan 7 95
(David Wachman, Ire) *chsd ldng pair: rdn and edgd rt 2f out: drvn and no ex over 1f out: wknd ins fnl f* **11/2**[2]
11 **6** *nse* **Cap O'Rushes**[37] 5976 2-9-0 0 FrankieDettori 9 95
(Mahmood Al Zarooni) *chsd ldrs: shuffled bk and n.m.r ent fnl 2f: swtchd rt and drvn over 1f out: kpt on but no threat to ldrs fnl f* **10/1**
1 **7** *3 1/2* **Flying Officer (USA)**[29] 6204 2-9-0 0[1] WilliamBuick 1 88
(John Gosden) *hld up in tch towards rr: rdn 3f out: no imp 2f out: wknd over 1f out* **11/1**
5125 **8** *1/2* **Makafeh**[35] 6027 2-9-0 88 KierenFallon 11 86
(Luca Cumani) *in tch: drvn and unable qck over 1f out: btn jst ins fnl f: sn wknd: eased towards fin* **33/1**
1302 **9** *3 1/2* **King Dragon (IRE)**[10] 6797 2-9-0 89 RyanMoore 6 79
(Brian Meehan) *hld up in tch towards rr: rdn and effrt wl over 1f out: no real prog: wknd fnl f* **40/1**
1 **10** *6* **Glenard**[30] 6164 2-9-0 0 MichaelHills 5 66
(Charles Hills) *stdd s: hld up in tch in rr: rdn and no hdwy ent 2f out: wl bhd fnl f* **20/1**
5031 **11** *nk* **Pinarius (IRE)**[8] 6841 2-9-0 76 (v) MartinLane 3 65
(Brian Meehan) *in tch: rdn and unable qck ent fnl 2f: lost pl and dropped to rr wl over 1f out: bhd fnl f* **100/1**

1m 37.83s (-0.77) **Going Correction** +0.10s/f (Good) **11** Ran SP% **116.0**
Speed ratings (Par 105): **107,106,103,102,101 101,98,97,94,88 87**
toteswingers 1&2 £2.90, 2&3 £5.00, 1&3 £3.80 CSF £7.59 TOTE £3.40: £1.30, £1.60, £2.30; EX 9.40 Trifecta £59.90 Pool: £2,228.60 - 27.49 winning tickets..
Owner Mrs J S Bolger **Bred** J S Bolger **Trained** Coolcullen, Co Carlow

FOCUS
This year's Derby third, Astrology, finished third in this race last year and this looked a good race with the future in mind. The winner impressed and there was promise from those behind, with the fourth setting the level.

NOTEBOOK
Trading Leather(IRE) ◆ could have a campaign geared around Epsom following this, having showed the right attitude in digging deep when tackled by the runner-up and seeing him off to win a shade cosily. The first two finished nicely clear and the he was paying a complement to Battle Of Marengo, who beat him on his debut, went on to take the Beresford Stakes next time out, and could well represent the Ballydoyle team in the Racing Post Trophy in a fortnight's time. He is by Teofilo out of a Sinndar mare so he should be suited by stepping up to middle distances next year, and Paddy Power go a best price 16-1 for the Derby. (tchd 11-4)
Montiridge(IRE) was keen early and got hampered 3f out. He didn't look comfortable running into the Dip either, but he still came there travelling like a winner, only to get outbattled in the closing stages. He's a talented colt but this may not have been his ideal track, and there will be other days for him. (tchd 11-4, 3-1 in a place)
Eye Of The Storm(IRE) ◆, a heavy-ground maiden winner on debut, was given a waiting ride and, despite getting unbalanced running into the Dip, made really good late progress out wide (not the place to be) once hitting the rising ground. Although he doesn't have a left eye, he could improve a lot from two to three and, being by Galileo out of a Shirley Heights mare, ought to get 1m4f standing on his head. (op 9-1 tchd 13-2)
Glory Awaits(IRE) excelled himself, but he did have the benefit of making the running on the rail, something which proved an advantage throughout the day. (tchd 50-1 in a place)
Galileo Rock(IRE) is bred to stay well, being a half-brother to Saddler's Rock. He lacked the required pace to remain competitive at the business end here, but should make up into a useful 3-y-o. (op 6-1 tchd 5-1)
Cap O'Rushes didn't get the clearest of runs but didn't really make up a great deal of ground once in the clear. He'd made the running in his previous two starts but took a lead this time, and perhaps he's happier when in front. (op 12-1)
Flying Officer(USA), who wore a hood this time, was drawn in stall one and was stuck on the outside of the pack for most of the race. That, combined with the easier ground is enough to excuse him this rather disappointing effort. (op 10-1 tchd 9-1)
Glenard was still green and found this all too much at this stage of his career. (op 16-1)
Pinarius(IRE)'s rider reported that the colt lost his action. Official explanation: jockey said colt lost its action

7054 DARLEY STKS (GROUP 3) 1m 1f
5:15 (5:16) (Class 1) 3-Y-O+

£31,190 (£11,825; £5,918; £2,948; £1,479; £742) **Stalls** High

Form RPR
0142 **1** **Mull Of Killough (IRE)**[14] 6674 6-9-3 103 JPO'Brien 8 113
(Jane Chapple-Hyam) *mde virtually all: rdn and wnt clr jst over 1f out: clr and r.o wl fnl f* **8/1**
6636 **2** *3* **Saigon**[15] 6634 3-8-13 105 KirstyMilczarek 11 106
(James Toller) *t.k.h: chsd ldrs: rdn and effrt over 2f out: drvn and chsd wnr jst ins fnl f: kpt on but no imp* **25/1**
2464 **3** *1* **Stipulate**[15] 6634 3-8-13 110 TomQueally 10 104
(Sir Henry Cecil) *in tch: nt clr run ent fnl 2f: swtchd rt and forced way out over 1f out: sn drvn: styd on same pce fnl f* **11/2**[2]
3110 **4** *1/2* **Trade Commissioner (IRE)**[58] 5278 4-9-3 105 WilliamBuick 7 103
(John Gosden) *wl in tch in midfield: effrt u.p to chse ldrs over 1f out: styd on same pce ins fnl f* **6/1**[3]

6131 **5** 3/4 **Bronze Angel (IRE)**[14] 6674 3-8-13 101......................(p) HayleyTurner 5 101+
(Marcus Tregoning) *jostled leaving stalls: hld up wl in tch in rr: rdn and nvr enough room fr over 1f out: hmpd 1f out: clr run and styd on fnl 100yds: no threat to wnr* **3/1**[1]
040 **6** 1/2 **Burano (IRE)**[14] 6674 3-8-13 105.................................... KierenFallon 12 100
(Brian Meehan) *hld up wl in tch in rr: pushed along and nt clr run wl over 1f out tl swtchd lft ins fnl f: r.o: nvr able to chal* **33/1**
-001 **7** 1 **Labarinto**[42] 5835 4-9-3 102.. RyanMoore 1 98
(Sir Michael Stoute) *w ldr: rdn and stl ev ch ent fnl 2f: outpcd by wnr over 1f out: lost 2nd jst ins fnl f: wknd fnl 100yds* **16/1**
1-66 **8** 1/2 **Mandaean**[21] 6508 3-8-13 110.................................... MickaelBarzalona 6 97
(Mahmood Al Zarooni) *jostled leaving stalls: in tch: rdn and effrt 2f out: unable qck and pushed rt over 1f out: wknd ins fnl f* **14/1**
6-02 **9** 3 **French Navy**[91] 4094 4-9-3 107.. FrankieDettori 3 90
(Mahmood Al Zarooni) *plld hrd: hld up in midfield tl stdd to rr after 2f: rdn and hdwy 2f out: no imp over 1f out: wknd 1f out* **6/1**[3]
5412 **10** 2 1/4 **Producer**[22] 6449 3-9-3 110.. RichardHughes 9 90
(Richard Hannon) *stdd s: hld up wl in tch in rr: rdn and effrt 2f out: no prog over 1f out: wknd 1f out* **16/1**
350 **11** 14 **Sos Brillante (CHI)**[71] 4764 7-9-0 76...................... FrankieMcDonald 13 52
(Terry Clement) *t.k.h: hld up wl in tch: losing pl and towards rr whn hmpd ent fnl 2f: sn bhd* **200/1**
4021 **12** 5 **Quick Wit**[28] 6242 5-9-3 108.. IanMongan 2 44
(Saeed Bin Suroor) *in tch towards rr: rdn and no rspnse 3f out: wl bhd over 1f out* **10/1**

1m 51.37s (-0.33) **Going Correction** +0.10s/f (Good)
WFA 3 from 4yo+ 4lb 12 Ran SP% **114.9**
Speed ratings (Par 113): **105,102,101,101,100 99,99,98,95,93 81,77**
toteswingers 1&2 £38.30, 2&3 £25.20, 1&3 £8.90 CSF £188.10 TOTE £8.20: £2.90, £6.80, £2.30; EX 266.40 Trifecta £1956.70 Part won. Pool: £2,644.21 - 0.20 winning tickets..
Owner Invictus **Bred** Owenstown Stud **Trained** Dalham, Suffolk

FOCUS
This Group 3 has been won by a mixture of solid performers at the level or upgraded handicappers, and one of the latter group prevailed. Tthe winner came up the stands' rail, which had appeared to have an advantage over the centre of the track throughout the day. The winner bettered his Cambridgeshire effort and the second is rated close to form.

NOTEBOOK
Mull Of Killough(IRE), a dual winner at 1m this year and runner-up to Bronze Angel in the Cambridgeshire, was 6lb better off with that rival here and duly reversed the form. He got to the rail after a furlong and raced upsides the leader until asserting running into the Dip. Clear over a furlong out, he stayed on for a deserved success on his first attempt at this level. He is in good form so might return here for the final meeting of the season. (op 9-1 tchd 10-1 in a place)
Saigon has been pretty consistent in Group and Listed company, but has not won this season. Stepping up in trip, he tracked the winner for much of the way but got a little outpaced before staying on well up the hill. There is a similar contest in him on this evidence.
Stipulate, a Listed winner over C&D and placed in a Group 3 over 1m2f, finished ahead of Saigon last time but got rather stuck in a pocket just as the winner kicked for home and that did not help his chance. Once in the clear though he didn't pick up as well as looked likely. (op 9-2)
Trade Commissioner(IRE) progressed really well to win a valuable Sandown handicap in July, but disappointed when stepped up to this level at Salisbury next time and had been off since. He raced more towards the outside than the first three but had his chance and could only maintain the one pace in the latter stages. (op 11-2)
Bronze Angel(IRE), who overcame a disadvantageous stall to take the Cambridgeshire after more than three months off, was up in grade here but 6lb was worse off with Mull of Killough. He raced more towards the centre and was unable to pick up once in the clear. He might not have fully recovered from his exertions a fortnight previously. (op 5-1)
Burano(IRE) was well beaten in the Cambridgeshire but had run well at Newbury before that. He travelled strongly out the back but had a wall of horses in front of him over 2f out. However, he did not respond immediately once a gap appeared, only staying on up the rising ground past beaten rivals.
Labarinto was up in grade here and made the running. However, he was in trouble as soon as he was tackled by the winner.
French Navy returned to form when runner-up in a Listed race at Newbury in July but had been absent since. He was keen early but travelled well into the race on the outside of his field, looking a real threat, only to drop away pretty quickly in the latter stages. (op 11-2 tchd 5-1)
T/Plt: £118.80 to a £1 stake. Pool: £172,248.19 - 1057.84 winning tickets. T/Qpdt: £9.50 to a £1 stake. Pool: £11,810.36 - 916.31 winning tickets. SP

7020 WOLVERHAMPTON (A.W) (L-H)
Saturday, October 13

OFFICIAL GOING: Standard
Wind: Light across Weather: Cloudy

7055 BETFRED STILL TREBLE ODDS ON LUCKY 15'S H'CAP 5f 216y(P)
5:45 (5:45) (Class 6) (0-60,60) 3-Y-O+ £2,181 (£644; £322) Stalls Low

Form RPR
0422 **1** **Amethyst Dawn (IRE)**[22] 6456 6-9-3 58..........................(t) SebSanders 1 69
(Alan McCabe) *sn pushed along to chse ldrs: rdn over 2f out: styd on u.p to ld wl ins fnl f* **5/1**[2]
4321 **2** 1 1/2 **Gran Canaria Queen**[8] 6836 3-8-10 59.......................(v) NedCurtis(7) 13 65
(Ian Semple) *chsd ldrs: led over 2f out: rdn clr over 1f out: hdd and unable qck wl ins fnl f* **16/1**
000- **3** nk **Menelik (IRE)**[358] 6983 3-9-4 60.. TomEaves 11 65+
(Tom Dascombe) *hld up: racd keenly: pushed along over 2f out: hdwy over 1f out: rdn and hung lft ins fnl f: r.o: nt rch ldrs* **10/11**[1]
3413 **4** 1 3/4 **Invigilator**[9] 6823 4-9-4 59...(t) PatrickMathers 8 58
(Derek Shaw) *s.s: hld up: rdn and r.o ins fnl f: nrst fin* **7/1**[3]
0020 **5** 1 1/4 **Methaaly (IRE)**[9] 6823 9-8-12 58.........................(be) NatashaEaton(5) 10 53
(Michael Mullineaux) *s.s: rdn over 1f out: r.o ins fnl f: nvr nrr* **25/1**
0005 **6** nk **Mr Optimistic**[8] 6836 4-8-11 57..............................(t) AshleyMorgan(5) 9 51
(Pat Murphy) *hld up: hdwy over 1f out: styd on* **28/1**
054 **7** 1 1/4 **Bang Tidy (IRE)**[9] 6806 3-8-13 58.................................. PaulPickard(3) 3 48
(Brian Ellison) *mid-div: rdn over 2f out: styd on ins fnl f: nvr on terms* **12/1**
6-34 **8** nse **Bengaline**[226] 748 3-9-3 59...(p) AdamKirby 6 49
(Scott Dixon) *chsd ldrs: rdn over 1f out: no ex fnl f* **66/1**
3012 **9** 1/2 **Red Shadow**[9] 6823 3-9-2 58...................................(p) MichaelO'Connell 4 47
(Alan Brown) *s.i.s: hld up: hdwy and nt clr run over 1f out: no ex fnl f* **8/1**
5030 **10** 1 1/2 **M J Woodward**[117] 3218 3-9-2 58.................................... SeanQuinlan 2 42
(Paul Green) *mid-div: drvn along and lost pl 1/2-way: n.d after* **50/1**
5512 **11** 3/4 **Portrush Storm**[29] 6194 7-9-3 58.................................... PatCosgrave 7 40
(Ray Peacock) *chsd ldrs tl rdn and wknd over 1f out* **25/1**
5050 **12** 2 1/2 **Punching**[35] 6053 8-9-0 60.. DavidKenny(5) 5 34
(Conor Dore) *chsd ldr tl rdn over 2f out: wknd over 1f out* **66/1**
0006 **13** 1 **Choc'A'Moca (IRE)**[28] 6264 5-9-4 59...........................(v) MickyFenton 12 29
(Paul Midgley) *led over 4f: rdn and wknd over 1f out* **50/1**

1m 14.24s (-0.76) **Going Correction** -0.125s/f (Stan)
WFA 3 from 4yo+ 1lb 13 Ran SP% **124.3**
Speed ratings (Par 101): **100,98,97,95,93 93,91,91,90,88 87,84,83**
toteswingers 1&2 £10.60, 2&3 £7.10, 1&3 £2.30 CSF £79.63 CT £141.15 TOTE £5.10: £1.90, £3.80, £1.10; EX 56.30 Trifecta £489.50 Part won. Pool: £661.49 - 0.20 winning tickets..
Owner A S Reid **Bred** W Kane **Trained** Averham Park, Notts

FOCUS
An interesting handicap for the grade, run at an honest pace. The winner was on a good mark and built on her recent form.
Red Shadow Official explanation: jockey said filly was slowly away

7056 BOOK TICKETS ONLINE AT WOLVERHAMPTON-RACECOURSE.CO.UK NURSERY 5f 216y(P)
6:15 (6:15) (Class 6) (0-65,65) 2-Y-O £2,181 (£644; £322) Stalls Low

Form RPR
6301 **1** **Ouzinkie (IRE)**[11] 6766 2-9-4 62... MartinHarley 1 64
(Mick Channon) *a.p: chsd ldr over 2f out: rdn over 1f out: styd on u.p to ld wl ins fnl f* **3/1**[1]
3020 **2** 3/4 **Cymeriad**[15] 6644 2-8-12 56.. LiamJones 13 56
(Michael Easterby) *led: rdn over 1f out: hdd wl ins fnl f: styd on* **10/1**
5000 **3** shd **Uknowwhatushouldo (IRE)**[25] 6337 2-9-7 65........ FergusSweeney 2 64
(J S Moore) *hld up: hdwy over 2f out: rdn over 1f out: r.o* **11/1**
1053 **4** hd **Not Now Blondie**[8] 6850 2-8-12 61............................ AshleyMorgan(5) 9 60
(Chris Dwyer) *chsd ldrs: rdn and bmpd over 1f out: r.o* **14/1**
3205 **5** nk **Fly Fisher (IRE)**[13] 6707 2-8-9 60................................(v[1]) NedCurtis(7) 12 58
(Ian Semple) *prom: racd keenly: pushed along over 2f out: rdn over 1f out: sn hung lft: r.o* **28/1**
0060 **6** 2 1/4 **Poetic Belle**[17] 6583 2-8-9 58.............................. MichaelJMMurphy(5) 4 49
(Alan Jarvis) *sn pushed along in rr: hdwy over 1f out: nt rch ldrs* **6/1**[3]
550 **7** shd **Melodee Princess (IRE)**[16] 6611 2-9-1 64................... DarrenEgan(5) 8 55
(Ronald Harris) *hld up in tch: plld hrd: rdn over 1f out: styd on* **12/1**
5500 **8** 1/2 **Bay Laurel (IRE)**[25] 6332 2-9-2 60.................................... SebSanders 6 49
(Harry Dunlop) *s.s: in rr: hdwy over 1f out: nt trble ldrs* **9/1**
5335 **9** 1 3/4 **Napinda**[38] 5940 2-8-10 54.. StevieDonohoe 5 38
(Philip McBride) *s.i.s: bhd 1/2-way: nvr nrr* **7/1**
2040 **10** 3 **Lucy Minaj**[20] 6511 2-8-11 55.. TomEaves 7 30
(Bryan Smart) *s.i.s: hld up: hdwy 1/2-way: plld hrd: rdn over 1f out: sn wknd* **20/1**
2363 **11** nse **Mrs Warren**[65] 4991 2-9-4 62.. WilliamCarson 3 37
(Charles Hills) *chsd ldr tl rdn over 2f out: wknd over 1f out* **11/2**[2]
0500 **12** 5 **Proventi**[70] 4816 2-9-2 60.. IPoullis 11 20
(Alan McCabe) *hld up: rdn over 2f out: sn wknd* **66/1**

1m 14.97s (-0.03) **Going Correction** -0.125s/f (Stan) 12 Ran SP% **118.7**
Speed ratings (Par 93): **95,94,93,93,93 90,90,89,87,83 83,76**
toteswingers 1&2 £8.80, 2&3 £17.10, 1&3 £5.00 CSF £33.42 CT £300.48 TOTE £3.70: £1.80, £4.70, £3.40; EX 40.60 Trifecta £373.80 Part won. Pool: £505.23 - 0.80 winning tickets..
Owner Box 41 **Bred** B Kennedy **Trained** West Ilsley, Berks

FOCUS
The pace was fair for this low-grade nursery, with little covering the front five at the line. The runner-up is among those who set the level.

NOTEBOOK
Ouzinkie(IRE) had taken advantage of a return to selling company when winning on his AW debut over C&D last time (first run since being gelded), and he confirmed his well-being with a gutsy success here. He remains on a handy mark judged on his form earlier in the year and holds a couple of entries in the coming days. (op 9-4 tchd 10-3)
Cymeriad, making her handicap debut, showed good pace to lead from her wide draw and enjoyed the run of the race out in front, but was caught by a well-handicapped rival late on. (tchd 11-1)
Uknowwhatushouldo(IRE) had not really progressed in three starts after a promising debut but showed a bit more here. She followed the winner into the straight, but was outpaced before staying on again near the line.
Not Now Blondie has yet to recapture the form of her nursery success at the track over the minimum trip in August, but ran better here and she´s on a mark she can go close off, when things drop right. (op 12-1)
Fly Fisher(IRE), wearing a visor for the first time, had to race wide from his poor draw but stayed on well and showed more than of late, on his third start for connections. (op 33-1)
Poetic Belle was outpaced 3f out over this shorter trip, but was finishing to good effect and this was a promising enough effort. (op 11-2 tchd 9-2)
Napinda Official explanation: jockey said filly hung right leaving stalls and did not face the kickback
Lucy Minaj Official explanation: jockey said filly hung right-handed
Mrs Warren, dropping to a 0-65 for the first time, looked to hold solid claims and was up with the pace early but weakened tamely when coming under pressure and is becoming a frustrating type. (op 7-1 tchd 15-2)

7057 DOWNLOAD OUR IPHONE APP MEDIAN AUCTION MAIDEN STKS 1m 141y(P)
6:45 (6:48) (Class 6) 2-Y-O £2,181 (£644; £322) Stalls Low

Form RPR
1 **Cafe Society (FR)** 2-9-3 0.. FergusSweeney 5 71+
(David Simcock) *hld up: hdwy over 1f out: shkn up to ld ins fnl f: r.o wl* **15/2**
05 **2** 1 1/2 **Khotan**[12] 6733 2-9-3 0... LukeMorris 8 68
(Sir Mark Prescott Bt) *chsd ldr tl led over 6f out: rdn over 1f out: hdd and unable qck ins fnl f* **25/1**
3 1 1/4 **Bin Singspiel** 2-9-3 0.. MartinDwyer 6 65+
(James Tate) *s.s: rn green in rr: rdn 3f out: hdwy over 2f out: r.o* **8/1**
5254 **4** 1 1/4 **Choral Prince (IRE)**[24] 6372 2-8-12 74............................ DarrenEgan(5) 4 63
(Mike Murphy) *chsd ldrs: rdn over 1f out: styd on same pce ins fnl f* **6/1**
5 3/4 **Mandy The Nag (USA)** 2-8-12 0................................ StevieDonohoe 7 56
(Ed Dunlop) *hld up in tch: rdn over 1f out: styd on same pce fnl f* **9/2**[2]
25 **6** 2 3/4 **Gabrial The Master (IRE)**[14] 6669 2-9-3 0......................... TomEaves 1 55
(Richard Fahey) *led: hdd over 6f out: chsd ldr tl rdn over 2f out: wknd fnl f* **5/1**[3]
7 5 **Bubbly Bailey** 2-9-3 0... LiamJones 2 45
(Alan Bailey) *chsd ldrs tl rdn and wknd over 1f out* **5/2**[1]
8 11 **Douglas Pasha (IRE)** 2-9-3 0.. KieranO'Neill 3 22
(Richard Hannon) *sn pushed along and prom: lost pl 4f out: rdn and wknd over 2f out* **7/1**

1m 51.19s (0.69) **Going Correction** -0.125s/f (Stan) 8 Ran SP% **116.9**
Speed ratings (Par 93): **91,89,88,87,86 84,79,70**
toteswingers 1&2 £20.40, 2&3 £13.30, 1&3 £8.50 CSF £166.31 TOTE £11.90: £3.10, £7.60, £2.90; EX 180.00 TRIFECTA Not won. Pool: £643.50..
Owner S Bamber, J Barnett & M Caine **Bred** Haras Du Quesnay **Trained** Newmarket, Suffolk

FOCUS
Just a fair maiden, run at a sound pace with the winner coming widest of all into the straight. However the time was poor. The level of the form is fluid, rated around the fourth.

NOTEBOOK

Cafe Society(FR) ◆, a 35,000euros yearling out of a 1m4f winner in France, was travelling well in rear at the 3f pole before coming with a sustained challenged out wide and was well on top at the line. The yard is more than capable of readying one first time but there should be more to come from him, especially over further. (op 11-1)

Khotan had shown little in two maidens prior to this at trips up to 1m2f, but made a brave bid from the front here. He looks a typical handicap type for the yard over longer trips. (tchd 20-1)

Bin Singspiel, a 30,000gns yearling half-brother to 1m5f winner Elegant Hawk, was recalcitrant entering the stalls and slowly into his stride but showed a willing attitude during the race and stayed on well to the line. This will have taught him plenty. (op 12-1)

Choral Prince(IRE), the most experienced runner in the field, lost out to more progressive types and will find things easier in handicaps. (op 8-1 tchd 9-1)

Mandy The Nag(USA), a £27,000 2-y-o and half-sister to two winners in America whose dam was from the family of top middle-distance performer Law Society, travelled nicely into the race but looked a shade green when asked for her effort and did not enjoy the clearest of passages up the straight. She can come on for this. (op 7-2 tchd 5-1)

Gabrial The Master(IRE), weak in the market beforehand, was outpaced up the straight and is now qualified for a mark. (op 11-4)

Bubbly Bailey, for whom there was a sustained move, is a 34,000gns half-brother to a number of winners. However, the gamble proved wide of the mark and he faded some way from home over a trip that may have been further than ideal. (op 7-1)

7058 BETFRED "BONUS KING BINGO" H'CAP — 1m 1f 103y(P)

7:15 (7:15) (Class 6) (0-55,60) 3-Y-0+ — **£2,181** (£483; £483) **Stalls** Low

Form — RPR

3301 **1** **Kathleensluckylad (IRE)**[7] 6892 3-9-6 **60**.............(t) GrahamGibbons 3 — 67
(Kevin Ryan) *mde all: rdn over 1f out: edgd rt ins fnl f: styd on gamely* **4/1**[2]

062 **2** ½ **Goal (IRE)**[5] 6941 4-9-3 **53**.......................(t[1]) AdamKirby 1 — 59
(Charles Smith) *trckd ldrs: rdn and ev ch fr over 1f out: r.o* **4/1**[2]

3331 **2** *dht* **Neige D'Antan**[38] 5938 3-9-1 **55**........................ LukeMorris 6 — 61
(Sir Mark Prescott Bt) *hld up: hdwy over 2f out: rdn and ev ch ins fnl f: r.o* **11/4**[1]

0400 **4** *nk* **Tartan Gunna**[38] 5941 6-9-4 **54**........................ PatCosgrave 2 — 59
(George Baker) *s.i.s: hld up: hdwy over 2f out: rdn over 1f out: r.o* **5/1**[3]

0002 **5** *shd* **Cobbs Quay**[10] 6773 4-9-3 **56**.................(b) SimonPearce(3) 11 — 61
(Daniel Kubler) *hld up: nt clr run over 2f out: hdwy over 1f out: r.o* **14/1**

50-0 **6** 2¼ **Golan Heights (IRE)**[30] 6187 6-8-11 **50**.................... IJBrennan(3) 5 — 50
(Adrian McGuinness, Ire) *prom: rdn over 2f out: styd on* **33/1**

0000 **7** 3¾ **Count Ceprano (IRE)**[14] 6690 8-9-3 **53**..................... JoeFanning 10 — 45
(Lydia Pearce) *prom: chsd wnr over 2f out tl rdn over 1f out: wknd ins fnl f* **25/1**

4056 **8** *hd* **Victorian Number (FR)**[10] 6778 4-8-12 **51**................ SophieDoyle(3) 8 — 43
(Geoffrey Deacon) *chsd wnr tl rdn over 2f out: wknd fnl f* **25/1**

24-0 **9** 2¼ **Vinniespride (IRE)**[133] 2726 5-9-3 **53**..................(tp) JamesSullivan 4 — 40
(Mark Michael McNiff, Ire) *hld up: rdn over 2f out: nvr trbld ldrs* **16/1**

6000 **10** 2½ **Rock Of Monet**[5] 6941 3-9-0 **54**.............................(vt) StevieDonohoe 7 — 36
(Ian Williams) *hld up: rdn over 2f out: n.d* **25/1**

2053 **11** 6 **Gulf Storm (IRE)**[14] 6660 3-9-1 **55**.............................(t[1]) TomEaves 13 — 24
(Bryan Smart) *hld up: hdwy over 3f out: sn rdn and wknd* **14/1**

00/2 **12** 99 **High 'n Dry (IRE)**[70] 4817 8-8-10 **53**...........................(t) NedCurtis(7) 12
(Roger Curtis) *s.s: a t.o* **20/1**

2m 0.96s (-0.74) **Going Correction** -0.125s/f (Stan)
WFA 3 from 4yo+ 4lb — **12** Ran SP% **121.8**
Speed ratings (Par 101): **98,97,97,97,97 95,91,91,89,87 82,**
PL: G £1.30; EX: K&G £9.90, K&N £8.60; TRIF: K&G&N £17.70, K&N&G £11.60; SF: K&G £9.72; TC: K&G&N £27.00 CSF £7.34 CT £24.16 TOTE £6.40: £1.50, £1.90; EX 9.90 Trifecta £17.70.toteswingers 1&2 £5.30, 2&2 £2.50, 1&2 £4.60
Owner Mrs Kathleen Flynn & Miss R A Galligan **Bred** Brendan Lavery **Trained** Hambleton, N Yorks

FOCUS

A low-grade contest run at a steady pace, with few able to close from behind and the winner making all under a strong ride . The form looks modest with a bunch finish. The winner confirmed his latest C&D win.

7059 PLAY "DAILY MILLION" AT BETFRED NURSERY (DIV I) — 7f 32y(P)

7:45 (7:47) (Class 5) (0-75,75) 2-Y-0 — **£2,911** (£866; £432; £216) **Stalls** High

Form — RPR

0363 **1** **Grilletto (USA)**[25] 6332 2-8-12 **66**.............................(b) PatCosgrave 5 — 69
(James Tate) *chsd ldrs: led over 1f out: sn hung lft: drvn out* **7/1**

4210 **2** 1 **Cappadocia (IRE)**[28] 6247 2-9-4 **72**..................... MartinHarley 12 — 73
(Mick Channon) *hld up: hdwy over 1f out: sn rdn: r.o* **8/1**

035 **3** ½ **Gravitational (IRE)**[36] 6015 2-8-12 **71**..................... DarrenEgan(5) 6 — 70
(Ed Dunlop) *trckd ldrs: plld hrd: rdn over 1f out: styd on* **7/2**[1]

2243 **4** 1 **Blue Nova**[28] 6253 2-9-0 **73**..................... MichaelJMMurphy(5) 3 — 70
(Jeremy Noseda) *chsd ldrs: shkn up and nt clr run over 1f out: rdn ins fnl f: nt run on* **5/1**[2]

0530 **5** *nk* **Something Magic**[30] 6160 2-8-13 **67**......................... LiamKeniry 1 — 63
(Sylvester Kirk) *mid-div: rdn over 1f out: r.o ins fnl f: nt trble ldrs* **25/1**

6565 **6** ¾ **Red Dragon (IRE)**[31] 6147 2-8-6 **60**......................... WilliamCarson 4 — 54
(Charles Hills) *hld up: rdn 3f out: styd on: nvr nrr* **10/1**

4123 **7** *nk* **Jumeirah Moon**[23] 6414 2-9-7 **75**..........................(b[1]) FergusSweeney 7 — 69
(David Simcock) *hld up: rdn over 1f out: styd on ins fnl f: nvr on terms* **6/1**[3]

6062 **8** 1 **Captain McCaw**[16] 6611 2-8-9 **70**...........(b) WilliamTwiston-Davies(7) 11 — 61
(Brian Meehan) *sn led: rdn and hdd over 1f out: hung lft and no ex ins fnl f* **11/1**

2430 **9** *nk* **Autumn Shadow (IRE)**[26] 6318 2-8-5 **59**..................... PatrickMathers 2 — 50
(Richard Fahey) *chsd ldr: chal 1/2-way: sn rdn: no ex ins fnl f* **25/1**

6600 **10** 1 **Haverstock**[21] 6491 2-9-0 **68**... JoeFanning 8 — 56
(Mark Johnston) *mid-div: drvn along 1/2-way: styd on same pce fnl 2f* **14/1**

5443 **11** *hd* **Black Dave (IRE)**[26] 6318 2-8-3 **57**............................... LukeMorris 10 — 45
(David Evans) *hld up: rdn 3f out: running on whn nt clr run ins fnl f: eased* **13/2**

1m 29.61s (0.01) **Going Correction** -0.125s/f (Stan) — **11** Ran SP% **121.9**
Speed ratings (Par 95): **94,92,92,91,90 89,89,88,88,86 86**
toteswingers 1&2 £12.00, 2&3 £10.50, 1&3 £13.80 CSF £64.42 CT £236.24 TOTE £10.20: £2.30, £2.80, £1.70; EX 102.50 Trifecta £361.40 Pool: £488.48 - 1.00 winning ticket..
Owner Sheikh Juma Dalmook Al Maktoum **Bred** Respite Farm Inc **Trained** Newmarket, Suffolk

FOCUS

Plenty of pace on for division one of this nursery, with the well-backed winner ideally positioned through the race. Ordinary form, with a compressed finish.

NOTEBOOK

Grilletto(USA) had run well over 6f on his handicap debut last time and stepped up in trip here, stayed on powerfully up the straight to land a bit of a gamble. He had hinted that this longer trip might suit and looks a progressive type for his promising handler. (op 14-1)

Cappadocia(IRE) got off the mark at the eighth attempt on his AW debut at Kempton last month and he ran another fine race back on the Polytrack, but had too much ground to make up on the winner. He looks a handy type on this surface for the winter. (tchd 10-1)

Gravitational(IRE), a handicap debutant, travelled kindly behind the winner into the straight, but did not see it out quite as well as the front two over this longer trip. (tchd 4-1)

Blue Nova has been keeping his form well but finding it difficult to win and he ran another solid race in defeat, but lacked the pace of the winner over this shorter trip. (op 4-1)

Something Magic had looked a shade regressive but showed more here, than off late. He got going when the race was over and may well be worth trying over further. (op 33-1)

Red Dragon(IRE) stayed on well on his first try over this far at Kempton last time and was again doing his best work late, once the race was over. (tchd 9-1 and 11-1)

Black Dave(IRE) Official explanation: jockey said colt was denied a clear run

7060 PLAY "DAILY MILLION" AT BETFRED NURSERY (DIV II) — 7f 32y(P)

8:15 (8:16) (Class 5) (0-75,75) 2-Y-0 — **£2,911** (£866; £432; £108; £108) **Stalls** High

Form — RPR

004 **1** **The Obvious Choice**[36] 6014 2-8-9 **63**........................ HarryBentley 1 — 69+
(Stuart Williams) *trckd ldrs: rdn over 1f out: led and edgd lft wl ins fnl f: r.o* **11/1**[3]

0433 **2** *hd* **Glossy Posse**[19] 6541 2-8-4 **58**............................... KieranO'Neill 9 — 64
(Richard Hannon) *hld up in tch: rdn to ld over 1f out: hdd wl ins fnl f: r.o* **14/1**

3615 **3** 2½ **Majestic Jess (IRE)**[13] 6699 2-8-13 **67**..................... HayleyTurner 8 — 67
(Luke Dace) *chsd ldrs: rdn over 1f out: hung lft ins fnl f: styd on same pce* **12/1**

6655 **4** 2 **Red Eclipse (IRE)**[1] 7026 2-7-12 **57**..................... NatashaEaton(5) 2 — 52
(Alan Bailey) *s.i.s: bmpd sn after s: hld up: hdwy over 2f out: rdn over 1f out: kpt on* **20/1**

0641 **4** *dht* **Sennockian Star**[29] 6189 2-9-3 **71**........................... JoeFanning 6 — 66
(Mark Johnston) *led: rdn and hdd over 1f out: no ex ins fnl f* **5/4**[1]

4400 **6** *nk* **Summer Isles**[21] 6490 2-9-0 **68**............................... LukeMorris 11 — 62
(Ed Vaughan) *s.i.s: hld up: rdn over 1f out: styd on ins fnl f: nvr nrr* **50/1**

510 **7** 1 **Skidby Mill (IRE)**[21] 6475 2-8-12 **66**..................... MichaelO'Connell 4 — 58
(John Quinn) *sn pushed along in rr: rdn and hung lft over 1f out: nvr on terms* **25/1**

3220 **8** ½ **This Is Nice (IRE)**[30] 6160 2-9-7 **75**..................... GrahamGibbons 5 — 66
(Tom Dascombe) *prom: pushed along 3f out: rdn over 1f out: wknd ins fnl f* **9/2**[2]

0433 **9** *nk* **Ighraa (IRE)**[28] 6227 2-9-4 **72**.............................(b[1]) TadhgO'Shea 3 — 62
(Brian Meehan) *s.i.s: hmpd sn after s: hld up: rdn over 1f out: n.d* **12/1**

2305 **10** ¾ **Royal Steps (IRE)**[16] 6604 2-9-5 **73**........................ MartinDwyer 12 — 61+
(James Tate) *s.s: a in rr* **14/1**

000 **11** 5 **Admirals Walk (IRE)**[36] 6015 2-9-1 **69**........................ LiamKeniry 10 — 45
(Sylvester Kirk) *hld up: rdn over 2f out: sn wknd: eased ins fnl f* **16/1**

0043 **12** ½ **Baltic Prince (IRE)**[22] 6451 2-7-7 **52**..................... DarrenEgan(5) 7 — 27
(Paul Green) *chsd ldr tl rdn over 2f out: wknd fnl f* **20/1**

1m 27.98s (-1.62) **Going Correction** -0.125s/f (Stan) — **12** Ran SP% **120.9**
Speed ratings (Par 95): **104,103,100,98,98 98,97,96,96,95 89,89**
toteswingers 1&2 £12.00, 2&3 £10.50, 1&3 £13.80 CSF £149.96 CT £1926.89 TOTE £13.70: £4.50, £4.80, £4.10; EX 196.80 Trifecta £362.50 Part won. Pool: £489.93 - 0.81 winning tickets..
Owner Qatar Racing Limited **Bred** Simon Tindall **Trained** Newmarket, Suffolk

FOCUS

The second leg of this nursery was run at a sound pace, with the front two pulling clear inside the final furlong. The winner may have more to offer and the form is straightforward behind.

NOTEBOOK

The Obvious Choice, got away in a handy position just behind the pace, from his inside draw on his handicap debut and saw the trip out well. The winner had tried to make all over 1m when last seen but was ridden with a touch more restraint here and that tactic paid dividends. This looks his trip and it would be no surprise to see him go on from this. (op 12-1 tchd 14-1)

Glossy Posse was more exposed than the winner but, stepping back up in trip, stayed on well to the line on only her second run on the surface. (op 12-1)

Majestic Jess(IRE) had landed a seller over 6f at the track on his penultimate start before disappointing last time at Epsom on his first start for connections, but bounced back to form here. He was outpaced by the front two a furlong out and, despite finishing strongly, had too much ground to make up. (op 11-1 tchd 9-1)

Red Eclipse(IRE) did best of those coming from off the pace, having her second run in 24 hours, but connections have yet to find her best trip. (op 16-1)

Sennockian Star stayed on well over 7f to score on his handicap debut last time and he was heavily supported to follow up here. It looked to be going to plan as he was able to dictate from the off but, surprisingly for a gamble from this yard, he found little when coming under pressure on his first start on the AW. (op 16-1)

This Is Nice(IRE), who finished second over C&D the last time she raced on the AW in August, was well supported to break her duck but found little when coming under pressure turning for home. (op 11-2 tchd 13-2 and 4-1)

7061 BOOK HORIZONS RESTAURANT AT WOLVERHAMPTON RACECOURSE MAIDEN STKS — 5f 20y(P)

8:45 (8:45) (Class 5) 3-Y-0+ — **£2,911** (£866; £432; £216) **Stalls** Low

Form — RPR

024- **1** **Lulla**[427] 5047 3-8-12 **81**.. HayleyTurner 2 — 58
(Marcus Tregoning) *sn pushed along to chse ldrs: shkn up to ld ins fnl f: rdn out* **6/5**[1]

0-32 **2** *nk* **Gaelic Wizard (IRE)**[27] 6287 4-8-10 **70**..................... JoshBaudains(7) 1 — 62
(Dominic Ffrench Davis) *led: rdn and hung rt fr over 1f out: hdd ins fnl f: r.o* **7/2**[2]

-424 **3** *shd* **Crazy Too (IRE)**[11] 6765 3-8-12 **63**........................ MartinLane 10 — 57
(David Simcock) *s.i.s: hld up: hdwy 1/2-way: rdn and ev ch ins fnl f: edgd rt: r.o* **7/2**[2]

4205 **4** 1½ **Silkee Supreme**[11] 6765 3-9-3 **65**........................ KieranO'Neill 8 — 57
(Richard Hannon) *hld up: pushed along over 3f out: hdwy over 1f out: sn rdn: styd on* **8/1**[3]

6324 **5** 1 **Green Mountain (IRE)**[18] 6563 3-8-12 **45**..............(vt) StevieDonohoe 7 — 48
(Philip McBride) *chsd ldr tl over 3f out: remained handy: rdn over 1f out: styd on same pce ins fnl f* **25/1**

6000 **6** 3½ **Love Club**[21] 6496 4-9-3 **44**.. WilliamCarson 6 — 40
(Brian Baugh) *prom: drvn along 1/2-way: hung lft and wknd fnl f* **50/1**

50 **7** ¾ **Winnetou**[9] 6827 3-8-10 **0**.................................. DanaZamecnikova(7) 5 — 38
(Frank Sheridan) *s.i.s: outpcd* **66/1**

2263 **8** 3¼ **Missile Attack (IRE)**[61] 5177 4-8-10 **56**..............(p) GeorgeChaloner(7) 9 — 26
(Ian Semple) *prom: chsd ldr over 3f out: pushed along and ev ch 2f out: wknd fnl f* **16/1**

1m 1.5s (-0.80) **Going Correction** -0.125s/f (Stan) — **8** Ran SP% **114.2**
Speed ratings (Par 103): **101,100,100,97,96 90,89,84**
toteswingers 1&2 £1.50, 2&3 £2.80, 1&3 £2.00 CSF £5.49 TOTE £2.50: £1.10, £1.20, £1.30; EX 7.60 Trifecta £17.50 Pool: £551.68 - 23.23 winning tickets..
Owner Mrs R B Kennard **Bred** Major And Mrs R B Kennard **Trained** Lambourn, Berks

FOCUS
A weakish maiden consisting of mainly exposed types, run at a fair pace with the runners spread across the track at the line. The poor fifth and slow time limit the form and the winner didn't need to match her best.

7062 BETFRED MOBILE LOTTO H'CAP 1m 4f 50y(P)
9:15 (9:16) (Class 6) (0-60,60) 3-Y-O **£2,181** (£644; £322) **Stalls** Low

Form RPR
1641 **1** **Critical Point**[26] 6305 3-9-5 **58**.....(b) LukeMorris 3 73+
(Sir Mark Prescott Bt) *chsd ldrs: shkn up to ld over 1f out: sn rdn clr and hung lft: eased nr fin* **5/1**[2]
3535 **2** *4* **Kashgar**[24] 6365 3-9-7 **60**..... StevieDonohoe 11 67
(Michael Bell) *chsd ldr: rdn and ev ch wl over 1f out: sn outpcd* **7/1**[3]
1221 **3** *1 1/4* **Norfolk Sky**[29] 6210 3-9-0 **60**..... ThomasBrown(7) 10 65+
(Chris Wall) *hld up in tch: rdn over 1f out: edgd lft and styd on same pce* **7/4**[1]
0026 **4** *3/4* **Always Eager**[14] 6690 3-9-2 **55**..... JoeFanning 7 59
(Mark Johnston) *led: rdn and hdd wl over 1f out: wknd ins fnl f* **8/1**
040 **5** *3* **Chella Thriller (SPA)**[58] 5280 3-9-7 **60**.....(bt[1]) FrankieMcDonald 5 59
(Alastair Lidderdale) *hld up: hdwy over 4f out: rdn over 2f out: wknd over 1f out* **28/1**
6020 **6** *4 1/2* **Cape Rainbow**[14] 6691 3-9-5 **58**..... DavidProbert 1 50
(Mark Usher) *chsd ldrs: rdn over 2f out: wknd over 1f out* **8/1**
0020 **7** *3 1/4* **Inniscastle Boy**[26] 6323 3-9-4 **57**..... MartinDwyer 8 44
(William Muir) *hld up: rdn over 2f out: n.d* **11/1**
0200 **8** *1 3/4* **Plus Fours (USA)**[21] 6474 3-9-5 **58**..... RobbieFitzpatrick 9 42
(Charles Smith) *hld up: rdn over 3f out: a in rr* **33/1**
0526 **9** *1 3/4* **Musically**[42] 5817 3-9-4 **57**..... MartinHarley 4 38
(Mick Channon) *chsd ldrs: pushed along and bmpd over 3f out: wknd over 2f out* **16/1**
2320 **10** *3* **Better Be Mine (IRE)**[24] 6365 3-9-3 **56**..... HayleyTurner 12 32
(John Dunlop) *hld up: a in rr: rdn over 2f out: sn lost tch* **7/1**[3]
603 **11** *4 1/2* **Cruachan (IRE)**[19] 6527 3-9-1 **54**..... TomEaves 6 23
(Ian Semple) *hld up: rdn and wknd over 3f out* **33/1**

2m 39.02s (-2.08) **Going Correction** -0.125s/f (Stan) **11** Ran SP% **123.8**
Speed ratings (Par 99): **101,98,97,97,95 92,89,88,87,85 82**
toteswingers 1&2 £5.20, 2&3 £2.40, 1&3 £4.20 CSF £41.57 CT £86.31 TOTE £5.60: £2.30, £2.50, £1.20; EX 48.80 Trifecta £105.70 Pool: £708.71 - 4.96 winning tickets..
Owner G Moore - Osborne House **Bred** Lofts Hall, M Philipson & Cheveley Park **Trained** Newmarket, Suffolk

FOCUS
A moderate handicap run at a steady pace, with the field well strung out at the line and the winner scoring impressively. Reasonable form for the grade.
T/Plt: £1,478.30 to a £1 stake. Pool: £82,116.62 - 40.55 winning tickets. T/Qpdt: £322.40 to a £1 stake. Pool: £9,978.00 - 22.90 winning tickets. CR

7028 YORK (L-H)
Saturday, October 13

OFFICIAL GOING: Soft (heavy in places; 5.5)
Wind: Virtually nil Weather: Fine and dry

7063 BET ON YOUR MOBILE WITH CORAL STKS (H'CAP) 5f
2:05 (2:05) (Class 3) (0-95,95) 3-Y-0+ **£8,409** (£2,502; £1,250; £625) **Stalls** Centre

Form RPR
0244 **1** **Pearl Blue (IRE)**[27] 6286 4-9-1 **89**..... GeorgeBaker 16 100
(Chris Wall) *hld up towards rr: swtchd rt to outer and hdwy over 1f out: rdn and str run ins fnl f: led last 50yds* **13/2**
0000 **2** *1 1/2* **Captain Dunne (IRE)**[14] 6666 7-9-7 **95**..... DavidAllan 9 101
(Tim Easterby) *stdd s and hld up in rr: swtchd rt and hdwy over 1f out: sn rdn and styd on strly ins fnl f: nrst fin* **25/1**
0500 **3** *shd* **Kaldoun Kingdom (IRE)**[21] 6466 7-9-3 **91**..... PaulHanagan 8 97
(Richard Fahey) *in tch: hdwy 2f out: rdn wl over 1f out: styd on wl fnl f: nrst fin* **5/1**[3]
3101 **4** *1/2* **Jamaican Bolt (IRE)**[22] 6427 4-9-4 **92**..... RobertWinston 4 96+
(Geoffrey Oldroyd) *cl up: rdn over 1f out: led ent fnl f: sn drvn: hdd & wknd last 50yds* **3/1**[1]
4033 **5** *nk* **Fitz Flyer (IRE)**[35] 6026 6-9-2 **90**.....(v) AdrianNicholls 11 93
(David Nicholls) *chsd ldrs: rdn and hdwy wl over 1f out: drvn and one pce ins fnl f* **9/1**
650 **6** *1/2* **Ancient Cross**[21] 6466 8-9-5 **93**.....(t) PaulMulrennan 19 94
(Michael Easterby) *chsd ldrs: rdn and hdwy wl over 1f out: drvn and one pce fnl f* **12/1**
1405 **7** *hd* **Steps (IRE)**[14] 6666 4-9-5 **93**.....(b) NeilCallan 15 93
(Roger Varian) *dwlt and towards rr: hdwy 2f out: sn rdn and chsd ldrs appr fnl f: sn drvn and one pce* **4/1**[2]
1605 **8** *1/2* **Singeur (IRE)**[11] 6755 5-9-5 **93**..... DanielTudhope 7 91
(Robin Bastiman) *a towards rr* **14/1**
3000 **9** *1 1/2* **Bosun Breese**[11] 6755 7-9-3 **91**..... GrahamGibbons 17 84
(David Barron) *chsd ldrs: hdwy 2f out: sn rdn and wknd over 1f out* **40/1**
-050 **10** *3/4* **Verinco**[83] 4367 6-9-4 **92**.....(vt) TomEaves 6 82
(Bryan Smart) *slt ld and set str pce: rdn along wl over 1f out: hdd ent fnl f: sn wknd* **14/1**
1010 **11** *9* **Trade Secret**[21] 6466 5-8-13 **87**..... DarryllHolland 10 45
(Mel Brittain) *a outpcd in rr* **16/1**

1m 1.19s (1.89) **Going Correction** +0.60s/f (Yiel) **11** Ran SP% **118.2**
Speed ratings (Par 107): **108,105,105,104,104 103,103,102,99,98 84**
toteswingers 1&2 £18.50, 2&3 £23.80, 1&3 £4.80 CSF £155.58 CT £896.44 TOTE £8.00: £2.10, £5.30, £1.90; EX 188.10 TRIFECTA Not won. Pool: £1,288.86..
Owner Archangels 2 **Bred** L Queally **Trained** Newmarket, Suffolk

FOCUS
Darryll Holland felt the ground was "holding and sticky" while Adrian Nicholls described it as "heavy". Nearly half of those originally declared were taken out of this decent sprint, but it still proved competitive, and the fast pace set it up for the closers. The winner is generally progressive and posted a length personal best.

NOTEBOOK
Pearl Blue(IRE) likes this sort of ground and scored under a patient, well-judged ride, bouncing back from a disappointing effort at Ffos Las in the process. This was the highest mark he's won off. (tchd 6-1)
Captain Dunne(IRE) came from further back than usual, staying on strongly and faring better than of late despite the ground being against him. He's slipped to a handy mark. (tchd 22-1)
Kaldoun Kingdom(IRE) was another closing fast at the finish and, although getting a good gallop to aim at, this still proved an inadequate test. (op 13-2)
Jamaican Bolt(IRE), up 7lb from Ayr, had no ground concerns and ran well considering he pushed the fast early gallop being set by Verinco. He can be rated better than the bare result. (tchd 10-3 and 7-2 in a place)
Fitz Flyer(IRE) continues to run well and will be happier back on drier ground. (op 10-1)
Steps(IRE), 3lb above his last win mark, failed to pick up as expected having been close enough if good enough.

7064 CORAL BACKING MACMILLAN CANCER SUPPORT STKS (H'CAP) 1m 208y
2:35 (2:36) (Class 2) (0-100,96) 3-Y-O **£12,938** (£3,850; £1,924; £962) **Stalls** Low

Form RPR
4020 **1** **Chapter Seven**[21] 6484 3-9-3 **92**..... FrederikTylicki 4 103
(Richard Fahey) *trckd ldrs: hdwy 3f out: chal 2f out: sn rdn and ev ch: drvn and styd on to ld wl ins fnl f: sltly hmpd nr fin: hld on wl* **3/1**[2]
211 **2** *hd* **Lahaag**[10] 6789 3-9-1 **90**..... PaulHanagan 2 101
(John Gosden) *t.k.h early: trckd ldr: hdwy and cl up over 2f out: rdn to chal wl over 1f out: edgd lft: sn drvn and slt ld whn hung bdly lft ins fnl f: hdd and bmpd wnr nr line: no ex* **11/8**[1]
0033 **3** *2 1/2* **Lady Macduff (IRE)**[5] 6921 3-8-8 **83**..... SilvestreDeSousa 8 88
(Mark Johnston) *led: rdn along 3f out: jnd 2f out: drvn and hdd ent fnl f: sn n.m.r and one pce* **7/1**[3]
4114 **4** *3 1/4* **Storm King**[23] 6400 3-9-4 **93**..... BrettDoyle 7 91
(Jane Chapple-Hyam) *trckd ldrs: effrt on outer over 3f out: rdn along over 2f out: sn one pce* **16/1**
244 **5** *2 3/4* **Swing Alone (IRE)**[13] 6701 3-8-10 **85**.....[1] RobertWinston 6 77
(Gay Kelleway) *hld up in rr: hdwy on inner to chse ldrs 3f out: rdn along over 2f out: sn one pce* **15/2**
3246 **6** *7* **Jack Who's He (IRE)**[36] 6010 3-8-10 **85**..... NeilCallan 5 61
(David Evans) *chsd ldrs: rdn along wl over 2f out: sn wknd* **16/1**
0161 **7** *5* **Dubai Sunshine (IRE)**[13] 6701 3-8-11 **86**..... StevieDonohoe 9 51
(Michael Bell) *hld up: hdwy over 3f out: rdn along wl over 2f out and sn wknd* **15/2**

1m 56.58s (4.58) **Going Correction** +0.70s/f (Yiel) **7** Ran SP% **114.9**
Speed ratings (Par 107): **107,106,104,101,99 93,88**
toteswingers 1&2 £2.00, 2&3 £2.80, 1&3 £4.70 CSF £7.61 CT £24.73 TOTE £4.10: £2.40, £1.40; EX 8.30 Trifecta £39.40 Pool: £1,807.99 - 33.91 winning tickets..
Owner T G & Mrs M E Holdcroft **Bred** Bearstone Stud **Trained** Musley Bank, N Yorks
■ Stewards' Enquiry : Frederik Tylicki two-day ban: used whip down shoulder in the forehand (Oct 29-30)

FOCUS
They appeared to go an even gallop in this and the front pair drew away late on. Sound form.

NOTEBOOK
Chapter Seven had contested a hot handicap at Newbury the time before and the slight drop in trip on softer ground enabled him to win for the third time this year. He should remain competitive in top handicaps, even after a rise. (op 4-1)
Lahaag, up 7lb for his Nottingham win, was unproven on ground slower than good to soft, but he handled it well and saw the race out gamely despite his tail spinning round under pressure. This represented another step forward and he's got the size to make up into a very useful 4-y-o. (op 15-8 tchd 2-1 in a place)
Lady Macduff(IRE) continues to run well on ground softer than ideal. Although she had a relatively easy time on the front, she was clearly struggling to pick her feet up out of the ground late on and remains capable of better from this mark when encountering a sounder surface.
Storm King didn't run badly from his new career-high mark, but he'll need to improve to win from it. He's rated 7lb lower on AW. (op 8-1)
Swing Alone(IRE) failed to reproduce his best in the first-time hood, probably finding the sticky ground against him. (tchd 7-1)
Jack Who's He(IRE) was keen and failed to pick up. (op 12-1 tchd 11-1)
Dubai Sunshine(IRE), up 4lb from Epsom, seemingly struggled on the ground. (op 7-1)

7065 CORAL.CO.UK ROCKINGHAM STKS (LISTED RACE) 6f
3:10 (3:14) (Class 1) 2-Y-O **£22,684** (£8,600; £4,304; £2,144; £1,076) **Stalls** Centre

Form RPR
1536 **1** **Royal Rascal**[21] 6467 2-8-9 101..... DavidAllan 6 96
(Tim Easterby) *trckd ldrs: hdwy 2f out: sn cl up: rdn to chal over 1f out: drvn to ld ins fnl f: kpt on strly* **3/1**[3]
1246 **2** *1 3/4* **Odooj (IRE)**[35] 6038 2-9-0 103..... PaulHanagan 1 96+
(William Haggas) *rrd and lost several lengths s: sn in tch: rdn to chse ldrs 2f out: drvn and kpt on fnl f* **2/1**[1]
1404 **3** *nse* **Lucky Beggar (IRE)**[7] 6865 2-9-0 98..... WilliamCarson 9 96
(Charles Hills) *cl up: led 2f out: sn rdn: drvn and hdd ins fnl f: eased and lost 2nd nr fin* **7/1**
113 **4** *1/2* **Queen Aggie (IRE)**[36] 6017 2-8-9 88..... PJMcDonald 3 89
(David Evans) *led: jnd 1/2-way: sn rdn along and hdd 2f out: drvn appr fnl f and kpt on same pce* **10/1**
0012 **5** *6* **Mary's Daughter**[21] 6467 2-8-9 95..... TonyHamilton 2 71
(Richard Fahey) *trckd ldng pair: hdwy and cl up 2f out: rdn along wl over 1f out: wknd ent fnl f* **5/2**[2]

1m 15.93s (4.03) **Going Correction** +0.60s/f (Yiel) **5** Ran SP% **108.5**
Speed ratings (Par 103): **97,94,94,93,85**
toteswingers 3&8 £4.90 CSF £9.12 TOTE £4.10: £2.00, £1.60; EX 9.00 Trifecta £53.10 Pool: £1,420.34 - 19.76 winning tickets..
Owner C H Stevens **Bred** Habton Farms **Trained** Great Habton, N Yorks
■ Stewards' Enquiry : William Carson ten-day ban: failing to rideout for 2nd (Oct 27,29-31, Nov 1-3,5-7)

FOCUS
Muddling 2yo form, with a couple not handling the ground and the runner-up losing his chance when rearing as the stalls opened. The winner is rated back to form in a race that lacked depth.

NOTEBOOK
Royal Rascal bounced back from a disappointing effort in the same grade at Ayr, responding well to pressure to make it 3-4 at the course, her one defeat coming when third in the Group 2 Lowther Stakes. She's a likeable type but will prove hard to place next season. Official explanation: trainer had no explanation for the apparent improvement in form (tchd 5-2)
Odooj(IRE) spread a plate on the way to the start and then lost any realistic chance on leaving the stalls. He did well to recover the ground and reach a challenging position, travelling well, but had used up his juice in getting there and his run flattened out, being fortunate to inherit second. He'd probably have won with more fortune. Official explanation: jockey said colt reared as gates opened (op 5-2 tchd 11-4 and 10-3 in a place)
Lucky Beggar(IRE) ran well in a weak Group 3 at Ascot the previous week and he'd have finished second here had his rider not dropped his hands for a few strides. (op 13-2 tchd 6-1)
Queen Aggie(IRE) has done really well considering she won a claimer on debut and she again deserves credit for sticking on despite appearing to not be in love with the ground. (op 15-2)

Mary's Daughter, ahead of the winner at Ayr, failed to give her running and possibly found the second experience of heavy testing ground too much. She's another who will be tough to place next season. (tchd 9-4)

7066 CORAL SPRINT TROPHY (H'CAP) 6f

3:45 (3:46) (Class 2) (0-105,106) 3-Y-O+

£46,687 (£13,980; £6,990; £3,495; £1,747; £877) **Stalls** Centre

Form RPR

3220 **1** **Regal Parade**[7] 6868 8-9-3 **103**.............................(t) MatthewLawson(5) 14 113
(Milton Bradley) *hld up in rr: gd hdwy on wd outside over 1f out: rdn and styd on strly ins fnl f: edgd lft last 100yds: styd on wl to ld nr fin* **14/1**

5230 **2** *shd* **Louis The Pious**[21] 6468 4-9-1 **96**.................................. DanielTudhope 8 106
(David O'Meara) *in tch: hdwy to chse ldrs over 2f out: rdn to chal ent fnl f: sn led and edgd lft: drvn and hung lft last 100yds: hdd nr fin* **6/1**[2]

6303 **3** *1 ¼* **Sirius Prospect (USA)**[25] 6346 4-9-7 **102**.......................(b) ShaneKelly 9 108
(Dean Ivory) *s.i.s and lost sveeral l s: in rr: gd hdwy wl over 1f out: sn rdn and styd on strly fnl f: nrst fin* **9/1**

0021 **4** *1 ¼* **Misplaced Fortune**[23] 6406 7-8-13 **94**..............................(v) DaleSwift 20 96
(Nigel Tinkler) *hld up towards rr: hdwy 2f out: rdn to chse ldrs over 1f out: styng on whn n.m.r ins fnl f: kpt on towards fin* **22/1**

3411 **5** *½* **Heeraat (IRE)**[34] 6075 3-9-5 **101**.................................... PaulHanagan 15 101+
(William Haggas) *cl up: led wl over 1f out: rdn and eged rt ent fnl f: sn drvn and hung lft: sn hdd & wknd* **7/2**[1]

0550 **6** *1 ½* **Dungannon**[70] 4802 5-9-2 **97**... LiamKeniry 4 92+
(Andrew Balding) *hld up: smooth hdwy over 2f out: sn chsng ldrs: rdn over 1f out and kpt on same pce* **14/1**

4101 **7** *nk* **Bubbly Bellini (IRE)**[13] 6716 5-8-10 **94**......................(p) IJBrennan(3) 16 88
(Adrian McGuinness, Ire) *hld up towards rr: hdwy 2f out: sn rdn and kpt on fnl f: nrst fin* **8/1**[3]

6150 **8** *1 ¼* **Johannes (IRE)**[21] 6468 9-8-7 **95**.......................... GeorgeChaloner(7) 13 85
(Richard Fahey) *towards rr: hdwy over 2f out: sn rdn and n.d* **20/1**

6004 **9** *1 ¼* **Mirza**[7] 6869 5-9-7 **102**... DarryllHolland 2 88
(Rae Guest) *trckd ldrs: hdwy wl over 1f out: rdn and ev ch ent fnl f: sn drvn and wknd* **16/1**

6005 **10** *½* **Miss Work Of Art**[7] 6878 3-8-13 **95**................................ FrederikTylicki 5 80
(Richard Fahey) *a towards rr* **20/1**

1505 **11** *nse* **Colonel Mak**[21] 6468 5-9-4 **99**..................................... GrahamGibbons 1 84
(David Barron) *prom: rdn 2f out: drvn and wknd appr fnl f* **10/1**

0510 **12** *2* **El Viento (FR)**[21] 6466 4-8-11 **92**..................................(b) TonyHamilton 6 70
(Richard Fahey) *led: rdn along over 2f out: hdd wl over 1f out and sn wknd* **25/1**

0060 **13** *7* **Brae Hill (IRE)**[7] 6868 6-9-2 **97**...................................... BarryMcHugh 12 53
(Richard Fahey) *in tch: rdn along 2f out: sn wknd* **16/1**

2201 **14** *1 ¼* **Mass Rally (IRE)**[21] 6466 5-9-4 **99**...........................(b) PaulMulrennan 18 51
(Michael Dods) *prom: rdn along wl over 1f out: sn drvn and wknd* **6/1**[2]

1m 14.04s (2.14) **Going Correction** +0.60s/f (Yiel)
WFA 3 from 4yo+ 1lb **14 Ran SP% 123.8**
Speed ratings (Par 109): **109,108,107,105,104 102,102,100,99,98 98,95,86,84**
toteswingers 1&2 £19.00, 2&3 £8.60, 1&3 £18.30 CSF £93.28 CT £822.19 TOTE £20.90: £5.30, £2.40, £3.10; EX 150.40 Trifecta £507.50 Pool: £1,714.61 - 2.50 winning tickets..
Owner Dab Hand Racing **Bred** Highclere Stud And Harry Herbert **Trained** Sedbury, Gloucs

FOCUS
They went hard enough up front early and the race set up the for the closers. Solid form, although the ground and pace played a part. The winner's best effort for over a year.

NOTEBOOK
Regal Parade, runner-up from 3lb lower in the Ayr Gold Cup, wasn't at his best over 7f at Ascot a week earlier but he produced a sustained run from the back here to just shade it. He may have been a tad fortunate, with the third looking unlucky, but it's hard to begrudge the 8yo his first success since landing the Group 1 Prix Maurice de Gheest back in 2010. (op 12-1)
Louis The Pious got considerably closer to the winner than he had done at Ayr, receiving a nice tow into the race and doing better with the headgear removed. (op 10-1)
Sirius Prospect(USA), last year's winner from 1lb lower, has failed to cut it at Group level this season, but there's no denying he was unlucky here returning to handicaps, rearing as the stalls opened and losing many lengths before finishing strongly. The concern going forward, however, is that this has become a trait since he's had the hood fitted. (tchd 8-1)
Misplaced Fortune was perhaps a little unlucky not to get closer, but she wouldn't have won. This was a good effort from her new 4lb higher mark. (op 20-1)
Heeraat(IRE), bidding for a hat-trick of course wins, was up 7lb and paid late on for racing on what was quite a strong pace. (op 9-2)
Dungannon was unable to pick up having travelled strongly, just keeping on at the one pace. He's got a race in him from this mark, but isn't the most reliable. (op 16-1)
Bubbly Bellini(IRE), 9lb higher than when winning with quite a bit in hand at the Curragh last time, was closing steadily without ever looking a threat. (op 7-1 tchd 6-1)
Mirza Official explanation: jockey said gelding lost its action
Mass Rally(IRE), ridden more forward than usual, failed to run to anything like the form of his Ayr Silver Cup win from 5lb higher, the way he dropped out suggesting something may have been amiss. Official explanation: trainer said gelding ran too free early (op 5-1)

7067 TEXT "MOBILE" TO "60006" CORAL E B F MAIDEN STKS 7f

4:20 (4:22) (Class 3) 2-Y-O **£7,439** (£2,213; £1,106; £553) **Stalls** Low

Form RPR

3 **1** **Mystery Bet (IRE)**[36] 6007 2-8-12 0................................ PaulHanagan 9 79
(Richard Fahey) *t.k.h early: trckd ldrs: hdwy over 2f out: swtchd lft and rdn along over 1f out: styd on wl to ld last 100yds* **5/2**[2]

002 **2** *2* **Lancelot Du Lac (ITY)**[24] 6377 2-9-3 83............................ BrettDoyle 1 79
(Dean Ivory) *trckd ldng pair: hdwy to chse ldr over 2f out: rdn and edgd rt over 1f out: swtchd lft and drvn ent fnl f: kpt on* **5/1**[3]

43 **3** *1 ¼* **You Da One (IRE)**[15] 6636 2-9-3 0.................................. LiamKeniry 4 76
(Andrew Balding) *wnt rt s: sn led: rdn along and edgd rt to stands' rail over 1f out: drvn ent fnl f: hdd & wknd last 100yds* **9/4**[1]

04 **4** *9* **Bitusa (USA)**[10] 6780 2-9-3 0.. RobertWinston 8 53
(Alan Swinbank) *sn chsng ldr: rdn along wl over 2f out: sn hung lft and wknd* **12/1**

0 **5** *1* **Lambert Pen (USA)**[9] 6818 2-8-12 0.......................... CharlesBishop(5) 11 51+
(Mick Channon) *wnt rt s: a in rr* **14/1**

6 *8* **Let Me In (IRE)** 2-9-3 0... AndrewMullen 6 31
(Nigel Tinkler) *hmpd s: a towards rr* **12/1**

7 *3 ¾* **Grayswood** 2-9-3 0.. GeorgeBaker 3 22
(William Muir) *a towards rr* **6/1**

1m 30.0s (4.70) **Going Correction** +0.60s/f (Yiel) **7 Ran SP% 112.3**
Speed ratings (Par 99): **97,94,93,83,81 72,68**
toteswingers 1&2 £2.80, 2&3 £3.70, 1&3 £1.90 CSF £14.82 TOTE £3.00: £2.00, £2.00; EX 9.60 Trifecta £15.80 Pool: £1,169.57 - 54.73 winning tickets..
Owner Mrs H Steel **Bred** Derek Veitch And Saleh Ali Hammadi **Trained** Musley Bank, N Yorks

FOCUS
No great depth to this juvenile maiden, with some of the more interesting contenders defecting, but it still provided a good test for these juveniles in the conditions. The first three were clear, showing fair form.

NOTEBOOK
Mystery Bet(IRE) confirmed the promise of her Haydock debut, benefiting from the step up in trip to outstay the strong-travelling placed runners. She has a bit of a knee action, suggesting some ease underfoot suits, and could develop into a fair type in handicaps next season. (tchd 9-4 and 11-4 in a place)
Lancelot Du Lac(ITY) is a strong-travelling type who's been committed too soon in earlier races. He was held on to longer this time, but the ground would have been testing enough and he couldn't stay on as strongly as the winner. It's a matter of time before he wins, whether it be a maiden or nursery. (op 4-1)
You Da One(IRE) travelled strongly in front but she hadn't encountered soft ground before and ultimately it proved too much of a stamina test. She's capable of winning a small maiden. (op 3-1)
Bitusa(USA) was well adrift of the first three but is now qualified for a mark and should appreciate drier ground. (op 9-1 tchd 14-1)
Lambert Pen(USA) Official explanation: trainer's rep said colt was unsuited by the soft (heavy in places) ground
Grayswood, a half-brother to numerous winners, most notably US Grade 1 winner Ticker Tape, was never involved but should leave this effort behind on better ground. (op 5-1 tchd 7-1)

7068 CORAL BACKING CHANGING FACES STKS (H'CAP) 2m 2f

4:55 (4:56) (Class 4) (0-85,84) 3-Y-O+ **£6,469** (£1,925; £962; £481) **Stalls** Low

Form RPR

0223 **1** **Mashaari (IRE)**[80] 4464 3-9-2 **84**....................................... PaulHanagan 3 94
(John Gosden) *trckd ldrs: hdwy over 3f out and sn cl up: rdn to chal 2f out: drvn and edgd lft ins fnl f: styd on to ld nr fin* **9/2**[2]

00/6 **2** *hd* **Cape Tribulation**[125] 2214 8-9-10 **80**............................... PJMcDonald 6 90
(Malcolm Jefferson) *a.p: led 3f out: rdn wl over 1f out: drvn ins fnl f: hdd and no ex towards fin* **6/1**

-656 **3** *1 ¾* **Valid Reason**[8] 6834 5-9-9 **79**... ShaneKelly 4 87
(Dean Ivory) *in tch: hdwy 5f out: chsd ldrs over 3f out: chal 2f out: sn rdn and ev ch tl drvn and one pce ins fnl f* **8/1**

052 **4** *3 ¼* **French Hollow**[22] 6428 7-9-10 **80**................................. FrederikTylicki 11 84
(Tim Fitzgerald) *hld up towards rr: stdy hdwy 7f out: trckd ldrs over 3f out: rdn along wl over 1f out: sn swtchd rt and no imp* **11/2**[3]

0-U3 **5** *shd* **Tiny Temper (IRE)**[13] 6706 4-8-10 **66** oh4.................... TonyHamilton 10 70
(Richard Fahey) *chsd ldrs: rdn along 3f out: drvn and one pce fnl 2f* **14/1**

3423 **6** *12* **Hawridge Star (IRE)**[36] 6019 10-9-5 **75**.......................... LiamKeniry 9 66
(Stuart Kittow) *hld up towards rr: sme hdwy over 4f out: sn rdn and nvr a factor* **10/1**

5000 **7** *17* **Becausewecan (USA)**[21] 6472 6-9-2 **72**................. SilvestreDeSousa 8 44
(Mark Johnston) *prom: led after 7f: rdn along over 4f out: hdd 3f out and sn wknd* **8/1**

0122 **8** *2* **Generous Dream**[10] 6784 4-8-10 **66** oh1......................... DavidAllan 12 36
(Mel Brittain) *cl up: effrt 4f out: sn rdn along and ev ch tl drvn 2f out and sn wknd* **12/1**

0606 **9** *18* **Fork Handles**[14] 6667 4-9-11 **81**.................................... GeorgeBaker 14 31
(Mick Channon) *a bhd* **16/1**

3241 **10** *61* **River Dragon (IRE)**[8] 6784 7-8-12 **68**............................. BarryMcHugh 1
(Tony Coyle) *led: pushed along and hdd after 7f: rdn along and lost pl 7f out: sn bhd: t.o fnl 4f* **4/1**[1]

4m 11.06s (15.66) **Going Correction** +0.70s/f (Yiel)
WFA 3 from 4yo+ 12lb **10 Ran SP% 119.4**
Speed ratings (Par 105): **93,92,92,90,90 85,77,76,68,41**
toteswingers 1&2 £6.00, 2&3 £8.40, 1&3 £6.70 CSF £32.60 CT £213.70 TOTE £5.00: £2.30, £2.70, £2.70; EX 37.40 Trifecta £130.10 Pool: £1,750.38 - 9.95 winning tickets..
Owner Hamdan Al Maktoum **Bred** Shadwell Estate Company Limited **Trained** Newmarket, Suffolk
■ Stewards' Enquiry : P J McDonald two-day ban: used whip above permitted level (Oct 29-30)
Paul Hanagan two-day ban: used whip above permitted level (Oct 29-30)

FOCUS
This was always likely to prove a dour test in the ground. The form makes a fair bit of sense amongst the first four, with the winner rated up 6lb.
River Dragon(IRE) Official explanation: jockey said gelding ran flat

7069 COLDSTREAM GUARDS ASSOCIATION CUP (HANDICAP STKS SUPPORTED BY MULBERRY HALL) 1m 2f 88y

5:30 (5:30) (Class 4) (0-85,85) 3-Y-O+ **£6,469** (£1,925; £962; £481) **Stalls** Low

Form RPR

5630 **1** **Bridle Belle**[21] 6476 4-9-5 **80**.. PaulHanagan 6 90
(Richard Fahey) *in tch: hdwy wl over 2f out: chsd ldrs wl over 1f out: sn rdn and chal ent fnl f: sn drvn and styd on gamely to ld last 50yds* **11/2**[3]

5345 **2** *½* **Crown Counsel (IRE)**[16] 6601 4-9-8 **83**................ SilvestreDeSousa 13 92
(Mark Johnston) *trckd ldrs: hdwy and cl up 3f out: rdn to ld jst over 1f out: drvn ins fnl f: hdd and no ex last 50yds* **8/1**

4322 **3** *2 ½* **Kay Gee Be (IRE)**[4] 6969 8-9-4 **82**................................. LeeTopliss(3) 16 86
(Richard Fahey) *in tch: hdwy 3f out: rdn to ld 2f out: drvn and hdd jst over 1f out: edgd lft and kpt on same pce fnl f* **13/2**

0511 **4** *hd* **Calaf**[11] 6757 4-9-7 **82**.. DaleSwift 3 86
(Brian Ellison) *hld up in rr: stdy hdwy 4f out: trckd ldrs 2f out: nt clr run and swtchd lft over 1f out: sn rdn and kpt on* **9/2**[2]

5005 **5** *4 ½* **Carragold**[7] 6884 6-8-12 **73**..(p) DavidAllan 4 68
(Mel Brittain) *prom: cl up 3f out: rdn along 2f out and ev ch tl drvn and one pce ent fnl f* **8/1**

5044 **6** *1 ½* **Tres Coronas (IRE)**[21] 6476 5-9-0 **80**............................. LMcNiff(5) 17 72
(David Barron) *hld up towards rr: stdy hdwy 3f out: swtchd rt and chal 2f out: sn rdn and ev ch tl wknd ins fnl f* **7/2**[1]

260 **7** *½* **Judicious**[21] 6476 5-8-12 **80**..................................... JacobButterfield(7) 20 72
(Ollie Pears) *cl up: rdn along wl over 2f out: wknd wl over 1f out* **25/1**

0004 **8** *½* **Kiwi Bay**[7] 6881 7-9-9 **84**.. PJMcDonald 1 75
(Michael Dods) *led: rdn along 3f out: drvn and hdd 2f out: grad wknd* **12/1**

610 **9** *2* **Nemushka**[42] 5820 3-9-1 **81**..................................(p) FrederikTylicki 10 68
(Richard Fahey) *hld up in rr: hdwy 4f out: rdn along 3f out: n.d* **16/1**

3106 **10** *½* **Fazza**[108] 3493 5-8-13 **81**.. DavidBergin(7) 15 67
(Edwin Tuer) *s.i.s and in rr: hdwy 4f out: chsd ldrs on outer wl over 2f out: sn rdn and wknd* **16/1**

3000 **11** *16* **Karaka Jack**[7] 6884 5-9-1 **76**.. AdrianNicholls 2 31
(David Nicholls) *chsd ldrs: rdn along wl over 3f out: sn wknd and bhd fnl 2f* **16/1**

2m 19.41s (6.91) **Going Correction** +0.70s/f (Yiel)
WFA 3 from 4yo+ 5lb **11 Ran SP% 120.5**
Speed ratings (Par 105): **100,99,97,97,93 92,92,91,90,89 77**
toteswingers 1&2 £10.00, 2&3 £8.30, 1&3 £8.20 CSF £50.47 CT £298.25 TOTE £6.20: £1.90, £2.70, £2.30; EX 36.30 Trifecta £283.20 Pool: £1,048.95 - 2.74 winning tickets..
Owner Mrs H Steel **Bred** Mrs C R Philipson & Mrs H G Lascelles **Trained** Musley Bank, N Yorks

FOCUS
The pace was quite a steady, in what was another depleted field, and any number held a chance in the straight as the runners started to bunch. Ultimately two drew on inside the final furlong. The form makes sense among the principals.
Nemushka Official explanation: trainer said filly was unsuited by the soft (heavy in places) ground
Karaka Jack Official explanation: jockey said gelding had no more to give
T/Jkpt: Part won. £40,934.80 to a £1 stake. Pool: £57,654.76 - 0.50 winning tickets. T/Plt: £156.10 to a £1 stake. Pool: £156,570.19 - 732.15 winning tickets. T/Qpdt: £41.80 to a £1 stake. Pool: £7,143.21 - 126.35 winning tickets. JR

7070 - 7072a (Foreign Racing) - See Raceform Interactive

6722 CAULFIELD (R-H)

Saturday, October 13

OFFICIAL GOING: Turf: good to soft changing to good after 4.15

7073a SPORTINGBET HERBERT POWER STKS (GROUP 2 H'CAP) (3YO+) (TURF) 1m 4f

6:50 (12:00) 3-Y-O+

£87,500 (£26,052; £13,026; £6,513; £3,618; £2,894)

RPR
1 **Shahwardi (FR)**[55] 5400 6-8-11 0 KerrinMcEvoy 13 107
(A De Royer-Dupre, France) **14/1**
2 *1* **Excluded (NZ)**[15] 5-8-7 0 (t) CraigAWilliams 9 101
(Robert Hickmott, Australia) **6/1**[2]
3 *1 ½* **Exceptionally (NZ)**[21] 6-8-7 0 (bt) DeanYendall 15 99
(Terry & Karina O'Sullivan, Australia) **13/2**[3]
4 *shd* **Ironstein (AUS)**[15] 7-8-11 0 BrentonAvdulla 5 103
(Gerald Ryan, Australia) **11/1**
5 *hd* **Silent Surround (AUS)**[21] 6-8-7 0 TimothyBell 1 99
(William Smart, Australia) **80/1**
6 *1 ½* **Precedence (NZ)**[15] 7-9-2 0 StevenArnold 6 105
(Bart Cummings, Australia) **14/1**
7 *1* **Gatewood**[48] 5650 4-8-11 0 CoreyBrown 4 99
(John Gosden) *sn settled in midfield on inner: shuffled bk and towards rr over 2f out: stl gng wl but nowhere to go 1 1/2f out: sn in the clr and rdn: styd on under hands and heels to go 7th cl home: n.d* **3/1**[1]
8 *1 ¾* **I'm Jake (NZ)**[360] 6967 7-8-7 0 (v) BenMelham 11 92
(David Brideoake & David Feek, Australia) **50/1**
9 *shd* **Reuben Percival (NZ)**[7] 6-8-8 0 (t) ChrisMunce 10 93
(Gai Waterhouse, Australia) **13/1**
10 *1 ¾* **Dance With Her (AUS)**[15] 6-8-9 0 (t) DwayneDunn 7 91
(David Brideoake & David Feek, Australia) **13/1**
11 *hd* **Bianmick (AUS)**[15] 6-8-10 0 DarrenGauci 14 91
(Michael Brady, Australia) **11/1**
12 *3* **Red Eye Special (NZ)**[360] 6967 6-8-7 0 (bt) MichaelWalker 2 84
(Michael Moroney, Australia) **100/1**
13 *2 ¼* **Mr O'Ceirin (NZ)**[21] 5-8-7 0 (b) GlenBoss 12 80
(Ciaron Maher, Australia) **8/1**
14 *shd* **Budai (GER)**[21] 6-8-7 0 (b) StevenKing 3 80
(David Hayes, Australia) **150/1**
15 *8* **Guns At Five (NZ)**[15] 5-8-7 0 (b) LukeNolen 8 67
(Peter G Moody, Australia) **30/1**
16 *10* **Auld Burns**[434] 4788 4-8-7 0 (p) NicholasHall 16 51
(David Hayes, Australia) **70/1**

2m 28.82s (148.82) **16** Ran SP% **117.5**
PARI-MUTUEL (NSW TAB - all including au$1 stakes): WIN 12.20 PLACE 3.90, 2.40, 2.80; DF 38.90; SF 75.50.
Owner Tony Bloom **Bred** H H The Aga Khan's Studs Sc **Trained** Chantilly, France

NOTEBOOK
Shahwardi(FR), formerly trained by Jeremy Gask, was only released from quarantine on the morning of racing, but showed no ill-effects. French trainers have won the last two runnings of the Melbourne Cup, with de Royer-Dupre successful in 2010 with Americain, and the trainer appears to have another live contender. As a result of his victory Shahwardi earns an automatic berth in the Caulfield Cup, though he is not certain to take up that engagement. The Melbourne Cup is the main target, and Shahwardi will be given a penalty on Monday.
Gatewood, a consistent and progressive colt, was sent off favourite but failed to get a clear run and can be expected to do better next time.

7074 - (Foreign Racing) - See Raceform Interactive

6725 SAN SIRO (R-H)

Saturday, October 13

OFFICIAL GOING: Turf: good

7075a PREMIO VERZIERE (MEM. ALDO CIRLA) (GROUP 3) (3YO+ FILLIES & MARES) (TURF) 1m 2f

2:50 (12:00) 3-Y-O+ **£23,333** (£10,266; £5,600; £2,800)

RPR
1 **Cartaya**[24] 4-9-0 0 UmbertoRispoli 7 103
(M Rulec, Germany) *midfield: swtchd outside and smooth hdwy 1 1/2f out: led ent fnl f: sn clr: won easing down* **9/2**
2 *2 ½* **French Quebec (IRE)**[84] 3-8-9 0 MEsposito 1 98
(Cestmir Olehla, Czech Republic) *trckd ldrs: rdn to hold pl 3 1/2f out: kpt on u.p fr 1 1/2f out: tk 2nd fnl 75yds: no ch w wnr* **7/1**
3 *¾* **Samba Brazil (GER)**[13] 6726 3-8-9 0 MircoDemuro 8 96
(A Wohler, Germany) *pressed ldr: chal on outside 2f out: led 1 1/2f out: sn rdn and hdd ent fnl f: no ex and lost 2nd 75yds out* **9/5**[1]
4 *¾* **Reyal (ITY)**[13] 4-9-0 0 CristianDemuro 5 95
(S Botti, Italy) *settled towards rr: prog u.p to chse ldrs fr 1/12f out: kpt on fnl f: nt pce to chal ldrs but tk 4th on line* **43/10**[3]
5 *nse* **Global Magic (GER)**[13] 6723 4-9-0 0 (p) EPedroza 3 94
(A Wohler, Germany) *settled towards rr: effrt to go 4th over 1f out: plugged on fnl f: lost 4th on line* **16/5**[2]
6 *2 ¼* **Aquila D'Oriente (ITY)**[111] 3426 3-8-9 0 LManiezzi 6 90
(S Botti, Italy) *hld up in last: rdn and no imp 2f out: n.d* **224/10**
7 *4* **Faciascura**[13] 3-8-11 0 FabioBranca 2 84
(S Botti, Italy) *led: rdn 2f out: hdd 1 1/2f out: wknd appr 1f out: eased* **83/10**
8 *7* **C'Est Moi (IRE)**[59] 4-9-0 0 PierantonioConvertino 4 68
(R Biondi, Italy) *trckd ldrs: rdn and nt qckn 2f out: wknd fr 1 1/2f out: eased fnl f* **10/1**

2m 3.8s (-2.90)
WFA 3 from 4yo+ 5lb **8** Ran SP% **133.2**
WIN (incl. 1 euro stake): 5.51. PLACES: 1.83, 2.13, 1.50. DF: 14.52.
Owner Gestut Burg Eberstein **Bred** Darpat S L **Trained** Germany

7076a GRAN CRITERIUM (GROUP 1) (2YO COLTS & FILLIES) (TURF) 1m

4:00 (12:00) 2-Y-O **£79,166** (£34,833; £19,000; £9,500)

RPR
1 **Law Enforcement (IRE)**[42] 5836 2-8-11 0 StephanePasquier 10 110
(Richard Hannon) *trckd ldr in 2nd: rdn over 3f out: hdwy to chal 2f out: led jst ins fnl f: styd on wl u.p to extend advantage cl home* **109/20**[3]
2 *1* **Sorella Bella (IRE)**[13] 6725 2-8-8 0 SamHitchcott 3 105
(Mick Channon) *broke wl to ld: 2 l clr and stl gng wl 3f out: rdn and strly pressed fr 2f out: hdd jst ins fnl f: kpt on wl u.p but no rspnse to wnr cl home: jst hld on for 2nd* **87/10**
3 *nse* **Pearl Flute (IRE)**[21] 6507 2-8-11 0 UmbertoRispoli 7 108
(F-H Graffard, France) *hld up in last trio: smooth hdwy over 3f out: rdn and wnt 3rd 1 1/2f out: styd on ins fnl f: almost snatched 2nd on post but nvr on terms w wnr* **17/10**[1]
4 *2* **Deauville Prince (FR)**[21] 6507 2-8-11 0 RichardKingscote 6 103
(Tom Dascombe) *midfield: rdn and brief effrt 2 1/2f out: sn outpcd by ldrs and fdd: plugged on u.p ins fnl f* **13/2**
5 *¾* **Virtual Game (IRE)**[20] 2-8-11 0 CristianDemuro 8 102
(S Botti, Italy) *stdd s and hld up in last: rdn 3f out: styd on to go 5th ins fnl f: nt pce to chal* **116/10**
6 *5* **Best Tango (ITY)**[20] 2-8-11 0 FabioBranca 4 91
(S Botti, Italy) *midfield: lost pl and dropped towards rr over 4f out: rdn and sme prog fr over 3f out: hung rt and flashed tail u.p: no ex and btn ent fnl f: eased* **30/1**
7 *2 ½* **Nabucco (GER)**[20] 2-8-11 0 MircoDemuro 1 84
(R Rohne, Germany) *prom on inner: rdn in cl 3rd 3f out: outpcd 2f out and fdd: btn ent fnl f: eased* **12/5**[2]
8 *2 ½* **Pearl Of Love (GER)**[45] 2-8-8 0 FilipMinarik 2 76
(T Potters, Germany) *midfield on inner: rdn 4f out: outpcd and btn over 2f out: fdd: eased ins fnl f* **166/10**
9 *8* **Demeteor (ITY)**[20] 2-8-11 0 LManiezzi 9 60
(R Menichetti, Italy) *hld up in last trio: rdn over 3f out: sn outpcd and btn: eased over 1f out* **88/1**
10 *½* **Castello Aragonese**[83] 2-8-11 0 PierantonioConvertino 12 59
(R Biondi, Italy) *plld hrd in midfield: rdn and sharp reminders over 3f out: btn and eased 2f out* **26/1**
11 *10* **Tiger Day**[28] 2-8-11 0 DarioVargiu 11 36
(B Grizzetti, Italy) *midfield on outer: rdn over 2 1/2f out: sn no ex and btn: eased over 1f out and sn last* **97/10**

1m 37.1s (-5.00) **11** Ran SP% **136.6**
WIN (incl. 1 euro stake): 6.45. PLACES: 2.07, 2.66, 1.49. DF: 24.96.
Owner M S Al Shahi **Bred** Mrs E J O'Grady **Trained** East Everleigh, Wilts

FOCUS
The form is up to scratch for the race.
NOTEBOOK
Law Enforcement(IRE) has done nothing but progress this season, and made the step up from nursery company to pick up this valuable prize. He could well return to Italy for the Italian Guineas next season and possibly the Italian Derby later on.
Sorella Bella(IRE), bidding for a hat-trick having won a Listed race here last time, made the running and dug deep when pressed by Law Enforcement 2f out, but the colt proved too strong.
Deauville Prince(FR) was just over a length behind today's third in a Longchamp Group 3 last time but finished a little further back on this better ground. The pair help set the level.

6571 GOODWOOD (R-H)

Sunday, October 14

OFFICIAL GOING: Soft (6.0)
Wind: Light, across Weather: Fine

7077 BETFRED BIGGER AND BETTER GOALS GALORE ALDERBROOK STKS (H'CAP) (FOR PROFESSIONAL NH JOCKEYS) 2m

2:00 (2:00) (Class 5) (0-70,73) 4-Y-O+ **£3,234** (£962; £481; £240) **Stalls** High

Form RPR
3-00 **1** **Tartan Jura**[14] 6706 4-11-9 **67** JasonMaguire 16 77
(Mark Johnston) *prom: rdn over 3f out: led u.p over 2f out: narrowly hdd over 1f out: edgd rt: bmpd runner-up and led again ins fnl f: forged clr* **16/1**
1243 **2** *1 ½* **Our Folly**[45] 5772 4-11-4 **62** (t) PaddyBrennan 2 70
(Stuart Kittow) *slowest away: hld up wl in rr: prog over 5f out: trckd ldrs 3f out: swtchd ins and hdwy to take narrow ld over 1f out: bmpd and hdd ins fnl f: rdn and nt qckn after* **8/1**
2-32 **3** *¾* **Sainglend**[42] 2575 7-11-4 **62** SeanFox 8 69
(Sean Curran) *prom: brought to chal on outer over 2f out: nt qckn over 1f out: styd on* **13/2**[3]
3311 **4** *10* **Presto Volante (IRE)**[11] 6802 4-12-1 **73** (p) LeightonAspell 11 68
(Amanda Perrett) *in tch in midfield: effrt 4f out: outpcd by ldrs 2f out: plugged on to take 4th nr fin* **7/2**[1]
5 *½* **Electric Tiger (GER)**[350] 5-11-2 **60** TommyPhelan 9 55
(David Bridgwater) *hld up wl in rr: prog and n.m.r 6f out: hdwy to trck ldrs over 3f out: cl 4th over 2f out: wknd over 1f out* **50/1**
0060 **6** *1* **Rulbin Realta**[118] 3222 5-10-7 **51** oh1 RichardKilloran 10 44
(Pat Phelan) *hld up wl in rr: lost tch w main gp 5f out and drvn: kpt on to pass wkng rivals fnl 3f* **66/1**
5246 **7** *¾* **Kings Troop**[14] 6703 6-11-7 **65** (v) RobertThornton 12 57
(Alan King) *in tch in midfield: rdn to chse ldrs over 3f out: no imp over 2f out: wknd* **9/1**
060 **8** *2* **Taigan (FR)**[109] 3484 5-11-9 **67** HarrySkelton 1 57
(Ian Williams) *trckd ldrs: gng strly 5f out: drvn over 2f out: sn wknd* **20/1**
1204 **9** *¾* **Waterford Star (IRE)**[24] 6407 4-11-10 **68** (v) TimmyMurphy 4 57
(Ian Williams) *trckd ldng pair: prog to ld 6f out: drvn and hdd over 2f out: wkng whn hmpd sn after* **8/1**
4215 **10** *6* **Three White Socks (IRE)**[47] 5718 5-11-11 **69** DannyCook 14 51
(Brian Ellison) *w ldr: drvn 5f out: wknd qckly over 2f out* **14/1**
5/6- **11** *nk* **Sarando**[232] 6998 7-11-2 **60** (t) DominicElsworth 5 42
(Paul Webber) *sn dropped to last: lost tch over 5f out: nvr on terms after* **25/1**

0/60 **12** *1 1/4* **Princely Hero (IRE)**[9] 3572 8-11-2 **60**........................(b) MarcGoldstein 6 40
(Chris Gordon) *s.i.s: rousted to go prom: lost pl 6f out: bhd fnl 4f* **50/1**
2-20 **13** *32* **Dance For Livvy (IRE)**[15] 6691 4-11-5 **63**........................ BarryKeniry 7
(Robin Dickin) *in tch tl wknd 6f out: sn t.o: eased fnl 2f* **22/1**
40-2 **14** *3 1/2* **Pocket Too**[159] 1952 9-10-12 **56**........................(p) AndrewGlassonbury 15
(Victor Dartnall) *mde most to 6f out: sn drvn: wknd rapidly over 3f out: t.o* **11/2**[2]
1600 **15** *38* **Ponte Di Rosa**[22] 6478 4-11-1 **59**.................................. JamesDavies 13
(Michael Appleby) *chsd ldrs tl wknd rapidly over 6f out: sn bhd: t.o and eased over 2f out* **33/1**

3m 42.47s (13.47) **Going Correction** +0.475s/f (Yiel) **15** Ran SP% **117.0**
Speed ratings (Par 103): **85,84,83,78,78 78,77,76,76,73 73,72,56,54,35**
toteswingers 1&2 £19.60, 2&3 £6.80, 1&3 £22.90 CSF £125.02 CT £927.81 TOTE £17.70: £4.00, £2.80, £2.40; EX 238.60 Trifecta £455.60 Part won. Pool: £615.71 - 0.10 winning tickets..
Owner Frank Bird **Bred** Newsells Park Stud **Trained** Middleham Moor, N Yorks
■ Stewards' Enquiry : Jason Maguire two-day ban: careless riding (Oct 29-30)
Tommy Phelan four-day ban: used whip above permitted level (Oct 29-Nov 1)

FOCUS
Following a dry night the going was soft. The top bend was dolled out 3yds, increasing distances by 8yds, and the lower bend was dolled out 3yds, increasing distances by 7yds. A staying handicap for jump jockeys, and a real test in the conditions.

7078 GREENE KING IPA MEDIAN AUCTION MAIDEN STKS 6f
2:35 (2:35) (Class 5) 2-Y-0 **£3,234** (£962; £481; £240) **Stalls** High

Form RPR
4 **1** **Don Marco**[23] 6443 2-9-3 0.. GeorgeBaker 4 85+
(Roger Charlton) *t.k.h: trckd ldrs: smooth prog to ld wl over 1f out: shkn up whn pressed ins fnl f: sn asserted: readily* **3/1**[1]
5 **2** *2 1/4* **Maid A Million**[26] 6335 2-8-12 0.................................... SebSanders 7 73
(David Elsworth) *s.s: t.k.h and sn in tch: rdn and prog over 2f out: wnt 2nd over 1f out: tried to chal fnl f: sn outpcd* **10/1**
0 **3** *3 1/4* **Hornboy**[16] 6636 2-9-3 0.. WilliamBuick 1 68
(Jeremy Noseda) *in tch on outer: shkn up and prog over 2f out: outpcd over 1f out: styd on to take 3rd nr fin* **7/2**[2]
4 *1 1/2* **Little Choosey** 2-8-12 0.. JohnFahy 2 59
(Clive Cox) *trckd ldr: led over 2f out to wl over 1f out: wknd fnl f* **33/1**
04 **5** *1 1/4* **Brownsea Brink**[11] 6795 2-9-3 0.................................. RichardHughes 6 60+
(Richard Hannon) *t.k.h: hld up in rr: shkn up and no prog 2f out: kpt on fnl f* **7/2**[2]
6 *3/4* **Apricot Sky** 2-9-3 0.. FergusSweeney 9 58
(Henry Candy) *racd against nr side rail: trckd ldrs: effrt 2f out: wknd jst over 1f out* **22/1**
7 *hd* **Carry On Sydney** 2-9-3 0.. PatDobbs 12 57+
(Richard Hannon) *dwlt: wl in rr: shkn up over 2f out: kpt on fr over 1f out: nrst fin* **12/1**
520 **8** *1/2* **Herbalist**[10] 6818 2-9-3 78... DaneO'Neill 10 56
(Henry Candy) *led to over 2f out: sn wknd* **6/1**[3]
0 **9** *6* **Edge Of Glory**[38] 5978 2-8-12 0...................................... JoeFanning 11 33+
(Richard Hannon) *s.s: t.k.h in rr: rdn and effrt over 2f out: wknd qckly over 1f out* **33/1**
10 *1 1/4* **Limoges** 2-8-12 0... LiamKeniry 13 29
(Gary Moore) *a in rr: wknd 2f out* **66/1**
6 **11** *nk* **Opus Cactus (USA)**[17] 6609 2-8-12 0................................ MartinHarley 5 28
(Marco Botti) *trckd ldrs tl wknd qckly 2f out* **25/1**
12 *15* **Guru Baby** 2-8-12 0... RichardThomas 3
(John E Long) *rn green: sn last: wknd bef 1/2-way: t.o* **200/1**

1m 15.64s (3.44) **Going Correction** +0.40s/f (Good) **12** Ran SP% **116.6**
Speed ratings (Par 95): **93,90,85,83,82 81,80,80,72,70 70,50**
toteswingers 1&2 £6.60, 2&3 £7.50, 1&3 £3.50 CSF £31.18 TOTE £3.90: £1.40, £2.40, £1.70; EX 33.40 Trifecta £130.10 Pool: £998.64 - 5.68 winning tickets..
Owner Lady Rothschild **Bred** The Rt Hon Lord Rothschild **Trained** Beckhampton, Wilts

FOCUS
This looked a fair maiden but due to the time of year a cautious approach has been taken. The winner did it well.

NOTEBOOK
Don Marco, whose promising debut effort had come on fast ground at Newbury, had questions to answer on this much softer surface, but his dam was a multiple winner in testing ground in France and he had no trouble with conditions, travelling well and quickening away to easily. He looks the type who could make up into a nice sprint handicapper next season.
Maid A Million was tardily away and keen early, but she came through to provide the only challenge, albeit brief, to the winner. She'll make her mark in handicaps in due course, but might be able to find a maiden before that. (op 11-1 tchd 12-1)
Hornboy, who was well backed, was drawn on the wide outside and outpaced by the first two in the closing stages, but he kept on reasonably well and there's better to come from him. (op 11-2)
Little Choosey, a half-sister to 7f winner Little Rainbow, seemed to know her job first time out and did best of the newcomers having raced up with the pace from the start. (op 40-1)
Brownsea Brink, dropped back in distance from 1m, just didn't settle in mid-pack and couldn't get competitive when the race got serious. He's eligible for a mark now and should have more to offer in handicaps next year. (op 3-1 tchd 11-4)
Apricot Sky, who only cost 4,000GBP, showed some ability on his debut. (op 25-1 tchd 20-1)
Carry On Sydney caught the eye keeping on nicely at the finish. He's a brother to 1m 2yo winner Plym and half-brother to 2000 Guineas third Frenchmans Bay, and he'll do better over a longer trip in time. (op 16-1)
Herbalist tried to make all but he hung right when pressure was applied and dropped right out. He might need better ground than this to show his best. (op 9-2 tchd 4-1)
Guru Baby Official explanation: trainer's rep said filly had sore shins

7079 BETFRED IRISH STALLION FARMS E B F NURSERY 7f
3:10 (3:10) (Class 4) (0-85,81) 2-Y-0 **£5,175** (£1,540; £769; £384) **Stalls** Low

Form RPR
0404 **1** **Empiricist (IRE)**[30] 6204 2-9-2 **76**.. PatDobbs 1 80
(Amanda Perrett) *trckd ldng trio: styd alone on far side in st and sn overall ldr: drvn over 1f out: styd on* **11/2**[3]
3610 **2** *1 1/4* **Aint Got A Scooby (IRE)**[44] 5786 2-8-4 **64**......................... JohnFahy 4 65
(Clive Cox) *t.k.h: hld up: c nr side st: plld out and prog over 1f out: r.o to ld gp nr fin* **8/1**
01 **3** *nk* **Surge Ahead (IRE)**[17] 6603 2-9-5 **79**............................... WilliamBuick 9 79
(Ed Walker) *led fr wdst draw: brought all but wnr to nr side in st and sn lost overall ld: racd against rail and drvn 2f out: lost gp ld nr fin* **11/4**[1]
3034 **4** *hd* **Summer Dream (IRE)**[43] 5818 2-9-1 **75**........................... MartinHarley 6 75
(Marco Botti) *t.k.h: hld up in tch: c nr side st: nt clr run briefly over 2f out: prog to press ldr over 1f out: upsides fnl f: nt qckn* **14/1**
4306 **5** *1* **Club House (IRE)**[18] 6572 2-8-3 **70**..........................[1] DanielCremin(7) 7 67
(Robert Mills) *racd awkwardly early: hld up: c nr side st: trapped bhd rivals against rail over 2f out to over 1f out: styd on but nvr able to chal* **25/1**
5510 **6** *2 1/4* **Colmar Kid (IRE)**[31] 6162 2-9-6 **80**.................................. RichardHughes 8 73
(Richard Hannon) *prom: c nr side st: drvn wl over 2f out: wknd over 1f out* **4/1**[2]
031 **7** *1 3/4* **Shebebi (USA)**[42] 5851 2-9-7 **81**...................................... PaulHanagan 5 68
(John Dunlop) *hld up in last: c nr side st: prog to chse ldrs over 1f out: sn wknd* **11/2**[3]
3100 **8** *nk* **Haatefina**[10] 6815 2-8-12 **72**... DavidProbert 3 58
(Mark Usher) *chsd ldr: c nr side st: lost 2nd over 1f out: wknd fnl f* **20/1**
5045 **9** *16* **Sinaadi (IRE)**[16] 6632 2-9-6 **80**....................................... NeilCallan 2 26
(Clive Brittain) *in tch: c nr side st: wknd qckly 2f out: t.o* **8/1**

1m 32.14s (5.14) **Going Correction** +0.475s/f (Yiel) **9** Ran SP% **114.9**
Speed ratings (Par 97): **89,87,87,87,85 83,81,80,62**
toteswingers 1&2 £8.40, 2&3 £5.00, 1&3 £5.20 CSF £48.49 CT £146.90 TOTE £6.30: £1.90, £2.20, £1.90; EX 51.20 Trifecta £154.70 Pool: £1,513.76 - 7.24 winning tickets..
Owner John Connolly & Odile Griffith **Bred** Drumlin Bloodstock **Trained** Pulborough, W Sussex

FOCUS
The field split as they entered the straight and the winner stayed alone on the far side. The runner-up is the bset guide.

NOTEBOOK
Empiricist(IRE), who stayed alone on the far side, just lasted home from the main bunch, who had crossed over to race on the stands' rail, and were closing fast at the line. The winner promised to be suited by the return to 7f, and his trainer was confident that the softer ground would suit him better, so it would be wrong to suggest that he won simply because his rider took the right route. Indeed, it's possible he won despite sticking to the far side. (op 8-1)
Aint Got A Scooby(IRE) bounced back from a below-par effort at Salisbury, again showing his liking for a soft surface. He 'won' his race on the stands' side but the winner had gone beyond recall on the far side. (op 10-1)
Surge Ahead(IRE), who made all at Pontefract last time, made a good first of trying to repeat the trick. The extra furlong wasn't a problem. (op 5-2)
Summer Dream(IRE), debuting in a handicap, might benefit from a drop back to 6f, as once again she didn't quite see her race out. (op 12-1 tchd 10-1)
Club House(IRE) shaped better in the first-time hood. (op 33-1)
Colmar Kid(IRE) was again below his best, perhaps finding the ground too testing. (op 9-2)
Shebebi(USA), who has had problems at the start before, went into the stalls last and behaved himself this time. A fast-ground maiden winner at Folkestone, he's by a sire whose progeny tend to prefer a decent surface, and this ground was probably not to his liking. (op 4-1)
Sinaadi(IRE) Official explanation: jockey said filly never travelled

7080 BETFRED "THE HOME OF GOALS GALORE" STKS (H'CAP) 6f
3:45 (3:46) (Class 3) (0-95,95) 3-Y-0+ **£8,409** (£2,502; £1,250; £625) **Stalls** High

Form RPR
1226 **1** **Prodigality**[29] 6244 4-8-11 **90**.. DarrenEgan(5) 5 99+
(Ronald Harris) *trckd ldrs: clsd over 2f out: led over 1f out: rdn and edgd lft after: styd on wl* **2/1**[1]
0300 **2** *1* **Sugar Beet**[28] 6286 4-9-2 **90**.. DavidProbert 2 96
(Ronald Harris) *chsd ldrs: rdn 2f out: chal 1f out: carried lft fnl f: a hld* **50/1**
0041 **3** *shd* **Ajjaadd (USA)**[20] 6543 6-8-11 **92**...............(p) WilliamTwiston-Davies(7) 9 98
(Ted Powell) *n.m.r s: wl in rr: prog over 2f out: shifted rt over 1f out u.p: styd on fnl f: nrst fin* **20/1**
6000 **4** *1/2* **Summerinthecity (IRE)**[6] 6938 5-8-11 **85**........................ LiamKeniry 14 89
(Ed de Giles) *trckd ldrs but nt on terms: shkn up over 2f out: drvn over 1f out: styd on fnl f: nrst fin* **20/1**
2605 **5** *1/2* **Gouray Girl (IRE)**[51] 5530 5-8-11 **85**................................ DaneO'Neill 1 87
(Henry Candy) *taken down early: slowly away: wl off the pce in last pair: stdy prog 2f out: clsd 1f out: kpt on same pce fnl f* **8/1**[3]
1030 **6** *3/4* **Fillionaire**[17] 6602 3-8-6 **81**... SamHitchcott 13 81
(Mick Channon) *chsd ldrs but nt on terms: drvn and struggling over 2f out: kpt on again fnl f* **20/1**
0260 **7** *nk* **Nasri**[15] 6659 6-8-13 **87**.. DarryllHolland 17 86
(Milton Bradley) *led to 1/2-way: sn u.p: one pce fnl 2f* **16/1**
3050 **8** *hd* **My Kingdom (IRE)**[10] 6820 6-8-8 **82**...........................(t) WilliamCarson 8 80
(Stuart Williams) *wl in rr: drvn 2f out: kpt on one pce u.p fr over 1f out: n.d* **16/1**
0000 **9** *1/2* **King Of Jazz (IRE)**[36] 6024 4-9-2 **90**............................(v) GeorgeBaker 7 87
(Michael Bell) *hld up wl in rr: stdy prog fr 1/2-way: chsd ldrs over 1f out: wl hld whn squeezed for room jst ins fnl f* **20/1**
4340 **10** *1/2* **Sohraab**[31] 6165 8-8-12 **86**...(v) RichardHughes 4 81
(Hughie Morrison) *w ldr: led 1/2-way: hdd & wknd over 1f out* **8/1**[3]
1250 **11** *1 3/4* **Farlow (IRE)**[78] 4611 4-9-1 **89**.. SebSanders 6 79
(Ralph Beckett) *wl in rr: u.p fr 1/2-way: prog 2f out: keeping on but hld whn hmpd over 1f out: nt rcvr* **20/1**
/040 **12** *1/2* **Head Of Steam (USA)**[33] 6119 5-9-3 **91**............................ PatDobbs 3 79
(Amanda Perrett) *towards rr: effrt 2f out: one pce and hld whn impeded over 1f out* **20/1**
4051 **13** *3 3/4* **Coolminx (IRE)**[21] 6515 5-8-10 **84**..............................(p) PaulHanagan 11 60
(Richard Fahey) *chsd ldrs to 1/2-way: sn lost pl and wknd* **8/1**[3]
6020 **14** *6* **R Woody**[12] 6767 5-8-10 **84**... WilliamBuick 16 41
(Robert Cowell) *a towards rr: wknd 2f out* **15/2**[2]
05 **15** *6* **Caratteraccio (IRE)**[26] 6346 4-9-7 **95**............................ MartinHarley 15 33
(Marco Botti) *s.i.s: rcvrd into midfield after 2f: wknd over 2f out: t.o* **33/1**
4000 **16** *2 1/4* **Bayleyf (IRE)**[71] 4802 3-9-1 **90**...................................... FergusSweeney 10 20
(John Best) *trckd ldrs tl wknd qckly over 2f out: t.o* **33/1**

1m 13.48s (1.28) **Going Correction** +0.40s/f (Good)
WFA 3 from 4yo+ 1lb **16** Ran SP% **126.6**
Speed ratings (Par 107): **107,105,105,104,104 103,102,102,101,101 98,98,93,85,77 74**
toteswingers 1&2 £27.30, 2&3 £125.90, 1&3 £9.80 CSF £154.35 CT £1753.11 TOTE £2.90: £1.10, £11.10, £5.20, £3.90; EX 156.80 Trifecta £1315.70 Part won. Pool: £1,778.00 - 0.63 winning tickets..
Owner Paul Moulton **Bred** Darley **Trained** Earlswood, Monmouths
■ Stewards' Enquiry : William Twiston-Davies 1st incid: three-day ban: careless riding (Oct 29-31); 2nd incid: caution, careless riding.

FOCUS
A big field sprint, but the market spoke strongly in favour of the winner.

NOTEBOOK
Prodigality was sent off a short price, and he landed the gamble despite edging left, almost all the way over to the stands' side, inside the last. Running off the same mark as when 'winning' the race on his side in the Portland last time, he deserved a change of fortune, and gained due reward for a strong of consistent efforts. He could have another run at Doncaster before the season is out. (op 5-2 tchd 3-1)
Sugar Beet, a stablemate of the winner, bounced back to form with conditions to suit on a track where she has run well in the past.
Ajjaadd(USA), who has done all his winning over 5f, ran well over a trip that's just beyond his ideal. (op 16-1)
Summerinthecity(IRE) backed up his fair effort at Wolverhampton last time when returning from almost four months off, and looks to be running into form.
Gouray Girl(IRE), fifth in this race last year, trailed the field early but was staying on at the finish. She struggles to win but her late-running style often gets her placed. (op 9-1)

Fillionaire, who has run well here in the past, put in a solid effort off a stiff mark. (tchd 22-1)
Nasri has always been a hard horse to win with. Official explanation: jockey said gelding hung left
My Kingdom (IRE) has now gone 22 starts on turf without a success.
Sohraab, with a visor on instead of blinkers, is more of a 5f horse, and after making the early running he dropped out. (op 10-1)
R Woody, who won this race two years ago, was well below his best. (op 11-2)

7081 BRITISH STALLION STUDS SUPPORTING BRITISH RACING E B F MAIDEN STKS 1m 1f

4:20 (4:21) (Class 4) 2-Y-O £4,851 (£1,443; £721 ; £360) Stalls Low

Form				RPR
23	1		**Nichols Canyon**25 6371 2 -9-30 WilliamBuick 2 (John Gosden) *rousted along to chse ldrs: pushed along over 3f out: prog to press ldr over 1f out: hrd rdn to ld ins fnl f: styd on strly* **10/3**2	79+
0	2	2	**Elidor**25 6371 2 -9-30 (v1) MartinHarley 7 (Mick Channon) *trckd ldrs: prog to ld 2f out: sn drvn: styd on but hdd and no ex ins fnl f* **20/1**	75
033	3	6	**Another Cocktail**23 6447 2 -9-381 DarryllHolland 5 (Hughie Morrison) *led after 1f: drvn and jnd 3f out: hdd 2f out: steadily wknd* **5/1**3	63
3	4	nk	**Excellent Result (IRE)**17 6596 2 -9-30 SilvestreDeSousa 11 (Saeed Bin Suroor) *trckd ldr after 1f: gng strly whn chalng and upsides 3f out: drvn 2f out: steadily wknd* **5/2**1	62
4	5	nse	**Mister Impatience**17 6607 2 -9-30 JoeFanning 4 (Mark Johnston) *led 1f: trckd ldng pair: easily outpcd fr over 2f out: kpt on again nr fin* **12/1**	62
05	6	5	**Flemish School**11 6791 2 -8-120 NeilCallan 9 (Gerard Butler) *in tch: drvn 3f out: no imp over 2f out: sn wknd* **12/1**	47
22	7	1 1/2	**Swing Easy**24 6412 2 -9-30 StevieDonohoe 10 (Robert Mills) *hld up in rr: effrt to chse ldrs 3f out: wknd 2f out* **8/1**	49+
	8	29	**White Month** 2 -9-30 DavidProbert 8 (Andrew Balding) *rn green in last trio: shkn up and wknd 3f out: t.o* **33/1**	
03	9	38	**Pentagram (USA)**20 6532 2 -9-30 (p) MickaelBarzalona 3 (Mahmood Al Zarooni) *sn lost prom pl: rdn in rr bef 1/2-way: sn wknd: wl t.o* **25/1**	
06	10	11	**A Ladies Man (IRE)**32 6491 2 -9-30 RichardHughes 1 (Richard Hannon) *a in rr: wknd over 3f out: wl t.o* **12/1**	

2m 0.44s (4.14) **Going Correction** +0.475s/f (Yiel) 10Ran SP% 114.1
Speed ratings (Par 97): **100,98,92,92,92 88,86,61,27,17**
toteswingers 1&2 £14.20, 2&3 £19.80, 1&3 £4.10 CSF £68.95 TOTE £4.40 : £1.40 , £7.40 , £1.90 ; EX 83.00 Trifecta £538.70 Pool: £3,465.29 - 4.76 winning tickets. .
Owner Rachel Hood & Elaine Lawlor **Bred** Rabbah Bloodstock Limited **Trained** Newmarket, Suffolk

FOCUS
Not a bad maiden, and a real test of stamina for these 2yos. The first two finished clear and the winner should progress next year.

NOTEBOOK
Nichols Canyon had been strong at the finish in both his previous starts, and this extra furlong coupled with a more testing surface promised to play to his strengths. By Authorized out of a Dalakhani mare, he's bred to stay well, and once Buick got him rolling the result was inevitable. He should make a useful 3yo. (tchd 3-1 and 7-2)
Elidor, who was visored this time, showed the benefit of his debut effort and ran a really promising race in second. He's a half-brother to an Irish Derby winner, so should get further next year, and given he's by Cape Cross it'll be a surprise if he doesn't appreciate getting back on a decent surface. (tchd 16-1 and 25-1)
Another Cocktail, who is bred to stay all day, was being niggled along some way out (reportedly unsuited by the soft ground), but kept plugging away. He'll get a trip next year. Official explanation: trainer's rep said colt was unsuited by the soft ground (op 9-2 tchd 4-1)
Excellent Result (IRE) travelled well enough on the shoulder of the leader, but when it came down to stamina and guts on this testing surface he was found wanting. He has a pedigree to suggest he'll do better at three. (op 9-4)
Mister Impatience was rallying at the finish. Both his pedigree and style of running suggest he'll be a staying handicapper next season. (op 14-1 tchd 16-1)
Flemish School found it tough going in the straight, but she's now eligible for a handicap mark and should do better in that sphere next year. (op 14-1)
A Ladies Man (IRE) Official explanation: jockey said colt did not feel right

7082 GOODWOOD RACEHORSE OWNERS GROUP STKS (H'CAP) 1m 4f

4:55 (4:55) (Class 3) (0-95,94) 3-Y-O £8,409 (£2,502; £1,250 ; £625) Stalls High

Form				RPR
1002	1		**Nicholascopernicus (IRE)**16 6625 3 -8-1386 DaneO'Neill 10 (Ed Walker) *hld up in last pair: stdy prog fr 3f out to trck ldrs over 1f out: produced to ld ins fnl f: sn clr: impressive* **7/2**1	101+
1046	2	2 1/4	**Princess Caetani (IRE)**32 6492 3 -8-280 oh1 DarrenEgan(5) 9 (David Simcock) *hld up in last pair: prog on wd outside over 3f out: rdn 2f out: clsd to ld 1f out: hdd and outpcd ins fnl f* **9/1**	90
3002	3	1 1/4	**Daneking**15 6662 3 -8-780 WilliamBuick 2 (John Gosden) *trckd ldng pair: squeezed through to ld 3f out: sn hrd pressed: hanging lft fr 2f out: hdd 1f out: one pce* **11/2**3	88
1	4	1	**Muharrer**24 6409 3 -8-780 PaulHanagan 5 (Marcus Tregoning) *racd in 7th and rn green: effrt over 3f out: chsd ldrs and rdn wl over 1f out: one pce* **8/1**	86+
2-1	5	2	**Danchai**20 6527 3 -8-1285 JoeFanning 4 (William Haggas) *trckd ldrs in 5th: prog to chal and upsides over 2f out to over 1f out: wknd* **9/2**2	88
0602	6	6	**Freddy Q (IRE)**18 6574 3 -8-881 SilvestreDeSousa 8 (Roger Teal) *a abt same pl: rdn and no prog 3f out: wl btn fnl 2f* **16/1**	75
0303	7	1 1/2	**Samba King**94 4009 3 -9-794 MickaelBarzalona 6 (Mahmood Al Zarooni) *hld up in 8th: effrt on outer over 3f out: shkn up and no prog wl over 2f out: wknd* **6/1**	85
6113	8	3 3/4	**The Quarterjack**18 6574 3 -8-780 oh4 DavidProbert 7 (Ron Hodges) *chsd ldng trio: rdn 3f out: wknd 2f out* **20/1**	65
2006	9	3	**Commitment**25 6380 3 -8-1184 PatDobbs 3 (Luca Cumani) *trckd ldr: led briefly over 3f out: wknd over 2f out* **12/1**	64
F446	10	15	**Star Date (IRE)**77 4621 3 -8-881 oh1 ow1 NeilCallan 1 (Gerard Butler) *dwlt but pushed up to ld and set solid pce: hdd over 3f out: hmpd sn after and wknd: t.o* **9/1**	37

2m 43.75s (5.35) **Going Correction** +0.475s/f (Yiel) 10Ran SP% 119.5
Speed ratings (Par 105): **101,99,98,98,96 92,91,89,87,77**
toteswingers 1&2 £8.20, 2&3 £9.30, 1&3 £5.20 CSF £36.74 CT £173.81 TOTE £4.90 : £1.90 , £2.80, £2.10 ; EX 39.00 Trifecta £213.10 Pool: £2,948.55 - 10.23 winning tickets. .
Owner Greenwood, Halsall and Pegum **Bred** Mrs E J O'Grady **Trained** Newmarket, Suffolk
■ Stewards' Enquiry : Pat Dobbs two-day ban: careless riding (Oct 29-30)

FOCUS
This looked a good quality handicap featuring a few improvers. It's probably form to be positive about.

NOTEBOOK
Nicholascopernicus(IRE) ◆, who bumped into one at Haydock last time, was given a patient ride, came through horses going well, then quickened up smartly inside the last to win going away. He's firmly on the upgrade, handles testing ground really well and could have a big prize in him. Perhaps the November Handicap will be considered. (op 4-1)
Princess Caetani (IRE) kept the winner company out the back early before being brought with her challenge up the centre of the track. Getting back on soft ground really suited her. (tchd 10-1)
Daneking, whose only win came at this track, did best of those that raced prominently. He's a consistent sort who appreciates cut in the ground, and helps set the level of the form. Official explanation: jockey said colt hung left (op 13-2)
Muharrer won his maiden over 2f shorter on fast ground, so had a bit to prove in these conditions on his handicap debut. He's well related, though, being out of an unraced half-sister to 1,000 Guineas and Coronation Stakes winner Ghanaati and high-class Mawatheeq, and he ran with plenty of encouragement, while still showing signs of greenness. There should be more to come from him. (op 11-1)
Danchai ◆ came there to have every chance 2f out, only to weaken out of things. He was stepping up 3f in distance on his handicap debut, and it found him out, but he showed more than enough to suggest he's on a competitive mark, perhaps back at 1m2f. (op 4-1 tchd 7-2)
Freddy Q (IRE) found the trip beyond him. He's probably at his best over 1m2f.
Samba King struggled to get involved. He's plenty high in the handicap and his two wins have come when making the running. (tchd 13-2)

7083 LAVANT HOUSE SCHOOL DIAMOND JUBILEE STKS (H'CAP) 1m

5:25 (5:27) (Class 4) (0-85,85) 3-Y-O+ £5,175 (£1,540; £769 ; £384) Stalls Low

Form				RPR
0220	1		**First Post (IRE)**22 6484 5 -9-179 DaneO'Neill 9 (Derek Haydn Jones) *hld up in 9th: nt clr run over 3f out: prog on outer over 2f out: led over 1f out gng wl: drvn and kpt on fnl f* **16/1**	89
2415	2	1/2	**Estebsaal (IRE)**39 5951 3 -9-182 PaulHanagan 16 (John Dunlop) *hld up in rr: stdy prog on outer over 2f out: wnt 2nd fnl f: hanging but pressed wnr nr fin: jst hld* **12/1**	90
0064	3	1 1/2	**Leviathan**16 6630 5 -8-1175 (t) NeilCallan 14 (Tony Newcombe) *hld up in 10th: prog on inner whn nowhere to go over 2f out to over 1f out: hdwy to dispute 2nd ent fnl f: edgd lft and styd on same pce* **9/1**	80
3006	4	3 1/4	**Take It To The Max**23 6426 5 -9-583 (p) GeorgeBaker 1 (Richard Fahey) *dwlt: hld up in last pair: rdn on wd outside 3f out: prog after: styd on to take 4th nr fin* **8/1**3	81
6402	5	nk	**Shamrocked (IRE)**22 6488 3 -8-572 SamHitchcott 4 (Mick Channon) *mde most at gd pce: hdd over 1f out: grad fdd* **25/1**	69
4031	6	1 3/4	**Duster**19 6566 5 -9-285 DarrenEgan(5) 2 (Hughie Morrison) *hld up in last trio: effrt and looking for room over 2f out: kpt on fnl 2f: nt pce to threaten* **8/1**3	80
5662	7	hd	**Shifting Star (IRE)**4 6705 7 -9-085 WilliamTwiston-Davies(7) 7 (John Bridger) *dwlt: hld up in last quartet: shkn up on outer over 3f out: kpt on fr over 2f out: nvr gng pce to threaten* **25/1**	77
41-0	8	1 3/4	**Tadabeer**240 177 4 -9-078 StevieDonohoe 11 (Ian Williams) *hld up in last: rdn wl over 2f out: styd on fr over 1f out: nrst fin* **50/1**	66
22-0	9	hd	**Blank Czech (IRE)**127 2942 3 -8-1077 PatDobbs 5 (Amanda Perrett) *hld up in 8th: looking for room over 2f out: kpt on one pce fr over 1f out* **22/1**	65
6500	10	1 1/2	**Honeymead (IRE)**14 6710 4 -9-280 MickaelBarzalona 8 (Richard Fahey) *trckd ldrs: rdn to dispute 2nd briefly wl over 1f out: sn wknd* **17/2**	64
0060	11	3/4	**Nazreef**16 6638 5 -9-179 (t) RichardHughes 10 (Hughie Morrison) *trckd ldng pair: rdn to dispute 2nd briefly wl over 1f out: sn fdd: eased fnl f* **12/1**	62
0210	12	1 3/4	**Maverik**36 6036 4 -9-785 SebSanders 15 (Ralph Beckett) *pressed ldr to 2f out: wknd and eased* **16/1**	64
-300	13	3	**Star Surprise**44 5794 4 -9-482 WilliamBuick 6 (Michael Bell) *a towards rr: rdn and no prog over 2f out* **14/1**	54
0040	14	3	**Polish World (USA)**15 6665 8 -9-179 MickyFenton 18 (Paul Midgley) *trckd ldng pair to over 2f out: eased whn btn over 1f out* **33/1**	44
0132	15	4	**Dolphin Rock**8 6881 5 -8-1175 SilvestreDeSousa 17 (Brian Ellison) *chsd ldrs: drvn 3f out: wknd over 2f out* **5/1**1	31
6143	16	1 1/4	**Copperwood**6 6932 7 -8-1175 JoeFanning 3 (Mark Johnston) *trckd ldrs: lost pl qckly 3f out: sn wl in rr* **13/2**2	28

1m 42.67s (2.77) **Going Correction** +0.475s/f (Yiel)
WFA 3 from 4yo+ 3lb 16Ran SP% 123.5
Speed ratings (Par 105): **105,104,103,99,99 97,97,95,95,94 93,91,88,85,81 80**
toteswingers 1&2 £36.60, 2&3 £16.00, 1&3 £26.30 CSF £187.50 CT £1856.04 TOTE £21.10 : £4.50, £2.50 , £2.50 , £2.30 ; EX 271.50 Trifecta £1168.60 Part won. Pool: £1,579.22 - 0.30 winning tickets. .
Owner Llewelyn, Runeckles **Bred** D Llewelyn & J Runeckles **Trained** Efail Isaf, Rhondda C Taff

FOCUS
A pretty open handicap and it paid to be ridden with a bit of patience.
Duster Official explanation: jockey said gelding hung right
Dolphin Rock Official explanation: jockey said gelding had no more to give
T/Jkpt: Not won. T/Plt: £139.20 to a £1 stake. Pool: £105,000.48 - 550.36 winning tickets.
T/Qpdt: £30.10 to £1. Pool: £8,422.24 - 206.85 w. tckts JN 7084a - 7090a (Foreign Racing) See RI

6906 DUSSELDORF (R-H)

Sunday, October 14

OFFICIAL GOING: Turf: very soft

7091a PREIS DES WINTERFAVORITEN (GROUP 3) (2YO) (TURF) 1m

2:20 (12:00) 2-Y-O

£70,833 (£21,458; £21,458 ; £8,583 ; £4,583 ; £2,250)

			RPR
1		**Limario (GER)**35 2 -9-20 APietsch 5 (R Dzubasz, Germany) *trckd ldr: led after 100yds: mde rest: shkn up and qckned 1 1/2f out: rdn ent fnl f: drew clr fr 150yds out: eased cl home* **83/10**	102+
2	2 1/2	**Anatol Artist (GER)**35 2 -9-20 KClijmans 9 (Uwe Ostmann, Germany) *carried lft s and sn adrift of rivals: pushed along to rcvr: chsd ldng gp on outside racing freely: rdn to press first two over 1 1/2f out: wnt 2nd over 1f out: kpt on u.p but nt pce of wnr: jnd for 2nd on line* **162/10**	97
2	dht	**Wildheart (IRE)** 2 -9-20 ADeVries 6 (M Figge, Germany) *trckd ldr on outside: 2nd and rdn over 1 1/2f out: lost 2nd over 1f out: kpt on u.p fnl f: got up to share 2nd on line* **57/10**	97

4 2 1/2 **Empire Hurricane (GER)**[35] 2-9-2 0 .... EPedroza 7 91
(A Wohler, Germany) *towards rr: moved into midfield 1/2-way: rdn and chsd ldng quartet appr fnl 1 1/2f: one pce fnl f* **41/10**

5 1 1/4 **Maurice (GER)** 2-9-2 0 .... EddyHardouin 8 88
(S Smrczek, Germany) *wnt lft s: settled towards rr: rdn and nt qckn under 2f out: styd on fnl f: nvr plcd to chal* **40/1**

6 1 **Daktani**[35] 2-9-2 0 .... EFrank 3 86
(Markus Klug, Germany) *smartly away: led tl hdd after 100yds: trckd ldr on ins: rdn and nt qckn 2 1/2f out: wknd over 1f out* **16/5[2]**

7 1/2 **Mauriac (GER)**[46] 5755 2-9-2 0 .... JBojko 4 85
(A Wohler, Germany) *in rr: sme prog 3f out: c wd fnl bnd: rdn and no imp 1 1/2f out: wknd ins fnl f* **163/10**

8 5 **Superplex (FR)**[17] 2-9-2 0 .... FilipMinarik 1 74
(M Figge, Germany) *midfield on ins: rdn and no imp over 2f out: bhd whn eased ins fnl f* **37/10[3]**

9 24 **Tres Blue (IRE)**[42] 2-9-2 0 .... MaximeGuyon 2 21
(H-A Pantall, France) *midfield: bmpd and nrly lost footing after 2f: in rr by 1/2-way: bhd whn heavily eased appr fnl f* **13/5[1]**

1m 44.3s (3.14) **9** Ran SP% **132.2**
WIN (incl. 10 euro stake): 93. PLACES: 25, 35 (Anatol Artist), 20 (Wildheart). SF: 1,393 (Limario & Anatol Artist), 412 (Limario & Wildheart)..
Owner Frau M Haller **Bred** Frau Martha Niebuhr **Trained** Germany

NOTEBOOK
Limario(GER) will probably be rated the top German two-year-old of 2012 after running out a very convincing winner. His jockey rode a confident race, leading after a furlong and making the rest of his way home, and was in no danger from the 2f marker. Although by a sprinter, he is a half-brother to a Listed class stayer, so could well get middle distances next year.

6298 WOODBINE (R-H)
Sunday, October 14
OFFICIAL GOING: Turf: good; polytrack: fast

7092a NEARCTIC STKS (GRADE 1) (3YO+) (TURF) 6f
8:04 (8:06) 3-Y-0+
£189,873 (£63,291; £31,645; £15,822; £6,329; £3,164)

RPR

1 **Next Question (USA)**[32] 4-8-5 0 .... (b) RADominguez 7 109
(Michael Trombetta, U.S.A) *disp ld on outer: edgd ahd 2f out: rdn ent fnl 1 1/2f: strly pressed again ins fnl f: fnd more and asserted cl home* **161/10**

2 1/2 **Night Carnation**[43] 5814 4-8-2 0 .... JRVelazquez 4 104+
(Andrew Balding) *midfield: rdn 2f out: r.o to go 2nd post: nt pce of wnr* **47/10[3]**

3 1/2 **Bear Tough Tiger (USA)**[15] 4-8-5 0 .... (b) JStein 1 105
(Reade Baker, Canada) *disp ld on inner: rdn in 2nd 2f out: rallied to re-press ldr ins fnl f: kpt on tl no ex cl home: dropped to 3rd last strides* **99/10**

4 1/2 **Big Band Sound (USA)**[28] 6300 5-8-9 0 .... TPizarro 8 108+
(Daniel J Vella, Canada) *hld up towards rr: rdn in last pair 2f out: edgd lft and r.o down wd outside to go 4th ins fnl f: fin wl but nvr able to chal* **29/10[1]**

5 2 1/2 **Stormy Rush (USA)**[49] 4-8-5 0 .... JMcAleney 3 96
(Lorne Richards, Canada) *midfield on inner: rdn 2f out: kpt on one pce ins fnl 1 1/2f: jst hld on for 5th* **201/10**

6 nse **As De Trebol (USA)**[77] 6-8-5 0 .... MircoDemuro 2 96
(M Delcher-Sanchez, Spain) *stdd and hld up towards rr on inner: rdn 2f out and sn outpcd: styd on ins fnl f: almost snatched 5th post* **33/1**

7 1 1/2 **Super Chunky (USA)**[41] 6-8-5 0 .... (b) SheldonRussell 10 91
(Kenneth M Cox, U.S.A) *prom: rdn over 2f out: kpt on tl no ex and btn ent fnl f: fdd* **33/1**

8 hd **Hammers Terror (USA)**[57] 3-8-4 0 .... (b) GKGomez 6 90
(Michael Stidham, U.S.A) *hld up in last: rdn and detached fr rest of field 2 1/2f out: plugged on to go 8th cl home: nvr a factor* **76/10**

9 3/4 **Grand Adventure (USA)**[49] 6-8-5 0 .... JJCastellano 5 88
(Malcolm Pierce, Canada) *midfield: rdn 3f out: keeping on whn nt clr run ent fnl f: swtchd ins and styd on cl home: nt rcvr* **167/20**

10 nse **Fire Lily (IRE)**[29] 6268 3-8-3 0 .... WayneLordan 11 87
(David Wachman, Ire) *slow to stride and hld up in last pair: rdn to try and improve on outer 2 1/2f out: lugged lft u.p ent fnl f: sn outpcd and btn: fdd* **31/10[2]**

11 2 **Artic Fern (CAN)**[28] 6300 5-8-5 0 .... LContreras 9 81
(Michael Keogh, Canada) *midfield on outer: rdn and hdwy to chal 2f out: kpt on tl no ex and btn ent fnl f: fdd and dropped to last cl home* **184/10**

1m 9.32s (69.32)
WFA 3 from 4yo+ 1lb **11** Ran SP% **120.7**
PARI-MUTUEL (all including $2 stakes): WIN 34.10; PLACE (1-2) 15.30, 7.80; SHOW (1-2-3) 10.70, 6.10, 8.00; SF 254.40.
Owner Three Diamonds Farm **Bred** Dr Lance G Bell **Trained** North America

NOTEBOOK
Next Question(USA)
Night Carnation finished well to take second, behind the all the way winner. She broke well and sat just off the pace but could not quicken in time to catch the winner.
Fire Lily(IRE) had little chance after fluffing the break and was unable to mount a serious challenge

7093a E. P. TAYLOR STKS (GRADE 1) (3YO+ FILLIES & MARES) (TURF) 1m 2f (T)
9:38 (9:41) 3-Y-0+
£379,746 (£126,582; £63,291; £31,645; £12,658; £6,329)

RPR

1 **Siyouma (IRE)**[15] 6673 4-8-12 0 .... GeraldMosse 3 113+
(F Doumen, France) **57/20[1]**

2 1 3/4 **Pagera (FR)**[43] 5844 4-8-12 0 .... OlivierPeslier 2 109
(H-A Pantall, France) **132/10**

3 nk **Dream Peace (IRE)**[15] 6695 4-8-12 0 .... RADominguez 5 108
(Chad C Brown, U.S.A) **3/1[2]**

4 3/4 **Kissable (IRE)**[41] 4-8-12 0 .... JRVelazquez 12 107+
(Roger L Attfield, Canada) **119/10**

5 1/2 **Havant**[23] 4-8-12 0 .... FrankieDettori 13 106+
(F Head, France) **239/10**

6 hd **Barefoot Lady (IRE)**[28] 6298 4-8-12 0 .... TonyHamilton 4 106
(Richard Fahey) **8/1**

7 nse **Moment Of Majesty (CAN)**[28] 6298 5-8-12 0 .... GOlguin 6 105
(Sue Leslie, Canada) **77/1**

8 nk **All Star Heart (CAN)**[28] 6298 5-8-12 0 .... BBlanc 7 105
(Ronald McAnally, U.S.A) **13/1**

9 3/4 **Stars To Shine (USA)**[28] 6298 5-8-12 0 .... ASolis 1 103
(Mark Frostad, Canada) **30/1**

10 2 **Princess Highway (USA)**[28] 6295 3-8-7 0 .... PatSmullen 9 99
(D K Weld, Ire) **23/5[3]**

11 1/2 **Trois Lunes (FR)**[54] 5472 3-8-7 0 .... Francois-XavierBertras 8 98
(F Rohaut, France) **35/1**

12 4 1/2 **Kapitale (GER)**[28] 6298 4-8-12 0 .... MircoDemuro 11 89
(A Wohler, Germany) **243/10**

13 17 3/4 **Vamo A Galupiar (CHI)**[175] 5-8-12 0 .... MESmith 10 54
(Neil Drysdale, U.S.A) **242/10**

2m 3.04s (-0.98)
WFA 3 from 4yo+ 5lb **13** Ran SP% **121.1**
PARI-MUTUEL (all including $2 stakes): WIN 7.70; PLACE (1-2) 4.80, 11.50; SHOW (1-2-3) 3.30, 6.90, 3.10; SF 71.70.
Owner Robert Jeffcock **Bred** Haras De Son Altesse L'Aga Khan Scea **Trained** Bouce, France

NOTEBOOK
Siyouma(IRE) was sent off favourite and scored emphatically from her compatriot. She was always well placed on the rail, just off the pace, before bursting through in the straight. He trainer now has Hong Kong in mind for the filly.
Havant finished well from the rear to take fifth.
Barefoot Lady(IRE), the winner of a Grade 2 here last month, ran her race but could not quite handle the step back up to this grade.
Princess Highway(USA), dropping in trip and on a faster surface, raced wide before fading in the stretch.

7094a PATTISON CANADIAN INTERNATIONAL STKS (GRADE 1) (3YO+) (TURF) 1m 4f (T)
10:44 (10:46) 3-Y-0+
£569,620 (£189,873; £94,936; £47,468; £18,987; £9,493)

RPR

1 **Joshua Tree (IRE)**[28] 6293 5-9-0 0 .... FrankieDettori 8 116
(Marco Botti) **87/20[2]**

2 1/2 **Dandino**[36] 6035 5-9-0 0 .... JimCrowley 2 115+
(James Fanshawe) **25/1**

3 1/2 **Forte Dei Marmi**[28] 6299 6-9-0 0 .... JRVelazquez 3 114
(Roger L Attfield, Canada) **167/20**

4 1 1/4 **Wigmore Hall (IRE)**[28] 6299 5-9-0 0 .... JamieSpencer 6 112
(Michael Bell) **23/4[3]**

5 1 **Air Support (USA)**[36] 4-9-0 0 .... JJCastellano 10 110
(Claude McGaughey III, U.S.A) **126/10**

6 1/2 **Imperial Monarch (IRE)**[92] 4121 3-8-7 0 .... RyanMoore 9 110
(A P O'Brien, Ire) **9/5[1]**

7 3/4 **Scalo**[28] 6299 5-9-0 0 .... (b) AStarke 4 108
(A Wohler, Germany) **22/1**

8 1/2 **Reliable Man**[23] 6464 4-9-0 0 .... OlivierPeslier 7 108
(A De Royer-Dupre, France) **87/20[2]**

9 3 1/4 **Prince Will I Am (USA)**[43] 5-9-0 0 .... RADominguez 5 102
(Michelle Nihei, U.S.A) **208/10**

10 2 3/4 **Lay Time**[22] 6482 4-8-11 0 .... JimmyFortune 1 95
(Andrew Balding) **46/1**

2m 30.89s (1.29)
WFA 3 from 4yo+ 7lb **10** Ran SP% **120.9**
PARI-MUTUEL (all including $2 stakes): WIN 10.70; PLACE (1-2) 6.10, 20.80; SHOW (1-2-3) 4.40, 11.30, 5.80; SF 120.80.
Owner K K Al Nabooda & K Albahou **Bred** Castlemartin Stud And Skymarc Farm **Trained** Newmarket, Suffolk

NOTEBOOK
Joshua Tree(IRE) reclaimed this event after winning two years ago for former trainer Aidan O'Brien and finishing second to Sarah Lynx in 2011. His rider, who had won the race twice before, rode his rivals to sleep. After sending Joshua Tree straight to the front on rain-softened ground, he set modest fractions. He then sprinted out of the far turn, immediately gaining a small break on his rivals, and that was to prove enough to get him home.
Dandino, came from off the pace and charged past former Luca Cumani-trained Forte Dei Marmi close home to snatch second. His rider though he would have won with a little further to go.
Wigmore Hall(IRE), who won the Northern Dancer here last month, stayed on into fourth place after rushing home from the rear.
Imperial Monarch(IRE) was well fancied but faded in the stretch.

6706 MUSSELBURGH (R-H)
Monday, October 15
OFFICIAL GOING: Soft (good to soft in places; 6.6)
Wind: Breezy, half against Weather: Cloudy, bright

7095 DRINKS DIRECT AT BATLEYS (S) H'CAP 1m 1f
1:40 (1:40) (Class 6) (0-65,63) 3-Y-0+ **£1,617** (£481; £240; £120) **Stalls** High

Form RPR

43 1 **Jordaura**[4] 7003 6-9-10 **63** .... RobertWinston 12 78
(Alan Berry) *t.k.h early: in tch: rdn 3f out: hdwy to ld over 1f out: rdn clr fnl f* **6/1[2]**

6006 2 10 **Bold Marc (IRE)**[28] 6313 10-9-0 **60** .... ConorHarrison(7) 11 53
(Mrs K Burke) *w ldr: led over 3f out: rdn and hdd over 1f out: kpt on fnl f: no ch w wnr* **18/1**

1062 3 nk **Monthly Medal**[12] 6785 9-9-7 **60** .... (t) AmyRyan 8 52
(Wilf Storey) *hld up: stdy hdwy over 2f out: rdn over 1f out: kpt on ins fnl f: nvr able to chal* **13/2[3]**

3000 4 2 3/4 **Nolecce**[12] 6785 5-9-1 **54** .... (p) RobbieFitzpatrick 1 40
(Richard Guest) *prom: drvn along over 2f out: kpt on same pce over 1f out* **33/1**

6040 5 3/4 **Eilean Mor**[7] 6941 4-9-1 **54** .... AndrewMullen 9 39
(R Mike Smith) *in tch: drvn along over 3f out: nt qckn wl over 1f out* **50/1**

0040 6 1/2 **Mangham (IRE)**[15] 6711 7-9-0 **56** ....[1] NeilFarley(3) 10 40
(George Foster) *s.i.s: effrt into midfield after 3f: rdn over 2f out: edgd rt and sn no imp* **20/1**

3003 7 1 1/2 **Madame Blavatsky (FR)**[21] 6528 4-9-3 **56** .... BarryMcHugh 13 36
(Karen McLintock) *in tch: drvn over 3f out: outpcd fnl 2f* **8/1**

3200 **8** 4 **Military Call**[15] 6711 5-9-2 **55**....(v) PJMcDonald 7 26
(Alistair Whillans) *hld up in midfield: rdn over 3f out: no imp fr 2f out* **10/1**
0620 **9** 4 **Goldenveil (IRE)**[30] 6262 4-9-0 **53**.... FrederikTylicki 2 16
(Richard Fahey) *bhd: drvn over 3f out: nvr able to chal* **15/2**
4143 **10** 3 3/4 **Future Wonder (IRE)**[11] 6814 3-9-0 **60**.... PaulPickard(3) 6 14
(Brian Ellison) *cl up: rdn 3f out: wknd wl over 1f out* **7/2**[1]
6000 **11** 4 1/2 **Glenluji**[13] 6758 7-9-1 **54**....(p) DanielTudhope 14
(Jim Goldie) *hld up: rdn along over 3f out: nvr able to chal* **40/1**
1105 **12** 5 **Valantino Oyster (IRE)**[35] 6103 5-9-7 **60**....(p) PatrickMathers 5
(Tracy Waggott) *s.i.s: bhd: struggling 1/2-way: nvr on terms* **18/1**
0260 **13** 1 1/2 **Goninodaethat**[13] 6756 4-9-2 **55**.... GrahamLee 3
(Jim Goldie) *t.k.h: led to over 3f out: rdn and wknd 2f out* **20/1**
5210 **14** 36 **Rasselas (IRE)**[7] 6941 5-9-6 **59**....(v) AdrianNicholls 4
(David Nicholls) *hld up on ins: struggling over 3f out: btn and eased fnl 2f* **16/1**

1m 58.47s (4.57) **Going Correction** +0.70s/f (Yiel)
WFA 3 from 4yo+ 4lb **14** Ran SP% **115.1**
Speed ratings (Par 101): **107,98,97,95,94 94,92,89,85,82 78,74,72,40**
toteswingers 1&2 £26.60, 1&3 £8.10, 2&3 £23.00 CSF £96.48 CT £723.11 TOTE £7.20: £2.80, £6.30, £1.50; EX 125.40.There was no bid for the winner.
Owner A B Parr **Bred** Pendley Farm **Trained** Cockerham, Lancs

FOCUS
Stands' rail moved to inner position. A modest selling handicap, run a decent pace, and it was turned into a procession by the top-weight Jordaura. Tricky form to pin down. The winner is rated in line with last winter's form.
Eilean Mor Official explanation: trainer said gelding was unsuited by the soft (good to soft in places) ground
Future Wonder(IRE) Official explanation: jockey said filly ran too free
Rasselas(IRE) Official explanation: jockey said gelding hung right throughout

7096 BRITISH STALLION STUDS SUPPORTING BRITISH RACING E B F MAIDEN STKS 1m
2:10 (2:11) (Class 4) 2-Y-0 **£5,175** (£1,540; £769; £384) **Stalls** Low

Form RPR
3 **1** **Leitrim Pass (USA)**[25] 6412 2-9-3 0.... PhillipMakin 4 77+
(William Haggas) *t.k.h: cl up: led gng wl 3f out: drvn 2f out: sn hrd pressed: styd on wl fnl f* **10/11**[1]
4 **2** 1 3/4 **Dolphin Village (IRE)**[22] 6512 2-9-3 0.... FrederikTylicki 6 74
(Richard Fahey) *hld up in tch: drvn and effrt 3f out: chsd wnr and edgd rt over 1f out: kpt on ins fnl f* **9/1**
23 **3** 3 1/2 **Rust (IRE)**[23] 6473 2-9-3 0.... PJMcDonald 3 66
(Ann Duffield) *t.k.h: chsd ldrs: outpcd over 3f out: rallied over 2f out: kpt on same pce fnl f* **9/2**[2]
43 **4** 14 **Ghur (USA)**[22] 6512 2-8-12 0.... JoeFanning 1 30
(Mark Johnston) *trckd ldrs tl rdn and wknd fr 2f out* **11/2**[3]
5 3 1/2 **Rainestorm (IRE)** 2-9-3 0.... AdrianNicholls 5 27+
(Mark Johnston) *s.i.s: rn green and sn wl bhd: sme late hdwy: nvr on terms* **16/1**
5 **6** hd **Hayley**[24] 6423 2-8-12 0.... GrahamLee 8 22
(Jim Goldie) *hld up bhd ldng gp: struggling over 2f out: sn btn* **50/1**
62 **7** 4 1/2 **Stagweekend (IRE)**[12] 6779 2-9-3 0.... MichaelO'Connell 2 17
(John Quinn) *led to 3f out: rdn and wknd 2f out* **6/1**
40 **8** 15 **Dark Marvel (IRE)**[27] 6336 2-8-12 0.... TomEaves 7
(Alan Berry) *towards rr: struggling over 3f out: sn lost tch: t.o* **150/1**

1m 46.92s (5.72) **Going Correction** +0.70s/f (Yiel) **8** Ran SP% **118.7**
Speed ratings (Par 97): **99,97,93,79,76 76,71,56**
toteswingers 1&2 £2.50, 1&3 £2.40, 2&3 £5.50 CSF £11.23 TOTE £2.60: £1.60, £1.60, £1.40; EX 11.30.
Owner Gallagher Equine Ltd **Bred** Indian Creek Et Al **Trained** Newmarket, Suffolk

FOCUS
An interesting juvenile maiden. The winner and second both showed improvement.

NOTEBOOK
Leitrim Pass(USA), who was heavily supported, won in determined fashion, confirming the promise he'd shown on his debut at Yarmouth last month. Purchased for 75,000gns at the Tattersalls Sales in October, he travelled powerfully through the early stages and knuckled down bravely to win a shade cosily. He'd looked sure to score handsomely when assuming control from 3f out but, like many in the first race, found these conditions more testing than the official description. A strapping type, he can only come on from this and rates as an exciting prospect for handicaps next season. (op 11-8 tchd 6-4)
Dolphin Village(IRE) ran an excellent race and clearly improved dramatically on the form he'd shown on heavy ground at Hamilton. He lugged in behind the winner when tiring inside the final furlong, but kept on steadily to pull clear of the remainder. Better ground and a drop to 7f may well pay dividends for him. (op 12-1)
Rust(IRE) was by no means disgraced, but he was readily left behind by the principals having raced keenly in the early stages. This was easily the softest ground he'd encountered and better should be expected back on a sounder surface. (op 4-1)
Ghur(USA) was disappointing. She had finished a long way clear of the runner-up last time and this represents a backward step. However, she is now qualified for handicaps and is another that may prefer drier ground. (tchd 5-1)

7097 BATLEYS SCOTLAND H'CAP 7f 30y
2:40 (2:41) (Class 3) (0-95,94) 3-Y-0+ **£7,115** (£2,117; £1,058; £529) **Stalls** Low

Form RPR
0550 **1** **Kingscroft (IRE)**[30] 6235 4-8-9 **82**.... JoeFanning 9 92
(Mark Johnston) *prom: hdwy on wd outside to ld over 2f out: rdn and hld on wl fnl f* **18/1**
6626 **2** 1 1/2 **Green Park (IRE)**[4] 6999 9-8-7 **80** oh1....(b) DavidAllan 12 86
(Declan Carroll) *t.k.h: hld up on outside: rdn and hdwy over 2f out: edgd rt and chsd wnr ins fnl f: r.o* **28/1**
0622 **3** hd **Capaill Liath (IRE)**[16] 6659 4-9-5 **92**....(p) AmyRyan 6 97
(Kevin Ryan) *hld up on outside: rdn over 2f out: hdwy over 1f out: kpt on: nvr able to chal* **4/1**[1]
0414 **4** 3/4 **Roninski (IRE)**[30] 6235 4-8-13 **86**.... TomEaves 7 90
(Bryan Smart) *t.k.h: cl up: rdn and ev ch over 2f out: one pce fnl f* **16/1**
3241 **5** 1 3/4 **Green Howard**[50] 5634 4-8-12 **85**.... RobertWinston 11 84
(Robin Bastiman) *towards rr: rdn over 2f out: edgd rt over 1f out: no imp* **6/1**
0141 **6** 3/4 **Common Touch (IRE)**[23] 6471 4-9-7 **94**....(p) FrederikTylicki 2 91
(Richard Fahey) *hld up: rdn and hdwy over 2f out: no imp over 1f out* **9/2**[2]
4000 **7** 1 **Powerful Presence (IRE)**[31] 6201 6-9-1 **88**.... DanielTudhope 8 82
(David O'Meara) *led to over 2f out: wknd over 1f out* **9/1**
0043 **8** 6 **Xilerator (IRE)**[16] 6659 5-9-3 **90**.... AdrianNicholls 3 69
(David Nicholls) *trckd ldrs tl rdn and wknd 2f out* **5/1**[3]
6016 **9** 7 **Clockmaker (IRE)**[16] 6659 6-8-13 **86**.... DuranFentiman 5 47
(Tim Easterby) *plld hrd early in midfield: struggling over 2f out: sn btn* **20/1**
0005 **10** 1 3/4 **Klynch**[16] 6665 6-8-13 **86**....(b) JamesSullivan 10 42
(Ruth Carr) *s.i.s and swtchd rt s: hld up: struggling over 2f out: sn btn* **20/1**
-040 **11** 1 3/4 **Diescentric (USA)**[16] 6676 5-9-2 **89**.... MickyFenton 4 41
(Julie Camacho) *plld hrd: trckd ldrs tl rdn and wknd over 2f out* **11/1**
0540 **12** 1 3/4 **New Leyf (IRE)**[23] 6465 6-8-10 **83**....(b) DaleSwift 1 30
(Colin Teague) *t.k.h: in tch tl rdn and wknd wl over 2f out* **20/1**

1m 32.82s (3.82) **Going Correction** +0.70s/f (Yiel) **12** Ran SP% **116.3**
Speed ratings (Par 107): **106,104,104,103,101 100,99,92,84,82 80,78**
toteswingers 1&2 £62.70, 1&3 £10.90, 2&3 £20.20 CSF £447.42 CT £2441.82 TOTE £17.00: £4.40, £7.20, £1.90; EX 287.50.
Owner Dr Marwan Koukash **Bred** J Beckett **Trained** Middleham Moor, N Yorks

FOCUS
A competitive handicap, run at a good pace. The form is rated around the first three.

NOTEBOOK
Kingscroft(IRE) had enjoyed a tremendous time of things in 2011, notching seven victories, but he'd found things much tougher off lofty marks this year. However, he'd gradually been working his way down the ratings and was able to take advantage of a mark which was 6lb below that of his last success at Chester. Versatile in terms of ground, he has an excellent record over this distance and saw this out really well to win under mainly hands and heels riding. Clearly working his way back towards peak form, he's likely to remain competitive in the coming weeks and should have more opportunities presented to him on the AW, a surface he's excelled on in the past. Official explanation: trainer's rep had no explanation for the apparent improvement in form (op 14-1 tchd 20-1)
Green Park(IRE) ran an a fine race. Yet to win beyond 6f, he stayed on encouragingly against the far rail without ever landing a blow at the winner. He's sure to go up a bit for this, though, and is already 7lb higher than when winning at Chester earlier in the year. (tchd 33-1)
Capaill Liath(IRE) doesn't look the easiest of rides, but he's performing creditably at present and backed up his somewhat unlucky defeat at Chester. The style in which he finished off suggests he'd appreciate a return to 1m. (op 6-1)
Roninski(IRE) ran well but failed to last home on this ground. He's proving very consistent and still appears on the upgrade. (op 18-1)
Green Howard kept on creditably on his first start after a short break. Racing off a career-high mark, he is one to keep an eye on in the coming weeks. (op 13-2 tchd 7-1)
Common Touch(IRE), 5lb higher, wasn't disgraced. (op 4-1)
Powerful Presence(IRE) raced with the choke out early on and did well to sustain his effort for as long as he did. (op 8-1)

7098 ISLE OF SKYE BLENDED SCOTCH WHISKY H'CAP (FOR THE WILLIE PARK TROPHY) 2m
3:15 (3:15) (Class 3) (0-90,89) 3-Y-0+ **£7,115** (£2,117; £1,058; £529) **Stalls** High

Form RPR
3020 **1** **Gordonsville**[23] 6493 9-9-5 **80**.... FrederikTylicki 13 89
(Jim Goldie) *hld up in midfield on outside: stdy hdwy over 4f out: led over 1f out: drvn and styd on wl* **7/1**[2]
5024 **2** nk **Come Here Yew (IRE)**[9] 6884 4-8-8 **72**.... NeilFarley(3) 8 80
(Declan Carroll) *midfield: hdwy and ev ch over 1f out: kpt on u.p fnl f: hld nr fin* **10/1**
0503 **3** 2 **Jonny Delta**[15] 6712 5-8-9 **70** oh1.... JoeFanning 11 75
(Jim Goldie) *hld up: stdy hdwy on outside over 2f out: chsng ldrs over 1f out: kpt on same pce fnl f* **8/1**[3]
1400 **4** 5 **Orsippus (USA)**[10] 6834 6-9-5 **80**.... AndrewMullen 10 79
(Michael Smith) *cl up: rdn to ld 3f out: hdd over 1f out: sn outpcd* **16/1**
5045 **5** 4 1/2 **Mica Mika (IRE)**[31] 6191 4-9-5 **80**....(p) DavidNolan 1 74
(Richard Fahey) *hld up: rdn 3f out: hdwy 2f out: nvr able to chal* **11/1**
-201 **6** 3 1/4 **Los Nadis (GER)**[24] 6428 8-9-7 **82**.... GrahamLee 2 72
(Jim Goldie) *hld up in midfield on ins: niggled after 5f: drvn over 3f out: sn outpcd: n.d after* **4/1**[1]
3530 **7** 1 1/2 **Itlaaq**[10] 6834 6-10-0 **89**....(t) GrahamGibbons 12 77
(Michael Easterby) *hld up: rdn along on outside over 3f out: sn n.d* **20/1**
3145 **8** shd **Awesome Pearl (USA)**[26] 6383 3-8-0 **72**....(b[1]) LukeMorris 5 60
(Sir Mark Prescott Bt) *cl up: ev ch and rdn over 3f out: wknd 2f out* **7/1**[2]
3603 **9** 1 3/4 **Tappanappa (IRE)**[25] 6415 5-9-8 **83**.... DaleSwift 9 69
(Brian Ellison) *dwlt: bhd: drvn over 3f out: nvr on terms* **7/1**[2]
/005 **10** 1/2 **Call It On (IRE)**[25] 6415 6-9-2 **77**.... PhillipMakin 6 62
(Philip Kirby) *led tl rdn and hdd 3f out: wknd 2f out* **16/1**
1300 **11** 15 **Cape Rising (IRE)**[23] 6492 5-9-3 **78**.... RobertWinston 4 45
(Alan Swinbank) *t.k.h: prom tl rdn and wknd qckly over 3f out: t.o* **10/1**
0100 **12** 18 **Herostatus**[37] 6031 5-9-11 **86**....(v) DanielTudhope 3 32
(David O'Meara) *cl up: rdn over 3f out: wknd wl over 2f out: t.o* **11/1**

3m 41.61s (8.11) **Going Correction** +0.70s/f (Yiel)
WFA 3 from 4yo+ 11lb **12** Ran SP% **120.0**
Speed ratings (Par 107): **107,106,105,103,101 99,98,98,97,97 90,81**
toteswingers 1&2 £19.80, 1&3 £11.90, 2&3 £9.90 CSF £76.22 CT £580.35 TOTE £11.40: £2.40, £5.00, £3.20; EX 111.10.
Owner Thomson Fyffe Racing **Bred** George Strawbridge **Trained** Uplawmoor, E Renfrews
■ Stewards' Enquiry : Neil Farley four-day ban: used whip above permitted level (Oct 29-Nov 1)

FOCUS
A strong staying handicap, run at a steady pace. Pretty straightforward form.

NOTEBOOK
Gordonsville won in gutsy fashion to enhance his already impressive record in the race. The 9yo, who had won this in 2009 prior to finishing second behind Los Nadis 12 months ago, was on a lengthy losing run on the Flat. However, he had posted a couple of good efforts on similar ground this year and he once again found conditions to his liking, as he rallied bravely to deny the persistent challenge of the runner-up. A winner twice over hurdles last winter, it's likely connections will look to return to that sphere in the coming weeks. (op 13-2 tchd 8-1)
Come Here Yew(IRE) had found shorter trips against him since winning over this distance at Newcastle in July and he duly returned to form. Making his challenge from a similar position to that of the winner, he took a while to hit top gear and could never quite get on terms. Still lightly-raced over staying trips, he remains open to further improvement.
Jonny Delta pulled clear of the remainder and ran a promising race on his first try over this trip on the Flat. A bumper winner on heavy ground last year, he looks sure to embark on a hurdling career before too long.
Orsippus(USA) made an early bid for glory but, having got embroiled in a duel, was running on empty with a furlong to run. (tchd 14-1 and 18-1)
Los Nadis(GER), last year's winner, ran poorly. He appeared to get outpaced as they turned for home and made very little in the way of headway. Official explanation: jockey said gelding never travelled (op 9-2 tchd 7-2)

7099 M & F FUNERAL SERVICES H'CAP 5f
3:45 (3:46) (Class 6) (0-60,60) 3-Y-0+ **£1,617** (£481; £240; £120) **Stalls** High

Form RPR
0040 **1** **Weetentherty**[35] 6104 5-8-9 **48**....(p) TomEaves 4 57
(Linda Perratt) *stdd in rr: hdwy and shkn up over 1f out: styd on wl to ld cl home* **40/1**

0042 **2** *hd* **Angelo Poliziano**[6] 6958 6-8-8 **52** .... LMcNiff(5) 2 60
(George Foster) *in tch: hdwy on outside over 1f out: rdn and led ins fnl f: edgd lft: hdd cl home* **13/2**[3]

5005 **3** *1 1/4* **Besty**[35] 6104 5-8-13 **52** ....(vt) PhillipMakin 9 56
(Paul Midgley) *mde most tl rdn and hdd ins fnl f: one pce whn hld towards fin* **6/1**[2]

6212 **4** *1 1/4* **Pavers Star**[28] 6314 3-9-0 **56** ....(p) NeilFarley(3) 13 55
(Noel Wilson) *cl up: rdn over 2f out: one pce fnl f* **13/2**[3]

3041 **5** *shd* **Distant Sun (USA)**[15] 6713 8-9-7 **60** ....(p) AmyRyan 7 59
(Linda Perratt) *prom: drvn over 2f out: kpt on same pce fnl f* **12/1**

6352 **6** *nk* **Foreign Rhythm (IRE)**[12] 6786 7-8-12 **58** .... KevinStott(7) 12 56
(Ron Barr) *bhd and outpcd: hdwy appr fnl f: kpt on same pce* **8/1**

0000 **7** *nse* **Captain Royale (IRE)**[9] 6887 7-9-7 **60** ....(p) BarryMcHugh 1 58
(Tracy Waggott) *cl up on outside: rdn over 2f out: one pce whn checked ins fnl f* **18/1**

0440 **8** *shd* **Saxonette**[15] 6713 4-8-12 **51** ....(v1) PJMcDonald 11 48
(Linda Perratt) *disp ld to 1f out: kpt on same pce* **25/1**

3606 **9** *3/4* **Monel**[35] 6104 4-8-12 **51** .... GrahamLee 3 46
(Jim Goldie) *bhd: drvn along 2f out: sme late hdwy: nvr on terms* **20/1**

3342 **10** *2 1/4* **Hadrians Rule (IRE)**[15] 6713 3-9-4 **57** ....(b1) DanielTudhope 6 44
(Tim Easterby) *trckd ldrs: drvn over 2f out: wknd appr fnl f* **3/1**[1]

0504 **11** *2 1/2* **Piste**[12] 6786 6-9-0 **53** ....(e) DuranFentiman 14 31
(Tina Jackson) *s.i.s: a outpcd and bhd* **20/1**

6024 **12** *12* **Absolute Fun (IRE)**[6] 6959 3-8-11 **50** .... DavidAllan 8
(Tim Easterby) *towards rr: struggling 1/2-way: sn btn* **9/1**

1m 3.08s (2.68) **Going Correction** +0.525s/f (Yiel) 12 Ran SP% **115.8**
Speed ratings (Par 101): **99,98,96,94,94 94,93,93,92,89 85,65**
toteswingers 1&2 £60.70, 1&3 £50.80, 2&3 £8.50 CSF £267.70 CT £1836.81 TOTE £44.40: £11.10, £2.90, £2.60; EX 345.30.
Owner H G Connor **Bred** New Hall Stud **Trained** East Kilbride, S Lanarks
■ Stewards' Enquiry : L McNiff one-day ban: careless riding (Oct 29); two-day ban: used whip above permitted level (Oct 30-31)

FOCUS
A moderate sprint handicap, run at a fierce pace. The race is rated around the winner's better efforts.
Pavers Star Official explanation: jockey said gelding hung right throughout
Piste Official explanation: jockey said mare anticipated start, reared and missed the break

7100 BESTPETS H'CAP (DIV I) 5f
4:20 (4:21) (Class 5) (0-75,74) 3-Y-0+ **£2,587** (£770; £384; £192) **Stalls** High

Form RPR

2203 **1** **Phoenix Clubs (IRE)**[18] 6605 3-9-4 **71** .... BarryMcHugh 3 79
(Paul Midgley) *hld up in midfield: hdwy over 1f out: led ins fnl f: all out* **12/1**

4332 **2** *shd* **Economic Crisis (IRE)**[4] 7001 3-9-3 **70** .... PaddyAspell 2 78
(Alan Berry) *prom: effrt and ev ch over 1f out: disp ld ins fnl f: kpt on: jst hld* **8/1**

0050 **3** *hd* **Oil Strike**[68] 4954 5-9-2 **69** .... GrahamGibbons 11 76
(Michael Easterby) *w ldr: led 1/2-way: rdn over 1f out: hdd ins fnl f: kpt on: hld towards fin* **3/1**[2]

5321 **4** *nk* **Ambitious Icarus**[12] 6788 3-9-1 **68** ....(e) RobbieFitzpatrick 9 74
(Richard Guest) *hld up: rdn and hdwy over 1f out: styd on wl fnl f: nrst fin* **5/1**[3]

6643 **5** *1 1/2* **Cocktail Charlie**[37] 6044 4-9-2 **74** ....(p) DarylByrne(5) 5 74
(Tim Easterby) *trckd ldrs: n.m.r briefly over 2f out: one pce fnl f* **11/4**[1]

0565 **6** *2 1/2* **Mercers Row**[18] 6605 5-8-12 **72** .... GemmaTutty(7) 4 63
(Karen Tutty) *in tch: drvn along over 2f out: no ex over 1f out* **20/1**

311 **7** *1/2* **Midnight Dynamo**[34] 6123 5-9-7 **74** .... GrahamLee 12 64
(Jim Goldie) *hld up towards rr: drvn along over 2f out: no imp fr over 1f out* **9/1**

0500 **8** *1 1/4* **Sunrise Dance**[12] 6782 3-8-7 **60** .... AndrewMullen 7 45
(Robert Johnson) *led to 1/2-way: rdn and wknd over 1f out* **50/1**

0-00 **9** *nk* **Major Muscari (IRE)**[68] 4963 4-8-11 **64** .... DavidAllan 10 48
(Ian McInnes) *dwlt: bhd and pushed along: nvr rchd ldrs* **50/1**

3013 **10** *2 3/4* **Mission Impossible**[9] 6886 7-8-13 **66** .... PatrickMathers 1 40
(Tracy Waggott) *bhd on outside: shortlived effrt over 2f out: wknd wl over 1f out* **10/1**

2420 **11** *1* **Ryan Style (IRE)**[48] 5703 6-9-3 **70** .... TomEaves 6 41
(Lisa Williamson) *dwlt: bhd: drvn along over 2f out: sn btn* **22/1**

1m 2.64s (2.24) **Going Correction** +0.525s/f (Yiel) 11 Ran SP% **119.3**
Speed ratings (Par 103): **103,102,102,102,99 95,94,92,92,87 86**
toteswingers 1&2 £11.30, 1&3 £11.30, 2&3 £7.80 CSF £101.75 CT £372.98 TOTE £17.80: £3.70, £2.60, £1.50; EX 96.00.
Owner Williams, Lindley, Turton, Bate **Bred** Mark & Pippa Hackett **Trained** Westow, N Yorks

FOCUS
A fair sprint handicap, run at a strong pace and a length faster than division II. A small personal best from the winner.
Sunrise Dance Official explanation: jockey said filly lost its action

7101 BESTPETS H'CAP (DIV II) 5f
4:50 (4:50) (Class 5) (0-75,74) 3-Y-0+ **£2,587** (£770; £384; £192) **Stalls** High

Form RPR

0040 **1** **Rothesay Chancer**[4] 7000 4-9-3 **70** .... GrahamLee 1 78
(Jim Goldie) *hld up in midfield on outside: hdwy over 1f out: led ins fnl f: hld on wl* **5/1**[3]

3442 **2** *nk* **Sandwith**[21] 6531 9-8-11 **69** ....(p) LMcNiff(5) 4 76
(George Foster) *w ldr: led over 1f out to ins fnl f: kpt on: hld nr fin* **9/1**

2335 **3** *hd* **Select Committee**[26] 6357 7-9-4 **71** ....(v) MichaelO'Connell 2 77
(John Quinn) *in tch: rdn and hdwy appr fnl f: kpt on: hld towards fin* **14/1**

5233 **4** *1* **Fear Nothing**[13] 6767 5-9-0 **74** .... DavidBergin(7) 5 77
(David O'Meara) *chsd ldrs: effrt and drvn 2f out: kpt on same pce wl ins fnl f* **7/2**[2]

6021 **5** *2 1/2* **I'll Be Good**[9] 6887 3-8-12 **72** .... KevinStott(7) 9 66
(Robert Johnson) *led at decent gallop: hdd over 1f out: no ex ins fnl f* **13/5**[1]

5350 **6** *shd* **Wicked Wilma (IRE)**[21] 6531 8-8-3 **63** .... JordanHibberd(7) 7 56
(Alan Berry) *missed break: bhd: rdn and hdwy over 1f out: no imp ins fnl f* **16/1**

0000 **7** *3 1/4* **Blown It (USA)**[28] 6314 6-8-12 **65** .... JoeFanning 8 47
(Keith Dalgleish) *bdly hmpd sn after s: bhd: drvn along 1/2-way: nvr rchd ldrs* **16/1**

004 **8** *1* **Go Go Green (IRE)**[45] 5801 6-9-3 **70** .... DanielTudhope 3 48
(Jim Goldie) *hld up: rdn along 1/2-way: nvr able to chal* **9/1**

0010 **9** *6* **Ingleby Star (IRE)**[26] 6358 7-9-0 **70** ....(p) PaulPickard(3) 6 26
(Ian McInnes) *in tch: drvn along 1/2-way: sn btn* **9/1**

1m 2.84s (2.44) **Going Correction** +0.525s/f (Yiel) 9 Ran SP% **115.1**
Speed ratings (Par 103): **101,100,100,98,94 94,89,87,78**
toteswingers 1&2 £6.90, 1&3 £11.70, 2&3 £9.30 CSF £48.94 CT £589.93 TOTE £6.80: £1.90, £2.30, £4.00; EX 37.80.
Owner Discovery Racing Club 2 **Bred** Mrs S R Kennedy **Trained** Uplawmoor, E Renfrews
■ Stewards' Enquiry : L McNiff four-day ban: careless riding (Nov 1-3,5)

FOCUS
The second division of this sprint handicap looked every bit as competitive as the first, but was a length slower. Similar form.

7102 TURFTV SHOWING PERTH AND KELSO AMATEUR RIDERS' H'CAP 2m
5:20 (5:20) (Class 6) (0-65,64) 3-Y-0+ **£1,559** (£483; £241; £121) **Stalls** High

Form RPR

0302 **1** **Cool Baranca (GER)**[10] 4867 6-10-4 **47** .... MissECSayer 7 56
(Dianne Sayer) *hld up and bhd: gd hdwy 3f out: led over 1f out: drfited rt: pushed out* **4/1**[1]

1023 **2** *3 1/2* **Stormy Morning**[28] 6315 6-11-1 **61** ....(p) MissHBethell(3) 9 66
(Philip Kirby) *t.k.h in midfield: hdwy to chse ldrs whn short of room briefly over 1f out: sn chsng wnr: no imp fnl f* **4/1**[1]

4504 **3** *hd* **Descaro (USA)**[6] 6956 6-10-7 **57** ....(v) MissRHeptonstall(7) 10 62
(David O'Meara) *trckd ldrs: led over 2f out: hdd over 1f out: kpt on same pce* **7/1**

2064 **4** *nk* **Terenzium (IRE)**[46] 5761 10-9-13 **47** ....(p) MissRSmith(5) 6 51
(Micky Hammond) *hld up: hdwy over 4f out: rdn over 2f out: kpt on fnl f: nvr able to chal* **16/1**

6050 **5** *1 1/4* **Altnaharra**[8] 4744 3-9-1 **48** ow3..(b1) MrsICGoldie(7) 13 51
(Jim Goldie) *in tch: rdn over 2f out: one pce fr over 1f out* **25/1**

3-04 **6** *18* **Soprano (GER)**[19] 5922 10-10-7 **57** .... MrsLGoldie(7) 1 38
(Jim Goldie) *hld up on ins: rdn and effrt 3f out: no imp fr 2f out* **8/1**

626 **7** *3/4* **Goodlukin Lucy**[13] 6758 5-9-11 **45** ....(t1) MissRobynGray(5) 5 25
(Dianne Sayer) *cl up: led to 1/2-way to over 2f out: sn wknd* **16/1**

6410 **8** *4* **Forrest Flyer (IRE)**[36] 6074 8-11-7 **64** .... MrsCBartley 3 40
(Jim Goldie) *led to 1/2-way: lost pl over 4f out: n.d after* **14/1**

4626 **9** *3/4* **Hoar Frost**[41] 5922 7-9-11 **45** ....(p) MissPhillipaTutty(5) 11 20
(Karen Tutty) *hld up on outside: hdwy and cl up after 5f: rdn and outpcd 3f out: sn btn* **25/1**

3460 **10** *6* **Millymonkin**[7] 6940 3-10-5 **59** ow1..(t) MissJCoward 8 27
(Michael Easterby) *cl up tl rdn and wknd fr 3f out* **6/1**[2]

124 **11** *12* **Grand Art (IRE)**[28] 6311 8-11-1 **58** ....(p) MissSBrotherton 2 11
(Noel Wilson) *hld up in tch: rdn over 3f out: wknd over 2f out* **13/2**[3]

0000 **12** *1* **Media Stars**[20] 6561 7-9-13 **45** ....(t) MissCWalton(3) 14
(Robert Johnson) *t.k.h: hld up in tch on outside: struggling over 3f out: sn btn* **66/1**

3m 49.64s (16.14) **Going Correction** +0.70s/f (Yiel)
WFA 3 from 4yo+ 11lb 12 Ran SP% **118.8**
Speed ratings (Par 101): **87,85,85,85,84 75,75,73,72,69 63,63**
toteswingers 1&2 £6.00, 1&3 £7.40, 2&3 £7.10 CSF £18.53 CT £110.32 TOTE £3.90: £1.50, £1.70, £3.60; EX 23.70.
Owner Dennis J Coppola **Bred** Stiftung Gestut Fahrhof **Trained** Hackthorpe, Cumbria

FOCUS
A low-grade amateur riders' handicap. The form is rated around the runner-up.
T/Jkpt: Not won. T/Plt: £903.80 to a £1 stake. Pool: £67,934.96 - 54.87 winning tickets T/Qpdt: £188.70 to a £1 stake. Pool: £5,559.61 - 21.80 winning tickets RY

6795 SALISBURY (R-H)
Monday, October 15

OFFICIAL GOING: Heavy (soft in places; 7.2)
Wind: mild breeze against Weather: cloudy becoming overcast with showers

7103 BATHWICK TYRES MAIDEN AUCTION STKS 6f 212y
1:50 (1:51) (Class 5) 2-Y-0 **£2,587** (£770; £384; £192) **Stalls** Low

Form RPR

0 **1** **Noble Gift**[23] 6481 2-8-13 0 .... WilliamBuick 7 77+
(John Dunlop) *cl up: pushed along and hdwy over 2f out: led ins fnl f: racd green: styd on wl: pushed out* **7/2**[2]

0 **2** *1 1/4* **Sweet Martoni**[21] 6534 2-8-8 0 .... NeilCallan 10 68
(William Knight) *trckd ldrs: rdn to ld 2f out: hdd ins fnl f: kpt on same pce* **9/1**

6 **3** *1/2* **Snowy Dawn**[11] 6818 2-8-2 0 .... JackDuern(7) 3 68+
(Reg Hollinshead) *trckd ldrs: rdn over 2f out: swtchd rt over 1f out: kpt on same pce fnl f* **5/1**

20 **4** *6* **Poor Duke (IRE)**[10] 6841 2-8-11 75 .... FergusSweeney 1 54
(Jamie Osborne) *trckd ldr: disp ld after 2f: rdn and hdd 2f out: fdd fnl 120yds* **10/3**[1]

460 **5** *1/2* **Red Four**[39] 5978 2-8-6 67 .... HayleyTurner 2 48
(George Baker) *hld up in tch: rdn over 2f out: nvr gng pce to get involved* **9/2**[3]

345 **6** *3/4* **Entrapping**[21] 6532 2-8-13 65 .... PatDobbs 6 53
(Richard Hannon) *led: jnd after 2f: rdn and hdd 2f out: sn hld: fdd fnl f* **13/2**

00 **7** *3 3/4* **See And Be Seen**[12] 6795 2-8-12 0 .... DaneO'Neill 9 42
(Sylvester Kirk) *hld up in tch: rdn over 3f out: wknd over 1f out* **20/1**

8 *3 1/4* **Zinnobar** 2-8-6 0 .... JohnFahy 5 28
(Jonathan Portman) *dwlt: pushed along over 4f out: a last: wknd 2f out* **14/1**

9 *6* **Bertie Moon** 2-8-8 0 .... SophieDoyle(3) 4 17
(Geoffrey Deacon) *s.i.s: hld up in tch: rdn over 2f out: wknd over 1f out* **66/1**

1m 32.3s (3.70) **Going Correction** +0.55s/f (Yiel) 9 Ran SP% **116.4**
Speed ratings (Par 95): **100,98,98,91,90 89,85,81,74**
toteswingers 1&2 £9.00, 1&3 £14.70, 2&3 £24.50 CSF £35.28 TOTE £4.40: £2.40, £3.30, £1.50; EX 35.40.
Owner Gail Brown Racing (V) **Bred** Theakston Stud **Trained** Arundel, W Sussex

FOCUS
Rail erected in order to use centre section of track but full width of course in use for last 2f. A fair juvenile auction maiden in which they went an honest gallop on ground officially described as heavy, soft in places. The winning time was over six seconds slower than standard. The first three clear and the race averages help with the level.

NOTEBOOK
Noble Gift weakened into a modest 12th of 18 in a better-class Newbury maiden on fast ground on his debut the previous month. He found marked improvement here, relishing the testing surface to come through from mid-division to take it up just inside the final furlong for a straightforward success. He looks a fair handicapper for next term who may need a soft surface to be seen to best effect. (op 9-2)
Sweet Martoni finished a moderate ninth of 13 over this trip at Kempton on her debut the previous month. She progressed notably on this testing ground, coming with what initially appeared a winning run 2f out, and she looks another fair prospect for handicaps at up to 1m on a soft surface. (op 16-1)
Snowy Dawn, a modest sixth at Warwick on soft ground on his debut 11 days earlier, gives the form some substance after an improved third placing, in which he was keeping on reasonably well at the end. He looks a fair handicapper at up to 1m2f for next term. (op 9-2)
Poor Duke(IRE), reportedly playing up in the preliminaries, once again failed to reproduce his second of seven from Yarmouth on his penultimate start. (op 7-2)
Red Four was never going the pace and disappointed. (tchd 4-1)

7104 BATHWICK TYRES E B F MAIDEN FILLIES' STKS — 6f 212y
2:20 (2:20) (Class 5) 2-Y-O — **£3,072** (£914; £456; £228) **Stalls** Low

Form — RPR
0 **1** **Trapeze**[123] 3074 2-9-0 0 ... WilliamBuick 3 — 77+
(John Gosden) *trckd ldr: rdn to ld over 1f out: kpt on: drvn out* **7/2**[3]
0 **2** ¾ **Estiqaama (USA)**[23] 6489 2-9-0 0 ... TadhgO'Shea 4 — 75+
(William Haggas) *sn led: rdn and swtchd to nrside rail 2f out: hdd over 1f out: styd on wl fnl 120yds: clsng on wnr at fin* **13/8**[1]
5 **3** 5 **Carry On Clapping (IRE)**[24] 6443 2-9-0 0 ... PatDobbs 5 — 62
(Richard Hannon) *s.i.s: t.k.h: sn trcking ldrs: c nrside rail and rdn 2f out: kpt on same pce* **2/1**[2]
4 6 **Perfect Beat** 2-9-0 0 ... RichardKingscote 2 — 46+
(Ralph Beckett) *dwlt: chsd ldng quartet: effrt over 2f out: fdd ins fnl f* **6/1**
0 **5** 16 **Sporting Club Girl**[21] 6535 2-9-0 0 ... NeilCallan 1
(William Knight) *s.i.s: trckd ldrs: rdn 3f out: wknd over 1f out* **40/1**

1m 33.01s (4.41) **Going Correction** +0.55s/f (Yiel) — **5** Ran SP% **110.4**
Speed ratings (Par 92): **96,95,89,82,64**
CSF £9.68 TOTE £5.50: £2.20, £1.30; EX 12.20.
Owner A E Oppenheimer **Bred** Hascombe & Valiant Studs & Cheveley Park **Trained** Newmarket, Suffolk

FOCUS
An average 2-y-o fillies maiden which matches up to the race averages. The first two may do better.

NOTEBOOK
Trapeze, who cost 240,000gns as a yearling and is a half-sister to the smart 6f-1m winner Leo, was returning from a four-month break since a poor start to her career at Nottingham in June. She raced up the centre of the track in isolation in the final part of the contest, and showed a willing attitude to get on top in the closing stages. She looks a fair filly in the making, but may need cut in the ground to be seen to best effect. (op 4-1 tchd 9-2)
Estiqaama(USA) finished a modest 12th of 17 in a better-class Newmarket maiden on fast ground on her debut the previous month. She handled these conditions well, but may prove versatile in that regard. She came over to race alone up the stands' rail over 1f out, but had to give best about 100yds from the line. She looks a fair 1m prospect for next term. (op 5-2)
Carry On Clapping(IRE) stayed on into fifth of 12 in a better-class Newbury maiden on fast ground on her debut the previous month, but couldn't get to grips with the front two here. (op 6-4 tchd 9-4)
Perfect Beat may benefit from this introduction over further in due course. (op 5-1)

7105 BATHWICK TYRES BOURNEMOUTH H'CAP (DIV I) — 6f 212y
2:50 (2:50) (Class 6) (0-60,60) 3-Y-O+ — **£1,940** (£577; £288; £144) **Stalls** Low

Form — RPR
0606 **1** **Bassett Road (IRE)**[12] 6774 4-9-6 **59** ... WilliamBuick 3 — 72
(Willie Musson) *mid-div: hdwy over 2f out: shkn up to ld over 1f out: kpt on strly: readily* **11/2**[3]
1606 **2** 2¾ **Querido (GER)**[30] 6252 8-9-5 **58** ... (tp) IanMongan 2 — 64
(Paddy Butler) *pushed along early: mid-div: rdn and hdwy over 2f out: ch over 1f out: kpt on ins fnl f but sn no ch w wnr* **10/1**
0-60 **3** 1¾ **Lordship (IRE)**[6] 6967 8-8-4 **50** ... JakePayne(7) 4 — 51
(Tony Carroll) *led: rdn 2f out: hdd over 1f out: no ex fnl f* **25/1**
4000 **4** 1¼ **White Flight**[12] 6774 3-9-0 **55** ... RichardKingscote 5 — 53
(Jonathan Portman) *prom: rdn and ev ch 2f out tl ent fnl f: fdd fnl 120yds* **18/1**
0000 **5** ½ **Oratorian (IRE)**[18] 6610 3-9-3 **58** ... PatDobbs 6 — 55
(Sylvester Kirk) *trckd ldrs: rdn over 2f out: kpt on same pce* **7/1**
2433 **6** ½ **George Thisby**[45] 5783 6-9-7 **60** ... (p) TomQueally 11 — 56
(Rod Millman) *towards rr: struggling and lost tch 4f out: sn hrd rdn: styd on fr over 1f out but nvr threatening* **4/1**[1]
-500 **7** 1 **Lord Deevert**[40] 5935 7-8-2 **48** oh1 ow2 ... (p) JackDuern(7) 7 — 41
(Bill Turner) *s.i.s: towards rr: hdwy 3f out: rdn over 2f out: ch over 1f out: fdd ins fnl f* **20/1**
344 **8** 1 **Bold Ring**[12] 6778 6-9-1 **54** ... JimmyQuinn 9 — 44
(Eric Wheeler) *trckd ldrs: effrt 2f out: wknd ent fnl f* **5/1**[2]
5656 **9** ½ **The Name Is Frank**[19] 6585 7-9-2 **55** ... (t) FergusSweeney 8 — 44
(Mark Gillard) *prom tl rdn 3f out: sn hld* **9/1**
000 **10** nk **Shaunas Spirit (IRE)**[27] 6334 4-9-1 **57** ... PatrickHills(3) 10 — 45
(Dean Ivory) *struggling 3f out: a towards rr* **15/2**
500/ **11** 1¼ **May Boy**[690] 6709 6-8-6 **48** ... SophieDoyle(3) 12 — 33
(Ron Hodges) *mid-div tl 3f out: sn swtchd to nrside rail and rdn: wknd over 1f out* **33/1**
0604 **12** 1 **Cheers Big Ears (IRE)**[38] 6000 6-8-4 **46** oh1 ... MarkCoumbe(3) 1 — 28
(Richard Price) *trckd ldrs: rdn over 2f out: wknd over 1f out* **20/1**

1m 32.15s (3.55) **Going Correction** +0.55s/f (Yiel)
WFA 3 from 4yo+ 2lb — **12** Ran SP% **117.0**
Speed ratings (Par 101): **101,97,95,94,93 93,92,91,90,90 88,87**
toteswingers 1&2 £4.60, 1&3 £27.10, 2&3 £28.00 CSF £55.21 CT £891.50 TOTE £7.90: £2.70, £4.20, £6.80; EX 69.80.
Owner The Poets **Bred** Michael Mullins **Trained** Newmarket, Suffolk

FOCUS
A moderate handicap, run in a similar time to division II. The winner finally took advantage of a reduced mark.
The Name Is Frank Official explanation: jockey said gelding hung right throughout

7106 BATHWICK TYRES BOURNEMOUTH H'CAP (DIV II) — 6f 212y
3:25 (3:25) (Class 6) (0-60,59) 3-Y-O+ — **£1,940** (£577; £288; £144) **Stalls** Low

Form — RPR
5401 **1** **Les Verguettes (IRE)**[6] 6967 4-9-3 **58** ... AshleyMorgan(3) 6 — 69
(Chris Wall) *travelled wl in mid-div: pushed along and hdwy 2f out: shkn up to ld ent fnl f: sn rdn: kpt on* **13/8**[1]
6402 **2** nk **See The Storm**[6] 6951 4-8-4 **45** ... RyanPowell(3) 3 — 55
(Ian Williams) *trckd ldr: led 2f out: sn rdn: edgd lft and hdd ent fnl f: kpt on fnl 120yds: hld fnl strides* **5/1**[3]
6505 **3** 3 **Blackamoor Harry**[13] 6758 3-8-0 **45** ... RachealKneller(5) 8 — 47
(Richard Ford) *mid-div: rdn over 2f out: no imp tl r.o ent fnl f: wnt 3rd towards fin* **28/1**
1563 **4** ¾ **One Last Dream**[14] 6739 3-9-2 **56** ... (b) RichardKingscote 12 — 56
(Ron Hodges) *racd keenly: trckd ldrs: rdn wl over 2f out: hung rt fr over 1f out: kpt on same pce* **8/1**
3566 **5** 1¼ **No Larking (IRE)**[6] 6967 4-9-4 **56** ... DaneO'Neill 4 — 53
(Henry Candy) *led: rdn and hdd 2f out: pressed ldrs tl ent fnl f: fdd fnl 120yds* **9/2**[2]
0200 **6** ½ **Custom House (IRE)**[5] 6982 4-9-5 **57** ...[1] JohnFahy 7 — 53
(John E Long) *v awkward and broke stalls open: in last pair: drvn 3f out: sme late prog: nvr trbld ldrs* **14/1**
0004 **7** 1 **Pose (IRE)**[6] 6951 5-8-8 **46** ... (t) AdamBeschizza 5 — 39
(Roger Ingram) *trckd ldrs: rdn over 2f out: wknd ent fnl f* **28/1**
0600 **8** 1¾ **Huzzah (IRE)**[6] 6967 7-9-3 **55** ... (p) MichaelStainton 10 — 43
(Paul Howling) *s.i.s: in last pair: rdn over 1f out: no imp* **16/1**
056 **9** ½ **Aujourd'Hui**[13] 6765 3-9-0 **54** ... PatDobbs 2 — 41
(Richard Hannon) *trckd ldrs tl rdn 3f out: wknd 2f out* **14/1**
0045 **10** 1 **Cadmium Loch**[56] 5427 4-8-12 **57** ... (p) JackDuern(7) 11 — 41
(Reg Hollinshead) *mid-div: rdn over 2f out: wknd over 1f out* **10/1**

1m 32.29s (3.69) **Going Correction** +0.55s/f (Yiel)
WFA 3 from 4yo+ 2lb — **10** Ran SP% **119.3**
Speed ratings (Par 101): **100,99,96,95,93 93,92,90,89,88**
toteswingers 1&2 £3.00, 1&3 £27.50, 2&3 £23.70 CSF £9.91 CT £166.16 TOTE £2.90: £1.10, £2.20, £5.90; EX 9.30.
Owner David Gilbert **Bred** Camogue Stud Ltd **Trained** Newmarket, Suffolk
■ Stewards' Enquiry : Ryan Powell twenty-five day ban: used whip above permitted level, 5th offence in 6mths (Nov 2-Dec 3)

FOCUS
The second division of a moderate handicap for 3yos and up, in which they once again went a fair gallop. The first two were both well in on recent runs.
Custom House(IRE) Official explanation: jockey said gelding hit its head on leaving stalls

7107 BATHWICK TYRES REDUCED ADMISSION RACEDAY CONDITIONS STKS — 6f 212y
4:00 (4:00) (Class 3) 3-Y-O+ — **£6,663** (£1,982; £990; £495) **Stalls** Low

Form — RPR
1246 **1** **Shamaal Nibras (USA)**[58] 5334 3-9-0 94 ... PatDobbs 1 — 99
(Richard Hannon) *trckd ldng trio: squeezed through gap to chal 2f out: sn rdn: tk narrow advantage ent fnl f: strly pressed: all out: won on nod* **11/4**[2]
3201 **2** shd **Gregorian (IRE)**[22] 6513 3-9-3 114 ... WilliamBuick 3 — 102
(John Gosden) *trckd ldng pair: drew upsides 2f out: rdn for str chal fr over 1f out: ev ch thrght fnl f: lost on nod* **2/5**[1]
6400 **3** 2½ **Red Seventy**[75] 4703 3-9-0 84 ... DaneO'Neill 4 — 92
(Richard Hannon) *disp ld: rdn whn hrd pressed fr 2f out: narrowly hdd ent fnl f: keeping on but looking hld in 1/2 l 3rd whn squeezed out fnl 140yds* **25/1**
1001 **4** 9 **Barons Spy (IRE)**[44] 5812 11-8-13 89 ... MarkCoumbe(3) 2 — 69
(Richard Price) *disp ld: rdn 2f out: sn hdd and hld: fdd fnl f* **20/1**[3]

1m 32.6s (4.00) **Going Correction** +0.55s/f (Yiel)
WFA 3 from 11yo 2lb — **4** Ran SP% **106.7**
Speed ratings (Par 107): **99,98,96,85**
CSF £4.23 TOTE £2.80; EX 4.60.
Owner Tariq S Al Tayer **Bred** Andrew Cowen & Gary Tolchin **Trained** East Everleigh, Wilts
■ Stewards' Enquiry : Pat Dobbs one-day ban: careless riding (Oct 31)

FOCUS
A muddling conditions event, and a relatively slow time. The winner is rated close to his handicap form.

NOTEBOOK
Shamaal Nibras(USA) was returning from a two-month break since a below-par display at Chester in August, but had previously looked progressive when fourth at Glorious Goodwood. He was already proven on soft ground, but had 17lb to find on these terms with the runner-up. That discrepancy on official BHA ratings did appear flattering beforehand and that played out so. The 3-y-o benefited from the stop-start nature of this race, and injected just enough speed to hold on narrowly in a driving finish. (op 7-2)
Gregorian(IRE) won a similar contest to this over an extended 1m on heavy ground at Hamilton the previous month, and that level of ability allied to his confirmed stamina should have counted for plenty. It is perfectly possible that he could have won this race if his jockey had ridden him in a more straightforward manner on the lead. That said, the winner may well have picked him up in any case and it is by no means cut and dried either way. (op 2-7)
Red Seventy was returning from an 11-week break and performed very respectably. (tchd 28-1)
Barons Spy(IRE) paid for doing too much too soon, but had plenty to find. (tchd 10-1)

7108 BATHWICK TYRES SALISBURY H'CAP — 1m 1f 198y
4:30 (4:30) (Class 5) (0-70,69) 3-Y-O — **£2,264** (£673; £336; £168) **Stalls** Low

Form — RPR
3311 **1** **Grand Liaison**[17] 6631 3-9-4 **66** ... IanMongan 5 — 74+
(John Berry) *mid-div: hdwy to trck ldrs 3f out: rdn to ld wl over 1f out: kpt on wl: comf* **5/2**[2]
6230 **2** 1¾ **Elegant Ophelia**[26] 6365 3-9-0 **62** ... BrettDoyle 6 — 66
(Dean Ivory) *trckd ldr tl rdn over 2f out: styd on same pce: regained 2nd ins fnl f* **22/1**
0613 **3** nk **Calculated Risk**[59] 5323 3-9-5 **67** ... WilliamBuick 7 — 71+
(Willie Musson) *hld up bhd: pushed along and hdwy 3f out: sn rdn: styd on same pce fr over 1f out: wnt 3rd towards fin* **7/4**[1]
003 **4** nk **Present Day**[63] 5152 3-8-7 **55** oh1 ... (b[1]) JohnFahy 2 — 58
(Clive Cox) *led: rdn over 2f out: hdd wl over 1f out: kpt on tl no ex and lost 2 pls ins fnl f* **28/1**
5346 **5** 1¼ **Any Other Day**[26] 6364 3-9-3 **65** ... NeilCallan 1 — 66
(William Knight) *trckd ldrs: rdn wl over 2f out: kpt on but nt pce to chal* **11/2**[3]
300 **6** 1¼ **The Noble Ord**[33] 6146 3-9-7 **69** ... (t) DaneO'Neill 8 — 67
(Sylvester Kirk) *towards rr: hdwy into midfield 6f out: rdn to chse ldrs over 2f out: fdd ins fnl f* **10/1**
0000 **7** ¾ **Operettist**[30] 6250 3-9-1 **63** ... PatDobbs 4 — 60
(Richard Hannon) *mid-div: rdn 3f out: nvr a danger: wknd fnl f* **10/1**
0-66 **8** 15 **Isola Bella**[120] 3193 3-8-4 **55** oh10 ... RyanPowell(3) 9 — 22
(Jonathan Portman) *trckd ldrs: rdn wl over 2f out: sn wknd* **40/1**

0-26 **9** *18* **Beaumont Cooper**[12] 6792 3-9-3 **65**.................................. TomQueally 3
(Tony Carroll) *wnt lft leaving stalls: struggling 3f out: a in rr: wknd over 2f out* **14/1**

2m 14.83s (4.93) **Going Correction** +0.475s/f (Yiel) **9** Ran SP% **115.4**
Speed ratings (Par 101): **99,97,97,97,96 95,94,82,68**
toteswingers 1&2 £6.30, 1&3 £1.70, 2&3 £3.10 CSF £57.72 CT £119.02 TOTE £4.10: £1.50, £4.20, £1.70; EX 72.60.
Owner Barrie Catchpole & Michael Meaney **Bred** Ashbrittle Stud **Trained** Newmarket, Suffolk

FOCUS
A modest 3-y-o handicap which looked sound run. The second and fourth lend doubts to the form.

7109 BATHWICK TYRES "SEASON FINALE" H'CAP 1m 6f 21y
5:00 (5:01) (Class 3) (0-95,88) 3-Y-O+ **£6,663** (£1,982; £990; £495) **Stalls** Far side

Form RPR

0000 **1** **The Betchworth Kid**[25] 6415 7-9-7 **82**.............................. HayleyTurner 2 97
(Michael Bell) *hld up bhd: pushed along fr over 5f out: hdwy fr 3f out: led over 1f out: drew rt away: easily* **11/2**[2]

016 **2** *8* **Stock Hill Fair**[23] 6472 4-9-2 **77**.. PatDobbs 9 81
(Brendan Powell) *led: rdn 2f out: hdd over 1f out: styd on but sn no ch w easy wnr* **15/2**[3]

0020 **3** *1 ½* **Dunhoy (IRE)**[59] 5306 4-9-5 **80**.. NeilCallan 4 82
(Tony Newcombe) *hld up towards rr: hdwy 3f out: swtchd rt and rdn over 2f out: styd on same pce* **14/1**

1320 **4** *1* **Suzi's A Class Act**[18] 6600 4-9-6 **81**........................(p) AdamBeschizza 11 82
(James Eustace) *trckd ldr: rdn over 2f out: styd on same pce* **8/1**

611 **5** *½* **Malekov (IRE)**[27] 6349 3-9-2 **86**.. TomQueally 1 86
(Sir Henry Cecil) *mid-div: hdwy 3f out: sn rdn: styd on same pce* **4/1**[1]

00P0 **6** *2* **Classic Vintage (USA)**[19] 6576 6-9-13 **88**.......................... IanMongan 10 85
(Amanda Perrett) *trckd ldrs: rdn 3f out: wknd fnl f* **33/1**

-064 **7** *nse* **Spifer (IRE)**[68] 4962 4-9-13 **88**.. KierenFallon 8 85
(Luca Cumani) *mid-div: pushed along 4f out: stdy prog but nt clrest of runs fr 3f out: rdn to chse ldrs over 1f out: wknd fnl f* **4/1**[1]

3300 **8** *1 ¾* **Purification (IRE)**[24] 6445 4-9-7 **82**...............................(b) WilliamBuick 5 76
(John Gosden) *mid-div: chsd ldrs 4f out: sn rdn: wknd ent fnl f* **15/2**[3]

46-1 **9** *6* **Into Wain (USA)**[212] 668 5-9-10 **85**.................................. KieranO'Neill 12 71
(Steve Gollings) *in tch tl rdn over 2f out: wknd over 1f out* **28/1**

U **10** *15* **Allied Answer**[3] 7034 4-9-3 **85**........................ WilliamTwiston-Davies(7) 3 50
(Steve Gollings) *mid-div: short of room and clipped heels after 4f: rdn over 3f out: wknd 2f out* **14/1**

60-5 **11** *8* **Phoenix Flight (IRE)**[244] 554 7-9-12 **87**.................... FergusSweeney 6 41
(James Evans) *hmpd after 4f: a bhd* **66/1**

5205 **P** **Woolfall Treasure**[10] 6834 7-9-13 **88**..............................(v) GeorgeBaker 7
(Gary Moore) *trcking ldrs whn looked to be struck into after 4f: immediately p.u* **14/1**

3m 11.42s (4.02) **Going Correction** +0.475s/f (Yiel)
WFA 3 from 4yo+ 9lb **12** Ran SP% **117.9**
Speed ratings (Par 107): **107,102,101,101,100 99,99,98,95,86 81,**
toteswingers 1&2 £5.20, 1&3 £21.00, 2&3 £28.50 CSF £45.58 CT £553.39 TOTE £4.50: £2.40, £3.10, £3.90; EX 55.00.
Owner W H Ponsonby **Bred** R P Williams **Trained** Newmarket, Suffolk

FOCUS
A fair staying handicap. The winner was well in on this year's best and has been rated around that.

NOTEBOOK
The Betchworth Kid had returned to former trainer Michael Bell's yard after an indifferent season on the Flat this summer for Alan King. The reasoning behind the move was to revitalise him with a return to his former surroundings, with a view to rising up the handicap sufficiently in order to get into the November Handicap at Doncaster next month, a race he finished runner-up in for today's trainer/jockey combination off 15lb higher in 2008. The first part of the plan worked like clockwork, as he demolished this field in a very taking manner. He should get into the Doncaster race now and, on this evidence, will play a leading role once more in that event given similar testing conditions. His owners have another live candidate in First Mohican. (op 13-2)
Stock Hill Fair gives the form real substance as a previous C&D winner off 4lb lower in August, and simply ran into one on this occasion. (op 8-1 tchd 9-1)
Dunhoy(IRE) was returning from a two-month break since a modest Newbury display. He had previously finished second over this C&D off a similar mark and should remain competitive off this sort of rating on turf or Polytrack. (op 20-1)
Suzi's A Class Act, who won over this C&D off 9lb lower in August, is entitled to be feeling the effects of a busy campaign and may need a break. (tchd 17-2)
Malekov(IRE) won his first start in a handicap over this trip at Yarmouth the previous month, but the ground may have been more of a factor than his subsequent 5lb rise in finishing out of the money on this occasion. (op 3-1)
Spifer(IRE), who was returning from a ten-week break, raced in mid-division before weakening out of contention around a furlong from home. (op 9-2)
Woolfall Treasure Official explanation: jockey said gelding stumbled and lost its action
T/Plt: £243.20 to a £1 stake. Pool: £47385.30 - 142.20 winning tickets T/Qpdt: £55.20 to a £1 stake. Pool: £4,633.70 - 62.10 winning tickets TM

6926 WINDSOR (R-H)
Monday, October 15

OFFICIAL GOING: Soft (heavy in places; 6.2)
All distances returned are by judge's eye; issues with timing equipment. A famous 10,168-1 seven-timer from eight rides for Richard Hughes.
Wind: Moderate, half behind Weather: Cloudy, occasional drizzle

7110 E B F JOE WARD HILL MEMORIAL MAIDEN STKS 6f
2:00 (2:00) (Class 5) 2-Y-O **£3,299** (£981; £490; £245) **Stalls** Low

Form RPR

66 **1** **Pivotal Movement**[12] 6787 2-9-3 0.............................. RichardHughes 4 76+
(Richard Hannon) *pressed ldr: shkn up to ld wl over 1f out: drew clr fnl f: comf* **13/8**[1]

0046 **2** *3 ¼* **Iris Blue**[63] 5160 2-8-12 60.. RobertHavlin 7 61
(John Gosden) *trckd ldrs: rdn 2f out: chsd wnr 1f out: no imp* **28/1**

4 **3** *½* **Secondo (FR)**[24] 6444 2-9-3 0.. RyanMoore 5 65
(Roger Charlton) *slowly away: t.k.h and hld up in last pair: prog on outer 2f out: rdn to press for 2nd fnl f: no ch w wnr* **13/8**[1]

04 **4** *3 ¼* **Provencal**[19] 6571 2-9-3 0.. JamesMillman 1 55
(Rod Millman) *chsd ldrs: pushed along bef 1/2-way: wknd over 1f out* **25/1**[3]

60 **5** *1 ¾* **Ishisoba**[21] 6534 2-8-12 0.. MartinHarley 2 45
(Alastair Lidderdale) *chsd ldrs tl wknd 2f out* **33/1**

003 **6** *nk* **Overrider**[56] 5418 2-9-3 78.. MichaelHills 3 49
(Charles Hills) *led to wl over 1f out: wknd* **8/1**[2]

0 **7** *shd* **Blue Twister**[61] 5235 2-9-3 0.. JimmyFortune 6 48
(Andrew Balding) *racd awkwardly early and bhd: in tch after 2f: shkn up 2f out: wknd over 1f out* **8/1**[2]

1m 14.42s (1.42) **Going Correction** +0.175s/f (Good) **7** Ran SP% **108.6**
Speed ratings (Par 95): **97,92,92,87,85 84,84**
toteswingers 1&2 £10.10, 1&3 £1.10, 2&3 £3.90 CSF £48.72 TOTE £2.10: £1.30, £7.60; EX 37.70.
Owner Sir A Ferguson,G Mason,R Wood & P Done **Bred** W And R Barnett Ltd **Trained** East Everleigh, Wilts

FOCUS
The ground was given as soft, heavy in places (GoingStick 6.2) and the racecourse was at its maximum width with the exception of the top bend, which was dolled out 6yds from the normal inner configuration, adding 20yds to race distances of 1m plus. Just an ordinary maiden and the runner-up will be key to the form. The winner is cpabale of doing a lot better next year.

NOTEBOOK
Pivotal Movement drew nicely clear inside the last. The 6f trip suited him, as did the ground, unsurprisingly as he's by Pivotal out of a Selkirk mare. The runner-up, who is rated 60, gives a marker for the form, and he ought not to be too harshly treated when going handicapping next year. (op 7-4 tchd 11-8)
Iris Blue, back from a two-month break, made it a one-two for her sire Pivotal. The ground suited her and she probably put up a career-best in defeat. (op 16-1)
Secondo(FR), in contrast, didn't build on his debut effort on this much softer ground. (op 7-4 tchd 15-8)
Provencal was a bit keen early, which didn't help his cause, but handicaps are now an option for him. (op 33-1)
Ishisoba is another now eligible for a mark. (op 28-1)
Overrider made the early running, but this ground wasn't for him. (op 6-1)

7111 DAVISBAKERYCARIBBEAN.COM NURSERY 1m 67y
2:30 (2:31) (Class 5) (0-75,74) 2-Y-O **£2,264** (£673; £336; £168) **Stalls** Low

Form RPR

6034 **1** **East Texas Red (IRE)**[12] 6793 2-8-10 **63**.................. RichardHughes 5 68
(Richard Hannon) *trckd ldr: led against rail wl over 2f out: sn rdn: kpt on wl fr over 1f out* **5/2**[1]

16 **2** *1 ¾* **Jebril (FR)**[14] 6732 2-9-6 **73**.. DarryllHolland 4 74
(Jonathan Portman) *s.s: settled in detached last: shkn up 1/2-way: prog u.p 2f out: styd on wl to take 2nd ins fnl f: unable to chal* **7/1**[3]

0014 **3** *1 ½* **Knight's Parade (IRE)**[14] 6732 2-8-1 **59**.................. DarrenEgan(5) 8 57
(Amanda Perrett) *racd wd: prog and prom 1/2-way: cl enough and rdn 3f out: one pce fnl 2f* **7/2**[2]

0625 **4** *1 ¼* **Rioja Day (IRE)**[35] 6096 2-9-2 **69**.. SebSanders 6 64
(J W Hills) *prom: cl enough and rdn 3f out: chsd wnr jst over 2f out: nt qckn over 1f out: lost 2nd ins fnl f* **7/1**[3]

13 **5** *nk* **Cheektocheek (IRE)**[42] 5890 2-9-2 **74**.................. TobyAtkinson(5) 1 68
(Marco Botti) *hld up towards rr: rdn over 3f out and sn lost tch w ldrs: tried to cl 2f out: one pce fnl f* **7/1**[3]

005 **6** *½* **Gabrial The Duke (IRE)**[17] 6644 2-8-11 **64**.................. FrannyNorton 7 59+
(Ian Williams) *hld up towards rr: rdn and no prog 3f out: one pce after* **14/1**

3220 **7** *½* **Missing Agent**[3] 7026 2-8-12 **65**..............................(v) SilvestreDeSousa 9 57
(David Evans) *fractious in stalls: led at gd pce: edgd off rail 1/2-way: hdd wl over 2f out: steadily wknd* **20/1**

044 **8** *13* **Al Muntazah (IRE)**[80] 4532 2-9-0 **67**.................................. MartinHarley 3 31+
(Ronald Harris) *t.k.h: hld up in tch: rdn wl over 2f out: sn wknd: t.o* **7/1**[3]

1m 47.06s (2.36) **Going Correction** +0.175s/f (Good) **8** Ran SP% **112.2**
Speed ratings (Par 95): **95,93,91,90,90 89,89,76**
toteswingers 1&2 £5.70, 1&3 £2.60, 2&3 £5.80 CSF £19.66 CT £60.16 TOTE £4.10: £1.60, £3.10, £1.20; EX 24.40 Trifecta £82.50 Pool: £803.24 - 7.20 winning tickets..
Owner Geoff Howard-Spink **Bred** Bricklow Stud **Trained** East Everleigh, Wilts

FOCUS
Just an average nursery. Improvement from the first two.

NOTEBOOK
East Texas Red(IRE) was well backed and got the job done pretty easily. The drop back to a mile proved to be in his favour, as did this testing surface - he's by Danehill Dancer out of a Sadler's Wells mare, so no surprise there. He's in the sales. (op 11-4 tchd 3-1)
Jebril(FR) won his maiden in soft ground at Chepstow, and appreciated getting his toe in again. He doesn't help himself with his slow starts, though. (op 13-2 tchd 6-1)
Knight's Parade(IRE), who finished in front of Jebril over 1m2f at Bath last time, couldn't confirm the form back in trip on this more testing surface. (op 11-2)
Rioja Day(IRE) came to have his chance, but didn't see his race out. Perhaps the ground was just too testing for him. (op 15-2 tchd 11-2)
Cheektocheek(IRE) was another who didn't look totally at home on the surface. (op 11-2 tchd 5-1)
Gabrial The Duke(IRE) still looked green. He can be expected to do better over further on a sounder surface next year. (op 12-1)

7112 LADBROKES GAME ON! MAIDEN STKS 1m 67y
3:05 (3:06) (Class 5) 3-Y-O+ **£2,264** (£673; £336; £168) **Stalls** Low

Form RPR

0 **1** **Embankment**[25] 6397 3-9-3 0.. RichardHughes 2 82
(Amanda Perrett) *trckd ldng pair: rdn 2f out: clsd fnl f: led last 100yds* **7/1**[3]

35 **2** *nk* **Surreal (IRE)**[42] 5889 3-8-12 73.................................. RyanMoore 12 76
(Sir Michael Stoute) *trckd ldr: rdn to chal over 2f out: narrow ld over 1f out: hdd last 100yds: styd on* **3/1**[2]

42 **3** *1 ¼* **Bishop's Castle (USA)**[7] 6925 3-9-3 0.................... SilvestreDeSousa 6 78
(Mark Johnston) *led: rdn along over 3f out: pressed and rdn over 2f out: hdd and one pce over 1f out* **8/11**[1]

6530 **4** *1 ¾* **Waveguide (IRE)**[49] 5671 3-8-12 66.................................. MartinLane 8 69
(David Simcock) *trckd ldrs: pushed along 3f out: outpcd and shkn up 2f out: styd on steadily after* **16/1**

0 **5** *2 ¾* **Gwenelda**[14] 6736 3-8-12 0.. JimmyFortune 9 63
(Andrew Balding) *trckd ldrs: in tch 3f out: pushed along and outpcd fr 2f out: shkn up and kpt on* **20/1**

56 **6** *shd* **Bladewood Girl**[19] 6582 4-9-1 0.................................. DavidProbert 3 62
(J R Jenkins) *trckd ldng trio: rdn 3f out: outpcd fr 2f out: kpt on* **25/1**

7 *13* **Merevale** 3-9-0 0.. DominicFox(3) 7 38
(Michael Appleby) *dwlt: nvr on terms w ldrs: rdn bef 1/2-way: sn lft bhd* **40/1**

00 **8** *¾* **Asia Minor (IRE)**[12] 6792 3-8-12 0.................................. RobertHavlin 11 31
(Dr Jon Scargill) *awkward s: wl bhd in last pair: nvr a factor* **50/1**

00 **9** *1 ¾* **Cape Sky**[14] 6736 5-9-1 0.. ChrisCatlin 4 27
(Roy Brotherton) *dwlt: a wl in rr: no ch fnl 3f* **100/1**

10 *½* **Tiny Thompson** 3-8-9 0.. SimonPearce(3) 1 26
(Lydia Pearce) *a off the pce: rdn bef 1/2-way: sn no ch* **100/1**

0 **11** *17* **Sassi Sioux**[17] 6643 3-8-12 0.. TedDurcan 10
(Tom Keddy) *in tch tl wknd rapidly over 3f out: t.o* **150/1**

12 38 **Blue Eyed Grey (IRE)** 4-9-6 0 .... J-PGuillambert 5
(Karen George) *dwlt: sn wl t.o* **100/1**

1m 47.53s (2.83) **Going Correction** +0.30s/f (Good)
WFA 3 from 4yo+ 3lb **12** Ran SP% **117.9**
Speed ratings (Par 103): **97,96,95,93,90 90,77,77,75,74 57,19**
toteswingers 1&2 £3.30, 1&3 £2.60, 2&3 £1.50 CSF £27.12 TOTE £9.20: £2.10, £1.20, £1.10; EX 32.70 Trifecta £40.80 Pool: £1,812.25 - 32.85 winning tickets..
Owner K Abdulla **Bred** Juddmonte Farms Ltd **Trained** Pulborough, W Sussex

FOCUS
No more than a fair maiden, and very few got involved. The fourth and sixth set the standard.

7113 LADBROKES MOBILE H'CAP (DIV I) 6f
3:35 (3:37) (Class 4) (0-80,79) 3-Y-0+ **£4,204** (£1,251; £625; £312) **Stalls** Low

Form RPR

500 **1** **Magic Secret**[19] 6577 4-9-5 **77** .... RichardHughes 14 96+
(Jeremy Gask) *cl up and a gng wl: pushed into ld jst over 1f out: drew rt away fnl f* **4/1**[1]

1210 **2** *5* **Jocasta Dawn**[54] 5486 3-9-0 **78** .... AmyScott(5) 9 81
(Henry Candy) *s.i.s: prog fr rr on outer over 3f out: rdn 2f out: no ch w wnr but kpt on to take 2nd nr fin* **15/2**

0344 **3** *hd* **Bathwick Bear (IRE)**[16] 6663 4-9-6 **78** .... KirstyMilczarek 1 80
(David Evans) *mde most to jst over 1f out: no ch w wnr fnl f: lost 2nd nr fin* **9/1**

1320 **4** *½* **Afkar (IRE)**[15] 6705 4-9-5 **77** ....(v) SilvestreDeSousa 10 78
(Clive Brittain) *w ldr to 2f out: hrd rdn and one pce after* **16/1**

4000 **5** *½* **O'Gorman**[23] 6488 3-9-4 **77** .... LiamKeniry 3 76
(Gary Brown) *hld up in midfield: jst pushed along fr 2f out: kpt on steadily: nrst fin* **33/1**

0004 **6** *½* **Rafaaf (IRE)**[11] 6820 4-9-3 **75** .... AndreaAtzeni 11 73
(Robert Eddery) *in tch in midfield: rdn over 2f out: kpt on one pce and nvr able to threaten* **13/2**[3]

603 **7** *½* **Cardinal**[19] 6577 7-9-1 **73** .... RyanMoore 15 69
(Robert Cowell) *awkward s: racd on outer in rr: tried to make prog 2f out: one pce over 1f out* **7/1**

1562 **8** *1 ½* **Forks**[30] 6256 5-9-0 **72** .... MickaelBarzalona 5 63
(Jane Chapple-Hyam) *sn lost decent position and towards rr 1/2-way: rdn and no real prog 2f out* **6/1**[2]

0616 **9** *hd* **Efistorm**[10] 6837 11-8-11 **74** .... MichaelJMMurphy(5) 8 65
(Joseph Tuite) *a in midfield: shkn up and no prog 2f out: n.d after* **16/1**

2462 **10** *nk* **Oh So Spicy**[26] 6378 5-9-1 **73** .... TedDurcan 6 63
(Chris Wall) *chsd ldrs: rdn over 2f out: hanging and fdd over 1f out* **10/1**

2100 **11** *2 ¾* **Orders From Rome (IRE)**[48] 5703 3-9-6 **79** .... JimmyFortune 2 60
(Eve Johnson Houghton) *hld up wl in rr: pushed along 2f out: nvr involved* **16/1**

6000 **12** *½* **Parisian Pyramid (IRE)**[16] 6663 6-9-7 **79** ....(t) StephenCraine 7 58
(Ian Williams) *a wl in rr: pushed along bef 1/2-way: no prog* **16/1**

00R0 **13** *2* **Monsieur Jamie**[174] 1581 4-9-5 **77** .... DavidProbert 4 50
(J R Jenkins) *dwlt: hld up in last: rdn 1/2-way: no real prog* **66/1**

0060 **14** *hd* **Kings 'n Dreams**[95] 3994 5-8-7 **65** oh1 ....(b) WilliamCarson 13 37
(Dean Ivory) *chsd ldrs on outer: shkn up 2f out: sn wknd qckly* **66/1**

1m 14.13s (1.13) **Going Correction** +0.30s/f (Good)
WFA 3 from 4yo+ 1lb **14** Ran SP% **120.4**
Speed ratings (Par 105): **104,97,97,96,95 95,94,92,92,91 88,87,84,84**
toteswingers 1&2 £8.60, 1&3 £12.70, 2&3 £14.10 CSF £32.93 CT £265.33 TOTE £3.80: £1.50, £2.90, £3.50; EX 41.40 Trifecta £422.40 Pool: £873.52 - 1.53 winning tickets..
Owner Carmel Stud **Bred** Carmel Stud **Trained** Sutton Veny, Wilts

FOCUS
This looked quite competitive on paper. It was the faster division and the form is taken at something like face value.

7114 LADBROKES MOBILE H'CAP (DIV II) 6f
4:10 (4:11) (Class 4) (0-80,79) 3-Y-0+ **£4,204** (£1,251; £625; £312) **Stalls** Low

Form RPR

1112 **1** **Links Drive Lady**[12] 6800 4-9-6 **78** .... RichardHughes 5 87
(Dean Ivory) *hld up in midfield: pushed along and prog 2f out: shkn up to chal fnl f: led last 100yds: rdn to assert nr fin* **5/2**[1]

0430 **2** *¾* **Perfect Pastime**[11] 6820 4-9-6 **78** ....(p) SebSanders 8 85
(Jim Boyle) *racd on outer: w ldrs: led jst over 2f out: drvn and hdd last 100yds: one pce* **10/1**

1311 **3** *nk* **Clear Spring (IRE)**[28] 6303 4-9-5 **77** .... FrannyNorton 12 83
(John Spearing) *trckd ldrs on outer: prog to chal over 1f out: upsides ins fnl f: nt qckn* **8/1**[2]

5321 **4** *hd* **Stonecrabstomorrow (IRE)**[19] 6578 9-8-3 **66**... MichaelJMMurphy(5) 2 71
(Michael Attwater) *wl in rr: rdn over 2f out: prog over 1f out: styd on fnl f: nrly snatched 3rd* **8/1**[2]

0105 **5** *½* **Belle Bayardo (IRE)**[19] 6578 4-8-2 **65** .... DarrenEgan(5) 15 69
(Ronald Harris) *towards rr: rdn and prog on outer 2f out: styd on fnl f: nrst fin* **16/1**

3223 **6** *1* **Rambo Will**[43] 5853 4-9-2 **74** .... DavidProbert 1 75
(J R Jenkins) *chsd ldrs: rdn 2f out: styd on same pce fr over 1f out: nvr able to chal* **14/1**

0101 **7** *nk* **Forest Edge (IRE)**[29] 6285 3-9-1 **74** ....(b) SilvestreDeSousa 6 74
(David Evans) *mde most to jst over 2f out: no ex fnl f* **12/1**

2502 **8** *nk* **Lupo D'Oro (IRE)**[7] 6930 3-9-1 **74** .... ChrisCatlin 14 73
(John Best) *w ldr on outer: upsides over 1f out: wknd ins fnl f* **25/1**

0651 **9** *8* **Galatian**[11] 6824 5-9-4 **76** .... JamesMillman 9 49
(Rod Millman) *chsd ldrs: no imp over 2f out: steadily wknd* **9/1**[3]

6003 **10** *nse* **Captain Scooby**[21] 6525 6-8-13 **74** .... DeclanCannon(3) 4 47
(Richard Guest) *a wl in rr: no ch fnl 2f* **14/1**

000 **11** *nk* **Layla's Hero (IRE)**[16] 6663 5-9-7 **79** ....(t) StephenCraine 13 51
(Ian Williams) *dwlt: a wl in rr: shkn up 2f out: wknd* **25/1**

0400 **12** *2 ¼* **Apollo D'Negro (IRE)**[38] 6008 4-9-5 **77** ....(v) EddieAhern 10 42
(Clive Cox) *hld up in rr: shkn up and no prog on outer over 2f out: eased fnl f* **12/1**

P006 **13** *4 ½* **Heyward Girl (IRE)**[49] 5662 3-8-13 **72** .... AndreaAtzeni 11 22
(Robert Eddery) *chsd ldrs tl rdn and wknd 2f out: eased fnl f* **20/1**

3060 **14** *2* **Tagula Night (IRE)**[19] 6577 6-9-5 **77** ....(bt) ShaneKelly 7 21
(Dean Ivory) *hld up in rr: jst pushed along and no prog 2f out: eased over 1f out* **14/1**

2300 **15** *4 ½* **Midnight Feast**[128] 2940 4-9-3 **75** .... WilliamCarson 3 5
(Lee Carter) *w ldrs against nr side rail: wknd u.p over 2f out: eased over 1f out* **20/1**

1m 14.8s (1.80) **Going Correction** +0.425s/f (Yiel)
WFA 3 from 4yo+ 1lb **15** Ran SP% **128.4**
Speed ratings (Par 105): **105,104,103,103,102 101,100,100,89,89 89,86,80,77,71**
toteswingers 1&2 £9.50, 1&3 £3.60, 2&3 £15.40 CSF £27.59 CT £189.76 TOTE £3.90: £2.20, £3.40, £2.80; EX 38.90 Trifecta £133.60 Pool: £989.74 - 5.48 winning tickets..
Owner It's Your Lucky Day **Bred** Peter Webb **Trained** Radlett, Herts

FOCUS
There was a good early pace here and they finished slowly, hence a winning time 0.67sec slower than the first division. Sound form, with a length personal best from the winner.
Apollo D'Negro(IRE) Official explanation: trainer said gelding was unsuited by the soft (heavy in places) ground
Tagula Night(IRE) Official explanation: jockey said gelding hung left

7115 LADBROKES ODDS ON! H'CAP 1m 67y
4:40 (4:40) (Class 5) (0-70,70) 3-Y-0+ **£2,264** (£673; £336; £168) **Stalls** Low

Form RPR

0305 **1** **Valley Queen**[3] 7015 3-8-11 **63** .... DavidProbert 4 69
(Mark Usher) *hld up tch: rdn and prog wl over 1f out: narrow ld ins fnl f: jst hld on* **15/2**

420U **2** *shd* **Heezararity**[12] 6801 4-9-2 **65** .... SilvestreDeSousa 3 71
(David Evans) *trckd ldrs: prog to ld wl over 1f out: narrowly hdd ins fnl f: styd on: jst failed* **10/1**

61 **3** *4 ½* **Ever Fortune (USA)**[65] 5113 3-9-2 **68** .... RichardHughes 8 63
(Rae Guest) *led to 1/2-way: drvn over 2f out: wnt 3rd over 1f out: no imp on ldng pair* **2/1**[1]

1225 **4** *2 ¾* **Cyril The Squirrel**[12] 6801 8-8-13 **62** .... DarryllHolland 2 51
(Karen George) *s.s and rousted along early in detached last: kpt on u.p fr over 2f out to take 4th ins fnl f* **5/1**[3]

5035 **5** *1 ½* **Mr Knightley (IRE)**[213] 916 3-9-4 **70** .... PatCosgrave 6 56
(Jim Boyle) *stdd s: hld up in detached last pair: clsd over 3f out: in tch on outer 2f out: shkn up and fdd* **40/1**

100 **6** *2 ½* **Catchanova (IRE)**[12] 6801 5-9-0 **63** ....(v1) JimmyFortune 7 43
(Eve Johnson Houghton) *trckd ldr: led 1/2-way: hdd & wknd wl over 1f out* **14/1**

2240 **7** *3* **Buckland (IRE)**[7] 6934 4-9-0 **70** .... NicoleNordblad(7) 5 43
(Hans Adielsson) *hld up in tch: prog on outer and wl on terms 2f out: wknd over 1f out* **7/1**

1315 **8** *71* **Lutine Charlie (IRE)**[7] 6932 5-8-9 **63** .... DarrenEgan(5) 1
(Pat Eddery) *trckd ldrs tl wknd qckly over 3f out: eased and wl t.o: b.b.v* **9/4**[2]

1m 47.08s (2.38) **Going Correction** +0.425s/f (Yiel)
WFA 3 from 4yo+ 3lb **8** Ran SP% **123.2**
Speed ratings (Par 103): **105,104,100,97,96 93,90,19**
toteswingers 1&2 £11.50, 1&3 £5.60, 2&3 £5.60 CSF £84.20 CT £211.58 TOTE £10.60: £3.10, £3.30, £1.10; EX 101.30 TRIFECTA Not won..
Owner Itchen Valley Stud **Bred** Itchen Valley Stud **Trained** Upper Lambourn, Berks

FOCUS
A fairly weak handicap, run in a modest time, and probably to be remembered as the only race on the card not won by Richard Hughes.
Cyril The Squirrel Official explanation: jockey said gelding missed the break
Lutine Charlie(IRE) Official explanation: vet said gelding bled from the nose

7116 BET IN PLAY WITH LADBROKES H'CAP 1m 2f 7y
5:10 (5:10) (Class 4) (0-85,82) 3-Y-0 **£4,204** (£1,251; £625; £312) **Stalls** Centre

Form RPR

-211 **1** **Duke Of Clarence (IRE)**[14] 6734 3-9-2 **77** .... RichardHughes 8 85+
(Richard Hannon) *trckd ldng trio: pushed along over 3f out: clsd to ld wl over 1f out but sn jnd: drvn and asserted last 100yds* **7/4**[1]

5510 **2** *½* **Sheila's Buddy**[74] 4735 3-9-0 **75** .... LiamKeniry 7 82
(J S Moore) *hld up disputing 5th: smooth prog over 2f out: jnd wnr over 1f out: drvn fnl f: nt qckn and hld last 100yds* **6/1**[3]

410 **3** *2 ½* **Intent (IRE)**[58] 5372 3-9-3 **78** .... JamieSpencer 6 80
(Michael Bell) *hld up disputing 5th: gng wl whn looking for room over 2f out: rdn to go 3rd jst ins fnl f: nt qckn and no imp* **10/1**

352 **4** *1* **Inthar (USA)**[19] 6580 3-9-7 **82** .... MickaelBarzalona 3 82+
(Saeed Bin Suroor) *hld up in last pair: looking for room fr over 2f out: effrt whn nowhere to go 1f out: swtchd lft and kpt on one pce* **11/4**[2]

5505 **5** *¾* **Sir Fredlot (IRE)**[14] 6734 3-8-10 **71** .... WilliamCarson 5 70
(Charles Hills) *led: rdn and hdd wl over 1f out: fdd* **10/1**

244 **6** *3* **Falkland (IRE)**[46] 5766 3-8-11 **72** ....(b) RobertHavlin 1 65
(John Gosden) *dwlt: hld up in last pair: pushed along to try to cl over 2f out: rdn and no hdwy over 1f out: fdd* **9/1**

1100 **7** *½* **Play Street**[24] 6450 3-9-1 **76** .... DarryllHolland 2 68
(Jonathan Portman) *t.k.h: trckd ldng pair: shkn up wl over 1f out: wknd tamely* **16/1**

2206 **8** *12* **Cooler Climes**[39] 5970 3-8-9 **70** ....(v1) SilvestreDeSousa 4 38
(Pat Eddery) *t.k.h: trckd ldr: rdn and wandered over 3f out: wknd qckly over 2f out* **25/1**

2m 13.7s (5.00) **Going Correction** +0.55s/f (Yiel) **8** Ran SP% **115.2**
Speed ratings (Par 103): **102,101,99,98,98 95,95,85**
toteswingers 1&2 £3.30, 1&3 £5.00, 2&3 £9.30 CSF £12.98 CT £81.20 TOTE £3.10: £1.10, £1.40, £3.40; EX 13.70 Trifecta £67.80 Pool: £2,180.71 - 23.80 winning tickets..
Owner D Dixon J Stunt J Fiyaz **Bred** Corduff Stud Ltd & J F Gribomont **Trained** East Everleigh, Wilts

FOCUS
Richard Hughes bounced back from defeat in the previous race to notch his sixth winner on the card.

7117 SKYBET.COM H'CAP 1m 3f 135y
5:40 (5:40) (Class 5) (0-70,68) 3-Y-0 **£2,264** (£673; £336; £168) **Stalls** Centre

Form RPR

6224 **1** **Mama Quilla (USA)**[31] 6190 3-9-7 **68** .... RichardHughes 7 75
(William Haggas) *led 3f: trckd ldr: led again over 3f out but jnd: drvn and styd on wl fr over 2f out* **15/8**[1]

2U00 **2** *2 ¼* **Viola Da Gamba (IRE)**[32] 6159 3-9-0 **61** .... EddieAhern 4 64
(William Knight) *trckd ldrs: gng wl in bhd them 3f out: effrt 2f out: drvn and styd on to take 2nd nr fin* **9/1**

4000 **3** *½* **Kozmina Bay**[17] 6626 3-8-7 **54** oh2 ....(v1) SamHitchcott 10 56
(Jonathan Portman) *trckd ldrs: prog to chal and w wnr 3f out: nt qckn wl over 1f out: kpt on* **14/1**

5620 **4** *hd* **Titus Bolt (IRE)**[5] 6988 3-8-13 **60** .... PatCosgrave 1 62
(Jim Boyle) *hld up in last early: stdy prog over 3f out: rdn to dispute 2nd over 1f out: nt qckn* **5/1**[3]

2343 **5** *13* **Collectable**[24] 6442 3-8-7 **54** oh4 ....(t) WilliamCarson 8 34
(Jonathan Portman) *hld up in tch: prog to chal and w wnr 3f out to 2f out: wknd over 1f out: eased* **6/1**

2110 **6** *36* **Attraction Ticket**[33] 6146 3-9-1 **67** .... DarrenEgan(5) 9
(David Simcock) *hld up in rr: prog 3f out: cl enough on wd outside over 2f out: sn wknd rapidly and eased: t.o* **10/3**[2]

5030 **7** *nk* **Cappielow Park**[27] 6349 3-8-8 **60**.............................. NatashaEaton(5) 2
(Fleur Hawes) *racd freely: led after 3f: hdd & wknd rapidly over 3f out: t.o*
22/1

0320 **8** *12* **Dewala**[11] 6807 3-8-4 **54**.............................. DominicFox(3) 6
(Michael Appleby) *in tch to 1/2-way: sn struggling: wl t.o fnl 3f* **20/1**

2m 35.72s (6.22) **Going Correction** +0.55s/f (Yiel) **8** Ran SP% **114.6**
Speed ratings (Par 101): **101,99,99,99,90 66,66,58**
toteswingers 1&2 £5.00, 1&3 £7.30, 2&3 £11.40 CSF £20.06 CT £182.86 TOTE £3.40: £1.10, £2.40, £4.50; EX 22.00 Trifecta £196.40 Pool: £2,941.02 - 11.08 winning tickets..
Owner Mr & Mrs G Middlebrook **Bred** Mr & Mrs Gary Middlebrook **Trained** Newmarket, Suffolk

FOCUS
A modest handicap. The winner probably didn't need to improve much on her maiden form.
T/Plt: £29.90 to a £1 stake. Pool: £71,332.31 - 1740.80 winning tickets T/Qpdt: £8.00 to a £1 stake. Pool: £7,436.41 - 619.35 winning tickets JN

7118 - 7121a (Foreign Racing) - See Raceform Interactive

6942 CHANTILLY (R-H)
Friday, October 12

OFFICIAL GOING: Turf: very soft; polytrack: standard

7122a PRIX ECLIPSE (GROUP 3) (2YO) (TURF) 6f
1:20 (12:00) 2-Y-O **£33,333** (£13,333; £10,000; £6,666; £3,333)

RPR

1 **Penny's Picnic (IRE)**[54] 5398 2-8-11 0.............................. ThierryJarnet 2 104
(D Guillemin, France) *restrained in midfield on inner: rdn to chal 1f out: sn led: wnt clr ins fnl f: readily* **19/10**[1]

2 *2 ½* **Interesting (IRE)**[30] 2-8-8 0.............................. FabriceVeron 10 94
(H-A Pantall, France) *prom on outer: rdn 1 1/2f out: led briefly 1f out: sn hdd and outpcd by wnr: kpt on: jst hld on for 2nd on nod* **9/1**

3 *nse* **Chef Oui Chef (FR)**[21] 6463 2-8-11 0.............................. Pierre-CharlesBoudot 6 96
(Y De Nicolay, France) *t.k.h: hld up in last pair: rdn and hdwy on outer 1 1/2f out: wnt 3rd jst ins fnl f: kpt on: jst denied 2nd on nod* **9/1**

4 *2* **Sage Melody (FR)**[31] 2-8-8 0.............................. MaximeGuyon 1 87
(P Demercastel, France) *prom on inner: rdn to chal 2f out: led 1 1/2f out: hdd 1f out: qckly outpcd and dropped to 4th: kpt on ins fnl f* **78/10**[3]

5 *1 ½* **Wedge Trust (IRE)**[55] 5379 2-8-8 0.............................. IoritzMendizabal 5 83
(J-C Rouget, France) *t.k.h: prom in centre: lost pl whn short of room and hmpd jst over 1f out: sn rdn and styd on to go 5th ins fnl f: nt rcvr* **8/1**

6 *¾* **Jadanna (IRE)**[13] 6672 2-8-8 0.............................. OlivierPeslier 8 81
(James Given) *sn disputing ld on outer: ld 3f out: rdn and hdd 1 1/2f out: sn no ex and btn: fdd and dropped to 6th ins fnl f* **5/1**[2]

7 *3* **Aksil (FR)**[31] 6128 2-8-8 0.............................. GregoryBenoist 9 72
(M Boutin, France) *midfield on outer: rdn 2f out: outpcd and btn ins fnl f: fdd* **20/1**

8 *3* **Lewisham**[33] 6078 2-8-11 0.............................. PatCosgrave 4 66
(Noel Quinlan) *drvn along early but nt pce to go gallop: hld up in last on inner: rdn 3f out: outpcd in rr 2f out: sn btn: tk remote 8th ins fnl f: nvr a factor* **17/2**

9 *1 ¾* **Atora Bere (FR)**[11] 2-8-8 0.............................. GeraldMosse 3 57
(M Boutin, France) *midfield: rdn and lost pl 2f out: sn outpcd and btn: eased ins fnl f* **28/1**

10 *7* **My Glitters (FR)**[46] 5697 2-8-8 0.............................. EddyHardouin 7 36
(P Demercastel, France) *sn disputing ld on rail: hdd 3f out: lost pl rapidly over 2f out: sn btn and eased: dropped to last ent fnl f* **36/1**

1m 14.5s (3.10) **10** Ran SP% **115.1**
WIN (incl. 1 euro stake): 2.90. PLACES: 1.60, 2.90, 2.40. DF: 15.20. SF: 19.30.
Owner G De St Seine & T Delegue **Bred** F Montauban **Trained** France

NOTEBOOK
Jadanna(IRE) has run well in soft ground before but was below her best here.
Lewisham, who had previous form on soft ground, was always struggling this time.

7123a PRIX TILBURY (CONDITIONS) (4YO+) (POLYTRACK) 6f 110y
1:50 (12:00) 4-Y-O+ **£11,666** (£4,666; £3,500; £2,333; £1,166)

RPR

1 **Dschahan (GER)**[47] 4-9-2 0.............................. AntoineHamelin 10 96
(F Vermeulen, France) **17/1**

2 *2 ½* **Amico Fritz (GER)**[105] 3603 6-9-2 0..............................(p) FabriceVeron 9 89
(H-A Pantall, France) **3/1**[2]

3 *nk* **Kajima**[99] 5-8-11 0.............................. ChristopheSoumillon 7 83
(R Pritchard-Gordon, France) **14/1**

4 *½* **Bravo Echo**[27] 6235 6-9-6 0.............................. J-PGuillambert 12 90
(Michael Attwater) *sn led on wd outside: shared ld bef end of bk st: rdn to go wl clr early in st: stl in front ent fnl f: u.p 100yds out: hdd 50yds out: r.o* **19/1**

5 *¾* **Action Chope (FR)**[62] 5118 4-8-10 0..............................(p) ThierryJarnet 11 78
(D Guillemin, France) **9/1**

6 *¾* **Heidikly (FR)**[24] 4-8-10 0.............................. FranckBlondel 13 76
(F Vermeulen, France) **44/5**

7 *hd* **Stand My Ground (IRE)**[84] 4316 5-9-2 0.............................. MaximeGuyon 1 82
(Mme Pia Brandt, France) **5/2**[1]

8 *1 ¾* **Valhillen**[14] 7-9-2 0.............................. HanaMouchova 6 76?
(T Schmeer, Germany) **65/1**

9 *1 ½* **Mogadishio (FR)**[14] 5-8-11 0.............................. AnthonyCrastus 2 67
(Mlle C Cardenne, France) **13/1**

10 *3* **Miss Fifty (IRE)**[14] 4-9-1 0.............................. GeraldMosse 8 62
(U Suter, France) **6/1**[3]

0 **Brown Colt (IRE)**[135] 7-8-11 0.............................. VincentVion 3
(Mme I T Oakes-Cottin, France) **52/1**

0 **One Set (IRE)**[651] 5-8-11 0.............................. ThierryThulliez 4
(Mme I T Oakes-Cottin, France) **57/1**

0 **So Well (FR)** 5-8-11 0.............................. MmeBrigitteJacques 5
(D Considerant, Belgium) **81/1**

1m 18.5s (78.50) **13** Ran SP% **118.8**
WIN (incl. 1 euro stake): 6.30 (Dschahan coupled with Heidikly). PLACES: 4.10, 2.00, 4.10. DF: 27.80. SF: 68.50.
Owner Jean-Pierre Vanden Heede **Bred** Gestut Fahrhof **Trained** France

NOTEBOOK
Bravo Echo made a brave bid from the front.

7124a PRIX DU RANELAGH (LISTED RACE) (3YO+) (TURF) 1m
2:20 (12:00) 3-Y-O+ **£21,666** (£8,666; £6,500; £4,333; £2,166)

RPR

1 **Chil The Kite**[13] 6674 3-9-0 0.............................. UmbertoRispoli 2 108
(Hughie Morrison) *hld up towards rr: swtchd towards outside early in st: qcknd wl u.p ent fnl f: chal for ld 100yds: tk ld 75yds out: r.o wl* **118/10**

2 *½* **Sulle Orme (FR)**[47] 5649 4-9-6 0.............................. GeraldMosse 6 110
(C Ferland, France) **48/10**[2]

3 *1 ½* **Celebrissime (IRE)**[47] 5649 7-9-6 0.............................. OlivierPeslier 5 107
(F Head, France) **10/1**

4 *1 ½* **Prince D'Alienor (IRE)**[96] 3900 4-9-6 0..............................(p) GregoryBenoist 7 103
(X Nakkachdji, France) **2/1**[1]

5 *2* **Simba (FR)**[27] 6273 4-9-3 0.............................. MarcLerner 9 96
(C Lerner, France) **22/1**

6 *½* **Ball Prince (IRE)**[40] 5-9-3 0.............................. FlavienPrat 1 94
(T Clout, France) **58/10**[3]

7 *snk* **Making Eyes (IRE)**[13] 6674 4-9-3 0.............................. IoritzMendizabal 8 94
(Hugo Palmer) *racd in 5th cl up bhd ldrs: rdn and swtchd towards outside 1 1/2f out: nt qckn: styd on one pce fnl f* **23/1**

8 *nk* **Balada Sale (ARG)**[60] 5183 4-9-0 0.............................. ChristopheSoumillon 3 90
(P Bary, France) **11/1**

9 *2 ½* **Konig Concorde (GER)**[26] 7-9-6 0..............................(p) FilipMinarik 11 91
(C Sprengel, Germany) **25/1**

10 *1 ¼* **Nid D'Amour (FR)**[20] 6506 6-9-3 0.............................. MaximeGuyon 4 85
(J-P Gallorini, France) **13/1**

0 **Gotlandia (FR)**[40] 5-9-0 0.............................. AntoineHamelin 10
(J-L Guillochon, France) **13/1**

1m 44.4s (6.40)
WFA 3 from 4yo+ 3lb **11** Ran SP% **117.2**
WIN (incl. 1 euro stake): 12.80. PLACES: 4.30, 2.00, 3.20. DF: 36.20. SF: 92.60.
Owner Hazel Lawrence & Graham Doyle **Bred** Whitsbury Manor Stud & Pigeon House Stud **Trained** East Ilsley, Berks

NOTEBOOK
Chil The Kite ran down Sulle Orme to land this Listed contest in good style. A tough sort, he coped with the sticky ground and will probably stay 1m2f.

6960 LEICESTER (R-H)
Tuesday, October 16

OFFICIAL GOING: Soft (good to soft in places; 7.5)
Wind: Blustery Weather: Cloudy with sunny spells

7125 WYMESWOLD CONDITIONS STKS 7f 9y
2:10 (2:11) (Class 3) 2-Y-O **£5,822** (£1,732; £865; £432) **Stalls High**

Form RPR

1 **1** **Van Der Neer**[26] 6411 2-9-2 0.............................. RichardHughes 4 95+
(Richard Hannon) *hld up in tch: shkn up over 2f out: led ins fnl f: sn clr: edgd rt and eased towards fin* **2/1**[2]

1 **2** *1 ¾* **Seek Again (USA)**[18] 6636 2-9-2 0..............................[1] WilliamBuick 6 87
(John Gosden) *trckd ldrs: plld hrd: shkn up over 2f out: rdn over 1f out: styd on same pce ins fnl f* **8/13**[1]

2016 **3** *¾* **Dark Emerald (IRE)**[25] 6447 2-8-13 **85**.............................. KierenFallon 1 82
(Brendan Powell) *chsd ldr tl led over 1f out: sn rdn and hung lft: hdd and no ex ins fnl f* **18/1**

01 **4** *nk* **Fat Gary**[159] 1997 2-9-2 **85**.............................. RichardKingscote 2 84
(Tom Dascombe) *sn led: rdn and hdd over 1f out: no ex ins fnl f* **14/1**[3]

1m 28.07s (1.87) **Going Correction** +0.25s/f (Good) **4** Ran SP% **107.2**
Speed ratings (Par 99): **99,97,96,95**
CSF £3.58 TOTE £2.10; EX 3.80.
Owner Saeed Manana **Bred** Jeremy Green And Sons **Trained** East Everleigh, Wilts

FOCUS
False rail from bend to winning post added 10yds to distances on Round course. Despite the two non-runners, this was still an interesting conditions event with the remaining quartet all previous winners, two of whom had won their only starts. The third and fourth set a believable level.

NOTEBOOK
Van Der Neer ◆, up a furlong from his successful debut in a Yarmouth maiden that is working out well, was on very different ground here, but after being switched right for his effort passing the 2f pole, his rider was able to take a pull and once asked to go and win his race, he fairly bolted up. The winning margin gives little indication of his superiority and he looks yet another smart juvenile prospect from the Hannon yard. (op 7-4)
Seek Again(USA) overcame greenness to make a winning debut from 18 rivals at Newmarket last month, but he didn't help himself at all here by taking a strong hold early in the first-time hood and he was left floundering by the winner when eventually asked for his effort. This slower ground may not have suited, however, and he is worth another chance if settling better. (op 5-6)
Dark Emerald(IRE) has faced some stiff tasks in his career to date and this looked to be another, so he probably did well to stay in the thick of the action for as long as he did. He lacks the scope of these rivals, however. (op 14-1)
Fat Gary hadn't been seen since winning on testing ground at Chester in May, but that form was boosted when four of the eight runners behind him that day won their next starts. Stepping up 2f in trip for this return, he also ran well for a long way and can be expected to have benefited from the outing. (op 11-1)

7126 WHISSENDINE (S) STKS 7f 9y
2:40 (2:40) (Class 6) 3-4-Y-O **£1,617** (£481; £240; £120) **Stalls High**

Form RPR

2662 **1** **Tunnager Grove**[22] 6542 3-8-10 **68**..............................(b[1]) RichardHughes 1 67
(Hughie Morrison) *trckd ldrs: shkn up to ld ins fnl f: hung rt: rdn out* **10/11**[1]

2430 **2** *½* **Barista (IRE)**[30] 6275 4-8-7 **57**.............................. CharlesBishop(5) 2 66
(Brian Forsey) *mid-div: hdwy 1/2-way: rdn to ld over 1f out: hung rt and hdd ins fnl f: styd on* **9/2**[2]

4600 **3** *6* **Foursquare Funtime**[24] 6502 3-9-1 **65**.............................. GrahamGibbons 7 55
(Reg Hollinshead) *s.i.s: sn prom: led over 4f out: rdn and hdd over 1f out: hung rt and wknd ins fnl f* **13/2**[3]

4366 **4** *1 ¼* **Storm Runner (IRE)**[67] 5052 4-9-3 **51**.............................. IanMongan 6 52
(George Margarson) *sn pushed along in rr: rdn over 2f out: hung rt u.p ins fnl f: n.d* **28/1**

0556 **5** *¾* **Decadence**[35] 6125 4-8-7 **45**.............................. MickaelBarzalona 3 40
(Nigel Tinkler) *chsd ldrs: rdn over 2f out: wknd over 1f out* **33/1**

5023 **6** *1 1/4* **Percythepinto (IRE)**33 6158 3-8-9 56 ow1(t) WilliamTwiston-Davies(7) 8 48
(George Baker) *s.i.s: hld up: hdwy over 2f out: rdn and wknd over 1f out* **15/2**
5400 **7** *7* **Qubuh (IRE)**53 5543 4-9-3 60................(p) TomEaves 4 28
(Linda Stubbs) *chsd ldrs: rdn 1/2-way: wknd over 2f out* **33/1**
-060 **8** *3 1/2* **Misty Eyes**27 6361 3-8-5 37................ JoeFanning 5
(Geoffrey Harker) *sn led: hdd over 4f out: rdn over 2f out: wknd over 1f out* **50/1**
4625 **9** *1* **Whats For Pudding (IRE)**14 6756 4-8-7 48.............. JamesSullivan 10
(Declan Carroll) *chsd ldrs: rdn 1/2-way: wknd over 2f out* **11/1**
-000 **10** *37* **Tribouley**13 6773 4-8-7 50................ LukeMorris 9
(Dean Ivory) *wnt rt s: sn outpcd: t.o fr 1/2-way* **66/1**

1m 27.28s (1.08) **Going Correction** +0.25s/f (Good)
WFA 3 from 4yo 2lb **10** Ran SP% **116.8**
Speed ratings (Par 101): **103,102,95,94,93 91,83,79,78,36**
toteswingers 1&2 £2.60, 2&3 £4.00, 1&3 £2.20 CSF £4.87 TOTE £2.20: £1.30, £1.40, £1.20; EX 6.80.There was no bid for the winner.
Owner M E Wates **Bred** M E Wates **Trained** East Ilsley, Berks

FOCUS
A poor seller, but a feeling of déjà vu with Richard Hughes making it nine wins from his last ten mounts, though he was aboard the odds-on favourite. The first two pulled a long way clear and the winner is rated 5lb off his C&D latest.
Foursquare Funtime Official explanation: jockey said gelding hung right

7127 ALBERT MARRIOTT 90 TOMORROW E B F MAIDEN STKS (C&G) 7f 9y
3:10 (3:12) (Class 4) 2-Y-O **£4,334** (£1,289; £644; £322) **Stalls** High

Form RPR
4 **1** **Hillstar**46 5792 2-9-0 0................ RyanMoore 6 81+
(Sir Michael Stoute) *trckd ldr: racd keenly: shkn up over 1f out: rdn ins fnl f: styd on to ld towards fin* **2/1**1
32 **2** *3/4* **Flashlight (IRE)**11 6846 2-9-0 0................ JoeFanning 12 78
(Mark Johnston) *led: rdn over 1f out: hdd towards fin* **9/2**3
322 **3** *2 3/4* **Pythagorean**20 6571 2-9-0 82................ GeorgeBaker 10 71
(Roger Charlton) *trckd ldrs: shkn up over 1f out: styd on same pce fnl f* **85/40**2
4 *1 3/4* **Aussie Lyrics (FR)** 2-9-0 0................ PatCosgrave 7 67+
(George Baker) *s.i.s: hdwy over 5f out: rdn over 2f out: no ex fnl f* **80/1**
5 *6* **Breden (IRE)** 2-9-0 0................ WilliamBuick 2 52+
(John Gosden) *s.s: hld up: styd on fr over 1f out: nvr on terms* **7/1**
6 *2 1/2* **Refuse To Mambo** 2-9-0 0................ MartinDwyer 1 46
(Reg Hollinshead) *mid-div: pushed along 3f out: n.d* **200/1**
7 *hd* **Public (IRE)** 2-9-0 0................ KierenFallon 9 45
(Luca Cumani) *chsd ldrs: pushed along 1/2-way: wknd over 1f out* **25/1**
8 *1 3/4* **Al Enbess (IRE)** 2-9-0 0................ TomQueally 5 41
(David Simcock) *mid-div: sn pushed along: nvr on terms* **28/1**
56 **9** *1/2* **Slip Of The Tongue**18 6645 2-9-0 0................ LukeMorris 4 40
(Sir Mark Prescott Bt) *hld up: rdn 1/2-way: n.d* **100/1**
10 *1* **Sword Of The Lord** 2-9-0 0................ JamieSpencer 8 37
(Michael Bell) *hld up: a towards rr* **33/1**
11 *5* **Prairie Prince (IRE)** 2-9-0 0................ JimmyFortune 13 25
(Andrew Balding) *s.i.s: a in rr* **40/1**
12 *3 1/2* **Platinum Proof (USA)** 2-9-0 0................ EddieAhern 11 16
(John Berry) *hld up: a in rr* **66/1**

1m 28.23s (2.03) **Going Correction** +0.25s/f (Good) **12** Ran SP% **112.9**
Speed ratings (Par 97): **98,97,94,92,85 82,82,80,79,78 72,68**
toteswingers 1&2 £3.10, 2&3 £2.10, 1&3 £2.00 CSF £10.14 TOTE £2.40: £1.10, £2.00, £1.10; EX 11.00.
Owner Sir Evelyn De Rothschild **Bred** Southcourt Stud **Trained** Newmarket, Suffolk

FOCUS
An interesting maiden, but very few ever got into it and the front four pulled clear. The winner built on debut promise and the second was close to form.

NOTEBOOK
Hillstar ◆ had very much caught the eye, despite market weakness, when fourth on his Sandown debut and a couple of winners have come out of that race. All the better for that experience, he got a nice tow from the runner-up here and although it took him a while to wear him down when asked, he showed a decent attitude to do so. He looks to hold a bright future. (op 15-8 tchd 9-4)
Flashlight(IRE) had shown progressive form in his first two starts and tried to make every yard. He kept on finding for pressure, but the winner just had the legs of him late on. He still looks to need a stiffer test and should develop into a nice handicapper at three. (op 4-1)
Pythagorean set the standard with an official mark of 82 having been placed in three maidens at top tracks (two in soft ground) including in the hood at Goodwood last time. However, he had also given the impression that he might not be straightforward and, having taken a fierce hold early, found little off the bridle and didn't seem to be enjoying himself in the last furlong. He has plenty of questions to answer now. (op 5-2 tchd 2-1)
Aussie Lyrics(FR) ◆, a 21,000euros 2yo and a half-brother to a winner at up to 1m2f in France, ran a most promising debut, pulling clear of the rest behind a trio with previous experience. He should win races. (op 100-1 tchd 50-1)
Breden(IRE), a 140,000gns half-brother to two winners at up to 7f including one at Listed level, merely plugged on from the back of the field for a remote fifth, but gave the impression that the experience was much needed. (tchd 6-1)

7128 WREAKE FILLIES' CONDITIONS STKS 1m 60y
3:40 (3:40) (Class 3) 3-Y-0+ **£6,931** (£2,074; £1,037; £519; £258) **Stalls** Low

Form RPR
6220 **1** **Cochabamba (IRE)**17 6667 4-8-12 82................ RyanMoore 5 90
(Roger Teal) *mde all: rdn over 1f out: jst hld on* **6/1**
4-26 **2** *nk* **Gifted Girl (IRE)**11 6831 3-8-9 85................ NeilCallan 6 89
(Paul Cole) *a.p: rdn to chse wnr and swtchd lft over 1f out: sn hung lft: r.o* **13/2**
0056 **3** *1 3/4* **Russian Rave**10 6870 6-8-12 88................ EddieAhern 2 85
(Jonathan Portman) *hld up: hdwy and nt clr run over 1f out: r.o: could nt rch ldrs* **11/4**2
405 **4** *shd* **Epernay**24 6470 5-8-12 79................(vt) JamieSpencer 3 85
(Ian Williams) *hld up: pushed along over 2f out: r.o ins fnl f: nrst fin* **10/1**
-000 **5** *1/2* **Crystal Gal (IRE)**10 6877 5-8-12 92................ IanMongan 1 84
(Lucy Wadham) *chsd wnr tl rdn over 1f out: hmpd sn after: styd on same pce ins fnl f* **9/2**3
2010 **6** *1 1/2* **My Queenie (IRE)**10 6870 3-8-9 95................ RichardHughes 4 80
(Richard Hannon) *hld up: hdwy over 2f out: rdn over 1f out: no ex ins fnl f* **2/1**1
1510 **7** *6* **Lolita Lebron (IRE)**49 5705 3-8-9 79................ JoeFanning 7 67
(Lawrence Mullaney) *chsd ldrs: rdn over 2f out: wknd over 1f out* **33/1**

1m 47.54s (2.44) **Going Correction** +0.35s/f (Good)
WFA 3 from 4yo+ 3lb **7** Ran SP% **117.8**
Speed ratings (Par 104): **101,100,98,98,98 96,90**
toteswingers 1&2 £4.30, 2&3 £3.50, 1&3 £4.30 CSF £45.64 TOTE £9.90: £4.00, £4.50; EX 39.80.
Owner The Rat Racers **Bred** Shortgrove Manor Stud **Trained** Ashtead, Surrey

FOCUS
A good fillies' conditions event, but the early pace wasn't that strong and the winner looked to have her own way out in front. Muddling form, the winner rated to this year's best.

NOTEBOOK
Cochabamba(IRE) ended a losing run of 22 since her successful racecourse debut and appreciated dropping in trip after failing to see out the extended 1m2f in heavy ground at Haydock last time. However, the key to this success was that she was left alone up front and kept on finding, while she also kept a straighter course than the runner-up on the run to the line. The fact that she had a bit to find on these terms suggests that the form may not be that reliable, especially given how the race was run. (op 7-1)
Gifted Girl(IRE), the least exposed in the field, was returning from another absence when failing to sparkle on testing ground at Ascot 11 days ago, but she should arguably have won this. Keen enough early, she had to rather force her way out of a pocket over a furlong from home, but then started to hang at a crucial stage and by the time she was gathered together the line was always going to beat her. She still doesn't look the finished article and may yet be capable of better. (tchd 15-2)
Russian Rave handles testing ground well, but could only make limited late progress from off the pace and never looked like winning. (op 3-1)
Epernay handles testing ground, but again she had plenty to find on these terms. Held up early, she was forced to come very wide to get a clear run over a furlong from home, but can't be described as unlucky. (op 16-1)
Crystal Gal(IRE), a Listed winner last season, didn't truly see her race out after racing in a handy position and is still to find her form this year. (tchd 5-1)
My Queenie(IRE) was the one most favoured by these weights, but an effort inside the last 2f came to little and her recent form has a very uneven look to it. (op 9-4 tchd 5-2)

7129 FOSSE WAY CLASSIFIED CLAIMING STKS 1m 3f 183y
4:10 (4:10) (Class 6) 3-5-Y-0 **£1,940** (£577; £288; £144) **Stalls** Low

Form RPR
5166 **1** **Guiletta (IRE)**53 5533 3-8-11 67................ RichardHughes 2 71
(Rae Guest) *trckd ldrs: rdn to ld over 1f out: drvn out* **9/2**
0400 **2** *1/2* **Bold Duke**36 6097 4-8-7 45................ ThomasBrown(7) 5 66
(Edward Bevan) *hld up: hdwy over 1f out: rdn ins fnl f: styd on* **66/1**
2101 **3** *1 1/4* **Bernisdale**8 6927 4-9-4 69................ JohnFahy 4 68
(John Flint) *led: rdn: edgd lft and hdd over 1f out: styd on same pce ins fnl f* **13/8**1
3562 **4** *1 1/4* **Breaking The Bank**13 6798 3-9-3 70................ MartinDwyer 3 72
(William Muir) *hld up in tch: chsd wnr over 3f out tl rdn over 1f out: no ex wl ins fnl f* **11/4**2
2010 **5** *44* **Finity Run (GER)**10 6891 3-8-9 70................ JoeFanning 1
(Mark Johnston) *chsd ldr tl rdn over 3f out: wknd over 2f out: t.o* **7/2**3

2m 39.13s (5.23) **Going Correction** +0.35s/f (Good)
WFA 3 from 4yo 7lb **5** Ran SP% **106.7**
Speed ratings (Par 101): **96,95,94,94,64**
CSF £100.98 TOTE £3.90: £1.50, £8.10; EX 50.50.Guiletta was claimed by J. L. Flint for £9000.
Owner The Hornets **Bred** The Hornets **Trained** Newmarket, Suffolk

FOCUS
A messy little claimer in which the two established front-runners probably didn't do each other many favours, while the proximity of the 45-rated runner-up does little for the form, which looks dubious.
Finity Run(GER) Official explanation: jockey said filly had no more to give

7130 IRISH STALLION FARMS E B F MAIDEN STKS 1m 60y
4:40 (4:40) (Class 4) 2-Y-O **£4,334** (£1,289; £644; £322) **Stalls** Low

Form RPR
5 **1** **Now Spun (USA)**24 6501 2-9-3 0................ MickaelBarzalona 2 80+
(Mahmood Al Zarooni) *hld up in tch: shkn up over 2f out: led over 1f out: hung rt ins fnl f: pushed clr* **11/4**2
2 *3 3/4* **Motion Lass** 2-8-12 0................ JimmyFortune 4 67+
(Ralph Beckett) *chsd ldrs: rdn over 1f out: styd on same pce ins fnl f* **10/1**
3 *3 1/4* **Gods Gift (IRE)** 2-9-3 0................ RichardHughes 3 65+
(Rae Guest) *s.i.s: rn green in rr: styd on fnl 2f: wnt 3rd wl ins fnl f: nvr nrr* **12/1**
4 *3/4* **Capitol Hill (IRE)**23 6519 2-9-3 0................ MartinHarley 7 63
(John Joseph Murphy, Ire) *chsd ldrs: led over 2f out: rdn and hdd over 1f out: wknd ins fnl f* **9/1**
0 **5** *6* **Boogie De Bispo**33 6153 2-8-12 0................ IanMongan 6 45
(Stuart Kittow) *led: rdn and hdd over 2f out: wknd over 1f out* **100/1**
0 **6** *1/2* **Deficit (IRE)**10 6876 2-9-3 0................ JamieSpencer 9 49
(Michael Bell) *chsd ldr: rdn over 3f out: wknd over 1f out* **6/4**1
7 *nk* **Bedouin Invader (IRE)** 2-9-3 0................ RyanMoore 5 48+
(Sir Michael Stoute) *hld up: pushed along 1/2-way: rdn over 2f out: nvr on terms* **11/2**3
8 *10* **Mallory Heights (IRE)** 2-9-3 0................ KierenFallon 1 26+
(Luca Cumani) *rn green and a bhd* **14/1**

1m 49.51s (4.41) **Going Correction** +0.35s/f (Good) **8** Ran SP% **116.5**
Speed ratings (Par 97): **91,87,84,83,77 76,76,66**
toteswingers 1&2 £5.80, 2&3 £7.10, 1&3 £6.70 CSF £30.80 TOTE £4.10: £1.30, £1.70, £3.60; EX 30.30.
Owner Godolphin **Bred** Hickstead Farm **Trained** Newmarket, Suffolk

FOCUS
This maiden has been won by some nice types including Opinion Poll in 2008 and Thomas Chippendale last year. The form has been rated at the lower end of the recent race averages, and the first three can rate higher.

NOTEBOOK
Now Spun(USA) ◆ had shown ability, despite running green, when fifth on last month's Wolverhampton debut, and despite stumbling on a couple of occasions at around halfway he came home in great style, hitting the front over a furlong from home and bounding clear. His sire isn't normally associated with soft-ground winners, so he may have won this despite the conditions and he is certainly one for the notebook. (tchd 5-2 and 3-1)
Motion Lass ◆, retained for 16,000gns as a yearling, is a half-sister to six winners including the Group 3 winner Enforcer. Not much went right for her here, as she took a keen grip early and then found herself stuck in a pocket on the inside just as the race was taking shape. She wouldn't have beaten the winner, but would have finished closer and this was a most encouraging debut. (op 7-1 tchd 11-1)
Gods Gift(IRE) ◆, out of a 7f juvenile winner who stayed much further, stayed on down the wide outside after missing the break and looking in need of the experience. Better can be expected. (op 11-1 tchd 14-1)

Capitol Hill(IRE), a well-beaten eighth on last month's Gowran Park debut, looked a possible winner when shooting to the front over 2f from home, but it wasn't long before the winner ranged alongside and he didn't get home. This was still an improvement from his debut. (op 7-1 tchd 10-1)

Deficit(IRE), well backed, had hinted at ability when seventh on his Newmarket debut ten days earlier. Although he was close enough early, sitting on the shoulder of the front-running Boogie de Bispo, his supporters knew their fate when he came under pressure fully 3f from home, from which point he gradually faded. Perhaps this came too soon. (op 5-2)

7131 STEWARDS H'CAP (DIV I) 1m 1f 218y

5:10 (5:10) (Class 5) (0-75,75) 3-Y-O+ **£2,587** (£770; £384; £192) **Stalls** Low

Form				RPR
6223	**1**		**Sky Khan**[33] 6181 3-9-3 **73**........ RyanMoore 7 (Ed Dunlop) *hld up: hdwy over 2f out: rdn to ld and hung rt ins fnl f: styd on wl* **5/1**[3]	00
4003	**2**	2 3/4	**Solfilia**[57] 5426 3-9-4 **74**........ DarryllHolland 4 (Hughie Morrison) *chsd ldrs: led over 1f out: rdn and hdd ins fnl f: styd on same pce* **14/1**	81
1142	**3**	4 1/2	**Cape Explorer**[27] 6359 3-9-5 **75**........ MartinDwyer 9 (James Tate) *chsd ldrs: led over 7f out: rdn and hdd over 1f out: wknd ins fnl f* **4/1**[2]	73
3322	**4**	shd	**Exning Halt**[18] 6639 3-9-5 **75**........ KierenFallon 8 (James Fanshawe) *s.i.s: sn pushed along in rr: hdwy over 2f out: rdn over 1f out: wknd ins fnl f* **13/8**[1]	73
20	**5**	3	**Chatterer (IRE)**[118] 3290 4-9-10 **75**........ JimmyFortune 5 (Marcus Tregoning) *hld up: rdn over 2f out: nvr nrr* **10/1**	67
-552	**6**	1/2	**Spyder**[13] 6794 4-9-5 **70**........(p) RichardHughes 10 (Jane Chapple-Hyam) *chsd ldr: led over 8f out tl over 7f out: rdn over 2f out: wknd over 1f out: hung rt ins fnl f* **5/1**[3]	61
4350	**7**	2 3/4	**Malih**[26] 6401 3-9-2 **72**........ FergusSweeney 6 (Jamie Osborne) *led: hdd over 8f out: remained handy: rdn over 2f out: wknd over 1f out* **20/1**	57
0000	**8**	3 1/4	**Amazing Blue Sky**[10] 6884 6-9-7 **72**........ JamesSullivan 3 (Ruth Carr) *chsd ldrs: lost pl over 7f out: rdn over 3f out: sn wknd* **33/1**	51

2m 10.41s (2.51) **Going Correction** +0.35s/f (Good)
WFA 3 from 4yo+ 5lb **8** Ran SP% **114.9**
Speed ratings (Par 103): **103,100,97,97,94 94,92,89**
toteswingers 1&2 £7.20, 2&3 £8.60, 1&3 £3.20 CSF £70.43 CT £306.25 TOTE £5.30: £1.60, £5.10, £1.10; EX 63.20.
Owner V I Araci **Bred** Heather Raw **Trained** Newmarket, Suffolk

FOCUS
The first division of this fair handicap looked pretty competitive on paper, but was dominated by the 3yos and resulted in something of a procession in the closing stages. It was the faster division and the winner built on his AW form.
Exning Halt Official explanation: trainer's rep had no explanation for the poor form shown

7132 STEWARDS H'CAP (DIV II) 1m 1f 218y

5:40 (5:40) (Class 5) (0-75,75) 3-Y-O+ **£2,587** (£770; £384; £192) **Stalls** Low

Form				RPR
1410	**1**		**The Lock Master (IRE)**[53] 5546 5-9-8 **73**........ TomQueally 7 (Michael Appleby) *a.p: pushed along over 4f out: jnd ldrs over 2f out: rdn to ld ins fnl f: jst hld on* **7/1**[3]	82
6410	**2**	hd	**Danube River**[6] 6988 3-9-5 **75**........ JoeFanning 11 (Mark Johnston) *chsd ldrs: rdn to ld over 1f out: hdd ins fnl f: styd on gamely* **7/2**[2]	84
4534	**3**	2 3/4	**Significant Move**[8] 6932 5-9-5 **70**........(t) FergusSweeney 6 (Stuart Kittow) *chsd ldr: led 7f out: rdn and hdd over 1f out: no ex ins fnl f* **3/1**[1]	74
3233	**4**	4	**Skyfire**[69] 4959 5-9-1 **66**........ MichaelStainton 10 (Nick Kent) *led 3f: chsd ldrs: rdn over 2f out: wknd fnl f* **8/1**	62
0-00	**5**	1 1/2	**Souter Point (USA)**[162] 1913 6-9-0 **70**........ LMcNiff(5) 8 (Peter Salmon) *hld up: rdn over 2f out: styd on: nvr trbld ldrs* **40/1**	63
-113	**6**	1/2	**Noble Jack (IRE)**[71] 4884 6-9-7 **72**........ J-PGuillambert 3 (Jo Hughes) *chsd ldrs: pushed along over 4f out: wknd over 1f out* **17/2**	64
0315	**7**	1/2	**Rosselli (IRE)**[87] 4325 3-9-0 **73**........ MichaelMetcalfe(3) 9 (Mrs K Burke) *hld up: rdn over 3f out: n.d* **7/1**[3]	64
0300	**8**	5	**Edgeworth (IRE)**[15] 6734 6-8-11 **69**........ JoshBaudains(7) 2 (David Bridgwater) *hld up: rdn over 3f out: wknd over 2f out* **18/1**	50
-506	**9**	17	**Young Lou**[17] 6662 3-8-12 **68**........ MartinDwyer 4 (Robin Dickin) *hld up: bhd fnl 4f: t.o* **25/1**	15
4-41	**10**	7	**Zafranagar (IRE)**[199] 1135 7-9-5 **75**........ GeorgeDowning(5) 5 (Tony Carroll) *hld up: plld hrd: hdwy over 3f out: rdn and wknd over 2f out: t.o* **10/1**	

2m 11.31s (3.41) **Going Correction** +0.35s/f (Good)
WFA 3 from 5yo+ 5lb **10** Ran SP% **114.5**
Speed ratings (Par 103): **100,99,97,94,93 92,92,88,74,69**
toteswingers 1&2 £4.90, 2&3 £3.40, 1&3 £3.50 CSF £31.10 CT £89.36 TOTE £10.80: £2.80, £1.10, £1.70; EX 31.90.
Owner K G Kitchen **Bred** Patrick F Kelly **Trained** Danethorpe, Notts

FOCUS
The slower of the two divisions by 0.9sec, and it looked the slightly lesser race. The first four were always prominent.
T/Plt: £272.30 to a £1 stake. Pool of £60614.40 -162.48 winning tickets. T/Qpdt: £63.40 to a £1 stake. Pool of £5826.32 - 67.90 winning tickets. CR

6779 NEWCASTLE (L-H)

Tuesday, October 16

7133 Meeting Abandoned - waterlogged

7055 WOLVERHAMPTON (A.W) (L-H)

Tuesday, October 16

OFFICIAL GOING: Standard
Wind: Strong behind Weather: Fine

7141 32RED H'CAP (DIV I) 7f 32y(P)

5:20 (5:20) (Class 5) (0-70,70) 3-Y-O+ **£2,264** (£673; £336; £168) **Stalls** High

Form				RPR
6300	**1**		**Lucky Money**[43] 5888 3-9-3 68........(b) LukeMorris 11 (Sir Mark Prescott Bt) *dwlt: hld up: rdn and hdwy on wd outside over 1f out: r.o strly fnl f: led fnl 50yds* **7/2**[1]	79
065	**2**	1 1/2	**Illustrious Prince (IRE)**[17] 6692 5-9-4 70........ NeilFarley(3) 10 (Declan Carroll) *midfield towards outer: rdn and hdwy over 1f out: led jst ins fnl f: kpt on: hdd fnl 50yds* **10/1**	77
0543	**3**	nse	**Handheld**[34] 6141 5-9-4 67........ LiamKeniry 5 (Ed de Giles) *dwlt: sn midfield on inner: rdn 2f out: sn chsd ldrs: kpt on ins fnl f* **9/2**[2]	74
0413	**4**	1/2	**Chester Aristocrat**[48] 5728 3-9-0 70........ JasonHart(5) 2 (Eric Alston) *chsd ldrs: rdn over 2f out: led 1f out: sn hdd: one pce ins fnl f* **10/1**	76
6053	**5**	1 1/2	**Who's Shirl**[17] 6687 6-9-6 69........ KellyHarrison 9 (Chris Fairhurst) *hld up: hdwy whn n.m.r 1f out: kpt on ins fnl f: nrest at fin* **10/1**	70
0304	**6**	1 1/2	**Dorlussa (IRE)**[59] 5336 3-8-12 68........ JackDuern(5) 3 (Mark Brisbourne) *prom: rdn to ld wl over 1f out: hdd 1f out: wknd* **16/1**	65
6443	**7**	shd	**Dark Lane**[38] 6053 6-9-1 64........ SilvestreDeSousa 1 (David Evans) *trckd ldrs: pushed along over 2f out: sn one pce* **20/1**	61
5000	**8**	1 3/4	**Viola D'Amour (IRE)**[19] 6610 3-9-2 67........ RichardKingscote 6 (Tom Dascombe) *led: rdn whn hdd wl over 1f out: grad wknd* **25/1**	59
204	**9**	4	**Lady Layla**[22] 6542 3-9-5 70........ TomEaves 4 (Bryan Smart) *trckd ldrs: rdn over 2f out: wknd over 1f out* **13/2**[3]	52
2405	**10**	1/2	**Duke Of Aricabeau (IRE)**[12] 6824 3-9-4 69........(b[1]) AdamKirby 8 (Mrs K Burke) *racd keenly in midfield: rdn over 2f out: wknd over 1f out* **11/1**	49
3540	**11**	3	**Ghost Train (IRE)**[12] 6825 3-8-11 67........(p) MichaelJMMurphy(5) 12 (Mark Johnston) *in tch on outer: rdn over 2f out: wknd over 1f out* **8/1**	39

1m 28.6s (-1.00) **Going Correction** -0.10s/f (Stan)
WFA 3 from 4yo+ 2lb **11** Ran SP% **114.9**
Speed ratings (Par 103): **101,99,99,98,96 95,95,93,88,87 84**
toteswingers: 1&2 £6.40, 2&3 £11.10, 1&3 £4.80 CSF £38.09 CT £162.50 TOTE £3.90: £3.00, £3.00, £1.60; EX 39.40 Trifecta £422.20 Part won. Pool £570.66 - 0.61 winning units..
Owner J M Brown **Bred** Whitley Stud **Trained** Newmarket, Suffolk

FOCUS
The pace was fair for this wide open handicap and those held up early dominated at the finish. The winner built on his 2yo form.
Who's Shirl Official explanation: jockey said mare was denied a clear run
Dark Lane Official explanation: jockey said gelding was denied a clear run
Duke Of Aricabeau(IRE) Official explanation: jockey said gelding ran too freely

7142 32RED H'CAP (DIV II) 7f 32y(P)

5:50 (5:50) (Class 5) (0-70,70) 3-Y-O+ **£2,264** (£673; £336; £168) **Stalls** High

Form				RPR
6006	**1**		**Majestic Dream (IRE)**[10] 6895 4-9-4 67........(v) GrahamGibbons 4 (Michael Easterby) *mde all: rdn 2f out: strly pressed fnl 50yds: hld on wl* **9/2**[2]	76
6244	**2**	1/2	**Bajan Bear**[24] 6495 4-9-5 68........ DaneO'Neill 8 (Michael Blanshard) *dwlt: hld up towards inner: hdwy over 1f out: chsd wnr jst ins fnl f: chal strly fnl 50yds: jst hld* **13/2**[3]	76
2233	**3**	1/2	**Fayr Fall (IRE)**[31] 6261 3-9-5 70........(v) DavidAllan 1 (Tim Easterby) *trckd ldrs: rdn 2f out: kpt on* **5/2**[1]	76
0410	**4**	nse	**Abhaath (USA)**[54] 5501 3-8-12 68........ DarrenEgan(5) 7 (Ronald Harris) *midfield: hdwy over 2f out: briefly short of room wl over 1f out: rdn to chse wnr appr fnl f: kpt on* **9/2**[2]	74
2006	**5**	1	**Satwa Laird**[10] 6894 6-9-7 70........ HayleyTurner 6 (Conor Dore) *in tch: rdn over 2f out: one pce* **16/1**	73
6400	**6**	4 1/2	**Wildcat Wizard (USA)**[12] 6824 6-9-4 67........ MickyFenton 5 (Paul Midgley) *slowly away: hld up: sme minor late hdwy: nvr threatened* **33/1**	58
5005	**7**	3/4	**All Right Now**[12] 6812 5-9-1 64........ AndreaAtzeni 11 (Derek Haydn Jones) *prom: rdn over 2f out: wknd appr fnl f* **20/1**	53
3223	**8**	1	**Loyal N Trusted**[10] 6895 4-8-13 65........[1] MarkCoumbe(3) 3 (Richard Price) *hld up in midfield: rdn 2f out: nvr threatened* **11/1**	52
5530	**9**	hd	**Daring Dream (GER)**[57] 5414 7-9-3 66........ GrahamLee 12 (Jim Goldie) *hld up: rdn over 2f out: sn btn* **20/1**	52
0504	**10**	1 3/4	**Safe House (IRE)**[33] 6171 3-9-1 66........ SilvestreDeSousa 9 (Mark Johnston) *trckd ldrs: pushed along 3f out: sn lost pl: wknd over 1f out* **14/1**	47
2000	**11**	3 1/2	**Pipers Piping (IRE)**[12] 6812 6-9-5 68........ AdamKirby 10 (John Butler) *hld up: nvr threatened* **50/1**	40

1m 28.44s (-1.16) **Going Correction** -0.10s/f (Stan)
WFA 3 from 4yo+ 2lb **11** Ran SP% **113.6**
Speed ratings (Par 103): **102,101,100,100,99 94,93,92,92,90 86**
toteswingers:1&2 £6.60, 2&3 £3.10, 1&3 £3.40 CSF £30.89 CT £89.30 TOTE £4.90: £1.60, £2.20, £1.10; EX 40.20 Trifecta £133.20 Pool £916.31 - 5.09 winning units..
Owner A Simpson, B Hoggarth & S Hull **Bred** Thomas Hassett **Trained** Sheriff Hutton, N Yorks

FOCUS
This was run at a steady pace, with the winner making all under a strong ride and the front five finishing some way clear. It was the faster division and the form makes sense.
Loyal N Trusted Official explanation: jockey said gelding suffered interference in running
Pipers Piping(IRE) Official explanation: jockey said gelding had no more to give

7143 32RED.COM MEDIAN AUCTION MAIDEN STKS 7f 32y(P)

6:20 (6:23) (Class 6) 2-Y-O **£1,704** (£503; £251) **Stalls** High

Form				RPR
	1		**Footstepsintherain (IRE)** 2-9-3 0........ TedDurcan 5 (David Lanigan) *dwlt: hld up in tch: nudged along and hdwy over 1f out: kpt on to ld fnl 50yds: shade cosily* **7/1**	77+
42	**2**	1/2	**Midnight Flower (IRE)**[25] 6453 2-8-12 0........ GrahamLee 4 (David Simcock) *led: rdn 2f out: one pce and wandered u.p ins fnl f: hdd fnl 50yds* **11/10**[1]	71
0	**3**	nse	**Al Manaal**[22] 6533 2-8-12 0........ SilvestreDeSousa 6 (Saeed Bin Suroor) *in tch: rdn over 2f out: chsd ldr over 1f out: kpt on fnl f* **9/2**[3]	71
04	**4**	3 3/4	**Vergality Ridge (IRE)**[7] 6945 2-9-3 0........ LukeMorris 3 (Ronald Harris) *trckd ldrs: rdn 2f out: no ex ins fnl f* **25/1**	67
0	**5**	1/2	**Nullarbor Sky (IRE)**[13] 6791 2-8-12 0........ EddieAhern 2 (Lucy Wadham) *hld up: pushed along over 2f out: kpt on one pce: nvr threatened* **12/1**	60
0	**6**	2 3/4	**Forward March**[13] 6796 2-9-3 0........(be[1]) GeorgeBaker 1 (Roger Charlton) *tk str hold: hld up in rr: swtchd to outside over 1f out: sn rdn and no imp* **4/1**[2]	59+
0	**7**	3	**Show More Faith**[6] 6977 2-9-3 0........ LiamKeniry 10 (Sylvester Kirk) *prom: rdn 2f out: wknd appr fnl f* **33/1**	51
0	**8**	8	**Honey Haven (IRE)**[153] 2163 2-8-12 0........ LiamJones 8 (Mark Brisbourne) *hld up: bhd 1/2-way* **66/1**	27

00 9 1 1/2 **Equinox**[27] 6355 2-8-12 0 TomEaves 7 23
(Bryan Smart) *prom towards outer tl wknd wl over 1f out* **100/1**

1m 29.78s (0.18) **Going Correction** -0.10s/f (Stan) **9** Ran SP% **115.3**
Speed ratings (Par 93): **94,93,93,89,88 85,81,72,71**
toteswingers:1&2 £2.60, 2&3 £1.80, 1&3 £4.30 CSF £14.93 TOTE £10.60: £2.00, £1.02, £1.70; EX 16.00 Trifecta £69.10 Pool £1,257.95 - 13.40 winning units..
Owner Favourites Racing **Bred** Ken Carroll **Trained** Upper Lambourn, Berks

FOCUS
An uncompetitive maiden run at a steady pace, with the front three home pulling clear late on. The bare form can't be rated any better.

NOTEBOOK
Footstepsintherain(IRE), whose dam was of little account but is a half-sister to a Group 3 winner and has produced two very useful 2yo performers (one placed in AW Group 3), was noted travelling kindly in midfield and picked up well up the straight, showing a willing attitude to hold on at the line. This did not look the strongest of contests but he looks a nice type for next season. (op 9-1 tchd 10-1)
Midnight Flower(IRE), had easily the best form of those who had run but was very weak in the market. Sent to the front from the off, despite having been caught late on over a furlong shorter when last seen, she travelled well enough but found little when coming under pressure, although was picking up again at the line. (op 5-6 tchd 8-11)
Al Manaal, didn´t show much when fitted with a hood (now removed) on her debut at Kempton three week ago, but showed more here although did not find much when driven, having looked the likely winner a furlong out. (op 5-1)
Vergality Ridge(IRE) ran well to a point. (op 22-1)
Nullarbor Sky(IRE), a half-sister to nine winners, including Listed-class Ghost Dance, played up entering the stalls and came under pressure some way out but was keeping on well enough to the line and should do better over further, in time. (op 20-1)
Forward March, did not settle on his debut and had the blinkers added to the eyeshield here, although that failed to do the trick, as he raced far too freely once again. The market support suggests he should be capable of better but he will need to learn to settle. Official explanation: jockey said gelding ran too freely (tchd 9-2)

7144 32RED CASINO H'CAP (DIV I) 5f 216y(P)
6:50 (6:50) (Class 4) (0-85,84) 3-Y-O+ **£4,528** (£1,347; £673; £336) **Stalls** Low

Form RPR
2520 1 **Song Of Parkes**[4] 7023 5-8-11 74 TedDurcan 8 85
(Eric Alston) *hld up in tch: pushed along and hdwy over 1f out: led ins fnl f: kpt on to go clr* **18/1**
0500 2 2 1/2 **Rasaman (IRE)**[17] 6665 8-9-0 77 GrahamLee 4 80
(Jim Goldie) *hld up in rr: pushed along 2f out: swtchd to outer appr fnl f: r.o wl: wnt 2nd nr fin: no ch w wnr* **7/1**
0150 3 1/2 **Orbit The Moon (IRE)**[39] 6008 4-9-2 79 (tp) TomEaves 6 80
(Michael Dods) *prom: led 2f: drvn over 1f out: hdd ins fnl f: sn no ch w wnr: lost 2nd nr fin* **11/2**[3]
0020 4 2 **Thirteen Shivers**[17] 6688 4-8-12 82 MatthewHopkins(7) 10 77
(Michael Easterby) *midfield on outer: rdn and hdwy to chse ldrs over 2f out: one pce fr over 1f out* **12/1**
0000 5 1/2 **Fred Willetts (IRE)**[12] 6820 4-9-7 84 (v) DavidProbert 7 77
(David C Griffiths) *led: rdn whn hdd 2f out: wknd ins fnl f* **7/1**
1102 6 2 1/4 **Sunny Side Up (IRE)**[19] 6605 3-8-13 77 TonyHamilton 2 63
(Richard Fahey) *trckd ldrs: drvn and hung lft over 1f out: wknd ins fnl f* **5/1**[2]
1203 7 3/4 **Button Moon (IRE)**[12] 6825 4-8-8 71 (p) SilvestreDeSousa 9 55
(Ian Wood) *chsd ldrs: wknd ins fnl f* **6/1**
5010 8 hd **Chiswick Bey (IRE)**[39] 6009 4-8-13 83 JacobButterfield(7) 1 66
(Ollie Pears) *dwlt: sn pushed along towards rr: nvr threatened* **11/2**[3]
2605 9 4 **Soap Wars**[31] 6234 7-9-4 81 AdamKirby 5 51
(Hugo Palmer) *racd keenly: trckd ldrs: rdn 2f out: wknd appr fnl f* **9/2**[1]

1m 12.57s (-2.43) **Going Correction** -0.10s/f (Stan) course record
WFA 3 from 4yo+ 1lb **9** Ran SP% **117.9**
Speed ratings (Par 105): **112,108,108,105,104 101,100,100,95**
toteswingers:1&2 £32.20, 2&3 £10.10, 1&3 £11.20 CSF £140.51 CT £804.12 TOTE £22.10: £3.50, £3.80, £2.20; EX 80.40 Trifecta £246.60 Pool £1,239.72 - 3.72 winning units..
Owner Joseph Heler **Bred** Joseph Heler **Trained** Longton, Lancs

FOCUS
Plenty of pace on for this handicap with the winner pulling clear late on. A clear personal best from the winner.

7145 32RED CASINO H'CAP (DIV II) 5f 216y(P)
7:20 (7:20) (Class 4) (0-85,84) 3-Y-O+ **£4,528** (£1,347; £673; £336) **Stalls** Low

Form RPR
4063 1 **Arctic Lynx (IRE)**[8] 6938 5-8-12 80 MichaelJMMurphy(5) 9 88
(Robert Cowell) *midfield: rdn and hdwy over 1f out: r.o fnl f: led post* **4/1**[3]
131 2 shd **Amoure Medici**[19] 6610 3-9-5 83 GrahamLee 2 91
(Ann Duffield) *chsd ldrs: rdn over 1f out: drvn to ld fnl 100yds: kpt on: hdd post* **10/3**[1]
0034 3 nk **Hopes N Dreams (IRE)**[17] 6665 4-9-1 78 AmyRyan 8 85
(Kevin Ryan) *dwlt: hld up: hdwy on outer over 1f out: chsd ldr jst ins fnl f: r.o: jst hld: rdr dropped whip crossing line* **8/1**
2062 4 1/2 **Noverre To Go (IRE)**[11] 6837 6-9-7 84 LukeMorris 4 89
(Ronald Harris) *dwlt: hld up in midfield: rdn and hdwy on inner over 1f out: kpt on* **7/2**[2]
5061 5 1/2 **Red Cape (FR)**[11] 6837 9-8-7 70 (b) JamesSullivan 1 74
(Ruth Carr) *led: drvn over 1f out: hdd fnl 100yds: no ex* **16/1**
1003 6 1 1/2 **Bop It**[39] 6005 3-9-3 81 TomEaves 3 80
(Bryan Smart) *in tch: briefly short of room over 1f out: sn rdn: one pce and no imp on ldrs* **22/1**
6014 7 nk **Ghostwing**[16] 6705 5-8-12 75 (vt) IanMongan 10 73
(Luke Dace) *prom towards outer: rdn 2f out: wknd ins fnl f* **22/1**
0-04 8 5 **Judd Street**[27] 6369 10-9-0 77 DaneO'Neill 7 59
(Eve Johnson Houghton) *s.i.s: hld up: nvr threatened* **16/1**
0300 9 1/2 **Diman Waters (IRE)**[17] 6665 5-8-9 72 KellyHarrison 5 52
(Eric Alston) *racd keenly: hld up: rdn over 1f out: nvr threatened* **28/1**
3502 10 2 3/4 **Sutton Veny (IRE)**[8] 6938 6-9-5 82 JamieSpencer 6 53
(Jeremy Gask) *prom: rdn wl over 1f out: sn wknd* **4/1**[3]

1m 13.21s (-1.79) **Going Correction** -0.10s/f (Stan)
WFA 3 from 4yo+ 1lb **10** Ran SP% **120.3**
Speed ratings (Par 105): **107,106,106,105,105 103,102,96,95,91**
toteswingers:1&2 £2.80, 2&3 £5.90, 1&3 £6.60 CSF £17.93 CT £106.56 TOTE £4.50: £1.20, £1.80, £2.20; EX 19.40 Trifecta £147.70 Pool £952.71 - 4.77 winning units..
Owner Heading For The Rocks Partnership **Bred** Derek Veitch And Saleh Ali Hammadi **Trained** Six Mile Bottom, Cambs

FOCUS
Plenty of in-form runners for the second division of this decent handicap that was run at a steady pace, with the front five well grouped at the post. It was the slower division. The winner is rated pretty much to his best.

7146 32RED SUPPORTING BRITISH RACING H'CAP 5f 216y(P)
7:50 (7:51) (Class 6) (0-60,59) 3-Y-O **£1,704** (£503; £251) **Stalls** Low

Form RPR
231 1 **George Fenton**[22] 6530 3-9-5 57 (p) J-PGuillambert 4 63
(Richard Guest) *hld up in tch: sme hdwy over 1f out: swtchd to ins jst ins fnl f: r.o strly to ld nr fin* **11/4**[1]
0045 2 nse **Kai**[8] 6937 3-9-1 53 (v) LukeMorris 12 59
(Alan McCabe) *chsd ldrs on outer: rdn over 1f out: r.o fnl f: jst failed* **10/1**
000 3 shd **Ghazeer (IRE)**[11] 6836 3-9-4 56 (v) SilvestreDeSousa 10 62
(Derek Shaw) *chsd ldrs: drvn over 1f out: sn ev ch: edgd rt jst ins fnl f: kpt on: jst hld* **14/1**
-030 4 1/2 **Monumental Man**[8] 6937 3-9-0 52 (p) LiamJones 8 56
(James Unett) *prom: led narrowly 4f out: rdn over 1f out: hdd nr fin* **16/1**
1432 5 hd **Lord Franklin**[14] 6756 3-8-12 55 JasonHart(5) 5 58
(Eric Alston) *led: hdd 4f out: remained prom: stl ev ch ins fnl f: one pce* **9/2**[2]
000 6 1 1/2 **Glennten**[34] 6151 3-9-5 57 LiamKeniry 11 55
(Sylvester Kirk) *midfield: hdwy to chse ldrs over 1f out: one pce ins fnl f* **28/1**
0-40 7 1 1/4 **Widow Flower (IRE)**[26] 6397 3-9-0 52 JamieSpencer 9 46
(Michael Bell) *prom: rdn and outpcd over 1f out: drvn and no imp ins fnl f* **12/1**
0306 8 1 **Trust Fund Babe (IRE)**[32] 6211 3-9-7 59 DavidAllan 13 50
(Tim Easterby) *midfield on outer: rdn over 2f out: no imp on ldrs* **11/1**
3114 9 1 1/2 **Verus Delicia (IRE)**[43] 5875 3-9-1 56 MarkCoumbe(3) 3 42
(Daniel Mark Loughnane) *hld up: nvr threatened* **16/1**
6045 10 1/2 **Irrational**[70] 4913 3-9-4 56 (v[1]) TomEaves 7 41
(Bryan Smart) *hld up: a towards rr* **16/1**
5050 11 3/4 **Lord Paget**[8] 6937 3-8-12 55 (p) JackDuern(5) 2 37
(Reg Hollinshead) *s.i.s: sn reminders in rr: nvr threatened* **33/1**
5030 12 3/4 **Alnair (IRE)**[5] 7001 3-9-4 59 (b) NeilFarley(3) 6 39
(Declan Carroll) *midfield on inner: rdn over 2f out: wknd over 1f out* **9/1**[3]
0000 13 3 3/4 **Nearly A Gift (IRE)**[31] 6264 3-9-0 52 (t) GrahamGibbons 1 20
(Tim Easterby) *hld up on inner: rdn over 2f out: wknd over 1f out* **14/1**

1m 14.68s (-0.32) **Going Correction** -0.10s/f (Stan) **13** Ran SP% **117.3**
Speed ratings (Par 99): **98,97,97,97,96 94,93,91,89,89 88,87,82**
toteswingers:1&2 £6.40, 2&3 £21.50, 1&3 £11.00 CSF £29.94 CT £342.19 TOTE £4.00: £1.70, £3.40, £5.10; EX 23.10 Trifecta £269.00 Pool £1,094.26 - 3.01 winning units..
Owner Maze Rattan Limited **Bred** R P Williams **Trained** Stainforth, S Yorks

FOCUS
A low-grade contest. The pace was honest although few able to close from behind with the front five home very well grouped. The front four were close to their marks at face value.

7147 £32 BONUS AT 32RED.COM H'CAP 1m 4f 50y(P)
8:20 (8:20) (Class 4) (0-85,85) 3-Y-O+ **£4,528** (£1,347; £505; £505) **Stalls** Low

Form RPR
4206 1 **Henry Clay**[11] 6832 3-9-2 82 SilvestreDeSousa 9 89
(Mark Johnston) *led at stdy pce: qcknd over 2f out: strly pressed fr over 1f out: hld on gamely ins fnl f* **7/2**[1]
2122 2 nk **Den Maschine**[18] 6642 7-9-2 80 DarrenEgan(5) 11 87
(Sean Curran) *in tch: rdn to chal over 1f out: kpt on but a jst hld* **11/2**[2]
625 3 hd **Pass Muster**[37] 6073 5-8-13 79 JacobButterfield(7) 5 85
(Ollie Pears) *trckd ldr: rdn and ev ch over 1f out: kpt on* **12/1**
6243 3 dht **Flying Power**[18] 6642 4-9-1 74 PaddyAspell 4 80
(John Norton) *racd keenly: in tch: rdn over 1f out: ev ch ins fnl f: kpt on* **16/1**
0201 5 3/4 **Borug (USA)**[16] 6702 4-9-11 84 NeilCallan 12 89
(James Tate) *hld up: rdn and hdwy over 1f out: kpt on fnl f: nt rch ldrs* **6/1**[3]
0663 6 1/2 **Spensley (IRE)**[13] 6776 6-9-12 85 KierenFallon 7 89
(James Fanshawe) *midfield: rdn 2f out: edgd lft over 1f out: kpt on ins fnl f: nt rch ldrs* **6/1**[3]
0506 7 1 1/4 **Cape Safari (IRE)**[7] 6964 3-8-11 82 (v) NatashaEaton(5) 6 84
(Alan Bailey) *midfield: hdwy to chse ldrs over 1f out: no ex ins fnl f* **22/1**
5340 8 1/2 **Anton Dolin (IRE)**[38] 6039 4-9-5 78 EddieAhern 2 79
(John Dunlop) *midfield: pushed along over 1f out: briefly short of room jst ins fnl f: no ch after* **12/1**
2042 9 3 3/4 **Dark Dune (IRE)**[24] 6476 4-9-5 78 DavidAllan 3 73
(Tim Easterby) *racd keenly: hld up: rdn over 1f out: nvr threatened* **15/2**
3620 10 1 1/2 **Gold Rules**[18] 6642 5-9-3 76 JamesSullivan 10 69
(Michael Easterby) *hld up in tch: rdn and brief hdwy over 1f out: wknd appr fnl f* **18/1**
6300 11 shd **My Lord**[8] 6932 4-9-2 75 IanMongan 8 68
(Luke Dace) *hld up in rr: a bhd* **40/1**
1210 12 5 **Illustrious Forest**[143] 2504 4-9-4 77 FrannyNorton 1 62
(John Mackie) *trckd ldr: lost pl over 1f out: wknd* **16/1**

2m 39.34s (-1.76) **Going Correction** -0.10s/f (Stan)
WFA 3 from 4yo+ 7lb **12** Ran SP% **117.1**
Speed ratings (Par 105): **101,100,100,100,100 99,99,98,96,95 95,91**PL 1.80 (Pass Muster), 2.80 (Flying Power); TC 104.52 (PM) 136.65 (FP); toteswingers:1&2 £3.80, 2&3 £4.90 (PM), 1&3 £3.10 (PM), 2&3 £5.00 (FP), 1&3 £10.50 (FP) CSF £21.42 TOTE £3.60: £1.40, £2.50; EX 22.90 TRIFECTA Trifecta 292.70 (PM), 292.70 (FP). Pool £791.127 Owner.

FOCUS
Little pace on for this decent handicap, which suited those up with the pace. The winner made all under a fine tactical ride. There was a bunch finish and the dead-heaters for third set the standard.
Illustrious Forest Official explanation: jockey said gelding hung left-handed

7148 32REDBET.COM H'CAP 1m 1f 103y(P)
8:50 (8:50) (Class 6) (0-60,59) 3-Y-O **£1,704** (£503; £251) **Stalls** Low

Form RPR
6004 1 **Hard Road**[41] 5938 3-9-0 52 TedDurcan 8 60+
(Chris Wall) *in tch: pushed along over 2f out: rdn to ld appr fnl f: kpt on* **2/1**[1]
0405 2 1 1/4 **Thane Of Cawdor (IRE)**[10] 6892 3-9-0 52 MickyFenton 4 58
(Joseph Tuite) *hld up: rdn and hdwy over 1f out: chsd wnr jst ins fnl f: kpt on* **16/1**
0334 3 3/4 **Love Grows Wild (USA)**[91] 4198 3-9-0 52 JamieSpencer 10 56+
(Michael Bell) *hld up: hdwy and stl gng wl 2f out: pushed along and swtchd to outer over 1f out: nt in clr tl ins fnl f: r.o wl* **11/2**[2]

0632 **4** 2 1/4 **Parque Atlantico**[12] 6829 3-9-7 59 FrannyNorton 13 58
(Ed McMahon) *midfield. rdn and hdwy to chse ldrs over 1f out: briefly short of room 1f out: kpt on* **6/1**[3]
0060 **5** 1 1/4 **Rogue Reporter (IRE)**[34] 6151 3-9-2 54 (b[1]) WilliamCarson 3 51
(Stuart Williams) *trckd ldrs: drvn and ev ch over 1f out: no ex ins fnl f* **6/1**[3]
-000 **6** 1/2 **Glaze**[82] 4486 3-8-13 51 DarryllHolland 6 47
(Hughie Morrison) *trckd ldr: rdn over 3f out: sn one pce* **50/1**
1500 **7** 1/2 **Camrock Star (IRE)**[12] 6814 3-9-2 54 GrahamLee 7 49
(Alastair Lidderdale) *midfield on outer: rdn over 2f out: nvr threatened ldrs* **25/1**
6546 **8** 4 1/2 **Barnacle**[10] 6892 3-9-0 52 (p) RussKennemore 5 37
(Pat Eddery) *prom: rdn to ld over 2f out: hdd appr fnl f: wknd* **33/1**
0031 **9** nk **Pass The Time**[21] 6569 3-8-8 49 (p) AmyBaker(3) 9 33
(Neil Mulholland) *in tch: rdn over 2f out: wknd over 1f out* **16/1**
6223 **10** 1 1/2 **Symphony Star (IRE)**[12] 6813 3-8-13 56 DarrenEgan(5) 1 37
(Paul D'Arcy) *hld up: a towards rr* **14/1**
0666 **11** 6 **Noosa Boy**[26] 6395 3-8-12 50 ow1 IanMongan 11 19
(Luke Dace) *midfield: rdn over 2f out: wknd over 1f out* **20/1**
5001 **12** 2 **First Glance**[30] 6281 3-8-8 49 DominicFox(3) 2 14
(Michael Appleby) *led: rdn whn hdd over 2f out: wknd* **14/1**
065 **13** 6 **The Yank**[183] 1415 3-9-1 58 GeorgeDowning(5) 12 10
(Tony Carroll) *swtchd lft s: hld up in rr: a bhd* **40/1**

2m 0.83s (-0.87) **Going Correction** -0.10s/f (Stan) **13 Ran SP% 118.3**
Speed ratings (Par 99): **99,97,97,95,94 93,93,89,88,87 82,80,75**
toteswingers: 1&2 £9.40, 2&3 £13.20, 1&3 £2.20: CSF £35.88 CT £159.13 TOTE £4.60: £1.70, £8.20, £1.10; EX 47.30 Trifecta £149.70 Pool £734.63 - 3.63 winning units..
Owner Ms Aida Fustoq **Bred** Deerfield Farm **Trained** Newmarket, Suffolk

FOCUS
A modest handicap. It was run at a steady pace and there were plenty in contention at the furlong pole. The winner's best run since one standout miaden effort.
T/Plt: £80.80 to a £1 stake. Pool £76,033.39 - 686.46 winning units. T/Qpdt: £50.70 to a £1 stake. Pool £9,336.00 - 136.00 winning units. AS

7149 - 7155a (Foreign Racing) - See Raceform Interactive

7005 KEMPTON (A.W) (R-H)
Wednesday, October 17

OFFICIAL GOING: Standard
Wind: Moderate, half behind Weather: Cloudy

7156 WIN BIG WITH BETDAQ MULTIPLES NURSERY 5f (P)
5:40 (5:42) (Class 6) (0-60,60) 2-Y-O **£1,617** (£481; £240; £120) **Stalls** Low

Form RPR
36 **1** **Modern Lady**[61] 5313 2-9-2 55 RobbieFitzpatrick 9 60
(Richard Guest) *trckd ldr: rdn to take narrow ld over 1f out: drvn to assert last 50yds* **7/1**
0003 **2** 1/2 **Prince Of Prophets (IRE)**[58] 5403 2-8-9 48 (t) WilliamCarson 8 51
(Stuart Williams) *dwlt: wl in rr: rdn 1/2-way: prog over 1f out: chsd ldng pair ins fnl f: styd on wl to take 2nd post* **5/1**[2]
0462 **3** hd **Marmot Bay (IRE)**[11] 6890 2-9-6 59 FergusSweeney 5 61
(Jamie Osborne) *led: drvn and narrowly hdd over 1f out: pressed wnr tl no ex last 50yds: lost 2nd post* **11/2**[3]
506 **4** 1 3/4 **Persian Marvel (IRE)**[58] 5403 2-8-13 52 (b[1]) PatCosgrave 3 48
(Jim Boyle) *chsd ldng pair: drvn over 1f out: nt qckn and no imp* **12/1**
064 **5** nk **Many Elements**[45] 5854 2-9-4 57 KierenFox 1 52
(Lee Carter) *chsd ldrs: hrd rdn 2f out: one pce and no imp fr over 1f out* **9/2**[1]
050 **6** shd **Constant Dream**[76] 4742 2-8-11 50 JimCrowley 2 45
(James Given) *in tch: rdn over 2f out: could nt qckn and no imp over 1f out: kpt on ins fnl f* **6/1**
006 **7** 5 **Delphica (IRE)**[42] 5948 2-9-4 57 (p) JamesDoyle 4 34
(Gary Moore) *chsd ldrs: rdn over 2f out: wknd over 1f out* **9/2**[1]
0000 **8** 3 **Jackpot**[69] 4990 2-8-6 45 KirstyMilczarek 10 11
(Brendan Powell) *dwlt: a in rr: bhd fnl 2f* **33/1**
500 **9** 1 **Baltic Sea (IRE)**[47] 5807 2-8-6 48 SophieDoyle(3) 6 10
(David Evans) *sn outpcd in last and pushed along: virtually t.o 1/2-way: rattled home last 100yds* **20/1**
3600 **10** 2 1/2 **Cashel's Missile (IRE)**[21] 6579 2-9-7 60 SamHitchcott 7 13
(John Spearing) *chsd ldrs on outer: rdn bef 1/2-way: wknd 2f out: sn wl bhd* **25/1**

59.78s (-0.72) **Going Correction** -0.20s/f (Stan) **10 Ran SP% 114.4**
Speed ratings (Par 93): **97,96,95,93,92 92,84,79,78,74**
toteswingers 1&2 £8.20, 1&3 £4.90, 2&3 £3.30 CSF £40.05 CT £206.94 TOTE £13.20: £4.30, £2.60, £1.02; EX 27.20 Trifecta £519.09 - 6.53 winning units..
Owner Maze Rattan Limited **Bred** Little Lodge Farm **Trained** Stainforth, S Yorks

FOCUS
A moderate nursery, with seven making their handicap debuts, and one run at a solid pace.

NOTEBOOK
Modern Lady relished this return to Polytrack and opened her account at the sixth attempt. She flopped on turf last time, but this was a return to the sort of form that saw her go close at Wolverhampton the time before and there was a fair bit to like about the way she saw it out off the home turn. There should be some more to come on this surface.
Prince Of Prophets(IRE), friendless in the betting, again got going all too late and is crying out for another furlong. He ought to collect when faced with one. (op 6-1 tchd 7-1)
Marmot Bay(IRE) made a decent fist of it under a positive ride and, second in a seller last time out, helps to set the standard. (op 9-2)
Persian Marvel(IRE) shaped better due to a 4lb drop in the handicap and application of first-time blinkers. His ideal trip remains uncertain, though. (op 14-1)
Many Elements, gambled on, had his chance to make the frame but mustered only the same pace under pressure. He may now prefer reverting to 6f. (op 4-1)
Constant Dream did her best to close, but lacked the pace to get involved and shaped as though the run would bring her on. She's begun life in nurseries on a workable mark and can improve. (op 8-1)
Delphica(IRE), in first-time cheekpieces, met support on this nursery debut but never threatened and may not be straightforward. (op 4-1)

7157 BACK OR LAY AT BETDAQ.COM H'CAP 5f (P)
6:10 (6:10) (Class 6) (0-55,56) 3-Y-O+ **£1,617** (£481; £240; £120) **Stalls** Low

Form RPR
R501 **1** **Ivestar (IRE)**[8] 6959 7-9-5 56 6ex (v) GrahamGibbons 6 65
(Michael Easterby) *chsd ldng pair: rdn and clsd to ld 1f out: sn jnd: fought on wl to assert last 75yds* **9/2**[3]
501 **2** 3/4 **Illustrious Lad (IRE)**[28] 6362 3-9-2 53 (p) PatCosgrave 10 59
(Jim Boyle) *trckd ldrs: rdn and clsd over 1f out: jnd wnr jst ins fnl f: fnd little and hld last 50yds* **4/1**[2]
05/0 **3** 3 **Burnt Cream**[19] 6640 5-9-1 52 (t) StevieDonohoe 8 48
(Martin Bosley) *awkward s: hld up: last tl prog over 1f out: styd on wl to take 3rd nr fin* **33/1**
0210 **4** 1/2 **Perfect Honour (IRE)**[8] 6959 6-9-3 54 (b) WilliamCarson 12 48
(Violet M Jordan) *w ldr to 1/2-way: lost 2nd and fdd over 1f out: b.b.v* **7/1**
2400 **5** nk **Mitie Mouse**[16] 6737 3-9-2 53 JamesDoyle 4 46
(Mike Murphy) *mde most: fought off chalr 2f out: hdd & wknd 1f out* **7/2**[1]
3250 **6** 1/2 **Blueberry Fizz (IRE)**[21] 6585 4-9-4 55 (b[1]) DaraghO'Donohoe 9 46
(John Ryan) *awkward s: rdn thrght and struggling in last trio: kpt on fnl f* **12/1**
-40 **7** 3/4 **Nafa (IRE)**[44] 5874 4-9-4 55 ShaneKelly 3 43
(Daniel Mark Loughnane) *nvr bttr than midfield: no prog over 1f out: fdd* **5/1**
2060 **8** nk **Ace Of Spies (IRE)**[9] 6937 7-8-13 55 DavidKenny(5) 1 42
(Conor Dore) *chsd ldrs: pushed along over 1f out and nt qckn: fdd fnl f* **20/1**
650 **9** 7 **Ladydolly**[34] 6180 4-9-2 53 [1] LukeMorris 5 15
(Roy Brotherton) *chsd ldrs: rdn 1/2-way: wknd over 1f out: eased* **7/1**

59.49s (-1.01) **Going Correction** -0.20s/f (Stan) **9 Ran SP% 117.5**
Speed ratings (Par 101): **100,98,94,93,92 91,90,90,79**
toteswingers 1&2 £1.90, 1&3 £2.50, 2&3 £4.60 CSF £23.32 CT £532.32 TOTE £2.70: £1.60, £2.80, £5.20; EX 14.20 Trifecta £296.80 Pool: £493.41 - 1.23 winning units..
Owner Mrs Krista Brown **Bred** Grenane House Stud & Hatta International Bloodstoc **Trained** Sheriff Hutton, N Yorks

FOCUS
A weak sprint handicap. The runner-up has been rated in line with his handicap form.

7158 BETDAQ MOBILE APPS CLAIMING STKS 1m (P)
6:40 (6:40) (Class 6) 3-Y-O **£1,617** (£481; £240; £120) **Stalls** Low

Form RPR
2111 **1** **Marford Missile (IRE)**[9] 6923 3-9-1 78 RichardKingscote 9 70
(Tom Dascombe) *led after 1f but unable to shake off runner-up: hrd rdn and hdd 2f out: led again jst ins fnl f: drvn out* **2/5**[1]
040 **2** nk **Eternal Gift (FR)**[12] 6840 3-9-6 70 (b) JimmyFortune 2 74
(Rae Guest) *led 1f: pressed wnr after: led again 2f out whn gng bttr: edgd lft over 1f out: hdd jst ins fnl f: could nt qckn after* **9/1**[3]
206 **3** 1 **Princess Maya**[35] 6152 3-8-12 61 JimCrowley 6 64
(Jo Crowley) *in tch: chsd clr ldng pair 1/2-way: hrd rdn over 2f out: no imp tl clsd fnl f: unable to chal* **10/1**
0603 **4** 2 1/4 **Island Melody (IRE)**[33] 6206 3-9-1 67 FergusSweeney 4 62
(J S Moore) *a abt same pl: rdn over 3f out: one pce and no imp* **8/1**[2]
550 **5** 3/4 **Desertcougar (IRE)**[14] 6774 3-8-2 57 ow1 MatthewLawson(5) 3 52
(Daniel Mark Loughnane) *awkward s: t.k.h: hld up in last pair: rdn over 2f out: modest late prog* **16/1**
3204 **6** 2 **Nevaeh**[26] 6433 3-8-10 62 (p) LukeMorris 7 50
(Pat Eddery) *sn dropped to last pair: hrd rdn 3f out: nvr on terms* **20/1**
3030 **7** hd **Desert Red (IRE)**[40] 5994 3-8-10 45 (b) JimmyQuinn 8 50
(Phil McEntee) *a in rr: rdn over 3f out: brief rally over 2f out: sn btn* **50/1**
00 **8** 8 **Darwinian**[27] 6398 3-8-8 0 DavidProbert 5 29
(Dave Morris) *chsd ldng pair to 1/2-way: sn wknd* **100/1**
0 **9** hd **Rose Madder**[130] 2935 3-8-9 0 SamHitchcott 1 30
(Roger Curtis) *awkward s: a in rr: rdn over 3f out: wknd 2f out* **25/1**

1m 38.25s (-1.55) **Going Correction** -0.20s/f (Stan) **9 Ran SP% 119.1**
Speed ratings (Par 99): **99,98,97,95,94 92,92,84,84**
toteswingers 1&2 £1.90, 2&3 £4.60, 1&3 £2.50 CSF £4.94 TOTE £1.40: £1.02, £2.10, £3.10; EX 5.80 Trifecta £20.30 Pool: £754.52 - 27.49 winning units..Marford Missile was claimed by A Weaver for £10000.
Owner The MHS 4x10 Partnership **Bred** Miss Mary Davidson & Mrs Steffi Von Schilcher **Trained** Malpas, Cheshire

FOCUS
Straightforward claiming form rated around the third.

7159 BETDAQ CASINO GAMES MAIDEN FILLIES' STKS (DIV I) 7f (P)
7:10 (7:10) (Class 5) 2-Y-O **£2,264** (£673; £336; £168) **Stalls** Low

Form RPR
3 **1** **Shuruq (USA)**[97] 4011 2-9-0 0 FrankieDettori 1 77+
(Saeed Bin Suroor) *mde all: rdn and pressed over 1f out: styd on wl and in command fnl f* **10/11**[1]
2 1 **Hidden Belief (IRE)** 2-9-0 0 JimCrowley 6 74
(Ralph Beckett) *trckd ldng pair: chsd wnr over 2f out: rdn and tried to chal over 1f out: safely hld fnl f* **7/1**[3]
2 **3** 3/4 **Hanzada (USA)**[40] 6017 2-9-0 0 JamesDoyle 12 72
(Ed Dunlop) *trckd ldng trio: wnt 3rd over 2f out: shkn up over 1f out: styd on but nvr able to chal* **4/1**[2]
4 3/4 **Cloudwalker (USA)** 2-9-0 0 LukeMorris 10 70+
(Ed Vaughan) *dwlt: hld up in 9th and off the pce: prog over 2f out: shkn up to take 4th 1f out: fair debut* **100/1**
5 1 1/4 **Wakeup Little Suzy (IRE)** 2-9-0 0 MartinHarley 11 67+
(Marco Botti) *dwlt: sn chsd ldrs in 6th: shkn up and kpt on same pce fnl 2f* **50/1**
6 1 3/4 **Qareenah (USA)** 2-9-0 0 PaulHanagan 8 62
(Sir Michael Stoute) *dwlt: sn in 7th but off the pce: shkn up over 2f out: effrt to dispute 4th briefly jst over 1f out: no prog after* **20/1**
7 1 1/4 **Modernstone** 2-9-0 0 EddieAhern 5 59
(William Knight) *dwlt: hld up in 8th and off the pce: shkn up 2f out: one pce and no threat* **66/1**
8 3/4 **Waverunner** 2-9-0 0 MickaelBarzalona 9 57+
(Mahmood Al Zarooni) *dwlt: wl off the pce in last quartet: sme prog and swtchd to inner over 1f out: kpt on same pce after* **9/1**
0 **9** 1 1/4 **Lilly White (USA)**[131] 2892 2-9-0 0 (t) KierenFallon 7 53
(Brian Meehan) *chsd wnr to over 2f out: wknd and lost pls fnl f* **33/1**
10 shd **Loraine** 2-9-0 0 FergusSweeney 4 53+
(Jamie Osborne) *dwlt: hld up in last pair but travelled quite wl: effrt on inner 2f out: nt clr run 1f out: styd on: nt disgracd* **100/1**
03 **11** 1/2 **Polly's Love (IRE)**[18] 6664 2-9-0 0 AdamKirby 3 52
(Clive Cox) *chsd ldng quartet: steadily wknd fnl 2f* **25/1**
12 6 **Cherry Malotte** 2-9-0 0 WilliamBuick 2 36
(John Gosden) *dwlt: rn green in last and wl off the pce: nvr a factor* **16/1**
13 3 3/4 **Kalithea** 2-9-0 0 PatCosgrave 14 25
(Jim Boyle) *dwlt: nvr bttr than 10th: rdn on outer over 2f out: no prog* **66/1**
14 1 **Noor Al Haya (IRE)** 2-9-0 0 DavidProbert 13 23
(Mark Usher) *s.s: a wl in rr: nvr a factor* **100/1**

1m 24.96s (-1.04) **Going Correction** -0.20s/f (Stan) **14 Ran SP% 120.2**
Speed ratings (Par 92): **97,95,95,94,92 90,89,88,87,86 86,79,75,74**
toteswingers 1&2 £3.70, 2&3 £6.70, 1&3 £1.80 CSF £7.18 TOTE £1.40: £1.02, £2.50, £1.60; EX 9.30 Trifecta £28.70 Pool: £668.64 - 17.24 winning units..
Owner Godolphin **Bred** Darley **Trained** Newmarket, Suffolk

The Form Book Flat, Raceform Ltd, Compton, RG20 6NL

■ Stewards' Enquiry : Fergus Sweeney one-day ban: careless riding (31 Oct)

FOCUS

A good 2yo fillies' maiden. The winner travelled well and didn't need to improve to score.

NOTEBOOK

Shuruq(USA) ran out a game winner and got off the mark at the second attempt, making light of a 97-day absence. It was her first outing since finishing third to high-class Certify over 6f on her Newmarket debut, when she was made favourite, and, from the plum draw, was given a straightforward ride en route to success. Her pedigree suggests this might be her optimum trip, but she ought to have little trouble getting a mile and is a Pattern-class prospect. (tchd 4-5)

Hidden Belief(IRE) ◆, from a yard previously 6-16 with 2yos here in this year, attracted support and posted a very promising debut effort. She flattened out near the finish, probably as a result of running freely, and looks a sure-fire winner of one of these in the coming weeks. (op 10-1)

Hanzada(USA) ◆ ran a big race on her debut here last month and did so again, but wasn't helped by her draw this time. She's useful and ought to be placed to strike before long. (op 7-2 tchd 9-2 in a place)

Cloudwalker(USA) ◆, first foal of a Listed-placed winner in the US, made an eyecatching debut. After a tardy start, she made stealthy headway on the inside from 2f out and was gaining on the principals approaching the finish. She's one to take from the race.

Wakeup Little Suzy(IRE) was found wanting from the furlong marker, but posted a pleasing debut effort and looks a fair prospect for longer trips next season.

Qareenah(USA) lacked a gear change, but she's from a yard whose newcomers most often need their initial experience these days and has scope to leave this behind in due course. Another furlong is probably what she needs already. (op 16-1)

Modernstone kept on under considerate handling and should repay the kindness before too long. She too may enjoy a stiffer test this year. (op 100-1)

Loraine, bred for middle-distances, was set a lot to do on her debut and caught the eye trying to make up her ground. She met some trouble doing so and is definitely one to keep tabs on.

7160 BETDAQ CASINO GAMES MAIDEN FILLIES' STKS (DIV II) 7f (P)

7:40 (7:42) (Class 5) 2-Y-O **£2,264** (£673; £336; £168) **Stalls** Low

Form RPR

23 **1** **Coincidently**[46] 5828 2-9-0 0 SamHitchcott 12 74+
(Alan Bailey) *mde all: set mod pce tl kicked on over 2f out: hrd pressed fnl f: hld on wl* **9/1**

2 ½ **Similu** 2-9-0 0 (t) KierenFallon 3 73+
(Brian Meehan) *dwlt: hld up in 8th and rn green: prog on outer fr 2f out: styd on fnl f to take 2nd nr fin* **25/1**

3 ½ **Zeva** 2-9-0 0 WilliamBuick 9 71+
(David Simcock) *t.k.h: chsd wnr: rdn 2f out: tried to chal fr over 1f out: hld fnl f: lost 2nd nr fin* **5/1**[2]

5 **4** nk **Rocksilla**[23] 6535 2-9-0 0 SebSanders 4 70
(Chris Wall) *chsd wnr: rdn over 2f out: kpt on but a hld ins fnl f* **33/1**

5 ¾ **Iffraaj Pink (IRE)** 2-9-0 0 JamieSpencer 7 69+
(Roger Varian) *trckd ldng trio: shkn up 2f out: hanging and green after: keeping on whn no room nr fin* **12/1**

6 2 ¼ **Bellitudo (IRE)** 2-8-9 0 TobyAtkinson(5) 2 62+
(Marco Botti) *dwlt: hld up in 7th: shkn up over 2f out: styd on same pce fr over 1f out: nt disgracd* **50/1**

0 **7** 1 **Reqaaba**[11] 6873 2-9-0 0 PaulHanagan 6 60
(John Gosden) *trckd ldrs in 5th: shkn up and nt qckn over 2f out: wl hld fr over 1f out* **1/1**[1]

8 2 ½ **Messageinabottle (USA)** 2-9-0 0 StevieDonohoe 13 53
(Michael Bell) *dwlt: a abt same pl: effrt but nt on terms w ldng gp 2f out: one pce* **66/1**

5 **9** 1 ¼ **Perfect Venture**[41] 5978 2-9-0 0 AdamKirby 5 50
(Clive Cox) *dwlt: sn chsd ldrs in 6th: prog on inner and in tch 2f out: wknd over 1f out* **33/1**

10 nse **Penang Power** 2-9-0 0 RobertWinston 14 49
(Charles Hills) *dwlt: rn green in last quartet: no real prog fnl 2f* **33/1**

11 2 **Magika** 2-9-0 0 MartinHarley 10 44
(Marco Botti) *sn hld up in last pair: pushed along and no prog over 2f out* **25/1**

12 1 ¼ **Sonnetation (IRE)** 2-9-0 0 PatCosgrave 1 41
(Jim Boyle) *sn rdn in rr: nvr a factor* **66/1**

13 4 **Hamla** 2-9-0 0[1] FrankieDettori 11 30
(Saeed Bin Suroor) *a wl in rr: wd bnd 3f out and struggling* **7/1**[3]

14 4 ½ **Tilly T (IRE)** 2-8-11 0 RyanPowell(3) 8 18
(J S Moore) *s.s: rn green and a bhd* **100/1**

1m 26.11s (0.11) **Going Correction** -0.20s/f (Stan) **14** Ran SP% **119.3**

Speed ratings (Par 92): **91,90,89,89,88 86,84,82,80,80 78,76,72,67**

toteswingers 1&2 £20.90, 2&3 £53.50, 1&3 £7.50 CSF £214.50 TOTE £15.50: £2.60, £6.40, £1.50; EX 336.40 Trifecta £372.20 Part won. Pool: £503.06 - 0.10 winning units..

Owner Tom Mohan & AJH **Bred** Langton Stud **Trained** Newmarket, Suffolk

FOCUS

This was a second slower than the opening division and there was a tight five-way finish.

NOTEBOOK

Coincidently, despite a poor draw, made it third time lucky with a gusty effort on this AW debut. She was there to be shot at off the home bend, but kept responding and her previous experience was a notable asset in the last 100yds. The extra furlong along with the sound surface played into her hands and her future looks bright. (op 10-1)

Similu ◆, tongue tied for her debut, made a bold bid down the centre of the track and would have probably collected had the penny dropped under pressure. This 150,00gns purchase is a good looker and should prove hard to beat next time. (op 33-1)

Zeva ◆ cost 180,000gns and has a lovely middle-distance pedigree. She held every chance on her debut and turned in a promising effort. Another furlong may suit ideally this year and she too ought to prove hard to beat on her next assignment. (op 11-2)

Rocksilla, well held in fifth on her debut here last time, tempers enthusiasm for the form somewhat. She was entitled to improve, though, and is worth the chance to prove herself a useful filly in the making

Iffraaj Pink(IRE) ◆, a 145,000gns half-sister to Breeders' Cup Juvenile Turf winner Vale Of York, ran a race full of promise on her debut. She ran green once asked for an effort and would have finished somewhat closer with the clearer passage inside the final furlong. She's another here that will hold strong claims next time. (tchd 14-1)

Bellitudo(IRE) looked her yard's second string and shaped as though she would come on plenty for the initial experience. Perhaps a drop back to 6f may suit in the short term. (tchd 66-1)

Reqaaba disappointed, but she ran too keen early on and this probably came too quickly after her very promising turf debut nine days earlier. She ought to be handed another chance. (tchd 10-11 and 11-10 in a place)

7161 DOWNLOAD THE FREE RACING PLUS APP MAIDEN FILLIES' STKS 6f (P)

8:10 (8:11) (Class 5) 2-Y-O **£2,264** (£673; £336; £168) **Stalls** Low

Form RPR

243 **1** **Flawless Beauty**[20] 6603 2-9-0 73 MichaelHills 1 77
(Hugo Palmer) *mde all: kicked on over 2f out: rdn out and hld on wl* **5/1**[2]

6 **2** ½ **Abated**[60] 5352 2-9-0 0 JamesDoyle 7 76+
(Roger Charlton) *hld up bhd ldrs: prog to go 3rd over 2f out: shkn up to chse wnr over 1f out: styd on but a hld fnl f* **11/8**[1]

3 1 ½ **Milly's Gift** 2-9-0 0 AdamKirby 8 71+
(Clive Cox) *hld up in 6th: prog 2f out: shkn up and styd on to take 3rd ins fnl f* **20/1**[3]

3 **4** 2 ½ **My Trust (IRE)**[9] 6936 2-9-0 0 FrankieDettori 2 64
(Saeed Bin Suroor) *trckd wnr: shkn up 2f out: nt qckn and lost 2nd over 1f out: wknd ins fnl f* **11/8**[1]

5 2 ¼ **Clearing** 2-9-0 0 PatCosgrave 9 57
(Jim Boyle) *sn chsd ldng pair but hanging lft: wd bnd 3f out and lost grnd: outpcd after* **50/1**

05 **6** 5 **Idle Curiosity (IRE)**[79] 4645 2-9-0 0 JimCrowley 4 42
(Jim Boyle) *chsd ldrs tl wknd jst over 2f out* **50/1**

040 **7** nk **My Claire**[28] 6360 2-0-7 59 DanielleMooney(7) 3 41
(Nigel Tinkler) *a in last pair: pushed along and struggling over 2f out* **33/1**

8 ¾ **Glenreef** 2-9-0 0 LukeMorris 6 39
(Pat Eddery) *dwlt: rn green in last: nvr on terms* **33/1**

1m 12.19s (-0.91) **Going Correction** -0.20s/f (Stan) **8** Ran SP% **115.4**

Speed ratings (Par 92): **98,97,95,92,89 82,81,80**

toteswingers 1&2 £1.80, 2&3 £7.30, 1&3 £6.50 CSF £12.08 TOTE £2.90: £1.02, £1.10, £5.00; EX 13.50 Trifecta £89.50 Pool: £885.58 - 7.32 winning units..

Owner Decadent Racing **Bred** Speers Bloodstock Ltd **Trained** Newmarket, Suffolk

FOCUS

A fair little 2yo fillies' sprint maiden. It was run at an uneven tempo, however, and the overall form may be worth treating with a degree of caution. Straightforward form, with the runner-up rated to her debut effort.

NOTEBOOK

Flawless Beauty dictated matters and, somewhat belatedly, opener her account with a ready display. She quickened nicely when kicking for home around 2f out and was in no danger from the furlong marker. Sprinting on this surface was right up her street and she ought to go on from this, but did have the run of things. (op 9-2)

Abated, better than the bare form on her Newbury debut, spoilt her cause by refusing to settle early and that blunted her finishing effort. A stronger pace would have probably seen her collecting, however, and this well-bred filly remains a very useful prospect. (op 6-4 tchd 5-4)

Milly's Gift ◆ has plenty of speed in her pedigree. She did her best work late on and looks sure to improve a deal for the debut experience.

My Trust(IRE) would have won with better luck on her debut at Wolverhampton nine days previously. Unsurprisingly popular, she was ridden a lot differently this time and faded tamely inside the final furlong. It probably came too soon for her. (op 6-4 tchd 13-8)

7162 REINDEER RACING CHRISTMAS PARTY AT KEMPTON MEDIAN AUCTION MAIDEN STKS 1m 4f (P)

8:40 (8:42) (Class 5) 3-5-Y-O **£2,264** (£673; £336; £168) **Stalls** Centre

Form RPR

563 **1** **Shea**[27] 6398 3-8-12 68 JimCrowley 6 69
(Ralph Beckett) *hld up bhd ldrs: prog to ld 2f out: drvn and edgd lft fr over 1f out: styd on* **7/2**[1]

60-4 **2** 1 ½ **Miss Blakeney**[16] 6736 3-8-12 68 HayleyTurner 7 66
(Marcus Tregoning) *mostly trckd ldng pair: rdn to chal 2f out: chsd wnr over 1f out: kpt on but could nt qckn* **9/2**[2]

5054 **3** 1 ½ **Thecornishcockney**[8] 6971 3-9-3 63 (t) AdamKirby 5 69
(John Ryan) *hld up in tch: rdn and prog to chse ldng pair over 1f out: could nt qckn and wl hld fnl f* **7/2**[1]

4 4 ½ **La Belle Doyenne**[79] 4-9-5 0 FergusSweeney 9 57
(Alan King) *cantered rdrless to post and fractious bef s: hld up in rr: prog 2f out: chsd ldng trio jst over 1f out: no imp* **33/1**

0 **5** 3 **Superstition**[119] 3279 3-8-12 0 EddieAhern 2 52
(James Fanshawe) *cl up: pushed along and wl outpcd fr 2f out: gng on again quite wl at fin* **16/1**

5020 **6** 1 ½ **Princess Steph (IRE)**[16] 6734 3-8-12 65 RobertWinston 1 50
(Heather Main) *led to 2f out: sn wknd* **8/1**[3]

63 **7** ½ **Jaja De Jau**[16] 6736 3-8-12 0 (t) JohnFahy 3 49
(Anthony Honeyball) *pressed ldr: rdn to chal over 2f out: wknd qckly wl over 1f out* **10/1**

3 **8** hd **Sauvage L'Il**[93] 4157 4-9-5 0 WilliamBuick 11 48
(Ed Dunlop) *in tch in midfield: urged along over 3f out: drvn and no prog 2f out: wknd* **8/1**[3]

9 2 ½ **Waving**[82] 4567 3-9-3 75 DavidProbert 12 49
(Tony Carroll) *hld up in last pair: shkn up and no prog over 2f out* **9/1**

04 **10** 21 **Icebreaker Two**[22] 6570 3-9-0 0 SimonPearce(3) 10 16
(John E Long) *dwlt and urged along early: a in last pair: lost tch over 3f out: t.o* **33/1**

2m 32.71s (-1.79) **Going Correction** -0.20s/f (Stan)

WFA 3 from 4yo 7lb **10** Ran SP% **115.7**

Speed ratings (Par 103): **97,96,95,92,90 89,88,88,86,72**

toteswingers 1&2 £3.70, 2&3 £4.20, 1&3 £2.90 CSF £18.88 TOTE £4.90: £1.40, £1.50, £2.40; EX 19.80 Trifecta £201.80 Pool: £417.25 - 1.53 winning units..

Owner Larksborough Stud Limited **Bred** Larksborough Stud Limited **Trained** Kimpton, Hants

FOCUS

A moderate maiden and it looked wide open. The principals came clear in the home straight and the third is the best guide to the level.

7163 COME JUMP RACING HERE ON SUNDAY H'CAP 1m (P)

9:10 (9:11) (Class 4) (0-85,90) 3-Y-O+ **£4,075** (£1,212; £606; £303) **Stalls** Low

Form RPR

0166 **1** **Prime Exhibit**[11] 6888 7-9-2 80 (t) ShaneKelly 9 89+
(Daniel Mark Loughnane) *hld up in last pair: gd prog through rivals fr over 1f out: rdn to ld ins fnl f: r.o wl* **33/1**

4100 **2** ¾ **Chapter And Verse (IRE)**[20] 6601 6-9-7 85 PatDobbs 5 92
(Mike Murphy) *dwlt: hld up in last pair: gd prog jst over 1f out: r.o wl to take 2nd last strides* **14/1**

2121 **3** nk **Alraased (USA)**[7] 6979 3-9-9 90 6ex PaulHanagan 8 96+
(John Dunlop) *t.k.h in midfield: stl t.k.h 3f out: rdn and prog 2f out: styd on to take 2nd briefly nr fin: outpcd* **11/8**[1]

2500 **4** nse **Takeitfromalady (IRE)**[17] 6701 3-9-4 85 (b) JimCrowley 13 91
(Ralph Beckett) *hld up in rr fr wd draw: prog on outer 2f out: styd on wl fnl f but nt gng pce to chal* **7/1**[3]

02 **5** 1 ¼ **Rio Grande**[36] 6124 3-9-4 85 (p) FrankieDettori 11 88+
(Ann Duffield) *led after 1f and set gd pce: drvn 2f out: hdd ins fnl f: lost pls nr fin* **12/1**

0655 **6** 1 ¾ **Cruiser**[23] 6538 4-9-7 85 MartinDwyer 7 84
(William Muir) *prom: rdn to dispute 2nd briefly over 1f out: fdd ins fnl f* **8/1**

0045 **7** 1 **Too Much Trouble**[11] 6879 6-9-7 85 (b1) LukeMorris 4 82
(Ed Vaughan) *cl up: effrt over 2f out: drvn to dispute 2nd briefly over 1f out: fdd fnl f* **25/1**

0132 **8** *nk* **Angelic Upstart (IRE)**[40] 6013 4-9-2 **80**...................... JimmyFortune 10 76
(Andrew Balding) *cl up: rdn to try to mount a chal 2f out: fdd over 1f out: sltly impeded ins fnl f* **5/1**[2]

10-1 **9** *2* **Outpost (IRE)**[13] 6812 4-9-2 **80**... FrannyNorton 2 72
(Alan Bailey) *led 1f: chsd ldr to 2f out: steadily wknd* **14/1**

200 **10** *4 ½* **Evervescent (IRE)**[118] 3294 3-9-4 **85**................................ LiamKeniry 3 66
(J S Moore) *hld up in midfield: effrt on inner over 2f out: no prog and wl hld whn hmpd 1f out* **50/1**

4-00 **11** *2 ¼* **Zebrano**[21] 6584 6-8-13 **80**.......................................(b) AshleyMorgan(3) 1 56
(Natalie Lloyd-Beavis) *dwlt: hld up in rr: shkn up and no prog over 2f out* **66/1**

3560 **12** *13* **Ariyfa (IRE)**[29] 6352 4-9-3 **81**..(tp) AdamKirby 6 27
(Noel Quinlan) *in tch in midfield: rdn 3f out: sn wknd and bhd* **20/1**

004- **13** *26* **Beauchamp Xerxes**[475] 3537 6-9-6 **84**..........................(t) JamesDoyle 12
(Hans Adielsson) *racd wd: sn prom: wknd wl over 2f out: t.o* **66/1**

1m 37.6s (-2.20) **Going Correction** -0.20s/f (Stan)
WFA 3 from 4yo+ 3lb **13** Ran SP% **119.9**
Speed ratings (Par 105): **103,102,101,101,100 98,97,97,95,91 88,75,49**
toteswingers 1&2 £16.20, 2&3 £8.50, 1&3 £25.80 CSF £419.74 CT £1081.41 TOTE £89.30: £12.80, £4.50, £1.60; EX 554.60 TRIFECTA Not won..
Owner D Fower & N J Titterton **Bred** Matthews Breeding And Racing Ltd **Trained** Baldwin's Gate, Staffs
■ Stewards' Enquiry : Liam Keniry two-day ban: careless riding (31st Oct - 1st Nov)

FOCUS
This was a fair handicap. The first four were all closers. The runner-up has been rated close to his recent C&D best, and the fourth has been rated close to his turf best.
T/Plt: £26.00 to a £1 stake. Pool of £58728.85 - 1646.73 winning tickets. T/Qpdt: £7.90 to a £1 stake. Pool of £7363.79 - 686.67 winning tickets. JN

6436 LINGFIELD (L-H)
Wednesday, October 17

OFFICIAL GOING: Standard to slow
Wind: fresh, behind Weather: dry, cloudy and breezy

7164 TAG WORLDWIDE NURSERY 6f (P)
2:00 (2:00) (Class 4) (0-85,83) 2-Y-O **£3,428** (£1,020; £509; £254) **Stalls** Low

Form RPR

5241 **1** **Pira Palace (IRE)**[23] 6541 2-8-13 **75**................................ RyanMoore 4 78
(Sir Michael Stoute) *chsd ldr: rdn wl over 1f out: drvn and styd on wl ins fnl f to ld last stride* **7/2**[2]

435 **2** *shd* **Tarbawi (IRE)**[29] 6330 2-8-10 **72**.............................. MickaelBarzalona 1 75
(Saeed Bin Suroor) *trckd ldrs: rdn to ld ent fnl f: hrd drvn fnl f: r.o wl tl hdd last stride* **3/1**[1]

1314 **3** *1 ½* **Alcando (IRE)**[14] 6799 2-9-4 **80**.. EddieAhern 5 78
(Denis Coakley) *t.k.h: hld up wl in tch: effrt u.p over 1f out: wnt 3rd fnl 100yds: no imp after* **9/1**

3031 **4** *nk* **Cut No Ice (IRE)**[45] 5854 2-9-2 **78**.....................................(b) NeilCallan 3 75
(Paul Cole) *led: rdn and c towards centre wl over 1f out: hdd ent fnl f: styd on same pce fnl f* **20/1**

3100 **5** *1* **Reliant Robin (IRE)**[11] 6883 2-8-13 **75**............................. JoeFanning 6 69
(Robert Mills) *hld up in tch in midfield: rdn and hdwy on inner over 1f out: styd on same pce fnl 100yds* **18/1**

0022 **6** *nk* **Extrasolar**[21] 6581 2-9-1 **77**..(t) AdamKirby 7 71+
(Amanda Perrett) *bmpd s: hld up towards rr: rdn and effrt over 1f out: kpt on ins fnl f: nvr trbld ldrs* **13/2**[3]

5301 **7** *hd* **Evoke (IRE)**[12] 6849 2-8-13 **75**... WilliamBuick 8 68
(Jeremy Noseda) *dwlt: rdn along in rr: hdwy 1f out: styd on ins fnl f: nvr trbld ldrs* **10/1**

2021 **8** *½* **Jubilee Diamond (IRE)**[31] 6276 2-9-6 **82**................. RichardHughes 11 73
(Richard Hannon) *stdd s: hld up towards rr: hdwy on outer 3f out: effrt and rdn bnd 2f out: styd on same pce and no imp fr over 1f out* **8/1**

1500 **9** *5* **Royal Aspiration (IRE)**[25] 6487 2-9-4 **80**............. AdamBeschizza 2 60+
(William Haggas) *in tch in midfield: rdn and shuffled bk whn nt clr run 2f out: wknd over 1f out: eased wl ins fnl f* **7/1**

2124 **10** *3 ½* **Khefyn (IRE)**[9] 6929 2-9-0 **76**.. LukeMorris 12 42+
(Ronald Harris) *s.i.s: sn swtchd lft: a bhd* **33/1**

1m 12.81s (0.91) **Going Correction** +0.20s/f (Slow) **10** Ran SP% **116.2**
Speed ratings (Par 97): **101,100,98,98,97 96,96,95,89,84**
toteswingers 1&2 £2.90, 1&3 £13.70, 2&3 £10.40 CSF £14.38 CT £86.41 TOTE £3.40: £1.10, £2.40, £3.60; EX 17.70.
Owner Miss T K Walters **Bred** Malm Partnership **Trained** Newmarket, Suffolk
■ The first race on the track on the new Polytrack surface.

FOCUS
The going for this first meeting since the surface was relaid was standard to slow. Clerk of the course Neil Mackenzie Ross expected it to ride slower to begin with. Ryan Moore who rode the first winner said "It rode nicely, probably a bit slower, but pretty similar to the old surface". A competitive nursery run at a steady pace with the field well strung out at the line. It paid to race prominently and the form is rated around the principals.

NOTEBOOK
Pira Palace(IRE) was suited by the drop to 6f on testing ground when winning last time at Leicester, and she stayed on best of all out wide here to get up near the line and land a bit of a gamble. She was off a 5lb higher mark, but is progressing with her racing and this trip looks to be her minimum. (op 5-1)
Tarbawi(IRE), racing on the AW for the first time and back in distance for his nursery debut, was well away from his inside draw and looked to have the race won when kicking clear up the straight, but was just caught on the line. (op 11-4 tchd 7-2)
Alcando(IRE) put up another solid effort, although he lacked the pace of the front two when asked before keeping on well again. (op 10-1)
Cut No Ice(IRE), helped set the early pace from her inside draw and looked like fading turning for home, but kept on to the line and this was a fair AW debut from the half-sister to former top sprinter Pipalong. (op 16-1 tchd 14-1)
Extrasolar was outpaced early but was closing best of all, suggesting the trip was on the short side. (op 11-1)
Evoke(IRE), 4lb higher than when winning on her handicap debut on heavy ground over 6f at Yarmouth last time, could not go the pace on his AW debut but kept on well to the line. (op 8-1 tchd 7-1)
Jubilee Diamond(IRE) got off the mark at the fourth time of asking when landing a weak Bath maiden, but couldn't find cover from her wide draw and weakened up the straight. (op 11-2)

7165 GAC SHIPPING AND LOGISTICS MAIDEN AUCTION STKS 1m (P)
2:30 (2:30) (Class 6) 2-Y-O **£1,704** (£503; £251) **Stalls** High

Form RPR

04 **1** **Close Together (IRE)**[13] 6816 2-8-6 0.......................... PaulHanagan 10 63+
(Robert Mills) *chsd ldrs: rdn to ld over 2f out: kpt on gamely u.p and hld on wl fnl f* **5/1**[2]

2 *hd* **High Time Too (IRE)** 2-8-8 0 ow1..............................[1] JamieSpencer 5 66+
(Hugo Palmer) *hld up in tch in midfield: nt clr run 2f out: swtchd lft and effrt over 1f out: ev ch u.p ins fnl f: kpt on* **6/1**[3]

00 **3** *hd* **Woza Moya (USA)**[20] 6609 2-8-12 0.............................. NickyMackay 3 68
(Gay Kelleway) *in tch: chsd ldrs and rdn over 1f out: ev ch ins fnl f: unable qck towards fin* **22/1**

46 **4** *¾* **Paddy's Saltantes (IRE)**[43] 5912 2-8-10 0....................... LukeMorris 6 64
(J S Moore) *in tch in midfield: rdn and effrt to chal ent fnl 2f: drvn and unable qck ent fnl f: one pce after* **13/2**

0 **5** *2 ¾* **Town Mouse**[21] 6572 2-9-0 0... RobertHavlin 1 62
(Hughie Morrison) *s.i.s: in tch towards rr: hdwy 1/2-way: chsd ldrs on outer bnd 2f out: drvn and styd on same pce fr over 1f out* **14/1**

003 **6** *½* **Paige Flyer**[26] 6437 2-8-5 60... MartinDwyer 11 52
(Michael Quinn) *chsd ldr tl led over 6f out: hdd and rdn over 2f out: stl pressing ldrs ent fnl f: no ex and wknd fnl 100yds* **16/1**

50 **7** *shd* **Terpsichore**[12] 6841 2-7-13 0.. DarrenEgan(5) 9 51
(Sylvester Kirk) *hld up in tch: rdn and effrt to press ldrs 2f out: unable qck ent fnl f: wknd ins fnl f* **28/1**

8 *5* **Secret Woman (IRE)** 2-8-6 0..................................... KirstyMilczarek 2 41
(Alan Jarvis) *in tch towards rr: rdn and struggling whn edgd rt over 2f out: wknd wl over 1f out* **16/1**

0 **9** *2 ¼* **Misteray**[16] 6733 2-8-5 0... JakePayne(7) 8 42
(Bill Turner) *led tl over 6f out: chsd ldrs after tl lost pl and rdn wl over 2f out: wknd wl over 1f out* **28/1**

0 **10** *nse* **Double Star**[13] 6817 2-8-9 0.. JohnFahy 7 39
(Jonathan Portman) *rn green and a towards rr: rdn over 3f out: wknd wl over 1f out* **40/1**

11 *2* **Jan De Heem** 2-8-9 0... JimCrowley 4 34
(Ralph Beckett) *rn green: sn bhd and rdn along: n.d* **2/1**[1]

0 **12** *6* **Gabrial The Tyrant (IRE)**[20] 6607 2-9-0 0........................ JoeFanning 12 26
(Mark Johnston) *dwlt: rcvrd to chse ldr over 5f out tl over 2f out: sn lost pl: wl bhd and eased ins fnl f* **10/1**

1m 41.15s (2.95) **Going Correction** +0.20s/f (Slow) **12** Ran SP% **118.8**
Speed ratings (Par 93): **93,92,92,91,89 88,88,83,81,81 79,73**
toteswingers 1&2 £4.80, 1&3 £8.30, 2&3 £20.30 CSF £33.69 TOTE £4.90: £2.40, £2.50, £7.30; EX 42.80.
Owner Miss J A Leighs & Mrs B B Mills **Bred** K B Lynch **Trained** Headley, Surrey

FOCUS
A wide open but weak maiden, run at a steady pace where once again it paid to race handy. The form looks modest and not a race to dwell on

NOTEBOOK
Close Together(IRE) had shown little in two starts but, stepping up in trip here, was well positioned throughout, got first run on the field and was just able to hold off the late challengers. This took little winning, but her pedigree suggests she could get further in time. (tchd 9-2 and 11-2)
High Time Too(IRE) ◆, whose rider put up 1lb overweight, was wearing a hood for this debut. She rates a somewhat unlucky loser as she was denied a clear passage entering the straight, which allowed the winner to get first run. (op 9-2)
Woza Moya(USA) was well held in Folkestone and Wolverhampton maidens, but showed more here stepping up in trip. He is now qualified for a mark and his handler could place him to good advantage at a lowly level. (op 16-1)
Paddy's Saltantes(IRE)'s two runs in 7f maidens had suggested this step up in trip would suit, and he was keeping on well to the line having been outpaced entering the straight. He continues to progress with each start. (op 8-1)
Jan De Heem was well supported on his debut but, having briefly been short of room down the far side, found little for pressure and was never in contention. (op 7-2)
Gabrial The Tyrant(IRE), who ran green when well beaten in a soft-ground 1m Pontefract maiden last month, had plenty of use made of him from his wide draw having been slowly away, but came under pressure some way out and dropped tamely away. (op 11-2 tchd 11-1)

7166 BAKER TILLY CLASSIFIED CLAIMING STKS 7f (P)
3:00 (3:04) (Class 6) 3-Y-O+ **£1,704** (£503; £251) **Stalls** Low

Form RPR

6400 **1** **Al Aqabah (IRE)**[14] 6801 7-8-12 65 ow1..........................(b) NeilCallan 12 75
(Brian Gubby) *t.k.h: chsd ldrs: rdn to chal over 1f out: led ins fnl f: hld on wl u.p* **16/1**

1330 **2** *½* **One Way Or Another (AUS)**[5] 7027 9-8-1 70...............(t) LukeMorris 7 63+
(David Evans) *hld up in tch in last quartet: rdn and effrt wl over 1f out: str run ins fnl f: wnt 2nd cl home* **4/1**[1]

43 **3** *½* **Zomerlust**[32] 6260 10-8-1 70..(v) JimmyQuinn 13 61
(John Quinn) *t.k.h: hld up wl in tch: swtchd ins and effrt wl over 1f out: ev ch 1f out: unable qck fnl 50yds* **8/1**[3]

0050 **4** *¾* **First Bid**[11] 6888 3-8-1 64.. NickyMackay 9 61
(James Given) *led: rdn and hrd pressed wl over 1f out: hdd ins fnl f: styd on same pce fnl 100yds* **16/1**

0305 **5** *nk* **Boudoir (IRE)**[19] 6641 3-8-1 70....................................... JamieMackay 6 60
(Ian Williams) *t.k.h: chsd ldr: rdn and ev ch over 1f out: unable qck ent fnl f: kpt on same pce fnl f* **16/1**

4600 **6** *nk* **Katy's Secret**[12] 6837 5-8-0 64...................................... RyanPowell(3) 10 60
(William Jarvis) *hld up in tch in last quartet: rdn and gd hdwy on inner to chal ent fnl f: no ex and btn fnl 100yds: wknd towards fin* **33/1**

1240 **7** *hd* **Kingswinford (IRE)**[18] 6692 6-8-9 69............................ PaulHanagan 2 65
(Alastair Lidderdale) *chsd ldrs: rdn to chal 1f out unable qck ins fnl f: wknd fnl 75yds* **6/1**[2]

0000 **8** *2* **Legal Legacy**[29] 6329 6-8-10 65................................... TobyAtkinson(5) 4 66
(Richard Rowe) *in tch in midfield: effrt u.p but no imp 2f out: plugged on same pce fnl f: nvr gng pce to chal* **33/1**

0000 **9** *3 ¾* **Orpen'Arry (IRE)**[86] 4411 4-8-11 64........................... RichardHughes 11 52
(Jimmy Fox) *in tch towards rr: reminders wl over 2f out: rdn and no hdwy over 1f out: nvr trbld ldrs* **10/1**

5104 **10** *3* **Offbeat Safaris (IRE)**[9] 6927 4-8-2 66............................ DarrenEgan(5) 14 39
(Ronald Harris) *sn detached in last and niggled along: lost tch wl over 1f out: n.d* **9/1**

-450 **11** *4 ½* **Vale Of Lingfield (IRE)**[15] 6765 3-8-13 65........................ JimCrowley 3 35
(John Best) *hld up in tch: lost pl qckly 2f out: wl bhd and eased ins fnl f* **25/1**

100- **R** **Storm Tide**526 1986 4-8-0 66..............................(t) JemmaMarshall(5) 1
(Pat Phelan) *unruly and led rdrless to post: ref to r: tk no part* **40/1**

1m 26.51s (1.71) **Going Correction** +0.20s/f (Slow)
WFA 3 from 4yo+ 2lb **12** Ran SP% **94.3**
Speed ratings (Par 101): **98,97,96,96,95 95,95,92,88,85 79,**
toteswingers 1&2 £18.20, 1&3 £47.00, 2&3 £2.80 CSF £49.45 TOTE £25.40: £6.40, £1.10, £1.20; EX 112.60.
Owner Brian Gubby **Bred** Ocal Bloodstock **Trained** Bagshot, Surrey

FOCUS
A tight claimer with only 6lb covering the 14 runners on officials ratings. The pace was not strong and the first six home were well grouped, with few able to close from off the pace. Muddling claiming form.

7167 NATWEST IRISH STALLION FARMS EBF MAIDEN STKS 7f (P)
3:35 (3:36) (Class 5) 2-Y-O **£3,234** (£962; £481; £240) **Stalls** Low

Form RPR
0 **1** **Correspondent**26 6443 2-9-3 0.. EddieAhern 8 82+
(Brian Meehan) *in tch: rdn and effrt to chse ldr 1f out: qcknd to ld ins fnl f: sn clr and r.o wl* **10/3**1

5 **2** 2 3/4 **Persepolis (IRE)**12 6845 2-9-3 0.................................... RyanMoore 12 75+
(Sir Michael Stoute) *off the pce towards rr: rdn: hdwy and edging rt over 1f out: styd on wl ins fnl f to snatch 2nd cl home: no threat to wnr* **13/2**

2 **3** hd **Lilac Tree**19 6645 2-9-3 0.................................... MickaelBarzalona 7 74
(Mahmood Al Zarooni) *chsd ldr tl swtchd rt and rdn to ld over 1f out: hdd and outpcd by wnr ins fnl f: styd on same pce and lost 2nd cl home* **6/1**

0 **4** 3 **Price Is Truth (USA)**75 4773 2-9-3 0........................... FrankieDettori 5 67+
(Mahmood Al Zarooni) *hld up in midfield: swtchd to outer 3f out: rdn and no hdwy whn edgd rt ent fnl f: no threat to wnr but styd on ins fnl f to go 4th cl home* **7/2**2

03 **5** nk **Tight Knit (USA)**19 6644 2-9-3 0.................................... MartinDwyer 1 66
(James Tate) *chsd ldng trio: rdn over 2f out: swtchd ins and drvn over 1f out: sn outpcd: wknd ins fnl f* **16/1**

34 **6** 3/4 **Noble Deed**40 6015 2-9-3 0.. WilliamBuick 10 64
(William Haggas) *chsd ldrs: rdn and effrt 2f out: drvn and no imp over 1f out: wknd fnl f* **11/2**3

7 1 1/4 **Tebbit (USA)** 2-9-3 0.. NeilCallan 14 61
(Roger Varian) *s.i.s: off the pce towards rr: rdn 2f out: styd on fnl f: nvr trbld ldrs* **40/1**

0 **8** 1 **Forging The Path (USA)**54 5562 2-9-3 0...................... PaulHanagan 2 62+
(Richard Fahey) *hld up in midfield: rdn and hdwy over 1f out: nt clr run ent fnl f tl ins fnl f: lost any ch and one pce after* **16/1**

0 **9** 1 **Short Squeeze (IRE)**25 6481 2-9-3 0............................. MichaelHills 4 55
(Hugo Palmer) *hld up off the pce towards rr: rdn and effrt over 1f out: no real prog: nvr trbld ldrs* **10/1**

10 hd **Teophilip (IRE)** 2-9-3 0..(t) AdamKirby 6 55
(Marco Botti) *s.i.s: rn green and sn pushed along in rr: sme hdwy fnl f: n.d* **40/1**

64 **11** 1/2 **Charm Cry (USA)**19 6644 2-8-12 0................................ JoeFanning 11 49
(Mark Johnston) *led and sn crossed to inner: clr after 1f: rdn and hdd over 1f out: btn 1f out and fdd fnl f* **22/1**

12 hd **Saxon Soldier** 2-9-3 0... TomMcLaughlin 3 53
(Ed Dunlop) *hld up off the pce in rr: sme hdwy on inner over 1f out: no prog 1f out: n.d* **66/1**

13 5 **Tigerish** 2-9-3 0.. JimCrowley 9 40
(Amanda Perrett) *rn green: racd off the pce in last trio: rdn and struggling over 2f out: bhd fnl 2f* **80/1**

1m 25.71s (0.91) **Going Correction** +0.20s/f (Slow) **13** Ran SP% **121.1**
Speed ratings (Par 95): **102,98,98,95,94 94,92,91,90,90 89,89,83**
CSF £24.83 TOTE £4.20: £2.20, £3.70, £2.40; EX 47.80.
Owner Mrs P Good **Bred** Mrs P Good **Trained** Manton, Wilts

FOCUS
Plenty of decent stables were represented in this maiden and the pace was honest with the field well strung out at the post. The form looks strong if somewhat fluid.

NOTEBOOK
Correspondent ♦, closely related to 6f-1m Group 2 winner Delegator, did not show much on his debut at Newbury but he had learnt plenty from that and ran out a most impressive winner here. He was noted travelling kindly behind the pace and picked up in fine style out wide in the shape of a decent type. He is with the right stable to progress and looks an exciting 3-y-o prospect. (op 7-2 tchd 9-2)

Persepolis(IRE) made a pleasing debut in a heavy ground 7f Yarmouth maiden and he ran another fine race over this inadequate trip. He was under pressure and near the back turning for home, but kept on finding for his rider and was doing all his best work late. He is another who looks a handy prospect over further next season. (op 9-1)

Lilac Tree, who looked the stable's second string, had run well when runner-up at Wolverhampton on his debut and he stepped up on that here, although he lacks the scope of the front two. (op 5-1 tchd 9-2)

Price Is Truth(USA), who cost $180,000 as a yearling and then $1,200,000 as a 2-y-o, ran green when beaten on his debut at Newmarket and again looked as though this outing would do him good. He was taken out wide down the back straight and took his time to pick up when asked, but was making pleasing progress late under an educating ride. (op 9-2)

Tight Knit(USA), stepped up on his debut effort with a fine run over 7f at Wolverhampton and he confirmed the promise of that run with another solid effort here. He should find things much easier now that he can be handicapped. (op 11-1)

Noble Deed, stepping up in trip after two promising efforts over 6f, raced closed to the pace but was not knocked about once his chance had gone. He looks a useful type for next season. (op 6-1)

Forging The Path(USA) ♦ was an eye-catcher who did not enjoy the clearest of passages when coming with his effort and he rates a fair bit better. (op 20-1)

Charm Cry(USA), the only filly in the field, made a bold bid from the front but paid for setting the strong early fractions late on. (op 14-1)

7168 EUROPA QUALITY PRINT H'CAP 1m 4f (P)
4:05 (4:06) (Class 2) (0-100,94) 3-Y-O **£10,221** (£3,041; £1,519; £759) **Stalls** Low

Form RPR
5221 **1** **Dr Yes (FR)**32 6228 3-9-7 **94**... IanMongan 4 105+
(Sir Henry Cecil) *hld up in midfield: hdwy over 3f out: rdn to chal 2f out: led over 1f out: styd on wl fnl f: rdn out* **5/2**1

421 **2** 1 1/4 **Fleeting Image**54 5554 3-8-4 **82**..........................(p) NatashaEaton(5) 10 90
(Alan Bailey) *led: sn clr: reduced advantage 5f out: pressed and drvn 2f out: hdd over 1f out: kpt on gamely but a hld by wnr fnl f* **25/1**

1110 **3** 2 1/2 **Enery (IRE)**18 6677 3-8-12 **85**.. NeilCallan 7 89
(Mark Johnston) *chsd ldrs: chsd ldr 3f out tl jst over 2f out: styd on same pce u.p fr over 1f out* **12/1**

1626 **4** 3 **Maria's Choice (IRE)**29 6348 3-8-11 **84**.......................... RyanMoore 6 83
(Sir Michael Stoute) *racd off the pce towards rr: rdn 4f out: drvn 2f out: styd on ins fnl f to go 4th cl home: nvr trbld ldrs* **10/1**

643 **5** 1/2 **Anjaz (USA)**28 6380 3-9-2 **89**... WilliamBuick 3 87
(Saeed Bin Suroor) *hld up off the pce towards rr: rdn and effrt whn hmpd and swtchd rt jst over 2f out: rallied and battling for 4th fnl f: kpt on but no threat to ldrs* **10/1**

5253 **6** hd **Come On Blue Chip (IRE)**21 6580 3-9-4 **91**...............(b) SebSanders 8 89
(Paul D'Arcy) *stdd s: hld up in rr: rdn and hdwy on outer to chse ldng trio over 2f out: outpcd 2f out: battling for 4th and wl hld fnl f* **20/1**

421 **7** 3 **Totalize**20 6615 3-8-13 **86**.. KierenFallon 11 79
(Luca Cumani) *pushed along leaving stalls: hld up in midfield: rdn and outpcd over 2f out: 5th and wl btn over 1f out: wknd* **8/1**

1252 **8** 2 **Muntasir (IRE)**39 6033 3-9-6 **93**...............................(p) FrankieDettori 5 83
(Saeed Bin Suroor) *stdd s: hld up off the pce towards rr: rdn and no real hdwy over 2f out: wl btn over 1f out* **13/2**3

0005 **9** 2 **Fennell Bay (IRE)**13 6819 3-9-1 **88**...............................(v1) JoeFanning 2 75
(Mark Johnston) *chsd ldrs: rdn over 2f out: sn struggling and wknd 2f out* **16/1**

3-1 **10** 11 **Representation (USA)**44 5889 3-9-0 **87**.................. MickaelBarzalona 9 56
(Mahmood Al Zarooni) *t.k.h: hld up off the pce towards rr: bhd and rdn over 3f out: sn struggling: bhd fnl 2f* **6/1**2

1150 **11** nk **Valiant**46 5835 3-9-7 **94**..(b1) RichardHughes 1 63
(William Haggas) *chsd ldr after 2f: reminders and rdn over 4f out: lost pl over 2f out: sn bhd: eased ins fnl f* **11/1**

2m 31.56s (-1.44) **Going Correction** +0.20s/f (Slow) **11** Ran SP% **116.0**
Speed ratings (Par 107): **112,111,109,107,107 107,105,103,102,95 94**
toteswingers 1&2 £43.70, 1&3 £6.20, 2&3 £43.70 CSF £75.05 CT £640.88 TOTE £4.40: £1.20, £7.30, £8.50; EX 120.80.
Owner Niarchos Family **Bred** Suc S Niarchos **Trained** Newmarket, Suffolk
■ Stewards' Enquiry : Natasha Eaton one-day ban: failed to keep straight from stalls (31 Oct)

FOCUS
A decent handicap run at a sound enough gallop. The winner is on the upgrade and the second, who went off hard, posted a personal best.

NOTEBOOK
Dr Yes(FR) ♦, landed his maiden in impressive style over this trip at Bath last time and was well backed here on his handicap debut. Always travelling sweetly, he came with his effort out wide 2f from home and, once taking up the running, never looked in any trouble. He has proved a progressive type and looks more than capable of stepping up in class next season. (op 3-1 tchd 7-2)

Fleeting Image made all to win at Newmarket last time and tried those tactics again. She drew clear down the far side and battled on well to the line under a clever ride, but found the higher mark against a progressive rival too much to overcome. (tchd 33-1)

Enery(IRE) had enjoyed a fine summer, but had questions to answer after disappointing at Newmarket off 1lb higher on his last start. He bounced back to form with a sound display, although will not find things easy off his current mark. (tchd 14-1)

Maria's Choice(IRE) was 3lb better off for a length defeat at the hands of Fleeting Image last time, but was not suited by how the race unfolded. Near the back, he swung wide into the straight before staying on all too late. He is lightly-raced and open to improvement. (op 16-1)

Come On Blue Chip(IRE), 9lb higher than when last successful and stepping up in trip, was taken wide through the contest and kept finding for pressure up the straight, although was tired late on. (op 16-1)

Muntasir(IRE) was noted travelling kindly in rear, but found little when coming off the bridle and this rates as slightly disappointing. (op 5-1 tchd 9-2)

7169 CHARTPLAN H'CAP 2m (P)
4:40 (4:40) (Class 6) (0-65,67) 3-Y-O+ **£1,704** (£503; £251) **Stalls** Low

Form RPR
3606 **1** **Marmas**16 6738 3-9-3 **64**.. PaulHanagan 1 72
(Marcus Tregoning) *chsd ldrs: swtchd rt and rdn over 4f out: drvn to ld over 1f out: clr w runner-up and hung rt fnl f: hld on u.p and asserted cl home* **2/1**1

2501 **2** 1/2 **Squad**6 7012 6-10-2 **67** 6ex...(v) NeilCallan 4 74
(Simon Dow) *hld up in last quartet: hdwy over 3f out: rdn to chal wl over 1f out: clr w wnr and edgd rt fnl f: no ex and btn cl home* **7/1**3

006 **3** 6 **Rollin 'n Tumblin**6 7012 8-8-9 **46** oh1............................ JimmyQuinn 10 46
(Michael Attwater) *stdd s: t.k.h: hld up in last pair: hdwy 3f out: drvn over 1f out: styd on to go 3rd ins fnl f: no threat to ldng pair* **33/1**

5500 **4** 1 1/4 **Showsinger**25 6474 3-7-13 **46**... NickyMackay 11 44
(Richard Fahey) *t.k.h early: hld up in midfield: rdn and effrt to chse ldrs 2f out: outpcd and btn 1f out: plugged on same pce ins fnl f* **16/1**

4223 **5** 1 1/2 **Galiotto (IRE)**24 5196 6-9-11 **62**......................................(v) RyanMoore 8 59
(Gary Moore) *chsd ldr: drvn to ld wl over 1f out: sn hdd and outpcd: 3rd and btn 1f out: wknd and lost 2 pls fnl f* **5/1**2

0054 **6** 2 **El Libertador (USA)**12 6838 6-9-5 **56**............................(b) LukeMorris 5 50
(Eric Wheeler) *hld up in midfield: shuffled bk towards rr over 3f out: hdwy into midfield and rdn 2f out: no imp over 1f out: wknd fnl f* **16/1**

4153 **7** 3/4 **Six Of Clubs**145 2468 6-9-3 **61**.................................(b) JakePayne(7) 12 54
(Bill Turner) *stdd and dropped in bhd after s: nt clr run over 3f out: rdn 3f out: sme hdwy 2f out: no imp and wl hld over 1f out* **10/1**

6035 **8** 2 3/4 **Ostentation**6 7012 5-10-0 **65**.. KierenFallon 7 55
(Gay Kelleway) *hld up in rr: swtchd rt and effrt wl over 2f out: no prog wl over 1f out: sn wknd* **5/1**2

565- **9** nk **Novel Dancer**320 7441 4-9-7 **58**...................................(e1) RobertHavlin 3 48
(Lydia Richards) *hld up in midfield: rdn and no hdwy on inner wl over 1f out: wknd ent fnl f* **28/1**

0045 **10** 1/2 **David's Folly (IRE)**46 5817 3-7-9 **47**........................... DarrenEgan(5) 6 36
(Bryn Palling) *chsd ldrs tl lost pl qckly over 3f out: bhd fnl 2f* **16/1**

0006 **11** 7 **Bennelong**8 6949 6-9-9 **65**.......................................(p) TobyAtkinson(5) 9 46
(Richard Rowe) *hld up in midfield: swtchd to outer and hdwy to ld over 5f out: sn clr: rdn and hdd 2f out: sn btn and fdd over 1f out* **25/1**

005- **12** 1 **Rachael's Ruby**488 3119 5-8-4 **46** oh1....................... NatashaEaton(5) 13 25
(Roger Teal) *t.k.h: hld up in midfield: rdn and struggling 3f out: sn bhd* **66/1**

5540 **13** 6 **Nesnaas (USA)**12 6838 11-8-4 **46** oh1................ MichaelJMMurphy(5) 2 18
(Alastair Lidderdale) *led tl over 5f out: lost pl 4f out: wl bhd fnl 2f* **50/1**

3m 30.33s (4.63) **Going Correction** +0.20s/f (Slow)
WFA 3 from 4yo+ 10lb **13** Ran SP% **119.6**
Speed ratings (Par 101): **96,95,92,92,91 90,90,88,88,88 84,84,81**
toteswingers 1&2 £5.50, 1&3 £31.60, 2&3 £33.10 CSF £15.26 CT £362.53 TOTE £3.20: £1.30, £1.90, £11.10; EX 23.80.
Owner Hamdan Al Maktoum **Bred** Shadwell Estate Company Limited **Trained** Lambourn, Berks

FOCUS
The pace was steady for this staying handicap with the front two pulling clear up the straight. The winner is rated up slightly on his recent form.

7170 GP LONDON H'CAP (DIV I) 1m (P)
5:10 (5:12) (Class 5) (0-75,75) 3-Y-O+ **£2,385** (£704; £352) **Stalls** High

Form RPR

4525 **1** **Schoolmaster**[22] [6566] 4-9-6 **74**.................................... JoeFanning 12 85
(Giles Bravery) *pressed ldrs: rdn and ev ch over 1f out: led jst ins fnl f: sn qcknd clr and in command fnl 100yds: r.o wl* **5/1**[2]

1235 **2** *2 ½* **Kinglami**[27] [6401] 3-8-13 **70**.................................... NeilCallan 5 75
(Brian Gubby) *t.k.h: chsd ldrs: rdn over 1f out: drvn and styd on ins fnl f to go 2nd last strides: no threat to wnr* **4/1**[1]

5020 **3** *hd* **Poetic Lord**[33] [6207] 3-9-4 **75**.................................... RichardHughes 1 79
(Richard Hannon) *led and dictated stdy gallop: rdn 2f out: drvn and hdd jst ins fnl f: no ex and sn outpcd by wnr: lost 2nd last strides* **6/1**

5632 **4** *nk* **Dozy Joe**[18] [6687] 4-9-3 **71**....................................(p) SebSanders 10 74
(Ian Wood) *t.k.h: hld up in tch towards rr: rdn over 1f out: styd on ins fnl f: gng on at fin but no threat to wnr* **14/1**

0124 **5** *hd* **Roy The Boy (USA)**[26] [6454] 4-9-5 **73**.................................... RyanMoore 3 76
(Alan Bailey) *t.k.h: sn pressing ldr: rdn and ev ch over 1f out: unable qck and one pce fnl f* **5/1**[2]

5345 **6** *½* **Srinagar Girl**[32] [6229] 3-9-3 **74**.................................... IanMongan 4 75
(Sir Henry Cecil) *t.k.h: hld up wl in tch in midfield: n.m.r over 2f out: drvn and effrt wl over 1f out: styd on same pce fnl f* **11/2**[3]

010 **7** *1 ¼* **Fever Few**[9] [6931] 3-9-2 **73**.................................... AdamKirby 9 71
(Jane Chapple-Hyam) *dwlt: in tch in rr: rdn over 2f out: styd on same pce and no imp over 1f out* **12/1**

610 **8** *2* **Morning Call**[25] [6488] 3-9-0 **71**.................................... DaneO'Neill 7 64
(Henry Candy) *hld up in tch in midfield: rdn and unable qck over 1f out: btn 1f out and wknd ins fnl f* **8/1**

0605 **9** *½* **Midas Moment**[11] [6895] 4-9-0 **68**.................................... PaulHanagan 8 59
(William Muir) *hld up in rr: rdn and effrt on outer over 1f out: kpt on but no real imp: n.d* **33/1**

0050 **10** *6* **George Baker (IRE)**[43] [5910] 5-9-3 **71**.................................... FrankieDettori 2 46
(George Baker) *broke wl: stdd and hld up wl in tch in midfield: shuffled bk towards rr and nt clr run jst over 2f out: wknd over 1f out* **25/1**

6150 **11** *18* **Bareback (IRE)**[215] [920] 3-8-10 **72**.................................... TobyAtkinson(5) 6
(John Best) *dwlt: wl in tch towards rr: rdn and struggling over 2f out: lost tch qckly 2f out: eased over 1f out* **66/1**

1m 39.9s (1.70) **Going Correction** +0.20s/f (Slow)
WFA 3 from 4yo+ 3lb 11 Ran SP% **116.8**
Speed ratings (Par 103): **99,96,96,96,95 95,94,92,91,85 67**
toteswingers 1&2 £5.40, 1&3 £5.20, 2&3 £4.60 CSF £24.75 CT £125.61 TOTE £6.10: £2.50, £2.10, £1.70; EX 38.40.
Owner Penny Farm **Bred** D D And Mrs Jean P Clee **Trained** Newmarket, Suffolk

FOCUS
A fair handicap run at a steady pace with the winner pulling clear to score impressively. The third helps set the standard.

7171 GP LONDON H'CAP (DIV II) 1m (P)
5:45 (5:45) (Class 5) (0-75,75) 3-Y-O+ **£2,385** (£704; £352) **Stalls** High

Form RPR

0400 **1** **L'Hirondelle (IRE)**[132] [2847] 8-9-0 **68**.................................... JoeFanning 6 76
(Michael Attwater) *broke v fast: mde virtually all: rdn and wnt clr 2f out: edging rt and idling ins fnl f: fnd ex whn pressed cl home* **33/1**

0605 **2** *nk* **Daruband**[23] [6545] 4-9-5 **73**....................................(v) JamieSpencer 10 80
(Michael Bell) *hld up in tch in rr: rdn and effrt on outer bnd 2f out: clsng on wnr and swtchd lft ins fnl f: str chal wl ins fnl f: hld towards fin* **17/2**

3256 **3** *1 ¼* **Feelthedifference**[27] [6401] 3-8-12 **69**.................................... IanMongan 11 73
(Sir Henry Cecil) *hld up in midfield: hdwy u.p over 1f out: chsd wnr and clsng ins fnl f: 3rd and styd on same pce fnl 100yds* **7/2**[2]

0012 **4** *1 ½* **Light From Mars**[9] [6934] 7-9-6 **74**....................................(t) EddieAhern 5 75
(Ian Williams) *hld up in midfield: hdwy and rdn over 1f out: drvn and kpt on same pce ins fnl f* **5/2**[1]

1-05 **5** *hd* **Orthodox Lad**[26] [6430] 4-9-3 **71**.................................... LiamKeniry 9 72
(Ed de Giles) *chsd ldrs: rdn 2f out: drvn and chsd clr ldr ent fnl f tl jst ins fnl f: one pce and lost 3 pls ins fnl f* **9/1**

2524 **6** *1 ¼* **Rocky Reef**[53] [5595] 3-8-11 **75**....................................(v) ThomasBrown(7) 7 73
(Andrew Balding) *t.k.h: hld up in tch: rdn and effrt whn swtchd lft jst over 1f out: styd on same pce ins fnl f* **9/2**[3]

3100 **7** *½* **Rezwaan**[16] [6735] 5-9-2 **70**.................................... FrankieMcDonald 8 67
(Murty McGrath) *hld up in rr: pushed aong over 2f out: styd on ins fnl f: nvr trbld ldrs* **33/1**

210 **8** *1 ¼* **Zing Wing**[28] [6367] 4-9-3 **71**.................................... AdamKirby 4 65
(David Evans) *hld up in tch in midfield: rdn and n.m.r over 2f out: drvn and no imp over 1f out: nvr able to chal* **20/1**

010 **9** *2* **King Vahe (IRE)**[52] [5625] 3-8-9 **71**.................................... MichaelJMMurphy(5) 2 60
(Alan Jarvis) *in tch in midfield: jostled on inner and outpcd bnd jst over 2f out: no prog and no threat to ldrs fr over 1f out* **12/1**

0302 **10** *5* **Hurricane Spirit (IRE)**[49] [5751] 8-9-0 **75**.................................... NicoleNordblad(7) 1 53
(Hans Adielsson) *t.k.h: pressed wnr tl unable qck 2f out: lost 2nd ent fnl f: fdd fnl f* **14/1**

0000 **11** *11* **Spirit Of Xaar (IRE)**[191] [1262] 6-9-0 **68**.................................... RobertHavlin 3 20
(Linda Jewell) *hld up in tch towards rr: rdn and lost tch 2f out: bhd and eased ins fnl f* **100/1**

1m 39.77s (1.57) **Going Correction** +0.20s/f (Slow)
WFA 3 from 4yo+ 3lb 11 Ran SP% **115.5**
Speed ratings (Par 103): **100,99,98,96,96 95,95,93,91,86 75**
toteswingers 1&2 £21.60, 1&3 £20.30, 2&3 £6.00 CSF £280.19 CT £1272.30 TOTE £21.00: £4.90, £2.80, £1.80; EX 190.40.
Owner Canisbay Bloodstock **Bred** Gainsborough Stud Management Ltd **Trained** Epsom, Surrey

FOCUS
The pace was honest for this concluding handicap, with the winner making all under a fine ride. He's rated to his best of the last year. It was slightly the faster division.

L'Hirondelle(IRE) Official explanation: trainer said, regarding the apparent improvement of form, that the gelding had benefited from a break and from being able to dominate today

T/Plt: £89.10 to a £1 stake. Pool: £60,974.95 - 499.48 winning tickets T/Qpdt: £9.10 to a £1 stake. Pool: £6,191.70 - 502.15 winning tickets SP

6983 NOTTINGHAM (L-H)
Wednesday, October 17

OFFICIAL GOING: Soft changing to soft (heavy in places) after race 2 (2:10)
Wind: moderate half against Weather: Sunny periods

7172 BRITISH STALLION STUDS SUPPORTING BRITISH RACING EBF MAIDEN STKS 1m 75y
1:40 (1:43) (Class 5) 2-Y-O **£3,234** (£962; £481; £240) **Stalls** Centre

Form RPR

02 **1** **Tawhid**[14] [6795] 2-9-3 0.................................... SilvestreDeSousa 7 90+
(Saeed Bin Suroor) *t.k.h and led 1f: trckd ldrs: smooth hdwy over 4f out: led wl over 2f out: sn pushed clr: styd on strly* **6/4**[1]

0 **2** *4* **Personable**[20] [6596] 2-8-12 0.................................... AntiocoMurgia(5) 5 82+
(Mahmood Al Zarooni) *towards rr: stdy hdwy 4f out: trckd ldrs 3f out: rdn to chse wnr ent fnl f: no imp* **9/1**

3 **3** *2 ½* **Zipp (IRE)**[26] [6448] 2-8-12 0.................................... DarryllHolland 2 71
(Charles Hills) *trckd ldrs: rdn along to chse ldng pair 3f out: kpt on same pce fnl 2f* **9/1**

5 **4** *1 ½* **Mujarrad (USA)**[14] [6795] 2-9-3 0.................................... TadhgO'Shea 9 73
(Marcus Tregoning) *prom: led over 4f out: rdn along 3f out: sn hdd and grad wknd* **8/1**[3]

0 **5** *5* **Song Light**[19] [6636] 2-9-3 0.................................... TedDurcan 13 62
(David Elsworth) *towards rr: hdwy 3f out: styd on appr fnl f: nrst fin* **25/1**

05 **6** *¾* **Vandross (IRE)**[12] [6844] 2-9-3 0....................................(b) FrannyNorton 11 60
(Chris Wall) *cl up: led after 1f: pushed along and hdd over 4f out: rdn 3f out and grad wknd* **100/1**

7 *2* **Morpheus** 2-9-3 0.................................... TomQueally 4 56+
(Sir Henry Cecil) *dwlt: towards rr: hdwy into midfield after 3f: in tch and effrt over 3f out: sn pushed along: rn green and no imp* **3/1**[2]

0 **8** *nse* **Tajheez (IRE)**[11] [6872] 2-9-3 0.................................... AndreaAtzeni 12 56
(Roger Varian) *towards rr: sme hdwy 3f out: sn pushed along and n.d* **40/1**

9 *2 ¼* **Argent Knight** 2-9-3 0.................................... GrahamLee 3 51
(William Jarvis) *a towards rr* **33/1**

0 **10** *6* **Darakti (IRE)**[34] [6164] 2-9-0 0.................................... DeclanCannon(3) 6 37
(Alan McCabe) *a in rr* **250/1**

0 **11** *½* **Bugsy**[14] [6796] 2-9-3 0.................................... PatDobbs 1 36
(Richard Hannon) *chsd ldrs: rdn along 4f out: sn wknd* **66/1**

12 *15* **Father And Son (IRE)** 2-9-3 0.................................... ChrisCatlin 10 3
(Marco Botti) *s.i.s: green and a bhd* **33/1**

1m 52.03s (3.03) **Going Correction** +0.775s/f (Yiel) 12 Ran SP% **111.2**
Speed ratings (Par 95): **98,94,91,90,85 84,82,82,79,73 73,58**
toteswingers 1&2 £3.80, 1&3 £2.50, 2&3 £7.10 CSF £14.15 TOTE £2.20: £1.10, £2.50, £2.10; EX 14.80 Trifecta £44.20 Pool £697.97 - 11.67 winning units..
Owner Godolphin **Bred** West Lodge Stud **Trained** Newmarket, Suffolk

FOCUS
Outer (Summer) straight tack used. The home straight at Nottingham splits into two courses, and they were back on the outer track for today's card following two meetings on the inner course. This was to provide fresher and drier ground (the inside track is close to being unraceable). After the first contest Silvestre De Sousa, Darryll Holland and Tadhg O'Shea reported the ground to be heavy. The first two are improving.

NOTEBOOK
Tawhid finished ahead of Mujarrad at Salisbury last time and more than confirmed those positions here. The Godolphin first string was well placed throughout and bounded clear when asked to. His head seemed a shade high in the final stages, but by then he was clear. (op 13-8)
Personable wasn't beaten far in what looked a fair maiden at Newmarket and built on that performance with a staying-on second. (op 10-1)
Zipp(IRE), up a furlong in distance after a promising debut at Newbury on good to firm ground, stayed on at the one pace - Darryll Holland reported that the filly hung left-handed. (op 10-1 tchd 11-1)
Mujarrad(USA) didn't get home after sitting handy throughout this time. His pedigree suggests a quicker surface may see him in a better light, especially Polytrack. (op 7-1 tchd 13-2)
Song Light ◆ caught the eye from the rear and has the scope to be better than he showed here. (op 33-1)
Morpheus, Frankel's half-brother and making his racecourse debut, looked green while chasing the leaders and possibly didn't handle the ground. (op 5-2 tchd 9-4)

7173 WINNING NUMBERS 01159 500500 DG CARS NURSERY 1m 75y
2:10 (2:11) (Class 5) (0-70,70) 2-Y-O **£2,264** (£673; £336; £168) **Stalls** Centre

Form RPR

0036 **1** **Precision Strike**[8] [6952] 2-8-1 **50**.................................... KellyHarrison 1 56+
(Richard Guest) *hld up in rr: hdwy 3f out: nt clr run 2f out: str run fr over 1f out to ld ins fnl f: kpt on strly* **33/1**

5624 **2** *2 ½* **Girl Of Cadiz**[21] [6583] 2-8-7 **63**.................................... RufusVergette(7) 9 63
(Richard Hannon) *a.p: cl up 4f out: rdn to ld 1f out: hdd and one pce ins fnl f* **16/1**

5063 **3** *½* **Kingsville**[64] [5206] 2-7-12 **47**.................................... FrannyNorton 5 47+
(Mark Johnston) *midfield: pushed along and n.m.r 3f out: sn swtchd to inner and rdn: styd on wl appr fnl f: nrst fin* **14/1**

260 **4** *1 ¼* **Reveille**[23] [6535] 2-9-5 **68**.................................... GeorgeBaker 7 64
(Hughie Morrison) *led: rdn along over 2f out: drvn and hdd 1f out: one pce* **11/1**

0002 **5** *½* **Mash Potato (IRE)**[15] [6753] 2-8-8 **57**.................................... TomEaves 3 52
(Michael Dods) *chsd ldrs on inner: rdn along wl over 2f out: drvn and one pce fr over 1f out* **13/2**[2]

0045 **6** *1 ½* **Romanoff (IRE)**[27] [6413] 2-8-8 **60**.................................... PatrickHills(3) 16 52
(Luca Cumani) *midfield: hdwy on outer 5f out: effrt to chal over 2f out: sn rdn and wknd over 1f out* **9/1**[3]

0600 **7** *1* **Sand Grouse**[26] [6451] 2-8-9 **58**.................................... ChrisCatlin 11 48
(Marco Botti) *s.i.s and bhd: hdwy over 3f out: rdn 2f out: kpt on: nvr nr ldrs* **9/1**[3]

6150 **8** *6* **Vino Collapso (IRE)**[26] [6451] 2-9-0 **63**.................................... GrahamLee 8 39
(James Given) *chsd ldrs on outer: rdn along 3f out: wknd 2f out* **14/1**

560 **9** *½* **Zero Game (IRE)**[25] [6501] 2-9-3 **66**.................................... HayleyTurner 6 41
(Michael Bell) *t.k.h: hld up: sme hdwy over 3f out: sn rdn along and n.d* **13/2**[2]

0504 **10** *2* **Another Ponty**[47] [5799] 2-8-2 **51**.................................... DuranFentiman 14 22
(Tim Easterby) *chsd ldrs: rdn along 3f out: sn wknd* **28/1**

5004 **11** *2 ½* **Pour La Victoire (IRE)**[19] [6628] 2-8-6 **55**.................................... AndrewMullen 10 20
(Nigel Tinkler) *t.k.h: cl up: rdn along over 3f out: sn wknd* **50/1**

634 **12** *2 ½* **Le Talisman (IRE)**[22] [6558] 2-9-7 **70**.................................... SilvestreDeSousa 13 30
(Mahmood Al Zarooni) *a towards rr* **5/1**[1]

5150 **13** *1 ½* **Beau Select (IRE)**[42] 5946 2-9-4 **67** AndreaAtzeni 2 24
(Robert Eddery) *in tch: rdn along over 3f out: sn wknd* **16/1**
040 **14** *21* **Captain's Dream (IRE)**[61] 5311 2-8-12 **61** MickyFenton 12
(Jedd O'Keeffe) *t.k.h: chsd ldrs: rdn along over 3f out: sn wknd* **33/1**
0030 **15** *dist* **Shooting Jacket (USA)**[28] 6363 2-9-0 **68** AntiocoMurgia(5) 4
(Mahmood Al Zarooni) *a towards rr: bhd whn heavily eased over 1f out* **10/1**

1m 54.37s (5.37) **Going Correction** +0.775s/f (Yiel) **15** Ran SP% **117.1**
Speed ratings (Par 95): **87,84,84,82,82 80,79,73,73,71 68,66,64,43,**
toteswingers 1&2 £122.10, 1&3 £39.20, 2&3 £30.50 CSF £469.67 CT £7672.68 TOTE £53.60: £10.20, £5.70, £3.50; EX 356.70 TRIFECTA Not won..
Owner Future Racing (Notts) Limited **Bred** Mickley Stud **Trained** Stainforth, S Yorks

FOCUS
Where you were positioned in the field didn't seem to matter as the race took shape, so the form ought to be reasonably reliable. There wasn't much depth to the race but Precision Strike won well.

NOTEBOOK
Precision Strike, up 2f in distance, didn't look the most obvious candidate for victory considering the balance of his form, but he could be spotted moving well over 2f out and came home strongly through the final stages. He is almost certainly just a moderate type who stays well. (op 25-1)
Girl Of Cadiz, back on turf, had shown consistent form since heading into handicaps and didn't quite get home after taking a while to edge to the front. She seems versatile with regards to ground. (op 20-1)
Kingsville, having only his second start on turf, flew home up the inside rail when the race was over. (op 12-1 tchd 16-1)
Reveille, up in distance for her handicap debut, ran pretty well considering she was giving plenty of weight away to the three that finished in front of her. (tchd 10-1 and 12-1)
Mash Potato(IRE) shaped nicely in heavy ground at Ayr, but didn't really repeat that here off a 3lb higher mark. (tchd 11-2)
Zero Game(IRE), making her handicap debut back on turf, never looked like being involved. (op 6-1 tchd 11-2)
Le Talisman(IRE), who had raced much more prominently previously, made no sort of show after being towards the back early. (op 6-1)

7174 ROSELAND BUSINESS PARK MAIDEN STKS 1m 2f 50y
2:40 (2:42) (Class 5) 3-Y-O **£2,264** (£673; £336; £168) **Stalls** Low

Form RPR
1 **Albasharah (USA)** 3-8-12 0 HarryBentley 8 81+
(Saeed Bin Suroor) *dwlt: midfield: pushed along over 3f out: sn angled towards outer: hdwy over 1f out: led jst ins fnl f: styd on wl to go clr* **9/1**
04 **2** *3 ¾* **Omar Khayyam**[17] 6704 3-9-3 0 (t) DavidProbert 3 79
(Andrew Balding) *dwlt: sn trckd ldrs: rdn 3f out: styd on one pce: wnt 2nd post* **11/1**
3 *nk* **Zeyran (IRE)** 3-8-12 0 TomQueally 7 74+
(Sir Henry Cecil) *dwlt: hld up in midfield: gd hdwy over 4f out: led on bit over 3f out: rdn over 1f out: hdd jst ins fnl f: no ex: lost 2nd post* **9/4**[1]
52 **4** *nk* **Miss Fortywinks**[22] 6570 3-8-12 0 RichardKingscote 9 73
(Paul Henderson) *hld up in midfield: hdwy 4f out: sn chsd ldrs: rdn over 2f out: kpt on one pce* **25/1**
4 **5** *6* **Indian Petal**[187] 1363 3-8-12 0 SilvestreDeSousa 14 62
(Mahmood Al Zarooni) *midfield: hdwy on outer 4f out: rdn and ev ch over 2f out: wknd appr fnl f* **6/1**[3]
0-30 **6** *6* **Big Johnny D (IRE)**[18] 6677 3-9-3 82 TedDurcan 10 55
(John Dunlop) *in tch: hdwy over 3f out: rdn and ev ch over 2f out: wknd over 1f out* **5/2**[2]
000 **7** *17* **Extremely Alert**[141] 2585 3-9-3 0 HayleyTurner 15 23
(Michael Bell) *hld up: drvn over 4f out: nvr threatened* **100/1**
323 **8** *2 ¼* **Claude Monet (BRZ)**[27] 6409 3-8-5 80 FrannyNorton 11 7
(Jeremy Noseda) *prom: rdn over 3f out: wknd over 2f out* **5/2**
0 **9** *3* **Merevale**[2] 7112 3-9-0 0 DominicFox(3) 2 13
(Michael Appleby) *led narrowly: hdd over 3f out: wknd* **50/1**
10 *1 ½* **Perforce** 3-9-3 0 GrahamLee 5 10
(Lucy Wadham) *midfield: pushed along over 4f out: wknd over 3f out* **16/1**
-06 **11** *9* **Italian Riviera**[20] 6614 3-9-3 0 ChrisCatlin 13
(Sir Mark Prescott Bt) *hld up: a towards rr* **100/1**
12 *8* **Rockalong (IRE)** 3-9-3 0 J-PGuillambert 1
(Luca Cumani) *trckd ldrs tl wknd 4f out* **33/1**
50 **13** *10* **Speedy Star (IRE)**[27] 6408 3-9-3 0 PaulMulrennan 4
(Tina Jackson) *w ldr tl wknd 4f out* **250/1**
56 **14** *2* **Minty Fox**[16] 6736 3-8-12 0 DarryllHolland 12
(Rae Guest) *hld up: a in rr* **33/1**
00 **15** *32* **Indie Wonder**[16] 6736 3-8-7 0 JackDuern(5) 6
(Reg Hollinshead) *slowly away: a bhd* **200/1**

2m 19.9s (5.60) **Going Correction** +0.775s/f (Yiel) **15** Ran SP% **122.4**
Speed ratings (Par 101): **98,95,94,94,89 84,71,69,67,65 58,52,44,42,17**
toteswingers 1&2 £17.20, 1&3 £6.60, 2&3 £7.20 CSF £101.73 TOTE £13.20: £3.70, £3.40, £1.10; EX 138.80 Trifecta £701.90 Part won. Pool £948.56 - 0.10 winning units..
Owner Godolphin **Bred** Darley **Trained** Newmarket, Suffolk

FOCUS
The ground was officially changed to soft, heavy in places before this contest.

7175 RYAN'S EVENT CLEANING SUPPORTING HORSE RACING UK H'CAP 1m 2f 50y
3:15 (3:17) (Class 3) (0-95,94) 3-Y-O+
£6,847 (£2,050; £1,025; £512; £256; £128) **Stalls** Low

Form RPR
1/1 **1** **First Mohican**[11] 6884 4-9-4 **88** TomQueally 13 105+
(Sir Henry Cecil) *trckd ldrs: smooth hdwy over 3f out: cl up 2f out: led appr fnl f: sn rdn and kpt on wl* **7/4**[1]
5051 **2** *3 ½* **Art Scholar (IRE)**[7] 6987 5-9-4 **88** 6ex GeorgeBaker 3 98
(Michael Appleby) *hld up: smooth hdwy on outer over 3f out: cl up 2f out: rdn to chal wl over 1f out and ev ch tl drvn and kpt on same pce fnl f* **15/2**[3]
1202 **3** *2 ½* **Swnymor (IRE)**[18] 6661 3-8-12 **87** LiamJones 7 92
(William Haggas) *hld up: hdwy 4f out: chsd ldrs over 2f out: rdn and n.m.r wl over 1f out: kpt on same pce fnl f* **9/2**[2]
0003 **4** *1* **Sirvino**[20] 6606 7-9-3 **92** LMcNiff(5) 6 95
(David Barron) *trckd ldrs: effrt over 2f out: rdn along whn n.m.r wl over 1f out: sn swtchd rt and one pce* **11/1**
4040 **5** *nk* **Stand To Reason (IRE)**[54] 5558 4-9-10 **94** (p) GrahamLee 16 97
(Mikael Magnusson) *a.p: cl up 1/2-way: rdn along over 2f out: drvn and edgd lft 1f out: one pce* **10/1**
2201 **6** *¾* **Las Verglas Star (IRE)**[20] 6606 4-9-7 **91** AmyRyan 14 92
(Richard Fahey) *cl up: led wl over 3f out: rdn along 2f out: drvn and hdd over 1f out: sn wknd* **12/1**
1000 **7** *3 ½* **Rock A Doodle Doo (IRE)**[53] 5600 5-9-6 **90** HarryBentley 10 85
(William Jarvis) *hld up: hdwy and in tch 4f out: rdn along to chse ldrs 3f out: wknd 2f out* **33/1**
6200 **8** *7* **Barren Brook**[11] 6884 5-8-11 **81** PaulMulrennan 8 62
(Michael Easterby) *s.i.s: a in rr* **25/1**
1124 **9** *2 ½* **Kalk Bay (IRE)**[20] 6606 5-9-2 **86** (t) JamesSullivan 2 63
(Michael Easterby) *rrd s and s.i.s: in rr tl sme late hdwy* **40/1**
0006 **10** *4 ½* **Mawaakef (IRE)**[20] 6601 4-9-4 **88** DarryllHolland 12 56
(J R Jenkins) *a towards rr* **40/1**
034 **11** *1 ¾* **Ellemujie**[62] 5268 7-8-12 **82** (p) TedDurcan 1 47
(Dean Ivory) *a towards rr* **33/1**
0156 **12** *10* **Bollin Greta**[70] 4962 7-9-3 **87** DavidAllan 15 33
(Tim Easterby) *a towards rr* **40/1**
4065 **13** *½* **Sandusky**[40] 6018 4-9-4 **88** SilvestreDeSousa 4 33
(Mahmood Al Zarooni) *chsd ldrs on inner: rdn along over 4f out: sn wknd* **11/1**
-500 **14** *7* **Hung Parliament (FR)**[139] 2642 4-8-13 **83** RichardKingscote 11 15
(Tom Dascombe) *led: rdn along 4f out: sn hdd & wknd* **50/1**
1300 **15** *11* **Brunston**[17] 6702 6-9-1 **85** SeanQuinlan 5
(Anthony Middleton) *chsd ldrs: rdn along 1/2-way: sn wknd and bhd fnl 3f* **100/1**

2m 17.48s (3.18) **Going Correction** +0.775s/f (Yiel)
WFA 3 from 4yo+ 5lb **15** Ran SP% **119.8**
Speed ratings (Par 107): **107,104,102,101,101 100,97,92,90,86 85,77,76,71,62**
toteswingers 1&2 £4.00, 1&3 £3.30, 2&3 £5.70 CSF £13.50 CT £53.54 TOTE £2.60: £1.50, £2.30, £1.80; EX 15.70 Trifecta £47.70 Pool £1,203.71 - 18.64 winning units..
Owner W H Ponsonby **Bred** Bottisham Heath Stud **Trained** Newmarket, Suffolk

FOCUS
A very decent contest, with the runner-up making the form look solid. There could well be more to come from the winner.

NOTEBOOK
First Mohican ◆ still looked a potential blot off a BHA mark of 88 and so it proved. There should be another handicap in him under similar conditions, and the November Handicap makes some appeal considering he ought to get his ground and should stay 1m4f. (tchd 13-8 and 15-8)
Art Scholar(IRE), up 5lb for his C&D success a week previously but still 1lb well in, is in cracking nick and helps to advertise the form. He was nicely clear of the third in ground he isn't proven on. (op 8-1)
Swnymor(IRE) was one of the least exposed of these, but didn't help his cause by being a little keen when chasing the leaders. It was still a good effort, however. (op 5-1)
Sirvino is only fairly treated and could do with coming down the weights a little more before his chance is obvious. (op 12-1 tchd 9-1)
Stand To Reason(IRE), down in distance, has run well in soft ground before and can't be faulted too much for this effort under top weight. He might make someone a useful hurdler if ever up for sale. (op 9-1)
Las Verglas Star(IRE), raised 3lb for his small-field Pontefract success, had his chance but couldn't go on. (op 11-1 tchd 10-1)
Rock A Doodle Doo(IRE), absent since the Ebor, could do with edging down the ratings a bit and finding a decent contest on Polytrack, considering four of his five successes have come on that surface.

7176 RYAN'S EVENT CLEANING SUPPORTING HORSE RACING UK MAIDEN AUCTION STKS 5f 13y
3:45 (3:46) (Class 5) 2-Y-O **£2,264** (£673; £336; £168) **Stalls** High

Form RPR
3023 **1** **Twilight Pearl**[8] 6953 2-8-5 60 (b) DuranFentiman 1 60
(Tim Easterby) *trckd ldrs towards outer: rdn 2f out: drvn ins fnl f: kpt on to ld nr fin* **8/1**
642 **2** *½* **Rangooned**[8] 6954 2-8-8 0 GrahamLee 5 61
(Ann Duffield) *w ldr: rdn over 1f out: drvn to ld fnl 100yds: hdd nr fin* **6/4**[1]
3542 **3** *½* **Bentleysoysterboy (IRE)**[7] 6983 2-9-0 66 (p) TedDurcan 6 65
(David Elsworth) *led narrowly: rdn 2f out: drvn ins fnl f: hdd fnl 100yds: no ex* **3/1**[2]
3502 **4** *1 ¾* **Ladweb**[12] 6850 2-8-9 64 TadhgO'Shea 2 56
(John Gallagher) *prom: pushed along and lost pl 1/2-way: kpt on ins fnl f: sltly short of room fnl 50yds* **9/1**
042 **5** *5* **Attenshun (IRE)**[11] 6889 2-9-0 74 (v) ChrisCatlin 3 41
(Tom Dascombe) *dwlt: sn pushed along towards rr: nvr threatened* **5/1**[3]
4 **6** *3* **Shatin Secret**[27] 6404 2-8-12 0 TomEaves 4 28
(Noel Wilson) *hld up in tch: pushed along 1/2-way: wknd over 1f out* **14/1**

1m 5.24s (3.74) **Going Correction** +0.625s/f (Yiel) **6** Ran SP% **109.4**
Speed ratings (Par 95): **91,90, , ,**
toteswingers 1&2 £2.90, 1&3 £3.20, 2&3 £1.30 CSF £19.55 TOTE £9.70: £4.60, £2.00; EX 13.00.
Owner D A West **Bred** Bumble Bloodstock Ltd **Trained** Great Habton, N Yorks

FOCUS
A low-grade, late-season sprint, and weak form.

NOTEBOOK
Twilight Pearl, the most experienced of these, had to dig deep after hitting a flat spot about 2f out. She probably ran up to her official mark, but certainly no more. (op 5-1)
Rangooned had shown fair form and almost collected a first victory. A small handicap can come her way as a juvenile. (op 11-4)
Bentleysoysterboy(IRE), who ran well over C&D a week previously, can have no excuses considering he had the rail to come up. (op 9-2 tchd 11-4)
Ladweb was keeping on nicely when short of room in the final stages. Had the John Gallagher horse got through the gap, he would have gone close to winning. (op 7-1 tchd 10-1)
Attenshun(IRE) never got involved. (op 10-3 tchd 11-2)

7177 FOR YOUR COMFORT DG CARS 01159 500500 H'CAP 5f 13y
4:20 (4:20) (Class 4) (0-85,84) 3-Y-O **£4,075** (£1,212; £606; £303) **Stalls** High

Form RPR
3631 **1** **Demora**[32] 6226 3-8-4 **70** oh1 DominicFox(3) 9 85
(Michael Appleby) *mde all: rdn clr over 1f out: edgd lft and kpt on wl fnl f* **10/1**
1024 **2** *3 ½* **El McGlynn (IRE)**[11] 6887 3-8-4 **74** HannahNunn(7) 6 76
(Peter Salmon) *a chsng wnr: rdn wl over 1f out: kpt on but no imp fnl f* **10/1**
10 **3** *¾* **Planetex (IRE)**[54] 5538 3-8-12 **75** BarryMcHugh 12 74
(John Quinn) *chsd ldng pair: rdn along 2f out: drvn over 1f out: kpt on same pce fnl f* **12/1**
2254 **4** *¾* **Bubbly Ballerina**[15] 6767 3-9-1 **78** GrahamLee 8 75
(Alan Bailey) *in tch: hdwy 2f out: rdn to chse ldrs over 1f out: no imp fnl f* **14/1**
305 **5** *½* **North Star Boy (IRE)**[15] 6768 3-9-4 **81** PatDobbs 14 76
(Richard Hannon) *hld up towards rr: hdwy on inner 2f out: rdn and kpt on fnl f* **14/1**

2124 **6** 1 ¾ **Milika**[116] 3396 3-9-6 **83** ChrisCatlin 7 72
(Rae Guest) *dwlt and in rr: pushed along and hdwy 2f out: rdn and kpt on fnl f: nt rch ldrs* **9/2**[1]

2163 **7** ½ **Rusty Rocket (IRE)**[18] 6665 3-9-3 **80** PaulMulrennan 10 67
(Paul Green) *chsd ldrs: rdn along 2f out: drvn over 1f out and grad wknd* **5/1**[2]

22 **8** 1 ½ **Tango Sky (IRE)**[65] 5165 3-9-7 **84** (p) GeorgeBaker 13 65
(Ralph Beckett) *a towards rr* **15/2**[3]

5065 **9** nk **Indian Tinker**[29] 6347 3-8-7 **70** HayleyTurner 4 50
(Robert Cowell) *chsd ldrs: rdn along 2f out: sn wknd* **22/1**

3330 **10** 6 **Beau Mistral (IRE)**[18] 6666 3-9-7 **84** SilvestreDeSousa 2 43
(Paul Green) *a towards rr* **9/1**

5026 **11** ½ **Indego Blues**[23] 6525 3-9-0 **77** PaulQuinn 1 34
(David Nicholls) *wnt lft s and in rr: hdwy on outer 2f out: sn rdn and wknd* **10/1**

4111 **12** ½ **Imperial Legend (IRE)**[30] 6314 3-8-6 **76** (p) ShirleyTeasdale(7) 3 31
(David Nicholls) *in tch: hdwy and in tch 2f out: sn rdn and wknd* **14/1**

1m 3.42s (1.92) **Going Correction** +0.625s/f (Yiel) **12** Ran SP% **115.9**
Speed ratings (Par 103): **105,99,98,97,96 93,92,90,89,80 79,78**
toteswingers 1&2 £14.20, 1&3 £19.60, 2&3 £28.80 CSF £103.82 CT £1233.37 TOTE £12.10: £4.40, £3.00, £3.60; EX 214.30 TRIFECTA Not won..
Owner JJMC Racing **Bred** A M Wragg **Trained** Danethorpe, Notts

FOCUS
This fair handicap was settled soon after the start, with few getting involved. It was the pick of the C&D times and the form could be rated higher at face value.

7178 BOOK YOUR BLACK AND WHITE CHRISTMAS PARTY H'CAP (DIV I) 5f 13y
4:50 (4:51) (Class 6) (0-65,65) 3-Y-0+ **£1,940** (£577; £288; £144) **Stalls** High

Form RPR

1366 **1** **Aubrietia**[8] 6961 3-9-5 **63** (b) TomQueally 7 74
(Alan McCabe) *sltly hmpd s: sn midfield: rdn to chse ldr over 1f out: led fnl 100yds: kpt on wl* **11/2**[2]

5040 **2** 1 ¾ **Piste**[2] 7099 6-8-9 **53** (e) SilvestreDeSousa 9 58
(Tina Jackson) *prom: led 1/2-way: rdn over 1f out: hdd fnl 100yds: sn no ch w wnr* **13/2**[3]

4602 **3** nk **Speedyfix**[12] 6836 5-8-13 **57** (t) BrettDoyle 4 61
(Christine Dunnett) *hld up in tch: rdn and hdwy on outer over 1f out: kpt on fnl f* **16/1**

2232 **4** 1 **Griffin Point (IRE)**[9] 6926 5-9-5 **63** (b) FrannyNorton 2 63
(William Muir) *chsd ldrs: rdn 1/2-way: kpt on one pce* **9/2**[1]

0060 **5** nk **Ginger Ted (IRE)**[14] 6788 5-9-6 **64** (tp) J-PGuillambert 12 63+
(Stuart Williams) *hld up towards stands' rail: hmpd 2f out and swtchd lft: rdn over 1f out: kpt on fnl 100yds: nrst fin* **8/1**

60-5 **6** ½ **Rock On Candy**[16] 6739 3-8-13 **57** ChrisCatlin 6 54
(John Spearing) *hld up in tch: pushed along whn n.m.r over 1f out tl ins fnl f: kpt on fnl 100yds* **16/1**

5343 **7** 1 ½ **Wreningham**[9] 6926 7-9-3 **61** RussKennemore 11 53
(Pat Eddery) *trckd ldrs against stands' rail: sltly short of room over 3f out: rdn over 1f out and sn no imp: wknd fnl 100yds* **15/2**

0010 **8** 1 **Dancing Maite**[18] 6687 7-8-7 **54** (b) MarkCoumbe(3) 5 42
(Roy Bowring) *midfield: rdn 1/2-way: wknd ins fnl f* **11/1**

3150 **9** nse **Majestic Manannan (IRE)**[11] 6887 3-9-7 **65** AndrewMullen 3 53
(David Nicholls) *sn led: rdn whn hdd 1/2-way: wknd over 1f out* **22/1**

6320 **10** 3 **Elegant Girl (IRE)**[13] 6806 3-9-4 **62** PaulMulrennan 8 39
(Tim Easterby) *dwlt: hld up: nvr threatened* **12/1**

4400 **11** ¾ **Commanche**[6] 7001 3-9-5 **63** (p) TomEaves 1 38
(Bryan Smart) *chsd ldrs towards outer: wknd over 1f out* **14/1**

050- **12** 1 ¼ **Tillys Tale**[342] 7355 5-9-6 **64** GrahamLee 10 34
(Paul Midgley) *trckd ldrs: rdn 1/2-way: wknd over 1f out* **12/1**

1m 4.17s (2.67) **Going Correction** +0.625s/f (Yiel) **12** Ran SP% **116.3**
Speed ratings (Par 101): **99,96,95,94,93 92,90,88,88,83 82,80**
toteswingers 1&2 £10.50, 1&3 £23.90, 2&3 £17.30 CSF £40.32 CT £547.64 TOTE £9.10: £3.40, £1.90, £5.60; EX 56.10 Trifecta £517.30 Pool £699.13 - 0.20 winning units..
Owner Mrs M J McCabe **Bred** C J Murfitt **Trained** Averham Park, Notts

FOCUS
The first division of the sprint handicap was run at a fair pace and in a decent time. The winner resumed her progress.

7179 BOOK YOUR BLACK AND WHITE CHRISTMAS PARTY H'CAP (DIV II) 5f 13y
5:20 (5:22) (Class 6) (0-65,65) 3-Y-0+ **£1,940** (£577; £288; £144) **Stalls** High

Form RPR

0301 **1** **Danzoe (IRE)**[22] 6563 5-9-5 **63** BrettDoyle 11 71
(Christine Dunnett) *trckd ldrs: hdwy over 2f out: rdn to ld over 1f out: drvn out* **11/1**

2061 **2** hd **Fama Mac**[8] 6958 5-8-10 **61** 6ex EvaMoscrop(7) 8 68
(Neville Bycroft) *a.p: cl up 2f out: rdn to chal ent fnl f: sn drvn and ev ch tl no ex nr fin* **11/4**[1]

0141 **3** hd **Havin' A Good Time (IRE)**[26] 6439 3-9-7 **65** AndreaAtzeni 12 72+
(Roger Varian) *trckd ldrs: hdwy 2f out: rdn to chal ent fnl f and ev ch tl no ex nr fin* **13/2**

0043 **4** 1 ½ **Ever Roses**[14] 6786 4-8-9 **53** (v) GrahamLee 4 54
(Paul Midgley) *towards rr: hdwy 2f out: sn rdn: styd on fnl f: nrst fin* **8/1**

4400 **5** ½ **Silver Wind**[59] 5389 7-9-6 **64** (p) IPoullis 10 63
(Alan McCabe) *dwlt and in rr: hdwy 2f out: swtchd lft and rdn over 1f out: styd on ins fnl f: nrst fin* **40/1**

0015 **6** nk **Lord Buffhead**[14] 6786 3-8-13 **60** DeclanCannon(3) 13 58
(Richard Guest) *prom: rdn along wl over 1f out: drvn and one pce fnl f* **10/1**

0004 **7** ¾ **Divertimenti (IRE)**[25] 6496 8-8-11 **58** (b) MarkCoumbe(3) 9 54
(Roy Bowring) *led: rdn along and hdd over 1f out: wknd ent fnl f* **22/1**

0415 **8** 1 **Amber Heights**[14] 6788 4-8-13 **62** AmyScott(5) 1 54
(Henry Candy) *cl up on outer: rdn along 2f out: sn wknd* **11/2**[3]

5630 **9** 1 **Duke Of Rainford**[49] 5740 5-8-7 **51** oh4 TomEaves 2 39
(Michael Herrington) *towards rr: sme hdwy whn n.m.r 2f out: sn rdn and btn* **66/1**

2000 **10** 1 ¾ **One Kool Dude**[14] 6788 3-8-13 **64** (v) ThomasHemsley(7) 3 46
(Michael Bell) *a in rr* **22/1**

3421 **11** 8 **Mr Mo Jo**[32] 6264 4-9-5 **63** DanielTudhope 6 16
(Lawrence Mullaney) *stmbld bdly s: sn cl up: rdn 2f out and sn wknd* **9/2**[2]

1m 4.95s (3.45) **Going Correction** +0.625s/f (Yiel) **11** Ran SP% **114.7**
Speed ratings (Par 101): **93,92,92,89,89 88,87,85,84,81 68**
CSF £39.01 CT £217.35 TOTE £18.10: £4.90, £1.20, £1.80; EX 37.60 Trifecta £112.80 Pool £1,000.80 - 6.56 winning units..
Owner One For All **Bred** Miss Anne Ormsby **Trained** Hingham, Norfolk
■ Stewards' Enquiry : Brett Doyle two-day ban: use of whip (31st Oct, 1 Nov)

FOCUS
Not much difference depth-wise from the first division, but it provided a much tighter finish. Ordinary form, with the winner probably the best guide.
T/Jkpt: £143,603.60 to a £1 stake. Pool: £202,258.61 - 1.00 winning ticket T/Plt: £643.60 to a £1 stake. Pool: £60,337.31 - 68.43 winning tickets T/Qpdt: £40.30 to a £1 stake. Pool: £5,679.62 - 104.20 winning tickets JR

7180 - 7181a (Foreign Racing) - See Raceform Interactive

6945 BRIGHTON (L-H)
Thursday, October 18

7182 Meeting Abandoned - Waterlogged

7156 KEMPTON (A.W) (R-H)
Thursday, October 18

OFFICIAL GOING: Standard
Wind: Virtually nil Weather: Light early, getting dark

7189 32REDBINGO.COM CLASSIFIED STKS 1m (P)
5:30 (5:32) (Class 6) 3-Y-0+ **£1,617** (£481; £240; £120) **Stalls** Low

Form RPR

2314 **1** **Pastoral Jet**[15] 6773 4-9-0 54 RyanPowell(3) 12 61+
(Richard Rowe) *hld up in rr: stdy hdwy 2f out: slt ld ins fnl f: sn rdn: hld on all out* **9/2**[2]

0000 **2** shd **Blackthorn Stick (IRE)**[65] 5212 3-9-0 35 (p) AdamKirby 10 60
(John Butler) *in rr: hdwy: nt clr run and swtchd lft ins fnl 2f: hrd drvn and str run fnl f: jst failed* **10/1**

0660 **3** nk **Squirrel Wood (IRE)**[15] 6778 4-9-3 53 (b) GeorgeBaker 3 59
(Mary Hambro) *s.i.s: in rr: gd hdwy fr 2f out: styd on wl fnl f: nt quite pce of ldng duo clsng stages* **14/1**

646 **4** 6 **Shahrazad (IRE)**[26] 6500 3-9-0 55 SilvestreDeSousa 6 45
(Patrick Gilligan) *led: hrd pressed fr 3f out tl hdd jst ins fnl f: sn outpcd by ldng duo* **10/1**

0050 **5** 1 **Litmus (USA)**[42] 5975 3-9-0 55 NeilCallan 2 43
(Simon Dow) *chsd ldrs: rdn 2f out: styd on same pce fnl f* **33/1**

0605 **6** ½ **Rogue Reporter (IRE)**[2] 7148 3-9-0 54 (b) JamesDoyle 4 42
(Stuart Williams) *chsd ldrs: rdn over 2f out: one pce fnl f* **9/4**[1]

-000 **7** ½ **Best In Show**[28] 6396 3-8-9 50 (t) MatthewLawson(5) 5 41
(Roger Curtis) *chsd ldrs: wnt 2nd wl over 1f out: wknd fnl f* **7/1**[3]

5006 **8** ½ **Monsieur Broughton**[190] 1309 4-9-3 53 KierenFallon 1 39
(Willie Musson) *chsd ldrs: rdn over 2f out: wknd fnl f* **7/1**[3]

50 **9** hd **Oceana Dreamer (IRE)**[76] 4754 3-9-0 48 (v[1]) JimmyFortune 11 39
(Andrew Balding) *s.i.s: in rr: drvn and hdwy on ins fr 2f out: nvr quite rchd ldrs and wknd fnl f* **7/1**[3]

0000 **10** ½ **Moody Dancer**[20] 6641 3-9-0 55 HayleyTurner 9 38
(William Muir) *chsd ldrs: rdn: hung rt and wknd fr 2f out* **25/1**

665 **11** 1 ¾ **Narapatisithu (FR)**[20] 6643 5-9-3 55 JamieMackay 13 34
(K F Clutterbuck) *chsd ldrs: rdn over 2f out: wknd over 1f out* **33/1**

3000 **12** shd **First Voice (IRE)**[49] 5764 3-9-0 52 JamesSullivan 8 34
(James Given) *t.k.h: trckd ldrs: one pce whn hmpd and wknd ins fnl 2f* **16/1**

000 **13** 9 **Ivan The Engine**[22] 6582 4-9-3 49 SebSanders 7 13
(Ian Wood) *chsd ldr: chal 3f out tl ins fnl 2f: wknd wl over 1f out* **25/1**

1m 38.89s (-0.91) **Going Correction** -0.20s/f (Stan)
WFA 3 from 4yo+ 3lb **13** Ran SP% **130.8**
Speed ratings (Par 101): **96,95,95,89,88 88,87,87,86,86 84,84,75**
Tote Swingers 1&2 £5.70, 2&3 £24.10, 1&3 £15.70 CSF £52.29 TOTE £3.10: £1.90, £4.60, £3.30; EX 58.40 TRIFECTA Not won..
Owner Andy Taylor **Bred** Pearl & David Moore **Trained** Sullington, W Sussex
■ Stewards' Enquiry : Adam Kirby one-day ban: careless riding (Nov 1)

FOCUS
Not too much to dwell on in a moderate classified event. A decent gallop suited those held up and the first three, who pulled clear, came down the centre.
First Voice(IRE) Official explanation: jockey said gelding ran too free

7190 32RED.COM NURSERY 1m (P)
6:00 (6:00) (Class 4) (0-85,84) 2-Y-0 **£3,428** (£1,020; £509; £254) **Stalls** Low

Form RPR

5001 **1** **Mushaakis (IRE)**[22] 6583 2-8-0 **63** SilvestreDeSousa 4 65
(Mark Johnston) *disp 2nd: drvn along 3f out: rallied u.p and styd on fnl f: led nr fin* **11/8**[1]

5240 **2** ½ **Arctic Admiral (IRE)**[9] 6946 2-8-7 **70** KieranO'Neill 6 71
(Richard Hannon) *sn led: drvn 2f out: hrd pressed fnl f: hdd and no ex nr fin* **16/1**

6321 **3** ½ **Magical Rose (IRE)**[29] 6356 2-8-13 **76** SebSanders 3 76
(Paul D'Arcy) *in rr but in tch: hdwy 2f out: disp cl 2nd ins fnl f: nt qckn clsng stages* **6/1**[3]

1446 **4** nk **Aussie Reigns (IRE)**[21] 6597 2-8-10 **73** (v[1]) JimCrowley 1 72
(William Knight) *chsd ldrs: rdn over 2f out: disp 2nd 1f out: styd on fnl f: nt qckn clsng stages* **3/1**[2]

022 **5** 1 **Mar Mar (IRE)**[24] 6534 2-9-4 **84** DarrenEgan(3) 7 81
(Saeed Bin Suroor) *in tch and t.k.h: rdn and hdwy over 2f out: styd on same pce fnl f* **3/1**[2]

1m 38.83s (-0.97) **Going Correction** -0.20s/f (Stan) **5** Ran SP% **112.3**
Speed ratings (Par 97): **96,95,95,94,93**
CSF £22.46 TOTE £3.00: £1.80, £5.80; EX 24.60.
Owner Hamdan Al Maktoum **Bred** Shadwell Estate Company Limited **Trained** Middleham Moor, N Yorks

FOCUS
A fair nursery but a steady gallop means the bare form isn't entirely reliable and the whole field finished in a heap. The winner came down the centre.

NOTEBOOK
Mushaakis(IRE) ◆ is a steadily progressive sort who had the run of the race and showed a good attitude to maintain his unbeaten record on Polytrack. He won't be going up too much for this and should be seen to much better effect granted a stronger gallop, and he appeals as the type to win more races. (op 7-4 tchd 2-1)
Arctic Admiral(IRE), back on Polytrack, was allowed an easy lead and ran as well as he ever has done. While this flatters him to an extent, he's in very good hands and remains capable of winning a small race. (tchd 10-1)
Magical Rose(IRE) came into this race as a steadily progressive sort on turf and she ran up to her best on this nursery and AW debut. She'll do better again on this surface when she gets a better gallop to aim at. (tchd 5-1)

Aussie Reigns(IRE), the most exposed of these, ran creditably in the first-time visor on this AW debut. A better gallop would also have suited but he'll have to raise his game to win a competitive nursery from his current mark. (op 7-2 tchd 4-1)
Mar Mar(IRE) wasn't beaten far on this nursery debut but didn't do herself any favours after failing to settle and drifting left under pressure. A stronger gallop would have suited better and she's lightly raced enough to be worth another chance. (op 5-2 tchd 2-1)

7191 32RED CASINO MAIDEN AUCTION STKS 7f (P)
6:30 (6:31) (Class 5) 2-Y-O **£2,264** (£673; £336; £168) **Stalls** Low

Form RPR
62 **1** **Birdlover**[12] 6871 2-8-4 0 .... MartinLane 13 72
(Ralph Beckett) *trckd ldr: led over 2f out: styd on u.p fnl f: hrd pressed cl home: all out* **4/7**[1]
5 **2** *nse* **Swift Bounty**[42] 5963 2-8-9 0 .... MichaelJMMurphy(5) 5 82
(Alan Jarvis) *trckd ldrs: swtchd sharply rt and collided w opponent over 2f out: sn drvn to chse wnr: str chal u.p ins fnl f: jst failed* **8/1**[3]
63 **3** *1 ½* **Jodies Jem**[13] 6846 2-8-12 0 .... JimCrowley 6 76
(William Jarvis) *chsd ldrs: drvn to take 3rd over 1f out: kpt on fnl f but nt pce of ldng duo* **6/1**[2]
4 *1 ¾* **Emperor Julius (IRE)** 2-8-11 0 .... JimmyFortune 9 71+
(Jo Crowley) *towards rr: hdwy fr 2f out: styd on wl to take 4th over 1f out: kpt on cl home* **33/1**
00 **5** *5* **Crystal Peaks**[15] 6790 2-8-8 0 .... JamesSullivan 4 54
(James Given) *in rr: hdwy fr 2f out: nvr gng pce to get into contention* **50/1**
6 *1 ½* **Halling's Wish** 2-8-12 0 .... JamesDoyle 10 54
(John Best) *s.i.s: in rr: styd on fr over 1f out: nvr a threat* **33/1**
0 **7** *1* **Dividend Dan (IRE)**[8] 6978 2-8-11 0 .... PatDobbs 11 50
(Mike Murphy) *in tch: drvn over 2f out: outpcd over 1f out* **33/1**
06 **8** *1 ¼* **Everreadyneddy**[48] 5784 2-8-11 0 .... (t) LiamKeniry 2 47
(J S Moore) *chsd ldrs: rdn over 2f out: sn btn* **66/1**
9 *¾* **Smart Alice** 2-8-7 0 .... HarryBentley 12 41
(Chris Wall) *in tch: pushed along 3f out: no ch fnl 2f* **20/1**
10 *hd* **Rabdaan** 2-9-0 0 .... HayleyTurner 8 47
(James Fanshawe) *s.i.s: in rr: sme late prog* **8/1**[3]
11 *2* **The Ginger Berry** 2-8-10 0 .... RobertHavlin 7 38
(Dr Jon Scargill) *s.i.s: in rr: mod prog fnl f* **66/1**
12 *2 ½* **My Renaissance** 2-8-12 0 .... ShaneKelly 1 33
(Ben Case) *in tch over 4f: wknd wl over 1f out* **33/1**
0 **13** *1 ¼* **Multi Fours**[66] 5153 2-8-6 0 .... MartinDwyer 3 24
(Daniel Kubler) *led tl hdd and bdly bmpd over 2f out: sn btn* **33/1**
14 *5* **Dream About You (IRE)** 2-8-0 0 .... DanielCremin(7) 14 11
(Robert Mills) *v.s.a: rn green and detached after 2f: no ch after* **66/1**

1m 24.82s (-1.18) **Going Correction** -0.20s/f (Stan) **14** Ran SP% **126.1**
Speed ratings (Par 95): **98,97,96,94,88 86,85,84,83,83 80,78,76,70**
Tote Swingers 1&2 £2.60, 2&3 £5.70, 1&3 £2.40 CSF £5.53 TOTE £1.40: £1.02, £2.60, £2.00; EX 7.50 Trifecta £23.30 Pool 775.68 - 24.54 winning units..
Owner Fortnum Racing **Bred** Mrs Robert Langton **Trained** Kimpton, Hants
■ Stewards' Enquiry : Michael J M Murphy two-day ban: careless riding (Nov 1-2)

FOCUS
A race lacking much in the way of strength in depth but fair form from the principals. The gallop was an ordinary one and the winner edged towards the far side in the closing stages. The balance of those down the field sets a fluid opening level.

NOTEBOOK
Birdlover looked to hold strong claims judged on her useful display at Ascot a few days earlier but, although she failed to match that effort on this AW debut over this longer trip, she showed a gritty attitude after racing with the choke out. She has a bit of scope and may do better. (op 5-6)
Swift Bounty, who showed ability at a modest level on his debut at Haydock, duly stepped up on that effort over this longer trip on this AW debut, despite hanging right. This race lacked anything in the way of strength but he should be able to pick up a small event at some point. (tchd 9-1)
Jodies Jem is a steadily progressive sort who ran his best race on this AW debut. The step into ordinary nursery company will suit and he should have no problems staying 1m. (op 5-1 tchd 9-2)
Emperor Julius(IRE), who cost 8,000GBP and who is a half-brother to a useful winner in Hong Kong, showed ability to fare the best of the newcomers and to fare the best of those held up. He should improve for this experience.
Halling's Wish, who cost 10,000gns as a yearling and is the second foal of a German 7f winner, herself a half-sister to very useful Flat stayer and smart hurdler/chaser Fair Along, wasn't totally disgraced and, while likely to remain vulnerable in this type of event, should improve for the run.
Rabdaan, a 17,000gns first foal of a very useful triple 1m winner, herself a grand-daughter of French 1,000 Guineas winner Ta Rib, was prominent in the market but was too green to do himself justice on this debut. He is entitled to come on for this. (op 7-1)

7192 £32 FREE AT 32RED.COM MAIDEN STKS 6f (P)
7:00 (7:00) (Class 5) 2-Y-O **£2,264** (£673; £336; £168) **Stalls** Low

Form RPR
32 **1** **Homage (IRE)**[27] 6443 2-9-3 0 .... WilliamBuick 8 80+
(Jeremy Noseda) *trckd ldrs: led appr fnl 2f: drvn over 1f out: pressed fnl 120yds: asserted clsng stages: readily* **11/10**[1]
0426 **2** *½* **Rock Up (IRE)**[34] 6203 2-9-3 75 .... RyanMoore 2 78
(David Elsworth) *t.k.h: chsd ldrs: drvn and one pce over 1f out: rallied ins fnl f: chal fnl 120yds: outpcd clsng stages* **11/2**[3]
0430 **3** *2 ¼* **Global Icon**[12] 6874 2-9-3 88 .... RichardHughes 4 71
(Richard Hannon) *trckd ldrs: pressed wnr 2f out: sn drvn: no ex ins fnl f: wknd fnl 120yds* **9/4**[2]
40 **4** *½* **David Jack**[42] 5963 2-9-3 0 .... TedDurcan 3 70
(Brian Meehan) *in tch: drvn and hdwy over 1f out: kpt on same pce ins fnl f* **8/1**
0 **5** *hd* **Shy Bride (IRE)**[26] 6486 2-8-12 0 .... JimCrowley 5 64+
(Alan Jarvis) *chsd ldrs: drvn and one pce 2f out: kpt on again ins fnl f: gng on cl home* **25/1**
6 **6** *8* **Great Crested (IRE)**[15] 6772 2-9-3 0 .... ShaneKelly 1 45
(Murty McGrath) *in rr: outpcd fr 1/2-way* **50/1**
7 *2* **Carrera** 2-9-3 0 .... SebSanders 7 39
(J W Hills) *s.i.s: outpcd* **25/1**
0 **8** *¾* **Superoo (IRE)**[12] 6889 2-9-3 0 .... SilvestreDeSousa 6 37
(Mark Johnston) *led tl hdd appr fnl 2f: sn btn* **33/1**

1m 12.82s (-0.28) **Going Correction** -0.20s/f (Stan) **8** Ran SP% **117.5**
Speed ratings (Par 95): **93,92,89,88,88 77,75,74**
Tote Swingers 1&2 £1.90, 2&3 £2.50, 1&3 £1.10 CSF £7.82 TOTE £3.20: £1.10, £2.60, £1.10; EX 6.60 Trifecta £8.40 Pool 979.31- 85.86 winning units..
Owner Highclere Thoroughbred Racing - Dalmeny **Bred** J Hanly **Trained** Newmarket, Suffolk

FOCUS
The second favourite proved a shade disappointing but useful form from the first two, who raced in the centre. The gallop was an ordinary one and the proximity of the fifth holds the overall form down.

NOTEBOOK
Homage(IRE) ◆, whose last run threw up several winners, is a steadily progressive sort who showed a good attitude on this AW debut to get off the mark at the third attempt. He should be equally effective over 7f, he's open to further improvement and he's very much the type to go in again. (op 5-4)
Rock Up(IRE) had the run of the race back up in distance and turned in an improved effort on this AW debut. He's shown more than enough to suggest he can make his mark in ordinary maiden company on Polytrack in the coming weeks. (tchd 4-1)
Global Icon had a good chance at the weights for this AW debut but didn't really settle and was disappointing back over sprint distances. While he should pick up a race, he's not the biggest and will do well to win a competitive handicap from his current mark of 88. (op 7-4 tchd 5-2)
David Jack, making his AW debut, returned to the form that saw him run creditably on his first racecourse appearance, but he's the type who may do better once switched to ordinary handicaps. (op 9-1)
Shy Bride(IRE), well beaten at Newbury on her debut the previous month, fared a good deal better on this AW debut but may be flattered by her proximity in this moderately run race. She's likely to remain vulnerable in this type of event.
Carrera, a Derby entry and 58,000gns yearling half-brother to this year's Group 1 (1m) and Grade 1 (1m1f) winner Samitar, and to 7f Group 3 scorer Najoom Dubai, didn't offer much on this debut but he may do better granted a stiffer test of stamina in due course. (op 33-1)

7193 32RED NURSERY 6f (P)
7:30 (7:30) (Class 3) (0-95,85) 2-Y-O **£5,822** (£1,732; £865; £432) **Stalls** Low

Form RPR
2102 **1** **Cappadocia (IRE)**[5] 7059 2-8-8 **72** .... MartinHarley 3 76
(Mick Channon) *in tch: drvn and hdwy to chse ldrs 2f out: led jst ins fnl f: styd on strly* **10/1**
51 **2** *1* **Agerzam**[15] 6772 2-9-7 **85** .... NeilCallan 7 86
(Roger Varian) *t.k.h: trckd ldrs: drvn to ld over 1f out: hdd jst ins fnl f: nt pce of wnr fnl 120yds* **9/4**[1]
011 **3** *nk* **Titled Gent**[50] 5743 2-9-7 **85** .... KierenFallon 5 85
(Brian Meehan) *in tch: drvn along 3f out: styd on u.p fnl f to cl on 2nd nr fin but no imp on wnr* **5/2**[2]
1460 **4** *1* **Jollification (IRE)**[26] 6487 2-9-2 **85** .... DavidKenny(5) 2 82
(George Baker) *in rr: pushed along and no prog over 2f out: styd on strly appr fnl f: fin wl clsng stages* **33/1**
6101 **5** *nk* **Excel Yourself (IRE)**[44] 5909 2-9-4 **82** .... MartinDwyer 8 78
(James Tate) *led after 1f: jnd over 3f out: kpt slt ld tl hdd over 1f out: btn ins fnl f* **14/1**
2142 **6** *2* **Black Monk (IRE)**[28] 6414 2-9-1 **79** .... RyanMoore 4 69
(Richard Hannon) *t.k.h: led 1f: chsd ldrs: rdn over 2f out: sn btn* **7/1**
01 **7** *1 ¼* **The Art Of Racing (IRE)**[39] 6071 2-9-0 **78** .... RichardHughes 6 64
(Richard Hannon) *s.i.s: sn trcking ldrs: chal over 3f out to 2f out: wknd over 1f out: eased whn hld* **3/1**[3]
360 **8** *1 ¼* **Uncomplicated**[8] 6984 2-8-13 **77** .... PatCosgrave 1 60
(Jim Boyle) *a outpcd* **50/1**

1m 11.8s (-1.30) **Going Correction** -0.20s/f (Stan) **8** Ran SP% **117.5**
Speed ratings (Par 99): **100,98,98,96,96 93,92,90**
Tote Swingers 1&2 £6.50, 2&3 £1.60, 1&3 £4.00 CSF £33.86 CT £77.02 TOTE £10.70: £2.20, £1.10, £1.30; EX 37.00 Trifecta £75.20 Pool 917.75 - 9.03 winning units..
Owner Dark Horse Racing Partnership SIx **Bred** Rathasker Stud **Trained** West Ilsley, Berks

FOCUS
A couple of progressive sorts in a useful nursery in which the gallop was no more than fair early on. The winner made his ground against the inside rail passing the intersection.

NOTEBOOK
Cappadocia(IRE) had looked fully exposed but he appreciated the drop back to sprinting and he posted his best effort to beat a couple of rivals who raced with the choke out early on. He's 2-2 over this C&D and should continue to give a good account on Polytrack. (tchd 8-1)
Agerzam ◆, whose C&D maiden win had been franked by the runner-up the previous week, raced freely in the early stages but matched the form of that win on this nursery debut. He's a strong sort with bags of physical scope and he should be able to add to his tally on this surface. (op 5-2 tchd 3-1)
Titled Gent, previously unbeaten on Polytrack, was another to race far too keenly in the early stages but he posted another creditable effort in terms of form from this 8lb higher mark. A stronger overall gallop would have suited and he should continue to give a good account. (tchd 9-4 and 11-4)
Jollification(IRE) bettered the form of her nursery debut on this first run on an artificial surface and, although her sole win came over 5f, she again left the impression that she'd be worth a try over 7f.
Excel Yourself(IRE), up 3lb for her narrow Leicester victory, had the run of the race and wasn't disgraced returned to Polytrack. She should continue to go well but is likely to remain vulnerable to an improver from this mark. (op 12-1)
The Art Of Racing(IRE), back up in trip, pulled too hard and not surprisingly didn't get home on this nursery and AW debut. The return to 5f should suit better but he really needs to learn to settle better. Official explanation: jockey said colt ran too free and had no more to give

7194 32REDBET.COM H'CAP (DIV I) 1m 4f (P)
8:00 (8:01) (Class 4) (0-85,84) 3-Y-O **£4,075** (£1,212; £606; £303) **Stalls** Centre

Form RPR
1523 **1** **Arch Villain (IRE)**[29] 6383 3-9-3 **80** .... (b[1]) JimCrowley 11 89
(Amanda Perrett) *s.i.s: led after 2f: rdn over 2f out: hrd pressed over 1f out and strly chal fr ins fnl f tl responded gamely to assert last strides* **7/2**[1]
010 **2** *nk* **Mawhub**[43] 5951 3-9-1 **78** .... SilvestreDeSousa 8 86
(Saeed Bin Suroor) *in rr: hdwy on inner over 2f out: str chal appr fnl f and upsides ins fnl f: styd chalng tl no ex last strides* **7/1**
2315 **3** *1* **Infinite Hope (USA)**[30] 6333 3-9-3 **80** .... KirstyMilczarek 9 86
(Luca Cumani) *chsd ldrs: pushed along over 2f out: sn rdn: one pce over 1f out: rallied and kpt on wl to take 3rd ins fnl f: nt rch ldng duo* **12/1**
6644 **4** *¾* **Shestheman**[15] 6776 3-9-0 **77** .... TedDurcan 1 82
(David Lanigan) *in tch: dropped to rr 5f out: drvn and hdwy over 2f out: styd on wl appr fnl f to take 4th: no imp on ldng trio* **7/2**[1]
6-10 **5** *2* **Dedication**[24] 6537 3-9-0 **77** .... (t) JamesDoyle 2 79
(Roger Charlton) *trckd ldrs: rdn over 2f out: no imp and styd on same pce u.p fnl f* **25/1**
6226 **6** *1 ¼* **Cape Savannah**[20] 6625 3-9-3 **80** .... MartinLane 3 80
(David Simcock) *in rr: rdn 4f out: styd on u.p fnl f: nvr a threat* **7/1**
5226 **7** *1 ¼* **Aazif (IRE)**[40] 6033 3-9-7 **84** .... PaulHanagan 5 82
(John Dunlop) *sn slt ld: hdd after 2f: chsd wnr to 7f out: styd chsng ldrs: chal u.p over 1f out: wknd ins fnl f* **4/1**[2]
5512 **8** *1 ¾* **Kelpie Blitz (IRE)**[41] 5990 3-8-7 **70** .... (t) JohnFahy 10 65
(Seamus Durack) *chsd ldrs: wnt 2nd 7f out: wknd ins fnl 2f* **16/1**
4434 **9** *14* **Cellist**[15] 6802 3-8-9 **72** .... (p) KierenFallon 4 45
(William Haggas) *in tch: drvn and hdwy 4f out: wknd 3f out* **6/1**[3]
4206 **10** *3 ¼* **Star For Life (USA)**[16] 6770 3-9-3 **80** .... (p) GeorgeBaker 7 47
(Mikael Magnusson) *a in rr* **33/1**

-606 **11** *nk* **Dandy (GER)**[22] 6574 3-8-11 **74**...................................... JimmyFortune 6 41
(Andrew Balding) *rdn over 4f out: a in rr* **25/1**

2m 30.52s (-3.98) **Going Correction** -0.20s/f (Stan) 11 Ran SP% **127.9**
Speed ratings (Par 103): **105,104,104,103,102 101,100,99,90,87 87**
Tote Swingers 1&2 £7.70, 2&3 £17.30, 1&3 £16.00 CSF £30.84 CT £281.42 TOTE £3.20: £2.00, £2.80, £4.00; EX 37.20 TRIFECTA Not won..

Owner Mr & Mrs F Cotton, Mr & Mrs P Conway **Bred** Summerhill Bloodstock **Trained** Pulborough, W Sussex

FOCUS
A useful handicap run at just a fair gallop. The principals came down the centre in the straight. The third earned a small personal best rating with the fourth to latest C&D form. This looks sound enough.

7195 32REDBET.COM H'CAP (DIV II) 1m 4f (P)
8:30 (8:32) (Class 4) (0-85,82) 3-Y-O **£4,075** (£1,212; £606; £303) **Stalls** Centre

Form RPR

5410 **1** **Castilo Del Diablo (IRE)**[40] 6025 3-9-6 **81**.................. JamieSpencer 4 93+
(David Simcock) *bhd: drvn along 4f out: gd hdwy over 1f out: qcknd to ld fnl 120yds* **7/4**[1]

1225 **2** *1 ¼* **Nordic Quest (IRE)**[18] 6712 3-9-4 **79**.................................. NeilCallan 2 89
(Gerard Butler) *bhd: hdwy 3f out: led ins fnl 2f: kpt on wl u.p tl hdd and outpcd fnl 120yds* **7/1**[3]

5215 **3** *shd* **Daliance (IRE)**[27] 6441 3-9-5 **80**............................ RichardKingscote 8 90
(Tom Dascombe) *hld up in rr: gd hdwy 2f out: str run to chal thrght fnl f: no ex clsng stages* **7/1**[3]

5041 **4** *2 ¾* **Wildomar**[7] 7011 3-8-12 **73** 6ex... BrettDoyle 3 78
(John Ryan) *bhd: hdwy 2f out: styd on wl to chse ldrs over 1f out: styd on same pce ins fnl f* **12/1**

34 **5** *4 ½* **Gabrial's King (IRE)**[19] 6662 3-8-8 **69**..................... SilvestreDeSousa 1 67
(Ian Williams) *in tch: hdwy over 2f out: edgd lft sn after: hung rt u.p over 1f out: sn wknd* **25/1**

1523 **6** *2 ½* **Spanish Wedding**[29] 6359 3-9-7 **82**.............................(b) AdamKirby 10 81+
(Marco Botti) *chsd ldrs: rdn and ev ch whn bmpd ins fnl 2f: nt rcvr* **11/2**[2]

3432 **7** *nse* **Grand Gold**[19] 6207 3-8-9 **70**...(t) JohnFahy 7 64
(Seamus Durack) *chsd ldrs: rdn over 2f out: wknd over 1f out* **25/1**

1036 **8** *2 ¼* **Keepax**[29] 6376 3-9-1 **76**... HarryBentley 5 67
(Chris Wall) *chsd ldrs: rdn and one pce whn bmpd ins fnl 2f: sn wknd* **8/1**

0-23 **9** *nk* **Inqadh (USA)**[21] 6615 3-9-2 **77**..........................(b[1]) MickaelBarzalona 11 67
(Saeed Bin Suroor) *chsd ldrs: drvn to ld over 2f out: veered lft: hdd & wknd ins fnl 2f* **16/1**

3060 **10** *6* **Cherry Street**[24] 6537 3-9-6 **81**.. DavidProbert 6 61
(Andrew Balding) *rdn along over 3f out: a towards rr* **33/1**

6110 **11** *9* **Joyful Spirit (IRE)**[20] 6647 3-9-2 **77**................................(b) TedDurcan 9 43
(John Dunlop) *sn led: hdd over 2f out: wkng whn bmpd ins fnl 2f* **20/1**

2m 30.38s (-4.12) **Going Correction** -0.20s/f (Stan) 11 Ran SP% **116.8**
Speed ratings (Par 103): **105,104,104,102,99 97,97,96,95,91 85**
Tote Swingers 1&2 £3.70, 2&3 £13.00, 1&3 £5.90 CSF £13.12 CT £70.51 TOTE £2.80: £1.30, £2.00, £2.70; EX 15.20 Trifecta £90.50 Pool 850.83 - 6.95 winning units..

Owner Sir Robert Ogden **Bred** Ennistown Stud **Trained** Newmarket, Suffolk

■ Stewards' Enquiry : John Fahy two-day ban: careless riding (Nov 1-2)

FOCUS
Division two of a useful handicap but the gallop was just on the ordinary side to the home turn and the winner, who came down the centre, deserves extra credit to win going away.

7196 32REDBINGO.COM H'CAP 2m (P)
9:00 (9:00) (Class 6) (0-60,60) 3-Y-O **£1,617** (£481; £240; £120) **Stalls** Low

Form RPR

-005 **1** **Glaisdale**[14] 6814 3-9-3 **56**... RobertHavlin 11 64+
(James Toller) *in tch: travelling wl whn hmpd 2f out: qcknd to ld ins fnl f* **14/1**

0036 **2** *¾* **Tokyo Brown (USA)**[19] 6691 3-9-2 **55**................................ NeilCallan 9 61
(Heather Main) *sn led: hdd 10f out: styd chsng ldrs: drvn over 2f out: styd on wl fnl f to take 2nd cl home: nt pce of wnr* **16/1**

050S **3** *½* **Red Mystique (IRE)**[62] 5330 3-8-11 **50**........................(b) RyanMoore 8 55
(Ed Dunlop) *sn chsng ldr: drvn over 2f out: led over 1f out: hdd and outpcd ins fnl f* **9/2**[3]

0606 **4** *3 ¾* **Regalo Rosado**[27] 6442 3-8-7 **46**.................................. NickyMackay 10 47
(Mike Murphy) *bhd: rapid hdwy to chse ldrs 5f out: rdn over 2f out: one pce fnl f* **25/1**

5621 **5** *1 ¼* **Smart Affair**[14] 6807 3-8-13 **52**..................................(be) SamHitchcott 7 51
(Alan Bailey) *in rr: drvn along 3f out: styd on over 1f out: kpt on clsng stages* **3/1**[2]

5352 **6** *nse* **Kashgar**[5] 7062 3-9-7 **60**.. StevieDonohoe 4 59
(Michael Bell) *chsd ldrs: led 10f out: rdn over 2f out: hdd over 1f out: sn btn* **7/4**[1]

6050 **7** *¾* **Lily Potts**[17] 6738 3-9-0 **58**...(p) JemmaMarshall[(5)] 2 56
(Chris Down) *chsd ldrs: drvn over 3f out: wknd over 1f out* **25/1**

0333 **8** *2 ½* **Zarosa (IRE)**[63] 5264 3-8-10 **49**...................................... JimmyQuinn 3 44
(John Berry) *in tch: pushed along 7f out: styd on over 2f out: wknd over 1f out* **12/1**

6000 **9** *3 ¼* **Corn Maiden**[9] 6948 3-8-8 **47**...................................... SilvestreDeSousa 1 39
(Mark Rimmer) *chsd ldrs: rdn 5f out: wknd 2f out* **33/1**

0003 **10** *3 ½* **Kozmina Bay**[3] 7117 3-8-13 **52**..(vt) JohnFahy 6 39
(Jonathan Portman) *bhd fr 1/2-way* **14/1**

5041 **11** *nse* **Maccabees**[9] 6948 3-8-6 **48**.. DarrenEgan[(3)] 5 35
(Roger Curtis) *t.k.h: a towards rr* **10/1**

3m 28.91s (-1.19) **Going Correction** -0.20s/f (Stan) 11 Ran SP% **126.2**
Speed ratings (Par 99): **94,93,93,91,90 90,90,89,87,85 85**
Tote Swingers 1&2 £45.00, 2&3 £14.20, 1&3 £12.20 CSF £226.75 CT £1189.49 TOTE £19.10: £7.50, £5.30, £2.30; EX 197.40 TRIFECTA Not won..

Owner Alan Gibson **Bred** Alan Gibson **Trained** Newmarket, Suffolk

FOCUS
A modest handicap in which the gallop was an ordinary one. The winner came down the centre.

Glaisdale Official explanation: trainer's rep said, regarding apparent improvement in form, that the filly had benefited from the step up in trip.

Kashgar Official explanation: jockey said gelding reared as stalls opened

T/Plt: £19.00 to a £1 stake. Pool £61,417.57. 2,353.88 winning tickets T/Qpdt: £3.20 to a £1 stake. Pool £9,217.70. 2,102.0 winning tickets ST

7141 WOLVERHAMPTON (A.W) (L-H)
Thursday, October 18

OFFICIAL GOING: Standard
Wind: medium, behind Weather: dry until rain for last 3 races

7197 32REDBET.COM H'CAP 5f 20y(P)
2:00 (2:00) (Class 5) (0-75,75) 3-Y-O+ **£2,264** (£673; £336; £168) **Stalls** Low

Form RPR

1654 **1** **Drawnfromthepast (IRE)**[14] 6824 7-9-5 **73**................ JamieSpencer 10 83
(Jamie Osborne) *chsd ldrs: rdn to ld 1f out: sn in command and styd on wl: rdn out* **11/2**[3]

4200 **2** *1 ¼* **Ryan Style (IRE)**[3] 7100 6-9-2 **70**....................................(v) PhillipMakin 2 75
(Lisa Williamson) *hld up in tch towards rr: rdn and hdwy on inner ent fnl f: styd on wl to snatch 2nd on post* **10/1**

3212 **3** *nse* **Mother Jones**[19] 6685 4-9-1 **69**... LukeMorris 5 74
(David Evans) *hld up in tch in midfield: rdn and hdwy over 1f out: chsd wnr jst ins fnl f: kpt on but no imp: lost 2nd on post* **9/1**

3402 **4** *1* **Ring For Baileys**[22] 6578 3-9-3 **71**................................. JoeFanning 13 72
(Chris Dwyer) *hld up in midfield on outer: hdwy u.p over 1f out: egded lft but kpt on ins fnl f* **9/1**

0060 **5** *¾* **Dancing Freddy (IRE)**[19] 6666 5-9-7 **75**..................(tp) WilliamCarson 8 74
(Violet M Jordan) *w ldr: rdn 2f out: unable qck u.p ent fnl f: one pce after* **14/1**

0600 **6** *nk* **Wooden King (IRE)**[19] 6688 7-9-5 **73**...................... TomMcLaughlin 11 70
(Malcolm Saunders) *hld up in tch in midfield: rdn and hdwy ent fnl f: drvn and kpt on same pce ins fnl f: eased towards fin* **20/1**

5000 **7** *¾* **Shawkantango**[15] 6788 5-8-13 **67**.................................(v) DaleSwift 9 62
(Derek Shaw) *taken down early: towards rr: rdn over 2f out: kpt on ins fnl f: nvr trbld ldrs* **25/1**

4024 **8** *½* **For Shia And Lula (IRE)**[21] 6610 3-9-4 **72**..................(p) MartinHarley 7 65
(Daniel Mark Loughnane) *in tch in midfield: rdn and effrt over 1f out: no imp and styd on same pce ins fnl f* **15/2**

1001 **9** *½* **Clubland (IRE)**[10] 6935 3-9-2 **70**.. AmyRyan 3 61
(Kevin Ryan) *led: drvn over 1f out: hdd 1f out: sn btn and wknd ins fnl f* **4/1**[1]

001 **10** *1 ¼* **Nawarah**[14] 6806 3-9-2 **70**... MartinDwyer 1 57
(Conrad Allen) *in tch in midfield on inner: rdn and effrt over 1f out: no imp: wknd ins fnl f* **5/1**[2]

4530 **11** *¾* **Berberana (IRE)**[22] 6578 4-9-0 **68**.................................(b[1]) RenatoSouza 6 52
(Jeremy Gask) *bhd: drvn and no prog whn edgd lft over 1f out: nvr trbld ldrs* **20/1**

5000 **12** *4 ½* **Bookiesindexdotnet**[27] 6439 3-9-1 **72**........................ DarrenEgan[(3)] 4 40
(J R Jenkins) *t.k.h: chsd ldrs: rdn and unable qck ent fnl 2f: wkng whn short of room 1f out: wknd and eased towards fin* **40/1**

5560 **13** *4 ½* **Nickel Silver**[19] 6685 7-8-13 **67**......................................(v) TomEaves 12 19
(Bryan Smart) *dwlt: sn rcvrd and in midfield on outer: wknd over 1f out: fdd fnl f: eased towards fin* **33/1**

1m 2.06s (-0.24) **Going Correction** -0.025s/f (Stan) 13 Ran SP% **118.3**
Speed ratings (Par 103): **100,98,97,96,95 94,93,92,91,89 88,81,74**
toteswingers 1&2 £14.50, 2&3 £18.40, 1&3 £6.10 CSF £54.34 CT £507.52 TOTE £8.00: £2.10, £4.00, £1.20; EX 80.50 TRIFECTA Not won..

Owner Mark Benton **Bred** D And Mrs D Veitch **Trained** Upper Lambourn, Berks

FOCUS
A fair sprint handicap for 3yos and up in which they were racing on standard Polytrack with a strong tailwind reported up the home straight. It's been rated around the runner-up and third pretty much to their marks.

7198 E.B.F./32RED CASINO MAIDEN STKS 5f 216y(P)
2:30 (2:30) (Class 5) 2-Y-O **£3,169** (£943; £471; £235) **Stalls** Low

Form RPR

4 **1** **Al Udeid (IRE)**[21] 6609 2-9-3 0... AmyRyan 8 80+
(Kevin Ryan) *mde all: rdn 2f out: in command and styd on wl fnl f: rdn out* **8/1**

024 **2** *1 ½* **Star Of Rohm**[40] 6032 2-9-3 81.. HayleyTurner 10 75
(Michael Bell) *chsd wnr thrght: drvn over 1f out: styd on same pce and a hld fnl f* **11/10**[1]

64 **3** *1 ½* **Space Artist (IRE)**[139] 2667 2-9-3 0................................. TomEaves 2 71
(Bryan Smart) *chsd ldng pair: rdn over 1f out: styd on same pce fnl f* **25/1**

000 **4** *1 ¼* **Forbidden Fruit (IRE)**[27] 6444 2-9-3 68........................(t) MartinDwyer 9 67
(Brian Meehan) *chsd ldrs: rdn and unable qck over 1f out: 4th and wl hld fnl f* **16/1**

4 **5** *2 ¾* **North Pole**[12] 6889 2-9-3 0.. LukeMorris 4 59+
(Sir Mark Prescott Bt) *chsd ldrs: rdn 1/2-way: outpcd and btn over 1f out: wknd ins fnl f* **7/1**[3]

6 *2* **Classy Trick (USA)** 2-9-3 0... HarryBentley 5 53+
(Richard Fahey) *dwlt: towards rr and sn pushed along: edgd lft and modest hdwy 1f out: nvr trbld ldrs* **14/1**

0000 **7** *1 ¼* **Lobelia**[12] 6871 2-8-12 51.. JoeFanning 7 44
(Brian Meehan) *hld up towards rr on outer: rdn and no prog over 1f out: wl btn fnl f* **50/1**

0 **8** *7* **Cuban Tash**[35] 6175 2-9-3 0...............................(t) RichardKingscote 6 28
(Tom Dascombe) *dwlt: a bhd: lost tch wl over 1f out* **20/1**

9 *2* **Prom Dress** 2-8-12 0.. EddieAhern 3 17
(Robert Cowell) *dwlt: a bhd: rdn and struggling ent fnl 2f: sn lost tch* **33/1**

224 **10** *2* **Emirates Echo**[121] 3244 2-9-3 78...................................... JamieSpencer 1 16
(David Simcock) *dwlt: sn rcvrd and in tch in midfield: rdn and no rspnse over 2f out: wknd over 1f out: bhd and eased fnl f* **9/2**[2]

1m 14.7s (-0.30) **Going Correction** -0.025s/f (Stan) 10 Ran SP% **115.5**
Speed ratings (Par 95): **101,99,97,95,91 89,87,78,75,72**
toteswingers 1&2 £3.20, 2&3 £8.90, 1&3 £16.20 CSF £16.42 TOTE £8.20: £2.70, £1.10, £8.20; EX 24.30 Trifecta £520.50 Part won. Pool: £703.50 - 0.91 winning tickets..

Owner Mubarak Al Naemi **Bred** Messrs Mark Hanly & James Hanly **Trained** Hambleton, N Yorks

FOCUS
A fair juvenile maiden. Suspect winner has more to offer and the fourth offers perspective.

NOTEBOOK
Al Udeid(IRE), a modest fourth over this C&D on his debut the previous month, shown he had derived considerable benefit from that initial experience with a straightforward pillar-to-post victory. He looks a fair type in the making. (op 10-1)

Star Of Rohm was returning from a six-week break and arrived with a BHA rating of 81, which made him the one to beat on the book. He was a shade below his best here but still gives the form plenty of substance, and should be able to win something similar. (op 6-4)

Space Artist(IRE) was returning from a near five-month break since a lesser second start at Newcastle in June. He produced peak form here on his third start. (op 20-1)

Forbidden Fruit(IRE), wearing a first-time tongue-tie, appeared to run slightly below his BHA rating of 68 on this fourth start.
North Pole failed to build on a modest C&D debut earlier this month but this half-brother to the speedy Krypton Factor can be expected to do better in handicaps after another run. (op 11-2)
Classy Trick(USA), who cost $85,000 as a yearling and is a half-brother to four winners in North America, dwelt at the start before making modest headway 1f out. He should show the benefit of this initial experience in due course. (op 12-1 tchd 10-1)
Emirates Echo, who got warm beforehand returning from a four-month break, proved disappointing. Official explanation: jockey said that the colt did not face the kick-back (op 4-1 tchd 5-1)

7199 E.B.F./£32 BONUS AT 32RED.COM MEDIAN AUCTION MAIDEN STKS 1m 141y(P)
3:00 (3:00) (Class 5) 2-Y-O **£3,169** (£943; £471; £235) **Stalls** Low

Form RPR
1 **Regal Hawk** 2-8-12 0 MartinDwyer 6 72+
(James Tate) *squeezed for room and lost pl sn after s: hld up in last trio after: clsd 3f out: rdn and qckng to ld on inner over 1f out: rn green and hung bdly rt 1f out: rdn and readily asserted fnl 100yds: comf* **11/2[3]**
0 2 1 1/2 **Aneedh**[20] 6636 2-9-3 0 LiamJones 4 72
(William Haggas) *pushed along in midfield leaving stalls: chsd ldrs 7f out: rdn to ld wl over 1f out: sn hdd and carried rt 1f out: kpt on same pce u.p fnl f* **4/1[2]**
2323 3 1/2 **Jullundar (IRE)**[10] 6919 2-9-3 68 MartinHarley 10 71
(Mick Channon) *hld up in tch: rdn and effrt on outer wl over 1f out: wnt 3rd 1f out: styd on same pce u.p fnl f* **7/2[1]**
4 4 2 3/4 **Subtle Difference**[64] 5230 2-8-12 0 LiamKeniry 7 60
(Andrew Balding) *t.k.h: hld up wl in tch: swtchd rt and rdn over 1f out: fnd little for press: wknd ins fnl f* **8/1**
00 5 4 1/2 **Bowland Princess**[15] 6791 2-8-12 0 TomMcLaughlin 3 53
(Ed Dunlop) *dwlt and rdn along leaving stalls: sn in tch in midfield: rdn and unable qck ent fnl 2f: wknd 1f out: eased fnl 75yds* **25/1**
5 6 2 1/4 **Train Hard**[8] 6985 2-9-3 0 JoeFanning 2 51
(Mark Johnston) *t.k.h: chsd ldr: rdn and ev ch ent fnl 2f: wknd over 1f out* **15/2**
0 7 5 **Isle Of Beauty**[15] 6791 2-8-12 0 RichardKingscote 8 36
(Tom Dascombe) *chsd ldrs: rdn and lost pl over 2f out: wknd wl over 1f out* **50/1**
3 8 3 1/2 **Hello Gorgeous**[80] 4637 2-8-12 0 TomEaves 5 28
(Keith Dalgleish) *a towards rr: rdn and lost tch over 2f out* **20/1**
646 9 2 1/2 **Pearl Ransom (IRE)**[25] 6512 2-9-3 67 JamieSpencer 1 33
(Kevin Ryan) *led: rdn and hung rt bnd over 3f out: drvn and hdd wl over 1f out: sn btn and dropped out: bhd and eased ins fnl f* **7/2[1]**
10 3 3/4 **Al Sulaimi (IRE)** 2-9-3 0 LukeMorris 9 20
(Ronald Harris) *v.s.a and rdn along leaving stalls: a in rr: rdn and lost tch over 2f out* **40/1**

1m 50.9s (0.40) **Going Correction** -0.025s/f (Stan) **10** Ran SP% **115.7**
Speed ratings (Par 95): **97,95,95,92,88 86,82,79,77,73**
toteswingers 1&2 £6.30, 2&3 £4.50, 1&3 £5.00 CSF £26.48 TOTE £7.00: £4.90, £1.80, £1.20; EX 39.70 Trifecta £48.60 Pool: £878.56 - 13.36 winning tickets..
Owner Saeed Manana **Bred** Hesmonds Stud Ltd **Trained** Newmarket, Suffolk
■ Stewards' Enquiry : Martin Dwyer Caution; careless riding.

FOCUS
A modest to fair juvenile auction maiden. The third limits the level.

NOTEBOOK
Regal Hawk, who cost 32,000gns in May, won comfortably once straightened up and looks a fair prospect over at least 1m2f next term. (op 10-3 tchd 6-1)
Aneedh ran moderately on his debut over 7f at Newmarket the previous month. He found improvement on this occasion, despite being carried right 1f out, but looks one for modest nursery handicaps from now on. (op 13-2)
Jullundar(IRE), who reportedly looked well beforehand, arrived with a BHA rating of 68 after a respectable third on his fourth start over 1m2f at Pontefract on good to soft ground this month. He performed slightly below that level on this Polytrack debut. (op 6-1)
Subtle Difference was returning from a two-month break since a fair 7f Kempton debut in August. She found little for pressure after racing keenly. (op 7-1 tchd 13-2)
Train Hard produced a respectable debut display over an extended 1m at Nottingham on good to soft ground this month. He took a keen hold before chasing the leaders, and paid for his earlier exertions in the closing stages. (op 11-2)
Pearl Ransom(IRE) led for much of the journey but hung right on the bend 3f out. He was quickly beaten once headed over 1f out. Official explanation: jockey said that the gelding hung right throughout (op 4-1)

7200 32RED SUPPORTING BRITISH RACING H'CAP 1m 1f 103y(P)
3:30 (3:31) (Class 6) (0-60,60) 3-Y-O+ **£1,617** (£481; £240; £120) **Stalls** Low

Form RPR
3244 1 **Barton Bounty**[82] 4594 5-9-5 56 DaleSwift 5 64
(Peter Niven) *towards rr: pushed along 6f out: rdn and effrt 3f out: hdwy u.p over 1f out: led ins fnl f: hld on wl cl home* **12/1**
0542 2 nk **Arctic Galaxy (CAN)**[9] 6962 3-9-4 59 WilliamBuick 4 66
(John Gosden) *dwlt and rdn along leaving stalls: racd in last trio: rdn and swtchd rt 2f out: hdwy over 1f out: hanging fire and no imp 1f out tl str burst to press ldrs towards fin: wnt 2nd but hld cl home* **11/2[3]**
0230 3 hd **Iulus**[23] 6561 4-9-7 58 MichaelO'Connell 9 65
(John Quinn) *chsd ldrs: effrt u.p on inner over 1f out: drvn to ld 1f out: sn hdd but kpt on u.p: no ex cl home* **14/1**
4004 4 2 1/4 **Tartan Gunna**[5] 7058 6-9-3 54 PatCosgrave 6 56
(George Baker) *rdn along leaving stalls: sn in tch in midfield: hdwy u.p to chse ldrs 1f out: styd on same pce fnl 150yds* **3/1[1]**
140 5 1 **Brown Pete (IRE)**[30] 6334 4-9-8 59 (e) WilliamCarson 2 59
(Violet M Jordan) *hld up in midfield: hdwy u.p over 1f out: styd on same pce and no imp ins fnl f* **25/1**
0063 6 3/4 **Koo And The Gang (IRE)**[16] 6756 5-9-8 59 BarryMcHugh 8 58
(Brian Ellison) *led: rdn 2f out: hdd 1f out: wknd ins fnl f* **11/2[3]**
0400 7 2 1/4 **Signora Frasi (IRE)**[9] 6950 7-9-4 55 DaneO'Neill 1 49
(Tony Newcombe) *hld up towards rr: drvn and sme hdwy over 1f out: no imp fnl f: nvr trbld ldrs* **22/1**
304 8 1/2 **Ela Gonda Mou**[8] 6988 5-9-6 57 RobertWinston 11 50
(Peter Charalambous) *taken down early: t.k.h: chsd ldr: rdn and ev ch 2f out: unable qck over 1f out: wknd 1f out* **7/2[2]**
3514 9 2 1/2 **Saucy Cat (IRE)**[204] 1062 3-9-5 60 [1] LukeMorris 7 48
(John Best) *in tch: rdn over 3f out: wknd u.p over 1f out* **14/1**
0200 10 2 3/4 **Sanad (IRE)**[53] 5633 3-9-5 60 TomEaves 13 42
(Anthony Carson) *stdd and dropped in bhd after s: hld up in last pair: pushed along wl over 1f out: rdn and no hdwy ent fnl f: n.d* **50/1**
5540 11 1 **Bussa**[6] 7015 4-9-6 57 TomMcLaughlin 10 37
(David Evans) *chsd ldrs: rdn to chal 2f out: no ex and wknd jst over 1f out: btn and eased fnl 100yds* **40/1**
0500 12 3/4 **Sasheen**[14] 6829 5-9-2 53 (p) JamieSpencer 12 31
(Jeremy Gask) *stdd and dropped in bhd after s: stl looked to be gng wl but stuck bhd wall of horses over 2f out: rdn no hdwy over 1f out: n.d* **20/1**
1006 13 8 **Cha Ching (IRE)**[38] 6092 3-9-2 57 EddieAhern 3 18
(J W Hills) *in tch in midfield: rdn and no rspnse 3f out: wknd wl over 1f out: wl bhd and eased ins fnl f* **33/1**

2m 1.8s (0.10) **Going Correction** -0.025s/f (Stan)
WFA 3 from 4yo+ 4lb **13** Ran SP% **119.3**
Speed ratings (Par 101): **98,97,97,95,94 94,92,91,89,86 86,85,78**
toteswingers 1&2 £6.30, 2&3 £16.10, 1&3 £20.70 CSF £70.66 CT £952.36 TOTE £10.40: £2.50, £1.60, £6.00; EX 88.20 Trifecta £586.80 Pool: £824.70 - 1.04 winning tickets..
Owner Francis Green Racing Ltd **Bred** Mrs M L Parry **Trained** Barton-le-Street, N Yorks

FOCUS
A moderate handicap for 3yos and up.

7201 32RED.COM H'CAP 1m 141y(P)
4:00 (4:02) (Class 6) (0-60,60) 3-Y-O **£1,617** (£481; £240; £120) **Stalls** Low

Form RPR
0002 1 **Geeaitch**[15] 6774 3-9-6 59 WilliamCarson 7 73
(Anthony Carson) *in tch: rdn and swtchd rt 2f out: rdn to chal and rn green ent fnl f: led and edgd lft fnl 100yds: r.o strly and drew clr towards fin* **4/1[2]**
6651 2 3 1/2 **Boonga Roogeta**[9] 6962 3-9-4 57 LukeMorris 2 63
(Peter Charalambous) *chsd ldr: rdn and ev ch 2f out: hrd drvn and led jst ins fnl f: hdd and outpcd fnl 100yds* **12/1**
5021 3 1 **Outlaw Torn (IRE)**[14] 6829 3-9-7 60 (e) RobbieFitzpatrick 13 64
(Richard Guest) *led and crossed to rail: rdn ent fnl 2f: hdd jst ins fnl f: one pce and outpcd by wnr fnl 100yds* **17/2**
000 4 1/2 **Tatting**[135] 2799 3-9-2 55 GrahamLee 8 58+
(Chris Dwyer) *hld up in last trio: nudged along ent fnl 2f: nt clr run and swtchd lft jst over 1f out: pushed along hands and heels and r.o wl ins fnl f: no threat to wnr* **16/1**
102 5 2 **Waspy**[32] 6281 3-9-6 59 (t) JamieSpencer 6 57
(George Baker) *hld up in tch in midfield: rdn 3f out: drvn and sme hdwy over 1f out: no imp ent fnl f: wknd ins fnl f* **8/1**
0260 6 1/2 **Queen Cassiopeia**[49] 5764 3-9-4 57 EddieAhern 3 54
(J R Jenkins) *chsd ldrs: rdn and unable qck 2f out: btn 1f out: wknd fnl f* **40/1**
4035 7 1 **Arctic Stryker**[14] 6827 3-9-7 60 [1] RobertWinston 4 55
(John Best) *t.k.h: hld up in midfield: effrt u.p and edgd rt over 1f out: no prog and wl hld fnl f* **9/1**
0600 8 2 3/4 **Guava**[36] 6152 3-8-7 53 ShirleyTeasdale(7) 9 41
(Shaun Harris) *chsd ldrs: rdn and unable qck over 2f out: wknd u.p over 1f out* **50/1**
5165 9 1 **Medam**[14] 6823 3-9-4 57 (t) MartinHarley 10 43
(Shaun Harris) *propped leaving stalls and v.s.a: a in rr: rdn 3f out: plugged on but n.d* **20/1**
0540 10 1 1/4 **Bang Tidy (IRE)**[5] 7055 3-9-3 56 BarryMcHugh 5 39
(Brian Ellison) *t.k.h: hld up in last trio: rdn and no hdwy wl over 1f out: wl btn fnl f* **7/1[3]**
464- 11 9 **Glen Ellyn**[356] 7132 3-9-7 60 JoeFanning 12 22
(Mark Johnston) *midfield on outer but niggled along: pushed along and hdwy to chse ldrs 3f out: rdn and no rspnse ent fnl 2f: wknd over 1f out: virtually p.u ins fnl f* **2/1[1]**

1m 50.14s (-0.36) **Going Correction** -0.025s/f (Stan) **11** Ran SP% **120.2**
Speed ratings (Par 99): **100,96,96,95,93 93,92,90,89,88 80**
toteswingers 1&2 £9.60, 2&3 £8.60, 1&3 £11.90 CSF £51.60 CT £402.58 TOTE £6.30: £2.30, £4.20, £3.30; EX 67.40 Trifecta £584.50 Pool: £797.77 - 1.01 winning tickets..
Owner George Houghton **Bred** G Houghton **Trained** Newmarket, Suffolk

FOCUS
A moderate 3yo handicap in which they went a steady gallop. The winner earned a clear personal-best rating.

7202 32RED H'CAP (DIV I) 7f 32y(P)
4:30 (4:31) (Class 5) (0-75,75) 3-Y-O+ **£2,264** (£673; £336; £168) **Stalls** High

Form RPR
1100 1 **Lucky Dan (IRE)**[19] 6665 6-9-6 74 FrannyNorton 7 81
(Paul Green) *t.k.h: chsd ldrs: drvn to ld 1f out: hld on gamely fnl f: all out* **28/1**
5511 2 nk **Pravda Street**[27] 6452 7-9-2 70 TomEaves 1 76
(Brian Ellison) *chsd ldr for 1f: styd chsng ldrs: drvn and ev ch fnl f: edgd rt u.p and unable qck towards fin* **3/1[1]**
45 3 3/4 **Frognal (IRE)**[30] 6329 6-8-8 62 (bt) WilliamCarson 11 66
(Violet M Jordan) *t.k.h: hld up wl in tch in midfield: nt clr run and swtchd rt over 1f out: rdn and chsd ldrs 1f out: kpt on same pce fnl 100yds* **20/1**
0000 4 hd **Crown Choice**[10] 6939 7-9-5 73 PhillipMakin 9 76
(Paul Midgley) *taken down early: stdd s: t.k.h: hld up in tch in rr: clsd and trcking ldrs whn nt clr run over 1f out: rdn and effrt jst ins fnl f: styd on same pce fnl 100yds* **10/1**
1031 5 3/4 **Chookie Avon**[10] 6934 5-9-7 75 (p) JoeFanning 10 76+
(Keith Dalgleish) *chsd ldrs but stuck wd early: grad stdd bk and in last trio 4f out: clsng whn nt clr run and hmpd over 1f out: shkn up and hdwy 1f out: kpt on but nvr able to chal* **4/1[2]**
0060 6 1 3/4 **Dark Falcon (IRE)**[44] 5915 3-8-9 65 EddieAhern 5 62
(James Tate) *led: stl gng wl 2f out: rdn over 1f out: hdd 1f out: no ex and wknd fnl 100yds* **6/1[3]**
0000 7 4 **Ralphy Boy (IRE)**[7] 7004 3-9-0 70 (p) AmyRyan 3 56
(Kevin Ryan) *hmpd and dropped to rr sn after s: rdn and no hdwy 3f out: plugged on but no threat to ldrs fr over 1f out* **8/1**
5005 8 hd **Stellar Express (IRE)**[8] 6986 3-8-13 69 (b) AndrewMullen 4 54
(Michael Appleby) *wnt lft s: rdn to chse ldr after 1f: rdn and ev ch ent fnl 2f: btn over 1f out: wknd fnl f* **7/1**
040 9 nk **Spin Again (IRE)**[30] 6329 7-9-2 70 BrettDoyle 6 55
(John Ryan) *chsd ldrs on outer: rdn and unable qck over 2f out: wknd over 1f out* **20/1**
6500 10 2 **Dhaular Dhar (IRE)**[12] 6881 10-8-10 64 (b[1]) GrahamLee 2 43
(Jim Goldie) *t.k.h: jostling match leaving stalls: hld up in midfield: hmpd and stmbld after 1f: rdn and no hdwy over 1f out: wknd fnl f* **8/1**

1m 28.93s (-0.67) **Going Correction** -0.025s/f (Stan)
WFA 3 from 5yo+ 2lb **10** Ran SP% **116.1**
Speed ratings (Par 103): **102,101,100,100,99 97,93,92,92,90**
toteswingers 1&2 £12.40, 2&3 £6.80, 1&3 £19.40 CSF £107.99 CT £1808.87 TOTE £20.90: £6.40, £1.80, £8.00; EX 78.10 TRIFECTA Not won..

Owner Paul Green (Oaklea) **Bred** Mountarmstrong Stud **Trained** Lydiate, Merseyside

FOCUS

This looks very ordinary form.

7203 32RED H'CAP (DIV II) 7f 32y(P)

5:00 (5:00) (Class 5) (0-75,75) 3-Y-0+ **£2,264** (£673; £336; £168) **Stalls** High

Form RPR

2535 **1** **Sunley Pride**[18] 6701 3-9-1 **71**........ SamHitchcott 7 83
(Mick Channon) *chsd ldrs: rdn to ld and qcknd clr 2f out: drvn and kpt on wl ins fnl f* **7/2**[1]

0506 **2** *2 1/4* **Mcmonagle (USA)**[10] 6934 4-9-2 **70**........(bt) RobertWinston 10 76
(Alan Brown) *t.k.h: hld up in tch: n.m.r over 2f out: rdn and hdwy to chse clr wnr wl over 1f out: kpt on but no imp ins fnl f* **12/1**

6066 **3** *shd* **Dance The Rain**[62] 5314 3-9-5 **75**........(p) TomEaves 5 81+
(Bryan Smart) *hld up towards rr of main gp: stl plenty to do whn swtchd rt and effrt over 2f out: styd on wl u.p ins fnl f: pressing for 2nd cl home: no threat to wnr* **6/1**[3]

0000 **4** *3/4* **Lastkingofscotland (IRE)**[6] 7022 6-8-9 **63**........(b) LukeMorris 6 67
(Conor Dore) *chsd ldrs: drvn and unable qck wl over 1f out: no threat to wnr and kpt on same pce fnl f* **20/1**

030 **5** *3/4* **Rulesn'regulations**[13] 6837 6-9-4 **75**........(v[1]) MichaelMetcalfe(3) 9 77
(Matthew Salaman) *short of room sn after s: hld up in tch: rdn and effrt on inner wl over 1f out: kpt on but no ch w wnr fnl f* **16/1**

0464 **6** *4 1/2* **Compton Prince**[28] 6401 3-8-10 **66**........(b) DaneO'Neill 11 55
(Clive Cox) *in tch: rdn and effrt to chse ldrs on outer over 2f out: unable qck and btn over 1f out: wknd fnl f* **4/1**[2]

2000 **7** *3* **Staff Sergeant**[7] 7000 5-9-4 **72**........ GrahamLee 2 53
(Jim Goldie) *chsd ldr after 1f: rdn to ld over 2f out: sn hdd and unable qck w wnr: wknd over 1f out* **15/2**

-000 **8** *3 1/2* **Master Of Ages (IRE)**[102] 3890 3-9-0 **70**........ JoeFanning 3 42
(Mark Johnston) *slowly away: sn detached in last pair: clsd to bk of main gp 3f out: sn btn and bhd over 1f out* **6/1**[3]

1020 **9** *3 1/4* **Rockme Cockney**[58] 5443 3-8-3 **62**........(p) RaulDaSilva(3) 1 25
(Jeremy Gask) *broke wl and led briefly: steadily lost pl: midfield and rdn 4f out: wknd 2f out* **20/1**

1553 **10** *2* **Joshua The First**[7] 7004 3-9-2 **72**........(p) PaulMulrennan 8 30
(Keith Dalgleish) *s.i.s: sn wl outpcd in rr: n.d* **9/1**

1363 **11** *1/2* **My Own Way Home**[26] 6498 4-8-12 **66**........ TomMcLaughlin 4 27
(David Evans) *sn led: rdn and hdd over 2f out: wknd qckly wl over 1f out: wl bhd and eased wl ins fnl f* **25/1**

1m 28.36s (-1.24) **Going Correction** -0.025s/f (Stan)
WFA 3 from 4yo+ 2lb **11** Ran SP% **119.5**
Speed ratings (Par 103): **106,103,103,102,101 96,93,89,85,83 82**
toteswingers 1&2 £15.30, 2&3 £13.50, 1&3 £5.70 CSF £45.80 CT £254.41 TOTE £3.50: £2.00, £5.20, £3.10; EX 46.00 Trifecta £397.20 Pool: £982.46 - 1.83 winning tickets..
Owner James Sunley **Bred** Sunley Stud **Trained** West Ilsley, Berks

FOCUS

The second division of a fair handicap for 3yos and up in which the winner recorded the best comparative time on the card. The form looks solid.

7204 32RED BINGO H'CAP 5f 216y(P)

5:35 (5:35) (Class 6) (0-55,55) 3-Y-0+ **£1,704** (£503; £251) **Stalls** Low

Form RPR

3004 **1** **Ryedale Dancer (IRE)**[15] 6782 4-9-1 **52**........ RobbieFitzpatrick 4 63
(Richard Guest) *stdd s: hld up in rr: hdwy 1/2-way: chsd ldrs and swtchd rt 1f out: str run to ld fnl 75yds: r.o wl and gng away at fin* **9/1**

0004 **2** *1 1/2* **Irie Ute**[8] 6982 4-9-4 **55**........ DaneO'Neill 6 61
(Sylvester Kirk) *chsd ldrs: rdn to press ldr whn carried rt and hmpd over 1f out: drvn to ld 1f out: edgd rt u.p and hdd fnl 75yds* **9/2**[1]

0000 **3** *3/4* **Music Festival (USA)**[38] 6106 5-9-1 **52**........ FrederikTylicki 10 56
(Jim Goldie) *hld up towards rr: nt clr run wl over 1f out: edging lft and hdwy ent fnl f: r.o wl fnl 100yds* **9/2**[1]

3633 **4** *1* **Dixie Gwalia**[86] 4422 4-8-9 **53**........ SiobhanMiller(7) 13 54
(David Simcock) *stuck wd early: towards rr: edging lft and hdwy over 1f out: styd on wl ins fnl f: nt rch ldrs* **20/1**

5026 **5** *1* **Majestic Breeze (IRE)**[10] 6937 3-8-8 **53**........(p) DavidSimmonson(7) 5 50
(Brian Ellison) *sn pushed along towards rr: hdwy into midfield 1/2-way: styd on same pce fnl f* **9/2**[1]

0000 **6** *shd* **North Central (USA)**[26] 6480 5-9-2 **53**........(p) JoeFanning 11 50
(Keith Dalgleish) *hld up towards rr: rdn and effrt over 1f out: edging lft and hdwy over 1f out: n.m.r jst ins fnl f: styd on: nvr able to chal* **10/1**

404 **7** *1/2* **Headstight (IRE)**[9] 6958 3-9-0 **52**........ MickyFenton 1 47
(Paul Midgley) *led: edgd rt and bmpd over 1f out: hdd 1f out: wknd ins fnl f* **8/1**[3]

5052 **8** *1* **Lisselton Cross**[22] 6585 4-9-2 **53**........(b) LukeMorris 2 45
(Martin Bosley) *chsd ldrs: drvn and pressed ldrs over 1f out: wknd ins fnl f* **7/1**[2]

6646 **9** *1* **Poseidon Grey (IRE)**[31] 6321 3-9-1 **53**........ LiamJones 7 42
(Ian Williams) *chsd ldrs: effrt and finding little whn sltly hmpd over 1f out: wknd 1f out* **14/1**

06-0 **10** *1 1/4* **Schoolboy Champ**[20] 6640 5-8-8 **52**........(vt) ShirleyTeasdale(7) 12 37
(Lisa Williamson) *rn wout declared tongue-tie: taken down early: a towards rr: rdn and no hdwy over 2f out: nvr trbld ldrs* **25/1**

2506 **11** *7* **Blueberry Fizz (IRE)**[1] 7157 4-9-4 **55**........(p) DaraghO'Donohoe 9 17
(John Ryan) *sn outpcd in rr: n.d* **16/1**

55-0 **12** *3/4* **Turn The Tide**[15] 6773 4-8-12 **52**........ SimonPearce(3) 8 12
(Dai Williams) *stdd s: hld up in rr: rdn and no hdwy 2f out: bhd fnl f* **50/1**

-500 **13** *3/4* **Dubai Rythm**[14] 6806 3-9-3 **55**........(b) AndrewMullen 3 13
(Michael Appleby) *pressed ldr: rdn ent fnl 2f: sn struggling: wknd over 1f out* **25/1**

1m 15.54s (0.54) **Going Correction** -0.025s/f (Stan)
WFA 3 from 4yo+ 1lb **13** Ran SP% **124.2**
Speed ratings (Par 101): **95,93,92,90,89 89,88,87,85,84 74,73,72**
toteswingers 1&2 £10.60, 2&3 £3.50, 1&3 £8.30 CSF £49.21 CT £221.34 TOTE £14.70: £4.50, £2.80, £1.70; EX 47.80 Trifecta £50.90 Pool £426.67 - 6.20 winning tickets..
Owner Future Racing (Notts) Limited **Bred** Max Morris **Trained** Stainforth, S Yorks

FOCUS

A moderate sprint handicap for 3yos and up. The winner has been rated close to this year's turf form, while the runner-up has been rated back to form.

Headstight(IRE) Official explanation: jockey said that the filly hung right-handed

Schoolboy Champ Official explanation: trainer said gelding ran without tongue strap that had come adrift and couldn't be re-fitted.

Turn The Tide Official explanation: joceky said that the filly was never travelling

T/Plt: £120.60 to a £1 stake. Pool: £61,165.82 - 370.20 winning tickets. T/Qpdt: £23.40 to a £1 stake. Pool: £5,617.81 - 177.46 winning tickets. SP

6664 HAYDOCK (L-H)

Friday, October 19

OFFICIAL GOING: Heavy

Wind: Nil Weather: Light Cloud

7205 BETFAIR CHASE 24TH NOVEMBER MAIDEN STKS 1m 2f 95y

1:55 (1:56) (Class 5) 2-Y-0 **£2,264** (£673; £336; £168) **Stalls** High

Form RPR

05 **1** **Rhombus (IRE)**[71] 4995 2-9-3 0........ RyanMoore 6 73+
(William Haggas) *hld up: hdwy to chse ldrs over 2f out: wnt 2nd wl over 1f out: chalng ins fnl f: styd on to ld towards fin* **4/1**[2]

022 **2** *1/2* **Esteaming**[7] 7033 2-9-3 0........ MartinHarley 5 72
(Mick Channon) *a.p: led over 3f out: hung lft ins fnl f: hdd and hld towards fin* **4/6**[1]

055 **3** *6* **Afro**[23] 6572 2-8-12 60........ ChrisCatlin 4 56
(Peter Hedger) *in rr: niggled along over 3f out: no imp u.p over 2f out: kpt on to take 3rd over 1f out: n.d to front two* **33/1**

0 **4** *2 1/4* **Angilina**[62] 5339 2-8-12 0........ RobertWinston 3 52
(Kevin Ryan) *led: pushed along 4f out: hdd over 3f out: wknd over 1f out* **12/1**

0 **5** *2 1/4* **Grendisar (IRE)**[13] 6876 2-9-3 0........ AdamKirby 2 52
(Marco Botti) *prom: pushed along briefly 5f out: ev ch 3f out: btn over 1f out: wknd fnl f* **7/1**[3]

6 *1 1/2* **Jebulani** 2-9-3 0........ DanielTudhope 1 50
(David O'Meara) *trckd ldrs: effrt 3f out: wl btn over 1f out* **16/1**

2m 22.22s (6.72) **Going Correction** +0.475s/f (Yiel) **6** Ran SP% **109.0**
Speed ratings (Par 95): **92,91,86,85,83 82**
toteswingers 1&2 £1.10, 2&3 £2.60, 1&3 £6.00 CSF £6.64 TOTE £3.40: £2.10, £1.10; EX 7.30.
Owner Sheikh Rashid Dalmook Al Maktoum **Bred** Ruskerne Ltd **Trained** Newmarket, Suffolk

FOCUS

All races on outer home straight. Races on Round course increased by 26yds except last race which increased by 31yds. A fair juvenile maiden in which they went a sensible gallop over this stiff extended 1m2f trip. The winning time was nearly 13 seconds slower than standard. The third helps set the level.

NOTEBOOK

Rhombus(IRE), who cost 90,000gns as a yearling and whose pedigree screams stamina on both sides, was returning from a ten-week break and had been gelded in the meantime. He produced modest form at up to 1m on both his previous starts on good to firm/good ground in July/August. His jockey Ryan Moore was content to sit and watch the action unfold for a spell up the home straight. He asked the serious questions from 2f out and stuck resolutely to the centre of the track. He outstayed the runner-up, getting on top well inside the final furlong on testing ground he clearly relishes. He looks a fair to decent middle-distance handicapper for next term. (op 9-2 tchd 7-2)

Esteaming arrived with a BHA rating of 75 and looks to have run to a similar mark once again faced with the stiffest stamina test of his career. He looks a fair 1m2f handicapper for next year on a better surface. (op 8-15)

Afro was a significant way behind the principals. She ran to an RPR of 56 on her third start over 1f shorter on soft ground at Goodwood the previous month, and may have improved slightly on that level here. (op 40-1)

Angilina was returning from a two-month break since a moderate 1m Doncaster debut on good ground in August. She showed improved form here but ultimately found this too much of a stamina test on the ground at this stage of her career. (op 14-1)

Grendisar(IRE) showed up early but weakened in these conditions from about 1f out. (op 9-1 tchd 13-2)

Jebulani, making his debut, was too keen early on and paid for it in the closing stages. (op 20-1 tchd 25-1)

7206 BACK OR LAY AT BETDAQ.COM NURSERY 5f

2:25 (2:26) (Class 2) 2-Y-0 **£7,633** (£2,271; £1,135; £567) **Stalls** Low

Form RPR

101 **1** **Dutch Masterpiece**[11] 6929 2-9-7 **86** 6ex........ RyanMoore 7 90+
(Gary Moore) *mde all: rdn over 1f out: edgd rt ins fnl f: kpt on wl* **4/6**[1]

0020 **2** *1 1/4* **Blue Lotus (IRE)**[13] 6883 2-8-13 **78** ow2........ DanielTudhope 3 77
(Tim Easterby) *trckd ldrs: chsd wnr over 2f out: kpt on u.p fnl f* **10/1**

1624 **3** *2 1/2* **Effie B**[7] 7028 2-9-5 **84**........ MartinHarley 6 74
(Mick Channon) *hld up: hdwy 2f out: rdn over 1f out: kpt on same pce* **8/1**[3]

125 **4** *1 3/4* **Tumblewind**[41] 6032 2-8-3 **68**........ PaulQuinn 1 52
(Richard Whitaker) *hld up: hdwy over 1f out: sn rdn and no imp ins fnl f* **22/1**

1501 **5** *2* **Secret Look**[34] 6238 2-9-7 **86**........ RobertWinston 4 63
(Ed McMahon) *trckd ldrs: lost pl 2f out: n.d after* **5/1**[2]

110 **6** *1* **Lady Phill**[121] 3269 2-9-5 **84**........ JoeFanning 2 58
(Bill Turner) *prom: rdn 2f out: wknd over 1f out* **14/1**

0140 **7** *9* **Somethingboutmary**[22] 6611 2-8-5 **70**........(p) AmyRyan 5 12
(Kevin Ryan) *in rr: pushed along over 2f out: edgd lft and outpcd over 1f out* **33/1**

1m 2.02s (1.22) **Going Correction** +0.225s/f (Good) **7** Ran SP% **110.8**
Speed ratings (Par 101): **99,97,93,90,87 85,71**
toteswingers 1&2 £2.70, 2&3 £4.60, 1&3 £2.20 CSF £7.80 TOTE £1.70: £1.20, £3.70; EX 9.10.
Owner R A Green **Bred** Bumble Bloodstock Ltd **Trained** Lower Beeding, W Sussex

FOCUS

A decent nursery sprint handicap in which they went an honest gallop on the testing ground. The winning time was over three seconds slower than standard, which does suggest the ground wasn't as bad as might have been expected on the straight course. The runner-up has been rated to his best.

NOTEBOOK

Dutch Masterpiece, who won readily off 6lb lower at Windsor last time, wanted to get on with things from the outset, racing towards the far side, and jockey Ryan Moore let him bowl on. He was asked for a winning effort well inside the 2f marker, and found plenty for pressure, despite edging to his left across the track. He is a good sprint prospect, and he's entered in a novice stakes over 1f further back on the Fibresand next week. (op 5-6)

Blue Lotus(IRE), who won his maiden over this 5f trip on soft ground in June, looks to have run right up to his best here back on testing ground, particularly with his jockey putting up 2lb overweight. (tchd 12-1)

Effie B, already competing in her 14th start, put in her usual game effort in third. (op 9-1)

Tumblewind, who was returning from a six-week break, performed respectably. (op 14-1)

Secret Look, a C&D winner on soft, did not run up to form on this occasion. (tchd 11-2)

7207 HAYDOCK PARK ANNUAL BADGEHOLDERS CONDITIONS STKS 7f

3:00 (3:00) (Class 3) 2-Y-0 **£5,822** (£1,732; £865; £432) **Stalls** Low

Form RPR

3036 **1** **Pure Excellence**[13] 6883 2-8-9 87........ JoeFanning 4 86
(Mark Johnston) *chsd ldr: rdn over 2f out: styd on to ld wl ins fnl f* **11/8**[1]

322 **2** 3/4 **Bravo Youmzain (IRE)**[25] 6540 2-9-0 88 .... AdamKirby 2 89
(Marco Botti) *led: rdn over 1f out: hdd wl ins fnl f* **7/2**[3]
1 **3** 2 1/4 **Hay Dude**[28] 6423 2-8-11 0 .... MichaelMetcalfe(3) 3 83
(Mrs K Burke) *hld up: effrt over 1f out: styd on same pce ins fnl f* **6/4**[2]
041 **4** 11 **Exzachary**[25] 6524 2-9-0 79 .... J-PGuillambert 1 55
(Jo Hughes) *hld up: pushed along over 3f out: btn over 1f out* **18/1**
1m 33.39s (2.69) **Going Correction** +0.475s/f (Yiel) **4** Ran SP% **109.6**
Speed ratings (Par 99): **103,102,99,87**
CSF £6.46 TOTE £2.70; EX 5.40.
Owner Excellence Racing **Bred** Peter Harris **Trained** Middleham Moor, N Yorks

FOCUS
A decent quality juvenile conditions contest in which they went a sensible gallop on the testing surface, and raced middle to far side entering the home straight. The runner-up looked unlucky and has been rated as improving 6lb.

NOTEBOOK
Pure Excellence, who arrived with a BHA rating of 87, produced a gritty second career victory, finally getting on top well inside the final furlong after being asked the question in behind the front-running runner-up 2f out. She looks a decent filly in the making, probably at up to 1m2f next term. (op 15-8)
Bravo Youmzain(IRE) arrived with a BHA rating of 88 but remains a maiden after five starts. He didn't go down through lack of application here, and appeared to stay 7f fine on the testing surface. He should win his maiden, and is a good handicapper in the making in any case, possibly at up to 1m for next term. (op 4-1 tchd 9-2)
Hay Dude, who won his debut readily over this trip on heavy ground at Ayr the previous month, loomed up going well about 3f out but failed to find as much as might have been anticipated. He remains an interesting prospective miler for next term. (op 5-4 tchd 6-5)

7208 HAYDOCK PARK'S RIO CARNIVAL CHRISTMAS PARTIES MAIDEN STKS 1m
3:35 (3:35) (Class 5) 2-Y-O **£2,264** (£673; £336; £168) **Stalls** Low

Form RPR
1 **Geordie Man** 2-9-3 0 .... RyanMoore 3 77+
(Pat Eddery) *chsd ldrs: pushed along over 3f out: led over 2f out: edgd rt fr over 1f out: edgd lft wl ins fnl f: styd on* **9/2**[3]
2 1/2 **Butterfly McQueen (USA)** 2-8-12 0 .... DavidProbert 5 71
(Andrew Balding) *chsd ldrs: effrt 2f out: wnt 2nd and hung lft over 1f out: styd on ins fnl f* **5/2**[2]
3 8 **Cool Runnings (IRE)** 2-9-3 0 .... RichardKingscote 6 57+
(Tom Dascombe) *s.i.s: bhd: kpt on ins fnl f: no ch w front two* **9/4**[1]
4 1 1/4 **Unknown Villain (IRE)** 2-9-3 0 .... StephenCraine 2 55
(Tom Dascombe) *hld up: hdwy 4f out: led briefly wl over 2f out: one pce fr over 1f out* **5/1**
00 **5** 6 **Silvio Dante (USA)**[36] 6175 2-9-3 0 .... DanielTudhope 4 41
(David O'Meara) *swtg: chsd ldr: led 3f out: sn hdd & wknd over 1f out* **11/1**
05 **6** 13 **Flying Nellie**[22] 6607 2-8-12 0 .... MickyFenton 1
(Tom Tate) *t.k.h: led: pushed along and hdd 3f out: wknd 2f out* **16/1**
1m 48.16s (4.46) **Going Correction** +0.475s/f (Yiel) **6** Ran SP% **108.4**
Speed ratings (Par 95): **96,95,87,86,80 67**
toteswingers 1&2 £2.50, 2&3 £2.20, 1&3 £2.60 CSF £14.99 TOTE £4.20: £1.30, £2.20; EX 11.40.
Owner Leo Daly **Bred** Hugh M Hurst **Trained** Nether Winchendon, Bucks

FOCUS
A modest juvenile maiden in terms of prior form. The winner was a bit wayward in front and has been rated to the race's average.

NOTEBOOK
Geordie Man cost 20,000GBP as a yearling and has a pretty stout pedigree. He was asked for his effort 3f out and was in the lead a furlong later. He had matters in hand thereafter, but did drift to his left, through inexperience, over 1f out, before being corrected by jockey Ryan Moore and edging to his right in the closing stages. He looks a nice prospective 1m2f/1m4f horse for next term. (op 11-2)
Butterfly McQueen(USA), who is closely related to a winner in the USA by Smart Strike, performed well here on her debut. She can win something similar and looks a decent prospective 1m/1m2f filly on better ground for next term. (op 7-2)
Cool Runnings(IRE) missed the break and raced green early in the race but kept on well enough into third, although some was behind the first two. He can build on this initial experience. (op 11-4 tchd 2-1)
Unknown Villain(IRE) produced a respectable debut display and should appreciate 1m on soft ground next term. (op 7-2)
Silvio Dante(USA), who was having his first start for a new trainer after leaving Kevin Ryan, weakened in the conditions about 2f out. (op 6-1)

7209 ARNOLD CLARK JEEP CHRYSLER NURSERY 1m
4:10 (4:11) (Class 2) 2-Y-O **£7,633** (£2,271; £1,135; £567) **Stalls** Low

Form RPR
1 **1** **Polar Chief**[87] 4427 2-8-12 74 .... PatrickMathers 2 76+
(Linda Stubbs) *hld up: effrt 2f out: led 1f out: hld on wl* **11/1**
2421 **2** nk **Dr Phibes (IRE)**[19] 6708 2-9-2 78 .... RobertWinston 3 79
(Alan Swinbank) *led: rdn over 1f out: sn hdd: rallied towards fin* **5/2**[2]
152 **3** 2 3/4 **Arthurs Secret**[43] 5969 2-9-7 83 .... MichaelO'Connell 4 78
(John Quinn) *w ldr: rdn and ev ch 2f out: u.p whn swtchd lft ins fnl f: one pce after* **3/1**[3]
61 **4** 5 **Allnecessaryforce (FR)**[16] 6779 2-8-9 71 .... FrederikTylicki 1 54
(Richard Fahey) *in rr: sn niggled along: rdn over 2f out: btn over 1f out* **2/1**[1]
2031 **5** 17 **Bix (IRE)**[26] 6512 2-8-13 75 ow2 .... DanielTudhope 5
(Alan Berry) *trckd ldrs: pushed along over 3f out: hung lft and wknd 2f out: eased whn wl btn over 1f out* **6/1**
1m 49.6s (5.90) **Going Correction** +0.475s/f (Yiel) **5** Ran SP% **109.5**
Speed ratings (Par 101): **89,88,85,80,63**
CSF £37.69 TOTE £8.60: £4.00, £1.60; EX 29.40.
Owner P & L Partners **Bred** J W Mitchell **Trained** Norton, N Yorks

FOCUS
A decent nursery rated around the runner-up to a small personal best.

NOTEBOOK
Polar Chief, returning from a three-month break, was competing off a fair initial mark of 74 and did well to win under these conditions, having pulled hard early on. He followed the two leaders over to the near side up the home straight, and his jockey chose to produce him on their outside, just off the rail, 2f out. He took over 1f out and held on gamely. He is a decent handicapper at up to 1m2f for next term. (op 6-1)
Dr Phibes(IRE) got off the mark at the seventh attempt in a 7f Musselburgh maiden on good to soft ground the previous month. He rallied gamely once headed a furlong out and looks a fair 1m handicapper in the making. (op 11-4 tchd 9-4)
Arthurs Secret was returning from a six-week break and it showed, in that when left by the front two over 1f out it looked as if he may lose out by a lot further than 3l. He may build on this respectable display in the final few weeks of the season. (op 9-2 tchd 11-4)
Allnecessaryforce(FR) was restless beforehand and his mind just wasn't on the job in hand. (op 11-4)

7210 MH CONSTRUCTION H'CAP 1m
4:45 (4:45) (Class 3) (0-95,95) 3-Y-O+ **£6,663** (£1,982; £990; £495) **Stalls** Low

Form RPR
1032 **1** **Benzanno (IRE)**[19] 6701 3-8-4 81 oh1 .... DavidProbert 9 93
(Andrew Balding) *midfield: hdwy over 3f out: led over 1f out: hung lft ent fnl f: sn clr: eased cl home* **9/1**
4211 **2** 4 **Chosen Character (IRE)**[21] 6630 4-8-12 91 ....(vt) NatashaEaton(5) 3 94
(Tom Dascombe) *led: rdn 2f out: hdd over 1f out: no ch w wnr ins fnl f* **4/1**[2]
0332 **3** shd **Toto Skyllachy**[31] 6338 7-8-13 87 .... DanielTudhope 6 90
(David O'Meara) *trckd ldrs: rdn 2f out: hung lft over 1f out: kpt on u.p fnl f* **10/1**
3452 **4** 1 **Crown Counsel (IRE)**[6] 7069 4-8-9 83 .... JoeFanning 5 83
(Mark Johnston) *w ldr tl rdn over 2f out and one pce fr over 1f out* **11/4**[1]
0044 **5** hd **Al Muheer (IRE)**[20] 6670 7-8-11 85 ....(b) JamesSullivan 11 85
(Ruth Carr) *hld up: rdn and hdwy over 1f out: styd on towards fin* **25/1**
0000 **6** 3/4 **Justonefortheroad**[55] 5572 6-8-11 92 .... GeorgeChaloner(7) 2 90
(Richard Fahey) *midfield: pushed along over 3f out: kpt on ins fnl f: nvr able to chal* **22/1**
0626 **7** 3 **Extraterrestrial**[21] 6630 8-8-12 86 .... FrederikTylicki 1 77
(Richard Fahey) *midfield: rdn and hdwy to chse ldrs 2f out: wknd ins fnl f* **11/1**
5650 **8** 1/2 **Kyllachy Star**[20] 6659 6-8-9 83 .... EddieAhern 4 73
(Richard Fahey) *trckd ldrs: rdn 3f out: wknd over 1f out* **16/1**
0000 **9** 1 1/4 **Viva Ronaldo (IRE)**[34] 6235 6-8-7 81 .... PatrickMathers 7 68
(Richard Fahey) *in rr: rdn 4f out: nvr on terms* **33/1**
0000 **10** 24 **Talwar (IRE)**[29] 6400 3-9-4 95 .... RyanMoore 13 27
(Jeremy Noseda) *towards rr: struggling over 2f out: nvr on terms* **20/1**
0003 **11** 1 1/4 **Tiger Reigns**[21] 6630 6-8-8 82 .... RobertWinston 8 11
(Michael Dods) *in tch: rdn over 2f out: wknd over 1f out* **6/1**[3]
2414 **12** 3/4 **Muffin McLeay (IRE)**[17] 6757 4-9-4 92 .... GrahamGibbons 14 20
(David Barron) *hld up: pushed along 2f out: nvr on terms* **16/1**
1m 46.06s (2.36) **Going Correction** +0.475s/f (Yiel)
WFA 3 from 4yo+ 3lb **12** Ran SP% **116.0**
Speed ratings (Par 107): **107,103,102,101,101 100,97,97,96,72 70,70**
toteswingers 1&2 £7.80, 2&3 £6.00, 1&3 £6.00 CSF £41.66 CT £378.18 TOTE £8.80: £2.30, £1.40, £2.70; EX 44.10 Trifecta £260.20 Pool: £1476.84 - 4.20 winning units..
Owner Martin & Valerie Slade & Partner **Bred** Nanallac Stud **Trained** Kingsclere, Hants
■ Stewards' Enquiry : David Probert caution: careless riding.

FOCUS
A good class handicap for 3yos and up in which the winner recorded the best comparative winning time on the card from the six races on the round course. The runner-up and third have been rated close to their marks.

NOTEBOOK
Benzanno(IRE) ◆ was racing off a 2lb higher mark than for a peak second over an extended 1m at Epsom the previous month. He raced in touch and came through on the outside of the pack, who were racing up the centre of the course in the straight, to quicken away over 1f out. He drifted to his left onto the far rail when tiring in the closing stages but produced a commanding second career victory. He is progressing well and may be able to find another opening before the season draws to a close. (op 14-1 tchd 10-1)
Chosen Character(IRE) was competing off a 21lb higher mark than for the first of his five successes this term, which came over this C&D in July. He produced his usual solid performance but ran into a progressive younger rival on this occasion.
Toto Skyllachy appears slightly high in the weights but is running consistently well without winning. (tchd 11-1)
Crown Counsel(IRE) finished a good second off this mark over a longer trip on softer ground just six days prior to this contest at York. He ran on one-paced into fourth from over 1f out dropped back to 1m here. (op 9-2)
Al Muheer(IRE) was held up and made some cheap late headway into fifth.
Justonefortheroad ran respectably returning from a two-month break. (op 25-1 tchd 28-1)
Talwar(IRE) Official explanation: trainer's rep said gelding was unsuited by the heavy ground
Tiger Reigns had good recent form with the second horse but performed disappointingly here. Official explanation: jockey said gelding ran too free (op 5-1)

7211 DOWNLOAD THE FREE RACING UK IPHONE APP H'CAP 2m 45y
5:20 (5:21) (Class 4) (0-85,84) 3-Y-O+ **£4,075** (£1,212; £606; £303) **Stalls** Low

Form RPR
2522 **1** **Yours Ever**[64] 5256 3-8-10 76 .... ChrisCatlin 5 85+
(Sir Mark Prescott Bt) *mde all: rdn wl over 1f out: styd on to draw clr and edgd lft ins fnl f: eased cl home* **7/4**[2]
20-4 **2** 7 **Zakatal**[49] 5798 6-9-8 78 .... RobertWinston 1 77
(Julie Camacho) *stdd s: hld up: hdwy 3f out: wnt 2nd 2f out: no ch w wnr fnl f* **9/1**
101 **3** 1 3/4 **New Youmzain (FR)**[48] 5830 3-9-4 84 .... MartinHarley 2 81
(Mick Channon) *chsd ldrs: rdn and outpcd over 2f out: kpt on modly to take 3rd wl ins fnl f* **6/4**[1]
4/61 **4** 1 3/4 **General Ting (IRE)**[160] 2086 7-8-13 69 ....(t) EddieAhern 3 64
(Lucy Wadham) *chsd wnr tl rdn 2f out and wknd fnl f* **5/1**[3]
066/ **5** 48 **Secret Dancer (IRE)**[265] 6563 7-9-2 72 .... DanielTudhope 4
(Alan Jones) *stdd s: hld up in rr: pushed along 4f out: lost tch 3f out: t.o* **20/1**
3m 46.92s (12.62) **Going Correction** +0.475s/f (Yiel)
WFA 3 from 6yo+ 10lb **5** Ran SP% **107.8**
Speed ratings (Par 105): **87,83,82,81,57**
CSF £15.56 TOTE £2.50: £1.70, £3.40; EX 13.90.
Owner Cheveley Park Stud **Bred** Mr & Mrs G Middlebrook **Trained** Newmarket, Suffolk

FOCUS
A fair staying handicap in which they went a sensible gallop in the testing ground. The winner, who made all, has been rated as running a small personal best.
T/Plt: £72.10 to a £1 stake. Pool of £49907.61 - 504.67 winning tickets. T/Qpdt: £55.40 to a £1 stake. Pool of £3125.31 - 41.68 winning tickets. DO

6880 REDCAR (L-H)
Friday, October 19
7212 Meeting Abandoned - Waterlogged

7197 WOLVERHAMPTON (A.W) (L-H)

Friday, October 19

OFFICIAL GOING: Standard

Wind: Almost nil Weather: Overcast

7218 32RED APPRENTICE H'CAP — 5f 216y(P)

5:50 (5:50) (Class 6) (0-65,65) 3-Y-0+ £1,704 (£503; £251) Stalls Low

Form RPR

0-00 **1** **Above Standard (IRE)**[54] 5618 4-8-12 64.........(t) DavidSimmonson(5) 8 84+
(Michael Easterby) *led early: chsd ldrs: led over 1f out: edgd lft and pushed clr fnl f* **7/4**[1]

0605 **2** *4* **Ginger Ted (IRE)**[2] 7178 5-9-3 64...............................(tp) CharlesBishop 9 71
(Stuart Williams) *hld up: hdwy over 1f out: r.o to go 2nd ins fnl f: no ch w wnr* **10/3**[2]

4430 **3** *1 3/4* **Dark Lane**[3] 7141 6-9-0 64.. NathanSweeney(3) 12 65
(David Evans) *prom: rdn over 2f out: no ex fnl f* **4/1**[3]

5625 **4** *nk* **Powerful Pierre**[7] 7022 5-9-2 63..(v) LMcNiff 11 63
(Ian McInnes) *mid-div: rdn over 2f out: styd on same pce fr over 1f out* **9/1**

2054 **5** *4 1/2* **Silkee Supreme**[6] 7061 3-8-10 65........................(b) MeganWhitehead(7) 1 51
(Richard Hannon) *sn pushed along and prom: rdn over 2f out: wknd fnl f* **16/1**

3000 **6** *1/2* **Choice Words (USA)**[11] 6926 4-9-1 65..................(t) ThomasBrown(3) 2 49
(Natalie Lloyd-Beavis) *prom: chsd ldr over 4f out: led wl over 1f out: sn hdd: wknd ins fnl f* **66/1**

2400 **7** *shd* **Man Of My Word**[130] 2981 3-8-11 64..........................(p) JordanUys(5) 10 48
(Scott Dixon) *prom: rdn over 2f out: wknd over 1f out* **40/1**

6022 **8** *1* **Mister Mackenzie**[17] 6765 3-9-3 65................................ TobyAtkinson 6 46
(John Best) *s.i.s: hld up: drvn along over 2f out: nvr on terms* **7/1**

0500 **9** *2* **Volcanic Dust (IRE)**[39] 6094 4-9-4 65....................(p) MatthewLawson 5 40
(Milton Bradley) *s.s: hld up: plld hrd: hdwy u.p over 2f out: wknd over 1f out* **33/1**

3536 **10** *1 1/2* **Chester'Slittlegem (IRE)**[128] 3044 3-8-9 64......... MatthewMcGhee(7) 7 34
(Lisa Williamson) *sn led: hdd wl over 1f out: sn wknd* **33/1**

2060 **11** *5* **Chjimes (IRE)**[41] 6053 8-9-2 63.......................................(b) DavidKenny 3 17
(Conor Dore) *hld up: rdn over 2f out: a in rr* **33/1**

0115 **F** **Juarla (IRE)**[49] 5808 4-9-3 64.. DarrenEgan 13
(Ronald Harris) *sn outpcd: bhd whn fell wl over 1f out: fatally injured* **11/1**

1m 13.64s (-1.36) **Going Correction** -0.125s/f (Stan)
WFA 3 from 4yo+ 1lb 12 Ran SP% **128.9**
Speed ratings (Par 101): **104,98,96,95,89 89,89,87,85,83 76,**
toteswingers 1&2 £4.70, 2&3 £7.10, 1&3 £6.50 CSF £7.99 CT £23.05 TOTE £5.20: £1.70, £1.70, £2.10; EX 17.70 Trifecta £112.00 Pool: £413.26 - 2.73 winning tickets..
Owner A Saha **Bred** Sandro Garavelli **Trained** Sheriff Hutton, N Yorks

FOCUS
There was a good gallop from the word go, which gives substance to the winner's visually impressive performance. He's been rated to his best.
Mister Mackenzie Official explanation: jockey said gelding anticipated the start

7219 BOOK HORIZONS RESTAURANT MEDIAN AUCTION MAIDEN STKS 5f 216y(P)

6:20 (7:03) (Class 6) 2-Y-0 £1,704 (£503; £251) Stalls Low

Form RPR

050 **1** **Work Ethic (IRE)**[16] 6787 2-9-3 68.................................. SebSanders 13 71
(Gerard Butler) *a.p: chsd ldr over 3f out: led over 1f out: rdn clr ins fnl f* **5/1**[3]

2060 **2** *2 3/4* **Pearl Noir**[9] 6980 2-9-3 71.. TomQueally 1 62
(Scott Dixon) *led: rdn and hdd over 1f out: styd on same pce ins fnl f* **7/4**[1]

3 *1* **Golden Pursuit** 2-9-3 0.. RichardKingscote 12 59+
(Tom Dascombe) *sn outpcd: hdwy over 1f out: r.o: nt rch ldrs* **8/1**

30 **4** *3/4* **Mr Paranoia**[16] 6787 2-9-3 0...(b[1]) MartinDwyer 7 57
(Conrad Allen) *sn chsng ldrs: rdn over 1f out: no ex ins fnl f* **7/2**[2]

5 *3 1/4* **Be On The Bell** 2-8-12 0... SeanQuinlan 8 41
(Jamie Osborne) *s.s: hdwy over 2f out: wknd fnl f* **33/1**

06 **6** *2 1/2* **She's Some Girl (IRE)**[13] 6889 2-8-12 0............................ AmyRyan 10 33
(Richard Fahey) *mid-div: sn pushed along: outpcd 1/2-way: n.d after* **50/1**

7 *1 3/4* **Ada Lovelace** 2-8-12 0... BrettDoyle 11 28
(Dean Ivory) *s.s: hdwy over 2f out: rdn and wknd over 1f out* **40/1**

8 *1 3/4* **Indian Lass (IRE)** 2-8-12 0.. LukeMorris 2 22
(John Best) *sn pushed along and prom: drvn along 1/2-way: wknd over 2f out* **20/1**

0 **9** *7* **Cash Rich**[25] 6533 2-9-3 0... AdamKirby 5
(Jamie Osborne) *s.s: outpcd* **20/1**

10 *nk* **Loulou Vuitton** 2-8-12 0.. WilliamCarson 4
(Brian Baugh) *s.s: a wl bhd* **66/1**

11 *6* **Ichimoku** 2-9-3 0.. TomEaves 9
(Bryan Smart) *racd keenly: trckd ldr tl over 3f out: sn rdn: wknd 2f out* **13/2**

12 *10* **Rovers Till I Die (IRE)** 2-9-0 0....................................... MarkCoumbe(3) 3
(Charles Smith) *s.s: outpcd* **80/1**

1m 15.32s (0.32) **Going Correction** -0.125s/f (Stan) 12 Ran SP% **119.3**
Speed ratings (Par 93): **92,88,87,86,81 78,76,73,64,63 55,42**
toteswingers 1&2 £2.70, 2&3 £5.40, 1&3 £4.70 CSF £13.40 TOTE £7.30: £2.60, £1.30, £2.00; EX 16.00 Trifecta £92.00 Pool: £708.10 - 5.69 winning tickets..
Owner K Quinn/ C Benham/ I Saunders **Bred** Philip Brady **Trained** Newmarket, Suffolk

FOCUS
This was 43 minutes late off owing to the absence of the ambulance which had taken jockey Darren Egan to hospital after his fall in the previous race. The fact that the first two home were the most experienced suggests that the form isn't great, but there were a few promising performances further down the field. The pace was good and the winner has been rated as running a personal best.

NOTEBOOK
Work Ethic(IRE), who had more experience than most of his rivals, had shown some promise on turf but this surface seemed to be ideal. The step up to 6f was in his favour, and on this evidence a return to 7f should be within his scope. (op 6-1)
Pearl Noir didn't appear to stay 7f last time, so the drop back in trip suited him. He is getting a bit exposed, but he has finished second in three of his six starts and is rated 71, so he might yet win a maiden. (op 5-2 tchd 11-4)
Golden Pursuit ◆, a 6,500gns Pastoral Pursuits half-brother to winners over multiple trips, made an eyecatching debut. There is Polytrack form in his family, and it would be no surprise to see him win at the second time of asking. (op 17-2 tchd 7-1)
Mr Paranoia, wearing first-time blinkers, made a satisfactory Polytrack debut but probably only replicated his turf form. 6f at this tempo stretches him at present, and he may be more at home in 5f nurseries for the time being.
Be On The Bell, out of a 6f Fibresand winner, and half-sister to two more sprint winners, is one to keep an eye on. She didn't do badly after missing the break and can do better with experience. (op 25-1)
She's Some Girl(IRE) looks unlikely to win a maiden, and she shouldn't get too high a mark now she is qualified for nurseries, so there may be a little better to come. (tchd 40-1)
Ada Lovelace, whose dam won over 1m on sand, showed promise considering the combination of a slow start and a wide stall. She should improve. (op 28-1)
Cash Rich Official explanation: jockey said colt missed the break
Loulou Vuitton Official explanation: jockey said filly reared leaving stalls

7220 32RED.COM NURSERY — 5f 20y(P)

6:50 (7:25) (Class 4) (0-80,79) 2-Y-0 £4,204 (£1,251; £625; £312) Stalls Low

Form RPR

0541 **1** **Rhagori Aur**[32] 6312 2-9-7 79.. TomEaves 5 85
(Bryan Smart) *s.i.s: hld up: plld hrd: hdwy over 1f out: r.o u.p to ld wl ins fnl f* **7/1**[3]

3125 **2** *1* **Dusty Storm (IRE)**[34] 6227 2-9-5 77.............................. SebSanders 12 79
(Ed McMahon) *sn chsng ldr: rdn to ld and hung lft over 1f out: hdd wl ins fnl f* **9/1**

1345 **3** *3/4* **Kodatish (IRE)**[16] 6799 2-8-12 70.............................. WilliamCarson 8 69
(Ronald Harris) *sn pushed along in rr: rdn over 1f out: r.o ins fnl f: nt rch ldrs* **16/1**

3135 **4** *1/2* **Secret Sign**[20] 6658 2-9-6 78..(v) KierenFallon 4 76
(Brian Meehan) *chsd ldrs: drvn along 1/2-way: sn outpcd: r.o ins fnl f* **7/2**[2]

0620 **5** *shd* **Cuisine (IRE)**[27] 6487 2-9-0 72...................................(b) PatCosgrave 13 69
(Andrew Balding) *sn outpcd: rdn over 1f out: r.o ins fnl f: nrst fin* **14/1**

1 **6** *1 3/4* **Time For Lambrini (IRE)**[151] 2349 2-9-6 78............................ AmyRyan 7 69
(Lisa Williamson) *sn outpcd: r.o ins fnl f: nvr nrr* **16/1**

616 **7** *nk* **Ovett**[13] 6871 2-9-3 75.. GeorgeBaker 2 65
(Gary Moore) *led early: chsd ldrs: rdn over 1f out: no ex ins fnl f* **2/1**[1]

3261 **8** *3/4* **La Sylphe**[15] 6809 2-9-1 78... LMcNiff(5) 6 65
(David Barron) *sn led: rdn and hdd over 1f out: wknd ins fnl f* **14/1**

0350 **9** *1 1/4* **Dust Whirl**[46] 5886 2-9-0 72... MartinDwyer 11 55
(Richard Hannon) *sn outpcd: rdn over 1f out: nvr on terms* **25/1**

4210 **10** *1/2* **Starlight Angel (IRE)**[9] 6984 2-9-2 74................................ LukeMorris 9 55
(Ronald Harris) *sn outpcd: rdn over 2f out: wknd ins fnl f* **25/1**

5122 **11** *1 1/4* **Vestibule**[31] 6332 2-8-13 76..(p) AmyScott(5) 1 52
(Eve Johnson Houghton) *chsd ldrs: drvn along 1/2-way: wknd fnl f* **10/1**

1m 2.03s (-0.27) **Going Correction** -0.125s/f (Stan) 11 Ran SP% **119.9**
Speed ratings (Par 97): **97,95,94,93,93 90,89,88,86,85 83**
toteswingers 1&2 £13.20, 2&3 £42.70, 1&3 £23.50 CSF £70.02 CT £988.35 TOTE £4.10: £3.00, £3.00, £3.30; EX 70.80 Trifecta £313.10 Part won. Pool: £423.16 - 0.20 winning tickets..
Owner Ceffyl Racing **Bred** Usk Valley Stud **Trained** Hambleton, N Yorks

FOCUS
A decent nursery, run at a solid 5f tempo. The level looks sound rated around the runner-up, third and fourth.

NOTEBOOK
Rhagori Aur has looked at home over 5f on turf, but this first Polytrack run suggests she will stay 6f no problem. She is on a roll now, and the way she finished suggests she has more improvement in her yet. (op 6-1 tchd 8-1)
Dusty Storm(IRE), a reliable sort, seemed to have timed her effort well, only to be nabbed by the strong-finishing winner. She should continue to give a good account of herself off this sort of mark. (op 8-1)
Kodatish(IRE) has repeatedly switched between 5f and 6f but on this evidence the longer trip should suit him at least as well from now on. This was an encouraging AW debut and he looks capable of winning on the surface.
Secret Sign tends to finish well over 5f, as he did again here, and 6f could become his better distance before long. (op 4-1)
Cuisine(IRE) did well from the widest stall, though coming home a bit too late. He could win an AW handicap given a better draw, with a step back up to 6f likely to be in his favour. (op 16-1)
Time For Lambrini(IRE), winner of a 5f maiden here on her only previous run, made a promising comeback after five months off and should do even better next time. (tchd 18-1)
Ovett's maiden win suggested this mark was a workable one, and he had already shown he acts on Polytrack, so this was a disappointing AW debut. He may need 6f these days. (op 5-2)

7221 BOOK TICKETS ONLINE AT WOLVERHAMPTON-RACECOURSE.CO.UK (S) STKS — 1m 141y(P)

7:20 (7:49) (Class 6) 3-5-Y-0 £1,704 (£503; £251) Stalls Low

Form RPR

1614 **1** **Justbookie Dot Com (IRE)**[13] 6894 4-9-6 72...............(b) AdamKirby 3 79
(David Evans) *hld up: shkn up over 2f out: hdwy over 1f out: rdn to ld ins fnl f: r.o* **13/8**[1]

2400 **2** *1 3/4* **Gunner Will (IRE)**[27] 6502 3-8-10 66............................ MartinDwyer 11 69
(Jamie Osborne) *chsd ldrs: pushed along over 3f out: rdn to ld over 1f out: hdd and unable qck ins fnl f* **6/1**[3]

0630 **3** *2 1/2* **Glass Mountain (IRE)**[7] 7027 4-9-0 68........................(v) KierenFallon 1 67
(Ian Williams) *a.p: gng wl whn nt clr run and hmpd over 1f out: styd on u.p: nvr able to chal* **15/8**[2]

0000 **4** *2 3/4* **Barathea Dancer (IRE)**[54] 5625 4-8-9 64.....................(b[1]) LukeMorris 8 52
(Gay Kelleway) *chsd ldr tl led 2f out: hmpd over 1f out: sn rdn and hdd: no ex ins fnl f* **7/1**

2440 **5** *1 3/4* **Carrie's Magic**[39] 6105 5-8-6 51...................................... JulieBurke(3) 12 48
(Alistair Whillans) *prom: racd keenly: pushed along over 5f out: rdn over 2f out: styd on same pce* **16/1**

0006 **6** *nk* **Poppy Golightly**[10] 6969 5-8-4 45..............................(b) JasonHart(5) 10 47
(Declan Carroll) *s.s: a in rr* **28/1**

3540 **7** *2 1/2* **Coastal Passage**[65] 5246 4-8-11 48............................ MarkCoumbe(3) 5 46
(Charles Smith) *led: rdn and hdd 2f out: wknd fnl f* **50/1**

6020 **8** *4 1/2* **Song Of Joy (IRE)**[59] 5459 3-8-5 52.............................. WilliamCarson 6 31
(Barry Leavy) *in rr: pushed along over 5f out: wknd over 2f out* **22/1**

1m 49.7s (-0.80) **Going Correction** -0.125s/f (Stan)
WFA 3 from 4yo+ 4lb 8 Ran SP% **115.3**
Speed ratings (Par 101): **98,96,94,91,90 89,87,83**
toteswingers 1&2 £3.40, 2&3 £3.70, 1&3 £1.10 CSF £11.94 TOTE £2.50: £1.30, £1.30, £1.10; EX 13.20 Trifecta £67.10 Pool: £689.61 - 7.60 winning tickets..There was no bid for the winner. Glass Mountain was claimed by Mr David Penman for £6,000.
Owner J A & S Wilcox **Bred** Haydock Park Stud **Trained** Pandy, Monmouths

FOCUS
A fair seller, with the first four all rated above 60. The medium tempo increased 4f out. The winner is more solid than most and the race has been rated around him.
Glass Mountain(IRE) Official explanation: jockey said gelding was denied a clear run

Poppy Golightly Official explanation: jockey said mare never travelled

7222 CELEBRATE CHRISTMAS AT WOLVERHAMPTON RACECOURSE CLASSIFIED STKS 1m 1f 103y(P)
7:50 (8:13) (Class 6) 3-Y-0+ £1,704 (£503; £251) Stalls Low

Form RPR
3312 1 **Neige D'Antan**[6] 7058 3-8-12 55 LukeMorris 5 66
(Sir Mark Prescott Bt) *a.p: led over 1f out: rdn clr fnl f* 11/10[1]
0054 2 3 3/4 **Taro Tywod (IRE)**[13] 6892 3-8-12 53 ShaneKelly 2 58
(Mark Brisbourne) *chsd ldrs: nt clr run over 2f out: rdn to chse wnr ins fnl f: edgd lft and no imp* 9/1
0635 3 3 1/4 **Essell**[10] 6948 3-8-12 55 SamHitchcott 3 51
(Mick Channon) *chsd ldr tl led over 2f out: rdn and hdd over 1f out: wknd ins fnl f* 13/2[3]
4054 4 2 1/4 **Neil's Pride**[11] 6924 3-8-12 55 FrederikTylicki 10 46
(Richard Fahey) *chsd ldrs: rdn over 2f out: edgd lft and wknd fnl f* 5/1[2]
-040 5 4 **Crucis Abbey (IRE)**[71] 4993 4-9-2 55 LiamJones 6 38
(Mark Brisbourne) *hld up: nt clr run over 2f out: nvr trbld ldrs* 33/1
6000 6 1/2 **Bubbly Bounty**[67] 5175 3-8-5 47 (b[1]) RobertTart(7) 12 37
(Alan Bailey) *hld up: hdwy 3f out: rdn and wknd over 1f out* 28/1
064- 7 2 1/4 **Lady Intrigue (IRE)**[422] 5372 4-8-9 47 GeorgeChaloner(7) 9 32
(Richard Fahey) *s.i.s: sn pushed along in rr: nvr on terms* 40/1
0-40 8 1 1/2 **Lady Author**[247] 571 3-8-12 39 PatrickMathers 11 29
(Richard Fahey) *mid-div: rdn over 2f out: sn wknd* 80/1
0010 9 2 3/4 **First Glance**[3] 7148 3-8-12 49 KierenFallon 8 23
(Michael Appleby) *hld up in tch: racd keenly: rdn over 2f out: sn wknd* 7/1
5050 10 1 1/4 **Variety Show (IRE)**[28] 6442 3-8-12 52 TomQueally 4 21
(Sir Henry Cecil) *sn pushed along and a in rr* 16/1
6000 11 4 **Leonards Pride (IRE)**[32] 6316 3-8-12 43 SeanQuinlan 1 12
(Daniel Mark Loughnane) *hld up: rdn over 3f out: wknd over 2f out* 66/1
000- 12 14 **Naturalmente (IRE)**[361] 7058 3-8-12 48 AmyRyan 7
(Kevin Ryan) *led: rdn and hdd over 2f out: sn wknd: t.o* 20/1

2m 0.25s (-1.45) **Going Correction** -0.125s/f (Stan)
WFA 3 from 4yo 4lb 12 Ran SP% 122.3
Speed ratings (Par 101): **101,97,94,92,89 88,86,85,83,81 78,65**
toteswingers 1&2 £3.00, 2&3 £1.50, 1&3 £4.10 CSF £11.81 TOTE £1.60: £1.10, £2.50, £2.60; EX 14.30 Trifecta £125.90 Pool: £711.45 - 4.18 winning tickets..
Owner Miss K Rausing **Bred** Miss K Rausing **Trained** Newmarket, Suffolk

FOCUS
A weak race with only the winner in any kind of form going into it. The third has been rated close to her recent handicap form.

7223 32RED CASINO NURSERY 7f 32y(P)
8:20 (8:40) (Class 6) (0-65,65) 2-Y-0 £1,704 (£503; £251) Stalls High

Form RPR
005 1 **El Mirage (IRE)**[8] 7007 2-9-5 63 ShaneKelly 6 72
(Dean Ivory) *hld up: hdwy over 2f out: chsd ldr over 1f out: nt clr run and swtchd rt ins fnl f: r.o to ld towards fin* 6/1
646 2 2 1/2 **Pearl Bounty (IRE)**[74] 4873 2-9-7 65 (v[1]) KierenFallon 2 67
(Andrew Balding) *chsd ldrs: shkn up to ld wl over 1f out: sn rdn and hung lft: hdd towards fin* 13/2
544 3 3 1/2 **Best To Better (IRE)**[23] 6581 2-9-4 62 AdamKirby 8 55
(Marco Botti) *outpcd: r.o u.p ins fnl f: nvr nrr* 7/2[2]
046 4 2 1/4 **Byron's Dream**[67] 5169 2-9-6 64 TomEaves 3 51
(Jedd O'Keeffe) *prom: rdn over 2f out: styd on same pce* 20/1
5006 5 2 **Hot Mustard**[29] 6413 2-9-4 62 HayleyTurner 5 43
(Michael Bell) *sn outpcd: nvr nrr* 10/3[1]
2200 6 3/4 **Missing Agent**[4] 7111 2-9-2 65 (v) NathanSweeney(5) 1 44+
(David Evans) *w ldr tl led 3f out: rdn and hdd wl over 1f out: sn wknd* 10/1
1502 7 4 **Slipstream Angel (IRE)**[8] 6998 2-9-5 63 (b) FrederikTylicki 10 32
(Richard Fahey) *s.i.s: outpcd* 5/1[3]
6040 8 4 **Al Khisa (IRE)**[10] 6952 2-9-6 64 (p) AmyRyan 4 22
(Kevin Ryan) *sn outpcd: bhd fnl 4f* 25/1
320 9 1 1/2 **Our Three Graces (IRE)**[58] 5484 2-9-7 65 GeorgeBaker 9 19
(Gary Moore) *prom: pushed along 4f out: sn hung lft: wknd 3f out* 12/1
0005 10 nk **Stand N Applaude**[10] 6953 2-9-6 64 AndrewMullen 7 17+
(David Nicholls) *sn led: rdn and hdd 3f out: wknd wl over 1f out* 33/1

1m 29.26s (-0.34) **Going Correction** -0.125s/f (Stan) 10 Ran SP% 117.9
Speed ratings (Par 93): **96,93,89,86,84 83,78,74,72,72**
toteswingers 1&2 £5.30, 2&3 £6.50, 1&3 £5.60 CSF £44.10 CT £163.17 TOTE £9.80: £1.90, £3.70, £1.20; EX 35.60 Trifecta £158.00 Pool: £514.86 - 2.41 winning tickets..
Owner Mrs Heather Yarrow **Bred** Jeddah Bloodstock **Trained** Radlett, Herts

FOCUS
The two leaders went a hectic gallop, with the field soon well strung out. The winner came from well back, while the runner-up raced closer to the pace and ran a personal best in the first-time visor.

NOTEBOOK
El Mirage(IRE), suited by the strong pace, was produced with perfect timing to win with a bit to spare. She looks at home on Polytrack and should go well again next time. Official explanation: trainer said, regarding apparent improvement in form, that the filly had benefited from the step up in trip and its first run in a handicap.
Pearl Bounty(IRE) made a good nursery debut in a first-time visor. This mark seems about right, and 7f could well be his trip even though he couldn't quite hold on this time. (op 7-1 tchd 15-2)
Best To Better(IRE) showed some ability in maidens, and this nursery debut suggests she can make her presence felt now she has a handicap mark. The fast pace offset her usual tendency to pull, and the way she finished suggests that a well-run 7f might suit. (tchd 3-1)
Byron's Dream will probably have to drop a few pounds to win, but this was a satisfactory nursery debut.
Hot Mustard, making his AW debut, was quickly taken off his feet by the crazy early gallop. He has yet to justify the market support for him here. (op 17-2)
Missing Agent ran himself into the ground by trying to dispute the lead at a furious tempo. (op 8-1 tchd 15-2)
Stand N Applaude, pressed by one rival, appeared to go off too fast and paid the penalty coming off the final bend. (op 28-1)

7224 32RED SUPPORTING BRITISH RACING H'CAP (DIV I) 7f 32y(P)
8:50 (9:05) (Class 6) (0-60,60) 3-Y-0+ £1,704 (£377; £377) Stalls High

Form RPR
0000 1 **Shaunas Spirit (IRE)**[4] 7105 4-9-3 59 (p) PatrickHills(3) 5 70
(Dean Ivory) *a.p: led over 1f out: rdn out* 18/1
0300 2 2 1/4 **Piccolo Express**[35] 6216 6-9-6 59 WilliamCarson 7 64
(Brian Baugh) *chsd ldrs: rdn over 1f out: styd on* 18/1
1600 2 dht **Circuitous**[11] 6937 4-9-0 53 (p) JoeFanning 1 58
(Keith Dalgleish) *led 1f: chsd ldrs: rdn over 1f out: styd on* 25/1
-150 4 1 1/2 **Monte Cassino (IRE)**[160] 2091 7-9-2 55 (e) TomEaves 9 56
(Bryan Smart) *hld up: hdwy u.p over 1f out: styd on same pce ins fnl f* 25/1
0566 5 1 1/4 **Lindoro**[15] 6823 7-9-5 58 (b) AmyRyan 8 56
(Brian Ellison) *hld up: hdwy over 1f out: nt rch ldrs* 9/2[2]
0052 6 1 1/2 **Darnathean**[9] 6982 3-9-3 58 SebSanders 2 52
(Paul D'Arcy) *sn pushed along in rr: sme hdwy over 1f out: no ex fnl f* 3/1[1]
04 7 2 1/4 **The Kicking Lord**[15] 6827 3-9-4 59 LiamJones 4 46
(Mark Brisbourne) *led 6f out: rdn and hdd over 1f out: wknd fnl f* 11/2
0450 8 hd **Cadmium Loch**[4] 7106 4-8-13 57 (p) JackDuern(5) 6 44
(Reg Hollinshead) *hld up: rdn over 1f out: n.d* 10/1
6200 9 4 1/2 **Not My Choice (IRE)**[45] 5915 7-9-1 54 (t) J-PGuillambert 10 29
(Paul Howling) *chsd ldr 6f out: rdn over 2f out: wknd over 1f out* 25/1
1006 10 1/2 **Athaakeel (IRE)**[10] 6951 6-9-1 54 HayleyTurner 12 27
(Ronald Harris) *chsd ldrs: rdn over 2f out: wknd over 1f out* 40/1
5000 11 3 1/4 **Fleetwoodsands (IRE)**[51] 5750 5-9-7 60 (t) LukeMorris 3 25
(Milton Bradley) *s.i.s: hld up: rdn over 2f out: a in rr* 7/1
-450 12 2 1/4 **Michael's Nook**[15] 6823 5-8-12 56 LMcNiff(5) 11 15
(David Barron) *s.i.s: hdwy 1/2-way: rdn and wknd over 2f out* 5/1[3]

1m 29.17s (-0.43) **Going Correction** -0.125s/f (Stan)
WFA 3 from 4yo+ 2lb 12 Ran SP% 121.3
Speed ratings (Par 101): **97,94,94,92,91 89,87,86,81,81 77,74**
PL: P 4.50, C 8.80. toteswingers 1&S £63.40, 2&2 £60.30, 1&P £56.60, EX: SS & PE £258.00, SS & C £284.10 CSF: SS & PE £148.70, TC SS & PE & C £3,979.00, SS & C &PE £4026.82 TOTE £19.50: £6.20 TRIFECTA Not won..
Owner John Connolly & Cynthia Smith **Bred** Miss Breda Wright **Trained** Radlett, Herts

FOCUS
A routine AW handicap won by a specialist on Polytrack. Piccolo Express, who dead-heated for second, has been rated close to his best.

7225 32RED SUPPORTING BRITISH RACING H'CAP (DIV II) 7f 32y(P)
9:20 (9:29) (Class 6) (0-60,60) 3-Y-0+ £1,704 (£503; £251) Stalls High

Form RPR
0006 1 **North Central (USA)**[1] 7204 5-9-0 53 (p) JoeFanning 12 60
(Keith Dalgleish) *chsd ldr 6f out: rdn to ld over 1f out: jst hld on* 8/1
0003 2 1/2 **Men Don't Cry (IRE)**[16] 6778 3-9-1 56 (b) ChrisCatlin 4 61
(Ed de Giles) *led 1f: chsd ldrs: rdn over 1f out: r.o* 8/1
300 3 1/2 **Lieutenant Dan (IRE)**[46] 5889 5-9-6 59 KierenFallon 10 63
(Michael Appleby) *sn prom: rdn over 2f out: r.o* 9/2[3]
5110 4 1 3/4 **Community (USA)**[36] 6157 4-9-7 60 AdamKirby 2 59
(Jamie Osborne) *prom: rdn over 1f out: styd on* 7/1
4404 5 1/2 **Keys Of Cyprus**[27] 6480 10-8-10 56 ShirleyTeasdale(7) 8 54
(David Nicholls) *led 6f out: rdn and hdd over 1f out: no ex ins fnl f* 4/1[2]
0-00 6 1/2 **Silence Is Easy**[69] 5099 3-9-4 59 MartinDwyer 11 56
(William Muir) *hld up: rdn over 2f out: nvr trbld ldrs* 20/1
2530 7 1/2 **Ereka (IRE)**[16] 6778 4-9-3 56 LukeMorris 5 51
(John Best) *mid-div: rdn over 2f out: no ex fnl f* 14/1
-322 8 3/4 **Forzarzi (IRE)**[21] 6640 8-8-11 53 PaulPickard(3) 6 46
(Hugh McWilliams) *hld up: rdn and hung lft over 1f out: n.d* 8/1
2061 9 1 3/4 **Trusting (IRE)**[16] 6778 3-9-2 57 (v) HayleyTurner 9 45
(Eve Johnson Houghton) *hld up: drvn along over 2f out: n.d* 7/2[1]
3000 10 1 3/4 **Mack's Sister**[165] 1934 5-9-2 58 PatrickHills(3) 1 42
(Dean Ivory) *hld up: rdn over 2f out: hdwy u.p over 1f out: wknd ins fnl f* 20/1

1m 30.18s (0.58) **Going Correction** -0.125s/f (Stan)
WFA 3 from 4yo+ 2lb 10 Ran SP% 122.4
Speed ratings (Par 101): **91,90,89,87,87 86,86,85,83,81**
toteswingers 1&2 £11.40, 2&3 £8.20, 1&3 £13.70 CSF £74.04 CT £334.40 TOTE £8.10: £2.40, £2.40, £1.70; EX 91.20 Trifecta £289.40 Part won. Pool: £391.17 - 0.63 winning tickets..
Owner Dogberry Racing **Bred** Tony Holmes & Walter Zent **Trained** Carluke, S Lanarks

FOCUS
This didn't take much winning. In contrast to the first division, it went to a runner with only one previous outing on Polytrack, and the time was a second slower. The runner-up has been rated to form, with the third up a bit on his maiden form.
T/Plt: £28.40 to a £1 stake. Pool: £94,537.89 - 2,423.96 winning tickets. T/Qpdt: £7.90 to a £1 stake. Pool: £8,957.09 - 837.00 winning tickets. CR

7226 - 7228a (Foreign Racing) - See Raceform Interactive

7035 DUNDALK (A.W) (L-H)
Friday, October 19

OFFICIAL GOING: Standard

7229a CROWNE PLAZA RACE & STAY PACKAGE H'CAP 7f (P)
7:30 (7:30) (60-95,88) 3-Y-0 £7,475 (£1,733; £758; £433)

RPR
1 **Spirituality (IRE)**[7] 7037 3-8-10 80 (b) LukeDempsey(10) 1 86+
(Thomas Carmody, Ire) *hld up in mid-div: hdwy under 2f out and rdn into 2nd jst ins fnl f: kpt on wl to ld fnl 50yds* 7/2[2]
2 nk **Captain Joy (IRE)**[21] 6653 3-9-12 86 MichaelHussey 4 91
(Tracey Collins, Ire) *hld up in tch: clsd gng wl to press ldr 2f out: led over 1f out: sn rdn and hdd fnl 50yds: kpt on* 5/2[1]
3 1/2 **Free Spin (IRE)**[34] 6267 3-9-5 79 ShaneFoley 7 83+
(M Halford, Ire) *hld up towards rr: hdwy 2f out: n.m.r and sn swtchd rt: r.o strly ins fnl f: nrst fin* 12/1
4 shd **Curia Regis**[7] 7037 3-8-11 71 (b) FergalLynch 13 74
(David Marnane, Ire) *slowly away: clsd gng wl on far side whn n.m.r ent fnl f: swtchd and r.o wl fnl f: nvr nrr* 12/1
5 1 1/4 **Khyber Pass**[7] 7037 3-8-11 71 WayneLordan 6 71
(Edward Lynam, Ire) *slowly away and racd in rr: last under 3f out: clsd gng wl fr 2f out whn n.m.r: kpt on wl ins fnl f: nrst fin* 20/1
6 1 1/4 **Beat The Ballot (IRE)**[99] 4031 3-9-2 76 EmmetMcNamara 5 73
(Tracey Collins, Ire) *chsd ldrs: rdn over 2f out and kpt on same pce fnl f* 14/1
7 1 1/2 **Arbitrageur (IRE)**[19] 6716 3-8-13 78 ConorHoban(5) 9 71
(Donal Kinsella, Ire) *hld up in tch: checked 1/2-way: ev ch 1 1/2f out: wkng whn hmpd ins fnl f: no ex* 14/1
8 1/2 **Catfromtherock (IRE)**[7] 7037 3-8-7 70 SamJames(3) 14 61
(David Marnane, Ire) *racd in mid-div: one pce fnl 2f* 20/1
9 3/4 **Strait Of Zanzibar (USA)**[14] 6862 3-9-9 86 RonanWhelan(3) 8 75
(K J Condon, Ire) *led: pushed along and jnd 3f out: sn hdd & wknd* 16/1
10 nk **Centrifugal (IRE)**[9] 6979 3-9-9 83 PatSmullen 11 71
(Mark Johnston) *chsd ldr in 2nd: on terms 3f out and led into st: qckly jnd and hdd under 1 1/2f out: wknd fnl f* 5/1[3]

11 ¾ **Atticus Finch (IRE)**[40] 6082 3-9-3 **77**....................... DeclanMcDonogh 2 63
(Edward Lynam, Ire) *cl up: t.k.h: wknd and n.d fr 2f out* **5/1**[3]

12 *shd* **Quote Of The Day (IRE)**[14] 6862 3-9-13 **87**.................(t) ChrisHayes 10 73
(Edward Lynam, Ire) *in rr of mid-div: rdn and one pce fnl 2f* **20/1**

13 ¾ **Springinmystep (IRE)**[14] 6830 3-10-0 **88**................. JohnnyMurtagh 3 72
(Michael Dods) *in rr of mid-div: n.d fr 2f out* **8/1**

14 *nk* **Go On Murt (IRE)**[53] 5693 3-9-1 **75**..........................(p) KevinManning 12 58
(Mrs John Harrington, Ire) *w.w towards rr: nvr a factor* **12/1**

1m 23.97s (83.97) **14** Ran SP% **151.8**
CSF £16.09 CT £112.90 TOTE £4.90: £1.60, £2.10, £4.10; DF 19.00.

Owner Andrew Tinkler **Bred** Fortbarrington Stud **Trained** the Curragh, Co Kildare

■ Stewards' Enquiry : Shane Foley two-day ban: careless riding (Nov 2,4)

FOCUS
Having got off the mark in first-time blinkers over the same course and trip a week previously, Spirituality followed up off a 7lb higher mark. This is rated around the fourth, fifth and sixth.

NOTEBOOK
Spirituality(IRE) arrived with a well-timed challenge entering the final furlong and ran on to get on top in the closing stages. (op 11-2 tchd 6-1)

Captain Joy(IRE) was always close up, hitting the front over 1f out before being grabbed late on. (op 7-2)

Free Spin(IRE) ◆ had trouble finding room to challenge before being switched right, hampering Arbitrageur, inside the final furlong and finishing well. He should win a handicap based on this effort.

Curia Regis, a maiden having his ninth start, had run third behind Spirituality here last time. He ran another solid race. Pushed along in mid-division turning for home, he didn't have the clearest of runs and kept on for pressure.

Khyber Pass, in the frame here on three of his five previous attempts, was making his handicap debut. He made progress from behind over the last 2f and was possibly unlucky not to finish a bit closer.

Go On Murt(IRE) Official explanation: trainer's rep said colt was found to be coughing

7230a IRISH STALLION FARMS EUROPEAN BREEDERS FUND FILLIES H'CAP 7f (P)
8:00 (8:01) (60-100,95) 3-Y-O+ **£13,541** (£3,958; £1,875; £625)

RPR

1 **Via Ballycroy (IRE)**[22] 6618 3-8-9 **76**............................(p) ShaneFoley 7 86+
(M Halford, Ire) *hld up in tch: t.k.h early: 5th under 3f out: pushed along over 1f out and hdwy on outer to ld fnl 150yds: drew clr: comf* **6/1**[3]

2 2 **Brown Butterfly**[21] 6654 4-8-11 **76**.......................(b) DeclanMcDonogh 3 81
(Kevin Prendergast, Ire) *chsd ldrs in 3rd: wnt 2nd 2f out: led briefly ins fnl f: sn hdd and kpt on same pce towards fin* **9/2**[2]

3 ½ **Precious Dream (USA)**[47] 5857 3-8-11 **78**................. WayneLordan 12 82+
(David Wachman, Ire) *w.w in rr: n.m.r and rdn over 1f out: r.o strly to go n.d 3rd over 50yds out: nrst fin* **8/1**

4 1 ½ **Imaginationrunwild (IRE)**[72] 4975 3-8-8 **80**............... ConorHoban(5) 1 80
(A Oliver, Ire) *chsd ldrs: hdwy 2f out: no imp ent fnl f: kpt on again towards fin* **7/2**[1]

5 *nse* **Core Element (IRE)**[14] 6854 5-9-1 **80**..................... EmmetMcNamara 8 79
(S Buggy, Ire) *chsd ldr: 2nd 3f out: almost on terms 2f out: rdn and no ex ins fnl f* **12/1**

6 *nk* **Dotada (IRE)**[426] 5294 7-8-7 **75**.. IJBrennan(3) 5 74
(Peter Casey, Ire) *led: rdn and strly pressed 2f out: hdd ins fnl f: no ex* **33/1**

7 1 **New Magic (IRE)**[30] 6385 5-9-3 **89**...............................(t) ColinKeane(7) 4 85
(Dermot Anthony McLoughlin, Ire) *hld up towards rr: rdn and one pce fr 2f out* **14/1**

8 *nk* **Geraldines Lass (IRE)**[54] 5640 4-8-1 **69** oh4............(t) LeighRoche(3) 6 64
(W McCreery, Ire) *hld up towards rr: sme late hdwy fnl f* **25/1**

9 3 ¼ **Knock Stars (IRE)**[111] 3648 4-9-4 **83**............................... ChrisHayes 11 69
(Patrick Martin, Ire) *a bhd: t.k.h: rdn and n.d fr 2f out* **14/1**

10 1 **Vocational (USA)**[14] 6835 3-10-0 **95**........................... JohnnyMurtagh 2 79
(Mark Johnston) *hld up in tch: t.k.h: 6th 3f out: sn pushed along and no imp fr 2f out: eased towards fin* **7/2**[1]

11 1 ¾ **Slim Chance (IRE)**[68] 5138 3-8-0 **77**......................(t) LukeDempsey(10) 9 56
(J G Coogan, Ire) *chsd ldrs: keen early: 7th over 3f out: sn pushed along and no imp under 2f out* **8/1**

12 2 **Dream Applause (IRE)**[22] 6622 4-8-5 **70**.................... NGMcCullagh 10 44
(K J Condon, Ire) *a towards rr: nvr a threat* **12/1**

1m 24.67s (84.67)
WFA 3 from 4yo+ 2lb **12** Ran SP% **134.6**
CSF £38.05 CT £236.96 TOTE £3.10: £2.10, £1.50, £3.40; DF 51.20.

Owner Rollx Syndicate **Bred** Keatly Overseas Ltd **Trained** Doneany, Co Kildare

FOCUS
Up in trip following her maiden win over 6f here last month, Via Ballycroy followed up in good style on her handicap debut.

NOTEBOOK
Via Ballycroy(IRE) began her effort under 2f out before hitting the front early in the final furlong. She ran out a comfortable winner and looks an improver. Winning trainer Michael Halford said "I was a bit concerned about the trip as she had shown plenty of speed, but she switched off nicely and did the job well." (op 9-2)

Brown Butterfly was back down in distance. She had blinkers back on and raced close up before going to the front over 1f out. However, she was unable to raise her effort when taken on by the winner. (op 8-1)

Precious Dream(USA), drawn high, made steady headway from behind over the last 2f and ran on well. Twice a winner, she should be capable of winning another handicap based on this performance. (op 6-1)

Imaginationrunwild(IRE) was trying this surface for the first time. She was a bit unlucky not to finish closer. (op 5-1)

Core Element(IRE) had run moderately in two starts since winning off a 7lb lower mark at Gowran Park last month. She ran a better race here and had every chance after turning for home in second place.

Vocational(USA) was tackling this trip for the first time. She was keen early on and was ridden and beaten early in the straight. (op 4-1 tchd 10-3)

7231 - 7233a (Foreign Racing) - See Raceform Interactive

MARSEILLE BORELY (L-H)
Friday, October 19

OFFICIAL GOING: Turf: good to soft

7234a PRIX ANDRE BABOIN (GRAND PRIX DES PROVINCES) (GROUP 3) (3YO+) (TURF) 1m 2f
1:20 (12:00) 3-Y-O+ **£33,333** (£13,333; £10,000; £6,666; £3,333)

RPR

1 **Mobaco (FR)**[42] 6058 3-8-8 0... RemiFradet 2 109
(F Rossi, France) *mde all: rdn and qcknd over 1 1/2f out: r.o u.p fnl f: jst hld on* **14/1**

2 *hd* **La Arenosa (IRE)**[64] 5289 3-8-5 0................................. MaximeGuyon 4 106
(A Fabre, France) *settled towards rr: scrubbed along over 2f out: hdwy on outside under 2f out: rdn and r.o wl fnl f: jst failed* **33/10**[2]

3 1 **Bassamba (FR)**[23] 6595 3-8-5 0.............................(b) StephanePasquier 5 104
(F Rohaut, France) *settled in rr: hrd rdn over 2f out: stuck bhd wall of horses fr 1 1/2f out: rdn and swtchd outside to be in clr ins fnl f: styd on strly fnl 100yds to take 3rd on line* **9/2**[3]

4 *nse* **Pink Gin (FR)**[47] 5871 5-8-13 0...................................... FabienLefebvre 1 107
(J-P Gauvin, France) *midfield on rail: rdn and chsd ldr fr 1 1/2f out: one pce fnl f: lost two pls late on* **11/1**

5 *hd* **Abdel (FR)**[27] 6506 4-8-13 0.. OlivierPeslier 8 107
(C Laffon-Parias, France) *t.k.h and chsd ldr: 2nd: rdn and nt qckn 2f out: one pce fr over 1f out: lost two pls late on* **7/1**

6 *shd* **Splendido (FR)**[30] 4-8-9 0.. ThierryThulliez 3 102
(F Rossi, France) *trckd ldrs on ins: rdn and one pce fr 1 1/2f out: no ex fnl f* **13/1**

7 1 **Gris Caro**[42] 6058 3-8-8 0.. FranckBlondel 6 104
(F Rossi, France) *midfield on outside: no imp fr ins fnl 2f* **5/2**[1]

8 6 **Bugie D'Amore**[65] 5249 3-8-8 0.................................... AntoineHamelin 7 92
(A De Royer-Dupre, France) *settled in rr: rdn and no imp fr 2f out: bhd fnl f* **58/10**

2m 3.34s (123.34)
WFA 3 from 4yo+ 5lb **8** Ran SP% **119.4**
WIN (incl. 1 euro stake): 2.40 (Mobaco coupled with Splendido & Gris Caro), PLACES: 2.40, 1.70, 1.90. DF: 27.80. SF: 45.60.

Owner Jean-Claude Seroul **Bred** J-C Seroul **Trained** France

NOTEBOOK
Mobaco(FR) probably didn't have to improve on last month's C&D Listed win to take this.

6865 ASCOT (R-H)
Saturday, October 20

OFFICIAL GOING: Soft (heavy in places on round course; stands' side 6.9, centre 7.0, far side 6.9, round 5.6)
Wind: Almost nil Weather: Overcast, brightening gradually

7235 QIPCO BRITISH CHAMPIONS LONG DISTANCE CUP (GROUP 3) 2m
1:45 (1:46) (Class 1) 3-Y-O+
£113,420 (£43,000; £21,520; £10,720; £5,380; £2,700) **Stalls** Low

Form RPR

1/3- 1 **Rite Of Passage**[510] 2534 8-9-7 0...................................... PatSmullen 3 117
(D K Weld, Ire) *awkward bef gng into stalls: hld up in last pair: rdn and gd prog on inner over 2f out: clsd on ldrs 1f out: eased off rail and fnd gap: r.o to ld nr fin* **8/1**

1144 2 *nk* **Aiken**[35] 6271 4-9-7 112.. WilliamBuick 7 116
(John Gosden) *trckd ldrs disputing 5th: rdn wl over 2f out: prog to chse ldr over 1f out: led jst ins fnl f and edgd rt: hdd nr fin* **4/1**[2]

4266 3 ½ **Askar Tau (FR)**[36] 6198 7-9-7 110...............................(v) GeorgeBaker 6 115
(Marcus Tregoning) *s.i.s: hld up in last: rdn and no prog wl over 2f out: gd hdwy over 1f out: clsd on ldrs fnl f: could nt qckn last 50yds* **33/1**

5042 4 1 ½ **Electrolyser (IRE)**[56] 5575 7-9-7 108............................... AdamKirby 9 113
(Clive Cox) *trckd ldng trio: rdn to chse ldr over 2f out to over 1f out: kpt on same pce* **33/1**

-106 5 *shd* **Fame And Glory**[35] 6271 6-9-7 116................................ JamieSpencer 5 113
(A P O'Brien, Ire) *trckd ldr: led wl over 2f out gng powerfully: drvn over 1f out: hdd jst ins fnl f: crowded for room sn after: fdd* **11/2**[3]

1054 6 1 ¼ **Saddler's Rock (IRE)**[13] 6914 4-9-7 115...................(t) JohnnyMurtagh 2 112
(John M Oxx, Ire) *trckd ldrs disputing 5th: rdn over 3f out: kpt on same pce and nvr able to chal* **10/1**

U-11 7 19 **Ile De Re (FR)**[112] 3625 6-9-7 105...................................... JimCrowley 8 89
(Donald McCain) *led at gd pce to wl over 2f out: sn wknd* **6/1**

2112 8 19 **Opinion Poll (IRE)**[121] 3293 6-9-7 116...................... MickaelBarzalona 4 66
(Mahmood Al Zarooni) *hld up in last trio: pushed along 6f out: prog on outer 2f out and threatened to cl on ldrs: wknd rapidly jst over 1f out and virtually p.u* **10/3**[1]

1303 9 47 **Colour Vision (FR)**[13] 6914 4-9-7 116.........................(p) FrankieDettori 1
(Saeed Bin Suroor) *trckd ldng pair tl wknd rapidly jst over 3f out: virtually p.u fnl 2f* **6/1**

3m 35.98s (6.98) **Going Correction** +0.775s/f (Yiel) **9** Ran SP% **113.1**
Speed ratings (Par 113): **113,112,112,111,111 111,101,92,68**
toteswingers 1&2 £8.20, 2&3 £15.40, 1&3 £32.00 CSF £39.17 TOTE £9.80: £2.90, £1.60, £8.50; EX 46.20 Trifecta £981.40 Pool: £3143.35 - 2.37 winning units..

Owner Dr R Lambe **Bred** Newsells Park Stud **Trained** The Curragh, Co Kildare

■ Stewards' Enquiry : Pat Smullen one-day ban: careless riding (Nov 3)
William Buick one-day ban: careless riding (Nov 3)

FOCUS
Most of the top stayers were present, with the last three winners of the Gold Cup, the first three from this year's Gold Cup and winners of the Goodwood Cup, Chester Cup and Northumberland Plate. It proved a war of attrition and produced possibly the training feat of the season. The riders confirmed the ground as better on the straight track. The winner has been rated 5lb off his Gold Cup winning effort, while the runner-up has been rated to form.

NOTEBOOK

Rite Of Passage, a former bumper and hurdles winner who won the Gold Cup in 2010, had only run once since his Gold Cup success of 2010, behind Fame and Glory in May last year. He had though, won three of four starts on soft and heavy ground. Heavily bandaged on both front legs, he was settled out the back early before making steady progress up the stands' rail in the straight. He had to wait for a gap, but once it came inside the last furlong his competitive instinct came in to play and he picked up well to go through it and settle the issue quickly. Maximum credit goes to all concerned, but with the future in mind much depends on how the gelding comes out of this. His trainer later hinted at a crack at Big Bucks in the World Hurdle next March, all being well, and that really would be something to savour.

Aiken ◆, who completed a six-timer between June 2011 and June 2012, including winning a Listed race over 1m4f of this track on heavy ground, bounced back from a break, after being well held in the Hardwicke, to go close in the Irish St Leger. Held up early, he was produced to take the lead at what looked the right time, although he did the fading Fame And Glory no favours in the process, but could not hold off the late surge of the winner. He looks the one to take out of this with next season's Cup races in mind. (tchd 7-2 and 9-2 in a place)

Askar Tau(FR) finished behind several of these this season and recorded his best effort when second to Saddler's Rock in the Goodwood Cup. His form suggested he was best on fast ground but he had rarely been tried on soft and never on heavy. He sat at the back for a long way but ran through tiring horses as he likes to do. He was upsides the winner inside the last furlong but that gelding produced more. This was still right up there with the best of his recent efforts.

Electrolyser(IRE), a C&D winner on fast ground, had won on soft, albeit in 2008. A close fourth in the Goodwood Cup, he handled the conditions pretty well, tracking the pace throughout and staying on without finding a change of gear in the straight.

Fame And Glory, who won the Gold Cup and this race in 2011, beating Opinion Poll both times, had not looked as good this year and had a bit to find with a number of these on recent efforts. He travelled well throughout and his rider looked full of confidence turning for home. However, when he hit the front he did not find as much as expected, drifted to the rail under pressure and faded out of contention in the last furlong. (op 6-1 tchd 13-2)

Saddler's Rock(IRE), winner of the Goodwood Cup and third in the Gold Cup, had a bit to find with a couple of these on Prix du Cadran form and had looked best on good ground or close to it. Held up early, he ran on in the straight but could not pick up sufficiently to mount a serious challenge. (tchd 9-1)

Ile De Re(FR) had improved since joining a new yard this year after a spell over hurdles and had won both starts, the Chester Cup and Northumberland Plate, the latter on heavy ground. He was up in grade here though and, after making much of the running, faded pretty quickly once headed. (op 13-2 tchd 7-1)

Opinion Poll(IRE) is normally a consistent stayer, having been runner-up in the Gold Cup and second in this last year. He had also won two of his three starts on soft and heavy ground and had not finished out of the frame in the last three years. However, he had suffered a setback since his last appearance and, after making an effort on the outside early in the straight, he was eased right off inside the final furlong as if something was amiss. (tchd 7-2 and 4-1 in a place)

Colour Vision(FR), who won the Gold Cup here on easy ground in June and finished third in this last year as a 3yo, had run third in the Prix du Cadran on heavy less than two weeks previously and went in first-time cheekpieces here. He might have been feeling the effects of a hard race there, as he was under pressure around 5f from home and was eased down in the last quarter-mile. Official explanation: trainer said gelding was unsuited by the soft (heavy in places) ground

7236 QIPCO BRITISH CHAMPIONS SPRINT STKS (GROUP 2) 6f

2:20 (2:23) (Class 1) 3-Y-O+

£141,775 (£53,750; £26,900; £13,400; £6,725; £3,375) **Stalls** High

Form RPR

1313 **1** **Maarek**[6] 7086 5-9-0 114 JamieSpencer 12 118
(David Peter Nagle, Ire) *hld up in last of nr side quartet: prog to ld overall over 1f out: hrd rdn and styd on* **5/1**[3]

0100 **2** *3/4* **Hawkeyethenoo (IRE)**[28] 6468 6-9-0 107 GrahamLee 9 116
(Jim Goldie) *hld up in last trio in centre: rdn and gd prog over 1f out: r.o to ld gp last 150yds: clsd on wnr nr fin* **25/1**

3033 **3** *1 3/4* **Sirius Prospect (USA)**[7] 7066 4-9-0 103 (p) ShaneKelly 6 110
(Dean Ivory) *rring in stalls but broke on terms: hld up in last trio in centre: rdn over 1f out: gd prog fnl f: r.o to take 3rd post* **12/1**

2120 **4** *hd* **Imperial Guest**[14] 6868 6-9-0 104 TomQueally 13 109
(George Margarson) *trckd nr side ldr: rdn to chal whn drifted rt over 1f out: one pce fnl f* **50/1**

3531 **5** *nse* **Society Rock (IRE)**[42] 6030 5-9-0 117 KierenFallon 7 109
(James Fanshawe) *hld up towards rr in centre: prog 2f out: drvn to ld gp briefly jst ins fnl f: one pce after* **7/2**[1]

2420 **6** *1* **The Cheka (IRE)**[28] 6468 6-9-0 109 (v) NeilCallan 15 106
(Eve Johnson Houghton) *led nr side quartet: overall ldr by 1/2-way: hdd and fdd over 1f out* **14/1**

0261 **7** *3/4* **Wizz Kid (IRE)**[13] 6908 4-8-11 114 (p) OlivierPeslier 8 101
(Robert Collet, France) *chsd ldrs in centre: rdn 2f out: no prog over 1f out: kpt on* **4/1**[2]

2-1 **8** *nk* **Slade Power (IRE)**[97] 4123 3-8-13 108 WayneLordan 2 103
(Edward Lynam, Ire) *s.s: racd centre: prog fr rr 1/2-way: chsd ldrs over 1f out: kpt on but nvr able to threaten* **7/1**

0500 **9** *1/2* **Elusivity (IRE)**[21] 6666 4-9-0 103 EddieAhern 10 101
(Brian Meehan) *trckd ldng trio in centre: rdn to chal over 1f out: fdd ins fnl f* **33/1**

1100 **10** *1* **Van Ellis**[29] 6449 3-8-13 107 JoeFanning 1 98
(Mark Johnston) *pressed ldrs in centre: led gp over 1f out to jst ins fnl f: wknd* **33/1**

400 **11** *nk* **Medicean Man**[105] 3877 6-9-0 109 (p) PatCosgrave 14 97
(Jeremy Gask) *chsd ldng pair nr side: rdn and no prog 2f out: sn btn* **40/1**

0356 **12** *2 3/4* **Restiadargent (FR)**[55] 5648 3-8-10 112 MaximeGuyon 3 85
(H-A Pantall, France) *pressed ldr in centre: led gp over 2f out to over 1f out: wknd fnl f* **8/1**

2010 **13** *1 3/4* **Libranno**[7] 7048 4-9-0 114 RichardHughes 4 82
(Richard Hannon) *chsd ldrs in centre: rdn and wknd qckly wl over 1f out* **20/1**

2256 **14** *3 1/2* **Royal Rock**[14] 6867 8-9-0 107 GeorgeBaker 11 71
(Chris Wall) *hld up in last trio in centre: shkn up 2f out: sn wknd* **33/1**

2051 **15** *2* **Jimmy Styles**[55] 5648 8-9-0 109 (p) FrankieDettori 5 65
(Clive Cox) *overall ldr in centre to 1/2-way: lost gp ld over 2f out: wknd rapidly* **33/1**

1m 15.99s (1.49) **Going Correction** +0.50s/f (Yiel)
WFA 3 from 4yo+ 1lb **15** Ran SP% **121.6**
Speed ratings (Par 115): **110,109,106,106,106 105,104,103,102,101 101,97,95,90,87**
toteswingers 1&2 £29.90, 2&3 £55.70, 1&3 £11.90 CSF £132.04 TOTE £7.50: £3.00, £7.80, £3.90; EX 233.20 Trifecta £2766.90 Pool: £81625.97 - 21.83 winning units..
Owner Lisbunny Syndicate **Bred** New England Stud & P J & P M Vela **Trained** Fethard, Co Tipperary

■ Stewards' Enquiry : Jamie Spencer four-day ban: used whip above permitted level (Nov 3,5-7)

FOCUS

A tricky puzzle to solve. They went a decent pace with most racing down the middle, but the stands' rail proved the place to be. The winner has been rated as running a small PB, while the runner-up and fourth help set the level.

NOTEBOOK

Maarek comfortably sealed the issue. He had disappointingly found one too good at the Curragh last weekend, but that was not a true reflection of his ability and, crucially, he does love soft ground. He got a nice lead on the near side and quickened smartly to take it up inside the final furlong. Indeed, he could have been called the winner some way out and, while he was probably helped by keeping stands' side, he won the race on merit. He has been a revelation this year when the mud is flying and it rates a career-best effort. There is very likely more to come from the late-maturing 6yo next year and he should always be seriously considered when getting his ground. Success at the top level should not be beyond him on this evidence. (op 7-1)

Hawkeyethenoo(IRE) had not shone the last twice, but had landed Stewards' Cup Glorious Goodwood in August and he bounced back with probably his finest effort in defeat, leading home the group that kept to the centre. It was the 6yo's 37th career outing, but only his third in Group company and this should spell and end to his handicap days. (op 33-1)

Sirius Prospect(USA) has been most frustrating to follow this season. Nothing was finishing stronger inside the final furlong, however, and it confirms him very much a Group performer. Getting his head in front will no doubt continue to prove tricky, though. (op 14-1)

Imperial Guest, a course specialist, produced a huge effort on the near side and he helps to put this form into perspective. He deserves to land a Group race.

Society Rock(IRE), who does enjoy this course, came good again in the Haydock Sprint Cup on contrasting ground last time out and had won the Golden Jubilee on an easy surface in 2011. He was always getting there too late down the centre and this was probably just one run too many for the season. (op 10-3 tchd 3-1)

The Cheka(IRE), another proven on deep ground, did his best towards the stands' side and ran well, but is probably a touch flattered. (op 16-1)

Wizz Kid(IRE), last year's second, posted a personal-best on Arc day in first-time cheekpieces over the minimum distance. She was never quite going the pace back up a furlong, though, and it may have been a case of second-time headgear not working out. (op 7-2)

Slade Power(IRE) threatened briefly down the middle, but flattened out when it mattered and getting so warm beforehand cannot have helped his cause. He could make this grade next year. (op 13-2)

Restiadargent(FR) was very interesting on her form behind Black Caviar here in June and came in for some support with ground in her favour. However, she did too much too soon and faded tamely from the furlong marker. (tchd 9-1)

7237 QIPCO BRITISH CHAMPIONS FILLIES' AND MARES' STKS (GROUP 2) 1m 4f

2:55 (2:55) (Class 1) 3-Y-O+

£151,702 (£57,513; £28,783; £14,338; £7,195; £3,611) **Stalls** Low

Form RPR

1-12 **1** **Sapphire (IRE)**[76] 4854 4-9-3 113 PatSmullen 4 118
(D K Weld, Ire) *hld up in 6th: prog over 2f out: rdn and clsd to ld 1f out: r.o wl* **5/2**[1]

3242 **2** *2 1/4* **Shirocco Star**[14] 6899 3-8-10 112 KierenFallon 2 114
(Hughie Morrison) *t.k.h: hld up in 5th: prog to go 3rd over 3f out and stl t.k.h: led over 2f out and committed for home: drvn and hdd 1f out: styd on same pce* **10/1**

110- **3** *2 3/4* **Dancing Rain (IRE)**[342] 7410 4-9-3 117 JohnnyMurtagh 6 110
(William Haggas) *led: narrowly hdd 6f out to over 4f out: rdn and hdd over 2f out: sn outpcd: kpt on* **7/1**[2]

1116 **4** *1 1/4* **Great Heavens**[13] 6912 3-8-10 117 WilliamBuick 3 108
(John Gosden) *trckd ldng trio: effrt and forced wd bnd 3f out: drvn and outpcd over 2f out: one pce after* **5/2**[1]

0061 **5** *1/2* **Semayyel (IRE)**[31] 6379 3-8-10 98 (b) FrederikTylicki 9 107?
(Clive Brittain) *hld up in last quartet: effrt on inner over 2f out: one pce and no imp on ldrs* **100/1**

0-05 **6** *shd* **Testosterone (IRE)**[105] 3856 4-9-3 112 FrankieDettori 10 107
(Ed Dunlop) *hld up in last pair: rdn and no prog over 2f out: n.d after: kpt on* **14/1**

1433 **7** *1/2* **Was (IRE)**[58] 5518 3-8-10 113 RyanMoore 5 106
(A P O'Brien, Ire) *pressed ldr: narrow ld 6f out to over 4f out: lost 2nd over 2f out: grad fdd* **10/1**

5-24 **8** *1* **Jehannedarc (IRE)**[23] 6598 4-9-3 107 AntoineHamelin 8 104
(A De Royer-Dupre, France) *hld up in last pair: shkn up and no prog 3f out: n.d after* **25/1**

1466 **9** *1* **Vow**[14] 6877 3-8-10 109 RichardHughes 7 103
(William Haggas) *restrained into last trio sn after s: shkn up and no prog wl over 2f out* **16/1**

-210 **10** *43* **La Pomme D'Amour**[34] 6295 4-9-3 113 MaximeGuyon 1
(A Fabre, France) *chsd ldng pair to over 3f out: wknd rapidly sn after: eased and t.o* **8/1**[3]

2m 37.32s (4.82) **Going Correction** +0.775s/f (Yiel)
WFA 3 from 4yo 7lb **10** Ran SP% **116.3**
Speed ratings (Par 112): **114,112,110,109,109 109,109,108,107,79**
toteswingers 1&2 £4.60, 2&3 £9.10, 1&3 £4.80 CSF £30.05 TOTE £3.40: £1.90, £2.80, £2.50; EX 24.00 Trifecta £127.70 Pool: £6589.04 - 38.16 winning units..
Owner Moyglare Stud Farm **Bred** Moyglare Stud Farm Ltd **Trained** The Curragh, Co Kildare

FOCUS

A very competitive Group 2 for fillies. The ultra-consistent second sets the standard. The third was not at her best following a long absence, while the winner has been rated as running a 3lb personal best.

NOTEBOOK

Sapphire(IRE) is a consistent and progressive filly who had won at up to Group 3 level but whose best effort was when second to Izzi Top in a 1m2f Group 1 at the Curragh on soft to heavy ground. A wide-margin winner of her three other races in the last year, all at this trip, she settled well behind the leaders and, once asked for her effort in the straight, the rest was pretty straightforward. This was only her 11th start and she looks to have more to offer, while the incentive for connections to keep her in training might be to win a Group 1 with her. (tchd 9-4)

Shirocco Star, runner-up to Was in the Oaks, Great Heavens in the Irish Oaks and touched off in a Group 2 at the Arc meeting, reversed form with those that re-opposed her here but was the bridesmaid once again. Proven on heavy ground but with the blinkers she wore last time left off, she tracked the pace and travelled well throughout, if perhaps rather keenly, until tackling the leader 2f out. She put up brief resistance when challenged by the winner, but had nothing in reserve for the last furlong. She deserves to pick up a Group race and might be worth dropping back to 1m2f at some point if she stays in training in 2013. That is apparently the plan. (op 9-1 tchd 8-1)

Dancing Rain(IRE) won the first running of this at Ascot in 2011 and was back again to defend her title. However, she had not run since finishing down the field in Japan last November, having had a few problems in the meantime. She made the running but steadied the pace coming out of Swinley Bottom before trying to kick again entering the straight. However, she could not pick as well as the principals, although she stuck on well for the minor placing. Providing she is none the worse, connections might consider another trip to the Far East, or even Dubai early next year, before she goes to stud. (tchd 13-2)

Great Heavens, a sister to Nathaniel who had progressed really well this season, winning the Lancashire and Irish Oaks, had been supplemented for the Arc to replace her brother and ran well to finish sixth. This race had been her original target but the Longchamp contest might have taken the edge off her, as she could stay on only at the one pace having come under pressure on the home turn. She can win more good races at this trip next season. (op 7-2 tchd 4-1 in a place)

Semayyel(IRE) won a fast-ground Listed race in re-applied blinkers last time but had been well beaten on her only try on soft, was stepping up in grade and had a lot to find. However, she kept on steadily in the straight and seems to have improved this autumn, aided by the headgear. (op 66-1)

Testosterone(IRE), a Group 2 winning ex-French filly who finished second in the Prix Vermeille in 2011, was sold for 1,200,000gns last autumn but had failed to show much for new connections on two starts in the first half of the season. However, she had form on soft ground and did not fare too badly, staying on steadily from the rear. (tchd 12-1)

Was(IRE), a surprise winner of the Oaks but in the frame in the Irish Oaks, Nassau and Yorkshire Oaks since, had a bit to find on that form and her best efforts had been on better ground than this. She was close up early but dropped away in the straight, suggesting this trip on the ground found her out. (op 8-1)

Jehannedarc(IRE) is a decent Listed/Group 3 performer and ran creditably at Goodwood and Newmarket on last two starts, but she was up in grade and could never land a blow, having been held up at the rear until the straight. (op 20-1)

Vow finished a close fourth in the Oaks on only her third start but had disappointed in the Ribblesdale and a Listed race since, and was again exposed in this better company. (tchd 20-1)

La Pomme D'Amour, a Group 2 winner on good ground at Deauville in August with the subsequent Arc winner behind, had scored on soft and very soft ground but, after racing close to the lead, dropped away and was eased in the straight.

7238 QUEEN ELIZABETH II STKS SPONSORED BY QIPCO (BRITISH CHAMPIONS MILE) (GROUP 1) — 1m (S)

3:30 (3:33) (Class 1) 3-Y-O+

£567,100 (£215,000; £107,600; £53,600; £26,900; £13,500) **Stalls** High

Form				RPR
1221	**1**		**Excelebration (IRE)**[69] 5141 4-9-3 125 ... JPO'Brien 6 (A P O'Brien, Ire) *hld up bhd ldrs: nt clr run over 2f out tl eased out over 1f out: qcknd to ld jst ins fnl f: sn rdn clr: impressive* **10/11**[1]	131+
0423	**2**	*3*	**Cityscape**[34] 6300 6-9-3 124 ... JamesDoyle 4 (Roger Charlton) *trckd ldng pair: wnt 2nd over 2f out: led over 1f out: hdd jst ins fnl f: r.o but easily outpcd* **5/1**[2]	123
2132	**3**	*3 ¼*	**Elusive Kate (USA)**[21] 6673 3-8-11 119 ... WilliamBuick 5 (John Gosden) *led: rdn and hdd over 1f out: kpt on but wl outpcd* **11/2**[3]	113
-124	**4**	*nk*	**Carlton House (USA)**[91] 4320 4-9-3 119 ... RyanMoore 7 (Sir Michael Stoute) *trckd ldrs: moved up to chal 2f out: sn rdn and wl outpcd* **7/1**	115
0120	**5**	*¾*	**Sovereign Debt (IRE)**[22] 6634 3-9-0 111 ... JamieSpencer 8 (Michael Bell) *stdd s: hld up in last pair: effrt over 2f out: kpt on one pce: n.d* **25/1**	113
3322	**6**	*hd*	**Side Glance**[22] 6634 5-9-3 115 ... JimmyFortune 3 (Andrew Balding) *t.k.h: trckd ldr to over 2f out: wknd over 1f out* **20/1**	113
2403	**7**	*3*	**Indomito (GER)**[48] 5869 6-9-3 112 ... TomQueally 2 (A Wohler, Germany) *hld up in last pair: rdn and no prog over 2f out* **50/1**	106
0100	**8**	*15*	**Most Improved (IRE)**[22] 6634 3-9-0 116 ...(v[1]) RichardHughes 1 (Brian Meehan) *in tch: rdn over 2f out: wknd rapidly wl over 1f out: t.o* **14/1**	71

1m 42.33s (1.53) **Going Correction** +0.50s/f (Yiel)
WFA 3 from 4yo+ 3lb — **8** Ran SP% **114.2**
Speed ratings (Par 117): **112,109,105,105,104 104,101,86**
toteswingers 1&2 £2.30, 2&3 £3.60, 1&3 £2.00 CSF £5.56 CT £15.92 TOTE £1.80: £1.02, £2.00, £2.10; EX 5.80 Trifecta £11.60 Pool: £29010.20 - 1845.48 winning units..
Owner Derrick Smith & Mrs John Magnier & Michael Tabor **Bred** Owenstown Stud **Trained** Ballydoyle, Co Tipperary

FOCUS
While only three of the eight-strong field had previously won at the top level, it was still a tight-looking running of this Group 1 and some of the best milers around lined up. They went just an average pace against the stands' side, but the form makes perfect sense. The runner-up is the best guide to the level, with the third below her earlier form.

NOTEBOOK
Excelebration(IRE), runner-up to Frankel in this event last year, has been given a new lease of life recently and stormed to success, following up his French success from old rival Cityscape. The second made a bold bid, but he loomed up going easily at the furlong marker and laughed at him when asked to win the race. The ground posed him no problems and there is no doubt he would be considered a champion himself had he not been around in the Frankel era. Surely a trip to California for the Breeders' Cup Mile will now figure and one should not be overly concerned about the likelihood of much quicker ground there. He was available in one place at 100-30 afterwards for that (soon snapped up), but generally most went around 5-2 and, with this looking his best display yet, he ought to take plenty of beating again as he will arrive full of confidence. (tchd 5-6 and evens in places)

Cityscape gave his all under a positive ride and bounced back to near his best, but was no match whatsoever for his old rival. He has had a busy campaign, but rates a rock-solid benchmark for this form and could well have run his last race before heading off to stud duties. (tchd 6-1)

Elusive Kate(USA) was a strong representative of the classic generation, one with a decent record in the race. She had something to prove on this deep surface, though, and was firmly put in her place after having the run of things against the rail. She ran close enough to her French form with the first pair and makes the form look straightforward. Her trainer later did not rule out renewing rivalry at Santa Anita next month where quicker ground will suit, although it's hard to see her reversing form all things being equal. (tchd 5-1)

Carlton House(USA) was a huge flop here on his previous outing here in July. His record fresh meant a revival was entirely possible, but he was undone by the modest tempo and this points towards 1m2f being his optimum distance. (op 15-2)

Sovereign Debt(IRE) is a smart performer on such ground and likes this venue. However, this was far too hot for him.

Side Glance has been an admirably consistent performer and finished close up to the winner at the Royal meeting here in June. However, Excelebration paid for trying to stick with Frankel that day and he shaped here as though the current campaign was taking its toll. (tchd 18-1)

Indomito(GER) refused to settle and was predictably well beaten. (op 40-1)

Most Improved(IRE), this year's St James's Palace winner, raced in a first-time visor and looks a long way off the horse that won at the Royal meeting. (op 16-1 tchd 12-1)

7239 QIPCO CHAMPION STKS (BRITISH CHAMPIONS MIDDLE DISTANCE) (GROUP 1) — 1m 2f

4:05 (4:11) (Class 1) 3-Y-O+

£737,230 (£279,500; £139,880; £69,680; £34,970; £17,550) **Stalls** Low

Form				RPR
1111	**1**		**Frankel**[59] 5490 4-9-3 140 ... TomQueally 3 (Sir Henry Cecil) *s.s: rcvrd into 4th after 3f: brought wd and prog over 2f out: cruised up to ld over 1f out: shkn up to assert fnl f* **2/11**[1]	136+
1121	**2**	*1 ¾*	**Cirrus Des Aigles (FR)**[14] 6898 6-9-3 130 ... OlivierPeslier 1 (Mme C Barande-Barbe, France) *led after 1f to over 5f out: led again wl over 2f out and kicked on: rdn and hdd over 1f out: styd on but readily hld* **9/2**[2]	132
-122	**3**	*2 ½*	**Nathaniel (IRE)**[42] 6063 4-9-3 126 ... WilliamBuick 6 (John Gosden) *sweating: trckd ldr after 2f to 6f out: rdn to chal over 2f out: btn off over 1f out: one pce* **9/1**[3]	127
1131	**4**	*3 ½*	**Pastorius (GER)**[17] 6805 3-8-12 122 ... FrankieDettori 5 (Mario Hofer, Germany) *hld up in last: effrt to go 4th 2f out: no imp on ldr after* **33/1**	120
3101	**5**	*4*	**Master Of Hounds (USA)**[48] 5869 4-9-3 115 ... RyanMoore 2 (William Haggas) *hld up and sn in 5th: rdn and wknd over 2f out* **80/1**	112
4645	**6**	*2 ½*	**Bullet Train**[59] 5490 5-9-3 113 ... IanMongan 4 (Sir Henry Cecil) *led 1f: restrained: moved up to ld again over 5f out to wl over 2f out: wknd* **100/1**	107

2m 10.22s (2.82) **Going Correction** +0.775s/f (Yiel)
WFA 3 from 4yo+ 5lb — **6** Ran SP% **118.0**
Speed ratings (Par 117): **119,117,115,112,109 107**
toteswingers 1&2 £1.10, 2&3 £1.40, 1&3 £1.20 CSF £1.77 TOTE £1.30: £1.02, £2.20; EX 2.10.
Owner K Abdulla **Bred** Juddmonte Farms Ltd **Trained** Newmarket, Suffolk

FOCUS
The best Champion Stakes for many a year and a fantastic result with Frankel signing off with a perfect record. He was a little below his best (7lb to be precise) on the testing ground, but the form looks solid rated around the runner-up to his latest PB and the third and fourth to around their previous best.

NOTEBOOK
Frankel was making his final appearance on the track and defending an unbeaten record stretching back 13 races. Faced with really testing ground for the first time and taking on a couple of top-notch performers, there were doubts earlier in the week about whether he would take part at all if the rain continued, but a dry night and a mild, rainless day convinced connections that the colt should take his chance. Supporters' confidence was boosted by the impressive victory of his habitual rival Excelebration in the preceding contest and the son of Galileo duly fulfilled his destiny. The race was not without its complications though, as connections have done such a good job settling this formerly excitable individual that he missed the break quite significantly when the stalls opened. The result was his pacemaker was taken back to settle the pace and try to give him a lead. However, Frankel was soon travelling sweetly in behind the pace and, when produced in the straight, his rider was still sitting comfortably before asking him to go past his main market rival. He picked up well when asked and soon had the French challenger's measure, but the winning distance was not as spectacularly wide as in many of his races and he also received a rare smack with the whip behind the saddle. Those points should not detract from this success though, as Cirrus Des Aigles is a seriously good horse on any ground but has a spectacular record on heavy. It will be interesting to see what the handicappers make of this, and it is entirely feasible that they will use the runner-up as the guide, indicating that Frankel ran a little below his peak rating. What really matters, though, is that this colt is one of the all-time greats, and whether it is argued he should have been tried at 1m4f or not (or even dropped back to 6f for that matter), it is likely to be a good few years before we see his like again. Credit must go to Sir Henry Cecil and all his team, his sporting owner Khalid Abdulla and to jockey Tom Queally, who has handled the pressure and expectation this season in an admirably cool manner. The colt has developed a terrific temperament, which was evidenced by how he handled the scenes afterwards, and that bodes well for his future as a stallion, and he could ultimately prove a worthy successor to his prepotent sire in that department. (op 1-5 tchd 1-4 in places and 1-6 in a place)

Cirrus Des Aigles(FR), a very consistent gelding who won this race in 2011 and had since taken the Dubai Sheema Classic, the Prix Ganay and Prix Dollar, at 130 was officially the highest rated rival Frankel had encountered. Also he had an outstanding record on very soft or heavy, his record on heavy being 3-3 and all by eight lengths or more. Not averse to making the running, he went on when Bullet Train was taken back and then let that rival go past before taking it up early in the straight, but try as he might, when the winner drew alongside he could not resist. He is probably the best guide to the level of this form but conversely might have achieved a personal-best in defeat. He seems likely to be off on his travels and can win more good races, so could well be aimed at the Hong Kong Cup, and/or the Sheema Classic again. (op 4-1 tchd 5-1, tchd 11-2 in a place)

Nathaniel(IRE) ran Frankel to half a length on their respective debuts (his only run on soft) but had gone on to win a King George in 2011 and an Eclipse in 2012; the only time he had previously finished out of the first two was when fifth in this race last season, when too keen early. He had been due to run in the Arc but missed that contest with a temperature although he appeared to run right up to his best here. Never far away, he challenged off the home turn but could not quite stay with the principals. It seems likely he will be retired to stud now, but could do really well if kept in training at five, with another King George and the Arc in mind. (op 10-1)

Pastorius(GER), the only 3yo in the field, is the winner of two German Group 1s, including the Deutsches Derby. However, his third to Danedream in the Grosser Preis von Baden indicated he had a bit to find with Nathaniel on a line through that filly, but he came into this 2-2 in Group races at this trip and had won on soft ground. Held up at the back, he ran on in the straight without threatening, but is the sort who could develop into a top international performer next season.

Master Of Hounds(USA) had won in Meydan early in the year and returned to action to win the Topkapi Trophy in Istanbul in September. However, both of those successes were a step down from this level, plus his best form had come on a sound surface and he had never encountered anything softer than good. It was no surprise he failed to make an impression. (op 66-1)

Bullet Train, who has done pacemaking duties for his younger sibling for the past year, seems best on a sound surface but proved amenable to restraint here after his stablemate's tardy start, which helped set the race up.

7240 QIPCO FUTURE STARS APPRENTICE H'CAP — 7f

4:45 (4:49) (Class 2) (0-100,99) 3-Y-O+ **£32,345** (£9,625; £4,810; £2,405) **Stalls** High

Form				RPR
3041	**1**		**Jack Dexter**[28] 6465 3-8-13 **93** ... GeorgeDowning(5) 1 (Jim Goldie) *hld up in last trio far side: gd prog jst over 2f out: r.o to ld overall jst ins fnl f: edgd lft u.p: jst lasted* **11/2**[2]	105+
5230	**2**	*hd*	**Loving Spirit**[21] 6674 4-9-2 **89** ... MichaelMetcalfe 12 (James Toller) *hld up towards rr far side: gd prog wl over 1f out: drifted to centre but r.o wl fnl f: jst failed: 2nd of 12 in gp* **16/1**	100+
5000	**3**	*½*	**Lightning Cloud (IRE)**[28] 6466 4-9-4 **91** ... JulieBurke 24 (Kevin Ryan) *w nr side ldr and racd against rail: led gp 3f out: clr of rivals over 1f out: styd on but jst denied: 1st of 14 in gp* **16/1**	101+
3401	**4**	*hd*	**Compton**[15] 6830 3-8-13 **93** ... WilliamTwiston-Davies(5) 14 (Ralph Beckett) *led far side gp: gng strly over 2f out: rdn and hdd jst ins fnl f: carried lft after: styd on: 3rd of 12 in gp* **12/1**	102
1032	**5**	*1*	**Redvers (IRE)**[21] 6676 4-8-13 **89** ...(b) MichaelJMMurphy(3) 6 (Ed Vaughan) *hld up in midfield far side: prog 2f out: styd on fnl f: nvr quite able to chal: 4th of 12 in gp* **16/1**	96
0404	**6**	*¾*	**Bertiewhittle**[21] 6676 4-9-3 **93** ... LMcNiff(3) 22 (David Barron) *hld up in rr nr side: prog 2f out: r.o to chse ldr fnl f: nrst fin: 2nd of 14 in gp* **16/1**	98
1622	**7**	*½*	**Highland Colori (IRE)**[28] 6466 4-9-3 **95** ... ThomasBrown(5) 7 (Andrew Balding) *trckd far side ldrs: wnt 2nd over 2f out to over 1f out: one pce fnl f: 5th of 12 in gp* **9/2**[1]	98
125	**8**	*½*	**Well Painted (IRE)**[112] 3607 3-9-5 **94** ...(t) AdamBeschizza 8 (William Haggas) *dwlt and squeezed out s: hld up in last on far side: gd prog over 1f out: styd on: nrst fin: 6th of 12 in gp* **10/1**[3]	96+

0030 **9** ½ **Johnny Castle**[21] 6676 4-9-4 **91** .... RyanPowell 26 92
(Amanda Perrett) *wl in tch nr side: rdn to chse ldr over 1f out tl fnl f: one pce: 3rd of 14 in gp* **33/1**

020 **10** *shd* **Atlantic Sport (USA)**[14] 6879 7-9-0 **90** .... DavidKenny(3) 28 90
(Mick Channon) *hld up nr side: prog 2f out: chsd ldrs 1f: styd on but n.d: 4th of 14 in gp* **16/1**

0302 **11** ½ **Boogie Shoes**[23] 6601 4-9-5 **95** .... CharlesBishop(3) 5 94
(Roger Varian) *chsd ldr far side to over 2f out: wknd over 1f out: 7th of 12 in gp* **25/1**

3-10 **12** ¾ **Forgotten Hero (IRE)**[184] 1470 3-9-0 **92** .... MatthewLawson(3) 27 89+
(Charles Hills) *chsd nr side ldrs: outpcd over 2f out: kpt on again fr over 1f out: 5th of 14 in gp* **22/1**

5003 **13** *hd* **Kaldoun Kingdom (IRE)**[7] 7063 7-8-13 **91** .... DarylByrne(5) 21 88
(Richard Fahey) *hld up in last on nr side: prog wl over 1f out: one pce fnl f: 6th of 14 in gp* **33/1**

5501 **14** 1 **Kingscroft (IRE)**[5] 7097 4-9-1 **88** 6ex .... KierenFox 25 82
(Mark Johnston) *trckd nr side ldrs: chsd ldr 2f out to over 1f out: fdd fnl f: 7th of 14 in gp* **20/1**

4600 **15** ¾ **Sir Reginald**[36] 6201 4-8-12 **90** .... GeorgeChaloner(5) 9 82
(Richard Fahey) *bmpd s: mostly in midfield far side: no prog 2f out: wl btn after: 8th of 12 in gp* **33/1**

0064 **16** ½ **Axiom**[14] 6879 8-8-13 **91** .... NoelGarbutt(5) 10 82
(Ed Walker) *a in rr far side: wl btn fnl 2f: 9th of 12 in gp* **20/1**

0200 **17** 1 ¾ **Anderiego (IRE)**[8] 7030 4-9-4 **94** .... NeilFarley(3) 11 80
(David O'Meara) *chsd ldrs far side: u.p 3f out: wknd 2f out: 10th of 12 in gp* **40/1**

6130 **18** 1 **The Confessor**[21] 6659 5-9-1 **91** .... AmyScott(3) 16 75
(Henry Candy) *racd on outer of nr side gp: pressed ldrs: rdn over 3f out: wknd qckly jst over 1f out: 8th of 14 in gp* **20/1**

0020 **19** 1 ¼ **White Frost (IRE)**[28] 6471 4-9-5 **92** .... DeclanCannon 18 72
(Charles Hills) *chsd nr side ldrs tl wknd wl over 1f out: 9th of 14 in gp* **40/1**

0121 **20** ½ **Zacynthus (IRE)**[43] 6011 4-9-4 **91** .... PatrickHills 29 70
(Luca Cumani) *towards rr nr side: rdn 3f out: sn struggling: 10th of 14 in gp* **11/1**

0406 **21** 4 ½ **Smarty Socks (IRE)**[21] 6676 8-9-2 **94** .... DavidBergin(5) 23 61
(David O'Meara) *hld up towards rr nr side: no prog 2f out: wl btn after: 11th of 14 in gp* **20/1**

1300 **22** ¾ **King Of Eden (IRE)**[49] 5827 6-8-9 **87** .... JasonHart(5) 4 53
(Eric Alston) *a in rr far side: no ch fnl 2f: 11th of 12 in gp* **66/1**

4030 **23** 1 **Citrus Star (USA)**[21] 6676 5-9-2 **92** .... TobyAtkinson(3) 15 55
(Chris Wall) *a in rr far side: bhd fnl 2f: last of 12 in gp* **50/1**

0150 **24** 1 **Rodrigo De Torres**[28] 6468 5-9-5 **97** .... ShirleyTeasdale(5) 19 57
(David Nicholls) *overall ldr nr side gp to 3f out: wknd qckly 2f out: 12th of 14 in gp* **50/1**

0214 **25** ½ **Misplaced Fortune**[7] 7066 7-9-0 **94** ....(v) DanielleMooney(7) 20 53
(Nigel Tinkler) *hld up in rr nr side: no prog over 2f out: wknd over 1f out: 13th of 14 in gp* **33/1**

5-14 **26** *hd* **My Freedom (IRE)**[182] 1523 4-9-12 **99** .... HarryBentley 17 57
(Saeed Bin Suroor) *racd on outer of nr side gp: trckd ldrs tl wknd qckly 2f out: last of 14 in gp* **25/1**

1m 29.48s (1.88) **Going Correction** +0.50s/f (Yiel)
WFA 3 from 4yo+ 2lb **26** Ran SP% **141.2**
Speed ratings (Par 109): **109,108,108,107,106 105,105,104,104,104 103,102,102,101,100 99,97,96,95,94 89,88,87,86,85 85**
toteswingers 1&2 £57.00, 2&3 £108.10, 1&3 £28.30 CSF £81.06 CT £1420.50 TOTE £6.30: £2.20, £5.70, £5.90, £2.70; EX 182.30 Trifecta £2087.30 Pool: £4823.42 - 1.71 winning units..
Owner Jim Goldie Racing Club **Bred** Jim Goldie **Trained** Uplawmoor, E Renfrews

FOCUS
While looking totally out of place on such a classy card, this was still a decent and ultra-competitive handicap for apprentice riders. They unsurprisingly split into two groups and, looking at the finish, there was no bias. Sound form. The winner continues to progress and is unbeaten on soft/heavy, while the runner-up was a little unlucky in running and the third, who has been rated close to his best, came clear on the stands' side.

NOTEBOOK
Jack Dexter ◆, whose yard sent out Hawkeythenoo to finish second in the Champion Sprint Stakes earlier on the card, confirmed himself a rapid improver and followed up his Ayr Bronze Cup success in decent fashion. Racing off a 9lb higher mark, he was well handled over this extra furlong and saw it out strongly on ground he loves. The handicapper will react accordingly again, but he looks another Pattern-class performer in the making for his yard. (op 6-1)
Loving Spirit ◆ was well beaten in the Cambridgeshire last time, but had been placed on his two previous outing on the AW and this straight track often suits Polytrack performers. He also goes well on soft ground and can find easier assignments, so surely can be placed to go one better again before long. (op 20-1)
Lightning Cloud(IRE) ran a huge race against the stands' rail. This was much better again from him back at a course he likes and he helps to set the standard.
Compton won over C&D off a 3lb lower mark last time out and cruised through the race. He was done from half a furlong out, but is clearly at the very top of his game and is one to note if turning up in one of the handicaps at next year's Royal meeting. (op 10-1)
Redvers(IRE) won here off 5lb lower in July and has held his form really well since. He again performed respectably and rates a solid benchmark. (op 20-1)
Bertiewhittle turned in a decent effort on the stands' side, but it was clear from the furlong marker he was not going to pick up Lightning Cloud. He looks held by the handicapper, but no doubt there is a race for him on one of the smaller tracks.
Highland Colori(IRE), a runner-up the last twice, had his chance on the far side, yet petered out inside the final furlong and this likeable 4yo shaped as though he's done enough for the year. (op 6-1)
T/Plt: £123.90 to £1 stake. Pool of £233559.73 - 1375.42 winning tickets. T/Qpdt: £5.10 to a £1 stake. Pool of £12764.53 - 1817.51 winning tickets. JN

6952 CATTERICK (L-H)
Saturday, October 20

OFFICIAL GOING: Soft (heavy in places; 6.6)
Wind: moderate 1/2 behind Weather: fine but breezy

7241 BET TOTESCOOP6 TEXT TOTE TO 89660 NOVICE STKS 5f
1:40 (1:40) (Class 5) 2-Y-O **£2,911** (£866; £432; £216) **Stalls** Low

Form RPR
1600 **1** **Strange Magic (IRE)**[14] 6883 2-8-11 75 .... TonyHamilton 3 78
(Richard Fahey) *trckd ldr: led appr fnl f: rdn out* **2/1**[1]

2015 **2** 3 **Palladius**[16] 6809 2-9-0 71 .... AmyRyan 2 70
(Kevin Ryan) *led: drvn over 2f out: hdd appr fnl f: kpt on same pce* **6/1**[3]

421 **3** 2 ¾ **Gallena**[8] 7014 2-9-0 71 .... LiamJones 5 60
(William Haggas) *chsd ldrs: drvn 3f out: kpt on one pce over 1f out* **2/1**[1]

0153 **4** 1 ¾ **Tharawal Lady (IRE)**[16] 6809 2-8-6 73 .... KevinLundie(7) 4 53
(John Quinn) *trckd ldrs: drvn over 2f out: one pce* **6/1**[3]

100 **5** 21 **My Boy Bill**[8] 7028 2-9-5 79 .... GrahamGibbons 6
(Michael Easterby) *dwlt: outpcd and lost pl over 3f out: sn bhd: t.o* **11/2**[2]

1m 2.28s (2.48) **Going Correction** +0.45s/f (Yiel) **5** Ran SP% **110.6**
Speed ratings (Par 95): **98,93,88,86,52**
CSF £14.32 TOTE £3.00: £1.70, £2.90; EX 17.60.
Owner Middleham Park Racing LX **Bred** J Cullinan **Trained** Musley Bank, N Yorks

FOCUS
Testing conditions but the rail in the home straight had been moved in three metres to provide ground not raced on since July 25th. Straightforward form rated through the runner-up.

NOTEBOOK
Strange Magic(IRE) was favoured by the weights so long as she bounced back from a couple of disappointing runs and Richard Fahey's filly did just that, seemingly relishing the drop back to the minimum trip for the first time. She showed enough speed to race on the sharp end with Palladius from the outset before drawing clear as they entered the final furlong to win with a fair amount in hand. Her career is back on track now and these conditions appear to suit her well. (op 11-4 tchd 3-1 in places)
Palladius showed lots of speed to bowl along in front but she was left behind by the stronger stayer in the final furlong. She had ground to make with the winner at these weights anyway, so wasn't really entitled to beat that rival, and so has run her race without showing any improvement. (op 11-2 tchd 5-1)
Gallena wasn't suited by the drop back to 5f. She just lacked the pace to stick with the front two and needs to return to 6f, where she ought to be competitive in nurseries off this sort of mark. (op 9-4 tchd 15-8)
Tharawal Lady(IRE) had nothing to offer in the final furlong and she seems to have gone off the boil. (op 9-2)

7242 TOTEPOOL.COM FILLIES' NURSERY 7f
2:15 (2:15) (Class 4) (0-85,85) 2-Y-O **£4,528** (£1,347; £673; £336) **Stalls** Centre

Form RPR
2520 **1** **Steer By The Stars (IRE)**[12] 6920 2-9-4 **82** .... SilvestreDeSousa 4 91
(Mark Johnston) *w ldrs 2f: drvn over 3f out: hdwy to ld over 2f out: edgd lft: drvn clr over 1f out: eased towards fin* **7/4**[1]

5243 **2** 6 **Storma Norma**[11] 6955 2-8-6 **70** .... DuranFentiman 2 63
(Tim Easterby) *chsd ldrs: wnt 2nd 2f out: no ch w wnr* **8/1**

1611 **3** 6 **Delores Rocket**[9] 6998 2-9-7 **85** ....(b) AmyRyan 3 63
(Kevin Ryan) *led: hdd over 2f out: wknd over 1f out* **7/2**[3]

2010 **4** 2 **Alexandrakollontai (IRE)**[18] 6753 2-7-13 **63** ....(b) JamesSullivan 1 36
(Alistair Whillans) *sn drvn in last: outpcd and reminders over 3f out: nvr a factor* **14/1**

5051 **5** 8 **Columella**[16] 6815 2-8-9 **73** ....(p) LiamJones 5 25
(William Haggas) *w ldrs: drvn over 3f out: hmpd over 2f out: sn wknd* **2/1**[2]

1m 30.45s (3.45) **Going Correction** +0.45s/f (Yiel) **5** Ran SP% **109.7**
Speed ratings (Par 94): **98,91,84,82,72**
CSF £15.15 TOTE £3.20: £1.80, £2.30; EX 11.40.
Owner Capt Alasdair & Mrs Eliza Ross **Bred** Ms E Flynn **Trained** Middleham Moor, N Yorks

FOCUS
Quite a competitive little nursery with two last-time-out winners, both of whom looked on the upgrade coming into this. The winner has been rated to a 8lb personal best.

NOTEBOOK
Steer By The Stars(IRE) put the race to bed with a sweeping move around the field on the home turn before storming up the straight to prove different gear to her rivals on these terms. Steer By The Stars had been slightly disappointing when well beaten by Delores Rocket at Pontefract last time but she looked a different horse here, showing a terrific change of gear to put these rivals to the sword on ground she clearly handles well. (op 3-1)
Storma Norma lacked any real change of gear but kept on much better than the rest for a clear second and she's not far away from landing that first career success. (op 7-1)
Delores Rocket bagged the rail out in front but didn't come anywhere near to seeing out this longer trip and may have done too much racing early on. (op 11-4)
Columella is proven under these conditions but she dropped out the back of the telly in the closing stages and, for whatever reason, was miles below par. Official explanation: trainer's rep had no explanation for the poor form shown (tchd 15-8 and 9-4)

7243 TOTESCOOP6 CATTERICK DASH (HANDICAP STKS) 5f
2:50 (2:51) (Class 2) (0-100,96) 3-Y-O+ **£12,938** (£3,850; £1,924; £962) **Stalls** Low

Form RPR
0210 **1** **Kingsgate Choice (IRE)**[35] 6244 5-9-4 **93** .... LiamKeniry 9 102
(Ed de Giles) *in rr stands' side: hdwy over 1f out: r.o ins fnl f: led post* **17/2**

6506 **2** *nse* **Ancient Cross**[7] 7063 8-9-2 **91** ....(t) PaulMulrennan 11 100
(Michael Easterby) *chsd ldrs stands' side: led that gp jst ins fnl f: hdd last stride* **9/1**

6100 **3** ½ **Even Stevens**[8] 7019 4-8-7 **82** oh1 ....(p) LukeMorris 3 89
(Scott Dixon) *led 4 others far side: kpt on wl fnl f: no ex towards fin: 1st of 5 that gp* **16/1**

360 **4** 2 ½ **Capone (IRE)**[37] 6165 7-8-13 **88** .... RobertWinston 2 86
(Garry Moss) *chsd ldr afr side: kpt on same pce fnl f: 2nd of 5 that gp* **14/1**

0035 **5** *nse* **Waseem Faris (IRE)**[8] 7019 3-8-7 **82** .... SamHitchcott 12 80
(Mick Channon) *racd stands' side: w ldrs: edgd lft and one pce fnl f* **14/1**

0500 **6** 1 ½ **Verinco**[7] 7063 6-9-0 **89** ....(vt) TomEaves 8 82
(Bryan Smart) *led stands' side gp: hdd jst ins fnl f: edgd rt: fdd* **8/1**[3]

5002 **7** *hd* **Partner (IRE)**[12] 6939 6-8-7 **82** ....(b) KellyHarrison 14 76
(Noel Wilson) *racd stands' side: mid-div: drvn over 2f out: swtchd lft over 1f out: keeping on whn nt clr run ins fnl f* **12/1**

400 **8** ¾ **Move In Time**[35] 6244 4-9-6 **95** ....(v) SilvestreDeSousa 15 84
(Bryan Smart) *w ldrs stands' side: wknd jst ins fnl f* **8/1**[3]

32U0 **9** *hd* **Flash City (ITY)**[21] 6689 4-8-9 **84** ....(v) DuranFentiman 10 72
(Bryan Smart) *racd stands' side: w ldrs: wknd jst ins fnl f* **20/1**

0300 **10** 1 ¼ **Jedward (IRE)**[21] 6666 5-8-9 **84** ....(p) AmyRyan 7 68
(Kevin Ryan) *racd stands' side: trckd ldrs over 1f out: sn wknd* **8/1**[3]

0000 **11** 1 ¾ **Bosun Breese**[7] 7063 7-9-0 **89** .... GrahamGibbons 6 67
(David Barron) *chsd ldrs stands' side: drvn over 2f out: wknd appr fnl f* **33/1**

004 **12** ¾ **Burning Thread (IRE)**[25] 6557 5-8-11 **86** .... JamesSullivan 5 61
(Tim Etherington) *racd far side: chsd ldrs: wknd over 1f out: 3rd of 5 that gp* **22/1**

0202 **13** *nk* **Arctic Feeling (IRE)**[18] 6755 4-8-12 **87** .... TonyHamilton 4 61
(Richard Fahey) *chsd ldrs far side: wknd over 1f out: 4th of 5 that gp* **15/2**[2]

3606 **14** 4 **Shoshoni Wind**[18] 6755 4-9-1 **90** ....(b[1]) PhillipMakin 13 50
(Kevin Ryan) *w ldrs stands' side: lost pl over 1f out: eased whn bhd* **40/1**

0033 **15** *10* **Ponty Acclaim (IRE)**[14] 6869 3-9-7 **96**........................ DanielTudhope 1 20
(Tim Easterby) *s.v.s: bhd far side: hdwy and in tch 2f out: sn wknd and eased: last of 5 that gp* **13/2**[1]

1m 1.89s (2.09) **Going Correction** +0.60s/f (Yiel) **15** Ran SP% **120.4**
Speed ratings (Par 109): **107,106,106,102,102 99,99,98,97,95 93,91,91,84,68**
Tote Swingers: 1&2 £27.20, 2&3 £48.50 CSF £78.68 CT £1240.81 TOTE £10.80: £3.40, £3.90, £7.00; EX 113.20 Trifecta £524.90 Part won. Pool of £709.35 - 0.10 winning units..
Owner T Gould **Bred** Michael Staunton **Trained** Ledbury, H'fords

FOCUS
A wide-open sprint handicap and not surprisingly the field split, with the majority electing to come towards the stands' side. There wasn't much between the leaders of the two groups at the line but it was the stands' side pair who edged it. The third has been rated to his turf best.

NOTEBOOK
Kingsgate Choice(IRE) got up on the line having come from a long way back. There looked to be a danger Kingsgate Choice might not get the gaps as he tried to make headway amongst a bunch of horses but he picked up smartly to take advantage of the gaps as they opened before scorching home to overcome a career-high mark. This has to go down as something very close to a career-best run from the winner, who seems to handle most ground, although he seems best on a sound surface. This was his last run of the season and he has the potential to do better again next term. (op 10-1 tchd 11-1)
Ancient Cross hasn't won this year but he went agonisingly close to changing that here and he ran a blinder. He is handicapped to strike again but there probably aren't any more opportunities for him this season.
Even Stevens fared much the best of the group of five to stick to the far side and he has run right up to is best. Given he has such a liking for Fibresand (rated 15lb higher on all-weather), there must be a good chance we'll see more of him over the winter. (op 18-1)
Capone(IRE) is another rated higher on the all-weather and this was only his second run since March, so it's likely he'll be kept on the go this winter. Connections will be pleased with this run as he's not a horse who appreciates testing conditions. (op 12-1)
Partner(IRE) Official explanation: jockey said gelding was denied a clear run
Burning Thread(IRE) Official explanation: trainer said gelding was unsuited by the soft (heavy in places) ground
Ponty Acclaim(IRE) completely blew the start and was always trailing her rivals on the far side. Official explanation: jockey said filly missed the break (op 6-1)

7244 TOTEPOOL MOBILE TEXT TOTE TO 89660 MEDIAN AUCTION MAIDEN STKS 7f
3:25 (3:25) (Class 6) 2-Y-O **£3,067** (£905; £453) **Stalls** Centre

Form RPR
023 **1** **Ready (IRE)**[16] 6818 2-9-3 73.. RobertWinston 4 72
(Garry Moss) *w ldr: t.k.h: led 4f out: drvn over 2f out: sn clr: styd on wl* **7/2**[2]
4 **2** *2* **Lilac Lace (IRE)**[14] 6880 2-8-12 0................................ DuranFentiman 2 62+
(Tim Easterby) *trckd ldrs: t.k.h: effrt over 2f out: chsd wnr over 1f out: no imp* **9/4**[1]
05 **3** *4 ½* **Lambert Pen (USA)**[7] 7067 2-9-3 0................................ SamHitchcott 5 55
(Mick Channon) *chsd ldrs: drvn over 2f out: edgd lft 1f out: one pce* **20/1**
34 **4** *5* **Sakhees Romance**[28] 6473 2-8-12 0........................ SilvestreDeSousa 9 37
(Noel Wilson) *led 3f: wkng whn swtchd rt 1f out* **9/1**
6 **5** *½* **Chocolate Block (IRE)**[23] 6603 2-8-12 0......................... LiamJones 3 36+
(William Haggas) *s.s: bhd tl kpt on fnl 2f* **9/2**[3]
6 *1* **Jackaddock** 2-9-3 0... GrahamGibbons 1 38
(James Bethell) *s.i.s: sn chsng ldrs: t.k.h: wknd over 1f out* **20/1**
7 *4 ½* **Szabo's Art** 2-8-12 0.. LukeMorris 6 22
(Sir Mark Prescott Bt) *s.i.s: sn drvn along: outpcd over 3f out: lost pl over 2f out* **11/2**
004 **8** *shd* **Red Charmer (IRE)**[31] 6356 2-9-3 72.......................... PaulMulrennan 8 26
(Ann Duffield) *chsd ldrs on outer: outpcd over 3f out: lost pl over 2f out* **16/1**
9 *2 ½* **Red Chubbs (IRE)** 2-8-12 0... PJMcDonald 7 15
(Ann Duffield) *s.i.s: a bhd* **33/1**

1m 32.39s (5.39) **Going Correction** +0.60s/f (Yiel) **9** Ran SP% **114.9**
Speed ratings (Par 93): **93,90,85,79,79 78,73,72,70**
Tote Swingers: 1&2 £2.20, 1&3 £5.00, 2&3 £10.30 CSF £11.38 TOTE £2.60: £1.10, £4.00, £3.50; EX 9.40.
Owner Ron Hull **Bred** Kilshannig Stud **Trained** Tickhill, S Yorks

FOCUS
A modest maiden, but straightforward form to rate, with the winner getting first run on the runner-up, who finished well.

NOTEBOOK
Ready(IRE) set the standard and the fact that he proved much the best tells its own story in terms of the quality of those well beaten off. All credit to the winner though as he bounced out to take a prominent position on the stands' rail before skipping clear early in the straight and being in no danger thereafter. It's doubtful he's had to better his two excellent recent runs in defeat but he clearly relishes slow ground and has the potential to do better again next term. (op 3-1)
Lilac Lace(IRE) took time to pick up, by which time the winner had flown, but she kept on well to pull clear of the rest and she confirmed the promise of her Redcar debut. She looks set to improve for a slightly stiffer test of stamina, or at least being able to race on a stiffer track.
Lambert Pen(USA) broke much better than on his first two starts and although no match for the front two, this was still a slight improvement in his form. More is needed though. (op 25-1)
Sakhees Romance didn't get home having been front rank early and maybe conditions were an issue given both previous runs had been on a sound surface. (op 14-1)
Chocolate Block(IRE) blew the start and was never a threat. (op 4-1 tchd early 5-1 in places)

7245 RACING POST FORM WITH TOTEPOOL MOBILE CLAIMING STKS 1m 3f 214y
4:00 (4:00) (Class 6) 3-Y-O+ **£2,181** (£644; £322) **Stalls** Centre

Form RPR
0330 **1** **Phase Shift**[33] 6323 4-8-10 52.................................... SilvestreDeSousa 9 64
(Brian Ellison) *trckd ldrs: t.k.h: chal over 3f out: led over 2f out: kpt on wl clsng stages* **16/1**
5553 **2** *2 ¼* **Arley Hall**[11] 6957 3-8-10 70... TonyHamilton 11 67
(Richard Fahey) *trckd ldrs: upside 3f out: kpt on same pce last 150yds* **6/4**[1]
0600 **3** *1* **Samsons Son**[42] 6039 8-8-13 80.................................. RossAtkinson(3) 3 65
(Terry Clement) *in rr: hdwy over 3f out: chsng ldrs over 2f out: kpt on ins fnl f* **11/1**
0600 **4** *¾* **Bright Applause**[41] 6076 4-9-8 67...................................... BarryMcHugh 7 70
(Tracy Waggott) *led 1f: chsd ldrs: edgd rt 2f out: one pce* **9/1**
5023 **5** *2* **Underwritten**[26] 6526 3-9-1 72...(b) TomEaves 8 66
(Donald McCain) *drvn to ld after 1f: hdd over 2f out: one pce* **11/2**[2]
0-46 **6** *5* **King Fingal (IRE)**[14] 6884 7-9-4 70.......................... MichaelO'Connell 10 54
(John Quinn) *sn chsng ldrs: drvn over 4f out: one pce fnl 2f* **12/1**
/400 **7** *14* **City Ground (USA)**[14] 6885 5-8-11 65.................... DavidSimmonson(7) 5 32
(Michael Easterby) *dwlt: hdwy over 6f out: drvn over 3f out: sn wknd* **50/1**
3044 **8** *2* **Politbureau**[14] 6885 5-9-2 51.. GrahamGibbons 6 27
(Michael Easterby) *mid-div: drvn over 3f out: wknd over 2f out* **40/1**
3050 **9** *3 ¼* **Tricksofthetrade (IRE)**[32] 6339 6-9-2 69..................... RobertWinston 4 22
(Alan Swinbank) *s.s: hld up detached in last: pushed along on outer over 5f out: sme hdwy over 3f out: sn wknd* **8/1**[3]
0344 **10** *8* **Nant Saeson (IRE)**[80] 4711 3-9-5 67.............................. PaulMulrennan 2 19
(John Quinn) *t.k.h in mid-div: drvn over 3f out: sn lost pl* **20/1**
2126 **11** *10* **Eijaaz (IRE)**[28] 6478 11-9-1 58...(p) PJMcDonald 1
(Geoffrey Harker) *in rr: drvn 4f out: nvr on terms: bhd and eased over 1f out* **8/1**[3]

2m 49.25s (10.35) **Going Correction** +0.60s/f (Yiel)
WFA 3 from 4yo+ 7lb **11** Ran SP% **118.7**
Speed ratings (Par 101): **89,87,86,86,85 81,72,71,68,63 56**
Tote Swingers: 1&2 £6.20, 1&3 £30.90, 2&3 £6.00 CSF £40.16 TOTE £23.50: £5.00, £1.60, £3.20; EX 76.00.
Owner Dan Gilbert **Bred** Natton House Thoroughbreds **Trained** Norton, N Yorks

FOCUS
A sound pace to this claimer but a surprise result even so. The level is set around the fourth.
Politbureau Official explanation: jockey said gelding had no more to give
Nant Saeson(IRE) Official explanation: jockey said gelding ran too free
Eijaaz(IRE) Official explanation: jockey said gelding never travelled

7246 BET TOTEPOOL TEXT TOTE TO 89660 H'CAP (DIV I) 7f
4:40 (4:41) (Class 5) (0-75,75) 3-Y-O+ **£2,911** (£866; £432; £216) **Stalls** Centre

Form RPR
460 **1** **Piceno (IRE)**[16] 6812 4-8-11 **65**......................................(p) PJMcDonald 3 80
(Scott Dixon) *mde virtually all: qcknd pce over 2f out: drvn clr fnl f* **15/2**
2410 **2** *6* **Llewellyn**[28] 6465 4-9-3 **71**.. AdrianNicholls 11 70
(David Nicholls) *chsd ldrs: wnt 2nd over 2f out: kpt on same pce appr fnl f* **9/2**[1]
3312 **3** *1 ¼* **Chookie Royale**[50] 5802 4-9-6 **74**......................................(p) TomEaves 2 70
(Keith Dalgleish) *chsd ldrs: 3rd over 2f out: styd on same pce over 1f out* **6/1**[3]
4025 **4** *2* **Shamrocked (IRE)**[6] 7083 3-9-2 **72**.............................. SamHitchcott 13 63
(Mick Channon) *rr-div: hdwy over 3f out: kpt on same pce fnl 2f* **13/2**
000 **5** *1 ¼* **Vale Of Clara (IRE)**[15] 6837 4-9-7 **75**............................ PaulMulrennan 5 63
(Peter Niven) *in rr: hdwy over 2f out: styd on ins fnl f* **50/1**
6000 **6** *hd* **Amazing Star (IRE)**[9] 7003 7-8-13 **67**......................... MichaelO'Connell 9 54
(Declan Carroll) *s.i.s: hdwy over 3f out: one pce fnl 2f* **16/1**
5544 **7** *nse* **Bunce (IRE)**[16] 6811 4-9-4 **72**...(t) DanielTudhope 12 59
(David O'Meara) *mid-div: hdwy over 3f out: one pce fnl 2f* **11/2**[2]
0050 **8** *hd* **On The Hoof**[28] 6502 3-8-13 **69**.................................... GrahamGibbons 10 56
(Michael Easterby) *chsd ldrs: drvn and outpcd over 3f out: kpt on fnl f: no threat* **25/1**
0026 **9** *10* **Emman Bee (IRE)**[17] 6789 3-9-5 **75**.......................... SilvestreDeSousa 6 36
(John Gallagher) *chsd ldrs: drvn over 3f out: wknd 2f out: sn eased* **6/1**[3]
0005 **10** *6* **Mandalay King (IRE)**[14] 6887 7-8-9 **66**........................(p) PaulPickard(3) 7
(Marjorie Fife) *in rr: lost pl over 2f out* **22/1**
0160 **11** *11* **First Class Favour (IRE)**[20] 6710 4-9-2 **70**................. RobertWinston 8
(Tim Easterby) *t.k.h: trckd ldrs: lost pl over 3f out: sn bhd: eased 2f out* **15/2**
0-00 **U** **Shotley Mac**[49] 5819 8-9-2 **70**.......................................(b) DuranFentiman 1
(Neville Bycroft) *stmbld and uns rdr leaving stalls* **40/1**

1m 31.56s (4.56) **Going Correction** +0.75s/f (Yiel)
WFA 3 from 4yo+ 2lb **12** Ran SP% **117.5**
Speed ratings (Par 103): **103,96,94,92,91 90,90,90,79,72 59,**
Tote Swingers: 1&2 £13.20, 1&3 £11.10, 2&3 £6.40 CSF £39.36 CT £222.13 TOTE £10.60: £3.10, £1.50, £2.20; EX 66.00.
Owner Paul J Dixon **Bred** Miss Wendy Fox **Trained** Babworth, Notts

FOCUS
The early speed proved crucial here as nothing got in a blow from off the pace.
Emman Bee(IRE) Official explanation: jockey said filly had no more to give

7247 BET TOTEPOOL TEXT TOTE TO 89660 H'CAP (DIV II) 7f
5:15 (5:16) (Class 5) (0-75,74) 3-Y-O+ **£2,911** (£866; £432; £216) **Stalls** Centre

Form RPR
3430 **1** **Conry (IRE)**[32] 6338 6-9-3 **70**.. StevieDonohoe 13 83
(Ian Williams) *in rr: hdwy on outer over 2f out: chsng ldng pair over 1f out: r.o to ld towards fin* **12/1**
0045 **2** *nk* **Flameoftheforest (IRE)**[23] 6610 5-9-7 **74**.......................(p) LiamKeniry 4 87
(Ed de Giles) *s.i.s: hld up in rr: gd hdwy on ins over 2f out: chsng ldr and carried lft over 1f out: led last 150yds: edgd rt: hdd and no ex towards fin* **11/2**[2]
5434 **3** *1 ¾* **Desert Creek (IRE)**[32] 6342 6-8-12 **65**........................... AdrianNicholls 6 73
(David Nicholls) *t.k.h in mid-div: gd hdwy on ins to ld over 2f out: wandered over 1f out: hdd ins fnl f: crowded and no ex* **9/2**[1]
3050 **4** *13* **Viking Warrior (IRE)**[21] 6687 5-9-1 **68**................................. TomEaves 3 42
(Michael Dods) *chsd ldrs: one pce fnl 2f* **7/1**[3]
5440 **5** *nse* **Serene Oasis (IRE)**[28] 6488 3-9-3 **72**.........................(v) SamHitchcott 11 46
(Mick Channon) *w ldrs: led 3f out: hdd over 2f out: wknd over 1f out* **11/2**[2]
1550 **6** *¾* **Cyflymder (IRE)**[12] 6934 6-9-5 **72**............................ MichaelO'Connell 8 44
(David C Griffiths) *s.i.s: hdwy over 3f out: one pce fnl 2f* **16/1**
0532 **7** *2* **Just The Tonic**[20] 6709 5-8-8 **64**.................................. PaulPickard(3) 12 31
(Marjorie Fife) *chsd ldrs: lost pl 2f out* **8/1**
0500 **8** *nk* **Boris Grigoriev (IRE)**[17] 6789 3-9-5 **74**......................... GrahamGibbons 2 40
(Michael Easterby) *in rr: nvr a factor* **10/1**
1125 **9** *9* **Meandmyshadow**[30] 6406 4-9-6 **73**................................. RobertWinston 10 16
(Alan Brown) *chsd ldrs: drvn over 3f out: wknd 2f out* **14/1**
0320 **10** *¾* **Sunnyside Tom (IRE)**[38] 6141 8-9-0 **67**............................ TonyHamilton 1
(Richard Fahey) *s.i.s: nvr on terms* **25/1**
4411 **11** *¾* **Talent Scout (IRE)**[30] 6410 6-8-11 **71**..........................(p) GemmaTutty(7) 9
(Tim Walford) *w ldrs: drvn 3f out: sn lost pl* **14/1**
0000 **12** *8* **L'Astre De Choisir (IRE)**[42] 6047 4-8-12 **65**.............. PaulMulrennan 7
(Michael Easterby) *s.i.s: in rr: bhd fnl 3f* **40/1**
1155 **13** *11* **Lady Del Sol**[26] 6531 4-9-2 **69**..................................... DanielTudhope 5
(Marjorie Fife) *led tl 3f out: wknd 2f out: eased fnl f* **22/1**

1m 31.89s (4.89) **Going Correction** +0.75s/f (Yiel)
WFA 3 from 4yo+ 2lb **13** Ran SP% **119.2**
Speed ratings (Par 103): **102,101,99,84,84 83,81,81,70,70 69,60,47**
Tote Swingers: 1&2 £24.00, 1&3 £16.70, 2&3 £4.50 CSF £74.97 CT £361.15 TOTE £18.70: £4.20, £1.80, £3.40; EX 125.80.
Owner T Birchall **Bred** Shay White **Trained** Portway, Worcs
■ Stewards' Enquiry : Adrian Nicholls one-day ban: careless riding (Nov 3)
Liam Keniry caution: careless riding.

FOCUS
A strong early gallop and the first three, who pulled a mile clear of the rest, all came from off the pace, with the winner coming from furthest back of the trio to run them down late. The third is the best guide to the level.

7248 FOLLOW TOTEPOOL ON FACEBOOK AND TWITTER "HANDS AND HEELS" APPRENTICE SERIES H'CAP (R.E.I.) 1m 5f 175y
5:45 (5:45) (Class 6) (0-60,63) 3-Y-O+ £2,181 (£644; £322) Stalls Low

Form RPR
5260 1 **Musically**[7] 7062 3-9-2 **57** .... PhilipPrince 1 65
(Mick Channon) *hld up in mid-div: hdwy over 3f out: 3rd 2f out: led appr fnl f: drvn clr last 100yds* **7/1**[3]
26-0 2 7 **Sea Cliff (IRE)**[117] 3440 8-8-13 **48** .... PaulMcGiff(3) 6 46
(Andrew Crook) *hld up in rr: hdwy over 3f out: 4th 2f out: kpt on to take 2nd last 100yds* **66/1**
-046 3 3 ¾ **Think**[73] 4958 5-9-0 **46** oh1 .... (t) DavidSimmonson 5 39
(Clive Mulhall) *trckd ldrs: t.k.h: wnt 3rd 4f out: 2nd over 2f out: upsides over 1f out: one pce* **25/1**
2221 4 3 ½ **Blue Dune**[11] 6956 3-9-8 **63** .... ConorHarrison 3 51
(Mark Johnston) *set str pce: drvn over 3f out: hdd appr fnl f: wknd last 100yds* **4/7**[1]
5363 5 12 **Valentine's Gift**[25] 6555 4-9-9 **55** .... JacobButterfield 10 26
(Neville Bycroft) *t.k.h in rr: drvn over 5f out: wknd over 2f out* **8/1**
0062 6 5 **Medieval Bishop (IRE)**[16] 6807 3-8-11 **52** .... GemmaTutty 4 16
(Tim Walford) *w ldr 4f: chsd ldrs: wknd 4f out: sn bhd* **5/1**[2]
0003 7 13 **Downtown Boy (IRE)**[73] 4958 4-8-11 **46** oh1 .... (b[1]) KevinStott(3) 2
(Ray Craggs) *trckd ldrs: upsides after 5f: drvn over 3f out: wknd 2f out: eased whn bhd ins fnl f* **25/1**

3m 19.33s (15.73) **Going Correction** +0.90s/f (Soft)
WFA 3 from 4yo+ 9lb 7 Ran SP% **113.1**
Speed ratings (Par 101): **91,87,84,82,76 73,65**
Tote Swingers: 1&2 £16.40, 1&3 £9.80, 2&3 £13.60 CSF £327.06 CT £10327.83 TOTE £5.60: £3.90, £15.50; EX 566.40.
Owner J P Repard **Bred** J Repard **Trained** West Ilsley, Berks
FOCUS
Very unreliable form.
T/Plt: £189.40 to a £1 stake. Pool: £45,423.60 - 175.00 winning tickets. T/Qpdt: £29.50 to a £1 stake. Pool: £3,937.88 - 98.69 winning tickets. WG

7218 WOLVERHAMPTON (A.W) (L-H)
Saturday, October 20

OFFICIAL GOING: Standard
Wind: Light behind Weather: Overcast

7249 32RED MEDIAN AUCTION MAIDEN STKS 1m 141y(P)
5:50 (5:51) (Class 6) 3-Y-O £2,181 (£644; £322) Stalls Low

Form RPR
3554 1 **Ty Gwr**[30] 6398 3-9-3 70 .... MartinLane 7 71
(David Simcock) *s.s: hld up: hdwy over 2f out: rdn to ld over 1f out: r.o* **2/1**[2]
4242 2 ½ **Arabic**[11] 6968 3-9-3 61 .... (p) HayleyTurner 8 70
(James Fanshawe) *a.p: chsd ldr over 4f out: rdn and ev ch over 1f out: edgd lft ins fnl f: r.o* **15/8**[1]
2203 3 2 **La Pampita (IRE)**[8] 7025 3-8-12 70 .... JimCrowley 2 60
(William Knight) *s.i.s: sn chsng ldrs: rdn over 1f out: edgd lft and styd on same pce ins fnl f* **3/1**[3]
5344 4 4 **Shore Performer (IRE)**[22] 6643 3-8-12 62 .... ShaneKelly 6 51
(William Haggas) *plld hrd: trckd ldr tl led over 6f out: clr over 5f out: rdn and hdd over 1f out: wknd ins fnl f* **7/1**
50 5 4 **Newington**[11] 6965 3-8-9 0 .... SimonPearce(3) 4 42
(Lydia Pearce) *hld up: hdwy u.p over 2f out: wknd over 1f out* **33/1**
00 6 21 **Fantastic Indian**[16] 6827 3-8-12 0 .... WilliamCarson 3
(Roy Brotherton) *led: hdd over 6f out: chsd ldrs tl rdn over 3f out: wknd over 2f out: t.o* **150/1**
5600 7 5 **Landaho**[52] 5738 3-8-12 40 .... [1] JoeFanning 1
(Hugh McWilliams) *s.s: a wl bhd: t.o* **100/1**
0 8 3 **Amantius**[11] 6965 3-9-3 0 .... ChrisCatlin 5
(John Spearing) *plld hrd and prom: lost pl 7f out: sn pushed along: wknd over 3f out: t.o* **40/1**

1m 50.37s (-0.13) **Going Correction** -0.10s/f (Stan) 8 Ran SP% **112.6**
Speed ratings (Par 99): **96,95,93,90,86 68,63,60**
toteswingers 1&2 £2.10, 1&3 £1.50, 2&3 £1.70 CSF £5.93 TOTE £4.00: £1.30, £1.10, £1.10; EX 10.10 Trifecta £29.60 Pool: £557.16 - 13.92 winning units..
Owner Mrs Ann Simcock **Bred** Mrs A E Simcock **Trained** Newmarket, Suffolk
FOCUS
An ordinary maiden rated around the first two.
Landaho Official explanation: jockey said filly was slowly away

7250 LIVE SCORES ON YOUR MOBILE AT FOOTBALLSCORES.COM H'CAP (DIV I) 1m 1f 103y(P)
6:20 (6:20) (Class 6) (0-65,72) 3-Y-O+ £2,181 (£644; £322) Stalls Low

Form RPR
5156 1 **Archina (IRE)**[12] 6941 3-8-12 **57** .... TedDurcan 4 66
(Chris Wall) *chsd ldrs: rdn to ld over 1f out: drvn out* **16/1**
0334 2 1 ¼ **Bold Cross (IRE)**[15] 6842 9-9-5 **65** .... RobertWilliams(5) 1 71
(Edward Bevan) *hld up: hdwy over 1f out: sn rdn: r.o* **12/1**
5632 3 ½ **Tenessee**[29] 6458 5-9-9 **64** .... PatCosgrave 6 69
(Jamie Osborne) *led: pushed along over 2f out: rdn and hdd over 1f out: styd on same pce ins fnl f* **3/1**[2]
2403 4 nk **Tiger Webb**[12] 6941 4-9-2 **57** .... PhillipMakin 8 61
(Michael Easterby) *hld up in tch: rdn over 1f out: r.o* **9/4**[1]
0320 5 1 **Chatterati (USA)**[9] 7003 3-9-6 **65** .... (v[1]) JoeFanning 2 67
(Mark Johnston) *prom: rdn over 2f out: styd on* **20/1**
2006 6 nk **Daniel Thomas (IRE)**[35] 6250 10-9-9 **64** .... (tp) WilliamCarson 9 66
(Violet M Jordan) *s.i.s: pushed along early in rr: drvn along over 3f out: r.o u.p ins fnl f: nrst fin* **16/1**
000 7 ¾ **Focail Eile**[43] 5990 7-9-5 **60** .... ShaneKelly 5 60
(Tim Pitt) *hld up: rdn over 1f out: nvr nrr* **20/1**
024 8 1 **Pearl War (USA)**[40] 6092 3-9-5 **64** .... JimCrowley 10 62
(William Haggas) *racd keenly: trckd ldrs: rdn and edgd lft over 1f out: no ex ins fnl f* **10/1**
365 9 2 **Ryedale Lass**[63] 5351 4-9-6 **61** .... AmyRyan 12 55
(Joseph Tuite) *s.i.s: racd keenly: hdwy over 6f out: rdn over 2f out: wknd fnl f* **11/1**
4101 10 3 **High Resolution**[9] 7003 5-9-12 **72** .... GarryWhillans(5) 11 59
(Linda Perratt) *s.i.s: hld up: rdn over 2f out: wknd over 1f out* **8/1**[3]
3054 11 1 ½ **Titus Star (IRE)**[10] 6502 3-9-4 **63** .... FergusSweeney 7 47
(J S Moore) *trckd ldr: racd keenly: rdn over 2f out: wknd over 1f out* **25/1**
1065 12 14 **Applaude**[21] 6690 7-8-10 **51** oh3 .... (b) MichaelStainton 3
(Chris Bealby) *hld up: drvn along and lost tch fnl 5f* **40/1**

2m 0.17s (-1.53) **Going Correction** -0.10s/f (Stan)
WFA 3 from 4yo+ 4lb 12 Ran SP% **119.6**
Speed ratings (Par 101): **102,100,100,100,99 99,98,97,95,93 91,79**
toteswingers 1&2 £34.30, 1&3 £15.70, 2&3 £8.50 CSF £186.26 CT £742.85 TOTE £20.70: £7.60, £2.80, £1.20; EX 313.10 TRIFECTA Not won..
Owner Hintlesham Thoroughbreds **Bred** Good Breeding **Trained** Newmarket, Suffolk
FOCUS
The first division of this modest handicap. The exposed runner-up sets the standard.

7251 LIVE SCORES ON YOUR MOBILE AT FOOTBALLSCORES.COM H'CAP (DIV II) 1m 1f 103y(P)
6:50 (6:50) (Class 6) (0-65,65) 3-Y-O+ £2,181 (£644; £322) Stalls Low

Form RPR
5060 1 **Tapis Libre**[17] 6794 4-8-12 **60** .... (b[1]) MatthewHopkins(7) 7 72
(Michael Easterby) *chsd ldr tl led over 6f out: rdn over 1f out: styd on wl* **12/1**
0540 2 2 ¼ **Mcbirney (USA)**[16] 6819 5-9-9 **64** .... SebSanders 2 71
(Paul D'Arcy) *a.p: rdn to chse wnr over 1f out: styd on* **5/2**[1]
3256 3 1 ¾ **Superciliary**[20] 6704 3-9-4 **63** .... JimCrowley 13 67
(Ralph Beckett) *chsd ldrs: wnt 2nd over 2f out tl rdn over 1f out: styd on same pce ins fnl f* **9/2**[2]
5504 4 1 ¼ **Son Vida (IRE)**[33] 6317 4-9-0 **62** .... (p) RobertTart(7) 10 63
(Alan Bailey) *prom: chsd ldr over 3f out tl rdn over 2f out: no ex fnl f* **16/1**
0055 5 1 **Greeley House**[37] 6174 4-9-3 **58** .... TedDurcan 9 57
(Chris Wall) *s.i.s: hld up: hdwy over 2f out: sn rdn: styd on same pce appr fnl f* **15/2**[3]
6646 6 ½ **Go On Gilbert**[122] 3275 3-8-12 **57** .... PaddyAspell 5 55
(John Wainwright) *mid-div: drvn along 3f out: styd on ins fnl f: nvr nrr* **40/1**
2544 7 1 ½ **Fishforcompliments**[8] 7022 8-9-10 **65** .... FrederikTylicki 11 60
(Richard Fahey) *hld up: rdn over 1f out: r.o ins fnl f: nrst fin* **17/2**
2142 8 nk **Celtic Step**[21] 6690 8-9-5 **60** .... DaleSwift 12 54
(Peter Niven) *hld up: rdn over 2f out: styd on ins fnl f: nvr nrr* **9/2**[2]
1306 9 4 ½ **Kyle Of Bute**[29] 6458 6-9-6 **61** .... WilliamCarson 6 46
(Brian Baugh) *mid-div: hdwy over 3f out: rdn over 2f out: wkng whn hung lft over 1f out* **12/1**
0060 10 3 **Transfer**[12] 6940 7-9-3 **58** .... (p) JoeFanning 8 36
(Richard Price) *sn pushed along and a in rr* **28/1**
4405 11 5 **Carrie's Magic**[1] 7221 5-8-10 **51** .... (v[1]) AmyRyan 3 19
(Alistair Whillans) *plld hrd: led: hdd over 6f out: chsd ldrs: rdn over 2f out: wknd wl over 1f out* **25/1**

1m 59.65s (-2.05) **Going Correction** -0.10s/f (Stan)
WFA 3 from 4yo+ 4lb 11 Ran SP% **118.2**
Speed ratings (Par 101): **105,103,101,100,99 99,97,97,93,90 86**
toteswingers 1&2 £12.30, 1&3 £10.50, 2&3 £3.70 CSF £41.68 CT £162.12 TOTE £12.70: £3.10, £2.30, £1.40; EX 74.40 Trifecta £351.60 Pool: £475.20 - 1.00 winning unit..
Owner Carpet Kings Syndicate **Bred** Sedgecroft Stud **Trained** Sheriff Hutton, N Yorks
FOCUS
The second leg was run 0.52secs faster than the preceding first division. The third and fourth have been rated close to their recent marks.

7252 32RED.COM H'CAP 1m 4f 50y(P)
7:20 (7:20) (Class 6) (0-60,60) 3-Y-O+ £2,181 (£644; £322) Stalls Low

Form RPR
535- 1 **Mutual Regard (IRE)**[352] 7240 3-9-3 **60** .... LukeMorris 1 70+
(Sir Mark Prescott Bt) *chsd ldrs: n.m.r and led over 1f out: edgd rt ins fnl f: drvn out* **11/4**[1]
0442 2 ¾ **Annelko**[23] 6616 5-9-5 **55** .... GrahamLee 7 64+
(Michael Blake) *hld up: hdwy and nt clr run over 1f out: rdn and r.o wl ins fnl f: nt rch wnr* **6/1**
6504 3 1 **Layla's Boy**[12] 6940 5-9-9 **59** .... (bp) FrederikTylicki 4 66
(John Mackie) *hld up: hdwy over 1f out: sn rdn: r.o* **16/1**
0004 4 1 ¼ **Unex Renoir**[109] 3722 4-9-7 **60** .... MarkCoumbe(3) 3 65
(Brian Ellison) *a.p: rdn and ev ch whn n.m.r over 1f out: styd on same pce ins fnl f* **3/1**[2]
-600 5 1 ½ **If You Whisper (IRE)**[142] 2637 4-9-8 **58** .... MartinDwyer 6 61
(Mike Murphy) *s.i.s: hdwy to trck ldr over 9f out: led over 2f out: rdn: edgd lft and hdd over 1f out: no ex ins fnl f* **40/1**
2501 6 2 ¼ **Schmooze (IRE)**[12] 6940 3-9-2 **59** .... DaleSwift 5 58
(Linda Perratt) *hld up: pushed along 5f out: hdwy and nt clr run over 1f out: swtchd rt: nvr trbld ldrs* **5/1**[3]
0025 7 1 **Cobbs Quay**[7] 7058 4-9-3 **56** .... (b) SimonPearce(3) 2 53
(Daniel Kubler) *chsd ldrs: rdn over 2f out: wknd fnl f* **14/1**
135 8 4 **Operateur (IRE)**[18] 6315 4-9-6 **56** .... PhillipMakin 9 52
(Ben Haslam) *led: rdn and hdd over 2f out: ev ch whn hmpd over 1f out: no ex* **14/1**
2400 9 3 ¼ **Fire In Babylon (IRE)**[11] 6949 4-9-6 **56** .... JimCrowley 12 42
(Michael Wigham) *s.i.s: hld up: a in rr: rdn over 1f out: wknd fnl f* **14/1**
-053 10 3 ¼ **Langley**[42] 6056 5-9-10 **60** .... (v) DavidProbert 11 41
(Tim Vaughan) *hld up: a in rr: rdn over 3f out: sn wknd* **16/1**
2214 11 11 **Iguacu**[34] 6278 8-9-0 **57** .... (p) DanielMuscutt(7) 8 20
(Richard Price) *mid-div: rdn and wknd over 3f out* **28/1**

2m 39.69s (-1.41) **Going Correction** -0.10s/f (Stan)
WFA 3 from 4yo+ 7lb 11 Ran SP% **120.3**
Speed ratings (Par 101): **100,99,98,98,97 95,94,92,90,87 80**
toteswingers 1&2 £4.60, 1&3 £12.90, 2&3 £12.20 CSF £20.21 CT £228.86 TOTE £4.40: £1.90, £2.90, £4.50; EX 26.70 Trifecta £153.90 Pool: £551.17 - 2.65 winning units..
Owner Moyglare Stud Farm **Bred** Moyglare Stud Farm Ltd **Trained** Newmarket, Suffolk
■ Stewards' Enquiry : Luke Morris two-day ban: used whip above shoulder height (Nov 3,5)
FOCUS
A moderate handicap. Fair form for the grade, though, with the winner unexposed and the runner-up running as well as ever to beat the rest.
Unex Renoir Official explanation: jockey said gelding suffered interference in running

7253 STAY AT THE WOLVERHAMPTON HOLIDAY INN MAIDEN STKS 5f 20y(P)
7:50 (7:52) (Class 5) 3-Y-O+ £2,911 (£866; £432; £216) Stalls Low

Form RPR
0333 1 **Levi Draper**[18] 6765 3-9-3 69 .... HayleyTurner 4 70
(James Fanshawe) *mde virtually all: rdn over 1f out: r.o* **6/4**[1]
-322 2 hd **Gaelic Wizard (IRE)**[7] 7061 4-8-10 70 .... JoshBaudains(7) 3 70
(Dominic Ffrench Davis) *w wnr: rdn ins fnl f: r.o* **2/1**[2]

550 3 1 ½ **Art Form**[16] 6806 3-8-12 67........(t) SebSanders 1 59
(Alan McCabe) *w wnr: rdn over 1f out: no ex towards fin* 7/2[3]
6-60 4 1 ¾ **Stans Deelyte**[55] 5624 3-8-5 47........ ShirleyTeasdale(7) 2 53
(Lisa Williamson) *chsd ldrs: rdn over 1f out: styd on same pce ins fnl f* 40/1
3 5 1 ½ **Saunta**[79] 4729 3-8-12 0........[1] MartinLane 6 48
(David Simcock) *s.i.s: hdwy 1/2-way: rdn over 1f out: no ex fnl f* 7/1
050 6 1 ¼ **Busy Bimbo (IRE)**[40] 6100 3-8-12 42........ AmyRyan 5 43
(Alan Berry) *s.i.s: outpcd: rdn and hung lft over 1f out: n.d* 66/1
7 17 **Mid Yorkshire Golf** 3-8-12 0........ RobbieFitzpatrick 7
(Peter Grayson) *s.s: outpcd* 125/1

1m 2.14s (-0.16) **Going Correction** -0.10s/f (Stan) 7 Ran SP% 112.8
Speed ratings (Par 103): **97,96,94,91,89 87,59**
toteswingers 1&2 £1.30, 1&3 £1.10, 2&3 £1.60 CSF £4.62 TOTE £2.30: £1.30, £1.30; EX 5.20.
Owner Andrew & Julia Turner **Bred** Cheveley Park Stud Ltd **Trained** Newmarket, Suffolk

FOCUS
A weak maiden. The runner-up has been rated to his turf form.
Mid Yorkshire Golf Official explanation: jockey said filly missed the break

7254 FOLEY STEELS CLAIMING STKS 5f 20y(P)
8:20 (8:21) (Class 6) 3-Y-0+ £2,181 (£644; £322) Stalls Low

Form RPR
1500 1 **Where's Reiley (USA)**[12] 6938 6-8-11 78........(b) FrankieMcDonald 4 77
(Alastair Lidderdale) *a.p: pushed along 1/2-way: rdn ins fnl f: r.o to ld nr fin* 8/1
0615 2 ½ **Red Cape (FR)**[4] 7145 9-8-5 70........(b) JamesSullivan 5 70
(Ruth Carr) *hld up in tch: rdn to ld wl ins fnl f: hdd nr fin* 5/1[3]
6040 3 ½ **Falasteen (IRE)**[8] 7023 5-8-9 73........ ChrisCatlin 11 72
(Milton Bradley) *led: rdn over 1f out: hdd wl ins fnl f* 12/1
0100 4 ½ **Dancing Maite**[3] 7178 7-8-12 70........(b) MarkCoumbe(3) 3 76
(Roy Bowring) *hld up: hdwy over 1f out: sn rdn: r.o* 33/1
0010 5 1 ½ **Clubland (IRE)**[2] 7197 3-8-5 70........ AmyRyan 1 61
(Kevin Ryan) *s.i.s: hld up: hdwy over 1f out: no ex wl ins fnl f* 3/1[2]
1100 6 2 **Lesley's Choice**[21] 6688 6-9-1 77........(b) JamesDoyle 6 63
(Sean Curran) *chsd ldr 1f: remained handy: rdn 1/2-way: no ex ins fnl f* 12/1
1460 7 3 **Julius Geezer (IRE)**[43] 6008 4-9-5 82........ RichardKingscote 2 57+
(Tom Dascombe) *s.i.s: in rr whn hmpd wl over 3f out: nvr on terms* 9/4[1]
0050 8 ½ **Powerful Wind (IRE)**[18] 6767 3-9-1 82........ LukeMorris 8 51
(Ronald Harris) *racd keenly: trckd ldr 4f out: rdn and ev ch over 1f out: wknd ins fnl f* 6/1
-335 9 2 **Nordic Light (USA)**[11] 6951 8-8-0 38........(t) JemmaMarshall(5) 7 34
(Mrs A Malzard, Jersey) *sn pushed along and prom: lost pl 4f out: sn bhd* 150/1

1m 1.2s (-1.10) **Going Correction** -0.10s/f (Stan) 9 Ran SP% 116.8
Speed ratings (Par 101): **104,103,102,101,99 96,91,90,87**
toteswingers 1&2 £7.10, 1&3 £11.70, 2&3 £17.30 CSF £48.27 TOTE £9.60: £2.10, £2.00, £2.90; EX 61.50 Trifecta £360.90 Part won. Pool: £487.74 - 0.30 winning units..Falasteen was subject to a friendly claim.
Owner Chris Beek & Steve Jakes **Bred** Overbrook Farm **Trained** Lambourn, Berks
■ Stewards' Enquiry : Jemma Marshall three-day ban: careless riding (Nov 3,5,6)

FOCUS
Some fair performers in this claimer and the leaders went off pretty quickly, leaving the race open for a finisher. The fourth limits the form.
Julius Geezer(IRE) Official explanation: jockey said gelding suffered interference in running

7255 32RED CASINO H'CAP 2m 119y(P)
8:50 (8:50) (Class 6) (0-60,54) 3-Y-0+ £2,181 (£644; £322) Stalls Low

Form RPR
0/22 1 **Blue Zealot (IRE)**[51] 5771 5-9-6 49........(t) RachaelGreen(3) 10 63
(Anthony Honeyball) *hld up: hdwy over 5f out: chsd ldr over 3f out: led on bit over 2f out: sn clr: styd on wl* 11/2[3]
0/ 2 8 **Iron Duke**[13] 3648 6-8-12 45........(t) PhilipPrince(7) 6 49
(Liam Corcoran) *mid-div: hdwy u.p over 2f out: wnt 2nd ins fnl f: no ch w wnr* 40/1
3500 3 3 ¾ **Waldsee (GER)**[16] 6821 7-9-13 53........(v[1]) JamesDoyle 7 53
(Sean Curran) *hld up: hdwy 11f out: chsd ldr over 6f out: led over 4f out: rdn and hdd over 2f out: wknd ins fnl f* 11/2[3]
6215 4 ½ **Smart Affair**[2] 7196 3-9-2 52........(be) SamHitchcott 4 51
(Alan Bailey) *hld up: hdwy u.p over 2f out: nt trble ldrs* 11/4[1]
0646 5 hd **Roughlyn**[56] 5589 3-8-9 45........(p) AmyRyan 5 44
(Lisa Williamson) *chsd ldrs: rdn over 3f out: hung lft and wknd over 1f out* 10/1
6040 6 ½ **Shirls Son Sam**[11] 6956 4-9-6 46........ KellyHarrison 11 44
(Chris Fairhurst) *hld up: hdwy over 5f out: rdn over 2f out: wknd over 1f out* 10/3[2]
5400 7 3 ¾ **Nesnaas (USA)**[3] 7169 11-9-5 45........ FrankieMcDonald 9 39
(Alastair Lidderdale) *hld up: rdn over 3f out: n.d* 40/1
0000 8 18 **Rare Coincidence**[58] 4867 11-9-5 45........ GrahamLee 8 17
(Alan Berry) *led: rdn and hdd over 4f out: wknd over 3f out: t.o* 40/1
-350 9 29 **Dazzling Begum**[11] 6948 7-9-2 45........(p) SimonPearce(3) 2
(Lydia Pearce) *prom: chsd ldr 14f out tl over 6f out: rdn and wknd over 4f out: t.o* 20/1
2050 10 25 **Pugnacious (IRE)**[16] 6807 3-9-4 54........(b) JoeFanning 1
(Mark Johnston) *chsd ldr over 2f: remained handy: pushed along over 7f out: wknd 5f out: sn t.o* 13/2

3m 40.2s (-1.60) **Going Correction** -0.10s/f (Stan)
WFA 3 from 4yo+ 10lb 10 Ran SP% 115.0
Speed ratings (Par 101): **99,95,93,93,93 92,91,82,69,57**
toteswingers 1&2 £71.00, 1&3 £5.40, 2&3 £71.00 CSF £206.12 CT £1250.31 TOTE £4.40: £1.80, £6.10, £1.80; EX 200.70 TRIFECTA Not won..
Owner Mrs Olivia Hoare **Bred** J Erhardt **Trained** Mosterton, Dorset

FOCUS
A weak staying handicap, and the winner has been rated as running 4lb better than his previous best.

7256 32RED SUPPORTING BRITISH RACING H'CAP 1m 141y(P)
9:20 (9:21) (Class 6) (0-65,65) 3-Y-0+ £2,181 (£644; £322) Stalls Low

Form RPR
0500 1 **Stylistickhill (IRE)**[40] 6106 4-9-3 61........(t) LukeMorris 6 70
(Scott Dixon) *hld up: hdwy over 2f out: rdn over 1f out: styd on u.p to ld wl ins fnl f* 17/2[3]
3263 2 ½ **Charlcot**[29] 6456 4-9-5 63........ TedDurcan 2 71
(James Bethell) *chsd ldr: rdn over 2f out: ev ch wl ins fnl f: r.o* 7/1[2]
2040 3 1 ¼ **Striker Torres (IRE)**[8] 7022 6-9-6 64........(v) GrahamLee 8 69
(Ian McInnes) *hld up: rdn over 1f out: r.o wl ins fnl f: nt rch ldrs* 11/1
3366 4 ½ **Silver Alliance**[17] 6794 4-9-7 65........ JimmyQuinn 3 72+
(Julia Feilden) *a.p: rdn over 1f out: running on whn hmpd wl ins fnl f: nt rcvr* 11/1
466- 5 shd **Avertis**[298] 7887 7-9-1 64........ AmyScott(5) 4 68
(Alastair Lidderdale) *a.p: rdn over 1f out: r.o* 18/1
306 6 ½ **Roger Ramjet (IRE)**[34] 6279 3-9-2 64........(bt[1]) JoeFanning 1 67
(Brian Meehan) *led: rdn over 1f out: hdd and edgd lft wl ins fnl f* 16/1
1000 7 shd **Flying Applause**[69] 5129 7-9-0 61........(b) MarkCoumbe(3) 9 63
(Roy Bowring) *hld up: hdwy over 2f out: sn rdn: outpcd wl over 1f out: r.o ins fnl f* 50/1
6015 8 2 **Cross The Boss (IRE)**[12] 6941 5-9-2 60........(t) PhillipMakin 10 58
(Ben Haslam) *hld up: rdn over 1f out: nvr nrr* 11/10[1]
0310 0 1 ¼ **Resplendent Alpha**[15] 6842 8-9-7 65........ FergusSweeney 5 60
(Jamie Osborne) *hld up: hdwy u.p over 1f out: no ex fnl f* 20/1
2320 10 1 **Ebony Clarets**[9] 7003 3-8-11 64........ GarryWhillans(5) 13 57
(Linda Perratt) *chsd ldrs: rdn over 2f out: wknd fnl f* 16/1
12-4 11 2 ¼ **Sovento (GER)**[269] 296 8-8-12 63........ NoraLooby(7) 7 50
(Alan McCabe) *prom: pushed along over 3f out: wknd over 1f out:* 18/1
0465 U **Rock Anthem (IRE)**[72] 5008 8-9-4 62........ MartinDwyer 11
(Mike Murphy) *tried to get under stalls and uns rdr as the gates opened* 9/1

1m 49.96s (-0.54) **Going Correction** -0.10s/f (Stan)
WFA 3 from 4yo+ 4lb 12 Ran SP% 126.3
Speed ratings (Par 101): **98,97,96,96,95 95,95,93,92,91 89,**
toteswingers 1&2 £11.40, 1&3 £19.60, 2&3 £9.10 CSF £71.49 CT £688.70 TOTE £5.80: £3.50, £1.70, £3.00; EX 96.20 Trifecta £164.30 Pool: £473.10 - 2.13 winning units..
Owner Paul Dixon & The Tickhill Racing Partner **Bred** Eamon Reilly **Trained** Babworth, Notts

FOCUS
A modest handicap. The third has been rated close to his recent best, with the fourth rated as having finished a narrow third with a clear run.
Cross The Boss(IRE) Official explanation: jockey said gelding ran too free
T/Plt: £37.40 to a £1 stake. Pool: £88,313.77 - 1,720.12 winning tickets T/Qpdt: £14.70 to a £1 stake. Pool: £7,419.05 - 373.36 winning tickets CR

7257 - 7263a (Foreign Racing) - See Raceform Interactive

7181 CAULFIELD (R-H)
Saturday, October 20

OFFICIAL GOING: Turf: good to soft changing to good after 4.00am

7264a BMW CAULFIELD CUP (GROUP 1 H'CAP) (3YO+) (TURF) 1m 4f
6:05 (12:00) 3-Y-0+
£1,085,526 (£246,710; £131,578; £72,368; £59,210; £49,342)

RPR
1 **Dunaden (FR)**[91] 4322 6-9-2 0........ CraigAWilliams 18 124+
(M Delzangles, France) *dropped in fr wd draw and hld up in last trio on inner: swtchd out and rdn to improve 2f out: styd on down wd outside to ld ins fnl 75yds: shade cosily* 13/1
2 ½ **Alcopop (AUS)**[7] 7070 8-8-4 0........ DominicTourneur 8 111
(Jake Stephens, Australia) *hld up in last quartet on outer: hdwy over 2f out: rdn to chal 1 1/2f out: led ent fnl f: hdd ins fnl 75yds: kpt on* 15/1
3 ¾ **Lights Of Heaven (NZ)**[28] 5-8-5 0........(p) LukeNolen 7 111
(Peter G Moody, Australia) *midfield: rdn 2f out: styd on to go 3rd fnl strides: nt pce of front pair* 10/1
4 hd **Americain (USA)**[62] 5400 7-9-2 0........ GeraldMosse 15 121+
(A De Royer-Dupre, France) *midfield on outer: rdn over 2f out: styd on to go 4th post: nt pce to chal* 20/1
5 shd **My Quest For Peace (IRE)**[56] 5575 4-8-6 0........ CoreyBrown 2 111
(Luca Cumani) *prom on inner: rdn to chal 2f out: led 1 1/2f out: hdd ent fnl f: kpt on: dropped to 5th post* 15/2[3]
6 1 ¼ **Zabeelionaire (NZ)**[14] 4-8-3 0........(p) CraigNewitt 1 106
(Leon Corstens, Australia) *midfield on inner: rdn over 1 1/2f out: styd on ins fnl f but nt pce to chal* 25/1
7 hd **Folding Gear (NZ)**[28] 5-8-3 0........ BenMelham 4 106+
(Lee & Shannon Hope, Australia) *stdd and settled in midfield: hdwy and stl gng okay whn nt clr run 1 1/2f out: shuffled bk: rdn ent fnl f: r.o to go 7th cl home: gng on at fin* 25/1
8 1 ¼ **Sneak A Peek (ITY)**[14] 4-8-5 0........ GlenBoss 9 106
(Peter G Moody, Australia) *midfield on outer: rdn over 2f out: ev ch whn hung lft and tightened rival 1 1/2f out: outpcd ent fnl f: fdd and dropped to 8th cl home* 14/1
9 nk **Winchester (USA)**[14] 7-8-10 0........(b) JamieMott 13 111+
(John D Sadler, Australia) *dropped in and hld up in last trio on outer: rdn 2 1/2f out: stl in rr over 1f out: plugged on to go 9th post: n.d* 50/1
10 shd **Sanagas (GER)**[7] 7070 6-8-7 0........(b) NicholasHall 3 107
(Bart Cummings, Australia) *midfield on inner: rdn 2f out: sn outpcd: plugged on: dropped to 10th post* 60/1
11 ½ **Secret Admirer (AUS)**[14] 5-8-5 0........(p) BrentonAvdulla 10 105
(Grahame Begg, Australia) *prom on outer: rdn 2f out: no ex and btn ent fnl f: fdd* 20/1
12 ½ **Niwot (AUS)**[14] 8-8-6 0........ DwayneDunn 6 105
(Michael, Wayne & John Hawkes, Australia) *midfield: rdn 3f out: plugged on ins fnl 1 1/2f: n.d* 20/1
13 ¾ **Jakkalberry (IRE)**[63] 5374 6-8-10 0........(t) CO'Donoghue 12 108
(Marco Botti) *midfield on outer: rdn and lost pl 2f out: outpcd and towards rr ent fnl f: styd on again cl home* 20/1
14 ¾ **Moudre (AUS)**[14] 7-8-4 0........(b) KerrinMcEvoy 5 100
(Ciaron Maher, Australia) *hld up towards rr on inner: rdn over 1 1/2f out: outpcd whn nt clr run ins fnl f: plugged on wout threatening whn in the clr* 60/1
15 1 ½ **Glencadam Gold (IRE)**[14] 4-8-6 0........ JimCassidy 17 100+
(Gai Waterhouse, Australia) *got all the way across fr wd draw to ld: rdn and strly pressed over 1 1/2f out: sn hdd and no ex: fdd* 17/5[1]
16 hd **Sabrage (AUS)**[7] 7070 4-8-0 0........(bt) ClareLindop 16 94
(Michael Moroney, Australia) *dropped in fr wd draw and hld up in last: rdn 2f out: plugged on but nvr a factor* 150/1
17 ½ **December Draw (IRE)**[14] 6-8-9 0........ MichaelRodd 11 102+
(Mark Kavanagh, Australia) *trckd ldr in 3rd on inner: swtchd out and rdn to chal over 1 1/2f out: no ex and btn ent fnl f: fdd* 6/1[2]
18 8 **Voila Ici (IRE)**[14] 7-8-9 0........ VladDuric 14 89+
(Peter G Moody, Australia) *trckd ldr in 2nd on inner: rdn 3f out: outpcd and lost pl over 1 1/2f out: sn btn and fdd: dropped to last ins fnl f* 17/1

2m 28.82s (148.82) 18 Ran SP% 116.1
PARI-MUTUEL (NSW TAB - all including au$1 stakes): WIN 13.00 PLACE 4.50, 3.80, 3.40; DF 110.20; SF 247.00.
Owner Pearl Bloodstock Ltd **Bred** Comte E Decazes **Trained** France

FOCUS
As could have been predicted, the early pace was hot as both Voila Ici and Glencadam Gold, previously unbeaten in four starts since going to Gai Waterhouse from Sir Henry Cecil, made positive moves from their wide draws to get to the head of affairs when hitting the first bend. That pair must have gone much too quick because they were out the back at the end. Those early fractions helped set up another sensational Australian performance by Dunaden.

NOTEBOOK
Dunaden(FR) Immediately dropped in after leaving the widest stall, Craig Williams remained patient in the rear and conjured an electric turn-of-foot out of his mount down the home straight to pass almost every rival on the outside. Speculation afterwards was that he'd be handed a 1kg-1.5kg (roughly 2-3lb) penalty for the Melbourne Cup, making him the clear top weight for Flemington, but even that burden may not stop this classy stayer repeating last year's win.
Alcopop(AUS) burst out of the pack about 200m out and had the rest beaten before being swallowed up. He'd finished second in a Group 1 on this previous start, helping to demonstrate the line-up had plenty of depth.
Lights Of Heaven(NZ) threaded herself through runners to be in a good position but couldn't quicken.
Americain(USA), who reportedly lost both front shoes, stayed on in decent style throughout the last few hundred metres. His participation here was in doubt right up until the last day due to potentially firm going, so this effort was particularly noteworthy. He'll go close in the Melbourne Cup, especially if there is a little bit of ease in the ground.
My Quest For Peace(IRE) was given an uncomplicated ride from a low stalls position and easily did best of the five who raced handily. As a prep for his main target it was a good one, but Corey Brown said subsequently he felt his mount was stargazing when at the head of affairs. One would presume that the Galileo colt will be held on to for a bit longer next time.
Winchester(USA) was going nowhere at the top of the home straight but made stealthy late ground. The longer straight at Flemington will help him if he repeated this effort.
Jakkalberry(IRE) held a good position early but was completely outpaced as the whole field quickened up. He ran all the way to the line for pressure but made no impression.

LE CROISE-LAROCHE
Saturday, October 20
OFFICIAL GOING: Turf: heavy

7265a PRIX LEON VOLTERRA (MAIDEN) (2YO) (TURF) 5f 110y
3:40 (12:00) 2-Y-0 £8,333 (£3,333; £2,500; £1,666; £833)

RPR
1 **Sorry Woman (FR)**39 6128 2-8-13 0 .... FabriceVeron 2 89
(H-A Pantall, France) **6/4**1
2 3 ½ **Rock With Me (FR)**19 2-9-2 0 .... AnthonyCrastus 7 80
(F Chappet, France) **78/10**
3 ¾ **Disko Dasko (FR)**22 6627 2-8-13 0 .... JohanVictoire 4 75
(Mrs K Burke) *broke fast: settled in 4th under hrd hold: rdn ent st: r.o wl u.p to go 3rd 50yds out* **9/2**2
4 1 ¼ **Kalevala (FR)**19 6751 2-8-13 0 .... LouisBeuzelin 1 71
(R Pritchard-Gordon, France) **9/1**
5 shd **Mirror Image**104 2-8-13 0 .... TheoBachelot 6 71
(S Wattel, France) **63/10**3
6 1 ¼ **The Monarck (FR)**70 2-9-2 0 .... VincentVion 8 69
(T Lallie, France) **18/1**
7 hd **Alice Neney (IRE)**19 6751 2-8-9 0 .... MarcLerner(4) 5 66
(C Lerner, France) **13/1**
8 nse **Gee Wizz (IRE)**17 2-8-13 0 .... SebastienMaillot 3 66
(Robert Collet, France) **8/1**
1m 6.1s (66.10) **8** Ran SP% **116.8**
WIN (incl. 1 euro stake): 2.50. PLACES: 1.40, 2.10, 1.90. DF: 11.70. SF: 14.50.
Owner Mlle Ingrid Pantall **Bred** Charkassan Racing Stud **Trained** France

7266a PRIX DE LA THIERACHE (CLAIMER) (3YO COLTS & GELDINGS) (TURF) 1m 2f 110y
4:45 (12:00) 3-Y-0 £6,250 (£2,500; £1,875; £1,250; £625)

RPR
1 **Prince Of Rules (GER)**7 3-9-4 0 ....(b) NJeanpierre 4 77
(C Lerner, France) **9/2**3
2 4 ½ **Priestley's Reward (IRE)**11 6962 3-9-3 0 ....(p) StephaneLaurent 3 67
(Mrs K Burke) *hld up towards rr on ins: mde gd prog down bk st: 4th ent st: r.o u.p to go 2nd 1 1/2f out: r.o wl fnl f* **13/2**
3 2 **Galenus (IRE)**33 3-9-0 0 .... YannickLetondeur 1 60
(F Vermeulen, France) **7/2**2
4 snk **Saloon Tramper (GER)**7 3-8-9 0 .... ChristianHanotel 10 55
(Mario Hofer, Germany) **7/1**
5 2 **Dark Ambition (IRE)**127 3-9-2 0 .... AshleyMorgan 5 58
(N Minner, Belgium) **27/1**
6 1 ¼ **The Dude (FR)**167 1900 3-9-6 0 .... GTemperini 7 59
(J Van Handenhove, France) **2/1**1
7 10 **Kurdy (FR)**7 3-8-9 0 ....(p) JimmyTastayre 9 29
(C Boutin, France) **53/1**
8 2 ½ **Pokalde (FR)** 3-8-11 0 ow2 ....(b) YohannBourgois 6 26
(P Favereaux, France) **105/1**
9 ¾ **Galileano (USA)** 3-9-2 0 ....(p) TonyFarina 8 30
(F Vermeulen, France) **26/1**
10 ½ **Ricasiendo (GER)** 3-9-2 0 .... AlexandreChampenois 11 29
(Dr A Bolte, Germany) **21/1**
0 **Rubio Bello (IRE)**150 3-8-9 0 ....(p) NathanKasztelan 12
(C Boutin, France) **87/1**
0 **Sandwati (FR)**212 3-8-9 0 .... LouisBeuzelin 2
(P Lefevre, France) **72/1**
2m 14.4s (134.40) **12** Ran SP% **116.7**
WIN (incl. 1 euro stake): 5.50. PLACES: 2.00, 2.20, 1.70. DF: 17.10. SF: 32.00.
Owner Gerard Augustin-Normand **Bred** Wilhelm Giedt **Trained** France

7267a PRIX DU MELANTOIS (CLAIMER) (3YO FILLIES) (TURF) 1m 2f 110y
5:45 (12:00) 3-Y-0 £6,250 (£2,500; £1,875; £1,250; £625)

RPR
1 **Joy To The World (IRE)**11 6962 3-8-9 0 .... AshleyMorgan 10 55
(Paul Cole) *broke fast: sn led: under restraint: wnt 2 l clr ent bk st: qcknd wl clr 1 1/2f out: nvr threatened: easily* **33/10**2
2 2 ½ **Alatasarai (IRE)**71 5074 3-8-13 0 ....(p) NJeanpierre 1 54
(Alex Fracas, France) **5/2**1
3 2 ½ **La Maria (FR)**7 3-8-9 0 .... TonyFarina 7 45
(C Lerner, France) **40/1**
4 ¾ **Shanylia (FR)**17 3-9-0 0 ....(p) WilliamsSaraiva 9 49
(S Wattel, France) **12/1**
5 snk **Esperance (FR)**17 3-8-13 0 .... YannickLetondeur 8 47
(S Wattel, France) **19/5**3
6 hd **Pepsy Chope (FR)**53 5726 3-8-13 0 .... JimmyTastayre 4 47
(C Boutin, France) **73/10**
7 ½ **Something Else (FR)**49 3-8-9 0 .... ChristianHanotel 3 42
(J-M Beguigne, France) **17/2**
8 3 **Vert De Mer (FR)**33 3-9-0 0 .... LouisBeuzelin 6 41
(P Lefevre, France) **11/1**
9 1 **Rashflower (FR)**303 3-8-13 0 .... GTemperini 5 38
(J Van Handenhove, France) **100/1**
10 dist **Lady Gade (FR)**49 3-8-9 0 .... TristanNormand 2
(G Doleuze, France) **60/1**
2m 16.3s (136.30) **10** Ran SP% **116.3**
WIN (incl. 1 euro stake): 4.30. PLACES: 1.90, 1.70, 5.50. DF: 5.80. SF: 12.20.
Owner Chris Wright & PFI Cole Ltd **Bred** Marston Stud **Trained** Whatcombe, Oxon

7014 BATH (L-H)
Sunday, October 21
OFFICIAL GOING: Soft (heavy in places; 5.3)
Wind: mild breeze half-behind Weather: cloudy with sunny periods

7268 BREEDERS CUP LIVE ONLY ON ATR/EBF MAIDEN STKS 5f 11y
1:30 (1:30) (Class 5) 2-Y-0 £3,234 (£962; £481; £240) Stalls Centre

Form RPR
35 1 **Keep The Dream**18 6772 2-9-3 0 ....(t) JimCrowley 4 69
(Paul Cole) *wnt lft s: trckd ldrs: chal wl over 1f out: sn rdn: led narrowly ent fnl f: jst hld on: all out* **11/4**3
0 2 nse **Silca's Dream**10 7006 2-9-3 0 .... RichardHughes 6 69
(Mick Channon) *led: rdn whn pressed wl over 1f out: narrowly hdd ent fnl f: sn edgd lft: rallied fnl 75yds: jst hld* **11/8**1
0560 3 9 **Frans Hals**24 6611 2-9-3 57 ....(b1) ChrisCatlin 3 37
(Dominic Ffrench Davis) *little slowly away and hmpd s: chsd ldrs: rdn over 2f out: sn one pce* **12/1**
03 4 ¾ **Skytrain**12 6970 2-9-3 0 .... JoeFanning 5 35
(Mark Johnston) *chsd ldr tl rdn over 2f out: sn one pce* **5/2**2
5400 5 5 **Sarahmanda**17 6822 2-8-12 55 ....(t) LukeMorris 1 12
(Peter Makin) *hmpd s: chsd ldrs: pushed along over 3f out: sn rdn: fdd fnl f* **33/1**
1m 5.48s (2.98) **Going Correction** +0.50s/f (Yiel) **5** Ran SP% **108.0**
Speed ratings (Par 95): **96,95,81,80,72**
toteswinger 2&3 £4.80 CSF £6.68 TOTE £4.00: £2.40, £1.60; EX 8.20.
Owner Mrs Fitri Hay **Bred** Bradmill Meats Ltd **Trained** Whatcombe, Oxon

FOCUS
It was dry overnight and the going was soft, heavy in places (GoingStick 5.3). Rail realignment meant that 12.5yds was added to race distances that included the bottom bend that runs into the home straight. A modest maiden, and a tight finish. Following a stewards' inquiry the result went the way of the first past the post. The winner has been rated as improving slightly.

NOTEBOOK
Keep The Dream was running on turf for the first time. His dam, who's by Selkirk, recorded her only win on soft ground, and the switch to this surface, coupled with a drop back to the minimum trip, clearly suited him. (op 5-2 tchd 3-1)
Silca's Dream, who had the benefit of racing on the stands' rail, was bumped by the winner inside the last, and he was only beaten a nose, but it was always unlikely that he'd be awarded the race. Closely related to 14-time sprint winner Green Manalishi, he'll make his mark sooner or later. (op 2-1)
Frans Hals, who had blinkers on for the first time, could have been expected to do a bit better back on soft ground, and he did have the rail to help, but he was well beaten off by the first two. (tchd 11-1)
Skytrain, who was well backed when only third on Polytrack last time, was struggling from some way out on this switch back to turf. Handicaps are now an option, though. (op 2-1)
Sarahmanda struggled to go the pace down in trip. (op 20-1)

7269 BATH LUXURY TOILET HIRE H'CAP 1m 5f 22y
2:00 (2:01) (Class 5) (0-75,75) 3-Y-0+ £2,911 (£866; £432; £216) Stalls High

Form RPR
4433 1 **Twelve Strings (IRE)**36 6263 3-9-4 75 .... KirstyMilczarek 8 85+
(Luca Cumani) *trckd ldrs: led over 2f out: sn rdn: kpt up to work whn idling fnl f: a in command* **6/1**3
2010 2 1 ½ **Villa Royale**23 6639 3-9-2 73 .... LukeMorris 5 78
(Harry Dunlop) *in tch: nudged along fr over 6f out: rdn over 3f out: hdwy fr over 2f out: styd on to chse wnr over 1f out: a being hld* **20/1**
1202 3 hd **Sunny Future (IRE)**9 7018 6-9-4 67 .... TomMcLaughlin 2 72
(Malcolm Saunders) *s.i.s: last: rdn over 3f out: styd on fr over 1f out: wnt 3rd nring fin* **25/1**
2365 4 ½ **Cyrus Sod**16 6843 3-9-1 72 .... DaneO'Neill 1 76
(Ed Dunlop) *trckd ldrs: rdn over 3f out: styd on same pce fnl 2f* **16/1**
262 5 ¾ **Madame St Clair (IRE)**18 6802 3-8-11 75 .... JoshBaudains(7) 7 78
(Roger Curtis) *hld up towards rr: rdn and stdy prog fr over 2f out: chsd ldrs over 1f out: kpt on same pce fnl f* **7/1**
4322 6 3 ¾ **Burnham**12 6964 3-9-4 75 .... RichardHughes 10 73
(Hughie Morrison) *trckd ldr: rdn over 4f out: kpt chsng ldrs tl no ex fnl f* **7/4**1
4/2- 7 nse **Oldrik (GER)**16 6410 9-9-9 75 ....(b) CPGeoghegan(3) 9 72
(Philip Hobbs) *in tch: rdn to chse ldrs wl over 2f out: nt clr run wl over 1f out: fdd fnl 100yds: nvr gng pce to get on terms* **14/1**
0032 8 2 **Stunning View (USA)**13 6924 3-8-13 70 .... WilliamBuick 6 64
(John Gosden) *led: rdn and hdd over 2f out: kpt chsng wnr tl wl over 1f out: wknd ins fnl f* **7/2**2
-P00 9 16 **Misk Khitaam (USA)**30 6440 4-8-12 61 oh1 .... LiamKeniry 14 31
(John Dunlop) *rdn over 3f out: a towards rr* **50/1**
5040 10 3 **Tidal Run**17 6819 4-9-10 73 .... GeorgeBaker 3 39
(Mick Channon) *hld up towards rr: effrt into midfield wl over 2f out: wknd wl over 1f out* **12/1**
5522 11 16 **Humungosaur**22 6660 3-8-13 70 .... JoeFanning 12 12
(Richard Ford) *chsd ldrs tl over 3f out: sn bhd* **25/1**
3m 4.73s (12.73) **Going Correction** +0.975s/f (Soft)
WFA 3 from 4yo+ 8lb **11** Ran SP% **120.0**
Speed ratings (Par 103): **99,98,97,97,97 94,94,93,83,81 72**
toteswingers 1&2 £20.60, 2&3 £53.50, 1&3 £16.50 CSF £124.11 CT £2794.32 TOTE £7.60: £2.10, £5.00, £4.10; EX 151.10 TRIFECTA Not won..
Owner S Stuckey **Bred** John & Anne-Marie O'Connor **Trained** Newmarket, Suffolk

FOCUS
The third is exposed and sets the intial standard, while the runner-up and fourth have been rated close to their marks.
Villa Royale Official explanation: jockey said filly hung left

7270 INSIGNIA RACING SYNDICATES FILLIES' H'CAP 1m 2f 46y
2:30 (2:31) (Class 5) (0-70,69) 3-Y-0+ £2,911 (£866; £432; £216) Stalls Low

Form RPR
6512 1 **Boonga Roogeta**[3] 7201 3-8-2 57 RosieJessop(5) 2 66
(Peter Charalambous) *trckd ldrs: led over 5f out: pushed clr 3f out: styd on wl: pushed out* 7/1
0502 2 1 1/2 **Elsie Bay**[36] 6231 3-8-4 59 RachealKneller(5) 1 65
(Mark Usher) *hld up towards rr: hdwy on inner over 3f out: sn rdn: chsd wnr ent fnl f: styd on but a being hld* 20/1
6604 3 hd **Broughtons Swinger**[83] 4652 5-9-1 60 JamieMackay 4 66
(Willie Musson) *in tch: rdn to chse wnr over 2f out tl ent fnl f: kpt on same pce* 25/1
4002 4 hd **Kampai**[12] 6949 4-9-3 62 RichardHughes 12 68
(Julia Feilden) *hld up towards rr: pushed along and stdy prog fr 3f out: rdn over 1f out: styd on ins fnl f: nt rch ldrs* 5/1[2]
-533 5 9 **Out Of Nothing**[20] 6734 9-9-10 69 KellyHarrison 8 58
(Dai Burchell) *disp ld tl over 5f out: chsd wnr tl rdn over 2f out: sn hld: fdd fnl f* 10/1
2213 6 3 1/4 **Gold Show**[41] 6092 3-9-5 69 GeorgeBaker 6 51
(Mick Channon) *mid-div: rdn over 2f out: nvr any imp: wknd fnl f* 4/1[1]
650 7 14 **Ryedale Lass**[1] 7250 4-9-2 61 LiamKeniry 5 17
(Joseph Tuite) *mid-div: rdn over 3f out: wknd over 1f out* 14/1
4505 8 13 **Eponastone (IRE)**[16] 6842 3-9-1 65 LukeMorris 11
(Gerard Butler) *mid-div tl lost pl on outer over 4f out: nvr bk on terms* 13/2[3]
3220 9 3 1/4 **Merry Jaunt (USA)**[24] 6613 3-9-3 67 WilliamBuick 7
(John Gosden) *nvr travelling: a towards rr* 4/1[1]
-100 10 1 1/4 **Lady Arabella (IRE)**[77] 4850 3-8-12 62 (p) FrankieMcDonald 9
(Alastair Lidderdale) *trckd ldrs: rdn over 4f out: wknd 3f out* 33/1
600 11 1 1/4 **Bov La Raconteuse**[12] 6962 3-8-7 57 JohnFahy 3
(Carroll Gray) *pushed along early to dispute ld: hdd over 5f out: rdn over 3f out: sn wknd* 100/1
033 12 4 **Ashkalara**[62] 5405 5-9-1 60 DaneO'Neill 10
(Stuart Howe) *chsd ldrs tl rdn over 3f out: wknd over 2f out* 12/1
2m 20.02s (9.02) **Going Correction** +0.975s/f (Soft)
WFA 3 from 4yo+ 5lb 12 Ran SP% **118.5**
Speed ratings (Par 100): **102,100,100,100,93 90,79,69,66,65 64,61**
toteswingers 1&2 £15.30, 2&3 £43.90, 1&3 £44.40 CSF £142.64 CT £3284.60 TOTE £8.30: £2.90, £5.30, £7.90; EX 113.00 TRIFECTA Not won..
Owner P Charalambous **Bred** Peter Charles **Trained** Newmarket, Suffolk
FOCUS
A positive ride paid dividends here. The third has been rated to this year's form.

7271 PROFAB WINDOWS H'CAP 2m 1f 34y
3:05 (3:05) (Class 5) (0-75,73) 3-Y-0 £2,911 (£866; £432; £216) Stalls Centre

Form RPR
3323 1 **Petaluma**[13] 6922 3-9-4 70 GeorgeBaker 3 79
(Mick Channon) *in tch: hdwy over 3f out: rdn to ld over 2f out: styd on strly: rdn out* 7/1[3]
6153 2 1 1/4 **Queen's Star**[75] 4918 3-8-9 61 DavidProbert 1 68
(Andrew Balding) *hld up: rdn wl over 2f out: no imp tl sed to stay on fr over 1f out: fin strly to go 2nd fnl 75yds: nt rch wnr* 7/1[3]
60-2 3 2 1/2 **Annaluna (IRE)**[10] 6280 3-8-4 56 LukeMorris 8 60
(David Evans) *trckd ldrs: rdn along briefly passing paddock entrnce 12f out: rdn over 3f out: styd on same pce fnl 2f* 10/3[1]
4124 4 1 3/4 **Somemothersdohavem**[16] 6834 3-9-7 73 (p) DaraghO'Donohoe 9 75
(John Ryan) *dwlt: in rr: gd hdwy on inner over 3f out: rdn to ld over 2f out: sn hdd: kpt chsng wnr tl no ex ins fnl f* 16/1
251 5 1/2 **Filatore (IRE)**[20] 6738 3-9-1 67 (p) ChrisCatlin 2 68
(Bernard Llewellyn) *trckd ldrs: rdn over 3f out: short of room over 2f out: one pce after* 9/1
0112 6 9 **Authentication**[12] 6957 3-9-0 66 JoeFanning 7 57
(Mark Johnston) *led tl over 5f out: regained ld over 3f out: rdn and hdd over 2f out: wknd over 1f out* 4/1[2]
5060 7 3 3/4 **Caphene**[43] 6033 3-9-0 66 DaneO'Neill 4 52
(John Dunlop) *rdn over 4f out: a towards rr* 25/1
0503 8 17 **Maria Letizia**[18] 6802 3-9-6 72 WilliamBuick 6 38
(John Gosden) *trckd ldr: struggling whn squeezed out over 3f out: sn btn* 4/1[2]
1165 9 68 **Kaiser Wilhelm (IRE)**[27] 6537 3-9-1 67 (t) RichardHughes 5
(Paul Cole) *in tch: jnd ldr 11f out: led over 5f out tl rdn over 3f out: qckly btn: virtually p.u* 14/1
4m 6.97s (15.07) **Going Correction** +0.975s/f (Soft) 9 Ran SP% **114.5**
Speed ratings (Par 101): **103,102,101,100,100 95,94,86,54**
toteswingers 1&2 £6.80, 2&3 £5.80, 1&3 £5.20 CSF £54.55 CT £192.97 TOTE £7.50: £2.60, £2.60, £1.50; EX 42.60 Trifecta £196.60 Pool: £930.14 - 3.50 winning tickets..
Owner Jon and Julia Aisbitt **Bred** Card Bloodstock **Trained** West Ilsley, Berks
FOCUS
Not a bad little staying handicap. The winner has been rated in line with her latest Pontefract effort.
Kaiser Wilhelm(IRE) Official explanation: jockey said colt stopped quickly

7272 1ST SECURITY SOLUTIONS IRISH EBF MEDIAN AUCTION MAIDEN STKS 5f 161y
3:35 (3:35) (Class 5) 2-Y-0 £3,234 (£962; £481; £240) Stalls Centre

Form RPR
5265 1 **French Press (IRE)**[15] 6880 2-9-3 73 RichardHughes 6 72+
(David Brown) *mde all: kpt up to work and in command fnl f: rdn out* 2/1[2]
0440 2 2 1/2 **Baltic Gin (IRE)**[55] 5654 2-8-12 55 TomMcLaughlin 7 59
(Malcolm Saunders) *trckd wnr: rdn in clr 2nd 2f out: kpt on but a being comf hld* 33/1
6 3 1 1/4 **Shore Step (IRE)**[65] 5325 2-9-3 0 WilliamBuick 1 59
(Mick Channon) *s.i.s: hld up in tch: hdwy over 2f out: sn rdn: kpt on same pce fr over 1f out* 15/8[1]
300 4 2 **Princess Sheila (IRE)**[13] 6936 2-8-12 65 LiamKeniry 5 48
(J S Moore) *hld up in tch: rdn over 2f out: sn one pce* 10/1
06 5 4 1/2 **Koharu**[35] 6276 2-8-12 0 (t) JimCrowley 3 33
(Peter Makin) *s.i.s: sn in tch: effrt over 2f out: wknd ent fnl f* 9/1
55 6 2 1/2 **Little Indian**[60] 5485 2-9-3 0 PatDobbs 8 30
(J R Jenkins) *hld up in tch: rdn 3f out: nvr gng pce to threaten* 14/1
653 7 1 **Edged Out**[127] 3138 2-8-12 75 LukeMorris 9 21
(Christopher Mason) *trckd wnr tl rdn wl over 2f out: wknd over 1f out* 5/1[3]
00 8 1/2 **Jonny Wombat**[12] 6954 2-8-10 0 VictorSantos(7) 4 25
(Richard Ford) *trckd wnr: rdn over 2f out: wknd over 1f out* 100/1
5 9 9 **Red Diesel (IRE)**[41] 6093 2-9-3 0 KellyHarrison 2
(Jo Hughes) *chsd wnr tl rdn over 2f out: wknd over 1f out* 33/1
1m 15.36s (4.16) **Going Correction** +0.50s/f (Yiel) 9 Ran SP% **117.4**
Speed ratings (Par 95): **92,88,87,84,78 75,73,73,61**
toteswingers 1&2 £8.70, 2&3 £13.00, 1&3 £1.80 CSF £68.50 TOTE £3.60: £1.30, £6.70, £1.20; EX 57.70 Trifecta £349.90 Pool: £1,125.48 - 2.38 winning tickets..
Owner J C Fretwell **Bred** A H And C E Robinson Partnership **Trained** Averham Park, Notts
FOCUS
Not a strong maiden. The winner and runner-up set the level.
NOTEBOOK
French Press(IRE) could do no more than win it comfortably. He'd done all his previous racing over 7f, but he's a brother to 5f Group 3 2yo winner Percolator, and the drop back in trip was no problem to him. He probably didn't need to improve on his previous best to score. (op 9-4)
Baltic Gin(IRE) has an official mark of 55 and hadn't run that well in her previous starts on soft ground, so this performance was a bit of a surprise. (op 25-1)
Shore Step(IRE), whose half-brother Balty Boys prefers a sound surface, didn't look at home in the conditions and failed to make the improvement from his debut that the market expected. (op 11-4)
Princess Sheila(IRE) kept on next to the stands' side rail. She's a sister to Princess Sinead, who was at her best over 7f-1m and was placed in the Irish 1,000 Guineas, so there's scope for improvement when she steps up in trip. (op 8-1)
Koharu, who wore a tongue-tie for the first time, is now eligible for a mark, and she ought to do better in handicaps. (op 8-1)
Edged Out, having her first outing since June and debuting for a new yard, ran as though in need of the run. (tchd 11-2)

7273 JOHN SMITHS H'CAP (DIV I) 5f 161y
4:10 (4:10) (Class 5) (0-75,80) 3-Y-0+ £2,911 (£866; £432; £216) Stalls Centre

Form RPR
1010 1 **Forest Edge (IRE)**[6] 7114 3-9-5 74 (b) RichardHughes 1 84
(David Evans) *kpt to farside rails: mde all: nudged 4 l clr 3f out: rdn ent fnl f: hld on wl: clever ride* 7/1[3]
5211 2 shd **Gull Rock**[12] 6961 3-8-9 64 DaneO'Neill 7 74+
(Henry Candy) *in tch: hdwy over 2f out: rdn to chse wnr over 1f out: r.o ins fnl f: jst hld* 9/4[2]
1111 3 2 3/4 **Gladiatrix**[9] 7019 3-9-6 80 MichaelJMMurphy(5) 5 81
(Rod Millman) *mid-div: hdwy over 2f out: rdn wl over 1f out disputing 2nd: kpt on same pce fnl f* 2/1[1]
2236 4 1 1/2 **Rambo Will**[6] 7114 4-9-6 74 PatDobbs 4 70
(J R Jenkins) *taken to s early: trckd ldrs: rdn to chse wnr briefly jst over 2f out: kpt on same pce* 14/1
3214 5 nk **Stonecrabstomorrow (IRE)**[6] 7114 9-8-9 66 MarkCoumbe(3) 2 61
(Michael Attwater) *s.i.s: in rr: rdn 2f out: kpt on but nvr any danger to ldrs* 16/1
3445 6 1 1/2 **Emiratesdotcom**[25] 6577 6-9-4 72 LiamKeniry 10 62
(Milton Bradley) *hld up: rdn over 2f out: sme late prog: n.d* 8/1
3064 7 1 **Lady Bayside**[12] 6961 4-9-0 68 TomMcLaughlin 9 54
(Malcolm Saunders) *chsd wnr: rdn wl over 2f out: wknd jst over 1f out* 9/1
5420 8 shd **Diamond Vine (IRE)**[41] 6094 4-9-1 69 (p) LukeMorris 3 55
(Ronald Harris) *chsd ldrs: rdn 3f out: wknd ent fnl f* 33/1
0010 9 10 **Dickie Le Davoir**[31] 6403 8-9-6 74 (b) RobbieFitzpatrick 8 27
(Richard Guest) *s.i.s: a towards rr: wknd fnl f* 28/1
1m 13.45s (2.25) **Going Correction** +0.50s/f (Yiel)
WFA 3 from 4yo+ 1lb 9 Ran SP% **116.7**
Speed ratings (Par 103): **105,104,101,99,98 96,95,95,82**
toteswingers 1&2 £3.50, 2&3 £2.00, 1&3 £3.80 CSF £23.38 CT £44.25 TOTE £7.00: £2.00, £1.50, £1.50; EX 25.80 Trifecta £109.10 Pool: £1,226.10 - 8.31 winning tickets..
Owner Peter Swinnerton **Bred** Alberto Panetta **Trained** Pandy, Monmouths
FOCUS
Richard Hughes made a race-winning move by electing to stay on the far side this time. The race is rated rather cautiously given that the winner possibly had a tactical edge, while the runner-up has done well to pull clear of the rest, and has been marked up.

7274 JOHN SMITHS H'CAP (DIV II) 5f 161y
4:40 (4:40) (Class 5) (0-75,75) 3-Y-0+ £2,911 (£866; £432; £216) Stalls Centre

Form RPR
3200 1 **Ashpan Sam**[25] 6577 3-9-3 72 LukeMorris 2 83
(John Spearing) *trckd ldr: rdn to ld over 1f out: r.o wl: rdn out* 9/1
1354 2 2 **Dream Catcher (FR)**[25] 6577 4-9-2 75 AmyScott(5) 5 79
(Henry Candy) *broke wl: led: rdn 2f out: hdd over 1f out: kpt on but sn hld by wnr* 3/1[1]
1055 3 3/4 **Belle Bayardo (IRE)**[6] 7114 4-8-11 65 WilliamCarson 8 67
(Ronald Harris) *chsd ldr: rdn jst over 2f out: kpt on same pce fnl f* 6/1[3]
0010 4 1/2 **Divine Call**[46] 5933 5-9-5 73 RichardKingscote 6 73
(Milton Bradley) *hld up: hdwy 2f out: sn rdn: kpt on to go 4th ins fnl f* 8/1
4342 5 1/2 **Represent (IRE)**[12] 6961 3-9-1 70 GeorgeBaker 10 69
(Mick Channon) *s.i.s: towards rr: hdwy over 2f out: rdn over 1f out: kpt on same pce fnl f* 4/1[2]
2123 6 6 **Mother Jones**[3] 7197 4-9-1 69 RichardHughes 4 48
(David Evans) *s.i.s: mid-div: rdn over 2f out: nt pce to threaten: wknd fnl f* 4/1[2]
2106 7 4 **Kyllachy Storm**[36] 6233 8-8-0 61 oh2 PhilipPrince(7) 7 27
(Ron Hodges) *dismntd and ld to s: mid-div: rdn over 2f out: no imp: wknd ent fnl f* 20/1
0600 8 1 3/4 **Pick A Little**[18] 6800 4-9-4 75 RyanClark(3) 3 35
(Michael Blake) *dwlt: sn struggling: a in rr* 20/1
0041 9 nk **Ryedale Dancer (IRE)**[3] 7204 4-9-0 68 6ex RobbieFitzpatrick 1 27
(Richard Guest) *mid-div: rdn over 2f out: wknd over 1f out* 12/1
1m 13.39s (2.19) **Going Correction** +0.50s/f (Yiel)
WFA 3 from 4yo+ 1lb 9 Ran SP% **117.6**
Speed ratings (Par 103): **105,102,101,100,100 92,86,84,83**
toteswingers 1&2 £6.70, 2&3 £5.40, 1&3 £8.70 CSF £36.92 CT £177.34 TOTE £13.10: £3.30, £1.20, £2.60; EX 49.90 Trifecta £487.60 Pool: £1,416.79 - 2.15 winning tickets..
Owner Advantage Chemicals Holdings Ltd **Bred** Advantage Chemicals Holdings Ltd **Trained** Kinnersley, Worcs
FOCUS
Marginally the quicker of the two divisions. They went quite steady early and it paid to race handily. It's been rated around the runner-up to his latest form.

Pick A Little Official explanation: jockey said gelding was slowly away

7275 **BREEDERS CUP LIVE ONLY ON ATR H'CAP** 5f 161y
5:15 (5:19) (Class 6) (0-58,58) 3-Y-0+ **£2,070** (£616; £307 ; £153) **Stalls** Centre

Form RPR
0655 **1** **Steel Rain**[20] 6737 4 -8-12**51** FrankieMcDonald 5 61
(Nikki Evans) *mid-div: hdwy over 2f out: sn rdn: str chal ent fnl f: led fnl stride* **7/1**[3]
0366 **2** *shd* **Ficelle (IRE)**[20] 6739 3 -9-4**58** WilliamCarson 14 68
(Ronald Harris) *s.i.s: bhd: hdwy fr 3f out: rdn over 2f out: led over 1f out: kpt on: hdd fnl stride* **10/1**
0503 **3** *1 1/2* **Dreams Of Glory**[20] 6737 4 -9-4**57** RichardKingscote 1 62
(Ron Hodges) *prom: rdn to ld over 2f out: hdd over 1f out: kpt on same pce* **11/2**[2]
3064 **4** *1* **Jawim**[20] 6737 3 -8-10**50** ow1 TomMcLaughlin 6 52
(Malcolm Saunders) *mid-div: hdwy on inner 3f out: sn rdn to chse ldrs: kpt on same pce fnl 2f* **18/1**
000 **5** *2* **Gracie's Games**[12] 6951 6 -8-10**56** JacobButterfield[(7)] 13 51
(Richard Price) *towards rr: rdn 3f out: styd on fnl 2f: nvr trbld ldrs* **14/1**
0400 **6** *shd* **Silly Billy (IRE)**[1] 6982 4 -8-8**47** (t) LiamKeniry 2 42
(Sylvester Kirk) *towards rr: rdn and stdy prog fr over 2f out: styd on wout threatening ldrs* **10/1**
0110 **7** *hd* **Sally's Swansong**[16] 6836 6 -9-5**58** (b) PatCosgrave 3 52
(Eric Alston) *s.i.s: bhd: rdn and stdy prog fr over 2f out: kpt on but nvr rchd ldrs* **11/1**
3050 **8** *1 1/2* **Efisio Princess**[127] 3151 9 -8-9**48** RichardThomas 10 37
(John E Long) *chsd ldrs: rdn over 2f out: sn one pce* **10/1**
460 **9** *1* **Gracie's Gift (IRE)**[32] 5775 10 -8-11**50** (v) KierenFox 17 36
(Richard Guest) *rdn over 2f out: a mid-div* **10/1**
404 **10** *1* **Alderton (IRE)**[36] 6254 3 -8-8**48** DavidProbert 4 31
(Martyn Meade) *towards rr: drvn and hdwy over 2f out: nvr trbld ldrs: wknd fnl f* **25/1**
5120 **11** *3 3/4* **Portrush Storm**[8] 7055 7 -9-0**58** CharlesBishop[(5)] 8 28
(Ray Peacock) *prom tl rdn over 2f out: sn btn* **16/1**
4300 **12** *3/4* **Yanza**[36] 6233 6 -8-6**50** RachealKneller[(5)] 12 18
(Pam Ford) *mid-div tl rdn over 2f out: sn towards rr* **33/1**
5005 **13** *1 1/2* **Replicator**[29] 6496 7 -8-7**46** oh1 (e) DominicFox 7 9
(Patrick Gilligan) *mid-div: rdn 3f out: wknd ent fnl f* **40/1**
0420 **14** *9* **Spic 'n Span**[20] 6737 7 -9-1**54** (b) LukeMorris 15
(Ronald Harris) *taken to s early: led tl rdn over 2f out: sn wknd* **12/1**
0063 **15** *9* **Ballinargh Girl (IRE)**[6] 6836 4 -9-5**58** (v[1]) RichardHughes 9
(Danielle McCormick) *prom: rdn over 2f out: sn wknd: eased whn btn* **7/2**[1]

1m 15.75s (4.55) **Going Correction** +0.50s/f (Yiel)
WFA 3 from 4yo+ 1lb **15Ran SP% 129.5**
Speed ratings (Par 101): **89,88,86,85,82 82,82,80,79,77 72,71,69,57,45**
toteswingers 1&2 £17.30, 2&3 £12.10, 1&3 £9.00 CSF £79.57 CT £438.43 TOTE £9.80 : £3.10 , £4.30, £2.20 ; EX 108.10 Trifecta £657.90 Part won. Pool: £889.18 - 0.63 winning tickets.
Owner John Berry (Gwent) **Bred** L T Roberts **Trained** Pandy, Monmouths

FOCUS
They were spread right across the track heading into the straight and there appeared to be no bias one way or another. The third has been rated to his latest effort over 5f here.
Sally's Swansong Official explanation: jockey said mare missed the break
T/Jkpt: Not won. T/Plt: £196.90 to a £1 stake. Pool: £90,998.53 - 337.36 winning tickets. T/Qpdt: £21.50 to £1. Pool: £6,926.17 - 237.70 w. tckts TM 7276a - 7280a (Foreign Racing) See RI

5865 BADEN-BADEN (L-H)
Sunday, October 21

OFFICIAL GOING: Turf: good

7281a **PREIS DER WINTERKONIGIN (GROUP 3) (2YO FILLIES) (TURF)** 1m
1:40 (1:41) 2-Y-0
£50,000 (£19,166; £9,166 ; £5,000 ; £2,500 ; £1,666)

RPR
1 **Swordhalf** 2 -9-2**0** AStarke 8 102
(A Wohler, Germany) *broke wl and trckd ldr: whole field c stands' side st: eased into ld over 2f out: sn rdn and qcknd fr under 2f out: r.o wl u.p fnl f: edgd lft fnl 75yds* **16/5**[2]
2 *1 1/4* **Akua'Da (GER)** 2 -9-2**0** JBojko 4 99
(A Wohler, Germany) *trckd ldng gp: chsd eventual wnr fr under 2f out: sn scrubbed along: rdn 1f out to press wnr tl no ex and hld fnl 75yds* **39/10**[3]
3 *1 3/4* **Viletta (GER)**[28] 6522 2 -9-2**0** KClijmans 3 95
(Uwe Ostmann, Germany) *towards rr in tch: hdwy u p fr under 2f out: kpt on fnl f: nt pce to chal* **3/1**[1]
4 *1 3/4* **Oriental Lady (GER)**[28] 6522 2 -9-2**0** EFrank 2 91
(Uwe Ostmann, Germany) *trckd ldrs: 4th and rdn over 2f out: outpcd 1 1/2f out: styd on u.p fnl f: nt threaten ldrs* **116/10**
5 *1/2* **Forever Beauty (GER)** 2 -9-2**0** ADeVries 1 90
(Mario Hofer, Germany) *racd keenly towards rr: in tch: midfield fr 1/2-way: short of room fr under 2f out: kpt on u.p fnl f: nvr able to chal* **5/1**
6 *1 1/4* **Zazera (FR)**[28] 6522 2 -9-2**0** MickaelBarzalona 6 87
(Mario Hofer, Germany) *w.w in last: scrubbed along over 2f out: hdwy to dispute 2nd under 2f out: ev ch 1f out: wknd fnl 150yds and lost three pls* **4/1**
7 *4 1/2* **Rosanna (GER)** 2 -9-2**0** THellier 7 77
(Uwe Ostmann, Germany) *smartly away and led: hdd over 2f out: sn rdn and wknd fnl 1 1/2f* **41/5**
8 *5* **Iberica (IRE)** 2 -9-2**0** FilipMinarik 5 66
(P Harley, Germany) *towards rr in tch: scrubbed along to hold pl 2 1/2f out: bhd fnl 2f* **176/10**

1m 42.58s (3.47) **8Ran SP% 130.1**
WIN (incl. 10 euro stake): 42. PLACES: 16, 18, 15. SF: 177 .
Owner Gestut Wittekindshof **Bred** Gestut Wittekindshof **Trained** Germany

7282a **HUBERTUS-LIEBRECHT-GEDACHTNISPREIS - LE DEFI DU GALOP (GROUP 3) (3YO+) (TURF)** 1m 4f
3:20 (3:24) 3-Y-0+
£26,666 (£9,166; £4,583 ; £2,500 ; £1,666 ; £1,250)

RPR
1 **Seismos (IRE)**[379] 6710 4 -9-0**0** AndreaAtzeni 5 105+
(A Wohler, Germany) *sn trcking ldr in 2nd on outer: rdn to ld over 2f out: strly pressed over 1 1/2f out: styd on strly u.p to go clr ins fnl f: v readily* **211/10**
2 *5* **Nightdance Paolo (GER)**[66] 5 -9-2**0** FredericSpanu 2 99
(A Schaerer, Switzerland) *prom on inner: rdn to chal over 1 1/2f out: ev ch tl outpcd and lft bhd by wnr ins fnl f: kpt on wl for 2nd cl home* **99/10**
3 *1 1/4* **Tidespring (IRE)**[35] 6290 4 -8-10**0** FilipMinarik 4 91+
(H-A Pantall, France) *midfield on inner: rdn over 2f out: styd on to go 3rd post: nt pce to chal* **48/10**[3]
4 *shd* **Santarius (GER)** 3 -8-9**0** AStarke 3 97
(P Harley, Germany) *midfield: rdn 2f out: 3rd and stl ev ch ent fnl f: sn outpcd by wnr: kpt on but dropped to 4th post* **83/10**
5 *1/2* **Flamingo Fantasy (GER)**[35] 6297 7 -9-0**0** (p) THellier 10 94
(S Smrczek, Germany) *dropped in fr wdst draw and hld up in last: rapid hdwy 2f out: rdn in 4th ent fnl f: kpt on but dropped to 5th cl home* **8/1**
6 *5* **Energia Davos (BRZ)**[49] 5865 4 -9-2**0** (b) SHellyn 6 88
(Fabricio Borges, Sweden) *hld up in last pair: rdn to try and improve over 2f out: sn outpcd: plugged on to go 6th post* **156/10**
7 *shd* **Sant'Alberto (ITY)**[36] 6273 4 -9-2**0** (p) MickaelBarzalona 7 88
(F Chappet, France) *midfield: rdn and outpcd over 2f out: plugged on wout threatening ins fnl 1 1/2f: dropped to 7th post* **104/10**
8 *4* **Andolini (GER)**[63] 5402 3 -8-11**0** JBojko 8 83
(A Wohler, Germany) *midfield on outer: rdn over 2f out: sn outpcd in rr: plugged on to go 8th ins fnl f* **13/5**[1]
9 *1/2* **Berlin Berlin**[21] 6723 3 -8-4**0** SilvestreDeSousa 9 76
(Markus Klug, Germany) *midfield on outer: rdn over 3f out: brief effrt over 2f out: sn outpcd and btn: fdd* **17/5**[2]
10 *14* **Maximool (GER)** 3 -8-9**0** APietsch 1 58
(R Dzubasz, Germany) *led: rdn and hdd over 2f out: qckly btn and wknd: dropped to last over 1f out and sn eased* **76/10**

2m 34.41s (0.95)
WFA 3 from 4yo+ 7lb **10Ran SP% 129.7**
WIN (incl. 10 euro stake): 221. PLACES: 55, 28, 25. SF: 2,046 .
Owner Gestut Karlshof **Bred** Gestut Karlshof **Trained** Germany

7180 LONGCHAMP (R-H)
Sunday, October 21

OFFICIAL GOING: Turf: heavy

7283a **PRIX DE CONDE (GROUP 3) (2YO) (TURF)** 1m 1f
1:30 (12:00) 2-Y-0 **£33,333** (£13,333; £10,000 ; £6,666 ; £3,333)

RPR
1 **Morandi (FR)**[39] 2 -8-11**0** GregoryBenoist 7 110+
(J-C Rouget, France) *trckd ldr in 2nd on outer: led gng wl over 2f out: rdn and sn wl clr: eased cl home: v easily* **5/4**[1]
2 *12* **Onedargent (FR)**[10] 2 -8-11**0** ThierryJarnet 6 83
(J-P Gallorini, France) *midfield on outer: rdn 2 1/2f out: wnt 2nd ent fnl f: styd on but no ch w v easy wnr* **8/1**
3 *2* **Lion D'Anvers (FR)**[37] 2 -8-11**0** RonanThomas 3 79
(J Van Handenhove, France) *midfield: rdn 2 1/2f out: sn outpcd: styd on ins fnl f and tk 3rd fnl strides* **7/1**
4 *nk* **Kourkam (FR)**[29] 2 -8-11**0** ThierryThulliez 1 78
(J-M Beguigne, France) *midfield on inner: rdn in 2nd 2f out: dropped to 3rd ent fnl f: no ex and relegated to 4th fnl strides* **9/2**[3]
5 *10* **Luhaif**[10] 7009 2 -8-11**0** SamHitchcott 2 58
(Mick Channon) *pushed along early to ld: rdn and hdd over 2f out: qckly btn and fdd* **7/2**[2]
6 *8* **Pont Neuilly (FR)**[24] 2 -8-11**0** Pierre-CharlesBoudot 5 42
(Y De Nicolay, France) *hld up in last pair: rdn to try and improve on outer over 2 1/2f out: sn outpcd and btn: fdd* **14/1**
7 *10* **Amigo Tonio (FR)**[8] 2 -8-11**0** TonyPiccone 4 22
(Robert Collet, France) *hld up in last: rdn 3f out: sn outpcd and btn: nvr a factor* **25/1**

2m 4.6s (13.00) **Going Correction** +1.525s/f (Heav) **7Ran SP% 119.0**
Speed ratings: **103,92,90,90,81 74,65**
WIN (incl. 1 euro stake): 2.50. PLACES: 1.90, 3.40. SF: 14.70 .
Owner Daniel-Yves Treves **Bred** E Puerari **Trained** Pau, France

NOTEBOOK
Morandi(FR) came into this with leading form claims and duly romped away in the testing conditions for quite an impressive success. Clearly well suited by heavy ground, this progressive type looks an obvious one for next month's Group 1 Criterium de Saint-Cloud.
Luhaif took them along early, but this ground was always going to prove too testing for the son of Cape Cross and he was quickly beaten.

7284a **PRIX DU CONSEIL DE PARIS (GROUP 2) (3YO+) (TURF)** 1m 4f
2:40 (12:00) 3-Y-0+ **£61,750** (£23,833; £11,375 ; £7,583 ; £3,791)

RPR
1 **Saga Dream (FR)**[15] 6898 6 -9-2**0** ThierryJarnet 4 111
(F Lemercier, France) *midfield on outer: smooth hdwy to chal 2 1/2f out: rdn to ld 2f out: edgd rt and styd on wl ins fnl 1 1/2f: strly pressed cl home but a doing enough* **6/1**
2 *snk* **Sediciosa (IRE)**[35] 6295 3 -8-8**0** GregoryBenoist 2 110
(Y Barberot, France) *midfield on inner: rdn over 2f out: wnt 2nd ent fnl f: styd on wl to chal cl home but a being hld by wnr* **5/1**
3 *4* **Gentle Storm (FR)**[31] 6422 3 -8-9**0** (p) Christophe-PatriceLemaire 5 105
(Y Barberot, France) *sn trcking ldr in 2nd on outer: jnd ldr 3f out: rdn and edgd ahd 2 1/2f out: sn hdd: outpcd and dropped to 3rd ent fnl f: plugged on* **12/1**
4 *8* **Dance Moves**[49] 5871 4 -9-2**0** MaximeGuyon 7 94
(A Fabre, France) *hld up in last trio on outer: rdn over 3f out: 4th and outpcd over 1f out: plugged on ins fnl f* **9/2**[3]

5 *7* **Chinchon (IRE)**[154] 2327 7-9-8 0................................ AnthonyCrastus 6 87
(C Laffon-Parias, France) *hld up in last: rdn 2 1/2f out: plugged on to go 5th ins fnl f: n.d* **10/3**[1]

6 *2 ½* **Remus De La Tour (FR)**[35] 6294 3-8-11 0...................... DavyBonilla 8 79
(K Borgel, France) *led and racd v wd early: sn cut across to join rest of field: jnd 3f out: rdn and hdd 2 1/2f out: sn btn and fdd: eased and dropped to 6th ins fnl f* **4/1**[2]

7 *20* **Albion**[29] 6508 3-8-9 0.. StephanePasquier 1 45
(A Fabre, France) *prom on inner: rdn 3f out: sn outpcd and btn: fdd and eased over 2f out: t.o* **7/1**

8 *4* **Victorinna (FR)**[25] 6595 4-8-13 0.................................. ThierryThulliez 3 35
(C Laffon-Parias, France) *hld up in last pair on inner: rdn in last 2 1/2f out: sn btn and eased: t.o* **16/1**

2m 47.62s (17.22) **Going Correction** +1.525s/f (Heav)
WFA 3 from 4yo+ 7lb **8** Ran SP% **118.3**
Speed ratings: **103,102,100,94,90 88,75,72**
WIN (incl. 1 euro stake): 7.60. PLACES: 2.10, 2.10, 3.70. DF: 22.50. SF: 47.00.
Owner Freddy Lemercier **Bred** A Audouinm, F Landais, A Oger & B Audouin **Trained** France

NOTEBOOK
Saga Dream(FR), blown away by Cirrus Des Aigles at the course the time before, proved suited by the longer trip and just held on to record a career-best. He's clearly suited by testing ground but it's doubtful he'll ever surpass this form.
Sediciosa(IRE) found this easier than the Prix Vermeille, just missing out despite the ground probably being soft enough. She remains capable of better.
Chinchon(IRE) proved disappointing on this first start since winning a big Group 1 at Kranji in May.

7075 SAN SIRO (R-H)
Sunday, October 21

OFFICIAL GOING: Turf: soft

7285a PREMIO DORMELLO (GROUP 3) (2YO FILLIES) (TURF) 1m
2:15 (12:00) 2-Y-O **£33,333** (£14,666; £8,000; £4,000)

RPR

1 **Punta Stella (IRE)**[35] 2-8-11 0.. MEsposito 2 103
(D Zarroli, Italy) *hld up towards rr: hdwy over 2f out: rdn and swtchd ins to chse ldr over 1f out: r.o wl u.p to ld cl home* **39/10**[2]

2 *nk* **Sorella Bella (IRE)**[8] 7076 2-8-11 0................................ MartinHarley 6 102
(Mick Channon) *led: qcknd over 2f out: sn rdn: r.o u.p fnl f: hdd cl home: no ex* **3/5**[1]

3 *3 ¾* **Shirley's Kitten (USA)** 2-8-11 0.. GBietolini 8 94
(Gianluca Bietolini, Italy) *settled in rr: rdn and hdwy on outside fr 2f out: styd on u.p fnl f to take 3rd cl home: nvr on terms w ldrs* **59/10**[3]

4 *nse* **Mangiapregaama (ITY)** 2-8-11 0.................................... DarioVargiu 7 94
(B Grizzetti, Italy) *midfield on outside: rdn and styd on fnl f: nt pce to chal* **67/1**

5 *snk* **Deflection (IRE)**[21] 6725 2-8-11 0.................................. FabioBranca 1 94
(S Botti, Italy) *trckd ldr: 2nd and ev ch 2 1/2f out: rdn and nt qckn over 2f out: one pce u.p fnl f: lost two pls cl home* **172/10**

6 *5* **Night Of Light (IRE)**[35] 2-8-11 0.................................... CFiocchi 9 83
(F Camici, Italy) *racd in 3rd: rdn and nt qckn over 2f out: wknd fr 1f out: eased fnl 100yds* **38/1**

7 *2 ½* **Road Tosky (IRE)**[21] 6725 2-8-11 0.............................. FrankieDettori 4 77
(A Peraino, Italy) *w.w towards rr: shortlived effrt u.p on ins 2f out: wknd over 1f out: eased fnl 100yds* **114/10**

8 *½* **Kentra (FR)**[21] 6725 2-8-11 0.. UmbertoRispoli 5 76
(G Botti, Italy) *racd keenly in midfield: rdn and wknd under 2f out: eased fnl 100yds* **41/5**

9 *1 ½* **Montevideo (GER)** 2-8-11 0.. CristianDemuro 3 73
(S Botti, Italy) *midfield on rail: chsd ldrs fr 2 1/2f out: wknd ins fnl 2f: bhd fr over 1f out: eased fnl 100yds* **113/10**

1m 40.6s (-1.50) **9** Ran SP% **134.0**
WIN (incl. 1 euro stake): 4.89. PLACES: 1.38, 1.11, 1.45. DF: 3.62.
Owner Daniele Zarroli **Bred** Azienda Agricola La Morosina Di Rua **Trained** Italy

7286a PREMIO DEL PIAZZALE (GROUP 3) (3YO+) (TURF) 1m
2:50 (12:00) 3-Y-O+ **£23,333** (£10,266; £5,600; £2,800)

RPR

1 **Douce Vie (IRE)**[323] 6-8-11 0.. FabioBranca 6 103
(S Botti, Italy) *midfield: hdwy on outside 2f out: chal for ld appr fnl f: r.o under hands and heels to ld cl home* **11/2**

2 *shd* **Combat Zone (IRE)**[14] 6906 6-9-2 0.............................. NRichter 4 107
(Mario Hofer, Germany) *racd keenly and pressed ldr on outside: sn settled bhd ldr: led over 2f out: rallied u.p whn chal fnl f: hdd cl home: no ex* **11/5**[2]

3 *1* **Sanjii Danon (GER)**[112] 6-8-11 0.................................... LManiezzi 3 100
(G Geisler, France) *trckd ldrs: chal ldrs towards outside 2f out: 3rd and ev ch between rivals over 1f out: n.m.r and dropped away fnl 100yds* **51/10**[3]

4 *½* **King's Hall**[14] 6906 4-9-0 0.. EPedroza 1 102
(A Wohler, Germany) *sn led on rail: shkn up and hdd over 2f out: one pce fnl f* **2/1**[1]

5 *2 ¼* **Malossol (USA)**[21] 6727 3-8-11 0.................................. UmbertoRispoli 7 97
(G Botti, Italy) *settled towards rr: shkn up and chsd ldng quartet under 2f out: rdn and one pce over 1f out: styd on fnl 150yds: nt pce to chal* **6/1**

6 *7* **Ransom Hope**[112] 7-8-11 0.. CristianDemuro 2 78
(L Riccardi, Italy) *midfield on ins: rdn and nt qckn over 2f out: bhd appr fnl f* **17/2**

7 *5* **Moustache (IRE)**[106] 3884 3-8-9 0.................................... MEsposito 5 67
(D Grilli, Italy) *hld up last: rdn and no imp fr 2f out: eased ins fnl f* **162/10**

1m 39.3s (-2.80)
WFA 3 from 4yo+ 3lb **7** Ran SP% **127.0**
WIN (incl. 1 euro stake): 6.53. PLACES: 2.50, 1.94. DF: 10.87.
Owner Effevi **Bred** Soc Finanza Locale Consulting **Trained** Italy

7287a GRAN PREMIO DEL JOCKEY CLUB ITALIANO (GROUP 1) (3YO+) (TURF) 1m 4f
4:00 (12:00) 3-Y-O+ **£79,166** (£34,833; £19,000; £9,500)

RPR

1 **Novellist (IRE)**[49] 5865 3-8-13 0.................................... EPedroza 1 120+
(A Wohler, Germany) *restrained in midfield on inner: rdn to improve 3f out: styd on to ld 1 1/2f out: stretched clr under hands and heels ins fnl f: easily* **8/13**[1]

2 *4 ½* **Retrieve (AUS)**[23] 6637 5-9-4 0.................................... FrankieDettori 2 111
(Saeed Bin Suroor) *hld up in last: rdn 3f out: styd on to go 2nd ent fnl f: kpt on but no ch w easy wnr* **16/5**[2]

3 *6* **Branderburgo (IRE)**[28] 6554 5-9-4 0.............................. MEsposito 5 102
(M Grassi, Italy) *trckd ldr in 2nd: rdn to ld 2 1/2f out: hdd 1 1/2f out and sn outpcd: dropped to 3rd ent fnl f: plugged on* **107/10**

4 *3 ½* **Araldo**[28] 6523 4-9-4 0.. MartinHarley 7 96
(P Harley, Germany) *hld up in last pair: rdn over 3f out: outpcd and btn over 1f out: plugged on for wl hld 4th ins fnl f* **41/10**[3]

5 *2 ¾* **Orsino (GER)**[28] 6554 5-9-4 0.. CristianDemuro 6 91
(R Rohne, Germany) *led: rdn and hdd 2 1/2f out: sn no ex and btn: steadily fdd* **63/10**

6 *8* **Lord Chaparral (IRE)**[21] 5-9-4 0.................................... DarioVargiu 3 78
(R Brogi, Italy) *midfield on outer: rdn and outpcd in last over 2f out: sn btn and fdd* **46/1**

2m 29.5s (-2.00)
WFA 3 from 4yo+ 7lb **6** Ran SP% **129.7**
WIN (incl. 1 euro stake): 1.61. PLACES: 1.27, 1.59. DF: 4.49.
Owner Dr Christoph Berglar **Bred** Christoph Berglar **Trained** Germany

FOCUS
Novellist became only the second 3yo this year to win a Group 1 open to older horses.

NOTEBOOK
Novellist(IRE) found this a good bit easier than the other Group 1s he's been contesting, having finished behind Danedream the time before, picking up smartly to readily draw clear of his elders. He looks capable of developing into a top older performer next season.
Retrieve(AUS), whose trainer has a fine record in this race, had a bit to find with the winner in terms of class and never got close. This level's a bit beyond him.

7288a PREMIO OMENONI (GROUP 3) (3YO+) (TURF) 5f
5:10 (12:00) 3-Y-O+ **£23,333** (£10,266; £5,600; £2,800)

RPR

1 **Noble Hachy**[21] 3-9-1 0.. CristianDemuro 6 111
(L Riccardi, Italy) *towards rr: rdn over 2f out: r.o to chal ins fnl f: led cl home: pushed out* **6/5**[1]

2 *1* **Dagda Mor (ITY)**[21] 5-9-0 0.. FabioBranca 2 106
(S Botti, Italy) *disp ld on outer: rdn and wnt on 1 1/2f out: strly pressed ins fnl f: no ex and hdd cl home* **5/2**[2]

3 *1 ¾* **Govinda (USA)**[14] 6908 5-9-4 0.. EPedroza 1 104
(A Wohler, Germany) *disp ld on outer: rdn and hdd 1 1/2f out: sn outpcd and dropped to 3rd: kpt on* **33/10**[3]

4 *¾* **Choisir Shadow (IRE)**[21] 3-8-10 0.................................. DarioVargiu 4 93
(B Grizzetti, Italy) *prom: rdn 2f out: outpcd ins fnl f: kpt on* **129/10**

5 *1* **Pabusar**[15] 6869 4-9-0 0.. MartinHarley 3 94
(Ralph Beckett) *midfield on inner: rdn over 2f out: kpt on one pce ins fnl f: nvr a threat* **41/5**

6 *3 ½* **Aristocrata (GER)**[21] 3-8-10 0.. LManiezzi 5 77
(R Rohne, Germany) *midfield on outer: dropped to last ent fnl f: shkn up and retk 5th cl home: nvr put under serious press* **38/1**

7 *½* **War Artist (AUS)**[21] 9-9-0 0.. UmbertoRispoli 8 79
(P Harley, Germany) *hld up in last: rdn 2f out: effrt to improve ent fnl f: sn btn: eased and dropped to last again cl home* **94/10**

59.1s (-0.10) **7** Ran SP% **127.5**
WIN (incl. 1 euro stake): 2.18. PLACES: 1.12, 1.20, 1.30. DF: 2.99.
Owner Allevamento La Nuova Sbarra **Bred** Allavemento La Nuova Sbarra **Trained** Italy

6919 PONTEFRACT (L-H)
Monday, October 22

OFFICIAL GOING: Heavy (soft in places; 7.2)
Wind: Virtually nil Weather: Heavy cloud and rain

7289 BET TOTEPLACEPOT TEXT TOTE TO 89660 NURSERY 1m 4y
2:20 (2:20) (Class 5) (0-75,74) 2-Y-O **£2,264** (£673; £336; £168) **Stalls** Low

Form RPR

4121 **1** **Charlie Em**[52] 5806 2-9-3 **70**.. GrahamLee 8 76
(Brendan Powell) *trckd ldr: cl up 1/2-way: led wl over 1f out: sn rdn clr and styd on wl* **7/1**

0041 **2** *4 ½* **Ingleby Symphony (IRE)**[20] 6753 2-8-8 **61**.................. TonyHamilton 1 57
(Richard Fahey) *trckd ldrs: hdwy 2f out: sn rdn: chsd wnr and edgd rt ins fnl f: no imp* **9/2**[3]

0433 **3** *3* **Scepticism (USA)**[13] 6946 2-8-10 **63**.............................. JoeFanning 2 53+
(Mark Johnston) *led: jnd 3f out: rdn along 2f out: hdd wl over 1f out: sn drvn and one pce* **7/1**

010 **4** *shd* **Topamichi**[19] 6793 2-8-10 **63**.. RobertWinston 5 52
(Mark H Tompkins) *stdd s: t.k.h and hld up in rr: hdwy on inner over 2f out: rdn to chse ldrs wl over 1f out: drvn and one pce fnl f* **3/1**[1]

0404 **5** *1 ¾* **Moorway (IRE)**[16] 6893 2-8-5 **58**.................................... HarryBentley 3 43
(Reg Hollinshead) *chsd ldrs: rdn along over 3f out: sn wknd* **6/1**

2056 **6** *10* **Notional Demand**[33] 6356 2-8-7 **60**................................ JamesSullivan 7 23
(Tim Easterby) *hld up in rr: sltly hmpd after s and t.k.h: effrt 3f out: sn rdn and nvr a factor* **16/1**

002 **7** *10* **Mutamaiz (IRE)**[14] 6919 2-8-13 **66**.................................. MartinDwyer 4 7
(James Tate) *hld up: effrt 3f out: sn rdn along and a in rr* **4/1**[2]

1330 **8** *7* **Silent Footsteps (IRE)**[43] 6070 2-9-7 **74**...................... PaulMulrennan 6
(Michael Dods) *hld up in tch: hdwy to chse ldrs after 3f: rdn along 3f out: sn wknd* **20/1**

1m 52.95s (7.05) **Going Correction** +0.975s/f (Soft) **8** Ran SP% **113.1**
Speed ratings (Par 95): **103,98,95,95,93 83,73,66**
toteswingers 1&2 £3.50, 1&3 £3.20, 2&3 £4.70 CSF £37.55 CT £230.53 TOTE £4.10: £1.10, £1.70, £2.30; EX 26.40.
Owner M Foley **Bred** Highfield Farm Llp **Trained** Upper Lambourn, Berks

FOCUS
After 5mm rain before racing the ground was changed to heavy, soft in places. The opening 1m nursery was run in a time 10secs slower than the RP standard, suggesting it was very testing. The jockeys in the opener were unanimous that it was heavy. A wide-open nursery. The principals were handy throughout and the first five finished clear. The runner-up has been rated to her Ayr form in deep ground.
NOTEBOOK
Charlie Em was having her first start for seven weeks having been snapped up after taking a claimer over 7f at Wolverhampton on her final start for Richard Fahey. She made light of the step up in trip, and the testing ground, to run out a most decisive winner. She lacks a little in size and scope and will go up in the ratings after this. (op 5-1 tchd 9-2)
Ingleby Symphony(IRE), raised 4lb after her 7f nursery win at Ayr, is all heart and will stay further than this at three. (op 5-1 tchd 11-2)
Scepticism(USA), third over seven at Brighton on his nursery bow, has size and scope. He was made to look very one-paced but is not bred for the soft and he will be interesting if kept going and sent on the AW. (op 5-1)
Topamichi, blinkered on his first three starts, was very keen. He will need to learn to settle much better if he is to progress. (op 7-2 tchd 4-1)
Moorway(IRE), fourth on the AW at Wolverhampton on his nursery bow, may be capable of something better on less testing ground. (op 8-1)

7290 TOTEPOOL MOBILE TEXT TOTE TO 89660 MAIDEN AUCTION STKS 6f
2:50 (2:52) (Class 5) 2-Y-O **£2,264** (£673; £336; £168) **Stalls** Low

Form			Horse	Jockey	RPR
05	1		**Yorkshireman (IRE)**[18] 6808 2-8-11 0 (David Brown) *led: rdn 2f out: drvn and hdd jst ins fnl f: rallied wl u.p to ld again last 40yds* **20/1**	RobertWinston 2	74
602	2	*hd*	**Medici Dancer**[19] 6781 2-8-7 72 (Tim Easterby) *prom: rdn to chse wnr wl over 1f out: styd on to ld jst ins fnl f: drvn: hdd and no ex last 40yds* **5/2**[2]	DavidAllan 12	69
0	3	*3 ½*	**Dewi Chinta (IRE)**[34] 6335 2-8-4 0 (Kevin Ryan) *in tch: hdwy 2f out: rdn to chse ldrs and carried sltly rt over 1f out: edgd lft and kpt on same pce fnl f* **28/1**	JulieBurke(3) 5	59
3	4	*hd*	**Divine Reward (USA)**[19] 6799 2-8-6 0 (Reg Hollinshead) *hld up towards rr: hdwy whn nt much 2f out and sn swtchd rt: effrt and nt clr run over 1f out: sn rdn: edgd rt and no imp fnl f* **9/4**[1]	JackDuern(5) 3	66+
06	5	*3 ¾*	**Cool And Clear (IRE)**[27] 6556 2-8-5 0 (Tim Easterby) *cl up: rdn along and outpcd over 2f out: plugged on fnl f* **66/1**	DarylByrne(5) 7	50
	6	*shd*	**Wotalad** 2-8-13 0 (Richard Whitaker) *towards rr: hdwy on inner 2f out: sn rdn and kpt on appr fnl f: nrst fin* **40/1**	PaulQuinn 1	52+
0	7	*1*	**Silvala Dance**[13] 6966 2-8-5 0 (Chris Wall) *stdd s and hld up in rr: hdwy 1/2-way: chsd ldrs 2f out: sn rdn and no imp* **20/1**	HarryBentley 6	41
4	8	*2*	**Faffa**[10] 7031 2-8-11 0 (Tim Easterby) *cl up: rdn along 2f out: edgd rt over 1f out and grad wknd* **12/1**	GrahamLee 4	41+
	9	*9*	**Duchess Of Dreams** 2-8-5 0 (Richard Guest) *t.k.h: chsd ldrs: rdn along wl over 2f out and sn wknd* **33/1**	KellyHarrison 9	8
6	10	*3 ¼*	**Dilady**[24] 6627 2-8-7 0 (Kevin Ryan) *dwlt: sn in tch on wd outside: rdn along wl over 2f out and sn wknd* **8/1**	AmyRyan 11	1
	11	*nse*	**Art Storm (IRE)** 2-8-12 0 (Richard Fahey) *dwlt: a in rr* **15/2**[3]	TonyHamilton 10	5+
05	12	*3 ¾*	**Accelerant (IRE)**[10] 7031 2-8-13 0 (Kevin Ryan) *dwlt: t.k.h: a towards rr* **20/1**	PhillipMakin 8	

1m 23.75s (6.85) **Going Correction** +0.975s/f (Soft) **12** Ran SP% **114.5**
Speed ratings (Par 95): **93,92,88,87,82 82,81,78,66,62 62,57**
toteswingers 1&2 £11.40, 1&3 £50.00, 2&3 £18.60 CSF £63.63 TOTE £25.60: £5.50, £1.10, £9.80; EX 106.40.
Owner Yorkshireman Partnership **Bred** Ossiana Partnership **Trained** Averham Park, Notts
FOCUS
No strength in depth in this 2yo maiden and the first two had it to themselves once in line for home. The time was over 9secs slower than RP standard. The runner-up showed her latest run was no fluke.
NOTEBOOK
Yorkshireman(IRE), only fifth on the AW on his second start when tried in a visor over 5f, seemed to appreciate the return to form. After showing ahead before the final turn with the rail to help he fought back to snatch the prize near the line.
Medici Dancer, rated 72 after giving a 1-5 shot a fright in a four-horse field in bad ground at Newcastle, took a narrow advantage inside the final furlong only to miss out at the line. She deserves to go one better. (op 9-4 tchd 11-4)
Dewi Chinta(IRE) stepped up on her first run and there ought to be even better to come in time. (op 25-1)
Divine Reward(USA), a 100-1 shot on his debut in a Class 2 event at Salisbury where his apprentice was unable to claim, found himself towards the rear. He had a troubled passage when trying to improve and could never get near the first two. He is well worth another chance. (op 3-1 tchd 10-3)
Cool And Clear(IRE) made a satisfactory bow but will not be seen to best advantage until next year.
Faffa, who took the eye in the paddock, will make a better 3yo. (op 14-1 tchd 11-1)
Art Storm(IRE), a newcomer from a yard that has sent out 47 juvenile winner this year, was well backed on the morning line but he never went a yard. Presumably he had been showing a lot more at home. (op 11-2)

7291 RACING POST FORM WITH TOTEPOOL MOBILE H'CAP (DIV I) 5f
3:20 (3:21) (Class 4) (0-85,85) 3-Y-O+ **£4,075** (£1,212; £606; £303) **Stalls** Low

Form			Horse	Jockey	RPR
0660	1		**Baby Strange**[14] 6939 8-8-13 77 (Derek Shaw) *trckd ldrs: hdwy 2f out: rdn to ld ins fnl f: kpt on* **14/1**	(v) MartinDwyer 15	87
0006	2	*¾*	**Master Bond**[10] 7023 3-8-9 73 (Bryan Smart) *trckd ldrs: hdwy 2f out: led wl over 1f out and sn rdn: hdd ins fnl f and kpt on same pce* **16/1**	(t) PaulMulrennan 7	80
1640	3	*1 ¾*	**Rylee Mooch**[31] 6427 4-8-12 76 (Richard Guest) *prom on inner: hdwy 2f out: sn rdn and ev ch tl drvn and one pce ins fnl f* **20/1**	(e) RobbieFitzpatrick 1	77
0034	4	*hd*	**Dickie's Lad (IRE)**[11] 7000 4-9-1 79 (Kevin Ryan) *towards rr: hdwy and wd st: rdn wl over 1f out: styd on fnl f: nrst fin* **10/1**	(t) AmyRyan 14	79
-123	5	*hd*	**Hello Stranger (IRE)**[11] 7001 3-8-7 71 oh3 (Tim Easterby) *chsd ldrs: rdn along wl over 1f out: kpt on same pce* **15/2**[3]	JamesSullivan 5	70
5000	6	*nk*	**Foxy Music**[23] 6666 8-9-7 85 (Eric Alston) *cl up on outer: rdn along 2f out: wd st: sn drvn and kpt on same pce* **22/1**	DavidAllan 10	83
5250	7	*½*	**Oldjoesaid**[44] 6044 8-8-13 77 (Paul Midgley) *s.i.s and bhd: hdwy 2f out: sn rdn: styd on fnl f: nrst fin* **20/1**	RussKennemore 16	73
5001	8	*¾*	**Solar Spirit (IRE)**[14] 6938 7-9-4 82 (Tracy Waggott) *hld up: hdwy on inner 2f out: rdn to chse ldrs wl over 1f out: sn drvn and kpt on same pce* **7/1**[2]	GrahamLee 3	76
632	9	*1 ¾*	**Breezolini**[11] 7000 4-8-11 75 (Geoffrey Harker) *in tch: rdn along 2f out: sn btn* **7/2**[1]	RobertWinston 4	62
10-0	10	*1*	**Dorback**[30] 6465 5-9-0 78 (David Nicholls) *nvr bttr than midfield* **20/1**	AdrianNicholls 2	62
-056	11	*½*	**Little Garcon (USA)**[20] 6767 5-9-1 84 (Robert Cowell) *dwlt: a in rr* **10/1**	MichaelJMMurphy(5) 6	66
103	12	*nk*	**Planetex (IRE)**[5] 7177 3-8-11 75 (John Quinn) *a towards rr* **10/1**	MichaelO'Connell 11	56
0030	13	*nk*	**Taurus Twins**[10] 7019 6-9-5 83 (Richard Price) *chsd ldrs: rdn along over 2f out: sn wknd* **22/1**	(b) JoeFanning 12	63
2306	14	*4*	**Master Rooney (IRE)**[28] 6543 6-9-6 84 (Bryan Smart) *led: rdn along and hdd wl over 1f out: sn wknd* **20/1**	PhillipMakin 8	49
0005	15	*7*	**Noodles Blue Boy**[28] 6543 6-8-10 81 (Ollie Pears) *s.i.s: sn rdn along and in tch 1/2-way: sn wknd* **10/1**	JacobButterfield(7) 9	21

1m 7.37s (4.07) **Going Correction** +0.975s/f (Soft) **15** Ran SP% **123.1**
Speed ratings (Par 105): **106,104,102,101,101 100,100,98,96,94 93,93,92,86,75**
toteswingers 1&2 £50.90, 1&3 £81.90, 2&3 £83.60 CSF £196.92 CT £4503.74 TOTE £19.30: £6.00, £6.50, £9.80; EX 417.00.
Owner Market Avenue Racing Club Ltd **Bred** Michael John Williamson **Trained** Sproxton, Leics
■ Stewards' Enquiry : Michael O'Connell two-day ban: careless riding (Nov 5-6)
FOCUS
They raced in two groups in this wide open sprint handicap. Half-a-dozen stuck to the inside route but the first two home came wide. The winner has been rated close to his best.
Foxy Music Official explanation: jockey said gelding hung right-handed
Breezolini Official explanation: jockey said filly ran flat

7292 TOTEPOOL.COM SILVER TANKARD STKS (LISTED RACE) 1m 4y
3:50 (3:50) (Class 1) 2-Y-O
£13,043 (£4,945; £2,474; £1,232; £618; £310) **Stalls** Low

Form			Horse	Jockey	RPR
1	1		**Willie The Whipper**[53] 5756 2-9-2 0 (Ann Duffield) *hld up in rr: hdwy on outer over 2f out: rdn to chse ldrs over 1f out: styd on to ld last 75yds* **7/1**	GrahamLee 2	92
212	2	*1 ¾*	**Oasis Cannes**[49] 5899 2-9-2 95 (Sir Mark Prescott Bt) *cl up: led over 2f out: rdn wl over 1f out: drvn ins fnl f: hdd and no ex last 75yds* **2/1**[1]	LukeMorris 3	88
3361	3	*1 ¼*	**Top Notch Tonto (IRE)**[30] 6469 2-9-2 98 (Ian McInnes) *trckd ldrs: pushed along and outpcd over 2f out: rdn wl over 1f out: styd on fnl f* **6/1**[3]	PatrickMathers 4	86
614	4	*¾*	**Allnecessaryforce (FR)**[3] 7209 2-9-2 71 (Richard Fahey) *trckd ldrs: pushed along and outpcd over 2f out: sn swtchd lft to inner: rdn and hdwy over 1f out: drvn to chal jst ins fnl f: ev ch tl edgd lft and one pce last 100yds* **33/1**	TonyHamilton 5	84
15	5	*1*	**Georgian Bay (IRE)**[38] 6200 2-9-2 0 (Mrs K Burke) *trckd ldrs: hdwy 3f out: rdn wl over 1f out: drvn and one pce appr fnl f* **17/2**	PhillipMakin 1	82
0222	6	*12*	**Esteaming**[3] 7205 2-9-2 75 (Mick Channon) *sn led: rdn along 3f out: sn hdd & wknd* **16/1**	SamHitchcott 7	55
01	7	*7*	**Pearl Reward (USA)**[25] 6607 2-9-2 0 (Stuart Williams) *trckd ldrs: hdwy and cl up on outer over 2f out: sn rdn and wknd* **9/4**[2]	HarryBentley 6	40

1m 53.48s (7.58) **Going Correction** +0.975s/f (Soft) **7** Ran SP% **110.2**
Speed ratings (Par 103): **101,99,98,97,96 84,77**
toteswingers 1&2 £2.70, 1&3 £5.00, 2&3 £2.90 CSF £19.89 TOTE £4.90: £3.40, £1.10; EX 28.30.
Owner Jimmy Kay **Bred** J S B Anderson **Trained** Constable Burton, N Yorks
FOCUS
First run 20 years ago this 1m Listed 2yo prize was won by subsequent St Leger winner Silver Patriarch in 1996. In the conditions it was a true test of stamina. Questionable form for the grade, with the runner-up rated to his British form.
NOTEBOOK
Willie The Whipper had won a 6f race confined to horses that had not previously run on his debut at Hamilton in late August. Settled at the back and brought widest of all, he really put his head down and battled to gain the upper hand. He has a very willing attitude and should go on to even better things at three. (op 6-1)
Oasis Cannes, now rated 95 after finishing runner-up in Listed company in France, had taken a nursery at Newmarket in August from a mark of 82. He went for home when straightening up but ultimately found the winner too strong. His nursery win came on quick ground and he looks a likely type for somewhere like Hong Kong. (op 5-2 tchd 11-4)
Top Notch Tonto(IRE), having his ninth start, is a really tough type who took a nursery at Ayr in September from a mark of 92. Tapped for toe turning in, he battled on to secure third spot and is a most admirable type. However, he is looking fully exposed now. (op 5-1)
Allnecessaryforce(FR), a bad-ground Newcastle maiden winner, managed only fourth when sent off favourite from a mark of just 71 at Haydock four days earlier. He left that effort behind and deserves marking up after being left to race alone against the far rail in the home straight.
Georgian Bay(IRE), closely matched with Top Notch Tonto on Doncaster nursery form, didn't improve for the step up in trip. He was found to have lost a front shoe. Official explanation: vet said colt lost a front plate (op 10-1 tchd 8-1)
Esteaming, bidding to give Mick Channon his fourth success in seven years, had just missed out in 1 1m2f maiden at Haydock four days earlier. He helped set the pace before dropping right away. (tchd 12-1)
Pearl Reward(USA), runaway winner of a C&D maiden, was a shade keen and stopped to nothing once in line for home. This was too bad to be true and connections could offer no explanation. Official explanation: trainer had no explanation for the poor form shown (tchd 2-1)

7293 TOTEQUICKPICK BLUFF COVE H'CAP 2m 1f 216y
4:20 (4:21) (Class 5) (0-75,75) 3-Y-O+ **£2,264** (£673; £336; £168) **Stalls** Low

Form			Horse	Jockey	RPR
0060	1		**Zefooha (FR)**[86] 4590 8-9-1 62 (Tim Walford) *mde all: rdn along 2f out: drvn ent fnl f: sn edgd rt and kpt on gamely* **20/1**	(p) PaddyAspell 1	71
0100	2	*1*	**Madam Lilibet (IRE)**[13] 6956 3-7-12 56 (Sharon Watt) *trckd ldrs: hdwy 4f out: rdn to chse wnr 2f out: chal over 1f out: drvn and ev ch ins fnl f: no ex last 100yds* **9/2**[3]	PaulQuinn 2	64
3000	3	*8*	**Inside Knowledge (USA)**[18] 6821 6-8-9 56 oh9 (Garry Woodward) *trckd wnr: pushed along 3f out: rdn 2f out: drvn and one pce fr over 1f out* **25/1**	LukeMorris 8	55

211 **4** 2 ¾ **Jawaab (IRE)**[32] 6407 8-10-0 **75**....................(v) PhillipMakin 10 71
(Philip Kirby) *trckd ldng pair: effrt 3f out: sn rdn along: drvn wl over 1f out and sn btn* **15/8**[1]

2150 **5** 1 **Tarantella Lady**[15] 4867 4-9-1 **62**....................(b[1]) PJMcDonald 7 57
(George Moore) *in tch: hdwy on outer over 4f out: rdn along wl over 2f out: drvn and btn wl over 1f out* **10/1**

1040 **6** 7 **Spanish Fork (IRE)**[24] 6407 3-8-5 **63**....................(v) SamHitchcott 5 50
(Mick Channon) *hld up in rr: sme hdwy over 4f out: rdn along 3f out: sn btn* **11/4**[2]

3000 **7** 5 **Blackstone Vegas**[32] 6407 6-9-1 **62**.................... JoeFanning 6 44
(Derek Shaw) *hld up in rr: effrt and sme hdwy 4f out: rdn along over 2f out: n.d* **5/1**

4m 29.9s (33.70) **Going Correction** +0.975s/f (Soft)
WFA 3 from 4yo+ 11lb **7** Ran SP% **114.0**
Speed ratings (Par 103): **64,63,60,58,58 55,53**
toteswingers 1&2 £10.70, 1&3 £11.80, 2&3 £8.20 CSF £105.47 CT £2275.60 TOTE £19.00: £6.70, £1.80; EX 121.40.
Owner Shaun Conway **Bred** Darley Stud Management Co Ltd **Trained** Sheriff Hutton, N Yorks

FOCUS
The gallop was sound and this was an extreme test of stamina in the ground. The winning time was nearly 40sec outside the RP standard. The runner-up has been rated to a small personal best.

7294 FOLLOW TOTEPOOL ON FACEBOOK AND TWITTER H'CAP 1m 2f 6y
4:50 (4:50) (Class 4) (0-85,85) 3-Y-0+ **£4,075** (£1,212; £606; £303) **Stalls** Low

Form RPR

-104 **1** **The Tiger**[24] 6639 4-9-1 **76**.................... GrahamLee 9 94+
(Ed Dunlop) *dwlt and in rr: stdy hdwy 1/2-way: chal on bit over 2f out: sn led and clr over 1f out: easily* **7/2**[1]

1240 **2** 4 ½ **Maybeagrey**[10] 7032 3-8-5 **71**.................... JamesSullivan 3 78
(Tim Easterby) *hld up: hdwy on inner over 2f out: rdn to chse wnr over 1f out: kpt on: no ch w wnr* **12/1**

U0 **3** 9 **Allied Answer**[7] 7109 4-9-10 **85**.................... FrederikTylicki 5 76
(Steve Gollings) *a.p: rdn along over 2f out: sn drvn and kpt on same pce* **20/1**

0055 **4** 1 **Carragold**[9] 7069 6-8-11 **72**....................(p) DavidAllan 7 61
(Mel Brittain) *in tch: hdwy to chse ldrs 3f out: rdn along over 2f out: drvn and one pce fr wl over 1f out* **11/1**

0460 **5** 2 ¼ **Trend Is My Friend (USA)**[13] 6964 3-8-12 **78**.................... JoeFanning 12 63
(Amanda Perrett) *dwlt and towards rr: smooth hdwy over 5f out: cl up 3f out: rdn over 2f out: grad wknd* **5/1**[2]

0012 **6** 1 ¼ **Follow The Flag (IRE)**[12] 6988 8-8-10 **71** oh3....................(v) LukeMorris 14 54
(Alan McCabe) *towards rr: rdn along bhd 1/2-way: styd on u.p fnl 2f: n.d* **16/1**

600 **7** 1 **Judicious**[9] 7069 5-8-10 **78**.................... JacobButterfield[(7)] 2 59
(Ollie Pears) *cl up: led 4f out: rdn along and hdd 2f out: grad wknd fr over 1f out* **20/1**

4100 **8** 14 **Dubaianswer**[204] 1158 4-9-5 **80**.................... BarryMcHugh 1 36
(Tony Coyle) *nvr bttr than midfield* **33/1**

1665 **9** 3 **Satanic Beat (IRE)**[14] 6921 3-9-5 **85**.................... PJMcDonald 13 35
(Jedd O'Keeffe) *in tch on outer: riddn along over 4f out: sn wknd* **10/1**

3060 **10** 3 ¼ **Tartan Gigha (IRE)**[30] 6476 7-9-4 **79**....................(p) DanielTudhope 4 23
(Geoffrey Harker) *chsd ldrs: rdn over 2f out: sn drvn and wknd* **25/1**

2355 **11** 4 ½ **Hakuna Matata**[16] 6881 5-8-12 **73**....................(p) PaulMulrennan 10
(Michael Dods) *a towards rr* **10/1**

0003 **12** 18 **West End Lad**[28] 6545 9-8-11 **72**....................(b) RobertWinston 11
(Roy Bowring) *prom: rdn along over 3f out: wknd wl over 2f out* **11/1**

0040 **13** 1 **Kiwi Bay**[9] 7069 7-9-8 **83**.................... TonyHamilton 6
(Michael Dods) *sn led: hdd 4f out: sn rdn along and wknd* **25/1**

5503 **14** 3 ¼ **Kathleen Frances**[16] 6884 5-9-1 **76**....................(p) MartinDwyer 8
(Mark H Tompkins) *in tch: hdwy to chse ldrs 4f out: rdn along 3f out and sn wknd* **7/1**[3]

2m 22.16s (8.46) **Going Correction** +0.975s/f (Soft)
WFA 3 from 4yo+ 5lb **14** Ran SP% **120.0**
Speed ratings (Par 105): **105,101,94,93,91 90,89,78,76,73 70,55,54,52**
toteswingers 1&2 £18.20, 1&3 £19.30, 2&3 £46.40 CSF £42.38 CT £748.96 TOTE £5.30: £2.00, £4.40, £5.40; EX 57.20.
Owner J R Weatherby **Bred** Preston Lodge Stud **Trained** Newmarket, Suffolk

FOCUS
A sound gallop, a facile winner and the first seven were clear of the remainder. It's been rated around the runner-up.
Kathleen Frances Official explanation: jockey said mare had no more to give

7295 RACING POST FORM WITH TOTEPOOL MOBILE H'CAP (DIV II) 5f
5:20 (5:20) (Class 4) (0-85,84) 3-Y-0+ **£4,075** (£1,212; £606; £303) **Stalls** Low

Form RPR

6226 **1** **Cheveton**[23] 6666 8-9-5 **82**.................... JoeFanning 14 91
(Richard Price) *midfield: hdwy and in tch 2f out: rdn to chse ldr ent fnl f: styd on wl to ld last 50yds* **10/3**[1]

0000 **2** ½ **Excel Bolt**[40] 6144 4-9-5 **82**.................... TonyHamilton 1 89
(Bryan Smart) *led: rdn and qcknd clr 2f out: drvn over 1f out: jnd ins fnl f: hdd and no ex last 50yds* **14/1**

2105 **3** 3 ¾ **Wild Sauce**[23] 6688 3-9-1 **78**....................(p) PhillipMakin 6 72
(Bryan Smart) *prom: rdn 2f out: chsd ldr over 1f out: sn drvn and kpt on same pce* **16/1**

0030 **4** hd **Captain Scooby**[7] 7114 6-8-11 **74**.................... AmyRyan 5 67
(Richard Guest) *towards rr: gd hdwy on inner 2f out: rdn wl over 1f out: styd on fnl f: nrst fin* **10/1**

4405 **5** 1 ¼ **Damika (IRE)**[20] 6767 9-9-7 **84**....................(v) MichaelStainton 13 72
(David Brown) *midfield: hdwy 1/2-way: rdn 2f out: kpt on appr fnl f: nt rch ldrs* **8/1**

2410 **6** hd **Da'Quonde (IRE)**[115] 3578 4-9-0 **77**.................... PaulMulrennan 11 65
(Bryan Smart) *chsd ldrs: rdn along 2f out: drvn wl over 1f out and sn one pce* **25/1**

1655 **7** ½ **Haajes**[14] 6938 8-8-12 **75**....................(v) MickyFenton 10 61
(Paul Midgley) *chsd ldrs: effrt 2f out: sn rdn and no imp fr over 1f out* **9/1**

1000 **8** 2 ¼ **Sir Geoffrey (IRE)**[31] 6427 6-8-7 **70**....................(p) LukeMorris 15 48
(Scott Dixon) *chsd ldrs on outer: rdn along over 2f out: sn wknd* **33/1**

0010 **9** ½ **Amenable (IRE)**[30] 6465 5-8-13 **83**.................... ShirleyTeasdale[(7)] 2 59
(David Nicholls) *cl up: rdn 2f out: wknd over 1f out* **8/1**

2310 **10** shd **Mount Hollow**[19] 6800 7-8-12 **80**....................(p) JackDuern[(5)] 12 56
(Reg Hollinshead) *dwlt: a in rr* **20/1**

3443 **11** ¾ **Bathwick Bear (IRE)**[7] 7113 4-9-1 **78**.................... DanielTudhope 3 51
(David Evans) *in tch: hdwy to chse ldrs 2f out: sn rdn and btn* **9/2**[2]

0033 **12** ¾ **Bouncy Bouncy (IRE)**[19] 6788 5-8-12 **75**....................(t) HayleyTurner 9 45
(Michael Bell) *dwlt: a towards rr* **7/1**[3]

-400 **13** 5 **Cornus**[37] 6260 10-8-4 **70** oh3....................(be) DeclanCannon[(3)] 7 22
(Alan McCabe) *dwlt: a in rr* **66/1**

1m 7.05s (3.75) **Going Correction** +0.975s/f (Soft) **13** Ran SP% **120.7**
Speed ratings (Par 105): **109,108,102,101,99 99,98,95,94,94 93,91,83**
toteswingers 1&2 £12.30, 1&3 £14.30, 2&3 £33.20 CSF £50.80 CT £691.84 TOTE £3.10: £1.70, £5.20, £7.00; EX 64.00.
Owner Mrs K Oseman **Bred** Miss K Rausing **Trained** Ullingswick, H'fords

FOCUS
The taxing surface found out most here. The winner raced wide and has been rated as stepping up slightly on this year's form.
Bouncy Bouncy(IRE) Official explanation: jockey said mare lost its tongue-strap
T/Jkpt: Not won. T/Plt: £15,743.00 to a £1 stake. Pool: £66,854.18 - 3.10 winning tickets T/Qpdt: £578.40 to a £1 stake. Pool: £5,315.08 - 6.80 winning tickets JR

7110 WINDSOR (R-H)
Monday, October 22

OFFICIAL GOING: Heavy (5.4)
Wind: Almost nil Weather: Murky

7296 ROFLOW ENVIRONMENTAL ENGINEERING MEDIAN AUCTION MAIDEN STKS 5f 10y
2:00 (2:00) (Class 5) 2-Y-0 **£2,264** (£673; £336; £168) **Stalls** Low

Form RPR

4652 **1** **Oscars Journey**[18] 6808 2-9-3 70.................... JimmyFortune 6 72
(J R Jenkins) *mde all: wnt to far side after 2f: rdn and styd on wl fnl f* **5/4**[1]

3320 **2** 1 ½ **Tregereth (IRE)**[36] 6276 2-8-12 63.................... RichardKingscote 4 62+
(Jonathan Portman) *chsd wnr: lft in ld of quartet on nr side after 2f: hung lft to far side fnl f: styd on but nvr quite on terms* **11/4**[2]

4 **3** 4 ½ **Captain Cruz (IRE)**[12] 6983 2-9-3 0.................... WilliamCarson 5 51
(Ronald Harris) *trckd ldng pair: styd nr side 3f out: hung lft to far side fr 2f out: wl hld in 3rd fnl f* **4/1**[3]

4 7 **Multitask** 2-9-3 0.................... JamieGoldstein 3 26
(Michael Madgwick) *dwlt: in tch in rr: followed wnr to far side after 2f: struggling fnl 2f* **40/1**

0 **5** ½ **Direct Trade**[19] 6772 2-8-12 0.................... DavidProbert 2 19
(Mark Usher) *t.k.h early: hld up in tch: styd nr side 3f out: sn outpcd and btn* **9/1**

6 17 **Sweet Piccolo** 2-9-3 0.................... IanMongan 1
(Paddy Butler) *s.i.s: sn outpcd: a bhd: t.o* **11/1**

1m 5.13s (4.83) **Going Correction** +0.725s/f (Yiel) **6** Ran SP% **111.9**
Speed ratings (Par 95): **90,87,80,69,68 41**
toteswingers 1&2 £1.40, 1&3 £1.40, 2&3 £1.60 CSF £4.86 TOTE £3.00: £1.10, £1.40; EX 4.70.
Owner R B Hill **Bred** R B Hill **Trained** Royston, Herts

FOCUS
The inner of the straight was dolled out eight yards at 6f and five yards at the winning post. The top bend was dolled out ten yards from normal inner configuration, adding 37 yards to race distances at 1m plus. A weak maiden and form to treat with caution as the field were spread out across the track in the closing stages, with Oscars Journey towards the far side, while runner-up Tregereth was positioned stands' side until drifting left late on. It's unclear what the winner achieved.

NOTEBOOK
Oscars Journey may be flattered by this win and his next run should tell us more. (tchd 6-5)
Tregereth(IRE), officially rated just 63, finished clear of the others. She looks up to winning a small race. (tchd 3-1)
Captain Cruz(IRE) ran to just a moderate level on his debut at Nottingham and he was again well held. (op 5-1)
Multitask, an already gelded brother to fair 7f-1m winner Multi Bene, didn't show a great deal but may yet do better. (op 50-1)

7297 HAPPY RETIREMENT JEREMY RIDGWAY CLAIMING STKS 6f
2:30 (2:30) (Class 5) 3-Y-0+ **£2,264** (£673; £336; £168) **Stalls** Low

Form RPR

0053 **1** **Victorian Bounty**[18] 6811 7-8-9 69.................... FergusSweeney 6 76
(Tony Newcombe) *pressed ldr over 4f out: rdn to ld over 1f out: kpt on fnl f* **12/1**

2534 **2** ½ **Ertikaan**[10] 7019 5-9-2 83.................... WilliamCarson 8 82
(Ronald Harris) *t.k.h: hld up bhd ldrs: rdn 2f out: pressed wnr jst over 1f out: kpt on but hld nr fin* **7/2**[2]

4565 **3** ½ **Mambo Spirit (IRE)**[36] 6277 8-8-7 66.................... ChrisCatlin 5 71
(Tony Newcombe) *t.k.h: hld up in rr: shkn up 2f out: prog over 1f out: styd on fnl f: gaining at fin* **16/1**

550 **4** shd **Fathsta (IRE)**[13] 6969 7-8-11 79.................... JimmyFortune 2 75
(Ian Williams) *hld up in tch: rdn 2f out: kpt on same pce fr over 1f out: nvr quite able to chal* **5/2**[1]

0065 **5** 1 **Toby Tyler**[11] 7000 6-8-6 70....................(v) MartinLane 10 66
(Paul Midgley) *stdd s: hld up in rr: drvn 2f out: kpt on one pce: nvr rchd ldrs* **4/1**[3]

0206 **6** 1 **Blue Jack**[23] 6689 7-8-7 81....................(tp) SilvestreDeSousa 1 64
(Alan McCabe) *hld up in tch: effrt over 2f out: cl enough over 1f out: fdd ins fnl f* **4/1**[3]

6160 **7** 1 ¾ **Efistorm**[7] 7113 11-8-4 74.................... AmyScott[(5)] 9 61
(Joseph Tuite) *led over 4f out: rdn over 2f out: hdd & wknd over 1f out* **8/1**

00 **8** 18 **Captain Hero (IRE)**[66] 5305 5-8-4 0....................(p) SimonPearce[(3)] 7
(Laura Mongan) *cl up tl wknd over 2f out: t.o* **100/1**

4000 **P** **Samba Night (IRE)**[53] 5774 3-8-5 57.................... DavidProbert 3
(James Eustace) *led to over 4f out: dropped out qckly: p.u 1/2-way: dismntd* **33/1**

1m 17.62s (4.62) **Going Correction** +0.725s/f (Yiel)
WFA 3 from 5yo+ 1lb **9** Ran SP% **119.4**
Speed ratings (Par 103): **98,97,96,96,95 93,91,67,**
toteswingers 1&2 £5.20, 1&3 £7.20, 2&3 £9.40 CSF £55.72 TOTE £16.80: £4.00, £1.10, £3.10; EX 72.30 Trifecta £352.50 Pool: £766.30 - 1.63 winning tickets..
Owner David Gilbert **Bred** Mrs P D Gray And H Farr **Trained** Yarnscombe, Devon

FOCUS
A modest claimer in which the main action unfolded far side. The winner has been rated as running his best race since last winter, but the third limits the form.
Samba Night(IRE) Official explanation: jockey said gelding lost its action

7298 R J CLYDE BUILDERS NURSERY 6f
3:00 (3:00) (Class 4) (0-85,78) 2-Y-0 **£3,557** (£1,058; £529; £264) **Stalls** Low

Form RPR

1005 **1** **Reliant Robin (IRE)**[5] 7164 2-9-4 **75**....................(v[1]) JimmyFortune 7 79
(Robert Mills) *cl up: led over 2f out tl wl over 1f out: hrd rdn to ld again ins fnl f: styd on wl* **11/2**

1240 **2** *2* **Khefyn (IRE)**^{5} 7164 2-9-4 **75**.......... WilliamCarson 6 73
(Ronald Harris) *trckd ldrs: prog over 2f out: led wl over 1f out: hdd and no ex ins fnl f* **12/1**

31 **3** *½* **Broughtons Charm (IRE)**^{14} 6936 2-9-4 **75**.......... WilliamBuick 2 72
(Willie Musson) *hld up in tch: prog to chal against far rail whn nt clr run wl over 1f out: renewed effrt to take 3rd ins fnl f: styd on* **5/1**

6162 **4** *3 ¼* **Front Page News**^{78} 4847 2-9-3 **74**.......... AdamBeschizza 1 61
(Robert Eddery) *s.s: hld up in rr: prog over 2f out: rdn to chse ldng pair over 1f out: wknd fnl f* **9/2**^{3}

0342 **5** *1 ½* **Dumbarton Rock**^{17} 6849 2-8-12 **69**..........(b^{1}) SilvestreDeSousa 9 51
(William Jarvis) *led to over 2f out: lost pl qckly and hanging: n.d fnl f* **4/1**^{2}

040 **6** *2* **Forceful Flame**^{53} 5765 2-8-12 **69**.......... PaoloSirigu 5 45
(Robert Eddery) *t.k.h: hld up in tch: rdn over 2f out: hanging and wknd over 1f out* **20/1**

301 **7** *nk* **Senator Bong**^{19} 6787 2-9-4 **75**.......... DaneO'Neill 8 50
(David Elsworth) *t.k.h: w ldr to 1/2-way: wknd u.p 2f out* **5/2**^{1}

0651 **8** *1 ¾* **Harrogate Fair**^{17} 6850 2-8-2 **59**.......... JamieMackay 3 29
(Michael Squance) *in tch: rdn 1/2-way: wknd 2f out* **16/1**

1m 17.85s (4.85) **Going Correction** +0.725s/f (Yiel) **8** Ran SP% **117.1**
Speed ratings (Par 97): **96,93,92,88,86 83,83,80**
toteswingers 1&2 £10.30, 1&3 £6.60, 2&3 £12.10 CSF £69.23 CT £354.63 TOTE £7.10: £1.60, £2.10, £2.30; EX 101.80 Trifecta £654.60 Part won. Pool: £872.91 - 0.40 winning tickets..
Owner Pinehurst Racing & Mrs B B Mills **Bred** Rathbarry Stud **Trained** Headley, Surrey

FOCUS
They raced far side in this fair nursery. This was a step up from the winner under a strong ride, but the form has been rated cautiously.

NOTEBOOK
Reliant Robin(IRE) hadn't gone on since winning his maiden in June, but he'd reportedly had excuses. He had been tried in blinkers without success, but took well to a first-time visor and he also had the advantage of the far rail in the closing stages. It remains to be seen whether he can build on this, and he reportedly now goes to the sales. (op 7-1)
Khefyn(IRE) was 10lb higher than when winning on soft ground at Chepstow in August and had no obvious excuse. (op 10-1 tchd 14-1)
Broughtons Charm(IRE) ◆ was a bit short of room when trying to challenge against the far rail and had to be switched. She probably would have been second with a clear run and this progressive sort, who had her first two starts on Polytrack, notably a Wolverhampton maiden win, is clearly versatile. (op 11-2 tchd 9-2)
Front Page News, returning from 78 days off, couldn't overcome a slow start, but the way she travelled through the race suggests she's a filly who may have more to offer.
Dumbarton Rock didn't take to the first-time blinkers, running well below the form he showed when second on heavy at Yarmouth last time. (tchd 7-2 and 9-2)
Senator Bong, successful in a 5f maiden on good to soft, was found out by these more demanding conditions. (op 11-4)

7299 DAVISBAKERYCARIBBEAN.COM H'CAP 5f 10y
3:30 (3:30) (Class 5) (0-70,70) 3-Y-O+ **£2,264** (£673; £336; £168) **Stalls** Low

Form RPR
0200 **1** **Whitecrest**^{19} 6788 4-9-5 **68**.......... ChrisCatlin 7 77
(John Spearing) *mde all: hrd rdn fnl f: hld on wl* **6/1**^{3}

0000 **2** *½* **Shawkantango**^{4} 7197 5-9-4 **67**..........(v) SilvestreDeSousa 3 74
(Derek Shaw) *taken down early: hld up: prog 1/2-way: drvn to chse wnr over 1f out: tried to chal fnl f: nt qckn last 100yds* **7/2**^{1}

4630 **3** *2 ½* **Speak The Truth (IRE)**^{26} 6578 6-9-1 **64**..........(p) PatCosgrave 5 62
(Jim Boyle) *hld up in tch: effrt 2f out: drvn and kpt on to take 3rd ins fnl f: one pce* **16/1**

5-06 **4** *nk* **Mr Hendrix**^{14} 6926 3-8-7 **56** oh3.......... WilliamCarson 6 53
(Mark Hoad) *pressed wnr to 2f out: lost 2nd over 1f out: one pce* **33/1**

0000 **5** *¾* **Dispol Grand (IRE)**^{16} 6886 6-8-13 **69**.......... NedCurtis$^{(7)}$ 8 63
(Paul Midgley) *hld up: in last 2f out: rdn and prog over 1f out: kpt on but nvr gng pce to threaten* **7/1**

1023 **6** *2 ¼* **Commandingpresence (USA)**^{26} 6578 6-9-0 **70**
WilliamTwiston-Davies$^{(7)}$ 10 56
(John Bridger) *prom: lost pl and drvn 2f out: nvr on terms after* **7/2**^{1}

5000 **7** *½* **Signifer (IRE)**^{26} 6578 3-9-4 **67**.......... MartinHarley 2 51
(Mick Channon) *t.k.h: hld up in rr: prog on outer 1/2-way: wandered u.p over 1f out: wknd* **9/2**^{2}

5000 **8** *1 ¼* **Welsh Inlet (IRE)**^{14} 6926 4-8-13 **62**.......... KieranO'Neill 1 42
(John Bridger) *chsd ldrs on outer: reminders bef 1/2-way: struggling fr 2f out* **16/1**

2200 **9** *1 ¾* **Courtland Avenue (IRE)**^{53} 5775 3-9-3 **66**.......... RichardKingscote 9 40
(Jonathan Portman) *in tch tl wknd wl over 1f out* **14/1**

1306 **10** *27* **Laura's Bairn**^{96} 4208 3-9-7 **70**..........(v) JimmyFortune 4
(J R Jenkins) *chsd ldrs tl wknd 2f out: eased over 1f out: t.o* **10/1**

1m 4.73s (4.43) **Going Correction** +0.725s/f (Yiel) **10** Ran SP% **119.9**
Speed ratings (Par 103): **93,92,88,87,86 82,82,80,77,34**
toteswingers 1&2 £4.30, 1&3 £13.80, 2&3 £10.00 CSF £28.14 CT £327.62 TOTE £8.10: £2.20, £1.20, £3.60; EX 38.70 TRIFECTA Pool: £1,172.21 - 2.88 winning tickets..
Owner G M Eales **Bred** J Spearing And Kate Ive **Trained** Kinnersley, Worcs

FOCUS
Again, they raced far side. Straightforward form rated around the winner to her best, and the runner-up to his turf best.
Laura's Bairn Official explanation: jockey said gelding lost its action

7300 ROYAL WINDSOR HUGHESIE SEVEN H'CAP 1m 2f 7y
4:00 (4:00) (Class 4) (0-85,81) 3-Y-O+ **£4,204** (£1,251; £625; £312) **Stalls** Centre

Form RPR
0652 **1** **Aldwick Bay (IRE)**^{14} 6933 4-9-9 **80**.......... PatDobbs 8 89
(Richard Hannon) *hld up off the pce in midfield: prog 4f out: led over 2f out: drvn and jnd over 1f out: kpt on wl* **5/1**^{2}

3042 **2** *¾* **Snow Trooper**^{14} 6932 4-9-5 **76**.......... ShaneKelly 9 84
(Dean Ivory) *hld up in rr: stdy prog 3f out: shkn up to chse ldng pair over 1f out: tried to chal between rivals fnl f: styd on to take 2nd last strides* **10/1**

2246 **3** *shd* **Choral Festival**^{18} 6819 6-8-9 **73**.......... WilliamTwiston-Davies$^{(7)}$ 6 80
(John Bridger) *hld up in midfield: trckd ldrs gng easily 3f out: wnt 2nd wl over 1f out and sn upsides: drvn and fnd nil after: lost 2nd last strides* **10/1**

2/2 **4** *2 ½* **Monte Cavallo (SAF)**^{44} 5306 7-9-9 **80**.......... GeorgeBaker 2 82
(Rebecca Curtis) *hld up towards rr: in tch 4f out: effrt on outer 2f out: styd on to take 4th fnl f: no imp on ldrs* **3/1**^{1}

6026 **5** *½* **Main Line**^{14} 6932 3-9-0 **76**.......... TedDurcan 1 77
(David Lanigan) *hld up towards rr: pushed along over 3f out: prog 2f out: kpt on one pce: n.d* **13/2**

6524 **6** *½* **Presburg (IRE)**^{26} 6573 3-9-0 **79**.......... MichaelMetcalfe$^{(3)}$ 3 79
(Joseph Tuite) *hld up wl in rr: stdy prog over 3f out: rdn over 2f out: no ex jst over 1f out* **25/1**

6026 **7** *7* **Freddy Q (IRE)**^{8} 7082 3-9-5 **81**.......... SilvestreDeSousa 12 67
(Roger Teal) *pressed ldr 2f: styd prom: rdn over 3f out: wknd 2f out* **20/1**

555 **8** *4* **Lieutenant Kojak**^{23} 6668 4-9-8 **79**.......... NeilCallan 11 57
(Peter Charalambous) *chsd clr ldrs: wknd over 2f out* **10/1**

01-0 **9** *3 ½* **Lancaster Gate**^{151} 2429 3-9-0 **76**.......... TomQueally 10 47
(Amanda Perrett) *nvr gng wl: dropped to last pair after 3f: lost tch 4f out* **12/1**

1545 **10** *3 ½* **Splendid Light**^{10} 7017 4-9-9 **80**.......... WilliamBuick 7 44
(John Gosden) *prog to ld after 2f and maintained str pce: rdn over 3f out: hdd & wknd over 2f out* **8/1**

121- **11** *97* **Avon River**^{376} 6785 5-9-4 **75**.......... JimmyFortune 4
(Dean Ivory) *a in last pair: wknd 4f out: wl t.o* **25/1**

0006 **12** *7* **Pivotman**^{12} 6987 4-9-5 **76**..........(t) JimCrowley 14
(Amanda Perrett) *led at str pce but hdd after 2f: wknd rapidly over 2f out: t.o and virtually p.u: b.b.v* **11/2**^{3}

2m 14.61s (5.91) **Going Correction** +0.725s/f (Yiel)
WFA 3 from 4yo+ 5lb **12** Ran SP% **128.9**
Speed ratings (Par 105): **105,104,104,102,101 101,95,92,89,87 9,3**
toteswingers 1&2 £12.60, 1&3 £14.40, 2&3 £22.20 CSF £58.07 CT £498.54 TOTE £5.40: £2.80, £4.80, £2.90; EX 62.20 Trifecta £429.60 Pool: £865.05 - 1.51 winning tickets..
Owner Mrs Ann Williams **Bred** Ailesbury Bloodstock **Trained** East Everleigh, Wilts

FOCUS
The lead was disputed, suiting those held up, and yet again on this card, the winner raced against the far rail in the straight. The runner-up and third have been rated close to their marks.
Pivotman Official explanation: vet said gelding bled from the nose

7301 BEN WOOLLACOTT MEMORIAL H'CAP 1m 3f 135y
4:30 (4:30) (Class 5) (0-70,69) 3-Y-O+ **£2,264** (£673; £336; £168) **Stalls** Centre

Form RPR
0600 **1** **Captain Cardington (IRE)**^{122} 2283 3-8-10 **60**.......... ChrisCatlin 12 71
(Sheena West) *pressed ldr: rdn over 3f out: responded to ld over 2f out and edgd lft: hrd pressed fr over 1f out: hld on most gamely* **9/1**

2400 **2** *nk* **Hidden Justice (IRE)**^{13} 6964 3-9-5 **69**.......... JimCrowley 3 79
(Amanda Perrett) *hld up in midfield: smooth prog over 3f out: rdn to chal over 1f out: pressed wnr hrd but could nt get by* **11/2**^{2}

0433 **3** *3 ¾* **Hurricane Hymnbook (USA)**^{18} 6819 7-9-7 **64**.......... StevieDonohoe 6 68
(Willie Musson) *hld up in rr: pushed along over 3f out: prog on outer 2f out: styd on to take 3rd nr fin* **9/2**^{1}

0400 **4** *1 ¼* **Cool Sky**^{24} 6647 3-9-3 **67**.......... NeilCallan 5 69
(William Knight) *trckd ldrs: prog to chal over 2f out: cl up whn hmpd against rail over 1f out: nt rcvr: lost 3rd nr fin* **10/1**

4210 **5** *1 ¾* **Cuckoo Rock (IRE)**^{78} 4843 5-9-5 **62**..........(p) RichardKingscote 10 61
(Jonathan Portman) *hld up in midfield: rdn and prog over 2f out: chsd ldrs over 1f out: fdd fnl f* **8/1**

201 **6** *5* **Beat Route**^{12} 6981 5-9-9 **66**.......... J-PGuillambert 4 56
(Michael Attwater) *chsd ldng trio: rdn over 3f out: fdd fnl 2f* **16/1**

-012 **7** *½* **Navajo Charm**^{47} 5939 3-8-13 **63**.......... KirstyMilczarek 2 55
(Alan Jarvis) *t.k.h: pressed ldng pair: chal over 2f out: hmpd twice wl over 1f out: fdd* **10/1**

2550 **8** *nk* **Eagle Nebula**^{51} 5838 8-9-12 **69**.......... IanMongan 13 58
(Brett Johnson) *wl in tch: rdn over 3f out: no imp on ldrs 2f out: fdd* **20/1**

0310 **9** *1 ½* **Mount Abora (IRE)**^{55} 5706 5-9-7 **64**.......... GeorgeBaker 11 50
(Laura Mongan) *dwlt: settled wl in rr: shkn up over 2f out: nvr involved* **18/1**

6141 **10** *1 ½* **Into The Wind**^{18} 6821 5-9-8 **65**.......... JamesMillman 9 49
(Rod Millman) *stdd s: hld up in last pair: shuffled along over 2f out: nvr remotely involved* **14/1**

1013 **11** *1 ¼* **Bernisdale**^{6} 7129 4-9-5 **69**.......... WilliamTwiston-Davies$^{(7)}$ 14 50
(John Flint) *led to over 2f out: n.m.r sn after and wknd qckly* **9/2**^{1}

5340 **12** *16* **Final Delivery**^{13} 6949 3-8-7 **57**..........(p) WilliamCarson 8 11
(Jim Boyle) *s.s: t.k.h in last pair: pushed along over 2f out: wknd: t.o* **50/1**

0321 **13** *13* **Shouda (IRE)**^{111} 3722 6-9-5 **62**.......... TomQueally 7
(Barney Curley) *hld up towards rr: rdn 4f out: sn wknd: t.o* **7/1**^{3}

2m 38.5s (9.00) **Going Correction** +0.725s/f (Yiel)
WFA 3 from 4yo+ 7lb **13** Ran SP% **128.1**
Speed ratings (Par 103): **99,98,96,95,94 90,90,90,89,88 87,76,68**
toteswingers 1&2 £17.40, 1&3 £16.80, 2&3 £8.40 CSF £62.19 CT £263.97 TOTE £14.40: £4.30, £2.70, £2.20; EX 109.20 Trifecta £595.10 Part won. Pool: £793.46 - 0.10 winning tickets..
Owner Tapestry Partnership **Bred** Brian Williamson **Trained** Falmer, E Sussex
■ Stewards' Enquiry : Chris Catlin two-day ban: careless riding (Nov 5-6)

FOCUS
The far side of the track was again the place to be in what looked an okay race for the grade. The winner has been rated as running his best race since his juvenile days.

7302 SKYBET.COM H'CAP 1m 67y
5:00 (5:00) (Class 5) (0-70,70) 3-Y-O+ **£2,264** (£673; £336; £168) **Stalls** Low

Form RPR
2331 **1** **Authoritarian**^{10} 7015 3-8-11 **70**.......... WilliamTwiston-Davies$^{(7)}$ 2 81
(Richard Hannon) *trckd ldrs: gng wl 3f out: rdn to ld over 1f out: drvn and styd on wl* **9/2**^{1}

6413 **2** *2* **Uncle Dermot (IRE)**^{13} 6950 4-9-7 **70**.......... TomQueally 13 77
(Brendan Powell) *dwlt: hld up in last pair: prog wl over 2f out: hrd rdn to chse wnr over 1f out: kpt on but no imp* **8/1**^{3}

20U2 **3** *¾* **Heezararity**^{7} 7115 4-9-2 **65**.......... SilvestreDeSousa 9 71+
(David Evans) *hld up in midfield: pushed along over 3f out: nt clr run 2f out: styd on u.p fr over 1f out to take 3rd last strides* **9/2**^{1}

2101 **4** *½* **Frozen Over**^{37} 6239 4-9-5 **68**.......... PatCosgrave 3 72+
(Stuart Kittow) *hld up towards rr: effrt whn hmpd wl over 2f out: prog after: chsd ldng pair ins fnl f: kpt on but lost 3rd last strides* **7/1**^{2}

0000 **5** *1 ¼* **Bloodsweatandtears**^{22} 6703 4-9-2 **65**..........(b) JimCrowley 4 66
(William Knight) *led: drvn and hdd over 1f out: fdd* **8/1**^{3}

4002 **6** *2* **Byrd In Hand (IRE)**^{13} 6950 5-8-9 **58**.......... LiamKeniry 8 54
(John Bridger) *hld up in midfield: gng strly 3f out: prog 2f out: effrt petered out over 1f out: fdd* **14/1**

1321 **7** *1 ½* **Saint Irene**^{13} 6950 3-8-11 **63**.......... DaneO'Neill 1 56
(Michael Blanshard) *settled in midfield: pushed along over 3f out: tried to make prog over 1f out: no hdwy after* **9/2**^{1}

0206 **8** *¾* **Push Me (IRE)**^{38} 6208 5-9-6 **69**.......... NeilCallan 7 60
(Jamie Poulton) *trckd ldrs: rdn over 2f out: steadily fdd* **14/1**

5060 **9** *hd* **King Of Wing (IRE)**^{21} 6734 3-9-3 **69**..........(b^{1}) GeorgeBaker 6 60
(Jim Boyle) *hld up wl in rr: shkn up over 2f out: no real prog* **50/1**

3666 **10** *¾* **Hereford Boy**^{13} 6950 8-9-0 **63**..........(v) MartinLane 12 52
(Dean Ivory) *hld up and sn last: shkn up over 2f out: no great prog* **33/1**

6062 **11** *3* **Querido (GER)**^{7} 7105 8-8-9 **58**..........(tp) RichardKingscote 5 40
(Paddy Butler) *chsd ldrs: lost pl over 2f out: sn wknd* **20/1**

050 **12** *3* **Katmai River (IRE)**[38] 6217 5-8-12 **61**........................(v) DavidProbert 11 36
(Mark Usher) *prom: chsd ldr over 2f out to wl over 1f out: wknd qckly* **25/1**

5055 **13** *1* **Salient**[13] 6950 8-8-8 **57**.. J-PGuillambert 10 30
(Michael Attwater) *t.k.h: chsd ldr to over 2f out: wknd and eased* **25/1**

-006 **14** *shd* **Berengar (IRE)**[13] 6973 3-9-4 **70**................................(p) JamieMackay 14 43
(Brian Meehan) *racd wd early and keen: prom tl wknd wl over 2f out* **25/1**

1m 51.69s (6.99) **Going Correction** +0.725s/f (Yiel)
WFA 3 from 4yo+ 3lb **14** Ran SP% **123.8**
Speed ratings (Par 103): **94,92,91,90,89 87,86,85,85,84 81,78,77,77**
toteswingers 1&2 £6.90, 1&3 £5.70, 2&3 £8.40 CSF £38.41 CT £181.52 TOTE £3.10: £1.10, £4.00, £2.10; EX 28.70 Trifecta £63.20 Pool: £865.81 - 10.26 winning tickets..
Owner Longview Stud & Bloodstock Ltd **Bred** Longview Stud & Bloodstock Ltd **Trained** East Everleigh, Wilts
■ Stewards' Enquiry : Silvestre De Sousa two-day ban: careless riding (Nov 5-6)

FOCUS
The action was far side once more, but in contrast to most of the earlier winners, Authoritarian had the race won by the time she reached the rail. The runner-up has been rated as running as well as ever, with the third to his latest effort.
T/Plt: £579.50 to a £1 stake. Pool: £62,082.19 - 78.20 winning tickets T/Qpdt: £172.00 to a £1 stake. Pool: £5,463.90 - 23.50 winning tickets JN

7164 LINGFIELD (L-H)
Tuesday, October 23

OFFICIAL GOING: Standard to slow
Wind: very light against Weather: dry, murky

7303 $150M BREEDERS' CUP POOLS APPRENTICE H'CAP — 1m 4f (P)
2:00 (2:00) (Class 6) (0-60,66) 3-Y-0+ **£1,704** (£503; £125; £125) **Stalls** Low

Form RPR

5345 **1** **Lady Bellatrix**[19] 6810 3-8-13 **57**.. DarylByrne(3) 3 64
(Mark H Tompkins) *mde all: rdn and kpt finding ex fr 2f out: forged clr ins fnl f: styd on wl* **33/1**

-042 **2** *1 ¼* **Langham Lily (USA)**[17] 6892 3-9-0 **58**.................. ThomasBrown(3) 10 66+
(Chris Wall) *chsd ldrs: rdn and effrt whn hmpd and snatched up over 1f out: lost pl: swtchd rt and rallied ins fnl f: styd on wl to snatch 2nd last strides* **15/8**[1]

4131 **3** *hd* **The Wonga Coup (IRE)**[38] 6230 5-9-4 **55**.................. JakePayne(3) 15 60
(Pat Phelan) *t.k.h early: hld up towards rr: hdwy 5f out: chsd ldrs over 2f out: rdn over 1f out: kpt on same pce ins fnl f* **7/1**

00 **3** *dht* **Parhelion**[24] 6691 5-9-6 **59**....................................(bt) RufusVergette(5) 13 64
(John Flint) *chsd wnr: rdn and swtchd lft over 1f out: styd on same pce ins fnl f* **40/1**

260 **5** *nk* **Young Jackie**[76] 4940 4-8-5 **46**................................ JordanVaughan(7) 12 50
(George Margarson) *hld up in midfield: rdn and effrt over 1f out: styd on wl fnl 100yds: could nt rch ldrs* **40/1**

030 **6** *shd* **Denton Dancer**[13] 6976 3-8-2 **48**.. RyanTate(5) 8 52
(James Eustace) *chsd ldrs: rdn and unable qck over 1f out: rallied and styd on again fnl 100yds* **33/1**

5364 **7** *¾* **Comedy House**[38] 6232 4-9-6 **57**................................ NatashaEaton(3) 7 60+
(Michael Madgwick) *hld up in rr: stl in last trio and rdn 2f out: hdwy over 1f out: r.o strly and swtchd rt towards fin: could nt rch ldrs: too much do* **9/2**[2]

-006 **8** *1* **Broxbourne (IRE)**[14] 6968 3-9-3 **58**......................... MichaelJMMurphy 4 59
(Mark Johnston) *in tch in midfield: rdn and hdwy on inner wl over 1f out: no imp u.p fnl f* **16/1**

0044 **9** *½* **Tartan Gunna**[5] 7200 6-9-6 **54**.. DavidKenny 11 54
(George Baker) *v.s.a and rdn leaving stalls: hld up in rr: rdn and hdwy over 1f out r.o fnl f: nvr trbld ldrs* **5/1**[3]

0450 **10** *nk* **Entrance**[28] 6562 4-9-1 **52**.. ShirleyTeasdale(3) 5 52
(Julia Feilden) *hld up in midfield: rdn and effrt ent fnl 2f: no imp tl styd on fnl 100yds: nvr gng pce to chal* **25/1**

0513 **11** *nk* **Lady Romanza (IRE)**[14] 6948 3-9-5 **60**..................(p) MatthewLawson 2 59
(Brendan Powell) *in tch in midfield: rdn and unable qck over 1f out: kpt on but nvr gng pce to chal* **14/1**

3160 **12** *6* **Oneiric**[12] 7012 4-9-10 **58**.. CharlesBishop 16 48
(Brett Johnson) *stdd s: t.k.h early: hld up in rr: effrt on outer bnd 2f out: no imp: n.d* **25/1**

0/5- **13** *6* **Silvermine Bay (IRE)**[473] 3799 5-8-9 **46** oh1.......... NicoleNordblad(3) 1 26
(Pat Eddery) *a towards rr: rdn and struggling over 2f out: bhd over 1f out* **50/1**

0015 **14** *6* **Dolly Colman (IRE)**[223] 895 4-8-12 **49**................. GeorgeDowning(3) 9 20
(Zoe Davison) *t.k.h early: hld up towards rr: gd hdwy on outer 5f out: pressed ldrs over 3f out: rdn and lost pl ent fnl 2f: sn wknd: bhd fnl f* **33/1**

-000 **15** *3* **Suhailah**[160] 2175 6-8-13 **47**.. TobyAtkinson 14 13
(Michael Attwater) *in tch in midfield: rdn and lost pl over 2f out: bhd fnl f* **33/1**

2m 34.61s (1.61) **Going Correction** +0.175s/f (Slow)
WFA 3 from 4yo+ 7lb **15** Ran SP% **121.0**
Speed ratings (Par 101): **101,100,100,100,99 99,99,98,98,98 97,93,89,85,83**
PL: Parhelion £6.30, The Wonga Cup £1.30 TRI: Lady Vellatrix /Langham Lily/P £1,331.01 LB/LL TWC: £262.05 toteswingers 1&2 £15.90, 1&Parhelion £94.30, 1&The Wonga Coup £19.60, 2&P £13.00, 2&TWC 1.90 CSF £88.61 TOTE £41.40: £6.60, £1.30; EX 177.90.
Owner John Brenchley **Bred** C A Cyzer **Trained** Newmarket, Suffolk
■ Stewards' Enquiry : Toby Atkinson one-day ban: failed to ride to draw (Nov 6)
Rufus Vergette one-day ban: failed to ride to draw (Nov 6)

FOCUS
This second fixture on the recently laid Polytack surface was again described as 'standard-to-slow'. A moderate handicap in which an ordinary gallop saw several finish in a heap and in which the winner raced close to the inside rail throughout. Dubious form considering the proximity of the third and sixth.
Tartan Gunna Official explanation: jockey said gelding was slowly away
Dolly Colman(IRE) Official explanation: jockey said filly hung right

7304 NEW LINGFIELD PARK OWNERS GROUP MAIDEN AUCTION STKS (DIV I) — 7f (P)
2:30 (2:30) (Class 6) 2-Y-0 **£1,704** (£503; £251) **Stalls** Low

Form RPR

04 **1** **Countryman**[13] 6977 2-9-1 0.. JimmyFortune 6 74
(Hughie Morrison) *racd keenly: trckd ldrs: wnt 2nd over 2f out: rdn and qcknd to ld ent fnl f: clr and r.o wl fnl 150yds* **5/2**[1]

2 *1 ½* **Ashamaly** 2-9-1 0.. MartinDwyer 11 70+
(James Tate) *chsd ldrs: rdn and rn green whn asked for effrt over 1f out: hdwy to chse clr wnr ins fnl f: no threat to wnr but r.o wl* **11/2**[3]

0200 **3** *1 ¾* **The Black Jacobin**[17] 6871 2-8-9 73..................................(b) LiamKeniry 1 60
(J S Moore) *hld up in tch: n.m.r on inner jst over 2f out: hdwy u.p jst over 1f out: swtchd rt and styd on fnl 100yds: no threat to wnr* **8/1**

6 **4** *¾* **Gigli (IRE)**[13] 6978 2-8-6 0.. AdamBeschizza 7 55
(William Haggas) *sn bustled along to chse ldr: led after 1f out: rdn 2f out: hdd and outpcd by wnr ent fnl f: wknd ins fnl f* **8/1**

5 *hd* **Jimmy The Snooze (IRE)** 2-8-13 0.............................. HarryBentley 9 61
(Stuart Williams) *hld up in tch: hdwy to chse ldrs over 2f out: rdn and unable qck wl over 1f out: btn and one pce fnl f* **25/1**

065 **6** *nse* **Gold Roll (IRE)**[128] 3191 2-8-11 70.................................... DaneO'Neill 2 59
(David Elsworth) *hld up in tch: stl gng okay 2f out: stuck bhd a wall of horses over 1f out: switching out rt 1f out: in the clr and r.o fnl 100yds: nvr able to chal* **3/1**[2]

00 **7** *hd* **Tuscan Fun**[11] 7033 2-9-1 0.. NeilCallan 8 62
(Roger Varian) *in tch: rdn and unable qck over 1f out: btn and styd on same pce u.p fnl f* **11/2**[3]

000 **8** *3 ½* **Madame Scarlett (IRE)**[25] 6645 2-7-13 52............. NathanSweeney(5) 5 42
(Jo Crowley) *led tl over 5f out: chsd ldr tl over 2f out: rdn and no ex over 1f out: wkng whn short of room jst ins fnl f* **66/1**

0305 **9** *1 ¼* **Red Adair (IRE)**[13] 6975 2-8-13 61.. PatDobbs 4 48
(Richard Hannon) *hld up in last pair: rdn and no rspnse 3f out: wknd u.p over 1f out* **25/1**

10 *1 ¼* **Wiggo** 2-8-9 0.. JimmyQuinn 3 41
(Julia Feilden) *v.s.a: detached and rn v green early on: clsd on to bk of field over 4f out: rdn and wknd wl over 1f out* **66/1**

1m 26.84s (2.04) **Going Correction** +0.175s/f (Slow) **10** Ran SP% **117.2**
Speed ratings (Par 93): **95,93,91,90,90 90,89,85,84,83**
toteswingers 1&2 £4.40, 2&3 £6.30, 1&3 £4.90 CSF £16.32 TOTE £3.10: £1.40, £1.80, £2.50; EX 20.60.
Owner H Scott-Barrett, S de Zoete & A Pickford **Bred** P And Mrs A G Venner **Trained** East Ilsley, Berks

FOCUS
Not a maiden that has a record of throwing up a decent sort and this form looks no better than fair. The gallop was an ordinary one and the winner edged to the far rail in the straight.

NOTEBOOK
Countryman has improved with every run and turned in his best effort to get off the mark after being well placed throughout. He had things in his favour but should stay 1m and there may be more to come in handicaps. (op 15-8)
Ashamaly ◆, who cost 20,000gns as a yearling and is a first foal of an unraced half-sister to 2000 Guineas winner Footstepsinthesand and to Group 1 Phoenix Stakes winner Pedro The Great, attracted support and shaped pleasingly, despite greenness, on this racecourse debut. He'll be better for this and should win something similar. (op 11-1 tchd 14-1)
The Black Jacobin, with the headgear again fitted, wasn't disgraced but again failed to match early promise on this AW debut. He's likely to remain vulnerable in this type of event and his current mark of 73 looks on the high side for handicaps. (op 6-1)
Gigli(IRE) had the run of the race and bettered the form of her debut but she was readily swept aside in the straight. She lacks much in the way of a change in gear and may do better over further once qualified for a mark. (op 9-1 tchd 15-2)
Jimmy The Snooze(IRE), who cost 30,000gns as a foal (price slipped to 12,000GBP at the Breeze-ups), is a half-brother to modest dual Polytrack winner (1m-1m2f) Little Bug, out of a maiden half-sister to a 1m2f Listed winner. He showed abilty without being knocked about on this racecourse debut and is entitled to improve. (op 33-1)
Gold Roll(IRE) failed to better his turf form upped in trip on this AW debut. He may not be entirely straightforward but may be suited by the step up to 1m and the switch into ordinary handicaps. (op 4-1)

7305 NEW LINGFIELD PARK OWNERS GROUP MAIDEN AUCTION STKS (DIV II) — 7f (P)
3:00 (3:00) (Class 6) 2-Y-0 **£1,704** (£503; £251) **Stalls** Low

Form RPR

0 **1** **Veeraya**[19] 6818 2-8-13 0.. AdamBeschizza 11 76+
(William Haggas) *t.k.h: trckd ldng pair: rdn and qcknd to chal over 1f out: led jst ins fnl f: r.o wl to assert fnl 75yds* **9/2**[3]

5202 **2** *1 ½* **Nenge Mboko**[14] 6945 2-9-1 76......................................(p) PatCosgrave 9 75
(George Baker) *sn chsng ldr: jnd ldr 3f out: led 2f out: jnd and drvn over 1f out: hdd jst ins fnl f: one pce fnl 100yds* **9/4**[1]

03 **3** *1 ¾* **David's Secret**[14] 6945 2-8-13 0.. JimmyFortune 5 68
(Hughie Morrison) *in tch in midfield: rdn and effrt 2f out: styd on to chse ldng pair fnl 100yds: no imp after* **6/1**

4 *½* **Lucky Mountain** 2-9-1 0.. JamesDoyle 3 69+
(Ed Dunlop) *dwlt: hld up in tch in rr: rdn and hdwy over 1f out: kpt on steadily ins fnl f* **16/1**

5 **5** *nk* **Nelina**[17] 6889 2-8-5 0.. MichaelJMMurphy(5) 1 63
(Robert Cowell) *in tch in midfield: rdn and unable qck over 1f out: styd on same pce u.p fnl f* **12/1**

4002 **6** *1 ½* **Age Of Bronze**[12] 7008 2-8-13 64.. PatDobbs 2 62
(Richard Hannon) *chsd ldrs: rdn and unable qck 2f out: wknd ins fnl f* **14/1**

7 *¾* **Mystery Woman (IRE)** 2-8-4 0.. ChrisCatlin 4 51+
(Peter Chapple-Hyam) *dropped to rr and pushed along 5f out: effrt on outer wl over 1f out: kpt on fnl f but nvr gng pce to chal* **11/4**[2]

8 *nk* **Tychaios** 2-8-11 0.. HarryBentley 8 57+
(Stuart Williams) *hld up in tch in rr: rdn and effrt over 1f out: styd on same pce ins fnl f* **40/1**

30 **9** *hd* **Don Eduardo**[17] 6871 2-8-9 0.. LiamKeniry 6 55
(J S Moore) *t.k.h: chsd ldrs early: dropped towards rr over 4f out: rdn and no imp over 1f out: kpt on same pce fnl f* **33/1**

00 **10** *½* **Prince Rakan (USA)**[18] 6846 2-8-13 0................................ DaneO'Neill 10 57
(Amy Weaver) *wnt rt and awkward leaving stalls: in tch: lost pl and rdn bnd 2f out: no imp after* **100/1**

11 *8* **Eton Miss (IRE)** 2-8-4 0.. NickyMackay 7 28
(Mike Murphy) *led tl 2f out: btn over 1f out: fdd fnl f* **50/1**

1m 27.47s (2.67) **Going Correction** +0.175s/f (Slow) **11** Ran SP% **118.5**
Speed ratings (Par 93): **91,89,87,86,86 84,83,83,83,82 73**
toteswingers 1&2 £6.50, 2&3 £3.30, 1&3 £8.10 CSF £14.91 TOTE £8.80: £3.50, £2.00, £1.10; EX 60.80.
Owner Ahamed Farook **Bred** Roan Rocket Partners **Trained** Newmarket, Suffolk

FOCUS
Division two of an ordinary maiden. The gallop was no more than fair and the well-backed winner raced down the centre in the straight. Straightforward form to rate, with the runner-up and sixth offering perspective.

NOTEBOOK
Veeraya, who hinted at ability in soft ground on his debut, attracted plenty of support and turned in a much-improved effort on this AW debut, despite racing with the choke out (as many from this yard do). He should stay 1m and there's probably better to come. (op 14-1)

Nenge Mboko, in first-time cheekpieces, had the run of the race and confirmed himself a fair sort on this AW debut. He's vulnerable to an improver in this grade but he looks sure to pick up a minor event on either this surface or back on turf. (op 15-8 tchd 11-4)
David's Secret bettered his turf form on this AW debut and should improve when switched to ordinary handicaps granted a stiffer overall test of stamina. (op 7-1 tchd 5-1)
Lucky Mountain ◆, a 20,000gns half-brother to moderate 1m winner Pacific Bay and to a 7f-1m winner in Italy, out of a 1m1f juvenile winner in France, showed ability despite running green on this racecourse debut. He'll stay 1m and can only improve. (op 20-1)
Nelina has a bit to recommend her on looks and she was again far from disgraced. Her pedigree suggests she'll be suited by 1m plus and she'll be one to keep an eye on granted a suitable test when qualified for a handicap mark. (op 8-1)
Mystery Woman(IRE) cost 5000GBP as a yearling and is a half-sister to 1m juvenile winner Vivaldi (also won over hurdles), as well as useful 6f Polytrack winner Three Decades, and very useful 1m winner Luxurious. She attracted plenty of support but, although she never showed on this racecourse debut, she is worth another chance. (tchd 5-2 and 3-1)
Eton Miss(IRE) Official explanation: jockey said filly hung left

7306 IRISH STALLION FARMS E B F MEDIAN AUCTION MAIDEN STKS 1m (P)
3:30 (3:30) (Class 5) 2-Y-O **£3,340** (£986; £493) **Stalls** High

Form RPR

3 **1** **Manazel (USA)**[11] 7021 2-9-3 0 (b) DaneO'Neill 1 72
(John Gosden) *dwlt and rdn along leaving stalls: chsd ldrs after 1f: led over 2f out and sn clr: rdn wl over 1f out: tiring fnl f but jst lasting home* **16/1**

6 **2** *hd* **Audacia (IRE)**[20] 6791 2-8-12 0 JimmyQuinn 2 67
(Hugo Palmer) *in tch: rdn to chse ldrs over 2f out: drvn and chsd clr ldr ins fnl f: styd on wl: could nt quite get up* **10/1**

55 **3** *1 1/4* **Gworn**[131] 3074 2-9-3 0 ChrisCatlin 7 69
(Ed Dunlop) *in tch: rdn 3f out: outpcd over 2f out: rallied and hdwy 1f out: styd on wl ins fnl f* **4/1**[2]

4 **4** *nk* **Kuantan One (IRE)**[11] 7033 2-9-3 0 ShaneKelly 12 68
(Paul Cole) *in tch in midfield: rdn and outpcd over 2f out: rallied u.p ent fnl f: kpt on wl fnl 100yds* **5/1**[3]

0 **5** *1 1/2* **Lyric Ballad**[20] 6791 2-8-12 0 RobertWinston 10 60
(Hughie Morrison) *t.k.h: led for 1f: chsd ldr after tl led again 3f out: sn hdd and outpcd by wnr: no imp u.p after: lost 2nd ins fnl f: plugged on same pce* **100/1**

6 *shd* **Cousin Melchior (IRE)** 2-9-3 0 NickyMackay 5 65
(John Gosden) *pushed along leaving stalls: in tch in midfield: rdn and outpcd jst over 2f out: no threat to wnr but kpt on steadily fr over 1f out* **16/1**

0223 **7** *3/4* **Ormindo (USA)**[14] 6972 2-9-3 76 MickaelBarzalona 3 63
(Mahmood Al Zarooni) *chsd ldrs: outpcd by wnr over 1f out: drvn and effrt on inner wl over 1f out: no imp: wknd ins fnl f* **10/3**[1]

4 **8** *3/4* **Mazaaher**[18] 6845 2-9-3 0 TadhgO'Shea 9 61+
(Marcus Tregoning) *s.i.s: t.k.h: hld up in rr: switching to outer 3f out: v wd bnd 2f out: sme hdwy over 1f out: kpt on fnl f but nvr threatened ldrs* **4/1**[2]

0 **9** *1 1/4* **Simple Joys**[20] 6796 2-8-12 0 JimmyFortune 6 53+
(Andrew Balding) *s.i.s: hld up in tch in last quartet: rdn and effrt wl over 1f out: kpt on ins fnl f: nvr trbld ldrs* **12/1**

40 **10** *1/2* **Ravens Nest**[15] 6928 2-9-3 0 MartinDwyer 11 57+
(Robert Mills) *t.k.h: hld up in tch in last trio: rdn and no hdwy wl over 1f out: styd on same pce fr over 1f out* **25/1**

11 *1/2* **Mosman** 2-9-3 0 FergusSweeney 8 56+
(Jamie Osborne) *s.i.s: hld up in tch in last quartet: rdn wl over 1f out: kpt on one pce and no real imp after* **40/1**

00 **12** *9* **Foxy Dancer (IRE)**[27] 6572 2-8-12 0 PatDobbs 4 30
(Richard Hannon) *led after 1f: hdd 3f out: wknd over 2f out: bhd fnl f* **50/1**

1m 40.54s (2.34) **Going Correction** +0.175s/f (Slow) **12 Ran SP% 117.5**
Speed ratings (Par 95): **95,94,93,93,91 91,90,90,88,88 87,78**
toteswingers 1&2 £11.10, 2&3 £10.00, 1&3 £9.00 CSF £161.86 TOTE £11.60: £3.60, £3.30, £1.20; EX 129.20.
Owner Hamdan Al Maktoum **Bred** Mr & Mrs Ralph Holcomb **Trained** Newmarket, Suffolk

FOCUS
No more than a fair maiden and one in which the winner, who came down the centre, quickened into a decisive lead turning for home.

NOTEBOOK
Manazel(USA) showed promise on his debut and bettered that effort under an enterprising ride with the headgear again fitted. The bare form of this race isn't anything special but he's in good hands, should stay 1m2f next year and remains open to improvement. (op 10-1 tchd 9-1)
Audacia(IRE) ◆ showed ability at a modest level on her debut and stepped up on that level against a rival who got first run turning for home. She should stay further, has a bit of scope and is capable of picking up an ordinary event. (op 7-1 tchd 11-1)
Gworn ran creditably to better his previous turf form and should do better over 1m2f in handicaps in due course. (op 9-2 tchd 5-1)
Kuantan One(IRE) was far from disgraced on this AW debut and should do better once qualified for a handicap mark. (op 9-2)
Lyric Ballad had the run of the race and fared a good deal better than on her debut, despite hanging left. She's likely to remain vulnerable in this type of event. (op 80-1)
Cousin Melchior(IRE), a 65,000gns foal who is the first foal of an unraced half-sister to 1m Matron (Group 3)/Sun Chariot (Group 2) winner Independence, from the family of Reference Point, proved easy in the market and was green but showed ability and is entitled to improve. (tchd 20-1)
Ormindo(USA) has proved a reliable yardstick but he wasn't at his best, despite being well placed throughout. He lacks much in the way of physical scope and isn't one to take too short a price about. (op 11-4 tchd 5-2)
Mazaaher attracted plenty of support but proved disappointing after a tardy start. It looks as though a much stiffer overall test of stamina will play more to his strengths. (op 8-1 tchd 7-2)

7307 GUARANTEED $2 MILLION JACKPOT POOL (S) STKS 6f (P)
4:00 (4:03) (Class 6) 3-Y-O **£1,704** (£503; £251) **Stalls** Low

Form RPR

3055 **1** **Boudoir (IRE)**[6] 7166 3-9-0 70 StevieDonohoe 3 62
(Ian Williams) *mde all: rdn over 1f out: kpt on wl ins fnl f: rdn out* **11/2**[2]

6050 **2** *3/4* **Whisky Bravo**[19] 6811 3-9-0 65 RobertWinston 6 60
(David Brown) *bmpd and hmpd leaving stalls: hld up in rr: hdwy on outer over 2f out: styd wl u.p ins fnl f: wnt 2nd last strides* **8/1**

4250 **3** *nk* **Mary Frith**[20] 6778 3-8-9 53 (p) JimCrowley 12 54
(William Knight) *flashing tail leaving stalls: sn chsng wnr: rdn and pressing wnr ent fnl f: kpt on but a hld: lost 2nd last strides* **11/2**[2]

3544 **4** *hd* **Ooi Long**[32] 6439 3-9-0 62 TobyAtkinson(5) 9 63
(Mark Rimmer) *hld up in tch: rdn and chsd ldrs 2f out: styd on same pce ins fnl f* **15/2**

0640 **5** *1/2* **Winter Hill**[22] 6737 3-8-9 57 (e[1]) RichardKingscote 10 52
(Tom Dascombe) *dwlt: hld up in last trio: rdn and hdwy on inner over 1f out: chsd ldrs 1f out: styng on same pce and hld whn hung rt towards fin* **4/1**[1]

0040 **6** *3/4* **Artful Lady (IRE)**[46] 5991 3-8-2 45 JordanVaughan(7) 11 49
(George Margarson) *in tch in last trio: rdn and effrt over 1f out: pushed along and hdwy ent fnl f: styd on but nvr gng pce to chal* **40/1**

2516 **7** *2* **Auntie Mabel**[63] 5446 3-8-7 61 (v) DanielMuscutt(7) 2 48
(Andrew Balding) *chsd ldrs: rdn and unable qck 2f out: btn and plugged on same pce ins fnl f* **11/2**[2]

0504 **8** *2 1/2* **First Bid**[6] 7166 3-9-5 64 NickyMackay 8 45
(James Given) *in tch: rdn and unable qck whn short of room 2f out: no prog over 1f out: wknd fnl f* **7/1**[3]

500 **9** *1/2* **Model Behaviour (IRE)**[22] 6737 3-8-9 43 ShaneKelly 7 33
(Daniel Mark Loughnane) *wnt lft s: hld up in tch towards rr: rdn and effrt over 1f out: no prog: nvr trbld ldrs* **100/1**

0300 **10** *3/4* **Desert Red (IRE)**[6] 7158 3-8-9 45 (b) JimmyQuinn 5 31
(Phil McEntee) *hld up in tch: swtchd rt and effrt over 1f out: no real prog: wknd ins fnl f* **50/1**

1m 13.3s (1.40) **Going Correction** +0.175s/f (Slow) **10 Ran SP% 106.9**
Speed ratings (Par 99): **97,96,95,95,94 93,91,87,87,86**
toteswingers 1&2 £8.30, 2&3 £7.20, 1&3 £4.20 CSF £42.15 TOTE £5.20: £1.40, £2.80, £2.30; EX 36.90.The winner was bought in for 4000gns.
Owner Paul Wildes **Bred** Airlie Stud **Trained** Portway, Worcs

FOCUS
A modest seller in which the gallop was fair. The winner came down the centre. The form isn't reliable, although the third is possibly the best guide.

7308 ANNUAL MEMBERS LOYALTY H'CAP 6f (P)
4:30 (4:32) (Class 5) (0-70,70) 3-Y-O+ **£2,385** (£704; £352) **Stalls** Low

Form RPR

6052 **1** **Ginger Ted (IRE)**[4] 7218 5-9-1 **64** (tp) J-PGuillambert 5 76+
(Stuart Williams) *rdn along in last trio: hdwy and travelling bttr over 2f out: rdn and wnt between horses jst ins fnl f: r.o wl u.p to ld cl home* **3/1**[1]

2303 **2** *nk* **Beat The Bell**[18] 6837 7-9-6 **69** (p) MartinDwyer 2 80
(Jamie Osborne) *led: rdn and drew 2 l clr jst over 1f out: kpt on wl u.p tl hdd and no ex cl home* **9/2**[2]

4050 **3** *2 3/4* **Duke Of Aricabeau (IRE)**[7] 7141 3-9-5 **69** RobertWinston 10 71
(Mrs K Burke) *s.i.s: racd in last pair: hdwy on outer over 2f out: drvn over 1f out: chsd ldng pair ins fnl f: no imp fnl 100yds* **16/1**

-152 **4** *3/4* **Running Mate (IRE)**[50] 5874 5-9-1 **64** (t) IanMongan 11 64
(Jo Crowley) *dismntd and led to s: hld up in rr: nt clr run 2f out: rdn and hdwy on inner over 1f out: styd on same pce and no imp ins fnl f* **7/1**

5200 **5** *shd* **Amazon Twilight**[15] 6934 4-9-7 **70** (v[1]) DavidProbert 12 69
(Brett Johnson) *pushed along in last quartet after 1f: hdwy into midfield over 2f out: drvn and styd on same pce fr over 1f out* **10/1**

1135 **6** *2 1/2* **Dorothy's Dancing (IRE)**[169] 2114 4-9-4 **67** FergusSweeney 9 58
(Gary Moore) *t.k.h: chsd ldrs on outer: rdn and unable qck 2f out: wknd 1f out* **10/1**

5640 **7** *nse* **Waabel**[26] 6610 5-9-4 **67** (t) MartinHarley 8 58
(Violet M Jordan) *in tch in midfield: rdn and lost pl over 2f out: no threat to ldrs fr over 1f out* **20/1**

400 **8** *1/2* **Flashbang**[34] 6369 4-9-4 **67** (bt) NeilCallan 3 57
(Paul Cole) *dwlt and rdn along leaving stalls: sn in tch in midfield: rdn and chsd ldr wl over 1f out: no imp: lost 2nd jst ins fnl f: wknd* **11/2**[3]

-230 **9** *1/2* **Compton Rainbow**[20] 6801 3-8-8 **65** (t) NicoleNordblad(7) 4 53
(Hans Adielsson) *taken down early: racd keenly: w ldr tl wl over 1f out: sn wknd: no ch whn sltly hmpd jst ins fnl f* **17/2**

2302 **10** *1* **Picansort**[53] 5791 5-9-5 **68** ShaneKelly 1 53
(Peter Crate) *chsd ldrs: rdn and unable qck 2f out: wknd ent fnl f* **16/1**

1m 12.37s (0.47) **Going Correction** +0.175s/f (Slow)
WFA 3 from 4yo+ 1lb **10 Ran SP% 116.3**
Speed ratings (Par 103): **103,102,98,97,97 94,94,93,93,91**
toteswingers 1&2 £3.50, 2&3 £13.80, 1&3 £12.50 CSF £16.01 CT £189.05 TOTE £4.10: £1.70, £2.30, £4.90; EX 17.70.
Owner Maze Rattan 2 **Bred** T Counihan **Trained** Newmarket, Suffolk

FOCUS
Mainly exposed sprinters in a modest handicap. The gallop was sound, the first two pulled clear and the winner raced centre-to-far side in the straight. The runner-up is the best guide to the level.

7309 BREEDERS' CUP LIVE ONLY ON ATR H'CAP 5f (P)
5:00 (5:01) (Class 5) (0-75,79) 3-Y-O+ **£2,385** (£704; £352) **Stalls** High

Form RPR

3532 **1** **Muhdiq (USA)**[67] 5296 3-9-5 **75** PatDobbs 9 82+
(Mike Murphy) *in tch in rr: hdwy whn nt clr run and swtchd rt 1f out: qcknd to chal ins fnl f: r.o wl to ld on post* **7/2**[1]

6541 **2** *nse* **Drawnfromthepast (IRE)**[5] 7197 7-9-9 **79** 6ex FergusSweeney 5 86
(Jamie Osborne) *trckd ldrs: swtchd rt over 1f out: rdn and effrt 1f out: edgd lft but r.o to ld ins fnl f: hdd on post* **7/2**[1]

4366 **3** *3/4* **Rebecca Romero**[34] 6370 5-9-4 **74** EddieAhern 8 78
(Denis Coakley) *restless in stalls: towards rr: swtchd rt and hdwy jst over 1f out: chsd ldrs ins fnl f: no imp towards fin* **13/2**[3]

6003 **4** *3/4* **Mac Gille Eoin**[11] 7023 8-9-4 **74** IanMongan 3 76
(Luke Dace) *in tch: rdn and hdwy whn n.m.r and squeezed jst ins fnl f: kpt on fnl 100yds* **7/1**

0400 **5** *1* **Fathom Five (IRE)**[45] 6026 8-9-2 **72** GeorgeBaker 7 70
(Gary Moore) *chsd ldrs: rdn and unable qck over 1f out: no ex ins fnl f: wknd towards fin* **12/1**

0240 **6** *shd* **For Shia And Lula (IRE)**[5] 7197 3-9-2 **72** (p) ShaneKelly 6 70
(Daniel Mark Loughnane) *hld up in tch: switching rt and hdwy over 1f out: swtchd for room and hmpd jst ins fnl f: styd on same pce after* **10/1**

3122 **7** *1/2* **I See You**[48] 5934 3-9-3 **73** (p) JimCrowley 1 69
(Peter Makin) *in tch: rdn and unable qck over 1f out: wknd wl ins fnl f* **6/1**[2]

0403 **8** *1/2* **Falasteen (IRE)**[3] 7254 5-9-3 **73** ChrisCatlin 4 67
(Milton Bradley) *led tl 2f out: sn unable qck u.p: wknd jst ins fnl f* **8/1**

1364 **9** *nk* **Billy Red**[75] 4980 8-9-3 **73** (b) DaneO'Neill 2 66
(J R Jenkins) *chsd ldr tl led 2f out: drvn 1f out: hdd ins fnl f: sn fdd and eased towards fin* **22/1**

5000 **10** *shd* **Desert Strike**[11] 7023 6-8-11 **72** (p) DavidKenny(5) 10 65
(Conor Dore) *taken down early: in tch in midfield on outer: rdn and no rspnse over 1f out: wknd 1f out* **40/1**

59.51s (0.71) **Going Correction** +0.175s/f (Slow) **10 Ran SP% 119.2**
Speed ratings (Par 103): **101,100,99,98,96 96,95,95,94,94**
toteswingers 1&2 £4.60, 2&3 £5.70, 1&3 £4.20 CSF £15.32 CT £77.50 TOTE £5.60: £1.90, £1.90, £1.30; EX 18.70.
Owner Ms Denise Tibbett **Bred** Shadwell Farm LLC **Trained** Westoning, Beds
■ Stewards' Enquiry : Pat Dobbs three-day ban: careless riding (Nov 6-8)

FOCUS
A fair handicap and one run at a decent gallop throughout. The winner raced centre-to-far side in the straight. Straightforward form rated around the runner-up and third.

Rebecca Romero Official explanation: jockey said mare became upset in stalls

7310 FOLLOW US ON TWITTER @LINGFIELDPARK H'CAP 1m 2f (P)

5:30 (5:31) (Class 5) (0-70,70) 3-Y-0+ **£2,385** (£704; £352) **Stalls** Low

Form RPR

1420 **1** **Bert The Alert**[137] 2886 4-9-3 **65** GeorgeBaker 14 75+
(Gary Moore) *trckd ldrs: jnd ldrs on bit 2f out: led over 1f out: rdn and kpt on ins fnl f* **9/1**

2005 **2** *1* **Harry Buckle**[12] 7011 3-9-0 **70** RaulDaSilva(3) 6 76
(Philip McBride) *led for 1f: chsd ldrs after: rdn and chsd wnr 1f out: kpt on u.p but a hld* **4/1**[1]

4630 **3** *1/2* **Hawaana (IRE)**[22] 6735 7-9-5 **67** RobertWinston 12 72
(Gay Kelleway) *in tch in midfield: hdwy to chse ldrs over 1f out: drvn and kpt on same pce ins fnl f* **7/1**[2]

6410 **4** *3/4* **Caterina**[22] 6734 3-9-3 **70** (b) PatDobbs 8 75
(Richard Hannon) *hld up in midfield: hdwy and nt clr run over 1f out tl 1f out: hdwy to chse ldrs and nt clr run again ins fnl f: kpt on but nvr able to chal* **8/1**[3]

1036 **5** *hd* **Officer In Command (USA)**[38] 6251 6-9-5 **67** (b) JamesDoyle 10 70
(Paul Rich) *hld up towards rr: hdwy on outer over 2f out: chsd ldrs u.p ins fnl f: styd on same pce fnl 100yds* **12/1**

0-00 **6** *3 3/4* **Apache Glory (USA)**[64] 5429 4-9-8 **70** LiamJones 5 66
(John Stimpson) *led rdrless to s: bhd in last trio: hdwy over 1f out: styd on same pce and no imp ins fnl f* **50/1**

0621 **7** *3/4* **Zenarinda**[17] 6885 5-9-2 **64** MartinDwyer 4 58
(Mark H Tompkins) *in tch in midfield: rdn and effrt on inner whn stuck bhd rival over 1f out: gap opened but all ch had gone ins fnl f: kpt on* **7/1**[2]

4620 **8** *1 1/4* **Hunt A Mistress (IRE)**[21] 6770 3-9-3 **70** (b[1]) ShaneKelly 1 62
(Paul Cole) *led after 1f: drvn 2f out: hdd over 1f out: wknd ins fnl f* **25/1**

0300 **9** *1/2* **Mafi (IRE)**[67] 5323 4-9-4 **66** FergusSweeney 13 57
(Mark Hoad) *in tch in midfield on outer: unable qck u.p over 1f out: wknd ins fnl f* **10/1**

5640 **10** *1* **Soweto Star (IRE)**[15] 6931 4-9-3 **65** DaneO'Neill 9 54
(John Best) *in tch in midfield: rdn and no imp over 1f out: styd on same pce fnl f* **14/1**

0040 **11** *3/4* **Ellie In The Pink (IRE)**[39] 6207 4-9-6 **68** IanMongan 2 55
(Pat Phelan) *s.i.s: bhd: clsd over 2f out: weaving through and trying to make hdwy ent fnl f: kpt on: n.d* **20/1**

0066 **12** *1/2* **Daniel Thomas (IRE)**[3] 7250 10-9-2 **64** (bt) MartinHarley 7 50
(Violet M Jordan) *in tch in midfield: rdn and struggling whn nt clr run and hmpd bnd 2f out: n.d after* **8/1**[3]

5400 **13** *nk* **Hip Hip Hooray**[13] 6981 6-9-2 **64** TomMcLaughlin 3 50
(Luke Dace) *s.i.s: bhd in last trio: rdn and no hdwy over 2f out: n.d* **33/1**

4100 **14** *2 1/4* **Shirataki (IRE)**[114] 3659 4-9-4 **66** ChrisCatlin 11 47
(Peter Hiatt) *chsd ldr over 8f out: ev ch and rdn 2f out: no ex and btn 1f out: sn wknd* **14/1**

2m 6.09s (-0.51) **Going Correction** +0.175s/f (Slow) 14 Ran SP% **120.8**
WFA 3 from 4yo+ 5lb
Speed ratings (Par 103): **109,108,107,107,107 104,103,102,102,101 100,100,100,98**
toteswingers 1&2 £9.70, 2&3 £4.00, 1&3 £17.30 CSF £43.25 CT £275.52 TOTE £11.00: £3.70, £2.20, £2.20; EX 61.90.
Owner Herbert Curwen Hinds & Waddingham **Bred** Pleasure Palace Racing **Trained** Lower Beeding, W Sussex

FOCUS
A modest handicap run at a fair gallop. The winner came down the centre. The third and fourth have been rated close to their recent turf form.
Zenarinda Official explanation: jockey said mare was denied a clear run
T/Plt: £44.60 to a £1 stake. Pool of £66198.77- 1081.31 winning tickets. T/Qpdt: £25.00 to a £1 stake. Pool of £4425.06 - 130.92 winning tickets. SP

6844 YARMOUTH (L-H)

Tuesday, October 23

OFFICIAL GOING: Heavy (5.2)
Wind: Light behind Weather: Foggy

7311 BRITISH STALLION STUDS SUPPORTING BRITISH RACING EBF MAIDEN STKS 6f 3y

1:50 (1:51) (Class 5) 2-Y-0 **£3,150** (£943; £471; £236; £117) **Stalls** Centre

Form RPR

2022 **1** **Huntsmans Close**[33] 6411 2-9-3 81 HayleyTurner 5 80
(Michael Bell) *mde all: shkn up over 1f out: sn clr* **2/1**[1]

52 **2** *4* **Maid A Million**[9] 7078 2-8-12 0 SebSanders 2 63
(David Elsworth) *s.i.s: hld up: hdwy to chse wnr over 2f out: rdn over 1f out: no ex ins fnl f* **9/4**[2]

3 *2* **First Sargeant** 2-9-3 0 (b[1]) SilvestreDeSousa 4 62+
(Marco Botti) *dwlt: outpcd: r.o ins fnl f: nrst fin* **10/1**

04 **4** *1/2* **Cape Of Hope (IRE)**[19] 6818 2-9-3 0 WilliamBuick 7 61
(Peter Chapple-Hyam) *trckd ldrs: racd keenly: wnt 2nd 1/2-way: sn rdn: styd on same pce fr over 1f out: lost 3rd nr fin* **11/2**[3]

60 **5** *9* **Raven's Rock (IRE)**[31] 6491 2-9-3 0 AndreaAtzeni 3 34
(Roger Varian) *chsd ldrs: rdn 1/2-way: wknd 2f out* **14/1**

3052 **6** *9* **Bold Prediction (IRE)**[27] 6579 2-9-3 76 RyanMoore 1 7
(Richard Hannon) *chsd wnr to 1/2-way: sn rdn: wknd 2f out* **7/1**

1m 17.22s (2.82) **Going Correction** +0.425s/f (Yiel) 6 Ran SP% **107.7**
Speed ratings (Par 95): **98,92,90,89,77 65**
toteswingers 1&2 £1.50, 2&3 £4.10, 1&3 £3.50 CSF £6.15 TOTE £2.70: £1.50, £1.50; EX 6.30.
Owner Sheikh Marwan Al Maktoum **Bred** Darley **Trained** Newmarket, Suffolk

FOCUS
The bottom bend was dolled out 2m to provide fresh ground, adding on 5m to all races round the bend. This did not look a bad maiden despite the small field size, and it was run at a fair pace, with the winner making all to win impressively. The winner has been rated as running a small personal best, with the runner-up a bit below form.

NOTEBOOK
Huntsmans Close has been held in high regard by connections and got off the mark at the fifth time of asking. This strong travelling type was sent to the front from the off and was never really threatened. It is hard to know what he would have found if facing a serious challenge but he looked more streetwise here and can go on from this next season. (tchd 15-8)
Maid A Million stepped up on her debut effort when runner-up at Goodwood last time (6f, soft) but was no match for the winner here. (op 5-2 tchd 11-4)
First Sargeant, slowly away, looked green from the off but was doing his best work late on and can be expected to come on a good deal. (op 12-1 tchd 14-1)
Cape Of Hope(IRE) travelled well enough behind the leaders but did not seem to act on the testing ground when coming under pressure. He has now qualified for handicaps. (op 6-1 tchd 5-1)
Bold Prediction(IRE), back up in trip, had not been progressing with his racing in recent starts and is another who looked unsuited by the conditions. Official explanation: trainer's rep said colt was unsuited by the heavy ground (op 5-1)

7312 BRITISH STALLION STUDS SUPPORTING BRITISH RACING EBF MAIDEN FILLIES' STKS 1m 3y

2:20 (2:20) (Class 5) 2-Y-0 **£3,150** (£943; £471; £236; £117) **Stalls** Centre

Form RPR

1 **Madame Defarge (IRE)** 2-9-0 0 TomQueally 2 79+
(Michael Bell) *s.i.s: hld up: hdwy over 3f out: jnd ldr over 2f out: shkn up to ld wl ins fnl f: styd on* **20/1**

3 **2** *1/2* **Nickels And Dimes (IRE)**[14] 6960 2-9-0 0 WilliamBuick 6 78
(John Gosden) *sn prom: pushed along over 3f out: sn chsng ldr: led over 2f out: rdn and hdd wl ins fnl f* **11/8**[1]

0 **3** *2* **Elik (IRE)**[20] 6790 2-9-0 0 RyanMoore 3 74
(Sir Michael Stoute) *chsd ldrs: rdn over 1f out: styd on same pce ins fnl f* **9/4**[2]

40 **4** *6* **Of Course Darling**[17] 6873 2-9-0 0 GrahamLee 4 60+
(Ed Dunlop) *chsd ldrs: rdn over 1f out: wknd ins fnl f* **9/2**[3]

00 **5** *10* **Tilstarr (IRE)**[53] 5792 2-9-0 0 AdamKirby 5 38
(Roger Teal) *led over 5f: rdn and wknd over 1f out* **40/1**

54 **6** *3 3/4* **Butterfly Dream**[25] 6645 2-9-0 0 SilvestreDeSousa 7 30
(William Haggas) *chsd ldr tl rdn over 3f out: wknd over 2f out* **12/1**

7 *nk* **Kensington Gardens** 2-9-0 0 HayleyTurner 1 29
(Michael Bell) *hld up: rdn and wknd over 3f out* **20/1**

1m 45.08s (4.48) **Going Correction** +0.575s/f (Yiel) 7 Ran SP% **110.7**
Speed ratings (Par 92): **100,99,97,91,81 77,77**
toteswingers 1&2 £6.80, 2&3 £2.40, 1&3 £6.70 CSF £45.30 TOTE £34.10: £11.60, £1.10; EX 73.10.
Owner W J Gredley **Bred** Middle Park Stud Ltd **Trained** Newmarket, Suffolk

FOCUS
Some big stables were represented in this fillies' maiden, which was run at an honest pace. The front three pulled clear and all look above average. This was a step up from the third, but the overall form looks sensible.

NOTEBOOK
Madame Defarge(IRE), who is closely related to 7f (at two) and 1m (Fibresand) winner Foolin Myself, and a half-sister to 7f-1m AW winner Comradeship and 7f-1m2f winner Unex El Greco, was not that well away but travelled sweetly and showed a willing attitude under pressure. Unsurprisingly she looked a shade unbalanced when asked to go and win her race on the heavy ground but was well on top at the line and looks a handy prospect for next season. (op 25-1)
Nickels And Dimes(IRE) ran a most promising debut when a staying on third over 7f at Leicester, suggesting this step up in trip would suit, and this was another respectable effort. (tchd 5-4)
Elik(IRE) ran green but with promise on her debut and she ran another fair race here. She travelled strongly, nearest to the far rail, and looked a real threat entering the final furlong, but was outstayed by the front two. She is just the type her trainer is so adept at improving. (op 11-4)
Of Course Darling looked to hold a solid chance judged on her debut effort when fourth at Newmarket (7f, soft) but had questions to answer after struggling in a valuable sales race when last seen. She travelled well enough but was left behind by the front three and looks more of a handicap type. (op 7-2)
Butterfly Dream had shown little in two maidens and, stepping up in trip, found little when coming under pressure some way from home. (op 14-1)

7313 CHRISTMAS PARTIES AT GREAT YARMOUTH RACECOURSE NURSERY 1m 3y

2:50 (2:51) (Class 6) (0-60,60) 2-Y-0 **£1,617** (£481; £240; £120) **Stalls** Centre

Form RPR

0300 **1** **Keep Calm**[36] 6318 2-9-7 **60** RyanMoore 10 66
(Richard Hannon) *racd towards stands' side: a.p: chsd ldr over 2f out: rdn over 1f out: led ins fnl f: drvn out* **12/1**

3544 **2** *nk* **Panama Cat (USA)**[14] 6953 2-9-2 **55** AmyRyan 11 60
(Kevin Ryan) *racd towards stands' side: chsd ldrs: led over 2f out: rdn and hdd ins fnl f: styd on: 2nd of 10 in gp* **7/1**[3]

065 **3** *2 1/2* **Caramel Sundae**[32] 6437 2-9-5 **58** (b[1]) AdamKirby 9 58
(Marco Botti) *racd towards stands' side: a.p: rdn over 2f out: styd on same pce fnl f: 3rd of 10 in gp* **12/1**

6500 **4** *5* **Trymyluck**[26] 6607 2-9-5 **58** MickyFenton 3 47
(Pam Sly) *racd towards far side: chsd ldr unitl rdn to ld that side over 1f out: edgd rt and wknd ins fnl f: 1st of 3 in gp* **33/1**

000 **5** *3/4* **Pennyweight**[34] 6371 2-8-12 **51** LukeMorris 7 38
(James Eustace) *racd towards stands' side: hld up in tch: rdn over 2f out: sn outpcd: 4th of 10 in gp* **16/1**

0066 **6** *2 1/2* **Garmelow Girl**[20] 6793 2-8-7 **46** (b) JamieMackay 6 28
(Kevin Ryan) *racd towards stands' side: chsd ldr tl rdn over 2f out: wknd over 1f out: 5th of 10 in gp* **12/1**

006 **7** *2 3/4* **Winslow Arizona (IRE)**[57] 5684 2-8-7 **46** HayleyTurner 1 22
(Michael Bell) *s.s: hld up: racd towards far side: hdwy over 2f out: rdn over 1f out: wknd fnl f: 2nd of 3 in that gp* **2/1**[1]

000 **8** *2 1/4* **Downright Dizzie**[42] 6114 2-9-3 **59** RyanClark(3) 8 30
(Tom Keddy) *racd towards stands' side: hld up: rdn over 2f out: nvr on terms: 6th of 10 in gp* **50/1**

0361 **9** *shd* **Precision Strike**[6] 7173 2-9-3 **56** 6ex RobbieFitzpatrick 5 26
(Richard Guest) *racd towards stands' side: hld up: sme hdwy 2f out: wknd over 1f out: 7th of 10 in gp* **9/2**[2]

0600 **10** *3 1/4* **Misty Secret (IRE)**[27] 6583 2-9-0 **53** AndreaAtzeni 13 16
(Jane Chapple-Hyam) *racd towards stands' side: in rr and pushed along 1/2-way: sn bhd: 8th of 10 in gp* **40/1**

0004 **11** *2 1/4* **Perseverent Pete (USA)**[14] 6946 2-9-1 **54** SebSanders 2 12
(Christine Dunnett) *racd towards far side: led that trio tl rdn: hdd & wknd over 1f out: last of 3 in gp* **15/2**

0000 **12** *7* **Karr Wa Farr (IRE)**[54] 5763 2-8-10 **49** (v[1]) MartinLane 4
(Ed Vaughan) *racd towards stands' side: hld up in tch: drvn along over 3f out: wknd over 2f out: 9th of 10 in gp* **33/1**

000 **13** *1 3/4* **Lilly May (IRE)**[13] 6978 2-8-7 **46** SilvestreDeSousa 12
(Phil McEntee) *racd towards stands' side: overall ldr tl rdn and hdd over 2f out: sn wknd: last of 10 in gp* **25/1**

1m 46.43s (5.83) **Going Correction** +0.575s/f (Yiel) 13 Ran SP% **118.9**
Speed ratings (Par 93): **93,92,90,85,84 81,79,76,76,73 71,64,62**
toteswingers 1&2 £6.70, 2&3 £11.50, 1&3 £15.30 CSF £89.07 CT £722.62 TOTE £18.80: £4.90, £1.10, £4.60; EX 47.80 Trifecta £533.40 Part won. Pool: £711.23 - 0.62 winning units..
Owner Richard Hitchcock Alan King **Bred** Aislabie Bloodstock Ltd **Trained** East Everleigh, Wilts

FOCUS
The pace was steady for this moderate nursery, but the field were strung out at the line and those racing up the stands' side seemed at a distinct advantage. The winner has been rated to a small personal best and the runner-up looks a stayer.

NOTEBOOK
Keep Calm had shown little in four starts, including in a nursery last time, but he was down to a 0-60 for the first time and just did enough in an exciting finish. He benefited from how the race unfolded and did not have much in hand at the line. (tchd 14-1)
Panama Cat(USA), stepping up in trip, was smartly away from her low draw and travelled well enough but lost out to a less-exposed type. (op 6-1)
Caramel Sundae, wearing blinkers for the first time on her nursery debut, stepped up on her maiden efforts but did not look that happy on the testing conditions. (op 9-1 tchd 14-1)
Trymyluck did best of the three runners who raced near the far rail, on her handicap debut. This was her best effort to date and she shaped as though further will suit in time.
Pennyweight was another making her handicap debut on the back of three maiden runs, all on good or quicker ground, and she shaped well enough. She came under pressure some way out but kept on all the way to the line, suggesting this trip is her minimum. (tchd 14-1)
Winslow Arizona(IRE) was slowly away and never able to get competitive, racing near the possibly unfavoured far side. The money suggests he has more to offer than he has shown so far and will be worth keeping an eye on, especially if the ground is less testing. Official explanation: jockey said filly was slowly away (op 9-2 tchd 5-1)
Precision Strike handled the soft ground well when winning at Nottingham last time but found little when coming under pressure, off a 6lb higher mark, in these even more testing conditions. (op 7-2 tchd 10-3)

7314 JENNINGSBET.COM FILLIES' H'CAP 7f 3y
3:20 (3:21) (Class 5) (0-70,70) 3-Y-0+ **£2,264** (£673; £336; £168) **Stalls** Centre

Form RPR
1005 **1** **Caramelita**[14] 6961 5-9-3 **66**....(v) FrederikTylicki 14 73
(J R Jenkins) *s.i.s: hld up: hdwy over 2f out: rdn to ld ins fnl f: r.o* **17/2**[3]
2251 **2** 1 3/4 **Clumber Place**[20] 6782 6-9-0 **63**.... GrahamLee 9 65
(James Given) *trckd ldrs: racd keenly: led over 1f out: rdn and hdd ins fnl f: styd on same pce* **4/1**[1]
2150 **3** 3/4 **Tahlia Ree (IRE)**[11] 7023 3-9-5 **70**.... HayleyTurner 1 71
(Michael Bell) *hld up: hdwy over 2f out: rdn over 1f out: r.o* **12/1**
5146 **4** 1/2 **Amis Reunis**[47] 5975 3-8-10 **61**.... WilliamCarson 7 60
(Anthony Carson) *trckd ldrs: plld hrd: rdn and ev ch over 1f out: styd on same pce ins fnl f* **16/1**
5003 **5** 3/4 **The New Black (IRE)**[19] 6810 3-8-2 **56**....(e) DeclanCannon(3) 10 53
(Gay Kelleway) *hld up: hdwy: nt clr run and swtchd rt ins fnl f: r.o: could nt rch ldrs* **40/1**
3663 **6** nk **Angel Cake (IRE)**[70] 5208 3-8-5 **56** oh11.... DominicFox 5 52
(Michael Appleby) *prom: rdn over 2f out: styd on* **25/1**
5020 **7** 1/2 **Batgirl**[24] 6687 5-8-13 **69**.... HannahNunn(7) 2 64
(John Berry) *hld up: hdwy over 2f out: rdn over 1f out: edgd lft and no ex ins fnl f* **10/1**
0003 **8** 1/2 **Lady Sledmere (IRE)**[20] 6782 4-8-11 **60**.... RussKennemore 13 54
(Paul Midgley) *sn outpcd: rdn over 1f out: r.o: nvr nrr* **14/1**
5000 **9** nse **Climaxfortackle (IRE)**[14] 6961 4-8-13 **62**....(v) SilvestreDeSousa 12 56
(Derek Shaw) *s.i.s: sn prom: led over 2f out tl over 1f out: no ex* **12/1**
0665 **10** 3/4 **Untold Melody**[20] 6782 3-8-9 **60**....(tp) AmyRyan 3 52
(Kevin Ryan) *chsd ldrs: rdn and ev ch over 1f out: wknd ins fnl f* **16/1**
0033 **11** 1/2 **Aarti (IRE)**[31] 6500 3-8-11 **62**.... WilliamBuick 4 52
(William Haggas) *w ldrs: rdn over 2f out: wknd ins fnl f* **11/1**
4553 **12** 1 1/2 **Santarini (IRE)**[35] 6328 3-9-3 **68**.... RyanMoore 11 55
(Richard Hannon) *hld up: rdn over 2f out: n.d* **17/2**[3]
00R/ **13** 3/4 **Glan Lady (IRE)**[48] 3054 6-8-7 **56** oh11.... AndrewMullen 8 41
(Michael Appleby) *chsd ldrs: drvn along 1/2-way: wknd over 2f out* **80/1**
1622 **14** 4 **Kashmiri Star**[32] 6436 3-8-8 **59**.... LukeMorris 15 33
(Michael Quinn) *led over 4f: wknd over 1f out* **14/1**
62/0 **15** 1/2 **Ceto**[71] 5148 5-8-7 **56**.... MartinLane 6 29
(Phil McEntee) *chsd ldrs tl rdn and wknd over 2f out* **80/1**
006 **16** 10 **Maria Vezzera**[12] 7005 3-8-5 **56** oh3.... AndreaAtzeni 16
(Marco Botti) *mid-div: rdn and wknd over 2f out* **13/2**[2]

1m 31.0s (4.40) **Going Correction** +0.725s/f (Yiel)
WFA 3 from 4yo+ 2lb **16** Ran SP% **121.0**
Speed ratings (Par 100): **103,101,100,99,98 98,97,97,97,96 95,94,93,88,88 76**
toteswingers 1&2 £6.60, 2&3 £15.40, 1&3 £21.90 CSF £41.11 CT £435.30 TOTE £9.50: £3.10, £1.40, £2.80, £4.20; EX 41.20 Trifecta £235.50 Pool: £942.24 - 3.00 winning units..
Owner La Senoritas **Bred** R B Hill **Trained** Royston, Herts
FOCUS
A wide-open handicap run at a steady pace, with eight in a line at the furlong pole, before the winner pulled clear late on. The form is modest, with doubts over plenty.
Climaxfortackle(IRE) Official explanation: jockey said filly hung right
Maria Vezzera Official explanation: jockey said filly stopped very quickly

7315 WEDDINGS AT GREAT YARMOUTH RACECOURSE H'CAP 1m 3f 101y
3:50 (3:51) (Class 5) (0-70,70) 3-Y-0+ **£2,264** (£673; £336; £168) **Stalls** Low

Form RPR
0404 **1** **Layline (IRE)**[18] 6848 5-9-10 **70**.... GrahamLee 5 78
(Gay Kelleway) *hld up: hdwy over 4f out: led over 1f out: sn rdn: jst hld on* **10/1**[3]
3053 **2** nk **Mediterranean Sea (IRE)**[56] 5718 6-9-10 **70**.... FrederikTylicki 4 77
(J R Jenkins) *hld up: hdwy over 2f out: rdn over 1f out: styd on wl* **16/1**
-442 **3** 6 **Minsky Mine (IRE)**[82] 4745 5-9-6 **66**.... WilliamBuick 10 63
(Michael Appleby) *chsd ldrs tl led over 2f out: rdn and hdd over 1f out: wknd ins fnl f* **9/2**[2]
5000 **4** 2 3/4 **Darsan (IRE)**[11] 7015 4-8-10 **56** oh2.... SilvestreDeSousa 6 49
(Phil McEntee) *sn prom: led over 9f out: rdn and hdd over 2f out: wknd over 1f out* **22/1**
41 **5** 8 **De Rigueur**[25] 6626 4-9-8 **68**....(t) AndreaAtzeni 2 48
(Marco Botti) *s.i.s: hld up: hdwy over 4f out: rdn and wknd over 1f out* **4/5**[1]
450 **6** 24 **Balcary Bay**[20] 6792 3-8-7 **59**.... LukeMorris 3
(James Eustace) *sn pushed along in rr: lost tch fr over 5f out: sn t.o* **33/1**
3306 **7** 1 **Lyric Poet (USA)**[49] 5908 5-9-2 **62**....(tp) WilliamCarson 8
(Anthony Carson) *chsd ldr 2f: remained handy: rdn and ev ch over 2f out: wknd wl over 1f out: t.o* **20/1**
6004 **8** 18 **The Ducking Stool**[20] 6794 5-9-1 **64**.... RyanClark(3) 7
(Julia Feilden) *led: hdd over 9f out: chsd ldrs tl rdn and wknd wl over 2f out: t.o* **14/1**
0000 **9** 5 **Steuben (GER)**[20] 6802 6-9-9 **69**.... TomQueally 1
(Barney Curley) *chsd ldrs: lost pl over 8f out: bhd fnl 5f: t.o* **20/1**
30-0 **10** 23 **Manshoor (IRE)**[234] 303 7-8-11 **57**.... HayleyTurner 9
(Lucy Wadham) *chsd ldrs: pushed along 7f out: wknd over 4f out: t.o* **25/1**

2m 40.4s (11.70) **Going Correction** +0.725s/f (Yiel)
WFA 3 from 4yo+ 6lb **10** Ran SP% **116.0**
Speed ratings (Par 103): **86,85,81,79,73 56,55,42,38,21**
toteswingers 1&2 £9.30, 2&3 £5.20, 1&3 £3.10 CSF £154.42 CT £822.79 TOTE £10.50: £2.20, £2.90, £1.50; EX 72.00 Trifecta £184.40 Pool: £1409.34 - 5.73 winning units..
Owner Matt Bartram, Bob Smith & Gay Kelleway **Bred** Mrs M E Slade **Trained** Exning, Suffolk
FOCUS
An uncompetitive handicap run at a messy pace, with the field strung out at the line. It has been rated around the runner-up to her AW form.

7316 INJURED JOCKEYS FUND H'CAP 6f 3y
4:20 (4:21) (Class 6) (0-60,60) 3-Y-0+ **£1,617** (£481; £240; £120) **Stalls** Centre

Form RPR
4022 **1** **See The Storm**[8] 7106 4-8-7 **49**.... RyanPowell(3) 11 60
(Ian Williams) *hld up: hdwy over 3f out: led over 1f out: pushed out* **3/1**[1]
0036 **2** nk **Seamus Shindig**[31] 6497 10-9-2 **60**.... AmyScott(5) 10 70
(Henry Candy) *hld up: hdwy over 2f out: rdn and ev ch fr over 1f out: styd on* **17/2**
5300 **3** 4 **Jonnie Skull (IRE)**[13] 6982 6-8-9 **55**.... ClaireMurray(7) 9 52
(Phil McEntee) *chsd ldrs: rdn over 2f out: styd on same pce fr over 1f out* **33/1**
1661 **4** nk **Mucky Molly**[14] 6951 4-9-4 **57**.... SebSanders 15 53
(Olivia Maylam) *prom: rdn over 2f out: styd on same pce fnl f* **7/1**[2]
0054 **5** 1/2 **Hatta Stream (IRE)**[46] 6002 6-9-4 **60**.... SimonPearce(3) 6 55
(Lydia Pearce) *hld up: hdwy over 2f out: led wl over 1f out: sn rdn and hdd: edgd rt and no ex ins fnl f* **12/1**
6334 **6** 1 1/2 **Dixie Gwalia**[5] 7204 4-8-7 **53**.... SiobhanMiller(7) 12 43
(David Simcock) *hld up: hdwy over 3f out: rdn over 2f out: no ex fnl f* **7/1**[2]
5000 **7** 1/2 **Dubai Rythm**[5] 7204 3-9-1 **55**....(bt) AndrewMullen 14 43
(Michael Appleby) *led: rdn over 2f out: hdd wl over 1f out: wknd ins fnl f* **33/1**
1053 **8** 3/4 **Novalist**[40] 6179 4-9-7 **60**....(b) FrederikTylicki 5 46
(Robin Bastiman) *chsd ldr: rdn and ev ch over 1f out: wknd ins fnl f* **9/1**
6000 **9** 1/2 **Summer Sun**[15] 6930 3-8-13 **53**.... LukeMorris 3 37
(Phil McEntee) *mid-div: hdwy over 2f out: rdn over 1f out: wknd fnl f* **40/1**
0504 **10** 1/2 **Black Douglas**[28] 6565 3-9-6 **60**....(p) GrahamLee 8 43
(William Jarvis) *chsd ldrs tl rdn and wknd over 1f out* **16/1**
5400 **11** 4 1/2 **Indiana Guest (IRE)**[14] 6967 3-9-0 **54**....(b) TomQueally 1 22
(George Margarson) *s.i.s: hld up: hdwy u.p over 2f out: wknd over 1f out* **33/1**
1250 **12** 6 **Plum Bay**[19] 6823 3-9-5 **59**.... WilliamCarson 16
(David Elsworth) *mid-div: hdwy 1/2-way: sn rdn: wknd 2f out* **15/2**[3]
003 **13** 2 1/2 **Ghazeer (IRE)**[7] 7146 3-9-4 **58**....(p) SilvestreDeSousa 7
(Derek Shaw) *chsd ldrs: rdn 1/2-way: wknd over 2f out* **12/1**
5040 **14** 1 1/4 **Simple Rhythm**[36] 6322 6-8-9 **48**....(p) DaraghO'Donohoe 2
(John Ryan) *prom over 3f* **33/1**
600 **15** 8 **Beach Candy (IRE)**[14] 6961 3-9-6 **60**....(p) AdamKirby 13
(Phil McEntee) *prom: rdn 1/2-way: wknd over 2f out* **16/1**

1m 18.23s (3.83) **Going Correction** +0.725s/f (Yiel)
WFA 3 from 4yo+ 1lb **15** Ran SP% **123.6**
Speed ratings (Par 101): **103,102,97,96,96 94,93,92,91,91 85,77,73,72,61**
toteswingers 1&2 £10.20, 2&3 £92.90, 1&3 £26.90 CSF £27.26 CT £732.31 TOTE £3.30: £2.00, £3.50, £9.30; EX 39.20 TRIFECTA Not won..
Owner Keating Bradley Fold Ltd **Bred** D R Botterill **Trained** Portway, Worcs
FOCUS
A modest if competitive sprint handicap run at a fair pace, with the front two pulling clear late on. The runner-up has been rated to this year's best.
Novalist Official explanation: jockey said gelding hung right
Beach Candy(IRE) Official explanation: jockey said filly had no more to give

7317 PLEASUREWOOD HILLS THEME PARK H'CAP (DIV I) 7f 3y
4:50 (4:52) (Class 6) (0-65,65) 3-Y-0+ **£1,617** (£481; £240; £120) **Stalls** Centre

Form RPR
4400 **1** **Zip Lock (IRE)**[26] 6610 6-9-2 **62**....[1] RyanClark(3) 6 70
(Tom Keddy) *chsd ldrs: led over 4f out: rdn over 1f out: styd on* **40/1**
0500 **2** 1/2 **Beautiful Day**[20] 6785 4-8-11 **54**.... AmyRyan 1 61
(Kevin Ryan) *a.p: chsd wnr over 4f out: rdn over 1f out: styd on* **7/2**[1]
0021 **3** 2 1/4 **Geeaitch**[5] 7201 3-9-6 **65** 6ex.... WilliamCarson 9 66+
(Anthony Carson) *in rr: drvn along over 4f out: nt clr run and swtchd lft over 3f out: hdwy u.p over 1f out: hung lft and r.o ins fnl f: could nt trble ldrs* **7/2**[1]
0410 **4** 3 1/4 **Olney Lass**[14] 6961 5-9-1 **61**.... SimonPearce(3) 2 54
(Lydia Pearce) *hld up: hdwy over 2f out: rdn over 1f out: no ex ins fnl f* **5/1**[3]
050 **5** 3/4 **Nurse Dominatrix (IRE)**[60] 5549 3-8-5 **50** oh1.... KellyHarrison 5 41
(Richard Guest) *s.s: rdn and hung lft over 1f out: n.d* **20/1**
2003 **6** 1 3/4 **Taizong (IRE)**[19] 6806 3-9-2 **61**.... MichaelO'Connell 3 47
(Ian Williams) *hld up: pushed along and bmpd over 3f out: hdwy over 2f out: wknd fnl f* **6/1**
4206 **7** 7 **Intomist (IRE)**[33] 6402 3-9-3 **62**....(p) TomQueally 4 30
(Jim Boyle) *led: hdd over 4f out: wknd over 2f out* **22/1**
0000 **8** 3/4 **Mystical Witch**[36] 6321 3-8-5 **50** oh5....(v[1]) DominicFox 11 16
(Christine Dunnett) *chsd ldrs: rdn over 2f out: sn wknd* **50/1**
3365 **9** 22 **Putin (IRE)**[46] 5996 4-8-7 **50** oh5....(bt) LukeMorris 7
(Phil McEntee) *chsd ldrs: drvn along 1/2-way: wknd over 2f out: t.o* **12/1**
1642 **10** 15 **Exceedexpectations (IRE)**[31] 6500 3-9-5 **64**.... HayleyTurner 8
(Michael Bell) *sn pushed along in rr: bhd fr 1/2-way: t.o* **9/2**[2]

1m 32.64s (6.04) **Going Correction** +0.725s/f (Yiel)
WFA 3 from 4yo+ 2lb **10** Ran SP% **114.8**
Speed ratings (Par 101): **94,93,90,87,86 84,76,75,50,33**
toteswingers 1&2 £28.30, 2&3 £3.20, 1&3 £21.60 CSF £168.80 CT £647.90 TOTE £54.70: £13.30, £1.60, £1.50; EX 339.00 TRIFECTA Not won..
Owner S T Ward **Bred** Major K R Thompson **Trained** Newmarket, Suffolk
FOCUS
A moderate contest run at a fair pace with the field again strung out at the finish. The runner-up has been rated to a similar level as last year's C&D effort.

7318 PLEASUREWOOD HILLS THEME PARK H'CAP (DIV II) 7f 3y
5:20 (5:21) (Class 6) (0-65,64) 3-Y-0+ **£1,617** (£481; £240; £120) **Stalls** Centre

Form RPR
56 **1** **Ishiamiracle**[71] 5149 3-9-0 **59**....(p) LukeMorris 4 68
(Phil McEntee) *racd centre: chsd ldrs: led over 2f out: rdn clr ins fnl f* **16/1**
2200 **2** 3 1/4 **Dream Walker (FR)**[30] 6514 3-9-5 **64**.... PatrickMathers 8 68
(Ian McInnes) *hld up: racd centre: hdwy over 2f out: short of room ovr 1f out: styd on: no ch w wnr* **4/1**[2]
3204 **3** 3/4 **Isingy Red (FR)**[20] 6801 4-9-5 **62**....(p) TomQueally 7 61
(Jim Boyle) *hld up: racd centre: hdwy over 2f out: rdn and hung rt over 1f out: no ex ins fnl f* **5/2**[1]
/22- **4** 1 3/4 **Hooligan Sean**[314] 7750 5-9-1 **63**.... AmyScott(5) 10 57
(Henry Candy) *racd stands' side: hld up: wnt centre 1/2-way: hdwy over 2f out: rdn over 1f out: no ex fnl f* **6/1**[3]

-603 **5** 3 1/4 **Lordship (IRE)**[8] 7105 8-8-2 **52** oh3 ow2.......................... JakePayne(7) 2 38
(Tony Carroll) *racd centre: chsd ldr: rdn and ev ch over 2f out: cl up whn hmpd over 1f out: sn wknd* **7/1**

0000 **6** 1 1/4 **Give Us A Belle (IRE)**[36] 6322 3-8-5 **50** oh3.................(vt) DominicFox 9 32
(Christine Dunnett) *racd stands' side: outpcd: nvr nrr* **33/1**

5000 **7** 7 **Mark Anthony (IRE)**[21] 6756 5-8-10 **53** oh2 ow3..(p) MichaelO'Connell 1 17
(Shaun Harris) *racd alone towards far side: led overall tl over 2f out: wknd over 1f out* **8/1**

400 **8** 8 **Spin Again (IRE)**[5] 7202 7-9-3 **60**........................ BrettDoyle 3
(John Ryan) *racd centre: sn pushed along in rr: bhd fnl 4f* **10/1**

00-6 **9** 3 1/2 **Teth**[14] 6965 3-9-3 **62**....................................... WilliamCarson 5
(Anthony Carson) *racd stands' side: in tch tl wknd 1/2-way* **8/1**

1m 31.98s (5.38) **Going Correction** +0.725s/f (Yiel)
WFA 3 from 4yo+ 2lb **9** Ran SP% **115.5**
Speed ratings (Par 101): **98,94,93,91,87 86,78,69,65**
toteswingers 1&2 £16.30, 2&3 £3.20, 1&3 £9.30 CSF £79.05 CT £218.93 TOTE £12.20: £3.60, £2.20, £1.20; EX 103.20 Trifecta £291.00 Pool: £915.68 - 2.36 winning units..
Owner Steve Jakes **Bred** M A L Evans **Trained** Newmarket, Suffolk

FOCUS
There was a fair pace for this modest handicap, with the winner pulling clear late on. The runner-up was hampered 2f out but has been rated to his best.
Lordship(IRE) Official explanation: jockey said gelding suffered interference in running
Mark Anthony(IRE) Official explanation: jockey said gelding hung badly right
T/Jkpt: Not won. T/Plt: £179.20 to a £1 stake. Pool of £71304.62 - 290.40 winning tickets. T/Qpdt: £63.30 to a £1 stake. Pool of £4846.70 - 56.64 winning tickets. CR

NANTES (R-H)
Tuesday, October 23

OFFICIAL GOING: Turf: heavy

7319a PRIX DES SABLONNETS (LISTED RACE) (2YO) (TURF) 1m
11:00 (12:00) 2-Y-O **£22,916** (£9,166; £6,875; £4,583; £2,291)

RPR

1 **Wingate**[18] 2-9-2 0.. FabriceVeron 4 96
(H-A Pantall, France) **23/10**[2]

2 6 **Beatrice**[44] 2-8-13 0.. AnthonyCrastus 3 80
(H-A Pantall, France) **9/2**[3]

3 2 **Alta Lilea (IRE)**[14] 6960 2-8-13 0.............................. JoeFanning 1 75
(Mark Johnston) *racd in 2nd on ins fr s: swtchd outside bef st: relegated to 3rd bef st: rdn but nt qckn 1 1/2f out: styd on one pce fnl f* **4/5**[1]

4 4 **Storm Tivoli (FR)** 2-9-2 0.. AdrienFouassier 2 70
(A Couetil, France) **7/1**

5 20 **Sparkie (FR)**[35] 2-9-2 0... MathieuAndrouin 5 26
(E J O'Neill, France) **29/1**

1m 46.4s (106.40) **5** Ran SP% **119.9**
WIN (incl. 1 euro stake): 3.30. PLACES: 1.70, 2.10. SF: 6.70.
Owner C Mimouni & Haras De Bernesq **Bred** Haras de Bernesq, A Bonin & Mme C Hennel de Beaupr **Trained** France

7320a GRAND PRIX DE NANTES (14TH ETAPE DU DEFI DU GALOP) (LISTED RACE) (3YO+) (TURF) 1m 4f
12:30 (12:00) 3-Y-O+ **£25,000** (£10,000; £7,500; £5,000; £2,500)

RPR

1 **Sir Graham Wade (IRE)**[18] 6833 3-8-8 0........................ JoeFanning 6 105
(Mark Johnston) *sn led on ins: hdd bef bk st: racd in 3rd: rdn to go 2nd bef st: r.o wl u.p to take ld 1 1/2f out: styd on wl* **21/10**[1]

2 1 1/2 **Opera Vert (FR)**[175] 4-9-1 0...........................(p) ArnaudBourgeais 1 102
(D Sepulchre, France) **15/1**

3 2 **Tigre D'Or (FR)**[50] 5900 6-9-5 0..............................(b) AdrienFouassier 3 103
(A Couetil, France) **9/1**

4 1/2 **Griraz (FR)**[159] 2223 7-9-5 0.. PhilippeSogorb 9 102
(P Sogorb, France) **11/1**

5 3/4 **Marceti (IRE)**[50] 5900 5-9-1 0...................................... GeraldAvranche 11 97
(E Leenders, France) **8/1**[3]

6 shd **Skyline Du Casse (FR)**[25] 6-9-1 0............................... MathieuAndrouin 7 97
(F Plouganou, France) **21/1**

7 dist **Kapirovska (FR)**[50] 5900 4-8-11 0................................ AntoineHamelin 2
(J-L Guillochon, France) **14/1**

8 hd **Crystifou (FR)**[84] 5-9-1 0.. JulienGuillochon 5
(Mme V Seignoux, France) **52/1**

9 2 1/2 **Tucumano (FR)**[10] 6-9-1 0.. AlexisBadel 4
(Y-M Porzier, France) **44/5**

10 20 **Snape Maltings (IRE)**[67] 5-9-1 0...........................(p) FabriceVeron 10
(H-A Pantall, France) **13/1**

11 15 **Aizavoski (IRE)**[50] 5900 6-9-10 0................................. AnthonyCrastus 8
(E Lellouche, France) **43/10**[2]

2m 43.44s (8.44) **11** Ran SP% **117.3**
WFA 3 from 4yo+ 7lb
WIN (incl. 1 euro stake): 3.10. PLACES: 1.90, 3.20, 2.50. DF: 24.90. SF: 27.70.
Owner Paul Dean **Bred** P D Savill **Trained** Middleham Moor, N Yorks

NOTEBOOK
Sir Graham Wade(IRE) built on his second place in similar company at Ascot to take his first Pattern race. He battled on strongly through the testing ground and will appreciate going back up in trip next year, when he should make up into a Cup horse.

7189 KEMPTON (A.W) (R-H)
Wednesday, October 24

OFFICIAL GOING: Standard
Wind: moderate, half against Weather: fine, cloudy

7321 WIN BIG WITH BETDAQ MULTIPLES H'CAP 1m 2f (P)
5:50 (5:50) (Class 6) (0-55,61) 3-Y-O+ **£1,617** (£481; £180; £180) **Stalls** Low

Form RPR

660 **1** **Bridge That Gap**[22] 6770 4-9-4 **52**........................... FergusSweeney 11 59
(Roger Ingram) *s.s: hld up in rr: hdwy over 1f out: str run to ld on line* **33/1**

3121 **2** hd **Neige D'Antan**[5] 7222 3-9-8 **61** 6ex.............................. LukeMorris 8 68+
(Sir Mark Prescott Bt) *trckd ldrs: led wl over 1f out and wnt 2 l clr: hrd drvn fnl f: jst ct* **8/11**[1]

0406 **3** nk **Irons On Fire (USA)**[39] 6255 4-9-7 **55**............................(p) AdamKirby 4 61
(Lee Carter) *led 1f: prom tl outpcd over 2f out: rallied and r.o fnl f* **12/1**

5000 **3** dht **Lightning Spirit**[34] 6395 4-9-2 **50**............................(p) GeorgeBaker 2 56
(Gary Moore) *hld up towards rr: hdwy on inner 2f out: styd on fnl f* **20/1**

0/ **5** 1 **Tyrur Ted**[817] 6602 7-9-4 **55**... SophieDoyle(3) 1 59
(Frank Sheridan) *hld up in rr: r.o over 1f out: nrst fin* **14/1**

3422 **6** 1 **Rapid Water**[21] 6778 6-9-7 **55**....................................(p) MartinLane 3 57
(Pat Eddery) *chsd ldrs: one pce fnl 2f* **8/1**[3]

6353 **7** 3/4 **Essell**[5] 7222 3-9-2 **55**... MartinHarley 9 56
(Mick Channon) *led after 1f tl 2f out: sn wknd* **6/1**[2]

03-0 **8** 1 1/4 **Boris The Bold**[13] 7005 3-9-2 **55**...................................1 LiamKeniry 6 53
(John Best) *sn pressing ldrs: led 2f out: sn hdd & wknd* **20/1**

005 **9** 5 **Cairanne**[29] 6569 4-9-1 **52**.. RyanClark(3) 10 40
(Tom Keddy) *in tch on outer tl wknd 2f out* **20/1**

2m 9.89s (1.89) **Going Correction** -0.025s/f (Stan)
WFA 3 from 4yo+ 5lb **9** Ran SP% **114.9**
Speed ratings (Par 101): **91,90,90,90,89 89,88,87,83**PLACE: Irons of Fire: £1.60, Lightning Spirit £3.10 TRICAST: Bridge That Gap/Neige D'Antan, Irons On Fire £174.84 BTG/NA/LS £282.26 toteswingers: 1&2 £26.20, 1&I Not won, 1&LS Not won, 2&I £0.50, 2&LS £7.20. TRIFECTA: B/N/L £220.90 CSF £55.60 TOTE £46.80: £14.3027, £Owner, £The Stargazers, £BredMichael Joy Trained Trifecta £Epsom, Surrey.

FOCUS
A messy race, with a steady pace (time over five seconds above standard) resulting in a bunch finish, and this form is muddling and probably isn't worth much, with the third the best guide.
Bridge That Gap Official explanation: trainer said, regarding the apparent improvement of form, that the colt appreciated the drop in distance and the weaker race, his first under handicap conditions
Tyrur Ted ◆ Official explanation: jockey said, regarding the running and riding that that her instructions were to sit where the gelding was comfortable and make the best of her way home. She added that the colt had been slowly into its stride, had showed signs of rustiness after his long absence and that the pace of the race was muddly and had developed into a sprint. She further added that the colt was initially outpaced when the tempo increased, before staying on in the latter stages despite being denied a clear run; trainer confirmed the instructions and stated that he was satisfied with the ride that Doyle gave

7322 BACK OR LAY AT BETDAQ.COM MEDIAN AUCTION MAIDEN STKS 6f (P)
6:20 (6:22) (Class 5) 3-4-Y-O **£2,264** (£673; £336; £168) **Stalls** Low

Form RPR

-036 **1** **Out Do**[21] 6800 3-9-3 81.. WilliamBuick 4 80+
(Luca Cumani) *hld up in rr: hdwy on bit to ld over 1f out: sn clr: easily* **2/5**[1]

0 **2** 3 1/4 **Gaelic Ice**[16] 6930 3-8-12 0...................................... DavidProbert 1 58
(Rod Millman) *towards rr: effrt 2f out: styd on fnl f: no ch w wnr* **50/1**

-0 **3** nk **Batchworth Firefly**[16] 6930 4-8-10 0.......................... PatrickHills(3) 10 57
(Dean Ivory) *bhd tl r.o fr over 1f out: nrst fin* **50/1**

3343 **4** shd **Generalyse**[68] 5308 3-9-3 71.....................................(p) JohnFahy 5 62
(Ben De Haan) *chsd ldrs: rdn and kpt on fr over 1f out: nt gng pce of wnr* **6/1**[2]

0220 **5** 1/2 **Mister Mackenzie**[5] 7218 3-9-3 65............................ GeorgeBaker 2 60
(John Best) *chsd ldrs: one pce appr fnl f* **8/1**[3]

0505 **6** 1 1/2 **Homeboy (IRE)**[16] 6930 4-8-13 64.............................. KatiaScallan(5) 6 55
(Marcus Tregoning) *mid-div: effrt and hung lft 2f out: nt rch ldrs* **16/1**

6425 **7** 1 1/2 **Enthrall (IRE)**[29] 6565 3-8-12 52...................................(be) LukeMorris 3 45
(Phil McEntee) *led tl wknd over 1f out* **50/1**

4040 **8** 1/2 **Alderton (IRE)**[3] 7275 3-8-12 48.................................. FergusSweeney 11 44
(Martyn Meade) *a towards rr* **66/1**

504 **9** 2 **Elusive Pursuit**[35] 6362 4-8-13 45.............................. AdamKirby 8 37
(Clive Cox) *mid-div: effrt over 2f out: wknd over 1f out* **25/1**

P4- **10** 3/4 **En Ete**[542] 1726 3-8-12 0... JimCrowley 9 35
(Ralph Beckett) *chsd ldr tl wknd 2f out* **16/1**

0 **11** 8 **Kerfuffle (IRE)**[16] 6930 3-8-12 0.................................. SebSanders 7
(Simon Dow) *chsd ldrs 4f* **50/1**

1m 12.11s (-0.99) **Going Correction** -0.025s/f (Stan)
WFA 3 from 4yo 1lb **11** Ran SP% **121.8**
Speed ratings (Par 103): **105,100,100,100,99 97,95,94,92,91 80**
toteswingers 1&2 £24.40, 2&3 £15.00, 1&3 £0.00 CSF £50.79 TOTE £1.40: £1.02, £7.10, £26.50; EX 41.50 Trifecta £611.80 Pool: £840.25 - 1.03 winning units..
Owner Leonidas Marinopoulos **Bred** Equibreed S R L **Trained** Newmarket, Suffolk
■ Stewards' Enquiry : Patrick Hills three-day ban: weighed in heavy (7-9 Nov)

FOCUS
In a maiden run at a fair pace, the 81-rated Out Do was different class to some modest rivals. The winner did not need to run to his best to score while the placed horses limit the form.

7323 BETDAQ MOBILE APPS/BRITISH STALLION STUDS EBF MAIDEN STKS (DIV I) 1m (P)
6:50 (6:51) (Class 5) 2-Y-O **£2,911** (£866; £432; £216) **Stalls** Low

Form RPR

1 **Secret Number** 2-9-3 .... SilvestreDeSousa 6 90+
(Saeed Bin Suroor) *s.s: sn in midfield: hdwy and swtchd lft 2f out: r.o to ld ins fnl f: rdn out* **2/1**[1]

0 **2** nk **Pether's Moon (IRE)**[28] 6572 2-9-3 .... RyanMoore 5 83
(Richard Hannon) *chsd ldrs: led 2f out tl ins fnl f: kpt on wl* **14/1**

04 **3** 4 **Portmonarch (IRE)**[18] 6872 2-9-3 .... TedDurcan 2 74
(David Lanigan) *trckd ldrs: rdn and one pce fnl 2f* **7/1**[3]

0 **4** 5 **Wallenberg**[40] 6204 2-9-3 ....(e) WilliamBuick 3 62
(John Gosden) *led tl 2f out: wknd jst over 1f out* **5/1**[2]

5 3/4 **Revise (IRE)** 2-9-3 .... AdamKirby 14 60+
(Marco Botti) *hld up in rr: sme hdwy on inner 2f out: styd on fnl f* **33/1**

6 3/4 **London Bridge (USA)** 2-9-3 .... LiamKeniry 1 59
(Mikael Magnusson) *chsd ldrs tl outpcd fnl 2f* **16/1**

0 **7** 1 1/4 **Soul Intent (IRE)**[32] 6486 2-9-3 .... SebSanders 7 56
(J W Hills) *prom tl wknd 2f out* **50/1**

5 **8** nk **Celebrated Talent (USA)**[21] 6796 2-9-3 .... MickaelBarzalona 12 55
(Mahmood Al Zarooni) *nvr beyond midfield* **5/1**[2]

9 2 1/2 **Jaladee** 2-9-3 .... NeilCallan 4 49
(Roger Varian) *dwlt: sn in midfield: no hdwy fnl 2f* **20/1**

10 nse **Count Curlin (USA)** 2-9-3 .... LukeMorris 9 49
(Gerard Butler) *chsd ldrs tl wknd over 2f out* **33/1**

0 **11** 3/4 **Great Ormond (IRE)**[26] 6644 2-9-3 .... MartinLane 8 47
(David Simcock) *a bhd* **66/1**

44 **12** 3/4 **Isis Blue**[21] 6772 2-9-3 .... JamesMillman 10 46
(Rod Millman) *in tch on outer: rdn 3f out: sn btn* **10/1**

00 **13** 8 **So Lyrical**[41] 6153 2-8-12 .... FergusSweeney 13 22
(Peter Makin) *a towards rr* **66/1**

0 **14** *16* **Frederick Alfred**[34] 6412 2-9-3 RobertWinston 11
(Mark H Tompkins) *t.k.h towards rr: n.d fnl 3f* **100/1**
1m 37.92s (-1.88) **Going Correction** -0.025s/f (Stan) **14** Ran SP% **117.4**
Speed ratings (Par 95): **108,107,103,98,97 97,95,95,93,93 92,91,83,67**
toteswingers 1&2 £26.70, 2&3 £10.90, 1&3 £3.10 CSF £31.38 TOTE £2.40: £1.02, £4.80, £4.20; EX 36.90 Trifecta £413.00 Part won. Pool: £550.71 - 0.61 winning units..
Owner Godolphin **Bred** Darley **Trained** Newmarket, Suffolk

FOCUS
An interesting maiden and it went to a potential Group horse, who did everything wrong but still won and is one to keep on-side.

NOTEBOOK
Secret Number ◆ overcame losing around 5l with a slow start, and his effort is all the more creditable considering the next three all raced close to the pace. He's a half-brother to Group 1 winning milers Dubai Destination and Librettist, and he's a name to keep in mind. (op 13-8)
Pether's Moon(IRE) was well beaten on his debut at Goodwood (1m1f, soft), but he went off favourite that day and proved here he has plenty of ability. He is flattered to finish so close to the winner, but was well clear of the others. (op 16-1)
Portmonarch(IRE) showed ability over this trip on soft turf on his second start and did so again. He might win an ordinary maiden, but he's now qualified for a handicap mark and looks the type to progress given time. (op 8-1)
Wallenberg raced keenly in the eye-shield on his debut, when midfield in a Sandown maiden, and this time he ran too free in front. He clearly has ability, but is best watched for now. (op 11-2)
Revise(IRE) is a half-brother to a few winners, out of a 1m1f Grade 3 winner in the US, and this was an encouraging introduction, keeping on well without being given a hard time.
Celebrated Talent(USA) didn't build on a mildly encouraging debut effort, not really applying himself. (tchd 9-2)
Isis Blue Official explanation: jockey said that the colt hung left on the bend

7324 BETDAQ MOBILE APPS/BRITISH STALLION STUDS EBF MAIDEN STKS (DIV II) 1m (P)
7:20 (7:22) (Class 5) 2-Y-O **£2,911** (£866; £432; £216) **Stalls** Low

Form				RPR
23	**1**		**Greatwood**[21] 6795 2-9-3 KierenFallon 1 (Luca Cumani) *hld up in midfield: hdwy 2f out: r.o to ld ins fnl f: drvn out* **15/8**[1]	77+
	2	*nk*	**Stasio (USA)** 2-9-3 WilliamBuick 3 (David Simcock) *plld hrd: prom: led over 1f out tl ins fnl f: rallied wl* **6/1**[3]	76
	3	*nk*	**Enobled** 2-9-3 RyanMoore 2 (Sir Michael Stoute) *hld up towards rr: hdwy 2f out: pressed ldrs ins fnl f: r.o* **14/1**	76+
4	**4**	*2 ½*	**Interior Minister**[32] 6501 2-9-3 LiamKeniry 12 (Mikael Magnusson) *prom: rdn 2f out: could nt qckn appr fnl f* **33/1**	70
4	**5**	*1*	**Layl (USA)**[18] 6876 2-9-3 MickaelBarzalona 14 (Mahmood Al Zarooni) *mid-div: styd on fnl 2f: nvr able to chal* **7/2**[2]	68
	6	*1 ¼*	**Takaathur (USA)** 2-9-3 (t) SilvestreDeSousa 6 (Saeed Bin Suroor) *dwlt: towards rr tl styd on fr over 1f out* **10/1**	65+
43	**7**	*nk*	**Harry Bosch**[110] 3824 2-9-3 NeilCallan 11 (Brian Meehan) *led and set modest pce: qcknd ent st: hdd & wknd over 1f out* **16/1**	64
3	**8**	*3*	**Kelvingrove (IRE)**[18] 6872 2-9-3 TomQueally 7 (Sir Henry Cecil) *mid-div: rdn and no hdwy fnl 2f* **8/1**	57
3	**9**	*2 ¼*	**Sadfig**[85] 4677 2-9-3 RobertWinston 5 (Clive Brittain) *trckd ldrs tl wknd 2f out* **33/1**	52
	10	*nk*	**Makin (IRE)** 2-9-3 (t) AdamKirby 9 (Marco Botti) *s.s: a bhd* **50/1**	51+
4	**11**	*1 ½*	**Fehaydi**[95] 4330 2-9-3 AdamBeschizza 10 (William Haggas) *a towards rr* **25/1**	48
6	**12**	*1 ¼*	**Nateeja (IRE)**[18] 6876 2-8-12 TadhgO'Shea 13 (Marcus Tregoning) *rdn 3f out: a bhd* **33/1**	40
0	**13**	*6*	**Bertie Moon**[9] 7103 2-9-0 SophieDoyle(3) 4 (Geoffrey Deacon) *plld hrd: chsd ldrs tl wknd over 2f out* **100/1**	31

1m 41.26s (1.46) **Going Correction** -0.025s/f (Stan) **13** Ran SP% **119.7**
Speed ratings (Par 95): **91,90,90,87,86 85,85,82,80,79 78,77,71**
toteswingers 1&2 £25.90, 2&3 £0.00, 1&3 £12.90 CSF £12.46 TOTE £3.70: £1.10, £2.40, £3.20; EX 15.90 Trifecta £164.70 Pool: £470.11 - 2.14 winning units..
Owner Highclere Thoroughbred Racing - Archer **Bred** The Kingwood Partnership **Trained** Newmarket, Suffolk

FOCUS
The pace was slow and the time was 3.34 seconds off the first division, as a result of which the form is not the most reliable.

NOTEBOOK
Greatwood didn't build on his useful debut effort when a beaten favourite at Salisbury next time, but he was reported to have been unsuited by ground on the soft side that day, and here he got the job done despite probably not being helped by the lack of pace. He has a really likeable attitude and is bred to improve with time and distance. (op 7-4 tchd 2-1)
Stasio(USA)'s sales prices increased significantly to 280,000gns this year, and he's related to winners in North America. He showed plenty of ability despite racing keenly. (op 9-2)
Enobled, a half-brother to useful sprinter Ladyship, out of dual Group 1 winning miler Peeress, kept on well from the steady pace and can go on from this. (op 16-1)
Interior Minister shaped okay on his debut at Wolverhampton and again showed ability, although he was well placed. He might be more of a handicap type. (op 25-1)
Layl(USA) didn't build on his Newmarket debut but wasn't helped by the slow pace and can be given another chance. (op 5-1)

7325 BETDAQ CASINO GAMES NURSERY 1m (P)
7:50 (7:50) (Class 4) (0-85,82) 2-Y-O **£3,428** (£1,020; £509; £254) **Stalls** Low

Form				RPR
41	**1**		**Cat O'Mountain (USA)**[56] 5742 2-9-7 **82** MickaelBarzalona 6 (Mahmood Al Zarooni) *little s.i.s: sn trcking ldr: rdn wl over 1f out: r.o ins fnl f: led fnl 75yds: pushed out* **2/1**[1]	87+
001	**2**	*hd*	**Muharrib (IRE)**[47] 5992 2-9-6 **81** SilvestreDeSousa 3 (Saeed Bin Suroor) *led: rdn wl over 1f out: r.o fnl f: hdd fnl 75yds: hld nring fin* **6/1**	86
1553	**3**	*2 ¼*	**Filfil (USA)**[21] 6775 2-9-5 **80** WilliamBuick 8 (Mahmood Al Zarooni) *hld up: rdn over 2f out: no imp tl r.o ins fnl f: wnt 3rd towards fin* **3/1**[2]	79
4104	**4**	*¾*	**Everleigh**[14] 6980 2-9-2 **77** RyanMoore 9 (Richard Hannon) *broke wl: sn lost pl: hdwy on outer to press ldrs 5f out: rdn wl over 2f out: kpt on same pce fnl f* **11/2**	75
3065	**5**	*2*	**Club House (IRE)**[10] 7079 2-8-2 **70** DanielCremin(7) 7 (Robert Mills) *s.i.s: towards rr: rdn wl over 2f out: sme late prog but nt gng pce to get involved* **25/1**	63
61	**6**	*nk*	**Sesentum**[15] 6947 2-9-4 **79** KierenFallon 5 (Luca Cumani) *in tch: rdn to chse ldrs over 2f out: no ex fnl 100yds* **4/1**[3]	72
535	**7**	*4*	**Causeway Foot (USA)**[46] 6043 2-8-10 **71** MichaelO'Connell 2 (Jedd O'Keeffe) *trckd ldrs: effrt over 2f out: wknd fnl f* **25/1**	54
6406	**8**	*4*	**Claude Greenwood**[20] 6815 2-9-1 **76** JamesDoyle 4 (Sylvester Kirk) *hld up but in tch: rdn over 2f out: sn outpcd: wknd ent fnl f* **25/1**	50

1m 40.08s (0.28) **Going Correction** -0.025s/f (Stan) **8** Ran SP% **119.5**
Speed ratings (Par 97): **97,96,94,93,91 91,87,83**
toteswingers 1&2 £3.60, 2&3 £2.20, 1&3 £1.40 CSF £15.15 CT £34.30 TOTE £2.10: £1.02, £3.70, £2.80; EX 13.40 Trifecta £105.20 Pool: £604.73 - 4.31 winning units..
Owner Godolphin **Bred** Darley **Trained** Newmarket, Suffolk
■ Stewards' Enquiry : Kieren Fallon caution: eased horse prematurely

FOCUS
The pace was slow so this is form to treat with a bit of caution, although it looks fairly straightforward.

NOTEBOOK
Cat O'Mountain(USA) had been off for 56 days since winning C&D maiden. He did well to follow up considering the second had the run of the race and also edged into his path late on. There's probably more to come. (op 5-2 tchd 3-1)
Muharrib(IRE) left his first two efforts well behind when a surprise winner of a 7f Brighton maiden last time, and this was another fair performance, but he may be a little flattered considering he was allowed to set such a modest pace. (op 11-2 tchd 5-1)
Filfil(USA) ruined his chance by refusing to settle and he did well to finish so close. (op 7-2)
Everleigh, up in trip, was caught wider than ideal in trying to sit close to the slow gallop. (op 7-1)
Sesentum did well to win his maiden at Brighton last time considering he challenged off the favoured stands' rail, but it was questionable whether this surface (sire 10% here) would suit as well as soft turf. He duly failed to build on that performance, but this wasn't a bad run - he would have been fifth had his jockey not stopped riding near the line - and he can do better. (op 7-2 tchd 9-2)

7326 DOWNLOAD THE FREE RACING PLUS APP CLASSIFIED STKS 7f (P)
8:20 (8:20) (Class 6) 3-Y-O+ **£1,617** (£481; £240; £120) **Stalls** Low

Form				RPR
6060	**1**		**Maggie Pink**[191] 1424 3-9-0 38 DominicFox 1 (Michael Appleby) *trckd ldrs: rdn to ld over 1f out: r.o: hld on wl fnl 120yds: pushed out* **20/1**	60
04	**2**	*½*	**Clapped**[88] 4583 3-9-0 55 TedDurcan 7 (Ed Vaughan) *s.i.s: sn in mid-div: hdwy over 2f out: nt clrest of runs over 1f out: qcknd up wl to chal ent fnl f: kpt on but being hld fnl 120yds* **8/1**	58
0010	**3**	*2*	**True Prince (USA)**[34] 6396 3-9-0 53 (v[1]) PatDobbs 5 (Amanda Perrett) *mid-div: hdwy over 2f out: sn rdn to press ldrs: ch ent fnl f: kpt on same pce* **6/1**[3]	53
-250	**4**	*1 ½*	**Scouting For Girls**[70] 5231 3-9-0 55 (p) RyanMoore 9 (Jim Boyle) *trckd ldrs: rdn wl over 2f out: kpt on same pce* **7/2**[1]	49
6600	**5**	*1*	**Tribal I D (IRE)**[14] 6982 3-9-0 55 (be) JimCrowley 4 (Jim Boyle) *mid-div: hdwy over 2f out: nt best of runs briefly over 1f out: sn rdn whn swtchd to far rails: kpt on but could nt quite rch ldrs* **9/2**[2]	46
4450	**6**	*1 ¾*	**Saint Boniface**[21] 6774 3-9-0 55 SebSanders 3 (Peter Makin) *hld up bhd: sme prog 2f out: no further imp fnl f* **6/1**[3]	42
0-00	**7**	*¾*	**Vermeyen**[13] 7005 3-8-11 50 SophieDoyle(3) 12 (Geoffrey Deacon) *sn prom: rdn and ev ch 2f out tl jst over 1f out: wknd* **25/1**	40
0000	**8**	*1 ½*	**Moody Dancer**[6] 7189 3-9-0 55 (b) HayleyTurner 6 (William Muir) *led: rdn 2f out: hdd over 1f out: wknd ins fnl f* **14/1**	35
-360	**9**	*3*	**Pastures New**[16] 6941 4-9-2 55 (b[1]) WilliamCarson 8 (Violet M Jordan) *sn pushed along in midfield: hdwy over 3f out: effrt over 2f out: wknd over 1f out* **7/1**	27
0600	**10**	*7*	**Kiss My Heart**[16] 6930 3-9-0 24 LukeMorris 11 (Eric Wheeler) *sn swtchd rt: towards rr: rdn 3f out: wknd over 1f out* **100/1**	
6660	**11**	*1 ¼*	**Noosa Boy**[8] 7148 3-9-0 49 IanMongan 2 (Luke Dace) *a towards rr: wknd over 1f out* **12/1**	
0-00	**12**	*2*	**Peters Pleasure**[15] 6951 3-9-0 32 (v[1]) EddieAhern 10 (Robert Cowell) *mid-div: effrt on outer over 3f out: wknd 2f out* **50/1**	

1m 25.47s (-0.53) **Going Correction** -0.025s/f (Stan)
WFA 3 from 4yo 2lb **12** Ran SP% **118.5**
Speed ratings (Par 101): **102,101,99,97,96 94,93,91,88,80 78,76**
toteswingers 1&2 £8.80, 2&3 £7.60, 1&3 £0.00 CSF £168.02 TOTE £22.70: £8.10, £3.60, £1.10; EX 186.00 TRIFECTA Not won..
Owner A W Bult **Bred** Harcourt Stud **Trained** Danethorpe, Notts

FOCUS
A moderate contest in which the form is fluid with the third the best guide.
Maggie Pink Official explanation: trainer said, regarding the apparent improvement of form, that the filly has matured and strengthened and this was a weak race

7327 TULLAMORE DEW H'CAP 7f (P)
8:50 (8:51) (Class 4) (0-85,85) 3-Y-O+ **£4,075** (£1,212; £606; £303) **Stalls** Low

Form				RPR
4450	**1**		**Numeral (IRE)**[14] 6979 4-9-4 **83** RyanMoore 12 (Richard Hannon) *a.p: led 2f out: sn hrd rdn: strly pressed thrght fnl f: jst hld on: all out* **7/1**	91
1002	**2**	*shd*	**Chapter And Verse (IRE)**[7] 7163 6-9-6 **85** PatDobbs 2 (Mike Murphy) *sn in mid-div on rails: swtchd off rails 3f out: r.o wl for str chal fnl 120yds: jst failed on nod* **4/1**[2]	93
1005	**3**	*hd*	**Shahzan (IRE)**[16] 6939 4-9-5 **84** NeilCallan 8 (Roger Varian) *hld up towards rr: hdwy whn nt clr run jst over 2f out: r.o strly ins fnl f: rapidly clsng on ldrs at fin* **8/1**	91
3010	**4**	*hd*	**Good Authority (IRE)**[21] 6800 5-9-5 **84** TomMcLaughlin 11 (Karen George) *mid-div: rdn over 2f out: hdwy over 1f out: r.o wl fnl f: clsng strly at fin* **8/1**	91
0330	**5**	*½*	**Way Too Hot**[19] 6830 3-9-3 **84** AdamKirby 7 (Clive Cox) *trckd ldrs: rdn over 2f out: ev ch ent fnl f: no ex fnl 75yds* **6/1**[3]	89
11-1	**6**	*1 ¼*	**Take Cover**[25] 6665 5-9-4 **83** RobertWinston 4 (David C Griffiths) *led: rdn and narrowly hdd 2f out: kpt on tl hung rt and no ex ins fnl f* **5/2**[1]	85
6620	**7**	*nse*	**Shifting Star (IRE)**[10] 7083 7-9-6 **85** IanMongan 6 (John Bridger) *chsd ldrs: rdn over 2f out: kpt on same pce fnl f* **25/1**	87
0500	**8**	*¾*	**My Kingdom (IRE)**[10] 7080 6-9-3 **82** (t) WilliamCarson 3 (Stuart Williams) *mid-div: effrt over 2f out: kpt on but nt gng pce to chal* **20/1**	82
-104	**9**	*2 ¼*	**Ongoodform (IRE)**[88] 4580 5-8-9 **81** LouisSteward(7) 13 (Paul D'Arcy) *trckd ldrs: rdn over 2f out: nt pce to threaten: wknd fnl f* **33/1**	75
0003	**10**	*nk*	**Kakatosi**[33] 6432 5-8-11 **83** DanielMuscutt(7) 1 (Andrew Balding) *trckd ldrs: rdn over 2f out: wknd fnl f* **7/1**	76
1000	**11**	*nk*	**Masai Moon**[14] 6979 8-9-2 **81** JamesMillman 14 (Rod Millman) *swtchd rt sn after s: a towards rr* **33/1**	73
3440	**12**	*nk*	**Lujeanie**[32] 6495 6-9-1 **83** (p) PatrickHills(3) 5 (Dean Ivory) *hld up towards rr: effrt to chse ldrs on far rails whn nt clrest of runs over 1f out: wknd fnl f* **33/1**	74

00 **13** *nk* **Oneladyowner**[61] 5557 4-9-4 **83** .... EddieAhern 10 73
(David Brown) *mid-div: rdn over 2f out: wknd fnl f* **25/1**

1m 25.66s (-0.34) **Going Correction** -0.025s/f (Stan)
WFA 3 from 4yo+ 2lb 13 Ran SP% **131.4**
Speed ratings (Par 105): **100,99,99,99,98 97,97,96,93,93 93,92,92**
toteswingers 1&2 £9.70, 2&3 £5.60, 1&3 £9.00 CSF £35.97 CT £246.86 TOTE £8.20: £2.50, £1.10, £3.40; EX 34.80 Trifecta £250.50 Pool: £608.10 - 1.82 winning units..
Owner Highclere Thoroughbred Racing-Flying Fox **Bred** Tinnakill Bloodstock & Forenaghts Stud **Trained** East Everleigh, Wilts
■ Stewards' Enquiry : Patrick Hills three-day ban: use of whip (10, 14, 15 Nov)

FOCUS
A fair handicap, but the pace was steady and the time was 0.19 seconds slower than the earlier nursery. The winner is rated to form with the runner-up to his recent best and the fourth and fifth close to recent marks.
Lujeanie Official explanation: jockey said that the gelding hung right

7328 GLENFIDDICH H'CAP — 1m (P)
9:20 (9:21) (Class 5) (0-75,75) 3-Y-0+ **£2,264** (£673; £336; £168) **Stalls** Low

Form RPR
6052 **1** **Daruband**[7] 7171 4-9-5 **73** ....(v) HayleyTurner 5 84
(Michael Bell) *s.i.s: towards rr: swtchd out and gd hdwy in centre fr 2f out: sn rdn: led ent fnl f: edgd sltly rt: r.o strly* **7/1**[3]
5445 **2** *1 1/4* **Methayel (IRE)**[41] 6176 4-9-5 **73** .... RobertWinston 2 81
(Clive Brittain) *mid-div: hdwy wl over 1f out: rdn and ev ch ent fnl f: wnt 2nd nring fin: nt gng pce of wnr* **10/1**
200 **3** *nk* **Roxelana (IRE)**[35] 6375 3-9-2 **73** ....(t) RyanMoore 7 80
(Jeremy Noseda) *chsd ldrs: rdn 2f out: ev ch ent fnl f: kpt on but nt gng pce of wnr: lost 2nd nring fin* **9/2**[1]
4256 **4** *2* **Paradise Spectre**[52] 5853 5-9-3 **71** .... LukeMorris 8 74
(Mrs K Burke) *disp ld: rdn into clr ld 2f out tl hdd ent fnl f: kpt on same pce* **12/1**
6324 **5** *hd* **Dozy Joe**[7] 7170 4-9-3 **71** ....(p) SebSanders 4 73
(Ian Wood) *mid-div: hdwy 2f out: sn rdn: kpt on same pce ins fnl f* **10/1**
0602 **6** *1* **Silverware (USA)**[18] 6894 4-9-7 **75** .... PatrickMathers 11 75
(Linda Stubbs) *disp ld tl rdn 2f out: one pce fnl f* **16/1**
2305 **7** *1/2* **Great Expectations**[71] 5214 4-9-3 **71** .... PatDobbs 13 70
(J R Jenkins) *s.i.s: in rr: pushed along 2f out: rdn and r.o fr over jst over 1f out: nvr trbld ldrs* **7/1**[3]
0024 **8** *1* **Switchback**[12] 7027 4-9-2 **70** .... PaulMulrennan 6 67
(Michael Easterby) *disp ld tl rdn 2f out: wknd ins fnl f* **11/2**[2]
0011 **9** *1* **Silver Bullitt**[33] 6430 4-9-5 **73** .... GeorgeBaker 12 67
(Gary Moore) *trckd ldrs: rdn 2f out: wknd fnl f* **11/2**[2]
0000 **10** *1 1/2* **Mullins Way (USA)**[16] 6931 4-9-4 **72** .... J-PGuillambert 1 63
(Jo Hughes) *unsettled and awkward leaving stalls: a towards rr* **20/1**
0140 **11** *1 1/2* **Ghostwing**[8] 7145 5-9-7 **75** ....(vt) IanMongan 3 62
(Luke Dace) *trckd ldrs: rdn over 2f out: wknd ent fnl f* **20/1**
2350 **12** *1/2* **Abigails Angel**[60] 5592 5-9-6 **74** .... AdamKirby 9 60
(Brett Johnson) *mid-div: rdn on outer over 2f out: wknd jst over 1f out* **16/1**

1m 37.84s (-1.96) **Going Correction** -0.025s/f (Stan)
WFA 3 from 4yo+ 3lb 12 Ran SP% **121.1**
Speed ratings (Par 103): **108,106,106,104,104 103,102,101,100,99 97,97**
toteswingers 1&2 £0.00, 2&3 £13.20, 1&3 £12.70 CSF £76.97 CT £356.83 TOTE £3.10: £1.30, £5.20, £1.90; EX 102.70 Trifecta £351.30 Part won. Pool: £468.51 - 0.10 winning units..
Owner Mrs June Bownes **Bred** Mickley Stud **Trained** Newmarket, Suffolk

FOCUS
A modest but competitive handicap and straightforward form, rated around the placed horses.
T/Jkpt: £25,432.80 to a £1 stake. Pool of £268,656.89 - 7.50 winning tickets. T/Plt: £23.60 to a £1 stake. Pool of £81754.49 - 2520.92 winning tickets. T/Qpdt: £17.60 to a £1 stake. Pool of £6329.48 - 265.30 winning tickets. TM

7048 NEWMARKET (R-H)
Wednesday, October 24

OFFICIAL GOING: Soft (6.7)
Wind: light across Weather: dry and murky

7329 THOROUGHBRED BREEDERS' ASSOCIATION MEDIAN AUCTION MAIDEN FILLIES' STKS — 7f
2:00 (2:01) (Class 5) 2-Y-0 **£3,234** (£962; £481; £240) **Stalls** Low

Form RPR
23 **1** **Desert Image**[15] 6966 2-9-0 0 .... MichaelHills 8 86+
(Charles Hills) *mde all: rdn and readily drew clr 2f out: in n.d after: eased cl home* **11/4**[2]
2 *4* **Mojo Miss (IRE)** 2-9-0 0 .... KierenFallon 4 76+
(Charles Hills) *hld up in midfield: sme hdwy 2f out: rdn and styd on fr over 1f out: wnt 2nd towards fin: no ch w wnr* **25/1**
3 **3** *3/4* **Capella's Song (IRE)**[21] 6791 2-9-0 0 .... HayleyTurner 12 74
(Michael Bell) *in tch: rdn and outpcd by wnr 2f out: wnt 2nd ent fnl f: plugged on but no imp: lost 2nd towards fin* **2/1**[1]
45 **4** *3 1/2* **Amulet**[14] 6978 2-9-0 0 .... MartinLane 14 65+
(David Simcock) *in tch in midfield: rdn 1/2-way: outpcd over 2f out: styd on steadily u.p fr over 1f out: wnt 4th fnl 75yds: no ch w wnr* **40/1**
5 *nk* **Sunbula (USA)** 2-9-0 0 .... FrankieDettori 10 64+
(Charles Hills) *towards rr: rdn and sme hdwy 2f out: styd on steadily u.p fnl f: no ch w wnr* **25/1**
6 *1 1/4* **Mudawala (USA)** 2-9-0 0 .... NeilCallan 6 61+
(Roger Varian) *midfield: rdn and outpcd over 2f out: rallied over 1f out: kpt on steadily fnl f: no ch w wnr* **10/1**
7 *3 1/2* **Saucy Minx (IRE)** 2-9-0 0 .... JimCrowley 2 51
(Amanda Perrett) *flashed tail leaving stalls: chsd ldrs: outpcd by wnr 2f out: wnt 2nd wl over 1f out tl ent fnl f: wknd* **33/1**
03 **8** *hd* **Tight Fit**[20] 6816 2-9-0 0 .... DaneO'Neill 9 51
(Henry Candy) *t.k.h: chsd wnr tl outpcd 2f out: sn lost 2nd and wl btn: wknd fnl f* **14/1**
00 **9** *4* **Edge Of Glory**[10] 7078 2-9-0 0 .... PatDobbs 3 41
(Richard Hannon) *in tch in midfield: rdn and outpcd ent fnl 2f: wknd u.p over 1f out* **66/1**
0 **10** *1 1/4* **Lavender Bay**[18] 6872 2-9-0 0 .... ShaneKelly 5 37
(Tim Pitt) *stdd after s: hld up in rr: rdn and no hdwy over 2f out: sn wl btn* **50/1**
11 *nk* **Dame Nellie Melba** 2-9-0 0 .... SilvestreDeSousa 7 36
(Mark Johnston) *rn green and pushed along early: in tch: hdwy to chse ldrs after 2f: wknd qckly over 2f out* **16/1**
12 *2 1/4* **Jareeda (USA)** 2-9-0 0 .... TadhgO'Shea 13 31
(Sir Michael Stoute) *stdd s and sn swtchd rt: a bhd* **14/1**
6 **13** *2 1/2* **Whatever You Do (IRE)**[48] 5977 2-9-0 0 .... RyanMoore 1 24
(Richard Hannon) *chsd ldrs: rdn and struggling 1/2-way: bhd over 1f out* **13/2**[3]
14 *1* **Rock Act (IRE)** 2-9-0 0 .... JimmyFortune 15 22
(Peter Chapple-Hyam) *rn green: a bhd* **25/1**

1m 29.24s (3.84) **Going Correction** +0.675s/f (Yiel) 14 Ran SP% **122.0**
Speed ratings (Par 92): **105,100,99,95,95 93,89,89,85,83 83,80,77,76**
toteswingers 1&2 £11.90, 2&3 £16.50, 1&3 £2.30 CSF £78.93 TOTE £2.70: £1.60, £6.80, £1.10; EX 90.20 Trifecta £224.00 Pool: £803.74 - 2.69 winning tickets..
Owner K Abdulla **Bred** Juddmonte Farms Ltd **Trained** Lambourn, Berks

FOCUS
It was dry overnight and the going was soft (GoingStick 6.5). The stalls were on the far side of the far side track. Those with previous experience dominated the betting, the winner was impressive and the third helps set the level.

NOTEBOOK
Desert Image, who'd shown more than enough on her debut (slightly disappointing second time) to suggest she could win a maiden of this class, made just about every yard to score by a wide margin. By Beat Hollow out of a sister to Zafonic, she'll have no trouble getting 1m next year. (tchd 5-2)
Mojo Miss(IRE), who raced on the far rail, was green and got outpaced as things quickened up, but she responded when given a slap and was keeping on well at the finish. Best of the newcomers, she's by Shirocco and a half-sister to five winners, and middle distances are going to suit her next year. (tchd 22-1)
Capella's Song(IRE), who was stepping down in trip, probably didn't improve on her debut effort, but she helps put a marker on the form. (op 13-8 tchd 9-4)
Amulet improved for the switch to softer ground and was keeping on at the finish. She gets a mark now and will be of more interest in handicaps. (op 66-1)
Sunbula(USA), whose dam is an unraced half-sister to US 1m2f and 1m4f Grade 3 winner Mustanfar, is bred for middle distances and quicker ground. Having been held up out the back, she was making quiet progress at the finish. (op 20-1)
Mudawala(USA), who has plenty of scope, was well supported from big prices, and although she failed to land a blow, largely due to greenness, she was keeping on at the finish and clearly has ability. She'll be all the better for this experience. (op 50-1)
Saucy Minx(IRE) got tired in the closing stages but she did show up well for a long way and is another who ought to come on for the run.
Tight Fit might have done better had she settled better. There's plenty of speed in her pedigree and a drop back to sprinting in handicaps wouldn't come as a surprise. (op 12-1 tchd 11-1)
Dame Nellie Melba Official explanation: jockey said that the filly ran green
Whatever You Do(IRE) was in trouble a long way out and perhaps the ground was to blame. (op 7-1 tchd 15-2)

7330 THOROUGHBRED BREEDERS' ASSOCIATION MAIDEN STKS (C&G) — 7f
2:30 (2:32) (Class 4) 2-Y-0 **£4,528** (£1,347; £673; £336) **Stalls** Low

Form RPR
1 **Goodwood Mirage (IRE)** 2-9-0 0 .... FrankieDettori 2 82+
(John Dunlop) *chsd ldrs: rdn 1/2-way: outpcd and looked btn 2f out: rallied gamely u.p to chse ldrs 1f out: led fnl 75yds: styd on wl* **12/1**
2 *3/4* **Legal Waves (IRE)** 2-9-0 0 .... KierenFallon 10 80+
(Brian Meehan) *in tch: rdn and effrt to chal 2f out: sustained duel w ldr tl led ins fnl f: sn hdd and one pce* **12/1**
4 **3** *1 1/4* **Yarroom (IRE)**[119] 3499 2-9-0 0 .... NeilCallan 8 77
(Roger Varian) *led: rdn and jnd 2f out: sustained duel w rival tl hdd ins fnl f: no ex* **5/1**[1]
4 *1 1/4* **Llaregyb (IRE)** 2-9-0 0 .... LiamKeniry 14 74
(David Elsworth) *t.k.h: chsd ldr tl ent fnl 2f: styd on same pce fr over 1f out* **33/1**
0 **5** *2* **Bold And Free**[18] 6876 2-9-0 0 .... WilliamCarson 3 69
(David Elsworth) *in tch: rdn and outpcd ent fnl 2f: kpt on ins fnl f* **50/1**
6 *1 1/2* **The Best Doctor (IRE)** 2-9-0 0 .... JamesDoyle 18 65+
(Jeremy Noseda) *in tch: rdn and unable qck ent fnl 2f: styd on same pce fr over 1f out* **6/1**[2]
7 *1* **Miraaj (IRE)** 2-9-0 0 .... RyanMoore 9 62
(Richard Hannon) *hld up in midfield: rdn and no hdwy over 2f out: no threat to ldrs but plugged on fnl f* **5/1**[1]
6 **8** *hd* **Admiralofthesea (USA)**[141] 2797 2-9-0 0 .... AndreaAtzeni 15 62
(Robert Eddery) *chsd ldrs: rdn and unable qck ent fnl 2f: wknd fnl f* **16/1**
9 *hd* **Rottingdean** 2-9-0 0 ....[1] WilliamBuick 12 63+
(John Gosden) *towards rr: hdwy past btn horses 2f out: styd on fnl f: nvr trbld ldrs* **6/1**[2]
10 *2 3/4* **Estibdaad (IRE)** 2-9-0 0 .... TadhgO'Shea 13 54
(Charles Hills) *s.i.s: t.k.h and sn in tch in midfield: rdn and no hdwy over 2f out: wknd over 1f out* **10/1**
11 *nk* **Dairam (USA)** 2-9-0 0 .... DaneO'Neill 6 53
(John Dunlop) *s.i.s: in rr: sme hdwy fr over 1f out: nvr trbld ldrs* **33/1**
12 *6* **Many Levels** 2-9-0 0 .... EddieAhern 1 37
(John Berry) *a towards rr: rdn and struggling over 2f out: no ch but plugged on fnl f* **66/1**
13 *hd* **Barnaby Brook (CAN)** 2-9-0 0 .... SebSanders 7 37
(Nick Littmoden) *in tch in midfield: rdn and no hdwy over 2f out: wknd wl over 1f out* **66/1**
14 *shd* **Roy Rocket (FR)** 2-8-7 0 .... HannahNunn[(7)] 4 37
(John Berry) *a towards rr: lost tch 2f out* **40/1**
15 *3 1/4* **Smileswithhiseyes (IRE)** 2-9-0 0 .... ChrisCatlin 5 28
(Gay Kelleway) *bhd: virtually t.o 2f out: plugged on fnl f* **100/1**
16 *2* **Blackball (USA)** 2-9-0 0 .... TedDurcan 17 23
(David Lanigan) *s.i.s: a in rr: lost tch 2f out: eased ins fnl f* **25/1**
17 *1 3/4* **Knight Owl** 2-9-0 0 .... JimCrowley 16 19
(James Fanshawe) *in tch in midfield: rdn and wknd over 2f out: wl bhd and eased ins fnl f* **9/1**[3]

1m 30.09s (4.69) **Going Correction** +0.675s/f (Yiel) 17 Ran SP% **120.4**
Speed ratings (Par 97): **100,99,97,96,94 92,91,90,90,87 87,80,80,80,76 74,72**
toteswingers 1&2 £14.70, 2&3 £13.70, 1&3 £12.20 CSF £138.38 TOTE £8.90: £2.70, £3.20, £2.00; EX 113.00 TRIFECTA Not won..
Owner Goodwood Racehorse Owners Group (19) Ltd **Bred** Mrs Chris Harrington **Trained** Arundel, W Sussex

FOCUS
Just like in the previous maiden the winner came up the far rail. The opening level is fluid but the winner can improve.

NOTEBOOK
Goodwood Mirage(IRE), who's a half-brother to winners over all sorts of distances, out of a mare who twice won over 1m4f, was slightly outpaced heading to the 2f marker, but once he hit the rising ground he began to kick into gear and finished well. He might take after his dam more than his sire. (op 11-1)

Legal Waves(IRE) ◆ picked up well to challenge the leader but couldn't hold off the winner's late challenge. Perhaps the winner had an edge in racing nearest the far rail, though, and it was still a good effort from Legal Waves, who hails from a stable that rarely sends out first-time-out winners. He ought to improve plenty for this. (op 14-1)

Yarroom(IRE) had the benefit of previous experience, albeit that debut outing came back in June, and he tried to put it to good use and make all. He didn't quite see it out, though, and it wouldn't be a surprise if this ground wasn't at all what he wants, for after all he is a son of Cape Cross and half-brother to smart fast-ground 2yo Saamidd. (op 4-1 tchd 7-2)

Llaregyb(IRE), prominent throughout, shaped with plenty of promise. He's another from a yard not known for having debutant winners so improvement is likely.

Bold And Free, from the same yard as the fourth, showed the benefit of his debut outing with a much improved effort. He was keeping on at the finish, and it might be that he takes after his dam, who's a half-sister to Group 3 1m2f winner Smokey Oakey, more than his sire, who was a sprinter. (op 66-1 tchd 40-1)

The Best Doctor(IRE) was drawn on the wide outside and got no cover racing on the outer of the pack. A 110,000gns purchase out of an unraced sister to Oaks winner Light Shift, he can do better. (tchd 11-2 and 7-1)

Miraaj(IRE), a half-brother to five winners including multiple 7f-1m1f winner Bolodenka, is by Iffraaj and could well do better over shorter and/or on quicker ground. (op 4-1 tchd 7-2)

Rottingdean, who wore a hood on his debut, was keeping on late. His dam was French Listed-placed and a 9.5f-1m4f winner, and he's likely to appreciate further in time. (op 12-1)

Estibdaad(IRE) raced a shade keenly, which didn't help him get home, but there's no shortage of speed in his pedigree and he'd be interesting dropped to 6f. (op 14-1)

7331 THOROUGHBRED BREEDERS' ASSOCIATION HOUGHTON CONDITIONS STKS 1m

3:05 (3:06) (Class 2) 2-Y-O £7,470 (£2,236; £1,118; £559; £279) Stalls Low

Form				RPR
3123	1		**Hoarding (USA)**[27] 6597 2-9-1 90 ...... WilliamBuick 2 *(John Gosden) racd on far side: pressed ldr tl led 1/2-way: rdn and wnt clr wl over 1f out: in n.d after: eased towards fin* **2/1**[2]	90
216	2	3	**Rhamnus**[103] 4058 2-9-1 89 ...... RyanMoore 3 *(Richard Hannon) racd in centre: awkward leaving stalls: hld up in rr: rdn and effrt over 2f out: battling for 2nd but no ch w wnr fr wl over 1f out: wnt 2nd towards fin* **11/1**	83
021	3	¾	**Master Ming (IRE)**[54] 5797 2-9-3 80 ...... FrankieDettori 5 *(Brian Meehan) racd in centre: overall ldr tl 1/2-way: chsd wnr tl drvn and outpcd 2f out: no ch w wnr and kpt on same pce after: lost 2nd towards fin* **11/2**[3]	84
5430	4	2½	**Ocean Applause**[27] 6599 2-8-12 88 ...... MichaelO'Connell 1 *(John Ryan) racd far side: hld up in rr: rdn and effrt over 2f out: no ch w wnr but pressing for pls 1f out: wknd ins fnl f* **22/1**	73
41	5	14	**So Beloved**[21] 6795 2-9-3 0 ...... JamesDoyle 4 *(Roger Charlton) stdd and stmbld leaving stalls: t.k.h: swtchd lft to r in centre sn after s: rdn and pressed ldrs over 2f out: wknd over 1f out: bhd and eased ins fnl f* **11/10**[1]	53

1m 45.16s (6.56) **Going Correction** +0.675s/f (Yiel) **5** Ran SP% **109.0**
Speed ratings (Par 101): **94,91,90,87,73**
CSF £20.70 TOTE £2.00: £1.60, £4.10; EX 15.90.
Owner H R H Princess Haya Of Jordan **Bred** Sc A R Di Paolo Agostini & Darley **Trained** Newmarket, Suffolk

FOCUS

Despite the evidence of the previous two races Frankie Dettori, aboard Master Ming, led So Beloved and Rhamnus to race wide of the far rail, while the winner stayed on the rail throughout. The winner had the run of the race and the third looks the key to the level.

NOTEBOOK

Hoarding(USA) had the run of the race, making the running on the rail, and pulled clear for an easy success. The bare form probably flatters him, and Ocean Applause, who tracked him on the far rail, is fraudulently rated 88, so getting a correct figure on the race might be a bit tricky. Nevertheless, the winner coped well with the ground (previous outings had all come on good or quicker) and confirmed himself a progressive colt. (op 5-2)

Rhamnus came through to beat Master Ming up the middle, but neither had a chance with the winner. The former got the trip well and clearly appreciates a testing surface. (op 7-1)

Master Ming(IRE) faced no easy task at the weights and didn't run badly in the circumstances. (tchd 5-1 and 6-1)

Ocean Applause is flattered by his mark and this ground possibly wasn't to his liking either. (op 20-1 tchd 25-1)

So Beloved sweated up, slipped leaving the stalls and didn't settle in the race itself. This wasn't his true form. Official explanation: jockey said that the colt slipped on leaving the stalls and ran too free (op 6-5 tchd Evens)

7332 BRITISH STALLION STUDS EBF TBA MAIDEN STKS (DIV I) 1m

3:40 (3:41) (Class 4) 2-Y-O £4,528 (£1,347; £673; £336) Stalls Low

Form				RPR
5	1		**Mujazif (IRE)**[26] 6636 2-9-3 0 ...... (t) KierenFallon 11 *(Brian Meehan) in tch in midfield: hdwy to ld jst over 2f out: sn rdn clr and in command: eased towards fin* **3/1**[2]	84+
	2	3	**Havana Cooler (IRE)** 2-9-0 0 ...... PatrickHills(3) 9 *(Luca Cumani) hld up in tch in rr: rdn and hdwy wl over 2f out: styd on to go 2nd 1f out: no imp on wnr but kpt on* **50/1**	76+
0	3	1¼	**Dashing Star**[18] 6876 2-9-3 0 ...... DaneO'Neill 2 *(David Elsworth) taken down early: chsd ldrs: rdn and outpcd whn edgd lft wl over 1f out: kpt on to go 3rd 1f out: styd on* **50/1**	74+
	4	2	**Hasheem** 2-9-3 0 ...... TadhgO'Shea 7 *(Roger Varian) s.i.s: hld up in tch: rdn and hdwy over 1f out: kpt on fnl f: no threat to wnr* **14/1**	69+
0	5	2¾	**Bursledon (IRE)**[46] 6020 2-9-3 0 ...... RyanMoore 4 *(Richard Hannon) t.k.h: in tch: effrt u.p 2f out: sme hdwy over 1f out: no imp 1f out: wknd ins fnl f* **7/1**[3]	63
2	6	2¼	**Ikhtisas (USA)**[21] 6796 2-9-3 0 ...... FrankieDettori 6 *(Saeed Bin Suroor) t.k.h: chsd ldr after 1f tl over 2f out: sn struggling: wkng whn hmpd over 1f out* **5/2**[1]	59
0	7	1¼	**Relentless (IRE)**[18] 6876 2-9-3 0 ...... WilliamBuick 10 *(John Gosden) led tl rdn and hdd jst over 2f out: btn over 1f out: lost 2nd 1f out and wknd fnl f* **17/2**	56
0	8	hd	**Thorpe (IRE)**[21] 6795 2-9-3 0 ...... JimCrowley 13 *(Ralph Beckett) chsd ldr for 1f: chsd ldrs after tl rdn and struggling over 2f out: wknd wl over 1f out* **11/1**	55
	9	shd	**Furibondo** 2-9-3 0 ...... TedDurcan 8 *(David Lanigan) in tch in rr: rdn and no hdwy over 2f out: wknd 2f out: nvr trbld ldrs* **9/1**	55+
	10	3¾	**Destiny Highway (FR)** 2-9-3 0 ...... JimmyFortune 12 *(Gay Kelleway) in tch in rr of main gp: rdn and struggling over 2f out: sn wknd* **66/1**	47
	11	2½	**No Truth (IRE)** 2-8-12 0 ...... MichaelHills 3 *(Charles Hills) v.s.a: rn green and detached in last: sme hdwy 3f out: sn bhd again* **10/1**	36+

1m 44.18s (5.58) **Going Correction** +0.675s/f (Yiel) **11** Ran SP% **116.1**
Speed ratings (Par 97): **99,96,94,92,90 87,86,86,86,82 79**
toteswingers 1&2 £22.60, 2&3 £90.70, 1&3 £90.70 CSF £145.79 TOTE £4.10: £1.80, £16.80, £8.90; EX 188.50 Trifecta £950.40 Part won. Pool: £1,267.28 - 0.63 winning tickets..
Owner Fawzi Abdulla Nass **Bred** Wardstown Stud Ltd **Trained** Manton, Wilts

FOCUS

The faster of the two divisions by 0.32sec, and this looked a good performance from the winner. The winner is value for more with the next three home shaping well.

NOTEBOOK

Mujazif(IRE), wearing a tongue-tie for the first time, raced on the outer of the pack and away from the favoured far rail, and yet quickened up well heading to the 2f marker and drew clear to win easily. His trainer clearly thinks a bit of him as he considers him a likely type for a Guineas trial in the spring, and it'll be interesting to see how he progresses over the winter. A mile should be right up his street anyway. (op 9-4)

Havana Cooler(IRE) ◆, friendless in the market on his debut for a yard whose juveniles usually need their first outing, raced very green in rear but, once switched and brought with his run, picked up nicely. He looks the type to make up into a decent middle-distance handicapper next year.

Dashing Star was a big price as well, but he was always well positioned just off the lead and on the far rail. He has plenty of size and scope, and ought to make up into a nice 3yo next year. Official explanation: jockey said that the colt hung left

Hasheem, whose dam is an unraced half-sister to smart 6f 2yo winner Suez, also benefited from racing on the far rail. However, he was too green to show what he's truly capable of, and he can only improve. (op 16-1)

Bursledon(IRE) was well supported on this second start, but he disappointed. Perhaps this ground wasn't for him. (op 9-1 tchd 10-1)

Ikhtisas(USA), who also raced keenly, was weakening when hampered. Given his pedigree he'll be of interest if given a spin on the AW. Official explanation: jockey said that the colt was unsuited by the soft ground (op 15-8)

Relentless(IRE) crossed over to lead on the rail but didn't really settle and failed to get home. Quicker ground might suit him in future. (op 10-1 tchd 11-1)

7333 BRITISH STALLION STUDS EBF TBA MAIDEN STKS (DIV II) 1m

4:10 (4:13) (Class 4) 2-Y-O £4,528 (£1,347; £673; £336) Stalls Low

Form				RPR
0	1		**Crop Report (USA)**[18] 6872 2-9-3 0 ...... RyanMoore 12 *(William Haggas) mde all: rdn and drew clr wl over 1f out: in command and styd on strly fnl f: comf* **9/2**	84+
	2	5	**Eshtiaal (USA)** 2-9-3 0 ...... TadhgO'Shea 2 *(Brian Meehan) in tch: rdn and effrt over 2f out: 3rd and no threat to wnr over 1f out: kpt on to go 2nd ins fnl f* **25/1**	73+
5	3	1¼	**Prairie Ranger**[16] 6928 2-9-3 0 ...... JimmyFortune 1 *(Andrew Balding) chsd wnr: rdn and unable qck wl over 1f out: styd on same pce fr over 1f out: lost 2nd ins fnl f* **10/3**[2]	71
5	4	¾	**Duke Of Perth**[18] 6872 2-9-3 0 ...... KierenFallon 6 *(Luca Cumani) chsd ldrs: rdn and outpcd over 2f out: 4th and wl hld fr over 1f out: plugged on* **7/2**[3]	69
	5	1	**Dance King** 2-9-3 0 ...... TedDurcan 7 *(David Lanigan) stdd and swtchd rt s: hld up in tch: rdn and effrt over 2f out: 5th and plugged on same pce fr over 1f out* **14/1**	67+
	6	4½	**Zain Eagle** 2-9-3 0 ...... FrankieDettori 8 *(Gerard Butler) in tch in midfield: rdn and outpcd 2f out: 6th and btn over 1f out: wknd fnl f* **12/1**	57
	7	¾	**Shemaal (IRE)** 2-9-3 0 ...... NeilCallan 4 *(Roger Varian) in tch in midfield: lost pl and rdn over 3f out: wknd 2f out: no ch over 1f out* **11/4**[1]	55
0	8	½	**Halperion**[18] 6872 2-9-3 0 ...... ChrisCatlin 5 *(David Elsworth) pushed along in last trio: rdn and no hdwy 3f out: wknd over 2f out: no ch over 1f out* **50/1**	54
	9	nse	**Street Map (USA)** 2-8-12 0 ...... (p) AntiocoMurgia(5) 10 *(Mahmood Al Zarooni) s.i.s: in tch in last quartet: rdn and sme hdwy 3f out: sn struggling: wknd 2f out: bhd fnl f* **16/1**	54
00	10	½	**Adeem (USA)**[32] 6481 2-9-3 0 ...... DaneO'Neill 3 *(John Dunlop) hld up in tch in last quartet: rdn and struggling 3f out: wknd over 2f out: no ch over 1f out* **22/1**	53

1m 44.5s (5.90) **Going Correction** +0.675s/f (Yiel) **10** Ran SP% **120.5**
Speed ratings (Par 97): **97,92,90,90,89 84,83,83,83,82**
toteswingers 1&2 £36.20, 2&3 £6.00, 1&3 £3.00 CSF £114.92 TOTE £7.00: £3.00, £7.20, £1.10; EX 121.30 Trifecta £159.70 Pool: £1,078.11 - 5.06 winning tickets..
Owner M J Tuckey **Bred** Liberation Farm **Trained** Newmarket, Suffolk

FOCUS

The slower of the two divisions by 0.32sec but the winner was impressive on this second start, with the form behind fluid.

NOTEBOOK

Crop Report(USA), a very late May foal, had clearly learnt plenty from his debut and made just about all on the far rail to win easily. He's a middle-distance prospect for next season and, given his pedigree, at some point he really ought to be given a chance to show what he can do on artificial surfaces. (op 4-1 tchd 7-2)

Eshtiaal(USA) ◆, who also raced on the rail, got a nice lead into the race and kept on well to do best of the newcomers. He's by Dynaformer, so will probably appreciate getting on a quicker surface (sire's progeny have a fantastic 19% strike-rate on good to firm, compared to 11% on soft), and coming from the yard he does, improvement is assured for this debut effort. (op 20-1)

Prairie Ranger ran a sound race, building on his debut effort, and should make up into a middle-distance handicapper next year. (op 7-2 tchd 4-1 in a place)

Duke Of Perth, bred to appreciate this sort of ground, couldn't confirm his debut form with Crop Report, when finishing two lengths in front of him. He did race two off the rail, though. (op 11-4)

Dance King, who cost 210,000gns and is a half-brother to US 8.5f Grade 2 winner Sun Boat, showed ability and ought to benefit from the outing. (op 12-1 tchd 8-1)

Zain Eagle, a half-brother to two winners in the US, didn't run badly on his debut given he raced towards the outer of the pack for most of the race. (op 14-1)

Shemaal(IRE), a half-brother to Modeyra, who won a 1m2f Listed race at this track, was far too green to do himself justice and ought to have learnt plenty from this. (op 9-1)

7334 THOROUGHBRED BREEDERS' ASSOCIATION FILLIES' H'CAP 1m

4:45 (4:48) (Class 2) (0-100,94) 3-Y-O+ £12,938 (£3,850; £1,924; £962) Stalls Low

Form				RPR
2120	1		**Hippy Hippy Shake**[18] 6877 3-9-1 88 ...... KierenFallon 8 *(Luca Cumani) racd in centre: in tch in midfield overall: rdn and hdwy 3f out: led over 1f out: kpt on wl fnl f: rdn out* **13/2**[3]	99+
-435	2	¾	**Raasekha**[74] 5101 4-9-10 94 ...... TadhgO'Shea 13 *(Charles Hills) racd in centre: overall ldr: rdn and hdd over 1f out: kpt on u.p but a hld fnl f: 2nd of 7 in gp* **14/1**	102

0110 **3** ¾ **Speedi Mouse**[46] 6023 3 -8-177 RaulDaSilva(3) 12 83
(Philip McBride) *racd in centre: chsd ldrs: 3rd and drvn over 1f out: styd on same pce ins fnl f: 3rd of 7 in gp* **10/1**

0311 **4** 2 **No Poppy (IRE)**[12] 7030 4 -9-892 FrankieDettori 14 94
(Tim Easterby) *racd in centre: hld up in tch: hdwy u.p over 1f out: styd on same pce ins fnl f: 4th of 7 in gp* **4/1**[1]

0500 **5** ¾ **Diverting**[88] 4579 4 -8-1282 HarryBentley 4 82
(William Jarvis) *racd far side: in tch in midfield overall: rdn and effrt over 1f out: led gp but nt on terms w ldrs over 1f out: kpt on fnl f: 1st of 8 in gp* **20/1**

2122 **6** nk **Subtle Knife**[19] 6830 3 -8-1083 WilliamCarson 1 82
(Giles Bravery) *racd far side: hld up in rr: rdn and hdwy over 2f out: drvn and pressing gp ldr but nt on terms w ldrs over 1f out: kpt on: 2nd of 8 in gp* **6/1**[2]

0560 **7** hd **Firdaws (USA)**[35] 6379 3 -9-491 (b) DaneO'Neill 16 90
(Roger Varian) *racd in centre: hld up in tch: rdn and effrt 2f out: no imp over 1f out: kpt on ins fnl f: nvr trbld ldrs: 5th of 7 in gp* **33/1**

3013 **8** 3 **Hurricane Lady (IRE)**[16] 6931 4 -8-1080 NickyMackay 9 72
(Mike Murphy) *racd in centre: stdd s: hld up in rr: sme hdwy u.p over 1f out: kpt on but nvr able to chal: 6th of 7 in gp* **25/1**

054 **9** 1½ **Epernay**[8] 7128 5 -8-979 (vt) MichaelO'Connell 2 67
(Ian Williams) *racd far side: towards rr and niggled along: rdn and swtchd lft over 1f out: kpt on ins fnl f: nvr trbld ldrs: 3rd of 8 in gp* **14/1**

5511 **10** nk **Raheeba**[27] 6613 3 -8-881 (b) JoeFanning 17 69
(Mark Johnston) *racd in centre: chsd overall ldr tl 2f out: wknd over 1f out: 7th of 7 in gp* **14/1**

1650 **11** 2¾ **Junket**[26] 6638 5 -8-676 JimmyQuinn 5 57
(Dr Jon Scargill) *racd far side: hld up towards rr: rdn and hdwy over 2f out: no imp and nt on terms w ldrs in centre over 1f out: wknd fnl f: 4th of 8 in gp* **9/1**

000 **12** 2 **Poisson D'Or**[19] 6830 3 -8-982 JamesDoyle 3 59
(Rae Guest) *racd far side: chsd ldr for 2f: styd prom: rdn ent fnl 2f: btn over 1f out: wknd fnl f: 5th of 8 in gp* **16/1**

4111 **13** 12 **Shena's Dream (IRE)**[35] 6381 3 -8-780 LiamJones 7 29
(William Haggas) *racd far side: led gp and chsd ldrs overall: rdn ent fnl 2f: wknd over 1f out: fdd fnl f: 6th of 8 in gp* **7/1**

2034 **14** 2½ **Tuscania**[65] 5420 4 -9-084 FrederikTylicki 6 27
(Lucy Wadham) *racd far side: chsd gp ldr and prom overall after 2f: rdn over 2f out: wknd over 1f out: fdd fnl f: 7th of 8 in gp* **14/1**

3330 **15** 8 **Red Larkspur (IRE)**[86] 4647 3 -7-1177 PhilipPrince(7) 11
(Roger Teal) *taken down early: racd far side: in tch tl 1/2-way: wl bhd fnl 2f: 8th of 8 in gp* **50/1**

1m 43.04s (4.44) **Going Correction** +0.675s/f (Yiel)
WFA 3 from 4yo+ 3lb **15**Ran SP% **125.3**
Speed ratings (Par 96): **104,103,102,100,99 99,99,96,94,94 91,89,77,75,67**
toteswingers 1&2 £14.10, 2&3 £0.00, 1&3 £22.30 CSF £93.92 CT £925.10 TOTE £4.70 : £1.80, £6.30, £4.10 ; EX 92.70 Trifecta £890.20 Part won. Pool: £1,187.06 - 0.61 winning tickets.
Owner Helena Springfield Ltd **Bred** Meon Valley Stud **Trained** Newmarket, Suffolk

FOCUS
A decent fillies' handicap. They split into two groups here and rather surprisingly, given the earlier results on the card, it was the bunch that raced up the centre of the track that came out on top. The winner recorded a personal best with the third pretty much to form.

NOTEBOOK
Hippy Hippy Shake appreciated the drop in class from Listed company and stayed on strongly to score. Although she'd done her previous racing over 1m2f, this stiff mile suited her well. (op 11-2 tchd 5-1)
Raasekha, who had an excuse last time when struck into (ground was fast as well), bounced back to her best in defeat, appreciating this softer ground. She could have more to offer if kept in training. (op 16-1)
Speedi Mouse, a three-time winner on good to firm this year, showed her versatility with a fine effort off a career-high mark on this much more testing surface. (op 20-1)
No Poppy (IRE) likes this sort of ground and has been in good form of late, but she just seemed to be found out by her latest 4lb rise in the handicap. (op 9-2 tchd 11-2)
Diverting came out best of those that raced on the far side, where the pace didn't look as strong. She has been eased slightly, 4lb since the beginning of the year to be precise, but could probably still do with a bit more leniency. (op 25-1)
Subtle Knife, second on the far side, was ridden to get the trip, and saw it out well enough without necessarily improving for it. (op 9-2)
Firdaws(USA), whose connections held Classic expectations for her at the end of last season, just didn't train on from two to three, and she achieved little in finishing fifth of seven in her group here. (op 28-1)
Red Larkspur (IRE) Official explanation: trainer said that the filly was unsuited by the soft ground

7335 THOROUGHBRED BREEDERS' ASSOCIATION NURSERY 1m 1f
5:20 (5:20) (Class 4) (0-85,85) 2-Y-0 **£3,881** (£1,155; £577 ; £288) **Stalls** Low

Form RPR

116 **1** **Shrewd**[60] 5579 2 -9-785 HayleyTurner 1 89+
(Michael Bell) *stdd s: hld up in last pair: hdwy over 2f out: rdn to chal over 1f out: led jst ins fnl f: styd on wl and gng away at fin* **11/4**[1]

6414 **2** 2¼ **Sennockian Star**[11] 7060 2 -8-771 JoeFanning 3 70
(Mark Johnston) *in tch: rdn and effrt to ld over 2f out: drvn and hrd pressed over 1f out: hdd jst ins fnl f: no ex and btn fnl 75yds* **10/3**[2]

430 **3** ½ **Monsieur Rieussec**[32] 6481 2 -8-1377 EddieAhern 8 75
(Jonathan Portman) *t.k.h: trckd ldrs tl wnt 2nd 2f out: rdn and ev ch over 1f out: no ex ins fnl f* **4/1**[3]

3340 **4** 7 **Rainbow Beauty**[25] 6675 2 -8-1074 (p) NickyMackay 2 58
(Gerard Butler) *t.k.h: chsd ldr: rdn and ev ch ent fnl 2f: outpcd and btn over 1f out: wl btn fnl f* **28/1**

556 **5** nk **Shamaheart (IRE)**[57] 5704 2 -8-471 RyanPowell(3) 6 54
(Richard Hannon) *in tch: rdn and effrt jst over 2f out: drvn and btn over 1f out: edgd lft and wknd fnl f* **11/2**

041 **6** 12 **Divine Angel (IRE)**[6] 6928 2 -8-468 JimmyQuinn 7 27
(Phil McEntee) *led tl rdn and hdd over 2f out: wknd over 1f out* **16/1**

0612 **7** 17 **Quintilian (IRE)**[61] 5552 2 -9-684 FrankieDettori 4 9
(Mahmood Al Zarooni) *stdd s: t.k.h: hld up in last pair: wknd ent fnl 2f: wl bhd fnl f: t.o* **9/2**

1m 56.73s (5.03) **Going Correction** +0.675s/f (Yiel) **7**Ran SP% **112.6**
Speed ratings (Par 97): **104,102,101,95,95 84,69**
toteswingers 1&2 £2.30, 2&3 £4.90, 1&3 £2.60 CSF £11.75 CT £34.63 TOTE £2.80 : £1.30, £3.10; EX 14.30 Trifecta £86.90 Pool: £1,185.45 - 10.22 winning tickets.
Owner Sheikh Marwan Al Maktoum **Bred** Darley **Trained** Newmarket, Suffolk

FOCUS
They all came up the centre of the track in this nursery, and it was quite a test in the conditions for these 2-y-os. The time was decent and the form looks sound.

NOTEBOOK
Shrewd disappointed on the July course on fast ground last time, but he'd been given a break since then and, back on a softer surface, he returned to form in good style, picking up well in the ground and going on to score comfortably. There could be a nice middle-distance handicap in him next year. (tchd 5-2 and 3-1 in a place)
Sennockian Star, who sweated up beforehand, improved for the step up in trip, as many do from his yard, and should get further still next year. (op 7-2 tchd 3-1)
Monsieur Rieussec, for whom there was market support on his handicap debut, also got warm beforehand, and raced keenly. He travelled well into contention and got the trip fine, but might have given the winner more of a race had he settled better early. (op 9-2)
Rainbow Beauty also raced a little keenly early and didn't get home as a result. (op 33-1 tchd 22-1)
Shamaheart(IRE), who like the third was well supported, may not have been at home on the ground. He's by Shamardal so might be worth a try on the AW (23% strike-rate). (op 7-1)
Divine Angel (IRE) didn't get home over this longer trip against tougher opposition. (op 10-1)
Quintilian(IRE), who isn't bred for this sort of ground, has been gelded since he last ran and could do with getting back on the Polytrack. (op 4-1 tchd 5-1)
T/Plt: £353.60 to a £1 stake. Pool: £61,052.30 - 126.03 winning tickets. T/Qpdt: £83.20 to a £1 stake. Pool: £4,926.22 - 43.80 winning tickets. SP

7336a - 7342a & 7343a (Foreign Racing) - See Raceform Interactive

5726
DEAUVILLE (R-H)
Wednesday, October 24
OFFICIAL GOING: Fibresand: standard; turf: very soft

7343a PRIX DES RESERVOIRS - HARAS D'ETREHAM (GROUP 3) (2YO FILLIES) (TURF) 1m (R)
1:50 (12:00) 2-Y-0 **£33,333** (£13,333; £10,000 ; £6,666 ; £3,333)

RPR

1 **Tasaday (USA)**[16] 2 -8-90 MaximeGuyon 4 104+
(A Fabre, France) *trckd ldrs gng wl: chal ldr ent fnl f: hands and heels to ld 100yds out: pushed out: comf* **2/5**[1]

2 1 **Cocktail Queen (IRE)**[31] 6790 2 -8-90 Christophe-PatriceLemaire 6 101
(David Elsworth) *broke wl and led: hdd narrowly over 3 1/2f out: styd prom: shkn up and led again 2 1/2f out: rdn over 1f out: hdd 100yds out: kpt on but no ex* **13/1**

3 3 **Meri Shika (FR)**[17] 6909 2 -8-90 ThierryJarnet 3 95
(J Bertran De Balanda, France) *trckd ldrs towards outside: 3rd and ev ch under 2f out: rdn and nt qckn 1 1/2f out: one pce u.p fnl f* **68/10**[3]

4 3 **Milena's Dream (IRE)**[37] 2 -8-90 OlivierPeslier 4 88
(Y De Nicolay, France) *chsd ldng gp: outpcd over 1 1/2f out: kpt on again ins fnl f: nvr on terms* **6/1**[2]

5 nk **Cassiopee (FR)**[40] 6225 2 -8-90 AntoineHamelin 1 87
(Y Barberot, France) *in rr: effrt towards outside appr 1 1/2f out: plugged on at same pce fnl f* **9/1**

6 6 **Delegation (FR)**[32] 2 -8-90 StephanePasquier 3 74
(M Rulec, Germany) *pressed ldr on ins: led narrowly over 3 1/2f out: hdd 2 1/2f out: sn rdn and nt qckn fr 2f out: wknd fnl f* **20/1**

1m 46.67s (5.87) **6**Ran SP% **120.4**
WIN (incl. 1 euro stake): 1.40. PLACES: 1.10, 2.30. SF: 11.50
Owner Godolphin SNC **Bred** Darley Stud Management Co Ltd **Trained** Chantilly, France

NOTEBOOK
Tasaday(USA) justified her short odds with a cosy success. By Nayef out of a mare who was a two-time Group 3 winner at around 1m2f, she should appreciate the Prix de Diane distance next year, and her rider said he thinks she could be a Classic filly next year.
Cocktail Queen (IRE) winner of a Nottingham maiden last time out, improved dramatically on this step up in class, and her trainer sees her as an Oaks type for next year.

7345a PRIX DU SAUBOUAS (CONDITIONS) (3YO) (FIBRESAND) 7f 110y
3:55 (12:00) 3-Y-0 **£12,083** (£4,833; £3,625 ; £2,416 ; £1,208)

RPR

1 **Spoil The Fun (FR)**[46] 6067 3 -9-30 JulienAuge 11 102
(C Ferland, France) **23/10**[1]

2 1½ **Silverheels (IRE)**[13] 7010 3 -8-130 OlivierPeslier 10 94
(Paul Cole) *racd in 2nd on outside on settling: rdn early in st: r.o u.p to take ld 1f out: r.o wl: hdd 100yds out: jst hld on for 2nd* **10/1**

3 hd **Jellicle (IRE)**[56] 3 -8-90 (b) FabriceVeron 8 90
(H-A Pantall, France) **34/1**

4 nk **Baby Cross**[88] 3 -8-130 JohanVictoire 5 93
(J-C Rouget, France) **73/10**

5 2½ **Al Malek (FR)**[9] 3 -8-130 FranckBlondel 2 87
(Mario Hofer, Germany) **9/1**

6 ¾ **Tibaldi (FR)**[42] 3 -8-90 StephanePasquier 3 81
(Mme C Head-Maarek, France) **7/1**

7 nk **Ideechic (FR)**[337] 3 -8-90 AntoineHamelin 6 80
(D Allard, France) **31/1**

8 hd **Hi Ya Pal (USA)**[305] 1171 3 -8-130 ThierryThulliez 9 83
(N Clement, France) **9/2**[2]

9 ¾ **Shomoukh (USA)**[189] 3 -8-90 MaximeGuyon 4 78
(F-H Graffard, France) **48/10**[3]

10 nk **Acappello (GER)**[20] 3 -8-130 TheoBachelot 7 81
(W Mongil, Germany) **37/1**

1m 30.09s (90.09) **10**Ran SP% **118.0**
WIN (incl. 1 euro stake): 3.30. PLACES: 1.70, 3.10, 5.30. DF: 15.60. SF: 27.90
Owner Prime Equestrian S.A.R.L. **Bred** Snig Elevage **Trained** France

GEELONG (L-H)
Wednesday, October 24
OFFICIAL GOING: Turf: good

7346a CENTREBET GEELONG CUP (GROUP 3 H'CAP) (3YO+) (TURF) 1m 4f
6:00 (12:00) 3-Y-0+
£128,289 (£35,526; £17,763 ; £8,881 ; £4,934 ; £3,947)

RPR

1 **Gatewood**[11] 7073 4 -8-100 GlenBoss 7 110+
(John Gosden) *trckd ldr in 2nd on outer: rdn to chal 2f out: led ent fnl f: edgd rt: styd on wl cl home: cosily* **11/5**[1]

2 3/4 **Chateau Margaux (AUS)**[12] 4-8-7 0 LukeNolen 2 106+
(Peter G Moody, Australia) *midfield on outer: rdn 3f out: bmpd by rival on turn into st: r.o to chal 1 1/2f out: sn outpcd by wnr: styd on ins fnl f: wnt 2nd post* **9/1**
3 shd **Brigantin (USA)**[66] 5400 5-9-1 0 UmbertoRispoli 1 114
(A Fabre, France) *prom in 3rd on inner: rdn 3f out: swtchd out and bmpd rival on turn into st: swtchd bk ins and styd on to go 2nd cl home: dropped to 3rd post* **5/2**[2]
4 1 **Back In Black (NZ)**[18] 7-8-7 0 CraigNewitt 4 104
(John Steffert, New Zealand) *led: set slow pce: rdn and strly pressed 2f out: hdd ent fnl f: no ex and dropped to 4th cl home* **60/1**
5 1 1/4 **Maluckyday (NZ)**[18] 6-9-3 0 (p) JimCassidy 3 112+
(Michael, Wayne & John Hawkes, Australia) *slow to stride and hld up in last on inner: rdn 3f out: styd on wl ins fnl f but nvr a threat* **6/1**
6 4 1/2 **Tac De Boistron (FR)**[102] 4120 5-9-3 0 CoreyBrown 5 105
(Michael Kent, Australia) *hld up in last trio on outer: rdn 3f out: outpcd over 1 1/2f out and on btn: fdd* **10/1**
7 shd **Exceptionally (NZ)**[11] 7073 6-8-7 0 (bt) DeanYendall 6 95
(Terry & Karina O'Sullivan, Australia) *hld up in last pair on outer: rdn in last 3f out and sn outpcd: plugged on wout threatening ins fnl 1 1/2f* **11/2**[3]

2m 34.1s (154.10) 7 Ran SP% **110.2**
PARI-MUTUEL (NSW TAB - all including au$1 stakes): WIN 3.10 PLACE 1.60, 4.10; DF 12.20; SF 17.30.
Owner G Strawbridge, Glenlogan Park Stud Et Al **Bred** George Strawbridge **Trained** Newmarket, Suffolk

FOCUS
This contest has produced the last two winners of the Melbourne Cup, but those renewals did contain more runners. The early pace was steady and the race turned into a sprint.

NOTEBOOK
Gatewood was well positioned throughout and struck for home at the right time before holding on gamely while challenged. His European form in 2012 was progressive and he's still lightly raced for his age, plus he handles both good and soft ground. His connections are hoping their runner gets a hefty penalty in order to make the line-up in Flemington. His victory also pays a handsome compliment to Shahwardi, who beat him at Caulfield last time.
Chateau Margaux(AUS) wasn't proven at this distance, and her effort backs up the impression that the early fractions weren't exactly testing.
Brigantin(USA), who was giving weight away to the front two, didn't shape badly all things considered, especially as he was knocked around a little in the final 3f. The Cozzene gelding had finished a place in front of Shahwardi when last seen in France during August so, with this effort under his belt, he can be expected to run well next month when the longer trip in the Melbourne Cup ought to suit.
Maluckyday(NZ), second to Americain in the 2010 Melbourne Cup, was ridden very much in the style of a horse trialling for bigger targets. He definitely caught the eye.
Tac De Boistron(FR), whose jockey rode Gatewood last time, was a strong stayer in his homeland on easy ground, so the way the race developed didn't suit.

6806 SOUTHWELL (L-H)
Thursday, October 25

OFFICIAL GOING: Standard
Wind: Light across Weather: Heavy cloud

7347 BRAMLEY APPLE H'CAP (DIV I) 1m (F)
1:30 (1:31) (Class 6) (0-65,65) 3-Y-O+ **£1,704** (£503; £251) **Stalls** Low

Form RPR
0031 1 **No Dominion (IRE)**[21] 6810 3-9-0 **61** GrahamLee 9 73
(James Given) *midfield: gd hdwy on outer over 3f out: cl up over 2f out: rdn to ld ent fnl f: styd on* **13/8**[1]
0062 2 1 **Bold Marc (IRE)**[10] 7095 10-8-12 **63** ow3 ConorHarrison(7) 2 73
(Mrs K Burke) *trckd ldrs: hdwy wl over 2f out: rdn to chse ldng pair over 1f out: kpt on u.p fnl f* **9/1**
504 3 1 1/4 **Eastern Hills**[34] 6452 7-9-7 **65** (p) IPoullis 7 72
(Alan McCabe) *cl up: led wl over 2f out: sn jnd and rdn: drvn and hdd ent fnl f: one pce* **8/1**[2]
2230 4 3 1/4 **Thrust Control (IRE)**[17] 6941 5-8-10 **54** (p) MichaelO'Connell 4 54
(Tracy Waggott) *led: rdn along 3f out: sn hdd: drvn and plugged on same pce fnl 2f* **14/1**
43 5 1/2 **Auto Mac**[40] 6258 4-9-4 **62** (p) LukeMorris 3 61
(Neville Bycroft) *dwlt: sn in tch: rdn along to chse ldrs wl over 2f out: kpt on same pce* **9/1**
0010 6 5 **Master Of Song**[88] 4627 5-9-2 **63** (p) MarkCoumbe(3) 5 50
(Roy Bowring) *s.i.s and in rr: hdwy 3f out: rdn along over 2f out: plugged on: nvr nr ldrs* **16/1**
5643 7 2 1/4 **Bonnie Prince Blue**[31] 6530 9-9-1 **59** DaleSwift 11 41
(Ian McInnes) *dwlt and bhd tl sme late hdwy* **28/1**
0-03 8 3/4 **Burns Night**[40] 6259 6-8-13 **64** JacobButterfield(7) 6 44
(Ollie Pears) *dwlt: a towards rr* **17/2**[3]
3000 9 4 **General Tufto**[22] 6794 7-8-6 **57** ow3 (b) DavidBergin(7) 13 28
(Charles Smith) *bhd and sn rdn along: nvr a factor* **28/1**
-000 10 2 3/4 **Thoroughly Red (IRE)**[70] 5258 7-8-4 **51** oh6 NeilFarley(3) 14 16
(Suzzanne France) *in tch: rdn along over 3f out: sn wknd* **100/1**
105- 11 1 3/4 **Riczar**[314] 7782 4-8-11 **55** RichardKingscote 1 16
(Tom Dascombe) *chsd ldr: rdn along 3f out: sn wknd* **16/1**
5335 12 hd **Tahnee Mara (IRE)**[33] 6477 3-9-3 **64** (p) AmyRyan 12 24
(Kevin Ryan) *prom: rdn along 3f out: drvn over 2f out and sn wknd* **9/1**
500 13 3 1/4 **Woteva**[68] 5345 6-8-6 **57** (p) DanielleMooney(7) 8 10
(Nigel Tinkler) *a in rr* **50/1**

1m 40.71s (-2.99) **Going Correction** -0.35s/f (Stan)
WFA 3 from 4yo+ 3lb 13 Ran SP% **118.0**
Speed ratings (Par 101): **100,99,97,94,94 89,86,86,82,79 77,77,74**
toteswingers 1&2 £4.60, 1&3 £3.80, 2&3 £6.90 CSF £15.74 CT £97.70 TOTE £2.00: £1.40, £2.90, £2.60; EX 14.80 Trifecta £123.20 Pool: £561.99 - 3.42 winning tickets..
Owner J Barson **Bred** N Cable & M Smith **Trained** Willoughton, Lincs

FOCUS
This was the first AW racing on the track for three weeks and the sand was harrowed beforehand. Division one of the 1m handicap. The form looks reasonable for the grade with the placed horses both well treated at present.
Riczar Official explanation: vet said filly bled from the nose

7348 BRAMLEY APPLE H'CAP (DIV II) 1m (F)
2:00 (2:03) (Class 6) (0-65,65) 3-Y-O+ **£1,704** (£503; £251) **Stalls** Low

Form RPR
3-02 1 **Royal Holiday (IRE)**[100] 4192 5-9-0 **58** (p) DanielTudhope 9 67
(Marjorie Fife) *sn trcking ldrs: hdwy and cl up over 3f out: led wl over 2f out: rdn over 1f out: styd on wl fnl f* **16/1**
0644 2 1 **River Ardeche**[45] 6105 7-9-1 **59** BarryMcHugh 14 66
(Tracy Waggott) *in tch on outer: gd hdwy 3f out: cl up 2f out: rdn to chal wl over 1f out: drvn and ev ch ent fnl f: kpt on same pce* **7/1**
004 3 5 **El Dececy (USA)**[40] 6230 8-9-5 **63** (tp) AdamKirby 2 59
(Charles Smith) *led: rdn along 3f out: sn hdd and drvn: kpt on same pce* **16/1**
6004 4 3/4 **The Blue Banana (IRE)**[149] 2589 3-9-4 **65** JamesSullivan 6 59
(Edwin Tuer) *chsd ldrs: rdn along 3f out: drvn over 2f out: kpt on same pce* **14/1**
0540 5 3/4 **Maz**[34] 6458 4-9-6 **64** SamHitchcott 10 56
(Alan Bailey) *chsd ldrs: rdn along wl over 2f out: sn one pce* **8/1**
0060 6 shd **Mubtadi**[44] 6127 4-9-7 **65** (t) LiamJones 7 57
(Ismail Mohammed) *s.i.s and in rr: hdwy over 3f out: rdn along wl over 2f out: kpt on: nrst fin* **6/1**[3]
4341 7 1/2 **Tony Hollis**[51] 5910 4-8-3 **54** ow1 GemmaTutty(7) 12 45
(Karen Tutty) *towards rr: effrt 3f out: sn rdn and sme hdwy 2f out: n.d* **8/1**
6-24 8 1/2 **Elusive Warrior (USA)**[94] 4406 9-8-6 **57** (p) NoraLooby(7) 5 47
(Alan McCabe) *prom on inner: rdn along 3f out: grad wknd* **16/1**
0404 9 1 3/4 **Chronic Flame (TUR)**[16] 6949 3-8-10 **57** (t) HayleyTurner 13 42
(Marcus Tregoning) *midfield: pushed along and outpcd over 3f out: in rr tl sme late hdwy* **4/1**[1]
0305 10 shd **This Ones For Eddy**[94] 4405 7-8-11 **55** LukeMorris 8 40
(John Balding) *in tch: rdn along wl over 3f out: sn wknd* **33/1**
0001 11 nk **Menadati (USA)**[42] 6157 4-9-3 **61** KirstyMilczarek 4 46
(Peter Hiatt) *a in rr* **5/1**[2]
0600 12 4 **Icy Blue**[14] 7003 4-9-2 **60** AmyRyan 3 35
(Richard Whitaker) *in tch: rdn along 3f out: sn drvn and wknd* **16/1**

1m 41.72s (-1.98) **Going Correction** -0.35s/f (Stan)
WFA 3 from 4yo+ 3lb 12 Ran SP% **118.8**
Speed ratings (Par 101): **95,94,89,88,87 87,86,86,84,84 84,80**
toteswingers 1&2 £12.10, 1&3 £27.60, 2&3 £27.90 CSF £124.25 CT £1863.30 TOTE £15.80: £3.20, £2.40, £4.20; EX 103.70 TRIFECTA Not won..
Owner Mrs Marion Turner **Bred** E Tynan **Trained** Stillington, N Yorks

FOCUS
Division two of the 1m handicap and it was a wide-open affair, run at a fast tempo. The form is average for the grade with the runner-up rated to his summer turf form.
Chronic Flame(TUR) Official explanation: trainer's rep had no explanation for the poor form shown
Menadati(USA) Official explanation: jockey said gelding did not face the kickback

7349 MIRROR PUNTERS CLUB MEDIAN AUCTION MAIDEN STKS 1m (F)
2:30 (2:30) (Class 6) 2-Y-O **£1,704** (£503; £251) **Stalls** Low

Form RPR
45 1 **Alwilda**[72] 5184 2-8-12 0 LukeMorris 2 66+
(Sir Mark Prescott Bt) *chsd ldrs: niggled along 1/2-way: pushed along to chse ldng pair 3f out: rdn to chal wl over 1f out: led jst ins fnl f: edgd lft and kpt on wl towards fin* **4/1**
05 2 1 1/4 **Codebreaker**[29] 6571 2-9-3 0 JimmyFortune 5 68
(Hughie Morrison) *sn led: rdn along 2f out: hdd jst ins fnl f: sn drvn and no ex last 100yds* **9/4**[2]
0454 3 nk **Roman Order (IRE)**[24] 6733 2-9-3 68 KierenFallon 6 68
(Brian Meehan) *prom: cl up 3f out: chal over 2f out: sn rdn and ev ch tl drvn and one pce ins fnl f* **2/1**[1]
3 4 3 1/2 **Dude Alert (IRE)**[20] 6844 2-9-3 0 WilliamBuick 7 60
(Peter Chapple-Hyam) *cl up on outer: rdn along 3f out: wknd wl over 1f out* **7/2**[3]
660 5 3/4 **Valley Of Wings**[16] 6945 2-9-3 62 ShaneKelly 3 58
(Robert Cowell) *cl up: rdn along over 3f out: sn outpcd and bhd* **25/1**
00 6 17 **Fiance Fiasco**[21] 6816 2-8-12 0 ChrisCatlin 1 16
(James Evans) *a towards rr: rdn along over 3f out: sn outpcd and bhd* **100/1**
054 7 6 **Princess Hollow**[110] 3842 2-8-12 54 BarryMcHugh 4 3
(Tony Coyle) *sn outpcd and a bhd* **25/1**

1m 42.31s (-1.39) **Going Correction** -0.35s/f (Stan) 7 Ran SP% **115.0**
Speed ratings (Par 93): **92,90,90,86,86 69,63**
toteswingers 1&2 £2.20, 1&3 £2.30, 2&3 £1.50 CSF £13.53 TOTE £3.90: £3.00, £1.50; EX 16.50.
Owner Miss K Rausing **Bred** Miss K Rausing **Trained** Newmarket, Suffolk

FOCUS
The market principals dominated in this maiden and the market leaders set a reasonable standard.

NOTEBOOK
Alwilda was urged along from the gate and never travelled with ease but kept responding for pressure to grind out a determined success. She disappointed when favourite at Ayr last time but showed her true colours here, and the further she went the better she looked. From a good family who improve with age and distance, she is likely to make up into a decent staying handicapper next season. (op 2-1)
Codebreaker has progressed with experience and was just worn down in the final furlong. He has a high knee action and is good enough to win a maiden on this surface. (op 5-1)
Roman Order(IRE) handled the Fibresand well on his AW debut but just got outstayed when it mattered. Now 0-5 in maidens, one would think handicaps beckon. (tchd 15-8 and 9-4)
Dude Alert(IRE) ran better than his finishing position suggests. He moved well until rounding for home and may be better over sprint trips. (op 9-2)

7350 BREEDERS' CUP LIVE ONLY ON ATR NOVICE STKS 6f (F)
3:05 (3:05) (Class 5) 2-Y-O **£2,264** (£673; £336; £168) **Stalls** Low

Form RPR
3000 1 **Secret Destination**[19] 6883 2-9-0 73 SilvestreDeSousa 1 71
(Brian Ellison) *cl up on inner: rdn along wl over 2f out: pushed up to chal over 1f out: rdn to ld ent fnl f: sn edgd rt: drvn out* **3/1**[2]
5000 2 1 1/4 **Bougaloo**[21] 6822 2-9-0 50 (v[1]) ShaneKelly 4 67
(Alan McCabe) *slt ld: rdn along and hdd over 2f out: cl up and ev ch ent fnl f: sn drvn and kpt on same pce* **50/1**
5156 3 2 1/4 **Double Your Money (IRE)**[15] 6980 2-9-5 82 JoeFanning 3 66
(Mark Johnston) *cl up: led over 2f out: sn rdn: drvn and hdd ent fnl f: sn btn* **1/3**[1]
2210 4 1 **Kicken Off (IRE)**[98] 4230 2-9-2 71 (p) AdamKirby 2 60
(Phil McEntee) *stdd s: hld up: effrt and n.m.r over 1f out: sn swtchd lft and rdn: flashed tail and no hdwy* **18/1**[3]

1m 15.48s (-1.02) **Going Correction** -0.35s/f (Stan) 4 Ran SP% **107.2**
Speed ratings (Par 95): **92,90,87,86**
CSF £43.61 TOTE £1.90; EX 21.70.
Owner Brian Ellison **Bred** Jtz International **Trained** Norton, N Yorks

FOCUS
Just the four runners for this novice event and it produced a surprise result. The winner is rated just below her best.

NOTEBOOK

Secret Destination kept on gamely to see off her three rivals. She hugged the rail before showing tenacity in the straight to fend off the big outsider. Her trainer does so well at Southwell and the horse has run well every time here. She will reportedly go to the sales next week. (op 11-4)

Bougaloo ran a stormer at a big price to take second. He was bustled along from the gate to race prominently and he helped the winner by softening up the favourite. The visor has sparked improvement from the gelding and if it works next time he could be posed for nursery success.

Double Your Money(IRE) bolted up on his Fibresand debut in August but hasn't gone forward from that maiden success. One may argue he was pestered for the lead on both flanks throughout, but he just didn't pick up when asked for maximum effort. This rates as his third disappointing effort in a row. (op 4-9)

Kicken Off(IRE) wasn't beaten far into fourth, having stayed on at the one pace. He is in good hands as his trainer has a decent record at this track. (op 9-1)

7351 ATTHERACES.COM BREEDERS' CUP SITE NOW LIVE H'CAP 5f (F)

3:35 (3:35) (Class 5) (0-65,65) 3-Y-O+ **£2,264** (£673; £336; £168) **Stalls** High

Form RPR

1413 **1** **Havin' A Good Time (IRE)**[8] 7179 3-9-7 **65** NeilCallan 3 87
(Roger Varian) *trckd ldrs: smooth hdwy and cl up over 2f out: led wl over 1f out: pushed clr appr fnl f: easily* **7/4**[1]

00 **2** *5* **Steel City Boy (IRE)**[59] 5681 9-8-12 **56** LukeMorris 2 60
(Garry Woodward) *in tch: hdwy 2f out: sn rdn: styd on ins fnl f: tk 2nd towards fin: no ch w wnr* **11/1**

060 **3** *hd* **Molly Jones**[16] 6961 3-8-11 **55** JohnFahy 11 58
(Derek Haydn Jones) *led: rdn along 2f out: sn hdd and kpt on same pce* **25/1**

0612 **4** *¾* **Fama Mac**[8] 7179 5-9-3 **61** DanielTudhope 9 62
(Neville Bycroft) *prom: rdn along 2f out: drvn over 1f out: sn one pce* **7/2**[2]

252- **5** *1* **Littlesuzie**[310] 7830 3-9-0 **65** (t) NicoleNordblad(7) 12 62
(Hans Adielsson) *chsd ldrs: hdwy and cl up 1/2-way: rdn wl over 1f out: wknd fnl f* **20/1**

2124 **6** *2* **Pavers Star**[10] 7099 3-8-9 **56** (p) NeilFarley(3) 1 46
(Noel Wilson) *s.i.s: hdwy on wd outside and in tch 2f out: sn rdn and wknd over 1f out* **15/2**

006 **7** *¾* **Made In The Shade**[16] 6959 3-8-0 **51** oh1 (p) DanielleMooney(7) 5 38
(Paul Midgley) *a towards rr* **33/1**

0204 **8** *4 ½* **Greek Islands (IRE)**[42] 6157 4-9-2 **60** (b) ChrisCatlin 6 31
(Ed de Giles) *sn outpcd and a bhd* **5/1**[3]

00-0 **9** *2 ½* **Micky Mac (IRE)**[16] 6958 8-8-7 **51** oh6 SilvestreDeSousa 10 13
(Colin Teague) *cl up 2f: sn lost pl and bhd* **50/1**

4000 **10** *1* **Irish Boy (IRE)**[20] 6837 4-9-2 **60** MickyFenton 7 18
(Paul Midgley) *sn outpcd and bhd* **16/1**

59.07s (-0.63) **Going Correction** -0.05s/f (Stan) 10 Ran SP% **114.7**

Speed ratings (Par 103): **103,95,94,93,91 88,87,80,76,74**

toteswingers 1&2 £6.50, 1&3 £12.30, 2&3 £37.50 CSF £21.30 CT £365.54 TOTE £1.90: £1.10, £4.80, £7.20; EX 22.70 Trifecta £665.60 Pool: £1,402.29 - 1.58 winning tickets..

Owner A D Spence **Bred** Twelve Oaks Stud Establishment **Trained** Newmarket, Suffolk

FOCUS

A sprint handicap which yielded an impressive winner. The level is a bit fluid but best rated around the placed horses.

Micky Mac(IRE) Official explanation: jockey said gelding hung left-handed

7352 $150M BREEDERS' CUP POOLS MAIDEN STKS 1m 4f (F)

4:05 (4:06) (Class 5) 3-Y-O+ **£2,385** (£704; £352) **Stalls** Low

Form RPR

5224 **1** **Infinitum**[23] 6770 3-8-12 80 (p) WilliamBuick 11 82
(John Gosden) *towards rr early: hdwy to trck ldrs after 4f: effrt 3f out: rdn to chal 2f out: led over 1f out: styd on wl* **6/5**[1]

464 **2** *2 ½* **Hallmark Star**[79] 4930 3-9-3 75 LukeMorris 8 83
(Gerard Butler) *trckd ldr: led 1/2-way: rdn over 2f out: drvn and hdd over 1f out: kpt on u.p fnl f* **11/4**[2]

3454 **3** *2 ¼* **Toptempo**[20] 6839 3-8-12 77 TedDurcan 7 74
(Mark H Tompkins) *trckd ldrs: hdwy to chse ldr over 3f out: rdn and ev ch over 2f out: drvn appr fnl f and one pce* **10/3**[3]

-606 **4** *8* **Straight Shot (IRE)**[40] 6228 3-9-3 67 (tp) GrahamLee 9 67
(Brian Meehan) *trckd ldrs: effrt and cl up 4f out: rdn along and ev ch over 2f out: sn drvn and wknd over 1f out* **9/1**

40 **5** *8* **All That Remains (IRE)**[20] 6839 7-9-7 0 PaulPickard(3) 10 54
(Brian Ellison) *in tch: rdn along over 4f out: drvn and outpcd fnl 3f* **28/1**

0 **6** *1 ¾* **Tram Express (FR)**[23] 6770 8-9-3 0 (t) WilliamTwiston-Davies(7) 6 51
(Shaun Lycett) *reminders after s: a in rr* **66/1**

0 **7** *8* **Slide Show**[16] 6957 4-9-5 59 DaleSwift 1 33
(Colin Teague) *chsd ldng pair on inner: rdn along over 5f out: sn wknd* **66/1**

0-50 **8** *1 ¼* **Neighbourhood (USA)**[54] 5811 4-9-10 41 ChrisCatlin 12 36
(James Evans) *a in rr* **50/1**

6 **9** *nk* **Thecornishwren (IRE)**[13] 7025 3-8-12 0 KirstyMilczarek 4 31
(John Ryan) *led: pushed along and hdd 1/2-way: rdn over 4f out: wknd 3f out* **66/1**

0- **10** *42* **Wise Lord**[430] 5325 3-9-0 0 AshleyMorgan(3) 2
(Natalie Lloyd-Beavis) *a in rr: t.o fnl 3f* **100/1**

2m 37.13s (-3.87) **Going Correction** -0.35s/f (Stan)

WFA 3 from 4yo+ 7lb 10 Ran SP% **116.1**

Speed ratings (Par 103): **98,96,94,89,84 83,77,76,76,48**

toteswingers 1&2 £1.40, 1&3 £1.90, 2&3 £2.40 CSF £4.53 TOTE £1.90: £1.10, £1.10, £1.50; EX 3.90 Trifecta £5.60 Pool: £1,432.40 - 190.59 winning tickets..

Owner Cheveley Park Stud **Bred** W And R Barnett Ltd **Trained** Newmarket, Suffolk

FOCUS

This middle-distance maiden brought the three market protagonists to the front. The form makes sense, although the winner did not need to match her best.

7353 GUARANTEED $2 MILLION JACKPOT POOL H'CAP 1m 4f (F)

4:40 (4:40) (Class 5) (0-75,75) 3-Y-O+ **£2,264** (£673; £336; £168) **Stalls** Low

Form RPR

0263 **1** **Saaboog**[21] 6812 3-9-0 **70** PatCosgrave 5 87
(James Tate) *trckd ldrs gng wl: smooth hdwy over 3f out: chal on bit over 2f out: led wl over 1f out: clr ent fnl f: kpt on strly* **9/1**

3404 **2** *9* **Honoured (IRE)**[19] 6891 5-8-12 **61** (p) HayleyTurner 3 64
(Michael Appleby) *led: rdn along wl over 2f out: sn jnd: drvn and hdd wl over 1f out: kpt on u.p fnl f: no ch w wnr* **14/1**

0000 **3** *nk* **Jacobs Son**[40] 6255 4-8-13 **62** GrahamLee 1 65
(Robert Mills) *trckd ldrs: effrt 4f out: rdn along and hdwy 3f out: drvn over 1f out: kpt on wl towards fin* **22/1**

2200 **4** *2 ½* **Honest Deal**[28] 6608 4-9-9 **72** RobertWinston 8 71
(Alan Swinbank) *hld up in tch: stdy hdwy 5f out: chsd ldrs wl over 2f out: sn rdn and one pce fr wl over 1f out* **7/1**

1423 **5** *5* **Cape Explorer**[9] 7131 3-9-5 **75** NeilCallan 14 66
(James Tate) *prom: rdn along over 3f out: wknd over 2f out* **9/2**[2]

0420 **6** *¾* **Sun Seal**[16] 6957 3-9-2 **72** JimmyFortune 6 61
(Hughie Morrison) *hld up in rr: hdwy 4f out: effrt on outer and in tch wl over 2f out: sn rdn and no imp* **10/1**

-005 **7** *1* **Souter Point (USA)**[9] 7132 6-9-7 **70** AdamBeschizza 7 58
(Peter Salmon) *hld up in rr: hdwy 4f out: rdn along 3f out: nvr nr ldrs* **16/1**

4102 **8** *21* **Danube River**[9] 7132 3-9-4 **74** SilvestreDeSousa 12 28
(Mark Johnston) *stdd and swtchd lft s: towards rr: hdwy and in tch 1/2-way: rdn along over 4f out: sn wknd: bhd and eased fnl 3f* **5/2**[1]

0/65 **9** *½* **Crystal Rock (IRE)**[20] 6340 7-9-8 **71** BarryMcHugh 9 24
(Tony Coyle) *a towards rr: bhd fnl 3f* **22/1**

0000 **10** *1 ¾* **Rayvin Black**[16] 6971 3-9-1 **71** (b[1]) TedDurcan 13 22
(Mark H Tompkins) *in tch: rdn along over 4f out: sn lost pl: bhd and eased fnl 3f* **10/1**[3]

3/1- **11** *5* **Agglestone Rock**[551] 1215 7-9-5 **75** WilliamTwiston-Davies(7) 4 18
(Philip Kirby) *a in rr: bhd fnl 3f* **25/1**

000 **12** *13* **Mazij**[22] 6794 4-9-10 **73** ChrisCatlin 11
(Peter Hiatt) *prom: rdn along and lost pl over 4f out: sn bhd and eased* **28/1**

0000 **13** *15* **Full Speed (GER)**[20] 6712 7-9-1 **64** MichaelO'Connell 2
(Philip Kirby) *reminders s: sn rdn along to chse ldrs: lost pl bef 1/2-way: bhd fnl 4f: t.o* **14/1**

2m 35.95s (-5.05) **Going Correction** -0.35s/f (Stan)

WFA 3 from 4yo+ 7lb 13 Ran SP% **126.9**

Speed ratings (Par 103): **102,96,95,94,90 90,89,75,75,74 70,62,52**

toteswingers 1&2 £24.80, 1&3 £41.80, 2&3 £29.10 CSF £129.74 CT £2720.88 TOTE £11.10: £2.80, £4.10, £6.90; EX 145.90 TRIFECTA Not won..

Owner Saif Ali **Bred** Rabbah Bloodstock Limited **Trained** Newmarket, Suffolk

FOCUS

A runaway winner of the 1m4f handicap with the second rated close to his turf form.

Danube River Official explanation: jockey said filly had no more to give

7354 BREEDERS' CUP LIVE ONLY ON ATR APPRENTICE H'CAP 6f (F)

5:10 (5:11) (Class 6) (0-55,55) 3-Y-O+ **£1,704** (£503; £251) **Stalls** Low

Form RPR

2244 **1** **Maltease Ah**[17] 6937 3-9-1 **53** DavidBergin 11 66
(Alan McCabe) *qckly away: mde all: rdn and jnd wl over 1f out: drvn and kpt on strly fnl f* **5/1**[2]

600 **2** *1 ¾* **Gracie's Gift (IRE)**[4] 7275 10-8-13 **50** (v) JasonHart 1 57
(Richard Guest) *trckd ldrs on inner: hdwy to chal 2f out: sn rdn and ev ch tl drvn and no ex ins fnl f* **6/1**[3]

0600 **3** *2 ½* **Ace Of Spies (IRE)**[8] 7157 7-9-3 **54** WilliamTwiston-Davies 12 53
(Conor Dore) *a.p: chsd ldng pair 2f out: sn rdn and one pce appr fnl f* **7/1**

0000 **4** *1* **Catalyze**[15] 6982 4-9-1 **52** (t[1]) JoshBaudains 8 48
(Charles Smith) *towards rr: wd st: hdwy over 2f out: sn rdn and styd on fnl f: nrst fin* **9/1**

1600 **5** *4* **Military Green (FR)**[16] 6958 3-8-7 **50** RachelRichardson(5) 2 33
(Tim Easterby) *chsd ldrs: rdn along over 2f out: grad wknd* **10/1**

02R **6** *4* **Rafella (IRE)**[16] 6967 4-9-0 **51** NoelGarbutt 10 21
(Michael Scudamore) *towards rr: sme hdwy over 2f out: nvr a factor* **16/1**

0305 **7** *1* **John Coffey (IRE)**[27] 6640 3-9-1 **53** (p) ShirleyTeasdale 9 20
(David Nicholls) *chsd ldrs: rdn along wl over 2f out: grad wknd* **3/1**[1]

0030 **8** *1 ¼* **Lady Nickandy (IRE)**[166] 2092 3-8-9 **50** (v) GemmaTutty(3) 13 13
(Karen Tutty) *dwlt: a towards rr* **33/1**

400 **9** *2 ¼* **Nafa (IRE)**[8] 7157 4-8-11 **55** LauraSimpson(7) 4 11
(Daniel Mark Loughnane) *towards rr: sme hdwy on inner over 2f out: sn rdn and wknd* **14/1**

6460 **10** *¾* **Poseidon Grey (IRE)**[7] 7204 3-9-1 **53** (p) GeorgeDowning 3 6
(Ian Williams) *chsd ldrs: rdn along 1/2-way: sn wknd* **12/1**

0460 **11** *hd* **Well Bank (IRE)**[85] 4711 3-9-3 **55** GeorgeChaloner 5 8
(Colin Teague) *dwlt: a in rr* **28/1**

0-00 **12** *11* **Toothache**[93] 4434 4-9-4 **55** NathanSweeney 7
(Garry Woodward) *dwlt: a in rr* **16/1**

1m 14.52s (-1.98) **Going Correction** -0.35s/f (Stan)

WFA 3 from 4yo+ 1lb 12 Ran SP% **120.1**

Speed ratings (Par 101): **99,96,93,92,86 81,80,78,75,74 74,59**

toteswingers 1&2 £6.30, 1&3 £5.10, 2&3 £7.40 CSF £35.64 CT £217.61 TOTE £4.70: £2.30, £3.00, £3.20; EX 22.00 Trifecta £49.90 Pool: £857.90 - 12.89 winning tickets..

Owner A S Reid **Bred** A S Reid **Trained** Averham Park, Notts

FOCUS

A low-grade apprentice handicap with the winner pretty much back to form and the second setting the standard.

T/Plt: £63.00 to a £1 stake. Pool: £59,701.92 - 691.05 winning tickets T/Qpdt: £16.10 to a £1 stake. Pool: £3,967.06 - 181.76 winning tickets JR

7249 WOLVERHAMPTON (A.W) (L-H)

Thursday, October 25

OFFICIAL GOING: Standard

Wind: Fresh against Weather: Overcast

7355 BREEDERS' CUP LIVE ONLY ON ATR CLAIMING STKS 5f 20y(P)

5:40 (5:41) (Class 6) 2-Y-O **£1,704** (£503; £251) **Stalls** Low

Form RPR

1101 **1** **Hardy Blue (IRE)**[15] 6975 2-9-2 66 FergusSweeney 7 68
(Jamie Osborne) *a.p: pushed along 1/2-way: rdn over 1f out: hung lft and styd on u.p to ld wl ins fnl f* **11/2**

1424 **2** *½* **Stripped Bear (IRE)**[19] 6890 2-8-8 62 RichardKingscote 3 58
(Tom Dascombe) *w ldr tl led over 1f out: rdn and hdd wl ins fnl f* **7/2**[2]

5001 **3** *4* **Mandy Layla (IRE)**[19] 6890 2-8-8 75 TomEaves 5 44
(Bryan Smart) *led: rdn and hdd over 1f out: no ex ins fnl f* **15/8**[1]

0216 **4** *1 ¼* **Chloe's Dream (IRE)**[28] 6611 2-9-2 65 (p) PJMcDonald 8 47
(Ann Duffield) *chsd ldrs: pushed along and hung rt 1/2-way: rdn over 1f out: styd on same pce* **13/2**

2510 **5** *1 ¾* **Coconut Kisses**[25] 6707 2-8-12 68 JoeFanning 6 37
(Bill Turner) *chsd ldrs: rdn over 1f out: wknd fnl f* **5/1**[3]

2050 **6** *4 ½* **Bamurru (IRE)**[55] 5786 2-9-3 68 (t[1]) SebSanders 1 26
(Peter Makin) *sn pushed along in rr: bhd fr 1/2-way* **22/1**

0040 **7** *1 ¼* **Strange Angel (IRE)**[41] 6212 2-8-8 64 SamHitchcott 4 12
(David Evans) *s.i.s: rdn and wknd 1/2-way* **40/1**

0000 **8** 17 **Jackpot**[8] 7156 2-8-1 38 RyanPowell(3) 2
(Brendan Powell) *sn outpcd* **80/1**

1m 1.54s (-0.76) **Going Correction** -0.125s/f (Stan) **8** Ran SP% **110.4**
Speed ratings (Par 93): **101,100,93,91,89 81,79,52**
toteswingers 1&2 £3.20, 1&3 £2.20, 2&3 £2.50 CSF £23.16 TOTE £5.10: £1.10, £1.40, £1.30; EX 23.30 Trifecta £35.20 Pool: £771.18 - 16.40 winning tickets..Hardy Blue was claimed by Miss D. S. McCormick for £8,000.
Owner Patrick Gage & Tony Taylor **Bred** Philip O'Dwyer **Trained** Upper Lambourn, Berks

FOCUS
Five previous winners in this claimer and the the runner-up sets the level backed up by the winner.

NOTEBOOK
Hardy Blue(IRE) is not that big but she is all heart and made it five wins from her last six starts. She really stuck her head down and battled to get the better of the front-running runner-up, who had 4lb in hand of her on official ratings. (op 7-2)
Stripped Bear(IRE) had accounted for Hardy Blue when taking a nursery at Kempton in August. She took them along and fought off the favourite but had to give best to the ultra-game winner near the line. (op 9-2 tchd 6-1)
Mandy Layla(IRE), fortunate winner of a C&D seller here on her previous start, sat upsides the leader but found little in the home straight. She had 17lb in hand of the winner and her rating of 75 greatly flatters her. (op 2-1 tchd 9-4 and 7-4)
Chloe's Dream(IRE), who had the worst of the draw, stuck on once in line for home after being tapped for toe and is worth a chance over 6f. (op 7-1 tchd 5-1)
Coconut Kisses, officially 6lb ahead of the winner, doesn't seem capable of running two races alike. (op 6-1 tchd 4-1)

7356 ATTHERACES.COM BREEDERS' CUP SITE NOW LIVE FILLIES' H'CAP 1m 141y(P)
6:10 (6:10) (Class 5) (0-75,75) 3-Y-O+ **£2,587** (£770; £384; £192) **Stalls** Low

Form RPR
5421 **1** **Miss Dashwood**[20] 6842 3-9-6 **75** EddieAhern 12 85+
(James Fanshawe) *hld up: edgd lft over 7f out: hdwy over 4f out: led over 1f out: edgd lft ins fnl f: drvn out* **13/8**[1]
2121 **2** 1 1/2 **Sigurwana (USA)**[45] 6102 3-9-3 **72** PaulHanagan 3 75
(William Haggas) *led early: chsd ldr: rdn and ev ch over 1f out: styd on* **6/1**[3]
025 **3** *shd* **Junior Diary (USA)**[50] 5931 3-9-1 **70** KierenFallon 10 73
(Brian Meehan) *chsd ldrs: rdn over 2f out: r.o* **11/1**
5-00 **4** *nse* **Adorable Choice (IRE)**[19] 6895 4-9-4 **69** (v) RichardKingscote 8 72
(Tom Dascombe) *sn pushed along to ld: rdn and hdd over 1f out: styd on same pce ins fnl f* **40/1**
6511 **5** 1/2 **Amba**[82] 4812 6-9-6 **71** WilliamCarson 4 73
(Violet M Jordan) *prom: hmpd over 7f out: sn lost pl: rdn over 3f out: hdwy u.p over 2f out: styd on* **22/1**
5335 **6** 1 1/4 **Ssafa**[16] 6969 4-9-6 **71** SebSanders 6 70
(J W Hills) *chsd ldrs: rdn over 2f out: no ex ins fnl f* **22/1**
2563 **7** 2 1/2 **Feelthedifference**[8] 7171 3-9-0 **69** TomQueally 9 62
(Sir Henry Cecil) *hld up: hmpd over 7f out: hdwy u.p over 2f out: nvr trbld ldrs* **5/1**[2]
6645 **8** 2 **Blackdown Fair**[20] 6840 3-9-3 **72** JamesMillman 13 61
(Rod Millman) *dwlt: in rr: r.o ins fnl f: nvr nrr* **22/1**
1520 **9** 3/4 **Elegant Flight**[33] 6488 3-8-10 **70** (v) MichaelJMMurphy(5) 5 57
(Alan Jarvis) *hld up: hmpd over 7f out: n.d after* **9/1**
060 **10** *nk* **Provisional**[82] 4821 4-9-10 **75** FergusSweeney 2 61
(Martyn Meade) *hld up: rdn over 2f out: a in rr* **33/1**
2340 **11** 3 1/4 **Alkadi (IRE)**[16] 6973 3-9-2 **71** JoeFanning 11 50
(Mark Johnston) *prom: rdn over 2f out: wknd over 1f out* **20/1**
10- **12** 1 1/2 **Cafe Express (IRE)**[404] 6146 3-9-1 **70** PhillipMakin 7 45
(Linda Perratt) *hld up: hmpd over 7f out: n.d* **25/1**
1003 **13** 2 1/2 **Silvas Romana (IRE)**[25] 6710 3-9-2 **71** PaulMulrennan 1 40
(Mark Brisbourne) *chsd ldrs: drvn along over 3f out: wknd over 2f out* **22/1**

1m 49.23s (-1.27) **Going Correction** -0.125s/f (Stan)
WFA 3 from 4yo+ 4lb **13** Ran SP% **118.8**
Speed ratings (Par 100): **100,98,98,98,98 96,94,92,92,92 89,87,85**
toteswingers 1&2 £2.10, 1&3 £5.50, 2&3 £7.60 CSF £9.12 CT £85.96 TOTE £2.50: £1.10, £2.10, £3.80; EX 11.80 Trifecta £22.60 Pool: £616.10 - 20.39 winning tickets..
Owner Helena Springfield Ltd **Bred** Meon Valley Stud **Trained** Newmarket, Suffolk
■ Stewards' Enquiry : Eddie Ahern three-day ban: careless riding (Nov 8-10)

FOCUS
A fair fillies' handicap and it paid to race close to the pace. The form is muddling with the placed horses the best guides.
Blackdown Fair Official explanation: jockey said filly was denied a clear run entering home straight

7357 32RED MEDIAN AUCTION MAIDEN STKS 1m 1f 103y(P)
6:40 (6:42) (Class 6) 2-Y-O **£1,704** (£503; £251) **Stalls** Low

Form RPR
1 **Gioia Di Vita** 2-9-3 0 AndreaAtzeni 12 72+
(Marco Botti) *a.p: rdn over 1f out: r.o to ld wl ins fnl f* **11/2**[3]
0340 **2** 1 1/4 **Chant (IRE)**[51] 5920 2-9-3 66 PJMcDonald 8 68
(Ann Duffield) *mid-div: lost pl over 6f out: hdwy over 2f out: rdn and swtchd lft ins fnl f: r.o* **8/1**
3233 **3** 1/2 **Jullundar (IRE)**[7] 7199 2-9-3 68 MartinHarley 13 67
(Mick Channon) *chsd ldrs: led 3f out: rdn over 1f out: hdd and unable qck wl ins fnl f* **2/1**[1]
055 **4** *shd* **Unison (IRE)**[20] 6841 2-9-3 68 SebSanders 10 67
(Peter Makin) *hld up: hdwy 4f out: jnd ldr over 2f out: rdn over 1f out: styd on same pce wl ins fnl f* **10/1**
6335 **5** 11 **It's Only Business**[71] 5236 2-8-10 65 JakePayne(7) 4 46
(Bill Turner) *sn led: rdn and hdd 3f out: sn hung rt: wknd wl over 1f out* **25/1**
55 **6** *nk* **Spieta (IRE)**[40] 6257 2-8-12 0 KierenFallon 1 40
(Luca Cumani) *sn pushed along and prom: rdn and wknd over 2f out* **10/3**[2]
5000 **7** 1/2 **Baltic Sea (IRE)**[8] 7156 2-8-12 48 SamHitchcott 9 39+
(David Evans) *sn pushed along in rr: drvn along over 3f out: wknd over 2f out* **66/1**
00 **8** 10 **Modern Society**[192] 1411 2-9-3 0 GrahamGibbons 2 25
(Alan McCabe) *sn w ldr tl rdn over 3f out: wknd over 2f out* **100/1**
0 **9** 1 1/4 **Greenfordgirl (IRE)**[13] 7021 2-8-12 0 MartinLane 11 18
(John Weymes) *s.i.s: outpcd* **100/1**
30 **10** 6 **Hello Gorgeous**[7] 7199 2-8-12 0 TomEaves 3 7
(Keith Dalgleish) *s.i.s: sn prom: lost pl and hmpd over 6f out: wknd 4f out: t.o* **33/1**
64 **11** 1 3/4 **Moaning Butcher**[17] 6919 2-9-3 0 JoeFanning 7 8
(Mark Johnston) *chsd ldrs tl rdn and wknd over 3f out: t.o* **12/1**
0 **12** 7 **Dinas Lane**[22] 6787 2-9-3 0 SeanQuinlan 6
(Paul Green) *in rr whn hmpd and hung rt over 7f out: hmpd again over 6f out: lost tch fnl 4f: t.o* **66/1**

2m 2.96s (1.26) **Going Correction** -0.125s/f (Stan) **12** Ran SP% **111.4**
Speed ratings (Par 93): **89,87,87,87,77 77,76,67,66,61 59,53**
toteswingers 1&2 £9.30, 1&3 £3.00, 2&3 £4.10 CSF £41.75 TOTE £4.30: £2.40, £3.00, £1.10; EX 60.40 Trifecta £206.30 Pool: £616.33 - 2.24 winning tickets..
Owner Mrs Lucie Botti **Bred** Hyphen Bloodstock **Trained** Newmarket, Suffolk

FOCUS
A fair 2-y-o median auction maiden - the first four well clear - and the winner is a newcomer bred to go on to much better things and the next four home set a modest if sound standard.

NOTEBOOK
Gioia Di Vita, a nice type, is from the damline of top-class performers Dylan Thomas, Queen's Logic and this year's 1000 Guineas winner Homecoming Queen. Drawn one from the outside, he travelled strongly and quickened up nicely to score in tidy fashion. He can expect a rating in the 70s and looks one to keep an eye on next year. (op 5-1)
Chant(IRE), racing off 66, clearly improved a fair bit for the step up in trip. Switched inside he stayed on in resolute fashion to snatch second near the line. His nursery mark will go up by about 7lb, so he could be worth pulling out again next week. (op 12-1)
Jullundar(IRE), who had the worst of the draw, went down fighting. His turn will surely come. (op 3-1 tchd 15-8)
Unison(IRE), dropped in and a shade keen, made a forward move on the wide outside halfway down the back stretch. Clearly suited by the step up in distance he seems to be learning to settle better. (tchd 9-1)
Spieta(IRE), absent six weeks after a disappointing effort at Newcastle on her second start, was hopelessly outpaced turning in and soon dropped right away. Hopefully she will do better at three. (op 11-4 tchd 5-2)

7358 $150M BREEDERS' CUP POOLS H'CAP (DIV I) 1m 1f 103y(P)
7:10 (7:11) (Class 5) (0-75,75) 3-Y-O **£2,264** (£673; £336; £168) **Stalls** Low

Form RPR
-002 **1** **Layali Dubai (USA)**[16] 6973 3-8-13 **67** SilvestreDeSousa 13 82+
(Saeed Bin Suroor) *a.p: led over 3f out: shkn up over 1f out: r.o wl: eased nr fin* **5/1**[2]
0046 **2** 2 1/4 **Rei D'Oro (USA)**[27] 6647 3-9-0 **68** (b[1]) MartinLane 11 75+
(David Simcock) *hld up: hdwy over 1f out: r.o: no ch w wnr* **20/1**
1042 **3** 1/2 **Sea Fever (IRE)**[13] 7027 3-9-4 **72** KierenFallon 3 78
(Luca Cumani) *trckd ldrs: shkn up over 3f out: rdn over 1f out: styd on same pce fnl f* **13/8**[1]
5443 **4** 1 1/2 **Xinbama (IRE)**[16] 6973 3-9-6 **74** SebSanders 7 77+
(J W Hills) *prom: chsd wnr 3f out: rdn over 2f out: no ex ins fnl f* **13/2**
5102 **5** 1 **Sheila's Buddy**[10] 7116 3-9-7 **75** FergusSweeney 6 76
(J S Moore) *hld up: hdwy over 2f out: rdn over 1f out: hung lft ins fnl f: nt rch ldrs* **10/1**
00 **6** 1/2 **Parley (USA)**[73] 5163 3-9-5 **73** JoeFanning 4 73
(Mark Johnston) *hld up: hdwy over 3f out: rdn over 1f out: no imp fnl f* **25/1**
4045 **7** 1/2 **Sir Trevor (IRE)**[16] 6973 3-9-1 **69** RichardKingscote 10 68
(Tom Dascombe) *hld up: rdn over 1f out: r.o ins fnl f: nvr nrr* **11/2**[3]
3006 **8** 1/2 **Welsh Nayber**[24] 6734 3-8-10 **64** (b) JamesDoyle 12 62
(Amanda Perrett) *s.i.s: swtchd lft sn after s: hld up: hdwy over 1f out: n.d* **16/1**
2535 **9** 1/2 **April Ciel**[13] 7018 3-8-12 **66** LukeMorris 8 63
(Ronald Harris) *chsd ldr: rdn 3f out: wknd fnl f* **14/1**
-005 **10** *shd* **Galilee Chapel (IRE)**[40] 6259 3-8-10 **64** PJMcDonald 5 60
(Alistair Whillans) *led: rdn and hdd over 3f out: wknd fnl f* **33/1**
1540 **11** 2 1/2 **Voice From Above (IRE)**[59] 5680 3-8-13 **67** DanielTudhope 1 58
(Patrick Holmes) *prom: lost pl over 3f out: wknd fnl f* **33/1**
006 **12** *hd* **The Noble Ord**[10] 7108 3-9-1 **69** (t) MartinHarley 9 60
(Sylvester Kirk) *hld up: hdwy 4f out: rdn and wknd over 1f out* **40/1**

2m 0.13s (-1.57) **Going Correction** -0.125s/f (Stan) **12** Ran SP% **122.0**
Speed ratings (Par 101): **101,99,98,97,96 95,95,95,94,94 92,92**
toteswingers 1&2 £27.70, 1&3 £2.30, 2&3 £8.80 CSF £108.13 CT £235.27 TOTE £10.40: £2.40, £7.40, £1.02; EX 95.30 Trifecta £233.20 Pool: £659.20 - 2.12 winning tickets..
Owner Godolphin **Bred** Darley **Trained** Newmarket, Suffolk

FOCUS
What looked a competitive handicap beforehand turned into a one-horse race. The winner looks a fair bit better than the bare form with the placed horses setting the level.

7359 $150M BREEDERS' CUP POOLS H'CAP (DIV II) 1m 1f 103y(P)
7:40 (7:40) (Class 5) (0-75,75) 3-Y-O **£2,264** (£673; £336; £168) **Stalls** Low

Form RPR
6221 **1** **Lean On Pete (IRE)**[34] 6458 3-8-12 **66** ShaneKelly 3 74
(Ollie Pears) *a.p: nt clr run wl over 1f out: shkn up to ld wl ins fnl f: jst hld on* **7/2**[2]
4310 **2** *nse* **Brimstone Hill (IRE)**[16] 6973 3-9-4 **72** WilliamCarson 9 80+
(Anthony Carson) *hld up: nt clr run over 1f out: rdn and r.o wl ins fnl f: jst failed* **14/1**
2-41 **3** 1 **Tawaasul**[146] 2665 3-9-6 **74** PaulHanagan 1 80
(William Haggas) *led: rdn over 1f out: hdd wl ins fnl f* **11/4**[1]
3420 **4** 3/4 **Rock Song**[16] 6973 3-8-10 **64** JamesDoyle 5 68
(Amanda Perrett) *chsd ldrs: rdn over 1f out: styd on* **8/1**
5140 **5** *shd* **Buster Brown (IRE)**[13] 7032 3-9-2 **70** DaleSwift 6 74
(James Given) *hld up: hdwy over 1f out: styd on* **15/2**
0530 **6** 1/2 **Opera Buff**[17] 6933 3-9-0 **68** MartinHarley 11 71
(Sylvester Kirk) *hld up: pushed along over 3f out: hdwy over 1f out: r.o* **18/1**
6034 **7** *hd* **Island Melody (IRE)**[8] 7158 3-8-13 **67** (b[1]) LukeMorris 2 70
(J S Moore) *chsd ldrs: pushed along over 3f out: rdn over 1f out: styd on same pce ins fnl f* **33/1**
0440 **8** 1/2 **Fairyinthewind (IRE)**[28] 6613 3-9-0 **68** SebSanders 12 70
(Paul D'Arcy) *stdd and swtchd lft sn after s: hld up: hdwy over 1f out: hmpd ins fnl f: styd on same pce* **28/1**
1402 **9** 1 3/4 **Charitable Act (FR)**[20] 6842 3-9-7 **75** PhillipMakin 4 73
(William Muir) *chsd ldr: rdn over 2f out: no ex ins fnl f* **7/1**[3]
4314 **10** 1 1/4 **Silke Top**[20] 6847 3-8-5 **64** MichaelJMMurphy(5) 8 59
(William Jarvis) *prom: rdn over 2f out: wknd fnl f* **12/1**
05-4 **11** 2 3/4 **Kuwait Star**[37] 6341 3-8-9 **63** SamHitchcott 10 53
(Jason Ward) *chsd ldrs: rdn over 2f out: wknd over 1f out* **33/1**
50U0 **12** 6 **Hikma (USA)**[20] 6843 3-9-1 **69** (b) JoeFanning 7 46
(Mark Johnston) *hld up: rdn over 2f out: wknd over 1f out* **25/1**

2m 0.18s (-1.52) **Going Correction** -0.125s/f (Stan) **12** Ran SP% **117.1**
Speed ratings (Par 101): **101,100,100,99,99 98,98,98,96,95 93,87**
toteswingers 1&2 £8.10, 1&3 £2.60, 2&3 £5.50 CSF £48.71 CT £152.17 TOTE £5.50: £1.60, £4.50, £1.10; EX 56.60 Trifecta £221.90 Pool: £547.35 - 1.85 winning tickets..
Owner Charles Wentworth **Bred** Mrs T Mahon **Trained** Norton, N Yorks

FOCUS
The complexion of the race changed late on and the winner is rated close to his recent winning mark.
Rock Song Official explanation: jockey said colt hung left-handed

7360 GUARANTEED $2 MILLION JACKPOT POOL H'CAP 7f 32y(P)
8:10 (8:10) (Class 5) (0-75,77) 3-Y-O+ **£2,264** (£673; £336; £168) **Stalls** High

Form RPR
260 **1** **Cut Across (IRE)**[21] 6824 4-9-2 **70** .... SebSanders 11 78
(Nick Littmoden) *pushed along early: sn chsng ldr: rdn over 1f out: styd on to ld wl ins fnl f: jst hld on* **10/1**
0315 **2** *hd* **Chookie Avon**[7] 7202 5-9-7 **75** .... (p) JoeFanning 8 83
(Keith Dalgleish) *chsd ldrs: rdn over 1f out: r.o* **8/1**[2]
0430 **3** *1* **Imperator Augustus (IRE)**[44] 6124 4-9-6 **74** .... PaulMulrennan 10 79
(Patrick Holmes) *led: rdn and hdd wl ins fnl f* **9/1**
0065 **4** *3/4* **Satwa Laird**[9] 7142 6-9-2 **70** .... HayleyTurner 1 73
(Conor Dore) *hld up: rdn and r.o wl ins fnl f: nt rch ldrs* **22/1**
0523 **5** *1 1/2* **Willies Wonder (IRE)**[20] 6840 3-9-0 **75** .... MatthewLawson(5) 9 74
(Charles Hills) *a.p: rdn over 2f out: no ex ins fnl f* **7/2**[2]
0014 **6** *3/4* **Jack Smudge**[13] 7023 4-9-5 **73** .... (v) GrahamLee 7 70
(James Given) *mid-div: hdwy over 2f out: rdn over 1f out: styd on same pce fnl f* **14/1**
500 **7** *nk* **Namwahjobo (IRE)**[14] 6999 4-9-3 **71** .... (v) DanielTudhope 4 67
(Jim Goldie) *hld up: r.o ins fnl f: nvr nrr* **22/1**
2305 **8** *1/2* **Swendab (IRE)**[13] 7023 4-9-2 **70** .... LukeMorris 6 65
(John O'Shea) *hld up: r.o ins fnl f: nrst fin* **33/1**
5351 **9** *shd* **Sunley Pride**[7] 7203 3-9-7 **77** 6ex .... SamHitchcott 3 71
(Mick Channon) *chsd ldrs: rdn over 1f out: no ex ins fnl f* **85/40**[1]
0000 **10** *1 3/4* **George Benjamin**[21] 6812 5-8-11 **70** .... (b[1]) AmyScott(5) 2 60
(Christopher Kellett) *mid-div: hdwy over 2f out: sn rdn: wknd ins fnl f* **66/1**
2442 **11** *3/4* **Silver Rime (FR)**[47] 6047 7-9-4 **72** .... PhillipMakin 5 60
(Linda Perratt) *hld up: a in rr* **17/2**
12-3 **12** *3/4* **Minortransgression (USA)**[280] 22 5-9-3 **71** .... AdamKirby 12 57
(Paul Rich) *hld up: nvr nr to chal* **20/1**

1m 28.09s (-1.51) **Going Correction** -0.125s/f (Stan)
WFA 3 from 4yo+ 2lb **12** Ran SP% **119.5**
Speed ratings (Par 103): **103,102,101,100,99 98,97,97,97,95 94,93**
toteswingers 1&2 £5.70, 1&3 £24.30, 2&3 £13.40 CSF £82.35 CT £757.50 TOTE £11.80: £6.20, £2.30, £3.60; EX 102.80 Trifecta £559.70 Part won. Pool: £746.37 - 0.20 winning tickets..
Owner Nigel Shields **Bred** D J And Mrs Brown **Trained** Newmarket, Suffolk
FOCUS
No hanging about here and the first three home raced up with the pace throughout. A personal best from the winner with the third to his recent turf best.

7361 32RED.COM MEDIAN AUCTION MAIDEN STKS 7f 32y(P)
8:40 (8:42) (Class 6) 3-5-Y-O **£1,704** (£503; £251) **Stalls** High

Form RPR
1 **Haftohaf** 3-9-3 0 .... AdamKirby 4 66+
(Marco Botti) *a.p: chsd ldr over 1f out: shkn up to ld ins fnl f: styd on* **9/4**[1]
6063 **2** *1 3/4* **Lucky Mark (IRE)**[17] 6937 3-9-3 52 .... StevieDonohoe 5 61
(Garry Moss) *led 6f out: rdn over 1f out: hdd and unable qck ins fnl f* **8/1**
3435 **3** *1/2* **Peak Storm**[13] 7025 3-9-3 63 .... LukeMorris 3 60
(John O'Shea) *chsd ldrs: rdn over 2f out: styd on same pce ins fnl f* **11/2**[3]
500 **4** *1 3/4* **Winnetou**[12] 7061 3-9-3 0 .... JamesDoyle 9 55
(Frank Sheridan) *in rr and reminder 5f out: hdwy 2f out: sn rdn: no ex wl ins fnl f* **33/1**
33 **5** *1 3/4* **Zenafire**[59] 5687 3-9-3 0 .... ShaneKelly 6 50
(Reg Hollinshead) *chsd ldrs: drvn along over 2f out: styd on same pce fr over 1f out* **3/1**[2]
6260 **6** *3/4* **Last Supper**[22] 6783 3-8-12 67 .... GrahamGibbons 1 43
(James Bethell) *chsd ldr tl rdn over 1f out: wknd ins fnl f* **13/2**
0006 **7** *2 3/4* **Sweet Grace**[77] 5014 3-8-12 43 .... (t) NickyMackay 7 36
(David Brown) *chsd ldrs: rdn over 1f out: wknd fnl f* **12/1**
8 *7* **Major Buckley (IRE)** 3-9-3 0 .... RobertWinston 10 22
(Alan Swinbank) *s.i.s: outpcd* **12/1**
050 **9** *9* **Absolute Bearing (IRE)**[82] 4798 3-9-3 47 .... PaulMulrennan 11
(Tim Etherington) *sn outpcd* **100/1**
4636 **10** *3/4* **Benidorm**[27] 6643 4-9-0 50 .... (v) AdamCarter(5) 2
(John Wainwright) *in rr: hdwy over 4f out: rdn and wknd over 1f out* **40/1**
0 **11** *3/4* **Mid Yorkshire Golf**[5] 7253 3-8-12 0 .... RobbieFitzpatrick 8
(Peter Grayson) *s.i.s: a in rr* **250/1**

1m 28.79s (-0.81) **Going Correction** -0.125s/f (Stan)
WFA 3 from 4yo 2lb **11** Ran SP% **117.8**
Speed ratings (Par 101): **99,97,96,94,92 91,88,80,70,69 68**
toteswingers 1&2 £6.90, 1&3 £3.60, 2&3 £5.00 CSF £21.12 TOTE £4.40: £1.10, £3.20, £2.20; EX 22.80 Trifecta £71.40 Pool: £500.25 - 5.25 winning tickets..
Owner Miss Catherine Loder **Bred** Ercan Dogan **Trained** Newmarket, Suffolk
FOCUS
A very modest maiden but an unraced winner of some potential. A modest maiden but a decent start from the winner with the third setting the level.
Last Supper Official explanation: jockey said filly lost its action
Sweet Grace Official explanation: jockey said filly hung left-handed

7362 BREEDERS' CUP LIVE ONLY ON ATR H'CAP 7f 32y(P)
9:10 (9:11) (Class 7) (0-50,55) 3-Y-O+ **£1,704** (£503; £251) **Stalls** High

Form RPR
4200 **1** **Renoir's Lady**[53] 5850 4-9-3 **50** .... HayleyTurner 11 58
(Simon Dow) *hld up in tch: shkn up over 1f out: r.o to ld nr fin* **14/1**
0221 **2** *1/2* **See The Storm**[2] 7316 4-9-5 **55** 6ex .... RyanPowell(3) 12 62
(Ian Williams) *s.i.s: hld up: hdwy 1/2-way: led over 1f out: rdn and edgd lft ins fnl f: hdd nr fin* **5/2**[1]
5000 **3** *1/2* **Reginald Claude**[29] 6585 4-8-12 **50** .... LeeNewnes(5) 10 56
(Mark Usher) *hld up: hdwy over 2f out: shkn up ins fnl f: r.o* **22/1**
0560 **4** *1 1/4* **Victorian Number (FR)**[12] 7058 4-9-3 **50** .... (p) GrahamLee 6 52
(Geoffrey Deacon) *chsd ldr tl led wl over 1f out: sn hdd: no ex ins fnl f* **9/2**[2]
0662 **5** *2* **Monsieur Pontaven**[60] 5632 5-9-2 **49** .... (b) DanielTudhope 2 46+
(Robin Bastiman) *s.i.s: hld up: hdwy over 1f out: nt rch ldrs* **5/2**[1]
1546 **6** *nk* **Avon Supreme**[21] 6829 4-8-9 **49** .... LouisSteward(7) 4 45
(Gay Kelleway) *led: hdd wl over 1f out: no ex ins fnl f* **16/1**
4003 **7** *3 1/2* **Media Jury**[27] 6640 5-8-10 **50** .... (p) KevinLundie(7) 9 37
(John Wainwright) *chsd ldrs: rdn over 2f out: wknd fnl f* **33/1**
0000 **8** *3/4* **Best In Show**[7] 7189 3-8-10 **50** .... (tp) MatthewLawson(5) 5 35
(Roger Curtis) *prom: rdn over 1f out: wknd ins fnl f* **28/1**
0046 **9** *2 1/2* **Vhujon (IRE)**[38] 6322 7-9-2 **49** .... RobbieFitzpatrick 3 27
(Peter Grayson) *hld up: nvr on terms* **20/1**
5200 **10** *4* **Bashama**[42] 6158 4-9-2 **49** .... (p) DavidProbert 8 16
(Nikki Evans) *prom: rdn 1/2-way: sn wknd* **25/1**
5454 **11** *4 1/2* **Forty Proof (IRE)**[31] 6546 4-9-2 **49** .... (t) AdamKirby 1
(David Evans) *prom: hmpd over 2f out: sn wknd* **10/1**[3]

1m 29.03s (-0.57) **Going Correction** -0.125s/f (Stan)
WFA 3 from 4yo+ 2lb **11** Ran SP% **116.3**
Speed ratings (Par 97): **98,97,96,95,93 92,88,87,85,80 75**
toteswingers 1&2 £5.10, 1&3 £39.50, 2&3 £15.30 CSF £45.37 CT £642.46 TOTE £16.70: £3.50, £1.30, £6.30; EX 62.80 Trifecta £427.10 Pool: £711.94 - 1.25 winning tickets..
Owner Malcolm & Alicia Aldis **Bred** Laundry Cottage Stud Farm **Trained** Epsom, Surrey
FOCUS
All the runners had an official rating of either 49 or 50. See The Storm, a winner in heavy ground at Yarmouth two days earlier, had to race from a mark of 55 under his 6lb penalty. The form is moderate although the second ran a personal best under his penalty.
Forty Proof(IRE) Official explanation: jockey said gelding suffered interference in running
T/Jkpt: Not won. T/Plt: £29.00 to a £1 stake. Pool: £80,728.67 - 2,029.85 winning tickets T/Qpdt: £22.20 to a £1 stake. Pool: £7,630.17 - 253.30 winning tickets CR

6242 DONCASTER (L-H)
Friday, October 26

OFFICIAL GOING: Soft (good to soft in places; 7.3)
Wind: Moderate half behind Weather: Cloudy

7363 E B F YORKSHIRE RADIO MAIDEN STKS 7f
1:40 (1:41) (Class 5) 2-Y-O **£3,299** (£981; £490; £245) **Stalls** High

Form RPR
1 **Singersongwriter** 2-8-12 0 .... GrahamLee 4 75+
(Ed Dunlop) *dwlt: hmpd and swtchd lft after 100yds: hdwy over 3f out: sn trcking ldrs: led appr fnl f: pushed out: smoothly* **9/2**[3]
026 **2** *2 3/4* **King Of Kudos (IRE)**[35] 6444 2-9-3 68 .... JimCrowley 5 72
(Richard Hannon) *sn trcking ldrs: chal over 2f out: led wl over 1f out: hdd appr fnl f: styd on same pce* **4/1**[2]
5 **3** *3 1/4* **Breden (IRE)**[10] 7127 2-9-3 0 .... WilliamBuick 15 65+
(John Gosden) *hld up in mid-div: hdwy over 2f out: edgd lft 1f out: kpt on one pce* **85/40**[1]
60 **4** *2* **War Lord (IRE)**[20] 6880 2-9-3 0 .... DanielTudhope 11 58+
(David O'Meara) *hld up in rr: effrt and nt clr run over 2f out: kpt on fnl f* **28/1**
5 *hd* **Algorithmic (IRE)** 2-9-3 0 .... TomQueally 10 58+
(Michael Bell) *dwlt: in rr and sn pushed along: kpt on fnl 2f: nvr nr ldrs* **4/1**[2]
0 **6** *3/4* **Sword Of The Lord**[10] 7127 2-9-3 0 .... HayleyTurner 3 56
(Michael Bell) *led over 5f out: hdd wl over 1f out: wknd fnl f* **25/1**
0 **7** *1 1/4* **Halfwaytocootehill (IRE)**[20] 6880 2-9-3 0 .... PaulMulrennan 2 53
(Ollie Pears) *swtchd rt after 100yds: sn chsng ldrs: one pce fnl 2f* **66/1**
8 *nk* **Thankyou Very Much** 2-8-12 0 .... GrahamGibbons 13 47
(James Bethell) *s.i.s: sn in tch: outpcd over 2f out: kpt on fnl f* **33/1**
0 **9** *3/4* **The Mighty Peg**[20] 6880 2-9-3 0 .... PhillipMakin 12 50
(Tim Walford) *chsd ldrs: lost pl wl over 1f out* **100/1**
6 **10** *1 3/4* **Let Me In (IRE)**[13] 7067 2-9-3 0 .... AndrewMullen 8 45
(Nigel Tinkler) *hld up: hdwy into mid-div over 3f out: wknd 2f out* **16/1**
04 **11** *nk* **Antonius**[29] 6603 2-9-3 0 .... TomEaves 7 45
(Linda Stubbs) *trckd ldrs: t.k.h: wknd over 1f out* **12/1**
0 **12** *2* **Loch Fyne Lady**[17] 6966 2-8-12 0 .... RussKennemore 1 34
(John Holt) *w ldrs: wknd 2f out* **100/1**
13 *3/4* **Finn Mac** 2-9-3 0 .... PaddyAspell 14 37
(John Norton) *s.i.s: in rr: bhd fnl 2f* **100/1**
0 **14** *27* **Rovers Till I Die (IRE)**[7] 7219 2-9-0 0 .... MarkCoumbe(3) 9
(Charles Smith) *t.k.h: led over 1f: lost pl over 3f out: sn bhd: t.o* **100/1**

1m 29.74s (3.44) **Going Correction** +0.175s/f (Good) **14** Ran SP% **119.4**
Speed ratings (Par 95): **87,83,80,77,77 76,75,75,74,72 71,69,68,37**
toteswwingers 1&2 £3.30, 2&3 £2.50, 1&3 £4.30 CSF £21.79 TOTE £6.80: £1.90, £1.20, £1.20; EX 30.10.
Owner Cliveden Stud **Bred** Cliveden Stud Ltd **Trained** Newmarket, Suffolk
FOCUS
An average maiden, rated around the second. The winner is capable of better than the bare form and several others showed promise.
NOTEBOOK
Singersongwriter ◆ raced widest of all without cover, but that didn't stop her from running out an easy debut winner on ground that evidently proved up her street. One of three fillies in the race, she's half-sister to most notably Group 2 winner Monitor Closely and also Mount Nelson, the 2009 Eclipse winner for Ballydoyle. One of her other siblings, Stone Of Scone, was a smart middle-distance winner for the same connections and, a horse with plenty of scope, she's one to look forward up in trip as a 3-y-o. (op 8-1 tchd 85-40)
King Of Kudos(IRE), rated 68, held every chance back up a furlong but was firmly put in his place by the promising winner. On this evidence there is a maiden to be won with him and he looks on a workable mark. (op 7-2)
Breden(IRE), well backed, travelled sweetly and had clearly come on for his Leicester debut ten days earlier. He petered out inside the final furlong, though, and may just prefer dropping to 6f in the short term. (op 3-1 tchd 2-1)
War Lord(IRE) ◆ was doing his best work late in the day and posted his most encouraging effort. He now qualifies for a mark and is well up to winning races. (op 25-1)
Algorithmic(IRE), whose yard's 2-y-os are going well at present, cost 340,000gns and is bred to be smart. The subject of support, he ultimately looked to need this initial experience and should last longer next time. (op 7-2)
Sword Of The Lord, his yard's second string, showed up well near the stands' rail for a long way. He ran close enough to his last-time-out debut form with Breden, but this was more promising and he's another that looks well worth a try over 6f. (op 28-1)

7364 E B F KAT COMMUNICATIONS KNOWLEDGE ABOUT TELECOMS MAIDEN FILLIES' STKS 1m (S)
2:10 (2:13) (Class 5) 2-Y-O **£3,299** (£981; £490; £245) **Stalls** High

Form RPR
4 **1** **The Lark**[23] 6790 2-9-0 0 .... HayleyTurner 10 77+
(Michael Bell) *hld up towards rr: stdy hdwy on outer 1/2-way: sn cl up: led 2f out: rdn appr fnl f: kpt on wl towards fin* **7/2**[1]
5 **2** *1/2* **Kalispell (IRE)**[23] 6790 2-9-0 0 .... WilliamBuick 12 76
(Mahmood Al Zarooni) *trckd ldrs: hdwy 2f out: rdn to chal ent fnl f and ev ch tl drvn and no ex last 50yds* **13/2**[3]
53 **3** *1/2* **Auction (IRE)**[23] 6790 2-9-0 0 .... GrahamLee 13 75
(Ed Dunlop) *a.p: cl up 2f out: rdn and ev ch ent fnl f tl no ex last 75yds* **9/1**
5 **4** *2 1/4* **Qawaafy (USA)**[63] 5551 2-9-0 0 .... PaulHanagan 4 70
(Roger Varian) *trckd ldrs: hdwy over 2f out: rdn along and sltly outpcd over 1f out: edgd lft and kpt on ins fnl f: nrst fin* **7/1**

5366 **5** ½ **Curl (IRE)**[65] 5484 2-9-0 66..................................(b¹) RichardKingscote 1 69
(Richard Hannon) *trckd ldrs: hdwy 3f out: rdn along 2f out: drvn and one pce appr fnl f* **20/1**

6 *hd* **Lemon Pearl** 2-9-0 0.. JimCrowley 11 68+
(Ralph Beckett) *hld up in rr: hdwy over 2f out: rdn to chse ldrs and edgd lft over 1f out: kpt on: nrst fin* **25/1**

7 *2* **Winter Snow (IRE)** 2-9-0 0.. FrankieDettori 2 64
(Saeed Bin Suroor) *wnt lft s: sn in tch: hdwy on wd outside to trck ldrs 3f out: effrt over 2f out: sn rdn and one pce* **5/1**²

22 **8** 1 ½ **Vicky Valentine**[28] 6627 2-9-0 0....................................... PhillipMakin 5 61
(Kevin Ryan) *cl up: effrt 2f out and ev ch: sn rdn and wkng whn n.m.r appr fnl f* **12/1**

04 **9** 4 ½ **Roanne (USA)**[17] 6960 2-9-0 0.. AdamKirby 6 51
(Clive Cox) *prom: led wl over 3f out: rdn along and hdd 2f out: wknd over 1f out* **16/1**

10 1 ¾ **Paris Rose** 2-9-0 0.. JoeFanning 8 47
(William Haggas) *in tch: hdwy to chse ldrs 3f out: cl up over 2f out: sn rdn and wknd* **8/1**

5 **11** 1 ¼ **Jillywinks**[17] 6966 2-9-0 0... TomQueally 9 44
(Scott Dixon) *t.k.h early: a towards rr* **25/1**

12 2 ½ **Katie Gale** 2-9-0 0.. ShaneKelly 7 39
(Tim Pitt) *a in rr* **33/1**

6 **13** *5* **Spirit Of Success**[91] 4546 2-9-0 0......................... SilvestreDeSousa 14 28
(Mahmood Al Zarooni) *a in rr* **16/1**

05 **14** 3 ¼ **Boogie De Bispo**[10] 7130 2-9-0 0...................................... ChrisCatlin 3 20
(Stuart Kittow) *led: rdn along 1/2-way: sn hdd & wknd* **200/1**

15 *15* **Fab Lolly (IRE)** 2-9-0 0.. GrahamGibbons 15
(James Bethell) *dwlt: sn in tch on outer: rdn along 1/2-way: sn wknd* **100/1**

1m 41.65s (2.35) **Going Correction** +0.175s/f (Good) **15** Ran SP% **122.2**
Speed ratings (Par 92): **95,94,94,91,91 91,89,87,83,81 80,77,72,69,54**
toteswingers 1&2 £5.90, 2&3 £8.90, 1&3 £6.30 CSF £24.21 TOTE £4.20: £1.80, £2.50, £3.00; EX 40.70.
Owner Lady Bamford **Bred** Lady Bamford **Trained** Newmarket, Suffolk

FOCUS
This is always a decent source of future winners. Rock-solid form with the fifth the key to the level.

NOTEBOOK
The Lark ground it out gamely from the furlong marker and opened her account at the second attempt. Her trainer's juveniles are going strongly at this late stage of the season and, well backed, this was a marked step up on her promising debut fourth at Nottingham 23 days previously. From a family her connections know all about, she ought to stay very well at three and could well turn up in an Oaks trial next year. (op 4-1)

Kalispell(IRE) finished one place behind the winner on her debut at Nottingham so she makes this form look straightforward. It was also a step up from her, despite failing to reverse form, and she ought to have no trouble going one better in something similar soon. (op 15-2)

Auction(IRE) finished just ahead of the first pair last time out, but she had the benefit of experience that day and just failed to confirm the form with her old rivals. No doubt she can win one of these, as she was nicely clear of the remainder, but she also now has the option of nurseries. (tchd 10-1)

Qawaafy(USA), a modest fifth on her Newmarket debut over 7f, was faced with slower ground on this return from a 63-day break. She looked to need all of this longer distance and will likely come on again for it. (op 9-1)

Curl(IRE) performed better again with the addition of first-time blinkers and got the longer trip well enough. She helps set the standard. (op 12-1)

Lemon Pearl ◆ stayed on promisingly under considerate handling. She's one to keep on side next time out and looks a useful middle-distance performer in the making. (tchd 22-1)

Winter Snow(IRE) hails from a yard with a decent record in this maiden and is out of a dam that did well for Godolphin. She's a very late foal though (May 20th), and this debut experience was needed. A sounder surface may also be required. (tchd 9-2 and 11-2)

7365 BET THROUGH THE RACING POST MOBILE APP NURSERY 1m (S)
2:40 (2:40) (Class 3) (0-95,89) 2-Y-O **£5,822** (£1,732; £865; £432) **Stalls** High

Form RPR
6116 **1** **Ronaldinho (IRE)**[23] 6775 2-9-4 86.................................... JimCrowley 3 88
(Richard Hannon) *hld up: hdwy 3f out: chal over 1f out: led last 150yds: edgd rt: hld on wl* **6/1**³

014 **2** ½ **Fat Gary**[10] 7125 2-9-3 85.. RichardKingscote 1 86
(Tom Dascombe) *w ldr: led over 2f out: hdd ins fnl f: keeping on same pce whn crowded in the clsng stages* **8/1**

6102 **3** ¾ **Aint Got A Scooby (IRE)**[12] 7079 2-7-10 67 oh2 ow1. RyanPowell(3) 2 66
(Clive Cox) *chsd ldrs: pushed along over 2f out: outpcd over 1f out: kpt on ins fnl f* **15/2**

5114 **4** 1 ½ **Penny Rose**[20] 6873 2-9-4 86.. JoeFanning 5 82
(Mark Johnston) *trckd ldrs: effrt over 2f out: drvn over 1f out: kpt on same pce* **15/8**²

3212 **5** *25* **Darkening (IRE)**[29] 6597 2-9-7 89.................................. FrankieDettori 4 40+
(Mahmood Al Zarooni) *led: qcknd pce over 2f out: sn hdd: wknd over 1f out: sn heavily eased: t.o: virtually p.u* **7/4**¹

1m 43.9s (4.60) **Going Correction** +0.175s/f (Good) **5** Ran SP% **108.3**
Speed ratings (Par 99): **84,83,82,81,56**
CSF £44.79 TOTE £8.20: £4.30, £4.10; EX 54.50.
Owner Macdonald,Wright,Creed,Smith & Jiggins **Bred** J Fallon **Trained** East Everleigh, Wilts
■ Stewards' Enquiry : Jim Crowley caution: careless riding.

FOCUS
Something of a turn-up in this fair little nursery and it proved a tactical affair. Late-season form.

NOTEBOOK
Ronaldinho(IRE) disappointed in his quest for the hat-trick at Kempton last time, but he bounced right back and posted a career-best effort. He raced furthest away from the stands' rail, which may well have been an advantage, but it was really his liking for soft ground that saw him home in front. He's got a cracking attitude and ought to get further next year. (op 13-2 tchd 7-1)

Fat Gary, rated 1lb inferior to the winner, was the only one to really push that rival inside the final furlong and turned in a decent effort in defeat. He got the extra furlong without fuss and obviously loves some cut underfoot. (op 10-1)

Aint Got A Scooby(IRE) would have been a little closer at the finish had he found a clearer passage nearing the final furlong. He raced off a feather weight on ground he enjoys, though, and helps to put the form into some perspective. (op 9-1)

Penny Rose was down in class and expected to relish the step up in trip. She got bogged down when asked to win the race, though, and this ground found her out. It may also be that she's had enough for the year. (op 13-8 tchd 6-4)

Darkening(IRE) was conceding upwards of 3lb all round, but he dropped out very quickly under pressure and surely the ground was to blame. Official explanation: trainer's rep had no explanation for the poor form shown (tchd 15-8)

7366 RACING POST/SIS BETTING SHOP MANAGER OF YEAR H'CAP 6f
3:15 (3:18) (Class 2) (0-105,105) 3-Y-O+ **£10,350** (£3,080; £1,539; £769) **Stalls** High

Form RPR
5600 **1** **Thunderball**[34] 6466 6-8-5 86..............................(p) SilvestreDeSousa 18 97
(Scott Dixon) *trckd ldrs: hdwy 2f out: sn rdn and edgd lft wl over 1f out: chal ent fnl f: sn drvn: edgd lft and kpt on to ld nr fin* **20/1**

5062 **2** *nk* **Ancient Cross**[6] 7243 8-8-10 91.............................(t) PaulMulrennan 15 101
(Michael Easterby) *trckd ldrs: hdwy 2f out: rdn to ld jst ins fnl f: sn drvn: hdd and no ex nr fin* **10/1**³

450 **3** 1 ¼ **Jonny Mudball**[20] 6882 6-9-1 96....................... (t) RichardKingscote 10 102
(Tom Dascombe) *prom: cl up 1/2-way: led wl over 1f out: sn rdn and hdd jst ins fnl f: drvn and kpt on* **12/1**

1312 **4** *hd* **Khubala (IRE)**[21] 6835 3-8-10 92...............................(b) FrankieDettori 16 99+
(Hugo Palmer) *hld up in rr: hdwy 2f out: rdn and styng on ins fnl f: n.m.r and swtchd rt last 100yds: kpt on: nrst fin* **4/1**¹

2500 **5** *hd* **Farlow (IRE)**[12] 7080 4-8-8 89.. JimCrowley 2 94
(Ralph Beckett) *midfield: hdwy on outer 2f out: rdn to chse ldrs over 1f out: drvn and ch ent fnl f: kpt on same pce* **20/1**

1000 **6** *2* **Shropshire (IRE)**[34] 6468 4-8-11 97...................... MatthewLawson(5) 11 95
(Charles Hills) *hld up: gd hdwy 2f out: sn rdn and styd on fnl f: nrst fin* **20/1**

5050 **7** *nk* **Colonel Mak**[13] 7066 5-8-12 98.. LMcNiff(5) 7 95
(David Barron) *trckd ldrs: hdwy over 2f out: rdn to chse ldrs over 1f out: drvn and one pce fnl f* **10/1**³

0005 **8** ½ **Gatepost (IRE)**[34] 6466 3-8-10 92.................................. PaulHanagan 14 88
(Richard Fahey) *in tch: pushed along and hdwy to chse ldrs 2f out: sn rdn and kpt on same pce fnl f* **11/1**

2261 **9** ¾ **Cheveton**[4] 7295 8-8-7 88 6ex... JoeFanning 1 81
(Richard Price) *prom: rdn along 2f out: drvn appr fnl f: kpt on same pce* **12/1**

2261 **10** ½ **Prodigality**[12] 7080 4-9-1 96 6ex.. GrahamLee 13 88
(Ronald Harris) *towards rr: hdwy 2f out: sn rdn and kpt on: nvr nr ldrs* **9/2**²

0000 **11** *2* **Grissom (IRE)**[34] 6466 6-8-9 90... DavidAllan 6 75
(Tim Easterby) *in tch: hdwy 2f out: rdn to chse ldrs over 1f out: wknd ent fnl f* **25/1**

0100 **12** *nk* **Trade Secret**[13] 7063 5-8-3 87... NeilFarley(3) 4 71
(Mel Brittain) *dwlt and bhd tl sme late hdwy* **50/1**

2600 **13** *hd* **Nasri**[12] 7080 6-8-6 87... HayleyTurner 9 71
(Milton Bradley) *prom: rdn along wl over 2f out: sn wknd* **20/1**

2225 **14** 2 ¾ **Vito Volterra (IRE)**[14] 7030 5-8-5 86............................. AndrewMullen 21 61
(Michael Smith) *chsd ldrs: rdn along wl over 2f out: sn wknd* **22/1**

0400 **15** *shd* **Head Of Steam (USA)**[12] 7080 5-8-10 91................(b¹) WilliamBuick 19 66
(Amanda Perrett) *led: rdn along 1/2-way: hdd wl over 1f out and sn wknd* **33/1**

0300 **16** *nk* **Secret Witness**[20] 6867 6-9-10 105................................(b) TomQueally 20 79
(Ronald Harris) *in tch: rdn along over 2f out: sn wknd* **20/1**

4000 **17** 2 ½ **Advanced**[27] 6659 9-7-12 86... PaulMcGiff(7) 5 52
(Kevin Ryan) *chsd ldrs: rdn along sn after 1/2-way: sn wknd* **25/1**

0335 **18** 1 ¼ **Fitz Flyer (IRE)**[13] 7063 6-8-8 89.................................(v) AdrianNicholls 22 51
(David Nicholls) *dwlt and towards rr: hdwy over 2f out: rdn wl over 1f out: sn btn* **20/1**

00U0 **19** 1 ¼ **West Leake Diman (IRE)**[21] 6835 3-9-2 98.............. RobertWinston 17 56
(Charles Hills) *cl up: rdn along over 2f out: sn wknd* **66/1**

1m 13.26s (-0.34) **Going Correction** +0.175s/f (Good)
WFA 3 from 4yo+ 1lb **19** Ran SP% **127.1**
Speed ratings (Par 109): **109,108,106,106,106 103,103,102,101,101 98,97,97,94,93 93,90,88,86**
toteswingers 1&2 £70.40, 2&3 £25.10, 1&3 £70.40 CSF £179.50 CT £2607.22 TOTE £24.20: £4.10, £2.80, £3.30, £1.70; EX 281.10.
Owner Paul J Dixon **Bred** Mrs Yvette Dixon **Trained** Babworth, Notts
■ Stewards' Enquiry : Silvestre De Sousa two-day ban: used whip above permitted level (Nov 9-10)

FOCUS
A decent and ultra-competitive sprint handicap. They went hard down the centre of the track and the first five came a little way clear. Straightforward form.

NOTEBOOK
Thunderball went for home some way out, but only got up near the finish. He's been somewhat in-and-out of late, but was 4lb lower than when last winning at Ascot in May and is a confirmed mud-lover. It was the 6yo's ninth career success and his trainer intends to keep him on the go.
Ancient Cross was agonisingly denied over the minimum trip at Catterick six days earlier and one has to feel for him again as it was the same story here. This trip on such ground is testing enough for him and he richly deserves to go one better again, but is now due a 4lb rise. (tchd 11-1)
Jonny Mudball showed his true colours again for the drop back a furlong and deserves to get his head back in front. He likely found the ground soft enough, too.
Khubala(IRE) fared best of those coming from off the pace at Ascot last time out, when running another blinder, and has since changed yards. Another 3lb higher, he tanked his way through the race, but ultimately got going too late in the day once again. Don't abandon him. (tchd 9-2)
Farlow(IRE) ◆ made a bold bid nearest to the far rail and this was much better again from him, returned to the C&D that saw his previous success off 3lb lower back in May. He looked well beforehand so could be about to strike again.
Prodigality was penalised for gaining a well-deserved second success of the season at Goodwood 12 days earlier and proved popular once more. After a tardy start, he was laboured some way out and this ground was probably more demanding than he cares for. (op 5-1)

7367 GENTING CLUB SHEFFIELD H'CAP 1m 6f 132y
3:50 (3:54) (Class 4) (0-85,88) 3-Y-O+ **£4,204** (£1,251; £625; £312) **Stalls** Low

Form RPR
0023 **1** **Daneking**[12] 7082 3-9-0 80... WilliamBuick 4 93
(John Gosden) *hld up towards rr: hdwy over 3f out: led over 1f out: styd on wl* **11/2**³

213 **2** 1 ¾ **Tiger Cliff (IRE)**[32] 6537 3-9-2 82.. TomQueally 2 92
(Sir Henry Cecil) *trckd ldrs: effrt over 2f out: chsd wnr fnl f: no real imp* **9/2**²

134 **3** 3 ¼ **Kiwayu**[37] 6359 3-9-0 80...(t) FrankieDettori 12 86
(Luca Cumani) *in rr div: hdwy over 3f out: wnt 3rd 1f out: kpt on same pce* **13/2**

5033 **4** *1* **Jonny Delta**[11] 7098 5-8-12 69... GrahamLee 14 74
(Jim Goldie) *hld up towards rr: hdwy over 3f out: chsng ldrs over 1f out: one pce* **16/1**

1550 **5** *hd* **Scarlet Whispers**[17] 6964 3-8-11 77...............................(p) MickyFenton 18 81
(Pam Sly) *chsd ldrs: led over 2f out: hdd over 1f out: one pce* **50/1**

6060 **6** 3 ½ **Fork Handles**[13] 7068 4-9-9 **80** .... PJMcDonald 15 80
(Mick Channon) *in rr: hdwy over 2f out: nvr nr ldrs* **40/1**

0600 **7** *nk* **Merchant Of Dubai**[28] 6642 7-9-7 **78** ....(v[1]) FrederikTylicki 10 78
(Jim Goldie) *led after 1f: hdd over 2f out: wknd over 1f out* **25/1**

4040 **8** ½ **Cosimo de Medici**[13] 7051 5-9-12 **83** ....(tp) RobertHavlin 8 82
(Hughie Morrison) *s.v.s: hdwy over 3f out: kpt on fnl 2f: nvr a factor* **20/1**

3111 **9** 2 ¼ **Porcini**[14] 7024 3-8-7 **76** .... RaulDaSilva(3) 20 72
(Philip McBride) *trckd ldrs on outer: t.k.h: dropped in rr after 4f: hdwy 3f out: no threat* **14/1**

0242 **10** ½ **Come Here Yew (IRE)**[11] 7098 4-8-12 **72** .... NeilFarley(3) 1 67
(Declan Carroll) *led 1f: chsd ldrs: drvn over 2f out: wknd over 1f out* **16/1**

4004 **11** *nk* **Orsippus (USA)**[11] 7098 6-9-9 **80** .... AndrewMullen 6 75
(Michael Smith) *in rr div: sme hdwy 9f out: drvn over 3f out: grad wknd* **33/1**

5221 **12** 1 ¼ **Yours Ever**[7] 7211 3-9-2 **82** 6ex .... ChrisCatlin 13 75
(Sir Mark Prescott Bt) *w ldrs: wknd 2f out* **6/1**

0500 **13** *12* **Activate**[107] 3953 5-9-8 **79** .... PaulMulrennan 5 57
(Michael Scudamore) *stdd s: hld up in rr: bhd fnl 3f* **40/1**

20 **14** *hd* **Hawkeshead**[21] 6834 5-9-4 **75** .... MichaelO'Connell 16 52
(Ian Williams) *chsd ldrs: reminders over 4f out: lost pl 3f out* **33/1**

0/0- **15** *6* **Bahrain Storm (IRE)**[28] 6654 9-9-7 **78** ....(b) PaulHanagan 3 48
(Noel Quinlan) *mid-div: effrt over 3f out: sn lost pl* **50/1**

0001 **16** *dist* **The Betchworth Kid**[11] 7109 7-10-3 **88** 6ex .... HayleyTurner 11
(Michael Bell) *t.k.h towards rr: pushed along over 5f out: heavily eased 4f out: sn virtually p.u and hopelessly t.o* **4/1**[1]

3m 14.01s (6.61) **Going Correction** +0.575s/f (Yiel)
WFA 3 from 4yo+ 9lb **16 Ran SP% 122.9**
Speed ratings (Par 105): **105,104,102,101,101 99,99,99,98,97 97,97,90,90,87**
toteswingers 1&2 £7.40, 2&3 £8.30, 1&3 £8.10 CSF £28.09 CT £168.97 TOTE £5.70: £1.20, £1.60, £2.50, £3.50; EX 28.90.
Owner Sir Eric Parker & Rachel Hood **Bred** Sir Eric Parker **Trained** Newmarket, Suffolk

FOCUS
While it's a shame Livery didn't turn up, this was still an absorbing staying handicap and it proved a decent test due to the solid pace on. Another step up from the winner.
Yours Ever Official explanation: trainer's rep said race came too soon for the filly
The Betchworth Kid Official explanation: trainer's rep said gelding ran too freely and stopped quickly

7368 LIDGET COMPTON H'CAP (DIV I) 1m 2f 60y
4:25 (4:27) (Class 5) (0-75,79) 3-Y-O+ **£2,264** (£673; £336; £168) **Stalls** Low

Form RPR

1200 **1** **My Mate Jake (IRE)**[14] 7027 4-9-4 **68** ....(b) GrahamLee 7 80
(James Given) *trckd ldrs: hdwy over 3f out: cl up 2f out: sn led and rdn clr appr fnl f: styd on strly* **25/1**

0664 **2** *5* **Aegaeus**[30] 6574 3-9-5 **74** ....(t) FrankieDettori 6 76
(Ed Dunlop) *stdd s and hld up in rr: t.k.h and rapid hdwy on outer 1/2-way: chsd ldr 4f out: led over 2f out: rdn and hdd wl over 1f out: kpt on: no ch w wnr* **9/4**[1]

4101 **3** 1 ½ **The Lock Master (IRE)**[10] 7132 5-10-1 **79** 6ex .... SilvestreDeSousa 1 78
(Michael Appleby) *trckd ldrs: hdwy over 3f out: rdn over 2f out: kpt on same pce* **7/2**[2]

0000 **4** 1 ¼ **Musnad (USA)**[10] 6638 4-9-9 **73** .... PaulHanagan 2 70
(Brian Ellison) *hld up towards rr: hdwy 4f out: rdn along over 2f out: kpt on fnl f: nrst fin* **7/1**[3]

2334 **5** 3 ¾ **Skyfire**[10] 7132 5-9-2 **66** ....(p) MichaelStainton 5 56
(Nick Kent) *sn led: rdn along over 3f out: hdd over 2f out and grad wknd* **10/1**

6430 **6** ½ **Miss Blink**[81] 4883 5-9-5 **69** .... DanielTudhope 11 58
(Robin Bastiman) *a in midfield* **8/1**

-055 **7** *hd* **Orthodox Lad**[9] 7171 4-9-7 **71** .... ChrisCatlin 8 59
(Ed de Giles) *chsd ldrs: rdn along 4f out: drvn wl over 2f out and sn wknd* **11/1**

5526 **8** *2* **Spyder**[10] 7131 4-9-3 **70** ....(b) RaulDaSilva(3) 3 55
(Jane Chapple-Hyam) *t.k.h: chsd ldr: rdn along 4f out: sn wknd* **9/1**

3062 **9** *10* **Change The Subject (USA)**[78] 5001 4-9-9 **73** .... AdamBeschizza 10 39
(Peter Salmon) *dwlt: a in rr* **14/1**

0600 **10** *32* **Kinyras (IRE)**[16] 6981 4-8-13 **63** .... PaulMulrennan 12
(Michael Easterby) *a in rr: bhd and eased fnl 2f* **16/1**

2m 14.9s (5.50) **Going Correction** +0.575s/f (Yiel)
WFA 3 from 4yo+ 5lb **10 Ran SP% 120.4**
Speed ratings (Par 103): **101,97,95,94,91 91,91,89,81,56**
toteswingers 1&2 £12.30, 2&3 £2.40, 1&3 £13.00 CSF £83.91 CT £262.07 TOTE £19.70: £5.30, £1.20, £1.20; EX 68.30.
Owner Alex Owen **Bred** Crandon Park Stud **Trained** Willoughton, Lincs

FOCUS
A modest handicap. It was run at a fair pace and they stuck to the middle again in the home straight. A clear personal best from out of the blue from the winner.

7369 LIDGET COMPTON H'CAP (DIV II) 1m 2f 60y
5:00 (5:00) (Class 5) (0-75,75) 3-Y-O+ **£2,264** (£673; £336; £168) **Stalls** Low

Form RPR

0002 **1** **Brockfield**[15] 7003 6-9-2 **67** .... DavidAllan 5 74
(Mel Brittain) *t.k.h in rr: hdwy to trck ldrs over 5f out: led over 3f out: hld on towards fin* **13/2**

0126 **2** ½ **Follow The Flag (IRE)**[4] 7294 8-8-10 **68** ....(v) DavidBergin(7) 8 74
(Alan McCabe) *hld up towards rr: drvn and hdwy over 2f out: 4th 1f out: styd on wl last 50yds* **5/1**[2]

3220 **3** ¾ **Mistress Of Rome**[34] 6472 3-9-1 **71** ....(p) PaulMulrennan 4 76
(Michael Dods) *led: hdd over 3f out: hung rt: kpt on fnl f* **11/2**[3]

0642 **4** *nk* **Uphold**[22] 6828 5-9-7 **72** ....(e) PaulHanagan 3 76
(Gay Kelleway) *hld up in rr: hdwy over 3f out: chsng ldrs over 2f out: kpt on same pce over 1f out* **11/2**[3]

3404 **5** *5* **Hydrant**[58] 5730 6-9-4 **69** .... FrankieDettori 6 64
(Peter Salmon) *trckd ldrs: drvn 4f out: wknd over 1f out* **9/2**[1]

0000 **6** *6* **El Bravo**[28] 6631 6-8-13 **64** ....(be[1]) RussKennemore 11 47
(Shaun Harris) *sn w ldr: drvn 3f out: wknd over 1f out* **33/1**

3-60 **7** *nk* **Sim Sala Bim**[18] 6933 4-9-5 **70** .... HarryBentley 9 53
(Stuart Williams) *mid-div: drvn to chse ldrs 3f out: wknd over 1f out* **10/1**

6040 **8** *5* **Pertemps Networks**[176] 1797 8-9-5 **70** .... GrahamGibbons 2 43
(Michael Easterby) *hld up towards rr: lost pl over 3f out* **10/1**

5030 **9** *11* **Exclusive Dancer**[81] 4868 3-8-9 **65** .... PJMcDonald 1 17
(George Moore) *t.k.h towards rr: lost pl over 3f out: sn bhd* **11/1**

41/ **10** *13* **Destination Aim**[1169] 5000 5-9-10 **75** .... DanielTudhope 7
(Frederick Watson) *t.k.h towards rr: hdwy over 5f out: drvn over 3f out: lost pl over 2f out: eased over 1f out: sn bhd* **50/1**

1100 **11** *dist* **Toymaker**[38] 6342 5-9-8 **73** ....(p) TomQueally 10
(James Given) *trckd ldrs: lost pl over 4f out: t.o whn virtually p.u 3f out: eventually completed* **14/1**

2m 16.11s (6.71) **Going Correction** +0.575s/f (Yiel)
WFA 3 from 4yo+ 5lb **11 Ran SP% 117.0**
Speed ratings (Par 103): **96,95,95,94,90 85,85,81,72,62**
toteswingers 1&2 £7.60, 2&3 £5.50, 1&3 £9.70 CSF £38.81 CT £192.61 TOTE £7.00: £3.20, £2.20, £1.10; EX 36.90.
Owner Mel Brittain **Bred** Cheveley Park Stud Ltd **Trained** Warthill, N Yorks

FOCUS
The second division of the modest 1m2f handicap. It was run at an average tempo and was the slower division. The winner didn't need to match his early-season form.
Toymaker Official explanation: trainer said gelding finished distressed

7370 ARTSIGN APPRENTICE H'CAP 1m (S)
5:30 (5:30) (Class 4) (0-85,85) 3-Y-O+ **£4,075** (£1,212; £606; £303) **Stalls** High

Form RPR

4034 **1** **Yojimbo (IRE)**[36] 6405 4-8-12 **80** .... RobertTart(5) 5 91
(Mick Channon) *trckd ldrs: hdwy to ld 3f out: rdn clr 2f out: styd on wl* **9/1**

0600 **2** 2 ½ **Dubai Hills**[20] 6882 6-9-3 **85** .... PeterSword(5) 10 90
(Bryan Smart) *hld up: hdwy 3f out: rdn to chse ldrs over 1f out: kpt on fnl f* **25/1**

4031 **3** 1 ¼ **She's A Character**[32] 6526 5-8-10 **73** .... LauraBarry 2 75
(Richard Fahey) *hld up in rr: stdy hdwy on outer 3f out: rdn to chse ldrs over 1f out: no imp ins fnl f: hld whn rdr dropped reins nr fin* **7/1**[3]

2604 **4** *hd* **Ruby Night (IRE)**[37] 6381 3-8-8 **81** .... ThomasHemsley(7) 15 83
(Michael Bell) *s.i.s and bhd: swtchd rt and hdwy over 2f out: rdn and styng on whn rdr dropped whip wl over 1f out: kpt on fnl f: nrst fin* **10/1**

1660 **5** *nk* **Hayek**[28] 6630 5-8-7 **75** ....(b) RachelRichardson(5) 4 76
(Tim Easterby) *in tch: hdwy 3f out: rdn to chse ldrs 2f out: kpt on same pce fnl f* **11/1**

0000 **6** *4* **Paramour**[38] 6338 5-9-1 **78** .... GeorgeDowning 12 70
(David O'Meara) *prom: effrt to chse wnr over 2f out: sn rdn and wknd over 1f out* **9/2**[2]

1060 **7** 1 ½ **Fazza**[13] 7069 5-9-1 **78** .... GeorgeChaloner 9 67
(Edwin Tuer) *dwlt: a towards rr* **16/1**

0316 **8** *nse* **Duster**[12] 7083 5-9-8 **85** .... NathanSweeney 3 73
(Hughie Morrison) *prom: rdn along 3f out: wknd 2f out* **9/1**

-314 **9** *nk* **Elspeth's Boy (USA)**[147] 2661 5-8-8 **76** .... MatthewHopkins(5) 1 64
(Philip Kirby) *t.k.h: chsd ldrs: rdn along 3f out: sn wknd* **11/1**

1400 **10** 3 ¼ **Majuro (IRE)**[16] 6979 8-9-1 **81** ....(t) RPWalsh(3) 6 61
(Charles Smith) *led: rdn along and hdd 3f out: sn wknd* **40/1**

4222 **11** *nk* **Robert The Painter (IRE)**[15] 7004 4-8-11 **74** ....(v) DavidBergin 14 54
(David O'Meara) *hld up in tch: hdwy 3f out: sn rdn and wknd over 2f out* **3/1**[1]

0000 **12** *1* **Oratory (IRE)**[36] 6405 6-9-0 **77** .... JacobButterfield 8 54
(Ollie Pears) *chsd ldrs: rdn along 3f out: sn wknd* **40/1**

5100 **13** *57* **Lolita Lebron (IRE)**[10] 7128 3-8-13 **79** .... DarylByrne 11
(Lawrence Mullaney) *s.i.s: a in rr: outpcd and bhd whn eased 2f out* **50/1**

1m 42.42s (3.12) **Going Correction** +0.175s/f (Good)
WFA 3 from 4yo+ 3lb **13 Ran SP% 118.0**
Speed ratings (Par 105): **91,88,87,87,86 82,81,81,80,77 77,76,19**
toteswingers 1&2 £35.40, 2&3 £30.00, 1&3 £15.60 CSF £219.79 CT £1712.98 TOTE £11.40: £4.10, £7.70, £3.20; EX 365.40.
Owner Jon and Julia Aisbitt **Bred** Peter Kelly And Ms Wendy Daly **Trained** West Ilsley, Berks
■ Stewards' Enquiry : Thomas Hemsley seven-day ban: failed to ride out for 3rd (9,10,14-17,19 Nov)

FOCUS
Not a bad handicap of its type. They went a modest pace down the middle and few landed a blow. The winner rates a small personal best.
Robert The Painter(IRE) Official explanation: jockey said gelding ran flat
Lolita Lebron(IRE) Official explanation: jockey said filly hung left throughout
T/Jkpt: Not won. T/Plt: £105.10 to a £1 stake. Pool of £74939.04 - 520.14 winning tickets.
T/Qpdt: £61.20 to a £1 stake. Pool of £4757.58 - 57.51 winning tickets. JR

6481 NEWBURY (L-H)
Friday, October 26

OFFICIAL GOING: Soft (heavy in places) changing to heavy after race 2 (2.20)
Wind: Brisk across Weather: Overcast

7371 JOIN HOT TO TROT RACING CLUB E B F MAIDEN STKS (DIV I) 6f 110y
1:50 (1:53) (Class 4) 2-Y-O **£4,398** (£1,309; £654; £327) **Stalls** Centre

Form RPR

0 **1** **Carry On Sydney**[12] 7078 2-9-3 0 .... RichardHughes 2 84
(Richard Hannon) *slt ld but jnd again and rdn wl over 1f out: kpt on gamely to assert fnl 75yds* **11/4**[1]

2 ½ **Zeus Magic** 2-9-3 0 .... DaneO'Neill 5 83+
(David Elsworth) *slowly away: in rr: pushed along: green and hdwy over 2f out: styd on wl fnl f: swtchd rt in clsng stages and r.o to take 2nd last strides: could nt rch wnr* **12/1**

3 *nk* **Absolutely So (IRE)** 2-9-3 0 .... JimmyFortune 1 82+
(Andrew Balding) *slowly away: t.k.h: hdwy to trck ldrs 1/2-way: jnd wnr travelling smoothly wl over 1f out: drvn and green ins fnl f: no ex fnl 75yds: lost 2nd last strides* **11/4**[1]

4 *5* **Collingbourneducis (IRE)** 2-9-3 0 .... PatDobbs 4 68
(Richard Hannon) *chsd ldrs: rdn over 2f out: outpcd wl over 1f out* **10/1**

04 **5** *3* **Lucky Di**[15] 7007 2-8-12 0 .... IanMongan 9 55
(Peter Hedger) *s.i.s: in rr: hdwy to cl up over 2f out: sn one pce* **20/1**

04 **6** *6* **Inaugural**[34] 6481 2-9-3 0 .... JamesDoyle 3 43
(Roger Charlton) *pressed wnr: drvn and stl upsides over 2f out: wknd ins fnl 2f* **7/2**[2]

7 *1* **King Of The Danes** 2-9-3 0 .... NeilCallan 11 41
(Mark Johnston) *chsd ldrs: rdn over 2f out and sn wknd* **9/1**[3]

8 2 ¾ **Freddy With A Y (IRE)** 2-9-3 0 .... GeorgeBaker 10 33
(Gary Moore) *in tch to 1/2-way* **33/1**

9 *4* **Chandelle Celeste** 2-8-12 0 .... EddieAhern 6 17
(Daniel Kubler) *t.k.h: in tch 3f* **40/1**

10 *1* **Burnt Fingers (IRE)** 2-8-13 0 ow1 .... JamesMillman 8 15
(Rod Millman) *broke wl: sn rdn and bhd* **100/1**

1m 23.89s (4.59) **Going Correction** +0.675s/f (Yiel) **10 Ran SP% 113.5**
Speed ratings (Par 97): **100,99,99,93,89 83,81,78,74,73**
toteswingers 1&2 £7.70, 2&3 £6.20, 1&3 £3.30 CSF £34.86 TOTE £3.90: £1.40, £3.20, £2.00; EX 38.40 Trifecta £105.50 Pool: £971.41 - 6.90 winning units..
Owner The Sydney Arms Partnership **Bred** Mrs James Wigan **Trained** East Everleigh, Wilts

FOCUS
Rail between 7f and 5f on Round course moved back in and distances were as advertised. The runners came centre-field in the first division of what looked a fair maiden, with those who raced more towards the far side of the group coming out well on top. The time was 0.28secs quicker than division two. The first three were clear and the winner improved considerably on his debut effort.

NOTEBOOK
Carry On Sydney put in some good work following a slow start on his Goodwood debut (6f) and, having been more alertly away this time, he held on well from a pair of newcomers. There's a good chance the placed runners would reverse form were they to meet again, but he's clearly progressing and showed a good attitude. (op 3-1)
Zeus Magic ◆, half-brother to a pair of 1m6f winners in Scott's View and Doctor Scott, out of a mare who also won at that trip, showed more than expected on debut, appearing to handle the ground well and finishing nicely having raced green in rear early. He ought to relish a longer trip and looks a ready-made maiden winner. (op 10-1)
Absolutely So(IRE) ◆, seemingly well thought of, suffered a major blow when missing the break and then racing keenly. The way he made ground, hard on the bridle, indeed suggests he was the best horse in the race, but those earlier exertions ultimately took a toll. Winning a 6f maiden should prove straightforward and he could develop into a useful 3yo sprinter. (op 9-4)
Collingbourneducis(IRE), a brother to 6f winner Hairspray, stayed on again having been outpaced and should benefit from the experience. He can win a small maiden. (op 14-1)
Lucky Di again showed promise and will be of interest switching to handicaps. (op 16-1)
Inaugural had been progressing but he had plenty to prove on a testing surface and may also have ended up racing on the slower part of the track.
King Of The Danes, a half-brother to six winners, most notably Group 1 scorer Spinning Queen, showed up well to a point, and he too may have been on the slowest ground. There should be plenty of improvement to come from him. (op 12-1 tchd 14-1)
Freddy With A Y(IRE), who cost 6,000euros and is bred to do better next year, made a brief show on what was probably the slowest ground and can leave this form behind. (op 28-1 tchd 20-1)

7372 JOIN HOT TO TROT RACING CLUB E B F MAIDEN STKS (DIV II) 6f 110y
2:20 (2:23) (Class 4) 2-Y-O **£4,398** (£1,309; £654; £327) **Stalls** Centre

Form RPR
0 **1** **Fort Knox**[23] 6772 2-9-3 0 ... PatDobbs 1 83+
(Richard Hannon) *s.i.s: in rr: pushed along: swtchd lft and gd hdwy over 1f out: qcknd smartly fnl f to ld fnl 150yds: comf* **13/2**[2]
2 1 ¾ **Beautiful View** 2-8-12 0 ... EddieAhern 4 74+
(Richard Hannon) *trckd ldrs: waiting for a run whn sltly outpcd ins fnl 2f: drvn and qcknd over 1f out: styd on wl to take 2nd fnl 120yds: nt gng pce of wnr* **8/1**[3]
20 **3** 2 ¼ **Sea Shanty (USA)**[70] 5304 2-9-3 0 ... RichardHughes 8 72
(Richard Hannon) *chsd ldr: drvn and narrow advantage appr fnl f: hdd and outpcd fnl 150yds* **1/1**[1]
0 **4** shd **My Gigi**[85] 4739 2-8-12 0 ... FergusSweeney 3 67
(Gary Moore) *t.k.h: chsd ldrs: drvn and slt ld 2f out: hdd appr fnl f: styd on same pce fnl 150yds* **40/1**
5 5 **Whiskeymack** 2-9-3 0 ... MartinHarley 5 58
(Mick Channon) *t.k.h: chsd ldrs: pushed along 3f out: outpcd fnl 2f* **16/1**
6 ¾ **Mawson** 2-9-3 0 ... JamesDoyle 6 56
(Roger Charlton) *in tch: pushed along over 2f out: sn swtchd rt: kpt on same pce* **10/1**
6 **7** 4 ½ **Maisie's Moon (USA)**[22] 6816 2-8-12 0 ... KierenFallon 2 39
(Hughie Morrison) *led: hdd 2f out: wknd qckly over 1f out* **12/1**
8 4 ½ **Secret Rebel** 2-9-3 0 ... GeorgeBaker 10 31
(Sylvester Kirk) *in tch: pushed along 3f out: btn whn pushed rt ins fnl f* **25/1**
9 1 **Oasis Spirit** 2-8-12 0 ... JimmyFortune 7 23
(Andrew Balding) *in tch: wkng whn pushed rt ins fnl 2f* **17/2**
10 19 **Veronica's Pursuit** 2-8-12 0 ... DaneO'Neill 9
(Peter Hedger) *s.i.s: in rr: pushed along and lost tch over 2f out* **66/1**

1m 24.17s (4.87) **Going Correction** +0.675s/f (Yiel) **10** Ran SP% **115.4**
Speed ratings (Par 97): **99,97,94,94,88 87,82,77,76,54**
toteswingers 1&2 £4.50, 2&3 £3.70, 1&3 £2.70 CSF £55.99 TOTE £7.80: £1.80, £2.50, £1.10; EX 47.80 Trifecta £103.90 Pool: £1079.17 - 7.79 winning units..
Owner Andrew Tinkler **Bred** A H Bennett **Trained** East Everleigh, Wilts
■ Stewards' Enquiry : James Doyle caution: careless riding.

FOCUS
The time was 0.28secs slower than division one, but they went noticeably slow early and there's little doubt the race produced the more impressive winner. Both he and the second can do better still. Richard Hannon was responsible for the first three.

NOTEBOOK
Fort Knox ◆, the supposed Richard Hannon second-string, produced a burst of speed rarely seen in such testing ground to draw nicely clear late on. A brother to the same connections' Dubawi Gold, who was runner-up to Frankel in the 2011 2,000 Guineas, he'd raced far too keenly on debut at Kempton, but settled better here despite the slow pace, and put in some effort when considering the next three home were never far away. It's worth mentioning he produced his run widest of all, on a part of the track that seemed favoured in division one, but he'd have won regardless of where he raced, and looks a smart prospect with next season in mind. (op 11-2 tchd 5-1)
Beautiful View ◆, the apparent Hannon third-string, is a half-sister to mudlark Ballesteros and she readily moved past the favourite, this despite having raced keenly in behind the leaders. Although no match for the winner, she shouldn't have much trouble winning an end-of-season fillies' maiden on this evidence. (op 12-1)
Sea Shanty(USA), off since disappointing in a 7f course maiden in August, again failed to build on the promise of his debut second, although the much softer ground on this occasion can probably be put forward as a valid excuse. (tchd 10-11 and 5-4)
My Gigi, last in a well-contested 7f fillies' maiden at Goodwood on debut, had been off 70 days and showed much improved form, travelling up okay and keeping on again in the manner of a horse set to be suited by further. (op 25-1)
Whiskeymack, whose dam was a Group-placed 6f AW winner, couldn't quicken having raced keenly but should improve for the experience and will benefit from a longer trip before long. (op 20-1 tchd 14-1)
Mawson, whose dam is an unraced daughter of Queensland Derby and Oaks winner Bravery, is expected to need better ground and should leave this form behind in time. (op 14-1)
Maisie's Moon(USA) has finished well beaten in two starts, but looks to have ability and will be of more interesting in handicaps on a sounder surface following another run. (op 25-1)
Oasis Spirit, a sister to Fearless Dream, placed up to 1m2f, offered little immediate promise but could be a different proposition on drier ground. (op 10-1 tchd 8-1)

7373 CHRISTAL MAIDEN STKS 1m (S)
2:50 (2:56) (Class 5) 2-Y-O **£2,264** (£673; £336; £168) **Stalls** Centre

Form RPR
00 **1** **Mombasa**[23] 6795 2-9-3 0 ... IanMongan 11 77
(John Dunlop) *trckd ldrs: chsd ldr and rdn appr fnl f: drvn to ld fnl 120yds: styd on wl* **13/2**[2]
02 **2** ½ **World Record (IRE)**[70] 5319 2-9-3 0 ... RichardHughes 7 76
(Richard Hannon) *led tl hdd over 3f out: styd trcking ldr tl drvn to ld again over 1f out: hdd fnl 120yds: one pce* **1/1**[1]
3 1 ¾ **Vicksburg** 2-8-12 0 ... JimmyFortune 12 67+
(Andrew Balding) *in rr: hdwy 3f out: styd on wl fr over 1f out to take 3rd fnl 120yds: could nt rch ldng duo* **12/1**
00 **4** 6 **Sweeping Rock (IRE)**[21] 6846 2-9-3 0 ... GeorgeBaker 10 59
(Marcus Tregoning) *trckd ldr: led over 3f out: hdd over 1f out: no ex ins fnl f and wknd fnl 150yds* **33/1**
60 **5** nk **Norphin**[56] 5793 2-9-3 0 ... EddieAhern 6 58+
(Denis Coakley) *chsd ldrs: pushed along 2f out: outpcd over 1f out* **40/1**
6 ¾ **Dragon City** 2-9-3 0 ... DaneO'Neill 5 57+
(Harry Dunlop) *s.i.s: in rr: hdwy over 2f out: nvr gng pce to rch ldrs: no prog fnl f* **16/1**
0 **7** hd **Seaside Rock (IRE)**[23] 6796 2-9-3 0 ... PatDobbs 8 56
(Richard Hannon) *chsd ldrs: rdn 3f out: styd on same pce fnl 2f* **14/1**
40 **8** nk **Star Of Mayfair (USA)**[48] 6020 2-8-12 0 ... MichaelJMMurphy[(5)] 2 56
(Alan Jarvis) *in tch: drvn and one pce fr over 2f out* **15/2**[3]
00 **9** 1 ½ **Teolagi (IRE)**[34] 6501 2-9-3 0 ... LiamKeniry 4 52
(J S Moore) *rdn in rr over 2f out: mod prog fnl f* **66/1**
10 2 ½ **Quest For More (IRE)** 2-9-3 0 ... JamesDoyle 9 47
(Roger Charlton) *rdn and green over 2f out: a in rr* **13/2**[2]
11 1 ¼ **Thought And Memory (IRE)** 2-9-3 0 ... MartinHarley 3 46+
(Mick Channon) *bhd fr 1/2-way* **12/1**
12 12 **Copper Rag** 2-8-12 0 ... RachealKneller[(5)] 1 18
(Mark Usher) *chsd ldrs over 5f* **125/1**

1m 46.47s (6.77) **Going Correction** +0.675s/f (Yiel) **12** Ran SP% **124.0**
Speed ratings (Par 95): **93,92,90,84,84 83,83,83,81,79 77,65**
toteswingers 1&2 £3.30, 2&3 £5.30, 1&3 £13.70 CSF £13.82 TOTE £8.50: £2.40, £1.10, £3.80; EX 22.60 Trifecta £783.40 Pool: £1253.51 - 1.20 winning units..
Owner Wis Green Partners **Bred** Lakin Bloodstock And H And W Thornton **Trained** Arundel, W Sussex

FOCUS
No great depth to this maiden, in which the first three were able to pull clear. The form is rated around the runner-up.

NOTEBOOK
Mombasa came in for plenty of support and the testing conditions just about made it enough of a test for him to triumph. He rates a decent middle-distance prospect for next season, when he'll be trained by Harry Dunlop. (op 12-1)
World Record(IRE), whose Newmarket second 70 days earlier had come on good to firm, didn't appear in love with the ground, but still ran another good and can win his maiden on a sounder surface. (op 11-10 tchd 10-11 and 5-4 in a place)
Vicksburg ◆, related to a pair of middle-distance winners, was the only filly in the race and ran full of promise. By a sire whose progeny tend to appreciate fast ground, this good-looking sort travelled nicely into the race and drew clear from the remainder, ultimately losing out to a pair of colts with previous experience. She can win her maiden and rates a useful 3yo prospect. (op 14-1 tchd 16-1)
Sweeping Rock(IRE) ran his best race yet and this half-brother to dual 1m4f winner Bay Story will be one for middle-distance handicaps next season. (op 25-1)
Norphin is another now qualified for a mark and he too will appreciate a stiffer test of stamina. (op 25-1)
Dragon City, a half-brother to 7f winner Esprit Danseur, made some late headway following a slow start and should improve, especially on a sounder surface. (op 25-1 tchd 33-1)
Seaside Rock(IRE) offered more than on debut but doesn't look capable of winning until he's in a handicap. (op 16-1 tchd 12-1)
Star Of Mayfair(USA), who raced keenly, is now qualified for a mark and should fare better in the handicap sphere. (op 6-1 tchd 8-1)
Quest For More(IRE), a half-brother to five winners, most notably US Grade 3 winner Macaw, looked green and was always struggling. He can leave this form behind on better ground with the run behind him. (op 7-1 tchd 6-1)
Thought And Memory(IRE), a half-brother to useful 1m3f winner Cool Judgement, failed to pick up but can surely do better on a sounder surface. Official explanation: vet said colt lost a right-hind shoe (op 16-1)

7374 SIR GERALD WHENT MEMORIAL NURSERY 6f 8y
3:25 (3:26) (Class 3) (0-95,89) 2-Y-O **£5,822** (£1,732; £865; £432) **Stalls** Centre

Form RPR
6243 **1** **Effie B**[7] 7206 2-9-2 **84** ... MartinHarley 4 88
(Mick Channon) *in rr: hdwy over 2f out: drvn to ld appr fnl f: styd on wl u.p: hld on all out* **16/1**
3143 **2** hd **Alcando (IRE)**[9] 7164 2-8-12 **80** ... EddieAhern 2 84
(Denis Coakley) *t.k.h: led 2f: styd pressing ldrs tl led again 2f out: hdd appr fnl f: hung rt: rallied fnl 100yds: could nt quite get bk up* **16/1**
3125 **3** 3 ¼ **Beedee**[15] 7009 2-9-1 **88** ... WilliamTwiston-Davies[(5)] 3 82
(Richard Hannon) *chsd ldrs: rdn over 2f out: styd on to take 3rd ins fnl f: no imp on ldng duo* **11/1**
1636 **4** 4 **Prince Regal**[34] 6487 2-8-7 **80** ... MichaelJMMurphy[(5)] 1 62
(Alan Jarvis) *pressed ldrs: str chal fr 2f out tl over 1f out: wknd ins fnl f* **8/1**
1042 **5** 1 ¼ **Shahdaroba (IRE)**[14] 7028 2-9-6 **88** ... JamesMillman 8 66
(Rod Millman) *pressed ldrs: led after 2f: rdn 3f out: hdd 2f out: wknd u.p appr fnl f* **5/1**[2]
4014 **6** 2 ¾ **Echion (IRE)**[41] 6227 2-8-8 **76** ... PatDobbs 5 46
(Richard Hannon) *chsd ldrs: drvn over 2f out: wknd over 1f out* **16/1**
5060 **7** 2 **Woodland Mill (IRE)**[20] 6883 2-8-8 **76** ... JimmyQuinn 6 40
(Richard Fahey) *in rr: drvn along fr 3f out: nvr gng pce to get into contention* **16/1**
3020 **8** 4 ½ **King Dragon (IRE)**[13] 7053 2-9-7 **89** ... KierenFallon 7 40
(Brian Meehan) *s.i.s: in rr: sme hdwy over 2f out: sn wknd* **6/1**[3]
6635 **9** 4 ½ **Dominate**[34] 6487 2-9-5 **87** ... RichardHughes 11 24
(Richard Hannon) *racd alone stands' side and disp ld tl rdn and wknd appr fnl 2f: eased whn no ch fnl f* **3/1**[1]
4262 **10** 19 **Rock Up (IRE)**[8] 7192 2-8-0 **75** ... NoelGarbutt[(7)] 9
(David Elsworth) *spd to 1/2-way* **12/1**
10 **11** 19 **Joey's Destiny (IRE)**[20] 6883 2-9-3 **85** ... PatCosgrave 10
(George Baker) *spd to 1/2-way: sn wknd* **8/1**

1m 17.18s (4.18) **Going Correction** +0.675s/f (Yiel) **11** Ran SP% **117.7**
Speed ratings (Par 99): **99,98,94,89,87 83,81,75,69,43 18**
toteswingers 1&2 £21.10, 2&3 £20.90, 1&3 £23.90 CSF £247.65 CT £1850.08 TOTE £17.60: £4.30, £4.70, £3.00; EX 235.10 Trifecta £861.50 Part won. Pool: £1148.75 - 0.80 winning units..
Owner R Bastian **Bred** R Bastian **Trained** West Ilsley, Berks

FOCUS
As in the first two races over a similar trip, those who raced on the far side of the main group came out on top, with Richard Hughes's decision to try and make all at a fast pace aboard Dominate under the stands' rail backfiring in a major way, the favourite being one of the first beaten. Personal bests from the first two but the form has not been rated too positively.

NOTEBOOK

Effie B is proven in testing ground and, having travelled up nicely on the far side of runners, she grittily dug in to just hold on. This is as far as she wants to go and she'll do well to defy much of a rise, but is very tough and can continue to give a good account on similar ground. (op 14-1)

Alcando(IRE), unproven on ground this soft, had run well from a similar mark on the Polytrack at Lingfield the time before but didn't quite have enough to get past the game winner. He drew a little way on from the remainder and can expect a rise.

Beedee ran well if seeming to find the drop to 6f, even on heavy ground, a little on the sharp side. She'll be happier back at 7f on a sounder surface. (tchd 10-1)

Prince Regal remains in the control of the handicapper from his current mark. (op 10-1 tchd 11-1)

Shahdaroba(IRE) failed to reproduce the form of her last-time-out York second on similar ground, perhaps going too fast early. (op 9-2)

King Dragon(IRE) didn't feature after a sluggish start. (op 11-1)

Dominate looked likely to be suited by the return to slower ground, but he was given little chance in going off quick on what was perhaps the slowest ground under the stands' rail. Official explanation: jockey said colt stopped quickly (op 11-4)

Joey's Destiny(IRE) raced towards the stands' rail early and was another beaten soon after halfway. (tchd 9-1)

7375 SMITH & WILLIAMSON FILLIES' H'CAP 1m 2f 6y

4:00 (4:00) (Class 4) (0-85,85) 3-Y-0+ **£4,075** (£1,212; £606; £303) **Stalls** Centre

Form RPR

0462 **1** **Princess Caetani (IRE)**[12] 7082 3-8-13 **79** DaneO'Neill 4 90
(David Simcock) *hld up in rr: stdy hdwy on inner over 2f out: drvn to ld over 1f out and sn 2 l clr: rdn ins fnl f: hld on all out* **4/1**[2]

2003 **2** *nse* **Misdemeanour (IRE)**[51] 5951 3-9-5 **85** RichardHughes 8 96+
(Richard Hannon) *hld up in rr: hdwy on outer wl over 1f out: drvn and qcknd but 2 l down jst ins fnl f: fin strly: jst failed* **7/1**[3]

4103 **3** *5* **Intent (IRE)**[11] 7116 3-8-12 **78** EddieAhern 10 80
(Michael Bell) *chsd ldrs: rdn over 2f out: styd on for wl-hld 3rd ins fnl f* **12/1**

3052 **4** *1* **The Giving Tree (IRE)**[25] 6735 3-8-10 **76** JamesDoyle 2 76
(Sylvester Kirk) *hld up in rr: hdwy on outside to chse ldrs 2f out: nvr quite gng pce to chal: wknd fnl f* **11/1**

0-62 **5** *1 ¼* **All Annalena (IRE)**[14] 7034 6-9-5 **85** MichaelJMMurphy(5) 14 82
(Lucy Wadham) *trckd ldr: led over 3f out: rdn over 2f out: hdd appr fnl f: sn wknd* **8/1**

-262 **6** *2 ½* **Gifted Girl (IRE)**[10] 7128 3-9-5 **85** NeilCallan 5 77
(Paul Cole) *t.k.h: hdwy whn bmpd ins fnl 2f: rdn and sme prog fnl f* **16/1**

2463 **7** *1* **Choral Festival**[4] 7300 6-8-9 **75** ow2 WilliamTwiston-Davies(5) 11 66
(John Bridger) *in rr: hdwy to trck ldrs over 2f out: sn rdn and btn* **10/1**

1001 **8** *9* **Our Gal**[21] 6847 4-9-7 **82** JimmyQuinn 12 55
(Noel Quinlan) *chsd ldrs: wkng whn bmpd ins fnl 2f* **14/1**

1660 **9** *hd* **Morant Bay (IRE)**[27] 6667 3-8-11 **77** StevieDonohoe 3 50
(Ian Williams) *in rr: pushed along and sme hdwy 3f out: nvr rchd ldrs and wknd 2f out* **66/1**

-163 **10** *13* **Dulkashe (IRE)**[16] 6987 3-9-1 **81** KierenFallon 1 29
(Luca Cumani) *chsd ldrs: rdn over 2f out: sn wknd* **10/3**[1]

1321 **11** *9* **Consider Yourself (USA)**[22] 6819 5-9-6 **81** (p) WilliamCarson 13 12
(Anthony Carson) *led tl hdd over 3f out: sn wknd* **8/1**

2m 16.09s (7.29) **Going Correction** +0.80s/f (Soft)
WFA 3 from 4yo+ 5lb 11 Ran SP% **117.0**
Speed ratings (Par 102): **102,101,97,97,96 94,93,86,86,75 68**
toteswingers 1&2 £7.30, 2&3 £14.10, 1&3 £11.10 CSF £32.08 CT £310.92 TOTE £5.10: £1.80, £3.70, £4.30; EX 40.40 Trifecta £294.90 Pool: £432.63 - 1.10 winning units..
Owner Favourites Racing **Bred** Barronstown Stud **Trained** Newmarket, Suffolk

■ Stewards' Enquiry : Eddie Ahern caution: entered wrong stall.

FOCUS

The tempo lifted significantly on turning into the straight and two of those held up ultimately drew clear. The winner backed up her Goodwood form and the second was possibly set a bit too much to do.

Gifted Girl(IRE) Official explanation: jockey said filly hung left and suffered interference in running

Our Gal Official explanation: jockey said filly suffered interference in running

7376 COLLINGWOOD FIRST ERVICE LTD H'CAP 1m 7y(R)

4:35 (4:35) (Class 5) (0-75,75) 3-Y-0 **£2,264** (£673; £336; £168) **Stalls** Centre

Form RPR

1533 **1** **Anya**[37] 6375 3-9-5 **73** DaneO'Neill 5 82
(Ed Walker) *hld up in tch: hdwy over 2f out: led over 1f out: drvn and styd on strly fnl f* **3/1**[1]

031 **2** *1 ½* **Sword In Hand**[30] 6582 3-9-2 **75** MichaelJMMurphy(5) 3 81+
(Alan Jarvis) *t.k.h: trckd ldr: chal fr over 2f out tl over 1f out: edgd rt u.p ins fnl f but kpt on: no imp on wnr* **11/2**[2]

0203 **3** *nk* **Poetic Lord**[9] 7170 3-9-2 **75** WilliamTwiston-Davies(5) 8 80
(Richard Hannon) *towards rr: hdwy over 2f out: styd on to take 3rd ins fnl f: styng on same pce whn hung rt in clsng stages* **8/1**

5434 **4** *3* **Tight Lipped (IRE)**[18] 6930 3-9-2 **70** NeilCallan 6 68
(James Eustace) *chsd ldrs: rdn over 3f out: one pce fnl 2f* **10/1**

3160 **5** *1 ¼* **Take Two**[97] 4323 3-9-7 **75** WilliamCarson 9 70
(John O'Shea) *rrd s and slowly away: rdn ins fnl 3f: styd on u.p fnl f: nvr a threat* **15/2**

3011 **6** *1 ½* **Capitol Gain (IRE)**[18] 6931 3-9-5 **73** (p) JamieMackay 1 65
(Brian Meehan) *sn led: rdn over 2f out: hdd over 1f out: sn btn* **11/2**[2]

0300 **7** *5* **Minstrels Gallery (IRE)**[69] 5358 3-9-7 **75** DarryllHolland 4 55
(J R Jenkins) *in rr: rdn over 3f out: mod prog in clsng stages* **14/1**

3251 **8** *14* **Christingle**[14] 7025 3-9-0 **68** LiamJones 7 16
(William Haggas) *chsd ldrs: rdn 3f out: hung lft and wknd qckly 2f out* **7/1**[3]

31 **9** *13* **Dynastic**[80] 4901 3-9-7 **75** RichardHughes 2
(Richard Hannon) *chsd ldrs: rdn over 3f out: wknd qckly 2f out* **16/1**

1m 44.66s (5.96) **Going Correction** +0.80s/f (Soft) 9 Ran SP% **112.8**
Speed ratings (Par 101): **102,100,100,97,95 94,89,75,62**
toteswingers 1&2 £5.80, 2&3 £6.30, 1&3 £5.90 CSF £18.63 CT £117.63 TOTE £3.10: £1.40, £2.00, £2.60; EX 23.10 Trifecta £46.10 Pool: £994.60 - 16.18 winning units..
Owner Mrs L Alexander **Bred** Mrs L M Alexander **Trained** Newmarket, Suffolk

■ Stewards' Enquiry : William Twiston-Davies two-day ban: used whip above permitted level (Nov 9-10)

FOCUS

The early pace appeared generous in this modest handicap. The third helps set the standard.

7377 RACECOURSE NEWBURY "HANDS AND HEELS" APPRENTICE SERIES FINAL H'CAP (RACING EXCELLENCE INITIATIVE) 2m

5:10 (5:10) (Class 5) (0-75,73) 4-Y-0+ **£2,264** (£673; £336; £168) **Stalls** High

Form RPR

2334 **1** **Tijori (IRE)**[22] 6821 4-8-8 **57** (p) DanielMuscutt 9 67
(Bernard Llewellyn) *in rr: hdwy over 4f out: slt ld fr 3f out: drvn clr fr over 1f out* **9/1**

0066 **2** *4* **Wily Fox**[14] 7018 5-8-7 **59** RyanTate(3) 1 64
(James Eustace) *chsd ldrs: rdn 3f out: styd on to take 2nd fnl f but no imp on wnr* **12/1**

3103 **3** *5* **Arch Event**[22] 6821 7-8-5 **54** oh2 (p) TimClark 10 53
(Bernard Llewellyn) *chsd ldrs: drvn to chal over 2f out: outpcd but wnr over 1f out: wknd into 3rd fnl f* **7/1**[3]

0000 **4** *2 ¾* **Becausewecan (USA)**[13] 7068 6-9-7 **70** MichaelJMMurphy 4 66
(Mark Johnston) *chsd ldrs: led ins fnl 4f: narrowly hdd 3f out: wknd 2f out* **11/4**[1]

0/0- **5** *4 ½* **Counting House (IRE)**[192] 2034 9-9-1 **64** RufusVergette 5 54
(Jim Old) *in rr: hdwy on outer 5f out: rdn and no prog fnl 4f* **12/1**

2536 **6** *24* **Not Til Monday (IRE)**[127] 3316 6-9-5 **68** (v) ThomasBrown 7 30
(J R Jenkins) *chsd ldrs: rdn 4f out: wknd over 3f out* **10/1**

2600 **7** *8* **Twice Bitten**[30] 6584 4-9-0 **63** PhilipPrince 6 15
(James Toller) *t.k.h towards rr: rdn 5f out: wknd 4f out* **6/1**[2]

1136 **8** *8* **Captain Bellamy (USA)**[199] 1282 4-9-10 **73** WilliamTwiston-Davies 11 15
(Hughie Morrison) *disp ld tl hdd ins fnl 4f: sn btn* **7/1**[3]

1360 **9** *6* **Gilded Age**[25] 6738 6-9-5 **68** (tp) NedCurtis 2
(Chris Gordon) *disp ld tl ins fnl 4f: sn wknd* **7/1**[3]

-005 **10** *41* **Kahfre**[241] 728 5-9-5 **68** (v) GemmaTutty 8
(Gary Moore) *a in rr: t.o fnl 4f* **20/1**

ms (-212.00) 10 Ran SP% **117.7**
toteswingers 1&2 £17.90, 2&3 £15.90, 1&3 £7.20 CSF £112.27 CT £805.72 TOTE £9.80: £3.20, £4.30, £1.60; EX 123.70 Trifecta £706.10 Part won. Pool: £941.48 - 0.26 winning units..
Owner G Robinson **Bred** Polish Belle Partnership **Trained** Fochriw, Caerphilly

FOCUS

Moderate staying form, with the field finishing quite well strung out in the ground. The winner's best form this season.

T/Plt: £160.70 to a £1 stake. Pool of £53087.01 - 241.12 winning tickets. T/Qpdt: £48.80 to a £1 stake. Pool of £4149.22 - 62.80 winning tickets. ST

7355 WOLVERHAMPTON (A.W) (L-H)

Friday, October 26

OFFICIAL GOING: Standard

Wind: Fresh against Weather: Overcast

7378 BET TOTEPLACEPOT TEXT TOTE TO 89660 CLASSIFIED STKS 5f 216y(P)

5:40 (5:40) (Class 6) 3-Y-0+ **£1,908** (£563; £281) **Stalls** Low

Form RPR

1 **My Good Brother (IRE)**[65] 5498 3-9-0 **48** AndreaAtzeni 11 63
(T G McCourt, Ire) *chsd ldr: rdn to ld ins fnl f: r.o* **11/1**

5401 **2** *2* **Gypsy Rider**[49] 6002 3-9-0 **55** LukeMorris 7 57
(Bryn Palling) *chsd ldrs: rdn over 2f out: styd on to go 2nd wl ins fnl f: nt trble wnr* **11/4**[2]

-000 **3** *½* **Lady Platinum Club**[46] 6104 4-9-1 **52** DaleSwift 5 55
(Linda Stubbs) *sn drvn along to go prom: rdn over 2f out: styd on* **9/4**[1]

5060 **4** *3 ½* **Blueberry Fizz (IRE)**[8] 7204 4-9-1 **55** (b) BrettDoyle 1 44
(John Ryan) *chsd ldrs: rdn over 1f out: styd on same pce* **7/1**

000 **5** *½* **Nafa (IRE)**[1] 7354 4-9-1 **55** ShaneKelly 4 43
(Daniel Mark Loughnane) *led: rdn: hdd & wknd ins fnl f* **6/1**[3]

5440 **6** *6* **Artillery Train (IRE)**[44] 6136 3-9-0 **52** JamesSullivan 3 23
(Tim Etherington) *mid-div: rdn 1/2-way: wknd over 2f out* **10/1**

5-00 **7** *¾* **Turn The Tide**[8] 7204 4-9-1 **52** JohnFahy 12 21
(Dai Williams) *sn outpcd* **66/1**

600 **8** *¾* **Rosa Lottie**[22] 6806 3-9-0 **41** (p) MartinDwyer 9 19
(David C Griffiths) *mid-div: rdn and wknd 1/2-way* **50/1**

-000 **9** *9* **Peters Pleasure**[2] 7326 3-9-0 **32** (v) AdamKirby 13
(Robert Cowell) *sn outpcd* **33/1**

006 **10** *6* **Smiley Miley (IRE)**[18] 6935 4-9-1 **24** SamHitchcott 2
(David Lewis) *sn pushed along in rr: bhd fnl 4f* **200/1**

10R **R** **Copper Falls**[30] 6585 3-8-7 **54** JoshBaudains(7) 8
(Brendan Powell) *ref to r* **22/1**

1m 14.46s (-0.54) **Going Correction** -0.075s/f (Stan)
WFA 3 from 4yo 1lb 11 Ran SP% **112.9**
Speed ratings (Par 101): **100,97,96,92,91 83,82,81,69,61**
toteswingers 1&2 £5.50, 2&3 £2.10, 1&3 £5.50 CSF £38.73 TOTE £12.70: £3.80, £1.40, £1.10; EX 56.00 Trifecta £561.60 Part won. Pool: £748.85 - 0.71 winning tickets..
Owner Oliver Curtis **Bred** Oghill House Stud **Trained** Stamullen, Co Meath

FOCUS

They leader went off hard in this classified event but not many got involved from off the pace and they finished quite well strung out. Obviously limited form, with the winner up 6lb on his best in Ireland.

My Good Brother(IRE) Official explanation: trainer's rep said, regarding apparent improvement in form, that the gelding was better suited by the quicker surface.

Copper Falls Official explanation: no further entries for flat races started from stalls to be accepted.

7379 FOLLOW US ON TWITTER @WOLVESRACES (S) STKS 5f 216y(P)

6:10 (6:12) (Class 6) 2-Y-0 **£1,704** (£503; £251) **Stalls** Low

Form RPR

4623 **1** **Marmot Bay (IRE)**[9] 7156 2-8-6 **59** MartinDwyer 1 61
(Jamie Osborne) *mde all: rdn over 1f out: edgd rt: styd on* **15/2**[3]

2343 **2** *¾* **Cracking Choice (IRE)**[38] 6336 2-8-11 **61** (p) TomEaves 2 64
(Michael Dods) *chsd wnr: rdn over 1f out: styd on* **10/1**

0640 **3** *½* **Archie Stevens**[29] 6609 2-8-11 **68** RichardKingscote 5 64
(Tom Dascombe) *hld up in tch: nt clr run wl over 1f out: r.o: nt rch ldrs* **2/1**[1]

2235 **4** *¾* **We Are City**[29] 6611 2-8-6 **64** LukeMorris 11 55
(Michael Bell) *prom: rdn over 2f out: styd on u.p* **9/4**[2]

0034 **5** *nk* **Tyson The Byson**[24] 6766 2-8-11 **52** (p) RobertWinston 13 59
(Mrs K Burke) *chsd ldrs: rdn over 1f out: styd on same pce ins fnl f* **28/1**

5054 **6** *1 ¼* **Sojourn**[22] 6826 2-8-6 **53** SamHitchcott 7 50
(Mick Channon) *mid-div: sn drvn along: hdwy u.p over 1f out: nt rch ldrs* **20/1**

0233 **7** *1 ¼* **Millie N Aire**[22] 6822 2-8-6 61.................................... JamesSullivan 9 47
(Danielle McCormick) *chsd ldrs: rdn 1/2-way: no ex fnl f* **14/1**

000 **8** *3 ¼* **Avanzare**[22] 6817 2-8-6 54.. AndreaAtzeni 8 37
(Charles Hills) *s.i.s: rdn over 2f out: nvr on terms* **14/1**

5030 **9** *1* **Only For You**[17] 6953 2-8-6 51.. MartinLane 4 34
(Alan Brown) *chsd ldrs: rdn over 2f out: wknd fnl f* **50/1**

46 **10** *6* **Hit The Note**[38] 6335 2-8-6 0.. AmyRyan 6 16
(Ann Duffield) *sn pushed along in rr: bhd fr 1/2-way* **22/1**

0 **11** *3 ½* **Bryter Layter**[20] 6890 2-8-6 0.. JackDuern(5) 12 10
(Christopher Kellett) *s.i.s: outpcd* **200/1**

0 **12** *10* **Red Chubbs (IRE)**[6] 7244 2-8-6 0..........................(p) PatrickMathers 10
(Ann Duffield) *sn outpcd* **80/1**

1m 14.9s (-0.10) **Going Correction** -0.075s/f (Stan) 12 Ran SP% **114.5**
Speed ratings (Par 93): **97,96,95,94,93 92,90,86,84,76 72,58**
toteswingers 1&2 £11.30, 2&3 £4.90, 1&3 £4.60 CSF £71.48 TOTF £7.40: £2.90, £2.40, £1.50; EX 41.10 Trifecta £136.60 Pool: £698.08 - 3.83 winning tickets..There was no bid for the winner. Archie Stevens was subject to a friendly claim for £6,000.
Owner J A Osborne **Bred** J C Bloodstock **Trained** Upper Lambourn, Berks

FOCUS
A modest 2yo seller. The pace was fair and the winner showed a good attitude to fight off the finishers. She didn't need to improve on her recent level.

NOTEBOOK
Marmot Bay(IRE), a close third off a mark of 59 in a Kempton nursery last time, travelled enthusiastically in the lead from her good draw and battled well to cash in on a drop to selling company. Her form has gone both ways in seven starts but she has been back on the way up on her last three runs and has raced almost exclusively on Polytrack. (op 13-2)
Cracking Choice(IRE) gave it a decent try under a prominent ride and can be marked up a bit because he took a strong hold early on. He is now 0-8 but is a fairly consistent type who is unexposed on Polytrack and could make a big impact in a minor sprint contest if he can settle a bit better. (op 9-1 tchd 8-1)
Archie Stevens, a well-backed favourite, didn't get much luck because he was short of room around the final turn before staying on strongly. It is still hard to pin down his optimum trip and he has a bit to prove off a current rating of 68 but he is still lightly raced and is well-connected on his dam's side. (tchd 7-4)
We Are City had been knocking on the door off marks in the 60s in sprint nurseries recently and had strong form claims dropped into a seller but she took a long time to get going out wide and couldn't threaten. (tchd 11-4)
Tyson The Byson has found some improvement since headgear has been applied and ran creditably from a wide draw with quite a bit to find on adjusted figures here. (op 25-1)
Sojoum stayed on well from an unpromising position dropped back to 6f. She is winless after 12 starts but has shown some more encouraging signs in 6f/7f sellers here on her last two runs. (tchd 25-1)
Avanzare Official explanation: jockey said filly never travelled

7380 BET TOTEQUADPOT TEXT TOTE TO 89660 H'CAP (DIV I) 1m 5f 194y(P)
6:40 (6:42) (Class 5) (0-75,75) 3-Y-0+ **£2,911** (£866; £432; £216) **Stalls** Low

Form RPR

0225 **1** **Aleksandar**[17] 6971 3-8-10 69.. PatrickHills(3) 10 75+
(Luca Cumani) *mid-div: hdwy over 3f out: led over 1f out: rdn out* **9/2**[3]

2556 **2** *hd* **Brouhaha**[21] 6838 8-9-2 63.. RichardKingscote 7 69
(Tom Dascombe) *chsd ldrs: rdn and ev ch fr over 1f out: styd on* **22/1**

0255 **3** *nse* **Fourth Generation (IRE)**[73] 5188 5-9-13 74................. RobertWinston 9 80
(Alan Swinbank) *hld up: hdwy over 1f out: rdn and ev ch ins fnl f: styd on* **12/1**

0305 **4** *1 ¼* **Toughness Danon**[20] 6891 6-9-7 68..............................(t) SebSanders 1 72
(Brendan Powell) *hld up: hdwy and nt clr run over 1f out: rdn and edgd lft ins fnl f: styd on* **6/1**

1 **5** *¾* **Passion Planet (IRE)**[54] 5864 4-9-4 65......................... JamesSullivan 2 68
(John C McConnell, Ire) *s.i.s: hld up: hdwy over 1f out: rdn and hung lft ins fnl f: nt rch ldrs* **33/1**

2122 **6** *1* **English Summer**[14] 7024 5-9-9 70................................(t) WilliamBuick 6 72
(David Simcock) *prom: nt clr run over 2f out: rdn over 1f out: styd on same pce ins fnl f* **3/1**[1]

1126 **7** *1* **Authentication**[5] 7271 3-8-10 66.. JoeFanning 12 66
(Mark Johnston) *led: rdn and hdd over 1f out: no ex ins fnl f* **4/1**[2]

3325 **8** *5* **Luctor Emergo (IRE)**[23] 6784 3-8-12 68..........................(v) TomEaves 8 66
(Keith Dalgleish) *prom: chsd ldr 8f out: chal over 3f out: rdn over 2f out: hmpd and no ex over 1f out* **12/1**

0050 **9** *1* **Almail (USA)**[57] 5772 6-9-9 70..................................... FergusSweeney 4 62
(Jamie Osborne) *hld up: hdwy over 4f out: rdn over 2f out: sn wknd* **22/1**

0304 **10** *1* **Kazbow (IRE)**[28] 6642 6-10-0 75..................................... TonyHamilton 11 66
(Chris Grant) *chsd ldr 6f: remained handy: rdn over 3f out: wknd over 1f out* **5/1**

3m 4.26s (-1.74) **Going Correction** -0.075s/f (Stan)
WFA 3 from 4yo+ 9lb 10 Ran SP% **121.2**
Speed ratings (Par 103): **101,100,100,100,99 99,98,95,95,94**
toteswingers 1&2 £12.00, 2&3 £37.50, 1&3 £15.20 CSF £103.30 CT £1131.94 TOTE £6.40: £1.50, £6.80, £3.60; EX 69.20 TRIFECTA Not won..
Owner Fittocks Stud **Bred** Fittocks Stud Ltd **Trained** Newmarket, Suffolk

FOCUS
A competitive handicap. The pace was not very strong and there was a tight finish. It was a second slower than division II and it's hard to be positive about the form.

7381 BET TOTEQUADPOT TEXT TOTE TO 89660 H'CAP (DIV II) 1m 5f 194y(P)
7:10 (7:12) (Class 5) (0-75,74) 3-Y-0+ **£2,911** (£866; £432; £216) **Stalls** Low

Form RPR

6013 **1** **Rythmic**[26] 6703 3-9-4 73.. JoeFanning 2 84+
(Mark Johnston) *hld up: hdwy and nt clr run over 1f out: r.o to ld wl ins fnl f* **8/1**

2221 **2** *1* **Peachez**[20] 6891 4-9-9 74..(p) AmyScott(5) 3 81
(Alastair Lidderdale) *dwlt: hld up: hdwy over 5f out: chsd ldr over 2f out: led over 1f out: rdn and hdd wl ins fnl f* **14/1**

-004 **3** *½* **Royal Entourage**[26] 6706 7-9-1 66........................... GarryWhillans(5) 8 72
(Philip Kirby) *hld up in tch: rdn and hung lft fr over 1f out: styd on* **11/1**

260 **4** *2 ¼* **Honourable Knight (IRE)**[55] 5816 4-9-9 69.................. GeorgeBaker 6 72
(Mark Usher) *led 1f: chsd ldrs: rdn and hmpd over 1f out: styd on same pce ins fnl f* **16/1**

320 **5** *¾* **Kames Park (IRE)**[14] 7024 10-9-3 63......................... RobbieFitzpatrick 4 65
(Richard Guest) *s.s: hld up: hdwy over 2f out: rdn over 1f out: styd on same pce ins fnl f* **33/1**

6 *nk* **Adatara (IRE)**[14] 7040 7-9-0 60..................................(b) ShaneKelly 10 62
(M M Lynch, Ire) *chsd ldrs: rdn and hung lft over 1f out: no ex fnl f* **50/1**

1602 **7** *2 ¾* **Hurakan (IRE)**[47] 6076 6-9-8 73.......................(p) RobertWilliams(5) 12 71
(Richard Price) *hld up: hdwy over 2f out: rdn over 1f out: no ex fnl f* **22/1**

-210 **8** *3 ½* **Welsh Bard (IRE)**[25] 6738 3-8-11 66................................... LukeMorris 5 59
(Sir Mark Prescott Bt) *mid-div: pushed along at several stages: drvn over 3f out: wknd fnl f* **5/2**[1]

2/66 **9** *½* **Cubism**[94] 4004 6-8-9 55 oh3...................................... FergusSweeney 1 47
(Anthony Middleton) *mid-div: lost pl over 4f out: sn bhd* **66/1**

0000 **10** *½* **Hector's Chance**[22] 6819 3-8-13 68........................(v[1]) RobertWinston 11 60
(Heather Main) *plld hrd: led over 11f out: rdn and hdd over 1f out: wknd fnl f* **25/1**

5213 **11** *hd* **Wayne Manor (IRE)**[25] 6738 3-9-2 71.................................. JimCrowley 9 62
(Ralph Beckett) *led after 1f: hdd over 11f out: chsd ldrs: rdn over 3f out: wknd over 2f out* **11/4**[2]

5032 **12** *14* **Saint Helena (IRE)**[38] 6333 4-9-10 70.............................. RyanMoore 7 42
(Harry Dunlop) *prom: rdn over 2f out: n.m.r and wknd over 1f out: eased* **6/1**[3]

3m 3.14s (-2.86) **Going Correction** -0.075s/f (Stan)
WFA 3 from 4yo+ 9lb 12 Ran SP% **116.1**
Speed ratings (Par 103): **105,104,104,102,102 102,100,98,98,98 98,90**
toteswingers 1&2 £17.50, 2&3 £16.60, 1&3 £21.20 CSF £104.73 CT £1233.77 TOTE £10.50: £2.70, £2.90, £4.40; EX 91.20 Trifecta £506.60 Part won. Pool: £675.50 - 0.40 winning tickets..
Owner Sheikh Hamdan Bin Mohammed Al Maktoum **Bred** Darley **Trained** Middleham Moor, N Yorks

FOCUS
There was another exciting finish in the second division of this handicap. It was the quicker leg by 1.12sec and the winner can do better still.

7382 BREEDERS' CUP LIVE ONLY ON ATR H'CAP 7f 32y(P)
7:40 (7:40) (Class 6) (0-60,60) 3-Y-0+ **£1,908** (£563; £281) **Stalls** High

Form RPR

1054 **1** **Elegant Muse**[28] 6641 4-9-6 59...(t) KierenFallon 3 67
(Michael Appleby) *mde all: shkn up over 1f out: rdn ins fnl f: styd on* **8/1**[3]

0301 **2** *½* **Athwaab**[30] 6585 5-9-6 59.. GeorgeBaker 6 66
(Noel Chance) *a.p: rdn to chse wnr ins fnl f: r.o* **8/1**[3]

4325 **3** *¾* **Lord Franklin**[10] 7146 3-8-9 55.. JasonHart(5) 4 60
(Eric Alston) *racd keenly: trckd wnr to 1/2-way: sn pushed along: rdn to chse wnr over 1f out tl ins fnl f: styd on* **7/2**[1]

0032 **4** *¾* **Men Don't Cry (IRE)**[7] 7225 3-9-1 56..............................(b) LiamKeniry 9 59
(Ed de Giles) *hld up: rdn over 2f out: r.o u.p ins fnl f: nrst fin* **9/2**[2]

4045 **5** *½* **Keys Of Cyprus**[7] 7225 10-9-3 56... PaulQuinn 8 58
(David Nicholls) *hld up: rdn over 1f out: r.o ins fnl f: nvr nrr* **9/1**

5505 **6** *1 ¼* **Desertcougar (IRE)**[9] 7158 3-9-2 57................................. SeanQuinlan 7 55
(Daniel Mark Loughnane) *hld up: hdwy over 2f out: rdn over 1f out: no ex ins fnl f* **20/1**

5000 **7** *½* **Odd Ball (IRE)**[58] 5750 5-9-6 59.. AmyRyan 2 56
(Lisa Williamson) *s.i.s: hld up: hdwy over 1f out: styd on same pce fnl f* **25/1**

0000 **8** *2 ¾* **Fleetwoodsands (IRE)**[7] 7224 5-9-7 60............(t[1]) RichardKingscote 10 49
(Milton Bradley) *hld up: rdn 1/2-way: nvr on terms* **8/1**[3]

026 **9** *nk* **Yes It's The Boy (USA)**[78] 5017 3-9-5 60.....................(b) LukeMorris 1 49
(Ed Walker) *prom: chsd wnr 1/2-way tl rdn over 1f out: wknd fnl f* **10/1**

30 **10** *nk* **Royal Selection (IRE)**[52] 5915 4-9-4 57..................... TomMcLaughlin 5 45
(Karen George) *prom: rdn over 2f out: wknd fnl f* **12/1**

0000 **11** *23* **Darrow (IRE)**[58] 5738 3-9-4 59.. DominicFox 12
(Wilf Storey) *chsd ldrs tl rdn and wknd over 2f out: t.o* **22/1**

-232 **12** *nse* **Chester Deelyte (IRE)**[256] 550 4-8-12 58........(v) ShirleyTeasdale(7) 11
(Lisa Williamson) *plld hrd and prom: rdn over 2f out: wknd wl over 1f out: t.o* **16/1**

1m 28.75s (-0.85) **Going Correction** -0.075s/f (Stan)
WFA 3 from 4yo+ 2lb 12 Ran SP% **119.4**
Speed ratings (Par 101): **101,100,99,98,98 96,96,93,92,92 66,65**
toteswingers 1&2 £19.70, 2&3 £9.00, 1&3 £5.20 CSF £69.10 CT £268.75 TOTE £9.60: £3.10, £2.90, £1.50; EX 51.40 Trifecta £211.20 Pool: £478.80 - 1.70 winning tickets..
Owner Terry Pryke **Bred** Genesis Green Stud Ltd **Trained** Danethorpe, Notts

FOCUS
The winner put in a dominant display under a good ride by Kieren Fallon in this low-grade handicap. The winner's best figure since she was a 2yo.

7383 TOTEPOOL MOBILE TEXT TOTE TO 89660 H'CAP 1m 1f 103y(P)
8:10 (8:10) (Class 6) (0-60,60) 3-Y-0+ **£1,908** (£563; £281) **Stalls** Low

Form RPR

0041 **1** **Hard Road**[10] 7148 3-9-4 58 6ex.. TedDurcan 2 69
(Chris Wall) *chsd ldrs: rdn to ld ins fnl f: r.o* **11/4**[1]

054 **2** *1 ¾* **Edgware Road**[29] 6616 4-9-8 58......................................(b) AdamKirby 10 65
(Sean Curran) *a.p: rdn over 1f out: r.o* **10/3**[2]

4034 **3** *1* **Tiger Webb**[6] 7250 4-9-7 57.. PaulMulrennan 13 62
(Michael Easterby) *led: rdn over 1f out: hdd and unable qck ins fnl f* **9/2**

050 **4** *¾* **Strawberry Flavour (GER)**[25] 6736 3-9-5 59.................. MartinDwyer 9 63
(James Tate) *hld up in tch: racd keenly: hmpd 8f out: pushed along over 2f out: rdn and hung rt ins fnl f: r.o* **40/1**

0000 **5** *nk* **Beautiful Lando (FR)**[23] 6804 4-9-9 59........................ RobertWinston 1 62
(Heather Main) *s.i.s: sn prom: rdn over 1f out: styd on same pce ins fnl f* **40/1**

0623 **6** *1* **Monthly Medal**[11] 7095 9-9-10 60..(t) DominicFox 4 61
(Wilf Storey) *hld up: swtchd rt and rdn over 1f out: edgd lft and r.o ins fnl f: nvr nrr* **18/1**

3602 **7** *2* **Retreat Content (IRE)**[24] 6758 4-9-2 57.................... GarryWhillans(5) 8 54
(Linda Perratt) *prom: rdn over 2f out: styd on same pce fr over 1f out* **20/1**

5422 **8** *¾* **Arctic Galaxy (CAN)**[8] 7200 3-9-5 59................................ WilliamBuick 7 54
(John Gosden) *hld up: hdwy over 3f out: rdn over 2f out: wknd fnl f* **7/2**[3]

300 **9** *2 ¾* **Another Squeeze**[23] 6792 4-9-7 57.............................. WilliamCarson 11 46
(Peter Hiatt) *chsd ldr 8f out tl rdn over 2f out: wknd over 1f out* **50/1**

0004 **10** *nse* **Nolecce**[11] 7095 5-9-7 57..(p) IPoullis 5 46
(Richard Guest) *hld up: rdn over 2f out: a in rr* **33/1**

1430 **11** *7* **Future Wonder (IRE)**[11] 7095 3-8-13 60............. DavidSimmonson(7) 6 35
(Brian Ellison) *hld up: rdn over 3f out: wknd over 2f out* **20/1**

/60- **12** *15* **Echo Dancer**[114] 1373 6-8-13 52.................................. MarkCoumbe(3) 12
(Trevor Wall) *s.i.s: sn pushed along in rr: wknd over 2f out: t.o* **100/1**

2m 0.85s (-0.85) **Going Correction** -0.075s/f (Stan)
WFA 3 from 4yo+ 4lb 12 Ran SP% **115.7**
Speed ratings (Par 101): **100,98,97,96,96 95,93,93,90,90 84,71**
toteswingers 1&2 £3.30, 2&3 £4.60, 1&3 £3.40 CSF £10.73 CT £39.20 TOTE £2.70: £1.60, £2.00, £1.90; EX 12.60 Trifecta £73.00 Pool: £778.99 - 8.00 winning tickets..
Owner Ms Aida Fustoq **Bred** Deerfield Farm **Trained** Newmarket, Suffolk
■ Stewards' Enquiry : Adam Kirby two-day ban: careless riding (Nov 9-10)

FOCUS
This looked a competitive handicap for the grade. The winner scored in good style from his main market rival and the form could be worth following.

7384 ATTHERACES.COM BREEDERS' CUP SITE NOW LIVE MEDIAN AUCTION MAIDEN STKS 1m 1f 103y(P)
8:40 (8:40) (Class 6) 3-5-Y-O **£1,908** (£563; £281) **Stalls** Low

Form RPR

20 **1** **Starfield**[23] 6792 3-9-3 0 WilliamBuick 2 86+
(John Gosden) *trckd ldrs: racd keenly: led over 1f out: shkn up and c clr ing fnl f: eased nr fin* **7/4**[1]

2-24 **2** *3 ¼* **Revered Citizen (USA)**[31] 5952 3-9-3 70 RyanMoore 9 79
(Sir Michael Stoute) *chsd ldr: pushed along over 2f out: rdn and ev ch over 1f out: styd on same pce ins fnl f* **5/2**[2]

232 **3** *1 ¼* **Fly Solo**[36] 6409 3-9-3 75 RobertWinston 8 76
(Alan Swinbank) *led: rdn and hdd over 1f out: no ex ins fnl f* **5/1**

3 **4** *1 ¼* **Syncopate**[22] 6827 3-9-3 0 KierenFallon 7 74
(Luca Cumani) *s.i.s: sn prom: pushed along over 2f out: styd on same pce appr fnl f* **11/4**[3]

0 **5** *8* **No Diamond**[21] 6839 5-9-7 0 (p) GeorgeBaker 1 57
(Michael Appleby) *hld up: nvr nrr* **100/1**

/000 **6** *21* **Super Smile (IRE)**[51] 5939 4-9-2 35 (t) AndrewMullen 6 8
(Michael Appleby) *plld hrd and prom: pushed along over 3f out: rdn and wknd over 2f out: t.o* **100/1**

7 *3 ¾* **Reverberate** 3-8-12 0 TomEaves 5
(Andrew Crook) *s.i.s: a in rr: wknd 3f out: t.o* **100/1**

0000 **8** *11* **Royal Gig**[62] 5589 3-8-12 22 JamesSullivan 3
(Tim Etherington) *mid-div tl wknd 3f out: t.o* **100/1**

2m 1.26s (-0.44) **Going Correction** -0.075s/f (Stan)
WFA 3 from 4yo+ 4lb **8** Ran SP% **112.2**
Speed ratings (Par 101): **98,95,94,92,85 67,63,54**
toteswingers 1&2 £2.80, 2&3 £2.60, 1&3 £1.70 CSF £6.17 TOTE £2.10: £1.10, £2.10, £2.40; EX 7.80 Trifecta £22.60 Pool: £673.76 - 22.27 winning tickets..
Owner Ms Rachel D S Hood **Bred** Dunchurch Lodge Stud Co **Trained** Newmarket, Suffolk

FOCUS
A decent maiden. The pace was very steady but the favourite powered clear from two rivals rated in the 70s. The winner is potentially on a good mark for handicaps.

7385 RACING POST FORM WITH TOTEPOOL MOBILE H'CAP 1m 141y(P)
9:10 (9:12) (Class 6) (0-55,59) 3-Y-O+ **£1,908** (£563; £281) **Stalls** Low

Form RPR

5000 **1** **Sasheen**[8] 7200 5-9-0 **53** (p) RaulDaSilva(3) 13 63
(Jeremy Gask) *a.p: chsd ldr over 5f out: led wl over 2f out: sn clr: styd on* **28/1**

622 **2** *1 ¾* **Goal (IRE)**[13] 7058 4-9-3 **53** (t) KierenFallon 3 59
(Charles Smith) *chsd ldrs: rdn over 1f out: r.o* **7/4**[1]

4324 **3** *nk* **Fortunate Bid (IRE)**[22] 6829 6-9-3 **53** (p) PatrickMathers 7 58
(Linda Stubbs) *hld up in tch: racd keenly: rdn to chse wnr over 1f out: nt run on* **12/1**

0660 **4** *nk* **Flipping**[24] 6758 5-9-3 **53** LukeMorris 2 58
(Eric Alston) *a.p: rdn over 2f out: r.o* **8/1**

4052 **5** *1 ½* **Thane Of Cawdor (IRE)**[10] 7148 3-8-12 **52** MickyFenton 11 53+
(Joseph Tuite) *s.i.s: hld up: hdwy over 1f out: r.o: nt rch ldrs* **4/1**[2]

3600 **6** *2 ¼* **Pastures New**[2] 7326 4-9-5 **55** (b) WilliamCarson 10 51
(Violet M Jordan) *s.i.s: sn pushed along in rr: styd on u.p fr over 1f out: nvr nrr* **40/1**

31 **7** *hd* **Praxios**[37] 6361 4-8-12 **51** (v) NeilFarley(3) 12 47
(Noel Wilson) *s.i.s: hld up: rdn over 2f out: nvr nrr* **5/1**[3]

5040 **8** *¾* **Rainsborough**[33] 3723 5-8-12 **48** (tp) LiamKeniry 5 42
(Peter Hedger) *hld up: rdn over 1f out: nvr on terms* **66/1**

0405 **9** *1 ½* **Crucis Abbey (IRE)**[7] 7222 4-9-5 **55** (p) LiamJones 4 45
(Mark Brisbourne) *racd keenly: led: hdd over 5f out: remained handy: nt clr run over 2f out: wknd over 1f out* **33/1**

6000 **10** *nk* **Broughton Place**[27] 6690 4-8-13 **49** JamieMackay 8 39
(Willie Musson) *plld hrd and prom: rdn over 3f out: wknd over 1f out* **50/1**

0405 **11** *3* **Eilean Mor**[11] 7095 4-9-2 **52** AndrewMullen 6 35
(R Mike Smith) *chsd ldrs: rdn over 3f out: wknd over 1f out* **28/1**

0061 **12** *2 ½* **North Central (USA)**[7] 7225 5-9-9 **59** 6ex (p) JoeFanning 1 36
(Keith Dalgleish) *chsd ldrs: pushed along over 3f out: wknd 2f out* **15/2**

0000 **13** *11* **Prohibition (IRE)**[30] 6586 6-9-5 **55** AdamKirby 9 7
(John Butler) *hld up: hdwy to ld over 5f out: hdd wl over 2f out: wknd over 1f out* **14/1**

1m 50.71s (0.21) **Going Correction** -0.075s/f (Stan)
WFA 3 from 4yo+ 4lb **13** Ran SP% **126.0**
Speed ratings (Par 101): **96,94,94,93,92 90,90,89,88,88 85,83,73**
toteswingers 1&2 £13.70, 2&3 £6.00, 1&3 £19.80 CSF £78.84 CT £705.50 TOTE £38.00: £5.90, £1.40, £3.30; EX 106.00 Trifecta £651.90 Part won. Pool: £869.26 - 0.10 winning tickets..
Owner Sasheen Partnership **Bred** Edward J G Young **Trained** Sutton Veny, Wilts

FOCUS
This minor handicap was run at a stop-start pace and the winner, who was well in, scored under a shrewd tactical ride. The form is a little shaky.
T/Plt: £252.50 to a £1 stake. Pool: £93,009.83 - 268.88 winning tickets. T/Qpdt: £85.80 to a £1 stake. Pool: £9,236.10 - 79.60 winning tickets. CR

7386 - 7389a (Foreign Racing) - See Raceform Interactive

7226 DUNDALK (A.W) (L-H)
Friday, October 26

OFFICIAL GOING: Standard

7390a MERCURY STKS (LISTED RACE) 5f (P)
8:00 (8:02) 2-Y-O+ **£21,666** (£6,333; £3,000; £1,000)

RPR

1 **Balmont Mast (IRE)**[21] 6854 4-9-11 101 JohnnyMurtagh 11 110+
(Edward Lynam, Ire) *w.w: prog on inner ent fnl 2f: wnt 5th appr fnl f: qcknd wl between horses to ld ins fnl 100yds* **7/2**[2]

2 *1* **Nocturnal Affair (SAF)**[21] 6854 6-9-11 110 (t) FergalLynch 12 107+
(David Marnane, Ire) *racd in mid-div: 9th 2f out: styd on strly on outer ent fnl f to go 2nd cl home* **13/2**

3 *¾* **Timeless Call (IRE)**[44] 6140 4-9-8 98 ChrisHayes 8 101
(Reginald Roberts, Ire) *broke wl: racd cl 3rd: pushed along to go 2nd 2f out: led ins fnl f tl hdd fnl 100yds: lost 2nd cl home* **20/1**

4 *nk* **Starspangledbanner (AUS)**[19] 6913 6-9-11 113 JPO'Brien 14 103+
(A P O'Brien, Ire) *trckd ldrs in 4th: pushed along and nt qckn over 1f out: kpt on same pce* **3/1**[1]

5 *hd* **Katla (IRE)**[12] 7086 4-9-11 102 SeamieHeffernan 1 96
(J F Grogan, Ire) *broke wl and racd in 2nd tl over 1f out: no ex ins fnl f* **12/1**

6 *½* **Zoola (IRE)**[35] 6424 2-8-4 99 NGMcCullagh 4 85
(Andrew Heffernan, Ire) *chsd ldrs tl no imp appr fnl f* **8/1**

7 *hd* **Liberating**[144] 2780 2-8-4 96 ShaneFoley 5 84
(Mrs John Harrington, Ire) *racd in rr: sme late hdwy* **25/1**

8 *nk* **Nero Emperor (IRE)**[343] 7467 3-9-11 96 WayneLordan 9 92
(T Stack, Ire) *sn led: hdd ins fnl f: sn wknd* **9/1**

9 *1 ¼* **Oor Jock (IRE)**[10] 7153 4-9-11 87 TadhgO'Shea 3 88
(John Patrick Shanahan, Ire) *bit slowly away: a in rr* **33/1**

10 *½* **Borderlescott**[19] 6908 10-10-0 PatSmullen 2 89
(Robin Bastiman) *hld up: pushed along over 2f out: sn no imp: eased* **10/1**

11 *nk* **Kingsgate Native (IRE)**[20] 6869 7-9-11 EmmetMcNamara 7 85
(Robert Cowell) *chsd ldrs whn n.m.r after 2f: no imp over 1f out* **6/1**[3]

12 *½* **Grey Danube (IRE)**[29] 6617 3-9-11 82 GaryCarroll 13 83
(D J Bunyan, Ire) *bit slowly away: a in rr* **25/1**

13 *17* **Experience (IRE)**[21] 6854 3-9-8 99 (p) WJLee 10 19
(David Wachman, Ire) *slowly away: a bhd* **22/1**

D *1 ¾* **Roicead (USA)**[44] 6140 5-9-11 101 (bt[1]) DeclanMcDonogh 6 97+
(W McCreery, Ire) *hld up towards rr: prog on inner whn nt clr run ins fnl f: kpt on clsng stages: fin 5th: disqualified and plcd last: rdr failed to weigh in* **25/1**

57.35s (57.35)
WFA 2 from 3yo+ 18lb **14** Ran SP% **136.3**
CSF £27.92 TOTE £6.00: £1.50, £2.60, £4.90; DF 26.90.
Owner Derek Iceton **Bred** Limestone & Tara Studs **Trained** Dunshaughlin, Co Meath

FOCUS
The 14 runners included three unpenalised Group 1 winners - the veteran Borderlescott, Kingsgate Native and Starspangledbanner - all of whom had something to prove at this stage of their careers. The standard is set around the third and tenth.

NOTEBOOK
Balmont Mast(IRE), twice a winner here and successful over 6f at the track a week previously, came out on top in course-record time. He pounced late, coming through between horses. The 6f Golden Rose Stakes, another Listed event, at Lingfield on November 17, was mentioned as a possible target but it subsequently transpired that he had picked up an injury. (op 4/1 tchd 9/2)
Nocturnal Affair(SAF), winner of this race a year ago, had finished second to Balmont Mast here a week previously. He got one and a half lengths closer on this occasion. He began to make headway under 2f out and ran on well inside the final furlong. (op 8/1)
Timeless Call(IRE), a three-time C&D winner, showed plenty of speed and was on the front end all the way. She had every chance until well inside the final furlong. (op 16/1)
Starspangledbanner(AUS), seeking a first win since returning from an unsuccessful spell at stud, had finished in rear in the Prix de la Foret on his previous start and was reverting to the minimum trip for the first time since finsihing second in the 2010 Nunthorpe Stakes. Always close up, he had every chance from 2f out and kept on without finding enough to get on terms inside the final furlong. According to trainer Aidan O'Brien, he will take his chance in the Breeders' Cup Sprint next weekend. (op 9/4)
Katla(IRE), a winner at this level at two, three and on her previous start at the Curragh, was always prominent and kept on in the closing stages having found no extra over 1f out. (op 14/1)
Zoola(IRE), one of two juveniles in the line-up, acquitted herself well. (op 14/1)
Nero Emperor(IRE), having his first run since scoring over this C&D in November, blazed away in front from the start and only gave best inside the final furlong.
Roicead(USA), having only his third run of the season, made headway from under 2f out and didn't get the run of the race. He finished fifth but was disqualified after his rider failed to weigh in. Official explanation: jockey said gelding reared up as stalls opened

7391 - 7394a (Foreign Racing) - See Raceform Interactive

7363 DONCASTER (L-H)
Saturday, October 27

OFFICIAL GOING: Soft (good to soft in places; 7.7)
Wind: Strong across Weather: Fine and dry

7395 UNIVERSAL RECYCLING APPRENTICE H'CAP (DIV I) 7f
1:25 (1:25) (Class 5) (0-75,75) 3-Y-O **£2,911** (£866; £432; £216) **Stalls** High

Form RPR

5246 **1** **Rocky Reef**[10] 7171 3-9-1 **74** (v) DanielMuscutt(5) 7 90
(Andrew Balding) *trckd ldrs: hdwy and cl up 1/2-way: led over 2f out: sn clr: easily* **5/1**[3]

4250 **2** *10* **Al's Memory (IRE)**[35] 6488 3-8-10 **67** NathanSweeney(3) 3 57
(David Evans) *hld up towards rr: swtchd to outer and hdwy 3f out: rdn over 2f out: styd on to take 2nd jst ins fnl f: no ch w wnr* **17/2**

222 **3** *2 ½* **Be My Rock**[24] 6792 3-9-7 **75** JamieJones 5 59
(Rae Guest) *hld up in rr: hdwy 2f out: sn rdn: styd on fnl f* **4/1**[2]

6230 **4** *1 ¾* **See Clearly**[24] 6782 3-9-1 **69** (p) DarylByrne 2 48
(Tim Easterby) *cl up: led 1/2-way: rdn along and hdd over 2f out: sn drvn and wknd appr fnl f* **8/1**

4000 **5** *½* **Man Of My Word**[8] 7218 3-8-2 **61** oh3 (p) JordanUys(5) 11 39
(Scott Dixon) *led: hdd 1/2-way: rdn along wl over 2f out: sn one pce* **33/1**

1550 **6** *½* **Red Trump (IRE)**[49] 6050 3-8-9 **63** MatthewLawson 12 39
(Charles Hills) *sn pushed along: in tch: rdn wl over 2f out: n.d* **11/1**

641 **7** *2 ¾* **Albert Tatlock (IRE)**[46] 6125 3-9-1 **72** ShirleyTeasdale(3) 1 41
(David Nicholls) *chsd ldrs: rdn along wl over 2f out: sn wknd* **15/2**

5024 **8** *1* **Cynthia Calhoun**[37] 6402 3-8-6 **65** RyanTate(5) 8 32
(Clive Cox) *chsd ldrs: rdn along bef 1/2-way: sn wknd* **14/1**

0155 **9** *1 ¼* **Baltic Bomber (IRE)**[56] 5831 3-8-3 **62** KevinLundie(5) 6 25
(John Quinn) *chsd ldrs: rdn along 3f out: sn wknd* **22/1**

6521 **10** *2 ½* **Gifted Dancer**[44] 6154 3-9-3 **71** AmyScott 10 28
(Henry Candy) *hld up in rr: effrt wl over 2f out: sn rdn and no hdwy* **7/2**[1]

3250 **11** *2 ¾* **Oakbrook**[47] 6105 3-8-7 **61** oh4 GarryWhillans 4 11
(Ann Duffield) *sligtly hmpd s: a in rr* **40/1**

1m 26.92s (0.62) **Going Correction** +0.20s/f (Good) **11** Ran SP% **117.0**
Speed ratings (Par 101): **104,92,89,87,87 86,83,82,80,78 74**
Tote Swingers: 1&2 £7.40, 1&3 £4.00, 2&3 £5.70 CSF £45.91 CT £187.49 TOTE £5.40: £1.90, £3.50, £1.70; EX 53.70 Trifecta £122.30 Pool: £510.52 - 3.13 winning tickets..
Owner Kingsclere Racing CLub **Bred** Gary Sanderson **Trained** Kingsclere, Hants

FOCUS
A weak handicap, confined to apprentice riders. The easy winner impressed in a standout time but the form in behind is moderate.

Cynthia Calhoun Official explanation: jockey said filly hung right throughout

7396 RACING POST IPAD APP H'CAP — 1m 4f

2:00 (2:00) (Class 2) (0-100,98) 3-Y-0+ **£12,938** (£3,850; £1,924; £962) **Stalls** Low

Form — RPR

1342 **1** **Party Line**[22] 6832 3-8-8 **87** .... MartinLane 20 — 98
(Mark Johnston) *chsd ldrs: hdwy on outer 4f out: led over 2f out: jnd and rdn over 1f out: drvn and styd on wl fnl f* **12/1**

0512 **2** *1 ½* **Art Scholar (IRE)**[10] 7175 5-9-4 **90** .... GeorgeBaker 12 — 99
(Michael Appleby) *hld up towards rr: stdy hdwy over 4f out: swtchd rt over 2f out: chal on bit over 1f out: rdn and ev ch ent fnl f: drvn and no ex last 100yds* **10/1**

0003 **3** *1 ¼* **Fulgur**[22] 6848 4-9-4 **90** .... KierenFallon 17 — 97
(Luca Cumani) *hld up in rr: stdy hdwy 5f out: swtchd to outer and effrt 3f out: rdn to chse ldrs wl over 1f out: kpt on same pce fnl f* **8/1**[3]

0034 **4** *1 ¼* **Sirvino**[10] 7176 7-9-5 **91** .... RichardHughes 2 — 96
(David Barron) *hld up on inner in midfield: hdwy over 4f out: swtchd rt 3f out: rdn 2f out: styd on fnl f: nrst fin* **12/1**

0000 **5** *1 ¼* **Right Step**[27] 6702 5-9-0 **86** .... RobertWinston 5 — 89
(Alan Jarvis) *in tch: hdwy to trck ldrs over 4f out: rdn wl over 2f out: drvn over 1f out: kpt on same pce fnl f* **40/1**

1321 **6** *shd* **Lady Kashaan (IRE)**[28] 6668 3-8-6 **85** .... JimmyQuinn 22 — 88
(Alan Swinbank) *in tch: hdwy over 3f out: rdn along and n.m.r wl over 2f out: kpt on appr fnl f: nrst fin* **11/1**

2543 **7** *½* **Ruacana**[29] 6625 3-8-10 **89** .... HayleyTurner 19 — 91
(Michael Bell) *trckd ldrs: hdwy to ld 3f out: rdn along and hdd over 2f out: sn drvn and grad wknd* **10/1**

0062 **8** *2 ¼* **Hillview Boy (IRE)**[16] 7002 8-9-2 **88** .... FrederikTylicki 14 — 86
(Jim Goldie) *midfield: hdwy on outer 4f out: effrt to chse wnr 2f out: sn rdn and grad wknd* **16/1**

000 **9** *hd* **Khawlah (IRE)**[119] 3632 4-9-11 **97** .... PhillipMakin 11 — 95
(Saeed Bin Suroor) *midfield on outer: hdwy 4f out: rdn along and in tch 3f out: drvn over 2f out and sn wknd* **66/1**

1250 **10** *10* **Life And Soul (IRE)**[77] 5079 5-9-6 **92** .... PaulMulrennan 13 — 74
(Amanda Perrett) *cl up on inner: disp ld over 4f out: rdn alon g 3f out: grad wknd* **50/1**

3030 **11** *nse* **Samba King**[13] 7082 3-9-1 **94** .... SilvestreDeSousa 6 — 76
(Mahmood Al Zarooni) *hld up: gd hdwy on inner to chse ldrs 3f out: rdn 2f out: sn wknd* **16/1**

6230 **12** *1 ½* **Scrapper Smith (IRE)**[28] 6668 6-9-6 **92** .... PJMcDonald 18 — 72
(Alistair Whillans) *stdd and swtchd lft s: hld up: a in rr* **20/1**

3000 **13** *1 ½* **Icon Dream (IRE)**[14] 7051 5-9-8 **94** .... GrahamLee 15 — 71
(Jim Goldie) *prom: rdn along over 3f out: sn wknd* **28/1**

1 **14** *2* **Proofreader**[127] 3349 3-8-11 **90** .... RobertHavlin 9 — 64
(John Gosden) *t.k.h: trckd ldrs: effrt 4f out: sn rdn along and wknd wl over 2f out* **4/1**[1]

3030 **15** *2 ¼* **Royal Peculiar**[22] 6832 4-9-1 **87** .... IanMongan 1 — 57
(Sir Henry Cecil) *chsd ldrs: rdn along over 3f out: sn wknd* **16/1**

0300 **16** *12* **Tepmokea (IRE)**[64] 5558 6-9-0 **89** .... MichaelMetcalfe(3) 16 — 40
(Mrs K Burke) *sn led: rdn along and jnd 4f out: drvn and hdd 3f out: sn wknd* **50/1**

0-00 **17** *9* **Cosmic Sun**[28] 6668 6-9-4 **90** .... DavidNolan 8 — 27
(Richard Fahey) *hld up: a towards rr* **66/1**

611- **18** *7* **Art History (IRE)**[135] 6528 4-9-6 **92** .... DanielTudhope 7 — 18
(David O'Meara) *midfield: rdn along over 4f out: sn wknd* **25/1**

2136 **19** *7* **Marshgate Lane (USA)**[28] 6677 3-9-1 **94** .... MickaelBarzalona 4
(Mahmood Al Zarooni) *hld up towards rr: swtchd to outer and hdwy 4f out: chsd ldrs wl over 2f out: sn rdn and wknd: eased fr wl over 1f out* **6/1**[2]

2000 **20** *87* **Crackentorp**[49] 6031 7-9-12 **98** .... DavidAllan 10
(Tim Easterby) *hld up in rr: rdn along over 3f out: sn lost tch: wl bhd and heavily eased fr over 1f out* **33/1**

0P06 **P** **Classic Vintage (USA)**[12] 7109 6-8-13 **85** ....(b) JimmyFortune 3
(Amanda Perrett) *midfield: lost pl bef 1/2-way: sn in rr: p.u over 4f out: b.b.v* **40/1**

2m 36.05s (1.15) **Going Correction** +0.325s/f (Good)
WFA 3 from 4yo+ 7lb — 21 Ran SP% **131.2**
Speed ratings (Par 109): **109,108,107,106,105 105,105,103,103,96 96,95,94,93,91 83,77,73,68,10**
Tote Swingers: 1&2 £13.50, 1&3 £19.00, 2&3 £9.70 CSF £122.84 CT £1050.86 TOTE £15.50: £3.30, £2.40, £2.90, £3.70; EX 131.60 Trifecta £789.80 Part won. Pool: £1,053.12 - 0.10 winning tickets..

Owner S R Counsell **Bred** Highclere Stud And Balmerino Bloodstock **Trained** Middleham Moor, N Yorks

FOCUS

A good handicap run at what seemed a fair pace. The form looks sound with the winner continuing her progress.

NOTEBOOK

Party Line, off the same mark as when runner-up to Fattsota (well held in the Group 3 St Simon Stakes at Newbury later on this day) at Ascot on her previous start, continued her progression with a game success. She may have more to offer.

Art Scholar(IRE), up 2lb for finishing second to the unbeaten First Mohican at Nottingham (1m2f, soft) last time, moved into the race going well but just didn't see it out quite as strongly as the winner. This was another career-best. (tchd 9-1)

Fulgur has dropped to a good mark and offered a bit more this time.

Sirvino couldn't reverse recent Nottingham placings with Art Scholar. (op 14-1)

Right Step ran better than of late with the visor left off. (op 50-1)

Lady Kashaan(IRE) ◆ is better than she showed. A winner over 1m6f on heavy at Haydock last time (off 5lb lower), she wasn't helped by losing her place early in the straight and lacked the speed to recover over this shorter trip, challenging more towards the inside than most.

Khawlah(IRE) ◆, who has struggled since winning a couple of UAE Classics in 2011, is being persevered with, and she travelled nicely and finished close enough to suggest she has a future on the race track. Better ground should help.

Samba King Official explanation: jockey said gelding had no more to give

Proofreader, gelded since making a winning debut at the Newmarket July course (1m2f, soft) in June, didn't run his race. (op 9-2)

Marshgate Lane(USA) ◆, better than he showed at Newmarket last time, raced in snatches but looked like staying on to have a big say until hanging badly left halfway up the straight. He was soon heavily eased (reported to have lost his action), but the suspicion remains we've yet to see the best of him, provided of course he's none the worse for this. Official explanation: jockey said colt lost its action (op 7-1)

Classic Vintage(USA) Official explanation: vet said gelding bled from the nose

7397 GENTING CASINOS LEVY BOARD H'CAP — 5f

2:30 (2:32) (Class 2) 3-Y-0+

£31,125 (£9,320; £4,660; £2,330; £1,165; £585) **Stalls** High

Form — RPR

0411 **1** **Jack Dexter**[7] 7240 3-9-1 **97** .... GrahamLee 22 — 108+
(Jim Goldie) *trckd ldrs stands' side: smooth hdwy 2f out: led over 1f out: rdn ins fnl f: kpt on wl* **4/1**[1]

1014 **2** *nk* **Jamaican Bolt (IRE)**[14] 7063 4-8-10 **92** .... SilvestreDeSousa 9 — 102+
(Geoffrey Oldroyd) *trckd ldrs stands' side: effrt wl over 1f out: rdn to chse wnr ins fnl f: kpt on: 2nd of 16 in gp* **9/1**[3]

2010 **3** *¾* **Mass Rally (IRE)**[14] 7066 5-9-3 **99** ....(b) PaulMulrennan 8 — 106
(Michael Dods) *trckd ldrs stands' side: hdwy wl over 1f out: swtchd lft and rdn ent fnl f: styd on wl towards fin: 3rd of 16 in gp* **16/1**

-004 **4** *1* **York Glory (USA)**[135] 3078 4-8-12 **94** ....(b) PhillipMakin 21 — 98
(Kevin Ryan) *trckd ldrs gng wl stands' side: hdwy and ev ch wl over 1f out: sn rdn and kpt on same pce fnl f: 4th of 16 in gp* **16/1**

0413 **5** *1 ¼* **Ajjaadd (USA)**[13] 7080 6-8-4 **93** ....(p) DavidBergin(7) 7 — 92
(Ted Powell) *dwlt and in rr stands' side: hdwy 2f out: sn rdn and styd on fnl f: nrst fin: 5th of 16 in gp* **20/1**

0300 **6** *hd* **Judge 'n Jury**[28] 6666 8-9-4 **100** ....(t) LukeMorris 11 — 98
(Ronald Harris) *cl up stands' side: rdn to ld 2f out: drvn and hdd over 1f out: wknd fnl f: 6th of 16 in gp* **40/1**

4101 **7** *½* **Doc Hay (USA)**[21] 6869 5-9-10 **106** .... DanielTudhope 19 — 103
(David O'Meara) *towards rr stands' side: hdwy over 2f out: sn rdn: styd on fnl f: nrst fin 7th of 16 in gp* **9/1**[3]

4050 **8** *1* **Steps (IRE)**[14] 7063 4-8-10 **92** .... AndreaAtzeni 10 — 85
(Roger Varian) *trckd ldrs stands' side: rdn wl over 1f out: no imp: 8th of 16 in gp* **10/1**

000 **9** *1 ¼* **Move In Time**[7] 7243 4-8-10 **92** ....(p) TomEaves 13 — 81
(Bryan Smart) *towards rr stands' side: hdwy 2f out: sn rdn and kpt on: n.d: 9th of 16 in gp* **33/1**

0330 **10** *1* **Ponty Acclaim (IRE)**[7] 7243 3-9-0 **96** .... KierenFallon 6 — 81
(Tim Easterby) *prom stands' side: rdn along over 2f out: sn wknd: 10th of 16 in gp* **20/1**

0002 **11** *¾* **Captain Dunne (IRE)**[14] 7063 7-8-13 **95** .... DavidAllan 17 — 77
(Tim Easterby) *a towards rr stands' side: 11th of 16 in gp* **16/1**

0030 **12** *1* **Kaldoun Kingdom (IRE)**[7] 7240 7-8-8 **90** .... BarryMcHugh 20 — 69
(Richard Fahey) *a towards rr stands' side: 12th of 16 in gp* **14/1**

314 **13** *hd* **Kyleakin Lass**[28] 6666 3-8-10 **92** .... JamesSullivan 15 — 70
(Ian Wood) *a towards rr stands' side: 13th of 16 in gp* **16/1**

3000 **14** *½* **Secret Witness**[1] 7366 6-9-9 **105** ....(b) HayleyTurner 12 — 81
(Ronald Harris) *in tch stands' side whn n.m.r over 2f out: sn rdn and wknd: 15th of 16 in gp* **33/1**

010 **14** *dht* **Cheviot (USA)**[35] 6468 6-9-8 **104** ....(p) IanMongan 18 — 80
(Ian Semple) *racd stands' side: trckd ldrs: rdn and edgd lft over 2f out: sn lost pl: 14th of 16 in gp* **33/1**

5506 **16** *nk* **Dungannon**[14] 7066 5-8-13 **95** .... JimmyFortune 5 — 70
(Andrew Balding) *hld up far side: hdwy 1/2-way: led that gp 2f out: sn rdn and no ch w stands' side gp: 1st of 5 in gp* **7/1**[2]

0-00 **17** *2 ½* **Moorhouse Lad**[49] 6028 9-8-8 **90** ....(b) MartinLane 14 — 56
(Garry Moss) *racd stands' side: w ldr: rdn over 2f out: lost pl over 1f out: 16th of 16 in gp* **40/1**

1011 **18** *7* **Ballista (IRE)**[46] 6116 4-9-8 **104** .... RichardKingscote 1 — 45
(Tom Dascombe) *led far side gp: rdn along 1/2-way: sn hdd & wknd: 2nd of 5 in gp* **12/1**

0040 **19** *1 ¾* **Mirza**[14] 7066 5-9-4 **100** .... RichardHughes 2 — 35
(Rae Guest) *chsd ldrs far side: rdn along over 2f out: sn wknd: 3rd of 5 in gp* **14/1**

-000 **20** *½* **Mister Manannan (IRE)**[49] 6028 5-8-9 **91** .... MartinDwyer 3 — 24
(David Nicholls) *dwlt: sn chsng ldr far side: rdn along and wknd over 2f out: 4th of 5 in gp* **100/1**

1002 **21** *2* **Tax Free (IRE)**[32] 6557 10-8-11 **93** .... AdrianNicholls 4 — 19
(David Nicholls) *trckd ldng pair far side: rdn along over 2f out: sn wknd: 5th of 5 in gp* **25/1**

1m 0.02s (-0.48) **Going Correction** +0.20s/f (Good) — 21 Ran SP% **134.2**
Speed ratings (Par 109): **111,110,109,107,105 105,104,103,101,99 98,96,96,95,95 95,91,79,77,76 73**
Tote Swingers: 1&2 £44.00, 1&3 £71.80, 2&3 £82.40 CSF £36.38 CT £568.42 TOTE £5.50: £1.70, £3.00, £5.60, £5.10; EX 68.30 Trifecta £1540.20 Pool: £63,048.31 - 30.70 winning tickets..

Owner Jim Goldie Racing Club **Bred** Jim Goldie **Trained** Uplawmoor, E Renfrews

FOCUS

The majority of these were positioned middle to stands' side, and the five who raced far side had no chance. It proved difficult to make up significant ground. The first two are on the upgrade.

NOTEBOOK

Jack Dexter made it a hat-trick of big-field handicap wins, adding to victories in the Ayr Bronze Cup (off 84) and the apprentices' race on Champions Day (93). He's beaten a total of 67 rivals on his last three starts, and it's a particularly impressive streak considering his wins have been gained between 5f-7f. While Group races don't always set up like these competitive handicaps, Jack Dexter is surely on his way to becoming a Pattern-class performer. (op 15-2)

Jamaican Bolt(IRE) was behind a couple of these when fourth at York on his previous start, but he went off too fast on that occasion and this was better. Lightly raced, he can go on improving when the ground is on the soft side. (tchd 17-2)

Mass Rally(IRE) returned to the sort of form he showed when winning the Ayr Silver Cup, keeping on after having to be switched. (op 14-1)

York Glory(USA) hasn't gone on from a promising campaign last year, and he'd been off for 135 days, but this was more like it. (op 14-1 tchd 20-1)

Ajjaadd(USA), who missed the break and was stuck widest of the main group when delivering his challenge, and he could yet do better. (op 16-1)

Doc Hay(USA) ◆, who won the Portland here earlier in the year and most recently an Ascot Listed event, got further back than ideal and had nothing to lead him into the race. (op 10-1)

Steps(IRE) was held off 3lb higher than when winning this last year. (op 14-1)

Cheviot(USA) Official explanation: jockey said gelding hung left throughout

Dungannon ◆, very well backed, was much the best of the five runners who raced far side. (op 8-1)

Mirza Official explanation: jockey said gelding hung left throughout

Mister Manannan(IRE) Official explanation: jockey said gelding hung left

7398 RACING POST TROPHY (GROUP 1) (ENTIRE COLTS & FILLIES) 1m (S)
3:05 (3:05) (Class 1) 2-Y-O

£122,493 (£46,440; £23,241; £11,577; £5,810; £2,916) **Stalls** High

Form RPR

1 **Kingsbarns (IRE)**[17] 6991 2-9-0 0 JPO'Brien 7 120+
(A P O'Brien, Ire) *trckd ldng pair: hdwy 3f out: led wl over 1f out: rdn and edgd lft ins fnl f: styd on wl* **15/8**[1]

11 **2** 1 3/4 **Van Der Neer**[11] 7125 2-9-0 0 RichardHughes 1 116+
(Richard Hannon) *hld up in tch: hdwy 1/2-way: effrt over 2f out: rdn to chse ldng pair and hung rt over 1f out: drvn ins fnl f: kpt on to take 2nd on line* **5/1**

1211 **3** shd **Steeler (IRE)**[28] 6671 2-9-0 112 KierenFallon 3 116
(Mark Johnston) *trckd ldr: led 3f out: rdn and hdd wl over 1f out: drvn and kpt on fnl f: lost 2nd fnl strides* **7/2**[3]

1 **4** 2 **First Cornerstone (IRE)**[62] 5642 2-9-0 0 ChrisHayes 4 112
(A Oliver, Ire) *trckd ldng pair: hdwy 3f out: rdn 2f out: sn drvn and one pce* **11/1**

21 **5** 3 1/2 **Trading Leather (IRE)**[14] 7053 2-9-0 0 KevinManning 5 104
(J S Bolger, Ire) *led: hdd 3f out and sn rdn along: wknd 2f out* **3/1**[2]

1126 **6** 6 **Sir Patrick Moore (FR)**[67] 5471 2-9-0 0 HayleyTurner 6 91
(Harry Dunlop) *in tch: rdn along over 3f out: sn outpcd* **50/1**

0354 **7** 7 **Birdman (IRE)**[28] 6671 2-9-0 105 MartinLane 2 75
(David Simcock) *dwlt: a in rr* **50/1**

1m 40.32s (1.02) **Going Correction** +0.20s/f (Good) 7 Ran SP% **110.9**
Speed ratings (Par 109): **102,100,100,98,94 88,81**
Tote Swingers: 1&2 £2.10, 1&3 £1.70, 2&3 £2.70 CSF £11.03 TOTE £2.60: £2.20, £2.70; EX 10.70.
Owner Mrs John Magnier & Michael Tabor & Derrick Smith **Bred** Mrs Ann Marie O'Brien **Trained** Ballydoyle, Co Tipperary

FOCUS
A solid running of this Group 1 prize. Five of the last 11 runnings of the Racing Post Trophy have produced a British Classic winner, with High Chaparral (2001), Motivator (2004), Authorized (2006) and Camelot (2011) going on to take the Derby, while Brian Boru (2002) won the St Leger. With the field racing up the middle of the track, the winner was helped by the third and fifth taking each other on, while the runner-up was reportedly unsuited by the ground, and the fourth looked short of race-fitness. This rates the second-best 2yo performance of the year and Kingsbarns looks a top 3yo prospect. The form is up to scratch for the race, with the third offering a solid guide.

NOTEBOOK
Kingsbarns(IRE), who landed a gamble, didn't win flashily and the race rather fell apart, but showed enough to suggest that he may have Classic aspirations. He had only started out 17 days earlier, when winning easily at Navan (1m, soft), and had to be supplemented, after which he was heavily punted (like stablemate Camelot 12 months earlier). It's also worth noting the last two horses who won this with just a debut maiden success to their name were Motivator and Camelot. He doesn't strike as an obvious Guineas type, looking more of a galloper than a speed horse, and while it's true Camelot managed to get away with the 1m trip at Newmarket, he only got up on the line despite unseasonably testing ground putting the emphasis on stamina. Kingsbarns also has a round action, suggesting quicker conditions may be a concern, although his jockey, who's usually worth listening to, has no worries on that score. Ladbrokes went a standout 8-1 about Aidan O'Brien's colt for both Newmarket and the Epsom Derby. (op 9-4)
Van Der Neer was also supplemented. He'd only won a couple of minor races over 6f-7f, but his connections really like him and weren't worried about the trip. The ground, though, did not seem to suit, and Richard Hannon's colt was never going well enough to challenge. He did well to keep on for second, especially as he hung right under pressure, and may yet do better. (op 9-2 tchd 11-2)
Steeler(IRE) wasn't helped by being taken on up front by the below-par Trading Leather, who had won the Autumn Stakes two weeks earlier. Mark Johnston's runner has the potential to improve again at three, when he may be with Godolphin. (tchd 10-3 and 4-1)
First Cornerstone(IRE) travelled second best but shaped like a horse in need of the run once off the bridle. He hadn't been seen since winning the Futurity Stakes in August. (op 10-1 tchd 9-1)
Trading Leather(IRE) dropped out rather tamely and probably found the ground too much. (op 10-3)
Sir Patrick Moore(FR) was outclassed. (tchd 66-1)
Birdman(IRE) offered nothing. (op 40-1)

7399 CROWNHOTEL-BAWTRY.COM NURSERY 7f
3:35 (3:36) (Class 3) (0-95,85) 2-Y-O **£7,439** (£2,213; £829; £829) **Stalls** High

Form RPR

01 **1** **Code Of Honor**[35] 6481 2-9-7 **85** FergusSweeney 2 89
(Henry Candy) *led: rdn along and hdd 2f out: drvn over 1f out: edgd rt wl ins fnl f: rallied wl fnl f to ld last 75yds* **7/1**[3]

0361 **2** 1 1/4 **Pure Excellence**[8] 7207 2-9-7 **85** SilvestreDeSousa 3 86
(Mark Johnston) *chsd ldr: pushed along and sltly outpcd 2f out: sn rdn: styd on u.p fnl f* **7/2**[1]

2231 **3** 1/2 **Intimidate**[22] 6845 2-9-3 **81** FrederikTylicki 12 81
(Jeremy Noseda) *chsd ldrs: hdwy 3f out: led 2f out: rdn and hung rt ent fnl f: sn drvn: hdd & wknd last 75yds* **7/2**[1]

3352 **3** dht **Elegant In Silk (USA)**[30] 6604 2-8-8 **72** (b[1]) ChrisHayes 7 72
(William Haggas) *s.i.s and in rr: hdwy wl over 2f out: rdn wl over 1f out: styd on fnl f: nrst fin* **16/1**

1306 **5** 4 **Diggory Delvet**[19] 6920 2-8-10 **74** BarryMcHugh 9 63
(Richard Fahey) *towards rr: hdwy wl over 2f out: rdn wl over 1f out: one pce* **17/2**

0231 **6** 3 **Ready (IRE)**[7] 7244 2-8-11 **75** RobertWinston 10 57
(Garry Moss) *in tch: effrt over 2f out: sn rdn and no imp* **4/1**[2]

0350 **7** 2 **Mirlo Blanco (IRE)**[35] 6475 2-8-3 **67** PatrickMathers 1 43
(Richard Fahey) *chsd ldrs: rdn along 3f out: sn wknd* **25/1**

3000 **8** 3 1/4 **Mickstathetricksta**[105] 4116 2-8-3 **67** JamesSullivan 5 35
(Scott Dixon) *chsd ldrs: rdn along 1/2-way: sn wknd* **33/1**

043 **9** 1 **Secret Beau**[92] 4532 2-8-9 **73** MartinLane 4 38
(Ralph Beckett) *in tch: hdwy to chse ldrs 3f out: sn rdn and wknd 2f out* **20/1**

2003 **10** 30 **King Oliver**[17] 6980 2-8-9 **73** RichardHughes 6
(Richard Hannon) *in tch: lost pl qckly over 3f out: sn bhd and eased* **12/1**

1m 28.74s (2.44) **Going Correction** +0.20s/f (Good) 10 Ran SP% **112.6**
Speed ratings (Par 99): **94,92,92,92,87 84,81,78,76,42**
Place: Intimidate £0.80 Elegant In Silk £1.30. Tricast: Code Of Honor, Pure Excellence, Intimidate £44.79, Code Of Honor, Pure Excellence, Elegant In Silk £167.62. Tote Swingers: 1&2 £3.80, C&I £2.20, C&E £4.90, P&I £1.20, P&E £3.60. CSF £28.56 TOTE £9.00: £2.70, £27, £Owner, £D B Clark/ J J ByrneBred J Byrne And Partners Trifecta £Trained Kingston Warren, Oxon n.
■ Stewards' Enquiry : Fergus Sweeney two-day ban: careless riding (Nov 10,14)

FOCUS
A modest nursery in which the winner and second, the topweights, were rated 10lb below the race ceiling. The form makes sense with the winner building on his maiden win.

NOTEBOOK
Code Of Honor produced a useful effort to follow up a 50-1 success gained in a Newbury maiden (7f, good to firm) on his second start. He clearly didn't mind the softer conditions and is a decent sort in the making. (tchd 13-2 and 8-1)
Pure Excellence, successful in a conditions race on testing ground at Haydock last time, ran right up to her best in defeat. (op 4-1 tchd 10-3)
Intimidate, off the mark in a Yarmouth maiden on bad ground on his previous start, threw away a good chance of following up by lugging right under pressure. (op 12-1)
Elegant In Silk(USA), runner-up in a 1m nursery on her previous start, missed the break in first-time blinkers but was finishing strongly when short of room near the line. She might have been second with a clear run. (op 12-1)
Ready(IRE) couldn't build on his success in an ordinary Catterick maiden. (op 9-2 tchd 5-1)

7400 PARK HILL HOSPITAL STKS (REGISTERED AS THE DONCASTER STAKES) (LISTED RACE) 6f
4:10 (4:11) (Class 1) 2-Y-O **£13,616** (£5,149; £2,573; £1,285) **Stalls** High

Form RPR

31 **1** **Invincible Warrior (IRE)**[31] 6581 2-9-1 85 KierenFallon 2 100+
(Brian Meehan) *trckd ldrs: hdwy on outer 2f out: rdn to chal ent fnl f: drvn to ld last 100yds: edgd rt and kpt on wl* **5/2**[2]

421 **2** 1/2 **Emell**[57] 5784 2-9-1 95 RichardHughes 1 99
(Richard Hannon) *prom: rdn wl over 1f out: drvn and n.m.r ins fnl f: kpt on gamely* **4/1**[3]

13 **3** hd **Taayel (IRE)**[35] 6483 2-9-1 0 TadhgO'Shea 5 98
(John Gosden) *chsd ldrs: rdn along wl over 1f out: led jst ins fnl f: sn drvn and hdd last 100yds: no ex* **2/1**[1]

4150 **4** 2 **Jillnextdoor (IRE)**[21] 6883 2-8-10 103 MartinDwyer 3 87+
(Mick Channon) *rrd and slowly away: hdwy 1/2-way: effrt to join ldrs on outer wl over 1f out: sn rdn and one pce fnl f* **8/1**

4043 **5** nk **Lucky Beggar (IRE)**[14] 7065 2-9-1 104 MichaelHills 8 91
(Charles Hills) *led: rdn along 2f out: drvn and hdd jst ins fnl f: wknd* **8/1**

134 **6** 17 **Dashing David (IRE)**[16] 7009 2-9-1 90 JimmyFortune 7 40
(Richard Hannon) *hld up: a in rr: rdn along and outpcd fr over 2f out* **12/1**

1m 14.78s (1.18) **Going Correction** +0.20s/f (Good) 6 Ran SP% **111.8**
Speed ratings (Par 103): **100,99,99,96,96 73**
Tote Swingers: 1&2 £2.20, 2&3 £1.60 CSF £12.73 TOTE £4.00: £2.70, £1.70; EX 16.20 Trifecta £13.20 Pool: £1,708.57 - 96.87 winning tickets..
Owner Car Colston Hall Stud **Bred** Car Colston Hall Stud **Trained** Manton, Wilts
■ Stewards' Enquiry : Tadhg O'Shea two-day ban: used whip above permitted level (Nov 10,14)

FOCUS
An ordinary juvenile Listed event, and again they raced middle to stands' side. Routine form for the grade.

NOTEBOOK
Invincible Warrior(IRE), whose first two starts came over 6f on the Kempton Polytrack, most recently winning a maiden, was good enough to cope with the step up in class. He's well regarded and his connections, who think he'll be better on quicker ground, suggested he may be aimed at a Guineas trial next year. (op 10-3)
Emell, absent since winning a Salisbury maiden (6f, good to soft) at the end of August, ran a decent race in defeat and could do better again next year. (tchd 7-2 and 5-1)
Taayel(IRE) didn't match the form of his Mill Reef third, perhaps being unsuited by the soft ground, while racing against the stands' rail may not have been the place to be. (tchd 15-8)
Jillnextdoor(IRE) did well to finish so close after losing several lengths when rearing in the stalls. (op 7-1)

7401 RACING POST SUPPORTS PROSTATE CANCER UK CONDITIONS STKS 7f
4:45 (4:45) (Class 3) 3-Y-O+

£8,092 (£2,423; £1,211; £605; £302; £152) **Stalls** High

Form RPR

3414 **1** **Captain Ramius (IRE)**[21] 6868 6-8-11 109 PhillipMakin 1 101
(Kevin Ryan) *cl up on outer: effrt 2f out: rdn to chal over 1f out: drvn to ld ins fnl f: edgd rt last 100yds: kpt on* **10/3**[2]

2000 **2** 1 1/2 **Justineo**[37] 6400 3-8-9 96 AndreaAtzeni 2 97
(Roger Varian) *led: rdn along 2f out: drvn over 1f out: hdd and n.m.r ins fnl f: no ex towards fin* **33/1**

0156 **3** 1/2 **Right To Dream (IRE)**[36] 6449 3-9-2 100 KierenFallon 3 103
(Brian Meehan) *hld up: hdwy over 2f out: rdn to chse ldrs over 1f out: drvn and n.m.r ins fnl f: kpt on fnl f* **16/1**

5241 **4** 10 **Skilful**[21] 6868 4-8-11 111 RobertHavlin 8 70
(John Gosden) *cl up: effrt and disp ld 3f out: rdn 2f out: sn drvn and btn over 1f out* **4/6**[1]

6555 **5** 1 1/4 **Webbow (IRE)**[21] 6882 10-8-11 95 MartinDwyer 7 67
(Julie Camacho) *chsd ldrs: rdn along wl over 2f out: sn wknd* **16/1**

-304 **6** 2 3/4 **Bronterre**[114] 3784 3-8-9 110 RichardHughes 6 60
(Richard Hannon) *hld up: a in rr* **8/1**[3]

0550 **7** 2 3/4 **Lord Ofthe Shadows (IRE)**[22] 6831 3-8-9 87 GrahamLee 5 52
(Richard Hannon) *hld up: a towards rr: rdn along and outpcd fnl 2f* **33/1**

51-0 **8** 11 **Monsieur Chevalier (IRE)**[21] 6869 5-8-11 111 JimmyFortune 4 24
(P J O'Gorman) *chsd ldrs: rdn along 3f out: sn wknd* **16/1**

1m 27.94s (1.64) **Going Correction** +0.20s/f (Good)
WFA 3 from 4yo+ 2lb 8 Ran SP% **117.7**
Speed ratings (Par 107): **98,96,95,84,82 79,76,64**
Tote Swingers 1&2 £13.60, 2&3 £25.90, 1&3 £6.30 CSF £98.90 TOTE £3.80: £1.50, £7.40, £3.10; EX 139.50 Trifecta £796.00 Pool: £1,507.20 - 1.42 winning tickets..
Owner Mrs Clodagh McStay **Bred** P G Lyons **Trained** Hambleton, N Yorks

FOCUS
Again, the action was middle to stands' side. A decent conditions event, but muddling form and the winner did not have to run near his best.

NOTEBOOK
Captain Ramius(IRE), this season's Ayr Gold Cup winner, didn't have to run to his official mark of 109 considering he had 13lb in hand over Justineo and 16lb in hand over Right To Dream. (op 9-2)
Justineo has been highly tried and would have been better off switching to a handicap, having dropped to a mark of 96.
Right To Dream(IRE) had a tough task conceding weight all round. He ran well but this isn't form to get carried away with.
Skilful, runner-up in this last year, may not have been on the best ground against the stands' rail, but he was basically just nowhere near the form he showed when defeating today's winner off 105 at Ascot last time. (op 5-6)

7402 UNIVERSAL RECYCLING APPRENTICE H'CAP (DIV II) 7f
5:20 (5:20) (Class 5) (0-75,75) 3-Y-O **£2,911** (£866; £432; £216) **Stalls** High

Form RPR

4405 **1** **Serene Oasis (IRE)**[7] 7247 3-9-3 71 (v) CharlesBishop 10 81
(Mick Channon) *mde all: rdn wl over 1f out: drvn ins fnl f: kpt on gamely* **9/2**[2]

6455 **2** *nk* **Dubious Escapade (IRE)**[90] 4624 3-8-13 **67**.......................... LMcNiff 3 76
(Ann Duffield) *in tch: hdwy to chse ldrs over 2f out: rdn to chse ldng pair over 1f out: styd on to chal ins fnl f and ev ch tl drvn and no ex nr fin* **8/1**

6002 **3** *2 ½* **Fortrose Academy (IRE)**[15] 7022 3-8-5 **64**.............. DanielMuscutt(5) 5 67
(Andrew Balding) *cl up: disp ld 2f out: rdn over 1f out and ev ch tl drvn and wknd fnl f* **13/2**

1215 **4** *5* **Mount Mayday (IRE)**[24] 6773 3-8-8 **65**.................... ThomasBrown(3) 7 55
(Stuart Williams) *t.k.h: chsd ldrs: rdn over 2f out: sn one pce* **4/1**[1]

0306 **5** *shd* **Quick Bite (IRE)**[16] 7004 3-9-2 **73**..............................(v) NoelGarbutt(3) 6 62
(Hugo Palmer) *dwlt: sn in tch: hdwy to chse ldrs over 3f out: rdn over 2f out and sn btn* **8/1**

2265 **6** *1 ¾* **Pashan Garh**[18] 6965 3-8-13 **70**............................. GeorgeDowning(3) 11 55
(Pat Eddery) *a towards rr* **8/1**

5355 **7** *4 ½* **Sabore**[33] 6542 3-8-4 **61** oh6... DavidBergin(3) 1 34
(Richard Fahey) *chsd ldrs: pushed along 1/2-way: sn rdn and wknd* **20/1**

0364 **8** *3 ½* **Sir Windsorlot (IRE)**[81] 4913 3-8-2 **61** oh3.................... KevinStott(5) 9 25
(John Quinn) *chsd ldrs: rdn along 3f out: sn wknd* **14/1**

-340 **9** *12* **Bengaline**[14] 7055 3-8-2 **61** oh4......................................(p) JordanUys(5) 2
(Scott Dixon) *t.k.h: prom: rdn along 3f out: sn wknd* **25/1**

0435 **10** *2 ¼* **Travis County (IRE)**[16] 7001 3-8-7 **66**.............................. RPWalsh(5) 4
(Brian Ellison) *s.i.s: a bhd* **5/1**[3]

1m 29.45s (3.15) **Going Correction** +0.20s/f (Good) **10** Ran SP% **116.8**
Speed ratings (Par 101): **90,89,86,81,80 78,73,69,56,53**
Tote Swingers 1&2 £7.30, 2&3 £9.60, 1&3 £6.10 CSF £40.49 TOTE £5.20: £1.90, £2.40, £2.40; EX 37.90 Trifecta £268.50 Pool: £1,436.56 - 4.01 winning tickets..
Owner Doric Racing **Bred** Round Hill Stud **Trained** West Ilsley, Berks
■ Stewards' Enquiry : L McNiff two-day ban: used whip above permitted level (Nov 10,14)

FOCUS
Few got into the second division of this modest apprentices' handicap. It was the slower division although the ground had worsened. The winner is rated back to her summer best.
T/Jkpt: Not won. T/Plt: £116.60 to a £1 stake. Pool: £118,950.23 - 744.46 winning tickets.
T/Qpdt: £17.70 to a £1 stake. Pool: £7,542.76 - 315.08 winning tickets. JR

7371 NEWBURY (L-H)
Saturday, October 27

OFFICIAL GOING: Heavy (soft in places; 5.4)
Wind: Brisk acrss Weather: Sunny

7403 SAXON-GATE.COM E B F MAIDEN FILLIES' STKS 1m (S)
1:40 (1:44) (Class 4) 2-Y-O **£4,398** (£1,309; £654; £327) **Stalls** Centre

Form RPR

2 **1** **Secret Gesture**[18] 6966 2-9-0 0.. JimCrowley 1 90+
(Ralph Beckett) *trckd ldrs: led ins fnl 2f and sn jnd: shkn up over 1f out: pushed clr ins fnl f* **11/8**[1]

2 *2 ¾* **I Say (IRE)** 2-9-0 0.. JoeFanning 3 81+
(William Haggas) *trckd ldrs: qcknd to chal fr 2f out: sn drvn outpcd by wnr ins fnl f but styd on wl for 2nd* **20/1**

3 *2 ¼* **Enaitch (IRE)** 2-9-0 0.. SamHitchcott 6 76+
(Mick Channon) *s.i.s: in rr: rdn over 3f out: swtchd lft to outer over 2f out: drvn and styd on to take 3rd appr fnl f: kpt on: nt rch ldng duo* **8/1**[3]

0 **4** *10* **Cherry Malotte**[10] 7159 2-9-0 0... WilliamBuick 10 54
(John Gosden) *chsd ldrs: drvn and hung lft fr over 2f out: wknd wl over 1f out* **10/1**

5 *½* **Absolutely Right (IRE)** 2-9-0 0... PatDobbs 16 53+
(Richard Hannon) *s.i.s: in rr: pushed along 3f out: hdwy over 1f out: kpt on fnl f but nvr any ch* **9/1**

6 *1 ¼* **Vega Dance (IRE)** 2-9-0 0.. AdamKirby 11 50+
(Clive Cox) *t.k.h: chsd ldrs early: stdd in mid-div whn hmpd over 2f out: kpt on again fnl f* **11/1**

7 *2 ¾* **Wild Anthem** 2-9-0 0... DaneO'Neill 5 44
(Hughie Morrison) *chsd ldrs: rdn 3f out: wknd 2f out* **25/1**

00 **8** *1 ¾* **Rock Diamond (IRE)**[22] 6841 2-9-0 0................................ LiamKeniry 7 40
(Sylvester Kirk) *chsd ldrs: rdn 3f out: wknd 2f out* **100/1**

02 **9** *1 ½* **Estiqaama (USA)**[12] 7104 2-9-0 0...................................... PatCosgrave 12 37
(William Haggas) *sn led: hdd & wknd ins fnl 2f* **7/2**[2]

0 **10** *2 ¾* **Impertinent**[18] 6960 2-9-0 0... JohnFahy 2 31
(Jonathan Portman) *chsd ldrs over 5f* **50/1**

11 *2 ¼* **Fanzine** 2-9-0 0... NickyMackay 14 26
(Hughie Morrison) *chsd ldrs 5f* **40/1**

00 **12** *3 ¼* **Kiwani Bay**[53] 5902 2-9-0 0... RussKennemore 4 19
(J W Hills) *sn bhd* **100/1**

13 *hd* **Royal Barge (IRE)** 2-9-0 0... TomQueally 9 18
(Eve Johnson Houghton) *slowly away: a in rr* **33/1**

14 *3 ½* **Sweet Louise (IRE)** 2-9-0 0.. KirstyMilczarek 15 11
(Paul Rich) *spd to 1/2-way* **100/1**

1m 47.51s (7.81) **Going Correction** +0.775s/f (Yiel) **14** Ran SP% **121.8**
Speed ratings (Par 94): **91,88,86,76,75 74,71,69,68,65 63,60,59,56**
Tote Swingers: 1&2 £11.10, 1&3 £2.40, 2&3 £36.90 CSF £38.29 TOTE £2.30: £1.10, £5.20, £2.80; EX 28.90 Trifecta £229.50 Pool: £930.45 - 3.04 winning tickets..
Owner Newsells Park Stud **Bred** Newsells Park Stud **Trained** Kimpton, Hants

FOCUS
The rail had been moved out overnight from the 7f point to the 5f marker on the Round course. Heavy ground and a strong wind ensured that conditions were very testing, and they finished well strung out in this opening fillies' maiden. The first three were well clear.

NOTEBOOK
Secret Gesture is clearly well regarded as she was well backed on her debut when finding one too good at Leicester, and she was sent off a solid favourite to go one better here. Always travelling comfortably, her rider never had to get particularly serious with her, just pushing her out for an easy win. She has the pedigree to make up into an Oaks filly next year and deserves to take her chance in a trial in the spring. Her trainer said he'd expect her to prefer better ground. (tchd 5-4)
I Say(IRE), a half-sister to 1m2f/1m4f winner Notalossonya, shaped well on her debut, being the only one to give Secret Gesture anything approaching a race. She should be able to win a maiden if connections persevere on the AW.
Enaitch(IRE) ◆, a 250,000gns half-sister to 6f-1m (including Fillies´ Mile and Falmouth) winner Simply Perfect, was very green early on but came through nicely to stay on for third, well clear of the rest. Her stable's juveniles tend to improve a bundle for their debut outings, so she's one to keep in mind. (op 12-1)
Cherry Malotte, green and well beaten on her debut, improved for that experience and the switch to soft turf, which was not unexpected given she's a daughter of Pivotal. (op 8-1)
Absolutely Right(IRE) showed signs of inexperience and didn't get the clearest of runs when trying to stay on from the back of the field, but this daughter of Teofilo should benefit from this outing. (op 20-1)
Vega Dance(IRE), who was hampered around 2f out, showed promise. (op 8-1)
Wild Anthem displayed some ability. (op 20-1)
Estiqaama(USA) was up there for a long way and might appreciate a sounder surface once going handicapping. (tchd 4-1)
Sweet Louise(IRE) Official explanation: jockey said filly lost left-hind shoe

7404 WORTHINGTON'S WHIZZ-KIDZ STKS (REGISTERED AS THE HORRIS HILL STAKES) (GROUP 3) (C&G) 7f (S)
2:15 (2:15) (Class 1) 2-Y-O

£20,982 (£7,955; £3,981; £1,983; £995; £499) **Stalls** Centre

Form RPR

021 **1** **Tawhid**[10] 7172 2-8-12 86.. JimCrowley 2 111+
(Saeed Bin Suroor) *trckd ldrs: led on bit over 1f out: qcknd clr fnl f: easily* **9/2**[2]

1210 **2** *4* **Alhebayeb (IRE)**[69] 5398 2-9-3 104................................... PaulHanagan 7 105
(Richard Hannon) *led: drvn over 2f out: hdd over 1f out: sn no ch w easy wnner but kpt on wl for 2nd* **5/1**[3]

1201 **3** *1 ¾* **Boomshackerlacker (IRE)**[36] 6463 2-8-12 99................ PatCosgrave 1 96
(George Baker) *t.k.h: trckd ldrs: rdn over 2f out: one pce fr over 1f out: carried rt clsng stages but kpt on to take 3rd clsng stages* **9/1**

41 **4** *½* **Half A Person (IRE)**[22] 6846 2-8-12 85.......................... JamieSpencer 5 95
(Peter Chapple-Hyam) *s.i.s: in rr: hdwy over 2f out: chsd ldrs and disp 3rd over 1f out: one pce ins fnl f: hung rt clsng stages and dropped to 4th* **8/1**

2462 **5** *2 ½* **Odooj (IRE)**[14] 7065 2-8-12 103... DaneO'Neill 4 89
(William Haggas) *in rr: rdn and hdwy over 2f out: nvr rchd ldrs: wknd fnl f* **9/2**[2]

123 **6** *3* **Glean**[30] 6599 2-8-12 102... RyanMoore 6 81
(Richard Hannon) *in tch: rdn over 2f out: sn btn* **7/2**[1]

3046 **7** *6* **Maxentius (IRE)**[20] 6910 2-8-12 107................................ WilliamBuick 8 66
(Peter Chapple-Hyam) *t.k.h: trckd ldr tl rdn wl over 2f out: sn btn* **13/2**

1104 **8** *¾* **Hasopop (IRE)**[49] 6038 2-8-12 97.. AdamKirby 3 64
(Marco Botti) *t.k.h: rdn and btn over 2f out* **14/1**

1m 29.64s (3.94) **Going Correction** +0.775s/f (Yiel) **8** Ran SP% **116.4**
Speed ratings (Par 105): **108,103,101,100,98 94,87,86**
Tote Swingers: 1&2 £2.40, 1&3 £3.00, 2&3 £4.10 CSF £27.74 TOTE £5.00: £1.90, £1.50, £1.90; EX 27.70 Trifecta £90.20 Pool: £729.95 - 6.06 winning tickets..
Owner Godolphin **Bred** West Lodge Stud **Trained** Newmarket, Suffolk

FOCUS
Probably not the strongest of Group 3 races ever run, and they did split into two groups, with the four who raced more wards the centre of the track eventually filling the first four places. However Tawhid impressed and rated towards the top of the race averages.

NOTEBOOK
Tawhid ◆ travelled like a dream and quickened away in the manner of a really smart colt. This sort of ground clearly brings out the best in him and he's going to be an interesting sort for next year. The French Guineas might be a suitable target for him, as Godolphin have Dawn Approach for the Newmarket version and there might be a better chance of getting some cut in the ground at Longchamp. Returning to a mile won't be a problem and, while he carries his head high, there's no questioning his attitude. (op 5-1)
Alhebayeb(IRE), who made the running up the centre of the track, was quickly left behind when the winner engaged top gear. As a result of winning the July Stakes (on soft ground) earlier in the year he had to give 5lb all round here, but that didn't come close to being the difference between victory and defeat. (tchd 11-2)
Boomshackerlacker(IRE) acts with plenty of cut in the ground, but he was quite keen early and, although he settled once getting a lead from Alhebayeb, his early exertions probably meant he had less left for the finish than ideal. (op 8-1)
Half A Person(IRE), winner of a heavy-ground maiden last time out, tracked the winner through but was left for dead when that one quickened up. Jamie Spencer reported that the colt hung right. Official explanation: jockey said colt hung right (op 9-1)
Odooj(IRE) was first home of those that initially raced in the group nearest the stands' side, but the step up in trip didn't seem to be of any great benefit. (op 5-1)
Glean, who's by Raven's Pass out of a mare who did all her winning on good to firm, probably found the ground too testing, and can be given another chance back on better ground. (op 9-2)
Maxentius(IRE) didn't settle through the early part of the race and his rider reported that the colt stopped quickly. Official explanation: jockey said colt stopped quickly (op 6-1 tchd 11-2)
Hasopop(IRE), although a winner of a three-runner race in testing conditions earlier in the year, probably doesn't want this ground really. (tchd 12-1)

7405 WORTHINGTON'S CHAMPION SHIELD NAVIGATION BREWERY STKS (REGISTERED THE ST SIMON STAKES) (GROUP 3) 1m 4f 5y
2:45 (2:45) (Class 1) 3-Y-O+

£31,190 (£11,825; £5,918; £2,948; £1,479; £742) **Stalls** Centre

Form RPR

0102 **1** **Hazel Lavery (IRE)**[44] 6163 3-8-7 102................................ EddieAhern 2 111
(Charles Hills) *in tch: pushed along 5f out: gd hdwy 3f out: led ins fnl 2f: styd on gamely u.p fnl f* **17/2**

2214 **2** *½* **Noble Mission**[66] 5489 3-8-13 113..................................... TomQueally 9 116
(Sir Henry Cecil) *mid-div: hdwy over 2f out: drvn to chse wnr appr fnl f: sn chalng but a hld by wnr* **7/2**[1]

3134 **3** *2 ½* **Songcraft (IRE)**[21] 6866 4-9-3 106.................................... TedDurcan 4 109
(Saeed Bin Suroor) *chsd ldrs: edgd rt and led over 2f out: hdd sn after: one pce fnl f* **28/1**

1135 **4** *1* **Khione**[30] 6598 3-8-7 94.. KirstyMilczarek 6 104
(Luca Cumani) *in rr: drvn along 3f out: styd on over 1f out: and swtchd lft ins fnl f: sn one pce* **20/1**

1102 **5** *hd* **Camborne**[21] 6866 4-9-3 108...................................(b[1]) WilliamBuick 10 107
(John Gosden) *hld up in rr: swtchd lft and hdwy 2f out: rdn: edging lft and fnd no ex fnl f* **6/1**[3]

4121 **6** *7* **Fattsota**[22] 6832 4-9-3 107.. AdamKirby 3 96
(Marco Botti) *chsd ldr: rdn 3f out: wknd 2f out* **7/1**

4406 **7** *5* **Salford Art (IRE)**[22] 6833 3-8-7 106................................. NickyMackay 11 85
(David Elsworth) *rdn along over 4f out: a towards rr* **40/1**

3133 **8** *shd* **Willing Foe (USA)**[21] 6866 5-9-3 107.............................. JamieSpencer 5 88
(Saeed Bin Suroor) *in rr: rdn and sme hdwy over 2f out: sn wknd* **11/1**

-141 **9** *4 ½* **Hawaafez**[21] 6866 4-9-3 110.. PaulHanagan 8 81
(Marcus Tregoning) *chsd ldrs: rdn: hmpd and wknd qckly appr fnl 2f* **7/2**[1]

3442 **10** *17* **Harris Tweed**[29] 6637 5-9-6 113... RyanMoore 1 56
(William Haggas) *led tl hdd over 2f out: sn wknd* **11/2**[2]

2m 44.33s (8.83) **Going Correction** +0.90s/f (Soft)
WFA 3 from 4yo+ 7lb **10** Ran SP% **116.1**
Speed ratings (Par 113): **106,105,104,103,103 98,95,95,92,80**
Tote Swingers: 1&2 £3.80, 1&3 £30.50, 2&3 £13.20 CSF £37.44 TOTE £10.30: £2.70, £1.50, £7.70; EX 49.40 Trifecta £1050.90 Pool: £1,569.48 - 1.12 winning tickets..
Owner R Morecombe, E O'Leary, R Scarborough **Bred** Longueville Bloodstock **Trained** Lambourn, Berks

FOCUS
They went a decent gallop given the conditions. Ordinary form for the grade with another step forward from Hazel Lavery.

NOTEBOOK

Hazel Lavery(IRE), who was second in the Park Hill last time out and clearly stays very well, saw it out best of all. She looks the type that could develop into a useful stayer next year, and she's in the sales. (op 10-1)

Noble Mission, back from a break, had the hood back on and ensured that the winner had to pull out all the stops. It wouldn't be a surprise to see him progress from three to four, although he'll need to, given the poor overall standard of the Classic generation this year.

Songcraft(IRE) turned Ascot form around with Hawaafez, who was below her best. He had a successful time of it in Meydan last winter and presumably another campaign out there will be the plan for him come the new year.

Khione, the least experienced runner in the line-up, was better away from the gates this time. She took another step forward on this first outing in Group company and looks the type to progress further at four.

Camborne, blinkered for the first time, was covered up and delivered late, but he again wandered about for pressure. (op 15-2 tchd 11-2 and 8-1 in a place)

Fattsota found nothing for pressure. He hadn't encountered ground this testing before, and perhaps it just wasn't to his liking. (op 13-2)

Willing Foe(USA) is by Dynaformer and his progeny tend to be far more effective on a fast surface. Jamie Spencer reported that the gelding was unsuited by the ground. Official explanation: jockey said gelding was unsuited by the heavy (soft in places) ground (tchd 12-1)

Hawaafez was disappointing as she won nicely in soft ground at Ascot last time, but she might just be the type who needs to be caught fresh. However, Marcus Tregoning reported that the filly was unsuited by the ground. Official explanation: jockey said filly was unsuited by the heavy (soft in places) ground

Harris Tweed, who could have done without being hassled up front, weakened quickly inside the final 2f. (tchd 5-1)

7406 BETFAIR. DON'T SETTLE FOR LESS RADLEY STKS (LISTED RACE) (FILLIES) 7f (S)

3:15 (3:17) (Class 1) 2-Y-0

£13,043 (£4,945; £2,474; £1,232; £618; £310) **Stalls** Centre

Form				RPR
416	**1**		**Need You Now (IRE)**[28] 6675 2-8-12 65....................(b[1]) JamieSpencer 6 (Peter Chapple-Hyam) *hmpd s: hld up in rr: swtchd rt and hdwy over 1f out: str run ins fnl f to ld fnl 100yds: pushed out* **33/1**	94
6535	**2**	*1*	**Momalorka**[14] 7052 2-8-12 98..(p) RyanMoore 2 (William Haggas) *in tch: hdwy 2f out: led over 1f out: kpt on u.p: hdd and one pce fnl 100yds* **7/2[3]**	91
231	**3**	*2¼*	**Lilbourne Eliza (IRE)**[28] 6657 2-8-12 75........................... DaneO'Neill 4 (Richard Hannon) *wnt rt s: trckd ldr: rdn 2f out: stl ev ch over 1f out: outpcd ins fnl f* **20/1**	85
10	**4**	*¾*	**Tantshi (IRE)**[51] 5979 2-8-12 81.. NeilCallan 3 (Roger Varian) *t.k.h: chsd ldrs: drvn to chal over 1f out: one pce fnl f* **14/1**	84
5201	**5**	*3¾*	**Steer By The Stars (IRE)**[7] 7242 2-8-12 90...................... JoeFanning 1 (Mark Johnston) *led: hdd over 1f out: wknd fnl f* **10/3[2]**	74
011	**6**	*3½*	**Victrix Ludorum (IRE)**[21] 6873 2-8-12 97............................ PatDobbs 8 (Richard Hannon) *t.k.h: trckd ldrs: rdn over 2f out: sn btn* **5/4[1]**	65
01	**7**	*2½*	**Trapeze**[12] 7104 2-8-12 76.. WilliamBuick 5 (John Gosden) *hmpd s: trckd ldrs: rdn 2f out: wknd over 1f out* **9/1**	59
2232	**8**	*44*	**Madame Elizabeth**[28] 6657 2-8-12 71....................... RussKennemore 7 (Reg Hollinshead) *t.k.h: a in rr: lost tch fnl 3f: t.o* **50/1**	

1m 30.68s (4.98) **Going Correction** +0.775s/f (Yiel) **8** Ran SP% **116.1**

Speed ratings (Par 100): **102,100,98,97,93 89,86,36**

Tote Swingers: 1&2 £18.60, 1&3 £16.10, 2&3 £7.50 CSF £145.44 TOTE £29.20: £4.90, £1.10, £5.20; EX 229.30 TRIFECTA Not won..

Owner Franconson Partners **Bred** John M Weld **Trained** Newmarket, Suffolk

FOCUS

They all came up the centre of the track this time and the winning time was 1.04sec slower than that recorded by Tawhid when impressively taking the Horris Hill earlier on the card. Decent form, but dubious all the same.

NOTEBOOK

Need You Now(IRE) caused a shock, the first-time blinkers and switch to soft ground bringing about significant improvement. She picked up well from the back of the field, there was no fluke about it, and the confidence in her on her first two starts (sent off short-price favourite both times) did reveal that, despite her bare form (officially rated 65 coming into the race), she is well regarded. (op 28-1)

Momalorka looked to have been brought with a well-timed challenge, only to be run down close home. She's a fairly reliable yardstick. (op 9-2)

Lilbourne Eliza(IRE) didn't achieve a great deal in beating Madame Elizabeth (last here) in a Chester maiden last time, but at least she'd shown an ability to handle this sort of ground. She ran a solid race and looks like she'll appreciate a little further next year.

Tantshi(IRE) didn't quite see her race out after racing a little keenly early. She coped well enough with the ground but will probably appreciate getting back on a sounder surface.

Steer By The Stars(IRE) tried to make all but she was swamped inside the final furlong. This might have come a bit quick after her Catterick win a week earlier. (op 9-2)

Victrix Ludorum(IRE) didn't settle well enough in the early stages and eventually paid the price. (op 11-10 tchd 11-8)

Trapeze found this competition a lot tougher than that she faced when winning her maiden 12 days earlier. (op 8-1 tchd 15-2)

Madame Elizabeth was lame on her right-fore. Official explanation: vet said filly was lame right-fore (op 40-1)

7407 BATHWICK TYRES H'CAP 1m 2f 6y

3:45 (3:46) (Class 2) (0-105,103) 3-Y-0+

£12,450 (£3,728; £1,864; £932; £466; £234) **Stalls** Centre

Form				RPR
3103	**1**		**Blue Surf**[35] 6484 3-8-11 93.. PatDobbs 1 (Amanda Perrett) *trckd ldrs: tk slt ld travelling smoothly ins fnl 2f: qcknd ins fnl f: drvn and styd on wl clsng stages and a doing enough* **7/1[3]**	104+
2015	**2**	*nk*	**Borug (USA)**[11] 7147 4-8-9 86 ow2...................................... NeilCallan 13 (James Tate) *stdd in rr: hdwy over 3f out: drvn and qcknd over 1f out: styd on to take 2nd fnl 75yds: gaining on wnr clsng stages but a hld* **16/1**	95
2314	**3**	*1¾*	**Sunpass**[17] 6987 3-8-3 85.. NickyMackay 8 (John Gosden) *towards rr but in tch: hdwy on inner to trck ldrs over 3f out: chal wnr fr ins fnl 2f tl outpcd ins fnl f: lost 2nd fnl 75yds* **8/1**	91
1010	**4**	*1½*	**Sir John Hawkwood (IRE)**[66] [illegible]-2 98................ RyanMoore 11 (Sir Michael Stoute) *in rr: pushed along over 3f out: styd on over 1f out: kpt on clsng stages: nvr gng pce to rch ldrs* **5/2[1]**	101+
2560	**5**	*1½*	**Licence To Till (USA)**[28] 6674 5-8-13 90........................... JoeFanning 4 (Mark Johnston) *led tl hdd ins fnl 2f: wknd fnl f* **12/1**	90
4032	**6**	*nk*	**Cool Macavity (IRE)**[15] 7017 4-8-10 87............................ EddieAhern 9 (Charles Hills) *in rr: pushed along over 2f out: hdwy sn after: kpt on ins fnl f: nt rch ldrs* **20/1**	86
2016	**7**	*nk*	**Las Verglas Star (IRE)**[10] 7175 4-9-0 91.......................... PaulHanagan 6 (Richard Fahey) *chsd ldrs: rdn 3f out: one pce fnl 2f* **12/1**	90
4121	**8**	*1¼*	**Little Rocky**[15] 7017 4-9-7 98... DaneO'Neill 14 (David Simcock) *chsd ldrs: rdn over 2f out: wknd appr fnl f* **13/2[2]**	94
0-02	**9**	*6*	**Credit Swap**[15] 7030 7-8-12 89... JimCrowley 3 (Michael Wigham) *hood off slowly and mised break: in rr: rdn over 2f out: sme prog fnl f but nvr gng pce to get into contention* **15/2**	74
0440	**10**	*2½*	**Navajo Chief**[28] 6674 5-9-7 103.............................. MichaelJMMurphy[(5)] 7 (Alan Jarvis) *chsd ldrs: rdn over 2f out: wknd qckly ins fnl f* **12/1**	83
1044	**11**	*5*	**Tigers Tale (IRE)**[21] 6875 3-8-2 84..................................(v) HarryBentley 5 (Roger Teal) *chsd ldrs: rdn 3f out: wknd over 2f out* **16/1**	55
2060	**12**	*26*	**Tameen**[84] 4821 4-8-9 86.. JamesDoyle 2 (Ed Dunlop) *a in rr: lost tch fnl 2f: eased whn no ch* **16/1**	

2m 15.53s (6.73) **Going Correction** +0.90s/f (Soft)

WFA 3 from 4yo+ 5lb **12** Ran SP% **122.8**

Speed ratings (Par 109): **109,108,107,106,104 104,104,103,98,96 92,71**

Tote Swingers: 1&2 £27.90, 1&3 £9.30, 2&3 £32.70 CSF £117.70 CT £930.70 TOTE £6.90: £2.40, £4.30, £2.50; EX 150.60 TRIFECTA Not won..

Owner John Connolly And Partners **Bred** Star Pointe Ltd,Brosnan And Williamson **Trained** Pulborough, W Sussex

FOCUS

It's hard to know if it was an advantage, but the first three all raced closest to the far rail in the straight. The winner is rated up 6lb on his C&D latest.

NOTEBOOK

Blue Surf travelled well in behind the pace and responded when asked to go and win his race. He showed he liked some ease at Goodwood and, while he hadn't run on ground this testing before, he clearly relished conditions and put up a personal best. (op 13-2)

Borug(USA), who ran well in a race not run to suit (steady pace) at Wolverhampton last time, confirmed his recent return to form with another solid effort. Equally effective on the AW, he could well win on that surface if found a race in the coming weeks. (op 14-1)

Sunpass, who was turned over at odds-on on last time out, looked to have his work cut out off a 7lb higher mark. He ran well in the circumstances, is relatively lightly raced and open to further improvement.

Sir John Hawkwood(IRE) ◆, just like at York, shaped as though finding the trip on the short side, and the ground didn't compensate enough for his lack of toe at the trip. He remains interesting for next year when a step up to 1m4f plus will suit, and races like the Ebor could come into play. (op 7-2)

Licence To Till(USA), back on his last winning mark, ran a sound race from the front.

Cool Macavity(IRE) put in some good late work. The latter could have done with a disputed lead setting things up for him. (op 16-1)

Las Verglas Star(IRE) was again held off his new mark.

Little Rocky found this tougher than when dominating a small field at Bath off 8lb lower last time. (op 7-1)

7408 WORTHINGTON'S CIPPENHAM RBL AND CIPPENHAM WMC EBF FILLIES' H'CAP 7f (S)

4:20 (4:22) (Class 3) (0-95,93) 3-Y-0+ **£8,409** (£2,502; £1,250; £625) **Stalls** Centre

Form				RPR
2213	**1**		**Whimsical (IRE)**[22] 6830 3-9-0 88....................................... RyanMoore 2 (Richard Hannon) *in rr: hdwy fr 2f out: drvn and qcknd fnl f: led fnl 50yds: styd on strly* **11/2[2]**	98
2500	**2**	*½*	**Galician**[43] 6201 3-9-1 89.. JoeFanning 14 (Mark Johnston) *chsd ldrs: chal 2f out: led sn after: hdd over 1f out: rallied ins fnl f to chse wnr clsng stages but nt pce of wnr* **8/1**	97
2240	**3**	*½*	**Tartiflette**[22] 6830 3-8-10 84 ow2...................................... SebSanders 1 (Ed McMahon) *chsd ldrs: chal ins fnl 2f: led over 1f out: rdn and kpt on fnl f: hdd and outpcd fnl 50yds* **8/1**	91
6055	**4**	*1¼*	**Gouray Girl (IRE)**[13] 7080 5-8-12 84................................. DaneO'Neill 12 (Henry Candy) *s.i.s: in rr: hdwy over 1f out: styd on fnl f nvr gng pce to rch ldrs* **7/1[3]**	88
0563	**5**	*hd*	**Russian Rave**[11] 7128 6-9-1 87.. JamesDoyle 4 (Jonathan Portman) *chsd ldrs: rdn over 2f out: one pce fnl f* **10/1**	90
1121	**6**	*nk*	**Links Drive Lady**[12] 7114 4-8-10 82..................................... JimCrowley 8 (Dean Ivory) *in rr: hdwy over 1f out: styd on wl fnl f: gng on cl home* **9/2[1]**	84
5000	**7**	*1½*	**Honeymead (IRE)**[13] 7083 4-8-7 79 oh2........................ HarryBentley 13 (Richard Fahey) *towards rr: hdwy 2f out: drvn to chse ldrs over 1f out: wknd ins fnl f* **10/1**	78
2003	**8**	*4*	**Dare To Dream**[35] 6488 3-8-8 82.. PatDobbs 5 (Richard Hannon) *in rr: rdn and sme hdwy over 2f out: wknd appr fnl f* **10/1**	70
1-00	**9**	*6*	**Cardigan (IRE)**[106] 4062 3-8-11 85................................... TomQueally 6 (William Haggas) *chsd ldrs: rdn over 2f out: sn btn* **18/1**	58
0500	**10**	*7*	**Dreamwriter (USA)**[27] 6705 3-8-8 82............................ NickyMackay 17 (Jim Boyle) *plld hrd: led and sn clr: jnd 2f out and wknd rapidly* **33/1**	36
0050	**11**	*1*	**Miss Work Of Art**[14] 7066 3-9-5 93................................. PaulHanagan 16 (Richard Fahey) *chsd ldrs: rdn 3f out: sn btn* **12/1**	45
1444	**12**	*11*	**Shesastar**[34] 6515 4-9-1 87.. GrahamGibbons 9 (David Barron) *a in rr: lost tch fnl 3f* **12/1**	10

1m 30.82s (5.12) **Going Correction** +0.775s/f (Yiel)

WFA 3 from 4yo+ 2lb **12** Ran SP% **119.2**

Speed ratings (Par 104): **101,100,99,98,98 97,96,91,84,76 75,63**

Tote Swingers: 1&2 £7.90, 1&3 £6.30, 2&3 £5.70 CSF £49.45 CT £361.09 TOTE £4.50: £2.10, £2.90, £2.90; EX 48.00 Trifecta £315.00 Pool: £1,041.93 - 2.48 winning tickets..

Owner Miss Yvonne Jacques **Bred** Churchtown House Stud **Trained** East Everleigh, Wilts

FOCUS

The early pace wasn't strong behind the ignored Dreamwriter, who went off far too quick, and the winning time was slower than the two juvenile pattern races earlier on the card. Straightforward fillies' form.

NOTEBOOK

Whimsical(IRE) got a nice bit of cover towards the far side of the group. She took a while to get on top but the impression was that she did it a shade cosily in the end. She remains progressive, can't go up much for this, and could find further success back on Polytrack, where she's unbeaten in two starts. (op 9-2)

Galician has yet to win beyond 6f but she showed here that she gets 7f fine, albeit this wasn't the strongest run race of all time. (op 10-1)

Tartiflette, who ran her best race of the campaign over this C&D back in April when only narrowly denied by a handicap snip in the shape of subsequent Group 1-placed Gregorian, once again showed her liking for the track, bouncing back from a below-par effort at Ascot. (op 9-1)

Gouray Girl(IRE), winner of this race two years ago, was finishing all too late. She doesn't find winning easy and could have done with a stronger pace to set things up for her. (op 13-2 tchd 15-2)

Russian Rave had her chance but her effort petered out inside the last. She remains on a fairly stiff mark. (op 8-1)

Links Drive Lady, up a furlong in distance, is another who would have appreciated a stronger gallop to run at. She was closing at the finish but the first three were beyond catching. It's possible she was at a disadvantage in trying to challenge nearest the stands' side rail. (op 6-1)

Dreamwriter(USA) ran too freely. Official explanation: jockey said filly ran too freely

7409 FESTIVAL RACING ON COURSE BOOKMAKERS LADY JOCKEYS' H'CAP (FOR LADY AMATEUR RIDERS) 1m 4f 5y
4:55 (4:56) (Class 5) (0-75,73) 4-Y-0+ **£2,807** (£870; £435; £217) **Stalls** Centre

Form RPR
2460 **1** **Kings Troop**[13] 7077 6-9-6 **63**.....(b) MissCBoxall(5) 7 74
(Alan King) *trckd ldrs: led appr fnl f: drvn out* **9/2**[3]
4002 **2** 1 1/4 **Bold Duke**[11] 7129 4-9-2 **59** oh2..... MissAliceMills(5) 2 68
(Edward Bevan) *sn led: pushed along 2f out: hdd appr fnl f: outpcd fnl 120yds but wl clr of 3rd* **14/1**
4145 **3** 10 **Iceman George**[28] 6691 8-9-5 **60**.....(v) MissJRRichards(3) 3 54
(Lydia Pearce) *in rr: hdwy 3f out: styd on for wl hld 3rd fnl 2f* **8/1**
3660 **4** 3 **Ice Nelly (IRE)**[23] 6819 4-9-7 **64**.....(b1) MissNDumelow(5) 8 54
(Hughie Morrison) *s.i.s: in rr: styd on for wl hld 4th fnl 2f* **11/1**
4844 **5** 6 **Whitby Jet (IRE)**[17] 6981 4-10-2 **71**..... MissHayleyMoore(3) 6 52
(Ed Vaughan) *t.k.h: in tch: rdn 3f out: wknd over 2f out* **7/1**
0500 **6** 4 1/2 **Four Nations (USA)**[24] 6776 4-10-5 **71**..... MissSBrotherton 4 45
(Amanda Perrett) *in tch: chsd ldrs 4f out: wknd fr 3f out* **7/2**[2]
6255 **7** 14 **Sir Boss (IRE)**[17] 6981 7-10-2 **71**..... MissMMullineaux(3) 1 24
(Michael Mullineaux) *chsd ldrs: wknd fr 3f out* **8/1**
2414 **8** 18 **Spin Cast**[23] 6819 4-10-4 **73**..... MissHBethell(3) 10
(Brian Ellison) *chsd ldrs: rdn 4f out: wknd 3f out* **10/3**[1]
0400 **9** 1/2 **Benandonner (USA)**[36] 6434 9-9-9 **66** ow2..... MissMBryant(5) 9
(Paddy Butler) *a in rr: lost tch over 4f out* **28/1**
0006 **10** 15 **Beggers Belief**[118] 3659 4-9-2 **59** oh7.....(b) MissNVorster(5) 5
(Eric Wheeler) *chsd ldrs: wknd rapidly over 3f out* **25/1**

2m 46.52s (11.02) **Going Correction** +0.90s/f (Soft) **10** Ran SP% **120.5**
Speed ratings (Par 103): **99,98,91,89,85 82,73,61,60,50**
Tote Swingers: 1&2 £7.10, 1&3 £3.30, 2&3 £8.70 CSF £67.90 TOTE £4.30: £1.60, £5.50, £3.30; EX 83.80 Trifecta £988.10 Part won. Pool: £1,317.56 - 0.62 winning tickets..
Owner W H Ponsonby **Bred** Wickfield Stud And Hartshill Stud **Trained** Barbury Castle, Wilts

FOCUS
The first two pulled clear in this lady amateur riders' handicap, but the form looks pretty ordinary. The winner had slipped to a good mark.

T/Plt: £1,224.80 to a £1 stake. Pool: £100,134.04 - 59.67 winning tickets. T/Qpdt: £243.60 to a £1 stake. Pool: £5,268.45 - 16.00 winning tickets. ST

7378 WOLVERHAMPTON (A.W) (L-H)
Saturday, October 27

OFFICIAL GOING: Standard
Wind: Fresh across Weather: Fine

7410 BREEDERS' CUP LIVE ONLY ON ATR MAIDEN AUCTION STKS 5f 216y(P)
5:45 (5:45) (Class 6) 2-Y-O **£2,181** (£644; £322) **Stalls** Low

Form RPR
0232 **1** **Almalekiah (IRE)**[22] 6853 2-8-6 70..... DavidProbert 6 75
(J S Moore) *sn chsng ldr: pushed along over 2f out: rdn to ld over 1f out: styd on wl* **5/2**[2]
5 **2** 3 3/4 **Red Tulip**[19] 6936 2-8-4 0..... HayleyTurner 5 62
(James Fanshawe) *chsd ldrs: rdn over 1f out: styd on to go 2nd post* **6/4**[1]
4426 **3** nse **Alhaarth Beauty (IRE)**[33] 6541 2-8-9 72..... LiamJones 1 67
(Ismail Mohammed) *led: rdn and hdd over 1f out: no ex ins fnl f: lost 2nd post* **12/1**
46 **4** 1 3/4 **Shatin Secret**[10] 7176 2-9-0 0..... DanielTudhope 12 66+
(Noel Wilson) *mid-div: hdwy over 1f out: r.o: nvr nr to chal* **28/1**
6336 **5** 1 1/4 **Daisie Cutter**[31] 6583 2-8-1 59..... SimonPearce(3) 7 53+
(Lydia Pearce) *hld up in tch: plld hrd: rdn over 1f out: r.o: nt trble ldrs* **33/1**
3 **6** 1/2 **Golden Pursuit**[8] 7219 2-8-11 0..... RichardKingscote 4 58+
(Tom Dascombe) *s.i.s: in rr tl r.o ins fnl f: nvr nrr* **4/1**[3]
5035 **7** hd **Gold Beau (FR)**[32] 6556 2-8-12 68..... TomEaves 3 59
(Linda Stubbs) *chsd ldrs: rdn over 2f out: sn outpcd* **20/1**
6004 **8** 3 3/4 **Kryena's Rose**[35] 6499 2-8-5 51..... SamHitchcott 11 40
(Mick Channon) *hld up: pushed along 2f out: nvr on terms* **66/1**
0050 **9** 2 **I'm Watching**[16] 7008 2-8-4 46..... KirstyMilczarek 8 33
(George Baker) *plld hrd and prom: rdn over 2f out: sn hung rt and wknd* **66/1**
50 **10** 7 **Val's Diamond (IRE)**[21] 6880 2-8-8 0..... PJMcDonald 2 16
(Ann Duffield) *s.i.s: sme hdwy over 2f out: wknd wl over 1f out* **80/1**

1m 14.49s (-0.51) **Going Correction** -0.125s/f (Stan) **10** Ran SP% **111.6**
Speed ratings (Par 93): **98,93,92,90,88 88,88,83,80,71**
toteswingers: 1&2 £1.10, 1&3 £3.90, 2&3 £4.70. CSF £5.91 TOTE £4.70: £1.30, £1.10, £2.10; EX 6.60 Trifecta £63.20 Pool: £914.07 - 10.84 winning units..
Owner Sheikh Abdullah Almalek Alsabah **Bred** Mark Hanly **Trained** Upper Lambourn, Berks

FOCUS
An ordinary 2yo maiden. The principals were always up there with the order changing little. A conservative view has been taken of the form.

NOTEBOOK
Almalekiah(IRE) finished a close second at Dundalk over 7f last time and that experience won her the day over this sharper test, which proved ideal. She cane make her mark in nurseries, despite a likely rise for this, and reverting to an extra furlong ought to be her optimum next year. (op 3-1 tchd 9-4)
Red Tulip looked comfortable just in behind turning for home, but let the leaders get away off the bend and was getting there too late inside the final furlong. Another furlong should suit her down to the ground. (op 5-4)
Alhaarth Beauty(IRE) was having a first outing since leaving Richard Hannon and turned in a decent effort under an aggressive ride. There must be a race for her on Polytrack. (op 11-1 tchd 14-1)
Shatin Secret was never seriously in the hunt, but turned in his best effort yet on this switch to Polytrack and debut over the extra furlong. He's now eligible for a mark. (op 33-1 tchd 25-1)

7411 FOLLOW LADBROKES ON TWITTER H'CAP (DIV I) 5f 216y(P)
6:15 (6:16) (Class 5) (0-75,80) 3-Y-0+ **£2,911** (£866; £432; £216) **Stalls** Low

Form RPR
0521 **1** **Ginger Ted (IRE)**[4] 7308 5-9-3 **71** 6ex.....(tp) J-PGuillambert 12 80+
(Stuart Williams) *mid-div: sn pushed along: nt clr run over 3f out: hdwy and swtchd rt over 1f out: r.o u.p to ld nr fin* **4/1**[2]
1202 **2** 3/4 **Avonvalley**[23] 6824 5-8-11 **65**..... RobbieFitzpatrick 8 72
(Peter Grayson) *hld up: hdwy over 1f out: rdn and r.o to go 2nd post: nt rch wnr* **10/1**
001 **3** hd **Above Standard (IRE)**[8] 7218 4-9-0 **75**.....(t) DavidSimmonson(7) 13 81+
(Michael Easterby) *s.i.s: sn chsng ldrs: led wl over 1f out: rdn and hdd nr fin* **5/2**[1]
5600 **4** 2 **Full Shilling (IRE)**[18] 6961 4-8-12 **66**..... LiamJones 5 66
(John Spearing) *s.i.s: outpcd: rdn and r.o ins fnl f: nt rch ldrs* **33/1**
5201 **5** 1/2 **Song Of Parkes**[11] 7144 5-9-12 **80**..... TedDurcan 9 78
(Eric Alston) *hld up: hdwy over 1f out: r.o: nrst fin* **5/1**[3]
5062 **6** nk **Mcmonagle (USA)**[9] 7203 4-9-2 **70**.....(bt) RobertWinston 10 67
(Alan Brown) *prom: rdn over 2f out: styd on same pce fnl f* **7/1**
4160 **7** 1 1/2 **Burnhope**[15] 7023 3-9-4 **73**..... LukeMorris 2 66
(Scott Dixon) *led: rdn and hdd wl over 1f out: no ex ins fnl f* **10/1**
6165 **8** 1/2 **Above The Stars**[21] 6886 4-9-0 **68**..... TonyHamilton 6 59
(Richard Fahey) *chsd ldrs: rdn over 2f out: no ex fnl f* **11/1**
2606 **9** 1 1/2 **Available (IRE)**[23] 6824 3-8-11 **66**..... DavidProbert 4 52
(John Mackie) *chsd ldr: rdn and ev ch over 2f out: hmpd over 1f out: wknd ins fnl f* **25/1**
14/ **10** 8 **Sextons House (IRE)**[178] 1762 4-8-8 **69**..... NoraLooby(7) 7 30
(Alan McCabe) *s.i.s: hld up: a bhd* **66/1**
000 **11** 5 **Alive And Kicking**[49] 6044 4-9-2 **70**.....(b1) JimmyQuinn 3 15
(James Bethell) *s.i.s: plld hrd and sn prom: rdn over 2f out: wknd wl over 1f out* **16/1**

1m 13.59s (-1.41) **Going Correction** -0.125s/f (Stan)
WFA 3 from 4yo+ 1lb **11** Ran SP% **118.4**
Speed ratings (Par 103): **104,103,102,100,99 99,97,96,94,83 77**
toteswingers: 1&2 £5.10, 1&3 £3.50, 2&3 £4.40. CSF £43.41 CT £120.64 TOTE £6.70: £2.40, £2.00, £1.30; EX 32.60 Trifecta £133.70 Pool: £822.26 - 4.61 winning units..
Owner Maze Rattan 2 **Bred** T Counihan **Trained** Newmarket, Suffolk

FOCUS
A modest sprint handicap, 0.86sec faster than division II. The winner reversed C&D form with the favourite.

Alive And Kicking Official explanation: jockey said gelding ran too free

7412 FOLLOW LADBROKES ON TWITTER H'CAP (DIV II) 5f 216y(P)
6:45 (6:46) (Class 5) (0-75,75) 3-Y-0+ **£2,911** (£866; £432; £216) **Stalls** Low

Form RPR
0430 **1** **Jinky**[16] 7004 4-9-0 **68**..... TomEaves 12 77
(Linda Perratt) *a.p: shkn up to ld over 1f out: rdn out* **10/1**
5646 **2** 1 **Red Senor (IRE)**[96] 4412 3-9-3 **72**..... RobertWinston 5 78
(Charles Hills) *hld up: hdwy over 1f out: r.o: nt rch wnr* **6/1**[3]
2002 **3** 1 **Ryan Style (IRE)**[9] 7197 6-9-2 **70**.....(v) SilvestreDeSousa 4 73
(Lisa Williamson) *a.p: racd keenly: rdn and ev ch 1f out: styd on same pce ins fnl f* **11/2**[2]
0165 **4** 1 **Chambles**[54] 5893 3-8-13 **68**.....(t) SebSanders 10 68+
(Alan McCabe) *s.s: hld up: hdwy over 1f out: n.m.r ins fnl f: r.o* **9/1**
0600 **5** 3/4 **Gabrial's Gift (IRE)**[25] 6768 3-9-6 **75**..... StevieDonohoe 7 72
(Ian Williams) *prom: chsd ldr over 2f out: rdn and ev ch over 1f out: no ex ins fnl f* **14/1**
110 **6** 1 3/4 **Mon Ami Jolie (USA)**[168] 2070 4-9-2 **75**.... WilliamTwiston-Davies(5) 13 67+
(Richard Hannon) *s.i.s: hld up: rdn over 1f out: nvr trbld ldrs* **15/8**[1]
6031 **7** 1/2 **Drive Home (USA)**[35] 6479 5-8-7 **64**.....(p) NeilFarley(3) 6 54
(Noel Wilson) *chsd ldrs: rdn over 2f out: wknd ins fnl f* **14/1**
0000 **8** 2 1/2 **L'Astre De Choisir (IRE)**[7] 7247 4-8-11 **65**.....(b1) JamesSullivan 11 47
(Michael Easterby) *led: rdn and hdd over 1f out: wknd ins fnl f* **33/1**
5550 **9** 3/4 **Dishy Guru**[44] 6173 3-9-4 **73**..... LukeMorris 2 53
(Michael Blanshard) *mid-div: n.m.r over 4f out: hdwy over 1f out: wknd ins fnl f* **10/1**
1000 **10** 1 3/4 **Gap Princess (IRE)**[19] 6934 8-9-2 **70**.....(p) PJMcDonald 8 44
(Geoffrey Harker) *prom: chsd ldr over 3f out tl rdn over 2f out: wknd over 1f out* **25/1**
0000 **11** 2 3/4 **Blown It (USA)**[12] 7101 6-9-1 **69**..... NeilCallan 9 34
(Keith Dalgleish) *hld up: rdn over 2f out: a in rr* **25/1**
6000 **12** 2 1/4 **Pick A Little**[6] 7274 4-9-4 **75**..... RyanClark(3) 3 33
(Michael Blake) *s.s: rdn over 2f out: a in rr* **20/1**
4606 **13** 3 1/4 **Topflight Princess**[81] 4920 3-8-12 **67**..... RichardKingscote 1 15
(Jeremy Gask) *sn pushed along towards rr: wknd over 2f out* **25/1**

1m 14.45s (-0.55) **Going Correction** -0.125s/f (Stan)
WFA 3 from 4yo+ 1lb **13** Ran SP% **125.2**
Speed ratings (Par 103): **98,96,95,94,93 90,90,86,85,83 79,76,72**
toteswingers: 1&2 £7.00, 1&3 £9.30, 2&3 £4.00. CSF £67.51 CT £387.07 TOTE £13.30: £3.90, £3.60, £2.60; EX 95.00 Trifecta £560.70 Part won. Pool: £747.63 - 0.40 winning units..
Owner John Murphy **Bred** J Breslin **Trained** East Kilbride, S Lanarks

FOCUS
The second division of the modest sprint handicap. It was 0.86secs slower than the preceding race and the form has been rated to average.

7413 WOLVERHAMPTON-RACECOURSE.CO.UK CLAIMING STKS 1m 4f 50y(P)
7:15 (7:15) (Class 6) 3-Y-0+ **£2,181** (£644; £322) **Stalls** Low

Form RPR
0101 **1** **A Little Bit Dusty**[17] 5967 4-9-5 80.....(p) JackDuern(5) 11 84
(Reg Hollinshead) *hld up: pushed along 7f out: hdwy over 4f out: drvn to ld over 3f out: styd on u.p* **12/1**
3334 **2** 1/2 **Boa**[34] 1011 7-9-1 72..... AmyRyan 6 74
(Reg Hollinshead) *a.p: rdn to chse wnr over 2f out: styd on* **6/1**[3]
6141 **3** 2 1/2 **Justbookie Dot Com (IRE)**[8] 7221 4-9-7 73.....(b) NeilCallan 10 76
(David Evans) *hld up: plld hrd: hdwy over 5f out: rdn over 2f out: styd on same pce ins fnl f* **13/2**
106/ **4** 1 3/4 **Tri Nations (UAE)**[6] 6078 7-9-6 74.....(vt) SeanQuinlan 8 72
(Anthony Middleton) *hld up: hdwy u.p over 1f out: nt rch ldrs* **50/1**
5060 **5** nk **Cape Safari (IRE)**[11] 7147 3-9-0 80.....(p) SamHitchcott 5 73
(Alan Bailey) *prom: chsd ldr over 7f out tl rdn over 3f out: outpcd wl over 1f out: styd on ins fnl f* **3/1**[2]
1400 **6** 1 **Pendragon (USA)**[29] 6638 9-9-10 77..... SilvestreDeSousa 4 74
(Brian Ellison) *prom: lost pl over 4f out: rallied over 1f out: no ex wl ins fnl f* **15/8**[1]
3122 **7** 1 3/4 **Xpres Maite**[18] 6967 9-9-5 73.....(b) MarkCoumbe(3) 7 69
(Roy Bowring) *s.i.s: hld up: hdwy over 4f out: rdn over 2f out: styd on same pce* **33/1**
5044 **8** 5 **Son Vida (IRE)**[7] 7251 4-8-13 60.....(p) RobertTart(7) 3 59
(Alan Bailey) *led: rdn and hdd over 3f out: wknd over 1f out* **40/1**
0000 **9** 3 3/4 **City Of The Kings (IRE)**[15] 7027 7-9-3 67..... JacobButterfield(7) 12 57
(Ollie Pears) *s.i.s: hld up: rdn and wknd over 2f out* **40/1**
0235 **10** 1 3/4 **Underwritten**[7] 7245 3-9-3 70.....(v) GrahamLee 2 55
(Donald McCain) *chsd ldr tl pushed along over 7f out: rdn over 4f out: sn wknd* **12/1**

2003 **11** 1 1/2 **Spey Song (IRE)**[23] 6828 4 -9-262..........(b) TedDurcan 1 44
(James Bethell) *hld up: a in rr: rdn and wknd over 3f out* **20/1**

2m 39.96s (-1.14)**Going Correction** -0.125s/f (Stan)
WFA 3 from 4yo+ 7lb 11Ran SP% 117.3
Speed ratings (Par 101): **98,97,96,94,94 93,92,89,86,85 84**
toteswingers: 1&2 £11.70, 1&3 £8.60, 2&3 £10.50. CSF £78.03 TOTE £10.30 : £2.00 , £2.30 , £1.90; EX 29.20 Trifecta £408.60 Part won. Pool: £544.93 - 0.62 winning units. .A Little Bit Dus was claimed by Conor Dore for £6,000. Cape Safari was claimed by Tom Malone for £12,000.
Owner John P Evitt **Bred** T O C S Limited **Trained** Upper Longdon, Staffs

FOCUS
A modest claimer. The form is slightly shaky but has been taken at face value for now.

7414 LIKE LADBROKES ON FACEBOOK NURSERY 1m 141y (P)
7:45 (7:45) (Class 6) (0-65,65) 2-Y-O **£2,181** (£644; £161 ; £161) **Stalls** Low

Form RPR
0020 **1** **Run It Twice (IRE)**[26] 6732 2 -9-261..........(b) MartinLane 4 68+
(Brian Meehan) *s.i.s: hld up: pushed along over 3f out: rdn and hung lft over 1f out: str run to ld wl ins fnl f: edgd lft and sn clr* **33/1**
0121 **2** 2 **Progenitor (IRE)**[21] 6893 2 -9-665.......... TedDurcan 10 68
(David Lanigan) *mid-div: hdwy over 2f out: rdn and ev ch wl ins fnl f: styd on same pce* **7/4**[1]
416 **3** 1 **Getaway Car**[44] 6156 2 -9-261.......... NeilCallan 9 62
(Gerard Butler) *hld up: hdwy on outer over 2f out: sn rdn: styd on* **6/1**[2]
01U3 **3** dht **Super Cookie**[15] 7026 2 -9-564.......... GrahamLee 11 65
(Philip McBride) *sn prom: rdn to ld over 1f out: hdd and unable qck wl ins fnl f* **7/1**[3]
1044 **5** 1 **Sekumkum (IRE)**[15] 7026 2 -9-665.......... JimmyQuinn 7 64
(Marco Botti) *mid-div: hdwy over 2f out: rdn over 1f out: styd on same pce ins fnl f* **6/1**[2]
0056 **6** 1 **Gabrial The Duke (IRE)**[12] 7111 2 -9-463.......... StevieDonohoe 12 60
(Ian Williams) *hld up: rdn over 1f out: hung lft and r.o ins fnl f: nt trble ldrs* **16/1**
1511 **7** 2 1/2 **Lea Valley Black**[16] 7008 2 -9-665.......... RichardKingscote 6 56
(Tom Dascombe) *chsd ldr tl rdn over 2f out: wknd ins fnl f* **12/1**
6242 **8** 1/2 **Girl Of Cadiz**[10] 7173 2 -9-165.......... WilliamTwiston-Davies(5) 5 55
(Richard Hannon) *chsd ldrs: rdn over 1f out: wknd ins fnl f* **14/1**
000 **9** 3/4 **Alfie's Rose**[22] 6845 2 -9-362.......... LiamJones 8 51
(William Haggas) *hld up: rdn over 1f out: nvr on terms* **25/1**
4620 **10** 1/2 **Gabrial The Boss (USA)**[15] 7026 2 -9-261.......... TomEaves 2 49
(David Simcock) *led: rdn and hdd over 1f out: wknd ins fnl f* **16/1**
506 **11** 4 1/2 **Pairumani Prince (IRE)**[22] 6841 2 -9-261.......... TomMcLaughlin 3 39
(Ed Dunlop) *prom: nt clr run and lost pl over 2f out: rallied over 1f out: wknd ins fnl f* **14/1**
2200 **12** 11 **Excellent Mariner (IRE)**[42] 6247 2 -9-665.......... SilvestreDeSousa 1 20
(Mark Johnston) *chsd ldrs: rdn 3f out: wknd 2f out* **16/1**

1m 49.88s (-0.62)**Going Correction** -0.125s/f (Stan) 12Ran SP% 122.9
Speed ratings (Par 93): **97,95,94,94,93 92,90,89,89,88 84,75**
PLACES: Super Cookie £1.10, Getaway Car £0.70, TRICAST: 1,2 & SC £250.80. 1,2 & GC £219.51. toteswinger: 1&2 £22.50, 1&SC £27.10, 1&GC £37.80, 2 & SC £2.30, 2& GC £2.30. CSF £94.18 TOTE £71.20 : £13.60 , £1.10 ; EX 200.20 TRIFECTA Not won. .
Owner John Dwyer **Bred** Yeomanstown Stud **Trained** Manton, Wilts

FOCUS
A competitive nursery and the form makes sense. The firt two may have more to offer.

NOTEBOOK
Run It Twice (IRE) readily landed his first success to date on this return to Polytrack. He was well beaten over 1m2f on turf last time, but had gone very close on his penultimate outing and returned to that sort of form here. He has some quirks, but clearly also a fair engine when in the mood. Official explanation: trainer's rep said, regarding apparent improvement in form, that the gelding may have benefited from the all-weather surface. (op 50-1)
Progenitor(IRE) held every chance in this bid to make it 3-4 in nurseries, but a combination of a 5lb higher mark and tricky draw found him out near the finish. He's not one to abandon yet. 2-1)
Getaway Car, whose yard does very well with 2-y-os here, ran close to his last-time-out form with the winner and rates a solid benchmark. (op 8-1)
Super Cookie probably ran up to her last-time-out performance over C&D and confirmed that form with Sekumkum. (op 8-1)

7415 ATTHERACES.COM BREEDERS' CUP SITE NOW LIVE CLAIMING STKS 1m 141y (P)
8:15 (8:15) (Class 6) 3-Y-0+ **£2,181** (£644; £322) **Stalls** Low

Form RPR
6206 **1** **Elijah Pepper (USA)**[21] 6881 7 -9-371.......... GrahamGibbons 10 77
(David Barron) *hld up: hdwy over 2f out: rdn to ld and edgd lft ins fnl f: r.o* **15/2**
3302 **2** 3/4 **One Way Or Another (AUS)**[16] 7166 9 -9-068..........(t) GrahamLee 5 72
(David Evans) *hld up: hdwy over 2f out: swtchd rt 1f out: sn rdn and r.o* **12/1**
0001 **3** 1/2 **Desert Vision**[18] 6969 8 -9-079..........(vt) MatthewHopkins(7) 9 78
(Michael Easterby) *led over 7f out: rdn and hdd ins fnl f: styd on same pce* **14/1**
0643 **4** 1 1/4 **Leviathan**[13] 7083 5 -9-1375..........(t) NeilCallan 8 81
(Tony Newcombe) *hld up: hdwy over 1f out: hmpd ins fnl f: styd on* **4/1**[2]
6300 **5** 1 1/2 **Thatcherite (IRE)**[15] 7027 4 -9-568..........(tp) StephenCraine 6 70
(Tony Coyle) *hld up: rdn over 1f out: r.o ins fnl f: nvr nrr* **50/1**
3240 **6** 1/2 **Aciano (IRE)**[21] 6894 4 -9-370..........(tp) SebSanders 12 67
(Brendan Powell) *chsd ldr: rdn over 2f out: no ex ins fnl f* **16/1**
7 shd **Demolition**[82] 4879 8 -9-1385.......... DanielTudhope 2 76
(Noel Wilson) *chsd ldrs: rdn over 1f out: no ex ins fnl f* **7/2**[1]
2023 **8** 1/2 **Brocklebank (IRE)**[26] 6752 3 -9-978..........(tp) AmyRyan 11 75
(Kevin Ryan) *hdwy over 6f out: rdn over 3f out: styd on same pce fr over 1f out* **20/1**
0256 **9** 1/2 **Bint Alzain (IRE)**[22] 6840 3 -9-474..........(t) LukeMorris 7 69
(Gerard Butler) *s.i.s: hld up: rdn over 1f out: styd on ins fnl f: nvr nrr* **14/1**
0060 **10** 3/4 **Berengar (IRE)**[5] 7302 3 -9-970..........(b[1]) MartinLane 4 72
(Brian Meehan) *hld up: rdn over 2f out: a iin rr* **16/1**
0063 **11** 1 3/4 **Indian Art (IRE)**[8] 6969 6 -8-674.......... MeganWhitehead(7) 1 54
(Sylvester Kirk) *hld up: hdwy over 1f out: wknd ins fnl f* **16/1**
6500 **12** 1/2 **Kyllachy Star**[8] 7210 6 -9-1180..........(p) TonyHamilton 3 65
(Richard Fahey) *led 1f: chsd ldrs: rdn over 2f out: wknd fnl f* **9/2**[3]
4333 **13** 66 **Aquilifer (IRE)**[151] 2581 4 -9-568.......... ShaneKelly 13
(Mrs K Burke) *prom tl n.m.r wl over 1f out: sn wknd and eased: t.o* **40/1**

1m 49.16s (-1.34)**Going Correction** -0.125s/f (Stan)
WFA 3 from 4yo+ 4lb 13Ran SP% 120.0
Speed ratings (Par 101): **100,99,98,97,96 95,95,95,95,94 92,92,33**
toteswingers: 1&2 £4.90, 1&3 £32.90, 2&3 £13.70. CSF £93.15 TOTE £9.50 : £4.50 , £5.00 , £5.60; EX 141.80 TRIFECTA Not won. .Elijah Pepper was claimed by Conor Dore for £7,000.
Owner Wensleydale Bacon Limited **Bred** Liberation Farm & Oratis Thoroughbreds **Trained** Maunby, N Yorks

FOCUS
Not a bad claimer, though the time was modest. The winner only needed to run to this year's form.
Aquilifer(IRE) Official explanation: jockey said gelding hung right-handed

7416 DOWNLOAD THE LADBROKES MOBILE APP FILLIES' H'CAP 1m 1f 103y (P)
8:45 (8:45) (Class 5) (0-75,74) 3-Y-O+ **£2,911** (£866; £432 ; £216) **Stalls** Low

Form RPR
05 **1** **Chatterer (IRE)**[11] 7131 4 -9-473.......... KatiaScallan(5) 7 84
(Marcus Tregoning) *chsd ldr tl led 3f out: shkn up over 1f out: styd on* **7/1**
5-60 **2** 1/2 **Easter Diva (IRE)**[illegible] [illegible] 5 -8-11[illegible].......... NickyMackay 12 75+
(Gerard Butler) *hld up: hdwy over 1f out: rdn and r.o to go 2nd wl ins fnl f: nt rch wnr* **20/1**
-204 **3** 2 1/4 **Amelia May**[30] 6613 3 -9-674.......... LukeMorris 2 79
(Ed Vaughan) *a.p: rdn to chse wnr over 1f out tl styd on same pce ins fnl f* **15/2**
1000 **4** 3 3/4 **Lady Arabella (IRE)**[6] 7270 3 -8-1367.......... GrahamLee 6 64
(Alastair Lidderdale) *prom: rdn over 2f out: no ex fnl f* **12/1**
0606 **5** shd **Cheers For Thea (IRE)**[30] 6613 7 -9-165..........(t) DanielTudhope 8 62
(Tim Easterby) *hld up: hdwy over 2f out: rdn over 1f out: no ex fnl f* **13/2**[3]
0050 **6** nk **Talk Of The North**[16] 7003 3 -8-1064..........(b) JimmyQuinn 3 60
(Hugo Palmer) *mid-div: hdwy over 2f out: rdn and edgd lft over 1f out: no ex fnl f* **11/2**[2]
0402 **7** hd **Ukrainian Princess**[21] 6895 3 -8-869.......... AmeliaGreen(7) 5 65+
(Sir Henry Cecil) *dwlt: hld up and bhd: styng on whn nt clr run ins fnl f: nvr trbld ldrs* **7/1**
0400 **8** 3/4 **Tidal Run**[6] 7269 4 -9-973.......... SamHitchcott 10 67
(Mick Channon) *hld up: drvn along over 4f out: nvr nrr* **16/1**
6200 **9** 1 1/2 **Hunt A Mistress (IRE)**[5] 7310 3 -9-270..........(t) SilvestreDeSousa 9 61
(Paul Cole) *sn led: pushed along and hdd 3f out: rdn and hung lft over 1f out: wknd fnl f* **9/1**
052 **10** 1 3/4 **Zaina (IRE)**[27] 6710 3 -9-472..........(p) NeilCallan 11 59
(Gerard Butler) *mid-div: rdn over 2f out: wknd over 1f out* **4/1**[1]
3630 **11** 11 **My Own Way Home**[9] 7203 4 -9-064.......... TomMcLaughlin 4 28
(David Evans) *hld up: a in rr: rdn and wknd over 2f out* **40/1**
-006 **12** 14 **Apache Glory (USA)**[4] 7310 4 -9-670.......... SeanQuinlan 1
(John Stimpson) *prom tl rdn and wknd over 2f out* **33/1**

1m 59.77s (-1.93)**Going Correction** -0.125s/f (Stan)
WFA 3 from 4yo+ 4lb 12Ran SP% 119.2
Speed ratings (Par 100): **103,102,100,97,97 96,96,96,94,93 83,70**
toteswingers: 1&2 £50.30, 1&3 £7.60, 2&3 £33.90. CSF £141.35 CT £1087.78 TOTE £6.60 : £2.40, £7.30 , £3.40 ; EX 207.70 TRIFECTA Not won. .
Owner Horne, Hoare, Gaskell & Partners **Bred** Airlie Stud And Sir Thomas Pilkington **Trained** Lambourn, Berks

FOCUS
A modest fillies' handicap, rated around the third. A 4lb personal best from the winner.

7417 LADBROKES GAME ON! H'CAP 1m 4f 50y (P)
9:15 (9:15) (Class 6) (0-65,66) 3-Y-0 **£2,181** (£644; £322) **Stalls** Low

Form RPR
0133 **1** **Kittens**[19] 6924 3 -9-361.......... MartinDwyer 2 69+
(William Muir) *hld up: rdn over 3f out: swtchd rt and hdwy over 1f out: r.o to ld nr fin* **7/2**[1]
0543 **2** 3/4 **Thecornishcockney**[10] 7162 3 -9-866..........(tp[1]) TomMcLaughlin 5 73
(John Ryan) *s.s: hld up: hdwy over 2f out: led on bit 1f out: shkn up and edgd lft: idled and hdd nr fin* **8/1**
002 **3** 4 **Bobs Her Uncle**[38] 6364 3 -9-664.......... TedDurcan 1 65+
(James Bethell) *hld up: hdwy over 1f out: sn rdn: styd on same pce ins fnl f* **13/2**
4 nk **Zambezi Tiger (IRE)**[16] 5694 3 -8-1256.......... ShaneKelly 12 56
(Mrs Prunella Dobbs, Ire) *prom: rdn to ld over 1f out: hdd 1f out: no ex* **16/1**
1005 **5** 2 1/4 **Rockgoat (IRE)**[32] 6555 3 -9-765.......... GrahamLee 7 62
(Ian McInnes) *hld up: hdwy over 2f out: sn rdn: styd on same pce fnl f* **16/1**
4053 **6** 1 **Quiet Appeal (IRE)**[9] 6940 3 -8-1155.......... SilvestreDeSousa 3 50
(Mark Johnston) *chsd ldrs: rdn over 2f out: wknd ins fnl f* **8/1**
405 **7** 3 **Chella Thriller (SPA)**[14] 7062 3 -8-1357..........(bt) RichardKingscote 8 47
(Alastair Lidderdale) *s.s: sn prom: chsd ldr over 4f out: led over 2f out: rdn and hdd over 1f out: wknd fnl f* **10/1**
4430 **8** nk **District Attorney (IRE)**[38] 6364 3 -9-563..........(b) LiamJones 10 53
(William Haggas) *led: rdn and hdd over 2f out: wknd fnl f* **6/1**[3]
0264 **9** shd **Always Eager**[14] 7062 3 -8-953.......... NeilCallan 6 42
(Mark Johnston) *chsd ldrs: rdn over 2f out: wknd over 1f out* **12/1**
5140 **10** 2 1/4 **Saucy Cat (IRE)**[9] 7200 3 -9-159.......... LukeMorris 11 45
(John Best) *hld up: pushed along over 6f out: rdn whn hmpd over 1f out: sn wknd* **33/1**
0350 **11** 3/4 **I'm Harry**[50] 5990 3 -8-1364.......... AaronJones(7) 4 49
(George Baker) *hld up: a in rr: bhd fnl 4f* **50/1**
3011 **12** 3 3/4 **Kathleensluckylad (IRE)**[14] 7058 3 -9-462..........(t) GrahamGibbons 9 41
(Kevin Ryan) *chsd ldrs: rdn over 3f out: wknd wl over 1f out* **5/1**[2]

2m 40.0s (-1.10)**Going Correction** -0.125s/f (Stan) 12Ran SP% 122.2
Speed ratings (Par 99): **98,97,94,94,93 92,90,90,90,88 88,85**
toteswingers: 1&2 £3.10, 1&3 £7.30, 2&3 £11.40. CSF £32.82 CT £180.58 TOTE £5.10 : £2.20 , £2.90, £2.30 ; EX 36.40 Trifecta £155.10 Pool: £421.95 - 2.04 winning units. .
Owner Muir Racing Partnership - Chester **Bred** Moyns Park Estate And Stud Ltd **Trained** Lambourn, Berks

FOCUS
A moderate 3-y-o handicap. The form is rated around the second, with little solid or convincing in behind.

T/Plt: £40.50 to a £1 stake. Pool: £80,090.76 - 1,441.66 winning tickets. T/Qpdt: £19.20 to a £1 stake. Pool: £7,739.10 - 297.60 w. tckts CR 7418a, 7420a-7422a, 7424a (Foreign Racing) See RI

6059 LEOPARDSTOWN (L-H)

Saturday, October 27

OFFICIAL GOING: Soft

7419a JRA KILLAVULLAN STKS (GROUP 3) 7f

2:40 (2:41) 2-Y-O **£25,729** (£7,520; £3,562; £1,187)

RPR

1 **Big Break**[49] 6059 2-9-0 .... PatSmullen 3 104+
(D K Weld, Ire) *trckd ldrs in 4th: short of room early in st and swtchd rt: qcknd wl to ld 1f out: sn clr: impressive* **10/11**[1]

2 3 ¾ **Beyond Thankful (IRE)**[6] 7278 2-9-3 91 .... RonanWhelan 7 96
(J S Bolger, Ire) *w.w: 5th appr home turn: sn pushed along and nt qckn w wnr 1f out: kpt on wl to go 2nd fnl 100yds* **10/1**

3 1 **Coolibah (IRE)**[12] 7118 2-9-0 .... DeclanMcDonogh 6 91
(Charles O'Brien, Ire) *bit slowly away and racd in rr: last home turn: styd on wl ins fnl f: nrst fin* **20/1**

4 shd **Canary Row (IRE)**[30] 6599 2-9-3 97 .... ShaneFoley 5 93
(P J Prendergast, Ire) *racd in cl 3rd: pushed along home turn: sn pressed ldr: nt qckn w wnr 1f out: kpt on one pce* **14/1**

5 2 **Dont Bother Me (IRE)**[56] 5833 2-9-3 .... WayneLordan 2 88
(Niall Moran, Ire) *racd in cl 2nd: led 2f out tl nt qckn w wnr 1f out: sn no ex* **12/1**

6 ½ **Dubaya**[17] 6992 2-9-0 .... GaryCarroll 8 84
(A Oliver, Ire) *hld up in 6th: pushed along appr home turn: sn no imp* **7/1**[3]

7 9 **Magician (IRE)**[13] 7084 2-9-3 .... SeamieHeffernan 4 80
(A P O'Brien, Ire) *sn led: hdd 2f out: stl in contention whn squeezed for room and snatched up over 1f out: sn eased* **15/8**[2]

1m 32.68s (3.98) **Going Correction** +0.75s/f (Yiel) **7 Ran SP% 127.9**
Speed ratings: **107,102,101,101,99 98,88**
CSF £14.23 TOTE £1.80: £1.02, £6.80; DF 11.20.
Owner K Abdulla **Bred** Juddmonte Farms Ltd **Trained** The Curragh, Co Kildare
■ Stewards' Enquiry : Shane Foley three-day ban; careless riding (16th,23rd,30th Nov).

FOCUS
The winner was quite impressive and is value for a bit extra, but the fourth gives perspective to the race.

NOTEBOOK
Big Break showed herself to be a smart filly and overcame a dislike for the soft surface to win this with some conviction. Tracking the pace, it took her some time to reach her full stride on the surface, and she chopped and changed her legs a couple of times early in the straight. When she eventually got on top, though, she strode out to the line and the gears she showed were far too much for her rivals to handle. Her trainer does have some decent ammunition in the 2yo filly department and the possibility of some nice selection headaches. (op evs tchd 9-10)
Beyond Thankful(IRE) is a reasonably progressive colt who stays well. He was off the bridle and struggling to make an impact turning in but stayed on well in the straight and already looks in need of a mile. He should be a nice colt for middle distances next season at a certain level. (op 10-1 tchd 11-1)
Coolibah(IRE) had been a Roscommon maiden winner prior to this and this represented further progression. She raced in rear and took some time to pick up but stayed on to pretty decent effect and can be expected to continue progressing. (op 16-1 tchd 14-1)
Canary Row(IRE) kept up his challenge for as long as he could having come off the bridle before turning in and perhaps this ground was soft enough for him at this sort of level. (op 12-1)
Dont Bother Me(IRE) ran a decent enough race but was a bit too free early on and didn't get home particularly well. (op 14-1 tchd 10-1)
Magician(IRE) was starting to fade but was badly squeezed up when the winner went to the front and his remote last-place finish was definitely exaggerated. (op 9-4)

7423a TRIGO STKS (LISTED RACE) 1m 2f

5:00 (5:01) 3-Y-O+ **£21,666** (£6,333; £3,000; £1,000)

RPR

1 **Famous Name**[48] 6079 7-10-0 119 .... PatSmullen 7 115+
(D K Weld, Ire) *trckd ldrs in 4th: travelled wl to press ldrs appr home turn: led 2f out: sn clr: easily* **1/5**[1]

2 3 ½ **Demurely (IRE)**[13] 7088 3-8-13 97 .... SeamieHeffernan 2 98
(A P O'Brien, Ire) *w.w: pushed along in 6th appr home turn: kpt on wl to chse wnr over 1f out: nvr on terms* **14/1**

3 ¾ **An Saincheann (IRE)**[139] 2962 3-8-13 ....(b) RonanWhelan 3 97
(J S Bolger, Ire) *t.k.h: chsd ldrs: 5th home turn: nt qckn w wnr ins fnl 2f but styd on wl fnl f* **25/1**

4 4 ½ **Macbeth (IRE)**[7] 7260 3-9-2 93 ....(t) ShaneFoley 10 91
(K J Condon, Ire) *hld up in rr: last home turn: kpt on fr over 1f out: nvr nrr* **20/1**

5 1 **Chrysanthemum (IRE)**[7] 7260 4-9-9 104 ....(b) WayneLordan 1 91
(David Wachman, Ire) *trckd ldrs in 3rd on inner: disp early in st tl nt qckn ins fnl 2f* **5/1**[2]

6 3 ½ **Colliding Worlds (IRE)**[97] 4378 3-8-13 103 .... JohnnyMurtagh 8 79
(John Patrick Shanahan, Ire) *hld up in rr: tk clsr order appr home turn: sn pushed along and no imp* **11/1**[3]

7 1 **Barack (IRE)**[7] 7260 6-9-7 98 ....(bt) BenCurtis 4 80
(W McCreery, Ire) *led tl hdd off home turn: wknd qckly ins fnl 2f* **14/1**

8 2 **Alla Speranza**[34] 6518 3-9-4 107 ....(t) RoryCleary 6 78
(J S Bolger, Ire) *racd in cl 2nd: disp off home turn tl hdd 2f out: sn no ex* **14/1**

2m 15.45s (7.25) **Going Correction** +0.75s/f (Yiel)
WFA 3 from 4yo+ 5lb **8 Ran SP% 136.9**
Speed ratings: **101,98,97,94,93 90,89,88**
CSF £8.55 TOTE £1.10: £1.10, £2.10, £4.30; DF 8.70.
Owner K Abdulla **Bred** Juddmonte Farms Ltd **Trained** The Curragh, Co Kildare

FOCUS
A fitting end to the career of a respected Irish Group performer. The runner-up sets the standard.

NOTEBOOK
Famous Name landed this race for the third time. It was won in the manner of many of his previous successes and his retirement is a pity as he seems to be racing with even more enthusiasm these days. That certainly was the case in this race. Pat Smullen couldn't hold on to him any longer as he went to the front probably earlier than desirable but he drew clear to win with plenty in hand. Farming soft races is something he did a lot of, but the horse's appetite for racing and consistently operating to a high level stands him apart in so many ways. It could be a while before we see one like him again. (op 2-7)
Demurely(IRE) managed to get into the frame in a race at this level once again and deserves to find a winning opportunity. She began to stay on and attempted to give effective chase to the winner over a furlong out but was outclassed.
An Saincheann(IRE) came into this race as a slight unknown quantity having run in two maidens earlier in the summer and she ran to a level that would give some hope she could win one of these. She stayed on well, perhaps not quite as well as the runner-up, but she did lack the experience of that filly and has more scope for improvement. She could be interesting next season. (op 25-1 tchd 22-1)
Macbeth(IRE) has been a shade disappointing this season and dropping him back in trip hasn't really led to any notable improvement. Held up off the pace he didn't have the speed to get involved, although he stayed on to reasonable effect.
Chrysanthemum(IRE) has been disappointing since the spring. She raced handily on the inside but it was disappointing the way in which she faded so tamely in the straight.

7394 MOONEE VALLEY (L-H)

Saturday, October 27

OFFICIAL GOING: Turf: good

7425a DRAKE INTERNATIONAL CUP (GROUP 2) (4YO+) (TURF) 1m 4f 110y

5:55 (12:00) 4-Y-O+

£113,815 (£29,605; £14,802; £7,401; £4,111; £3,289)

RPR

1 **Vatuvei (AUS)**[140] 2956 4-8-7 0 ....(p) LukeNolen 1 105+
(Peter G Moody, Australia) **12/1**

2 1 ½ **Reuben Percival (NZ)**[14] 7073 6-8-11 0 ....(t) NashRawiller 8 105
(Gai Waterhouse, Australia) **17/2**

3 2 **Ironstein (AUS)**[14] 7073 7-8-13 0 ....(p) BrentonAvdulla 3 104
(Gerald Ryan, Australia) **4/1**[3]

4 hd **Precedence (NZ)**[14] 7073 7-9-0 0 .... JamesMcDonald 7 105
(Bart Cummings, Australia) **19/5**[2]

5 3 **Unusual Suspect (USA)**[13] 8-9-2 0 ....(v) BradRawiller 2 102
(Michael Kent, Australia) **60/1**

6 1 ¼ **Shenzhou Steeds (NZ)**[35] 5-8-13 0 .... KerrinMcEvoy 5 97
(Michael Moroney, Australia) **12/1**

7 1 ½ **Ibicenco (GER)**[63] 5599 4-8-9 0 .... CraigNewitt 4 91
(Luca Cumani) *disp ld on inner: hdd and dropped to 3rd after 5f: short of room and shuffled bk to last 3f out: rdn over 2f out: sn outpcd and btn: plugged on* **13/2**

8 4 **Midas Touch**[14] 7070 5-8-9 0 ....(t) HughBowman 9 85
(Robert Hickmott, Australia) **16/5**[1]

9 3 ½ **Rialya (AUS)**[35] 5-9-0 0 ....(p) DamienOliver 6 85
(Lloyd Kennewell, Australia) **20/1**

2m 35.73s (155.73) **9 Ran SP% 110.3**
PARI-MUTUEL (NSW TAB - all including au$1 stakes): WIN 9.50 PLACE 2.70, 2.30, 1.60; DF 40.20; SF 75.30.
Owner Sitralos Racing Syndicate, C Sharpe et al **Bred** Caradale Pty Ltd **Trained** Australia

7426a SPORTINGBET COX PLATE (GROUP 1) (3YO+) (TURF) 1m 2f 44y

7:15 (12:00) 3-Y-O+

£1,217,105 (£289,473; £144,736; £85,526; £72,368; £65,789)

RPR

1 **Ocean Park (NZ)**[14] 7070 4-9-1 0 ....(b) GlenBoss 9 122
(Gary Hennessy, New Zealand) *settled in rr of midfield: rdn to improve 3f out: hdwy on wd outside to chal over 1f out: led ins fnl 50yds: drvn out* **5/1**[3]

2 nk **All Too Hard (AUS)**[14] 7072 3-7-11 0 ....(p) ChrisMunce 3 119
(Michael, Wayne & John Hawkes, Australia) *prom on inner: swtchd out and rdn to chal 2f out: led over 1f out: strly pressed thrght fnl f: hdd ins fnl 50yds* **8/1**

3 3 ¾ **Pierro (AUS)**[14] 7072 3-7-11 0 ....(b) CoreyBrown 7 112
(Gai Waterhouse, Australia) *prom early: stdd and sn settled in midfield: rdn 3f out: styd on to go 3rd ins fnl 100yds: no ch w front pair* **9/2**[2]

4 hd **Ethiopia (AUS)**[21] 4-9-1 0 ....(b[1]) RhysMcLeod 6 113
(Pat Carey, Australia) *pushed along to go forward early and led first turn: sn hdd and trckd ldr in 2nd on outer: rdn 3f out: outpcd by ldrs and dropped to 4th ent fnl f: kpt on* **17/1**

5 nk **Shoot Out (AUS)**[21] 6-9-4 0 ....(b) HughBowman 4 116
(Chris Waller, Australia) *hld up towards rr: hdwy into midfield over 5f out: rdn over 3f out: styd on to go 5th ins fnl 50yds: nt pce to chal* **16/1**

6 hd **Southern Speed (AUS)**[21] 5-9-0 0 ....(b) LukeNolen 13 111+
(Leon Macdonald & Andrew Gluyas, Australia) *dropped in fr wd draw and hld up in last pair: rdn in last over 2f out: styd on to go 6th cl home: fin wl but nvr a threat* **40/1**

7 1 ¼ **Green Moon (IRE)**[21] 5-9-4 0 .... CraigAWilliams 5 113
(Robert Hickmott, Australia) *midfield on outer: rdn 3f out and sn outpcd: styd on to go 7th post: n.d* **4/1**[1]

8 shd **Proisir (AUS)**[21] 3-7-11 0 .... CraigNewitt 10 107
(Gai Waterhouse, Australia) *prom early: led after first turn: rdn over 2f out: strly pressed and hdd over 1f out: sn no ex and fdd: dropped to 8th post* **9/1**

9 hd **Sincero (AUS)**[14] 7070 5-9-4 0 ....(b) MichaelRodd 12 112
(Stephen Farley, Australia) *hld up towards rr: rdn 3f out: styd on to go 9th fnl strides: nt pce to chal* **30/1**

10 shd **Happy Trails (AUS)**[21] 5-9-4 0 ....(p) KerrinMcEvoy 8 112
(Paul Beshara, Australia) *led on run to first turn: sn hdd but remained prom: rdn 3f out: sn outpcd by ldrs: kpt on tl no ex ins fnl f: fdd and dropped to 10th fnl strides* **60/1**

11 1 **More Joyous (NZ)**[14] 7071 6-9-0 0 .... NashRawiller 11 106
(Gai Waterhouse, Australia) *prom on outer: rdn over 2f out: kpt on tl no ex and btn ins fnl f: fdd* **15/2**

12 shd **Linton (AUS)**[21] 6-9-4 0 .... StevenArnold 14 110
(John D Sadler, Australia) *dropped in fr wdst draw and hld up in last: rdn 3f out: plugged on: nvr a factor* **100/1**

13 1 ½ **Glass Harmonium (IRE)**[14] 7071 6-9-4 0 ....(t) JamesMcDonald 2 107
(Michael Moroney, Australia) *sltly slow to stride and pushed along to rcvr: midfield: rdn 3f out: sn outpcd* **80/1**

14 2 ¼ **Rekindled Interest (AUS)**[21] 5-9-4 0 ....(b) DwayneDunn 1 102
(Jim Conlan, Australia) *midfield on inner: rdn over 3f out: sn outpcd and btn: fdd and dropped to last ent fnl f* **25/1**

2m 4.14s (124.14)
WFA 3 from 4yo+ 5lb **14 Ran SP% 112.5**
PARI-MUTUEL (NSW TAB - all including au$1 stakes): WIN 6.50 PLACE 2.20, 2.70, 1.80; DF 31.20; SF 67.80.
Owner A Wong, S Yan & G Hennessy **Bred** Trelawney Thoroughbred Ltd **Trained** New Zealand

FOCUS
This has often been referred to as 'the race where legends are made', and the 2012 renewal looked fairly strong in depth. The early pace was decent around the tight track but plenty of runners held some sort of chance over 2f out.

NOTEBOOK
Ocean Park (NZ)had some fantastic performances under his belt since returning from New Zealand. Both his recent victories have come at Group 1 level under Glen Boss in good races, and he beat Caulfield Cup runner-up Alcopop last time. His jockey made sure he came through to have a clear run by going around the whole field as the tempo lifted, and he fought on gamely for pressure to just get up.
All Too Hard (AUS) Black Caviar's half-brother, went really close to gaining victory for a generation that doesn't have a great record in this race (only four 3yos had won since 1980). Well ridden off a low weight, the colt has plenty of heart and made the winner fight really hard to overcome him.
Pierro(AUS) could not reverse Caulfield Guineas form with All Too Hard. The Gai Waterhouse 3yo was one-paced late on and never seemed like winning.
Ethiopia(AUS), last year's Australian Derby winner, predictably stayed on nicely over a trip short of his best. The feeling afterwards was that he would go for the Melbourne Cup next.
Shoot Out (AUS) who easily beat All Too Hard in the George Main over 1m while giving plenty of weight away, caught the eye finishing well, albeit all too late.
Southern Speed (AUS)was last turning in but finished well.
Green Moon (IRE)had struck up a decent partnership with Craig Williams so this was a particularly tame effort. The jockey said that his mount didn't feel right some way out.
More Joyous (NZ)'s trainer controversially chose a wide stall at the barrier draw despite having first pick. That tactic backfired and the top-class mare was never a threat.

7285 SAN SIRO (R-H)
Saturday, October 27
OFFICIAL GOING: Turf: heavy

7427a ST LEGER ITALIANO (GROUP 3) (3YO+) (TURF) — **1m 6f**
3:55 (12:00) 3-Y-O+ **£23,333** (£10,266; £5,600 ; £2,800)

RPR

1 **Donn Halling (IRE)**[41] 6290 4 -8-130 VJanacek 5 107
(V Luka Jr, Czech Republic) *settled towards rr: tk clsr order 3f out: 4th and rdn over 2f out: styd on to ld narrowly between horses 1f out: rn gamely u.p: hld on wl* **30/1**

2 *shd* **Altano (GER)**[41] 6290 6 -9-10 EPedroza 2 109
(A Wohler, Germany) *midfield: scrubbed along to chse ldrs over 3f out: drvn to ld ins fnl 2f: rdn and hdd on ins of two rivals 1f out: r.o wl fnl f: inched clsr all way to line: nt quite get up* **7/10**[1]

3 *snk* **Slowfoot (GER)**[420] 4 -8-130 AStarke 8 106
(Markus Klug, Germany) *trckd ldrs: prog on outside under 2f out: chal narrow ldr on outside 1f out: kpt on but no ex fnl 75yds* **127/10**

4 *5* **Earlsalsa (GER)**[41] 6290 8 -8-130 CristianDemuro 7 99
(C Von Der Recke, Germany) *hld up towards rr: rdn and styd on fnl 1 1/2f: nvr on terms* **143/10**

5 *nk* **Wilddrossel (GER)**[41] 6290 3 -8-20 FilipMinarik 9 97
(Markus Klug, Germany) *prom on wd outside: led after 1 1/2f and swtchd ins to rail: hdd over 3f out: sn rdn and nt qckn: wknd fnl f* **63/10**[3]

6 *4* **Sopran Montieri (IRE)**[39] 2968 3 -8-50 DarioVargiu 6 94
(B Grizzetti, Italy) *v keen in midfield: hrd rdn and no imp 2f out: plugged on tl eased fnl 75yds* **113/10**

7 *2* **Sanogo (GER)**[97] 4 -8-130 JBojko 3 91
(A Wohler, Germany) *led: hdd after 1 1/2f: trckd ldr: led again over 3f out: hdd ins fnl 2f: styd prom tl wknd over 1f out* **205/10**

8 *dist* **Caudillo (GER)**[90] 4634 9 -8-130 LManiezzi 4
(Dr A Bolte, Germany) *w.w in last two pls: rdn and no imp 2 1/2f out: sn wknd: eased ins fnl f* **111/10**

9 *dist* **Vashti (FR)**[37] 3 -8-20 UmbertoRispoli 1
(M Delzangles, France) *settled in last two pls on ins: hdwy to trck ldrs 1/2-way: rdn and wknd fr 2f out: eased ins fnl f* **33/10**[2]

3m 7.0s (187.00)
WFA 3 from 4yo+ 9lb **9**Ran SP% **133.9**
WIN (incl. 1 euro stake): 30.55. PLACES: 5.14, 1.24, 2.43. DF: 21.53.
Owner DS Maentiva **Bred** Lynch Bages Ltd **Trained** Czech Rep.

7428a (Foreign Racing) See RI

2323 CAPANNELLE (R-H)
Sunday, October 28
OFFICIAL GOING: Turf: heavy

7429a PREMIO LYDIA TESIO LONGINES (GROUP 1) (3YO+ FILLIES & MARES) (TURF) — **1m 2f**
3:55 (12:00) 3-Y-O+ **£79,166** (£34,833; £19,000 ; £9,500)

RPR

1 **Sortilege (IRE)**[43] 6273 4 -9-00 AndreaAtzeni 10 107
(A Wohler, Germany) *midfield: rdn to chal 2f out: led ins fnl f: drvn out* **125/10**

2 *1* **Cherry Collect (IRE)**[35] 3 -8-100 FabioBranca 8 106
(S Botti, Italy) *hld up towards rr: rdn 3f out: styd on to go 2nd wl ins fnl f* **5/2**[1]

3 *1* **Nova Hawk**[28] 6726 4 -9-00 OlivierPeslier 9 103+
(Rod Collet, France) *hld up in last: rdn 2f out: styd on to go 3rd fnl strides* **9/2**

4 *shd* **Sajjhaa**[164] 2209 5 -9-00 FrankieDettori 2 103
(Saeed Bin Suroor) *sn trcking clr ldr in 2nd: smooth hdwy to chal gng wl 2f out: rdn to ld over 1f out: strly pressed and hdd ins fnl f: no ex and dropped to 4th fnl strides* **17/5**[2]

5 *1/2* **Wedding Fair**[18] 5 -9-00 (b) MickaelBarzalona 7 102
(E Botti, Italy) *midfield: rdn 3f out: kpt on one pce ins fnl 2f* **122/10**

6 *1* **Cartaya**[15] 7075 4 -9-00 JamieSpencer 1 100
(M Rulec, Germany) *midfield: rdn 2f out: outpcd over 1f out: styd on wout threatening ins fnl f* **91/10**

7 *2 1/4* **Opera Gal (IRE)**[36] 6470 5 -9-00 JimmyFortune 5 95
(Andrew Balding) *led and sn clr: rdn and strly pressed 2f out: hdd over 1f out: sn btn and fdd* **41/10**[3]

8 *1* **Etoile D'Argent (ITY)**[28] 3 -8-100 MEsposito 4 94
(G Mosconi, Italy) *midfield: rdn to chal 2f out: stl ev ch ent fnl f: sn no ex and btn: fdd: eased and dropped to 8th cl home* **84/1**

9 *1 1/2* **Quiza Quiza Quiza**[21] 6911 6 -9-00 DarioVargiu 11 90
(L Riccardi, Italy) *prom: rdn and brief effrt to chal 2f out: outpcd and btn over 1f out: fdd* **59/10**

10 *6* **Aquamarine (JPN)**[35] 6554 4 -9-00 ThomasHuet 6 78
(M Delzangles, France) *hld up towards rr: rdn 3f out: no ex and btn over 1f out: eased ent fnl f* **101/10**

11 *8* **Oeuvre D'Art (IRE)**[14] 4 -9-00 CristianDemuro 3 62
(L Riccardi, Italy) *hld up: rdn 3f out: last and btn over 1f out: eased* **38/1**

2m 7.7s (4.40)
WFA 3 from 4yo+ 5lb **11**Ran SP% **141.2**
WIN (incl. 1 euro stake): 13.50. PLACES: 3.20, 1.40, 1.80. DF: 145.60.
Owner Gestut Karlshof **Bred** Wertheimer Et Frere **Trained** Germany

NOTEBOOK
Sajjhaa hit the front approaching the final furlong but could not see it out in what developed into a bit of a sprint.
Opera Gal (IRE) who went off in front, couldn't repeat the form she showed when successful at Ayr last time.

7283 LONGCHAMP (R-H)
Sunday, October 28
OFFICIAL GOING: Turf: heavy

7430a CRITERIUM DE VITESSE (LISTED RACE) (2YO) (TURF) — **5f (S)**
1:30 (12:00) 2-Y-O **£22,916** (£9,166; £6,875 ; £4,583 ; £2,291)

RPR

1 **Disko Dasko (FR)**[8] 7265 2 -8-130 RichardKingscote 6 95
(Mrs K Burke) *broke wl on outside to r 2nd: rdn 2f out: chal for ld 1 1/2f out: tk ld 250yds out: styd on wl* **40/1**

2 *3/4* **Strange Magic (IRE)**[8] 7241 2 -8-130 FrederikTylicki 2 92
(Richard Fahey) *broke wl on ins: racd 3rd: styd on wl fr 2f out: clsd on eventual wnr ins fnl 100yds* **11/1**

3 *2 1/2* **The Brothers War (USA)**[8] 2 -9-20 MaximeGuyon 3 86
(J-C Rouget, France) **1/2**[1]

4 *shd* **Rime A Rien**[74] 5248 2 -8-130 ThierryJarnet 1 83
(F Rohaut, France) **48/10**[2]

5 *2* **Plaza Mayor (FR)**[47] 2 -8-130 FranckBlondel 5 76
(F Rossi, France) **7/1**[3]

6 *12* **Cucuma (FR)**[91] 4632 2 -8-130 StephanePasquier 7 33
(P Bary, France) **9/1**

7 *2* **Tricky Week (FR)**[37] 6463 2 -8-130 UmbertoRispoli 4 25
(C Baillet, France) **28/1**

1m 1.26s (4.96)**Going Correction** +1.075s/f (Soft) **7**Ran SP% **120.6**
Speed ratings: **103,101,97,97,94 75,72**
WIN (incl. 1 euro stake): 41.00. PLACES: 12.20, 6.10. SF: 250.50.
Owner Hubert John Strecker **Bred** Jean - Pierre Quinson **Trained** Middleham Moor, N Yorks

NOTEBOOK
Disko Dasko (FR) third in a conditions race at Le Croise-Laroche last time out, caused something of a surprise, and led home a one-two for British trained runners.
Strange Magic (IRE) a winner at Catterick last time out, stepped up dramatically on that form to chase her compatriot home.

7431a PRIX ROYAL-OAK (GROUP 1) (3YO+) (TURF) — **1m 7f 110y**
2:45 (12:00) 3-Y-O+ **£119,041** (£47,625; £23,812 ; £11,895 ; £5,958)

RPR

1 **Les Beaufs (FR)**[22] 6896 3 -8-90 JulienGuillochon 3 113+
(Mme V Seignoux, France) *mde all: sn clr: given a breather and c bk to rivals fnl turn: shkn up and wnt clr under 2f out: r.o wl u.p fnl f* **9/1**

2 *4 1/2* **Silver Valny (FR)**[43] 6864 6 -9-40 ThomasMessina 8 107
(Mlle M-L Mortier, France) *towards rr: hdwy on rail under 3f out: 2nd and rdn 1 1/2f out: kpt on u.p fnl f: no ch w wnr* **40/1**

3 *1 1/4* **Rollex Borget (FR)**[38] 6422 3 -8-90 ThierryJarnet 7 106
(J Bertran De Balanda, France) *towards rr: tk clsr order on outside 2 1/2f out: styd on into 3rd over 1f out: one pce u.p fnl f* **16/1**

4 *1 1/2* **Verema (FR)**[22] 6896 3 -8-60 MaximeGuyon 5 101
(A De Royer-Dupre, France) *midfield: shkn up over 2f out: hrd rdn and wnt 4th over 1f out: plugged on fnl f* **15/2**[3]

5 *6* **Dalkala (USA)**[22] 6899 3 -8-60 Christophe-PatriceLemaire 1 94
(A De Royer-Dupre, France) *led main gp bhd clr ldr: 2nd and rdn 2f out: nt qckn: wknd appr fnl f* **7/4**[1]

6 *1 3/4* **Miss Lago (IRE)**[21] 6914 4 -9-10 (b) GregoryBenoist 6 91
(E Lellouche, France) *slowly away: hld up in rr: rdn and short-lived effrt on outside over 2f out: no imp on ldrs: nvr in contention* **10/1**

7 *8* **Quiz Mistress**[23] 6864 4 -9-10 UmbertoRispoli 4 81
(Hughie Morrison) *prom in main gp bhd clr ldr: 3rd and ev ch 2f out: sn rdn and nt qckn: wknd u.p fnl 1 1/2f* **14/1**

8 *snk* **Brown Panther**[43] 6271 4 -9-40 RichardKingscote 9 84
(Tom Dascombe) *prom on outside in main gp bhd clr ldr: rdn 2 1/2f out: wknd u.p over 1 1/2f out* **3/1**[2]

9 *dist* **Hurricane Higgins (IRE)**[15] 7051 4 -9-40 JoeFanning 2
(Mark Johnston) *prom in main gp bhd clr ldr: rdn and lost pl 2 1/2f out: sn bhd: eased rt down and t.o fr 1 1/2f out* **12/1**

3m 36.22s (14.72)**Going Correction** +1.35s/f (Soft)
WFA 3 from 4yo+ 9lb **9**Ran SP% **114.9**
Speed ratings: **117,114,114,113,110 109,105,105,**
WIN (incl. 1 euro stake): 7.50. PLACES: 2.40, 7.90, 4.10. DF: 115,70. SF: 196.30.
Owner Stephane Seignoux **Bred** Mme Christina Kolungia **Trained** France

FOCUS
Not a strong race for the level, but it did see a potentially nice staying prospect confirm he is on an upward curve. The fourth has been rated to par.

NOTEBOOK
Les Beaufs (FR)ran right away from his rivals in the home straight after gaining a nice advantage early. He'd put up a career-best effort when second in the Prix Chaudenay last time, and is seemingly a dangerous opponent when allowed to dominate. Whether he can do the same against classier opposition remains to be seen. The winning trainer said afterwards that her gelding is finished for this year but will have a programme built around all the good staying events next season.
Silver Valny (FR) ninth of 14 in this race last season and comfortably held by Quiz Mistress on recent form at Saint-Cloud, hasn't won in Listed company let alone at Group level, so his effort helps to confirm the result as modest.
Rollex Borget (FR)had a bit of work to do with Verema on their Prix De Letece meeting in September but reversed those placings. The former had only finished fifth in a 1m4f Listed event last time.

Dalkala(USA) travelled nicely for a long way towards the head of affairs before blatantly not getting home.

Quiz Mistress was in front of Silver Valny last time but didn't get home over this trip.

Brown Panther, who missed a good opportunity at Ascot recently to take up this option, deserved plenty of respect if running near his best but he never looked comfortable as the race started to take shape and was readily held.

Hurricane Higgins(IRE) could have been given a chance on his Doncaster Cup form but he isn't the most consistent of horses and dropped out tamely once under serious pressure.

7700a PRIX DU MONTPARNASSE (CLAIMER) (2YO) (TURF) 7f

3:15 (12:00) 2-Y-O **£11,250** (£4,500; £3,375; £2,250; £1,125)

RPR

1 **Pont Marie (FR)**[9] 2-8-11 0 (b) GregoryBenoist 1 78
(F Chappet, France) **33/10**[1]

2 3 **Shaslika (FR)**[22] 2-8-11 0 StephanePasquier 2 71
(D Prod'Homme, France) **4/1**[2]

3 nk **City Chope (FR)**[9] 2-8-8 0 JulienAuge 5 67
(C Boutin, France) **10/1**

4 1 1/4 **Princesse Leila (FR)**[118] 2-8-8 0 (b[1]) MorganDelalande 8 64
(Y Barberot, France) **10/1**

5 1/2 **Excellent Touch (IRE)**[37] 2-8-9 0 CesarPasserat(6) 3 69
(C Lerner, France) **11/1**

6 3/4 **Mesha Dream (FR)**[9] 2-8-8 0 (b) MatthieuAutier 9 61
(S Wattel, France) **5/1**

7 1 1/2 **Glorious Melody (FR)**[65] 5570 2-9-1 0 EddyHardouin 7 64
(Robert Collet, France) **23/1**

8 2 1/2 **La Vermandoise (FR)**[9] 2-8-8 0 TheoBachelot 10 51
(Y Barberot, France) **17/1**

9 1/2 **Sorelite (FR)** 2-8-11 0 ManonScandella(4) 6 56
(T De Lauriere, France) **36/1**

10 5 **Krupskaya (FR)**[25] 6780 2-8-13 0 RichardKingscote 4 42
(Mrs K Burke) *racd 4th on outside: rdn early in st: no rspnse u.p: wknd* **43/10**[3]

1m 30.09s (9.39) **10** Ran SP% **117.7**

WIN (incl. 1 euro stake): 4.30. PLACES: 1.80, 1.80, 2.40. DF: 7.90. SF: 15.50.

Owner Patrick Barbe **Bred** Pat Barbe & J Beres **Trained** France

7701a PRIX DES BOULEAUX (CLAIMER) (4YO+) (TURF) 1m

3:45 (12:00) 4-Y-O+ **£6,666** (£2,666; £2,000; £1,333; £666)

RPR

1 **Musikverein (FR)**[15] 5-8-11 0 RonanThomas 3 75
(J Phelippon, France) **143/10**

2 1 1/2 **Psy Chic (FR)**[15] 8-9-2 0 SebastienMaillot 1 77
(E Wianny, France) **16/1**

3 2 1/2 **Mount Berry (FR)**[448] 5-9-2 0 (p) FabriceVeron 4 71
(E Leenders, France) **24/1**

4 1 **Madly In Love (FR)**[17] 4-9-2 0 ThibaultSpeicher(5) 17 74
(F-X Belvisi, France) **41/1**

5 nse **L'Ami Gaby (FR)**[15] 5-9-2 0 ThierryJarnet 11 68
(R Chotard, France) **4/1**[1]

6 1 3/4 **Bread Loft (FR)**[174] 4-9-2 0 CarlaO'Halloran 7 64
(Mlle M Henry, France) **69/1**

7 3/4 **Bold Marc (IRE)**[3] 7347 10-8-11 0 (p) RichardKingscote 10 58
(Mrs K Burke) *racd midfield on ins: mde gd prog 2f out to go 3rd: no ex u.p 1f out: styd on one pce* **16/1**

8 3/4 **Boarding Pass (FR)**[38] 4-8-11 0 (b) Pierre-CharlesBoudot 18 56
(A Lyon, France) **47/1**

9 5 **Beringson (FR)**[15] 6-9-6 0 MatthieuAutier 19 53
(Mlle H Mennessier, France) **15/1**

10 1 1/4 **Sabys Gem (IRE)**[15] 4-8-11 0 (p) BriceRaballand 12 42
(Mlle F Bizot, France) **112/1**

0 **All Ways To Rome (FR)**[11] 8-9-2 0 (b) CyrilleStefan 8
(H P Rosport, Germany) **15/1**

0 **Deacon Blue (FR)**[174] 7-8-4 0 SoufyaneMoulin(7) 9
(C Boutin, France) **37/1**

0 **Accord Secret (FR)**[17] 6-9-3 0 (p) MarcLerner(3) 13
(C Lerner, France) **13/2**[2]

0 **Chopsoave (FR)**[528] 4-9-3 0 (p) ManonScandella(3) 2
(Mme C Dufreche, France) **12/1**

0 **Daliamoon (FR)**[17] 5-9-6 0 MaximeGuyon 14
(F Lemercier, France) **8/1**[3]

0 **Shamardanse (IRE)**[63] 5649 4-8-13 0 (b) TheoBachelot 16
(S Wattel, France) **12/1**

0 **World Cup (GER)** 5-8-11 0 FabienLefebvre 15
(Frau Nina Bach, Germany) **14/1**

0 **Okebibi (FR)**[393] 4-9-2 0 AntoineHamelin 6
(J-M Lefebvre, France) **22/1**

0 **Cat Spirit (FR)**[11] 4-9-2 0 JohanVictoire 5
(C Boutin, France) **33/1**

1m 48.29s (9.89) **19** Ran SP% **118.0**

WIN (incl. 1 euro stake): 15.30. PLACES: 5.00, 5.50, 8.00. DF: 100.60. SF: 318.20.

Owner Julien Phelippon **Bred** R Monnier & Mme S Lefebvre **Trained** France

7125 LEICESTER (R-H)

Monday, October 29

OFFICIAL GOING: Soft (6.7)

Wind: Light across Weather: Overcast

7432 HAYMARKET NURSERY (DIV I) 7f 9y

12:50 (12:50) (Class 6) (0-65,65) 2-Y-O **£1,940** (£577; £288; £144) **Stalls** High

Form RPR

060 1 **Intrigo**[18] 7006 2-8-13 57 RichardHughes 5 65
(Richard Hannon) *s.i.s: sn prom: led 5f out: shkn up over 1f out: sn clr: comf* **5/1**[2]

000 2 4 **Equitissa (IRE)**[53] 5978 2-9-6 64 JimmyFortune 2 63
(Richard Hannon) *hld up: hdwy over 2f out: rdn to chse wnr over 1f out: no imp* **22/1**

0546 3 4 **Sojoum**[3] 7379 2-8-9 53 SamHitchcott 3 41
(Mick Channon) *chsd ldrs: rdn over 2f out: styd on same pce fr over 1f out* **15/2**

054 4 1/2 **Beautifulwildthing**[40] 6355 2-9-7 65 AdrianNicholls 4 52
(Peter Salmon) *chsd ldrs: rdn over 2f out: styd on same pce appr fnl f* **25/1**

2006 5 3/4 **Missing Agent**[10] 7223 2-9-2 60 (v) NeilCallan 1 45
(David Evans) *sn prom: rdn over 2f out: styd on same pce appr fnl f* **7/1**[3]

0534 6 2 **Amelia Jay**[20] 6952 2-8-8 52 JoeFanning 12 32
(Danielle McCormick) *hld up: hdwy over 2f out: rdn and hung rt fr over 1f out: sn wknd* **11/1**

1042 7 nse **Poetic Princess**[33] 6583 2-9-4 62 KellyHarrison 10 42
(Jo Hughes) *led 2f: chsd ldrs: rdn over 2f out: wknd wl over 1f out* **7/1**[3]

050 8 15 **Canadian Red**[53] 5963 2-9-3 61 (b[1]) RichardKingscote 7 3
(Tom Dascombe) *chsd ldrs: rdn 1/2-way: wknd over 2f out* **11/1**

5604 9 9 **Sakhee's Ichigou**[24] 6841 2-8-12 56 NickyMackay 11
(Michael Blanshard) *sn pushed along in rr: wknd 3f out: t.o* **22/1**

0002 10 4 1/2 **Bougaloo**[4] 7350 2-8-6 50 DavidProbert 8
(Alan McCabe) *chsd ldrs: rdn 1/2-way: wknd over 2f out: t.o* **9/2**[1]

000 11 1 **Poetic Star**[126] 3436 2-8-7 51 ChrisCatlin 6
(Ben Haslam) *s.i.s: a in rr: bhd fr 1/2-way: t.o* **33/1**

0043 12 1 1/4 **Marguerite St Just**[83] 4934 2-9-1 59 SebSanders 9
(Olivia Maylam) *mid-div: rdn and wknd 3f out: t.o* **15/2**

1m 28.98s (2.78) **Going Correction** +0.20s/f (Good) **12** Ran SP% **115.5**

Speed ratings (Par 93): **92,87,82,82,81 79,79,61,51,46 45,43**

Tote Swingers 1&2 £12.60, 2&3 £38.90, 1&3 £10.40 CSF £113.70 CT £818.41 TOTE £4.90: £2.00, £7.40, £4.10; EX 62.40.

Owner Gillian, Lady Howard De Walden **Bred** Gillian Lady Howard De Walden **Trained** East Everleigh, Wilts

FOCUS

False rail from top of hill on back straight to winning post added 13m to races on Round course. After 3mm of rain overnight the ground had eased to soft all round with Richard Hughes, after riding the opening winner, reporting it was riding "very soft". On paper this looked a trappy, if modest, little contest, but the winner did it well. Late-season form, not one to take too seriously.

NOTEBOOK

Intrigo, on his nursery debut, had the race sewn up a couple of furlongs out and was just pushed clear for a comfortable success. His form was nothing to shout about leading up to this but he had shaped better in a couple of AW maidens when dropped back in trip and slipped in here off a good-looking mark of 59. Encountering soft ground for the first time, which he handled well, he should be capable of following up. This Medicean 2yo will now be heading to the sales on Wednesday. Official explanation: trainer's rep said, regarding apparent improvement in form, that the colt benefited from running on soft ground for the first time. (op 11-2 tchd 6-1)

Equitissa(IRE), the stable's second string, had a similar profile to the winner but was fighting a losing battle from a fair way out. She kept on well enough and should find a similar opportunity in the near future. (op 25-1)

Sojoum had been beaten in a seller recently and was up against it back in nursery company. He stayed on well enough but remains a maiden after 13 attempts. (op 8-1)

Beautifulwildthing has been steadily progressive in three maidens but looks to be on a stiff enough mark now sent handicapping.

Missing Agent has been rather busy of late and holds few secrets. (op 8-1)

Poetic Princess Official explanation: jockey said filly hung right

Bougaloo had shown improved form in first-time visor last week but with the headgear left off, he could never get competitive. Official explanation: jockey said gelding lost a shoe and never travelled (op 5-1 tchd 11-2)

7433 HOBY MEDIAN AUCTION MAIDEN FILLIES' STKS 5f 218y

1:20 (1:21) (Class 5) 2-Y-O **£2,264** (£673; £336; £168) **Stalls** High

Form RPR

040 1 **Take The Lead**[81] 5003 2-9-0 66 RichardHughes 1 64
(Richard Hannon) *led over 2f: chsd ldr: rdn over 2f out: led over 1f out: pushed out* **11/4**[1]

2 3/4 **Miss Avonbridge (IRE)** 2-9-0 0 RichardKingscote 6 62+
(Tom Dascombe) *chsd ldrs: outpcd over 3f out: rallied over 1f out: r.o to go 2nd post: nt rch wnr* **5/1**

0 3 shd **Mojo Bear**[38] 6453 2-9-0 0 LiamKeniry 7 61
(Sylvester Kirk) *sn pushed along in rr: hdwy over 2f out: rdn to chse wnr ins fnl f: lost 2nd post* **50/1**

4 1 1/2 **Ningbo Express (IRE)** 2-9-0 0 J-PGuillambert 4 57+
(Rae Guest) *s.i.s: sn pushed along in rr: hdwy over 2f out: styd on* **6/1**

03 5 2 1/4 **Dewi Chinta (IRE)**[7] 7290 2-9-0 0 AmyRyan 5 50
(Kevin Ryan) *chsd ldrs: rdn over 2f out: wknd wl ins fnl f* **3/1**[2]

023 6 1 **Puteri Nur Laila (IRE)**[23] 6889 2-9-0 67 (b) NeilCallan 8 47
(Paul Cole) *chsd ldr tl led over 3f out: rdn and hdd over 1f out: wknd ins fnl f* **4/1**[3]

7 8 **Camilla De Rossi** 2-9-0 0 ChrisCatlin 2 23
(Rae Guest) *s.i.s: rn green and outpcd* **16/1**

0 8 22 **Dalhousie Lassie**[171] 2047 2-9-0 0 (bt[1]) NickyMackay 3
(James Unett) *s.i.s: sn prom: rdn over 3f out: wknd wl over 2f out* **50/1**

1m 16.01s (3.01) **Going Correction** +0.40s/f (Good) **8** Ran SP% **112.4**

Speed ratings (Par 92): **95,94,93,91,88 87,76,47**

Tote Swingers 1&2 £3.60, 2&3 £19.20, 1&3 £13.80 CSF £16.32 TOTE £2.40: £1.10, £3.20, £8.80; EX 13.70.

Owner Lady Whent **Bred** Lady Whent **Trained** East Everleigh, Wilts

FOCUS

A weak maiden for fillies run at a decent pace in the conditions.

NOTEBOOK

Take The Lead had to bounce back after a disappointing effort in a decent contest at Sandown and was returning after a two-month absence. Always prominent she was pushed into the lead over a furlong out and scored with something in hand. Although not one of the stables leading lights, she shaped as though she'll get further in time and rates an interesting prospect for the future. (tchd 9-4)

Miss Avonbridge(IRE) made an encouraging debut after racing a little green and ran on strongly inside the final furlong to snatch second in the final strides. She's a half-sister to the Listed-placed 2yo Dr Planet and she looks the one to take out of the race. (op 11-4)

Mojo Bear needed the experience when beaten a fair way on debut and this was far more encouraging. She could not quite lay down a serious challenge to the winner but kept on inside the final furlong before being mugged for the runner-up spot nearing the finish. If building upon this she should find a little opening. (op 66-1)

Ningbo Express(IRE) shaped with promise after missing the break. She too was rather green during the race but connections should be pleased with this effort. Official explanation: jockey said filly ran green (op 9-1)

Dewi Chinta(IRE) arguably held the most progressive profile after a couple of maiden efforts and was proven in conditions, but after chasing the pace for much of the way she failed to get home. (op 9-2)

Puteri Nur Laila(IRE) set the standard (rated 65) but had never encountered ground as testing as this and after setting the pace for over four furlongs folded tamely. (op 9-2 tchd 6-1)

7434 IRISH STALLION FARMS EBF MAIDEN STKS 5f 218y

1:50 (1:50) (Class 4) 2-Y-O **£4,334** (£1,289; £644; £322) **Stalls** High

Form				RPR
0	1		**Barbs Princess**[158] 2426 2-8-12 0 ... RichardHughes 1 (Charles Hills) *racd alone towards centre and mde virtually all: rdn over 1f out: r.o* **11/2**[3]	70
02	2	*2*	**Silca's Dream**[8] 7268 2-9-3 0 ... MartinHarley 9 (Mick Channon) *chsd wnr: rdn and ev ch over 2f out: hung rt over 1f out: styd on same pce fnl f* **7/4**[1]	69
60	3	*nk*	**Betzyoucan**[84] 4877 2-8-12 0 ... JoeFanning 10 (Mark Johnston) *chsd ldrs: rdn and ev ch over 2f out: styd on same pce fnl f* **16/1**	63
	4	*6*	**Paddy Burke** 2-9-3 0 ... FergusSweeney 6 (Stuart Kittow) *dwlt: outpcd: r.o ins fnl f: nvr nrr* **40/1**	50+
4424	5	*hd*	**Exotic Guest**[39] 6414 2-9-3 77 ... EddieAhern 4 (George Margarson) *prom: rdn over 2f out: wknd over 1f out* **7/2**[2]	50
	6	*1*	**Mont Signal** 2-9-3 0 ... RichardKingscote 2 (Daniel Kubler) *sn pushed along and prom: rdn 1/2-way: wknd over 1f out* **13/2**	47
	7	*5*	**Moe's Place (IRE)** 2-9-3 0 ... PhillipMakin 8 (Kevin Ryan) *chsd ldrs: rdn over 2f out: wknd over 1f out* **9/1**	32
	8	*5*	**Ocean Power (IRE)** 2-9-3 0 ... RobertHavlin 5 (Richard Phillips) *s.s: outpcd* **100/1**	17
4	9	*1 ¼*	**Robyn**[25] 6808 2-8-12 0 ... NickyMackay 3 (Scott Dixon) *chsd ldrs: rdn over 2f out: sn wknd* **16/1**	8

1m 16.04s (3.04) **Going Correction** +0.40s/f (Good) **9** Ran SP% **112.5**
Speed ratings (Par 97): **95,92,91,83,83 82,75,69,67**
Tote Swingers 1&2 £3.10, 2&3 £6.40, 1&3 £7.60 CSF £14.99 TOTE £5.50: £2.70, £1.20, £3.80; EX 15.60.
Owner Mrs Barbara James **Bred** Mrs R Wilson **Trained** Lambourn, Berks

FOCUS
A fair pace for this maiden in the conditions and not many got into it, with the principals all sitting prominently throughout. Pretty weak, late-season form.

NOTEBOOK
Barbs Princess was given an enterprising ride by Richard Hughes, who switched her to race alone in the centre of the course from the start. She held a slight advantage throughout the race before staying on stoutly to assert from over a furlong out. She missed the break on debut but clearly had gained from the experience and this was a likeable performance. She's a well-related filly who is open to plenty of improvement and shouldn't be too harshly treated by the handicapper for the future. (op 5-1 tchd 9-2)
Silca's Dream was proven in the conditions and had strong claims to open his account after being touched off by the narrowest of margins last time. He had his chance here after sitting prominently throughout and was basically just outstayed by the winner. Another respectable effort, he should find an opportunity now qualified for a mark. (op 9-4)
Betzyoucan had not shown a great deal in her two runs to date but this was a far better effort and she seemed suited by the testing conditions. A pleasing effort, she should build upon this. (op 8-1)
Paddy Burke caught the eye on this his debut for after completely missing the break and, despite having plenty to do from the 3f marker, ran on well to snatch fourth in the closing stages. He cna go on form this as he gains in experience. (tchd 50-1)
Exotic Guest was below form on nursery debut and again was a little disappointing on this return to maiden company. However, he can be given another chance as this was the most testing ground he has encountered. (op 3-1)
Robyn Official explanation: jockey said filly ran too free

7435 SIS LIVE H'CAP 1m 60y

2:20 (2:20) (Class 2) (0-100,94) 3-Y-O+ **£10,221** (£3,041; £1,519; £759) **Stalls** Low

Form				RPR
0006	1		**Justonefortheroad**[10] 7210 6-9-3 90 ... TonyHamilton 4 (Richard Fahey) *hld up: hdwy over 1f out: styd on u.p to ld post* **10/1**	98
2461	2	*shd*	**Shamaal Nibras (USA)**[14] 7107 3-9-4 94 ... RichardHughes 5 (Richard Hannon) *trckd ldrs: nt clr run and swtchd lft over 1f out: rdn to ld ins fnl f: hdd post* **15/8**[1]	101
1410	3	*1 ½*	**Osteopathic Remedy (IRE)**[17] 7030 8-9-0 94 ... ConnorNichol(7) 6 (Michael Dods) *plld hrd and prom: rdn and ev ch ins fnl f: styd on same pce* **10/1**	98
0420	4	*2 ¼*	**Weapon Of Choice (IRE)**[51] 6036 4-9-2 89 ... NeilCallan 1 (Stuart Kittow) *set stdy pce tl qcknd over 3f out: rdn over 1f out: hdd and no ex ins fnl f* **9/2**[3]	88
0200	5	*1 ½*	**Atlantic Sport (USA)**[9] 7240 7-9-2 89 ... MartinHarley 7 (Mick Channon) *chsd ldrs: rdn over 2f out: no ex fnl f* **15/2**	84
3323	6	*shd*	**Toto Skyllachy**[10] 7210 7-9-0 87 ... DanielTudhope 2 (David O'Meara) *chsd ldr: rdn over 2f out: no ex ins fnl f* **9/2**[3]	82
6223	7	*8*	**Capaill Liath (IRE)**[14] 7097 4-9-5 92 ... (p) AmyRyan 3 (Kevin Ryan) *hld up: pushed along over 3f out: rdn and wknd over 2f out* **3/1**[2]	69

1m 50.08s (4.98) **Going Correction** +0.60s/f (Yiel)
WFA 3 from 4yo+ 3lb **7** Ran SP% **126.1**
Speed ratings (Par 109): **99,98,97,95,93 93,85**
Tote Swingers 1&2 £6.30, 2&3 £7.40, 1&3 £10.80 CSF £32.78 TOTE £17.20: £8.10, £1.10; EX 50.80.
Owner The Pontoon Partnership **Bred** Wellsummers Farm & Hammarsfield B'Stock **Trained** Musley Bank, N Yorks
■ Stewards' Enquiry : Richard Hughes caution: careless riding.

FOCUS
A competitive handicap with just an ordinary pace being dictated before the tempo increased over 3f out, with six of the seven runners holding some sort of chance entering the final furlong. The winner was still a few pounds off his spring best.

NOTEBOOK
Justonefortheroad has been contesting some fairly hot races over the summer and gained a deserved and gutsy success here. After being held up at the back of the pack an opening kindly appeared entering the final furlong, and having the rail might well have helped him wear down the runner-up in the shadow of the post. He had slipped to a handy mark but is a capable performer on his day and should handle the inevitable rise. (op 12-1 tchd 14-1)
Shamaal Nibras(USA) goes well on testing ground, as shown when landing a conditions stakes last time. He travelled well for much of the race and looked to be the one to beat after switching off the rails for his challenge entering the final furlong. He was collared on the line but this was another decent effort stepping back up to 1m. (tchd 7-4 and 2-1)
Osteopathic Remedy(IRE) is another proven in conditions and posted a respectable effort. He moved through to lay down his challenge a furlong out but could only stay on at the same pace. He keeps creeping up the weights. (tchd 11-1)
Weapon Of Choice(IRE) dictated the pace and to his credit kept finding when challenged over a furlong out. He was beaten in a hot contest on the AW recently but he remains in good heart and can continue to make his presence felt. (op 6-1 tchd 13-2)
Atlantic Sport(USA) is mainly campaigned over 7f but added to his sole success back in 2008 when scoring at Haydock in July, however he had something to prove stepping back up to a mile. He was close enough just over a furlong out but his effort flattened out inside the final furlong. A fair effort nonetheless. (op 7-1 tchd 6-1)
Toto Skyllachy has been consistent this season and had his chance but he might well be in the grip of the handicapper at present. (op 6-1)
Capaill Liath(IRE) was struggling as soon as the pace increased and could never get involved. (op 4-1 tchd 9-2)

7436 HAMISH'S DIAMOND DAY H'CAP (FOR GENTLEMEN AMATEUR RIDERS) 7f 9y

2:50 (2:50) (Class 5) (0-70,77) 3-Y-O+ **£2,305** (£709; £354) **Stalls** High

Form				RPR
4343	1		**Desert Creek (IRE)**[9] 7247 6-11-3 65 ... MrSCrawford 2 (David Nicholls) *hld up in tch: led over 1f out: sn rdn and hung lft: styd on wl* **11/4**[1]	79
6621	2	*5*	**Tunnager Grove**[13] 7126 3-10-13 68 ... (b) MrRPooles(5) 10 (Hughie Morrison) *chsd ldrs: ev ch over 1f out: styd on same pce ins fnl f* **12/1**	69
0000	3	*1 ½*	**Mazovian (USA)**[25] 6811 4-10-2 55 ... MrKevinJones(5) 3 (Michael Chapman) *mid-div: outpcd 1/2-way: hdwy over 1f out: styd on* **40/1**	52
5665	4	*hd*	**Lindoro**[10] 7224 7-10-12 65 ... (b) MrDLevey(5) 8 (Brian Ellison) *led: rdn and hdd 2f out: styd on same pce fnl f* **14/1**	62
350	5	*2 ¼*	**Ted's Brother (IRE)**[39] 6410 4-11-0 65 ...[1] MrSDrinkwater(3) 5 (Richard Guest) *s.i.s: hld up: hdwy over 1f out: no ex ins fnl f* **7/1**[3]	56
0004	6	*½*	**Caledonia Prince**[25] 6812 4-10-4 55 oh6 ... (p) MrCMartin(3) 16 (Jo Hughes) *hld up: hung rt fr over 4f out: hdwy 1/2-way: styd on same pce fnl 2f* **20/1**	44
0012	7	*2*	**Elusive Hawk (IRE)**[82] 4969 8-11-6 68 ... MrDLQueally 11 (Barney Curley) *chsd ldr: led 2f out: sn hdd: wknd ins fnl f* **5/1**[2]	52
0414	8	*¾*	**Shomberg**[31] 5501 3-10-4 57 ... MrNdeBoinville(3) 15 (Dai Burchell) *hld up: rdn over 2f out: nvr nrr* **20/1**	39
3000	9	*1 ½*	**Pull The Pin (IRE)**[21] 6937 3-10-0 55 oh6 ... (tp) MrTCheesman(5) 7 (William Kinsey) *prom: rdn 1/2-way: wknd over 1f out* **22/1**	33
2502	10	*1*	**Al's Memory (IRE)**[2] 7395 3-11-3 67 ... MrFWindsorClive 13 (David Evans) *chsd ldrs: rdn 1/2-way: wknd 2f out* **8/1**	43
043	11	*1 ¼*	**Eastern Hills**[4] 7347 7-10-12 65 ... (tp) MrRHatch(5) 14 (Alan McCabe) *prom: rdn over 2f out: wknd wl over 1f out* **8/1**	38
5310	12	*shd*	**Hoppy's Flyer (FR)**[29] 6709 4-10-12 65 ... (v) MrNSlatter(5) 1 (Paul Midgley) *prom: rdn over 2f out: sn wknd* **28/1**	37
0000	13	*1*	**Pelmanism**[23] 6886 5-11-2 69 ... MrJohnWilley(5) 12 (Brian Ellison) *prom: rdn 1/2-way: wknd over 2f out* **14/1**	39
22-4	14	*1 ¼*	**Hooligan Sean**[6] 7318 5-10-10 63 ... MrFMitchell(5) 18 (Henry Candy) *hmpd s: hld up: rdn over 2f out: a in rr* **14/1**	29
3000	15	*1*	**Khajaaly (IRE)**[20] 6950 5-10-12 60 ... MrRBirkett 17 (Julia Feilden) *s.i.s: hdwy 1/2-way: rdn and wknd over 1f out* **33/1**	24
2-40	16	*7*	**Sovento (GER)**[9] 7256 8-10-9 62 ... MrJSherwood(5) 9 (Alan McCabe) *prom: sn pushed along: lost pl over 5f out: sn bhd* **33/1**	8
260	17	*38*	**Fistful Of Dollars (IRE)**[261] 518 3-10-11 68 ... MrGrahamCarson(7) 6 (David Nicholls) *bhd fnl 4f: t.o* **33/1**	

1m 30.77s (4.57) **Going Correction** +0.60s/f (Yiel)
WFA 3 from 4yo+ 2lb **17** Ran SP% **134.3**
Speed ratings (Par 103): **97,91,89,89,86 86,83,83,81,80 78,78,77,76,74 66,23**
Tote Swingers 1&2 £8.70, 2&3 £99.60, 1&3 £33.40 CSF £37.19 CT £1221.76 TOTE £2.80: £1.20, £2.80, £7.00, £3.80; EX 46.80.
Owner D W Barker & D Nicholls **Bred** Mount Coote Stud And M H Dixon **Trained** Sessay, N Yorks
■ Stewards' Enquiry : Mr John Willey four-day ban: used whip above permitted level (tbn)

FOCUS
A competitive amateur riders' handicap where a solid pace was set. The winner was formerly smart and had been hinting at better, but this form has been rated a bit cautiously.

7437 GUMLEY CLAIMING STKS 7f 9y

3:20 (3:20) (Class 6) 3-4-Y-O **£1,940** (£577; £288; £144) **Stalls** High

Form				RPR
040	1		**Lady Layla**[13] 7141 3-7-12 68 ... (p) JimmyQuinn 1 (Bryan Smart) *a.p: pushed along over 2f out: rdn over 1f out: styd on u.p to ld wl ins fnl f* **6/1**[3]	61
4102	2	*2*	**Llewellyn**[9] 7246 4-8-13 70 ... AdrianNicholls 2 (David Nicholls) *sn led: hdd over 5f out: chsd ldr to 1/2-way: wnt 2nd again over 2f out: rdn over 1f out: styd on* **2/1**[1]	69
0402	3	*shd*	**Eternal Gift (FR)**[12] 7158 3-9-1 72 ... (b) JimmyFortune 8 (Rae Guest) *s.i.s: sn prom: led over 5f out: rdn over 1f out: hdd and unable qck wl ins fnl f* **9/1**	73
4302	4	*nk*	**Barista (IRE)**[13] 7126 4-8-7 58 ... SamHitchcott 5 (Brian Forsey) *mid-div: sn pushed along: hdwy over 4f out: edgd rt 1/2-way: rdn over 2f out: styd on* **13/2**	62
3662	5	*1 ½*	**Ficelle (IRE)**[8] 7275 3-7-10 58 ow1 ... RyanPowell(3) 9 (Ronald Harris) *hld up: hdwy over 2f out: rdn over 1f out: styd on* **14/1**	52
6024	6	*5*	**Liliargh (IRE)**[18] 7004 3-8-4 72 ... ChrisCatlin 6 (Ben Haslam) *hld up: bhd 1/2-way: kpt on ins fnl f: nvr nrr* **6/1**[3]	44
0000	7	*3*	**Cathcart Castle**[20] 6969 4-8-5 42 ... (e[1]) AmyRyan 12 (Simon West) *sn bhd: nvr nrr* **100/1**	36
4020	8	*4 ½*	**Rigolleto (IRE)**[26] 6800 4-9-7 76 ... RichardHughes 7 (Anabel K Murphy) *prom: rdn over 2f out: wknd over 1f out* **11/2**[2]	40
0-56	9	*2 ¾*	**Ave Sofia**[46] 6178 3-7-5 48 ... NoraLooby(7) 3 (John Holt) *chsd ldrs: rdn 1/2-way: wknd over 2f out* **66/1**	12
5006	10	*½*	**Monzino (USA)**[25] 6812 4-8-13 50 ... (p) RussKennemore 11 (Michael Chapman) *s.s: outpcd* **66/1**	23
3040	11	*4*	**More Bottle (IRE)**[59] 5803 3-7-12 49 ... NickyMackay 4 (Tom Tate) *mid-div: hdwy over 4f out: hmpd over 3f out: sn rdn: wknd over 2f out* **28/1**	
5400	12	*2 ½*	**Bussa**[11] 7200 4-8-5 54 ... (t) KirstyMilczarek 10 (David Evans) *rn wout declared tongue strap: prom: chsd ldr 1/2-way tl rdn over 2f out: wknd wl over 1f out* **50/1**	

1m 29.78s (3.58) **Going Correction** +0.60s/f (Yiel)
WFA 3 from 4yo 2lb **12** Ran SP% **116.7**
Speed ratings (Par 101): **103,100,100,100,98 92,89,84,81,80 75,73**
Tote Swingers 1&2 £4.30, 2&3 £4.60, 1&3 £8.90 CSF £17.73 TOTE £7.50: £2.60, £1.60, £2.90; EX 22.70.Lady Layla was claimed by Jo Hughes for £6,000
Owner Dr Marwan Koukash **Bred** H Q Spooner **Trained** Hambleton, N Yorks

FOCUS
A modest time and very moderate form, the winner not needing to improve on last month's C&D selling form.

Bussa Official explanation: trainer said gelding had a breathing problem

7438 SIR GORDON RICHARDS CONDITIONS STKS 1m 3f 183y

3:50 (3:50) (Class 3) 3-Y-0+ **£6,931** (£2,074; £1,037; £519; £258) **Stalls** Low

Form				RPR
-300	**1**		**Cracking Lass (IRE)**[32] 6600 5-8-11 98........................ TonyHamilton 2	102
			(Richard Fahey) *hld up: hdwy over 3f out: chsd ldr over 1f out: rdn to ld wl ins fnl f: styd on* **5/1**[3]	
0402	**2**	*nk*	**Mijhaar**[17] 7029 4-9-2 104........................ NeilCallan 3	107
			(Roger Varian) *led: shkn up and edgd lft over 1f out: rdn and hdd wl ins fnl f: styd on* **9/4**[2]	
3-12	**3**	*1 3/4*	**Model Pupil**[172] 1995 3-8-13 107........................ RichardHughes 5	108
			(Charles Hills) *sn trcking ldr: shkn up over 3f out: rdn over 2f out: styd on same pce ins fnl f* **8/11**[1]	
525-	**4**	*6*	**Genzy (FR)**[401] 4-9-2 102........................ JimCrowley 4	94
			(Ian Williams) *hld up: plld hrd: hdwy over 2f out: wknd ins fnl f* **20/1**	
1013	**5**	*6*	**The Lock Master (IRE)**[3] 7368 5-8-9 77........................ DanielMuscutt(7) 1	85
			(Michael Appleby) *s.i.s: sn chsng ldrs: pushed along 4f out: wknd 2f out* **33/1**	

2m 40.11s (6.21) **Going Correction** +0.60s/f (Yiel)
WFA 3 from 4yo+ 7lb **5** Ran SP% **113.0**
Speed ratings (Par 107): **103,102,101,97,93**
CSF £17.02 TOTE £8.70: £3.00, £1.50; EX 17.80.

Owner Mel Roberts and Ms Nicola Meese **Bred** Thomas Doherty **Trained** Musley Bank, N Yorks

FOCUS

Just a fair pace for this decent conditions stakes. The winner only needed to run to form with the next two not at their best.

NOTEBOOK

Cracking Lass(IRE) had been a little disappointing after an encouraging comeback in Listed company in August. She had been found wanting in a Group 2 next time and ran no sort of race in the Jockey Club Rose Bowl at Newmarket last month. She stayed on determinedly here to run out a brave winner with connections left feeling that the small field and how the race was run played to her strengths. Official explanation: trainer's rep said, regarding apparent improvement in form, that on the mare 's previous run, it failed to stay the 2m trip. (op 11-2 tchd 6-1)

Mijhaar dictated the pace and was the last to come under pressure over a furlong out. He stayed on well enough but was just outgunned by the determined late surge of the winner inside the final furlong. He ran a fine race to finish third in the Wolferton at Royal Ascot but his form has been rather patchy since although posting some respectable efforts in between. (tchd 2-1 and 11-4)

Model Pupil, the Chester Vase runner-up, had been off since suffering a setback and missing his Royal Ascot engagement but he looked ready to do himself justice in the preliminaries. He laid down his challenge a fair way out but he was made to look rather one-paced and shaped as though a further step up in trip would suit. It would be fair to say that he would have preferred better ground on his return as the conditions were becoming a little holding and he remains a horse of potential assuming he stays in training as a 4yo. (op Evens)

Genzy(FR), ex-French, ran a fine race on his return to action after a break of 491 days and he is entitled to come on for the race, a sentiment in which his connections mentioned before the race. He would be an exciting prospect if attentions were turned to hurdling. (op 16-1 tchd 22-1)

The Lock Master(IRE) was facing a huge task on official figures and got comfortably brushed aside when the pace increased over three furlong out. (op 18-1)

7439 HAYMARKET NURSERY (DIV II) 7f 9y

4:20 (4:20) (Class 6) (0-65,65) 2-Y-0 **£1,940** (£577; £288; £144) **Stalls** High

Form				RPR
4332	**1**		**Glossy Posse**[16] 7060 2-9-4 62........................ RichardHughes 3	65+
			(Richard Hannon) *chsd ldr: rdn to ld over 1f out: styd on* **11/8**[1]	
4606	**2**	*nk*	**Stupenda**[20] 6946 2-8-9 53........................(v[1]) EddieAhern 7	55
			(Denis Coakley) *s.i.s: hld up: hdwy over 2f out: edgd rt: rdn and ev ch fr over 1f out: nt run on* **20/1**	
1	**3**	*5*	**Laughing Rock (IRE)**[48] 6115 2-9-5 63........................[1] AdrianNicholls 4	53
			(Phil McEntee) *hld up: pushed along and hdwy whn n.m.r 4f out: rdn over 1f out: styd on same pce fnl f* **9/2**[2]	
303	**4**	*1 1/4*	**Bell'Arte (IRE)**[18] 6997 2-9-7 65........................ JoeFanning 1	52
			(Mark Johnston) *prom: n.m.r and lost pl 4f out: rallied over 1f out: no ex fnl f* **9/2**[2]	
000	**5**	*1*	**See And Be Seen**[14] 7103 2-8-13 57........................ LiamKeniry 8	41
			(Sylvester Kirk) *prom: pushed along 1/2-way: rdn over 1f out: styd on same pce* **22/1**	
5020	**6**	*3/4*	**Slipstream Angel (IRE)**[10] 7223 2-9-2 60........................ TonyHamilton 5	42
			(Richard Fahey) *hld up: bhd and pushed along 4f out: nvr on terms* **6/1**[3]	
3530	**7**	*hd*	**Plexolini**[20] 6953 2-8-7 51........................ NickyMackay 2	33
			(Jo Hughes) *led: rdn and hdd over 1f out: wknd fnl f* **22/1**	
5265	**8**	*10*	**Otto The First**[24] 6850 2-8-12 56........................ FergusSweeney 10	13
			(John Best) *racd alone tl jnd the main gp 5f out: chsd ldrs: rdn over 2f out: sn wknd* **28/1**	
0535	**9**	*nk*	**Tiger's Home**[123] 3533 2-9-3 61........................ JimmyQuinn 6	17
			(Julia Feilden) *s.i.s: hdwy 1/2-way: rdn whn hmpd wl over 1f out: sn wknd* **22/1**	

1m 30.68s (4.48) **Going Correction** +0.60s/f (Yiel) **9** Ran SP% **114.0**
Speed ratings (Par 93): **98,97,91,90,89 88,88,76,76**
Tote Swingers 1&2 £6.30, 2&3 £17.20, 1&3 £2.10 CSF £36.47 CT £102.51 TOTE £2.10: £1.30, £5.50, £1.50; EX 33.50.

Owner J G Davis **Bred** J G Davis & Star Pointe Ltd **Trained** East Everleigh, Wilts

FOCUS

The winner seems to be thriving but the bare form can't be rated any higher.

NOTEBOOK

Glossy Posse was up 4lb for her recent Wolverhampton run but showed a good attitude to repel the challenge of the runner-up inside the final furlong and was on top at the finish. She's a consistent and versatile filly who the handicapper appears to have about right, so any significant rise would make life tougher. (op 6-4 tchd 5-4)

Stupenda was being tried in a first-time visor after some laboured efforts in nurseries and this was a better effort. She battled on well when laying down a strong challenge inside the final furlong, only giving best nearing the finish. (tchd 22-1)

Laughing Rock(IRE) was a winner of a C&D seller on debut but that form hasn't really worked out and he was starting life in handicaps off a high enough mark of 63. He was racing in a hood for the first time could only keep on at the same pace after coming under strong pressure from a fair way out. (op 7-2 tchd 5-1)

Bell'Arte(IRE) didn't appear to get home in soft ground over a mile last time. He could never find the pace to get involved dropping back in trip but stayed on in the closing stages well enough to suggest it might be worthwhile trying a mile again. (op 5-1)

T/Jkpt: Not won. T/Plt: £97.60 to a £1 stake. Pool: £62,890.70 - 470.30 winning tickets. T/Qpdt: £9.80 to a £1 stake. Pool: £6,774.50 - 509.80 winning tickets. CR

[6880] REDCAR (L-H)

Monday, October 29

OFFICIAL GOING: Heavy (6.3)

Wind: Moderate against Weather: Cloudy

7440 BRITISH STALLION STUDS SUPPORTING BRITISH RACING EBF MAIDEN FILLIES' STKS 6f

12:40 (12:40) (Class 5) 2-Y-0 **£2,975** (£885; £442) **Stalls** Centre

Form				RPR
6022	**1**		**Medici Dancer**[7] 7290 2-9-0 72........................ DavidAllan 7	69+
			(Tim Easterby) *mde all: pushed clr wl over 1f out: unchal* **1/12**[1]	
4650	**2**	*7*	**Mace The Ace**[20] 6953 2-8-9 50........................(b) DarylByrne(5) 6	43
			(Lawrence Mullaney) *chsd wnr: rdn along and outpcd 3f out: plugged on u.p appr fnl f: no ch w wnr* **66/1**[3]	
	3	*4*	**Doodles** 2-8-7 0........................ ShirleyTeasdale(7) 3	31
			(David Nicholls) *dwlt: hdwy to chse wnr 1/2-way: effrt and cl up over 2f out: sn rdn and wknd* **17/2**[2]	

1m 20.12s (8.32) **Going Correction** +1.15s/f (Soft) **3** Ran SP% **104.4**
Speed ratings (Par 92): **90,80,75**
CSF £7.07 TOTE £1.10; EX 3.70.

Owner Ryedale Partners No 3 **Bred** Selwood Bloodstock **Trained** Great Habton, N Yorks

FOCUS

The running rail was be moved in four metres between the straight 8f and 6 3/4f mark. It had no impact on the 7f race. A field decimated by non-runners lined up for a fair juvenile fillies' maiden in which they went an honest gallop on ground officially described as heavy. A bit of a non-event as the market suggested. The winning time was over ten seconds slower than standard.

NOTEBOOK

Medici Dancer had posted consecutive RPR's of 69 when runner-up over this 6f trip on heavy ground at Newcastle/Pontefract the last twice this month. She didn't have to improve on that form here, stretching clear in a pleasing fashion off her own solid fractions once asked for her effort over 1f out. She looks a fair handicapper for up to 1m for next term. (op 1-8)

Mace The Ace remains a maiden after eleven starts and ran below her current BHA rating of 50. (op 40-1)

Doodles started slowly on this debut but took closer order, after racing keenly, 2f out. She weakened thereafter and will have learnt plenty going forward. (op 15-2 tchd 9-1)

7441 VOLTIGEUR RESTAURANT 2 COURSE SPECIAL £10.95 NURSERY 5f

1:10 (1:11) (Class 6) (0-65,65) 2-Y-0 **£1,617** (£481; £240; £120) **Stalls** Centre

Form				RPR
3042	**1**		**Dream Vale (IRE)**[20] 6952 2-9-1 64........................ AdamCarter(5) 5	67
			(Tim Easterby) *wnt rt s: trckd ldrs: swtchd rt and hdwy over 1f out: sn rdn and styd on ins fnl f to ld last 50yds* **9/2**[2]	
603U	**2**	*1/2*	**Grand Jipeck (IRE)**[20] 6952 2-8-10 54........................(t) PatrickMathers 7	55
			(Ian McInnes) *hmpd s: sn chsng ldrs: hdwy 2f out: rdn to ld over 1f out: drvn and hdd last 50yds: no ex* **14/1**	
5100	**3**	*nk*	**Skidby Mill (IRE)**[16] 7060 2-9-6 64........................ MichaelO'Connell 2	64
			(John Quinn) *wnt rt s: in tch: pushed along and sltly outpcd over 2f out: sn rdn and hdwy over 1f out: styd on wl fnl f* **13/2**[3]	
065	**4**	*1 1/4*	**Beacon Tarn**[26] 6787 2-9-3 61........................ TedDurcan 4	57
			(Eric Alston) *led 1f: trckd ldrs: effrt and hdwy on inner over 1f out: cl up and ev ch ent fnl f: sn rdn and one pce* **7/2**[1]	
4252	**5**	*1 1/4*	**Perfect Words (IRE)**[20] 6953 2-9-4 65........................ PaulPickard(3) 10	56
			(Marjorie Fife) *wnt lft s: cl up: led after 1f: rdn along 2f out: edgd lft and hdd over 1f out: sn drvn and one pce* **9/1**	
600	**6**	*nse*	**Angel Grigio**[31] 6627 2-8-1 45........................(v) JamesSullivan 3	36
			(Bryan Smart) *hmpd s: a in rr* **10/1**	
0001	**7**	*1/2*	**Mill End Dancer**[87] 4767 2-8-6 50........................ BarryMcHugh 1	39
			(Michael Easterby) *prom: rdn along 1/2-way: sn wknd* **8/1**	
000	**8**	*4 1/2*	**Troy Boy**[17] 7031 2-8-11 55........................ RobertWinston 9	38
			(Robin Bastiman) *hmpd s: a towards rr* **9/2**[2]	
0636	**9**	*2 1/4*	**Salvatore Fury (IRE)**[55] 5920 2-9-2 60........................ TomEaves 8	25
			(Keith Dalgleish) *prom: cl up 1/2-way: rdn along wl over 1f out: sn wknd* **12/1**	

1m 5.51s (6.91) **Going Correction** +1.15s/f (Soft) **9** Ran SP% **116.5**
Speed ratings (Par 93): **90,89,88,86,84 84,83,76,73**
Tote Swingers 1&2 £11.30, 2&3 £14.10, 1&3 £8.20 CSF £65.31 CT £412.92 TOTE £3.20: £1.10, £4.40, £3.80; EX 67.80 TRIFECTA Not won..

Owner Middleham Park Racing LII & Partner **Bred** Jaykayeen Breeding **Trained** Great Habton, N Yorks

■ Stewards' Enquiry : Adam Carter two-day ban: used whip above permitted level (Nov 14-15)

FOCUS

A modest nursery handicap in which they went a fair gallop on the very testing ground, and the winning time was over eight seconds slower than standard. An end-of-season feel to the form.

NOTEBOOK

Dream Vale(IRE) was headed close home when finishing runner-up off a 3lb lower mark in a 6f soft-ground Catterick nursery this month. She raced prominently, travelling well just behind the leaders, and went on to win readily enough once switched out to produced her challenge about 1f from home. She looks a fair sprint handicapper for next term. (op 5-1 tchd 11-2)

Grand Jipeck(IRE) was worn down well inside the final furlong after coming through from off the pace. He looks capable of winning a moderate sprint handicap off a mark in the low-mid 50s. (op 12-1)

Skidby Mill(IRE) won her maiden over 6f on good ground at Thirsk the previous month, and got going just too late from off the pace over this 1f shorter trip on a much more testing surface. (op 10-1)

Beacon Tarn raced up with the early pace but couldn't sustain her effort. (op 10-3 tchd 4-1 in a place)

Perfect Words(IRE) raced prominently but drifted to his left and out of contention when tiring over 1f out. Official explanation: jockey said colt hung left (op 13-2 tchd 11-2)

Angel Grigio (op 14-1)

Mill End Dancer, who was returning from a three-month break since winning off 5lb lower on good ground at Musselburgh, was never involved after being hampered. (op 7-1)

Troy Boy wouldn't have liked the ground. (op 6-1 tchd 4-1 and 13-2 in a place)

7442 EUROPEAN BREEDERS' FUND - DOUBLE TRIGGER MAIDEN STKS (FOR THE DOUBLE TRIGGER TROPHY) 1m 1f

1:40 (1:41) (Class 5) 2-Y-0 **£2,975** (£885; £442; £221) **Stalls** Low

Form				RPR
3232	**1**		**Disclaimer**[23] 6880 2-9-3 79........................ IanMongan 2	76
			(Sir Henry Cecil) *trckd ldrs on inner: smooth hdwy over 3f out: taken wd to chal wl over 2f out: sn rdn: drvn and wandered wl over 1f out: kpt on u.p to ld ins fnl f* **5/6**[1]	

0 **2** *1 ¼* **Oakham**[86] 4813 2-8-12 0............................ AntiocoMurgia(5) 8 74+
(Mahmood Al Zarooni) *wnt rt s: led after 1f: rdn along 3f out: drvn over 1f out: hdd ins fnl f: kpt on same pce* **6/1**[3]

04 **3** *8* **Borodino (IRE)**[17] 7021 2-9-3 0............................ BarryMcHugh 7 58
(Richard Fahey) *trckd ldrs: hdwy over 3f out: sn rdn along and plugged on same pce fnl 2f* **33/1**

33 **4** *9* **Backstage Tour**[20] 6947 2-9-3 0............................ MickaelBarzalona 1 40
(Mahmood Al Zarooni) *hld up in rr: rdn along wl over 3f out: sn outpcd* **11/4**[2]

56 **5** *2 ¾* **Train Hard**[11] 7199 2-9-3 0............................ SilvestreDeSousa 6 34
(Mark Johnston) *led 1f: trckd ldr: rdn along 4f out: drvn 3f out and sn wknd* **9/1**

0 **6** *13* **Distant Sunrise**[19] 6985 2-8-12 0............................ GrahamLee 5 3
(Ann Duffield) *a in rr: outpcd and bhd fr over 3f out* **66/1**

2m 6.88s (13.88) **Going Correction** +1.475s/f (Soft) **6** Ran SP% **109.9**
Speed ratings (Par 95): **97,95,88,80,78 66**
Tote Swingers 1&2 £2.20, 2&3 £8.40, 1&3 £4.10 CSF £6.22 TOTE £2.30: £1.40, £3.30; EX 8.40 Trifecta £36.50 Pool: £711.17 - 14.58 winning tickets..
Owner K Abdulla **Bred** Juddmonte Farms Ltd **Trained** Newmarket, Suffolk

FOCUS
A fair juvenile maiden in which they went a sensible gallop on the heavy ground. The first two were clear but this is not form to take too literally.

NOTEBOOK
Disclaimer, who is a half-brother to a decent 1m2f winner out of a well-related 1m2f/Listed 1m6f winning dam, arrived with a BHA rating of 79 after finishing a fair second over 7f on soft ground here on his fifth start this month. He proved good enough, getting the better of a protracted duel with the runner-up inside the final furlong, despite still showing signs of inexperience when initially asked to go on over 1f out. He looks a fair middle-distance handicapper for next term. (op 10-11 tchd 4-5 and evens in a place)
Oakham was returning from a three-month break since a poor debut on quick ground at Lingfield in August. He is bred to appreciate middle-distances on soft ground, and ran well here under these testing conditions for a 2yo. He should continue to progress at up to 1m4f next term. (op 8-1 tchd 9-1)
Borodino(IRE) improved on his second start over 7f at Wolverhampton this month, and ran to a similar level over this 2f longer trip, although much better ground will suit going forward. (op 20-1)
Backstage Tour, who reportedly looked well, performed disappointingly.
Train Hard struggled under these conditions. (op 17-2 tchd 10-1)

7443 SUBSCRIBE TO RACING UK (S) STKS 1m 2f
2:10 (2:10) (Class 6) 3-5-Y-0 **£1,704** (£503; £251) **Stalls** Low

Form RPR

0004 **1** **Barathea Dancer (IRE)**[10] 7221 4-8-10 59...................(bt) GrahamLee 2 54
(Gay Kelleway) *led: pushed clr 4f out: rdn 2f out: hdd over 1f out: drvn and rallied ins fnl f: led nr fin* **11/4**[1]

6230 **2** *shd* **Petrocelli**[20] 6956 5-9-1 53............................(t) DominicFox 5 59
(Wilf Storey) *hld up in rr: stdy hdwy over 4f out: chsd wnr wl over 2f out: sn rdn and styd on to take slt ld over 1f out: drvn ins fnl f: hdd and no ex towards fin* **3/1**[2]

-000 **3** *11* **Dancing Paddy (IRE)**[63] 5679 4-8-10 41.................. GarryWhillans(5) 7 37
(Alan Swinbank) *trckd ldrs: hdwy over 3f out: sn rdn and plugged on one pce* **9/1**

6000 **4** *nk* **Gangsterbanksters (FR)**[19] 6976 3-8-10 54........(p) MichaelO'Connell 4 36
(Mrs K Burke) *chsd ldrs: rdn along wl over 3f out: sn drvn and plugged on one pce* **11/2**[3]

000- **5** *38* **Charity Fair**[404] 6264 5-8-3 35............................ KevinStott(7) 3
(Ron Barr) *a towards rr: outpcd and bhd fnl 3f* **66/1**

0000 **6** *37* **Bertie Blu Boy**[112] 3914 4-9-1 40............................ BarryMcHugh 8
(Lisa Williamson) *a in rr: bhd fnl 4f* **33/1**

5404 **7** *48* **Frederickthegreat**[25] 6813 3-8-10 60...................... SilvestreDeSousa 9
(David O'Meara) *trckd ldr tl hung bdly rt bnd after 4f: sn rdn and lost pl: bhd fnl 3f* **11/4**[1]

2m 24.36s (17.26) **Going Correction** +1.475s/f (Soft)
WFA 3 from 4yo+ 5lb **7** Ran SP% **108.2**
Speed ratings (Par 101): **89,88,80,79,49 19,**
Tote Swingers 1&2 £3.10, 2&3 £5.70, 1&3 £3.00 CSF £9.99 TOTE £5.00: £3.80, £1.10; EX 13.10 Trifecta £151.90 Pool: £510.58 - 2.52 winning tickets..There was no bid for the winner. There were no claims.
Owner Miss Gay Kelleway **Bred** B Wallace And M Lydon **Trained** Exning, Suffolk

FOCUS
A poor seller run in desperate ground. The first two were clear, with the second setting the standard.

7444 MARKET CROSS JEWELLERS H'CAP 1m 6f 19y
2:40 (2:40) (Class 5) (0-70,69) 3-Y-0 **£2,264** (£673; £336; £168) **Stalls** Low

Form RPR

4410 **1** **Dorry K (IRE)**[17] 7032 3-9-7 69............................ GrahamGibbons 1 78+
(David Barron) *hld up in rr: hdwy over 5f out: swtchd rt and effrt to chal 3f out: sn led: rdn clr wl over 1f out: eased towards fin* **4/1**[3]

-306 **2** *4* **My Destination (IRE)**[137] 3072 3-9-5 67............................ DavidAllan 5 68
(Declan Carroll) *trckd ldng pair: hdwy to chse ldr 1/2-way: effrt and cl up over 3f out: sn rdn: chsd wnr fnl 2f: no imp* **6/1**

2151 **3** *5* **Red Tyke (IRE)**[22] 6516 3-8-13 61............................ MichaelO'Connell 6 55
(John Quinn) *led: pushed along and jnd over 3f out: rdn and hdd wl over 2f out: sn drvn and wknd over 1f out* **11/8**[1]

0416 **4** *50* **Panettone (IRE)**[44] 6232 3-9-6 68............................[1] DominicFox 4
(Roger Varian) *trckd ldr: pushed along 1/2-way: sn lost pl and bhd fr over 4f out* **9/4**[2]

3m 28.32s (23.62) **Going Correction** +1.475s/f (Soft) **4** Ran SP% **107.2**
Speed ratings (Par 101): **91,88,85,57**
CSF £22.73 TOTE £1.70; EX 16.50.
Owner Twinacre Nurseries Ltd **Bred** Twinacre Nurseries Ltd **Trained** Maunby, N Yorks

FOCUS
A weak 3yo staying handicap in which they went a steady gallop on the heavy ground. It took little winning.
Panettone(IRE) Official explanation: trainer's rep said filly was unsuited by the heavy ground

7445 BOOK YOUR CHRISTMAS PARTIES @ REDCAR RACECOURSE MAIDEN STKS 7f
3:10 (3:11) (Class 5) 3-Y-0+ **£2,264** (£673; £336; £168) **Stalls** Centre

Form RPR

5-40 **1** **Kuwait Star**[4] 7359 3-9-3 63............................ TedDurcan 3 71
(Jason Ward) *in tch on outer: hdwy to chse ldrs 3f out: effrt 2f out: rdn to ld and edgd lft ins fnl f: kpt on* **7/1**[3]

03-2 **2** *1 ¾* **Snooky**[66] 5549 3-9-3 73............................ BarryMcHugh 9 66
(Richard Fahey) *prom: hdwy to trck ldr 1/2-way: effrt 2f out: sn led and rdn: drvn and hdd ins fnl f: kpt on same pce* **5/2**[1]

603 **3** *9* **Quan (IRE)**[21] 6925 3-8-12 58............................ GarryWhillans(5) 7 43
(Alan Swinbank) *led: rdn along 3f out: hdd wl over 1f out: sn drvn and plugged on one pce* **13/2**[2]

0602 **4** *nk* **Gladsome**[26] 6783 4-9-0 64............................ DominicFox 2 37
(Jason Ward) *in tch: hdwy and pushed along 1/2-way: rdn to chse ldrs 2f out: sn drvn and plugged on same pce* **5/2**[1]

5 *4* **Zilzie (IRE)** 3-8-12 0............................ TomEaves 6 27
(Ann Duffield) *hld up towards rr tl styd on fnl 2f: n.d* **25/1**

0260 **6** *5* **Lady Bentinck (IRE)**[61] 5728 3-8-5 50............................ KevinStott(7) 15 14
(Alan Berry) *dwlt and towards rr: rdn and hdwy over 2f out: kpt on: n.d* **80/1**

7 *nk* **Copper To Gold** 3-8-12 0............................ MichaelO'Connell 13 13
(Robin Bastiman) *s.i.s and rr tl styd on fnl 2f: n.d* **14/1**

8 *shd* **Ebony Express** 3-9-3 0............................ RobertWinston 12 18
(Alan Swinbank) *towards rr: hdwy wl over 2f out: styng on whn hmpd appr fnl f: n.d* **16/1**

9 *¾* **Adam's Ale** 3-9-3 0............................ MickyFenton 8 16
(Paul Midgley) *chsd ldrs: rdn along over 2f out: sn wknd and hung lft appr fnl f* **100/1**

00 **10** *5* **Bondi Beach Boy**[26] 6792 3-9-3 0............................ PaddyAspell 10
(James Turner) *chsd ldrs: rdn along wl over 2f out: sn wknd* **100/1**

5 **11** *1 ¾* **Imperial Bond**[61] 5734 3-9-3 0............................ GrahamLee 17
(Jedd O'Keeffe) *a towards rr* **25/1**

5 **12** *7* **Mrsb**[35] 6527 3-8-12 0............................ PaulMulrennan 14
(Mrs K Burke) *nvr bttr than midfield* **33/1**

6000 **13** *½* **Peteron**[83] 4911 4-9-2 42............................ DeclanCannon(3) 11
(Colin Teague) *a towards rr* **100/1**

14 *3 ¼* **Miss Bunter** 3-8-12 0............................ SilvestreDeSousa 16
(David O'Meara) *in tch: rdn along over 3f out: sn wknd* **8/1**

15 *1* **Extol** 3-9-3 0............................ DaleSwift 4
(Colin Teague) *s.i.s: a bhd* **100/1**

16 *11* **Miss Bossy Boots** 3-8-12 0............................ PatrickMathers 18
(Tracy Waggott) *dwlt: midfield: rdn along 1/2-way: sn outpcd and bhd* **66/1**

1m 33.14s (8.64) **Going Correction** +1.15s/f (Soft)
WFA 3 from 4yo 2lb **16** Ran SP% **124.0**
Speed ratings (Par 103): **96,94,83,83,78 73,72,72,71,66 64,56,55,51,50 38**
Tote Swingers 1&2 £5.70, 2&3 £5.30, 1&3 £8.90 CSF £24.21 TOTE £9.50: £2.00, £1.30, £2.30; EX 34.50 Trifecta £128.90 Pool: £318.05 - 1.85 winning tickets..
Owner Miss Vivian Pratt **Bred** H & V Pratt **Trained** Middleham, N Yorks

FOCUS
A weak maiden run in bad ground and rated cautiously. The first two were well clear.
Miss Bunter Official explanation: jockey said filly hung left-handed

7446 FOLLOW REDCARRACING ON FACEBOOK & TWITTER APPRENTICE H'CAP (DIV I) 6f
3:40 (3:40) (Class 6) (0-65,65) 3-Y-0+ **£1,617** (£481; £240; £120) **Stalls** Centre

Form RPR

6124 **1** **Fama Mac**[4] 7351 5-9-2 **65**............................ EvaMoscrop(5) 16 74
(Neville Bycroft) *cl up: led over 2f out: rdn ent fnl f: styd on wl* **9/2**[1]

0006 **2** *2* **Tenancy (IRE)**[43] 6288 8-8-2 **51** oh3............................(b) JordanUys(5) 13 54
(Shaun Harris) *in tch: hdwy over 2f out: rdn to chse wnr over 1f out: no imp ins fnl f* **33/1**

0220 **3** *1* **Windygoul Lad**[26] 6786 3-9-0 **59**............................ GarryWhillans 11 59
(Keith Dalgleish) *in tch: h4eadway to chse ldrs over 2f out: rdn over 1f out: edgd lft and kpt on fnl f* **13/2**[2]

600 **4** *1 ½* **Greenhead High**[75] 5245 4-8-10 **57**............................ ShirleyTeasdale(3) 12 52
(David Nicholls) *led: rdn along and hdd over 2f out: drvn over 1f out: one pce ent fnl f* **28/1**

0135 **5** *nk* **Celestial Dawn**[36] 6514 3-9-3 **65** ow4............................ DavidBergin(3) 10 59
(John Weymes) *midfield: hdwy 2f out: sn rdn to chse ldrs: no imp fnl f* **10/1**

6000 **6** *nk* **Hab Reeh**[20] 6958 4-8-2 **51** oh3............................(bt) MatthewHopkins(5) 17 44
(Ruth Carr) *dwlt and in rr: hdwy 1/2-way: chsd ldrs and n.m.r wl over 1f out: kpt on ins fnl f: nrst fin* **33/1**

4326 **7** *1 ¾* **Strong Man**[25] 6811 4-9-3 **64**............................(bt) DavidSimmonson(3) 5 51
(Michael Easterby) *chsd ldrs: rdn 2f out: sn drvn and grad wknd* **8/1**[3]

6405 **8** *4 ½* **Ace Master**[20] 6967 4-8-6 **55**............................ PhilipPrince(5) 4 28
(Roy Bowring) *in tch: rdn over 2f out: grad wknd* **16/1**

4500 **9** *1 ¼* **Michael's Nook**[10] 7224 5-8-10 **54** ow2............................ LMcNiff 18 23
(David Barron) *nvr bttr than midfield* **16/1**

0410 **10** *1 ¼* **Ryedale Dancer (IRE)**[8] 7274 4-9-1 **62**............................ JasonHart(3) 14 27
(Richard Guest) *chsd ldrs: rdn over 2f out: grad wknd* **12/1**

5205 **11** *1 ¾* **Holy Angel (IRE)**[40] 6358 3-9-4 **63**............................ DarylByrne 8 22
(Tim Easterby) *nvr bttr than midfield* **25/1**

561 **12** *2 ¾* **Northern Bolt**[35] 6529 7-9-6 **64**............................ MatthewLawson 1 15
(Ian McInnes) *dwlt and sn rdn along: a towards rr* **9/1**

4406 **13** *½* **Artillery Train (IRE)**[3] 7378 3-8-0 **52**............................ JoeyHaynes(7) 7 1
(Tim Etherington) *a towards rr* **50/1**

3020 **14** *¾* **Morna's Glory**[76] 5185 3-9-3 **62**............................ AdamCarter 15 9
(Jason Ward) *in tch: rdn along 1/2-way: sn wknd* **33/1**

6305 **15** *5* **Cannon Bolt (IRE)**[42] 6309 4-8-5 **52**............................(b) JacobButterfield(3) 3
(Robin Bastiman) *chsd ldrs: rdn along 1/2-way: sn wknd* **12/1**

0402 **16** *½* **Piste**[12] 7178 6-8-7 **54**............................(e) RachealKneller(3) 19
(Tina Jackson) *in rr fr 1/2-way* **16/1**

-605 **17** *1 ¾* **Feel The Heat**[70] 5416 5-9-2 **65**............................(v) PeterSword(5) 20
(Bryan Smart) *dwlt: a in rr* **12/1**

5-00 **18** *16* **Miss Pronounce**[151] 2618 4-8-4 **51** oh6............................ GeorgeChaloner(3) 6
(Linda Perratt) *a towards rr* **66/1**

00 **19** *1 ½* **Double Carpet (IRE)**[170] 2091 9-8-9 **53**............................ CharlesBishop 2
(Garry Woodward) *prom: rdn along over 2f out: sn wknd* **33/1**

1m 18.54s (6.74) **Going Correction** +1.15s/f (Soft)
WFA 3 from 4yo+ 1lb **19** Ran SP% **125.0**
Speed ratings (Par 101): **101,98,97,95,94 94,91,85,84,82 80,76,75,74,68 67,65,43,41**
Tote Swingers 1&2 £49.60, 2&3 £60.70, 1&3 £6.70 CSF £170.72 CT £991.37 TOTE £4.70: £1.30, £6.50, £1.90, £6.90; EX 198.70 TRIFECTA Not won..
Owner Mrs C M Whatley **Bred** N Bycroft **Trained** Brandsby, N Yorks
■ Stewards' Enquiry : Matthew Lawson two-day ban: used whip above permitted level (Nov 14-15)
L McNiff two-day ban: weighed in 2lb heavy (Nov 14-15)
David Bergin two-day ban: weighed in 4lb heavy (Nov 14-15)

FOCUS
The first division of a modest sprint handicap for apprentice riders in which the winner recorded the best comparative time on the card. Modest form, rated a bit cautiously.

7447 FOLLOW REDCARRACING ON FACEBOOK & TWITTER APPRENTICE H'CAP (DIV II) 6f
4:10 (4:16) (Class 6) (0-65,65) 3-Y-0+ **£1,617** (£481; £240; £120) **Stalls** Centre

Form RPR

5005 **1** **Half A Crown (IRE)**[39] 6403 7-9-0 **63**.......................... HannahNunn(5) 3 71
(Peter Salmon) *trckd ldrs: hdwy to chse ldng pair and swtchd rt over 1f out: rdn to ld ent fnl f: kpt on gamely towards fin* **7/1**[1]

1154 **2** *nk* **Orwellian**[35] 6530 3-9-0 **64**.......................... PeterSword(5) 6 71
(Bryan Smart) *dwlt and towards rr: rdn along and bhd 2f out: gd hdwy over 1f out: str run ins fnl f: jst failed* **7/1**[1]

3010 **3** *½* **Mango Music**[26] 6782 9-9-0 **64**.......................... MatthewLawson 17 69
(David Thompson) *dwlt and towards rr: hdwy on outer 2f out: rdn over 1f out: styd on to chal ins fnl f: ev ch tl drvn and nt qckn last 100yds* **20/1**

6000 **4** *1* **Prince James**[37] 6497 5-8-10 **57**.......................... DavidSimmonson(3) 2 59
(Michael Easterby) *towards rr: pushed along 1/2-way: hdwy on wd outside 2f out: sn rdn and kpt on fnl f* **11/1**

46-0 **5** *¾* **Tadalavil**[176] 1875 7-9-1 **59**.......................... LMcNiff 14 59
(Linda Perratt) *hld up: gd hdwy over 2f out: chsd ldrs whn nt clr run over 1f out: swtchd rt and rdn: styd on wl fnl f: nrst finyp* **20/1**

6530 **6** *2* **Keep It Dark**[26] 6785 3-9-3 **65**.......................... DavidBergin(3) 18 58
(Tony Coyle) *trckd ldrs: cl up 1/2-way: chal 2f out: sn rdn and ev ch tl wknd ent fnl f* **25/1**

0-00 **7** *¾* **Zoom In**[117] 3753 4-8-4 **51** oh6..........................(bt[1]) NoelGarbutt(3) 7 42
(Lee James) *towards rr: pushed along 1/2-way: rdn and hdwy 2f out: kpt on fnl f: nrst fin* **66/1**

0000 **8** *shd* **Cara's Request (AUS)**[42] 6309 7-8-5 **52**.......................... ShirleyTeasdale(3) 11 43
(David Nicholls) *led: rdn along 2f out: hdd ent fnl f: sn wknd* **9/1**[3]

3526 **9** *hd* **Foreign Rhythm (IRE)**[14] 7099 7-8-8 **57**.......................... KevinStott(5) 9 47
(Ron Barr) *midfield: rdn 2f out: kpt on fnl f: n.d* **10/1**

0040 **10** *2¼* **Divertimenti (IRE)**[12] 7179 8-8-6 **55**..........................(b) PhilipPrince(5) 5 38
(Roy Bowring) *prom: rdn along wl over 2f out: grad wknd* **25/1**

0000 **11** *½* **Errigal Lad**[39] 6403 7-8-8 **52**.......................... CharlesBishop 13 33
(Garry Woodward) *dwlt and towards rr: sme hdwy 2f out: sn rdn and nvr dangeros* **12/1**

0005 **12** *hd* **Gracie's Games**[8] 7275 6-8-9 **56**.......................... JacobButterfield(3) 1 37
(Richard Price) *towards rr: hdwy on wd outside over 2f out: sn rdn and n.d* **16/1**

0415 **13** *¾* **Distant Sun (USA)**[14] 7099 8-9-2 **60**..........................(p) GarryWhillans 19 38
(Linda Perratt) *chsd ldrs: rdn along over 2f out: drvn and wknd wl over 1f out* **16/1**

3000 **14** *1* **Secret City (IRE)**[61] 5737 6-9-7 **65**..........................(b) DarylByrne 10 40
(Robin Bastiman) *a in rr* **20/1**

-006 **15** *hd* **Wood Nymph (IRE)**[25] 6806 3-8-2 **52**.......................... RachelRichardson(5) 4 26
(Tim Easterby) *prom: rdn along 1/2-way: sn wknd* **25/1**

006 **16** *1½* **Red Roar (IRE)**[32] 6605 5-8-11 **62**.......................... JordanHibberd(7) 8 32
(Alan Berry) *in tch: rdn along 1/2-way: sn wknd* **25/1**

6002 **17** *27* **Gracie's Gift (IRE)**[4] 7354 10-8-4 **51** oh1..........................(v) JasonHart(3) 15
(Richard Guest) *dwlt: a in rr: bhd and eased fnl 2f* **15/2**[2]

1m 19.96s (8.16) **Going Correction** +1.15s/f (Soft)
WFA 3 from 4yo+ 1lb **17** Ran SP% **114.8**
Speed ratings (Par 101): **91,90,89,88,87 84,83,83,83,80 79,79,78,77,77 75,39**
Tote Swingers 1&2 £9.50, 2&3 £23.90, 1&3 £34.40 CSF £39.34 CT £726.33 TOTE £8.80: £2.40, £1.80, £4.80, £3.30; EX 48.40 Trifecta £480.80 Part won. Pool: 641.12 - 0.80 winning tickets..
Owner Viscount Environmental **Bred** Burns Farm Stud **Trained** Kirk Deighton, W Yorks
■ Bridge Valley was withdrawn (8/1, unruly in stalls). Deduct 10p in the £ under R4.
■ Stewards' Enquiry : Hannah Nunn two-day ban: use of whip (20-21 November)
David Simmonson four-day ban: used whip above permitted level (Nov 14-17)

FOCUS
The second division of a modest sprint handicap for apprentice riders in which the winner recorded a significantly slower time than that of Fama Mac in the first instalment. The pace may have been overstrong. The form is rated around the placed horses.
Gracie's Gift(IRE) Official explanation: jockey said gelding missed the break
T/Plt: £110.70 to a £1 stake. Pool: £35,887.91 - 236.59 winning tickets. T/Qpdt: £35.10 to a £1 stake. Pool: £2,973.04 - 62.60 winning tickets. JR

7448 - (Foreign Racing) - See Raceform Interactive

7013 SAINT-CLOUD (L-H)
Monday, October 29

OFFICIAL GOING: Turf: heavy

7449a PRIX DE FLORE (GROUP 3) (3YO+ FILLIES & MARES) (TURF) 1m 2f 110y
1:35 (12:00) 3-Y-0+ **£33,333** (£13,333; £10,000; £6,666; £3,333)

RPR

1 **Lil'Wing (IRE)**[31] 3-8-7 0.......................... Christophe-PatriceLemaire 4 110
(A De Royer-Dupre, France) *trckd ldrs: qcknd to press ldr 2f out: led 1 1/2f out: rdn and r.o wl fnl f* **29/10**[1]

2 *¾* **La Peinture (FR)**[155] 2532 3-8-7 0.......................... FranckBlondel 1 109
(A De Royer-Dupre, France) *hld up towards rr: hdwy on ins 2f out: 2nd and rdn over 1f out: chal wnr tl no ex fnl 50yds* **53/10**[3]

3 *1¼* **Omana (FR)**[26] 6803 3-8-7 0.......................... FabriceVeron 7 107
(H-A Pantall, France) *front rnk in centre: trckd ldr after 2f: styd prom: hmpd and hemmed in bhd horses on rail 2f out: styd on u.p fnl f: tk 3rd cl home* **34/1**

4 *snk* **Midnight Soprano (IRE)**[15] 7088 5-8-11 0.......................... OlivierPeslier 5 104
(P D Deegan, Ire) *front rnk on ins: trckd ldr after 2f: shkn up to ld 2f out: hdd 1 1/2f out: kpt on at same pce fnl f: lost 3rd cl home* **7/1**

5 *3½* **Andromeda Galaxy (FR)**[36] 6518 4-8-11 0.......................... TomQueally 6 97
(Sir Henry Cecil) *awkward leaving stalls and wnt rt: settled in midfield: outpcd and scrubbed along 3f out: styd on to go 4th over 1 1/2f out: one pce fnl f* **18/1**

6 *nse* **Haya Landa (FR)**[22] 6912 4-8-11 0.......................... ThierryThulliez 10 97
(Mme L Audon, France) *trckd ldrs: shuffled bk and trapped on rail whn field c stands's side 2 1/2f out: swtchd ins and rdn 1 1/2f out: kpt on fnl f: nt pce to chal* **3/1**[2]

7 *2* **Aghareed (USA)**[57] 5870 3-8-7 0.......................... FabienLefebvre 2 95
(J E Hammond, France) *settled in rr: last and rdn 2f out: no imp tl r.o fnl f: nvr plcd to chal* **19/1**

8 *½* **Last Born (FR)**[26] 6803 3-8-7 0.......................... FlavienPrat 3 94
(A Fabre, France) *settled towards rr: prog to chse ldrs over 1 1/2f out: sn rdn and nt qckn: wknd fnl f* **15/1**

9 *2* **Nobilis**[42] 6327 3-8-7 0.......................... MaximeGuyon 9 91
(A Fabre, France) *front rnk on outside: wnt on after 2f: led whole field to stands' side st: sn rdn and hdd 2f out: wknd fnl 1 1/2f* **8/1**

10 *1¼* **Shaqira**[15] 4-8-11 0.......................... THellier 8 86
(W Figge, Germany) *settled towards rr: rdn and no imp fr over 1 1/2f out: wknd fnl f* **12/1**

2m 24.3s (4.70)
WFA 3 from 4yo+ 5lb **10** Ran SP% **117.2**
WIN (incl. 1 euro stake): 3.20 (Lil'Wing coupled with Andromeda Galaxy). PLACES: 1.80, 2.40, 6.10. DF: 9.40. SF: 20.40.
Owner Ecurie Wildenstein **Bred** Dayton Investments Ltd **Trained** Chantilly, France

NOTEBOOK
Lil'Wing(IRE) retained her unbeaten record on this step up in class and her trainer was full of praise. She will stay in training at four and this daughter of Galileo could well develop into a Group 1 performer next year.
La Peinture(FR) was at a disadvantage to her stablemate in that she hadn't run since May, so in the circumstances this was a good effort, and she too will be kept in training as a 4yo. Alain De Royer-Dupre said afterwards that the winner and La Peinutre work together and there isn't much between them.
Andromeda Galaxy(FR) was again below her best on her second start for this yard.
Haya Landa(FR), the Arc fourth, got no run and can be excused this effort.

7241 CATTERICK (L-H)
Tuesday, October 30

OFFICIAL GOING: Soft (6.8)
Wind: Light across Weather: Sunny periods

7450 CATTERICKBRIDGE.CO.UK MEDIAN AUCTION MAIDEN STKS 5f 212y
12:50 (12:50) (Class 6) 2-Y-0 **£2,045** (£603; £302) **Stalls** Low

Form RPR

1 **General Direction (IRE)**[9] 7276 2-9-3 0.......................... PaulMulrennan 5 74+
(Reginald Roberts, Ire) *slt ld: pushed clr wl over 1f out: rdn and kpt on fnl f* **7/4**[1]

2 **2** *1½* **Brooke's Bounty**[28] 6754 2-9-3 0.......................... TonyHamilton 9 69
(Richard Fahey) *trckd ldng pair: effrt to chse wnr 2f out: sn rdn and no imp fnl f* **3/1**[3]

2 **3** *7* **Marcus Caesar (IRE)**[61] 5756 2-9-3 0.......................... GrahamGibbons 12 48+
(David Barron) *in tch: hdwy over 2f out: rdn along wl over 1f out: sn one pce* **5/2**[2]

60 **4** *2½* **Diddy Eric**[21] 6954 2-8-12 0.......................... GarryWhillans(5) 8 40+
(Micky Hammond) *bhd: rdn along bef 1/2-way: styd on fnl 2f: nvr nr ldrs* **80/1**

00 **5** *1* **Superoo (IRE)**[12] 7192 2-9-3 0.......................... JoeFanning 4 37
(Mark Johnston) *cl up on inner: rdn along over 2f out: wknd over 1f out* **16/1**

40 **6** *2* **Faffa**[8] 7290 2-9-3 0.......................... DavidAllan 6 31
(Tim Easterby) *chsd ldrs: rdn along over 2f out: sn edgd lft and wknd* **9/1**

7 *¾* **Heights Ridge** 2-8-12 0.......................... DarylByrne(5) 7 29
(Tim Easterby) *s.i.s: sn rdn along and outpcd: a bhd* **33/1**

00 **8** *4½* **Don't Tell**[52] 6042 2-8-12 0.......................... TomEaves 2 10
(George Moore) *dwlt and keen in rr: hdwy and in tch 1/2-way: rdn along over 2f out: sn wknd* **66/1**

1m 18.84s (5.24) **Going Correction** +0.775s/f (Yiel) **8** Ran SP% **111.5**
Speed ratings (Par 93): **96,94,84,81,80 77,76,70**
Tote Swingers 1&2 £1.90, 2&3 £2.80, 1&3 £2.40 CSF £6.83 TOTE £2.50: £1.10, £1.90, £1.20; EX 7.50 Trifecta £9.00 Pool: £536.92 - 44.59 winning tickets..
Owner John James Feane **Bred** M Phelan & Lawman Syndicate **Trained** Rathangan, Co Kildare

FOCUS
No strength in depth in this 2yo median auction maiden, the first two pulling clear. The winner is rated to his Irish form.

NOTEBOOK
General Direction(IRE), who stepped up on his initial effort when chasing home an Aidan O'Brien-trained favourite at Naas, recording a RPR of 74, travelled strongly and took this with the minimum of fuss. He lacks size, but clearly handles soft ground well. (op 11-8)
Brooke's Bounty, conceding the winner 4lb when runner-up in a maiden auction event at Ayr in bad ground on his debut a month earlier, improved on that outing without ever seriously threatening the winner. He is sure to be found an opportunity to go one better. (op 10-3 tchd 7-2)
Marcus Caesar(IRE), no match for a subsequent Listed winner in a newcomers' race at Hamilton two months earlier, kept tabs on the winner only to fade in the final 2f. He is the type to do better at three. (op 10-3)
Diddy Eric, quite a big backward-type, stayed on after turning for home detached. He is the type to do much better in handicaps over a mile plus at three. (op 66-1)
Superoo(IRE), who had shown little in two starts on the all-weather, shaped a fraction better without ever threatening to take a hand. (op 12-1)
Faffa is another likely to fare better in handicap company at three. (op 10-1)
Heights Ridge, slow to break and tailed off at halfway on his debut, was far from disgraced in the end, but clearly has a lot to learn.

7451 GO RACING AT WETHERBY THIS FRIDAY H'CAP 5f 212y
1:20 (1:20) (Class 4) (0-85,81) 3-Y-0 **£4,204** (£1,251; £625; £312) **Stalls** Low

Form RPR

2362 **1** **Half A Billion (IRE)**[26] 6811 3-8-8 **75**.......................... ConnorNichol(7) 5 84
(Michael Dods) *t.k.h: cl up: led after 1f: rdn over 1f out: hld on wl towards fin* **7/1**[3]

2001 **2** *nse* **Ashpan Sam**[9] 7274 3-9-4 **78** 6ex.......................... GrahamLee 2 87
(John Spearing) *in tch: hdwy 2f out: rdn over 1f out: chsd wnr ins fnl f: drvn and kpt on wl: jst failed* **7/2**[1]

2210 **3** *3¼* **Blue Shoes (IRE)**[37] 6514 3-8-10 **70**.......................... DavidAllan 4 68
(Tim Easterby) *cl up on inner: disp ld 1/2-way: rdn along 2f out: drvn and one pce fnl f* **10/1**

630 **4** *3¾* **Rusty Rocket (IRE)**[13] 7177 3-9-6 **80**.......................... JoeFanning 9 66
(Paul Green) *led 1f: trckd ldrs: pushed along and sltly outpcd over 2f out: sn rdn: kpt on fnl f* **6/1**[2]

0355 **5** *hd* **Waseem Faris (IRE)**[10] 7243 3-9-2 **81**.......................... CharlesBishop(5) 8 67
(Mick Channon) *hld up in rr: hdwy over 2f out: rdn over 1f out: kpt on fnl f: nrst fin* **7/1**[3]

1110 **6** *½* **Imperial Legend (IRE)**[13] 7177 3-8-9 **76**..........................(p) ShirleyTeasdale(7) 6 60
(David Nicholls) *prom: rdn wl over 1f out: wknd ent fnl f* **33/1**

0260 **7** *2¾* **Indego Blues**[13] 7177 3-9-1 **75**.......................... PaulQuinn 3 50
(David Nicholls) *a towards rr* **10/1**

1004 **8** *2* **Takealookatmenow (IRE)**[64] 5676 3-8-11 **71**..........................(p) AndrewMullen 10 40
(David Nicholls) *a towards rr* **25/1**

-266 **9** 3/4 **Key Ambition**[22] 6938 3-9-1 **75**......(tp) RussKennemore 7 42
(Garry Moss) *cl up: rdn along 1/2-way: sn wknd* **8/1**
2031 **10** shd **Phoenix Clubs (IRE)**[15] 7100 3-9-1 **75**...... TonyHamilton 1 41
(Paul Midgley) *chsd ldrs on inner: rdn along over 2f out: sn wknd* **12/1**
3322 **11** 7 **Economic Crisis (IRE)**[15] 7100 3-8-13 **73**...... PaddyAspell 11 17
(Alan Berry) *a in rr* **11/1**
1m 17.91s (4.31) **Going Correction** +0.775s/f (Yiel) 11 Ran SP% **113.6**
Speed ratings (Par 103): **102,101,97,92,92 91,88,85,84,84 74**
Tote Swingers 1&2 £3.80, 2&3 £7.00, 1&3 £10.00 CSF £30.51 CT £244.51 TOTE £4.40: £1.10, £1.30, £4.70; EX 38.60 Trifecta £414.50 Part won. Pool: £552.68 - 0.60 winning tickets..
Owner I Galletley, B Stenson, M Dods **Bred** Mount Coote Stud **Trained** Denton, Co Durham

FOCUS
A competitive sprint handicap, but few became seriously involved and again the first two finished clear. The winner is rated in line with his latest Southwell form.
Waseem Faris(IRE) Official explanation: trainer's rep said gelding was unsuited by the soft ground

7452 WEATHERBYS HAMILTON INSURANCE H'CAP (DIV I) 7f
1:50 (1:50) (Class 4) (0-85,85) 3-Y-0+ **£4,528** (£1,347; £673; £336) **Stalls** Centre

Form RPR
4301 **1** **Conry (IRE)**[10] 7247 6-8-10 **74**...... StevieDonohoe 3 88
(Ian Williams) *hld up towards rr: hdwy and in tch 2f out: swtchd rt and effrt over 1f out: rdn to ld ins fnl f: sn clr* **7/2[1]**
5010 **2** 7 **Kingscroft (IRE)**[10] 7240 4-9-7 **85**...... JoeFanning 1 81
(Mark Johnston) *trckd ldrs: hdwy and cl up 2f out: rdn to ld 1f out: hdd ins fnl f: kpt on same pce* **9/2[3]**
601 **3** 1 3/4 **Piceno (IRE)**[10] 7246 4-8-11 **75**......(p) RobertWinston 9 66
(Scott Dixon) *chsd ldng pair: rdn along 2f out: drvn over 1f out: kpt on same pce* **4/1[2]**
0400 **4** 1 3/4 **Atlantis Star**[30] 6705 5-9-2 **80**...... PaulMulrennan 2 67
(James Tate) *sn led: hdd over 3f out and sn rdn along: drvn wl over 1f out and sn one pce* **13/2**
0110 **5** nk **Fieldgunner Kirkup (GER)**[19] 7000 4-9-5 **83**...... GrahamGibbons 10 69
(David Barron) *chsd ldrs: rdn along over 2f out: sn one pce* **10/1**
6100 **6** 1/2 **Lucky Numbers (IRE)**[31] 6665 6-9-2 **80**......(e) DanielTudhope 8 65
(David O'Meara) *towards rr: hdwy on wd outside 2f out: sn rdn and no imp* **22/1**
0050 **7** 1 1/4 **Klynch**[15] 7097 6-9-6 **84**......(b) DaleSwift 6 65
(Ruth Carr) *cl up: led 3f out: rdn wl over 1f out: hdd and edgd lft 1f out: sn wknd* **22/1**
0000 **8** 1/2 **Viva Ronaldo (IRE)**[11] 7210 6-9-0 **78**...... TonyHamilton 5 58
(Richard Fahey) *a in rr* **8/1**
0010 **9** 3/4 **Solar Spirit (IRE)**[8] 7291 7-9-4 **82**...... GrahamLee 7 60
(Tracy Waggott) *trckd ldrs: effrt 2f out: sn rdn and wknd over 1f out* **17/2**
5000 **10** 1 1/2 **Boris Grigoriev (IRE)**[10] 7247 3-8-6 **72**...... JamesSullivan 4 46
(Michael Easterby) *a bhd* **28/1**
1m 31.49s (4.49) **Going Correction** +0.775s/f (Yiel)
WFA 3 from 4yo+ 2lb 10 Ran SP% **116.6**
Speed ratings (Par 105): **105,97,95,93,92 92,90,90,89,87**
Tote Swingers 1&2 £4.10, 2&3 £3.00, 1&3 £2.70 CSF £18.71 CT £66.75 TOTE £4.80: £1.90, £1.30, £1.50; EX 19.90 Trifecta £33.10 Pool: £946.67 - 21.42 winning tickets..
Owner T Birchall **Bred** Shay White **Trained** Portway, Worcs
■ Stewards' Enquiry : Stevie Donohoe two-day ban: careless riding (Nov 14-15)

FOCUS
They went a good gallop in the conditions and the runaway winner came from off the pace, while the next three home were in the thick of things from the off. It was the faster division and the wide-margin winner is rated back to his old best.

7453 WEATHERBYS HAMILTON INSURANCE H'CAP (DIV II) 7f
2:20 (2:20) (Class 4) (0-85,85) 3-Y-0+ **£4,528** (£1,347; £673; £336) **Stalls** Centre

Form RPR
4400 **1** **Nameitwhatyoulike**[18] 7032 3-8-11 **77**...... PaulMulrennan 2 88
(Michael Easterby) *trckd ldrs: hdwy 2f out: swtchd rt over 1f out: led ent fnl f: sn rdn and styd on wl* **5/2[1]**
6262 **2** 1 3/4 **Green Park (IRE)**[15] 7097 9-9-2 **80**......(b) DavidAllan 1 86
(Declan Carroll) *towards rr and rdn along after 3f: gd hdwy 2f out: chsd ldrs over 1f out: rdn to chse wnr ins fnl f: no imp towards fin* **15/2**
0024 **3** 1 3/4 **Dr Red Eye**[31] 6659 4-9-5 **83**......(p) RobertWinston 3 84
(Scott Dixon) *chsd ldr: led 2f out: rdn over 1f out: hdd ent fnl f: kpt on same pce* **7/2[2]**
0400 **4** 2 1/4 **Polish World (USA)**[16] 7083 8-8-13 **77**...... MickyFenton 7 73
(Paul Midgley) *racd wd 3f: led: rdn along and hdd 2f out: grad wknd* **25/1**
0000 **5** 4 **Layla's Hero (IRE)**[15] 7114 5-8-11 **75**...... StevieDonohoe 4 60
(Ian Williams) *bhd and outpcd 1/2-way: wd st and rdn along: styd on fnl 2f: n.d* **16/1**
6336 **6** 1/2 **Beckermet (IRE)**[19] 7000 10-9-3 **81**...... JamesSullivan 9 65
(Ruth Carr) *chsd ldrs: rdn along over 2f out: grad wknd* **12/1**
0040 **7** 5 **Roker Park (IRE)**[31] 6663 7-8-12 **83**......(b) DavidBergin(7) 5 54
(David O'Meara) *a in rr* **17/2**
0020 **8** 1 1/2 **Orpsie Boy (IRE)**[42] 6338 9-9-1 **79**...... DaleSwift 8 46
(Ruth Carr) *a in rr* **16/1**
6002 **9** 4 **Dubai Hills**[4] 7370 6-9-7 **85**...... TomEaves 6 42
(Bryan Smart) *a in rr* **9/2[3]**
1m 31.93s (4.93) **Going Correction** +0.775s/f (Yiel)
WFA 3 from 4yo+ 2lb 9 Ran SP% **114.6**
Speed ratings (Par 105): **102,100,98,95,90 90,84,82,78**
Tote Swingers 1&2 £4.70, 2&3 £3.00, 1&3 £2.80 CSF £21.72 CT £65.10 TOTE £2.50: £1.10, £2.80, £2.60; EX 20.80 Trifecta £45.50 Pool: £1,311.07 - 21.59 winning tickets..
Owner S Bowett, S Hollings & S Hull **Bred** A E Smith And Co **Trained** Sheriff Hutton, N Yorks
■ Stewards' Enquiry : Micky Fenton one-day ban: careless riding (Nov 14)

FOCUS
The slightly slower division, but still sound run. Possibly setting the trend for later in the day, the winner came wide to make his effort towards the stands' rail. The second sets the standard.

7454 WEATHERBYS FOREIGN EXCHANGE H'CAP 1m 7f 177y
2:50 (2:50) (Class 5) (0-70,70) 3-Y-0+ **£2,587** (£770; £384; £192) **Stalls** Centre

Form RPR
0-15 **1** **Mason Hindmarsh**[30] 6706 5-9-8 **64**...... GrahamLee 9 73
(Karen McLintock) *sn led and set stdy pce: pushed along 2f out: rdn fnl f: styd on wl: readily* **3/1[1]**
5144 **2** 1 1/2 **Ctappers**[12] 6738 3-8-6 **63** ow2...... CharlesBishop(5) 2 70
(Mick Channon) *hld up towards rr: hdwy 4f out: rdn 2f out: styd on u.p to chse wnr ent fnl f: sn no imp* **7/2[2]**
60 **3** 6 **Ad Value (IRE)**[83] 4955 4-8-13 **60**...... GarryWhillans(5) 5 60
(Alan Swinbank) *trckd ldng pair: hdwy to chse wnr 3f out: rdn 2f out: kpt on one pce* **13/2[3]**
0056 **4** 2 **Ferney Boy**[27] 6784 6-8-9 **51** oh3...... MichaelStainton 7 49
(Chris Fairhurst) *trckd ldrs: hdwy over 3f out: rdn along over 2f out and sn one pce* **16/1**
2020 **5** 4 1/2 **Vittachi**[23] 6076 5-8-13 **62**...... DavidBergin(7) 11 54
(Alistair Whillans) *s.i.s and bhd: hdwy on wd outside over 5f out: chsd ldrs 4f out: rdn along 3f out: sn one pce* **10/1**
/530 **6** 1 **Shaker Style (USA)**[45] 6262 6-9-2 **58**...... JamesSullivan 1 49
(Barry Murtagh) *in tch: hdwy to chse ldrs 1/2-way: rdn along 4f out: drvn wl over 2f out and plugged on one pce* **16/1**
440P **7** nse **Jan Smuts (IRE)**[27] 6784 4-8-13 **55**......(tp) PaddyAspell 10 46
(Wilf Storey) *chsd ldrs: rdn along over 4f out: sn outpcd* **18/1**
5060 **8** 5 **Mohawk Ridge**[21] 6957 6-9-12 **68**......(p) TomEaves 8 53
(Michael Dods) *prom: pushed along 4f out: rdn wl over 2f out: sn wknd* **13/2[3]**
1-03 **9** 43 **Sphinx (FR)**[27] 6784 14-10-0 **70**......(b) PaulMulrennan 13
(Edwin Tuer) *hld up in rr: effrt and sme hdwy 5f out: sn rdn along and wknd: bhd and eased fnl 2f* **7/1**
021/ **10** 5 **Ibn Hiyyan (USA)**[313] 1145 5-9-2 **58**...... DanielTudhope 12
(Ferdy Murphy) *hld up towards rr: hdwy to chse ldrs after 6f: rdn along 6f out: sn lost pl and bhd: t.o fnl 3f* **18/1**
0-60 **11** 83 **Muzey's Princess**[33] 6614 6-8-6 **51** oh6...... JulieBurke(3) 4
(Michael Mullineaux) *midfield: rdn along over 6f out: sn lost pl and bhd: t.o fnl 4f* **100/1**
3m 51.26s (19.26) **Going Correction** +0.775s/f (Yiel)
WFA 3 from 4yo+ 10lb 11 Ran SP% **118.8**
Speed ratings (Par 103): **82,81,78,77,75 74,74,71,50,47 6**
Tote Swingers 1&2 £3.10, 2&3 £5.70, 1&3 £5.80 CSF £13.46 CT £64.19 TOTE £4.80: £1.80, £1.10, £2.70; EX 16.00 Trifecta £134.30 Pool: £1,006.84 - 5.62 winning tickets..
Owner Brian Chicken **Bred** Newsells Park Stud **Trained** Ingoe, Northumberland

FOCUS
A real test of stamina in the ground. Modest form but the winner may do better.
Sphinx(FR) Official explanation: trainer's rep said gelding was unsuited by the track

7455 RACING UK ON SKY 432 H'CAP 1m 3f 214y
3:20 (3:22) (Class 4) (0-85,85) 3-Y-0+ **£4,431** (£1,308; £654) **Stalls** Centre

Form RPR
1041 **1** **The Tiger**[8] 7294 4-9-9 **82** 6ex...... GrahamLee 5 94+
(Ed Dunlop) *hld up: hdwy on outer and in tch 1/2-way: effrt and cl up 3f out: led wl over 1f out: rdn ins fnl f: styd on strly towards fin* **8/11[1]**
6-10 **2** 1 3/4 **Into Wain (USA)**[15] 7109 5-9-9 **82**...... JoeFanning 3 91
(Steve Gollings) *trckd ldrs: hdwy 3f out: rdn to chal appr fnl f: ev ch tl drvn and no ex last 50yds* **16/1**
1210 **3** 3 3/4 **Azrag (USA)**[31] 6691 4-8-12 **71** oh1......(p) PaulMulrennan 11 74
(Gerard Butler) *chsd ldrs: hdwy to ld 3f out: sn rdn and hdd wl over 1f out: drvn and kpt on same pce fr over 1f out* **16/1**
2214 **4** 4 1/2 **Only Orsenfoolsies**[18] 7032 3-8-9 **75**...... MichaelO'Connell 10 71
(Micky Hammond) *midfield: hdwy and in tch 5f out: rdn along to chse ldrs 3f out: cl up over 2f out: sn rdn and wknd over 1f out* **8/1[2]**
0446 **5** 3 3/4 **Tres Coronas (IRE)**[17] 7069 5-9-5 **78**...... GrahamGibbons 4 68
(David Barron) *hld up in tch: effrt on inner 4f out: rdn along 3f out: sn one pce* **10/1[3]**
0034 **6** 1 1/4 **Focail Maith**[29] 6735 4-8-13 **72**...... RussKennemore 6 60
(John Ryan) *hld up towards rr: hdwy 4f out: rdn along wl over 2f out: n.d* **20/1**
3005 **7** 11 **Euston Square**[19] 7003 6-8-12 **71** oh3...... DaleSwift 2 41
(Alistair Whillans) *a towards rr* **40/1**
4064 **8** 10 **Swinging Hawk (GER)**[46] 6191 6-9-3 **76**...... StevieDonohoe 7 30
(Ian Williams) *prom: led over 4f out: rdn along and hdd 3f out: sn wknd* **8/1[2]**
0600 **9** 4 1/2 **Tartan Gigha (IRE)**[8] 7294 7-9-6 **79**...... DanielTudhope 1 26
(Geoffrey Harker) *cl up: led after 3f: rdn along and hdd over 4f out: sn wknd* **50/1**
5110 **10** 56 **Lifetime (IRE)**[145] 2214 4-9-1 **77**...... PaulPickard(3) 8
(Brian Ellison) *led 3f: prom tl lost pl over 5f out: sn bhd* **20/1**
1000 **11** 1/2 **Persian Peril**[109] 4072 8-9-12 **85**...... RobertWinston 12
(Alan Swinbank) *a in rr: t.o fnl 4f* **40/1**
2m 49.03s (10.13) **Going Correction** +0.775s/f (Yiel)
WFA 3 from 4yo+ 7lb 11 Ran SP% **117.3**
Speed ratings (Par 105): **97,95,93,90,87 87,79,73,70,32 32**
Tote Swingers 1&2 £5.20, 2&3 £13.60, 1&3 £4.50 CSF £13.18 CT £115.40 TOTE £1.50: £1.20, £3.20, £3.60; EX 16.70 Trifecta £108.60 Pool: £1,403.43 - 9.69 winning tickets..
Owner J R Weatherby **Bred** Preston Lodge Stud **Trained** Newmarket, Suffolk

FOCUS
They went a sound gallop in this 1m4f handicap, again the first two pulling clear. The winner matched his Pontefract form.

7456 JUMP SEASON NEXT ON DECEMBER 5TH H'CAP (DIV I) 5f
3:50 (3:53) (Class 6) (0-65,65) 3-Y-0+ **£2,045** (£603; £302) **Stalls** Low

Form RPR
300 **1** **M J Woodward**[17] 7055 3-8-12 **56**...... JoeFanning 15 65
(Paul Green) *cl up stands' side: led that gp and overall ldr after 2f: rdn over 1f out: kpt on wl* **22/1**
0422 **2** 1/2 **Angelo Poliziano**[15] 7099 6-9-0 **58**...... GrahamLee 12 65
(George Foster) *trckd ldrs stands' side: hdwy wl over 1f out: rdn to chse wnr ins fnl f: kpt on: 2nd of 9 in gp* **6/1[2]**
1241 **3** 1 3/4 **Fama Mac**[1] 7446 5-9-0 **65**...... EvaMoscrop(7) 1 66+
(Neville Bycroft) *led far side gp and overall ldr for 2f: prom: rdn and ev ch ent fnl f: kpt on same pce: 1st of 3 in gp* **11/8[1]**
3200 **4** nk **Elegant Girl (IRE)**[13] 7178 3-9-1 **59**...... DanielTudhope 13 59
(Tim Easterby) *prom stands' side: effrt and ev ch wl over 1f out: sn rdn and one pce ins fnl f: 3rd of 9 in gp* **16/1**
500 **5** 1 **Lees Anthem**[56] 5923 5-8-7 **51** oh1...... AndrewMullen 9 47
(Michael Smith) *in tch: stands' side: hdwy 2f out: sn rdn and kpt on same pce fnl f: 4th of 9 in gp* **15/2[3]**
5011 **6** 1/2 **Ivestar (IRE)**[13] 7157 7-9-4 **62**......(v) GrahamGibbons 7 56
(Michael Easterby) *led stands' side gp for 2f: prom tl rdn and wknd appr fnl f: 5th of 9 in gp* **9/1**
6046 **7** nse **Sophie's Beau (USA)**[71] 5416 5-8-0 **51** oh1......(bt) GemmaTutty(7) 4 45
(Michael Chapman) *chsd ldr far side gp: hdwy 2f out: sn rdn and one pce fnl f: 2nd of 3 in gp* **33/1**
4020 **8** 2 **Piste**[1] 7446 6-8-10 **54**......(e) PaulMulrennan 11 41
(Tina Jackson) *chsd ldrs stands' side: rdn along 2f out: sn wknd: 6th of 9 in gp* **16/1**
3303 **9** 3 1/2 **Baybshambles (IRE)**[21] 6958 8-8-11 **55**...... DaleSwift 10 29
(Ron Barr) *a in rr stands' side: 7th of 9 in gp* **14/1**

0434 **10** 3/4 **Ever Roses**13 7179 4-8-9 **53**....(v) MichaelO'Connell 5 25
(Paul Midgley) *dwlt: a in rr stands' side: 8th of 9 in gp* **12/1**
2054 **11** 3/4 **Bailadeira**174 1990 4-8-13 **57**....1 JamesSullivan 2 26
(Tim Etherington) *chsd ldng pair far side: rdn along 2f out: sn outpcd: 3rd of 3 in gp* **18/1**
50-0 **12** 1/2 **Tillys Tale**13 7178 5-8-9 **60**.... DanielleMooney(7) 14 27
(Paul Midgley) *a in rr stands' side: 9th of 9 in gp* **33/1**
1m 3.2s (3.40) **Going Correction** +0.725s/f (Yiel) **12 Ran SP% 119.8**
Speed ratings (Par 101): **101,100,97,96,95 94,94,91,85,84 83,82**
Tote Swingers 1&2 £17.90, 2&3 £3.20, 1&3 £10.80 CSF £148.31 CT £313.03 TOTE £37.90: £9.40, £1.10, £1.10; EX 267.00 Trifecta £1136.60 Part won. Pool: £1,515.49 - 0.62 winning tickets..
Owner E Sciarrillo **Bred** Paul Green **Trained** Lydiate, Merseyside

FOCUS
The slightly faster division, but only modest form. The three lowest drawn runners stuck to the far side. The winner, drawn highest of all, made all under the stands' side rail and postcd a cleai eprsonal best.
Piste Official explanation: jockey said mare missed the break

7457 JUMP SEASON NEXT ON DECEMBER 5TH H'CAP (DIV II) 5f
4:20 (4:21) (Class 6) (0-65,63) 3-Y-O+ **£2,045** (£603; £302) **Stalls** Low

Form RPR
0-56 **1** **Rock On Candy**13 7178 3-9-0 **56**.... RobertWinston 12 69
(John Spearing) *in tch: hdwy to ld over 2f out: rdn clr over 1f out: kpt on strly* **9/2**1
5416 **2** 3 **Middleton Flyer (IRE)**19 7001 3-9-7 **63**....(b) RussKennemore 3 65
(Paul Midgley) *prom: rdn wl over 1f out: drvn to chse wnr ins fnl f: no imp* **16/1**
436 **3** shd **Sharp Shoes**27 6786 5-8-9 **51**.... PaddyAspell 9 53
(Christopher Wilson) *chsd ldrs: rdn along 2f out: styd on u.p fnl f* **12/1**
2325 **4** 1/2 **Dazzlin Bluebell (IRE)**21 6958 3-8-7 **49**....(b) DavidAllan 6 49
(Tim Easterby) *led: rdn along and edgd lft over 2f out: sn hdd: drvn and wknd over 1f out* **7/1**3
0000 **5** hd **Captain Royale (IRE)**15 7099 7-8-12 **59**....(p) GarryWhillans(5) 2 58
(Tracy Waggott) *prom: rdn along on wd outside 2f out: drvn ent fnl f: sn wknd* **16/1**
0053 **6** 1 1/2 **Besty**15 7099 5-8-12 **54**....(bt1) GrahamLee 14 48
(Paul Midgley) *cl up: ev ch over 2f out: sn rdn and wknd over 1f out* **9/2**1
3212 **7** 1/2 **Gran Canaria Queen**17 7055 3-8-5 **54**....(v) GeorgeChaloner(7) 4 46
(Ian Semple) *towards rr: hdwy 2f out: sn rdn and no imp fnl f* **8/1**
3506 **8** 1 1/2 **Wicked Wilma (IRE)**15 7101 8-8-11 **60**.... JordanHibberd(7) 13 47
(Alan Berry) *chsd ldrs: rdn 2f out: sn btn* **16/1**
013 **9** 1 3/4 **On The High Tops (IRE)**62 5740 4-9-4 **60**.... DaleSwift 15 40
(Colin Teague) *in tch: rdn along bef 1/2-way: sn wknd* **16/1**
2260 **10** hd **Two Turtle Doves (IRE)**21 6961 6-9-2 **58**.... SeanQuinlan 5 38
(Michael Mullineaux) *prom: rdn along 1/2-way: sn wknd* **20/1**
11 nk **Phils Wish (IRE)**139 3056 3-8-8 **50**....(p) JamesSullivan 7 28
(John C McConnell, Ire) *in tch: effrt whn n.m.r and lost pl 1/2-way: bhd after* **6/1**2
-000 **12** 2 **Major Muscari (IRE)**15 7100 4-9-4 **60**.... PatrickMathers 11 31
(Ian McInnes) *in tch: rdn along 1/2-way: sn lost pl and bhd* **33/1**
0060 **13** 1 1/4 **Choc'A'Moca (IRE)**17 7055 5-9-1 **57**....(v) MickyFenton 1 24
(Paul Midgley) *prom on wd outside: rdn along 1/2-way: sn wknd* **20/1**
5663 **14** 1/2 **Cataract**21 6959 3-8-2 **51** oh4 ow2.... DavidBergin(7) 10 16
(John Weymes) *dwlt: a in rr* **25/1**
0000 **15** 2 3/4 **Forever Janey**76 5247 3-8-7 **49** oh4.... JoeFanning 8
(Paul Green) *prom: rdn along 1/2-way: sn lost pl and bhd* **66/1**
1m 3.41s (3.61) **Going Correction** +0.725s/f (Yiel) **15 Ran SP% 123.3**
Speed ratings (Par 101): **100,95,95,94,93 91,90,88,85,85 84,81,79,78,74**
Tote Swingers 1&2 £18.80, 2&3 £48.50, 1&3 £15.10 CSF £75.67 CT £847.64 TOTE £4.50: £2.50, £7.10, £4.40; EX 118.30 TRIFECTA Not won..
Owner Tom Hayes **Bred** T M Hayes **Trained** Kinnersley, Worcs

FOCUS
Division two of this low-grade sprint handicap and more of the same. The comfortable winner raced stands' side, while the second and third were in a group of four who raced towards the far side. The form is rated around the second.
Rock On Candy Official explanation: trainer said, regarding apparent improvement in form, that the filly had a clearer run.
Besty Official explanation: jockey said gelding hung left
T/Plt: £7.20 to a £1 stake. Pool: £46,073.57 - 4,654.21 winning tickets. T/Qpdt: £3.80 to a £1 stake. Pool: £3,671.39 - 707.14 winning tickets. JR

7410 WOLVERHAMPTON (A.W) (L-H)
Tuesday, October 30

OFFICIAL GOING: Standard
Wind: Light behind Weather: Overcast

7458 32RED MAIDEN STKS (DIV I) 7f 32y(P)
4:40 (4:42) (Class 5) 2-Y-O **£2,264** (£673; £336; £168) **Stalls** High

Form RPR
4 **1** **Unknown Villain (IRE)**11 7208 2-9-3 0.... RichardKingscote 6 75+
(Tom Dascombe) *chsd ldrs: wnt 2nd 2f out: rdn to ld wl ins fnl f: jst hld on* **9/2**2
2 nse **Horsted Keynes (FR)** 2-9-3 0.... JamieSpencer 3 76+
(Roger Varian) *dwlt: hld up: swtchd rt and hdwy over 1f out: hung lft ins fnl f: r.o wl* **11/10**1
4446 **3** hd **Bartack (IRE)**42 6344 2-9-0 73.... PatrickHills(3) 1 74
(Luca Cumani) *a.p: led over 1f out: rdn and hdd wl ins fnl f* **8/1**
0 **4** 3 **Bright Glow**42 6343 2-8-12 0.... TedDurcan 11 62
(David Lanigan) *s.i.s: hld up: hdwy over 2f out: rdn over 1f out: styd on* **6/1**3
30 **5** nk **Midnight Warrior**42 6330 2-9-3 0.... MartinDwyer 7 66
(James Tate) *a.p: rdn over 2f out: styd on same pce fnl f* **8/1**
02 **6** nse **Orions Hero (IRE)**80 5083 2-9-3 0.... DavidNolan 10 66
(Richard Fahey) *chsd ldrs: rdn 2f out: no ex ins fnl f* **8/1**
7 1 3/4 **Bapak Muda (USA)** 2-9-3 0.... AmyRyan 8 62
(Kevin Ryan) *led: rdn and hdd over 1f out: wknd ins fnl f* **14/1**
00 **8** 1/2 **Marju's Quest (IRE)**34 6571 2-9-3 0.... DaneO'Neill 2 61
(David Simcock) *hld up: hdwy over 1f out: no imp fnl f* **20/1**
9 4 1/2 **Sewn Up** 2-9-3 0.... GeorgeBaker 5 50
(Reg Hollinshead) *hld up: pushed along over 2f out: nvr on terms* **50/1**
00 **10** 1 1/4 **Lilly White (USA)**13 7159 2-8-12 0....(bt1) JamieMackay 4 42
(Brian Meehan) *chsd ldr tl rdn 2f out: wknd fnl f* **25/1**
11 5 **Little Eli** 2-9-3 0.... ShaneKelly 9 34
(Eric Alston) *hld up: a in rr: rdn and wknd over 2f out* **50/1**
1m 29.27s (-0.33) **Going Correction** -0.125s/f (Stan) **11 Ran SP% 132.6**
Speed ratings (Par 95): **96,95,95,92,91 91,89,89,84,82 77**
Tote Swingers 1&2 £1.80, 2&3 £5.40, 1&3 £6.20 CSF £10.89 TOTE £6.20: £1.80, £1.20, £2.60; EX 14.70 Trifecta £64.10 Pool: £1,047.23 - 12.25 winning tickets..
Owner Panarea Racing **Bred** Mrs Jan O'Dwyer **Trained** Malpas, Cheshire

FOCUS
An interesting maiden, from which one of the beaten horses will go into many a notebook. The proximity of the third suggest the form is pretty solid.

NOTEBOOK
Unknown Villain(IRE)'s experience proved crucial as the grey son of Verglas stepped up nicely on his Haydock debut, where the heavy ground proved all too much. This quicker surface saw him in a much better light and, having raced in a handy position throughout, he battled on well up the straight to hold on in a three-way finish, with the trio clear. he deserves plenty of credit and is a nice prospect for next year, but the overriding feeling from this race has to be that the best horse finished second (op 5-1)
Horsted Keynes(FR) ◆ was extremely well-backed and would surely have won had so much not gone wrong, and he will be a warm order wherever he goes next. This Derby entrant was totally disorganised as he left the gates and was immediately trailing the field and up against it. He compounded matters by racing freely at the back of the field, although much of that may have been down to greenness, and he was forced to make his move widest of all as the field straightened up for home. He still had enough of an engine to sweep by most of the field and go agonisingly close to landing hefty market support. He is clearly quite talented and a similar contest looks a formality before he goes on to better things. (op 7-4)
Bartack(IRE) is much more exposed having already had four runs, but he went down fighting up the inside and the switch to Polytrack has suited this colt. He is rated 73, which helps to evaluate the strength of this form. (op 13-2)
Bright Glow showed some improvement, making some headway out wide from off the pace and she can do better again. (op 8-1)
Midnight Warrior once again failed to build on his promising debut but he was keeping on at the finish and a stiffer test might help. (op 10-1)
Orions Hero(IRE) had no excuses, for having had every chance, he dropped away disappointingly. (op 4-1)

7459 32RED MAIDEN STKS (DIV II) 7f 32y(P)
5:10 (5:15) (Class 5) 2-Y-O **£2,264** (£673; £336; £168) **Stalls** High

Form RPR
32 **1** **Mundahesh (IRE)**19 7007 2-9-3 0.... DaneO'Neill 6 80+
(William Haggas) *hld up: hdwy 1/2-way: led over 1f out: hung lft ins fnl f: sn clr* **1/3**1
2 5 **Declamation (IRE)** 2-9-3 0.... NeilCallan 11 65
(Mark Johnston) *chsd ldrs: led wl over 1f out: sn rdn and hdd: no ex fnl f* **6/1**2
3 3/4 **Pink Anemone** 2-8-12 0.... TedDurcan 3 58
(David Lanigan) *outpcd: hdwy over 2f out: shkn up over 1f out: styd on same pce* **25/1**
06 **4** shd **Love Marmalade (IRE)**35 6558 2-9-3 0.... AmyRyan 7 63
(Kevin Ryan) *sn pushed along and prom: rdn and ev ch wl over 1f out: no ex ins fnl f* **20/1**
00 **5** 1 1/4 **Star Spun (USA)**50 6099 2-9-3 0.... JamieSpencer 2 60
(David Barron) *led: rdn and hdd wl over 1f out: wknd ins fnl f* **8/1**3
000 **6** 1 1/4 **July Waits (USA)**27 6790 2-8-12 0....(b1) LukeMorris 8 52+
(Sir Mark Prescott Bt) *chsd ldr tl drvn along 3f out: styd on same pce fnl 2f* **100/1**
7 2 **Manchestar** 2-9-3 0.... DavidNolan 9 52+
(Richard Fahey) *s.i.s: outpcd: styd on appr fnl f: nvr on terms* **22/1**
00 **8** 16 **Cash Rich**11 7219 2-9-3 0.... FergusSweeney 5 12
(Jamie Osborne) *chsd ldrs tl wknd 1/2-way* **50/1**
56 **9** 24 **Loucal**25 6844 2-9-3 0.... ChrisCatlin 10
(Noel Quinlan) *sn outpcd: t.o* **33/1**
1m 29.26s (-0.34) **Going Correction** -0.125s/f (Stan) **9 Ran SP% 119.3**
Speed ratings (Par 95): **96,90,89,89,87 86,84,65,38**
Tote Swingers 1&2 £1.60, 2&3 £6.90, 1&3 £3.70 CSF £2.55 TOTE £1.20: £1.02, £1.40, £6.00; EX 4.00 Trifecta £46.10 Pool: £1,456.85 - 23.69 winning tickets..
Owner Hamdan Al Maktoum **Bred** Shadwell Estate Company Limited **Trained** Newmarket, Suffolk

FOCUS
This had less depth than the first division. There was a clear-cut winner and the fourth and fifth look the best guides.

NOTEBOOK
Mundahesh(IRE) proved different class, coming clear in the final furlong having been patiently ridden in what looked quite a strongly run race. He made smooth headway as the leaders began to feel the heat around the home turn, before clearing away in the straight to score in quite stylish fashion and confirm the promise of his previous two runs. He looks a useful tool for next season where 1m+ looks within range on breeding.
Declamation(IRE)\n\x\x shaped best of the newcomers, running with some promise. Any improvement on this will see him hard to beat in this company, especially as he will be unlikely to bump into another one of the quality of Mundahesh in a winter Wolverhampton maiden.
Pink Anemone is bred to want a much stiffer test in time and she shaped like this was too sharp, as she didn't have the pace to lie up but kept plugging away. She looks a sure-fire improver when going up in trip.
Love Marmalade(IRE) had every chance but was blown away in the straight and is still to show enough promise to make him of interest. (op 25-1)
Star Spun(USA), stepping up in trip, went quite hard up front and didn't get home. He might be of more interest back over 6f.

7460 32RED.COM MEDIAN AUCTION MAIDEN STKS 1m 141y(P)
5:40 (5:43) (Class 6) 2-Y-O **£1,704** (£503; £251) **Stalls** Low

Form RPR
4262 **1** **Glory City (IRE)**21 6972 2-9-3 78....(t) AdamKirby 7 77
(Marco Botti) *led: rdn: edgd rt and hdd over 1f out: rallied to ld nr fin* **6/4**2
322 **2** nk **Sicur**20 6985 2-9-0 79.... PatrickHills(3) 8 76
(Luca Cumani) *chsd ldrs: led and edgd lft over 1f out: rdn: hung rt and hdd nr fin* **11/10**1
00 **3** hd **King Muro**27 6795 2-9-3 0.... DavidProbert 4 76+
(Andrew Balding) *chsd ldrs: rdn: hmpd and ev ch fr over 1f out: r.o* **9/1**3
5 **4** 5 **Mandy The Nag (USA)**17 7057 2-8-12 0.... DaneO'Neill 5 60
(Ed Dunlop) *hld up: hdwy over 2f out: rdn over 1f out: nt trble ldrs* **10/1**
5 1 1/4 **Common Courtesy** 2-8-12 0.... JamieSpencer 2 57
(Michael Bell) *s.i.s: hld up: r.o ins fnl f: nvr nrr* **16/1**
0 **6** 2 3/4 **Alzavola**48 6132 2-8-12 0.... LukeMorris 10 51
(Sir Mark Prescott Bt) *s.i.s: sn pushed along in rr: rdn over 3f out: n.d* **20/1**
0 **7** 1 **Messageinabottle (USA)**13 7160 2-8-12 0.... TedDurcan 11 49
(Michael Bell) *prom: rdn over 2f out: wknd over 1f out* **25/1**

05 **8** 3 1/4 **Mjaal (IRE)**[27] 6779 2-8-9 0 RaulDaSilva(3) 12 42
(John Weymes) *chsd ldr tl rdn 3f out: wknd over 1f out* **250/1**
00 **9** 9 **Honey Haven (IRE)**[14] 7143 2-8-12 0 RobbieFitzpatrick 1 22
(Mark Brisbourne) *a in rr: bhd fnl 3f* **100/1**
00 **10** 1/2 **Greenfordgirl (IRE)**[5] 7357 2-8-12 0 ChrisCatlin 3 21
(John Weymes) *s.i.s: a in rr* **250/1**
1m 51.21s (0.71) **Going Correction** -0.125s/f (Stan) 10 Ran SP% **123.0**
Speed ratings (Par 93): **91,90,90,86,85 82,81,78,70,70**
Tote Swingers 1&2 £1.10, 2&3 £2.30, 1&3 £3.00 CSF £3.64 TOTE £1.70: £1.10, £1.10, £2.50; EX 4.70 Trifecta £11.10 Pool: £1,683.02 - 113.02 winning tickets..
Owner Fung Lok Li **Bred** Eamon D Delany **Trained** Newmarket, Suffolk

FOCUS
Little depth to this maiden but the right horses dominated with the front three in the betting coming nicely clear. The trio came close together in the straight but there wasn't enough interference for it to have had any significant effect on the outcome. The first three were clear but the form is rated slightly negatively with the winner to his mark and the second just below.

NOTEBOOK
Glory City(IRE) saw this out strongest to edge back ahead close home having been headed inside the final furlong. His sire's progeny often prove strong stayers so it's no surprise he kept on strongly in the closing stages, and he looks the type to do well in middle-distance handicaps next term. (op 13-8 tchd 7-4)
Sicur edged ahead in the final furlong and looked the most likely winner, but his momentum petered out a touch and he edged right in the closing stages. He was only beaten a neck, though, and has clearly run right up to form, so that first success shouldn't be long in coming. Official explanation: jockey said colt hung right closing stages (tchd 5-4 in places)
King Muro ◆, for whom there was some interesting market support, had finished down the field in two stronger maidens than this, and he ran easily his best race so far, sticking on well in between the big two and finishing 5l clear of the rest. He also looks like a maiden winner in waiting and there is plenty in his pedigree that suggests he'll do better still over middle distances next year. (op 12-1 tchd 8-1)
Mandy The Nag(USA) showed some promisebut was no match for the front three, although she looks to have enough ability to make her mark in low-grade events down the line. (op 9-1)

7461 32RED CASINO H'CAP — 1m 1f 103y(P)
6:10 (6:11) (Class 4) (0-85,85) 3-Y-0+ £4,204 (£1,251; £625; £312) Stalls Low

Form RPR
341 **1** **Afraah (USA)**[39] 6457 3-8-13 78 DaneO'Neill 8 88
(Roger Varian) *hld up in tch: rdn and edgd lft over 1f out: styd on u.p to ld nr fin* **7/1**
1021 **2** hd **Saharia (IRE)**[31] 6692 5-9-2 77 (v) ShaneKelly 4 86
(Michael Attwater) *hld up: hdwy over 2f out: shkn up to ld wl ins fnl f: rdn and hdd nr fin* **6/1**[3]
0566 **3** 1 1/4 **Spanish Plume**[20] 6976 4-8-9 75 JackDuern(5) 13 81
(Reg Hollinshead) *hmpd s: hld up: hdwy over 3f out: led over 2f out: rdn over 1f out: hdd and unable qck wl ins fnl f* **28/1**
6610 **4** 1 **Patriotic (IRE)**[41] 6381 4-9-4 82 RaulDaSilva(3) 6 86
(Chris Dwyer) *chsd ldrs: rdn over 3f out: styd on u.p* **10/1**
3515 **5** nk **I Confess**[19] 7004 7-8-9 77 (b) JordanNason(7) 10 81
(Geoffrey Harker) *a.p: pushed along and edgd lft wl over 2f out: sn ev ch: styd on* **40/1**
2000 **6** 3 **Knowe Head (NZ)**[31] 6692 5-8-13 74 (p) LiamJones 5 71
(James Unett) *prom: rdn over 2f out: styd on same pce fnl f* **16/1**
4600 **7** 1/2 **Thunderstruck**[62] 5752 7-9-5 80 (p) IanMongan 9 76
(Scott Dixon) *s.s: hld up: hdwy u.p over 1f out: nvr nrr* **25/1**
0340 **8** nk **Final Drive (IRE)**[36] 6538 6-9-5 80 (p) LiamKeniry 7 76
(John Butler) *hld up: rdn over 2f out: n.d* **20/1**
1420 **9** 1 1/2 **Night And Dance (IRE)**[79] 5129 4-9-10 85 AdamKirby 2 78+
(Clive Cox) *chsd ldrs: hmpd and lost pl over 2f out: nt rcvr* **5/1**[2]
1400 **10** 1 1/2 **Standpoint**[20] 6987 6-9-3 78 LukeMorris 12 67
(Conor Dore) *hmpd s: hld up: rdn over 2f out: nvr on terms* **25/1**
1320 **11** 22 **Kung Hei Fat Choy (USA)**[55] 5942 3-8-12 77 (b) JimCrowley 11 20
(James Given) *wnt rt s: sn chsng ldr: led over 7f out: rdn and hdd over 2f out: sn wknd* **7/1**
0333 **12** 1 1/2 **Lady Macduff (IRE)**[17] 7064 3-9-5 84 NeilCallan 1 24
(Mark Johnston) *chsd ldr tl rdn 3f out: wknd wl over 1f out* **5/1**[2]
6444 **13** 17 **Shestheman**[12] 7194 3-8-12 77 TedDurcan 3 +
(David Lanigan) *mid-div: pushed along and hmpd over 3f out: hmpd again wl over 2f out: sn bhd* **7/2**[1]
1m 59.17s (-2.53) **Going Correction** -0.125s/f (Stan)
WFA 3 from 4yo+ 4lb 13 Ran SP% **128.2**
Speed ratings (Par 105): **106,105,104,103,103 100,100,100,98,97 77,76,61**
Tote Swingers 1&2 £5.00, 2&3 £51.30, 1&3 £42.00 CSF £49.18 CT £1152.73 TOTE £10.70: £2.80, £2.40, £10.90; EX 34.60 Trifecta £713.80 Part won. Pool: £951.76 - 0.10 winning tickets..
Owner Hamdan Al Maktoum **Bred** Shadwell Farm LLC **Trained** Newmarket, Suffolk
■ Stewards' Enquiry : Jack Duern two-day ban: used whip above permitted level arm over shoulder height (Nov 14-15)

FOCUS
A strongly run event in which the finish was dominated by horses who were held up off the pace, with the early leaders dropping right away. The form is rated around the runner-up.
Night And Dance(IRE) Official explanation: jockey said filly was hampered in running
Kung Hei Fat Choy(USA) Official explanation: jockey said gelding ran too free
Shestheman Official explanation: jockey said filly was hampered on final bend

7462 32RED SUPPORTING BRITISH RACING NURSERY (DIV I) — 5f 216y(P)
6:40 (6:40) (Class 5) (0-75,75) 2-Y-0 £2,264 (£673; £336; £168) Stalls Low

Form RPR
040 **1** **Dream Ally (IRE)**[46] 6203 2-9-1 69 PhillipMakin 9 72
(Jedd O'Keeffe) *hld up: hdwy over 2f out: rdn and edgd lft ins fnl f: r.o to ld nr fin* **8/1**
0501 **2** nk **Work Ethic (IRE)**[11] 7219 2-9-4 72 SebSanders 3 74
(Gerard Butler) *chsd ldrs: led over 1f out: sn rdn: edgd lft ins fnl f: hdd nr fin* **3/1**[1]
0456 **3** nse **Romanoff (IRE)**[13] 7173 2-8-4 58 KirstyMilczarek 1 60+
(Luca Cumani) *hld up: nt clr run over 2f out: hdwy over 1f out: rdn ins fnl f: r.o* **9/2**[3]
0425 **4** 2 3/4 **Attenshun (IRE)**[13] 7176 2-9-5 73 (v) RichardKingscote 4 67
(Tom Dascombe) *led 5f out: hdd 1/2-way: rdn and ev ch over 1f out: no ex ins fnl f* **8/1**
6205 **5** 1/2 **Cuisine (IRE)**[11] 7220 2-9-2 70 (b) DavidProbert 7 62
(Andrew Balding) *s.i.s: hld up: hdwy over 2f out: rdn over 1f out: styd on same pce ins fnl f* **4/1**[2]
0602 **6** 1 1/2 **Pearl Noir**[11] 7219 2-8-11 65 IanMongan 10 53
(Scott Dixon) *led 1f: chsd ldr tl led again 1/2-way: rdn and hdd over 1f out: no ex ins fnl f* **11/2**
000 **7** 6 **Fat Bottom Girl**[42] 6335 2-7-13 53 ow1 NickyMackay 6 23
(Michael Easterby) *prom: rdn over 1f out: wknd fnl f* **50/1**
16 **8** 2 3/4 **Time For Lambrini (IRE)**[11] 7220 2-9-7 75 AmyRyan 2 36
(Lisa Williamson) *chsd ldrs: rdn 1/2-way: wknd over 1f out* **20/1**
044 **9** 1/2 **Vergality Ridge (IRE)**[14] 7143 2-9-0 68 LukeMorris 8 28
(Ronald Harris) *s.s: a in rr: wknd wl over 1f out* **10/1**
1m 14.58s (-0.42) **Going Correction** -0.125s/f (Stan) 9 Ran SP% **116.6**
Speed ratings (Par 95): **97,96,96,92,92 90,82,78,77**
Tote Swingers 1&2 £6.40, 2&3 £7.00, 1&3 £12.80 CSF £32.60 CT £124.22 TOTE £10.10: £2.40, £1.20, £1.90; EX 44.60 Trifecta £685.50 Pool: £914.09 - 1.00 winning ticket..
Owner Caron & Paul Chapman **Bred** Noel & Roger O'Callaghan **Trained** Middleham Moor, N Yorks

FOCUS
A sound pace to this nusery and the form looks solid, if just fair, for the grade.

NOTEBOOK
Dream Ally(IRE) didn't have an ideal trip out wide and gave away ground when he made headway around the outside, but he stuck to his task in determined style to edge ahead in the closing stages and get off the mark. Given the way things panned out, he looks value for a bit more than the winning margin and is one to keep on the right side of, even off a slightly higher mark. (tchd 15-2)
Work Ethic(IRE) had a dream trip and travelled strongly just behind the pace before the gap opened perfectly early in the straight. He ran well but doesn't look as progressive as the winner. (op 10-3 tchd 7-2)
Romanoff(IRE) ◆ posted an eyecatching run, being held up on the inside before being pulled out to make a challenge. However, he had to switch back to the inside to get the gap and just had too much ground to make up. This trip was always likely to prove too sharp for him but he's one to be interested in over 7f. Official explanation: jockey said colt was denied a clear run (op 11-2 tchd 6-1)
Attenshun(IRE) helped to set a sound gallop but was a sitting duck early in the straight. He looks speedy enough to be worth another try at the minimum trip, especially on Polytrack. (tchd 7-1)

7463 32RED SUPPORTING BRITISH RACING NURSERY (DIV II) — 5f 216y(P)
7:10 (7:10) (Class 5) (0-75,74) 2-Y-0 £2,264 (£673; £336; £168) Stalls Low

Form RPR
3621 **1** **Blazing Knight (IRE)**[33] 6611 2-9-2 69 JimCrowley 8 76+
(Ralph Beckett) *sn pushed along towards rr: hdwy over 2f out: led over 1f out: rdn and edgd lft ins fnl f: r.o* **7/4**[1]
0066 **2** 1 3/4 **My Sweet Lord**[62] 5749 2-7-13 52 JamieMackay 10 53+
(Mark Usher) *s.s: hdwy over 1f out: rdn to chse wnr and hung lft ins fnl f: no ex towards fin* **20/1**
0144 **3** 2 1/4 **Ayasha**[36] 6541 2-9-0 67 TomEaves 5 65
(Bryan Smart) *hld up in tch: racd keenly: nt clr run over 1f out: r.o to go 3rd post* **7/1**[3]
0530 **4** hd **Little Miss Zuri (IRE)**[84] 4934 2-7-13 52 oh4 ow1 NickyMackay 1 46
(Sylvester Kirk) *chsd ldrs: rdn over 1f out: styd on* **40/1**
041 **5** nse **Grace Hull**[24] 6889 2-9-2 69 FergusSweeney 3 63
(J S Moore) *chsd ldrs: rdn and ev ch over 1f out: no ex ins fnl f* **12/1**
0202 **6** 2 3/4 **Cymeriad**[17] 7056 2-8-3 56 LukeMorris 2 42
(Michael Easterby) *chsd ldr tl rdn over 1f out: wknd ins fnl f* **10/1**
5230 **7** 1 1/4 **Multisure**[48] 6130 2-8-12 65 PhillipMakin 4 47
(Richard Fahey) *chsd ldrs: rdn over 2f out: wknd fnl f* **20/1**
5223 **8** 3 1/2 **Layla's Oasis**[21] 6954 2-9-3 70 JamieSpencer 9 41
(Jamie Osborne) *led: rdn and hdd over 1f out: sn wknd* **11/4**[2]
1005 **9** 11 **My Boy Bill**[10] 7241 2-8-12 72 DavidSimmonson(7) 6 10
(Michael Easterby) *s.i.s: outpcd* **9/1**
1m 15.24s (0.24) **Going Correction** -0.125s/f (Stan) 9 Ran SP% **114.3**
Speed ratings (Par 95): **93,90,87,87,87 83,82,77,62**
Tote Swingers 1&2 £11.50, 2&3 £28.50, 1&3 £3.70 CSF £41.97 CT £202.62 TOTE £2.70: £1.30, £3.80, £2.10; EX 37.90 Trifecta £213.20 Pool: £961.11 - 3.38 winning tickets..
Owner Circuit Racing **Bred** Tally-Ho Stud **Trained** Kimpton, Hants

FOCUS
A strong pace helped set things up for horses coming from behind. The runner-up sets the level.

NOTEBOOK
Blazing Knight(IRE) ◆, for whom there was plenty of market support, travelled smoothly before picking up in taking style to sweep by the field and score in decisive style. Raised 3lb for his win over C&D last month, he looks progressive colt and should have no problem with an extra furlong. He looks up to completing the hat-trick. (op 9-4 tchd 5-2)
My Sweet Lord's performance merits respect because he looked to have no chance after blowing the start. He came from a long way back to chase the winner up the straight and, although he was making no inroads in the final half furlong, he had done a lot of running to get into that position. He looks to be getting the hang of things. (tchd 22-1)
Ayasha travelled nicely, but the winner had flown by the time she got going. She ran on in the closing stages and showed enough to suggest she can win races on this surface. (op 15-2 tchd 8-1)
Layla's Oasis was the biggest disappointment, as having set too strong a pace she dropped away at the business end. (op 2-1)
My Boy Bill Official explanation: jockey said gelding would not face the kickback

7464 £32 BONUS AT 32RED.COM H'CAP — 5f 216y(P)
7:40 (7:40) (Class 4) (0-80,80) 3-Y-0+ £4,204 (£1,251; £625; £312) Stalls Low

Form RPR
3032 **1** **Beat The Bell**[7] 7308 7-8-10 69 (p) MartinDwyer 2 80
(Jamie Osborne) *chsd ldrs: rdn to ld over 1f out: r.o* **4/1**[2]
3100 **2** 2 **Mount Hollow**[8] 7295 7-9-2 80 (p) JackDuern(5) 4 85
(Reg Hollinshead) *a.p: shkn up over 1f out: styd on* **16/1**
1000 **3** 1/2 **Taffe**[22] 6938 3-9-4 78 JimCrowley 9 81
(James Given) *chsd ldrs: rdn over 1f out: r.o* **6/1**
0343 **4** 1/2 **Hopes N Dreams (IRE)**[14] 7145 4-9-6 79 AmyRyan 8 81
(Kevin Ryan) *chsd ldrs: rdn over 1f out: kpt on* **11/4**[1]
3000 **5** nse **Diman Waters (IRE)**[14] 7145 5-8-11 70 (b) ShaneKelly 1 72
(Eric Alston) *hld up: hdwy over 1f out: sn rdn: styd on* **25/1**
5504 **6** hd **Fathsta (IRE)**[8] 7297 7-9-6 79 TedDurcan 10 80
(Ian Williams) *s.i.s: hld up: rdn over 1f out: r.o ins fnl f: nrst fin* **10/1**
1000 **7** 3/4 **Italian Tom (IRE)**[31] 6665 5-9-7 80 LukeMorris 6 79
(Ronald Harris) *hld up: rdn over 2f out: r.o ins fnl f: nt rch ldrs* **14/1**
5506 **8** hd **Cyflymder (IRE)**[10] 7247 6-8-12 71 KirstyMilczarek 5 69
(David C Griffiths) *chsd ldrs: rdn over 2f out: no ex ins fnl f* **16/1**
0000 **9** 1 1/2 **Parisian Pyramid (IRE)**[15] 7113 6-9-2 75 JamieSpencer 7 68
(Ian Williams) *led: rdn and hdd over 1f out: wknd ins fnl f* **11/2**[3]
5052 **10** 1/2 **Bandstand**[45] 6260 6-9-6 79 TomEaves 12 71
(Bryan Smart) *hld up: plld hrd: rdn over 1f out: nvr on terms* **9/1**
1001 **11** 2 1/2 **Lucky Dan (IRE)**[12] 7202 6-9-4 77 PhillipMakin 3 61
(Paul Green) *hld up: rdn over 1f out: n.d* **11/1**
0-00 **12** 3 1/2 **Secret Millionaire (IRE)**[18] 7019 5-9-0 78 GeorgeDowning(5) 11 50
(Tony Carroll) *s.i.s: a in rr* **50/1**
1m 13.69s (-1.31) **Going Correction** -0.125s/f (Stan)
WFA 3 from 4yo+ 1lb 12 Ran SP% **128.0**
Speed ratings (Par 105): **103,100,99,99,98 98,97,97,95,94 91,86**
Tote Swingers 1&2 £14.10, 2&3 £27.20, 1&3 £5.90 CSF £72.73 CT £405.63 TOTE £3.60: £2.10, £6.10, £2.30; EX 66.90 TRIFECTA Not won..
Owner Leslie Marshall **Bred** D J P Turner **Trained** Upper Lambourn, Berks

FOCUS
A reasonable race for the grade and won with some authority. The time was decent and this is sound if ordinary form.
Lucky Dan(IRE) Official explanation: jockey said gelding ran too freely

7465 32REDBET.COM H'CAP 5f 216y(P)
8:10 (8:11) (Class 6) (0-52,52) 3-Y-O+ **£1,704** (£503; £251) Stalls Low

Form RPR
653 **1** **Flamborough Breeze**[77] 5212 3-9-4 52........................(t) TedDurcan 5 63
(Ed Vaughan) *s.i.s: sn pushed along in rr: rdn over 1f out: str run ins fnl f to ld post* **9/1**[3]
0632 **2** *nk* **Lucky Mark (IRE)**[5] 7361 3-9-4 52........................ StevieDonohoe 11 62+
(Garry Moss) *s.i.s: rcvrd to ld 5f out: rdn ins fnl f: hdd post* **6/4**[1]
005 **3** *3/4* **Venetias Dream (IRE)**[78] 5166 3-9-2 50........................(t) AdamKirby 2 58+
(Stuart Williams) *broke wl: sn lost pl: rdn over 1f out: nt clr run and r.o ins fnl f: nrst fin* **13/2**[2]
0-00 **4** *nk* **Kaylee**[69] 6479 3-9-2 50........................ GeorgeBaker 1 57
(Gary Moore) *hld up in tch: hmpd over 4f out: rdn over 1f out: r.o* **14/1**
0030 **5** *1 3/4* **Media Jury**[5] 7362 5-8-10 50........................(v) KevinLundie[(7)] 12 51
(John Wainwright) *chsd ldrs: rdn over 2f out: styd on same pce fnl f* **25/1**
5401 **6** *1* **Yungaburra (IRE)**[47] 6179 8-9-4 51........................(tp) KirstyMilczarek 6 49
(David C Griffiths) *chsd ldrs: rdn over 1f out: no ex fnl f* **10/1**
0060 **7** *1 1/4* **Athaakeel (IRE)**[11] 7224 6-9-5 52........................ LukeMorris 10 46
(Ronald Harris) *chsd ldrs: rdn over 1f out: wknd ins fnl f* **20/1**
0463 **8** *2 1/4* **Rightcar**[38] 6496 5-9-4 51........................ RobbieFitzpatrick 4 38
(Peter Grayson) *s.i.s: hmpd over 2f out: nvr nrr* **12/1**
-400 **9** *1 1/4* **Widow Flower (IRE)**[14] 7146 3-9-2 50........................ JamieSpencer 7 33
(Michael Bell) *prom: rdn over 2f out: wknd fnl f* **14/1**
1020 **10** *nk* **Avonlini**[22] 6937 6-9-4 51........................ TomEaves 8 33
(Brian Baugh) *led 1f: chsd ldr tl rdn over 2f out: wknd fnl f* **10/1**
-604 **11** *2 1/2* **Stans Deelyte**[10] 7253 3-8-11 52........................ ShirleyTeasdale[(7)] 9 26
(Lisa Williamson) *s.i.s: rdn 1/2-way: a in rr* **25/1**
3245 **P** **Green Mountain (IRE)**[17] 7061 3-9-2 50........................(vt) ShaneKelly 3
(Philip McBride) *mid-div tl p.u and dismntd over 2f out* **16/1**

1m 15.18s (0.18) **Going Correction** -0.125s/f (Stan)
WFA 3 from 5yo+ 1lb **12 Ran SP% 120.9**
Speed ratings (Par 101): **93,92,91,91,88 87,85,82,81,80 77,**
Tote Swingers 1&2 £6.10, 2&3 £3.10, 1&3 £8.60 CSF £22.62 CT £99.41 TOTE £11.30: £2.00, £1.10, £2.50; EX 33.50 Trifecta £325.60 Pool: £620.82 - 1.43 winning tickets..
Owner A M Pickering **Bred** Windymains Farm Ltd **Trained** Newmarket, Suffolk

FOCUS
A weak handicap but an exciting finish and fair form for the grade.
Rightcar Official explanation: jockey said gelding hung right-handed
Green Mountain(IRE) Official explanation: jockey said filly lost its action but returned sound
T/Plt: £15.00 to a £1 stake. Pool: £69,039.66 - 3,340.71 winning tickets. T/Qpdt: £7.20 to a £1 stake. Pool: £8,882.13 - 907.11 winning tickets. CR

7311 YARMOUTH (L-H)
Tuesday, October 30

OFFICIAL GOING: Heavy (5.3)
Wind: medium, across Weather: dry and bright

7466 IRISH STALLION FARMS E B F MAIDEN STKS 7f 3y
1:10 (1:12) (Class 5) 2-Y-O **£2,911** (£866; £432; £216) **Stalls** Centre

Form RPR
0 **1** **Teophilip (IRE)**[13] 7167 2-9-3 0........................(t) MartinHarley 5 83+
(Marco Botti) *w ldr tl led over 5f out: mde rest: readily drew clr and in command fr over 1f out: v easily* **4/1**[3]
2 *6* **Charter (IRE)** 2-9-3 0........................ HayleyTurner 1 68+
(Michael Bell) *in tch: rdn over 2f out: chsd clr wnr over 1f out: kpt on for clr 2nd but no ch w wnr* **5/1**
0 **3** *3 1/2* **Just Wondering (IRE)**[21] 6960 2-8-9 0........................ AshleyMorgan[(3)] 4 54
(Ed Dunlop) *chsd ldrs: rdn and chsd clr wnr ent fnl 2f: sn outpcd and btn: lost 2nd over 1f out: wl btn after* **10/3**[2]
06 **4** *1/2* **Deficit (IRE)**[14] 7130 2-9-3 0........................ EddieAhern 6 58
(Michael Bell) *in tch in rr: rdn and effrt over 2f out: no imp tl styd on past btn horses 1f out: no ch w wnr* **3/1**[1]
00 **5** *6* **Hidden Asset**[81] 5040 2-9-3 0........................ TomQueally 3 43
(Michael Appleby) *led tl over 5f out: chsd wnr tl ent fnl 2f: sn wknd* **7/1**
6 *1* **Sakash** 2-9-3 0........................ DarryllHolland 7 40
(J R Jenkins) *rn green thrght: in tch: rdn and outpcd over 2f out: edgd lft and wknd over 1f out* **15/2**
7 *16* **I Need A Dollar** 2-9-3 0........................ JimmyQuinn 2
(J R Jenkins) *a bhd: lost tch over 2f out: t.o* **33/1**

1m 33.09s (6.49) **Going Correction** +0.875s/f (Soft) **7 Ran SP% 112.0**
Speed ratings (Par 95): **97,90,86,85,78 77,59**
Tote Swingers 1&2 £4.40, 2&3 £2.60, 1&3 £3.40 CSF £23.02 TOTE £5.40: £2.70, £1.10; EX 26.30.
Owner Giuliano Manfredini **Bred** Mount Coote Stud, Richard Pegum & M Bell Racing **Trained** Newmarket, Suffolk

FOCUS
Bottom bend moved out 2m. A modest juvenile maiden, in terms of prior form, in which they went a very steady gallop on ground officially described a heavy. The jockeys later reported that the ground was riding as proper, heavy ground. The winner's effort has been taken at face value.

NOTEBOOK
Teophilip(IRE) cost £26,000 as a yearling and is a half-brother to six winners, including 5f-6f Listed winner One Putra and decent 1m2f winner Rondelet, out of a well-related French 6f 2yo winner. He showed definite ability, despite running green, on his debut over this 7f trip at Lingfield on Polytrack this month. He eased into an uncontested lead after about 2f here and never saw another rival, showing useful accleration just inside the 2f marker to stretch clear of his rivals. He looks a decent miling prospect for next term, and relished this ground. (op 13-2 tchd 7-1)
Charter(IRE), who cost 64,000euros as a yearing and is a half-brother to very useful dual 7f turf/Polytrack winner Astonishment, reportedly looked the pick of these in the paddock. He came through from midfield into a never-nearer and well-beaten second. He can build on this display next time. (op 7-2)
Just Wondering(IRE) has failed to build on a modest Leicester debut this month in any significant manner. (op 3-1 tchd 11-4)
Deficit(IRE) made modest late gains into a never-nearer fourth. He will need at least 1m2f next year. (op 7-2 tchd 11-4)

7467 BURLINGTON PALM HOTEL NURSERY 7f 3y
1:40 (1:40) (Class 5) (0-75,70) 2-Y-O **£2,264** (£673; £336; £168) **Stalls** Centre

Form RPR
0606 **1** **Strong Conviction**[34] 6571 2-9-3 66........................ SilvestreDeSousa 6 70
(Mick Channon) *hld up in tch: rdn and effrt to chal over 1f out: led 1f out: edgd lft but styd on u.p fnl f* **3/1**[3]
6554 **2** *1 1/2* **Red Eclipse (IRE)**[17] 7060 2-8-7 56........................ AndreaAtzeni 4 56
(Alan Bailey) *led: hdd over 2f out: drvn and ev ch over 1f out: no ex and one pce fnl 100yds* **2/1**[1]
003 **3** *2 3/4* **Woza Moya (USA)**[13] 7165 2-9-7 70........................ NickyMackay 5 64
(Gay Kelleway) *w ldr: led over 2f out: sn rdn and edgd lft: hdd and slily outpcd whn short of room wl over 1f out: one pce after* **4/1**
1005 **4** *1 1/2* **Warrant Officer**[19] 7008 2-8-13 62........................ MartinHarley 1 52
(Mick Channon) *chsd ldrs: rdn and ev ch over 1f out: wknd ins fnl f* **9/4**[2]

1m 33.84s (7.24) **Going Correction** +0.875s/f (Soft) **4 Ran SP% 109.1**
Speed ratings (Par 95): **93,91,88,86**
Tote Swinger 3&6 £3.20 CSF £9.29 TOTE £4.70; EX 6.00.
Owner Materna, Dunleavy, Barrett **Bred** M Barrett **Trained** West Ilsley, Berks

FOCUS
A fair nursery in which they went a steady gallop on very testing ground. Seemingly straightforward form.

NOTEBOOK
Strong Conviction produced peak form on the second of his nine starts when staying on well into second behind Sir Prancealot over a furlong shorter at Bath in May. He returned to form here, travelling well before coming through from last to first well inside the 2f marker and winning decisively. He should get at least 1m next term in fair handicaps. (op 7-2 tchd 11-4)
Red Eclipse(IRE), who reportedly looked well beforehand, attempted to make all at her own tempo and rallied when headed over 2f out, but had to give best to the winner inside the final furlong. She may pick up a moderate handicap off a mark in the mid-50s at some stage. (op 9-4)
Woza Moya(USA) took up the baton over 2f out, but edged to his left when asked to go on and proved one-paced thereafter. (op 3-1 tchd 5-1)
Warrant Officer weakened disappointingly inside the final furlong. (tchd 5-2)

7468 BRITISH STALLION STUDS SUPPORTING BRITISH RACING E B F MAIDEN STKS 1m 3y
2:10 (2:11) (Class 5) 2-Y-O **£2,911** (£866; £432; £216) **Stalls** Centre

Form RPR
1 **Mutashaded (USA)** 2-9-3 0........................ AndreaAtzeni 4 75+
(Roger Varian) *s.i.s and rn green early: in tch in rr: smooth hdwy 2f out: pushed along to ld over 1f out: in command whn pressed and fnd ex under hands and heels riding to assert fnl 75yds: comf* **9/4**[2]
52 **2** *1 1/4* **High Troja (IRE)**[25] 6845 2-9-3 0........................ EddieAhern 3 70
(Ed Dunlop) *led: rdn and hdd over 1f out: looked hld tl rallied u.p and pressed wnr ins fnl f: sn brushed aside and one pce towards fin* **2/1**[1]
3 **3** *2 3/4* **Gods Gift (IRE)**[14] 7130 2-9-3 0........................ TomQueally 5 64
(Rae Guest) *t.k.h: trckd ldrs: rdn and effrt to press ldrs over 1f out: btn 1f out and plugged on same pce fnl f* **5/2**[3]
4 *4 1/2* **Himalayan Peak** 2-8-10 0........................ RyanTate[(7)] 1 54
(James Eustace) *in tch: rdn and pressed ldrs 2f out: btn ent fnl f: wknd* **7/1**
06 **5** *1* **Planchette**[39] 6437 2-8-12 0........................ BrettDoyle 2 47
(Jane Chapple-Hyam) *t.k.h: chsd ldr tl over 1f out: sn drvn and no ex: wknd fnl f* **25/1**

1m 49.89s (9.29) **Going Correction** +0.875s/f (Soft) **5 Ran SP% 109.0**
Speed ratings (Par 95): **88,86,84,79,78**
CSF £7.00 TOTE £3.30: £1.60, £1.10; EX 7.10.
Owner Hamdan Al Maktoum **Bred** Shadwell Farm LLC **Trained** Newmarket, Suffolk

FOCUS
A modest juvenile maiden, in terms of prior form, in which they went a sensible gallop on the heavy ground. The winner looks capable of better than the bare form.

NOTEBOOK
Mutashaded(USA), first foal of Sortita, useful over 1m1f/1m2f and a sister to three Group 1 winners including German Derby winner Samum, holds a Derby entry. He was reportedly carrying plenty of condition on this debut and was held up in the last place after a slow start, but came through to win nicely after quickening into the lead about 1f out. He looks a decent middle-distance prospect for next term. (op 5-1 tchd 11-2)
High Troja(IRE), who reportedly looked well in the paddock, improved to finish a respectable second over 1f shorter here on similar ground on his second start this month. He improved his level of form over this extra furlong and looks capable of winning a similar contest. He is a fair middle-distance handicapper in the making in any case. (op 5-4)
Gods Gift(IRE) finished a never-nearer third of eight over this trip on soft ground at Leicester on his debut this month. He ran to a similar level on this occasion. (tchd 2-1)
Himalayan Peak, a half-brother to Group 3 1m4f winner Orcadian, performed moderately on this debut and looks more of a longer term project. (tchd 13-2 and 8-1)

7469 TRAFALGAR RESTAURANT AT GREAT YARMOUTH RACECOURSE H'CAP 1m 3y
2:40 (2:40) (Class 5) (0-70,67) 3-Y-O+ **£2,264** (£673; £336; £168) **Stalls** Centre

Form RPR
613 **1** **Ever Fortune (USA)**[15] 7115 3-9-4 67........................ TomQueally 2 78+
(Rae Guest) *hld up in last trio: pushed along and hdwy whn nt clr run ent fnl 2f: swtchd rt and hdwy nrest stands' rail over 1f out: pushed into ld ins fnl f: sn in command: pushed out* **6/1**
0035 **2** *2* **The New Black (IRE)**[7] 7314 3-8-4 56........................(e) DeclanCannon[(3)] 6 62
(Gay Kelleway) *racd in last trio: rdn and hdwy to ld 2f out: hdd and one pce ins fnl f* **15/2**
3051 **3** *5* **Valley Queen**[15] 7115 3-9-4 67........................ HayleyTurner 8 62
(Mark Usher) *in tch: rdn and effrt over 2f out: drvn and ev ch 2f out: no ex and btn 1f out: wknd ins fnl f* **9/2**[3]
000 **4** *4 1/2* **Focail Eile**[10] 7250 7-8-12 58........................ BrettDoyle 7 42
(John Ryan) *in tch: pressed ldrs and drvn 2f out: btn over 1f out: wknd fnl f* **4/1**[2]
0R/0 **5** *3/4* **Glan Lady (IRE)**[7] 7314 6-8-7 53 oh8........................ DominicFox 5 35
(Michael Appleby) *chsd ldr: rdn and led jst over 2f out: sn hdd and btn: wknd over 1f out* **40/1**
5221 **6** *7* **Balti's Sister (IRE)**[39] 6456 3-8-11 65........................ NatashaEaton[(5)] 4 31
(Terry Clement) *hood removed late and v.s.a: in rr: hdwy and chsd ldrs u.p 2f out: wknd over 1f out: fdd fnl f* **9/2**[3]
61 **7** *12* **Ishiamiracle**[7] 7318 3-9-2 65 6ex........................(p) SilvestreDeSousa 3
(Phil McEntee) *led: rdn and hdd jst over 2f out: sn btn: bhd and virtually p.u fr over 1f out: t.o* **10/3**[1]

-326 8 46 **Frosty Friday**[197] 1423 4-9-1 **61** .... DarryllHolland 1
(J R Jenkins) *in tch tl 1/2-way: sn dropped out: t.o and virtually p.u fnl 2f* **16/1**

1m 46.85s (6.25) **Going Correction** +0.875s/f (Soft)
WFA 3 from 4yo+ 3lb **8** Ran SP% **113.8**
Speed ratings (Par 103): **103,101,96,91,90 83,71,25**
Tote Swingers 1&2 £8.30, 2&3 £3.80, 1&3 £6.10 CSF £49.31 CT £221.77 TOTE £7.40: £3.80, £3.30, £1.30; EX 42.10.
Owner Fung Lok Li **Bred** Lantern Hill Farm Llc **Trained** Newmarket, Suffolk

FOCUS
A modest handicap for 3yos and up in which they went an honest gallop in the attritional conditions. The form is rated around the runner-up.
Balti's Sister(IRE) Official explanation: jockey said filly was slowly away as blindfold was tucked in tightly and difficult to remove
Ishiamiracle Official explanation: trainer had no explanation for the poor form shown

7470 GREAT YARMOUTH TOURIST AUTHORITY H'CAP 1m 1f
3:10 (3:12) (Class 6) (0-60,64) 3-Y-O £1,617 (£481; £240; £120) **Stalls** Low

Form RPR
5121 1 **Boonga Roogeta**[9] 7270 3-9-6 **64** 6ex .... RosieJessop(5) 1 77+
(Peter Charalambous) *mde all: sn clr: rdn and kpt on fr 2f out: tiring ins fnl f but a doing enough: unchal* **7/2**[1]

5022 2 1 1/2 **Elsie Bay**[9] 7270 3-9-1 **59** .... RachealKneller(5) 7 66
(Mark Usher) *chsd ldrs: chsd clr wnr 5f out: no imp tl kpt on ins fnl f: nvr seriously threatened wnr* **15/2**

3062 3 1 1/2 **Inffiraaj (IRE)**[18] 7015 3-8-12 **51** .... MartinHarley 12 55
(Mick Channon) *hld up off the pce in midfield: effrt and wnt modest 4th 2f out: kpt on steadily and wnt 3rd ins fnl f: no threat to wnr* **6/1**[3]

5053 4 2 1/4 **Blackamoor Harry**[15] 7106 3-8-2 **46** oh1 .... NatashaEaton(5) 9 45
(Richard Ford) *squeezed for room leaving stalls: hld up off pce towards rr: hdwy to go modest 3rd 2f out: plugged on but no threat to wnr: lost 3rd ins fnl f* **16/1**

6636 5 3 1/2 **Angel Cake (IRE)**[7] 7314 3-8-7 **46** oh1 .... DominicFox 13 37
(Michael Appleby) *racd off the pce in midfield: rdn and effrt over 2f out: styd on same pce and no imp after* **11/2**[2]

0604 6 2 3/4 **Connishka**[26] 6810 3-8-8 **47** .... AndreaAtzeni 4 32
(Alan Bailey) *racd off the pce in midfield: rdn and no prog 3f out: plugged on but n.d* **25/1**

0300 7 1 **My Manekineko**[26] 6810 3-9-4 **57** .... DarryllHolland 3 40
(J R Jenkins) *hld up off the pce towards rr: rdn and sme hdwy over 2f out: styd on: nvr trbld ldrs* **25/1**

3343 8 3/4 **Love Grows Wild (USA)**[14] 7148 3-8-13 **52** .... HayleyTurner 11 33
(Michael Bell) *chsd ldrs: rdn and no prog 3f out: btn 2f out: sn wknd* **6/1**[3]

0500 9 2 1/2 **Hawaiian Storm**[27] 6785 3-9-4 **60** .... MichaelMetcalfe(3) 2 36
(Mrs K Burke) *hld up off the pce towards rr: rdn and sme hdwy over 2f out: no hdwy fnl 2f: nvr trbld ldrs* **28/1**

0505 10 5 **Nurse Dominatrix (IRE)**[7] 7317 3-8-10 **49** .... KellyHarrison 5 14
(Richard Guest) *t.k.h: hld up off the pce in rr: rdn and no hdwy 3f out: n.d* **20/1**

4345 11 3 3/4 **Yojojo (IRE)**[65] 5623 3-9-5 **58** .... EddieAhern 6 15
(Gay Kelleway) *chsd wnr tl 5f out: rdn and btn 3f out: steadily lost pl: bhd fnl f* **12/1**

0300 12 1 1/2 **Cappielow Park**[15] 7117 3-9-2 **55** .... SilvestreDeSousa 14 8
(Fleur Hawes) *stdd and swtchd lft after s: a bhd: n.d* **40/1**

0006 13 1/2 **Attain**[41] 6365 3-9-5 **58** ....(b) TomQueally 10 10
(Julia Feilden) *hld up off the pce in midfield: rdn and no real prog 3f out: n.d* **12/1**

0625 14 23 **Tresabella**[26] 6813 3-8-7 **49** ....(b) RyanPowell(3) 8
(Michael Appleby) *rdn along leaving stalls: racd off the pce in midfield: hdwy 1/2-way: btn 3f out: sn wknd: t.o fnl f* **33/1**

2m 3.4s (7.60) **Going Correction** +0.875s/f (Soft) **14** Ran SP% **120.5**
Speed ratings (Par 99): **101,99,98,96,93 90,89,89,87,82 79,77,77,57**
Tote Swingers 1&2 £6.30, 2&3 £8.70, 1&3 £4.30 CSF £26.71 CT £160.45 TOTE £4.40: £2.00, £3.30, £2.80; EX 29.30.
Owner P Charalambous **Bred** Peter Charles **Trained** Newmarket, Suffolk

FOCUS
A modest 3yo handicap in which they went an even tempo on the very testing ground. The winner confirmed Bath form with the second despite the 4lb worse terms.
Tresabella Official explanation: jockey said filly never travelled

7471 INJURED JOCKEYS FUND H'CAP 5f 43y
3:40 (3:40) (Class 6) (0-60,60) 3-Y-O+ £1,617 (£481; £240; £120) **Stalls** Centre

Form RPR
2350 1 **Auntie Kathryn (IRE)**[21] 6968 3-8-11 **50** .... SilvestreDeSousa 7 62
(Peter Chapple-Hyam) *bhd: rdn and hdwy towards stands' side over 1f out: led ins fnl f: sn clr and r.o wl* **3/1**[2]

0400 2 4 **Simple Rhythm**[7] 7316 6-8-2 **48** ....(p) CarolineKelly(7) 5 46
(John Ryan) *led: rdn ent fnl f: hdd and outpcd by wnr ins fnl f: hld on for 2nd cl home* **20/1**

0156 3 nk **Lord Buffhead**[13] 7179 3-9-2 **60** .... JasonHart(5) 6 57
(Richard Guest) *chsd ldr: rdn and unable qck over 1f out: styd on same pce ins fnl f* **13/8**[1]

0502 4 nk **Itum**[27] 6771 5-8-7 **46** oh1 .... BrettDoyle 8 41
(Christine Dunnett) *hood removed late and slowly away: sn rcvrd and in tch in midfield: rdn and chsd ldrs over 1f out: styd on same pce ins fnl f* **10/1**

-064 5 5 **Mr Hendrix**[8] 7299 3-9-0 **53** .... RobertHavlin 3 30
(Mark Hoad) *in tch: rdn and no rspnse 2f out: wknd over 1f out* **5/1**[3]

6000 6 1 1/4 **Beach Candy (IRE)**[7] 7316 3-9-0 **60** .... ClaireMurray(7) 2 33
(Phil McEntee) *taken down early: s.i.s: swtchd to r against stands' rail: a bhd: n.d* **16/1**

1626 7 6 **Whiskey Junction**[35] 6563 8-9-1 **54** .... SeanLevey 4
(Michael Quinn) *chsd ldrs: rdn and struggling 1/2-way: bhd over 1f out* **9/1**

0500 8 2 **Fiona's Spirit (IRE)**[29] 6737 5-8-7 **46** oh1 .... AndreaAtzeni 1
(Daniel Mark Loughnane) *in tch: rdn and struggling ent fnl 2f: sn wknd and bhd fnl f* **25/1**

1m 7.14s (4.44) **Going Correction** +0.875s/f (Soft) **8** Ran SP% **113.3**
Speed ratings (Par 101): **99,92,92,91,83 81,72,68**
Tote Swingers 1&2 £12.00, 2&3 £6.30, 1&3 £2.20 CSF £57.36 CT £126.70 TOTE £3.20: £1.30, £4.60, £1.30; EX 66.30.
Owner P W Chapple-Hyam **Bred** Norelands Bloodstock, J Hanly & H Lascelles **Trained** Newmarket, Suffolk

FOCUS
A moderate sprint handicap for 3yos plus in which they went a fair gallop on the heavy ground. A clear personal best from the winner.

Itum Official explanation: jockey said gelding was slowly away as blindfold was tucked in tightly and difficult to remove

7472 SCROBY SANDS WIND FARM H'CAP 1m 6f 17y
4:10 (4:10) (Class 6) (0-55,55) 4-Y-O+ £1,617 (£481; £240; £120) **Stalls** High

Form RPR
056- 1 **Beyeh (IRE)**[185] 7839 4-9-1 **54** .... DominicFox 2 64+
(Michael Appleby) *hld up in last trio: clsd on ldrs 4f out: rdn to ld 2f out: sn clr and in command: heavily eased towards fin* **4/1**[2]

0550 2 2 **Baan (USA)**[26] 6821 9-8-9 **55** .... RyanTate(7) 8 58
(James Eustace) *racd in last pair: rdn and effrt 4f out: wnt 3rd over 1f out: plugged on to chse wnr wl ins fnl f: kpt on but flattered by proximity to wnr* **6/1**[3]

0004 3 1/2 **Darsan (IRE)**[7] 7315 4-9-1 **54** .... SilvestreDeSousa 9 56
(Phil McEntee) *in tch in midfield: wnt 2nd 4f out: rdn and chsd wnr wl over 1f out: sn outpcd and hld: plugged on same pce after: lost 2nd wl ins fnl f* **5/2**[1]

2000 4 7 **Penderyn**[35] 6561 5-8-0 **46** oh1 .... NoelGarbutt(7) 10 39
(Charles Smith) *chsd ldr tl led 1/2-way: clr 6f out tl rdn and hdd 2f out: wknd over 1f out* **14/1**

0340 5 3/4 **Satwa Ballerina**[21] 6948 4-8-6 **50** ....(bt) TobyAtkinson(5) 7 41
(Mark Rimmer) *chsd ldrs: wnt 3rd 4f out tl 2f out: edgd lft and wknd u.p over 1f out* **9/1**

2650 6 19 **Royal Defence (IRE)**[21] 6948 6-8-11 **50** .... SeanLevey 6 15
(Michael Quinn) *led tl 1/2-way: chsd ldr after tl 4f out: sn dropped out: t.o fnl 2f* **11/1**

00 7 9 **Dunaskin (IRE)**[21] 6956 12-8-7 **46** ....(b) KellyHarrison 5
(Richard Guest) *chsd ldrs tl 4f out: sn dropped out and bhd: t.o over 2f out* **9/1**

0500 8 31 **Harry Lime**[42] 6334 4-8-7 **46** oh1 .... JimmyQuinn 3
(Fleur Hawes) *s.i.s: bhd: rdn and lost tch over 3f out: t.o over 2f out* **28/1**

1060 9 53 **Sommersturm (GER)**[43] 6305 8-9-1 **54** .... TomQueally 1
(Barney Curley) *in tch in midfield: rdn 10f out: dropped to last 7f out: sn lost tch: wl t.o fnl 5f* **6/1**[3]

3m 22.35s (14.75) **Going Correction** +0.875s/f (Soft) **9** Ran SP% **115.6**
Speed ratings (Par 101): **92,90,90,86,86 75,70,52,22**
Tote Swingers 1&2 £5.50, 2&3 £3.80, 1&3 £3.00 CSF £28.29 CT £71.24 TOTE £6.20: £2.10, £1.40, £1.10; EX 29.40.
Owner Terry Pryke **Bred** Michael McGlynn **Trained** Danethorpe, Notts

FOCUS
A moderate staying handicap for older horses. The time was very slow despite what looked a fair pace, and the form is rated around the runner-up.
Sommersturm(GER) Official explanation: trainer had no explanation for the poor form shown
T/Plt: £257.80 to a £1 stake. Pool: £48,760.10 - 138.05 winning tickets. T/Qpdt: £12.60 to a £1 stake. Pool: £4,957.68 - 290.05 winning tickets. SP

7321 KEMPTON (A.W) (R-H)
Wednesday, October 31

OFFICIAL GOING: Standard
Wind: Strong, half behind Weather: Mostly overcast, drizzle from race 6 onwards

7473 WIN BIG WITH BETDAQ MULTIPLES RACING H'CAP (DIV I) 1m 2f (P)
4:35 (4:35) (Class 6) (0-65,71) 3-Y-O+ £1,617 (£481; £240; £120) **Stalls** Low

Form RPR
U400 1 **Royal Etiquette (IRE)**[23] 6933 5-9-7 **62** ....(v) KirstyMilczarek 8 70
(Lawney Hill) *hld up in last pair: rapid prog on wd outside over 3f out to press ldrs over 2f out: drvn to ld jst ins fnl f: styd on* **12/1**

2441 2 1 **Barton Bounty**[17] 7200 5-9-4 **59** .... DaleSwift 6 65
(Peter Niven) *pushed along in last bef 1/2-way: stl in last pair and hrd rdn over 1f out: gd prog after: r.o to take 2nd last stride* **11/2**[2]

330 3 shd **Ashkalara**[10] 7270 5-9-5 **60** .... HarryBentley 2 67
(Stuart Howe) *towards rr: hmpd after 3f: urged along over 2f out: prog on outer over 1f out: r.o to press for 2nd last stride* **8/1**[3]

4201 4 shd **Bert The Alert**[8] 7310 4-10-2 **71** 6ex .... GeorgeBaker 12 77
(Gary Moore) *led after 2f: shkn up over 1f out: hdd and nt qckn jst ins fnl f: lost 2 pls last stride* **6/4**[1]

3100 5 1 **Resplendent Alpha**[11] 7256 8-9-8 **63** .... FergusSweeney 14 67
(Jamie Osborne) *dwlt: rapid prog on outer to chse ldr 1/2-way: lost 2nd over 2f out: one pce after* **25/1**

20-0 6 1 1/4 **Bolanderi (USA)**[30] 6734 7-9-5 **63** .... KieranO'Neill(3) 11 64
(Andy Turnell) *rn wout declared tongue tie: racd on outer in midfield: prog over 3f out: chsd ldr over 2f out to over 1f out: wknd:* **66/1**

6400 7 1 3/4 **Soweto Star (IRE)**[8] 7310 4-9-10 **65** .... LukeMorris 13 63
(John Best) *prom: rdn 3f out: sn lost pl: no imp on ldrs over 1f out* **20/1**

5400 8 1/2 **Marvo**[30] 6735 8-9-4 **64** ....(p) RobertWilliams(5) 5 61
(Dai Burchell) *hld up in rr: prog on outer over 2f out: rdn and fnd nil over 1f out: btn after* **50/1**

0660 9 nk **Daniel Thomas (IRE)**[8] 7310 10-9-2 **62** ....(bt) CharlesBishop(5) 1 59
(Violet M Jordan) *hld up: lost pl after 4f: dropped to last pair 3f out: stl there over 1f out: modest late prog* **12/1**

0300 10 shd **Frosty Secret**[33] 6647 3-9-2 **62** ....(p) MartinDwyer 7 58
(Jane Chapple-Hyam) *hld up in midfield: rdn over 2f out: no prog whn nt clr run over 1f out* **25/1**

0206 11 1 1/2 **Princess Steph (IRE)**[14] 7162 3-9-3 **63** .... DarryllHolland 3 57
(Heather Main) *led 2f: chsd ldr to 1/2-way: sn pushed along: wknd over 2f out* **10/1**

40 12 1 **Dicey Vows (USA)**[83] 5001 4-9-2 **62** .... MichaelJMMurphy(5) 4 54
(Alan Jarvis) *t.k.h: prom: lost pl wl over 2f out: sn struggling* **10/1**

2m 5.88s (-2.12) **Going Correction** -0.10s/f (Stan)
WFA 3 from 4yo+ 5lb **12** Ran SP% **116.0**
Speed ratings (Par 101): **104,103,103,103,102 101,99,99,99,99 97,97**
Tote Swingers: 1&2 £8.90, 1&3 £15.20, 2&3 £5.10 CSF £70.94 CT £567.44 TOTE £12.30: £3.40, £1.50, £1.80; EX 103.80 Trifecta £497.10 Part won. Pool: £654.93 - 0.62 winning units..
Owner John Bull & Alan Hill **Bred** Windflower Overseas Holdings Inc **Trained** Aston Rowant, Oxon

FOCUS
A modest handicap.
Ashkalara Official explanation: jockey said mare suffered interference in running.

Bolanderi(USA) Official explanation: trainer reported gelding ran without tongue strap because it had come adrift in the stalls.

7474 WIN BIG WITH BETDAQ MULTIPLES RACING H'CAP (DIV II) 1m 2f (P)
5:05 (5:05) (Class 6) (0-65,65) 3-Y-O+ **£1,617** (£481; £240; £120) **Stalls** Low

Form RPR
4436 **1** **Having A Ball**[28] 6773 8-9-2 **57** .... JohnFahy 4 67+
(Peter Cundell) *wl in tch: only one of ldrs gng wl 3f out: prog to go 2nd wl over 1f out: drvn to cl and led 150yds out: styd on wl* **14/1**
6323 **2** *1 ¼* **Tenessee**[11] 7250 5-9-9 **64** .... JimCrowley 3 72
(Jamie Osborne) *rousted along to ld at gd pce: urged along 3f out: more than 2 l clr over 1f out: 5hdd and nt qckn last 150yds* **7/4**[1]
0205 **3** *4* **Landesherr (GER)**[28] 6794 5-9-3 **63** .... MichaelJMMurphy[(5)] 13 63
(Steve Gollings) *hld up in midfield: rdn and prog on outer fr 3f out: forced wd bnd 2f out: styd on to take 3rd fnl f: no ch* **4/1**[2]
0000 **4** *1 ¼* **Orpen'Arry (IRE)**[14] 7166 4-9-7 **62** .... KieranO'Neill 2 60
(Jimmy Fox) *hld up in last pair: pushed along 1/2-way: drvn 3f out: stl wl in rr over 1f out: styd on after to take 4th nr fin* **20/1**
5405 **5** *1 ½* **Maz**[6] 7348 4-9-9 **64** ....(v[1]) SamHitchcott 5 59
(Alan Bailey) *chsd ldr 2f: styd prom: drvn 3f out: fdd over 1f out* **14/1**
4/0- **6** *¾* **Educated Son**[150] 2586 4-9-1 **63** .... RyanTate[(7)] 9 56
(Ben De Haan) *trckd ldrs: rdn 3f out: n.m.r and looked awkward over 1f out: kpt on nr fin* **33/1**
4500 **7** *½* **Vale Of Lingfield (IRE)**[14] 7166 3-8-12 **58** .... LukeMorris 6 50
(John Best) *towards rr: rdn 3f out: effrt on inner over 1f out: no great prog* **25/1**
0205 **8** *nk* **Finlodex**[22] 6949 5-9-5 **60** .... FrankieMcDonald 10 52
(Murty McGrath) *trckd ldng trio: rdn wl over 2f out: no prog over 1f out: fdd* **25/1**
0000 **9** *1* **Legal Legacy**[14] 7166 6-9-5 **65** .... TobyAtkinson[(5)] 8 55
(Richard Rowe) *s.s: wl in rr: rdn 3f out: no ch after: plugged on* **20/1**
50-0 **10** *nk* **Evergreen Forest (IRE)**[25] 6891 4-9-7 **65** .... RyanClark[(3)] 14 59+
(Tom Keddy) *dropped in fr wd and hld up in last: pushed along briefly 1/2-way: gng bttr but stl last 3f out: no ch but styng on whn no room thrght fnl f* **10/1**
5503 **11** *½* **Highlife Dancer**[22] 6949 4-9-1 **61** ....(v) CharlesBishop[(5)] 1 49
(Mick Channon) *hld up in midfield: rdn 3f out and no prog: wknd fnl f* **8/1**[3]
0600 **12** *1* **King Of Wing (IRE)**[9] 7302 3-8-11 **62** ....(b) NathanAlison[(5)] 11 49
(Jim Boyle) *chsd ldr after 2f to wl over 1f out: wknd qckly* **33/1**
0530 **13** *2 ¾* **Langley**[11] 7252 5-9-3 **58** ....(t) DavidProbert 12 39
(Tim Vaughan) *nvr bttr than midfield: wknd jst over 2f out* **12/1**

2m 5.72s (-2.28) **Going Correction** -0.10s/f (Stan)
WFA 3 from 4yo+ 5lb **13** Ran SP% **120.7**
Speed ratings (Par 101): **105,104,100,99,98 98,97,97,96,96 95,95,92**
Tote Swingers: 1&2 £5.80, 1&3 £8.30, 2&3 £2.20 CSF £35.74 CT £123.43 TOTE £24.60: £4.20, £1.40, £2.00; EX 65.70 Trifecta £196.30 Pool: £952.80 - 3.64 winning units..
Owner P D Cundell **Bred** R G Percival **Trained** Compton, Berks
■ Peter Cundell's first winner since taking out a licence again.

FOCUS
This second division was run 0.16 secs faster than the first leg.
Evergreen Forest(IRE) Official explanation: jockey said gelding was denied a clear run.

7475 BACK OR LAY AT BETDAQ.COM H'CAP 1m 2f (P)
5:35 (5:36) (Class 4) (0-85,85) 3-Y-O **£4,075** (£1,212; £606; £303) **Stalls** Low

Form RPR
1 **1** **Albasharah (USA)**[14] 7174 3-9-2 **80** .... HarryBentley 8 88+
(Saeed Bin Suroor) *trckd ldng trio: shkn up and clsd to ld 1f out: r.o wl* **11/4**[2]
4211 **2** *1* **Rhagori**[61] 5796 3-9-4 **82** .... JimCrowley 2 88+
(Ralph Beckett) *trckd ldng pair: waited tl jst over 1f out to chal on inner: r.o but nt pce of wnr last 100yds* **9/4**[1]
2061 **3** *2* **Henry Clay**[15] 7147 3-9-6 **84** .... MartinLane 4 86
(Mark Johnston) *led: drvn and hrd pressed over 2f out: hdd and outpcd 1f out* **5/1**[3]
0343 **4** *shd* **Savanna Days (IRE)**[42] 6376 3-9-1 **79** .... MartinHarley 1 81
(Mick Channon) *hld up in last trio: rdn over 2f out: kpt on fnl f: nrly snatched 3rd* **9/1**
015 **5** *hd* **Magma**[47] 6205 3-9-0 **78** .... DavidProbert 7 80
(Andrew Balding) *trckd ldr: drvn to chal wl over 2f out: upsides over 1f out: outpcd fnl f* **8/1**
166 **6** *1 ½* **Perfect Delight**[102] 4342 3-9-0 **78** .... JohnFahy 3 77
(Clive Cox) *wl in tch: drvn 3f out and sn struggling: nvr on terms after* **20/1**
501 **7** *nk* **Viewpoint (IRE)**[28] 6792 3-9-7 **85** .... SeanLevey 5 83
(Richard Hannon) *slowly away and reminders s: hld up in last trio: rdn over 2f out: hanging and no prog over 1f out* **16/1**
3-10 **8** *44* **Representation (USA)**[14] 7168 3-9-7 **85** ....(t) MickaelBarzalona 9
(Mahmood Al Zarooni) *dwlt: nvr gng that wl: a in last trio: wknd over 2f out: eased over 1f out: t.o* **9/1**

2m 5.18s (-2.82) **Going Correction** -0.10s/f (Stan) **8** Ran SP% **115.9**
Speed ratings (Par 103): **107,106,104,104,104 103,102,67**
Tote Swingers: 1&2 £2.20, 1&3 £2.80, 2&3 £3.10 CSF £9.53 CT £28.38 TOTE £2.50: £1.10, £1.10, £2.60; EX 9.60 Trifecta £29.00 Pool: £1,204.95 - 31.16 winning units..
Owner Godolphin **Bred** Darley **Trained** Newmarket, Suffolk

FOCUS
A decent handicap for 3yos and not surprisingly run 0.54secs faster than the quicker of the two divisions of the Class 6 handicap that preceded it.
Representation(USA) Official explanation: jockey said colt was never travelling.

7476 BETDAQ MOBILE APPS NURSERY 6f (P)
6:05 (6:05) (Class 6) (0-65,65) 2-Y-O **£1,617** (£481; £240; £120) **Stalls** Low

Form RPR
3011 **1** **Ouzinkie (IRE)**[18] 7056 2-9-6 **64** .... MartinHarley 8 69
(Mick Channon) *dwlt: hld up towards rr: prog over 2f out: clsd to ld jst over 1f out: rdn and styd on wl: readily* **5/1**[2]
6453 **2** *1 ¼* **Eastern Dragon (IRE)**[35] 6583 2-9-4 **62** ....(v) PaulMulrennan 1 63
(Michael Scudamore) *trckd ldrs: rdn 2f out: nt qckn as wnr wnt by over 1f out: styd on to take 2nd ins fnl f* **6/1**[3]
050 **3** *nk* **Gracious George (IRE)**[27] 6818 2-9-7 **65** .... KieranO'Neill 7 65
(Jimmy Fox) *settled in last trio: urged along and stl there 2f out: gd prog on outer jst over 1f out: r.o to take 3rd nr fin* **7/1**
504 **4** *½* **Sakhee's Rose**[23] 6936 2-9-7 **65** .... GeorgeBaker 11 64
(Roger Charlton) *chsd ldr: rdn to ld 2f out: hdd and one pce jst over 1f out* **8/1**
0306 **5** *nk* **Our Sweet Art**[26] 6849 2-9-4 **62** .... JimCrowley 3 60
(John Best) *hld up in last trio: shkn up over 2f out: styd on fr over 1f out: nrst fin* **16/1**
4021 **6** *½* **Iwilsayzisonlyonce**[22] 6953 2-9-2 **63** .... MichaelMetcalfe[(3)] 2 59
(Joseph Tuite) *chsd ldr: chal on inner and upsides 2f out to over 1f out: one pce fnl f* **6/1**[3]
6603 **7** *½* **Solvanna**[27] 6808 2-9-2 **60** ....[1] DarryllHolland 5 55
(Heather Main) *trckd ldrs: rdn over 2f out: stl chsng but no imp over 1f out: one pce* **20/1**
0000 **8** *2 ¼* **Sunny Hollow**[21] 6977 2-9-7 **65** .... KirstyMilczarek 10 53
(James Toller) *racd wd towards rr: rdn over 2f out: no prog over 1f out* **16/1**
5024 **9** *1 ¼* **Ladweb**[14] 7176 2-9-6 **64** .... StevieDonohoe 9 48
(John Gallagher) *in tch towards rr: rdn over 2f out: no prog over 1f out: fdd* **16/1**
025 **10** *4 ½* **Compton Silver**[34] 6609 2-9-0 **65** .... NicoleNordblad[(7)] 4 36
(Hans Adielsson) *plld v hrd: sn restrained into last and hrd to steer: a bhd* **12/1**
640 **11** *2 ¼* **Charm Cry (USA)**[14] 7167 2-9-7 **65** .... MartinLane 6 29
(Mark Johnston) *led to 2f out: wknd rapidly* **4/1**[1]

1m 13.57s (0.47) **Going Correction** -0.10s/f (Stan) **11** Ran SP% **119.0**
Speed ratings (Par 93): **92,90,89,89,88 88,87,84,82,76 73**
Tote Swingers: 1&2 £5.10, 1&3 £10.00, 2&3 £9.00 CSF £35.60 CT £217.45 TOTE £6.10: £2.00, £1.40, £3.30; EX 32.60 Trifecta £332.10 Pool: £801.69 - 1.81 winning units..
Owner Box 41 **Bred** B Kennedy **Trained** West Ilsley, Berks

FOCUS
A moderate nursery but quite competitive, with only 5lb covering the entire field on official ratings, and they finished in a bunch behind the progressive winner.

NOTEBOOK
Ouzinkie(IRE) had 12 unsuccessful starts on turf before taking a seller on his first try on this surface and first run since being gelded. He completed the hat-trick in taking fashion here, sweeping through from the rear, and looks one to keep on-side on Polytrack until he is beaten. He is in the sales this week and could be a decent buy at a reasonable price. (op 4-1)
Eastern Dragon(IRE) has had a number of chances without winning, but has not been beaten far in recent starts on this surface and probably sets the standard. (tchd 11-2)
Gracious George(IRE), making his handicap and AW debut, was being ridden along on the home turn, around halfway, before staying on well. He can build on this and a longer trip might suit. (op 9-1 tchd 10-1 in a place)
Sakhee's Rose ran another decent race on this handicap debut and seems suited by Polytrack. (tchd 7-1)
Our Sweet Art had run her best previous race on Polytrack and performed with credit here, looking as if another furlong would be in her favour. (op 20-1)
Iwilsayzisonlyonce, 4lb higher for his Catterick win over this trip, switched to lead at the intersection of the courses but could not sustain his effort and faded. (op 11-2 tchd 5-1)
Solvanna, up in trip and wearing a hood for the first time, ran well considering she was quite keen early on. (op 33-1)
Sunny Hollow Official explanation: jockey said filly hung left.
Charm Cry(USA), sent off favourite on this handicap debut, was disappointing as she dropped away very quickly after leading until the quarter-mile pole. (op 9-2)

7477 BETDAQ CASINO GAMES MAIDEN STKS 7f (P)
6:35 (6:37) (Class 5) 3-Y-O+ **£2,264** (£673; £336; £168) **Stalls** Low

Form RPR
22 **1** **Tropics (USA)**[20] 7005 4-9-5 0 .... JimCrowley 4 83
(Dean Ivory) *trckd ldr: led 2f out gng easily: reminder and flashed tail 1f out: sn drew clr* **1/2**[1]
3-22 **2** *4* **Kalokagathia (IRE)**[142] 2974 3-9-3 74 .... FergusSweeney 11 70
(Jo Crowley) *led: rdn and hdd 2f out: one pce and no ch w wnr fnl f* **10/1**
4 **3** *1 ½* **Queen Of Skies (IRE)**[40] 6457 3-8-12 0 .... LukeMorris 2 61
(Clive Cox) *chsd ldrs: rdn to go 3rd 2f out but outpcd: kpt on* **9/1**[3]
4 *¾* **Pategonia** 3-9-3 0 .... RobertHavlin 10 64+
(John Gosden) *in tch in midfield: outpcd and shkn up 2f out: kpt on one pce after* **11/1**
05 **5** *hd* **Bowstar**[138] 3107 3-8-12 0 .... J-PGuillambert 7 58
(Michael Attwater) *chsd ldng pair: rdn 1/2-way: lost 3rd and outpcd 2f out: kpt on u.p* **33/1**
6 *shd* **Willow Beck** 3-8-12 0 .... NickyMackay 5 58
(John Gosden) *wl in tch: pushed along on inner over 2f out: sn outpcd: kpt on* **11/2**[2]
-045 **7** *¾* **It's My Time**[48] 6154 3-8-12 65 .... MartinLane 6 56
(David Simcock) *towards rr: rdn over 2f out: latched on to chsng gp over 1f out: one pce after* **25/1**
8 *14* **Balmoral Castle** 3-9-3 0 .... MartinHarley 3 23
(Jonathan Portman) *s.s: a bhd: t.o* **50/1**
00 **9** *7* **La Giaconda**[28] 6792 3-8-12 0 ....(t) JohnFahy 1
(Clive Cox) *sn in last pair: struggling 3f out: t.o* **50/1**
10 *5* **Boyzee** 4-9-5 0 .... LiamKeniry 9
(Linda Jewell) *s.s: racd wd in rr: wknd 1/2-way: t.o* **66/1**

1m 24.5s (-1.50) **Going Correction** -0.10s/f (Stan)
WFA 3 from 4yo 2lb **10** Ran SP% **121.7**
Speed ratings (Par 103): **104,99,97,96,96 96,95,79,71,65**
Tote Swingers: 1&2 £1.50, 1&3 £2.50, 2&3 £8.30 CSF £6.94 TOTE £2.00: £1.10, £2.60, £3.10; EX 6.30 Trifecta £14.90 Pool: £1,016.81 - 51.10 winning units..
Owner Dean Ivory **Bred** D Konecny, S Branch & A Branch **Trained** Radlett, Herts

FOCUS
An ordinary older horse maiden that was run in heavy rain but the wind was behind the runners in the straight and the time was fairly good.

7478 DOWNLOAD THE FREE RACING PLUS APP NURSERY 7f (P)
7:05 (7:05) (Class 3) (0-95,90) 2-Y-O **£5,822** (£1,732; £865; £432) **Stalls** Low

Form RPR
1 **1** **Secretinthepark**[65] 5684 2-8-10 **79** .... SeanLevey 9 83+
(Ed McMahon) *t.k.h: trckd ldr: shkn up to ld over 1f out: at least 2 l clr ins fnl f: a holding on nr fin* **5/2**[1]
1346 **2** *½* **Dashing David (IRE)**[4] 7400 2-9-7 **90** .... JimmyFortune 2 93
(Richard Hannon) *hld up in last: plenty to do after pce qcknd 3f out and pushed along: drvn and str run on outer jst over 1f out: tk 2nd last 100yds: clsd on wnr fin* **7/1**[3]
4464 **3** *2* **Aussie Reigns (IRE)**[13] 7190 2-8-3 **72** ....(v) HarryBentley 6 69
(William Knight) *mostly in 3rd: rdn and outpcd by ldng pair 2f out: styd on same pce after* **10/1**
2003 **4** *¾* **The Black Jacobin**[8] 7304 2-8-0 **69** ....(b) DavidProbert 7 64
(J S Moore) *sn led and set modeerate pce first 2f: wound it up fr 3f out: hdd u.p over 1f out: fdd ins fnl f* **25/1**

1021 **5** ½ **Cappadocia (IRE)**[13] 7193 2-8-8 **77**................................ MartinHarley 4 71
(Mick Channon) *t.k.h: hld up in midfield: shkn up over 1f out: kpt on same pce: nvr able to chal* **3/1**[2]

2200 **6** *nse* **This Is Nice (IRE)**[18] 7060 2-8-5 **74** ow1..................(v[1]) MartinDwyer 8 68
(Tom Dascombe) *trckd ldng trio: outpcd and rdn 2f out: kpt on one pce after* **7/1**[3]

1160 **7** 2 ½ **Opt Out**[25] 6883 2-8-12 **81**.. MartinLane 3 68
(Mark Johnston) *trckd ldrs: rdn on inner over 2f out: no imp over 1f out: wknd* **14/1**

0515 **8** 1 ½ **Zain Spirit (USA)**[22] 6972 2-8-3 **72**.................................. LukeMorris 1 55
(Gerard Butler) *hld up in rr: rdn over 2f out: no prog and wl btn over 1f out* **14/1**

0610 **9** 3 **Rich Forever (IRE)**[25] 6883 2-8-8 **77**...................... MickaelBarzalona 5 52
(James Bethell) *hld up in rr: rdn and fnd nil over 2f out: wknd and eased over 1f out* **10/1**

1m 25.98s (-0.02) **Going Correction** -0.10s/f (Stan) **9** Ran SP% **113.9**
Speed ratings (Par 99): **96,95,93,92,91 91,88,87,83**
Tote Swingers 1&2 £5.80, 2&3 £7.40, 1&3 £7.20 CSF £20.20 CT £148.49 TOTE £3.40: £1.60, £2.30, £2.90; EX 20.60 Trifecta £137.90 Pool: £779.79 - 4.24 winning units..
Owner Mia Racing **Bred** Mia Racing **Trained** Lichfield, Staffs

FOCUS
The feature race and a pretty good nursery, despite the top weight being 5lb below the race ceiling.

NOTEBOOK
Secretintheparik, who took has maiden on fast ground in August, followed up on this handicap debut. He was able to race prominently from his outside draw, seeing plenty of daylight, but picked up well when asked to win his race and looks capable of further progress. (op 11-4 tchd 3-1)
Dashing David(IRE), in contrast to the winner, was held up out the back before sweeping down the outside in the last 2f. He was racing off a mark of 90 here and might have won had the wind not been behind the runners in the straight. (op 6-1 tchd 11-2)
Aussie Reigns(IRE) is a fairly solid marker and ran his race despite the drop in trip, but the principals were a class above. (op 12-1 tchd 8-1)
The Black Jacobin made the running but could not hold off the winner. He kept going though and there is a small race in him on Polytrack, possibly at 6f.
Cappadocia(IRE), both of whose wins came over 6f of this course, does stay this trip though but failed to land a blow having been held up, and he is probably high enough in the handicap now. (tchd 11-4)
This Is Nice(IRE), wearing a visor for the first time, ran reasonably without being able to pick up significantly for pressure. (tchd 8-1)

7479 SPORTINGLIFE.COM H'CAP 1m 4f (P)
7:35 (7:39) (Class 6) (0-55,55) 3-Y-0+ **£1,617** (£481; £240; £120) **Stalls** Centre

Form RPR

44 **1** **Uncle Roger (IRE)**[27] 6814 3-8-13 **54**....................(v[1]) JimmyFortune 11 62
(Eve Johnson Houghton) *racd keenly: led at modest pce 3f: trckd ldr after: rdn to ld 2f out: hung lft over 1f out: drvn out* **7/1**[3]

0165 **2** 1 **Five Hearts**[66] 5638 4-8-11 **50**.. DarylByrne(5) 7 57
(Mark H Tompkins) *tk v t.k.h in midfield: shkn up and prog on outer 2f out: chsd wnr 1f out: styd on but a hld* **16/1**

0440 **3** 1 **Tartan Gunna**[8] 7303 6-9-5 **53**.. SeanLevey 9 58
(George Baker) *reluctant to enter stalls: s.s: sn t.k.h and hld up towards rr: drvn and prog 2f out: styd on to take 3rd last strides: nvr able to chal* **5/1**[1]

5406 **4** *shd* **Saloon (USA)**[66] 5637 8-8-7 **48**..........................(p) IanBurns(7) 12 53
(Jane Chapple-Hyam) *prom: rdn over 2f out: chsd wnr over 1f out and looked a threat: fnd nil and wl hld fnl f* **16/1**

4000 **5** 2 ¾ **Fire In Babylon (IRE)**[11] 7252 4-9-6 **54**..................(be) JimCrowley 4 55
(Michael Wigham) *hld up in midfield: nt clr run over 2f out and lost pl: gd prog over 1f out: effrt flattened out tamely fnl f* **5/1**[1]

4610 **6** ¾ **Chasin' Rainbows**[22] 6948 4-8-12 **53**...................... ThomasBrown(7) 1 53
(Sylvester Kirk) *hld up towards rr: gng wl enough 3f out: effrt on inner and drvn over 1f out: one pce and no threat* **7/1**[3]

0/05 **7** 1 ¼ **Gladstone (IRE)**[23] 6927 4-8-12 **51**............................ DavidKenny(5) 5 49
(John Panvert) *dwlt: hld up in rr: rdn over 2f out: prog over 1f out: one pce and no hdwy fnl f* **50/1**

0410 **8** *hd* **Maccabees**[13] 7196 3-8-7 **55**... NedCurtis(7) 14 52
(Roger Curtis) *s.v.s: hld up in last: shkn up and looked less than keen over 2f out: modest late prog* **14/1**

2605 **9** *hd* **Young Jackie**[8] 7303 4-8-12 **46**.................................. FrederikTylicki 10 43
(George Margarson) *racd wd towards rr: rdn over 2f out: no prog over 1f out: wl btn after* **11/2**[2]

530/ **10** *hd* **Whiepa Snappa (IRE)**[753] 6020 5-9-1 **54**............... JemmaMarshall(5) 6 51
(Pat Phelan) *dwlt: hld up in last pair: nudged along over 2f out: taken to inner over 1f out: pushed along and kpt on steadily at one pce* **12/1**

4063 **11** 2 ½ **Irons On Fire (USA)**[7] 7321 4-9-0 **55**........................(p) AaronChave(7) 3 48
(Lee Carter) *hld up in midfield: pushed along and no prog 2f out: wknd over 1f out* **12/1**

4530 **12** ½ **Tinkerbell Will**[54] 6004 5-9-2 **50**............................... RichardThomas 13 42
(John E Long) *t.k.h: led after 3f: hdd & wknd 2f out* **9/1**

000 **13** 6 **Mad Ginger Alice**[27] 6829 4-9-1 **49**.............................. RobertWinston 8 32
(Olivia Maylam) *t.k.h early: prom: rdn over 2f out: wknd qckly wl over 1f out* **16/1**

0150 **14** 1 ½ **Dolly Colman (IRE)**[8] 7303 4-9-1 **49**................................. LukeMorris 2 30
(Zoe Davison) *trckd ldrs: wknd qckly 2f out* **33/1**

2m 35.48s (0.98) **Going Correction** -0.10s/f (Stan)
WFA 3 from 4yo+ 7lb **14** Ran SP% **128.3**
Speed ratings (Par 101): **92,91,90,90,88 88,87,87,87,87 85,85,81,80**
Tote Swingers: 1&2 £23.40, 1&3 £7.10, 2&3 £24.40 CSF £122.03 CT £629.15 TOTE £9.40: £3.10, £6.90, £2.20; EX 105.10 Trifecta £399.20 Part won. Pool: £532.36 - 0.40 winning units..
Owner Mrs J E O'Halloran **Bred** Mrs J O'Halloran **Trained** Blewbury, Oxon
■ Stewards' Enquiry : Jimmy Fortune two-day ban; careless riding (14th-15th Nov).

FOCUS
A maximum field for this very moderate handicap and the pace looked ordinary.

7480 SPORTINGLIFE.COM RACING H'CAP 1m (P)
8:05 (8:06) (Class 5) (0-70,70) 3-Y-0+ **£2,264** (£673; £336; £168) **Stalls** Low

Form RPR

00 **1** **Diplomatic (IRE)**[98] 4469 7-8-11 **66**............................. HarryPoulton(5) 5 74
(Michael Squance) *hld up in midfield: nt clr run briefly over 3f out: plld out wd and prog 2f out: rdn to ld ins fnl f: styd on* **25/1**

0365 **2** ½ **Officer In Command (USA)**[8] 7310 6-9-3 **67**..................(b) JohnFahy 4 74
(Paul Rich) *dwlt: hld up in rr: hrd rdn and prog on inner over 1f out: r.o fnl f: jst failed* **8/1**

0623 **3** ½ **Good Luck Charm**[35] 6582 3-9-3 **70**................................ GeorgeBaker 6 75
(Gary Moore) *cl up on inner: led 2f out: sn drvn: hdd ins fnl f: styd on* **3/1**[1]

0500 **4** ½ **George Baker (IRE)**[14] 7170 5-9-4 **68**.............................. SeanLevey 2 73
(George Baker) *hld up in midfield: prog 2f out: clsd to chal fnl f: one pce last 100yds* **25/1**

0654 **5** 1 ½ **Satwa Laird**[6] 7360 6-9-5 **69**..................................... KirstyMilczarek 7 70
(Conor Dore) *trckd ldrs: rdn and prog to chal over 1f out: nt qckn and fdd fnl f* **6/1**[2]

0005 **6** *nk* **Uncle Fred**[47] 6209 7-9-5 **69**.. JimCrowley 1 70
(Patrick Chamings) *dwlt: hld up in rr: prog on inner over 2f out: clsd on ldrs u.p over 1f out: fdd ins fnl f* **7/1**[3]

0652 **7** 1 ¾ **Illustrious Prince (IRE)**[15] 7141 5-9-1 **70**..................... JasonHart(5) 9 67
(Declan Carroll) *prom: cl up but rdn whn squeezed out 2f out: tried to rally over 1f out: no ex* **10/1**

3000 **8** 1 ¾ **Edgeworth (IRE)**[15] 7132 6-8-9 **66**........................... JoshBaudains(7) 8 59
(David Bridgwater) *dwlt: hld up wl in rr: hung lft and no prog over 2f out: plugged on fnl f* **16/1**

3416 **9** *nk* **Siouxperhero (IRE)**[26] 6843 3-9-2 **69**.....................(b) MartinDwyer 12 60
(William Muir) *chsd ldr to over 2f out: losing pl whn short of room over 1f out* **7/1**[3]

0066 **10** 1 ¾ **Golden Desert (IRE)**[32] 6687 8-9-3 **67**........................... SebSanders 10 55
(Simon Dow) *dwlt: t.k.h in rr: jst pushed along fr over 2f out: lft bhd by ldng gp over 1f out* **7/1**[3]

1500 **11** ½ **Bareback (IRE)**[14] 7170 3-9-3 **70**................................... LukeMorris 3 56
(John Best) *led to 2f out: sn wknd* **25/1**

1000 **12** 9 **Rezwaan**[14] 7171 5-9-5 **69**..(b) LiamKeniry 13 35
(Murty McGrath) *racd wd: trckd ldrs: steadily wknd over 2f out: t.o* **16/1**

00-R **13** 3 ¼ **Storm Tide**[14] 7166 4-8-11 **66**.............................. JemmaMarshall(5) 11 24
(Pat Phelan) *s.s: hld up in rr: hung lft over 2f out and nrly on nr side rail: t.o: b roke blood vessel* **40/1**

1m 39.01s (-0.79) **Going Correction** -0.10s/f (Stan)
WFA 3 from 4yo+ 3lb **13** Ran SP% **122.7**
Speed ratings (Par 103): **99,98,98,97,96 95,93,92,91,90 89,80,77**
Tote Swingers 1&2 £49.00, 2&3 £4.30, 1&3 £27.30 CSF £212.53 CT £793.56 TOTE £49.60: £10.10, £2.90, £1.60; EX 436.50 TRIFECTA Not won..
Owner Miss K Squance **Bred** Darley **Trained** Newmarket, Suffolk
■ Stewards' Enquiry : John Fahy two-day ban; used whip above permitted level (14th-15th Nov).

FOCUS
An ordinary handicap but a steady pace resulted in a close, driving finish.
Storm Tide Official explanation: vet said filly bled from nose.
T/Jkpt: £56,923.50 to a £1 stake. Pool: £280,609.22 - 3.50 winning tickets. T/Plt: £17.20 to a £1 stake. Pool: £76,036.33 - 3,224.65 winning tickets. T/Qpdt: £4.60 to a £1 stake. Pool: £8,644.59 - 1,372.30 winning tickets. JN

7303 LINGFIELD (L-H)
Wednesday, October 31

OFFICIAL GOING: Standard to slow
Wind: fresh, behind Weather: dry and breezy

7481 BREEDERS' CUP LIVE ONLY ON ATR MAIDEN STKS 5f (P)
12:30 (12:31) (Class 5) 2-Y-0 **£2,385** (£704; £352) **Stalls** High

Form RPR

4 **1** **Multitask**[9] 7296 2-9-3 0... JamieGoldstein 10 70
(Michael Madgwick) *mde all: rdn and clr over 1f out: styd on wl* **100/1**

00 **2** 1 ½ **Blessing Box**[20] 7007 2-8-12 0....................................... TedDurcan 8 60
(Chris Wall) *in tch in rr: rdn and hdwy over 1f out: styd on wl ins fnl f: to go 2nd nr fin: no threat to wnr* **3/1**[2]

45 **3** ½ **North Pole**[13] 7198 2-9-3 0... LukeMorris 4 63
(Sir Mark Prescott Bt) *chsd ldrs: rdn over 1f out: kpt on u.p ins fnl f: wnt 3rd nr fin: no threat to wnr* **11/2**[3]

22 **4** *nk* **Free Island**[22] 6970 2-8-12 0...................................... PatCosgrave 9 57
(James Tate) *in tch: rdn and effrt over 1f out: chsd wnr fnl 150yds: styd on same pce and lost 2 pls towards fin* **7/4**[1]

00 **5** 2 **Tom Hall**[20] 7007 2-9-3 0.. GeorgeBaker 2 55
(John Best) *chsd ldr: ev ch and rdn over 1f out: sn no ex and btn 1f out: wknd ins fnl f* **16/1**

4300 **6** 3 ¾ **Sand And Deliver**[92] 4687 2-8-12 75................................. EddieAhern 3 36
(Gary Moore) *s.i.s: in tch in rr: rdn an struggling ent fnl 2f: sn wknd* **8/1**

43 **7** 2 ½ **Captain Cruz (IRE)**[9] 7296 2-9-3 0.......................... RichardKingscote 7 32
(Ronald Harris) *chsd ldrs: rdn and struggling over 2f out: wknd 2f out* **15/2**

59.03s (0.23) **Going Correction** +0.025s/f (Slow) **7** Ran SP% **106.5**
Speed ratings (Par 95): **99,96,95,95,92 86,82**
Tote Swingers: 1&2 £24.20, 1&3 £19.00, 2&3 £2.90 CSF £329.24 TOTE £61.30: £20.40, £2.20; EX 353.30.
Owner Mrs L N Harmes **Bred** Mrs L N Harmes **Trained** Denmead, Hants
■ Hand In Glove was withdrawn (14/1, ref to ent stalls). Deduct 5p in the £ under R4.

FOCUS
With the new Polytrack surface still bedding in, the going was described as Standard to Slow. A moderate maiden to start proceedings and the sort of result to immediately have punters on their knees.

NOTEBOOK
Multitask had finished around 7l behind Captain Cruz when fourth of six on his Windsor debut nine days earlier, but for some reason he improved a ton for these totally different conditions and comprehensively turned that form around under a front-running ride. It's not hard to treat the form with caution, but he obviously liked this surface and will surely be back. (op 66-1)
Blessing Box, unplaced in her first two starts but not without showing some ability, was dropped out last early before staying on late, despite tending to hang in behind rivals in the straight. She now gets a mark which opens up a few more options. (op 7-2)
North Pole was dropping in trip and that seemed to count against him, as he was always having to be niggled along to go the pace before staying on, though it transpired that he had lost his right hind shoe. He also now gets a mark and will appreciate a return to further. Official explanation: vet said colt lost right hind shoe. (op 5-1 tchd 4-1)
Free Island looked the one to beat having finished runner-up in her first two starts, but despite holding a good position on the outside just behind the leaders she didn't pick up as had seemed likely. This was a step backwards, but she can also now be handicapped. (op 6-4)
Sand And Deliver, absent since finishing last of ten in the Molecomb, was making her debut for the yard but faded disappointingly from the home bend. (op 9-1 tchd 10-1 and 7-1)
Captain Cruz(IRE) was reported not to have handled the bends. Official explanation: jockey said colt failed to handle the bends. (op 12-1 tchd 7-1)

7482 LINGFIELD PARK H'CAP 6f (P)
1:00 (1:00) (Class 6) (0-58,58) 3-Y-0+ **£1,704** (£503; £251) **Stalls** Low

Form RPR

2010 **1** **Demoiselle Bond**[21] 6982 4-9-7 **58**.................................. RobertHavlin 2 66
(Lydia Richards) *mounted on crse: led: rdn and c towards centre wl over 1f out: hdd jst ins fnl f: rallied u.p to ld again last strides* **15/2**

2504 **2** *hd* **Loyal Royal (IRE)**[26] 6836 9-9-5 **56** (bt) RichardKingscote 8 63
(Milton Bradley) *stdd s: t.k.h: hld up in rr: hdwy into midfield 1/2-way: swtchd lft and trckd ldrs 2f out: rdn and qcknd to ld jst ins fnl f: sn drvn: hdd and no ex last strides* **7/1**[3]

0124 **3** *1 ¼* **Strategic Action (IRE)**[35] 6585 3-9-4 **56** (tp) SebSanders 9 60
(Linda Jewell) *in tch in midfield: rdn wl over 1f out: kpt on u.p to go 3rd wl ins fnl f: styd on* **12/1**

012 **4** *1 ¼* **Illustrious Lad (IRE)**[14] 7157 3-9-4 **56** (p) PatCosgrave 1 56
(Jim Boyle) *chsd ldrs: effrt u.p over 1f out: drvn and styd on same pce ins fnl f: lost 3rd wl ins fnl f* **5/1**[2]

0120 **5** *½* **Red Shadow**[18] 7055 3-9-6 **58** (p) DaleSwift 12 56+
(Alan Brown) *stuck wd: bhd: effrt and v wd bnd 2f out: lost pl and plenty to do over 1f out: rallied and styd on wl ins fnl f: nt rch ldrs* **4/1**[1]

4005 **6** *¾* **Sherjawy (IRE)**[82] 5047 8-9-1 **52** KirstyMilczarek 11 48+
(Zoe Davison) *hld up in rr: sme hdwy and nt clr run bnd 2f out: hdwy over 1f out: kpt on fnl f: nvr trbld ldrs* **40/1**

4006 **7** *½* **Silly Billy (IRE)**[10] 7275 4-8-12 **54** (t) JemmaMarshall(5) 7 49
(Sylvester Kirk) *in tch: rdn and unable qck over 1f out: btn and styd on same pce fnl f* **10/1**

0500 **8** *1 ¼* **Punching**[18] 7055 8-9-7 **58** HayleyTurner 3 49
(Conor Dore) *chsd ldr tl over 1f out: sn rdn and unable qck: wl hld and styd on same pce fnl f* **20/1**

0440 **9** *nse* **Mey Blossom**[22] 6961 7-9-7 **58** (p) PaulHanagan 10 49+
(Richard Whitaker) *mounted on crse and taken down early: t.k.h: hld up towards rr: rdn and effrt over 1f out: kpt on ins fnl f: nvr trbld ldrs* **8/1**

0000 **10** *2* **Red Rhythm**[30] 6737 5-9-4 **55** (t) FergusSweeney 6 40
(Mark Hoad) *t.k.h: chsd ldrs: rdn and unable qck over 1f out: sn wknd* **33/1**

5300 **11** *2* **Ereka (IRE)**[12] 7225 4-9-4 **55** LukeMorris 5 37
(John Best) *hld up in rr: pushed along and struggling whn hmpd ent fnl 2f: rdn and no hdwy wl over 1f out: sn wknd* **12/1**

4000 **12** *7* **Tidy Affair (IRE)**[95] 4584 3-9-6 **58** LiamKeniry 4 16
(Murty McGrath) *in tch in midfield: rdn and lost pl over 2f out: hmpd ent fnl 2f: bhd over 1f out: wknd fnl f* **7/1**[3]

1m 11.85s (-0.05) **Going Correction** +0.025s/f (Slow)
WFA 3 from 4yo+ 1lb **12** Ran SP% **119.2**
Speed ratings (Par 101): **101,100,99,97,96 95,95,93,93,90 88,78**
Tote Swingers: 1&2 £16.20, 1&3 £9.80, 2&3 £7.20 CSF £58.37 CT £640.49 TOTE £4.50: £2.50, £2.80, £3.30; EX 74.50.
Owner The Demoiselle Bond Partnership **Bred** Mrs Lydia Richards **Trained** Funtington, W Sussex
■ Stewards' Enquiry : Richard Kingscote two-day ban; careless riding (14th-15th Nov).

FOCUS
A modest sprint handicap.

7483 BREATHE SPA AT LINGFIELD PARK MARRIOTT FILLIES' H'CAP 6f (P)
1:30 (1:32) (Class 5) (0-75,75) 3-Y-O+ **£2,385** (£704; £352) **Stalls** Low

Form RPR

2200 **1** **Millibar (IRE)**[25] 6878 3-9-2 **73** (b) DarryllHolland 7 84
(Nick Littmoden) *dwlt: sn rcvrd and in tch in midfield: hmpd over 4f out: swtchd rt and effrt wl over 1f out: drvn to ld fnl 100yds: r.o wl* **9/1**

2030 **2** *2* **Button Moon (IRE)**[15] 7144 4-8-13 **69** (p) SebSanders 6 74
(Ian Wood) *chsd ldrs: wnt 2nd over 2f out: drvn and ev ch ent fnl f: led ins fnl f: sn hdd and one pce* **8/1**

6036 **3** *1 ½* **Isola Verde**[42] 6378 3-8-11 **68** (v) HayleyTurner 2 68
(James Fanshawe) *taken down early: jostling w rival leaving stalls: hld up in rr: hdwy u.p 1f out: styd on but no threat to wnr* **7/2**[1]

1503 **4** *¾* **Diamond Blue**[42] 6357 4-9-0 **70** AmyRyan 11 68+
(Richard Whitaker) *hmpd and dropped to last after 1f: hdwy bur v wd bnd 2f out: styd on wl ins fnl f: nvr trbld ldrs* **11/2**[2]

0200 **5** *1* **Yurituni**[57] 5906 5-9-5 **75** (v) FergusSweeney 5 70
(Eve Johnson Houghton) *taken down early: chsd ldr tl led 1/2-way: rdn over 1f out: hdd ins fnl f: fdd fnl 100yds* **14/1**

5130 **6** *1* **Charming (IRE)**[19] 7019 3-8-12 **69** EddieAhern 1 61
(Olivia Maylam) *in tch in midfield: rdn and fnd little over 1f out: styd on same pce and no threat to ldrs fnl f* **25/1**

1250 **7** *¾* **Meandmyshadow**[11] 7247 4-9-2 **72** DaleSwift 9 62
(Alan Brown) *chsd ldrs: rdn and lost pl over 2f out: no threat to ldrs after but kpt on fnl f* **7/1**[3]

1000 **8** *nk* **Dancing Welcome**[96] 4533 6-9-5 **75** (b) LukeMorris 8 64
(Milton Bradley) *in tch in midfield: rdn over 3f out: no imp and one pce fr over 1f out* **25/1**

1000 **9** *½* **Best Be Careful (IRE)**[46] 6226 4-8-12 **73** RachealKneller(5) 12 60+
(Mark Usher) *swtchd lft after s: dropped to rr after 1f: rdn and kpt on fnl f: nvr trbld ldrs* **16/1**

0113 **10** *1 ¼* **Ziefhd**[48] 6173 3-9-1 **75** (p) MarkCoumbe(3) 4 59
(Tim McCarthy) *led tl 1/2-way: rdn and struggling 2f out: wknd over 1f out* **8/1**

0136 **11** *hd* **Dressed In Lace**[119] 3762 3-9-0 **71** LiamKeniry 3 54
(Jo Crowley) *jostling match w rival leaving stalls: in tch in midfield: rdn and no hdwy wl over 1f out: sn wknd* **16/1**

3010 **12** *9* **Tiger Cub**[42] 6378 3-9-0 **71** (vt) MickaelBarzalona 10 27
(Mrs Ilka Gansera-Leveque) *v keen to post: hld up in rr: hmpd after 1f out: rdn and no hdwy over 2f out: bhd over 1f out* **12/1**

1m 11.76s (-0.14) **Going Correction** +0.025s/f (Slow)
WFA 3 from 4yo+ 1lb **12** Ran SP% **116.1**
Speed ratings (Par 100): **101,98,96,95,94 92,91,91,90,88 88,76**
Tote Swingers: 1&2 £17.60, 1&3 £9.30, 2&3 £6.00 CSF £77.55 CT £303.06 TOTE £16.00: £3.10, £2.70, £2.80; EX 106.70.
Owner Mrs Linda Francis **Bred** Martin Francis **Trained** Newmarket, Suffolk

FOCUS
No more than a fair fillies' sprint handicap and it paid to race handily.

7484 ATTHERACES.COM BREEDERS' CUP SITE NOW LIVE H'CAP (DIV I) 7f (P)
2:05 (2:07) (Class 5) (0-75,76) 3-Y-O+ **£2,385** (£704; £352) **Stalls** Low

Form RPR

1100 **1** **Scottish Lake**[31] 6705 4-9-6 **75** KirstyMilczarek 12 82
(Olivia Maylam) *chsd ldr: rdn to press ldr 2f out: led 1f out: hld on wl fnl f* **15/2**[3]

3245 **2** *nk* **Dozy Joe**[7] 7328 4-9-2 **71** (p) SebSanders 6 77
(Ian Wood) *hld up in tch in midfield: n.m.r ent fnl 2f: swtchd rt and hdwy jst ins fnl f: pressed wnr fnl 75yds: hld cl home* **9/1**

0041 **3** *nk* **Atlantis Crossing (IRE)**[40] 6455 3-8-11 **68** PatCosgrave 5 72
(Jim Boyle) *wnt lft s: sn niggled along towards rr: gd hdwy u.p 1f out: pressing wnr fnl 100yds: kpt on but hld towards fin* **8/1**

0100 **4** *¾* **Fever Few**[14] 7170 3-8-13 **70** RobertHavlin 11 72
(Jane Chapple-Hyam) *t.k.h: chsd ldrs: rdn and effrt over 1f out: kpt on same pce ins fnl f* **9/1**

3610 **5** *nse* **First Class**[57] 5910 4-8-9 **64** TedDurcan 3 67
(Rae Guest) *in tch in midfield on inner: rdn and hdwy over 1f out: kpt on same pce ins fnl f* **5/1**[1]

0450 **6** *nse* **The Strig**[42] 6370 5-9-1 **70** J-PGuillambert 10 73
(Stuart Williams) *in tch in midfield: rdn over 2f out: hdwy to chse ldrs 1f out: styd on same pce ins fnl f* **33/1**

320 **7** *½* **Sunshine Always (IRE)**[35] 6577 6-8-10 **68** MarkCoumbe(3) 9 70
(Michael Attwater) *hld up in last trio: rdn and hdwy 2f out: kpt on ins fnl f: unable to chal* **11/1**

0004 **8** *nk* **Crown Choice**[13] 7202 7-9-4 **73** MartinLane 4 74
(Paul Midgley) *taken down early: stdd s: hld up in rr: effrt on outer over 1f out: styd on wl ins fnl f: nt rch ldrs* **11/2**[2]

601 **9** *¾* **Sandbetweenourtoes (IRE)**[40] 6436 3-8-8 **72** (p) NedCurtis(7) 8 70
(Roger Curtis) *hld up in tch in last trio: stuck bhd a wall of horses over 1f out: hdwy but nvr enough room thrght fnl f: kpt on but unable to chal* **12/1**

00-0 **10** *hd* **Spartic**[49] 6145 4-8-7 **62** SeanLevey 2 61
(Alan McCabe) *led: rdn wl over 1f out: drvn and hdd 1f out: wknd ins fnl f* **40/1**

1535 **11** *½* **Lady Mango (IRE)**[55] 5972 4-8-11 **66** LukeMorris 7 63
(Ronald Harris) *in tch in midfield: rdn and unable qck 2f out: styd on same pce u.p fr over 1f out* **16/1**

1012 **12** *½* **Eager To Bow (IRE)**[54] 5993 6-9-3 **72** GeorgeBaker 14 68
(Patrick Chamings) *in tch in midfield but stuck wd: rdn and no hdwy over 1f out: wknd ins fnl f* **15/2**[3]

4001 **13** *½* **Al Aqabah (IRE)**[14] 7166 7-9-3 **72** (b) NeilCallan 1 72
(Brian Gubby) *chsd ldrs: rdn and unable qck over 1f out: wknd ins fnl f: btn and eased towards fin* **20/1**

1m 24.62s (-0.18) **Going Correction** +0.025s/f (Slow)
WFA 3 from 4yo+ 2lb **13** Ran SP% **118.7**
Speed ratings (Par 103): **102,101,101,100,100 100,99,99,98,98 97,97,96**
Tote Swingers: 1&2 £14.50, 1&3 £20.60, 2&3 £12.80 CSF £71.50 CT £578.82 TOTE £12.10: £3.40, £3.20, £4.20; EX 93.00.
Owner A C Maylam **Bred** Farmers Hill Stud **Trained** Epsom, Surrey

FOCUS
A modest but competitive handicap in which the principals finished in a heap.
Sandbetweenourtoes(IRE) Official explanation: jockey said gelding did not face the kickback.

7485 ATTHERACES.COM BREEDERS' CUP SITE NOW LIVE H'CAP (DIV II) 7f (P)
2:40 (2:40) (Class 5) (0-75,75) 3-Y-O+ **£2,385** (£704; £352) **Stalls** Low

Form RPR

0635 **1** **Saskia's Dream**[32] 6687 4-8-13 **68** RobertHavlin 7 77
(Jane Chapple-Hyam) *t.k.h early: chsd ldr tl wnt 2nd 3f out: rdn to ld over 1f out: kpt on wl fnl f* **7/1**[3]

0465 **2** *¾* **Aldermoor (USA)**[48] 6172 6-9-5 **74** NickyMackay 12 81+
(Stuart Williams) *hld up in midfield: rdn and hdwy over 1f out: r.o wl ins fnl f to go 2nd towards fin: nt rch wnr* **9/1**

0004 **3** *nk* **Lastkingofscotland (IRE)**[13] 7203 6-8-8 **63** (b) HayleyTurner 3 69
(Conor Dore) *in tch: effrt and drvn to chse ldrs over 1f out: chsd wnr ins fnl f: styd on but lost 2nd towards fin* **14/1**

2145 **4** *½* **Stonecrabstomorrow (IRE)**[10] 7273 9-8-8 **66** MarkCoumbe(3) 6 71
(Michael Attwater) *towards rr: hdwy on inner bnd 2f out: drvn and chsd ldrs 1f out: kpt on same pce ins fnl f* **20/1**

2442 **5** *1* **Bajan Bear**[15] 7142 4-9-0 **69** MartinLane 8 71
(Michael Blanshard) *bhd: rdn and hdwy ent fnl f: styd on wl fnl f: nt rch ldrs* **9/2**[1]

0355 **6** *shd* **Mr Knightley (IRE)**[16] 7115 3-8-11 **68** PatCosgrave 10 69
(Jim Boyle) *chsd ldrs: rdn and unable qck over 1f out: styd on same pce fnl f* **14/1**

0610 **7** *½* **The Tichborne (IRE)**[39] 6495 4-9-3 **72** (v) EddieAhern 5 73
(Roger Teal) *in tch in midfield: rdn and unable qck over 1f out: styd on same pce and no imp fnl f* **7/1**[3]

4420 **8** *¾* **Leelu**[22] 6951 6-8-6 **61** oh1 LukeMorris 14 59
(David Arbuthnot) *led and grad crossed to inner rail: rdn ent fnl 2f: hdd over 1f out: lost 2nd ins fnl f: wknd fnl 100yds* **25/1**

000 **9** *¾* **Spin Again (IRE)**[8] 7318 7-8-13 **68** MickaelBarzalona 11 64
(John Ryan) *hld up in rr: rdn and hdwy 1f out: styd on fnl f: nvr trbld ldrs* **33/1**

-502 **10** *1 ¼* **Opus Dei**[77] 5245 5-8-11 **71** NathanSweeney(5) 13 64
(Alan McCabe) *dwlt: sn rcvrd and in tch in midfield over 4f out: rdn and unable qck over 1f out: wknd fnl f* **16/1**

0-00 **11** *nk* **Elsie's Orphan**[23] 6934 5-9-1 **70** GeorgeBaker 1 62
(Patrick Chamings) *in tch in midfield: swtchd rt arnd wkng rival 2f out: sn rdn and no hdwy: wknd 1f out* **20/1**

6003 **12** *2* **Big Wave (IRE)**[23] 6934 4-9-1 **70** FrederikTylicki 9 57
(Alison Hutchinson) *rrd as stalls opened and s.i.s: t.k.h: hld up in rr: wd bnd 2f out: pushed along and plugged on fnl f: n.d* **14/1**

6510 **13** *5* **Galatian**[16] 7114 5-9-6 **75** JamesMillman 4 48
(Rod Millman) *bhd and rdn 4f out: wknd over 1f out: bhd fnl f* **6/1**[2]

1250 **14** *2 ½* **Halling Dancer**[23] 6932 3-9-4 **75**[1] DarryllHolland 2 41
(Lee Carter) *chsd ldr tl 3f out: rdn and lost pl 2f out: bhd fnl f* **8/1**

1m 24.63s (-0.17) **Going Correction** +0.025s/f (Slow)
WFA 3 from 4yo+ 2lb **14** Ran SP% **120.8**
Speed ratings (Par 103): **101,100,99,99,98 97,97,96,95,94 93,91,85,83**
Tote Swingers: 1&2 £12.10, 1&3 £16.10, 2&3 £24.60 CSF £65.28 CT £895.44 TOTE £7.30: £2.20, £3.70, £4.20; EX 74.50.
Owner Peter Bottomley & Jane Chapple-Hyam **Bred** Psb Holdings Ltd **Trained** Dalham, Suffolk
■ Stewards' Enquiry : Mark Coumbe two-day ban; used whip above permitted level (14th-15th Nov).

FOCUS
Another contest in which the winner enjoyed the run of the race in a prominent position. The time was almost identical to the first division.

7486 $150M BREEDERS' CUP POOLS H'CAP 1m (P)
3:10 (3:10) (Class 6) (0-60,60) 4-Y-O+ **£1,704** (£503; £251) **Stalls** High

Form RPR

566 **1** **Bladewood Girl**[16] 7112 4-9-5 **60** FrederikTylicki 9 68+
(J R Jenkins) *broke okay but grad stdd bk to rr after 2f: gd hdwy on inner over 1f out: led jst ins fnl f: hld on wl cl home* **5/1**[2]

5305 **2** *½* **Warbond**[28] 6774 4-9-3 **58** JamieGoldstein 5 65
(Michael Madgwick) *hld up in tch in last quartet: swtchd to outer 3f out and wd bnd 2f out: rdn and hdwy over 1f out: pressed wnr wl ins fnl f: r.o but hld cl home* **11/1**

3404 **3** ½ **Barachiel**[21] 6976 4-9-3 **58** RobertHavlin 4 64
(Luke Dace) *chsd ldr tl led 7f out: hdd 6f out and chsd ldr after: rdn to ld and edgd lft u.p over 1f out: hdd jst ins fnl f: kpt on same pce after* **5/1**[2]

0550 **4** 2 ¼ **Salient**[9] 7302 8-9-2 **57** J-PGuillambert 3 58
(Michael Attwater) *led for 1f: chsd ldrs after: carried lft but drvn to press ldr over 1f out: unable qck 1f out: wknd ins fnl f* **15/2**

0026 **5** hd **Byrd In Hand (IRE)**[9] 7302 5-9-3 **58** SeanLevey 12 58
(John Bridger) *dwlt: sn in tch in midfield: edgd out rt and effrt wl over 1f out: no imp 1f out and one pce fnl f* **6/1**[3]

405 **6** 1 ¼ **Brown Pete (IRE)**[13] 7200 4-8-11 **57** (e) CharlesBishop(5) 10 54
(Violet M Jordan) *in tch: rdn and unable qck 2f out: one pce and no imp fnl f* **6/1**[3]

4650 **7** 1 ½ **Saucy Buck (IRE)**[56] 5941 4-9-2 **57** (p) NeilCallan 11 51
(Zoe Davison) *s.i.s: bhd and sn rdn along: hdwy into midfield 3f out: drvn and unable qck 2f out: no imp over 1f out: btn and eased wl ins fnl f* **20/1**

0300 **8** 1 ½ **Spirit Of Gondree (IRE)**[28] 6773 4-9-4 **59** (b) LukeMorris 7 49
(Milton Bradley) *taken down early: t.k.h: chsd ldrs tl led 6f out: drvn and hdd wl over 1f out: wknd ent fnl f: wl btn and eased wl ins fnl f* **9/2**[1]

0500 **9** ¾ **Cut The Cackle (IRE)**[22] 6961 6-8-12 **60** (bt) NoraLooby(7) 8 49
(Violet M Jordan) *t.k.h: hld up in tch in midfield: shuffled bk towards rr over 2f out: pushed along and no hdwy over 1f out* **33/1**

0-30 **10** ½ **Pytheas (USA)**[292] 154 5-8-13 **60** (p) MarkCoumbe(3) 2 45
(Michael Attwater) *hld up in tch in last quartet: rdn and no hdwy wl over 1f out: bhd fnl f* **20/1**

1m 38.73s (0.53) **Going Correction** +0.025s/f (Slow) **10** Ran SP% **112.6**
Speed ratings (Par 101): **98,97,97,94,94 93,91,90,89,89**
Tote Swingers: 1&2 £9.10, 1&3 £6.20, 2&3 £8.60 CSF £54.51 CT £286.11 TOTE £4.80: £1.60, £3.20, £2.10; EX 30.40.
Owner Byron Boys **Bred** Southill Stud **Trained** Royston, Herts

FOCUS
A moderate handicap.
Bladewood Girl Official explanation: trainers representative said regarding apparent improvement in form that the filly had run well in her three maidens and this was her first run in a handicap.

7487 LINGFIELD PARK MARRIOTT HOTEL & COUNTRY CLUB H'CAP 1m 4f (P)
3:45 (3:45) (Class 3) (0-95,92) 3-Y-O+ £6,663 (£1,982; £990; £495) Stalls Low

Form RPR

-311 **1** **Estedaama (IRE)**[166] 2258 3-8-8 **81** TedDurcan 9 91+
(Marcus Tregoning) *hld up in tch in last quartet: hdwy to chse ldrs 3f out: rdn and wnt clr w ldr 2f out: led 1f out: drvn and styd on wl to assert fnl 75yds* **5/1**[3]

212 **2** 1 ½ **Fleeting Image**[14] 7168 3-8-8 **86** (p) NatashaEaton(5) 10 94
(Alan Bailey) *led: rdn and wnt clr w wnr 2f out: hdd 1f out: kpt battling on gamely tl no ex and btn fnl 75yds* **4/1**[1]

1103 **3** 4 **Enery (IRE)**[14] 7168 3-8-12 **85** NeilCallan 8 87
(Mark Johnston) *chsd ldrs: rdn and outpcd by ldng pair 2f out: kpt on same pce and no threat to ldrs after* **9/2**[2]

2153 **4** ½ **Daliance (IRE)**[13] 7195 3-8-10 **83** RichardKingscote 7 84
(Tom Dascombe) *hld up in rr: swtchd to outer 3f out: wnt modest 5th 2f out: styd on wl ins fnl f and pressing for 3rd cl home* **4/1**[1]

2520 **5** 1 ¾ **Muntasir (IRE)**[14] 7168 3-9-2 **89** (p) MickaelBarzalona 5 88
(Saeed Bin Suroor) *hld up in tch: hdwy to chse ldr over 5f out tl unable qck u.p ent fnl 2f: sn outpcd and btn: wknd 1f out* **9/2**[2]

0120 **6** 10 **Ukrainian (IRE)**[23] 6933 3-8-9 **82** (v) LiamJones 1 66
(Mark Johnston) *in tch tl dropped to rr and rdn 4f out: bhd fnl 2f* **12/1**

4050 **7** 9 **Emma's Gift (IRE)**[42] 6379 4-9-8 **88** (b) JimmyQuinn 4 58
(Julia Feilden) *hld up in tch in last quartet: reminders and rdn 5f out: outpcd and* **50/1**

6521 **8** ½ **Aldwick Bay (IRE)**[9] 7300 4-9-6 **86** 6ex SeanLevey 3 55
(Richard Hannon) *in tch: rdn 4f out: outpcd by ldrs and btn over 2f out: 6th and wl btn over 1f out: wknd* **12/1**

0410 **9** 20 **Emerald Wilderness (IRE)**[26] 6848 8-9-12 **92** FrederikTylicki 2 31
(Mark Rimmer) *t.k.h: chsd ldr tl over 5f out: rdn and dropped out over 3f out: t.o and eased ins fnl f* **25/1**

2m 28.38s (-4.62) **Going Correction** +0.025s/f (Slow)
WFA 3 from 4yo+ 7lb **9** Ran SP% **114.2**
Speed ratings (Par 107): **116,115,112,112,110 104,98,97,84**
Tote Swingers: 1&2 £3.40, 1&3 £3.60, 2&3 £4.90 CSF £25.02 CT £95.66 TOTE £4.50: £1.40, £1.10, £2.50; EX 19.80.
Owner Hamdan Al Maktoum **Bred** Shadwell Estate Company Limited **Trained** Lambourn, Berks

FOCUS
By far the best contest on the card and a solidly run race over the trip. The finish was dominated by two fillies.

NOTEBOOK
Estedaama(IRE) ◆, bidding for a hat-trick after 166 days off, was held up early but travelled smoothly into contention racing down towards the final bend. She had to dig deep to get the better of a tough and streetwise rival, but impressed with the way she went about it and she was well on top at the line. She remains unexposed and it will be fascinating to see where she goes next as there is surely plenty more to come. (tchd 9-2)
Fleeting Image, raised 4lb following a cracking effort in defeat over C&D a fortnight earlier, again attempted to run her rivals into the ground. She wouldn't give in without a fight when pressed by the winner after turning in, but eventually had to give best to a more progressive rival. She is wonderfully consistent, but may face another rise for this. (tchd 5-1)
Enery(IRE), closely matched with Fleeting Image on their meeting over C&D 14 days earlier, had every chance but looked to be struggling when meeting trouble on the home bend and was beaten a similar margin by his old rival at the line. (op 11-2)
Daliance(IRE), up another 3lb, was given awful lot to do and never had a prayer of making up the ground in time. He may prefer the stiffer 1m4f at Wolverhampton. (op 7-2)
Muntasir(IRE), who finished well behind a couple of these over C&D last time, was sent to take up a more prominent position at halfway, but looked to have run his race when meeting trouble turning for home. (op 7-1)

7488 FOLLOW US ON TWITTER @LINGFIELDPARK MAIDEN STKS 1m 2f (P)
4:15 (4:15) (Class 5) 3-Y-O+ £2,385 (£704; £352) Stalls Low

Form RPR

6 **1** **Ehtedaam (USA)**[41] 6397 3-9-3 0 TedDurcan 7 78
(Saeed Bin Suroor) *chsd ldrs: hdwy to join ldrs 3f out: led and wnt clr w rival over 2f out: styd on to assert and edgd lft ins fnl f* **2/1**[2]

62 **2** 1 ½ **Light Shine**[101] 4366 3-8-12 0 RobertHavlin 9 70
(John Gosden) *chsd ldr: upside ldr 3f out: drew clr w wnr over 2f out: ev ch tl no ex and btn ins fnl f: one pce after* **5/2**[3]

3 **3** 8 **Zeyran (IRE)**[14] 7174 3-8-12 0 TomQueally 5 55
(Sir Henry Cecil) *led tl rdn and hdd over 2f out: sn btn: wknd 2f out* **11/10**[1]

-056 **4** 3 ¼ **Awesome Rock (IRE)**[78] 5198 3-9-3 43 SebSanders 1 54
(Louise Best) *t.k.h: hld up in midfield: rdn and chsd ldng trio 3f out: sn outpcd and wl hld fnl 2f* **100/1**

00-0 **5** 3 ¾ **Tymismoni (IRE)**[20] 7005 4-9-0 45 MarkCoumbe(3) 10 42
(Michael Attwater) *in tch in midfield: rdn and outpcd over 3f out: 6th and wl btn over 2f out: plugged on* **100/1**

00/0 **6** nk **May Boy**[16] 7105 6-9-1 44 PhilipPrince(7) 4 46
(Ron Hodges) *chsd ldrs tl rdn and struggling over 3f out: sn wknd: 5th and wl btn 2f out* **100/1**

7 17 **Twilight Legend (IRE)** 3-8-12 0 JimmyQuinn 3 9
(Seamus Mullins) *hld up in last trio: lost tch over 3f out: t.o over 2f* **50/1**

0000 **8** 3 **Karistar (IRE)**[72] 5408 3-8-12 44 LiamJones 6
(Tom Keddy) *bhd: rdn and lost tch over 3f out: t.o over 2f out* **100/1**

0 **9** 2 **Neeka**[23] 6927 4-9-3 0 JamieGoldstein 11
(Zoe Davison) *s.i.s: hld up in last trio: lost tch 4f out: t.o over 2f out* **100/1**

0 **10** 25 **Flow Jo (IRE)**[27] 6827 4-9-3 0 J-PGuillambert 8
(Karen George) *t.k.h: chsd ldrs 4f out: steadily lost pl: bhd 3f out: wl t.o over 1f out* **33/1**

2m 5.67s (-0.93) **Going Correction** +0.025s/f (Slow)
WFA 3 from 4yo+ 5lb **10** Ran SP% **119.4**
Speed ratings (Par 103): **104,102,96,93,90 90,76,74,72,52**
Tote Swingers: 1&2 £1.30, 2&3 £1.10 CSF £7.68 TOTE £4.30: £1.30, £1.10, £1.02; EX 9.20.
Owner Godolphin **Bred** Grapestock Llc **Trained** Newmarket, Suffolk

FOCUS
Only three really mattered in this uncompetitive maiden. The pace appeared decent thanks to the third horse.
Twilight Legend(IRE) Official explanation: jockey said filly ran too free.
T/Plt: £1,735.00 to a £1 stake. Pool: £45,967.79 - 19.34 winning tickets. T/Qpdt: £85.50 to a £1 stake. Pool: £6,823.71 - 59.00 winning tickets. SP

7172 NOTTINGHAM (L-H)
Wednesday, October 31

OFFICIAL GOING: Soft (good to soft in places; 7.2)
Wind: Moderate against Weather: Overcast

7489 TROJAN HORSE H'CAP 5f 13y
12:20 (12:22) (Class 5) (0-75,75) 3-Y-O+ £2,264 (£673; £336; £168) Stalls High

Form RPR

5020 **1** **Lupo D'Oro (IRE)**[16] 7114 3-9-4 **72** RobertWinston 8 83
(John Best) *hld up in tch: smooth hdwy wl over 1f out: rdn to ld ins fnl f: sn clr: kpt on* **12/1**

1220 **2** 2 ½ **I See You**[8] 7309 3-9-5 **73** (p) JimmyFortune 7 75
(Peter Makin) *hld up: hdwy over 1f out: rdn and styd on to chse wnr ins fnl f: no imp towards fin* **16/1**

6550 **3** 1 ½ **Haajes**[9] 7295 8-9-7 **75** MickyFenton 10 71
(Paul Midgley) *trckd ldrs: hdwy 2f out: rdn to ld appr fnl f: sn drvn: hdd ins fnl f and one pce* **14/1**

2001 **4** 1 ¾ **Whitecrest**[9] 7299 4-9-6 **74** 6ex ChrisCatlin 9 63
(John Spearing) *chsd ldrs: rdn along wl over 1f out: kpt on same pce* **16/1**

0R00 **5** hd **Monsieur Jamie**[16] 7113 4-9-4 **72** IanMongan 11 61
(J R Jenkins) *midfield: hdwy 2f out: sn rdn: no imp fnl f* **50/1**

14/0 **6** ¾ **Sextons House (IRE)**[4] 7411 4-9-1 **69** MartinHarley 14 55
(Alan McCabe) *in rr: hdwy wl over 1f out: sn rdn and kpt on fnl f: nrst fin* **80/1**

3011 **7** nk **Danzoe (IRE)**[14] 7179 5-9-0 **68** TomMcLaughlin 6 53
(Christine Dunnett) *midfield: hdwy over 1f out: n.m.r and swtchd lft ent fnl f: sn rdn and kpt on same pce* **16/1**

3214 **8** nse **Ambitious Icarus**[16] 7100 3-9-2 **70** (e) RobbieFitzpatrick 16 56
(Richard Guest) *in rr tl sme late hdwy* **6/1**[2]

4422 **9** nk **Sandwith**[16] 7101 9-8-13 **72** (p) GarryWhillans(5) 17 56
(George Foster) *chsd ldng paiur: effrt 2f out: sn rdn and ev ch tl edgd lft jst ins fnl f and sn wknd* **16/1**

030 **10** ½ **Cardinal**[16] 7113 7-9-4 **72** JimCrowley 13 54
(Robert Cowell) *in tch on outer: rdn along 2f out: n.d* **7/1**[3]

5300 **11** ½ **Berberana (IRE)**[13] 7197 4-8-13 **67** (p) GrahamLee 5 47
(Jeremy Gask) *chsd ldrs: rdn along over 2f out: sn wknd* **20/1**

0005 **12** nk **Dispol Grand (IRE)**[9] 7299 6-8-8 **69** (v) DanielleMooney(7) 3 48
(Paul Midgley) *a in rr* **33/1**

3661 **13** nse **Aubrietia**[14] 7178 3-8-8 **69** (b) DavidBergin(7) 2 49
(Alan McCabe) *chsd ldrs: rdn along 2f out: sn wknd* **7/2**[1]

0304 **14** nk **Captain Scooby**[9] 7295 6-9-0 **73** JasonHart(5) 15 51
(Richard Guest) *a towards rr* **10/1**

0242 **15** 1 ¼ **El McGlynn (IRE)**[14] 7177 3-8-13 **74** HannahNunn(7) 1 48
(Peter Salmon) *cl up: disp ld 1/2-way: led 2f out: sn rdn and hdd appr fnl f: wknd qckly* **10/1**

0215 **16** 5 **I'll Be Good**[16] 7101 3-8-11 **72** KevinStott(7) 4 28
(Robert Johnson) *slt ld: pushed along 1/2-way: rdn and hdd over 2f out: wknd over 1f out* **16/1**

1m 3.98s (2.48) **Going Correction** +0.675s/f (Yiel) **16** Ran SP% **121.9**
Speed ratings (Par 103): **103,99,96,93,93 92,91,91,91,90 89,89,89,88,86 78**
Tote Swingers: 1&2 £16.40, 1&3 £25.20, 2&3 £37.40 CSF £185.83 CT £2721.61 TOTE £17.50: £3.80, £4.90, £4.30, £5.20; EX 238.50 TRIFECTA Not won..
Owner S Malcolm M Winwright P Tindall **Bred** Mrs E Fitzsimons **Trained** Hucking, Kent

FOCUS
Cathedral bend out 3yds, Northern bend in 3yds. A typically competitive sprint handicap, run on drying ground.
Sandwith Official explanation: jockey said gelding hung left.

7490 FORTIOAKS H'CAP 2m 9y
12:50 (12:52) (Class 6) (0-65,66) 3-Y-O+ £1,617 (£481; £240; £120) Stalls Low

Form RPR

3330 **1** **Zarosa (IRE)**[13] 7196 3-7-9 **48** NoelGarbutt(7) 9 59
(John Berry) *in tch: hdwy over 3f out: led over 2f out: rdn clr over 1f out: kpt on: comf* **10/1**

1532 **2** 5 **Queen's Star**[10] 7271 3-9-1 **61** DavidProbert 11 65
(Andrew Balding) *midfield: rdn 3f out: styd on fnl 2f: wnt 2nd ins fnl f: no ch w wnr* **2/1**[1]

0146 **3** ¾ **Eastern Magic**[27] 6821 5-9-3 **58** JackDuern(5) 7 61
(Reg Hollinshead) *midfield: hdwy over 3f out: rdn and ev ch over 2f out: sn one pce and no ch w wnr: lost 2nd ins fnl f* **9/1**[3]

0450 **4** 4 **David's Folly (IRE)**[14] 7169 3-7-13 **48** ow3 RyanPowell(3) 1 46
(Bryn Palling) *trckd ldrs: rdn over 3f out: sn outpcd by ldrs: plugged on fnl 2f* **14/1**

The Form Book Flat, Raceform Ltd, Compton, RG20 6NL

6001 **5** 1 1/4 **Captain Cardington (IRE)**[9] 7301 3-9-6 **66** 6ex............. ChrisCatlin 10 63
(Sheena West) *prom: led 4f out: rdn whn hdd over 2f out: wknd over 1f out* **4/1**[2]
065/ **6** 1/2 **Elysian Heights (IRE)**[767] 6365 4-9-5 **55**........................(t) GrahamLee 5 51
(Nigel Twiston-Davies) *hld up: hdwy 3f out: rdn over 2f out: plugged on: nvr threatened ldrs* **9/1**[3]
0003 **7** 7 **Inside Knowledge (USA)**[9] 7293 6-8-11 **47**.................. MickyFenton 14 35
(Garry Woodward) *led: hdd 4f out: wknd over 2f out* **25/1**
000 **8** 11 **Dunaskin (IRE)**[1] 7472 12-8-5 **46**..................................(b) JasonHart(5) 2 21
(Richard Guest) *trckd ldrs: pushed along over 3f out: sn wknd* **50/1**
2601 **9** 5 **Musically**[11] 7248 3-9-4 **64**.. MartinHarley 3 33
(Mick Channon) *hld up: rdn over 3f out: nvr threatened* **10/1**
4440 **10** 24 **Avison (IRE)**[25] 6885 4-9-2 **52** ow2....................................... DavidNolan 8
(Richard Fahey) *hld up in midfield: rdn over 3f out: sn btn* **25/1**
0-50 **11** 2 **Sunny Bank**[19] 7016 3-8-8 **57**.................................... SimonPearce(3) 15
(Andrew Balding) *hld up in midfield: rdn 4f out: sn btn* **14/1**
3660 **12** 3/4 **Gavi**[26] 6838 6-9-3 **53**.. TomMcLaughlin 12
(Karen George) *trckd ldrs towards outer: rdn over 3f out: sn wknd* **28/1**

3m 45.33s (10.83) **Going Correction** +0.85s/f (Soft)
WFA 3 from 4yo+ 10lb **12** Ran SP% **117.9**
Speed ratings (Par 101): **96,93,93,91,90 90,86,81,78,66 65,65**
Tote Swingers: 1&2 £5.70, 1&3 £14.50, 2&3 £3.10 CSF £29.01 CT £194.89 TOTE £17.20: £4.30, £1.10, £3.30; EX 45.80 Trifecta £156.00 Part won. Pool: £205.05 - 0.20 winning units..
Owner Roger Vicarage **Bred** Keatly Overseas Ltd **Trained** Newmarket, Suffolk

FOCUS
A modest staying handicap run at a steady pace.
Inside Knowledge(USA) Official explanation: jockey said gelding hung right.

7491 FORTIGUINEAS (S) STKS 1m 75y
1:20 (1:22) (Class 6) 2-Y-O **£1,617** (£481; £240; £120) **Stalls** Centre

Form RPR
450 **1** **Rakticate (IRE)**[40] 6437 2-8-6 60...................................... AndreaAtzeni 4 62
(J S Moore) *hld up: hreadway 4f out: pushed along to chse ldrs 3f out: rdn and cl up over 2f out: led wl over 1f out: drvn out* **5/2**[1]
0500 **2** 5 **Unidexter (IRE)**[20] 7008 2-8-11 57................................ SamHitchcott 12 56
(Mick Channon) *midfield: hdwy 1/2-way: rdn along and cl up over 2f out: drvn to chse wnr wl over 1f out: sn drvn and no imp* **7/1**[3]
0 **3** 3/4 **Tilly T (IRE)**[14] 7160 2-8-3 0...................................... RyanPowell(3) 2 49
(J S Moore) *dwlt and towards rr: hdwy 4f out: rdn along 3f out: styd on fnl 2f: nrst fin* **20/1**
0430 **4** 4 1/2 **Baltic Prince (IRE)**[18] 7060 2-8-11 52...................... SilvestreDeSousa 6 44
(Paul Green) *trckd ldng pair: hdwy 3f out: rdn to ld over 2f out: drvn and hdd wl over 1f out: sn one pce* **11/2**[2]
3500 **5** 6 **Fruity Bun**[35] 6583 2-8-6 47.. DominicFox 3 26
(Matthew Salaman) *chsd ldrs: rdn along over 3f out: sn one pce* **22/1**
3605 **6** 4 1/2 **Lucky Suit (IRE)**[34] 6612 2-8-11 53............................ DavidProbert 11 21
(Ronald Harris) *chsd ldrs: hdwy 4f out: cl up wl over 2f out: sn rdn and wknd* **8/1**
046 **7** 2 **Sad But True (IRE)**[27] 6826 2-8-11 43..........................(v) MartinHarley 7 17
(Alan McCabe) *led: rdn along over 3f out: hdd wl over 2f out: grad wknd* **12/1**
3300 **8** 3/4 **Strawberry Duck (IRE)**[40] 6435 2-8-6 51.......................... ChrisCatlin 9 10
(Amy Weaver) *chsd ldr: cl up after 3f: rdn along 1/2-way: sn wknd* **10/1**
9 hd **Amelia Hull** 2-8-3 0.. SimonPearce(3) 1 10
(J S Moore) *midfield: rdn along 1/2-way: sn outpcd* **16/1**
00 **10** 3 3/4 **Gabrial The Tyrant (IRE)**[14] 7165 2-8-11 0...................... JoeFanning 5 7
(Mark Johnston) *s.i.s: a in rr* **9/1**
11 1 **Naughty Indian (IRE)** 2-8-11 0.............................. FrankieMcDonald 8 4
(Paul Fitzsimons) *rdn along after 3f: a towards rr* **16/1**
12 2 3/4 **Sarahs Pal** 2-8-3 0.. RaulDaSilva(3) 10
(Mandy Rowland) *s.i.s: a bhd* **20/1**

1m 54.35s (5.35) **Going Correction** +0.85s/f (Soft) **12** Ran SP% **120.0**
Speed ratings (Par 93): **90,85,84,79,73 69,67,66,66,62 61,58**
Tote Swingers: 1&2 £4.80, 1&3 £17.50, 2&3 £45.80 CSF £19.09 TOTE £2.20: £1.10, £1.30, £11.00; EX 23.20 Trifecta £317.40 Part won. Pool: £423.31 - 0.90 winning units..No bid for winner.
Owner G V March & J S Moore **Bred** Geoffrey And Mrs E Thompson **Trained** Upper Lambourn, Berks

FOCUS
A poor juvenile seller run at a decent pace.

NOTEBOOK
Rakticate(IRE) justified strong market confidence. The winner, one of the least exposed in the field, had shown ability on a similar surface to this at Goodwood in August and he confirmed his liking for conditions, albeit in extremely workmanlike fashion. Under pressure fully 3f from home, he looked to have it all to do but, pulled to the outside to challenge, stuck on tenaciously and eventually won with plenty in hand. Rated 60 coming into this, he's unlikely to be too heavily penalised and may well be capable of better once stepped up to middle-distances. (op 7-2)
Unidexter(IRE) ran a sound race but failed to see this out as well as the winner. He rolled around once working his way to the front and could probably do with better ground. (tchd 13-2)
Tilly T(IRE) was seemingly going nowhere, but she responded well to strong driving without ever being close enough to challenge. (op 33-1)
Baltic Prince(IRE) finished tired and appeared not to last home on his first try at 1m. He was going as well as anything 2f out and a drop back in distance is anticipated. (op 7-1 tchd 15-2)

7492 E B F FORTIGOLD CUP OATH MAIDEN STKS (C&G) 1m 75y
1:55 (1:58) (Class 4) 2-Y-O **£4,528** (£1,347; £673; £336) **Stalls** Centre

Form RPR
45 **1** **Mister Impatience**[17] 7081 2-9-0 0................................... JoeFanning 12 81+
(Mark Johnston) *trckd ldng pair: cl up 1/2-way: led 3f out: rdn clr wl over 1f out: easily* **6/1**[3]
00 **2** 6 **Chocala (IRE)**[50] 6114 2-9-0 0.. AdamKirby 14 67
(Alan King) *trckd ldrs: hdwy over 3f out: rdn along over 2f out: styd on to chse wnr over 1f out: sooin drvn and kpt on: no ch w wnr* **66/1**
0 **3** 3/4 **Guilded Spirit**[28] 6795 2-9-0 0.. IanMongan 10 65
(Stuart Kittow) *hld up: hdwy 4f out: rdn to chse ldrs over 2f out: kpt on appr fnl f: nrst fin* **33/1**
02 **4** 4 1/2 **Elidor**[17] 7081 2-9-0 0..(v) MartinHarley 1 55
(Mick Channon) *trckd ldrs on inner: hdwy over 3f out: rdn along wl over 2f out: sn one pce* **15/8**[1]
0 **5** nse **White Month**[17] 7081 2-9-0 0.. JimmyFortune 2 55
(Andrew Balding) *led: hdd and pushed along 1/2-way: rdn wl over 2f out and grad wknd* **16/1**
6 1 3/4 **Marlborough House** 2-9-0 0.. SamHitchcott 8 51
(Mark Johnston) *midfield: hdwy and in tch 1/2-way: effrt 3f out: sn rdn along and n.d* **33/1**
7 2 1/4 **Powder Hound** 2-8-7 0.. DanielMuscutt(7) 7 46
(Andrew Balding) *midfield: rdn along over 3f out: n.d* **33/1**
00 **8** 3 1/4 **Misteray**[14] 7165 2-8-7 0.. JakePayne(7) 9 39
(Bill Turner) *cl up: led 4f out: rdn and hdd 3f out: sn wknd* **125/1**
9 7 **Rancher (IRE)** 2-9-0 0.. ChrisCatlin 13 24
(Harry Dunlop) *a towards rr* **40/1**
4 **10** 3/4 **Sizzler**[23] 6928 2-9-0 0.. JimCrowley 4 22
(Ralph Beckett) *dwlt: a towards rr* **10/3**[2]
11 1 3/4 **Ballinderry Boy** 2-9-0 0.. DavidProbert 6 18
(Andrew Balding) *s.i.s: a bhd* **28/1**
12 1 1/2 **Muhtaram** 2-9-0 0.. SilvestreDeSousa 3 15
(Saeed Bin Suroor) *dwlt: green and a bhd* **14/1**
05 **13** 1/2 **Sir Frank Morgan (IRE)**[20] 6997 2-9-0 0....................(b[1]) GrahamLee 11 14
(Mark Johnston) *a towards rr* **50/1**
2 **14** 25 **Intermix (IRE)**[21] 6978 2-8-11 0...................................... RaulDaSilva(3) 5
(Paul Cole) *plld hrd: chsd ldng pair: rdn along over 4f out: sn wknd: bhd and eased fnl 2f* **6/1**[3]

1m 52.28s (3.28) **Going Correction** +0.85s/f (Soft) **14** Ran SP% **117.9**
Speed ratings (Par 97): **100,94,93,88,88 86,84,81,74,73 71,70,69,44**
Tote Swingers: Not won. CSF £364.09 TOTE £5.60: £1.60, £18.70, £12.90; EX 452.30 TRIFECTA Not won..
Owner The Originals **Bred** The Kathryn Stud Ltd **Trained** Middleham Moor, N Yorks

FOCUS
An informative juvenile maiden, run in testing conditions.

NOTEBOOK
Mister Impatience came clear to win with any amount in hand. The winner had finished a long way behind Elidor on their meeting at Goodwood earlier this month but he turned that form on its head and looks a nice staying prospect for connections to go to war with next season. Always travelling well towards the lead, he fairly breezed clear and was value for a deal more than eventual winning margin. Distances in this type of ground can often be exaggerated but it's likely he'll be given a mark in the high 70s at the very least, such was the authority of this success. However, he remains open to bags of improvement and is clearly well suited to getting his toe in. (op 8-1)
Chocala(IRE) hadn't shown a great deal previously, but this was the softest ground he'd encountered and he clearly relished it. Not given an unduly hard time once his winning chance had gone, he should be very competitive in handicaps off his anticipated mark. (op 40-1)
Guilded Spirit was another significant improver. He'd clearly learnt plenty for his debut and pulled nicely clear of the remainder. He could well be seen on the AW before too long with handicaps surely on the agenda for him on turf next season. (op 25-1)
Elidor was bitterly disappointing and has seemingly regressed since his encouraging Goodwood second, when he had today's winner behind. Sporting a visor for the second time, he's probably not straightforward. (op 5-2)
White Month shaped with a deal more promise than he had on debut, though is only limited on this evidence. A step up to middle-distances may extract further improvement however. (op 50-1)
Sizzler appeared not to have any real excuses for this poor showing and is one to have reservations about. (op 3-1 tchd 11-4)
Muhtaram looked all at sea throughout and will need to step up greatly on this if he's to get competitive. (op 13-2)
Intermix(IRE) was still in contention when the saddle slipped forward. He should be given another chance. Official explanation: jockey said saddle slipped. (op 15-2)

7493 FORTINATIONAL H'CAP 1m 75y
2:30 (2:30) (Class 4) (0-85,84) 3-Y-O+ **£4,075** (£1,212; £606; £303) **Stalls** Centre

Form RPR
1321 **1** **Myboyalfie (USA)**[23] 6932 5-9-7 **84**...............................(v) IanMongan 10 93
(J R Jenkins) *mde most: rdn 2f out: styd on gamely fnl f* **8/1**
4132 **2** 1 1/2 **Uncle Dermot (IRE)**[9] 7302 4-8-7 **70**............................ ChrisCatlin 3 76
(Brendan Powell) *trckd ldrs: hdwy and cl up 1/2-way: rdn along over 2f out and sltly outpcd over 1f out: kpt on u.p fnl f: tk 2nd nr fin* **9/1**
4524 **3** 1/2 **Crown Counsel (IRE)**[12] 7210 4-9-7 **84**.......................... JoeFanning 6 89
(Mark Johnston) *cl up: effrt over 2f out: rdn along wl over 1f out: drvn and kpt on same pce fnl f* **5/1**[2]
0 **4** 1 **The Osteopath (IRE)**[72] 5414 9-8-11 **74**......................... PJMcDonald 7 76
(John Davies) *trckd ldrs: hdwy 4f out: rdn along and outpcd 2f out: styd on fnl f: nrst fin* **20/1**
2201 **5** 2 1/4 **First Post (IRE)**[17] 7083 5-9-6 **83**...................................... AndreaAtzeni 5 80
(Derek Haydn Jones) *hld up towards rr: hdwy on inner 3f out: rdn 2f out: chsd ldrs over 1f out: sn drvn and no imp* **5/1**[2]
0030 **6** 3/4 **West End Lad**[9] 7294 9-8-3 **72** ow1.............................(b) DavidBergin(7) 9 69
(Roy Bowring) *prom: hdwy on outer to chse ldng pair 1/2-way: rdn along 3f out: sn wknd* **15/2**[3]
0000 **7** 1 1/4 **Flying Applause**[11] 7256 7-8-12 **75**................................(b) DominicFox 4 68
(Roy Bowring) *dwlt: a in rr* **50/1**
1614 **8** 1/2 **Moheebb (IRE)**[20] 7003 8-8-10 **73**............................(e[1]) RobertWinston 2 65
(Robert Johnson) *a towards rr* **20/1**
6260 **9** 1/2 **Extraterrestrial**[12] 7210 8-9-7 **84**...................................... DavidNolan 8 75
(Richard Fahey) *hld up in rr: sme hdwy 1/2-way: sn rdn along and nvr a factor* **16/1**
5221 **10** 1 3/4 **A'Juba**[23] 6925 3-8-11 **77**..(b[1]) SilvestreDeSousa 1 63
(Saeed Bin Suroor) *trckd ldrs: hdwy over 3f out: rdn to chse wnr 2f out: drvn over 1f out: wkng whn edgd rt ent fnl f: wknd qckly and eased* **9/4**[1]

1m 51.33s (2.33) **Going Correction** +0.85s/f (Soft)
WFA 3 from 4yo+ 3lb **10** Ran SP% **114.3**
Speed ratings (Par 105): **105,103,103,102,99 99,97,97,96,95**
Tote Swingers: 1&2 £6.90, 1&3 £5.20, 2&3 £6.60 CSF £73.97 CT £407.49 TOTE £10.50: £2.90, £3.00, £1.10; EX 53.40 Trifecta £561.70 Pool: £763.92 - 1.02 winning units..
Owner D Badham **Bred** Robert Pierz & Robert Brooks **Trained** Royston, Herts

FOCUS
A competitive handicap run at a steady pace in tiring conditions.
A'Juba Official explanation: jockey said gelding became unbalanced in the closing stages.

7494 FORTIGUARDIAN MAIDEN STKS 1m 75y
3:00 (3:03) (Class 5) 3-Y-O **£2,264** (£673; £336; £168) **Stalls** Centre

Form RPR
22 **1** **Last Fighter (IRE)**[22] 6965 3-9-3 0.......................... SilvestreDeSousa 4 78
(Saeed Bin Suroor) *sn in tch: pushed along and hdwy over 2f out: led over 1f out: drvn and edgd lft ins fnl f: hld on towards fin* **15/8**[1]
2 1/2 **Hassle (IRE)** 3-9-3 0.. AdamKirby 5 77+
(Clive Cox) *dwlt: hld up in tch: pushed along over 3f out: hdwy over 1f out: chsd wnr jst ins fnl f: kpt on but a jst hld* **7/2**[3]
3530 **3** hd **Safarjal (IRE)**[62] 5766 3-8-12 74.. GrahamLee 3 71
(Charles Hills) *led: rdn and one pce whn hdd over 1f out: kpt on again towards fin* **9/2**
352 **4** 1 3/4 **Surreal (IRE)**[16] 7112 3-8-12 73...................................... JimmyFortune 2 68
(Sir Michael Stoute) *racd keenly: trckd ldr: rdn over 2f out: sn one pce* **10/3**[2]

03 **5** *2 1/4* **Basingstoke (IRE)**[22] 6965 3-8-10 0 DanielMuscutt(7) 6 68
(Andrew Balding) *trckd ldr: rdn over 2f out: sn one pce: no ex ins fnl f* **8/1**
00 **6** *36* **Merevale**[14] 7174 3-9-3 0 DominicFox 1
(Michael Appleby) *hld up: bhd fnl 4f* **80/1**
1m 52.99s (3.99) **Going Correction** +0.85s/f (Soft) **6** Ran SP% **110.6**
Speed ratings (Par 101): **97,96,96,94,92 56**
Tote Swingers: 1&2 £2.10, 1&3 £1.90, 2&3 £2.80 CSF £8.44 TOTE £2.80: £1.60, £2.50; EX 10.50.
Owner Godolphin **Bred** Yeomanstown Lodge Stud **Trained** Newmarket, Suffolk
FOCUS
Just a fair end-of-season maiden.

7495 FINAL FORTIFURLONG AJA LADIES' GRAND FINALE H'CAP (FOR LADY AMATEUR RIDERS) (DIV I) 1m 2f 50y
3:35 (3:35) (Class 6) (0-65,65) 3-Y-0+ **£1,559** (£483; £241; £121) **Stalls** Low

Form RPR
6236 **1** **Monthly Medal**[5] 7383 9-9-10 **59** (t) MissSMDoolan(5) 3 70
(Wilf Storey) *hld up in rr: stdy hdwy 3f out: trckd ldrs 2f out: chsd ldr over 1f out: rdn to ld ins fnl f: kpt on* **5/1**[2]
1231 **2** *1 3/4* **Tawseef (IRE)**[22] 6949 4-10-7 **65** MissSBrotherton 4 73
(Roy Brotherton) *dwlt: sn midfield: hdwy 4f out: led over 2f out: rdn ent fnl f: sn hdd and one pce* **6/4**[1]
0236 **3** *6* **Maybeme**[21] 6988 6-9-3 **52** [1] MissAliceMills(5) 1 49
(Neville Bycroft) *cl up: led after 2f: rdn along over 3f out: hdd over 2f out and kpt on same pce* **13/2**[3]
2254 **4** *1* **Cyril The Squirrel**[16] 7115 8-10-3 **61** MissGAndrews 12 56
(Karen George) *hld up in rr: hdwy over 4f out: rdn along wl over 2f out: kpt on same pce* **10/1**
4054 **5** *1 3/4* **Graceful Act**[36] 6561 4-9-5 **54** MissVBarr(5) 7 46
(Ron Barr) *chsd ldrs: rdn along 3f out: grad wknd fnl 2f* **20/1**
0304 **6** *1 1/4* **Harare**[34] 6608 11-9-11 **60** (v) MissPhillipaTutty(5) 2 50
(Karen Tutty) *dwlt: towards rr: rfiudden along on inner and bhd 3f out: sn swtchd rt and kpt on fr over 1f out: nrst fin* **33/1**
0644 **7** *1 1/2* **Fonterutoli (IRE)**[28] 6774 5-9-0 **51** oh4 (e) MissRBIngram(7) 9 38
(Roger Ingram) *towards rr: sme hdwy on wd outside over 3f out: sn rdn and n.d* **16/1**
34 **8** *1/2* **Present Day**[16] 7108 3-9-3 **55** (b) MissRachelKing(3) 13 41
(Clive Cox) *trckd ldrs on inner: effrt 3f out: rdn along over 2f out: sn btn* **7/1**
5050 **9** *hd* **Dzesmin (POL)**[36] 6562 10-9-2 **53** oh2 ow2 (p) MrsAGuest(7) 11 39
(Richard Guest) *nvr bttr than midfield* **25/1**
0300 **10** *12* **Flag Of Glory**[87] 4844 5-9-9 **60** MissMEdden(7) 8 24
(Peter Hiatt) *led 2f: cl up: rdn along over 3f out: sn wknd* **20/1**
-000 **11** *2 1/4* **Highland Cadett**[45] 6280 5-9-0 **51** oh6 MissSLBowen(7) 6 11
(Pam Ford) *in tch: rdn along over 3f out: sn wknd* **100/1**
6505 **12** *1/2* **Kieron's Rock (IRE)**[36] 6562 3-8-10 **52** oh6 ow1 MissEmmaBedford(7) 5 11
(Jedd O'Keeffe) *chsd ldrs: rdn along over 4f out: sn wknd* **50/1**
2m 20.71s (6.41) **Going Correction** +0.85s/f (Soft)
WFA 3 from 4yo+ 5lb **12** Ran SP% **116.3**
Speed ratings (Par 101): **97,95,90,90,88 87,86,86,85,76 74,74**
Tote Swingers: 1&2 £3.40, 1&3 £4.90, 2&3 £2.60 CSF £11.64 CT £49.42 TOTE £4.90: £1.70, £1.40, £1.70; EX 18.50 Trifecta £68.90 Pool: £588.98 - 6.41 winning units..
Owner Gremlin Racing **Bred** G S Shropshire **Trained** Muggleswick, Co Durham
FOCUS
A moderate lady riders' handicap, run at a brisk pace given the testing conditions.

7496 FINAL FORTIFURLONG AJA LADIES' GRAND FINALE H'CAP (FOR LADY AMATEUR RIDERS) (DIV II) 1m 2f 50y
4:05 (4:05) (Class 6) (0-65,61) 3-Y-0+ **£1,559** (£483; £241; £121) **Stalls** Low

Form RPR
0656 **1** **Shamo Hill Theatre**[46] 6258 5-9-0 **47** (p) MissVickiWood(7) 8 54
(Lawrence Mullaney) *midfield: rdn and hdwy over 2f out: chal appr fnl f: kpt on: led post* **14/1**
542 **2** *shd* **Edgware Road**[5] 7383 4-9-11 **58** (b) MissBHampson(7) 3 65
(Sean Curran) *trckd ldrs: led over 3f out: rdn over 2f out: strly pressed appr fnl f: kpt on: hdd post* **4/1**[2]
0006 **3** *3 1/2* **Hoonose**[27] 6813 3-8-13 **47** MissRachelKing(3) 6 48
(Pat Eddery) *midfield: rdn over 3f out: kpt on: wnt 3rd ins fnl f: no threat ldng pair* **14/1**
240 **4** *nk* **Captain Oats (IRE)**[27] 6821 9-9-7 **54** MissSLBowen(7) 10 54
(Pam Ford) *v.s.a: hld up in rr: stl wl bhd over 2f out: r.o wl fnl f: nrst fin* **50/1**
3430 **5** *1* **South Cape**[28] 6801 9-10-3 **60** MissHayleyMoore(3) 11 58
(Gary Moore) *hld up: rdn over 2f out: kpt on fnl f: nvr threatened ldrs* **13/2**
00 **6** *hd* **Kingaroo (IRE)**[28] 6794 6-9-8 **53** MissRSmith(5) 1 51
(Garry Woodward) *led: hdd over 3f out: sn rdn and outpcd: plugged on again fnl f* **28/1**
5023 **7** *1* **Hernando Torres**[33] 6631 4-10-0 **61** MissAHesketh(7) 9 57
(Michael Easterby) *slowly away: hld up: hdwy over 3f out: sn chsd ldrs: no ex ins fnl f* **11/2**[3]
0400 **8** *hd* **Ptolomeos**[60] 5824 9-9-3 **50** MissEmmaBedford(7) 5 46
(Sean Regan) *in tch: rdn and outpcd over 3f out: plugged on again fnl f* **11/1**
4042 **9** *1 1/4* **Honoured (IRE)**[6] 7353 5-10-7 **61** (p) MissSBrotherton 2 54
(Michael Appleby) *midfield: hdwy 4f out: rdn and ev ch 3f out: wknd ins fnl f* **3/1**[1]
0040 **10** *1 3/4* **Nolecce**[5] 7383 5-9-5 **52** (p) MrsAGuest(7) 4 42
(Richard Guest) *trckd ldrs: rdn over 3f out: sn struggling* **22/1**
0246 **11** *1/2* **Corrib (IRE)**[19] 7015 9-9-2 **47** oh2 (p) MissAliceMills(5) 12 36
(Bryn Palling) *trckd ldrs on outer: rdn over 3f out: sn wknd* **25/1**
0505 **12** *8* **Al Furat (USA)**[39] 6478 4-10-1 **60** MissVBarr(5) 7 35
(Ron Barr) *v.s.a: hld up in rr: brief hdwy on inner over 4f out: wknd over 3f out* **12/1**
2m 24.14s (9.84) **Going Correction** +0.85s/f (Soft)
WFA 3 from 4yo+ 5lb **12** Ran SP% **116.7**
Speed ratings (Par 101): **84,83,81,80,80 79,79,78,77,76 76,69**
Tote Swingers: 1&2 £15.90, 1&3 £25.60, 2&3 £6.80 CSF £65.66 CT £815.52 TOTE £22.20: £4.80, £2.10, £3.90; EX 89.70 TRIFECTA Not won..
Owner Ross Heatherill **Bred** Karen Watson **Trained** Great Habton, N Yorks
■ Vicki Wood's first winner, on just her second ride.
FOCUS
There was more depth to the second division of this lady riders' handicap
Al Furat(USA) Official explanation: trainers representative said gelding was unsuited by going soft (good to soft in places).
T/Plt: £2,749.20 to a £1 stake. Pool: £35,476.92 - 9.42 winning tickets. T/Qpdt: £127.90 to a £1 stake. Pool: £4,011.23 - 2.00 winning tickets. JR

7473 KEMPTON (A.W) (R-H)
Thursday, November 1

OFFICIAL GOING: Standard
Wind: Moderate, across Weather: Clear

7497 32REDBET.COM MAIDEN STKS (DIV I) 6f (P)
4:40 (4:40) (Class 5) 2-Y-0 **£2,264** (£673; £336; £168) **Stalls** Low

Form RPR
1 **Foxtrot Jubilee (IRE)** 2-9-3 0 RichardThomas 1 72
(Ralph Beckett) *mde all: kicked on over 2f out: 2 l clr 1f out: jst lasted* **14/1**
4 **2** *shd* **Floating Along (IRE)**[75] 5357 2-8-12 0 LiamJones 5 67
(William Haggas) *t.k.h: hld up in midfield: rdn and prog over 1f out: chsd wnr jst ins fnl f: clsd fin: jst failed* **3/1**[2]
23 **3** *nse* **Secret Missile**[35] 6609 2-9-3 0 MartinDwyer 7 72
(William Muir) *trckd ldrs: rdn over 1f out: prog to dispute 2nd fnl f: styd on nr fin: jst hld* **9/2**[3]
20 **4** *1 3/4* **Desert Sunrise**[125] 3560 2-8-12 0 TomEaves 3 61
(Sir Michael Stoute) *trckd ldng pair: chsd wnr 2f out to jst ins fnl f: one pce* **14/1**
2 **5** *shd* **Serenity Spa**[104] 4282 2-8-12 0 JimmyFortune 9 61
(Roger Charlton) *hld up in last trio: prog on inner 2f out: shkn up over 1f out: disp 2nd briefly 1f out: one pce after* **3/1**[2]
0 **6** *1 1/2* **Malaysian Boleh**[29] 6772 2-9-3 0 SebSanders 8 62
(Simon Dow) *hld up in last trio: shkn up and rn green 2f out: one pce and no imp after* **66/1**
7 *hd* **Bastion (USA)** 2-9-3 0 NeilCallan 2 61
(Roger Varian) *s.s: in tch in last: pushed along over 2f out: one pce and no imp on ldrs* **11/4**[1]
00 **8** *3 3/4* **Bapak Besar (CAN)**[55] 6015 2-9-3 0 FergusSweeney 4 50
(Kevin Ryan) *chsd wnr to 2f out: wknd* **33/1**
1m 12.65s (-0.45) **Going Correction** -0.125s/f (Stan) **8** Ran SP% **112.6**
Speed ratings (Par 96): **98,97,97,95,95 93,93,88**
Tote Swingers 1&2 £9.20, 2&3 £3.80, 1&3 £9.60 CSF £54.26 TOTE £12.80: £2.70, £2.00, £1.30; EX 69.10 Trifecta £392.80 Pool: £3,488.41 - 6.66 winning tickets..
Owner Foxtrot Racing Partnership IV **Bred** Patrick Roche **Trained** Kimpton, Hants
FOCUS
A modest maiden. The winner enjoyed a soft lead but the form has been rated at face value.
NOTEBOOK
Foxtrot Jubilee(IRE), who has already been gelded, looks to have achieved a fair level of form on his debut here. Pinging the gates and making all, this half-brother to 7f/1m winner Just On Fire, whose sales price increased from 10,000euros as a yearling to 18,000GBP as a 2yo, clearly knew his job first time up, and the question is whether there's much improvement to come short-term. (tchd 12-1)
Floating Along(IRE) was rather awkward from the stalls and then raced keenly in mid-pack. She still only came up a little short, though, and might have done better off a contested lead. (op 5-2)
Secret Missile, who was stuck on the outside all the way round, kept on well and might have been in front a few yards after the line. He can go handicapping now, but there might still be a maiden in him if connections choose to persevere. (op 5-1)
Desert Sunrise, having her third run, had a nice enough trail into the race but was outpaced when it mattered. Nurseries are now open to her. (op 8-1)
Serenity Spa, off the track since finishing second in a stronger maiden at Ascot on her debut in July, didn't settle well enough through the early stages and could make no impression inside the last. (tchd 7-2)
Bastion(USA) lost plenty of ground with a slow start and, racing greenly, never got in a blow. He should come on for the experience. (op 4-1)

7498 32REDBET.COM MAIDEN STKS (DIV II) 6f (P)
5:10 (5:11) (Class 5) 2-Y-0 **£2,264** (£673; £336; £168) **Stalls** Low

Form RPR
6 **1** **Tartary (IRE)**[21] 7007 2-9-3 0 GeorgeBaker 9 74+
(Roger Charlton) *t.k.h: hld up in 6th: prog 2f out: shkn up over 1f out: clsd to ld last 150yds: pushed out: readily* **11/4**[2]
0 **2** *1/2* **Red Valerian (IRE)**[27] 6845 2-9-3 0 EddieAhern 5 70
(Charles Hills) *trckd ldng trio: rdn and prog wl over 1f out: upsides ldr as wnr wnt by 150yds out: styd on* **33/1**
322 **3** *1 1/2* **Sky Garden**[44] 6343 2-8-12 77 LiamJones 6 60
(William Haggas) *led: rdn and hdd 2f out: sn outpcd: kpt on again last 100yds* **2/1**[1]
6 **4** *shd* **Apricot Sky**[18] 7078 2-9-3 0 FergusSweeney 7 65
(Henry Candy) *trckd ldr: shkn up to ld 2f out: hdd & wknd last 150yds* **8/1**
5 *3/4* **Consign** 2-9-3 0 JimmyFortune 2 62+
(Jeremy Noseda) *dwlt: rn green in last pair early: nudged along and kpt on steadily fnl 2f: nrst fin* **8/1**
6 *4 1/2* **Dee Aitch Dove** 2-8-12 0 MartinDwyer 4 44
(George Baker) *s.s: a in last pair: nvr a factor* **33/1**
7 *hd* **Birdie King** 2-9-3 0 LukeMorris 8 48
(John Best) *s.s: sn in 5th: rdn over 2f out: sltly impeded sn after: wknd over 1f out* **33/1**
5540 **U** **Millers Wharf (IRE)**[35] 6597 2-9-3 73 SeanLevey 3 67
(Richard Hannon) *chsd ldng pair: cl 3rd whn stmbld and uns rdr 2f out* **3/1**[3]
1m 12.89s (-0.21) **Going Correction** -0.125s/f (Stan) **8** Ran SP% **116.0**
Speed ratings (Par 96): **96,95,93,93,92 86,85,**
Tote Swingers 1&2 £18.00, 2&3 £8.50, 1&3 £1.90 CSF £86.74 TOTE £5.60: £1.60, £7.20, £1.10; EX 127.70 Trifecta £767.40 Pool: £5,781.26 - 5.65 winning tickets..
Owner Lady Rothschild **Bred** The Rt Hon Lord Rothschild **Trained** Beckhampton, Wilts
FOCUS
This looked the weaker of the two divisions, and the winning time was 0.24sec slower. The winner scored with a bit in hand.
NOTEBOOK
Tartary(IRE) raced keenly and carried his head a little high, but he responded perfectly well when asked to go and win his race, so it's hard to criticise his attitude. There ought to be more to come from him. (op 9-2)
Red Valerian(IRE) struggled to show any ability on his debut, but that was on heavy ground, and the switch to this surface brought about plenty of improvement. He looks a likely nursery type after one more outing.
Sky Garden again made the running, but she was headed with 2f to run. Rallying at the finish, despite her speedy pedigree she might be worth a try over another furlong. (op 6-4)
Apricot Sky quickened up quite well to lead, but didn't see his race out, and Sky Garden rallied past him at the finish. It was his heels that the faller clipped, so that probably didn't help. (tchd 10-1)
Consign, a 68,000gns purchase, was green early and had to be niggled along to keep in touch at the back of the field. Staying on nicely for hands-and-heels riding at the finish, he should come on quite a bit for this introduction.

Millers Wharf(IRE) was creeping into contention and hadn't been asked for his effort when he clipped heels with Apricot Sky and unseated his rider. He'd have been in the mix.

7499 32REDBINGO.COM (S) STKS — 1m 3f (P)

5:40 (5:41) (Class 6) 3-Y-O — **£1,617** (£481; £240; £120) **Stalls** Low

Form — RPR

2213 **1** **Norfolk Sky**[19] 7062 3-9-0 60 SebSanders 8 63+
(Chris Wall) *trckd ldrs: wnt 2nd over 2f out: rdn to ld over 1f out: wl in command fnl f* **11/10**[1]

0000 **2** 1 3/4 **Sir Dylan**[29] 6798 3-9-0 54 LukeMorris 11 58
(Ronald Harris) *t.k.h: hld up in last: prog on outer 1/2-way and hanging lft: rdn to chse ldng pair 2f out: styd on to take 2nd last 50yds: n.d to wnr* **33/1**

5130 **3** 3/4 **Lady Romanza (IRE)**[9] 7303 3-9-0 60 GrahamLee 9 57
(Brendan Powell) *wd first bnd but prog to ld after 3f: drvn and hdd over 1f out: kpt on same pce* **6/1**[3]

4002 **4** 2 **Gunner Will (IRE)**[13] 7221 3-9-0 64 AdamKirby 1 54
(Jamie Osborne) *settled towards rr: shkn up over 2f out: prog over 1f out: wnt 4th last 150yds: n.d* **3/1**[2]

05 **5** 1 1/2 **Superstición**[15] 7162 3-8-9 0 EddieAhern 13 46+
(James Fanshawe) *prom: chsd ldr 1/2-way to over 2f out: nt qckn and sn btn: one pce after* **8/1**

0006 **6** nk **Glaze**[16] 7148 3-8-9 48 RobertHavlin 4 46
(Hughie Morrison) *prom: rdn over 3f out: outpcd 2f out: no imp on ldrs after* **25/1**

0334 **7** 2 1/2 **Here Comes Jeanie**[23] 6948 3-8-4 45 NatashaEaton(5) 7 42
(Michael Madgwick) *t.k.h: hld up bhd ldrs: rdn over 3f out: outpcd fnl 2f* **14/1**

3003 **8** 7 **Dangerous To Know**[37] 6569 3-8-9 49 NickyMackay 3 34
(Hughie Morrison) *hld up in tch: prog to go 4th over 3f out: shkn up over 2f out: wknd over 1f out: eased* **20/1**

6600 **9** 6 **Noosa Boy**[8] 7326 3-9-0 46 IanMongan 2 26
(Luke Dace) *hld up in last trio: drvn and no prog over 2f out: wl btn after* **33/1**

0500 **10** 1 3/4 **Make Me Smyle**[20] 7025 3-9-0 40 (b) FergusSweeney 5 23
(Stuart Kittow) *a towards rr: wknd over 2f out: sn wl bhd* **66/1**

06- **11** 50 **Greek Music**[436] 5351 3-8-9 0 SeanLevey 12
(John Bridger) *led 3f: chsd ldr to 5f out: wknd rapidly over 3f out: wl t.o* **66/1**

2m 20.73s (-1.17) **Going Correction** -0.125s/f (Stan) **11** Ran SP% **122.2**
Speed ratings (Par 98): **99,97,97,95,94 94,92,87,83,81 45**
Tote Swingers 1&2 £10.70, 2&3 £18.40, 1&3 £2.40 CSF £59.46 TOTE £1.90: £1.10, £5.60, £1.70; EX 26.30 Trifecta £179.70 Pool: £4,397.58 - 18.35 winning tickets..The winner was bought by Laura Mongan for £3,800.
Owner FarandWide Partners **Bred** Farmers Hill Stud **Trained** Newmarket, Suffolk

FOCUS
This wasn't going to take much winning. The winner stood out and was well on top in the end.
Sir Dylan Official explanation: jockey said gelding hung badly left

7500 32REDPOKER.COM H'CAP — 1m (P)

6:10 (6:11) (Class 6) (0-55,55) 3-Y-0+ — **£1,617** (£481; £240; £120) **Stalls** Low

Form — RPR

3300 **1** **Whinging Willie (IRE)**[23] 6950 3-9-3 55 GeorgeBaker 11 64+
(Gary Moore) *restrained into rr sn after s: gng smoothly over 2f out: prog and weaved through rivals over 1f out: sustained effrt to ld last 100yds: readily* **14/1**

0003 **2** 1 1/4 **Aragorn Rouge**[28] 6829 4-9-2 52 JoeFanning 10 59+
(Keith Dalgleish) *trckd ldr after 1f: led 2f out gng easily: booted 2 l clr over 1f out and looked sure to win: collared and nt qckn last 100yds* **7/4**[1]

006 **3** shd **Vitznau (IRE)**[269] 450 8-9-3 53 (tp) AdamKirby 5 59
(John Butler) *hld up in rr: gng wl over 2f out: rdn and prog over 1f out: styd on fnl f: nrly tk 2nd* **8/1**

0501 **4** 2 1/2 **Ermyntrude**[47] 6252 5-9-3 53 (v) IanMongan 8 53
(Pat Phelan) *dwlt: rousted along early: drvn towards rr over 2f out and no prog: styd on over 1f out: tk 4th ins fnl f: no ch* **7/1**[3]

0000 **5** nk **Gallantry**[47] 6252 10-9-2 52 JimmyQuinn 14 51
(Paul Howling) *awkward s: wl in rr: prog on inner over 2f out: nvr on terms w ldrs but styd on* **33/1**

3664 **6** 3/4 **Storm Runner (IRE)**[16] 7126 4-9-1 54 RyanPowell(3) 12 52
(George Margarson) *hld up in rr and racd wd: gng wl enough but stl only 13th 2f out: drvn over 1f out: kpt on fnl f: no hope* **10/1**

6000 **7** 1/2 **Dichoh**[75] 5349 9-9-2 52 (v) JamieGoldstein 9 49
(Michael Madgwick) *sn prom: drvn to chse ldr wl over 1f out: no imp and lost 2nd jst over 1f out: fdd* **50/1**

3552 **8** 3/4 **Exopuntia**[42] 6395 6-9-2 52 GrahamLee 1 47
(Julia Feilden) *hld up towards rr on inner: nt clrest of runs 2f out and over 1f out: jst pushed along and sme prog fnl f: nvr involved* **8/1**

0625 **9** nk **Divine Rule (IRE)**[29] 6778 4-9-2 52 (v) AmirQuinn 13 46
(Laura Mongan) *hld up in rr: prog on outer bef 1/2-way: trckd ldrs gng easily over 2f out: rdn and fnd nil over 1f out* **20/1**

0020 **10** shd **Rufus Stone (USA)**[29] 6773 4-8-12 55 (p) IanBurns(7) 3 49
(Jane Chapple-Hyam) *trckd ldrs: rdn over 2f out: nt qckn wl over 1f out: steadily lost pl* **20/1**

3-00 **11** 5 **Boris The Bold**[8] 7321 3-9-3 55 LiamKeniry 2 37
(John Best) *led 150yds: keen and restrained bhd ldrs: drvn over 2f out: wknd over 1f out* **25/1**

0620 **12** 6 **Querido (GER)**[10] 7302 8-9-4 54 (tp) EddieAhern 4 23
(Paddy Butler) *pushed up to go prom: rdn over 2f out: wknd qckly over 1f out* **25/1**

0000 **13** 1 3/4 **Just Five (IRE)**[80] 5175 6-9-2 55 (v) RaulDaSilva(3) 6 20
(John Weymes) *pushed up to ld after 150yds: hdd & wknd rapidly 2f out* **20/1**

614 **14** 4 1/2 **Pink Lips**[23] 6967 4-9-4 54 DarryllHolland 7 8
(J R Jenkins) *chsd ldrs 3f: wknd 1/2-way: t.o 3f out* **5/1**[2]

1m 38.46s (-1.34) **Going Correction** -0.125s/f (Stan)
WFA 3 from 4yo+ 2lb **14** Ran SP% **130.4**
Speed ratings (Par 101): **101,99,99,97,96 96,95,94,94,94 89,83,81,77**
Tote Swingers 1&2 £12.50, 2&3 £8.00, 1&3 £16.00 CSF £38.65 CT £241.34 TOTE £11.60: £2.90, £1.90, £2.80; EX 77.00 Trifecta £1008.30 Pool: £1,788.09 - 1.33 winning tickets..
Owner P B Moorhead **Bred** Joe Rogers **Trained** Lower Beeding, W Sussex

FOCUS
The pace wasn't bad here and most of those involved in the finish came from well back.

7501 32RED CASINO NURSERY — 1m (P)

6:40 (6:40) (Class 4) (0-85,84) 2-Y-0 — **£3,428** (£1,020; £509; £254) **Stalls** Low

Form — RPR

6120 **1** **Quintilian (IRE)**[8] 7335 2-9-7 84 MickaelBarzalona 2 87
(Mahmood Al Zarooni) *led after 1f: mde rest and set mod pce: wound it up over 2f out: drvn over 1f out: styd on wl* **11/2**[3]

4440 **2** 1 1/4 **Party Royal**[68] 5602 2-9-3 80 JoeFanning 5 80
(Mark Johnston) *reluctant ldr 1f: trckd wnr after: rdn and nt qckn 2f out: wl hld after: clung on for 2nd* **12/1**

3036 **3** nse **Requested**[85] 4951 2-9-0 77 SilvestreDeSousa 7 77+
(Mahmood Al Zarooni) *t.k.h: hld up in last pair in modly run event: detached in last 2f out: drvn and gd prog over 1f out: r.o and nrly snatched 2nd* **6/1**

21 **4** nk **Infinite Magic (USA)**[34] 6645 2-9-5 82 JimmyFortune 4 81
(Jeremy Noseda) *dwlt and rousted along early: settled in last pair in modly run event: prog 2f out: rdn to chse ldng pair 1f out: kpt on but nvr able to chal: lost 3rd last strides* **7/4**[1]

1500 **5** 1 **Beau Select (IRE)**[15] 7173 2-8-2 65 LukeMorris 6 62
(Robert Eddery) *trckd ldrs: rdn wl over 2f out and struggling: kpt on again fr over 1f out: nvr able to chal* **33/1**

2544 **6** 4 **Choral Prince (IRE)**[19] 7057 2-8-5 68 MartinDwyer 10 56
(Mike Murphy) *t.k.h: trckd ldng pair and racd wd: nt qckn over 2f out: wknd over 1f out* **20/1**

1332 **7** 3/4 **Danz Choice (IRE)**[28] 6815 2-8-10 73 SeanLevey 9 59
(Richard Hannon) *t.k.h: hld up in tch: nt qckn over 2f out: wknd jst over 1f out* **7/1**

1 **8** 1 **Footstepsintherain (IRE)**[16] 7143 2-9-0 77 TedDurcan 3 61
(David Lanigan) *trckd ldrs: nt qckn whn pce lifted 2f out: wknd jst over 1f out* **7/2**[2]

1m 39.63s (-0.17) **Going Correction** -0.125s/f (Stan) **8** Ran SP% **116.2**
Speed ratings (Par 98): **95,93,93,93,92 88,87,86**
Tote Swingers 1&2 £15.60, 2&3 £14.50, 1&3 £3.80 CSF £68.63 CT £413.05 TOTE £4.20: £1.70, £3.40, £2.00; EX 59.70 Trifecta £265.80 Pool: £3,576.31 - 10.09 winning tickets..
Owner Marmoom Racing **Bred** Mrs C Regalado-Gonzalez **Trained** Newmarket, Suffolk

FOCUS
The early gallop was steady here but the form is straightforward.

NOTEBOOK
Quintilian(IRE) took full advantage of being allowed the run of things out in front. Quickening up approaching the cutaway, he soon had the rest in trouble and saw off the second quite cosily. The soft ground was all against him at Newmarket last time and this surface clearly suits him much better. (op 7-2)
Party Royal was the winner's closest pursuer throughout in a race lacking early pace. His stamina for this trip was in question beforehand and this performance (he'd dropped to fourth soon after the line) by no means proves he stays. (op 16-1)
Requested ◆ looked the unlucky horse in the race as he finished with a rattle from the back of the field to reach the frame. In a race run at a regular pace he would probably have won. This was his first start at 1m and his first outing on Polytrack, and it was no surprise to see him improve given the stamina in his pedigree and the record of his sire's progeny on the AW. He can win a similar race. (op 8-1)
Infinite Magic(USA) was another who was held up out the back. He got first run on the third, but still, it was a solid effort in a race not run to suit. (op 2-1)
Beau Select(IRE) ran a better race trying Polytrack for the first time, but the bare form probably flatters him a touch.
Danz Choice(IRE) was stepping up to 1m for the first time and proved disappointing, but he wasn't suited by the way the race was run, failing to settle off the modest gallop. (op 9-1)
Footstepsintherain(IRE) was another unsuited by the way the race was run. (op 3-1 tchd 4-1)

7502 32RED H'CAP — 1m (P)

7:10 (7:11) (Class 3) (0-95,95) 3-Y-0+
£6,411 (£1,919; £959; £479; £239; £120) **Stalls** Low

Form — RPR

2340 **1** **Santefisio**[70] 5517 6-8-12 86 (b) JimmyFortune 8 96+
(Keith Dalgleish) *slowly away: hld up in last pair: scythed through field fr over 1f out gng easily: brought between rivals to ld w decisive burst last 100yds: impressive* **16/1**

1301 **2** 3/4 **Basseterre (IRE)**[35] 6601 3-8-9 85 GrahamLee 2 92
(Charles Hills) *hld up in mdfield on inner: prog 2f out: rdn to chal over 1f out: upsides ins fnl f: outpcd by wnr last 100yds* **9/2**[2]

1106 **3** shd **Dance Company**[43] 6375 3-8-10 86 EddieAhern 7 93
(William Knight) *trckd ldrs: rdn over 2f out: styd on wl fr over 1f out: nrly tk 2nd* **25/1**

1531 **4** 1/2 **True To Form (IRE)**[239] 817 5-9-6 94 (p) DavidProbert 13 100
(Martyn Meade) *trckd ldrs: rdn and prog to ld narrowly over 1f out: hdd and no ex last 100yds* **33/1**

2466 **5** 1 1/2 **Jack Who's He (IRE)**[19] 7064 3-8-7 83 KirstyMilczarek 9 85
(David Evans) *in tch on outer: rdn 3f out: kpt on u.p fnl 2f: nt pce to threaten* **20/1**

5500 **6** nk **Lord Ofthe Shadows (IRE)**[5] 7401 3-8-11 87 SeanLevey 4 89
(Richard Hannon) *hld up in rr: nudged along over 2f out: pushed along and only 13th over 1f out: rdn and r.o fnl f: gng on at fin* **33/1**

-001 **7** 1 1/4 **Shamir**[38] 6539 5-9-0 88 IanMongan 14 87
(Jo Crowley) *hld up in midfield: rdn over 2f out: tried to cl on ldrs over 1f out: one pce* **20/1**

21 **8** nk **Volcanic Wind (USA)**[21] 7005 3-8-11 87 SilvestreDeSousa 10 85+
(Saeed Bin Suroor) *mostly trckd ldr: rdn to chal and upsides over 1f out: wknd ins fnl f* **11/8**[1]

0022 **9** hd **Rakaan (IRE)**[26] 6888 5-9-0 88 FergusSweeney 1 86
(Jamie Osborne) *hld up in rr: effrt on inner over 2f out: tried to cl over 1f out: one pce fnl f* **20/1**

0060 **10** nk **Albaqaa**[40] 6494 7-8-12 86 KieranO'Neill 11 83
(P J O'Gorman) *dwlt: t.k.h and hld up wl in rr: drvn over 2f out: no real imp over 1f out* **16/1**

-340 **11** 1/2 **Robin Hoods Bay**[96] 4578 4-8-13 87 LukeMorris 5 83
(Ed Vaughan) *prom: rdn over 2f out: stl cl up over 1f out: wknd fnl f* **12/1**

5005 **12** 3/4 **The Rectifier (USA)**[124] 3640 5-9-7 95 (t) MickyFenton 12 89
(Seamus Durack) *led at str pce to over 1f out: wknd qckly fnl f* **40/1**

00U0 **13** 9 **Loyalty**[34] 6630 5-9-7 95 (v) JoeFanning 6 68
(Derek Shaw) *slowly away then swvd bdly: virtually t.o after 1f: nvr able to rcvr* **20/1**

-661 **14** 3 ¾ **Kiz Kulesi**[75] 5365 3-8-12 **88** MickaelBarzalona 3 53+
(Mahmood Al Zarooni) *prom: rdn over 2f out: wknd rapidly over 1f out: heavily eased* **8/1**[3]

1m 37.06s (-2.74) **Going Correction** -0.125s/f (Stan)
WFA 3 from 4yo+ 2lb **14** Ran SP% **122.1**
Speed ratings (Par 107): **108,107,107,106,105 104,103,103,103,102 102,101,92,88**
Tote Swingers 1&2 £15.50, 2&3 £27.40, 1&3 £119.60 CSF £77.85 CT £1881.47 TOTE £22.20: £4.90, £1.70, £6.90; EX 106.20 Trifecta £363.60 Pool: £969.77 - 2.00 winning tickets..
Owner Weldspec Glasgow Limited **Bred** D Brocklehurst **Trained** Carluke, S Lanarks
■ Stewards' Enquiry : Silvestre De Sousa one-day ban: careless riding (Nov 15)

FOCUS
A good, competitive handicap run at a decent gallop, with the pace collapsing late. Straightforward form.

NOTEBOOK
Santefisio found things falling just right for him as he came from the back of the field travelling well, quickened between horses and won easily. He wouldn't necessarily be one to trust to repeat this, as he's not one for a battle when challenged, but he's now won once and placed four times in his ten starts since joining Keith Dalgleish, and it won't be the handicapper's reaction that stops him winning again. (op 20-1)
Basseterre(IRE) had run well in his previous two starts on Polytrack and this was another solid effort. He's a reliable sort and a good guide to the level of the form. (tchd 7-2)
Dance Company saw the mile out well but the handicapper might just have his measure for the time being.
True To Form(IRE), debuting for a new stable and dropping back in distance, ran a promising race given he hadn't run since March. He has a cracking record at this track and at Wolverhampton, and will surely soon be adding to his tally.
Jack Who's He(IRE) was another who benefited from sitting well off the early pace.
Volcanic Wind(USA), who was caught wide, was there to be shot at up front. (op 6-4 tchd 5-4)
Loyalty Official explanation: jockey said gelding was slowly away
Kiz Kulesi raced keenly too close to the pace and carried his head awkwardly. (op 6-1)

7503 32RED.COM RACING H'CAP 6f (P)
7:40 (7:41) (Class 3) (0-95,95) 3-Y-0+
£6,411 (£1,919; £959; £479; £239; £120) **Stalls** Low

Form RPR
604 **1** **Capone (IRE)**[12] 7243 7-9-7 **95** HayleyTurner 6 103
(Garry Moss) *chsd clr ldrs: rdn and no prog over 2f out: grad clsd over 1f out: styd on strly fnl f to ld last 75yds* **11/2**[3]
1410 **2** 1 ¼ **Amadeus Wolfe Tone (IRE)**[40] 6466 3-9-5 **93** (p) AdamKirby 1 97
(Jamie Osborne) *hld up in last and wl off the pce: urged along over 2f out: drvn and prog over 1f out: r.o wl fnl f: tk 2nd last stride* **4/1**[2]
3126 **3** *hd* **Ihtifal**[68] 5576 3-9-2 **90** (t) MickaelBarzalona 12 94+
(Saeed Bin Suroor) *ponied to s: fast away fr wd draw: led at blistering pce and spreadeagled field: rdn 2f out: fended off rivals tl hdd last 75yds: lost 2nd fnl stride* **8/1**
6104 **4** 1 ¼ **Barnet Fair**[47] 6244 4-9-4 **92** SilvestreDeSousa 9 92
(Richard Guest) *t.k.h: hld up in rr: prog over 2f out: clsd on ldrs 1f out: kpt on same pce u.p* **3/1**[1]
43 **5** ½ **Swiss Cross**[51] 6116 5-9-4 **92** (t) DavidProbert 8 90
(Phil McEntee) *hld up in midfield: rdn over 2f out: sme prog over 1f out but nvr on terms: kpt on* **8/1**
141 **6** ¾ **Last Sovereign**[33] 6685 8-8-9 **90** (b) JacobButterfield(7) 5 86
(Ollie Pears) *disp 2nd bhd clr ldr and wl ahd of rest: drvn over 2f out: tried to cl over 1f out: fdd ins fnl f* **10/1**
0000 **7** ½ **Elna Bright**[54] 6026 7-9-2 **90** IanMongan 3 85
(Peter Crate) *chsd clr ldng trio: drvn and effrt over 2f out: no imp over 1f out: fdd* **16/1**
3002 **8** ½ **Sugar Beet**[18] 7080 4-9-3 **91** LukeMorris 4 84
(Ronald Harris) *hld up in rr: rdn and prog over 2f out: tried to cl on ldrs over 1f out: no prog fnl f* **12/1**
1104 **9** 1 ½ **Bravo Echo**[20] 7123 6-9-7 **95** J-PGuillambert 2 84
(Michael Attwater) *disp 2nd bhd clr ldr and wl ahd of rest: drvn over 2f out: tried to cl over 1f out: wknd fnl f* **14/1**
0610 **10** 2 ¾ **Seek The Fair Land**[173] 2070 6-9-2 **90** (b) GrahamLee 10 70
(Jim Boyle) *racd wd in rr: rdn and no prog over 2f out: wl btn over 1f out* **33/1**
000 **11** *11* **Vocational (USA)**[13] 7230 3-9-7 **95** JoeFanning 7 42
(Mark Johnston) *chsd clr ldrs: wknd over 2f out: eased over 1f out: t.o* **20/1**

1m 10.77s (-2.33) **Going Correction** -0.125s/f (Stan) course record **11** Ran SP% **119.6**
Speed ratings (Par 107): **110,108,108,106,105 104,104,103,101,97 83**
Tote Swingers 1&2 £5.80, 2&3 £6.50, 1&3 £12.50 CSF £28.30 CT £182.28 TOTE £5.50: £2.40, £1.80, £2.10; EX 29.50 Trifecta £113.10 Pool: £834.48 - 5.53 winning tickets..
Owner Brooklands Racing **Bred** S J Macdonald **Trained** Tickhill, S Yorks

FOCUS
A decent handicap run at a strong pace that resulted in the course record being lowered by 0.25sec. The winner is rated back to his best.

NOTEBOOK
Capone(IRE) had the race run just as he likes it and finished strongly to record his fifth win from 14 starts on the AW. He's a better horse on this surface than he is on turf and his trainer said he might consider running him in a Listed race again later in the month - he already has a place finish at that level from Lingfield in February. (op 5-1)
Amadeus Wolfe Tone(IRE) was in last place at halfway but finished strongly thanks to the fast early pace. His new mark is not going to be easy to defy, unless he's granted a similarly good gallop to run at. (op 11-2)
Ihtifal ◆ ran a big race in defeat. She had far too much use made of her and it was a terrific effort to finish placed in the circumstances as those who raced close up to her through the early parts dropped right out. She's not entirely straightforward but she has plenty of ability and should be capable of winning one of these. (op 9-1)
Barnet Fair was another to pick up the pieces late having been held up off the strong gallop. (tchd 11-4)
Swiss Cross also benefited from the overly strong pace up front. (op 10-1)
Last Sovereign dropped out having sat too close to the scorching heels of Ihtifal. (op 9-1)

7504 £32 FREE AT 32RED.COM H'CAP 7f (P)
8:10 (8:13) (Class 6) (0-55,55) 3-Y-0+ **£1,617** (£481; £240; £120) **Stalls** Low

Form RPR
6002 **1** **Circuitous**[13] 7224 4-9-4 **53** (p) JoeFanning 8 61
(Keith Dalgleish) *trckd ldr: rdn to ld over 1f out: fnd enough and hld on fnl f* **3/1**[1]
0400 **2** ¾ **Bahri Sheen (IRE)**[29] 6778 4-9-3 **52** GeorgeBaker 2 58
(John Best) *restless stalls: hld up in last: prog on inner 2f out: rdn to go 2nd last 100yds: kpt on but nvr really chal* **6/1**[3]
0000 **3** *nk* **Mack's Sister**[13] 7225 5-9-6 **55** DarryllHolland 6 60
(Dean Ivory) *chsd ldng pair: rdn 2f out: chsd wnr 1f out: hld after and lost 2nd last 100yds* **12/1**
3003 **4** ½ **Jonnie Skull (IRE)**[9] 7316 6-9-6 **55** (vt) LukeMorris 1 59
(Phil McEntee) *hld up in midfield: rdn over 2f out: chsd ldrs but hanging and nt qckn over 1f out: styd on nr fin* **8/1**
0600 **5** *nse* **Doctor Hilary**[163] 2373 10-9-4 **53** (v) RobertHavlin 12 57
(Mark Hoad) *hld up towards rr: prog on inner over 2f out: rdn to dispute 2nd 1f out: one pce after* **50/1**
2006 **6** ¾ **Custom House (IRE)**[17] 7106 4-9-6 **55** FrankieMcDonald 10 57
(John E Long) *hld up in midfield: rdn 2f out: nt qckn over 1f out: kpt on same pce after* **14/1**
0000 **7** *nk* **Emma Jean (IRE)**[27] 6836 3-8-13 **52** (bt) SophieDoyle(3) 9 52
(Frank Sheridan) *dwlt: hld up in rr: shkn up over 2f out: kpt on fr over 1f out: nvr gng pce to threaten* **33/1**
4 **8** 1 ¼ **The Kernigal (IRE)**[36] 6586 3-9-0 **53** (t) AshleyMorgan(3) 11 49
(Pat Murphy) *racd wd: in tch: rdn and no prog on outer 2f out: no threat after* **10/1**
0452 **9** *nse* **Kai**[16] 7146 3-9-4 **54** (v) SeanLevey 5 50
(Alan McCabe) *chsd ldrs: rdn over 2f out: no rspnse and no prog over 1f out: wl hld after* **5/1**[2]
5600 **10** *shd* **One Cool Chick**[42] 6396 4-9-2 **51** MickyFenton 13 48
(John Bridger) *dwlt: hld up in last trio: rdn and no prog on outer 2f out: one pce after* **16/1**
0056 **11** *1* **Mr Optimistic**[19] 7055 4-9-6 **55** (t) DavidProbert 7 49
(Pat Murphy) *led to over 1f out: wknd qckly fnl f* **6/1**[3]
2000 **12** 2 ½ **Not My Choice (IRE)**[13] 7224 7-9-3 **52** (t) J-PGuillambert 4 40+
(Paul Howling) *reluctant to enter stalls: prom: hrd rdn over 2f out: sn btn: eased fnl f* **14/1**

1m 25.95s (-0.05) **Going Correction** -0.125s/f (Stan)
WFA 3 from 4yo+ 1lb **12** Ran SP% **122.3**
Speed ratings (Par 101): **95,94,93,93,93 92,91,90,90,90 89,86**
Tote Swingers 1&2 £5.30, 2&3 £22.70, 1&3 £6.70 CSF £21.26 CT £199.25 TOTE £4.30: £1.90, £3.00, £4.00; EX 21.30 Trifecta £262.10 Pool: £775.90 - 2.22 winning tickets..
Owner A R M Galbraith **Bred** Deepwood Farm Stud **Trained** Carluke, S Lanarks
■ Stewards' Enquiry : Darryll Holland two-day ban: used whip above permitted level (Nov 15-16)

FOCUS
An ordinary handicap where they finished in a heap. The bare form is surely no better than this.
T/Plt: £210.80 to a £1 stake. Pool: £64,130.34 - 222.06 winning tickets. T/Qpdt: £57.00 to a £1 stake. Pool: £9,659.40 - 125.20 winning tickets. JN

7481 LINGFIELD (L-H)
Thursday, November 1

OFFICIAL GOING: Standard to slow
Wind: medium, behind Weather: dry

7505 E B F WEATHERBYS HAMILTON INSURANCE MAIDEN FILLIES' STKS (DIV I) 7f (P)
12:50 (12:51) (Class 5) 2-Y-0 **£3,234** (£962; £481; £240) **Stalls** Low

Form RPR
1 **Mrs Bannock (IRE)** 2-9-0 0 MickaelBarzalona 9 75+
(Mahmood Al Zarooni) *hld up in tch towards rr: hdwy and pushed rt bnd 2f out: hdwy over 1f out: str run u.p ins fnl f to ld fnl 50yds: gng away at fin* **5/1**[2]
6 **2** ¾ **Hekaayaat (USA)**[44] 6343 2-9-0 0 PaulHanagan 1 73+
(Roger Varian) *in tch in midfield: rdn and hdwy 2f out: rdn to chal 1f out: led ins fnl f: r.o tl hdd and no ex fnl 50yds* **9/2**[1]
6 **3** 2 ½ **Bellitudo (IRE)**[15] 7160 2-9-0 0 AdamKirby 6 66
(Marco Botti) *dwlt: sn in tch: rn green and hung rt bnd 2f out: hdwy 1f out and pressed ldrs briefly ins fnl f: outpcd by ldng pair fnl 100yds: kpt on* **11/2**[3]
00 **4** ½ **Princess Patsky (USA)**[28] 6816 2-9-0 0 HayleyTurner 7 65
(Michael Bell) *led: flashed tail u.p and hung lft 1f out: sn hdd and no ex* **25/1**
05 **5** 1 ¼ **Nullarbor Sky (IRE)**[16] 7143 2-9-0 0 EddieAhern 12 62+
(Lucy Wadham) *hld up in last trio: stl plenty to do and hdwy ent fnl f: styd on wl and gng on fin: nvr trbld ldrs* **25/1**
5 **6** *nk* **Puligny (IRE)**[23] 6960 2-9-0 0 RobertWinston 8 62
(Charles Hills) *chsd ldrs: rdn and unable qck whn sltly hmpd over 1f out: wknd ins fnl f* **8/1**
7 *shd* **Sweet Vintage (IRE)** 2-9-0 0 MartinLane 13 61
(J W Hills) *dwlt: swtchd lft after s: hld up in last trio: hdwy and swtchd lft over 1f out: no imp ins fnl f* **33/1**
0000 **8** ½ **Pivotal Silence**[23] 6946 2-9-0 63 IanMongan 4 60
(Amanda Perrett) *rdn leaving stalls: sn pressing ldr: rdn and outpcd whn sltly hmpd jst over 1f out: wknd ins fnl f* **40/1**
9 ¾ **Fusion (IRE)** 2-9-0 0 JoeFanning 2 57
(Mark Johnston) *chsd ldrs: rdn wl over 2f out: wknd ins fnl f* **13/2**
10 1 ½ **First Secretary** 2-9-0 0 JimmyFortune 11 54
(Roger Charlton) *in tch in midfield on outer: wdst of all and lost pl bnd 2f out: no imp and no threat to ldrs after* **8/1**
11 ½ **Lady Of Yue** 2-9-0 0 GrahamLee 10 52
(Ed Dunlop) *s.i.s: bhd: sme hdwy over 1f out: kpt on but nvr trbld ldrs* **25/1**
3 **12** 2 ½ **A Touch Of Fashion (USA)**[38] 6534 2-9-0 0 LukeMorris 3 46
(Gerard Butler) *chsd ldrs: rdn 3f out: struggling u.p and lost pl ent fnl 2f: wknd over 1f out* **7/1**
0 **13** *hd* **Soubrette**[23] 6960 2-9-0 0 TomQueally 5 45
(George Margarson) *hld up in tch: nt clr run and shuffled bk jst over 2f out: bhd and no hdwy over 1f out* **100/1**

1m 25.33s (0.53) **Going Correction** 0.0s/f (Stan) **13** Ran SP% **116.2**
Speed ratings (Par 93): **96,95,92,91,90 89,89,89,88,86 86,83,83**
Tote Swingers 1&2 £4.70, 2&3 £6.40, 1&3 £7.30 CSF £24.94 TOTE £5.50: £1.80, £2.30, £2.00; EX 25.20 Trifecta £153.90 Pool: £707.97 - 3.45 winning tickets..
Owner Godolphin **Bred** Darley **Trained** Newmarket, Suffolk

FOCUS
The first division and a modest juvenile fillies' maiden, in terms of prior form, in which they went a fair gallop racing on officially standard-to-slow Polytrack, with a tailwind reported up the home straight. The bare form is worth little better than this.

NOTEBOOK
Mrs Bannock(IRE) is a half-sister to 5f-6f 2yo Listed-class winner Bannock and is out of a UAE Oaks winner on dirt. She produced a useful winning debut here from an unhelpful draw, coming wide but making headway around the home turn, before quickening to a comfortable success well inside the final furlong. She took her stable's strike-rate with juveniles here in recent seasons to 38% (8-21), and looks a decent miling prospect for next term. (tchd 13-2)

Hekaayaat(USA) was returning from a six-week break since a respectable 6f Yarmouth debut on quick ground in September. She came through to lead inside the 1f pole but had no answer to the winner in the last 50 yards. This was a better display and she looks capable of winning a similar contest at up to 1m. (op 4-1 tchd 11-2)
Bellitudo(IRE), who cost 50,000gns in May, was far from disgraced when sixth over this trip at Kempton on debut the previous month. She produced an improved performance here and is capable of winning a similar contest over this trip. Adam Kirby, her rider, reported that the filly hung right. Official explanation: jockey said filly hung right (op 15-2 tchd 8-1)
Princess Patsky(USA) attempted to make all but flashed her tail and hung left when asked to go on 1f out.
Nullarbor Sky(IRE) made notably strong headway from the rear up the home straight into a never-nearer fifth.
Fusion(IRE) attempted to keep tabs on the leaders from a low draw but weakened inside the final furlong. (tchd 7-1)
A Touch Of Fashion(USA) reportedly looked well in the paddock but disappointed in the race itself. (op 6-1 tchd 11-2)

7506 E B F WEATHERBYS HAMILTON INSURANCE MAIDEN FILLIES' STKS (DIV II) 7f (P)
1:20 (1:24) (Class 5) 2-Y-0 **£3,234** (£962; £481; £240) **Stalls** Low

Form RPR
05 **1** **Shy Bride (IRE)**[14] 7192 2-9-0 0 .... RobertWinston 6 72
(Alan Jarvis) *t.k.h: chsd ldr: rdn over 1f out: led ins fnl f: styd on wl* **25/1**
2 ¾ **Iridescence** 2-9-0 0 .... JimmyFortune 8 70+
(Jeremy Noseda) *chsd ldrs: rdn and outpcd 2f out: looked hld 1f out: rallied and r.o strly fnl 100yds: wnt 2nd towards fin* **10/1**
3 ¾ **La Belle Epoque (USA)** 2-9-0 0 .... LukeMorris 5 68+
(Gerard Butler) *chsd ldrs: rdn and effrt to press ldr 1f out: edgd lft u.p jst ins fnl f: one pce fnl 100yds* **50/1**
2 **4** nk **Thakana**[23] 6960 2-9-0 0 .... PaulHanagan 11 67
(Marcus Tregoning) *hld up in midfield: rdn and no prog whn wd bnd 2f out: rallied and styd on wl ins fnl f: nt rch ldrs* **2/1**[1]
5 nk **Tomintoul Magic (IRE)** 2-9-0 0 ....[1] TomQueally 10 69+
(Sir Henry Cecil) *dwlt: t.k.h and hld up in tch: effrt to press ldrs whn squeezed for room and hmpd jst ins fnl f: styd on same pce after* **8/1**
2 **6** ¾ **Hidden Belief (IRE)**[15] 7159 2-9-0 0 .... MartinLane 3 64
(Ralph Beckett) *led: rdn wl over 1f out: hdd and no ex ins fnl f: wknd towards fin* **11/4**[2]
7 1 **Lovesome** 2-9-0 0 .... HayleyTurner 7 62+
(Michael Bell) *v.s.a: bhd and rdn early: clsd onto bk of field and travelling bttr 3f out: styd on wl fnl f* **50/1**
65 **8** 1 **Elusive Gold (IRE)**[57] 5932 2-9-0 0 .... SebSanders 4 59
(J W Hills) *hld up in last quartet: rdn and hdwy into midfield 2f out: styd on same pce and no imp fnl f* **40/1**
9 1 **Aloha** 2-9-0 0 .... NeilCallan 13 56
(Roger Varian) *in tch in last quartet: rdn and no imp over 2f out: kpt on ins fnl f but nvr trbld ldrs* **33/1**
10 4 **World Map (IRE)** 2-9-0 0 .... SilvestreDeSousa 1 45
(Saeed Bin Suroor) *s.i.s: a in rr: rdn and no hdwy 2f out: n.d* **4/1**[3]
06 **11** 24 **Phoebe's Perfect**[66] 5656 2-9-0 0 .... AdamKirby 9
(Neil Mulholland) *in tch early: lost pl and rdn 4f out: bhd fnl 2f* **200/1**

1m 25.54s (0.74) **Going Correction** 0.0s/f (Stan) **11** Ran SP% **113.8**
Speed ratings (Par 93): **95,94,93,92,92 91,90,89,88,83 56**
Tote Swingers 1&2 £13.50, 2&3 £39.40, 1&3 £40.00 CSF £236.54 TOTE £40.00: £7.50, £4.30, £17.20; EX 404.40 TRIFECTA Not won..
Owner Christopher Shankland & Ann Jarvis **Bred** Barronstown Stud **Trained** Twyford, Bucks

FOCUS
The second division and a fair juvenile fillies' maiden in which the winning time was marginally slower than the first instalment, despite a decent pace. The bare form is likely modest.

NOTEBOOK
Shy Bride(IRE) progressed markedly when keeping on into a modest but promising fifth over 1f shorter at Kempton on her second start the previous month. She raced prominently throughout and found plenty for pressure up the home straight to record her first success. She looks a fair 1m handicap prospect for next season. (tchd 20-1)
Iridescence, who is a sister to 6f-1m winner Princess Of Orange and half-sister to 7f-1m2f winner Icebuster, finished well into a decent second here on debut and should be able to win a similar contest. She looks capable of making up into a good 1m-1m2f handicapper for next term. (op 12-1 tchd 7-1)
La Belle Epoque(USA), who cost 30,000gns as a yearling, produced a decent debut display here from an always handy position over a 7f trip, which may continue to suit her going forward. (op 40-1)
Thakana, who reportedly looked well in the paddock and ran a fair race when second over this 7f trip at Leicester on debut the previous month, was forced to race wide around the home turn from a poor initial draw but picked up well in the home straight. She is capable of winning a similar contest at up to 1m. (op 7-2)
Tomintoul Magic(IRE), who cost 52,000gns as a yearling, was wearing a hood on this debut. She quickly made up for a slow start and showed plenty of ability, despite a troubled passage through the race. (op 4-1)
Hidden Belief(IRE) attempted to make all but found little for pressure up the home straight. (op 5-2 tchd 10-3)
Lovesome showed ability and will appreciate further in time.
World Map(IRE) was always struggling after a slow start. Official explanation: jockey said filly was slowly away and did not face the kickback (op 5-1 tchd 7-2)

7507 BRITISH STALLION STUDS SUPPORTING BRITISH RACING E B F MAIDEN STKS 7f (P)
1:50 (1:54) (Class 5) 2-Y-0 **£3,234** (£962; £481; £240) **Stalls** Low

Form RPR
1 **Chengho (USA)** 2-9-3 0 .... JimmyFortune 8 80+
(Sir Michael Stoute) *racd off the pce in last trio: stl plenty to do and rdn over 1f out: hdwy ent fnl f: str run to ld wl ins fnl f: gng away at fin* **25/1**
3 **2** ¾ **Watcheroftheskies**[21] 7006 2-9-3 0 .... SebSanders 9 77
(J W Hills) *hld up in tch: rdn and effrt to chse ldrs 2f out: ev ch ins fnl f: led fnl 100yds: r.o tl hdd and no ex cl home* **25/1**
3 ¾ **Emperical** 2-9-3 0 .... TomQueally 12 75
(Sir Henry Cecil) *chsd ldrs: wnt 2nd over 4f out: rdn and hdwy to chal ins fnl f: no ex and one pce fnl 100yds* **13/2**[3]
3 **4** 1 ¾ **Future Reference (IRE)**[29] 6772 2-9-3 0 .... SilvestreDeSousa 6 70
(Saeed Bin Suroor) *chsd ldrs: rdn and unable qck 2f out: kpt on to chse ldrs ins fnl f: no imp fnl 100yds* **4/7**[1]
02 **5** ¾ **Anjuna Beach (USA)**[71] 5478 2-9-3 0 .... GeorgeBaker 1 70+
(Gary Moore) *t.k.h: hld up in tch: swtchd to outer over 3f out: nt handling bnd and lost pl 2f out: looked wl btn over 1f out: pushed along hands and heels and styd on wl ins fnl f* **16/1**
04 **6** ¾ **Price Is Truth (USA)**[15] 7167 2-9-3 0 ....(p) MickaelBarzalona 13 66
(Mahmood Al Zarooni) *led: rdn 2f out: drvn and hrd pressed ins fnl f: hdd fnl 100yds: fdd towards fin* **11/2**[2]
06 **7** shd **Plutocracy (IRE)**[24] 6928 2-9-3 0 .... TedDurcan 7 69+
(David Lanigan) *off the pce in last pair and rdn along: no hdwy and hanging rt fr 2f out: hdwy and swtchd lft jst ins fnl f: styd on wl fnl 100yds* **25/1**
8 1 ¾ **Sabre Rock** 2-9-3 0 .... LukeMorris 4 61
(John Best) *dwlt: sn in tch in midfield: nt clr run 2f out: swtchd rt and no hdwy u.p over 1f out: wl hld fnl f* **33/1**
0 **9** 3 **Tigerish**[15] 7167 2-9-3 0 .... SeanLevey 11 53
(Amanda Perrett) *t.k.h: chsd ldr tl over 4f out: styd chsng ldrs tl over 1f out: fdd fnl f* **100/1**
10 3 ¼ **Musical Moon** 2-8-12 0 .... DavidKenny(5) 5 44
(Lady Herries) *s.i.s: rn green and sn rdn along in rr: n.d* **100/1**

1m 25.56s (0.76) **Going Correction** 0.0s/f (Stan) **10** Ran SP% **114.7**
Speed ratings (Par 96): **95,94,93,91,90 89,89,87,84,80**
Tote Swingers 1&2 £19.30, 2&3 £7.20, 1&3 £14.40 CSF £468.91 TOTE £26.90: £5.20, £4.90, £2.10; EX 262.00 TRIFECTA Not won..
Owner Robert Ng **Bred** Barnett Enterprises **Trained** Newmarket, Suffolk

FOCUS
A fair juvenile maiden. The winner did it well and the form is straightforward.

NOTEBOOK
Chengho(USA), who cost 80,000gns in May and is a half-brother to eight winners, notably US 1m1f Grade 1 winner/Dubai World Cup runner-up Harlan's Holiday, came with a withering late run up the home straight from well off the pace to record a taking debut success. He looks a useful 1m-1m2f prospect for next term. (op 16-1)
Watcheroftheskies stepped up significantly here on his modest but mildly promising debut third of nine over 1f shorter at Kempton the previous month. He looks capable of winning a similar contest over this 7f trip. (op 16-1)
Emperical, who is closely related to smart 1m1f-1m2f winner Jet Away for the same connections, made headway to challenge inside the 1f marker here on debut but proved one paced in the closing stages. He should appreciate a longer trip next year. (op 7-1 tchd 6-1)
Future Reference(IRE) proved slightly disappointing over this 7f trip after an encouraging 6f debut at Kempton the previous month. (op 10-11)
Anjuna Beach(USA) was returning from a ten-week break since a fair second on his second start over 1f further at Kempton in August. A return to 1m and a right-handed track may suit in modest to fair handicaps going forward. Official explanation: jockey said colt hung right (op 11-1)
Price Is Truth(USA) attempted to make all in first-time cheekpieces but faded again once headed inside the final furlong. (op 4-1)
Plutocracy(IRE) came home strongly from well off the pace inside the final furlong. (op 33-1)
Tigerish Official explanation: jockey said gelding ran too free

7508 LINGFIELD PARK MARRIOTT HOTEL & COUNTRY CLUB H'CAP 7f (P)
2:20 (2:22) (Class 3) (0-95,95) 3-Y-0+ **£6,663** (£1,982; £990; £495) **Stalls** Low

Form RPR
0004 **1** **Haamaat (IRE)**[35] 6602 4-8-13 **87** .... PaulHanagan 12 95
(William Haggas) *t.k.h: chsd ldr 5f out: rdn to chal over 1f out: led 1f out: idled and drvn ins fnl f: kpt on wl* **5/1**[1]
1206 **2** nk **Elusive Flame**[49] 6165 3-8-13 **88** .... LiamKeniry 14 94
(David Elsworth) *chsd ldrs: rdn and effrt over 1f out: hdwy u.p 1f out: ev ch fnl 100yds: hld towards fin* **14/1**
4144 **3** ¾ **Roninski (IRE)**[17] 7097 4-8-12 **86** .... TomEaves 13 91
(Bryan Smart) *t.k.h: hld up in tch in midfield: rdn and effrt over 1f out: styd on to go 3rd wl ins fnl f* **14/1**
0051 **4** 1 **Lockantanks**[26] 6888 5-9-2 **90** .... TomQueally 10 92
(Michael Appleby) *hld up in tch in midfield: rdn and effrt over 1f out: drvn and styd on wl ins fnl f* **16/1**
0102 **5** nse **Kingscroft (IRE)**[2] 7452 4-8-11 **85** .... JoeFanning 3 87
(Mark Johnston) *chsd ldrs: rdn 2f out: styd on same pce u.p ins fnl f* **13/2**[3]
-040 **6** ½ **Poetic Dancer**[33] 6676 3-8-13 **88** .... AdamKirby 2 88
(Clive Cox) *broke fast and led for 1f: chsd ldrs after: effrt u.p wl over 1f out: styd on same pce ins fnl f* **16/1**
4060 **7** ¾ **Forceful Appeal (USA)**[92] 4703 4-8-12 **86** .... HayleyTurner 9 85
(Simon Dow) *chsd ldr tl led after 1f: rdn and qcknd ent fnl 2f: drvn and hdd 1f out: wknd wl ins fnl f* **6/1**[2]
0000 **8** nk **King Of Jazz (IRE)**[18] 7080 4-9-0 **88** ....(v) LukeMorris 11 86
(Michael Bell) *stdd and swtchd lft after s: t.k.h: hld up in tch: drvn and effrt over 1f out: kpt on same pce ins fnl f* **25/1**
4000 **9** ¾ **Red Art (IRE)**[33] 6676 3-8-13 **88** .... RobertWinston 6 84
(Charles Hills) *chsd ldrs: rdn and unable qck over 1f out: no ex 1f out: wknd ins fnl f* **25/1**
0030 **10** shd **Gold City (IRE)**[33] 6676 3-9-6 **95** ....(t) MickaelBarzalona 5 90
(Saeed Bin Suroor) *s.i.s: bhd: pushed along over 4f out: rdn and effrt 2f out: styd on ins fnl f: nvr trbld ldrs* **6/1**[2]
05-5 **11** nk **Ceremonial Jade (UAE)**[67] 5634 9-9-3 **91** ....(t) JimmyQuinn 8 90+
(Marco Botti) *in tch in rr: rdn and effrt wl over 1f out: styd on ins fnl f but nvr goling pce to chal* **20/1**
004 **12** 1 **Theladyinquestion**[43] 6373 5-8-13 **87** .... JimmyFortune 4 79
(Andrew Balding) *hld up in tch in last quartet: rdn and effrt over 1f out: kpt on but no real imp* **22/1**
0300 **13** nk **Johnny Castle**[12] 7240 4-9-2 **90** .... SeanLevey 1 81
(Amanda Perrett) *hld up in midfield on inner: rdn and no imp over 1f out: wknd ins fnl f* **15/2**
0240 **14** 2 ¼ **Mr David (USA)**[48] 6192 5-8-13 **87** .... EddieAhern 7 72
(Jamie Osborne) *a towards rr but in tch: rdn and no prog wl over 1f out: n.d* **11/1**

1m 23.57s (-1.23) **Going Correction** 0.0s/f (Stan)
WFA 3 from 4yo+ 1lb **14** Ran SP% **120.6**
Speed ratings (Par 107): **107,106,105,104,104 104,103,102,101,101 101,100,100,97**
Tote Swingers 1&2 £13.80, 2&3 £15.40, 1&3 £10.40 CSF £71.67 CT £651.07 TOTE £5.60: £2.00, £4.80, £4.40; EX 80.00 Trifecta £269.00 Pool: £1,449.25 - 4.04 winning tickets..
Owner Hamdan Al Maktoum **Bred** Hunscote House Farm Stud **Trained** Newmarket, Suffolk

FOCUS
A good quality handicap for 3yos and up in which the winner not surprisingly recorded easily the best comparative time from the first four races, all over 7f, on this card. The third helps govern the level.

NOTEBOOK
Haamaat(IRE) shaped better at Newmarket five weeks prior to this contest and is fully effective from 6f-7f on Polytrack. She was competing off 5lb higher than for her previous peak-winning effort over 1f shorter at Kempton in May. She led 1f from the line but appeared to think she had done enough, before being rousted to keep up to her work, and go on to win well. She should remain competitive under these conditions once reassessed for her fourth career victory. (op 15-2)
Elusive Flame was returning from a seven-week break on her AW debut. This was a good effort in a close second and she looks capable of winning a similar contest over this trip on Polytrack. (tchd 16-1)

Roninski(IRE) performed with credit and would be of interest over 1m back at this venue. (op 11-1)
Lockantanks arrived in form after winning a decent 7f claimer at Wolverhampton the previous month, and he kept up the good work. A return to 1m here would suit. (op 11-1)
Kingscroft(IRE) performed very respectably in fifth. (op 11-2 tchd 5-1)
Forceful Appeal(USA), who was returning from a three-month break, led after 1f but weakened after being headed 1f out. (op 7-1 tchd 15-2)
Gold City(IRE), who was racing for the first time since a gelding operation, started slowly and made late gains in the final furlong. (op 10-1)

7509 E B F NORMANDIE STUD FLEUR DE LYS FILLIES' STKS (LISTED RACE) 1m (P)
2:50 (2:52) (Class 1) 3-Y-0+

£18,714 (£7,095; £3,550; £1,768; £887; £445) **Stalls** High

Form RPR

2053 **1** **Sentaril**[26] 6870 3-8-12 103 GrahamLee 6 101+
(William Haggas) *taken down early: hmpd sn after s and dropped to last pair: in tch: swtchd lft and hdwy to chse ldrs jst ins fnl f: n.m.r fnl 100yds tl gap opened and qcknd smartly to ld nr fin* **10/3**[2]

2100 **2** *hd* **Burke's Rock**[26] 6875 3-8-12 90 (p) JimmyFortune 10 99
(Jeremy Noseda) *chsd ldrs: drvn and hdwy to chal 1f out: led ins fnl f: styd on wl tl hdd and no ex nr fin* **14/1**

65 **3** *1¼* **Love Your Looks**[53] 6085 4-9-0 90 EddieAhern 9 96
(Mike Murphy) *t.k.h: hld up in tch: hdwy on outer to join ldrs over 2f out: rdn to ld over 1f out: hdd and one pce ins fnl f* **25/1**

1114 **4** *hd* **Baheeja**[26] 6878 3-8-12 95 NeilCallan 8 95
(Roger Varian) *t.k.h: hld up wl in tch towards rr: rdn and effrt on outer over 1f out: styd on wl u.p ins fnl f* **13/2**[3]

4340 **5** *nk* **Instance**[26] 6870 4-9-0 94 (p) TomQueally 3 97+
(Jeremy Noseda) *wl in tch towards rr: effrt on inner and nt clr run ent fnl f: swtchd rt and sme hdwy ins fnl f: nt clr run and swtchd rt again fnl 75yds: styd on cl home* **16/1**

0406 **6** *½* **Libys Dream (IRE)**[34] 6633 4-9-3 95 RichardKingscote 7 96+
(Tom Dascombe) *hld up in tch: nt clr run over 1f out: styd on ins fnl f: unable to chal* **12/1**

1436 **7** *shd* **Appealing (IRE)**[49] 6161 3-8-12 98 MartinHarley 1 93
(Marco Botti) *in tch: rdn and hdwy to chse ldrs over 1f out: styd on same pce ins fnl f* **20/1**

3211 **8** *¾* **Forgive**[43] 6375 3-8-12 90 SeanLevey 5 91
(Richard Hannon) *chsd ldrs: rdn and unable qck over 1f out: one pce and btn ins fnl f* **12/1**

3031 **9** *2½* **Moone's My Name**[26] 6879 4-9-0 107 PaulHanagan 12 86
(Ralph Beckett) *dwlt and pushed along leaving stalls: hdwy to chse ldrs 6f out: rdn to ld 2f out: hdd and unable qck over 1f out: wknd ins fnl f* **11/4**[1]

560 **10** *2¾* **Night Lily (IRE)**[61] 5834 6-9-0 98 SilvestreDeSousa 2 79
(Paul D'Arcy) *led tl rdn and hdd 2f out: sn drvn and unable qck: wknd ins fnl f* **8/1**

2500 **11** *3½* **Villeneuve**[49] 6161 3-8-12 94 MartinDwyer 11 71
(William Muir) *chsd ldrs: ev ch u.p over 1f out: fdd ins fnl f* **66/1**

2300 **12** *3¼* **Valencha**[26] 6870 5-9-0 95 HayleyTurner 4 78+
(Hughie Morrison) *t.k.h: hld up wl in tch in midfield: stl cl enough but nt clr run and hmpd over 1f out: nt clr run thrght fnl f and eased* **16/1**

1m 36.17s (-2.03) **Going Correction** 0.0s/f (Stan)
WFA 3 from 4yo+ 2lb 12 Ran SP% 118.1
Speed ratings (Par 108): **110,109,108,108,108 107,107,106,104,101 97,94**
Tote Swingers 1&2 £11.00, 2&3 £52.80, 1&3 £19.90 CSF £48.35 TOTE £4.60: £1.40, £4.40, £7.30; EX 52.30 Trifecta £1237.90 Part won. Pool: £1,650.54 - 0.70 winning tickets..
Owner Lael Stable **Bred** Lael Stables **Trained** Newmarket, Suffolk

FOCUS
A competitive Listed fillies' contest for 3yos and up, but the pace was steady and this isn't form to take too literally. The winner did not need to be at her best.

NOTEBOOK
Sentaril produced peak form when running on to finish second in the Group 3 Jersey Stakes at Royal Ascot in June. She was stepped up to 1m here for the first time and had to show a smart turn-of-foot to come through a gap between horses near the line, after a troubled passage through the race. She looks capable of winning in Group company at up to 1m (op 5-2)
Burke's Rock is suited by these conditions and, though flattered by her proximity to the winner, ran right up to her best and earned valuable black type in the process. (op 25-1)
Love Your Looks, who was returning from a near eight-week break, appreciates these conditions and ran her usual solid race in third, also increasing her paddock value by earning black type. (op 16-1)
Baheeja has shown very progressive form this season and performed well here once again on her second start in Listed company, especially as she came very wide into the straight. (op 15-2 tchd 6-1)
Instance, who ran very well in a 7f Doncaster Group 3 on her penultimate start in September, suffered a troubled passage through this race, and needs marking up on this first start at 1m. (tchd 20-1)
Libys Dream(IRE), who was a carrying a 3lb penalty for her 7f Listed Wolverhampton success in March, ran well once again, despite being denied a clear run over 1f out. (op 14-1 tchd 11-1)
Moone's My Name dwelt from a poor draw before making ground to the leaders after a couple of furlongs, but paid for an uneven trip when headed and weakening over 1f out. (op 7-2)
Night Lily(IRE) attempted to make all but was headed 2f out and found little thereafter. (op 15-2 tchd 10-1)
Valencha Official explanation: jockey said mare was denied a clear run

7510 E B F DUAL CLASSIC WINNING SIRE COCKNEY REBEL RIVER EDEN FILLIES' STKS (LISTED RACE) 1m 5f (P)
3:20 (3:22) (Class 1) 3-Y-0+

£18,714 (£7,095; £3,550; £1,768; £887; £445) **Stalls** Low

Form RPR

-215 **1** **Tempest Fugit (IRE)**[27] 6833 3-8-9 90 NickyMackay 5 99
(John Gosden) *in tch: rdn and effrt to chse ldr wl over 1f out: led ins fnl f: hld on wl cl home* **16/1**

1031 **2** *nk* **Rumh (GER)**[58] 5905 4-9-2 99 SilvestreDeSousa 7 99
(Saeed Bin Suroor) *led: rdn ent fnl 2f: drvn over 1f out: hdd ins fnl f: kpt on wl but hld cl home* **9/2**[2]

1524 **3** *nse* **Aniseed (IRE)**[26] 6877 3-8-9 94 GrahamLee 8 99+
(William Haggas) *hld up in rr: gd hdwy and swtchd lft over 1f out: str run ins fnl f: clsng qckly towards fin: nt quite rch ldrs* **14/1**

111 **4** *1* **Surprise Moment (IRE)**[40] 6492 3-8-9 96 MickaelBarzalona 3 98+
(Saeed Bin Suroor) *bmpd leaving stalls: hld up in midfield: swtchd rt and effrt but stl plenty to do ent fnl 2f: drvn over 1f out: styd on wl ins fnl f: rch ldrs* **7/4**[1]

56 **5** *3¼* **Jiwen (CAN)**[43] 6379 4-9-2 86 PaulHanagan 14 93
(Roger Varian) *hld up in midfield: effrt u.p ent fnl 2f: plugged on ins fnl f but nvr gng pce to chal* **33/1**

410 **6** *¾* **Roxy Flyer (IRE)**[35] 6598 5-9-2 98 SeanLevey 9 92
(Amanda Perrett) *hld up in tch in midfield: 6th and rdn ent fnl 2f: no imp over 1f out: one pce and btn fnl f* **12/1**

3342 **7** *hd* **Albamara**[35] 6598 3-8-9 97 LukeMorris 10 92
(Sir Mark Prescott Bt) *chsd ldrs: rdn over 3f out: drvn and unable qck 2f out: btn ent fnl f: wknd fnl 150yds* **11/2**[3]

0011 **8** *¾* **Polygon (USA)**[26] 6877 4-9-5 103 (b) RobertHavlin 6 94
(John Gosden) *sn rdn along to chse ldrs: wnt 2nd 5f out tl wl over 1f out: sn struggling u.p: wknd fnl f* **8/1**

055 **9** *4½* **Western Pearl**[110] 4111 5-9-2 90 [1] EddieAhern 1 84
(William Knight) *hld up towards rr: rdn and effrt over 2f out: no imp wl over 1f out: wknd over 1f out* **25/1**

0316 **10** *¾* **Livia's Dream (IRE)**[24] 6933 3-8-9 76 HarryBentley 4 83
(Ed Walker) *t.k.h: hld up towards rr: rdn and no hdwy over 2f out: wknd wl over 1f out* **80/1**

/030 **11** *1½* **Miss Starlight**[26] 6877 5-9-2 88 TomQueally 12 81
(Ibrahim Saeed Al Malki, Qatar) *hld up in midfield tl dropped to last quartet 9f out: rdn and struggling whn hmpd and swtchd lft over 2f out: wknd 2f out* **66/1**

1045 **12** *4½* **Momentary**[39] 6518 3-8-12 102 (v[1]) HayleyTurner 2 78
(Michael Bell) *wnt rt and bmpd rival leaving stalls: hld up towards rr: rdn and short-lived effrt on inner ent fnl 2f: wknd wl over 1f out* **25/1**

3-14 **13** *33* **Sunday Bess (JPN)**[43] 6379 4-9-2 87 RichardKingscote 11 29
(Tom Dascombe) *in tch: rdn and lost pl 4f out: t.o and eased fnl 2f* **33/1**

5364 **14** *12* **Good Morning Star (IRE)**[27] 6833 3-8-12 95 JoeFanning 13 15
(Mark Johnston) *chsd ldr tl 5f out: sn dropped out: t.o fnl 3f* **25/1**

2m 41.3s (-4.70) **Going Correction** 0.0s/f (Stan)
WFA 3 from 4yo+ 7lb 14 Ran SP% 121.4
Speed ratings (Par 108): **114,113,113,113,111 110,110,110,107,106 105,103,82,75**
Tote Swingers 1&2 £12.30, 2&3 £15.70, 1&3 £22.30 CSF £82.66 TOTE £21.00: £5.10, £1.80, £3.70; EX 98.60 TRIFECTA Not won..
Owner A E Oppenheimer **Bred** Michael Woodlock And Seamus Kennedy **Trained** Newmarket, Suffolk

FOCUS
An interesting middle-distance Listed fillies' contest for 3yos and up in which the winner recorded easily the best comparative time on the card. The bare form makes sense.

NOTEBOOK
Tempest Fugit(IRE) won her maiden impressively over 1f shorter at Kempton on her penultimate start in September, and she confirmed that promise on this occasion on her second start in Listed company under suitable conditions. She raced handily before going on over 1f out, and showed a very willing attitude to hold on in the finish. She looks capable of further success in this sort of company.
Rumh(GER) was returning from a two-month break since winning a 2m Goodwood handicap in September. She is equally effective under these conditions, and in this Listed company. She attempted to make all but couldn't quite get back up once headed inside the final furlong. (op 5-1 tchd 4-1)
Aniseed(IRE) has been running respectably at this level and appreciates these conditions. She was held up before making stealthy late headway up the home straight, and very nearly getting to the leaders.
Surprise Moment(IRE) was returning from a six-week break, entering Listed company, after winning her first three races at up to 1m4f on turf. She was given plenty to do after being bumped leaving the stalls, and ran very respectably. (op 2-1)
Albamara had very few excuses having both been close to the lead for a long way. (op 6-1 tchd 7-1)
Polygon(USA) was close to the pace early, but didn't appear to get home. (tchd 9-1)
Miss Starlight Official explanation: trainer's rep said mare was struck into right-hind.

7511 LINGFIELD PARK MARRIOTT HOTEL H'CAP 1m 2f (P)
3:50 (3:51) (Class 5) (0-75,75) 3-Y-0+ **£2,385** (£704; £352) **Stalls** Low

Form RPR

0021 **1** **Layali Dubai (USA)**[7] 7358 3-9-4 73 6ex SilvestreDeSousa 4 84+
(Saeed Bin Suroor) *in tch: rdn to chse ldrs over 2f out: chal ent fnl f: led ins fnl f: r.o wl* **13/8**[1]

0032 **2** *1½* **Solfilia**[16] 7131 3-9-6 75 NickyMackay 3 83
(Hughie Morrison) *chsd ldrs: rdn to chse ldng trio over 2f out: swtchd lft over 1f out: ev ch ent fnl f: chsd wnr and hung rt fnl 100yds: one pce* **17/2**[3]

5120 **3** *2¼* **Kelpie Blitz (IRE)**[14] 7194 3-9-1 70 (t) MickyFenton 10 74+
(Seamus Durack) *hld up in midfield: rdn and effrt whn wd bnd 2f out: styd on wl fnl f to go 3rd towards fin: no threat to ldng pair* **16/1**

5343 **4** *1* **Significant Move**[16] 7132 5-9-4 69 (t) IanMongan 13 71
(Stuart Kittow) *led: rdn over 2f out: hdd ins fnl f: wknd fnl 100yds* **10/1**

2-00 **5** *½* **Blank Czech (IRE)**[18] 7083 3-9-5 74 AdamKirby 12 75
(Amanda Perrett) *chsd ldr: rdn and ev ch 2f out tl no ex and btn ins fnl f: wknd fnl 100yds* **16/1**

0614 **6** *shd* **Semeen**[55] 5990 3-9-0 69 PaulHanagan 1 70
(Luca Cumani) *in tch in midfield: effrt u.p on inner ent fnl 2f: styd on same pce and no imp after* **11/4**[2]

6303 **7** *¾* **Hawaana (IRE)**[9] 7310 7-9-2 67 RobertWinston 8 66
(Gay Kelleway) *hld up towards rr: hdwy into midfield 7f out: rdn over 2f out: styd on ins fnl f: nvr trbld ldrs* **16/1**

142- **8** *3½* **Winning Spark (USA)**[172] 7601 5-9-8 73 LiamKeniry 5 66
(Gary Moore) *hld up towards rr: rdn and sme hdwy on inner wl over 1f out: no imp 1f out: nvr trbld ldrs* **25/1**

0330 **9** *2¼* **Sedgwick**[26] 6891 10-9-1 66 RussKennemore 2 54
(Shaun Harris) *hld up in midfield: rdn and no imp over 2f out: plugged on but nvr trbld ldrs* **40/1**

5500 **10** *4½* **Eagle Nebula**[10] 7301 8-9-4 69 DavidProbert 6 49
(Brett Johnson) *hld up in rr: rdn and no hdwy over 2f out: bhd fnl 2f* **66/1**

6000 **11** *2½* **Simayill**[22] 6987 4-9-9 74 TomMcLaughlin 14 49
(John Berry) *hld up in rr: rdn and no hdwy over 2f out: n.d* **33/1**

100 **12** *½* **Marine Girl**[107] 4199 3-9-1 70 TomQueally 7 44
(Stuart Kittow) *t.k.h: chsd ldrs tl rdn and lost pl over 2f out: wknd 2f out: bhd fnl f* **33/1**

30-0 **13** *1¼* **Ligurian Sea**[29] 6792 3-8-12 67 TedDurcan 11 39
(Chris Wall) *hld up in rr: rdn and no rspnse over 2f out: sn bhd* **25/1**

2m 5.5s (-1.10) **Going Correction** 0.0s/f (Stan)
WFA 3 from 4yo+ 4lb 13 Ran SP% 119.5
Speed ratings (Par 103): **104,102,101,100,99 99,99,96,94,90 88,88,87**
Tote Swingers 1&2 £4.30, 2&3 £22.80, 1&3 £11.20 CSF £15.13 CT £171.25 TOTE £2.20: £1.60, £2.40, £3.50; EX 12.80 Trifecta £172.60 Pool: £1,043.05 - 4.53 winning tickets..
Owner Godolphin **Bred** Darley **Trained** Newmarket, Suffolk

FOCUS
A fair handicap for 3yos and up run at a steady pace to halfway. The winner probably has more to offer.

7512 LINGFIELD PARK OWNERS GROUP LAUNCHES TODAY APPRENTICE H'CAP 7f (P)
4:20 (4:20) (Class 6) (0-60,60) 3-Y-O+ £1,704 (£503; £251) Stalls Low

Form RPR
0610 1 **North Central (USA)**[6] 7385 5-9-0 56...(p) JasonHart(3) 7 62
(Keith Dalgleish) *prom in main gp: rdn and clsd on ldr jst over 1f out: led ins fnl f: kpt on wl* 11/2[2]
0526 2 nk **Darnathean**[13] 7224 3-9-1 60... LouisSteward(5) 11 64
(Paul D'Arcy) *hld up off the pce in midfield: rdn and hdwy over 1f out: styd on wl ins fnl f to go 2nd towards fin: nt quite rch wnr* 5/1[1]
0406 3 shd **Artful Lady (IRE)**[9] 7307 3-7-13 46 oh1... JordanVaughan(7) 0 50
(George Margarson) *wl off the pce towards rr: rdn and hdwy on outer over 1f out: styd on strly ins fnl f: nt rch ldrs* 11/1
066 4 3/4 **Delightful Sleep**[248] 724 4-8-2 46... MatthewHopkins(5) 4 49
(David Evans) *hld up off the pce in midfield: rdn and hdwy on inner over 1f out: styd on wl ins fnl f to go 3rd towards fin* 6/1[3]
6-00 5 3/4 **Schoolboy Champ**[14] 7204 5-8-8 50...(vt) JackDuern(3) 12 51
(Lisa Williamson) *chsd clr ldr lost 2nd wl over 1f out but sn clsng on ldr: styd on same pce ins fnl f* 33/1
0035 6 hd **Mary's Pet**[36] 6585 5-8-13 59... AaronChave(7) 13 59+
(Lee Carter) *dwlt: sn rdn along to ld and crossed to rail: clr over 5f out: stl wl clr and rdn 2f out: tiring ent fnl f: hdd ins fnl f: fdd towards fin* 16/1
000 7 hd **Silvee**[50] 6145 5-9-6 59... CharlesBishop 1 59
(John Bridger) *chsd ldng pair: chsd clr ldr wl over 1f out: clsd and ev ch briefly ins fnl f: wknd towards fin* 10/1
5543 8 1 1/2 **Jackie Love (IRE)**[45] 6321 4-8-7 49...(v) ThomasBrown(3) 5 45
(Olivia Maylam) *hld up off the pce towards rr: rdn and clsd over 1f out: styng on whn bdly hmpd ins fnl f: nt rcvr and no hdwy after* 11/2[2]
0030 9 1/2 **Bedibyes**[34] 6646 4-8-10 49... DavidKenny 2 43
(Richard Mitchell) *s.i.s: wl off the pce in rr: hdwy over 1f out: styng on but no threat to ldrs whn nt clr run and swtchd rt wl ins fnl f: no impresssion after* 16/1
0006 10 1 3/4 **Give Us A Belle (IRE)**[9] 7318 3-8-2 47... HannahNunn(5) 9 35
(Christine Dunnett) *hld up wl off the pce in rr: rdn and kpt on fnl f: nvr trbld ldrs* 33/1
6055 11 1 **Memphis Man**[49] 6158 9-8-5 49... PhilipPrince(5) 10 36
(David Evans) *taken down early: wl bhd: nt clr run on inner bnd ent fnl 2f: swtchd rt 2f out: styd on fnl f: nvr trbld ldrs* 16/1
-000 12 1 3/4 **Lady On Top (IRE)**[23] 6951 4-8-4 46... NoelGarbutt(3) 8 28
(Nerys Dutfield) *handy in main gp: rdn and lost pl 2f out: bhd and plugged on same pce fnl f* 40/1
0000 13 20 **Rio Royale (IRE)**[49] 6158 6-9-3 59...(p) WilliamTwiston-Davies(3) 3
(Amanda Perrett) *racd off the pce in midfield: rdn and lost pl over 2f out: wl bhd fnl f* 13/2

1m 26.03s (1.23) **Going Correction** 0.0s/f (Stan)
WFA 3 from 4yo+ 1lb 13 Ran SP% 118.4
Speed ratings (Par 101): **92,91,91,90,89 89,89,87,87,85 83,81,59**
Tote Swingers 1&2 £4.30, 2&3 £22.80, 1&3 £11.20 CSF £32.32 CT £296.68 TOTE £7.60: £2.70, £1.60, £3.60; EX 29.40 Trifecta £506.20 Pool: £891.01 - 1.32 winning tickets..
Owner Dogberry Racing **Bred** Tony Holmes & Walter Zent **Trained** Carluke, S Lanarks
■ Stewards' Enquiry : Jack Duern two-day ban: careless riding (Nov 16-17); four-day ban: used whip above shoulder height (Nov 19-22)

FOCUS
A modest apprentice riders' handicap, run at a fast pace with a bunch finish.
Memphis Man Official explanation: jockey said gelding ran too free
T/Jkpt: Not won. T/Plt: £7,101.50 to a £1 stake. Pool: £59,341.88 - 6.10 winning tickets. T/Qpdt: £169.40 to a £1 stake. Pool: £6,617.80 - 28.90 winning tickets. SP

7428 CAPANNELLE (R-H)
Thursday, November 1
OFFICIAL GOING: Turf: heavy

7513a PREMIO GUIDO BERARDELLI (GROUP 3) (2YO) (TURF) 1m 1f
3:00 (12:00) 2-Y-O £23,333 (£10,266; £5,600; £2,800)

RPR
1 **Never Say Never (ITY)**[123] 2-8-11 0... DarioVargiu 3 102
(S Botti, Italy) *mde all: 5 l clr 3 1/2f out: rdn 2f out: r.o gamely and drifted lft u.p fnl f: hld on wl* 158/10
2 snk **Castello Aragonese**[19] 7076 2-8-11 0... PierantonioConvertino 6 102
(R Biondi, Italy) *racd keenly: chsd ldr: rdn and disp 2nd 1 1/2f out: r.o to chal ins fnl f: styd on but nvr quite getting there* 19/5[3]
3 2 **Wish Come True (IRE)**[123] 2-8-11 0... CristianDemuro 4 98
(S Botti, Italy) *hld up: hdwy fr rr 2f out: styd on u.p fnl f: nvr on terms* 11/10[1]
4 3/4 **Best Tango (ITY)**[19] 7076 2-8-11 0... GBietolini 5 97
(Gianluca Bietolini, Italy) *towards rr: effrt to chse ldrs over 2f out: disp 2nd and styng on u.p fr 1 1/2f out: wknd fnl 150yds* 11/2
5 3 **Biz The Nurse (IRE)** 2-8-11 0... FabioBranca 2 91
(S Botti, Italy) *dwlt: hld up towards rr: hrd rdn and short-lived effrt 2 1/2f out: no further imp fr 1 1/2f out: eased fnl 100yds* 12/5[2]
6 5 **Demeteor (ITY)**[19] 7076 2-8-11 0... CFiocchi 1 81
(R Menichetti, Italy) *chsd ldrs: rdn and nt qckn 2f out: sn wl btn eased fnl f* 185/10
7 dist **Slow Cavern (IRE)** 2-8-11 0... MPasquale 7
(Affe D'Agostino, Italy) *trckd ldng gp: rdn and lost pl 3f out: bhd whn heavily eased fnl f* 157/10

1m 56.57s (1.87) 7 Ran SP% 130.3
WIN (incl. 1 euro stake): 16.81. PLACES: 4.73, 2.70. DF: 44.39.
Owner Scuderia Andy Capp **Bred** Scuderia Lazzeri Marcello **Trained** Italy

7449 SAINT-CLOUD (L-H)
Thursday, November 1
OFFICIAL GOING: Turf: heavy

7514a CRITERIUM INTERNATIONAL (GROUP 1) (2YO COLTS & FILLIES) (TURF) 1m
1:50 (12:00) 2-Y-O £119,041 (£47,625; £23,812; £11,895; £5,958)

RPR
1 **Loch Garman (IRE)**[8] 7337 2-9-0 0... KevinManning 2 111+
(J S Bolger, Ire) *racd in 3rd on settling: relegated to 5th on ins bef st: r.o u.p: swtchd to outside and qcknd wl 2f out: wnt 3rd under continual press 2f out: tk 2nd 1f out: kpt on wl ins fnl f to take ld 10yds ou* 11/2[3]
2 1/2 **Anna's Pearl**[26] 6874 2-9-0 0...(b[1]) JimCrowley 1 110
(Ralph Beckett) *led fr s: wnt wl clr ent st: stl w clr ld 1f out: r.o wl: ct and hdd 10yds out* 13/1
3 1 1/4 **Us Law (IRE)**[21] 7013 2-9-0 0... ChristopheSoumillon 4 107
(P Bary, France) *plld hrd in 2nd on outside: swtchd to ins bef st and relegated to 3rd: chsd ldr and wnt 2nd 2f out: r.o u.p: hdd for 2nd 1f out: styd on* 3/1[2]
4 3 1/2 **Triple Threat (FR)**[27] 2-9-0 0... MaximeGuyon 5 100
(A Fabre, France) *hld up towards rr: rdn early in st: wnt 3rd u.p 2f out: hdd for 3rd and nt qckn fr 1 1/2f out: styd on one pce fnl f* 6/4[1]
5 4 **Kenhope (FR)**[21] 7013 2-8-10 0... OlivierPeslier 6 87
(H-A Pantall, France) *midfield fr s: wnt 2nd on outside bef st: rdn but no ex fr 2f out: styd on one pce fnl 1 1/2f* 13/2
6 7 **Pearl Flute (IRE)**[19] 7076 2-9-0 0... JohnnyMurtagh 3 75
(F-H Graffard, France) *hld up in rr: rdn but no ex ent st: sn btn* 11/2[3]

1m 52.7s (5.20) 6 Ran SP% 116.2
WIN (incl. 1 euro stake): 6.50. PLACES: 3.20, 4.70. SF: 48.10.
Owner Mrs J S Bolger **Bred** J S Bolger **Trained** Coolcullen, Co Carlow

FOCUS
Not the strongest juvenile Group 1 and three of the home-trained contingent had form linking in with each other, but the heavy ground and strong wind proved a factor here, as the foreign raiders filled the first two places. The form is rated at the bottom end of the race averages, but Loch Garman is clearly an exciting prospect.

NOTEBOOK
Loch Garman(IRE), who only made his debut the previous week, was held up and looked to be in trouble turning for home, but found plenty for pressure and gradually wore down the long-time leader. Clearly at home in the conditions, he has plenty of size about him and could make up into a decent 3yo, providing he goes on from this hard race.
Anna's Pearl, runner-up in two maidens before finishing fourth in a sales race on his most recent start, for which he earned a rating of 94, had blinkers on for the first time and they nearly resulted in him making all to get off the mark. He set a fair pace in the conditions and found more early in the straight but was legless when the winner came by near the finish.
Us Law(IRE) had form with the last two to finish here, having taken a Group 3 from Kenhope over C&D. He was never far away on ground he was proven on, but was one-paced under pressure in the straight.
Triple Threat(FR), who beat a subsequent winner when getting off the mark over C&D on very soft ground, was never travelling that well and, after being ridden to close up turning for home, failed to find any more.
Kenhope(FR), runner-up to US Law over C&D on similar ground last time, did not help her chances by racing too keenly early on.
Pearl Flute(IRE), who beat today's third when winning a Group 3 at Longchamp in September, totally failed to handle the testing conditions and was at the back throughout.

7515a PRIX PERTH (GROUP 3) (3YO+) (TURF) 1m
2:20 (12:00) 3-Y-O+ £33,333 (£13,333; £10,000; £6,666; £3,333)

RPR
1 **Don Bosco (FR)**[26] 6898 5-9-4 0... FlavienPrat 8 112
(D Smaga, France) *led: hdd over 4f out: c nr side in st: rdn over 2f out: styd on to regain ld ins fnl f: drvn out* 26/1
2 2 **Evaporation (FR)**[26] 6897 5-8-11 0... OlivierPeslier 7 100
(C Laffon-Parias, France) *prom thrght: c nr side in st: rdn 2f out: styd on to chal ins fnl f: wnt 2nd cl home: hld by wnr* 7/2[3]
3 1 3/4 **Sarkiyla (FR)**[26] 6897 3-8-11 0... AntoineHamelin 3 98
(A De Royer-Dupre, France) *midfield on inner: styd far side in st: rdn over 2f out and briefly outpcd: rallied and styd on to go 3rd wl ins fnl f* 10/1
4 1/2 **Pollyana (IRE)**[11] 3-8-8 0...(p) MaximeGuyon 5 94
(D Prod'Homme, France) *hld up towards rr: styd far side in st: rdn and hdwy over 2f out: styd on to ld over 1f out: hdd ins fnl f: no ex and dropped to 4th cl home* 14/5[1]
5 2 1/2 **Prince D'Alienor (IRE)**[20] 7124 4-9-1 0...(p) GregoryBenoist 1 93
(X Nakkachdji, France) *hld up towards rr: styd far side in st: rdn and lost pl 2 1/2f out: plugged on to go 5th post: nt pce to chal* 9/1
6 shd **Takar (IRE)**[77] 5286 3-9-1 0... StephanePasquier 10 95
(Rod Collet, France) *hld up and sn last: styd far side in st: rdn 2 1/2f out: plugged on to go 5th cl home: dropped to 6th post* 24/1
7 3/4 **Sommerabend**[25] 6913 5-9-1 0... GaetanMasure 4 92
(U Stoltefuss, Germany) *midfield on inner: styd far side in st: rdn 2 1/2f out: kpt on tl no ex ins fnl f: lost 2 pls and dropped to 7th cl home* 27/1
8 1 1/4 **Chil The Kite**[20] 7124 3-8-11 0... UmbertoRispoli 11 87
(Hughie Morrison) *hld up in last pair: styd far side in st: rdn over 2f out: outpcd ent fnl f and sn no ex: eased whn btn* 18/1
9 3 **Sulle Orme (FR)**[20] 7124 4-9-1 0... ThierryThulliez 6 82
(C Ferland, France) *midfield: styd far side in st: rdn 2 1/2f out: outpcd and btn ent fnl f: fdd* 22/1
10 5 **Dux Scholar**[26] 6897 4-9-1 0... ChristopheSoumillon 9 70
(A Savujev, Czech Republic) *midfield: styd far side in st: rdn 2 1/2f out: led over 1 1/2f out: strly pressed and hdd over 1f out: sn no ex and fdd: eased whn btn* 33/10[2]
11 **Alianthus (GER)**[25] 6906 7-9-4 0... AlexisBadel 2
(W Giedt, Germany) *prom: led over 4f out: styd far side in st: rdn 2 1/2f out: strly pressed and hdd over 1 1/2f out: qckly btn and fdd: dropped to last and eased ins fnl f* 15/1

1m 50.8s (3.30)
WFA 3 from 4yo+ 2lb 11 Ran SP% 118.0
WIN (incl. 1 euro stake): 26.90. PLACES: 5.10, 1.80, 2.80. DF: 57.20. SF: 151.80.
Owner Omar El Sharif **Bred** Haras D'Etreham, Vision Bloodstock Ltd **Trained** Lamorlaye, France

NOTEBOOK
Don Bosco(FR) raced wide throughout, and he and the second were the only ones to tack over to the stands' rail in the straight.

Chil The Kite never figured and despite his Chantilly win perhaps he doesn't want the ground quite this soft.

[7329] NEWMARKET (R-H)
Friday, November 2

OFFICIAL GOING: Soft (6.2)
Wind: Fresh across Weather: Fine

7516 EBF EXPRESS COFFEE CARS MAIDEN STKS 6f
12:40 (12:40) (Class 4) 2-Y-O **£4,528** (£1,347; £673; £336) **Stalls** Low

Form RPR
0 **1** **Winter Song (IRE)**[30] 6787 2-8-12 0 MichaelHills 1 66
(Charles Hills) *led over 2f: chsd ldr: rdn over 2f out: styd on u.p to ld and hung lft nr fin* **11/4**[2]
0004 **2** *hd* **Forbidden Fruit (IRE)**[15] 7198 2-8-12 68..(t) WilliamTwiston-Davies(5) 5 70
(Brian Meehan) *chsd wnr tl led over 3f out: rdn over 1f out: hdd nr fin* **4/1**[3]
63 **3** *1* **Shore Step (IRE)**[12] 7272 2-9-3 0 MartinHarley 2 67
(Mick Channon) *edgd lft s: plld hrd and prom: rdn over 1f out: styd on* **5/2**[1]
4 *2 ½* **Smokethatthunders (IRE)** 2-9-3 0 RobertHavlin 4 60
(James Toller) *hmpd s: prom: rdn over 1f out: styd on same pce* **5/1**
6 **5** *2 ½* **Wotalad**[11] 7290 2-9-3 0 AmyRyan 6 52
(Richard Whitaker) *prom: rdn over 2f out: wknd ins fnl f* **11/2**
6 *7* **Sweet Talking Guy (IRE)** 2-9-0 0 (t) SimonPearce(3) 8 31
(Lydia Pearce) *hld up: rdn over 2f out: edgd rt and wknd over 1f out* **16/1**

1m 16.2s (4.00) **Going Correction** +0.40s/f (Good) **6** Ran **SP%** **113.2**
Speed ratings (Par 98): **89,88,87,84,80 71**
toteswingers 1&2 £3.00, 1&3 £2.90, 2&3 £1.50 CSF £14.28 TOTE £4.00: £2.40, £2.00; EX 13.40 Trifecta £48.70 Pool: £566.37 - 8.71 winning tickets..
Owner Mrs E O'Leary **Bred** Sunderland Holdings Inc **Trained** Lambourn, Berks
■ A winner for Michael Hills on his final day before retirement. He rode his first winner in 1979.
■ Stewards' Enquiry : Michael Hills four-day ban: used whip above permitted level (Nov 16-17,19-20)

FOCUS
Stands' side course used with stalls on far side, except 1m4f and 2m: centre. A weak maiden for the track, rated through the runner-up.

NOTEBOOK
Winter Song(IRE) was representing a yard that has taken this race several times in the past. A 110,000gns purchase, out of a mare who won over 5f, and a half-sister to 5f (inc Group 3 at 2yrs and 4yrs) winner Enticing and Group-placed 1m Listed winner Sentaril, she knew her job this time, in contrast to her debut, and bounced out from the gates. She rallied well for pressure after being headed 3f out and clearly appreciated the ground, but the bare form is nothing special using the placed horses as a guide. (op 5-2 tchd 3-1)
Forbidden Fruit(IRE) had shown only modest ability in four previous starts and the return to testing ground wasn't sure to suit. He travelled best to 2f out, but struggled when let down. (op 10-3 tchd 3-1)
Shore Step(IRE), proven under the conditions, would probably have done better had he settled through the early stages. (op 9-4 tchd 85-40)
Smokethatthunders(IRE) ran all right considering his lack of previous experience. (op 12-1)
Wotalad didn't really build on his debut effort. He might do better on a faster surface. (op 8-1)
Sweet Talking Guy(IRE) Official explanation: jockey said gelding ran green

7517 EBF WARRENS OF WARWICK MAIDEN STKS 7f
1:10 (1:13) (Class 4) 2-Y-O **£4,528** (£1,347; £673; £336) **Stalls** Low

Form RPR
5 **1** **Amralah (IRE)**[103] 4362 2-9-0 0 MartinHarley 5 83
(Mick Channon) *chsd ldr: led 1/2-way: rdn and hdd over 1f out: rallied to ld nr fin* **6/4**[1]
40 **2** *shd* **Fehaydi**[9] 7324 2-9-0 0 MichaelHills 4 83
(William Haggas) *led to 1/2-way: chsd ldr tl led again over 1f out: sn rdn and edgd lft: hdd nr fin* **14/1**
3 *2 ¾* **Hasaad (USA)** 2-9-0 0 PaulHanagan 1 76+
(Brian Meehan) *a.p: rdn over 1f out: styd on* **11/1**
6 **4** *3* **Cousin Melchior (IRE)**[10] 7306 2-9-0 0 RobertHavlin 10 68
(John Gosden) *hld up: hdwy 1/2-way: rdn over 1f out: no ex fnl f* **11/2**[2]
0 **5** *1* **Putra Eton (IRE)**[28] 6846 2-9-0 0 NeilCallan 6 66
(Roger Varian) *chsd ldrs: rdn over 2f out: styd on same pce fr over 1f out* **6/1**[3]
63 **6** *7* **Snowy Dawn**[18] 7103 2-8-9 0 JackDuern(5) 7 48+
(Reg Hollinshead) *mid-div: rdn and wknd over 2f out* **9/1**
6 **7** *3* **Refuse To Mambo**[17] 7127 2-9-0 0 MartinDwyer 11 41
(Reg Hollinshead) *sn pushed along in rr: sme hdwy over 2f out: edgd rt and wknd wl over 1f out* **40/1**
8 *3* **Doctor's Gift** 2-9-0 0 DavidProbert 3 33
(Andrew Balding) *s.i.s: sn prom: lost pl over 4f out: wknd over 2f out* **12/1**
9 *1 ½* **Great Demeanor (USA)** 2-9-0 0 LiamKeniry 2 30
(David Elsworth) *s.s: sn pushed along in rr: wknd over 2f out* **16/1**
0 **10** *1* **Prairie Prince (IRE)**[17] 7127 2-9-0 0 JimmyFortune 9 27
(Andrew Balding) *prom: rdn over 2f out: wknd wl over 1f out* **20/1**
00 **11** *6* **Shining Cross (IRE)**[25] 6928 2-9-0 0 IanMongan 8 12
(George Margarson) *prom: pushed along 1/2-way: wknd over 2f out* **100/1**
0 **12** *14* **Tychaios**[10] 7305 2-9-0 0 HarryBentley 12
(Stuart Williams) *a in rr: lost tch fnl 3f: t.o* **66/1**

1m 28.27s (2.87) **Going Correction** +0.40s/f (Good) **12** Ran **SP%** **117.9**
Speed ratings (Par 98): **99,98,95,92,91 83,79,76,74,73 66,50**
toteswingers 1&2 £3.50, 1&3 £5.20, 2&3 £18.10 CSF £24.70 TOTE £2.00: £1.30, £2.30, £3.40; EX 18.50 Trifecta £65.40 Pool: £596.97 - 6.84 winning tickets..
Owner Prince A A Faisal **Bred** Nawara Stud Co Ltd **Trained** West Ilsley, Berks

FOCUS
The first two duked it out from some way out. The time was decent and the winner built on debut promise.

NOTEBOOK
Amralah(IRE), a well regarded colt, gained the verdict. Given a break after finishing fifth to subsequent Mill Reef winner Moohaajim on his debut, this ground is not what he wants and the bare form is nothing too special, but he battled well to get see off the runner-up, and he should make a better 3yo. (tchd 11-8)
Fehaydi was disappointing on his second start, not progressing from a fair debut effort, but he's a half-brother to Fillies' Mile winner Red Bloom, and this was more like it. He ought to make up into a useful handicapper over further next year. (op 11-1)
Hasaad(USA) ran a race of promise on his debut. His dam is out of a US 7f Grade 1 winner and he could well take a Polytrack maiden before the end of the year granted normal improvement from this yard. (op 16-1)
Cousin Melchior(IRE) was drawn in stall ten and, while the main action developed towards the far rail, he raced nearer the centre of the track until edging right inside the final 3f. He'll be of more interest in handicaps after one more run. (op 6-1 tchd 7-1)
Putra Eton(IRE) stepped up on his debut effort and finished well clear of the rest in fifth, but he's another who looks more of a handicap type. (op 13-2)
Snowy Dawn is by Notnowcato out of a mare who placed over 1m7f, and he's going to need a much longer trip to show his best in handicaps next year. (op 6-1)

7518 EBF EXPRESS CAFES BOSRA SHAM FILLIES' STKS (LISTED RACE) 6f
1:40 (1:42) (Class 1) 2-Y-O
£13,043 (£4,945; £2,474; £925; £925; £310) **Stalls** Low

Form RPR
3101 **1** **Melbourne Memories**[27] 6871 2-8-12 85 PaulHanagan 3 93
(Clive Cox) *racd far side: w ldrs: overall ldr 2f out: rdn out* **9/1**
2431 **2** *1 ½* **Effie B**[7] 7374 2-8-12 82 NeilCallan 14 88+
(Mick Channon) *racd stands' side: mid-div: hdwy over 2f out: swtchd lft over 1f out: rdn to ld her side ins fnl f: r.o: no ch w wnr far side: 1st of 8 in gp* **9/1**
12 **3** *hd* **Hoodna (IRE)**[62] 5828 2-8-12 0 MickaelBarzalona 2 87
(Saeed Bin Suroor) *racd far side: w ldr tl overall ldr over 3f out: rdn and hdd 2f out: styd on same pce ins fnl f: 2nd of 8 in gp* **7/1**[3]
1164 **4** *1 ½* **City Image (IRE)**[76] 5379 2-9-1 100 TomQueally 1 86
(Richard Hannon) *racd far side: a.p: rdn over 1f out: styd on same pce: 3rd of 8 in gp* **5/1**[2]
21 **4** *dht* **Exactement (IRE)**[22] 7007 2-8-12 80 JimCrowley 16 83
(Mrs K Burke) *racd stands' side: chsd ldr tl led that gp 2f out: rdn and hdd 1f out: styd on same pce: 2nd of 8 in gp* **14/1**
4310 **6** *½* **Woodlandsway**[34] 6675 2-8-12 77 HayleyTurner 8 81
(Richard Hannon) *racd far side: s.i.s: hld up: rdn over 2f out: styd on u.p fr over 1f out: nvr nrr: 4th of 8 in gp* **25/1**
1504 **7** *1 ¼* **Jillnextdoor (IRE)**[6] 7400 2-8-12 103 MartinHarley 12 78
(Mick Channon) *racd stands' side: hld up: hdwy over 2f out: rdn to ld 1f out: hdd and no ex ins fnl f: 3rd of 8 in gp* **8/1**
2431 **8** *3* **Flawless Beauty**[16] 7161 2-8-12 80 MichaelHills 6 69
(Hugo Palmer) *racd far side: overall ldr tl hdd over 3f out: rdn over 1f out: sn wknd: 5th of 8 in gp* **16/1**
0415 **9** *½* **Grace Hull**[3] 7463 2-8-12 69 LiamKeniry 7 67
(J S Moore) *racd far side: hld up: hdwy over 2f out: rdn and wknd fnl f: 6th of 8 in gp* **100/1**
01 **10** *1 ¾* **Eminently**[35] 6627 2-8-12 71 SeanLevey 13 62
(Richard Hannon) *racd stands' side: prom: lost pl 4f out: rdn over 2f out: wknd over 1f out: 4th of 8 in gp* **25/1**
0651 **11** *nse* **Lady Ibrox**[34] 6658 2-8-12 89 DaleSwift 15 62
(Alan Brown) *racd stands' side: hld up: hdwy over 2f out: rdn over 1f out: sn wknd: 5th of 8 in gp* **16/1**
001 **12** *1 ¾* **Tassel**[39] 6540 2-8-12 89 JimmyFortune 10 57
(Richard Hannon) *racd stands' side: chsd ldrs: rdn and ev ch wl over 1f out: wknd fnl f: 6th of 8 in gp* **16/1**
3215 **13** *¾* **Pearl Sea (IRE)**[71] 5516 2-8-12 95 GrahamLee 17 54
(David Brown) *led stands' side: rdn and hdd 2f out: wknd over 1f out: 7th of 8 in gp* **4/1**[1]
2106 **14** *2 ¼* **Faithfilly (IRE)**[42] 6424 2-9-1 96 LukeMorris 11 51
(Ed Walker) *racd stands' side: hld up: rdn over 2f out: wknd over 1f out: last of 8 in gp* **33/1**
2 **15** *3 ½* **Rebelde (IRE)**[25] 6936 2-8-12 0 MartinDwyer 9 37
(Conrad Allen) *racd far side: prom: rdn over 2f out: wknd over 1f out: 7th of 8 in gp* **66/1**
125 **16** *3 ¾* **Scatty Cat (IRE)**[13] 7258 2-8-12 79 (t) MichaelHussey 4 26
(Peter McCreery, Ire) *racd far side: s.i.s: a in rr: rdn and wknd over 2f out: last of 8 in gp* **33/1**

1m 14.72s (2.52) **Going Correction** +0.40s/f (Good) **16** Ran **SP%** **120.6**
Speed ratings (Par 101): **99,97,96,94,94 94,92,88,87,85 85,83,82,79,74 69**
toteswingers 1&2 £12.90, 1&3 £10.50, 2&3 £10.50 CSF £81.85 TOTE £10.00: £3.20, £3.40, £2.70; EX 85.50 Trifecta £649.80 Part won. Pool: £866.52 - 0.58 winning tickets..
Owner M P Coleman & R J Coleman **Bred** M P Coleman & R J Coleman **Trained** Lambourn, Berks
■ Stewards' Enquiry : Paul Hanagan caution: careless riding.

FOCUS
A really competitive Listed race, and the field split into two equal groups. Three of the first four came from the far-side bunch. The form looks below par for the grade.

NOTEBOOK
Melbourne Memories was hanging on somewhat on the climb to the line, but she had enough in hand and held off the closing pack fairly cosily. Clearly suited by plenty of give in the ground, the Fred Darling was mentioned as a possible starting off point next year, and she has a fair chance of getting her ground at Newbury in April, but the extra furlong will be a question mark. (op 12-1)
Effie B finished well to 'win' the race on the stands' side. Winner of a heavy-ground nursery at Newbury last time out, she's had a long old season, but takes her racing really well and this was a career-best in defeat. (op 11-1)
Hoodna(IRE), one of the least experienced fillies in the line-up, was returning from a two-month break and ran well to finish second on the far side. A winner on Polytrack on her debut, this ground might have been plenty soft enough for her. (op 8-1)
City Image(IRE), fourth in a 7f French Group 3 last time out, had a 3lb penalty to carry due to a win at this level earlier in the campaign. She could never quite get in blow, and the drop back to 6f seemed to find her out. (op 6-1)
Exactement(IRE) is by dirt sire Speightstown, but her dam won on soft ground and she coped pretty well with conditions, keeping on to finish second on the stands' side. There's more to come from her, especially back on Polytrack. (op 6-1)
Woodlandsway kept plugging away, but she never looked that happy on the ground. She'll be of more interest if given another try on the Polytrack. (op 40-1)
Jillnextdoor(IRE) looks flattered by her rating based on her close-up fifth in the Cheveley Park, a piece of form which is in theory a stone better than anything else she's done. She's by Henrythenavigator, though, and as a result it'll be a surprise if she doesn't appreciate a return to a quicker surface. (op 6-1)
Pearl Sea(IRE) was very disappointing, but presumably she just found conditions too testing. (tchd 9-2)

7519 EBF THAI STREET CAFE FILLIES' H'CAP 1m 4f
2:10 (2:14) (Class 3) (0-90,89) 3-Y-O+
£6,411 (£1,919; £959; £479; £239; £120) **Stalls** Centre

Form RPR
6301 **1** **Bridle Belle**[20] 7069 4-9-5 **84** PaulHanagan 9 92
(Richard Fahey) *hld up: hdwy over 3f out: led over 1f out: rdn out* **9/1**
2014 **2** *¾* **Varnish**[35] 6625 3-8-10 **81** SeanLevey 1 88
(Richard Hannon) *chsd ldrs: rdn over 2f out: styd on* **17/2**[3]

0524 **3** *nk* **The Giving Tree (IRE)**[7] 7375 3-8-5 **76** MartinDwyer 3 82
(Sylvester Kirk) *hld up: swtchd lft and hdwy over 1f out: r.o* **14/1**
2540 **4** *1 1/4* **Qushchi**[36] 6598 4-9-10 **89** GrahamLee 11 94
(William Jarvis) *chsd ldrs: led over 2f out: rdn and hdd over 1f out: styd on same pce ins fnl f* **16/1**
1201 **5** *2 1/2* **Require**[24] 6964 3-9-2 **87** KirstyMilczarek 7 88
(Luca Cumani) *chsd ldrs: led over 6f out: rdn and hdd over 2f out: no ex fnl f* **9/2**[1]
2000 **6** *1 3/4* **Always The Lady**[34] 6667 4-8-12 **77** (p) NeilCallan 5 75
(Clive Cox) *led over 5f: rdn over 2f out: no ex fnl f* **16/1**
2201 **7** *2 1/4* **Abundantly**[25] 6924 3-8-4 **75** oh2 ChrisCatlin 6 70
(Hughie Morrison) *hld up: rdn over 4f out: hdwy u.p over 2f out: wknd over 1f out* **17/2**[3]
2213 **8** *1/2* **Bedazzled**[34] 6667 3-9-0 **85** HayleyTurner 8 79
(James Fanshawe) *hld up: hdwy 1/2-way: rdn over 1f out: wknd and eased ins fnl f* **9/2**[1]
2153 **9** *9* **Gosbeck**[41] 6492 4-9-7 **86** FergusSweeney 4 67
(Henry Candy) *prom: rdn over 2f out: sn wknd* **9/1**
2502 **10** *7* **Jane Lachatte (IRE)**[28] 6847 3-8-4 **75** HarryBentley 10 45
(Stuart Williams) *hld up: hdwy over 4f out: wknd 2f out* **16/1**
2304 **11** *1* **Rio's Rosanna (IRE)**[48] 6248 5-9-9 **88** AmyRyan 2 57
(Richard Whitaker) *hld up: rdn and wknd over 3f out* **5/1**[2]

2m 38.13s (6.13) **Going Correction** +0.40s/f (Good)
WFA 3 from 4yo+ 6lb **11** Ran SP% **118.4**
Speed ratings (Par 104): **95,94,94,93,91 90,89,88,82,78 77**
toteswingers 1&2 £12.30, 1&3 £20.20, 2&3 £18.10 CSF £83.88 CT £1073.18 TOTE £9.00: £3.20, £2.40, £4.70; EX 91.90 Trifecta £897.80 Part won. Pool: £1,197.11 - 0.20 winning tickets..

Owner Mrs H Steel **Bred** Mrs C R Philipson & Mrs H G Lascelles **Trained** Musley Bank, N Yorks
■ Stewards' Enquiry : Sean Levey four-day ban: used whip above permitted level (16-17,19-20)

FOCUS
Competitive stuff in which they went 9-2 the field. The winner and third are good guides to the form.

NOTEBOOK
Bridle Belle returned to winning ways at York last time and the extra 2f here was only going to suit her even better, as she just about stays 1m6f. Very much at home in soft ground, she got the job done well. (op 8-1)
Varnish may have found 1m6f in heavy ground taxing her a bit too much last time, but these conditions proved fine for her and she probably ran another personal best in defeat. (op 8-1 tchd 9-1)
The Giving Tree(IRE) had never run over a distance this far before, but she got it well and was never better than at the finish. This opens up some new options. (op 16-1 tchd 12-1)
Qushchi has only finished placed once in ten starts this season, but she's run well enough, including in Listed company, to ensure that the handicapper has only dropped her 7lb. Quicker ground suits her ideally. (op 14-1 tchd 12-1)
Require found things tougher up in class, but her rider reported that she ran flat and perhaps she's just had enough for the year. Official explanation: jockey said filly ran flat (tchd 5-1 and 11-2 in a place)
Always The Lady, wearing cheekpieces for the first time, didn't see her race out and is probably better over 1m2f. (op 20-1)
Abundantly, racing from 2lb out of the handicap, had more on her plate in this company and ground this soft ground was new to her as well. (op 9-1 tchd 8-1)
Bedazzled got unbalanced running into the Dip and didn't look happy on the ground. (op 5-1 tchd 11-2)
Rio's Rosanna(IRE) Official explanation: jockey said mare never travelled

7520 EXPRESS CAFES RACING EXCELLENCE APPRENTICE JOCKEYS' TRAINING SERIES FINAL (H'CAP) 1m
2:45 (2:46) (Class 4) (0-85,84) 3-Y-O **£4,075** (£1,212; £606; £303) **Stalls** Low

Form RPR
1211 **1** **Boonga Roogeta**[3] 7470 3-8-4 **70** 12ex HannahNunn(3) 2 78+
(Peter Charalambous) *hld up: hdwy 5f out: led over 2f out: rdn out* **2/1**[1]
0400 **2** *1/2* **Masters Blazing**[23] 6986 3-8-0 **70** oh3 BradleyBosley(7) 8 76
(John Ryan) *a.p: chsd wnr over 1f out: styd on* **20/1**
2445 **3** *2 1/2* **Swing Alone (IRE)**[20] 7064 3-9-2 **84** LouisSteward(5) 1 84
(Gay Kelleway) *hld up: hdwy over 3f out: rdn over 1f out: styd on same pce ins fnl f* **11/2**[3]
1-50 **4** *3 3/4* **Dakota Canyon (IRE)**[63] 5802 3-8-12 **75** GeorgeChaloner 4 67
(Richard Fahey) *chsd ldrs: rdn over 3f out: styd on same pce fnl 2f* **12/1**
0302 **5** *2 3/4* **Mr Spiggott (IRE)**[25] 6931 3-9-5 **82** DavidBergin 7 68
(Joseph Tuite) *sn prom: rdn over 2f out: wknd over 1f out* **11/4**[2]
1400 **6** *1/2* **Centrifugal (IRE)**[14] 7229 3-9-6 **83** JasonHart 6 68
(Mark Johnston) *led: rdn and hdd over 2f out: wknd over 1f out* **8/1**
0060 **7** *19* **Amber Silk (IRE)**[44] 6375 3-9-0 **77** WilliamTwiston-Davies 5 20
(Charles Hills) *chsd ldrs tl wknd over 3f out* **15/2**

1m 42.42s (3.82) **Going Correction** +0.40s/f (Good) **7** Ran SP% **110.7**
Speed ratings (Par 104): **96,95,93,89,86 86,67**
toteswingers 1&2 £7.30, 1&3 £2.70, 2&3 £9.30 CSF £38.99 CT £181.24 TOTE £2.30: £1.30, £12.30; EX 47.70 Trifecta £446.20 Pool: £1,309.01 - 2.20 winning tickets..
Owner P Charalambous **Bred** Peter Charles **Trained** Newmarket, Suffolk

FOCUS
An ordinary race. The form has limiations but looks sound enough.
Amber Silk(IRE) Official explanation: trainer's rep said filly was unsuited by the soft ground

7521 NGK SPARK PLUGS CONDITIONS STKS 6f
3:20 (3:20) (Class 3) 2-3-Y-O
£6,411 (£1,919; £959; £479; £239; £120) **Stalls** Low

Form RPR
1341 **1** **Ninjago**[30] 6777 2-8-6 99 SeanLevey 5 88+
(Richard Hannon) *s.i.s: hld up: hdwy over 1f out: swtchd rt sn after: r.o to ld wl ins fnl f* **1/1**[1]
1246 **2** *nk* **Miliika**[16] 7177 3-9-6 83 ChrisCatlin 4 82
(Rae Guest) *chsd ldrs: led over 1f out: rdn and hdd wl ins fnl f* **11/4**[2]
-645 **3** *2 1/2* **Brick Tops**[147] 2893 3-9-6 76 TomQueally 6 75
(David Simcock) *hld up: pushed along 1/2-way: hdwy over 1f out: sn rdn: styd on same pce ins fnl f* **7/1**
6220 **4** *3 1/2* **Kashmiri Star**[10] 7314 3-9-3 59 (v[1]) AdamKirby 3 61
(Michael Quinn) *led over 3f: sn rdn: hmpd and no ex ins fnl f* **50/1**
4114 **5** *2 1/4* **Love Island**[43] 6406 3-9-3 76 AmyRyan 2 54
(Richard Whitaker) *chsd ldr tl led over 2f out: rdn and hdd over 1f out: hmpd and wknd ins fnl f* **9/2**[3]
2104 **6** *hd* **Kicken Off (IRE)**[8] 7350 2-8-3 71 (p) JimmyQuinn 1 56
(Phil McEntee) *prom tl rdn and wknd over 1f out* **33/1**

1m 15.43s (3.23) **Going Correction** +0.40s/f (Good) **6** Ran SP% **112.3**
Speed ratings: **94,93,90,85,82 82**
toteswingers 1&2 £1.90, 1&3 £2.10, 2&3 £2.60 CSF £3.98 TOTE £1.80: £1.10, £1.30; EX 4.60.
Owner J Palmer-Brown & Potensis Ltd **Bred** Newsells Park Stud **Trained** East Everleigh, Wilts
■ Stewards' Enquiry : Sean Levey two-day ban: improper riding (Nov 21-22)

FOCUS
A race that has been dominated by 2yos, with nine of the last ten now having been won by a juvenile. The winner was the clear pick of the weights and this looks form to be negative about overall.

NOTEBOOK
Ninjago, one of two 2yos in the race, held an outstanding chance at the weights but was weak in the betting, presumably on account of the soft ground, which he hadn't encountered before. He handled it well, though, and looked to win a shade cosily, idling a little once hitting the front. He gave his trainer a third win in the race in the last six years. (op 5-6 tchd 5-4)
Miliika appreciated the return to 6f, and clearly acts well with cut. There was no disgrace in being seen off by a 2yo who was well treated by the race conditions. (op 3-1 tchd 9-4)
Brick Tops didn't run badly considering she'd been off the track since June. (op 10-1 tchd 13-2)
Kashmiri Star, visored for the first time, was outclassed. (op 33-1)
Love Island didn't handle the conditions and failed to get home. (op 6-1)

7522 MILOS SEAFOOD & NORFOLK ICE CREAM H'CAP 2m
3:55 (3:57) (Class 3) (0-90,89) 3-Y-O+ **£6,663** (£1,982; £990; £495) **Stalls** Centre

Form RPR
-022 **1** **Ardlui (IRE)**[28] 6834 4-10-0 **89** FergusSweeney 10 97
(Alan King) *a.p: chsd ldr over 2f out: styd on u.p to ld wl ins fnl f* **11/4**[1]
0 **2** *3/4* **Sohar**[36] 6598 4-9-4 **79** KirstyMilczarek 3 86
(James Toller) *chsd ldrs: led 3f out: rdn over 1f out: edgd lft and hdd wl ins fnl f* **12/1**
1 **3** *9* **Lieutenant Miller**[25] 6922 6-9-3 **78** TomQueally 4 74
(Nicky Henderson) *prom: rdn over 2f out: wknd fnl f* **7/2**[2]
0-42 **4** *1* **Zakatal**[14] 7211 6-9-5 **80** DaleSwift 9 75
(Julie Camacho) *mid-div: hdwy over 5f out: rdn over 2f out: styd on same pce fnl 2f* **25/1**
4543 **5** *1 1/2* **Toptempo**[8] 7352 3-8-7 **77** HarryBentley 2 70
(Mark H Tompkins) *chsd ldrs: rdn over 3f out: wknd over 1f out* **9/1**
/-00 **6** *2* **Ocean's Minstrel**[28] 6834 6-9-11 **86** MichaelO'Connell 13 77
(John Ryan) *hld up in tch: rdn over 2f out: wknd over 1f out* **25/1**
01 **7** *16* **Kleitomachos (IRE)**[111] 4096 4-9-6 **81** AdamKirby 16 53
(Stuart Kittow) *mid-div: hdwy over 4f out: wknd 2f out: t.o* **12/1**
1000 **8** *2* **Epsom Salts**[41] 6493 7-8-7 **73** JemmaMarshall(5) 11 42
(Pat Phelan) *led: rdn and hdd 3f out: wknd wl over 1f out: t.o* **66/1**
1244 **9** *3* **Somemothersdohavem**[12] 7271 3-8-3 **73** (p) KieranO'Neill 1 39
(John Ryan) *hld up: rdn and hung rt fr over 4f out: wknd over 2f out: t.o* **16/1**
5300 **10** *4* **Nafaath (IRE)**[20] 7051 6-9-12 **87** MickaelBarzalona 7 48
(Neil King) *hld up: rdn over 3f out: wknd over 2f out: t.o* **14/1**
4236 **11** *6* **Hawridge Star (IRE)**[20] 7068 10-8-13 **74** IanMongan 14 28
(Stuart Kittow) *hld up: rdn over 4f out: wknd over 3f out: t.o* **12/1**
0640 **12** *1* **Dark Ranger**[20] 7051 6-9-8 **83** SeanLevey 6 36
(Tim Pitt) *s.s: hld up: hdwy over 6f out: wknd 4f out: t.o* **8/1**[3]
6003 **13** *1 1/4* **Samsons Son**[13] 7245 8-8-7 **73** RosieJessop(5) 12 24
(Terry Clement) *mid-div: wknd 4f out: t.o* **40/1**
25 **14** *25* **Bilidn**[98] 4528 4-9-12 **87** PaulHanagan 5 8
(Noel Quinlan) *hld up: a in rr: bhd fnl 5f: t.o* **14/1**

3m 33.94s (3.44) **Going Correction** +0.40s/f (Good)
WFA 3 from 4yo+ 9lb **14** Ran SP% **123.9**
Speed ratings (Par 107): **107,106,102,101,100 99,91,90,89,87 84,83,83,70**
toteswingers 1&2 £12.00, 1&3 £3.40, 2&3 £12.60 CSF £37.27 CT £124.38 TOTE £3.60: £1.60, £4.80, £2.10; EX 52.50 Trifecta £283.50 Pool: £1,493.37 - 3.95 winning tickets..
Owner Thomas Barr **Bred** Sunderland Holdings Ltd **Trained** Barbury Castle, Wilts
■ Stewards' Enquiry : Kirsty Milczarek two-day ban: used whip above permitted level (Nov 16-17)

FOCUS
The first two came clear in this staying handicap. Straightforward form.

NOTEBOOK
Ardlui(IRE) gained due reward for a couple of near-misses in his previous two starts. As the leader edged left for pressure, he found his stride on the climb to the line and just saw it out best of all. He'll presumably go back hurdling now, and a step up from 2m in that sphere ought to suit him. (op 3-1 tchd 7-2)
Sohar had her ground and appreciated the step up in trip, but she was just seen off by a stronger stayer late on. She beat the rest pointless, though, and ought to be able to win something similar next spring. (op 10-1 tchd 14-1)
Lieutenant Miller, who took a conditions race at Pontefract on his Flat debut last month, looked to have been given a fair mark for his handicap debut, but he might just have found this ground a bit too taxing. (tchd 3-1)
Zakatal was keeping on again at the finish and looks to have loads of stamina. He's already won at 2m6f over hurdles and probably has more to offer in that sphere.
Toptempo is already due to be dropped 4lb, which should help. (op 14-1 tchd 8-1)
Ocean's Minstrel ran a better race than at Ascot, but he remains plenty high enough in the weights. (op 20-1)
Somemothersdohavem Official explanation: jockey said gelding hung right
Bilidn Official explanation: jockey said filly stopped quickly
T/Plt: £185.20 to a £1 stake. Pool: £52,292.91 - 206.06 winning tickets T/Qpdt: £48.60 to a £1 stake. Pool: £4,465.90 - 67.86 winning tickets CR

7458 WOLVERHAMPTON (A.W) (L-H)
Friday, November 2

OFFICIAL GOING: Standard
Wind: Moderate, behind Weather: Cloudy

7523 BREEDERS' CUP LIVE ONLY ON ATR NOVICE STKS 7f 32y(P)
4:15 (4:15) (Class 5) 2-Y-O **£2,264** (£673; £336; £168) **Stalls** High

Form RPR
01 **1** **Correspondent**[16] 7167 2-9-5 0 EddieAhern 4 89+
(Brian Meehan) *hld up in 3rd: rdn over 2f out: r.o to ld ins fnl f: sn pushed clr* **8/15**[1]
140 **2** *2 1/4* **Bottle Blonde**[25] 6920 2-9-0 78 SebSanders 1 78
(Ed McMahon) *led: rdn over 2f out: edgd rt 1f out: hdd and unable qck ins fnl f* **14/1**[3]
12 **3** *nk* **Spokeswoman (IRE)**[30] 6777 2-9-0 0 SilvestreDeSousa 3 79
(Saeed Bin Suroor) *chsd ldr: hrd rdn whn n.m.r ent fnl f: lost 2nd pl and one pce ins fnl f* **9/4**[2]
0051 **4** *2 3/4* **El Mirage (IRE)**[14] 7223 2-8-11 70 ShaneKelly 5 68
(Dean Ivory) *hld up in rr: rdn over 2f out: unable to trble first 3* **20/1**

1m 28.4s (-1.20) **Going Correction** -0.05s/f (Stan) **4** Ran SP% **107.4**
Speed ratings (Par 96): **104,101,101,97**
CSF £8.32 TOTE £1.40; EX 6.40.
Owner Mrs P Good **Bred** Mrs P Good **Trained** Manton, Wilts
■ Stewards' Enquiry : Seb Sanders caution: careless riding.

FOCUS
An interesting novice event despite the small field. The winner confirmed the promise of his Lingfield win, with the third a few pounds below form.

NOTEBOOK
Correspondent followed up last month's Lingfield maiden win. Off the mark with a fluent victory at the Surrey venue 16 days ago, he was backed as if defeat was out of the question and those that got involved in the gamble had very few anxious moments as he always looked to have the eventual runner-up in his sights. Conceding weight all round, he's clearly a useful prospect and looks destined for a step up in class after this. Fast ground on turf is likely to suit. (op 4-6)
Bottle Blonde ran well, though was readily brushed aside by the confidently ridden winner inside the final furlong. A shock winner on her debut over 6f at this track in August, she benefited from an enterprising ride on this occasion and, as a result, was probably flattered by her proximity to Correspondent. Wandering around under pressure, it may be that connections will return to sprint distances before too long. (op 16-1)
Spokeswoman(IRE) was done no favours by the drifting runner-up, but was by no means unlucky. She was in the ideal position to strike off the home bend but lacked the necessary pace to challenge. She was another trying this trip for the first time and, on this evidence, may do better once up another furlong. (op 2-1)
El Mirage(IRE) looked to have plenty on her plate on paper and was basically outclassed. (op 14-1)

7524 ATTHERACES.COM BREEDERS' CUP SITE NOW LIVE FILLIES' H'CAP — 7f 32y(P)
4:45 (4:45) (Class 5) (0-75,75) 3-Y-0+ — **£2,587** (£770; £384; £192) **Stalls** High

Form — RPR

4210 **1** **Finesse**[24] 6961 3-9-0 **69** ... JimCrowley 1 — 79+
(Ralph Beckett) *trckd ldrs gng wl: rdn to ld jst over 1f out: drvn out* **11/4**[1]

0000 **2** ¾ **Sugarformyhoney (IRE)**[49] 6209 3-8-9 **69** ...(p) CharlesBishop(5) 4 — 76+
(Seamus Durack) *dwlt: sn rdn up in tch: effrt on inner over 2f out: rdn to chal over 1f out: unable qck ins fnl f* **6/1**

4011 **3** 1 **Les Verguettes (IRE)**[18] 7106 4-8-10 **67** ... AshleyMorgan(3) 6 — 73
(Chris Wall) *chsd ldrs: rdn and styd on same pce fnl 2f* **7/2**[2]

0535 **4** 1 ¾ **Who's Shirl**[17] 7141 6-9-1 **69** ... KellyHarrison 8 — 71
(Chris Fairhurst) *towards rr: rdn over 2f out: styd on: nt gng pce to chal* **9/2**[3]

0603 **5** nk **Imaginary World (IRE)**[21] 7022 4-8-9 **63** ...(p) LukeMorris 7 — 64
(John Balding) *midfield on outer: rdn and rn wd on bnd over 2f out: styd on fnl f* **8/1**

0051 **6** ½ **Caramelita**[10] 7314 5-9-4 **72** 6ex ...(v) FrederikTylicki 9 — 72
(J R Jenkins) *hld up in rr: rdn 2f out: sme late hdwy* **8/1**

5000 **7** ¾ **Sunrise Dance**[18] 7100 3-8-6 **61** oh4 ... AndrewMullen 3 — 58
(Robert Johnson) *led tl wknd jst over 1f out* **40/1**

0000 **8** 2 ¾ **Poker Hospital**[74] 5426 3-8-8 **63** ... ShaneKelly 5 — 53
(John Stimpson) *mid-div: rdn over 2f out: wknd over 1f out* **40/1**

00 **9** 5 **Golconde (IRE)**[25] 6939 3-9-6 **75** ... EddieAhern 2 — 53
(Robert Cowell) *chsd ldr tl over 2f out: wknd wl over 1f out* **22/1**

0300 **10** 1 **Qeethaara (USA)**[78] 5259 8-8-9 **68** ...(p) JackDuern(5) 10 — 44
(Mark Brisbourne) *a bhd* **33/1**

1m 29.1s (-0.50) **Going Correction** -0.05s/f (Stan)
WFA 3 from 4yo+ 1lb — **10** Ran SP% **115.7**
Speed ratings (Par 100): **100,99,98,96,95 95,94,91,85,84**
toteswingers: 1&2 £5.90, 2&3 £4.70, 1&3 £2.90 CSF £18.75 CT £59.01 TOTE £4.00: £2.60, £2.60, £1.10; EX 31.40 Trifecta £125.30 Pool: £1,073.28 - 6.42 winning tickets..
Owner P K Gardner **Bred** Springcombe Park Stud **Trained** Kimpton, Hants

FOCUS
A fair fillies' handicap, run at a steady pace. The winner probably has more to offer while this was the second's best run on Polytrack.

7525 ENJOY THE PUNTERS PACKAGE GROUP OFFER MEDIAN AUCTION MAIDEN STKS — 7f 32y(P)
5:15 (5:16) (Class 6) 2-Y-0 — **£1,704** (£503; £251) **Stalls** High

Form — RPR

642 **1** **Aye Aye Skipper (IRE)**[23] 6977 2-9-3 74 ... JimCrowley 7 — 74
(Dean Ivory) *chsd ldr: led wl over 1f out: hld on wl whn pressed by runner-up ins fnl f* **7/2**[2]

42 **2** hd **Magique (IRE)**[29] 6816 2-8-12 0 ... GrahamLee 9 — 69
(Jeremy Noseda) *plld hrd: in tch on outer: wd into st: rdn to press wnr fnl f: r.o: jst hld* **4/5**[1]

3 3 ¼ **Minimee** 2-9-3 0 ... NeilCallan 1 — 66+
(Roger Varian) *trckd ldrs: rdn 2f out: one pce appr fnl f* **6/1**[3]

40 **4** 1 **Ella Motiva (IRE)**[76] 5331 2-8-12 0 ... RobbieFitzpatrick 10 — 58
(Mark Brisbourne) *mid-div: outpcd and rn wd ent st: rallied and r.o ins fnl f* **40/1**

0 **5** ½ **Carrera**[15] 7192 2-9-3 0 ... SebSanders 4 — 62
(J W Hills) *chsd ldrs: rdn 3f out: no ex over 1f out* **25/1**

6323 **6** nse **Imperial Spirit**[71] 5503 2-9-3 73 ... MartinHarley 3 — 62
(Mick Channon) *led tl wl over 1f out: wknd ent fnl f* **15/2**

0 **7** 2 ½ **Good As New**[41] 6501 2-8-12 0 ... TedDurcan 2 — 51+
(Chris Wall) *s.s: sn in midfield on inner: shkn up and rn green fnl 2f: no imp* **66/1**

00 **8** 4 ½ **Shesthecaptain (IRE)**[45] 6335 2-8-12 0 ... LukeMorris 8 — 40
(John Weymes) *prom tl wknd over 2f out* **200/1**

00 **9** 1 ¾ **Hazza The Jazza**[125] 3611 2-9-3 0 ... J-PGuillambert 11 — 40
(Richard Guest) *sn bhd: rdn 3f out: n.d* **66/1**

10 4 ½ **Call Me Marilyn (USA)** 2-8-12 0 ... HayleyTurner 5 — 24
(Michael Bell) *s.s: rdn over 2f out: a bhd* **20/1**

0 **P** **Smart Alice**[15] 7191 2-8-9 0 ... AshleyMorgan(3) 6
(Chris Wall) *sn towards rr: eased and p.u 4f out: sddle slipped* **40/1**

1m 31.41s (1.81) **Going Correction** -0.05s/f (Stan) — **11** Ran SP% **120.8**
Speed ratings (Par 94): **87,86,83,81,81 81,78,73,71,66**
toteswingers: 1&2 £1.30, 2&3 £2.30, 1&3 £3.10 CSF £6.56 TOTE £3.40: £1.10, £1.10, £1.20; EX 9.80 Trifecta £29.30 Pool: £1,330.07 - 33.99 winning tickets..
Owner Heather Yarrow & Lesley Ivory **Bred** Ballyhane Stud **Trained** Radlett, Herts

FOCUS
A fair maiden, run at a steady pace, and the finish was dominated by the market principals. Straightforward form.

NOTEBOOK
Aye Aye Skipper(IRE) did enough to get off the mark. Setting the standard with a mark of 74, he had turned in a career best effort over this trip at Kempton last time and was able to build on that here. To the fore throughout, he travelled stylishly to the front and stuck to his guns well to deny the battling runner-up, with the pair clear of an interesting newcomer. However, it's unlikely that the assessor will adjust his mark too much after this and he should remain competitive in 7f handicaps over the coming months. (op 9-2)
Magique(IRE) only just lost out but she's becoming frustrating with this her second odds-on defeat in as many runs. Keener than ideal through the early part of the race, she did well to find as much as she did in the finish. She will surely be capable of picking up a race, but backing her at similarly short prices will come with a health warning attached. (op 10-11 tchd Evens)
Minimee stayed on late to fill the frame. He's clearly no world beater, but should improve for the experience. (op 13-2)
Ella Motiva(IRE) was also putting in some good late work and could be handily treated in handicaps after this. Disappointing at Chester last time, she showed much more on this occasion and can be expected to do even better once tackling middle-distances. (op 33-1)
Imperial Spirit, returning to the track after two months off, enjoyed the run of the race out in front but failed to pick up. He looks high enough in the handicap on this evidence and may soon be dropped in grade.
Call Me Marilyn(USA) Official explanation: jockey said filly suffered interference in running
Smart Alice Official explanation: jockey said saddle slipped

7526 COMMITTEE PUBS SPECTACULAR NURSERY — 5f 20y(P)
5:45 (5:45) (Class 6) (0-60,66) 2-Y-0 — **£1,704** (£503; £251) **Stalls** Low

Form — RPR

6510 **1** **Harrogate Fair**[11] 7298 2-9-6 **59** ... LiamJones 4 — 61
(Michael Squance) *chsd ldrs: effrt over 2f out: led ins fnl f: rdn out and hld on wl* **11/2**[3]

61 **2** hd **Modern Lady**[16] 7156 2-9-6 **59** ... RobbieFitzpatrick 10 — 60
(Richard Guest) *led: hrd rdn and hdd ins fnl f: rallied wl* **3/1**[1]

0010 **3** 3 ¼ **Mill End Dancer**[4] 7441 2-8-11 **50** ... JamesSullivan 11 — 39
(Michael Easterby) *dwlt: wd thrght: chsd ldrs: hrd rdn over 1f out: one pce* **8/1**

5603 **4** nk **Frans Hals**[12] 7268 2-9-4 **57** ...(be) NeilCallan 5 — 45
(Dominic Ffrench Davis) *s.i.s and rdn early: outpcd in 6th: styd on u.p fnl 2f* **7/2**[2]

5000 **5** 3 ¾ **Proventi**[20] 7056 2-9-1 **54** ...(p) SebSanders 2 — 29
(Alan McCabe) *pressed ldr tl over 2f out: wknd jst over 1f out* **25/1**

054 **6** ½ **Lexi's Beauty (IRE)**[24] 6970 2-9-4 **57** ... StevieDonohoe 9 — 30
(Ian Williams) *chsd ldrs tl wknd over 1f out* **7/1**

0445 **7** 1 ¾ **Michael's Song (IRE)**[29] 6822 2-9-0 **53** ... MartinHarley 7 — 20
(Mick Channon) *sn bhd: shkn up 2f out: nvr nr to chal* **11/2**[3]

006 **8** 3 ½ **Royal Jenray**[44] 6360 2-8-11 **50** ...(p) GrahamLee 1 — 4
(Jedd O'Keeffe) *dwlt: outpcd: a bhd* **14/1**

0006 **9** shd **Cos I Can**[28] 6850 2-8-6 **45** ... SilvestreDeSousa 6
(Derek Shaw) *outpcd and lost pl after 1f: struggling after* **40/1**

1m 2.8s (0.50) **Going Correction** -0.05s/f (Stan) — **9** Ran SP% **114.6**
Speed ratings (Par 94): **94,93,88,88,82 81,78,72,72**
toteswingers: 1&2 £3.40, 2&3 £6.30, 1&3 £8.10 CSF £22.17 CT £131.91 TOTE £7.20: £2.40, £1.30, £3.10; EX 23.20 Trifecta £169.90 Pool: £1,171.79 - 5.17 winning tickets..
Owner Kevin Daniel Crabb **Bred** Kevin Daniel Crabb **Trained** Newmarket, Suffolk

FOCUS
A moderate nursery, but it served up a thrilling finish. Low-grade, late-season form, with the first two clear.

NOTEBOOK
Harrogate Fair clung on to win from the rallying runner-up. He had got off the mark in heavy ground at Yarmouth at the beginning of last month before running no sort of race over 6f in similar conditions at Windsor last time. However, clearly better was expected of her here and she justified some good late support, albeit in workmanlike fashion. The form is nothing to write home about but this was a big improvement on the form she'd shown on her two previous AW starts at Kempton, and it should open up further opportunities for her over the winter. (op 15-2 tchd 8-1)
Modern Lady fell on her sword and was arguably a shade unlucky not to follow-up her Kempton victory having pulled hard out in front once crossing from her wide stall. She battled on tenaciously once headed and may be able to defy a small rise if found a similarly weak event. (op 5-2 tchd 9-4)
Mill End Dancer, another poorly drawn, was forced to race wide throughout and deserves some credit for this. While readily left behind by the principals, she responded gamely to pressure and should not be written off next time given her lowly mark. (op 6-1)
Frans Hals was taken off his feet early on, despite the steady pace, and he'll surely require a stiffer test of stamina if he's to be competitive. (op 11-2)
Lexi's Beauty(IRE) ran moderately on this, her handicap debut, and is clearly very limited. (op 11-2)

7527 $150M BREEDERS' CUP POOLS H'CAP — 1m 1f 103y(P)
6:15 (6:17) (Class 6) (0-60,60) 3-Y-0 — **£1,704** (£503; £251) **Stalls** Low

Form — RPR

0004 **1** **Tatting**[15] 7201 3-9-2 **55** ... GrahamLee 4 — 63
(Chris Dwyer) *mid-div: rdn and hdwy wl over 1f out: styd on to ld fnl 50yds* **9/2**[2]

0613 **2** ½ **Scarlett Fever**[72] 5482 3-9-2 **55** ...(b) HayleyTurner 10 — 62
(Marcus Tregoning) *chsd ldrs: rdn 3f out: wnt 2nd 1f out: kpt on u.p* **8/1**

0542 **3** ¾ **Taro Tywod (IRE)**[14] 7222 3-9-1 **54** ... ShaneKelly 6 — 60
(Mark Brisbourne) *led: rdn 2 l ahd ent st: hdd and no ex fnl 50yds* **11/2**[3]

0000 **4** ½ **Hill Of Dreams (IRE)**[64] 5764 3-8-11 **50** ... EddieAhern 12 — 55
(Dean Ivory) *chsd ldr: hrd rdn and lost 2nd 1f out: one pce* **25/1**

0004 **5** 3 **Destiny Awaits (IRE)**[21] 7025 3-9-2 **55** ...(p) TomEaves 13 — 54
(Ian Semple) *in tch: rdn 3f out: one pce* **33/1**

5033 **6** 6 **Rhossili Bay**[27] 6892 3-8-13 **52** ... MartinHarley 9 — 40
(Alastair Lidderdale) *towards rr: rdn 3f out: styd on fnl f* **9/2**[2]

1561 **7** ½ **Archina (IRE)**[13] 7250 3-9-7 **60** ... TedDurcan 7 — 47
(Chris Wall) *mid-div: n.m.r 7f out: rdn and no hdwy fnl 3f* **4/1**[1]

3444 **8** hd **Shore Performer (IRE)**[13] 7249 3-9-4 **57** ... KellyHarrison 1 — 43
(William Haggas) *hld up in rr: pushed along and sme hdwy on inner fnl 2f: nvr nr to chal* **22/1**

063 **9** nk **Brandy Snapping**[240] 816 3-9-3 **56** ... PaulMulrennan 3 — 42
(Mark Brisbourne) *chsd ldrs tl outpcd 3f out* **50/1**

3200 **10** ½ **Landown Littlerock**[148] 2860 3-9-1 **59** ...[1] JackDuern(5) 11 — 44
(Reg Hollinshead) *towards rr: rdn 4f out: nvr nr ldrs* **16/1**

6610 **11** 2 ¾ **Penang Pegasus**[68] 5623 3-8-13 **52** ... RobertWinston 5 — 32
(David O'Meara) *towards rr: rdn and n.d fnl 3f* **8/1**

045 **12** 12 **Trevose (IRE)**[47] 6279 3-9-4 **57** ... LukeMorris 2 — 14
(Roy Brotherton) *prom: rdn 4f out: wknd 3f out* **40/1**

460 **13** 35 **Donatia**[25] 6925 3-8-7 **46** oh1 ... AdrianNicholls 8
(David Nicholls) *hld up in rr: struggling over 4f out: wl bhd and eased fnl 2f* **25/1**

1m 59.66s (-2.04) **Going Correction** -0.05s/f (Stan) — **13** Ran SP% **119.2**
Speed ratings (Par 98): **107,106,105,105,102 97,97,96,96,96 93,83,51**
toteswingers: 1&2 £6.40, 2&3 £6.40, 1&3 £7.40 CSF £36.90 CT £205.54 TOTE £3.70: £2.00, £2.70, £2.10; EX 49.20 Trifecta £258.00 Pool: £980.74 - 2.85 winning tickets..
Owner Mrs K W Sneath **Bred** Darley **Trained** Six Mile Bottom, Cambs

FOCUS
Only a modest 3yo event, run at a fair pace, but there was plenty to like about the performance of the winner. Low-grade, straightforward form.

7528 GUARANTEED $2 MILLION JACKPOT POOL H'CAP 2m 119y (P)
6:45 (6:45) (Class 6) (0-60,60) 3-Y-0+ £1,704 (£503; £251) Stalls Low

Form RPR
1530 1 **Six Of Clubs**[16] 7169 6 -9-1260 .....(b) LukeMorris 8 67
(Bill Turner) *towards rr: rdn and hdwy over 2f out: styd on u.p to ld fnl strides* **9/1**
4422 2 *shd* **Annelko**[13] 7252 5 -9-957 ..... GrahamLee 3 64
(Michael Blake) *trckd ldrs: got through on inner gng wl 2f out: led jst over 1f out: hrd rdn fnl f: jst ct* **11/4**[2]
/6-0 3 *3/4* **Sarando**[19] 7077 7 -9-856 .....(tp) TedDurcan 13 62
(Paul Webber) *sn trcking ldr: drvn to chal 2f out: kpt on u.p* **8/1**
221 4 *1 3/4* **Blue Zealot (IRE)**[3] 7255 5 -9-556 ..... RachaelGreen(3) 7 60
(Anthony Honeyball) *hld up in rr: rdn and hdwy 2f out: nrest at fin* **2/1**[1]
5003 5 *2 1/2* **Waldsee (GER)**[13] 7255 7 -9-351 .....(b[1]) PaulMulrennan 4 52
(Sean Curran) *in tch: rdn to chse ldrs 3f out: no ex over 1f out* **20/1**
0362 6 *hd* **Tokyo Brown (USA)**[5] 7196 3 -9-158 ..... NeilCallan 1 59
(Heather Main) *led: hrd rdn and hdd jst over 1f out: wknd fnl f* **6/1**[3]
1240 7 *6* **Grand Art (IRE)**[8] 7102 8 -9-957 .....(p) SilvestreDeSousa 6 50
(Noel Wilson) *hld up in rr: rdn over 3f out: nvr trbld ldrs* **14/1**
5430 8 *4 1/2* **Crimson Monarch (USA)**[106] 4244 8 -8-1047 ..... RyanClark(3) 10 35
(Peter Hiatt) *mid-div on outer: wd and hrd rdn 3f out: sn lost pl* **40/1**
9 *28* **Southfork**[28] 4566 3 -9-158 .....(p) SebSanders 12 12
(Barry Brennan) *prom tl wknd over 3f out: eased whn no ch over 1f out* **50/1**
0040 10 *5* **Sea Change (IRE)**[21] 7024 5 -9-1058 .....(v[1]) FrederikTylicki 2 6
(Jim Goldie) *mid-div: outpcd over 3f out: sn struggling: bhd and eased fnl 2f* **25/1**
5/4- 11 *30* **Sagunt (GER)**[564] 308 9 -9-755 ..... SeanQuinlan 9
(Sean Curran) *hld up in rr: outpcd and lost tch 4f out: sn wl bhd* **33/1**

3m 41.41s (-0.39) **Going Correction** -0.05s/f (Stan)
WFA 3 from 5yo+ 9lb 11Ran SP% **118.0**
Speed ratings (Par 101): **98,97,97,96,95 95,92,90,77,75 60**
toteswingers: 1&2 £5.80, 2&3 £7.30, 1&3 £18.80 CSF £32.43 CT £212.77 TOTE £9.30 : £2.30, £1.20, £2.40 ; EX 40.90 Trifecta £161.20 Pool: £692.34 - 3.22 winning tickets.
Owner Gongolfin **Bred** R V Young **Trained** Sigwells, Somerset

FOCUS
Just a low-grade staying handicap, but it produced yet another stirring finish on the card. Straightforward form.

7529 BREEDERS' CUP LIVE ONLY ON ATR H'CAP (DIV I) 1m 141y (P)
7:15 (7:15) (Class 5) (0-70,74) 3-Y-0+ £2,264 (£673; £336 ; £168) Stalls Low

Form RPR
0213 1 **Outlaw Torn (IRE)**[5] 7201 3 -8-960 .....(e) RobbieFitzpatrick 3 67
(Richard Guest) *mde all: hrd rdn over 1f out: hld on gamely* **17/2**
5440 2 *hd* **Fishforcompliments**[13] 7251 8 -9-264 ..... FrederikTylicki 4 71
(Richard Fahey) *hld up in rr: hdwy 2f out: drvn to chal ins fnl f: jst hld* **12/1**
2-03 3 *1/2* **Wordiness**[102] 4411 4 -8-1063 .....(t) WilliamTwiston-Davies(5) 2 69
(Seamus Durack) *in tch: rdn over 2f out: styd on wl fr over 1f out: clsng at fin* **6/1**[3]
2001 4 *2* **My Mate Jake (IRE)** 7368 4 -9-1274 6ex .....(b) GrahamLee 1 76
(James Given) *chsd ldrs: hrd rdn and kpt on same pce fnl 2f* **5/2**[1]
514 5 *1 3/4* **Idol Deputy (FR)**[70] 2173 6 -8-1366 ..... RachealKneller(5) 9 64
(Mark Usher) *chsd ldrs on outer: wnt 2nd over 2f out tl over 1f out: no ex* **12/1**
5000 6 *1/2* **Dhaular Dhar (IRE)**[5] 7202 10 -9-062 ..... TedDurcan 8 59
(Jim Goldie) *sltly hmpd and stdd s: hld up in rr: rdn 2f out: sme hdwy and edgd lft ins fnl f: nt rch ldrs* **16/1**
3433 7 *2 1/4* **Lovage**[21] 7015 3 -9-065 ..... SeanLevey 5 57
(Roger Charlton) *chsd wnr tl over 2f out: sn lost pl: 7th and btn whn carried lft ins fnl f* **3/1**[2]
3046 8 *3 1/2* **Berlusca (IRE)**[17] 7141 3 -9-267 ..... ShaneKelly 7 52
(Mark Brisbourne) *wd: in tch tl lost pl on outer 3f out: n.d after* **8/1**
4006 9 *4 1/2* **Wildcat Wizard (USA)**[17] 7142 6 -9-365 ..... MickyFenton 6 41
(Paul Midgley) *s.i.s: towards rr: rdn 4f out: sn struggling* **40/1**

1m 49.42s (-1.08) **Going Correction** -0.05s/f (Stan)
WFA 3 from 4yo+ 3lb 9Ran SP% **113.2**
Speed ratings (Par 103): **102,101,101,99,98 97,95,92,88**
toteswingers: 1&2 £22.20, 2&3 £6.60, 1&3 £9.20 CSF £102.11 CT £656.17 TOTE £11.90 : £2.30, £5.10, £2.50 ; EX 95.50 Trifecta £558.90 Pool: £1,199.88 - 1.61 winning tickets.
Owner James S Kennerley **Bred** Derek Veitch & Rory O'Brien **Trained** Stainforth, S Yorks
■ Stewards' Enquiry : Frederik Tylicki two-day ban: used whip above permitted level (Nov 16-17)

FOCUS
A fair handicap, run at a steady pace, and an all-the-way victory for the well-supported winner. The runner-up helps limit the level.

7530 BREEDERS' CUP LIVE ONLY ON ATR H'CAP (DIV II) 1m 141y (P)
7:45 (7:45) (Class 5) (0-70,70) 3-Y-0+ £2,264 (£673; £336 ; £168) Stalls Low

Form RPR
000 1 **Space War**[30] 6785 5 -9-265 ..... GrahamGibbons 7 75+
(Michael Easterby) *hld up in 5th: jnd ldrs 2f out: drvn to ld ins fnl f* **9/2**[3]
4224 2 *1/2* **Christmas Light**[35] 6638 5 -9-770 ..... SilvestreDeSousa 8 79
(Brian Ellison) *towards rr: gd hdwy on inner ent st: styd on to take 2nd nr fin: a hld* **2/1**[2]
465U 3 *3/4* **Rock Anthem (IRE)**[3] 7256 8 -8-1362 ..... SeanLevey 9 69
(Mike Murphy) *chsd ldrs: led ent st: hrd rdn and hdd ins fnl f: no ex* **14/1**
4511 4 *8* **Silver Lace (IRE)**[31] 6151 3 -9-066 ..... TedDurcan 6 57
(Chris Wall) *hld up in 6th: effrt and swtchd outside 2f out: wnt modest 4th ins fnl f: nvr able to chal* **13/8**[1]
0000 5 *3* **Northern Fling**[33] 6711 8 -9-467 ..... GrahamLee 10 51
(Jim Goldie) *awkward leaving stalls: bhd: rdn and struggling over 4f out: passed btn horses fr over 1f out* **25/1**
2230 6 *2 1/4* **Loyal N Trusted**[17] 7142 4 -9-164 ..... ShaneKelly 3 44
(Richard Price) *trckd ldrs: bdly hmpd and lost pl 2f out: nt rcvr* **12/1**
0600 7 *2 1/4* **Whitechapel**[28] 6843 5 -8-359 .....(t) DanielMuscutt(7) 4 34
(Keith Goldsworthy) *led after 1f and set decent pce: hdd & wknd ent st* **28/1**
0000 8 *2 3/4* **Mistress Shy**[28] 6843 5 -8-056 oh11 .....(t) NoelGarbutt(7) 5 25
(Michael Appleby) *led 1f: pressed ldr tl wknd qckly wl over 1f out* **50/1**

1m 49.53s (-0.97) **Going Correction** -0.05s/f (Stan)
WFA 3 from 4yo+ 3lb 8Ran SP% **113.2**
Speed ratings (Par 103): **102,101,100,93,91 89,87,84**
toteswingers: 1&2 £3.40, 2&3 £5.70, 1&3 £5.10 CSF £13.57 CT £113.20 TOTE £5.80 : £2.20, £1.30, £3.80 ; EX 13.50 Trifecta £248.00 Pool: £942.68 - 2.85 winning tickets.
Owner B Padgett **Bred** Shutford Stud And O F Waller **Trained** Sheriff Hutton, N Yorks

FOCUS
The second division of this handicap. With the market leader running no sort of race, things were made easier for the well-supported winner. Decent form with the first three clear.
T/Plt: £28.80 to a £1 stake. Pool £65,175.97 - 1,650.29 winning units. T/Qpdt: £10.60 to a £1 stake. Pool £9,304.09 - 648.16 w. units LM 7531a - 7544a (Foreign Racing) See RI

6915 SANTA ANITA (L-H)
Friday, November 2

OFFICIAL GOING: Dirt: fast; turf: firm

7545a BREEDERS' CUP JUVENILE SPRINT (CONDITIONS) (2YO) (DIRT) 6f (D)
8:06 (12:00) 2-Y-0 £174,193 (£58,064; £31,935 ; £19,354 ; £9,677)

RPR
1 **Hightail (USA)**[27] 6904 2 -8-100 .....(b) RMaragh 1 107
(D Wayne Lukas, U.S.A) *stdd and sn trcking ldrs on inner: rdn 1 1/2f out: r.o to chal on rail ins fnl f: edgd ahd ins fnl 100yds: drvn and jst prevailed* **20/1**
2 *nse* **Merit Man (USA)**[27] 2 -8-100 .....(b) PValenzuela 3 107
(R Hess Jr, U.S.A) *broke wl and sn disputing ld: led after 2f: rdn and strly pressed fr 2f out: hdd ins fnl 100yds: rallied u.p but jst denied* **4/7**[1]
3 *2 1/4* **Sweet Shirley Mae (USA)**[61] 5867 2 -8-70 ..... JRosario 5 97
(Wesley A Ward, U.S.A) *stdd and hld up in last but wl in tch: rdn over 1 1/2f out: r.o to go 3rd cl home: nt pce of front pair* **9/2**[2]
4 *1 1/4* **Hazardous (USA)**[19] 2 -8-100 ..... EMaldonado 4 96
(Carl O'Callaghan, U.S.A) *prom on wd outside: rdn to chal 2f out: kpt on tl no ex ins fnl f: dropped to 4th cl home* **10/1**
5 *8 1/2* **Ceiling Kitty**[34] 6672 2 -8-70 ..... JRVelazquez 2 66
(Tom Dascombe) *pushed along to dispute ld early: hdd after 2f: rdn and lost pl 2f out: last and struggling on turn into st: sn wl bhd and btn* **6/1**[3]

1m 9.75s (1.49) 5Ran SP% **110.0**
PARI-MUTUEL (all including $2 stakes): WIN 32.80; PLACE (1-2) 7.20, 2.40; SHOW (1-2-3) 3.40, 2.10, 2.40; SF 50.60 .
Owner Bluegrass Hall LLC **Bred** Green Hills Farm Inc **Trained** USA

FOCUS
A poor advert for the Breeders' Cup, five runners representing the smallest field in the meeting's history and the prize going to an eight-race maiden. It's events like this that dilute the fixture, although in fairness both Super Ninety Nine (cast in his box in the morning) and South Floyd (withdrawn at the start on the Vet's advice) had been due to line up as well, and last year the inaugural running was a decent enough contest. Splits of 22.41 and 45.94 showed the pace was not overly quick.

NOTEBOOK
Hightail(USA) was the only one of the four US-trained runners who had experience of racing without Lasix (now banned in 2yo races at the Breeders' Cup). Put bluntly, there can't have been many less worthy winners of a Breeders' Cup race than Hightail, who saved ground all the way against a rail that was certainly not playing slow and was helped by an outrageously bad ride on the runner-up. (op 16-1)
Merit Man (USA)'s rider allowed the winner a gap against the inside rail early in the straight and proved ineffective in a driving finish, even momentarily appearing to stop pushing after receiving a slight bump. (op 8-11)
Sweet Shirley Mae (USA) could have done with stronger fractions to chase on this drop in trip and we probably haven't see the best of her. (op 7-1)
Hazardous(USA) found this tougher than the C&D claimer he won last time. (op 9-1)
Ceiling Kitty faded after showing speed, probably not getting over the dirt surface. (op 11-2)

7546a BREEDERS' CUP MARATHON (GRADE 2) (3YO+) (DIRT) 1m 6f
8:46 (12:00) 3-Y-0+ £193,548 (£64,516; £35,483 ; £19,354 ; £9,677)

RPR
1 **Calidoscopio (ARG)**[132] 9 -9-00 ..... AGryder 6 111
(Guillermo J Frenkel Santillan, Argentina) *sltly slow to stride: hld up in detached last: hdwy to join main body of field 3f out: rdn and styd on to chal 1f out: led ins fnl f and sn clr: rdn out* **14/1**
2 *4 1/4* **Grassy (USA)**[32] 6 -9-00 ..... GKGomez 4 105
(Martin F Jones, U.S.A) *midfield: rdn and hdwy into 3rd over 3f out: plugged on to go 2nd cl home: nt pce of wnr* **16/1**
3 *1/2* **Atigun (USA)**[34] 6697 3 -8-100 ..... MESmith 1 108
(Kenneth McPeek, U.S.A) *prom: jnd ldr over 6f out: led 5f out: rdn and strly pressed fr over 2f out: hdd ins fnl f: no ex and dropped to 3rd cl home* **3/1**[1]
4 *5 1/4* **Juniper Pass (USA)**[19] 5 -9-00 ..... FrankieDettori 14 97
(Thomas Ray Bell II, U.S.A) *prom: wnt 2nd over 3f out: rdn to chal over 2f out: kpt on tl no ex and dropped to 4th ent fnl f: fdd* **16/1**
5 *1 1/2* **Not Abroad (USA)**[27] 5 -9-00 .....(b) NPetro 7 95
(Michael P Petro, U.S.A) *hld up last in main body of field: hdwy into midfield over 4f out: rdn in 4th 2f out: dropped to 5th ent fnl f and sn outpcd: plugged on* **8/1**[3]
6 *1* **Balladry (USA)**[33] 6731 4 -9-00 ..... JamesGraham 3 94
(Eoin Harty, U.S.A) *midfield on inner: rdn over 3f out and sn outpcd: swtchd out and plugged on in st: wnt 6th ins fnl f* **25/1**
7 *1 1/4* **Eldaafer (USA)**[27] 7 -9-00 .....(b) RSantanaJr 10 92
(Diane Alvarado, U.S.A) *midfield: rdn over 3f out: sn outpcd: plugged on: n.d* **10/1**
8 *1/2* **Romp (ARG)**[25] 8 -9-00 ..... JRosario 8 91
(Kristin Mulhall, U.S.A) *midfield: rdn over 3f out: sn outpcd: plugged on wout threatening ins fnl 1 1/2f* **50/1**
9 *30* **Commander (USA)**[24] 4 -9-00 ..... MGutierrez 11 49
(Troy Taylor, Canada) *led: sn hdd and trckd ldrs: rdn and outpcd 3f out: sn btn and fdd: eased in st and t.o* **10/1**
10 *2 1/4* **Almudena (PER)**[161] 5 -8-110 ..... JValdiviaJr 9 43
(J Suarez Villarroel, Peru) *hld up: rdn and detached fr main body over field 3f out: sn btn: t.o* **20/1**
11 *10 1/2* **Jaycito (USA)**[12] 4 -9-00 .....(b) JTalamo 5 31
(Bob Baffert, U.S.A) *sltly slow to stride and towards rr early: sent forward and sn led: jnd over 6f out: hdd 5f out: lost pl rapidly over 3f out: rdn and sn btn: t.o* **8/1**[3]
P **Fame And Glory**[13] 7235 6 -9-00 .....(v[1]) JamieSpencer 2
(A P O'Brien, Ire) *midfield on outer: rdn and reminders over 6f out: sn lost pl and btn: t.o whn p.u* **4/1**[2]

P **Sense Of Purpose (IRE)**[54] 6083 5-8-11 0 .... PatSmullen 13
(D K Weld, Ire) *midfield: rdn and lost pl over 6f out: sn btn: t.o whn p.u* **12/1**

2m 57.25s (177.25)
WFA 3 from 4yo+ 8lb **13** Ran SP% **122.1**
PARI-MUTUEL (all including $2 stakes): WIN 36.40; PLACE (1-2) 16.00, 12.40; SHOW (1-2-3) 9.60, 7.60, 3.40; SF 505.00.

Owner Dona Pancha **Bred** Haras La Quebrada **Trained** Argentina

FOCUS

If the Juvenile Sprint is of questionable worth to the Breeders' Cup, then the Marathon has no place at all at this meeting. The US horses are rarely bred to stay, while the Europeans are rarely bred for dirt, and it went to a South American-trained plodder who, having been tailed off early, stayed on to become the oldest winner of a race at this fixture.

NOTEBOOK

Calidoscopio(ARG) hadn't run since winning a Group 2 in Argentina in June. His jockey was reportedly riding to instructions, but he still deserves credit for his part in this success, not rushing the old horse and then saving ground by sticking towards the inside when making his move.

Grassy(USA) had to prove himself on dirt, but he'd shown he gets 1m4f well. He probably didn't achieve much.

Atigun(USA) had produced his best Beyer figures over 1m2f and ran out of stamina after being forwardly ridden. (op 7-2)

Juniper Pass(USA) showed up well without the blinkers.

Eldaafer(USA) won this in 2010 at Churchill Downs, but he's not the same horse at Santa Anita. (op 8-1)

Fame And Glory was a top-class stayer on turf, but he hadn't been at his best lately and, in a surprising move, was now switched to dirt. He used Lasix and had headgear added, but seemed to hate the experience. (op 10-1)

Sense Of Purpose(IRE), like Fame And Glory, she is a turf runner and didn't take to dirt. (op 10-1)

7547a BREEDERS' CUP JUVENILE FILLIES TURF (GRADE 1) (2YO FILLIES) (TURF) 1m (T)

9:28 (12:00) 2-Y-O **£348,387** (£116,129; £63,870; £38,709; £19,354)

RPR

1 **Flotilla (FR)**[26] 6909 2-8-10 0 .... Christophe-PatriceLemaire 4 110
(M Delzangles, France) **8/1**

2 1 1/4 **Watsdachances (IRE)**[25] 2-8-10 0 .... JJCastellano 6 107
(Chad C Brown, U.S.A) **6/1**[3]

3 1/2 **Summer Of Fun (USA)**[22] 2-8-10 0 .... RADominguez 2 106
(George Weaver, U.S.A) **40/1**

4 1 **Tara From The Cape (USA)**[28] 2-8-10 0 .... JRVelazquez 8 103
(Todd Pletcher, U.S.A) **16/1**

5 hd **The Gold Cheongsam (IRE)**[27] 6873 2-8-10 0 ....(b[1]) WilliamBuick 12 103
(Jeremy Noseda) **16/1**

6 1 **Waterway Run (USA)**[35] 6632 2-8-10 0 .... FrankieDettori 10 101
(Ralph Beckett) **10/1**

7 3/4 **Moonwalk (USA)**[22] 2-8-10 0 .... CLanerie 11 99
(Dale Romans, U.S.A) **40/1**

8 3/4 **Sky Lantern (IRE)**[54] 6081 2-8-10 0 .... RichardHughes 3 103+
(Richard Hannon) **5/2**[1]

9 hd **Nancy O (IRE)**[27] 6900 2-8-10 0 .... DJMoran 9 98
(Carolyn M Costigan, U.S.A) **33/1**

10 nk **Infanta Branca (USA)**[21] 7038 2-8-10 0 .... RyanMoore 15 96
(A P O'Brien, Ire) **20/1**

11 1/2 **Flashy Ways (USA)**[24] 2-8-10 0 ....(b) JTalamo 13 95
(Richard Baltas, U.S.A) **10/1**

12 1/2 **Kitten's Point (USA)**[22] 2-8-10 0 .... RBejarano 1 93
(H Graham Motion, U.S.A) **20/1**

13 1/2 **Spring Venture (USA)**[27] 2-8-10 0 ....(b) PHusbands 5 92
(Mark Casse, Canada) **7/2**[2]

14 1/2 **Oscar Party (USA)**[22] 2-8-10 0 .... KDesormeaux 7 91
(Wayne Catalano, U.S.A) **50/1**

1m 34.64s (0.77) **14** Ran SP% **125.4**
PARI-MUTUEL (all including $2 stakes): WIN 24.80; PLACE (1-2) 10.80, 6.40; SHOW (1-2-3) 7.80, 5.40, 19.40; SF 171.00.

Owner H H Sheikh Mohammed Bin Khalifa Al Thani **Bred** E Puerari, Oceanic Bloodstock & Mme A Gravereaux **Trained** France

FOCUS

The home team didn't look a great bunch beforehand and most of them had been racing on Lasix, which they now had to do without. Interestingly, the front two had both previously won without the anti-bleeding medication, and all things considered this probably isn't form to get carried away with, but it was hard not to be impressed by Flotilla. They went 23.14 for the first quarter and 47.39 for the half-mile, so not an overly strong pace given the conditions, and things got a bit messy in the straight.

NOTEBOOK

Flotilla(FR), who was a bit keen under restraint, had to wait longer than ideal for a gap and was unbalanced when being switched into the clear, but she showed a tremendous finishing burst to win easily. She had been quietly progressive on bad ground in France (better than she showed last twice, including when fourth in the Marcel Boussac) and was bred to appreciate these vastly different conditions. Indeed, both her sire and dam enjoyed success in California after switching from France, and prior to this five of Mizzen Mast's top six progeny (according to RPRs) had all won on firm turf in the US. There's talk of Flotilla returning to Europe with the Classics in mind, but a safer bet would be to keep her stateside where she can mop up a fair few more Grade 1s.

Watsdachances(IRE), a maiden winner for Ger Lyons, had won both her starts since switching to the US and confirmed herself a pretty smart filly, although she's flattered to get so close to Flotilla.

Summer Of Fun(USA), who was coming off Lasix, was denied a clear run until it was too late, although she just looked to be flattening out at the line and might not have been any better than her placing indicates.

Tara From The Cape(USA), another who had been using Lasix, was allowed a soft enough time up front and had her chance. (op 20-1)

The Gold Cheongsam(IRE), upped in trip, proved hard work in the first-time headgear and only ran on when the race was all over.

Waterway Run(USA) enjoyed a ground-saving trip in a good position, but she was a little short of room when first looking to challenge and soon flattened out. She was up in distance from 7f after winning an ordinary running of the Oh So Sharp at Newmarket.

Sky Lantern(IRE), the Moyglare winner, got no run at all in the straight. It's impossible to say where she might have finished. (op 11-4)

Infanta Branca(USA) was hopelessly placed after being dropped in from her wide stall and we probably haven't seen the best of her yet.

Spring Venture(USA), who came into this unbeaten in three, ran like a horse with a problem, maybe missing the Lasix.

7548a GREY GOOSE BREEDERS' CUP JUVENILE FILLIES (GRADE 1) (2YO FILLIES) (DIRT) 1m 110y(D)

10:08 (12:00) 2-Y-O **£696,774** (£232,258; £127,741; £77,419; £38,709)

RPR

1 **Beholder (USA)**[29] 2-8-10 0 .... GKGomez 1 116
(Richard E Mandella, U.S.A) **9/2**[2]

2 1 **Executiveprivilege (USA)**[34] 6698 2-8-10 0 .... RBejarano 2 114
(Bob Baffert, U.S.A) **13/8**[1]

3 4 1/4 **Dreaming Of Julia (USA)**[27] 6900 2-8-10 0 .... JRVelazquez 5 105
(Todd Pletcher, U.S.A) **5/1**[3]

4 2 1/4 **Kauai Katie (USA)**[33] 2-8-10 0 .... RosieNapravnik 8 100
(Todd Pletcher, U.S.A) **9/2**[2]

5 5 1/4 **Spring In The Air (CAN)**[28] 2-8-10 0 .... PHusbands 3 88
(Mark Casse, Canada) **6/1**

6 2 1/2 **Broken Spell (USA)**[28] 2-8-10 0 ....(b) RMaragh 7 83
(D Wayne Lukas, U.S.A) **20/1**

7 7 1/4 **Renee's Queen (USA)**[59] 2-8-10 0 .... CNakatani 4 67
(Eric J Guillot, U.S.A) **40/1**

8 1 1/2 **Almost An Angel (USA)**[28] 2-8-10 0 .... JRosario 6 63
(Wesley A Ward, U.S.A) **50/1**

1m 43.61s (1.19) **8** Ran SP% **114.6**
PARI-MUTUEL (all including $2 stakes): WIN 9.80; PLACE (1-2) 4.60, 3.40; SHOW (1-2-3) 3.00, 2.40, 3.20; SF 26.60.

Owner Spendthrift Farm LLC **Bred** Clarkland Farm **Trained** USA

FOCUS

Form to be a bit wary of as all of these had been racing on Lasix, which was banned for this contest, and the winner dominated (going fair splits of 22.62 and 46.47) against the inside rail on a track that may have aided such tactics. The winner is improving fast and the second is rated to his mark.

NOTEBOOK

Beholder(USA) was also helped by her nearest rival wandering around under pressure and this was reminiscent of Hansen's front-running victory in the colts' version of this race in 2011. That one had also seen his nearest rival veer off a straight line, and much like Hansen the suspicion is Beholder will find it tougher going next year. Her first preference had been the Juvenile Sprint and there's more speed than stamina in her pedigree. (op 11-2)

Executiveprivilege(USA) was 5-5, including a narrow verdict over Beholder and most recently a C&D Grade 1, but she threw away a good opportunity of extending her winning sequence by continually edging right under pressure. Perhaps she needs Lasix. (op 7-4)

Dreaming Of Julia(USA) came into this off the back of a gruelling effort in the Frizette and she never looked happy. It's to her credit she was able to keep on for third. (op 4-1)

Kauai Katie(USA), representing the same connections as the third, had also won all of her starts to date but she was upped to a trip her breeding suggested would find her out and she duly failed to stay. (op 5-1)

Spring In The Air(CAN), a Grade 1 winner on the Keeneland Polytrack on her previous start, didn't seem to handle the dirt.

7549a BREEDERS' CUP FILLY & MARE TURF (GRADE 1) (3YO+ FILLIES & MARES) (TURF) 1m 2f (T)

10:48 (12:00) 3-Y-O+ **£696,774** (£232,258; £127,741; £77,419; £38,709)

RPR

1 **Zagora (FR)**[34] 6695 5-8-12 0 .... JJCastellano 2 116
(Chad C Brown, U.S.A) **9/1**

2 3/4 **Marketing Mix (CAN)**[33] 6730 4-8-12 0 .... GKGomez 9 114
(Thomas F Proctor, U.S.A) **8/1**[3]

3 1/2 **The Fugue**[71] 5518 3-8-8 0 .... WilliamBuick 4 115+
(John Gosden) **11/8**[1]

4 1/2 **Ridasiyna (FR)**[26] 6911 3-8-8 0 .... Christophe-PatriceLemaire 10 112+
(M Delzangles, France) **9/2**[2]

5 3/4 **Lady Of Shamrock (USA)**[75] 5401 3-8-8 0 .... MESmith 6 111
(John W Sadler, U.S.A) **16/1**

6 nse **I'm A Dreamer (IRE)**[34] 6695 5-8-12 0 .... RichardHughes 11 110
(David Simcock) **14/1**

7 nk **Up (IRE)**[34] 6673 3-8-8 0 .... RyanMoore 7 110
(A P O'Brien, Ire) **16/1**

8 1 1/2 **Star Billing (USA)**[33] 6729 4-8-12 0 .... VEspinoza 1 107
(John Shirreffs, U.S.A) **33/1**

9 1/2 **In Lingerie (USA)**[26] 6907 3-8-8 0 .... JRVelazquez 12 106
(Todd Pletcher, U.S.A) **16/1**

10 1 3/4 **Nahrain**[34] 6695 4-8-12 0 ....(b[1]) FrankieDettori 8 102
(Roger Varian) **8/1**[3]

11 1/2 **Stormy Lucy (USA)**[33] 6730 3-8-8 0 .... MPedroza 3 101
(Frank Lucarelli, U.S.A) **66/1**

1m 59.7s (0.42)
WFA 3 from 4yo+ 4lb **11** Ran SP% **121.3**
PARI-MUTUEL (all including $2 stakes): WIN 20.40; PLACE (1-2) 7.80, 6.00; SHOW (1-2-3) 5.00, 3.80, 2.80; SF 95.80.

Owner Martin S Schwartz **Bred** E Puerari & Oceanic Bloodstock **Trained** USA

FOCUS

A steady pace (24.70 for the first quarter, 48.72 for the half) around this tight circuit resulted in a messy race and the bare form is worth little.

NOTEBOOK

Zagora(FR) was helped by an outstanding ride from Javier Castellano, racing close enough to the modest gallop before keeping The Fugue hemmed in after switching into the clear. The ex-French-trained winner had run out of stamina when caught late by Nahrain on easy ground in the Flower Bowl last time, but prior to that she'd broken a course record over the extended 1m at Saratoga and her speed was the key. She is highly unlikely to ever better this achievement and is due to go the Keeneland sales. (op 10-1)

Marketing Mix(CAN) was held up off a half-mile split of 45.78 when winning a weak Grade 1 over C&D on her previous start, but she was never likely to get such a quick pace this time and her jockey shrewdly had her forwardly placed. She ran well and has a fine record on turf, currently 7-11.

The Fugue, who was last seen finishing runner-up in the Yorkshire Oaks, was stuck on the inside when looking to make her move and never had enough room to challenge. She probably would have won with a clear run, but it would be silly to blame her rider as the nature of this race simply left the filly a hostage to fortune. (op 6-4)

Ridasiyna(FR), who came here after winning the Prix de l'Opera on desperate ground, was faced with much more of a speed test and got going too late after racing out the back and having to be switched with her effort. (op 11-2)

Lady Of Shamrock(USA) raced in last after being short of room soon after the start and had insufficient room against the inside rail when looking to challenge. She's better than she showed. (op 14-1)

I'm A Dreamer(IRE) looked to have something to offer when continually short of room in the straight.

Up(IRE) wasn't good enough.

Nahrain, last year's runner-up who defeated Zagora on much easier ground when taking the Flower Bowl, didn't settle with the headgear added. (op 7-1)

7550a BREEDERS' CUP LADIES' CLASSIC (GRADE 1) (3YO+ FILLIES & MARES) (DIRT) 1m 1f (D)

11:30 (12:00) 3-Y-0+ **£696,774** (£232,258; £127,741; £77,419; £38,709)

RPR

1 **Royal Delta (USA)**[34] 6693 4-8-12 0 .... MESmith 6 123
(William Mott, U.S.A) **9/4**[1]

2 1 1/2 **My Miss Aurelia (USA)**[41] 6509 3-8-9 0 .... CNakatani 2 120
(Steven Asmussen, U.S.A) **6/1**

3 1 1/4 **Include Me Out (USA)**[33] 6729 4-8-12 0 .... JTalamo 7 117
(Ronald W Ellis, U.S.A) **4/1**[3]

4 6 1/4 **Grace Hall (USA)**[27] 3-8-9 0 .... JJCastellano 1 104
(Anthony Dutrow, U.S.A) **14/1**

5 1/2 **Love And Pride (USA)**[33] 6729 4-8-12 0 .... JRVelazquez 8 103
(Todd Pletcher, U.S.A) **14/1**

6 hd **Awesome Feather (USA)**[43] 4-8-12 0 .... JASanchez 5 103
(Chad C Brown, U.S.A) **3/1**[2]

7 1 3/4 **Class Included (USA)**[25] 4-8-12 0 ....(b) RBaze 3 99
(Jim Penney, U.S.A) **40/1**

P **Questing**[41] 6509 3-8-9 0 .... IOrtizJr 4
(Kiaran McLaughlin, U.S.A) **7/1**

1m 48.8s (-0.10)
WFA 3 from 4yo 3lb **8** Ran SP% **118.3**
PARI-MUTUEL (all including $2 stakes): WIN 5.40; PLACE (1-2) 3.60, 5.80; SHOW (1-2-3) 2.60, 4.00, 5.20; SF 30.40.
Owner Besilu Stables **Bred** Palides Investments NV Inc **Trained** USA

FOCUS

This had the potential to be one of the great Breeders' Cup races - it featured three past champions of this fixture - but while it was indeed a thriller, it did not unfold as expected. A couple of the main players failed to give their true running and the form does not look anything special.

NOTEBOOK

Royal Delta(USA) wasn't expected to take them along, but last year's winner did so, cutting out strong fractions of 22.69, 45.81 and 1:09.80. She looked vulnerable for much of the closing stages, but the track may have helped her (possibly favoured inside speed), while she has stamina for further, and she just kept on rolling to complete a double in the Ladies Classic. This doesn't represent her best form, but it was a gutsy performance. She may go to Dubai next year. (op 5-2)
My Miss Aurelia(USA), last year's Breeders' Cup Juvenile Fillies winner, didn't return until August but came into this unbeaten in six, and she travelled best. However, she had to wait for a run and looked intimidated when having to challenge between the winner and third. Her bid flattened out late on, but this was a fine effort from one so light on race conditioning and we might not have seen the best of her. (op 5-1)
Include Me Out(USA) just wasn't good enough after going wide into the straight. (op 10-1)
Grace Hall(USA), runner-up to My Miss Aurelia in last year's Juvenile Fillies, found nothing for pressure.
Love And Pride(USA), unable to dominate, seemed to show she's flattered by her recent profile. (op 9-1)
Awesome Feather(USA) came into this unbeaten in ten, including the 2010 Juvenile Fillies, but she's had her problems and never looked comfortable. (op 11-4)
Questing was expected to take the field along, but she broke slowly and was never going prior to being pulled up early in the back straight. Something may have been bothering her (reportedly had a problem with her left eye), but she had a really hard race when sustaining strong fractions in the Alabama earlier in the season, and on her only start since then she ran flat when a close second to My Miss Aurelia. That big win seems to have left its mark. (op 6-1)

3714 COMPIEGNE (L-H)

Friday, November 2

OFFICIAL GOING: Turf: heavy

7551a PRIX ALEXANDRE D'ORSETTI (CONDITIONS) (4YO+) (AMATEUR RIDERS) (TURF) 7f

12:30 (12:00) 4-Y-0+ **£9,166** (£3,666; £2,750; £1,833; £916)

RPR

1 **Planet Elder**[30] 6804 4-10-7 0 ow3 .... MrChristopheGuimard 5 94
(X Nakkachdji, France) **17/10**[1]

2 1 **Heidikly (FR)**[21] 7123 4-9-12 0 .... KatjaMarkwalder 7 82
(F Vermeulen, France) **14/1**

3 snk **Blazon (FR)**[41] 5-10-1 0 ....(b[1]) MrFlorentGuy 4 85
(P Van De Poele, France) **4/1**[3]

4 3 **Amico Fritz (GER)**[21] 7123 6-10-1 0 ......(p) MrJean-PhilippeBoisgontier 1 76
(H-A Pantall, France) **3/1**[2]

5 3/4 **Tariq Too**[41] 6468 5-10-8 0 .... MissSallyAnnGrassick 8 81
(Amy Weaver) *w.w in rr: sme hdwy over 1 1/2f out: kpt on fnl f: nvr on terms* **10/1**

6 1 1/2 **Dancing Dynamite (GER)**[22] 4-10-4 0 .... MikaelMescam 6 73
(S Cerulis, France) **68/10**

7 2 1/2 **Guy De Normandie (FR)**[197] 5-10-1 0 .... MrYannickMergirie 2 64
(F Chappet, France) **26/1**

8 15 **Nokov (GER)**[128] 5-10-4 0 ....(b) JonathanLux 3 26
(F Meckes, France) **24/1**

1m 35.56s (95.56) **8** Ran SP% **118.3**
PARI-MUTUEL (all including 1 euro stakes): WIN 2.70; PLACE 1.40, 2.80, 1.80; DF 16.00; SF 26.70.
Owner Antoine Boucher **Bred** Suc S Niarchos **Trained** France

7516 NEWMARKET (R-H)

Saturday, November 3

OFFICIAL GOING: Soft (6.3)

Wind: Fresh across Weather: Overcast

7552 IRISH STALLION FARMS E B F MAIDEN FILLIES' STKS (DIV I) 7f

12:15 (12:16) (Class 4) 2-Y-0 **£4,528** (£1,347; £673; £336) **Stalls** High

Form RPR

0 1 **Oilinda**[91] 4818 2-9-0 0 ....[1] HayleyTurner 9 75
(Michael Bell) *chsd ldr: led over 1f out: rdn out* **11/2**[3]

2 1 3/4 **Shamiana** 2-9-0 0 .... NeilCallan 1 71
(Gerard Butler) *hld up: hdwy over 1f out: sn rdn: r.o* **9/1**

3 1/2 **Sillabub (USA)** 2-9-0 0 .... NickyMackay 2 69
(John Gosden) *a.p: rdn over 1f out: styd on* **9/2**[1]

0 4 hd **Dutch Gal**[28] 6880 2-9-0 0 .... AmirQuinn 11 69
(John Holt) *sn led: rdn and hdd over 1f out: styd on same pce ins fnl f* **20/1**

5 shd **Buona Fortuna** 2-9-0 0 .... DavidProbert 8 69
(Andrew Balding) *a.p: rdn over 1f out: styd on same pce ins fnl f* **8/1**

0 6 1/2 **Candoluminescence**[31] 6795 2-8-9 0 .... WilliamTwiston-Davies[(5)] 10 67
(Roger Charlton) *chsd ldrs: rdn over 1f out: no ex ins fnl f* **13/2**

0 7 6 **No Truth (IRE)**[10] 7332 2-9-0 0 .... FergusSweeney 5 52
(Charles Hills) *s.i.s: rdn over 2f out: a in rr* **15/2**

8 3/4 **Vitruvian Lady** 2-9-0 0 .... GrahamLee 3 51
(Noel Quinlan) *hld up: rdn: hung lft and wknd over 1f out* **5/1**[2]

0 9 3 3/4 **Tracks Of My Tears**[22] 7020 2-9-0 0 .... LiamKeniry 7 41
(Giles Bravery) *hld up: a in rr: wknd 2f out* **100/1**

10 4 **Endura** 2-9-0 0 .... TedDurcan 6 31
(John Dunlop) *s.i.s: a in rr: rdn and wknd 2f out* **8/1**

0 11 5 **Zinnobar**[19] 7103 2-9-0 0 .... JohnFahy 4 19
(Jonathan Portman) *s.i.s: sn pushed along in rr: wknd over 2f out* **50/1**

1m 30.63s (5.23) **Going Correction** +0.50s/f (Yiel) **11** Ran SP% **115.3**
Speed ratings (Par 95): **90,88,87,87,87 86,79,78,74,69 64**
toteswingers 1&2 £19.10, 2&3 £10.20, 1&3 £2.60 CSF £52.32 TOTE £5.20: £2.50, £2.80, £1.60; EX 51.30 Trifecta £266.20 Pool: £436.60 - 1.23 winning units..
Owner Karmaa Racing Limited **Bred** Highclere Stud And Floors Farming **Trained** Newmarket, Suffolk

FOCUS

Racing on this final day of the course's season was staged on the stands' side track and, with the stalls on the stands' rail, the runners raced up that side. The time was moderate and the jockeys reported the ground as being "soft" and "sticky".\n\x\x The first leg of this fillies' maiden, divisions of which have been won by such good fillies at Sariska and The Fugue, and this year's 1,000 Guineas runner-up Starscope in the last five years. The time and the previous form of those involved suggest this was the weaker of the two divisions, and the form is rated towards the bottom end of the race averages.

NOTEBOOK

Oilinda had exhibited minor promise on her debut on fast ground on the July Course in August, but had a hood fitted this time and was reluctant to go to post. However, she was seen in a much better light in the race, being close to the pace throughout and settling the issue once sent to the front running into the Dip. Her breeding suggests she will get a little further in time. (op 9-2 tchd 6-1)
Shamiana ◆, a half-sister to a 7f AW winner, made an encouraging debut and is probably the filly to take out of this race. Held up early, she as the only one to make significant headway in the closing stages, racing widest of all, and should know a lot more next time. (op 8-1)
Sillabub(USA), whose trainer won both divisions of this last season, is out of an unraced half-sister to a Grade 1 winner and was sent off favourite. She had to race on the outside of her field and saw plenty of daylight, but stuck to her task and was not beaten far. She should know more next time. (op 7-2)
Dutch Gal was getting the hang of things late on her debut and was sharper this time, making the running and keeping on under pressure once headed. She could be of interest once handicapped. (tchd 18-1)
Buona Fortuna, a half-sister by Oasis Dream to the stayer Daneking, tracked the pace on this debut before keeping on steadily and can be expected to do better of further next season. (op 17-2 tchd 9-1)
Candoluminescence, a half-sister to Firestreak and the middle-distance stayer Moidore, had finished well beaten on her debut in a Salisbury maiden that is working out quite well and built on that here. She can do better in handicaps over further. (op 16-1)
No Truth(IRE) missed the break and never got involved. (op 13-2 tchd 8-1)
Vitruvian Lady failed to pick up under pressure. (op 7-1)

7553 IRISH STALLION FARMS E B F MAIDEN FILLIES' STKS (DIV II) 7f

12:45 (12:45) (Class 4) 2-Y-0 **£4,528** (£1,347; £673; £336) **Stalls** High

Form RPR

2 1 **Beautiful View**[8] 7372 2-9-0 0 .... EddieAhern 7 86+
(Richard Hannon) *chsd ldrs: led over 1f out: edgd lft ins fnl f: r.o wl* **15/8**[1]

4 2 3 1/4 **Omoor (IRE)**[59] 5947 2-9-0 0 .... PaulHanagan 9 76
(John Dunlop) *chsd ldr tl led 2f out: rdn and hdd over 1f out: styd on same pce fnl f* **3/1**[2]

3 4 1/2 **Precinct** 2-9-0 0 .... GrahamLee 2 65
(James Eustace) *prom: rdn over 1f out: styd on same pce fnl f* **25/1**

04 4 2 1/2 **My Gigi**[8] 7372 2-9-0 0 .... FergusSweeney 1 58
(Gary Moore) *hld up: hdwy over 2f out: rdn over 1f out: no ex fnl f* **14/1**

5 3 1/2 **Za'Hara (IRE)** 2-9-0 0 .... SilvestreDeSousa 3 50+
(Saeed Bin Suroor) *hld up: hdwy over 1f out: wknd fnl f* **11/2**[3]

44 6 shd **Society Pearl (IRE)**[35] 6664 2-9-0 0 .... JoeFanning 10 49
(Charles Hills) *led: rdn and hdd 2f out: wknd over 1f out* **6/1**

7 nk **Sugar Coated (IRE)** 2-9-0 0 .... HayleyTurner 4 49+
(Michael Bell) *s.s: hld up: nt clr run 4f out: nvr nr to chal* **9/1**

65 8 10 **Chocolate Block (IRE)**[14] 7244 2-9-0 0 .... LiamJones 5 24
(William Haggas) *prom: pushed along 1/2-way: rdn and wknd over 2f out* **33/1**

0 9 11 **Dream About You (IRE)**[16] 7191 2-9-0 0 .... TomEaves 11
(Robert Mills) *s.s: swtchd rt over 4f out: lost tch over 2f out: t.o* **100/1**

10 hd **Grey Poppett** 2-9-0 0 .... AndreaAtzeni 6
(Chris Dwyer) *hld up: pushed along over 4f out: wknd 3f out: t.o* **100/1**

1m 28.44s (3.04) **Going Correction** +0.50s/f (Yiel) **10** Ran SP% **114.9**
Speed ratings (Par 95): **102,98,93,90,86 86,85,74,61,61**
toteswingers 1&2 £2.60, 2&3 £17.70, 1&3 £11.40 CSF £7.15 TOTE £2.80: £1.10, £1.40, £5.60; EX 9.00 Trifecta £227.40 Pool: £712.56 - 2.35 winning units..
Owner Mrs P Good **Bred** Exors Of The Late J R Good **Trained** East Everleigh, Wilts

FOCUS

This looked the stronger division with a few already having shown ability. That view was backed up by the winning time, which was 2.19 seconds faster than the first leg, the winner building on a good debut. They finished well spread out.

NOTEBOOK

Beautiful View set a decent standard, having split a couple of colts from the same stable when runner-up over half a furlong shorter on her Newbury debut eight days earlier. She had no problem with the testing ground there and it was obvious from some way out that she was going to go one better here, as she was still on the bridle when looming alongside over 2f out and she found plenty when committed a furlong later. She ought to continue to improve and, given her liking for an easy surface, she may be just the type for one of the Classic trials early next season. (op 6-4)
Omoor(IRE) finished fourth on her Lingfield debut in September on much quicker ground over today's trip, but the form of that race hasn't really worked out. Always handy, she had every chance when hitting the front over 2f out, but the winner was always running all over her and she couldn't match the favourite for finishing pace. She may be more of a handicap prospect for next season. (op 4-1)
Precinct ◆, a half-sister to the smart Metropolitan Man (a winner at up to 1m and Group 2 placed), stayed on for a respectable third and fared much the best of the four newcomers. She is likely to come on for this and she has a future. (tchd 20-1)

My Gigi, over 2l behind Beautiful View at Newbury, was rather stuck out wide from her low draw here and was beaten much further by her old rival here, but she now gets a mark and handicaps will be where her future lies. (op 12-1)
Za'Hara(IRE), a half-sister to three winners at up to 1m4f including the Arlington Million winner Debussy, ran green and didn't show much immediate promise. She is entitled to improve, though. (op 7-1)
Society Pearl(IRE) was surrounded by subsequent winners when a promising fourth on fast ground on her Doncaster debut, but didn't fare so well on testing ground at Haydock next time so it wasn't hard to hold reservations about her under these conditions. She dropped right away after making much of the running, but is worth another chance on a sounder surface. (op 7-1 tchd 15-2)
Sugar Coated(IRE), a 40,000euros half-sister to a 1m winner, blew the start, but did show a hint of ability late on. (tchd 10-1)
Grey Poppett Official explanation: jockey said filly ran very green

7554 LAUNDRY COTTAGE STUD FARM ZETLAND CONDITIONS STKS 1m 2f

1:20 (1:20) (Class 3) 2-Y-O £7,470 (£2,236; £1,118) **Stalls** High

Form RPR
3521 **1** **Restraint Of Trade (IRE)**[26] 6919 2-9-0 82............ SilvestreDeSousa 3 96
(Mahmood Al Zarooni) *w ldr tl led over 3f out: rdn over 1f out: styd on u.p* **9/4**[2]
116 **2** ½ **Cap O'Rushes**[21] 7053 2-9-0 95.................. MickaelBarzalona 2 95
(Mahmood Al Zarooni) *hld up: pushed along over 4f out: hdwy to chse wnr over 1f out: sn rdn: styd on* **4/7**[1]
3531 **3** 8 **Linguine (FR)**[25] 6963 2-9-3 88.......................... MickyFenton 1 84
(Seamus Durack) *led: pushed along and hdd over 3f out: wknd fnl f* **8/1**[3]
2m 9.69s (3.89) **Going Correction** +0.50s/f (Yiel) **3** Ran SP% **105.5**
Speed ratings (Par 100): **104,103,97**
CSF £3.97 TOTE £2.70; EX 4.30.
Owner Marmoom Racing **Bred** Kildaragh Stud **Trained** Newmarket, Suffolk

FOCUS
A disappointing turnout for this conditions stakes run over the longest trip juveniles tackle. Mahmood Al Zarooni won this in 2011 and was responsible for two of the trio taking part this time. That pair fought out the finish but the result was not as either the betting or official ratings suggested it would be. The form fits with the race's usual standard.

NOTEBOOK
Restraint Of Trade(IRE), a wide-margin winner on his first try at this trip and on soft ground last time, had the lowest official rating but raced close up and nearest the rail and, after going on around 4f from home, kept finding extra to hold off his stablemate. This ground clearly suits and he should get further next year. (op 5-2)
Cap O'Rushes, a winner on good ground and Polytrack, recorded a personal best when finishing sixth in a Group 3 on easy ground here last month. Sent off at odds-on, he seemed to race in snatches before making his challenge and could not get past his stable companion up the hill. He was probably unsuited by the ground and had a hard race here. (tchd 1-2, 4-6 and 8-13 in places)
Linguine(FR), making his debut for new connections having been bought for 77,000gns earlier in the week, had a bit to find on ratings especially as he was carrying a penalty for his success over this trip on his last start. He made the running but was ridden and headed by the winner 4f out and finished well beaten. (op 15-2 tchd 9-1)

7555 E B F PIPER-HEIDSIECK MONTROSE FILLIES' STKS (LISTED RACE) 1m

1:55 (1:55) (Class 1) 2-Y-O
£13,043 (£4,945; £2,474; £1,232; £618; £310) **Stalls** High

Form RPR
3612 **1** **Pure Excellence**[7] 7399 2-8-12 87.......................... JoeFanning 4 99
(Mark Johnston) *chsd ldr tl led over 1f out: styd on wl* **5/1**[3]
231 **2** 1½ **Desert Image**[10] 7329 2-8-12 85.......................... PaulHanagan 5 96
(Charles Hills) *led: rdn: hung rt and hdd over 1f out: styd on same pce ins fnl f* **15/8**[1]
14 **3** 3¼ **Power Of Light (IRE)**[36] 6632 2-8-12 0.................. MickaelBarzalona 3 89
(Mahmood Al Zarooni) *chsd ldrs: rdn over 1f out: no ex fnl f* **9/2**[2]
1 **4** 5 **Hollowina**[35] 6664 2-8-12 0.......................... RobertWinston 7 78
(David Brown) *prom: lost pl over 3f out: sn bhd: r.o towards fin* **12/1**
4 **5** nse **Cloudwalker (USA)**[17] 7159 2-8-12 0.......................... GrahamLee 2 77
(Ed Vaughan) *hld up: hdwy over 2f out: rdn and wknd over 1f out* **33/1**
2 **6** 4 **Similu**[17] 7160 2-8-12 0.......................... (t) MartinLane 6 69
(Brian Meehan) *prom: pushed along over 4f out: wknd over 1f out* **9/1**
2 **7** 1¼ **Jadesnumberone (IRE)**[28] 6872 2-8-12 0.................. HayleyTurner 8 66
(Michael Bell) *chsd ldrs: rdn over 2f out: wknd over 1f out* **5/1**[3]
5631 **8** 2 **Becky Lou (USA)**[63] 5825 2-8-12 85.......................(p) JimmyFortune 1 61
(Jeremy Noseda) *hld up: pushed along over 3f out: sn wknd* **16/1**
1m 41.52s (2.92) **Going Correction** +0.50s/f (Yiel) **8** Ran SP% **112.8**
Speed ratings (Par 101): **105,103,100,95,95 91,89,87**
toteswingers 1&2 £3.00, 2&3 £2.60, 1&3 £3.30 CSF £14.38 TOTE £5.60: £2.00, £1.20, £1.70; EX 16.40 Trifecta £31.70 Pool: £1,636.65 - 38.61 winning units..
Owner Excellence Racing **Bred** Peter Harris **Trained** Middleham Moor, N Yorks

FOCUS
This Listed contest has been won by some high-class juvenile fillies in recent years with Passage Of Time, Timepiece and Blue Bunting among the winners since 2006. This year's renewal became a war of attrition in the conditions and those that raced handily from the start dominated. The third helps with the form.

NOTEBOOK
Pure Excellence was much more exposed than her seven rivals (this being her eighth start), but she is consistent and handles testing ground well. Trying 1m for the first time, she was always on the shoulder of the leader and, in a style that has become synonymous with runners from the yard, ground away at the favourite before wearing her down inside the last. Although further success as a 3-y-o can hardly be ruled out, this win will have enhanced her value greatly. (op 11-2)
Desert Image handled the soft ground well when bolting up in a 7f maiden here ten days earlier and again tried to make all, but the winner would never go away and outstayed her up the hill. (tchd 7-4)
Power Of Light(IRE) arguably had the best form coming into this having finishing fourth in the Group 3 Oh So Sharp Stakes here last time, but she raced keenly on the outside of the leaders early and was found wanting for pace once off the bridle inside the last 2f. (op 4-1)
Hollowina, who had no problem with the testing ground when winning a six-runner maiden over this trip on her Haydock debut in September, ran a rather strange race. She looked likely to finish a tailed-off last when losing her place just after halfway, but took off again up the hill and grabbed an unlikely, if remote, fourth. She may well improve with experience and is likely to appreciate middle distances next term. Official explanation: trainer said filly was unsuited by the track (op 9-1)
Cloudwalker(USA), an eyecatching fourth of 14 when sent off at 100-1 for her Kempton debut last month, stayed on from off the pace without threatening the leaders, but this was quite a jump up in class at this stage of her career. She should make her mark in due course.
Similu ran a most promising debut when narrowly beaten at Kempton last month (Cloudwalker was fourth in the other division), but she was off the bridle and going nowhere at halfway here. Perhaps this ground isn't what she wants and she is worth another chance. (op 10-1 tchd 8-1)
Jadesnumberone(IRE) ran a fine debut against the boys when runner-up in a soft ground C&D maiden early last month, but was off the bridle and beaten off coming to the last 2f in this much stronger event. (op 6-1 tchd 13-2 and 7-1 in a place)
Becky Lou(USA), up to 1m for the first time and tried in cheekpieces, was never in the race at any stage. (op 14-1)

7556 BETFRED "THE BONUS KING" H'CAP 1m

2:30 (2:31) (Class 3) (0-95,92) 3-Y-O+
£8,092 (£2,423; £1,211; £605; £302; £152) **Stalls** High

Form RPR
0100 **1** **Wannabe King**[22] 7030 6-9-3 88.......................(p) SilvestreDeSousa 3 97
(Geoffrey Harker) *chsd ldrs: led over 3f out: rdn and edgd lft ins fnl f: jst hld on* **33/1**
-020 **2** shd **Credit Swap**[7] 7407 7-9-4 89.......................... JimCrowley 8 98
(Michael Wigham) *hld up in tch: rdn over 2f out: r.o wl towards fin* **4/1**[2]
3641 **3** ¾ **Jake's Destiny (IRE)**[29] 6831 3-9-5 92.......................(t) PaulHanagan 10 99
(George Baker) *led over 4f: rdn over 2f out: r.o* **11/4**[1]
0640 **4** 1¼ **Bancnuanaheireann (IRE)**[22] 7030 5-9-7 92.................. LiamKeniry 1 96
(Michael Appleby) *sn prom: rdn over 1f out: styd on same pce ins fnl f* **7/1**
6316 **5** hd **Boots And Spurs**[26] 6921 3-8-7 80.......................(v) SeanLevey 9 84
(Mrs K Burke) *chsd ldrs: rdn over 1f out: styd on same pce ins fnl f* **14/1**
6004 **6** ½ **Vainglory (USA)**[22] 7030 8-8-9 87.......................... SiobhanMiller(7) 2 90
(David Simcock) *hld up: hdwy u.p over 1f out: kpt on* **14/1**
4103 **7** 5 **Jo'Burg (USA)**[28] 6881 8-8-12 90.......................... DavidBergin(7) 7 82
(David O'Meara) *s.i.s: hdwy 1/2-way: rdn over 1f out: wknd fnl f* **16/1**
0602 **8** 1¾ **Classic Colori (IRE)**[36] 6638 5-9-2 87.......................... GrahamLee 4 75
(David O'Meara) *prom: rdn over 3f out: wknd over 2f out* **9/2**[3]
004 **9** nk **Titus Mills (IRE)**[29] 6831 4-9-3 88.......................(v) MartinLane 5 75
(Brian Meehan) *hld up: racd keenly: wknd over 2f out* **16/1**
2603 **10** 1½ **Directorship**[37] 6601 6-9-7 92.......................... GeorgeBaker 6 76
(Patrick Chamings) *hld up: rdn over 2f out: sn wknd* **17/2**
1m 41.76s (3.16) **Going Correction** +0.50s/f (Yiel)
WFA 3 from 4yo+ 2lb **10** Ran SP% **115.9**
Speed ratings (Par 107): **104,103,103,101,101 101,96,94,94,92**
toteswingers 1&2 £24.90, 1&3 £10.40, 2&3 £3.20 CSF £160.37 CT £507.69 TOTE £38.60: £6.80, £2.00, £1.60; EX 301.90 Trifecta £928.50 Pool: £2,005.70 - 1.62 winning units..
Owner Mr & Mrs H Nensey, Saif Nensey **Bred** Chippenham Lodge Stud Ltd **Trained** Thirkleby, N Yorks

FOCUS
A good class handicap but the field was the smallest in the last ten years, although that said it looked a competitive contest. The subsequent Group-race performer Farhh took this last season but there did not appear anything with the same potential in this year's line-up. They appeared to go a sound gallop and it produced a thrilling finish, although the time was 0.24secs slower than the preceding juvenile fillies' Listed race. Straightforward form.

NOTEBOOK
Wannabe King was discounted in the market as all his previous wins had been on a sound surface. However, he was wearing cheekpieces for the first time since finishing unplaced in this race in 2010, and was 7lb below his peak winning mark, despite having scored in the interim. Always in the leading group, after getting to the front over 1f out, he stuck on up the hill to just hold the late surge of the second.
Credit Swap has rediscovered his form since rejoining Michael Wigham and returning to the Flat, and he put a below-par effort at Newbury behind him (when the hood was removed late) to lose out only narrowly. He tracked the pace and took a long while to pick up under pressure, but the rising ground helped and he finished strongly, but was just denied. (op 5-1 tchd 7-2)
Jake's Destiny(IRE) ◆ has made up into a consistent handicapper this season and rallied well up the hill, having been headed around 2f out. He looks the sort who could make an impression in something like the Suffolk Handicap back here in the spring. (op 5-2 tchd 3-1 and 10-3 in a place)
Bancnuanaheireann(IRE), who ran a fine race when fourth in the Cambridgeshire before disappointing on heavy at York, performed much better on a course that suits him, being up with the pace from the start and sticking on for pressure. He deserves to pick up a decent handicap, but might have to wait until next year now. (op 17-2 tchd 9-1)
Boots And Spurs, whose last win came off 6lb lower in a lesser grade, but on heavy ground, ran pretty well again, only fading up the hill. He could well improve again with another winter behind him. (op 20-1)
Vainglory(USA), who has dropped below his last winning mark, ran a fair race considering he was posted wide throughout, and gave the impression another try over further might be in his favour. (op 9-1)
Classic Colori(IRE), who was up 5lb having been narrowly beaten in the Silver Cambridgeshire, has form on this ground but didn't help his chances by being too keen early on. (op 6-1 tchd 13-2)
Titus Mills(IRE)'s rider reported that the gelding hung badly left. Official explanation: jockey said gelding hung badly left (op 12-1)
Directorship's trainer reported that the gelding was unsuited by the soft ground. Official explanation: trainer said gelding was unsuited by the soft ground (op 8-1)

7557 PIPER-HEIDSIECK JAMES SEYMOUR STKS (LISTED RACE) 1m 2f

3:05 (3:07) (Class 1) 3-Y-O+
£18,714 (£7,095; £3,550; £1,768; £887; £445) **Stalls** High

Form RPR
1421 **1** **Mull Of Killough (IRE)**[21] 7054 6-9-8 110.................. GeorgeBaker 4 116
(Jane Chapple-Hyam) *chsd ldr tl led over 3f out: rdn out* **11/2**[3]
1601 **2** 2½ **Hajras (IRE)**[42] 6484 3-8-12 105.......................... PaulHanagan 5 105
(Mark Johnston) *hld up: hdwy over 2f out: rdn to chse wnr and hung lft over 1f out: styd on same pce ins fnl f* **11/4**[1]
221/ **3** 3¼ **Rainbow Peak (IRE)**[748] 6977 6-9-2 112.................. SilvestreDeSousa 2 99
(Saeed Bin Suroor) *s.i.s: hld up: hdwy over 2f out: sn rdn: styd on same pce fr over 1f out* **4/1**[2]
5215 **4** hd **Proud Chieftain**[36] 6637 4-9-2 95.......................... DarryllHolland 8 99
(Clifford Lines) *led: rdn and hdd over 3f out: styd on same pce appr fnl f* **22/1**
5221 **5** 3¼ **Primevere (IRE)**[38] 6575 4-9-0 107.......................(v) JimmyFortune 6 91
(Roger Charlton) *prom: rdn over 2f out: wknd fnl f* **11/4**[1]
0406 **6** 1¼ **Burano (IRE)**[21] 7054 3-8-12 103.......................... MartinLane 7 91
(Brian Meehan) *chsd ldrs: rdn over 2f out: wknd over 1f out* **16/1**
0031 **7** 12 **Prince Siegfried (FR)**[22] 7029 6-9-2 107.................. MickaelBarzalona 3 69
(Saeed Bin Suroor) *s.i.s: racd keenly and sn prom: rdn over 3f out: wknd 2f out* **7/1**
524 **8** 6 **Miss Fortywinks**[17] 7174 3-8-7 70.......................... LiamKeniry 1 53
(Paul Henderson) *hld up: rdn and wknd 3f out* **150/1**
2m 7.65s (1.85) **Going Correction** +0.50s/f (Yiel)
WFA 3 from 4yo+ 4lb **8** Ran SP% **112.1**
Speed ratings (Par 111): **112,110,107,107,104 103,94,89**
toteswingers 1&2 £3.10, 2&3 £2.50, 1&3 £3.90 CSF £20.16 TOTE £5.70: £2.00, £1.50, £1.90; EX 19.80 Trifecta £55.10 Pool: £1,875.52 - 25.49 winning units..
Owner Invictus **Bred** Owenstown Stud **Trained** Dalham, Suffolk

FOCUS
The classic generation had taken the last three runnings of this Listed race, but this year was one for the older generation. The pace was solid in the conditions and the runners finished well spread out. Decent Listed form for the time of year.

NOTEBOOK

Mull Of Killough(IRE) had to carry a 6lb penalty for winning a Group 3 contest here three weeks earlier and his only previous attempt at the trip was when third on the Lingfield Polytrack a year ago. He wasn't ridden as though stamina was thought to be an issue, though, disputing the lead from the off and finding plenty when in front on his own over 2f from home. He has thrived for his current yard in recent months and he may not have finished yet. (op 5-1 tchd 9-2)

Hajras(IRE), winner of three handicaps this year including a valuable event at Newbury last time, was given a contrasting ride to Mull Of Killough, being produced wide from well off the pace to chase the winner up the hill. He hung when winning at Newbury and didn't display the most attractive of head-carriages in the closing stages here either, but it may be that he doesn't want the ground like this despite his Ripon success on a testing surface in the spring. (op 7-2 tchd 4-1 in a place)

Rainbow Peak(IRE), a Group 1 winner in Italy for the late Michael Jarvis, was making his debut for Godolphin after an absence of 748 days and he was solid enough in the betting to suggest that the run wasn't thought to be needed. However, although he ran on well enough up the stands' rail to grab third, he never really looked like winning. It will be interesting to see where he turns up next. (tchd 10-3)

Proud Chieftain was back down to a more suitable trip, but he had come up short in three previous tries in Listed company and was seen off after matching strides with the winner for nearly a mile. This wasn't a bad effort at the weights, however. (op 25-1)

Primevere(IRE), carrying a 3lb penalty having won a soft-ground Goodwood Listed event last time when equipped with a first-time visor, didn't get home here and found the headgear not working so well a second time. (tchd 3-1 in places)

Burano(IRE) raced handily until over 2f from home and finished behind Mull Of Killough for the third consecutive race. (op 12-1)

Prince Siegfried(FR), lightly raced this year, finished runner-up in this in 2009 and 2010, but having taken a keen hold early eventually dropped right out. His rider reported that the gelding hung right. Official explanation: jockey said gelding hung right (op 11-2)

Miss Fortywinks had shown ability in three maidens, but is rated just 70 and duly found this an impossible task. (op 200-1)

7558 BETFRED BEN MARSHALL STKS (LISTED RACE) 1m
3:40 (3:41) (Class 1) 3-Y-O+

£18,714 (£7,095; £3,550; £1,768; £887; £445) **Stalls High**

Form RPR

-020 **1** **French Navy**[21] 7054 4-9-0 107 MickaelBarzalona 9 110
(Mahmood Al Zarooni) *chsd ldrs: shkn up to ld: r.o wl* **9/2**[2]

0002 **2** *3* **Red Jazz (USA)**[21] 7048 5-9-3 112 RobertWinston 7 106
(Charles Hills) *chsd ldr tl led over 2f out: rdn and edgd lft over 1f out: sn hdd: styd on same pce ins fnl f* **6/1**[3]

2511 **3** *3/4* **Fire Ship**[26] 6921 3-8-12 97 JimCrowley 6 101
(William Knight) *hld up: hdwy u.p 2f out: r.o: could nt rch ldrs* **9/2**[2]

5005 **4** *1* **Diverting**[10] 7334 4-8-9 80 GrahamLee 12 94
(William Jarvis) *prom: rdn and edgd rt over 1f out: r.o* **40/1**

22-3 **5** *1/2* **Entangle**[20] 6-8-12 109 EddieAhern 10 96
(Rune Haugen, Norway) *led over 5f: rdn and hmpd over 1f out: styd on same pce fnl f* **7/1**

1104 **6** *1 1/2* **Trade Commissioner (IRE)**[21] 7054 4-9-0 104 (p) RobertHavlin 3 95
(John Gosden) *prom: rdn over 1f out: wknd fnl f* **4/1**[1]

1354 **7** *6* **Dance And Dance (IRE)**[28] 6882 6-9-0 108 JimmyFortune 4 82
(Ed Vaughan) *hld up: hdwy over 2f out: rdn and wknd over 1f out* **12/1**

1-5 **8** *2 1/4* **Swedish Sailor**[52] 6142 3-8-12 0 PaulHanagan 5 77
(Mahmood Al Zarooni) *hld up: rdn over 2f out: nvr on terms* **12/1**

4324 **9** *2 1/2* **Mrs Greeley**[28] 6870 4-8-9 85 TedDurcan 11 66
(Eve Johnson Houghton) *hld up: rdn over 3f out: wknd over 2f out* **40/1**

66-1 **10** *9* **Mia Madonna**[162] 2455 4-8-9 63 TomEaves 2 46
(Bryan Smart) *hld up: a in rr: rdn and wknd over 2f out* **100/1**

0210 **11** *2 3/4* **Quick Wit**[21] 7054 5-9-0 108 SilvestreDeSousa 8 45
(Saeed Bin Suroor) *prom: pushed along over 4f out: wknd over 2f out* **8/1**

1m 40.37s (1.77) **Going Correction** +0.50s/f (Yiel)
WFA 3 from 4yo+ 2lb **11 Ran SP% 115.5**
Speed ratings (Par 111): **111,108,107,106,105 104,98,96,93,84 81**
toteswingers 1&2 £6.40, 2&3 £6.10, 1&3 £5.20 CSF £30.85 TOTE £5.30: £1.60, £2.00, £2.30; EX 35.30 Trifecta £228.20 Pool: £2,458.64 - 8.08 winning units..
Owner Godolphin **Bred** Darley **Trained** Newmarket, Suffolk

FOCUS

Mixed levels of ability judged on official ratings in this Listed contest but the field raced up the centre of the track and the time was 1.15 secs faster than the quicker of the earlier races over the trip. Solid form, the winner only a fraction below his best.

NOTEBOOK

French Navy goes well on soft ground, and although he had disappointed in a Group 3 at the last meeting might have needed the run after three months off. He was ridden along soon after halfway but picked up well this time, coming to lead in the Dip and pulling clear for a fairly comfortable success. With his preference for soft ground it seems unlikely that he will go to Dubai for the Carnival, unless the plan is to run him on synthetics. (op 11-2)

Red Jazz(USA), who went close in the Group 2 Challenge Stakes here last time, had a 3lb penalty to carry for his Listed win in the spring. He was produced running into the Dip, but was almost immediately taken on by the winner and could not respond. He is ideally suited by 7f on better ground. The trainer reported that the horse lost a shoe. Official explanation: trainer said horse lost a shoe (op 5-1)

Fire Ship, bidding for a hat-trick on this rise in grade, having won a couple of soft-ground handicaps, should not suffer too much ratings-wise as a result of this and might be able to make his mark at this level next season.

Diverting, who had a lot to find on official ratings, having gained her last success in a Pontefract handicap off a mark of 82 over a year ago, ran a decent race which might not do her rating much good. (op 33-1)

Entangle, a prolific winner in Scandinavia, performed creditably, making the running and sticking to her task once headed. (tchd 13-2 and 15-2)

Trade Commissioner(IRE), wearing cheekpieces for the first time, has now been beaten three times at Group and Listed level since taking a valuable handicap at Sandown in July and has been unable to make the transition. It might be that he is better suited by a turning track. (tchd 9-2)

Dance And Dance(IRE) has won on soft but seems happier on a sounder surface these days. (op 11-1 tchd 10-1)

Swedish Sailor, who went down early, never got into contention and has something to prove now. (op 14-1 tchd 16-1)

Quick Wit, whose trainer had won the two previous runnings of this Listed race, came under pressure some way from home and faded. (op 11-1)

7559 JAYNE REID SMILES ON MEMORIAL H'CAP 7f
4:10 (4:13) (Class 4) (0-85,85) 3-Y-O+ £5,175 (£1,540; £769; £384) **Stalls High**

Form RPR

4004 **1** **Sam Nombulist**[23] 6999 4-9-3 81 (v) RobertWinston 12 90
(Richard Whitaker) *led main gp: overall ldr 3f out: rdn and hung lft over 1f out: styd on* **8/1**

2656 **2** *nk* **Pashan Garh**[7] 7402 3-8-6 71 oh4 JoeFanning 18 79
(Pat Eddery) *hdwy over 5f out: chsd wnr over 2f out: rdn and carried lft over 1f out: styd on* **25/1**

1014 **3** *4* **Frozen Over**[12] 7302 4-8-7 71 oh3 SilvestreDeSousa 16 69
(Stuart Kittow) *sn prom: rdn and swtchd rt over 1f out: styd on* **11/2**[1]

1060 **4** *nk* **Warfare**[34] 6701 3-8-13 78 AmyRyan 4 76
(Kevin Ryan) *racd far side: overall ldr 5f: rdn over 1f out: no ex ins fnl f* **12/1**

2400 **5** *3/4* **Kingswinford (IRE)**[17] 7166 6-8-10 74 KirstyMilczarek 1 70
(Alastair Lidderdale) *racd far side tl hdwy and hung lft over 1f out: styd on same pce ins fnl f* **20/1**

4003 **6** *3/4* **Red Seventy**[19] 7107 3-9-5 84 JimmyFortune 11 78
(Richard Hannon) *chsd ldrs: rdn over 2f out: styd on same pce fr over 1f out* **9/1**

0201 **7** *1 1/2* **Bond Fastrac**[23] 7000 5-9-7 85 TonyHamilton 3 76
(Geoffrey Oldroyd) *hld up: hdwy u.p over 1f out: could nt trble ldrs* **20/1**

6225 **8** *nse* **Rough Rock (IRE)**[45] 6381 7-8-7 71 oh1 HayleyTurner 8 61
(Chris Dwyer) *chsd ldrs: rdn over 2f out: no ex ins fnl f* **16/1**

000 **9** *nse* **Bay Knight (IRE)**[31] 6800 6-9-5 83 JohnFahy 6 73
(Sean Curran) *hld up: rdn over 1f out: nvr nrr* **12/1**

2110 **10** *3/4* **Trojan Rocket (IRE)**[30] 6820 4-9-1 79 MickaelBarzalona 14 67
(Michael Wigham) *mid-div: hdwy u.p over 1f out: wknd ins fnl f* **6/1**[2]

2063 **11** *2 3/4* **Russian Ice**[45] 6367 4-8-11 75 (b) ShaneKelly 10 56
(Dean Ivory) *n.m.r at s: sn pushed along in rr: nvr on terms* **20/1**

3140 **12** *1/2* **Bunraku**[72] 5520 3-8-13 78 PaulHanagan 13 58
(Charles Hills) *hld up: hdwy over 2f out: rdn and wknd over 1f out* **7/1**[3]

3003 **13** *3 1/2* **Master Mylo (IRE)**[39] 6566 5-9-1 79 EddieAhern 17 50
(Robert Cowell) *prom: rdn over 2f out: wknd wl over 1f out* **14/1**

3113 **14** *shd* **Comrade Bond**[46] 6338 4-9-0 78 TedDurcan 15 49
(Mark H Tompkins) *prom: rdn over 1f out: wknd and eased ins fnl f* **11/1**

0000 **15** *nk* **Masked Dance (IRE)**[71] 5530 5-8-13 77 (tp) TomQueally 5 47
(Scott Dixon) *prom: rdn over 2f out: wknd over 1f out* **16/1**

1000 **16** *3* **Orders From Rome (IRE)**[19] 7113 3-8-12 77 (p) GrahamLee 7 40
(Eve Johnson Houghton) *hld up: rdn over 2f out: sn wknd* **25/1**

1m 28.67s (3.27) **Going Correction** +0.50s/f (Yiel)
WFA 3 from 4yo+ 1lb **16 Ran SP% 127.4**
Speed ratings (Par 105): **101,100,96,95,94 94,92,92,92,91 88,87,83,83,83 79**
toteswingers 1&2 £50.00, 2&3 £28.00, 1&3 £12.20 CSF £207.85 CT £1209.81 TOTE £9.20: £2.60, £5.60, £2.20, £3.70; EX 273.80 Trifecta £1089.90 Part won. Pool: £1,453.32 - 0.40 winning units..
Owner Robert Macgregor **Bred** R F And S D Knipe **Trained** Scarcroft, W Yorks

FOCUS

A fair handicap and a competitive one, although not that many got into it. The main group went up the centre, while a couple raced against the far rail and, as they finished fourth and fifth, it didn't seem to be much of a disadvantage. Several of these were inclined to roll around in the soft ground late on. The winner is rated back to his best.

Russian Ice Official explanation: jockey said filly never travelled

T/Plt: £38.40 to a £1 stake. Pool of £59053.27 - 1121.08 winning tickets. T/Qpdt: £16.90 to a £1 stake. Pool of £4004.56 -174.71 winning tickets. CR

881 FLEMINGTON (L-H)

Saturday, November 3

OFFICIAL GOING: Turf: good to soft changing to good after 00.20

7560a LEXUS STKS (GROUP 3 H'CAP) (3YO+) (TURF) 1m 4f 110y
1:00 (12:00) 3-Y-O+

£99,671 (£29,605; £14,802; £7,401; £4,111; £3,289)

RPR

1 **Kelinni (IRE)**[28] 4-9-0 0 (p) NashRawiller 9 111
(Chris Waller, Australia) **17/2**

2 *nk* **Dare To Dream (IRE)**[28] 4-8-9 0 (b[1]) JamesMcDonald 10 106
(Bart Cummings, Australia) **15/2**[3]

3 *1* **Exceptionally (NZ)**[10] 7346 6-8-9 0 (bt) DeanYendall 4 104
(Terry & Karina O'Sullivan, Australia) **9/1**

4 *3/4* **Ibicenco (GER)**[7] 7425 4-8-13 0 (b) KerrinMcEvoy 2 107
(Luca Cumani) *midfield on rail: hemmed in 3f out: nowhere to go over 2f out and again appr fnl f: in clr and styd on fnl 100yds to go 4th cl home* **40/1**

5 *1/2* **Dame Claire (NZ)**[14] 5-8-9 0 (b) PeterMertens 6 102
(Pat Carey, Australia) **20/1**

6 *hd* **Gatewood**[10] 7346 4-9-2 0 GlenBoss 3 109
(John Gosden) *trckd ldng gp: 4th and ev ch over 1 1/2f out: sn rdn and nt qckn: kpt on at same pce fnl f* **2/1**[1]

7 *1/2* **Reuben Percival (NZ)**[7] 7425 6-8-10 0 (t) VladDuric 5 102
(Gai Waterhouse, Australia) **13/1**

8 *1* **Sabrage (AUS)**[14] 7264 4-8-9 0 (bt) DamienOliver 7 98
(Michael Moroney, Australia) **60/1**

9 *shd* **Fictional Account (IRE)**[28] 7-8-9 0 MarkZahra 1 99
(David Hayes, Australia) **50/1**

10 *1/2* **Peal Of Bells (AUS)**[28] 5-8-9 0 JimCassidy 8 99
(Gwenda Markwell, Australia) **50/1**

11 *shd* **Tanby (AUS)**[28] 6-9-2 0 (t) HughBowman 13 106
(Robert Hickmott, Australia) **14/1**

12 *3/4* **Permit**[28] 5-9-1 0 (t) CoreyBrown 11 103
(Chris Waller, Australia) **50/1**

13 *1 3/4* **Excluded (NZ)**[21] 7073 5-8-10 0 (t) CraigAWilliams 12 96
(Robert Hickmott, Australia) **9/2**[2]

2m 37.67s (157.67) **13 Ran SP% 112.3**
PARI-MUTUEL (NSW TAB - all including au 1 stakes): WIN 8.50 PLACE 2.60, 2.70, 3.10; DF 40.30; SF 80.30.
Owner F Cook, Mrs C Cook Et Al **Bred** Newberry Stud Farm Ltd **Trained** Australia

NOTEBOOK

Ibicenco(GER) missed the start and soon ended up on the fence, which isn't where he wanted to be, so he ran a good race under the circumstances.

Gatewood had nothing more to give on reaching the straight and reportedly wouldn't let himself down on the ground.

7561 -7564a (Foreign Racing) - See Raceform Interactive

7427 SAN SIRO (R-H)

Saturday, November 3

OFFICIAL GOING: Turf: heavy

7565a PREMIO CHIUSURA (GROUP 3) (2YO+) (TURF) 7f

3:35 (12:00) 2-Y-O+ **£23,333** (£10,266; £5,600 ; £2,800)

RPR

1 **Malagenia (IRE)**[377] 7047 4 -9-10 .... FabioBranca 1 103
(L Riccardi, Italy) *w.w towards rr stands' side: hdwy to chse ldrs 1 1/2f out: swtchd rnd rival and r.o to ld fnl 100yds: sn clr: won easing down* **41/10[3]**

2 2 1/2 **Konig Concorde (GER)**[22] 7124 7 -9-40 .... FilipMinarik 8 99
(C Sprengel, Germany) *midfield: swtchd to stands' rail after 2f: rdn and qcknd to dispute ld 1 1/2f out: led 1f out: r.o u.p: hdd 100yds out: no ch w wnr* **152/100[1]**

3 5 **Mister Big Shuffle (GER)**[36] 6942 2 -7-120 .... JimmyQuinn 9 84
(M Figge, Germany) *prom on outside: disp ld 1 1/2f out: rdn and hdd 1f out: one pce fnl f* **17/4**

4 1 **Rosendhal (IRE)**[118] 3901 5 -9-40 ....(b) UmbertoRispoli 4 83
(G Botti, Italy) *trckd ldrs racing freely: 5th and u.p 1 1/2f out: nt qckn: plugged on at same pce fnl f* **13/5[2]**

5 3/4 **Choisir Shadow (IRE)**[13] 7288 3 -9-10 .... GArena 3 79
(B Grizzetti, Italy) *led main gp towards centre of trck: rdn and hdd 1 1/2f out: no ex* **66/10**

6 3 **Cavenaco (ITY)**[34] 5 -9-40 .... PierantonioConvertino 6 73
(A Marcialis, Italy) *towards rr: rdn and no imp fr 2f out* **183/10**

7 8 **Killachy Loose**[34] 6726 3 -9-10 .... DarioVargiu 5 49
(B Grizzetti, Italy) *towards rr: nvr in contention: bhd fr 1 1/2f out: eased ins fnl f* **66/10**

8 3 **Traditional Chic (IRE)**[11] 4 -9-40 .... CristianDemuro 7 43
(L Riccardi, Italy) *hld up in tch towards outside: rdn and nt qckn over 1 1/2f out: sn wknd: eased ins fnl f* **41/10[3]**

9 5 **Zack Tiger (IRE)**[34] 3 -9-40 .... MEsposito 2 30
(P Schaerer, Switzerland) *racd freely bhd ldrs: rdn and wknd over 2f out: bhd whn eased ins fnl f* **17/1**

1m 26.7s (-1.50) **9**Ran SP% **162.8**

WIN (incl. 1 euro stake): 5.06 (Malagenia coupled with Traditional Chic). PLACES: 4.45, 1.55, 2.19. DF: 24.30 .

Owner Allevamento La Nuova Sbarra **Bred** Allevamento La Nuova Sbarra **Trained** Italy

7545 SANTA ANITA (L-H)

Saturday, November 3

OFFICIAL GOING: Dirt: fast; turf: firm

7566a TWILIGHT DERBY (FORMERLY OAK TREE DERBY) (GRADE 2) (3YO) (TURF) 1m 1f

12:15 (12:16) 3-Y-O **£58,064** (£19,354; £11,612 ; £5,806 ; £1,935)

RPR

1 **Grandeur (IRE)**[43] 6446 3 -8-60 .... WilliamBuick 7 108
(Jeremy Noseda) *stmbld s: settled in last on rail: hdwy 2 1/2f out: r.o u.p to chal between horses ins fnl f: led cl home and bmpd w runner-up on line* **53/10**

2 1/2 **Speaking Of Which (IRE)**[56] 6062 3 -8-100 ....(b) PatSmullen 2 111
(D K Weld, Ire) *trckd ldng gp: tk clsr order on outside over 2f out: led over 1 1/2f out: r.o ent fnl f: edgd rt and hdd cl home: bmpd on line* **13/5[1]**

3 1 **Smart Ellis (USA)**[61] 3 -8-60 .... CNakatani 4 105
(Richard E Mandella, U.S.A) **54/10**

4 nk **All Squared Away (USA)**[31] 3 -8-80 .... GKGomez 5 106
(Peter Miller, U.S.A) **233/10**

5 1/2 **My Best Brother (USA)**[61] 3 -8-100 ....(b) MGarcia 8 107
(Julio C Canani, U.S.A) **27/10[2]**

6 3 1/4 **Power Foot (USA)**[61] 3 -8-60 .... EMaldonado 3 96
(Richard E Mandella, U.S.A) **171/10**

7 1/2 **Old Time Hockey (USA)**[61] 3 -8-100 .... JTalamo 6 99
(Thomas F Proctor, U.S.A) **47/10[3]**

8 1 3/4 **Huntsville (USA)** 3 -8-60 ....(b) JJHernandez 9 92
(Barry Abrams, U.S.A) **30/1**

9 4 1/4 **Hoist (USA)**[54] 3 -8-60 .... MGutierrez 10 83
(Troy Taylor, Canada) **33/1**

1m 46.78s (106.78) **9**Ran SP% **119.7**

PARI-MUTUEL (all including $2 stakes): WIN 12.60; PLACE (1-2) 6.00, 4.40; SHOW (1-2-3) 3.60, 3.40, 4.20; SF 35.60 .

Owner Miss Yvonne Jacques **Bred** Mrs Cherry Faeste **Trained** Newmarket, Suffolk

NOTEBOOK

Grandeur(IRE) trailed the field after stumbling leaving the stalls, but still produced a telling turn of foot to score. He will now be aimed at the Hollywood Derby in the 25th of the month.

7567a BREEDERS' CUP JUVENILE TURF SPRINT PREVIEW STKS (CONDITIONS) (2YO) (TURF) 6f 110y

5:35 (5:38) 2-Y-O **£38,709** (£12,903; £7,741 ; £3,870 ; £1,290)

RPR

1 **Gabriel Charles (USA)**[34] 6728 2 -8-60 ....(b) JTalamo 5 105+
(Jeff Mullins, U.S.A) **49/10[3]**

2 3 1/2 **Den's Legacy (USA)**[26] 2 -8-60 ....(b) GKGomez 9 95+
(Bob Baffert, U.S.A) **9/2[2]**

3 1 **Mico Margarita (USA)**[72] 2 -8-60 .... JRosario 10 93
(Steven Asmussen, U.S.A) **53/10**

4 1/2 **Kafister (USA)** 2 -8-40 ....(b) TBaze 4 89
(Peter Miller, U.S.A) **29/1**

5 nk **Moulin De Mougin (USA)**[36] 2 -8-60 .... CNakatani 7 90
(Richard E Mandella, U.S.A) **77/10**

6 1 1/4 **One Firm Cat (USA)**[47] 2 -8-60 ....(b) KKrigger 6 87
(Peter Miller, U.S.A) **99/10**

7 hd **Upward Spiral**[35] 6672 2 -8-30 .... RBejarano 2 83
(Tom Dascombe) *slow to stride: sn rcvrd and racd in midfield on inner: rdn on turn into st: sn outpcd: kpt on but n.d* **11/2**

8 1 1/4 **Snow King (USA)**[56] 6020 2 -8-60 .... WilliamBuick 3 83
(John Gosden) *slow to stride and racd in last trio: rdn 2f out and sn outpcd: kpt on but nvr a factor* **37/10[1]**

9 nk **Scherer Magic (USA)**[28] 2 -8-100 .... JRVelazquez 1 86
(John W Sadler, U.S.A) **162/10**

10 3 1/4 **No Rachmones (USA)**[28] 2 -8-40 .... MGarcia 8 71
(Peter Miller, U.S.A) **49/1**

1m 12.22s (72.22) **10**Ran SP% **119.5**

PARI-MUTUEL (all including $2 stakes): WIN 11.80; PLACE (1-2) 5.80, 5.00; SHOW (1-2-3) 4.40, 3.40, 3.80; SF 66.40 .

Owner Sam Britt & Michael House **Bred** Doris E Tummilo **Trained** USA

7568a BREEDERS' CUP JUVENILE TURF (GRADE 1) (2YO COLTS & GELDINGS) (TURF) 1m (T)

6:50 (6:51) 2-Y-O **£348,387** (£116,129; £63,870 ; £38,709 ; £19,354)

RPR

1 **George Vancouver (USA)**[21] 7050 2 -8-100 .... RyanMoore 3 117
(A P O'Brien, Ire) *broke wl: stdd and settled in midfield on inner: travelling wl on heels of ldrs on turn into st: slipped through gap between rivals to ld ent fnl f: rdn and r.o strly* **6/1[2]**

2 1 1/4 **Noble Tune (USA)**[26] 2 -8-100 .... RADominguez 9 114
(Chad C Brown, U.S.A) *hld up in tch on inner: rdn on turn into st: swtchd out and r.o to go 2nd ins fnl f: kpt on wout matching wnr cl home* **6/1[2]**

3 nk **Balance The Books (USA)**[27] 2 -8-100 .... JRLeparoux 8 113
(Chad C Brown, U.S.A) *sltly slow to stride and hld up towards rr: hdwy into midfield on turn into st: nt clr run over 1f out: swtchd out and rdn ent fnl f: r.o to go 3rd cl home: fin wl but nvr able to chal* **10/1**

4 1 1/4 **Dundonnell (USA)**[49] 6243 2 -8-100 .... JamesDoyle 6 110+
(Roger Charlton) *midfield: t.k.h: awkward and rn wd first bnd: rapid hdwy onto heels of ldrs 3f out: swtchd out and rdn on turn into st: r.o to chal over 1f out: sn outpcd: dropped to 4th cl home* **7/2[1]**

5 hd **Gervinho (USA)**[26] 2 -8-100 .... RBejarano 4 110
(Carla Gaines, U.S.A) *prom on inner: jnd ldrs over 2f out: rdn on turn into st: stl ev ch whn hdd ent fnl f: sn no ex and fdd: dropped to 5th cl home* **12/1**

6 3 **Artigiano (USA)**[35] 6671 2 -8-100 .... FrankieDettori 2 102
(Mahmood Al Zarooni) *sltly slow to stride and sn towards rr on inner: rdn and hdwy on turn into st: sn outpcd: kpt on wout threatening ins fnl f: wnt 6th fnl strides* **6/1[2]**

7 nk **Lines Of Battle (USA)**[22] 7038 2 -8-100 ....(b[1]) RichardHughes 14 102
(A P O'Brien, Ire) *sent forward fr wdst draw and sn prom on outer: t.k.h: rdn over 2f out: no ex ins fnl f: dropped to 7th fnl strides* **20/1**

8 3/4 **Joha (USA)**[28] 6904 2 -8-100 .... JJCastellano 10 100
(Michael J Maker, U.S.A) *midfield: rdn and looking for room on turn into st: sn outpcd and btn: plugged on* **10/1**

9 3/4 **Brown Almighty (USA)**[27] 2 -8-100 .... KDesormeaux 7 98
(Tim Ice, U.S.A) *prom: hdwy on outer to join ldrs over 2f out: rdn on turn into st: hdd whn bdly hmpd and snatched up ent fnl f: nt rcvr and fdd* **20/1**

10 1 1/4 **Fantastic Moon**[35] 6671 2 -8-100 .... KierenFallon 5 95
(Jeremy Noseda) *slow to stride and racd in last: rdn over 2f out: plugged on and sme late hdwy but nvr a factor* **9/1[3]**

11 1 **Dry Summer (USA)**[34] 6728 2 -8-100 .... JTalamo 11 93
(Jeff Mullins, U.S.A) *hld up towards rr: rdn on turn into st: sn no ex and btn: nvr a factor* **33/1**

12 1 1/4 **Summit County (USA)**[27] 2 -8-100 .... CNakatani 1 90
(Dale Romans, U.S.A) *led: jnd over 2f out: rdn and hdd on turn into st: no ex and btn ent fnl f: eased and fdd* **50/1**

13 1 3/4 **Know More (USA)**[34] 6728 2 -8-100 .... GKGomez 13 85
(Doug O'Neill, U.S.A) *hld up towards rr: briefly rdn 2f out: eased w jockey looking down on turn into st: sn no ex and btn* **20/1**

14 hd **I'm Boundtoscore (USA)**[49] 2 -8-100 .... SarahRook 12 85
(Troy Rankin, U.S.A) *got across fr wd draw to trck ldr: lost pl rapidly 2f out: rdn and sn btn* **33/1**

1m 33.78s (-0.09) **14**Ran SP% **123.1**

PARI-MUTUEL (all including $2 stakes): WIN 20.60; PLACE (1-2) 11.00, 6.00; SHOW (1-2-3) 7.20, 3.80, 6.00; SF 125.60 .

Owner Mrs John Magnier & Michael Tabor & Derrick Smith **Bred** Capital Bloodstock **Trained** Ballydoyle, Co Tipperary

FOCUS

Three of the five previous runnings of the Juvenile Turf had fallen to European raiders, and they were well represented again. Aidan O'Brien, who trained the 2011 winner Wrote, was doubly represented and George Vancouver gave him another success. British form suggests this was a good renewal of what can be a weak Group 1.

NOTEBOOK

George Vancouver (USA) runner-up in the Prix Morny and third in the Dewhurst, he had never raced on fast turf before but the surface suited his sire Henrythenavigator and he seemed to really act on it. Given a fine ride, he was settled on the rail from his good draw and then squeezed through a narrow gap early in the straight before being driven clear, getting a decisive first run on the late closers. Presumably next year's Classics will be in connections' minds now, and it is likely they will be hoping for a dry spring. He is currently around 20-1 for the 2,000 Guineas.

Noble Tune (USA) unbeaten on two starts in the east, had first run on his stable companion but the winner got the jump on both of them and they never looked like reeling him in. He looks a decent prospect for next year.

Balance The Books (USA)a winner at both Grade 2 and Grade 3 level in the east with several of today's rivals behind, missed the break but that was not as big a problem as it might have been, as he is usually held up. He did come from a long way back though and, not helped by getting an interrupted passage in the straight, could never quite get there.

Dundonnell(USA), well suited by a sound surface on turf, had the best form of the British runners but was keen early and nearly went straight on at the first turn, affecting his own chance and hampering a couple of his rivals. However, he recovered to make good ground at the end the back straight, only to be ridden to make his challenge and then paying for earlier efforts in the closing stages. He looks to have plenty of ability and could well be a force next year when more mature, providing this hard race does not leave its mark.

Gervinho(USA), unbeaten in two starts at a lower level, including one over C&D, was always in the leading group from his low draw and, after showing in front briefly early in the straight, only backed out of it in the last furlong.

Artigiano(USA) had proved himself a solid Group 2 performer in Britain, most recently finishing second in the Royal Lodge over this trip. However, he was slowly into his stride from his good draw and, despite running on steadily, failed to land a blow.

Lines Of Battle (USA)whose sire's progeny have a good record here, had been held in Group races on turf earlier in the season, but had taken a Polytrack Listed event at Dundalk following a break. With blinkers replacing the cheekpieces he wore there, he had a tough task from the widest draw of all, but ran a fine race, doing a lot of running early and racing keenly, then only fading late on. He might be the sort that could do well in Dubai over the winter.

Joha(USA), the only Grade 1 winner in the line-up (on Polytrack), also had form on turf. He had led in the past but was settled from his double-figure draw before making a move towards the end of the back straight. However, he was under pressure on the home turn and could not find a change of gear.

Fantastic Moon, who looked unlucky when finishing behind Artigiano in the Royal Lodge, totally blew the start and never got into the race.

Know More(USA), runner-up in Grade 1s on turf and Polytrack on his previous two starts, was making his turf debut but, drawn wide, his chance was seriously compromised when carried even wider by Dundonnell on the first bend.

I'm Boundtoscore(USA) did a lot of running early from his wide draw and paid for it from the home turn.

7569a BREEDERS' CUP FILLY & MARE SPRINT (GRADE 1) (3YO+ FILLIES & MARES) (DIRT) 7f

7:35 (7:36) 3-Y-0+ £348,387 (£116,129; £63,870; £38,709; £19,354)

RPR

1 **Groupie Doll (USA)**[20] 4-8-12 0........................(b) RMaragh 9 121
(William Bradley, U.S.A) *drvn to go forward early: midfield on outer: rdn and hdwy over 2f out: r.o to ld over 1f out: wnt clr ins fnl f: rdn out: v readily* **4/6**[1]

2 4 ½ **Dust And Diamonds (USA)**[42] 4-8-12 0.................. JRLeparoux 3 109
(Steven Asmussen, U.S.A) *pressed ldr on outer: rdn to ld on turn into st: hdd over 1f out and qckly lft bhd by wnr: kpt on wl for 2nd ins fnl f* **5/1**[2]

3 3 ¾ **Switch (USA)**[34] 6729 5-8-12 0.................. GKGomez 10 99
(John W Sadler, U.S.A) *dropped in fr wdst draw and hld up in detached last: rdn 2f out: r.o down wd outside to go 3rd ins fnl f: nvr remotely dangerous* **14/1**

4 1 **Belle Of The Hall (USA)**[31] 5-8-12 0........................(b) IOrtizJr 2 96
(Thomas Albertrani, U.S.A) *hld up towards rr on inner: rdn over 2f out: plugged on to go 4th ins fnl f: nvr a threat* **40/1**

5 ¾ **Rumor (USA)**[27] 4-8-12 0.................................. MESmith 5 94
(Richard E Mandella, U.S.A) *hld up towards rr: rdn over 3f out and sn outpcd: plugged on to go 5th ins fnl f: nvr a threat* **16/1**

6 2 ¾ **Musical Romance (USA)**[28] 5-8-12 0........................(b) JCLeyva 8 87
(William Kaplan, U.S.A) *midfield: rdn and outpcd 2f out: plugged on wout threatening in st* **11/1**

7 2 ¼ **Turbulent Descent (USA)**[42] 4-8-12 0.................. JRVelazquez 6 81
(Todd Pletcher, U.S.A) *prom: rdn and outpcd on turn into st: sn no ex and btn: fdd* **7/1**[3]

8 ½ **Teddy's Promise (USA)**[21] 4-8-12 0.................. JTalamo 1 79
(Ronald W Ellis, U.S.A) *led: rdn and hdd on turn into st: sn no ex and btn: fdd* **25/1**

9 1 **Great Hot (BRZ)**[27] 4-8-12 0.................. EMaldonado 7 77
(A C Avila, U.S.A) *midfield: rdn 3f out and sn outpcd: btn on turn into st* **50/1**

10 2 ¼ **Strike The Moon (USA)**[28] 4-8-12 0........................(b) JLezcano 4 71
(Michael Trombetta, U.S.A) *prom: lost pl 3f out: rdn 2f out: sn no ex and btn: dropped to last ins fnl f* **40/1**

1m 20.72s (80.72) **10** Ran SP% **120.7**

PARI-MUTUEL (all including $2 stakes): WIN 3.40; PLACE (1-2) 2.60, 4.20; SHOW (1-2-3) 2.10, 3.20, 3.60; SF 12.00.

Owner Fred F & William B Bradley et al **Bred** Fred & William Bradley **Trained** USA

FOCUS

This went to a top-class filly in the shape of Groupie Doll. She's rated to her mark.

NOTEBOOK

Groupie Doll(USA) improved her record in blinkers to 5-5 despite the quick track not suiting her run style and the improving second enjoying a favourable trip. The winner had to be driven along early but gradually warmed up and had this won when ranging upsides Dust And Diamonds at the top of the straight.

Dust And Diamonds(USA) was up in trip from 6.5f but stamina wasn't the issue - she was just beaten by a much better rival and if anything she's flattered to finish so close.

Switch(USA) had finished runner-up in this race for the last two years, but the track wasn't playing to suit her late-running style and she was never seen with a chance this time.

Belle Of The Hall(USA) achieved little in plugging on into fourth.

7570a BREEDERS' CUP DIRT MILE (GRADE 1) (3YO+) (DIRT) 1m

8:14 (8:15) 3-Y-0+ £348,387 (£116,129; £63,870; £38,709; £19,354)

RPR

1 **Tapizar (USA)**[35] 4-9-0 0.................. CNakatani 8 118
(Steven Asmussen, U.S.A) *pressed ldr on outside: led 2f out: sn rdn and r.o: drew clr ent fnl f: pushed out fnl 100yds* **20/1**

2 2 ¼ **Rail Trip (USA)**[34] 6731 7-9-0 0.................. JValdiviaJr 1 113
(Ronald W Ellis, U.S.A) *broke wl: sn settled towards rr: hrd rdn and prog over 1 1/2f out: r.o to go 2nd 150yds out: no imp fnl 100yds: nvr on terms w wnr* **10/1**

3 1 ¾ **Delegation (USA)**[20] 3-8-11 0.................. PHusbands 2 108
(Mark Casse, Canada) *trckd ldr on rail: cl 3rd 1 1/2f out: nt qckn whn asked: kpt on at same pce fnl f* **16/1**

4 ½ **John Scott (USA)**[20] 5-9-0 0.................. VEspinoza 4 108
(Carla Gaines, U.S.A) *settled in rr: hdwy on outside 3f out: hrd rdn and c wd fnl bnd: no imp 1 1/2f out: styd on u.p ins fnl f to go 4th cl home: nt pce to chal* **12/1**

5 ½ **Jersey Town (USA)**[35] 6-9-0 0.................. JJCastellano 3 107
(Barclay Tagg, U.S.A) *broke wl: trckd ldrs: 3rd and ev ch but hemmed in 2f out: sn swtchd outside and nt qckn u.p 1 1/2f out: one pce fnl f* **5/1**[3]

6 1 ¼ **Emcee (USA)**[63] 5846 4-9-0 0.................. AGarcia 7 104
(Kiaran McLaughlin, U.S.A) *sn led: rdn and hdd 2f out: wknd u.p over 1f out* **5/2**[1]

7 1 **Shackleford (USA)**[35] 4-9-0 0.................. RADominguez 6 102+
(Dale Romans, U.S.A) *propped leaving stalls and lft bhd wall of horses: trckd ldrs on outside after 3f: hrd rdn 2f out: nt qckn: fdd ins fnl f* **10/3**[2]

8 1 ¾ **Fed Biz (USA)**[28] 3-8-11 0.................. JTalamo 5 96
(Bob Baffert, U.S.A) *towards rr but in tch: rdn and nt qckn over 2f out: nvr in contention* **5/1**[3]

9 6 ¼ **Second City (USA)**[28] 3-8-11 0........................(b) MGutierrez 9 82
(B Cecil, U.S.A) *hld up towards rr: lost grnd far bnd: rdn and bhd 2f out: no imp* **33/1**

1m 35.34s (95.34)

WFA 3 from 4yo+ 2lb **9** Ran SP% **115.4**

PARI-MUTUEL (all including $2 stakes): WIN 32.60; PLACE (1-2) 13.60, 8.40; SHOW (1-2-3) 8.20, 5.80, 8.20; SF 245.60.

Owner Winchell Thoroughbreds LLC **Bred** Winchell Thoroughbreds LLC **Trained** USA

FOCUS

This race fell apart with the two main players failing to give their true running.

NOTEBOOK

Tapizar(USA) benefited most from the unexpected set up, sitting next to Emcee through modest enough fractions (considering how quick the track was riding) of 22.77 and 46.58. He had been well beaten in the Kelso last time, but that came on a wet surface when he couldn't get his own way, and he had won two of his previous four starts here. With the benefit of hindsight, perhaps this wasn't such a big shock after all, although his chance was further aided by the runner-up and third both suffering poor trips.

Rail Trip(USA) does most of his racing on synthetics and came into this 0-5 on dirt, but he stayed on well having been poorly placed.

Delegation(USA), debuting on dirt, couldn't dominate as he had when winning a Polytrack Grade 3 at Woodbine on his previous start, but he would probably have finished quite a bit closer had he been able to get a run when seemingly travelling well turning into the straight. He had lost his momentum when belatedly in the open.

John Scott(USA) had a wide trip into the straight and then didn't get the clearest of runs, but this is not form to get carried away with.

Emcee(USA) just didn't relax in front on this step up in trip and first try around two turns.

Shackleford(USA), a one-dimensional front-runner, had no chance of getting to the lead after stumbling at the start.

7571a BREEDERS' CUP TURF SPRINT (GRADE 1) (3YO+) (TURF) 6f 110y

8:57 (9:01) 3-Y-0+ £348,387 (£116,129; £63,870; £38,709; £19,354)

RPR

1 **Mizdirection (USA)**[159] 4-8-11 0.................. MESmith 11 111+
(Mike Puype, U.S.A) *midfield: rdn 2f out: r.o down wd outside to chal ins fnl f: led cl home: drvn out* **7/1**[2]

2 ½ **Unbridled's Note (USA)**[35] 3-8-12 0.................. CNakatani 13 112
(Steven Asmussen, U.S.A) *midfield: rdn on turn into st: r.o to chal ins fnl f: led ins fnl 100yds: hdd cl home* **9/2**[1]

3 1 ¼ **Reneesgotzip (USA)**[27] 6915 3-8-9 0........................(b) GKGomez 7 105
(Peter Miller, U.S.A) *prom: rdn 2f out: lugged lft u.p 1 1/2f out and bmpd rival: r.o to chal ins fnl f: led briefly 100yds out: sn hdd and outpcd by front pair: kpt on* **12/1**

4 1 ¼ **Great Mills (USA)**[28] 4-9-0 0.................. RBejarano 3 106
(Steven Asmussen, U.S.A) *broke wl and sn trcking ldr in 2nd: rdn on turn into st: bmpd by rival 1 1/2f out: r.o to chal ent fnl f: ev ch tl no ex and fdd ins fnl 100yds* **20/1**

5 hd **Great Attack (USA)**[182] 5-9-0 0........................(b) JRosario 8 105+
(Wesley A Ward, U.S.A) *hld up towards rr: rdn on turn into st: r.o to go 5th cl home: nt pce to chal* **16/1**

6 nk **Corporate Jungle (USA)**[28] 6905 4-9-0 0.................. JJCastellano 10 104+
(Chad C Brown, U.S.A) *midfield: rdn over 2f out: r.o to go 6th cl home: nt pce to chal* **8/1**

7 ¾ **Next Question (USA)**[20] 7092 4-9-0 0........................(b) RADominguez 5 102+
(Michael Trombetta, U.S.A) *hld up towards rr: rdn on turn into st: kpt on wout threatening ins fnl f: lost two pls cl home* **12/1**

8 ½ **Tale Of A Champion (USA)**[35] 4-9-0 0........................(b[1]) TBaze 4 101
(Kristin Mulhall, U.S.A) *midfield: rdn on turn into st: kpt on wout threatening ins fnl f* **33/1**

9 ½ **Upgrade (USA)**[22] 5-9-0 0........................(b) RMaragh 6 99
(Michelle Nihei, U.S.A) *sn last: rdn on turn into st: r.o and sme late hdwy but nvr a factor* **25/1**

10 2 ¼ **Starspangledbanner (AUS)**[8] 7390 6-9-0 0.................. JosephO'Brien 14 93
(A P O'Brien, Ire) *broke wl and led: set fast pce: rdn 1 1/2f out: strly pressed and hdd ins fnl f: no ex and fdd: lost multiple positions cl home* **11/1**

11 ½ **Camp Victory (USA)**[27] 6915 5-9-0 0........................(b) JRLeparoux 2 91
(Mike Mitchell, U.S.A) *slow to stride and racd towards rr: rdn over 2f out: sn btn: nvr a factor* **12/1**

12 hd **Chosen Miracle (USA)**[35] 4-9-0 0.................. MGarcia 12 91
(Jerry Hollendorfer, U.S.A) *broke wl and trckd ldr: lost pl and shuffled bk on rail 3f out: rdn on turn into st: sn outpcd: btn ins fnl f: fdd* **25/1**

13 1 ½ **California Flag (USA)**[196] 8-9-0 0........................(b) JTalamo 1 86
(Brian Koriner, U.S.A) *midfield: rdn on turn into st: outpcd and btn ent fnl f: eased* **15/2**[3]

14 1 ¼ **Bridgetown (USA)**[28] 5-9-0 0.................. JRVelazquez 9 83
(Todd Pletcher, U.S.A) *midfield: rdn over 2f out: no ex and beten ent fnl f: fdd and dropped to last* **7/1**[2]

1m 11.39s (71.39) **14** Ran SP% **118.7**

PARI-MUTUEL (all including $2 stakes): WIN 15.80; PLACE (1-2) 7.40, 5.80; SHOW (1-2-3) 5.00, 4.40, 7.00; SF 80.20.

Owner Jungle Racing LLC, Danny Grohs et al **Bred** Joseph J Perrotta **Trained** USA

FOCUS

The four previous renewals of the Turf Sprint had all fallen to US-trained runner. The early pace on this quirky downhill track, that has a right-handed dog-leg and skirts the car park, was very strong and they broke the track record, with the first two coming from behind.

NOTEBOOK

Mizdirection(USA), having her first start since May, was 2-2 on the track coming into this and maintained her record, coming from well off the pace to sweep to the front well inside the last furlong. She is pretty versatile, having made all around here previously, and it will be interesting to see if she is kept in training with a repeat success in mind.

Unbridled's Note(USA), a C&D winner last time on his switch to turf from dirt, was held up before being produced at what looked the ideal moment, only to be run down by the late surge of the filly down the outside. He looks the sort who could be back with a major chance next season, and he might even get a mile in time.

Reneesgotzip(USA), better known as a dirt and synthetics performer, put up a terrific performance on this turf debut. She was never far away and, despite hanging left under pressure, kept finding and was only worn down by the late closers. Just a 3yo, she could be back for more next year, possibly in the dirt event.

Great Mills(USA) is a pretty consistent sort around some of the lesser US tracks but ran a fine race here, showing up from the start and overcoming a bump in the straight to keep going for fourth.

Great Attack(USA), who is well suited by being held up in his races, stayed on but was never close enough to make an impression.

Corporate Jungle(USA), better known as a miler, stayed on late but did not have the raw speed to get involved.

Starspangledbanner(AUS) tried to make the best of his draw, which gave him the advantage of the right-handed curve early, but he went too fast. He's likely to race again next year.

California Flag(USA), who won this in 2009, was back again. His win was over C&D and his defeats in the two latest runnings were both over 5f at Churchill Downs. However, he could never get to the front, and after appearing close enough to deliver a challenge turning in, he faded in the straight.

Bridgetown(USA), who had been in good form this season, ran no sort of race and dropped away as if something was amiss.

7572a GREY GOOSE BREEDERS' CUP JUVENILE (GRADE 1) (2YO COLTS & GELDINGS) (DIRT) 1m 110y (D)

9:36 (9:38) 2-Y-O **£696,774** (£232,258; £127,741 ; £77,419 ; £38,709)

Pos	Dist	Horse (Trainer)	Age-Wgt	Jockey / Draw	SP	RPR
1		**Shanghai Bobby (USA)**[28] [6901] (Todd Pletcher, U.S.A)	2 -8-10[0]	(b) RosieNapravnik 4	7/4[1]	117+
2	*hd*	**He's Had Enough (USA)**[28] [6904] (Doug O'Neill, U.S.A)	2 -8-10[0]	(b) MGutierrez 3	33/1	114+
3	[illegible]	**Capo Bastone (USA)**[34] [6728] (John W Sadler, U.S.A)	2 -8-10[0]	JRosario 7	11/1	108
4	*1 ¾*	**Fortify (USA)**[28] [6901] (Kiaran McLaughlin, U.S.A)	2 -8-10[0]	RADominguez 8	15/2[3]	104
5	*1*	**Power Broker (USA)**[34] [6728] (Bob Baffert, U.S.A)	2 -8-10[0]	(b) RBejarano 9	5/2[2]	102
6	*nk*	**Dynamic Sky (CAN)**[28] [6904] (Mark Casse, Canada)	2 -8-10[0]	LContreras 6	12/1	101
7	*½*	**Speak Logistics (USA)**[21] (Edward Plesa Jr, U.S.A)	2 -8-10[0]	(b) ASerpa 2	20/1	100
8	*10 ¼*	**Title Contender (USA)**[35] (Bob Baffert, U.S.A)	2 -8-10[0]	(b) MGarcia 1	8/1	77
9	*9 ½*	**Monument (USA)**[21] (John W Sadler, U.S.A)	2 -8-10[0]	JTalamo 5	20/1	55

1m 44.58s (2.16) **9**Ran SP% **114.6**

PARI-MUTUEL (all including $2 stakes): WIN 4.60; PLACE (1-2) 3.40, 12.60; SHOW (1-2-3) 2.60, 7.40, 5.00; SF 90.80 .

Owner Starlight Racing, Mrs J Magnier, M Tabor & D Smith **Bred** Stonehaven Steadings **Trained** USA

FOCUS

Title Contender set too strong a pace, reaching the half-mile point in 45.55 (just over a second quicker than the pacesetter in the Dirt Mile), and consequently the final time was desperate. There was only around four lengths covering the first eight with a furlong to go, as the runners tired, and it's hard to consider this anything like top-class form (also taking into account the Lasix ban), but Shanghai Bobby needs his effort upgrading. He didn't need to improve on his solid pre-race credentials.

NOTEBOOK

Shanghai Bobby (USA)was fired into a clear lead rounding the final bend, but that was a poor move as he'd been racing bang up with the hot fractions and had previously shown a tendency to idle in front. Having allowed his rivals back into the contest early in the straight, when he looked in trouble, he kept doing just enough to hold on. He is now 5-5, adding to his victory in the Champagne, and just about proved he has the legs for two turns, but at this early stage he makes little appeal for the Kentucky Derby.

He's Had Enough (USA)just failed despite having nowhere to go when apparently full of running around the turn into the straight, but while being messed about can't have helped, it was no bad thing he had his effort delayed and he did draw alongside the tiring winner with a full furlong left to run. On that basis, it might be dangerous to suggest he was anything other than second best, but this was still a good run on his dirt debut and he strikes as being a hardy sort who could cope with the demands of a Triple Crown campaign.

Capo Bastone (USA)reversed recent form with the below-par Power Broker, and that's despite bleeding according to his connections.

Fortify(USA) had finished behind Shanghai Bobby on his last two starts and never really looked like turning the form around, despite being the only runner used to competing without Lasix.

Power Broker (USA)might be flattered by a C&D win on his previous start. He hadn't looked anything out of the ordinary on different surfaces prior to that success, and here he just wasn't sharp enough.

7573a BREEDERS' CUP TURF (GRADE 1) (3YO+) (TURF) 1m 4f (T)

10:18 (10:20) 3-Y-O+ **£1,045,161** (£348,387; £191,612; £116,129; £58,064)

Pos	Dist	Horse (Trainer)	Age-Wgt	Jockey / Draw	SP	RPR
1		**Little Mike (USA)**[35] [6696] (Dale Romans, U.S.A)	5 -9-0[0]	RADominguez 7	25/1	121
2	*½*	**Point Of Entry (USA)**[35] [6696] (Claude McGaughey III, U.S.A)	4 -9-0[0]	(b) JRVelazquez 1	4/1[2]	120+
3	*¾*	**St Nicholas Abbey (IRE)**[27] [6912] (A P O'Brien, Ire)	5 -9-0[0]	JosephO'Brien 3	5/2[1]	119+
4	*1*	**Trailblazer (JPN)**[28] (Yasutoshi Ikee, Japan)	5 -9-0[0]	YutakaTake 12	9/2[3]	117
5	*nk*	**Shareta (IRE)**[27] [6912] (A De Royer-Dupre, France)	4 -8-11[0]	Christophe-PatriceLemaire 5	4/1[2]	114+
6	*2 ¼*	**Kindergarden Kid (USA)**[16] (Peter Miller, U.S.A)	5 -9-0[0]	JRLeparoux 8	50/1	113
7	*hd*	**Cogito (USA)**[28] [6902] (Doug O'Neill, U.S.A)	3 -8-10[0]	(b) FrankieDettori 6	25/1	115
8	*¾*	**Slim Shadey**[33] (Simon Callaghan, U.S.A)	4 -9-0[0]	(b) GKGomez 11	25/1	112
9	*1 ½*	**Dullahan (USA)**[28] [6902] (Dale Romans, U.S.A)	3 -8-10[0]	JRosario 9	16/1	111
10	*½*	**Treasure Beach**[35] [6696] (A P O'Brien, Ire)	4 -9-0[0]	JamieSpencer 4	16/1	109
11	*½*	**Optimizer (USA)**[42] (D Wayne Lukas, U.S.A)	3 -8-10[0]	JKCourt 10	33/1	110
12	*3 ¼*	**Turbo Compressor (USA)**[33] (Todd Pletcher, U.S.A)	4 -9-0[0]	JBravo 2	50/1	103

2m 22.83s (-3.82)

WFA 3 from 4yo+ 6lb **12**Ran SP% **116.9**

PARI-MUTUEL (all including $2 stakes): WIN 36.60; PLACE (1-2) 12.20, 4.20; SHOW (1-2-3) 7.80, 3.00, 3.80; SF 136.40 .

Owner Priscilla Vaccarezza **Bred** Carlo E Vaccarezza **Trained** USA

FOCUS

This race, more than any other at the meeting, has been dominated by challengers from Europe, with six of the previous seven being trained in either Britain, Ireland or France. The challenge was smaller than has sometimes been the case, but last year's winner St Nicholas Abbey was back to defend his title. The time was fast and the form is rated around the winner and the sixth.

NOTEBOOK

Little Mike (USA) who had done most of his racing at a mile, had won the Arlington Million in August, but did not get home when making the running on easy ground on his first try at this trip on his previous outing. However, connections opted for this race instead of the Mile and, having taken a lead until the straight, he battled on for a determined success. This versatile gelding could be back to defend his title next year.

Point Of Entry (USA)who had been fine form this season in the east, was short of room early here and, although he was cutting into the winner's advantage near the finish, his effort came a little too late.

St Nicholas Abbey (IRE)held up off the pace, he came from out of the pack in the straight to chase the leaders but never looked like reeling them in. He came into this last year on the back of an Arc run, but the ground was much softer at Longchamp this time and maybe the combination of that and the tighter track here found him out. He may stay in training.

Trailblazer(JPN), a Japanese challenger who had gained experience of the track when a late-finishing second over a much shorter trip early last month, was well fancied here. However, his rider got a good pitch but tended to race a few horse-widths wide of the inside rail, and then made his effort rounding the home turn, which caused his mount to run wider still. Not surprisingly the horse had no more to give in the closing stages.

Shareta(IRE) was the only runner not on Lasix. Ahead of today's third in the Arc, she was expected to appreciate the better ground but might have found it too fast, as she could only stay on late. Like St Nicholas Abbey though, it is possible the Longchamp race had taken the edge off her.

Treasure Beach, second to today's runner-up in the Turf Classic in September, has done a lot of travelling this year and might have preferred more give in the ground, as he was never really going. He's likely to race again next year.

7574a XPRESSBET BREEDERS' CUP SPRINT (GRADE 1) (3YO+) (DIRT) 6f (D)

10:58 (11:01) 3-Y-O+ **£522,580** (£174,193; £95,806 ; £58,064 ; £29,032)

Pos	Dist	Horse (Trainer)	Age-Wgt	Jockey / Draw	SP	RPR
1		**Trinniberg (USA)**[42] (Shivananda Parbhoo, U.S.A)	3 -8-12[0]	(b) WMartinez 9	20/1	123
2	*¾*	**The Lumber Guy (USA)**[35] [6694] (Michael Hushion, U.S.A)	3 -8-12[0]	JRVelazquez 7	5/1[2]	121
3	*2 ¼*	**Smiling Tiger (USA)**[26] (Jeff Bonde, U.S.A)	5 -9-0[0]	RADominguez 10	20/1	116
4	*hd*	**Sum Of The Parts (USA)**[28] (Thomas Amoss, U.S.A)	3 -8-12[0]	JRLeparoux 1	20/1	113
5	*1*	**Justin Phillip (USA)**[35] [6694] (Steven Asmussen, U.S.A)	4 -9-0[0]	(b) RBejarano 5	25/1	112+
6	*1 ½*	**Fast Bullet (USA)**[357] (Bob Baffert, U.S.A)	4 -9-0[0]	(b) JTalamo 6	11/1	107
7	*½*	**Coil (USA)**[27] [6915] (Bob Baffert, U.S.A)	4 -9-0[0]	(b) MGarcia 4	5/1[2]	106+
8	*hd*	**Amazombie (USA)**[27] [6915] (Bill Spawr, U.S.A)	6 -9-0[0]	MESmith 11	4/1[1]	105
9	*nse*	**Jimmy Creed (USA)**[27] [6915] (Richard E Mandella, U.S.A)	3 -8-12[0]	GKGomez 2	7/1[3]	103+
10	*1 ¼*	**Hamazing Destiny (USA)**[63] [5846] (D Wayne Lukas, U.S.A)	6 -9-0[0]	JRosario 12	33/1	101+
11	*1 ¼*	**Gantry (USA)**[56] (Ron Faucheux, U.S.A)	5 -9-0[0]	JJCastellano 3	16/1	97+
12	*2 ¼*	**Capital Account (USA)**[27] [6915] (Bob Baffert, U.S.A)	5 -9-0[0]	(b) DFlores 8	7/1[3]	90+
13	*2 ¼*	**Boxeur Des Rues (USA)**[35] (Doug O'Neill, U.S.A)	4 -9-0[0]	MGutierrez 14	66/1	82+
14	*1 ¼*	**Poseidon's Warrior (USA)**[35] [6694] (Robert E Reid Jr, U.S.A)	4 -9-0[0]	IOrtizJr 13	25/1	78+

1m 7.98s (-0.28) **14**Ran SP% **119.0**

PARI-MUTUEL (all including $2 stakes): WIN 29.40; PLACE (1-2) 13.20, 6.40; SHOW (1-2-3) 11.00, 5.00, 12.20; SF 203.40 .

Owner Sherry Parbhoo **Bred** J M Stables Inc **Trained** USA

FOCUS

Despite taking each other on through quick fractions of 21.41 and 43.73, Trinniberg and Sum Of The Parts managed to finish first and fourth respectively and both should be capable of even better when able to dominate outright.

NOTEBOOK

Trinniberg(USA), who finished down the field in this year's Kentucky Derby, is all speed and had blinkers on for the first time. He managed to win despite being taken on by the fourth.

The Lumber Guy (USA)came into this unbeaten in four runs at up to 1m, most recently recording a big win in the Grade 1 Vosburgh at this trip. This was a solid effort in defeat and he should still have more to offer.

Smiling Tiger (USA)returned to form to repeat his third-place finish in this race from 2010.

Sum Of The Parts (USA)is even better than fourth place indicates, as he disputed the lead with the winner.

Justin Phillip (USA)only ran on past beaten horses and is now 1-14 on fast dirt.

Amazombie(USA), last year's winner, wasn't at his best in his prep race and just didn't fire.

7575a BREEDERS' CUP MILE (GRADE 1) (3YO+) (TURF) 1m (T)

11:40 (12:00) 3-Y-O+ **£696,774** (£232,258; £127,741 ; £77,419 ; £38,709)

Pos	Dist	Horse (Trainer)	Age-Wgt	Jockey / Draw	SP	RPR
1		**Wise Dan (USA)**[28] [6905] (Charles Lopresti, U.S.A)	5 -9-0[0]	JRVelazquez 2	9/4[2]	127+
2	*1 ½*	**Animal Kingdom (USA)**[259] (H Graham Motion, U.S.A)	4 -9-0[0]	(b) RBejarano 5	14/1	123+
3	*½*	**Obviously (IRE)**[28] (Mike Mitchell, U.S.A)	4 -9-0[0]	JTalamo 3	11/1	121
4	*nse*	**Excelebration (IRE)**[14] [7238] (A P O'Brien, Ire)	4 -9-0[0]	JosephO'Brien 6	11/8[1]	121+
5	*1*	**Mr. Commons (USA)**[28] (John Shirreffs, U.S.A)	4 -9-0[0]	(b) BBlanc 1	40/1	119
6	*1 ½*	**Jeranimo (USA)**[68] (Michael Pender, U.S.A)	6 -9-0[0]	GKGomez 4	40/1	116+
7	*1 ¼*	**Suggestive Boy (ARG)**[34] [6731] (Ronald McAnally, U.S.A)	4 -9-0[0]	MESmith 8	50/1	113
8	*½*	**Moonlight Cloud**[48] [6296] (F Head, France)	4 -8-11[0]	ThierryJarnet 9	4/1[3]	109+
9	*hd*	**Willcox Inn (USA)**[28] [6905] (Michael Stidham, U.S.A)	4 -9-0[0]	(b) JamesGraham 7	66/1	111+

1m 31.78s (-2.09) **9**Ran SP% **116.2**

PARI-MUTUEL (all including $2 stakes): WIN 5.60; PLACE (1-2) 3.00, 6.60; SHOW (1-2-3) 2.80, 4.60, 4.20; SF 54.60 .

Owner Morton Fink **Bred** Mort Fink **Trained** USA

FOCUS

The turf mile has been equally shared between North American winners and challengers from France in recent years, with Goldikova having been responsible for three of their five successes.

NOTEBOOK

Wise Dan (USA)had been in terrific form since returning from a break in August, winning his three starts, the last two in Grade 1 company. He got a good lead into the race and, once asked to go and win early in the straight, the result was never in doubt, the gelding keeping on strongly to break the course record. It will take a good one to beat him if he returns in similar form next year.

Animal Kingdom (USA) the 2011 Kentucky Derby winner, was having his first start since February but was produced fighting fit and looked somewhat unlucky. Held up off the pace, he was short of room turning for home and had to wait for a gap to appear, and once it did he finished strongly. Presumably he will remain in training if none the worse and he will surely find easier tasks than this.

Obviously(IRE), a C&D winner when beating Trailblazer early last month, made the running as usual and tried to kick clear early in the straight, but the winner had him in his sights and he had nothing in reserve for the last half-furlong.
Excelebration(IRE), an impressive winner of the Queen Elizabeth II Stakes last time, had only been beaten by one horse other than Frankel since his racecourse debut. However, after tracking the leaders, he seemed to get a little outpaced leaving the back straight, and, although he moved onto the heels of the leaders turning for home, failed to pick up in the straight, looking a little uncomfortable on the fast ground.
Mr. Commons (USA) not beaten far by today's third in his two previous starts, ran pretty close to that form and helps set the standard.
Moonlight Cloud, a filly with plenty of speed, came into this relatively fresh after winning the Moulin, but her only moderate run had been on her only previous encounter with fast turf and she failed to get involved, having been held up.

7566 SANTA ANITA (L-H)

Sunday, November 4

OFFICIAL GOING: Dirt: fast; turf: firm

7576a BREEDERS' CUP CLASSIC (GRADE 1) (3YO+) (DIRT) 1m 2f (D)

12:35 (12:43) 3-Y-O+ **£1,741,935** (£580,645; £319,354; £193,548; £96,774)

RPR

1 **Fort Larned (USA)**[86] 6697 4 -9-00 (b) BHernandezJr 4 128
(Ian Wilkes, U.S.A) *led after 75yds: mde rest: wnt 2 l clr over 3 1/2f out: rdn and chal by runner-up fr 1 1/2f out: responded gamely fnl f: hld on wl* **9/1**

2 1/2 **Mucho Macho Man (USA)**[64] 5847 4 -9-00 MESmith 11 127
(Kathy Ritvo, U.S.A) *broke best fr wd draw and led first 75yds: sn hdd and trckd ldr on outside: chsd wnr fr 2 1/2f out: rdn and chal thrght fnl f: nvr quite getting there* **6/1**[2]

3 6 1/2 **Flat Out (USA)**[36] 6697 6 -9-00 JRosario 2 114
(William Mott, U.S.A) *settled in rr of main pack: hdwy on outside over 2 1/2f out: c wd fnl bnd: wnt 3rd bhd two clr ldrs over 1 1/2f out: hrd rdn and styd on: no imp on ldrs fnl f* **8/1**

4 3/4 **Ron The Greek (USA)**[36] 6697 5 -9-00 JLezcano 10 113
(William Mott, U.S.A) *hld up 3rd last and detached fr main pack: prog 3 1/2f out: 8th and styng on 1 1/2f out: wnt 4th fnl 100yds: nvr in contention* **7/1**[3]

5 nk **Richard's Kid (USA)**[35] 6731 7 -9-00 (b) GKGomez 9 112
(Doug O'Neill, U.S.A) *in rr: hdwy on rail 2 1/2f out: 6th and styng on 1 1/2f out: swtchd outside over 1f out: kpt on fnl f but run flattened out last 100yds: n.d* **16/1**

6 2 3/4 **Nonios (USA)**[35] 6731 3 -8-100 MPedroza 8 106
(Jerry Hollendorfer, U.S.A) *wl away: midfield on heels of ldng gp: outpcd 3f out: styd on to chse plcd horses 1 1/2f out: one pce fnl f* **25/1**

7 4 1/4 **Game On Dude (USA)**[35] 6731 5 -9-00 (b) RBejarano 5 98
(Bob Baffert, U.S.A) *modly away: midfield on heels of ldng gp: 3rd and in tch on outside 3f out: rdn and nt go on w front two 2 1/2f out: grad wknd fnl 1 1/2f* **5/4**[1]

8 2 1/2 **Pool Play (CAN)**[29] 7 -9-00 MMena 1 93
(Mark Casse, Canada) *settled next to last detached fr main pack: hdwy on outside fr 3 1/2f out: plugged on u.p fnl 1 1/2f: nvr a factor* **40/1**

9 3 1/4 **Handsome Mike (USA)**[43] 3 -8-100 (b) MGutierrez 7 86
(Doug O'Neill, U.S.A) *chsd ldrs: lost pl and rdn over 3 1/2f out: 6th and u.p 2f out: wknd fnl 1 1/2f* **25/1**

10 14 1/2 **To Honor And Serve (USA)**[43] 4 -9-00 JRVelazquez 12 57
(William Mott, U.S.A) *trckd ldng pair on outside: outpcd 3 1/2f out: towards rr and wl btn fr 2f out* **16/1**

11 2 1/4 **Brilliant Speed (USA)**[57] 4 -9-00 (b[1]) JAlvarado 6 53
(Thomas Albertrani, U.S.A) *towards rr of main gp: rdn and btn fr 3f out* **33/1**

12 7 1/4 **Alpha (USA)**[43] 3 -8-100 RADominguez 3 38
(Kiaran McLaughlin, U.S.A) *chsd ldrs on rail: lost pl over 4f out: wl btn fnl 2f* **25/1**

2m 0.11s (0.23)
WFA 3 from 4yo+ 4lb 12Ran SP% **121.0**
PARI-MUTUEL (all including $2 stakes): WIN 20.80; PLACE (1-2) 9.80, 6.60; SHOW (1-2-3) 6.80, 4.60, 5.20; SF 125.40 .
Owner Janis R Whitham **Bred** Janis R Whitham **Trained** USA

FOCUS
A sub-par Classic in which the winner and runner-up raced one-two more or less throughout, taking advantage of sensible fractions (23.20, 46.50, 1:10.12) on a speed-favouring track, and they had the race to themselves from the final bend. The time was impressive (winner awarded provisional Beyer speed figure of 117), but it was achieved cheaply. The first two were well clear.

NOTEBOOK
Fort Larned (USA) just like the last two winners of the Classic, had been beaten in the Jockey Club Gold Cup on his most recent outing, and in total the last four horses to have won this race on dirt all contested that Grade 1 contest at Belmont. Clearly, Fort Larned had come on a good deal for his prep, but the pace scenario/track bias helped him see out a trip he wasn't sure to stay, while the runner-up's suspect attitude gave him the edge in a thrilling battle.
Mucho Macho Man (USA) hadn't exactly impressed with his battling qualities when just denied by To Honor And Serve in the Woodward on his previous start and he couldn't get the job done this time either.
Flat Out (USA) was a well-beaten third, but nevertheless deserves a deal of credit. He's essentially a high-class plodder, so this set up gave him no hope, but he stuck to his task.
Ron The Greek (USA) stayed on from even further back but wasn't good enough.
Richard's Kid (USA) plugged on past beaten horses from last.
Game On Dude (USA) trainer wasn't happy with Rafael Bejarano's ride, believing the horse's main asset is his speed and that he needed to be ridden forwardly. The favourite, runner-up in this last year at Churchill Downs, came here with a 5-5 record at Santa Anita but was never going after making a sluggish start.

7577a GOLDIKOVA STKS (FORMERLY LAS PALMAS STAKES) (GRADE 2) (3YO+ FILLIES & MARES) (TURF) 1m (T)

11:38 (12:00) 3-Y-O+ **£58,064** (£19,354; £11,612 ; £5,806 ; £1,935)

RPR

1 **Rhythm Of Light**[64] 5849 4 -8-120 GKGomez 3 106
(Tom Dascombe) **12/5**[1]

2 1 1/2 **A Jealous Woman (USA)**[36] 6 -8-70 BBlanc 8 98
(Francis Meza, U.S.A) **37/10**[2]

3 2 1/2 **Vivo Per Lei (USA)**[35] 6730 5 -8-70 MESmith 1 92
(John Shirreffs, U.S.A) **7/1**

4 3/4 **I Dazzle (USA)**[35] 6730 4 -8-90 ow2 PValenzuela 7 92
(Jack Van Berg, U.S.A) **198/10**

5 3/4 **Hard To Resist (USA)**[46] 4 -8-70 JRLeparoux 6 88
(Peter Eurton, U.S.A) **43/5**

6 1/2 **Byrony (IRE)**[61] 4 -8-70 RBejarano 4 87
(John W Sadler, U.S.A) **39/10**[3]

7 1 1/4 **Let's Go Cheyenne (USA)**[35] 6730 4 -8-70 TBaze 2 84
(Vladimir Cerin, U.S.A) **37/10**[2]

1m 33.42s (-0.45) 7Ran SP% **120.1**
PARI-MUTUEL (all including $2 stakes): WIN 6.80; PLACE (1-2) 4.60, 5.40; SHOW (1-2-3) 3.40, 3.80, 4.40; SF 28.80 .
Owner Lowe Silver Deal **Bred** Hermes Services Ltd **Trained** Malpas, Cheshire

NOTEBOOK
Rhythm Of Light came with a strong late run from off the pace to win going away. She will now stay in the US to be trained by Simon Callaghan.

7578 - 7583a (Foreign Racing) - See Raceform Interactive

7418 LEOPARDSTOWN (L-H)

Sunday, November 4

OFFICIAL GOING: Soft (soft to heavy in places)

7584a LEOPARDSTOWN NOVEMBER H'CAP (PREMIER HANDICAP) 2m

4:05 (4:07) 3-Y-O+

£30,000 (£9,500; £4,500 ; £1,500 ; £1,000 ; £500)

RPR

1 **Face Value**[11] 7342 4 -8-272 (p) IJBrennan(3) 13 80
(Adrian McGuinness, Ire) *led: 6 l clr 1/2-way: pushed along and reduced advantage appr st: hdd under 2f out: rallied ins fnl f to ld again cl home: gamely* **12/1**

2 nk **Albert Bridge**[22] 7051 4 -9-586 JimCrowley 18 94
(Ralph Beckett) *chsd ldr: 6 l 2nd 1/2-way: niggled along 5f out: clsd to ld narrowly under 2f out: strly pressed ins fnl f and hdd cl home: jst failed* **4/1**[1]

3 3 **Shu Lewis (IRE)**[30] 6863 6 -9-1195 ShaneGorey(3) 14 100
(Ms M Dowdall Blake, Ire) *chsd ldrs: 3rd 1/2-way: brought wd into st and sn lost pl: kpt on wl again ins fnl f to go 3rd fnl strides* **14/1**

4 1/2 **Lough Ferrib (IRE)**[21] 7089 11 -8-572 WayneLordan 8 76
(J L Hassett, Ire) *hld up in tch: racd in mid-div 1/2-way: hdwy appr st and wnt n.d 4th fnl strides: nvr nrr* **7/1**[3]

5 1/2 **Bondage (IRE)**[15] 5397 5 -8-1387 (t) ColinKeane(7) 9 91
(Gordon Elliott, Ire) *hld up: hdwy fr 3f out on inner: wnt 6th u.p 1 1/2f out and kpt on same pce fnl f* **8/1**

6 1/2 **Dibella (IRE)**[91] 4666 5 -8-074 (p) SamanthaBell(7) 6 77
(Ms Joanna Morgan, Ire) *racd in mid-div: prog fr under 4f out: effrt on inner into st: sn rdn in 3rd and no ex ins fnl f* **22/1**

7 1 1/4 **Double Double (FR)**[21] 7089 6 -8-1279 DeclanMcDonogh 3 81
(Charles O'Brien, Ire) *hld up in rr: niggled along 4f out: sme late hdwy u.p fr 2f out: nrst fin* **16/1**

8 hd **Beau Michael**[8] 7424 8 -8-781 (tp) MarcMonaghan(7) 2 82
(Adrian McGuinness, Ire) *prom on far side early: 4th 1/2-way: rdn in 5th over 2f out and wknd ins fnl f* **25/1**

9 3 3/4 **Tantalising (IRE)**[21] 7089 4 -8-979 (p) RonanWhelan(3) 16 76
(P J Prendergast, Ire) *nvr bttr than mid-div: kpt on fnl f* **14/1**

10 5 1/2 **Leroy Parker (IRE)**[9] 7280 4 -8-074 ShaneGray(7) 5 65
(Noel Meade, Ire) *chsd ldrs: 6th 1/2-way: pushed along in 4th bef st and one pce fnl 2f* **16/1**

11 5 1/2 **Show Court (IRE)**[62] 5898 3 -8-1392 LeighRoche(3) 10 77
(D K Weld, Ire) *hld up in tch: pushed along in 8th under 2f out and no ex ent fnl f* **5/1**[2]

12 1 **Cry For The Moon (USA)** 7448 6 -9-586 WJLee 7 70
(J H Culloty, Ire) *hld up towards rr: hdwy fr 4f out into 9th under 2f out: sn no ex: wknd fnl f* **16/1**

13 3/4 **Giant's Quest (AUS)**[10] 6224 6 -8-777 SamJames(3) 11 60
(H Rogers, Ire) *hld up towards rr: nvr a threat* **16/1**

14 12 **Deutschland (USA)**[29] 6224 9 -8-976 (t) MichaelHussey 19 46
(W P Mullins, Ire) *nvr bttr than mid-div: eased fnl f* **16/1**

15 24 **Clare Glen (IRE)**[8] 7424 6 -9-1192 (t) EmmetMcNamara 12 36
(A Oliver, Ire) *chsd ldrs: 5th 1/2-way: rdn and wknd fr under 4f out: eased* **33/1**

16 22 **Admiral Barry (IRE)**[8] 7424 7 -9-384 JohnnyMurtagh 4 4
(Eoin Griffin, Ire) *hld up in mid-div: pushed along over 4f out and sn no imp: eased* **12/1**

17 6 1/2 **Citizenship**[8] 7424 6 -8-976 (b) NGMcCullagh 17
(Mrs John Harrington, Ire) *hld up towards rr: rdn 4f out and no imp: nvr a factor* **7/1**[3]

18 6 1/2 **The Four Elms (IRE)**[21] 7342 4 -8-976 ChrisHayes 15
(John J Walsh, Ire) *hld up in tch: 7th 1/2-way: rdn and wknd fr 4f out: eased* **10/1**

3m 46.1s (15.10) **Going Correction** +0.875s/f (Soft)
WFA 3 from 4yo+ 9lb 18Ran SP% **151.1**
Speed ratings: **97,96,95,95,94 94,93,93,92,89 86,86,85,79,67 56,53,50**
Pick Six: Not won. CSF £71.10 CT £752.50 TOTE £17.70 : £3.40 , £1.60 , £5.50 , £2.50 ; DF 110.30 .

Owner Sean F Gallagher **Bred** Biddestone Stud **Trained** Lusk, Co Dublin

FOCUS
A competitive end-of-season staying handicap although there was no real jumping star in the line-up and the withdrawal of the promising Call Me Bubbles took another bit of gloss away from it. The pace was generous but slowed up before the home turn in a canny move by the winning jockey.

NOTEBOOK
Face Value looked dead and buried 1f out. He made this into a thorough test of stamina and was half a dozen lengths clear down the back straight. That lead was quickly whittled away 2f out and he looked to be treading water passing the 1f pole when headed. However, he somehow managed to find reserves and got back up to nab the runner-up close home. It was a fine effort from a horse that has really availed of his lenient Flat rating over the last month. He'll go back hurdling now but may find life tougher in that sphere due to his lofty mark.
Albert Bridge, seventh in the Cesarewitch, was backed into favouritism and looked sure to land the gamble when hitting the front 1f out. He seemed to have the winner's measure at that stage but just came out the wrong side of a thrilling tussle in the closing stages. An excellent effort. (op 9-2)
Shu Lewis (IRE) was never too far away and was kept to the outside down the back straight. She looked to be going backwards rounding the final bend but got a second wind in the home straight and finished well to grab third. It was a fine effort off top-weight and one that will leave her spot-on ahead of the jumps campaign.
Lough Ferrib (IRE) was only just better than mid-division turning for home but did stick to his task well and remains in good heart. (op 8-1)

Bondage(IRE) was given plenty do and stayed on passed beaten horses in the home straight without ever really threatening the principals. (op 7-1 tchd 13-2)
Dibella(IRE) travelled sweetly into the home straight and looked primed to mount a major challenge 1f out. However, he failed to get home and didn't even manage to get a chuck of the place money. (op 25-1)
Show Court(IRE), representing Dermot Weld who won two of the last three runnings of the race, was never able to land a telling blow and was disappointing. (op 13-2 tchd 7-1)
Citizenship Official explanation: jockey said gelding hung badly right
T/Jkpt: @1,900.40. Pool of @7,601.80 - 3.00 winning units. T/Plt: @437.00. Pool of @25,757.63 - 44.20 winning units. BF

7585 - (Foreign Racing) - See Raceform Interactive

[7513]CAPANNELLE (R-H)
Sunday, November 4

OFFICIAL GOING: Turf: heavy

7586a PREMIO ROMA GBI RACING (GROUP 1) (3YO+) (TURF) 1m 2f
2:35 (12:00) 3-Y-0+ £79,166 (£34,833; £19,000; £9,500)

RPR
1 **Hunter's Light (IRE)**[29] 6898 4-9-2 0........................ SilvestreDeSousa 1 112+
(Saeed Bin Suroor) *trckd ldr travelling wl: eased into ld towards ins rail over 2 1/2f out: hung lft 1 1/2f out: stened for a few strides then hung across to stands' rail appr fnl f: r.o strly ins fnl f: eased cl home* **98/100**[1]
2 2 **Feuerblitz (GER)**[42] 6523 3-9-0 0........................ OlivierPeslier 5 110
(M Figge, Germany) *trckd ldrs: qcknd to ld far side over 1f out: r.o wl but no ch w wnr* **7/2**[2]
3 2 **Occhio Della Mente (IRE)**[14] 5-9-2 0..................(p) MickaelBarzalona 6 104
(E Botti, Italy) *in rr: hdwy 2f out: styd on appr fnl f: nt pce to chal* **28/1**
4 2 ½ **Waldpark (GER)**[42] 6523 4-9-2 0........................ EPedroza 3 99
(A Wohler, Germany) *midfield: rdn and short of room over 2f out: swtchd ins and sltly hmpd 1 1/2f out: styd on ins fnl f: nt pce to chal* **42/10**[3]
5 1 ¾ **Branderburgo (IRE)**[14] 7287 5-9-2 0........................ MEsposito 4 96
(M Grassi, Italy) *led: hdd over 2 1/2f out: styd prom u.p: plugged on at same pce fnl f* **10/1**
6 ¾ **Durban Thunder (GER)**[32] 6805 6-9-2 0........................ MartinHarley 7 94
(P Harley, Germany) *prom on outside: qcknd to ld narrowly under 3f out: hdd over 2 1/2f out: wknd 1 1/2f out* **48/10**
7 3 **Ostinato (GER)**[32] 6805 4-9-2 0........................(b) KKerekes 2 88
(Sandor Kovacs, Hungary) *towards rr: last whn rdn and no imp 2f out: styd on ins fnl f: nvr in contention* **115/10**

2m 3.38s (0.08)
WFA 3 from 4yo+ 4lb 7 Ran SP% **129.7**
WIN (incl. 1 euro stake): 1.98. PLACES: 1.30, 1.69. DF: 3.33.
Owner Godolphin **Bred** Darley **Trained** Newmarket, Suffolk
■ Silvestre De Sousa's first Group 1 winner for Godolphin.

NOTEBOOK
Hunter's Light(IRE) managed to win his first Group 1 despite hanging all the way over to the stands' rail. He will now head for the big international meeting in Hong Kong next month and will stay in training next year.

7587a PREMIO RIBOT (GROUP 2) (3YO+) (TURF) 1m
3:10 (12:00) 3-Y-0+ £39,583 (£17,416; £9,500; £4,750)

RPR
1 **King Air (FR)**[35] 6727 5-9-2 0........................ StephanePasquier 3 109
(R Pritchard-Gordon, France) *midfield: rdn 3f out: r.o to ld 1 1/2f out: styd on wl and sn clr: readily* **39/10**[3]
2 2 **Saint Bernard**[147] 2969 3-9-1 0........................ SSulas 5 105
(D Camuffo, Italy) *hld up: rdn 2f out: styd on to go 2nd ins fnl f: no ch w wnr* **78/1**
3 ¾ **Douce Vie (IRE)**[14] 7286 6-9-2 0........................ FabioBranca 7 103
(S Botti, Italy) *midfield on inner: swtchd out and rdn to improve 3f out: styd on to go 3rd wl ins fnl f: nt pce to chal* **4/1**
4 ½ **Point Blank (GER)**[28] 6906 4-9-2 0........................ StefanieHofer 2 102
(Mario Hofer, Germany) *trckd ldr: rdn 3f out: wnt 2nd 1 1/2f out: qckly outpcd by wnr: styd on but dropped to 4th wl ins fnl f* **36/5**
5 2 ½ **Monami (GER)**[35] 6727 3-8-11 0........................ EPedroza 4 93
(A Wohler, Germany) *prom: rdn 3f out: sn outpcd: plugged on* **13/5**[1]
6 2 **Cielo Canarias (IRE)**[77] 4-9-2 0........................ J-LMartinez 6 91
(E Leon Penate, Spain) *midfield: rdn 3f out: sn outpcd: plugged on* **15/2**
7 1 ¾ **Malossol (USA)**[14] 7286 3-9-1 0........................ DarioVargiu 8 88
(G Botti, Italy) *midfield on outer: rdn over 2f out: outpcd and btn ent fnl f: plugged on* **114/10**
8 3 **Ransom Hope**[14] 7286 7-9-2 0........................ CristianDemuro 13 80
(L Riccardi, Italy) *hld up in last: rdn 3f out: sme late hdwy but nvr a factor* **92/10**
9 1 ½ **Combat Zone (IRE)**[14] 7286 6-9-4 0........................ OlivierPeslier 11 79
(Mario Hofer, Germany) *hld up: rdn 3f out: btn 2f out: nvr a factor* **19/5**[2]
10 2 ½ **Principe Adepto (USA)**[126] 4-9-2 0........................ MickaelBarzalona 12 71
(E Botti, Italy) *led: rdn 3f out: hdd 1 1/2f out and sn btn: fdd* **92/10**
11 2 ½ **Le Vie Infinite (IRE)**[175] 5-9-2 0........................ AndreaMezzatesta 1 65
(R Brogi, Italy) *prom on inner: rdn 3f out: outpcd 2f out: sn no ex and btn: fdd* **56/1**
12 10 **Silver Arrow (ITY)**[35] 7-9-2 0........................ CFiocchi 9 42
(R Menichetti, Italy) *a towards rr: last and btn over 2f out: nvr a factor* **14/1**

1m 39.03s (-0.77)
WFA 3 from 4yo+ 2lb 12 Ran SP% **150.3**
WIN (incl. 1 euro stake): 4.90. PLACES: 2.54, 18.78, 2.50. DF: 286.20.
Owner Pearl Bloodstock Ltd **Bred** A-P Larrieu & Chevin Bloodstock Ltd **Trained** France

[6723]HANOVER (L-H)
Sunday, November 4

OFFICIAL GOING: Turf: good

7588a CAMPANOLOGIST-CUP (LISTED RACE) (FILLIES) (TURF) 7f
12:30 (12:37) 2-Y-0 £10,000 (£3,666; £2,000; £1,000)

RPR
1 **Dancing Shuffle (GER)** 2-9-2 0........................ DPorcu 1 87
(S Smrczek, Germany) **101/10**
2 shd **Give Way Nelson (IRE)**[37] 6644 2-9-2 0........................ JoeFanning 7 86
(Brian Meehan) *broke wl and led: rdn and qcknd clr under 2f out: rdn and r.o fr 1f out: hrd pressed thrght fnl f: hdd fnl strides* **53/10**
3 shd **Charlie Em**[13] 7289 2-9-2 0........................ JohnFahy 8 86
(Brendan Powell) *broke wl: trckd ldr on outside: rdn and briefly outpcd under 2f out: rallied and pressed ldr thrght fnl f: no ex cl home* **31/10**[2]
4 ½ **Isioma**[67] 5755 2-9-2 0........................ AndreBest 5 85
(Mario Hofer, Germany) **149/10**
5 11 **Librettista (FR)** 2-9-2 0........................ PJWerning 2 56
(I G Ivanov, Bulgaria) **3/1**[1]
6 2 ½ **Agama (GER)**[56] 2-9-2 0........................ FilipMinarik 4 50
(C Sprengel, Germany) **7/2**[3]
7 hd **Vesper (GER)**[51] 6225 2-9-2 0........................ AStarke 3 49
(M Munch, Germany) **94/10**
8 1 **Sydney City (GER)** 2-9-2 0........................ DennisSchiergen 9 46
(W Mongil, Germany) **27/1**
9 4 **La Sabara** 2-9-2 0........................ JBojko 6 36
(A Wohler, Germany) **49/10**

1m 37.72s (97.72) 9 Ran SP% **132.9**
WIN (incl. 10 euro stake): 111. PLACES: 26, 25, 16. SF: 1118.
Owner Frau L Godde **Bred** Stud Rheinberg AG **Trained** Germany

[7523]WOLVERHAMPTON (A.W) (L-H)
Monday, November 5

OFFICIAL GOING: Standard
Wind: Fresh across Weather: Fine

7589 HOTEL & CONFERENCING AT WOLVERHAMPTON H'CAP (DIV I) 5f 216y(P)
1:45 (1:45) (Class 6) (0-65,65) 3-Y-0+ £1,704 (£503; £251) Stalls Low

Form RPR
6000 1 **Gung Ho Jack**[32] 6825 3-9-6 **65**........................ JamesDoyle 9 75
(John Best) *mid-div: hdwy over 2f out: r.o to ld nr fin* **11/2**[2]
-000 2 nk **Passionada**[27] 6961 3-9-3 **62**........................ SeanLevey 1 71
(Ed McMahon) *sn led: rdn over 1f out: hdd nr fin* **12/1**
6400 3 nk **Waabel**[13] 7308 5-9-1 **65**........................(t) CharlesBishop[(5)] 3 73
(Violet M Jordan) *chsd ldrs: rdn and ev ch ins fnl f: r.o* **10/1**
0100 4 nk **Dickie Le Davoir**[15] 7273 8-9-3 **62**........................(b) RobbieFitzpatrick 6 69
(Richard Guest) *sn pushed along in rr: r.o ins fnl f: nt rch ldrs* **10/1**
6254 5 3 ½ **Powerful Pierre**[17] 7218 5-9-4 **63**........................(v) DaleSwift 13 60
(Ian McInnes) *prom: lost pl 4f out: rdn over 2f out: edgd lft and r.o ins fnl f* **7/1**[3]
-020 6 ½ **Sir Nod**[51] 6264 10-9-6 **65**........................ BarryMcHugh 10 63
(Julie Camacho) *s.i.s: hld up: hdwy and nt clr run over 2f out: hmpd wl over 1f out: sn rdn: styd on: nt trble ldrs* **8/1**
0000 7 2 ½ **Dashwood**[28] 6926 5-9-0 **62**........................ RyanClark[(3)] 12 50
(Anthony Carson) *sn pushed along in rr: rdn over 2f out: nvr on terms* **15/2**
3000 8 hd **Cape Of Storms**[182] 1910 9-9-2 **61**........................(b) AdamKirby 4 48
(Roy Brotherton) *s.i.s: sn prom: rdn over 1f out: wknd fnl f* **28/1**
2150 9 shd **Amosite**[62] 5915 6-9-5 **64**........................(p) FrederikTylicki 7 51
(J R Jenkins) *mid-div: sn pushed along: rdn 1/2-way: wknd over 1f out* **20/1**
140- 10 3 **Yellow Dandy (IRE)**[17] 7226 4-9-5 **64**........................ AndreaAtzeni 8 42
(Liam McAteer, Ire) *prom: rdn over 2f out: wknd fnl f* **7/2**[1]
0600 11 ½ **Chjimes (IRE)**[17] 7218 8-9-2 **61**........................(b) HayleyTurner 11 37
(Conor Dore) *chsd ldrs: rdn over 2f out: wknd wl over 1f out* **40/1**
3400 12 hd **Wiltshire Life (IRE)**[39] 6610 3-9-2 **64**........................(p) RaulDaSilva[(3)] 5 40
(Jeremy Gask) *chsd ldrs tl rdn and wknd over 1f out* **12/1**
1300 13 64 **Seventeen Seventy**[94] 4777 3-9-3 **62**........................ LiamKeniry 2
(Alan Coogan) *sn outpcd: bhd fnl 4f: t.o* **25/1**

1m 13.82s (-1.18) **Going Correction** -0.15s/f (Stan) 13 Ran SP% **121.0**
Speed ratings (Par 101): **101,100,100,99,95 94,91,90,90,86 86,85,**
toteswingers 1&2 £14.70, 1&3 £13.10, 2&3 £15.70 CSF £67.60 CT £676.90 TOTE £7.40: £2.00, £6.40, £3.10; EX 76.90 Trifecta £366.30 Part won. Pool: £488.41 - 0.62 winning units..
Owner John Fletcher **Bred** D R Tucker **Trained** Hucking, Kent

FOCUS
The time of this modest handicap was 0.63 seconds quicker than the second division. A rather rough, messy race, with the form rated around the runner-up.
Yellow Dandy(IRE) Official explanation: trainer said filly was unsuited by the Polytrack

7590 HOTEL & CONFERENCING AT WOLVERHAMPTON H'CAP (DIV II) 5f 216y(P)
2:15 (2:16) (Class 6) (0-65,65) 3-Y-0+ £1,704 (£503; £251) Stalls Low

Form RPR
4303 1 **Dark Lane**[17] 7218 6-9-5 **63**........................ AdamKirby 6 72
(David Evans) *a.p: r.o u.p to ld wl ins fnl f* **5/1**[2]
0043 2 nse **Lastkingofscotland (IRE)**[5] 7485 6-9-5 **63**........................(b) HayleyTurner 2 72
(Conor Dore) *s.i.s: hld up: hdwy over 1f out: rdn and edgd lft ins fnl f: r.o* **7/2**[1]
0152 3 ½ **Catalinas Diamond (IRE)**[102] 4493 4-9-4 **62**........................(t) SebSanders 9 69
(Pat Murphy) *chsd ldr: led 1f out: rdn and hdd wl ins fnl f* **20/1**
5306 4 ¾ **Keep It Dark**[7] 7447 3-9-7 **65**........................ BarryMcHugh 3 70
(Tony Coyle) *a.p: rdn and edgd lft ins fnl f: styd on* **8/1**
1534 5 hd **Trending (IRE)**[32] 6825 3-9-1 **62**........................(b) RaulDaSilva[(3)] 10 66
(Jeremy Gask) *hld up: plld hrd: hdwy over 1f out: sn rdn: r.o* **15/2**
4040 6 2 ¾ **Fenella Fudge**[53] 6176 4-9-6 **64**........................(v) MartinDwyer 1 60
(Derek Shaw) *mid-div: pushed along over 2f out: rdn and hung lft fr over 1f out: styd on: nt rch ldrs* **14/1**
3301 7 ½ **Belinsky (IRE)**[60] 5971 5-9-6 **64**........................(v) JimCrowley 5 58
(Julie Camacho) *hld up: rdn over 1f out: styd on ins fnl f: nvr nrr* **9/1**
3012 8 1 **Athwaab**[10] 7382 5-9-3 **61**........................ GeorgeBaker 11 52
(Noel Chance) *chsd ldrs: lost pl wl over 3f out: n.d after* **7/1**[3]
1-2 9 2 ½ **Just Breathe (IRE)**[292] 201 3-9-7 **65**........................ KirstyMilczarek 4 49
(Olivia Maylam) *chsd ldrs: rdn over 2f out: hmpd and wknd ins fnl f* **7/1**[3]
5160 10 ¾ **Auntie Mabel**[13] 7307 3-9-2 **60**........................(v) DavidProbert 13 42
(Andrew Balding) *mid-div: sn pushed along: lost pl over 3f out: n.d after* **25/1**
3210 11 1 **Miss Polly Plum**[47] 6378 5-9-4 **62**........................(p) AndreaAtzeni 12 41
(Chris Dwyer) *led: rdn and hdd 1f out: sn wknd* **25/1**
0050 12 ½ **Ishetoo**[32] 6825 8-9-4 **62**........................ RobbieFitzpatrick 7 39
(Peter Grayson) *prom: pushed along 1/2-way: rdn and wknd 2f out* **50/1**

1m 14.45s (-0.55) **Going Correction** -0.15s/f (Stan) 12 Ran SP% **117.8**
Speed ratings (Par 101): **97,96,96,95,95 91,90,89,86,85 83,83**
toteswingers 1&2 £6.20, 1&3 £14.80, 2&3 £15.00 CSF £21.61 CT £329.90 TOTE £6.10: £2.00, £2.10, £5.60; EX 19.80 Trifecta £180.80 Pool: £723.49 - 3.00 winning units..

The Form Book Flat, Raceform Ltd, Compton, RG20 6NL

Owner Jason Tucker **Bred** David Jamison Bloodstock **Trained** Pandy, Monmouths
FOCUS
A slower time than the first division by 0.63 seconds. Straightforward form, rated around the runner-up.

7591 WOLVERHAMPTON-RACECOURSE.CO.UK (S) STKS 5f 20y(P)
2:50 (2:50) (Class 6) 3-5-Y-O £1,704 (£503; £251) Stalls Low

Form RPR
4004 **1** **Alaskan Bullet (IRE)**31 6837 3-9-3 80 GeorgeBaker 8 85
(Brian Ellison) *hld up: hdwy 1/2-way: chsd ldr over 1f out: r.o to ld wl ins fnl f: sn clr* **4/6**1
0500 **2** 5 **Powerful Wind (IRE)**16 7254 3-9-9 80 (p) JamesDoyle 9 73
(Ronald Harris) *led and sn clr: rdn: hdd and no ex wl ins fnl f* **4/1**2
2200 **3** 1 3/4 **Funcheon Vale (IRE)**31 6836 3-8-12 58 RobertHavlin 2 56
(Hughie Morrison) *chsd ldr tl rdn over 1f out: styd on same pce* **20/1**
5000 **4** 3/4 **Volcanic Dust (IRE)**17 7218 4-8-12 62 (b1) LiamKeniry 12 53
(Milton Bradley) *s.i.s: hld up: nt clr run wl over 2f out: swtchd rt sn after: rdn and r.o ins fnl f: nvr nrr* **28/1**
0264 **5** 1 1/2 **First Fast Now (IRE)**28 6935 3-8-5 49 DanielleMooney(7) 3 48
(Nigel Tinkler) *sn pushed along in rr: hdwy 1/2-way: nt clr run wl over 1f out: nvr on terms* **50/1**
4100 **6** 1 3/4 **Ice Trooper**32 6825 4-9-9 68 (p) DarryllHolland 11 52
(Linda Stubbs) *prom: rdn over 1f out: wknd fnl f* **10/1**3
06 **7** nk **Myjestic Melody (IRE)**46 6403 4-8-12 48 MartinLane 1 40
(Noel Wilson) *prom: rdn 1/2-way: wknd over 1f out* **25/1**
0502 **8** 1/2 **Nine Before Ten (IRE)**44 6496 4-8-9 57 (t) MarkCoumbe(3) 5 38
(Charles Smith) *hld up: rdn over 1f out: n.d* **18/1**
00 **9** 1 **Rose Madder**19 7158 3-8-12 0 FrankieMcDonald 6 35
(Roger Curtis) *sn pushed along and a in rr* **50/1**
2440 **10** 2 1/4 **Deveze (IRE)**154 2760 4-9-4 49 (b) HayleyTurner 4 33
(Milton Bradley) *chsd ldrs: rdn 1/2-way: wknd over 1f out* **50/1**
0006 **11** 2 3/4 **Simpson Millar**45 6429 3-9-3 45 (b1) KellyHarrison 10 22
(Noel Wilson) *s.i.s: outpcd* **80/1**
0006 **12** hd **Choice Words (USA)**17 7218 4-9-0 61 (t) AshleyMorgan(3) 7 21
(Natalie Lloyd-Beavis) *chsd ldrs: rdn 1/2-way: wknd wl over 1f out* **20/1**
1m 1.16s (-1.14) **Going Correction** -0.15s/f (Stan) 12 Ran SP% 118.3
Speed ratings (Par 101): **103,95,92,91,88 85,85,84,82,79 74,74**
toteswingers 1&2 £1.90, 1&3 £4.70, 2&3 £6.60 CSF £2.80 TOTE £1.60: £1.02, £2.50, £3.80; EX 4.30 Trifecta £27.70 Pool: £1,331.62 - 35.97 winning units..The winner was bought in for 6,500gns. Powerful Wind was subject to a friendly claim.
Owner M Khan X2 **Bred** Pat Heffernan **Trained** Norton, N Yorks
FOCUS
This only concerned the front two, but the time was just 0.15 seconds slower than the later Class 4 handicap. Things were set up nicely for the winner.

7592 ENJOY THE PUNTERS PACKAGE GROUP OFFER MAIDEN AUCTION STKS 1m 141y(P)
3:20 (3:21) (Class 5) 2-Y-O £2,264 (£673; £336; £168) Stalls Low

Form RPR
3404 **1** **Rainbow Beauty**12 7335 2-8-11 71 (tp) NickyMackay 2 66
(Gerard Butler) *led 1f: chsd ldrs: r.o u.p to ld nr fin* **10/3**2
0 **2** nk **Inessa Armand (IRE)**31 6841 2-8-7 0 AndreaAtzeni 11 61
(J S Moore) *chsd ldrs: led over 2f out: rdn and hung lft ins fnl f: hdd nr fin* **16/1**
2 **3** 1 1/2 **High Time Too (IRE)**19 7165 2-8-7 0 JimmyQuinn 6 58
(Hugo Palmer) *s.i.s: hdwy over 6f out: rdn and ev ch ins fnl f: styd on same pce* **10/3**2
0000 **4** 1 3/4 **Admirals Walk (IRE)**23 7060 2-9-1 66 JamesDoyle 1 63
(Sylvester Kirk) *hld up: hdwy over 2f out: rdn over 1f out: styng on whn hmpd ins fnl f: nvr able to chal* **8/1**
053 **5** 1 3/4 **Lucky Black Star (IRE)**31 6841 2-9-2 67 SeanLevey 7 60
(George Baker) *led over 7f out: rdn and hdd over 2f out: wknd wl ins fnl f* **7/1**3
0666 **6** 1 **Garmelow Girl**13 7313 2-8-7 42 (b) AmyRyan 5 49
(Kevin Ryan) *chsd ldrs: rdn over 2f out: wknd fnl f* **25/1**
00 **7** nse **Damian One**33 6796 2-8-13 0 (v) LiamKeniry 3 55
(Joseph Tuite) *chsd ldrs: rdn over 3f out: wknd over 1f out* **28/1**
063 **8** shd **Taxiformissbyron**33 6781 2-8-4 52 JamesSullivan 4 45+
(Ollie Pears) *hld up: rdn over 3f out: n.d* **33/1**
0 **9** 15 **Belatorio (IRE)**26 6985 2-8-9 0 DaleSwift 10 19
(James Given) *hld up: rdn 1/2-way: bhd fnl 3f* **40/1**
5 **P** **Rainestorm (IRE)**21 7096 2-9-2 0 JoeFanning 8
(Mark Johnston) *s.i.s: sn pushed along in rr: no ch whn broke leg and p.u wl ins fnl f: fatally injured* **11/4**1
1m 51.5s (1.00) **Going Correction** -0.15s/f (Stan) 10 Ran SP% 115.0
Speed ratings (Par 96): **89,88,87,85,84 83,83,83,69,**
toteswingers 1&2 £6.90, 1&3 £2.90, 2&3 £5.60 CSF £50.74 TOTE £6.00: £1.60, £5.70, £1.10; EX 51.40 Trifecta £178.50 Pool: £1,664.40 - 6.99 winning units..
Owner D O'Donohoe & J Cavanagh **Bred** Mascalls Stud **Trained** Newmarket, Suffolk
FOCUS
A weak 2-y-o maiden but the form makes sense.
NOTEBOOK
Rainbow Beauty, rated 71, gain her first win on her seventh start. She had a tongue-tie on for the first time, but didn't need to improve and things are likely to be tougher from now on. (op 5-2 tchd 7-2)
Inessa Armand(IRE) was behind Lucky Black Star on her debut over C&D but she improved on that form, showing enough to suggest she can win a small race if continuing to go the right way. (op 10-1 tchd 20-1)
High Time Too(IRE) went without the hood she had fitted when second on her debut at Lingfield and failed to progress. (op 11-4 tchd 7-2)
Admirals Walk(IRE) was keeping on when hampered with just under a furlong to run. That cost him his chance, but it's doubtful he'd have troubled the winner and he had enjoyed a ground-saving trip, so it might be dangerous to get carried way. (op 17-2 tchd 7-1)
Lucky Black Star(IRE) was below the form he showed when third over C&D (today's runner-up behind) on his previous start. (op 8-1 tchd 10-1 and 6-1)
Rainestorm(IRE), who looked too green to do himself justice on his debut at Musselburgh, was never going this time either and sadly broke his leg in the straight. (op 11-2)

7593 HOLIDAY INN WOLVERHAMPTON H'CAP 1m 141y(P)
3:55 (3:55) (Class 6) (0-60,60) 3-Y-O+ £1,704 (£503; £251) Stalls Low

Form RPR
0032 **1** **Aragorn Rouge**4 7500 4-8-13 52 JoeFanning 10 63+
(Keith Dalgleish) *chsd ldrs: shkn up to ld over 1f out: r.o* **11/8**1
6604 **2** 3/4 **Flipping**10 7385 5-8-13 52 DavidAllan 2 61+
(Eric Alston) *prom: nt clr run and lost pl over 3f out: rallied over 1f out: r.o* **11/1**
1104 **3** 3 1/4 **Community (USA)**17 7225 4-9-1 59 LeonnaMayor(5) 3 61
(Jamie Osborne) *prom: outpcd over 2f out: styd on to go 3rd post* **25/1**
335 **4** nk **Zenafire**11 7361 3-8-11 58 JackDuern(5) 12 59
(Reg Hollinshead) *s.i.s: hld up: hdwy over 3f out: rdn over 1f out: styd on same pce fnl f* **20/1**
6222 **5** nk **Goal (IRE)**10 7385 4-9-0 53 (tp) AdamKirby 9 53
(Charles Smith) *sn chsng ldr: led over 2f out: rdn and hdd over 1f out: no ex ins fnl f* **11/2**2
0260 **6** 1/2 **Calypso Cay**27 6967 4-9-4 57 AdamBeschizza 7 56
(Peter Salmon) *led: rdn and hdd over 2f out: ev ch over 1f out: no ex ins fnl f* **16/1**
0601 **7** 3/4 **Maggie Pink**12 7326 3-9-0 56 DominicFox 6 53
(Michael Appleby) *hld up: n.m.r and stmbld after 1f: rdn over 2f out: r.o ins fnl f: nvr nrr* **14/1**
4314 **8** 3/4 **Dubai Celebration**36 6711 4-9-6 59 PaddyAspell 1 55
(Julie Camacho) *chsd ldrs: rdn over 1f out: wknd ins fnl f* **8/1**3
0000 **9** 1 1/4 **Odd Ball (IRE)**10 7382 5-9-2 55 AmyRyan 8 48
(Lisa Williamson) *s.i.s: hld up: shkn up over 1f out: nvr on terms* **25/1**
6324 **10** hd **Parque Atlantico**20 7148 3-9-3 59 SeanLevey 5 51
(Ed McMahon) *prom: rdn over 2f out: wknd ins fnl f* **8/1**3
0455 **11** 1 1/4 **Keys Of Cyprus**10 7382 10-9-1 54 AdrianNicholls 4 43
(David Nicholls) *hld up: pushed along over 3f out: n.d* **28/1**
3060 **12** 3 **Kyle Of Bute**16 7251 6-9-7 60 (p) KellyHarrison 13 42
(Brian Baugh) *hld up: a in rr* **40/1**
1m 49.13s (-1.37) **Going Correction** -0.15s/f (Stan)
WFA 3 from 4yo+ 3lb 12 Ran SP% 118.9
Speed ratings (Par 101): **100,99,96,96,95 95,94,94,93,92 91,89**
toteswingers 1&2 £5.30, 1&3 £12.50, 2&3 £31.80 CSF £16.29 CT £278.64 TOTE £2.60: £1.30, £4.70, £4.80; EX 21.20 Trifecta £203.40 Pool: £1,470.06 - 5.42 winning units..
Owner Keith Dalgleish **Bred** Gerard Kerin **Trained** Carluke, S Lanarks
FOCUS
A moderate handicap run at what looked just an ordinary pace. Quite an interesting race for the level with the first two clear.

7594 SPONSOR A RACE BY CALLING 01902 390000 MAIDEN STKS 1m 4f 50y(P)
4:25 (4:25) (Class 5) 3-Y-O+ £2,264 (£673; £336; £168) Stalls Low

Form RPR
66-2 **1** **Epic Storm (IRE)**39 6614 4-9-10 76 JamesDoyle 9 75
(Sean Curran) *hld up and bhd: hdwy over 2f out: rdn to ld over 1f out: edgd lft: styd on* **4/1**2
0044 **2** 1 1/4 **Unex Renoir**16 7252 4-9-7 58 MarkCoumbe(3) 5 73
(Brian Ellison) *a.p: led over 2f out: rdn and hdd over 1f out: styd on same pce ins fnl f* **9/1**
2-44 **3** hd **Pacific Heights (IRE)**24 7016 3-9-4 78 (p) ShaneKelly 10 73
(Tim Pitt) *chsd ldrs: rdn and ev ch over 1f out: styd on same pce ins fnl f* **11/2**3
40 **4** 6 **Entitlement**68 5753 3-8-13 0 JimCrowley 4 58
(James Fanshawe) *hld up: hdwy over 2f out: rdn over 1f out: wknd fnl f* **18/1**
433 **5** 2 **Maun Vrat (IRE)**31 6839 3-8-13 77 GrahamLee 3 55
(Ed Dunlop) *chsd ldrs: rdn over 3f out: wknd over 1f out* **6/5**1
6 **6** 3/4 **Ginger Fizz**25 7011 5-9-5 0 MartinDwyer 8 54
(Ben Case) *chsd ldr: jinked rt over 8f out: led over 4f out: rdn and hdd over 2f out: wknd over 1f out* **12/1**
06 **7** 1 3/4 **Tram Express (FR)**11 7352 8-9-5 0 (t) LeonnaMayor(5) 7 56
(Shaun Lycett) *s.i.s: hld up and bhd: drvn along over 2f out: nvr on terms* **100/1**
4- **8** 24 **Wolf Heart (IRE)**410 6286 4-9-10 0 J-PGuillambert 6 17
(Lucinda Russell) *s.i.s: hld up: rdn and wknd over 3f out: t.o* **12/1**
00 **9** 11 **Slide Show**11 7352 4-9-5 54 (b1) DaleSwift 1
(Colin Teague) *led: rdn and hdd over 4f out: wknd over 3f out: t.o* **100/1**
2m 37.97s (-3.13) **Going Correction** -0.15s/f (Stan)
WFA 3 from 4yo+ 6lb 9 Ran SP% 113.5
Speed ratings (Par 103): **104,103,103,99,97 97,96,80,72**
toteswingers 1&2 £5.80, 1&3 £4.50, 2&3 £8.30 CSF £38.90 TOTE £2.80: £1.10, £3.20, £1.90; EX 37.40 Trifecta £184.50 Pool: £1,853.00 - 7.53 winning units..
Owner L M Power **Bred** Lynch Bages Ltd **Trained** Hatford, Oxon
FOCUS
The form of this maiden probably isn't worth much, but is straightforward enough. The first three were clear.

7595 WOLVERHAMPTON-RACECOURSE.CO.UK H'CAP 5f 20y(P)
4:55 (4:56) (Class 4) (0-85,85) 3-Y-O+ £5,175 (£1,540; £769; £384) Stalls Low

Form RPR
4200 **1** **Church Music (IRE)**45 6427 3-9-3 81 (p) PaulMulrennan 3 89
(Michael Scudamore) *chsd ldrs: pushed along 1/2-way: r.o u.p to ld wl ins fnl f* **28/1**
5412 **2** nk **Drawnfromthepast (IRE)**13 7309 7-9-3 81 FergusSweeney 1 88
(Jamie Osborne) *chsd ldrs: led over 1f out: rdn and hdd wl ins fnl f: r.o* **6/1**
4055 **3** 3/4 **Damika (IRE)**14 7295 9-9-5 83 (v) MichaelStainton 6 87
(David Brown) *sn pushed along in rr: hdwy over 1f out: r.o* **20/1**
5520 **4** 1 1/2 **Clear Praise (USA)**34 6767 5-9-6 84 SebSanders 13 83
(Simon Dow) *sn pushed along towards rr: rdn over 1f out: r.o ins fnl f: nt rch ldrs* **15/2**
6U20 **5** 1 3/4 **Pea Shooter**37 6688 3-9-5 83 (t) AmyRyan 4 75
(Kevin Ryan) *led: rdn: edgd rt and hdd over 1f out: no ex ins fnl f* **11/2**3
1600 **6** nk **Hamoody (USA)**44 6465 8-9-2 80 AdrianNicholls 7 71
(David Nicholls) *s.s: bhd and reminders 4f out: hung lft and r.o ins fnl f: nvr nrr* **20/1**
6601 **7** 2 1/2 **Baby Strange**14 7291 8-9-3 81 (v) MartinDwyer 8 63
(Derek Shaw) *s.i.s: rdn over 1f out: nvr on terms* **12/1**
-154 **8** 1 **Queen Grace (IRE)**37 6689 5-9-4 82 JimCrowley 9 61
(Michael J Browne, Ire) *prom: rdn 2f out: wknd fnl f* **10/1**
1103 **9** 1/2 **Island Legend (IRE)**185 1828 6-9-7 85 (p) HayleyTurner 12 62
(Milton Bradley) *sn chsng ldr: rdn and ev ch over 1f out: wknd ins fnl f* **20/1**
0020 **10** nse **Partner (IRE)**16 7243 6-9-4 82 (b) GrahamLee 10 59
(Noel Wilson) *s.i.s: outpcd* **9/2**2
0000 **11** 1 **Khawatim**28 6938 4-9-4 82 MartinLane 5 55
(Noel Quinlan) *sn outpcd* **40/1**
1004 **12** 1/2 **Decision By One**28 6939 3-9-5 83 (t) StephenCraine 2 54
(Tom Dascombe) *chsd ldrs: rdn 1/2-way: wknd over 1f out* **7/2**1
1m 1.01s (-1.29) **Going Correction** -0.15s/f (Stan) 12 Ran SP% 118.8
Speed ratings (Par 105): **104,103,102,99,97 96,92,91,90,90 88,87**
toteswingers 1&2 £12.70, 1&3 £45.80, 2&3 £19.00 CSF £178.08 CT £3498.01 TOTE £25.40: £8.30, £1.40, £6.00; EX 278.50 TRIFECTA Not won..

Owner JCG Chua & CK Ong **Bred** Mrs Ellen Lyons **Trained** Bromsash, H'fords

FOCUS

A fair sprint handicap run at a good pace. Straightforward form.

Queen Grace(IRE) Official explanation: trainer said, on return, the mare was found to be coughing and had a very high temperature.

7596 BOOK HORIZONS RESTAURANT AT WOLVERHAMPTON RACECOURSE H'CAP 1m 4f 50y(P)

5:25 (5:25) (Class 6) (0-65,65) 3-Y-O+ **£1,704** (£503; £251) **Stalls** Low

Form RPR

026 **1** **Badea**[31] 6842 3-9-3 **65**....(v) TonyHamilton 11 76
(Richard Fahey) *a.p: led over 2f out: sn rdn clr: eased nr fin* **5/1**[2]

620- **2** *3 ½* **Viva Diva**[17] 7232 4-9-9 **65**.... JamesSullivan 4 71+
(John C McConnell, Ire) *hld up: hdwy over 2f out: rdn to go 2nd ins fnl f: no ch w wnr* **13/2**[3]

0320 **3** *3* **Holden Eagle**[53] 6170 7-9-2 **65**.... IanBurns(7) 3 66
(Tony Newcombe) *chsd ldrs: rdn over 2f out: styd on* **7/1**

205 **4** *shd* **Kames Park (IRE)**[10] 7381 10-9-6 **62**.... RobbieFitzpatrick 12 63
(Richard Guest) *s.i.s: hld up: rdn and r.o ins fnl f: nrst fin* **16/1**

050 **5** *¾* **Strike Force**[45] 6458 8-9-7 **63**....(t) TomEaves 2 63
(Alison Hutchinson) *hld up: hdwy over 1f out: nt trble ldrs* **22/1**

2042 **6** *hd* **Jalors (IRE)**[31] 6838 4-9-9 **65**.... JamesDoyle 7 65
(Ronald Harris) *chsd ldrs: led 4f out: rdn and hdd over 2f out: wknd fnl f* **7/2**[1]

1401 **7** *nse* **Pindar (GER)**[14] 4817 8-9-4 **60**.... TomQueally 5 60
(Barney Curley) *led: hdd 6f out: chsd ldrs: rdn over 2f out: styd on same pce fr over 1f out* **5/1**[2]

1000 **8** *1* **Shirataki (IRE)**[13] 7310 4-9-9 **65**.... JimCrowley 6 63
(Peter Hiatt) *chsd ldrs: rdn over 2f out: wknd fnl f* **10/1**

4400 **9** *8* **Before Bruce**[26] 6981 5-9-5 **61**....(tp) SeanLevey 1 47
(Brendan Powell) *hld up: rdn over 3f out: wknd over 2f out* **28/1**

2302 **10** *5* **Elegant Ophelia**[21] 7108 3-9-2 **64**.... DarryllHolland 9 43
(Dean Ivory) *hld up: drvn along over 3f out: wknd over 2f out* **10/1**

-403 **11** *¾* **Mesariya (IRE)**[30] 6885 4-9-4 **60**.... BarryMcHugh 8 37
(Tony Coyle) *s.i.s: hld up: a in rr: rdn and wknd over 2f out* **28/1**

0060 **12** *22* **Bennelong**[19] 7169 6-9-6 **62**....(p) AmirQuinn 10 6
(Richard Rowe) *sn prom: led 6f out: hdd 4f out: sn rdn and wknd: t.o* **28/1**

2m 38.3s (-2.80) **Going Correction** -0.15s/f (Stan)

WFA 3 from 4yo+ 6lb **12** Ran SP% **120.1**

Speed ratings (Par 101): **103,100,98,98,98 97,97,97,91,88 88,73**

toteswingers 1&2 £4.50, 1&3 £6.30, 2&3 £10.50 CSF £36.30 CT £225.51 TOTE £6.70: £2.60, £4.00, £2.30; EX 47.00 Trifecta £391.70 Pool: £1,582.59 - 3.03 winning units..

Owner Dr Marwan Koukash **Bred** N J Hughes **Trained** Musley Bank, N Yorks

FOCUS

This form looks pretty limited, and could be rated a bit higher. They didn't seem to go that strong a pace.

Jalors(IRE) Official explanation: vet said gelding finished lame left-fore

T/Jkpt: £8,875.00 to a £1 stake. Pool: £25,000.0 - 2.00 winning tickets T/Plt: £140.30 to a £1 stake. Pool: £67,914.61 - 353.13 winning tickets T/Qpdt: £19.10 to a £1 stake. Pool: £7,355.90 - 284.40 winning tickets CR

7122 CHANTILLY (R-H)

Monday, November 5

OFFICIAL GOING: Turf: very soft; polytrack: standard

7597a PRIX WELLS (MAIDEN) (2YO) (POLYTRACK) 7f

1:35 (12:00) 2-Y-O **£10,000** (£4,000; £3,000; £2,000; £1,000)

RPR

1 **Looking At Glory (IRE)**[35] 2-9-2 0.... MaximeGuyon 5 75
(A Fabre, France) **59/10**[3]

2 *1* **Kiss Me Goodbye**[23] 2-8-13 0.... ThierryThulliez 14 69
(P Bary, France) **48/10**[2]

3 *snk* **Maurice (GER)**[22] 7091 2-9-2 0.... EddyHardouin 10 72
(S Smrczek, Germany) **48/10**[2]

4 *¾* **Le Deluge (FR)**[126] 3714 2-9-2 0.... OlivierPeslier 7 70
(John Best) *racd in 3rd towards outside: wnt 2nd bef st: rdn 1 1/2f out: r.o u.p: ev ch 1f out: relegated to 4th 100yds out: r.o* **14/1**

5 *shd* **Karadargent (FR)**[178] 2-9-2 0.... FabriceVeron 3 69
(H-A Pantall, France) **10/1**

6 *snk* **Catushaba (IRE)** 2-8-9 0.... MarcLerner(4) 2 66
(C Lerner, France) **11/1**

7 *shd* **Lady American (FR)**[12] 2-8-13 0.... FabienLefebvre 11 66
(Mlle V Dissaux, France) **72/1**

8 *nse* **Minxilinx**[35] 2-8-13 0.... StephanePasquier 12 65
(Mme C Head-Maarek, France) **14/5**[1]

9 *snk* **The Monarck (FR)**[16] 7265 2-9-2 0.... VincentVion 8 68
(T Lallie, France) **52/1**

10 *hd* **Ars d'Ortige (FR)**[15] 2-9-2 0.... AntoineHamelin 1 68
(Mme P Butel, France) **29/1**

0 **Midnight Dancer (FR)**[65] 2-9-2 0.... AnthonyCrastus 6
(F Chappet, France) **17/1**

0 **La Banche (FR)**[85] 2-8-13 0.... FreddyDiFede 4
(C Des Mazis, France) **125/1**

0 **Silver Blue (FR)**[15] 2-8-10 0.... CesarPasserat(6) 9
(C Boillot, France) **100/1**

0 **Tamarissimo (GER)**[11] 2-8-13 0.... RudyPimbonnet(3) 15
(M Nigge, France) **81/1**

0 **Ysper (FR)**[11] 2-8-13 0.... Francois-XavierBertras 13
(M Nigge, France) **83/1**

1m 26.1s (86.10) **15** Ran SP% **115.7**

WIN (incl. 1 euro stake): 6.90. PLACES: 2.40, 2.10, 2.50. DF: 21.60. SF: 46.00.

Owner Rothschild Family **Bred** Famille Rothschild **Trained** Chantilly, France

FOCUS

The first ten were covered by less than 10 lengths.

NOTEBOOK

Le Deluge(FR) improved on his debut effort.

7440 REDCAR (L-H)

Tuesday, November 6

OFFICIAL GOING: Heavy (6.8)

Race 1 Flag start, races 2/3 flip start due to the ground conditions in that area of the track.

Wind: moderate 1/2 behind Weather: rain 1st 4 races

7598 IRISH STALLION FARMS E B F MAIDEN STKS 7f

1:00 (1:03) (Class 5) 2-Y-O **£2,975** (£885; £442; £221)

Form RPR

1 **Cinderslipper (IRE)** 2-8-12 0.... PJMcDonald 12 66
(Ann Duffield) *in rr div: hdwy and rn green over 3f out: styd on wl to ld jst ins fnl f: drvn out* **10/1**

45 **2** *2 ¼* **Hawk High (IRE)**[25] 7033 2-9-3 0.... DavidAllan 4 66
(Tim Easterby) *chsd ldrs: kpt on same pce ins fnl f* **7/4**[1]

3 *nk* **Chevalgris** 2-9-3 0.... RobertWinston 7 65+
(Alan Swinbank) *dwlt: in rr and sn drvn along: hdwy over 2f out: styd on wl ins fnl f* **4/1**[2]

00 **4** *nk* **The Mighty Peg**[11] 7363 2-9-3 0.... GrahamGibbons 6 64
(Tim Walford) *best away fr flag s: led: hdd over 1f out: kpt on same pce* **25/1**

6 **5** *2 ¼* **Prokeel (IRE)**[38] 6669 2-8-12 0.... DarylByrne(5) 13 59
(Tim Easterby) *chsd ldrs: led over 1f out: hdd jst ins fnl f: wknd last 50yds* **12/1**

06 **6** *3* **Sword Of The Lord**[11] 7363 2-9-3 0.... HayleyTurner 11 51
(Michael Bell) *hld up in mid-div: hdwy to trck ldrs 4f out: wknd over 1f out* **9/2**[3]

00 **7** *1 ¾* **Threepence**[28] 6954 2-9-3 0.... PaulQuinn 1 47
(Richard Whitaker) *in rr div: hdwy over 3f out: wknd 2f out* **50/1**

00 **8** *4* **Halfwaytocootehill (IRE)**[11] 7363 2-8-10 0.... JacobButterfield(7) 10 37
(Ollie Pears) *in rr: drvn over 3f out: bhd fnl 2f* **16/1**

9 *3 ¾* **Big Storm Coming** 2-9-0 0.... PaulPickard(3) 8 27
(Brian Ellison) *sn chsng ldrs: wknd 2f out: bhd whn eased ins fnl f* **9/1**

10 *11* **Niknad** 2-8-5 0.... RPWalsh(7) 3
(Brian Ellison) *chsd ldrs: wknd 3f out: eased over 1f out* **20/1**

1m 34.6s (10.10) **Going Correction** +1.375s/f (Soft) **10** Ran SP% **117.8**

Speed ratings (Par 96): **97,94,94,93,91 87,85,81,76,64**

toteswingers 1&2 £5.60, 2&3 £2.50, 1&3 £5.50 CSF £27.65 TOTE £11.30: £3.10, £1.10, £1.90; EX 45.40 Trifecta £103.10 Pool: £312.12 - 2.27 winning units..

Owner Mrs Ann Starkie & Partners **Bred** John Cullinan **Trained** Constable Burton, N Yorks

FOCUS

There was no further rain overnight and after an early-morning inspection the meeting was given the go-ahead. The official going was heavy and the 7f and 1m races, for which there were no stalls, were reduced to 14 runners to allow for dolling to be placed around areas of unraceable ground. A flip start to this ordinary maiden in which all the runners got off on terms. Rnd-of-season form, rated on the negative side.

NOTEBOOK

Cinderslipper(IRE), a 5,500euros purchase, saw it out best of all to make a winning debut. Out of a 1m4f winner, she's bred to be suited by middle distances and her stamina was an asset given the testing conditions. This was a nice performance and she can make her mark in handicaps. (op 9-1)

Hawk High(IRE) set a modest standard on his two runs in heavy-ground maidens over 1m. Down in trip, he kept on well enough after coming under pressure at the halfway stage but proved no match for the winner. (tchd 13-8 and 2-1)

Chevalgris is a half-brother to a couple of winners, notably useful sprinter Head Space, but has stamina on his dam's side. He showed his inexperience and was under pressure a long way from home before finishing best of all with a sustained run up the near side. He clearly has ability and a stiffer test is probably what he needs. (tchd 10-3)

The Mighty Peg showed up well for a long way and this was his best effort after being well held in his two previous starts. (tchd 20-1)

Prokeel(IRE) travelled best of all and had his chance entering the final furlong before finishing one-paced under pressure. (op 14-1)

Sword Of The Lord didn't appear to get home in the testing conditions. (tchd 5-1)

7599 HOLD YOUR CHRISTMAS PARTY HERE (S) STKS 1m

1:30 (1:31) (Class 6) 3-5-Y-O **£1,704** (£503; £251)

Form RPR

42 **1** **Spin A Wish**[70] 5708 4-8-9 48.... PaulQuinn 2 55
(Richard Whitaker) *chsd ldrs: led over 1f out: jst hld on* **6/1**[3]

3440 **2** *hd* **Nant Saeson (IRE)**[17] 7245 3-8-12 64.... BarryMcHugh 8 60
(John Quinn) *hld up towards rr: hdwy 3f out: swtchd rt over 1f out: styd on ins fnl f: jst hld* **7/1**

3550 **3** *½* **Jupiter Fidius**[35] 6758 5-8-13 56....(p) GemmaTutty(7) 4 65
(Karen Tutty) *towards rr: hdwy over 4f out: chsng ldrs over 3f out: upsides fnl f: no ex in clsng stages* **10/1**

2302 **4** *2* **Petrocelli**[8] 7443 5-9-0 53....(t) DominicFox 5 55
(Wilf Storey) *chsd ldrs: drvn over 3f out: hmpd over 1f out: kpt on ins fnl f* **3/1**[1]

0041 **5** *3* **Barathea Dancer (IRE)**[8] 7443 4-9-1 59....(bt) GrahamLee 3 49
(Gay Kelleway) *t.k.h: led: hdd over 1f out: sn wknd* **7/2**[2]

330 **6** *1* **Spread Boy (IRE)**[28] 6959 5-8-13 50.... JordanHibberd(7) 1 52
(Alan Berry) *trckd ldr: drvn over 3f out: outpcd over 2f out: no threat after* **25/1**

4126 **7** *4* **Goldmadchen (GER)**[26] 7003 4-8-9 57.... TomEaves 6 32
(Keith Dalgleish) *hld up in mid-div: drvn over 3f out: wknd over 1f out* **7/2**[2]

60-6 **8** *29* **Gertmegalush (IRE)**[57] 6105 5-9-0 52.... RobertWinston 7
(Noel Wilson) *s.i.s: racd alone towards stands' side: bhd fnl 3f: t.o whn eased over 1f out* **20/1**

1m 51.4s (13.40) **Going Correction** +1.375s/f (Soft)

WFA 3 from 4yo+ 2lb **8** Ran SP% **113.9**

Speed ratings (Par 101): **88,87,87,85,82 81,77,48**

toteswingers 1&2 £5.50, 2&3 £10.20, 1&3 £10.70 CSF £46.70 TOTE £9.60: £2.10, £2.80, £4.50; EX 62.20 Trifecta £245.10 Part won. Pool: £326.89 - 0.10 winning units..There was no bid for the winner.

Owner R M Whitaker **Bred** Hellwood Stud Farm **Trained** Scarcroft, W Yorks

■ Stewards' Enquiry : Barry McHugh fifteen day ban: used whip above permitted level, 5th offence since 8th May (Nov 23 - Dec 10)

FOCUS

A poor seller in which all the runners got off on terms after a flag start.

Spin A Wish Official explanation: two-day ban: careless riding (20-21 November)

Nant Saeson(IRE) Official explanation: two-day ban: careless riding (20-21 Nov)

Jupiter Fidius Official explanation: two-day ban: careless riding (20-21 November)

7600 SUBSCRIBE TO RACING UK H'CAP — 7f

2:00 (2:00) (Class 5) (0-70,70) 3-Y-O — £2,264 (£673; £336; £168)

Form — RPR

-401 **1** **Kuwait Star**[8] 7445 3-9-6 **69** 6ex ... TonyHamilton 3 — 76
(Jason Ward) *mid-div: hdwy over 2f out: edgd lft over 1f out: styd on fnl f: led nr fin* **7/2**[1]

4350 **2** *nk* **Travis County (IRE)**[10] 7402 3-8-11 **63** ... PaulPickard(3) 11 — 69
(Brian Ellison) *wnt rt s: sn w ldrs: led over 1f out: hung rt: hdd nr fin* **14/1**

5003 **3** *1¼* **Come Hither**[34] 6783 3-8-12 **61** ... PhillipMakin 9 — 64
(David O'Meara) *s.i.s: in rr: hdwy over 2f out: kpt on same pce ins fnl f* **12/1**

-006 **4** *1* **Crossley**[29] 6925 3-8-11 **60** ... BarryMcHugh 12 — 61
(Geoffrey Oldroyd) *hld up towards rr: hdwy over 2f out: kpt on same pce fnl f* **25/1**

3060 **5** *4½* **Trust Fund Babe (IRE)**[21] 7146 3-8-8 **57** ... DavidAllan 2 — 46
(Tim Easterby) *t.k.h: led: hdd over 1f out: sn wknd* **20/1**

0500 **6** *1¼* **On The Hoof**[17] 7246 3-9-2 **65** ... GrahamGibbons 13 — 51
(Michael Easterby) *w ldrs: wknd over 1f out* **11/1**

0352 **7** *1* **The New Black (IRE)**[7] 7469 3-8-4 **56** oh2 ...(e) DeclanCannon(3) 6 — 40
(Gay Kelleway) *hld up in rr: hdwy over 3f out: one pce fnl 2f* **8/1**

2002 **8** *nk* **Dream Walker (FR)**[14] 7318 3-9-1 **64** ... DaleSwift 10 — 47
(Ian McInnes) *mid-div: sn drvn along: one pce fnl 2f* **9/1**

1542 **9** *8* **Orwellian**[8] 7447 3-9-1 **64** ... TomEaves 8 — 27
(Bryan Smart) *in rr: sn drvn along: bhd fnl 2f* **9/2**[2]

4060 **10** *4½* **Artillery Train (IRE)**[8] 7446 3-8-4 **56** oh6 ...(p) NeilFarley(3) 14 — 8
(Tim Etherington) *chsd ldrs: lost pl 2f out* **33/1**

1503 **11** *11* **Tahlia Ree (IRE)**[14] 7314 3-9-7 **70** ... HayleyTurner 4
(Michael Bell) *trckd ldrs: effrt over 2f out: wknd over 1f out: sn eased* **11/2**[3]

-350 **12** *15* **Alice Rose (IRE)**[97] 4711 3-9-2 **65** ...(t) RobertWinston 1
(Rae Guest) *chsd ldrs: lost pl over 1f out: sn heavily eased* **7/1**

1m 33.8s (9.30) **Going Correction** +1.375s/f (Soft) — **12** Ran SP% **123.6**
Speed ratings (Par 102): **101,100,99,98,92 91,90,90,80,75 63,46**
toteswingers 1&2 £6.70, 2&3 £44.30, 1&3 £7.60 CSF £56.02 CT £557.98 TOTE £6.10: £2.00, £6.80, £4.50; EX 75.40 Trifecta £227.30 Part won. Pool: £303.17 - 0.62 winning units..
Owner Miss Vivian Pratt **Bred** H & V Pratt **Trained** Middleham, N Yorks

FOCUS
A flag start to this fair handicap which was run at an honest gallop in the conditions. The winner stepped up on his recent maiden form over C&D.
Travis County(IRE) Official explanation: seven-day ban: use of whip (20- 24, 26-27 Nov)

7601 ANNUAL BADGES MAKE GREAT CHRISTMAS PRESENTS H'CAP — 1m 2f

2:30 (2:31) (Class 3) (0-95,90) 3-Y-O+ — £6,663 (£1,982; £990; £495) Stalls Low

Form — RPR

3223 **1** **Kay Gee Be (IRE)**[24] 7069 8-9-1 **81** ... RobertWinston 4 — 88
(Alan Berry) *trckd ldrs: effrt on ins over 2f out: led appr fnl f: drvn out* **7/1**

6424 **2** *1¼* **Uphold**[11] 7369 5-8-7 **76** oh5 ...(e) DeclanCannon(3) 1 — 81
(Gay Kelleway) *led: hdd appr fnl f: kpt on same pce last 75yds* **12/1**

0160 **3** *¾* **Las Verglas Star (IRE)**[10] 7407 4-9-3 **90** ... GeorgeChaloner(7) 10 — 93
(Richard Fahey) *mid-div: hdwy 4f out: chsng ldrs over 2f out: kpt on same pce ins fnl f* **6/1**

5605 **4** *8* **Licence To Till (USA)**[10] 7407 5-9-9 **89** ... FrannyNorton 3 — 78
(Mark Johnston) *chsd ldrs: chal over 2f out: wknd appr fnl f* **11/4**[1]

4041 **5** *4* **Layline (IRE)**[14] 7315 5-8-10 **76** oh1 ... GrahamLee 8 — 58
(Gay Kelleway) *s.i.s: hld up in rr: effrt over 3f out: wknd 2f out* **9/2**[3]

1043 **6** *27* **Maven**[25] 7034 4-9-4 **84** ... DavidAllan 6 — 17
(Tim Easterby) *s.s: hdwy over 3f out: sn rdn lost pl 2f out: heavily eased ins fnl f: t.o* **4/1**[2]

6033 **7** *3¼* **Gala Casino Star (IRE)**[26] 7002 7-8-13 **86** ...(v) JordanNason(7) 9 — 13
(Geoffrey Harker) *chsd ldrs: lost pl over 2f out: eased whn bhd: t.o* **7/1**

0400 **8** *15* **Kiwi Bay**[15] 7294 7-9-1 **81** ... TomEaves 5
(Michael Dods) *t.k.h: w ldr: drvn and wknd 4f out: sn bhd: t.o* **20/1**

2m 19.82s (12.72) **Going Correction** +1.45s/f (Soft) — **8** Ran SP% **116.6**
Speed ratings (Par 107): **107,106,105,99,95 74,71,59**
toteswingers 1&2 £6.10, 2&3 £10.40, 1&3 £6.50 CSF £86.64 CT £536.20 TOTE £6.90: £1.70, £5.20, £3.60; EX 97.10 TRIFECTA Not won..
Owner Alan Berry **Bred** Pursuit Of Truth Syndicate **Trained** Cockerham, Lancs

FOCUS
A decent handicap but an unsatisfactory result with the field finishing well strung out on the heavy ground. Straightforward form.

NOTEBOOK
Kay Gee Be(IRE), having his first run for Alan Berry, travelled well and showed a good attitude. He got to the front entering the final furlong and gradually pulled clear of the game runner-up. His last two wins came in claimers but he was 5lb below his last winning handicap mark and made no mistake under conditions that hold no fears for him. (tchd 9-1 in a place)
Uphold was suited by a return to front-running tactics and ran a cracker from 5lb out of the handicap. He emerges with plenty of credit as he made the running and kept on strongly when challenged, only finding the winner too good. (op 16-1)
Las Verglas Star(IRE) is holding his form well and this was another solid effort. He looked a threat when delivered with his challenge 3f out but couldn't quite get on terms with the front two. (op 5-1)
Licence To Till(USA), 1lb below his last winning mark, was ridden to challenge 2f out but couldn't quicken on this extreme going. He may appreciate the return to less testing conditions. (op 4-1)
Maven had landed her two turf wins on fast ground but had form on heavy and was expected to be suited by this drop in trip after finishing third at York over 1m4f last month. She ran no sort of race after a slow start and her jockey reported that she lost her action. Official explanation: jockey said that the filly lost her action (op 7-2 tchd 10-3)

7602 VOLTIGEUR RESTAURANT 2 COURSE SPECIAL £10.95 CLAIMING STKS — 1m 2f

3:00 (3:01) (Class 6) 3-4-Y-O — £1,704 (£503; £251) Stalls Low

Form — RPR

5532 **1** **Arley Hall**[17] 7245 3-8-12 70 ... TonyHamilton 1 — 76
(Richard Fahey) *trckd ldrs: led over 1f out: forged clr* **7/4**[1]

3642 **2** *5* **Priestley's Reward (IRE)**[17] 7266 3-8-13 68 ...(p) RobertWinston 4 — 68
(Mrs K Burke) *led: drvn 4f out: hdd over 1f out: one pce* **11/4**[3]

5000 **3** *8* **Hawaiian Storm**[7] 7470 3-8-3 60 ... DeclanCannon(3) 3 — 47
(Mrs K Burke) *t.k.h: sn trcking ldrs: effrt over 2f out: edgd lft and wknd appr fnl f* **16/1**

3301 **4** *3¾* **Phase Shift**[17] 7245 4-9-2 60 ... GrahamLee 5 — 46
(Brian Ellison) *trckd ldrs: effrt over 3f out: wknd 2f out* **5/2**[2]

000 **5** *16* **Darrow (IRE)**[11] 7382 3-8-8 46 ... DominicFox 6 — 13
(Wilf Storey) *hld up in last: hdwy over 4f out: wknd over 2f out: eased whn bhd ins fnl f* **40/1**

6300 **6** *½* **Korngold**[25] 7018 4-8-10 60 ... JacobButterfield(7) 2 — 17
(Ollie Pears) *chsd ldrs: drvn and lost pl over 6f out: bhd fnl 3f* **8/1**

2m 23.39s (16.29) **Going Correction** +1.45s/f (Soft)
WFA 3 from 4yo 4lb — **6** Ran SP% **111.0**
Speed ratings (Par 101): **92,88,81,78,65 65**
toteswingers 1&2 £2.10, 2&3 £6.00, 1&3 £5.40 CSF £6.70 TOTE £2.40: £1.70, £2.00; EX 4.90.The winner was claimed by M. Khan for £12,000.
Owner David W Armstrong **Bred** Plantation Stud **Trained** Musley Bank, N Yorks

FOCUS
This looked a competitive claimer on paper, despite the small field. Only the first two ran their races.
Phase Shift Official explanation: trainer said that the filly was unsuited by the shorter trip in this race

7603 REDCARRACING ON FACEBOOK & TWITTER H'CAP — 1m 6f 19y

3:30 (3:30) (Class 6) (0-65,65) 3-Y-O+ — £1,704 (£503; £251) Stalls Low

Form — RPR

/2-2 **1** **Categorical**[186] 1822 9-10-0 **65** ... PhillipMakin 10 — 77
(Keith Reveley) *dwlt: t.k.h in rr: hdwy after 3f: led wl over 2f out: forged clr over 1f out: eased in clsng stages* **9/2**[2]

4000 **2** *12* **Maska Pony (IRE)**[52] 6262 8-9-4 **55** ... GrahamLee 13 — 49
(George Moore) *mid-div: jnd ldrs 7f out: wnt 2nd over 2f out: kpt on: no ch w wnr* **15/2**

1002 **3** *3¾* **Madam Lilibet (IRE)**[15] 7293 3-8-13 **58** ... PaulQuinn 15 — 47
(Sharon Watt) *t.k.h in rr: hdwy into mid-div after 4f: chsng ldrs 7f out: wnt 3rd over 2f out: kpt on same pce* **6/1**[3]

-0 **4** *1¼* **Denison Flyer**[33] 6821 5-8-6 **46** ...(p) DeclanCannon(3) 1 — 34
(Lawrence Mullaney) *chsd ldrs: effrt on ins over 3f out: kpt on ins fnl f: tk 4th nr fin* **20/1**

1505 **5** *nk* **Tarantella Lady**[15] 7293 4-9-10 **61** ...(b) PJMcDonald 7 — 48
(George Moore) *in rr: detached in last and drvn 6f out: kpt on fnl 3f: tk 5th cl home: nvr a factor* **16/1**

5336 **6** *¾* **Stanley Rigby**[42] 6561 6-9-3 **54** ... BarryMcHugh 16 — 40
(Richard Fahey) *in rr: hdwy 4f out: sn chsng ldrs: 4th over 2f out: edgd lft and wknd last 150yds* **16/1**

0/00 **7** *¾* **Ruff Diamond (USA)**[172] 2242 7-9-2 **53** ... DaleSwift 2 — 38
(David Thompson) *led: hdd wl over 2f out: wkng whn hmpd and swtchd rt ins fnl f* **40/1**

0406 **8** *3¼* **Shirls Son Sam**[17] 7255 4-8-9 **46** oh1 ... KellyHarrison 4 — 27
(Chris Fairhurst) *t.k.h in rr: effrt over 3f out: nvr a factor* **9/1**

64-0 **9** *15* **Lady Intrigue (IRE)**[18] 7222 4-8-9 **46** oh1 ... TonyHamilton 8 — 7
(Richard Fahey) *chsd ldrs: lost pl over 3f out: bhd whn eased fnl f: t.o* **14/1**

0601 **10** *16* **Zefooha (FR)**[15] 7293 8-10-0 **65** ...(p) PaddyAspell 14 — 6
(Tim Walford) *chsd ldr: drvn over 7f out: lost pl over 4f out: bhd whn eased over 1f out: t.o* **10/1**

603 **11** *14* **Ad Value (IRE)**[7] 7454 4-9-4 **60** ... GarryWhillans(5) 9
(Alan Swinbank) *mid-div: lost pl over 3f out: eased over 1f out: t.o* **6/1**[3]

012/ **12** *13* **Essexbridge**[261] 3146 5-9-7 **58** ... GrahamGibbons 6
(David O'Meara) *chsd ldrs: lost pl over 3f out: bhd whn eased over 1f out: t.o* **4/1**[1]

3m 27.49s (22.79) **Going Correction** +1.45s/f (Soft)
WFA 3 from 4yo+ 8lb — **12** Ran SP% **123.2**
Speed ratings (Par 101): **92,85,83,82,82 81,81,79,70,61 53,46**
toteswingers 1&2 £8.90, 2&3 £14.10, 1&3 £5.60 CSF £40.08 CT £211.01 TOTE £6.40: £3.20, £3.90, £2.30; EX 49.60 TRIFECTA Not won..
Owner Rug, Grub & Pub Partnership **Bred** Darley **Trained** Lingdale, Redcar & Cleveland

FOCUS
A modest staying handicap which was turned into a procession. The winner could be worth 3lb more but this isn't a race to be positive about.
Zefooha(FR) Official explanation: jockey said that the mare was never travelling

7604 THANKS & SEE YOU NEXT SEASON H'CAP — 6f

4:00 (4:05) (Class 6) (0-60,60) 3-Y-O+ — £1,704 (£503; £251) Stalls High

Form — RPR

0004 **1** **Prince James**[8] 7447 5-8-11 **57** ... DavidSimmonson(7) 12 — 65
(Michael Easterby) *mde virtually all: styd on wl ins fnl f: drvn out* **9/1**

0005 **2** *1¼* **Captain Royale (IRE)**[7] 7457 7-9-6 **59** ...(p) BarryMcHugh 6 — 63
(Tracy Waggott) *trckd ldrs: chal over 2f out: styd on same pce last 75yds* **16/1**

2203 **3** *nse* **Windygoul Lad**[8] 7446 3-9-6 **59** ... AndrewMullen 11 — 63
(Keith Dalgleish) *trckd ldrs: effrt 2f out: styd on towards fin* **9/2**[1]

005 **4** *1* **Lees Anthem**[7] 7456 5-8-11 **50** ... GrahamLee 14 — 51
(Michael Smith) *trckd ldrs: kpt on same pce fnl f* **13/2**[3]

0006 **5** *2¼* **Hab Reeh**[8] 7446 4-8-9 **48** ...(bt) PJMcDonald 5 — 42
(Ruth Carr) *dwlt: hdwy over 2f out: nvr a threat* **8/1**

0060 **6** *½* **Sweet Grace**[12] 7361 3-8-7 **46** oh1 ...(b[1]) FrannyNorton 15 — 39
(David Brown) *s.s: in rr: hdwy whn nt clr run and swtchd rt appr fnl f: styng on at fin* **16/1**

0656 **7** *hd* **Charles Parnell (IRE)**[134] 3442 9-8-8 **47** ... MichaelStainton 8 — 39
(Simon Griffiths) *s.s: bhd: kpt on fnl 2f: nvr nr ldrs* **28/1**

6-05 **8** *hd* **Tadalavil**[8] 7447 7-9-6 **59** ... PhillipMakin 3 — 51
(Linda Perratt) *chsd ldrs: one pce over 1f out* **8/1**

2500 **9** *4½* **Oakbrook**[10] 7395 3-9-4 **57** ...(v[1]) GrahamGibbons 10 — 35
(Ann Duffield) *chsd ldrs: edgd lft and lost pl over 1f out* **25/1**

5040 **10** *½* **First Bid**[14] 7307 3-9-7 **60** ... DaleSwift 9 — 37
(James Given) *chsd ldrs: drvn over 2f out: wknd appr fnl f* **20/1**

6614 **11** *1¾* **Mucky Molly**[14] 7316 4-9-4 **57** ... DominicFox 16 — 28
(Alison Hutchinson) *in rr: rdn over 3f out: sme hdwy over 1f out: nvr a factor* **6/1**[2]

1000 **12** *1¼* **Jerry Ellen (IRE)**[28] 6959 3-8-7 **46** ...(b) DavidAllan 13 — 14
(Tim Easterby) *trckd ldrs: hung lft and wknd over 1f out* **20/1**

3255 **13** *2¾* **Isle Of Ellis (IRE)**[28] 6959 5-8-4 **46** ...(v) JulieBurke(3) 7 — 5
(Ron Barr) *s.i.s: nvr on terms* **20/1**

4240 **14** *½* **Bartley**[47] 6403 3-9-7 **60** ...(p) TomEaves 18 — 18
(Bryan Smart) *stmbld s: nvr on terms* **14/1**

0630 **15** *11* **Ballinargh Girl (IRE)**[16] 7275 4-9-3 **56** ... RobertWinston 1
(Danielle McCormick) *w ldrs: hung lft and lost pl over 1f out: sn heavily eased* **20/1**

0060 **16** *25* **Simpson Millar**[1] 7591 3-8-7 **46** oh1 ... KellyHarrison 4
(Noel Wilson) *chsd ldrs: hung lft and lost pl 3f out: bhd whn eased over 1f out: t.o* **33/1**

6005 P **Military Green (FR)**[12] 7354 3-8-10 **49**........................ TonyHamilton 17
(Tim Easterby) *in rr: heavily eased 2f out: sn p.u* **16/1**
1m 19.87s (8.07) **Going Correction** +1.375s/f (Soft) 17 Ran SP% **131.6**
Speed ratings (Par 101): **101,99,99,97,94 94,94,93,87,87 84,83,79,78,64 30,**
toteswingers 1&2 £43.80, 2&3 £25.00, 1&3 £11.80 CSF £140.26 CT £756.90 TOTE £9.50: £2.00, £5.40, £2.10, £3.60; EX 319.00 Trifecta £650.60 Part won. Pool: £867.59 - 0.40 winning units..
Owner A Saha **Bred** A C M Spalding **Trained** Sheriff Hutton, N Yorks

FOCUS
A modest sprint handicap run in awful ground. Straightforward form.
Sweet Grace Official explanation: jockey said that the filly was denied a clear run
Bartley Official explanation: jockey said that the gelding stumbled on leaving the stall
Ballinargh Girl(IRE) Official explanation: jockey said that the filly hung left
Simpson Millar Official explanation: jockey said that the gelding hung left
Military Green(FR) Official explanation: jockey said that the gelding lost its action
T/Plt: £242.20 to a £1 stake. Pool of £41743.32 - 125.80 winning tickets. T/Qpdt: £33.80 to a £1 stake. Pool of £3763.94 - 82.20 winning tickets. WG

7347 SOUTHWELL (L-H)
Tuesday, November 6

OFFICIAL GOING: Standard
Wind: Moderate halfd behind Weather: Heavy cloud and rain

7605 32RED SUPPORTING BRITISH RACING H'CAP (DIV I) 1m (F)
12:40 (12:41) (Class 6) (0-52,52) 3-Y-0+ **£1,704** (£503; £251) **Stalls** Low

Form RPR
0630 1 **Gay Gallivanter**[28] 6950 4-8-10 **46** oh1........................(p) AndreaAtzeni 5 55
(Michael Quinn) *trckd ldng pair: effrt to chse ldr 3f out: rdn along over 2f out: drvn and styd on to ld ins fnl f* **16/1**
00-5 2 2 **Geronimo Chief (IRE)**[33] 6829 4-9-2 **52**..................(v) FrederikTylicki 3 57
(Ben Haslam) *led: rdn and edgd lft wl over 1f out: drvn and hdd ins fnl f: edgd rt and one pce* **11/4**[2]
0363 3 2 ½ **Chez Vrony**[47] 6396 6-8-10 **46**.. DavidProbert 8 45
(Dave Morris) *prom: rdn along on outer over 3f out: drvn 2f out: kpt on same pce* **3/1**[3]
0650 4 1 ½ **Applaude**[17] 7250 7-8-11 **47**.......................................(b) PaulMulrennan 9 43
(Chris Bealby) *in tch: hdwy to chse ldrs 3f out: rdn over 2f out and sn one pce* **17/2**
2154 5 ½ **Smart Affair**[17] 7255 3-8-6 **51**.......................................(be) RobertTart(7) 6 45+
(Alan Bailey) *s.i.s and rdn along in rr: bhd tl hdwy 3f out: styd on u.p fnl 2f: nrst fin* **5/2**[1]
0600 6 5 **Orpen Wide (IRE)**[42] 6562 10-8-8 **47** oh1 ow1..........(bt) RyanClark(3) 10 30
(Michael Chapman) *in tch: sn rdn along on outer: lost pl bef 1/2-way and sn bhd* **33/1**
3000 7 ¾ **Desert Red (IRE)**[14] 7307 3-8-8 **46** oh1........................(be) LukeMorris 2 27
(Phil McEntee) *chsd ldr: rdn along over 3f out: sn wknd* **28/1**
2044 8 ¾ **Heading To First**[147] 2998 5-8-10 **46**........................... KirstyMilczarek 4 25
(Paddy Butler) *towards rr: sme hdwy over 3f out: sn rdn and wknd* **16/1**
0000 9 15 **Mark Anthony (IRE)**[14] 7318 5-8-3 **46** oh1..................(p) JordanUys(7) 1
(Shaun Harris) *trckd ldrs on inner: rdn along wl over 3f out: sn wknd and bhd* **25/1**
1m 42.5s (-1.20) **Going Correction** -0.175s/f (Stan)
WFA 3 from 4yo+ 2lb 9 Ran SP% **112.8**
Speed ratings (Par 101): **99,97,94,93,92 87,86,86,71**
toteswingers 1&2 £6.30, 2&3 £2.70, 1&3 £3.80 CSF £57.57 CT £172.96 TOTE £17.40: £3.40, £2.60, £1.10; EX 92.60.
Owner Andy Viner **Bred** Cheveley Park Stud Ltd **Trained** Newmarket, Suffolk

FOCUS
Handicaps don't come much weaker than this. Only the first two mattered from some way out.
Smart Affair Official explanation: jockey said that the filly was slowly away

7606 32REDPOKER.COM NURSERY 7f (F)
1:10 (1:10) (Class 6) (0-60,60) 2-Y-O **£1,704** (£503; £251) **Stalls** Low

Form RPR
060 1 **Apache Rising**[42] 6558 2-9-1 **54**.................................. PaulMulrennan 8 59+
(Bryan Smart) *trckd ldrs: smooth hdwy on outer and cl up 3f out: chal over 2f out: led wl over 1f out and sn rdn: kpt on wl fnl f* **9/4**[1]
000 2 1 ½ **Prince Rakan (USA)**[14] 7305 2-9-7 **60**..............................(b[1]) AdamKirby 6 59
(Amy Weaver) *dwlt: hdwy to trck ldrs 1/2-way: effrt 2f out: sn rdn: styd on to chse wnr ins fnl f: no imp towards fin* **10/1**
6030 3 ½ **Solvanna**[6] 7476 2-9-7 **60**.. DarryllHolland 4 58
(Heather Main) *led: rdn along and jnd wl over 2f out: hdd wl over 1f out: drvn and one pce ent fnl f* **6/1**
0060 4 1 ¾ **Birdy Boy (USA)**[85] 5161 2-8-6 **45**................................ JoeFanning 1 38
(Mark Johnston) *trckd ldrs on inner: rdn along 3f out: drvn 2f out and sn one pce* **11/2**[3]
0000 5 2 ½ **Shades Of Light**[27] 6977 2-8-11 **50**................................ SebSanders 2 37
(Peter Makin) *dwlt: towards rr: sme hdwy 3f out: sn rdn and n.d* **25/1**
2400 6 4 ½ **Lincolnrose (IRE)**[33] 6822 2-9-1 **54**.................................(v[1]) LukeMorris 7 29
(Alan McCabe) *in tch: hdwy on outer to chse ldrs 3f out: rdn over 2f out and sn wknd* **5/1**[2]
5304 7 13 **Little Miss Zuri (IRE)**[7] 7463 2-8-8 **47**........................... NickyMackay 5
(Sylvester Kirk) *chsd ldrs on outer: rdn along 1/2-way: sn wknd* **9/1**
065 8 3 **Cool And Clear (IRE)**[15] 7290 2-9-2 **55**............................ TedDurcan 3
(Tim Easterby) *prom 2f: rdn along and lost pl bef 1/2-way: sn bhd* **5/1**[2]
1m 30.1s (-0.20) **Going Correction** -0.175s/f (Stan) 8 Ran SP% **116.7**
Speed ratings (Par 94): **94,92,91,89,86 81,66,63**
toteswingers 1&2 £6.40, 2&3 £8.20, 1&3 £4.90 CSF £27.13 CT £122.01 TOTE £3.30: £1.40, £2.20, £1.50; EX 38.00.
Owner The Smart Distant Music Partnership **Bred** Southill Stud **Trained** Hambleton, N Yorks

FOCUS
A low-grade nursery and, although a few of these are still capable of better, the winner aside, this isn't form to get too excited about. The winner was value for a little extra.

NOTEBOOK
Apache Rising was well backed throughout the day and he duly stepped up a good deal on his three maiden runs to get off the mark. His task was made trickier by being drawn widest but the Sleeping Indian colt travelled strongly and was the only one not to be asked any serious question by the top of the straight. He found more than enough to get the job done, if looking a little green still, and this surface looks the making of him. He could easily win again around here. Official explanation: trainer's representative said, regarding the apparent improvement of form, that this run did not necessarily represent an improvement in form and he added that the colt was the top-rated in the race (op 11-4)
Prince Rakan(USA), for whom things didn't go right early on, saw his race out in quite tidy style up the straight and the combination of first-time blinkers, a switch to handicaps and Fibresand for the first time definitely brought about improvement from this colt. If he can go on from this he can get off the mark. (op 7-1)
Solvanna kept on having always been close up, but she isn't improving. (op 9-2 tchd 13-2)
Birdy Boy(USA), for whom the switch to Fibresand only brought marginal improvement, looks very modest at this stage. (op 6-1 tchd 7-1)

7607 32RED.COM H'CAP 7f (F)
1:40 (1:40) (Class 5) (0-75,75) 3-Y-O+ **£2,264** (£673; £336; £168) **Stalls** Low

Form RPR
2333 1 **Fayr Fall (IRE)**[21] 7142 3-9-1 **70**....................................(v) TedDurcan 13 78
(Tim Easterby) *cl up: chal on bit over 2f out: slt ld 1 1/2f out: sn shkn up: rdn ent fnl f: kpt on wl* **5/1**[2]
013 2 nk **Piceno (IRE)**[7] 7452 4-9-7 **75**...(p) LukeMorris 1 83
(Scott Dixon) *slt ld: rdn along over 2f out: hdd 1 1/2f out: cl up: drvn ent fnl f and ev ch tl no ex last 50yds* **8/1**
5020 3 3 **Opus Dei**[6] 7485 5-9-2 **70**..(p) SebSanders 14 70
(Alan McCabe) *in tch: hdwy on outer 1/2-way: rdn to chse ldrs 2f out: kpt on same pce fnl f* **14/1**
3200 4 1 ¼ **Sunnyside Tom (IRE)**[17] 7247 8-8-9 **63**....................... FrederikTylicki 5 60
(Richard Fahey) *trckd ldrs: cl up 3f out: rdn 2f out: kpt on same pce fnl f* **14/1**
1405 5 hd **Only Ten Per Cent (IRE)**[33] 6811 4-9-6 **74**.................. DarryllHolland 8 71+
(J R Jenkins) *towards rr: smooth hdwy to trck ldrs 3f out: effrt 2f out: rdn and one pce appr fnl f* **6/1**[3]
4002 6 1 ¼ **Sehnsucht (IRE)**[33] 6810 3-9-1 **70**...............................(p) ShaneKelly 12 62
(Alan McCabe) *chsd ldrs: rdn along over 2f out: sn no imp* **9/2**[1]
2660 7 hd **Key Ambition**[7] 7451 3-9-6 **75**..................................(tp) RussKennemore 7 67
(Garry Moss) *chsd ldrs: rdn along wl over 2f out: sn one pce* **22/1**
0150 8 1 ¾ **Avonrose**[54] 6172 5-9-6 **74**..(v) JoeFanning 11 62
(Derek Shaw) *t.k.h early: hld up towards rr: hdwy 1/2-way: in tch and rdn over 2f out: sn no imp* **10/1**
0005 9 8 **Vale Of Clara (IRE)**[17] 7246 4-9-4 **72**........................... PaulMulrennan 6 40
(Peter Niven) *a in rr: bhd fr 1/2-way* **33/1**
2-30 10 ¾ **Minortransgression (USA)**[12] 7360 5-9-0 **68**................. AdamKirby 9 34
(Paul Rich) *cl up: rdn along wl over 2f out: sn wknd* **10/1**
3140 11 3 ¼ **Elspeth's Boy (USA)**[11] 7370 5-9-7 **75**........................... JimmyQuinn 2 32
(Philip Kirby) *chsd ldrs on inner: rdn along 3f out: sn wknd* **9/1**
0003 12 2 ½ **Nasharra (IRE)**[26] 6999 4-9-2 **70**..................................(p) AmyRyan 4 21
(Kevin Ryan) *hmpd s: hdwy on inner 1/2-way: rdn along wl over 2f out and sn wknd* **10/1**
1m 27.76s (-2.54) **Going Correction** -0.175s/f (Stan)
WFA 3 from 4yo+ 1lb 12 Ran SP% **118.1**
Speed ratings (Par 103): **107,106,103,101,101 100,99,97,88,87 84,81**
toteswingers 1&2 £2.90, 2&3 £18.20, 1&3 £17.10 CSF £44.69 CT £537.43 TOTE £6.20: £2.00, £1.60, £4.20; EX 35.00.
Owner Reality Partnerships **Bred** M Sinanan **Trained** Great Habton, N Yorks

FOCUS
Quite a competitive handicap with a raft of course winners in opposition. The winner may have more to offer here.
Avonrose Official explanation: jockey said that the mare was denied a clear run
Elspeth's Boy(USA) Official explanation: trainer's representative said that the gelding bled from the nose
Nasharra(IRE) Official explanation: jockey said that the gelding lost his action

7608 32REDBET.COM CLAIMING STKS 1m 3f (F)
2:10 (2:11) (Class 6) 3-Y-O+ **£1,704** (£503; £251) **Stalls** Low

Form RPR
-111 1 **La Estrella (USA)**[167] 2403 9-9-10 89................................ AdamKirby 8 82+
(Don Cantillon) *trckd ldrs on outer: hdwy 4f out: cl up over 2f out: rdn to chal and bmpd wl over 1f out: drvn and edgd lft 1f out: kpt on to ld and hung lft wl ins fnl f: kpt on* **2/7**[1]
4006 2 1 ½ **Pendragon (USA)**[10] 7413 9-9-2 75............................ PaulMulrennan 5 71+
(Brian Ellison) *trckd ldrs: hdwy 4f out: cl up 3f out: led over 2f out: sn rdn and edgd rt: drvn and hmpd 1f out: hdd and consistently hmpd ins fnl f: n.m.r and no ex last 40yds* **4/1**[2]
2052 3 3 ¼ **Lakeman (IRE)**[71] 5672 6-8-10 55.................................... RyanClark(3) 7 63
(Brian Ellison) *trckd ldr: led 4f out: rdn along 3f out: hdd over 2f out and kpt on same pce* **28/1**
1220 4 ½ **Xpres Maite**[10] 7413 9-8-12 71..................................(v) MarkCoumbe(3) 3 64
(Roy Bowring) *led: rdn along and hdd 4f out: sn wknd* **20/1**
/ 5 9 **Low Key (IRE)**[358] 5-8-13 88.. MickyFenton 4 48
(John Butler) *chsd ldng pair on inner: rdn along 5f out: sn wknd* **18/1**[3]
1400 6 40 **King Of Windsor (IRE)**[37] 6706 5-8-13 73.................. AdamCarter(5) 6
(John Wainwright) *sn outpcd and bhd: t.o fnl 4f* **33/1**
2m 26.35s (-1.65) **Going Correction** -0.175s/f (Stan) 6 Ran SP% **114.2**
Speed ratings (Par 101): **99,97,95,95,88 59**
toteswingers 1&2 £1.40, 2&3 £5.80, 1&3 £2.60 CSF £1.79 TOTE £1.50: £1.10, £2.00; EX 2.40.
Owner Don Cantillon **Bred** Five Horses Ltd And Theatrical Syndicate **Trained** Newmarket, Suffolk
■ La Estrella's 13th straight win at Southwell, breaking the record for consecutive wins at one course.

FOCUS
This was all about La Estrella. The form is limited by the third.

7609 E B F 32RED MAIDEN STKS 5f (F)
2:40 (2:41) (Class 5) 2-Y-O **£3,234** (£962; £481; £240) **Stalls** High

Form RPR
0506 1 **Constant Dream**[20] 7156 2-8-12 48................................ JamesSullivan 3 62
(James Given) *chsd ldrs: hdwy 2f out: rdn to ld over 1f out: styd on wl u.p towards fin* **20/1**
36 2 hd **Lexington Place**[28] 6954 2-9-3 0.. DavidNolan 8 66
(Richard Fahey) *prom: effrt to chal wl over 1f out: sn rdn and ev ch: could nt qckn towards fin* **9/1**
42 3 1 **Lilac Lace (IRE)**[17] 7244 2-8-12 0.................................... TedDurcan 10 57+
(Tim Easterby) *chsd ldrs: hdwy 2f out: rdn over 1f out: drvn and kpt on fnl f* **9/4**[1]
40 4 1 ½ **Robyn**[8] 7434 2-8-12 0.. NickyMackay 1 52
(Scott Dixon) *towards rr: hdwy 1/2-way: rdn along wl over 1f out: kpt on fnl f: nrst fin* **11/2**[3]
0345 5 ½ **Tyson The Byson**[11] 7379 2-9-0 59....................(p) MichaelMetcalfe(3) 7 55
(Mrs K Burke) *led: rdn along 2f out: drvn and hdd over 1f out: grad wknd* **8/1**
6006 6 hd **Angel Grigio**[8] 7441 2-8-12 45...(v) JimmyQuinn 2 49
(Bryan Smart) *dwlt and towards rr: hdwy 2f out: sn rdn and kpt on fnl f: nrst fin* **25/1**

0 **7** *nk* **Ichimoku**[18] 7219 2-9-3 0........ PaulMulrennan 6 53
(Bryan Smart) *cl up: rdn along wl over 1f out: grad wknd* **9/1**

0 **8** *3 ¾* **Underwhelm**[64] 5887 2-8-12 0........ SebSanders 9 35
(Alan McCabe) *cl up: rdn along 2f out: grad wknd* **22/1**

0400 **9** *2 ¾* **I'Ve No Money (IRE)**[69] 5749 2-9-3 50........ KirstyMilczarek 4 30
(David C Griffiths) *s.i.s: a in rr* **40/1**

453 **10** *6* **North Pole**[6] 7481 2-9-3 0........ LukeMorris 11 8
(Sir Mark Prescott Bt) *sn rdn along and a outpcd in rr* **3/1**[2]

00 **11** *9* **Rovers Till I Die (IRE)**[11] 7363 2-9-0 0........(tp) MarkCoumbe(3) 5
(Charles Smith) *dwlt: sn rdn and outpcd in rr: bhd fr 1/2-way* **100/1**

58.62s (-1.08) **Going Correction** -0.275s/f (Stan) **11** Ran SP% **118.6**
Speed ratings (Par 96): **97,96,95,92,91 91,91,85,80,71 56**
toteswingers 1&2 £14.50, 2&3 £5.10, 1&3 £11.30 CSF £181.36 TOTE £30.70: £5.50, £1.10, £2.10; EX 428.80.
Owner Dolton Grange **Bred** J Ellis **Trained** Willoughton, Lincs

FOCUS
A poor maiden on the face of it and, with the front two in the betting proving totally unsuited by the drop back to the minimum trip, this is not form to place too much faith in.

NOTEBOOK
Constant Dream would never be entitled to win a maiden with an official rating of just 48 but she clearly showed improved form on her first try on Fibresand. She had enough pace to keep in touch early and the further she went the stronger she looked, seeing this out nicely and shaping as though she'll be seen to better effect up to 6f. This surface could be the making of her. (op 25-1)
Lexington Place went backwards at Catterick last time, but he bounced back here to confirm the promise of his Haydock debut. Like the winner, he looks like he'll be better back up in trip. (op 10-1 tchd 12-1)
Lilac Lace(IRE) got going late in the day and finished best of all, but she couldn't live with the early gallop and clearly needs further. (op 5-2 tchd 11-4)
Robyn got a bit outpaced mid-race before sticking on well again in the closing stages, and there are races to be won with her. (op 10-1 tchd 11-1)
I'Ve No Money(IRE) Official explanation: jockey said that the gelding reared at the start
North Pole was unsuited by the drop back to 5f. Official explanation: jockey said that the colt was never travelling (op 9-4)

7610 £32 BONUS AT 32RED.COM H'CAP 2m (F)
3:10 (3:10) (Class 5) (0-75,72) 3-Y-0+ **£2,264** (£673; £336; £168) **Stalls** Low

Form RPR

0426 **1** **Irish Jugger (USA)**[203] 1429 5-8-13 **57**........ DarryllHolland 5 63+
(Michael Appleby) *hld up in tch: smooth hdwy over 4f out: chal on outer over 2f out: led wl over 1f out: eased towards fin: readily* **11/2**

0460 **2** *¾* **Nice Rose**[38] 6662 3-9-5 **72**........ AdrianNicholls 3 75
(Mark Johnston) *prom: led over 3f out: sn rdn and hdd over 2f out: drvn and kpt on fnl f* **9/2**[3]

-151 **3** *nk* **Mason Hindmarsh**[7] 7454 5-9-12 **70** 6ex........ FrederikTylicki 6 73
(Karen McLintock) *trckd ldrs: pushed along and lost pl briefly after 6f: hdwy over 6f out: led 5f out to 4f out: led again wl over 2f out: sn rdn and hdd wl over 1f out: kpt on same pce* **5/2**[1]

5662 **4** *16* **Benartic (IRE)**[52] 6255 8-9-8 **66**........ LukeMorris 4 50
(Harry Dunlop) *prom: rdn along over 3f out: sn wknd* **7/2**[2]

0060 **5** *2 ¾* **Monzino (USA)**[8] 7437 4-9-0 **61**........(p) RyanClark(3) 1 42
(Michael Chapman) *hld up in rr: stdy hdwy 7f out: led 4f out: rdn and hdd 3f out: sn drvn and wknd* **33/1**

/1-0 **6** *11* **Agglestone Rock**[12] 7353 7-9-5 **70**........ EvaMoscrop(7) 7 37
(Philip Kirby) *racd wd: prom: rdn along 6f out: wknd over 4f out* **17/2**

656 **7** *4 ½* **Carnac (IRE)**[113] 4145 6-9-3 **61**........(p) ShaneKelly 8 23
(Alan McCabe) *prom: rdn along 6f out: sn wknd* **14/1**

-050 **8** *16* **Liberate**[34] 6802 9-9-12 **70**........ PaulMulrennan 2 13
(Anabel K Murphy) *prom: lost pl after 5f: sn in rr: bhd fnl 6f* **12/1**

0043 **9** *25* **El Dececy (USA)**[12] 7348 8-9-0 **61**........(tp) MarkCoumbe(3) 9
(Charles Smith) *t.k.h: mde most tl hdd over 4f out and sn wknd* **22/1**

3m 40.99s (-4.51) **Going Correction** -0.175s/f (Stan)
WFA 3 from 4yo+ 9lb **9** Ran SP% **116.5**
Speed ratings (Par 103): **104,103,103,95,94 88,86,78,65**
toteswingers 1&2 £5.10, 2&3 £2.50, 1&3 £3.50 CSF £30.77 CT £77.31 TOTE £10.00: £1.80, £2.20, £1.50; EX 25.30.
Owner Dallas Racing **Bred** Richard S Kaster & Frederick C Wieting **Trained** Danethorpe, Notts

FOCUS
Some familiar faces on show here in what was a run-of-the-mill staying handicap, but the writing was on the wall a long way out. The winner was well in on his old form.
Benartic(IRE) Official explanation: jockey said that the gelding bled from the nose

7611 32REDCASINO.COM MAIDEN STKS 5f (F)
3:40 (3:40) (Class 5) 3-Y-0+ **£2,385** (£704; £352) **Stalls** High

Form RPR

3254 **1** **Dazzlin Bluebell (IRE)**[7] 7457 3-8-12 49........(b) TedDurcan 9 58
(Tim Easterby) *trckd ldrs: hdwy wl over 1f out: rdn ent fnl f: styd on wl to ld nr line* **6/1**

6435 **2** *nse* **Jermatt**[33] 6806 3-9-3 57........ FrederikTylicki 7 63
(J R Jenkins) *led: rdn over 1f out: drvn ins fnl f: hdd nr line* **8/1**

-232 **3** *2* **Place That Face**[33] 6806 3-8-12 60........ RobertHavlin 2 51
(Hughie Morrison) *a.p: effrt and cl up over 1f out: rdn and ev ch ent fnl f: kpt on same pce* **5/2**[1]

0503 **4** *1 ¾* **College Doll**[34] 6771 3-8-12 48........ TomMcLaughlin 1 44
(Christine Dunnett) *racd towards far rail: cl up: effrt and ev ch 2f out: sn rdn and wknd appr fnl f* **33/1**

3222 **5** *nk* **Gaelic Wizard (IRE)**[17] 7253 4-8-10 69........ JoshBaudains(7) 10 48
(Dominic Ffrench Davis) *chsd ldrs: rdn along wl over 1f out: kpt on same pce appr fnl f* **11/4**[2]

33 **6** *shd* **Ella Fitzgerald (IRE)**[29] 6930 3-8-12 0........ NickyMackay 8 43
(Rae Guest) *in tch: hdwy 2f out: rdn to chse ldrs over 1f out: no imp fnl f* **5/1**[3]

4244 **7** *¾* **Finefrenzyrolling (IRE)**[139] 3285 4-8-9 56.......(b) MichaelMetcalfe(3) 12 40
(Mrs K Burke) *chsd ldrs: rdn along 2f out: sn edgd lft and one pce* **16/1**

0500 **8** *2 ½* **Lady By Red (IRE)**[104] 4454 4-8-12 44........ PaulMulrennan 3 31
(Ann Duffield) *midfield: hdwy 2f out: sn rdn and wknd over 1f out* **40/1**

605/ **9** *1 ¼* **Island Express (IRE)**[1252] 2588 5-8-12 52........(bt[1]) AnnStokell(5) 13 32
(Ann Stokell) *dwlt: a towards rr* **150/1**

5400 **10** *3* **Coastal Passage**[18] 7221 4-9-0 47........(bt[1]) MarkCoumbe(3) 4 21
(Charles Smith) *stmbld s: a towards rr* **33/1**

0-00 **11** *1 ¾* **Totally Trusted**[127] 3694 4-8-12 47........ MickyFenton 11 10
(Scott Dixon) *dwlt: a in rr* **25/1**

0005 **12** *3 ¾* **Bonbon Bonnie**[52] 6254 4-8-9 41........(be) RyanClark(3) 6
(Phil McEntee) *hmpd s and in rr: edgd lft to far rail after 2f: sn rdn and bhd* **100/1**

58.01s (-1.69) **Going Correction** -0.275s/f (Stan) **12** Ran SP% **117.0**
Speed ratings (Par 103): **102,101,98,95,95 95,94,90,88,83 80,74**
toteswingers 1&2 £6.00, 2&3 £5.70, 1&3 £3.40 CSF £49.77 TOTE £5.00: £1.10, £3.20, £2.50; EX 41.70.
Owner Craig Wilson **Bred** Neville O'Byrne & John Weld **Trained** Great Habton, N Yorks

FOCUS
Weak maiden form.
Coastal Passage Official explanation: jockey said that the gelding stumbled leaving the stalls
Totally Trusted Official explanation: jockey said that the filly missed the break
Bonbon Bonnie Official explanation: jockey said that the filly was never travelling

7612 32RED SUPPORTING BRITISH RACING H'CAP (DIV II) 1m (F)
4:10 (4:10) (Class 6) (0-52,50) 3-Y-0+ **£1,704** (£503; £251) **Stalls** Low

Form RPR

5050 **1** **Nurse Dominatrix (IRE)**[7] 7470 3-8-11 **47**........ RobbieFitzpatrick 1 52
(Richard Guest) *towards rr: pushed along 1/2-way: hdwy 3f out: rdn 2f out: styd on appr fnl f: sn drvn and led last 50yds* **6/1**[3]

0000 **2** *nk* **Pull The Pin (IRE)**[8] 7436 3-8-13 **49**........(tp) DarryllHolland 7 53
(William Kinsey) *prom: led after 3f: rdn over 2f out: drvn ins fnl f: hdd and no ex last 50yds* **4/1**[2]

4000 **3** *6* **Fairy Mist (IRE)**[134] 3442 5-8-12 **46**........(p) MickyFenton 3 36
(Brian Rothwell) *set str pce: hdd after 3f: cl up: rdn over 2f out and ev ch tl drvn and wknd ent fnl f* **12/1**

0000 **4** *1 ¾* **Cathcart Castle**[8] 7437 4-8-4 **45**........(e) ShirleyTeasdale(7) 8 31
(Simon West) *bhd: hdwy wl over 2f out: sn rdn and kpt on: nvr nr ldrs* **9/1**

0004 **5** *1 ½* **Catalyze**[12] 7354 4-8-13 **50**........(t) MarkCoumbe(3) 6 33
(Charles Smith) *prom on outer: chsd ldng pair 3f out: rdn over 2f out: grad wknd* **9/4**[1]

03-0 **6** *6* **Generous Genella**[186] 1830 4-9-1 **49**........(e[1]) JimmyQuinn 4 18
(Julia Feilden) *chsd ldrs: rdn along wl over 2f out: sn wknd* **10/1**

2000 **7** *4* **Bashama**[12] 7362 4-8-11 **45**........(p) DavidProbert 5 5
(Nikki Evans) *chsd ldrs: rdn along over 3f out: sn wknd* **6/1**[3]

0- **8** *2 ½* **Indian St Jovite (IRE)**[244] 545 5-8-11 **45**........ ShaneKelly 9
(Seamus Fahey, Ire) *in tch on outer: rdn along over 3f out: sn wknd* **16/1**

000- **9** *38* **Femme D'Espere**[405] 6459 6-8-12 **46** ow1........ TomMcLaughlin 2
(Christopher Kellett) *prom: rdn along 1/2-way: sn wknd* **50/1**

1m 43.7s **Going Correction** -0.175s/f (Stan)
WFA 3 from 4yo+ 2lb **9** Ran SP% **114.0**
Speed ratings (Par 101): **93,92,86,84,83 77,73,70,32**
toteswingers 1&2 £3.20, 2&3 £4.50, 1&3 £8.30 CSF £29.80 CT £280.23 TOTE £6.30: £2.30, £1.40, £2.90; EX 37.80.
Owner Future Racing (Notts) Limited **Bred** Michael O'Brien **Trained** Stainforth, S Yorks

FOCUS
A shocking contest, at least run at a good tempo.
Nurse Dominatrix(IRE) Official explanation: trainer's representative said, reagarding the apparent improvement of form, that this was the filly's first run on the all-weather and he added that it was a weak race on this occasion
T/Plt: £33.60 to a £1 stake. Pool of £45671.82 - 1.00 winning tickets. T/Qpdt: £6.10 to £1 stake. Pool of £4275.50 - 2.00 winning tickets. JR

7589 WOLVERHAMPTON (A.W) (L-H)
Tuesday, November 6

OFFICIAL GOING: Standard
Wind: Fresh behind Weather: Overcast

7613 32RED CASINO MAIDEN STKS 5f 216y(P)
4:30 (4:32) (Class 5) 2-Y-0 **£2,264** (£673; £336; £168) **Stalls** Low

Form RPR

1 **Equity Risk (USA)** 2-9-3 0........ NeilCallan 6 74+
(Kevin Ryan) *chsd ldrs: led over 1f out: shkn up and r.o wl* **7/2**[2]

2 *2 ½* **Catch The Cider** 2-8-10 0........ NicoleNordblad(7) 3 67+
(Hans Adielsson) *s.s: hld up: plld hrd: hdwy on outer over 2f out: chsd wnr fnl f: r.o* **14/1**

3 *1 ¼* **Macaabra (IRE)** 2-8-12 0........ AndreaAtzeni 9 58
(James Tate) *a.p: shkn up over 1f out: r.o* **16/1**

4 *2 ¼* **Gebayl** 2-8-12 0........ MartinDwyer 5 51
(James Tate) *chsd ldrs: rdn over 1f out: no ex fnl f* **13/2**[3]

0 **5** *2* **Sewn Up**[7] 7458 2-9-3 0........ GeorgeBaker 2 50
(Reg Hollinshead) *s.i.s: hld up: rdn and edgd lft over 1f out: styd on ins fnl f: nvr nrr* **8/1**

0 **6** *½* **Loulou Vuitton**[18] 7219 2-8-12 0........ J-PGuillambert 7 44
(Brian Baugh) *sn pushed along and prom: nt clr run over 2f out: rdn over 1f out: wknd fnl f* **66/1**

2334 **7** *1 ¼* **Polish Crown**[26] 6998 2-8-12 74........ JoeFanning 1 40
(Mark Johnston) *led 5f out: rdn and hdd over 1f out: wknd ins fnl f* **1/1**[1]

050 **8** *2* **Southern Sapphire**[59] 6042 2-9-3 0........ PatrickMathers 4 39
(Linda Stubbs) *led 1f: chsd ldr: ev ch 2f out: sn rdn: wknd fnl f* **33/1**

0 **9** *5* **Ri Na Si**[41] 6581 2-9-3 0........ IanMongan 8 24
(Pat Phelan) *hld up: rdn over 2f out: sn wknd* **20/1**

1m 13.72s (-1.28) **Going Correction** -0.15s/f (Stan) **9** Ran SP% **118.4**
Speed ratings (Par 96): **102,98,97,94,91 90,89,86,79**
toteswingers 1&2 £9.80, 2&3 £15.80, 1&3 £7.30 CSF £50.68 TOTE £2.80: £1.40, £4.70, £4.70; EX 56.40 Trifecta £496.60 Pool: £1556.20 - 2.35 winning units..
Owner Clipper Logistics **Bred** Crosshaven Bloodstock Et Al **Trained** Hambleton, N Yorks

FOCUS
A modest juvenile maiden, run at a solid pace. It lacked depth but there was plenty to like about the front pair.

NOTEBOOK
Equity Risk(USA) ran out a taking debut winner. He failed to get any cover early and showed his inexperience. However, he picked up the bridle 3f out and was soon in control off the home bend. This US-bred $65,000 purchase clearly has gears and should improve for the run, so his future looks bright. (op 5-1)
Catch The Cider proved distinctly green early on, but showed he has an engine by making up ground near the home turn and running on promisingly late in the day. He could take some beating next time, especially if facing another furlong. (op 16-1 tchd 20-1)
Macaabra(IRE) looked the yard's second string, but she finished ahead of her one-paced stablemate, and relished the step up in distance. (op 12-1)
Gebayl, a stablemate of the third, was one-paced. (op 4-1)

Polish Crown got bogged down on turf the last twice, but her previous form on sound surfaces unsurprisingly saw her sent off a short price back on Polytrack. She looked like she had done more than enough for the year as she faded tamely off the home turn.

7614 32RED.COM NURSERY — 7f 32y(P)
5:00 (5:01) (Class 4) (0-85,84) 2-Y-O — £3,881 (£1,155; £577; £288) Stalls High

Form — RPR

5533 1 — **Filfil (USA)**[13] 7325 2-9-2 **79** .... MickaelBarzalona 6 — 86
(Mahmood Al Zarooni) *chsd ldrs: led over 4f out: rdn clr fr over 1f out* — 11/10[1]

0566 2 4 ½ **Makinson Lane (IRE)**[28] 6972 2-8-4 **67** ow1 .... PatrickMathers 4 — 63
(Richard Fahey) *a.p: chsd wnr over 2f out: rdn over 1f out: sn outpcd* — 15/2

0306 3 ¾ **Secret Symphony**[64] 5886 2-8-5 **68** .... (t) MartinLane 1 — 62
(Sylvester Kirk) *s.i.s: sn pushed along in rr: hdwy u.p over 2f out: styd on same pce fr over 1f out* — 16/1

561 4 1 ½ **Mystical Man**[109] 4310 2-9-7 **84** .... MartinDwyer 5 — 74
(James Tate) *led 6f out tl over 4f out: rdn over 2f out: wknd fnl f* — 13/2[3]

41 5 nk **Al Udeid (IRE)**[19] 7198 2-9-2 **79** .... AmyRyan 2 — 69
(Kevin Ryan) *led 1f: chsd ldrs: rdn over 2f out: wknd fnl f* — 11/4[2]

0000 6 9 **Mickstathetricksta**[10] 7399 2-8-0 **63** .... AndreaAtzeni 3 — 31
(Scott Dixon) *sn pushed along towards rr: bhd fr 1/2-way* — 25/1

1m 28.23s (-1.37) **Going Correction** -0.15s/f (Stan) — 6 Ran SP% **109.1**
Speed ratings (Par 98): **101,95,95,93,92 83**
toteswingers 1&2 £2.30, 2&3 £5.80, 1&3 £3.40 CSF £9.49 TOTE £1.60: £1.20, £8.80; EX 12.50.
Owner Godolphin **Bred** Fares Farm Llc **Trained** Newmarket, Suffolk

FOCUS
An ordinary nursery, run at a decent pace. The winner was dominant and the form is rated a tad negatively.

NOTEBOOK
Filfil(USA), strongly supported, took the race by the scruff of the neck after halfway and saw it out comfortably when sent for home. He was took keen over 1m on his previous outing and had shaped as though would be his optimum trip when also placed over that distance the time before. The stronger pace enabled him to relax and he's a good bit better than this class, but the handicapper will have his say. (op 6-4 tchd Evens)
Makinson Lane(IRE) was no match for the winner, but he moved smoothly before being put in his place and this was just about his best effort yet. He'd been dropped 5lb and can surely find a race on Polytrack this year. (op 10-1)
Secret Symphony, sweating beforehand, got taken off his feet early on and was still green. He kept on to suggest this is now his trip, though, and is entitled to come on for the run.
Mystical Man made it third time lucky over 6f at Pontefract when last seen in July. Conceding upwards of 5lb all round on this AW/nursery debut, he couldn't dominate this time and was beaten a long way out. (tchd 6-1)
Al Udeid(IRE), whose yard won the opening 2yo maiden, took a walk in the market prior to this nursery debut. He wasn't helped when taken on for the lead and failed to prove his stamina for the extra furlong. (op 13-8 tchd 3-1)
Mickstathetricksta Official explanation: jockey said that the gelding was never travelling

7615 32REDBET.COM H'CAP (DIV I) — 7f 32y(P)
5:30 (5:30) (Class 6) (0-55,55) 3-Y-O — £1,704 (£503; £251) Stalls High

Form — RPR

0002 1 — **Blackthorn Stick (IRE)**[19] 7189 3-9-7 55 .... AdamKirby 9 — 67+
(John Butler) *a.p: rdn to ld over 1f out: r.o u.p* — 4/1[2]

6056 2 1 ½ **Rogue Reporter (IRE)**[19] 7189 3-9-3 51 .... (v[1]) NeilCallan 1 — 59
(Stuart Williams) *a.p: rdn to chse wnr whn rdr dropped whip 1f out: r.o* — 9/2[3]

3253 3 2 ¼ **Lord Franklin**[11] 7382 3-9-2 55 .... JasonHart(5) 5 — 57
(Eric Alston) *chsd ldrs: rdn to go 2nd over 2f out: ev ch over 1f out: styd on same pce ins fnl f* — 10/3[1]

6365 4 shd **Angel Cake (IRE)**[7] 7470 3-9-4 52 .... TomQueally 4 — 54
(Michael Appleby) *hld up: drvn along 1/2-way: r.o u.p ins fnl f: could nt rch ldrs* — 10/1

0400 5 ¾ **Findhornbay**[57] 6104 3-8-13 47 .... JoeFanning 3 — 47
(Keith Dalgleish) *hld up: hdwy over 1f out: shkn up and n.m.r ins fnl f: styd on same pce* — 16/1

6000 6 1 ¼ **Guava**[19] 7201 3-9-1 49 .... (b[1]) RussKennemore 8 — 46
(Shaun Harris) *sn drvn along to chse ldr: rdn over 2f out: no ex fnl f* — 50/1

245P 7 nk **Green Mountain (IRE)**[7] 7465 3-8-13 50 .... (v) RaulDaSilva(3) 2 — 46
(Philip McBride) *led: rdn and hdd over 1f out: wknd ins fnl f* — 20/1

0005 8 ¾ **Invincible Dream (IRE)**[29] 6926 3-9-0 48 .... (v) IanMongan 11 — 42
(Pat Phelan) *hld up: hdwy u.p over 1f out: no ex ins fnl f* — 16/1

004 9 3 ¾ **Winnetou**[12] 7361 3-9-7 55 .... (b) MartinDwyer 7 — 39
(Frank Sheridan) *hld up: pushed along 1/2-way: rdn over 1f out: wknd ins fnl f* — 14/1

0500 10 hd **Sandy Lane (IRE)**[55] 6152 3-9-6 54 .... GeorgeBaker 10 — 37
(Amy Weaver) *prom: rdn over 2f out: wknd over 1f out* — 9/2[3]

6010 11 1 ¾ **Compton Crofter**[68] 5770 3-8-11 52 .... (t) NicoleNordblad(7) 6 — 30
(Hans Adielsson) *hld up: plld hrd: a in rr* — 20/1

5000 12 1 **Pindrop**[65] 5850 3-9-0 48 .... JohnFahy 12 — 24
(Clive Cox) *hld up: rdn and wknd over 1f out* — 33/1

1m 28.45s (-1.15) **Going Correction** -0.15s/f (Stan) — 12 Ran SP% **121.4**
Speed ratings (Par 98): **100,98,95,95,94 93,92,92,87,87 85,84**
toteswingers 1&2 £4.20, 2&3 £3.10, 1&3 £2.60 CSF £21.95 CT £69.07 TOTE £3.70: £1.60, £1.10, £1.90; EX 12.90 Trifecta £40.40 Pool: £890.36 - 16.51 winning units..
Owner W J Dunphy **Bred** F Prendergast **Trained** Newmarket, Suffolk

FOCUS
A moderate 3yo handicap, run at an average pace. The second helps set the standard.

7616 32REDBET.COM H'CAP (DIV II) — 7f 32y(P)
6:00 (6:00) (Class 6) (0-55,55) 3-Y-O — £1,704 (£503; £251) Stalls High

Form — RPR

605 1 — **Coach Montana (IRE)**[47] 6396 3-9-0 48 .... (b) FrederikTylicki 8 — 55
(Jane Chapple-Hyam) *chsd ldrs: led 2f out: rdn over 1f out: jst hld on* 6/1[3]

0 2 shd **Phils Wish (IRE)**[7] 7457 3-9-2 50 .... AmyRyan 9 — 57
(John C McConnell, Ire) *hld up: plld hrd: hdwy over 2f out: rdn and hung lft fr over 1f out: r.o* — 20/1

6001 3 nk **Precision Five**[88] 5050 3-8-13 50 .... (p) RaulDaSilva(3) 2 — 56
(Jeremy Gask) *hld up: nt clr run over 2f out: hdwy over 1f out: sn rdn: r.o* — 9/1

3530 4 1 **Essell**[13] 7321 3-9-4 52 .... MartinHarley 5 — 56
(Mick Channon) *mid-div: hdwy over 2f out: rdn and hung lft ins fnl f: styd on* — 13/2

0006 5 1 ½ **Glennten**[21] 7146 3-9-7 55 .... GeorgeBaker 4 — 55
(Sylvester Kirk) *chsd ldrs: rdn over 1f out: styd on same pce ins fnl f* 6/1[3]

040 6 ¾ **The Kicking Lord**[18] 7224 3-9-7 55 .... AdamBeschizza 10 — 53
(Mark Brisbourne) *hld up: hdwy over 2f out: outpcd wl over 1f out: r.o towards fin* — 11/2[2]

0500 7 ½ **Lord Paget**[21] 7146 3-8-13 52 .... (p) JackDuern(5) 11 — 49
(Reg Hollinshead) *s.i.s: hld up: rdn over 1f out: r.o ins fnl f: nvr nrr* — 40/1

4012 8 ½ **Gypsy Rider**[11] 7378 3-9-7 55 .... LukeMorris 7 — 51
(Bryn Palling) *chsd ldrs: rdn over 2f out: no ex fnl f* — 6/1[3]

9 hd **Doublebarreljimmy (IRE)**[53] 6221 3-8-13 47 .... (b) TomQueally 12 — 43
(John Butler) *hld up: pushed along 1/2-way: rdn over 2f out: nvr nrr* — 5/1[1]

0050 10 2 ¾ **Louis Hull**[33] 6813 3-9-1 49 .... (v[1]) NeilCallan 1 — 38
(Garry Moss) *led: rdn and hdd 2f out: wknd ins fnl f* — 12/1

000 11 6 **Whatsofunny (IRE)**[48] 6361 3-8-13 47 .... (b[1]) JamesSullivan 3 — 21
(Ruth Carr) *hld up: a in rr: rdn and wknd wl over 1f out* — 20/1

1m 29.31s (-0.29) **Going Correction** -0.15s/f (Stan) — 11 Ran SP% **117.9**
Speed ratings (Par 98): **95,94,94,93,91 90,90,89,89,86 79**
toteswingers 1&2 £44.10, 2&3 £50.60, 1&3 £8.40 CSF £121.62 CT £1098.98 TOTE £10.10: £3.90, £8.10, £4.50; EX 195.60 TRIFECTA Not won..
Owner Carl Moore **Bred** Summerhill & J Osborne **Trained** Dalham, Suffolk

FOCUS
The second division of the moderate 7f 3yo handicap and it looked wide-open. Ordinary form which makes sense.

7617 32RED H'CAP — 1m 5f 194y(P)
6:30 (6:30) (Class 4) (0-80,80) 3-Y-O+ — £2,937 (£2,937; £673; £336) Stalls Low

Form — RPR

2212 1 — **Peachez**[11] 7381 4-9-9 75 .... (p) GeorgeBaker 9 — 82
(Alastair Lidderdale) *hld up: hdwy over 1f out: r.o to dead-heat on line* 7/1

0415 1 dht **Foster's Road**[18] 5637 3-8-7 67 .... AndreaAtzeni 3 — 74
(Mick Channon) *chsd ldrs: rdn to ld over 1f out: jnd on line* — 25/1

0131 3 nk **Rythmic**[11] 7381 3-9-2 76 .... JoeFanning 10 — 83
(Mark Johnston) *chsd ldrs: rdn over 1f out: r.o* — 2/1[1]

1424 4 nk **Scarlet Belle**[47] 6416 3-8-10 70 .... MartinDwyer 8 — 76
(Marcus Tregoning) *chsd ldr: rdn to ld wl over 1f out: sn hdd: styd on* — 5/1[3]

0053 5 ¾ **Icebuster**[41] 6584 4-9-13 79 .... JamesMillman 5 — 86+
(Rod Millman) *s.i.s: hld up: plld hrd: nt clr run over 1f out: r.o ins fnl f: nvr nr to chal* — 3/1[2]

15 6 1 **Passion Planet (IRE)**[11] 7380 4-8-12 64 .... JamesSullivan 7 — 68
(John C McConnell, Ire) *prom: racd keenly: rdn over 1f out: hung lft ins fnl f: styd on same pce* — 20/1

1011 7 ¾ **A Little Bit Dusty**[10] 7413 4-10-0 80 .... (p) TomQueally 4 — 83
(Conor Dore) *hld up: hdwy over 2f out: rdn over 1f out: styd on same pce fnl f* — 16/1

460 8 6 **Star Date (IRE)**[23] 7082 3-9-3 77 .... (tp) LukeMorris 2 — 71
(Gerard Butler) *hld up: nt clr run over 2f out: hdwy over 1f out: wknd fnl f* — 8/1

562- 9 3 ¾ **Raktiman (IRE)**[175] 7002 5-9-4 70 .... AdamKirby 6 — 59
(Chris Bealby) *led: rdn 2f out: sn hdd: wknd fnl f* — 33/1

3m 3.7s (-2.30) **Going Correction** -0.15s/f (Stan)
WFA 3 from 4yo+ 8lb — 9 Ran SP% **116.0**
Speed ratings (Par 105): **100,100,99,99,99 98,98,94,92**WIN: Peachez £3.70, Foster's Road £14.80 PL: Peachez £2.60, Foster's Road £6.50, R £1.02. EX: P/FR £36.80 FR/P £55.00 CSF: P/FR £82.00, FR/P £93.34 TRI: P/FR/Rythmic £238.80 FR/P/R £258.72 toteswingers FR&P £14.00, P&3 £2.50, FR& 3 £5.30: £27, £Owner, £Dave and Gill Hedley, £BredG Hedley & Mike Channon Bloodstock Limited Trained Trifecta £West Ilsley, Berks.
Owner Sally Doyle & Chris Beek **Bred** Mrs Sally Doyle **Trained** Lambourn, Berks

FOCUS
A modest staying handicap. It was run at an ordinary pace and that resulted in a dead-heat and a blanket finish.

7618 32RED SUPPORTING BRITISH RACING H'CAP — 1m 141y(P)
7:00 (7:01) (Class 5) (0-75,75) 3-Y-O+ — £2,264 (£673; £336; £168) Stalls Low

Form — RPR

6026 1 — **Silverware (USA)**[13] 7328 4-9-6 74 .... PatrickMathers 2 — 82
(Linda Stubbs) *chsd ldrs: rdn to ld 1f out: r.o* — 10/1

4005 2 ½ **Kingswinford (IRE)**[3] 7559 6-8-7 68 .... SemiraPashai(7) 3 — 75+
(Alastair Lidderdale) *hld up: hdwy over 3f out: nt clr run 1f out: r.o* — 16/1

0210 3 hd **Inpursuitoffreedom**[25] 7022 5-8-8 65 .... RaulDaSilva(3) 11 — 72
(Philip McBride) *hld up: rdn over 2f out: hdwy over 1f out: r.o* — 10/1

0402 4 1 ¼ **My Single Malt (IRE)**[38] 6692 4-9-4 72 .... PaulMulrennan 12 — 76
(Julie Camacho) *hld up: hdwy u.p over 1f out: r.o* — 7/2[2]

0300 5 ¾ **Ventura Sands (IRE)**[26] 7004 4-9-1 69 .... FrederikTylicki 1 — 71
(Richard Fahey) *chsd ldrs: rdn over 1f out: styd on* — 25/1

-004 6 ¾ **Adorable Choice (IRE)**[12] 7356 4-9-1 69 .... (v) StephenCraine 4 — 70
(Tom Dascombe) *led: rdn and hdd 1f out: wknd towards fin* — 14/1

5001 7 2 ¼ **Stylistickhill (IRE)**[17] 7256 4-8-10 64 .... (t) LukeMorris 6 — 60
(Scott Dixon) *mid-div: rdn over 2f out: wknd ins fnl f* — 13/2[3]

3400 8 1 ¾ **Alkadi (IRE)**[12] 7356 3-8-12 69 .... JoeFanning 8 — 61
(Mark Johnston) *chsd ldrs: rdn over 1f out: wknd ins fnl f* — 7/1

3020 9 hd **Hurricane Spirit (IRE)**[20] 7171 8-9-5 73 .... GeorgeBaker 5 — 65
(Hans Adielsson) *s.i.s: a in rr* — 14/1

5663 10 ½ **Spanish Plume**[7] 7461 4-9-2 75 ....[1] JackDuern(5) 7 — 66
(Reg Hollinshead) *sn outpcd: hdwy over 3f out: pushed along on outer over 2f out: wknd over 1f out* — 3/1[1]

0000 11 7 **Pipers Piping (IRE)**[21] 7142 6-8-11 65 .... FrankieMcDonald 9 — 41
(John Butler) *hld up: pushed along over 2f out: a in rr* — 33/1

106- 12 20 **Shelovestobougie**[341] 7589 4-8-8 62 .... AdamBeschizza 10
(Mark Brisbourne) *prom tl rdn and wknd over 2f out: t.o* — 50/1

1m 48.66s (-1.84) **Going Correction** -0.15s/f (Stan)
WFA 3 from 4yo+ 3lb — 12 Ran SP% **119.2**
Speed ratings (Par 103): **102,101,101,100,99 98,96,95,95,94 88,70**
toteswingers 1&2 £18.80, 2&3 £45.40, 1&3 £12.80 CSF £157.17 CT £1675.61 TOTE £15.10: £3.90, £7.90, £4.30; EX 127.10 TRIFECTA Not won..
Owner Paul & Linda Dixon **Bred** Alliand Equine **Trained** Norton, N Yorks

FOCUS
This was another open handicap. Straightforward form.
Adorable Choice(IRE) Official explanation: jockey that the filly ran too freely
Spanish Plume Official explanation: jockey said that the gelding resented it's hood

7619 £32 BONUS AT 32RED.COM H'CAP (DIV I) — 1m 1f 103y(P)
7:30 (7:31) (Class 6) (0-60,66) 3-Y-O+ — £1,704 (£503; £251) Stalls Low

Form — RPR

2111 1 — **Boonga Roogeta**[4] 7520 3-9-10 66 6ex .... LukeMorris 6 — 78+
(Peter Charalambous) *a.p: chsd ldr over 2f out: led over 1f out: drvn out* — 11/8[1]

313 **2** 2 1/4 **The Wonga Coup (IRE)**[14] 7303 5-9-2 55 .... IanMongan 10 63
(Pat Phelan) *mid-div: hdwy over 2f out: rdn over 1f out: r.o* **6/1**[3]
4412 **3** 1 1/4 **Barton Bounty**[6] 7473 5-9-6 59 .... PaulMulrennan 7 64
(Peter Niven) *prom: rdn over 2f out: styd on same pce ins fnl f* **7/2**[2]
0006 **4** 2 1/4 **El Bravo**[11] 7369 6-9-7 60 ....(b) RussKennemore 9 60
(Shaun Harris) *led after 1f: rdn and hdd over 1f out: no ex ins fnl f* **8/1**
0336 **5** nk **Rhossili Bay**[4] 7527 3-8-10 52 ....(p) FrankieMcDonald 1 52
(Alastair Lidderdale) *s.i.s and given reminders sn after s: hld up: drvn along over 3f out: r.o ins fnl f: nrst fin* **10/1**
2-0 **6** 1 1/2 **Pacey Outswinger (IRE)**[302] 104 5-8-7 46 oh1.......... JamesSullivan 4 42
(John C McConnell, Ire) *chsd ldrs: rdn over 2f out: wknd fnl f* **25/1**
056 **7** 1/2 **Brown Pete (IRE)**[6] 7486 4-9-4 57 .... MartinHarley 5 52
(Violet M Jordan) *s.i.s: hld up: rdn over 2f out: n.d* **12/1**
0006 **8** 3/4 **Bertie Blu Boy**[8] 7443 4-8-0 46 oh1........................(v) ShirleyTeasdale(7) 2 40
(Lisa Williamson) *led 1f: chsd ldr tl rdn over 2f out: wknd fnl f* **40/1**
3005 **9** nk **Doc Hill**[46] 6442 3-8-4 46 oh1.. NickyMackay 3 39
(Michael Blanshard) *mid-div: rdn over 2f out: wknd fnl f* **33/1**
2/00 **10** 9 **Ceto**[14] 7314 5-9-2 55 ....(p) AdamKirby 11 29
(Phil McEntee) *hld up: rdn over 3f out: wknd over 2f out* **50/1**
6000 **11** 12 **Landaho**[17] 7249 3-8-4 46 oh1 .... JamieMackay 8
(Hugh McWilliams) *s.i.s: hld up: rdn over 3f out: wknd over 2f out* **66/1**

1m 59.96s (-1.74) **Going Correction** -0.15s/f (Stan)
WFA 3 from 4yo+ 3lb 11 Ran SP% **119.2**
Speed ratings (Par 101): **101,99,97,95,95 94,93,93,92,84 74**
toteswingers 1&2 £2.40, 2&3 £3.90, 1&3 £2.40 CSF £9.79 CT £25.49 TOTE £2.50: £1.20, £2.30, £1.70; EX 11.40 Trifecta £17.30 Pool: £969.15 - 41.79 winning units..
Owner P Charalambous **Bred** Peter Charles **Trained** Newmarket, Suffolk

FOCUS
This moderate handicap was run at a fair gallop and the form looks solid for the class. The winner continues to progress.

7620 £32 BONUS AT 32RED.COM H'CAP (DIV II) 1m 1f 103y(P)
8:00 (8:00) (Class 6) (0-60,60) 3-Y-0+ **£1,704** (£503; £251) **Stalls** Low

Form RPR
0231 **1** **Dandarrell**[52] 6258 5-9-2 55 .... FrederikTylicki 4 63+
(Julie Camacho) *chsd ldrs: rdn and hung lft fr over 1f out: nt clr run sn after: styd on u.p to ld wl ins fnl f* **9/2**[3]
5422 **2** 1 1/2 **Edgware Road**[6] 7496 4-9-7 60 ....(b) AdamKirby 9 65
(Sean Curran) *a.p: chsd ldr over 3f out: rdn to ld over 1f out: sn hung lft: hdd and unable qck wl ins fnl f* **6/4**[1]
2460 **3** 2 **Corrib (IRE)**[6] 7496 9-8-7 46 oh1 ....(p) LukeMorris 5 47
(Bryn Palling) *hld up: hdwy u.p over 1f out: r.o: could nt rch ldrs* **20/1**
0001 **4** 1/2 **Sasheen**[11] 7385 5-9-1 57 ....(p) RaulDaSilva(3) 10 57
(Jeremy Gask) *chsd ldrs: led over 6f out: rdn and hdd over 1f out: no ex ins fnl f* **8/1**
004 **5** nk **Bandy Bob**[94] 4807 3-8-4 46 oh1 .... JamieMackay 11 46
(Iain Jardine) *hld up: rdn over 3f out: styd on u.p fr over 1f out: nvr nrr* **33/1**
3003 **6** 2 3/4 **Lieutenant Dan (IRE)**[18] 7225 5-9-6 59 ....(p) TomQueally 7 53
(Michael Appleby) *mid-div: rdn over 3f out: hung lft over 1f out: styd on same pce fnl f* **4/1**[2]
50-0 **7** 4 **Chik's Dream**[40] 6616 5-8-8 47 .... AndreaAtzeni 3 34
(Derek Haydn Jones) *mid-div: rdn over 2f out: sn wknd* **12/1**
050 **8** 1/2 **Cairanne**[13] 7321 4-8-11 50 .... MartinLane 8 36
(Tom Keddy) *s.i.s: a in rr* **33/1**
-000 **9** 2 1/4 **Retromania (IRE)**[48] 6365 3-8-5 47 oh1 ow1 ....(b[1]) JohnFahy 6 29
(John Best) *led: hdd over 6f out: chsd ldr tl over 3f out: sn rdn: wknd wl over 1f out* **33/1**
0000 **10** 1 **Bridal Medic**[82] 5261 3-7-11 46 oh1.............................(t) NoelGarbutt(7) 2 26
(Barry Leavy) *hld up: pushed along over 3f out: sn wknd* **50/1**
2140 **11** 4 **Iguacu**[17] 7252 8-8-9 55 ....(p) DanielMuscutt(7) 1 27
(Richard Price) *chsd ldrs tl rdn and wknd over 2f out* **16/1**

2m 0.38s (-1.32) **Going Correction** -0.15s/f (Stan)
WFA 3 from 4yo+ 3lb 11 Ran SP% **118.4**
Speed ratings (Par 101): **99,97,95,95,95 92,89,88,86,85 82**
toteswingers 1&2 £2.80, 2&3 £7.80, 1&3 £9.80 CSF £11.10 CT £124.28 TOTE £2.40: £1.10, £1.30, £5.30; EX 15.20 Trifecta £112.10 Pool: £1067.24 - 7.14 winning units..
Owner Jocelyn Waller **Bred** Peter Onslow **Trained** Norton, N Yorks

FOCUS
The second division of the 0-60 handicap. There was a solid pace on, but nothing landed a blow from out the back. The winner can better this in the short term.
T/Jkpt: Not won. T/Plt: £888.00 to a £1 stake. Pool of £67391.54 - 55.40 winning tickets. T/Qpdt: £102.00 to a £1 stake. Pool of £11832.27 - 85.80 winning tickets. CR

7560 FLEMINGTON (L-H)
Tuesday, November 6

OFFICIAL GOING: Turf: good

7621a EMIRATES MELBOURNE CUP (GROUP 1 H'CAP) (3YO+) (TURF) 2m
4:00 (12:00) 3-Y-0+
£2,500,000 (£592,105; £296,052; £164,473; £115,131; £82,236)

RPR
1 **Green Moon (IRE)**[10] 7426 5-8-6 0 .... BrettPrebble 5 117
(Robert Hickmott, Australia) *sn prom on inner: checked on run to first turn: sn rcvrd and travelled wl in bhd ldrs: swtchd out and rdn to chal 2f out: edgd lft and r.o to ld over 1f out: styd on wl ins fnl f: drvn out* **19/1**
2 1 **Fiorente (IRE)**[51] 6293 4-8-6 0 ....(b[1]) JamesMcDonald 2 116
(Gai Waterhouse, Australia) *sltly slow to stride: prom in midfield on outer: travelled wl into st: rdn 2f out: styd on to go 2nd ent fnl 100yds: chsd wnr cl home but nt pce to chal* **30/1**
3 1 1/4 **Jakkalberry (IRE)**[17] 7264 6-8-10 0 ....(t) CO'Donoghue 19 119
(Marco Botti) *dropped in fr wd draw and hld up in tch in midfield: hdwy on rail fr 3f out: rdn over 2f out: styd on to go 3rd cl home: no ch w wnr* **80/1**
4 3/4 **Kelinni (IRE)**[3] 7560 4-8-0 0 ....(p) GlenBoss 10 108
(Chris Waller, Australia) *sn prom: cut across to rail on run to first bnd squeezing out eventual wnr and settled in 3rd: rdn to chal 2f out: disputing 2nd and stl ev ch ent fnl f: sn outpcd by front pair: dropped to 4th cl home* **18/1**
5 nk **Mount Athos (IRE)**[80] 5354 5-8-7 0 .... RyanMoore 8 114+
(Luca Cumani) *sltly slow to stride: sn towards rr: prog into midfield on outer on run to first turn: bmpd 3f out and again whn rdn over 2f out: styd on down wd outside to go 5th cl home: gng on at fin but nvr able to chal* **13/2**[2]
6 3/4 **Glencadam Gold (IRE)**[17] 7264 4-8-6 0 .... TommyBerry 7 113
(Gai Waterhouse, Australia) *led: set mod pce: stl lobbing along in front on turn into st: rdn 2f out: hdd over 1f out: sn no ex and fdd: dropped to 6th cl home* **40/1**
7 3/4 **Mourayan (IRE)**[31] 6-8-6 0 ....(b) HughBowman 3 112
(Robert Hickmott, Australia) *wnt rt s but broke wl: prom on inner: swtchd out and hdwy to chal on turn into st: rdn 2f out: outpcd by ldrs over 1f out: kpt on but dropped to 7th wl ins fnl f* **25/1**
8 1 **Red Cadeaux**[117] 4010 6-8-10 0 .... MichaelRodd 18 115+
(Ed Dunlop) *sltly slow to stride: dropped in fr wd draw and hld up towards rr: rdn on turn into st: styd on down wd outside to go 8th fnl strides: nvr able to chal* **17/2**[3]
9 hd **Precedence (NZ)**[10] 7425 7-8-5 0 .... BlakeShinn 20 110
(Bart Cummings, Australia) *broke wl and sn prom but trapped wd: stdd on run to first turn and settled in midfield: rdn on turn into st: swtchd ins and styd on to go 9th fnl strides but n.d* **100/1**
10 hd **My Quest For Peace (IRE)**[17] 7264 4-8-6 0 .... CoreyBrown 1 110
(Luca Cumani) *broke wl but stdd in bhd ldrs: short of room on rail on run to first turn: sn settled in midfield on inner: rdn 3f out: styd on one pce in st: dropped to 10th fnl strides* **17/1**
11 1/2 **Americain (USA)**[17] 7264 7-9-2 0 .... DamienOliver 12 120
(A De Royer-Dupre, France) *midfield on inner: bmpd rival whn rdn and swtchd out 3f out and again whn looking for clr run over 2f out: swtchd bk ins and styd on one pce ins fnl 1 1/2f: nvr a threat* **13/2**[2]
12 1 **Cavalryman**[40] 6600 6-8-7 0 .... FrankieDettori 6 110
(Saeed Bin Suroor) *hld up towards rr on inner: rdn and hdwy on turn into st: plugged on but n.d: eased whn btn cl home* **30/1**
13 nk **Voila Ici (IRE)**[17] 7264 7-8-9 0 .... VladDuric 13 111
(Peter G Moody, Australia) *midfield: swtchd out and rdn on turn into st: sn outpcd: plugged on but n.d* **100/1**
14 2 **Dunaden (FR)**[17] 7264 6-9-4 0 .... CraigAWilliams 16 118
(M Delzangles, France) *dropped in and hld up towards rr on outer: pushed along over 3f out: drvn to try and improve on turn into st: plugged on and sme v mod late hdwy but nvr remotely dangerous* **6/1**[1]
15 shd **Niwot (AUS)**[17] 7264 8-8-6 0 .... DwayneDunn 15 106
(Michael, Wayne & John Hawkes, Australia) *broke wl but stdd and sn settled in rr of midfield on inner: rdn on turn into st: sn outpcd: plugged on but wl btn* **70/1**
16 3/4 **Lights Of Heaven (NZ)**[17] 7264 5-8-5 0 ....(p) LukeNolen 17 104
(Peter G Moody, Australia) *sn trcking ldr in 2nd: rdn on turn into st: no ex and btn 1 1/2f out: fdd and sn eased* **19/1**
17 hd **Winchester (USA)**[3] 7562 7-8-10 0 ....(b) JamieMott 22 109
(John D Sadler, Australia) *dropped in fr wd draw and hld up in last trio on inner: rdn on turn into st: outpcd and btn ent fnl f: nvr a factor* **60/1**
18 1/2 **Sanagas (GER)**[17] 7264 6-8-7 0 ....(b) NicholasHall 4 105
(Bart Cummings, Australia) *squeezed s: midfield on outer: rdn on turn into st: no ex and btn 1f out: fdd* **50/1**
19 1/2 **Maluckyday (NZ)**[13] 7346 6-8-6 0 ....(p) JimCassidy 9 104
(Michael, Wayne & John Hawkes, Australia) *towards rr thrght: rdn on turn into st and sn btn: nvr a factor* **16/1**
20 shd **Galileo's Choice (IRE)**[89] 5027 6-8-6 0 .... PatSmullen 11 104
(D K Weld, Ire) *broke wl and sn prom on outer: rdn 3f out: brief effrt to chal on turn into st: sn outpcd: no ex and btn 1f out: fdd* **15/1**
21 shd **Unusual Suspect (USA)**[10] 7425 8-8-5 0 ....(b) GlynSchofield 23 103
(Michael Kent, Australia) *broke wl but stdd and dropped in fr wd draw and hld up in last trio on outer: rdn on turn into st: sn outpcd and btn: nvr a factor* **150/1**
22 hd **Zabeelionaire (NZ)**[3] 7562 4-8-3 0 ....(p) CraigNewitt 24 100
(Leon Corstens, Australia) *dropped in fr wdst draw and hld up in last: rdn over 2f out and sn btn: nvr a factor* **50/1**
23 1 1/4 **Tac De Boistron (FR)**[13] 7346 5-8-6 0 .... ODoleuze 21 102
(Michael Kent, Australia) *dropped in fr wd draw and hld up towards rr: rdn on turn into st: sn outpcd and btn: nvr a factor* **100/1**
24 50 **Ethiopia (AUS)**[10] 7426 4-8-6 0 ....(b) RhysMcLeod 14 47
(Pat Carey, Australia) *sn prom on outer: rdn and lost pl rapidly over 3f out: eased and tailed rt off on turn into st* **20/1**

3m 20.45s (0.81) 24 Ran SP% **113.8**
PARI-MUTUEL (NSW TAB - all including au$1 stakes): WIN 20.80; PLACE 6.60, 12.70, 15.30; DF 533.50; SF 852.70.
Owner N C Williams & Mr & Mrs L J Williams **Bred** Goldsmith Bloodstock Partnership **Trained** Australia
■ Nine of the first ten have raced in either Britain or Ireland.

FOCUS
This edition of the Melbourne Cup looked strong on paper, but will be remembered for any number of runners not getting seriously involved after sitting too far off the leaders. The initial pace was fair but it soon slowed down after the first bend and got even steadier a mile out. Although circumstances dictated a large portion of these would be 'unlucky', only a few jockeys on fancied mounts, in one of the world's most high-profile events, emerge from it with much credit for adapting to the way it developed.

NOTEBOOK
Green Moon(IRE), who once beat a subsequent Dubai World Cup winner in a Newbury handicap when in the care of Harry Dunlop, didn't really show much in the Cox Plate recently after looking to hold sound claims, but returned to the sort of form that saw him land the Turnbull Stakes prior to that. A horse with two victories and a place at the course from five previous starts, he was close up throughout and kicked on about 200 metres out to gained a decisive advantage. From that point, considering he has speed in his armoury, he was not going to be caught.
Fiorente(IRE) was a really difficult contender to weigh up on his debut for Gai Waterhouse. He was very good when at his best for Sir Michael Stoute but has never been the most consistent and new connections opted for blinkers straightaway. James McDonald, having his first ride in the race, tracked the winner into a good position but couldn't get to him once he quickened away, which wasn't a surprise given it turned into a sprint. That said, it was a run full of promise and one would expect to see him back for this next year.
Jakkalberry(IRE) didn't show much in the Caulfield Cup but, under one of the better rides in the race, proved that performance all wrong with an effort more in keeping with his best. Connections may take up their invitation to the Japan Cup.
Kelinni(IRE), who landed one of his two races for Amanda Perrett back in 2010, got into this after landing the Lexus Stakes on Saturday. His form over the last couple of months was decent and Glen Boss was excellent on his mount, never being far away on a gelding with little weight.

Mount Athos(IRE) had always looked to be a horse with plenty of ability no matter who was training him, although Luca Cumani does seem to have got a bit extra out of the gelding this season. His ability to handle fast conditions and a big field were already confirmed but, like many here, he simply had too much ground to make up on turning in to win. The gelding battled on in willing style, passing lots of rivals after getting thrown wide (he got bumped twice at different times by Americain) and one can't help but feel he was potentially the best horse on the day but things conspired against him. He could go to Japan next.
Glencadam Gold(IRE), a really disappointing favourite for the Caulfield Cup and absent from the Lexus on Saturday with a hoof injury, was responsible for the uneven fractions out front, which probably contributed to his final position. He appeared a likely winner in the home straight but his stamina ebbed away.
Red Cadeaux got pushed wide turning in and didn't have the time from that point to get involved.
My Quest For Peace(IRE) had an awkward barrier draw to emerge from but doesn't have too many excuses after being fairly well placed in a stacking field, although he wouldn't have enjoyed the dash to the line. Luca Cumani said afterwards that the gelding could head to Hong Kong next.
Americain(USA) was kept close to the rail early and encountered a couple of problems when attempting to make ground. However, that made no difference to him winning and the decision to change jockeys failed miserably. In fact, one could argue that had Gerald Mosse still been aboard, he'd have been more aware his horse was going to be badly outpaced on ground that was plenty quick enough for him.
Cavalryman was almost last turning in and made up lot of ground before his effort flattened out. Frankie Dettori was easy on his mount late on and his reaction after the race of 'no good' summed it up perfectly.
Dunaden(FR) never had a chance of defending his 2011 victory from his position off the final bend under top weight. It's fair to say his performance lacked his usual sparkle, as even when he was in the clear, he didn't really make any significant ground.
Galileo's Choice(IRE), who hadn't raced since winning the Ballyroan Stakes in August, was one of the best placed of the European contingent from the outset, but Pat Smullen reported afterwards that his mount wouldn't let himself down on the ground.

6974 MAISONS-LAFFITTE (R-H)

Tuesday, November 6

OFFICIAL GOING: Turf: heavy

7622a PRIX MIESQUE (GROUP 3) (2YO FILLIES) (TURF) 7f (S)

1:20 (12:00) 2-Y-O **£33,333** (£13,333; £10,000; £6,666; £3,333)

RPR

1 **Aquatinta (GER)**[18] 2-8-11 0 .... OlivierPeslier 2 104
(H-A Pantall, France) *hld up in rr on stands' side: qcknd wl to join ldrs 1f out: r.o wl to ld 100yds out: comf* **33/10**[2]

2 *1* **Show Gorb (SPA)**[58] 2-8-11 0 .... PhilippeSogorb 7 102
(P Sogorb, France) *followed ldr in centre swtchd outside horses 1 1/2f: qcknd wl to ld 1 1/2f out: hdd 100yds out: r.o* **63/10**

3 *1 ½* **Holy Dazzle**[7] 2-8-11 0 .... RonanThomas 5 98
(J E Pease, France) *prom fr s in stands' side gp: nt qckn and outpcd 1 1/2f out: rallied and fin wl ins fnl f to go 3rd 50yds out* **10/1**

4 *1 ¼* **Melody Of Love**[24] 7052 2-9-1 0 .... EddieAhern 3 99
(Ann Duffield) *a.p in stands' side gp: wnt 3rd u.p ent fnl f: r.o wl: lost 3rd 50yds out: jst hld on for 4th* **23/10**[1]

5 *shd* **Dauphine Russe (FR)**[22] 2-8-11 0 .... ThomasHuet 1 95
(F Doumen, France) *hld up in rr of gp in centre: r.o u.p on outside fnl f: jst missed 4th* **11/1**

6 *¾* **Queen Aggie (IRE)**[24] 7065 2-8-11 0 .... WayneLordan 4 93
(David Evans) *racd in cl 3rd on stands;'side: rdn 2f out: r.o u.p: no ex ins fnl f* **18/1**

7 *5* **Kensea (FR)**[29] 6942 2-8-11 0 .... FabriceVeron 6 80
(H-A Pantall, France) *prom fr s: led stands' side gp: rdn but no ex ent fnl f: fdd: eased 100yds out* **13/2**

8 *4* **You Will See (FR)**[24] 2-8-11 0 .... MaximeGuyon 8 70
(Mario Hofer, Germany) *led gp in centre: rdn and hdd by eventual runner-up 1 1/2 f out: no ex: sn wknd: eased ins fnl f* **6/1**[3]

1m 32.7s (4.70) **8** Ran SP% **117.6**
WIN (incl. 1 euro stake): 4.30. PLACES: 1.80, 2.20, 2.60. DF: 14.10. SF: 22.50.
Owner Haras De Bernesq **Bred** Gestut Karlshof **Trained** France

FOCUS
The form fits with the race averages.
NOTEBOOK
Aquatinta(GER), described as "small but courageous" by her trainer, produced an impressive late burst in the bad ground.
Melody Of Love, a winner in similar ground at Ayr, faded in the latter stages.
Queen Aggie(IRE) was well held on this rise in grade.

7623a CRITERIUM DE MAISONS-LAFFITTE (GROUP 2) (2YO) (TURF) 6f (S)

1:50 (12:00) 2-Y-O **£90,250** (£34,833; £16,625; £11,083; £5,541)

RPR

1 **Penny's Picnic (IRE)**[25] 7122 2-9-0 0 .... AntoineHamelin 3 112
(D Guillemin, France) *hld up towards rr on rail but wl in tch: rdn and hdwy under 1 1/2f out: qcknd to ld 100yds out: comf* **23/5**[2]

2 *1* **Viztoria (IRE)**[37] 6715 2-8-10 0 .... JohnnyMurtagh 10 105
(Edward Lynam, Ire) *prom on outside: led 1 1/2f out: hdd 100yds out: no ex* **13/10**[1]

3 *1 ¼* **Boomshackerlacker (IRE)**[10] 7404 2-9-0 0 .... MaximeGuyon 5 105
(George Baker) *midfield: rdn over 1f out: styd on to press ldr: nt qckn fnl 100yds* **10/1**

4 *hd* **Three Sea Captains (IRE)**[43] 6550 2-9-0 0 .... WayneLordan 6 104
(David Wachman, Ire) *towards rr but wl in tch: styd on to be 4th and ev ch under 1 1/2f out: rdn and kpt on at same pce fnl f* **58/10**[3]

5 *1 ¼* **Snowday (FR)**[30] 6910 2-9-0 0 .... OlivierPeslier 2 101
(C Laffon-Parias, France) *trckd ldr: rdn and nt qckn 1 1/2f out: kpt on at one pce fnl f* **68/10**

6 *3 ½* **Linngaro (FR)**[29] 6942 2-9-0 0 .... UmbertoRispoli 7 90
(Mario Hofer, Germany) *w.w in rr but wl in tch: sme prog over 1 1/2f out: one pce tl fdd fnl 100yds* **32/1**

7 *1* **Chef Oui Chef (FR)**[25] 7122 2-9-0 0 .... Pierre-CharlesBoudot 8 87
(Y De Nicolay, France) *chsd ldrs: rdn and wknd fnl 1 1/2f* **15/1**

8 *½* **Sorry Woman (FR)**[17] 7265 2-8-10 0 .... FabriceVeron 1 82
(H-A Pantall, France) *led: hdd 1 1/2f out: sn wknd* **30/1**

9 *9* **Gordol Du Mes (USA)**[30] 2-9-0 0 ....(p) GBietolini 4 59
(Gianluca Bietolini, Italy) *pressed ldrs: rdn and wknd fr 1 1/2f out: eased ins fnl f* **18/1**

1m 14.4s (1.00) **9** Ran SP% **115.7**
WIN (incl. 1 euro stake): 5.60. PLACES: 1.70, 1.40, 2.20. DF: 6.40. SF: 20.00.
Owner G De St Seine & T Delegue **Bred** F Montauban **Trained** France

FOCUS
The form is rated at the bottom end of the race averages.
NOTEBOOK
Penny's Picnic(IRE) surged to a success that was a good deal more comfortable than the margin of a length suggests. He will probably come back here for the Prix Djebel in April.
Viztoria(IRE) appeared to have most of her rivals in trouble when hitting the front two furlongs out, but the winner pulled away in the last half-furlong. This was a good effort following two easy wins at home, and the Irish Guineas remains her aim.
Boomshackerlacker(IRE) ran really well on ground he "hated", according to his jockey.
Three Sea Captains(IRE) has run in heavy ground on all five of his turf starts.

7624a PRIX DE SEINE-ET-OISE (GROUP 3) (3YO+) (TURF) 6f (S)

2:20 (12:00) 3-Y-O+ **£33,333** (£13,333; £10,000; £6,666; £3,333)

RPR

1 **Myasun (FR)**[29] 6943 5-8-11 0 .... MaximeGuyon 7 107
(C Baillet, France) *midfield in stands' side gp: gd hdwy under 1 1/2f out: rdn and qcknd to ld 150yds out: r.o wl* **128/10**

2 *½* **Maarek**[17] 7236 5-9-2 0 .... SeamieHeffernan 14 111
(David Peter Nagle, Ire) *towards rr outside gp: hdwy under 2f out: briefly short of room over 1f out: swtchd outside and r.o u.p to press wnr 100yds out: no ex cl home* **2/1**[1]

3 *¾* **Sabratah**[29] 6943 4-8-8 0 .... FabriceVeron 6 100
(H-A Pantall, France) *led stands' side gp and overall: hdd under 1 1/2f out: styd prom but sltly outpcd 1f out: kpt on wl fnl f* **19/1**

4 *nk* **Fred Lalloupet**[29] 6943 5-8-11 0 .... FlavienPrat 5 102
(D Smaga, France) *chsd ldrs on stands' side: hrd rdn over 1f out: kpt on fnl f* **24/1**

5 *snk* **Ferro Sensation (GER)**[51] 6-9-2 0 .... SHellyn 3 107
(J Pubben, Holland) *hld up towards rr in stands' side gp: hdwy 1 1/2f out: styd on fnl f: nt pce to chal* **44/1**

6 *nk* **Totxo (IRE)**[28] 4-8-11 0 ....(b) JulienAuge 8 101
(R Avial Lopez, Spain) *towards rr: hrd rdn and styd on under 1 1/2f out: nvr on terms* **19/1**

7 *1* **Ballesteros**[30] 6908 3-8-11 0 .... EddieAhern 15 98
(Brian Meehan) *a.p in outside gp: led overall under 1 1/2f out: sn rdn: hdd 150yds out: wknd fnl 100yds* **9/1**[3]

8 *1 ½* **Iver Bridge Lad**[31] 6867 5-8-11 0 ....(b) StephanePasquier 4 93
(John Ryan) *trckd ldr in stands' side gp: rdn and nt qckn 1 1/2f out: wknd wl ins fnl f* **12/1**

9 *7* **Restiadargent (FR)**[17] 7236 3-8-8 0 .... UmbertoRispoli 2 68
(H-A Pantall, France) *midfield in stands' side gp: one pce u.p fr 1 1/2f out* **11/1**

10 *snk* **Khubala (IRE)**[11] 7366 3-8-11 0 ....(b) JamesDoyle 12 70
(Hugo Palmer) *towards rr: no imp fr under 2f out* **25/1**

11 **Regal Parade**[24] 7066 8-8-11 0 .... MatthewLawson 1 70
(Milton Bradley) *a among bkmarkers: no imp u.p fnl 2f: n.d* **8/1**[2]

12 **Gammarth (FR)**[29] 6943 4-8-11 0 .... JohanVictoire 11 70
(H-A Pantall, France) *chsd ldrs: hrd rdn and no imp over 1f out: wknd and heavily eased ins fnl f* **15/1**

13 **Barbayam**[72] 5648 3-8-8 0 .... OlivierPeslier 13 67
(F Head, France) **13/1**

14 **Pleine Forme (USA)**[44] 4-8-8 0 .... AntoineHamelin 10 67
(A De Royer-Dupre, France) *nvr in contention* **15/1**

15 **Swiss Dream**[31] 6878 4-8-8 0 .... LiamKeniry 9 67
(David Elsworth) *led outside gp: rdn and grad wknd fr under 1 1/2f out: heavily eased fnl f* **45/1**

1m 14.6s (1.20) **15** Ran SP% **119.6**
WIN (incl. 1 euro stake): 13.80. PLACES: 3.50, 1.70, 4.50. DF: 30.40. SF: 78.20.
Owner Ecurie Jarlan **Bred** Sarl Ecurie Jarlan **Trained** France

NOTEBOOK
Myasun(FR) handled ground conditions well to gain a first win in this grade.
Maarek, winner of the British Champions Sprint at Ascot, ran well from an unfavourable draw but couldn't peg back the winner. He's well at home in testing ground.
Ballesteros, the Abbaye fourth, had his ground and showed up well for a long way, but his stamina was waning late on.

7497 KEMPTON (A.W) (R-H)

Wednesday, November 7

OFFICIAL GOING: Standard
Wind: Moderate, across Weather: Cloudy

7625 WIN BIG WITH BETDAQ MULTIPLES MEDIAN AUCTION MAIDEN STKS 1m 2f (P)

4:25 (4:25) (Class 6) 3-4-Y-0 **£1,617** (£481; £240; £120) **Stalls** Low

Form RPR

1 **Villoresi (IRE)** 3-9-3 0 ....[1] HayleyTurner 4 75+
(James Fanshawe) *rn green early in last: wl in tch: prog on outer 2f out to ld over 1f out: pushed wl clr fnl f* **3/1**[2]

-005 2 *6* **Blank Czech (IRE)**[6] 7511 3-9-3 74 ....(b[1]) RichardHughes 1 62
(Amanda Perrett) *led at gd pce: breather 1/2-way: shkn up and hdd over 1f out: no rspnse and sn btn: jst clung on for 2nd* **8/15**[1]

4 3 *shd* **La Belle Doyenne**[21] 7162 4-9-2 0 .... FergusSweeney 3 57
(Alan King) *trckd ldng pair: shkn up and outpcd over 1f out: kpt on fnl f: nrly snatched 2nd* **9/1**[3]

- 4 *2 ¾* **Giantstepsahead (IRE)** 3-8-12 0 ....[1] HarryPoulton[(5)] 2 57
(Terry Clement) *t.k.h: hld up in last pair: stopped pulling and dropped off remainder over 3f out: pushed along and nvr on terms after* **33/1**

365 5 *5* **Trulee Scrumptious**[52] 6274 3-8-12 52 ....(b) RobertWinston 5 42
(Peter Charalambous) *trckd ldr: pushed up to chal 4f out to over 2f out: wknd rapidly* **14/1**

2m 5.29s (-2.71) **Going Correction** -0.125s/f (Stan)
WFA 3 from 4yo 4lb **5** Ran SP% **109.8**
Speed ratings (Par 101): **105,100,100,97,93**
CSF £4.99 TOTE £3.10: £1.50, £1.10; EX 6.40.
Owner Mr & Mrs W J Williams **Bred** B Kennedy **Trained** Newmarket, Suffolk

The Form Book Flat, Raceform Ltd, Compton, RG20 6NL

FOCUS
A weak maiden run at a fair pace. The winner can do better than the bare form.

7626 BACK OR LAY AT BETDAQ.COM H'CAP 1m 2f (P)
4:55 (4:55) (Class 4) (0-85,85) 3-Y-O+ **£4,075** (£1,212; £606; £303) **Stalls** Low

Form RPR
4200 **1** **Night And Dance (IRE)**[8] 7461 4-9-10 **85** AdamKirby 3 93
(Clive Cox) *wl plcd in slowly run contest bhd ldng pair: shkn up and prog to ld 1f out: drvn out* **10/1**[3]
3524 **2** ½ **Inthar (USA)**[23] 7116 3-9-3 **82** MickaelBarzalona 9 89+
(Saeed Bin Suroor) *hld up in rr in slowly run event: n.m.r over 1f out: plld out and r.o wl to take 2nd nr fin: too much to do* **11/8**[1]
1006 **3** ½ **Franco Is My Name**[74] 5595 6-9-10 **85** (p) IanMongan 6 91
(Peter Hedger) *trckd ldrs and wl in tch: shkn up and hung fire over 1f out: r.o to take 2nd ins fnl f: hld by wnr and lost 2nd nr fin* **20/1**
0340 **4** ½ **Tuscania**[14] 7334 4-9-7 **82** FrederikTylicki 2 87+
(Lucy Wadham) *hld up in rr in slowly run r: nt clr run over 1f out: squeezed through sn after: r.o to take 4th nr fin: no ch* **10/1**[3]
340 **5** *nk* **Ellemujie**[21] 7175 7-9-6 **81** (p) MartinLane 1 86
(Dean Ivory) *hld up in midfield: effrt over 1f out: styd on same pce fnl f: nvr able to chal* **12/1**
1020 **6** 1 ¼ **Danube River**[13] 7353 3-8-13 **78** FrannyNorton 10 80
(Mark Johnston) *led after 1f whn nthing else wanted to: wound it up fr 3f out: hdd & wknd 1f out* **12/1**
0203 **7** ½ **Sakhee's Pearl**[54] 6207 6-8-9 **75** NathanSweeney(5) 8 78+
(Jo Crowley) *hld up in last pair in slowly run event: swtchd ins and nt clr run over 1f out: prog and trying to cl whn hmpd ins fnl f: nt rcvr* **8/1**[2]
61- **8** ½ **Parigino (FR)**[254] 4-9-5 **80** GeorgeBaker 5 82+
(Nick Gifford) *hld up in rr in slowly run event: nt clr run over 1f out: prog whn hmpd 1f out: nt rcvr* **50/1**
0060 **9** ¾ **Mawaakef (IRE)**[21] 7175 4-9-10 **85** DarryllHolland 11 84
(J R Jenkins) *hld up in last pair in slowly run event and racd wd: v wd into st and stl last: r.o fnl f: no ch* **10/1**[3]
1300 **10** 1 ¾ **Casual Mover (IRE)**[174] 2199 4-9-1 **76** FergusSweeney 4 72
(John Best) *reluctant ldr 1f: chsd ldr after tl wknd qckly over 1f out* **16/1**
4056 **11** 1 ½ **Fantasy Gladiator**[69] 5768 6-9-2 **77** (p) JimmyQuinn 7 70
(Robert Cowell) *hld up towards rr: nt qckn on outer wl over 1f out: no prog after* **25/1**
0010 **12** 11 **Islesman**[35] 6804 4-9-3 **78** RichardHughes 12 50
(Heather Main) *racd wd early: prom tl wknd over 1f out: eased: t.o* **14/1**

2m 6.27s (-1.73) **Going Correction** -0.125s/f (Stan)
WFA 3 from 4yo+ 4lb **12** Ran SP% **119.0**
Speed ratings (Par 105): **101,100,100,99,99 98,98,97,97,95 94,85**
toteswingers: 1&2 £5.30, 1&3 £40.20, 2&3 £10.80 CSF £23.60 CT £288.44 TOTE £12.00: £2.80, £1.40, £6.70; EX 34.50 TRIFECTA Not won..
Owner H E Sheikh Sultan Bin Khalifa Al Nahyan **Bred** Round Hill Stud **Trained** Lambourn, Berks

FOCUS
A competitive handicap, despite the lopsided look of the market. The pace was slow and the race had a messy look to it.
Parigino(FR) Official explanation: jockey said gelding was denied a clear run.
Islesman Official explanation: jockey said gelding moved poorly behind.

7627 BRITISH STALLION STUDS SUPPORTING BRITISH RACING EBF MAIDEN STKS (DIV I) 7f (P)
5:25 (5:29) (Class 5) 2-Y-O **£3,169** (£943; £471; £235) **Stalls** Low

Form RPR
0 **1** **Rottingdean**[14] 7330 2-9-3 0 WilliamBuick 8 73+
(John Gosden) *hld up in midfield: plld out over 2f out: prog over 1f out: chsd ldr ins fnl f: drvn and r.o to ld post* **5/2**[2]
4352 **2** *nse* **Tarbawi (IRE)**[21] 7164 2-9-3 75 (p) MickaelBarzalona 4 73
(Saeed Bin Suroor) *trckd ldrs: prog and pushed into ld over 1f out: rdn fnl f: hdd post* **7/4**[1]
0 **3** 1 ¾ **Mac's Superstar (FR)**[48] 6411 2-9-3 0 MartinLane 3 68
(James Fanshawe) *trckd ldrs: tried to chal on inner over 1f out: styd on same pce after* **20/1**
0 **4** ½ **Tebbit (USA)**[21] 7167 2-9-3 0 NeilCallan 7 67
(Roger Varian) *dwlt: hld up in midfield: effrt over 2f out: shkn up and prog over 1f out: kpt on to take 4th last strides* **10/1**
0 **5** *nk* **Sabre Rock**[6] 7507 2-9-3 0 GeorgeBaker 1 66
(John Best) *led to over 1f out: one pce fnl f* **16/1**
6 ¾ **Visit Copenhagen (USA)** 2-8-12 0 MartinHarley 9 59+
(Mrs K Burke) *wl in rr: shkn up over 2f out: prog jst over 1f out: styd on fnl f: nrst fin* **14/1**
40 **7** ¾ **Mazaaher**[15] 7306 2-9-3 0 PaulHanagan 11 62+
(Marcus Tregoning) *dwlt: hld up in last pair: pushed along over 2f out: sme prog over 1f out: no hdwy fnl f: possible improver* **14/1**
0 **8** 1 ½ **King Of The Danes**[12] 7371 2-9-3 0 FrannyNorton 5 58
(Mark Johnston) *chsd ldr to 2f out: steadily wknd* **25/1**
9 1 **Atlantis City (FR)** 2-9-3 0 RichardHughes 2 55
(Richard Hannon) *difficult to load into stalls: dwlt: wl in rr: pushed along over 2f out: mod prog whn nt clr run over 1f out: n.d after* **8/1**[3]
10 2 ¼ **Captain Caroline** 2-8-12 0 FergusSweeney 6 44
(Mike Murphy) *difficult to load into stalls: s.s then swvd: mostly in last: nvr a factor* **100/1**
00 **11** 1 ½ **Ebony Roc (IRE)**[34] 6818 2-9-3 0 AdamKirby 10 45
(Amanda Perrett) *prom on outer: wknd over 2f out* **66/1**

1m 25.34s (-0.66) **Going Correction** -0.125s/f (Stan) **11** Ran SP% **115.4**
Speed ratings (Par 96): **98,97,95,95,95 94,93,91,90,87 86**
toteswingers: 1&2 £1.70, 1&3 £20.20, 2&3 £11.00 CSF £6.81 TOTE £3.50: £1.40, £1.10, £7.50; EX 8.40 Trifecta £210.00 Pool: £2,405.88 - 8.59 winning units..
Owner Denford Stud **Bred** Denford Stud Ltd **Trained** Newmarket, Suffolk

FOCUS
An interesting juvenile maiden run at a fair pace. The field was compressed and the bare form is modest.

NOTEBOOK
Rottingdean confirmed the promise he'd shown at Newmarket on his debut. The winner, sporting a first-time hood, travelled well in midfield for much of this but looked to be playing for minor honours as the eventual runner-up skipped clear in the straight. However, pulled out widest of all, he really stuck to his guns and was able to put his head in front where it mattered most. A never-nearer 9th of 17 at Newmarket a fortnight previously, this distance looks a bare minimum for him. He's unlikely to be seen again this year but is very much one to keep in mind for middle-distance handicaps next term. (op 3-1)
Tarbawi(IRE) set the standard on all known form and he appeared to have the race sewn up when carting his way to the front in his first-time cheekpieces. There was a suspicion that he wasn't doing a lot to help his jockey however and, while clearly talented, he may require further headgear applied if he's to open his account. (op 6-4 tchd 11-8)
Mac's Superstar(FR) was by no means disgraced and stepped up considerably on his Yarmouth debut. He took well to this surface and may be worth trying back over 6f. (op 33-1)
Tebbit(USA) looks something of a longer-term project but connections will surely be pleased with this effort. He went as well as anything for much of the race but lacked the pace of the principals. (op 8-1)
Visit Copenhagen(USA) ran on late without ever threatening. (op 16-1 tchd 20-1)
Mazaaher didn't get the clearest of runs and is better than the bare form suggests. He'll now go handicapping.

7628 BRITISH STALLION STUDS SUPPORTING BRITISH RACING EBF MAIDEN STKS (DIV II) 7f (P)
5:55 (5:58) (Class 5) 2-Y-O **£3,169** (£943; £471; £235) **Stalls** Low

Form RPR
23 **1** **Lilac Tree**[21] 7167 2-9-3 0 MickaelBarzalona 8 77
(Mahmood Al Zarooni) *led after 1f: mde rest: kicked on over 2f out: styd on wl fnl f* **3/1**[2]
52 **2** ¾ **Swift Bounty**[20] 7191 2-9-3 0 RobertWinston 1 75+
(Alan Jarvis) *racd freely: led 1f: stdd into 3rd after 2f: nt qckn and outpcd by ldng pair over 2f out: styd on wl to take 2nd ins fnl f: gaining fin* **4/1**[3]
04 **3** 1 **Wallenberg**[14] 7323 2-9-3 0 (e) WilliamBuick 5 72
(John Gosden) *trckd wnr after 2f: tried to kick on w him over 2f out and clr of rest: nt qckn over 1f out: hld after: lost 2nd ins fnl f* **8/1**
05 **4** 2 **Lyric Ballad**[15] 7306 2-8-12 0 RobertHavlin 4 62+
(Hughie Morrison) *settled in rr: pushed along and prog fr 2f out: no ch w ldrs but styd on steadily fnl f* **50/1**
0 **5** *nk* **Grayswood**[25] 7067 2-9-3 0 MartinDwyer 2 66
(William Muir) *trckd ldrs: outpcd over 2f out: shkn up and kpt on fr over 1f out* **25/1**
3 **6** 2 **Twary (USA)**[89] 5042 2-9-3 0 PaulHanagan 10 61
(Roger Varian) *s.s: t.k.h on wd outside and prom over 4f out: nt qckn and outpcd over 2f out: wknd over 1f out* **6/4**[1]
60 **7** *shd* **Nateeja (IRE)**[14] 7324 2-8-12 0 HayleyTurner 9 55+
(Marcus Tregoning) *dwlt: hld up in last: pushed along over 2f out: nvr a factor but kpt on steadily fr over 1f out: nt disgracd* **33/1**
0 **8** 1 ¼ **Knight Owl**[14] 7330 2-9-3 0 MartinLane 7 57
(James Fanshawe) *dwlt: wl in rr: rdn and struggling wl over 2f out: kpt on fr over 1f out* **12/1**
6 **9** 2 ¼ **Halling's Wish**[20] 7191 2-9-3 0 GeorgeBaker 3 51
(John Best) *trckd ldrs: outpcd over 2f out: wknd over 1f out* **33/1**
0 **10** 4 **Gold Weight**[35] 6772 2-9-3 0 JamieGoldstein 11 40
(Michael Madgwick) *towards rr: no prog over 2f out: wknd wl over 1f out* **100/1**
11 4 **Putmeintheswindle** 2-9-3 0 IanMongan 6 29
(Peter Hedger) *towards rr: wknd over 2f out: sn bhd* **100/1**

1m 26.04s (0.04) **Going Correction** -0.125s/f (Stan) **11** Ran SP% **117.5**
Speed ratings (Par 96): **94,93,92,89,89 87,86,85,82,78 73**
toteswingers: 1&2 £3.10, 1&3 £3.90, 2&3 £6.50 CSF £14.74 TOTE £3.60: £1.70, £1.30, £1.80; EX 15.10 Trifecta £54.80 Pool: £2,110.80 - 28.85 winning units..
Owner Godolphin **Bred** Biddestone Stud Ltd **Trained** Newmarket, Suffolk

FOCUS
The second division of this maiden looked equally as competitive as the first and it saw a taking performance. The winner posted a slight personal best and the second possibly should have won.

NOTEBOOK
Lilac Tree paid a handsome compliment to Correspondent, who had beaten him readily at Lingfield last time. The 70,000gns colt was given a positive ride on this occasion and, having settled nicely out in front, put the race to bed with a smart turn of foot from 2f out. Visibly tiring inside the final furlong, this is probably as far as he'd like to go at this stage of his career and it would be no surprise should connections opt to drop him back to 6f for his next start. (op 5-2 tchd 9-4)
Swift Bounty ran an eyecatching race, running on strongly from out of the pack to close down the winner. He had finished with a similar burst over C&D last time and surely has a race in him. Now qualified for handicaps, it will be interesting to see if he's persevered with over this distance. (op 3-1 tchd 9-2)
Wallenberg continues to improve with racing and he was seen in a much better light back over this trip, having failed to see out a mile here last time. (tchd 7-1)
Lyric Ballad made up a mountain of ground from the rear and is definitely worth keeping tabs on if taking the handicap route.
Twary(USA) was disappointing. He, like on debut, blew the start but failed to find anything for pressure on a surface that should have suited. (op 5-2)

7629 BETDAQ MOBILE APPS H'CAP 2m (P)
6:25 (6:29) (Class 6) (0-60,58) 3-Y-O+ **£1,617** (£481; £240; £120) **Stalls** Low

Form RPR
-060 **1** **Italian Riviera**[21] 7174 3-8-10 **51** LukeMorris 5 64+
(Sir Mark Prescott Bt) *hld up bhd ldrs: prog to ld over 2f out: edgd lft and narrowly hdd over 1f out: hrd rdn and responded to ld again ins fnl f: forged clr* **6/1**[2]
6343 **2** 1 ¾ **Celtic Charlie (FR)**[27] 7012 7-9-5 **51** IanMongan 9 59
(Pat Phelan) *hld up in midfield: prog over 3f out to chal 2f out: narrow ld over 1f out: hdd and no ex ins fnl f* **9/1**
0024 **3** 2 **Kampai**[17] 7270 4-9-9 **55** RichardHughes 11 61
(Julia Feilden) *hld up wl in rr: prog fr 4f out: rdn to chse ldng pair 2f out and cl enough: one pce over 1f out* **4/1**[1]
0063 **4** 3 ½ **Rollin 'n Tumblin**[21] 7169 8-8-13 **45** JimmyQuinn 10 46
(Michael Attwater) *hld up in last trio: plenty to do fr 6f out: effrt whn hmpd 3f out: gd prog on inner 2f out: wnt 4th over 1f out: no imp after* **20/1**
3640 **5** ¾ **Comedy House**[15] 7303 4-9-11 **57** JamieGoldstein 2 58
(Michael Madgwick) *hld up in rr: rdn wl over 2f out: styd on fnl 2f: n.d to ldrs* **6/1**[2]
3054 **6** 6 **Astroscarlet**[34] 6807 3-9-3 **58** PaulHanagan 14 51
(Mark H Tompkins) *prom: chsd ldr after 6f: drvn 3f out: wknd 2f out* **7/1**[3]
65-0 **7** ¾ **Novel Dancer**[21] 7169 4-9-9 **55** (e) RobertHavlin 8 47
(Lydia Richards) *hld up in midfield: prog to trck ldrs over 3f out gng strly: drvn and struggling whn sltly impeded over 2f out: drifted lft and wknd* **25/1**
5-46 **8** 2 ¼ **Tower**[10] 2242 5-9-5 **51** (e) GeorgeBaker 7 41
(Martin Keighley) *reluctant to enter stalls: hld up in last pair: lft bhd whn pce qcknd after 1/2-way: no ch after: passed wkng rivals fnl 2f* **8/1**
/660 **9** 3 ¼ **Cubism**[12] 7381 6-9-4 **50** (vt) SeanQuinlan 12 36
(Anthony Middleton) *t.k.h: prom: wknd 3f out* **50/1**
3626 **10** 4 **Tokyo Brown (USA)**[5] 7528 3-9-3 **58** (v[1]) NeilCallan 13 39
(Heather Main) *plld way into ld after 1f: set mod pce tl past 1/2-way: hdd & wknd qckly over 2f out* **6/1**[2]
506/ **11** 1 ½ **Llamadas**[2118] 192 10-9-9 **55** KirstyMilczarek 4 34
(Olivia Maylam) *led 1f: styd prom tl wknd 3f out* **33/1**
60-0 **12** 1 ¼ **Burnbrake**[48] 6399 7-8-13 **45** DarryllHolland 3 23
(Richard Rowe) *hld up in midfield: rdn and no prog 3f out: sn wknd* **50/1**

0/2 **13** *5* **Iron Duke**[18] 7255 6-8-6 **45**....................(t) PhilipPrince(7) 6 17
(Liam Corcoran) *prom on outer tl wknd rapidly over 3f out* **20/1**

1666 **14** *43* **Chapter Nine (IRE)**[51] 6305 6-9-6 **52**.................... LiamKeniry 1
(Mike Hammond) *tk fierce hold: hld up in last: wknd over 3f out: wl t.o* **50/1**

3m 30.81s (0.71) **Going Correction** -0.125s/f (Stan)
WFA 3 from 4yo+ 9lb **14** Ran SP% **118.7**
Speed ratings (Par 101): **93,92,91,89,89 86,85,84,82,80 80,79,77,55**
toteswingers: 1&2 £14.00, 1&3 £6.10, 2&3 £8.50 CSF £53.57 CT £241.36 TOTE £9.00: £3.00, £2.90, £1.70; EX 65.50 Trifecta £214.20 Pool: £1,657.07 - 5.80 winning units..
Owner J L C Pearce **Bred** J L C Pearce **Trained** Newmarket, Suffolk
■ Stewards' Enquiry : Jamie Goldstein three-day ban; careless riding (21st-23rd Nov).

FOCUS
A poor staying handicap which was steadily run. The winner was an understandable improver.
Italian Riviera Official explanation: trainers representative said gelding had run too keenly in two its races and was suited by this step up in trip.
Rollin 'n Tumblin Official explanation: jockey said gelding suffered interference in running.

7630 CONGRATULATIONS CHAMPION JOCKEY RICHARD HUGHES FLOODLIT STKS (LISTED RACE) 1m 4f (P)
6:55 (6:58) (Class 1) 3-Y-O+
£18,714 (£7,095; £3,550; £1,768; £887; £445) **Stalls** Centre

Form RPR

2120 **1** **Spring Of Fame (USA)**[47] 6446 6-9-3 112.................... MickaelBarzalona 8 110
(Saeed Bin Suroor) *hld up in last trio: stdy prog on outer over 2f out: shkn up and r.o to ld last 150yds: sn in command: readily* **11/2**[2]

6336 **2** *1 ½* **Modun (IRE)**[53] 6236 5-9-3 108.................... SilvestreDeSousa 3 108
(Saeed Bin Suroor) *trckd ldrs: drvn and prog over 2f out to ld over 1f out: hdd and one pce last 150yds* **11/4**[1]

4111 **3** *½* **Viking Storm**[53] 6248 4-9-3 102.................... PaulHanagan 2 107
(Harry Dunlop) *led 1f: trckd ldrs after: rdn to chal and upsides wl over 1f out: kpt on same pce after* **11/4**[1]

1533 **4** *3 ¼* **Media Hype**[59] 6091 5-9-3 101.................... MartinHarley 4 102
(Mrs K Burke) *led after 1f: allowed to stride on after 4f: hdd over 1f out: wknd* **9/1**[3]

6030 **5** *1 ½* **Tappanappa (IRE)**[23] 7098 5-9-3 91....................(b) WilliamBuick 1 99
(Brian Ellison) *s.s: in tch in last trio: rdn 3f out: hanging and lft bhd over 2f out: nvr on terms after* **25/1**

1126 **6** *nk* **Sequence (IRE)**[41] 6598 3-8-8 100 ow2.................... RichardHughes 5 96
(Sir Michael Stoute) *trckd ldr after 2f: shkn up and nt qckn over 2f out: steadily wknd over 1f out* **11/4**[1]

250- **7** *dist* **Nebula Storm (IRE)**[14] 3418 5-9-3 100.................... GeorgeBaker 7
(Gary Moore) *hld up last: lost tch bef 1/2-way: wl t.o whn virtually p.u fnl 2f* **100/1**

2m 28.99s (-5.51) **Going Correction** -0.125s/f (Stan) course record
WFA 3 from 4yo+ 6lb **7** Ran SP% **110.2**
Speed ratings (Par 111): **113,112,111,109,108 108,42**
toteswingers: 1&2 £2.70, 1&3 £2.40, 2&3 £2.00 CSF £19.44 TOTE £7.00: £2.40, £1.80; EX 19.90 Trifecta £77.30 Pool: £2,413.48 - 23.40 winning units..
Owner Godolphin **Bred** Brushwood Stable **Trained** Newmarket, Suffolk

FOCUS
A really good turnout for this Listed feature, which was run in a course record time. The winner looks as good as ever.

NOTEBOOK
Spring Of Fame(USA) had done well in three starts at the Dubai Carnival in the spring, but he'd failed to translate that level of form back to turf when beating just one home on his British return at Newbury in September. However, back on his favoured surface, he created a favourable impression, coming from off the pace to win going away. He did have stamina to prove at this distance but clearly relished this extra furlong and, on this evidence, may well be able to cope with marathon distances. Opportunities in Britain are limited for him so he'll head back to sunnier climes. (tchd 5-1)
Modun(IRE) ran a solid race, although he remains winless from six starts in 2012. While carrying the first colours of Godolphin, he had a bit to find with the winner on these terms and appeared to run right up to his best. (tchd 3-1)
Viking Storm continues to go the right way. A winner of four of his last five races, he by no means looked out of place in this grade and could still have more to offer. (tchd 5-2)
Media Hype kept on well having set the gallop. Usually held up, he took well to these tactics and was by no means disgraced, especially if noting his first win of the year in April had come off a mark of only 70. (op 8-1 tchd 10-1)
Tappanappa(IRE) never landed a blow but was closer at the finish than at any other stage. (op 33-1)
Sequence(IRE) dropped out disappointingly. She faced no easy task here however and may not have taken to the surface. (op 3-1)
Nebula Storm(IRE) Official explanation: jockey said gelding was never travelling.

7631 PETER SLATTERY BIG BIRTHDAY H'CAP 1m (P)
7:25 (7:29) (Class 3) (0-95,95) 3-Y-O+ **£6,663** (£1,982; £990; £495) **Stalls** Low

Form RPR

315- **1** **Validus**[396] 6692 3-9-5 **95**.................... KirstyMilczarek 4 107+
(Luca Cumani) *hld up in 8th: prog fr 2f out: sustained effrt to ld last 100yds: r.o wl* **14/1**

5314 **2** *1 ¼* **True To Form (IRE)**[6] 7502 5-9-6 **94**....................(p) DavidProbert 3 102
(Martyn Meade) *led 2f: trckd ldng pair sn after: clsd to ld again over 1f out: hdd and outpcd last 100yds* **20/1**

-204 **3** *1 ½* **Terdaad (IRE)**[103] 4557 4-9-3 **91**....................(tp) SilvestreDeSousa 8 96
(Saeed Bin Suroor) *tk v t.k.h: led after 2f: hdd and one pce over 1f out* **10/1**

0022 **4** *nk* **Chapter And Verse (IRE)**[14] 7327 6-8-11 **85**.................... RichardHughes 14 89
(Mike Murphy) *hld up in last: prog wl over 1f out: shkn up and styd on fnl f: nt pce to threaten* **14/1**

0-1 **5** *nk* **Net Whizz (USA)**[48] 6397 3-8-8 **84**.................... WilliamBuick 6 87+
(Jeremy Noseda) *dwlt: hld up in 7th: taken out wd and rdn over 2f out: stl green and nt qckn: styd on fr over 1f out: nt rch ldrs* **5/6**[1]

6604 **6** *2 ¼* **George Guru**[60] 6036 5-9-2 **93**.................... MarkCoumbe(3) 5 91
(Michael Attwater) *reluctant to enter stalls: t.k.h: prom: drvn over 2f out: wknd jst over 1f out* **7/1**[2]

1360 **7** *2* **Invisible Hunter (USA)**[60] 6046 3-9-3 **93**...........(t) MickaelBarzalona 10 87
(Saeed Bin Suroor) *racd wd early: prog to chse ldr over 5f out: rdn and nt qckn over 2f out: wknd over 1f out* **8/1**[3]

0103 **8** *nk* **Shavansky**[26] 7017 8-9-0 **88**.................... JamesMillman 12 81
(Rod Millman) *dwlt: hld up in last: taken to far rail and shuffled along fnl 2f: nvr involved* **14/1**

2013 **9** *¾* **Rustic Deacon**[28] 6979 5-8-8 **85**.................... RaulDaSilva(3) 13 76+
(Willie Musson) *t.k.h: prom on outer: rdn over 2f out: wknd wl over 1f out* **12/1**

- **10** *¾* **Eighty Eight Red**[422] 4-8-12 **86**.................... LukeMorris 1 75
(Ed Walker) *dwlt: sn chsd ldrs in 6th: drvn over 2f out: wknd over 1f out* **66/1**

1m 37.65s (-2.15) **Going Correction** -0.125s/f (Stan)
WFA 3 from 4yo+ 2lb **10** Ran SP% **121.2**
Speed ratings (Par 107): **105,103,102,101,101 99,97,97,96,95**
toteswingers: 1&2 £17.40, 1&3 £10.20, 2&3 £6.70 CSF £268.55 CT £2922.00 TOTE £21.90: £4.50, £4.00, £2.30; EX 347.60 Trifecta £1022.70 Part won. Pool: £1,363.67 - 0.30 winning units..
Owner S Stuckey **Bred** Stuart Stuckey **Trained** Newmarket, Suffolk

FOCUS
A decent 1m handicap, run at an early crawl. Solid form, and the winner is a good prospect.

NOTEBOOK
Validus came from off the pace to win on his return from a 396-day absence. The 3yo, who had suffered a nasty rib injury after finishing fifth of eight in a Newmarket Group 3, showed no rustiness and burst clear inside the final furlong to win convincingly. A wide margin winner of a maiden over C&D here in September 2011, he's clearly well suited to this surface and appears to have a bright future ahead of him. He, like the previous Listed winner, probably won't have too many opportunities over the winter months in Britain given his lofty rating, and it's likely that connections will be forced to look abroad should they wish to keep him going. Dubai looks the obvious target for him at this stage. (op 25-1)
True To Form(IRE) has a tremendous record on this surface and he turned in yet another excellent effort. This was only his second start since March and there could still be a bit more improvement to come from him. A winner over 1m2f here earlier in the year, he did well to keep pace with these in the straight. (op 14-1)
Terdaad(IRE) was handed the early lead on sufferance and did well in the circumstances. He tried to pinch it as they turned for home but was readily left behind by the principals.
Chapter And Verse(IRE) would not have been suited by the tactical nature of this and deserves credit. He's weighted up to the hilt but remains in good heart and is always dangerous around here. (op 10-1)
Net Whizz(USA) failed to shine but showed enough to suggest he'll be competitive in similar races off his mark. He took a while to hit top gear and was another undone by the funereal tempo. (tchd 4-5 and 10-11)

7632 DOWNLOAD THE FREE RACING PLUS APP H'CAP 1m 4f (P)
7:55 (7:57) (Class 6) (0-55,55) 3-Y-O **£1,617** (£481; £240; £120) **Stalls** Centre

Form RPR

0002 **1** **Sir Dylan**[6] 7499 3-9-1 **54**.................... LukeMorris 6 64
(Ronald Harris) *hld up in last: gd prog 3f out but stl plenty to do: sustained hdwy to chse clr ldr ins fnl f: drvn and r.o to ld post* **6/1**[2]

0564 **2** *shd* **Awesome Rock (IRE)**[7] 7488 3-8-7 **46** oh1.................... FrannyNorton 3 56
(Louise Best) *hld up wl in rr: rapid prog on outer fr 1/2-way to chse clr ldr wl over 3f out: clsd to ld over 2f out: 3 l ahd 1f out: ct post* **33/1**

5423 **3** *3* **Taro Tywod (IRE)**[5] 7527 3-9-1 **54**.................... ShaneKelly 8 59
(Mark Brisbourne) *wl in tch in chsng gp: drvn on outer over 2f out: prog to chse clr ldr over 1f out: one pce and lost 2nd ins fnl f* **9/4**[1]

0000 **4** *2 ¼* **Corn Maiden**[20] 7196 3-8-7 **46** oh1....................(b[1]) SilvestreDeSousa 14 48
(Mark Rimmer) *fast away fr wdst draw: led and clr w one rival after 3f: clr on her own fr 1/2-way: hdd over 2f out: sn btn but kpt on* **33/1**

6425 **5** *½* **Merchants Return**[33] 6838 3-8-9 **51**....................(v) SimonPearce(3) 11 52
(Lydia Pearce) *s.i.s and short of room sn after: wl in rr: rapid prog on outer fr 4f out to chse ldng pair 3f out: fdd and lost 3rd over 1f out* **8/1**

00-0 **6** *3 ¼* **Midnight Bahia (IRE)**[42] 6582 3-8-8 **47** oh1 ow1.......... DarryllHolland 2 43
(Dean Ivory) *hld up wl in rr: stl long way adrift 3f out: pushed along and prog over 2f out: nvr nrr* **16/1**

0005 **7** *3 ¼* **Ecechelra**[119] 3965 3-8-7 **46** oh1.................... JimmyQuinn 7 36
(Dean Ivory) *wl there in chsng gp: rdn over 3f out: steadily wknd over 2f out* **33/1**

0546 **8** *1 ¼* **Suedehead**[41] 6616 3-9-1 **54**.................... MartinDwyer 9 42
(William Muir) *prom in chsng gp: wnt 2nd v briefly 4f out: sltly hmpd over 3f out: fdd* **7/1**[3]

600 **9** *6* **Spanish Trail**[28] 6988 3-8-4 **46**.................... RaulDaSilva(3) 4 25
(Christopher Kellett) *a towards rr: rdn and no prog 3f out* **100/1**

063 **10** *9* **Poetry Writer**[53] 6230 3-9-0 **53**.................... FergusSweeney 13 17
(Michael Blanshard) *v wd bnd after 3f: sn prom: rdn in 4th briefly over 3f out: short of room sn after: wknd qckly* **9/1**

0460 **11** *½* **Eanans Bay (IRE)**[33] 6838 3-8-13 **52**.................... PaulHanagan 1 16
(Mark H Tompkins) *prom in chsng gp tl wknd qckly 3f out* **9/1**

0540 **12** *1* **Nowdoro**[34] 6807 3-8-7 **46** oh1....................(p) MartinLane 10
(Julie Camacho) *wd bnd after 3f: in tch in chsng gp: wknd over 3f out: bhd fnl 2f* **12/1**

0060 **13** *25* **The Ploughman**[53] 6255 3-8-7 **46** oh1.................... KieranO'Neill 5
(John Bridger) *in tch tl wknd qckly over 3f out: wl t.o* **33/1**

2000 **14** *¾* **Plus Fours (USA)**[25] 7062 3-8-11 **55**.................... JackDuern(5) 12
(Charles Smith) *chsd ldr and clr of rest after 3f: pushed along 1/2-way: wknd rapidly and lost 2nd 4f out: t.o* **20/1**

2m 33.09s (-1.41) **Going Correction** -0.125s/f (Stan) **14** Ran SP% **119.8**
Speed ratings (Par 98): **99,98,96,95,95 92,90,89,85,79 79,78,62,61**
toteswingers: 1&2 £27.90, 1&3 £2.50, 2&3 £23.60 CSF £203.36 CT £582.02 TOTE £8.90: £2.50, £6.70, £1.10; EX 163.90 Trifecta £666.10 Pool: £1,101.36 - 1.24 winning units..
Owner David & Gwyn Joseph/Ridge House Stables **Bred** Cavendish Bloodstock **Trained** Earlswood, Monmouths

FOCUS
A moderate handicap run at a brisk pace. Ordinary form.
T/Jkpt: Part won. £17,750.00 to a £1 stake. Pool: £25,000.00. 0.50 winning tickets. T/Plt: £10.50 to a £1 stake. Pool £61,652.64. 4,247.72 winning tickets. T/Qpdt: £7.70 to a £1 stake. Pool: £7,257.33. 692.70 winning tickets. JN

7489 NOTTINGHAM (L-H)
Wednesday, November 7

OFFICIAL GOING: Soft (6.7)
Wind: Moderate, half against Weather: Fine

7633 DIRECT 365 SUPPORTING OUR BUSINESS WORLD H'CAP (DIV I) 5f 13y
12:10 (12:11) (Class 6) (0-55,56) 3-Y-O+ **£1,940** (£577; £288; £144) **Stalls** High

Form RPR

6551 **1** **Steel Rain**[17] 7275 4-9-4 **55**.................... FrankieMcDonald 2 63+
(Nikki Evans) *hld up in rr: gd hdwy 1/2-way: chsd ldrs over 1f out: sn rdn and styd on to ld last 100yds* **9/2**[2]

54 **2** *1 ¼* **First Rebellion**[78] 5446 3-8-9 **46** oh1.................... DavidProbert 9 50
(Tony Carroll) *cl up: rdn to ld wl over 1f out: drvn ins fnl f: hdd and nt qckn last 100yds* **12/1**

1004 **3** *2* **Dancing Maite**[18] 7254 7-9-0 **54**....................(b) MarkCoumbe(3) 10 50
(Roy Bowring) *sn led: rdn along 2f out: sn hdd: kpt on same pce* **13/2**[3]

3501 **4** ¾ **Auntie Kathryn (IRE)**[8] 7471 3-9-5 **56** 6ex.............. SilvestreDeSousa 5 50
(Peter Chapple-Hyam) *trckd ldrs: hdwy 2f out: sn rdn and one pce appr fnl f* **2/1**[1]

002 **5** ¾ **Steel City Boy (IRE)**[13] 7351 9-8-11 **48**.............................. LukeMorris 7 39
(Garry Woodward) *in tch: hdwy 2f out: sn rdn and no imp appr fnl f* **8/1**

000- **6** 4 **Yougoigo**[510] 3075 4-8-11 **48**.. FrederikTylicki 6 25
(Lawrence Mullaney) *t.k.h: trckd ldrs: swtchd rt to stands' rail and hdwy 3f out: rdn 2f out: sn wknd* **8/1**

6300 **7** nk **Duke Of Rainford**[21] 7179 5-8-10 **47**.................................. TomEaves 4 22
(Michael Herrington) *chsd ldrs: rdn along over 2f out: sn wknd* **28/1**

000 **8** 3½ **Overwhelm**[58] 6105 4-9-0 **51**..(t) NeilCallan 1 14
(Alan McCabe) *s.i.s: a in rr* **16/1**

4501 **9** 2¾ **Bitter Lemon**[65] 5875 3-9-1 **52**...................................(p) FergusSweeney 3 5
(Tony Newcombe) *chsd ldrs on outer: rdn along 1/2-way: sn wknd* **10/1**

1m 4.89s (3.39) **Going Correction** +0.825s/f (Soft) **9** Ran SP% **113.2**
Speed ratings (Par 101): **101,99,95,94,93 87,86,80,76**
toteswingers: 1&2 £10.80, 1&3 £6.40, 2&3 £16.60 CSF £55.50 CT £349.34 TOTE £4.70: £1.40, £3.40, £2.60; EX 89.80 Trifecta £349.70 Part won. Pool: £466.36 - 0.10 winning units..
Owner John Berry (Gwent) **Bred** L T Roberts **Trained** Pandy, Monmouths

FOCUS
Bottom bend out 2m for fresh ground and drop in at 4f marker. The first division of this moderate handicap looked stronger than the following contest, as it containing three last-time-out winners. End-of-season form, but the winner could do a little better.
Bitter Lemon Official explanation: jockey said filly was never travelling.

7634 DIRECT 365 SUPPORTING OUR BUSINESS WORLD H'CAP (DIV II) 5f 13y
12:40 (12:41) (Class 6) (0-55,55) 3-Y-O+ **£1,940** (£577; £288; £144) **Stalls** High

Form RPR

4134 **1** **Invigilator**[25] 7055 4-9-0 **51**...(t) MartinDwyer 8 59
(Derek Shaw) *hld up towards rr: hdwy 2f out: effrt over 1f out: sn rdn and str run ins fnl f to ld last 50yds* **7/2**[1]

0062 **2** ½ **Tenancy (IRE)**[9] 7446 8-8-4 **48**... JordanUys(7) 6 54
(Shaun Harris) *led: rdn clr ent fnl f: hdd and no ex last 50yds* **4/1**[2]

0000 **3** 1¾ **Errigal Lad**[9] 7447 7-9-1 **52**.. KellyHarrison 5 52
(Garry Woodward) *dwlt and in rr: swtchd rt and hdwy 2f out: sn rdn: styd on wl fnl f: nrst fin* **10/1**

00-2 **4** 2 **Rio Sands**[29] 6959 7-8-9 **46** oh1... AmyRyan 7 39
(Richard Whitaker) *in tch: hdwy 2f out: rdn to chse ldrs over 1f out: one pce fnl f* **14/1**

0200 **5** 3½ **Piste**[8] 7456 6-9-3 **54**...(e) PaulMulrennan 4 34
(Tina Jackson) *trckd ldrs: hdwy to chse ldr over 1f out: sn rdn and wknd fnl f* **9/1**

0006 **6** 1 **Adventure Story**[37] 6737 5-8-13 **55**........................ GeorgeDowning(5) 1 32
(Tony Carroll) *s.i.s and bhd tl sme late hdwy* **15/2**[3]

0400 **7** shd **Divertimenti (IRE)**[9] 7447 8-9-4 **55**.........................(b) RussKennemore 2 31
(Roy Bowring) *cl up on outer: rdn along wl over 1f out: sn wknd* **14/1**

4002 **8** 6 **Simple Rhythm**[8] 7471 6-8-3 **47**................................(p) CarolineKelly(7) 10 2
(John Ryan) *racd wd: in tch: rdn along and edgd lft over 2f out: sn wknd* **14/1**

0000 **9** 3¾ **Jerry Ellen (IRE)**[1] 7604 3-8-9 **46**.......................................(b) DavidAllan 3
(Tim Easterby) *cl up: rdn along 2f out: sn wknd* **8/1**

2360 **10** nk **Alpha Tauri (USA)**[53] 6233 6-8-11 **51**.......................(t) MarkCoumbe(3) 9
(Charles Smith) *prom: rdn along 2f out: sn wknd* **9/1**

1m 5.85s (4.35) **Going Correction** +0.825s/f (Soft) **10** Ran SP% **114.2**
Speed ratings (Par 101): **94,93,90,87,81 80,79,70,64,63**
toteswingers: 1&2 £3.00, 1&3 £11.40, 2&3 £8.60 CSF £16.84 CT £125.58 TOTE £4.10: £1.30, £2.20, £3.90; EX 19.80 Trifecta £220.30 Pool: £531.83 - 1.81 winning units..
Owner The Warren Partnership **Bred** Granham Farm And P Hearson Bloodstock **Trained** Sproxton, Leics

FOCUS
The top four in the weights hadn't finished any closer than sixth on their last two outings, so this lived up to its moderate status. Unlike in the preceding division, the field came up the centre of the track. The runner-up sets the level.

7635 DIRECT WASTE REMOVAL AND MANAGEMENT NURSERY 5f 13y
1:10 (1:11) (Class 4) (0-85,85) 2-Y-O **£3,428** (£1,020; £509; £254) **Stalls** High

Form RPR

6521 **1** **Oscars Journey**[16] 7296 2-8-6 **70**....................................... JoeFanning 5 73
(J R Jenkins) *cl up: led wl over 1f out: rdn appr fnl f: sn drvn and hld on gamely* **6/1**[3]

010 **2** shd **Senator Bong**[16] 7298 2-8-11 **75**... LiamKeniry 1 78
(David Elsworth) *in tch: hdwy on outer 2f out: rdn to chal ins fnl f: drvn and nt qckn nr line* **13/2**

5015 **3** nk **Secret Look**[19] 7206 2-9-7 **85**.. FrannyNorton 8 87
(Ed McMahon) *trckd ldrs: hdwy wl over 1f out: effrt and nt much ent fnl f: sn rdn and kpt on* **7/1**

10 **4** 1 **Poppy Bond**[56] 6130 2-7-13 **63**.. DominicFox 3 61+
(Chris Fairhurst) *chsd ldrs: rdn along: green and outpcd 1/2-way: hdwy over 1f out: kpt on wl fnl f: nrst fin* **12/1**

0541 **5** ½ **Shiatsu**[54] 6203 2-9-0 **78**.. EddieAhern 4 74
(Richard Hannon) *dwlt and in rr: hdwy 2f out: sn rdn and kpt on fnl f: nrst fin* **12/1**

0202 **6** ¾ **Blue Lotus (IRE)**[19] 7206 2-8-9 **78**................................... DarylByrne(5) 6 71
(Tim Easterby) *dwlt and in rr: rdn wl over 1f out: kpt on fnl f: nrst fin* **3/1**[1]

4213 **7** ½ **Balinka**[28] 6984 2-8-5 **69**.. SilvestreDeSousa 2 61
(Mel Brittain) *led and sn swtchd rt to stands' rail: rdn 2f out: sn hdd and grad wknd* **5/1**[2]

5012 **8** nk **Work Ethic (IRE)**[8] 7462 2-8-8 **72**...................................... LukeMorris 9 63
(Gerard Butler) *chsd ldrs: rdn along 2f out: drvn and wknd over 1f out* **7/1**

1m 4.8s (3.30) **Going Correction** +0.825s/f (Soft) **8** Ran SP% **109.7**
Speed ratings (Par 98): **102,101,101,99,98 97,96,96**
CSF £40.64 CT £258.14 TOTE £5.20: £1.60, £2.70, £3.80; EX 43.20 Trifecta £471.90 Part won. Pool: £629.31 - 0.62 winning units..
Owner R B Hill **Bred** R B Hill **Trained** Royston, Herts

FOCUS
Quite a few of these had run well on their previous outing so, in soft ground, this is probably reasonable form. As was the case in the opener, the field head towards the stands' rail soon after the start. Straightforward form.

NOTEBOOK
Oscars Journey, making his nursery debut, travelled strongly close to the pace and went on at the right time to just about secure success. Still open to improvement, some ease in the ground appears to be required considering his best efforts. (op 5-1 tchd 15-2)
Senator Bong, who only ran because the ground was suitable, had won at the course previously and almost got to the winner. His performance helps to confirm the form as being fair. (op 11-2)
Secret Look got a little short of room when the tempo increased but showed a good attitude under his big weight inside the final furlong. The handicapper probably has him about right but he can continue to run well. (op 8-1 tchd 13-2)
Poppy Bond was keeping on nicely in the final furlong after being behind. (tchd 16-1)
Shiatsu ◆ was an eyecatcher from off the pace, although the representative of that trainer reported afterwards that the colt was slowly away and was unsuited by the soft ground. Official explanation: trainers representative said colt was slowly away and unsuited by soft ground. (op 10-1)
Blue Lotus(IRE) plugged on up the stands' rail and may need further in this class. (op 11-4)
Balinka showed early speed but was soon beaten when joined. (op 7-1 tchd 9-2)

7636 B & M INSTALLATIONS MAIDEN STKS (DIV I) 1m 75y
1:40 (1:40) (Class 5) 2-Y-O **£2,264** (£673; £336; £168) **Stalls** Centre

Form RPR

03 **1** **Dashing Star**[14] 7332 2-9-3 0... LiamKeniry 6 84+
(David Elsworth) *trckd ldrs: smooth hdwy 3f out: led wl over 1f out: rdn clr appr fnl f: styd on* **9/4**[1]

2 4 **Arabian Skies (IRE)** 2-9-3 0.................................... SilvestreDeSousa 8 74+
(Saeed Bin Suroor) *hld up towards rr: stdy hdwy on inner over 3f out: swtchd rt and rdn wl over 1f out: styd on to chse wnr ent fnl f: no imp* **11/4**[2]

00 **3** 7 **Tajheez (IRE)**[21] 7172 2-9-3 0.. NeilCallan 3 59
(Roger Varian) *trckd ldrs: hdwy to ld over 2f out: sn rdn and hdd wl over 1f out: drvn and wknd appr fnl f* **16/1**

6 **4** 1 **Zain Eagle**[14] 7333 2-9-3 0.. LukeMorris 12 57
(Gerard Butler) *towards rr: hdwy on outer 4f out: rdn along and edging lft thrght fnl 3f: styd on: nrst fin* **11/1**

0 **5** 3¾ **Dame Nellie Melba**[14] 7329 2-8-12 0................................ JoeFanning 5 43
(Mark Johnston) *led: rdn along over 3f out: hdd over 2f out and grad wknd* **14/1**

6 ¾ **Shwaiman (IRE)** 2-9-3 0... EddieAhern 7 47
(James Fanshawe) *s.i.s and in rr: sme hdwy 3f out: n.d* **8/1**[3]

0 **7** 2½ **Miss Tiger Lily**[29] 6960 2-8-12 0.................................. DavidProbert 14 36
(Harry Dunlop) *chsd ldrs on outer: rdn along 4f out: sn wknd* **20/1**

0 **8** 1¼ **Spats Colombo**[41] 6603 2-9-3 0...................................... PJMcDonald 11 38
(Micky Hammond) *s.i.s: a in rr* **66/1**

6 **9** shd **Jebulani**[19] 7205 2-9-3 0.. GrahamLee 2 38
(David O'Meara) *dwlt: sn in tch: rdn along over 3f out: sn wknd* **20/1**

60 **10** 1½ **Admiralofthesea (USA)**[14] 7330 2-9-3 0...................... AndreaAtzeni 10 35
(Robert Eddery) *chsd ldr: rdn along 3f out: drvn over 2f out and sn wknd* **17/2**

0 **11** 6 **Heights Ridge**[8] 7450 2-8-12 0....................................... AdamCarter(5) 1 22
(Tim Easterby) *chsd ldrs on inner: rdn along over 4f out: sn wknd* **100/1**

0 **12** 1 **Roy Rocket (FR)**[14] 7330 2-8-10 0................................. HannahNunn(7) 4 20
(John Berry) *s.i.s: a in rr* **66/1**

0544 **13** 16 **Beautifulwildthing**[9] 7432 2-8-9 63 ow2.............................. LMcNiff(5) 13
(Peter Salmon) *a in rr: bhd fnl 3f* **33/1**

1m 54.54s (5.54) **Going Correction** +1.25s/f (Soft) **13** Ran SP% **116.4**
Speed ratings (Par 96): **105,101,94,93,89 88,86,84,84,83 77,76,60**
toteswingers: 1&2 £3.00, 1&3 £9.50, 2&3 £10.40 CSF £7.37 TOTE £2.70: £1.30, £1.10, £5.30; EX 8.20 Trifecta £88.60 Pool: £552.04 - 4.67 winning units..
Owner J C Smith **Bred** Littleton Stud **Trained** Newmarket, Suffolk

FOCUS
This didn't look a particularly strong maiden but the horse with the best previous form won comfortably. The form could be rated a little higher.

NOTEBOOK
Dashing Star had run well at Newmarket on his previous start and came right away from his rivals here once Liam Keniry sent his mount on. The colt can only keep improving considering his frame but it could be that he needs ease in the ground to be at his most effective. (tchd 2-1 and 5-2)
Arabian Skies(IRE), a 75,000euros yearling closely related to the useful at her best Mooretown Lady, was a little green early but was clear second-best on the day. Normal improvement should see him claim something similar. (op 3-1 tchd 7-2)
Tajheez(IRE) had only shown modest form before but this looked a little better. Handicaps are now an option. (op 25-1)
Zain Eagle still appeared in need of the experience but built on his debut at Newmarket and is heading in the right direction. (tchd 10-1)
Dame Nellie Melba led until fading but it still appeared to be an improvement on her debut effort. (tchd 12-1 and 16-1)
Shwaiman(IRE) ◆, an Authorized colt out of an unraced sister to 1m1f Group 1 winner Best Of The Bests, had a sheepskin noseband on for his first outing and didn't make much impression until running on late. He may need a bit more time but this seemed promising. (tchd 15-2)
Beautifulwildthing Official explanation: trainer said filly was unsuited by soft ground.

7637 B & M INSTALLATIONS MAIDEN STKS (DIV II) 1m 75y
2:10 (2:11) (Class 5) 2-Y-O **£2,264** (£673; £336; £168) **Stalls** Centre

Form RPR

1 **Muhtaris (IRE)** 2-9-3 0... SilvestreDeSousa 3 74+
(Saeed Bin Suroor) *s.i.s and in rr: pushed along into midfield 4f out: rdn along 3f out: n.m.r 2f out: styd on strly u.p ent fnl f: led last 40yds* **9/2**[2]

05 **2** ½ **Song Light**[21] 7172 2-9-3 0.. SebSanders 4 73
(David Elsworth) *dwlt and towards rr: hdwy over 3f out: swtchd rt and rdn 2f out: styd on to chal ins fnl f: led briefly last 75yds: sn hdd and no ex* **14/1**

03 **3** ½ **Duroble Man**[33] 6845 2-9-3 0.. NeilCallan 8 71
(Roger Varian) *led: rdn along wl over 2f out: drvn over 1f out: hdd and no ex wl ins fnl f* **14/1**

4 1¼ **Boite (IRE)** 2-9-3 0.. RobertHavlin 13 69+
(Peter Chapple-Hyam) *trckd ldrs: smooth hdwy to chse ldr 3f out: rdn wl over 1f out: one pce fnl f* **7/1**

5 1¼ **Magic Hurricane (IRE)** 2-9-3 0.. EddieAhern 14 66
(James Fanshawe) *in tch: effrt on outer 3f out: rdn along over 2f out: kpt on fnl f: nrst fin* **6/1**[3]

0 **6** 2¼ **Furibondo**[14] 7332 2-9-3 0.. TedDurcan 11 61+
(David Lanigan) *chsd ldrs: rdn along 3f out: kpt on same pce fnl 2f* **12/1**

4 **7** ¾ **Llaregyb (IRE)**[14] 7330 2-9-3 0... LiamKeniry 7 59
(David Elsworth) *t.k.h: trckd ldrs: hdwy to chse ldr 2f out: sn rdn and wknd over 1f out* **3/1**[1]

0 **8** 2 **Rancher (IRE)**[7] 7492 2-9-3 0.. ChrisCatlin 2 55
(Harry Dunlop) *s.i.s: a in rr* **100/1**

2 **9** 1¼ **Motion Lass**[22] 7130 2-8-12 0...................................... PaulMulrennan 9 47
(Ralph Beckett) *in tch: hdwy 1/2-way: chsd ldrs 3f out: rdn over 2f out: drvn and wknd wl over 1f out* **6/1**[3]

0220 **10** 1 **Woody Bay**[35] 6793 2-9-3 72... GrahamLee 12 50
(James Given) *a towards rr* **14/1**

5000 **11** 3½ **Royal Caper**[42] 6583 2-9-3 58..................................... KieranO'Neill 1 42
(John Ryan) *prom on inner: rdn along 3f out: wknd 2f out* **150/1**

0 **12** *11* **Tallaay (IRE)**[28] [6985] 2-9-3 0................................ JoeFanning 6 18
(Mark Johnston) *s.i.s: a in rr* **40/1**

1m 56.54s (7.54) **Going Correction** +1.25s/f (Soft) **12** Ran SP% **116.0**
Speed ratings (Par 96): **95,94,94,92,91 89,88,86,85,84 80,69**
toteswingers: 1&2 £12.60, 1&3 £11.60, 2&3 £33.00 CSF £64.31 TOTE £5.40: £1.10, £6.40, £3.80; EX 101.90 TRIFECTA Not won..
Owner Godolphin **Bred** Rabbah Bloodstock Limited **Trained** Newmarket, Suffolk

FOCUS
Probably on a par depth-wise with the preceding division but run in a two-second slower time. The field was compressed and the level is guessy.

NOTEBOOK
Muhtaris(IRE) ◆, who cost 240,000gns yearling and is a brother to a Black Arrow (a well-fancied runner for this year's German Derby), made a visually impressive debut after coming from off the gallop despite looking green. He has the size to keep improving and the breeding to be at least smart. (op 6-1)

Song Light came with his effort wide of the field and mastered the third close to the line but found the winner sneak past him up the inside rail. He is progressing with each outing. (tchd 16-1)

Duroble Man ◆ led and kept on respectably for pressure back up in trip. Nicely bred, it'll surely be handicaps next. (tchd 11-1)

Boite(IRE), a half-brother to several winners abroad, notably Santa Biatra and Anisei, was prominent on his debut and made a perfectly satisfactory start to his career, rallying nicely late on. (op 9-1 tchd 10-1)

Magic Hurricane(IRE) ◆, a half-brother to useful Irish miler Maybe Grace, shaped as though in need of further but he will be sharper for the run. (tchd 8-1)

Furibondo ◆ wasn't given a hard time in the final stages and is no doubt better than he showed here. His half-brother Amerigo stayed 2m5f on the Flat.

Llaregyb(IRE) took a strong hold just in behind the leader early and that told inside the final furlong when he started to weaken. (op 7-2 tchd 11-4)

Motion Lass, who was a little keen again early, was thereabouts 3f out but didn't quicken and came home at the one pace thereafter. Official explanation: jockey said filly had no more to give. (op 9-2 tchd 13-2)

7638 DIRECT 365 SMALL BUSINESS WASHROOM SERVICE CONDITIONS STKS 1m 75y
2:40 (2:40) (Class 3) 3-Y-O+ **£7,158** (£2,143; £1,071; £535; £267) **Stalls** Centre

Form RPR
2003 **1** **St Moritz (IRE)**[46] [6470] 6-8-10 97................................ AdrianNicholls 4 74+
(David Nicholls) *mde all: rdn 2f out: drvn ins fnl f and kpt on strly* **13/8**[2]

004 **2** *1 3/4* **Focail Eile**[8] [7469] 7-8-10 58................................ JoeFanning 3 70
(John Ryan) *trckd ldng pair: hdwy over 2f out: rdn to chse wnr over 1f out: drvn and edgd lft fnl f: no imp towards fin* **12/1**[3]

5/ **3** *1* **Day Of Destiny (IRE)**[25] [6682] 7-8-10 0................................ GrahamLee 1 68+
(James Given) *hld up in rr: hdwy 3f out: swtchd rt and rdn wl over 1f out: styd on fnl f: nrst fin* **18/1**

-000 **4** *1 3/4* **Colonial (IRE)**[32] [6882] 5-8-10 103................................ SilvestreDeSousa 2 64
(Saeed Bin Suroor) *trckd wnr: effrt over 2f out: rdn along wl over 1f out: sn btn* **5/6**[1]

3306 **5** *9* **Spread Boy (IRE)**[1] [7599] 5-8-3 50................................ JordanHibberd(7) 5 44
(Alan Berry) *chsd ldrs on outer: rdn along over 3f out: sn wknd* **125/1**

1m 55.55s (6.55) **Going Correction** +1.25s/f (Soft) **5** Ran SP% **106.4**
Speed ratings (Par 107): **100,98,97,95,86**
CSF £17.46 TOTE £2.60: £1.70, £2.80; EX 10.90.
Owner Billy Hughes **Bred** Newsells Park Stud **Trained** Sessay, N Yorks

FOCUS
Barring something unforeseen happening, only two could have been considered here. One really disappointed, though, which left the way clear for the other. The second is the key to the form.

NOTEBOOK
St Moritz(IRE), a shade disappointing on his last three outings, he was rushed up to lead and comfortably held everything at bay when the dash for the line started. He wasn't best in at the weights, and certainly didn't run to his BHA rating of 97, but still managed to claim a first success since landing a Listed contest back in May 2011. (op 5-4)

Focail Eile ran a cracker on these terms but hopefully the handicapper won't punish him for the performance. (op 16-1)

Day Of Destiny(IRE), a modest sort over hurdles who was last seen pulling up in a chase, stayed on well but this undoubtedly wasn't a true reflection of his ability as he'd be getting a rating in the 90s now, which would be wide of the mark. (op 12-1 tchd 11-1)

Colonial(IRE) is clearly regressing at a rapid rate and can't be seriously considered until showing much more. (op 11-10 tchd 4-5)

7639 DIRECT 365 BUSINESS NECESSITIES H'CAP 1m 75y
3:15 (3:15) (Class 4) (0-85,87) 3-Y-O+ **£4,075** (£1,212; £606; £303) **Stalls** Centre

Form RPR
4001 **1** **Nameitwhatyoulike**[8] [7453] 3-9-3 83 6ex................................ PaulMulrennan 2 92
(Michael Easterby) *trckd ldrs: hdwy 3f out: chsd ldr wl over 1f out: sn rdn: drvn to chal ent fnl f: kpt on to ld last 75yds* **11/4**[1]

1322 **2** *3/4* **Uncle Dermot (IRE)**[7] [7493] 4-8-8 72................................ ChrisCatlin 1 79
(Brendan Powell) *trckd ldr: led 3f out: rdn along wl over 1f out: jnd and drvn ent fnl f: hdd and no ex last 75yds* **9/2**[2]

4002 **3** *1 1/2* **Masters Blazing**[5] [7520] 3-8-5 71 oh4................................ KieranO'Neill 12 75
(John Ryan) *hld up in tch: hdwy 3f out: rdn 2f out: kpt on u.p fnl f* **9/2**[2]

0306 **4** *1 1/4* **West End Lad**[7] [7493] 9-8-6 73 ow2................................(b) MarkCoumbe(3) 9 74
(Roy Bowring) *led: rdn along and hdd 3f out: drvn wl over 1f out: kpt on same pce* **12/1**

04 **5** *1 3/4* **The Osteopath (IRE)**[7] [7493] 9-8-10 74................................ PJMcDonald 13 71
(John Davies) *chsd ldrs: rdn along and sltly outpcd 2f out: kpt on u.p fnl f* **8/1**[3]

6605 **6** *1* **Hayek**[12] [7370] 5-8-7 76 ow2................................(b) AdamCarter(5) 8 71
(Tim Easterby) *a towards rr* **11/1**

0020 **7** *nk* **Dubai Hills**[8] [7453] 6-9-0 85................................ PeterSword(7) 4 80
(Bryan Smart) *a towards rr* **25/1**

6000 **8** *3* **Judicious**[16] [7294] 5-8-5 76................................ JacobButterfield(7) 11 64
(Ollie Pears) *prom: rdn along over 3f out: sn wknd* **9/1**

1200 **9** *3 1/4* **May Be Some Time**[37] [6734] 4-8-8 72................................(t) EddieAhern 3 53
(Stuart Kittow) *dwlt: a towards rr* **8/1**[3]

1m 54.45s (5.45) **Going Correction** +1.25s/f (Soft)
WFA 3 from 4yo+ 2lb **9** Ran SP% **115.1**
Speed ratings (Par 105): **105,104,102,101,99 98,98,95,92**
toteswingers: 1&2 £3.80, 1&3 £3.20, 2&3 £3.70 CSF £14.85 CT £53.38 TOTE £3.70: £1.60, £1.60, £2.20; EX 16.10 Trifecta £19.60 Pool: £954.96 - 36.39 winning units..
Owner S Bowett, S Hollings & S Hull **Bred** A E Smith And Co **Trained** Sheriff Hutton, N Yorks

FOCUS
A fair-looking contest that contained two runners who had won over C&D in the past. The early pace appeared sound thanks to veteran West End Lad, who fought on nicely once passed. Straightforward form.

7640 AJA GENTLEMEN AMATEUR H'CAP 1m 2f 50y
3:50 (3:50) (Class 5) (0-75,75) 3-Y-O+ **£2,183** (£677; £338; £169) **Stalls** Low

Form RPR
0022 **1** **Bold Duke**[11] [7409] 4-10-3 62................................ MrPJohn(5) 14 73+
(Edward Bevan) *trckd ldrs: hdwy 3f out: led wl over 1f out: rdn appr fnl f: styd on strly* **8/1**

1363 **2** *2 1/2* **Astra Hall**[30] [6933] 3-10-2 65................................ MrCharlieDuckworth(5) 5 71
(Ralph Beckett) *hld up [illegible] hdwy over 3f out: chsd ldrs 2f out: sn rdn and hung lft over 1f out: chsd wnr ins fnl f: no imp* **11/4**[1]

431 **3** *4 1/2* **Jordaura**[23] [7095] 6-10-9 70................................ MrRHogg(7) 13 68
(Alan Berry) *t.k.h: led after 2f: rdn 3f out: hdd wl over 1f out: kpt on same pce appr fnl f* **15/2**

0346 **4** *2 1/4* **Focail Maith**[8] [7455] 4-11-4 72................................(p) MrAJBerry 2 66
(John Ryan) *trckd ldrs: hdwy 3f out: rdn 2f out: kpt on same pce* **10/1**

1262 **5** *hd* **Follow The Flag (IRE)**[12] [7369] 8-11-1 69................................(v) MrPCollington 12 62
(Alan McCabe) *t.k.h early: trckd ldrs: effrt 3f out: rdn along 2f out: kpt on same pce* **13/2**[3]

0U23 **6** *1* **Heezararity**[16] [7302] 4-11-0 68................................ MrFWindsorClive 10 60
(David Evans) *t.k.h early: led 2f: cl up: rdn along and ev ch over 2f out: drvn wl over 1f out and sn wknd* **11/1**

0000 **7** *1/2* **Oratory (IRE)**[12] [7370] 6-11-2 75................................ MrJHamilton(5) 4 66
(Ollie Pears) *midfield: hdwy and in tch 3f: rdn along over 2f out: sn one pce* **50/1**

1522 **8** *nse* **Bountiful Girl**[81] [5336] 3-10-6 71................................ MrAFrench(7) 15 62
(John Wainwright) *a towards rr* **20/1**

2361 **9** *nk* **Monthly Medal**[7] [7495] 9-10-5 64 6ex................................(t) MrWEasterby(5) 6 54
(Wilf Storey) *hld up and bhd: hdwy on inner 3f out: rdn to chse ldrs over 2f out: sn btn* **9/2**[2]

6140 **10** *2 1/2* **Moheebb (IRE)**[7] [7493] 8-11-2 73................................(p) MrMEnnis(3) 11 59
(Robert Johnson) *a towards rr* **20/1**

2430 **11** *1/2* **Turjuman (USA)**[29] [6949] 7-10-0 61................................(p) MrDSMcLaughlin(7) 1 46
(Alan Bailey) *dwlt: t.k.h and sn chsng ldrs on inner: rdn along over 3f out and sn wknd* **50/1**

0000 **12** *2* **Flying Applause**[7] [7493] 7-11-4 75................................(b) MrCMartin(3) 9 56
(Roy Bowring) *dwlt: a towards rr* **33/1**

0400 **13** *22* **Yourinthewill (USA)**[156] [2767] 4-10-2 63................................ MrSClarke(7) 3 5
(Daniel Mark Loughnane) *s.i.s: a bhd* **66/1**

2m 26.96s (12.66) **Going Correction** +1.25s/f (Soft)
WFA 3 from 4yo+ 4lb **13** Ran SP% **116.4**
Speed ratings (Par 103): **88,86,82,80,80 79,79,79,78,76 76,74,57**
toteswingers: 1&2 £5.80, 1&3 £16.40, 2&3 £7.50 CSF £27.45 CT £175.14 TOTE £9.80: £2.70, £1.30, £3.50; EX 45.80 Trifecta £596.20 Part won. Pool: £795.03 - 0.40 winning units..
Owner E G Bevan **Bred** Pullen Farm Stud **Trained** Ullingswick, H'fords

FOCUS
Plenty of these were in reasonable heart but the early gallop was modest to say the least and one got the impression it was a 3f dash to the line. The suspicion is that not too many gave their running.

Flying Applause Official explanation: jockey said gelding moved poorly.

T/Plt: £198.80 to a £1 stake. Pool: £34,308.09. 125.98 winning tickets. T/Qpdt: £34.30 to a £1 stake. Pool: £3,370.36. 72.58 winning tickets. JR

7505 LINGFIELD (L-H)
Thursday, November 8

OFFICIAL GOING: Standard to slow
Wind: modest, across Weather: dry

7641 FREE BETTING WITH FREEBETS.CO.UK MAIDEN AUCTION STKS (DIV I) 1m (P)
12:40 (12:40) (Class 6) 2-Y-O **£1,704** (£503; £251) **Stalls** High

Form RPR
220 **1** **Swing Easy**[25] [7081] 2-8-13 76................................ GrahamLee 7 71
(Robert Mills) *chsd ldrs: rdn to chse ldng pair 2f out: styd on fr over 1f out to chse ldr jst ins fnl f: led fnl 100yds: styd on wl* **4/7**[1]

2 *1 1/4* **Aficionado** 2-8-11 0................................ WilliamBuick 6 66+
(Ed Dunlop) *dwlt: in tch in last pair: pushed along 4f out: rdn and effrt wl over 1f out: str run ins fnl f: wnt 2nd towards fin* **14/1**

0 **3** *1/2* **Barnaby Brook (CAN)**[15] [7330] 2-8-12 0................................ IanMongan 1 66
(Nick Littmoden) *in tch in last trio: rdn and effrt wl over 1f out: styd on ins fnl f: wnt 2nd briefly wl ins fnl f: kpt on* **50/1**

4 *3/4* **Sam Spade (IRE)** 2-9-0 0................................ JimmyFortune 2 66+
(Richard Hannon) *t.k.h: hld up in tch: rdn and effrt 2f out: kpt on u.p ins fnl f* **10/1**

5 *1* **Sofi's Spirit (IRE)** 2-8-2 0................................ SimonPearce(3) 9 55
(J S Moore) *racd keenly: chsd ldrs tl led after 2f: clr and rdn ent fnl f: hdd and no ex fnl 100yds: wknd towards fin* **50/1**

05 **6** *1 1/4* **Town Mouse**[22] [7165] 2-8-12 0................................ RobertHavlin 5 59
(Hughie Morrison) *t.k.h: chsd ldr: rdn and unable qck wl over 1f out: wknd ins fnl f* **7/1**[2]

5640 **7** *hd* **Roland**[51] [6337] 2-8-10 47................................ AmyRyan 8 57?
(Kevin Ryan) *led for 2f: chsd ldr: rdn and unable qck 2f out: wknd ins fnl f* **25/1**

0 **8** *9* **Loraine**[22] [7159] 2-8-9 0................................ FergusSweeney 3 35
(Jamie Osborne) *stdd s: hld up in last pair: rdn and no rspnse wl over 1f out: bhd fnl f: burst blood vessel* **8/1**[3]

9 *nse* **Spirit Man** 2-9-0 0................................ SebSanders 4 40
(Paul D'Arcy) *chsd ldrs: shuffled bk and pushed along after 1f: swtchd rt and in midfield 6f out: rdn over 3f out: lost pl and bhd wl over 1f out: no ch after* **20/1**

1m 38.53s (0.33) **Going Correction** +0.025s/f (Slow) **9** Ran SP% **115.6**
Speed ratings (Par 94): **99,97,97,96,95 94,94,85,85**
toteswingers 1&2 £3.10, 2&3 £34.00, 1&3 £12.30 CSF £9.70 TOTE £1.80: £1.10, £1.80, £15.10; EX 8.90 Trifecta £215.90 Pool: £691.03 - 2.40 winning units..
Owner Mrs B B Mills & J Harley **Bred** Lady Bamford **Trained** Headley, Surrey

FOCUS
Still early days with the new Polytrack surface and the going was officially described as standard to slow. Probably no more than a fair maiden for the track. The winner probably didn't need to match his pre-race form.

NOTEBOOK

Swing Easy set the standard with an official mark of 76 having finished runner-up in his first two starts before failing to cope with the longer trip and soft ground at Goodwood. He got himself pretty warm and briefly came off the bridle when trapped out wide on the home bend, he did this nicely and was well on top after leading half a furlong out. He should continued to pay his way in handicaps. (op 8-11)

Aficionado ◆, a 10,000gns yearling out of a winner at up to 1m5f in France, is the one to take from the race. He raced green at the back of the field at various stages and was forced very wide off the home bend, but finished in some style down the outside to grab second. It shouldn't be long before he goes one better and he should appreciate further. (op 16-1 tchd 12-1)

Barnaby Brook(CAN), well beaten on last month's Newmarket debut, was off the bridle some way out but stayed on well in the latter stages. This was a lot better and there looks to be a race in him. (op 40-1)

Sam Spade(IRE), a 26,000gns half-brother to a winning sprinter in Norway out of a 1m4f winner, was another doing his best work at the end, and on this evidence he will appreciate a bit further. (op 7-1)

Sofi's Spirit(IRE), a half-sister to a couple of winners (including on the AW) at up to 7f, was sent to the front after 3f and it looked for a stride or two that she may have stolen it when kicking clear off the final bend, but she stuck to the inside and was swamped well inside the last. This was an encouraging enough debut. (op 40-1)

Town Mouse showed improved form on his second start over C&D last month, but was a bit disappointing here as he was in a good position for most of the journey. He will have a few more options now that he gets a mark. (op 6-1)

Loraine bled from the nose. Official explanation: vet said filly broke blood vessel. (tchd 9-1)

7642 FREE BETTING WITH FREEBETS.CO.UK MAIDEN AUCTION STKS (DIV II) 1m (P)

1:10 (1:10) (Class 6) 2-Y-O **£1,704** (£503; £251) **Stalls** High

Form				RPR
4	**1**		**Aussie Lyrics (FR)**[23] 7127 2-9-0 0 ... JimCrowley 1 (George Baker) *led tl over 6f out: chsd ldr after tl led again over 2f out: rdn clr over 1f out: r.o wl: comf* **7/4**[1]	77+
464	**2**	2 ¼	**Paddy's Saltantes (IRE)**[22] 7165 2-8-10 66 ... DarryllHolland 6 (J S Moore) *chsd ldrs: rdn to press wnr over 2f out: unable qck over 1f out: wl hld by wnr but hld on for 2nd fnl f* **14/1**	67
033	**3**	nk	**David's Secret**[16] 7305 2-8-11 68 ... JimmyFortune 3 (Hughie Morrison) *in tch in midfield: rdn and effrt to chse ldrs whn hung rt bnd 2f out: kpt on to press for 2nd fnl f* **4/1**[3]	67
4	**4**	1 ½	**Lucky Mountain**[16] 7305 2-8-13 0 ... WilliamBuick 8 (Ed Dunlop) *in tch in midfield: rdn and effrt to chse ldrs on inner 2f out: outpcd and btn 1f out: styd on same pce ins fnl f* **2/1**[2]	66
0	**5**	7	**Booktheband (IRE)**[55] 6204 2-8-12 0 ... KirstyMilczarek 9 (Clive Brittain) *dwlt: sn rcvrd to ld over 6f out: hdd and rdn over 2f out: wknd over 1f out* **33/1**	49
	6	2 ¼	**Aegean Whispers** 2-8-4 0 ... KieranO'Neill 5 (Richard Hannon) *chsd ldrs: rdn and lost pl over 2f out: wl btn over 1f out* **14/1**	36
	7	1	**Jd Rockefeller** 2-8-2 0 ... LouisSteward(7) 2 (Paul D'Arcy) *t.k.h: hld up in midfield: lost pl and outpcd 3f out: wl btn fnl 2f* **25/1**	38
	8	3 ¾	**Candyman Can (IRE)** 2-8-10 0 ... LiamKeniry 4 (Dominic Ffrench Davis) *dwlt: a in rr: rdn 4f out: struggling and outpcd 3f out: bhd fnl 2f* **50/1**	31

1m 39.22s (1.02) **Going Correction** +0.025s/f (Slow) **8** Ran SP% **111.8**

Speed ratings (Par 94): **95,92,92,90,83 81,80,76**

toteswingers 1&2 £3.50, 2&3 £3.30, 1&3 £2.30 CSF £25.40 TOTE £2.00: £1.10, £3.50, £1.10; EX 14.70 Trifecta £67.80 Pool: £835.27 - 9.23 winning units..

Owner Michael Watt, J A McGrath, The Anzacs **Bred** Hugh Hogg **Trained** Manton, Wilts

FOCUS

They finished much more spread out in this division, but the winning time was 0.69 seconds slower than the first leg. Ordinary form rated around the second and third.

NOTEBOOK

Aussie Lyrics(FR) ◆ had shown definite promise when chasing home a trio with previous experience on last month's Leicester debut and duly built on that. Never far away, he was taken on by the runner-up rounding the home bend, but easily saw him off and came home in style. He can continue to improve. (op 2-1 tchd 13-8)

Paddy's Saltantes(IRE), rated 66 after showing improved form in his first three starts, also raced close to the pace but was inclined to run in snatches. He was still in with every chance turning in, but started to hang in the straight and couldn't live with the winner. He may be better off in a nursery. (op 12-1)

David's Secret, rated 68 after also showing progressive form in his first three starts, came from further back than the front pair and stayed on without ever looking likely to get there. He was closely matched with the runner-up on official ratings so has run his race. (op 7-2)

Lucky Mountain ran a debut full of promise when just behind David's Secret here last month, but it was disappointing that he couldn't reverse the form. He looked like playing a part when moving closer turning for home, but hung towards the inside rail in the straight and was never doing enough. (op 9-4 tchd 5-2)

7643 FREEBETS.CO.UK FREE BETS H'CAP 1m (P)

1:40 (1:43) (Class 6) (0-60,60) 3-Y-O+ **£1,704** (£503; £251) **Stalls** High

Form				RPR
0500	**1**		**Chrissycross (IRE)**[30] 6949 3-9-5 **60** ...(b) AdamKirby 11 (Roger Teal) *dwlt: sn rcvrd to chse ldr after 1f: rdn to ld 2f out: clr ent fnl f: r.o wl* **20/1**	70
6440	**2**	3	**Fonterutoli (IRE)**[8] 7495 5-9-3 **56** ...(e) RobertHavlin 2 (Roger Ingram) *in tch in last quartet: weaving through and hdwy over 1f out: chsd wnr jst ins fnl f: styd on but no threat to wnr* **12/1**	58
0000	**3**	½	**Cativo Cavallino**[36] 6773 9-9-0 **56** ... NataliaGemelova(3) 4 (John E Long) *bustled along early: in tch towards rr: hdwy and rdn over 2f out: styd on press for 2nd ins fnl f: kpt on but no threat to wnr* **16/1**	57
124	**4**	½	**Belle Park**[27] 7015 5-9-1 **54** ... DarryllHolland 8 (Karen George) *in tch in midfield: rdn and effrt wl over 1f out: no threat to wnr but kpt on u.p fnl f* **13/2**[2]	54
0236	**5**	hd	**Percythepinto (IRE)**[23] 7126 3-9-1 **56** ...(t) KirstyMilczarek 7 (George Baker) *t.k.h: hld up in tch: switching rt and effrt 2f out: styd on u.p ins fnl f: no threat to wnr* **9/1**	55
5445	**6**	1 ¼	**Source Of Light (IRE)**[30] 6968 3-9-2 **57** ...(p) MartinHarley 12 (Daniel Mark Loughnane) *chsd ldrs: rdn and unable qck over 1f out: styd on same pce and wl hld fnl f* **5/1**[1]	53
0050	**7**	1	**Italian Lady (USA)**[59] 6103 3-9-2 **57** ...(v[1]) RobertWinston 10 (Alan Jarvis) *led: rdn and hdd 2f out: sn outpcd by wnr and wl hld whn lost 2nd jst ins fnl f: wknd* **14/1**	51
0324	**8**	nk	**Men Don't Cry (IRE)**[13] 7382 3-9-2 **57** ...(b) LiamKeniry 1 (Ed de Giles) *in tch in midfield: rdn and unable qck over 1f out: sltly hmpd ent fnl f: wl hld and one pce fnl f* **14/1**	50
2043	**9**	1	**Isingy Red (FR)**[16] 7318 4-9-6 **59** ...(p) GrahamLee 3 (Jim Boyle) *in tch: rdn over 4f out: no hdwy u.p wl over 1f out: n.d fnl f* **7/1**[3]	50
-006	**10**	nk	**Silence Is Easy**[20] 7225 3-9-2 **57** ... JimCrowley 6 (William Muir) *hld up in rr: stl in last and swtchd rt bnd 2f out: no imp over 1f out* **16/1**	47
0265	**11**	2	**Byrd In Hand (IRE)**[8] 7486 5-9-0 **58** ...(v[1]) WilliamTwiston-Davies(5) 5 (John Bridger) *chsd ldr for 1f: chsd ldrs after tl rdn and unable qck ent fnl 2f: wknd jst over 1f: fdd fnl f* **11/1**	44

1m 37.97s (-0.23) **Going Correction** +0.025s/f (Slow)

WFA 3 from 4yo+ 2lb **11** Ran SP% **98.4**

Speed ratings (Par 101): **102,99,98,98,97 96,95,95,94,93 91**

toteswingers 1&2 £34.30, 2&3 £34.10, 1&3 £37.50 CSF £164.14 CT £2075.16 TOTE £25.40: £6.70, £3.10, £3.40; EX 268.10 TRIFECTA Not won..

Owner John Morton **Bred** David Watson & Shane Horan **Trained** Ashtead, Surrey

■ Stewards' Enquiry : Kieren Fallon five-day ban; appeared to strike his mount over the head as the gelding was being led back after being withdrawn (22nd-27th Nov).

FOCUS

A moderate handicap, weakened further when the fancied Two Sugars was withdrawn after refusing to enter the stalls (4/1F, deduct 20p in the £ under R4). The winner is rated basically back to her best.

7644 FREEBETS.CO.UK H'CAP 1m 2f (P)

2:10 (2:11) (Class 5) (0-75,75) 3-Y-O **£2,385** (£704; £352) **Stalls** Low

Form				RPR
1025	**1**		**Sheila's Buddy**[14] 7358 3-9-6 **74** ... LiamKeniry 5 (J S Moore) *in tch in midfield: rdn over 2f out: hdwy u.p to chal 1f out: led fnl 100yds: hld on cl home: all out* **12/1**	81
4400	**2**	hd	**Fairyinthewind (IRE)**[14] 7359 3-8-12 **66** ... SebSanders 1 (Paul D'Arcy) *hld up in tch in rr: rdn and hdwy 2f out: drvn 1f out: str run ins fnl f: pressing wnr cl home: could nt quite get up* **20/1**	73
6642	**3**	nk	**Aegeaus**[13] 7368 3-9-7 **75** ...(t) GrahamLee 8 (Ed Dunlop) *hld up wl in tch in last trio: stl plenty to do whn swtchd lft over 1f out: gd hdwy ins fnl f: r.o wl: could nt quite rch ldrs* **11/2**[2]	81+
1203	**4**	nk	**Kelpie Blitz (IRE)**[7] 7511 3-9-2 **70** ...(t) MickyFenton 6 (Seamus Durack) *in tch: rdn and effrt to chal over 1f out: led ins fnl f: sn hdd and styd on same pce towards fin* **7/1**	75
0-42	**5**	¾	**Miss Blakeney**[22] 7162 3-8-12 **66** ...(p) HayleyTurner 9 (Marcus Tregoning) *wnt lft s: chsd ldr for 2f: styd handy: chsd ldrs and rdn over 1f out: swtchd lft and styd on same pce ins fnl f* **12/1**	70
0604	**6**	hd	**Aquilonius (IRE)**[55] 6206 3-9-6 **74** ...(t[1]) JimCrowley 7 (Stuart Williams) *chsd ldr tl led 8f out: rdn ent fnl 2f: hdd ins fnl f: no ex and one pce fnl 100yds* **13/2**[3]	78
0356	**7**	1 ¼	**Berwin (IRE)**[29] 6981 3-9-2 **70** ... MartinHarley 4 (Sylvester Kirk) *in tch towards rr: hdwy over 2f out: kpt on same pce u.p ins fnl f* **16/1**	71
2033	**8**	nk	**Poetic Lord**[13] 7376 3-9-2 **75** ... WilliamTwiston-Davies(5) 2 (Richard Hannon) *in tch in midfield: rdn and effrt 2f out: styd on same pce fnl f* **8/1**	75
1212	**9**	hd	**Sigurwana (USA)**[14] 7356 3-9-4 **72** ... PaulHanagan 12 (William Haggas) *midfield early: stdy hdwy to chse ldr 5f out tl jst over 1f out: no ex and btn whn sltly hmpd ins fnl f: wknd towards fin* **5/1**[1]	72
3000	**10**	17	**Minstrels Gallery (IRE)**[13] 7376 3-9-0 **68** ... DarryllHolland 11 (J R Jenkins) *dwlt and hmpd s: t.k.h: hld up in rr early: hdwy into midfield 5f out: rdn and btn over 2f out: bhd and eased fnl f* **20/1**	34
3-40	**11**	7	**Caitlin**[76] 5555 3-9-2 **70** ... JimmyFortune 3 (Andrew Balding) *led for 2f: chsd ldrs tl rdn and dropped to rr over 2f out: bhd and eased fnl f* **33/1**	22
-602	**12**	4	**Easter Diva (IRE)**[12] 7416 3-9-0 **68** ... NickyMackay 10 (Gerard Butler) *pushed rt s: hld up in tch: rdn over 2f out: sn btn: bhd and eased fnl f* **15/2**	12

2m 4.49s (-2.11) **Going Correction** +0.025s/f (Slow) **12** Ran SP% **114.5**

Speed ratings (Par 102): **109,108,108,108,107 107,106,106,106,92 87,83**

toteswingers 1&2 £18.70, 2&3 £18.40, 1&3 £10.70 CSF £227.00 CT £1465.85 TOTE £14.10: £6.80, £6.40, £1.50; EX 409.70 TRIFECTA Not won..

Owner Ray Styles **Bred** Mrs Anita R Dodd **Trained** Upper Lambourn, Berks

FOCUS

A modest handicap and a typical Lingfield bunched finish. The early pace was ordinary, but the first three all came from behind. The winner is rated to his recent best.

Minstrels Gallery(IRE) Official explanation: jockey said gelding was never travelling.

Easter Diva(IRE) Official explanation: jockey said filly was never travelling.

7645 LINGFIELDPARK.CO.UK H'CAP 7f (P)

2:40 (2:41) (Class 4) (0-85,84) 3-Y-O+ **£4,075** (£1,212; £606; £303) **Stalls** Low

Form				RPR
5251	**1**		**Schoolmaster**[22] 7170 4-9-3 **80** ... AdamKirby 1 (Giles Bravery) *mde all: dictated stdy gallop tl rdn and qcknd clr wl over 1f out: kpt on and a holding on towards fin* **5/1**[2]	87
3413	**2**	½	**Delft**[31] 6939 3-9-4 **82** ... WilliamBuick 3 (Jeremy Noseda) *chsd ldng pair: rdn 2f out: chsd clr wnr 1f out: kpt on u.p to press wnr towards fin* **11/2**[3]	87
0053	**3**	nk	**Shahzan (IRE)**[15] 7327 4-9-7 **84** ... NeilCallan 10 (Roger Varian) *swtchd lft s: t.k.h: hld up in midfield: rdn wl over 1f out: styd on wl ins fnl f: nvr quite looked like rching wnr* **9/2**[1]	89+
0000	**4**	shd	**Advanced**[13] 7366 9-9-6 **83** ... AmyRyan 8 (Kevin Ryan) *chsd wnr: rdn and unable qck w wnr wl over 1f out: lost 2nd 1f out: kpt on* **16/1**	88
1216	**5**	½	**Links Drive Lady**[12] 7408 4-9-5 **82** ... KierenFallon 6 (Dean Ivory) *hld up in tch in last quartet: hdwy on inner over 1f out: styd on same pce ins fnl f* **9/1**	86+
6255	**6**	½	**Wahylah (IRE)**[47] 6488 3-9-2 **80** ... FrederikTylicki 11 (Clive Brittain) *in tch in last quartet: wd bnd 2f out: stl plenty to do and hdwy ent fnl f: styd on wl: unable to chal* **15/2**	81+
0104	**7**	½	**Good Authority (IRE)**[15] 7327 5-9-7 **84** ... TomMcLaughlin 5 (Karen George) *in tch in midfield: rdn ent fnl 2f: hdwy 1f out: kpt on u.p but no threat to wnr* **11/1**	85
1040	**8**	½	**Ongoodform (IRE)**[15] 7327 5-9-2 **79** ...(b) GrahamLee 13 (Paul D'Arcy) *t.k.h: chsd ldng trio: hung lft bnd 2f out and sn outpcd by wnr: styd on same pce fnl f* **25/1**	79
6200	**9**	hd	**Shifting Star (IRE)**[15] 7327 7-9-1 **83** ... WilliamTwiston-Davies(5) 2 (John Bridger) *in tch: rdn and unable qck 2f out: one pce and no imp fr over 1f out* **25/1**	82
0102	**10**	½	**Mahadee (IRE)**[45] 6538 7-9-3 **80** ...(b) LiamKeniry 9 (Ed de Giles) *carried lft s: hld up in tch in last trio: effrt u.p and edging lft 1f out: styd on but no threat to wnr* **25/1**	78+

005 **11** *nk* **Tidentime (USA)**[39] 6705 3-9-4 **82** .... MartinHarley 7 79
(Mick Channon) *in tch: rdn over 2f out: outpcd and btn over 1f out: wknd ins fnl f* **10/1**

03-0 **12** *1* **Wilfred Pickles (IRE)**[100] 4689 6-9-6 **83** .... IanMongan 14 77
(Jo Crowley) *hld up in tch in midfield: rdn and no hdwy whn hung lft over 1f out: plugged on same pce fnl f* **12/1**

0000 **13** *2* **Titan Triumph**[45] 6538 8-9-2 **79** ....(t) JimCrowley 12 68
(William Knight) *stdd and dropped in bhd after s: hld up in rr: effrt on inner over 1f out: no imp* **50/1**

1m 24.29s (-0.51) **Going Correction** +0.025s/f (Slow) **13** Ran SP% **116.5**
WFA 3 from 4yo+ 1lb
Speed ratings (Par 105): **103,102,102,101,101 100,100,99,99,98 98,97,95**
toteswingers 1&2 £4.60, 2&3 £4.10, 1&3 £5.30 CSF £30.36 CT £137.19 TOTE £5.30: £2.70, £1.40, £1.90; EX 38.90 Trifecta £101.00 Pool: £734.00 - 5.44 winning units..
Owner Penny Farm **Bred** D D And Mrs Jean P Clee **Trained** Newmarket, Suffolk

FOCUS
A good handicap and again the early tempo wasn't that strong, but on this occasion it was crucial to be up with the pace. Another muddling bunched finish.

7646 LINGFIELD PARK OWNERS GROUP H'CAP 6f (P)
3:10 (3:10) (Class 4) (0-85,84) 3-Y-0+ **£4,075** (£1,212; £606; £303) **Stalls** Low

Form RPR

5321 **1** **Muhdiq (USA)**[16] 7309 3-9-1 **78** .... NeilCallan 1 85
(Mike Murphy) *chsd ldrs: rdn ent fnl 2f: chsd ldr and drvn 1f out: carried rt but sustained chal fnl f to ld towards fin: hld on cl home* **4/1**[1]

3100 **2** *hd* **Rowe Park**[61] 6026 9-9-7 **84** .... LiamKeniry 3 90
(Linda Jewell) *led: rdn and qcknd clr over 1f out: edgd rt but kpt on wl ins fnl f tl hdd towards fin: kpt on gamely* **20/1**

3434 **3** *½* **Hopes N Dreams (IRE)**[9] 7464 4-9-2 **79** .... AmyRyan 5 84
(Kevin Ryan) *taken down early: stdd s: hld up in tch in rr: n.m.r ent fnl 2f: swtchd lft and effrt on inner over 1f out: hdwy 1f out: chsd ldrs ins fnl f: no imp towards fin* **7/1**

3055 **4** *nk* **North Star Boy (IRE)**[22] 7177 3-8-11 **79** ...... WilliamTwiston-Davies(5) 2 83
(Richard Hannon) *in tch in midfield: rdn and hdwy over 1f out: chsd ldrs ins fnl f: kpt on* **12/1**

4400 **5** *hd* **Lujeanie**[15] 7327 6-9-4 **81** ....(p) MartinLane 4 84
(Dean Ivory) *t.k.h: hld up in tch in midfield: effrt and drvn jst over 1f out: kpt on same pce ins fnl f* **8/1**

0145 **6** *¾* **Another Try (IRE)**[36] 6800 7-9-6 **83** .... RobertWinston 7 84
(Alan Jarvis) *chsd ldr: rdn wl over 1f out: lost 2nd and unable qck 1f out: styd on same pce after* **9/2**[2]

0631 **7** *2 ¼* **Arctic Lynx (IRE)**[23] 7145 5-8-13 **83** .... HannahNunn(7) 9 77
(Robert Cowell) *t.k.h: hld up in tch in midfield: rdn and unable qck over 1f out: hld and one pce fnl f* **5/1**[3]

5000 **8** *1 ¾* **Dreamwriter (USA)**[12] 7408 3-9-2 **79** ....[1] GrahamLee 10 68
(Jim Boyle) *hld up in rr: rdn and effrt over 1f out: no real imp: nvr trbld ldrs* **20/1**

0560 **9** *nk* **Little Garcon (USA)**[17] 7291 5-9-6 **83** .... WilliamBuick 6 71
(Robert Cowell) *taken down early: hld up in tch towards rr: rdn and effrt jst over 1f out: sn no imp: n.d* **5/1**[3]

3064 **10** *2* **Celtic Sultan (IRE)**[67] 5852 8-8-7 **77** .... SemiraPashai(7) 8 59
(Alastair Lidderdale) *taken down early: restless in stalls and rrd as stalls opened: t.k.h: hld up in rr: hdwy into midfield on outer 1/2-way: lost pl bnd 2f out: n.d after* **20/1**

1m 12.13s (0.23) **Going Correction** +0.025s/f (Slow) **10** Ran SP% **117.1**
Speed ratings (Par 105): **99,98,98,97,97 96,93,91,90,88**
toteswingers 1&2 £11.20, 2&3 £26.20, 1&3 £4.30 CSF £87.04 CT £536.37 TOTE £4.60: £2.00, £9.00, £2.60; EX 39.70 Trifecta £717.40 Part won. Pool: £956.55 - 0.72 winning units..
Owner Ms Denise Tibbett **Bred** Shadwell Farm LLC **Trained** Westoning, Beds

FOCUS
A fair sprint handicap, but they went no pace and this was another race where you needed to be prominent. The front six finished in a heap and it's hard to rate this form any higher.

7647 FOLLOW @LINGFIELDPARK ON TWITTER MAIDEN STKS 1m (P)
3:40 (3:40) (Class 5) 3-Y-O **£2,385** (£704; £352) **Stalls** High

Form RPR

1 **Hanseatic** 3-9-3 0 .... WilliamBuick 7 79+
(John Gosden) *dwlt: sn rcvrd to press ldr: rdn and rn green but clr w ldr over 2f out: led narrowly 2f out: forged ahd ins fnl f: styd on wl* **5/4**[1]

0 **2** *2* **Rockalong (IRE)**[22] 7174 3-9-3 0 .... KierenFallon 2 74+
(Luca Cumani) *pressed ldrs tl led after 1f: wnt clr w wnr jst over 2f out: hdd 2f out but ev ch after tl ins fnl f: no ex fnl 100yds* **11/2**[3]

4505 **3** *1 ¾* **Stormbound (IRE)**[28] 7005 3-9-3 75 .... GrahamLee 4 69
(Paul Cole) *t.k.h: hld up in tch: outpcd over 2f out: rallied u.p and styd on wl ins fnl f* **5/1**[2]

03 **4** *1* **Spark Of Genius**[28] 7005 3-8-12 0 .... HayleyTurner 1 62
(James Toller) *chsd ldrs: rdn and outpcd ent fnl 2f: 3rd and no imp over 1f out: kpt on same pce ins fnl f* **12/1**

56 **5** *1* **Shawka**[69] 5795 3-8-12 0 .... PaulHanagan 3 60
(Charles Hills) *stdd after s: hld up in tch: rdn and outpcd by ldng pair jst over 2f out: styd on same pce ins fnl f* **11/2**[3]

6 *2 ½* **Morinda** 3-8-12 0 .... JimmyFortune 8 54
(Ed Walker) *t.k.h: in tch: rdn and outpcd over 2f out: no threat to ldrs fr over 1f out* **25/1**

063 **7** *nk* **Made Of More**[111] 4301 3-9-3 64 ....[1] RobertHavlin 5 58
(Roger Ingram) *t.k.h: led for 1f: chsd ldrs after tl rdn and lost pl over 2f: no threat to ldrs fr over 1f out* **14/1**

8 *26* **El Calafate (USA)** 3-9-3 0 .... GeorgeBaker 6
(John Best) *v.s.a: a detached in last: lost tch over 2f out: t.o* **20/1**

1m 38.28s (0.08) **Going Correction** +0.025s/f (Slow) **8** Ran SP% **114.8**
Speed ratings (Par 102): **100,98,96,95,94 91,91,65**
toteswingers 1&2 £3.60, 2&3 £7.30, 1&3 £2.30 CSF £8.51 TOTE £1.80: £1.10, £2.10, £1.80; EX 8.20 Trifecta £42.70 Pool: £1013.66 - 17.79 winning units..
Owner K Abdulla **Bred** Juddmonte Farms Ltd **Trained** Newmarket, Suffolk

FOCUS
There wasn't a great deal of depth to this maiden and it only concerned the front two from a long way out. The first two both have the scope to do better.

7648 JUMPING AT LINGFIELD NEXT TUESDAY H'CAP 5f (P)
4:10 (4:11) (Class 5) (0-75,75) 3-Y-0+ **£2,385** (£704; £352) **Stalls** High

Form RPR

0402 **1** **Sonko (IRE)**[31] 6935 3-9-7 **75** ....(p) JimmyFortune 3 84
(Tim Pitt) *sn led: rdn and wnt clr over 1f out: drvn ins fnl f: tiring towards fin but a holding on* **16/1**

0502 **2** *½* **Beauty Pageant (IRE)**[54] 6226 5-9-7 **75** .... RobertWinston 9 82
(Ed McMahon) *in tch: rdn and unable qck over 1f out: rallied u.p ins fnl f: styd on strly to press wnr cl home* **9/2**[2]

6403 **3** *½* **Rylee Mooch**[17] 7291 4-9-2 **75** ....(e) JasonHart(5) 6 80
(Richard Guest) *broke fast and led briefly: sn chsng ldng pair: chsd wnr 1/2-way and sn rdn: outpcd over 1f out: kpt on ins fnl f: lost 2nd cl home* **10/3**[1]

6146 **4** *nk* **Tom Sawyer**[33] 6886 4-9-4 **72** ....(b) GrahamLee 2 76
(Julie Camacho) *t.k.h: sn chsng wnr: rdn ent fnl f: kpt on but nvr quite gng pce to chal* **13/2**

0605 **5** *¾* **Dancing Freddy (IRE)**[21] 7197 5-9-6 **74** ....(tp) WilliamCarson 1 75
(Violet M Jordan) *in tch in midfield: rdn ent fnl 2f: styd on same pce ins fnl f* **12/1**

4005 **6** *1* **Fathom Five (IRE)**[16] 7309 8-9-2 **70** .... GeorgeBaker 10 68
(Gary Moore) *stdd s: hld up in last pair: rdn and sme hdwy ent fnl f: kpt on but nvr trbld ldrs* **5/1**[3]

3640 **7** *nse* **Billy Red**[16] 7309 8-9-3 **71** ....(b) FergusSweeney 5 69
(J R Jenkins) *dwlt: a towards rr: rdn and edgd lft over 1f out: kpt on but nvr trbld ldrs* **14/1**

1400 **8** *1* **Ghostwing**[15] 7328 5-9-4 **72** ....(bt) IanMongan 8 66
(Luke Dace) *hld up in last pair: sme hdwy on inner over 1f out: no imp fnl f* **13/2**

2005 **9** *½* **Yurituni**[8] 7483 5-9-7 **75** ....(v) KierenFallon 4 67
(Eve Johnson Houghton) *in tch in midfield: rdn and struggling 1/2-way: lost pl 2f out: styd on same pce and n.d after* **12/1**

0000 **10** *3* **Desert Strike**[16] 7309 6-9-2 **70** ....(p) HayleyTurner 7 51
(Conor Dore) *in tch in midfield: wd and lost pl bnd 2f out: bhd fnl f* **20/1**

58.88s (0.08) **Going Correction** +0.025s/f (Slow) **10** Ran SP% **117.3**
Speed ratings (Par 103): **100,99,98,97,96 95,95,93,92,87**
toteswingers 1&2 £6.00, 2&3 £3.70, 1&3 £5.90 CSF £87.19 CT £313.03 TOTE £14.70: £4.70, £2.10, £1.10; EX 29.10 Trifecta £64.90 Pool: £1266.82 - 14.62 winning units..
Owner Dr Marwan Koukash **Bred** Tally-Ho Stud **Trained** Newmarket, Suffolk

FOCUS
A modest sprint handicap and another race dominated by the pace-setters. The order barely changed throughout the contest. The bare form could be rated slightly better.
Beauty Pageant(IRE) Official explanation: vet said mare lost a left hind shoe.
T/Jkpt: Not won. T/Plt: £455.70 to a £1 stake. Pool of £51822.44 - 83.01 winning tickets. T/Qpdt: £181.50 to a £1 stake. Pool of £5299.82 - 21.60 winning tickets. SP

7613 WOLVERHAMPTON (A.W) (L-H)
Thursday, November 8

OFFICIAL GOING: Standard
Wind: Fresh half-behind Weather: Overcast

7649 £32 BONUS AT 32RED.COM NURSERY (DIV I) 5f 216y(P)
4:20 (4:20) (Class 6) (0-65,65) 2-Y-O **£1,704** (£503; £251) **Stalls** Low

Form RPR

005 **1** **Monsieur Royale**[99] 4710 2-9-1 **59** ....(b1) SilvestreDeSousa 5 69+
(Geoffrey Oldroyd) *hld up: hdwy over 3f out: rdn to ld over 1f out: r.o wl* **13/8**[1]

5406 **2** *4* **Katy Spirit (IRE)**[28] 7006 2-8-11 **55** .... FrannyNorton 4 53
(Michael Blanshard) *sn pushed along in rr: hdwy over 2f out: rdn to chse wnr 1f out: styd on same pce* **12/1**

2055 **3** *2* **Fly Fisher (IRE)**[26] 7056 2-9-1 **59** ....(v) TonyHamilton 10 51
(Ian Semple) *a.p: rdn and hung lft over 1f out: no ex fnl f* **10/1**

5520 **4** *½* **Frosted Off**[42] 6611 2-9-2 **60** .... AndreaAtzeni 7 51
(John Spearing) *mid-div: hdwy over 2f out: sn rdn: styng on same pce whn hmpd ins fnl f* **28/1**

500 **5** *1* **Melodee Princess (IRE)**[26] 7056 2-9-4 **62** ....(b1) LukeMorris 1 50
(Ronald Harris) *prom: chsd ldr over 3f out tl rdn over 1f out: hung lft and wknd ins fnl f* **14/1**

0005 **6** *nk* **Proventi**[6] 7526 2-8-10 **54** ....(v1) DavidProbert 2 41
(Alan McCabe) *sn led: rdn and hdd over 1f out: wknd ins fnl f* **50/1**

6000 **7** *1 ¾* **Fit For A King (IRE)**[43] 6583 2-9-2 **60** ....(b1) TomQueally 8 41
(John Best) *hld up: rdn over 2f out: nvr on terms* **4/1**[2]

040 **8** *1 ¾* **Antonius**[17] 7363 2-9-7 **65** .... TomEaves 3 41
(Linda Stubbs) *chsd ldr tl pushed along over 3f out: rdn over 1f out: wknd fnl f* **11/2**[3]

3355 **9** *½* **It's Only Business**[14] 7357 2-8-12 **63** .... JakePayne(7) 9 38
(Bill Turner) *chsd ldrs: sn pushed along: lost pl and drvn along 1/2-way: wknd over 2f out* **14/1**

666 **10** *4* **Lady Jean**[33] 6890 2-8-4 **48** ow1 .... ChrisCatlin 6 11
(Reg Hollinshead) *s.i.s: outpcd* **25/1**

1m 15.4s (0.40) **Going Correction** -0.075s/f (Stan) **10** Ran SP% **112.9**
Speed ratings (Par 94): **94,88,86,85,84 83,81,78,78,72**
toteswingers 1&2 £7.50, 2&3 £8.40, 1&3 £6.10 CSF £21.87 CT £152.15 TOTE £2.30: £1.10, £5.20, £3.00; EX 20.40 Trifecta £128.20 Pool: £791.54 - 4.63 winning units..
Owner Casino Royale Racing **Bred** Bond Thoroughbred Corporation **Trained** Brawby, N Yorks

FOCUS
The track was Gallop Mastered after the fourth race. A modest nursery run at a good gallop which went to the well-backed favourite. Good progress from the winner, but pretty weak in behind.

NOTEBOOK
Monsieur Royale was steadily progressive in three maiden starts on turf and made a winning handicap/AW debut in first-time blinkers on his return from 99 days off. He travelled well off the pace and once delivered entering the straight he pulled clear to win with plenty in hand. Still only lightly raced, he may well be capable of better on this surface. Official explanation: trainer's representative said regarding apparent improvement in form that the colt benefited from the application of blinkers, seemed to appreciate the all-weather and a weak race. (op 2-1 tchd 9-4 and 6-4)
Katy Spirit(IRE) was under pressure a long way from home, but to her credit she responded well and ran on gamely up the far rail to pull a couple of lengths clear of the third. (op 8-1)
Fly Fisher(IRE) returned to form in a first-time visor (retained) over C&D 26 days earlier and wasn't disgraced, despite racing wide throughout from the widest draw. (op 8-1)
Frosted Off disappointed on his AW debut last time over C&D and although this was an improvement, it was still below his best turf form. (op 25-1 tchd 20-1)
Melodee Princess(IRE) appeared sharper for the first-time blinkers and was ridden closer to the front this time, but was only one-paced in the straight. (op 15-2)

Fit For A King(IRE) didn't show any improvement for the application of blinkers on his return from 43 days off. (op 13-2 tchd 7-1)

7650 £32 BONUS AT 32RED.COM NURSERY (DIV II) 5f 216y(P)
4:50 (4:50) (Class 6) (0-65,64) 2-Y-O £1,704 (£503; £251) Stalls Low

Form RPR
6403 **1** **Archie Stevens**13 7379 2-9-6 **63** RichardKingscote 2 77+
(Tom Dascombe) *chsd ldrs: rdn to ld wl ins fnl f: r.o* **11/4**1
6231 **2** 3 ¼ **Marmot Bay (IRE)**13 7379 2-9-3 **60** MartinDwyer 9 63
(Jamie Osborne) *sn led: rdn over 1f out: hdd and unable qck wl ins fnl f* **9/2**2
0534 **3** 2 ¼ **Not Now Blondie**26 7056 2-9-4 **61** AndreaAtzeni 3 58
(Chris Dwyer) *chsd ldrs: rdn over 2f out: styd on same pce fr over 1f out* **8/1**
065 **4** 1 ¾ **Koharu**18 7272 2-8-13 **56** (t) TomQueally 7 47
(Peter Makin) *sn pushed along in rr: r.o ins fnl f* **7/1**
0662 **5** nk **My Sweet Lord**9 7463 2-8-9 **52** DavidProbert 8 42
(Mark Usher) *in rr: pushed along 1/2-way: hdwy u.p fr over 1f out: nvr nrr* **9/2**2
0146 **6** ¾ **Senora Lobo (IRE)**93 4927 2-8-12 **55** TomEaves 1 43
(Lisa Williamson) *prom: rdn over 2f out: wknd over 1f out* **40/1**
0604 **7** 2 **Birdy Boy (USA)**2 7606 2-8-2 **45** JoeFanning 4 27
(Mark Johnston) *chsd ldr: rdn over 2f out: wknd fnl f* **6/1**3
5004 **8** 1 **Eyeline**29 6975 2-9-1 **58** RussKennemore 10 37
(Reg Hollinshead) *hld up in tch: racd keenly: drvn along 1/2-way: wknd wl over 1f out* **33/1**
6005 **9** ½ **Amirah (IRE)**48 6438 2-9-7 **64** LukeMorris 6 42
(Tony Carroll) *mid-div: drvn along 1/2-way: wknd 2f out* **14/1**
066 **10** nse **World Freight Girl**148 3040 2-9-2 **59** JimmyQuinn 5 36
(Dean Ivory) *s.i.s: outpcd* **20/1**

1m 14.76s (-0.24) **Going Correction** -0.075s/f (Stan) **10** Ran SP% **117.7**
Speed ratings (Par 94): **98,93,90,88,87 86,84,82,82,82**
toteswingers 1&2 £4.10, 2&3 £8.40, 1&3 £5.10 CSF £14.80 CT £90.47 TOTE £4.70: £2.40, £2.30, £1.70; EX 13.90 Trifecta £26.40 Pool: £1218.39 - 34.56 winning units..
Owner Black House Boys **Bred** Howard Barton Stud **Trained** Malpas, Cheshire

FOCUS
Division two of this 6f nursery and it looked a stronger division that the first one. The pace was generous although those ridden prominently were favoured. The winner impressed and could do better again. The second and third help with the form.

NOTEBOOK
Archie Stevens benefited from a nice tow into the race and reversed recent C&D form with Marmot Bay to open his account at the sixth attempt. He was arguably unlucky not to score last time but he had no problems here and and quickened away stylishly once hitting the front inside the final furlong. (tchd 9-4)
Marmot Bay(IRE) did well to get to the lead from her wide draw and, although no match for the winner, deserves credit for a strong front-running effort. She's capable of winning again and remains in form. (op 4-1 tchd 5-1)
Not Now Blondie, a previous winner at this track over 5f, ran wide entering the straight but finished clear of the remainder. She has little in hand off her current mark but should continue to give a good account, especially if returning to this venue. (op 15-2)
Koharu wasn't disgraced on this first run on Polytrack. She was under pressure in rear on the bend entering the straight but kept on to finish in the frame on this handicap debut.
My Sweet Lord ran well last time over C&D after a slow start, and he was again sluggish when the stalls opened before finishing well on the outside. He has ability and is one to keep an eye on.
Birdy Boy(USA) attracted support back down in trip, but weakened in the straight after racing prominently. This may have come too soon after running at Southwell two days earlier.

7651 32REDBET.COM CLAIMING STKS 5f 216y(P)
5:20 (5:20) (Class 6) 3-Y-O+ £1,704 (£503; £251) Stalls Low

Form RPR
0624 **1** **Noverre To Go (IRE)**23 7145 6-9-4 84 LukeMorris 4 91
(Ronald Harris) *a.p: hrd rdn to ld 1f out: styd on u.p* **7/2**1
416 **2** ¾ **Last Sovereign**7 7503 8-9-0 90 (b) JacobButterfield(7) 6 92
(Ollie Pears) *a.p: edgd rt over 2f out: rdn over 1f out: sn ev ch: styd on* **7/2**1
4600 **3** nk **Julius Geezer (IRE)**19 7254 4-9-4 82 RichardKingscote 5 88
(Tom Dascombe) *trckd ldrs: rdn and ev ch 1f out: styd on* **9/1**
0040 **4** ¾ **Valery Borzov (IRE)**82 5356 8-9-7 85 (v) TonyHamilton 12 88
(Richard Fahey) *hld up: rdn and r.o wl ins fnl f: could nt rch ldrs* **9/2**3
6152 **5** ¾ **Red Cape (FR)**19 7254 9-8-11 70 (b) JamesSullivan 8 76
(Ruth Carr) *led: rdn and hdd 1f out: no ex wl ins fnl f* **18/1**
2066 **6** 1 ¼ **Blue Jack**17 7297 7-8-11 78 (tp) SebSanders 1 72
(Alan McCabe) *hld up: pushed along over 2f out: styd on fr over 1f out: could nt trble ldrs* **20/1**
1006 **7** 4 ½ **Lesley's Choice**19 7254 6-9-2 75 (b) JohnFahy 9 62
(Sean Curran) *chsd ldr tl rdn over 1f out: wknd fnl f* **50/1**
5-00 **8** ½ **Al Khan (IRE)**139 3348 3-9-7 88 PaulMulrennan 7 66
(Michael Easterby) *s.i.s: outpcd: styd on towards fin: nvr nrr* **20/1**
5001 **9** shd **Where's Reiley (USA)**19 7254 6-8-12 78 (b) FrankieMcDonald 11 57
(Alastair Lidderdale) *mid-div: rdn and hung lft over 2f out: wknd over 1f out* **12/1**
0344 **10** 1 ¾ **Dickie's Lad (IRE)**17 7291 4-9-4 78 (t) PhillipMakin 2 57
(Kevin Ryan) *hld up: shkn up over 1f out: no rspnse* **4/1**2

1m 13.81s (-1.19) **Going Correction** -0.075s/f (Stan) **10** Ran SP% **117.1**
Speed ratings (Par 101): **104,103,102,101,100 98,92,92,92,89**
toteswingers 1&2 £4.10, 2&3 £8.40, 1&3 £5.10 CSF £15.39 TOTE £4.00: £2.50, £1.10, £3.70; EX 14.80 Trifecta £101.60 Pool: £1313.27 - 9.72 winning units..Noverre To Go was subject to a friendly claim.
Owner Robert & Nina Bailey **Bred** Gestut Gorlsdorf **Trained** Earlswood, Monmouths

FOCUS
A competitive claimer in which the lowest-rated runner was racing off a mark of 70. The pace was strong and the form is straightforward.

7652 32RED.COM H'CAP 1m 5f 194y(P)
5:50 (5:50) (Class 5) (0-70,70) 3-Y-O+ £2,264 (£673; £336; £168) Stalls Low

Form RPR
345 **1** **Gabrial's King (IRE)**21 7195 3-9-3 **67** (p) StevieDonohoe 1 75
(Ian Williams) *chsd ldrs: shkn up over 1f out: rdn to ld wl ins fnl f: styd on* **7/2**2
1143 **2** nse **Laser Blazer**33 6891 4-9-7 **66** (p) RaulDaSilva(3) 10 74
(Jeremy Gask) *hld up: plld hrd: hdwy over 5f out: chsd ldr over 1f out: rdn and ev ch ins fnl f: styd on* **5/1**3
0400 **3** 1 ½ **Pertemps Networks**13 7369 8-9-13 **69** GrahamGibbons 7 75
(Michael Easterby) *set stdy pce tl qcknd 3f out: rdn over 1f out: hdd and unable qck wl ins fnl f* **8/1**
6225 **4** 2 ¼ **Pelham Crescent (IRE)**38 6735 9-9-2 **58** LukeMorris 9 60
(Bryn Palling) *hld up: hdwy over 7f out: chsd ldr over 2f out tl rdn over 1f out* **10/1**
0546 **5** ½ **El Libertador (USA)**22 7169 6-8-13 **55** (b) ShaneKelly 6 57
(Eric Wheeler) *chsd ldrs tl lost pl over 5f out: rdn and hung lft over 1f out: styd on* **25/1**
5012 **6** hd **Squad**22 7169 6-9-9 **70** (v) TobyAtkinson(5) 11 71
(Simon Dow) *s.i.s: hld up: drvn along 3f out: styd on fr over 1f out: nt rch ldrs* **15/2**
-U35 **7** 5 **Tiny Temper (IRE)**26 7068 4-9-8 **64** TonyHamilton 5 58
(Richard Fahey) *chsd ldr tl rdn over 2f out: wknd fnl f* **15/2**
3054 **8** ¾ **Toughness Danon**13 7380 6-9-12 **68** (t) SebSanders 8 61
(Brendan Powell) *hld up: rdn over 2f out: sme hdwy over 1f out: wknd fnl f* **10/3**1
06/4 **9** 11 **Tri Nations (UAE)**12 7413 7-10-0 **70** (vt) SeanQuinlan 3 46
(Anthony Middleton) *hld up: hdwy over 3f out: rdn and wknd over 2f out* **22/1**

3m 6.77s (0.77) **Going Correction** -0.075s/f (Stan)
WFA 3 from 4yo+ 8lb **9** Ran SP% **113.9**
Speed ratings (Par 103): **94,93,93,91,91 91,88,88,81**
toteswingers 1&2 £4.20, 2&3 £10.00, 1&3 £6.30 CSF £21.08 CT £128.75 TOTE £4.20: £1.90, £1.10, £4.80; EX 22.80 Trifecta £294.80 Pool: £1387.97 - 3.53 winning units..
Owner Dr Marwan Koukash **Bred** Danella Partnership **Trained** Portway, Worcs

FOCUS
A fair staying handicap but the pace was only modest. The winner raced centre-to-far-side in the straight and recorded a small personal best.
Toughness Danon Official explanation: jockey said gelding hung left in the closing stages.

7653 32REDPOKER.COM MAIDEN AUCTION STKS 5f 216y(P)
6:20 (6:22) (Class 6) 2-Y-O £1,704 (£503; £251) Stalls Low

Form RPR
2022 **1** **Nenge Mboko**16 7305 2-9-3 75 LukeMorris 9 74
(George Baker) *led early: chsd ldrs: pushed along 1/2-way: wnt 2nd over 2f out: sn drvn along: styd on u.p to ld nr fin* **4/6**1
666 **2** ½ **Midnight Dream (FR)**29 6977 2-8-12 68 PatrickMathers 6 68
(Linda Stubbs) *sn led: rdn over 1f out: hdd nr fin* **5/1**3
0406 **3** nk **Forceful Flame**17 7298 2-8-11 66 AndreaAtzeni 2 66
(Robert Eddery) *chsd ldrs: rdn over 1f out: r.o* **3/1**2
0 **4** nk **Ada Lovelace**20 7219 2-8-5 0 JimmyQuinn 1 59
(Dean Ivory) *hld up: hdwy over 2f out: rdn and ev ch ins fnl f: unable qck nr fin* **20/1**
00 **5** 3 ½ **Multi Fours**21 7191 2-8-4 0 SimonPearce(3) 5 50
(Daniel Kubler) *hld up: hdwy over 1f out: could nt trble ldrs* **20/1**
0 **6** 5 **Duchess Of Dreams**17 7290 2-8-9 0 ow2 RobbieFitzpatrick 4 37
(Richard Guest) *hld up: pushed along over 2f out: nvr on terms* **33/1**
0 **7** nk **Posh Secret**30 6954 2-8-11 0 BarryMcHugh 3 38
(John Quinn) *prom: racd keenly: wknd over 1f out* **25/1**
50 **8** 4 ½ **Mr Vendman (IRE)**35 6818 2-8-11 0 StevieDonohoe 8 25
(Ian Williams) *s.i.s: outpcd* **16/1**
0 **9** 1 **Eton Miss (IRE)**16 7305 2-8-6 0 JoeFanning 7 17
(Mike Murphy) *sn prom: rdn and wknd over 1f out* **50/1**

1m 15.48s (0.48) **Going Correction** -0.075s/f (Stan) **9** Ran SP% **125.8**
Speed ratings (Par 94): **93,92,91,91,86 80,79,73,72**
toteswingers 1&2 £2.20, 2&3 £3.10, 1&3 £1.20 CSF £4.84 TOTE £1.50: £1.02, £1.30, £1.30; EX 5.10 Trifecta £7.20 Pool: £1860.84 - 192.89 winning units..
Owner Russell Conrad Vail Wheeler Hippychick **Bred** Pigeon House Stud **Trained** Manton, Wilts

FOCUS
An ordinary maiden which lacked strength in depth. It was run at a sound gallop and the first four home were covered by a length. The principals set the level.

NOTEBOOK
Nenge Mboko had leading form claims having finished runner-up in three of his previous four starts including on his Polytrack debut at Lingfield 16 days earlier in first-time cheekpieces which were discarded this time. He had to be driven entering the straight and only got up close home under a strong ride from Luke Morris to open his account at the sixth attempt. He'll be put away now for a 3yo campaign next season and will probably be suited by stepping back up in trip. (op 8-15 tchd 8-11)
Midnight Dream(FR) adopted similar front-running tactics as when recording an improved effort at Kempton on his previous start over a furlong further. He stuck to his task well but was worn down in the final strides. (op 11-2)
Forceful Flame, who had run well when fourth in a Newmarket maiden over 7f on his second start, put a below-par par run in heavy ground firmly behind him back on Polytrack. (op 7-2)
Ada Lovelace stepped up considerably on her debut run over C&D and deserves credit against more experienced rivals. On this evidence she may be capable of landing a similar contest. (op 28-1)

7654 32RED CASINO MAIDEN STKS 7f 32y(P)
6:50 (6:52) (Class 5) 3-Y-O+ £2,264 (£673; £336; £168) Stalls High

Form RPR
-202 **1** **Kenny Powers**229 1032 3-9-3 106 (t) RichardKingscote 2 89+
(Tom Dascombe) *trckd ldrs: racd keenly: led over 2f out: shkn up and c clr fr over 1f out* **1/5**1
3202 **2** 8 **Green Mitas (ITY)**35 6827 3-9-3 64 AdamKirby 3 68
(Frank Sheridan) *a.p: chsd wnr over 2f out: sn rdn: no ex fnl f* **8/1**3
63 **3** 1 **Ifan (IRE)**103 4582 4-9-4 0 LukeMorris 11 65
(Bryn Palling) *hld up: hdwy over 2f out: sn rdn: styd on same pce appr fnl f* **16/1**
0432 **4** 1 ½ **Premier Choice**65 5919 3-9-3 63 (p) SilvestreDeSousa 1 61
(Tim Easterby) *chsd ldrs: rdn over 2f out: sn outpcd* **6/1**2
5 **5** ¾ **Zilzie (IRE)**10 7445 3-8-12 0 PJMcDonald 10 54
(Ann Duffield) *prom: rdn over 2f out: sn outpcd* **33/1**
05 **6** 5 **No Diamond**13 7384 5-9-4 0 (p) TomQueally 6 45
(Michael Appleby) *s.i.s: outpcd* **33/1**
7 8 **Harrier Exhibition (IRE)**24 7120 3-8-12 0 ShaneKelly 5 19
(Seamus Fahey, Ire) *s.s: outpcd* **50/1**
6 **8** 7 **Miss Jo B**54 6254 3-8-9 0 RyanClark(3) 4
(Phil McEntee) *sn pushed along towards rr: bhd fnl 4f: t.o* **66/1**
0- **9** 11 **Lady Libby Lamb**371 7245 4-8-13 0 MartinDwyer 9
(David C Griffiths) *chsd ldrs: rdn 1/2-way: wknd over 2f out: t.o* **100/1**
3/0- **10** 1 ¼ **Fast Samurai (USA)**607 850 4-8-11 0 JoeyHaynes(7) 8
(Tony Carroll) *led: rdn and hdd over 2f out: sn wknd: t.o* **33/1**
00 **11** 11 **Amantius**19 7249 3-9-3 0 ChrisCatlin 7
(John Spearing) *sn outpcd: t.o* **40/1**

1m 28.67s (-0.93) **Going Correction** -0.075s/f (Stan)
WFA 3 from 4yo+ 1lb **11** Ran SP% **130.3**
Speed ratings (Par 103): **102,92,91,90,89 83,74,66,53,52 39**
toteswingers 1&2 £2.10, 2&3 £4.40, 1&3 £3.10 CSF £3.43 TOTE £1.10: £1.02, £1.40, £3.20; EX 3.90 Trifecta £19.00 Pool: £1783.93 - 70.19 winning units..

Owner First Manor **Bred** Bearstone Stud **Trained** Malpas, Cheshire
FOCUS
As the betting suggested this modest maiden was turned into a procession by the short-priced favourite. The second to fourth set the level.

7655 32RED H'CAP 1m 4f 50y (P)
7:20 (7:20) (Class 4) (0-85,85) 3-Y-O **£4,075** (£1,212; £606 ; £303) **Stalls** Low

Form RPR
0211 **1** **Layali Dubai (USA)**[7] 7511 3-9-2[80] 6ex................ SilvestreDeSousa 10 90+
(Saeed Bin Suroor) *hld up: hdwy and hung lft over 1f out: sn rdn: r.o to ld wl ins fnl f: readily* **6/4**[1]
1313 **2** ¾ **Rythmic**[2] 7617 3-8-12[76].. JoeFanning 1 84
(Mark Johnston) *set stdy pce tl qcknd 3f out: rdn and hdd wl ins fnl f* **6/1**
0261 **3** 1 ¼ **Badea**[3] 7596 3-8-7[71] 6ex...................................(v) BarryMcHugh 2 77
(Richard Fahey) *a.p: chsd ldr 3f out: rdn over 1f out: styd on u.p* **5/1**[3]
0656 **4** 1 ½ **Addazero**[42] 6615 3-8-7[71].. JohnFahy 5 75
(Alastair Lidderdale) *chsd ldrs: rdn over 1f out: styd on* **50/1**
3153 **5** 2 ¼ **Infinite Hope (USA)**[21] 7194 3-9-3[81]........................ KirstyMilczarek 9 81
(Luca Cumani) *racd keenly and sn trcking ldrs: wnt 2nd over 7f out tl pushed along 3f out: no ex fnl f* **11/2**
4000 **6** 5 **Silent Moment (USA)**[17] 6492 3-9-7[85].................. MickaelBarzalona 3 78
(Saeed Bin Suroor) *prom: pushed along over 3f out: wknd over 1f out* **9/1**
0000 **7** 1 ½ **Hector's Chance**[13] 7381 3-8-0[71] oh4..............................(p) RyanTate(7) 6 62
(Heather Main) *hld up: rdn over 2f out: nvr on terms* **66/1**
0605 **8** 15 **Cape Safari (IRE)**[12] 7413 3-8-8[79]........................... ChloeIngram(7) 8 47
(Tim Vaughan) *hld up and a bhd* **50/1**
2252 **9** nk **Nordic Quest (IRE)**[21] 7195 3-9-4[82]................................ NeilCallan 7 50
(Gerard Butler) *plld hrd and prom: rdn over 2f out: wknd wl over 1f out* **10/3**[2]

2m 38.63s (-2.47)**Going Correction** -0.075s/f (Stan) 9Ran SP%**124.8**
Speed ratings (Par 104): **105,104,103,102,101 97,96,86,86**
toteswingers 1&2 £2.00, 2&3 £6.20, 1&3 £3.70 CSF £12.60 CT £40.32 TOTE £2.60 : £1.50, £2.30, £1.90 ; EX 12.00 Trifecta £30.70 Pool: £1292.47 - 31.48 winning units.
Owner Godolphin **Bred** Darley **Trained** Newmarket, Suffolk
FOCUS
A decent handicap which was run at a steady pace. The winner came wide on the bend entering the straight and challenged down the centre-to-far-side. He has more to offer, and the form makes sense.

7656 32RED SUPPORTING BRITISH RACING MAIDEN FILLIES' STKS 1m 141y (P)
7:50 (7:51) (Class 5) 3-Y-O+ **£2,264** (£673; £336 ; £168) **Stalls** Low

Form RPR
3220 **1** **Four Leaves (IRE)**[71] 5747 3-8-12[76]..............................(p) AdamKirby 1 82
(Marco Botti) *mde all: set stdy pce tl qcknd over 2f out: clr over 1f out: sn rdn and hung lft: styd on* **2/1**[2]
3456 **2** 2 ¼ **Srinagar Girl**[22] 7170 3-8-12[73]..[1] TomQueally 8 77
(Sir Henry Cecil) *hld up: hdwy over 3f out: rdn to go 2nd over 1f out: styd on: could nt rch wnr* **7/4**[1]
00 **3** 6 **Guarda Pampa**[154] 2849 3-8-12[0].................................. AdamBeschizza 5 63
(William Haggas) *prom: rdn over 2f out: sn outpcd* **14/1**
2043 **4** ½ **Amelia May**[12] 7416 3-8-12[73]..(b[1]) LukeMorris 9 62
(Ed Vaughan) *chsd wnr over 7f out: rdn and hung rt over 2f out: wknd over 1f out* **11/4**[3]
02- **5** 6 **Queen Of Epirus**[510] 3119 4-9-1[0].. TomEaves 4 48
(Brian Rothwell) *hld up: rdn over 2f out: nvr on terms* **33/1**
6 hd **Alezanna** 3-8-12[0]... KirstyMilczarek 2 48
(James Toller) *chsd wnr 1f: remained handy: rdn whn hmpd over 2f out: sn wknd* **28/1**
0/ **7** nk **Fashion Flow**[937] 1355 5-9-1[0]................................. SilvestreDeSousa 6 47
(Michael Wigham) *hld up: a in rr* **16/1**
0006 **8** 11 **Super Smile (IRE)**[13] 7384 4-9-1[34]............................(t) AndrewMullen 7 22
(Michael Appleby) *chsd ldrs: rdn over 2f out: sn wknd* **80/1**
00-0 **9** 13 **Femme D'Espere**[2] 7612 6-9-1[10].. ChrisCatlin 3
(Christopher Kellett) *s.i.s and hmpd s: a in rr: bhd fnl 3f: t.o* **80/1**

1m 50.09s (-0.41)**Going Correction** -0.075s/f (Stan)
WFA 3 from 4yo+ 3lb 9Ran SP%**117.8**
Speed ratings (Par 100): **98,96,90,90,84 84,84,74,63**
toteswingers 1&2 £1.30, 2&3 £6.40, 1&3 £6.60 CSF £5.93 TOTE £3.10 : £1.30, £1.30, £4.10; EX 6.50 Trifecta £40.90 Pool: £1720.14 - 31.51 winning units.
Owner H E Sheikh Sultan Bin Khalifa Al Nahyan **Bred** Sheikh Sultan Bin Khalifa Al Nayhan **Trained** Newmarket, Suffolk
FOCUS
An ordinary maiden in which the winner benefited from a fine tactical ride by Adam Kirby. The favouirite is not rated far below form.
T/Plt: £9.40 to a £1 stake. Pool: £65080.29 - 5048.22 winning tickets. T/Qpdt: £4.60 to a £1 stake. Pool of £7658.18 - 1211.16 w. tckts CR 7657a - 7664a (Foreign Racing) See RI

[6595]TOULOUSE
Thursday, November 8
OFFICIAL GOING: Turf: soft

7665a PRIX FILLE DE L'AIR (GROUP 3) (3YO+ FILLIES & MARES) (TURF) 1m 2f 110y
2:20 (12:00) 3-Y-O+ **£33,333** (£13,333; £10,000 ; £6,666 ; £3,333)

RPR
1 **Casaca**[18] 6-8-11[0].. JeremyCrocquevieille 11 106
(J-M Osorio, Spain) *hld up towards rr: hdwy on outside over 1 1/2f out: r.o wl fnl f: led 50yds out: won easing down* **164/10**
2 1 ¾ **Baino Rock (FR)**[36] 6803 3-8-8[0]...................... Jean-BernardEyquem 7 105
(J-C Rouget, France) *midfield: prog on outside 1 1/2f out: hrd rdn and edgd lft over 1f out: r.o to chal ldr 120yds out: jst mastered ldr as wnr wnt by 50yds out: kpt on wl* **23/10**[1]
3 nk **Brasileira**[43] 6595 4-8-11[0].. AntoineHamelin 9 102
(J-M Beguigne, France) *trckd ldrs: chal on outside 1 1/2f out: disputing 2nd appr fnl f: rdn and qcknd to ld under 1f out: r.o u.p: hdd 50yds out and lost 2nd sn after: no ex* **11/2**[3]
4 2 ½ **Jetfire**[28] 4-8-11[0]... StephanePasquier 2 98
(D Prod'Homme, France) *midfield: rowed along to hold pl over 3f out: outpcd over 1 1/2f out: styd on u.p fnl 150yds: nt rch ldrs* **17/2**
5 nse **Salona (GER)**[48] 4-8-11[0].. RonanThomas 10 97
(J-P Carvalho, Germany) *hld up in rr: hdwy over 1f out: styd on u.p fnl f: nvr on terms* **21/1**
6 nk **Clunia (IRE)**[68] 5845 4-8-11[0]...................................... AnthonyCrastus 3 97
(C Laffon-Parias, France) *trckd ldr on rail: rdn and outpcd under 2f out: kpt on at one pce fnl f* **18/1**
7 nk **Bassamba (FR)**[20] 7234 3-8-8[0]....................(b) Francois-XavierBertras 4 98
(F Rohaut, France) *rel to r: rdn and sn 5 l adrift: fnd stride settled among bkmarkers after 2 1/2f: midfield appr 1/2-way: moved up to press ldr over 2f out: rdn and led over 1 1/2f out: hdd under 1f out: sn wknd* **33/10**[2]
8 1 ¼ **Un Jour (FR)**[28] 4-8-11[0]... SebastienMaillot 8 94
(Mlle Valerie Boussin, France) *settled towards rr: rowed along to hold position 3f out: lost pl and bhd fr 2f out: styd on u.p ins fnl f: n.d* **48/1**
9 2 **Gloomy Sunday (FR)**[43] 6595 3-8-8[0]................................ JohanVictoire 1 92
(C Ferland, France) *midfield: rdn and effrt on ins to dispute 2nd appr fnl f: sn wknd and eased whn btn fnl 100yds* **17/2**
10 5 **Night Serenade (IRE)**[43] 6595 5-8-11[0]...........................(b) JulienAuge 5 80
(H-A Pantall, France) *prom on outside: pressed ldr over 2f out: sn rdn: wknd under 1 1/2f out* **52/1**
11 5 **Monicker**[43] 3-8-8[0].. FabriceVeron 6 72
(H-A Pantall, France) *led: hdd over 1 1/2f out: wknd appr fnl f* **14/1**

2m 15.6s (135.60)
WFA 3 from 4yo+ 4lb 11Ran SP%**116.1**
WIN (incl. 1 euro stake) 17.40. PLACES: 3.10, 1.50, 2.00. DF: 22.80. SF: 56.90
Owner Mme Africa Cuadra-Lores **Bred** Almagro De Actividades Comerci **Trained** Spain

NOTEBOOK
Casaca, a Spanish-trained raider, swept past the favourite to win with plenty in hand.

[7649]WOLVERHAMPTON (A.W) (L-H)
Friday, November 9
OFFICIAL GOING: Standard
Wind: Fresh behind Weather: Overcast turning showery after race 4

7666 32RED.COM APPRENTICE H'CAP 5f 216y (P)
4:20 (4:20) (Class 5) (0-70,70) 3-Y-O+ **£2,911** (£866; £432 ; £216) **Stalls** Low

Form RPR
0005 **1** **Diman Waters (IRE)**[10] 7464 5-8-13[70]........................(b) JasonHart(5) 1 78
(Eric Alston) *s.i.s: sn pushed along and prom: shkn up over 2f out: styd on to ld wl ins fnl f* **11/1**
0302 **2** ¾ **Another Citizen (IRE)**[36] 6825 4-8-9[68].....................(b) GaryMahon(7) 6 74
(Tim Easterby) *chsd ldrs: led 1/2-way: shkn up and clr over 1f out: rdr dropped reins wl ins fnl f: sn hdd and unable qck* **5/2**[1]
0051 **3** nk **Half A Crown (IRE)**[4] 7447 7-9-3[69] 6ex................. AdamBeschizza 13 74
(Peter Salmon) *hld up: rdn and r.o wl ins fnl f: nrst fin* **20/1**
0626 **4** ¾ **Mcmonagle (USA)**[13] 7411 4-8-13[70].............(tp) DavidSimmonson(5) 9 73
(Alan Brown) *led 1f: chsd ldrs: rdn over 1f out: r.o* **6/1**[3]
0531 **5** ¾ **Victorian Bounty**[18] 7297 7-9-4[70]................................. AshleyMorgan 12 71
(Tony Newcombe) *prom: outpcd over 2f out: rdn over 1f out: r.o* **9/1**
1654 **6** ¾ **Chambles**[13] 7412 3-8-11[68]... NoraLooby(5) 4 67
(Alan McCabe) *hld up: nt clr run over 1f out: styd on ins fnl f: nvr nrr* **4/1**[2]
2304 **7** ½ **See Clearly**[13] 7395 3-8-13[68].......................................(p) DarylByrne(3) 5 65
(Tim Easterby) *chsd ldrs: pushed along over 2f out: styd on same pce fnl f* **8/1**
00-0 **8** 2 ¾ **Johnstown Lad (IRE)**[300] 178 8-9-2[68]..................(t) DeclanCannon 11 57
(Daniel Mark Loughnane) *sn pushed along in rr: bhd 4f out: styd on u.p fnl f: nvr nrr* **50/1**
3050 **9** 2 ¼ **Swendab (IRE)**[15] 7360 4-9-2[68]...(v) RyanClark 2 50
(John O'Shea) *s.i.s: sn pushed along in rr: nvr on terms* **16/1**
2000 **10** 3 ½ **Befortyfour**[55] 6226 7-9-3[69]...(e[1]) AmyRyan 7 40
(Charles Smith) *s.i.s: outpcd* **33/1**
2406 **11** ½ **For Shia And Lula (IRE)**[3] 7309 3-9-1[70].........(p) MatthewLawson(3) 8 40
(Daniel Mark Loughnane) *hld up: rdn 1/2-way: sn bhd* **12/1**
0450 **12** 4 ½ **Steelcut**[85] 5272 8-8-13[70]...(p) JackDuern(5) 3 26
(Mark Buckley) *led 5f out: hdd 1/2-way: wknd fnl f* **28/1**

1m 15.02s (0.02)**Going Correction** +0.025s/f (Slow) 12Ran SP%**119.0**
Speed ratings (Par 103): **100,99,98,97,96 95,94,91,88,83 82,76**
Swingers 1&2 £7.50, 2&3 £6.90, 1&3 £31.70 CSF £37.45 CT £573.25 TOTE £13.40 : £3.70, £1.10, £5.10 ; EX 41.10 Trifecta £376.00 Pool: £932.54 - 1.86 winning units.
Owner Buist, Long, Thompson **Bred** Mrs Chris Harrington **Trained** Longton, Lancs
■ Stewards' Enquiry : David Simmonson two-day ban: used whip above permitted level (Nov 23-24)
FOCUS
Track Gallop Mastered after fourth race. A modest handicap, and straightforward form. The pace was pretty honest.

7667 32RED CASINO MAIDEN STKS (DIV I) 5f 216y (P)
4:50 (4:50) (Class 5) 3-Y-O **£2,587** (£770; £384 ; £192) **Stalls** Low

Form RPR
0 **1** **Living Leader**[32] 6930 3-9-3[0].. TomMcLaughlin 3 78+
(Nick Littmoden) *chsd ldrs: pushed along over 2f out: rdn to ld wl ins fnl f: hung rt: r.o* **2/1**[1]
430 **2** 2 **Bull Bay**[31] 6965 3-8-10[62]... IanBurns(7) 4 70
(Jane Chapple-Hyam) *led: rdn: hung rt and hdd wl ins fnl f: styd on same pce* **11/2**
3422 **3** 2 **Tidal's Baby**[39] 6739 3-9-3[67].. DavidProbert 6 64
(Tony Carroll) *chsd ldr: rdn and hung lft ins fnl f: styd on same pce* **9/4**[2]
4243 **4** 1 ¾ **Crazy Too (IRE)**[27] 7061 3-8-12[63]................................ GrahamLee 2 53
(David Simcock) *hld up in tch: plld hrd: rdn over 1f out: no ex fnl f* **3/1**[3]
5 2 ½ **Flumps** 3-8-12[0].. ShaneKelly 10 45
(John Stimpson) *s.i.s: sn pushed along in rr: styd on fr over 1f out: nvr nrr* **66/1**
0 **6** 2 **Sherry Cherie (IRE)**[213] 1274 3-8-12[0]......................[1] PatrickMathers 9 39
(Richard Fahey) *hld up: plld hrd: hdwy over 4f out: pushed along over 2f out: wknd over 1f out* **14/1**
06 **7** 1 **Stoneacre Hull (IRE)**[68] 5177 3-8-12[0]...................... RobbieFitzpatrick 1 35
(Peter Grayson) *prom: lost pl 4f out: wknd over 2f out* **100/1**
5344 **8** ½ **Brown Volcano (IRE)**[54] 6287 3-9-3[60]............................ LukeMorris 5 39
(John O'Shea) *chsd ldrs: lost pl and drvn along 1/2-way: wknd over 1f out* **33/1**
9 1 ½ **Ioannou** 3-9-3[0].. JimmyQuinn 8 34
(Noel Quinlan) *s.s: outpcd* **33/1**

1m 15.24s (0.24)**Going Correction** +0.025s/f (Slow) 9Ran SP%**119.5**
Speed ratings (Par 102): **99,96,93,91,88 85,84,83,81**
Swingers 1&2 £3.60, 2&3 £3.60, 1&3 £2.40 CSF £14.08 TOTE £2.90 : £1.80, £1.60, £1.40 ; EX 20.60 Trifecta £115.80 Pool: £1,913.06 - 12.39 winning units.
Owner Nigel Shields **Bred** D J And Mrs Deer **Trained** Newmarket, Suffolk

FOCUS
In what was a weak maiden, the market spoke strongly in favour of the winner. He can do better, but the form is rated on the negative side.

7668 32RED CASINO MAIDEN STKS (DIV II) 5f 216y(P)
5:20 (5:21) (Class 5) 3-Y-O £2,587 (£770; £384; £192) Stalls Low

Form RPR
3434 1 **Generalyse**[16] 7322 3-9-3 70 (b[1]) JohnFahy 8 72
(Ben De Haan) *led 5f out: rdn and edgd rt 1f out: styd on* **5/1**[3]
24 2 1 ½ **Far East**[29] 7005 3-8-12 0 LukeMorris 3 63
(Clive Cox) *trckd ldrs: racd keenly: wnt 2nd over 2f out: rdn over 1f out: styd on* **7/2**[2]
3 hd **Polar Venture** 3-9-3 0 GrahamLee 4 67+
(William Haggas) *hld up: hdwy over 2f out: rdn over 1f out: styd on* **2/1**[1]
63 4 2 **Game All (IRE)**[52] 6345 3-8-12 0 JimmyQuinn 5 56+
(Hugo Palmer) *hld up: shkn up and edgd lft over 1f out: styd on: nt trble ldrs* **16/1**
0204 5 nk **Foot Tapper**[81] 5427 3-9-3 63 TedDurcan 9 60
(Chris Wall) *a.p: rdn over 1f out: styd on* **13/2**
3000 6 1 **Red Ramesses (IRE)**[140] 3343 3-9-3 70 [1] GeorgeBaker 2 58
(John Best) *prom: nt clr run over 2f out: sn rdn: styd on same pce fnl f* **10/1**
6-00 7 ½ **Silver Marizah (IRE)**[104] 4583 3-8-12 59 [1] RobertHavlin 6 51
(Roger Ingram) *led 1f: chsd wnr tl rdn over 2f out: no ex fnl f* **40/1**
53 8 4 ½ **Transfix**[55] 6254 3-8-12 0 (b[1]) JoeFanning 1 37
(Ed Vaughan) *s.i.s: a in rr* **13/2**
1m 14.9s (-0.10) **Going Correction** +0.025s/f (Slow) **8** Ran SP% **116.3**
Speed ratings (Par 102): **101,99,98,96,95 94,93,87**
Swingers 1&2 £3.40, 2&3 £2.00, 1&3 £3.70 CSF £23.30 TOTE £5.90: £2.20, £1.10, £1.60; EX 26.60 Trifecta £65.90 Pool: £1,092.20 - 12.43 winning units..
Owner Mrs D Vaughan **Bred** Mrs D Vaughan **Trained** Lambourn, Berks
FOCUS
The winning time was 0.34sec quicker than the first division. Four of the nine runners were trying a new form of headgear for the first time, and one of their number came home in front. The winner didn't need to match his best in this modest race.

7669 32RED SUPPORTING BRITISH RACING MEDIAN AUCTION MAIDEN STKS 5f 20y(P)
5:50 (5:51) (Class 6) 2-Y-O £1,704 (£503; £251) Stalls Low

Form RPR
643 1 **Space Artist (IRE)**[22] 7198 2-9-3 71 TomEaves 6 76
(Bryan Smart) *chsd ldr: pushed along over 2f out: rdn over 1f out: styd on u.p to ld wl ins fnl f* **11/8**[1]
4263 2 1 ¾ **Alhaarth Beauty (IRE)**[13] 7410 2-8-12 69 LiamJones 1 65
(Ismail Mohammed) *led: rdn over 1f out: hdd and unable qck wl ins fnl f* **2/1**[2]
60 3 2 ¾ **Con Leche**[36] 6808 2-9-3 0 GrahamLee 3 60
(Scott Dixon) *chsd ldrs: rdn over 2f out: sn outpcd: styd on nr fin* **50/1**
4 10 **Beauchamp Sunset** 2-9-3 0 GeorgeBaker 5 24
(Hans Adielsson) *s.i.s: nvr nr to chal* **12/1**[3]
5 2 **Beauchamp Astra** 2-8-5 0 NicoleNordblad[(7)] 7 12
(Hans Adielsson) *s.s: nvr nr to chal* **28/1**
1m 2.39s (0.09) **Going Correction** +0.025s/f (Slow) **5** Ran SP% **88.5**
Speed ratings (Par 94): **100,97,92,76,73**
Imperial Spirit (7-2) was withdrawn. Rule 4 applies to all bets. Deduction - 20p in the pound. CSF £2.54 TOTE £1.70: £1.10, £1.20; EX 3.00.
Owner The Smart Dame Laura Partnership **Bred** Rathasker Stud **Trained** Hambleton, N Yorks
FOCUS
A two-horse race from the turn in. The runner-up is the bset guide.
NOTEBOOK
Space Artist(IRE) saw the trip out strongest. He was being pushed along at halfway, but kept the leader in his sights and he was the one with the stamina to see it out at the finish. He's nothing special, but he's a half-brother to multiple winning sprinter Your Gifted, and he ought to pay his way in sprint handicaps. (op 7-4 tchd 5-4)
Alhaarth Beauty(IRE), dropping to the minimum trip for the first time, travelled well in the lead and looked to have the winner in trouble on the turn in, but, as has been the case for her over 6f and 7f, she didn't see her race out. (op 15-8)
Con Leche hadn't beaten a rival home in his two previous starts and he was soon left behind by the first two on the turn into the straight here. (op 40-1)
Beauchamp Sunset reared up in the stalls and when the gates opened he was slowly away. He raced detached from the other three and never got in a blow, but is bred to appreciate further in time. (op 16-1 tchd 10-1)
Beauchamp Astra, who veered right at the start, is, like her stablemate, bred to want a longer trip. (tchd 25-1 and 33-1)

7670 DAVID MORRIS 60TH BIRTHDAY H'CAP 7f 32y(P)
6:20 (6:21) (Class 6) (0-62,62) 3-Y-O+ £1,704 (£503; £251) Stalls High

Form RPR
53 1 **Frognal (IRE)**[22] 7202 6-9-4 **62** (bt) WilliamCarson 4 70
(Violet M Jordan) *hld up: hdwy over 2f out: nt clr run over 1f out: rdn to ld wl ins fnl f: edgd rt: styd on* **6/1**[2]
500 2 nk **Katmai River (IRE)**[18] 7302 5-9-0 **58** (v) DavidProbert 3 65
(Mark Usher) *chsd ldrs: rdn over 1f out: ev ch ins fnl f: sn hung rt: styd on* **8/1**[3]
4353 3 1 ½ **Peak Storm**[15] 7361 3-9-0 **59** (p) LukeMorris 9 62
(John O'Shea) *hld up: hdwy over 1f out: running on whn hmpd wl ins fnl f* **8/1**[3]
0000 4 1 ¼ **Zaheeb**[65] 5941 4-9-4 **62** (b) DaleSwift 6 63
(Dave Morris) *chsd ldr tl led over 2f out: rdn and hdd wl ins fnl f: no ex* **8/1**[3]
-000 5 1 **Mountrath**[37] 6801 5-9-4 **62** (v) GeorgeBaker 11 60
(Gary Moore) *chsd ldrs: ev ch over 2f out: sn rdn: styd on same pce fnl f* **5/1**[1]
3002 6 hd **Piccolo Express**[21] 7224 6-9-1 **59** J-PGuillambert 7 57
(Brian Baugh) *hld up: nt clr run fr over 1f out tl swtchd rt ins fnl f: nvr able to chal* **12/1**
0310 7 3 **Drive Home (USA)**[13] 7412 5-9-1 **62** (p) NeilFarley[(3)] 10 52
(Noel Wilson) *mid-div: drvn along 1/2-way: n.d* **12/1**
4306 8 nk **Regal Acclaim (IRE)**[81] 5415 3-8-8 **58** (p) JasonHart[(5)] 8 47
(Declan Carroll) *prom: rdn over 2f out: wknd fnl f* **10/1**
0330 9 1 **Hey Fiddle Fiddle (IRE)**[108] 4420 3-9-2 **61** (b) RobertWinston 2 47
(Charles Hills) *led: rdn and hdd over 2f out: wknd fnl f* **12/1**
0541 10 ¾ **Elegant Muse**[14] 7382 4-9-4 **62** (t) GrahamLee 1 47
(Michael Appleby) *chsd ldrs tl rdn over 2f out: sn wknd* **5/1**[1]
2000 11 1 ½ **Sanad (IRE)**[22] 7200 3-8-10 **58** (p) RyanClark[(3)] 12 39
(Anthony Carson) *s.i.s: hdwy over 5f out: rdn over 2f out: wknd fnl f* **40/1**
5000 12 6 **Cut The Cackle (IRE)**[9] 7486 6-9-2 **60** (bt) MartinHarley 5 27
(Violet M Jordan) *s.i.s: outpcd* **40/1**
1m 29.16s (-0.44) **Going Correction** +0.025s/f (Slow)
WFA 3 from 4yo+ 1lb **12** Ran SP% **118.0**
Speed ratings (Par 101): **103,102,100,99,98 98,94,94,93,92 90,83**
Swingers 1&2 £7.60, 2&3 £16.20, 1&3 £9.60 CSF £53.21 CT £391.81 TOTE £7.50: £2.50, £2.60, £2.60; EX 75.20 Trifecta £532.30 Part won. Pool: £709.75 - 0.10 winning units..
Owner Rakebackmypoker.com **Bred** Bryan Ryan **Trained** Moreton Morrell, Warwicks
FOCUS
A modest handicap and the field finished compressed. The form might prove a bit better.

7671 £32 BONUS AT 32RED.COM CLASSIFIED STKS 1m 141y(P)
6:50 (6:50) (Class 6) 3-Y-O+ £1,704 (£503; £251) Stalls Low

Form RPR
0623 1 **Inffiraaj (IRE)**[10] 7470 3-9-0 53 MartinHarley 6 57
(Mick Channon) *a.p: rdn over 1f out: styd on u.p to ld post* **7/2**[2]
3001 2 nse **Whinging Willie (IRE)**[8] 7500 3-9-6 55 GeorgeBaker 7 63
(Gary Moore) *hld up: hdwy over 1f out: rdn to ld wl ins fnl f: hdd post* **5/4**[1]
0545 3 1 ½ **Graceful Act**[9] 7495 4-9-3 54 DaleSwift 11 53
(Ron Barr) *stmbld s: sn prom: rdn and ev ch ins fnl f: styd on same pce* **14/1**
42 4 1 ¼ **Clapped**[16] 7326 3-9-0 55 (p) TedDurcan 8 51
(Ed Vaughan) *led: rdn and edgd lft over 1f out: hdd and no ex wl ins fnl f* **6/1**[3]
0/06 5 2 **May Boy**[9] 7488 6-8-10 44 PhilipPrince[(7)] 5 46
(Ron Hodges) *chsd ldr tl rdn over 2f out: nt clr run over 1f out: styd on fnl f* **16/1**
4050 6 ¾ **Crucis Abbey (IRE)**[14] 7385 4-9-3 52 (p) WilliamCarson 9 44
(Mark Brisbourne) *hld up: hdwy over 3f out: rdn over 1f out: no ex fnl f* **25/1**
5000 7 ¾ **Lord Paget**[3] 7616 3-8-9 52 (p) JackDuern[(5)] 4 44
(Reg Hollinshead) *s.i.s: hld up: hdwy over 2f out: rdn over 1f out: no ex fnl f* **20/1**
3640 8 hd **Sir Windsorlot (IRE)**[13] 7402 3-9-0 55 TomEaves 2 43
(John Quinn) *chsd ldrs: nt clr run over 2f out: rdn over 1f out: wknd fnl f* **20/1**
500/ 9 1 ¾ **Apache Moon**[615] 836 6-9-3 50 LukeMorris 12 39
(Alastair Lidderdale) *hld up: rdn over 2f out: n.d* **50/1**
3410 10 2 ½ **Tony Hollis**[15] 7348 4-8-10 52 GemmaTutty[(7)] 3 33
(Karen Tutty) *hld up: pushed along over 3f out: a in rr* **12/1**
4600 11 1 **Well Bank (IRE)**[15] 7354 3-9-0 50 GrahamLee 1 32
(Colin Teague) *prom: rdn over 2f out: sn wknd* **50/1**
1m 50.76s (0.26) **Going Correction** +0.025s/f (Slow)
WFA 3 from 4yo+ 3lb **11** Ran SP% **118.5**
Speed ratings (Par 101): **99,98,97,96,94 94,93,93,91,89 88**
Swingers 1&2 £1.90, 2&3 £4.50, 1&3 £5.60 CSF £7.73 TOTE £5.30: £1.50, £1.10, £4.20; EX 8.90 Trifecta £44.90 Pool: £657.49 - 10.98 winning units..
Owner Billy Parish **Bred** Incense Partnership **Trained** West Ilsley, Berks
FOCUS
All but one of these were rated within 6lb of each other on adjusted official ratings, but the market suggested it was far less competitive than that, and it was the first two in the betting that came to the fore, with little between them at the line. A steady tempo and straightforward form.

7672 32RED H'CAP 1m 4f 50y(P)
7:20 (7:21) (Class 4) (0-85,84) 3-Y-O+ £4,075 (£1,212; £606; £303) Stalls Low

Form RPR
2433 1 **Flying Power**[24] 7147 4-9-1 **75** PaddyAspell 3 84
(John Norton) *chsd ldrs: led over 1f out: edgd lft: styd on* **11/1**
2553 2 nk **Fourth Generation (IRE)**[14] 7380 5-9-2 **76** RobertWinston 7 85+
(Alan Swinbank) *hld up: hdwy over 1f out: shkn up ins fnl f: styd on* **10/1**
253 3 1 **Pass Muster**[24] 7147 5-9-6 **80** FrederikTylicki 1 87
(Ollie Pears) *chsd ldrs: rdn over 1f out: styd on same pce ins fnl f* **7/2**[2]
2330 4 2 ¼ **Mizbah**[69] 5838 3-8-12 **78** TedDurcan 9 81
(Saeed Bin Suroor) *hld up: hdwy over 2f out: rdn over 1f out: no imp fnl f* **11/2**[3]
6020 5 1 ¼ **Hurakan (IRE)**[14] 7381 6-8-5 **72** (p) DanielMuscutt[(7)] 5 73
(Richard Price) *hld up: hdwy over 2f out: sn rdn: edgd lft fnl f: styd on same pce* **40/1**
0102 6 hd **Mawhub**[22] 7194 3-9-0 **80** MickaelBarzalona 10 81
(Saeed Bin Suroor) *hld up: pushed along over 2f out: hdwy u.p over 1f out: nt trble ldrs* **1/1**[1]
-600 7 1 ½ **Carter**[13] 6642 6-9-0 **74** (v) StevieDonohoe 12 72
(Ian Williams) *hld up: rdn over 3f out: r.o ins fnl f: nvr nrr* **40/1**
2100 8 3 ¼ **Illustrious Forest**[24] 7147 4-9-1 **75** FrannyNorton 2 68
(John Mackie) *led: rdn and hdd over 1f out: wknd ins fnl f* **20/1**
3342 9 ½ **Boa**[13] 7413 7-8-11 **71** AmyRyan 6 63
(Reg Hollinshead) *mid-div: hdwy over 3f out: rdn over 2f out: nt clr run over 1f out: sn wknd* **20/1**
2036 10 4 **Queen's Estate (GER)**[29] 7002 3-8-10 **76** JoeFanning 8 62
(Mark Johnston) *chsd ldr after 1f tl rdn over 2f out: wknd fnl f* **11/1**
-000 11 hd **Cosmic Sun**[13] 7396 6-9-1 **82** EireannCagney[(7)] 4 68
(Richard Fahey) *s.i.s: a in rr* **40/1**
3000 12 6 **Brunston**[23] 7175 6-9-10 **84** SeanQuinlan 11 60
(Anthony Middleton) *chsd ldrs: rdn over 3f out: wknd over 2f out* **66/1**
2m 38.57s (-2.53) **Going Correction** +0.025s/f (Slow)
WFA 3 from 4yo+ 6lb **12** Ran SP% **128.5**
Speed ratings (Par 105): **109,108,108,106,105 105,104,102,102,99 99,95**
Swingers 1&2 £23.10, 2&3 £13.10, 1&3 £6.90 CSF £168.88 CT £760.81 TOTE £14.60: £4.30, £5.80, £1.70; EX 141.90 Trifecta £693.20 Part won. Pool: £924.30 - 0.30 winning units..
Owner Jaffa Racing Syndicate **Bred** Rabbah Bloodstock Limited **Trained** High Hoyland, S Yorks
FOCUS
The best race on the card. The winner is consistent and the form is straightforward.

7673 32REDBET.COM H'CAP 5f 20y(P)
7:50 (7:52) (Class 6) (0-60,60) 3-Y-O+ £1,704 (£503; £251) Stalls Low

Form RPR
4222 1 **Angelo Poliziano**[10] 7456 6-9-5 **58** GrahamLee 5 66
(George Foster) *hld up: hdwy over 1f out: rdn to ld wl ins fnl f: r.o* **11/4**[1]
5361 2 ½ **Here Now And Why (IRE)**[32] 6937 5-9-7 **60** (p) TomEaves 13 66
(Ian Semple) *hld up in tch: rdn over 1f out: r.o* **13/2**
1246 3 ½ **Pavers Star**[15] 7351 3-9-2 **55** (p) WilliamCarson 12 59
(Noel Wilson) *chsd ldr: rdn over 1f out: ev ch ins fnl f: styd on* **20/1**
5020 4 hd **Nine Before Ten (IRE)**[4] 7591 4-9-4 **57** RobertWinston 1 61
(Charles Smith) *chsd ldrs: rdn over 1f out: led ins fnl f: sn hdd and unable qck* **33/1**

6023 **5** 3/4 **Speedyfix**23 7178 5-9-4 **57**........(t) TomMcLaughlin 2 58
(Christine Dunnett) *hld up: hdwy 2f out: rdn and ev ch ins fnl f: styd on same pce* **11/1**
6322 **6** 1/2 **Lucky Mark (IRE)**10 7465 3-9-7 **60**........ StevieDonohoe 4 59
(Garry Moss) *a.p: rdn over 1f out: r.o* **9/2**2
-505 **7** 1/2 **Jolly Ranch**156 2809 6-9-5 **58**........ FergusSweeney 7 55
(Tony Newcombe) *led: rdn over 1f out: hdd and no ex ins fnl f* **14/1**
0650 **8** 1 1/2 **Legal Eagle (IRE)**36 6823 7-9-5 **58**........(p) SeanQuinlan 11 50
(Paul Green) *sn outpcd: r.o ins fnl f: nvr nrr* **33/1**
2040 **9** hd **Ballarina**35 6836 6-9-0 **53**........ DavidAllan 10 44
(Eric Alston) *hld up: rdn over 1f out: nvr trbld ldrs* **16/1**
603 **10** hd **Molly Jones**15 7351 3-9-2 **55**........ LiamKeniry 9 46
(Derek Haydn Jones) *chsd ldrs: rdn 1/2-way: nt clr run 1f out: no ex* **20/1**
2120 **11** hd **Gran Canaria Queen**10 7457 3-9-2 **60**........(v) LMcNiff(5) 3 50
(Ian Semple) *hld up: rdn over 1f out: edgd rt ins fnl f: n.d* **11/2**3
423 **12** 1/2 **Arch Walker (IRE)**78 5504 5-9-7 **60**........(b) LukeMorris 8 48
(John Weymes) *hld up: rdn over 1f out: no ex fnl f* **14/1**

1m 2.74s (0.44) **Going Correction** +0.025s/f (Slow) 12 Ran SP% **116.5**
Speed ratings (Par 101): **97,96,95,95,93 93,92,89,89,89 88,88**
Swingers 1&2 £6.40, 2&3 £32.80, 1&3 £12.30 CSF £18.86 CT £296.83 TOTE £4.20: £1.60, £2.60, £5.70; EX 22.80 Trifecta £511.50 Part won. Pool: £682.11 - 0.20 winning units..
Owner William A Powrie **Bred** Bumble Bs, C Liesack & Mrs S Nicholls **Trained** Haddington, East Lothian

FOCUS
The market proved a good guide here. A low-grade sprint with a compressed finish. The first pair can both rate higher.
Gran Canaria Queen Official explanation: jockey said filly became upset in stalls
T/Jkpt: Part won. £23,014.70 to a £1 stake. Pool: £32,415.00 - 0.50 winning tickets. T/Plt: £25.60 to a £1 stake. Pool: £86,580.00 - 2,465.52 winning tickets. T/Qpdt: £4.70 to a £1 stake. Pool: £10,707.00 - 1,659.76 winning tickets. CR

7674 - 7679a (Foreign Racing) - See Raceform Interactive

7531 DUNDALK (A.W) (L-H)
Friday, November 9

OFFICIAL GOING: Standard

7680a IRISH STALLION FARMS EUROPEAN BREEDERS FUND COOLEY FILLIES STKS (LISTED RACE) 1m (P)
9:00 (9:02) 3-Y-O+ **£27,083** (£7,916; £3,750; £1,250)

RPR
1 **Lily's Angel (IRE)**14 7386 3-9-0 102........ GaryCarroll 5 98+
(G M Lyons, Ire) *trckd ldrs in 4th: clsd travelling wl 2f out: led over 1f out and qcknd clr: easily* **8/11**1
2 2 1/2 **Precious Stone (IRE)**13 7422 3-9-0 84........ WayneLordan 1 91
(David Wachman, Ire) *racd in 3rd on inner: led briefly ins fnl 2f: sn hdd and nt qckn w wnr ins fnl f* **6/1**2
3 3/4 **New Magic (IRE)**14 7386 5-9-2 89........(bt1) NGMcCullagh 3 90+
(Dermot Anthony McLoughlin, Ire) *chsd ldrs: pushed along 2f out: nt qckn w wnr but kpt on wl ins fnl f* **25/1**
4 1 1/4 **Romantic Stroll (IRE)**141 3321 3-9-0 69........ WJLee 2 87
(T Stack, Ire) *racd in mid-div: nvr on terms but kpt on wl fnl f* **40/1**
5 1 **Libys Dream (IRE)**8 7509 4-9-5........ JohnnyMurtagh 12 87
(Tom Dascombe) *racd in mid-div: swtchd rt 1f out: kpt on fnl f: nvr nrr* **15/2**3
6 1/2 **Aaraas**14 7386 3-9-0 96........(b) DeclanMcDonogh 11 83
(Kevin Prendergast, Ire) *racd in cl 2nd: pressed ldr 2f out: wknd ent fnl f* **20/1**
7 nk **Colorful Notion (IRE)**51 6367 3-9-0........ CO'Donoghue 4 83
(Marco Botti) *hld up towards rr: swtchd to outer ins fnl 2f: kpt on fnl f: nvr nrr* **14/1**
8 1 1/2 **Night Lily (IRE)**8 7509 6-9-2........ PatSmullen 9 79
(Paul D'Arcy) *trckd ldrs: wnt 5th 1/2-way: pushed along early in st: no ex over 1f out* **8/1**
9 1 3/4 **Cnocan Diva (IRE)**26 7087 4-9-2 77........ ShaneFoley 6 75
(T Stack, Ire) *hld up in rr: nvr a threat: modest late hdwy* **50/1**
10 3/4 **Core Element (IRE)**5 7581 5-9-2 84........ FergalLynch 10 73
(S Buggy, Ire) *sn led: hdd ins fnl 2f: sn wknd* **33/1**
11 3 1/4 **Alsium (IRE)**152 2959 3-9-0 76........ ChrisHayes 7 66
(P D Deegan, Ire) *a in rr* **28/1**
12 1 1/4 **Devotion (IRE)**5 7581 3-9-0 93........(b) SeamieHeffernan 8 63
(A P O'Brien, Ire) *a in rr* **16/1**
13 2 1/4 **No Trimmings (IRE)**74 5693 6-9-2 71........(bt) ColinKeane 13 58
(Gerard Keane, Ire) *racd in mid-div: no threat early in st* **50/1**

1m 35.94s (95.94)
WFA 3 from 4yo+ 2lb 13 Ran SP% **129.0**
CSF £5.48 TOTE £1.70: £1.40, £1.90, £4.30; DF 7.20.
Owner Clodagh Mitchell **Bred** N And Mrs N Nugent **Trained** Dunsany, Co. Meath

FOCUS
Take the winner out of this Listed race and it would have been something of a bicycle race for the grade. The form is rated around the third and sixth.

NOTEBOOK
Lily's Angel(IRE) made it 3-3 for her trainer and won it like an odds-on favourite should. Racing handily, her rider had a ton of filly underneath him throughout and she didn't disappoint when he asked for effort, quickening up smartly and leaving inferior rivals toiling. It was a good performance from a filly that belongs in at least one higher grade than this. (op 4-6)
Precious Stone(IRE) ran a cracking race. She raced prominently throughout with the inside rail to help her and picked up well in the straight. She was no match for the winner but that wasn't a disgrace and she can probably progress further. (op 8-1 tchd 11-2)
New Magic(IRE)'s rating was a bit short of what was required to be placed in Listed company normally. She was off the bridle before turning in but ran on well enough.
Romantic Stroll(IRE) hadn't been seen out since June and to her credit she ran on quite well on the inside from mid-division without threatening. She probably would be suited by further, and while she looked an exposed maiden when winning back in the summer, could well be progressive.
Libys Dream(IRE) did best of the cross-channel raiders and ran on from slightly off the pace. (op 7-1)
Aaraas has been disappointing since the very early summer. This trip is probably on the short side for Aaraas and she got no closer to the winner than she did here a couple of weeks previously after travelling well for much of the way.

7681 - (Foreign Racing) - See Raceform Interactive

7597 CHANTILLY (R-H)
Friday, November 9

OFFICIAL GOING: Polytrack: standard

7682a PRIX DES COURTILS (CONDITIONS) (2YO) (POLYTRACK) 6f 110y
11:00 (12:00) 2-Y-O **£12,083** (£4,833; £3,625; £2,416; £1,208)

RPR
1 **Complimentor (IRE)**59 6128 2-8-13 0........ UmbertoRispoli 1 92
(X Thomas-Demeaulte, France) **7/5**1
2 1/2 **Paiza (IRE)**32 6942 2-8-13 0........ MaximeGuyon 3 91
(H-A Pantall, France) **5/2**2
3 nk **Rapideur (FR)**35 2-8-13 0........ AntoineHamelin 6 90
(S Smrczek, Germany) **11/1**
4 1/2 **Bayargal (USA)** 2-8-2 0........ MlleAmelieFoulon(7) 8 85
(A Fabre, France) **25/1**
5 1 3/4 **Asteria (FR)**69 2-8-9 0........ RonanThomas 5 80
(J E Pease, France) **14/1**
6 3/4 **La Belliere (IRE)**17 2-9-0 0........ JohanVictoire 4 83
(J-C Rouget, France) **4/1**3
7 2 **Lewamy (IRE)**107 4476 2-8-13 0........ OlivierPeslier 7 76
(John Best) *hld up towards rr: rdn bef st: no ex u.p 1 1/2f out: styd on fnl f* **18/1**
8 nk **Gee Wizz (IRE)**20 7265 2-8-9 0........ ThierryThulliez 2 72
(Robert Collet, France) **31/1**

1m 18.7s (78.70) 8 Ran SP% **117.5**
WIN (incl. 1 euro stake): 2.40. PLACES: 1.10, 1.20, 1.70. DF: 3.30. SF: 6.00.
Owner Prime Equestrian S.A.R.L. **Bred** Grangecon Stud **Trained** France

7683a PRIX COLOMBER (MAIDEN) (2YO) (POLYTRACK) 1m
11:30 (12:00) 2-Y-O **£10,000** (£4,000; £3,000; £2,000; £1,000)

RPR
1 **Dastarhon (IRE)**16 2-9-2 0........ UmbertoRispoli 9 83
(Mme Pia Brandt, France) **19/10**1
2 2 **Banu (GER)**23 2-8-13 0........ AlexisBadel 4 75
(J-P Carvalho, Germany) **8/1**
3 nk **Don't Be**29 2-8-13 0........ RonanThomas 3 75
(F-H Graffard, France) **28/1**
4 snk **Mister Tee (FR)**19 2-9-2 0........ FlavienPrat 7 77
(D Smaga, France) **43/10**3
5 1 **Sojitzen (FR)** 2-8-7 0........ MlleAmelieFoulon(6) 2 72
(X Nakkachdji, France) **9/1**
6 3/4 **Davanti (FR)**29 2-9-2 0........ TheoBachelot 8 73
(Mlle B Renk, France) **53/1**
7 1 1/4 **Dear Nofa (IRE)**39 6751 2-8-13 0........ MaximeGuyon 1 67
(A Fabre, France) **3/1**2
8 shd **Aurore Bere (FR)**170 2-8-13 0........ ThierryThulliez 5 67
(Mme C Head-Maarek, France) **22/1**
9 3 **Habeshia** 2-9-2 0........ OlivierPeslier 6 63
(John Best) *racd midfield towards outside: proged to 4th bef st: 3rd and rdn 1 1/2f out: no ex: grad fdd* **16/1**
10 1 3/4 **Guinevilla (FR)** 2-9-2 0........ JulienAuge 10 59
(L A Urbano-Grajales, France) **57/1**

1m 39.7s (99.70) 10 Ran SP% **116.7**
WIN (incl. 1 euro stake): 2.90. PLACES: 1.40, 2.30, 5.60. DF: 10.00. SF: 18.10.
Owner Avaz Ismoilov **Bred** Ecurie Skymarc Farm **Trained** France

7395 DONCASTER (L-H)
Saturday, November 10

OFFICIAL GOING: Good (good to soft in places; 8.1)
Weather: Cloudy with sunny periods

7684 BETFRED "BIGGER AND BETTER" GOALS GALORE APPRENTICE H'CAP (DIV I) 7f
11:50 (11:52) (Class 5) (0-75,76) 3-Y-O+ **£2,911** (£866; £432; £216) **Stalls** High

Form RPR
3431 **1** **Desert Creek (IRE)**12 7436 6-9-1 **74**........ ShirleyTeasdale(5) 8 86+
(David Nicholls) *trckd ldrs: led appr fnl f: edgd lft: all out* **6/1**2
3050 **2** nk **Great Expectations**17 7328 4-8-12 **69**........ DarylByrne(3) 6 80
(J R Jenkins) *hld up towards rr: smooth hdwy over 2f out: chal jst ins fnl f: carried lft: no ex nr fin* **8/1**3
6520 **3** 4 **Illustrious Prince (IRE)**10 7480 5-8-9 **70**........ LukeLeadbitter(7) 9 71
(Declan Carroll) *led: hdd appr fnl f: one pce* **16/1**
6562 **4** 1 1/2 **Pashan Garh**7 7559 3-9-4 **76**........ CharlesBishop(3) 14 72
(Pat Eddery) *chsd ldrs: kpt on same pce to take 4th last 150yds* **10/1**
2304 **5** 2 **Colbyor**30 7001 3-8-7 **67**........ LauraBarry(5) 3 58
(Richard Fahey) *chsd ldrs: one pce fnl 2f* **16/1**
1004 **6** 1 1/2 **Dickie Le Davoir**5 7589 8-9-0 **73**........(b) JasonHart(5) 19 61
(Richard Guest) *trckd one other stands' side: swtchd lft to main gp 4f out: kpt on fnl f* **16/1**
5020 **7** nk **Al's Memory (IRE)**12 7436 3-8-6 **66**........(v1) NathanSweeney(5) 12 52
(David Evans) *s.s: in rr: kpt on fnl 2f: nvr a factor* **18/1**
5056 **8** nse **Homeboy (IRE)**17 7322 4-8-0 **61**........ CharlieBennett(7) 11 48
(Marcus Tregoning) *in rr: hdwy over 4f out: one pce fnl 2f* **25/1**
0052 **9** 1/2 **Kingswinford (IRE)**4 7618 6-8-11 **72**........ SemiraPashai(7) 15 58
(Alastair Lidderdale) *trckd ldrs: effrt over 2f out: sn outpcd* **12/1**
2413 **10** 1 1/4 **Fama Mac**11 7456 5-8-10 **71**........ EvaMoscrop(7) 16 53
(Neville Bycroft) *chsd ldrs: drvn over 2f out: wknd wl over 1f out* **10/1**
2061 **11** 1 1/4 **Elijah Pepper (USA)**14 7415 7-9-1 **69**........ JulieBurke 7 48
(Conor Dore) *in rr and sn drvn along: nvr a factor* **14/1**
00-0 **12** 1 3/4 **Casela Park (IRE)**61 6108 7-8-8 **67**........ DavidBergin(5) 2 42
(David O'Meara) *s.i.s: hdwy far side over 3f out: wknd 2f out* **5/1**1
0005 **13** 3/4 **Layla's Hero (IRE)**11 7453 5-8-11 **70**........(p) GeorgeDowning(5) 5 43
(Ian Williams) *mid-div: drvn over 2f out: hung lft and sn btn* **12/1**
001 **14** 2 **Sabratha (IRE)**39 6756 4-8-11 **68**........ GarryWhillans(3) 17 35
(Linda Perratt) *hld up towards rr: hdwy to trck ldrs over 4f out: wknd fnl 2f* **20/1**
30-6 **15** 1 1/2 **Kingarrick**47 6544 4-8-7 **64**........ NeilFarley(3) 4 28
(Noel Wilson) *s.i.s: sn chsng ldrs: lost pl over 2f out* **50/1**

533 **16** *2* **Dundrum Dancer (IRE)**[48] 4942 5-8-11 **65**.................... RaulDaSilva 13 23
(Alex Hales) *mid-div: drvn over 3f out: wknd 2f out* **25/1**
100 **17** *2 ¾* **Layla's King**[37] 6812 4-8-6 **63**................................ MatthewLawson(3) 18 14
(David C Griffiths) *racd stands' side: bhd fnl 2f* **33/1**
0000 **18** *6* **Pelmanism**[12] 7436 5-8-13 **67**..(p) RyanClark 10
(Brian Ellison) *in rr and sn drvn along: bhd fnl 2f* **16/1**
4/06 **19** *10* **Sextons House (IRE)**[10] 7489 4-8-5 **64**......................... NoraLooby(5) 1
(Alan McCabe) *chsd ldrs: lost pl over 3f out: sn bhd* **33/1**

1m 28.92s (2.62) **Going Correction** +0.30s/f (Good)
WFA 3 from 4yo+ 1lb **19** Ran SP% **131.4**
Speed ratings (Par 103): **97,96,92,90,88 86,86,85,85,83 82,80,79,77,75 73,70,63,51**
toteswingers 1&2 £8.70, 1&3 £14.00, 2&3 £37.10 CSF £52.22 CT £767.08 TOTE £5.40: £2.00, £3.90, £2.70; EX 45.40 TRIFECTA Not won..
Owner D W Barker & D Nicholls **Bred** Mount Coote Stud And M H Dixon **Trained** Sessay, N Yorks
■ Stewards' Enquiry : Shirley Teasdale two-day ban: careless riding (Nov 24,26)

FOCUS
There was hardly any rain overnight and the ground was given as good, good to soft in places (GoingStick 8.1). Apprentices who rode in the first race agreed with the description. Most of the field came up the centre of the track, including the first two, who had a nice tow into the race, and inside the final half furlong they had the race between them. Sound form.
Layla's King Official explanation: jockey said gelding hung badly left-handed

7685 BETFRED "BIGGER AND BETTER" GOALS GALORE APPRENTICE H'CAP (DIV II) 7f
12:20 (12:21) (Class 5) (0-75,75) 3-Y-0+ **£2,911** (£866; £432; £216) **Stalls** High

Form RPR
3123 **1** **Chookie Royale**[21] 7246 4-9-0 **73**..................................(p) JasonHart(5) 5 82
(Keith Dalgleish) *towards rr: pushed along 1/2-way: rdn along over 2f out: styng on to chal whn carried rt ent fnl f: styd on wl u.p to ld nr fin* **13/2**[1]
0000 **2** *½* **George Benjamin**[16] 7360 5-8-8 **65**.............................. LeonnaMayor(3) 3 73
(Christopher Kellett) *towards rr: stdy hdwy 3f out: chsd ldrs 2f out: rdn to ld jst over 1f out: drvn ins fnl f: hdd and no ex towards fin* **50/1**
0121 **3** *1 ¼* **Fame Again**[35] 6894 4-8-9 **70**............................ MatthewHopkins(7) 9 75
(Michael Easterby) *prom: hdwy wl over 2f out: rdn and cl up whn hung rt over 1f out: drvn and ev ch ins fnl f: wknd towards fin* **7/1**[2]
0156 **4** *nk* **Nezami (IRE)**[38] 6785 7-8-10 **69**..................................(b) JackDuern(5) 15 73
(Patrick Clinton) *in tch: pushed along over 2f out: swtchd lft and rdn over 1f out: styd on ins fnl f: nrst fin* **20/1**
0545 **5** *¾* **Silkee Supreme**[22] 7218 3-8-3 **63**...........................(b) RufusVergette(5) 2 65
(Richard Hannon) *led: rdn along and edgd rt over 2f out: hdd jst over 1f out: sn hung rt ent fnl f and one pce* **33/1**
0313 **6** *2 ¼* **She's A Character**[15] 7370 5-9-0 **73**................................ LauraBarry(5) 7 69+
(Richard Fahey) *towards rr: pushed along 1/2-way: styd on fnl 2f: nrst fin* **8/1**[3]
4005 **7** *2 ¼* **Silver Wind**[24] 7179 7-8-10 **64**..(b) AmyRyan 16 54
(Alan McCabe) *in tch on outer: hdwy over 2f out: rdn and ch over 1f out: wknd ent fnl f* **9/1**
0-10 **8** *½* **Outpost (IRE)**[24] 7163 4-9-2 **75**.................................... NatashaEaton(5) 8 63
(Alan Bailey) *chsd ldrs: rdn along and outpcd over 2f out: kpt on fnl f* **14/1**
4001 **9** *2 ¼* **Zip Lock (IRE)**[18] 7317 6-8-12 **66**.. RyanClark 11 48
(Tom Keddy) *trckd ldrs: hdwy over 2f out: rdn and ev ch wl over 1f out: sn drvn and wknd* **25/1**
2250 **10** *hd* **Rough Rock (IRE)**[7] 7559 7-9-1 **69**.............................. AdamBeschizza 4 51
(Chris Dwyer) *in rr: pushed along and sme hdwy over 2f out: sn rdn and nvr nr ldrs* **20/1**
6654 **11** *3* **Lindoro**[12] 7436 7-8-5 **64**..(b) RPWalsh(5) 1 38
(Brian Ellison) *hld up in rr: hdwy on outer over 2f out: sn rdn and n.d* **16/1**
0113 **12** *7* **Les Verguettes (IRE)**[8] 7524 4-8-9 **63**............................. AshleyMorgan 10 18
(Chris Wall) *hld up in midfield: rdn along 3f out: nvr a factor* **7/1**[2]
4420 **13** *nk* **Silver Rime (FR)**[16] 7360 7-9-1 **72**........................... GarryWhillans(3) 14 26+
(Linda Perratt) *s.i.s: a in rr* **14/1**
066 **14** *2* **Jake The Snake (IRE)**[56] 6256 11-8-10 **69**.......... GeorgeDowning(5) 18 17
(Tony Carroll) *in tch on wd outside: pushed along over 3f out: sn wknd* **20/1**
2512 **15** *8* **Clumber Place**[18] 7314 6-8-11 **65**..................................... RaulDaSilva 12
(James Given) *nvr bttr than midfield* **8/1**[3]
5600 **16** *6* **Horatio Carter**[53] 6342 7-8-9 **68**.................................. DavidBergin(5) 17
(David O'Meara) *in tch: rdn along over 3f out: sn wknd* **16/1**
6351 **17** *1 ¾* **Saskia's Dream**[10] 7485 4-8-12 **71**...................................... IanBurns(5) 13
(Jane Chapple-Hyam) *chsd ldrs: rdn along 3f out: sn wknd* **12/1**
030- **18** *1* **Kerchak (USA)**[511] 3184 5-8-6 **67**.................................. RichardOliver(7) 6
(Brian Ellison) *a in rr: hung rt to stands' rail 1/2-way: sn bhd* **33/1**

1m 30.88s (4.58) **Going Correction** +0.30s/f (Good)
WFA 3 from 4yo+ 1lb **18** Ran SP% **129.3**
Speed ratings (Par 103): **85,84,83,82,81 79,76,76,73,73 69,61,61,59,50 43,41,40**
toteswingers 1&2 £74.20, 1&3 £7.50, 2&3 £207.20 CSF £342.66 CT £2390.56 TOTE £7.40: £2.30, £11.20, £2.50, £4.90; EX 406.20 TRIFECTA Not won..
Owner Raeburn Brick Limited **Bred** D And J Raeburn **Trained** Carluke, S Lanarks
■ Stewards' Enquiry : Matthew Hopkins two-day ban: careless riding (Nov 24,26); four-day ban: used whip above permitted level (Nov 27-30)

FOCUS
The main action unfolded centre-field in division two. The winner is rated back to his 2011 turf best.
Zip Lock(IRE) Official explanation: jockey said gelding had no more to give
Silver Rime(FR) Official explanation: jockey said gelding was slowly away

7686 BETFRED COCK O'THE NORTH EBF MAIDEN STKS 6f
12:50 (12:51) (Class 5) 2-Y-O **£3,816** (£1,135; £567; £283) **Stalls** High

Form RPR
0225 **1** **Mar Mar (IRE)**[23] 7190 2-8-12 84..................................(v[1]) WilliamBuick 14 86
(Saeed Bin Suroor) *trckd ldrs stands' side: smooth hdwy to ld 2f out: edgd lft and wnt clr fnl f* **7/2**[2]
322 **2** *4* **Flashlight (IRE)**[25] 7127 2-9-3 82.. JoeFanning 7 78
(Mark Johnston) *led: hdd 2f out: styd on same pce* **11/8**[1]
3 *2* **Cape Peron** 2-9-3 0.. RichardHughes 12 72+
(Henry Candy) *s.i.s: t.k.h and sn midfield: styd on fnl 2f: tk 3rd last 100yds* **8/1**
34 **4** *1* **Future Reference (IRE)**[9] 7507 2-9-3 0..............(p) MickaelBarzalona 2 69
(Saeed Bin Suroor) *chsd ldrs far side: one pce fnl 2f* **6/1**[3]
5 *6* **Tanawar (IRE)** 2-9-3 0.. GrahamLee 1 51+
(William Haggas) *hld up in rr: styd on fnl 2f: nvr nr ldrs* **8/1**
0 **6** *1 ¼* **Bapak Muda (USA)**[11] 7458 2-9-3 0.. AmyRyan 11 47+
(Kevin Ryan) *chsd ldrs: wknd over 1f out* **25/1**
00 **7** *1* **Silvala Dance**[19] 7290 2-8-12 0... TedDurcan 15 39
(Chris Wall) *chsd ldrs: wknd 2f out* **50/1**
8 *shd* **Zed Candy Girl** 2-8-12 0... ShaneKelly 9 39
(John Stimpson) *s.s: kpt on fnl 2f: nvr a factor* **100/1**
0 **9** *1 ¼* **Bubbly Bailey**[28] 7057 2-8-12 0.................................. NatashaEaton(5) 10 40
(Alan Bailey) *chsd ldrs: hung lft and wknd over 1f out* **25/1**
000 **10** *6* **Downright Dizzie**[18] 7313 2-8-9 56.................................. RyanClark(3) 13 17
(Tom Keddy) *in rr: bhd fnl 2f* **100/1**
0 **11** *1* **Many Levels**[17] 7330 2-9-3 0.. TomMcLaughlin 3 19
(John Berry) *mid-div: lost pl over 2f out* **100/1**
5 **12** *¾* **Whiskeymack**[15] 7372 2-9-3 0... MartinHarley 5 17
(Mick Channon) *mid-div: lost pl over 2f out* **16/1**
13 *5* **Sensiz (IRE)** 2-8-12 0.. NeilCallan 8
(Roger Varian) *s.i.s: bucked twice sn after s: in rr whn hmpd over 1f out: eased and sn bhd* **14/1**
0 **14** *9* **Haarmonic**[46] 6556 2-9-3 0... RobertWinston 4
(Richard Whitaker) *s.i.s: in rr whn hmpd over 1f out* **100/1**
U **Wishing Bridge** 2-9-3 0... LukeMorris 6
(Pat Eddery) *chsd ldrs: wkng whn hmpd and uns rdr over 1f out* **66/1**

1m 14.85s (1.25) **Going Correction** +0.30s/f (Good) **15** Ran SP% **128.5**
Speed ratings (Par 96): **103,97,95,93,85 84,82,82,80,72 71,70,63,51,**
toteswingers 1&2 £2.50, 1&3 £6.10, 2&3 £4.60 CSF £8.95 TOTE £4.50: £2.10, £1.20, £2.90; EX 11.10 TRIFECTA Pool: £1,207.69 - 15.43 winning units..
Owner Godolphin **Bred** Kilcarn Stud **Trained** Newmarket, Suffolk

FOCUS
Not a bad maiden, and an impressive performance from the winner. The race lacked depth though and it's unwise to get carried away with the form.

NOTEBOOK
Mar Mar(IRE) ◆ had a visor on for the first time on this drop back to sprinting. When asked to quicken the response was immediate and she quickly put distance between herself and the runner-up. Using the second and fourth as a guide, she's put up a useful performance, and it'll be interesting to see how she develops over the winter. Clearly speed is her thing, and it wouldn't be a surprise to see her develop into a pattern level performer next season. (op 7-1)
Flashlight(IRE) hadn't quite got home in his previous two starts over 7f but, boasting an official rating of 82, he looked the one to beat back in trip. When it came to it, though, he was left standing by the winner, who quickened right away. He bumped into one here, but he can get off the mark on the AW if connections persist with him this year. (op 13-8 tchd 7-4)
Cape Peron ◆ is by Beat Hollow out of a mare who won over 7f at two and twice over 1m2f at three, so this trip looked on the short side for him, but there was some market support and he ran with plenty of credit to finish placed on his debut. He'll be interesting when upped in distance. (op 6-1)
Future Reference(IRE), beaten at odds-on last time, had cheekpieces fitted here. Outpaced when his stablemate kicked clear, he looks to need further, and can be given another chance in handicap company when granted a stiffer test. (op 5-1)
Tanawar(IRE), a 125,000gns purchase out of a mare who won over 1m1f in Germany, was keeping on nicely at the finish. Given his pedigree, one would imagine that the quicker the ground the better he'll be. (op 12-1)
Bapak Muda(USA), dropped back a furlong in distance, showed speed to 2f out before weakening. He's bred for further, and will be of more interest once eligible for handicaps. Official explanation: jockey said gelding never travelled

7687 BETFRED "THE HOME OF GOALS GALORE" NURSERY 6f
1:25 (1:27) (Class 4) (0-85,84) 2-Y-O **£4,398** (£1,309; £654; £327) **Stalls** High

Form RPR
0012 **1** **Muharrib (IRE)**[17] 7325 2-9-7 **84**............................. MickaelBarzalona 10 91
(Saeed Bin Suroor) *trckd ldrs: smooth hdwy over 2f out: led wl over 1f out: rdn clr ent fnl f: readily* **5/1**[1]
3310 **2** *2* **Indignant**[78] 5563 2-9-5 **82**.. RichardHughes 16 83
(Richard Hannon) *led: rdn along 2f out: sn hdd: drvn and kpt on same pce fnl f* **5/1**[1]
3341 **3** *hd* **Shrimpton**[29] 7031 2-8-12 **75**.. MartinHarley 12 75
(Mick Channon) *hld up in rr: stdy hdwy wl over 2f out: rdn to chse ldrs over 1f out: kpt on u.p fnl f: nrst fin* **10/1**
0034 **4** *3 ¼* **The Black Jacobin**[10] 7478 2-8-3 **66**..........................(b) DavidProbert 13 57
(J S Moore) *dwlt and towards rr: hdwy 1/2-way: rdn to chse ldrs over 1f out: nrst fin* **10/1**
2402 **5** *¾* **Khefyn (IRE)**[19] 7298 2-8-11 **74**.. LukeMorris 3 62
(Ronald Harris) *hld up: hdwy on outer 1/2-way: rdn to chse ldrs 2f out: wknd fnl f* **12/1**
0221 **6** *2 ½* **Medici Dancer**[12] 7440 2-8-9 **72**... DavidAllan 14 53
(Tim Easterby) *in rr tl styd on fnl 2f: nrst fin* **11/1**
4246 **6** *dht* **Star Request**[32] 6953 2-7-13 **62**.. NickyMackay 2 43
(Keith Dalgleish) *prom on outer: effrt over 2f out: sn rdn and wknd over 1f out* **10/1**
440 **8** *¾* **Fife Jo**[91] 5083 2-8-0 **63** oh1 ow2.. FrannyNorton 6 42
(Jim Goldie) *cl up: rdn along wl over 2f out: sn wknd* **20/1**
3410 **9** *nk* **Bond Club**[29] 7028 2-8-9 **72**.. TomEaves 18 50
(Geoffrey Oldroyd) *in tch: rdn along wl over 2f out: sn wknd* **25/1**
565 **10** *2 ½* **Lucky Lodge**[76] 5620 2-8-5 **68**... PaulHanagan 9 38
(Mel Brittain) *cl up: rdn along over 2f out: grad wknd* **33/1**
6211 **11** *½* **Blazing Knight (IRE)**[11] 7463 2-8-13 **76**............................ JimCrowley 11 45
(Ralph Beckett) *in tch: hdwy 1/2-way: rdn to chse ldrs 2f out: drvn and wknd appr fnl f* **8/1**[3]
6360 **12** *½* **Salvatore Fury (IRE)**[12] 7441 2-7-12 **61** oh3................... JimmyQuinn 4 28
(Keith Dalgleish) *in tch: rdn along wl over 2f out: sn wknd* **66/1**
1 **13** *nk* **Run Fat Lass Run**[205] 1474 2-9-3 **80**................................. PhillipMakin 5 46
(Kevin Ryan) *dwlt: a in rr: bhd fnl 2f* **7/1**[2]
1624 **14** *1 ¼* **Front Page News**[19] 7298 2-8-10 **73**................................ AndreaAtzeni 7 36
(Robert Eddery) *t.k.h: prom: rdn along 1/2-way: sn wknd* **14/1**
4520 **15** *1* **Projectisle (IRE)**[58] 6160 2-8-9 **72**...................................... GrahamLee 8 32
(Kevin Ryan) *midfield: rdn along wl over 2f out: sn wknd* **33/1**
051 **16** *6* **Yorkshireman (IRE)**[19] 7290 2-9-0 **77**........................... RobertWinston 15 19
(David Brown) *chsd ldrs: rdn along 1/2-way: wknd over 2f out* **16/1**

1m 15.91s (2.31) **Going Correction** +0.30s/f (Good) **16** Ran SP% **128.8**
Speed ratings (Par 98): **96,93,93,88,87 84,84,83,83,79 79,78,77,76,74 66**
toteswingers 1&2 £6.90, 1&3 £9.90, 2&3 £17.40 CSF £27.97 CT £255.23 TOTE £4.70: £1.80, £2.00, £3.30, £2.30; EX 26.60 Trifecta £481.60 Pool: £1,714.80 - 2.67 winning units..
Owner Godolphin **Bred** Lady Richard Wellesley **Trained** Newmarket, Suffolk

FOCUS
A competitive-looking nursery that saw those who raced nearer the stands' side come out on top. The first three were clear and this is solid, straightforward form.

NOTEBOOK
Muharrib(IRE), who'd won his maiden over 7f and was just run out of it late in a 1m nursery at Kempton, seemed happier returned to this distance, travelling strongly and readily asserting to win with any amount in hand. A much improved sort, his versatility ought to stand him in good stead and it would be no surprise to see him head off to race in Dubai for the winter months. (op 9-2 tchd 4-1)

Indignant ran no sort of race on his nursery debut at York, but a horse can always be forgiven a poor run there, and this effort was more in keeping with the level of ability he showed when winning his maiden. She can make a useful 3yo handicapper. (op 10-1)
Shrimpton, winner of a 5f heavy-ground maiden at York, is just as effective at this longer distance and she was going on nicely from the rear. (op 8-1 tchd 11-1)
The Black Jacobin is an exposed maiden but he was going on better than most at the finish. (op 12-1)
Khefyn(IRE) raced more towards the far side and this effort confirmed she's going to remain vulnerable from her current sort of rating.
Medici Dancer was never involved, but at least reversed Pontefract form with Yorkshireman. (op 12-1 tchd 10-1)
Blazing Knight(IRE) Official explanation: trainer's rep said colt was unsuited by the good (good to soft places) ground
Run Fat Lass Run, off since winning a 5f maiden on debut back in April, offered little on this nursery debut. (op 17-2)
Yorkshireman(IRE) was one of the first under pressure and ran a shocker. Official explanation: jockey said colt ran flat (op 14-1)

7688 BETFRED EBF GILLIES FILLIES' STKS (LISTED RACE) 1m 2f 60y

2:00 (2:01) (Class 1) 3-Y-0+ **£19,536** (£7,388; £3,692; £1,844) **Stalls** Low

Form RPR

-302 **1** **Cubanita**[45] 6576 3-8-10 92 ... JimCrowley 8 105
(Ralph Beckett) *hld up in mid-div: smooth hdwy over 3f out: wnt 2nd over 1f out: styd on to ld nr fin* **8/1**

0-24 **2** ½ **Sajjhaa**[13] 7429 5-9-0 111 ... MickaelBarzalona 6 104
(Saeed Bin Suroor) *trckd ldrs: drvn and rapid hdwy to ld over 2f out: 4 l clr 1f out: hdd towards fin* **7/4**[1]

1- **3** 1 ¼ **Reckoning (IRE)**[386] 6985 3-8-10 90 ... RichardHughes 7 102
(Jeremy Noseda) *hld up in mid-div: hdwy over 2f out: styd on to take 3rd jst ins fnl f* **11/1**

4352 **4** 4 **Raasekha**[17] 7334 4-9-0 98 ... PaulHanagan 9 94
(Charles Hills) *led after 1f: hdd over 2f out: wknd over 1f out* **16/1**

1114 **5** 1 ½ **Surprise Moment (IRE)**[9] 7510 3-8-10 96 ... JimmyFortune 3 91
(Saeed Bin Suroor) *mid-div: effrt over 2f out: nvr a threat* **4/1**[2]

521 **6** 3 ¼ **Wannabe Loved**[29] 7016 3-8-10 88 ... WilliamBuick 5 85
(John Gosden) *trckd ldrs: effrt 3f out: wknd 2f out* **8/1**

1111 **7** 2 ¼ **Boonga Roogeta**[4] 7619 3-8-10 76 ... LukeMorris 12 81
(Peter Charalambous) *led 1f: chsd ldrs: wknd 2f out* **33/1**

6125 **8** 4 **Strathnaver**[82] 5420 3-8-10 81 ... GrahamLee 13 73
(Ed Dunlop) *hld up in rr: effrt 3f out: nvr a factor* **66/1**

-622 **9** 5 **Dorcas Lane**[35] 6877 4-9-0 99 ...(p) TedDurcan 4 64
(David Lanigan) *s.i.s: in rr: effrt 3f out: sn wknd* **5/1**[3]

1661 **10** 7 **Guiletta (IRE)**[25] 7129 3-8-10 67 ... JohnFahy 2 50
(John Flint) *hld up in rr: pushed along 4f out: bhd fnl 2f* **100/1**

000 **11** ½ **Khawlah (IRE)**[14] 7396 4-9-0 93 ... PhillipMakin 11 49
(Saeed Bin Suroor) *hld up in rr: outpcd over 3f out: sn bhd* **33/1**

6105 **12** 23 **Dinvar Diva**[35] 6877 3-8-10 93 ... NickyMackay 1 6
(John Gosden) *t.k.h: trckd ldrs: lost pl 3f out: eased over 1f out: virtually p.u: t.o* **25/1**

2m 10.4s (1.00) **Going Correction** +0.30s/f (Good)
WFA 3 from 4yo+ 4lb 12 Ran SP% **121.7**
Speed ratings (Par 108): **108,107,106,103,102 99,97,94,90,85 84,66**
toteswingers 1&2 £3.70, 1&3 £9.80, 2&3 £6.90 CSF £22.31 TOTE £9.30: £2.60, £1.20, £3.60; EX 29.40 Trifecta £546.40 Pool: £2,025.49 - 2.78 winning units..
Owner Miss K Rausing **Bred** Miss K Rausing **Trained** Kimpton, Hants

FOCUS
A well-contested Listed event that saw three draw clear, the gallop set being a decent one. The form is rated around the race avaerges and the runner-up.

NOTEBOOK
Cubanita, a good second to an unexposed type from 2lb lower on her handicap debut at Goodwood, had finished third in the Cheshire Oaks earlier in the season and this just proved enough of a test. She was having only her third starts of the season and with any improvement from three to four, may be able to make a breakthrough at Group level against her own sex. (tchd 9-1)
Sajjhaa, slightly disappointing in an Italian Group 1 last time, was happier back on better ground and made a sweeping move to go clear, but she started to idle and was ultimately worn down. She'd almost certainly have won had she been held on to for longer. (tchd 2-1)
Reckoning(IRE) ◆, off since winning a course maiden 13 months earlier, followed the winner through but the lack of a recent run told inside the final furlong. She's clearly capable of winning at this level and rates a very useful 4yo prospect. (op 10-1 tchd 12-1)
Raasekha was quickly brushed aside, but did keep plodding away.
Surprise Moment(IRE), done for speed in a slowly-run race at Lingfield latest, was down in trip and simply lacked the pace to challenge. (op 6-1)
Wannabe Loved chased the early pace and was quickly beaten once coming under pressure. (op 9-1 tchd 7-1)
Boonga Roogeta has been a huge improver, winning a seller at Leicester last month and scoring a further four times in the past two weeks in handicaps, as recently as at Wolverhampton four days earlier. This was a step too far, though.
Dorcas Lane was disappointing considering she brought solid form at the level into the race. This clearly wasn't her true form. Official explanation: trainer's rep said filly was unsuited by the good (good to soft places) ground (op 6-1 tchd 9-2)

7689 BETFRED NOVEMBER H'CAP 1m 4f

2:35 (2:39) (Class 2) 3-Y-0+

£40,462 (£12,116; £6,058; £3,029; £1,514; £760) **Stalls** Low

Form RPR

5122 **1** **Art Scholar (IRE)**[14] 7396 5-8-7 93 ... FrannyNorton 9 102
(Michael Appleby) *hld up towards rr: smooth hdwy 3f out: trckd ldrs wl over 1f out: rdn ent fnl f: led last 75yds: styd on* **20/1**

4312 **2** ¾ **Communicator**[70] 5826 4-8-8 94 ... DavidProbert 5 102
(Andrew Balding) *midfield: hdwy and in tch over 4f out: rdn to chse ldrs 2f out: drvn to ld briefly ins fnl f: hdd and no ex last 75yds* **14/1**

134 **3** 1 **Voodoo Prince**[36] 6832 4-8-9 95 ...(p) GrahamLee 6 102
(Ed Dunlop) *in tch: hdwy 4f out: chsd ldrs 2f out: rdn over 1f out: ev ch ent fnl f: hld whn n.m.r last 75yds* **16/1**

0300 **4** 3 ¼ **Samba King**[14] 7396 3-8-1 93 ... NickyMackay 2 95
(Mahmood Al Zarooni) *set stdy pce: qcknd over 4f out: rdn along 3f out: hdd over 2f out: sltly outpcd over 1f out: rallied ins fnl f: tk 4th on line* **40/1**

105 **5** nk **Hanoverian Baron**[36] 6832 7-8-0 86 ... DominicFox 1 87
(Tony Newcombe) *trckd ldng pair: hdwy to ld over 2f out: rdn over 1f out: edgd rt and hdd ins fnl f: wknd: lost 4th on line* **40/1**

0344 **6** 1 ¼ **Sirvino**[14] 7396 7-8-4 90 ... AmyRyan 14 89
(David Barron) *chsd ldrs: rdn and cl up 3f out: drvn 2f out and grad wknd* **25/1**

3412 **7** ¾ **Retrieve (AUS)**[20] 7287 5-9-10 110 ... MickaelBarzalona 10 108
(Saeed Bin Suroor) *trckd ldrs: hdwy 3f out: rdn 2f out: kpt on same pce* **16/1**

6014 **8** ¾ **Kirthill (IRE)**[49] 6484 4-9-3 103 ... KierenFallon 7 100
(Luca Cumani) *hld up in midfield: hdwy 3f out: sn rdn and no imp fr over 1f out* **7/1**[2]

3326 **9** 1 ½ **Clayton**[35] 6875 3-8-2 94 ... JimmyQuinn 15 89
(Kevin Ryan) *trckd ldrs: hdwy 3f out: rdn 2f out: sn drvn and wknd* **9/1**[3]

3421 **10** nse **Party Line**[14] 7396 3-8-0 92 ... JoeFanning 13 87
(Mark Johnston) *chsd ldrs: hdwy 3f out: rdn along over 2f out: sn drvn and wknd* **12/1**

1031 **11** ¾ **Blue Surf**[14] 7407 3-8-7 99 ... JimCrowley 12 93
(Amanda Perrett) *nvr bttr than midfield* **11/1**

1/11 **12** 1 **First Mohican**[24] 7175 4-9-0 100 ... TomQueally 21 92+
(Sir Henry Cecil) *t.k.h early: hld up towards rr: effrt on outer over 3f out: sn rdn and btn* **3/1**[1]

0021 **13** ½ **Nicholascopernicus (IRE)**[27] 7082 3-8-3 95 ... LukeMorris 18 86+
(Ed Walker) *nvr bttr than midfield* **10/1**

0005 **14** shd **Crystal Gal (IRE)**[25] 7128 5-8-6 92 ... HayleyTurner 16 83
(Lucy Wadham) *nvr bttr than midfield* **66/1**

0-04 **15** hd **Darley Sun (IRE)**[33] 6922 6-8-8 94 ... WilliamBuick 3 85
(Saeed Bin Suroor) *a in rr* **33/1**

0411 **16** 2 **The Tiger**[11] 7455 4-8-5 91 ... ChrisCatlin 19 79+
(Ed Dunlop) *t.k.h early: hld up: a in rr* **18/1**

0620 **17** shd **Hillview Boy (IRE)**[14] 7396 8-8-1 87 ... AndreaAtzeni 11 75
(Jim Goldie) *hld up: a bhd* **33/1**

3011 **18** 1 ¼ **Bridle Belle**[8] 7519 4-8-2 88 ... PaulHanagan 17 74
(Richard Fahey) *midfield: hdwy over 3f out: sn rdn and wknd 2f out* **25/1**

2300 **19** 2 ¾ **Scrapper Smith (IRE)**[14] 7396 6-8-2 91 ... JulieBurke(3) 20 73+
(Alistair Whillans) *hld up: a bhd* **66/1**

1343 **20** 2 **Songcraft (IRE)**[14] 7405 4-9-6 106 ... TedDurcan 22 85+
(Saeed Bin Suroor) *a in rr* **28/1**

0050 **21** 2 ¼ **War Poet**[78] 5558 5-8-5 91 ... JohnFahy 23 66+
(David O'Meara) *a towards rr* **28/1**

1560 **22** ½ **Bollin Greta**[24] 7175 7-7-13 85 ... JamesSullivan 8 60
(Tim Easterby) *t.k.h early: a in rr* **66/1**

11-0 **23** 17 **Art History (IRE)**[14] 7396 4-8-5 91 ...(b[1]) BarryMcHugh 4 40
(David O'Meara) *prom: rdn along over 4f out: sn wknd* **100/1**

2m 35.04s (0.14) **Going Correction** +0.30s/f (Good)
WFA 3 from 4yo+ 6lb 23 Ran SP% **131.9**
Speed ratings (Par 109): **111,110,109,107,107 106,106,105,104,104 104,103,103,103,102 101,101,100,98,97 96,95,84**
toteswingers 1&2 £34.60, 1&3 £134.20, 2&3 £110.20 CSF £265.31 CT £4590.41 TOTE £21.40: £3.60, £3.50, £4.80, £12.30; EX 283.50 Trifecta £6481.30 Pool: £63,085.15 - 7.30 winning units..
Owner Mrs J Scrivens **Bred** John Ramsbottom **Trained** Danethorpe, Notts

FOCUS
The usual big field lined up for this valuable handicap, but the pace wasn't strong and it paid to save ground around the inner. Those drawn out wide were at a disadvantage. The winner is quietly progressive and the form makes sense.

NOTEBOOK
Art Scholar(IRE) enjoyed a nice run through the race, saving ground on the rail. Brought with a well-timed challenge, he saw the trip out well on this better ground, and once again showed a real liking for this track – he now has three wins and a second place from six starts here. His trainer is hoping to take him to Dubai for the carnival in the new year. (op 18-1 tchd 16-1)
Communicator, back from a break, also saved ground on the inner. He got first run on the winner, but couldn't quite make it stick. (op 16-1)
Voodoo Prince, who had cheekpieces on for the first time, got the trip well, and the 5lb he was put up for finishing third in a Listed race two starts back may well have been the difference. (op 20-1)
Samba King, having his third run back from a break, had a fairly easy time of it in front and was able to rally late past the weakening Hanoverian Baron to take fourth. (op 50-1)
Hanoverian Baron, who finished fourth off 5lb higher last year, was sent for home with over 2f to run and paid the price inside the last. (op 33-1)
Sirvino, who has slipped to a fair mark, had a chance at the weights, but he had a bit of use made of him early to get a prominent position (normally ridden with more patience) and eventually faded. (op 20-1 tchd 33-1)
Retrieve(AUS), who finished second in an Italian Group 1 last time, posted a sound effort off a challenging mark of 110. (op 14-1)
Kirthill(IRE) was disappointing, failing to pick up for pressure. A stronger gallop might have seen him in a better light. (op 8-1)
Clayton got caught a little wider than ideal, and raced a shade keenly. He was brought to have his chance in the straight, but there was nothing in the locker when pressure was applied. (tchd 11-1)
Party Line beat Art Scholar over this C&D last time out, but she was 5lb higher in the weights this time and the ground wasn't as testing. (tchd 10-1)
Blue Surf is another who ran a career-best in the mud last time, but here he was faced with different conditions and a career-high mark. (op 12-1)
First Mohican had impressed in winning both starts since returning from injury, but this represented another rise in class, the ground was quicker, and off a 12lb higher mark than for his last win, and from stall 21 (first five were all drawn in single figures), he got caught wide, and then ran green in the straight, wandering under pressure. He's still very lightly raced and there should be better to come from him next year. Official explanation: trainer's rep said gelding was unsuited by the good (good to soft places) ground (op 7-2 tchd 11-4)
Nicholascopernicus(IRE), who was weak in the betting, struggled to get involved from the back of the field. A stronger pace and softer ground would have suited him better. (op 11-1 tchd 12-1)

7690 BETFRED "BONUS KING BINGO" WENTWORTH STKS (LISTED RACE) 6f

3:10 (3:13) (Class 1) 3-Y-0+ **£19,536** (£7,388; £3,692; £1,844) **Stalls** High

Form RPR

4403 **1** **Eton Rifles (IRE)**[35] 6867 7-9-3 108 ... WilliamCarson 12 110
(Stuart Williams) *trckd ldrs: led 1f out: kpt on wl* **7/1**[3]

4122 **2** 1 **Ultrasonic (USA)**[35] 6878 3-8-12 102 ... RichardHughes 7 102+
(Sir Michael Stoute) *hld up towards rr: hdwy over 2f out: styd on wl appr fnl f: tk 2nd towards fin* **7/1**[3]

0002 **3** 1 ½ **Justineo**[14] 7401 3-9-3 97 ... NeilCallan 11 103
(Roger Varian) *w ldr: led over 2f out: hdd 1f out: kpt on same pce* **20/1**

0333 **4** ¾ **Sirius Prospect (USA)**[21] 7236 4-9-3 108 ...(p) ShaneKelly 3 100
(Dean Ivory) *hld up in rr: effrt and n.m.r over 1f out: styd on strly last 100yds* **9/2**[2]

4206 **5** 2 **The Cheka (IRE)**[21] 7236 6-9-6 108 ...(v) JimmyFortune 18 97
(Eve Johnson Houghton) *mid-div: hdwy to chse ldrs over 2f out: kpt on fnl f* **10/1**

6001 **6** hd **Thunderball**[15] 7366 6-9-3 91 ...(p) TomQueally 2 94
(Scott Dixon) *chsd ldrs: kpt on same pce appr fnl f* **33/1**

3000 **7** hd **Ladies Are Forever**[35] 6878 4-8-12 100 ... TomEaves 16 88
(Geoffrey Oldroyd) *chsd ldrs: one pce fnl 2f* **25/1**

0103 **8** ½ **Mass Rally (IRE)**[4] 7397 5 -9-3100 (b) PaulMulrennan 9 92
(Michael Dods) *dwlt: hdwy over 2f out: kpt on ins fnl f: nvr trbld ldrs* **12/1**

1003 **9** 1¼ **Even Stevens**[21] 7243 4 -9-385 (p) MartinHarley 17 88
(Scott Dixon) *led: hdd over 2f out: wknd appr fnl f* **80/1**

4111 **10** 1½ **Jack Dexter**[14] 7397 3 -9-3102 GrahamLee 10 83
(Jim Goldie) *mid-div: effrt over 2f out: sn hrd drvn: fdd last 100yds* **4/1**[1]

0554 **11** 1 **Gouray Girl (IRE)**[4] 7408 5 -8-1283 DaleSwift 8 75
(Brian Ellison) *in rr: kpt on fnl 2f: nvr a factor* **66/1**

0044 **12** 1¼ **York Glory (USA)**[4] 7397 4 -9-393 (b) PhillipMakin 5 77
(Kevin Ryan) *chsd ldrs: wknd over 1f out* **12/1**

1010 **13** 1¼ **Doc Hay (USA)**[4] 7397 5 -9-6106 JoeFanning 14 76
(David O'Meara) *s.i.s: t.k.h: swtchd rt and hdwy stands' side over 3f out: wknd over 1f out* **16/1**

3000 **14** 1 **Valencha**[9] 7509 5 -8-1295 WilliamBuick 6 65
(Hughie Morrison) *t.k.h in rr: effrt over 2f out: n.m.r over 1f out: sn wknd* **16/1**

6332 **15** shd **Best Trip (IRE)**[37] 6820 5 -9-381 BarryMcHugh 4 70
(Brian Ellison) *chsd ldrs on outer: lost pl over 1f out* **40/1**

1500 **16** ½ **Johannes (IRE)**[28] 7066 9 -9-394 PaulHanagan 1 68
(Richard Fahey) *s.i.s: a in rr* **33/1**

2000 **17** 4½ **Place In My Heart**[35] 6878 3 -8-1292 LukeMorris 15 50
(George Baker) *dwlt: mid-div: lost pl over 2f out* **66/1**

3046 **18** 1 **Katla (IRE)**[15] 7390 4 -9-1102 WJLee 13 50
(J F Grogan, Ire) *mid-div: effrt over 2f out: sn wknd* **25/1**

1-16 **19** 3¾ **Take Cover**[17] 7327 5 -9-383 MartinDwyer 19 40
(David C Griffiths) *mid-div: t.k.h: effrt over 2f out: sn wknd* **40/1**

1m 13.25s (-0.35)**Going Correction** +0.30s/f (Good) **19**Ran SP% **126.9**
Speed ratings (Par 111): **114,112,110,109,107 106,106,105,104,102 100,99,97,96,96 95,89,88,83**
toteswingers 1&2 £54.20, 1&3 £2.00, 2&3 Not won. CSF £51.59 TOTE £8.30 : £2.70 , £2.60 , £7.80; EX 44.20 Trifecta £1729.10 Pool: £3,527.39 - 1.53 winning units.
Owner The Eton Riflemen **Bred** Grangecon Stud **Trained** Newmarket, Suffolk

FOCUS
Not many got competitive here. The winner is rated to his recent level in a race where it was beneficial to be near the speed.

NOTEBOOK
Eton Rifles (IRE) who was an unlucky-in-running fourth in this last year, built on his recent third in a Group 3 at Ascot to get into the winner's enclosure for the first time this year, on the final day of the turf season. This is his level, and 6f with a bit of ease in the ground seem to be his conditions. (op 8-1)
Ultrasonic(USA), who was buried in the pack early, let the winner and third get first run on her, but she picked up well once asked to bridge the gap and was finishing well at the line. Her pedigree suggests the quicker the ground the better she'll like it. (tchd 6-1)
Justineo bounced back to form over 7f here last time and backed that up with a really good effort from the front over this shorter distance. He could well end up going up another pound or two for this, though. (op 22-1 tchd 25-1)
Sirius Prospect (USA)won this race last year but not for the first time this season he found himself staying on all too late at the finish. He started the year rated 110 and is now rated only 2lb lower, but apart from his third place at Ascot last time it has been a disappointing campaign. (op 5-1)
The Cheka (IRE)has probably just had enough for the year. He's one to keep in mind for his seasonal return, though, as his form figures on his reappearance read 11321. (op 12-1)
Thunderball faced no easy task at the weights and ran about as well as could be expected.
Ladies Are Forever was again below her best. She just hasn't hit the heights of her 3yo career this time around. (tchd 22-1)
Jack Dexter has been competing in tough handicaps. He wasn't at his best here, and this was probably just one race too many at the end of a long season. (op 9-2)

7691 BETFRED "THE BONUS KING" H'CAP 7f
3:45 (3:47) (Class 2) (0-105,102) 3-Y-O **£12,938** (£3,850; £1,924 ; £962) **Stalls** High

Form RPR

2403 **1** **Tartiflette**[14] 7408 3 -8-584 FrannyNorton 2 92
(Ed McMahon) *in tch far side: hdwy wl over 2f out: rdn and hung rt jst ins fnl f: led last 75yds: kpt on* **10/1**

1130 **2** ¾ **Jack's Revenge (IRE)**[42] 6674 4 -8-1189 (bt) JimmyFortune 5 96
(George Baker) *hld up far side: hdwy over 1f out: sn rdn and styd on wl fnl f: jst hld: 2nd of 10 in gp* **12/1**

0000 **3** nk **Grissom (IRE)**[15] 7366 6 -8-987 DavidAllan 10 93
(Tim Easterby) *trckd ldrs far side: hdwy 2f out: rdn to ld jst over 1f out: drvn ins fnl f: hdd and one pce last 75yds: 3rd of 10 in gp* **33/1**

1443 **4** 1½ **Roninski (IRE)**[9] 7508 4 -8-987 JimmyQuinn 11 90
(Bryan Smart) *hld up in tch far side: hdwy 2f out: rdn over 1f out and ev ch whn bdly hmpd jst ins fnl f: kpt on: 4th of 10 in gp* **25/1**

3211 **5** nk **Myboyalfie (USA)**[10] 7493 5 -8-1189 (v) FrederikTylicki 9 91
(J R Jenkins) *cl up far side: led 2f out: sn rdn and hdd jst over 1f out: hld whn hmpd jst ins fnl f: 5th of 10 in gp* **14/1**

5000 **6** 1¾ **Prince Of Johanne (IRE)**[42] 6674 6 -9-10102 (p) JohnFahy 20 99+
(Tom Tate) *in rr stands' side: swtchd lft and hdwy 3f out: rdn 2f out: styd on appr fnl f: nrst fin 1st of 10 in gp* **25/1**

4612 **7** nk **Shamaal Nibras (USA)**[12] 7435 3 -9-497 RichardHughes 13 92+
(Richard Hannon) *hld up in rr stands' side: hdwy 2f out: sn rdn: kpt on: nrst fin: 2nd of 10 in gp* **8/1**[3]

0041 **8** hd **Sam Nombulist**[7] 7559 4 -8-987 (v) RobertWinston 3 83
(Richard Whitaker) *overall ldr far side: rdn along and hdd 2f out: wknd appr fnl f: 6th of 10 in gp* **25/1**

1250 **9** 1 **Well Painted (IRE)**[21] 7240 3 -9-194 (t) AdamBeschizza 16 86
(William Haggas) *trckd ldrs stands' side: effrt and n.m.r over 2f out: sn rdn and btn: 3rd of 10 in gp* **5/1**[1]

2302 **10** shd **Louis The Pious**[28] 7066 4 -9-8100 GrahamLee 14 93+
(David O'Meara) *trckd ldrs stands' side: rdn along over 2f out: sn btn: 4th of 10 in gp* **11/2**[2]

0500 **11** 1 **Colonel Mak**[15] 7366 5 -9-597 GrahamGibbons 17 87
(David Barron) *trckd ldrs stands' side: rdn along over 2f out: sn wknd: 5th of 10 in gp* **33/1**

6220 **12** 1 **Highland Colori (IRE)**[21] 7240 4 -9-395 DavidProbert 12 83
(Andrew Balding) *led stands' side gp: rdn along over 2f out: sn wknd: 6th of 10 in gp* **8/1**[3]

5100 **13** 3¼ **El Viento (FR)**[28] 7066 4 -8-1391 (v[1]) TonyHamilton 1 70
(Richard Fahey) *chsd ldrs far side: rdn along over 2f out: sn wknd: 7th of 10 in gp* **33/1**

1025 **14** 1¼ **Kingscroft (IRE)**[9] 7508 4 -8-684 JoeFanning 6 60
(Mark Johnston) *chsd ldrs far side: rdn along over 2f out: sn wknd: 8th of 10 in gp* **16/1**

-006 **15** 4½ **Irish Heartbeat (IRE)**[154] 2931 7 -8-987 PaulHanagan 18 51
(Richard Fahey) *prom stands' side: rdn along over 2f out: sn wknd: 7th of 10 in gp* **12/1**

4103 **16** ½ **Osteopathic Remedy (IRE)**[12] 7435 8 -8-994 ConnorNichol[(7)] 22 57
(Michael Dods) *a in rr stands' side: 8th of 10 in gp* **50/1**

-140 **17** 4½ **My Freedom (IRE)**[21] 7240 4 -9-597 (p) TedDurcan 8 48
(Saeed Bin Suroor) *in tch far side: rdn along over 2f out: sn wknd: 9th of 10 in gp* **33/1**

1001 **18** 2¼ **Wannabe King**[7] 7556 6 -8-691 (v) JordanNason[(7)] 4 36
(Geoffrey Harker) *dwlt: sn chsng ldrs far side: rdn along wl over 2f out and sn wknd: last of 10 in gp* **25/1**

3000 **19** ¾ **Docofthebay (IRE)**[30] 7010 8 -8-785 (b) PJMcDonald 15 28
(Scott Dixon) *chsd ldrs stands' side: rdn along wl over 2f out: sn wknd: 9th of 10 in gp* **12/1**

210 **20** 2¼ **Volcanic Wind (USA)**[9] 7502 3 -8-887 WilliamBuick 19 24
(Saeed Bin Suroor) *chsd ldrs stands' side: rdn along wl over 2f out: sn wknd last of 10 in gp* **14/1**

1m 27.21s (0.91)**Going Correction** +0.30s/f (Good)
WFA 3 from 4yo+ 1lb **20**Ran SP% **134.8**
Speed ratings (Par 109): **106,105,104,103,102 100,100,100,99,98 97,96,92,91,86 85,80,78,77,74**
toteswingers 1&2 £54.20, 1&3 £2.00, 2&3 Not won CSF £121.08 CT £3956.23 TOTE £14.00 : £2.80, £2.80 , £7.60 , £7.00 ; EX 232.10 TRIFECTA Not won. .
Owner A Buxton **Bred** Andrew Buxton **Trained** Lichfield, Staffs
■ Stewards' Enquiry : Franny Norton three-day ban: careless riding (Nov 24,26,27)

FOCUS
The field split into two groups, with the far-side runners holding the advantage throughout. Straightforward form.

NOTEBOOK
Tartiflette picked up best, staying on well to gain a deserved, albeit belated, first win of the season. A course winner who enjoys some cut in the ground, she'd twice finished runner-up from 1lb lower earlier in the year, so this was hardly a surprise success, and she can continue to give a good account in handicaps next year, assuming she's kept in training. (op 14-1)
Jack's Revenge (IRE) down in trip having finished a fine eighth in the Cambridgeshire, was duly doing his best work late, staying on well next to the far rail without having the winner's finishing kick. (tchd 14-1)
Grissom(IRE), a previous C&D winner, is on a fair mark and handles these conditions, but he couldn't quite see it out having challenged more down the centre. (tchd 40-1)
Roninski(IRE), 7lb above his last win mark, wasn't helped by some late interference, but wouldn't have won. (op 22-1)
Myboyalfie(USA), down in trip but up another 5lb, didn't have the early pace to dominate and was already held when hampered late on.
Prince Of Johanne (IRE)s edging back down the weights and fared best of the stands' side runners, albeit he was never in with a chance. (tchd 28-1)
Shamaal Nibras (USA)never got close enough to challenge. (tchd 7-1)
Well Painted (IRE)failed to pick up having briefly had to wait for a run and was disappointing. (tchd 4-1)
Louis The Pious travelled up well before finding little. (op 8-1)
Highland Colori (IRE)was another stands' side runner to disappoint. (op 11-1)
T/Jkpt: Not won. T/Plt: £177.60 to a £1 stake. Pool: £108934.45 - 447.71 winning tickets T/Qpdt: £32.00 to £1. Pool: £9574.16 - 221.06 w. tckts JR 7692a, 7694a-7695a (Foreign Racing) See RI

7514 SAINT-CLOUD (L-H)
Saturday, November 10

OFFICIAL GOING: Turf: heavy

7693a CRITERIUM DE SAINT-CLOUD (GROUP 1) (2YO COLTS & FILLIES) (TURF) 1m 2f
1:00 (12:00) 2-Y-O **£119,041** (£47,625; £23,812 ; £11,895 ; £5,958)

RPR

1 **Morandi (FR)**[20] 7283 2 -9-00 MaximeGuyon 4 117+
(J-C Rouget, France) *settled in 2nd: rdn to ld 2 1/2f out: sn wnt clr: extended ld ins fnl f: eased fnl 100yds: v easily* **7/10**[1]

2 7 **Willie The Whipper**[19] 7292 2 -9-00 JamieSpencer 2 102
(Ann Duffield) *settled 3rd: rdn 2 1/2f out: wnt 2nd 2f out: r.o wl fnl f to go clr 2nd: no ch w wnr* **7/2**[2]

3 3 **Miss You Too**[35] 6873 2 -8-100 IanMongan 5 93
(David Simcock) *racd towards rr: wnt 5th ent st: r.o wl 2f out: styd on fnl f to take 3rd 100yds out* **18/1**

4 1 **Sempre Medici (FR)**[24] 2 -9-00 AlexisBadel 6 95
(Mme M Bollack-Badel, France) *towards rr fr s: sent up to go 3rd on outside bef end of bk st: rdn 2f out: r.o fnl f: wnt 4th 50yds out* **14/1**

5 nk **Kapstadt (FR)**[28] 2 -9-00 UmbertoRispoli 3 95
(F Doumen, France) *racd 4th: r.o u.p 2f out: styd on wl: lost 3rd 100yds out* **11/1**

6 4 **Cassiopee (FR)**[17] 7343 2 -8-100 AntoineHamelin 7 83
(Y Barberot, France) *hld up towards rr: rdn but no ex fr 2f out: sn btn* **31/1**

7 12 **Princedargent (FR)**[25] 2 -9-00 OlivierPeslier 8 66
(H-A Pantall, France) *hld up towards rr: rdn but no ex fr 2f out: sn btn: eased* **19/1**

8 dist **Wingate**[18] 7319 2 -9-00 FabriceVeron 1
(H-A Pantall, France) *sn led: set gd pce: hdd 2 1/2f out: sn wknd in st: t.o: eased* **17/2**[3]

2m 25.3s (9.30) **8**Ran SP% **120.0**
WIN (incl. 1 euro stake): 1.70. PLACES: 1.20, 1.40, 2.70. DF: 3.20. SF: 4.00 .
Owner Daniel-Yves Treves **Bred** E Puerari **Trained** Pau, France

FOCUS
This wouldn't have looked out of place as a Group 3, with it lacking even more depth than usual and none of Europe's elite yard's being represented. There was a solid early pace and the winner was value for an extra length. The form is rated cautiously.

NOTEBOOK
Morandi(FR), who trounced the opposition by 12l in a 1m1f heavy-ground Group 3 at Longchamp last month, produced a visually impressive display. He was bred to improve for the extra yardage and he again revelled in the ground, taking over early in the straight and asserting with ease. A fine, big sort, it remains to be seen whether he can prove himself as effective on quicker ground next spring, but he clearly rates a very smart prospect for next season.
Willie The Whipper accounted for a useful type in a 1m Listed event at Pontefract on similar ground, but couldn't handle the dominant winner on this rise in grade. His dam won up to 1m6f and he very much looks the type to benefit from 1m4f and more next season.
Miss You Too is bred to stay well and she got going late to gain some very valuable black type. It's doubtful she'll ever be able to top this achievement.
Sempre Medici (FR) a once-raced maiden winner, still looked green and should do better as a 3yo.
Wingate

7663 FLEMINGTON (L-H)
Saturday, November 10

OFFICIAL GOING: Turf: good to soft changing to good before patinack farm classic

7696a QUEEN ELIZABETH STKS (GROUP 3 H'CAP) (3YO+) (TURF) 1m 5f
5:30 (12:00) 3-Y-O+

£99,671 (£29,605; £14,802 ; £7,401 ; £4,111 ; £3,289)

RPR

1 **Puissance De Lune (IRE)**[10] 4 -8-8⁰ ...(t) GlenBoss 7 110+
(Darren Weir, Australia) **2/1**[1]

2 5 **Ironstein (AUS)**[14] 7425 7 -8-11⁰ ... BrentonAvdulla 9 106
(Gerald Ryan, Australia) **25/1**

3 2 1/2 **Tanby (AUS)**[7] 7560 6 -8-13⁰ ...(t) HughBowman 4 104
(Robert Hickmott, Australia) **20/1**

4 1 **Dare To Dream (IRE)** 7560 4 -8-8⁰ ...(b) DamienOliver 12 97+
(Bart Cummings, Australia) **13/2**[3]

5 3/4 **Lost In The Moment (IRE)** 6600 5 -9-2⁰ ...(p) KerrinMcEvoy 8 104
(Saeed Bin Suroor) *hld up in last quartet on outer: rdn over 3f out: styd on to go 5th cl home: fin wl but n.d* **15/1**

6 1 1/4 **Lightinthenite (AUS)**[4] 5 -8-9⁰ ... CraigAWilliams 2 95
(J O'Shea, Australia) **20/1**

7 1/2 **Shahwardi (FR)**[28] 7073 6 -9-2⁰ ... MichaelRodd 5 102
(A De Royer-Dupre, France) **4/1**[2]

8 hd **Moudre (AUS)**[21] 7264 7 -9-1⁰ ...(b) StevenArnold 3 100
(Ciaron Maher, Australia) **40/1**

9 hd **Folding Gear (NZ)**[21] 7264 5 -8-13⁰ ... BenMelham 1 98
(Lee & Shannon Hope, Australia) **10/1**

10 1/2 **Vatuvei (AUS)**[14] 7425 4 -8-9⁰ ...(p) VladDuric 11 93
(Peter G Moody, Australia) **14/1**

11 1 3/4 **Streaky Fella (AUS)**[3] 7 -8-8⁰ ...(bt) DwayneDunn 10 90
(Aaron Purcell, Australia) **100/1**

12 1 3/4 **Miss With Attitude (AUS)**[10] 6 -8-8⁰ ...(b) JimCassidy 13 87
(Mick Price, Australia) **150/1**

13 25 **Excluded (NZ)**[7] 7560 5 -8-8⁰ ...(t) NicholasHall 14 49
(Robert Hickmott, Australia) **17/1**

P **The Verminator (AUS)**[21] 6 -8-13⁰ ...(b) CraigNewitt 6
(Chris Waller, Australia) **30/1**

2m 44.23s (164.23) **14**Ran SP% **114.9**

PARI-MUTUEL (NSW TAB - all including au$1 stakes): WIN 2.90; PLACE 1.50, 3.40, 5.70; DF 36.20; SF 51.20 .

Owner Limerick Lane Syndicate **Bred** Round Hill Stud **Trained** Australia

NOTEBOOK

Lost In The Moment (IRE) who missed the cut for the Melbourne Cup, was never a threat over a trip short of his best.

7585 CAPANNELLE (R-H)
Sunday, November 11

OFFICIAL GOING: Turf: heavy

7697a PREMIO CARLO E FRANCESCO ALOISI (GROUP 3) (2YO+) (TURF) 6f
3:45 (12:00) 2-Y-O+ **£16,800** (£16,800; £5,600 ; £2,800)

RPR

1 **Rosendhal (IRE)**[8] 7565 5 -9-4⁰ ...(b) SSulas 2 109
(G Botti, Italy) *trckd ldrs: hdwy on rail over 1 1/2f out: chal ins fnl f: r.o wl in hd-to-hd w Blu Constellation fnl 150yds: dead-heat* **94/10**

1 dht **Blu Constellation (ITY)**[372] 7311 4 -9-4⁰ ... DarioVargiu 7 109
(R Biondi, Italy) *pressed ldr: led appr 1 1/2f out: jnd on ins fnl f: r.o wl in hd-to-hd w Rosendhal fnl 150yds: dead-heat* **604/100**

3 3 **Noble Hachy**[21] 7288 3 -9-5⁰ ... CristianDemuro 5 100
(L Riccardi, Italy) *midfield: effrt to press ldrs 2f out: 3rd and hrd rdn 1 1/2f out: kpt on u.p but unable qck fnl f* **87/100**[1]

4 1 **Chiara Wells (IRE)** 3 -9-1⁰ ... MVargiu 8 93
(A Floris, Italy) *prom on outside: outpcd and lost pl 1/2-way: styd on again to chse ldrs 1 1/2f out: sn rdn: one pce under hrd driving fnl f* **204/10**

5 shd **Dagda Mor (ITY)**[21] 7288 5 -9-4⁰ ... FabioBranca 1 96
(S Botti, Italy) *led narrowly towards rail: rdn and hdd appr 1 1/2f out: kpt on same pce fnl f* **462/100**[3]

6 3/4 **Blue Soave (FR)**[35] 6913 4 -9-8⁰ ... ThierryThulliez 9 97
(F Chappet, France) *midfield on outside: prog to press ldrs over 2f out: sn rdn and nt qckn over 1f out: one pce fnl f* **13/4**[2]

7 nk **Alfkona (GER)**[56] 4 -9-1⁰ ... MEsposito 6 90
(Jozef Roszival, Hungary) *chsd ldng gp: rdn and no imp over 1f out: nt rdn out fnl 150yds* **185/10**

8 8 **Samysilver (USA)**[364] 7408 4 -9-4⁰ ... GBietolini 3 67
(Gianluca Bietolini, Italy) *a in rr: bhd whn eased ins fnl f* **29/1**

9 7 **Lipfix (ITY)**[119] 4 -9-4⁰ ... CFiocchi 4 45
(G Pucciatti, Italy) *a in rr: bhd and no imp u.p fr 2f out: eased fnl f* **56/1**

1m 9.85s (-0.45) **9**Ran SP% **133.5**

WIN (incl. 1 euro stake): 3.67 (Blu Constellation), 4.96 (Rosendhal). PLACES: 1.93 (Blue Constellation), 2.08 (Rosendhal), 1.19. DF: 34.78 .

Owner Allevamento Pian Di Neve SRL **Bred** Allevamento Pian Di Neve Srl **Trained** Italy

Owner Incolinx **Bred** Luciani Loreto **Trained** Italy

1553 KREFELD (R-H)
Sunday, November 11

OFFICIAL GOING: Turf: good to soft

7698a GP DER WOHNSTATTE KREFELD WOHNUNGS-AKTIENGESELLSCHAFT - HERZOG VON RATIBOR-RENNEN (GROUP 3) (2YO) 1m 110y
1:30 (12:00) 2-Y-O

£26,666 (£9,166; £4,583 ; £2,500 ; £1,666 ; £1,250)

RPR

1 **Flamingo Star (GER)**[22] 2 -8-13⁰ ... APietsch 8 98
(R Dzubasz, Germany) *led after 100yds: rdn over 2f out: hdd 1 1/2f out: cl 3rd in between horses and hrd rdn 1f out: rallied u.p to regain ld fnl 50yds: gamely* **164/10**

2 nse **Protectionist (GER)**[63] 2 -8-13⁰ ... EPedroza 6 98
(A Wohler, Germany) *dwlt and rowed along to go early pce: towards rr on outside: gd hdwy over 2f out: shkn up and led narrowly 1 1/2f out: rdn and r.o fnl f: hdd 50yds out: no ex* **6/4**[1]

3 3/4 **Beatrice**[19] 7319 2 -8-13⁰ ... FabriceVeron 2 96
(H-A Pantall, France) *led 100yds: hdd and trckd ldr on rail: rdn and wnt 2nd on rail 1f out: r.o u.p fnl f: no ex fnl 50yds* **66/10**

4 1 1/2 **Big Memory (FR)**[24] 2 -9-2⁰ ... AntoineHamelin 4 96
(J-P Carvalho, Germany) *trckd ldng gp: 3rd and ev ch under 2f out: sn hrd rdn: one pce fnl f* **77/10**

5 2 **Stellato**[35] 2 -8-13⁰ ... JBojko 3 88
(A Wohler, Germany) *racd keenly towards rr: rdn and gd prog on heels of ldrs whn squeezed out and snatched up under 2f out: rdn and no imp fr over 1f out* **63/10**

6 1/2 **Anatol Artist (GER)**[28] 7091 2 -9-2⁰ ... KClijmans 5 90
(Uwe Ostmann, Germany) *towards rr: hdwy on rail but short of room and checked 2f out: sn in clr but no imp u.p: one pce fr over 1f out: fdd fnl 100yds* **19/5**[2]

7 5 **Mister Westminster**[10] 2 -9-2⁰ ... MiguelLopez 1 79
(S Smrczek, Germany) *sn adrift at rr: sme hdwy on outside over 1 1/2f out: nvr in contention* **98/10**

8 3 **Spellbound (FR)**[30] 2 -8-13⁰ ... FilipMinarik 7 70
(M Munch, Germany) *midfield: rdn and short-lived effrt on rail over 1 1/2f out: sn wknd: eased ins fnl f* **195/10**

9 9 **Forever Beauty (GER)**[21] 7281 2 -8-13⁰ ... AStarke 9 50
(Mario Hofer, Germany) *trckd ldr on outside: rdn and nt qckn under 2f out: wknd appr last 1 1/2f: eased ins fnl f* **6/1**[3]

1m 49.68s (3.08) **9**Ran SP% **133.4**

WIN (incl. 10 euro stake): 174. PLACES: 29, 14, 19. SF: 495 .

Owner Frau M Haller **Bred** Frau Marlene Haller **Trained** Germany

7682 CHANTILLY (R-H)
Monday, November 12

OFFICIAL GOING: Polytrack: standard

7699a PRIX DE L'ALLEE MASSINE (CLAIMER) (2YO) (POLYTRACK) 6f 110y
11:30 (12:00) 2-Y-O **£11,250** (£4,500; £3,375 ; £2,250 ; £1,125)

RPR

1 **Carlton Blue (IRE)**[33] 6980 2 -9-8⁰ ... ChristopheSoumillon 5 81
(Paul Cole) *broke fast to ld: rdn 1 1/2f out to go clr: r.o wl fnl f: wnt further clr: easily* **13/5**[1]

2 3 **Starki (FR)**[19] 2 -8-11⁰ ... FabriceVeron 2 62
(H-A Pantall, France) **13/1**

3 nse **Roman Order (IRE)**[18] 7349 2 -8-11⁰ ... MartinDwyer 1 62
(Brian Meehan) *broke wl to r in 2nd on ins: relegated to 4th 2f out: rallied and r.o wl to go 2nd 1f out: r.o wl but hdd for 2nd on line* **10/1**

4 2 **Contesurmoi (FR)**[19] 2 -8-11⁰ ... RonanThomas 11 56
(A Bonin, France) **53/10**[3]

5 nse **Meshaheera (FR)**[20] 2 -8-11⁰ ... SoufyaneMoulin(4) 3 60
(F Sanchez, France) **60/1**

6 1 1/2 **Lily Merrill**[19] 2 -8-13⁰ ... AntoineHamelin 10 54
(T Lemer, France) **13/1**

7 1/2 **Rock With Me (FR)**[13] 7265 2 -9-1⁰ ... AnthonyCrastus 6 54
(F Chappet, France) **21/1**

8 3/4 **Kalevala (FR)**[23] 7265 2 -8-9⁰ ... CesarPasserat(6) 8 52
(R Pritchard-Gordon, France) **32/1**

9 1 **Short Final (FR)** 2 -8-8⁰ ... ThierryThulliez 15 43
(Mario Hofer, Germany) **15/1**

10 1 1/4 **Liberty River (FR)** 2 -8-11⁰ ...(p) FlavienPrat 4 42
(G Botti, Italy) **37/1**

0 **Atora Bere (FR)**[21] 7122 2 -8-13⁰ ... StephanePasquier 13
(M Boutin, France) **43/10**[2]

0 **So Irish (IRE)**[77] 2 -9-1⁰ ... OlivierPeslier 12
(Robert Collet, France) **10/1**

0 **Flicka (FR)**[14] 2 -8-8⁰ ...(b[1]) JohanVictoire 7
(J Van Handenhove, France) **32/1**

0 **Alice Neney (IRE)**[23] 7265 2 -8-5⁰ ... MlleAmelieFoulon(3) 9
(C Lerner, France) **74/1**

1m 18.3s (78.30) **14**Ran SP% **117.4**

WIN (incl. 1 euro stake): 3.60. PLACES: 2.00, 3.20, 2.70. DF: 51.10. SF: 73.70 .

Owner Meyrick, Dunnington-Jefferson & Wright **Bred** Eoghan Grogan **Trained** Whatcombe, Oxon

NOTEBOOK

Carlton Blue (IRE) made all the running to win easily.

7700a - 7701a See Page 1371

7625 KEMPTON (A.W) (R-H)

Wednesday, November 14

OFFICIAL GOING: Standard

Wind: Virtually nil

7702 WIN BIG WITH BETDAQ MULTIPLES APPRENTICE CLASSIFIED CLAIMING STKS 1m 2f (P)

4:25 (4:25) (Class 6) 3-Y-O **£1,617** (£481; £240; £120) Stalls Low

Form RPR
6 **1** **Purple 'n Gold (IRE)**[109] [4603] 3-9-0 70 ....(v) NathanAlison 1 70
(Jim Boyle) *mde all: qcknd 4 l clr 3f out: in n.d after: easily* **2/1**[2]
1623 **2** *3 ¾* **Renegotiate**[35] [6976] 3-9-2 67 .... DanielMuscutt(5) 2 70
(Andrew Balding) *trckd wnr tl easily outpcd and btn over 2f out: wl hld and hanging in st* **1/1**[1]
350 **3** *2 ¾* **Anychanceofabirdie (USA)**[34] [7011] 3-8-13 65(t) WilliamTwiston-Davies(3) 3 60
(David Simcock) *hld up in 3rd: wknd over 2f out* **6/1**[3]
4140 **4** *13* **Shomberg**[16] [7436] 3-8-9 56 .... RachealKneller(3) 4 31
(Dai Burchell) *in tch in 4th tl wknd qckly over 2f out: sn bhd* **8/1**
2m 7.16s (-0.84) **Going Correction** -0.05s/f (Stan) **4** Ran SP% **108.7**
Speed ratings (Par 98): **101,98,95,85**
The winner was claimed by David Pipe for £8,000. CSF £4.44 TOTE £4.20; EX 4.50.
Owner M Khan X2 **Bred** Stonethorn Stud Farms Ltd **Trained** Epsom, Surrey

FOCUS
The going was standard with the rails positioned up the inside. Quite an interesting claimer restricted to runners rated 70 or less, run at a fair pace with the winner making all to win convincingly. The form may not be quite as good as rated.
Anychanceofabirdie(USA) Official explanation: jockey said gelding hung right.

7703 BACK OR LAY AT BETDAQ.COM H'CAP 5f (P)

4:55 (4:55) (Class 7) (0-50,50) 3-Y-O+ **£1,455** (£433; £216; £108) Stalls Low

Form RPR
4200 **1** **Brandywell Boy (IRE)**[47] [6640] 9-9-3 50 .... SilvestreDeSousa 9 57
(Dominic Ffrench Davis) *charged stall open fractionally early: chsd ldr: rdn 1/2-way: styd on u.p to ld last strides* **10/1**
5024 **2** *hd* **Itum**[15] [7471] 5-9-1 48 .... SebSanders 5 54
(Christine Dunnett) *led: rdn over 1f out: hdd and no ex last strides* **6/1**[2]
5000 **3** *2 ¾* **Crown Dependency (IRE)**[33] [7015] 3-8-10 50 .... PhilipPrince(7) 6 46
(David Evans) *chsd ldrs: rdn over 1f out: styd on u.p fnl f to take 3rd nr fin but no imp on ldng duo* **11/2**[1]
4400 **4** *¾* **Deveze (IRE)**[9] [7591] 4-9-2 49 ....(b) LiamKeniry 1 43
(Milton Bradley) *plld hrd: chsd ldrs in 3rd: rdn and no imp over 1f out: no ex and dropped to 4th nr fin* **20/1**
0030 **5** *shd* **Adaeze (IRE)**[42] [6771] 4-9-0 47 ....(v) EddieAhern 4 40
(Jonathan Portman) *chsd ldrs: drvn and styd on fr over 1f out but nvr gng pce to get into contention* **25/1**
004 **6** *hd* **Pharoh Jake**[42] [6771] 4-8-9 47 .... WilliamTwiston-Davies(5) 11 40
(John Bridger) *in rr: racd wd into st and hdwy over 1f out: kpt on clsng stages* **20/1**
06-4 **7** *1* **Brian Sprout**[308] [118] 4-9-2 49 .... DarryllHolland 2 38
(John Weymes) *chsd ldrs: drvn 2f out: styd on one pce* **8/1**
5034 **8** *shd* **College Doll**[8] [7611] 3-9-1 48 .... TomMcLaughlin 3 37
(Christine Dunnett) *slowly away: in rr: pushed along 2f out: mod prog fnl f* **8/1**
3000 **9** *½* **Duke Of Rainford**[7] [7633] 5-9-0 47 .... JamieSpencer 10 34
(Michael Herrington) *towards rr: pushed along and styd on same pce fnl 2f* **11/2**[1]
0460 **10** *nse* **Vhujon (IRE)**[20] [7362] 7-9-0 47 .... RobbieFitzpatrick 8 34
(Peter Grayson) *outpcd: mod prog clsng stages* **7/1**[3]
0056 **11** *nse* **Sherjawy (IRE)**[14] [7482] 8-8-13 49 .... SimonPearce(3) 12 35
(Zoe Davison) *hld up in rr and outpcd: mod prog fnl f* **14/1**
45P0 **12** *nse* **Green Mountain (IRE)**[8] [7615] 3-9-0 50 ....(v) RaulDaSilva(3) 7 36
(Philip McBride) *slowly away: t.k.h: outpcd most of way* **10/1**
1m 0.39s (-0.11) **Going Correction** -0.05s/f (Stan) **12** Ran SP% **118.0**
Speed ratings (Par 97): **98,97,93,92,91 91,90,89,89,88 88,88**
Tote Swingers 1&2 £14.30, 2&3 £8.20, 1&3 £11.60 CSF £66.60 CT £369.88 TOTE £8.80: £3.40, £1.80, £3.10; EX 56.00 Trifecta £1130.70 Pool: £2,879.54 - 1.91 winning tickets..
Owner D J Ffrench Davis **Bred** Mountarmstrong Stud **Trained** Lambourn, Berks

FOCUS
A low-grade sprint handicap run at a steady pace with those racing up with the gallop at a distinct advantage. The form is rated around the front pair.

7704 BETDAQ MOBILE APPS H'CAP 5f (P)

5:25 (5:26) (Class 3) (0-95,93) 3-Y-O+ **£6,663** (£1,982; £990; £495) Stalls Low

Form RPR
6 **1** **Ubetterbegood (ARG)**[64] [6116] 4-9-6 92 .... NeilCallan 10 101
(Robert Cowell) *chsd ldrs: drvn and styd on strly fnl f to ld cl home* **25/1**
1263 **2** *½* **Ihtifal**[13] [7503] 3-9-7 93 ....(t) SilvestreDeSousa 3 100
(Saeed Bin Suroor) *s.i.s: sn chsng ldrs: drvn to ld 1f out: hdd cl home* **11/8**[1]
4135 **3** *hd* **Ajjaadd (USA)**[18] [7397] 6-9-2 93 .... WilliamTwiston-Davies(5) 2 99
(Ted Powell) *s.i.s: in rr: hdwy on outside over 1f out: str run fnl f: fin wl* **14/1**
000 **4** *1 ¼* **Moorhouse Lad**[18] [7397] 9-9-1 87 .... AdamKirby 4 89
(Garry Moss) *led tl hdd 1f out: wknd fnl 100yds* **14/1**
5204 **5** *1 ¼* **Clear Praise (USA)**[9] [7595] 5-8-12 84 .... SebSanders 6 81
(Simon Dow) *in tch: rdn and hdwy over 1f out: kpt on same pce clsng stages* **7/1**[3]
002 **6** *1 ¼* **Harrison George (IRE)**[35] [6979] 7-9-1 87 ....(t) DarryllHolland 1 80
(P J O'Gorman) *in rr: pushed along and hdwy appr fnl f: fin wl: nt rch ldrs* **6/1**[2]
1150 **7** *nk* **Electric Qatar**[118] [4234] 3-8-12 84 .... JamieSpencer 5 76
(Tom Dascombe) *in rr: pushed along and hdwy over 1f out: r.o clsng stages* **12/1**
4001 **8** *shd* **Whozthecat (IRE)**[46] [6689] 5-8-11 86 ....(b) NeilFarley(3) 8 77
(Declan Carroll) *chsd ldrs: rdn 2f out: wknd fnl f* **16/1**
1030 **9** *1 ½* **Island Legend (IRE)**[9] [7595] 6-8-13 85 ....(p) LiamKeniry 9 71
(Milton Bradley) *chsd ldr: rdn 2f out: wknd appr fnl f* **33/1**
000 **10** *½* **Move In Time**[18] [7397] 4-9-3 89 ....(v) TomEaves 7 73
(Bryan Smart) *chsd ldrs: rdn 1/2-way: wknd over 1f out* **7/1**[3]
0200 **11** *2 ¼* **Le Toreador**[51] [6543] 7-9-3 89 ....(tp) EddieAhern 11 65
(Kevin Ryan) *chsd ldrs to 1/2-way* **25/1**
040 **12** *5* **Burning Thread (IRE)**[25] [7243] 5-8-13 85 .... JimmyQuinn 12 43
(Tim Etherington) *outpcd* **50/1**
58.59s (-1.91) **Going Correction** -0.05s/f (Stan) **12** Ran SP% **120.9**
Speed ratings (Par 107): **113,112,111,109,107 105,105,105,102,102 98,90**
Tote Swingers 1&2 £11.70, 2&3 £7.00, 1&3 £69.60 CSF £59.39 CT £562.29 TOTE £46.80: £9.00, £1.10, £3.60; EX 143.80 Trifecta £1665.60 Pool: £5,307.79 - 2.39 winning tickets..
Owner Malih Lahej Al Basti **Bred** Tnt Argentina S A **Trained** Six Mile Bottom, Cambs

FOCUS
A decent, competitive sprint, run at a fast pace. The winner's form is hard to pin down and the second produced another big run.

NOTEBOOK
Ubetterbegood(ARG), a handicap debutant, having only his second start since coming from Argentina, was driven some way out but picked up in pleasing fashion inside the final furlong and showed a willing attitude to hold on when pressed near the line. He is with a handler who excels with his sprinters and one can expect him to go on from this. (op 50-1)
Ihtifal, who had plenty of use made of her over 6f here last time, was always nicely positioned and looked the likely winner when moving ahead up the far rail but was outpaced late on by an unexposed type, and this rates a fair enough effort. (op 6-4 tchd 13-8 in a place)
Ajjaadd(USA) missed the break and had plenty on when turning for home but he came with a blistering burst out wide although could not catch the leaders. He will be a useful sort if kept going over the winter. (op 11-1)
Moorhouse Lad, who had shown little in three starts this season, produced a return to form. While his handler is unlikely to garner much improvement from this 9yo, he is lightly raced on the AW and would be off interest in a 0-90 in the coming weeks. (op 25-1)
Clear Praise(USA) has been a credit to connections this season and he ran another sound race but is 10lb higher than when last successful and found this 5f trip round here, on the short side. (tchd 8-1)
Harrison George(IRE), who was short-headed over 7f here last month, was outpaced in rear approaching the final furlong but fairly flew late on this third AW start, and will surely be of interest when stepped up in trip. (tchd 7-1)
Whozthecat(IRE), 6lb higher then when winning over the minimum at Wolverhampton last time, found little for pressure on his first start at the track. (op 12-1)

7705 BETDAQ CASINO GAMES/BRITISH STALLION STUDS E B F MAIDEN STKS (DIV I) 7f (P)

5:55 (5:57) (Class 5) 2-Y-O **£3,169** (£943; £471; £235) Stalls Low

Form RPR
2 **1** **Melvin The Grate (IRE)**[57] [6330] 2-9-3 0 .... JamieSpencer 1 77
(Andrew Balding) *trckd ldr: pushed along appr fnl f: styd on wl under hand driving to ld nr fin* **11/10**[1]
00 **2** *½* **Short Squeeze (IRE)**[28] [7167] 2-9-3 0 .... JimCrowley 4 76
(Hugo Palmer) *t.k.h: led: drvn 2f out: styd on wl: hdd and outpcd nr fin* **10/1**
3 *2 ½* **One Pekan (IRE)** 2-9-3 0 .... NeilCallan 8 69+
(Roger Varian) *t.k.h: chsd ldrs: drvn 2f out: styd on to take 3rd 1f out but nvr gng pce of ldng duo* **6/1**[3]
4 *¾* **Captain Starlight (IRE)** 2-9-3 0 .... EddieAhern 7 67+
(Jo Crowley) *s.i.s: towards rr: hdwy fr 2f out: styd on to take 4th 1f out: nvr gng pce to rch ldrs* **33/1**
2 **5** *2 ½* **Zeus Magic**[19] [7371] 2-9-3 0 .... SebSanders 11 60
(David Elsworth) *in rr: rdn over 2f out: styd on fnl f but nvr a threat* **3/1**[2]
6 **6** *1* **Mawson**[19] [7372] 2-9-3 0 .... GeorgeBaker 6 57
(Roger Charlton) *t.k.h: chsd ldrs: rdn 2f out: wknd 1f out* **8/1**
7 *1 ½* **Jakey (IRE)** 2-9-3 0 .... IanMongan 5 53
(Pat Phelan) *s.i.s: in rr: pushed along over 2f out: sme prog fnl f* **25/1**
8 *4 ½* **Speronella** 2-8-12 0 .... RobertHavlin 3 36
(Hughie Morrison) *s.i.s: a in rr* **33/1**
00 **9** *2* **Burma Days (USA)**[42] [6796] 2-9-3 0 .... MartinHarley 9 36
(Sylvester Kirk) *chsd ldrs tl ins fnl 3f* **100/1**
6 **10** *13* **Sweet Piccolo**[23] [7296] 2-9-3 0 .... AdamKirby 10
(Paddy Butler) *outpcd* **100/1**
1m 26.89s (0.89) **Going Correction** -0.05s/f (Stan) **10** Ran SP% **118.8**
Speed ratings (Par 96): **92,91,88,87,84 83,82,76,74,59**
Tote Swingers 1&2 £2.90, 2&3 £13.30, 1&3 £3.10 CSF £13.81 TOTE £2.10: £1.10, £2.50, £1.70; EX 15.10 Trifecta £59.30 Pool: £6,037.60 - 76.31 winning tickets..
Owner Mrs Fitri Hay **Bred** Barronstown Stud **Trained** Kingsclere, Hants

FOCUS
Some interesting types in Divison I of this maiden, run at a messy gallop with once again those up with the pace dominating at the finish. No more than fair form, the first pair dominating.

NOTEBOOK
Melvin The Grate(IRE) ran a most encouraging debut at Folkestone (7f, good to firm) last time and put the benefit of that experience to good use with a hard-fought victory here, to land a bit of a gamble. With many of his market rivals under-performing, the form is questionable but he is with the right yard to continue his progression nest season. (op 5-4 tchd 11-8)
Short Squeeze(IRE) benefited by how the race unfolded but stepped up markedly on what he had shown in two previous starts, finishing some way clear of the third. He is now qualified for a mark and his breeding suggests he may want further in time.
One Pekan(IRE), a 125,000gns 2yo whose dam was placed in America and is a sister to Brave Tin Soldier, an 8.5f Grade 3 winner in America, did best of the newcomers and will have learnt plenty from this. He was keen enough through the race but showed a willing attitude and stayed on all the way to the line. (op 8-1 tchd 9-1)
Captain Starlight(IRE), a 10,000euros yearling and half-brother to 7f-1m2f winner Sky Diamond, ran a sound debut for a yard not noted for their newcomers. He can be placed to good advantage to land a small maiden.
Zeus Magic, a half-brother to a pair of 1m6f winners, ran better than expected over an inadequate-looking 6.5f (soft) on his debut last time but did not really build on that here. Weak in the market, he was doing all his best work late on and looks to be crying out for further. (op 7-4)
Mawson, whose dam is an unraced daughter of Queensland Derby and Oaks winner Bravery, shaped well in a soft-ground 7f Newbury maiden on his debut and again performed with promise here, under an educating ride and will be better in time. (op 11-1)

7706 BETDAQ CASINO GAMES/BRITISH STALLION STUDS E B F MAIDEN STKS (DIV II) 7f (P)

6:25 (6:25) (Class 5) 2-Y-O **£3,169** (£943; £471; £235) Stalls Low

Form RPR
2 **1** **Horsted Keynes (FR)**[15] [7458] 2-9-3 0 .... JamieSpencer 8 76+
(Roger Varian) *broke wl: t.k.h and stdd to trck ldrs: rdn over 1f out: styd on to ld ins fnl f: pushed along and a doing enough* **1/3**[1]
0 **2** *nk* **Secret Rebel**[19] [7372] 2-9-3 0 .... LiamKeniry 9 75
(Sylvester Kirk) *t.k.h: chsd ldr: led over 2f out: sn rdn and styd on: hdd ins fnl f: nt pce of wnr but rallied wl to cl nr fin* **16/1**
50 **3** *1 ½* **Poitin**[53] [6489] 2-8-12 0 .... JimCrowley 6 66
(Harry Dunlop) *chsd ldrs: rdn over 1f out: styd on for one pce 3rd fnl f* **14/1**
0 **4** *1 ¼* **Quest For More (IRE)**[19] [7373] 2-9-3 0 .... GeorgeBaker 2 68+
(Roger Charlton) *chsd ldrs: rdn 2f out: styd on same pce appr fnl f* **12/1**[3]

00 5 ½ **Tigerish**[13] 7507 2-9-3 0 ... EddieAhern 10 66
(Amanda Perrett) *t.k.h: chsd ldrs: rdn over 1f out: styd on same pce over 1f out* **50/1**

6 2 ½ **Lucilla** 2-8-12 0 ... DavidProbert 3 55
(Pat Murphy) *in rr: rdn over 2f out: styd on ins fnl f: nvr a threat* **50/1**

3 7 nk **First Sargeant**[22] 7311 2-9-3 0 ... (b) SilvestreDeSousa 7 59+
(Marco Botti) *t.k.h and stdd in rr: hrd rdn appr fnl 2f: mod prog ins fnl f* **5/1**[2]

00 8 1 ½ **Seaside Rock (IRE)**[19] 7373 2-9-3 0 ... KieranO'Neill 4 55
(Richard Hannon) *in rr: rdn over 2f out: a outpcd* **14/1**

00 9 ¾ **Lavender Bay**[21] 7329 2-8-12 0 ... JimmyQuinn 5 48
(Tim Pitt) *sn led: hdd over 2f out: wknd appr fnl f: eased whn no ch clsng stages* **50/1**

00 10 1 ½ **Great Ormond (IRE)**[21] 7323 2-9-3 0 ... MartinLane 1 49
(David Simcock) *outpcd* **50/1**

1m 26.91s (0.91) **Going Correction** -0.05s/f (Stan) **10 Ran SP% 126.4**
Speed ratings (Par 96): **92,91,89,88,87 85,84,83,82,80**
Tote Swingers 1&2 £5.60, 2&3 £8.00, 1&3 £3.30 CSF £9.86 TOTE £2.00: £1.02, £6.20, £4.40; EX 17.60 Trifecta £151.40 Pool: £7,613.63 - 37.71 winning tickets..
Owner Mrs Fitri Hay **Bred** Oceanic Bloodstock & Mme A Gravereaux **Trained** Newmarket, Suffolk

FOCUS
Division II of this maiden was run at a steady pace, with the short-priced favourite all out to score. The favourite has more to offer given a stronger gallop.

NOTEBOOK
Horsted Keynes(FR), who ran a race full of promise when runner-up on his debut, looked to face an easy task here but once again things did not go as planned. Very keen through the early part of the contest, his rider was at pains to settle him and he took his time to pick up off the steady pace, with his class just telling in the end. Obviously held in high regard at home, he has plenty to learn about the game but could develop into a decent enough type next season. (op 4-11 tchd 2-5)
Secret Rebel stepped up on his debut effort and made the favourite pull out all the stops. As in previous races, it proved advantageous to race up with the pace but his yard is adept at improving these types. (tchd 14-1)
Poitin was staying on well enough over this shorter trip and she will find things easier now qualified for a mark.
Quest For More(IRE) stepped up on his debut effort on heavy ground, but was outpaced inside the final furlong and his breeding suggests he will be seen to better effect over further.
First Sargeant, who had the blinkers retained, proved most disappointing. He looked to be getting the hang of things in the closing stages on his debut, having raced green, but was once again all at sea here early on. He was doing his best work inside the final furlong once again and may be seen to better effect over further, once handicapped. (tchd 9-2)

7707 TIME ORDER CARDS IN RACING PLUS MEDIAN AUCTION MAIDEN STKS 1m (P)
6:55 (6:56) (Class 6) 2-Y-O £1,617 (£481; £240; £120) Stalls Low

Form / RPR

44 1 **Kuantan One (IRE)**[22] 7306 2-9-3 0 ... SilvestreDeSousa 12 76
(Paul Cole) *mde all: rdn fr over 1f out: styd on strly clsng stages* **9/2**[2]

4 2 2 ¾ **Emperor Julius (IRE)**[27] 7191 2-9-3 0 ... JimCrowley 10 70
(Jo Crowley) *chsd ldrs: t.k.h: drvn 2f out: chsd wnr fnl f: no imp* **9/2**[2]

3 nk **Spillway** 2-9-3 0 ... LiamKeniry 9 69+
(Eve Johnson Houghton) *s.i.s: rcvring whn hmpd after 1f: drvn and gd hdwy over 1f out: fin strly: gng on clsng stages* **50/1**

04 4 1 ¼ **Couloir Extreme (IRE)**[36] 6947 2-9-3 0 ... GeorgeBaker 14 66
(Gary Moore) *chsd ldrs: rdn over 2f out: wknd fnl 100yds* **16/1**

5 nse **Staffhoss** 2-9-3 0 ... JoeFanning 1 66+
(Mark Johnston) *sn towards rr: pushed along over 2f out: hdwy over 1f out: kpt on wl clsng stages: nt rch ldrs* **16/1**

44 6 ¾ **Subtle Difference**[27] 7199 2-8-12 0 ... DavidProbert 6 59
(Andrew Balding) *chsd ldrs: pushed along 2f out: wknd fnl f* **12/1**

7 1 **Lion Beacon** 2-9-3 0 ... EddieAhern 13 62
(Amanda Perrett) *sn in tch: chsd ldrs and pushed along 3f out: wknd ins fnl f* **33/1**

8 ¾ **Misfer** 2-9-3 0 ... IanMongan 7 60+
(Sir Henry Cecil) *s.i.s: in rr: pushed along over 2f out: styd on ins fnl f: gng on clsng stages* **9/1**[3]

9 nk **Perpetual Ambition** 2-9-3 0 ... SebSanders 8 60
(Paul D'Arcy) *chsd ldrs: rdn 3f out: sn outpcd: styd on again fnl f* **25/1**

10 ¾ **Suspension** 2-8-12 0 ... RobertHavlin 3 53
(Hughie Morrison) *broke wl: sn towards rr: hdwy whn nt clr run over 2f out: kpt on same pce* **33/1**

11 6 **Cherry Tiger** 2-9-3 0 ... KirstyMilczarek 2 44
(James Toller) *pushed along: green and in tch early: rdn over 3f out: wknd ins fnl 2f* **20/1**

12 2 ¼ **Big Moza** 2-8-12 0 ... JimmyQuinn 5 34
(John Best) *s.i.s: in rr and outpcd* **50/1**

13 5 **Sweet Force** 2-9-3 0 ... AdamKirby 4 27
(Marco Botti) *hmpd and in rr after 1f: no ch after* **4/1**[1]

14 15 **Daring Dragon** 2-9-3 0 ... NeilCallan 11
(Ed Walker) *sn mid-div: rdn 3f out: green: hung rt and wknd wl over 2f out* **9/2**[2]

1m 39.74s (-0.06) **Going Correction** -0.05s/f (Stan) **14 Ran SP% 122.4**
Speed ratings (Par 94): **98,95,94,93,93 92,91,91,90,90 84,81,76,61**
Tote Swingers 1&2 £5.90, 2&3 £52.00, 1&3 £38.30 CSF £23.70 TOTE £5.30: £1.70, £1.80, £4.90; EX 19.90 Trifecta £106.00 Pool: £2,366.75 - 16.74 winning tickets..
Owner H R H Sultan Ahmad Shah **Bred** Manister House Stud **Trained** Whatcombe, Oxon

FOCUS
A wide-open maiden run at a fairly steady pace with the winner making all from his wide draw, under a fine ride. Modest form behind the winner.

NOTEBOOK
Kuantan One(IRE) had shown fair form on two starts over 1m, staying on well at Lingfield on his last start, and his rider was determined to make this a real test. Sent for home 4f out, he kept responding and was well on top at the line and he could well improve over further. (tchd 11-2)
Emperor Julius(IRE), a half-brother to a useful winner in Hong Kong, did best of those held up when fourth here on this debut (7f) and was travelling best turning for home here but he was outstayed by the winner up the straight. (op 7-2)
Spillway, a half-brother to 1m juvenile winner Remember Rocky, whose dam was a 6f juvenile winner and half-sister to 7f Listed winner Medley, ran a most promising debut. He could be noted travelling kindly near the back of the pack and did not enjoy the best of passages up the straight but stayed on best of all, under hands and heels, for a yard not known for their debutants.
Couloir Extreme(IRE) raced prominently but was outpaced inside the final furlong on his AW debut. He looks to be progressing with his racing and is now qualified for a mark. (op 25-1)
Staffhoss, a brother to 1m4f/13.7f selling winner Always Dixie and half-brother to useful 5f/6f juvenile, later 7f-9.4f AW winner Parkview Love and decent 6f 2yo winner Always Fruitful, was unable to take advantage of his inside draw and was badly baulked early on as well as when making his move up the straight. He should be credited for finishing so close up. (tchd 14-1)
Subtle Difference travelled well enough in behind the pace but found little for pressure and she will find things easier now handicapped. (op 8-1)

Cherry Tiger Official explanation: jockey said colt ran green.
Sweet Force, whose dam was an unraced half-sister to 1m4f AW winner Sweet Origin and Italian 1m1f/1m3f winner Lusorio, was hampered early on from which he was never able to recover. Official explanation: jockey said colt suffered interference after start and ran green. (op 6-1)

7708 SPORTINGLIFE.COM NURSERY 1m (P)
7:25 (7:26) (Class 6) (0-60,60) 2-Y-O £1,617 (£481; £240; £120) Stalls Low

Form / RPR

000 1 **Teolagi (IRE)**[19] 7373 2-9-5 60 ... JamieSpencer 8 65
(J S Moore) *in rr: rdn and hung rt over 2f out: hung lft to wd outside sn after and last: rdn and rapid hdwy over 1f out: styd on u.p and hung rt clsng stagest: led last stride* **4/1**[2]

065 2 nse **Red Eight (USA)**[75] 5797 2-9-5 60 ... AdamKirby 13 65
(John Butler) *led after 1f: rdn 2 l clr jst ins fnl f: ct last stride* **4/1**[2]

6200 3 1 ¾ **Gabrial The Boss (USA)**[18] 7414 2-9-3 58 ... (t) JimCrowley 4 59
(David Simcock) *in tch early: stdd in rr after 2f: gd hdwy on ins over 2f out to chse ldr appr fnl f: one pce into 3rd fnl 120yds* **6/1**[3]

4430 4 1 ¼ **Black Dave (IRE)**[32] 7059 2-9-2 57 ... LukeMorris 5 55
(David Evans) *in rr: rdn 2f out: styd on u.p fnl f to take one pce 4th clsng stages* **7/1**

5060 5 shd **Pairumani Prince (IRE)**[18] 7414 2-9-4 59 ... TomMcLaughlin 9 57
(Ed Dunlop) *in rr: hdwy wl over 1f out: styd on u.p fnl f: nvr gng pce to rch ldrs: hung rt and one pce clsng stages* **12/1**

060 6 1 ½ **Sovereign Power**[53] 6486 2-9-5 60 ... MartinLane 10 54
(Paul Cole) *in rr: rdn appr fnl 2f: kpt on u.p fnl f: nvr rchd ldrs* **33/1**

005 7 2 **Crystal Peaks**[27] 7191 2-9-4 59 ... TomEaves 6 49
(James Given) *chsd ldrs: rdn over 2f out: outpcd over 1f out* **12/1**

000 8 nk **Kastini**[35] 6978 2-9-2 57 ... EddieAhern 11 46
(Denis Coakley) *chsd ldr after 1f: rdn over 2f out: wknd lost 2nd appr fnl f: wknd fnl 120yds* **16/1**

0003 9 1 ¾ **Shearian**[34] 7008 2-8-12 58 ... GeorgeDowning(5) 3 43
(Tony Carroll) *hld up in rr: sme hdwy fr 2f out but nvr gng pce to rch ldrs* **20/1**

006 10 ½ **North Weald (IRE)**[41] 6817 2-9-5 60 ... SebSanders 7 44
(J W Hills) *chsd ldrs: rdn over 2f out: wknd over 1f out* **20/1**

0002 11 1 **Prince Rakan (USA)**[8] 7606 2-9-5 60 ... (b) IanMongan 12 42
(Amy Weaver) *led 1f: styd chsng ldrs: wknd ins fnl 2f* **14/1**

434 12 7 **Ghur (USA)**[30] 7096 2-9-3 58 ... PaulHanagan 1 23
(Mark Johnston) *chsd ldrs: wknd over 2f out: wl btn whn hmpd appr fnl f: eased* **7/2**[1]

1m 40.94s (1.14) **Going Correction** -0.05s/f (Stan) **12 Ran SP% 129.4**
Speed ratings (Par 94): **92,91,90,88,88 87,85,85,83,82 81,74**
Tote Swingers 1&2 £5.60, 2&3 £5.90, 1&3 £8.80 CSF £21.99 CT £103.39 TOTE £8.30: £2.40, £1.80, £4.10; EX 25.70 Trifecta £111.10 Pool: £1,032.96 - 6.97 winning tickets..
Owner Mrs Fitri Hay **Bred** Mrs Fitriani Hay **Trained** Upper Lambourn, Berks
■ Stewards' Enquiry : Jamie Spencer two-day ban: used whip above permitted level (28th-29th Nov).

FOCUS
Plenty of unexposed types in this nursery, run at an honest pace with the winner passing the whole field out wide, to score under an inspired ride. The winner may have more to offer short term with the balance of the third to the sixth setting the level.

NOTEBOOK
Teolagi(IRE), on an evening where runners struggled to come from behind, earns extra credit for this effort on his handicap debut. He was not that well away and looked unbalanced out wide when coming round the home bend but came with a strong late run to get up on the post. He can progress from this and holds an entry early next week, for which he would be of interest, if turned out under a penalty. Official explanation: trainer said regarding apparent improvement in form that colt is a late maturing horse and was suited by the all-weather. (op 9-2 tchd 5-1)
Red Eight(USA) was well supported on his first run for John Butler, running in a handicap for the first time and he made a bold bid from the front but was just caught on the line by a potentially well-handicapped type. (op 5-1 tchd 3-1)
Gabrial The Boss(USA) has proved a shade disappointing this season but ran well enough here wearing a tongue strap for the first time, but looks vulnerable to less exposed types. (op 7-1)
Black Dave(IRE) was doing his best work late on trying this trip for the first time, and this opens up more options for connections. (op 6-1)
Pairumani Prince(IRE) had shown little in four starts over a variety of trips (5f-9f) but was staying on to good effect on his first try over 1m. (op 20-1)
Sovereign Power was near the back 2f out but came with a fine late run on his handicap/AW debut and this was his most promising effort to date.
Ghur(USA), Paul Hanagan's only ride of the meeting, proved disappointing. She was nicely positioned up the rail but found precious little once driven and dropped tamely away as though something was amiss. (op 5-1 tchd 11-2)

7709 SPORTINGLIFE.COM RACING CONDITIONS STKS 7f (P)
7:55 (7:55) (Class 4) 3-Y-O+ £4,075 (£1,212; £606; £303) Stalls Low

Form / RPR

0041 1 **Belgian Bill**[34] 7010 4-8-11 104 ... (t) JimCrowley 4 103
(George Baker) *trckd ldr: shkn up to ld 2f out: drvn fnl f and hld on wl clsng stages* **8/11**[1]

3401 2 ½ **Santefisio**[13] 7502 6-8-11 91 ... (b) JoeFanning 5 102
(Keith Dalgleish) *stdd s: hld up in last pl: swtchd rt and gd hdwy over 1f out: styd on u.p to chse wnr ins fnl f but a jst hld* **8/1**[3]

5344 3 nk **Burj Alzain (IRE)**[34] 7010 4-8-11 98 ... (tp) JamieSpencer 1 101
(Gerard Butler) *trckd ldrs in 3rd: drvn to dispute 2nd jst ins fnl f: nvr quite gng pce to get to wnr and dropped to 3rd clsng stages* **7/2**[2]

4000 4 3 ½ **Global City (IRE)**[108] 4629 6-8-11 106 ... (t) SilvestreDeSousa 3 92
(Saeed Bin Suroor) *plld hrd and chsd ldrs in cl 4th: wnt 3rd over 2f out and sn rdn: wknd over 1f out* **8/1**[3]

35 5 hd **Swiss Cross**[13] 7503 5-8-11 91 ... (t) LukeMorris 2 91
(Phil McEntee) *rn wout declared tongue-tie: sn led: hdd 2f out: rdn over 1f out: wknd ins fnl f* **16/1**

1m 25.71s (-0.29) **Going Correction** -0.05s/f (Stan)
WFA 3 from 4yo+ 1lb **5 Ran SP% 108.2**
Speed ratings (Par 105): **99,98,98,94,93**
Tote Swinger 1&4 £8.10 CSF £6.89 TOTE £1.50: £1.10, £2.10; EX 6.00.
Owner PJL, Cooper & Baker **Bred** Wickfield Stud And Hartshill Stud **Trained** Manton, Wilts

FOCUS
A decent contest, run at a steady pace with the winner perfectly positioned throughout. The winner was fully entitled to win on these terms and the runner-up earns credit.
T/Jkpt: Not won. T/Plt: £87.40 to a £1 stake. Pool: £58,552.52 - 488.50 winning tickets. T/Qpdt: £5.90 to a £1 stake. Pool: £8,491.01 - 1053.32 winning tickets. ST

[7605]SOUTHWELL (L-H)
Wednesday, November 14

OFFICIAL GOING: Standard

Wind: Virtually nil Weather: Overcast

7710 32REDPOKER.COM H'CAP (DIV I) 1m 6f (F)
12:20 (12:20) (Class 6) (0-60,63) 3-Y-0+ £1,704 (£503; £251) Stalls Low

Form RPR

500 **1** **Neighbourhood (USA)**[20] 7352 4-9-0 **45**........................ ChrisCatlin 3 51
(James Evans) *hld up in tch: hdwy 4f out: trckd ldrs 3f out: rdn to ld wl over 1f out: drvn out* **25/1**

0030 **2** ¾ **Inside Knowledge (USA)**[14] 7490 6-9-4 **49**..............(b[1]) LukeMorris 7 54
(Garry Woodward) *led: rdn along 3f out: hdd wl over 1f out: drvn and kpt on fnl f* **14/1**

0003 **3** ¾ **Dancing Paddy (IRE)**[16] 7443 4-8-9 **45**.................. GarryWhillans(5) 6 49
(Alan Swinbank) *trckd ldng pair: hdwy and cl up 1/2-way: rdn along over 2f out: sn ev ch: drvn and one pce fnl f* **12/1**

4261 **4** 2¼ **Irish Jugger (USA)**[8] 7610 5-9-13 **63** 6ex.............. CharlesBishop(5) 2 64
(Michael Appleby) *trckd ldr on inner: effrt over 3f out: rdn along over 2f out: btn over 1f out* **10/11**[1]

055 **5** 3¼ **Superstiction**[13] 7499 3-8-11 **50**................................ FrannyNorton 4 47
(James Fanshawe) *hld up in rr: hdwy over 4f out: chsd ldrs 3f out: rdn along over 2f out: swtchd rt to outer over 1f out: no imp* **4/1**[2]

6 6 **War (IRE)**[16] 4273 6-9-2 **47**...(bt) ShaneKelly 8 36
(J A Nash, Ire) *trckd ldrs: hdwy over 4f out: rdn along 3f out: sn carried hd high and wknd* **7/1**[3]

000- **7** 7 **I'Lldoit**[513] 3235 5-9-5 **50**...(p) TedDurcan 1 30
(Michael Scudamore) *trckd ldrs: rdn along over 4f out: sn wknd* **9/1**

4000 **8** 2¼ **Magnitude**[52] 4189 7-9-0 **45**...(b) WilliamCarson 5 22
(Brian Baugh) *dwlt and sn rdn along in rr: hdwy and in tch after 5f: rdn along over 4f out: chsd ldrs 3f out: sn wknd* **40/1**

3m 8.65s (0.35) **Going Correction** -0.275s/f (Stan)
WFA 3 from 4yo+ 8lb **8** Ran SP% **115.5**
Speed ratings (Par 101): **88,87,87,85,84 80,76,75**
Tote Swingers 1&2 £13.90, 2&3 £11.60, 1&3 £23.10 CSF £324.13 CT £4360.66 TOTE £33.00: £7.10, £4.50, £2.20; EX 212.10 TRIFECTA Not won..
Owner James Evans Racing **Bred** Mr & Mrs Gary Middlebrook **Trained** Broadwas, Worcs

FOCUS
A moderate staying handicap and a result that would have left many punters scratching their heads. The pace was ordinary. Unconvincing form, rated a shade negatively.
Neighbourhood(USA) Official explanation: trainer said regarding apparent improvement in form that gelding benefited from a step up in trip.
Irish Jugger(USA) Official explanation: vet said gelding finished lame.

7711 32REDBET.COM MAIDEN AUCTION STKS 5f (F)
12:50 (12:52) (Class 6) 2-Y-O £1,704 (£503; £251) Stalls High

Form RPR

3 **1** **Small Fury (IRE)**[59] 6276 2-8-6 0................................ FrannyNorton 3 58
(Jo Hughes) *dwlt: sn in tch: hdwy over 2f out: cl up over 1f out: rdn to ld ins fnl f: edgd rt and styd on* **9/2**[3]

6026 **2** 1¼ **Pearl Noir**[15] 7462 2-8-13 65.. LukeMorris 4 61
(Scott Dixon) *a.p: rdn over 1f out: drvn and kpt on same pce fnl f* **15/8**[1]

0300 **3** nse **Only For You**[19] 7379 2-8-3 50 ow2............................ RaulDaSilva(3) 2 51
(Alan Brown) *cl up: rdn to ld over 1f out: drvn and hdd ins fnl f: kpt on same pce* **28/1**

406 **4** hd **Faffa**[15] 7450 2-8-13 52...(b[1]) TedDurcan 1 60
(Tim Easterby) *dwlt and in rr: hdwy on wd outside over 2f out: sn rdn and styd on appr fnl f: nrst fin* **6/1**

0056 **5** 2½ **Proventi**[6] 7649 2-8-4 52..(v) NoraLooby(7) 8 49
(Alan McCabe) *led: rdn along over 2f out: drvn and hdd over 1f out: wknd ent fnl f* **33/1**

6 hd **Tartan Blue** 2-8-1 0.. HannahNunn(7) 5 45
(Robert Cowell) *chsd ldrs: rdn 2f out: edgd lft and wknd over 1f out* **20/1**

404 **7** nse **Robyn**[8] 7609 2-8-6 0.. AdamBeschizza 6 43
(Scott Dixon) *towards rr: sme hdwy 2f out: sn rdn and n.d* **7/2**[2]

0 **8** 1 **Secret Empress**[142] 3436 2-8-6 0.. JimmyQuinn 9 39
(Bryan Smart) *a towards rr* **7/1**

50 **9** ¾ **Red Diesel (IRE)**[24] 7272 2-8-4 0.......................... JemmaMarshall(5) 10 39
(Jo Hughes) *a in rr* **66/1**

59.46s (-0.24) **Going Correction** -0.275s/f (Stan) **9** Ran SP% **114.6**
Speed ratings (Par 94): **94,92,91,91,87 87,87,85,84**
Tote Swingers 1&2 £2.30, 2&3 £12.50, 1&3 £8.80 CSF £12.80 TOTE £4.30: £1.50, £2.10, £5.60; EX 11.40 Trifecta £149.60 Pool: £690.53 - 3.46 winning tickets..
Owner Joseph Hearne, D Bird, H Downs, J Hughes **Bred** Tally-Ho Stud **Trained** Lambourn, Berks
■ Stewards' Enquiry : Raul Da Silva three-day ban; weighted in 2lb over (28th-30th Nov).

FOCUS
A weak juvenile maiden auction dominated by those that raced up the centre, with the first four home starting from the four lowest stalls. The form makes sense.

NOTEBOOK
Small Fury(IRE) had shown plenty of promise when third on firm ground on her Bath debut in September, but was on a very different surface here. She didn't break from the stalls at all well, but despite that she was still able to run down her rivals and hit the front well inside the last. This wasn't much of a race, but she is entitled to improve again. (op 10-3)
Pearl Noir, second three times from seven previous starts on turf/Polytrack, had every chance and plugged on, but he was 6lb well-in with the third and beat her a nose, so probably didn't run up to his mark. (op 2-1 tchd 7-4)
Only For You, rated 50 and winless after ten previous attempts including in selling company, had every chance when hitting the front over a furlong out, but proved no match for the winner. This was her best effort yet, but her proximity does little for the form. Her rider was found to have weighed in 2lb heavy.
Faffa, rated 52 after finishing unplaced in three turf maidens, was tried in blinkers and stayed on towards the far side of the track to finish alongside the placed horses. She may be worth a try in a nursery. (op 11-1 tchd 12-1)
Proventi made most of the running until swamped over a furlong out and is yet to make the frame in nine attempts. (op 20-1)

7712 32RED MAIDEN STKS 1m (F)
1:20 (1:20) (Class 5) 3-Y-0+ £2,385 (£704; £352) Stalls Low

Form RPR

3-22 **1** **Snooky**[16] 7445 3-9-3 70... TonyHamilton 5 70
(Richard Fahey) *towards rr: hdwy and in tch over 4f out: chsd ldrs 3f out: cl up over 2f out: rdn to ld over 1f out: kpt on* **5/4**[1]

4040 **2** 2 **Frederickthegreat**[16] 7443 3-9-3 59.............................(b[1]) GrahamLee 7 65
(David O'Meara) *trckd ldrs: smooth hdwy 3f out: led over 2f out: sn rdn and hdd over 1f out: drvn and one pce fnl f* **10/1**[3]

3200 **3** ¾ **Dewala**[30] 7117 3-8-12 52... AndrewMullen 2 59
(Michael Appleby) *cl up: led after 1f: rdn along 3f out: hdd over 2f out: drvn wl over 1f out: kpt on fnl f* **20/1**

0026 **4** shd **Sehnsucht (IRE)**[8] 7607 3-9-3 70...................................(be) ShaneKelly 6 63
(Alan McCabe) *led 1f: trckd ldr: hdwy and cl up 3f out: rdn and ev ch 2f out: sn hung lft: drvn and one pce appr fnl f* **6/4**[2]

3260 **5** 10 **Frosty Friday**[15] 7469 4-9-0 60.................................. FrederikTylicki 4 35
(J R Jenkins) *chsd ldrs: rdn along 2f out: sn one pce* **10/1**[3]

0 **6** 5 **Major Buckley (IRE)**[20] 7361 3-9-3 0........................... RobertWinston 9 29
(Alan Swinbank) *dwlt and swvd bdly rt s: v green and wl bhd racing wd: sme hdwy over 3f out: nvr a factor* **20/1**

400- **7** 14 **Emley Moor**[407] 6599 3-8-12 46.. KellyHarrison 3
(Chris Fairhurst) *towards rr: outpcd and bhd fr 1/2-way* **66/1**

8 10 **Running On Faith** 4-9-5 0.. LukeMorris 1
(Garry Woodward) *towards rr: outpcd and bhd fr 1/2-way* **66/1**

0000 **9** 7 **Icing Sugar**[56] 6361 4-9-0 35.. PatrickMathers 8
(Mike Sowersby) *chsd ldrs 3f: sn lost pl and bhd fnl 3f* **100/1**

1m 40.7s (-3.00) **Going Correction** -0.275s/f (Stan)
WFA 3 from 4yo 2lb **9** Ran SP% **116.1**
Speed ratings (Par 103): **104,102,101,101,91 86,72,62,55**
Tote Swingers 1&2 £2.40, 2&3 £8.00, 1&3 £5.20 CSF £14.02 TOTE £1.80: £1.10, £2.00, £4.90; EX 10.60 Trifecta £130.80 Pool: £668.08 - 3.83 winning tickets..
Owner Mrs Janis Macpherson **Bred** Dunchurch Lodge Stud Co **Trained** Musley Bank, N Yorks
■ Stewards' Enquiry : Andrew Mullen two-day ban; used whip above permitted level 28th-29th Nov).

FOCUS
A modest maiden in which the front four pulled well clear of the rest. Straightforward form.
Major Buckley(IRE) Official explanation: jokey said gelding hung badly right

7713 32RED.COM NURSERY 6f (F)
1:50 (1:51) (Class 5) (0-70,70) 2-Y-O £2,385 (£704; £352) Stalls Low

Form RPR

000 **1** **Seemenomore**[68] 5992 2-8-4 **53**.......................................(v[1]) MartinLane 8 73
(Michael Bell) *awkward s and in rr: rapid hdwy to ld after 1 1/2f: rdn 2f out and sn qcknd clr: easily* **10/1**

1443 **2** 9 **Ayasha**[15] 7463 2-9-2 **65**.. GrahamLee 4 58
(Bryan Smart) *trckd ldrs: hdwy 3f out: rdn 2f out: sn drvn and kpt on same pce* **9/2**[3]

603 **3** hd **Betzyoucan**[16] 7434 2-9-3 **66**.. JoeFanning 6 58
(Mark Johnston) *led 1 1/2f: chsd wnr: rdn along 2f out: sn drvn and one pce* **9/2**[3]

6034 **4** ¾ **Frans Hals**[12] 7526 2-8-4 **53**..(be) ChrisCatlin 3 43
(Dominic Ffrench Davis) *towards rr early: hdwy on wd outside 1/2-way: rdn along over 2f out: kpt on same pce* **12/1**

533 **5** nk **Carina Palace**[47] 6645 2-9-4 **67**...................................... MartinDwyer 7 56
(Jamie Osborne) *outpcd and in rr 1/2-way: rdn along and hdwy on inner over 2f out: kpt on fnl f: nrst fin* **4/1**[2]

6533 **6** 1¼ **Windforpower (IRE)**[39] 6890 2-9-7 **70**.........................(p) LukeMorris 1 56
(Ronald Harris) *in tch: hdwy to chse ldrs 1/2-way: rdn along over 2f out: sn wknd* **17/2**

0020 **7** nk **Bougaloo**[16] 7432 2-9-7 **70**...(v) ShaneKelly 5 55
(Alan McCabe) *chsd ldrs: rdn along 1/2-way: sn wknd* **20/1**

000 **8** 3¼ **Bronte Belle**[147] 3286 2-8-1 **50**.................................. AndrewMullen 9 25
(Jedd O'Keeffe) *prom: rdn along over 3f out: sn lost pl and bhd* **25/1**

4532 **9** 1¾ **Eastern Dragon (IRE)**[14] 7476 2-9-1 **64**......................(v) TedDurcan 2 34
(Michael Scudamore) *in rr: rdn along 3f out: sme hdwy 2f out: sn wknd* **7/2**[1]

1m 15.19s (-1.31) **Going Correction** -0.275s/f (Stan) **9** Ran SP% **114.5**
Speed ratings (Par 96): **97,85,84,83,83 81,81,76,74**
Tote Swingers 1&2 £21.10, 2&3 £3.70, 1&3 £7.90 CSF £54.10 CT £234.65 TOTE £10.90: £3.90, £2.50, £2.10; EX 67.70 Trifecta £269.40 Pool: £869.48 - 2.42 winning tickets..
Owner K J P Gundlach **Bred** A S Reid **Trained** Newmarket, Suffolk

FOCUS
A modest nursery which was completely torn apart by the winner. The relevance of the form is questionable, but could possibly be worth 3lb better.

NOTEBOOK
Seemenomore, well beaten in three turf maidens, was making his nursery/AW debuts in a first-time visor, but didn't go off unbacked. Slow to stride, he didn't look all that keen to race in the early stages and had managed to get pretty warm, but he carted himself to the front over half a mile from home. However, instead of going off too quick and falling in a heap, he just kept on pulling further and further clear and ended up winning by a street. He holds an entry back here next Tuesday and will probably have to take up that engagement as the handicapper won't be merciful, but a lot depends on the headgear working again. The Stewards held an enquiry to consider the apparent improvement in form; the trainer's representative stated that the gelding appeared to appreciate both his first-time visor and first run on Fibresand. Official explanation: trainer's representative said regarding apparent improvement in form that the gelding appeared to appreciate both his first-time visor and first run on fibresand. (op 16-1)
Ayasha, down another 2lb on this switch to Fibresand, kept plugging on to win the separate race for second and can be counted unlucky to have bumped into one. She should be able to win a similar event around here. (op 4-1 tchd 5-1)
Betzyoucan, making her nursery debut having shown her first sign of ability in the last of her three starts in turf maidens, was happy to get a lead from the winner after making the early running, but like all the others she was totally outclassed by him. There should be another day for her. (op 4-1 tchd 5-1)
Frans Hals, back up to 6f off a 4lb lower mark, was taken very wide and never managed to land a blow. (tchd 14-1)
Eastern Dragon(IRE) has been running well in defeat in Polytrack nurseries lately, but never got into the race at all this time and the different surface would be the obvious excuse. (tchd 10-3)

7714 £32 BONUS AT 32RED.COM (S) STKS 1m (F)
2:20 (2:20) (Class 6) 2-Y-O £1,704 (£503; £251) Stalls Low

Form RPR

0416 **1** **Divine Angel (IRE)**[21] 7335 2-8-12 66.................................. LukeMorris 4 59
(Phil McEntee) *mde most: jnd and rdn wl over 1f out: drvn ent fnl f: kpt on wl* **5/2**[2]

0036 **2** 2 **Holding Fast (IRE)**[97] 5009 2-8-11 50...................... RobertWinston 5 53
(Tobias B P Coles) *dwlt: t.k.h and trckd ldrs: smooth hdwy over 2f out: chal wl over 1f out: rdn and ev ch ent fnl f: sn drvn and one pce* **16/1**

0060 **3** 4½ **Cerys**[47] 6645 2-8-6 0...(p) WilliamCarson 6 38
(Derek Haydn Jones) *in tch: rdn along wl over 2f out: kpt on appr fnl f:* **50/1**

4501 **4** ¾ **Rakticate (IRE)**[14] 7491 2-8-12 60 AndreaAtzeni 2 42+
(J S Moore) *s.i.s and bhd: rdn along bef 1/2-way: kpt on u.p fnl 2f: nrst fin* **7/4**[1]

6400 **5** 3 ¼ **Roland**[6] 7641 2-8-4 47 (p) PaulMcGiff(7) 1 34
(Kevin Ryan) *cl up on inner: rdn along wl over 2f out: drvn and hung bdly rt to stands' rail over 1f out and sn wknd* **6/1**[3]

000 **6** 2 **Portside Blue**[75] 5797 2-8-11 51 (p) BarryMcHugh 7 29
(Tony Coyle) *cl up: rdn along wl over 2f out: sn wknd* **6/1**[3]

30 **7** 57 **Didnt I Do Well**[34] 7008 2-8-11 0 (p[1]) AdamBeschizza 3
(Julia Feilden) *in tch: rdn along and outpcd after 2f: sn bhd* **12/1**

1m 42.39s (-1.31) **Going Correction** -0.275s/f (Stan) **7** Ran SP% **109.0**
Speed ratings (Par 94): **95,93,88,87,84 82,25**
Tote Swingers 1&2 £3.80, 2&3 £11.60, 1&3 £7.20 CSF £35.78 TOTE £2.80: £1.40, £8.90; EX 46.10.There was no bid for the winner and there were no claims.
Owner Steve Jakes **Bred** Yeomanstown Stud **Trained** Newmarket, Suffolk

FOCUS
A moderate seller. The winner had the run of things, and didn't need to hit his maiden form to win.

NOTEBOOK
Divine Angel(IRE), who failed to see out the extra furlong in a Newmarket nursery last time after winning a Windsor maiden over this trip, was the one to beat on these terms dropped into a seller. Always up there, once she had seen off the wayward Roland after disputing the advantage with him for much of the way, she then found plenty to hold off her only remaining danger. She did little more than she was entitled to at the weights, but seemed to take to the surface well enough. (tchd 9-4 and 11-4)
Holding Fast(IRE), dropped into a seller and gelded since last seen three months earlier, travelled well behind the leaders and looked a possible danger passing the 2f pole, but the filly held too many guns for him. He would have been 15lb better off with her in a handicap, so this wasn't a bad effort in the context of the race. (tchd 14-1 and 18-1)
Cerys had shown nothing in four starts in maidens and achieved little in running on into a remote third here. (op 66-1)
Rakticate(IRE) was backed to win a Nottingham seller a fortnight ago and duly bolted up, but on this occasion she blew the start after rearing as the stalls opened and her efforts to get into the race came to nothing. Official explanation: jockey said filly was slowly away. (tchd 15-8)

7715 32RED CASINO H'CAP — 1m (F)
2:50 (2:51) (Class 4) (0-85,85) 3-Y-0+ **£4,204** (£1,251; £625; £312) **Stalls** Low

Form RPR
4311 **1** **Desert Creek (IRE)**[4] 7684 6-8-3 74 ShirleyTeasdale(7) 14 86
(David Nicholls) *trckd ldrs: smooth hdwy 3f out: chal wl over 1f out: rdn to ld appr fnl f: kpt on* **7/2**[1]

1254 **2** ¾ **Jack Of Diamonds (IRE)**[53] 6488 3-8-13 79 RobertWinston 9 89
(Roger Teal) *hld up: hdwy 1/2-way: chsd ldrs wl over 2f out: rdn and ev ch over 1f out: drvn and kpt on fnl f* **15/2**

2130 **3** ½ **Dubawi Island (FR)**[37] 6921 3-9-5 85 (v[1]) MartinDwyer 11 94
(James Tate) *led: rdn over 2f out: hung bdly lft to stands' rails over 1f out: hdd appr fnl f: sn drvn and one pce* **4/1**[2]

1320 **4** 2 ¾ **Dolphin Rock**[31] 7083 5-8-10 74 DaleSwift 4 77
(Brian Ellison) *chsd ldrs: rdn along wl over 2f out: drvn and one pce fr over 1f out* **14/1**

3200 **5** ½ **Kung Hei Fat Choy (USA)**[15] 7461 3-8-11 77 (b) GrahamLee 6 78
(James Given) *midfield: hdwy 3f out: rdn to chse ldrs 2f out: sn drvn and no imp appr fnl f* **7/1**[3]

2625 **6** 2 ¾ **Follow The Flag (IRE)**[7] 7640 8-8-13 77 (be) ShaneKelly 1 72
(Alan McCabe) *towards rr and sn swtchd rt to r wd: rdn along 3f out: styd on fnl 2f: nrst fin* **33/1**

0050 **7** 1 ¼ **Mingun Bell (USA)**[37] 6931 5-9-7 85 ChrisCatlin 2 77
(Ed de Giles) *chsd ldrs: rdn along wl over 2f out: sn wknd* **17/2**

124/ **8** 2 **Diamond Penny (IRE)**[788] 6174 4-9-2 80 WilliamCarson 13 68
(Seamus Durack) *stdd s and hld up: sn outpcd and bhd tl sme hdwy on inner fnl 2f: nvr nr ldrs* **40/1**

000 **9** 2 ¼ **Dunn'o (IRE)**[53] 6471 7-9-5 83 (t) AndrewMullen 12 65
(David Nicholls) *a towards rr* **25/1**

5002 **10** ½ **Beautiful Day**[22] 7317 4-9-1 79 PhillipMakin 3 60
(Kevin Ryan) *chsd ldr: rdn along wl over 2f out: sn drvn and wknd* **17/2**

1000 **11** shd **Toymaker**[19] 7369 5-8-8 72 (p) LukeMorris 8 53
(James Given) *dwlt: racd wd: a in rr* **25/1**

1000 **12** ½ **Dubaianswer**[23] 7294 4-9-7 85 BarryMcHugh 10 65
(Tony Coyle) *a towards rr* **16/1**

0006 **13** 48 **Paramour**[19] 7370 5-8-12 76 TedDurcan 5
(David O'Meara) *in tch on inner: rdn along 1/2-way: sn lost pl and bhd whn eased fnl 2f* **12/1**

1m 40.5s (-3.20) **Going Correction** -0.275s/f (Stan)
WFA 3 from 4yo+ 2lb **13** Ran SP% **120.9**
Speed ratings (Par 105): **105,104,103,101,100 97,96,94,92,91 91,91,43**
Tote Swingers 1&2 £6.50, 2&3 £5.60, 1&3 £3.70 CSF £29.01 CT £112.15 TOTE £4.00: £1.80, £2.90, £1.90; EX 28.30 Trifecta £112.80 Pool: £767.63 - 5.10 winning tickets..
Owner D W Barker & D Nicholls **Bred** Mount Coote Stud And M H Dixon **Trained** Sessay, N Yorks

FOCUS
A decent and competitive handicap, run at a solid pace. The form is rated through the second and third.
Dubawi Island(FR) Official explanation: jockey said gelding hung right.

7716 THANKS TO CAR PARK STAFF @SOUTHWELL-RACECOURSE H'CAP — 6f (F)
3:20 (3:22) (Class 4) (0-85,83) 3-Y-0+ **£4,294** (£1,268; £634) **Stalls** Low

Form RPR
-100 **1** **Outpost (IRE)**[4] 7685 4-9-4 80 FrannyNorton 1 92
(Alan Bailey) *mde all: jnd 2f out and sn rdn: drvn over 1f out: kpt on gamely ins fnl f* **6/1**[3]

-160 **2** shd **Take Cover**[4] 7690 5-9-7 83 WilliamCarson 3 95
(David C Griffiths) *hld up in tch: smooth hdwy to trck ldrs 1/2-way: effrt 2f out: sn chal: rdn over 1f out: drvn ins fnl f and ev ch tl no ex nr fin* **10/3**[1]

2351 **3** 3 ¾ **Waking Warrior**[41] 6811 4-8-9 78 (tp) KevinStott(7) 2 78
(Kevin Ryan) *trckd ldrs on inner: hdwy to chse ldng pair wl over 1f out: sn rdn and no imp fnl f* **11/2**[2]

1001 **4** 2 **Scottish Lake**[14] 7484 4-9-2 78 (b) KirstyMilczarek 8 72
(Olivia Maylam) *prom: chsd wnr 1/2-way: rdn along 2f out: drvn and one pce fr over 1f out* **12/1**

6004 **5** 3 ¾ **Greenhead High**[16] 7446 4-8-0 69 oh2 ShirleyTeasdale(7) 11 52
(David Nicholls) *prom on outer: rdn along 2f out: grad wknd appr fnl f* **25/1**

300 **6** 1 ½ **Mon Brav**[18] 6338 5-8-11 73 GrahamLee 7 52
(Brian Ellison) *hld up towards rr: hdwy 2f out: sn rdn and kpt on fnl f: nvr nr ldrs* **14/1**

0100 **7** ½ **Amenable (IRE)**[23] 7295 5-9-6 82 AndrewMullen 12 59
(David Nicholls) *midfield: hdwy on outer to chse ldrs over 2f out: rdn wl over 1f out and sn btn* **6/1**[3]

0200 **8** 2 ½ **R Woody**[31] 7080 5-9-6 82 FrederikTylicki 4 52
(Robert Cowell) *prom: rdn along wl over 2f out: grad wknd* **9/1**

0321 **9** 2 **Beat The Bell**[15] 7464 7-9-0 76 (p) MartinDwyer 9 40
(Jamie Osborne) *dwlt: a in rr* **9/1**

0046 **10** nk **Rafaaf (IRE)**[30] 7113 4-8-12 74 TedDurcan 5 37
(Richard Phillips) *sn outpcd and a in rr* **16/1**

0000 **11** ½ **Sir Geoffrey (IRE)**[23] 7295 6-9-1 77 RobertWinston 10 38
(Scott Dixon) *a towards rr* **33/1**

1m 13.59s (-2.91) **Going Correction** -0.275s/f (Stan) **11** Ran SP% **114.1**
Speed ratings (Par 105): **108,107,102,100,95 93,92,89,86,86 85**
Tote Swingers 1&2 £4.40, 2&3 £3.40, 1&3 £5.50 CSF £25.39 CT £108.20 TOTE £7.90: £2.70, £1.10, £2.70; EX 26.50 Trifecta £73.10 Pool: £962.03 - 9.87 winning tickets..
Owner Rathordan Partnership **Bred** Martin Dunne **Trained** Newmarket, Suffolk

FOCUS
A decent sprint handicap run in a fair time, with a cracking finish. The winner has a good record on this surface.

7717 32REDPOKER.COM H'CAP (DIV II) — 1m 6f (F)
3:50 (3:50) (Class 6) (0-60,58) 3-Y-0+ **£1,704** (£503; £251) **Stalls** Low

Form RPR
0601 **1** **Italian Riviera**[7] 7629 3-9-3 57 6ex LukeMorris 3 67+
(Sir Mark Prescott Bt) *led 2f: trckd ldr tl led again over 4f out: rdn and jnd over 2f out: drvn over 1f out: kpt on wl towards fin* **4/9**[1]

006 **2** 1 ¼ **Caunay**[33] 7016 5-9-9 58 (tp) AmyBaker(3) 5 65
(Neil Mulholland) *trckd ldrs: hdwy over 3f out: rdn to chse wnr over 2f out: sn drvn to chal and ev ch tl no ex wl ins fnl f* **14/1**

4000 **3** 10 **Nesnaas (USA)**[5] 7255 11-8-13 45 (tp) FrankieMcDonald 2 39
(Alastair Lidderdale) *trckd ldrs: hdwy 4f out: rdn along 3f out: sn drvn and plugged on one pce fnl 2f* **25/1**

0000 **4** 1 **Dunaskin (IRE)**[14] 7490 12-8-8 45 (b) JasonHart(5) 4 38
(Richard Guest) *dwlt: hdwy to ld after 2f: rdn along and hdd over 4f out: drvn and plugged on same pce fnl 3f* **14/1**

0043 **5** 5 **Darsan (IRE)**[15] 7472 4-9-7 53 ChrisCatlin 8 39
(Phil McEntee) *trckd ldng pair: effrt 4f out: rdn along 3f out and sn wknd* **6/1**[2]

6-02 **6** 1 ¼ **Sea Cliff (IRE)**[25] 7248 8-8-9 48 PaulMcGiff(7) 6 33
(Andrew Crook) *sn outpcd and bhd: rdn along and wd st: sme hdwy fnl 2f: nvr a factor* **8/1**[3]

0000 **7** 18 **Tanjung Agas (IRE)**[38] 5811 4-8-8 45 (b) LeonnaMayor(5) 1 6
(Christopher Kellett) *sn outpcd and bhd: t.o fr 1/2-way* **50/1**

0405 **8** 23 **Shakespeare Dancer**[92] 5198 3-7-12 45 HannahNunn(7) 9
(James Evans) *a towards rr: outpcd and bhd fr 1/2-way: t.o fnl 4f* **16/1**

-004 **U** **Sing Alana Sing**[258] 741 4-8-6 45 (t) JakePayne(7) 7
(Bill Turner) *chsd ldrs whn stmbld and uns rdr after 2f* **20/1**

3m 6.08s (-2.22) **Going Correction** -0.275s/f (Stan)
WFA 3 from 4yo+ 8lb **9** Ran SP% **124.4**
Speed ratings (Par 101): **95,94,88,88,85 84,74,61,**
Tote Swingers 1&2 £4.00, 2&3 £17.00, 1&3 £7.30 CSF £9.93 CT £97.41 TOTE £1.70: £1.30, £3.20, £5.80; EX 12.10 Trifecta £180.10 Pool: £1,095.35 - 4.56 winning tickets..
Owner J L C Pearce **Bred** J L C Pearce **Trained** Newmarket, Suffolk

FOCUS
The winning time was 2.57 seconds faster than the first division and the front pair pulled clear. The winner is almost sure to do better again and the runner-up is key to the form.
Sing Alana Sing Official explanation: three-day ban; careless riding (28th-30th Nov).
T/Plt: £723.70 to a £1 stake. Pool: £50,067.08 - 50.50 winning tickets. T/Qpdt: £20.40 to a £1 stake. Pool: £7,107.38 - 256.73 winning tickets. JR

7702 KEMPTON (A.W) (R-H)
Thursday, November 15

OFFICIAL GOING: Standard
Wind: Almost nil Weather: Overcast

7718 THANKS JAMES AND GOOD LUCK CLAIMING STKS — 1m 4f (P)
4:25 (4:26) (Class 6) 3-Y-0 **£1,617** (£481; £240; £120) **Stalls** Centre

Form RPR
5541 **1** **Ty Gwr**[26] 7249 3-8-12 70 MartinLane 3 71+
(David Simcock) *stdd s: t.k.h: hld up in last: smooth prog over 2f out: rdn to ld 1f out: drvn clr* **7/4**[1]

1303 **2** 3 ¼ **Lady Romanza (IRE)**[14] 7499 3-8-4 57 (p) KirstyMilczarek 7 58
(Brendan Powell) *led: rdn over 2f out: hdd 1f out: no ch w wnr after: clung on for 2nd* **9/1**

441 **3** shd **Uncle Roger (IRE)**[15] 7479 3-8-10 57 (v) WilliamBuick 4 64
(Eve Johnson Houghton) *chsd ldr to over 4f out: styd handy: rdn over 2f out: kpt on to press for 2nd fnl f* **7/1**

-500 **4** 2 ½ **Sunny Bank**[15] 7490 3-8-8 55 (t) DavidProbert 2 58
(Andrew Balding) *chsd ldrs: pushed along over 4f out: nt qckn u.p over 2f out: plugged on* **20/1**

2131 **5** nk **Norfolk Sky**[14] 7499 3-8-7 61 FergusSweeney 5 57
(Laura Mongan) *wl in tch: chsd ldr over 4f out: rdn wl over 2f out: lost 2nd and wknd over 1f out* **11/4**[2]

0242 **6** 30 **Mohair**[35] 7011 3-8-9 67 JimCrowley 6 14
(Luke Dace) *hld up in 5th: brief effrt over 3f out: wknd rapidly wl over 2f out: eased and t.o* **4/1**[3]

2m 33.64s (-0.86) **Going Correction** -0.075s/f (Stan) **6** Ran SP% **110.3**
Speed ratings (Par 98): **99,96,96,95,94 74**
toteswingers: 1&2 £3.80, 1&3 £2.40, 2&3 £4.30. CSF £17.31 TOTE £4.70: £2.00, £3.60; EX 23.30.Ty Gwr was claimed by C E Weare for £10,000.
Owner Mrs Ann Simcock **Bred** Mrs A E Simcock **Trained** Newmarket, Suffolk

FOCUS
Straightforward claiming form.

7719 32REDPOKER.COM MEDIAN AUCTION MAIDEN STKS — 7f (P)
4:55 (4:57) (Class 6) 3-5-Y-0 **£1,617** (£481; £240; £120) **Stalls** Low

Form RPR
- **1** **Dance Express (IRE)** 3-8-12 0 WilliamBuick 4 79+
(Clive Cox) *dwlt: settled in last: prog wl over 2f out: pushed along and clsd rapidly over 1f out: led ins fnl f: jst nudged along and in command after* **10/1**[3]

-222 **2** 1 ¼ **Kalokagathia (IRE)**[15] 7477 3-9-3 74 FergusSweeney 5 78
(Jo Crowley) *cl up: trckd ldr 4f out: led 2f out gng strly: styd on but hdd and readily hld ins fnl f* **4/7**[1]

0560 **3** *5* **Homeboy (IRE)**[5] 7684 4-8-13 64 KatiaScallan(5) 7 64
(Marcus Tregoning) *t.k.h: prog on outer to ld after 2f: hdd 2f out: lost 2nd and wl btn over 1f out* **20/1**

2225 **4** *9* **Gaelic Wizard (IRE)**[9] 7611 4-9-4 69 AdamKirby 2 40
(Dominic Ffrench Davis) *led 2f: lost 2nd after 3f: sn struggling* **5/1**[2]

02 **5** *1* **Gaelic Ice**[22] 7322 3-8-12 0 DavidProbert 6 32
(Rod Millman) *a in rr: drvn and struggling wl over 2f out: sn bhd* **10/1**[3]

-03 **6** *4 ½* **Batchworth Firefly**[22] 7322 4-8-13 0 JimCrowley 1 20
(Dean Ivory) *a towards rr: drvn wl over 2f out: sn bhd* **12/1**

1m 24.85s (-1.15) **Going Correction** -0.075s/f (Stan)
WFA 3 from 4yo 1lb **6 Ran SP% 111.0**
Speed ratings (Par 101): **103,101,95,85,84 79**
toteswingers: 1&2 £2.60, 1&3 £11.10, 2&3 £3.20. CSF £16.06 TOTE £5.40: £2.30, £1.10; EX 18.50.
Owner Mrs T L Cox **Bred** P McCartan & Paddy Twomey **Trained** Lambourn, Berks

FOCUS
Straightforward maiden form and a respectable winning time.

7720 32RED CASINO BRITISH STALLION STUDS EBF MAIDEN FILLIES' STKS (DIV I) 1m (P)
5:25 (5:27) (Class 5) 2-Y-O **£3,169** (£943; £471; £235) **Stalls** Low

Form RPR

1 **Al Jamal** 2-9-0 0 TedDurcan 9 75+
(Saeed Bin Suroor) *wl plcd: shkn up and prog over 1f out: led 150yds out: r.o wl: decisively* **9/2**[2]

2 *1 ½* **Auld Alliance (IRE)** 2-9-0 0 ShaneKelly 10 72+
(Sir Michael Stoute) *hld up in rr: gd prog on inner over 2f out: rdn and styd on to take 2nd ins fnl f: no ch w wnr* **14/1**

5 **3** *hd* **Absolutely Right (IRE)**[19] 7403 2-9-0 0 KieranO'Neill 8 71
(Richard Hannon) *prom: shkn up 3f out: rdn and styd on fr over 1f out to press for 2nd nr fin* **9/2**[2]

46 **4** *1 ¼* **Chittenden (USA)**[52] 6534 2-9-0 0 EddieAhern 4 68
(Mahmood Al Zarooni) *chsd ldrs: pushed along over 2f out: nt qckn over 1f out: styd on ins fnl f* **9/1**

2006 **5** *hd* **This Is Nice (IRE)**[15] 7478 2-9-0 71 (v) HayleyTurner 2 68
(Tom Dascombe) *led: kicked on over 2f out: hdd and no ex last 150yds* **9/1**

6 *shd* **Everlasting Light** 2-9-0 0 AdamKirby 6 68+
(Luca Cumani) *hld up but sn in midfield: shkn up 2f out: styd on steadily fr over 1f out: nrst fin* **33/1**

7 *½* **India's Song** 2-9-0 0 MartinLane 3 67+
(David Simcock) *in tch in midfield: shkn up over 2f out: effrt on inner whn n.m.r over 1f out: kpt on fnl 150yds* **33/1**

8 *¾* **Ingot Of Gold** 2-9-0 0 JimCrowley 13 65
(Ralph Beckett) *chsd ldr: rdn and no imp 2f out: lost 2nd and fdd 1f out* **6/1**[3]

24 **9** *4* **Thakana**[14] 7506 2-9-0 0 PaulHanagan 11 56
(Marcus Tregoning) *s.i.s: t.k.h and hld up in rr: shkn up and hanging over 2f out: no prog and wl btn over 1f out* **7/2**[1]

10 *5* **Point Of Control** 2-9-0 0 JamieSpencer 1 44
(Michael Bell) *s.i.s: a in rr: shkn up over 3f out and no real prog* **14/1**

0 **11** *2 ¾* **Veronica's Pursuit**[20] 7372 2-9-0 0 FergusSweeney 5 38
(Peter Hedger) *s.i.s: a wl in rr: shkn up and no prog over 2f out* **100/1**

04 **12** *2 ½* **Cherry Malotte**[19] 7403 2-9-0 0 WilliamBuick 12 32
(John Gosden) *racd on outer: chsd ldrs: wknd qckly jst over 2f out* **16/1**

1m 40.07s (0.27) **Going Correction** -0.075s/f (Stan) **12 Ran SP% 119.0**
Speed ratings (Par 93): **95,93,93,92,91 91,91,90,86,81 78,76**
toteswingers: 1&2 £17.70, 1&3 £5.40, 2&3 £16.00. CSF £65.54 TOTE £5.40: £1.80, £3.70, £2.40; EX 75.20 Trifecta £203.60 Pool: £3,119.23 - 11.49 winning units..
Owner Godolphin **Bred** Darley **Trained** Newmarket, Suffolk

FOCUS
Probably a fair 2-y-o fillies' maiden.

NOTEBOOK
Al Jamal got her career off to a perfect start and completed the task in ready fashion. Se got a lovely sit through the race and saw it out professionally enough for a newcomer. Half-sister to the juvenile winner over this trip, she looks sure to stay further next year and rates a very useful prospect. (op 13-2 tchd 7-1)
Auld Alliance(IRE) proved very easy to back ahead of this racecourse debut and turned in a promising effort. From a highly successful family her trainer knows all about, she already looks to want a stiffer test, but ought to be hard to stop if turning out again this winter. (op 12-1)
Absolutely Right(IRE) was well backed near the off on this switch to Polytrack and showed her true colours with an improved effort. She can land one of these if kept on the go. (op 7-1)
Chittenden(USA) travelled smoothly on the inside, but lacked a turn of foot when asked for an effort and probably wants a stiffer test. She's now eligible for a mark. (op 8-1)
This Is Nice(IRE) sets the level with a mark of 71, even though she's probably up against it in handicaps off such a rating. (op 7-1)
Everlasting Light ◆ caught the eye staying on under hands-and-heels riding near the finish and posted a pleasing debut display. There's speed on her dam's side, but she looks to have inherited the sire's influence more and clearly stays well. She's one to keep tabs on. (op 25-1)
India's Song, whose dam won over 1m4f, showed ability on the inside down the home straight and ought to improve.
Ingot Of Gold faded after showing up nicely off the home bend. She too ought to come on a deal. (op 9-1 tchd 10-1)
Thakana looked sure to enjoy the extra furlong. Having again dwelt from the gates, she pulled far too hard and had thus run her race before the final furlong. She looks one to be wary of, but nurseries are at least now an option. (op 11-4 tchd 5-2)

7721 32RED CASINO BRITISH STALLION STUDS EBF MAIDEN FILLIES' STKS (DIV II) 1m (P)
5:55 (5:55) (Class 5) 2-Y-O **£3,169** (£943; £471; £235) **Stalls** Low

Form RPR

1 **Ribbons** 2-9-0 0 HayleyTurner 10 74+
(James Fanshawe) *mostly chsd ldr after 1f: pushed along over 2f out: led over 1f out: shkn up and styd on wl* **20/1**

36 **2** *2 ½* **Centred (IRE)**[65] 6117 2-9-0 0 WilliamBuick 4 70+
(Sir Michael Stoute) *prom early but shuffled bk to midfield over 5f out: rdn and prog on inner over 2f out: styd on to take 2nd nr fin: no ch w wnr* **3/1**[2]

00 **3** *½* **Dream About You (IRE)**[12] 7553 2-9-0 0 (p) RobertHavlin 3 67
(Robert Mills) *led 1f: styd prom: chal on inner 2f out: chsd wnr over 1f out: wl hld fnl f: lost 2nd nr fin* **100/1**

0 **4** *nk* **Waverunner**[29] 7159 2-9-0 0 PaulHanagan 2 66
(Mahmood Al Zarooni) *pushed up to ld after 1f: rdn and hdd over 1f out: nt qckn and sn wl hld* **9/2**[3]

5 *2* **Fast Pace** 2-9-0 0 EddieAhern 12 64+
(Amanda Perrett) *prom: shkn up over 2f out: trying to cl whn nt clr run over 1f out: stl ch of a pl whn nt clr run and snatched up ins fnl f: nt rcvr* **33/1**

54 **6** *½* **Rocksilla**[29] 7160 2-9-0 0 SebSanders 7 60
(Chris Wall) *trckd ldrs: prog to dispute 2nd 2f out: fdd over 1f out* **8/1**

7 *¾* **Lunette (IRE)** 2-9-0 0 JimCrowley 8 59
(Ralph Beckett) *hld up in midfield: pushed along in 7th over 2f out and nt on terms w ldrs: no hdwy after* **9/4**[1]

8 *1 ¾* **Gamble** 2-9-0 0 JamieSpencer 1 55+
(Michael Bell) *t.k.h: hld up bhd ldrs: messed abt after 2f and dropped to rr: no prog over 2f out: styd on fnl f* **8/1**

9 *nk* **Easy Life** 2-8-7 0 [1] CharlieBennett(7) 9 54
(Marcus Tregoning) *restrained into last trio sn after s and off the pce: prog whn wd bnd 3f out and lost grnd: nvr on terms after: styd on fnl f: nt disgracd* **66/1**

10 *nse* **Poste Restante** 2-9-0 0 MartinLane 6 54
(David Simcock) *v s.i.s: hld up in rr: last of main gp over 2f out and wl off the pce: pushed along and styd on fnl f* **33/1**

0 **11** *4* **Lady Of Yue**[14] 7505 2-9-0 0 TomMcLaughlin 13 45
(Ed Dunlop) *nvr bttr than midfield: lft bhd fnl 3f* **66/1**

12 *¾* **Ely Valley** 2-9-0 0 WilliamCarson 5 43
(William Muir) *a towards rr: n.d fnl 3f* **66/1**

13 *20* **Sugar Rock** 2-9-0 0 DavidProbert 11
(Andrew Balding) *v s.i.s: plld v hrd and prog on wd outside over 5f out: hanging bdly bnd over 3f out and sn dropped out: t.o* **25/1**

1m 40.14s (0.34) **Going Correction** -0.075s/f (Stan) **13 Ran SP% 116.1**
Speed ratings (Par 93): **95,92,92,91,89 89,88,86,86,86 82,81,61**
toteswingers: 1&2 £9.30, 1&3 £50.80, 2&3 £17.30. CSF £74.58 TOTE £19.80: £5.30, £1.10, £17.30; EX 103.90 TRIFECTA Not won..
Owner Elite Racing Club **Bred** Elite Racing Club **Trained** Newmarket, Suffolk
■ Stewards' Enquiry : William Buick two-day ban: careless riding (Nov 29-30)

FOCUS
The second division of the 2-y-o fillies' maiden. They went a sound pace and the runner-up sets the standard.

NOTEBOOK
Ribbons ◆ was unfancied according to the market, but she raced professionally throughout and ran out a ready debut winner. Her dam, a sister to connections' top miler Soviet Song, also won over this C&D at two and so the surface obviously suits. A step up in trip ought to be within her compass at three and she looks a lovely prospect. (op 16-1)
Centred(IRE) would have gone very close with a more straightforward passage. She was allowed to lose a decent early position and then found all sorts of trouble on the inside when making up ground. This was an opportunity missed. (op 2-1)
Dream About You(IRE) found a decent passage round the inside and showed massively improved form in first-time cheekpieces. She has an engine and now qualifies for nurseries, but this won't have helped her prospective mark.
Waverunner did too much from the front, but this was still a step up on her course debut form over 7f last month. (op 11-2 tchd 7-1)
Fast Pace ◆ was not helped by her wide draw and is better than the bare form as she too met trouble towards the inside late on. She's stoutly bred and looks sure to improve. (op 25-1)
Rocksilla ran close to her previous level and saw out the extra furlong well enough. Nurseries are now an option for her. (tchd 7-1)
Lunette(IRE) attracted strong support for this debut outing, but was done with a furlong out and looked to need it. (op 3-1)
Sugar Rock Official explanation: jockey said filly hung left

7722 32REDBET.COM H'CAP 1m (P)
6:25 (6:30) (Class 5) (0-75,75) 3-Y-O+ **£2,264** (£673; £336; £168) **Stalls** Low

Form RPR

5004 **1** **George Baker (IRE)**[15] 7480 5-9-0 **68** WilliamBuick 1 76
(George Baker) *led 1f: trckd ldrs after: wnt 2nd over 2f out and rdn: clsd to ld last 150yds: styd on* **8/1**

01 **2** *1 ¼* **Diplomatic (IRE)**[15] 7480 7-8-9 **68** HarryPoulton(5) 2 73
(Michael Squance) *hld up in midfield: rdn and prog over 2f out: chsd ldrs over 1f out: styd on to take 2nd last strides* **11/1**

0002 **3** *½* **Sugarformyhoney (IRE)**[13] 7524 3-8-10 **71** (p) CharlesBishop(5) 7 75
(Seamus Durack) *racd freely: led after 1f: kicked on 3f out: looked like holding on over 1f out: hdd 150yds out: wknd nr fin* **8/1**

0630 **4** *shd* **Russian Ice**[12] 7559 4-9-7 **75** (b) JimCrowley 5 79
(Dean Ivory) *hld up in last pair: prog over 2f out: drvn over 1f out: kpt on fnl f: nrly snatched 3rd* **7/1**[3]

2211 **5** *¾* **Lean On Pete (IRE)**[21] 7359 3-9-0 **70** ShaneKelly 8 72+
(Ollie Pears) *stdd s: hld up in last pair: stl there 2f out: swtchd to r in isolation on inner and prog over 1f out: rdn and styd on fnl f: no ch to chal* **2/1**[1]

0046 **6** *½* **Caledonia Prince**[17] 7436 4-8-13 **67** (p) FrannyNorton 4 68
(Jo Hughes) *prom: shkn up and fnd nil over 2f out: one pce and no imp over 1f out* **20/1**

6500 **7** *1* **Junket**[22] 7334 5-9-7 **75** RobertHavlin 11 74+
(Dr Jon Scargill) *dwlt and rousted along early in rr: prog on wd outside over 3f out to chse ldrs over 2f out: no hdwy after: fdd over 1f out* **9/2**[2]

3556 **8** *2* **Mr Knightley (IRE)**[15] 7485 3-8-10 **66** EddieAhern 13 60
(Jim Boyle) *towards rr: rdn and no prog over 2f out: n.d fr over 1f out* **20/1**

-000 **9** *1* **Zebrano**[29] 7163 6-9-7 **75** AdamKirby 14 67
(Natalie Lloyd-Beavis) *hld up initially but prog to chse ldr after 2f: lost 2nd over 2f out: wknd over 1f out* **25/1**

5400 **10** *15* **Big Bay (USA)**[78] 5741 6-8-13 **67** (p) TedDurcan 6 24
(Jane Chapple-Hyam) *in tch tl wknd jst over 2f out: t.o* **14/1**

1m 40.63s (0.83) **Going Correction** -0.075s/f (Stan)
WFA 3 from 4yo+ 2lb **10 Ran SP% 114.6**
Speed ratings (Par 103): **92,90,90,90,89 88,87,85,84,69**
toteswingers: 1&2 £5.50, 1&3 £4.70, 2&3 £6.40. CSF £82.98 CT £645.10 TOTE £6.80: £2.10, £2.10, £2.40; EX 34.80 Trifecta £248.50 Pool: £2,654.66 - 8.01 winning units..
Owner Popbitch Racing Club **Bred** Mull Enterprises Ltd **Trained** Manton, Wilts
■ Amba was withdrawn (14/1, ref to ent stalls). Deduct 5p in the £ under R4.

FOCUS
This moderate handicap was run at a steady early pace and it unsurprisingly paid to race handily.

7723 32RED NURSERY 6f (P)
6:55 (6:55) (Class 4) (0-85,85) 2-Y-O **£3,428** (£1,020; £509; £254) **Stalls** Low

Form RPR

6255 **1** **Tommy's Secret**[40] 6871 2-9-0 **85** IanBurns(7) 7 87
(Jane Chapple-Hyam) *settled in last pair: rdn and prog over 2f out: chsd ldrs u.p over 1f out: styd on to ld last 75yds: jst hld on* **13/2**[3]

0503 **2** *nk* **Gracious George (IRE)**^{15} 7476 2-8-2 **66**.......................... LukeMorris 4 68
(Jimmy Fox) *n.m.r s and racd in last pair: rdn and prog on inner 2f out: styd on to chal last 50yds: jst hld* **7/1**

6153 **3** *½* **Majestic Jess (IRE)**^{33} 7060 2-7-11 **68**........................ JoeyHaynes$^{(7)}$ 3 68
(Luke Dace) *led at brisk pce: rdn over 2f out: edgd lft over 1f out: hdd and no ex last 75yds* **12/1**

3522 **4** *1* **Tarbawi (IRE)**^{8} 7627 2-8-11 **75**....................................(v^{1}) WilliamBuick 5 72
(Saeed Bin Suroor) *trckd ldr: wd bnds 4f out and 3f out: rdn to chal over 1f out: fnd nil and hld ins fnl f* **8/11**^{1}

044 **5** *2¼* **Provencal**^{31} 7110 2-8-3 **67**.. DavidProbert 6 57
(Rod Millman) *chsd ldng pair: rdn over 2f out: sn dropped to last and btn* **20/1**

010 **6** *hd* **Eminently**^{13} 7518 2-8-7 **71**.. KieranO'Neill 1 61
(Richard Hannon) *chsd ldng pair: rdn over 2f out: hanging and nt qckn: lost pl and btn over 1f out* **6/1**^{2}

1m 12.65s (-0.45) **Going Correction** -0.075s/f (Stan) **6** Ran SP% **110.5**
Speed ratings (Par 98): **100,99,98,97,94 94**
toteswingers: 1&2 £3.00, 1&3 £6.70, 2&3 £6.30. CSF £47.00 TOTE £3.80: £1.30, £2.30; EX 51.40.
Owner Mrs Jane Chapple-Hyam **Bred** Henry And Mrs Rosemary Moszkowicz **Trained** Dalham, Suffolk

FOCUS
A modest nursery, run at a solid pace.

NOTEBOOK
Tommy's Secret got up near the finish and landed his first win since taking his maiden at Goodwood in May. He'd been pretty highly tried since then, including when a beaten favourite on soft at Ascot last time, and would have conceded upwards of 10lb here without his rider's claim. That proved crucial as he dug deep near the finish and, while a rise will make things harder for him, it may be another furlong suits now. (op 5-1 tchd 7-1)

Gracious George(IRE) was markedly outpaced early, but the race rather collapsed in front of him a furlong out and he stayed on strongly on the inside, just missing out. He's appreciated the recent switch to this surface and can no doubt pick up a race this winter. (op 11-1)

Majestic Jess(IRE), back down a furlong, deserves credit as he fought to fight off the warm favourite a furlong out and kept on gamely near the finish. (op 10-1)

Tarbawi(IRE) unsurprisingly proved popular reverting to 6f after his near miss at the course eight days earlier and went in a first-time visor. He was produced with every chance, but didnt enjoy getting into a battle with the third and ultimately the run probably came soon enough for him. Official explanation: jockey said gelding hung left (op 10-11)

Provencal was well held on this nursery debut but is still learning his trade. (tchd 16-1)

Eminently was disappointing back down from Listed company. She's bred to act on the AW and may need time to strengthen up. (op 9-2)

7724 32RED.COM NURSERY 7f (P)
7:25 (7:25) (Class 6) (0-65,65) 2-Y-O **£1,617** (£481; £240; £120) **Stalls** Low

Form RPR

0065 **1** **Missing Agent**^{17} 7432 2-8-7 **58**....................................(v) EoinWalsh$^{(7)}$ 11 64
(David Evans) *mde all: sn clr: rdn wl over 1f out: tired fnl f but won unchal* **7/1**^{3}

5005 **2** *1½* **Beau Select (IRE)**^{14} 7501 2-9-5 **63**............................(b^{1}) AndreaAtzeni 8 65+
(Robert Eddery) *bmpd s: hld up in last: gd prog fr 2f out: wnt 2nd jst ins fnl f: clsd on wnr but no ch to chal* **9/2**^{1}

005 **3** *3¾* **Tilstarr (IRE)**^{23} 7312 2-9-4 **62**... AdamKirby 1 55
(Roger Teal) *hld up in midfield: nt clr run briefly over 2f out: rdn and prog over 1f out: styd on to take 3rd last 75yds* **7/1**^{3}

004 **4** *1¾* **Princess Sheila (IRE)**^{25} 7272 2-9-4 **62**............................ LiamKeniry 3 49
(J S Moore) *prom in chsng gp: wnt 2nd bhd clr wnr 2f out: no imp and lost 2nd jst ins fnl f* **6/1**^{2}

605 **5** *nse* **Ishisoba**^{31} 7110 2-9-6 **64**.. MartinHarley 10 51
(Alastair Lidderdale) *t.k.h: hld up in rr: rdn and no prog over 2f out: styd on fr over 1f out: n.d* **14/1**

13 **6** *1¾* **Laughing Rock (IRE)**^{17} 7439 2-9-3 **61**............................ ChrisCatlin 4 43
(Phil McEntee) *t.k.h: prom in chsng gp: rdn over 2f out: fdd fnl f* **6/1**^{2}

4006 **7** *½* **Summer Isles**^{33} 7060 2-9-7 **65**...(t) MartinLane 5 46
(Ed Vaughan) *hld up in rr: shkn up over 2f out: no real prog* **8/1**

0430 **8** *½* **Marguerite St Just**^{17} 7432 2-9-1 **59**................................ SebSanders 2 39
(Olivia Maylam) *hld up in last trio: rdn and no prog whn hmpd over 1f out* **33/1**

0440 **9** *1¼* **Vergality Ridge (IRE)**^{16} 7462 2-9-5 **63**............................ LukeMorris 9 39
(Ronald Harris) *wnt rt s: sn in midfield: rdn 3f out: no prog and wl btn 2f out* **16/1**

0026 **10** *nk* **Age Of Bronze**^{23} 7305 2-9-1 **64**.................... WilliamTwiston-Davies$^{(5)}$ 7 39
(Richard Hannon) *racd on outer in chsng gp: u.p by 1/2-way: wknd over 2f out* **7/1**^{3}

5140 **11** *1¼* **Windsor Rose (IRE)**^{40} 6893 2-9-0 **58**............................ FrannyNorton 6 30
(Mark Brisbourne) *chsd clr wnr to 2f out: wknd qckly* **25/1**

1m 25.75s (-0.25) **Going Correction** -0.075s/f (Stan) **11** Ran SP% **114.7**
Speed ratings (Par 94): **98,96,92,90,89 87,87,86,85,85 83**
toteswingers: 1&2 £5.70, 1&3 £8.30, 2&3 £10.20. CSF £37.50 CT £233.43 TOTE £12.80: £3.00, £1.80, £3.70; EX 49.90 Trifecta £601.60 Part won. Pool: £802.25 - 0.62 winning units..
Owner Mrs E Evans **Bred** Jason Puckey **Trained** Pandy, Monmouths
■ Eoin Walsh's first ride in Britain.

FOCUS
A weak nursery and an all-the-way winner. Suspect form.

NOTEBOOK
Missing Agent went clear into the home straight and had enough left in reserve to hold off the runner-up's late challenge. It seemed likely that he would fold 1f out as he had gone so hard early, but the others clearly allowed him too much rope. He's really a plater and the form is obviously suspect, but one cannot fault his effort. This was his jockey's first ride in Britain since switching from Dermot Weld's operation in Ireland. (op 9-1)

Beau Select(IRE) met support back from 1m with a first-time visor enlisted and he kept on from well back to finish a clear second-best. This could well have been his big day as much now depends on the headgear continuing to work out. (op 5-1 tchd 11-2)

Tilstarr(IRE) ◆had shown little in three previous outings. However, she's bred to be better than her opening mark of 62 and she stayed on nicely from an impossible position. She ought to build on this. (op 8-1)

Princess Sheila(IRE) did not help her chances of seeing out the extra furlong by running somewhat freely (op 7-1 tchd 11-2)

Ishisoba showed her mark is probably a workable one as she stayed on with some purpose from out the back on this nursery debut. (op 16-1 tchd 12-1)

Marguerite St Just Official explanation: jockey said filly was denied a clear run

7725 £32 FREE AT 32RED.COM H'CAP 7f (P)
7:55 (7:56) (Class 5) (0-70,70) 3-Y-O+ **£2,264** (£673; £336; £168) **Stalls** Low

Form RPR

6233 **1** **Good Luck Charm**^{15} 7480 3-9-5 **70**................................ GeorgeBaker 4 80
(Gary Moore) *hld up towards rr: smooth prog over 2f out: led over 1f out: rdn fnl f: fnd enough* **9/2**^{2}

0413 **2** *½* **Atlantis Crossing (IRE)**^{15} 7484 3-9-4 **69**........................ EddieAhern 2 77
(Jim Boyle) *hld up in midfield: prog towards inner 2f out: drvn to chse wnr 150yds out: clsd nr fin but a hld* **8/1**^{3}

200 **3** *2* **Sunshine Always (IRE)**^{15} 7484 6-9-3 **67**.................. KirstyMilczarek 6 70
(Michael Attwater) *hld up in last trio: prog on inner over 2f out: rdn to chse wnr briefly 1f out: one pce after* **16/1**

4506 **4** *nse* **The Strig**^{15} 7484 5-9-6 **70**.. WilliamCarson 1 73
(Stuart Williams) *trckd ldng pair: drvn to chal over 1f out: nt qckn and one pce fnl f* **25/1**

-640 **5** *nk* **Relentless Harry (IRE)**^{41} 6840 3-9-5 **70**........................(t) JimCrowley 9 72+
(George Baker) *hld up wl in rr: effrt on outer over 2f out: styd on fr over 1f out: nvr able to chal* **9/2**^{2}

2352 **6** *shd* **Kinglami**^{29} 7170 3-9-5 **70**.. FrannyNorton 11 72
(Brian Gubby) *prom: hrd rdn to try to chal over 1f out: nt qckn: one pce fnl f* **3/1**^{1}

0520 **7** *shd* **Kingswinford (IRE)**^{5} 7684 6-8-10 **67**........................ SemiraPashai$^{(7)}$ 14 69
(Alastair Lidderdale) *hld up in rr fr wd draw: brought wdst of all in st: nudged along and kpt on fr over 1f out: nrst fin* **20/1**

531 **8** *1* **Frognal (IRE)**^{6} 7670 6-9-4 **68** 6ex................................(bt) MartinHarley 13 67
(Violet M Jordan) *stdd s fr wd draw and hld up in last trio: prog 2f out: drvn and nt qckn over 1f out: no hdwy after* **20/1**

0363 **9** *1* **Isola Verde**^{15} 7483 3-9-2 **67**..(b^{1}) HayleyTurner 7 63
(James Fanshawe) *hld up in rr: trapped bhd rivals and dropped to last 2f out: no ch after but styd on fnl f* **8/1**^{3}

1500 **10** *¾* **Tenbridge**^{55} 6454 3-9-4 **69**..(p) AndreaAtzeni 12 63
(Derek Haydn Jones) *chsd ldr: rdn over 2f out: stl chalng over 1f out: wknd fnl f* **33/1**

-300 **11** *½* **Minortransgression (USA)**^{9} 7607 5-9-4 **68**.................... AdamKirby 3 61
(Paul Rich) *led to over 1f out: wknd fnl f* **50/1**

0000 **12** *2¾* **Kakapuka**^{47} 6692 5-9-5 **69**..^{1} SebSanders 5 54
(Anabel K Murphy) *trckd ldrs: rdn over 2f out: lost pl and wknd over 1f out* **16/1**

0005 **13** *3½* **Oratorian (IRE)**^{31} 7105 3-9-4 **69**.. LiamKeniry 8 45
(Sylvester Kirk) *in tch in midfield: rdn over 2f out: sn wknd* **20/1**

4104 **14** *1¾* **Abhaath (USA)**^{30} 7142 3-9-3 **68**.. LukeMorris 10 39
(Ronald Harris) *racd on outer in midfield: wknd over 2f out* **10/1**

1m 25.34s (-0.66) **Going Correction** -0.075s/f (Stan)
WFA 3 from 5yo+ 1lb **14** Ran SP% **127.5**
Speed ratings (Par 103): **100,99,97,97,96 96,96,95,94,93 92,89,85,83**
toteswingers: 1&2 £7.50, 1&3 £6.40, 2&3 £52.30. CSF £38.93 CT £554.27 TOTE £5.30: £1.80, £3.70, £5.20; EX 59.10 Trifecta £793.20 Pool: £1,057.60 - 0.63 winning units..
Owner Heart Of The South Racing **Bred** John And Caroline Penny **Trained** Lower Beeding, W Sussex

FOCUS
This was run at an ordinary pace and it saw any amount in with a chance 1f out.
Isola Verde Official explanation: jockey said filly was denied a clear run
T/Plt: £462.60 to a £1 stake. Pool: £62,078.63 - 97.95 winning tickets. T/Qpdt: £108.30 to a £1 stake. Pool: £8,972.58 - 61.30 winning tickets. JN

7710 SOUTHWELL (L-H)
Thursday, November 15

OFFICIAL GOING: Standard
Wind: Virtually nil Weather: Fine and dry

7726 GAME IS UP H'CAP (DIV I) 5f (F)
12:20 (12:21) (Class 4) (0-85,85) 3-Y-O+ **£4,075** (£1,212; £606; £303) **Stalls** High

Form RPR

3000 **1** **Royal Bajan (USA)**^{47} 6689 4-8-12 **76**............................(b^{1}) GrahamLee 8 87
(James Given) *mde all: rdn clr appr fnl f: readily* **14/1**

4122 **2** *1¾* **Drawnfromthepast (IRE)**^{10} 7595 7-9-3 **81**.............. FergusSweeney 1 86
(Jamie Osborne) *prom on outer: effrt 2f out: rdn over 1f out: styd on to chse wnr ins fnl f: no imp* **11/4**^{1}

2544 **3** *1¾* **Bubbly Ballerina**^{29} 7177 3-8-13 **77**.............................. FrannyNorton 4 75
(Alan Bailey) *cl up: rdn and ev ch over 1f out: sn drvn and one pce fnl f* **10/1**

050 **4** *2¼* **Six Wives**^{34} 7019 5-9-4 **82**.. LukeMorris 9 72
(Scott Dixon) *cl up: rdn along wl over 1f out: edgd lft and wknd ent fnl f* **8/1**

0010 **5** *1½* **Where's Reiley (USA)**^{7} 7651 6-8-9 **78**..................(b) LeonnaMayor$^{(5)}$ 7 63
(Alastair Lidderdale) *s.i.s and bhd: rdn and hdwy 2f out: styd on fnl f: nrst fin* **9/1**

4033 **6** *¾* **Rylee Mooch**^{7} 7648 4-8-6 **75**...(e) JasonHart$^{(5)}$ 5 57
(Richard Guest) *chsd ldrs: rdn along 2f out: drvn and wknd over 1f out* **7/1**^{3}

0300 **7** *¾* **Taurus Twins**^{24} 7291 6-8-12 **76**....................................(b) JoeFanning 2 56
(Richard Price) *prom: rdn along over 2f out: grad wknd* **16/1**

0006 **8** *½* **Foxy Music**^{24} 7291 8-9-2 **80**.. GrahamGibbons 6 58
(Eric Alston) *dwlt: sn pushed along to chse ldrs: rdn along overe 2f out: sn wknd* **12/1**

6060 **9** *¾* **Shoshoni Wind**^{26} 7243 4-9-4 **85**....................................(p) JulieBurke$^{(3)}$ 11 60
(Kevin Ryan) *dwlt: swtchd lft sn after s: a in rr* **25/1**

R005 **10** *1¾* **Monsieur Jamie**^{15} 7489 4-8-12 **76**................................ FrederikTylicki 3 45
(J R Jenkins) *dwlt and swtchd lft s: racd wd: in tch: rdn along over 2f out: sn wknd* **11/2**^{2}

5503 **11** *4* **Haajes**^{15} 7489 8-8-9 **73**.. MickyFenton 10 27
(Paul Midgley) *in tch rdn along and lost pl after 2f: sn outpcd and bhd* **25/1**

58.04s (-1.66) **Going Correction** -0.125s/f (Stan) **11** Ran SP% **112.7**
Speed ratings (Par 105): **108,105,102,98,96 95,94,93,92,89 82**
Tote Swingers 1&2 £13.20, 2&3 £4.10, 1&3 £35.60 CSF £50.20 CT £415.49 TOTE £19.50: £4.70, £1.40, £2.80; EX 73.20 Trifecta £635.80 Part won. Pool: £847.79 - 0.63 winning tickets..
Owner Danethorpe Racing Partnership **Bred** West Wind Farm **Trained** Willoughton, Lincs

FOCUS
The first three home raced up with the pace throughout.

7727 BOOK SEASONS RESTAURANT AT SOUTHWELL RACECOURSE CLAIMING STKS — 6f (F)
12:50 (12:50) (Class 6) 2-Y-O — £1,617 (£481; £240; £120) Stalls Low

Form | | | | RPR
1625 **1** **Equitania**[38] 6929 2-9-0 84 .... GrahamLee 2 76+
(David O'Meara) *mde most: shkn up 1/ 2f out: rdn ent fnl f: styd on* **4/7**[1]
1046 **2** 2 1/4 **Kicken Off (IRE)**[13] 7521 2-8-7 68 ....(b[1]) JimmyQuinn 1 59
(Phil McEntee) *trckd ldrs: hdwy on inner 3f out: chal 2f out: sn rdn and ev ch tl drvn ent fnl f and kpt on same pce* **10/1**
5336 **3** shd **Windforpower (IRE)**[1] 7713 2-8-13 70 ....(p) LukeMorris 3 65
(Ronald Harris) *trckd ldrs: hdwy over 2f out: rdn wl over 1f out: kpt on same pce fnl f* **6/1**[3]
5200 **4** 2 3/4 **Projectisle (IRE)**[5] 7687 2-8-6 72 ....(p) JulieBurke(3) 5 51
(Kevin Ryan) *trckd ldrs: effrt on outer 3f out: rdn 2f out: sn one pce* **9/2**[2]
5 1 3/4 **Squawk** 2-8-5 0 .... AndrewMullen 4 43
(Bill Turner) *cl up: rdn along 3f out: wknd 2f out* **50/1**

1m 16.8s (0.30) **Going Correction** -0.10s/f (Stan) — 5 Ran SP% **107.2**
Speed ratings (Par 94): **94,91,90,87,84**
CSF £6.63 TOTE £1.40: £1.30, £3.60; EX 6.50.The winner was claimed by Mr John Stocker for £16,000.
Owner Middleham Park Racing XLIII **Bred** Longdon Stud **Trained** Nawton, N Yorks

FOCUS
A straightforward task for the odds-on favourite. The second and third suggest the bare form is no better.

NOTEBOOK
Equitania was having her first outing for David O'Meara after changing hands at the sales for 10,000gns. Winner of a nursery at Lingfield from a mark of 71, she is now rated 84. She had upwards of 8lb in hand on her all-weather bow and took this with the minimum of fuss. She was claimed for £16,000. (op 8-13 tchd 8-15)
Kicken Off(IRE), who has looked less than straightforward at times, had first-time blinkers replacing cheekpieces. She had 9lb to find with the winner and, after travelling strongly, proved no real match.
Windforpower(IRE) had finished well beaten in a C&D nursery the previous day from a mark of 70, suggesting the runner-up did not run to his official mark of 68. (op 7-1 tchd 15-2)
Projectisle(IRE), who had 8lb to find with the winner, was making a quick reappearance. Fitted with first-time cheekpieces, she wanted to do nothing but hang left and is going the wrong way. (tchd 4-1)
Squawk, who cost just 1,000gns as a yearling, knew her job but tired in the closing stages. On this evidence she might take a seller. (op 20-1)

7728 LIKE US ON FACEBOOK SOUTHWELL RACECOURSE MAIDEN AUCTION STKS — 7f (F)
1:20 (1:20) (Class 6) 2-Y-O — £1,617 (£481; £240; £120) Stalls Low

Form | | | | RPR
423 **1** **Lilac Lace (IRE)**[9] 7609 2-8-4 0 .... PaulQuinn 2 64+
(Tim Easterby) *trckd ldr: cl up 3f out: led over 2f out and sn rdn: styd on u.p fnl f* **11/10**[1]
55 **2** 2 1/2 **Nelina**[23] 7305 2-8-7 0 .... MichaelJMMurphy(5) 6 65
(Robert Cowell) *trckd ldng pair: hdwy 3f out: cl up 2f out: sn rdn: edgd lft and drvn appr fnl f: one pce* **7/4**[2]
0000 **3** 1 1/4 **Una Bella Cosa**[43] 6791 2-8-4 48 ....(p) FrannyNorton 1 53
(Alan McCabe) *led: rdn along 3f out: hdd over 2f out: sn drvn and one pce* **5/1**[3]
00 **4** 9 **Darakti (IRE)**[29] 7172 2-8-11 0 .... GrahamGibbons 4 37
(Alan McCabe) *sluggish s and sn swtchd wd: rdn along: outpcd and bhd after 2f: sme late hdwy* **33/1**
5000 **5** 1/2 **Cielo Rojo (IRE)**[64] 6147 2-9-3 40 ....(p) DavidNolan 5 42
(Richard Fahey) *in tch: rdn along bef 1/2-way: sn outpcd* **33/1**
0 **6** 4 1/2 **Niknad**[9] 7598 2-7-11 0 .... RPWalsh(7) 3 17
(Brian Ellison) *dwlt: a in rr* **25/1**
6502 **7** 3 1/2 **Mace The Ace**[17] 7440 2-8-4 50 ....(b) LukeMorris 7 8
(Lawrence Mullaney) *chsd ldrs: rdn along 1/2-way: sn outpcd and bhd fnl 2f* **16/1**

1m 28.54s (-1.76) **Going Correction** -0.10s/f (Stan) — 7 Ran SP% **116.3**
Speed ratings (Par 94): **106,103,101,91,90 85,81**
Tote Swingers 1&2 £1.50, 2&3 £2.10, 1&3 £1.90 CSF £3.30 TOTE £2.40: £1.10, £1.30; EX 3.60 Trifecta £17.50 Pool: £961.40 - 41.07 winning tickets..
Owner S A Heley **Bred** Robert Ryan, Brendan Quinn & Joan Quinn **Trained** Great Habton, N Yorks

FOCUS
A poor 2yo maiden auction race proved easy meat for the favourite. Weak but solid form, the winner basically to his turf mark.

NOTEBOOK
Lilac Lace(IRE) had achieved an RPR of 64 when fourth over this trip on her racecourse debut at Redcar in October. Placed over 7f at Catterick and 5f here since, she made no mistake. It all now depends on what mark she is pitched on her handicap bow. (op 4-6 tchd 8-13)
Nelina, who had showed ability in two previous outings on Polytrack, is quite a big, sturdy type and she may well improve again with handicaps now an option. (op 9-4 tchd 10-3)
Una Bella Cosa, rated just 48 after four previous starts, wore first-time cheekpieces on her first try on Fibresand. (op 14-1)
Darakti(IRE), who had shown little in two back-end outings on turf, claimed a distant fourth on the line after being last of all with 2f left to run. He may need a big step up in trip. (op 40-1 tchd 50-1)

7729 PLAY GOLF AT SOUTHWELL GOLF CLUB MAIDEN STKS — 7f (F)
1:50 (1:50) (Class 5) 3-Y-O — £2,264 (£673; £336; £168) Stalls Low

Form | | | | RPR
6033 **1** **Quan (IRE)**[17] 7445 3-9-3 57 .... RobertWinston 13 56
(Alan Swinbank) *cl up: slt ld over 2f out: sn rdn: drvn ent fnl f: kpt on wl towards fin* **2/1**[1]
0000 **2** nk **Mystical Witch**[23] 7317 3-8-12 40 ....(v) TomMcLaughlin 8 50
(Christine Dunnett) *chsd ldrs on outer: hdwy wl over 2f out: rdn to chal over 1f out: drvn and ev ch ins fnl f: no ex towards fin* **100/1**
0606 **3** hd **Sweet Grace**[9] 7604 3-8-12 43 ....(b) FrannyNorton 7 50
(David Brown) *trckd ldrs: hdwy 3f out: rdn wl over 1f out and sn ev ch: drvn ins fnl f: edgd lft and no ex last 50yds* **13/2**
3064 **4** 5 **Keep It Dark**[10] 7590 3-9-3 64 .... GrahamLee 1 42
(Tony Coyle) *trckd ldrs on inner: effrt 3f out: sn rdn and outpcd wl over 1f out: kpt on to take mod 4th towards fin* **3/1**[2]
0 **5** 1/2 **Miss Bunter**[17] 7445 3-8-12 0 .... GrahamGibbons 10 35
(David O'Meara) *led: rdn along and hdd over 2f out: drvn over 1f out and ev ch tl wknd ins fnl f* **12/1**
0060 **6** nk **Give Us A Belle (IRE)**[14] 7512 3-9-3 44 .... JimmyQuinn 11 40
(Christine Dunnett) *towards rr: hdwy 3f out: sn rdn and kpt on fnl 2f: nrst fin* **50/1**
0 **7** 3 **Balmoral Castle**[15] 7477 3-9-3 0 .... StephenCraine 9 32
(Jonathan Portman) *a in rr* **66/1**
0 **8** hd **Dr Victoria**[42] 6827 3-8-12 0 .... AndrewMullen 2 26
(John Norton) *a in rr* **66/1**
0000 **9** 3 3/4 **Summer Sun**[23] 7316 3-8-7 50 .... LeonnaMayor(5) 12 17
(Phil McEntee) *chsd ldrs: rdn along 1/2-way: sn wknd* **12/1**
2606 **10** 1 **Queen Cassiopeia**[28] 7201 3-8-12 55 .... FrederikTylicki 3 14
(J R Jenkins) *towards rr on inner: swtchd rt to outer 1/2-way: sn rdn along and nvr a factor* **9/2**[3]
000 **11** 2 1/4 **Kuraanda**[75] 5823 3-8-12 40 .... PatrickMathers 4 8
(John Wainwright) *s.i.s: a bhd* **66/1**
0 **12** 6 **Adam's Ale**[17] 7445 3-9-3 0 .... MickyFenton 6
(Paul Midgley) *a in rr: bhd fnl 2f* **20/1**

1m 29.83s (-0.47) **Going Correction** -0.10s/f (Stan) — 12 Ran SP% **117.4**
Speed ratings (Par 102): **98,97,97,91,91 90,87,87,82,81 79,72**
Tote Swingers 1&2 £17.20, 2&3 £35.00, 1&3 £3.50 CSF £270.56 TOTE £3.50: £1.40, £12.30, £2.30; EX 259.50 TRIFECTA Not won..
Owner S P C Woods **Bred** Oscar Stud **Trained** Melsonby, N Yorks

FOCUS
A dire maiden and a tight, three-way finish.

7730 GAME IS UP H'CAP (DIV II) — 5f (F)
2:20 (2:20) (Class 4) (0-85,83) 3-Y-O+ — £4,075 (£1,212; £606; £303) Stalls Low

Form | | | | RPR
0-00 **1** **Dorback**[24] 7291 5-9-0 76 .... FrannyNorton 4 86
(David Nicholls) *trckd ldrs: n.m.r and swtchd lft over 1f out: rdn and qcknd wl ent fnl f: led last 100yds* **8/1**[3]
0005 **2** 1/2 **O'Gorman**[31] 7113 3-9-0 76 .... LiamKeniry 7 84
(Gary Brown) *hld up in rr: gd hdwy over 1f out: styd on ins fnl f: nrst fin* **25/1**
3404 **3** 1 **Sleepy Blue Ocean**[38] 6938 6-9-0 76 ....(p) LukeMorris 5 81
(John Balding) *cl up: led over 2f out: jnd and rdn over 1f out: carried rt ent fnl f: drvn: hdd and no ex last 100yds* **6/1**[2]
2364 **4** 1 1/4 **Rambo Will**[25] 7273 4-8-11 73 .... FrederikTylicki 11 73
(J R Jenkins) *led: rdn along and hdd over 2f out: grad wknd appr fnl f* **8/1**[3]
4131 **5** 1 **Havin' A Good Time (IRE)**[21] 7351 3-9-1 77 .... NeilCallan 1 74
(Roger Varian) *racd wd: t.k.h: in tch: hdwy 2f out: edgd rt and rdn to chal over 1f out and ev ch: drvn and wknd qckly ent fnl f* **11/8**[1]
0003 **6** nk **Taffe**[16] 7464 3-9-2 78 .... JoeFanning 8 73
(Amy Weaver) *cl up: rdn along 2f out: hld whn n.m.r over 1f out* **11/1**
2500 **7** nk **Oldjoesaid**[24] 7291 8-8-13 75 .... MickyFenton 10 69
(Paul Midgley) *chsd ldrs: rdn along wl over 1f out: sn one pce* **33/1**
6055 **8** shd **Dancing Freddy (IRE)**[7] 7648 5-8-12 74 ....(tp) WilliamCarson 2 68
(Violet M Jordan) *prom on outer: rdn along wl over 1f out: grad wknd* **17/2**
0553 **9** shd **Damika (IRE)**[10] 7595 9-9-7 83 ....(be) MichaelStainton 6 77
(David Brown) *a towards rr* **12/1**
6010 **10** 7 **Baby Strange**[10] 7595 8-9-5 81 ....(v) MartinDwyer 9 49
(Derek Shaw) *towards rr: rdn along over 2f out: sn bhd* **22/1**

58.74s (-0.96) **Going Correction** -0.125s/f (Stan) — 10 Ran SP% **116.3**
Speed ratings (Par 105): **102,101,99,97,96 95,95,94,94,83**
Tote Swingers 1&2 £30.30, 2&3 £18.90, 1&3 £8.20 CSF £189.14 CT £1283.76 TOTE £11.00: £2.50, £7.70, £2.30; EX 272.60 TRIFECTA Not won..
Owner Ms Sara Hattersley **Bred** Winterbeck Manor Stud **Trained** Sessay, N Yorks

FOCUS
There was plenty of pace on here and the first two home came from behind.

7731 DOWNLOAD OUR IPHONE APP H'CAP — 1m 4f (F)
2:50 (2:50) (Class 6) (0-60,60) 3-Y-O+ — £1,704 (£503; £251) Stalls Low

Form | | | | RPR
1260 **1** **Goldmadchen (GER)**[9] 7599 4-9-7 57 .... JoeFanning 8 66+
(Keith Dalgleish) *hld up: stdy hdwy 1/2-way: trckd ldrs over 3f out: effrt to chse ldr over 1f out: rdn to ld appr fnl f: styd on strly* **9/1**
0523 **2** 3 1/4 **Lakeman (IRE)**[9] 7608 6-9-2 55 .... RyanClark(3) 12 59
(Brian Ellison) *trckd ldrs on outer: effrt over 3f out: rdn along over 2f out: styd on u.p fnl f* **6/1**[3]
U002 **3** hd **Viola Da Gamba (IRE)**[31] 7117 3-9-4 60 .... NeilCallan 14 64
(William Knight) *a.p: effrt over 3f out: rdn over 2f out and ev ch: drvn wl over 1f out and kpt on same pce* **11/2**[2]
5043 **4** 1/2 **Layla's Boy**[26] 7252 5-9-10 60 ....(bt) FrannyNorton 2 63
(John Mackie) *in tch: hdwy to trck ldrs 1/2-way: cl up over 3f out: led wl over 2f out: rdn wl over 1f out: hdd appr fnl f: sn drvn and wknd* **7/2**[1]
0000 **5** 3 1/4 **General Tufto**[21] 7347 7-9-3 53 ....(b) RobbieFitzpatrick 10 51
(Charles Smith) *towards rr: hdwy over 3f out: rdn to chse ldrs wl over 1f out: sn edgd lft and no imp* **22/1**
006 **6** 8 **Kingaroo (IRE)**[4] 7496 6-9-9 59 .... LukeMorris 1 45
(Garry Woodward) *cl up: rdn along over 4f out: wknd over 3f out* **12/1**
-054 **7** 5 **Leitrim King (IRE)**[117] 3233 3-9-3 59 ....(be) LiamKeniry 5 38
(Murty McGrath) *chsd ldrs: rdn along over 4f out: sn wknd* **40/1**
12/0 **8** 3/4 **Essexbridge**[9] 7603 5-9-8 58 ....(b) GrahamLee 11 35
(David O'Meara) *prom: cl up 1/2-way: led over 4f out: rdn along over 3f out: hdd wl over 2f out and sn wknd* **13/2**
6 **9** 3 1/4 **War (IRE)**[1] 7710 6-8-11 47 ....(bt) ChrisCatlin 13 20
(J A Nash, Ire) *a towards rr* **20/1**
0605 **10** 1 3/4 **Monzino (USA)**[9] 7610 4-9-10 60 ....(p) AdamBeschizza 7 30
(Michael Chapman) *a in rr: rdn along and bhd fr 1/2-way* **8/1**
03/0 **11** 15 **Miss Kingwood**[34] 7018 5-9-10 60 .... J-PGuillambert 9 7
(Jo Hughes) *led: rdn along and hdd over 4f out: sn wknd and bhd fnl 2f* **16/1**
4000 **12** 1 1/2 **Ptolomeos**[15] 7496 9-8-6 47 ....(p) AmyScott(5) 6
(Sean Regan) *a in rr: bhd fnl 3f* **28/1**
00-0 **13** 39 **Investment World (IRE)**[56] 6399 4-8-8 51 .... DanielMuscutt(7) 3
(Tim Vaughan) *chsd ldrs: rdn along 5f out: sn wknd* **16/1**

2m 40.34s (-0.66) **Going Correction** -0.10s/f (Stan)
WFA 3 from 4yo+ 6lb — 13 Ran SP% **120.8**
Speed ratings (Par 101): **98,95,95,95,93 87,84,84,81,80 70,69,43**
Tote Swingers 1&2 £11.50, 2&3 £6.40, 1&3 £10.70 CSF £60.07 CT £332.97 TOTE £8.70: £3.10, £3.20, £2.40; EX 46.60 Trifecta £270.60 Pool: £584.67 - 1.62 winning tickets..
Owner G L S Partnership **Bred** Gestut Gorlsdorf **Trained** Carluke, S Lanarks

FOCUS
Plenty keen to have a piece of the action and there was no hanging about in this open looking low-grade handicap.

7732 BOOK TICKETS ONLINE AT SOUTHWELL-RACECOURSE.CO.UK CLAIMING STKS 7f (F)
3:20 (3:20) (Class 6) 3-Y-0+ **£1,617** (£481; £240 ; £120) **Stalls** Low

Form RPR
0140 **1** **Flying Pickets (IRE)**[92] 5243 3 -8-1368...............(be) GrahamGibbons 11 71
(Alan McCabe) *midfield: hdwy 1/2-way: chsd ldrs over 2f out: rdn to ld 1 1/2f out: drvn and edgd lft fnl f: kpt on* **20/1**
1022 **2** *1* **Llewellyn**[17] 7437 4 -9-160.. ShirleyTeasdale(7) 12 77
(David Nicholls) *prom: effrt over 2f out: rdn over 1f out: styd on to chse wnr ins fnl f: kpt on* **11/2**[2]
0400 **3** *nk* **Corporal Maddox**[47] 6659 5 -9-788............. WilliamTwiston-Davies(5) 2 86+
(Jamie Osborne) *dwlt and bhd: swtchd to outer 1/2-way: wd st and hdwy over 2f out: sn rdn and styd on wl fnl f: nrst fin* **9/2**[1]
0430 **4** *2* **Eastern Hills**[17] 7436 7 -8-1265...(p) IPoullis 7 61
(Alan McCabe) *trckd ldr: hdwy over 2f out: rdn wl over 1f out: kpt on same pce appr fnl f* **8/1**
5 *shd* **Daisy Mountain (IRE)**[13] 7535 5 -8-1165.......................(t) ChrisCatlin 13 60
(J A Nash, Ire) *prom on outer: rdn along over 2f out: drvn and one pce fr over 1f out* **14/1**
6540 **6** *1* **Lindoro**[5] 7685 7 -8-356...(b) JulieBurke(3) 8 53
(Brian Ellison) *midfield: hdwy over 3f out: rdn to chse ldrs 2f out: no imp appr fnl f* **14/1**
3600 **7** *hd* **Alpha Tauri (USA)**[9] 7634 6 -9-179..........................(t) DanielMuscutt(7) 9 68
(Charles Smith) *led: rdn along over 2f out: hdd 1 1/2f out and sn wknd* **14/1**
0154 **8** *2 1/2* **Imprimis Tagula (IRE)**[76] 2398 8 -9-478...............(p) RobertWinston 14 58
(Alan Bailey) *nvr bttr than midfield* **9/1**
4004 **9** *hd* **Rio Cobolo (IRE)**[46] 6709 6 -9-1262.............................(p) MartinDwyer 1 65
(David Nicholls) *chsd ldrs on inner: rdn along wl over 2f out: sn wknd* **18/1**
0000 **10** *1 3/4* **Masai Moon**[22] 7327 8 -9-679......................................(b) JamesMillman 5 54
(Rod Millman) *a in rr* **6/1**[3]
0230 **11** *6* **Brocklebank (IRE)**[19] 7415 3 -9-777.............................(tp) GrahamLee 4 40
(Kevin Ryan) *a in rr* **9/1**
0401 **12** *2* **Lady Layla**[17] 7437 3 -8-1067.......................................(p) J-PGuillambert 6 24
(Jo Hughes) *dwlt: a in rr* **8/1**

1m 28.74s (-1.56)**Going Correction** -0.10s/f (Stan)
WFA 3 from 4yo+ 1lb 12Ran SP%120.1
Speed ratings (Par 101): **104,102,102,100,100 98,98,95,95,93 86,84**
Tote Swingers 1&2 £16.90, 2&3 £6.60, 1&3 £25.90 CSF £128.22 TOTE £27.70 : £7.50 , £2.60 £2.00; EX 222.10 TRIFECTA Not won. .Corporal Maddox was subject to a friendly claim for £12,000, Lady Layla was claimed by Lady Herries for £7,000 and Lindoro was claimed by Mr J M Curran for £2,000.
Owner Tariq Al Nisf **Bred** Richard Frayne **Trained** Averham Park, Notts

FOCUS
The usual bunch of suspects in this wide-open claimer.

7733 SOUTHWELL ALL-WEATHER "HANDS AND HEELS" APPRENTICE SERIES H'CAP (PART OF THE RACING EXCELLENCE) 7f (F)
3:50 (3:52) (Class 6) (0-60,60) 3-Y-0+ **£1,704** (£503; £251) **Stalls** Low

Form RPR
6003 **1** **Ace Of Spies (IRE)**[1] 7354 7 -9-053................................ PhilipPrince 4 63
(Conor Dore) *mde all: pushed clr wl over 1f out: rdn and kpt on strly fnl f* **20/1**
-240 **2** *2 1/4* **Elusive Warrior (USA)**[21] 7348 9 -9-356...................(p) DanielMuscutt 6 60
(Alan McCabe) *trckd ldrs: hdwy to chse wnr wl over 1f out: rdn ent fnl f and no imp* **16/1**
1504 **3** *1 3/4* **Monte Cassino (IRE)**[27] 7224 7 -9-154..............................(e) TimClark 3 54
(Bryan Smart) *in tch: hdwy on inner whn nt clr run 2f out: sn swtchd rt and rdn: styd on wl fnl f: nrst fin* **12/1**
0636 **4** *nk* **Koo And The Gang (IRE)**[28] 7200 5 -9-558....................... RPWalsh 13 57
(Brian Ellison) *towards rr: hdwy 3f out: pushed along 2f out: sn rdn and no imp fnl f* **9/4**[1]
0005 **5** *1 1/4* **Man Of My Word**[19] 7395 3 -9-160..............................(p) JordanUys(5) 14 55
(Scott Dixon) *towards rr: hdwy on outer 1/2-way: rdn 2f out: styd on appr fnl f: nrst fin* **8/1**[3]
0034 **6** *1/2* **Jonnie Skull (IRE)**[14] 7504 6 -8-854..............................(vt) JoshQuinn(7) 5 48
(Phil McEntee) *in tch: hdwy to chse ldrs wl over 2f out: sn rdn along and one pce fr wl over 1f out* **16/1**
6030 **7** *3/4* **Boy The Bell**[37] 6967 5 -8-1357.. KevinStott(5) 11 49
(Ollie Pears) *dwlt and towards rr: wd st: hdwy 2f out: styd on appr fnl f: nrst fin* **12/1**
2606 **8** *1* **Calypso Cay**[10] 7593 4 -8-1357.................................. LukeLeadbitter(5) 8 47
(Peter Salmon) *dwlt: sn chsd ldrs: cl up 1/2-way: rdn over 2f out: wknd over 1f out* **8/1**[3]
4040 **9** *hd* **Arachnophobia (IRE)**[94] 5179 6 -8-1359...............(b[1]) KirstenSmith(7) 7 48
(Martin Bosley) *towards rr: wd st: hdwy on outer 2f out: sn rdn and styd on fnl f: nrst fin* **33/1**
6042 **10** *4* **Scarlet Rocks (IRE)**[82] 5590 4 -9-457.. HannahNunn 10 36
(Ron Barr) *dwlt: a in rr* **14/1**
0622 **11** *1 3/4* **Tenancy (IRE)**[8] 7634 8 -9-154 ow2...........................(v[1]) ConorHarrison 9 28
(Shaun Harris) *chsd ldrs on outer: rdn along wl over 2f out: sn wknd* **16/1**
0440 **12** *4* **Son Vida (IRE)**[9] 7413 4 -9-058............................(v) RobertTart(5) 2 22
(Alan Bailey) *chsd ldrs on inner: pushed along 3f out: sn wknd* **9/2**[2]
-400 **13** *8* **Sovento (GER)**[17] 7436 8 -9-760.. GemmaTutty 12 3
(Alan McCabe) *a in rr: bhd fnl 2f* **40/1**
0-00 **14** *2 3/4* **Concrete Jungle (IRE)**[60] 5653 4 -8-753.............................. AaronJones(7) 1
(Bill Turner) *a in rr: bhd fnl 2f* **50/1**

1m 29.69s (-0.61)**Going Correction** -0.10s/f (Stan)
WFA 3 from 4yo+ 1lb 14Ran SP%123.0
Speed ratings (Par 101): **99,96,94,94,92 92,91,90,89,85 83,78,69,66**
Tote Swingers 1&2 £27.60, 2&3 £19.40, 1&3 £23.80 CSF £307.67 CT £3990.06 TOTE £23.30 : £5.80, £3.10 , £3.80 ; EX 169.00 TRIFECTA Not won. .
Owner Mrs Louise Marsh **Bred** Gainsborough Stud Management Ltd **Trained** Hubbert's Bridge, Lincs
■ Stewards' Enquiry : Luke Leadbitter seven-day ban: used whip contrary to rules (Nov 29-Dec 1,3-6)

FOCUS
Visually they seemed to go off very quick in this low-grade 'hands and heels' apprentice handicap, yet the winner was in the firing line throughout.
T/Plt: £52.80 to a £1 stake. Pool: £47,780.49 - 660.36 winning tickets. T/Qpdt: £20.40 to a £1 stake. Pool: £3,913.10 - 141.50 winning tickets. JR

7693 SAINT-CLOUD (L-H)
Thursday, November 15
OFFICIAL GOING: Turf: heavy

7735a PRIX DENISY (LISTED RACE) (3YO+) (TURF) 1m 7f 110y
2:50 (12:00) 3-Y-0+ **£21,666** (£8,666; £6,500 ; £4,333 ; £2,166)

RPR
1 **Silver Valny (FR)**[18] 7431 6 -9-10............................. ThomasMessina 1 106
(Mlle M-L Mortier, France) **13/5**[2]
2 *3 1/2* **Skyline Du Casse (FR)**[33] 7320 6 -9-10............. Jean-BaptisteHamel 7 102
(F Plouganou, France) **16/1**
3 *1/2* **Tidespring (IRE)**[25] 7282 4 -8-110.................................. FabriceVeron 6 97
(H-A Pantall, France) **15/2**
4 *2 1/2* **Western Pearl**[14] 7510 5 -8-110...................................... TheoBachelot 3 94
(William Knight) *racd midfield: rdn 2f out: r.o u.p ent fnl f: styd on wl to go 4th 75yds out* **29/1**
5 *1* **Jehannedarc (IRE)**[26] 7237 4 -8-110.............................. AntoineHamelin 5 93
(A De Royer-Dupre, France) **15/2**
6 *1/2* **Gentoo (FR)**[39] 6914 8 -9-10...............................(b) StephanePasquier 4 97
(A Lyon, France) **68/10**
7 *20* **Oh Beautiful**[22] 7344 3 -8-70.................................... AurelienLemaitre 8 74
(F Head, France) **5/2**[1]
8 *dist* **Valamar (FR)**[23] 3 -8-70.. MaximeGuyon 2
(A De Royer-Dupre, France) **11/2**[3]

3m 49.7s (11.00)
WFA 3 from 4yo+ 8lb 8Ran SP%117.3
WIN (incl. 1 euro stake): 3.60. PLACES: 1.60, 3.40, 2.30. DF: 28.50. SF: 36.50 .
Owner L Baudron & Mlle H Dichamp **Bred** Tony Salva & Mme Charlotte Thoreau **Trained** France

NOTEBOOK
Western Pearl, fifth in this last year, got one place closer this time, helped by the return to testing ground on turf.

7734a & 7736a - (Foreign Racing) - See Raceform Interactive

7641 LINGFIELD (L-H)
Friday, November 16
OFFICIAL GOING: Standard
Wind: virtually nil Weather: dry, foggy

7737 BET TOTEPLACEPOT AT TOTEPOOL.COM NURSERY 7f (P)
12:00 (12:00) (Class 4) (0-85,79) 2-Y-0 **£3,428** (£1,020; £509 ; £254) **Stalls** Low

Form RPR
2316 **1** **Ready (IRE)**[20] 7399 2 -9-173.. AdamKirby 2 75
(Garry Moss) *hld up in tch in rr: rdn and effrt 2f out: swtchd rt over 1f out: drvn and str run ins fnl f to ld fnl 50yds: r.o wl* **12/1**
2204 **2** *1/2* **Martial Art (IRE)**[43] 6815 2 -9-779.. DavidProbert 1 80
(Andrew Balding) *hld up in tch: rdn over 1f out: hdwy u.p and chal ins fnl f: led wl ins fnl f: hdd and no ex fnl 50yds* **3/1**[2]
4031 **3** *nk* **Archie Stevens**[8] 7650 2 -8-1169 6ex.......................... RichardKingscote 4 71
(Tom Dascombe) *t.k.h: hld up wl in tch: rdn and effrt over 1f out: swtchd rt and chal between horses ins fnl f: one pce towards fin* **10/11**[1]
6421 **4** *1 1/4* **Aye Aye Skipper (IRE)**[4] 7525 2 -9-779.................................. JimCrowley 3 76
(Dean Ivory) *chsd ldrs: ev ch and rdn 2f out: led fnl 150yds tl hdd wl ins fnl f: no ex: btn and eased cl home* **13/2**[3]
2402 **5** *1 3/4* **Arctic Admiral (IRE)**[29] 7190 2 -8-570............................ RufusVergette(7) 7 62
(Richard Hannon) *s.i.s: sn rcvrd and chsd ldr after 1f out: ev ch 2f out: rdn to ld over 1f out: hdd fnl 150yds: wknd towards fin* **11/1**
5305 **6** *1 1/2* **Something Magic**[34] 7059 2 -8-866.. LiamKeniry 6 54
(Sylvester Kirk) *led: rdn ent fnl 2f: hdd over 1f out: wknd ins fnl f* **28/1**

1m 25.12s (0.32)**Going Correction** 0.0s/f (Stan) 6Ran SP%110.2
Speed ratings (Par 98): **98,97,97,95,93 91**
CSF £45.82 TOTE £14.10 : £4.30 , £1.30 ; EX 39.70 .
Owner Ron Hull **Bred** Kilshannig Stud **Trained** Tickhill, S Yorks

FOCUS
An interesting nursery in which they went a steady early pace, the tempo increasing before the straight. Straightforward form, the runner-up helping the level.

NOTEBOOK
Ready(IRE) failed to build on the form of his maiden win when well held on his nursery debut last time, but proved suited by the switch to Polytrack. The result looked unlikely as he was under strong pressure on the bend into the straight, but picked up really well from off the pace down the outside to gain a narrow victory. (op 10-1 tchd 14-1)
Martial Art (IRE)had shown ability in maidens and when in the frame on his nursery debut in soft ground on his previous start, and ran well on this AW debut. He didn't go unbacked and proved effective on the surface, so this should open more options for him. (op 4-1)
Archie Stevens, penalised 6lb for winning on his nursery debut at Wolverhampton eight days earlier, had to wait for a gap in the straight but his chance wasn't compromised. This was his first start over 7f and he didn't fail through a lack of stamina. He should continue to give a good account. (op 5-6 tchd 4-5)
Aye Aye Skipper (IRE)who narrowly won his maiden at Wolverhampton 14 days earlier, was forced three wide entering the straight and made a creditable handicap debut. He just lacked the pace of the principals inside the final furlong. (op 6-1 tchd 11-2 and 7-1)
Arctic Admiral (IRE)benefited from the run of the race when second over 1m at Kempton last time and he was again ridden prominently, but found little for pressure and was one-paced close home. His jockey reported that he hung left in the straight. Official explanation: jockey said colt hung left in straight. (op 12-1)

7738 BRITISH STALLION STUDS SUPPORTING BRITISH RACING EBF MAIDEN STKS 5f (P)
12:30 (12:32) (Class 5) 2-Y-0 **£3,169** (£943; £471 ; £235) **Stalls** High

Form RPR
233 **1** **Secret Missile**[15] 7497 2 -9-378.. MartinDwyer 8 83
(William Muir) *pressed ldr: rdn over 1f out: led 1f out: sn in command: comf* **7/4**[1]
522 **2** *2* **Maid A Million**[24] 7311 2 -8-1274... SebSanders 4 71
(David Elsworth) *chsd ldrs: lft chsng ldng pair and rdn 2f out: styd on to go 2nd wl ins fnl f: no threat to wnr* **7/4**[1]
0 **3** *1* **Freddy With A Y (IRE)**[7] 7371 2 -9-30..................................... GeorgeBaker 7 72
(Gary Moore) *led: rdn wl over 1f out: hdd and no ex 1f out: styd on same pce and lost 2nd wl ins fnl f* **12/1**[3]

4 1 ¾ **Royal Acquisition** 2-9-3 0 JimCrowley 9 66
(Robert Cowell) *hld up in tch in midfield: rdn over 1f out: kpt on ins fnl f* **6/1**[2]

0240 5 2 **Ladweb**[16] 7476 2-8-12 62 MichaelJMMurphy[(5)] 5 59
(John Gallagher) *sn pushed along in midfield: rdn and unable qck over 1f out: wl hld and styd on same pce fnl f* **25/1**

3033 6 1 ½ **Pal Of The Cat**[37] 6975 2-9-3 73 FrannyNorton 10 54
(Brian Gubby) *pressed ldrs tl hung rt and lost pl bnd 2f out: lost any ch and styd on same pce after* **14/1**

7 ¾ **Lady Cooper** 2-8-12 0 JamieMackay 6 46
(Willie Musson) *in tch in rr of main gp: sn pushed along along: rdn and outpcd over 2f out: wl hld and one pce after* **33/1**

0 8 1 **Chandelle Celeste**[21] 7371 2-8-12 0 RichardKingscote 3 42
(Daniel Kubler) *a in last pair: nvr trbld ldrs* **66/1**

5000 9 ½ **Sally Bruce**[51] 6581 2-8-5 47 JenniferFerguson[(7)] 2 40
(Louise Best) *sn pushed along and outpcd in last: n.d* **100/1**

58.83s (0.03) **Going Correction** 0.0s/f (Stan) **9** Ran SP% **110.6**
Speed ratings (Par 96): **99,95,94,91,88 85,84,83,82**
Tote Swingers: 1&2 £1.40, 1&3 £3.60, 2&3 £4.40 CSF £4.20 TOTE £2.50: £1.10, £1.20, £4.30; EX 4.70 Trifecta £28.40 Pool: £527.48 - 13.92 winning units..
Owner Muir Racing Partnership - Manchester **Bred** Whitsbury Manor Stud **Trained** Lambourn, Berks

FOCUS
Little depth to this maiden, but they went a decent pace with a contested lead. The form is rated cautiously.

NOTEBOOK
Secret Missile, who set the standard with an official mark of 78 having been placed in all three starts on Polytrack, including when narrowly beaten over 6f at Kempton 15 days earlier, proved good enough to open his account at the fourth attempt. Down in trip, he was ridden positively and, despite helping to set a strong gallop, saw it out strongly all the way to the line. (op 13-8 tchd 6-4 and 2-1)
Maid A Million, runner-up the last twice in easy-ground maidens, was down in trip on this AW debut and lacked the natural pace of the winner. She kept on well and shaped as though she would appreciate a step back up in trip. (op 5-2 tchd 11-4)
Freddy With A Y(IRE) was well held on his debut in a soft ground Newbury maiden, but the switch to this surface and drop down in trip brought about some improvement. He served it up to the winner for much of the race and wasn't seen off until inside the final furlong. (op 14-1 tchd 16-1)
Royal Acquisition, a 45,000GBP 2yo out of a useful 6f 2yo winner and half-brother to four winners at up to 1m4f, made an encouraging debut. He showed signs of inexperience, but kept on nicely and it was a run that suggested he would improve significantly for the experience. (op 11-2 tchd 9-2)
Pal Of The Cat Official explanation: jockey said gelding hung right throughout

7739 BET TOTEQUADPOT AT TOTEPOOL.COM MAIDEN STKS 1m 4f (P)
1:00 (1:04) (Class 5) 3-Y-O+ **£2,385** (£704; £352) **Stalls** Low

Form RPR

3322 1 **Suegioo (FR)**[59] 6339 3-9-3 84 (p) AdamKirby 1 89
(Marco Botti) *chsd ldrs: rdn to chse ldng pair 4f out: led over 1f out: sn clr: v easily* **2/5**[1]

62 2 9 **Elysian**[47] 6704 3-8-12 0 WilliamBuick 2 69
(Sir Michael Stoute) *led tl rdn and hdd over 1f out: sn btn but kpt on for clr 2nd* **3/1**[2]

43 3 9 **La Belle Doyenne**[9] 7625 4-9-4 0 FergusSweeney 9 55
(Alan King) *taken down early and led to post: in tch: chsd ldr 4f out tl over 2f out: sn outpcd and wl btn fnl 2f* **14/1**

55 4 ¾ **Murphy (IRE)**[114] 4465 10-9-4 0 (t) JemmaMarshall[(5)] 10 59
(Nick Gifford) *hld up towards rr: sme hdwy and modest 5th 3f out: no real imp after but plugged on to press for modest 3rd towards fin* **33/1**

023 5 6 **Matured**[50] 6614 3-8-12 75 JimCrowley 11 44
(Ralph Beckett) *hld up in midfield: rdn and struggling 4f out: wl btn fnl 3f* **6/1**[3]

6000 6 7 **Ice Apple**[36] 7012 4-9-1 35 NataliaGemelova[(3)] 3 33
(John E Long) *bhd and sn niggled along: rdn and struggling over 4f out: wl btn fnl 3f: plugged on past btn horses fr over 1f out* **66/1**

60 7 2 **Thecornishwren (IRE)**[22] 7352 3-8-12 0 FrannyNorton 6 30
(John Ryan) *chsd ldrs: rdn and lost pl over 4f out: wl btn fnl 3f* **66/1**

0-05 8 ¾ **Tymismoni (IRE)**[16] 7488 4-9-4 45 TomMcLaughlin 5 29
(Michael Attwater) *towards rr: rdn 7f out: bhd fnl 3f* **66/1**

0/ 9 shd **Artful Dodger**[1106] 7276 5-9-9 0 SebSanders 7 33
(Olivia Maylam) *hld up in midfield: rdn and lost pl over 4f out: bhd fnl 3f* **66/1**

000 10 nk **Let's Confer**[36] 7011 3-8-12 0 J-PGuillambert 4 28
(Michael Attwater) *chsd ldr tl 4f out: sn lost pl: bhd over 2f out: eased ins fnl f* **66/1**

0-00 11 dist **Aaranyow (IRE)**[177] 2386 4-9-4 40 MichaelJMMurphy[(5)] 8
(Terry Clement) *in tch in midfield: rdn and dropped to rr over 4f out: t.o fnl 3f* **66/1**

2m 30.21s (-2.79) **Going Correction** 0.0s/f (Stan)
WFA 3 from 4yo+ 6lb **11** Ran SP% **129.3**
Speed ratings (Par 103): **109,103,97,96,92 87,86,86,85,85**
Tote Swingers: 1&2 £1.40, 1&3 £3.40, 2&3 £4.70 CSF £2.28 TOTE £1.60: £1.02, £1.30, £2.90; EX 2.90 Trifecta £10.70 Pool: £2,839.73 - 62.76 winning units..
Owner Scuderia Rencati Srl **Bred** Rabbah Bloodstock Ltd **Trained** Newmarket, Suffolk

FOCUS
An uncompetitive maiden run at a steady pace, the favourite took advantage of what looked a golden opportunity.

7740 BRITISH STALLION STUDS SUPPORTING BRITISH RACING EBF FILLIES' H'CAP 1m 2f (P)
1:35 (1:35) (Class 3) (0-90,86) 3-Y-O **£6,663** (£1,982; £990; £495) **Stalls** Low

Form RPR

2111 1 **Layali Dubai (USA)**[8] 7655 3-9-11 86 6ex SilvestreDeSousa 5 91+
(Saeed Bin Suroor) *chsd ldng pair tl wnt 2nd over 5f out: rdn ent fnl 2f: edgd lft but chal fnl 100yds: led fnl 50yds: rdn out* **5/4**[1]

2201 2 hd **Four Leaves (IRE)**[8] 7656 3-9-7 82 6ex (p) AdamKirby 1 87
(Marco Botti) *led: sn hdd: chsd ldr tl over 5f out: rdn ent fnl 2f: ev ch fnl f: kpt on: wnt 2nd on post* **9/1**

411 3 nse **Afraah (USA)**[17] 7461 3-9-7 82 PaulHanagan 4 87
(Roger Varian) *sn led: rdn and qcknd ent fnl 2f: hrd pressed ent fnl f: hdd and lost 2 pls fnl 50yds* **9/4**[2]

413 4 2 ¼ **Tawaasul**[22] 7359 3-8-13 74 JimCrowley 2 74
(William Haggas) *chsd ldng trio: effrt and hung lft u.p 1f out: styd on same pce ins fnl f* **4/1**[3]

-340 5 3 ¾ **Soho Rocks**[78] 5769 3-8-9 68 ow2 [1] RobertHavlin 6 63
(James Toller) *stdd and dropped in bhd s: hld up in tch: rdn and effrt over 2f out: wknd ent fnl f* **20/1**

2m 7.71s (1.11) **Going Correction** 0.0s/f (Stan) **5** Ran SP% **110.0**
Speed ratings (Par 103): **95,94,94,93,90**
CSF £12.75 TOTE £2.20: £1.10, £2.80; EX 7.70.
Owner Godolphin **Bred** Darley **Trained** Newmarket, Suffolk

FOCUS
Only a small field, but a competitive handicap featuring three last-time-out winners. The pace was steady, which resulted in a very close finish between the first three.

NOTEBOOK
Layali Dubai(USA) looked ahead of the handicapper despite a 6lb penalty for her recent Wolverhampton success and she landed the four-timer in tenacious style. This form can be upgraded as she wasn't suited by the slow pace back down in trip, and in the end she did well to win. She's a smashing filly with a faultless attitude and there ought to be more to come from her, especially given a stiffer test. She's now 4-5 in handicaps. (tchd 13-8)
Four Leaves(IRE), with the cheekpieces retained, opened her account at the sixth attempt in maiden company on her previous start and ran a cracker under a 6lb penalty back in a handicap. She showed a good turn of foot and looks capable of winning more races. (op 7-1 tchd 10-1)
Afraah(USA), with the hood retained and 4lb higher than when winning on her handicap debut 17 days earlier, was allowed an uncontested lead and at one stage it looked like she may have stolen it from the front once Paul Hanagan kicked for home on the bend entering the straight. She didn't shirk the issue, was only run out of it close home, and remains in good form. (op 3-1 tchd 2-1)
Tawaasul, who ran creditably on her return from a break when third on her handicap debut at Wolverhampton 22 days previously, just lacked the tactical speed to get involved. (op 7-2)
Soho Rocks, having her second start on the AW, fared okay in a first-time hood although she was ultimately outclassed. (tchd 25-1)

7741 LINGFIELDPARK.CO.UK H'CAP (DIV I) 6f (P)
2:10 (2:11) (Class 5) (0-75,75) 3-Y-O+ **£2,385** (£704; £352) **Stalls** Low

Form RPR

4652 1 **Aldermoor (USA)**[16] 7485 6-9-7 75 WilliamCarson 8 83
(Stuart Williams) *in tch in midfield: hdwy u.p ent fnl f: led fnl 100yds: r.o wl* **7/2**[1]

0432 2 ½ **Lastkingofscotland (IRE)**[11] 7590 6-8-10 64 (b) PaulHanagan 2 70
(Conor Dore) *chsd ldrs: rdn and effrt on inner over 1f out: chsd wnr ins fnl f: r.o* **11/2**

6100 3 ½ **The Tichborne (IRE)**[16] 7485 4-9-3 71 (v) AdamKirby 9 76
(Roger Teal) *bhd: reminder over 4f out: hdwy u.p jst ins fnl f: r.o wl: nt quite rch ldrs* **5/1**[3]

6300 4 ½ **My Own Way Home**[20] 7416 4-8-10 64 ow1 TomMcLaughlin 1 67
(David Evans) *hld up in rr: c wd and effrt bnd 2f out: styd on wl u.p ins fnl f: nt rch ldrs* **50/1**

6600 5 hd **Key Ambition**[10] 7607 3-9-5 73 (tp) SebSanders 11 76
(Garry Moss) *rdn leaving stalls: sn pressing ldr: ev ch and rdn 2f out: led jst ins fnl f: hdd and one pce fnl 100yds* **20/1**

0000 6 nk **Parisian Pyramid (IRE)**[17] 7464 6-8-13 72 WilliamTwiston-Davies[(5)] 6 74
(Ian Williams) *led: rdn 2f out: hdd jst ins fnl f: no ex and styd on same pce fnl 100yds* **14/1**

0545 7 ¾ **Hatta Stream (IRE)**[24] 7316 6-9-4 75 SimonPearce[(3)] 4 74
(Lydia Pearce) *in tch in midfield: short of room and dropped into last quartet: rdn and effrt jst over 1f out: kpt on ins fnl f* **20/1**

6303 8 hd **Speak The Truth (IRE)**[25] 7299 6-8-7 66 (p) NathanAlison[(5)] 5 65
(Jim Boyle) *stdd s: hld up in last quartet: clsng and looking for run over 1f out: swtchd lft 1f out: kpt on but nvr able to chal* **16/1**

0260 9 shd **Emman Bee (IRE)**[27] 7246 3-9-0 73 MichaelJMMurphy[(5)] 7 71
(John Gallagher) *in tch in midfield: rdn and trying to switch rt over 1f out: styd on same pce and no imp fnl f* **7/1**

4600 10 shd **Saucy Brown (IRE)**[104] 4829 6-9-1 69 (t) FrannyNorton 10 67
(Kevin Ryan) *chsd ldrs: nt clr run 2f out: nvr much room after: lost pl and keeping on same pce whn nt clr run again wl ins fnl f* **9/2**[2]

0300 11 ½ **Cardinal**[16] 7489 7-9-3 71 JimCrowley 12 67
(Robert Cowell) *chsd ldrs: rdn and unable qck over 1f out: wknd ins fnl f* **12/1**

0236 12 ½ **Commandingpresence (USA)**[25] 7299 6-8-11 65 RichardKingscote 3 60
(John Bridger) *in tch in midfield: rdn and unable qck on inner 2f out: wknd ins fnl f* **25/1**

1m 11.74s (-0.16) **Going Correction** 0.0s/f (Stan) **12** Ran SP% **120.5**
Speed ratings (Par 103): **101,100,99,99,98 98,97,97,96,96 96,95**
Tote Swingers: 1&2 £2.40, 1&3 £5.60, 2&3 £4.40 CSF £21.78 CT £99.88 TOTE £3.90: £1.40, £2.00, £2.10; EX 13.00 Trifecta £57.70 Pool: £1,008.78 - 13.11 winning units..
Owner Darren Hudson-Wood **Bred** Gulf Coast Farms LLC **Trained** Newmarket, Suffolk

FOCUS
A fair handicap run at a good pace which suited the closers.

7742 LINGFIELDPARK.CO.UK H'CAP (DIV II) 6f (P)
2:45 (2:47) (Class 5) (0-75,75) 3-Y-O+ **£2,385** (£704; £352) **Stalls** Low

Form RPR

0034 1 **Mac Gille Eoin**[24] 7309 8-9-6 74 JimCrowley 10 83
(Luke Dace) *hld up in tch: rdn and qcknd over 1f out: led ins fnl f: r.o wl* **5/1**[2]

2202 2 1 **I See You**[16] 7489 3-9-3 71 (p) SilvestreDeSousa 7 77
(Peter Makin) *chsd ldng trio: rdn and unable qck 2f out: kpt on u.p ins fnl f* **6/1**[3]

0130 3 ¾ **We Have A Dream**[35] 7023 7-9-7 75 WilliamCarson 6 79
(William Muir) *led: sn hdd: chsd ldr: rdn wl over 1f out: kpt on same pce u.p ins fnl f* **15/2**

2601 4 1 **Cut Across (IRE)**[22] 7360 4-9-5 73 SebSanders 8 73+
(Nick Littmoden) *s.i.s: bhd and sn pushed along: hdwy into midfield over 2f out: kpt on ins fnl f: nvr trbld ldrs* **9/4**[1]

0302 5 ¾ **Button Moon (IRE)**[16] 7483 4-8-11 70 (p) MichaelJMMurphy[(5)] 1 68
(Paul Fitzsimons) *chsd ldrs: rdn and effrt on inner over 1f out: led 1f out tl ins fnl f: wknd ins fnl f* **8/1**

6400 6 nse **Billy Red**[8] 7648 8-9-3 71 (b) FergusSweeney 9 69
(J R Jenkins) *sn led and racd keenly: rdn and hdd 1f out: wknd fnl 100yds* **20/1**

1454 7 nse **Stonecrabstomorrow (IRE)**[16] 7485 9-8-9 66 MarkCoumbe[(3)] 3 64
(Michael Attwater) *bhd: clsng and n.m.r ent fnl 2f: kpt on u.p fnl f: nvr able to chal* **12/1**

0000 8 1 ½ **Welsh Inlet (IRE)**[25] 7299 4-8-7 61 oh6 KieranO'Neill 5 54
(John Bridger) *racd in midfield: rdn and effrt ent fnl 2f: styd on same pce fr over 1f out: nvr trbld ldrs* **50/1**

0 9 3 **Amour Fou (IRE)**[31] 7153 4-8-10 64 ChrisCatlin 2 47
(W T Farrell, Ire) *restless in stalls: s.i.s: bhd: n.d* **16/1**

1356 10 1 **Dorothy's Dancing (IRE)**[24] 7308 4-8-12 66 AdamBeschizza 12 46
(Gary Moore) *t.k.h: hld up in rr: rdn wl over 1f out: no imp* **10/1**

5400 **11** *1 ¾* **Justbookies Dotnet**[78] 5775 3-8-11 **65**.......................(v) FrannyNorton 4 39
(Louise Best) *in tch early: steadily lost pl: bhd over 1f out* **33/1**

1m 11.46s (-0.44) **Going Correction** 0.0s/f (Stan) 11 Ran SP% **116.9**
Speed ratings (Par 103): **102,100,99,98,97 97,97,95,91,89 87**
Tote Swingers: 1&2 £5.10, 1&3 £7.10, 2&3 £8.10 CSF £34.21 CT £224.89 TOTE £5.00: £2.90, £1.20, £3.50; EX 25.40 Trifecta £390.40 Pool: £952.62 - 1.83 winning units..
Owner M C S D Racing Partnership **Bred** M C S D Racing Ltd **Trained** Five Oaks, W Sussex

FOCUS
The steady pace made it difficult to make up late ground and those ridden prominently were favoured.
I See You Official explanation: jockey said filly hung left.
Cut Across(IRE) Official explanation: trainer said gelding was slowly away.
Amour Fou(IRE) Official explanation: jockey said filly got upset in stalls and missed the break.

7743 BET TOTEEXACTA AT TOTEPOOL.COM H'CAP 1m (P)
3:20 (3:22) (Class 5) (0-75,74) 3-Y-0+ **£2,385** (£704; £352) **Stalls** High

Form RPR
003 **1** **Roxelana (IRE)**[23] 7328 3-9-4 **73**.....................................(t) WilliamBuick 9 82+
(Jeremy Noseda) *stdd after s: hld up in last trio: stl towards rr and stuck bhd a wall horses 2f out: swtchd rt and effrt over 1f out: str run to ld wl ins fnl f* **9/4**[1]
2400 **2** *¾* **Buckland (IRE)**[32] 7115 4-8-12 **72**.......................... NicoleNordblad[(7)] 12 79
(Hans Adielsson) *hld up in last pair: c wd and hdwy 2f out: r.o wl ins fnl f* **20/1**
6045 **3** *1* **Mister Musicmaster**[42] 6837 3-9-5 **74**...................... RichardKingscote 3 79
(Ron Hodges) *in tch: rdn and effrt on inner over 1f out: edging out rt and kpt on wl ins fnl f* **10/1**
1245 **4** *nse* **Roy The Boy (USA)**[30] 7170 4-9-6 **73**........................... FrannyNorton 1 78
(Alan Bailey) *led: clr and rdn wl over 1f out: edgd rt and hdd wl ins fnl f* **6/1**[2]
6545 **5** *hd* **Satwa Laird**[16] 7480 6-8-10 **68**.. DavidKenny[(5)] 7 72
(Conor Dore) *in tch in midfield: rdn and effrt to chse ldrs ent fnl f: kpt on same pce ins fnl f* **20/1**
3022 **6** *hd* **One Way Or Another (AUS)**[20] 7415 9-9-0 **67**......... TomMcLaughlin 2 71
(David Evans) *hld up in tch in midfield: n.m.r and stl gng wl 2f out: rdn and hdwy ent fnl f: no imp fnl 100yds* **5/1**[3]
4001 **7** *2* **L'Hirondelle (IRE)**[30] 7171 8-9-4 **71**............................ J-PGuillambert 5 70
(Michael Attwater) *chsd ldr: rdn 3f out: wknd ins fnl f* **16/1**
0400 **8** *1* **Ellie In The Pink (IRE)**[24] 7310 4-8-9 **67**............. JemmaMarshall[(5)] 10 64
(Pat Phelan) *s.i.s: bhd: rdn 2f out: styng but no threat to ldrs whn nt clr run and switching rt ins fnl f: kpt on* **25/1**
410 **9** *¾* **Paphos**[64] 6171 5-9-2 **69**..(v) PaulHanagan 11 64
(Stuart Williams) *chsd ldrs: rdn and unable qck wl over 1f out: wknd jst ins fnl f* **15/2**
4425 **10** *nk* **Bajan Bear**[16] 7485 4-9-2 **69**.. JimCrowley 8 73+
(Michael Blanshard) *hld up in tch: clsd and wl in tch whn nt clr run over 1f out: swtchd lft 1f out: sn nt clr run again and nt pushed after* **13/2**[3]
3222 **11** *1 ¼* **Uncle Dermot (IRE)**[9] 7639 4-9-5 **72**.................................. ChrisCatlin 4 63
(Brendan Powell) *chsd ldrs: rdn and unable qck 2f out: wknd ins fnl f* **8/1**
4000 **12** *nk* **Benandonner (USA)**[20] 7409 9-9-6 **73**........................ FergusSweeney 6 64
(Paddy Butler) *in tch in midfield: rdn and lost pl wl over 1f out: bhd ins fnl f* **40/1**

1m 37.7s (-0.50) **Going Correction** 0.0s/f (Stan)
WFA 3 from 4yo+ 2lb 12 Ran SP% **116.8**
Speed ratings (Par 103): **102,101,100,100,100 99,97,96,96,95 94,94**
Tote Swingers: 1&2 £21.10, 1&3 £6.60, 2&3 £39.50 CSF £57.12 CT £388.74 TOTE £3.30: £1.70, £9.60, £4.00; EX 75.90 TRIFECTA Not won..
Owner P Makin **Bred** Stowell Park Stud **Trained** Newmarket, Suffolk

FOCUS
A modest handicap, but the pace was strong and four of the first five home were held up in the early stages.
Bajan Bear ◆ Official explanation: jockey said gelding was denied a clear run on more than one occasion.

7744 BET TOTEEXACTA APPRENTICE H'CAP 1m 5f (P)
3:55 (3:55) (Class 5) (0-70,70) 3-Y-0+ **£2,385** (£704; £352) **Stalls** Low

Form RPR
35-1 **1** **Mutual Regard (IRE)**[27] 7252 3-9-0 **65**............................... TimClark 11 77+
(Sir Mark Prescott Bt) *chsd ldr tl led over 2f out: rdn and asserted ent fnl f: idling in front and rdn out cl home* **11/8**[1]
1226 **2** *nk* **English Summer**[21] 7380 5-9-12 **70**.............................(t) AliceHaynes 10 76
(David Simcock) *in tch: effrt to chse clr pair over 1f out: styd on strly ins fnl f: wnt 2nd and pressing wnr cl home* **5/1**[2]
3432 **3** *¾* **Celtic Charlie (FR)**[9] 7629 7-8-12 **56** oh5...................... RufusVergette 6 61
(Pat Phelan) *in tch in midfield: n.m.r and outpcd 2f out: rallied and swtchd rt ins fnl f: styd on wl fnl 100yds* **6/1**[3]
5465 **4** *½* **El Libertador (USA)**[8] 7652 6-8-5 **56** oh1..................(b) JoeyHaynes[(7)] 3 60
(Eric Wheeler) *chsd ldrs: chsd wnr on inner 2f out: drvn and unable qck over 1f out: styd on same pce fnl f: lost 2 pls towards fin* **25/1**
5432 **5** *1* **Thecornishcockney**[20] 7417 3-8-11 **69**..............(tp) BradleyBosley[(7)] 8 72
(John Ryan) *stdd s: hld up wl off the pce in rr: stdy hdwy over 4f out: outpcd 2f out: rallied and r.o strly ins fnl f: nt rch ldrs* **10/1**
4210 **6** *1* **Swift Blade (IRE)**[56] 6430 4-9-4 **69**.....................(p) JoshQuinn[(7)] 1 70
(Lady Herries) *t.k.h: hld up off the pce in last trio: hdwy into midfield 5f out: outpcd bnd 2f out: rallied and kpt on ins fnl f: nt rch ldrs* **16/1**
3500 **7** *nk* **I'm Harry**[20] 7417 3-8-4 **62**.......................................(t) AaronJones[(7)] 5 63
(George Baker) *chsd ldrs: rdn and outpcd 2f out: kpt on same pce fr over 1f out* **50/1**
0524 **8** *2 ¾* **Rodrigo De Freitas (IRE)**[36] 7012 5-8-13 **57**................(v) PhilipPrince 4 54
(Jim Boyle) *hld up in midfield on inner: rdn and unable qck 2f out: no imp and wl hld after* **20/1**
5000 **9** *3 ½* **Eagle Nebula**[15] 7511 8-9-8 **66**......................................(p) HannahNunn 12 57
(Brett Johnson) *hld up off the pce in last trio: nvr trbld ldrs* **40/1**
5233 **10** *2 ½* **Ampleforth**[77] 5798 4-9-9 **70**...(v) JoshCrane[(3)] 14 58
(Ian Williams) *hld up in last trio: rdn and no imp wl over 1f out: wl btn and hung lft ins fnl f* **15/2**
-032 **11** *2 ¼* **Missionaire (USA)**[15] 519 5-8-6 **57**......................... AidenBlakemore[(7)] 2 41
(Tony Carroll) *led tl over 2f out: wknd qckly over 1f out* **33/1**
1453 **12** *5* **Iceman George**[20] 7409 8-8-13 **59**.................................(v) CarolineKelly[(7)] 13 36
(Lydia Pearce) *racd wd: in tch in midfield: lost pl bnd 4f out: bhd fnl 2f* **25/1**

2m 46.07s (0.07) **Going Correction** 0.0s/f (Stan)
WFA 3 from 4yo+ 7lb 12 Ran SP% **119.6**
Speed ratings (Par 103): **99,98,98,98,97 96,96,94,92,91 89,86**
Tote Swingers: 1&2 £3.10, 1&3 £3.60, 2&3 £6.50 CSF £7.30 CT £32.87 TOTE £2.00: £1.20, £1.80, £2.40; EX 8.90 Trifecta £34.70 Pool: £1,478.30 - 31.94 winning units..
Owner Moyglare Stud Farm **Bred** Moyglare Stud Farm Ltd **Trained** Newmarket, Suffolk

■ Stewards' Enquiry : Josh Crane five-day ban; used whip when out of contention (1st,3rd-5th Dec).

FOCUS
A moderate handicap run at a steady pace. The visibility was poor with a sea of fog having descended on the track.
T/Plt: £29.90 to a £1 stake. Pool: £40,830.00 - 995.99 winning tickets. T/Qpdt: £5.70 to a £1 stake. Pool: £4,863.00 - 630.01 winning tickets. SP

7666 WOLVERHAMPTON (A.W) (L-H)
Friday, November 16

OFFICIAL GOING: Standard
Wind: Almost nil Weather: Overcast turning misty

7745 32RED SUPPORTING BRITISH RACING NURSERY 5f 20y(P)
4:15 (4:16) (Class 5) (0-75,74) 2-Y-O **£2,264** (£673; £336; £168) **Stalls** Low

Form RPR
2230 **1** **Layla's Oasis**[17] 7463 2-9-0 **67**... JamieSpencer 4 73
(Jamie Osborne) *stdd s: hld up: hdwy over 1f out: shkn up to ld wl ins fnl f: r.o* **13/2**
12 **2** *2* **Modern Lady**[14] 7526 2-8-10 **63**................................. RobbieFitzpatrick 1 62
(Richard Guest) *chsd ldr: rdn over 1f out: ev ch and hung rt ins fnl f: styd on same pce* **9/1**
160 **3** *1* **Ovett**[28] 7220 2-9-5 **72**... GeorgeBaker 5 67
(Gary Moore) *hld up: pushed along 1/2-way: rdn over 1f out: r.o ins fnl f: nvr nrr* **3/1**[1]
2026 **4** *shd* **Cymeriad**[17] 7463 2-8-3 **56**.. NickyMackay 3 51
(Michael Easterby) *sn led: rdn over 1f out: hdd and no ex wl ins fnl f* **18/1**
6432 **5** *nk* **Indian Affair**[35] 7014 2-9-0 **67**.. LiamKeniry 7 61
(Milton Bradley) *chsd ldrs: rdn over 1f out: styd on* **7/1**
5101 **6** *2 ¼* **Harrogate Fair**[14] 7526 2-8-11 **64**...................................... AndreaAtzeni 9 50
(Michael Squance) *in rr: pushed along 3f out: rdn over 1f out: nt trble ldrs* **10/1**
221 **7** *¾* **Smart Daisy K**[38] 6970 2-9-7 **74**.. ShaneKelly 2 57
(Reg Hollinshead) *hld up in tch: rdn over 1f out: wknd ins fnl f* **5/1**[3]
3453 **8** *hd* **Kodatish (IRE)**[28] 7220 2-9-2 **69**.. LukeMorris 6 51
(Ronald Harris) *hld up: rdn 1/2-way: n.d* **9/2**[2]
0423 **9** *1 ½* **Someone's Darling**[38] 6952 2-8-10 **63**............................... GrahamLee 10 40
(Jim Goldie) *a in rr* **25/1**
4000 **10** *5* **Mossgo (IRE)**[39] 6929 2-9-5 **72**.. JimmyQuinn 8 31
(John Best) *s.i.s and hmpd s: sn prom: rdn and wknd over 1f out* **33/1**

1m 2.29s (-0.01) **Going Correction** 0.0s/f (Stan) 10 Ran SP% **116.8**
Speed ratings (Par 96): **100,96,95,95,94 90,89,89,87,79**
Tote Swingers: 1&2 £10.20, 1&3 £3.70, 2&3 £7.90 CSF £63.76 CT £212.52 TOTE £7.60: £2.40, £2.70, £1.60; EX 45.30 Trifecta £265.50 Pool: £615,99 - 1.74 winning units.
Owner Dr Marwan Koukash **Bred** P T Tellwright **Trained** Upper Lambourn, Berks

FOCUS
They went quite quick here. Straightforward form behind the winner, who might have more to offer.

NOTEBOOK
Layla's Oasis ◆, in a change of tactics, was out the back early. Having her second start for Jamie Osborne, she appreciated being dropped in rather than making it, and came through strongly at the finish. She might have more to offer now that the right way to ride her has been discovered. (op 7-1 tchd 11-2)
Modern Lady, narrowly beaten over the C&D a fortnight earlier, was 4lb higher and ran another sound race, doing best of those that raced prominently. (op 11-2)
Ovett couldn't pick up like the winner, despite having the race run to suit. He looks too high in the weights. (op 9-2 tchd 11-4)
Cymeriad was down in distance, but she still had the speed to lead this lot. She went pretty quick early, though, and just didn't see it out. (op 14-1)
Indian Affair, another dropping back in trip, wasn't best away, edging right as he exited the stalls, and couldn't get to the front. (op 8-1)
Smart Daisy K was disappointing on her handicap debut, but she raced keenly in behind on the rail and as a result had nothing left for the finish. (op 3-1)
Kodatish(IRE)'s rider reported that the colt hung right-handed. Official explanation: jockey said colt hung right-handed. (op 9-1)

7746 32REDPOKER.COM H'CAP 5f 20y(P)
4:45 (4:46) (Class 6) (0-55,55) 3-Y-0+ **£1,704** (£503; £251) **Stalls** Low

Form RPR
0400 **1** **Ballarina**[7] 7673 6-9-0 **53**.. GrahamGibbons 2 61
(Eric Alston) *mde all: rdn and edgd rt ins fnl f: styd on* **9/2**[3]
2463 **2** *½* **Pavers Star**[7] 7673 3-9-2 **55**...................................(p) RobertWinston 11 61
(Noel Wilson) *chsd ldrs: rdn over 1f out: r.o* **10/3**[1]
005 **3** *½* **Nafa (IRE)**[21] 7378 4-8-13 **52**.. ShaneKelly 5 56
(Daniel Mark Loughnane) *chsd ldr: rdn over 1f out: styd on: lost 2nd post* **15/2**
0-24 **4** *1* **Rio Sands**[9] 7634 7-8-7 **46** oh1... PaulQuinn 6 47
(Richard Whitaker) *mid-div: sn pushed along: hdwy u.p over 1f out: r.o: nt rch ldrs* **16/1**
0006 **5** *¾* **Love Club**[34] 7061 4-8-7 **46** oh1.................................... PatrickMathers 12 44
(Brian Baugh) *hood removed slighly late: sn prom: outpcd 1/2-way: r.o u.p ins fnl f* **40/1**
5/03 **6** *½* **Burnt Cream**[30] 7157 5-8-13 **52**...(t) MartinLane 8 48
(Martin Bosley) *s.i.s: hld up: rdn over 1f out: r.o: nt trble ldrs* **10/1**
5040 **7** *nse* **Elusive Pursuit**[23] 7322 4-8-7 **46** oh1................................. EddieAhern 7 42
(Clive Cox) *s.i.s and hmpd s: hdwy u.p over 1f out: nvr on terms* **4/1**[2]
4630 **8** *1 ¾* **Rightcar**[17] 7465 5-8-11 **50**.. RobbieFitzpatrick 4 40
(Peter Grayson) *s.i.s: in rr and drvn along over 3f out: nvr nrr* **6/1**
4004 **9** *5* **Deveze (IRE)**[2] 7703 4-8-10 **49**...(b) LukeMorris 3 21
(Milton Bradley) *chsd ldrs: pushed along 1/2-way: rdn over 1f out: wknd fnl f* **12/1**
6040 **10** *2* **Stans Deelyte**[17] 7465 3-8-1 **47**................................ ShirleyTeasdale[(7)] 1 11
(Lisa Williamson) *prom: rdn 1/2-way: wknd over 1f out* **16/1**
0/0- **11** *2* **Reach For The Sky (IRE)**[533] 2631 5-8-7 **46**................. JimmyQuinn 13
(Hugh McWilliams) *hld up: bhd fr 1/2-way* **66/1**

1m 2.87s (0.57) **Going Correction** 0.0s/f (Stan) 11 Ran SP% **119.8**
Speed ratings (Par 101): **95,94,93,91,90 89,89,86,78,75 72**
Tote Swingers: 1&2 £4.40, 1&3 £7.70, 2&3 £6.70 CSF £20.29 CT £114.64 TOTE £5.00: £2.20, £1.50, £2.70; EX 20.60 Trifecta £102.80 Pool: £1,054.98 - 7.69 winning units..
Owner Mrs P O Morris **Bred** Mrs D Du Feu And Trickledown Stud **Trained** Longton, Lancs

FOCUS
Few got involved here, with those held up struggling to land a blow.

The Form Book Flat, Raceform Ltd, Compton, RG20 6NL

Ballarina Official explanation: trainer said regarding apparent improvement in form that a change of tactics on her last run had been unsuccessful and the mare appreciated a return to making the running.

7747 32REDBET.COM H'CAP (DIV I) 5f 216y(P)

5:15 (5:17) (Class 6) (0-55,55) 3-Y-0+ **£1,704** (£503; £251) **Stalls** Low

Form				RPR
4400	**1**		**Mey Blossom**[16] 7482 7-9-2 **55**....................(p) RobertWinston 1 (Richard Whitaker) *hld up: hdwy over 2f out: led ins fnl f: r.o* **12/1**	65
6260	**2**	¾	**Whiskey Junction**[17] 7471 8-9-0 **53**.................... AndreaAtzeni 2 (Michael Quinn) *chsd ldrs: rdn over 2f out: styd on u.p* **8/1**	61
0065	**3**	*hd*	**Hab Reeh**[10] 7604 4-8-6 **48**....................(bt) JulieBurke[(3)] 7 (Ruth Carr) *s.i.s: hld up: rdn and r.o ins fnl f: nt rch ldrs* **11/1**	55+
0003	**4**	*nk*	**Music Festival (USA)**[29] 7204 5-8-13 **52**.................... GrahamLee 10 (Jim Goldie) *hld up: pushed along over 2f out: rdn and r.o wl ins fnl f: nt rch ldrs* **4/1**[1]	58
0600	**5**	¾	**Athaakeel (IRE)**[17] 7465 6-8-11 **50**.................... DavidProbert 13 (Ronald Harris) *chsd ldr tl led over 3f out: rdn over 1f out: hdd and no ex ins fnl f* **25/1**	54
0450	**6**	½	**Irrational**[31] 7146 3-9-0 **53**....................(e[1]) JimmyQuinn 4 (Bryan Smart) *hld up: nt clr run 2f out: hdwy over 1f out: nt trble ldrs* **25/1**	55
0660	**7**	*nk*	**Sairaam (IRE)**[66] 6127 6-8-10 **49**.................... MartinLane 3 (Charles Smith) *prom: drvn along 1/2-way: sn outpcd: r.o ins fnl f* **28/1**	50
-600	**8**	*1*	**Ionwy**[70] 6002 3-8-11 **50**.................... TedDurcan 8 (Derek Haydn Jones) *chsd ldrs: rdn over 1f out: styd on same pce fnl f* **40/1**	48
0003	**9**	*1*	**Lady Platinum Club**[21] 7378 4-9-1 **54**....................(p) DaleSwift 11 (Linda Stubbs) *mid-div: drvn along 1/2-way: nvr trbld ldrs* **8/1**	49
0120	**10**	*3 ¼*	**Gypsy Rider**[10] 7616 3-9-2 **55**....................(p) LukeMorris 5 (Bryn Palling) *sn led: hdd over 3f out: chsd ldr tl rdn over 1f out: wknd ins fnl f* **11/2**[2]	40
0000	**11**	*1 ¾*	**Major Muscari (IRE)**[17] 7457 4-9-2 **55**.................... PatrickMathers 6 (Ian McInnes) *s.s: hdwy u.p over 1f out: wknd ins fnl f* **16/1**	34
4540	**12**	*nse*	**Forty Proof (IRE)**[22] 7362 4-8-8 **47**....................(vt) GrahamGibbons 9 (David Evans) *s.i.s: a in rr* **15/2**	26
0536	**13**	*2 ¼*	**Besty**[17] 7457 5-9-0 **53**....................(vt) JamieSpencer 12 (Paul Midgley) *plld hrd: hdwy over 4f out: hung lft: wknd and eased fnl f* **7/1**[3]	25

1m 15.67s (0.67) **Going Correction** 0.0s/f (Stan) **13** Ran SP% **117.4**
Speed ratings (Par 101): **95,94,93,93,92 91,91,89,88,84 81,81,78**
Tote Swingers: 1&2 £12.80, 1&3 £19.30, 2&3 £21.50 CSF £98.82 CT £1128.31 TOTE £12.90: £3.70, £4.20, £4.90; EX 98.30 TRIFECTA Not won..
Owner Waz Developments Ltd **Bred** Hellwood Stud Farm **Trained** Scarcroft, W Yorks

FOCUS
A tight handicap.
Besty Official explanation: jockey said gelding hung left-handed.

7748 32REDBET.COM H'CAP (DIV II) 5f 216y(P)

5:45 (5:48) (Class 6) (0-55,55) 3-Y-0+ **£1,704** (£503; £251) **Stalls** Low

Form				RPR
0003	**1**		**Reginald Claude**[22] 7362 4-8-6 **50**.................... RachealKneller[(5)] 9 (Mark Usher) *hld up: hdwy over 2f out: shkn up to ld nr fin* **4/1**[2]	59
0003	**2**	*1 ¼*	**Mack's Sister**[15] 7504 5-9-2 **55**....................(p) TedDurcan 4 (Dean Ivory) *chsd ldrs: led over 2f out: rdn ins fnl f: hdd nr fin* **15/2**[3]	60
3346	**3**	*nk*	**Dixie Gwalia**[24] 7316 4-8-6 **52**.................... SiobhanMiller[(7)] 10 (David Simcock) *hld up: hdwy over 1f out: r.o to go 3rd nr fin: nt rch ldrs* **14/1**	56
0550	**4**	½	**Temple Road (IRE)**[134] 3791 4-9-2 **55**.................... GrahamLee 6 (Milton Bradley) *hld up: r.o ins fnl f: nrst fin* **8/1**	57+
0604	**5**	½	**Blueberry Fizz (IRE)**[21] 7378 4-8-13 **52**....................(b) JohnFahy 12 (John Ryan) *chsd ldrs: rdn and ev ch ins fnl f: no ex towards fin* **28/1**	53
0520	**6**	*2*	**Lisselton Cross**[29] 7204 4-9-0 **53**....................(b) MartinLane 7 (Martin Bosley) *in rr and drvn along 1/2-way: r.o ins fnl f: nvr nrr* **14/1**	47
060	**7**	*1 ½*	**Myjestic Melody (IRE)**[11] 7591 4-8-9 **48**.................... RobertWinston 8 (Noel Wilson) *prom: rdn over 2f out: no ex fnl f* **25/1**	38
5430	**8**	*1 ½*	**Jackie Love (IRE)**[15] 7512 4-8-3 **49**....................(b) ShirleyTeasdale[(7)] 11 (Olivia Maylam) *hld up: hdwy 1/2-way: sn rdn: wknd fnl f* **9/1**	34
-560	**9**	*9*	**Ave Sofia**[18] 7437 3-8-7 **46** oh1.................... DominicFox 1 (John Holt) *a in rr* **22/1**	
06-0	**10**	*13*	**Monte Mayor One**[73] 5923 5-9-0 **53**....................(p) LukeMorris 2 (Mrs K Burke) *led early: chsd ldrs: drvn along over 2f out: wknd over 1f out* **20/1**	
0560	**11**	*14*	**Mr Optimistic**[15] 7504 4-8-11 **53**....................(t) AshleyMorgan[(3)] 3 (Pat Murphy) *chsd ldr: hmpd 4f out: cl up whn hmpd wl over 1f out: eased* **8/1**	+
0003	**F**		**Crown Dependency (IRE)**[2] 7703 3-8-11 **50**.......... GrahamGibbons 5 (David Evans) *sn pushed along to ld: edgd lft 4f out: pushed along and hdd over 2f out: wkng whn hmpd wl over 1f out: fell sn after: fatally injured* **3/1**[1]	

1m 15.29s (0.29) **Going Correction** 0.0s/f (Stan) **12** Ran SP% **118.7**
Speed ratings (Par 101): **98,96,95,95,94 91,89,87,75,58 39,**
Tote Swingers: 1&2 £4.70, 1&3 £12.90, 2&3 £8.60 CSF £32.22 CT £393.39 TOTE £6.80: £2.50, £1.20, £4.00; EX 39.60 Trifecta £88.40 Pool £785.06 - 6.74 winning units..
Owner High Five Racing **Bred** Whitsbury Manor Stud **Trained** Upper Lambourn, Berks

FOCUS
The quicker of the two divisions by 0.38sec.
Mr Optimistic Official explanation: jockey said gelding suffered interference in running.

7749 32RED CASINO MAIDEN STKS 7f 32y(P)

6:15 (6:16) (Class 5) 2-Y-0 **£2,264** (£673; £336; £168) **Stalls** High

Form				RPR
43	**1**		**Yarroom (IRE)**[23] 7330 2-9-3 0.................... AndreaAtzeni 4 (Roger Varian) *mde virtually all: racd keenly: pushed clr fr over 1f out: easily* **1/1**[1]	87+
	2	*7*	**Prophets Pride** 2-9-3 0.................... SebSanders 2 (Jeremy Noseda) *chsd wnr over 5f out: rdn over 2f out: outpcd fr over 1f out* **16/1**	70
05	**3**	*2*	**Sewn Up**[10] 7613 2-9-3 0.................... ShaneKelly 6 (Reg Hollinshead) *prom: rdn over 2f out: sn outpcd* **66/1**	65
02	**4**	*2*	**Not Rigg (USA)**[36] 7006 2-9-3 0....................(t) JamieSpencer 1 (Andrew Balding) *chsd ldr tl over 5f out: remained handy: rdn over 2f out: wknd over 1f out* **11/4**[2]	60
	5	½	**Silver Dixie (USA)** 2-9-3 0.................... GrahamLee 12 (Jeremy Noseda) *s.i.s: hld up: shkn up over 1f out: nvr nrr* **16/1**	59+
2	**6**	*nk*	**Ashamaly**[24] 7304 2-9-3 0.................... MartinDwyer 8 (James Tate) *trckd ldrs: rdn over 2f out: wknd over 1f out* **11/2**[3]	58
0	**7**	*1*	**Blackball (USA)**[23] 7330 2-9-3 0.................... TedDurcan 7 (David Lanigan) *mid-div: lost pl over 4f out: sn pushed along: wknd over 2f out* **25/1**	56+
	8	*hd*	**Masaadr** 2-9-3 0.................... MartinLane 10 (James Tate) *s.i.s: hld up: wknd over 3f out* **50/1**	55
6	**9**	½	**Classy Trick (USA)**[29] 7198 2-9-3 0.................... DavidNolan 9 (Richard Fahey) *hld up: shkn up and edgd lft 2f out: sn wknd* **33/1**	54
0	**10**	*6*	**Copper Rag**[21] 7373 2-8-12 0.................... RachealKneller[(5)] 3 (Mark Usher) *s.i.s: hdwy 1/2-way: wknd 2f out* **100/1**	39

1m 29.88s (0.28) **Going Correction** 0.0s/f (Stan) **10** Ran SP% **115.0**
Speed ratings (Par 96): **98,90,87,85,84 84,83,83,82,75**
Tote Swingers: 1&2 £4.50, 1&3 £17.50, 2&3 £54.20 CSF £19.39 TOTE £2.20: £1.10, £4.00, £11.90; EX 26.70 Trifecta £278.80 Pool: £832.86 - 2.24 winning units..
Owner Sheikh Ahmed Al Maktoum **Bred** Darley **Trained** Newmarket, Suffolk

FOCUS
A useful winner but it's doubtful if he had to improve too much, the race lacking depth.

NOTEBOOK
Yarroom(IRE) won the battle for the lead going to the first turn, and then was allowed the run of things out in front. He drew well clear in the straight and looks to have improved for the return to Polytrack, which wasn't unexpected considering his pedigree. (op 5-6)
Prophets Pride, the first foal of an unraced mare, was the winner's closest pursuer for most of the race, but just had no answer when that one kicked clear in the straight. Very weak in the betting beforehand, clearly not much was expected of him, so it wasn't a bad debut effort, and he should build on it. (op 20-1)
Sewn Up was keeping on quite nicely at the finish. There's stamina on the dam's side and he ought to appreciate further when he goes handicapping.
Not Rigg(USA) didn't match his Kempton form but he's another who can now go the handicap route, and better should be seen of him in that sphere. (op 3-1 tchd 5-2)
Silver Dixie(USA), dropped in from stall 12, was switched wide around the turn into the straight, then back towards the rail once in line for home. He made quiet headway late and this brother to graded-placed US 2yo winner Dixiewin can do better.
Ashamaly, scrubbed along on the turn in, still looked green and edged left for pressure. This was a step back from his debut run. (op 9-2)
Masaadr Official explanation: jockey said colt was denied a clear run.

7750 32RED.COM MAIDEN STKS 1m 141y(P)

6:45 (6:46) (Class 5) 2-Y-0 **£2,264** (£673; £336; £168) **Stalls** Low

Form				RPR
6	**1**		**Contributer (IRE)**[126] 4066 2-9-3 0.................... GrahamLee 10 (Ed Dunlop) *chsd ldrs: led wl over 1f out: shkn up and r.o* **15/8**[1]	81+
	2	*2 ½*	**Thouwra (IRE)** 2-9-3 0.................... TedDurcan 3 (Saeed Bin Suroor) *a.p: nt clr run wl over 1f out: chsd wnr fnl f: no imp* **7/2**[2]	79+
06	**3**	*4 ½*	**Ersaal**[91] 5304 2-9-3 0.................... AndreaAtzeni 4 (Roger Varian) *led: hdd 7f out: chsd ldr: rdn and ev ch wl over 1f out: wknd ins fnl f* **9/2**[3]	66
	4	*1 ¾*	**Mount Tiger** 2-9-3 0.................... MartinDwyer 5 (James Tate) *led 7f out: rdn and hdd wl over 1f out: wknd fnl f* **8/1**	63
5	**5**	*2*	**Revise (IRE)**[23] 7323 2-9-3 0.................... AdamKirby 6 (Marco Botti) *s.i.s: hld up: drvn along over 3f out: styd on u.p ins fnl f: nvr nrr* **12/1**	58+
42	**6**	*2*	**Dolphin Village (IRE)**[32] 7096 2-9-3 0.................... DavidNolan 8 (Richard Fahey) *hld up: pushed along 4f out: hdwy over 2f out: wknd over 1f out* **25/1**	54
	7	*1 ¾*	**Venue** 2-9-3 0.................... EddieAhern 7 (Sir Henry Cecil) *s.i.s: pushed along over 3f out: a in rr* **6/1**	51+
60	**8**	*nk*	**Refuse To Mambo**[14] 7517 2-9-3 0.................... ShaneKelly 9 (Reg Hollinshead) *chsd ldrs: rdn over 2f out: wknd over 1f out* **100/1**	50
0	**9**	*2 ¼*	**Ballinderry Boy**[16] 7492 2-9-3 0.................... DavidProbert 11 (Andrew Balding) *hld up: rdn over 3f out: wknd over 2f out* **80/1**	45

1m 49.08s (-1.42) **Going Correction** 0.0s/f (Stan) **9** Ran SP% **114.3**
Speed ratings (Par 96): **106,103,99,98,96 94,93,92,90**
Tote Swingers: 1&2 £2.30, 2&3 £4.10, 1&3 £2.40 CSF £8.27 TOTE £2.30: £1.10, £2.10, £1.90; EX 7.70 Trifecta £26.00 Pool £674.74 - 19.44 winning units.
Owner George Bolton **Bred** Petra Bloodstock Agency Ltd **Trained** Newmarket, Suffolk

FOCUS
The winner looks to have a fair bit more to offer and the second looks a ready-made maiden winner.

NOTEBOOK
Contributer(IRE) ◆ contested a strong maiden when he made his debut back in July, and this was always going to be much easier going providing he was at his best following a 126-day absence. He made his move wide around the bend leaving the back straight and, while that wouldn't normally be a wise thing to do, on this occasion it proved an advantage, as the runner-up got held up in a pocket on the rail and by the time he was out in the clear Contributer was away and gone. He's out of a French Group 3 winner and he should make up into a useful middle-distance handicapper next season. (op 7-4 tchd 2-1)
Thouwra(IRE) was going well on the turn but he was short of room as the winner was sent to the front, and that one got the jump on him. He finished clear of the rest, though, and this half-brother to ten-time winner Benandonner can soon go one better on this surface. (op 4-1)
Ersaal, one-paced in the closing stages, probably ran to a similar level as for his first two starts over 7f. He can go handicapping now. (op 7-1 tchd 15-2)
Mount Tiger, who's bred to stay well, made a promising start to his career. (op 11-2)
Revise(IRE) made some late progress from the back. He's another who looks like he'll need further in handicaps next year. (op 14-1 tchd 10-1)
Dolphin Village(IRE), bred to improve for the switch from soft/heavy ground to Polytrack, was under pressure a long way out and never got in a blow. He's now eligible for a mark, though, and better can be expected from him in handicaps. (op 16-1 tchd 14-1)
Venue, tall and unfurnished, was slowly away and ran green in rear. A half-brother to several smart winners, he probably just needs more time. (op 5-1)

7751 32RED H'CAP 1m 1f 103y(P)

7:15 (7:16) (Class 3) (0-95,92) 3-Y-0+ **£6,663** (£1,982; £990; £495) **Stalls** Low

Form				RPR
35	**1**		**Anjaz (USA)**[30] 7168 3-9-0 **88**.................... SilvestreDeSousa 3 (Saeed Bin Suroor) *a.p: chsd ldr over 2f out: led over 1f out: r.o* **7/2**[1]	103+
2536	**2**	*1 ¾*	**Come On Blue Chip (IRE)**[30] 7168 3-9-2 **90**..........(b) SebSanders 10 (Paul D'Arcy) *s.i.s: hld up: hdwy over 1f out: rdn to go 2nd wl ins fnl f: nt rch wnr* **6/1**[2]	100
1105	**3**	*4*	**Grey Mirage**[140] 3563 3-9-0 **88**.................... AdamKirby 4 (Marco Botti) *chsd ldr tl led 3f out: rdn and hdd over 1f out: no ex ins fnl f* **7/2**[1]	90
533	**4**	*2 ¼*	**Pass Muster**[7] 7672 5-8-9 **80**.................... ShaneKelly 5 (Ollie Pears) *hld up in tch: rdn over 1f out: styd on same pce* **6/1**[2]	77
1320	**5**	*1*	**Angelic Upstart (IRE)**[30] 7163 4-8-9 **80**.................... DavidProbert 11 (Andrew Balding) *hld up: pushed along over 4f out: styd on u.p fnl f: nvr nrr* **10/1**[3]	75

3464 **6** 1½ **Focail Maith**[9] 7640 4 -8-7**78** oh1 ....(b) JohnFahy 7 70
(John Ryan) *drvn along in rr early: n.d* **10/1**[3]

2015 **7** 1 **First Post (IRE)**[6] 7493 5 -8-12**83** .... AndreaAtzeni 13 73
(Derek Haydn Jones) *chsd ldrs: rdn over 2f out: wknd fnl f* **20/1**

6104 **8** 1¼ **Patriotic (IRE)**[17] 7461 4 -8-6**80** .... AshleyMorgan(3) 12 67
(Chris Dwyer) *hld up: hdwy over 3f out: rdn and wknd over 1f out* **10/1**[3]

0U00 **9** 1½ **Loyalty**[15] 7502 5 -9-5**90** ....(v) PatrickMathers 9 74
(Derek Shaw) *hld up: rdn over 1f out: nvr on terms* **50/1**

6630 **10** 5 **Spanish Plume**[10] 7618 4 -8-7**78** oh3 .... LukeMorris 1 51
(Reg Hollinshead) *chsd ldrs: rdn over 3f out: wknd over 2f out* **33/1**

-000 **11** ¾ **Pekan Star**[76] 5835 5 -9-0**85** .... DominicFox 2 57
(Roger Varian) *led: rdn and hdd 3f out: wkng whn hung lft over 1f out* **20/1**

0-00 **12** 13 **Polar Kite (IRE)**[26] 3128 4 -9-2**87** .... DavidNolan 8 31
(Richard Fahey) *hld up in tch: pushed along over 2f out: sn wknd* **40/1**

1m 58.74s (-2.96) **Going Correction** 0.0s/f (Stan)
WFA 3 from 4yo+ 3lb 12Ran SP% 117.2
Speed ratings (Par 107): **113,111,107,105,105 103,102,101,100,95 95,83**
Tote Swingers: 1&2 £4.60, 1&3 £4.00, 2&3 £5.70 CSF £22.39 CT £79.05 TOTE £2.10 : £1.10, £2.60, £1.60 ; EX 19.70 Trifecta £266.70 Pool: £1,234.26 - 3.47 winning units.
Owner Godolphin **Bred** Darley **Trained** Newmarket, Suffolk

FOCUS
A good-quality handicap dominated by the three 3yos in the line-up.

NOTEBOOK
Anjaz(USA), who was dropping in grade and back 2f in distance, won nicely. She quickened up well to go to the front and was always cosily holding off the runner-up, who'd finished much closer to her over 1m4f at Lingfield last time out. The drop back in trip was clearly a positive and, having only had seven starts, there should be more to come from her. (op 3-1)
Come On Blue Chip (IRE)who has done all his winning at this track, finished narrowly behind Anjaz over 1m4f at Lingfield last time. He came from well back to chase her home again, but she had much more in hand over him at the finish this time. (op 7-1 tchd 15-2 and 11-2)
Grey Mirage had been gelded since he last ran in June. The absence wasn't a great concern as he's won fresh before, and he made a bold bid, kicking off the front turning in. The winner comfortably had his measure, though, and he might just need a little help from the handicapper. (op 4-1 tchd 3-1)
Pass Muster, back in distance, put up a solid effort in a better race, but the handicapper looks to have his measure for the time being. (op 9-2)
Angelic Upstart (IRE)didn't get the clearest of runs in the straight, but he's another who remains vulnerable off his current mark. (op 9-1)
Focail Maith, back on the Polytrack and with blinkers replacing cheekpieces, found the race was over by the time he was in the clear. He was keeping on at the finish and is on a similar mark to when successful at Kempton in January. (op 11-1)

7752 £32 BONUS AT 32RED.COM CLASSIFIED STKS 1m 1f 103y (P)
7:45 (7:45) (Class 6) 3-Y-O+ **£1,704** (£503; £251) **Stalls** Low

Form RPR

4233 **1** **Taro Tywod (IRE)**[9] 7632 3 -8-12**54** .... ShaneKelly 1 60
(Mark Brisbourne) *led: hdd 8f out: chsd ldrs: rdn to ld ins fnl f: styd on* **3/1**[1]

0004 **2** ¾ **Hill Of Dreams (IRE)**[14] 7527 3 -8-12**49** .... EddieAhern 11 58
(Dean Ivory) *hld up: hdwy over 2f out: rdn to ld over 1f out: hdd ins fnl f: styd on* **5/1**[2]

0040 **3** 3¼ **Winnetou**[10] 7615 3 -8-12**55** .... MartinDwyer 13 52
(Frank Sheridan) *s.i.s: sn prom: rdn and ev ch over 1f out: no ex ins fnl f* **40/1**

/065 **4** 1¼ **May Boy**[7] 7671 6 -9-1**44** .... SilvestreDeSousa 9 49
(Ron Hodges) *chsd ldr over 7f out: led over 2f out: rdn and hdd over 1f out: no ex ins fnl f* **8/1**

6006 **5** 2 **Pastures New**[21] 7385 4 -9-1**52** ....(b) LukeMorris 3 45
(Violet M Jordan) *prom: drvn along over 5f out: wknd fnl f* **22/1**

3233 **6** 2 **Miss Ella Jade**[44] 6785 3 -8-12**55** .... PaulQuinn 7 41
(Richard Whitaker) *sn pushed along in rr: nvr on terms* **6/1**[3]

0 **7** 2½ **Doublebarreljimmy (IRE)**[10] 7616 3 -8-12**47** .... JimmyQuinn 8 35
(John Butler) *hld up: sme hdwy u.p over 2f out: wknd over 1f out* **16/1**

6423 **8** 3½ **Sweet Liberta (IRE)**[60] 6305 3 -8-5**53** .... DanielMuscutt(7) 4 28
(Andrew Balding) *led 8f out: rdn and hdd over 2f out: wknd over 1f out* **3/1**[1]

630 **9** 2 **Poetry Writer**[9] 7632 3 -8-12**53** .... LiamKeniry 12 24
(Michael Blanshard) *hld up: a in rr* **20/1**

0000 **10** 30 **Plus Fours (USA)**[9] 7632 3 -8-12**55** ....(v[1]) AndreaAtzeni 6
(Charles Smith) *hld up: rdn over 3f out: sn wknd* **16/1**

2m 1.95s (0.25) **Going Correction** 0.0s/f (Stan)
WFA 3 from 4yo+ 3lb 10Ran SP% 115.4
Speed ratings (Par 101): **98,97,94,93,91 89,87,84,82,56**
Tote Swingers: 1&2 £4.30, 2&3 £57.60, 1&3 £35.90 CSF £17.26 TOTE £2.10 : £1.10, £2.80, £10.50; EX 18.90 Trifecta £407.30 Part won. Pool: £543.10 - 0.40 winning units.
Owner Rasio Cymru Racing 1 **Bred** Pat Fullam **Trained** Great Ness, Shropshire

FOCUS
An ordinary heat.
Plus Fours (USA) Official explanation: jockey said gelding stopped quickly.
T/Plt: £131.90 to a £1 stake. Pool: £61,592.92 - 340.65 winning tickets. T/Qpdt: £18.10 to a £1 stake. Pool: £9,340.90 - 381 w. tckts CR 7753a - 7766a (Foreign Racing) see RI

7737 LINGFIELD (L-H)
Saturday, November 17

OFFICIAL GOING: Standard
Wind: Light, across Weather: dry

7767 BET ON TODAY'S FOOTBALL AT BLUESQ.COM H'CAP (DIV I) 1m 2f (P)
12:00 (12:00) (Class 6) (0-65,65) 3-Y-O+ **£2,181** (£644; £322) **Stalls** Low

Form RPR

2200 **1** **Merry Jaunt (USA)**[27] 7270 3 -9-6**65** .... WilliamBuick 8 73
(John Gosden) *hld up in tch: rdn and effrt over 2f out: led 1f out: edgd lft u.p ins fnl f: r.o wl: rdn out* **4/1**[1]

3030 **2** ½ **Hawaana (IRE)**[16] 7511 7 -9-10**65** .... RobertWinston 9 72
(Gay Kelleway) *hld up in midfield: rdn and hdwy ent fnl 2f: ev ch whn bmpd ins fnl f: styd on same pce and hld after* **4/1**[1]

0366 **3** nk **Sail Home**[58] 6416 5 -9-10**65** .... AdamBeschizza 6 71
(Julia Feilden) *chsd ldrs: drvn to press ldrs 1f out: kpt on same pce u.p fnl 75yds* **10/1**

0000 **4** nk **Edgeworth (IRE)**[17] 7480 6 -9-1**63** .... JoshBaudains(7) 1 69
(David Bridgwater) *hld up wl in tch: rdn and effrt on inner over 1f out: pressed ldrs ins fnl f: kpt on same pce fnl 100yds* **12/1**

0000 **5** 1¼ **Legal Legacy**[17] 7474 6 -9-8**63** .... EddieAhern 5 66
(Richard Rowe) *s.i.s: hld up towards rr: rdn and hdwy over 1f out: swtchd rt ins fnl f: styd on wl: nt rch ldrs* **20/1**

3000 **6** shd **Mafi (IRE)**[25] 7310 4 -9-9**64** .... WilliamCarson 10 67
(Mark Hoad) *hld up in tch towards rr: hdwy on outer 3 f out: kpt on same pce u.p fnl f* **16/1**

206 **7** ½ **Scary Movie (IRE)**[127] 818 7 -9-6**61** ....(p) MartinHarley 11 63
(Shaun Harley, Ire) *t.k.h: hld up in tch towards rr: effrt u.p over 1f out: swtchd rt ent fnl f: styd on: nt rch ldrs* **8/1**[3]

2660 **8** ½ **Santadelacruze**[88] 5441 3 -9-3**62** ....(p) GeorgeBaker 3 69+
(Gary Moore) *t.k.h: hld up in tch in midfield: hdwy to trck ldrs: and gng wl: whn nt clr run over 1f out: stl waiting for gap whn squeezed and hmpd ins fnl f: nt rcvr and nt pushed after* **8/1**[3]

0004 **9** shd **Orpen'Arry (IRE)**[17] 7474 4 -9-5**60** .... KieranO'Neill 13 61
(Jimmy Fox) *hld up in tch in rr: swtchd rt and effrt over 1f out: styd on but nvr gng pce to rch ldrs* **12/1**

010 **10** ½ **Indian Violet (IRE)**[185] 2173 6 -9-8**63** ....(p) LiamKeniry 14 63
(Zoe Davison) *chsd ldr: rdn to ld over 1f out: hdd 1f out: wknd ins fnl f* **66/1**

4000 **11** ¾ **Sovento (GER)**[2] 7733 8 -8-12**60** .... NoraLooby(7) 7 58
(Alan McCabe) *sn led: rdn and hdd over 1f out: wknd ins fnl f* **50/1**

2060 **12** 1½ **Princess Steph (IRE)**[7] 7473 3 -9-2**61** ....(t) SilvestreDeSousa 2 56
(Heather Main) *chsd ldrs: rdn 3f out: no ex u.p over 1f out: wknd fnl f* **20/1**

4430 **13** 6 **Derfenna Art (IRE)**[40] 6932 3 -9-6**65** ....(bt[1]) JimCrowley 12 48
(Seamus Durack) *s.i.s: nvr gng wl and niggled along in rr: rdn 4f out: wknd over 1f out* **11/2**[2]

2m 6.98s (0.38) **Going Correction** +0.05s/f (Slow)
WFA 3 from 4yo+ 4lb 13Ran SP% 120.9
Speed ratings (Par 101): **100,99,99,99,98 98,97,97,97,96 96,94,90**
Tote Swingers 1&2 £5.80, 2&3 £4.90, 1&3 £6.00 CSF £18.35 CT £153.53 TOTE £4.90 : £2.00, £1.60, £3.50 ; EX 22.40 Trifecta £89.30 Pool £171.51 - 1.44 winning units.
Owner K Abdulla **Bred** Juddmonte Farms Inc **Trained** Newmarket, Suffolk

FOCUS
A moderate handicap to start the card and they didn't go very quick.
Legal Legacy Official explanation: jockey said gelding was denied a clear run.
Mafi(IRE) Official explanation: jockey said gelding hung left.
Santadelacruze ◆ Official explanation: jockey said colt was denied a clear run.

7768 BET ON TODAY'S FOOTBALL AT BLUESQ.COM H'CAP (DIV II) 1m 2f (P)
12:30 (12:30) (Class 6) (0-65,65) 3-Y-O+ **£2,181** (£644; £322) **Stalls** Low

Form RPR

2023 **1** **Ishikawa (IRE)**[43] 6843 4 -9-10**65** .... FergusSweeney 3 75
(Alan King) *t.k.h: trckd ldrs: rdn and wnt between horses to chal ent fnl f: led ins fnl f: r.o wl* **6/1**

3210 **2** ½ **Thecornishcowboy**[39] 6973 3 -9-3**62** ....(t) AdamKirby 9 71
(John Ryan) *in tch: rdn and effrt to chal over 1f out: led 1f out: hdd ins fnl f: kpt on but a hld after* **10/1**

6210 **3** 1¼ **Zenarinda**[25] 7310 5 -9-9**64** .... GeorgeBaker 14 71
(Mark H Tompkins) *stdd after s: hld up in rr: hdwy 3f out: v wd bnd 2f out: drvn: edging lft but styd on wl fnl f to go 3rd towards fin* **16/1**

-033 **4** ½ **Wordiness**[15] 7529 4 -9-3**63** ....(t) WilliamTwiston-Davies(5) 6 69
(Seamus Durack) *hld up in tch: rdn and effrt on inner over 1f out: chsd ldrs fnl 100yds: no imp after and lost 3rd towards fin* **5/1**[2]

-030 **5** 1¼ **Burns Night**[23] 7347 6 -9-8**63** .... PaulHanagan 12 66
(Ollie Pears) *chsd ldng trio: rdn and effrt to press ldrs 2f out: drvn and unable qck over 1f out: wknd ins fnl f* **11/2**[3]

0004 **6** nse **Lady Arabella (IRE)**[21] 7416 3 -9-6**65** .... MartinHarley 8 68
(Alastair Lidderdale) *hld up towards rr: hdwy and swtchd lft ent fnl f: kpt on ins fnl f: nvr trbld ldrs* **25/1**

0505 **7** shd **Strike Force**[12] 7596 8 -9-1**61** ....(t) NatashaEaton(5) 2 64
(Alison Hutchinson) *led and set stdy gallop: rdn and hrd pressed ent fnl 2f: hdd 1f out: no ex and wknd ins fnl f* **20/1**

1005 **8** ½ **Resplendent Alpha**[17] 7473 8 -9-7**62** .... WilliamBuick 1 64
(Jamie Osborne) *rdr struggling to remove hood and slowly away: bhd: switching rt and hdwy wl over 1f out: kpt on u.p fnl f: nvr trbld ldrs* **11/1**

5324 **9** nk **Manomine**[59] 6365 3 -9-5**64** .... SilvestreDeSousa 10 65
(Clive Brittain) *in tch in midfield: rdn and unable qck over 2f out: drvn and styd on same pce fr over 1f out* **4/1**[1]

0222 **10** ½ **Elsie Bay**[18] 7470 3 -8-12**62** .... RachealKneller(5) 13 62
(Mark Usher) *hld up in midfield: rdn and effrt ent fnl 2f: styd on same pce and no real imp fr over 1f out* **11/1**

630 **11** 2¾ **Made Of More**[9] 7647 3 -9-5**64** .... LiamKeniry 4 59
(Roger Ingram) *hld up in midfield: rdn and lost pl over 2f out: towards rr but stl in tch tl wknd ent fnl f* **50/1**

-500 **12** ½ **Lady Barastar (IRE)**[36] 7018 4 -9-5**60** .... JimCrowley 7 54
(Amanda Perrett) *chsd ldr: rdn and ev ch 2f out tl ent fnl f: fdd ins fnl f* **25/1**

2650 **13** 2¾ **Byrd In Hand (IRE)**[9] 7643 5 -9-0**55** .... LukeMorris 5 43
(John Bridger) *hld up in tch towards rr: rdn and no real imp over 1f out: nvr trbld ldrs* **40/1**

0-00 **14** ¾ **Evergreen Forest (IRE)**[17] 7474 4 -9-7**65** .... RyanClark(3) 11 52
(Tom Keddy) *hld up in midfield: dropped towards rr but stl in tch 1/2-way: rdn over 2f out: no prog* **20/1**

2m 6.96s (0.36) **Going Correction** +0.05s/f (Slow)
WFA 3 from 4yo+ 4lb 14Ran SP% 119.6
Speed ratings (Par 101): **100,99,98,98,97 97,97,96,96,96 93,93,91,90**
Tote Swingers 1&2 £14.30, 2&3 £25.20, 1&3 £9.20 CSF £58.14 CT £923.46 TOTE £5.30 : £2.20, £4.20, £3.20 ; EX 71.00 TRIFECTA Not won.
Owner ROA Racing Partnership V **Bred** Ken Carroll **Trained** Barbury Castle, Wilts

FOCUS
Again they didn't appear to go that quick early and it was an advantage to be handy. The wining time was 0.02 seconds faster than the first division.
Resplendent Alpha Official explanation: jockey said gelding was slowly away.

7769 GET STRAIGHT TO THE BET AT BLUESQ.COM CLAIMING STKS 1m (P)
1:05 (1:05) (Class 6) 3-Y-O **£2,181** (£644; £322) **Stalls** High

Form RPR

2300 **1** **Brocklebank (IRE)**[2] 7732 3 -9-0**77** ....(tp) PhillipMakin 1 71
(Kevin Ryan) *t.k.h: chsd ldr tl over 4f out: rdn to chse ldr again 2f out: drvn to ld 1f out: styd on wl* **9/2**[3]

2560 **2** 1½ **Bint Alzain (IRE)**[21] 7415 3 -8-7**72** ....(t) LukeMorris 7 61
(Gerard Butler) *taken down early: dwlt: hld up in tch in rr: rdn and hdwy over 1f out: kpt on u.p to go 2nd cl home* **3/1**[2]

0060 **3** nk **Silence Is Easy**[9] 7643 3 -8-3**53** .... WilliamCarson 5 56
(William Muir) *led: rdn and c towards centre wl over 1f out: hdd 1f out: styd on same pce ins fnl f: lost 2nd cl home* **16/1**

2204 **4** *nk* **Kashmiri Star**[15] 7521 3-8-9 59......................................(v) AndreaAtzeni 2 61
(Michael Quinn) *t.k.h: hld up wl in tch: rdn and chsd ldng pair 2f out: styd on same pce u.p fnl f* **14/1**

0540 **5** *2¾* **Titus Star (IRE)**[28] 7250 3-8-12 60.. LiamKeniry 4 58
(J S Moore) *t.k.h: hld up in tch in rr: rdn and effrt wl over 1f out: no imp 1f out: one pce after* **8/1**

55 **6** *nk* **Trulee Scrumptious**[10] 7625 3-8-7 50..............................(b) KieranO'Neill 8 52
(Peter Charalambous) *t.k.h: chsd ldrs: steadily lost pl and towards rr whn rdn over 2f out: no prog and styd on same pce fr over 1f out* **25/1**

000 **7** *3¾* **Darwinian**[31] 7158 3-8-2 30.. JimmyQuinn 6 38?
(Dave Morris) *hld up towards rr: hdwy to chse ldr over 4f out tl 2f out: wknd over 1f out* **100/1**

0000 **8** *7* **Ewell Place (IRE)**[43] 6835 3-9-5 90................................ JamieSpencer 3 47
(David Nicholls) *stdd s: hld up in last pair: hdwy on inner into midfield after 2f out: lost pl and rdn over 2f out: no rspnse: btn 1f out: eased ins fnl f* **5/4**[1]

1m 38.65s (0.45) **Going Correction** +0.05s/f (Slow) **8** Ran SP% **116.1**
Speed ratings (Par 98): **99,97,97,96,94 93,90,83**
Tote Swingers 1&2 £3.10, 2&3 £10.10, 1&3 £9.90 CSF £18.75 TOTE £6.40: £1.20, £1.70, £3.10; EX 19.10 Trifecta £90.40 Pool £472.52 - 3.92 winning units..
Owner Mrs Margaret Forsyth **Bred** Vincent Reen **Trained** Hambleton, N Yorks

FOCUS
With the early pace very modest for this claimer, a few were inclined to pull. With the favourite running a shocker, the form probably amounts to little.
Titus Star(IRE) Official explanation: jockey said gelding ran too freely.

7770 BET AT BLUESQ.COM MEDIAN AUCTION MAIDEN STKS 6f (P)
1:40 (1:40) (Class 6) 3-5-Y-O **£2,181** (£644; £322) **Stalls** Low

Form RPR

4223 **1** **Tidal's Baby**[8] 7667 3-8-12 65.................................. GeorgeDowning(5) 7 62+
(Tony Carroll) *rrd as stalls opened and s.i.s: hld up bhd: hdwy ent fnl f: pushed along and qcknd to ld fnl 75yds: sn in command: comf* **5/2**[1]

6622 **2** *1¼* **Miakora**[88] 5454 4-8-12 55.. AndreaAtzeni 5 53
(Michael Quinn) *chsd ldr: rdn and ev ch 2f out: styd on same pce ins fnl f: wnt 2nd last strides* **14/1**

0000 **3** *nse* **Summer Sun**[2] 7729 3-8-12 50... LukeMorris 3 53
(Phil McEntee) *t.k.h: chsd ldrs: rdn and pressed ldrs 2f out: styd on same pce u.p fr over 1f out* **33/1**

0006 **4** *hd* **Red Ramesses (IRE)**[8] 7668 3-9-3 65............................ GeorgeBaker 2 57
(John Best) *led: rdn and c towards centre wl over 1f out: hdd and no ex fnl 75yds: lost 2 pls cl home* **7/2**[3]

5603 **5** *2* **Homeboy (IRE)**[2] 7719 4-8-12 63..............................(b) KatiaScallan(5) 4 51
(Marcus Tregoning) *taken down early: t.k.h: chsd ldrs over 4f out: rdn and fnd nil over 1f out: wknd ins fnl f* **7/2**[3]

6 *3¼* **My Colleen (USA)** 3-8-12 0.. ChrisCatlin 6 36
(Rae Guest) *in tch in last pair: pushed along 4f out: wknd over 1f out* **11/4**[2]

1m 12.3s (0.40) **Going Correction** +0.05s/f (Slow) **6** Ran SP% **109.3**
Speed ratings (Par 101): **99,97,97,97,94 90**
Tote Swingers 1&2 £1.40, 2&3 £6.90, 1&3 £7.20 CSF £32.87 TOTE £3.10: £2.20, £3.80; EX 13.00.
Owner Mrs Bernadette Quinn **Bred** Mr & Mrs J Quinn **Trained** Cropthorne, Worcs

FOCUS
A poor older-horse maiden with one newcomer against fives horses that had managed to avoid winning in 70 races between them.

7771 BLUE SQUARE BET CHURCHILL STKS (LISTED RACE) 1m 2f (P)
2:15 (2:15) (Class 1) 3-Y-O+
£18,714 (£7,095; £3,550; £1,768; £887; £445) **Stalls** Low

Form RPR

23-3 **1** **Farraaj (IRE)**[202] 1698 3-8-12 108.................................. AndreaAtzeni 10 107+
(Roger Varian) *chsd ldng pair: rdn to ld over 2f out: edgd rt over 1f out: styd on wl fnl f: rdn out* **11/8**[1]

25-4 **2** *1* **Genzy (FR)**[19] 7438 4-9-2 100... JimCrowley 2 105
(Ian Williams) *hld up in tch: hdwy over 2f out: chsd ldrs and drvn over 1f out: chsd wnr ins fnl f: no imp towards fin* **8/1**[3]

262 **3** *1¼* **Circumvent**[56] 6470 5-9-2 103.. PaulHanagan 6 103
(Paul Cole) *in tch: clsd on ldrs over 2f out: rdn and pressed wnr over 1f out: no ex ins fnl f: lost 2nd ins fnl f and wknd towards fin* **3/1**[2]

3030 **4** *2¾* **Tinshu (IRE)**[56] 6484 6-8-11 93....................................(p) WilliamCarson 8 92
(Derek Haydn Jones) *stdd s: hld up in last trio: clsd and nt clr run jst over 2f out: squeezed between horses and hdwy 2f out: styd on same pce u.p fnl f* **12/1**

3142 **5** *hd* **True To Form (IRE)**[10] 7631 5-9-2 96...........................(p) DavidProbert 3 97
(Martyn Meade) *hld up in midfield: clsd on ldrs over 2f out: drvn and styd on same pce fr over 1f out* **14/1**

6404 **6** *2½* **Bancnuanaheireann (IRE)**[14] 7556 5-9-2 91................ GeorgeBaker 1 94
(Michael Appleby) *hld up in midfield: clsd over 2f out: rdn and bdly hmpd on inner bnd 2f out: no imp over 1f out* **9/1**

2115 **7** *nse* **Quixote**[43] 6848 3-8-12 83...(t) RobertWinston 5 92
(Clive Brittain) *stdd s: t.k.h: hld up in rr: clsd on ldrs over 2f out: rdn and no imp fr over 1f out* **20/1**

0010 **8** *6* **Our Gal**[22] 7375 4-8-11 82.. JimmyQuinn 9 75
(Noel Quinlan) *dwlt: sn rcvrd and in midfield: lost pl and rdn 3f out: wknd 2f out* **100/1**

-140 **9** *3¼* **Sunday Bess (JPN)**[16] 7510 4-8-11 87.................(v) RichardKingscote 7 68
(Tom Dascombe) *led tl 7f out: clr w ldr after tl lost pl qckly over 2f out: bhd fnl f* **33/1**

4100 **10** *1½* **Emerald Wilderness (IRE)**[17] 7487 8-9-2 89...........(tp) JamieSpencer 4 70
(Mark Rimmer) *t.k.h: chsd ldr tl led 7f out: sn clr w ldr: rdn and hdd over 2f out: wknd over 1f out: bhd and eased ins fnl f* **25/1**

2m 2.37s (-4.23) **Going Correction** +0.05s/f (Slow)
WFA 3 from 4yo+ 4lb **10** Ran SP% **115.1**
Speed ratings (Par 111): **118,117,116,114,113 111,111,107,104,103**
toteswingers 1&2 £5.10, 1&3 £2.80, 2&3 £8.10 CSF £12.49 TOTE £2.00: £1.10, £3.00, £2.00; EX 13.00 Trifecta £54.80 Pool £1,045.57 - 14.29 winning units..
Owner Sheikh Ahmed Al Maktoum **Bred** Darley **Trained** Newmarket, Suffolk

FOCUS
Refreshingly for a race like this, there was no hanging about with Emerald Wilderness and Sunday Bess taking each other on for most of the way, clear of the rest. It didn't help them, though, as they eventually finished last and last but one. The classic generation had taken three of the four previous runnings of this Listed contest and that sequence was extended.

NOTEBOOK
Farraaj(IRE), gelded since finishing third in the Italian 2000 Guineas back in April, was up 2f in trip for this AW debut and had there been any chinks in his stamina, then this race would have exposed them. Leading the main group adrift of the two clear leaders, he was sent to the front rounding the home bend as that pair wilted and, despite hanging away to his right under pressure late on, was always doing enough. The Winter Derby back here in March does look the ideal target. Official explanation: jockey said gelding hung left from final bend making it difficult for him to ride out. (op 2-1)
Genzy(FR), a smart performer in France who ran Meandre to a head at Longchamp in May of last year, was entitled to need the run on his debut for the yard at Leicester last month following a 16-month absence, and he stepped up considerably from that. He had every chance after making headway into a challenging position rounding the home bend and kept on well, despite racing closer to the inside than his two main rivals. There are races to be won with him over here. (tchd 17-2)
Circumvent, narrowly beaten in this last year and a close third in the Winter Derby back in March, had every chance from the final bend and although hampered by the winner well inside the last furlong, he looked held at that point. He just seems to fall short in races like this around here. Official explanation: jockey said gelding suffered interference in the straight. (op 5-2)
Tinshu(IRE) is well suited to these conditions having won another Listed event over C&D last December and finished runner-up in the Winter Derby Trial back here in February. Given a waiting ride, she ran into a bit of traffic when trying to get closer turning for home and by the time she was in the clear, the front three had got away. She still has the ability to win a nice race around here at some point. (op 11-1 tchd 14-1)
True To Form(IRE) looked as good as ever in two starts for this yard earlier this month following a break, and finished closer to Tinshu than when they met here back in February, despite being 3lb worse off. He should continue to give his new connections plenty of fun. (op 10-1)
Bancnuanaheireann(IRE), beaten all 11 starts since a successful racecourse debut, including when a fine fourth in the Cambridgeshire, ran creditably but doesn't look the easiest to place. (op 17-2 tchd 10-1)
Quixote has winning form here and was in good heart on turf this autumn, but he had up to 25lb to find with his nine rivals and found this too tough an ask. (op 22-1)

7772 BLUE SQUARE BET GOLDEN ROSE STKS (LISTED RACE) 6f (P)
2:50 (2:50) (Class 1) 3-Y-O+
£18,714 (£7,095; £3,550; £1,768; £887; £445) **Stalls** Low

Form RPR

0110 **1** **Ballista (IRE)**[21] 7397 4-9-2 104................................ RichardKingscote 6 113
(Tom Dascombe) *mde all: rdn and wnt clr over 1f out: in command fnl f: r.o wl* **7/1**[3]

0000 **2** *2* **Ladies Are Forever**[7] 7690 4-8-11 100..................... SilvestreDeSousa 3 102
(Geoffrey Oldroyd) *in tch: rdn and effrt ent fnl 2f: styd on to chse clr wnr ins fnl f: kpt on but no threat to wnr* **16/1**

2116 **3** *nk* **Hezmah**[42] 6878 4-8-11 99.. PaulHanagan 7 101+
(John Gosden) *dwlt: hld up in last trio: stl plenty to do and hdwy 1f out: str run fnl f and presing for 2nd cl home: no threat to wnr* **4/1**[2]

4005 **4** *1* **Duchess Dora (IRE)**[51] 6602 5-8-11 96.......................... WilliamBuick 1 98
(David Simcock) *t.k.h: chsd ldrs: rdn and outpcd by wnr over 1f out: chsd clr wnr jst ins fnl f: no imp and lost 2 pls fnl 100yds* **33/1**

3443 **5** *shd* **Burj Alzain (IRE)**[3] 7709 4-9-2 98...................................(b[1]) LukeMorris 5 103
(Gerard Butler) *hld up in tch: rdn and effrt whn n.m.r over 1f out: sn swtchd rt: kpt on but no ch w wnr* **12/1**

132 **6** *nse* **Artistic Jewel (IRE)**[60] 6346 3-8-11 100..................... GrahamGibbons 9 97
(Ed McMahon) *in tch on outer: rdn and unable qck whn carried rt over 1f out: styd on same pce after* **12/1**

0000 **7** *hd* **Iver Bridge Lad**[11] 7624 5-9-2 105.................................(b) AdamKirby 11 102
(John Ryan) *stdd s: hld up in last trio: rdn and hdwy on outer over 1f out: kpt on but nvr a threat to wnr* **16/1**

0400 **8** *hd* **Fratellino**[63] 6244 5-9-4 100..(t) MartinHarley 12 103
(Alan McCabe) *chsd wnr: rdn and unable qck over 2f out: lost 2nd jst ins fnl f: no ex* **33/1**

041 **9** *1* **Capone (IRE)**[16] 7503 7-9-2 102... ShaneKelly 4 98
(Garry Moss) *in tch in midfield: rdn and styd on same pce fr wl over 1f out* **7/1**[3]

3000 **10** *½* **Secret Asset (IRE)**[41] 6908 7-9-2 102............................. GeorgeBaker 2 96
(Jane Chapple-Hyam) *hld up in tch: rdn and unable qck over 1f out: one pce and wl hld fnl f* **16/1**

1004 **11** *1¼* **Dandy Boy (ITY)**[70] 6030 6-9-2 111............................. JamieSpencer 10 92
(David Marnane, Ire) *stdd and dropped in bhd after s: hld up in rr: rdn and effrt on inner over 1f out: no prog* **9/4**[1]

30 **12** *½* **Pandar**[40] 6943 3-9-2 107.. JimCrowley 8 91
(Robert Cowell) *hld up in tch towards rr: lost pl wl over 1f out: wknd fnl f* **16/1**

1m 10.35s (-1.55) **Going Correction** +0.05s/f (Slow) **12** Ran SP% **120.6**
Speed ratings (Par 111): **112,109,108,107,107 107,107,106,105,104 103,102**
toteswingers 1&2 £22.50, 1&3 £4.50, 2&3 £16.40 CSF £115.54 TOTE £9.20: £2.80, £6.30, £1.90; EX 143.70 Trifecta £814.90 Part won. Pool £1,086.57 - 0.50 winning units..
Owner Well Done Top Man Partnership **Bred** Sj Partnership **Trained** Malpas, Cheshire

FOCUS
A decent Listed sprint.

NOTEBOOK
Ballista(IRE), making his AW debut, found himself drawn on the wrong side at Doncaster last time, but had previously been in good form and was back on song here. Making every yard as he likes to do, his rider did the right thing in bringing him out into the centre of the track on turning in and it was soon obvious that he wasn't going to be caught. He has done nothing but improve this year. (tchd 6-1)
Ladies Are Forever was also making her AW debut, having shown regressive form on turf this year, and ran a blinder. Racing in midfield before staying on all the way to the line, she is well worth another try on an artificial surface if an opportunity can be found. (op 18-1 tchd 20-1)
Hezmah, another making her AW debut, had been running well prior to pulling her chance away in a soft-ground Newmarket Listed event last time, but on this occasion she hampered herself with a slow start and, at this level, that was always going to be hard to overcome. She did her best to get involved and finished with a rattle, but it always looked as though she was going to run out of time. (op 13-2)
Duchess Dora(IRE), yet another making her AW debut, had yet to prove she truly stays this far, but it would be harsh to blame a lack of stamina for this defeat as she ran a cracker having been close to the pace from the start. (op 28-1)
Burj Alzain(IRE), blinkered for the first time, was another to finish well having given himself plenty to do and he ideally needs at least another furlong. (op 16-1)
Artistic Jewel(IRE) has been running well on turf this year and can be given some extra credit for this AW debut, as she was always being forced to race wider than ideal. (op 10-1)
Iver Bridge Lad, well held in a couple of soft-ground Group 3s since reappearing last month, tried to come from well back and was forced very wide off the final bend before finishing strongly. He is probably being readied for another Meydan campaign and this should have set him up nicely.
Fratellino, under a 2lb penalty for winning a 5f Listed event here back in March, showed his usual early speed, but didn't get home and is now 0-13 over this trip.

Dandy Boy(ITY), winner of this year's Wokingham and last seen finishing fourth in the Group 1 Betfred Sprint Cup at Haydock, was the one to beat on official ratings, but he never made any impression from the back of the field and even being kept close to the inside rail isn't enough to explain this timid effort. His trainer reported that the horse ran too free on a turning track. Official explanation: trainer said horse ran too freely on the turning track. (op 5-2)

7773 ENOUGH SAID JUST BET AT BLUESQ.COM EBF NOVICE STKS 1m (P)

3:20 (3:21) (Class 4) 2-Y-O **£4,398** (£1,309; £654; £327) **Stalls** High

Form				RPR
2	**1**		**Stasio (USA)**[24] 7324 2-9-0 0 ... WilliamBuick 4 (David Simcock) *chsd ldrs: swtchd ins and effrt over 1f out: led 1f out: sn in command and r.o wl: comf* **11/10**[1]	84+
	2	2 ¼	**Secret Talent** 2-9-0 0 ... JimCrowley 1 (Hughie Morrison) *rn green: hld up in rr: clsd and swtchd rt ent fnl f: styd on to chse clr wnr fnl 100yds: kpt on* **33/1**	79+
0142	**3**	2	**Fat Gary**[22] 7365 2-9-5 87 ... GeorgeBaker 2 (Tom Dascombe) *chsd ldr: rdn and ev ch ent fnl 2f: led over 1f out: hdd and outpcd by wnr 1f out: lost 2nd fnl 100yds* **11/4**[2]	79
01	**4**	3 ¼	**Teophilip (IRE)**[18] 7466 2-9-5 0 ... (t) AdamKirby 5 (Marco Botti) *dwlt: a same pl: rdn and unable qck over 2f out: wknd 1f out* **4/1**[3]	72
51	**5**	2 ½	**Bapak Sayang (USA)**[72] 5963 2-9-5 0 ... PhillipMakin 3 (Kevin Ryan) *led: rdn and hrd pressed ent fnl 2f: hdd over 1f out: sn wknd* **8/1**	66

1m 38.05s (-0.15) **Going Correction** +0.05s/f (Slow) 5 Ran SP% **108.3**
Speed ratings (Par 98): **102,99,97,94,92**
CSF £29.72 TOTE £1.80: £1.10, £10.00; EX 23.90.
Owner H E Sheikh Sultan Bin Khalifa Al Nahyan **Bred** Hinkle Farms & Thomas T Ladt **Trained** Newmarket, Suffolk

FOCUS
Just the five runners, but the four to have run before had all shown decent form. There's a good chance the winner can prove a fair bit better than the bare form.

NOTEBOOK
Stasio(USA) ◆ had shown plenty of promise when running a more-experienced rival to a neck on his Kempton debut last month and duly went one better here, despite taking a hold through the early stages. He had little choice but to make his effort up the inside once into the home straight, but it didn't matter in this small field and he was running all over his rivals once hitting the front a furlong out. He can win bigger prizes than this and looks a nice prospect. (op 5-4)
Secret Talent ◆, a half-brother to the winning sprinter (including on Polytrack) Amazing Win, was held up last in the early stages, but stayed on nicely into second inside the last furlong despite showing signs of greenness. It was some effort to finish ahead of three previous winners on debut and connections can only have been encouraged by this. (op 16-1)
Fat Gary had shown decent form in soft-ground events on turf and had every chance under pressure starting up the home straight, but lacked a decisive turn of foot. His mark of 87 provides the benchmark. (op 3-1 tchd 10-3)
Teophilip(IRE), back on Polytrack after bolting up by 6l in a heavy-ground Yarmouth maiden, looked nothing like as effective under these conditions. (tchd 3-1)
Bapak Sayang(USA), up 2f in trip and another back on Polytrack after springing a 50-1 surprise in a Haydock maiden in September, enjoyed the run of the race in front but didn't see his race out. (op 13-2)

7774 BLUE SQUARE SPRINT SERIES RETURNS JANUARY H'CAP 1m (P)

3:55 (3:55) (Class 2) (0-100,100) 3-Y-O+ **£12,938** (£3,850; £1,924; £962) **Stalls** High

Form				RPR
5061	**1**		**Solar Deity (IRE)**[46] 6768 3-8-8 89 ow1 ... MartinHarley 3 (Marco Botti) *hld up in tch: rdn and effrt to chse ldrs 2f out: drvn and styd on wl fnl f to ld fnl 75yds* **11/4**[2]	98+
1144	**2**	½	**Storm King**[35] 7064 3-8-12 93 ... JamieSpencer 7 (Jane Chapple-Hyam) *hld up in midfield: hdwy u.p over 1f out: hrd drvn and styd on wl fnl f to go 2nd cl home* **5/2**[1]	101+
0514	**3**	nk	**Lockantanks**[16] 7508 5-8-10 89 ... WilliamBuick 9 (Michael Appleby) *hld up in last quartet: hdwy on outer over 1f out: styd on strly u.p ins fnl f to go 3rd last stride* **7/1**[3]	96
6046	**4**	shd	**George Guru**[10] 7631 5-8-9 91 ... MarkCoumbe(3) 10 (Michael Attwater) *t.k.h: hld up in tch: hdwy over 3f out: rdn and ev ch ent fnl 2f: led 1f out: hdd and no ex fnl 75yds* **11/1**	98
0406	**5**	1	**Poetic Dancer**[16] 7508 3-8-6 87 ... PaulHanagan 6 (Clive Cox) *chsd ldrs tl led over 2f out: sn rdn: hdd 1f out: no ex and btn fnl 100yds* **9/1**	91
0640	**6**	½	**Axiom**[28] 7240 8-8-10 89 ... JimCrowley 4 (Ed Walker) *hld up in midfield: rdn and effrt wl over 1f out: styng on when swtchd rt 1f out: kpt on* **15/2**	92
1-00	**7**	¾	**Monsieur Chevalier (IRE)**[21] 7401 5-9-2 100 ... NatashaEaton(5) 2 (P J O'Gorman) *sddle slipped sn after s: chsd ldr tl led 6f out: hdd over 2f out: rdr only able to push along and styd on same pce fr over 1f out* **40/1**	102
0224	**8**	shd	**Chapter And Verse (IRE)**[10] 7631 6-8-7 86 oh1 ... AndreaAtzeni 11 (Mike Murphy) *stdd s: hld up in rr: effrt on inner over 1f out: styd on fnl f: nvr trbld ldrs* **10/1**	87
55	**9**	2 ½	**Swiss Cross**[3] 7709 5-8-7 91 ... (t) LeonnaMayor(5) 1 (Phil McEntee) *racd keenly: led for 2f: pressed ldr after tl over 2f out: sn rdn and lost pl 2f out: wl hld whn swtchd rt wl ins fnl f* **25/1**	87
0300	**10**	½	**Mia's Boy**[43] 6831 8-9-5 98 ... GeorgeBaker 12 (Chris Dwyer) *stdd s: hld up in rr: rdn and no prog wl over 1f out: kpt on ins fnl f: n.d* **28/1**	92
2/00	**11**	4 ½	**Bobbyscot (IRE)**[136] 3766 5-8-7 86 oh1 ... ChrisCatlin 5 (Gary Moore) *a bhd: rdn and no hdwy 2f out: n.d* **66/1**	70
0000	**12**	2 ¼	**Elna Bright**[16] 7503 7-8-8 87 ... JimmyQuinn 8 (Peter Crate) *t.k.h: hld up in tch: rdn and struggling jst over 2f out: wknd over 1f out: eased ins fnl f* **33/1**	66

1m 37.07s (-1.13) **Going Correction** +0.05s/f (Slow) 12 Ran SP% **121.1**
WFA 3 from 5yo+ 2lb
Speed ratings (Par 109): **107,106,106,106,105 104,103,103,101,100 96,94**
Toteswingers 1&2 £3.70, 1&3 £5.20, 2&3 £5.70 CSF £9.80 CT £45.14 TOTE £3.60: £1.50, £1.50, £2.50; EX 14.20 Trifecta £63.70 Pool £1,067.42 - 12.56 winning units..
Owner G Manfredini & A Tinkler **Bred** Castlemartin Stud And Skymarc Farm **Trained** Newmarket, Suffolk

FOCUS
A valuable and competitive handicap. Two of the three 3yos fought out the finish.

NOTEBOOK
Solar Deity(IRE) ◆, back up in trip, was raised 6lb for last month's Wolverhampton win and had another 1lb overweight to carry as well. Never far away, it took him a little time to click into gear once under pressure, but he eventually did so and forged his way to the front a few strides from the line. He still doesn't have that many miles on the clock and can rate higher. (op 5-2 tchd 3-1)
Storm King ◆ came from further back than the winner and his final flourish was always going to fall just short. He is now 15lb higher than for the second of two wins over this trip at Kempton in August, but this effort shows that he is perfectly capable of defying this sort of mark. (op 4-1)
Lockantanks, back up to his ideal trip, tried to come from well off the pace and finished strongly down the wide outside, if just too late. He was off the same mark as when winning over C&D last December and this was a decent effort against a couple of progressive 3yos. (op 13-2)
George Guru, 3lb higher than when winning over C&D back in March, was forced to take a wide trip but had every chance when joining issue off the final bend. Just about in front entering the last furlong, he held that position until run right out of the placings in the last few strides. This was another good effort. (tchd 10-1)
Poetic Dancer had yet to prove that she stays this far, but she had her chance when disputing the lead with George Guru off the final bend and stuck at it despite being kept close to the inside rail. There will be other days.
Axiom, beaten just under 2l by George Guru over C&D in March and a stone better off, plugged on but was unable to reverse that form. (op 7-1)
Monsieur Chevalier(IRE), a high-class performer for Richard Hannon in his younger days, didn't look the same horse in two starts for his new yard last month after 392 days off and this was his first try beyond 7f. Considering he was keen enough in front before losing the advantage over 2f from home and his saddle had slipped, he didn't completely fall in a hole as might have been expected and it may be that he does retain some ability. Official explanation: jockey said saddle slipped. (tchd 50-1)
Chapter And Verse(IRE), sixth in this race last year on his only previous visit here, stayed on late against the inside rail but looks much more effective at Kempton. (op 14-1)
T/Plt: £54.20 to a £1 stake. Pool: £52,532.54. 706.43 winning tickets T/Qpdt: £11.20 to a £1 stake. Pool: £4,153.83. 272.14 winning tickets SP

7745 WOLVERHAMPTON (A.W) (L-H)

Saturday, November 17

OFFICIAL GOING: Standard
Wind: Light behind Weather: Cloudy

7775 STAN FISHER H'CAP 5f 20y(P)

5:50 (5:50) (Class 5) (0-70,70) 3-Y-O+ **£2,911** (£866; £432; £216) **Stalls** Low

Form				RPR
4024	**1**		**Ring For Baileys**[30] 7197 3-9-5 70 ... JoeFanning 2 (Chris Dwyer) *led: hdd over 3f out: led again 1/2-way: rdn over 1f out: styd on wl* **9/2**[2]	86
1650	**2**	3	**Above The Stars**[21] 7411 4-8-9 67 ... EireannCagney(7) 1 (Richard Fahey) *sn pushed along and prom: chsd wnr over 1f out: styd on same pce ins fnl f* **12/1**	72
0002	**3**	1	**Shawkantango**[26] 7299 5-9-5 70 ... (v) DaleSwift 9 (Derek Shaw) *hld up: pushed along over 3f out: hdwy over 1f out: sn rdn: styd on* **14/1**	72
0045	**4**	shd	**Greenhead High**[3] 7716 4-8-9 67 ... ShirleyTeasdale(7) 12 (David Nicholls) *s.i.s: hld up: shkn up over 1f out: r.o wl ins fnl f: nt rch ldrs* **13/2**[3]	68
1236	**5**	½	**Mother Jones**[27] 7274 4-9-4 69 ... TomMcLaughlin 11 (David Evans) *hld up: swtchd lft and hdwy over 1f out: r.o: nt rch ldrs* **16/1**	68
0000	**6**	nse	**Master Of Disguise**[101] 4963 6-9-5 70 ... WilliamCarson 5 (Brian Baugh) *chsd wnr tl led over 3f out: pushed along and hdd 1/2-way* **15/2**	69
4500	**7**	2 ¾	**Steelcut**[8] 7666 8-9-3 68 ... (p) TedDurcan 6 (Mark Buckley) *trckd ldrs: shkn up over 1f out: wknd ins fnl f* **25/1**	57
0210	**8**	nse	**Roy's Legacy**[48] 6713 3-9-2 67 ... FrannyNorton 8 (Shaun Harris) *prom: rdn 1/2-way: wknd ins fnl f* **18/1**	56
1306	**9**	½	**Charming (IRE)**[17] 7483 3-9-2 67 ... SebSanders 7 (Olivia Maylam) *mid-div: rdn over 1f out: wknd ins fnl f* **8/1**	54
0006	**10**	1	**Amadeus Denton (IRE)**[59] 6357 3-8-12 70 ... ConnorNichol(7) 4 (Michael Dods) *chsd ldrs: rdn 1/2-way: wknd over 1f out* **17/2**	54
-000	**11**	2 ½	**Secret Millionaire (IRE)**[18] 7464 5-9-5 70 ... StephenCraine 10 (Tony Carroll) *hld up: a in rr* **50/1**	45
0000	**12**	nk	**Bookiesindexdotnet**[30] 7197 3-9-5 70 ... (vt[1]) EddieAhern 3 (J R Jenkins) *chsd ldrs: rdn over 1f out: wknd fnl f* **33/1**	44
412	**13**	nse	**Avon Breeze**[64] 6211 3-9-2 67 ... RobertWinston 13 (Richard Whitaker) *s.s: pushed along early then plld hrd after 1f: rdn over 1f out: a in rr* **4/1**[1]	41

1m 1.22s (-1.08) **Going Correction** -0.05s/f (Stan) 13 Ran SP% **119.2**
Speed ratings (Par 103): **106,101,99,99,98 98,94,94,93,91 87,87,87**
toteswingers 1&2 £13.50, 1&3 £6.80, 2&3 £51.10 CSF £56.66 CT £730.41 TOTE £4.60: £1.50, £3.90, £4.40; EX 82.10 Trifecta £255.80 Pool £620.84 - 1.82 winning units..
Owner G R Bailey Ltd (Baileys Horse Feeds) **Bred** P And Mrs A G Venner **Trained** Six Mile Bottom, Cambs

FOCUS
It paid to be be prominent here.
Avon Breeze Official explanation: jockey said filly was slowly away.

7776 WOLVERHAMPTON CELEBRITY HAIRDRESSING ROYSTON BLYTHE H'CAP 7f 32y(P)

6:20 (6:20) (Class 6) (0-65,65) 3-Y-O **£2,181** (£644; £322) **Stalls** High

Form				RPR
2216	**1**		**Balti's Sister (IRE)**[18] 7469 3-9-6 65 ... RobertWinston 1 (Terry Clement) *hld up: hdwy 2f out: shkn up to ld 1f out: r.o wl* **5/1**[2]	76
2022	**2**	2 ¼	**Green Mitas (ITY)**[9] 7654 3-9-5 64 ... SilvestreDeSousa 5 (Frank Sheridan) *trckd ldrs: racd keenly: rdn over 1f out: styd on same pce ins fnl f* **13/2**[3]	69
0023	**3**	½	**Fortrose Academy (IRE)**[21] 7402 3-9-5 64 ... DavidProbert 9 (Andrew Balding) *hld up in tch: rdn and ev ch over 1f out: styd on same pce ins fnl f* **13/2**[3]	68
0060	**4**	1 ½	**The Noble Ord**[23] 7358 3-9-6 65 ... (t) LiamKeniry 10 (Sylvester Kirk) *hld up: r.o ins fnl f: nvr nrr* **40/1**	65
1464	**5**	1 ¼	**Amis Reunis**[25] 7314 3-9-2 61 ... WilliamCarson 8 (Anthony Carson) *hld up: rdn over 2f out: styd on ins fnl f: nvr on terms* **22/1**	57
00-3	**6**	nk	**Menelik (IRE)**[35] 7055 3-9-2 61 ... RichardKingscote 3 (Tom Dascombe) *prom: rdn over 2f out: styd on same pce fr over 1f out* **1/1**[1]	56
001	**7**	1 ¾	**M J Woodward**[18] 7456 3-9-3 62 ... JoeFanning 7 (Paul Green) *led 6f out: rdn and hdd 1f out: wknd ins fnl f* **33/1**	53
2300	**8**	½	**Compton Rainbow**[25] 7308 3-8-12 64 ... (t) NicoleNordblad(7) 11 (Hans Adielsson) *chsd ldrs: ev ch over 1f out: wknd ins fnl f* **40/1**	53
0020	**9**	1 ¼	**Dream Walker (FR)**[11] 7600 3-9-4 63 ... DaleSwift 2 (Ian McInnes) *led 1f: w ldr: rdn over 2f out: ev ch over 1f out: wknd ins fnl f* **25/1**	49

0413 **10** *hd* **Graylyn Valentino**[63] [6251] 3-9-6 **65**.................................... LukeMorris 6 50
(Robin Dickin) *hld up: rdn over 1f out: a in rr* **11/1**

1m 29.11s (-0.49) **Going Correction** -0.05s/f (Stan) **10** Ran SP% **117.7**
Speed ratings (Par 98): **100,97,96,95,93 93,91,90,89,89**
toteswingers 1&2 £4.40, 1&3 £4.80, 2&3 £6.00 CSF £35.15 CT £218.14 TOTE £4.70: £1.70, £1.80, £1.90; EX 29.40 Trifecta £105.70 Pool £831.50 - 5.90 winning units..

Owner Mrs Michelle Smith **Bred** P Monaghan, J Collins & G Dillon **Trained** Newmarket, Suffolk

FOCUS
With the unexposed Menelik proving disappointing, this became wide open.

Compton Rainbow Official explanation: jockey said filly had no more to give.

7777 EUROPEAN BREEDERS' FUND MAIDEN FILLIES' STKS (DIV I) 7f 32y(P)
6:50 (6:50) (Class 5) 2-Y-O **£3,137** (£933; £466; £233) **Stalls** High

Form RPR
5 **1** **Be On The Bell**[29] [7219] 2-9-0 0.................................. FergusSweeney 3 74+
(Jamie Osborne) *hld up: hdwy over 2f out: shkn up to ld ins fnl f: r.o* **20/1**
204 **2** *1 ¾* **Desert Sunrise**[16] [7497] 2-9-0 67.. DavidProbert 9 70
(Sir Michael Stoute) *chsd ldr tl led 3f out: rdn and hdd ins fnl f: styd on same pce* **3/1**[2]
63 **3** *2 ¾* **La Danza**[54] [6535] 2-9-0 0.. FrannyNorton 6 63
(Alan Bailey) *led: racd keenly: hdd 3f out: rdn over 1f out: no ex ins fnl f* **3/1**[2]
03 **4** *¾* **Mojo Bear**[19] [7433] 2-9-0 0... LiamKeniry 7 61
(Sylvester Kirk) *w ldrs: plld hrd: stdd over 5f out: rdn over 2f out: styd on same pce fr over 1f out* **25/1**
0 **5** *1 ½* **Fusion (IRE)**[16] [7505] 2-9-0 0... JoeFanning 4 58
(Mark Johnston) *chsd ldrs: pushed along 1/2-way: outpcd over 2f out: n.d after* **7/4**[1]
0654 **6** *nk* **Beacon Tarn**[19] [7441] 2-9-0 60...................................... GrahamGibbons 8 57
(Eric Alston) *prom: rdn over 2f out: hung lft and wknd fnl f* **11/1**
7 *shd* **Portrait** 2-9-0 0.. LukeMorris 5 57
(Sir Mark Prescott Bt) *hld up: pushed along over 2f out: n.d* **13/2**[3]
00 **8** *29* **Tracks Of My Tears**[14] [7552] 2-9-0 0............................ WilliamCarson 1
(Giles Bravery) *bhd fnl 5f: t.o* **100/1**

1m 30.15s (0.55) **Going Correction** -0.05s/f (Stan) **8** Ran SP% **117.6**
Speed ratings (Par 93): **94,92,88,88,86 85,85,52**
toteswingers 1&2 £11.60, 1&3 £12.40, 2&3 £1.60 CSF £80.65 TOTE £29.10: £3.60, £1.50, £1.60; EX 116.10 Trifecta £397.30 Pool £858.29 - 1.62 winning units..

Owner M K P Turner **Bred** Michael Turner **Trained** Upper Lambourn, Berks

FOCUS
Probably just ordinary maiden form but a bit of a surprise result. The runner-up and the time offer some perspective.

NOTEBOOK
Be On The Bell took a major step forward from her debut here last month to win with a degree of authority. Despite still being quite green early, she began to make eyecatching headway leaving the back straight and she was clearly travelling best turning in, so it was only a case of whether she would find off the bridle to win. She picked up nicely and looks capable of going on from here. Her pedigree is mostly about speed, so it's unlikely she'll go up much in trip. (op 25-1)

Desert Sunrise hasn't gone on from her encouraging debut but this was a solid enough first try at the trip having been close to the speed throughout. She does look vulnerable in this company though. (op 5-2)

La Danza was ridden more aggressively than when showing much improved form at Kempton last time and it didn't really work as she dropped away in the straight. She might turn out to be a bit better than she was able to show here. (op 5-2)

Mojo Bear was quite keen early and that may have been a factor in her not getting competitive at the business end. Official explanation: jockey said filly hung left-handed. (op 16-1)

Fusion(IRE), a half-sister to Attraction, who has now run poorly on both starts. (op 3-1)

Portrait didn't show too much but looks much more of a longer-term project. (op 8-1 tchd 17-2 and 6-1)

7778 EUROPEAN BREEDERS' FUND MAIDEN FILLIES' STKS (DIV II) 7f 32y(P)
7:20 (7:22) (Class 5) 2-Y-O **£3,137** (£933; £466; £233) **Stalls** High

Form RPR
2 **1** **Miss Avonbridge (IRE)**[19] [7433] 2-9-0 0.................. RichardKingscote 1 69+
(Tom Dascombe) *mde virtually all: rdn over 1f out: r.o* **15/8**[1]
04 **2** *½* **Bright Glow**[18] [7458] 2-9-0 0.. TedDurcan 6 68+
(David Lanigan) *trckd ldrs: rdn to chse wnr and edgd lft ins fnl f: r.o* **9/4**[2]
0 **3** *1 ¾* **Sweet Vintage (IRE)**[16] [7505] 2-9-0 0................................ MartinLane 3 64
(J W Hills) *chsd wnr: rdn and ev ch over 1f out: styd on same pce ins fnl f* **6/1**
4 *½* **Liliana (IRE)** 2-9-0 0.. SilvestreDeSousa 4 62+
(Peter Chapple-Hyam) *hld up: rdn over 1f out: r.o: nt rch ldrs* **9/2**[3]
5 *1 ¼* **Sandaura (IRE)** 2-9-0 0.. AdamKirby 5 59
(Clive Cox) *chsd ldrs: rdn over 2f out: no ex fnl f* **16/1**
6 *4 ½* **Bouyrin (IRE)** 2-9-0 0.. FergusSweeney 2 48
(Michael Bell) *s.s: hld up: rdn over 1f out: wknd fnl f* **12/1**
03 **7** *6* **Just Wondering (IRE)**[18] [7466] 2-8-11 0.................. AshleyMorgan(3) 9 34
(Ed Dunlop) *hld up: hung rt and wknd 2f out* **18/1**

1m 30.14s (0.54) **Going Correction** -0.05s/f (Stan) **7** Ran SP% **116.9**
Speed ratings (Par 93): **94,93,91,90,89 84,77**
toteswingers 1&2 £1.50, 1&3 £3.40, 2&3 £2.80 CSF £6.61 TOTE £2.80: £1.70, £1.60; EX 7.80 Trifecta £47.30 Pool £1,063.22 - 16.85 winning units..

Owner Deva Racing Avonbridge Partnership **Bred** T Whitehead **Trained** Malpas, Cheshire

FOCUS
An ordinary fillies' maiden in which the winner improved from her debut promise.

NOTEBOOK
Miss Avonbridge(IRE) attracted most of the market attention, having shaped with promise at Leicester on her debut, and she justified the support to go one better thanks to quite a taking display of resolution. She was kept honest on the front end from the start by the attentions of the third and the pair looked to have softened each other up for the closers in the straight, but she found plenty up the inside and wasn't going to be denied. She has the potential to go on from here but the form is nothing special. (op 7-4 tchd 11-8 and 2-1)

Bright Glow ◆ got the perfect trail through and looked as if she was poised to pick off the winner when challenging down the middle of the track, but she just found that rival too resilient. She came clear of the remainder though and shouldn't be long in going one better. (op 7-2 tchd 9-2)

Sweet Vintage(IRE) couldn't maintain her challenge in the final furlong, but this nicely bred filly probably stepped up on what she did first time and remains open to improvement. (op 8-1 tchd 9-1)

Liliana(IRE) kept on quite nicely from off the pace and any improvement on this will make her a player in similar company next time. (tchd 4-1)

Sandaura(IRE)'s debut run here was not devoid of promise. (op 14-1)

Bouyrin(IRE) started slowly and needs to improve markedly on what she showed here. (op 8-1)

7779 FIND US ON FACEBOOK NURSERY 1m 141y(P)
7:50 (7:50) (Class 5) (0-70,70) 2-Y-O **£2,911** (£866; £432; £216) **Stalls** Low

Form RPR
553 **1** **Gworn**[25] [7306] 2-9-7 **70**.. GrahamLee 11 81+
(Ed Dunlop) *hld up: hdwy on outer over 2f out: led over 1f out: rdn clr* **11/4**[1]
056 **2** *5* **Prospera (IRE)**[39] [6960] 2-9-4 **67**.............................. RichardKingscote 5 68
(Ralph Beckett) *chsd ldr: rdn over 2f out: styd on same pce fr over 1f out* **7/1**
5565 **3** *¾* **Shamaheart (IRE)**[24] [7335] 2-9-0 **68**........... WilliamTwiston-Davies(5) 10 68
(Richard Hannon) *hld up: nt clr run over 2f out: r.o u.p ins fnl f: nt rch ldrs* **13/2**[3]
0651 **4** *½* **Missing Agent**[2] [7724] 2-9-1 **64** 6ex.......................(v) SilvestreDeSousa 2 62
(David Evans) *led: rdn and hdd over 1f out: no ex ins fnl f* **13/2**[3]
3563 **5** *nk* **Corton Lad**[37] [6998] 2-8-9 **58**.. JoeFanning 12 55
(Keith Dalgleish) *hld up: forced to r wd tl 6f out: hdwy over 1f out: sn rdn and hung lft: styd on same pce fnl f* **16/1**
6300 **6** *2* **Walter White (IRE)**[47] [6732] 2-9-3 **66**............................(p) DavidProbert 9 59
(Andrew Balding) *in rr: drvn along 4f out: n.d* **14/1**
0656 **7** *4 ½* **Gold Roll (IRE)**[25] [7304] 2-9-4 **67**.. DaleSwift 3 51
(Ruth Carr) *s.i.s: hdwy 6f out: rdn and nt clr run over 2f out: wknd over 1f out* **25/1**
404 **8** *nk* **Ella Motiva (IRE)**[15] [7525] 2-9-2 **65**............................ RobbieFitzpatrick 4 48
(Mark Brisbourne) *chsd ldrs: rdn over 3f out: edgd rt and wknd over 1f out* **14/1**
0554 **9** *1 ¼* **Unison (IRE)**[23] [7357] 2-9-6 **69**.. SebSanders 7 49
(Peter Makin) *chsd ldrs: rdn over 2f out: wknd over 1f out* **18/1**
500 **10** *2 ¼* **Terpsichore**[31] [7165] 2-8-2 **51**.. FrannyNorton 6 27
(Sylvester Kirk) *mid-div: drvn along over 2f out: hmpd and wknd over 1f out* **50/1**
0033 **11** *4* **Woza Moya (USA)**[18] [7467] 2-9-4 **67**.................................. LukeMorris 1 34
(Gay Kelleway) *chsd ldrs: rdn over 2f out: wknd wl over 1f out* **16/1**
064 **12** *¾* **Love Marmalade (IRE)**[18] [7459] 2-9-3 **66**......................... PhillipMakin 8 32
(Kevin Ryan) *drvn along 4f out: a in rr* **4/1**[2]

1m 49.46s (-1.04) **Going Correction** -0.05s/f (Stan) **12** Ran SP% **122.0**
Speed ratings (Par 96): **102,97,96,96,96 94,90,90,89,87 83,82**
toteswingers 1&2 £6.10, 1&3 £7.70, 2&3 £6.60 CSF £22.92 CT £120.88 TOTE £2.40: £1.10, £3.20, £3.10; EX 27.40 Trifecta £143.30 Pool £477.78 - 2.50 winning units..

Owner N Martin **Bred** Azienda Agricola F Lli Nencini **Trained** Newmarket, Suffolk

FOCUS
A modest nursery but nothing modest about the performance of the winner, who proved a good bit better than the grade.

NOTEBOOK
Gworn ◆ bolted up despite being trapped wide all the way around and he looks way ahead of his current mark of 70. Always travelling smoothly, he cruised around the field before showing a smart turn of foot to shoot clear at the top of the straight to prove different class to his rivals. He'll have to go up in grade but, if connections can find a race for him before he is reassessed, he'll be very hard to beat. (op 5-2)

Prospera(IRE) kept plugging away having been close up throughout and was a bit unlucky to bump into such a well-treated rival. He looks up to winning off this sort of mark. (op 13-2 tchd 6-1)

Shamaheart(IRE) ◆, switching to Polytrack from turf, was the biggest finisher from off the pace after being interrupted in his run on the bend and he looks one to be interested in next time. (op 11-1)

Missing Agent, under a penalty for his Kempton success, was again ridden quite aggressively but this longer trip stretched his stamina too far. (op 4-1)

Corton Lad, making his Polytrack debut, was suited to testing ground on turf so might be worth a try at Southwell. (op 28-1)

7780 BRITISH STALLION STUDS SUPPORTING BRITISH RACING EBF MAIDEN STKS 1m 1f 103y(P)
8:20 (8:21) (Class 5) 2-Y-O **£3,137** (£933; £466; £233) **Stalls** Low

Form RPR
4 **1** **Press Room (USA)**[58] [6412] 2-9-3 0....................... SilvestreDeSousa 11 70+
(Mahmood Al Zarooni) *chsd ldr tl led 2f out: clr over 1f out: rdn towards fin: jst hld on* **2/1**[1]
3 **2** *nk* **Bin Singspiel**[35] [7057] 2-9-3 0.. MartinDwyer 1 69+
(James Tate) *hld up: swtchd rt and hdwy over 1f out: edgd lft and r.o strly ins fnl f: jst failed* **7/2**[2]
06 **3** *4* **Posh Boy (IRE)**[38] [6985] 2-9-3 0.. GeorgeBaker 6 61
(Chris Wall) *a.p: rdn over 1f out: styd on same pce fnl f* **16/1**
0 **4** *shd* **Argent Knight**[31] [7172] 2-9-3 0.. GrahamLee 2 61
(William Jarvis) *a.p: rdn over 2f out: styd on same pce fnl f* **20/1**
5 **5** *1 ½* **Common Courtesy**[18] [7460] 2-8-12 0............................... LukeMorris 10 53
(Michael Bell) *hld up: racd keenly: swtchd rt over 1f out: r.o ins fnl f: nvr on terms* **10/1**
6 *1* **Majeed** 2-9-3 0.. MartinLane 8 56+
(David Simcock) *dwlt: rn green in rr: drvn along over 2f out: r.o ins fnl f: nvr nrr* **13/2**
0 **7** *½* **Father And Son (IRE)**[31] [7172] 2-9-3 0.............................. AdamKirby 3 56
(Marco Botti) *s.i.s: hld up: rdn over 2f out: nvr trbld ldrs* **33/1**
0 **8** *1* **Faither**[89] [5410] 2-9-3 0.. JoeFanning 13 54
(Keith Dalgleish) *chsd ldrs: rdn over 2f out: wknd over 1f out* **25/1**
5 **9** *3 ¼* **Buona Fortuna**[14] [7552] 2-8-12 0...................................... DavidProbert 5 42
(Andrew Balding) *led: rdn and hdd 2f out: wknd ins fnl f* **9/2**[3]
04 **10** *nk* **Angilina**[29] [7205] 2-8-12 0.. PhillipMakin 9 42+
(Kevin Ryan) *chsd ldrs: drvn along over 4f out: wknd wl over 1f out* **28/1**
0 **11** *5* **Katie Gale**[22] [7364] 2-8-12 0.. ShaneKelly 4 32
(Tim Pitt) *chsd ldrs: rdn over 3f out: wknd wl over 1f out* **66/1**
12 *82* **Sings Poet** 2-9-3 0.. GrahamGibbons 12
(James Tate) *sn pushed along in rr: bhd fnl 4f: t.o* **50/1**

2m 2.41s (0.71) **Going Correction** -0.05s/f (Stan) **12** Ran SP% **120.5**
Speed ratings (Par 96): **94,93,90,90,88 87,87,86,83,83 78,6**
toteswingers 1&2 £2.70, 1&3 £12.70, 2&3 £7.20 CSF £8.23 TOTE £3.30: £1.50, £2.10, £3.90; EX 10.40 Trifecta £167.40 Pool £497.81 - 2.23 winning units..

Owner Godolphin **Bred** Darley **Trained** Newmarket, Suffolk

FOCUS
Quite an interesting maiden with several potentially useful performers on show and the pace looked sound. The front two pulled clear but the form looks only ordinary.

NOTEBOOK
Press Room(USA) ◆ had shaped with only medium promise on his debut at Yarmouth but the switch to Polytrack for this second start proved ideal for this Street Cry colt and he blew these away with a lethal turn of foot early in the straight. Although his advantage was eroded in the closing stages the race was already in safe keeping and there ought to be plenty more races to be won with him. (op 11-4)

Bin Singspiel flew home having raced off the pace and was gaining hand over fist in the final half-furlong, but the line was always coming too soon for him. He already looks as if he needs another furlong and looks a certainty to go one better sooner rather than later. (op 11-4)
Posh Boy(IRE) made good headway out wide but then his effort flattened out a bit in the straight and he could keep on only at the one pace. He qualifies for a mark now and his future probably lies in mid to low-grade handicaps. (op 25-1)
Argent Knight improved on what he did on debut, without really threatening. He kept on to suggest he might do better over further next year, a point backed up by his pedigree. (op 33-1)
Common Courtesy, just as on debut, put in her best work in the closing stages and she'll do better when handicapped and upped in trip. (op 12-1)
Majeed also made some late headway after being out the back but he looked very green and in need of the experience and much better can be expected next time. (op 14-1)
Buona Fortuna set a decent pace but dropped away disappointingly once headed. (op 3-1 tchd 11-4)

7781 EAST2WEST RESTAURANT SUPPORTS BALLS TO CANCER H'CAP 1m 141y(P)
8:50 (8:50) (Class 6) (0-60,63) 3-Y-O+ £2,181 (£644; £322) Stalls Low

Form RPR
0000 1 **Ensnare**63 6252 7-8-10 **49**..........(b1) JamieMackay 7 59
(Willie Musson) *awkward leaving stalls: bhd: hdwy over 1f out: r.o to ld nr fin* 16/1
0321 2 nk **Aragorn Rouge**12 7593 4-9-6 **59**.......... JoeFanning 12 68
(Keith Dalgleish) *hld up: hdwy over 2f out: shkn up to ld wl ins fnl f: hdd nr fin* 6/4[1]
0042 3 2 **Focail Eile**10 7638 7-9-10 **63**.......... AdamKirby 13 67
(John Ryan) *hld up: hdwy over 2f out: rdn over 1f out: styd on* 6/1[3]
3354 4 shd **Zenafire**12 7593 3-9-2 **58**.......... GrahamLee 4 62
(Reg Hollinshead) *mid-div: hdwy over 4f out: led over 1f out: rdn and hdd wl ins fnl f* 6/1[3]
4104 5 2 3/4 **Olney Lass**25 7317 5-9-4 **60**.......... SimonPearce(3) 6 58
(Lydia Pearce) *hld up: hdwy over 2f out: sn rdn: no ex ins fnl f* 33/1
0000 6 5 **Dansili Dutch (IRE)**44 6813 3-8-13 **55**.......... FrannyNorton 3 41
(Andrew Crook) *hld up: hmpd over 2f out: nvr nrr* 66/1
4035 7 8 **Dhhamaan (IRE)**106 4779 7-8-12 **51**..........(b) DaleSwift 8 19
(Ruth Carr) *led: rdn and hdd over 1f out: wknd fnl f* 50/1
-005 8 2 3/4 **Schoolboy Champ**16 7512 5-8-3 **49**..........(vt) ShirleyTeasdale(7) 11 10
(Lisa Williamson) *chsd ldrs: rdn over 2f out: wknd over 1f out* 66/1
340 9 1 3/4 **Present Day**17 7495 3-8-12 **54**..........(b) LukeMorris 9 11
(Clive Cox) *prom: drvn along 1/2-way: edgd lft and wknd over 2f out* 20/1
6042 10 1/2 **Flipping**12 7593 5-9-3 **56**..........(b1) GrahamGibbons 5 12
(Eric Alston) *chsd ldrs: rdn over 2f out: wknd over 1f out* 7/2[2]
4456 11 2 3/4 **Source Of Light (IRE)**9 7643 3-8-13 **55**..........(b1) StephenCraine 10
(Daniel Mark Loughnane) *s.i.s: hld up: rdn over 2f out: sn wknd* 20/1
40-0 12 7 **Hector Spectre (IRE)**68 6097 6-8-9 **48**..........(p) RobertWinston 2
(Nikki Evans) *chsd ldr: rdn over 2f out: wknd wl over 1f out* 66/1
0000 13 22 **Poker Hospital**15 7524 3-9-2 **58**.......... 1 ShaneKelly 1
(John Stimpson) *mid-div: wkng whn hmpd over 2f out* 50/1

1m 50.08s (-0.42) **Going Correction** -0.05s/f (Stan)
WFA 3 from 4yo+ 3lb 13 Ran SP% **117.5**
Speed ratings (Par 101): **99,98,96,96,94 89,82,80,78,78 75,69,50**
toteswingers 1&2 £6.30, 1&3 £16.70, 2&3 £3.30 CSF £37.64 CT £173.74 TOTE £31.00: £4.70, £1.40, £2.60; EX 76.60 TRIFECTA Not won..
Owner C Owen **Bred** Cheveley Park Stud Ltd **Trained** Newmarket, Suffolk

FOCUS
Just a few interesting runners in an otherwise weak handicap.
Ensnare Official explanation: trainer said regarding apparent improvement in form that gelding had benefited form the application of blinkers.

7782 STAY AT THE WOLVERHAMPTON HOLIDAY INN MAIDEN STKS 1m 141y(P)
9:20 (9:21) (Class 5) 3-Y-O+ £2,911 (£866; £432; £216) Stalls Low

Form RPR
45 1 **Guest Of Honour (IRE)**40 6925 3-9-3 0.......... AdamKirby 1 80+
(Marco Botti) *trckd ldr: shkn up to ld over 1f out: rdn out* 1/1[1]
264 2 1 1/4 **Eltifaat (IRE)**64 6215 3-9-3 73.......... DavidProbert 4 77
(Sir Michael Stoute) *s.i.s: hld up: hdwy over 2f out: rdn to chse wnr over 1f out: styd on* 7/2[2]
43 3 6 **Queen Of Skies (IRE)**17 7477 3-8-12 0.......... LukeMorris 9 58
(Clive Cox) *led: rdn and hdd over 1f out: wknd ins fnl f* 4/1[3]
5303 4 3/4 **Safarjal (IRE)**17 7494 3-8-12 74.......... GrahamLee 10 56
(Charles Hills) *hld up in tch: rdn over 2f out: wknd over 1f out* 5/1
0- 5 1/2 **Lord Golan**424 6242 4-9-6 0.......... WilliamCarson 7 60
(Violet M Jordan) *s.i.s: hld up: r.o ins fnl f: nvr nrr* 100/1
3600 6 2 1/2 **Aureolin Gulf**56 6500 3-9-3 57.......... GrahamGibbons 6 55
(Reg Hollinshead) *prom: racd keenly: rdn over 2f out: wknd over 1f out* 50/1
0/0 7 10 **Fashion Flow**9 7656 5-9-1 0.......... JoeFanning 5 27
(Michael Wigham) *hld up: rdn over 3f out: wknd over 2f out* 40/1
0550 8 15 **Colamandis**65 6179 5-9-1 40..........(b) RobbieFitzpatrick 8
(Hugh McWilliams) *chsd ldrs: rdn over 3f out: wknd over 2f out: t.o* 125/1
634 9 11 **Mexican Mick**91 5335 3-9-3 75.......... SilvestreDeSousa 2
(Ian Williams) *mid-div: sn pushed along: rdn and lost pl 5f out: wknd over 3f out: t.o* 10/1

1m 50.25s (-0.25) **Going Correction** -0.05s/f (Stan)
WFA 3 from 4yo+ 3lb 9 Ran SP% **124.2**
Speed ratings (Par 103): **99,97,92,91,91 89,80,67,57**
toteswingers 1&2 £1.50, 1&3 £2.70, 2&3 £3.90 CSF £5.37 TOTE £2.40: £1.10, £1.20, £1.70; EX 6.70 TRIFECTA Pool £1,120.66 - 40.52 winning units..
Owner Mrs Lucie Botti **Bred** Azienda Agricola Gennaro Stimola **Trained** Newmarket, Suffolk

T/Plt: £27.70 to a £1 stake. Pool: £96,858.60 - 2,550.70 winning tickets T/Qpdt: £3.80 to a £1 stake. Pool: £9,572.20 - 1,830.36 winning tickets CR

SANDOWN (AUS) (L-H)
Saturday, November 17
OFFICIAL GOING: Turf: good

7783a SPORTINGBET SANDOWN CUP (LISTED H'CAP) (3YO+) (TURF) 2m
2:30 (12:00) 3-Y-O+
£59,210 (£17,763; £8,881; £4,440; £2,467; £1,184)

RPR
1 **Ibicenco (GER)**14 7560 4-9-0 0..........(b) GlenBoss 2
(Luca Cumani) *hld up towards rr on outer: hdwy fr over 6f out and sn prom: rdn on turn into st: led 1 1/2f out: styd on wl* 5/2[2]
2 3/4 **Reuben Percival (NZ)**14 7560 6-8-11 0..........(t) VladDuric 12
(Gai Waterhouse, Australia) 17/2
3 1 1/4 **Unusual Suspect (USA)**11 7621 8-9-2 0..........(b) BradRawiller 11
(Michael Kent, Australia) 50/1
4 shd **I'm Jake (NZ)**35 7073 7-8-8 0.......... DeanYendall 3
(David Brideoake & David Feek, Australia) 30/1
5 1 1/4 **Miss With Attitude (AUS)**7 7696 6-8-8 0..........(b) CraigNewitt 1
(Mick Price, Australia) 80/1
6 1 **Verdant**476 4532 5-8-8 0..........(tp) DwayneDunn 6
(Robert Smerdon, Australia) 21/10[1]
7 3 1/4 **Ironstein (AUS)**7 7696 7-9-2 0.......... KerrinMcEvoy 8
(Gerald Ryan, Australia) 7/1[3]
8 1 1/2 **Spechenka (AUS)**17 7-8-8 0..........(t) StevenKing 9
(Ben Ahrens, Australia) 70/1
9 shd **Crafty Cruiser (AUS)** 5-8-9 0 ow1.......... BlakeShinn 4
(Bryce Stanaway, Australia) 9/1
10 hd **Akzar (IRE)**835 4769 5-8-8 0..........(b) DanielMoor 7
(Rob Blacker, Australia) 80/1
11 2 3/4 **Fictional Account (IRE)**14 7560 7-8-8 0.......... ChadSchofield 5
(David Hayes, Australia) 16/1
12 8 **Back In Black (NZ)**14 7562 7-8-8 0..........(b) MichaelWalker 10
(John Steffert, New Zealand) 40/1

3m 26.86s (206.86) 12 Ran SP% **111.2**
PARI-MUTUEL (NSW TAB - all including au$1 stakes): WIN 3.60; PLACE 1.60, 2.00, 10.90; DF 15.00; SF 26.10.
Owner Oti Racing, J Higgins Et Al **Bred** Gestut Schlenderhan **Trained** Newmarket, Suffolk

NOTEBOOK
Ibicenco(GER) will go to his new Australian home with a more impressive cv than the one he arrived in Melbourne with following his win in the Listed Sandown Cup. He had finished seventh in the Moonee Valley Cup and then a luckless fourth in the Lexus Stakes. On the back of his last run he started favourite here and, according to jockey Glen Boss, had the race sewn up after 800m. The colt will remain in Melbourne to be trained by Peter Moody, who will aim him at next autumn's Sydney Cup.

1900 FRANKFURT (L-H)
Sunday, November 18
OFFICIAL GOING: Turf: soft

7784a HESSEN-POKAL (GROUP 3) (3YO+) (TURF) 1m 2f
2:00 (12:00) 3-Y-O+
£26,666 (£9,166; £4,583; £2,500; £1,666; £1,250)

RPR
1 **Seismos (IRE)**28 7282 4-9-4 0.......... AndreaAtzeni 3 104+
(A Wohler, Germany) *4th on ins: rowed along and hdwy on inner 2 1/2f out: chal ldr under 1 1/2f out: r.o u.p to take narrow ld ent fnl f: drvn out: eased cl home* 18/5[3]
2 2 **Petit Chevalier (FR)**26 4-9-0 0.......... AStarke 9 96+
(W Mongil, Germany) *settled in last travelling wl: gd hdwy on outside 2f out: hrd rdn 1 1/2f out to go 3rd: styd on fnl f: wnt 2nd 50yds out: nvr on terms* 9/1
3 1 **Quinindo (GER)**58 6464 4-9-2 0.......... SHellyn 5 96
(Elfie Schnakenberg, Germany) *led: rdn over 1 1/2f out: r.o: hdd ent fnl f: one pce u.p* 125/10
4 5 **Point Blank (GER)**14 7587 4-9-0 0.......... StefanieHofer 1 84
(Mario Hofer, Germany) *hld up towards rr: hdwy on inner to chse ldrs fr over 2f out: sn rdn and nt qckn over 1f out: fdd ins fnl f* 103/10
5 9 **Calipatria**49 6723 5-9-1 0.......... FabriceVeron 6 67
(H-A Pantall, France) *hld up towards rr: hrd rdn and short-lived effrt under 2f out: wl bhd fnl 1 1/2f* 19/10[1]
6 7 **King's Hall**28 7286 4-9-4 0..........(p) EPedroza 8 56
(A Wohler, Germany) *midfield: rdn and no imp 2f out: wknd fnl 1 1/2* 23/5
7 3 1/2 **Durban Thunder (GER)**14 7586 6-9-2 0.......... MartinHarley 4 47
(P Harley, Germany) *trckd ldr: hrd rdn and nt qckn over 2f out: wknd fr 1 1/2f out: eased ins fnl f* 27/10[2]
8 11 **Red Ghost (GER)**15 3-8-10 0..........(b) FilipMinarik 7 23
(S Smrczek, Germany) *trckd ldrs: rdn and lost pl fr 3f out: eased fnl f: t.o* 215/10

2m 14.57s (6.00)
WFA 3 from 4yo+ 4lb 8 Ran SP% **131.8**
WIN (incl. 10 euro stake): 46. PLACES: 25, 33, 36. SF: 475.
Owner Gestut Karlshof **Bred** Gestut Karlshof **Trained** Germany

7775 WOLVERHAMPTON (A.W) (L-H)
Monday, November 19
OFFICIAL GOING: Standard
Wind: Fresh, half-behind Weather: Overcast and Rain

7785 SPONSOR A RACE BY CALLING 01902 390000 NURSERY 1m 1f 103y(P)
2:00 (2:00) (Class 6) (0-65,64) 2-Y-O £1,617 (£481; £240; £120) Stalls Low

Form RPR
3001 1 **Keep Calm**27 7313 2-9-2 **64**.......... WilliamTwiston-Davies(5) 9 69
(Richard Hannon) *in tch: led over 2f out: rdn over 1f out: edgd rt ins fnl f: kpt on* 8/1
5014 2 1/2 **Rakticate (IRE)**5 7714 2-9-3 **60**.......... AndreaAtzeni 8 64
(J S Moore) *trckd ldrs: effrt over 2f out: wnt 2nd over 1f out: carried rt wl ins fnl f: pressed wnr cl home but hld* 10/1
6000 3 1 1/4 **Sand Grouse**33 7173 2-8-13 **56**..........(b) SilvestreDeSousa 3 58
(Marco Botti) *racd keenly in midfield: hdwy on outer over 1f out: styd on chsng ldrs whn carried rt wl ins fnl f: a hld* 6/1[3]
6002 4 2 **Flying Tempo**47 6793 2-8-9 **52**.......... JimmyQuinn 1 50
(Ed Dunlop) *midfield: pushed along briefly over 3f out: hdwy on inner whn nt clr run over 1f out: styd on: no imp on ldrs ins fnl f* 17/2
566 5 nk **Gabrial The Duke (IRE)**23 7414 2-9-3 **60**.......... StevieDonohoe 7 57
(Ian Williams) *rdn along s: midfield: hdwy ent fnl f: styd on ins fnl f: nt gng pce to trble ldrs* 5/1[1]
6666 6 2 **Garmelow Girl**14 7592 2-8-7 **50**..........(b) LukeMorris 2 44
(Stuart Kittow) *trckd ldrs: rdn over 1f out: one pce fnl f* 50/1

0005 **7** *shd* **See And Be Seen**[21] 7439 2-8-11 **54** .... LiamKeniry 13 47
(Sylvester Kirk) *in rr: struggling gng nowhere over 3f out: stl bhd over 1f out: styd on ins fnl f: nrst fin* **40/1**

000 **8** *3/4* **Kiwani Bay**[23] 7403 2-8-9 **52** .... SebSanders 12 44
(J W Hills) *hld up: hdwy into midfield 5f out: u.p over 2f out: wknd over 1f out* **20/1**

0006 **9** *hd* **Pleasant Moment**[38] 7021 2-8-7 **50** .... RichardKingscote 6 42
(Tom Dascombe) *w ldr tl rdn over 2f out: kpt on same pce over 1f out: no imp: wknd wl ins fnl f* **16/1**

5002 **10** *nk* **Unidexter (IRE)**[19] 7491 2-9-0 **57** .... MartinHarley 11 48
(Mick Channon) *hld up: pushed along over 2f out: nvr a threat* **20/1**

2003 **11** *1/2* **Gabrial The Boss (USA)**[5] 7708 2-9-1 **58** ....(t) GrahamLee 5 48
(David Simcock) *hld up: hdwy whn nt clr run and hmpd over 1f out: kpt on wout threatening fnl f* **11/2**[2]

0633 **12** *6* **Kingsville**[33] 7173 2-8-4 **47** .... JoeFanning 4 26
(Mark Johnston) *led: rdn and hdd over 2f out: hld whn n.m.r and hmpd ent fnl f: sn eased* **7/1**

506 **13** *17* **Orla's Rainbow (IRE)**[70] 6096 2-9-3 **60** ....(b) FrannyNorton 10 6
(John Berry) *towards rr: rdn whn n.m.r on inner and hmpd wl over 2f out: wl bhd after: t.o* **11/1**

2m 3.1s (1.40) **Going Correction** +0.025s/f (Slow) **13** Ran SP% **117.7**
Speed ratings (Par 94): **94,93,92,90,90 88,88,87,87,87 86,81,66**
toteswingers 1&2 £14.20, 2&3 £17.70, 1&3 £14.00 CSF £80.59 CT £518.75 TOTE £5.60: £3.50, £4.70, £3.00; EX 88.10 Trifecta £354.50 Part won. Pool: £472.74 - 0.80 winning units..
Owner Richard Hitchcock Alan King **Bred** Aislabie Bloodstock Ltd **Trained** East Everleigh, Wilts
■ Stewards' Enquiry : William Twiston-Davies two-day ban; careless riding (Dec 3-4)

FOCUS
A modest nursery run in a slow time. Straightforward form.

NOTEBOOK
Keep Calm followed up his Yarmouth win (1m, heavy) off 4lb higher. He had a wide trip, but that was no bad thing on this card and he was always doing enough late on, despite edging right (had to survive a stewards' enquiry). A rise in the weights will force him up in grade, but he's clearly going the right way. (op 17-2 tchd 9-1)
Rakticate(IRE) was well short of her best when a beaten favourite in a Fibresand seller on her previous start, but this surface proved more suitable and she ran up to her best. She was carried slightly right near the line, but it made no difference to the result. (op 12-1)
Sand Grouse, with blinkers re-fitted, came from a bit further back than the front two but even so this wasn't particularly encouraging. (op 15-2)
Flying Tempo was blinkered for the first time when runner-up on his nursery debut at Nottingham (1m2f, good to soft), but he'd been off for 47 days since then and returned without the headgear. His performance can be upgraded as he didn't have much room when challenging against the inside rail in the straight (possibly not the place to be on this card; first three raced wider). (op 10-1 tchd 12-1 and 8-1)
Gabrial The Duke(IRE), up in trip, was driven along on leaving the stalls and soon ran into trouble. That can't have helped and he never had a meaningful say. (op 9-2)
See And Be Seen was soon well behind but he made late headway and can probably do better as he gets the idea.
Gabrial The Boss(USA) was continually short of room from the home bend until around a furlong out, having also been hampered soon after the start. The Vet reported the gelding suffered an injury to his left fore leg. Official explanation: jockey said gelding was denied a clear run; vet said gelding had suffered an injury to its left-fore (tchd 5-1)

7786 DOWNLOAD OUR IPHONE APP CLAIMING STKS 1m 141y(P)
2:30 (2:30) (Class 6) 2-Y-O **£1,704** (£503; £251) **Stalls** Low

Form RPR

5 **1** **Diletta Tommasa (IRE)**[46] 6816 2-8-9 0 .... AndreaAtzeni 4 61
(Marco Botti) *hld up: hdwy on outer over 1f out: r.o to ld and bump rival wl ins fnl f: in command fnl strides* **7/2**[3]

3063 **2** *1/2* **Secret Symphony**[13] 7614 2-8-11 66 .... LiamKeniry 7 62
(Sylvester Kirk) *trckd ldrs: effrt over 1f out: chalng whn bmpd wl ins fnl f: styd on: hld fnl strides* **11/4**[2]

0100 **3** *nk* **Myzamour**[67] 6156 2-7-12 49 ....(b) SimonPearce[(3)] 6 51
(J S Moore) *t.k.h: sn w ldr: rdn whn chalng over 1f out: led briefly ins fnl f: kpt on same pce fnl strides* **20/1**

0 **4** *1 3/4* **Amelia Hull**[19] 7491 2-8-2 0 .... JimmyQuinn 3 48
(J S Moore) *sn led: rdn over 1f out: hdd ins fnl f: no ex fnl 75yds* **66/1**

4060 **5** *12* **Claude Greenwood**[26] 7325 2-8-12 74 .... StevieDonohoe 5 33
(Jamie Osborne) *hld up: pushed along over 3f out: sn outpcd: no imp over 1f out: lost tch w front quartet ins fnl f* **15/8**[1]

00 **6** *nk* **Bugsy**[33] 7172 2-8-9 0 .... EddieAhern 2 29
(Richard Hannon) *trckd ldrs: lost pl over 3f out: sn bhd* **11/2**

03 **7** *46* **Tilly T (IRE)**[19] 7491 2-8-3 0 .... LukeMorris 1
(J S Moore) *s.i.s: in rr: rdn 4f out: t.o* **10/1**

1m 51.21s (0.71) **Going Correction** +0.025s/f (Slow) **7** Ran SP% **114.4**
Speed ratings (Par 94): **97,96,96,94,84 83,42**
.Diletta Tommasa was claimed by J. T. Stimpson for £13000.\n\x\x
Owner Immobiliare Casa Paola SRL **Bred** Ms Sheila Lavery **Trained** Newmarket, Suffolk
■ Stewards' Enquiry : Jimmy Quinn two-day ban; used whip above permitted level (Dec 3-4)

FOCUS
A moderate claimer run in a slow time. The first two set the level.

NOTEBOOK
Diletta Tommasa(IRE) improved a good deal on her debut at Warwick (7f, soft) 46 days earlier, challenging widest of all (not a bad move at this meeting). Whether she's worth her £13,000 price tag (claimed by John Stimpson) remains to be seen, but being so lightly raced means she could yet leave this ordinary form behind. (op 5-1 tchd 11-2 and 10-3)
Secret Symphony, who was stepped up to his furthest trip to date and went without the tongue-tie this time, didn't find extra when his jockey went for the whip inside the final furlong. He did not look to run to his official mark of 66. (op 5-2 tchd 9-4 and 3-1)
Myzamour, returning from 67 days off, challenged more towards the inside than the front two and would have been 7lb better off with the runner-up in a handicap. Simon Pearce reported the filly hung left-handed. Official explanation: jockey said filly hung left-handed. (op 11-1 tchd 25-1)
Amelia Hull showed more than on her debut at Nottingham, possibly in spite of racing against the inside rail. (tchd 80-1)
Claude Greenwood, bought out of Sylvester Kirk's yard for 14,000gns since last seen, was reported to have stopped very quickly. Official explanation: jockey said colt stopped quickly; vet said colt lost its right-fore shoe. (op 13-8 tchd 2-1)

7787 "JOHN TRUSCOTT AND FRIENDS ANNUAL DAY" MAIDEN FILLIES' STKS 7f 32y(P)
3:00 (3:03) (Class 5) 3-Y-O+ **£2,264** (£673; £336; £168) **Stalls** High

Form RPR

6 **1** **Willow Beck**[19] 7477 3-8-12 0 .... NickyMackay 2 66+
(John Gosden) *s.i.s: hld up: hmpd on bnd over 6f out: stl rn green: pushed along 2f out: swtchd rt 1f out: prog arnd the whole field ins fnl f: str run to ld cl home* **5/4**[2]

4562 **2** *3/4* **Srinagar Girl**[11] 7656 3-8-12 73 .... EddieAhern 5 56
(Sir Henry Cecil) *chsd ldrs: rdn to ld on inner over 1f out but a hrd pressed: hdd and outpcd by wnr cl home* **10/11**[1]

0450 **3** *shd* **It's My Time**[19] 7477 3-8-12 62 .... PhillipMakin 7 56
(David Simcock) *hld up: hdwy to chse ldrs over 2f out: styd on to chal ins fnl f: outpcd by wnr cl home* **9/1**[3]

0200 **4** *1 3/4* **Big Sylv (IRE)**[90] 5446 3-8-12 46 ....(p) DavidProbert 11 51
(James Unett) *wnt lft at s: led: rdn over 2f out: hdd over 1f out: kpt on same pce fnl 75yds* **100/1**

0 **5** *1 1/4* **Outside Art**[224] 1257 3-8-9 0 .... RaulDaSilva[(3)] 9 48
(Paul Fitzsimons) *dwlt: hmpd s: sn prom: chalng 2f out: rdn and stl ch over 1f out: no ex fnl 75yds* **66/1**

0 **6** *7* **Copper To Gold**[21] 7445 3-8-12 0 .... SilvestreDeSousa 10 29
(Robin Bastiman) *hmpd s: chsd ldrs: racd keenly wout cover on outer: rdn and lost pl over 2f out: bhd over 1f out* **40/1**

06 **7** *hd* **Sherry Cherie (IRE)**[10] 7667 3-8-12 0 .... PatrickMathers 3 28
(Richard Fahey) *hld up: struggling over 2f out: wl btn* **66/1**

1m 30.6s (1.00) **Going Correction** +0.025s/f (Slow)
WFA 3 from 5yo 1lb **7** Ran SP% **113.2**
Speed ratings (Par 100): **95,94,94,92,90 82,82**
toteswingers 1&2 £1.10, 2&3 £1.70, 1&3 £1.80 CSF £2.50 TOTE £2.10: £1.50, £1.10; EX 2.70 Trifecta £7.40 Pool: £681.36 - 68.98 winning units..
Owner H R H Princess Haya Of Jordan **Bred** Worksop Manor Stud **Trained** Newmarket, Suffolk
■ Stewards' Enquiry : Eddie Ahern three-day ban; used whip without giving filly time to respond (Dec 3-5)

FOCUS
Just an ordinary pace at best. The fourth limits the level.

7788 BOOK TICKETS ONLINE AT WOLVERHAMPTON-RACECOURSE.CO.UK (S) STKS 7f 32y(P)
3:30 (3:30) (Class 6) 3-Y-O+ **£1,704** (£503; £251) **Stalls** High

Form RPR

525P **1** **Tarooq (USA)**[149] 3405 6-9-1 89 .... WilliamCarson 3 83
(Stuart Williams) *mde all: shkn up over 1f out: a in command: pushed out and r.o ins fnl f* **1/2**[1]

0124 **2** *2 1/4* **Light From Mars**[33] 7171 7-9-7 77 ....(t) StevieDonohoe 6 83
(Ian Williams) *racd in 2nd pl: unable to go w wnr over 1f out: no imp fnl f* **2/1**[2]

2360 **3** *9* **Berbice (IRE)**[50] 6711 7-9-1 65 .... GrahamLee 1 53
(Linda Perratt) *plld hrd: hld up bhd ldrs: outpcd over 1f out: wl btn* **14/1**[3]

0000 **4** *5* **Lady On Top (IRE)**[18] 7512 4-8-3 43 .... NoelGarbutt[(7)] 4 34
(Nerys Dutfield) *hld up: pushed along 3f out: wl outpcd fnl 2f* **100/1**

1m 31.34s (1.74) **Going Correction** +0.025s/f (Slow)
WFA 3 from 4yo+ 1lb **4** Ran SP% **107.7**
Speed ratings (Par 101): **91,88,78,72**
CSF £1.72 TOTE £2.10; EX 2.00.There was no bid for the winner. Light From Mars was claimed by R. A. Harris for £6000.
Owner H Chamberlain, I Pearce **Bred** Kirsten Rausing **Trained** Newmarket, Suffolk

FOCUS
An unconvincing win from Tarooq, who set a very slow pace. He didn't need to match his best.

7789 BOOK HOSPITALITY IN HORIZONS H'CAP (DIV I) 7f 32y(P)
4:00 (4:01) (Class 4) (0-85,85) 3-Y-O+ **£4,075** (£1,212; £606; £303) **Stalls** High

Form RPR

0010 **1** **Cockney Dancer**[58] 6488 3-9-2 **80** .... RobertWinston 4 88
(Charles Hills) *trckd ldrs: effrt over 1f out: styd on to ld wl ins fnl f: rdn out* **4/1**[2]

1055 **2** *3/4* **Jungle Bay**[46] 6820 5-8-6 **76** ....(b) IanBurns[(7)] 7 82
(Jane Chapple-Hyam) *in tch: impr to ld 1f out: hdd wl ins fnl f: hld cl home* **11/2**[3]

321 **3** *nk* **Fabled City (USA)**[50] 6705 3-9-1 **79** ....(t) AdamKirby 9 84
(Clive Cox) *midfield: pushed along over 3f out: hdwy 2f out: chalng ins fnl f: styd on: hld cl home* **6/1**

2053 **4** *2 1/2* **Showboating (IRE)**[46] 6820 4-9-1 **78** ....(tp) MartinHarley 3 76
(Alan McCabe) *hld up: hmpd on bnd over 6f out: rdn and hdwy over 1f out: styd on ins fnl f: unable to rch ldrs* **7/1**

0005 **5** *1* **Fred Willetts (IRE)**[34] 7144 4-9-5 **82** .... GrahamGibbons 12 78
(Mark Brisbourne) *led: rdn over 1f out: sn hdd: no ex fnl 100yds* **25/1**

0010 **6** *3/4* **Lucky Dan (IRE)**[20] 7464 6-9-0 **77** .... FrannyNorton 8 71
(Paul Green) *prom: ev ch 2f out: rdn over 1f out: one pce ins fnl f* **25/1**

0231 **7** *1 1/2* **Restaurateur (IRE)**[45] 6840 3-9-0 **78** ....(b) DavidProbert 11 68
(Andrew Balding) *midfield: rdn over 1f out: one pce and no imp* **3/1**[1]

5046 **8** *2 3/4* **Fathsta (IRE)**[20] 7464 7-9-1 **78** .... StevieDonohoe 5 60
(Ian Williams) *s.i.s: n.m.r on bnd 6f out: sn lost pl: rdn over 2f out: no imp* **20/1**

0004 **9** *3/4* **Summerinthecity (IRE)**[36] 7080 5-8-13 **81** .... ShirleyTeasdale[(5)] 10 61
(David Nicholls) *towards rr: rdn over 2f out: nvr a threat* **14/1**

0200 **10** *1 3/4* **Dubai Hills**[12] 7639 6-9-1 **85** .... PeterSword[(7)] 1 60
(Bryan Smart) *hmpd on bnd over 6f out: a bhd* **25/1**

0104 **11** *3 1/2* **Divine Call**[29] 7274 5-9-2 79 .... RichardKingscote 2 45
(Milton Bradley) *prom: rdn over 1f out: wknd fnl f* **14/1**

1m 28.15s (-1.45) **Going Correction** +0.025s/f (Slow)
WFA 3 from 4yo+ 1lb **11** Ran SP% **116.8**
Speed ratings (Par 105): **109,108,107,104,103 102,101,98,97,95 91**
toteswingers 1&2 £6.00, 2&3 £7.20, 1&3 £4.40 CSF £24.59 CT £127.78 TOTE £5.40: £2.70, £2.00, £2.50; EX 31.00 Trifecta £111.90 Pool: £837.01 - 5.61 winning units..
Owner Phil Cunningham **Bred** P M Cunningham **Trained** Lambourn, Berks

FOCUS
A fair handicap run in a similar time to the second division. Pace held up and few got involved. The winner has had fewer chances than most.

7790 BOOK HOSPITALITY IN HORIZONS H'CAP (DIV II) 7f 32y(P)
4:30 (4:30) (Class 4) (0-85,84) 3-Y-O+ **£4,075** (£1,212; £606; £303) **Stalls** High

Form RPR

0250 **1** **Kingscroft (IRE)**[9] 7691 4-9-7 **83** .... JoeFanning 7 93
(Mark Johnston) *midfield: hdwy over 3f out: led wl over 1f out: styd on ins fnl f: a doing enough cl home* **9/2**[3]

5002 **2** *1* **Rasaman (IRE)**[34] 7144 8-9-1 **77** .... GrahamLee 4 84
(Jim Goldie) *hld up: hdwy over 1f out: styd on to take 2nd wl ins fnl f: nvr able to chal wnr* **14/1**

2611 **3** *1 1/4* **Light Burst (USA)**[63] 6302 3-9-3 **80** .... ShaneKelly 11 84
(Ismail Mohammed) *hld up: hdwy over 2f out: chsd wnr over 1f out: no imp whn lost 2nd wl ins fnl f: one pce cl home* **3/1**[1]

0404 **4** *3 1/2* **Valery Borzov (IRE)**[11] 7651 8-9-8 **84** ....(v) TonyHamilton 5 78
(Richard Fahey) *bmpd s: trckd ldrs: rdn over 2f out: could nt qckn over 1f out: kpt on towards fin* **8/1**

0604 **5** *nse* **Warfare**[16] [7559] 3-8-13 **76**.. PhillipMakin 3 70
(Kevin Ryan) *midfield: rdn over 1f out: kpt on ins fnl f: nvr able to chal* **7/2**[2]

0000 **6** *nk* **Azrael**[114] [4580] 4-9-2 **78**.. SebSanders 10 71
(Alan McCabe) *w ldr: led 2f out: rdn and hdd wl over 1f out: wknd wl ins fnl f* **25/1**

0030 **7** *1* **Kakatosi**[26] [7327] 5-9-6 **82**.. DavidProbert 1 73
(Andrew Balding) *racd keenly: handy on inner: pushed along over 2f out: rdn over 1f out: wknd wl ins fnl f* **12/1**

050 **8** *nk* **Tidentime (USA)**[11] [7645] 3-9-2 **79**.. MartinHarley 9 69
(Mick Channon) *midfield: rdn over 1f out: one pce ins fnl f* **12/1**

000 **9** *5* **Evervescent (IRE)**[33] [7163] 3-9-5 **82**.. LiamKeniry 12 58
(J S Moore) *in tch: effrt whn chsng ldrs 2f out: rdn and wknd over 1f out* **40/1**

2100 **10** *nk* **Frequency**[39] [7000] 5-9-1 **77**..(b) RobertWinston 2 52
(Keith Dalgleish) *s.s: hld up: plld rt over 1f out: nvr on terms to threaten* **16/1**

3400 **11** *1 ¾* **Final Drive (IRE)**[20] [7461] 6-9-2 **78**..(p) AdamKirby 8 49
(John Butler) *missed break: a bhd: outpcd over 4f out: nvr on terms* **12/1**

0115 **12** *½* **Smalljohn**[59] [6454] 6-9-0 **76**..(v) TomEaves 6 45
(Bryan Smart) *bmpd s: led: hdd 2f out: rdn and wknd over 1f out* **16/1**

1m 28.08s (-1.52) **Going Correction** +0.025s/f (Slow)
WFA 3 from 4yo+ 1lb **12** Ran SP% **124.3**
Speed ratings (Par 105): **109,107,106,102,102 102,100,100,94,94 92,91**
toteswingers 1&2 £11.50, 2&3 £8.90, 1&3 £3.60 CSF £69.83 CT £228.20 TOTE £3.10: £1.20, £3.00, £2.00; EX 57.60 Trifecta £222.40 Pool: £1103.20 - 3.72 winning units..
Owner Dr Marwan Koukash **Bred** J Beckett **Trained** Middleham Moor, N Yorks
■ Stewards' Enquiry : Tom Eaves £290.00 fine; used mobile phone outside the designated area.

FOCUS
The time was marginally quicker than the first division and this was yet another race in which it paid to challenge wide. Sound form.
Frequency Official explanation: jockey said gelding was denied a clear run.

7791 GREAT OFFERS AT WOLVERHAMPTON-RACECOURSE.CO.UK H'CAP 2m 119y(P)
5:00 (5:01) (Class 5) (0-75,72) 3-Y-O+ **£2,264** (£673; £336; £168) **Stalls** Low

Form RPR

2440 **1** **Somemothersdohavem**[17] [7522] 3-9-5 **72**..................(p) AdamKirby 12 81
(John Ryan) *hld up: hdwy 2f out: prog on outer to ld ins fnl f: edgd lft towards fin whn in command* **9/2**

451 **2** *1* **Gabrial's King (IRE)**[11] [7652] 3-9-3 **70**..................(p) StevieDonohoe 4 78
(Ian Williams) *trckd ldrs: styd on through gap to chal ins fnl f: tk 2nd cl home but hld by wnr* **7/2**[2]

3 *nk* **Formal Bid (IRE)**[24] [7392] 5-9-5 **63**..................(bt) GrahamLee 2 70
(Gordon Elliott, Ire) *hld up in midfield: hdwy towards inner over 1f out: chalng ins fnl f: styd on: hld cl home* **4/1**[3]

-001 **4** *nk* **Tartan Jura**[36] [7077] 4-10-0 **72**.. JoeFanning 3 79
(Mark Johnston) *led after 1f: pushed along and hdd over 4f out: regained ld 2f out: rdn and hrd pressed over 1f out: hdd ins fnl f: one pce cl home* **11/4**[1]

5301 **5** *2 ¼* **Six Of Clubs**[17] [7528] 6-9-5 **63**..................(b) LukeMorris 6 67
(Bill Turner) *midfield: hdwy over 3f out: rdn and ch over 1f out: kpt on same pce fnl 100yds* **12/1**

2130 **6** *½* **Looks Like Rain**[47] [6784] 3-8-13 **66**.. SilvestreDeSousa 11 70
(Brian Ellison) *hld up: rdn over 3f out: prog ins fnl f: styd on but unable to chal* **8/1**

62-0 **7** *2 ¾* **Raktiman (IRE)**[13] [7617] 5-9-10 **68**..................(b[1]) LiamKeniry 5 68
(Chris Bealby) *midfield: hdwy over 4f out: chsd ldrs 2f out: rdn over 1f out: wknd ins fnl f* **50/1**

1463 **8** *nk* **Eastern Magic**[19] [7490] 5-8-9 **58**.. ShirleyTeasdale(5) 9 58
(Reg Hollinshead) *s.s: hld up: rdn over 3f out: swtchd lft ins fnl f: kpt on but nvr able to chal* **16/1**

0050 **9** *1 ¾* **Souter Point (USA)**[25] [7353] 6-9-7 **65**.. AdamBeschizza 8 63
(Peter Salmon) *trckd ldrs: led 4f out: hdd 2f out: wknd ins fnl f* **40/1**

0050 **10** *3 ½* **Kahfre**[24] [7377] 5-9-7 **65**..................(vt) DavidProbert 10 59
(Gary Moore) *prom: rdn over 3f out: wknd 2f out* **40/1**

1420 **11** *5* **Geanie Mac (IRE)**[11] [6311] 3-8-9 **62**..................(b) TomEaves 1 50
(Linda Perratt) *led for 1f: remained prom: rdn and wknd over 2f out* **40/1**

110- **12** *17* **Brabazon (IRE)**[56] [5864] 9-9-7 **65**..................(bt) MartinHarley 7 32
(Shaun Harley, Ire) *hld up: struggling and wl bhd over 3f out: lost tch* **20/1**

3m 41.6s (-0.20) **Going Correction** +0.025s/f (Slow)
WFA 3 from 4yo+ 9lb **12** Ran SP% **125.8**
Speed ratings (Par 103): **101,100,100,100,99 98,97,97,96,95 92,84**
toteswingers 1&2 £4.60, 2&3 £4.80, 1&3 £5.60 CSF £21.16 CT £71.84 TOTE £6.50: £2.00, £1.20, £2.30; EX 22.60 Trifecta £192.60 Pool: £1427.86 - 5.56 winning units..
Owner The Somemothers Partnership **Bred** John And Susan Davis **Trained** Newmarket, Suffolk

FOCUS
A modest staying handicap run at a steady pace, and another race in which the winner challenged away from the inside rail. Straightforward form.
Looks Like Rain Official explanation: jockey said filly hung left-handed.

7792 FOLLOW US ON TWITTER @WOLVESRACES H'CAP 1m 4f 50y(P)
5:30 (5:30) (Class 5) (0-75,75) 3-Y-O+ **£2,264** (£673; £336; £168) **Stalls** Low

Form RPR

3420 **1** **Boa**[10] [7672] 7-9-0 **70**.. ShirleyTeasdale(5) 10 78
(Reg Hollinshead) *hld up: hdwy on outer 3f out: r.o to ld wl ins fnl f: in command cl home* **25/1**

2004 **2** *1* **Honest Deal**[25] [7353] 4-9-6 **71**.. RobertWinston 3 77
(Alan Swinbank) *led: rdn ins fnl f: sn hdd: hld cl home* **7/1**

2550 **3** *¾* **Sir Boss (IRE)**[23] [7409] 7-9-0 **70**.. NatashaEaton(5) 5 75
(Michael Mullineaux) *s.i.s: hld up: hdwy over 1f out: styd on ins fnl f: unable to chal front two* **25/1**

4306 **4** *¾* **Miss Blink**[24] [7368] 5-9-3 **68**.. SilvestreDeSousa 7 72
(Robin Bastiman) *midfield: pushed along and outpcd over 3f out: hdwy over 1f out: styd on towards fin: could nt quite get to ldrs* **22/1**

431 **5** *hd* **Candelita**[251] [581] 5-8-13 **64**.. J-PGuillambert 9 68
(Jo Hughes) *hld up: hdwy over 3f out: chsd ldrs over 2f out: cl up over 1f out: styd on same pce ins fnl f* **25/1**

2613 **6** *½* **Badea**[11] [7655] 3-9-1 **72**..................(v) TonyHamilton 1 75
(Richard Fahey) *hld up: rdn over 2f out: hdwy over 1f out: styd on towards fin: unable to chal ldrs* **3/1**[3]

4045 **7** *½* **Hydrant**[24] [7369] 6-9-3 **68**.. AdamBeschizza 11 70
(Peter Salmon) *prom: rdn 2f out: could nt qckn over 1f out: kpt on same pce ins fnl f* **16/1**

6000 **8** *2 ¾* **Merchant Of Dubai**[24] [7367] 7-9-10 **75**..................(v) FrederikTylicki 4 73
(Jim Goldie) *midfield: hdwy over 3f out: sn chsd ldrs: wknd ins fnl f* **11/4**[2]

0100 **9** *nk* **Cadgers Brig**[39] [7003] 4-9-2 **67**..................(p) JoeFanning 8 64
(Keith Dalgleish) *hld up: hdwy 7f out: wnt 2nd 6f out: lost 2nd wl over 1f out: wknd ins fnl f* **33/1**

400/ **10** *1 ¾* **Silverlord (FR)**[17] [7537] 8-9-5 **70**..................(t) GrahamLee 2 64
(Gordon Elliott, Ire) *sn dropped to midfield: rdn and wknd over 1f out* **5/2**[1]

1000 **11** *10* **Illustrious Forest**[10] [7672] 4-9-8 **73**.. FrannyNorton 12 51
(John Mackie) *prom: rdn 3f out: sn wknd* **8/1**

133/ **12** *hd* **Augustus John (IRE)**[969] [996] 9-9-0 **65**.. TomEaves 6 43
(Roy Brotherton) *hld up: struggling over 2f out: nvr on terms* **50/1**

2m 40.28s (-0.82) **Going Correction** +0.025s/f (Slow)
WFA 3 from 4yo+ 6lb **12** Ran SP% **130.5**
Speed ratings (Par 103): **103,102,101,101,101 100,100,98,98,97 90,90**
toteswingers 1&2 £17.40, 2&3 £24.40, 1&3 £35.30 CSF £195.83 CT £4477.89 TOTE £12.80: £2.40, £2.80, £5.40; EX 112.60 TRIFECTA Not won..
Owner Geoff Lloyd **Bred** R Hollinshead **Trained** Upper Longdon, Staffs

FOCUS
As was the theme on this card, the inside rail looked best avoided. An ordinary pace and straightforward form.
Illustrious Forest Official explanation: jockey said gelding hung left-handed.
T/Jkpt: £43,155.60 to a £1 stake. Pool of £303,913.06 - 5.00 winning tickets. T/Plt: £46.60 to a £1 stake. Pool of £84770.44 - 1325.34 winning tickets. T/Qpdt: £7.70 to a £1 stake. Pool of £7781.66 - 746.90 winning tickets. DO

7726 SOUTHWELL (L-H)
Tuesday, November 20

OFFICIAL GOING: Standard
Wind: Fresh across Weather: Heavy cloud

7793 BOOK SEASONS RESTAURANT AT SOUTHWELL RACECOURSE H'CAP (DIV I) 1m 4f (F)
12:20 (12:20) (Class 6) (0-55,55) 3-Y-O+ **£1,704** (£503; £251) **Stalls** Low

Form RPR

6030 **1** **Bocamix (FR)**[42] [6956] 6-9-4 **52**..................(v) TomEaves 8 59
(Andrew Crook) *a.p: chsd ldr over 4f out: rdn wl over 2f out: drvn wl over 1f out: styd on fnl f to ld on line* **16/1**

0004 **2** *nse* **Dunaskin (IRE)**[6] [7717] 12-8-7 **46** oh1..................(b) JasonHart(5) 2 53
(Richard Guest) *prom: led after 4f: rdn 3f out: drvn wl over 1f out: hdd on line* **20/1**

000 **3** *hd* **Honest Strike (USA)**[43] [6940] 5-9-2 **50**..................(b) ShaneKelly 1 56
(Daniel Mark Loughnane) *hld up and bhd: hdwy 4f out: rdn along wl over 2f out: styd on wl to chse ldng pair whn swtchd lft ins fnl f: drvn and kpt on wl towards fin* **7/1**[3]

4504 **4** *3 ¼* **David's Folly (IRE)**[20] [7490] 3-8-3 **46** oh1.. RaulDaSilva(3) 7 47
(Bryn Palling) *midfield: hdwy 5f out: chsd ldrs 3f out: rdn to chse ldng pair over 2f out: drvn wl over 1f out: one pce appr fnl f* **12/1**

4400 **5** *11* **Magic Haze**[84] [3440] 6-9-5 **53**..................(p) SilvestreDeSousa 14 36
(Sally Hall) *in tch: hdwy to chse ldrs over 4f out: rdn along over 3f out: drvn and no imp fnl 2f* **7/1**[3]

-00 **6** *10* **Manshoor (IRE)**[28] [7315] 7-9-7 **55**.. LukeMorris 5 22
(Lucy Wadham) *towards rr and rdn along after 2f: sn bhd* **20/1**

006 **7** *½* **Linroyale Boy (USA)**[172] [2669] 4-9-6 **54**.. RobertWinston 10 21
(Alan Swinbank) *hld up: a in rr* **3/1**[1]

4100 **8** *4* **Maccabees**[20] [7479] 3-8-12 **52**.. FrederikTylicki 9 12
(Roger Curtis) *nvr bttr than midfield* **7/1**[3]

1220 **9** *12* **Emperors Waltz (IRE)**[104] [4941] 3-9-1 **55**.. GrahamLee 4
(Ralph Smith) *led 1 1/2f: chsd ldrs: rdn along 1/2-way: sn lost pl and bhd* **16/1**

00/0 **10** *2* **Apache Moon**[11] [7671] 6-8-13 **47**.. JimmyQuinn 6
(Alastair Lidderdale) *midfield: hdwy to chse ldrs after 4f: rdn along and wknd over 4f out* **33/1**

060 **11** *2 ½* **Alaskan Prince (IRE)**[67] [6215] 7-8-12 **46** oh1.. AdamBeschizza 3
(Peter Salmon) *chsd ldrs: led after 1 1/2f: hdd after 4f: cl up tl rdn along 4f out and sn wknd* **66/1**

3405 **12** *nk* **Satwa Ballerina**[21] [7472] 4-8-9 **48**..................(bt) TobyAtkinson(5) 13
(Mark Rimmer) *midfield: rdn along 1/2-way: sn outpcd and bhd* **33/1**

4-00 **13** *79* **Lady Intrigue (IRE)**[14] [7603] 4-8-12 **46** oh1.. TonyHamilton 12
(Richard Fahey) *dwlt: a in rr: bhd fnl 4f: t.o and eased fnl 2f* **20/1**

1652 **P** **Five Hearts**[20] [7479] 4-9-3 **51**.. GeorgeBaker 11
(Mark H Tompkins) *chsd ldrs: rdn along and lost pl 1/2-way: sn bhd and p.u 4f out* **6/1**[2]

2m 39.31s (-1.69) **Going Correction** -0.125s/f (Stan)
WFA 3 from 4yo+ 6lb **14** Ran SP% **117.9**
Speed ratings (Par 101): **100,99,99,97,90 83,83,80,72,71 69,69,16,**
Tote Swingers 1&2 £52.80, 2&3 £24.90, 1&3 £16.20 CSF £307.45 CT £2440.00 TOTE £23.20: £7.80, £8.00, £4.50; EX 276.90 TRIFECTA Not won..
Owner Mrs Helen Sinclair **Bred** Baron Guy De Rothschild **Trained** Middleham Moor, N Yorks
■ Stewards' Enquiry : Shane Kelly two-day ban: careless riding (Dec 4-5)

FOCUS
A weak handicap in which few ever got into it, but it produced a thrilling finish with little covering the first three at the line. The form is rated around the runner-up.
Bocamix(FR) Official explanation: trainer said, regarding apparent improvement in form, that the gelding benfited from a return to Fibresand
Magic Haze Official explanation: jockey said gelding had no more to give
Linroyale Boy(USA) Official explanation: jockey said gelding never travelled
Five Hearts Official explanation: jockey said filly lost its action but returned sound

7794 32RED.COM H'CAP 6f (F)
12:50 (12:51) (Class 6) (0-65,65) 3-Y-O+ **£1,704** (£503; £251) **Stalls** Low

Form RPR

-054 **1** **Spitfire**[120] [4406] 7-9-4 **62**..................(t) FrederikTylicki 9 73
(J R Jenkins) *towards rr: hdwy over 2f out: rdn to chse ldrs over 1f out: drvn ent fnl f: styd on strly to ld nr fin* **5/1**[2]

2050 **2** *½* **Holy Angel (IRE)**[22] [7446] 3-8-11 **60**..................(e[1]) AdamCarter(5) 3 69
(Tim Easterby) *in tch: hdwy 1/2-way: chal 2f out: rdn to ld wl over 1f out: edgd rt to stands' rail and clr ins fnl f: eased and hdd nr fin* **16/1**

0116 **3** *2 ½* **Ivestar (IRE)**[21] [7456] 7-9-4 **62**..................(v) GrahamGibbons 2 63
(Michael Easterby) *chsd ldrs on inner: rdn along over 2f out: drvn over 1f out: kpt on same pce fnl f* **22/1**

025 **4** *nk* **Steel City Boy (IRE)**[13] [7633] 9-8-5 **56**.. GeorgeChaloner(7) 13 56
(Garry Woodward) *in tch on outer: hdwy over 2f out: sn rdn and kpt on fnl f: nrst fin* **28/1**

0553 **5** *¾* **Belle Bayardo (IRE)**[30] [7274] 4-9-7 **65**.. LukeMorris 14 63
(Ronald Harris) *midfield: hdwy 2f out: sn rdn and kpt on fnl f: nrst fin* **7/1**[3]

3226 **6** *nk* **Lucky Mark (IRE)**[11] 7673 3-9-0 **58** MartinLane 5 55
(Garry Moss) *sn rdn along towards rr: hdwy to trck ldrs after 2f: rdn over 2f out: kpt on same pce* **8/1**

4650 **7** *nk* **No Mean Trick (USA)**[196] 1954 6-9-6 **64** MickyFenton 1 60
(Paul Midgley) *led: rdn along 2f out: drvn and hdd over 1f out: sn wknd* **20/1**

2441 **8** *2 1/2* **Maltease Ah**[26] 7354 3-9-1 **59** SilvestreDeSousa 6 47
(Alan McCabe) *prom: effrt over 2f out and ev ch: sn rdn and wknd wl over 1f out* **11/4**[1]

0500 **9** *nk* **Ishetoo**[15] 7590 8-9-0 **58** DominicFox 12 45
(Peter Grayson) *a towards rr* **66/1**

0052 **10** *nse* **Captain Royale (IRE)**[14] 7604 7-9-1 **59** (p) GrahamLee 4 46
(Tracy Waggott) *cl up: effrt over 2f out: sn rdn and ev ch tl wknd appr fnl f* **9/1**

6006 **11** *1* **Katy's Secret**[34] 7166 5-9-0 **63** ShirleyTeasdale(5) 10 46
(William Jarvis) *a in rr* **8/1**

0000 **12** *5* **Cape Of Storms**[15] 7589 9-9-1 **59** (b) TomEaves 8 26
(Roy Brotherton) *chsd ldrs on outer: rdn along wl over 2f out: sn wknd* **33/1**

2040 **13** *1 1/4* **Greek Islands (IRE)**[26] 7351 4-8-13 **57** (b) LiamKeniry 11 20
(Ed de Giles) *in tch: rdn along bef 1/2-way: sn wknd* **20/1**

5610 **14** *10* **Northern Bolt**[22] 7446 7-9-1 **59** (e[1]) PatrickMathers 7
(Ian McInnes) *rrd and lost several l s: a bhd* **28/1**

1m 16.31s (-0.19) **Going Correction** -0.125s/f (Stan) **14** Ran SP% **119.1**
Speed ratings (Par 101): **96,95,92,91,90 90,89,86,86,86 84,78,76,63**
Tote Swingers 1&2 £18.50, 2&3 £29.70, 1&3 £25.00 CSF £72.94 CT £1670.88 TOTE £5.90: £2.40, £6.40, £7.70; EX 83.80 Trifecta £258.20 Part won. Pool: £344.33 - 0.40 winning tickets..
Owner Mrs Wendy Jenkins **Bred** R B Hill **Trained** Royston, Herts

FOCUS
A moderate sprint handicap. The winner is rated similarly to C&D efforts this time last year.
Maltease Ah Official explanation: jockey said filly hung right
Captain Royale(IRE) Official explanation: trainer said gelding bled from the nose

7795 32RED.COM (S) STKS 7f (F)
1:20 (1:20) (Class 6) 2-Y-O **£1,704** (£503; £251) **Stalls** Low

Form RPR

2004 **1** **Projectisle (IRE)**[5] 7727 2-8-12 70 (b[1]) PhillipMakin 2 71
(Kevin Ryan) *mde all: rdn clr over 2f out: kpt on* **5/1**

3550 **2** *10* **It's Only Business**[12] 7649 2-8-5 60 JakePayne(7) 5 45
(Bill Turner) *chsd wnr: rdn wl over 2f out: sn one pce* **8/1**

504 **3** *2 1/4* **Lady Raffa**[64] 6310 2-8-7 47 TomEaves 7 34
(Michael Dods) *dwlt: sn chsng ldrs: rdn along wl over 2f out: sn drvn and one pce* **18/1**

0260 **4** *1 3/4* **Age Of Bronze**[5] 7724 2-8-12 64 LiamKeniry 4 34
(Richard Hannon) *sn outpcd and bhd tl sme late hdwy* **9/4**[1]

0 **5** *1 1/4* **Art Storm (IRE)**[29] 7290 2-8-12 0 TonyHamilton 6 31
(Richard Fahey) *dwlt: sn outpcd: a in rr* **7/2**[3]

0462 **6** *4* **Kicken Off (IRE)**[5] 7727 2-9-3 68 (b) JimmyQuinn 3 26
(Phil McEntee) *trckd ldrs: hdwy 3f out: rdn over 2f out and sn btn* **3/1**[2]

4000 **7** *4 1/2* **I'Ve No Money (IRE)**[14] 7609 2-8-12 45 KirstyMilczarek 1 9
(David C Griffiths) *chsd ldrs: rdn wl over 2f out: sn wknd* **40/1**

1m 29.12s (-1.18) **Going Correction** -0.125s/f (Stan) **7** Ran SP% **113.5**
Speed ratings (Par 94): **101,89,87,85,83 79,73**
Tote Swingers 1&2 £4.80, 2&3 £8.10, 1&3 £6.20 CSF £42.57 TOTE £3.50: £1.10, £4.80; EX 45.50.There was no bid for the winner.
Owner Mrs Angie Bailey **Bred** K B Lynch **Trained** Hambleton, N Yorks

FOCUS
A poor seller and one-way traffic. The winner only needed to get back to some of her early-season form.

NOTEBOOK
Projectisle(IRE) had finished around 3l behind Kicken Off in first-time cheekpieces over 6f here five days earlier and was 6lb better off, but she was tried in blinkers this time and the contrast could hardly have been greater. Quickly away, she just went further and further clear up the home straight and absolutely bolted up, but it remains to be seen if she will repeat this performance in the same headgear. (op 5-2)
It's Only Business, tried on Fibresand after losing his way on turf/Polytrack, raced closest to the winner early and although under pressure a long way out, still managed to hold off the rest. In reality, there was no second. (op 12-1 tchd 7-1)
Lady Raffa, rated just 47 after being well held in two maidens and a seller, achieved little in finishing third. (op 20-1 tchd 25-1 and 16-1)
Age Of Bronze, making his Fibresand debut, had a chance at the weights but he was being ridden along from the start and appeared to hate the surface. (op 5-2 tchd 15-8)
Art Storm(IRE) attracted support on his Pontefract debut last month, but ran a stinker on the heavy ground and didn't seem to be enjoying himself at all here either. (op 7-1)
Kicken Off(IRE) was blinkered for the first time when finishing ahead of the winner here the previous week, but never got into the race at all this time. (tchd 11-4 and 10-3)

7796 MARGARET RICE MEMORIAL MEDIAN AUCTION MAIDEN STKS 1m (F)
1:50 (1:51) (Class 5) 2-Y-O **£2,264** (£673; £336; £168) **Stalls** Low

Form RPR

54 **1** **Mandy The Nag (USA)**[21] 7460 2-8-12 0 GrahamLee 7 68+
(Ed Dunlop) *trckd ldrs on outer: hdwy wl over 2f out: chal over 1f out: rdn to ld jst ins fnl f: styd on* **7/2**[2]

025 **2** *1 1/4* **Anjuna Beach (USA)**[19] 7507 2-9-3 72 GeorgeBaker 3 70
(Gary Moore) *cl up on inner: led 1/2-way: rdn along wl over 1f out: jnd and drvn 1f out: sn hdd and one pce* **8/15**[1]

0 **3** *2* **Mosman**[28] 7306 2-9-3 0 FergusSweeney 5 66
(Jamie Osborne) *trckd ldrs: hdwy 3f out: rdn 2f out: drvn and one pce appr fnl f* **10/1**[3]

06 **4** *2 1/4* **Alzavola**[21] 7460 2-8-12 0 LukeMorris 8 58+
(Sir Mark Prescott Bt) *prom: rdn along 3f out: edgd lft wl over 1f out and sn one pce* **20/1**

5 *2 3/4* **Handiwork** 2-9-3 0 StevieDonohoe 1 55+
(Michael Bell) *in tch: pushed along and rn green over 3f out: edgd rt over 1f out: kpt on fnl f* **10/1**[3]

6 *11* **Hartlebury** 2-9-3 0 TedDurcan 4 31
(James Bethell) *in tch: rdn along 3f out: green and sn wknd* **10/1**[3]

004 **7** *nk* **Darakti (IRE)**[5] 7728 2-9-3 0 GrahamGibbons 2 30
(Alan McCabe) *reminders s: a in rr* **33/1**

00 **8** *2 1/2* **Roy Rocket (FR)**[13] 7636 2-9-3 0 RobertHavlin 6 25
(John Berry) *led: hdd 1/2-way: cl up and rdn 3f out: drvn over 2f out and sn wknd* **66/1**

1m 42.67s (-1.03) **Going Correction** -0.125s/f (Stan) **8** Ran SP% **123.9**
Speed ratings (Par 96): **100,98,96,94,91 80,80,77**
Tote Swingers 1&2 £1.70, 2&3 £2.60 CSF £6.17 TOTE £3.00: £1.10, £1.10, £3.60; EX 9.70 Trifecta £55.20 Pool: £1,080.96 - 14.68 winning tickets..
Owner Dr Marwan Koukash **Bred** Randal Family Trust Et Al **Trained** Newmarket, Suffolk

FOCUS
The betting suggested that this was a two-horse race and the pair duly dominated. Ordinary maiden form.

NOTEBOOK
Mandy The Nag(USA), who had shown ability in a couple of Wolverhampton maidens last month, raced widest throughout and having been brought with her effort starting up the home straight, saw her race out best. She can progress again and would be of obvious interest in a nursery back here. (op 11-4)
Anjuna Beach(USA)'s BHA rating of 72 set the standard and he appeared to be travelling much better than his rivals after leading at halfway. However, he didn't force home the advantage and couldn't quicken when the filly came to challenge entering the last furlong. (op 4-5 tchd 5-6)
Mosman beat only one home on his Lingfield debut last month and this was much better. He looks the type to come into his own in handicaps after one more run. (op 12-1 tchd 9-1)
Alzavola, well held in her first two starts including behind Mandy The Nag at Wolverhampton last time, showed a little more on this occasion and is likely to come into her own in handicaps over further now that she gets a mark.
Handiwork, a half-brother to three winners at up to 1m4f, offered only limited promise on this debut, but he is entitled to improve.

7797 32RED.COM NURSERY 6f (F)
2:20 (2:21) (Class 6) (0-60,59) 2-Y-O **£1,704** (£503; £251) **Stalls** Low

Form RPR

0001 **1** **Seemenomore**[6] 7713 2-9-9 **59** 6ex (v) MartinLane 7 66
(Michael Bell) *dwlt: sn cl up: led 4f out: rdn along wl over 1f out: drvn and hung rt ent fnl f: kpt on* **4/9**[1]

3003 **2** *1* **Only For You**[6] 7711 2-9-0 **50** SilvestreDeSousa 9 54
(Alan Brown) *prom: hdwy to chse wnr 2f out: rdn to chal over 1f out: ev ch and drvn ins fnl f: kpt on same pce* **14/1**

005 **3** *3 1/4* **Hazard Warning (IRE)**[53] 6628 2-8-9 **45** (b) TedDurcan 5 39
(Tim Easterby) *in tch: hdwy over 2f out: rdn wl over 1f out: kpt on fnl f: nrst fin* **33/1**

0066 **4** *3/4* **Angel Grigio**[14] 7609 2-9-2 **52** (v) JimmyQuinn 1 44
(Bryan Smart) *chsd ldrs: rdn along over 2f out: kpt on same pce* **10/1**[2]

556 **5** *1 3/4* **Little Indian**[30] 7272 2-9-5 **55** FrederikTylicki 2 42+
(J R Jenkins) *chsd ldrs on inner: rdn along over 2f out: wknd appr fnl f* **10/1**[2]

065 **6** *3/4* **Hanga Roa (IRE)**[64] 6301 2-8-9 **45** FergusSweeney 10 30
(Gary Moore) *dwlt and in rr: hdwy over 2f out: sn rdn and kpt on fnl f: nrst fin* **33/1**

000 **7** *1 1/2* **Edge Of Glory**[27] 7329 2-8-9 **45** KieranO'Neill 4 25+
(Richard Hannon) *nvr nr ldrs* **10/1**[2]

0645 **8** *2 1/4* **Many Elements**[34] 7156 2-8-12 **55** (p) AaronChave(7) 6 28
(Lee Carter) *racd wd: a towards rr* **12/1**[3]

6056 **9** *1 1/2* **Lucky Suit (IRE)**[20] 7491 2-9-1 **51** LukeMorris 8 20
(Ronald Harris) *led 2f: cl up: rdn along wl over 2f out: sn wknd* **33/1**

0000 **10** *hd* **Fat Bottom Girl**[21] 7462 2-8-13 **49** NickyMackay 11 17
(Michael Easterby) *chsd ldrs on outer: rdn along 3f out: sn wknd* **40/1**

1m 16.88s (0.38) **Going Correction** -0.125s/f (Stan) **10** Ran SP% **122.1**
Speed ratings (Par 94): **92,90,86,85,83 82,80,77,75,74**
Tote Swingers 1&2 £3.50, 2&3 £36.30, 1&3 £7.50 CSF £8.93 CT £120.74 TOTE £1.30: £1.10, £2.20, £7.70; EX 8.30 Trifecta £141.60 Pool: £1,406.84 - 7.45 winning tickets..
Owner K J P Gundlach **Bred** A S Reid **Trained** Newmarket, Suffolk

FOCUS
A moderate nursery which totally revolved around one horse. The winner was a few lengths below last week's C&D romp.

NOTEBOOK
Seemenomore was carrying a 6lb penalty after winning a C&D nursery with embarrassing ease in a first-time visor six days earlier, and was all the rage to follow up. In front inside the first 2f, just like the previous week, everything seemed to be going smoothly starting up the home straight as he appeared to be travelling nicely in front. However, he started to hang badly away to his right coming to the last furlong and gave the runner-up a chance, but fortunately he still had enough in hand. Again he had got himself warm and, with an 11lb rise already imminent even before this performance, life is about to get an awful lot harder. (op 4-7)
Only For You was never far away and although intimidated by the hanging favourite inside the last furlong, she looked held at the time. She is now 0-12. (tchd 16-1)
Hazard Warning(IRE), making his nursery debut after failing to beat a rival in his first three starts, ran on well from the middle of the field to record by far his best effort to date. He looks well worth another try here.
Angel Grigio was shoved up 7lb for finishing too close to a much higher-rated rival in a 5f maiden here last time (third has won since) and although not disgraced ths time, didn't suggest that he is progressing. (op 8-1)
Little Indian, making his nursery/Fibresand debuts after showing a little ability in three turf maidens, plugged on after coming off the bridle at halfway and still has a bit of scope. (op 16-1)

7798 32RED CASINO (S) STKS 1m (F)
2:50 (2:50) (Class 6) 3-Y-O+ **£1,704** (£503; £251) **Stalls** Low

Form RPR

6220 **1** **Bold Marc (IRE)**[23] 7701 10-9-0 65 LukeMorris 11 72
(Mrs K Burke) *trckd ldrs: hdwy and cl up 2f out: rdn and slt ld over 1f out: sn drvn: edgd lft ins fnl f: kpt on gamely* **5/1**[3]

6442 **2** *1 1/2* **River Ardeche**[26] 7348 7-9-0 60 GrahamLee 6 69
(Tracy Waggott) *trckd ldrs: hdwy on inner over 3f out and sn cl up: rdn to chal 2f out and ev ch: drvn ins fnl f: no ex last 75yds* **4/1**[2]

4304 **3** *1* **Eastern Hills**[5] 7732 7-9-0 65 (p) IPoullis 9 67
(Alan McCabe) *cl up: led after 2f: rdn along over 2f out: drvn and hdd over 1f out: ev ch ins fnl f: n.m.r and no ex last 100yds* **13/2**

5200 **4** *5* **Sir George (IRE)**[52] 6687 7-8-7 67 JacobButterfield(7) 3 55
(Ollie Pears) *towards rr: pushed along over 3f out: hdwy over 2f out: sn rdn: styd on appr fnl f: nrst fin* **8/1**

0502 **5** *1 1/4* **Whisky Bravo**[28] 7307 3-8-12 63 (p) ShaneKelly 14 52
(Tim Pitt) *prom on outer: rdn along wl over 2f out: drvn wl over 1f out: grad wknd* **16/1**

3650 **6** *2* **Putin (IRE)**[28] 7317 4-9-0 43 (bt) JimmyQuinn 7 48
(Phil McEntee) *dwlt: sn w ldrs: cl up 3f out: rdn along over 2f out and grad wknd* **50/1**

0006 **7** *1/2* **Guava**[14] 7615 3-8-2 45 (b) ShirleyTeasdale(5) 1 42
(Shaun Harris) *led 2f: cl up on inner: rdn along over 3f out: wknd wl over 2f out* **66/1**

0033 **8** *2* **Come Hither**[14] 7600 3-8-13 61 (b[1]) SilvestreDeSousa 12 43
(David O'Meara) *cl up on outer: rdn along over 2f out: sn wknd* **10/3**[1]

0501 **9** *1* **Nurse Dominatrix (IRE)**[14] 7612 3-8-13 49 RobbieFitzpatrick 13 41
(Richard Guest) *a in rr* **25/1**

4006 **10** *hd* **King Of Windsor (IRE)**[14] 7608 5-9-1 70 AdamCarter(5) 10 45
(John Wainwright) *dwlt: a in rr* **33/1**

2004 **11** *1/2* **Sunnyside Tom (IRE)**[14] 7607 8-9-0 61 (p) TonyHamilton 5 38
(Richard Fahey) *a in rr* **7/1**

0001 **12** *30* **Lothair (IRE)**[129] 4087 3-9-4 52 RobertWinston 8
(Alan Swinbank) *prom: rdn along bef 1/2-way: sn lost pl and bhd* **18/1**
005 **13** *3/4* **Darrow (IRE)**[14] 7602 3-8-12 52 (t) DominicFox 2
(Wilf Storey) *a in rr* **100/1**
1m 42.56s (-1.14) **Going Correction** -0.125s/f (Stan)
WFA 3 from 4yo+ 2lb 13 Ran SP% **119.1**
Speed ratings (Par 101): **100,98,97,92,91 89,88,86,85,85 85,55,54**
Tote Swingers 1&2 £4.90, 2&3 £7.40, 1&3 £6.40 CSF £24.45 TOTE £6.00: £1.80, £1.60, £3.50; EX 23.10 Trifecta £196.40 Pool: £1,030.04 - 3.93 winning tickets..There was no bid for the winner.
Owner Mrs Elaine M Burke **Bred** Eamon D Delany **Trained** Middleham Moor, N Yorks

FOCUS
A modest seller, though quite a competitive one. The winner was close to this year's C&D form.

7799 32RED H'CAP 1m (F)
3:20 (3:20) (Class 5) (0-70,74) 3-Y-O+ **£2,385** (£704; £352) **Stalls** Low

Form RPR
-021 **1** **Royal Holiday (IRE)**[26] 7348 5-8-12 61 (p) PhillipMakin 2 69
(Marjorie Fife) *mde most: rdn 2f out: drvn over 1f out: kpt on gamely towards fin* **16/1**
0311 **2** *nk* **No Dominion (IRE)**[26] 7347 3-9-2 67 GrahamLee 4 75
(James Given) *in tch: hdwy over 2f out: rdn to chse ldrs over 1f out: drvn and kpt on to chal ins fnl f: no ex towards fin* **7/4**[1]
4402 **3** *nk* **Fishforcompliments**[18] 7529 8-9-2 65 FrederikTylicki 5 72
(Richard Fahey) *midfield: hdwy 3f out: chsd ldrs wl over 1f out: swtchd lft and rdn ent fnl f: kpt on wl towards fin* **10/1**[3]
5203 **4** *nk* **Illustrious Prince (IRE)**[10] 7684 5-9-0 70 LukeLeadbitter(7) 9 76
(Declan Carroll) *prom: cl up over 3f out: chal over 2f out and sn rdn: ev ch tl drvn ins fnl f and wknd last 50yds* **12/1**
1401 **5** *2* **Flying Pickets (IRE)**[5] 7732 3-9-4 74 6ex(be) WilliamTwiston-Davies(5) 6 76
(Alan McCabe) *bhd: hdwy wl over 2f out: sn rdn: styd on appr fnl f: nrst fin* **16/1**
0000 **6** *hd* **Mullins Way (USA)**[27] 7328 4-9-7 70 J-PGuillambert 8 71
(Jo Hughes) *in tch: rdn along wl over 2f out: kpt on fnl f: nrst fin* **14/1**
0-00 **7** *2* **Casela Park (IRE)**[10] 7684 7-9-2 65 (b) SilvestreDeSousa 1 62
(David O'Meara) *dwlt: sn in tch: hdwy to chse ldrs 1/2-way: rdn along over 2f out: grad wknd* **7/1**[2]
6264 **8** *3 1/4* **Mcmonagle (USA)**[11] 7666 4-9-7 70 (tp) DaleSwift 3 59
(Alan Brown) *prom: rdn along over 3f out: sn wknd* **18/1**
632 **9** *11* **Charlcot**[31] 7256 4-9-2 65 TedDurcan 10 29
(James Bethell) *in tch on wd outside: rdn along 3f out: sn wknd* **12/1**
3005 **10** *1 3/4* **Ventura Sands (IRE)**[14] 7618 4-9-5 68 TonyHamilton 11 28
(Richard Fahey) *chsd ldrs on outer: rdn along 3f out: sn wknd* **12/1**
0000 **11** *9* **Pipers Piping (IRE)**[14] 7618 6-8-13 62 LiamKeniry 14
(John Butler) *a in rr* **33/1**
0050 **12** *nk* **Dream Win**[111] 4715 6-9-0 63 (t) TomEaves 12
(Brian Ellison) *dwlt: a in rr* **33/1**
435 **13** *9* **Auto Mac**[26] 7347 4-8-12 61 (b) LukeMorris 7
(Neville Bycroft) *a in rr: bhd fnl 3f* **10/1**[3]
1m 42.13s (-1.57) **Going Correction** -0.125s/f (Stan)
WFA 3 from 4yo+ 2lb 13 Ran SP% **119.7**
Speed ratings (Par 103): **102,101,101,101,99 98,96,93,82,80 71,71,62**
Tote Swingers 1&2 £7.20, 2&3 £6.20, 1&3 £19.30 CSF £44.09 CT £285.44 TOTE £17.30: £3.60, £1.40, £2.80; EX 52.10 Trifecta £252.60 Pool: £1,077.88 - 3.20 winning tickets..
Owner Mrs Marion Turner **Bred** E Tynan **Trained** Stillington, N Yorks

FOCUS
A fair handicap. A small personal best from the winner.
Charlcot Official explanation: jockey said gelding suffered interference leaving stalls

7800 BOOK SEASONS RESTAURANT AT SOUTHWELL RACECOURSE H'CAP (DIV II) 1m 4f (F)
3:50 (3:50) (Class 6) (0-55,55) 3-Y-O+ **£1,704** (£503; £251) **Stalls** Low

Form RPR
0430 **1** **Tobrata**[53] 6626 6-9-7 55 SilvestreDeSousa 11 65
(Mel Brittain) *hld up towards rr: stdy hdwy on outer 1/2-way: chsd ldrs 3f out: rdn over 2f out: drvn to chse ldr ent fnl f: styd on wl to ld last 50yds* **5/2**[1]
2003 **2** *nk* **Dewala**[6] 7712 3-8-12 52 AndrewMullen 1 61
(Michael Appleby) *led: rdn along over 2f out: drvn over 1f out: jnd ent fnl f: hdd and no ex last 50yds* **8/1**
0544 **3** *2 1/4* **Neil's Pride**[32] 7222 3-8-12 52 FrederikTylicki 8 58
(Richard Fahey) *trckd ldrs: hdwy 4f out: rdn along wl over 2f out: drvn and ch over 1f out: kpt on same pce* **4/1**[2]
0045 **4** *1 1/4* **Destiny Awaits (IRE)**[18] 7527 3-8-13 53 (p) TomEaves 10 57
(George Foster) *hld up: stdy hdwy over 5f out: chsd ldrs 3f out: drvn 2f out: styd on u.p fnl f* **9/1**
0564 **5** *1* **Spring Secret**[39] 7018 6-9-3 51 LukeMorris 4 53
(Bryn Palling) *prom: chsd ldr 1/2-way: rdn along wl over 2f out: drvn wl over 1f out: grad wknd* **16/1**
0-06 **6** *16* **Midnight Bahia (IRE)**[13] 7632 3-8-6 46 oh1 JimmyQuinn 7 22
(Dean Ivory) *trckd ldrs on inner: effrt over 4f out: rdn along 3f out: drvn over 2f out and sn wknd* **6/1**[3]
4300 **7** *4* **Crimson Monarch (USA)**[7] 7528 8-8-12 46 oh1 ChrisCatlin 2 16
(Peter Hiatt) *a towards rr* **40/1**
0005 **8** *12* **General Tufto**[5] 7731 7-9-5 53 (b) RobbieFitzpatrick 14
(Charles Smith) *a bhd* **16/1**
/000 **9** *1/2* **Ceto**[14] 7619 5-9-0 48 (be[1]) GrahamLee 13
(Phil McEntee) *in tch: hdwy to chse ldrs 1/2-way: rdn along over 4f out: sn wknd* **40/1**
2000 **10** *13* **Landown Littlerock**[18] 7527 3-9-1 55 GrahamGibbons 12
(Reg Hollinshead) *a in rr* **8/1**
-234 **11** *8* **Nippy Nikki**[217] 1433 4-9-2 50 PhillipMakin 9
(John Norton) *a bhd* **20/1**
600- **12** *2 1/4* **Revitalise**[426] 6260 3-8-9 49 MickyFenton 6
(Paul Midgley) *prom: rdn along 1/2-way: sn lost pl and bhd* **25/1**
4030 **13** *7* **Mesariya (IRE)**[15] 7596 4-9-5 53 [1] StephenCraine 5
(Tony Coyle) *s.i.s and in rr: hdwy to chse ldrs after 4f: rdn along 1/2-way: sn outpcd and bhd fnl 4f* **40/1**
2m 38.73s (-2.27) **Going Correction** -0.125s/f (Stan)
WFA 3 from 4yo+ 6lb 13 Ran SP% **122.8**
Speed ratings (Par 101): **102,101,100,99,98 88,85,77,77,68 63,61,56**
Tote Swingers 1&2 £5.10, 2&3 £9.60, 1&3 £2.70 CSF £22.43 CT £79.14 TOTE £2.90: £1.10, £3.20, £1.70; EX 31.30 Trifecta £227.80 Pool: £1,327.55 - 4.37 winning tickets..
Owner Mel Brittain **Bred** J S B Anderson **Trained** Warthill, N Yorks

FOCUS
The winning time was 0.58 seconds faster than the first division and it looked the more convincing form.
T/Jkpt: Not won. T/Plt: £181.10 to a £1 stake. Pool: £54,074.59 - 217.93 winning tickets. T/Qpdt: £7.00 to a £1 stake. Pool: £6,141.56 - 645.2 winning tickets. JR

7801 - 7802a (Foreign Racing) - See Raceform Interactive

7699 CHANTILLY (R-H)
Tuesday, November 20
OFFICIAL GOING: Turf: heavy; polytrack: standard

7803a PRIX DE LA PORTE DES VIGNES (CONDITIONS) (3YO) (POLYTRACK) 6f 110y
1:50 (12:00) 3-Y-O **£12,083** (£4,833; £3,625; £2,416; £1,208)

RPR
1 **Silverheels (IRE)**[27] 7345 3-8-13 0 ChristopheSoumillon 11 94
(Paul Cole) *trckd ldr: disp ld over 2f out: shkn up and led appr fnl f: sn clr: pushed out: comf* **17/10**[1]
2 *2 1/2* **Paraggi**[45] 3-8-13 0 MaximeGuyon 15 87
(Mme Pia Brandt, France) **15/1**
3 *1/2* **American Saga (FR)**[21] 3-8-9 0 GregoryBenoist 1 81
(M Delzangles, France) **10/1**
4 *1 1/2* **Jellicle (IRE)**[27] 7345 3-8-9 0 (b) FabriceVeron 14 77
(H-A Pantall, France) **10/1**
5 *nk* **Katherine Deux (FR)**[24] 3-8-9 0 AlexisBadel 2 76
(Mme M Bollack-Badel, France) **44/5**[3]
6 *hd* **Turcoman's (FR)**[8] 3-8-13 0 ThierryJarnet 6 80
(A Junk, France) **12/1**
7 *1/2* **Ma Victoryan (FR)**[26] 3-9-0 0 AurelienLemaitre 12 79
(C Baillet, France) **16/1**
8 *1* **Whip Des Aigles (FR)** 3-8-13 0 FredericSpanu 7 75
(Mme C Barande-Barbe, France) **76/1**
9 *1/2* **Amberley (FR)**[24] 3-8-13 0 TonyFarina 3 74
(Mlle S-V Tarrou, France) **113/1**
10 *1 3/4* **Lou Bega** 3-8-13 0 KClijmans 9 69
(Frau M Weber, Germany) **84/1**
0 **Kapitala (FR)**[8] 3-8-9 0 JohanVictoire 13
(J-P Carvalho, Germany) **32/1**
0 **Paris Blue (FR)**[26] 3-8-13 0 (p) Pierre-CharlesBoudot 5
(J-L Pelletan, France) **35/1**
0 **Brillante Etoile (FR)**[63] 3-8-9 0 (b) StephanePasquier 4
(Y Durepaire, Spain) **21/1**
0 **Alexandre D'Or (FR)**[174] 3-8-13 0 BriceRaballand 10
(Mme C Head-Maarek, France) **44/1**
0 **Viking Quest (FR)**[15] 3-8-13 0 AntoineHamelin 8
(C Boutin, France) **53/10**[2]
1m 20.63s (80.63) 15 Ran SP% **117.0**
WIN (incl. 1 euro stake): 2.70. PLACES: 1.80, 4.20, 3.20. DF: 20.50. SF: 24.80.
Owner P F I Cole Ltd **Bred** Castlemartin Stud And Skymarc Farm **Trained** Whatcombe, Oxon

NOTEBOOK
Silverheels(IRE) has taken well to artificial surfaces of late and looks capable of following up this success.

7718 KEMPTON (A.W) (R-H)
Wednesday, November 21
OFFICIAL GOING: Standard
Wind: Strong, across (away from stands), becoming moderate Weather: Rain before racing; becoming dry

7804 WIN BIG WITH BETDAQ MULTIPLES MEDIAN AUCTION MAIDEN STKS 5f (P)
4:00 (4:04) (Class 6) 3-5-Y-O **£1,617** (£481; £240; £120) **Stalls** Low

Form RPR
2323 **1** **Place That Face**[15] 7611 3-8-12 57 RobertHavlin 3 60
(Hughie Morrison) *pushed up to ld: mde all: shkn up and in command 1f out: rdn out* **5/4**[1]
0003 **2** *2 1/4* **Summer Sun**[4] 7770 3-8-12 50 LukeMorris 8 52
(Phil McEntee) *dropped in bhd ldng pair fr wd draw: rdn to chse wnr 2f out: no imp fnl f* **7/2**[2]
00 **3** *3/4* **Kerfuffle (IRE)**[28] 7322 3-8-12 0 SebSanders 4 49
(Simon Dow) *sn last: pushed along 1/2-way: styd on fr jst over 1f out: tk 3rd last strides* **66/1**
5P00 **4** *nk* **Green Mountain (IRE)**[7] 7703 3-8-12 46 (vt) WilliamCarson 5 48
(Philip McBride) *v reluctant to enter stalls: chsd wnr to 2f out: nt qckn and wl hld after* **16/1**
00 **5** *3* **Caboodle**[225] 1274 3-8-12 0 JimCrowley 7 37
(Tom Dascombe) *chsd ldng trio: pushed along after 2f: no prog over 1f out* **4/1**[3]
0050 **6** *1* **Ishi**[147] 3489 3-8-12 51 JamesMillman 2 34
(Rod Millman) *sn pushed along in last pair: nvr on terms* **5/1**
1m 0.42s (-0.08) **Going Correction** -0.05s/f (Stan) 6 Ran SP% **110.7**
Speed ratings (Par 101): **98,94,93,92,87 86**
toteswingers 1&2 £2.00, 2&3 £10.50, 1&3 £9.70 CSF £5.70 TOTE £1.90: £1.30, £2.20; EX 5.00 Trifecta £30.00 Pool: £1923.29 - 48.04 winning units..
Owner R J Cornelius **Bred** R J Cornelius **Trained** East Ilsley, Berks

FOCUS
Due to downpours throughout the day the surface was expected to be riding somewhat quicker than is often the case due to being compacted and that was backed up by Luke Morris after riding in the opener. There was no hanging about in this weak sprint maiden and the winner is rated in line with this year's form backed up by the second and fourth.

7805 BACK OR LAY AT BETDAQ.COM H'CAP 1m 2f (P)
4:30 (4:31) (Class 5) (0-75,75) 3-Y-O+ **£2,264** (£673; £336; £168) **Stalls** Low

Form RPR
0026 **1** **Ancient Greece**[44] 6931 5-9-9 74 (t) LukeMorris 11 83
(George Baker) *trckd ldng pair: rdn to ld over 1f out: hrd pressed fnl f: hld on wl* **20/1**
4002 **2** *1/2* **Fairyinthewind (IRE)**[13] 7644 3-8-12 67 SebSanders 3 75
(Paul D'Arcy) *trckd ldng quartet: prog to press wnr jst over 1f out: drvn and nt find enough fnl f: kpt on* **7/1**[3]

3102 **3** ¾ **Brimstone Hill (IRE)**[27] 7359 3-9-5 **74**........................ WilliamCarson 2 83+
(Anthony Carson) *trckd ldrs: looking for room fr 2f out tl swtchd lft jst over 1f out: r.o to take 3rd ins fnl f: clsng at fin* **6/1**[2]

2030 **4** 2 **Sakhee's Pearl**[14] 7626 6-9-5 **75**........................ NathanSweeney(5) 6 78
(Jo Crowley) *s.i.s: hld up in last quartet: prog on outer fr 3f out: continued hdwy and threatened to cl on ldrs jst over 1f out: one pce after* **6/1**[2]

4333 **5** 2 **Hurricane Hymnbook (USA)**[30] 7301 7-9-3 **68**.......... StevieDonohoe 7 67+
(Willie Musson) *hld up in rr: poorly plcd 2f out: pushed along and prog over 1f out: reminder and r.o fnl f: too much to do* **8/1**

0110 **6** 2 ¾ **Silver Bullitt**[28] 7328 4-9-7 **72**........................ GeorgeBaker 4 65
(Gary Moore) *led to over 1f out: wknd fnl f* **9/1**

0330 **7** ½ **Poetic Lord**[13] 7644 3-9-0 **74**........................(b) WilliamTwiston-Davies(5) 1 66
(Richard Hannon) *trckd ldng pair to jst over 1f out: wknd fnl f* **8/1**

0056 **8** nk **Uncle Fred**[21] 7480 7-9-2 **67**........................ JimCrowley 5 58
(Patrick Chamings) *a abt same pl on inner: shkn up and no prog 2f out: pushed along and one pce fnl f* **10/1**

0414 **9** 1 ¼ **Wildomar**[34] 7195 3-9-6 **75**........................(p) AdamKirby 12 64
(John Ryan) *dwlt: mostly in last pair: shoved along 4f out and no prog: modest hdwy on wd outside over 1f out: nvr in it* **9/2**[1]

0000 **10** 1 ¼ **Rezwaan**[21] 7480 5-9-1 **66**........................(be) ShaneKelly 9 52
(Murty McGrath) *hld up in 9th: shkn up and no prog 2f out: no ch whn rdn fnl f* **33/1**

060- **11** ¾ **Strewth (IRE)**[391] 7120 4-9-1 **66**........................ ChrisCatlin 10 51
(John Best) *dwlt: mostly in last pair: effrt on outer 3f out: no prog and wl btn 2f out* **33/1**

500 **12** hd **Understory (USA)**[61] 6440 5-9-6 **71**........................ GrahamLee 13 56
(Tim McCarthy) *qckly across fr wd draw to trck ldr: wknd qckly wl over 1f out* **25/1**

3000 **13** shd **Casual Mover (IRE)**[14] 7626 4-9-9 **74**........................[1] FergusSweeney 8 58
(John Best) *nvr bttr than midfield: pushed along 1/2-way: wl btn over 1f out: eased* **20/1**

2m 6.14s (-1.86) **Going Correction** -0.05s/f (Stan)
WFA 3 from 4yo+ 4lb **13** Ran SP% **119.8**
Speed ratings (Par 103): **105,104,104,102,100 98,98,97,96,95 95,95,95**
toteswingers 1&2 £35.30, 2&3 £5.60, 1&3 £14.90 CSF £146.29 CT £957.55 TOTE £30.60: £8.20, £2.50, £2.90; EX 174.50 TRIFECTA Not won..
Owner Inkin, Inkin, Byng, Baker & Partners **Bred** Darley **Trained** Manton, Wilts

FOCUS
This looked wide-open but the form looks sound amongst the principals. It was run at a fair pace, but the first pair dominated late on after skipping away from the furlong marker.

7806 BRITISH STALLION STUDS SUPPORTING BRITISH RACING E B F MAIDEN STKS (DIV I) 7f (P)
5:00 (5:01) (Class 5) 2-Y-O **£3,234** (£962; £481; £240) **Stalls** Low

Form RPR

045 **1** **Brownsea Brink**[38] 7078 2-9-3 74........................ GeorgeBaker 7 74
(Richard Hannon) *trckd ldng trio: shkn up to go 3rd wl over 1f out: clsd after: styd on wl to ld last 50yds* **6/1**[3]

55 **2** ½ **Rangi**[82] 5792 2-9-3 0........................ RobertHavlin 3 73
(John Gosden) *led: kicked on over 2f out: drvn over 1f out: hdd and one pce last 50yds* **10/11**[1]

65 **3** ½ **Avatar Star (IRE)**[48] 6818 2-9-3 0........................ AdamKirby 9 71
(Marco Botti) *trckd ldr: rdn 2f out: chal 1f out: could nt qckn and lost 2nd last 100yds* **5/1**[2]

4 1 ¾ **El Buen Turista** 2-9-3 0........................ DavidProbert 5 67+
(Andrew Balding) *dwlt: t.k.h: hld up disputing 5th: shkn up jst over 2f out: prog to go 4th 1f out: styd on fnl f: nrst fin* **5/1**[2]

05 **5** 5 **Bold And Free**[28] 7330 2-9-3 0........................ LiamKeniry 8 54
(David Elsworth) *stdd s: hld up disputing 5th: reminder wl over 1f out: no imp on ldrs* **14/1**

0 **6** 2 ¼ **Ocean Power (IRE)**[23] 7434 2-9-3 0........................ FergusSweeney 2 48
(Richard Phillips) *a in rr: no prog over 2f out: wl hld after* **100/1**

6 **7** ¾ **Mont Signal**[23] 7434 2-9-3 0........................ RobertWinston 4 46
(Daniel Kubler) *chsd ldng pair to wl over 1f out: wknd* **20/1**

00 **8** hd **Rancher (IRE)**[14] 7637 2-9-3 0........................ ChrisCatlin 6 46
(Harry Dunlop) *mostly in last and racd wd: struggling over 2f out* **40/1**

66 **9** hd **Great Crested (IRE)**[34] 7192 2-9-3 0........................ ShaneKelly 1 45
(Murty McGrath) *in tch disputing 5th to over 2f out: sn btn* **100/1**

1m 26.14s (0.14) **Going Correction** -0.05s/f (Stan) **9** Ran SP% **115.9**
Speed ratings (Par 96): **97,96,95,93,88 85,84,84,84**
toteswingers 1&2 £2.20, 2&3 £1.90, 1&3 £4.10 CSF £11.76 TOTE £9.40: £2.50, £1.02, £1.40; EX 13.00 Trifecta £55.40 Pool: £1309.03 - 17.70 winning units..
Owner The Heffer Syndicate **Bred** Carmel Stud **Trained** East Everleigh, Wilts

FOCUS
Jockeyship played a big part in this juvenile maiden. Straightforward enough form and the winner has the scope to go forward from this.

NOTEBOOK
Brownsea Brink got up late to shed his maiden tag at the fourth attempt. He flopped dropped to 6f at Goodwood last time and was back up a furlong for this AW debut. He again took time to settle, but did get a decent tow into the race from 2f out and pounced late in the day. This looks his optimum trip and, now he's shown a liking for Polytrack, could build on this if kept on the go. (op 7-1)
Rangi was the form pick after his two previous turf efforts and was expected to collect on this AW debut. He looked well after his break, but was a reluctant leader after jumping to the front and ultimately teed this up for the winner. It was a game effort and he's not one to abandon. (op 8-11)
Avatar Star(IRE) shadowed the leader and while he was always held inside the final furlong, this was his best effort yet switched to Polytrack. He's sure to get further as he matures and when qualifies for a mark. (op 6-1)
El Buen Turista ◆, whose dam was a Listed-placed 2yo winner over this trip, attracted money beforehand He proved too green to do himself full justice, refusing to settle early, but finished with promise and is the one to take from the race. (op 11-2)
Bold And Free, on his AW debut, proved very easy to back and was never in the hunt. He has scope and it wouldn't at all surprise to see improvement when he switches to a handicap, for which he now becomes eligible.

7807 BRITISH STALLION STUDS SUPPORTING BRITISH RACING E B F MAIDEN STKS (DIV II) 7f (P)
5:30 (5:31) (Class 5) 2-Y-O **£3,234** (£962; £481; £240) **Stalls** Low

Form RPR

1 **Plunder** 2-9-3 0........................ PhillipMakin 3 78+
(Kevin Ryan) *mde all: kicked on over 2f out: rdn and edgd lft fnl f: kpt on wl* **4/1**[3]

0 **2** 1 **Great Demeanor (USA)**[19] 7517 2-9-3 0........................ GrahamLee 4 75
(David Elsworth) *t.k.h: trckd wnr: shkn up 2f out: styd on fnl f but a hld* **33/1**

32 **3** 1 ½ **Watcheroftheskies**[20] 7507 2-9-3 0........................ SebSanders 6 72
(J W Hills) *chsd ldng trio: wnt 3rd 2f out: rdn to dispute 2nd jst over 1f out: could nt qckn fnl f* **5/2**[1]

4 2 ¼ **Groove On (IRE)** 2-9-3 0........................(t) MartinHarley 1 66
(Marco Botti) *wl in tch: effrt whn short of room: rn green and lost grnd 2f out: wl hld in 4th fr over 1f out but kpt on* **12/1**

5 3 ¼ **Plenum (GER)** 2-9-3 0........................ TedDurcan 7 57+
(David Lanigan) *slowly away: hld up in last: effrt on inner 2f out: no prog over 1f out: sn wknd: bttr for r* **3/1**[2]

6 shd **Al Sahraa** 2-8-12 0........................ LukeMorris 5 52
(John Butler) *chsd ldng pair to 2f out: rdn and steadily wknd* **25/1**

4 **7** nk **Sam Spade (IRE)**[13] 7641 2-9-3 0........................ GeorgeBaker 9 56
(Richard Hannon) *slowly away: racd on outer and hld up: nudged along over 2f out: steadily lost grnd* **3/1**[2]

60 **8** 2 ¼ **Classy Trick (USA)**[5] 7749 2-9-3 0........................ PaulHanagan 2 50
(Richard Fahey) *a towards rr: shkn up over 2f out: sn btn* **33/1**

1m 27.04s (1.04) **Going Correction** -0.05s/f (Stan) **8** Ran SP% **116.0**
Speed ratings (Par 96): **92,90,89,86,82 82,82,79**
toteswingers 1&2 £15.10, 2&3 £9.00, 1&3 £1.90 CSF £121.09 TOTE £4.00: £1.70, £8.70, £1.10; EX 116.40 Trifecta £903.20 Part won. Pool: £1204.38 - 0.40 winning units..
Owner Graham Hillen & Fitzpatrick **Bred** Millsec Limited **Trained** Hambleton, N Yorks

FOCUS
The second division of the 2yo maiden and yet again racing handily was a must, with those held up having little chance. It's hard form to pin down but this looked a pretty good effort from the winner.

NOTEBOOK
Plunder was supported earlier in the day, but advertised his inexperience in the preliminaries and drifted out. He got a very easy lead through the contest and, while he found plenty when asked for everything, was really gifted the race. The son of Zamindar still took some pulling up, though, and it will be interesting to see what mark he gets. (op 10-3 tchd 3-1)
Great Demeanor(USA) has a US pedigree and showed a lot more on this switch to Polytrack. He was also suited by racing near the lead, however, and may be a little flattered. (op 25-1)
Watcheroftheskies held every chance was done with half a furlong out and again found a few too good. He can find a weak maiden and now qualifies for nurseries, but the handicapper already knows a fair bit about him. (op 9-4)
Groove On(IRE), tongue tied for his debut, travelled kindly and would have gone closer off a stronger pace. This cheap purchase clearly has a future. (op 16-1)
Plenum(GER), who cost 330,000gns and is out of a Group 3 winner, was fancied to go well on this racecourse debut but his chance was apparent a long way out as he sat last off the ordinary pace. He ought to come on plenty for the run and leave this form behind. (op 5-2)
Sam Spade(IRE) attracted support dropping down a furlong, but he also found himself badly placed in the race and lacked a turn of foot. (op 6-1)

7808 BETDAQ CASINO GAMES NURSERY 7f (P)
6:00 (6:00) (Class 6) (0-65,64) 2-Y-O **£1,617** (£481; £240; £120) **Stalls** Low

Form RPR

0000 **1** **Royal Caper**[14] 7637 2-8-10 **53**........................ JohnFahy 2 59
(John Ryan) *t.k.h: trckd ldng pair: rousted along to ld 2f out and wnt for home: drvn and styd on fnl f* **33/1**

2420 **2** 1 **Girl Of Cadiz**[25] 7414 2-9-2 **64**........................ WilliamTwiston-Davies(5) 5 67
(Richard Hannon) *trckd ldrs: prog wl over 1f out: drvn to chse wnr ins fnl f: styd on but unable to chal* **7/1**

0362 **3** 1 ¼ **Holding Fast (IRE)**[7] 7714 2-8-7 **50**........................ JoeFanning 1 50
(Tobias B P Coles) *plld hrd early: hld up bhd ldrs: prog over 2f out: chsd wnr over 1f out to ins fnl f: one pce* **6/1**[3]

000 **4** 2 ¼ **Derwentwater (IRE)**[62] 6411 2-9-5 **62**........................ NickyMackay 13 56+
(John Gosden) *hld up in last pair: prog jst over 2f out: rchd 4th fnl f but no hdwy after* **6/4**[1]

0000 **5** hd **Darkest Night (IRE)**[48] 6822 2-8-11 **54**........................ FergusSweeney 6 48
(Jamie Osborne) *t.k.h: racd in 2nd pl to over 1f out: fdd fnl f* **10/1**

000 **6** ¾ **Elvin**[98] 5235 2-8-11 **54**........................ JimCrowley 14 47+
(Amanda Perrett) *t.k.h: hld up in rr: effrt but hanging rt over 2f out and no prog: kpt on fnl f* **5/1**[2]

000 **7** nk **Black Truffle (FR)**[93] 5424 2-8-7 **50**........................ DavidProbert 3 41
(Mark Usher) *hld up in rr: prog on inner 2f out: no hdwy fnl f* **20/1**

066 **8** 1 **She's Some Girl (IRE)**[33] 7219 2-8-9 **52**........................ PaulHanagan 10 40+
(Richard Fahey) *dwlt: hld up in last: effrt over 2f out: hung rt over 1f out: sme late prog* **25/1**

00 **9** nk **Our Three Graces (IRE)**[33] 7223 2-9-4 **61**........................ GeorgeBaker 11 49
(Gary Moore) *trckd ldrs on outer: shkn up and could nt qckn over 2f out: pushed along and steadily lost pl after* **16/1**

5463 **10** 1 **Sojoum**[23] 7432 2-8-9 **52**........................ MartinHarley 7 37
(Mick Channon) *plld hrd early: hld up towards rr: effrt 2f out: no prog over 1f out: fdd* **14/1**

4062 **11** 1 ½ **Katy Spirit (IRE)**[13] 7649 2-9-0 **57**........................ TedDurcan 8 38
(Michael Blanshard) *wl in tch on outer: rdn over 2f out: wknd over 1f out* **33/1**

5050 **12** 7 **Hats Off**[48] 6822 2-8-9 **52**........................ RobertWinston 9 15
(John Best) *led to 2f out: wknd rapidly* **25/1**

1m 26.77s (0.77) **Going Correction** -0.05s/f (Stan) **12** Ran SP% **123.4**
Speed ratings (Par 94): **93,91,90,87,87 86,86,85,84,83 82,74**
toteswingers 1&2 £66.60, 2&3 £4.50, 1&3 £55.00 CSF £246.64 CT £1150.17 TOTE £72.80: £17.90, £1.40, £1.90; EX 793.00 TRIFECTA Not won..
Owner Kilco (International) Ltd **Bred** P And Mrs A G Venner **Trained** Newmarket, Suffolk

FOCUS
This moderate nursery was run at a muddling pace and once more the pace bias towards those racing handy played out. The surprise winner bounced back to his early-season form.

NOTEBOOK
Royal Caper saw it out gamely from the furlong marker and opened his account at the eighth attempt. He had flopped on his last four outings, but his fifth to a useful sort at Newmarket in August showed he had an engine. John Fahy gave him a decent ride and he showed a nice attitude once in front. He had the run of the race, but may have a little more to offer on this surface. Official explanation: trainer said, regarding the apparent improvement of form, that the gelding was better suited by the all-weather surface rather than the soft going at Nottingham last time
Girl Of Cadiz was another racing prominently and she bounced back to near her best, rating a sound enough benchmark. (op 6-1 tchd 11-2)
Holding Fast(IRE), related to Polytrack winners, would have finished closer had he not pulled so hard through the early parts and he too can do better on the AW. He's now due a 4lb rise, though. (op 5-1)

Derwentwater(IRE), making his nursery and AW debut and gambled on, is a deal better than the bare form. He had an impossible task racing so far back and made a promising mid-race move. (op 2-1)

7809 BETDAQ MOBILE APPS HYDE STKS (LISTED RACE) 1m (P)
6:30 (6:31) (Class 1) 3-Y-0+

£18,714 (£7,095; £3,550; £1,768; £887; £445) **Stalls** Low

Form				RPR
4-10	**1**		**Pearl Mix (IRE)**[39] 7048 3-9-0 103 .... JimCrowley 8	113
			(Ralph Beckett) *trckd ldr after 2f: led over 2f out: stretched on sn after: r.o strly fnl f* **7/2**[2]
0411	**2**	*2*	**Belgian Bill**[7] 7709 4-9-2 104 .... (t) TedDurcan 7	108
			(George Baker) *wl plcd bhd ldrs: rdn to chse wnr over 1f out: readily lft bhd fnl f* **9/2**[3]
3334	**3**	*¾*	**Sirius Prospect (USA)**[11] 7690 4-9-2 108 .... GrahamLee 2	107
			(Dean Ivory) *hld up in midfield: prog on inner 2f out: drvn to take 3rd 1f out: styd on same pce* **8/1**
4120	**4**	*1*	**Producer**[39] 7054 3-9-4 110 .... GeorgeBaker 9	108
			(Richard Hannon) *prom on outer: cl up jst over 2f out: rdn and could nt qckn over 1f out: outpcd* **8/1**
15-1	**5**	*½*	**Validus**[14] 7631 3-9-0 101 .... KirstyMilczarek 3	103
			(Luca Cumani) *hld up towards rr: prog over 2f out: rdn over 1f out: styd on same pce* **3/1**[1]
0000	**6**	*1*	**Valencha**[11] 7690 5-8-11 93 .... RobertHavlin 11	96
			(Hughie Morrison) *dropped in fr wd draw and hld up wl in rr: stdy prog over 2f out: chsd ldrs over 1f out: shkn up and could nt qckn* **20/1**
3405	**7**	*½*	**Instance**[20] 7509 4-8-11 94 .... (p) PaulHanagan 14	95
			(Jeremy Noseda) *dropped in fr wd draw and hld up in last pair: prog on inner over 2f out: chsd ldrs over 1f out: no hdwy after* **16/1**
0665	**8**	*2*	**Libys Dream (IRE)**[12] 7680 4-8-13 95 .... LiamKeniry 6	92
			(Tom Dascombe) *hld up in midfield: cl enough and pushed along over 2f out: wknd over 1f out* **20/1**
0031	**9**	*nk*	**St Moritz (IRE)**[14] 7638 6-9-2 97 .... AdrianNicholls 5	94
			(David Nicholls) *t.k.h and hld up in last: shkn up over 2f out: modest late prog* **33/1**
2556	**10**	*1 ¼*	**Wahylah (IRE)**[13] 7645 3-8-9 80 .... FrederikTylicki 1	87
			(Clive Brittain) *led 1f: styd prom tl wknd qckly over 1f out* **50/1**
1063	**11**	*½*	**Dance Company**[20] 7502 3-8-9 87 .... LukeMorris 4	85
			(William Knight) *led after 1f to over 2f out: wknd qckly over 1f out* **33/1**
4141	**12**	*¾*	**Captain Ramius (IRE)**[25] 7401 6-9-2 109 .... PhillipMakin 13	89
			(Kevin Ryan) *racd wd towards rr: rdn and no prog over 2f out: sn btn* **16/1**
0054	**13**	*4*	**Diverting**[18] 7558 4-8-11 85 .... JoeFanning 10	75
			(William Jarvis) *t.k.h: racd wdst of all and prom: lost pl and pushed along fr over 2f out* **66/1**

1m 37.76s (-2.04) **Going Correction** -0.05s/f (Stan)
WFA 3 from 4yo+ 2lb **13** Ran SP% **118.3**
Speed ratings (Par 111): **108,106,105,104,103 102,102,100,99,98 98,97,93**
toteswingers 1&2 £4.80, 2&3 £4.70, 1&3 £7.20 CSF £17.83 TOTE £4.10: £1.50, £2.10, £2.30; EX 26.20 Trifecta £122.50 Pool: £1500.06 - 9.18 winning units..
Owner Pearl Bloodstock Ltd **Bred** Jean-Etienne Dubois **Trained** Kimpton, Hants

FOCUS
A decent Listed prize and reasonable, if slightly muddling, form for the grade, as it turned into a dash nearing 2f out after an uneven early pace.

NOTEBOOK
Pearl Mix(IRE) ◆ showed his true colours again, under a fine tactical ride, and made it three wins out of four at this venue. Connections put his previous Newmarket disappointment down to him bouncing and he was much better judged on his powerful comeback success in a decent C&D handicap in September off 98. His jockey was alive to the pace bias and that suited him as he does like to get on with it. He was always going to be very hard to reel in as the race panned out, but he's a lightly raced and improving 3yo no doubt. Indeed he ought to get further as he matures and remains one to follow. Venturing to Dubai could be on his agenda. (op 9-2)
Belgian Bill had plenty go his way when making it two from two over 7f here in a tactical affair a week earlier, ridden then by the jockey of the winner here. He too proved suited by racing prominently, posting an improved effort in defeat, but the winner got first run and he was giving that progressive rival 2lb. He's now due for a return trip to Dubai. (op 5-1)
Sirius Prospect(USA) has become fiendishly hard to win with, and this was an interesting effort. It was his first outing over a mile since flopping on his handicap debut here in 2011 (won maiden over 7f here the time before) and he went more enthusiastically. He showed no signs of quirks and would strongly appeal if connections can find him something over 7f during the winter. (op 6-1)
Producer lined up with the highest BHA rating, but was conceding weight all round. His jockey was also alive to the pace bias and had him close up, which saw him hold every chance on this AW debut. No doubt his optimum distance is 7f, however. (op 10-1)
Validus ◆ won readily off 95 over C&D when making it two from two here on his belated return a fortnight earlier. Well backed for this sterner test, he was always likely to find it tough if again coming from off the pace, which he attempted to do, and the best of him is very likely still to be seen.

7810 RACING PLUS - THE BEST WEEKEND ACTION H'CAP 1m 4f (P)
7:00 (7:01) (Class 4) (0-80,80) 3-Y-0+ **£4,075** (£1,212; £606; £303) **Stalls** Centre

Form				RPR
5003	**1**		**Miss Aix**[47] 6847 4-9-7 78 .... LukeMorris 12	86
			(Michael Bell) *hld up in 8th: prog over 2f out: chsd ldng pair over 1f out: sustained effrt fnl f to ld nr fin* **33/1**
3160	**2**	*½*	**Livia's Dream (IRE)**[20] 7510 3-9-2 79 .... GrahamLee 2	86
			(Ed Walker) *trckd ldr: led 3f out: hrd pressed over 1f out: fought on wl but hdd nr fin* **7/1**[3]
2016	**3**	*1*	**Beat Route**[30] 7301 5-9-2 73 .... J-PGuillambert 8	78
			(Michael Attwater) *hld up bhd ldrs: gng wl: prog to chse ldr over 2f out: str chal over 1f out: could nt qckn ins fnl f and sn lost 2nd* **20/1**
5532	**4**	*1 ¼*	**Fourth Generation (IRE)**[12] 7672 5-9-7 78 .... RobertWinston 10	81
			(Alan Swinbank) *hld up in 9th: looking for room over 2f out: urged along and prog wl over 1f out: styd on to take 4th last stride* **7/1**[3]
412	**5**	*nse*	**Moderator**[43] 6971 3-9-2 79 .... GeorgeBaker 3	82
			(Gary Moore) *trckd ldng pair: lost pl sltly over 2f out: renewed effrt wl over 1f out: one pce fnl f* **11/4**[1]
0455	**6**	*1 ¾*	**Mica Mika (IRE)**[37] 7098 4-9-7 78 .... PaulHanagan 13	79
			(Richard Fahey) *hld up in rr: rdn and effrt over 2f out: kpt on same pce fnl 2f: no real threat* **16/1**
0535	**7**	*½*	**Icebuster**[15] 7617 4-9-8 79 .... JamesMillman 5	79
			(Rod Millman) *stdd s: hld up in last trio: gng wl but same pl over 2f out: shuffled along and kpt on fnl 2f: nvr involved* **4/1**[2]
1214	**8**	*½*	**Stand Guard**[209] 1632 8-9-6 77 .... LiamKeniry 4	76
			(John Butler) *t.k.h: trckd ldng trio: wl there u.p 2f out: steadily fdd* **33/1**
1	**9**	*2 ¼*	**No Such Number**[72] 6098 4-9-3 74 .... JimCrowley 9	69
			(Julia Feilden) *hld up in midfield: looking for room over 2f out: sme prog wl over 1f out: wknd fnl f* **8/1**
3405	**10**	*¾*	**Ellemujie**[14] 7626 7-9-6 80 .... (p) PatrickHills(3) 6	74
			(Dean Ivory) *trckd ldng quartet: effrt on inner over 2f out: no prog over 1f out: wknd* **12/1**
3300	**11**	*3*	**Where's Susie**[56] 6584 7-9-4 75 .... ChrisCatlin 11	64
			(Michael Madgwick) *hld up in last: brought wd in st: sn no prog and btn* **50/1**
0006	**12**	*3 ¾*	**Always The Lady**[19] 7519 4-9-3 74 .... (p) AdamKirby 1	57
			(Clive Cox) *led to 3f out: sn wknd* **16/1**
3-	**13**	*11*	**Six Silver Lane**[69] 6185 4-9-8 79 .... JoeFanning 14	45
			(Derek Shaw) *stdd s: hld up in last trio: no prog 3f out: sn wknd: t.o* **33/1**

2m 31.4s (-3.10) **Going Correction** -0.05s/f (Stan)
WFA 3 from 4yo+ 6lb **13** Ran SP% **117.8**
Speed ratings (Par 105): **108,107,107,106,106 104,104,104,102,102 100,97,90**
toteswingers 1&2 £28.00, 2&3 £35.30, 1&3 £46.70 CSF £238.21 CT £4727.60 TOTE £30.90: £10.40, £3.20, £4.50; EX 301.70 TRIFECTA Not won..
Owner J L C Pearce **Bred** J L C Pearce **Trained** Newmarket, Suffolk
■ Stewards' Enquiry : George Baker two-day ban: failed to ride out for fourth place (5-6 Dec)

FOCUS
This competitive handicap was run at a sound early pace, but it slackened somewhat on the far side. The form still appears straightforward, despite the surprise winner.

7811 BOXINGDAYRACES.CO.UK H'CAP 1m 4f (P)
7:30 (7:32) (Class 6) (0-65,65) 3-Y-0 **£1,617** (£481; £240; £120) **Stalls** Centre

Form				RPR
5-11	**1**		**Mutual Regard (IRE)**[5] 7744 3-9-7 65 .... LukeMorris 3	83+
			(Sir Mark Prescott Bt) *trckd ldng trio: shkn up over 2f out: prog to chal over 1f out: led ins fnl f: drvn but wl on top nr fin* **8/11**[1]
-425	**2**	*1 ¼*	**Miss Blakeney**[13] 7644 3-9-7 65 .... (v[1]) GeorgeBaker 8	78
			(Marcus Tregoning) *trckd ldng trio: prog to ld wl over 1f out: edgd lft sn after: hdd ins fnl f: styd on but readily hld* **6/1**[3]
4004	**3**	*2 ¾*	**Cool Sky**[30] 7301 3-9-7 65 .... JimCrowley 10	74
			(William Knight) *hld up in 9th: shkn up over 2f out: gd prog over 1f out: r.o to take 3rd ins fnl f: no ch but nrst fin* **9/2**[2]
3451	**4**	*4 ½*	**Lady Bellatrix**[29] 7303 3-8-10 59 .... DarylByrne(5) 11	61
			(Mark H Tompkins) *led at gd pce: hdd wl over 1f out: wknd fnl f* **12/1**
0120	**5**	*2 ¾*	**Navajo Charm**[30] 7301 3-9-5 63 .... RobertWinston 12	60
			(Alan Jarvis) *t.k.h: trckd ldr after 3f to over 2f out: steadily wknd* **14/1**
6500	**6**	*nk*	**Mariet**[77] 5931 3-9-2 60 .... GrahamLee 4	57
			(Suzy Smith) *hld up in last trio: shuffled along fr over 2f out: styd on quite takingly fnl f* **50/1**
5000	**7**	*¾*	**I'm Harry**[5] 7744 3-8-11 62 .... (t) AaronJones(7) 6	58
			(George Baker) *awkward s: tk sme time to organise and dropped to last briefly: prog fr 8f out to chse ldrs over 4f out: outpcd fnl 2f* **25/1**
560	**8**	*½*	**Minty Fox**[35] 7174 3-9-6 64 .... TedDurcan 7	59
			(Rae Guest) *a abt same pl: outpcd fr over 2f out: no ch after* **25/1**
0063	**9**	*1 ½*	**Hoonose**[21] 7496 3-8-7 51 oh5 .... JoeFanning 5	44
			(Pat Eddery) *in tch in midfield: drvn over 3f out: struggling over 2f out* **20/1**
0050	**10**	*6*	**Shot In The Dark (IRE)**[49] 6801 3-9-4 62 .... (v[1]) RobertHavlin 2	45
			(Jonathan Geake) *stdd s: hld up in last pair: drvn and no prog over 2f out* **33/1**
0050	**11**	*1*	**Ececheira**[14] 7632 3-8-7 51 oh6 .... JimmyQuinn 9	32
			(Dean Ivory) *in tch in midfield: drvn over 3f out: wknd over 2f out* **66/1**
0050	**12**	*6*	**Doc Hill**[15] 7619 3-8-7 51 oh6 .... NickyMackay 1	23
			(Michael Blanshard) *t.k.h: chsd ldr 3f: styd prom to over 2f out: wknd rapidly and eased* **100/1**
0600	**13**	*4*	**The Ploughman**[14] 7632 3-8-7 51 oh6 .... KieranO'Neill 13	16
			(John Bridger) *hld up in last pair: nvr any prog: wl bhd fnl 2f* **100/1**

2m 32.95s (-1.55) **Going Correction** -0.05s/f (Stan) **13** Ran SP% **125.6**
Speed ratings (Par 98): **103,102,100,97,95 95,94,94,93,89 88,84,82**
toteswingers 1&2 £1.80, 2&3 £4.10, 1&3 £2.30 CSF £5.40 CT £14.97 TOTE £2.00: £1.40, £1.60, £1.40; EX 6.60 Trifecta £18.50 Pool: £1329.49 - 53.77 winning units..
Owner Moyglare Stud Farm **Bred** Moyglare Stud Farm Ltd **Trained** Newmarket, Suffolk

FOCUS
A moderate handicap. It was another race in which the pace slowed up on the far side and few landed a serious blow, but the form is solid, rated around the first three.
T/Plt: £15.10 to a £1 stake. Pool of £61225.53 -2957.99 winning tickets. T/Qpdt: £5.80 to a £1 stake. Pool: £7614.81, 967.95 winning tickets JN

7767 LINGFIELD (L-H)
Wednesday, November 21

OFFICIAL GOING: Standard
Wind: medium, half behind, strong from race 5 Weather: rain, heavy from race 5

7812 BETFRED MOBILE LOTTO CLAIMING STKS 7f (P)
12:00 (12:00) (Class 6) 2-Y-0 **£1,704** (£503; £251) **Stalls** Low

Form				RPR
0262	**1**		**King Of Kudos (IRE)**[26] 7363 2-8-12 68 .... KieranO'Neill 5	71
			(Richard Hannon) *chsd ldrs: rdn ent fnl 2f: led ins fnl f: sn in command: r.o wl* **5/4**[1]
56	**2**	*2 ¼*	**Elusive Thought (IRE)**[70] 6134 2-8-6 0 .... LukeMorris 6	59+
			(J S Moore) *in tch in rr: rdn 4f out: outpcd and wd bnd 2f out: drvn and rallied 1f out: chsd wnr wl ins fnl f: kpt on* **16/1**
1533	**3**	*1 ¼*	**Majestic Jess (IRE)**[6] 7723 2-8-3 68 .... JoeyHaynes(7) 4	59
			(Luke Dace) *t.k.h: pressed ldr: rdn and ev ch 2f out: drvn to ld over 1f out: hdd and one pce ins fnl f* **9/4**[2]
5	**4**	*1 ½*	**Sofi's Spirit (IRE)**[13] 7641 2-7-12 0 ....[1] SimonPearce(3) 2	46
			(J S Moore) *led: rdn ent fnl 2f: hdd over 1f out: wknd ins fnl f* **5/1**[3]
34	**5**	*4 ½*	**Dude Alert (IRE)**[27] 7349 2-8-10 0 .... SilvestreDeSousa 1	43
			(Peter Chapple-Hyam) *chsd ldrs: rdn over 3f out: drvn and outpcd 2f out: sn wknd* **7/1**

1m 25.0s (0.20) **Going Correction** -0.025s/f (Stan) **5** Ran SP% **110.3**
Speed ratings (Par 94): **97,94,93,91,86**
Tote Swinger 1&4 £9.00 CSF £20.02 TOTE £1.80: £1.70, £4.20; EX 16.60.
Owner R Hannon **Bred** Citadel Stud **Trained** East Everleigh, Wilts

FOCUS
Ordinary form. The race set up nicely for the winner.

NOTEBOOK
King Of Kudos(IRE) went for home plenty soon enough, helping to set things up for the top-weight, who'd sat in behind. He did look the one to beat beforehand, but things couldn't have been teed up any nicer for him. (op 11-8 tchd 6-4)

Elusive Thought(IRE), debuting for a new yard, got outpaced but finished best of all. He should have more to offer on this surface over a mile. (op 20-1)
Majestic Jess(IRE) held sound claims, but he was taken on in front by Sofi's Spirit and the pair ended up setting the race up for those ridden more patiently. (tchd 2-1)
Sofi's Spirit(IRE) went too hard and set it up for the others. (op 9-2 tchd 4-1)
Dude Alert(IRE) didn't improve for the switch to Polytrack or for the drop in trip. (op 8-1)

7813 BRITISH STALLION STUDS SUPPORTING BRITISH RACING E B F MAIDEN STKS 6f (P)

12:30 (12:31) (Class 5) 2-Y-O **£3,169** (£943; £471; £235) **Stalls** Low

Form				RPR
3	**1**		**Absolutely So (IRE)**[26] 7371 2-9-3 0 ... DavidProbert 10 (Andrew Balding) *t.k.h: chsd ldrs: wnt 3rd 2f out: rdn and qcknd to ld jst ins fnl f: in command and idling fnl 100yds: comf* **4/5**[1]	78+
230	**2**	1 ¼	**Whipper Snapper (IRE)**[113] 4688 2-9-3 73 ... JimCrowley 11 (William Knight) *hld up in tch in midfield on outer: rdn and hdwy over 1f out: chsd wnr wl ins fnl f: kpt on* **5/1**[2]	69
	3	*hd*	**Kohlaan (IRE)** 2-9-3 0 ... AndreaAtzeni 7 (Roger Varian) *s.i.s: bhd: gd hdwy on inner over 1f out: chsd ldrs ins fnl f: styd on* **8/1**	71+
0036	**4**	1 ½	**Overrider**[37] 7110 2-9-3 75 ... RobertWinston 4 (Charles Hills) *in tch towards rr: rdn and hdwy but edging lft over 1f out: kpt on ins fnl f but no threat to wnr* **6/1**[3]	67+
0	**5**	1 ¾	**Birdie King**[20] 7498 2-9-3 0 ... GeorgeBaker 12 (John Best) *led and sn crossed to inner: rdn and hung rt 2f out: rn green u.p over 1f out: hdd ins fnl f: lost 2nd and wknd wl ins fnl f* **50/1**	59
	6	*nk*	**Timeless Appeal (IRE)** 2-8-12 0 ... SilvestreDeSousa 9 (Peter Chapple-Hyam) *in tch: effrt u.p over 1f out: styd on same pce ins fnl f* **25/1**	53
60	**7**	*nk*	**Maisie's Moon (USA)**[26] 7372 2-8-12 0 ... RobertHavlin 2 (Hughie Morrison) *chsd ldrs: rdn and unable qck 2f out: wknd jst ins fnl f* **66/1**	52
	8	¾	**Indigo Moon** 2-8-12 0 ... ShaneKelly 6 (Denis Coakley) *wnt lft s: in tch in midfield: rdn and styd on same pce fr over 1f out: burst blood vessel* **20/1**	50
05	**9**	½	**Direct Trade**[30] 7296 2-8-12 0 ... LiamKeniry 3 (Mark Usher) *t.k.h: hld up in tch: rdn and struggling ent fnl 2f: wknd 1f out* **100/1**	48
00	**10**	1 ¾	**Underwhelm**[15] 7609 2-8-12 0 ... (t) SebSanders 8 (Alan McCabe) *w ldr: rdn over 2f out: no ex over 1f out: fdd ins fnl f* **100/1**	43
0	**11**	10	**Guru Baby**[38] 7078 2-8-12 0 ... RichardThomas 1 (John E Long) *in tch in midfield early: dropped towards rr and struggling 1/2-way: bhd fnl f* **200/1**	13
	12	2 ¾	**Instinctual** 2-9-3 0 ... KirstyMilczarek 5 (Brendan Powell) *bdly bmpd and pushed lft s: slowly away: a bhd* **80/1**	10

1m 12.3s (0.40) **Going Correction** -0.025s/f (Stan) **12** Ran SP% **113.4**
Speed ratings (Par 96): **96,94,94,92,89 89,88,87,87,84 71,67**
Tote Swingers 1&2 £2.40, 2&3 £3.90, 1&3 £2.70 CSF £4.29 TOTE £1.70: £1.10, £1.30, £1.80; EX 5.70 Trifecta £14.30 Pool: £623.37 - 32.63 winning tickets..
Owner Jackie & George Smith **Bred** L Mulryan **Trained** Kingsclere, Hants

FOCUS
No more than a fair maiden, but the winner and third are better than the facts. The steady pace governs the merit of the form.

NOTEBOOK
Absolutely So(IRE) was keen early, but he had plenty left in the tank turning in, and he quickened up in taking style, winning with his ears pricked. He had more in hand over his rivals than the winning margin suggests, looks a really nice prospect for next year, as he has plenty of size and scope, and his rider was very complimentary. He's one to put in the notebook. (tchd 4-6)
Whipper Snapper(IRE), who'd been gelded since he last ran in July, was trapped widest of all, and ran well against a taking winner. He has the ability to take an AW maiden. (tchd 11-2)
Kohlaan(IRE), a 105,000gns half-brother to Moyglare Stud Stakes winner Termagant, was slowly away and raced in rear, before heading to the inside rail (not the place to be) entering the straight. He shaped with plenty of promise in the circumstances and should be winning soon. (op 9-1 tchd 10-1)
Overrider, who could be given a chance in this company on his best form, didn't help his cause by hanging left up the straight. Official explanation: jockey said that the gelding hung left in the straight (op 11-2)
Birdie King stepped up on her debut effort, showing good early speed to get to the front from the outside stall.
Timeless Appeal(IRE), who's closely related to 5.5f winner Al Janadeirya and is a half-sister to 5f 2yo winner Tioman Legend, showed ability on her debut and ought to build on this.
Indigo Moon Official explanation: vet said the filly bled from the nose
Instinctual Official explanation: jockey said that the gelding ran green

7814 BETFRED STILL TREBLE ODDS ON LUCKY 15'S NURSERY 1m (P)

1:00 (1:00) (Class 5) (0-75,74) 2-Y-O **£2,385** (£704; £352) **Stalls** High

Form				RPR
2434	**1**		**Blue Nova**[39] 7059 2-9-5 72 ... PaulHanagan 5 (Jeremy Noseda) *t.k.h: hld up in tch in midfield: rdn to chse ldrs and hung rt bnd 2f out: rallied u.p over 1f out: led wl ins fnl f: drvn out* **7/1**	75
336	**2**	*nk*	**Lyric Piece**[85] 5715 2-9-5 72 ... LukeMorris 4 (Sir Mark Prescott Bt) *chsd ldrs: rdn 4f out: drvn and sltly outpcd 2f out: rallied u.p 1f out: pressing wnr cl home: styd on* **5/1**[2]	74
503	**3**	¾	**Emulating (IRE)**[56] 6571 2-8-11 69 ... WilliamTwiston-Davies[(5)] 8 (Richard Hannon) *t.k.h: hld up wl in tch in last trio: hdwy into midfield 3f out: v wd and lost pl bnd 2f out: rallied 1f out: styd on strly ins fnl f* **10/3**[1]	70
0655	**4**	*nse*	**Club House (IRE)**[28] 7325 2-8-13 66 ... GrahamLee 6 (Robert Mills) *t.k.h: hld up wl in tch in last trio: hdwy wl over 1f out: rdn and effrt 1f out: styd on wl towards fin* **5/1**[2]	66
0632	**5**	*shd*	**Ivanhoe**[44] 6928 2-9-3 70 ... FergusSweeney 3 (Michael Blanshard) *t.k.h: led tl over 6f out: pressed ldr after: rdn and ev ch 2f out: led over 1f out: hdd and no ex wl ins fnl f* **8/1**	70
0022	**6**	½	**Sunblazer (IRE)**[47] 6841 2-9-7 74 ... MartinDwyer 1 (William Muir) *pushed along early: led over 6f out: drvn and hdd over 1f out: stl ev ch tl no ex and btn wl ins fnl f* **13/2**[3]	73
0600	**7**	½	**Epsom Flyer**[85] 5702 2-7-12 51 ... JimmyQuinn 7 (Pat Phelan) *t.k.h: hld up in tch towards rr: rdn and effrt over 1f out: kpt on ins fnl f but nvr gng pce to rch ldrs* **33/1**	49
0201	**8**	½	**Run It Twice (IRE)**[25] 7414 2-9-0 67 ... KirstyMilczarek 9 (David Evans) *stdd and dropped in bhd after s: t.k.h: hld up in tch in rr: rdn and effrt jst over 1f out: kpt on but wl hld whn swtchd rt wl ins fnl f* **8/1**	64
044	**9**	2	**My Gigi**[18] 7553 2-9-1 68 ... ShaneKelly 2 (Gary Moore) *chsd ldrs: drvn and unable qck ent fnl f: wknd fnl 150yds* **14/1**	60

1m 39.17s (0.97) **Going Correction** -0.025s/f (Stan) **9** Ran SP% **114.1**
Speed ratings (Par 96): **94,93,92,92,92 92,91,91,89**
Tote Swingers 1&2 £9.60, 2&3 £2.60, 1&3 £8.00 CSF £41.32 CT £138.76 TOTE £8.80: £2.50, £2.00, £1.40; EX 28.20 Trifecta £49.20 Pool: £365.31 - 5.56 winning tickets..
Owner Newsells Park Stud **Bred** Newsells Park Stud **Trained** Newmarket, Suffolk

FOCUS
A competitive if messy nursery, and easy enough form to assess around the first four.

NOTEBOOK
Blue Nova just about hung on at the line. Although a shade keen early, the return to a mile proved to be in her favour and she stuck her neck out close home. (op 13-2 tchd 8-1)
Lyric Piece, up 2f in distance for her handicap debut, still looks green. She was being niggled along early and didn't handle the bend into the straight at all well, but she really got motoring once in line for home. She can only improve. (op 11-2 tchd 9-2)
Emulating(IRE) gave ground away racing on the outside and was carried even wider rounding the turn into the straight. He finished well having been in last place with a furlong to run, and can surely win something similar. (op 7-2 tchd 9-2)
Club House(IRE), with Graham Lee taking over in the saddle from a 7lb claimer, kept on well but again found a few too good. (op 15-2)
Ivanhoe was another who raced a shade keenly, but he was well placed turning in and had every chance. (op 7-1)
Sunblazer(IRE) led them into the home straight but edging left onto the slow inside rail didn't help his cause at all. (op 11-2 tchd 9-2)
Run It Twice(IRE) Official explanation: jockey said that the gelding hung left up the straight
My Gigi, who was the subject of a jockey change, was weak in the market on her handicap debut. She tracked the leader and stuck to the unfavoured inside rail in the straight. Official explanation: trainer said that the racecourse provided the wrong number cloth (tchd 12-1)

7815 THAKEHAM HOMES LINGFIELD H'CAP (DIV I) 1m (P)

1:30 (1:30) (Class 6) (0-55,55) 3-Y-O+ **£1,704** (£503; £251) **Stalls** High

Form				RPR
2365	**1**		**Percythepinto (IRE)**[13] 7643 3-9-3 55 ... (t) JimCrowley 8 (George Baker) *hld up in midfield: chsd ldrs over 2f out: rdn and qcknd to ld jst ins fnl f: styd on wl: rdn out* **7/2**[1]	65
0562	**2**	1 ¼	**Rogue Reporter (IRE)**[15] 7615 3-9-2 54 ... (v) AdamKirby 5 (Stuart Williams) *in tch: rdn and effrt to chse ldng pair 2f out: pressing ldr and hung lft ent fnl f: no threat to wnr fnl 100yds but kpt on to go 2nd cl home* **7/2**[1]	61
0060	**3**	*nk*	**Silly Billy (IRE)**[21] 7482 4-8-12 53 ... (v[1]) JemmaMarshall[(5)] 4 (Pat Phelan) *chsd ldr tl led 2f out: rdn over 1f out: hdd and no ex jst ins fnl f: plugged on same pce after: lost 2nd cl home* **20/1**	59
0003	**4**	4 ½	**Cativo Cavallino**[13] 7643 9-9-2 55 ... NataliaGemelova[(3)] 7 (John E Long) *pushed along in last trio: rdn and hdwy into midfield but stl off the pce 3f out: kpt on to go 4th ins fnl f: nvr trbld ldrs* **7/1**[3]	51
600-	**5**	½	**Compton Bell**[422] 6400 3-9-3 55 ... (t) GeorgeBaker 1 (Hans Adielsson) *t.k.h early: lost pl and pushed along over 2f out: rn green bnd 2f out: edging lft and kpt on ins fnl f: no threat to ldrs* **20/1**	50
354	**6**	½	**Sudden Wish (IRE)**[169] 2802 3-9-3 55 ... KirstyMilczarek 6 (David Evans) *racd off the pce in last trio: rdn and stl plenty to do over 2f out: styd on fnl f: nvr trbld ldrs* **4/1**[2]	49
5504	**7**	¾	**Salient**[21] 7486 8-9-5 55 ... (p) J-PGuillambert 3 (Michael Attwater) *led: rdn and hdd 2f out: wknd over 1f out: wl btn and eased wl ins fnl f* **8/1**	47
5000	**8**	2 ½	**Vale Of Lingfield (IRE)**[21] 7474 3-9-2 54 ... LukeMorris 9 (John Best) *t.k.h: chsd ldrs: rdn and struggling ent fnl 2f: wknd over 1f out* **16/1**	40
0000	**9**	*shd*	**Cut The Cackle (IRE)**[12] 7670 6-9-5 55 ... (tp) WilliamCarson 10 (Violet M Jordan) *stdd and dropped in bhd after s: a in rr: rdn and effrt but stl plenty to do over 2f out: no imp* **25/1**	41
6140	**10**	7	**Pink Lips**[20] 7500 4-9-2 52 ... (be[1]) FrederikTylicki 12 (J R Jenkins) *stdd s: hdwy into midfield after 2f: rdn and lost pl over 2f out: bhd fnl f* **11/1**	22
62-0	**11**	¾	**Esteem Lord**[49] 6774 6-9-3 53 ... (b) RobertHavlin 2 (Zoe Davison) *t.k.h: chsd ldrs tl jst over 2f out: sn wknd: bhd fnl f* **40/1**	21

1m 37.65s (-0.55) **Going Correction** -0.025s/f (Stan)
WFA 3 from 4yo+ 2lb **11** Ran SP% **118.1**
Speed ratings (Par 101): **101,99,99,94,94 93,93,90,90,83 82**
Tote Swingers 1&2 £3.80, 2&3 £10.80, 1&3 £19.60 CSF £14.82 CT £215.12 TOTE £4.10: £1.10, £1.30, £8.10; EX 18.50 Trifecta £325.70 Pool: £486.41 - 1.12 winning tickets..
Owner Seaton Partnership **Bred** Stone Ridge Farm **Trained** Manton, Wilts

FOCUS
There was a fair pace on here and it was the pick of the three 1m times. Sound form.
Esteem Lord Official explanation: vet said that the gelding lost an off fore shoe

7816 THAKEHAM HOMES LINGFIELD H'CAP (DIV II) 1m (P)

2:00 (2:02) (Class 6) (0-55,55) 3-Y-O+ **£1,704** (£503; £251) **Stalls** High

Form				RPR
6646	**1**		**Storm Runner (IRE)**[20] 7500 4-9-3 53 ... GrahamLee 4 (George Margarson) *hld up in rr: rdn and gd hdwy over 1f out: drvn to ld ins fnl f: styd on wl* **4/1**[1]	61
5520	**2**	¾	**Exopuntia**[20] 7500 6-9-2 52 ... AdamBeschizza 8 (Julia Feilden) *hld up towards rr: rdn and effrt on outer over 1f out: stl plenty to do and hdwy 1f out: str run fnl f: wnt 2nd cl home: nt rch wnr* **8/1**[2]	58
6200	**3**	*nk*	**Querido (GER)**[20] 7500 8-8-11 52 ... (tp) WilliamTwiston-Davies[(5)] 5 (Paddy Butler) *hld up towards rr: clsd and in tch whn nt clr run over 1f out: hdwy ent fnl f: chsd wnr fnl 100yds: styd on same pce: lost 2nd cl home* **33/1**	57
3240	**4**	¾	**Men Don't Cry (IRE)**[13] 7643 3-9-3 55 ... (b) LiamKeniry 2 (Ed de Giles) *chsd ldr tl led 2f out: rdn over 1f out: hdd ins fnl f: styd on same pce after* **14/1**	59+
0630	**5**	2 ¼	**Irons On Fire (USA)**[21] 7479 4-8-12 55 ... (p) AaronChave[(7)] 6 (Lee Carter) *racd in midfield: hdwy on inner to chse ldrs 1f out: no imp and wknd fnl 100yds* **20/1**	53
3400	**6**	1	**Do More Business (IRE)**[30] 6778 5-9-2 52 ... RenatoSouza 10 (Alison Batchelor) *chsd ldrs: rdn styd on same pce fr over 1f out* **25/1**	48
0560	**7**	½	**Brown Pete (IRE)**[15] 7619 4-9-4 54 ... MartinHarley 12 (Violet M Jordan) *led and sn crossed to inner: clr 5f out: rdn and hdd 2f out: btn jst over 1f out: wknd ins fnl f* **10/1**[3]	49
4440	**8**	2 ¾	**Shore Performer (IRE)**[19] 7527 3-9-2 54 ... JimCrowley 9 (William Haggas) *t.k.h: hld up in midfield: rdn and fnd nil over 1f out: sn btn: wknd and eased ins fnl f* **4/1**[1]	43

0066 **9** ½ **Custom House (IRE)**[20] 7504 4-9-3 **53** JohnFahy 3 40
(John E Long) *chsd ldrs: rdn and unable qck wl over 1f out: wknd fnl f* **20/1**

4002 **10** 1 ¼ **Bahri Sheen (IRE)**[20] 7504 4-9-3 **53** LukeMorris 7 38
(John Best) *t.k.h: hld up in rr: rdn and no hdwy over 2f out: bhd fnl f* **8/1**[2]

6603 **11** 2 ½ **Squirrel Wood (IRE)**[34] 7189 4-9-5 **55** (b) GeorgeBaker 11 34
(Mary Hambro) *stdd s: hld up in rr: n.d* **4/1**[1]

1m 38.67s (0.47) **Going Correction** -0.025s/f (Stan)
WFA 3 from 4yo+ 2lb **11** Ran SP% **114.3**
Speed ratings (Par 101): **96,95,94,94,91 90,90,87,87,85 83**
Tote Swingers 1&2 £8.70, 2&3 £35.90, 1&3 £28.40 CSF £33.57 CT £915.29 TOTE £3.20: £1.20, £3.70, £10.00; EX 42.40 Trifecta £334.10 Pool: £717.27 - 1.61 winning tickets..
Owner Pitfield Partnership **Bred** Kevin Foley **Trained** Newmarket, Suffolk

FOCUS
The early leader Brown Pete set a strong pace, and the first three came from the back of the field. The winning time was 1.02sec slower than the first division. The winner's best form since the summer.

7817 BETFRED "THE BONUS KING" H'CAP 6f (P)
2:30 (2:32) (Class 3) (0-95,95) 3-Y-0+ **£6,663** (£1,982; £990; £495) **Stalls** Low

Form RPR

0440 **1** **York Glory (USA)**[11] 7690 4-9-4 **92** (b) PhillipMakin 4 105
(Kevin Ryan) *mde all: rdn and drifted rt fr over 1f out: styd on wl and a holding runner-up fnl f: rdn out* **7/2**[1]

550 **2** ½ **Swiss Cross**[4] 7774 5-9-3 **91** (t) GeorgeBaker 9 102
(Phil McEntee) *chsd ldrs: wnt 2nd 2f out: pressed wnr and carried lft fr over 1f out: kpt on but a hld* **14/1**

0041 **3** 4 **Haamaat (IRE)**[20] 7508 4-9-2 **90** PaulHanagan 10 88
(William Haggas) *t.k.h: hld up in tch: rdn and effrt over 1f out: chsd ldng pair over 1f out: styd on same pce* **7/2**[1]

4000 **4** ¾ **Head Of Steam (USA)**[26] 7366 5-8-13 **87** GrahamLee 8 83
(Amanda Perrett) *hld up towards rr: rdn and effrt over 1f out: styd on ins fnl f: no threat to ldrs* **10/1**[3]

5060 **5** nk **Dungannon**[25] 7397 5-9-7 **95** LiamKeniry 12 90
(Andrew Balding) *hld up in last trio: rdn and hdwy jst over 1f out: styd on same pce and no imp ins fnl f: nvr trbld ldrs* **6/1**[2]

0016 **6** 1 **Thunderball**[11] 7690 6-9-3 **91** (p) SilvestreDeSousa 3 83
(Scott Dixon) *chsd ldrs: rdn and outpcd by ldng pair wl over 1f out: wknd ins fnl f* **6/1**[2]

6241 **7** nk **Noverre To Go (IRE)**[13] 7651 6-8-11 **85** LukeMorris 5 76
(Ronald Harris) *chsd ldrs: rdn and unable qck 2f out: wknd ins fnl f* **12/1**

0000 **8** ¾ **Docofthebay (IRE)**[11] 7691 8-9-2 **90** (b) MartinHarley 1 78
(Scott Dixon) *bhd: rdn 1/2-way: plugged on ins fnl f but n.d* **20/1**

0043 **9** 1 **Sulis Minerva (IRE)**[125] 4231 5-8-10 **87** [1] RaulDaSilva(3) 2 72
(Jeremy Gask) *in tch in midfield: rdn and no prog over 2f out: wknd 1f out* **22/1**

6100 **10** ½ **Seek The Fair Land**[20] 7503 6-9-1 **89** (b) WilliamCarson 11 72
(Jim Boyle) *a towards rr: rdn and wd bnd 2f out: no prog and wl hld after* **25/1**

0020 **11** 25 **Sugar Beet**[20] 7503 4-9-2 **90** DavidProbert 6
(Ronald Harris) *chsd wnr tl 2f out: sn lost pl: wl bhd and virtually p.u ins fnl f: dismntd immediately after fin* **25/1**

1m 9.93s (-1.97) **Going Correction** -0.025s/f (Stan) **11** Ran SP% **113.3**
Speed ratings (Par 107): **112,111,106,105,104 103,102,101,100,99 66**
Tote Swingers 1&2 £11.40, 2&3 £6.40, 1&3 £4.90 CSF £50.18 CT £183.40 TOTE £4.10: £1.30, £6.30, £1.20; EX 70.60 Trifecta £205.00 Pool: £880.44 - 3.22 winning tickets..
Owner Salman Rashed & Mohamed Khalifa **Bred** Paget Bloodstock & Horse France **Trained** Hambleton, N Yorks

FOCUS
A good quality handicap, but with Even Stevens withdrawn after he burst the stalls, there was a question over who would make the running. In the end the winner made all, and few became involved. The winner's best form this year.

NOTEBOOK
York Glory(USA) made every yard. Kicking off the turn, he edged right and intimidated the second out of giving him a tougher race. Lightly raced this term, he's dirt bred, and could have more to offer on the AW surfaces. (op 4-1)
Swiss Cross was the only one to give the winner any sort of race, but he was carried right by him in the closing stages, which didn't help his cause. The return to sprinting suited him.
Haamaat(IRE), back a furlong in distance, raced keenly again and was caught wide from her double-figure draw. The first two got away from her running down the hill but she kept on well. She has a good record on this surface and probably has another win in her off this sort of mark. (op 11-4)
Head Of Steam(USA) has dropped to an attractive mark and ran a promising race on his AW debut. A return to 7f or a more positive ride over this trip could see him get off the mark for current connections. (op 16-1)
Dungannon, again unlucky with the draw, struggled to get into it from off the pace. A disputed lead up front would have helped him. (op 5-1 tchd 7-1)
Thunderball is weighted up to the hilt now. (op 17-2)
Noverre To Go(IRE) found things tough back in handicap company. (op 11-1 tchd 10-1)
Sugar Beet Official explanation: jockey said that the filly lost her action

7818 BETFRED "BONUS KING BINGO" MAIDEN STKS 1m 2f (P)
3:00 (3:01) (Class 5) 3-Y-0+ **£2,385** (£704; £352) **Stalls** Low

Form RPR

6423 **1** **Aegaeus**[13] 7644 3-9-3 75 GrahamLee 3 78+
(Ed Dunlop) *chsd ldrs: effrt to chal jst over 1f out: rdn to ld wl ins fnl f: pushed out towards fin* **5/4**[1]

0052 **2** ¾ **Harry Buckle**[29] 7310 3-9-0 70 RaulDaSilva(3) 2 76
(Philip McBride) *led for 2f: chsd ldr after tl led again over 3f out: rdn and hrd pressed over 1f out: hdd and one pce wl ins fnl f* **3/1**[2]

0-3 **3** 1 ½ **Honour**[61] 6457 3-8-12 0 ShaneKelly 1 68
(Sir Michael Stoute) *in tch: chsd ldrs over 3f out: rdn and unable qck over 1f out: 3rd and styd on same pce ins fnl f* **7/2**[3]

5053 **4** 4 **Stormbound (IRE)**[13] 7647 3-9-3 70 SilvestreDeSousa 9 65
(Paul Cole) *chsd ldr for 2f: chsd ldr again over 3f out tl over 1f out: wknd u.p ins fnl f* **5/1**

5 21 **Notabadgirl** 3-8-12 0 DavidProbert 8 18
(Simon Dow) *s.i.s: sn pushed along and off the pce in last pair: no ch but past btn horses over 2f out: no imp: eased wl ins fnl f* **66/1**

6 4 **Tobago** 4-9-2 0 DavidKenny(5) 7 15
(Lady Herries) *s.i.s: a bhd and rdn along thrght: lost tch over 3f out: past btn horses fnl 2f* **50/1**

60 **7** ½ **Miss Jo B**[13] 7654 3-8-12 0 JimmyQuinn 4
(Phil McEntee) *hld up towards rr: rdn and lost tch over 2f out: fdd over 1f out* **100/1**

50/ **8** 40 **Bravo Belle (IRE)**[737] 7462 5-8-11 0 NathanAlison(5) 6
(Paddy Butler) *racd keenly: hdwy to ld after 2f: hdd and dropped out rapidly over 3f out: t.o and virtually p.u fnl 2f* **150/1**

0 **9** 2 ¼ **El Calafate (USA)**[13] 7647 3-9-3 0 GeorgeBaker 5
(John Best) *t.k.h: chsd ldrs tl lost pl rapidly 4f out: t.o and virtually p.u fnl 2f* **100/1**

2m 5.27s (-1.33) **Going Correction** -0.025s/f (Stan)
WFA 3 from 4yo+ 4lb **9** Ran SP% **114.4**
Speed ratings (Par 103): **104,103,102,99,82 79,78,46,44**
Tote Swingers 1&2 £1.70, 2&3 £2.10, 1&3 £1.30 CSF £5.23 TOTE £3.00: £1.10, £1.60, £1.10; EX 6.00 Trifecta £12.30 Pool: £1,216.27 - 74.02 winning tickets..
Owner Lord Derby **Bred** Stanley Estate And Stud Co **Trained** Newmarket, Suffolk

FOCUS
A modest late-season maiden and the winner didn't need to improve.

7819 BETFRED GOALS GALORE AMATEUR RIDERS' H'CAP 1m 4f (P)
3:30 (3:30) (Class 6) (0-65,65) 3-Y-0+ **£2,305** (£709; £354) **Stalls** Low

Form RPR

0243 **1** **Kampai**[14] 7629 4-10-0 **56** ShelleyBirkett(5) 3 65
(Julia Feilden) *hld up in tch: hdwy to chse ldrs 2f out: rdn to chal over 1f out: led 1f out: edgd rt but styd on wl: rdn out* **5/1**[1]

5-00 **2** 2 ¼ **Novel Dancer**[14] 7629 4-10-1 **52** (e) MrSWalker 9 57
(Lydia Richards) *hld up in tch in midfield: hdwy over 2f out: rdn and ev ch 1f out: unable qck and sltly hmpd ins fnl f: no ex fnl 100yds* **5/1**[1]

3300 **3** nk **Sedgwick**[20] 7511 10-10-9 **65** MrFMitchell(5) 6 70
(Shaun Harris) *hld up in tch in rr: hdwy 3f out: drvn to chse ldrs 1f out: kpt on u.p* **12/1**

054 **4** nk **Kames Park (IRE)**[16] 7596 10-10-3 **61** MrsAGuest(7) 15 65
(Richard Guest) *stdd s: hld up in rr: hdwy on inner over 4f out: nt clr run and shuffled bk 3f out: switching rt and hdwy 2f out: pushed along and styd on wl ins fnl f: gng on fin* **12/1**

1534 **5** ¾ **Cosmic Halo**[71] 6118 3-10-2 **64** MrJHamilton(5) 11 67
(Richard Fahey) *in tch on outer: rdn to chse ldr 2f out tl jst over 1f out: styd on same pce ins fnl f* **5/1**[1]

0004 **6** 1 **Edgeworth (IRE)**[4] 7767 6-10-9 **63** MrJHodson(3) 14 64
(David Bridgwater) *hld up in tch in midfield: effrt and sltly hmpd ent fnl 2f: styd on same pce fr over 1f out* **10/1**

003 **7** 1 ½ **Parhelion**[29] 7303 5-10-3 **59** (bt) MrBGibbs(5) 2 58
(John Flint) *chsd ldrs tl led 3f out: drvn 2f out: hdd 1f out: wknd ins fnl f* **11/2**[2]

1540 **8** 1 ¼ **Asterales**[81] 5811 5-9-13 **57** MissJGordon(7) 12 54
(Jo Hughes) *hld up in tch towards rr: hdwy and chsng ldrs over 2f out: wknd 1f out* **50/1**

3000 **9** 2 **Flag Of Glory**[21] 7495 5-10-0 **58** MissMEdden(7) 7 52
(Peter Hiatt) *chsd ldrs: rdn and unable qck over 2f out: wknd over 1f out* **40/1**

4300 **10** 1 **Turjuman (USA)**[8] 7640 7-10-1 **59** (p) MrDSMcLaughlin(7) 8 51
(Alan Bailey) *a towards rr but in tch: rdn and no real imp 3f out: plugged on but n.d* **33/1**

33/0 **11** 2 ¼ **Murfreesboro**[25] 6843 9-10-4 **62** MissRDorrell(7) 4 50
(Raymond York) *in tch: lost pl and towards rr 4f out: pushed along and no hdwy 2f out* **33/1**

4000 **12** 1 ¾ **Before Bruce**[16] 7596 5-10-0 **58** (bt) MrJNPilkington(7) 10 44
(Brendan Powell) *mde most tl 3f out: rdn over 2f out: wknd wl over 1f out* **33/1**

0062 **13** 9 **Caunay**[7] 7717 5-10-2 **58** (tp) MrMatthewBarber(5) 5 29
(Neil Mulholland) *in tch: lost pl and rdn 4f out: bhd fnl f* **11/1**

4222 **14** 14 **Edgware Road**[15] 7620 4-10-2 **60** (p) MissBHampson(7) 1 9
(Sean Curran) *pressed ldr on inner tl 3f out: sn wknd: bhd fnl f: t.o* **8/1**[3]

6036 **15** 8 **Surrey Dream (IRE)**[134] 3938 3-9-10 **60** MissAimeeMKing(7) 16
(Charlie Mann) *racd wd thrght: a bhd: lost tch 4f out: t.o fnl 2f* **66/1**

2m 33.88s (0.88) **Going Correction** -0.025s/f (Stan)
WFA 3 from 4yo+ 6lb **15** Ran SP% **124.0**
Speed ratings (Par 101): **96,94,94,94,93 92,91,91,89,89 87,86,80,71,65**
Tote Swingers 1&2 £5.00, 2&3 £19.60, 1&3 £18.90 CSF £28.73 CT £295.86 TOTE £3.80: £1.30, £2.30, £5.80; EX 42.10 Trifecta £400.00 Pool: £597.36 - 1.12 winning tickets..
Owner Peter M Crane **Bred** Miss A J Rawding & P M Crane **Trained** Exning, Suffolk

FOCUS
An ordinary handicap for amateur riders. The winner was close to her turf mark, with the third and fourth setting the standard.
Asterales Official explanation: jockey said that she had slightly mistimed the removal of the blind and that it was her first ride; jockey said that the mare was slowly away. jockey said that she had slightly mistimed the removal of the blind and that it was her first ride; jockey said that the mare was slowly away.
T/Jkpt: £2,468.70 to a £1 stake. Pool: £8,692.61 - 2.50 winning tickets. T/Plt: £37.30 to a £1 stake. Pool: £41,984.68 - 820.36 winning tickets. T/Qpdt: £18.10 to a £1 stake. Pool: £5,940.11 - 242.25 winning tickets. SP

7804 KEMPTON (A.W) (R-H)
Thursday, November 22

OFFICIAL GOING: Standard
Wind: fresh, half behind Weather: dry, breezy

7820 32REDBINGO.COM CLAIMING STKS 6f (P)
4:10 (4:10) (Class 6) 3-Y-0+ **£1,617** (£481; £240; £120) **Stalls** Low

Form RPR

342 **1** **Ertikaan**[31] 7297 5-9-7 82 (p[1]) LukeMorris 2 89
(Ronald Harris) *chsd ldng pair: rdn and chal over 1f out: led 1f out: in command and rdn out fnl f* **7/4**[1]

3210 **2** 1 ½ **Beat The Bell**[8] 7716 7-9-1 76 (p) MartinDwyer 4 78
(Jamie Osborne) *chsd ldr: rdn 2f out: chsd wnr ins fnl f: styd on same pce and no imp* **7/2**[3]

0000 **3** 1 ¼ **Masai Moon**[7] 7732 8-9-3 79 (p) JamesMillman 10 76
(Rod Millman) *sn pushed along in 4th: rdn ent fnl 2f: styd on to go 3rd ins fnl f: no imp fnl 100yds* **14/1**

0341 **4** 1 **Mac Gille Eoin**[6] 7742 8-9-9 74 JimCrowley 5 79
(Luke Dace) *awkward leaving stalls: hld up in last pair: rdn and clsng whn nt clr run 1f out: styd on same pce ins fnl f* **2/1**[2]

4000 **5** 1 **Sir Mozart (IRE)**[62] 6452 9-8-13 68 JoeFanning 1 66
(Ronald Harris) *led: rdn and hdd 1f out: btn and eased wl ins fnl f* **25/1**

5653 **6** *11* **Mambo Spirit (IRE)**[31] 7297 8-8-13 66 ChrisCatlin 3 31
(Tony Newcombe) *slowly away: a bhd: lost tch 2f out* **8/1**

1m 12.04s (-1.06) **Going Correction** -0.05s/f (Stan) **6** Ran SP% **113.5**
Speed ratings (Par 101): **105,103,101,100,98 84**
toteswingers 1&2 £1.70, 1&3 £4.60, 2&3 £5.70 CSF £8.49 TOTE £2.60: £1.30, £2.10; EX 7.80 Trifecta £33.50 Pool: £1,130.74 - 25.28 winning tickets..Ertikaan was claimed by Mr B G Powell for £10,000.

Owner Robert & Nina Bailey **Bred** Floors Farming And Dominic Burke **Trained** Earlswood, Monmouths

FOCUS
The form is fair, despite the small field, but it's probably not worth being too positive about this bunch, the first two being the best guides to the level.
Sir Mozart(IRE) Official explanation: jockey said gelding lost its action in final furlong

7821 32REDPOKER.COM NURSERY 6f (P)
4:40 (4:40) (Class 6) (0-65,65) 2-Y-O £1,617 (£481; £240; £120) Stalls Low

Form RPR

5044 **1** **Sakhee's Rose**[22] 7476 2-9-7 65 GeorgeBaker 9 71+
(Roger Charlton) *stdd and dropped in bhd s: clsd ent fnl 2f: rdn and hdwy over 1f out: chal ins fnl f: rdn to ld wl ins fnl f: idled towards fin* **3/1**[1]

3040 **2** *½* **Little Miss Zuri (IRE)**[16] 7606 2-8-0 47 SimonPearce(3) 5 52
(Sylvester Kirk) *chsd ldr: rdn to ld 2f out: hrd pressed and drvn 1f out: hdd ins fnl f: kpt on* **25/1**

064 **3** *½* **Persian Marvel (IRE)**[36] 7156 2-8-1 50 (b) NathanAlison(5) 2 53
(Jim Boyle) *chsd ldrs: rdn 2f out: ev ch 1f out: led briefly ins fnl f: sn hdd and no ex towards fin* **6/1**[3]

4400 **4** *2¾* **Vergality Ridge (IRE)**[7] 7724 2-9-5 63 (b[1]) LukeMorris 10 58
(Ronald Harris) *t.k.h: hld up in tch towards rr: rdn and hanging rt over 2f out: hdwy u.p over 1f out: no imp ins fnl f* **20/1**

0546 **5** *hd* **Lexi's Beauty (IRE)**[20] 7526 2-8-4 48 JimmyQuinn 6 42
(Ian Williams) *in tch: effrt to press ldrs 2f out: drvn and unable qck over 1f out: wknd ins fnl f* **25/1**

6625 **6** *1¾* **My Sweet Lord**[14] 7650 2-8-10 54 DavidProbert 7 43
(Mark Usher) *in tch in midfield: rdn and lost pl over 3f out: rallied u.p over 1f out: styd on same pce ins fnl f* **6/1**[3]

0000 **7** *¾* **Fit For A King (IRE)**[14] 7649 2-8-12 56 (b) RobertWinston 3 45
(John Best) *led tl rdn and hdd 2f out: wknd u.p over 1f out: wl hld whn n.m.r and eased ins fnl f* **10/1**

3065 **8** *½* **Our Sweet Art**[22] 7476 2-9-4 62 [1] ChrisCatlin 11 47
(John Best) *chsd ldrs: rdn and unable qck jst over 2f out: wknd over 1f out* **9/1**

0350 **9** *nk* **Gold Beau (FR)**[26] 7410 2-9-7 65 GrahamLee 4 53+
(Linda Stubbs) *in tch in midfield: nt clr run on inner over 2f out: sme hdwy over 1f out: nt clr again and eased ins fnl f* **5/1**[2]

0250 **10** *2½* **Compton Silver**[22] 7476 2-9-7 65 JimCrowley 1 42
(Hans Adielsson) *t.k.h: hld up in tch in midfield: rdn and btn ent fnl 2f: wknd over 1f out* **8/1**

000 **11** *hd* **Lilly White (USA)**[23] 7458 2-8-13 62 (bt) WilliamTwiston-Davies(5) 8 38
(Brian Meehan) *in tch in midfield: lost pl and rdn over 3f out: bhd and no hdwy u.p 2f out* **10/1**

1m 13.33s (0.23) **Going Correction** -0.05s/f (Stan) **11** Ran SP% **122.0**
Speed ratings (Par 94): **96,95,94,91,90 88,87,86,86,83 82**
toteswingers 1&2 £19.50, 1&3 £3.40, 2&3 £21.60 CSF £92.61 CT £439.13 TOTE £1.90: £1.02, £7.90, £3.60; EX 105.50 Trifecta £524.10 Part won. Pool: £698.84 - 0.60 winning tickets..

Owner J R Dwyer **Bred** R F And S D Knipe **Trained** Beckhampton, Wilts

FOCUS
A moderate nursery best rated through the third.

NOTEBOOK
Sakhee's Rose benefited from a nice George Baker ride, being given time to find her stride after an awkward start and then producing a sustained challenge. A rise in the weights will force her up in class and that may well prevent the follow up. (tchd 11-4)
Little Miss Zuri(IRE), dropped in trip and returned to Polytrack, was a bit keen early but she found plenty for pressure, battling back past the third near the line only to find the winner too good.
Persian Marvel(IRE), back up in trip in second-time blinkers, didn't really go through with his challenge against the inside rail, perhaps not quite staying.
Vergality Ridge(IRE) showed a bit more in first-time blinkers but was never seriously involved.
Gold Beau(FR) might have been a few lengths closer with a clear run, but this didn't look a run to get carried away with. (op 7-1)

7822 32REDBET.COM MEDIAN AUCTION MAIDEN STKS 1m (P)
5:10 (5:10) (Class 6) 3-5-Y-O £1,617 (£481; £240; £120) Stalls Low

Form RPR

052 **1** **Hint Of Promise**[41] 7025 3-8-12 62 GrahamLee 5 74
(Roger Charlton) *in tch: clsd smoothly to ld 2f out: sn clr: r.o wl: rdn out* **11/10**[1]

034 **2** *2¾* **Spark Of Genius**[14] 7647 3-8-12 63 RobertHavlin 4 67
(James Toller) *hld up in tch in midfield: rdn and effrt to chse ldr over 1f out: no imp but r.o for clr 2nd* **7/2**[3]

5455 **3** *6* **Silkee Supreme**[12] 7685 3-9-3 62 (b) KieranO'Neill 1 58
(Richard Hannon) *chsd ldrs: rdn and effrt jst over 2f out: outpcd and btn 2f out: 3rd and wl hld fr over 1f out* **3/1**[2]

5536 **4** *4* **Johnny Splash (IRE)**[12] 6927 3-9-3 44 (b) AdamKirby 6 48
(Roger Teal) *led for 1f: chsd ldr after tl rdn and outpcd by wnr 2f out: sn wknd* **25/1**

5 *3¼* **Handsome Molly** 3-8-12 0 LiamKeniry 8 35
(David Elsworth) *s.i.s: bhd: rn green: rdn and outpcd over 2f out: pushed along and styd on past btn horses fnl f* **11/1**

500 **6** *¾* **Touching History (IRE)**[45] 6925 3-9-3 45 GeorgeBaker 3 38
(Tim Etherington) *led after 1f: rdn and hdd 2f out: sn outpcd and btn: wknd over 1f out* **50/1**

7 *2* **Sugar Lips** 3-8-12 0 LukeMorris 2 29
(Simon Dow) *s.i.s: sn rdn along in last pair: lost tch over 2f out* **16/1**

000- **8** *1¼* **Back For Tea (IRE)**[348] 7712 4-9-5 43 (t) ChrisCatlin 7 31
(Phil McEntee) *stdd after s: hld up in last trio: rdn and no hdwy over 2f out: sn wknd* **66/1**

1m 39.39s (-0.41) **Going Correction** -0.05s/f (Stan)
WFA 3 from 4yo 2lb **8** Ran SP% **116.4**
Speed ratings (Par 101): **100,97,91,87,84 83,81,80**
toteswingers 1&2 £1.70, 1&3 £1.20, 2&3 £2.20 CSF £5.29 TOTE £1.90: £1.02, £1.40, £1.20; EX 4.90 Trifecta £7.10 Pool: £1,244.30 - 130.22 winning tickets..

Owner K Abdulla **Bred** Juddmonte Farms Ltd **Trained** Beckhampton, Wilts

FOCUS
A weak maiden, although the winner took another step forward and the runner-up sets the standard.

7823 32RED CASINO H'CAP (DIV I) 1m (P)
5:40 (5:40) (Class 4) (0-85,85) 3-Y-O+ £4,075 (£1,212; £606; £303) Stalls Low

Form RPR

01 **1** **Embankment**[38] 7112 3-8-13 79 JoeFanning 6 91
(William Jarvis) *dwlt: sn in tch in midfield: rdn and gd hdwy to ld 1f out: r.o strly* **10/1**

0220 **2** *1½* **Rakaan (IRE)**[21] 7502 5-9-7 85 GeorgeBaker 4 94
(Jamie Osborne) *stdd s: hld up in rr: swtchd lft and effrt 2f out: hdwy over 1f out: r.o ins fnl f: wnt 2nd towards fin* **7/1**[3]

221 **3** *nk* **Tropics (USA)**[22] 7477 4-9-5 83 JimCrowley 5 91
(Dean Ivory) *t.k.h: hld up in tch: rdn and effrt over 1f out: pressed wnr 1f out: r.o same pce ins fnl f: lost 2nd towards fin* **5/4**[1]

0560 **4** *3¼* **Fantasy Gladiator**[15] 7626 6-8-11 75 (p) GrahamLee 2 76
(Robert Cowell) *hld up in tch in midfield: rdn and effrt on inner over 1f out: no imp and styd on same pce fnl f* **14/1**

2511 **5** *nk* **Schoolmaster**[14] 7645 4-9-5 83 AdamKirby 7 83
(Giles Bravery) *chsd ldr over 6f out: rdn to ld 2f out: hdd 1f out: sn outpcd and wknd ins fnl f* **7/2**[2]

0212 **6** *½* **Saharia (IRE)**[23] 7461 5-9-2 80 (v) ShaneKelly 10 79
(Michael Attwater) *stdd after s: hld up in last pair: rdn and sme hdwy over 1f out: no imp fnl f: nvr trbld ldrs* **10/1**

0100 **7** *3½* **Islesman**[15] 7626 4-8-13 77 RobertWinston 3 68
(Heather Main) *hld up in tch towards rr: swtchd lft and effrt over 1f out: no prog 1f out: wknd fnl f* **25/1**

1020 **8** *hd* **Mahadee (IRE)**[14] 7645 7-9-2 80 (b) LiamKeniry 8 70
(Ed de Giles) *hld up in tch in midfield: lost pl and rdn 2f out: wknd over 1f out* **25/1**

2000 **9** *1¾* **Shifting Star (IRE)**[14] 7645 7-9-4 82 ChrisCatlin 1 68
(John Bridger) *chsd ldr tl over 6f out: styd chsng ldrs tl wknd u.p over 1f out* **33/1**

036 **10** *nk* **Red Seventy**[19] 7559 3-8-9 80 (v[1]) WilliamTwiston-Davies(5) 9 66
(Richard Hannon) *led tl rdn and hdd 2f out: wknd over 1f out* **16/1**

3 **11** *1¾* **Saoi (USA)**[148] 3503 5-8-12 76 EddieAhern 11 58
(William Knight) *chsd ldrs: rdn and struggling over 2f out: wknd 2f out: bhd and eased wl ins fnl f* **16/1**

1m 38.8s (-1.00) **Going Correction** -0.05s/f (Stan)
WFA 3 from 4yo+ 2lb **11** Ran SP% **126.4**
Speed ratings (Par 105): **103,101,101,97,97 97,93,93,91,91 89**
toteswingers 1&2 £15.40, 1&3 £5.70, 2&3 £2.90 CSF £82.65 CT £152.31 TOTE £9.90: £3.50, £1.90, £1.40; EX 81.00 Trifecta £200.10 Pool: £974.02 - 3.65 winning tickets..

Owner Canisbay Bloodstock **Bred** Juddmonte Farms Ltd **Trained** Newmarket, Suffolk

FOCUS
A fair handicap which is rated fairly positively through the runner-up.
Islesman Official explanation: jockey said gelding lost its action

7824 32RED CASINO H'CAP (DIV II) 1m (P)
6:10 (6:11) (Class 4) (0-85,85) 3-Y-O+ £4,075 (£1,212; £606; £303) Stalls Low

Form RPR

2542 **1** **Jack Of Diamonds (IRE)**[8] 7715 3-8-13 79 RobertWinston 10 88
(Roger Teal) *chsd ldrs: rdn to chal 2f out: led over 1f out: hld on gamely cl home: all out* **11/4**[1]

5043 **2** *shd* **Bank On Me**[64] 6381 3-9-2 82 LukeMorris 9 90
(Philip McBride) *pushed along leaving stalls: in tch in midfield: hdwy u.p over 1f out: chsd wnr ins fnl f: r.o wl and clsng grad fnl 100yds: jst hld* **7/1**

5006 **3** *1¼* **Lord Ofthe Shadows (IRE)**[21] 7502 3-9-5 85 GeorgeBaker 8 90
(Richard Hannon) *chsd ldr tl led 2f out: sn rdn and hdd over 1f out: lost 2nd and styd on same pce ins fnl f* **11/2**[3]

1661 **4** *3¾* **Prime Exhibit**[36] 7163 7-9-5 83 (t) ShaneKelly 4 80
(Daniel Mark Loughnane) *hld up in last trio: swtchd rt and gd hdwy 2f out: chsd ldrs and drvn over 1f out: no hdwy 1f out: wknd ins fnl f* **12/1**

6113 **5** *1¾* **Light Burst (USA)**[3] 7790 3-9-0 80 AndreaAtzeni 7 72
(Ismail Mohammed) *chsd ldrs: rdn and effrt 2f out: no imp ent fnl f: wknd ins fnl f* **11/4**[1]

1 **6** *4* **Selkie's Friend**[124] 4341 3-8-12 78 JimCrowley 3 61
(Henry Candy) *hld up in tch in midfield: swtchd rt and effrt ent fnl 2f: no hdwy and sn outpcd: wknd over 1f out* **7/2**[2]

01/0 **7** *2¾* **Everybody Knows**[84] 5768 7-8-8 77 NathanSweeney(5) 2 54
(Jo Crowley) *led tl 2f out: sn lost pl u.p: wknd over 1f out* **33/1**

0000 **8** *4½* **Brunston**[13] 7672 6-9-3 81 LiamKeniry 5 48
(Anthony Middleton) *stdd s: hld up in rr: rdn and no rspnse over 2f out: bhd over 1f out* **33/1**

04-0 **9** *3¾* **Beauchamp Xerxes**[36] 7163 6-9-0 78 RichardKingscote 1 36
(Hans Adielsson) *hld up in last pair: rdn and no hdwy jst over 2f out: bhd over 1f out* **50/1**

1m 38.44s (-1.36) **Going Correction** -0.05s/f (Stan)
WFA 3 from 4yo+ 2lb **9** Ran SP% **119.0**
Speed ratings (Par 105): **104,103,102,98,97 93,90,85,82**
toteswingers 1&2 £5.10, 1&3 £1.20, 2&3 £10.30 CSF £23.38 CT £96.59 TOTE £3.00: £1.10, £2.90, £2.40; EX 20.90 Trifecta £160.90 Pool: £1,115.86 - 5.20 winning tickets..

Owner Inside Track Racing Club **Bred** Gigginstown House Stud **Trained** Ashtead, Surrey

FOCUS
The time was 0.36 seconds quicker than the first division and the form looks sound rated around the first three.

7825 32RED H'CAP 1m 4f (P)
6:40 (6:42) (Class 3) (0-95,95) 3-Y-O+ £6,663 (£1,982; £990; £495) Stalls Centre

Form RPR

-102 **1** **Into Wain (USA)**[23] 7455 5-9-0 85 JoeFanning 2 93
(Steve Gollings) *chsd ldrs tl wnt 2nd 3f out: rdn and ev ch over 2f out: led over 1f out: styd on wl: rdn out* **7/1**

06 **2** *2½* **Be Perfect (USA)**[47] 6879 3-9-4 95 (t) MartinHarley 9 99
(Marco Botti) *chsd ldr tl led over 3f out: rdn and clr w wnr over 2f out: hdd over 1f out: no ex and btn ins fnl f: jst hld on for 2nd* **10/1**

6636 **3** *nse* **Spensley (IRE)**[37] 7147 6-9-0 85 EddieAhern 8 89
(James Fanshawe) *hld up in tch in midfield: rdn and chsd clr ldng pair over 1f out: styd on ins fnl f: pressing for 2nd nr fin* **6/1**[3]

1055 **4** *hd* **Hanoverian Baron**[12] 7689 7-9-0 85 SebSanders 4 89
(Tony Newcombe) *hld up in midfield: swtchd lft and effrt ent fnl 2f: battling for 3rd over 1f out: styd on ins fnl f: pressing for 2nd cl home* **14/1**

3111 **5** *7* **Estedaama (IRE)**[22] 7487 3-8-12 **89** .... PaulHanagan 5 84
(Marcus Tregoning) *in tch in midfield: rdn over 4f out: 5th and stl plenty to do whn drvn 2f out: no imp* **5/4**[1]

-056 **6** *4 ½* **Greylami (IRE)**[117] 4578 7-9-3 **88** .... AdamKirby 3 73
(Clive Cox) *hld up in last pair: rdn 3f out: no hdwy and wknd over 2f out: wl btn fnl 2f* **11/2**[2]

022/ **7** *7* **Desert Recluse (IRE)**[756] 7196 5-9-5 **90** .... LukeMorris 1 64
(Pat Eddery) *hld up in rr: rdn 3f out: sn struggling and wknd: bhd fnl 2f* **25/1**

0300 **8** *19* **Royal Peculiar**[26] 7396 4-9-1 **86** ....(t) GeorgeBaker 7 30
(Michael Appleby) *led tl hdd and rdn over 3f out: wknd over 2f out: t.o and eased ins fnl f* **6/1**[3]

2m 31.49s (-3.01) **Going Correction** -0.05s/f (Stan)
WFA 3 from 4yo+ 6lb **8** Ran SP% **120.5**
Speed ratings (Par 107): **108,106,106,106,101 98,93,81**
toteswingers 1&2 £11.20, 1&3 £5.90, 2&3 £11.50 CSF £77.12 CT £452.31 TOTE £9.30: £2.40, £3.80, £2.10; EX 76.60 Trifecta £904.10 Pool: £1,506.95 - 1.25 winning tickets..
Owner P J Martin **Bred** Don M Robinson **Trained** Scamblesby, Lincs

FOCUS
The top weight was rated 5lb below the race ceiling and the favourite flopped, so the form isn't as strong as it might have been and not totally convincing. The third looks the best guide.

NOTEBOOK
Into Wain(USA) came into this off the back of a useful effort on turf and readily improved his Polytrack record to 4-8. He's a versatile sort (also a dual winner over hurdles) and has more to offer. (op 8-1 tchd 6-1)

Be Perfect(USA), having just his third start since coming over from France, failed to convince he really needs a trip this far. (tchd 9-1)

Spensley(IRE) is held off this mark. (tchd 7-1)

Hanoverian Baron, fifth in the November Handicap last time, was never doing enough. (op 12-1)

Estedaama(IRE) had won her last three, most recently on the Lingfield Polytrack off 8lb lower, but she was beaten a long way out this time. Paul Hanagan reported the filly moved poorly and hung right throughout. Official explanation: jockey said filly moved poorly and hung right throughout (tchd 11-8)

7826 32BONUS H'CAP 7f (P)
7:10 (7:10) (Class 3) (0-95,95) 3-Y-0+ **£6,663** (£1,982; £990; £495) **Stalls** Low

Form RPR

0400 **1** **Diescentric (USA)**[38] 7097 5-8-13 **87** .... RobertWinston 5 97+
(Julie Camacho) *hld up towards rr: str run on outer over 1f out: led ins fnl f: r.o strly and sn clr: readily* **33/1**

5555 **2** *1 ½* **Webbow (IRE)**[26] 7401 10-9-5 **93** .... GeorgeBaker 1 99
(Julie Camacho) *in tch: rdn to ld over 1f out: hdd and outpcd by wnr ins fnl f: hld on for 2nd towards fin* **16/1**

4434 **3** *nk* **Roninski (IRE)**[12] 7691 4-8-13 **87** .... JimmyQuinn 12 92+
(Bryan Smart) *stdd s: t.k.h: hld up in midfield: rdn and swtchd lft over 1f out: hdwy to chse ldrs ins fnl f: styd on but no threat to wnr* **8/1**

2501 **4** *1 ¾* **Kingscroft (IRE)**[3] 7790 4-9-1 **89** 6ex .... JoeFanning 6 89
(Mark Johnston) *in tch: effrt u.p over 2f out: chsd ldr briefly jst over 1f out: styd on same pce ins fnl f* **9/2**[3]

0050 **5** *1 ¼* **The Rectifier (USA)**[21] 7502 5-9-2 **90** ....(t) MickyFenton 4 87
(Seamus Durack) *hld up in midfield: rdn and hdwy on inner jst over 2f out: no imp 1f out and styd on same pce fnl f* **16/1**

0516 **5** *dht* **Triple Charm**[42] 7010 4-9-2 **90** ....(p) GrahamLee 2 87+
(Jeremy Noseda) *hld up in last trio: clsd ent fnl 2f: rdn and hdwy over 1f out: swtchd lft 1f out: styd on ins fnl f: nvr trbld ldrs* **2/1**[1]

5053 **7** *½* **Hurry Up George**[48] 6835 3-9-6 **95** .... JimCrowley 8 91
(Ralph Beckett) *chsd ldrs: rdn and chsd ldrs wl over 1f out: drvn and unable qck over 1f out: wknd ins fnl f* **5/2**[2]

1040 **8** *2 ¾* **Bravo Echo**[21] 7503 6-9-6 **94** .... J-PGuillambert 9 82
(Michael Attwater) *chsd ldr tl 2f out: sn drvn and unable qck: wknd over 1f out: btn whn sltly hmpd jst ins fnl f* **20/1**

0060 **9** *2 ½* **Irish Heartbeat (IRE)**[12] 7691 7-8-11 **85** .... PaulHanagan 7 67
(Richard Fahey) *hld up in midfield: rdn and effrt whn n.m.r briefly ent fnl 2f: rdn and no hdwy over 1f out: sn wknd* **20/1**

5540 **10** *2 ½* **Gouray Girl (IRE)**[12] 7690 5-8-9 **83** .... TomEaves 3 58
(Brian Ellison) *stdd s: hld up in rr: rdn and no hdwy ent fnl 2f: n.d* **25/1**

1500 **11** *4* **Rodrigo De Torres**[33] 7240 5-9-7 **95** .... AdrianNicholls 11 59
(David Nicholls) *led tl rdn and hdd over 1f out: sn wknd: bhd and eased wl ins fnl f* **33/1**

0600 **12** *nk* **Forceful Appeal (USA)**[21] 7508 4-8-10 **84** .... LukeMorris 10 47
(Simon Dow) *chsd ldrs: rdn and struggling over 2f out: wknd wl over 1f out: bhd and eased wl ins fnl f* **16/1**

1m 24.63s (-1.37) **Going Correction** -0.05s/f (Stan)
WFA 3 from 4yo+ 1lb **12** Ran SP% **128.1**
Speed ratings (Par 107): **105,103,102,100,99 99,98,95,92,90 85,85**
toteswingers 1&2 £71.30, 1&3 £129.70, 2&3 £10.90 CSF £487.86 CT £4673.97 TOTE £54.90: £14.80, £4.90, £3.10; EX 186.90 TRIFECTA Not won..
Owner Axom (XVIII) **Bred** Morgan's Ford Farm **Trained** Norton, N Yorks

FOCUS
A one-two for Julie Camacho in this competitive handicap and the winner is rated back to his 3yo form, backed up by his stablemate.

NOTEBOOK
Diescentric(USA) has been lightly raced since winning the Wood Ditton for Sir Henry Cecil, but he took well to Polytrack at the first attempt, travelling nicely under restraint before finding plenty when delivered with a well-timed challenge. He probably has the ability to rate a fair bit higher on this surface. (op 50-1)

Webbow(IRE) was runner-up and a winner on just two previous Polytrack starts (also successful on Fibresand) and again showed a liking for the surface, only being reeled in by his stablemate after hitting the front soon enough. (op 20-1)

Roninski(IRE) was keen enough (without cover early) and did well to get so close. He's probably still improving. (op 10-1)

Kingscroft(IRE) ran well under the penalty picked up for his Wolverhampton success three days earlier. (tchd 4-1)

The Rectifier(USA) didn't try to dominate but offered encouragement on just his second start for this yard. (tchd 3-1)

Triple Charm didn't apply herself with cheekpieces replacing the visor and looks ready for blinkers. (tchd 3-1)

Hurry Up George hadn't been seen for 48 days and failed to prove his stamina on this first run beyond 6.5f. (op 11-4 tchd 3-1)

Rodrigo De Torres Official explanation: jockey said gelding ran too free

7827 £32 FREE AT 32RED.COM H'CAP 7f (P)
7:40 (7:40) (Class 5) (0-75,75) 3-Y-0+ **£2,264** (£673; £336; £168) **Stalls** Low

Form RPR

0120 **1** **Eager To Bow (IRE)**[22] 7484 6-9-3 **71** .... GeorgeBaker 6 79
(Patrick Chamings) *hld up in tch in rr: rdn and hdwy on inner 2f out: chal ins fnl f: r.o wl to ld towards fin* **7/1**

305 **2** *½* **Rulesn'regulations**[35] 7203 6-9-6 **74** ....(v) AdamKirby 9 81
(Matthew Salaman) *chsd ldr tl led over 2f out: sn rdn: drvn and hrd pressed 1f out: hdd ins fnl f: sn led again tl hdd and no ex towards fin* **6/1**[3]

2564 **3** *hd* **Paradise Spectre**[29] 7328 5-9-2 **70** .... MartinHarley 4 76
(Mrs K Burke) *chsd ldrs: rdn and effrt to chse ldr wl over 1f out: ev ch 1f out: led ins fnl f: sn hdd and styd on same pce towards fin* **7/2**[1]

6304 **4** *1 ¼* **Russian Ice**[7] 7722 4-9-7 **75** ....(b) JimCrowley 13 78
(Dean Ivory) *hld up in tch towards rr: rdn and hdwy wl over 1f out: styng on whn swtchd lft 1f out: styd on wl to snatch 4th on post: nt rch ldrs* **9/2**[2]

0023 **5** *nse* **Sugarformyhoney (IRE)**[7] 7722 3-8-11 **71** ....(p) CharlesBishop[(5)] 5 73
(Seamus Durack) *in tch: rdn to chse ldrs and edgd rt ent fnl f: styd on same pce ins fnl f* **6/1**[3]

5064 **6** *4 ½* **The Strig**[7] 7725 5-9-2 **70** ....[1] J-PGuillambert 3 60
(Stuart Williams) *in tch in midfield: rdn and effrt ent fnl 2f: no imp over 1f out: wknd fnl f* **12/1**

3510 **7** *¾* **Saskia's Dream**[12] 7685 4-9-3 **71** .... RobertHavlin 8 59
(Jane Chapple-Hyam) *led tl over 2f out: sn rdn and unable qck: wknd ent fnl f* **10/1**

3000 **8** *¾* **Midnight Feast**[38] 7114 4-9-4 **72** ....(t) LukeMorris 1 58
(Lee Carter) *in tch in midfield: rdn and unable qck ent fnl 2f: wknd jst over 1f out* **20/1**

4000 **9** *½* **Ghostwing**[14] 7648 5-8-9 **70** ....(v) JoeyHaynes[(7)] 2 55
(Luke Dace) *in tch in midfield: rdn and no hdwy 2f out: sn btn and wknd jst over 1f out* **20/1**

6000 **10** *½* **Point North (IRE)**[68] 6256 5-9-7 **75** .... RobertWinston 10 59
(John Balding) *stdd s: t.k.h: hld up in tch towards rr: rdn and effrt ent fnl 2f: no hdwy and wknd over 1f out* **8/1**

-040 **11** *¾* **Judd Street**[37] 7145 10-9-7 **75** .... GrahamLee 12 57
(Eve Johnson Houghton) *dwlt: in tch in midfield: rdn and no hdwy ent fnl 2f: wknd over 1f out* **20/1**

0030 **12** *11* **Big Wave (IRE)**[22] 7485 4-9-1 **69** .... AdamBeschizza 14 21
(Alison Hutchinson) *t.k.h: hld up in midfield on outer: rdn and wknd 2f out: bhd and eased ins fnl f* **33/1**

1m 25.89s (-0.11) **Going Correction** -0.05s/f (Stan)
WFA 3 from 4yo+ 1lb **12** Ran SP% **126.6**
Speed ratings (Par 103): **98,97,97,95,95 90,89,88,88,87 86,74**
toteswingers 1&2 £7.70, 1&3 £5.80, 2&3 £6.20 CSF £49.44 CT £178.94 TOTE £10.20: £2.30, £3.50, £1.90; EX 63.50 Trifecta £159.80 Pool: £667.25 - 3.13 winning tickets..
Owner Mrs J E L Wright **Bred** Stone Ridge Farm **Trained** Baughurst, Hants

FOCUS
A modest but competitive handicap with the winner recording a personal best and the second rated slightly up on this year's form.
T/Jkpt: £633.20 to a £1 stake. Pool: £6,243.69 - 7.00 winning tickets T/Plt: £42.60 to a £1 stake. Pool: £88,202.97 - 1,508.94 winning tickets T/Qpdt: £12.50 to a £1 stake. Pool: £8,495.63 - 502.56 winning tickets SP

1125 FONTAINEBLEAU
Thursday, November 22
OFFICIAL GOING: Turf: very soft

7828a PRIX ZEDDAAN (LISTED RACE) (2YO) (TURF) 6f
12:20 (12:00) 2-Y-O **£22,916** (£9,166; £6,875; £4,583; £2,291)

RPR

1 **Gengis (FR)**[45] 6942 2-8-11 0 .... StephanePasquier 7 100
(G Doleuze, France) **6/1**[3]

2 *1* **Wedge Trust (IRE)**[41] 7122 2-8-8 0 .... FranckBlondel 11 94
(J-C Rouget, France) **16/1**

3 *1 ¼* **Sage Melody (FR)**[41] 7122 2-8-13 0 .... AnthonyCrastus 6 96
(P Demercastel, France) **21/1**

4 *1 ½* **Strange Magic (IRE)**[25] 7430 2-8-9 0 ow1 .... FrederikTylicki 9 87
(Richard Fahey) *broke wl: prom: rowed along to press ldr 2 1/2f out: styd 2nd u.p tl fdd ins fnl f* **78/10**

5 *½* **Via Chope (FR)**[30] 2-8-8 0 .... AntoineHamelin 2 85
(Y Barberot, France) **10/1**

6 *1* **Vilna (FR)**[23] 2-8-8 0 .... GregoryBenoist 10 82
(Y Barberot, France) **10/1**

7 *3* **Effie B**[20] 7518 2-8-9 0 ow1 .... MartinHarley 5 74
(Mick Channon) *towards rr but wl in tch: rdn and sme hdwy to chse ldng gp over 2f out: no further imp: wknd ins fnl f* **3/1**[1]

8 *1 ¾* **Chef Oui Chef (FR)**[16] 7623 2-9-2 0 .... Pierre-CharlesBoudot 8 75
(Y De Nicolay, France) **17/2**

9 *1 ½* **Medeleck (FR)**[50] 2-8-11 0 .... ThomasHuet 3 66
(Mme C De La Soudiere-Niault, France) **41/1**

10 *10* **Kenhope (FR)**[21] 7514 2-8-13 0 .... MaximeGuyon 4 38
(H-A Pantall, France) **33/10**[2]

1m 11.3s (71.30) **10** Ran SP% **115.4**
WIN (incl. 1 euro stake): 7.00. PLACES: 3.00, 4.80, 5.80. DF: 40.20. SF: 88.70.
Owner Mlle Claire Stephenson **Bred** Edy S.R.L. **Trained** France

NOTEBOOK
Strange Magic(IRE), placed at this level over 5f last time, probably did not get home over this longer trip.
Effie B goes well on this sort of ground but never got seriously competitive.

7829a PRIX CONTESSINA (LISTED RACE) (3YO+) (TURF) 6f
1:20 (12:00) 3-Y-0+ **£21,666** (£8,666; £6,500; £4,333; £2,166)

RPR

1 **Eton Rifles (IRE)**[12] 7690 7-9-2 0 .... WilliamCarson 3 111
(Stuart Williams) *w ldrs travelling strly: led over 1 1/2f out: shkn up and r.o wl ent fnl f: asserted fnl 100yds* **21/10**[1]

2 *2* **Personified (GER)**[31] 5-8-8 0 ....(p) MaximeGuyon 2 97
(Mme J Bidgood, France) **11/1**

3 *nk* **Fred Lalloupet**[16] 7624 5-9-2 0 .... GregoryBenoist 1 104
(D Smaga, France) **7/2**[3]

4	hd	**Flash Mash (USA)**[45] 6943 4-8-13 0........................ ThomasMessina 4 (X Nakkachdji, France) **11/1**	100
5	3	**Abu Sidra (FR)**[17] 3-8-11 0........................ MickaelForest 7 (J-F Bernard, France) **14/5**[2]	98+
6	3	**Totxo (IRE)**[16] 7624 4-8-11 0........................(b) Francois-XavierBertras 8 (R Avial Lopez, Spain) **14/1**	88+
7	3	**Namera (GER)**[45] 6943 3-8-8 0........................ TheoBachelot 6 (P Vovcenko, Germany) **51/1**	76+
8	1 1/4	**Best Of Order (IRE)**[44] 5-8-11 0........................(b) AdrienFouassier 9 (E J O'Neill, France) **20/1**	75+
9	7	**Huma Bird**[88] 5647 3-8-8 0........................(p) StephanePasquier 5 (H-A Pantall, France) **16/1**	49+

1m 10.5s (70.50) **9** Ran SP% **116.7**
WIN (incl. 1 euro stake): 3.10. PLACES: 1.50, 2.60, 1.70. DF: 16.80. SF: 20.60.
Owner The Eton Riflemen **Bred** Grangecon Stud **Trained** Newmarket, Suffolk

NOTEBOOK
Eton Rifles(IRE)repeated his 2011 victory, when he accounted for Fred Lalloupet and Personified, the same two horses that chased him home again. It's clearly the right time of year for the son of Pivotal, who was a close third to Mince at Ascot before scoring at Listed level at Doncaster last time out.

7830 - 7836a (Foreign Racing) - See Raceform Interactive

7785 WOLVERHAMPTON (A.W) (L-H)

Friday, November 23

OFFICIAL GOING: Standard
Wind: Fresh against Weather: Fine

7837 32REDBET.COM APPRENTICE H'CAP 5f 216y(P)
4:10 (4:11) (Class 6) (0-52,56) 3-Y-O+ £1,704 (£503; £251) Stalls Low

Form				RPR
4063	1		**Artful Lady (IRE)**[22] 7512 3-8-7 **48**........................ JordanVaughan(7) 7 (George Margarson) *mid-div: hdwy over 2f out: shkn up to ld wl ins fnl f: r.o* **16/1**	57
-004	2	1/2	**Kaylee**[24] 7465 3-8-13 **50**........................ RyanTate(3) 9 (Gary Moore) *chsd ldrs: pushed along over 1f out: led ins fnl f: sn rdn and hdd: edgd rt: styd on* **14/1**	57
0060	3	nk	**Under Par**[171] 2796 4-8-10 **49**........................(t) MatthewHopkins(5) 12 (Michael Easterby) *sn chsng ldr: edgd lft over 5f out: rdn and n.m.r over 1f out: r.o* **9/2**[1]	55
0031	4	1/2	**Reginald Claude**[7] 7748 4-9-1 **56** 6ex........................ EmilyMelbourn(7) 8 (Mark Usher) *mid-div: hdwy over 2f out: nt clr run over 1f out: r.o: nt trble ldrs* **9/2**[1]	60
603/	5	1	**Cookie Crumbles (IRE)**[7] 7754 5-9-2 **50**........................(t) PhilipPrince 3 (Adrian McGuinness, Ire) *mid-div: hmpd over 2f out: rdn and r.o ins fnl f: nrst fin* **6/1**[2]	51+
6045	6	1/2	**Blueberry Fizz (IRE)**[7] 7748 4-8-11 **52**........................(v) BradleyBosley(7) 13 (John Ryan) *sn led and crossed over fr wd draw: rdn and hung lft over 1f out: hdd and no ex* **28/1**	52
6005	7	1 1/2	**Athaakeel (IRE)**[7] 7747 6-9-2 **50**........................ HannahNunn 10 (Ronald Harris) *chsd ldrs: rdn over 1f out: no ex ins fnl f* **20/1**	45
3463	8	1 1/4	**Dixie Gwalia**[7] 7748 4-8-11 **52**........................ SiobhanMiller(7) 2 (David Simcock) *hld up: racd keenly: rdn over 1f out: nvr nrr* **12/1**[3]	43
0053	9	1	**Venetias Dream (IRE)**[24] 7465 3-8-12 **51**........................(t) LouisSteward(5) 6 (Stuart Williams) *sn pushed along towards rr: nvr on terms* **9/2**[1]	39
/036	10	shd	**Burnt Cream**[7] 7746 5-8-11 **52**........................(t) KirstenSmith(7) 4 (Martin Bosley) *s.i.s: hld up: hmpd 5f out: a in rr* **25/1**	39
30-0	11	6	**Doyouknowwhoiam**[48] 6892 3-8-13 **52**........................(p) KevinStott(5) 5 (Geoffrey Oldroyd) *s.s: a in rr* **33/1**	20
051	U		**Coach Montana (IRE)**[17] 7616 3-8-9 **50**........................(b) JoshQuinn(7) 1 (Jane Chapple-Hyam) *mid-div whn hmpd and uns rdr 5f out* **6/1**[2]	

1m 15.23s (0.23) **Going Correction** -0.075s/f (Stan) **12** Ran SP% **118.4**
Speed ratings (Par 101): **95,94,93,93,91 91,89,87,86,86 78,**
toteswingers: 1&2 £19.20, 1&3 £19.70, 2&3 £15.80. CSF £210.39 CT £1185.29 TOTE £20.30: £5.90, £4.10, £2.50; EX 161.80 Trifecta £1080.80 Part won. Pool: £1,441.17 - 0.63 winning units..
Owner Graham Lodge Partnership **Bred** Michael Begley **Trained** Newmarket, Suffolk
■ Jordan Vaughan's first winner.
■ Stewards' Enquiry : Matthew Hopkins five-day ban: careless riding (Dec 7-12)

FOCUS
Restricted to inexperienced apprentices, this was a messy race with Coach Montana losing his rider when badly squeezed against the rail soon after the start (a few others met trouble at the same time), and the loose horse then got in the way in the closing stages. A personal-best from the winner and the form looks reasonable.

7838 32RED SUPPORTING BRITISH RACING MAIDEN STKS 5f 216y(P)
4:40 (4:41) (Class 5) 3-4-Y-O £2,264 (£673; £336; £168) Stalls Low

Form				RPR
4002	1		**Buckland (IRE)**[7] 7743 4-8-10 72........................ NicoleNordblad(7) 1 (Hans Adielsson) *hld up: hdwy over 1f out: rdn to ld ins fnl f: r.o* **11/4**[2]	76
	2	1 1/4	**Appease** 3-9-3 0........................ GrahamGibbons 9 (Dean Ivory) *sn led: hdd 1/2-way: rdn to ld again over 1f out: hdd and unable qck ins fnl f* **14/1**	72
2045	3	2	**Foot Tapper**[14] 7668 3-9-3 62........................ GeorgeBaker 8 (Chris Wall) *led early: chsd ldr tl led 1/2-way: rdn and hdd over 1f out: styd on same pce ins fnl f* **5/1**	66
35	4	3/4	**Saunta**[34] 7253 3-8-12 0........................ PhillipMakin 6 (David Simcock) *hmpd sn after s: plld hrd and sn prom: rdn over 1f out: no ex ins fnl f* **14/1**	58
04	5	1/2	**Rich Again (IRE)**[188] 2262 3-9-3 0........................ RobertWinston 7 (James Bethell) *prom: rdn over 1f out: no ex ins fnl f* **9/4**[1]	62
0	6	1 3/4	**Ioannou**[14] 7667 3-9-3 0........................ StevieDonohoe 2 (Noel Quinlan) *in rr: shkn up over 1f out: nvr nr to chal* **66/1**	56
-000	7	5	**Totally Trusted**[17] 7611 4-8-12 45........................(p) GrahamLee 4 (Scott Dixon) *chsd ldrs: rdn over 2f out: wknd over 1f out* **25/1**	35
506	8	3 1/2	**Busy Bimbo (IRE)**[34] 7253 3-8-12 45........................ TomEaves 5 (Alan Berry) *hld up: rdn and wknd over 1f out* **125/1**	24
020-	9	hd	**Hexagonal (IRE)**[7] 7757 3-9-3 73........................ LukeMorris 3 (Adrian McGuinness, Ire) *chsd ldrs: rdn over 2f out: wknd over 1f out* **7/2**[3]	28

1m 14.77s (-0.23) **Going Correction** -0.075s/f (Stan) **9** Ran SP% **115.8**
Speed ratings (Par 103): **98,96,93,92,92 89,83,78,78**
toteswingers: 1&2 £9.00, 1&3 £3.20, 2&3 £8.00. CSF £39.86 TOTE £2.70: £1.10, £3.20, £1.70; EX 37.00 Trifecta £148.60 Pool: £1,936.21 - 9.77 winning units..
Owner P S McNally **Bred** Airlie Stud And Sir Thomas Pilkington **Trained** Kingston Lisle, Oxon

FOCUS
Not much of a race, but it should produce the odd winner, with the runner-up in particular shaping nicely. the form is taken at face value with the winner, third and fifth close to their marks.

7839 32RED.COM H'CAP 1m 5f 194y(P)
5:10 (5:11) (Class 5) (0-75,74) 3-Y-O+ £2,264 (£673; £336; £168) Stalls Low

Form				RPR
111	1		**Mutual Regard (IRE)**[2] 7811 3-9-3 **71** 6ex........................ LukeMorris 9 (Sir Mark Prescott Bt) *trckd ldrs: led 3f out: shkn up over 1f out: styd on wl* **4/5**[1]	96+
4325	2	2 1/4	**Thecornishcockney**[7] 7744 3-9-1 **69**........................(tp) RobertWinston 10 (John Ryan) *dwlt: hdwy 10f out: chsd wnr over 2f out: rdn over 1f out: no imp fnl f* **15/2**[3]	89
1432	3	15	**Laser Blazer**[15] 7652 4-9-8 **68**........................(p) GeorgeBaker 4 (Jeremy Gask) *sn led: hdd 8f out: chsd ldr tl led again over 3f out: sn hdd and rdn: wknd 2f out* **10/1**	67
2262	4	1/2	**English Summer**[7] 7744 5-9-3 **70**........................(t) AliceHaynes(7) 6 (David Simcock) *hld up: hdwy and nt clr run over 2f out: nvr trbld ldrs* **4/1**[2]	68+
0640	5	3/4	**Swinging Hawk (GER)**[24] 7455 6-10-0 **74**........................ StevieDonohoe 3 (Ian Williams) *hld up: rdn over 1f out: nvr on terms* **12/1**	71
30-0	6	4 1/2	**Kerchak (USA)**[13] 7685 5-9-5 **65**........................ DaleSwift 2 (Brian Ellison) *hld up: pushed along over 4f out: rdn and wknd over 2f out* **50/1**	56
635-	7	3 3/4	**Jezza**[371] 7461 6-9-9 **69**........................ TomMcLaughlin 1 (Karen George) *s.s: outpcd: nvr on terms* **50/1**	55
01-3	8	4 1/2	**Ninfea (IRE)**[181] 2502 4-9-7 **67**........................(p) GrahamLee 12 (David Bridgwater) *prom: rdn over 3f out: wknd over 2f out: t.o* **25/1**	46
	9	2 1/2	**Cool Kid**[134] 4027 4-8-10 **56**........................(b) TomEaves 11 (Eoin Griffin, Ire) *s.s: a towards rr: rdn over 3f out: sn wknd: t.o* **66/1**	32
-245	10	7	**White Diamond**[185] 2363 5-9-7 **67**........................ AndrewMullen 8 (Michael Appleby) *chsd ldrs: wnt 2nd 10f out: led 8f out: rdn and hdd over 3f out: wknd over 2f out: t.o* **33/1**	33
604	11	9	**Honourable Knight (IRE)**[28] 7381 4-9-8 **68**........................ DavidProbert 5 (Mark Usher) *chsd ldr 6f: remained handy: rdn over 4f out: wknd over 2f out: t.o* **25/1**	22

3m 0.1s (-5.90) **Going Correction** -0.075s/f (Stan)
WFA 3 from 4yo+ 8lb **11** Ran SP% **120.2**
Speed ratings (Par 103): **113,111,103,102,102 99,97,95,93,89 84**
toteswingers: 1&2 £2.90, 1&3 £2.40, 2&3 £3.90. CSF £7.21 CT £39.78 TOTE £1.40: £1.02, £2.40, £2.70; EX 7.80 Trifecta £27.00 Pool: £2,119.03 - 58.85 winning units..
Owner Moyglare Stud Farm **Bred** Moyglare Stud Farm Ltd **Trained** Newmarket, Suffolk
■ Stewards' Enquiry : Luke Morris one-day ban: careless riding (Dec 7)

FOCUS
The pace was quicker than normal for a staying handicap on Polytrack and the front two pulled a long way clear. The level is fluid although the winner continues to progress.

7840 32REDPOKER.COM MAIDEN AUCTION STKS 7f 32y(P)
5:40 (5:41) (Class 6) 2-Y-O £1,617 (£481; £240; £120) Stalls High

Form				RPR
633	1		**Jodies Jem**[36] 7191 2-8-11 75........................ GrahamLee 10 (William Jarvis) *trckd ldrs: wnt 2nd over 2f out: shkn up to ld ins fnl f: r.o wl* **4/5**[1]	72
	2	4	**Last Minute Lisa (IRE)**[28] 7389 2-8-4 0........................ LukeMorris 11 (S Donohoe, Ire) *led: rdn over 1f out: hdd and unable qck ins fnl f* **33/1**	55
006	3	3 3/4	**Dha Chara (IRE)**[175] 2663 2-8-11 35........................ GrahamGibbons 1 (Reg Hollinshead) *chsd ldr tl pushed along over 2f out: sn outpcd* **25/1**	53
0	4	nk	**Rex Whistler (IRE)**[88] 5668 2-8-13 0........................ RobertWinston 2 (Julie Camacho) *prom: rdn over 2f out: sn outpcd* **18/1**	54
	5	1	**Lady Malet** 2-8-8 0........................ AdamBeschizza 4 (William Haggas) *hld up: hdwy over 1f out: no ex fnl f* **3/1**[2]	47+
0P	6	5	**Smart Alice**[21] 7525 2-8-6 0........................ AndrewMullen 9 (Chris Wall) *hld up: pushed along over 2f out: nvr on terms* **25/1**	33+
00	7	1 1/4	**Many Levels**[13] 7686 2-8-13 0........................ TomMcLaughlin 3 (John Berry) *mid-div: pushed along 3f out: wkng whn hung lft over 1f out* **16/1**	37
2432	8	1/2	**Storma Norma**[34] 7242 2-8-6 69........................[1] PaulQuinn 5 (Tim Easterby) *prom: rdn over 2f out: wknd over 1f out* **4/1**[3]	28
0	9	1	**Noor Al Haya (IRE)**[37] 7159 2-8-8 0........................[1] DavidProbert 6 (Mark Usher) *s.s: a in rr* **50/1**	28
00	10	3 3/4	**Bryter Layter**[28] 7379 2-8-4 0........................ JackDuern(5) 8 (Christopher Kellett) *s.i.s: a in rr* **200/1**	20

1m 29.86s (0.26) **Going Correction** -0.075s/f (Stan) **10** Ran SP% **124.8**
Speed ratings (Par 94): **95,90,86,85,84 78,77,76,75,71**
toteswingers: 1&2 £7.60, 1&3 £5.00, 2&3 £12.40. CSF £48.47 TOTE £1.80: £1.10, £6.50, £6.70; EX 23.10 Trifecta £336.80 Pool: £1,549.28 - 3.45 winning units..
Owner Mrs M C Banks **Bred** Wickfield Stud And Hartshill Stud **Trained** Newmarket, Suffolk

FOCUS
A weak maiden run at a slow pace, thanks to the 52-rated Last Minute Lisa, who is probably a bit flattered, and it consequently proved hard to make up ground. The winner was not far off his official mark but the form behind is weak.

NOTEBOOK
Jodies Jem was well placed and the only moment of concern came when he had to switch to the inside after the runner-up edged into the centre of the course off the final bend, but he quickly asserted. He's going the right way and should make a fair handicapper. (op 6-5)
Last Minute Lisa(IRE) had the run of the race and is probably flattered.
Dha Chara(IRE) earned an official rating of 35 after three 5f-6f runs earlier in the year, but he returned from 175 days off with an improved performance and should now be given a mark that can get him into handicaps. (op 33-1)
Rex Whistler(IRE), well beaten on his debut three months earlier, was a bit keen early but showed ability. (op 20-1)
Lady Malet, the first foal of a 1m2f winner, could make no impression on this racecourse debut, but the lack of pace gave her little hope and she can probably leave the form well behind. (tchd 10-3)
Storma Norma is out of a Polytrack winner, but was nowhere near her best on this switch from turf. (op 3-1)

7841 £32 BONUS AT 32RED.COM H'CAP 1m 1f 103y(P)
6:10 (6:11) (Class 6) (0-60,60) 3-Y-O+ £1,704 (£503; £251) Stalls Low

Form				RPR
6600	1		**Daniel Thomas (IRE)**[23] 7473 10-9-6 **59**........................(tp) WilliamCarson 11 (Violet M Jordan) *dwlt: hld up: hdwy over 1f out: rdn to ld wl ins fnl f: r.o* **10/1**	69
0005	2	1/2	**Mountrath**[14] 7670 5-9-7 **60**........................(v) GeorgeBaker 3 (Gary Moore) *hld up: hdwy over 1f out: rdn and swtchd lft ins fnl f: r.o* **12/1**	69

0041 **3** ½ **Tatting**[21] 7527 3-9-3 **59** .... GrahamLee 10 67+
(Chris Dwyer) *hld up: hdwy over 2f out: led over 1f out: rdn and hdd wl ins fnl f* **15/8**[1]

5610 **4** ¾ **Archina (IRE)**[21] 7527 3-9-4 **60** .... TedDurcan 5 66
(Chris Wall) *hld up: hdwy over 2f out: rdn and n.m.r over 1f out: styd on same pce ins fnl f* **11/1**

1043 **5** 4 **Community (USA)**[18] 7593 4-9-1 **59** .... LeonnaMayor(5) 9 57
(Jamie Osborne) *broke wl: stdd and lost pl over 7f out: hdwy over 3f out: led wl over 1f out: sn rdn and hdd: no ex ins fnl f* **20/1**

056 **6** nk **No Diamond**[15] 7654 5-9-1 **54** ....(p) LukeMorris 1 51
(Michael Appleby) *s.s: bhd: rdn over 1f out: r.o ins fnl f: nrst fin* **28/1**

2311 **7** nk **Dandarrell**[17] 7620 5-9-6 **59** .... FrederikTylicki 2 56
(Julie Camacho) *hld up: rdn over 1f out: r.o ins fnl f: nvr trbld ldrs* **11/2**[3]

5600 **8** 3¾ **Brown Pete (IRE)**[2] 7816 4-9-1 **54** .... MartinHarley 6 43
(Violet M Jordan) *sn led: clr over 3f out: rdn and hdd wl over 1f out: wknd ins fnl f* **20/1**

3212 **9** 2 **Aragorn Rouge**[6] 7781 4-9-1 **59** .... AdamCarter(5) 12 44
(Keith Dalgleish) *chsd ldrs: rdn over 2f out: n.m.r over 1f out: sn wknd* **4/1**[2]

12-4 **10** 3¾ **Compton Bird**[129] 4186 3-8-11 **60** ....(t[1]) NicoleNordblad(7) 13 37
(Hans Adielsson) *hld up: a in rr* **33/1**

1244 **11** nk **Belle Park**[15] 7643 5-9-0 **53** .... TomMcLaughlin 8 29
(Karen George) *prom: rdn over 3f out: wknd and eased fnl f* **20/1**

-006 **12** 7 **Smirfy's Silver**[253] 909 8-9-4 **57** .... JoeFanning 4 18
(Michael Mullineaux) *chsd ldr tl rdn over 2f out: wknd over 1f out* **40/1**

13 25 **La Zam (FR)**[207] 3-9-4 **60** .... GrahamGibbons 7
(Reg Hollinshead) *chsd ldrs: rdn over 3f out: wknd over 2f out: t.o* **40/1**

1m 59.99s (-1.71) **Going Correction** -0.075s/f (Stan)
WFA 3 from 4yo+ 3lb **13** Ran SP% **120.8**
Speed ratings (Par 101): **104,103,103,102,98 98,98,95,93,89 89,83,61**
toteswingers: 1&2 £10.00, 1&3 £7.00, 2&3 £7.80. CSF £113.15 CT £325.40 TOTE £11.90: £3.10, £4.80, £1.10; EX 137.50 Trifecta £210.80 Pool: £1,208.66 - 4.30 winning units..
Owner Rakebackmypoker.com **Bred** Lawn Stud **Trained** Moreton Morrell, Warwicks

FOCUS
Brown Pete took the field along at an overly strong pace (first seven finishers waited with) and Daniel Thomas, representing the same/owner trainer combination, stayed on best. The first two are rated to last winter's best marks with the fourth back to last month's C&D win.
Compton Bird Official explanation: Jockey said filly hung right-handed
La Zam(FR) Official explanation: Jockey said filly stopped quickly

7842 32RED H'CAP 1m 1f 103y(P)

6:40 (6:43) (Class 4) (0-85,85) 3-Y-0+ **£4,075** (£1,212; £606; £303) **Stalls** Low

Form RPR

3400 **1** **Robin Hoods Bay**[22] 7502 4-9-7 **85** .... LukeMorris 4 97
(Ed Vaughan) *a.p: chsd ldr over 1f out: sn shkn up and edgd lft: styd on to ld wl ins fnl f* **5/1**[2]

1210 **2** ¾ **Multi Bene**[42] 7032 3-8-11 **78** .... GrahamGibbons 1 88
(Ed McMahon) *led: rdn over 1f out: hdd wl ins fnl f* **12/1**

0422 **3** 2¼ **Snow Trooper**[32] 7300 4-8-13 **77** .... TedDurcan 2 82
(Dean Ivory) *hld up: hdwy over 2f out: rdn over 1f out: r.o* **11/1**

1040 **4** ¾ **Patriotic (IRE)**[7] 7751 4-9-2 **80** .... GrahamLee 9 84
(Chris Dwyer) *hld up: hdwy over 1f out: rdn and edgd rt ent fnl f: r.o* **6/1**

41-3 **5** 2¼ **Ajeeb (USA)**[81] 5888 4-9-2 **80** .... GeorgeBaker 13 83+
(David Simcock) *hld up: nt clr run wl over 1f out: hdwy and nt clr run 1f out: r.o: nt rch ldrs* **7/1**

2023 **6** shd **Docs Legacy (IRE)**[42] 7032 3-8-10 **77** .... TonyHamilton 8 76
(Richard Fahey) *mid-div: hdwy over 2f out: rdn and hung lft fr over 1f out: styd on same pce* **4/1**[1]

4646 **7** 1¼ **Focail Maith**[7] 7751 4-8-12 **76** ....(p) StevieDonohoe 6 72
(John Ryan) *hld up: hdwy over 2f out: rdn over 1f out: no ex fnl f* **16/1**

0261 **8** 2½ **Silverware (USA)**[17] 7618 4-8-13 **77** .... PatrickMathers 10 68
(Linda Stubbs) *trckd ldrs: racd keenly: wnt 2nd 4f out: rdn over 1f out: wknd fnl f* **33/1**

4000 **9** 1 **Standpoint**[24] 7461 6-8-8 **77** .... DavidKenny(5) 5 66
(Conor Dore) *hld up: rdn over 1f out: n.d* **33/1**

6300 **10** nse **Spanish Plume**[7] 7751 4-8-6 **75** .... JackDuern(5) 12 64
(Reg Hollinshead) *hld up: nvr on terms* **25/1**

0055 **11** ½ **Fred Willetts (IRE)**[4] 7789 4-9-4 **82** .... TomMcLaughlin 11 70
(Mark Brisbourne) *sn pushed along to chse ldr: lost 2nd 4f out: sn rdn: wknd over 1f out* **20/1**

-411 **12** nk **Star Links (USA)**[63] 6462 6-9-3 **81** ....(b) RobertWinston 7 68
(S Donohoe, Ire) *prom: rdn over 3f out: wknd over 1f out* **11/2**[3]

2-05 **13** 18 **Chosen Forever**[253] 907 7-9-0 **78** .... TomEaves 3 27
(Geoffrey Oldroyd) *prom tl wknd 3f out* **33/1**

1m 58.0s (-3.70) **Going Correction** -0.075s/f (Stan)
WFA 3 from 4yo+ 3lb **13** Ran SP% **118.2**
Speed ratings (Par 105): **113,112,110,109,107 107,106,104,103,103 102,102,86**
toteswingers: 1&2 £19.10, 1&3 £11.80, 2&3 £16.20. CSF £58.41 CT £622.63 TOTE £3.70: £2.30, £3.90, £3.10; EX 72.30 Trifecta £841.70 Part won. Pool: £1,122,39 - 0.30 winning units..
Owner A M Pickering **Bred** Palm Tree Thoroughbreds **Trained** Newmarket, Suffolk

FOCUS
A fair handicap and the form looks sound rated around the third and fourth.
Silverware(USA) Official explanation: Jockey said gelding hung right-handed

7843 32RED CASINO H'CAP (DIV I) 1m 141y(P)

7:10 (7:11) (Class 5) (0-75,75) 3-Y-0+ **£2,264** (£673; £336; £168) **Stalls** Low

Form RPR

1-00 **1** **Trois Vallees (USA)**[156] 3280 3-9-4 **75** .... JoeFanning 10 84+
(James Tate) *trckd ldrs: led over 1f out: shkn up and r.o wl: comf* **9/2**[2]

2 2¼ **Gran Maestro (USA)**[39] 3-9-2 **73** ....(b) DaleSwift 1 77
(Ruth Carr) *chsd ldrs: rdn over 2f out: styd on same pce ins fnl f* **25/1**

600 **3** ½ **Morant Bay (IRE)**[28] 7375 3-9-2 **73** .... StevieDonohoe 7 76
(Ian Williams) *sn led: hdd over 7f out: chsd ldr tl led again over 2f out: rdn and hdd over 1f out: styd on same pce ins fnl f* **33/1**

4 nse **Ferryview Place**[14] 7679 3-8-6 **63** ....(b) LukeMorris 8 66
(Eoin Griffin, Ire) *hld up: hdwy u.p over 1f out: hung lft ins fnl f: nt rch ldrs* **13/2**

6065 **5** shd **Cheers For Thea (IRE)**[27] 7416 7-8-9 **63** ....(bt) TomEaves 5 65
(Tim Easterby) *hld up: hdwy over 1f out: nt rch ldrs* **10/1**

145 **6** ½ **Idol Deputy (FR)**[21] 7529 6-8-7 **66** .... RachealKneller(5) 6 67
(Mark Usher) *prom: pushed along and swtchd lft over 1f out: styd on same pce fnl f* **13/2**

4250 **7** ¾ **Bajan Bear**[7] 7743 4-9-1 **69** .... DavidProbert 9 68
(Michael Blanshard) *hld up: hdwy over 2f out: rdn over 1f out: styd on same pce fnl f* **5/1**[3]

4000 **8** 1½ **Marvo**[23] 7473 8-8-8 **62** ....(b) KellyHarrison 2 58
(Dai Burchell) *s.i.s: nvr nrr* **40/1**

21-0 **9** 3¼ **Avon River**[32] 7300 5-9-5 **73** .... TedDurcan 3 62
(Dean Ivory) *hld up: nvr on terms* **14/1**

33-1 **10** 18 **Yeomanoftheguard**[50] 6827 3-8-9 **66** .... TonyHamilton 4 13
(Richard Fahey) *chsd ldr: led over 7f out: hdd over 2f out: rdn and wknd over 1f out* **9/4**[1]

1m 50.71s (0.21) **Going Correction** -0.075s/f (Stan)
WFA 3 from 4yo+ 3lb **10** Ran SP% **117.3**
Speed ratings (Par 103): **96,94,93,93,93 92,92,90,88,72**
toteswingers: 1&2 £25.20, 1&3 £17.10, 2&3 £31.20. CSF £111.83 CT £3358.15 TOTE £5.40: £2.00, £3.40, £11.00; EX 115.60 TRIFECTA Not won..
Owner Saif Ali **Bred** Stone Farm **Trained** Newmarket, Suffolk

FOCUS
Hand-timed sectionals showed the pace was quite a bit slower than the second division (final time over a second slower), yet Trois Vallees, who was potentially well handicapped, was able to draw clear of a bunch finish for the minor honours. The winner is on good mark with the form behind fluid.
Yeomanoftheguard Official explanation: Jockey said gelding stopped quickly; vet said gelding had irregular heartbeat

7844 32RED CASINO H'CAP (DIV II) 1m 141y(P)

7:40 (7:41) (Class 5) (0-75,72) 3-Y-0+ **£2,264** (£673; £336; £168) **Stalls** Low

Form RPR

5006 **1** **On The Hoof**[17] 7600 3-8-2 **63** .... MatthewHopkins(7) 2 73
(Michael Easterby) *mde all: rdn and edgd rt over 1f out: jst hld on* **12/1**

6046 **2** nse **Aquilonius (IRE)**[15] 7644 3-9-4 **72** ....(t) WilliamCarson 6 82
(Stuart Williams) *trckd wnr: racd keenly: rdn over 1f out: r.o* **11/10**[1]

4024 **3** 1¾ **My Single Malt (IRE)**[17] 7618 4-9-7 **72** .... GrahamLee 7 78
(Julie Camacho) *mid-div: hdwy over 2f out: rdn over 1f out: styd on* **5/2**[2]

5200 **4** ½ **Kingswinford (IRE)**[8] 7725 6-9-5 **70** .... GeorgeBaker 5 75
(Alastair Lidderdale) *hld up: hdwy over 1f out: rdn and hung lft ins fnl f: nt trble ldrs* **8/1**[3]

65U3 **5** 1¾ **Rock Anthem (IRE)**[21] 7530 8-8-11 **62** .... KieranO'Neill 8 63
(Mike Murphy) *s.i.s: hld up: rdn over 1f out: nvr nrr* **10/1**

0610 **6** ½ **Elijah Pepper (USA)**[13] 7684 7-9-1 **71** .... DavidKenny(5) 3 71
(Conor Dore) *hld up: rdn over 1f out: nt trble ldrs* **11/1**

0010 **7** 3¼ **Stylistickhill (IRE)**[17] 7618 4-8-13 **64** ....(t) LukeMorris 9 56
(Scott Dixon) *chsd ldrs: rdn over 1f out: wknd fnl f* **25/1**

6303 **8** 4½ **Glass Mountain (IRE)**[35] 7221 4-9-2 **67** ....(v) GrahamGibbons 4 49
(John Mackie) *chsd ldrs: rdn over 2f out: wknd fnl f* **12/1**

1m 49.43s (-1.07) **Going Correction** -0.075s/f (Stan)
WFA 3 from 4yo+ 3lb **8** Ran SP% **124.0**
Speed ratings (Par 103): **101,100,99,98,97 96,94,90**
toteswingers: 1&2 £4.20, 1&3 £6.30, 2&3 £2.00. CSF £28.04 CT £50.21 TOTE £6.50: £4.80, £1.10, £1.20; EX 36.00 Trifecta £139.60 Pool: £646.30 - 3.47 winning units..
Owner A Chandler & L Westwood **Bred** Whitsbury Manor Stud & Pigeon House Stud **Trained** Sheriff Hutton, N Yorks

FOCUS
A quicker pace than in the first division and the final time was 1.28 seconds faster, but the winner and runner-up raced one-two for most of the way. The first two had dropped to goos marks with the third and fourth the best guides to the level.
Glass Mountain(IRE) Official explanation: vet said gelding bled from the nose
T/Plt: £104.20 to a £1 stake. Pool: £87,035.19 - 609.49 winning tickets. T/Qpdt: £14.20 to a £1 stake. Pool: £12,379.17 - 641.52 winning tickets. CR

7845 - 7851a (Foreign Racing) - See Raceform Interactive

[7753]DUNDALK (A.W) (L-H)

Friday, November 23

OFFICIAL GOING: Standard

7852a DUNDALK STADIUM - LIGHT UP YOUR NIGHT H'CAP 1m 4f (P)

9:25 (9:33) 3-Y-0+ **£7,475** (£1,733; £758; £433)

RPR

1 **Aladdins Cave**[16] 7424 8-9-1 **82** ....(p) RonanWhelan(3) 3 86
(C A Murphy, Ire) *hld up in tch: 6th 1/2-way: hdwy into st to dispute 3rd 2f out: rdn ent fnl f to ld fnl 75yds: kpt on* **12/1**

2 ½ **King Of Aran (IRE)**[27] 7424 5-9-2 **80** .... NGMcCullagh 5 83
(M J Grassick, Ire) *hld up in rr of mid-div: hdwy fr over 2f out: n.m.r in 5th and swtchd rt ins fnl f: kpt on wl towards fin: nvr nrr* **14/1**

3 hd **Solo Performer (IRE)**[28] 7391 7-9-10 **88** ....(b) ChrisHayes 12 91
(H Rogers, Ire) *mid-div: gd hdwy to ld bef 1m out: extended advantage and over 6 l clr 3f out: rdn and strly pressed ent fnl f: hdd fnl 75yds and no ex cl home* **14/1**

4 ¾ **Cul Baire (IRE)**[40] 7089 4-9-6 **84** .... KevinManning 9 85
(J S Bolger, Ire) *hld up in rr of mid-div: edgd rt over 2f out and kpt on u.p fnl f wout troubling principals* **4/1**[1]

5 ¾ **Denny Crane**[28] 7391 6-9-6 **84** .... WayneLordan 1 84
(Edward Lynam, Ire) *hld up in mid-div: prog into st and wnt 4th 1 1/2f out: kpt on same pce fnl f* **11/2**[3]

6 ¾ **Discovery Bay**[28] 7391 4-9-1 **79** .... WJLee 11 78
(C F Swan, Ire) *hld up towards rr: hdwy gng wl fr 2f out whn short of room ent fnl f: swtchd and kpt on towards fin* **9/1**

7 1¼ **The Fox Tully (IRE)**[14] 7681 7-8-9 **78** .... ColinKeane(5) 14 75
(Gerard Keane, Ire) *towards rr: sme late hdwy fr 2f out: nvr a threat* **16/1**

8 hd **Zalanga (IRE)**[42] 7040 3-8-7 **82** ....(t) ConorHoban(5) 13 79
(M Halford, Ire) *nvr bttr than mid-div: kpt on fnl f* **11/2**[3]

9 hd **Prince Chaparral (IRE)**[29] 4666 6-8-12 **79** .... LeighRoche(3) 2 75
(Patrick J Flynn, Ire) *disp early: 4th 1/2-way: rdn in 2nd 2f out and sn no ex* **7/1**

10 1¼ **Beau Michael**[5] 7584 8-8-13 **80** ....(tp) IJBrennan(3) 8 74
(Adrian McGuinness, Ire) *sn led: hdd bef 8f out and racd in 2nd tl wknd fr over 2f out* **20/1**

11 nk **Nanton (USA)**[62] 6493 10-9-9 **87** .... JosephO'Brien 10 81
(Jim Goldie) *w.w in rr: rdn whn hmpd over 2f out and n.d after* **9/2**[2]

12 2 **Admiral Barry (IRE)**[19] 7584 7-9-3 **81** ....(bt[1]) DeclanMcDonogh 4 72
(Eoin Griffin, Ire) *t.k.h: disp early: 3rd 1/2-way: rdn into st and sn no ex* **25/1**

13 nk **The Giving Tree (IRE)**[21] 7519 3-8-7 **77** .... RoryCleary 7 67
(Sylvester Kirk) *nvr bttr than mid-div: pushed along and no ex whn hmpd over 2f out* **7/1**

The Form Book Flat, Raceform Ltd, Compton, RG20 6NL

14 7 **Birzali (FR)**[35] 5930 5-9-3 **81**............(t) FergalLynch 6 60
(John Joseph Hanlon, Ire) *hld up in tch: 5th 1/2-way: pushed along and wknd fr 4f out: eased* **25/1**

2m 30.6s (150.60)
WFA 3 from 4yo+ 6lb **14** Ran SP% **143.3**
Pick Six: Not won. Daily Double: Not won. CSF £196.78 CT £2443.26 TOTE £16.70: £3.60, £6.50, £4.70; DF 245.50.
Owner Treasure Hunters Syndicate **Bred** The Queen **Trained** Gorey, Co Wexford

FOCUS
Probably just a fair handicap, in which Solo Performer was 6l clear turning in. The placed horses help set the level.

NOTEBOOK
Aladdins Cave was 8lb lower than when he last raced at this venue early last month and this versatile performer posted his sixth Flat win and his second over this course and trip, throwing down his challenge from one and a half furlongs out and getting on top well inside the final furlong.
King Of Aran(IRE), twice successful on turf and also a winner over hurdles, had been placed several times here and, on the evidence of this effort, should be able to win a race back here. Held up, he began to close 2f out and when switched right entering the final furlong he ran on well to go second close home.
Solo Performer(IRE), five of whose nine wins have been achieved here, had been very slowly away when third over a slightly shorter trip at the same venue last month. Dashed to the front after about 3f, he was ridden clear well before the straight but the pack began to close under 2f out and he was reeled in well inside the final furlong.
Cul Baire(IRE), winner of a bumper and a 1m6f maiden, was sampling this surface for the first time. He made headway turning for home and stayed on steadily under pressure in the closing stages. (op 5/1)
Denny Crane, a four-time course winner but without a victory for over a year, had shown signs of a return to form here last time. Racing on the inner in midfield, he worked his way forward in the straight but could find no extra inside the final furlong.
T/Jkpt: Not won. T/Plt: @145.10. Pool of @33,641.86 - 173.79 winning units. BF

7853 - (Foreign Racing) - See Raceform Interactive

7812 LINGFIELD (L-H)
Saturday, November 24

OFFICIAL GOING: Standard
Wind: Moderate, across Weather: Rain

7854 32RED SUPPORTING BRITISH RACING (S) STKS 1m (P)
11:40 (11:42) (Class 6) 2-Y-O **£2,181** (£644; £322) **Stalls** High

Form RPR
04 **1** **Amelia Hull**[5] 7786 2-8-6 .... JimmyQuinn 5 54
(J S Moore) *towards rr: hdwy on inner ent st: led ins fnl f: drvn out* **20/1**
00 **2** *nk* **Bubbly Bailey**[14] 7686 2-8-11 .... GrahamLee 9 58+
(Alan Bailey) *towards rr: pushed along 3f out: hdwy over 1f out: pressed wnr fnl f: kpt on u.p* **10/3**[1]
5253 **3** *2 1/4* **Lucy Bee**[49] 6893 2-8-11 **51**............ JoeFanning 10 53
(Keith Dalgleish) *wd: t.k.h: in tch: clsd on ldrs 3f out: outpcd over 1f out: styd on again fnl f* **13/2**[3]
003 **4** *nse* **Dream About You (IRE)**[9] 7721 2-8-7 **69** ow1............(p) RobertHavlin 7 49
(Robert Mills) *chsd ldrs: sltly wd into st: narrow ld 1f out: sn hdd: one pce* **7/2**[2]
5034 **5** *2* **Maypole Joe (IRE)**[130] 4195 2-8-11 **51**............ SilvestreDeSousa 4 48
(David Evans) *prom: wnt 2nd 4f out: chal 2f out: sltly wd into st: no ex fnl f* **40/1**
2604 **6** *hd* **Age Of Bronze**[4] 7795 2-8-11 **62**............ SeanLevey 3 48
(Richard Hannon) *led: sltly wd into st: hrd rdn and hdd 1f out: no ex* **8/1**
0020 **7** *1 1/4* **Unidexter (IRE)**[5] 7785 2-8-6 **57**............ CharlesBishop(5) 1 45
(Mick Channon) *prom tl wknd jst over 1f out* **12/1**
50 **8** *3 1/4* **Whiskeymack**[14] 7686 2-8-11 .... MartinHarley 6 37
(Mick Channon) *in tch: hrd rdn 3f out: sn outpcd* **7/2**[2]
1003 **9** *4* **Myzamour**[5] 7786 2-8-11 **49**............(b) LukeMorris 8 28
(J S Moore) *towards rr: rdn over 4f out: n.d fnl 3f* **14/1**
4005 **10** *1* **Sarahmanda**[34] 7268 2-8-6 **49**............(tp) ChrisCatlin 2 21
(Peter Makin) *a in rr: drvn along and n.d fnl 3f* **80/1**

1m 38.55s (0.35) **Going Correction** 0.0s/f (Stan) **10** Ran SP% **114.8**
Speed ratings (Par 94): **98,97,95,95,93 93,91,88,84,83**
Tote Swingers 1&2 £29.50, 2&3 £8.20, 1&3 £12.30 CSF £83.69 TOTE £21.40: £6.30, £1.70, £1.90; EX 182.90 Trifecta £249.10 Part won. Pool: £332.21 - 0.10 winning tickets..There was no bid for the winner. Bubbly Bailey was subject to a friendly claim.
Owner Ron Hull **Bred** New Hall Stud **Trained** Upper Lambourn, Berks

FOCUS
A moderate seller witha small step forward from the winner, while the third and fifth offer the best guide to the level.

NOTEBOOK
Amelia Hull just held off the gambled-on Bubbly Bailey. She had shaped better than the bare result when fourth in a Wolverhampton claimer on her second start (inside was riding really slow that day) and here she made the most of a ground-saving trip, in the process reversing placings with Myazamour. (op 12-1)
Bubbly Bailey had been well beaten in a couple of maidens, but it's interesting to note he was made favourite for his debut, and the money came for him again. Back up in trip, he just took too long to get the idea, and while this is moderate form, there was a bit more to him physically than most of these. A 34,000gns purchase, he was the subject of two claims, one of which was from his own connections and they managed to keep him. (op 8-1)
Lucy Bee, returning from 49 days off, had a wide trip and is better than she showed. Her connections put in a friendly claim, so presumably believe there might be more to come. (tchd 6-1 and 7-1)
Dream About You(IRE) had upwards of 11lb in hand over those with official ratings (carried 1lb overweight), but she got pushed wide into the straight and failed to see her race out. (op 15-8 tchd 9-2)
Maypole Joe(IRE) might come on for this first run in 130 days. (op 25-1)

7855 BRITISH STALLION STUDS SUPPORTING BRITISH RACING E B F MAIDEN STKS 5f (P)
12:10 (12:11) (Class 5) 2-Y-O **£3,816** (£1,135; £567; £283) **Stalls** High

Form RPR
4 **1** **Royal Acquisition**[8] 7738 2-9-3 0............ JimCrowley 4 72
(Robert Cowell) *sn led: edgd rt away fr rail and jnd by runner-up ins fnl f: sn bk on top: drvn out* **4/7**[1]
04 **2** *3/4* **Ada Lovelace**[16] 7653 2-8-12 0............ JimmyQuinn 1 64
(Dean Ivory) *chsd ldng pair: shkn up over 2f out: got through on rail and jnd wnr ins fnl f: unable qck again nr fin* **12/1**[3]
603 **3** *2 3/4* **Con Leche**[15] 7669 2-9-3 **62**............ SilvestreDeSousa 7 59
(Scott Dixon) *broke wl: pressed wnr: rdn over 2f out: one pce appr fnl f* **20/1**
4 **4** *1 3/4* **Lager Time (IRE)** 2-9-3 0............ AdamKirby 2 53+
(David Evans) *hung rt thrght: in tch: wnt v wd and lost pl on home turn: r.o ins fnl f* **14/1**
22 **5** *2 1/4* **Rangooned**[38] 7176 2-8-12 **66**............ GrahamLee 8 40
(Ann Duffield) *chsd ldrs: pushed along 3f out: wknd wl over 1f out* **11/4**[2]
5 **6** *1/2* **Beauchamp Astra**[15] 7669 2-8-12 0............ J-PGuillambert 5 38
(Hans Adielsson) *pushed along and sn bhd: nvr rchd ldrs* **100/1**
4 **7** *1/2* **Beauchamp Sunset**[15] 7669 2-9-3 0............ GeorgeBaker 6 41
(Hans Adielsson) *t.k.h in 6th: pushed along and n.d fnl 2f* **50/1**
8 *nk* **Somerton Star** 2-9-3 0............ LukeMorris 3 40
(Pat Eddery) *s.s: rn green in rr: n.d* **25/1**

59.82s (1.02) **Going Correction** 0.0s/f (Stan) **8** Ran SP% **116.2**
Speed ratings (Par 96): **91,89,85,82,79 78,77,76**
Tote Swingers 1&2 £3.00, 2&3 £5.40, 1&3 £4.20 CSF £9.11 TOTE £1.70: £1.02, £2.40, £3.60; EX 11.00 Trifecta £62.70 Pool: £564.63 - 6.75 winning tickets..
Owner J Sargeant **Bred** Dunchurch Lodge Stud Co **Trained** Six Mile Bottom, Cambs

FOCUS
The bare form looks just modest, but a few of these are open to significant improvement. The winner and fourth look capable of better.

NOTEBOOK
Royal Acquisition confirmed the promise he showed when fourth in a similar race over C&D on his debut eight days earlier. He's bred to be quite decent and could leave this form behind in time. (op 5-6 tchd 10-11)
Ada Lovelace, dropped in trip, had her chance and was just held by a better one. She can win an ordinary sprint maiden, and handicaps are now an option as well. (op 9-1)
Con Leche again ran respectably, but he might benefit from some headgear to sharpen him up. (op 16-1)
Lager Time(IRE) ◆ is a half-brother to a few winners including a couple of decent sorts, and he's out of a close relation to Group-class sprinter Danehurst. Green to post, it was a surprise to see him finish so close after he hung right and gave away many lengths by failing to handle the bend into the straight. He evidently has a lot of learning to do, but could be alright. Official explanation: Jockey said colt hung right (tchd 16-1)
Rangooned was inclined to go out to her right, noticeably on the first bend, and didn't run to her earlier form. (op 5-2 tchd 9-4)
Beauchamp Astra ◆ was particularly eyecatching, still looking green early and not being given anything like a hard ride in the straight.
Beauchamp Sunset ◆ showed ability and should do better over further once handicapped.
Somerton Star ◆, whose siblings include Ascalon, Captain John Nixon and Resentful Angel, should do better in due course. He started slowly and ran green, but showed a powerful round action in the straight.

7856 32RED CONDITIONS STKS 7f (P)
12:45 (12:46) (Class 3) 2-Y-O **£7,439** (£2,213; £1,106; £553) **Stalls** Low

Form RPR
3161 **1** **Ready (IRE)**[8] 7737 2-9-0 **72**............ AdamKirby 1 82
(Garry Moss) *hld up: effrt on outer ent st: r.o to ld ent fnl f: rdn clr: readily* **9/4**[2]
3320 **2** *2* **Danz Choice (IRE)**[23] 7501 2-9-0 **73**............ SeanLevey 3 77
(Richard Hannon) *in tch: rdn to chse ldrs on inner over 1f out: kpt on to take 2nd ins fnl f* **16/1**
6251 **3** *3/4* **Equitania**[9] 7727 2-8-9 **84**............ GrahamLee 2 70
(Alan Bailey) *led 2f: remained w ldrs: led wl over 1f out tl ent fnl f: one pce* **9/2**
02 **4** *3/4* **Secret Rebel**[10] 7706 2-9-0 0............ LiamKeniry 4 73
(Sylvester Kirk) *hld up: effrt 2f out: styd on same pce: no imp* **7/2**[3]
1423 **5** *1* **Fat Gary**[7] 7773 2-9-3 **87**............ RichardKingscote 5 73
(Tom Dascombe) *rdn to chse ldr sn after s: led over 2f out tl wl over 1f out: no ex fnl f* **2/1**[1]
41 **6** *21* **Multitask**[24] 7481 2-9-3 **73**............ JamieGoldstein 6 19
(Michael Madgwick) *t.k.h: led after 2f tl over 2f out: sn wknd* **25/1**

1m 23.79s (-1.01) **Going Correction** 0.0s/f (Stan) **6** Ran SP% **114.2**
Speed ratings (Par 100): **105,102,101,101,99 75**
Tote Swingers 1&2 £3.70, 2&3 £5.50, 1&3 £2.20 CSF £34.73 TOTE £3.40: £1.70, £3.60; EX 29.20.
Owner Ron Hull **Bred** Kilshannig Stud **Trained** Tickhill, S Yorks

FOCUS
The visual impression was the pace picked up plenty soon enough and the first two, who both came into this rated in the 70s, were the last two to challenge. The time was almost a second quicker than following Class 6 handicap for older horses and this was a step up from the winner.

NOTEBOOK
Ready(IRE) is now 2-2 on Polytrack, following a C&D nursery win gained off 73 eight days earlier. (op 5-2 tchd 11-4)
Danz Choice(IRE), officially rated only 73, looks pretty well exposed, but this was a lot better than his recent Polytrack debut at Kempton. (op 9-1)
Equitania, who was claimed for £16,000 after winning over 6f on Fibresand for David O'Meara last time, couldn't sustain her bid after having plenty of use made of her under these different conditions. (op 7-2 tchd 5-1)
Secret Rebel took too long to pick, not really building on her recent second at Kempton with the shorter straight not appearing to suit. (op 4-1 tchd 9-2)
Fat Gary gets 1m, so connections seemingly wanted to make use of his stamina, but even so he looked to make his move too soon. He's now been below form on both starts here. (op 5-2)
Multitask ran too free. Official explanation: Jockey said gelding ran too free (op 20-1 tchd 33-1)

7857 B & CE'S 70TH ANNIVERSARY H'CAP 7f (P)
1:20 (1:20) (Class 6) (0-65,66) 3-Y-O+ **£2,181** (£644; £322) **Stalls** Low

Form RPR
0660 **1** **Golden Desert (IRE)**[24] 7480 8-9-2 **64**............ GrahamLee 5 72
(Simon Dow) *s.s: hld up in rr: rapid hdwy 1f out: fnd clr run through and str run to ld fnl stride* **6/1**[3]
2630 **2** *hd* **Muhandis (IRE)**[43] 7022 4-9-2 **64**............(b) J-PGuillambert 9 71
(Nick Littmoden) *s.s: sn chsng ldrs: narrow ld 1f out: jst ct* **14/1**
6061 **3** *nk* **Bassett Road (IRE)**[40] 7105 4-9-3 **65**............ JoeFanning 12 71
(Keith Dalgleish) *t.k.h on outer: in tch: drvn to join ldrs ins fnl f: r.o* **11/2**[2]
000 **4** *1/2* **Spin Again (IRE)**[24] 7485 7-9-3 **65**............ AdamKirby 7 70
(John Ryan) *towards rr: gd hdwy fnl f: fin wl* **10/1**
3660 **5** *1/2* **The Mongoose**[222] 1418 4-8-10 **65**............(t) PhilipPrince(7) 6 68
(David Evans) *towards rr: styd on fr over 1f out: nrst fin* **20/1**
5310 **6** *3/4* **Frognal (IRE)**[9] 7725 6-9-3 **65**............(bt) WilliamCarson 2 66
(Violet M Jordan) *stdd s: hld up towards rr: r.o fnl f: nvr nrr* **11/1**
0001 **7** *nse* **Shaunas Spirit (IRE)**[36] 7224 4-8-13 **64**............(p) PatrickHills(3) 10 65
(Dean Ivory) *chsd ldrs: one pce appr fnl f* **25/1**
4000 **8** *shd* **Cornus**[33] 7295 10-9-3 **65**............(be) MartinHarley 4 66
(Alan McCabe) *mid-div: effrt 2f out: styd on same pce* **66/1**
4322 **9** *hd* **Lastkingofscotland (IRE)**[8] 7741 6-9-4 **66**............(b) LukeMorris 14 67
(Conor Dore) *chsd ldr most of way: wknd ins fnl f* **7/1**

0005 **10** *hd* **Bloodsweatandtears**[33] 7302 4-9-2 **64**............................ JimCrowley 8 64
(William Knight) *prom: hrd rdn over 1f out: wknd ins fnl f* **7/2**[1]

0034 **11** *1* **Hawk Moth (IRE)**[82] 5893 4-9-3 **65**............................ RobertWinston 11 62
(John Spearing) *mid-div: rdn and no imp fnl 2f* **14/1**

-000 **12** *nk* **Elsie's Orphan**[24] 7485 5-9-3 **65**............................ GeorgeBaker 1 61
(Patrick Chamings) *in tch: rdn and fdd over 1f out: hld whn n.m.r ins fnl f* **16/1**

-000 **13** *3/4* **Da Ponte**[184] 2413 4-8-12 **65**............................(p) DavidKenny(5) 13 59
(Michael Scudamore) *a in rr: rdn and n.d fnl 2f* **33/1**

4003 **14** *nse* **Waabel**[19] 7589 5-8-12 **65**............................(t) CharlesBishop(5) 3 59
(Violet M Jordan) *led at decent pce: hdd & wknd qckly ent fnl f* **12/1**

1m 24.73s (-0.07) **Going Correction** 0.0s/f (Stan) **14** Ran SP% **121.8**
Speed ratings (Par 101): **100,99,99,98,98 97,97,97,97,96 95,95,94,94**
Tote Swingers 1&2 £21.00, 2&3 £14.60, 1&3 £9.80 CSF £84.91 CT £511.12 TOTE £10.10: £2.90, £5.00, £2.00; EX 143.40 Trifecta £424.70 Part won. Pool: £566.30 - 0.40 winning tickets..
Owner T G Parker **Bred** Mervyn Stewkesbury **Trained** Epsom, Surrey

FOCUS
Typically for a Lingfield handicap, a bunch finish and this form is ordinary and isn't worth much.
Elsie's Orphan Official explanation: Jockey said mare suffered interference in running

7858 BRITISH STALLION STUDS E.B.F./32RED.COM FILLIES' H'CAP 1m (P)
1:55 (1:56) (Class 4) (0-85,85) 3-Y-0+ **£5,175** (£1,540; £769; £384) **Stalls** High

Form RPR

2626 **1** **Gifted Girl (IRE)**[29] 7375 3-9-5 **85**............................ SilvestreDeSousa 3 97
(Paul Cole) *mde all: kicked 2 l clr 4f out: pushed further clr and in command fnl 2f: comf* **5/2**[1]

1023 **2** *4 1/2* **Rugosa**[105] 5107 3-8-12 **78**............................ RobertWinston 8 83+
(Charles Hills) *hld up towards rr: nt clr run arnd home turn: gd hdwy over 1f out: r.o to take 2nd ins fnl f* **10/3**[2]

0046 **3** *1 3/4* **Adorable Choice (IRE)**[18] 7618 4-8-2 **71** oh3........(v) NatashaEaton(5) 4 69
(Tom Dascombe) *w wnr for 4f: sltly outpcd 3f out: lost 2nd ins fnl f* **12/1**

0006 **4** *3/4* **Deire Na Sli (IRE)**[55] 6702 4-9-2 **80**............................(b) LukeMorris 2 76
(Martyn Meade) *chsd ldrs: outpcd fnl 3f* **25/1**

0516 **5** *3/4* **Caramelita**[22] 7524 5-8-9 **73** ow1............................(v) GrahamLee 7 68
(J R Jenkins) *hld up in rr: hdwy on inner ent st: unable to sustain run* **14/1**

2600 **6** *2 1/4* **Emman Bee (IRE)**[8] 7741 3-8-5 **71**............................ JoeFanning 9 60
(John Gallagher) *towards rr on outer: rdn and nt trble ldrs fnl 2f* **8/1**

540 **7** *3/4* **Epernay**[31] 7334 5-8-13 **77**............................(vt) StevieDonohoe 5 65
(Ian Williams) *s.i.s: in tch tl rdn and outpcd fnl 2f* **13/2**

522 **8** *1 1/4* **Young Dottie**[72] 6172 6-8-8 **77**............................ JemmaMarshall(5) 10 62
(Pat Phelan) *t.k.h: pressed ldrs tl wknd 3f out* **11/2**[3]

9 *15* **Kindia (IRE)**[411] 4-9-3 **81**............................(v[1]) JimCrowley 1 31
(Michael Attwater) *chsd ldrs: wknd 3f out: sn bhd* **25/1**

1m 36.04s (-2.16) **Going Correction** 0.0s/f (Stan)
WFA 3 from 4yo+ 2lb **9** Ran SP% **113.5**
Speed ratings (Par 102): **110,105,103,103,102 100,99,98,83**
Tote Swingers 1&2 £2.30, 2&3 £8.60, 1&3 £7.10 CSF £10.51 CT £79.49 TOTE £2.80: £1.20, £2.00, £3.70; EX 10.30 Trifecta £132.00 Pool: £986.26 - 5.60 winning tickets..
Owner A D Spence **Bred** Airlie Stud **Trained** Whatcombe, Oxon

FOCUS
A weak fillies' handicap for the class in which the runner-up is rated to form at face value.
Kindia(IRE) Official explanation: Jockey said filly moved poorly down the hill and stopped quickly

7859 32RED CASINO H'CAP (DIV I) 5f (P)
2:25 (2:25) (Class 4) (0-85,85) 3-Y-0+ **£5,175** (£1,540; £769; £384) **Stalls** High

Form RPR

4021 **1** **Sonko (IRE)**[16] 7648 3-9-0 **78**............................(p) ShaneKelly 5 87
(Tim Pitt) *mde all: rdn over 2 l ahd over 1f out: hld on fnl f* **7/1**

2001 **2** *1/2* **Millibar (IRE)**[24] 7483 3-9-2 **80**............................(b) TomMcLaughlin 6 87
(Nick Littmoden) *dwlt: sn in tch on outer: rdn 2f out: clsd on wnr fnl f: wnt 2nd nr fin: a hld* **10/1**

1222 **3** *1/2* **Drawnfromthepast (IRE)**[9] 7726 7-9-5 **83**............................ AdamKirby 9 88
(Jamie Osborne) *chsd ldrs: drvn into 2nd over 1f out: styd on fnl f* **3/1**[1]

5443 **4** *3/4* **Bubbly Ballerina**[9] 7726 3-8-12 **76**............................ GrahamLee 8 80
(Alan Bailey) *chsd ldrs: stmbld over 2f out: rdn and kpt on same pce* **5/1**[3]

0000 **5** *nk* **Speightowns Kid (USA)**[50] 6837 4-8-7 **71** oh6............................ JoeFanning 2 73
(Jo Hughes) *chsd wnr tl no ex over 1f out* **20/1**

-001 **6** *1 1/4* **Dorback**[9] 7730 5-9-2 **80**............................ GeorgeBaker 3 77
(David Nicholls) *towards rr most of way: shkn up over 1f out: styng on at fin* **7/2**[2]

1002 **7** *1 1/2* **Rowe Park**[16] 7646 9-9-7 **85**............................(p) LiamKeniry 4 77
(Linda Jewell) *mid-div: hrd rdn and no imp over 1f out* **5/1**[3]

0000 **8** *1 1/2* **Khawatim**[19] 7595 4-9-0 **78**............................ StevieDonohoe 10 64
(Noel Quinlan) *hld up and bhd: shkn up over 1f out: nvr nr ldrs* **40/1**

000 **9** *8* **Cadeaux Pearl**[43] 7019 4-9-4 **82**............................(b) SilvestreDeSousa 7 40
(Scott Dixon) *a towards rr: lost tch 2f out* **12/1**

58.63s (-0.17) **Going Correction** 0.0s/f (Stan) **9** Ran SP% **117.0**
Speed ratings (Par 105): **101,100,99,98,97 95,93,90,78**
Tote Swingers 1&2 £6.90, 2&3 £7.90, 1&3 £3.20 CSF £75.19 CT £257.29 TOTE £6.20: £2.00, £3.60, £1.20; EX 59.40 Trifecta £217.50 Pool: £646.86 - 2.23 winning tickets..
Owner Dr Marwan Koukash **Bred** Tally-Ho Stud **Trained** Newmarket, Suffolk

FOCUS
The time was 0.44 seconds faster than the other division. The winner is rated close to his latest C&D win backed up by the placed horses.
Bubbly Ballerina Official explanation: Jockey said filly clipped heels on the home bend
Cadeaux Pearl Official explanation: Jockey said gelding moved poorly

7860 32RED CASINO H'CAP (DIV II) 5f (P)
3:00 (3:00) (Class 4) (0-85,83) 3-Y-0+ **£5,175** (£1,540; £769; £384) **Stalls** High

Form RPR

0336 **1** **Rylee Mooch**[9] 7726 4-8-12 **74**............................(e) RobbieFitzpatrick 6 83
(Richard Guest) *hld up in rr: hdwy on inner ent st: led ins fnl f: drvn out* **8/1**

0241 **2** *1/2* **Ring For Baileys**[7] 7775 3-9-2 **78**............................ JoeFanning 2 85+
(Chris Dwyer) *rdn to ld: hdd ins fnl f: kpt on u.p* **7/2**[2]

0101 **3** *nk* **Forest Edge (IRE)**[34] 7273 3-9-2 **78**............................(b) MartinHarley 4 84
(David Evans) *in tch: rdn 2f out: edgd lft and nt clr run over 1f out: r.o wl nr fin* **9/2**[3]

504 **4** *3/4* **Six Wives**[9] 7726 5-9-4 **80**............................ SilvestreDeSousa 9 83
(Scott Dixon) *sn w ldrs on outer: one pce ent fnl f* **5/1**

0056 **5** *1 1/2* **Fathom Five (IRE)**[16] 7648 8-8-7 **69** oh1............................ WilliamCarson 1 67
(Gary Moore) *chsd ldrs: rdn 2f out: one pce* **9/2**[3]

0001 **6** *4 1/2* **Royal Bajan (USA)**[9] 7726 4-9-7 **83**............................(b) GrahamLee 7 65
(James Given) *prom tl wknd jst over 1f out* **5/2**[1]

0300 **7** *3 1/4* **Island Legend (IRE)**[10] 7704 6-9-6 **82**............................(p) ChrisCatlin 8 52
(Milton Bradley) *dwlt: pushed along towards rr on outer: n.d fnl 2f* **12/1**

59.07s (0.27) **Going Correction** 0.0s/f (Stan) **7** Ran SP% **122.6**
Speed ratings (Par 105): **97,96,95,94,92 84,79**
Tote Swingers 1&2 £5.70, 2&3 £3.20, 1&3 £10.50 CSF £39.17 CT £147.43 TOTE £8.80: £3.50, £2.30; EX 25.10 Trifecta £345.10 Pool: £598.30 - 1.30 winning tickets..
Owner Katie Hughes,Julie McCarlie,Sheila White **Bred** Mrs Sheila White **Trained** Stainforth, S Yorks

FOCUS
A slower time than the first division. The winner and third were helped by coming off the pace and the second did best of those to race up with the pace.
Six Wives Official explanation: Jockey said mare hung left

7861 £32 BONUS AT 32RED.COM H'CAP 6f (P)
3:35 (3:35) (Class 6) (0-60,60) 3-Y-0+ **£2,181** (£644; £322) **Stalls** Low

Form RPR

0030 **1** **Glastonberry**[117] 4653 4-9-2 **57**............................ GeorgeBaker 10 69
(Geoffrey Deacon) *mid-div: hdwy 2f out: r.o to ld fnl 100yds* **8/1**

0-00 **2** *2* **Spartic**[24] 7484 4-9-3 **58**............................ SeanLevey 2 64
(Alan McCabe) *led: rdn over 2 l clr over 1f out: hdd and no ex fnl 100yds* **11/2**[3]

6000 **3** *shd* **Chjimes (IRE)**[19] 7589 8-9-3 **58**............................(b) LiamKeniry 9 64
(Conor Dore) *in tch: drvn to chse ldrs ent fnl f: styd on* **14/1**

1243 **4** *1/2* **Strategic Action (IRE)**[24] 7482 3-9-2 **57**............................(tp) RobertHavlin 6 61
(Linda Jewell) *chsd ldrs: effrt 2f out: one pce fnl f* **5/1**[2]

5042 **5** *1/2* **Loyal Royal (IRE)**[24] 7482 9-9-5 **60**............................(bt) GrahamLee 11 62
(Milton Bradley) *t.k.h in midfield on outer: styd on u.p fnl 2f* **7/1**

2266 **6** *hd* **Lucky Mark (IRE)**[4] 7794 3-9-3 **58**............................ JimmyQuinn 1 60
(Garry Moss) *prom: chsd ldr 3f out tl over 1f out: one pce* **9/2**[1]

0600 **7** *2* **Kings 'n Dreams**[40] 7113 5-9-2 **57**............................ JimCrowley 12 52
(Dean Ivory) *hld up in rr of midfield: shkn up and sme hdwy over 1f out: no imp* **8/1**

0050 **8** *nk* **Frock (IRE)**[268] 743 3-8-12 **58**............................ LeeNewnes(5) 4 52
(Sylvester Kirk) *sn wl bhd: shkn up over 1f out: styd on wl fnl f* **33/1**

/060 **9** *nk* **Sextons House (IRE)**[14] 7684 4-9-5 **60**............................ MartinHarley 5 54
(Alan McCabe) *t.k.h towards rr: rdn 2f out: nvr trbld ldrs* **10/1**

4100 **10** *1 1/4* **Ryedale Dancer (IRE)**[26] 7446 4-9-2 **57**............................ RobbieFitzpatrick 7 47
(Richard Guest) *dwlt: bhd: pushed along 3f out: sme hdwy on inner ent st: no further prog* **16/1**

0204 **11** *1/2* **Nine Before Ten (IRE)**[15] 7673 4-9-2 **57**............................(t) SilvestreDeSousa 8 45
(Charles Smith) *chsd ldrs: rdn over 2f out: sn wknd* **20/1**

0540 **12** *1/2* **Bailadeira**[25] 7456 4-9-2 **60**............................ PatrickHills(3) 3 46
(Tim Etherington) *chsd ldr tl 3f out: wknd over 1f out: 6th and btn whn hmpd ins fnl f* **33/1**

1m 11.91s (0.01) **Going Correction** 0.0s/f (Stan) **12** Ran SP% **117.2**
Speed ratings (Par 101): **99,96,96,95,94 94,91,91,91,89 88,88**
Tote Swingers 1&2 £16.70, 2&3 £14.40, 1&3 £34.80 CSF £49.90 CT £615.12 TOTE £11.10: £3.50, £2.90, £3.50; EX 73.60 TRIFECTA Not won..
Owner Jim Kelly **Bred** Geoffrey Deacon **Trained** Upper Basildon, Berks

FOCUS
A moderate sprint handicap in which the fourth and fifth are rated close to their latest C&D form and help set the standard.
Nine Before Ten(IRE) Official explanation: Jockey said mare hung right
T/Plt: £202.20 to a £1 stake. Pool: £56,801.80 - 205.01 winning tickets. T/Qpdt: £45.20 to a £1 stake. Pool: £5,828.90 - 95.30 winning tickets. LM

7837 WOLVERHAMPTON (A.W) (L-H)
Saturday, November 24

OFFICIAL GOING: Standard
Wind: Light, across Weather: Raining

7862 32RED SUPPORTING BRITISH RACING H'CAP 2m 119y(P)
5:50 (5:50) (Class 6) (0-60,65) 3-Y-0+ **£2,070** (£616; £307; £153) **Stalls** Low

Form RPR

6011 **1** **Italian Riviera**[10] 7717 3-9-8 **65**............................ LukeMorris 12 77
(Sir Mark Prescott Bt) *hld up: hdwy over 6f out: rdn to chse ldr over 2f out: styd on u.p to ld wl ins fnl f* **10/11**[1]

52/1 **2** *nk* **Goldan Jess (IRE)**[21] 6399 8-9-0 **48**............................ AdamKirby 3 60
(Philip Kirby) *led 1f: chsd ldr tl over 9f out: remained handy: wnt 2nd again over 4f out: led wl over 2f out: rdn over 1f out: hdd wl ins fnl f* **11/1**

404 **3** *3 3/4* **Entitlement**[19] 7594 3-9-1 **58**............................ MartinLane 11 65
(James Fanshawe) *hld up: pushed along 6f out: hdwy over 2f out: sn rdn: styd on: nt rch ldrs* **11/2**[3]

0-23 **4** *7* **Annaluna (IRE)**[34] 7271 3-8-13 **56**............................(v) GrahamGibbons 1 57
(David Evans) *led after 1f: rdn and hdd wl over 2f out: wknd over 1f out* **10/1**

2343 **5** *18* **Sheila's Castle**[70] 6262 8-9-2 **57**............................ ConorHarrison(7) 10 34
(Sean Regan) *s.i.s: hld up: hdwy over 5f out: hung lft and wknd wl over 3f out* **20/1**

214 **6** *hd* **Blue Zealot (IRE)**[22] 7528 5-9-5 **56**............................(t) RachaelGreen(3) 13 33
(Anthony Honeyball) *hld up: hdwy over 6f out: sn pushed along: wknd 4f out* **4/1**[2]

65/6 **7** *10* **Elysian Heights (IRE)**[24] 7490 4-9-0 **53**....(t) WilliamTwiston-Davies(5) 2 18
(Nigel Twiston-Davies) *prom: pushed along over 5f out: rdn and wknd over 3f out: t.o* **28/1**

0000 **8** *6* **Before Bruce**[3] 7819 5-9-10 **58**............................(bt) RichardKingscote 9 16
(Brendan Powell) *chsd ldrs: wnt 2nd over 9f out tl over 4f out: sn rdn: wknd over 2f out: t.o* **40/1**

3m 39.07s (-2.73) **Going Correction** -0.125s/f (Stan)
WFA 3 from 4yo+ 9lb **8** Ran SP% **115.8**
Speed ratings (Par 101): **101,100,99,95,87 87,82,79**
toteswingers: 1&2 £3.10, 1&3 £2.10, 2&3 £6.00 CSF £12.46 CT £38.82 TOTE £1.90: £1.30, £1.70, £1.50; EX 9.00 Trifecta £27.90 Pool: £1,231.28 - 33.03 winning units..
Owner J L C Pearce **Bred** J L C Pearce **Trained** Newmarket, Suffolk
■ Stewards' Enquiry : Luke Morris two-day ban: used whip above shoulder height (Dec 8,10)

FOCUS
A moderate staying handicap, hit by non-runners. The winner is still learning and the second is ratec close to his best Flat form since his early days.

7863 32RED.COM H'CAP (DIV I) 5f 216y(P)
6:20 (6:21) (Class 5) (0-70,70) 3-Y-0+ **£2,911** (£866; £432; £108; £108) **Stalls** Low

Form RPR

2365 **1** **Mother Jones**[7] 7775 4-8-12 **68**............................ EoinWalsh(7) 6 78
(David Evans) *s.i.s: hld up: hdwy 2f out: led ins fnl f: r.o* **10/1**

1525 **2** *2* **Red Cape (FR)**[16] 7651 9-9-7 **70**..(b) DaleSwift 7 74
(Ruth Carr) *sn pushed along to ld: hdd over 3f out: rdn to ld over 1f out: hdd and unable qck ins fnl f* **7/1**
0454 **3** *nk* **Greenhead High**[7] 7775 4-9-2 **65**.................................. AdrianNicholls 1 68
(David Nicholls) *w ldr tl led over 3f out: rdn and hdd over 1f out: styd on same pce ins fnl f* **6/1**[3]
1235 **4** *nk* **Hello Stranger (IRE)**[33] 7291 3-9-6 **69**................................ TedDurcan 4 71+
(Tim Easterby) *s.i.s: sn pushed along in rr: hdwy over 1f out: r.o: nt rch ldrs* **3/1**[1]
4060 **4** *dht* **For Shia And Lula (IRE)**[15] 7666 3-9-5 **68**..................(be[1]) ShaneKelly 3 70
(Daniel Mark Loughnane) *a.p: rdn 1/2-way: styd on u.p* **22/1**
6000 **6** *2* **Saucy Brown (IRE)**[8] 7741 6-9-3 **66**..............................(t) PhillipMakin 5 61
(Kevin Ryan) *sn pushed along and prom: rdn and nt clr run over 1f out: no imp fnl f* **4/1**[2]
5350 **7** *1 3/4* **Lady Mango (IRE)**[24] 7404 4-9-2 **65**.................................. LukeMorris 2 55
(Ronald Harris) *mid-div: sn pushed along: outpcd 4f out: styd on ins fnl f* **14/1**
0050 **8** *nk* **Vale Of Clara (IRE)**[18] 7607 4-9-5 **68**.................................. TomEaves 9 57
(Peter Niven) *sn pushed along in rr: nvr nrr* **50/1**
000 **9** *1/2* **Golconde (IRE)**[22] 7524 3-9-0 **68**..................(p) MichaelJMMurphy(5) 13 55
(Robert Cowell) *prom: rdn over 2f out: wknd fnl f* **28/1**
0010 **10** *1/2* **Zip Lock (IRE)**[14] 7685 6-9-4 **70**...................................... RyanClark(3) 12 55
(Tom Keddy) *chsd ldrs: rdn over 2f out: wknd fnl f* **28/1**
0041 **11** *1 1/4* **Prince James**[18] 7604 5-9-4 **67**................................ GrahamGibbons 11 48
(Michael Easterby) *broke wl: sn lost pl: nvr on terms afterwards* **8/1**
0000 **12** *5* **Blown It (USA)**[28] 7412 6-9-4 **67**.. JoeFanning 8 32
(Keith Dalgleish) *prom: rdn over 2f out: wknd over 1f out* **16/1**

1m 14.49s (-0.51) **Going Correction** -0.125s/f (Stan) **12** Ran SP% **117.7**
Speed ratings (Par 103): **98,95,94,94,94 91,89,89,88,87 86,79**
toteswingers: 1&2 £14.20, 1&3 £13.60, 2&3 £8.60 CSF £74.79 CT £470.30 TOTE £10.00: £3.00, £2.40, £2.00; EX 60.80 Trifecta £256.00 Pool: £624.74 - 1.83 winning units..
Owner Mike Nolan **Bred** New Hall Stud **Trained** Pandy, Monmouths

FOCUS
A modest sprint handicap run slightly slower than division I. Few got involved, and this is straightforward form.

7864 32RED.COM H'CAP (DIV II) 5f 216y(P)
6:50 (6:52) (Class 5) (0-70,70) 3-Y-O+ **£2,911** (£866; £432; £216) **Stalls** Low

Form RPR
0001 **1** **Gung Ho Jack**[19] 7589 3-9-4 **67**...................................... GeorgeBaker 10 75
(John Best) *chsd ldr tl led over 1f out: rdn out* **5/1**[2]
3022 **2** *hd* **Another Citizen (IRE)**[15] 7666 4-9-6 **69**..........................(b) TedDurcan 9 76
(Tim Easterby) *chsd ldrs: rdn over 1f out: r.o* **3/1**[1]
0344 **3** *1/2* **Restless Bay (IRE)**[63] 6498 4-9-5 **68**..........................(v) MartinHarley 7 73
(Mrs K Burke) *hld up: hdwy over 1f out: swtchd rt ins fnl f: r.o: nt rch ldrs* **15/2**
4302 **4** *1 1/4* **Bull Bay**[16] 7007 3-8-9 **65**.. IanBurns(7) 13 66
(Jane Chapple-Hyam) *chsd ldrs: ev ch over 1f out: styd on same pce ins fnl f* **9/1**
0000 **5** *3/4* **Desert Strike**[16] 7648 6-9-4 **67**..(p) AdamKirby 2 66
(Conor Dore) *hld up in tch: nt clr run fr over 1f out tl r.o ins fnl f: nvr able to chal* **20/1**
0110 **6** *hd* **Danzoe (IRE)**[24] 7489 5-9-5 **68**.................................... TomMcLaughlin 4 66
(Christine Dunnett) *prom: rdn over 1f out: styd on same pce ins fnl f* **28/1**
3031 **7** *nse* **Dark Lane**[19] 7590 6-9-3 **66**.. AndreaAtzeni 3 64
(David Evans) *mid-div: rdn over 1f out: r.o ins fnl f: nvr trbld ldrs* **6/1**[3]
0023 **8** *1/2* **Ryan Style (IRE)**[28] 7412 6-9-7 **70**..................................(v) TomEaves 11 67
(Lisa Williamson) *s.i.s: hld up: hdwy over 1f out: sn rdn: r.o: nt rch ldrs* **18/1**
3600 **9** *3/4* **Colourbearer (IRE)**[130] 4187 5-9-2 **65**.................(t) RichardKingscote 12 59
(Milton Bradley) *mid-div: hdwy over 2f out: rdn over 1f out: styd on same pce fnl f* **25/1**
4200 **10** *1 3/4* **Diamond Vine (IRE)**[34] 7273 4-9-5 **68**............................(p) LukeMorris 8 57
(Ronald Harris) *broke wl: lost pl 5f out: n.d after* **16/1**
0006 **11** *1 1/2* **Master Of Disguise**[7] 7775 6-9-5 **68**.............................. WilliamCarson 1 52
(Brian Baugh) *sn led: rdn and hdd over 1f out: wknd ins fnl f* **12/1**
0-00 **12** *1 3/4* **Johnstown Lad (IRE)**[15] 7666 8-9-2 **65**............................(t) ShaneKelly 6 43
(Daniel Mark Loughnane) *sn pushed along in rr: n.d* **50/1**
6004 **13** *1/2* **Full Shilling (IRE)**[28] 7411 4-9-3 **66**.............................. RobertWinston 5 43
(John Spearing) *s.i.s: in rr: hdwy over 1f out: wknd fnl f* **11/1**

1m 14.1s (-0.90) **Going Correction** -0.125s/f (Stan) **13** Ran SP% **118.9**
Speed ratings (Par 103): **101,100,100,98,97 97,97,96,95,93 91,88,88**
toteswingers: 1&2 £4.00, 1&3 £8.80, 2&3 £5.60 CSF £19.28 CT £113.90 TOTE £6.60: £2.10, £1.80, £2.40; EX 27.40 Trifecta £80.20 Pool: £607.84 - 5.68 winning units..
Owner John Fletcher **Bred** D R Tucker **Trained** Hucking, Kent

FOCUS
The second and slightly faster division of the 6f handicap, and straightforward form judged around the second.

7865 32REDPOKER.COM (S) STKS 5f 216y(P)
7:20 (7:20) (Class 6) 2-Y-O **£2,070** (£616; £307; £153) **Stalls** Low

Form RPR
2312 **1** *shd* **Marmot Bay (IRE)**[16] 7650 2-8-13 60 ow1.......................... AdamKirby 3 62
(Jamie Osborne) *chsd ldr 1f: remained handy: wnt 2nd again 2f out: sn rdn: edgd lft over 1f out: sn ev ch carried rt wl ins fnl f: styd on: fin 2nd: plcd 1st* **11/8**[1]
3363 **2** **Windforpower (IRE)**[9] 7727 2-9-3 68..............................(p) LukeMorris 4 66
(Ronald Harris) *sn prom: rdn over 2f out: led 1f out: styd on u.p: hung rt wl ins fnl f: all out: fin 1st: plcd 2nd* **7/2**[2]
2650 **3** *2 1/2* **Otto The First**[26] 7439 2-8-12 54..............................(p) GrahamGibbons 7 53
(John Best) *chsd ldr 5f out tl rdn 2f out: styd on same pce ins fnl f* **40/1**
5 **4** *1/2* **Squawk**[9] 7727 2-8-7 0.. AndrewMullen 6 47
(Bill Turner) *sn pushed along towards rr: drvn along 1/2-way: r.o ins fnl f: nt rch ldrs* **25/1**
0060 **5** *1 1/4* **Summer Isles**[9] 7724 2-8-7 63..(p) MartinLane 5 43
(Ed Vaughan) *led: hung rt over 2f out: rdn and hdd 1f out: no ex* **5/1**
0000 **6** *3* **Sunny Hollow**[24] 7476 2-8-7 60.. JoeFanning 1 34
(James Toller) *s.i.s: outpcd: hdwy over 1f out: no ex fnl f* **4/1**[3]
1000 **7** *4 1/2* **Harleys Rocket**[80] 5940 2-8-12 60............................ RichardKingscote 2 25
(Brendan Powell) *in tch: lost pl over 4f out: bhd fr 1/2-way* **14/1**

1m 15.43s (0.43) **Going Correction** -0.125s/f (Stan) **7** Ran SP% **113.9**
Speed ratings (Par 94): **91,92,88,87,86 82,76**
toteswingers: 1&2 £1.40, 1&3 £9.40, 2&3 £14.60 CSF £6.35 TOTE £2.40: £1.50, £1.50; EX 5.90.There was no bid for the winner.
Owner J A Osborne **Bred** J C Bloodstock **Trained** Upper Lambourn, Berks
■ Stewards' Enquiry : Luke Morris three-day ban: careless riding (Dec 11-13)

FOCUS
A moderate 2-y-o seller and the stewards reversed placings of the first pair in the subsequent enquiry. The first two set the level which is limited by the third.

NOTEBOOK
Marmot Bay(IRE) was carried right by the leader near the finish and that was enopugh to see him handed the race by the stewards. He has now won his last two outings over C&D in this company. (tchd 11-10 and 6-4)
Windforpower(IRE) passed the post in front, but had hung right near the finish and the stewards deemed that was enough to hand the verdict to the second. He's effective on both this surface and Polytrack and can surely be placed to gain compensation in this class. (op 9-2)
Otto The First travelled kindly just off the pace, but lacked a change of gear under pressure and may prefer reverting to 7f in this sort of company. (op 28-1)
Squawk left the impression she ought to a pick up a race in this grade over a stiffer test. (op 28-1)

7866 32RED CASINO NURSERY 5f 216y(P)
7:50 (7:51) (Class 5) (0-75,75) 2-Y-O **£2,911** (£866; £432; £216) **Stalls** Low

Form RPR
6431 **1** **Space Artist (IRE)**[15] 7669 2-9-7 **75**...................................... TomEaves 7 77
(Bryan Smart) *sn led: hrd rdn ins fnl f: all out* **11/4**[1]
2042 **2** *nk* **Desert Sunrise**[7] 7777 2-9-2 **70**.. DavidProbert 3 71+
(Sir Michael Stoute) *chsd ldrs: swtchd lft over 1f out: sn rdn: r.o* **7/2**[3]
4325 **3** *shd* **Indian Affair**[8] 7745 2-8-12 **66**.................................. RichardKingscote 5 67
(Milton Bradley) *led early: chsd wnr: rdn and ev ch 1f out: r.o: rdr dropped whip wl ins fnl f* **11/2**
1603 **4** *3/4* **Ovett**[8] 7745 2-9-3 **71**.. GeorgeBaker 6 70
(Gary Moore) *broke wl: sn stdd and lost pl: hdwy over 2f out: rdn over 1f out: styd on* **10/3**[2]
0225 **5** *4 1/2* **Spicy (IRE)**[64] 6453 2-9-6 **74**.. AdamKirby 1 59
(Marco Botti) *chsd ldrs: rdn over 1f out: wknd wl ins fnl f* **9/2**
6400 **6** *5* **Charm Cry (USA)**[24] 7476 2-8-8 **62**.................................. JoeFanning 4 32
(Mark Johnston) *hld up: effrt over 2f out: wknd over 1f out* **14/1**

1m 14.7s (-0.30) **Going Correction** -0.125s/f (Stan) **6** Ran SP% **112.2**
Speed ratings (Par 96): **97,96,96,95,89 82**
toteswingers: 1&2 £1.20, 1&3 £3.00, 2&3 £3.40 CSF £12.60 TOTE £3.60: £2.60, £1.10; EX 9.40.
Owner The Smart Dame Laura Partnership **Bred** Rathasker Stud **Trained** Hambleton, N Yorks

FOCUS
An ordinary nursery that saw a tight finish and straightforward form rated around the placed horses.

NOTEBOOK
Space Artist(IRE) took the bull by the horns early doors and battled near the finish to follow up his maiden success over 5f here 19 days earlier. He has evidently started off in handicaps on a good mark and is open to improvement over this trip. (op 10-3)
Desert Sunrise was back down a furlong for this switch to a handicap and just failed. It shouldn't be long before she's off the mark. (op 5-2)
Indian Affair was only just held and one has to think the rider losing his whip made a difference. No doubt he can be placed to shed his maiden tag this winter. (op 11 1)
Ovett lost ground after being taken back after a flying break and that may have cost him as he was not beaten at all far. (op 4-1)

7867 32REDBET.COM CLAIMING STKS 1m 141y(P)
8:20 (8:20) (Class 6) 3-Y-O+ **£2,070** (£616; £307; £153) **Stalls** Low

Form RPR
0013 **1** **Desert Vision**[28] 7415 8-9-1 77..................................(vt) GrahamGibbons 1 86
(Michael Easterby) *a.p: chsd ldr over 2f out: led over 1f out: hrd rdn and hung lft ins fnl f: styd on* **13/2**
0-00 **2** *1 1/2* **Super Say (IRE)**[36] 7233 6-9-5 92..(t) AdamKirby 4 79
(Jamie Osborne) *chsd ldrs: rdn over 1f out: styd on* **13/8**[1]
4000 **3** *2 1/2* **Majuro (IRE)**[29] 7370 8-9-1 84..................................(tp) RobertWinston 8 69
(Charles Smith) *sn pushed along to ld: rdn and hdd over 1f out: styd on same pce ins fnl f* **6/1**[3]
6020 **4** *1* **Classic Colori (IRE)**[7] 7556 5-9-7 85................................ GrahamLee 6 73
(David O'Meara) *hld up: hdwy over 2f out: rdn over 1f out: styd on same pce fnl f* **9/5**[2]
0160 **5** *9* **Honey Of A Kitten (USA)**[49] 6895 4-8-6 65.................... EoinWalsh(7) 3 44
(David Evans) *hld up: lost tch fr 1/2-way* **18/1**
0014 **6** *9* **Sasheen**[18] 7620 5-8-2 57..(p) RaulDaSilva(3) 7 15
(Jeremy Gask) *prom: chsd ldr 4f out tl rdn over 2f out: sn wknd* **25/1**
7 *19* **Acton Jenson** 3-9-0 0.. J-PGuillambert 2
(Brian Baugh) *s.s: a in rr: bhd fr 1/2-way: t.o* **66/1**
1404 **8** *4* **Shomberg**[10] 7702 3-8-7 54..(p) KellyHarrison 9
(Dai Burchell) *chsd ldr tl rdn 4f out: wknd 3f out: t.o* **50/1**

1m 47.91s (-2.59) **Going Correction** -0.125s/f (Stan)
WFA 3 from 4yo+ 3lb **8** Ran SP% **114.0**
Speed ratings (Par 101): **106,104,102,101,93 85,68,65**
toteswingers: 1&2 £1.30, 1&3 £6.80, 2&3 £2.80 CSF £17.35 TOTE £8.20: £1.90, £1.10, £2.00; EX 17.50 Trifecta £334.40 Pool: £570.79 - 1.30 winning units..
Owner A Black,R Edmonds,J Holdroyd,J Quickfall **Bred** Gainsborough Stud Management Ltd **Trained** Sheriff Hutton, N Yorks

FOCUS
It paid to race handily in this decent claimer. The winner's best figure for two years, but there are doubts over the form.
Honey Of A Kitten(USA) Official explanation: Jockey said, regarding running and riding, that his orders were to settle gelding in early stages, it raced keenly, and blew up in the back straight; trainer confirmed, adding that the gelding is difficult to train

7868 32RED E B F MAIDEN STKS 1m 141y(P)
8:50 (8:51) (Class 5) 2-Y-O **£3,784** (£1,126; £562; £281) **Stalls** Low

Form RPR
035 **1** **Tight Knit (USA)**[38] 7167 2-9-3 73.. JoeFanning 6 74+
(James Tate) *mde all: pushed clr fr over 1f out: comf* **2/1**[1]
0 **2** *4 1/2* **Makin (IRE)**[31] 7324 2-9-3 0...(t) AdamKirby 3 65
(Marco Botti) *a.p: rdn to chse wnr over 1f out: styd on same pce fnl f* **14/1**
05 **3** *1* **Grayswood**[17] 7628 2-9-3 0.. WilliamCarson 2 62
(William Muir) *mid-div: hdwy over 2f out: rdn over 1f out: styd on to go 3rd towards fin: nvr nrr* **15/2**
4 *1/2* **Chief Executive (IRE)** 2-9-3 0.. LiamKeniry 11 61
(Mikael Magnusson) *chsd wnr tl pushed along over 1f out: no ex fnl f* **8/1**
02 **5** *1* **Inessa Armand (IRE)**[19] 7592 2-8-12 0.............................. AndreaAtzeni 1 54
(J S Moore) *chsd ldrs: pushed along over 2f out: no ex fnl f* **8/1**
6 *nk* **Good Evans** 2-9-3 0.. RichardKingscote 4 59+
(Tom Dascombe) *s.i.s: hld up: hdwy over 1f out: nt trble ldrs* **7/1**[3]
05 **7** *hd* **Grendisar (IRE)**[36] 7205 2-8-12 0.. TobyAtkinson(5) 5 58
(Marco Botti) *mid-div: rdn over 3f out: hmpd over 1f out: nvr trbld ldrs* **25/1**

8 *hd* **Rainford Glory (IRE)**2 -9-30 .... GrahamLee 8 60+
(Ed Dunlop) *s.i.s: hld up: styd on fnl f: nvr on terms* **6/1**[2]

0 9 *1* **Mallory Heights (IRE)**[9] 7130 2 -9-00 .... PatrickHills(3) 7 60+
(Luca Cumani) *hld up: pushed along whn n.m.r wl over 3f out: n.d* **33/1**

00 10 *hd* **Rhyolite (IRE)**[71] 6214 2 -9-30 .... MartinHarley 10 55
(Marco Botti) *prom: rdn over 2f out: wknd fnl f* **14/1**

0 11 *4 1/2* **Portrait**[7] 7777 2 -8-120 .... LukeMorris 9 41
(Sir Mark Prescott Bt) *hld up: pushed along over 3f out: a in rr* **40/1**

1m 50.13s (-0.37) **Going Correction** -0.125s/f (Stan) 11Ran SP% 116.7
Speed ratings (Par 96): **96,92,91,90,89 89,89,89,88,88 84**
toteswingers: 1&2 £10.10, 1&3 £4.60, 2&3 £24.40 CSF £32.36 TOTE £3.10 : £1.40 , £4.00 , £2.20; EX 35.50 TRIFECTA Not won.
Owner Saeed Manana **Bred** Rabbah Bloodstock Ltd **Trained** Newmarket, Suffolk

FOCUS
An ordinary 2-y-o maiden with the winner rated to 7f course form.

NOTEBOOK
Tight Knit (USA) came home a comfortable winner on his fourth outing. He looked really happy bowling along from the front over the stiffer test and is open to progression over this sort of distance, but will have to improve again to defy a likely rise in handicap company. (tchd 5-2)
Makin(IRE) was firmly put in his place by the winner, but improved a deal on his Kempton debut and will be eligible for a mark after his next assignment. (tchd 12-1)
Grayswood stayed on late and can be ridden more positively now connections know he gets this far. Nurseries are now an option. (op 17-2 tchd 7-1)
Chief Executive (IRE)◆ is well bred and posted a respectable debut effort. He should land a maiden. (op 10-1)
Mallory Heights (IRE) Official explanation: Jockey said colt was denied a clear run

7869 £32 BONUS AT 32RED.COM H'CAP 1m 4f 50y (P)
9:20 (9:20) (Class 6) (0-60,60) 3-Y-O+ £2,070 (£616; £307 ; £153) Stalls Low

Form RPR

3300 1 **Chookie Hamilton**[55] 6712 8 -9-657 .... JoeFanning 11 68
(Keith Dalgleish) *chsd ldrs: led 5f out: hdd over 2f out: sn led again: rdn and edgd rt ins fnl f: styd on* **9/2**[2]

2333 2 *nk* **White Deer (USA)**[10] 6838 8 -9-253 .... (v) RobertWinston 7 63
(Geoffrey Harker) *hld up: hdwy over 2f out: chsd wnr gng wl ins fnl f: cajoled along and styd on towards fin* **15/2**[3]

0064 3 *4 1/2* **El Bravo**[18] 7619 6 -9-258 .... (v[1]) MichaelJMMurphy(5) 9 61
(Shaun Harris) *s.i.s: hld up: hdwy over 6f out: chsd wnr over 4f out: led over 2f out: sn rdn and hdd: no ex ins fnl f* **15/2**[3]

/36- 4 *1/2* **Stetson**[580] 1542 6 -9-657 .... MartinHarley 12 59
(Ian Williams) *hld up: hdwy u.p over 1f out: nt rch ldrs* **25/1**

6005 5 *2* **If You Whisper (IRE)**[9] 7252 4 -9-455 .... AndreaAtzeni 4 54
(Mike Murphy) *chsd ldrs: rdn over 3f out: wknd fnl f* **15/2**[3]

4222 6 *3 1/4* **Annelko**[22] 7528 5 -9-859 .... GrahamLee 10 53
(Michael Blake) *chsd ldrs: led 6f out: hdd 5f out: rdn over 1f out: wknd fnl f* **5/2**[1]

4123 7 *7* **Barton Bounty**[18] 7619 5 -9-859 .... DaleSwift 5 41
(Peter Niven) *hld up: hdwy over 2f out: rdn and wknd over 1f out* **14/1**

4435 8 *3* **Quiet Route (IRE)**[38] 6821 3 -9-360 .... PhillipMakin 3 38
(Brian Ellison) *hld up: nvr on terms* **14/1**

0050 9 *3 3/4* **Galilee Chapel (IRE)**[30] 7358 3 -9-360 .... GrahamGibbons 1 32
(Alistair Whillans) *led to 1/2-way: pushed along over 4f out: rdn and wknd wl over 2f out* **18/1**

02-5 10 *9* **Queen Of Epirus**[16] 7656 4 -9-960 .... TomEaves 2 17
(Brian Rothwell) *chsd ldrs: rdn over 4f out: wknd over 3f out: t.o* **50/1**

0021 11 *16* **Sir Dylan**[17] 7632 3 -9-360 .... LukeMorris 8
(Ronald Harris) *s.i.s: hld up: plld hrd: hdwy over 7f out: hung lft and lost pl over 4f out: wkng whn hmpd 3f out: t.o* **9/1**

2m 39.6s (-1.50) **Going Correction** -0.125s/f (Stan)
WFA 3 from 4yo+ 6lb 11Ran SP% 116.5
Speed ratings (Par 101): **100,99,96,96,95 92,88,86,83,77 67**
toteswingers: 1&2 £9.30, 1&3 £10.80, 2&3 £11.90 CSF £37.90 CT £248.87 TOTE £3.40 : £2.10, £2.40, £3.40 ; EX 52.30 Trifecta £401.50 Part won. Pool: £535.44 - 0.72 winning units.
Owner Straightline Construction Ltd **Bred** D And J Raeburn **Trained** Carluke, S Lanarks

FOCUS
An open handicap in which two pulled clear. The winner had dropped to a good mark and the second, who arguably should have won, is rated close to this year's best.
White Deer (USA) Official explanation: Jockey said, regarding riding, that the gelding is a difficult ride, he was unable to obtain a position tracking the leader and ultimate winner when asked to quicken it did not respond and was slightly intimidated by the winner edging to its right approaching the line
Sir Dylan Official explanation: Jockey said gelding hung
T/Plt: £17.50 to a £1 stake. Pool: £122,942.52. 5,107.26 winning tickets. T/Qpdt: £3.60 to a £1 stake. Pool: £8,185.94. 1,659.68 w. tckts CR 7870a - 7871a (Foreign Racing) See RI

TOKYO (L-H)
Sunday, November 25

OFFICIAL GOING: Turf: firm

7872a JAPAN CUP (GRADE 1) (3YO+) (TURF) 1m 4f
6:40 (12:00) 3-Y-O+ £2,115,551 (£842,816; £529,868 ; £317,036 ; £208,576)

RPR

1 **Gentildonna (JPN)**[42] 3 -8-50 .... YasunariIwata 15 126
(Sei Ishizaka, Japan) *got across fr wd draw and sn trcking ldr in 3rd on inner: shuffled bk against rail on turn into st: rdn over 2f out: swtchd out to chal and bmpd rival 1f out: styd on wl to ld cl home* **56/10**[3]

2 *nse* **Orfevre (JPN)**[49] 6912 4 -9-00 .... KenichiIkezoe 17 129
(Yasutoshi Ikee, Japan) *hld up towards rr on outer: smooth hdwy over 3f out: rdn to chal whn bmpd by rival 1f out: led jst ins fnl f: styd on wl but hdd cl home* **1/1**[1]

3 *2 1/2* **Rulership (JPN)**[28] 5 -9-00 .... CraigAWilliams 13 125
(Katsuhiko Sumii, Japan) *slow to stride and racd towards rr on inner: swtchd to wd outside and rdn on turn into st: styd on to go 3rd fnl strides* **22/5**[2]

4 *hd* **Dark Shadow (JPN)**[28] 5 -9-00 .... MircoDemuro 10 125
(Noriyuki Hori, Japan) *hld up in last quartet: hdwy on turn into st: rdn 2f out: r.o to go 3rd ins fnl 100yds: dropped to 4th fnl strides* **176/10**

5 *2 1/2* **Fenomeno (JPN)**[28] 3 -8-90 .... MasayoshiEbina 4 123
(Hirofumi Toda, Japan) *prom on inner: swtchd out and rdn 3f out: outpcd by ldrs ent fnl f: plugged on: wnt 5th cl home* **7/1**

6 *hd* **Tosen Jordan (JPN)**[28] 6 -9-00 .... ChristopheSoumillon 16 120
(Yasutoshi Ikee, Japan) *got across fr wd draw and sn trcking ldr in 2nd on outer: rdn 3f out: outpcd over 1f out: fdd and dropped to 6th cl home* **55/1**

7 *3/4* **Beat Black (JPN)**[21] 5 -9-00 .... Syulshibashi 1 119
(Hitoshi Nakamura, Japan) *led: at least 8 l clr 4f out: rdn and diminishing advantage fr over 2f out: strly pressed and hdd ent fnl f: no ex and fdd* **42/1**

8 *nk* **Red Cadeaux**[19] 7621 6 -9-00 .... GeraldMosse 6 119
(Ed Dunlop) *midfield: rdn over 3f out and sn outpcd: styd on wout threatening ins fnl 2f* **152/1**

9 *nk* **Eishin Flash (JPN)**[28] 5 -9-00 .... Christophe-PatriceLemaire 8 118
(Hideaki Fujiwara, Japan) *midfield: travelled strly: ev ch whn rdn 2f out: outpcd ins fnl f: fdd* **129/10**

10 *1 1/4* **Jaguar Mail (JPN)**[28] 8 -9-00 .... (b) WilliamBuick 3 116
(Noriyuki Hori, Japan) *hld up in last pair on inner: rdn on turn into st: styd on but n.d* **65/1**

11 *1 1/4* **Jakkalberry (IRE)**[19] 7621 6 -9-00 .... CO'Donoghue 11 114
(Marco Botti) *hld up in last trio: rdn and hdwy on outer over 3f out: outpcd and btn ent fnl f: fdd* **158/1**

12 *3/4* **Mount Athos (IRE)**[19] 7621 5 -9-00 .... RyanMoore 5 113
(Luca Cumani) *midfield on inner: t.k.h: rdn on turn into st: sn outpcd: plugged on but nvr a factor* **88/1**

13 *1/2* **Solemia (IRE)**[49] 6912 4 -8-90 .... OlivierPeslier 14 108
(C Laffon-Parias, France) *prom: rdn 3f out: no ex and btn 2f out: steadily fdd* **217/10**

14 *1 1/4* **Oken Bruce Lee (JPN)**[21] 7 -9-00 .... SuguruHamanaka 9 110
(Hidetaka Otonashi, Japan) *midfield: rdn over 3f out: outpcd and btn over 1f out: fdd* **206/1**

15 *1/2* **Meisho Kampaku (JPN)**[28] 5 -9-00 .... HiroyukiUchida 7 109
(Yoshiyuki Arakawa, Japan) *hld up in last: rdn on turn into st: sn btn: nvr a factor* **153/1**

16 *2 1/2* **Rose Kingdom (JPN)**[28] 5 -9-00 .... YutakaTake 12 105
(Kojiro Hashiguchi, Japan) *midfield: hdwy to be prom on turn into st: rdn 2f out and fnd little: qckly btn and fdd* **47/1**

17 *dist* **Sri Putra**[95] 5490 6 -9-00 .... NeilCallan 2
(Roger Varian) *midfield on inner: rdn over 3f out and sn outpcd: fdd and dropped to last ent fnl f: eased* **200/1**

2m 23.1s (-2.40)
WFA 3 from 4yo+ 6lb 17Ran SP% 124.9
PARI-MUTUEL (all including 100 ypj stake): WIN 660; SHOW 170, 120, 140; DF 700; SF 1580
Owner Sunday Racing Co Ltd **Bred** Northern Racing Co Ltd **Trained** Japan

FOCUS
This looked a classy renewal of an extremely valuable contest. The early pace seemed decent.

NOTEBOOK
Gentildonna(JPN) completed the fillies' Triple Crown this season in her homeland, including the Japanese Oaks over C&D by 5l, and was ideally placed towards the head of the chasing pack to be in a good position when the race really started to take shape. She did need a really hard ride to get to the front and her rider forcibly got the pair out of a pocket late on before galloping on bravely to win. It wasn't a surprise to see a stewards' inquiry called soon after, and, while she kept the prize, her jockey was banned for two days for interference to the runner-up.
Orfevre(JPN) was delivered at the right time and narrowly denied in a tight finish. However, despite giving weight away and somehow, considering the margin of defeat, not getting the race in the stewards' room, one got the feeling again that the chestnut son of Stay Gold may have spurned a big victory which was there for the taking. He appeared to want to edge towards the inside rail while duelling with the winner, and Kenichi Ikezoe was far less animated in the saddle than Yasunari Iwata in the final 100 yards. It seems strange considering what happened at Longchamp that connections didn't experiment with some sort of headgear.
Rulership(JPN) came with his effort really wide along with Dark Shadow, and just got the better of that battle.
Dark Shadow (JPN) travelled strongly for quite some way before his effort flattened out.
Fenomeno(JPN), the only 3yo colt in the line-up, kept on after being prominent in the chasing bunch. He had finished in front of Rulership and Dark Shadow last time on the same terms, so this is probably a better reflection of his true ability.
Beat Black (JPN) made full use of his inside draw. He stole a healthy advantage turning into the home straight but his earlier exertions told late on.
Red Cadeaux did best of the visitors and kept on nicely before being squeezed up at the end. Connections said afterwards that the gelding was struck into on the first bend but will hopefully head to Hong Kong next.
Jakkalberry(IRE) made no meaningful impression.
Mount Athos (IRE) will surely be better over further next season.
Solemia(IRE) was well below her Arc form, but the ground was completely different, she was drawn wide, and it's quite possible she hadn't recovered from the hard race she had at Longchamp.
Sri Putra likes fast ground but isn't up to this level.

7873 - (Foreign Racing) - See Raceform Interactive

[7793] SOUTHWELL (L-H)
Monday, November 26

7874 Meeting Abandoned - waterlogged

[7873] HOLLYWOOD PARK (L-H)
Monday, November 26

OFFICIAL GOING: Turf: firm

7882a HOLLYWOOD DERBY (GRADE 1) (3YO) (TURF) 1m 2f
12:35 (12:43) 3-Y-O £96,774 (£32,258; £19,354 ; £9,677 ; £3,225)

RPR

1 **Unbridled Command (USA)**[37] 3 -8-100 .... JJCastellano 3 113
(Thomas Bush, U.S.A) *towards rr of main pack on rail: hdwy on outside 4f out: led 1 1/2f out: clr ins fnl f: r.o wl* **7/1**

2 *1 1/2* **Grandeur (IRE)**[23] 7566 3 -8-100 .... GKGomez 4 110
(Jeremy Noseda) *last detached fr main pack: stl last but making hdwy on wd outside over 1 1/2f out: r.o strly u.p fr 1 1/2f out: wnt 2nd cl home: nrest at fin* **7/2**[1]

3 *hd* **Lucky Chappy (IRE)**[65] 3 -8-100 .... JRLeparoux 10 110
(H Graham Motion, U.S.A) *settled next to last detached fr main pack: pushed along and hdwy on outside 2 1/2f out: r.o u.p to go 2nd 100yds out: kpt on wl but lost 2nd cl home* **15/1**

4 2 ½ **Rjwa (IRE)**[50] 6911 3-8-7 0 .... ThierryJarnet 8 102
(F Rohaut, France) *midfield: tk clsr order under 2f out: 6th and styng on appr 1f out: kpt on u.p: nt pce to chal* **133/10**

5 1 ½ **Power Foot (USA)**[23] 7566 3-8-10 0 .... EMaldonado 7 102
(Richard E Mandella, U.S.A) *hld up: hdwy on outside 2f out: rdn and nt qckn 1 1/2f out: one pce fnl f* **61/1**

6 nk **Summer Front (USA)**[51] 6902 3-8-10 0 .... RADominguez 13 101
(Christophe Clement, U.S.A) *towards rr of main pack: kpt on fr 1 1/2f out: nvr on terms* **43/10**[2]

7 nse **My Best Brother (USA)**[23] 7566 3-8-10 0 ....(b) MGarcia 9 101
(Julio C Canani, U.S.A) *pressed ldr: led after 3f: hdd 1 1/2f out: wknd ins fnl f* **87/10**

8 ½ **All Squared Away (USA)**[23] 7566 3-8-10 0 .... RBejarano 12 100
(Peter Miller, U.S.A) *midfield: rdn and short-lived effrt 2f out: no imp fr over 1 1/2f out* **45/1**

9 1 ¾ **Big Bane Theory (USA)**[24] 3-8-10 0 .... JTalamo 1 96
(Carla Gaines, U.S.A) *chsd ldng gp on inner: rdn and nt qckn over 1 1/2f out: fdd ins fnl f* **185/10**

10 1 ¼ **Handsome Mike (USA)**[22] 7576 3-8-10 0 .... MGutierrez 2 94
(Doug O'Neill, U.S.A) *prom: rdn and wknd fr over 1 1/2f out* **132/10**

11 1 ¼ **Golden Ticket (USA)**[65] 3-8-10 0 .... MESmith 6 91
(Kenneth McPeek, U.S.A) *led: hdd after 3f: remained prom tl wknd u.p ins fnl 2f* **132/10**

12 4 **Smart Ellis (USA)**[23] 7566 3-8-10 0 .... CNakatani 5 83
(Richard E Mandella, U.S.A) *a towards rr: nvr a factor* **34/1**

13 4 ¾ **General Logan (USA)**[31] 3-8-10 0 .... ECastro 14 74
(H Graham Motion, U.S.A) *trckd ldng gp: short of room and lost pl 2f out: swtchd outside and no imp fr 1 1/2f out* **62/1**

14 15 **Speaking Of Which (IRE)**[23] 7566 3-8-10 0 ....(b) PatSmullen 11 44
(D K Weld, Ire) *trckd ldrs: 5th and travelling wl 3f out: pressing ldrs whn clipped heels and all but fell under 2f out: eased immediately* **6/1**[3]

2m 1.07s (121.07) **14** Ran SP% **118.9**
PARI-MUTUEL (all including $2 stakes): WIN 16.00; PLACE (1-2) 7.20, 4.80; SHOW (1-2-3) 6.00, 3.60, 7.60; DF 34.00; SF 70.20.
Owner Lewis G Lakin **Bred** Sequel Thoroughbreds LLC **Trained** North America

7793 SOUTHWELL (L-H)
Tuesday, November 27
7883 Meeting Abandoned - waterlogged

7820 KEMPTON (A.W) (R-H)
Wednesday, November 28

OFFICIAL GOING: Standard
Wind: Moderate ahead

7891 WIN BIG WITH BETDAQ MULTIPLES CLAIMING STKS 5f (P)
4:00 (4:01) (Class 6) 2-Y-O **£1,617** (£481; £240; £120) **Stalls** Low

Form RPR

6 **1** **Tartan Blue**[14] 7711 2-8-8 0 .... SilvestreDeSousa 1 58
(Robert Cowell) *mde all: pushed along 2f out: kpt on strly fnl f* **7/1**[2]

6450 **2** 1 ¾ **Many Elements**[8] 7797 2-8-11 55 ....(p) LukeMorris 3 55
(Lee Carter) *chsd wnr thrght: drvn along fr 1/2-way: no imp fr over 1f out* **11/1**[3]

006 **3** ½ **Fiance Fiasco**[34] 7349 2-7-8 38 .... JoeyHaynes(7) 2 43
(Luke Dace) *chsd ldrs in 3rd: pushed along over 2f out: one pce fr over 1f out* **33/1**

2301 **4** ½ **Layla's Oasis**[12] 7745 2-9-2 74 .... AdamKirby 5 56
(Jamie Osborne) *stdd into 4th: pushed along 1/2-way: rdn over 1f out and fnd no ex u.p* **1/4**[1]

536 **5** 6 **Miss Starry Eyed**[141] 3937 2-8-0 47 .... JimmyQuinn 4 19
(Derek Shaw) *s.i.s: a outpcd in last pl* **16/1**

1m 0.53s (0.03) **Going Correction** -0.125s/f (Stan) **5** Ran SP% **109.7**
Speed ratings (Par 94): **94,91,90,89,80**
CSF £65.31 TOTE £4.70: £2.90, £4.20; EX 22.40.
Owner Khalifa Dasmal & Bottisham Heath Stud **Bred** Manor Farm Stud (rutland) **Trained** Six Mile Bottom, Cambs

FOCUS
Quite a turn-up in this claimer and very weak form as a result.

NOTEBOOK
Tartan Blue didn't show a great deal on her debut, but that was on Fibresand, and not every horse acts on that surface. With that experience under her belt, she improved for the switch to Polytrack, and made every yard. A half-sister to four winners, including Pickett, who was runner-up in the Group 3 Molecomb Stakes at two, she might have more to offer on this surface. (op 6-1)
Many Elements appreciated getting back on the Polytrack but couldn't match the winner's speed inside the last. (op 12-1)
Fiance Fiasco, beaten out of sight in her previous three starts over further, ran a much better race dropped in trip and grade on her debut for a new stable. (op 25-1)
Layla's Oasis, the clear pick at the weights, ran well below her Wolverhampton form. In trouble from the turn in, never picked up in the straight, and her rider's only explanation was that the filly was unsuited by the track. Perhaps she'll bounce back when returned to a left-handed track.
Official explanation: trainer said filly was unsuited by the track.

7892 BACK OR LAY AT BETDAQ.COM H'CAP (DIV I) 1m 2f (P)
4:30 (4:30) (Class 5) (0-70,70) 3-Y-O+ **£2,264** (£673; £336; £168) **Stalls** Low

Form RPR

1564 **1** **Daffydowndilly**[50] 6950 4-9-4 67 ....(bt) RobertHavlin 4 77
(Hughie Morrison) *led 1f: trckd ldr tl drvn to chal fr wl over 1f out: styd upsides tl led again fnl 50yds: drvn out* **8/1**[2]

0022 **2** nk **Fairyinthewind (IRE)**[7] 7805 3-9-0 67 ....(p) SebSanders 6 76
(Paul D'Arcy) *towards rr: gd hdwy 3f out: slt ld wl over 1f out but remained hrd pressed tl hdd and no ex fnl 50yds* **9/4**[1]

3663 **3** 5 **Sail Home**[11] 7767 5-9-3 66 .... AdamBeschizza 9 65
(Julia Feilden) *chsd ldrs: rdn 2f out: styd on same pce for wl hld 3rd ins fnl f* **20/1**

003 **4** ¾ **Guarda Pampa**[20] 7656 3-8-10 63 .... SilvestreDeSousa 10 61
(William Haggas) *led after 1f: rdn over 2f out: hdd wl over 1f: wknd fnl f* **8/1**[2]

3400 **5** 1 **Final Delivery**[37] 7301 3-7-12 56 oh1 ....(v) NathanAlison(5) 8 52
(Jim Boyle) *slowly away: in rr: stl plenty to do fr 2f out: styd on wl fnl f but nvr any ch* **50/1**

4361 **6** nk **Having A Ball**[28] 7474 8-8-13 62 .... JohnFahy 7 57
(Peter Cundell) *mid-div tl rdn and dropped to rr 3f out: sn hrd drvn: styd on again fr over 1f out* **10/1**[3]

4001 **7** 1 ¾ **Royal Etiquette (IRE)**[28] 7473 5-8-11 65 ....(v) LeonnaMayor(5) 5 57
(Lawney Hill) *in rr: hdwy towards outside 3f out: nvr gng pce to rch ldrs and wl hld fr over 1f out* **8/1**[2]

4216 **8** 5 **Shalambar (IRE)**[178] 1418 6-9-6 69 .... JimCrowley 3 51
(Tony Carroll) *s.i.s: a in rr* **20/1**

2014 **9** 9 **Bert The Alert**[28] 7473 4-9-7 70 .... GeorgeBaker 2 34
(Gary Moore) *chsd ldrs tl wknd qckly 2f out* **9/4**[1]

2m 5.52s (-2.48) **Going Correction** -0.125s/f (Stan)
WFA 3 from 4yo+ 4lb **9** Ran SP% **115.4**
Speed ratings (Par 103): **104,103,99,99,98 98,96,92,85**
toteswingers 1&2 £3.90, 1&3 £11.30, 2&3 £8.90 CSF £25.80 CT £353.32 TOTE £9.90: £3.20, £1.10, £4.80; EX 38.70 Trifecta £598.50 Pool: £1,141.32 - 1.43 winning tickets..
Owner Lady Blyth **Bred** D Curran **Trained** East Ilsley, Berks

FOCUS
A modest handicap, but the first two came nicely clear. A personal best from the winner, in a faster time than the second division.
Final Delivery Official explanation: jockey said gelding was slowly away.
Bert The Alert Official explanation: jockey said gelding stopped quickly.

7893 BACK OR LAY AT BETDAQ.COM H'CAP (DIV II) 1m 2f (P)
5:00 (5:00) (Class 5) (0-70,70) 3-Y-O+ **£2,264** (£673; £336; £168) **Stalls** Low

Form RPR

2034 **1** **Kelpie Blitz (IRE)**[20] 7644 3-9-3 70 ....(t) MickyFenton 7 82
(Seamus Durack) *hld up in rr: hdwy ins fnl 2f: str run to ld fnl 120yds: r.o strly* **6/1**[3]

1212 **2** 2 **Neige D'Antan**[35] 7321 3-8-8 61 .... LukeMorris 4 69
(Sir Mark Prescott Bt) *chsd ldrs: wnt 2nd 5f out: drvn to ld jst ins fnl f: hdd and outpcd fnl 120yds* **7/2**[1]

3652 **3** 1 ½ **Officer In Command (USA)**[28] 7480 6-9-5 68 ....(b) JohnFahy 1 73
(Paul Rich) *s.i.s: in rr: hdwy towards outside over 1f out: styd on to take 3rd fnl 150yds* **10/1**

0302 **4** ½ **Hawaana (IRE)**[11] 7767 7-9-4 67 .... RobertWinston 2 71
(Gay Kelleway) *chsd ldrs: rdn 2f out: one pce fnl f* **10/1**

12 **5** 1 ¼ **Diplomatic (IRE)**[13] 7722 7-9-1 69 .... HarryPoulton(5) 5 73
(Michael Squance) *in rr: hdwy on ins whn nt clr run wl over 1f out: swtchd lft and hdwy fnl f: kpt on cl home* **8/1**

-600 **6** 2 **Sim Sala Bim**[33] 7369 4-9-4 67 .... WilliamCarson 8 65
(Stuart Williams) *in tch: rdn 3f out: hung rt u.p and btn fnl 2f* **4/1**[2]

0000 **7** ½ **Shirataki (IRE)**[23] 7596 4-9-0 63 .... KirstyMilczarek 6 60
(Peter Hiatt) *led after 1f: hdd jst ins fnl f: wknd rapidly fnl 120yds* **10/1**

0013 **8** 2 ¾ **Bramshill Lass**[70] 6365 3-9-0 67 ....(b) JimCrowley 3 58
(Amanda Perrett) *led 1f: chsd ldrs tl wknd qckly fr 2f out* **7/1**

5001 **9** 6 **Chrissycross (IRE)**[20] 7643 3-9-0 67 ow1 ....(b) AdamKirby 9 46
(Roger Teal) *chsd ldrs: rdn and wknd over 2f out* **14/1**

2m 6.21s (-1.79) **Going Correction** -0.125s/f (Stan)
WFA 3 from 4yo+ 4lb **9** Ran SP% **114.1**
Speed ratings (Par 103): **102,100,99,98,97 96,95,93,88**
toteswingers 1&2 £4.40, 1&3 £9.20, 2&3 £5.00 CSF £26.93 CT £205.94 TOTE £7.80: £2.30, £1.10, £3.90; EX 30.50 Trifecta £429.30 Pool: £6,004.97 - 10.49 winning tickets..
Owner Mrs Anne Cowley **Bred** Irish National Stud **Trained** Baydon, Wilts

FOCUS
There was a decent gallop on here and it paid to be held up. The winning time was 0.69sec slower than the first division. The winner looked capable of this figure two runs ago.

7894 BETDAQ MOBILE APPS BRITISH STALLION STUDS E B F MAIDEN STKS 6f (P)
5:30 (5:32) (Class 5) 2-Y-O **£3,234** (£962; £481; £240) **Stalls** Low

Form RPR

30 **1** **Rivellino**[68] 6424 2-9-3 0 .... JimCrowley 1 81+
(Mrs K Burke) *trckd ldrs: qcknd on inner over 2f out to ld over 1f out: pushed clr: comf* **5/4**[1]

25 **2** 2 ¼ **Serenity Spa**[27] 7497 2-8-12 0 .... GrahamLee 3 66
(Roger Charlton) *trckd ldrs: pushed along over 1f out: styd on wl to take 2nd fnl 100yds but no ch w wnr* **9/2**[3]

540U **3** ½ **Millers Wharf (IRE)**[27] 7498 2-9-3 73 .... RichardHughes 7 70
(Richard Hannon) *led: drvn over 2f out: hdd over 1f out: one pce and dropped to 3rd fnl 100yds* **11/4**[2]

06 **4** 3 ¼ **Malaysian Boleh**[27] 7497 2-9-3 0 .... SebSanders 8 60
(Simon Dow) *chsd ldr: rdn over 2f out: wknd fnl 120yds* **16/1**

60 **5** 4 ½ **Mont Signal**[7] 7806 2-9-3 0 ....(t) MartinDwyer 4 47
(Daniel Kubler) *in tch: rdn and one pce fnl 2f* **33/1**

05 **6** nk **Birdie King**[7] 7813 2-9-3 0 .... LukeMorris 11 46
(John Best) *in rr: pushed along 2f out: kpt on fnl f: nvr a threat* **25/1**

00 **7** nk **Aphrodite Spirit (IRE)**[56] 6772 2-8-12 0 .... JimmyQuinn 6 40
(Pat Eddery) *chsd ldrs: rdn over 2f out: sn btn* **100/1**

8 ½ **Woodland Fleur** 2-8-12 0 .... DavidProbert 9 38
(Tony Carroll) *s.i.s: outpcd most of way* **100/1**

9 4 ½ **Dubai Applause** 2-8-12 0 .... WilliamCarson 5 25
(Charles Hills) *s.i.s: outpcd* **14/1**

10 2 ¼ **Fire Fairy (USA)** 2-8-12 0 .... RobertWinston 2 18
(Charles Hills) *bhd fr 1/2-way* **10/1**

1m 12.88s (-0.22) **Going Correction** -0.125s/f (Stan) **10** Ran SP% **119.7**
Speed ratings (Par 96): **96,93,92,88,82 81,81,80,74,71**
toteswingers 1&2 £2.50, 1&3 £1.90, 2&3 £3.20 CSF £7.38 TOTE £2.90: £1.50, £1.90, £1.10; EX 11.90 Trifecta £16.70 Pool: £5,376.98 - 241.46 winning tickets..
Owner Mrs Melba Bryce **Bred** Castlemartin Sky & Skymarc Farm **Trained** Middleham Moor, N Yorks

FOCUS
A drop in class did the trick for Rivellino and the form behind looks sound with the third, fourth and fifth setting the level.

NOTEBOOK
Rivellino was well backed on his return from a little break. Always going nicely in behind the leader, he quickened well once asked to take the race at the cutaway. With an exposed, 73-rated rival, back in third, he can expect a mark around 80, and, considering the regard in which he's held by connections, he's likely to pay his way in handicaps. (op 15-8 tchd 2-1)
Serenity Spa, like the winner, travelled well into contention, but the colt got first run on her. She stayed on well inside the last, and while handicaps are now an option, she might still be found a little maiden before having her attentions switched. (op 7-2 tchd 3-1)
Millers Wharf(IRE), who was unlucky to stumble and unseat when going well here last time, had every chance, but the winner just had too many gears for him in the closing stages. (op 9-4)
Malaysian Boleh didn't run badly, despite only beating two home, over this C&D last time, and this was another sound effort. He can go the handicap route now and things ought to be easier for him in that sphere. (tchd 20-1)

Mont Signal, whose dam is an unraced half-sister to Group 1 winners Divine Proportions and Whipper, cost 55,000gns as a yearling. He hasn't shown much in three starts to date, but at least the handicap route is now open to him. (op 50-1)

7895 BETDAQ CASINO GAMES WILD FLOWER STKS (LISTED RACE) 1m 4f (P)
6:00 (6:02) (Class 1) 3-Y-0+

£18,714 (£7,095; £3,550; £1,768; £887; £445) **Stalls** Centre

Form | RPR
5334 1 **Media Hype**[21] 7630 5-9-6 101 MartinHarley 1 104+
(Mrs K Burke) *t.k.h: trckd ldrs: led ins fnl 2f: drvn clr ins fnl f: comf* **3/1**[2]
4106 2 3 ¾ **Roxy Flyer (IRE)**[27] 7510 5-9-1 97 JimCrowley 4 93
(Amanda Perrett) *in tch: hdwy to chse ldrs fr 5f out: styd on u.p fnl f to take 2nd fnl 150yds but no ch w wnr* **4/1**
4420 3 1 ½ **Harris Tweed**[32] 7405 5-9-10 107 GrahamLee 9 100
(William Haggas) *sn led: hdd over 5f out: styd trcking ldr: drvn to chse wnr ins fnl 2f: no ex and dropped to 3rd fnl 150yds* **5/2**[1]
3122 4 shd **Communicator**[18] 7689 4-9-6 98 DavidProbert 6 95+
(Andrew Balding) *in rr: hdwy over 2f out: styd on u.p fnl f to cl on 3rd last strides but nvr a threat* **7/2**[3]
0322 5 2 ¾ **Solfilia**[27] 7511 3-8-9 78 NickyMackay 8 86
(Hughie Morrison) *t.k.h: trckd ldr tl led over 5f out: drvn ins fnl 3f: hdd ins fnl 2f: wknd fnl f* **25/1**
4140 6 nk **Wildomar**[7] 7805 3-9-0 75 AdamKirby 7 91?
(John Ryan) *in rr and pushed along after 2f: rdn 4f out: styd on u.p fr over 1f out but nvr a threat* **66/1**
5404 7 4 **Qushchi**[26] 7519 4-9-1 88 RichardHughes 2 79
(William Jarvis) *sn wl there: rdn 2f out: sn btn* **10/1**
1221 8 nk **Art Scholar (IRE)**[18] 7689 5-9-6 99 GeorgeBaker 3 84
(Michael Appleby) *hld up in rr: hdwy over 2f out bt nvr rchd ldrs: wknd over 1f out* **6/1**
5220 9 7 **Bountiful Girl**[21] 7640 3-8-9 69 LukeMorris 5 67
(John Wainwright) *a in rr* **100/1**

2m 32.02s (-2.48) **Going Correction** -0.125s/f (Stan)
WFA 3 from 4yo+ 6lb **9** Ran SP% **125.5**
Speed ratings (Par 111): **103,100,99,99,97 97,94,94,89**
toteswingers 1&2 £4.50, 1&3 £4.10, 2&3 £3.90 CSF £17.01 TOTE £6.40: £2.00, £2.40, £1.10; EX 37.90 Trifecta £107.20 Pool: £5,437.81 - 38.02 winning tickets..
Owner Light Valley Stud & Mrs E Burke **Bred** Meon Valley Stud **Trained** Middleham Moor, N Yorks
■ Stewards' Enquiry : Nicky Mackay caution; entered wrong stall.

FOCUS
A pretty ropey Listed race. During the early stages it looked like Harris Tweed would get an easy lead, but he was soon taken on by the keen-going Solfilia, and that led to an increase in the pace, and the race was set up for those sitting in behind the leading pair. The winner did it nicely, but the bare form has been rated cautiously.

NOTEBOOK
Media Hype travelled strongly into contention and strode clear once asked to go on, recording a personal best in the process. He's up to competing out in Dubai if that's the way connections want to go with him. (op 7-2 tchd 5-1)
Roxy Flyer(IRE) ran on well for second without threatening to trouble the winner. She seems to reserve her best for Goodwood and this track (previous best five RPRs had been recorded at those two courses). She's in the December Sales. (op 11-2)
Harris Tweed had his race ruined to an extent by being taken on in front and, while he still plugged on for third under his penalty, he's become quite a disappointing sort. (op 7-2 tchd 4-1)
Communicator, runner-up in the November Handicap, was keeping on nicely at the finish. He's a consistent sort and ran with credit on this step up in class. (tchd 3-1)
Solfilia wouldn't settle for her rider and, having pulled herself to the front, and then gone clear on the turn in, she was a sitting duck in the straight. Official explanation: jockey said filly ran too free. (tchd 33-1)
Art Scholar(IRE), the November Handicap winner, ran no sort of race. He's better on turf than on the AW, but this was still disappointing. (op 5-1)

7896 RACING PLUS - EVERY SATURDAY MEDIAN AUCTION MAIDEN STKS 7f (P)
6:30 (6:31) (Class 6) 3-5-Y-0 **£1,617** (£481; £240; £120) **Stalls** Low

Form | RPR
02 1 **Rockalong (IRE)**[20] 7647 3-9-3 0 AdamKirby 7 86+
(Luca Cumani) *trckd ldr: rdn to ld appr fnl f: pushed out* **6/4**[1]
2222 2 2 ¼ **Kalokagathia (IRE)**[13] 7719 3-9-3 74 IanMongan 8 80
(Jo Crowley) *wnt rt s: led: rdn 2f out: hdd appr fnl f: sn outpcd* **6/4**[1]
0052 3 3 ¼ **Blank Czech (IRE)**[21] 7625 3-9-3 70 JimCrowley 4 71
(Amanda Perrett) *chsd ldrs: rdn take one pce 3rd appr fnl 2f but nvr any ch w ldng duo* **4/1**[2]
4 7 **Bubblina** 5-8-8 0 LeonnaMayor[(5)] 5 47
(Alastair Lidderdale) *s.i.s: in rr: mod hdwy fr over 1f out* **50/1**
5 1 **Zaminate** 3-8-12 0 DavidProbert 6 45
(Andrew Balding) *in rr: drvn and sme hdwy over 1f out: nvr nr ldrs* **12/1**[3]
0002 6 4 ½ **Mystical Witch**[13] 7729 3-8-12 48 (v) TomMcLaughlin 2 32
(Christine Dunnett) *chsd ldrs tl wknd over 2f out* **50/1**
0 7 5 **Twilight Legend (IRE)**[28] 7488 3-8-12 0 LiamKeniry 1 19
(Seamus Mullins) *chsd ldrs to 3f out* **100/1**
0-5 8 5 **Lord Golan**[11] 7782 4-9-4 0 WilliamCarson 3
(Violet M Jordan) *s.i.s: a in rr* **33/1**

1m 24.59s (-1.41) **Going Correction** -0.125s/f (Stan)
WFA 3 from 4yo+ 1lb **8** Ran SP% **115.5**
Speed ratings (Par 101): **103,100,96,88,87 82,76,71**
toteswingers 1&2 £1.20, 1&3 £1.10, 2&3 £1.40 CSF £3.80 TOTE £3.30: £1.20, £1.10, £1.60; EX 6.20 Trifecta £15.20 Pool: £8,024.58 - 395.13 winning tickets..
Owner Nagy El Azar **Bred** Churchtown House Stud **Trained** Newmarket, Suffolk

FOCUS
Modest stuff, but it was well run in a reasonable time, so a slightly positive view has been taken of the form.

7897 SPORTINGLIFE.COM H'CAP 6f (P)
7:00 (7:02) (Class 2) (0-100,101) 3-Y-0+ **£10,221** (£3,041; £1,519; £759) **Stalls** Low

Form | RPR
0405 1 **Whaileyy (IRE)**[70] 6382 4-9-4 97 (b) MartinHarley 8 108
(Marco Botti) *trckd ldrs: led appr fnl f: drvn out* **11/2**
0000 2 1 ¼ **Iver Bridge Lad**[11] 7772 5-9-8 101 (b) AdamKirby 5 108
(John Ryan) *in rr: drvn and hdwy over 1f out: styd on wl fnl f to take 2nd cl home: no imp on wnr* **5/2**[1]
5502 3 nk **Swiss Cross**[7] 7817 5-8-10 89 (t) LukeMorris 2 95
(Phil McEntee) *trckd ldr: led ins fnl 2f: hdd appr fnl f: one pce then lost 2nd cl home* **7/2**[2]
0000 4 ¾ **Bajan Tryst (USA)**[54] 6854 6-9-3 96 (b) GrahamLee 6 100
(Kevin Ryan) *in rr: drvn and hdwy appr fnl f: kpt on clsng stages* **9/1**
1353 5 1 ¼ **Ajjaadd (USA)**[14] 7704 6-9-3 96 (p) KieranO'Neill 7 96
(Ted Powell) *t.k.h: chsd ldrs: rdn and styd on same pce fr over 1f out* **12/1**
1001 6 3 ½ **Outpost (IRE)**[14] 7716 4-8-8 87 AndreaAtzeni 9 75
(Alan Bailey) *sn led: hdd ins fnl 2f: wknd over 1f out* **12/1**
61 7 3 ¾ **Ubetterbegood (ARG)**[14] 7704 4-9-4 97 JimCrowley 3 73
(Robert Cowell) *in tch: pushed along 3f out: hdwy to cl on ldrs appr fnl 2f: sn wknd* **4/1**[3]

1m 11.13s (-1.97) **Going Correction** -0.125s/f (Stan) **7** Ran SP% **111.6**
Speed ratings (Par 109): **108,106,105,104,103 98,93**
toteswingers 1&2 £3.90, 1&3 £4.30, 2&3 £4.00 CSF £18.67 CT £52.85 TOTE £7.50: £3.60, £1.90; EX 27.70 Trifecta £140.90 Pool: £5,511.43 - 29.32 winning tickets..
Owner Saleh Al Homaizi & Imad Al Sagar **Bred** Iona Equine **Trained** Newmarket, Suffolk

FOCUS
This looked a good handicap, they went an honest pace and the third, coming off a cracking effort at Lingfield, gives the form a solid look. The winner rates a length personal best.

NOTEBOOK
Whaileyy(IRE) appreciated getting back on the Polytrack. He showed improved form on the surface last winter and confirmed himself to be even better now, defying a mark of 97 on his return from a little break. He'll have fewer opportunities this time around and might be one for Dubai, but he could soon be deserving of a shot at Listed prizes. (op 6-1 tchd 7-1)
Iver Bridge Lad, who caught the eye at Lingfield last time, was well backed throughout the day. Held up, he didn't quite have the pace of the winner but posted a solid effort and he'll no doubt once again pick up some decent prize-money out in Dubai in the coming months. (op 7-2)
Swiss Cross, who only found York Glory (winner again since) too strong at Lingfield a week earlier, ran another big race in defeat and helps set the level of the form. (op 3-1 tchd 4-1)
Bajan Tryst(USA), who has slipped back to his last winning mark, shaped much better this time. (op 12-1)
Ajjaadd(USA) wasn't at all disgraced off a career-high mark, especially considering he's done all his winning over the minimum trip. (op 8-1)
Outpost(IRE), who is more effective on Fibresand, was rousted along from the outside stall to get to the front and perhaps he paid for that early effort later on. (op 14-1 tchd 10-1)
Ubetterbegood(ARG), a shock winner over 5f here last time, was disappointing, being beaten before stamina came into play. (op 7-2)

7898 SPORTINGLIFE.COM RACING ALL WEATHER "HANDS AND HEELS" APPRENTICE SERIES H'CAP 1m (P)
7:30 (7:31) (Class 7) (0-50,50) 3-Y-0+ **£1,455** (£433; £216; £108) **Stalls** Low

Form | RPR
0000 1 **Breakheart (IRE)**[107] 5164 5-8-9 50 JoeyHaynes[(5)] 6 59
(Andrew Balding) *slowly away: in rr tl stdy hdwy over 2f out: led fnl 150yds: pushed out* **11/4**[1]
6250 2 ¾ **Divine Rule (IRE)**[27] 7500 4-8-11 50 (v) CharlotteJenner[(3)] 13 57
(Laura Mongan) *slowly away: in rr: wd into st 3f out: styd on wl fr over 1f out: r.o fnl f to take 2nd cl home: no imp on wnr* **7/1**
4000 3 ½ **Bussa**[30] 7437 4-9-0 50 (t) PhilipPrince 12 56
(David Evans) *chsd ldrs: led appr fnl 2f: sn hrd pressed hdd fnl 150yds: lost 2nd cl home* **25/1**
0100 4 1 ¾ **Compton Crofter**[22] 7615 3-8-12 50 (t) DanielMuscutt 3 52
(Hans Adielsson) *chsd ldrs: pushed along and ev ch 1f out: outpcd fnl 120yds* **25/1**
0403 5 shd **Winnetou**[12] 7752 3-8-7 50 DanaZamecnikova[(5)] 8 52
(Frank Sheridan) *in rr: pushed along and hdwy fr 2f out: styd on ins fnl f: nt rch ldrs* **10/1**
0400 6 hd **Takitwo**[56] 6778 9-8-11 50 RyanTate[(3)] 14 51
(Peter Cundell) *chsd ldrs: pushed along over 2f out: styd on same pce fnl f* **20/1**
5640 7 shd **Northern Spy (USA)**[60] 6690 8-8-9 50 AaronChave[(5)] 5 51
(Simon Dow) *sn in tch: pushed along over 2f out: kpt on fnl f: nt rch ldrs* **8/1**
-000 8 ½ **Boris The Bold**[27] 7500 3-8-12 50 TimClark 1 50
(John Best) *sn led: hdd appr fnl 2f: wknd fnl f* **16/1**
4500 9 1 ½ **Entrance**[36] 7303 4-9-0 50 GemmaTutty 4 46
(Julia Feilden) *in rr: hdwy and hung rt fr over 2f out: nvr rchd ldrs* **14/1**
4300 10 shd **Jackie Love (IRE)**[12] 7748 4-8-12 48 AliceHaynes 9 44
(Olivia Maylam) *in rr: sme prog fr over 1f out* **6/1**[3]
0002 11 1 **Pull The Pin (IRE)**[22] 7612 3-8-9 50 LukeLeadbitter[(3)] 2 44
(Declan Carroll) *t.k.h: pressed ldr and sddle slipped after 2f: chal 4f out tl over 2f out: wknd over 1f out* **3/1**[2]
0-00 12 8 **Saffron Park**[123] 4582 3-8-12 50 [1] HannahNunn 7 26
(John Best) *s.i.s: c wd into st: a in rr* **25/1**
0/00 13 5 **Sun Dream**[253] 972 5-8-9 50 AidenBlakemore[(5)] 10 14
(Tony Carroll) *slowly away: a bhd* **50/1**

1m 39.82s (0.02) **Going Correction** -0.125s/f (Stan)
WFA 3 from 4yo+ 2lb **13** Ran SP% **129.5**
Speed ratings (Par 97): **94,93,92,91,90 90,90,90,88,88 87,79,74**
toteswingers 1&2 £7.10, 1&3 £43.50, 2&3 £23.60 CSF £23.13 CT £445.12 TOTE £3.70: £2.60, £2.10, £9.80; EX 31.50 TRIFECTA Not won..
Owner I A Balding **Bred** Littleton Stud **Trained** Kingsclere, Hants
■ The first winner for Joey Haynes.

FOCUS
The first two came from well off the pace in this apprentice handicap. Modest form.
T/Plt: £64.50 to a £1 stake. Pool: £57,370.98 - 648.82 winning tickets T/Qpdt: £3.00 to a £1 stake. Pool: £9,513.28 - 2,280.83 winning tickets ST

7854 LINGFIELD (L-H)
Wednesday, November 28

OFFICIAL GOING: Standard
Wind: fairly light, against Weather: showers

7899 BRITISH STALLION STUDS SUPPORTING BRITISH RACING E B F MAIDEN STKS (DIV I) 1m (P)
12:00 (12:00) (Class 5) 2-Y-0 **£3,169** (£943; £471; £235) **Stalls** High

Form | RPR
1 **Mighty Yar (IRE)** 2-9-3 0 EddieAhern 10 72+
(Sir Henry Cecil) *dwlt: hld up in last trio: hdwy to chse ldrs on outer 4f out: rdn and wd bnd 2f out: styd on wl ins fnl f to ld towards fin* **11/1**
02 2 ½ **Soaring Spirits (IRE)**[61] 6644 2-9-3 0 AndreaAtzeni 7 70
(Roger Varian) *chsd ldr: rdn and ev ch 2f out: drvn to ld 1f out: kpt on tl hdd and no ex towards fin* **6/5**[1]
44 3 hd **Interior Minister**[35] 7324 2-9-3 0 LiamKeniry 8 70
(Mikael Magnusson) *led: rdn wl over 1f out: hdd 1f out: drvn and stl ev ch thrght fnl f: unable qck towards fin* **6/1**[3]

0 **4** *nk* **Magika**[42] 7160 2-8-12 0 .... MartinHarley 2 64
(Marco Botti) *in tch: rdn and effrt to press ldrs 1f out: no ex and styd on same pce fnl 100yds* **66/1**

5 *1 1/4* **Ningara** 2-9-3 0 .... DavidProbert 9 66+
(Andrew Balding) *hld up in tch towards rr: hdwy ent fnl 2f: chsd ldrs 1f out: nt clrest of runs and one pce ins fnl f* **20/1**

6 *3/4* **Don Padeja** 2-9-0 0 .... PatrickHills(3) 3 65+
(Luca Cumani) *hld up in tch towards rr: swtchd rt to outer and hdwy over 2f out: styd on ins fnl f: nt rch ldrs* **33/1**

043 **7** *nse* **Wallenberg**[21] 7628 2-9-3 76 .... (e) RobertHavlin 11 65
(John Gosden) *taken down early: chsd ldrs: rdn and unable qck 2f out: btn 1f out and one pce after* **5/1**[2]

8 *1 3/4* **Dusky Lark** 2-9-3 0 .... GeorgeBaker 5 61+
(Hughie Morrison) *rn green: s.i.s: in tch in rr: pushed along and hdwy 2f out: styd on steadily ins fnl f: nt trble ldrs* **20/1**

44 **9** *shd* **Lucky Mountain**[20] 7642 2-9-3 0 .... GrahamLee 6 60
(Ed Dunlop) *hld up in tch towards rr: rdn and effrt towards inner 2f out: styd on same pce and no imp fnl f* **13/2**

10 *7* **Give Me High Five** 2-8-12 0 .... SeanLevey 4 39
(Richard Hannon) *dwlt: a towards rr: rdn and struggling 3f out: bhd over 1f out* **33/1**

0 **11** *2 3/4* **Platinum Proof (USA)**[43] 7127 2-9-3 0 .... TomMcLaughlin 1 38
(John Berry) *chsd ldrs tl rdn and lost pl over 2f out: bhd over 1f out* **100/1**

0 **12** *2 1/4* **Instinctual**[7] 7813 2-9-3 0 .... KirstyMilczarek 12 33
(Brendan Powell) *chsd ldrs: rdn and wknd ent fnl 2f: bhd over 1f out* **200/1**

1m 38.31s (0.11) **Going Correction** -0.025s/f (Stan) **12** Ran SP% **116.5**
Speed ratings (Par 96): **98,97,97,97,95 95,94,93,93,86 83,81**
Tote swingers 1&2 £4.00, 1&3 £13.50, 2&3 £4.00, CSF £23.08 TOTE £18.80: £5.50, £1.10, £2.90; EX 32.80 Trifecta £213.60 Pool: £319.02 - 1.12 winning tickets..
Owner R A H Evans **Bred** Gerry Flannery Developments **Trained** Newmarket, Suffolk

FOCUS
Some powerful stables were involved for Division I of this maiden, run at a fair pace with the winner coming wide to win on his debut. Few were able to close from off the pace and the placed horses help set the level.

NOTEBOOK
Mighty Yar(IRE), a 45,000gns half-brother to the useful 1m/1m2f winner Karawana and 1m4f winner Ocean Bluff, was keen enough and green in rear early, but came with a wide move over 4f out and having been slightly outpaced turning for home, stayed on powerfully up the straight, to win in the style of a decent type. This trip looks to be his minimum and he can surely build on this as a 3yo. (op 12-1 tchd 14-1)
Soaring Spirits(IRE), who built on his debut when runner-up at Wolverhampton last time, was well-backed to win here, stepping up in trip. He was perfectly positioned throughout but was outstayed by the potentially useful winner late on. (op 5-4 tchd 11-10)
Interior Minister showed good pace to get to the front from his draw and kept on well to the line but was worn down late on. (op 8-1)
Magika showed little on her debut over 7f at Kempton six weeks previously but ran much better here, stepped up in trip. She is with the right stable to keep progressing.
Ningara, a 65,000gns half-brother to Group-placed 7f juvenile winner I Love Me, did best of those coming from off the pace having been unable to find an early position from his wide draw and this rates a promising debut. (op 14-1)
Don Padeja, a half-brother to 1m4f AW winner La Concorde, was doing his best work late on out wide, over this inadequate looking trip.
Wallenberg, the most experienced runner in the field, ran his best race when dropped to 7f last time, and having raced up with the pace here, did not convince that he stayed this 1m trip. (tchd 9-2)

7900 BRITISH STALLION STUDS SUPPORTING BRITISH RACING E B F MAIDEN STKS (DIV II) 1m (P)
12:30 (12:31) (Class 5) 2-Y-O **£3,169** (£943; £471; £235) **Stalls** High

Form RPR

25 **1** **Zeus Magic**[14] 7705 2-9-3 0 .... LiamKeniry 6 77+
(David Elsworth) *chsd ldrs: rdn to ld wl over 1f out: edgd lft 1f out: kpt on wl ins fnl f to assert towards fin* **4/1**[2]

00 **2** *3/4* **Khudoua**[138] 4066 2-9-3 0 .... RobertHavlin 5 75
(John Gosden) *in tch: effrt to chal on outer bnd 2f out: chal u.p and edgd lft ent fnl f: no ex and btn towards fin* **4/1**[2]

0 **3** *1 3/4* **Lion Beacon**[14] 7707 2-9-3 0 .... JimCrowley 1 71
(Amanda Perrett) *chsd ldrs: rdn and effrt 2f out: chsd ldng pair fnl 100yds: no imp and one pce after* **20/1**

4 *1/2* **Demonic** 2-9-3 0 .... EddieAhern 7 72+
(Sir Henry Cecil) *rn green: in tch in midfield: rdn wl over 2f out: styng on and clsng on ldrs whn hung bdly lft ent fnl f: swtchd rt and racd awkwardly ins fnl f: kpt on but unable to chal* **6/4**[1]

0 **5** *3* **Perpetual Ambition**[14] 7707 2-9-3 0 .... (b[1]) SebSanders 10 63
(Paul D'Arcy) *pressed ldr: upsides wnr and rdn wl over 1f out: no ex and carried lft 1f out: wknd ins fnl f* **33/1**

6 *1 1/2* **Exclusive Waters (IRE)** 2-9-3 0 .... AdamKirby 2 60
(William Knight) *s.i.s: pushed along early: bhd: rdn and outpcd ent fnl 2f: no threat to ldrs but kpt on again ins fnl f* **33/1**

00 **7** *1 1/4* **Lady Of Yue**[13] 7721 2-8-12 0 .... GrahamLee 11 52
(Ed Dunlop) *stdd s: t.k.h: hld up towards rr: rdn and hdwy over 2f out: drvn and wknd ent fnl f* **100/1**

8 *3/4* **Star Of Namibia (IRE)** 2-9-3 0 .... LukeMorris 8 55
(J S Moore) *bhd: rdn 4f out: outpcd wl over 2f out: plugged on but no threat to ldrs after* **33/1**

00 **9** *3/4* **Faither**[11] 7780 2-8-12 0 .... JasonHart(5) 4 53
(Keith Dalgleish) *dwlt: sn in tch in midfield: rdn and struggling over 2f out: wknd over 1f out* **100/1**

04 **10** *1/2* **Tebbit (USA)**[21] 7627 2-9-3 0 .... AndreaAtzeni 9 52
(Roger Varian) *t.k.h: led tl wl over 1f out: sn rdn and btn: fdd ins fnl f* **5/1**[3]

1m 37.51s (-0.69) **Going Correction** -0.025s/f (Stan) **10** Ran SP% **112.2**
Speed ratings (Par 96): **102,101,99,99,96 94,93,92,91,91**
Tote swingers 1&2 £2.30, 1&3 £0.00, 2&3 £6.70 CSF £18.23 TOTE £3.60: £1.10, £2.00, £6.00; EX 20.20 Trifecta £129.40 Pool: £541.84 - 3.14 winning tickets..
Owner J C Smith **Bred** The Kingwood Partnership **Trained** Newmarket, Suffolk

FOCUS
The pace was solid for division two of this maiden, with the front pair well on top at the line. The winner returned to something like his debut form.

NOTEBOOK
Zeus Magic showed promise over an inadequate 7f on his debut and again found that trip on the short side when disappointing at Kempton last time, but stepping up in trip here stayed on well to the line to win cosily enough. He is bred to want further and looks a fair enough type for middle distance handicaps next season.
Khudoua, running for the first time since being gelded, showed some promise on his second start when staying on well in a decent 7f Newmarket maiden in July (soft) and stepped up on that here. He was a shade unbalanced turning for home, but kept on well up the straight although the lack of a recent run may have told late on. (op 3-1 tchd 11-4)
Lion Beacon travelled well for a long way before weakening on his debut over this trip at Kempton, but kept on much better here for a yard whose runners tend to improve with experience. (tchd 16-1)
Demonic, a January foal out of a well-connected 7f winner who has bred five winners including the high-class Phoenix Tower (7f-1m1f, including Group 3) and two juvenile winners, was the one to take out of the race. Green throughout the contest, he travelled well in parts and looked to be coming with an effort up the straight before hanging his chance away. He can be expected to have learnt plenty from this. (op 7-4 tchd 2-1)
Perpetual Ambition raced up with the pace before fading late on. (op 50-1)
Tebbit(USA) set the pace, but dropped away disappointingly up the straight and may have paid for doing too much early over this longer trip. Official explanation: jockey said colt stopped quickly. (op 9-2 tchd 4-1)

7901 BETFRED "THE HOME OF GOALS GALORE" CLAIMING STKS 7f (P)
1:00 (1:00) (Class 6) 3-Y-O+ **£1,704** (£503; £251) **Stalls** Low

Form RPR

003 **1** **Corporal Maddox**[13] 7732 5-9-6 86 .... AdamKirby 9 91+
(Jamie Osborne) *s.i.s: in tch in rr: stl last and swtchd sharply rt over 1f out: str run 1f out: led wl ins fnl f: gng away at fin* **5/4**[1]

0003 **2** *1* **Majuro (IRE)**[4] 7867 8-8-13 84 .... (t) RobertWinston 8 81
(Charles Smith) *t.k.h: sn pressing ldr: led 2f out: rdn over 1f out: clr ins fnl f: hdd and no ex wl ins fnl f* **9/2**[2]

3001 **3** *1* **Brocklebank (IRE)**[11] 7769 3-9-0 76 .... (tp) GrahamLee 13 81
(Kevin Ryan) *chsd ldrs: rdn and outpcd 2f out: kpt on again u.p ins fnl f* **10/1**

3152 **4** *2 1/2* **Chookie Avon**[34] 7360 5-9-6 77 .... (p) WilliamCarson 4 79
(Keith Dalgleish) *broke wl: sn stdd into midfield: effrt and nt clr run over 1f out tl 1f out: drvn and styd on same pce ins fnl f* **8/1**[3]

2452 **5** *nk* **Dozy Joe**[28] 7484 4-8-13 73 .... (p) SebSanders 11 71
(Paul Fitzsimons) *in tch in midfield: rdn and unable qck ent fnl 2f: styd on same pce ins fnl f* **14/1**

0500 **6** *3/4* **April Fool**[81] 6051 8-9-0 77 .... (b) LukeMorris 5 70
(Ronald Harris) *sn led: rdn and hdd 2f out: btn 1f out: wknd ins fnl f* **10/1**

0400 **7** *nk* **Ongoodform (IRE)**[20] 7645 5-9-3 78 .... EddieAhern 10 72
(Paul D'Arcy) *hld up in tch in last trio: rdn and effrt wl over 1f out: kpt on but nvr gng pce to trble ldrs* **14/1**

1540 **8** *1/2* **Imprimis Tagula (IRE)**[13] 7732 8-8-10 76 .... (v) NatashaEaton(5) 12 69
(Alan Bailey) *in tch: rdn and unable qck ent fnl 2f: plugged on same pce and btn fr over 1f out* **25/1**

3330 **9** *1 1/4* **Aquilifer (IRE)**[32] 7415 4-8-13 66 .... ShaneKelly 6 63
(Mrs K Burke) *hld up in tch in last trio: effrt and nt clr run over 1f out: no imp: nvr able to chal* **40/1**

0010 **10** *2 3/4* **Al Aqabah (IRE)**[28] 7484 7-8-6 70 .... (b) SilvestreDeSousa 1 49
(Brian Gubby) *in tch towards rr: rdn and effrt over 1f out: no imp: wl hld and eased fnl 100yds* **16/1**

0050 **11** *10* **Replicator**[38] 7275 7-8-8 44 ow1 .... (e) RyanClark(3) 2 27
(Patrick Gilligan) *t.k.h: in tch: rdn and wknd over 2f out: bhd fnl f* **200/1**

1m 23.39s (-1.41) **Going Correction** -0.025s/f (Stan)
WFA 3 from 4yo+ 1lb **11** Ran SP% **117.9**
Speed ratings (Par 101): **107,105,104,101,101 100,100,99,98,95 83**
Tote swingers 1&2 £2.60, 1&3 £3.70, 2&3 £9.90 CSF £6.55 TOTE £2.00: £1.60, £1.70, £3.60; EX 10.40 Trifecta £71.40 Pool: £674.60 - 7.08 winning tickets..Corporal Maddox was claimed by Ron Harris for £15,000.
Owner Dr Marwan Koukash **Bred** Theobalds Stud **Trained** Upper Lambourn, Berks

FOCUS
An open-looking claimer with plenty of in-form runners, run at a sound gallop which suited those coming from off the pace. The form is rated around the winner to last winter's handicap form.
Al Aqabah(IRE) Official explanation: jockey said mare moved poorly.

7902 BETFRED MOBILE SPORTS H'CAP 6f (P)
1:30 (1:32) (Class 5) (0-75,75) 3-Y-O+ **£2,385** (£704; £352) **Stalls** Low

Form RPR

0646 **1** **The Strig**[6] 7827 5-9-2 **70** .... (v) WilliamCarson 6 79
(Stuart Williams) *t.k.h: hld up in tch towards rr: rdn and hdwy over 1f out: chal 1f out: led ins fnl f: styd on wl: rdn out* **4/1**[1]

2100 **2** *3/4* **Roy's Legacy**[11] 7775 3-8-7 **66** .... (t) MichaelJMMurphy(5) 3 73
(Shaun Harris) *in tch on inner: styd towards inner bnd 2f out and led over 1f out: hdd and styd on same pce ins fnl f* **25/1**

0000 **3** *3/4* **Dancing Welcome**[28] 7483 6-9-5 **73** .... (b) GrahamLee 4 77
(Milton Bradley) *in tch in midfield: effrt to press ldrs over 1f out: no ex and styng on same pce whn n.m.r ins fnl f* **16/1**

2000 **4** *1* **Diamond Vine (IRE)**[4] 7864 4-9-0 **68** .... (p) LukeMorris 10 69
(Ronald Harris) *in tch in midfield: effrt ent fnl 2f: kpt on u.p ins fnl f* **8/1**[3]

5450 **5** *shd* **Hatta Stream (IRE)**[12] 7741 6-9-1 **72** .... SimonPearce(3) 7 73+
(Lydia Pearce) *hld up in tch towards rr: hdwy on outer bnd 2f out: pushed rt wl over 1f out: racing on stands' rail and styd on wl ins fnl f: nt rch ldrs* **7/1**[2]

0550 **6** *nse* **Dancing Freddy (IRE)**[13] 7730 5-9-3 **71** .... (tp) MartinHarley 5 72
(Violet M Jordan) *t.k.h: hld up in tch in rr: rdn and gd hdwy wl over 1f out: drvn and styd on same pce ins fnl f* **12/1**

1303 **7** *3/4* **We Have A Dream**[12] 7742 7-9-7 **75** .... MartinDwyer 9 73
(William Muir) *sn bustled along to chse ldr: carried rt bnd 2f out: sn unable qck and btn 1f out: one pce after* **4/1**[1]

4226 **8** *3/4* **The Dancing Lord**[240] 1169 3-8-5 **66** .... JakePayne(7) 2 62
(Bill Turner) *led: c towards centre 2f out: sn hdd and unable qck: btn and one pce fnl f* **50/1**

3025 **9** *2 1/4* **Button Moon (IRE)**[12] 7742 4-9-1 **69** .... (p) SebSanders 11 58
(Paul Fitzsimons) *chsd ldrs: carried rt bnd 2f out: swtchd rt and outpcd wl over 1f out: wknd ent fnl f* **12/1**

640 **10** *1/2* **Celtic Sultan (IRE)**[20] 7646 8-8-13 **74** .... SemiraPashai(7) 8 61
(Alastair Lidderdale) *taken down early: rdr slow removing hood and v.s.a: a bhd* **25/1**

1410 **11** *4 1/2* **Torres Del Paine**[63] 6577 5-9-7 **75** .... AdamKirby 1 48
(Brett Johnson) *in tch tl rdn and lost pl over 2f out: bhd fnl f* **4/1**[1]

1m 11.61s (-0.29) **Going Correction** -0.025s/f (Stan) **11** Ran SP% **114.5**
Speed ratings (Par 103): **100,99,98,96,96 96,95,94,91,90 84**
Tote swingers 1&2 £30.00, 1&3 £18.20, 2&3 £34.20 CSF £112.81 CT £1435.50 TOTE £6.50: £2.10, £10.10, £5.10; EX 111.90 TRIFECTA Not won..
Owner Brian Piper & David Cobill **Bred** Old Mill Stud **Trained** Newmarket, Suffolk

FOCUS
A competitive sprint handicap, run at a decent gallop which suited those coming from off the pace, with the front three home all racing towards the far side. Pretty straightforward form.

The Dancing Lord Official explanation: jockey said gelding hung right.

7903 BETFRED 'THE BONUS KING' MAIDEN STKS — 6f (P)

2:00 (2:00) (Class 5) 3-Y-O — **£2,385** (£704; £352) **Stalls** Low

Form — RPR

3 **1** **Polar Venture**[19] 7668 3-9-3 0 AdamBeschizza 4 62+
(William Haggas) *hld up in tch: rdn and qcknd to chal over 1f out: led 1f out: styd on wl* **30/100**[1]

0032 **2** 1 ¼ **Summer Sun**[7] 7804 3-8-12 53 LukeMorris 6 53
(Phil McEntee) *chsd ldrs tl wnt 2nd over 2f out: drvn to ld wl over 1f out: hdd 1f out: styd on same pce ins fnl f* **7/1**[2]

0060 **3** shd **Christopher Chua (IRE)**[126] 4467 3-9-3 57 SebSanders 8 58
(Simon Dow) *taken down early: t.k.h: hld up in midfield: rdn and chsd ldrs 2f out: kpt on ins fnl f* **8/1**[3]

05 **4** 2 ¼ **Outside Art**[9] 7787 3-8-7 0 MichaelJMMurphy(5) 5 45
(Paul Fitzsimons) *t.k.h: hld up in last pair: rdn and effrt over 1f out: kpt on ins fnl f: nvr trbld ldrs* **8/1**[3]

4240 **5** 1 **King's Future**[69] 6402 3-9-3 55 WilliamCarson 9 47
(Lee Carter) *led: hdd and drvn wl over 1f out: wknd ins fnl f* **12/1**

6 ½ **Guilietta Girl (IRE)**[49] 6989 3-8-12 0 [1] KirstyMilczarek 1 41
(David Evans) *chsd ldr tl over 2f out: stl pressing ldrs and drvn over 1f out: wknd ins fnl f* **40/1**

5 **7** 1 ¼ **Flumps**[19] 7667 3-8-12 0 ShaneKelly 2 37
(John Stimpson) *dwlt and sn pushed along in rr: rdn and no imp 2f out: wl hld whn swtchd rt ins fnl f* **25/1**

0-00 **8** 1 ¼ **La Passionata**[57] 6765 3-8-12 41 MartinHarley 7 33
(Jeremy Gask) *stdd s: hld up in tch: hdwy over 3f out: rdn and struggling ent fnl 2f: wknd over 1f out* **66/1**

0400 **9** 4 ½ **Johnson's Cat (IRE)**[202] 2010 3-9-3 42 GrahamLee 3 23
(Daniel Mark Loughnane) *in tch: lost pl and drvn over 2f out: bhd fnl f* **33/1**

1m 12.91s (1.01) **Going Correction** -0.025s/f (Stan) 9 Ran SP% **130.1**

Speed ratings (Par 102): **92,90,90,87,85 85,83,81,75**

Tote swingers 1&2 £1.40, 1&3 £2.50, 2&3 £3.00 CSF £4.13 TOTE £1.50: £1.02, £1.40, £1.70; EX 4.60 Trifecta £15.50 Pool: £1031.42 - 49.67 winning tickets..

Owner Cheveley Park Stud **Bred** F C T Wilson **Trained** Newmarket, Suffolk

FOCUS

A weak, uncompetitive maiden, run at a steady pace, which suited those up with the gallop. The winner didn't need to match his debut run.

7904 DORMANSLAND H'CAP — 1m 2f (P)

2:35 (2:35) (Class 2) (0-100,98) 3-Y-O+ **£10,221** (£3,041; £1,519; £759) **Stalls** Low

Form — RPR

0304 **1** **Tinshu (IRE)**[11] 7771 6-9-4 92 (p) WilliamCarson 6 101
(Derek Haydn Jones) *t.k.h: hld up in midfield: rdn and effrt ent fnl 2f: led over 1f out: hld on wl ins fnl f: rdn out* **5/1**

4001 **2** nk **Robin Hoods Bay**[5] 7842 4-9-3 91 6ex LukeMorris 8 99+
(Ed Vaughan) *hld up in tch in midfield: hdwy to chse ldrs and wd bnd 2f out: chsd wnr 1f out: kpt on wl u.p fnl 100yds* **10/3**[1]

1000 **3** 1 ¼ **Emerald Wilderness (IRE)**[11] 7771 8-8-11 85 FrederikTylicki 7 91
(Mark Rimmer) *stdd s: hld up in tch in last pair: nt clr run and hmpd 2f out: swtchd rt and rallied over 1f out: styd on wl ins fnl f* **25/1**

0600 **4** hd **Nazreef**[25] 7083 5-9-9 97 (t) RobertWinston 4 103
(Hughie Morrison) *t.k.h: chsd ldr: rdn 3f out: unable qck ent fnl f: styd on same pce after* **14/1**

201 **5** ½ **Starfield**[33] 7384 3-8-10 88 RobertHavlin 9 93
(John Gosden) *stdd s: t.k.h: hld up in last pair: effrt 2f out: swtchd lft and hdwy over 1f out: styd on same pce and no imp fnl 100yds* **9/2**

0640 **6** 2 ½ **Spifer (IRE)**[44] 7109 4-8-13 87 AdamKirby 3 87
(Marco Botti) *led and set stdy gallop: qcknd 3f out: hdd and drvn wl over 1f out: nt qckn u.p: wknd ins fnl f* **7/2**[2]

5362 **7** hd **Come On Blue Chip (IRE)**[12] 7751 3-8-13 91 (b) SebSanders 2 90
(Paul D'Arcy) *t.k.h: hld up in tch in midfield: shuffled bk and rdn over 2f out: no imp over 1f out and wknd 1f out* **4/1**[3]

0500 **8** 4 **Emma's Gift (IRE)**[28] 7487 4-8-12 86 (v[1]) AdamBeschizza 5 77
(Julia Feilden) *chsd ldrs tl unable qck u.p jst over 2f out: wknd ent fnl f* **40/1**

2m 6.64s (0.04) **Going Correction** -0.025s/f (Stan)

WFA 3 from 4yo+ 4lb 8 Ran SP% **113.1**

Speed ratings (Par 109): **98,97,96,96,96 94,94,90**

Tote swingers 1&2 £2.90, 1&3 £22.90, 2&3 £6.10 CSF £21.53 CT £373.35 TOTE £5.40: £1.50, £2.20, £10.40; EX 22.60 Trifecta £414.60 Pool: £1,249.61 - 2.26 winning tickets..

Owner Llewelyn, Runeckles **Bred** Mrs M L Parry & P M Steele-Mortimer **Trained** Efail Isaf, Rhondda C Taff

FOCUS

An unsatisfactory pace for this decent contest which led to a sprint finish up the straight. There are doubts over the form, which is rated around the winner.

NOTEBOOK

Tinshu(IRE), 12lb higher than when landing this contest in 2011 and unlucky in the Listed Churchill Stakes over C&D last time, was ridden more prominently than of late and enjoyed a dream passage up the inner turning into the straight, and was just able to hold off the challenge of the runner-up. She clearly excels under these conditions and possesses a fine turn of foot, which proved crucial in this steadily run affair. (op 4-1)

Robin Hoods Bay can consider himself a shade unlucky, as he was cruising when forced wide as the pace quickened turning for home and that allowed the winner to get first run on him. He enjoys a fine record on the AW, but would have preferred a better pace to aim at. (op 7-2)

Emerald Wilderness(IRE) ◆, who was well treated off a 7lb lower mark than for the last of his three C&D wins in January, had questions to answer on the back of two poor recent efforts and he ran a most eye-catching race. Held up in rear off the steady pace, he came with a fine run out wide when the race was all over and this was a more encouraging effort. (tchd 33-1)

Nazreef, on whom Robert Winston was 2-2 prior to this effort, was plenty keen enough and unable to find cover, so deserves credit for battling on well to the line. (tchd 16-1)

Starfield, making his handicap debut, was another unsuited by the steady early fractions, but he showed decent pace to close on the leaders up the straight, although his effort folded rather tamely late on over this longer trip. (op 5-1 tchd 4-1)

Spifer(IRE), having his first run for Marco Botti, helped set the gallop but was readily outpaced inside the final 2f over this shorter trip. He can be expected to come on for this. (op 5-1)

7905 LINGFIELD MARRIOTT HOTEL & COUNTRY CLUB H'CAP — 1m 2f (P)

3:10 (3:11) (Class 6) (0-65,65) 3-Y-O+ **£1,704** (£503; £251) **Stalls** Low

Form — RPR

5050 **1** **Strike Force**[11] 7768 8-8-11 60 (t) NatashaEaton(5) 7 68
(Alison Hutchinson) *chsd ldrs: rdn and effrt to ld 2f out: kpt on wl ins fnl f: all out* **20/1**

0050 **2** nk **Resplendent Alpha**[11] 7768 8-9-4 62 MartinDwyer 13 69
(Jamie Osborne) *slowly away: swtchd lft and rdn leaving stalls: in tch in last quartet: rdn over 2f out: styng on whn swtchd rt over 1f out: str run fnl f: wnt 2nd last strides: nt quite rch wnr* **12/1**

2102 **3** hd **Thecornishcowboy**[11] 7768 3-9-3 65 (t) JohnFahy 1 72
(John Ryan) *wl in tch in midfield: nt clr run briefly on inner 2f out: rdn and effrt to chse wnr over 1f out: ev ch fnl f: no ex cl home* **9/2**[3]

0046 **4** ½ **Lady Arabella (IRE)**[11] 7768 3-9-2 64 GrahamLee 14 70
(Alastair Lidderdale) *hld up towards rr: hdwy on outer over 2f out: rdn and chsd ldrs ins fnl f: kpt on* **16/1**

2053 **5** 1 **Landesherr (GER)**[28] 7474 5-8-13 62 MichaelJMMurphy(5) 11 66
(Steve Gollings) *hld up in tch in midfield: rdn and hdwy between horses over 1f out: chsd ldrs and drvn ins fnl f: styd on same pce fnl 100yds* **4/1**[2]

0006 **6** 2 ½ **Mafi (IRE)**[11] 7767 4-9-5 63 WilliamCarson 12 62
(Mark Hoad) *stdd s: hld up in last pair: hdwy and switching lft over 1f out: drvn and no imp ins fnl f* **16/1**

0005 **7** ¾ **Legal Legacy**[11] 7767 6-9-5 63 EddieAhern 3 61
(Richard Rowe) *dwlt: sn rcvrd and chsng ldrs: effrt u.p ent fnl 2f: unable qck over 1f out: wknd ins fnl f* **10/1**

0052 **8** ½ **Mountrath**[5] 7841 5-9-2 60 (v) GeorgeBaker 9 57
(Gary Moore) *t.k.h: stdd s: hld up in last pair: rdn and effrt ent fnl 2f: sme hdwy over 1f out: rdn and styd on same pce ins fnl f* **3/1**[1]

-000 **9** 1 **Evergreen Forest (IRE)**[11] 7768 4-9-0 61 RyanClark(3) 6 56
(Tom Keddy) *racd in last quartet: rdn over 4f out: struggling and no hdwy u.p 2f out: kpt on ins fnl f: no threat to ldrs* **33/1**

4000 **10** ¾ **Soweto Star (IRE)**[28] 7473 4-9-2 60 FrederikTylicki 10 53
(John Best) *chsd ldrs: wnt 2nd 5f out: pressing ldr and rdn over 3f out: stl pressing ldr ent fnl 2f: sn outpcd and btn: wknd fnl f* **10/1**

0-06 **11** 2 **Bolanderi (USA)**[28] 7473 7-9-3 61 (t) KieranO'Neill 5 50
(Andy Turnell) *chsd ldr tl 5f out: styd chsng ldrs tl unable qck u.p 2f out: wknd 1f out* **33/1**

0060 **12** 1 ¼ **Apache Glory (USA)**[32] 7416 4-9-7 65 ShaneKelly 4 52
(John Stimpson) *hld up in midfield: rdn and no imp on inner over 1f out: wknd ins fnl f* **50/1**

0065 **13** 2 ¾ **Archelao (IRE)**[165] 3154 4-9-4 62 AmirQuinn 2 43
(Richard Rowe) *led tl 2f out: sn btn: wknd qckly ent fnl f* **16/1**

2m 5.81s (-0.79) **Going Correction** -0.025s/f (Stan)

WFA 3 from 4yo+ 4lb 13 Ran SP% **119.3**

Speed ratings (Par 101): **102,101,101,101,100 98,97,97,96,96 94,93,91**

Tote swingers 1&2 £19.80, 1&3 £43.70, 2&3 £6.00 CSF £235.29 CT £1283.74 TOTE £33.70: £7.00, £4.10, £1.40; EX 385.00 Trifecta £584.00 Part won. Pool: £778.77 - 0.10 winning tickets..

Owner Miss A L Hutchinson **Bred** Cheveley Park Stud Ltd **Trained** Exning, Suffolk

FOCUS

A moderate handicap, run at an honest pace with little covering the front four at the line. Very ordinary form.

7906 BETFRED HAT TRICK HEAVEN/DOUBLE DELIGHT APPRENTICE H'CAP — 7f (P)

3:40 (3:40) (Class 6) (0-58,63) 3-Y-O+ **£1,704** (£503; £251) **Stalls** Low

Form — RPR

2212 **1** **See The Storm**[34] 7362 4-9-2 56 CharlesBishop(3) 4 65
(Ian Williams) *t.k.h: chsd ldrs: rdn to chal over 1f out: led ins fnl f: hld on cl home: all out* **9/2**[2]

0603 **2** hd **Silly Billy (IRE)**[7] 7815 4-8-11 53 (v) JakePayne(5) 13 61
(Pat Phelan) *chsd ldrs: rdn and effrt wl over 1f out: pressed ldr ins fnl f: kpt on and clsng grad fnl 100yds: nt quite rch ldrs* **15/2**

0301 **3** shd **Glastonberry**[4] 7861 4-9-5 63 6ex RyanTate(7) 11 71+
(Geoffrey Deacon) *hld up in tch in midfield on outer: effrt u.p over 1f out: hdwy 1f out: edgd lft and pressing ldrs wl ins fnl f: r.o: nt quite rch ldrs* **7/1**[3]

3060 **4** ½ **Regal Acclaim (IRE)**[19] 7670 3-8-12 55 JasonHart(5) 8 62
(Declan Carroll) *led: rdn ent fnl 2f: kpt battling on tl hdd ins fnl f: no ex cl home* **10/1**

0000 **5** 1 **Welsh Inlet (IRE)**[12] 7742 4-8-12 54 WilliamTwiston-Davies(5) 5 58
(John Bridger) *in tch in midfield: effrt u.p over 1f out: chsd ldrs and drvn 1f out: kpt on* **40/1**

-300 **6** 1 **Pytheas (USA)**[28] 7486 5-9-4 55 (v[1]) RyanClark 7 56
(Michael Attwater) *dwlt: sn in tch in midfield: rdn over 2f out: kpt on ins fnl f: nvr quite gng pce to threaten ldrs* **33/1**

5622 **7** ½ **Rogue Reporter (IRE)**[7] 7815 3-9-2 54 (v) AshleyMorgan 3 54
(Stuart Williams) *hld up in tch in midfield: swtchd rt and effrt u.p 2f out: drvn and styd on same pce ins fnl f* **4/1**[1]

0000 **8** 1 ½ **Fleetwoodsands (IRE)**[33] 7382 5-9-5 56 (t) PatrickHills 10 52
(Milton Bradley) *t.k.h: hld up in tch towards rr: rdn and effrt over 1f out: styd on but nvr trbld ldrs* **22/1**

0-60 **9** ½ **Teth**[36] 7318 3-8-12 57 RobertTart(7) 12 52
(Anthony Carson) *sn outpcd in last pair: pushed along 4f out: c wd bnd 2f out: styd on ins fnl f: nvr trbld ldrs* **20/1**

6531 **10** ½ **Flamborough Breeze**[29] 7465 3-8-13 56 (t) NicoleNordblad(5) 14 49
(Ed Vaughan) *stdd and dropped in bhd after s: wl off the pce in last: nudged along and clsd on inner over 1f out: styd on but n.d* **9/1**

0103 **11** ½ **Mango Music**[30] 7447 9-9-2 56 MatthewLawson(3) 6 48
(David Thompson) *chsd ldr tl 2f out: sn unable qck u.p: wknd fnl f* **9/1**

1000 **12** ¾ **Rise To Glory (IRE)**[12] 2373 4-9-2 56 (t) MichaelJMMurphy(3) 2 46
(Shaun Harris) *chsd ldrs: rdn 3f out: kpt on tl btn ent fnl f: wknd fnl f* **25/1**

0021 **13** nk **Circuitous**[27] 7504 4-9-2 56 (p) TobyAtkinson(3) 1 45
(Keith Dalgleish) *in tch in midfield: n.m.r and hmpd over 5f out: rdn and struggling over 2f out: wknd wl over 1f out* **12/1**

0000 **14** 15 **Red Rhythm**[28] 7482 5-9-1 55 ow2 (t) JamieJones(3) 9 4
(Mark Hoad) *awkward leaving stalls and slowly away: hld up in rr of main gp: wknd 2f out: wl bhd and eased fnl f* **100/1**

1m 24.4s (-0.40) **Going Correction** -0.025s/f (Stan)

WFA 3 from 4yo+ 1lb 14 Ran SP% **118.6**

Speed ratings (Par 101): **101,100,100,100,98 97,97,95,94,94 93,92,92,75**

Tote swingers 1&2 £7.10, 2&3 £14.20, 1&3 £7.10 CSF £34.46 CT £241.95 TOTE £5.60: £2.00, £4.00, £2.00; EX 30.60 Trifecta £240.80 Pool: £758.00 - 2.36 winning tickets..

Owner Keating Bradley Fold Ltd **Bred** D R Botterill **Trained** Portway, Worcs

FOCUS

This weak handicap, confined to apprentice riders, was run at a fair pace with three almost in line passing the post. Sound form, with a small personal best from the winner.

T/Plt: £32.70 to a £1 stake. Pool: £64,044.93 - 1428.81 winning tickets T/Qpdt: £12.90 to a £1 stake. Pool: £5,750.72 - 329.34 winning tickets SP

[7793]SOUTHWELL (L-H)
Wednesday, November 28
7907 Meeting Abandoned - waterlogged

[7862]WOLVERHAMPTON (A.W) (L-H)
Wednesday, November 28

OFFICIAL GOING: Standard
Wind: Fresh against Weather: Fine

7914 £32 BONUS AT 32RED.COM H'CAP (DIV I) 5f 216y(P)
1:10 (1:10) (Class 6) (0-65,65) 3-Y-O+ **£1,704** (£503; £251) **Stalls** Low

Form RPR
0005 **1** **Speightowns Kid (USA)**[4] 7859 4-9-7 65 JoeFanning 2 76+
(Jo Hughes) *led 5f out: shkn up over 1f out: clr fnl f: eased nr fin* **4/1**[2]
0000 **2** *1* **Pelmanism**[18] 7684 5-9-5 63 (b) DaleSwift 4 70
(Brian Ellison) *s.i.s: sn pushed along in rr: hdwy over 2f out: r.o u.p: no ch w wnr* **11/4**[1]
0050 **3** *1 ½* **Silver Wind**[18] 7685 7-9-2 60 (b) JimmyFortune 5 63
(Alan McCabe) *s.i.s: sn pushed along in rr: hdwy u.p over 1f out: r.o: nt rch ldrs* **4/1**[2]
0456 **4** *hd* **Blueberry Fizz (IRE)**[5] 7837 4-8-7 51 oh1 (v) MartinLane 7 53
(John Ryan) *prom: rdn over 1f out: hung lft ins fnl f: styd on* **9/1**[3]
254 **5** *2* **Steel City Boy (IRE)**[8] 7794 9-8-6 57 ow1 GeorgeChaloner(7) 12 53
(Garry Woodward) *prom: rdn over 2f out: styd on same pce fnl f* **20/1**
3400 **6** *2 ½* **Bengaline**[32] 7402 3-8-11 55 (b) RichardKingscote 6 43
(Scott Dixon) *chsd ldrs: rdn over 2f out: wknd ins fnl f* **12/1**
0340 **7** *1 ¼* **College Doll**[14] 7703 3-8-7 51 oh4 DominicFox 11 35
(Christine Dunnett) *chsd ldrs: ev ch 2f out: sn rdn: wknd fnl f* **33/1**
1200 **8** *½* **Gran Canaria Queen**[19] 7673 3-9-2 60 (v) TomEaves 13 42
(David O'Meara) *led 1f: chsd ldrs: rdn over 1f out: wknd ins fnl f* **11/1**
0400 **9** *½* **Elusive Pursuit**[12] 7746 4-8-2 53 oh6 ow2 JenniferFerguson(7) 1 33
(Clive Cox) *chsd ldr: pushed along over 2f out: wknd fnl f* **33/1**
6100 **10** *½* **Northern Bolt**[8] 7794 7-9-1 59 (b) PatrickMathers 9 38
(Ian McInnes) *sn outpcd* **50/1**
5025 **11** *¾* **Whisky Bravo**[8] 7798 3-8-12 63 (p) GeorgeBuckell(7) 10 39
(Tim Pitt) *s.i.s: sn pushed along and a in rr* **9/1**[3]
0020 **12** *7* **Simple Rhythm**[21] 7634 6-8-0 51 oh6 (p) BradleyBosley(7) 3
(John Ryan) *s.i.s: effrt over 2f out: sn wknd* **50/1**

1m 13.96s (-1.04) **Going Correction** -0.20s/f (Stan) **12** Ran SP% **117.3**
Speed ratings (Par 101): **98,96,94,94,91 88,86,86,85,84 83,74**
Tote swingers 1&2 £3.90, 1&3 £4.70, 2&3 £4.80 CSF £14.41 CT £46.12 TOTE £3.80: £2.00, £1.10, £2.20; EX 23.80.
Owner R P Phillips **Bred** Sandyview Farm **Trained** Lambourn, Berks
■ Stewards' Enquiry : Dale Swift two-day ban; used whip above shoulder hight (12th-13th Dec).

FOCUS
Division one of a modest sprint handicap, and slightly the quicker leg. The winner looks as good as ever and the right horses were involved.

7915 £32 BONUS AT 32RED.COM H'CAP (DIV II) 5f 216y(P)
1:40 (1:41) (Class 6) (0-65,65) 3-Y-O+ **£1,704** (£503; £251) **Stalls** Low

Form RPR
0046 **1** **Dickie Le Davoir**[18] 7684 8-9-4 62 (b) RobbieFitzpatrick 8 71
(Richard Guest) *s.i.s: sn drvn along in rr: hdwy over 1f out: rdn and r.o to ld wl ins fnl f* **13/2**
4001 **2** *1* **Mey Blossom**[12] 7747 7-9-1 59 (p) GrahamGibbons 2 65
(Richard Whitaker) *a.p: pushed along over 2f out: rdn to chse ldr and edgd rt 1f out: ev ch wl ins fnl f: styd on* **10/1**
0235 **3** *½* **Speedyfix**[19] 7673 5-8-12 56 (t) TomEaves 12 60
(Christine Dunnett) *broke wl: sn lost pl: hdwy over 1f out: sn rdn: r.o* **16/1**
3004 **4** *nk* **My Own Way Home**[12] 7741 4-8-12 63 EoinWalsh(7) 4 66
(David Evans) *mid-div: hdwy over 1f out: sn rdn: r.o towards fin* **4/1**[2]
0653 **5** *nk* **Hab Reeh**[12] 7747 4-8-7 51 oh1 (bt) AmyRyan 6 53+
(Ruth Carr) *led: rdn clr over 1f out: hdd and unable qck wl ins fnl f* **9/1**
1523 **6** *hd* **Catalinas Diamond (IRE)**[23] 7590 4-9-5 63 (t) JoeFanning 7 65
(Pat Murphy) *mid-div: hdwy over 2f out: rdn over 1f out: styd on* **7/2**[1]
030 **7** *1 ¼* **Ghazeer (IRE)**[36] 7316 3-8-13 57 (v) DaleSwift 3 55
(Derek Shaw) *prom: rdn over 2f out: swtchd lft over 1f out: styd on* **16/1**
5400 **8** *1* **Bang Tidy (IRE)**[41] 7201 3-8-10 54 (bt[1]) MartinLane 10 49+
(Brian Ellison) *sn pushed along to chse ldr 5f out: rdn over 2f out: hmpd and no ex 1f out* **5/1**[3]
3205 **9** *2 ¼* **Whipphound**[169] 3016 4-8-11 60 RachealKneller(5) 5 47
(Mark Brisbourne) *prom: rdn over 2f out: wknd fnl f* **17/2**
5600 **10** *2* **Ave Sofia**[12] 7748 3-8-7 51 oh6 (b[1]) DominicFox 1 32
(John Holt) *sn pushed along towards rr: lost tch over 2f out* **100/1**
5000 **11** *1 ¼* **Diddums**[138] 4061 6-8-3 54 oh6 ow3 (e[1]) CarolineKelly(7) 11 31
(John Ryan) *s.i.s: hld up: a bhd* **40/1**

1m 14.08s (-0.92) **Going Correction** -0.20s/f (Stan) **11** Ran SP% **117.0**
Speed ratings (Par 101): **98,96,96,95,95 94,93,91,88,86 84**
Tote Swingers 1&2 £14.90, 2&3 £21.60, 1&3 £29.60 CSF £69.56 CT £1020.03 TOTE £12.10: £2.40, £3.90, £7.50; EX 81.60.
Owner Future Racing (Notts) Limited **Bred** P And Mrs A G Venner **Trained** Stainforth, S Yorks

FOCUS
This was run at a strong gallop, but the overall time was slightly slower than that for division one. The first two help with the standard.

7916 32RED CASINO MEDIAN AUCTION MAIDEN FILLIES' STKS 7f 32y(P)
2:10 (2:10) (Class 6) 2-Y-O **£1,940** (£577; £288; £144) **Stalls** High

Form RPR
5000 **1** **Bay Laurel (IRE)**[46] 7056 2-9-0 57 RichardKingscote 6 62
(Mrs K Burke) *chsd ldrs: nt clr run over 1f out: led ins fnl f: rdn out* **7/1**[2]
54 **2** *1 ¼* **Sofi's Spirit (IRE)**[7] 7812 2-8-9 0 RachealKneller(5) 8 59
(J S Moore) *chsd ldr: rdn: hung rt and ev ch fr over 1f out: styd on same pce ins fnl f* **12/1**
03 **3** *¾* **Sweet Vintage (IRE)**[11] 7778 2-9-0 0 JimmyFortune 3 57
(J W Hills) *led: rdn over 1f out: hdd and edgd rt ins fnl f: styd on same pce* **2/1**[1]
4 *nk* **Barbsiz (IRE)** 2-9-0 0 JoeFanning 5 56
(Mark H Tompkins) *hld up: pushed along over 2f out: hdwy and hung lft over 1f out: edgd rt ins fnl f: styd on* **25/1**
5 *¾* **Xaloc (IRE)** 2-9-0 0 TonyHamilton 1 55+
(Richard Fahey) *s.i.s: hld up: r.o ins fnl f: nt rch ldrs* **9/1**
044 **6** *nk* **Princess Sheila (IRE)**[13] 7724 2-9-0 60 (p) GrahamGibbons 4 54
(J S Moore) *chsd ldrs: rdn over 1f out: no ex ins fnl f* **8/1**[3]
0 **7** *3 ½* **Mariella**[55] 6817 2-9-0 0 MartinLane 7 45
(Peter Chapple-Hyam) *s.i.s: in rr: pushed along over 2f out: n.d* **2/1**[1]

1m 29.62s (0.02) **Going Correction** -0.20s/f (Stan) **7** Ran SP% **111.8**
Speed ratings (Par 91): **91,89,88,88,87 87,83**
Tote swingers 1&2 £11.60, 1&3 £4.40, 2&3 £3.50 CSF £78.70 TOTE £4.60: £5.80, £5.40; EX 77.20.
Owner Mrs Elaine M Burke **Bred** D Veitch & R O'Callaghan **Trained** Middleham Moor, N Yorks

FOCUS
A decidedly modest fillies' maiden. The principals all drifted to the stands' side in the straight and the form is rated on the negative side.

NOTEBOOK
Bay Laurel(IRE) came widest of all to win going away. Having her first run since being sold out of Harry Dunlop's yard for 3,500GBP, the winner had not built on some promising early efforts and came here with a BHA mark of 57. The return to 7f suited her. (op 5-1 tchd 8-1)
Sofi's Spirit(IRE), not fitted with a hood this time, was never far from the pace and stuck on for second. A small race should come her way. (tchd 11-1)
Sweet Vintage(IRE), whose trainer's cold spell continues, stuck on for pressure after setting the pace but had to give best late on. She had also been third over C&D on her previous start and probably ran close to that form. (op 13-8 tchd 6-4)
Barbsiz(IRE) is a half-sister to Potaro, a Group 3 winner in France for Brian Meehan. Staying on without being able to mount a challenge, she looked somewhat green and will know more next time. (tchd 20-1)
Xaloc(IRE) is a half-sister to a couple of winners out of a winning miler. There were clear signs that she was getting the hang of things late on and better can be expected with the experience behind her. (tchd 8-1 and 11-1)
Princess Sheila(IRE), tried in first-time cheekpieces, had her chance but her stamina was perhaps running out late on. (op 9-1 tchd 15-2)
Mariella, who had shown a hint of promise on her debut at Warwick two months back, was disappointing. She missed the break and could never get into it. (op 11-4 tchd 3-1)

7917 32REDPOKER.COM H'CAP 7f 32y(P)
2:45 (2:45) (Class 6) (0-62,62) 3-Y-O+ **£1,704** (£503; £251) **Stalls** High

Form RPR
6010 **1** **Maggie Pink**[23] 7593 3-8-13 55 DominicFox 11 63+
(Michael Appleby) *chsd ldrs: led 5f out: rdn clr over 2f out: hld on* **8/1**
5043 **2** *¾* **Monte Cassino (IRE)**[13] 7733 7-8-12 53 (e) TomEaves 4 59
(Bryan Smart) *mid-div: pushed along over 4f out: hdwy u.p over 2f out: r.o* **6/1**[2]
-136 **3** *½* **Buxton**[253] 972 8-9-5 60 (t) PhillipMakin 3 64
(Roger Ingram) *hld up: hdwy u.p over 1f out: r.o: nt rch ldrs* **14/1**
1500 **4** *½* **Amosite**[23] 7589 6-9-7 62 (p) JoeFanning 1 65
(J R Jenkins) *led: racd keenly: hdd 5f out: chsd wnr: rdn over 2f out: lost 2nd ins fnl f: kpt on* **28/1**
6364 **5** *1 ½* **Koo And The Gang (IRE)**[13] 7733 5-9-2 57 DaleSwift 12 56
(Brian Ellison) *prom: pushed along 1/2-way: rdn over 1f out: styd on* **4/1**[1]
0026 **6** *hd* **Piccolo Express**[19] 7670 6-9-4 59 J-PGuillambert 2 57
(Brian Baugh) *chsd ldrs: pushed along 3f out: rdn over 1f out: no ex ins fnl f* **15/2**[3]
0300 **7** *hd* **Boy The Bell**[13] 7733 5-9-0 55 TonyHamilton 8 53
(Ollie Pears) *chsd ldrs: rdn over 2f out: no ex fnl f* **20/1**
4413 **8** *1 ½* **Wyndham Wave**[49] 6982 3-9-1 57 (p) JamesMillman 10 51
(Rod Millman) *hld up: rdn over 2f out: nvr trbld ldrs* **4/1**[1]
0055 **9** *3 ¾* **Man Of My Word**[13] 7733 3-9-2 58 (p) IanMongan 6 42
(Scott Dixon) *chsd ldrs: rdn over 2f out: wknd over 1f out* **9/1**
1000 **10** *2 ¾* **Ryedale Dancer (IRE)**[4] 7861 4-9-2 57 RobbieFitzpatrick 7 33
(Richard Guest) *s.s a in rr: pushed along over 2f out: eased whn no ch fnl f* **8/1**
4000 **11** *1* **Justbookies Dotnet**[12] 7742 3-9-6 62 (v) MartinLane 9 36
(Louise Best) *mid-div: pushed along 1/2-way: wknd over 2f out* **40/1**

1m 28.66s (-0.94) **Going Correction** -0.20s/f (Stan)
WFA 3 from 4yo+ 1lb **11** Ran SP% **115.6**
Speed ratings (Par 101): **97,96,95,95,93 93,92,91,86,83 82**
Tote swingers 1&2 £13.80, 1&3 £18.20, 2&3 £8.10 CSF £53.23 CT £675.47 TOTE £19.30: £5.20, £1.40, £4.00; EX 66.50.
Owner A W Bult **Bred** Harcourt Stud **Trained** Danethorpe, Notts

FOCUS
Very ordinary handicap form, although the winner is perhaps worth a bit more than the bare figure.

7918 32RED H'CAP 5f 20y(P)
3:20 (3:20) (Class 3) (0-95,98) 3-Y-O+ **£6,792** (£2,021; £1,010; £505) **Stalls** Low

Form RPR
4401 **1** **York Glory (USA)**[7] 7817 4-9-13 98 6ex (b) PhillipMakin 4 107
(Kevin Ryan) *trckd ldrs: led 1f out: rdn out* **11/10**[1]
5044 **2** *nk* **Six Wives**[4] 7860 5-8-9 80 (p) RichardKingscote 6 88
(Scott Dixon) *chsd ldr tl led over 3f out: rdn and hdd 1f out: r.o* **20/1**
0041 **3** *1 ½* **Alaskan Bullet (IRE)**[23] 7591 3-8-9 80 MartinLane 9 83
(Brian Ellison) *s.i.s: hld up: hdwy over 1f out: hung lft ins fnl f: r.o: nt rch ldrs* **11/2**[2]
162 **4** *hd* **Last Sovereign**[20] 7651 8-8-10 88 (b) JacobButterfield(7) 1 90
(Ollie Pears) *hld up: edgd rt wl over 1f out: rdn and r.o ins fnl f: nt rch ldrs* **9/1**
0004 **5** *shd* **Moorhouse Lad**[14] 7704 9-9-2 87 IanMongan 8 89
(Garry Moss) *led: hdd over 3f out: chsd ldr tl rdn over 1f out: styd on* **14/1**
0010 **6** *3* **Whozthecat (IRE)**[14] 7704 5-9-1 86 (b) JoeFanning 2 77
(Declan Carroll) *prom: rdn over 1f out: styd on same pce* **7/1**[3]
3361 **7** *½* **Rylee Mooch**[4] 7860 4-8-9 80 6ex (e) RobbieFitzpatrick 7 69
(Richard Guest) *chsd ldrs: rdn over 1f out: styd on same pce fnl f* **20/1**
220 **8** *3 ½* **Profile Star (IRE)**[80] 6075 3-8-10 81 GrahamGibbons 3 57
(David Barron) *sn pushed along in rr: hmpd wl over 1f out: nvr on terms* **12/1**
20 **9** *8* **Tango Sky (IRE)**[42] 7177 3-8-13 84 AdrianNicholls 5 32
(David Nicholls) *s.i.s: outpcd* **25/1**

1m 0.56s (-1.74) **Going Correction** -0.20s/f (Stan) **9** Ran SP% **113.2**
Speed ratings (Par 107): **105,104,102,101,101 96,96,90,77**
Tote swingers 1&2 £6.20, 1&3 £3.20, 2&3 £12.90 CSF £29.02 CT £90.01 TOTE £1.80: £1.20, £4.80, £2.10; EX 18.40.
Owner Salman Rashed & Mohamed Khalifa **Bred** Paget Bloodstock & Horse France **Trained** Hambleton, N Yorks

FOCUS
A decent sprint handicap, if not the strongest for the grade, in which few became involved. The winner is back to his best.

NOTEBOOK

York Glory(USA) followed up under the penalty for his recent Lingfield win. Adopting different tactics on this drop back to 5f, he didn't do much in front and won a shade more easily than the margin suggests. He's still relatively unexposed on artificial surfaces and there should be more to come from him. There's a possibility he could go to the Dubai carnival. (tchd 5-4)

Six Wives, back in cheekpieces, went freely to post. She rallied well to go down fighting, but has now been beaten all seven times she has raced off 80 or higher. (op 22-1)

Alaskan Bullet(IRE), winner of a C&D seller earlier this month on his debut for the Ellison stable, and running from an unchanged mark, made good late progress despite appearing to be hanging. (op 5-1 tchd 9-2 and 6-1)

Last Sovereign, dropped 2lb since finishing runner-up in a 6f claimer here, made late progress and remains in good heart. (op 13-2)

Moorhouse Lad backed up his decent effort at Kempton and was still third with a few yards to go. (op 16-1 tchd 18-1)

7919 32REDBINGO.COM NURSERY — 1m 141y(P)
3:50 (3:50) (Class 6) (0-65,64) 2-Y-O — £1,704 (£503; £251) Stalls Low

Form — RPR

0050 **1** **Crystal Peaks**[14] 7708 2-8-13 56 .... DaleSwift 2 — 60
(James Given) *sn pushed along and prom: rdn to chse ldr over 2f out: led and edgd rt ins fnl f: hrd rdn: styd on* **20/1**

5635 **2** *1* **Corton Lad**[11] 7779 2-9-0 57 ....(p) JoeFanning 9 — 59
(Keith Dalgleish) *chsd ldrs: rdn over 1f out: r.o* **3/1**[1]

6005 **3** *nk* **Flywheel (IRE)**[63] 6583 2-8-8 51 ....(bt[1]) MartinLane 1 — 52
(Brian Meehan) *hld up in tch: rdn over 1f out: r.o* **15/2**

3006 **4** *½* **Walter White (IRE)**[11] 7779 2-9-7 64 ....(p) JimmyFortune 10 — 64
(Andrew Balding) *a.p: rdn over 1f out: r.o* **6/1**[3]

4005 **5** *2¼* **Roland**[14] 7714 2-8-12 55 ....(b[1]) AmyRyan 3 — 50
(Kevin Ryan) *led: rdn over 1f out: hung rt: hdd and no ex ins fnl f* **20/1**

0660 **6** *2¾* **She's Some Girl (IRE)**[7] 7808 2-8-9 52 .... TonyHamilton 12 — 42
(Richard Fahey) *hld up: nt clr run over 2f out: nvr nrr* **50/1**

0001 **7** *1¾* **Royal Caper**[7] 7808 2-9-2 59 6ex .... StevieDonohoe 5 — 45
(John Ryan) *prom tl rdn and wknd over 2f out* **12/1**

665 **8** *½* **Gabrial The Duke (IRE)**[9] 7785 2-9-3 60 ....(v[1]) TomEaves 11 — 45
(Ian Williams) *hld up: rdn over 2f out: nvr on terms* **7/1**

5324 **9** *1* **Poetic Verse**[76] 6156 2-9-0 57 .... JamesMillman 7 — 40
(Rod Millman) *prom: lost pl over 7f out: n.d after* **12/1**

4040 **10** *3¾* **Ella Motiva (IRE)**[11] 7779 2-9-6 63 .... RobbieFitzpatrick 6 — 38
(Mark Brisbourne) *hld up: rdn over 2f out: a in rr* **20/1**

0652 **11** *5* **Red Eight (USA)**[14] 7708 2-9-7 64 .... PhillipMakin 8 — 29
(John Butler) *chsd ldr tl drvn along 3f out: wknd 2f out* **7/2**[2]

1m 49.01s (-1.49) **Going Correction** -0.20s/f (Stan) — 11 Ran SP% **117.4**
Speed ratings (Par 94): **98,97,96,96,94 91,90,89,89,85 81**
Tote swingers 1&2 £15.30, 2&3 £4.20, 1&3 £26.80 CSF £76.28 CT £519.54 TOTE £27.60: £4.50, £1.90, £1.10; EX 137.40.
Owner Danethorpe Racing Partnership **Bred** Mrs Hugh Maitland-Jones **Trained** Willoughton, Lincs
■ Stewards' Enquiry : Dale Swift two-day ban; used whip above shoulder (14th-15th Dec).

FOCUS

Low-grade nursery form, with a couple of the leading candidates failing to give their running. The winner is back to form and sets the level.

NOTEBOOK

Crystal Peaks had not shown a whole lot in four previous tries, including her nursery bow, but she was 3lb lower here and the longer trip brought about some improvement. She didn't have much to spare at the end, having been under pressure before the home turn. Official explanation: trainers representative said regarding apparent improvement in form that filly appeared to benefit on this occasion from a favourable draw and the race being run to suit. (op 16-1)

Corton Lad came in for support and he ran creditably in the first-time cheekpieces. He ought to win a nursery. (op 9-2)

Flywheel(IRE), upped in trip and with blinkers added to the tongue tie, travelled quite well before running on for pressure near the inside rail. (tchd 6-1)

Walter White(IRE) is exposed and has been beaten in six nurseries now. He hung to his right in the straight but did stay on. (op 10-1)

Roland, having hung badly in cheekpieces at Southwell, did a similar thing in the blinkers here. He was still in front at the time, after looking set to make the frame at least turning for home. Official explanation: jockey said gelding hung right.

Royal Caper, penalised for his Kempton win, was in trouble before the straight. Stevie Donohoe reported that his mount was never travelling. Official explanation: jockey said gelding was never travelling. (op 11-1 tchd 14-1)

Red Eight(USA) had Crystal Peaks well behind when beaten a nose on his nursery debut at Kempton, but dropped away to finish last here. Phillip Makin reported that the colt stopped very quickly. Official explanation: jockey said colt stopped very quickly. (op 9-4)

7920 32RED.COM H'CAP — 1m 141y(P)
4:20 (4:21) (Class 4) (0-85,85) 3-Y-O+ — £4,204 (£1,251; £625; £312) Stalls Low

Form — RPR

1231 **1** **Chookie Royale**[18] 7685 4-9-0 78 ....(p) TomEaves 9 — 91
(Keith Dalgleish) *hld up: hdwy over 3f out: rdn to ld ins fnl f* **15/2**

1303 **2** *1½* **Dubawi Island (FR)**[14] 7715 3-9-4 85 ....(b) JoeFanning 1 — 95
(James Tate) *chsd ldr tl led over 2f out: rdn and hung rt fr over 1f out: hdd ins fnl f: styd on same pce* **2/1**[1]

3205 **3** *1¼* **Angelic Upstart (IRE)**[12] 7751 4-9-1 79 .... MichaelStainton 8 — 86
(Andrew Balding) *chsd ldrs: rdn over 1f out: hmpd sn after: hung lft ins fnl f: styd on* **15/2**

6614 **4** *2½* **Prime Exhibit**[6] 7824 7-9-5 83 ....(t) RichardKingscote 5 — 84
(Daniel Mark Loughnane) *hld up: hdwy over 1f out: r.o: nt rch ldrs* **9/1**

6256 **5** *1½* **Follow The Flag (IRE)**[14] 7715 8-8-12 76 ....(v) GrahamGibbons 4 — 74
(Alan McCabe) *hld up: rdn over 2f out: hmpd over 1f out: n.d* **25/1**

665 **6** *¾* **Jack Who's He (IRE)**[27] 7502 3-8-7 81 .... EoinWalsh[(7)] 2 — 77
(David Evans) *prom: rdn over 2f out: wknd over 1f out* **4/1**[2]

3111 **7** *1¾* **Desert Creek (IRE)**[14] 7715 6-8-10 79 .... ShirleyTeasdale[(5)] 11 — 71
(David Nicholls) *trckd ldrs: racd keenly: shkn up over 1f out: wknd fnl f* **7/1**[3]

0062 **8** *4½* **Pendragon (USA)**[22] 7608 9-8-10 74 .... DaleSwift 3 — 56
(Brian Ellison) *hld up: rdn over 1f out: wknd fnl f* **20/1**

0020 **9** *6* **Beautiful Day**[14] 7715 4-8-13 77 ....(b) PhillipMakin 7 — 45
(Kevin Ryan) *led: rdn and hdd over 2f out: wknd over 1f out* **28/1**

3100 **10** *14* **Icelander (USA)**[154] 3492 3-8-10 77 .... J-PGuillambert 6 — 13
(Jo Hughes) *sn pushed along in rr: bhd fnl 3f* **28/1**

1m 47.28s (-3.22) **Going Correction** -0.20s/f (Stan)
WFA 3 from 4yo+ 3lb — 10 Ran SP% **114.9**
Speed ratings (Par 105): **106,104,103,101,100 99,97,93,88,76**
Tote swingers 1&2 £3.70, 1&3 £12.20, 2&3 £4.50 CSF £21.47 CT £118.13 TOTE £6.80: £2.20, £1.40, £1.80; EX 24.70.
Owner Raeburn Brick Limited **Bred** D And J Raeburn **Trained** Carluke, S Lanarks

FOCUS

They went a brisk pace in this fair handicap. The form seems sound enough, rated around the third.

7921 32REDBBET.COM H'CAP — 1m 4f 50y(P)
4:50 (4:50) (Class 6) (0-60,60) 3-Y-O — £1,704 (£503; £251) Stalls Low

Form — RPR

0422 **1** **Langham Lily (USA)**[36] 7303 3-9-6 59 .... StevieDonohoe 10 — 69
(Chris Wall) *hld up: hdwy over 4f out: pushed along over 2f out: rdn over 1f out: styd on to ld post* **6/4**[1]

0032 **2** *shd* **Dewala**[8] 7800 3-9-0 53 .... DominicFox 11 — 62
(Michael Appleby) *chsd ldr tl led 4f out: rdn over 2f out: hung lft ins fnl f: hdd post* **6/1**[3]

0060 **3** *3¾* **Guava**[8] 7798 3-8-7 46 oh1 .... JamieMackay 7 — 49
(Shaun Harris) *hld up: rdn over 2f out: r.o ins fnl f: nt rch ldrs* **50/1**

0000 **4** *1¼* **Landown Littlerock**[8] 7800 3-8-11 55 .... JackDuern[(5)] 8 — 56
(Reg Hollinshead) *chsd ldrs: rdn over 3f out: styd on same pce appr fnl f* **50/1**

5004 **5** *1¼* **Sunny Bank**[13] 7718 3-9-2 55 ....(t) JimmyFortune 3 — 54
(Andrew Balding) *chsd ldrs: rdn over 2f out: sn outpcd* **8/1**

2331 **6** *2¼* **Taro Tywod (IRE)**[12] 7752 3-9-4 57 .... GrahamGibbons 2 — 52
(Mark Brisbourne) *led 8f: chsd ldr: rdn and ev ch over 1f out: wknd ins fnl f* **7/2**[2]

0630 **7** *6* **Brandy Snapping**[26] 7527 3-8-13 52 .... RobbieFitzpatrick 12 — 38
(Mark Brisbourne) *hld up: rdn over 3f out: nvr on terms* **50/1**

4350 **8** *nk* **Quiet Route (IRE)**[4] 7869 3-9-7 60 ....(b[1]) DaleSwift 6 — 45
(Brian Ellison) *hld up: rdn over 2f out: nvr on terms* **11/1**

0350 **9** *2¼* **Chankillo**[40] 6474 3-9-6 59 .... JoeFanning 5 — 41
(Mark H Tompkins) *hld up in tch: rdn over 3f out: wknd over 2f out* **8/1**

0 **10** *1* **La Zam (FR)**[5] 7841 3-9-7 60 .... RussKennemore 9 — 40
(Reg Hollinshead) *stdd s: hld up: plld hrd: rdn over 2f out: a in rr* **40/1**

2m 38.14s (-2.96) **Going Correction** -0.20s/f (Stan) — 10 Ran SP% **115.4**
Speed ratings (Par 98): **101,100,98,97,96 95,91,91,89,88**
Tote swingers 1&2 £3.30, 1&3 £14.60, 2&3 £16.50 CSF £10.62 CT £295.41 TOTE £2.70: £1.60, £2.00, £7.00; EX 11.00.
Owner Peter Botham **Bred** Nato **Trained** Newmarket, Suffolk

FOCUS

A very moderate handicap for 3yos, but the pace was sound and the first two, who were clear, are improving at a lowly level.

T/Jkpt: Not won. T/Plt: £789.20 to a £1 stake. Pool: £69,715.22 - 64.48 winning tickets T/Qpdt: £217.70 to a £1 stake. Pool: £5974.21 - 20.30 winning tickets CR

7891 KEMPTON (A.W) (R-H)
Thursday, November 29

OFFICIAL GOING: Standard
Wind: virtually nil Weather: dry, chilly

7922 32REDBINGO.COM CLAIMING STKS — 1m (P)
4:05 (4:05) (Class 6) 2-Y-O — £1,617 (£481; £240; £120) Stalls Low

Form — RPR

6514 **1** **Missing Agent**[12] 7779 2-8-0 63 ....(v) PhilipPrince[(7)] 2 — 65
(David Evans) *mde all: clr w runner-up 2f out: styd on wl fnl f: eased cl home* **2/1**[2]

0632 **2** *2* **Secret Symphony**[10] 7786 2-8-10 66 ....(t) LiamKeniry 3 — 63
(Sylvester Kirk) *chsd wnr thrght: rdn to press wnr 1f out: edgd rt and fnd little u.p: btn fnl 100yds* **11/2**[3]

00 **3** *4½* **Mick Dundee (IRE)**[159] 3387 2-9-5 0 .... SebSanders 6 — 62
(J W Hills) *s.i.s: in tch in rr: outpcd wl over 2f out: swtchd lft and hdwy over 2f out: chsd ldng pair over 1f out: kpt on but no imp* **50/1**

0200 **4** *1* **Unidexter (IRE)**[5] 7854 2-8-7 57 ....(v[1]) AndreaAtzeni 4 — 48
(Mick Channon) *in tch in midfield: rdn and outpcd over 3f out: no threat to ldrs but plugged on fnl f* **16/1**

0 **5** *2½* **Doctor's Gift**[27] 7517 2-8-11 0 .... DavidProbert 5 — 46
(Andrew Balding) *chsd ldrs tl lost pl and bhd 4f out: n.d after* **9/1**

135 **6** *4* **Cheektocheek (IRE)**[45] 7111 2-9-2 74 .... AdamKirby 1 — 42
(Marco Botti) *dwlt: rcvrd to chse ldrs after 2f: rdn and outpcd over 2f out: fdd fnl f* **11/8**[1]

1m 38.56s (-1.24) **Going Correction** -0.15s/f (Stan) — 6 Ran SP% **108.7**
Speed ratings (Par 94): **100,98,93,92,90 86**
Tote Swingers 1&2 £1.50, 2&3 £7.60, 1&3 £13.80 CSF £12.32 TOTE £3.50: £1.90, £1.60; EX 11.70.There were no claims.
Owner Mrs E Evans **Bred** Jason Puckey **Trained** Pandy, Monmouths

FOCUS

Few got seriously involved in this weak 2-y-o claimer and the form is straightforward with the first two and the fourth all close to recent marks.

NOTEBOOK

Missing Agent added to his nursery success over 7f here two runs back with a game effort from the front. He had to prove himself fully over this far, but was able to boss the race and kept finding after getting a smack 2f out. This is his sort of class, but he's now 2-2 at the course and remains capable of further success during the winter. (tchd 7-4 and 9-4)

Secret Symphony looked the one to side with nearing the final furlong, but he lacked the resolution of the winner and again found one too good. He sets the level. (op 9-2)

Mick Dundee(IRE) shaped as though he would come on for the run on this switch to Polytrack. He's now found his level. (op 33-1)

Cheektocheek(IRE) was best in at the weights down in class but never looked happy after missing the break and gave up quickly once pressure was applied. He's one to avoid. (op 5-4)

7923 32REDPOKER.COM MAIDEN AUCTION STKS (DIV I) — 1m (P)
4:35 (4:35) (Class 6) 2-Y-O — £1,617 (£481; £240; £120) Stalls Low

Form — RPR

0 **1** **Smileswithhiseyes (IRE)**[36] 7330 2-8-11 0 .... RobertWinston 3 — 70+
(Gay Kelleway) *pushed along leaving stalls: hld up in tch in midfield: rdn and hdwy to press ldr over 1f out: drew clr w rival and led ins fnl f: styd on wl* **33/1**

0 **2** *¾* **Misfer**[15] 7707 2-8-13 0 .... IanMongan 11 — 70+
(Sir Henry Cecil) *chsd ldr over 6f out: rdn to ld over 2f out: drvn and hrd pressed over 1f out: clr w wnr 1f out: hdd and styd on same pce ins fnl f* **6/4**[1]

0 **3** *4½* **Mystery Woman (IRE)**[37] 7305 2-8-5 0 .... MartinDwyer 9 — 52
(Peter Chapple-Hyam) *hld up in last trio: hdwy over 2f out: chsd ldng pair over 1f out: outpcd and btn 1f out: pushed along and kpt on for clr 3rd* **8/1**[3]

0 **4** *2* **Hello Sailor**[52] 6928 2-8-11 0..............(b[1]) JimCrowley 10 53
(Ralph Beckett) *t.k.h: hld up towards rr: rdn and struggling over 3f out: no ch w ldrs but hdwy u.p over 1f out: styd on fnl f* **8/1**[3]

025 **5** *½* **Inessa Armand (IRE)**[5] 7868 2-8-7 0.............. AndreaAtzeni 2 48
(J S Moore) *led for 1f: chsd ldrs: rdn and unable qck 2f out: btn 1f out: wknd ins fnl f* **9/2**[2]

6 **6** *hd* **Aegean Whispers**[21] 7642 2-8-4 0.............. KieranO'Neill 6 44+
(Richard Hannon) *s.i.s: rdn along in rr: hdwy u.p over 1f out: styd on fnl f: nvr trbld ldrs* **25/1**

7 *nk* **On With The Dance (IRE)** 2-9-0 0.............. TedDurcan 4 54
(Ed Vaughan) *s.i.s: bhd: hdwy on inner ent fnl 2f: no prog and btn 1f out: wknd ins fnl f* **14/1**

0 **8** *3¾* **Candyman Can (IRE)**[21] 7642 2-8-10 0.............. LiamKeniry 5 41
(Dominic Ffrench Davis) *chsd ldrs: rdn and outpcd ent fnl f: wknd over 1f out* **100/1**

9 *nk* **Poem (IRE)** 2-8-9 0.............. DavidProbert 1 39
(Andrew Balding) *hld up in tch in midfield: nt clr run and swtchd lft over 2f out: sn rdn and outpcd: wknd over 1f out* **8/1**[3]

64 **10** *16* **Gigli (IRE)**[37] 7304 2-8-7 0..............(b[1]) AdamBeschizza 8
(William Haggas) *racd freely: led after 1f: hdd and rdn over 2f out: fdd over 1f out: wl bhd and eased ins fnl f* **8/1**[3]

6040 **11** *2¼* **Sakhee's Ichigou**[31] 7432 2-8-4 56.............. NickyMackay 7
(Michael Blanshard) *in tch in midfield: rdn and struggling whn hung rt over 2f out: sn wknd: bhd fnl f* **66/1**

1m 38.69s (-1.11) **Going Correction** -0.15s/f (Stan) **11** Ran SP% **118.6**
Speed ratings (Par 94): **99,98,93,91,91 91,90,87,86,70 68**
Tote Swingers 1&2 £14.90, 2&3 £3.30, 1&3 £39.30 CSF £82.79 TOTE £53.60: £10.60, £1.70, £2.20; EX 181.30 Trifecta £1108.50 Part won. Pool: £1,478.05 - 0.62 winning tickets..
Owner Chris Peach & Matt Bartram **Bred** B Walsh **Trained** Exning, Suffolk

FOCUS
They went quick enough in this modest 2-y-o maiden and the first pair came well clear. The form could be better than rated.

NOTEBOOK
Smileswithhiseyes(IRE) showed the clear benefit of his Newmarket debut last month and produced a hugely improved effort to score. He was a lot more professional and made his effort that bit later than the runner-up, which made the difference nearing the finish. The extra furlong helped and it will be interesting to see what mark he's allotted.
Misfer ◆ was the best horse in this race. He raced a lot more alertly than was the case over C&D on his debut 15 days earlier, but did plenty getting across from the outside stall and also found himself in front sooner than looked ideal in the home straight. His rider getting tangled up with his whip late on also didn't help, but he was in trouble at that point. This imposing colt should be well up to making amends if out again this winter. (op 2-1)
Mystery Woman(IRE) ran well below market expectations on her Lingfield debut and was still too green here to do herself full justice. She kept on well enough late, though, and looks more of one for handicaps after her next outing. (tchd 6-1)
Hello Sailor got no cover out wide and hit a flat spot 5f out. However, he was doing some decent late work in first-time blinkers and is evidently going the right way. (op 10-1)
Inessa Armand(IRE) looked to find this coming too soon. (op 7-2 tchd 5-1)
Aegean Whispers got going late on and is one to note when switching to handicaps. (op 33-1)
On With The Dance(IRE) ◆, half-brother to stable star Dance And Dance, got well behind early, but made a promising move on the inside 2f out before tiring and ought to improve plenty for this debut experience. (op 16-1)

7924 32REDPOKER.COM MAIDEN AUCTION STKS (DIV II) 1m (P)
5:05 (5:05) (Class 6) 2-Y-O £1,617 (£481; £240; £120) Stalls Low

Form RPR

4642 **1** **Paddy's Saltantes (IRE)**[21] 7642 2-8-10 67.............. AndreaAtzeni 6 68
(J S Moore) *in tch towards rr: rdn over 3f out: hdwy u.p over 1f out: chal ins fnl f: led fnl 75yds: r.o wl* **8/1**

2 *½* **Stepping Ahead (FR)** 2-8-11 0.............. RobertWinston 5 68
(Mrs K Burke) *dwlt and rdn along early: hdwy to ld after 2f: rdn over 2f out: hrd pressed ins fnl f: hdd and one pce fnl 75yds* **7/1**[3]

4 **3** *shd* **Captain Starlight (IRE)**[15] 7705 2-8-12 0.............. EddieAhern 4 69
(Jo Crowley) *broke wl: t.k.h and sn stdd bk into midfield: hdwy on outer to chal wl over 1f out: awkward hd carriage u.p: no ex wl ins fnl f* **5/2**[1]

050 **4** *1¼* **Night's Watch**[70] 6412 2-9-0 0.............. JoeFanning 3 68+
(William Jarvis) *t.k.h: hmpd and dropped to rr after 1f: hdwy and edging lft over 1f out: chsd ldng trio ins fnl f: kpt on* **20/1**

52 **5** *3* **Red Tulip**[33] 7410 2-8-4 0.............. LukeMorris 10 51
(James Fanshawe) *in tch in midfield: rdn and effrt to chal over 1f out: sn struggling: wknd ins fnl f* **9/2**[2]

0 **6** *¾* **Jan De Heem**[43] 7165 2-8-9 0.............. JimCrowley 1 54
(Ralph Beckett) *in tch in midfield: rdn and effrt 2f out: no imp 1f out: kpt on same pce after* **8/1**

0 **7** *nk* **Jd Rockefeller**[21] 7642 2-8-2 0.............. LouisSteward[(7)] 8 53
(Paul D'Arcy) *in tch towards rr: rdn and no hdwy over 2f out: styd on past btn horses ins fnl f: nvr trbld ldrs* **66/1**

2 **8** *shd* **Shamiana**[26] 7552 2-8-7 0.............. NickyMackay 2 51
(Gerard Butler) *chsd ldrs: rdn and unable qck ent fnl 2f: btn over 1f out: wknd fnl f* **5/2**[1]

9 *½* **Hail To Princess** 2-8-5 0.............. JohnFahy 9 48+
(Patrick Chamings) *v.s.a: clsd and in tch in rr after 2f: hdwy on outer over 3f out: rdn and hung rt jst over 2f out: wknd over 1f out* **66/1**

0 **10** *5* **Suspension**[15] 7707 2-8-5 0.............. DavidProbert 7 37
(Hughie Morrison) *led for 2f: styd chsng ldr tl wl over 1f out: sn btn: fdd ent fnl f* **14/1**

1m 39.71s (-0.09) **Going Correction** -0.15s/f (Stan) **10** Ran SP% **124.5**
Speed ratings (Par 94): **94,93,93,92,89 88,88,88,87,82**
Tote Swingers 1&2 £9.00, 2&3 £4.80, 1&3 £4.80 CSF £66.39 TOTE £10.00: £2.70, £2.60, £1.50; EX 72.10 Trifecta £374.10 Pool: £1,930.54 - 3.87 winning tickets..
Owner Wall To Wall Partnership **Bred** Tom And Hazel Russell **Trained** Upper Lambourn, Berks

FOCUS
This second division of the juvenile maiden was run at an ordinary tempo and it paid to race handily, but the winner came from near last to first in the home straight. The form looks ordinary although the winner deserves extra credit.

NOTEBOOK
Paddy's Saltantes(IRE), rated 67, posted a personal best at Lingfield last time out and improved again to land this. He looked to need every yard of the trip, which suggests he'll peak at around 1m2f next year. (op 12-1)
Stepping Ahead(FR), already gelded, was seemingly unfancied for his debut but his yard sent out a treble the previous day, two of them at this venue. He ran a solid race from the front and was not beaten at all far. There should be a maiden for him. (op 14-1)
Captain Starlight(IRE) ran fourth over 7f in a better maiden here on his debut. He held every chance and got the longer trip without trouble. However, as was the case first time up, he advertised a high head carriage under pressure and now has a little to prove on that front. (op 7-2)
Night's Watch, on his AW debut, was doing his best work late on this return from a 70-day break. It was certainly his best effort yet. (op 33-1)
Red Tulip has plenty of stamina on her dam's side. She flattened out after having a chance and probably found it too testing at this stage. (op 11-2 tchd 6-1)
Shamiana was a huge market drifter. She faded tamely over the extra furlong and was well below the promise of her Newmarket debut. (op 6-4 tchd 4-1)

7925 32REDBET.COM H'CAP 1m (P)
5:35 (5:36) (Class 6) (0-65,65) 3-Y-0+ £1,617 (£481; £240; £120) Stalls Low

Form RPR

0423 **1** **Focail Eile**[12] 7781 7-9-3 63.............. AdamKirby 1 71
(John Ryan) *chsd ldrs: rdn and effrt to chal over 1f out: led ins fnl f: kpt on wl u.p: collapsed fatally after line* **3/1**[1]

66-5 **2** *½* **Avertis**[40] 7256 7-8-12 63.............. AmyScott[(5)] 2 70
(Alastair Lidderdale) *led: rdn and hrd pressed ent fnl 2f: battled on wl tl hdd and one pce ins fnl f* **10/1**

055 **3** *hd* **Bowstar**[29] 7477 3-9-2 64.............. J-PGuillambert 12 71
(Michael Attwater) *chsd ldrs: rdn and effrt 2f out: chsd ldrs 1f out: kpt on wl u.p ins fnl f* **9/1**[3]

5661 **4** *hd* **Bladewood Girl**[29] 7486 4-9-3 63.............. FrederikTylicki 10 69+
(J R Jenkins) *hld up in tch in midfield: hdwy to chse ldrs whn nt clr run and swtchd rt 1f out: kpt on u.p ins fnl f* **3/1**[1]

320 **5** *¾* **Conducting**[73] 6302 4-9-5 65.............. RobertWinston 11 69
(Gay Kelleway) *stdd after s: hld up in tch in rr: nt clr run 3f out: hdwy and swtchd rt ent fnl f: kpt on: nt rch ldrs* **10/1**

0240 **6** *1* **Sir Bruno (FR)**[48] 7022 5-9-4 64..............(p) LukeMorris 6 66
(Bryn Palling) *dwlt: hld up in tch towards rr: hdwy over 2f out: styd on same pce u.p ins fnl f* **10/1**

0403 **7** *2¾* **Striker Torres (IRE)**[40] 7256 6-9-4 64..............(v) GeorgeBaker 8 60
(Ian McInnes) *chsd ldr tl wl over 1f out: sn rdn and unable qck: btn and one pce fnl f* **7/1**[2]

0460 **8** *2½* **Berlusca (IRE)**[27] 7529 3-9-2 64.............. JoeFanning 9 54
(Mark Brisbourne) *stdd after s: t.k.h: hld up in tch in midfield: rdn and effrt over 2f out: no imp over 1f out: wknd fnl f* **16/1**

6035 **9** *1½* **Imaginary World (IRE)**[27] 7524 4-9-2 62..............(p) IanMongan 7 49
(John Balding) *hld up in tch towards rr: rdn and hdwy on inner over 2f out: no imp over 1f out: wknd fnl f* **10/1**

3000 **10** *2½* **Qeethaara (USA)**[27] 7524 8-9-0 65..............(p) JackDuern[(5)] 3 46
(Mark Brisbourne) *dwlt: hld up in tch in rr: dropped to last 4f out: swtchd to outer and hdwy over 3f out: rdn and wknd over 2f out* **25/1**

5250 **11** *3½* **Mataajir (USA)**[229] 1384 4-9-3 63.............. MartinDwyer 4 36
(Derek Shaw) *in tch in midfield: rdn and outpcd 2f out: sn wknd* **20/1**

100 **12** *18* **Indian Violet (IRE)**[12] 7767 6-9-2 62..............(p) LiamKeniry 13
(Zoe Davison) *chsd ldrs tl wl over 2f out: sn dropped out: bhd fnl 2f: t.o* **33/1**

1m 38.23s (-1.57) **Going Correction** -0.15s/f (Stan)
WFA 3 from 4yo+ 2lb **12** Ran SP% **126.3**
Speed ratings (Par 101): **101,100,100,100,99 98,95,93,91,89 85,67**
Tote Swingers 1&2 £8.00, 2&3 £28.00, 1&3 £7.50 CSF £37.15 CT £260.41 TOTE £3.60: £1.70, £3.50, £4.00; EX 41.70 Trifecta £756.60 Part won. Pool: £1,008.86 - 0.81 winning tickets..
Owner Cathal Fegan **Bred** D Robb **Trained** Newmarket, Suffolk

FOCUS
They went a solid early pace in this moderate handicap, but the tempo steadied nearing the home turn and the principals were always handy. The winner is rated to this year's form, while the third and fourth ran personal bests and the fifth is rated to his summer form.

7926 £32 FREE AT 32RED.COM MEDIAN AUCTION MAIDEN STKS 7f (P)
6:05 (6:06) (Class 5) 2-Y-O £2,264 (£673; £336; £168) Stalls Low

Form RPR

1 **Mystical Sapphire** 2-8-12 0.............. LiamKeniry 13 67+
(Jo Crowley) *s.i.s: hld up in tch in rr: swtchd rt and gd hdwy over 1f out: str run to ld fnl 100yds: hld on wl* **10/1**

03 **2** *hd* **Mac's Superstar (FR)**[22] 7627 2-9-3 0.............. MartinLane 7 71
(James Fanshawe) *chsd ldrs: rdn to chal over 1f out: led jst ins fnl f: hdd fnl 100yds: r.o wl but a jst hld* **9/2**[2]

3 *2¼* **Rome** 2-9-3 0.............. IanMongan 3 65+
(Sir Henry Cecil) *led: jinked lft over 5f out: rdn and qcknd over 2f out: hdd jst ins fnl f: no ex and outpcd fnl 100yds* **8/1**[3]

0 **4** *2¼* **Atlantis City (FR)**[22] 7627 2-9-3 0.............. SeanLevey 2 59+
(Richard Hannon) *dwlt: sn rdn along and rcvrd to r in tch in midfield: drvn and swtchd lft over 1f out: no hdwy and wl hld fnl f* **14/1**

5 *¾* **Two No Bids (IRE)** 2-9-3 0.............. SebSanders 1 57
(J W Hills) *chsd ldrs: rdn and unable qck ent fnl 2f: outpcd by ldrs and btn 1f out: plugged on same pce after* **50/1**

2042 **6** *nk* **Martial Art (IRE)**[13] 7737 2-9-3 82.............. JimmyFortune 4 57
(Andrew Balding) *chsd ldr: pushed lft and hmpd over 5f out: ev ch and rdn 2f out: hld hd awkwardly and fnd little over 1f out: wknd fnl f* **4/6**[1]

3236 **7** *2¾* **Imperial Spirit**[27] 7525 2-8-12 72.............. CharlesBishop[(5)] 9 49
(Mick Channon) *t.k.h: hld up in tch in midfield: rdn and outpcd ent fnl 2f: wknd over 1f out* **25/1**

0 **8** *1¾* **Aloha**[28] 7506 2-8-12 0.............. AndreaAtzeni 5 40
(Roger Varian) *hld up in tch towards rr: rdn and outpcd over 2f out: no threat to ldrs fnl 2f* **20/1**

00 **9** *1½* **Good As New**[27] 7525 2-8-12 0.............. TedDurcan 10 36
(Chris Wall) *rn green: short of room s: in tch towards rr: rdn and hdwy on inner over 2f out: wknd qckly over 1f out* **66/1**

10 *shd* **Balatina** 2-8-12 0.............. LukeMorris 6 36
(Chris Dwyer) *in tch in midfield: rdn and unable qck jst over 2f out: wknd over 1f out* **66/1**

11 *2¼* **Running Bull (IRE)** 2-9-3 0.............. RobertWinston 8 35
(Linda Jewell) *s.i.s: in tch in rr: rdn and wknd over 2f out: bhd fnl f* **100/1**

12 *1* **Hannahs Turn** 2-8-9 0.............. AshleyMorgan[(3)] 12 27
(Chris Dwyer) *t.k.h: hld up in tch in rr: wknd over 2f out* **66/1**

60 **13** *2½* **Sweet Piccolo**[15] 7705 2-9-3 0..............(p) AdamKirby 11 26
(Paddy Butler) *chsd ldrs tl over 2f out: sn wknd: bhd fnl f* **100/1**

1m 27.64s (1.64) **Going Correction** -0.15s/f (Stan) **13** Ran SP% **122.1**
Speed ratings (Par 96): **84,83,81,78,77 77,74,72,70,70 67,66,63**
Tote Swingers 1&2 £7.10, 2&3 £5.30, 1&3 £12.00 CSF £53.70 TOTE £13.10: £4.50, £1.50, £3.20; EX 93.70 Trifecta £588.40 Pool: £1,278.91 - 1.63 winning tickets..
Owner Mrs Liz Nelson **Bred** Mrs R I Nelson **Trained** Whitcombe, Dorset

FOCUS
This maiden was run at a sound pace and the form, which is ordinary, is rated through the runner-up.

NOTEBOOK
Mystical Sapphire produced a strong burst on the inside to get up near the finish and make a winning debut. She was last early on, but the early fractions helped and she showed a neat turn of foot once switched to the far rail. This is made more meritorious as she was drawn widest of all and she looks sure to get another furlong down the line.

Mac's Superstar(FR) was third over C&D last time and, just going down late, improved a little on that here. He rates the benchmark and is now eligible for a mark. (op 5-1)

Rome knew his job on this racecourse debut and posted a decent effort from the front. He ought to come on nicely.

Atlantis City(FR) stayed on steadily late in the day and improved a deal on his debut outing 22 days previously. He has scope and is one to keep tabs on. Official explanation: jockey said colt was slowly away (op 16-1)

Two No Bids(IRE) went well from the inside draw and turned in a promising debut effort. It looks as though another furlong will suit him.

Martial Art(IRE) went down to a subsequent winner over this trip at Lingfield last time and proved all the rage. His rider failed to settle him early, though, and unsurprisingly he had nothing to offer when it mattered.

7927 32 BONUS H'CAP — 2m (P)

6:35 (6:35) (Class 5) (0-75,78) 3-Y-O+ — £2,264 (£673; £336; £168) Stalls Low

Form — RPR

512 **1** **Gabrial's King (IRE)**[10] 7791 3-9-0 **70** (p) StevieDonohoe 4 — 76
(Ian Williams) *chsd ldrs: rdn and effrt over 1f out: pushed into ld ins fnl f: pulling himself up towards fin but a gng to hold on: pushed out* **11/4**[1]

6040 **2** ½ **Honourable Knight (IRE)**[6] 7839 4-9-7 **68** LiamKeniry 10 — 73+
(Mark Usher) *stdd s: hld up in last pair: swtchd lft and effrt 2f out: hdwy u.p 1f out: styd on strly to press wnr cl home* **33/1**

/000 **3** hd **Ascalon**[52] 6933 8-9-8 **69** JoeFanning 7 — 74
(Pat Eddery) *chsd ldr: rdn to chal and edgd rt 2f out: led over 1f out: hdd ins fnl f: kpt on same pce after: lost 2nd last strides* **10/1**

0126 **4** nk **Squad**[21] 7652 6-9-9 **70** (v) EddieAhern 8 — 75
(Simon Dow) *hld up in tch towards rr: rdn and hdwy over 1f out: chsd ldrs ins fnl f: kpt on* **20/1**

4401 **5** 1 **Somemothersdohavem**[10] 7791 3-9-8 **78** 6ex (p) AdamKirby 11 — 82+
(John Ryan) *stdd s: hld up in last pair: rdn and hung rt over 2f out: sme hdwy and pushed lft 2f out: hung rt and styd on wl fnl f: nt rch ldrs* **3/1**[2]

4323 **6** 1¾ **Celtic Charlie (FR)**[13] 7744 7-8-4 **56** JemmaMarshall[(5)] 2 — 58
(Pat Phelan) *taken down early: hld up in tch in last trio: hdwy on inner ent fnl 2f: chsd ldrs 1f out: sn no imp: wknd towards fin* **7/1**[3]

4151 **7** ½ **Foster's Road**[12] 7617 3-8-13 **69** AndreaAtzeni 3 — 70
(Mick Channon) *in tch in midfield: rdn and unable qck 2f out: styd on same pce u.p fr over 1f out* **9/1**

2210 **8** ½ **The Absent Mare**[50] 1505 4-9-6 **67** LukeMorris 5 — 67
(Robin Dickin) *in tch in midfield: drvn and unable qck ent fnl 2f: styd on same pce u.p fr over 1f out* **12/1**

2123 **9** ¾ **Hesperides**[69] 6440 3-9-0 **70** DavidProbert 6 — 69
(Harry Dunlop) *led: rdn and hrd pressed whn bmpd 2f out: sn hdd: wknd 1f out* **12/1**

3000 **10** 2¼ **Where's Susie**[8] 7810 7-10-0 **75** GeorgeBaker 1 — 72
(Michael Madgwick) *chsd ldrs: rdn and effrt 2f out: unable qck over 1f out: btn whn short of room jst ins fnl f: wknd* **12/1**

0066 **11** 9 **Hawridge King**[57] 6802 10-9-4 **65** (p) IanMongan 12 — 51
(Stuart Kittow) *hld up in tch towards rr: rdn and struggling 3f out: sn wknd* **25/1**

-516 **12** 12 **Boston Blue**[154] 3535 5-10-0 **75** JimCrowley 9 — 47
(Tony Carroll) *hld up in tch in midfield: rdn and struggling 4f out: bhd over 2f out* **25/1**

3m 34.88s (4.78) **Going Correction** -0.15s/f (Stan)
WFA 3 from 4yo+ 9lb — **12** Ran SP% **121.7**
Speed ratings (Par 103): **82,81,81,81,81 80,79,79,79,78 73,67**
Tote Swingers 1&2 £23.70, 2&3 £56.30, 1&3 £9.10 CSF £107.94 CT £826.02 TOTE £3.10: £1.80, £11.80, £4.00; EX 108.60 Trifecta £803.40 Part won. Pool: £1,071.26 - 0.62 winning tickets..
Owner Dr Marwan Koukash **Bred** Danella Partnership **Trained** Portway, Worcs

FOCUS
Racing handily was a must in this steadily run staying handicap. The form is ordinary rated around the runner-up and fourth.

7928 32RED H'CAP — 6f (P)

7:05 (7:05) (Class 4) (0-85,85) 3-Y-O+ — £4,075 (£1,212; £606; £303) Stalls Low

Form — RPR

2410 **1** **Noverre To Go (IRE)**[8] 7817 6-9-7 **85** LukeMorris 2 — 94
(Ronald Harris) *chsd ldrs: effrt u.p over 1f out: drvn to ld wl ins fnl f: hld on cl home* **11/2**[2]

0052 **2** hd **O'Gorman**[14] 7730 3-9-0 **78** LiamKeniry 5 — 86
(Gary Brown) *stdd s: hld up in rr: gd hdwy jst over 1f out: swtchd rt and str run fnl f: nt quite rch wnr* **8/1**

030 **3** ¾ **Seeking Magic**[77] 6165 4-9-7 **85** (t) AdamKirby 8 — 91
(Clive Cox) *t.k.h: hld up in midfield tl dashed up to ld over 4f out: sn clr: stl clr and rdn over 1f out: kpt on wl tl hdd and no ex wl ins fnl f* **3/1**[1]

6310 **4** 1¾ **Arctic Lynx (IRE)**[21] 7646 5-9-0 **83** MichaelJMMurphy[(5)] 4 — 83
(Robert Cowell) *hld up in tch in midfield: hdwy u.p jst over 1f out: kpt on fnl f but nvr gng pce to chal* **7/1**[3]

4005 **5** hd **Lujeanie**[21] 7646 6-9-2 **80** JimCrowley 1 — 80
(Dean Ivory) *chsd ldrs: rdn and effrt on inner 2f out: no ex jst ins fnl f: wknd towards fin* **7/1**[3]

5530 **6** nk **Damika (IRE)**[14] 7730 9-9-5 **83** (v) MichaelStainton 3 — 82
(David Brown) *in tch in midfield: rdn and unable qck 2f out: styd on same pce u.p fnl f* **10/1**

2045 **7** ½ **Clear Praise (USA)**[15] 7704 5-9-4 **82** SebSanders 10 — 79
(Simon Dow) *stdd and dropped in bhd after s: hld up in rr: hdwy 2f out: no imp 1f out: wknd ins fnl f* **17/2**

032 **8** 2½ **Time Medicean**[48] 7019 6-8-13 **77** RobertWinston 7 — 66
(Tony Carroll) *hld up in last trio: rdn and hdwy wl over 1f out: no prog 1f out: wknd ins fnl f* **16/1**

3030 **9** 7 **We Have A Dream**[1] 7902 7-8-11 **75** MartinDwyer 6 — 42
(William Muir) *led tl over 4f out: chsd ldr tl over 1f out: wknd qckly* **7/1**[3]

0036 **10** 2¼ **Taffe**[14] 7730 3-9-0 **78** JoeFanning 9 — 38
(Amy Weaver) *t.k.h: chsd ldrs tl 2f out: sn wknd: bhd fnl f* **14/1**

1m 10.87s (-2.23) **Going Correction** -0.15s/f (Stan) — **10** Ran SP% **121.2**
Speed ratings (Par 105): **108,107,106,104,104 103,103,99,90,87**
Tote Swingers 1&2 £12.20, 2&3 £11.20, 1&3 £3.60 CSF £51.10 CT £162.89 TOTE £7.60: £3.20, £3.20, £1.60; EX 68.50 Trifecta £300.00 Pool: £640.18 - 1.60 winning tickets..
Owner Robert & Nina Bailey **Bred** Gestut Gorlsdorf **Trained** Earlswood, Monmouths

FOCUS
A fair sprint handicap. The pace sharply increased around halfway and the form looks sound rated around the first three.

7929 32RED CASINO APPRENTICE H'CAP — 6f (P)

7:35 (7:36) (Class 7) (0-50,50) 3-Y-O+ — £1,455 (£433; £216; £108) Stalls Low

Form — RPR

5 **1** **Rose Garnet (IRE)**[94] 5692 4-8-8 **47** RyanTate[(5)] 6 — 55
(Tony Carroll) *mde all: rdn and fnd ex over 1f out: styd on wl fnl f* **3/1**[2]

0046 **2** ¾ **Pharoh Jake**[15] 7703 4-8-12 **46** WilliamTwiston-Davies 10 — 52
(John Bridger) *t.k.h: hld up in tch towards rr: rdn and effrt over 1f out: chsd wnr fnl 100yds: kpt on* **16/1**

0550 **3** 1 **Memphis Man**[28] 7512 9-8-8 **47** EoinWalsh[(5)] 4 — 49
(David Evans) *taken down early: t.k.h: hld up in midfield: hmpd after 1f: rdn and hdwy wl over 1f out: chsd wnr 1f out tl fnl 100yds: no ex* **7/1**

0440 **4** ¾ **Fantasy Fighter (IRE)**[90] 5808 7-9-2 **50** JackDuern 12 — 50
(John E Long) *stdd s: t.k.h: hld up in tch in last trio: hmpd after 1f: rdn and hdwy 2f out: chsd ldrs and styd on same pce ins fnl f* **33/1**

-046 **5** 1¾ **Loved To Bits**[85] 5937 4-8-9 **50** JoeyHaynes[(7)] 8 — 44
(Eric Wheeler) *stdd s: hld up in detached last: swtchd ins and hdwy 2f out: drvn over 1f out: styd on same pce fnl f* **20/1**

4564 **6** 1 **Blueberry Fizz (IRE)**[1] 7914 4-9-2 **50** (v) NatashaEaton 3 — 41
(John Ryan) *chsd ldrs: rdn to chse wnr 2f out tl 1f out: wknd ins fnl f* **4/1**[3]

0560 **7** ½ **Sherjawy (IRE)**[15] 7703 8-9-0 **48** ThomasBrown 1 — 38
(Zoe Davison) *hld up in tch in midfield: squeezed for room and bmpd rail after 1f: dropped to last trio but stl in tch: rdn and hdwy 2f out: no imp over 1f out: wknd ins fnl f* **14/1**

0050 **8** 1½ **Athaakeel (IRE)**[6] 7837 6-8-13 **50** (b) DanielMuscutt[(3)] 5 — 35
(Ronald Harris) *chsd ldrs: lost pl u.p ent fnl 2f: no imp and wl hld after* **14/1**

6000 **9** 1¾ **One Cool Chick**[28] 7504 4-9-0 **48** JakePayne 7 — 27
(John Bridger) *t.k.h: chsd wnr tl 2f out: sn wknd: bhd fnl f* **14/1**

0042 **10** 1¼ **Kaylee**[6] 7837 3-9-2 **50** NedCurtis 2 — 25
(Gary Moore) *chsd ldrs: barging match w rival and hmpd after 1f: rdn and unable qck 2f out: wknd over 1f out* **11/4**[1]

1m 12.59s (-0.51) **Going Correction** -0.15s/f (Stan) — **10** Ran SP% **117.8**
Speed ratings (Par 97): **97,96,94,93,91 90,89,87,85,83**
Tote Swingers 1&2 £13.90, 2&3 £13.40, 1&3 £7.40 CSF £50.86 CT £323.63 TOTE £4.90: £2.90, £3.80, £2.70; EX 83.20 Trifecta £704.20 Part won. Pool: £939.04 - 0.62 winning tickets..
Owner Nicholls Family **Bred** The Duke Of Roxburghe's Stud **Trained** Cropthorne, Worcs
■ Stewards' Enquiry : Ryan Tate four-day ban: careless riding (Dec 13-15,17)

FOCUS
This bottom-drawer sprint handicap was run at an average pace. The winner is rated close to the best of her Irish form, while the runner-up was near his best mark on this surface.
T/Plt: £406.00 to a £1 stake. Pool: £69,668.78 - 125.26 winning tickets. T/Qpdt: £69.30 to a £1 stake. Pool: £9,352.28 - 99.80 winning tickets. SP

7914 WOLVERHAMPTON (A.W) (L-H)

Friday, November 30

OFFICIAL GOING: Standard
Wind: Almost nil Weather: Overcast

7930 LIKE US ON FACEBOOK WOLVERHAMPTON RACECOURSE NURSERY — 5f 20y(P)

3:55 (3:56) (Class 6) (0-65,64) 2-Y-O — £1,704 (£503; £251) Stalls Low

Form — RPR

040 **1** **Greenery (IRE)**[58] 6787 2-9-7 **64** GeorgeBaker 1 — 74+
(Roger Charlton) *hld up: hdwy over 1f out: nt clr run and swtchd rt ins fnl f: sn led: r.o wl: readily* **7/4**[1]

0344 **2** 1½ **Frans Hals**[16] 7713 2-8-9 **52** SilvestreDeSousa 4 — 52
(Dominic Ffrench Davis) *sn pushed along and prom: drvn 1/2-way: r.o to go 2nd post: no ch w wnr* **7/1**

122 **3** hd **Modern Lady**[14] 7745 2-9-7 **64** RobbieFitzpatrick 5 — 63
(Richard Guest) *led: rdn over 1f out: hdd and unable qck wl ins fnl f: lost 2nd post* **9/2**[2]

005 **4** 1 **Tom Hall**[30] 7481 2-9-4 **61** LukeMorris 8 — 57
(John Best) *sn pushed along in rr: rdn and r.o wl ins fnl f: could nt rch ldrs* **16/1**

0000 **5** ½ **Fat Bottom Girl**[10] 7797 2-8-6 **49** NickyMackay 3 — 43
(Michael Easterby) *sn prom: pushed along 1/2-way: styd on* **50/1**

5465 **6** 1 **Lexi's Beauty (IRE)**[8] 7821 2-8-5 **48** JimmyQuinn 11 — 38
(Ian Williams) *mid-div: hdwy and edgd lft over 3f out: rdn over 1f out: no ex ins fnl f* **25/1**

0402 **7** shd **Little Miss Zuri (IRE)**[8] 7821 2-8-1 **47** SimonPearce[(3)] 10 — 37
(Sylvester Kirk) *chsd ldrs: pushed along 1/2-way: rdn over 1f out: no ex ins fnl f* **14/1**

1016 **8** hd **Harrogate Fair**[14] 7745 2-9-7 **64** AndreaAtzeni 2 — 53
(Michael Squance) *prom: pushed along over 3f out: rdn and swtchd lft over 1f out: no ex ins fnl f* **5/1**[3]

6033 **9** ½ **Con Leche**[6] 7855 2-9-5 **62** (p) IanMongan 7 — 49
(Scott Dixon) *chsd ldr tl rdn over 1f out: wknd ins fnl f* **12/1**

0605 **10** ¾ **Summer Isles**[6] 7865 2-9-6 **63** (bt[1]) MartinLane 9 — 48
(Ed Vaughan) *hld up: rdn over 1f out: n.d* **28/1**

5365 **11** 13 **Miss Starry Eyed**[2] 7891 2-8-5 **48** ow1 MartinDwyer 6 —
(Derek Shaw) *mid-div: hmpd and lost pl over 3f out: n.d after* **50/1**

1m 2.16s (-0.14) **Going Correction** -0.05s/f (Stan) — **11** Ran SP% **115.2**
Speed ratings (Par 94): **99,96,96,94,93 92,92,91,91,89 69**
toteswingers 1&2 £3.30, 2&3 £4.90, 1&3 £2.50 CSF £13.48 CT £46.68 TOTE £2.90: £1.10, £1.50, £2.10; EX 15.50 Trifecta £39.50 Pool: £606.06 - 11.49 winning units..
Owner D J Deer **Bred** D J And Mrs Deer **Trained** Beckhampton, Wilts

FOCUS
A moderate nursery run at a good pace and straightforward form rated around the placed horses.

NOTEBOOK
Greenery(IRE) had shown ability in three sprint maidens and proved well handicapped after a two-month break. She was a bit keen early and had to weave her way through rivals in the straight, but was basically just a fair bit better than a moderate bunch, and she ought to cope with slightly better opposition. (op 6-4)

Frans Hals, without any headgear this time, was flat out for most of the way but kept on. He might be worth another try at 6f. (op 8-1)

Modern Lady was forced to go off plenty fast enough in a race where the other three runners who made the top four all raced off the speed. She's only moderate but is improving. (op 4-1 tchd 5-1)

Tom Hall was caught wide early and couldn't go the pace at all, but he finished quite well. He may step up on this over another furlong. (op 20-1)

Fat Bottom Girl was keen early, but still didn't fare too badly considering she chased a strong gallop, and this was her most encouraging performance to-date.

Lexi's Beauty(IRE), poorly drawn, was caught wide early and might yet be capable of better. She still reversed recent 6f Kempton placings with Little Miss Zuri. (op 40-1)
Harrogate Fair wasn't that well balanced going into the first run and never looked in a good rhythm. He might be best excused. (op 15-2 tchd 8-1)

7931 DOWNLOAD OUR IPHONE APP MEDIAN AUCTION MAIDEN STKS 5f 216y(P)
4:25 (4:26) (Class 6) 2-Y-O **£1,704** (£503; £251) **Stalls** Low

Form RPR
1 **Gift Of Music (IRE)** 2-8-12 0 LukeMorris 2 73
(James Eustace) *chsd ldrs: wnt 2nd over 1f out: shkn up to ld ins fnl f: edgd rt: r.o* **3/1**[3]
23 2 *nk* **Boxing Shadows**[181] 2686 2-9-3 0 TomEaves 4 77
(Bryan Smart) *led: rdn and hdd ins fnl f: r.o* **7/4**[1]
20 3 *3 1/4* **Clear Loch**[87] 5911 2-9-3 0 NickyMackay 1 67
(John Spearing) *hld up: hdwy u.p over 1f out: styd on: could nt trble ldrs* **7/1**
06 4 *nk* **Loulou Vuitton**[24] 7613 2-8-12 0 GrahamLee 6 61+
(Brian Baugh) *s.s: drvn along over 1f out: styd on ins fnl f: nvr nrr* **40/1**
5 *hd* **Alfaisaliah (IRE)** 2-8-12 0 DavidProbert 7 61
(J S Moore) *chsd ldr tl rdn over 1f out: no ex fnl f* **14/1**
6326 6 *9* **Finaz**[160] 3401 2-9-3 70 AdamKirby 3 39
(Noel Quinlan) *sn pushed along and prom: wknd fnl f* **9/4**[2]
7 *1 1/2* **Copper Leyf** 2-9-3 0 IanMongan 5 34+
(Jeremy Gask) *s.s: hdwy over 2f out: rdn over 1f out: wknd fnl f* **33/1**

1m 16.37s (1.37) **Going Correction** -0.05s/f (Stan) 7 Ran SP% **116.7**
Speed ratings (Par 94): **88,87,83,82,82 70,68**
toteswingers 1&2 £2.20, 2&3 £2.50, 1&3 £3.50 CSF £9.02 TOTE £4.90: £4.90, £1.10; EX 14.30.
Owner J C Smith **Bred** Littleton Stud **Trained** Newmarket, Suffolk

FOCUS
The form looks just ordinary (modest pace and time slower than following juvenile claimer), but it went to a fair prospect, with the runner-up the best guide to the level.

NOTEBOOK
Gift Of Music(IRE) is the first foal of four-time 5f winner (including Listed) Loch Verdi, who is a daughter of Group-1 winning sprinter Lochsong. Her trainer's first successful juvenile newcomer since 2007, she showed a straightforward attitude and ought to rate higher in due course. (op 11-2)
Boxing Shadows showed plenty of ability in a couple of early season maidens, but his second start was not an improvement on his first and he'd been off for six months and been gelded. This was an encouraging enough return and he can find a similarly weak race, with handicaps also now an option. (tchd 5-2)
Clear Loch didn't go on from a pleasing debut at 6f when reported to have run too free upped to 7f on his second start, and he'd been off for three months since then. He shaped okay on this first Polytrack outing and can now switch to handicaps. (op 13-2 tchd 15-2)
Loulou Vuitton, who has raced exclusively over this C&D so far, took another step in the right direction, keeping on after losing significant ground by rearing as the stalls opened. She's now qualified for a handicap mark. (op 50-1)
Alfaisaliah(IRE), a 12,500euros first foal of a 7f winner, showed speed before fading and has ability. (op 16-1)
Finaz ran no sort of race on his debut for this yard/first Polytrack start after a 160-day break. (op 2-1)

7932 HOTEL & CONFERENCING AT WOLVERHAMPTON CLAIMING STKS 5f 216y(P)
4:55 (4:55) (Class 6) 2-Y-O **£1,704** (£503; £251) **Stalls** Low

Form RPR
3122 1 **Marmot Bay (IRE)**[6] 7865 2-8-5 60 MartinDwyer 3 60
(Jamie Osborne) *plld hrd: mde all: set stdy pce tl qcknd over 2f out: rdn ins fnl f: r.o* **1/1**[1]
3631 2 *nk* **Windforpower (IRE)**[6] 7865 2-8-12 68 (b) LukeMorris 1 66
(Ronald Harris) *a.p: chsd wnr over 1f out: rdn and ev ch ins fnl f: could nt qckn towards fin* **3/1**[2]
0 3 *3 1/2* **Traps Army (IRE)**[45] 7152 2-8-10 0 KieranO'Neill 4 54
(W McCreery, Ire) *chsd wnr: rdn over 2f out: lost 2nd over 1f out: styd on same pce fnl f* **7/1**
3 4 *1* **Doodles**[32] 7440 2-8-3 0 ow1 AdrianNicholls 2 44
(David Nicholls) *s.i.s: rdn 1/2-way: nvr trbld ldrs* **33/1**
0605 5 *1 3/4* **Claude Greenwood**[11] 7786 2-9-0 74 JamieSpencer 5 49
(Jamie Osborne) *hld up: rdn over 2f out: sn outpcd* **5/1**[3]

1m 16.14s (1.14) **Going Correction** -0.05s/f (Stan) 5 Ran SP% **107.1**
Speed ratings (Par 94): **90,89,84,83,81**
CSF £3.92 TOTE £2.10: £1.30, £1.20; EX 4.50.Marmot Bay was claimed by A. J. D. Lidderdale for £6000.
Owner J A Osborne **Bred** J C Bloodstock **Trained** Upper Lambourn, Berks

FOCUS
A modest claimer but straightforward form.

NOTEBOOK
Marmot Bay(IRE), 3lb better off with her old rival Windforpower, was keen enough but her attitude saw her gain a third C&D victory. She was claimed by Alastair Lidderdale for £6,000. (op 10-11)
Windforpower(IRE) finished a short-head in front of the winner when first past the post in a C&D seller last time, but lost the race in the stewards' room (hung under pressure, didn't help the second) and this time he didn't go through with his effort. (op 5-2)
Traps Army(IRE) had plenty to find with the front two at the weights. (op 11-1)
Doodles was always struggling after a slow start. (op 25-1)
Claude Greenwood, reported to have stopped quickly and lost a shoe last time, was never going on this drop in trip. (op 6-1 tchd 13-2 and 9-2)

7933 BOOK HORIZONS RESTAURANT MAIDEN STKS 1m 5f 194y(P)
5:25 (5:26) (Class 5) 3-Y-O+ **£2,264** (£673; £336; £168) **Stalls** Low

Form RPR
3252 1 **Thecornishcockney**[7] 7839 3-9-3 69 (tp) AdamKirby 2 74
(John Ryan) *s.s: hld up: hdwy over 2f out: rdn to ld 1f out: hung lft: styd on wl* **15/8**[2]
25-0 2 *3 1/4* **Vimiero (USA)**[45] 6073 5-9-11 77 GeorgeBaker 6 69
(Jonjo O'Neill) *hld up: hdwy over 2f out: rdn over 1f out: styd on to go 2nd post* **5/1**[3]
042 3 *shd* **Omar Khayyam**[44] 7174 3-9-3 77 (t) DavidProbert 4 69
(Andrew Balding) *trckd ldrs: racd keenly: rdn over 1f out: styd on same pce fnl f* **5/4**[1]
66 4 *shd* **Ginger Fizz**[25] 7594 5-9-6 0 MartinDwyer 7 64
(Ben Case) *prom: led over 10f out: rdn and hdd over 1f out: styd on same pce* **22/1**
0 5 *6* **Waving**[15] 7162 3-9-3 72 GrahamLee 9 61
(Tony Carroll) *led: hdd over 10f out: remained handy: chsd ldr 3f out: rdn over 1f out: wknd ins fnl f* **25/1**
0 6 *3* **Dubai Emerald (USA)**[176] 2849 3-8-9 0 AshleyMorgan(3) 1 51
(Chris Dwyer) *s.i.s: rdn over 2f out: sme hdwy over 1f out: wknd fnl f* **125/1**
066/ 7 *10* **Nouailhas**[380] 4932 6-9-6 42 JackDuern(5) 5 42
(Reg Hollinshead) *plld hrd and prom: rdn over 3f out: wknd wl over 1f out* **40/1**
-400 8 *1* **Lady Author**[42] 7222 3-8-12 39 TonyHamilton 3 36
(Richard Fahey) *hld up in tch: plld hrd: rdn and wknd 4f out* **100/1**
9 *nk* **Primo Blanca** 3-9-3 0 TomEaves 10 41
(Michael Mullineaux) *mid-div: hdwy 4f out: sn rdn: wknd over 2f out* **80/1**
0000 10 *2 1/2* **Bridal Medic**[24] 7620 3-9-0 32 (t) RyanClark(3) 8 37
(Barry Leavy) *hld up: rdn and wknd over 3f out* **200/1**
30 11 *nk* **Sauvage L'Il**[44] 7162 4-9-6 0 SilvestreDeSousa 11 32
(Ed Dunlop) *prom: chsd ldr 10f out tl rdn over 3f out: wknd wl over 1f out* **16/1**

3m 9.47s (3.47) **Going Correction** -0.05s/f (Stan)
WFA 3 from 4yo+ 8lb 11 Ran SP% **115.9**
Speed ratings (Par 103): **88,86,86,86,82 80,75,74,74,73 72**
toteswingers 1&2 £1.70, 2&3 £2.70, 1&3 £1.40 CSF £11.11 TOTE £2.90: £1.10, £1.30, £1.10; EX 12.00 Trifecta £16.80 Pool £1,724.71 - 76.87 winning units..
Owner C Letcher & J Ryan **Bred** D Robb **Trained** Newmarket, Suffolk

FOCUS
Ordinary form, as one would expect for a staying maiden at this time of year, and the pace was slow. The winner did not need to run to his latest mark to score but the form behind looks fluid.

7934 WOLVERHAMPTON HOLIDAY INN H'CAP 1m 141y(P)
5:55 (5:55) (Class 3) (0-95,95) 3-Y-O+ **£6,490** (£1,942; £971; £486; £242) **Stalls** Low

Form RPR
2202 1 **Rakaan (IRE)**[8] 7823 5-8-11 **85** TedDurcan 1 93+
(Jamie Osborne) *hld up: rdn: hung lft and r.o ins fnl f: led post* **11/4**[1]
106 2 *shd* **Alfred Hutchinson**[71] 6405 4-8-7 **81** oh2 TomEaves 5 88
(Geoffrey Oldroyd) *chsd ldrs: led over 1f out: rdn ins fnl f: hdd post* **13/2**
5014 3 *hd* **Kingscroft (IRE)**[8] 7826 4-9-1 **89** 6ex JoeFanning 4 96
(Mark Johnston) *chsd ldr: rdn and ev ch ins fnl f: r.o* **7/2**[2]
3000 4 *1 3/4* **Mia's Boy**[13] 7774 8-9-7 **95** GeorgeBaker 3 98
(Chris Dwyer) *hld up: hdwy over 1f out: r.o* **5/1**
5143 5 *1/2* **Lockantanks**[13] 7774 5-9-1 **89** LukeMorris 8 91
(Michael Appleby) *chsd ldrs: rdn over 1f out: styng on same pce whn hmpd wl ins fnl f* **9/2**[3]
0004 6 *3/4* **Advanced**[22] 7645 9-8-9 **83** AmyRyan 9 83
(Kevin Ryan) *led: rdn and hdd over 1f out: no ex ins fnl f* **9/1**
U000 7 *4* **Loyalty**[14] 7751 5-8-10 **84** (v) MartinDwyer 6 75
(Derek Shaw) *s.i.s: hld up: rdn over 2f out: hung lft and wknd fnl f* **22/1**

1m 48.79s (-1.71) **Going Correction** -0.05s/f (Stan)
WFA 3 from 4yo+ 3lb 7 Ran SP% **111.4**
Speed ratings (Par 107): **105,104,104,103,102 102,98**
toteswingers 1&2 £4.10, 2&3 £4.30, 1&3 £3.40 CSF £19.83 CT £60.74 TOTE £3.80: £2.90, £4.20; EX 19.90 Trifecta £85.20 Pool: £518.62 - 4.56 winning units..
Owner J A Osborne **Bred** L Mulryan & M Fahy **Trained** Upper Lambourn, Berks

FOCUS
Not that strong a race for the grade, but still fair enough form, rated through the third and backed up by the winner.

NOTEBOOK
Rakaan(IRE) ended a losing run dating back to a success at Meydan in February 2011, despite hanging left when delivered with his challenge. He was 16lb lower, including being 2lb well-in following his second at Kempton the previous week.
Alfred Hutchinson, who won his maiden over the extended 1m1f here on his only previous Polytrack start, just failed from 2lb out of the handicap after a 71-day break. He's lightly raced and open to further improvement. (op 7-1 tchd 8-1)
Kingscroft(IRE) has never won beyond an extended 7f but he didn't seem to fail through lack of stamina. He was 1lb wrong under his penalty and this is about as good as he is. (op 4-1 tchd 10-3)
Mia's Boy challenged towards the inside, away from the main action. He's dropped to a workable mark. (tchd 6-1)
Lockantanks had Rakaan behind in second when winning a 7f claimer here in October, but he was 9lb worse off with the Osborne runner. He was held when short of room late on. (op 3-1)

7935 GEORGE MORRIS H'CAP (DIV I) 7f 32y(P)
6:25 (6:27) (Class 5) (0-75,75) 3-Y-O+ **£2,264** (£673; £336; £168) **Stalls** High

Form RPR
01 1 **Living Leader**[21] 7667 3-9-2 **71** TomMcLaughlin 4 85+
(Nick Littmoden) *a.p: shkn up to ld over 1f out: rdn and edgd rt ins fnl f: r.o* **15/8**[1]
2454 2 *2 1/4* **Roy The Boy (USA)**[14] 7743 4-9-5 **73** AdamKirby 10 81
(Alan Bailey) *chsd ldrs: rdn over 1f out: styd on* **7/2**[2]
0000 3 *1 1/4* **Khajaaly (IRE)**[32] 7436 5-9-2 **70** JimmyQuinn 8 75
(Julia Feilden) *hld up: hdwy over 1f out: sn rdn: styd on same pce ins fnl f* **33/1**
0132 4 *nk* **Piceno (IRE)**[24] 7607 4-9-7 **75** (p) IanMongan 7 79
(Scott Dixon) *chsd ldrs: led 1/2-way: shkn up over 2f out: hdd over 1f out: no ex ins fnl f* **12/1**
0243 5 *3/4* **My Single Malt (IRE)**[7] 7844 4-9-4 **72** (p) GrahamLee 6 74
(Julie Camacho) *hld up: hdwy u.p over 1f out: could nt rch ldrs* **7/1**[3]
4303 6 *1 1/4* **Imperator Augustus (IRE)**[36] 7360 4-9-6 **74** PhillipMakin 9 72
(Patrick Holmes) *chsd ldr to 1/2-way: rdn over 1f out: wknd ins fnl f* **8/1**
1040 7 *2 3/4* **Abhaath (USA)**[15] 7725 3-8-13 **68** LukeMorris 11 59
(Ronald Harris) *hld up: pushed along 3f out: rdn and hung lft fr over 1f out: n.d* **16/1**
/0-0 8 *2 3/4* **Geraldines Lass (IRE)**[42] 7230 4-8-7 **61** (t) KieranO'Neill 2 45
(W McCreery, Ire) *hld up: hdwy over 2f out: rdn and wknd over 1f out* **12/1**
403- 9 *2 1/4* **Lord Of The Dance (IRE)**[398] 7176 6-8-9 **63** TomEaves 3 40
(Michael Mullineaux) *hld up: rdn over 2f out: a in rr* **50/1**
-000 10 *1* **Fairlie Dinkum**[61] 6709 4-8-10 **64** RobertHavlin 5 39
(Andrew Crook) *hld up: rdn over 2f out: sn wknd* **66/1**
0222 11 *2* **Llewellyn**[15] 7732 4-9-3 **71** AdrianNicholls 1 40
(David Nicholls) *led to 1/2-way: sn rdn: wknd over 1f out* **11/1**

1m 28.47s (-1.13) **Going Correction** -0.05s/f (Stan)
WFA 3 from 4yo+ 1lb 11 Ran SP% **116.6**
Speed ratings (Par 103): **104,101,100,99,98 97,94,91,88,87 85**
toteswingers 1&2 £2.80, 2&3 £27.70, 1&3 £15.30 CSF £7.86 CT £160.09 TOTE £3.40: £2.00, £1.50, £6.20; EX 11.40 Trifecta £271.80 Pool: £975.05 - 2.69 winning units..
Owner Nigel Shields **Bred** D J And Mrs Deer **Trained** Newmarket, Suffolk

FOCUS
The pace was good and this looks decent form for the level rated around the placed horses.

7936 GEORGE MORRIS H'CAP (DIV II) 7f 32y (P)
6:55 (7:09) (Class 5) (0-75,74) 3-Y-0+ **£2,264** (£673; £336; £168) **Stalls** High

Form | | | | RPR
1 **1** **Haftohaf**[36] 7361 3 -8-13[67] AdamKirby 3 79+
(Marco Botti) *chsd ldrs: rdn over 1f out: edgd rt: r.o u.p to ld wl ins fnl f* **5/4**[1]
6014 **2** 1 ¾ **Cut Across (IRE)**[14] 7742 4 -9-6[73] SebSanders 9 80
(Nick Littmoden) *chsd ldr 6f out: led over 2f out: rdn over 1f out: hdd and unable qck wl ins fnl f* **6/1**[3]
3331 **3** ½ **Fayr Fall (IRE)**[24] 7607 3 -9-4[72] (v) TedDurcan 1 78
(Tim Easterby) *hld up: hdwy over 1f out: sn rdn: r.o* **9/2**[2]
3443 **4** ½ **Restless Bay (IRE)**[9] 7864 4 -9-1[68] (v) GrahamLee 6 73
(Mrs K Burke) *hld up: hdwy over 2f out: rdn over 1f out: styd on* **9/2**[2]
5410 **5** 4 **Elegant Muse**[21] 7670 4 -8-9[62] (t) LukeMorris 7 56
(Michael Appleby) *led 6f out: rdn and hdd over 2f out: wknd ins fnl f* **20/1**
0000 **6** 8 **Secret Millionaire (IRE)**[3] 7775 5 -8-10[63] DavidProbert 8 35
(Tony Carroll) *prom: rdn over 2f out: sn wknd* **66/1**
006 **7** 2 ¼ **Cool Marble (IRE)**[95] 5674 5 -9-3[70] LiamKeniry 5 36
(Jeremy Gask) *hld up: rdn over 2f out: sn wknd* **10/1**
005 **8** 7 **Gabrial's Gift (IRE)**[34] 7412 3 -9-5[73] JamieSpencer 2 20
(Ian Williams) *led: hdd 6f out: chsd ldrs: rdn over 1f out: sn wknd and eased* **8/1**

1m 27.7s (-1.90) **Going Correction** -0.05s/f (Stan)
WFA 3 from 4yo+ 1lb 8Ran SP% **121.6**
Speed ratings (Par 103): **108,106,105,104,100 91,88,80**
toteswingers 1&2 £3.20, 2&3 £3.20, 1&3 £1.70 CSF £10.32 CT £28.64 TOTE £2.60 : £1.10, £2.10, £2.20 ; EX 12.50 Trifecta £22.40 Pool: £906.97 - 30.35 winning units.
Owner Miss Catherine Loder **Bred** Ercan Dogan **Trained** Newmarket, Suffolk

FOCUS
On a cold, misty evening, there was an inspection prior to this race after some jockeys reported the Polytrack was balling up. The tractors harrowed the surface and racing continued approximately 15 minutes behind schedule. Like the first division, a fair race for the grade won by a progressive sort. The time was 0.77 seconds faster than the other leg, but that may be misleading considering the track needed plenty of work in between the two races. however, the form looks solid rated around the third and fourth.

7937 WOLVERHAMPTON-RACECOURSE.CO.UK H'CAP 5f 20y (P)
7:25 (7:37) (Class 5) (0-75,74) 3-Y-0+ **£2,264** (£673; £336; £168) **Stalls** Low

Form | | | | RPR
0222 **1** **Another Citizen (IRE)**[9] 7864 4 -9-2[69] (b) TedDurcan 13 81
(Tim Easterby) *chsd ldrs: led 1/2-way: r.o wl* **4/1**[1]
5000 **2** 3 ½ **Steelcut**[13] 7775 8 -8-13[66] (p) JimmyQuinn 8 67
(Mark Buckley) *hld up in tch: plld hrd: chsd wnr over 1f out: sn rdn: edgd lft and styd on same pce fnl f* **40/1**
0060 **3** 1 ¾ **Amadeus Denton (IRE)**[13] 7775 3 -9-1[68] PhillipMakin 3 63
(Michael Dods) *chsd ldrs: rdn 1/2-way: styd on same pce fr over 1f out* **16/1**
4341 **4** ¾ **Generalyse**[21] 7668 3 -9-4[71] (b) JohnFahy 12 64
(Ben De Haan) *hld up: hdwy over 1f out: nt rch ldrs* **6/1**[3]
6502 **5** ¾ **Above The Stars**[13] 7775 4 -8-13[66] TonyHamilton 5 56
(Richard Fahey) *prom: rdn 1/2-way: no ex fnl f* **7/1**
3000 **6** ¾ **Taurus Twins**[15] 7726 6 -9-7[74] LukeMorris 2 62
(Richard Price) *led early: chsd ldrs: rdn and wknd over 1f out* **12/1**
2022 **7** nk **Avonvalley**[34] 7411 5 -9-2[69] AdamKirby 1 56+
(Peter Grayson) *sn pushed along in rr: sme hdwy whn nt clr run over 1f out: n.d* **4/1**[1]
0000 **8** nk **Sir Geoffrey (IRE)**[16] 7716 6 -9-3[70] (p) IanMongan 10 56
(Scott Dixon) *sn led: rdn and hdd 1/2-way: wknd fnl f* **11/1**
0006 **9** 3 **Parisian Pyramid (IRE)**[14] 7741 6 -9-3[70] JamieSpencer 6 46+
(Ian Williams) *hmpd sn after s: nvr on terms* **5/1**[2]
1464 **10** ½ **Tom Sawyer**[22] 7648 4 -9-5[72] (b) GrahamLee 7 47
(Julie Camacho) *prom: rdn 2f out: sn wknd* **13/2**
0004 **11** 20 **Upper Lambourn (IRE)**[37] 4141 4 -9-5[72] JoeFanning 4
(Christopher Kellett) *s.i.s: outpcd* **40/1**

1m 1.38s (-0.92) **Going Correction** -0.05s/f (Stan) 11Ran SP% **123.6**
Speed ratings (Par 103): **105,99,96,95,94 93,92,92,87,86 54**
toteswingers 1&2 £16.70, 2&3 £45.50, 1&3 £15.50 CSF £177.09 CT £2387.74 TOTE £5.30 : £2.30, £13.10 , £3.60 ; EX 153.60 Trifecta £588.50 Pool £973.15 - 1.24 winning units .
Owner Middleham Park Racing V & Partners **Bred** Sandro Garavelli **Trained** Great Habton, N Yorks

FOCUS
Form to treat with real caution. While the meeting survived an inspection prior to the preceding race, the kickback looked horrendous, especially for those not close up behind other horses (or in front), and the riders on Parisian Pyramid (squeezed out soon after start) and Upper Lambourn (started slowly), who were both soon well behind, had little choice but to take their mounts extremely wide. That pair were left with no chance. Unsurprisingly, this went to a horse who avoided the kickback by helping force the pace.
T/Plt: £8.00 to a £1 stake. Pool £73,596.07 - 6,681.24 winning units. T/Qpdt: £4.80 to a £1 stake. Pool £8,595.99 - 1,316.00 w. units CR 7938a - 7951a (Foreign Racing) See RI

[7930]WOLVERHAMPTON (A.W) (L-H)
Saturday, December 1

OFFICIAL GOING: Standard (meeting was abandoned after race 3 (6.50) due to the surface becoming unsafe)
Wind: Light across Weather: Fine

7952 32RED.COM MAIDEN STKS 5f 20y (P)
5:50 (5:51) (Class 5) 3-Y-0+ **£2,911** (£866; £432; £216) **Stalls** Low

Form | | | | RPR
05 **1** **Miss Bunter**[16] 7729 3 -8-12[0] SilvestreDeSousa 2 61
(David O'Meara) *chsd ldrs: n.m.r 1/2-way: rdn to ld ins fnl f: r.o* **20/1**
4352 **2** ¾ **Jermatt**[25] 7611 3 -9-3[58] GrahamLee 12 63
(J R Jenkins) *chsd ldrs: rdn over 1f out: r.o* **9/4**[2]
354 **3** hd **Saunta**[8] 7838 3 -8-12[55] PhillipMakin 5 57+
(David Simcock) *s.i.s: hld up: hdwy over 1f out: swtchd rt: rdn and hung lft ins fnl f: r.o* **5/1**[3]
4 2 ¾ **Steely Grace (IRE)**[191] 2434 3 -8-12[62] ShaneFoley 11 47
(M Halford, Ire) *hld up in tch: rdn over 1f out: styd on same pce ins fnl f* **2/1**[1]
0 **5** hd **Resonare**[54] 6930 3 -9-3[0] WilliamCarson 4 52+
(Stuart Williams) *sn pushed along in rr: r.o ins fnl f: nvr nrr* **6/1**
2003 **6** hd **Funcheon Vale (IRE)**[26] 7591 3 -8-12[57] RobertHavlin 8 46
(Hughie Morrison) *sn pushed along to ld: rdn over 1f out: hdd and no ex ins fnl f* **10/1**
6 **7** 1 ½ **Guilietta Girl (IRE)**[9] 7903 3 -8-12[0] (b[1]) LukeMorris 6 41
(David Evans) *chsd ldrs: rdn over 1f out: no ex ins fnl f* **40/1**
00-6 **8** 3 ¼ **Desert Spree**[89] 5878 3 -8-12[46] SebSanders 10 29
(Jeremy Gask) *mid-div: sn drvn along: n.d* **100/1**
0-0 **9** 2 ¼ **Lady Libby Lamb**[23] 7654 4 -8-12[0] DavidProbert 9 21
(David C Griffiths) *chsd ldrs: rdn 1/2-way: wknd fnl f* **100/1**
5/0 **10** ½ **Island Express (IRE)**[25] 7611 5 -8-12[50] (bt) AnnStokell[(5)] 7 24
(Ann Stokell) *sn outpcd* **100/1**
50 **11** 3 ¼ **Flumps**[3] 7903 3 -8-12[0] ShaneKelly 3
(John Stimpson) *dwlt: outpcd* **66/1**
66-0 **12** 2 ½ **Georgian Silver**[328] 101 4 -8-12[40] TomEaves 13
(George Foster) *mid-div: drvn along 3f out: wknd 1/2-way* **100/1**

1m 2.29s (-0.01) **Going Correction** -0.075s/f (Stan) 12Ran SP% **116.8**
Speed ratings (Par 103): **97,95,95,91,90 90,88,82,79,78 73,69**
toteswingers 1&2 £7.00, 2&3 £2.70, 1&3 £8.30 CSF £63.71 TOTE £19.60 : £4.40 , £1.40 , £1.50 ; EX 82.90 Trifecta £84.60 Pool: £788.84 - 6.99 winning units.
Owner D Fravigar Miss K Dixon & Mrs R Mitchell **Bred** Bumble Bloodstock Ltd **Trained** Nawton, N Yorks

FOCUS
This didn't take much winning. It's been rated around the second and third.

7953 JOHN COCHRANE 50TH BIRTHDAY CELEBRATION MAIDEN STKS 5f 20y (P)
6:20 (6:21) (Class 5) 2-Y-O **£2,911** (£866; £432; £216) **Stalls** Low

Form | | | | RPR
6662 **1** **Midnight Dream (FR)**[23] 7653 2 -9-3[68] GrahamLee 2 74
(Linda Stubbs) *led early: trckd ldrs: wnt 2nd over 1f out: rdn to ld ins fnl f: r.o* **13/2**[3]
2 1 ¼ **Golden Flower**[36] 7389 2 -8-12[0] SilvestreDeSousa 3 65
(David O'Meara) *sn led: rdn over 1f out: hdd ins fnl f: styd on same pce* **9/4**[2]
3 3 ½ **Saga Lout** 2 -9-3[0] RichardKingscote 8 59
(Tom Dascombe) *prom: pushed along 3f out: hmpd 2f out: styd on: could nt trble ldrs* **10/1**
024 **4** 2 ½ **Not Rigg (USA)**[15] 7749 2 -9-3[75] (t) JamieSpencer 1 48
(Andrew Balding) *s.i.s: sn drvn along and prom: rdn over 1f out: no ex fnl f* **7/4**[1]
0 **5** 2 ¼ **Little Eli**[32] 7458 2 -9-3[0] ShaneKelly 4 40
(Eric Alston) *sn chsng ldr: rdn over 1f out: wknd fnl f* **80/1**
6 3 **La Luz Del Sol** 2 -8-12[0] TonyHamilton 9 24
(Richard Fahey) *s.i.s: outpcd: r.o ins fnl f: nvr nrr* **16/1**
7 3 **Shamglas Queen**[8] 7845 2 -8-12[0] LukeMorris 10 13
(John C McConnell, Ire) *in tch: pushed along 1/2-way: rdn and wknd over 1f out* **25/1**
4 **8** ½ **Lager Time (IRE)**[7] 7855 2 -9-3[0] AdamKirby 6 16
(David Evans) *sn outpcd* **9/1**
00 **9** 4 ½ **Ichimoku**[25] 7609 2 -9-3[0] (t) TomEaves 7
(Bryan Smart) *prom: hmpd and wknd 2f out* **22/1**
10 6 **Lucky Morgan** 2 -9-3[0] StephenCraine 5
(Daniel Mark Loughnane) *s.i.s: outpcd* **66/1**

1m 1.78s (-0.52) **Going Correction** -0.075s/f (Stan) 10Ran SP% **116.4**
Speed ratings (Par 96): **101,99,93,89,85 81,76,75,68,58**
toteswingers 1&2 £2.40, 2&3 £7.20, 1&3 £16.70 CSF £20.93 TOTE £6.40 : £1.50 , £1.40 , £4.00 ; EX 20.30 Trifecta £526.90 Part won. Pool: £702.56 - 0.20 winning units. .
Owner O J Williams **Bred** Bruno Camus-Denais **Trained** Norton, N Yorks

FOCUS
Just a modest maiden. The winner put up an improved effort back over 5f and the runner-up hasn't been rated too far off her best on her first start for David O'Meara.

NOTEBOOK
Midnight Dream (FR) dropped back to 5f, travelled strongly in behind the pace on the rail, and found enough once switched to get off the mark at the fifth attempt. He can expect to go up in the weights on the back of this, which will make things harder when he switches to handicaps, but he's unexposed over this distance and might have more to offer. (op 6-1 tchd 10-1)
Golden Flower ran well in defeat at Dundalk last time out, and this was another solid effort on her debut for a new stable. The shorter trip wasn't a problem and, in finishing well clear of the rest, proved she can win a similarly ordinary maiden. (op 13-8 tchd 11-8)
Saga Lout ◆, a half-brother to a couple of winners, including seven-time winning sprinter Taurus Twins, was caught wide round the bend and got hampered on the turn in. He was staying on while hanging, probably through greenness, and ought to do better next time. (op 14-1 tchd 16-1)
Not Rigg (USA) was being shoved along from an early stage and the drop back to 5f backfired. (op 9-4)
Little Eli had clearly learnt a lot from his debut and showed bright early speed this time, before weakening. His dam was a speedball and he'll be interesting once handicapped. (op 66-1)

7954 32RED H'CAP 1m 4f 50y (P)
6:50 (6:50) (Class 5) (0-70,73) 3-Y-0+ **£2,911** (£866; £432; £216) **Stalls** Low

Form | | | | RPR
4003 **1** **Pertemps Networks**[23] 7652 8 -9-9[69] GrahamGibbons 8 81
(Michael Easterby) *mde all: rdn over 2f out: clr fr over 1f out: eased nr fin* **7/2**[2]
4252 **2** 3 ¾ **Miss Blakeney**[10] 7811 3 -9-4[69] (v) GeorgeBaker 2 74
(Marcus Tregoning) *chsd wnr: rdn over 2f out: styd on same pce fr over 1f out* **3/1**[1]
0540 **3** hd **Toughness Danon**[23] 7652 6 -9-7[67] (t) SebSanders 6 72
(Brendan Powell) *hld up: hdwy over 3f out: rdn over 2f out: styd on* **8/1**
6232 **4** 2 ¼ **Renegotiate**[17] 7702 3 -9-2[67] JimmyFortune 3 68
(Andrew Balding) *hld up: hdwy over 2f out: rdn over 1f out: eased whn hld wl ins fnl f* **11/1**
5 8 **Nashville (IRE)**[83] 6084 3 -9-3[68] JamieSpencer 12 57
(Ian Williams) *s.i.s: hdwy over 9f out: rdn and wknd over 2f out* **9/1**
5220 **6** ½ **Humungosaur**[41] 7269 3 -9-2[67] GrahamLee 1 55
(Richard Ford) *prom: hmpd after 1f: rdn and wknd over 2f out* **25/1**
5503 **7** 4 ½ **Sir Boss (IRE)**[2] 7792 7 -9-5[70] NatashaEaton[(5)] 7 51
(Michael Mullineaux) *hld up: effrt over 2f out: sn wknd* **14/1**
4201 **8** 9 **Boa**[12] 7792 7 -9-8[73] NicoleNordblad[(5)] 5 39
(Reg Hollinshead) *hld up: a in rr: wknd 3f out* **10/1**
053- **9** 7 **Gloucester**[32] 3533 9 -9-10[70] JamieGoldstein 9 25
(Michael Scudamore) *s.i.s: a in rr: wknd 3f out: t.o* **40/1**
05-2 **10** 12 **White Fusion**[220] 10 4 -9-10[70] SilvestreDeSousa 4
(David O'Meara) *prom: drvn along 6f out: wknd over 3f out: t.o* **11/2**[3]

3560 **11** *40* **Berwin (IRE)**[23] 7644 3-9-4 **69** ... LiamKeniry 11
(Sylvester Kirk) *chsd ldrs tl rdn and wknd 3f out: t.o* **20/1**

2m 39.15s (-1.95) **Going Correction** -0.075s/f (Stan)
WFA 3 from 4yo+ 5lb **11** Ran SP% **118.9**
Speed ratings (Par 103): **103,100,100,98,93 93,90,84,79,71 44**
toteswingers 1&2 £3.70, 2&3 £7.20, 1&3 £8.60 CSF £14.25 CT £79.36 TOTE £3.50: £1.20, £1.90, £3.90; EX 20.50 Trifecta £244.70 Pool: £822.40 - 2.52 winning units..
Owner E A Brook **Bred** H G Llewellyn **Trained** Sheriff Hutton, N Yorks

FOCUS
With the kickback pretty bad (meeting was abandoned after this race) the winner dominated from the front. He's been rated pretty much back to his best, with the third rated to his recent form.

7955 £32 BONUS AT 32RED.COM (S) STKS 1m 1f 103y(P)
() (Class 6) 3-Y-O+ £

7956 32RED SUPPORTING BRITISH RACING H'CAP 1m 1f 103y(P)
() (Class 6) (0-55,) 3-Y-O+ £

7957 32RED CASINO MAIDEN STKS 7f 32y(P)
() (Class 5) 2-Y-O £

7958 32REDBET.COM H'CAP (DIV I) 7f 32y(P)
() (Class 6) (0-55,) 3-Y-O+ £

7959 32REDBET.COM H'CAP (DIV II) 7f 32y(P)
() (Class 6) (0-55,) 3-Y-O+ £

T/Plt: £5.00 to a £1 stake. Pool: £126697.02 - 18456.27 winning tickets T/Qpdt: £1.20 to a £1 stake. Pool: £9351.50- 5431.82 winning tickets. CR

7922 KEMPTON (A.W) (R-H)
Monday, December 3

OFFICIAL GOING: Standard
Wind: medium, half behind Weather: overcast

7960 BETFRED "THE HOME OF GOALS GALORE" H'CAP 1m 2f (P)
2:20 (2:20) (Class 6) (0-60,60) 3-Y-O+ **£1,617** (£481; £240; £120) **Stalls** Low

Form RPR
132 **1** **The Wonga Coup (IRE)**[27] 7619 5-9-4 **57** ... IanMongan 4 67+
(Pat Phelan) *hld up wl in tch in midfield: swtchd lft and effrt over 1f out: chsd clr ldr 1f out: r.o wl u.p to ld towards fin* **5/2**[1]

4043 **2** *hd* **Barachiel**[33] 7486 4-9-0 **58** ... NicoleNordblad(5) 1 67
(Luke Dace) *led and set stdy gallop: pushed along and wnt clr over 1f out: pushed along hands and heels ins fnl f: hdd and no ex towards fin* **4/1**[2]

560 **3** *2 1/2* **Tallevu (IRE)**[73] 6442 3-9-1 **57** ... JimmyFortune 3 61
(Noel Chance) *t.k.h: rdn and effrt over 1f out: chsd ldng pair and one pce ins fnl f* **14/1**

0060 **4** *3/4* **Beggers Belief**[37] 7409 4-8-11 **57** ...(b) JoeyHaynes(7) 6 60+
(Eric Wheeler) *stdd s: hld up in tch in last quartet: rdn and effrt whn swtchd rt over 1f out: kpt on ins fnl f* **12/1**

0040 **5** *1* **Calypso Magic (IRE)**[65] 6690 4-9-1 **54** ...(t) GrahamLee 10 55
(Olivia Maylam) *hld up wl in tch in midfield: rdn and effrt to chse ldrs over 1f out: no ex and one pce fnl f* **7/1**[3]

0006 **6** *2 1/4* **Snowy Valley**[54] 6982 3-9-1 **57** ... MartinDwyer 2 53
(Simon Earle) *chsd ldrs: rdn 3f out: kpt on u.p tl no ex ent fnl f: wknd ins fnl f* **16/1**

0520 **7** *3/4* **Youm Jamil (USA)**[67] 6616 5-9-6 **59** ... JimCrowley 9 54
(Tony Carroll) *hld up in midfield: rdn and effrt wl over 1f out: no imp over 1f out: wknd fnl f* **12/1**

2220 **8** *nk* **Edgware Road**[12] 7819 4-9-7 **60** ...(p) JohnFahy 5 54
(Sean Curran) *v.s.a: hld up in rr: rdn and sme hdwy over 2f out: styd on same pce and no imp fnl f* **12/1**

30-0 **9** *1/2* **Jodawes (USA)**[18] 6949 5-9-4 **57** ... GeorgeBaker 12 50
(Gary Moore) *chsd ldr: rdn and unable qck wl over 1f out: lost 2nd 1f out: sn wknd* **8/1**

5344 **10** *3 1/4* **Time Square (FR)**[10] 944 5-9-5 **58** ...(t) AdamKirby 8 45
(Tony Carroll) *stdd s: hld up in tch in last quartet: rdn and effrt wl over 1f out: no imp and sn wknd* **8/1**

0/20 **11** *nk* **High 'n Dry (IRE)**[51] 7058 8-8-7 **53** ...(p) NedCurtis(7) 11 39
(Roger Curtis) *stdd s: hld up in tch in last quartet: wd bnd and rdn 2f out: sn edgd rt and no hdwy: wl btn fnl f* **50/1**

0600 **12** *16* **Great Charm (IRE)**[60] 6811 7-9-1 **59** ... HarryPoulton(5) 7 13
(Sheena West) *awkward leaving stalls: t.k.h: hld up wl in tch in midfield: rdn and wknd 2f out: bhd fnl f* **25/1**

2m 9.46s (1.46) **Going Correction** -0.025s/f (Stan)
WFA 3 from 4yo+ 3lb **12** Ran SP% **124.7**
Speed ratings (Par 101): **93,92,90,90,89 87,87,86,86,83 83,70**
Tote swingers 1&2 £3.70, 1&3 £12.20, 2&3 £12.40 CSF £12.58 CT £123.51 TOTE £2.80: £1.60, £1.80, £5.10; EX 9.20 Trifecta £118.20 Pool: £ 1,415.70 - 8.98 winning units..
Owner Celtic Contractors Limited **Bred** Harry Sweeney **Trained** Epsom, Surrey

FOCUS
A moderate handicap run at a messy pace, with the first two home fighting out an exciting finish. The first two are rated to personal bests.

7961 BETFRED MOBILE LOTTO CLAIMING STKS 7f (P)
2:50 (2:50) (Class 5) 3-Y-O+ **£2,264** (£673; £336; £168) **Stalls** Low

Form RPR
-000 **1** **Polar Kite (IRE)**[17] 7751 4-8-13 83 ... TonyHamilton 3 83
(Richard Fahey) *chsd ldr tl led over 3f out: rdn and clr over 1f out: in command fnl f and a doing enough to hold on* **6/1**

4055 **2** *1* **Only Ten Per Cent (IRE)**[27] 7607 4-9-1 73 ... DarryllHolland 8 82
(J R Jenkins) *hld up in tch in rr: rdn and effrt on inner wl over 1f out: chsd clr wnr jst ins fnl f: switching lft and styd on wl but nvr gng to rch wnr* **11/2**[3]

1000 **3** *5* **Frequency**[14] 7790 5-9-7 77 ...(b) JimmyFortune 1 75
(Keith Dalgleish) *t.k.h: hld up in tch in midfield: rdn and effrt to chse clr wnr wl over 1f out: no imp: wknd fnl f* **6/1**

5400 **4** *4* **Imprimis Tagula (IRE)**[5] 7901 8-8-13 76 ...(v) GrahamLee 7 56
(Alan Bailey) *t.k.h: chsd ldrs: rdn and unable qck ent fnl 2f: wknd over 1f out* **7/2**[2]

5000 **5** *4* **Lord Deevert**[49] 7105 7-8-6 45 ...(p) AndrewMullen 4 38
(Bill Turner) *rdn along leaving stalls: sn led: hdd over 3f out: lost 2nd and drvn wl over 1f out: sn wknd* **50/1**

6 *nk* **Fairy Wing (IRE)**[79] 6267 5-9-0 81 ...(p) AdamKirby 9 45
(Conor Dore) *taken down early: in tch: hdwy on outer to chse ldrs 1/2-way: rdn and fnd nil over 2f out: wknd 2f out* **11/8**[1]

5450 **7** *1 1/4* **Le King Beau (USA)**[110] 5229 3-8-10 62 ...(v) SeanLevey 6 38
(John Bridger) *hld up in tch in last pair: rdn and struggling over 2f out: sn wknd* **25/1**

1m 26.08s (0.08) **Going Correction** -0.025s/f (Stan) **7** Ran SP% **114.1**
Speed ratings (Par 103): **98,96,91,86,82 81,80**
Tote swingers 1&2 £4.40, 1&3 £3.80, 2&3 £4.50 CSF £38.13 TOTE £9.90: £3.80, £3.90; EX 43.60 Trifecta £149.90 Pool: £ 1,223.94 - 6.12 winning units..No claims.
Owner Mr And Mrs J D Cotton **Bred** Holborn Trust Co **Trained** Musley Bank, N Yorks

FOCUS
This complexion of this race changed with the late withdrawal (stuck in traffic) of favourite and likely pace angle April Fool. The gallop was fair with the field finishing well strung out. It's unclear whether this form is entirely solid with the winner showing his best form for a year and the second running to his best at face value.

7962 BETFRED "THE BONUS KING" MAIDEN STKS (DIV I) 1m (P)
3:20 (3:21) (Class 5) 2-Y-O **£2,264** (£673; £336; £168) **Stalls** Low

Form RPR
4 **1** **El Buen Turista**[12] 7806 2-9-3 0 ... JimmyFortune 8 84+
(Andrew Balding) *sn led and mde rest: rdn and qcknd clr wl over 1f out: in n.d and r.o wl fnl f: readily* **11/4**[2]

62 **2** *4 1/2* **Saved By The Bell (IRE)**[80] 6204 2-9-3 0 ... MartinLane 1 74+
(Brian Meehan) *chsd ldrs: rdn and effrt 2f out: chsd clr wnr ent fnl f: r.o for clr 2nd but no imp on wnr* **7/4**[1]

3 *3 3/4* **Emerging** 2-9-3 0 ... LiamKeniry 3 65+
(David Elsworth) *hld up in tch towards rr: rdn and hdwy into modest 4th 2f out: kpt on to go 3rd fnl 100yds: no ch w wnr* **25/1**

5 **4** *1 1/2* **Silver Dixie (USA)**[17] 7749 2-9-3 0 ... GrahamLee 6 62+
(Jeremy Noseda) *hld up in tch in midfield: rdn and lost pl wl over 2f out: trying to rally whn edgd rt 2f out: no ch w wnr but kpt on ins fnl f* **9/2**[3]

26 **5** *nk* **Ashamaly**[17] 7749 2-9-3 0 ... IanMongan 10 61
(James Tate) *pressed wnr tl rdn and outpcd by wnr wl over 1f out: 3rd and wl hld jst ins fnl f: wknd fnl 150yds* **14/1**

6 *1* **Little Buxted (USA)** 2-9-3 0 ... JimCrowley 7 59
(Robert Mills) *stdd after s: hld up in tch in last pair: swtchd rt and effrt 2f out: no imp and styd on same pce after* **16/1**

5 **7** *2 3/4* **Plenum (GER)**[12] 7807 2-9-3 0 ... TedDurcan 5 53
(David Lanigan) *hld up in tch in midfield: rdn and outpcd ent fnl 2f: sn outpcd and wl btn 1f out* **8/1**

8 *1 1/2* **Tebee's Oasis** 2-8-12 0 ... RobertHavlin 2 44
(John Gosden) *dwlt: in tch in rr: rdn and outpcd over 2f out: wl btn over 1f out* **16/1**

9 *3 1/2* **Rosaceous** 2-8-12 0 ... RichardKingscote 9 36
(Daniel Kubler) *broke wl: stdd after s and chsd ldrs: rdn and struggling over 2f out: bhd over 1f out* **100/1**

0 **10** *2* **Sweet Force**[19] 7707 2-9-3 0 ... AdamKirby 4 37
(Marco Botti) *chsd ldrs: lost pl over 2f out: wknd u.p 2f out: bhd fnl f* **25/1**

1m 39.18s (-0.62) **Going Correction** -0.025s/f (Stan) **10** Ran SP% **119.4**
Speed ratings (Par 96): **102,97,93,92,91 90,88,86,83,81**
Tote swingers 1&2 £1.80, 1&3 £16.60, 2&3 £9.20, CSF £8.04 TOTE £3.20: £1.10, £1.50, £8.00; EX 11.40 Trifecta £149.50 Pool: £ 1,518.95 - 7.62 winning units..
Owner N M Watts **Bred** Newsells Park Stud **Trained** Kingsclere, Hants

FOCUS
Some decent stables in opposition for this maiden, run at a steady pace with the winner making all. As in the previous race, those racing up the far rail looked at an advantage. The winner built on his promising debut and the second was below his debut form.

NOTEBOOK
El Buen Turista, a half-brother to a 1m winner in Spain and out of a Listed-placed 1m 2yo winner, ran green but with promise when fourth in a 7f maiden here on his debut last month and he showed the benefit of that run. Smartly away, he dictated the pace and produced a fine turn of foot to put the race to bed over a furlong out. He got run of the race but with the favourite back in second, the form looks solid enough. (tchd 3-1)
Saved By The Bell(IRE) ran well on his second start when runner-up at Sandown in September and again ran with credit on his first AW outing. He looks capable of landing a maiden over the winter but is now qualified for a mark. (op 2-1)
Emerging, a 65,000gns yearling and half-brother to seven winners, out of a Listed-placed French 1m winner, was weak in the market but kept on well to the line, having looked outpaced at the 2f marker. From a yard whose juveniles tend to improve with experience, this was a fair debut. (op 20-1)
Silver Dixie(USA) found the 7f too sharp on his debut at Wolverhampton and again shaped as though this 1m trip was on the short side. He was staying on well late and one would expect his shrewd yard to garner more improvement out of him. (op 5-1 tchd 11-2)
Ashamaly, who ran well on his debut before disappointing last time out, raced up with the pace but weakened inside the final furlong over this longer trip. (op 20-1)
Plenum(GER), who ran green on his debut, looked a shade burly here and ran as though finding this too short. One would expect to see plenty of improvement next season. (tchd 7-1)

7963 BETFRED "THE BONUS KING" MAIDEN STKS (DIV II) 1m (P)
3:50 (3:51) (Class 5) 2-Y-O **£2,264** (£673; £336; £168) **Stalls** Low

Form RPR
3 **1** **Sillabub (USA)**[30] 7552 2-8-12 0 ... RobertHavlin 4 74+
(John Gosden) *chsd ldng trio: effrt and smooth hdwy to ld wl over 1f out: sn shkn up and qcknd clr: comf* **5/4**[1]

2 *2 1/2* **Tinghir (IRE)** 2-9-3 0 ... TedDurcan 3 73+
(David Lanigan) *hld up in midfield: rdn and effrt ent fnl 2f: styd on to chse clr wnr ent fnl f: no threat to wnr but styd on for clr 2nd* **8/1**

00 **3** *4* **Knight Owl**[26] 7628 2-9-3 0 ... JimCrowley 1 63
(James Fanshawe) *hld up in tch in rr of main gp: rdn and hdwy on inner 2f out: wnt 3rd 1f out: no ex and wknd fnl 100yds* **5/1**[3]

04 **4** *1* **Argent Knight**[16] 7780 2-9-3 0 ... GrahamLee 8 61
(William Jarvis) *chsd ldrs: rdn over 2f out: chsd clr wnr and no imp wl over 1f out: lost 2nd ent fnl f: wl hld and plugged on same pce after* **4/1**[2]

5 *nk* **Bin Manduro** 2-9-3 0 ...[1] MartinLane 2 60+
(James Tate) *t.k.h: hld up in tch in rr of main gp: rdn and outpcd 2f out: no ch w wnr and edgd rt 1f out: styd on same pce after* **10/1**

6 *hd* **Camachoice (IRE)** 2-9-3 0 ...(t) AdamKirby 6 60+
(Marco Botti) *hld up in midfield: rdn and struggling ent fnl 2f: outpcd and wl btn over 1f out: plugged on* **25/1**

5 **7** *1* **Handiwork**[13] 7796 2-9-3 0 ... GeorgeBaker 9 57
(Michael Bell) *chsd ldrs: rdn and unable qck over 2f out: outpcd and btn over 1f out: wknd fnl f* **12/1**

00 **8** *13* **Ri Na Si**[27] 7613 2-9-3 0 ... IanMongan 7 27
(Pat Phelan) *led tl wl over 1f out: sn btn and wknd: fdd ins fnl f* **66/1**

9 41 **Dark Diamond (IRE)** 2-8-12 0............................ MichaelJMMurphy(5) 5
(Robert Cowell) *s.i.s: rn green and rdn along in detached last thrght: lost tch 1/2-way: t.o* **33/1**

1m 40.44s (0.64) **Going Correction** -0.025s/f (Stan) **9** Ran SP% **117.3**
Speed ratings (Par 96): **95,92,88,87,87 87,86,73,32**
Tote swingers 1&2 £4.10, 1&3 £2.90, 2&3 £5.50 CSF £12.40 TOTE £1.60: £1.02, £2.60, £1.70; EX 16.10 Trifecta £49.90 Pool: £ 1,300.24 - 19.51 winning units..
Owner H R H Princess Haya Of Jordan **Bred** Grade 1 Bloodstock Et Al **Trained** Newmarket, Suffolk

FOCUS
Not the strongest maiden, but the first pair came clear. It was run at an honest pace with those racing up the far rail dominating, and the winner looking above average.

NOTEBOOK
Sillabub(USA), the only filly in the field, stayed on well enough when third on her debut at Newmarket (7f, soft) and looked the one to beat here. Always handily placed, her jockey was confident throughout and once sent to the front, she quickened under minimal pressure in the style of a nice type. (op 6-4 tchd 7-4)
Tinghir(IRE), a half-brother to seven winners, most notably the high-class French performer Policy Maker, ran a race full of promise on his debut. Hailing from a yard whose runners improve with experience, he travelled kindly throughout but was outpaced by the winner, although finished well clear of the third. (tchd 9-1)
Knight Owl showed improved form on his third start stepped up in trip here, and one would expect him to be placed to good advantage in handicaps over further. (op 11-2 tchd 4-1)
Argent Knight stayed on well enough when fourth at Wolverhampton (1m1f) on his last start but, having raced handily, was outpaced up the straight over this shorter trip, suggesting he wants further. (op 9-2 tchd 7-2)
Bin Manduro, who raced green in rear in a first-time hood, made some progress up the straight and this experience should not be lost on him. (op 8-1)
Camachoice(IRE), a third foal of a middle-distance winner in Germany and wearing a tongue strap on his debut, kept on well enough under an educating ride and he should come on for this. (op 16-1)

7964 BETFRED NEW "30 MINUTE LIMIT" COUPON H'CAP — 1m (P)
4:20 (4:21) (Class 6) (0-60,60) 3-Y-0+ **£1,617** (£481; £240; £120) **Stalls** Low

Form — RPR

4226 **1** **Rapid Water**[40] 7321 6-9-2 **55**..[1] JimmyFortune 3 — 62
(Pat Eddery) *hld up in tch in midfield: hdwy 3f out: rdn to chse ldng pair over 1f out: kpt on u.p to ld last strides* **10/1**

0004 **2** *hd* **Zaheeb**[24] 7670 4-9-7 **60**..(b) AdamBeschizza 4 — 67
(Dave Morris) *led: clr 3f out: drvn wl over 1f out: pressed fnl 100yds: kpt on tl hdd and no ex last strides* **5/1**[2]

2050 **3** *nse* **Finlodex**[33] 7474 5-9-3 **56**.. FrankieMcDonald 11 — 62
(Murty McGrath) *s.i.s and drvn along early: in rr: swtchd lft and effrt over 2f out: hdwy but stl plenty to do 1f out: styd on wl u.p: nt quite rch ldng pair* **25/1**

043 **4** *hd* **Green Earth (IRE)**[61] 6773 5-9-7 **60**..............................(v[1]) IanMongan 7 — 66
(Pat Phelan) *in tch in midfield: rdn and effrt to chse ldrs over 2f out: chsd clr ldr over 1f out: styd on to press wnr fnl f: kpt on but lost 2 pls cl home* **7/1**[3]

6461 **5** *hd* **Storm Runner (IRE)**[12] 7816 4-9-2 **55**.............................. GrahamLee 8 — 61
(George Margarson) *off the pce in last trio and pushed along: hdwy 2f out: styd on wl u.p ins fnl f: nt quite rch ldrs* **5/2**[1]

0036 **6** *6* **Lieutenant Dan (IRE)**[27] 7620 5-9-5 **58**.......................... GeorgeBaker 2 — 50
(Michael Appleby) *hld up off the pce in last quartet: rdn and hdwy 2f out: edging rt and no imp ent fnl f: plugged on but wl hld after* **10/1**

-036 **7** *5* **Play The Blues (IRE)**[76] 6334 5-8-9 **55**.........................(t) NedCurtis(7) 9 — 35
(Roger Curtis) *chsd ldrs: wnt 2nd 3f out: sn rdn and no imp on ldr: lost 2nd over 1f out: fdd fnl f* **33/1**

300 **8** *1* **Made Of More**[16] 7768 3-9-6 **60**..................................... RobertHavlin 14 — 38
(Roger Ingram) *in tch in midfield: rdn and no imp whn edgd rt over 2f out: wknd over 1f out* **20/1**

0050 **9** *3* **Bitaphon (IRE)**[60] 6810 3-9-6 **60**.................................. AndrewMullen 5 — 31
(Michael Appleby) *chsd ldr tl 3f out: sn drvn and struggling: wknd 2f out* **8/1**

0222 **10** *shd* **Songbird Blues**[189] 2548 3-9-4 **58**................................. DavidProbert 12 — 29
(Mark Usher) *hld up in tch in midfield: rdn and no imp whn hung rt over 2f out: wknd wl over 1f out* **14/1**

110/ **11** *2 1/4* **Love Pegasus (USA)**[551] 2627 6-9-2 **60**..........(p) MichaelJMMurphy(5) 6 — 26
(Paddy Butler) *hld up off the pce in last quartet: rdn and no hdwy over 2f out: sn wknd* **10/1**

1-00 **12** *1 3/4* **Miriam's Song**[137] 4235 3-9-6 **60**...................................(v[1]) AdamKirby 13 — 22
(Stuart Kittow) *s.i.s: sn pushed along: a bhd: lost tch u.p over 2f out* **50/1**

560- **13** *1* **Fromthestables Com (IRE)**[515] 3780 3-9-6 **60**.............. SebSanders 1 — 19
(Brendan Powell) *in tch in midfield: rdn and struggling over 2f out: wknd 2f out* **33/1**

0040 **14** *3* **Sunnyside Tom (IRE)**[13] 7798 8-9-6 **59**....................... TonyHamilton 10 — 11
(Richard Fahey) *taken down early: chsd ldrs on outer: rdn and wknd over 2f out: bhd fnl f* **16/1**

1m 39.78s (-0.02) **Going Correction** -0.025s/f (Stan)
WFA 3 from 4yo+ 1lb **14** Ran SP% **125.1**
Speed ratings (Par 101): **99,98,98,98,98 92,87,86,83,83 81,79,78,75**
Tote swingers 1&2 £10.20, 1&3 £44.30, 2&3 £36.10 CSF £58.59 CT £1291.96 TOTE £7.90: £2.80, £2.40, £12.40; EX 83.50 Trifecta £1138.50 Part won. Pool: £ 1,518.12 - 0.31 winning units..
Owner Miss Emma L Owen **Bred** Littleton Stud **Trained** Nether Winchendon, Bucks
■ Stewards' Enquiry : Ian Mongan Seven-day ban: excessive use of the whip (Dec 17-22, 26)

FOCUS
A wide-open handicap with just 5lb covering the 14 runners, run at a fair pace with five virtually in a line at the finish and clear of the remainder. Ordinary form, but sound.

7965 BETFRED "BONUS KING BINGO" NURSERY — 7f (P)
4:50 (4:50) (Class 5) (0-75,75) 2-Y-0 **£2,264** (£673; £252; £252) **Stalls** Low

Form — RPR

5032 **1** **Gracious George (IRE)**[18] 7723 2-8-13 **67**...................... JimCrowley 2 — 70
(Jimmy Fox) *hld up in tch in midfield: rdn and effrt 2f out: hdwy into 4th over 1f out: str run 1f out to ld fnl 75yds: idling in front: rdn out* **2/1**[1]

0053 **2** *1/2* **Tilstarr (IRE)**[18] 7724 2-8-7 **61**....................................... MartinLane 4 — 63
(Roger Teal) *chsd ldrs tl wnt 2nd 1/2-way: rdn and sltly outpcd 2f out: rallied ent fnl f: led ins fnl f: hdd and styd on same pce fnl 75yds* **16/1**

0065 **3** *2* **This Is Nice (IRE)**[18] 7720 2-9-2 **70**......................(v) RichardKingscote 6 — 67
(Tom Dascombe) *led: rdn and qcknd clr 2f out: pressed and drvn 1f out: hdd and no ex ins fnl f: wknd towards fin* **7/2**[2]

15 **3** *dht* **Mick Duggan**[61] 6797 2-9-5 **73**...................................... DavidProbert 3 — 70
(Simon Hodgson) *sn bhd in last pair and pushed along: stl plenty to do but hdwy u.p 2f out: styd on strly ins fnl f: nt rch ldng pair* **20/1**

5662 **5** *1 1/4* **Makinson Lane (IRE)**[27] 7614 2-8-13 **67**......................... TonyHamilton 5 — 60
(Richard Fahey) *taken down early: racd keenly: chsd ldrs: wnt 3rd and rdn over 2f out: no imp over 1f out: plugged on same pce fnl f* **9/1**

0445 **6** *nk* **Provencal**[18] 7723 2-8-4 **63**..................................... MichaelJMMurphy(5) 1 — 55
(Rod Millman) *hld up in tch in last quartet: hdwy over 2f out: effrt u.p on inner 2f out: no imp and styd on same pce fr over 1f out* **8/1**

5320 **7** *2 1/4* **Eastern Dragon (IRE)**[19] 7713 2-8-10 **64**.......................(v) GrahamLee 7 — 51
(Michael Scudamore) *hld up in tch towards rr: rdn and hdwy ent fnl 2f: no imp over 1f out: wknd fnl f* **9/1**

500 **8** *1/2* **Bountiful Bess**[61] 6790 2-8-12 **66**..................................... LiamKeniry 10 — 51
(Pam Sly) *in tch in midfield: rdn and unable qck ent fnl 2f: plugged on but n.d after* **33/1**

51 **9** *2 1/4* **Be On The Bell**[16] 7777 2-9-7 **75**................................... MartinDwyer 11 — 54
(Jamie Osborne) *stdd and dropped in bhd after s: hld up off the pce in last pair: rdn and effrt 2f out: no imp: nvr trbld ldrs* **7/1**[3]

2604 **10** *54* **Reveille**[47] 7173 2-8-13 **67**.. JimmyFortune 9
(Hughie Morrison) *chsd ldrs tl 1/2-way: rdn and lost pl whn wandered over 2f out: sn bhd: t.o fnl f* **25/1**

1m 26.23s (0.23) **Going Correction** -0.025s/f (Stan) **10** Ran SP% **116.6**
CSF £36.30 TOTE £2.20: £1.10, £5.60; EX 34.50 TRIFECTA Pool £1,516.41 GG-T-MD £568.60 1.027 Owner.

FOCUS
Plenty of in-form runners lined up for this nursery, run at a sound pace with the winner coming late to win well. The form is only ordinary.

NOTEBOOK
Gracious George(IRE) was outpaced early before staying on well over 6f here last time and finished well again, over this extra furlong. He looked briefly outpaced once more when coming under pressure, but kept on under a strong drive that saw him collect. (op 5-2)
Tilstarr(IRE) was always nicely berthed behind the pace and looked the likely winner when moving ahead a furlong out but was worn down late on. This was her best effort to date and she remains open to further improvement. (op 14-1)
This Is Nice(IRE) ensured it was a truly run affair but is receiving little respite from the handicapper for being beaten. There is little doubting her resolution, but she tends to find a couple too good off this current rating. (tchd 4-1)
Mick Duggan looked to have plenty on off this mark on his handicap debut, but he ran an encouraging race making excellent late headway from the rear, inside the final furlong. (tchd 4-1)
Makinson Lane(IRE) ran well off this mark at Wolverhampton last time but was outpaced inside the final furlong on this occasion. (op 12-1 tchd 14-1)
Provencal was unable to take advantage of his inside berth and did not enjoy the clearest of passages but stayed on well enough to the line suggesting he can prove competitive off this mark. (tchd 7-1)
Eastern Dragon(IRE) was keeping on well enough for pressure without ever looking dangerous over a trip that looks on the short side. (tchd 8-1)
Reveille Official explanation: jockey said filly stopped quickly

7966 BETFRED STILL TREBLE ODDS ON LUCKY 15'S H'CAP — 7f (P)
5:20 (5:21) (Class 4) (0-85,85) 3-Y-0+ **£4,075** (£1,212; £606; £303) **Stalls** Low

Form — RPR

0004 **1** **Head Of Steam (USA)**[12] 7817 5-9-7 **85**............................ GrahamLee 6 — 96+
(Amanda Perrett) *hld up in midfield: nt clr run and shuffled bk 2f out: swtchd lft over 1f out: hdwy 1f out: str run to ld fnl 75yds: r.o wl* **11/2**[2]

4542 **2** *1/2* **Roy The Boy (USA)**[3] 7935 4-8-9 **73**................................. LiamKeniry 5 — 82
(Alan Bailey) *stdd s: hld up in rr: stl plenty to do 2f out: rdn and gd hdwy jst over 1f out: chal wl ins fnl f: no ex and hld cl home* **11/2**[2]

1-1U **3** *3/4* **Haaf A Sixpence**[211] 1894 3-9-1 **79**............................... JimCrowley 14 — 86+
(Ralph Beckett) *chsd ldr tl led wl over 1f out: drvn ent fnl f: hdd and one pce fnl 75yds* **6/1**[3]

0041 **4** *3/4* **George Baker (IRE)**[18] 7722 5-8-8 **72**............................ MartinDwyer 1 — 77
(George Baker) *hld up in tch in midfield: rdn and hdwy 2f out: pressed ldrs 1f out: styd on same pce ins fnl f* **20/1**

1040 **5** *1 1/4* **Good Authority (IRE)**[25] 7645 5-9-6 **84**..................... TomMcLaughlin 2 — 86
(Karen George) *chsd ldrs: rdn and ev ch over 1f out: drvn and no ex jst ins fnl f: wknd fnl 75yds* **12/1**

4132 **6** *3/4* **Atlantis Crossing (IRE)**[18] 7725 3-8-4 **73**.................. NathanAlison(5) 4 — 73+
(Jim Boyle) *restless in stalls: s.i.s: hld up in rr: hdwy and nt clr run wl over 1f out: swtchd rt and styd on ins fnl f: nt trble ldrs* **20/1**

0130 **7** *1 1/2* **Rustic Deacon**[26] 7631 5-9-7 **85**.................................... JamieMackay 13 — 81
(Willie Musson) *t.k.h: chsd ldrs: rdn to chse ldrs over 1f out: no ex 1f out: wknd ins fnl f* **6/1**[3]

0560 **8** *hd* **Prince Of Burma (IRE)**[152] 3767 4-9-5 **83**....................... IanMongan 11 — 78
(Jeremy Gask) *hld up in tch towards rr: rdn and hdwy jst over 1f out: styd on fnl f: nt rch ldrs* **33/1**

4132 **9** *1 3/4* **Delft**[25] 7645 3-9-5 **83**.. JimmyFortune 3 — 74
(Jeremy Noseda) *hld up in tch in midfield: rdn and effrt ent fnl 2f: drvn and no hdwy over 1f out: wknd ins fnl f* **2/1**[1]

0040 **10** *2 1/4* **Summerinthecity (IRE)**[14] 7789 5-9-0 **78**........................ AdamKirby 10 — 63
(David Nicholls) *t.k.h: hld up towards rr on outer: rdn and effrt over 2f out: no imp over 1f out: wknd fnl f* **25/1**

0000 **11** *3/4* **Shifting Star (IRE)**[11] 7823 7-9-2 **80**............................... SeanLevey 7 — 63
(John Bridger) *chsd ldrs: rdn and unable qck over 2f out: wknd over 1f out* **33/1**

0600 **12** *9* **Irish Heartbeat (IRE)**[11] 7826 7-9-4 **82**.....................(v[1]) TonyHamilton 8 — 40
(Richard Fahey) *racd keenly: led tl wl over 1f out: sn wknd* **33/1**

600 **13** *39* **Caldercruix (USA)**[101] 5557 5-8-11 **78**...................(v) SimonPearce(3) 12
(James Evans) *v.s.a and virtually ref to r: t.o thrght* **20/1**

5604 **14** *2 1/4* **Fantasy Gladiator**[11] 7823 6-8-5 **74**..................(p) MichaelJMMurphy(5) 9
(Robert Cowell) *sddle slipped and rdr lost irons sn after s: sn t.o* **11/1**

1m 24.69s (-1.31) **Going Correction** -0.025s/f (Stan) **14** Ran SP% **135.7**
Speed ratings (Par 105): **106,105,104,103,102 101,99,99,97,94 94,83,39,36**
Tote swingers 1&2 £6.80, 1&3 £11.80, 2&3 £8.40 CSF £37.35 CT £202.87 TOTE £7.40: £3.00, £2.50, £2.30; EX 39.40 Trifecta £475.60 Pool: £ 1,541.20 - 2.43 winning units..
Owner George Materna **Bred** Juddmonte Farms Inc **Trained** Pulborough, W Sussex

FOCUS
Plenty of incident for this competitive handicap, run at a sound pace with the front two home coming latest and wide. Solid-looking form.

7967 BETFRED "HAT-TRICK HEAVEN" H'CAP — 6f (P)
5:50 (5:50) (Class 5) (0-70,70) 3-Y-0+ **£2,264** (£673; £336; £168) **Stalls** Low

Form — RPR

0233 **1** **Fortrose Academy (IRE)**[16] 7776 3-9-0 **63**...................... DavidProbert 4 — 74
(Andrew Balding) *chsd ldrs: rdn to ld ent fnl f: hrd pressed and hld on gamely cl home* **4/1**[1]

3220 **2** *nk* **Lastkingofscotland (IRE)**[9] 7857 6-9-3 **66**...................(b) AdamKirby 9 — 76
(Conor Dore) *hld up towards rr: effrt and switching lft over 1f out: str run ins fnl f: pressing wnr cl home: nt quite rch wnr* **6/1**[3]

5533 **3** ½ **Welease Bwian (IRE)**[73] 6439 3 -9-1 **64** RichardKingscote 8 72
(Stuart Williams) *stdd s: hld up in tch in midfield: rdn and hdwy over 1f out: chsd wnr ins fnl f: kpt on but lost 2nd towards fin* **6/1**[3]

3030 **4** ¾ **Speak The Truth (IRE)**[7] 7741 6 -9-0 **63** (p) SebSanders 2 69
(Jim Boyle) *in tch in midfield: effrt on inner 2f out: chsd wnr over 1f out tl ins fnl f: styd on same pce fnl 100yds* **14/1**

0060 **5** 2 ¼ **Parisian Pyramid (IRE)**[9] 7937 6 -9-7 **70** GrahamLee 7 69
(Ian Williams) *hld up towards rr: rdn and effrt over 1f out: hdwy ent fnl f: styd on but no threat to ldrs* **4/1**[1]

3010 **6** 1 ¼ **Belinsky (IRE)**[28] 7590 5 -9-0 **63** JimCrowley 11 58
(Julie Camacho) *pushed lft after s: hld up towards rr: hdwy on inner over 1f out: styd on: nvr trbld ldrs* **14/1**

3560 **7** 1 ½ **Dorothy's Dancing (IRE)**[17] 7742 4 -9-1 **64** (p) GeorgeBaker 3 54
(Gary Moore) *led and sn clr: rdn wl over 1f out: hdd ent fnl f: wknd fnl 150yds* **9/1**

0460 **8** ¾ **Rafaaf (IRE)**[19] 7716 4 -9-7 **70** SeanQuinlan 5 58
(Richard Phillips) *in tch in midfield: rdn and unable qck over 2f out: styd on same pce and wl hld fr over 1f out* **33/1**

1600 **9** ½ **Efistorm**[42] 7297 11 -8-11 **65** NicoleNordblad(5) 10 51+
(Joseph Tuite) *hld up off the pce in rr: hdwy towards inner over 1f out: styng on but no threat to ldrs whn nt clr run and eased ins fnl f* **33/1**

1002 **10** 1 **Roy's Legacy**[5] 7902 3 -8-12 **66** (t) MichaelJMMurphy(5) 6 49
(Shaun Harris) *chsd ldr tl over 1f out: wknd ins fnl f* **9/2**[2]

1360 **11** ¾ **Dressed In Lace**[33] 7483 3 -9-7 **70** IanMongan 1 50
(Jo Crowley) *chsd ldrs tl 2f out: wknd u.p ent fnl f* **25/1**

0050 **12** shd **Oratorian (IRE)**[18] 7725 3 -9-1 **64** LiamKeniry 12 44
(Sylvester Kirk) *edgd rt and bmpd rival sn after s: in tch towards rr: rdn and no hdwy over 2f out: wknd over 1f out* **33/1**

1m 12.08s (-1.02) **Going Correction** -0.025s/f (Stan) 12Ran SP% **122.8**
Speed ratings (Par 103): **105,104,103,102,99 98,96,95,94,93 92,92**
Tote swingers 1&2 £5.20, 1&3 £5.30, 2&3 £12.50 CSF £28.16 CT £145.66 TOTE £5.30 : £2.00, £2.10, £2.60 ; EX 25.10 Trifecta £138.20 Pool: £ 1,284.84 - 6.97 winning units. .
Owner Evan M Sutherland **Bred** L K I Bloodstock & Diomed Bloodstock **Trained** Kingsclere, Hants
■ Stewards' Enquiry : Jim Crowley two-day ban: careless riding (Dec 17-18)

FOCUS
Another open looking handicap to conclude the card, run at a solid pace with the winner all out to hold on at the line. The time was decent and a slightly positive view has been taken of the form.
T/Jkpt: Part won. £8,383.00 to a £1 stake. Pool: £11,,807.14. 0.50 winning units. T/Plt: £149.10 to a £1 stake. Pool: £59,087.45. 289.22 winning units. T/Qpdt: £9.80 to a £1 stake. Pool: £5,966.97. 449.48 winning units. SP

7952 WOLVERHAMPTON (A.W) (L-H)
Monday, December 3

OFFICIAL GOING: Standard
Wind: Fresh behind Weather: Fine

7968 DOWNLOAD OUR IPHONE APP H'CAP FOR AMATEUR RIDERS 1m 5f 194y (P)
1:25 (1:25) (Class 6) (0-65,65) 3-Y-0+ **£1,646** (£506; £253) **Stalls** Low

Form RPR

3001 **1** **Chookie Hamilton**[9] 7869 8 -10-10 **61** MrSWalker 13 74+
(Keith Dalgleish) *chsd ldrs: led over 2f out: rdn clr fr over 1f out: comf* **11/8**[1]

0544 **2** 4 **Kames Park (IRE)**[12] 7819 10 -10-3 **61** MrsAGuest(7) 4 68
(Richard Guest) *s.i.s: hld up: hdwy over 2f out: wnt 2nd ins fnl f: no ch w wnr* **8/1**[3]

3003 **3** 3 ¾ **Sedgwick**[12] 7819 10 -10-7 **65** MrWFeatherstone(7) 2 67
(Shaun Harris) *hld up: hdwy over 4f out: rdn over 1f out: styd on same pce* **12/1**

3203 **4** ¾ **Holden Eagle**[28] 7596 7 -10-8 **64** MrFMitchell(5) 10 65
(Tony Newcombe) *led 3f: chsd ldr tl led again over 3f out: rdn over 1f out: styd on same pce* **6/1**[2]

4315 **5** 2 ¼ **Candelita**[14] 7792 5 -10-8 **64** MrFTett(5) 9 62
(Jo Hughes) *prom: racd keenly: pushed along over 2f out: wknd ins fnl f* **8/1**[3]

0000 **6** 2 ½ **Before Bruce**[9] 7862 5 -9-11 **55** (p) MrJNPilkington(7) 11 49
(Brendan Powell) *racd keenly: prom: led 11f out: hdd over 3f out: wknd wl over 1f out* **66/1**

5304 **7** nk **Shy**[83] 6126 7 -10-0 **56** (b) MissPhillipaTutty(5) 7 50
(Karen Tutty) *hld up: pushed along over 4f out: rdn over 1f out: nvr on terms* **12/1**

33/0 **8** hd **Augustus John (IRE)**[14] 7792 9 -10-6 **60** MrCMartin(3) 8 53
(Roy Brotherton) *hld up: nvr on terms* **18/1**

5200 **9** ½ **Ravi River (IRE)**[80] 6131 8 -10-11 **62** MrColmMcCormack 12 55
(Alistair Whillans) *prom: rdn over 3f out: wknd over 2f out* **33/1**

5400 **10** 2 ¾ **Asterales**[12] 7819 5 -9-12 **56** MissJGordon(7) 3 45
(Jo Hughes) *s.i.s: hdwy 6f out: wknd over 2f out* **40/1**

6113 **11** 14 **Bute Street**[143] 4061 7 -10-13 **64** MissSBrotherton 1 33
(Ron Hodges) *chsd ldrs: pushed along over 4f out: wknd 3f out: t.o* **8/1**[3]

3m 3.18s (-2.82) **Going Correction** -0.15s/f (Stan) 11Ran SP% **117.2**
Speed ratings (Par 101): **102,99,97,97,95 94,94,94,93,92 84**
Tote swingers 1&2 £4.20, 1&3 £7.20, 2&3 £15.30 CSF £12.66 CT £97.23 TOTE £2.00 : £1.70, £2.20, £3.80 ; EX 12.20 Trifecta £86.00 Pool: £ 1,018.82 - 8.88 winning units. .
Owner Straightline Construction Ltd **Bred** D And J Raeburn **Trained** Carluke, S Lanarks

FOCUS
A weak staying handicap which didn't look strong run. The time was decent and the form is rated around the runner-up.
Shy Official explanation: vet said mare pulled up lame right-fore

7969 LIKE US ON FACEBOOK WOLVERHAMPTON RACECOURSE H'CAP (DIV I) 5f 20y (P)
1:55 (1:55) (Class 6) (0-65,65) 3-Y-0+ **£1,704** (£503; £251) **Stalls** Low

Form RPR

0002 **1** **Passionada**[28] 7589 3 -9-5 **63** RobertWinston 11 73
(Ed McMahon) *chsd ldrs: rdn to ld 1f out: edgd lft: r.o* **5/2**[1]

4543 **2** 1 ½ **Greenhead High**[9] 7863 4 -9-7 **65** AdrianNicholls 12 70
(David Nicholls) *chsd ldrs: rdn over 1f out: r.o* **5/1**[2]

1163 **3** nk **Ivestar (IRE)**[13] 7794 7 -9-4 **62** (v) GrahamGibbons 10 66
(Michael Easterby) *a.p: rdn over 1f out: r.o* **15/2**

0013 **4** 1 ½ **Novabridge**[69] 6563 4 -9-4 **65** (b) CPGeoghegan(3) 1 64
(Neil Mulholland) *sn pushed along: led 4f out: rdn and hdd 1f out: styd on same pce* **6/1**[3]

1100 **5** 1 ½ **Sally's Swansong**[43] 7275 6 -9-0 **58** (b) ShaneKelly 4 51
(Eric Alston) *chsd ldrs: rdn over 1f out: no ex fnl f* **14/1**

6000 **6** ¾ **Colourbearer (IRE)**[9] 7864 5 -9-5 **63** (t) LukeMorris 3 54
(Milton Bradley) *sn pushed along in rr: hdwy u.p over 1f out: nt trble ldrs* **6/1**[3]

2320 **7** 2 **Chester Deelyte (IRE)**[38] 7382 4 -9-0 **58** (v) AmyRyan 7 41
(Lisa Williamson) *sn outpcd: r.o ins fnl f: nvr nrr* **33/1**

4-46 **8** ½ **Cri Na Mara (IRE)**[128] 4592 4 -8-7 **51** oh1 (t[1]) AndreaAtzeni 5 33
(Mark Michael McNiff, Ire) *mid-div: drvn along 1/2-way: n.d* **16/1**

1-20 **9** 4 ½ **Just Breathe (IRE)**[28] 7590 3 -9-6 **64** KirstyMilczarek 9 29
(Olivia Maylam) *sn outpcd* **10/1**

2040 **10** ½ **Nine Before Ten (IRE)**[5] 7861 4 -8-13 **57** (b) RobbieFitzpatrick 2 21
(Charles Smith) *led 1f: chsd ldr: rdn and wknd over 1f out* **20/1**

3215 **11** 10 **My Meteor**[91] 5876 5 -9-7 **65** ChrisCatlin 8
(Tony Newcombe) *hmpd sn after s: outpcd* **18/1**

1m 1.12s (-1.18) **Going Correction** -0.15s/f (Stan) 11Ran SP% **120.2**
Speed ratings (Par 101): **103,100,100,97,95 94,90,90,82,82 66**
Tote swingers 1&2 £3.10, 1&3 £6.00, 2&3 £6.60 CSF £14.79 CT £82.49 TOTE £3.00 : £1.10, £2.50, £2.60 ; EX 15.20 Trifecta £70.70 Pool: £ 1,091.26 - 11.56 winning units. .
Owner Mia Racing **Bred** Mia Racing **Trained** Lichfield, Staffs

FOCUS
A moderate sprint handicap run slightly faster than division II. Straightforward form.
Just Breathe (IRE) Official explanation: jockey said filly suffered interference shortly after start

7970 LIKE US ON FACEBOOK WOLVERHAMPTON RACECOURSE H'CAP (DIV II) 5f 20y (P)
2:30 (2:30) (Class 6) (0-65,65) 3-Y-0+ **£1,704** (£503; £251) **Stalls** Low

Form RPR

2221 **1** **Angelo Poliziano**[24] 7673 6 -9-4 **62** TomEaves 9 70
(George Foster) *hld up in tch: shkn up over 1f out: rdn to ld wl ins fnl f: r.o* **7/2**[2]

2324 **2** nk **Griffin Point (IRE)**[47] 7178 5 -9-5 **63** (b) StevieDonohoe 3 70
(William Muir) *chsd ldrs: rdn and ev ch wl ins fnl f: r.o* **6/1**[3]

0000 **3** 1 ¼ **Blown It (USA)**[9] 7863 6 -9-6 **64** ShaneKelly 1 67
(Keith Dalgleish) *hld up in tch: shkn up and ev ch ins fnl f: nt qckn* **10/1**

5405 **4** ½ **Atlantic Beach**[250] 1069 7 -9-7 **65** (b) RobertWinston 10 66
(Milton Bradley) *led 1f: chsd ldrs: rdn to ld ins fnl f: sn hdd and unable qck* **20/1**

0005 **5** nse **Desert Strike**[9] 7864 6 -9-7 **65** (p) LukeMorris 11 66
(Conor Dore) *a.p: rdn and hung rt 1/2-way: styd on* **7/1**

5400 **6** 1 **Bailadeira**[9] 7861 4 -9-0 **58** JamesSullivan 2 55
(Tim Etherington) *chsd ldr tl led 2f out: sn hung rt: hdd and no ex ins fnl f* **22/1**

0004 **7** 1 ¼ **Volcanic Dust (IRE)**[28] 7591 4 -9-2 **60** (b) ChrisCatlin 5 53
(Milton Bradley) *s.i.s: rdn 1/2-way: n.d* **12/1**

0603 **8** 2 ½ **Under Par**[10] 7837 4 -8-8 **52** oh2 ow1 (t) GrahamGibbons 7 36
(Michael Easterby) *led 4f out: hdd 2f out: ev ch whn hmpd sn after: wknd ins fnl f* **10/3**[1]

0000 **9** 2 **Befortyfour**[24] 7666 7 -9-7 **65** [1] RobbieFitzpatrick 8 42
(Charles Smith) *s.i.s: outpcd* **22/1**

0600 **10** 2 ¼ **Sextons House (IRE)**[5] 7861 4 -8-13 **57** WilliamCarson 6 25
(Alan McCabe) *s.i.s: outpcd* **6/1**[3]

1500 **11** ½ **Chateau Lola**[183] 2730 3 -8-8 **52** (v) SilvestreDeSousa 12 19
(Derek Shaw) *dwlt: swtchd lft sn after s: outpcd* **40/1**

1m 1.39s (-0.91) **Going Correction** -0.15s/f (Stan) 11Ran SP% **119.1**
Speed ratings (Par 101): **101,100,98,97,97 94,94,90,86,83 82**
Tote swingers 1&2 £3.30, 1&3 £9.30, 2&3 £9.40 CSF £23.83 CT £199.00 TOTE £4.70 : £1.40, £1.40, £5.50 ; EX 15.20 Trifecta £165.10 Pool: £ 1,294.42 - 165.10 winning units. .
Owner William A Powrie **Bred** Bumble Bs, C Liesack & Mrs S Nicholls **Trained** Haddington, East Lothian

FOCUS
The second division of the moderate 5f handicap, and slightly the faster. Sound, straightforward form.

7971 SPONSOR A RACE BY CALLING 01902 390000 CLAIMING STKS 1m 1f 103y (P)
3:00 (3:00) (Class 6) 2-Y-0 **£1,704** (£503; £251) **Stalls** Low

Form RPR

2533 **1** **Lucy Bee**[9] 7854 2 -8-4 **54** SilvestreDeSousa 5 57
(Keith Dalgleish) *wnt rt s: sn chsng ldrs: rdn to ld wl ins fnl f: r.o* **9/2**[3]

0142 **2** ¾ **Rakticate (IRE)**[14] 7785 2 -8-4 **62** AndreaAtzeni 2 55
(J S Moore) *chsd ldrs: pushed along over 3f out: rdn and ev ch wl ins fnl f: edgd rt: styd on* **6/5**[1]

4161 **3** ¾ **Divine Angel (IRE)**[19] 7714 2 -8-4 **65** LukeMorris 6 54
(Phil McEntee) *hmpd s: a.p: chsd ldr over 6f out: rdn over 2f out: led ins fnl f: sn hdd and unable qck* **5/2**[2]

0345 **4** 4 ½ **Maypole Joe (IRE)**[9] 7854 2 -8-7 **51** (v[1]) KirstyMilczarek 8 48
(David Evans) *sn led: rdn over 1f out: hdd & wknd ins fnl f* **16/1**

000 **5** 4 **Honey Haven (IRE)**[94] 7460 2 -8-0 **40** JamesSullivan 7 34
(Mark Brisbourne) *sn pushed along in rr: rdn over 3f out: hung lft and wknd over 2f out* **100/1**

600 **6** 6 **Refuse To Mambo**[17] 7750 2 -8-12 **55** MatthewHopkins(7) 1 41
(Reg Hollinshead) *hld up: pushed along 5f out: wknd over 2f out* **11/1**

0603 **7** 2 ½ **Cerys**[19] 7714 2 -8-3 **47** (p) WilliamCarson 4 21
(Derek Haydn Jones) *chsd ldr tl over 6f out: rdn over 3f out: wknd over 1f out* **33/1**

2m 0.74s (-0.96) **Going Correction** -0.15s/f (Stan) 2y crse rec 7Ran SP% **110.4**
Speed ratings (Par 94): **98,97,96,92,89 83,81**
Tote swingers 1&2 £1.60, 1&3 £2.10, 2&3 £1.40 CSF £9.57 TOTE £3.00 : £1.40, £1.30 ; EX 10.70 Trifecta £23.90 Pool: £ 2,190.56 - 68.68 winning units. .No claims.
Owner Mrs Lucille Bone **Bred** Sandy Bone **Trained** Carluke, S Lanarks

FOCUS
The early pace was strong in this 2yo claimer. Three in a line inside the final furlong. The winner is rated back to her best and the fourth and fifth offer perspective.

NOTEBOOK
Lucy Bee, off the mark in a heavy-ground maiden at Hamilton in July, is rated just 54. She had plenty to find with the two market leaders but, making her final effort widest of all, she stuck her head in front near the line. Her stable is flying at present. (op 4-1 tchd 7-2)
Rakticate(IRE), below form when only fourth behind Divine Angel on Fibresand at Southwell, had finished runner-up in a C&D nursery on her previous start. She was under pressure fully half a mile from home yet was only just held. She had 8lb in hand of the winner on official figures so it is doubtful if she ran up to her mark. (op 5-4 tchd Evens)
Divine Angel (IRE) winner of a soft-ground maiden and a Fibresand seller, had 11lb in hands of the winner on official ratings. She came up just short in the end but seems not as effective at present on Polytrack. (tchd 11-4)

Maypole Joe(IRE), in a first-time visor, won the early battle for the lead. After dropping anchor he wound it up exiting the back straight but in the end proved no match for the first three. (op 14-1)

7972 WOLVERHAMPTON-RACECOURSE.CO.UK H'CAP — 2m 119y(P)
3:30 (3:30) (Class 5) (0-75,80) 3-Y-0+ — **£2,264** (£673; £336; £168) **Stalls** Low

Form / RPR

2521 **1** **Thecornishcockney**[3] 7933 3-9-11 **80** 6ex..............(tp) RobertWinston 7 90+
(John Ryan) *s.i.s: hld up: plld hrd: hdwy 12f out: led wl over 1f out: shkn up: hung lft and sn clr: comf* **7/2**[3]

0014 **2** 1 ¾ **Tartan Jura**[14] 7791 4-9-12 **73**.................................. SilvestreDeSousa 6 79
(Mark Johnston) *chsd ldr to 1/2-way: sn pushed along: rdn over 1f out: hung lft ins fnl f: styd on* **11/4**[2]

124- **3** nk **Priors Gold**[350] 7818 5-10-0 **75**... TomEaves 2 81
(Ollie Pears) *a.p: swtchd rt over 1f out: sn rdn: styd on* **20/1**

0111 **4** 3 ½ **Italian Riviera**[9] 7862 3-9-2 **71**....................................... LukeMorris 3 73
(Sir Mark Prescott Bt) *set stdy pce tl hdd over 5f out: led again 4f out: rdn over 2f out: hdd wl over 1f out: styd on same pce* **11/10**[1]

1442 **5** ¾ **Ctappers**[34] 7454 3-8-9 **64**.. AndreaAtzeni 1 65
(Mick Channon) *chsd ldrs: rdn over 3f out: no ex fr over 1f out* **16/1**

3040 **6** 3 ¼ **Kazbow (IRE)**[38] 7380 6-9-6 **74**..................................(t) VictorSantos(7) 4 71
(Richard Ford) *hld up: bhd 7f out: tk clsr order over 2f out: wknd over 1f out* **40/1**

6405 **7** 6 **Swinging Hawk (GER)**[10] 7839 6-9-12 **73**.................. StevieDonohoe 5 63
(Ian Williams) *hld up: hdwy to chse ldr 8f out: led over 5f out tl 4f out: rdn and wknd over 1f out* **10/1**

3m 43.59s (1.79) **Going Correction** -0.15s/f (Stan)
WFA 3 from 4yo+ 8lb — **7** Ran SP% **118.7**
Speed ratings (Par 103): **89,88,88,86,86 84,81**
Tote swingers 1&2 £1.70, 1&3 £6.90, 2&3 £5.20 CSF £14.38 CT £169.28 TOTE £3.80: £1.90, £1.30; EX 11.60 Trifecta £140.10 Pool: £ 2,015.83 - 10.79 winning units..
Owner C Letcher & J Ryan **Bred** D Robb **Trained** Newmarket, Suffolk

FOCUS
A steadily run staying handicap, and rather muddling form. The winner is rated a bit better than the bare figures.

7973 STAY AT THE HOLIDAY INN WOLVERHAMPTON NURSERY — 1m 141y(P)
4:00 (4:01) (Class 6) (0-65,65) 2-Y-0 — **£1,704** (£503; £251) **Stalls** Low

Form / RPR

6352 **1** **Corton Lad**[5] 7919 2-8-13 **57**...(p) TomEaves 6 62
(Keith Dalgleish) *chsd ldrs: led 5f out: drvn out* **13/8**[1]

053 **2** ¾ **Sewn Up**[17] 7749 2-9-7 **65**... ShaneKelly 9 68
(Reg Hollinshead) *s.s: hld up: hdwy over 5f out: chsd wnr over 2f out: rdn over 1f out: r.o* **8/1**

600 **3** 3 ¼ **Classy Trick (USA)**[12] 7807 2-8-13 **57**......................... WilliamCarson 8 54
(Richard Fahey) *chsd ldrs: rdn over 1f out: hung lft ins fnl f: styd on u.p* **12/1**

054 **4** shd **Lyric Ballad**[26] 7628 2-9-7 **65**.. ChrisCatlin 10 61
(Hughie Morrison) *hld up: hdwy over 1f out: n.m.r ins fnl f: styd on: nt trble ldrs* **7/2**[2]

2120 **5** 1 ¼ **Spithead**[52] 7026 2-9-7 **65**.. LukeMorris 5 59
(Ian McInnes) *prom: racd keenly: rdn over 2f out: edgd rt and no ex ins fnl f* **14/1**

4300 **6** 1 ¼ **Marguerite St Just**[18] 7724 2-8-13 **57**........................ KirstyMilczarek 11 48
(Olivia Maylam) *chsd ldrs: rdn over 1f out: no ex fnl f* **33/1**

0050 **7** ¾ **See And Be Seen**[14] 7785 2-8-6 **50**................................... NickyMackay 2 40
(Sylvester Kirk) *prom: rdn over 3f out: nt clr run 2f out: wknd over 1f out* **25/1**

500 **8** 1 **Mr Vendman (IRE)**[25] 7653 2-8-7 **51** ow3...................... StevieDonohoe 7 38
(Ian Williams) *s.i.s: hld up: rdn over 2f out: n.d* **20/1**

0653 **9** shd **Caramel Sundae**[41] 7313 2-9-0 **58**.................................. AndreaAtzeni 4 45
(Robert Eddery) *hld up: rdn over 3f out: nvr on terms* **12/1**

606 **10** 1 **By A Wiska**[118] 4907 2-9-1 **59**.. JamesSullivan 3 44
(Ann Duffield) *hld up: rdn over 3f out: n.d* **33/1**

6330 **11** 4 **Kingsville**[14] 7785 2-8-3 **47**... SilvestreDeSousa 1 24
(Mark Johnston) *led: hdd 5f out: rdn over 2f out: wknd over 1f out* **7/1**[3]

1m 51.21s (0.71) **Going Correction** -0.15s/f (Stan) — **11** Ran SP% **120.5**
Speed ratings (Par 94): **90,89,86,86,85 84,83,82,82,81 78**
Tote swingers 1&2 £4.60, 1&3 £6.80, 2&3 £9.30 CSF £15.13 CT £120.62 TOTE £3.30: £1.60, £2.00, £4.80; EX 19.90 Trifecta £204.30 Pool: £ 1,547.27 - 5.68 winning units..
Owner J Hutton **Bred** Frank Brady And Brian Scanlon **Trained** Carluke, S Lanarks

FOCUS
A weak nursery, run at a fair pace. The winner has a bit more to offer in weak races like these.

NOTEBOOK
Corton Lad, runner-up in first-time cheekpieces over this C&D five days earlier, opened his account at the eighth attempt with a gutsy display, completing a hat-trick on the card for his trainer. (op 9-4 tchd 5-2)
Sewn Up, up in trip on his nursery bow, reared leaving the stalls. After going head-to-head he came off just second-best. He is clearly going the right away and deserves to go one better. (op 9-1 tchd 7-1)
Classy Trick(USA), another making his first appearance in handicap company, showed improved form stepped up in distance. There may be even better to come. (op 20-1)
Lyric Ballad, making her nursery bow after two eye-catching efforts in maidens over shorter, had just one behind her with 3f left to run. With half-a-dozen in front of her once in line for home she stayed on in encouraging fashion. She will benefit from a more positive ride. (op 5-2)

7974 HOTEL & CONFERENCING AT WOLVERHAMPTON RACECOURSE NURSERY — 7f 32y(P)
4:30 (4:32) (Class 6) (0-60,60) 2-Y-0 — **£1,704** (£503; £251) **Stalls** High

Form / RPR

5656 **1** **Red Dragon (IRE)**[51] 7059 2-9-4 **57**............................. RobertWinston 9 61
(Charles Hills) *a.p: chsd ldr 1/2-way: led over 1f out: rdn out* **8/1**

0066 **2** 2 **Blazeofenchantment (USA)**[60] 6822 2-9-3 **56**.............. PhillipMakin 1 55
(Noel Quinlan) *hld up in tch: rdn over 1f out: styd on* **7/4**[1]

0005 **3** hd **Darkest Night (IRE)**[12] 7808 2-9-1 **54**............................ ShaneKelly 2 53
(Jamie Osborne) *trckd ldrs: racd keenly: rdn ins fnl f: styd on* **22/1**

5343 **4** 1 ¼ **Not Now Blondie**[25] 7650 2-9-7 **60**................................ AndreaAtzeni 5 56
(Chris Dwyer) *mid-div: hdwy over 2f out: rdn over 1f out: styd on: nt trble ldrs* **12/1**

0040 **5** nk **Eyeline**[25] 7650 2-9-0 **58**.. JackDuern(5) 12 53
(Reg Hollinshead) *chsd ldrs: led over 5f out: rdn and hdd over 1f out: no ex ins fnl f* **100/1**

446 **6** hd **Subtle Difference**[19] 7707 2-9-7 **60**................................ LukeMorris 4 54
(Andrew Balding) *hld up: hdwy 2f out: rdn over 1f out: styd on: nt rch ldrs* **9/2**[3]

0630 **7** ¾ **Taxiformissbyron**[28] 7592 2-8-13 **52**.................................. TomEaves 8 44
(Michael Herrington) *hld up: hdwy over 1f out: nt rch ldrs* **50/1**

002 **8** nk **Bubbly Bailey**[9] 7854 2-9-6 **59**................................... SilvestreDeSousa 3 51
(Alan Bailey) *hld up: hdwy over 1f out: r.o: nt rch ldrs* **5/2**[2]

0030 **9** 1 ¼ **Shearian**[19] 7708 2-9-3 **56**.. KirstyMilczarek 7 45
(Tony Carroll) *hld up: rdn over 1f out: nvr on terms* **20/1**

4304 **10** 4 ½ **Baltic Prince (IRE)**[33] 7491 2-8-13 **52**.......................... JamesSullivan 11 30
(Paul Green) *hld up: rdn over 1f out: n.d* **33/1**

1400 **11** 10 **Windsor Rose (IRE)**[18] 7724 2-9-2 **55**..................... RobbieFitzpatrick 6 8
(Mark Brisbourne) *trckd ldrs: racd keenly: rdn and wknd over 1f out* **80/1**

4064 **12** 6 **Faffa**[19] 7711 2-9-5 **58**...(b) GrahamGibbons 10
(Tim Easterby) *led: hdd over 5f out: chsd ldrs to 1/2-way: sn rdn: wknd over 1f out* **20/1**

1m 29.59s (-0.01) **Going Correction** -0.15s/f (Stan) — **12** Ran SP% **122.9**
Speed ratings (Par 94): **94,91,91,90,89 89,88,88,86,81 70,63**
Tote swingers 1&2 £4.40, 1&3 £16.60, 2&3 £9.10 CSF £21.94 CT £320.83 TOTE £7.90: £2.30, £1.20, £7.60; EX 24.20 Trifecta £998.30 Part won. Pool: £ 1,331.07 - .62 winning units..
Owner R J Arculli & Des Anderson **Bred** N Hartery **Trained** Lambourn, Berks

FOCUS
A moderate nursery in which the form has a straightforward feel.

NOTEBOOK
Red Dragon(IRE), a 60,000gns yearling, had been dropped 5lb since making his handicap debut two outings ago. He was in the right place throughout and once sent on always looked in command. This looks his level. Official explanation: trainer's rep said, regarding apparent improvement in form, that the colt had benefited from being loaded last and being ridden closer to the pace. (op 11-1)
Blazeofenchantment(USA) ◆, who changed hands for £43,000 at the Breeze-Up sales, was gambled on on just his second start for this yard. Trapped on the inner and short of room on the home turn, he stayed on once in clear water to claim second spot. He can surely recoup losses at this low level. (op Evens)
Darkest Night(IRE), who had performed respectably on his first two starts in nursery company, seemed to run his best race yet (op 28-1)
Not Now Blondie, a winner over 5f here in August, was attempting 7f for the first time. It didn't seem to bring about any improvement. (op 14-1)
Eyeline, who had the worst of the draw, had cut little ice in three previous starts in nursery company. (op 80-1)
Subtle Difference, whose dam has already bred eight winners, didn't seem to get home over a mile on her third and final start in maiden company. She was putting in her best work at the finish here and is worth another try over further. (op 6-1 tchd 13-2)

7975 THE BLACK COUNTRY'S ONLY RACECOURSE FILLIES' H'CAP — 7f 32y(P)
5:00 (5:01) (Class 5) (0-75,73) 3-Y-0+ — **£2,385** (£704; £352) **Stalls** High

Form / RPR

2161 **1** **Balti's Sister (IRE)**[16] 7776 3-9-4 **70**......................... RobertWinston 6 82
(Terry Clement) *hld up: hdwy wl over 1f out: led 1f out: shkn up and r.o* **15/8**[2]

0230 **2** 2 ¾ **Travelling**[87] 5990 3-9-1 **67**.. WilliamCarson 2 71
(Tony Carroll) *hld up: hdwy u.p over 1f out: r.o to go 2nd wl ins fnl f: nt trble wnr* **22/1**

1500 **3** 1 **Avonrose**[27] 7607 5-9-7 **73**..(v) SilvestreDeSousa 7 74
(Derek Shaw) *led 6f out: rdn and hdd 1f out: styd on same pce* **8/1**

4552 **4** nk **Dubious Escapade (IRE)**[37] 7402 3-9-4 **70**...................... TomEaves 5 70
(Ann Duffield) *prom: rdn and hung lft fr over 1f out: styd on* **6/1**[3]

3231 **5** 1 ¼ **Ebble**[62] 6765 3-9-4 **70**... NickyMackay 4 67
(John Gosden) *led 1f: chsd ldrs: rdn over 1f out: no ex ins fnl f* **6/4**[1]

1-00 **6** 10 **Slewtoo**[59] 6840 3-9-2 **68**... GrahamGibbons 9 38
(Michael Easterby) *dwlt: hdwy to chse ldr over 5f out: rdn over 1f out: wknd fnl f* **25/1**

5000 **7** 13 **Tenbridge**[18] 7725 3-9-1 **67**..(p) AndreaAtzeni 1
(Derek Haydn Jones) *hld up: pushed along over 3f out: wknd over 1f out* **12/1**

1m 28.02s (-1.58) **Going Correction** -0.15s/f (Stan) — **7** Ran SP% **116.1**
Speed ratings (Par 100): **103,99,98,98,96 85,70**
Tote swingers 1&2 £8.00, 1&3 £2.30, 2&3 £8.00 CSF £40.84 CT £276.01 TOTE £2.40: £1.20, £5.20; EX 15.90 Trifecta £149.50 Pool: £ 1,951.65 - 9.79 winning units..
Owner Mrs Michelle Smith **Bred** P Monaghan, J Collins & G Dillon **Trained** Newmarket, Suffolk

FOCUS
A modest fillies' handicap run in an ordinary time. The winner is progressive.
Dubious Escapade(IRE) Official explanation: jockey said filly hung left-handed
Tenbridge Official explanation: jockey said filly never travelled
T/Plt: £21.80 to a £1 stake. Pool: £63,090.09. 2108.96 winning units. T/Qpdt: £7.70 to a £1 stake. Pool: £5,201.16. 494.60 winning units. CR

7968 WOLVERHAMPTON (A.W) (L-H)
Tuesday, December 4

OFFICIAL GOING: Standard
Wind: breezy behind Weather: fine

7976 ALL WEATHER "HANDS AND HEELS" APPRENTICE SERIES H'CAP (RACING EXCELLENCE INITIATIVE) — 1m 1f 103y(P)
1:40 (1:41) (Class 5) (0-75,73) 3-Y-0+ — **£2,264** (£673; £336; £168) **Stalls** Low

Form / RPR

0500 **1** **Dream Win**[14] 7799 6-8-5 **60**.. PaulBooth(3) 6 68
(Brian Ellison) *trckd ldr: chal over 1f out: led ins fnl f: drvn out* **28/1**

2122 **2** ¾ **Neige D'Antan**[6] 7893 3-8-4 **61**...................................... JoeyHaynes(3) 1 67
(Sir Mark Prescott Bt) *set stdy pce: increased gallop over 2f out: jnd over 1f out: hdd and no ex last 100yds* **9/4**[1]

6106 **3** ¾ **Elijah Pepper (USA)**[11] 7844 7-9-3 **69**............................... RyanWhile 4 73
(Conor Dore) *trckd ldrs: effrt 2f out: kpt on same pce fnl f* **20/1**

2004 **4** ¾ **Kingswinford (IRE)**[11] 7844 6-8-11 **68**........................ SemiraPashai(5) 8 71
(Alastair Lidderdale) *t.k.h in rr: hdwy on inner over 1f out: kpt on same pce fnl f* **11/1**

0006 **5** nk **Knowe Head (NZ)**[35] 7461 5-9-6 **72**.................................(p) PatMillman 9 74
(James Unett) *hld up in mid-div: hdwy to trck ldrs over 6f out: one pce over 1f out* **6/1**[3]

2 **6** hd **Gran Maestro (USA)**[11] 7843 3-9-5 **73**.........................(b) GemmaTutty 10 75
(Ruth Carr) *t.k.h: trckd ldrs: one pce over 1f out* **16/1**

1120 **7** ½ **Cabal**[194] 1439 5-8-4 **59**..(b) PaulMcGiff(3) 5 60
(Andrew Crook) *hld up in rr: drvn and outpcd over 2f out: kpt on fnl f* **40/1**

3031 **8** ½ **One Scoop Or Two**[53] 7027 6-9-0 **71**...........................(p) JoshQuinn(5) 7 71
(Reg Hollinshead) *hld up in rr: effrt over 1f out: nvr a factor* **9/2**[2]
2m 7.37s (5.67) **Going Correction** -0.05s/f (Stan)
WFA 3 from 4yo+ 2lb **8** Ran SP% **88.1**
Speed ratings (Par 103): **72,71,70,70,69 69,69,68**
Tote swingers 1&2 £7.60, 1&3 £35.70, 2&3 £7.80 CSF £50.76 CT £476.65 TOTE £37.60: £7.20, £1.10, £3.70; EX 76.10 Trifecta £339.40 Part won. Pool: £ 452.59 - 0.10 winning units..
Owner Koo's Racing Club **Bred** Juddmonte Farms Ltd **Trained** Norton, N Yorks
FOCUS
Fame Again, who was expected to make the running, was withdrawn after sitting down in his stall and as a consequence the pace was slow. Whips were not allowed to be used by these inexperienced riders and, all things considered, this is unreliable form, although it has been assessed at face value. The first two were the front pair throughout.

7977 WOLVERHAMPTON HOLIDAY INN (S) STKS 7f 32y(P)
2:10 (2:10) (Class 6) 2-Y-O **£1,704** (£503; £251) **Stalls** High

Form RPR
542 **1** **Sofi's Spirit (IRE)**[6] 7916 2-8-7 0.. LiamKeniry 8 58
(J S Moore) *trckd ldrs: styd on to ld jst ins fnl f: hld on towards fin* **4/1**[3]
053 **2** *nk* **Lambert Pen (USA)**[45] 7244 2-8-7 62.................... CharlesBishop(5) 10 62
(Mick Channon) *hld up in rr: hdwy over 2f out: plld wd over 1f out: styd on wl* **9/4**[2]
0041 **3** *1* **Projectisle (IRE)**[14] 7795 2-8-12 72.................................(b) PhillipMakin 1 60
(Kevin Ryan) *wnt rt s: w ldr: led over 3f out: hdd jst ins fnl f: kpt on same pce* **1/1**[1]
2300 **4** *6* **Multisure**[35] 7463 2-8-12 63... TonyHamilton 9 45
(Richard Fahey) *trckd ldrs: drvn and outpcd over 2f out: kpt on fnl f* **12/1**
6660 **5** ¾ **Lady Jean**[26] 7649 2-8-4 43 ow2.. JackDuern(5) 5 40
(Reg Hollinshead) *s.i.s: in rr: hdwy over 2f out: nvr a factor* **40/1**
0560 **6** ½ **Lucky Suit (IRE)**[14] 7797 2-8-12 48.................................... LukeMorris 4 42
(Ronald Harris) *trckd ldrs: effrt over 2f out: one pce over 1f out* **33/1**
500 **7** 1 ¾ **Red Diesel (IRE)**[20] 7711 2-8-7 45.......................... JemmaMarshall(5) 7 38
(Jo Hughes) *led: hdd over 3f out: wknd fnl f: eased towards fin* **50/1**
050 **8** *14* **Mjaal (IRE)**[35] 7460 2-8-7 49... AndreaAtzeni 6
(John Weymes) *rr-div: reminders over 4f out: lost pl over 2f out: bhd whn eased ins fnl f* **50/1**
0 **9** *9* **Wiggo**[42] 7304 2-8-12 0... AdamBeschizza 3
(Julia Feilden) *bmpd s: in rr: lost pl 4f out: sn wl bhd* **25/1**
1m 30.05s (0.45) **Going Correction** -0.05s/f (Stan) **9** Ran SP% **121.6**
Speed ratings (Par 94): **95,94,93,86,85 85,83,67,56**
Tote swingers 1&2 £1.40, 1&3 £2.00, 2&3 £1.70 CSF £13.80 TOTE £3.70: £1.60, £1.02, £1.30; EX 12.00 Trifecta £21.10 Pool: £ 1,093.33 - 38.75 winning units..There was no bid for the winner.
Owner J S Moore **Bred** Yvonne & Gerard Kennedy **Trained** Upper Lambourn, Berks
FOCUS
A moderate juvenile seller. The form makes plenty of sense around the front pair and the fifth.
NOTEBOOK
Sofi's Spirit(IRE), runner-up in a C&D maiden on her previous start, travelled best but only did enough off the bridle. The way she moved through the race suggests she may yet rate a bit higher. (op 7-2 tchd 3-1)
Lambert Pen(USA), debuting on Polytrack after 45 days off, showed enough to suggest he can pick up one of these, keeping on after the winner got first run. (op 3-1)
Projectisle(IRE), a 10l winner from the front in a 7f Fibresand seller last time, had a penalty to contend with and wasn't as effective on Polytrack after being hassled up front. (op 4-5 tchd 11-10)
Multisure was up in trip but still got going too late.
Mjaal(IRE) Official explanation: Jockey said filly was never travelling.

7978 BOOK WOLVERHAMPTON HOSPITALITY MAIDEN STKS 7f 32y(P)
2:40 (2:40) (Class 5) 3-Y-0+ **£2,264** (£673; £336; £168) **Stalls** High

Form RPR
0342 **1** **Spark Of Genius**[12] 7822 3-8-12 63.................................. RobertHavlin 4 73+
(James Toller) *mde all: drvn wl clr over 1f out: heavily eased last 75yds* **8/13**[1]
3 **2** *8* **Infortual (TUR)**[304] 429 3-8-12 0................................... RobertWinston 1 47
(Charles Hills) *wnt lft s: sn trcking ldrs: chsd wnr over 2f out: no ch w wnr* **2/1**[2]
0000 **3** *4* **Captain Cavallo**[57] 6930 5-9-3 45...................................(vt) LukeMorris 7 42
(Nicky Vaughan) *trckd ldrs: drvn over 2f out: one pce* **33/1**
4 ¾ **Just River** 3-9-3 0..(t) FrankieMcDonald 8 40
(Natalie Lloyd-Beavis) *s.i.s: in rr: hdwy 3f out: styd on ins fnl f* **14/1**
0 **5** ½ **Acton Jenson**[10] 7867 3-9-3 0... J-PGuillambert 6 38
(Brian Baugh) *trckd ldrs: t.k.h: wknd wl over 1f out* **28/1**
0 **6** *14* **Reverberate**[39] 7384 3-8-12 0... TomEaves 5
(Andrew Crook) *sn chsng ldrs on outer: outpcd over 2f out: sn wknd* **33/1**
0040 **7** 1 ½ **Naafetha (IRE)**[78] 6308 4-8-12 45......................................[1] GrahamLee 2
(George Foster) *mid-div: drvn over 4f out: lost pl over 3f out* **9/1**[3]
8 1 ¾ **Fountain Girl** 3-8-9 0.. MarkCoumbe(3) 3
(Edward Bevan) *s.i.s: in rr: drvn 4f out: hung lft and sn bhd* **28/1**
1m 28.58s (-1.02) **Going Correction** -0.05s/f (Stan) **8** Ran SP% **124.7**
Speed ratings (Par 103): **103,93,89,88,87 71,70,68**
Tote swingers 1&2 £1.40, 1&3 £8.50, 2&3 £8.60 CSF £2.27 TOTE £1.60: £1.02, £1.02, £12.90; EX 3.00 Trifecta £29.10 Pool: £ 1,523.11 - 39.25 winning units..
Owner N J Charrington **Bred** Elsdon Farms **Trained** Newmarket, Suffolk
FOCUS
A weak maiden alltold, but the winner impressed in a fair comparative time.
Spark Of Genius Official explanation: She now goes to the Newmarket sales on Thursday and I will be sad to lose her as I think there might well be a bit more to come. - James Toller, trainer.
Fountain Girl Official explanation: Jockey said filly hung left throughout

7979 DINE IN HORIZONS MEDIAN AUCTION MAIDEN STKS 7f 32y(P)
3:10 (3:11) (Class 6) 2-Y-O **£1,704** (£503; £251) **Stalls** High

Form RPR
2 **1** **Prophets Pride**[18] 7749 2-9-3 0.. GrahamLee 3 72+
(Jeremy Noseda) *chsd ldrs: pushed along over 3f out: drvn to ld over 1f out: forged clr* **1/2**[1]
3 **2** 2 ¼ **Minimee**[32] 7525 2-9-3 0.. AndreaAtzeni 1 64+
(Roger Varian) *mde most: hdd over 1f out: kpt on same pce* **2/1**[2]
6000 **3** 3 ½ **Misty Secret (IRE)**[42] 7313 2-8-12 49.......................... RichardKingscote 7 50
(Tom Dascombe) *chsd ldrs on outer: drvn over 3f out: one pce fnl 2f* **20/1**[3]
00 **4** 4 ½ **Spats Colombo**[27] 7636 2-9-3 0.. TomEaves 2 44
(Micky Hammond) *in rr: effrt 3f out: sn outpcd: kpt on fnl f* **100/1**
5 1 ½ **Blue Missile** 2-8-10 0... RyanWhile(7) 4 41
(Bill Turner) *dwlt: hdwy on outside to chse ldrs over 4f out: edgd lft and wknd over 1f out* **28/1**
0 **6** 2 ¾ **Ely Valley**[19] 7721 2-8-12 0... MartinDwyer 5 29
(William Muir) *t.k.h: sn w ldr: wknd wl over 1f out* **20/1**[3]
550 **7** 1 ¼ **Belle Voir**[60] 6844 2-8-12 45.. RobertWinston 6 26
(Gay Kelleway) *in rr: effrt over 3f out: lost pl 2f out* **33/1**
1m 29.71s (0.11) **Going Correction** -0.05s/f (Stan) **7** Ran SP% **116.9**
Speed ratings (Par 94): **97,94,90,85,83 80,79**
Tote swingers 1&2 £1.10, 1&3 £2.30, 2&3 £4.40 CSF £1.67 TOTE £1.40: £1.10, £1.10; EX 2.40 Trifecta £7.50 Pool: £ 1,300.27 - 129.96 winning units..
Owner Saeed Suhail **Bred** Rabbah Bloodstock Limited **Trained** Newmarket, Suffolk
■ Graham Lee's 100th winner in his maiden year on the Flat.
FOCUS
They didn't look to go that quick and the bare form is very ordinary and rated a shade negatively. The winner should have more to offer.
NOTEBOOK
Prophets Pride confirmed the promise he showed when a well-held second behind a useful sort over C&D on his debut, winning cosily despite still looking green. He's open to plenty more improvement. (op 4-6)
Minimee, like the winner, had shown ability over C&D on his debut and he did so again, but he simply wasn't quite good enough. (op 7-4)
Misty Secret(IRE) came into this rated just 49, but she was debuting for a new trainer and shaped okay. (tchd 25-1)
Spats Colombo, well held in a couple of turf maidens, again showed little but handicaps are now an option.

7980 HOTEL & CONFERENCING AT WOLVERHAMPTON H'CAP 1m 5f 194y(P)
3:40 (3:40) (Class 5) (0-75,80) 3-Y-0+ **£2,264** (£673; £336; £168) **Stalls** Low

Form RPR
2140 **1** **Stand Guard**[13] 7810 8-10-0 **75**... AdamKirby 1 85
(John Butler) *mid-div: effrt over 2f out: chsng ldng pair whn swtchd wd appr fnl f: styd on to ld nr fin* **7/1**[3]
0011 **2** *nk* **Chookie Hamilton**[1] 7968 8-9-6 **67** 6ex.................................. TomEaves 2 77
(Keith Dalgleish) *trckd ldr: led jst ins fnl f: edgd rt: no ex and hdd towards fin* **5/4**[1]
0031 **3** 4 ½ **Pertemps Networks**[3] 7954 8-10-0 **75** 6ex................. GrahamGibbons 3 78
(Michael Easterby) *led: qcknd pce 4f out: hdd jst ins fnl f: kpt on same pce* **7/4**[2]
560/ **4** *4* **Fairmile**[4] 7945 10-9-11 **75**....................................(t) AndrewPThornton(3) 5 73
(C Moore, Ire) *t.k.h towards rr: hdwy over 2f out: one pce* **25/1**
0205 **5** 1 ¼ **Vittachi**[24] 7454 5-8-8 **60**.. GarryWhillans(5) 7 56
(Alistair Whillans) *dwlt: hdwy to chse ldrs after 3f: hung lft over 1f out: one pce* **14/1**
35-0 **6** 2 ¼ **Jezza**[11] 7839 6-9-4 **65**.. TomMcLaughlin 4 58
(Karen George) *dwlt: hld up in rr: drvn over 3f out: nvr a factor* **14/1**
3004 **7** 1 ¾ **Maison Brillet (IRE)**[198] 1925 5-9-4 **65**...........................(p) RobertHavlin 8 55
(Clive Drew) *hld up in rr: hdwy over 2f out: sn wknd* **20/1**
1400 **8** *7* **Rocky Rebel**[53] 7024 4-9-7 **68**...(b) LiamKeniry 6 49
(Chris Bealby) *trckd ldrs: drvn over 3f out: wknd 2f out: sn bhd* **33/1**
3m 2.99s (-3.01) **Going Correction** -0.05s/f (Stan)
WFA 3 from 4yo+ 7lb **8** Ran SP% **118.2**
Speed ratings (Par 103): **106,105,103,100,100 98,97,93**
Tote swingers 1&2 £3.10, 1&3 £3.10, 2&3 £1.60 CSF £16.51 CT £22.94 TOTE £4.50: £1.40, £1.02, £1.60; EX 25.00 Trifecta £21.01 Pool: £ 1,513.43 - 54.00 winning units..
Owner J Butler **Bred** Juddmonte Farms Ltd **Trained** Newmarket, Suffolk
FOCUS
Not a bad race for the class, run at a decent pace. The first two were clear, and this rates the winner's best run since autumn 2010.

7981 DOWNLOAD OUR IPHONE APP MEDIAN AUCTION MAIDEN STKS 1m 141y(P)
4:10 (4:11) (Class 6) 3-5-Y-0 **£1,704** (£503; £251) **Stalls** Low

Form RPR
6 **1** **Alezanna**[26] 7656 3-8-12 0... KirstyMilczarek 1 53
(James Toller) *mde all: hung rt over 1f out: sn wnt clr: styd on strly* **12/1**
0000 **2** *4* **Mistress Shy**[32] 7530 5-9-0 45....................................(t) AndrewMullen 8 44
(Michael Appleby) *chsd ldrs: hung rt and kpt on to take 2nd nr fin* **25/1**
0606 **3** ½ **Give Us A Belle (IRE)**[19] 7729 3-9-3 42.................(t) TomMcLaughlin 10 48
(Christine Dunnett) *swtchd lft after s: w ldrs: wnt 2nd 4f out: chal wl over 1f out: kpt on same pce* **33/1**
4 *2* **Veyepea**[120] 4898 3-8-12 0.. LiamKeniry 9 38
(Sylvester Kirk) *hld up in rr: effrt 3f out: kpt on fnl f: nrst fin* **5/2**[1]
5 ¾ **Baile Atha Cliath (IRE)** 3-8-10 0........................... MichaelKenny(7) 6 42
(Declan Carroll) *t.k.h in mid-div: effrt over 2f out: hung lft over 1f out: kpt on: nvr a factor* **25/1**
6 2 ¾ **Exclusive Predator** 3-9-3 0.. TomEaves 5 35
(Geoffrey Oldroyd) *s.s: sme hdwy on outer over 2f out: nvr on terms* **11/2**[3]
0640 **7** *hd* **Only A Round (IRE)**[100] 5623 3-9-3 41............................ TonyHamilton 7 35
(Micky Hammond) *hld up in mid-div: outpcd over 2f out: no threat after* **50/1**
55 **8** 3 ½ **Zilzie (IRE)**[26] 7654 3-8-12 0... GrahamLee 3 22
(Ann Duffield) *w ldrs: drvn 3f out: sn lost pl* **5/2**[1]
9 1 ¼ **Stormy Glaz (FR)** 3-9-3 0... LukeMorris 2 24
(Mrs K Burke) *s.i.s: reminders over 4f out: nvr a factor* **7/2**[2]
0000 **10** 4 ½ **Spoken Words**[53] 7025 3-8-9 43..............................(p) MarkCoumbe(3) 4 9
(Hugh McWilliams) *chsd ldrs: lost pl over 2f out: sn bhd* **66/1**
1m 50.37s (-0.13) **Going Correction** -0.05s/f (Stan)
WFA 3 from 5yo 2lb **10** Ran SP% **116.5**
Speed ratings (Par 101): **98,94,94,92,91 89,88,85,84,80**
Tote swingers 1&2 £19.90, 1&3 £14.40, 2&3 £24.40 CSF £264.25 TOTE £21.60: £4.00, £7.50, £8.50; EX 161.00 Trifecta £1390.00 Part won. Pool: £ 1,853.37 - 0.82 winning units..
Owner Skeltools Ltd **Bred** A B Phipps **Trained** Newmarket, Suffolk
FOCUS
It paid to be handy in what was a really moderate maiden, as the pace was only steady. The form has been rated around the poor second and third.

7982 SPONSOR A RACE BY CALLING 01902 390000 H'CAP (DIV I) 1m 141y(P)
4:40 (4:40) (Class 6) (0-55,55) 3-Y-0+ **£1,704** (£503; £251) **Stalls** Low

Form RPR
0000 **1** **Count Ceprano (IRE)**[52] 7058 8-8-8 **50**................... SimonPearce(3) 2 57
(Lydia Pearce) *hld up in rr: last and pushed along over 3f out: gd hdwy on inner over 1f out: styd on to ld last 50yds* **14/1**
5406 **2** ½ **Lindoro**[19] 7732 7-9-2 **55**... AdamKirby 7 61
(Sean Curran) *hld up in rr: effrt and c wd over 1f out: hung lft and styd on ins fnl f: jst hld* **4/1**[2]
5304 **3** *nk* **Essell**[28] 7616 3-8-6 **51** ow1.. CharlesBishop(5) 1 57
(Mick Channon) *led 3f: chsd ldrs: upsides on inner over 1f out: kpt on same pce last 50yds* **5/1**[3]
2004 **4** ½ **Big Sylv (IRE)**[15] 7787 3-8-9 **50**.....................................(p) DavidProbert 11 54
(James Unett) *in rr: hdwy on outside to join ldrs over 5f out: keeping on same pce whn hmpd clsng stages* **14/1**

3651 **5** *nk* **Safwaan**[256] 1014 5-8-12 **51** JamieMackay 5 54
(Willie Musson) *chsd ldrs: hmpd bnd after 1f: led 2f out: hdd last 50yds: no ex* **3/1**[1]
0664 **6** *1 3/4* **Delightful Sleep**[33] 7512 4-8-7 **46** KirstyMilczarek 3 47
(David Evans) *mid-div: outpcd 4f out: hdwy 2f out: sn chsng ldrs: one pce whn n.m.r and eased nr fin* **4/1**[2]
0006 **7** *3 1/4* **Dansili Dutch (IRE)**[17] 7781 3-8-11 **52** RobertHavlin 6 44
(Andrew Crook) *dwlt: in rr: hdwy 2f out: edgd rt: nvr nr ldrs* **25/1**
0603 **8** *nk* **Silence Is Easy**[17] 7769 3-8-12 **53** MartinDwyer 10 44
(William Muir) *trckd ldrs: led after 3f: hdd 2f out: sn wknd* **9/1**
0505 **9** *1* **Litmus (USA)**[47] 7189 3-8-11 **52** GrahamLee 4 41
(Simon Dow) *sn chsng ldrs: hmpd bnd after 1f: lost pl over 2f out* **16/1**
0000 **10** *nk* **Poker Hospital**[17] 7781 3-8-13 **54** LukeMorris 8 42
(John Stimpson) *prom hmpd bnd after 1f: sn in rr: hdwy over 4f out: wknd over 2f out* **33/1**

1m 50.48s (-0.02) **Going Correction** -0.05s/f (Stan)
WFA 3 from 4yo+ 2lb **10** Ran SP% **117.7**
Speed ratings (Par 101): **98,97,97,96,96 95,92,91,90,90**
Tote swingers 1&2 £9.70, 1&3 £13.00, 2&3 £4.80 CSF £70.02 CT £335.78 TOTE £15.20: £4.70, £1.40, £1.20; EX 97.90 Trifecta £1062.80 Part won. Pool: £ 1,417.13 - 0.60 winning units..
Owner Mrs Louise Marsh **Bred** Pendley Farm **Trained** Newmarket, Suffolk
■ Stewards' Enquiry : Adam Kirby one-day ban: careless riding (Dec 18)
FOCUS
Ordinary form to this muddling race. The winner's best run since the spring.

7983 SPONSOR A RACE BY CALLING 01902 390000 H'CAP (DIV II) 1m 141y(P)
5:10 (5:13) (Class 6) (0-55,55) 3-Y-0+ **£1,704** (£503; £251) **Stalls** Low

Form RPR
3654 **1** **Angel Cake (IRE)**[28] 7615 3-8-9 **50** AndrewMullen 13 58
(Michael Appleby) *chsd ldrs on outer: led over 1f out: hld on towards fin* **6/1**[3]
3546 **2** *3/4* **Sudden Wish (IRE)**[13] 7815 3-8-13 **54** KirstyMilczarek 10 60
(David Evans) *hld up in rr: effrt 3f out: hdwy over 1f out: swtchd lft and styd on ins fnl f: no ex nr fin* **9/1**
0013 **3** *nk* **Precision Five**[28] 7616 3-8-7 **51** (p) RaulDaSilva(3) 3 56
(Jeremy Gask) *trckd ldrs: t.k.h: upsides over 1f out: kpt on same pce last 50yds* **4/1**[2]
3243 **4** *3/4* **Fortunate Bid (IRE)**[39] 7385 6-9-0 **53** (p) TonyHamilton 4 57
(Linda Stubbs) *hld up in mid-div: hdwy over 3f out: n.m.r and swtchd rt over 1f out: styd on same pce ins fnl f* **6/1**[3]
05 **5** *nk* **Royal Sea (IRE)**[77] 6341 3-8-12 **53** (v[1]) GrahamLee 5 56
(David O'Meara) *gave problems loading: trckd ldrs towards outer: hung rt and kpt on one pce fnl f* **9/4**[1]
0003 **6** *1 1/4* **Lightning Spirit**[41] 7321 4-8-11 **50** (p) FergusSweeney 7 50
(Gary Moore) *in rr: hdwy over 2f out: kpt on fnl f: nvr a threat* **12/1**
0000 **7** *1 1/2* **Just Five (IRE)**[33] 7500 6-8-13 **52** (v) LukeMorris 1 49
(John Weymes) *trckd ldrs: drvn over 3f out: one pce and hung rt over 1f out* **14/1**
0350 **8** *1/2* **Dhhamaan (IRE)**[17] 7781 7-8-11 **50** (b) JamesSullivan 2 45
(Ruth Carr) *t.k.h: led hdd over 1f out: sn wknd* **25/1**
3-06 **9** *1/2* **Generous Genella**[28] 7612 4-8-7 **46** (b[1]) AdamBeschizza 12 40
(Julia Feilden) *s.i.s: hdwy on outside over 4f out: one pce fnl 2f* **40/1**
4560 **10** *5* **Source Of Light (IRE)**[17] 7781 3-8-9 **53** AndrewPThornton(3) 6 36
(Daniel Mark Loughnane) *mid-div: effrt over 2f out: lost pl over 1f out: eased towards fin* **12/1**
0266 **11** *5* **Titan Diamond (IRE)**[140] 4193 4-8-2 **46** RachealKneller(5) 9 17
(Mark Usher) *trckd ldrs: drvn over 4f out: sn lost pl and bhd: eased towards fin* **22/1**
6504 **12** *nk* **Applaude**[28] 7605 7-8-8 **47** ow1 (b) LiamKeniry 8 18
(Chris Bealby) *s.i.s: a in rr: eased whn bhd towards fin* **25/1**

1m 49.67s (-0.83) **Going Correction** -0.05s/f (Stan)
WFA 3 from 4yo+ 2lb **12** Ran SP% **125.9**
Speed ratings (Par 101): **101,100,100,99,99 98,96,96,95,91 86,86**
Tote swingers 1&2 £15.20, 1&3 £7.60, 2&3 £7.60 CSF £60.23 CT £253.69 TOTE £8.30: £2.60, £3.00, £2.10; EX 89.10 Trifecta £407.00 Pool: £ 1,981.04 - 3.65 winning units..
Owner W Sewell **Bred** Stephanie Hanly **Trained** Danethorpe, Notts
FOCUS
More interesting than the first division and the quickest of three races at the trip. Ordinary form for the grade.
T/Plt: £13.80 to a £1 stake. Pool: £61,020.65. 3226.81 winning units. T/Qpdt: £7.10 to a £1 stake. Pool: £4,354.12. 448.70 winning units. WG

7343 DEAUVILLE (R-H)
Tuesday, December 4
OFFICIAL GOING: Fibresand: standard

7984a PRIX SOLEIL (CONDITIONS) (2YO COLTS & GELDINGS) (FIBRESAND) 7f 110y
9:20 (12:00) 2-Y-0 **£14,166** (£5,666; £4,250; £2,833; £1,416)

RPR
1 **Seche (FR)**[102] 2-9-0 0 MaximeGuyon 7 84
(L A Urbano-Grajales, France) **11/10**[1]
2 *1* **Pont Neuilly (FR)**[44] 7283 2-8-11 0 ow1 Pierre-CharlesBoudot 11 78
(Y De Nicolay, France) **29/1**
3 *1/2* **Linngaro (FR)**[28] 7623 2-9-4 0 FilipMinarik 3 84
(Mario Hofer, Germany) **43/10**[2]
4 *hd* **Chika Dream (FR)** 2-8-7 0 GregoryBenoist 4 73
(Y Barberot, France) **23/1**
5 *snk* **Admire Fuji (IRE)**[29] 2-9-0 0 FabriceVeron 14 79
(S Kobayashi, France) **72/1**
6 *2* **Prince De Perse (FR)**[35] 2-9-0 0 Francois-XavierBertras 10 74
(Rod Collet, France) **23/1**
7 *3/4* **San Juan (FR)**[73] 6507 2-9-1 0 (b) MarcLerner(3) 5 77
(C Lerner, France) **26/1**
8 *snk* **The Monarck (FR)**[29] 7597 2-8-10 0 VincentVion 9 68
(T Lallie, France) **63/1**
9 *snk* **Early Emperor** 2-9-0 0 RonanThomas 2 72
(Carmen Bocskai, Switzerland) **20/1**
10 *3/4* **Attention Baileys (FR)**[102] 2-9-0 0 AdrienFouassier 6 70
(E J O'Neill, France) **71/1**
0 **Pont Marie (FR)**[7] 2-8-8 0 (b) AntoineCoutier(6) 1
(F Chappet, France) **23/1**
0 **Kalicamix**[99] 5698 2-9-0 0 ThierryThulliez 8
(Paul Cole) *broke wl: racd 2nd in mid-trck: swtchd to ins and dropped to 3rd bef st: rdn 2f out: no ex: styd on one pce fnl f* **10/1**[3]
0 **Plovdiv (FR)**[35] 2-9-0 0 AlexandreRoussel 13
(E Leenders, France) **15/1**
0 **Princedargent (FR)**[24] 7693 2-9-0 0 ThierryJarnet 12
(H-A Pantall, France) **18/1**

1m 29.9s (89.90) **14** Ran SP% **115.7**
WIN (incl. 1 euro stake): 2.10. PLACES: 1.30, 4.30, 1.80. DF: 33.00. SF: 52.20.
Owner Jean-Pierre-Joseph Dubois **Bred** D Farm LLC **Trained** Pau, France

7985a PRIX LYPHARD (LISTED RACE) (3YO+) (FIBRESAND) 1m 1f 110y
2:05 (12:00) 3-Y-0+ **£21,666** (£8,666; £6,500; £4,333; £2,166)

RPR
1 **Silver Pond (FR)**[48] 5-8-13 0 ThierryJarnet 11 105
(P Bary, France) **18/5**[1]
2 *4 1/2* **Simba (FR)**[53] 7124 4-8-13 0 MarcLerner 5 96
(C Lerner, France) **12/1**
3 *1 1/4* **Rhenania (IRE)**[14] 5-8-9 0 FlavienPrat 9 89
(M Nigge, France) **14/1**
4 *1 1/4* **Silver Green (FR)**[35] 5-8-13 0 Francois-XavierBertras 7 90
(F Rohaut, France) **68/10**[3]
5 *1/2* **Curro Perote (FR)**[42] 5-8-13 0 JulienAuge 1 89
(L A Urbano-Grajales, France) **13/1**
6 *shd* **Pigeon Catcher (IRE)**[14] 3-8-11 0 MaximeGuyon 4 90
(Mme Pia Brandt, France) **7/1**
7 *1* **Malossol (USA)**[30] 7587 3-9-4 0 (p) Pierre-CharlesBoudot 15 95
(G Botti, Italy) **33/1**
8 *3/4* **Sargasses (FR)**[14] 6-8-9 0 GregoryBenoist 6 82
(Mlle V Dissaux, France) **21/1**
9 *1/2* **Stand My Ground (IRE)**[14] 7802 5-8-13 0 ThomasMessina 8 85
(Mme Pia Brandt, France) **56/1**
10 *snk* **Anaxis (FR)**[514] 5-8-13 0 JeromeCabre 14 84
(S Wattel, France) **21/1**
0 **Balaythous (FR)**[42] 6-8-13 0 (b) FabienLefebvre 13
(Mlle B Renk, France) **14/1**
0 **Execution (IRE)**[145] 5-8-13 0 JohanVictoire 2
(Mme N Verheyen, Belgium) **34/1**
0 **Circumvent**[17] 7771 5-8-13 0 (p) LouisBeuzelin 12
(Paul Cole) *led: hdd over 1 1/2f out: sn rdn and wknd* **5/1**[2]
0 **Divine Music (IRE)**[42] 5-8-9 0 (b) RonanThomas 3
(P Van De Poele, France) **42/1**
0 **Calipatria**[16] 7784 5-9-2 0 FabriceVeron 10
(H-A Pantall, France) **18/1**

1m 55.89s (115.89)
WFA 3 from 4yo+ 2lb **15** Ran SP% **116.1**
WIN (incl. 1 euro stake): 4.60. PLACES: 2.20, 3.10, 5.30. DF: 28.80. SF: 43.40..
Owner Saeed Nasser Al Romaithi **Bred** Earl Haras Du Quesnay **Trained** Chantilly, France

7960 KEMPTON (A.W) (R-H)
Wednesday, December 5
OFFICIAL GOING: Standard
Wind: Moderate, across Weather: Cold and clear

7986 WIN BIG WITH BETDAQ MULTIPLES H'CAP 1m 2f (P)
3:50 (3:52) (Class 4) (0-85,85) 3-Y-0+ **£4,075** (£1,212; £606; £303) **Stalls** Low

Form RPR
0600 **1** **Mawaakef (IRE)**[28] 7626 4-9-5 **83** SilvestreDeSousa 8 93
(J R Jenkins) *trckd ldrs: wnt 2nd over 1f out: rdn to ld ins fnl f* **8/1**
010 **2** *3/4* **Viewpoint (IRE)**[35] 7475 3-9-3 **84** SeanLevey 1 93
(Richard Hannon) *trckd ldr: led over 2f out tl ins fnl f: kpt on* **7/1**[3]
0261 **3** *2* **Ancient Greece**[14] 7805 5-8-13 **77** (t) LukeMorris 13 82
(George Baker) *in tch: effrt 3f out: kpt on u.p fnl 2f* **5/1**[2]
3032 **4** *nk* **Dubawi Island (FR)**[7] 7920 3-9-4 **85** (b) JimmyFortune 4 89
(James Tate) *led tl 7f out: rdn 4f out: one pce appr fnl f* **6/4**[1]
61-0 **5** *3/4* **Parigino (FR)**[28] 7626 4-9-0 **78** RichardKingscote 6 80+
(Nick Gifford) *mid-div: rdn and styd on fr over 1f out: nrest at fin* **16/1**
3404 **6** *1 1/4* **Tuscania**[28] 7626 4-9-4 **82** AndreaAtzeni 10 82
(Lucy Wadham) *bhd: rdn and hdwy 2f out: no imp over 1f out* **5/1**[2]
/000 **7** *1* **Bobbyscot (IRE)**[18] 7774 5-9-0 **78** FergusSweeney 9 76
(Gary Moore) *bhd: pushed along 2f out: styd on wl fnl f* **50/1**
-504 **8** *1/2* **Dakota Canyon (IRE)**[33] 7520 3-8-7 **74** ow1 TomEaves 2 71
(Richard Fahey) *chsd ldrs: outpcd 3f out: steadily fdd* **20/1**
0000 **9** *3/4* **Brunston**[13] 7824 6-9-0 **78** (p) LiamKeniry 3 73
(Anthony Middleton) *hld up in midfield: shkn up over 1f out: no rspnse and sn lost pl* **66/1**
4200 **10** *1 1/4* **Destiny Of Dreams**[61] 6847 4-9-1 **79** IanMongan 11 72
(Jo Crowley) *prom: led and increased tempo 7f out: hdd over 2f out: wknd over 1f out* **25/1**
0 **11** *11* **Kindia (IRE)**[11] 7858 4-9-0 **78** (v) WilliamCarson 12 49
(Michael Attwater) *mid-div: rdn 4f out: sn struggling: bhd whn eased fnl f* **66/1**
3-0 **12** *3 3/4* **Six Silver Lane**[14] 7810 4-9-0 **78** MartinDwyer 7 41
(Derek Shaw) *bhd: rdn over 3f out: no ch whn rn wd on fnl bnd* **50/1**

2m 4.95s (-3.05) **Going Correction** -0.05s/f (Stan)
WFA 3 from 4yo+ 3lb **12** Ran SP% **118.3**
Speed ratings (Par 105): **110,109,107,107,106 105,105,104,104,103 94,91**
Tote Swingers 1&2 £7.90, 2&3 £6.60, 1&3 £6.80 CSF £59.19 CT £311.56 TOTE £8.70: £2.20, £2.50, £1.50; EX 63.10 Trifecta £483.40 Pool: £986.16 - 1.53 winning tickets..
Owner The Three Honest Men **Bred** J Egan, J Corcoran And J Judd **Trained** Royston, Herts
FOCUS
A fair 1m2f handicap, run at a steady pace. Not the strongest for the grade but the form makes enough sense at face value.

7987 BETDAQ MOBILE APPS/BRITISH STALLION STUDS EBF MAIDEN FILLIES' STKS 6f (P)
4:20 (4:21) (Class 5) 2-Y-0 **£3,169** (£943; £471; £235) **Stalls** Low

Form RPR
1 **Khobaraa** 2-9-0 0 RobertHavlin 3 77+
(John Gosden) *trckd ldrs: effrt and n.m.r over 1f out: qcknd to ld fnl 100yds: pushed out* **3/1**[2]

63 **2** *1 3/4* **Bellitudo (IRE)**[34] 7505 2-9-0 0 .... SebSanders 1 69
(Marco Botti) *prom: led over 1f out: hrd rdn and hdd fnl 100yds* **9/2**[3]

6 **3** *1 1/2* **Bouyrin (IRE)**[18] 7778 2-9-0 0 .... StevieDonohoe 5 65
(Michael Bell) *mid-div: hdwy 2f out: unable qck fnl f* **25/1**

4 *1/2* **Two In The Pink (IRE)** 2-9-0 0 .... MartinLane 4 63+
(Hugo Palmer) *bhd: hdwy on far rail over 1f out: kpt on same pce fnl f* **25/1**

5 *1 1/4* **Last Hooray** 2-9-0 0 .... LiamKeniry 6 59+
(David Elsworth) *towards rr: pushed along and styd on fnl 2f: nvr nrr* **20/1**

50 **6** *1/2* **Perfect Venture**[49] 7160 2-9-0 0 .... AdamKirby 7 58
(Clive Cox) *led tl over 1f out: wknd fnl f* **10/1**

2 **7** *1 1/4* **Sherinn**[111] 5267 2-9-0 0 .... AndreaAtzeni 9 54
(Roger Varian) *pressed ldr: chal 2f out: wknd over 1f out* **11/8**[1]

00 **8** *1 1/2* **Chandelle Celeste**[19] 7738 2-9-0 0 .... RichardKingscote 8 50
(Daniel Kubler) *dwlt: on prom: wknd wl over 1f out* **100/1**

9 *shd* **Al Gharrafa** 2-9-0 0 .... SilvestreDeSousa 12 49
(Marco Botti) *towards rr: rdn over 2f out: n.d whn hung lft over 1f out* **25/1**

10 *1* **Compton Albion (IRE)** 2-9-0 0 .... IanMongan 11 46
(Jeremy Gask) *a in rr* **50/1**

11 *2 1/4* **Rectory Lane** 2-9-0 0 .... JimmyFortune 10 39
(Eve Johnson Houghton) *chsd ldrs on outer: wknd 2f out* **20/1**

1m 13.56s (0.46) **Going Correction** -0.05s/f (Stan) **11** Ran SP% **118.4**
Speed ratings (Par 93): **94,91,89,89,87 86,85,83,82,81 78**
Tote Swingers 1&2 £3.00, 2&3 £16.90, 1&3 £13.60 CSF £15.45 TOTE £3.70: £1.20, £1.60, £6.00; EX 21.30 Trifecta £197.10 Pool: £1,308.90 - 4.98 winning tickets..
Owner Hamdan Al Maktoum **Bred** Shadwell Estate Company Limited **Trained** Newmarket, Suffolk

FOCUS
An informative juvenile contest. The bare form looks ordinary but the winner did it well.

NOTEBOOK
Khobaraa defied inexperience to win with plenty in hand. John Gosden has enjoyed a fair amount of success with his juveniles at this venue in recent seasons and there was much to like about the way in which the winner went about her job. Solid in the market, she always appeared to be going best and picked up pleasingly once finding daylight. She came clear under only hands and heels riding and appears to have a bright future. She's entitled to come on a fair bit for this and should have no problem coping with a step up to 7f. (tchd 7-2)
Bellitudo(IRE) had shown ability in a couple of starts over 7f and arguably produced a career-best here on this drop back in trip. She was ultimately no match for the winner but showed more than enough to suggest she'll be a player in handicaps next year. (tchd 5-1)
Bouyrin(IRE) had run only moderately on her debut over 7f at Wolverhampton but appeared to take a significant step forward. She tracked the winner through but probably paid for her early keenness in the final furlong. (op 33-1)
Two In The Pink(IRE) ran encouragingly, despite her inflated odds. The £32,000 purchase was short of room for much of the home straight and will have learnt plenty for this. (op 33-1)
Last Hooray put in some good late work. Green throughout, she can be expected to step up considerably on this effort. (op 25-1)
Sherinn failed to justify strong market confidence and now has questions to answer. Off the track since finishing a good second at Newmarket in August, she had no obvious excuses and was made to look very one-paced. (op 6-4 tchd 6-5)

7988 BACK OR LAY AT BETDAQ.COM MAIDEN STKS 6f (P)
4:50 (4:52) (Class 5) 3-Y-O+ **£2,264** (£673; £336; £168) **Stalls** Low

Form RPR

3024 **1** **Bull Bay**[11] 7864 3-9-3 65 .... LukeMorris 3 64
(Jane Chapple-Hyam) *prom: led wl over 1f out: edgd lft ins fnl f: hld on wl* **5/4**[1]

24 **2** *hd* **Clapped**[26] 7671 3-9-3 54 .... JimmyFortune 1 63
(Ed Vaughan) *hld up towards rr: hdwy and fnd gap over 1f out: str chal ins fnl f: nt quite able to get past* **6/1**[3]

3-30 **3** *3/4* **Stepturn**[208] 2045 3-9-3 65 .... IanMongan 5 61
(Michael Wigham) *in tch: rdn to join ldrs over 1f out: kpt on fnl f* **2/1**[2]

0064 **4** *1 3/4* **Red Ramesses (IRE)**[18] 7770 3-9-3 62 .... FergusSweeney 9 55
(John Best) *pressed ldr: rdn 2f out: one pce* **7/1**

5364 **5** *1* **Johnny Splash (IRE)**[13] 7822 3-9-3 46 .... AdamKirby 2 52
(Roger Teal) *led tl wl over 1f out: wknd fnl f* **25/1**

0600 **6** *1/2* **Artillery Train (IRE)**[29] 7600 3-9-3 48 ....(b[1]) JamesSullivan 7 50
(Tim Etherington) *chsd ldrs: rdn over 2f out: sn outpcd* **33/1**

0506 **7** *1 3/4* **Ishi**[14] 7804 3-8-12 48 .... JamesMillman 8 40
(Rod Millman) *t.k.h in 6th: rdn over 2f out: nt trble ldrs* **50/1**

0 **8** *9* **Boyzee**[35] 7477 4-9-3 0 ....(p) LiamKeniry 6 16
(Linda Jewell) *dwlt: a outpcd in rr* **66/1**

1m 13.24s (0.14) **Going Correction** -0.05s/f (Stan) **8** Ran SP% **114.8**
Speed ratings (Par 103): **97,96,95,93,92 91,89,77**
Tote Swingers 1&2 £2.60, 2&3 £1.80, 1&3 £1.70 CSF £9.29 TOTE £2.30: £1.10, £1.20, £1.20; EX 6.60 Trifecta £15.50 Pool: £2,155.59 - 103.96 winning tickets..
Owner Mrs Julie Martin **Bred** Julie Routledge-Martin **Trained** Dalham, Suffolk

FOCUS
A weak maiden by the track's usual standards. The winner did not need to quite match his recent Wolverhampton form.

7989 BETDAQ CASINO GAMES NURSERY 1m (P)
5:20 (5:22) (Class 5) (0-75,75) 2-Y-O **£2,264** (£673; £336; £168) **Stalls** Low

Form RPR

426 **1** **Canadian Run (IRE)**[97] 5765 2-9-4 72 .... JimmyFortune 4 76
(Robert Mills) *t.k.h: chsd ldrs: led over 1f out: rdn out* **7/1**

046 **2** *1 3/4* **Raging Bear (USA)**[94] 5851 2-9-4 72 .... SeanLevey 5 72
(Richard Hannon) *s.i.s: in rr: hrd rdn and hdwy over 1f out: styd on to take 2nd ins fnl f* **7/2**[3]

033 **3** *1* **Duroble Man**[28] 7637 2-9-4 72 ....(p) AndreaAtzeni 8 70
(Roger Varian) *prom: led wl over 1f out: sn hdd: one pce* **8/1**

3362 **4** *1/2* **Lyric Piece**[14] 7814 2-9-5 73 .... LukeMorris 7 70
(Sir Mark Prescott Bt) *towards rr: drvn along fr 1/2-way: styd on fr over 1f out* **11/4**[1]

0052 **5** *nk* **Beau Select (IRE)**[20] 7724 2-8-11 65 ....(b) MartinLane 3 62
(Robert Eddery) *in rr: hdwy over 1f out: 4th and hld whn nt clr run ins fnl f* **4/1**

3456 **6** *1 3/4* **Entrapping**[51] 7103 2-8-9 63 .... KieranO'Neill 1 55
(Richard Hannon) *t.k.h: chsd ldr 4f: outpcd fnl 2f* **25/1**

653 **7** *6* **Avatar Star (IRE)**[14] 7806 2-9-7 75 .... AdamKirby 6 53
(Marco Botti) *hld up in 5th: rdn over 2f out: wknd wl over 1f out* **3/1**[2]

654 **8** *1 3/4* **Koharu**[27] 7650 2-8-0 54 ....(t) SilvestreDeSousa 2 28
(Peter Makin) *led: rdn 3f out: hdd wl over 1f out: sn wknd* **25/1**

1m 39.06s (-0.74) **Going Correction** -0.05s/f (Stan) **8** Ran SP% **125.2**
Speed ratings (Par 96): **101,99,98,97,97 95,89,87**
Tote Swingers 1&2 £6.10, 2&3 £3.80, 1&3 £9.90 CSF £34.93 CT £208.74 TOTE £10.80: £3.00, £2.20, £3.10; EX 41.40 Trifecta £395.80 Pool: £1,615.26 - 3.06 winning tickets..
Owner Brendan Kerr **Bred** Stuart Weld **Trained** Headley, Surrey

FOCUS
A fair nursery, run at a steady pace. Straightforward form, the winner to his mark.

NOTEBOOK
Canadian Run(IRE), who has been gelded, made light of a three-month absence. The winner, tackling 1m for the first occasion, was keen enough through the early stages and the fact that he was able to find so much at the business end of the race suggests that he was value for a shade more than the official margin of victory. He has a long, raking stride and threatens to be even more effective over middle-distances on a more galloping track. (op 8-1 tchd 9-1)
Raging Bear(USA), representing the powerful yard of Richard Hannon, ran well but looks to be crying out for more of a test of stamina. Out the back with 2f to run, he passed all bar the winner and doesn't appear too badly treated. (op 4-1)
Duroble Man kept on creditably but was probably fortunate to finish third. He was up with the pace throughout but lacked the necessary change of gear to go with the principals. A step up in trip may see him in a better light. (tchd 11-2)
Lyric Piece is clearly not straightforward. Forced wide throughout, she was off the bridle at a very early stage before making late headway. She's another one that will benefit for a more demanding test of stamina. (op 4-1)
Beau Select(IRE) was badly impeded inside the final furlong. (tchd 9-2)
Avatar Star(IRE) was a big disappointment and ran as if in need of a break. (op 7-2 tchd 4-1)

7990 RACING PLUS - THE BEST WEEKEND ACTION H'CAP 6f (P)
5:50 (5:51) (Class 6) (0-60,60) 3-Y-O+ **£1,617** (£481; £240; £120) **Stalls** Low

Form RPR

4000 **1** **Commanche**[49] 7178 3-9-5 59 .... AdamKirby 2 72
(Patrick Chamings) *in tch: clsd on ldrs 2f out: led over 1f out: drvn clr* **7/2**[1]

0425 **2** *1 3/4* **Loyal Royal (IRE)**[11] 7861 9-9-5 59 ....(bt) GrahamLee 7 66
(Milton Bradley) *stdd s: hld up towards rr: hdwy on bit 2f out: cajoled along over 1f out: wnt 2nd ins fnl f: nt trble wnr* **8/1**

0343 **3** *1 1/4* **Baby Dottie**[79] 6307 5-9-2 56 ....(t) IanMongan 3 59
(Pat Phelan) *led 1f: chsd ldr: one pce appr fnl f* **9/2**[2]

5040 **4** *1 1/4* **Sannibel**[88] 6053 4-9-6 60 .... LukeMorris 5 59
(Graeme McPherson) *chsd ldrs: outpcd over 1f out: styd on again ins fnl f* **14/1**

000 **5** *2* **Silvee**[34] 7512 5-9-4 58 .... SeanLevey 6 51
(John Bridger) *prom tl wknd over 1f out* **7/1**

2000 **6** *1* **Madame Kintyre**[126] 4708 4-8-13 60 .... PatMillman(7) 9 49
(Rod Millman) *in rr: hmpd after 2f: plenty to do after and sn pushed along: sme late hdwy* **33/1**

4200 **7** *hd* **Leelu**[35] 7485 6-9-4 58 .... LiamKeniry 10 47
(David Arbuthnot) *led after 1f tl wknd over 1f out* **8/1**

0604 **8** *1* **Lady Kildare (IRE)**[107] 5416 4-9-2 56 .... TomEaves 8 42
(Jedd O'Keeffe) *chsd ldrs tl hrd rdn and wknd 2f out* **25/1**

0120 **9** *1 1/4* **Athwaab**[30] 7590 5-9-6 60 .... JimmyFortune 12 42
(Noel Chance) *in rr: hmpd after 2f: bhd after* **8/1**

303- **10** *6* **Onceaponatime (IRE)**[568] 2179 7-9-4 58 .... JamieMackay 1 20
(Michael Squance) *in rr: hmpd after 2f: wl bhd after* **12/1**

0300 **U** **Ghazeer (IRE)**[7] 7915 3-9-3 57 ....(v) SilvestreDeSousa 4
(Derek Shaw) *mid-div tl short of room: stmbld and uns rdr after 2f: fatally injured* **6/1**[3]

1m 13.14s (0.04) **Going Correction** -0.05s/f (Stan) **11** Ran SP% **121.7**
Speed ratings (Par 101): **97,94,93,91,88 87,87,85,84,76**
Tote Swingers 1&2 £4.40, 2&3 £3.20, 1&3 £4.30 CSF £33.19 CT £134.23 TOTE £6.10: £1.10, £2.50, £2.10; EX 46.20 Trifecta £333.10 Pool: £1,168.25 - 2.63 winning tickets..
Owner K W Tyrrell **Bred** Paramount Bloodstock **Trained** Baughurst, Hants

FOCUS
A modest handicap, run at a stern pace. The winner is rated back to something like his 2yo form.

7991 BOXINGDAYRACES.CO.UK H'CAP 1m 4f (P)
6:20 (6:24) (Class 6) (0-55,55) 3-Y-O+ **£1,617** (£481; £240; £120) **Stalls** Centre

Form RPR

5240 **1** **Rodrigo De Freitas (IRE)**[19] 7744 5-9-5 55 ....(v) WilliamCarson 11 64
(Jim Boyle) *dwlt and rdn early: sn in tch: led wl over 1f out and rdn over 2 l ahd: drvn along fnl f: jst hld on* **14/1**

6405 **2** *nse* **Comedy House**[28] 7629 4-9-5 55 .... AdamKirby 13 64
(Michael Madgwick) *in tch: effrt over 2f out: wnt 2nd over 1f out: clsd on wnr fnl f: jst failed* **2/1**[1]

4654 **3** *5* **El Libertador (USA)**[19] 7744 6-9-5 55 ....(b) LukeMorris 8 56
(Eric Wheeler) *mid-div: hdwy over 2f out: one pce appr fnl f* **7/1**[3]

500 **4** *5* **Life Of Laughter (USA)**[200] 2288 4-9-2 52 .... StevieDonohoe 2 45
(Willie Musson) *bhd: rdn and hdwy over 1f out: nvr nrr* **10/1**

11/ **5** *3/4* **Mondego (GER)**[19] 7758 10-9-1 54 .... AndrewPThornton(3) 6 46
(C Moore, Ire) *mid-div: effrt over 2f out: no imp* **12/1**

0-00 **6** *3/4* **Sinchiroka (FR)**[75] 6456 6-9-2 52 .... JamieGoldstein 9 43
(Ralph Smith) *disp ld: led over 2f out tl wknd wl over 1f out* **16/1**

430- **7** *2 1/4* **Dane Cottage**[39] 6873 5-9-2 52 .... GrahamLee 12 39
(Richard Ford) *stdd s: hld up in rr: rdn over 2f out: nvr rchd ldrs* **50/1**

5000 **8** *7* **Lady Barastar (IRE)**[18] 7768 4-9-5 55 .... AdamBeschizza 5 31
(Amanda Perrett) *prom tl wknd over 2f out* **20/1**

06/0 **9** *3* **Llamadas**[28] 7629 10-9-3 53 .... KirstyMilczarek 1 24
(Olivia Maylam) *disp ld tl over 2f out: sn wknd* **33/1**

0/5 **10** *7* **Tyrur Ted**[42] 7321 7-9-5 55 .... LiamKeniry 14 15
(Frank Sheridan) *sn wl bhd* **4/1**[2]

-353 **11** *5* **Herschel (IRE)**[39] 519 6-8-10 53 .... NedCurtis(7) 4
(Gary Moore) *s.s: towards rr: rdn 4f out: n.d after* **20/1**

0005 **12** *14* **Fire In Babylon (IRE)**[35] 7479 4-9-2 52 .... MartinLane 10
(Noel Quinlan) *chsd ldrs: rdn 4f out: wknd over 2f out: eased* **12/1**

0/00 **13** *19* **Fashion Flow**[18] 7782 5-9-5 55 .... RobertWinston 3
(Michael Wigham) *prom tl wknd and lost pl 3f out: virtually p.u 2f out* **33/1**

2m 32.51s (-1.99) **Going Correction** -0.05s/f (Stan) **13** Ran SP% **120.2**
Speed ratings (Par 101): **104,103,100,97,96 96,94,90,88,83 80,70,58**
Tote Swingers 1&2 £5.20, 2&3 £3.30, 1&3 £6.70 CSF £40.05 CT £226.73 TOTE £12.00: £4.10, £1.10, £1.20; EX 40.80 Trifecta £51.80 Pool: £766.67 - 11.10 winning tickets..
Owner The Rodrigo De Freitas Partnership **Bred** Castlemartin Stud And Skymarc Farm **Trained** Epsom, Surrey

FOCUS
A weak handicap run at a sound pace. The first pair were clear and the winner is rated up a length on this year's form.

7992 BOOK W.H.W.F. TICKETS ON 0844 579 3008 H'CAP (DIV I) 7f (P)
6:50 (6:52) (Class 6) (0-60,60) 3-Y-O+ **£1,617** (£481; £240; £120) **Stalls** Low

Form RPR

0005 **1** **Gallantry**[34] 7500 10-8-12 51 .... JimmyQuinn 5 63
(Paul Howling) *in tch: led wl over 1f out: drvn out* **16/1**

2121 **2** 1 **See The Storm**[7] 7906 4-9-0 **56** ...... RyanPowell(3) 3 65
(Ian Williams) *hld up towards rr: smooth hdwy 2f out: r.o to take 2nd ins fnl f* **2/1**[1]

4645 **3** 3 **Amis Reunis**[18] 7776 3-9-7 **60** ...... WilliamCarson 6 61
(Anthony Carson) *chsd ldrs: rdn to chal 2f out: one pce fnl f* **12/1**

0004 **4** ¾ **White Flight**[51] 7105 3-9-0 **53** ...... LukeMorris 12 52+
(Jane Chapple-Hyam) *hld up towards rr: rdn and r.o fnl 2f: nrest at fin* **25/1**

0366 **5** hd **Lieutenant Dan (IRE)**[2] 7964 5-9-5 **58** ...... AndrewMullen 7 56
(Michael Appleby) *chsd ldrs: hrd rdn over 1f out: one pce* **12/1**

4553 **6** ½ **Silkee Supreme**[13] 7822 3-9-2 **60** ......(b) WilliamTwiston-Davies(5) 9 57
(Richard Hannon) *bhd: rdn 3f out: sme late hdwy* **8/1**[3]

0314 **7** ¾ **Reginald Claude**[12] 7837 4-8-12 **56** ...... LeeNewnes(5) 10 51
(Mark Usher) *hld up in midfield: rdn and sme hdwy over 1f out: no imp* **8/1**[3]

1363 **8** 1¼ **Buxton**[7] 7917 8-9-7 **60** ......(t) JimmyFortune 1 52
(Roger Ingram) *hld up in midfield: effrt 2f out: no imp over 1f out* **14/1**

0450 **9** ½ **Flying Kitty**[84] 6152 3-8-8 **47** ...... KieranO'Neill 13 37
(John Bridger) *stdd s: t.k.h in rr: rdn 3f out: n.d* **66/1**

1453 **10** 1¼ **Comadoir (IRE)**[79] 6306 6-9-2 **60** ......(p) NathanSweeney(5) 4 47
(Jo Crowley) *chsd ldr tl wknd 2f out* **14/1**

3006 **11** 1½ **Pytheas (USA)**[7] 7906 5-8-13 **55** ......(v) RyanClark(3) 8 38
(Michael Attwater) *led tl wl over 1f out: sn wknd* **20/1**

0/-0 **12** 7 **Aegean King**[289] 636 6-8-10 **49** ...... AndreaAtzeni 11 13
(Michael Wigham) *prom tl wknd qckly over 2f out* **3/1**[2]

1m 25.44s (-0.56) **Going Correction** -0.05s/f (Stan) 12 Ran SP% **125.3**
Speed ratings (Par 101): **101,99,96,95,95 94,93,92,91,90 88,80**
Tote Swingers 1&2 £14.90, 2&3 £8.70, 1&3 £35.60 CSF £50.07 CT £433.30 TOTE £29.00: £5.30, £1.70, £3.60; EX 98.20 TRIFECTA Not won..
Owner J Wright D Patrick P D Woodward **Bred** Cheveley Park Stud Ltd **Trained** Lee-On-The-Solent, Hants

FOCUS
A competitive if low-grade handicap. It was the fastwer division and the form looks sound.
Aegean King Official explanation: jockey said that the gelding stopped quickly

7993 BOOK W.H.W.F. TICKETS ON 0844 579 3008 H'CAP (DIV II) 7f (P)
7:20 (7:20) (Class 6) (0-60,60) 3-Y-O+ £1,617 (£481; £240; £120) Stalls Low

Form RPR

0005 **1** **Welsh Inlet (IRE)**[7] 7906 4-8-10 **54** ...... WilliamTwiston-Davies(5) 14 63
(John Bridger) *t.k.h towards rr: gd hdwy over 1f out: edgd rt ins fnl f: r.o to ld on line* **14/1**

3052 **2** shd **Warbond**[35] 7486 4-9-6 **59** ...... JamieGoldstein 9 67
(Michael Madgwick) *mid-div: hdwy 2f out: led ins fnl f: hrd rdn and edgd rt: jst ct* **5/1**[2]

6000 **3** 1 **Huzzah (IRE)**[51] 7106 7-8-11 **50** ...... JimmyQuinn 1 56
(Paul Howling) *in tch: drvn to chal ent fnl f: kpt on* **16/1**

0003 **4** 1 **Bussa**[7] 7898 4-8-4 **50** ......(t) EoinWalsh(7) 12 53
(David Evans) *chsd ldrs: led 2f out tl ins fnl f: one pce* **8/1**

3520 **5** shd **The New Black (IRE)**[29] 7600 3-9-2 **55** ......(e) RobertWinston 8 58
(Gay Kelleway) *towards rr: rdn and struggling 3f out: styd on wl fnl f: nrest at fin* **6/1**[3]

0500 **6** 1¾ **Bitaphon (IRE)**[2] 7964 3-9-7 **60** ...... AndrewMullen 3 58
(Michael Appleby) *led tl 2f out: no ex ent fnl f* **14/1**

002 **7** 1½ **Katmai River (IRE)**[26] 7670 5-9-7 **60** ......(v) DavidProbert 4 54
(Mark Usher) *towards rr: rdn over 2f out: nvr rchd ldrs* **2/1**[1]

0050 **8** ½ **Schoolboy Champ**[18] 7781 5-8-9 **48** ......(vt) AndreaAtzeni 6 41
(Lisa Williamson) *prom tl wknd over 1f out* **33/1**

-036 **9** ½ **Batchworth Firefly**[20] 7719 4-9-7 **60** ...... GrahamLee 5 51
(Dean Ivory) *mid-div: rdn over 2f out: no imp* **25/1**

0000 **10** 1¾ **Pipers Piping (IRE)**[15] 7799 6-9-5 **58** ...... AdamKirby 2 45
(John Butler) *dwlt: hld up towards rr: nt clr run over 1f out: nvr in chalng position* **7/1**

0000 **11** nk **Rise To Glory (IRE)**[7] 7906 4-9-3 **56** ......(t) DominicFox 10 42
(Shaun Harris) *bhd: sme hdwy on inner 2f out: sn wknd* **14/1**

506- **12** 3 **Chorister Girl**[362] 7697 3-8-8 **47** ...... KieranO'Neill 7 25
(Richard Ford) *prom tl wknd over 2f out* **33/1**

000 **13** 3½ **Smoky Cloud (IRE)**[137] 4332 5-9-0 **53** ...... LukeMorris 11 21
(Dave Morris) *t.k.h: chsd ldr tl over 2f out: sn wknd* **14/1**

1m 25.88s (-0.12) **Going Correction** -0.05s/f (Stan) 13 Ran SP% **130.2**
Speed ratings (Par 101): **98,97,96,95,95 93,91,91,90,88 88,84,80**
Tote Swingers 1&2 £9.80, 2&3 £18.00, 1&3 £20.80 CSF £88.71 CT £1208.25 TOTE £19.30: £5.80, £1.40, £7.70; EX 110.10 Trifecta £424.30 Part won. Pool: £565.76 - 0.62 winning tickets..
Owner Kevin J Walls **Bred** Patrick Gleeson **Trained** Liphook, Hants

FOCUS
Another poor if very competitive handicap. It was a bit slower than division one and the form is similar.
T/Jkpt: Not won. T/Plt: £84.80 to a £1 stake. Pool: £69,349.69 - 596.44 winning tickets. T/Qpdt: £12.40 to a £1 stake. Pool: £9,153.19 - 545.31 winning tickets. LM

7899 LINGFIELD (L-H)
Wednesday, December 5

OFFICIAL GOING: Standard
Wind: light, against Weather: dry, cold

7994 ATTHERACES.COM EXCLUSIVE BARRY GERAGHTY BLOG NURSERY 1m (P)
12:00 (12:00) (Class 4) (0-85,85) 2-Y-O £3,428 (£1,020; £509; £254) Stalls High

Form RPR

431 **1** **Yarroom (IRE)**[19] 7749 2-9-7 **85** ...... AndreaAtzeni 2 91+
(Roger Varian) *broke wl: stdd to chse ldrs and t.k.h: rdn and effrt to ld ent fnl f: r.o wl and gng away at fin* **10/11**[1]

2010 **2** 1¼ **Run It Twice (IRE)**[14] 7814 2-8-3 **67** ...... KirstyMilczarek 5 69
(David Evans) *dwlt: hld up in tch in rr: rdn and hdwy 2f out: ev ch 1f out: no ex and one pce fnl 75yds* **12/1**

4402 **3** 1¾ **Party Royal**[34] 7501 2-9-3 **81** ...... SilvestreDeSousa 7 79
(Mark Johnston) *sn bustled along to press ldr tl led 5f out: rdn 2f out: hdd ent fnl f: styd on same pce ins fnl f* **7/1**[3]

2621 **4** 1 **King Of Kudos (IRE)**[14] 7812 2-8-8 **72** ...... KieranO'Neill 8 68
(Scott Dixon) *broke wl: stdd bk and hld up in tch in midfield: effrt and carried wd bnd wl over 1f out: rallied and styd on ins fnl f* **10/1**

0313 **5** nk **Archie Stevens**[19] 7737 2-8-8 **72** ...... RichardKingscote 3 67
(Tom Dascombe) *chsd ldrs: rdn whn carried wd and outpcd bnd wl over 1f out: kpt on but no threat to ldrs fnl f* **9/2**[2]

4304 **6** 1½ **Ocean Applause**[42] 7331 2-9-7 **85** ...... JohnFahy 1 77
(John Ryan) *in tch towards rr: rdn and hdwy on inner over 1f out: no imp 1f out: wknd ins fnl f* **16/1**

0226 **7** ½ **Sunblazer (IRE)**[14] 7814 2-8-8 **72** ......(b[1]) MartinDwyer 4 63
(William Muir) *in tch towards rr: effrt u.p over 1f out: no real imp: wknd ins fnl f* **16/1**

10 **8** hd **Run Fat Lass Run**[25] 7687 2-8-11 **75** ...... AmyRyan 6 65
(Kevin Ryan) *led tl 5f out: styd w ldr tl edgd rt bnd wl over 1f out: lost pl and no prog over 1f out: edgd lft and wknd ins fnl f* **25/1**

1m 36.33s (-1.87) **Going Correction** -0.05s/f (Stan) 2y crse rec 8 Ran SP% **115.5**
Speed ratings (Par 98): **107,105,104,103,102 101,100,100**
Tote Swingers 1&2 £4.90, 2&3 £8.30, 1&3 £2.40 CSF £13.87 CT £52.41 TOTE £1.50: £1.20, £3.90, £1.60; EX 12.20 Trifecta £65.10 Pool: £509.94 - 5.87 winning tickets..
Owner Sheikh Ahmed Al Maktoum **Bred** Darley **Trained** Newmarket, Suffolk

FOCUS
A juvenile course record was set in this nursery, the previous best being lowered by 0.05sec. Straightforward form which should prove reliable, and the winner should have a bit more to offer.

NOTEBOOK
Yarroom(IRE) won his maiden at Wolverhampton with plenty to spare and, despite being given more to do here off an opening mark of 85, was well supported and got the job done handily, holding off the runner-up well in the straight. The step up to a mile was very much in his favour and there should be more improvement to come. (op 4-5 tchd 8-11 and Evens)
Run It Twice(IRE) settled better this time due to a solid gallop, and came to have every chance in the straight. He was unlucky to bump into a well-handicapped and unexposed rival. (tchd 10-1 and 14-1)
Party Royal, up there throughout, kept battling away after being headed. Second at Kempton last time, he's a good marker for the form. (op 8-1)
King Of Kudos(IRE), debuting for his new stable after winning a 7f claimer here last time, was pushed very wide on the turn in, which made things difficult. He didn't fail through lack of stamina. (op 11-1 tchd 12-1)
Archie Stevens, up another furlong in distance, was also carried wide on the bend into the straight. He didn't improve for the longer trip. (op 7-1)

7995 MARSH GREEN CLAIMING STKS 5f (P)
12:30 (12:30) (Class 6) 3-Y-O+ £1,704 (£503; £251) Stalls High

Form RPR

2223 **1** **Drawnfromthepast (IRE)**[11] 7859 7-8-7 83 ...... FergusSweeney 6 84
(Jamie Osborne) *chsd ldrs: rdn and effrt over 1f out: chal 1f out: led wl ins fnl f: styd on wl: rdn out* **9/4**[1]

0055 **2** 1 **Lujeanie**[6] 7928 6-8-11 80 ......(p) GrahamLee 2 84
(Dean Ivory) *stdd after s: racd off the pce in last trio: rdn and hdwy but stl plenty to do over 1f out: swtchd rt and r.o wl ins fnl f: wnt 2nd towards fin* **5/2**[2]

5025 **3** ¾ **Above The Stars**[5] 7937 4-8-1 66 ...... JamesSullivan 5 72
(Richard Fahey) *in tch in midfield: rdn and effrt whn edgd lft ent fnl f: styd on fnl 100yds to go 3rd cl home* **16/1**

0211 **4** ½ **Sonko (IRE)**[11] 7859 3-8-9 82 ......(p) SilvestreDeSousa 7 78
(Tim Pitt) *chsd ldr tl rdn to ld over 1f out: sn hrd pressed: hdd wl ins fnl f: no ex and lost 2 pls towards fin* **3/1**[3]

5246 **5** 1 **Haadeeth**[82] 6194 5-8-4 65 ...... KirstyMilczarek 3 69
(David Evans) *in tch in midfield: rdn and outpcd 2f out: rallied u.p ent fnl f: no imp fnl 100yds* **20/1**

0105 **6** 2¼ **Where's Reiley (USA)**[20] 7726 6-8-2 76 ow3 ......(b) LeonnaMayor(5) 9 64
(Alastair Lidderdale) *hld up in midfield on outer: wd bnd and outpcd wl over 1f out: no prog over 1f out* **9/1**

0050 **7** nse **Yurituni**[27] 7648 5-7-13 72 ......(b) SimonPearce(3) 8 59
(Eve Johnson Houghton) *taken down early: chsd ldrs: struggling and u.p wl over 1f out: wknd 1f out* **40/1**

5002 **8** ¾ **Powerful Wind (IRE)**[30] 7591 3-9-0 78 ...... LukeMorris 4 68
(Ronald Harris) *led tl rdn and hdd over 1f out: fdd ins fnl f* **20/1**

0060 **9** 3 **Lesley's Choice**[27] 7651 6-8-9 72 ......(p) JohnFahy 1 53
(Sean Curran) *a off the pce in last trio: wknd wl over 1f out* **33/1**

400 **10** 2½ **Celtic Sultan (IRE)**[7] 7902 8-8-4 74 ...... SemiraPashai(7) 10 46
(Alastair Lidderdale) *taken down early: v.s.a: detached in last: clsd over 3f out: pushed along over 2f out: wknd wl over 1f out* **66/1**

57.72s (-1.08) **Going Correction** -0.05s/f (Stan) 10 Ran SP% **116.6**
Speed ratings (Par 101): **106,104,103,102,100 97,97,95,91,87**
Tote Swingers 1&2 £2.00, 2&3 £10.70, 1&3 £6.20 CSF £7.56 TOTE £3.70: £1.10, £1.70, £6.90; EX 10.40 Trifecta £74.40 Pool: £495.37 - 4.99 winning tickets..Drawnfromthepast was claimed by Mr Mustafa Khan for £8,000 and Sonko was claimed by Mr John Khan for £15,000.
Owner Mark Benton **Bred** D And Mrs D Veitch **Trained** Upper Lambourn, Berks

FOCUS
Not a bad claimer. The winner was best in and did not need to quite match his recent handicap best.
Yurituni Official explanation: jockey said that the mare hung right
Lesley's Choice Official explanation: jockey said that the gelding anticipated the start and was slowly away

7996 FOREST ROW MAIDEN STKS 1m (P)
1:00 (1:01) (Class 5) 3-Y-O+ £2,385 (£704; £352) Stalls High

Form RPR

53 **1** **Desert Berry**[63] 6792 3-8-12 0 ...... TedDurcan 7 71
(Chris Wall) *mde all: rdn wl over 1f out: drvn and hld on wl fnl 100yds: all out* **4/1**[3]

6 **2** shd **High Net Worth**[58] 6930 3-9-3 0 ...... LukeMorris 8 76+
(Ed Walker) *t.k.h: chsd wnr tl over 6f out: chsd ldrs after: swtchd rt and effrt over 1f out: drvn and chal fnl 100yds: r.o: jst hld* **9/4**[1]

5622 **3** nk **Srinagar Girl**[16] 7787 3-8-12 72 ...... IanMongan 2 70
(Sir Henry Cecil) *t.k.h: chsd ldrs: rdn and ev ch ent fnl f: drvn ins fnl f: no ex cl home* **7/2**[2]

0523 **4** ½ **Blank Czech (IRE)**[7] 7896 3-9-3 70 ...... AdamKirby 9 74
(Amanda Perrett) *chsd ldrs tl wnt 2nd over 6f out: rdn and unable qck over 1f out: rallied ins fnl f and pressing ldrs whn hit on nose by rivals whip fnl 50yds: one pce after* **4/1**[3]

0553 **5** 1 **Bowstar**[6] 7925 3-8-12 64 ...... J-PGuillambert 3 67
(Michael Attwater) *t.k.h: hld up in tch: rdn over 2f out: outpcd wl over 1f out: swtchd rt and rallied 1f out: kpt on but nvr gng to rch ldrs* **9/2**

6 11 **Staigue Fort**[40] 4-9-4 0 ...... LiamKeniry 10 46
(Emma Lavelle) *v.s.a: bhd: clsd and in tch after 2f: drvn and wknd wl over 1f out* **66/1**

0000 **7** 3½ **Doyle's Dream**[140] 4214 3-8-9 29 ...... SimonPearce(3) 4 33
(Michael Madgwick) *in tch in last pair: rdn and wknd wl over 1f out* **150/1**

4 **8** ¾ **Bubblina**[7] 7896 5-8-8 0 .... LeonnaMayor(5) 5 32
(Alastair Lidderdale) *s.i.s: sn in tch in midfield: hdwy to chse ldrs 3f out: rdn 2f out: wknd and btn 1f out: eased ins fnl f* **40/1**

1m 37.7s (-0.50) **Going Correction** -0.05s/f (Stan)
WFA 3 from 4yo+ 1lb 8 Ran SP% **115.8**
Speed ratings (Par 103): **100,99,99,99,98 87,83,82**
Tote Swingers 1&2 £5.50, 2&3 £3.40, 1&3 £3.40 CSF £13.64 TOTE £4.50: £2.50, £1.10, £1.10; EX 20.40 Trifecta £48.10 Pool: £668.51 - 10.41 winning tickets..
Owner Mrs A L J White **Bred** Mrs J A Chapman And Darley **Trained** Newmarket, Suffolk

FOCUS
A modest maiden which was steadily run. There's every chance the inner can rate a bit higher.
Bubblina Official explanation: jockey said that the mare suffered a cut to her right hind leg

7997 LINGFIELDPARK.CO.UK H'CAP 1m (P)
1:30 (1:30) (Class 5) (0-75,75) 3-Y-O+ **£2,385** (£704; £352) **Stalls** High

Form RPR

0302 **1** **Hometown Glory**[61] 6840 3-9-6 **75** .... (t) MartinLane 7 88
(Brian Meehan) *chsd ldrs: gap opened on inner and rdn to ld wl over 1f out: in command 1f out: kpt on: rdn out* **11/2**[2]

0000 **2** 1¼ **Lowther**[111] 5269 7-9-5 **73** .... (b) IanMongan 10 83
(Lee Carter) *hld up wl in tch: hdwy to press ldr and carried sltly rt wl over 1f out: chsd clr wnr and rdn over 1f out: kpt on but nvr looked like rching wnr* **9/2**[1]

6045 **3** 2¾ **Warfare**[16] 7790 3-9-5 **74** .... AmyRyan 8 78
(Kevin Ryan) *led: rdn: edgd rt and hdd bnd wl over 1f out: 3rd and styd on same pce fnl f* **9/2**[1]

0453 **4** shd **Mister Musicmaster**[19] 7743 3-9-5 **74** .... RichardKingscote 9 77
(Ron Hodges) *chsd ldr tl 6f out: styd chsng ldrs: outpcd and drvn wl over 1f out: kpt on but no threat to ldrs fnl f* **8/1**[3]

6405 **5** ¾ **Relentless Harry (IRE)**[20] 7725 3-9-0 **69** .... (t) LukeMorris 4 71
(George Baker) *in tch in midfield: effrt u.p on inner over 1f out: drvn and styd on same pce fnl f* **9/2**[1]

0021 **6** ½ **Buckland (IRE)**[12] 7838 4-9-1 **74** .... NicoleNordblad(5) 6 75+
(Hans Adielsson) *stdd after s: t.k.h: hld up in tch in midfield: nt clr run over 2f out: switching rt and effrt over 1f out: styd on ins fnl f: no threat to ldrs* **10/1**

3044 **7** 1¾ **Russian Ice**[13] 7827 4-9-7 **75** .... (b) GrahamLee 2 72
(Dean Ivory) *hld up in tch in midfield: rdn and effrt over 1f out: no imp and wl hld fnl f* **14/1**

6523 **8** hd **Officer In Command (USA)**[7] 7893 6-9-0 **68** .... (b) JohnFahy 5 64
(Paul Rich) *s.i.s: in rr tl hdwy into midfield 4f out: rdn and struggling 2f out: wknd over 1f out* **10/1**

0000 **9** 2¾ **Titan Triumph**[27] 7645 8-9-7 **75** .... (t) AdamKirby 3 65
(William Knight) *dwlt: hld up in rr: stl plenty to do whn bdly hmpd wl over 1f out: nt rcvr: n.d* **20/1**

4-00 **10** 2½ **Beauchamp Xerxes**[13] 7824 6-9-5 **73** .... (t) J-PGuillambert 11 57
(Hans Adielsson) *stdd s: t.k.h: hld up in rr: rdn and wknd wl over 1f out* **66/1**

1-00 **11** 1¼ **Avon River**[12] 7843 5-9-2 **70** .... TedDurcan 1 51
(Dean Ivory) *hld up in last quartet: rdn and struggling over 2f out: wknd wl over 1f out* **50/1**

6236 **12** 1¼ **Cathedral**[118] 5008 3-9-4 **73** .... RobertWinston 12 51
(Michael Wigham) *s.i.s: racd freely: hdwy to chse ldr 6f out tl over 2f out: sn wknd* **11/1**

1m 36.01s (-2.19) **Going Correction** -0.05s/f (Stan)
WFA 3 from 4yo+ 1lb 12 Ran SP% **122.4**
Speed ratings (Par 103): **108,106,104,103,103 102,100,100,97,95 94,92**
Tote Swingers 1&2 £6.10, 2&3 £6.40, 1&3 £6.90 CSF £31.14 CT £124.73 TOTE £4.00: £2.50, £2.30, £1.70; EX 43.40 Trifecta £105.90 Pool: £357.40 - 2.53 winning tickets..
Owner Mascalls Stud **Bred** Mascalls Stud **Trained** Manton, Wilts

FOCUS
This looked quite competitive on paper but few got involved. A slightly positive view has been taken of the form.
Cathedral Official explanation: jockey said that the colt missed the break

7998 GOAT CROSS H'CAP 7f (P)
2:00 (2:01) (Class 5) (0-70,70) 3-Y-O+ **£2,385** (£704; £352) **Stalls** Low

Form RPR

2003 **1** **Sunshine Always (IRE)**[20] 7725 6-9-4 **67** .... SebSanders 9 76
(Michael Attwater) *hld up in tch in midfield: nt clr run wl over 1f out: rdn and hdwy over 1f out: r.o wl to ld wl ins fnl f* **12/1**

6420 **2** ¾ **Exceedexpectations (IRE)**[43] 7317 3-9-4 **67** .... MartinLane 12 74
(Michael Bell) *led and set stdy gallop: rdn and fnd ex 2f out: kpt on u.p tl hdd and no ex wl ins fnl f* **15/2**[3]

5400 **3** 1 **Chevise (IRE)**[75] 6434 4-9-4 **67** .... WilliamCarson 13 71
(Steve Woodman) *pressed ldr: rdn and sltly outpcd 2f out: kpt on u.p ins fnl f* **40/1**

4023 **4** hd **Fishforcompliments**[15] 7799 8-9-3 **66** .... (p) TonyHamilton 4 70
(Richard Fahey) *chsd ldrs: rdn and sltly outpcd wl over 1f out: rallied and edgd rt u.p 1f out: kpt on* **8/1**

-620 **5** ¾ **Excellent Jem**[106] 5454 3-9-7 **70** .... AdamKirby 1 74+
(Jane Chapple-Hyam) *hld up in tch in midfield: rdn over 1f out: styng on whn nt clr run and hmpd 1f out: styd on same pce ins fnl f* **4/1**[1]

301 **6** ½ **Purley Queen (IRE)**[83] 6172 3-9-2 **65** .... DavidProbert 5 65
(Sylvester Kirk) *chsd ldrs: rdn and unable qck over 1f out: styd on same pce u.p fnl f* **12/1**

6601 **7** hd **Golden Desert (IRE)**[11] 7857 8-9-4 **67** .... GrahamLee 7 67+
(Simon Dow) *stdd stat: hld up in tch towards rr: hdwy and swtchd lft 1f out: r.o but nvr gng pce to rch ldrs* **4/1**[1]

0004 **8** ½ **Spin Again (IRE)**[11] 7857 7-9-2 **65** .... JohnFahy 2 63
(John Ryan) *in tch in midfield: effrt u.p on inner over 1f out: one pce and no imp fnl f* **15/2**[3]

6660 **9** ¾ **Hereford Boy**[44] 7302 8-9-4 **67** .... (v) TedDurcan 3 63
(Dean Ivory) *stdd s: hld up in tch in rr: swtchd rt and effrt over 1f out: kpt on but no real imp* **16/1**

2650 **10** 3¼ **Linkable**[55] 7011 3-9-2 **65** .... KirstyMilczarek 10 53
(Brendan Powell) *hld up in last pair: rdn and no hdwy over 1f out: n.d* **16/1**

0100 **11** nse **Zip Lock (IRE)**[11] 7863 6-9-0 **66** .... RyanClark(3) 6 54
(Tom Keddy) *stdd s: t.k.h: hld up in tch towards rr: rdn and no hdwy wl over 1f out* **33/1**

0006 **12** ¾ **Mullins Way (USA)**[15] 7799 4-9-6 **69** .... J-PGuillambert 8 55
(Jo Hughes) *stdd s: hld up in tch in rr: rdn and struggling 2f out: sn wknd* **6/1**[2]

1m 25.93s (1.13) **Going Correction** -0.05s/f (Stan) 12 Ran SP% **121.5**
Speed ratings (Par 103): **91,90,89,88,87 87,87,86,85,81 81,81**
Tote Swingers 1&2 £12.00, 2&3 £42.00, 1&3 £31.40 CSF £101.67 CT £2247.43 TOTE £13.50: £3.60, £3.70, £13.00; EX 103.20 TRIFECTA Not won..
Owner Miss Maureen Stopher **Bred** Moyglare Stud Farm Ltd **Trained** Epsom, Surrey

FOCUS
They didn't go a great gallop here and few became involved. The winner's best form since he was a 4yo.

7999 HINDLEAP H'CAP (DIV I) 1m 4f (P)
2:30 (2:30) (Class 4) (0-85,85) 3-Y-O+ **£4,075** (£1,212; £606; £303) **Stalls** Low

Form RPR

30-0 **1** **Alazan (IRE)**[36] 5665 6-8-13 **74** .... LukeMorris 3 83
(Philip Hobbs) *hld up in tch in midfield: hdwy to chse ldrs 2f out: swtchd rt and drvn to chal ins fnl f: r.o wl to ld fnl 50yds* **16/1**

0003 **2** nk **Emerald Wilderness (IRE)**[7] 7904 8-9-10 **85** .... TedDurcan 2 93
(Mark Rimmer) *hld up in tch in last trio: hdwy on inner over 1f out: rdn to ld fnl 100yds: hdd and no ex fnl 50yds* **11/1**

4242 **3** 1¼ **Uphold**[29] 7601 5-9-0 **75** .... (e) RobertWinston 9 81
(Gay Kelleway) *led: rdn and hrd pressed 2f out: kpt on u.p tl hdd fnl 100yds: no ex and outpcd towards fin* **7/1**

125 **4** ¾ **Moderator**[14] 7810 3-8-13 **79** .... FergusSweeney 4 84
(Gary Moore) *chsd ldr for 1f: chsd ldng pair after tl rdn and ev ch 2f out: no ex fnl 100yds: wknd towards fin* **10/3**[2]

1-35 **5** ½ **Ajeeb (USA)**[12] 7842 4-9-5 **80** .... JamieSpencer 5 84
(David Simcock) *stdd s: hld up in detached last: clsd up to bk of field over 4f out: hdwy on inner 2f out: chsd ldrs but stuck bhd horses 1f out: swtchd rt and kpt on same pce fnl 100yds* **5/1**[3]

0/0- **6** 2¾ **The Pier (IRE)**[76] 7378 6-8-8 **72** .... (b) SimonPearce(3) 6 72
(David Pipe) *t.k.h: hld up in tch in midfield: rdn and unable qck over 1f out: btn and styng on same pce whn sltly hmpd jst ins fnl f* **16/1**

10 **7** ¾ **Canary Wharf (IRE)**[57] 6964 3-8-11 **77** .... (b) SilvestreDeSousa 10 76
(Marco Botti) *t.k.h: chsd ldr after 2f tl 2f out: wknd u.p ent fnl f* **13/2**

1602 **8** 1¾ **Livia's Dream (IRE)**[14] 7810 3-9-1 **81** .... GrahamLee 7 77
(Ed Walker) *chsd ldrs: rdn and struggling 2f out: wknd u.p jst over 1f out* **3/1**[1]

6050 **9** 15 **Cape Safari (IRE)**[27] 7655 3-8-4 **77** .... ChloeIngram(7) 8 49
(Tim Vaughan) *in tch in midfield tl dropped to rr 4f out: lost tch 3f out* **66/1**

2m 29.31s (-3.69) **Going Correction** -0.05s/f (Stan)
WFA 3 from 4yo+ 5lb 9 Ran SP% **112.2**
Speed ratings (Par 105): **110,109,108,108,108 106,105,104,94**
Tote Swingers 1&2 £14.90, 2&3 £6.90, 1&3 £11.50 CSF £171.72 CT £1342.68 TOTE £30.40: £6.30, £3.20, £2.90; EX 88.80 Trifecta £528.10 Part won. Pool: £704.18 - 0.80 winning tickets..
Owner Mrs Caren Walsh **Bred** D G Iceton **Trained** Withycombe, Somerset

FOCUS
They went a good pace here and it was the quicker division by 3.7sec. There was a bit of a turn-up but the winner was well in on his old form.

8000 HINDLEAP H'CAP (DIV II) 1m 4f (P)
3:00 (3:00) (Class 4) (0-85,80) 3-Y-O+ **£4,075** (£1,212; £606; £303) **Stalls** Low

Form RPR

6460 **1** **Focail Maith**[12] 7842 4-9-4 **74** .... (p) JamieSpencer 10 82
(John Ryan) *hld up in tch in last pair: rdn and effrt whn pushed wd bnd 2f out: hdwy and edgd lft u.p fnl f: led fnl 100yds: hld on wl* **6/1**[2]

-321 **2** hd **Noble Silk**[91] 5952 3-9-2 **77** .... GrahamLee 3 85
(Lucy Wadham) *hld up in tch in midfield: rdn and gd hdwy on inner over 1f out: ev ch ins fnl f: r.o wl but jst hld* **11/4**[1]

0000 **3** 1¾ **Standpoint**[12] 7842 6-9-5 **75** .... KirstyMilczarek 9 81
(Conor Dore) *stdd and dropped in bhd after s: t.k.h: hld up in tch in last pair: rdn and hdwy whn barging match w rival 1f out: r.o fnl 100yds to snatch 3rd last strides* **40/1**

6-21 **4** hd **Epic Storm (IRE)**[30] 7594 4-9-6 **76** .... AdamKirby 5 81
(Sean Curran) *t.k.h: chsd ldrs: rdn and effrt whn edgd lft ent fnl f: styng on same pce and hld whn hmpd towards fin* **11/4**[1]

6136 **5** hd **Badea**[16] 7792 3-8-11 **72** .... (v) TonyHamilton 2 76
(Richard Fahey) *led: rdn and hrd pressed 2f out: kpt on u.p tl hdd and no ex fnl 100yds* **9/1**

666 **6** shd **Perfect Delight**[35] 7475 3-9-1 **76** .... JohnFahy 1 80
(Clive Cox) *chsd ldr: rdn and ev ch 2f out: kpt on u.p tl no ex fnl 100yds: btn whn short of room towards fin* **14/1**

0600 **7** nk **Admirable Duque (IRE)**[91] 5936 6-9-0 **77** .... JoshBaudains(7) 8 81
(Dominic Ffrench Davis) *hld up in tch in last trio: hdwy to chse ldrs and carried rt bnd wl over 1f out: kpt on same pce ins fnl f* **33/1**

3564 **8** ½ **Nave (USA)**[54] 7024 5-9-2 **72** .... MartinLane 4 75
(David Simcock) *chsd ldrs: rdn over 2f out: lost pl u.p over 1f out: styd on same pce and hld fnl f* **15/2**

0163 **9** 3½ **Beat Route**[14] 7810 5-9-3 **73** .... J-PGuillambert 7 70
(Michael Attwater) *t.k.h: hld up in tch in midfield: rdn and unable qck over 1f out: n.m.r and wknd 1f out* **7/1**[3]

2m 33.01s (0.01) **Going Correction** -0.05s/f (Stan)
WFA 3 from 4yo+ 5lb 9 Ran SP% **113.9**
Speed ratings (Par 105): **97,96,95,95,95 95,95,94,92**
Tote Swingers 1&2 £5.10, 2&3 £15.90, 1&3 £24.90 CSF £22.53 CT £601.67 TOTE £6.50: £2.20, £1.90, £9.70; EX 22.30 Trifecta £504.80 Part won. Pool: £673.16 - 0.10 winning tickets..
Owner Cathal Fegan **Bred** D Robb **Trained** Newmarket, Suffolk

FOCUS
The weaker of the two divisions. The winning time was 3.7sec slower, and they covered the final 2f only 1sec quicker than those in the earlier event, despite saving energy going around 3sec slower for the first 7f and 2sec slower for the next 3f. The first three came from the rear and the winner built on recent promise from a good yard.

8001 TANDRIDGE AMATEUR RIDERS' H'CAP 2m (P)
3:30 (3:31) (Class 6) (0-60,60) 3-Y-O+ **£1,646** (£506; £253) **Stalls** Low

Form RPR

6465 **1** **Roughlyn**[46] 7255 3-9-6 **46** oh1 .... (b[1]) MissSBrotherton 1 54
(Lisa Williamson) *led tl 9f out: chsd ldr after tl led again 3f out: rdn and 2 l clr over 1f out: kpt on: rdn out* **25/1**

50S3 **2** 2 **Red Mystique (IRE)**[48] 7196 3-9-4 **51** .... (b) MissChelseyBanks(7) 13 57
(Philip Hide) *t.k.h: chsd ldr tl led 9f out: hdd 3f out: rdn and styd on same pce fr over 1f out* **8/1**[3]

5502 **3** *nk* **Baan (USA)**[36] 7472 9-10-2 **55** MrStevieSanders(7) 14 60+
(James Eustace) *t.k.h: hld up in tch in rr: hdwy into midfield and rdn 2f out: kpt on ins fnl f and pressed for 2nd cl home: no threat to wnr* **10/1**

0630 **4** *1 1/2* **Hoonose**[14] 7811 3-9-3 **46** (b[1]) MissRachelKing(3) 7 49
(Pat Eddery) *chsd ldrs: rdn and unable qck over 2f out: plugged on ins fnl f* **16/1**

554 **5** *1* **Murphy (IRE)**[19] 7739 10-10-11 **57** (t) MrSWalker 12 59+
(Nick Gifford) *t.k.h: hld up in tch towards rr: hdwy into midfield over 4f out: chsd ldng trio and rdn over 2f out: no imp tl kpt on ins fnl f* **11/4[1]**

0035 **6** *1 3/4* **Waldsee (GER)**[33] 7528 7-9-11 **50** MissBHampson(7) 9 50
(Sean Curran) *hld up in tch in midfield on outer: outpcd over 2f out: kpt on but no threat to wnr fnl f* **12/1**

2235 **7** *1* **Galiotto (IRE)**[49] 7169 6-10-7 **60** (v) MrGGorman(7) 5 59
(Gary Moore) *in tch in midfield: outpcd and rdn over 2f out: kpt on again ins fnl f but no threat to ldrs* **17/2**

0634 **8** *2 1/4* **Rollin 'n Tumblin**[28] 7629 8-10-0 **46** oh1 MrFWindsorClive 8 42
(Michael Attwater) *s.i.s: t.k.h: hld up in tch in rr: hdwy into midfield and drvn over 2f out: no prog and wl hld fnl 2f* **11/1**

020- **9** *5* **Rock With You**[516] 3817 5-10-4 **55** MrFMitchell(5) 6 45
(Pat Phelan) *t.k.h: chsd ldrs: rdn and unable qck wl over 2f out: wknd 2f out* **9/2[2]**

6050 **10** *2 1/2* **Young Jackie**[35] 7479 4-9-9 **46** oh1 MissKMargarson(5) 11 33
(George Margarson) *t.k.h: hld up in tch towards rr: rdn and outpcd over 2f out: wl hld and plugged on same pce after* **16/1**

0006 **11** *19* **Carlton Scroop (FR)**[187] 2653 9-9-9 **46** (p) MissMBryant(5) 3 10
(Paddy Butler) *chsd ldrs tl 3f out: sn struggling: bhd and eased ins fnl f: t.o* **66/1**

0360 **12** *9* **Surrey Dream (IRE)**[14] 7819 3-9-8 **55** MissAimeeMKing(7) 10 9
(Charlie Mann) *chsd ldrs tl lost pl qckly 4f out: bhd fnl 2f* **66/1**

0500 **P** **Kahfre**[16] 7791 5-10-9 **60** (vt) MrMatthewBarber(5) 2
(Gary Moore) *s.i.s: sn in tch in midfield: eased and p.u 9f out: dismntd* **8/1[3]**

3m 26.52s (0.82) **Going Correction** -0.05s/f (Stan)
WFA 3 from 4yo+ 8lb **13** Ran SP% **121.3**
Speed ratings (Par 101): **95,94,93,93,92 91,91,90,87,86 76,72,**
Tote Swingers 1&2 £27.10, 2&3 £15.00, 1&3 £28.00 CSF £215.66 CT £2157.84 TOTE £41.90: £11.20, £4.50, £3.90; EX 216.20 TRIFECTA Not won..
Owner Chester Racing Club Ltd **Bred** Goldford Stud And D O Pickering **Trained** Saighton, Cheshire

FOCUS
An ordinary race. It was slowly run with the first two always in the front pair. The winner is rated back to his early 3yo form.
Kahfre Official explanation: jockey said that the gelding lost its action
T/Plt: £171.50 to a £1 stake. Pool: £48,572.09 - 206.70 winning tickets. T/Qpdt: £73.90 to a £1 stake. Pool: £5,028.14 - 50.30 winning tickets. SP

8002 - (Foreign Racing) - See Raceform Interactive

7994 LINGFIELD (L-H)
Thursday, December 6

OFFICIAL GOING: Standard
Wind: Nil Weather: Cloudy and Cold

8003 32REDBET.COM (S) STKS 1m (P)
11:55 (11:55) (Class 6) 2-Y-O **£1,704** (£503; £251) **Stalls** High

Form RPR

0055 **1** **Roland**[8] 7919 2-8-12 53 (b) GrahamLee 9 60
(Kevin Ryan) *a.p: rdn 2f out: led over 1f out: r.o ins fnl f: in command ins fnl 110yds* **11/2[3]**

1613 **2** *1 1/2* **Divine Angel (IRE)**[3] 7971 2-8-12 65 LukeMorris 2 57
(Phil McEntee) *chsd ldrs: rdn 2f out: styd on ins fnl f: tk 2nd fnl stride: no imp on wnr* **7/2[1]**

0034 **3** *hd* **Dream About You (IRE)**[12] 7854 2-8-7 65 RobertHavlin 1 52
(Robert Mills) *led: rdn and hdd over 1f out: kpt on u.p tl no ex towards fin* **7/1**

3454 **4** *nse* **Maypole Joe (IRE)**[3] 7971 2-8-5 51 (v) EoinWalsh(7) 7 56
(David Evans) *in tch: rdn and nt qckn over 1f out: styd on ins fnl f: edgd rt towards fin: no imp on wnr* **14/1**

0330 **5** *1/2* **Woza Moya (USA)**[19] 7779 2-8-12 65 RobertWinston 6 55
(Gay Kelleway) *hld up: effrt to chse ldrs over 1f out: swtchd rt wl ins fnl f: kpt on towards fin: nvr able to chal* **4/1[2]**

041 **6** *3/4* **Amelia Hull**[12] 7854 2-8-12 55 JimmyQuinn 8 54+
(J S Moore) *sn pushed along towards rr: styd on u.p ins fnl f: nvr gng pce to chal but nrst fin* **6/1**

50 **7** *13* **Buona Fortuna**[19] 7780 2-8-7 0 DavidProbert 3 19
(Andrew Balding) *prom: rdn over 3f out: wknd over 2f out* **7/2[1]**

8 *4 1/2* **Immaculate Heart (IRE)** 2-8-7 0 FrankieMcDonald 4 8
(Natalie Lloyd-Beavis) *s.i.s: nvr really travelled in rr: lft wl bhd over 2f out* **66/1**

6666 **9** *3 1/2* **Garmelow Girl**[17] 7785 2-8-7 47 (b) SilvestreDeSousa 5
(Stuart Kittow) *midfield: rdn and wknd over 2f out: eased whn wl btn ins fnl f* **33/1**

1m 36.8s (-1.40) **Going Correction** -0.15s/f (Stan) **9** Ran SP% **117.7**
Speed ratings (Par 94): **101,99,99,99,98 98,85,80,77**
Tote swingers 1&2 £5.90, 1&3 £9.00, 2&3 £5.20 CSF £25.63 TOTE £11.80: £2.20, £3.20, £2.00; EX 45.00 Trifecta £439.00 Part won. Pool: £585.42 - .94 winning units..there was no bid for the winner.
Owner Mrs Angie Bailey **Bred** Minster Stud And Bickerton Racing **Trained** Hambleton, N Yorks

FOCUS
A low-grade juvenile seller, run at a steady pace. Clearly modest form.

NOTEBOOK
Roland was breaking his duck at the ninth time of asking. He was by no means well treated on these terms, but he showed more resolve than most and eventually came clear to win decisively, despite a high head carriage. Beaten a long way behind Divine Angel on their last meeting at Southwell, he was clearly more at home on Polytrack. (op 8-1)
Divine Angel(IRE) continues to perform creditably. Third in a claimer at Wolverhampton just three days previously, she appeared to run right up to her best under her penalty. It's possible that Fibresand suits best, but with Southwell out of action until at least February, she'll have to be kept to this quicker surface. (op 3-1)
Dream About You(IRE) was allowed the run of the race out in front, but was unable to sustain her challenge. She looked one of the more favourably treated coming into this and could well be dropped a few pounds as a result.
Maypole Joe(IRE) wasn't beaten far. (op 16-1)
Woza Moya(USA) was also not beaten that far. (op 7-1)
Amelia Hull stayed on well having been slowly away and outpaced in the early part of the race. Official explanation: vet said filly bled from the nose (op 4-1)
Buona Fortuna was one the first beaten and will struggle to win a race on this evidence. Official explanation: jockey said filly never travelled (op 11-4)

8004 £32 BONUS AT 32RED.COM H'CAP (DIV I) 7f (P)
12:25 (12:26) (Class 6) (0-65,65) 3-Y-O+ **£1,704** (£503; £251) **Stalls** Low

Form RPR

2666 **1** **Lucky Mark (IRE)**[12] 7861 3-8-13 57 JimmyQuinn 4 67
(Garry Moss) *chsd ldrs: wnt 2nd over 2f out: rdn over 1f out: led wl ins fnl f: r.o* **8/1**

0330 **2** *1* **Hoover**[84] 6172 4-9-5 63 (t) GrahamLee 11 70
(Jim Boyle) *racd keenly: chsd ldr: led 3f out: rdn over 1f out: hdd wl ins fnl f: no ex cl home* **6/1[3]**

0010 **3** *1/2* **Shaunas Spirit (IRE)**[12] 7857 4-9-3 64 PatrickHills(3) 1 70
(Dean Ivory) *in tch: effrt to chse ldrs over 1f out: styd on u.p ins fnl f: a hld* **10/1**

6000 **4** *1* **Efistorm**[3] 7967 11-9-2 65 NicoleNordblad(5) 9 68
(Joseph Tuite) *hld up towards rr: plld wd top of st wl over 1f out: prog ins fnl f: r.o: gng on at fin* **8/1**

0040 **5** *3/4* **Spin Again (IRE)**[1] 7998 7-9-7 65 AdamKirby 2 66
(John Ryan) *midfield: hdwy 2f out: chsd ldrs over 1f out: kpt on same pce and no further imp fnl 100yds* **7/2[1]**

3106 **6** *nk* **Frognal (IRE)**[12] 7857 6-9-6 64 (bt) WilliamCarson 8 64
(Violet M Jordan) *swtchd lft sn after s: hld up: rdn and hdwy over 1f out: kpt on ins fnl f: nvr able to chal* **9/2[2]**

0000 **7** *4 1/2* **Totally Trusted**[13] 7838 4-8-7 51 oh6 (p) LukeMorris 5 39
(Scott Dixon) *missed break: hld up: pushed along over 2f out: one pce fnl f: nvr able to chal* **33/1**

0560 **8** *8* **Inquisitress**[163] 3470 8-8-7 51 oh6 KieranO'Neill 10 17
(John Bridger) *missed break: hld up: niggled along over 3f out: nvr on terms* **66/1**

0101 **9** *1* **Demoiselle Bond**[36] 7482 4-9-4 62 RobertHavlin 3 26
(Lydia Richards) *led: rdn and hdd 3f out: wknd over 1f out: eased whn wl btn ins fnl f* **8/1**

006 **10** *2 3/4* **Beach Candy (IRE)**[37] 7471 3-8-3 52 (be) LeonnaMayor(5) 6
(Phil McEntee) *racd keenly on outer: chsd ldrs: wnt cl 2nd briefly wl over 2f out: sn hung bdly rt and lost pl off fnl bnd: bhd after* **25/1**

-001 **11** *7* **Intiqaal (IRE)**[231] 1487 5-9-5 63 (t) MartinDwyer 7
(Derek Shaw) *towards rr: pushed along 4f out: nvr on terms* **13/2**

1m 22.94s (-1.86) **Going Correction** -0.15s/f (Stan) **11** Ran SP% **118.7**
Speed ratings (Par 101): **104,102,102,101,100 99,94,85,84,81 73**
Tote swingers 1&2 £4.20, 1&3 £12.00, 2&3 £16.30 CSF £55.21 CT £499.77 TOTE £10.30: £1.90, £2.50, £3.50; EX 55.30 TRIFECTA Not won..
Owner Ron Hull **Bred** Mrs Lisa Kelly **Trained** Tickhill, S Yorks

FOCUS
There wasn't as much pace on as looked likely on paper and it paid to race handily. It was slightly the faster division. The winner rates a length personal best.
Beach Candy(IRE) Official explanation: jockey said filly hung right

8005 £32 BONUS AT 32RED.COM H'CAP (DIV II) 7f (P)
12:55 (12:55) (Class 6) (0-65,65) 3-Y-O+ **£1,704** (£503; £251) **Stalls** Low

Form RPR

6302 **1** **Muhandis (IRE)**[12] 7857 4-9-7 65 (b) SebSanders 3 73
(Nick Littmoden) *missed break: hld up: hdwy on inner 2f out: rdn over 1f out: edgd rt whn running on ins fnl f: led cl home* **3/1[1]**

5560 **2** *1/2* **Mr Knightley (IRE)**[21] 7722 3-9-6 64 (b) GrahamLee 1 70
(Jim Boyle) *led: kicked abt 2 l clr over 1f out: worn down cl home* **5/1[2]**

3 *hd* **Norwegian Reward (IRE)**[116] 4-8-7 51 oh6 SilvestreDeSousa 7 57
(Michael Wigham) *hmpd sn after s: towards rr: nt clr run on inner 2f out: hdwy over 1f out: sn plld out: r.o ins fnl f: fin wl* **7/1**

0604 **4** *1 3/4* **The Noble Ord**[19] 7776 3-9-5 63 (t) LiamKeniry 2 64
(Sylvester Kirk) *chsd ldrs: rdn over 1f out: styd on same pce ins fnl f* **13/2**

3240 **5** *1 1/2* **Dvinsky (USA)**[76] 6456 11-9-6 64 (b) JimmyQuinn 4 61
(Paul Howling) *rdn along s: sn chsd ldr: nt qckn w ldr over 1f out: lost 2nd ins fnl f: wknd fnl 75yds* **14/1**

346 **6** *2 3/4* **Jonnie Skull (IRE)**[21] 7733 6-8-9 53 (vt) KirstyMilczarek 9 43
(Phil McEntee) *racd keenly on outer: chsd ldrs: rdn over 1f out: one pce fnl f* **11/1**

4006 **7** *1 1/4* **Bengaline**[8] 7914 3-8-8 52 (b) NickyMackay 11 38
(Scott Dixon) *towards rr: u.p over 2f out: nvr on terms w ldrs* **33/1**

0000 **8** *shd* **Diddums**[8] 7915 6-8-0 51 oh6 (e) CarolineKelly(7) 10 37
(John Ryan) *missed break: pushed along wl over 1f out: nvr on terms w ldrs* **50/1**

3500 **9** *1* **Lady Mango (IRE)**[12] 7863 4-9-5 63 LukeMorris 5 46
(Ronald Harris) *chsd ldrs: pushed along briefly 5f out: rdn and wknd over 1f out* **11/2[3]**

2500 **10** *2 1/2* **Mataajir (USA)**[7] 7925 4-9-3 61 (t) MartinDwyer 8 37
(Derek Shaw) *chsd ldrs tl rdn and wknd 2f out* **8/1**

610 **11** *1 3/4* **Ishiamiracle**[37] 7469 3-9-2 65 (p) LeonnaMayor(5) 6 37
(Phil McEntee) *hld up towards rr: pushed along on wd outside on bnd 2f out: outpcd after* **14/1**

1m 23.16s (-1.64) **Going Correction** -0.15s/f (Stan) **11** Ran SP% **120.6**
Speed ratings (Par 101): **103,102,102,100,98 95,93,93,92,89 87**
Tote swingers 1&2 £4.10, 1&3 £4.40 , 2&3 £8.70 CSF £18.01 CT £101.27 TOTE £3.40: £1.60, £2.10, £2.90; EX 18.70 Trifecta £68.00 Pool: £519.13 - 5.72 winning units..
Owner A A Goodman **Bred** Shadwell Estate Co Ltd **Trained** Newmarket, Suffolk

FOCUS
There was considerably more pace on than in the first division, though it was 0.22sec slower. The winner looks the best guide to the form.

8006 32RED SUPPORTING BRITISH RACING MAIDEN STKS 6f (P)
1:25 (1:25) (Class 5) 2-Y-O **£2,264** (£673; £336; £168) **Stalls** Low

Form RPR

5222 **1** **Maid A Million**[20] 7738 2-8-12 73 SebSanders 3 71
(David Elsworth) *wnt rt s: mde all: qcknd over 1f out: sn rdn: r.o wl fnl f and sn wl in command* **5/2[2]**

0 **2** *3* **Go Far**[131] 4595 2-9-3 0 LukeMorris 1 67
(Alan Bailey) *prom: rdn and nt qckn over 1f out: styd on to take 2nd wl ins fnl f: no ch w wnr* **12/1**

4 **3** *hd* **Groove On (IRE)**[15] 7807 2-9-3 0 (t) AdamKirby 4 66
(Marco Botti) *forced rt s: hld up: rdn and outpcd over 1f out: prog ins fnl f: styd on towards fin: nt trble wnr* **9/2[3]**

0426 **4** *1* **Martial Art (IRE)**[7] 7926 2-9-3 82 JimmyFortune 6 63
(Andrew Balding) *racd keenly: prom: rdn and nt qckn over 1f out: no ex wl ins fnl f* **6/4[1]**

5 *1/2* **Calmer Waters (USA)** 2-8-12 0 LiamKeniry 7 57
(David Elsworth) *hld up towards rr: styd on ins fnl f: nvr nr to chal* **5/1**

50 **6** 2 3/4 **Exit Clause**[57] 6978 2-9-3 0 .... RobertWinston 8 54
(Tony Carroll) *hld up: hdwy on outer to chse ldrs 3f out: one pce fnl f* **33/1**

40 **7** 2 1/2 **Beauchamp Sunset**[12] 7855 2-9-3 0 .... RichardKingscote 2 46
(Hans Adielsson) *racd keenly: handy: lost pl 2f out: outpcd fnl f* **50/1**

56 **8** 7 **Beauchamp Astra**[12] 7855 2-8-7 0 .... NicoleNordblad(5) 5 20
(Hans Adielsson) *forced rt s: a bhd: nvr on terms* **50/1**

1m 12.89s (0.99) **Going Correction** -0.15s/f (Stan) **8** Ran SP% **118.0**
Speed ratings (Par 96): **87,83,82,81,80 77,73,64**
Tote swingers 1&2 £5.60, 1&3 £2.60, 2&3 £5.60 CSF £32.26 TOTE £3.60: £1.10, £5.10, £1.20; EX 27.20 Trifecta £515.20 Pool: £ 961.77 - 1.40 winning units..

Owner Khalifa Dasmal **Bred** Barton Bloodstock **Trained** Newmarket, Suffolk

FOCUS
Only a handful could be seriously fancied for this juvenile maiden. The winner had some of the better form on offer.

NOTEBOOK
Maid A Million proved much the best. She had a fair bit to find with the market leader on these terms, but she never looked in any danger once handed an easy lead. Second on her last three starts, including when dropped to 5f here the previous month, she looked much happier over this additional furlong. She threatens to be considerably better than her current rating of 72 and it's likely the ease of this success would not have gone unnoticed by the assessor. (op 7-4)

Go Far had shown little on his debut at Newmarket in the summer, but he took a significant step forward on this occasion. Bumped and chivvied along from 3f out, he stuck on well and is sure to appreciate a stiffer test of stamina. (op 16-1)

Groove On(IRE) ◆ finished best of all and will surely be capable of picking up a small race this winter. He once again showed signs of greenness, but really grabbed hold of the bridle close home and should be capable of further improvement. (op 11-2 tchd 4-1)

Martial Art(IRE) was a major disappointment and looks one to avoid. Keen in the early stages, he carried his head awkwardly throughout and didn't appear to be putting it all in. A mark of 82 will surely prove beyond him in handicaps and it may be that connections will have to drop him in grade if he's to get off the mark. Some headgear might help. (op 2-1)

Calmer Waters(USA) showed promise on this debut. Slowly away, he made some progress without being knocked around. (op 3-1)

8007 32REDPOKER.COM NURSERY 6f (P)
1:55 (1:58) (Class 6) (0-65,64) 2-Y-O **£1,704** (£503; £251) Stalls Low

Form RPR

6256 **1** **My Sweet Lord**[14] 7821 2-8-8 51 .... RichardKingscote 4 54
(Mark Usher) *hld up in rr: hdwy on inner over 1f out: r.o ins fnl f: led post* **8/1**

31 **2** nse **Small Fury (IRE)**[22] 7711 2-9-5 62 .... J-PGuillambert 8 65
(Jo Hughes) *w ldr: rdn over 1f out: styng on whn led and edgd rt ins fnl f: all out cl home: hdd post* **9/2**[2]

0620 **3** 2 **Katy Spirit (IRE)**[15] 7808 2-9-0 57 .... LiamKeniry 1 54
(Michael Blanshard) *midfield: hdwy on inner 2f out: styd on ins fnl f: nt pce to chal front pair* **33/1**

0643 **4** 3/4 **Persian Marvel (IRE)**[14] 7821 2-8-4 52 .... (b) NathanAlison(5) 11 47
(Jim Boyle) *led: rdn over 1f out: bmpd and hdd ins fnl f: no ex towards fin* **8/1**

0000 **5** 1 1/4 **Fit For A King (IRE)**[14] 7821 2-8-10 53 .... (b) RobertWinston 3 44
(John Best) *racd keenly: prom: rdn over 1f out: nt qckn: kpt on same pce ins fnl f* **16/1**

050 **6** 1 **Direct Trade**[15] 7813 2-8-12 55 .... DavidProbert 2 43
(Mark Usher) *hld up in midfield: rdn over 1f out: kpt on ins fnl f: nvr able to chal* **33/1**

5020 **7** 1/2 **Loki's Strike**[79] 6337 2-9-4 61 .... (v[1]) LukeMorris 6 47
(Mrs K Burke) *s.s: in rr: hdwy u.p over 1f out: no imp ins fnl f* **7/4**[1]

304 **8** 1/2 **Outbid**[71] 6579 2-9-4 61 .... FergusSweeney 9 46
(Jamie Osborne) *hld up: shkn up over 1f out: kpt on wout troubling ldrs ins fnl f* **15/2**

4040 **9** 1 1/4 **Robyn**[22] 7711 2-8-9 52 .... NickyMackay 5 33
(Scott Dixon) *in tch: effrt to chse ldrs 2f out: outpcd over 1f out: no imp after* **25/1**

0660 **10** 1 3/4 **World Freight Girl**[28] 7650 2-8-13 56 .... JimmyQuinn 12 32
(Dean Ivory) *towards rr: rdn 3f out: nvr on terms* **50/1**

1221 **11** 5 **Marmot Bay (IRE)**[6] 7932 2-9-7 64 .... FrankieMcDonald 7 25
(Alastair Lidderdale) *racd keenly on outer: chsd ldrs: rdn and wknd wl over 1f out* **11/2**[3]

1466 **12** 14 **Senora Lobo (IRE)**[28] 7650 2-8-9 52 .... SilvestreDeSousa 10
(Lisa Williamson) *racd on outer: chsd ldrs tl wknd over 2f out* **25/1**

1m 11.35s (-0.55) **Going Correction** -0.15s/f (Stan) **12** Ran SP% **125.3**
Speed ratings (Par 94): **97,96,94,93,91 90,89,88,87,84 78,59**
Tote swingers 1&2 £9.20, 1&3 £37.00, 2&3 £30.50 CSF £44.37 CT £1190.21 TOTE £7.70: £2.00, £1.40, £10.50; EX 54.00 Trifecta £1058.90 Part won. Pool: £1,411.88 - 0.20 winning units..

Owner The Ridgeway Alchemist's **Bred** Ridgeway Bloodstock **Trained** Upper Lambourn, Berks

FOCUS
A low-grade nursery, but it served up a tremendous finish. Weak form, but improvement from the runner-up.

NOTEBOOK
My Sweet Lord snatched victory in the shadow of the post. He had shown ability in a handful of starts on this surface, but he left behind a modest display at Kempton last time on his first appearance at this venue. The form probably doesn't amount a great deal but he did well in win, having been held up in a tactically run affair, and he's unlikely to be too heavily penalised. (op 10-1)

Small Fury(IRE) was always up with the pace and looked set to follow-up last month's Southwell win when making her way to the front. However, having been involved in a scrap with the eventual fourth, she just failed to last home. Still unexposed, she appears equally effective on Polytrack as on Fibresand. (op 4-1)

Katy Spirit(IRE) was taken off her feet when the race developed, but stayed on again close home. She appeared not to see out 7f at Kempton last time, but may be suited by a return that trip around this sharper track.

Persian Marvel(IRE) ran a brave race, but paid for his early exuberance in the straight. Fractious in the stalls, he's clearly got ability but will need to settle better if he's to be winning. (op 9-1 tchd 10-1)

Loki's Strike, the subject of significant market confidence, failed to get involved after missing the break. He made limited headway, however, and continues to disappoint. (op 2-1)

Marmot Bay(IRE) was beaten a long way out. She could never get to the front and failed to handle the bends. A return to Wolverhampton in lesser company might be on the cards. Official explanation: jockey said filly ran too free and failed to handle the bend (op 5-1)

Senora Lobo(IRE) Official explanation: jockey said filly had no more to give

8008 32RED H'CAP 6f (P)
2:25 (2:25) (Class 3) (0-95,95) 3-Y-0+ **£6,663** (£1,982; £990; £495) Stalls Low

Form RPR

5023 **1** **Swiss Cross**[8] 7897 5-9-6 94 .... (t) DavidProbert 4 102
(Phil McEntee) *chsd ldr: rdn to ld over 1f out: r.o ins fnl f: in control cl home* **11/2**[3]

0000 **2** 1 **Elna Bright**[19] 7774 7-8-11 85 .... JimmyQuinn 8 90
(Peter Crate) *a.p: effrt to take 2nd 1f out: tried to chal ins fnl f: one pce fnl strides* **20/1**

031 **3** hd **Corporal Maddox**[8] 7901 5-8-12 86 .... LukeMorris 1 90
(Ronald Harris) *s.i.s: pushed along to r in midfield: rdn and edgd rt whn no imp one ldrs over 1f out: prog wl ins fnl f: clsng at fin* **6/1**

0430 **4** hd **Sulis Minerva (IRE)**[15] 7817 5-8-8 85 .... RaulDaSilva(3) 10 89
(Jeremy Gask) *chsd ldrs: nt qckn over 1f out: styd on ins fnl f but a hld* **20/1**

1650 **5** nk **Woolfall Sovereign (IRE)**[208] 2071 6-8-13 87 .... IanMongan 6 90
(George Margarson) *hld up: hdwy ins fnl f: r.o: nt quite able to chal* **20/1**

0004 **6** 1 1/4 **Bajan Tryst (USA)**[8] 7897 6-9-7 95 .... (b) GrahamLee 9 94
(Kevin Ryan) *hld up: rdn and styd on ins fnl f: nvr able to rch ldrs* **9/2**[2]

2021 **7** nse **Mezzotint (IRE)**[159] 3639 3-9-2 90 .... AdamKirby 2 88
(Marco Botti) *hld up: hmpd early on jst bef 1st bnd: rdn over 1f out: styd on u.p ins fnl f: nvr able to trble ldrs* **11/8**[1]

0030 **8** 1 1/4 **Even Stevens**[26] 7690 4-9-7 95 .... (p) RobertWinston 3 89
(Scott Dixon) *led: pushed along over 2f out: rdn and hdd over 1f out: wknd fnl 100yds* **12/1**

2015 **9** 3/4 **Song Of Parkes**[40] 7411 5-8-7 81 oh1 .... DominicFox 5 73
(Peter Grayson) *racd keenly in midfield: hmpd over 4f out: pushed along over 2f out: btn over 1f out* **20/1**

1m 10.48s (-1.42) **Going Correction** -0.15s/f (Stan) **9** Ran SP% **116.7**
Speed ratings (Par 107): **103,101,101,101,100 99,99,97,96**
Tote swingers 1&2 £19.30, 1&3 £3.60, 2&3 £23.00 CSF £109.45 CT £677.16 TOTE £3.30: £1.20, £7.50, £2.20; EX 120.10 Trifecta £424.10 Pool: £ 1,221.51 - 2.16 winning units..

Owner Steve Jakes **Bred** Lordship Stud **Trained** Newmarket, Suffolk

FOCUS
A good turnout for the feature handicap and much to like about the way in which the winner went about it. The favourite disappointed and few got involved. The winner is rated back to his old best.

NOTEBOOK
Swiss Cross scampered clear for a first win for current connections. The 5yo hadn't won since the Derby meeting at Epsom last year, but he's been performing well in similarly competitive handicaps this term and most certainly wasn't winning out of turn. Racing from 5lb higher than when third at Kempton eight days previously, it took arguably a career-best to win this. This sharper track appears to suit him better than Kempton but his lofty rating means opportunities will be thin on the ground for him this winter. He is, though, entered in a valuable 5f handicap here next week and should make a bold bid under a penalty. (op 4-1)

Elna Bright laid down a stern challenge, but was burned off inside the final 100 yards. A smart performer on this surface, this was his best run for some time and should set him up nicely for the remainder of the campaign. (op 16-1)

Corporal Maddox found this much tougher than the claimer he won last week, but he was by no means disgraced. Closer at the finish than at any other stage, he would likely have appreciated a stronger early pace. (op 8-1)

Sulis Minerva(IRE) would also have appreciated a stronger gallop. (op 16-1)

Woolfall Sovereign(IRE), off the track for 208 days, looks to have continued the progression he made at the start of the year.

Mezzotint(IRE) was heavily backed, despite his 159-day absence. However, he was warm and edgy in the preliminaries and never looked like getting involved. (op 13-8)

8009 32RED.COM H'CAP 5f (P)
2:55 (2:55) (Class 4) (0-85,95) 3-Y-0+ **£4,075** (£1,212; £454; £454) Stalls High

Form RPR

4434 **1** **Bubbly Ballerina**[12] 7859 3-8-6 75 .... NatashaEaton(5) 7 82
(Alan Bailey) *chsd ldrs: effrt to chal ins fnl f: r.o to ld towards fin* **8/1**

0045 **2** 1/2 **Moorhouse Lad**[8] 7918 9-9-7 85 .... AdamKirby 9 90
(Garry Moss) *led narrowly: rdn 1f out: strly pressed ins fnl f: hdd and hld towards fin* **11/2**[3]

0106 **3** hd **Titus Gent**[172] 3188 7-9-2 83 .... RaulDaSilva(3) 6 87
(Jeremy Gask) *chsd ldrs: chalng ins fnl f: r.o u.p but jst hld* **33/1**

31 **3** dht **My Son Max**[59] 6939 4-9-0 83 .... WilliamTwiston-Davies(5) 1 90+
(P J O'Gorman) *in tch: nt clr run 1f out: rdr stopped riding briefly ins fnl f: swtchd rt ins fnl 100yds: r.o and clsd fnl strides* **7/2**[1]

0442 **5** 1 1/4 **Six Wives**[8] 7918 5-9-4 82 .... (p) IanMongan 2 82
(Scott Dixon) *w ldr: rdn over 1f out: stl ev ch ins fnl f tl no ex fnl 50yds* **5/1**[2]

0413 **6** 1 **Alaskan Bullet (IRE)**[8] 7918 3-9-2 80 .... GrahamLee 10 76
(Brian Ellison) *hld up in rr: rdn and styd on ins fnl f: nvr able to trble ldrs* **7/2**[1]

3651 **7** nk **Mother Jones**[12] 7863 4-8-3 74 .... EoinWalsh(7) 4 69
(David Evans) *in rr: hdwy into midfield over 3f out: rdn and outpcd over 1f out: nvr able to get to ldrs ins fnl f* **20/1**

1315 **8** nk **Havin' A Good Time (IRE)**[21] 7730 3-8-13 77 .... AndreaAtzeni 3 71
(Roger Varian) *hld up: rdn and no imp on ldrs over 1f out: styd on same pce ins fnl f* **6/1**

0006 **9** 3/4 **Taurus Twins**[6] 7937 6-8-7 71 oh1 .... (b) SilvestreDeSousa 8 62
(Richard Price) *in tch: rdn and no imp over 1f out: wknd fnl 50yds: eased whn btn cl home* **25/1**

5506 **10** 1 1/4 **Dancing Freddy (IRE)**[8] 7902 5-8-7 71 oh1 .... (bt) WilliamCarson 5 58
(Violet M Jordan) *a pushed along in rr: nvr on terms* **14/1**

57.68s (-1.12) **Going Correction** -0.15s/f (Stan) **10** Ran SP% **120.1**
Speed ratings (Par 105): **102,101,100,100,98 97,96,96,95,93**PL: My Son Max 0.60, Titus Gent 5.50. Tote swingers 1&2 £13.60, 1&3 (MSM) £4.90, 2&3 (MSM) £3.10 1&3 (TG) £22.30, 2&3 (TG) £16.40 CSF £51.94 CT £698.95 TOTE £13.00: £4.00, £2.80; EX 76.10 TRIFECTA Part won. Pool: £1,027.36. BB-ML-MSM £289.60 - 1.33 winnin27 Owner.

FOCUS
A blanket finish to this decent sprint handicap. Ordinary form with the winner pretty much to his best.

My Son Max Official explanation: jockey said gelding was denied a clear run

8010 32RED CASINO APPRENTICE H'CAP 1m (P)
3:25 (3:25) (Class 5) (0-70,68) 3-Y-0+ **£2,264** (£673; £336; £168) Stalls High

Form RPR

1605 **1** **Honey Of A Kitten (USA)**[12] 7867 4-8-10 64 .... (v) EoinWalsh(7) 6 74
(David Evans) *hld up: hdwy 2f out: rdn over 1f out: r.o to ld ins fnl f: wl in command towards fin* **7/1**

4615 **2** 1½ **Storm Runner (IRE)**[9] 7964 4 -8-155 JordanVaughan(7) 7 62
(George Margarson) *midfield: hdwy on inner under 2f out: led 1f out: hdd ins fnl f: unable to qck w wnr towards fin* **2/1**[1]

4402 **3** 1¼ **Fonterutoli (IRE)**[28] 7643 5 -8-956 (e) AdamBeschizza 2 60
(Roger Ingram) *midfield: nt qckn over 1f out: hdwy ins fnl f: r.o cl home: nvr gng to get there* **5/1**[2]

6400 **4** 1 **May's Boy**[83] 6208 4 -8-1163 (p) RachealKneller(5) 10 65
(Mark Usher) *prom: effrt over 1f out: sn trying to chal: kpt on u.p ins fnl f but nt pce of ldrs* **12/1**

0050 **5** ¾ **Ventura Sands (IRE)**[16] 7799 4 -9-066 GeorgeChaloner(5) 1 66
(Richard Fahey) *racd keenly: prom: pushed along over 2f out: rdn and nt qckn over 1f out: styd on same pce ins fnl f* **8/1**

3300 **6** ½ **Aquilifer (IRE)**[8] 7901 4 -9-065 ow1 (v[1]) ConorHarrison(5) 3 65
(Mrs K Burke) *chsd ldrs: led 3f out: rdn and hdd 1f out: no ex fnl 50yds* **6/1**[3]

6506 **7** ¾ **Putin (IRE)**[16] 7798 4 -8-754 oh9 (bt) RaulDaSilva 9 51
(Phil McEntee) *racd freely: led: hdd 3f out: rdn and stl ev ch over 1f out: no ex fnl 75yds* **33/1**

-666 **8** hd **Flying Phoenix**[21] 1907 4 -8-254 oh2 NatashaEaton(5) 11 51
(Dai Burchell) *prom early: in tch: outpcd over 1f out: n.d after* **12/1**

0000 **9** 5 **Marvo**[13] 7843 8 -8-1360 (b) AshleyMorgan 4 45
(Dai Burchell) *s.i.s: hld up: pushed along over 1f out: no imp* **33/1**

0550 **10** 2 **Man Of My Word**[8] 7917 3 -8-156 (p) JordanUys(7) 8 37
(Scott Dixon) *midfield: rdn and lost pl 3f out: sn bhd* **25/1**

06- **11** 72 **Dan's Martha**[441] 6285 4 -9-364 RyanClark 5
(Robin Dickin) *a u.p and bhd: lost tch over 4f out: t.o* **10/1**

1m 36.99s (-1.21) **Going Correction** -0.15s/f (Stan)
WFA 3 from 4yo+ 1lb **11**Ran SP% **122.1**
Speed ratings (Par 103): **100,98,97,96,95 95,94,94,89,87** **15**Tote swingers 1&2 £5.90, 1&3 £8.10, 2&3 £2.70 CSF £Tote swingers 1&2 £5.90, 1&3 £8.10, 2&3 £2.70 .
Owner Mrs E Evans **Bred** Kenneth L Ramsey And Sarah K Ramsey **Trained** Pandy, Monmouths

FOCUS
A fair apprentice handicap, run at a stern pace but in a modest overall time. The second in third are rated in line with their recent marks.
T/Jkpt: Not won. T/Plt: £297.70 to a £1 stake. Pool: £58,769.78 - 144.11 winning tickets. T/Qpdt: £25.10 to £1. Pool: £7895.45 - 232.45 w. tckts DO

8011a - 8015a (Foreign Racing) See RI

8003 LINGFIELD (L-H)
Friday, December 7

OFFICIAL GOING: Standard
Wind: medium,against Weather: dry, cold

8016 LIMPIO FACILITIES MANAGEMENT NURSERY 6f (P)
11:50 (11:50) (Class 5) (0-75,75) 2-Y-O **£2,385** (£704; £352) **Stalls** Low

Form RPR

6034 **1** **Ovett**[13] 7866 2 -9-270 (p) FergusSweeney 8 76
(Gary Moore) *racd freely: mde all: rdn and 2 l clr over 1f out: styd on wl: rdn out* **10/1**[3]

4530 **2** 1½ **Kodatish (IRE)**[21] 7745 2 -9-068 WilliamCarson 7 69
(Ronald Harris) *t.k.h: chsd wnr thrght: rdn 2f out: styd on same pce and no imp fnl f* **12/1**

2104 **3** shd **Seven Of Clubs (IRE)**[58] 6984 2 -9-775 (b) AdamKirby 6 76
(Noel Quinlan) *chsd ldng pair thrght: rdn and effrt ent fnl 2f: styd on same pce u.p fnl f* **4/1**[2]

0422 **4** 2 **Desert Sunrise**[13] 7866 2 -9-270 JimmyFortune 1 66
(Sir Michael Stoute) *in tch in midfield: rdn and effrt to chse ldng trio 2f out: no imp u.p fr over 1f out* **4/1**[2]

0650 **5** 4 **Our Sweet Art**[15] 7821 2 -8-862 ChrisCatlin 2 45
(John Best) *t.k.h: hld up in rr: pushed along 4f out: rdn and wknd wl over 1f out: no ch but styd on past btn horses fnl f* **33/1**

6033 **6** hd **Betzyoucan**[23] 7713 2 -8-1266 SilvestreDeSousa 5 48
(Mark Johnston) *in tch in midfield: rdn and struggling 2f out: wknd u.p over 1f out* **12/1**

0441 **7** 2¼ **Sakhee's Rose**[15] 7821 2 -9-270 GeorgeBaker 4 45
(Roger Charlton) *uns rdr gng to post but sn ct: dwlt: in tch in last pair: rdn and effrt whn edgd lft and bmpd rival wl over 1f out: no imp after: wknd fnl f* **5/2**[1]

3425 **8** 1¼ **Dumbarton Rock**[46] 7298 2 -9-169 (b) GrahamLee 3 41
(William Jarvis) *in tch in last trio: effrt and rdn whn edgd rt and bmpd rival wl over 1f out: no prog over 1f out: wknd fnl f* **4/1**[2]

1m 11.54s (-0.36) **Going Correction** -0.025s/f (Stan) **8**Ran SP% **116.0**
Speed ratings (Par 96): **101,99,98,96,90 90,87,85**
toteswingers 1&2 £15.90, 1&3 £6.70, 2&3 £7.40 CSF £121.15 CT £450.07 TOTE £14.40 : £5.30, £6.30, £1.80 ; EX 177.90 TRIFECTA Not won. .
Owner 8 Wealth Management **Bred** Whatton Manor Stud **Trained** Lower Beeding, W Sussex

FOCUS
A moderate nursery in which the pace was just fair and where it paid to race handily. The form stacks up pretty well.

NOTEBOOK
Ovett, who was wearing first-time cheekpieces, bounced out of the gates from a wide draw, quickly settled once on the lead and never saw another rival. He looked ideally suited by 6f on this track and should remain ultra competitive once reassessed for this success under similar conditions this winter, provided the headgear continues to have the desired effect. (tchd 8-1)
Kodatish(IRE) did well to finish second after racing too freely early in the contest. (op 14-1 tchd 16-1 and 10-1)
Seven Of Clubs (IRE)was returning from a two-month break and looks on a fair mark for a winter campaign.
Desert Sunrise held a good position to mount a challenge, but never made any significant progress in the home straight. (op 3-1)
Sakhee's Rose reportedly looked well, but unseated jockey George Baker on the way down to the start and never got into this contest from a hold-up position.

8017 BRITISH STALLION STUDS E.B.F./32RED.COM MAIDEN FILLIES' STKS (DIV I) 1m (P)
12:20 (12:21) (Class 5) 2-Y-O **£3,169** (£943; £471 ; £235) **Stalls** High

Form RPR

1 **Azma (USA)** 2 -9-00 MartinDwyer 2 72+
(Conrad Allen) *hld up wl in tch in midfield: rdn and hdwy to chse ldr ent fnl f: rn green and edgd rt but r.o strly to ld towards fin* **25/1**

00 **2** ½ **Sweet As Honey**[79] 6366 2 -9-00 SeanLevey 10 71
(Richard Hannon) *led and grad crossed to inner: rdn and wnt clr over 1f out: looked wnr tl tired wl ins fnl f and hdd towards fin* **10/1**

3 2 **Debdebdeb** 2 -9-00 JimmyFortune 5 66+
(Andrew Balding) *dwlt: sn bustled along and rcvrd to chse ldr after 2f: drvn and unable qck over 1f out: kpt on same pce ins fnl f* **15/2**

5 **4** hd **Fast Pace**[22] 7721 2 -9-00 GrahamLee 9 66
(Amanda Perrett) *t.k.h: chsd ldrs: effrt and racd awkwardly bnd 2f out: rdn: hld hd high and nt qckn over 1f out: j. shadow ins fnl f: one pce* **11/4**[1]

5 nk **Gertrude Versed** 2 -9-00 MarcHalford 8 65+
(John Gosden) *in tch towards rr: hdwy to chse ldrs over 2f out: rdn and unable qck 2f out: swtchd lft and kpt on ins fnl f* **4/1**[3]

6 hd **Soryah (IRE)** 2 -8-120 ow1 PatrickHills(3) 11 66+
(Luca Cumani) *t.k.h: hld up in tch in midfield: rdn and outpcd 2f out: rallied and kpt on ins fnl f: no threat to wnr* **10/1**

7 2¾ **Nur Jahan (IRE)** 2 -9-00 TedDurcan 4 58+
(David Lanigan) *dwlt: in tch in rr: rdn and effrt but stl plenty to do over 2f out: no imp tl kpt on ins fnl f: nvr trbld ldrs* **7/2**[2]

8 2¼ **Mesmerized (IRE)** 2 -9-00 AdamKirby 6 53+
(Marco Botti) *s.i.s: t.k.h: hld up in rr: rdn and no imp over 2f out: plugged on but no threat to ldrs fr over 1f out* **20/1**

00 **9** 1¼ **Portrait**[13] 7868 2 -9-00 ChrisCatlin 7 50
(Sir Mark Prescott Bt) *chsd ldrs: rdn and losing pl 3f out: wknd 2f out* **100/1**

10 ¾ **Pearla** 2 -9-00 KellyHarrison 1 49
(William Haggas) *dwlt: hld up in tch in rr: rdn and no prog over 2f out: kpt on same pce and wl hld fr over 1f out* **50/1**

002 **11** 1 **Serenata (IRE)**[64] 6817 2 -9-071 SilvestreDeSousa 3 46
(Paul Cole) *in tch in midfield: rdn and lost pl over 2f out: wknd over 1f out: bhd fnl f* **7/1**

1m 36.95s (-1.25) **Going Correction** -0.025s/f (Stan) **11**Ran SP% **122.9**
Speed ratings (Par 93): **105,104,102,102,102 101,99,96,95,94 93**
toteswingers 1&2 £64.10, 1&3 £19.40, 2&3 £16.60 CSF £259.37 TOTE £46.40 : £8.70, £5.00, £2.60; EX 831.80 TRIFECTA Not won. .
Owner A Al Hajri **Bred** Robert Raphaelson **Trained** Newmarket, Suffolk

FOCUS
This first division of a fair juvenile fillies' maiden. The runner-up is the key to the level.

NOTEBOOK
Azma(USA), who was a 38,000gns purchase in April, is the third foal out a well related 1m/8.5f turf stakes winner in the US. She settled in behind the leaders in the early stages and set about her task of chasing down the enterprisingly ridden runner-up with relish in the home straight. She looks a fairly decent prospect at around this trip or slightly further for next term.
Sweet As Honey found late market support returning from an 11-week break. She attempted to make all from a wide draw, and made a good fist of doing just that after jockey Sean Levey injected pace into the contest 3f out. It will be interesting to see what mark she gets for handicaps after this improved effort. (op 20-1 tchd 25-1)
Debdebdeb recovered quickly from a slow start, but proved one-paced in the home straight. (op 12-1)
Fast Pace reportedly looked well beforehand, but failed to build on a respectable Kempton debut the previous month and was still very green. (op 5-2 tchd 3-1)
Gertrude Versed, who is a half-sister to Lancashire Oaks winner Gertrude Bell for the same connections, came through quite pleasingly into fifth from the rear. (op 7-2)
Soryah(IRE) ◆ cost 100,000gns as a yearling and has a nice middle-distance pedigree. She kept on well close home. (op 16-1)
Nur Jahan (IRE)was a 180,000gns purchase as a yearling and has a decent 1m-1m2f pedigree. She lost a few lengths at the start, but was another to make some headway in the final furlong. (op 11-4 tchd 5-2)

8018 BRITISH STALLION STUDS E.B.F./32RED.COM MAIDEN FILLIES' STKS (DIV II) 1m (P)
12:50 (12:50) (Class 5) 2-Y-O **£3,169** (£943; £471 ; £235) **Stalls** High

Form RPR

1 **Streak** 2 -9-00 TedDurcan 9 64+
(David Lanigan) *s.i.s: in tch in rr: rdn and hdwy wl over 1f out: chal ins fnl f: rn green but r.o under hands and heels to ld towards fin* **8/1**

0 **2** ½ **Give Me High Five**[9] 7899 2 -9-00 SeanLevey 6 63
(Richard Hannon) *chsd ldr tl led 3f out: rdn wl over 1f out: kpt on u.p: hrd pressed fnl 100yds: hdd and no ex towards fin* **6/1**

3 hd **Special Meaning** 2 -9-00 SilvestreDeSousa 7 63
(Mark Johnston) *rn green: pressed ldrs: rdn and ev ch whn edgd rt bnd wl over 1f out: unable qck and styd on same pce ins fnl f* **11/4**[1]

0 **4** 1¼ **Easy Life**[22] 7721 2 -9-00 MartinDwyer 5 60+
(Marcus Tregoning) *hld up wl in tch: nt clr run and hmpd over 3f out: carried rt and outpcd bnd wl over 1f out: rallied and edgd lft 1f out: styd on same pce fnl 100yds* **7/1**

5 1½ **Familliarity** 2 -9-00 AndreaAtzeni 1 57
(Roger Varian) *chsd ldrs: rdn and effrt wl over 1f out: unable qck ent fnl f: wknd towards fin* **9/2**[3]

0 **6** nk **Poste Restante**[22] 7721 2 -9-00 MartinLane 10 56+
(David Simcock) *s.i.s: rn green: in tch in rr: rdn 5f out: outpcd and rn green bnd 2f out: rallied and styd on ins fnl f: no threat to ldrs* **12/1**

0 **7** ¾ **Salute To Seville (IRE)**[76] 3074 2 -9-00 LiamKeniry 8 54
(J S Moore) *hld up in tch in last quartet: rdn and unable qck wl over 1f out: edgd lft and styd on same pce fnl f* **33/1**

633 **8** 1½ **La Danza**[20] 7777 2 -8-970 NatashaEaton(5) 2 51
(Alan Bailey) *wl in tch in midfield: rdn and lost pl over 2f out: bhd and no imp fnl 2f* **7/2**[2]

0 **9** 70 **Actonetaketwo**[149] 3959 2 -9-00 WilliamCarson 3
(Ron Hodges) *t.k.h: led tl 3f out: sn lost pl and dropping out whn short of room and hit rail over 2f out: t.o fnl 2f* **33/1**

1m 39.14s (0.94) **Going Correction** -0.025s/f (Stan) **9**Ran SP% **118.5**
Speed ratings (Par 93): **94,93,93,92,90 90,89,88,18**
toteswingers 1&2 £10.30, 1&3 £5.80, 2&3 £4.60 CSF £56.76 TOTE £8.90 : £3.20, £2.10, £1.40 ; EX 79.90 TRIFECTA Not won.
Owner B E Nielsen **Bred** The Brook Stud Co Ltd **Trained** Upper Lambourn, Berks

FOCUS
The second division of a fair juvenile fillies' maiden in which the winner recorded a significantly slower time than in the first instalment. It's hard to rate the form higher than the first leg but it could be worth 10-12lb more.

NOTEBOOK
Streak ◆, who cost 32,000gns as a yearling, missed the break but was able to tag on to the rear of the pack with the early pace not really picking up until 3f out. She came through to win well enough, but the field were still quite bunched at the finish. She will improve for the experience and a looks a fair handicapper for next term at up to 1m2f. (op 10-1)
Give Me High Five was well placed to take up the pace gauntlet 3f out and improved markedly on her debut over the same C&D the previous month. (op 8-1)
Special Meaning ◆ was an 150,000gns purchase as a yearling and is a half-sister to 1000 Guineas winner Speciosa. She showed understandable inexperience in an always prominent position and should build on this display. (tchd 3-1)

Easy Life built on her Kempton debut run the previous month in a retained hood, but had a troubled passage through the race. She can continue to progress over further. (op 10-1)
Familliarity would have been better served by a more honest gallop on debut. (op 4-1 tchd 5-1)
La Danza performed disappointingly. (op 11-4)

8019 FRED AND RON GIBSON MEMORIAL CLAIMING STKS 1m 2f (P)
1:20 (1:20) (Class 6) 3-Y-0+ £1,704 (£503; £251) Stalls Low

Form RPR
-002 1 **Super Say (IRE)**[13] 7867 6-9-4 90 (t) JamieSpencer 1 75+
(Jamie Osborne) *hld up wl in tch: trcking ldrs and travelling wl whn nt clr run 2f out: gap opened and rdn to chal 1f out: rdn and hands and heels and qcknd to ld ins fnl f: comf* 4/6[1]
/04- 2 ¾ **Noguchi (IRE)**[394] 7328 7-9-8 78 TomMcLaughlin 8 77
(Michael Murphy) *dwlt: t.k.h: hld up in tch in rr: rdn and hdwy on outer 3f out: chsd ldrs and drvn over 1f out: kpt on ins fnl f: wnt 2nd last strides* 7/1[3]
-220 3 nk **Tornado Force (IRE)**[132] 4596 4-9-8 87 JimmyFortune 9 77
(Chris Dwyer) *chsd ldrs: rdn to chal 2f out: drvn to ld jst over 1f out: hdd and one pce ins fnl f: lost 2nd last strides* 7/2[2]
0410 4 1 ¾ **Aviso (GER)**[33] 2498 8-9-0 63 AdamKirby 6 65
(David Evans) *hld up in tch in midfield: rdn and effrt over 1f out: kpt on u.p ins fnl f* 14/1
-360 5 1 ¼ **Foxhaven**[147] 4061 10-9-4 68 (v) GeorgeBaker 2 67
(Patrick Chamings) *w ldr: rdn over 1f out: drvn and no ex ins fnl f: wknd fnl 100yds* 16/1
3503 6 1 ¾ **Anychanceofabirdie (USA)**[23] 7702 3-8-5 62 MartinLane 3 53
(David Simcock) *chsd ldrs: rdn and lost pl bnd 2f out: rallied u.p over 1f out: no imp ins fnl f* 25/1
10-0 7 nse **Electrician**[27] 6768 3-8-8 85 GeorgeBuckell(7) 4 63
(Tim Pitt) *led: rdn wl over 1f out: hdd jst over 1f out: wknd ins fnl f* 33/1
000 8 1 ½ **Mad Ginger Alice**[37] 7479 4-7-12 46 NathanAlison(5) 5 45
(Olivia Maylam) *hld up in tch in last trio: rdn and effrt on inner over 1f out: no imp and styd on same pce fnl f* 66/1
-060 9 hd **Bolanderi (USA)**[9] 7905 7-8-8 61 (t) KieranO'Neill 7 50
(Andy Turnell) *in tch in midfield: rdn and struggling 2f out: outpcd and drvn over 1f out: one pce and wl hld fnl f* 50/1
0050 10 40 **Legal Legacy**[9] 7905 6-9-2 63 AmirQuinn 10
(Richard Rowe) *hld up in tch in rr: stl rr but wl in tch whn sddle slipped ent fnl 2f: sn eased and lost tch: t.o* 25/1

2m 6.57s (-0.03) **Going Correction** -0.025s/f (Stan)
WFA 3 from 4yo+ 3lb 10 Ran SP% 121.3
Speed ratings (Par 101): **99,98,98,96,95 94,94,93,92,60**
toteswingers 1&2 £2.20, 1&3 £1.50, 2&3 £4.10 CSF £6.16 TOTE £1.70: £1.10, £2.00, £1.60; EX 5.50 Trifecta £14.90 Pool: £932.05 - 46.61 winning units..Super Say was claimed by Mr Steven Nightingale for £10,000.
Owner Dr Marwan Koukash **Bred** Peter Jones And G G Jones **Trained** Upper Lambourn, Berks

FOCUS
Not a bad claimer, but it was slowly run and the form is rated cautiously.
Legal Legacy Official explanation: jockey said saddle slipped.

8020 32RED CASINO H'CAP 1m 2f (P)
1:55 (1:56) (Class 5) (0-75,75) 3-Y-0+ £2,385 (£704; £352) Stalls Low

Form RPR
0000 1 **Casual Mover (IRE)**[16] 7805 4-9-3 71 GeorgeBaker 6 78+
(John Best) *hld up in tch in last trio: rdn and effrt whn nt clr run wl over 1f out: swtchd lft and hdwy 1f out: rn wl u.p to ld on post* 7/1[3]
0304 2 nse **Sakhee's Pearl**[16] 7805 6-9-6 74 IanMongan 3 81
(Jo Crowley) *hld up in tch in midfield: hdwy on inner over 2f out: drvn and pressed ldrs 1f out: ev ch ins fnl f: led wl ins fnl f: hdd on post* 5/1[2]
30 3 shd **Saoi (USA)**[15] 7823 5-9-6 74 ShaneKelly 1 81
(William Knight) *hld up in tch in midfield: hdwy over 2f out: rdn and chsd ldrs over 1f out: styd on strly u.p ins fnl f: snatched 3rd last stride* 20/1
0-33 4 shd **Honour**[16] 7818 3-8-13 70 JimmyFortune 7 77
(Sir Michael Stoute) *chsd ldr tl 7f out: styd chsng ldrs tl wnt 2nd again over 2f out: sn drvn and ev ch after tl no ex and lost 2 pls last strides* 9/2[1]
0450 5 ½ **Hydrant**[18] 7792 6-8-12 66 AdamBeschizza 8 72
(Peter Salmon) *led tl 6f out: chsd ldr after tl led again over 2f out: sn hrd pressed and drvn: battled on wl tl hdd and no ex wl ins fnl f* 7/1[3]
2103 6 ½ **Zenarinda**[20] 7768 5-8-11 65 MartinDwyer 5 70
(Mark H Tompkins) *chsd ldrs: rdn and chsd ldng pair 2f out: kpt on same pce u.p ins fnl f* 10/1
1063 7 1 **Elijah Pepper (USA)**[3] 7976 7-9-1 69 AdamKirby 9 72
(Conor Dore) *hld up in tch in midfield: hdwy u.p ent fnl f: r.o but nvr gng to rch ldrs* 12/1
0010 8 ¾ **Menadati (USA)**[43] 7348 4-8-7 61 KirstyMilczarek 2 62
(Peter Hiatt) *short of room s and s.i.s: t.k.h: hld up in tch in rr: rdn and effrt wl over 1f out: styd on ins fnl f: nvr trbld ldrs* 20/1
/35- 9 ½ **Al Amaan**[17] 315 7-9-0 68 FergusSweeney 13 68
(Gary Moore) *hld up in tch towards rr: rdn and effrt over 1f out: styd on u.p ins fnl f: nvr trbld ldrs* 50/1
1205 10 ½ **Navajo Charm**[16] 7811 3-8-5 62 MartinLane 4 61
(Alan Jarvis) *chsd ldrs: rdn and unable qck whn hung rt bnd 2f out: kpt on u.p ins fnl f* 12/1
6/40 11 7 **Tri Nations (UAE)**[29] 7652 7-8-13 67 (vt) LiamKeniry 11 52
(Anthony Middleton) *hld up in tch in last trio: rdn and no imp over 1f out: wknd 1f out* 50/1
3165 12 1 ¾ **St Ignatius**[7] 6703 5-9-7 75 (p) GrahamLee 10 57
(Alan Bailey) *in tch in midfield: pushed along and hdwy 5f out: rdn over 3f out: wknd 2f out* 7/1[3]
4000 13 nk **Final Drive (IRE)**[18] 7790 6-9-7 75 (tp) StevieDonohoe 14 56
(John Butler) *stdd s: t.k.h: hld up in detached last: rdn over 2f out: lost tch 2f out* 14/1
4600 14 1 ¼ **Star Date (IRE)**[31] 7617 3-9-3 74 (b[1]) NickyMackay 12 53
(Gerard Butler) *t.k.h: chsd ldrs: wnt 2nd 7f out tl led 6f out: rdn and hdd over 2f out: sn lost pl: wl btn and eased fnl f* 7/1[3]

2m 4.4s (-2.20) **Going Correction** -0.025s/f (Stan)
WFA 3 from 4yo+ 3lb 14 Ran SP% 129.4
Speed ratings (Par 103): **107,106,106,106,106 106,105,104,104,103 98,96,96,95**
toteswingers 1&2 £8.60, 1&3 £39.90, 2&3 £36.30 CSF £43.66 CT £698.85 TOTE £8.30: £2.20, £2.60, £7.00; EX 65.80 Trifecta £793.20 Part won. Pool: £1,057.70 - 0.10 winning units..
Owner Brian Goodyear & Rhonda Wilson **Bred** M S And C S Griffiths **Trained** Hucking, Kent

FOCUS
A tight handicap with a bunch finish, and the bare form is only ordinary.

Casual Mover(IRE) Official explanation: trainer said regarding apparent improvement in form that gelding was better suited by fitting of hood.

8021 32RED SUPPORTING BRITISH RACING MAIDEN STKS 7f (P)
2:30 (2:30) (Class 5) 3-Y-0+ £2,385 (£704; £352) Stalls Low

Form RPR
5305 1 **Flavius Victor (IRE)**[72] 6582 3-9-3 66 GeorgeBaker 5 66
(Patrick Chamings) *stdd s: hld up in rr: gd hdwy on outer to chse ldrs whn hung rt and wnt v wd bnd 2f out: rdn and rallied to ld over 1f out: kpt on fnl f: rdn out* 6/5[1]
6605 2 1 ¼ **The Mongoose**[13] 7857 4-9-3 64 (t) AdamKirby 6 63
(David Evans) *hld up in last pair: swtchd rt and effrt wl over 1f out: chsd wnr 1f out: styd on same pce and a hld fnl f* 6/4[2]
06- 3 3 ¾ **Marshall Art**[22] 7709 3-9-3 0 KirstyMilczarek 2 53
(David Evans) *led: rdn and hdd over 1f out: outpcd and btn 1f out: plugged on fnl f* 50/1
0322 4 ½ **Summer Sun**[9] 7903 3-8-12 52 GrahamLee 7 46
(Phil McEntee) *t.k.h: chsd ldrs: rdn and ev ch briefly over 1f out: sn outpcd and btn 1f out: plugged on* 6/1[3]
00-0 5 4 **Back For Tea (IRE)**[15] 7822 4-9-3 41 (b[1]) TomMcLaughlin 4 40
(Phil McEntee) *chsd ldr: rdn and ev ch 2f out: sn struggling and btn: wknd over 1f out* 100/1
2405 6 2 ¼ **King's Future**[9] 7903 3-9-3 55 WilliamCarson 1 34
(Lee Carter) *rdn along leaving stalls: chsd ldrs: rdn and unable qck 2f out: wknd over 1f out* 10/1

1m 24.49s (-0.31) **Going Correction** -0.025s/f (Stan) 6 Ran SP% 111.8
Speed ratings (Par 103): **100,98,94,93,89 86**
toteswingers 1&2 £1.10, 1&3 £10.30, 2&3 £7.20 CSF £3.22 TOTE £2.00: £1.40, £1.10; EX 4.60 Trifecta £39.00 Pool: £1,716.06 - 32.97 winning units..
Owner P R Chamings F T Lee **Bred** Western Bloodstock **Trained** Baughurst, Hants

FOCUS
A very modest maiden in which they went a decent contested pace, enabling the form principals to come to the fore in the final furlong. Shaky form, rated cautiously around the winner.

8022 32RED SUPPORTS THE GERAINT JONES BENEFIT H'CAP 6f (P)
3:05 (3:05) (Class 4) (0-85,83) 3-Y-0+ £4,075 (£1,212; £606; £303) Stalls Low

Form RPR
1013 1 **Forest Edge (IRE)**[13] 7860 3-9-2 78 (b) AdamKirby 3 92
(David Evans) *mde all: rdn and qcknd clr 2f out: in command and rn wl fnl f* 11/4[2]
0552 2 2 **Lujeanie**[2] 7995 6-9-4 80 (p) GrahamLee 2 88
(Dean Ivory) *t.k.h: chsd ldrs tl effrt to chse wnr 2f out: rdn wl over 1f out: kpt on but comf hld fnl f* 9/4[1]
0000 3 3 ¾ **Italian Tom (IRE)**[38] 7464 5-9-2 78 WilliamCarson 6 74
(Ronald Harris) *chsd ldrs: rdn and unable qck ent fnl 2f: wl hld and one pce fr over 1f out* 16/1
0012 4 1 ¼ **Millibar (IRE)**[13] 7859 3-9-6 82 (b) TomMcLaughlin 1 74
(Nick Littmoden) *awkward leaving stalls: hld up in last pair: rdn and effrt ent fnl 2f: wl hld and styd on same pce fr over 1f out* 9/2
2022 5 ½ **I See You**[21] 7742 3-8-12 74 ow1 (p) JimmyFortune 4 64
(Peter Makin) *chsd ldr tl 2f out: c wd and lost pl wl over 1f out: wl hld after* 8/1
0 6 1 ½ **Albaqaa**[36] 7502 7-9-7 83 KieranO'Neill 5 68
(P J O'Gorman) *t.k.h: hld up in last pair: hung bdly rt and v wd bnd 2f out: nt rcvr and no ch after: hung lft fnl f* 7/2[3]

1m 11.18s (-0.72) **Going Correction** -0.025s/f (Stan) 6 Ran SP% 114.8
Speed ratings (Par 105): **103,100,95,93,93 91**
toteswingers 1&2 £2.30, 1&3 £4.60, 2&3 £7.50 CSF £9.71 TOTE £2.50: £1.10, £3.10; EX 11.80 Trifecta £97.90 Pool: £1,127.95 - 8.64 winning units..
Owner Peter Swinnerton **Bred** Alberto Panetta **Trained** Pandy, Monmouths

FOCUS
A weak handicap where the winner dictated. The time was ordinary but the winner rates a small personal best.

8023 £32 BONUS AT 32RED.COM H'CAP 1m 4f (P)
3:40 (3:40) (Class 6) (0-65,66) 3-Y-0+ £1,704 (£503; £251) Stalls Low

Form RPR
1023 1 **Thecornishcowboy**[9] 7905 3-9-5 65 (t) AdamKirby 14 72
(John Ryan) *hld up in tch in midfield: rdn and effrt to ld ent fnl f: idling in front fnl 100yds: jst lasted hame* 3/1[1]
0501 2 shd **Strike Force**[9] 7905 8-9-6 66 6ex (t) NatashaEaton(5) 8 73
(Alison Hutchinson) *hld up in tch towards rr: swtchd to outer and effrt over 1f out: str run ins fnl f: pressing wnr cl home: jst failed* 14/1
4450 3 ¾ **Joe The Coat**[168] 3345 3-9-5 65 MartinDwyer 12 71
(Mark H Tompkins) *t.k.h: chsd ldrs tl wnt 2nd 7f out: rdn and ev ch 2f out: unable qck 1f out u.p over 1f out: one pce ins fnl f* 25/1
0000 4 ¾ **Eagle Nebula**[21] 7744 8-9-9 64 IanMongan 13 68
(Brett Johnson) *rdn along leaving stalls: in tch in midfield: hdwy to chse ldrs 5f out: rdn and ev ch 2f out: styd on same pce fnl f* 25/1
0023 5 nk **Viola Da Gamba (IRE)**[22] 7731 3-9-1 61 (b[1]) ShaneKelly 4 65
(William Knight) *t.k.h: hld up wl in tch: rdn and sltly outpcd over 1f out: rallied and kpt on fnl 100yds* 10/1
6104 6 nk **Archina (IRE)**[14] 7841 3-9-0 60 TedDurcan 9 63
(Chris Wall) *t.k.h: chsd ldr tl 7f out: chsd ldrs after: swtchd ins and pressed ldrs u.p over 1f out: one pce ins fnl f* 9/2[3]
1-30 7 shd **Ninfea (IRE)**[14] 7839 4-9-10 65 (t) LiamKeniry 5 68
(David Bridgwater) *t.k.h: hld up in tch towards rr: rdn over 2f out: hdwy u.p fnl f: styd on wl fnl 100yds: nt rch ldrs* 14/1
30/0 8 nk **Whiepa Snappa (IRE)**[37] 7479 5-8-6 52 JemmaMarshall(5) 11 55
(Pat Phelan) *dwlt: sn in tch in midfield: rdn and unable qck wl over 1f out: kpt on fnl f but nt pce to chal* 20/1
5006 9 nk **Mariet**[16] 7811 3-8-13 59 GrahamLee 10 61
(Suzy Smith) *led: rdn and hrd pressed 2f out: hdd ent fnl f: no ex and one pce fnl f: btn whn short of room cl home* 20/1
0600 10 shd **Bennelong**[32] 7596 6-9-3 58 (p) AmirQuinn 7 60
(Richard Rowe) *stdd s: hld up in tch in rr: rdn and effrt over 1f out: styd on wl fnl 100yds: nt rch ldrs* 33/1
2431 11 nk **Kampai**[16] 7819 4-8-13 61 ShelleyBirkett(7) 3 63
(Julia Feilden) *hld up in tch towards rr: rdn and effrt on inner over 1f out: kpt on but nvr looked like threatening ldrs: short of room towards fin* 5/1
0000 12 ½ **Shirataki (IRE)**[9] 7893 4-9-8 63 ChrisCatlin 6 64
(Peter Hiatt) *t.k.h: chsd ldrs tl rdn and lost pl jst over 2f out: styd on same pce fr over 1f out: btn whn short of room ins fnl f* 20/1

0210 **13** ¾ **Sir Dylan**[13] 7869 3-9-0 60 WilliamCarson 1 60
(Ronald Harris) *stdd s: t.k.h: hld up bhd: clsd on to rr of field 7f out: effrt and trying to switch rt over 1f out: nvr enough room and no real hdwy fnl f* **25/1**

60-0 **14** 1¾ **Strewth (IRE)**[16] 7805 4-9-9 64 GeorgeBaker 2 61
(John Best) *t.k.h: hld up in midfield: shuffled bk to rr but stl wl in tch over 2f out: rdn and no imp 1f out: wl hld and eased towards fin* **4/1**[2]

2m 33.35s (0.35) **Going Correction** -0.025s/f (Stan)
WFA 3 from 4yo+ 5lb **14** Ran SP% **131.0**
Speed ratings (Par 101): **97,96,96,95,95 95,95,95,95,95 94,94,93,92**
toteswingers 1&2 £9.90, 1&3 £21.90, 2&3 £38.50 CSF £47.31 CT £952.95 TOTE £3.60: £1.20, £5.50, £9.30; EX 53.20 Trifecta £873.50 Pool: £1,560.80 - 1.34 winning units..
Owner C Letcher & J Ryan **Bred** Hadi Al Tajir **Trained** Newmarket, Suffolk

FOCUS
An ordinary pace resulted in a bunched finish here. Muddling, unreliable form.
T/Plt: £1,839.90 to a £1 stake. Pool: £51,569.42 - 20.46 winning tickets T/Qpdt: £8.50 to a £1 stake. Pool: £8,045.52 - 696.42 winning tickets SP

8024 - 8031a (Foreign Racing) - See Raceform Interactive

8016 LINGFIELD (L-H)
Saturday, December 8

OFFICIAL GOING: Standard
Wind: Nil Weather: Fine

8032 32RED SUPPORTING BRITISH RACING NURSERY — 1m 2f (P)
11:35 (11:35) (Class 5) (0-75,72) 2-Y-O — **£2,911** (£866; £432; £216) **Stalls** Low

Form RPR

6421 **1** **Paddy's Saltantes (IRE)**[9] 7924 2-9-2 67 AndreaAtzeni 8 70
(J S Moore) *a.p: rdn over 3f out: led ins fnl f: styd on* **5/1**[2]

050 **2** ½ **Grendisar (IRE)**[14] 7868 2-9-0 65 AdamKirby 9 67+
(Marco Botti) *hld up: hdwy 2f out: sn rdn: r.o ins fnl f: nt rch wnr* **4/1**[1]

6003 **3** hd **Classy Trick (USA)**[5] 7973 2-8-6 57 WilliamCarson 1 59
(Richard Fahey) *led: hdd over 6f out: chsd ldrs: rdn to ld over 1f out: hdd and unable qck ins fnl f* **10/1**

440 **4** 3½ **Lucky Mountain**[10] 7899 2-9-3 68 IanMongan 4 63
(Scott Dixon) *sn pushed along and prom: lost pl 4f out: hdwy over 1f out: styd on same pce ins fnl f* **16/1**

0064 **5** 2 **Walter White (IRE)**[10] 7919 2-8-13 64 (p) JimmyFortune 6 55
(Andrew Balding) *chsd ldrs: led over 6f out: rdn and hdd over 1f out: no ex fnl f* **4/1**[1]

6000 **6** 2¾ **Epsom Flyer**[17] 7814 2-8-0 51 oh1 ow2 SilvestreDeSousa 3 37
(Pat Phelan) *hld up: pushed along 5f out: rdn and hung lft over 1f out: nvr on terms* **8/1**

6554 **7** 1½ **Club House (IRE)**[17] 7814 2-9-0 65 GrahamLee 5 48
(Robert Mills) *prom: chsd ldr over 3f out tl rdn 2f out: wknd fnl f* **4/1**[1]

2260 **8** 11 **Sunblazer (IRE)**[3] 7994 2-9-7 72 MartinDwyer 2 34
(William Muir) *chsd ldrs: pushed along over 4f out: rdn and wknd over 1f out* **7/1**[3]

2m 4.49s (-2.11) **Going Correction** -0.125s/f (Stan) **8** Ran SP% **115.3**
Speed ratings (Par 96): **103,102,102,99,98 95,94,85**
Tote Swingers: 1&2 £4.90, 1&3 £2.60, 2&3 £8.60 CSF £25.52 CT £192.34 TOTE £6.50: £2.50, £1.90, £2.80; EX 51.70 Trifecta £248.70 Part won. Pool: £331.69 - 0.30 winning units..
Owner Wall To Wall Partnership **Bred** Tom And Hazel Russell **Trained** Upper Lambourn, Berks

FOCUS
Ordinary nursery form, the race lacking depth.

NOTEBOOK
Paddy's Saltantes(IRE), quietly progressive, saw out the extra two furlongs to follow up his recent Kempton maiden win. He didn't travel as smoothly as one would ideally like but he kept finding down the outside before kicking clear in the straight and having just enough to hold on from the fast finisher. This is probably as far as he needs to go in terms of trip, but he's a horse very much going the right way and there is every chance he can hold his own off slightly higher marks. (op 4-1)
Grendisar(IRE) can probably be considered slightly unlucky given he was caught in a pocket at a crucial stage and the winner got first run on him. He finished strongly down the outside but the line was always coming too soon. This was his best run so far and he looks well up to winning a race off this sort of mark. (op 6-1)
Classy Trick(USA) had every chance around the inside and ran with credit, albeit without screaming that he'll be getting off the mark soon. (op 8-1)
Lucky Mountain was again fairly one-paced at the business end, the switch to handicaps failing to revive his fortunes. He hasn't gone on from a promising debut run. (op 10-1)
Walter White(IRE) Official explanation: jockey said colt hung right.

8033 32RED EBF MAIDEN STKS — 7f (P)
12:05 (12:07) (Class 5) 2-Y-O — **£3,137** (£933; £466; £116; £116) **Stalls** Low

Form RPR

5 **1** **Staffhoss**[24] 7707 2-9-3 0 SilvestreDeSousa 13 74+
(Mark Johnston) *chsd ldr: rdn over 2f out: styd on u.p to ld nr fin* **6/1**

5 **2** ½ **Lady Malet**[15] 7840 2-8-12 0 AdamBeschizza 5 68
(William Haggas) *sn led: clr 2f out: rdn and hdd nr fin* **25/1**

5 **3** 1 **Consign**[37] 7498 2-9-3 0 JimmyFortune 11 70
(Jeremy Noseda) *mid-div: pushed along 4f out: hdwy and edgd rt over 2f out: sn rdn: styd on* **2/1**[1]

50 **4** 1½ **Plenum (GER)**[5] 7962 2-9-3 0 TedDurcan 8 66
(David Lanigan) *s.i.s: sn pushed along in rr: hdwy over 2f out: sn carried rt: r.o ins fnl f: nvr nrr* **16/1**

4 dht **Rapscallion Deep (IRE)** 2-9-3 0 PhillipMakin 3 66+
(Kevin Ryan) *mid-div: hdwy and hung rt fr over 2f out: r.o ins fnl f: nt rch ldrs* **7/2**[2]

02 **6** ½ **Great Demeanor (USA)**[17] 7807 2-9-3 0 LiamKeniry 1 65
(David Elsworth) *chsd ldrs: rdn over 2f out: no ex ins fnl f* **5/1**[3]

30 **7** shd **First Sargeant**[24] 7706 2-9-3 0 (b) GrahamLee 6 65+
(Marco Botti) *trckd ldrs: plld hrd: shkn up over 1f out: styd on* **12/1**

8 1¾ **Hurry Home Poppa (IRE)** 2-9-3 0 RichardKingscote 7 60
(Tom Dascombe) *prom: rdn over 2f out: styd on same pce fr over 1f out* **16/1**

60 **9** 2½ **Spirit Of Success**[43] 7364 2-8-12 0 StevieDonohoe 12 48
(Michael Bell) *s.i.s: bhd tl styd on ins fnl f: nvr nrr* **33/1**

10 ½ **Passionate Diva (USA)** 2-8-12 0 ChrisCatlin 9 48
(Ed Vaughan) *sn pushed along in rr: hdwy 1/2-way: hmpd and wknd over 2f out* **20/1**

11 nse **Striking Echo** 2-9-3 0 ShaneKelly 4 52
(Reg Hollinshead) *mid-div: lost pl after 1f: n.d after* **66/1**

12 1¼ **Handsome Stranger (IRE)**[175] 3171 2-9-3 0 AdamKirby 2 49
(David Evans) *hld up: pushed along 4f out: a in rr* **33/1**

00 **13** 6 **Instinctual**[10] 7899 2-9-3 0 KirstyMilczarek 10 33
(Brendan Powell) *a in rr* **66/1**

1m 24.95s (0.15) **Going Correction** -0.125s/f (Stan) **13** Ran SP% **123.4**
Speed ratings (Par 96): **94,93,92,90,90 90,89,87,85,84 84,82,76**
Tote Swingers: 1&2 £15.30, 1&3 £4.40, 2&3 £20.90 CSF £157.94 TOTE £7.20: £2.50, £9.20, £1.40; EX 62.80 Trifecta £231.00 Part won. Pool: £308.07 - 0.50 winning units..
Owner Emjayaarrghh Syndicate **Bred** Mark Johnston Racing Ltd **Trained** Middleham Moor, N Yorks

■ Stewards' Enquiry : Silvestre De Sousa one-day ban; not keeping straight from stalls (22nd Dec).

FOCUS
An open-looking maiden run at what appeared a sound enough pace. The first four improved and the form could be worth a bit more.

NOTEBOOK
Staffhoss overcame the wide draw on his second start and he stepped up on his debut effort to see his race out strongly and pick up the front-runner in the closing stages. This Lucky Story colt clearly likes this surface and he's a nice prospect for handicaps through the winter, if connections choose to keep him on the go. (op 7-1)
Lady Malet very nearly took this from the front. She hadn't shown much on debut but this represented marked improvement.
Consign attracted support which suggested he was going to step up considerably on his promising debut run at Kempton but it's debatable whether he even improved on that run in fairness. It's still early days for this Dutch Art colt. (op 11-4 tchd 7-4)
Plenum(GER), never nearer on this quick reappearance, is eligible for handicaps now. (op 5-2)
Rapscallion Deep(IRE) showed some promise on his debut. He raced very wide off the home bend but kept on well enough. (op 5-2)
Great Demeanor(USA) looked to have the perfect sit just behind the speed but he found disappointingly little at the business end and was unable to confirm the promise of his second start. (op 4-1 tchd 7-2)

8034 32RED CASINO H'CAP — 7f (P)
12:40 (12:40) (Class 5) (0-75,75) 3-Y-0+ — **£2,911** (£866; £432; £216) **Stalls** Low

Form RPR

2005 **1** **Kung Hei Fat Choy (USA)**[24] 7715 3-9-7 75 (b) GrahamLee 6 84
(James Given) *chsd ldrs: rdn to ld ins fnl f: r.o* **5/1**[3]

0003 **2** 1½ **Masai Moon**[16] 7820 8-8-13 74 PatMillman(7) 7 79
(Rod Millman) *hld up: hdwy over 2f out: r.o to go 2nd ins fnl f: nt trble wnr* **12/1**

0605 **3** nk **Parisian Pyramid (IRE)**[5] 7967 6-9-1 69 JamieSpencer 9 73
(Ian Williams) *hld up: rdn over 1f out: r.o ins fnl f: nrst fin* **4/1**[2]

0203 **4** 2¾ **Opus Dei**[32] 7607 5-9-1 69 JimmyFortune 10 66
(Alan McCabe) *dwlt: hld up: rdn and r.o ins fnl f: nt rch ldrs* **10/1**

0006 **5** hd **Azrael**[19] 7790 4-9-7 75 SebSanders 8 71
(Alan McCabe) *prom: chsd ldr over 2f out: rdn and ev ch fr over 1f out tl no ex ins fnl f* **7/2**[1]

100 **6** shd **Paphos**[22] 7743 5-8-13 67 (v) DavidProbert 2 63
(Stuart Williams) *prom: rdn over 2f out: no imp fnl f* **4/1**[2]

0006 **7** 1 **Saucy Brown (IRE)**[14] 7863 6-8-10 64 (p) SilvestreDeSousa 1 57
(Kevin Ryan) *led: rdn over 1f out: hdd and no ex ins fnl f* **10/1**

3045 **8** ½ **Colbyor**[28] 7684 3-8-12 66 TomEaves 5 58
(Richard Fahey) *hld up: hmpd over 2f out: n.d* **12/1**

0044 **9** 2¼ **My Own Way Home**[10] 7915 4-8-9 63 KirstyMilczarek 4 49
(David Evans) *chsd ldr tl rdn over 2f out: wknd over 1f out* **16/1**

1m 23.03s (-1.77) **Going Correction** -0.125s/f (Stan) **9** Ran SP% **118.3**
Speed ratings (Par 103): **105,103,102,99,99 98,97,95,95**
Tote Swingers: 1&2 £11.30, 1&3 £4.60, 2&3 £11.70 CSF £64.37 CT £265.84 TOTE £4.20: £1.80, £4.20, £1.60; EX 91.20 Trifecta £196.10 Part won. Pool: £261.58 - 0.10 winning units..
Owner Danethorpe Racing Partnership **Bred** Gilgai Farm **Trained** Willoughton, Lincs

FOCUS
Run-of-the-mill handicap form, judged around the second and third.
Paphos Official explanation: jockey said gelding was never travelling.

8035 £32 BONUS AT 32RED.COM H'CAP — 2m (P)
1:10 (1:10) (Class 6) (0-65,68) 3-Y-0+ — **£2,070** (£616; £307; £153) **Stalls** Low

Form RPR

3015 **1** **Six Of Clubs**[19] 7791 6-9-12 63 (b) GrahamLee 9 70
(Bill Turner) *s.i.s: hld up: racd keenly: hdwy over 4f out: chsd ldr over 1f out: led ins fnl f: styd on wl* **7/2**[1]

0560 **2** 2 **Perfect Shot (IRE)**[248] 1184 6-8-10 50 MarkCoumbe(3) 1 54
(Michael Attwater) *chsd ldrs: led 6f out: clr 4f out: rdn over 1f out: hdd and unable qck ins fnl f* **6/1**[3]

0023 **3** ¾ **Masters Blazing**[31] 7639 3-9-3 62 AdamKirby 2 65
(John Ryan) *hld up and bhd: rdn over 1f out: r.o ins fnl f: nt rch ldrs* **4/1**[2]

001 **4** 1 **Neighbourhood (USA)**[24] 7710 4-8-12 49 ChrisCatlin 4 51
(James Evans) *hld up: hdwy over 3f out: rdn over 1f out: styd on same pce fnl f* **20/1**

6340 **5** 1 **Rollin 'n Tumblin**[3] 8001 8-8-9 46 oh1 JimmyQuinn 5 47
(Michael Attwater) *hld up: pushed along over 3f out: styd on ins fnl f: nvr on terms* **6/1**[3]

060 **6** nk **Tram Express (FR)**[33] 7594 8-8-13 55 (t) WilliamTwiston-Davies(5) 11 55
(Shaun Lycett) *prom: chsd ldr over 3f out tl rdn over 1f out: no ex ins fnl f* **16/1**

-002 **7** nk **Novel Dancer**[17] 7819 4-9-2 53 (e) RobertHavlin 3 53
(Lydia Richards) *hld up: hdwy over 5f out: n.m.r and pushed along over 3f out: rdn over 1f out: styd on same pce* **8/1**

0-00 **8** 1¼ **Burnbrake**[31] 7629 7-8-9 46 oh1 (b) LiamKeniry 7 45
(Richard Rowe) *slowly in to stride: hld up: n.d* **50/1**

3/0- **9** 8 **Sonara (IRE)**[187] 3730 8-10-0 68 ow3 RichardEvans(3) 8 57
(David Evans) *chsd ldrs: lost pl over 5f out: rdn over 3f out: wknd over 2f out* **33/1**

0222 **10** 18 **Akula (IRE)**[42] 6478 5-9-8 59 MartinDwyer 10 26
(Mark H Tompkins) *chsd ldr: rdn over 3f out: wknd over 2f out: t.o* **4/1**[2]

0000 **11** 27 **Tanjung Agas (IRE)**[24] 7717 4-8-9 46 oh1 (b) JohnFahy 6
(Christopher Kellett) *led 10f: sn rdn: wknd over 3f out: t.o* **66/1**

3m 22.59s (-3.11) **Going Correction** -0.125s/f (Stan)
WFA 3 from 4yo+ 8lb **11** Ran SP% **118.9**
Speed ratings (Par 101): **102,101,100,100,99 99,99,98,94,85 72**
Tote Swingers: 1&2 £11.30, 1&3 £5.10, 2&3 £13.10 CSF £24.37 CT £88.74 TOTE £4.50: £2.10, £3.90, £1.50; EX 16.50 Trifecta £71.80 Pool: £433.06 - 4.52 winning units..
Owner Gongolfin **Bred** R V Young **Trained** Sigwells, Somerset

FOCUS
Not a particularly competitive staying event, and muddling, weakish form.

8036 32REDPOKER.COM (S) STKS — 6f (P)
1:40 (1:40) (Class 6) 3-Y-0+ £2,070 (£616; £307; £153) Stalls Low

Form RPR
460 **1** **Fathsta (IRE)**[19] 7789 7-9-6 77 .... JamieSpencer 7 74
(Ian Williams) *s.i.s: hld up: shkn up over 1f out: str run to ld nr fin: readily* **7/2**[2]
6006 **2** *1* **Hamoody (USA)**[33] 7595 8-9-6 79 .... JimmyFortune 4 71
(David Nicholls) *chsd ldr: led over 1f out: rdn and edgd rt ins fnl f: hdd nr fin* **6/1**[3]
0310 **3** *1/2* **Dark Lane**[14] 7864 6-9-6 66 .... AdamKirby 2 69
(David Evans) *trckd ldrs: pushed along over 1f out: rdn and running on whn hmpd towards fin* **8/1**
2102 **4** *3/4* **Beat The Bell**[16] 7820 7-9-6 75 .... (p) MartinDwyer 6 67
(Jamie Osborne) *chsd ldrs: rdn over 1f out: styng on whn hmpd towards fin* **5/2**[1]
0040 **5** *3* **Pose (IRE)**[54] 7106 5-8-9 45 .... (t) AdamBeschizza 10 46
(Roger Ingram) *slowly in to stride: outpcd: r.o ins fnl f: nvr nrr* **66/1**
1000 **6** *1 1/2* **Amenable (IRE)**[24] 7716 5-9-6 80 .... TedDurcan 1 52
(David Nicholls) *led: rdn and hdd over 1f out: no ex ins fnl f* **7/2**[2]
2260 **7** *nk* **The Dancing Lord**[10] 7902 3-8-9 64 ow2 .... RyanWhile(7) 8 47
(Bill Turner) *sn pushed along to chse ldrs: rdn over 2f out: sn outpcd* **25/1**
5360 **8** *nk* **Chester'Slittlegem (IRE)**[50] 7218 3-8-9 62 .... AndreaAtzeni 5 39
(Lisa Williamson) *hld up: rdn over 2f out: n.d* **25/1**
5400 **9** *1* **Ghost Train (IRE)**[53] 7141 3-9-6 65 .... (p) SilvestreDeSousa 3 47
(Mark Johnston) *prom: n.m.r and lost pl after 1f: n.d after* **8/1**
6000 **10** *29* **Ionwy**[22] 7747 3-8-9 47 .... WilliamCarson 9
(Derek Haydn Jones) *sn pushed along and prom: lost pl 4f out: rdn and wknd over 2f out: t.o* **66/1**

1m 11.21s (-0.69) **Going Correction** -0.125s/f (Stan) 10 Ran SP% 120.2
Speed ratings (Par 101): **99,97,97,96,92 90,89,89,87,49**
Tote Swingers: 1&2 £4.10, 1&3 £5.60, 2&3 £8.00 CSF £24.97 TOTE £4.10: £1.70, £1.90, £2.60; EX 27.70 Trifecta £174.50 Pool: £453.84 - 1.95 winning units..There was no bid for the winner. Amenable was claimed by Steven Arnold for 6,000gns.
Owner Dr Marwan Koukash **Bred** Brian Miller **Trained** Portway, Worcs

FOCUS
Quite a warm race for the grade and the pace was strong. The form is rated cautiously around the third and fifth.

8037 32RED.COM MAIDEN STKS — 1m 4f (P)
2:15 (2:15) (Class 5) 3-Y-0+ £2,911 (£866; £432; £216) Stalls Low

Form RPR
0423 **1** **Omar Khayyam**[8] 7933 3-9-3 75 .... (t) DavidProbert 5 68+
(Andrew Balding) *chsd ldr: shkn up over 2f out: rdn to ld 1f out: styd on wl* **2/1**[2]
2- **2** *2* **Hepworth**[414] 6985 3-8-12 0 .... RobertHavlin 1 60+
(John Gosden) *chsd ldrs: reminder over 4f out: rdn over 1f out: styd on to go 2nd wl ins fnl f: nt trble wnr* **6/5**[1]
622 **3** *1 1/4* **Elysian**[22] 7739 3-8-12 66 .... JimmyFortune 3 58+
(Sir Michael Stoute) *led: rdn and hdd 1f out: styd on same pce* **3/1**[3]
0000 **4** *3* **Let's Confer**[22] 7739 3-8-12 34 .... (p) JimmyQuinn 7 53?
(Michael Attwater) *plld hrd and prom: rdn over 2f out: styd on same pce appr fnl f* **100/1**
0-04 **5** *3 1/4* **Gabrial's Hope (FR)**[70] 6660 3-9-3 18 .... JamieSpencer 4 53
(Ian Williams) *stdd s: hld up: racd keenly: rdn over 1f out: nvr on terms* **33/1**
0065 **6** *6* **Pastures New**[22] 7752 4-9-8 47 .... (t) WilliamCarson 6 43
(Violet M Jordan) *hld up: rdn over 2f out: wknd wl over 1f out* **100/1**
7 *6* **Jaques Vert (FR)**[609] 6-9-8 0 .... GrahamLee 2 34
(Danielle McCormick) *dwlt: hld up: rdn over 3f out: sn wknd* **25/1**

2m 31.64s (-1.36) **Going Correction** -0.125s/f (Stan)
WFA 3 from 4yo+ 5lb 7 Ran SP% 112.6
Speed ratings (Par 103): **99,97,96,94,92 88,84**
Tote Swingers: 1&2 £1.20, 1&3 £1.50, 2&3 £1.90 CSF £4.61 TOTE £3.00: £1.10, £2.20; EX 7.40 Trifecta £11.60 Pool: £811.37 - 52.42 winning units..
Owner J L C Pearce **Bred** Fittocks Stud **Trained** Kingsclere, Hants

FOCUS
Little depth to this maiden and the market principals were the only ones that mattered at the business end. It was slowly run though, and the form is rated cautiously.

8038 32REDBET.COM H'CAP (DIV I) — 1m (P)
2:50 (2:50) (Class 6) (0-60,61) 3-Y-0+ £2,070 (£616; £307; £153) Stalls High

Form RPR
3 **1** **Norwegian Reward (IRE)**[2] 8005 4-8-7 45 .... SilvestreDeSousa 5 52+
(Michael Wigham) *a.p: shkn up over 1f out: led ins fnl f: r.o* **10/11**[1]
4462 **2** *1 1/4* **Ermyn Flyer**[82] 6302 3-9-0 53 .... IanMongan 1 57
(Pat Phelan) *led 1f: chsd ldr tl 5f out: remained handy: rdn to ld over 1f out: hdd ins fnl f: styd on* **16/1**
5462 **3** *nk* **Sudden Wish (IRE)**[4] 7983 3-9-1 54 .... KirstyMilczarek 3 57
(David Evans) *prom: lost pl 6f out: hdwy over 1f out: r.o* **9/2**[2]
4023 **4** *nse* **Fonterutoli (IRE)**[2] 8010 5-9-4 56 .... (e) RobertHavlin 6 61+
(Roger Ingram) *hld up: hdwy over 1f out: nt clr run sn after: r.o* **5/1**[3]
0035 **5** *nk* **Meydan Style (USA)**[82] 6316 6-8-2 45 .... [1] RachealKneller(5) 4 47
(Richard Ford) *s.i.s: sn prom: rdn over 1f out: styd on* **50/1**
6- **6** *1 1/4* **Egretta (IRE)**[36] 7536 3-9-6 59 .... (p) MartinDwyer 8 58
(Richard Brabazon, Ire) *hld up: hdwy and nt clr run 1f out: swtchd lft: r.o: nt rch ldrs* **8/1**
2261 **7** *nk* **Rapid Water**[5] 7964 6-9-9 61 6ex .... JimmyFortune 2 60
(Pat Eddery) *prom: chsd ldr 5f out tl rdn over 1f out: no ex ins fnl f* **10/1**
0-00 **8** *1* **Chik's Dream**[32] 7620 5-8-7 45 .... WilliamCarson 7 41
(Derek Haydn Jones) *led 1f: chsd ldr tl 5f out: remained handy: rdn over 2f out: no ex fnl f* **33/1**
0030 **9** *8* **Tous Les Deux**[263] 966 9-8-8 46 .... RichardThomas 9 23
(Dr Jeremy Naylor) *s.i.s: a in rr: rdn and wknd over 1f out* **50/1**

1m 38.36s (0.16) **Going Correction** -0.125s/f (Stan)
WFA 3 from 4yo+ 1lb 9 Ran SP% 120.2
Speed ratings (Par 101): **94,92,92,92,92 90,90,89,81**
Tote Swingers: 1&2 £4.30, 1&3 £2.20, 2&3 £6.00 CSF £19.97 CT £50.89 TOTE £1.50: £1.02, £4.90, £1.70; EX 20.70 Trifecta £50.10 Pool: £630.36 - 9.42 winning units..
Owner Tapas Partnership **Bred** Sean O'Sullivan **Trained** Newmarket, Suffolk

FOCUS
A weak handicap and the slower division. A bunch finish and muddling form.

Fonterutoli(IRE) Official explanation: jockey said gelding was denied a clear run.

8039 32REDBET.COM H'CAP (DIV II) — 1m (P)
3:25 (3:26) (Class 6) (0-60,60) 3-Y-0+ £2,070 (£616; £307; £153) Stalls High

Form RPR
0060 **1** **Bertie Blu Boy**[32] 7619 4-8-7 46 oh1 .... (b[1]) TomEaves 8 59
(Lisa Williamson) *mde all: clr 2f out: rdn out* **16/1**
5310 **2** *3 3/4* **Flamborough Breeze**[10] 7906 3-9-2 56 .... (t) TedDurcan 9 60
(Ed Vaughan) *s.i.s: hld up: hdwy over 2f out: rdn to go 2nd ins fnl f: no ch w wnr* **4/1**[2]
6032 **3** *1 1/4* **Silly Billy (IRE)**[10] 7906 4-9-1 54 .... (v) IanMongan 2 56
(Pat Phelan) *hld up in tch: nt clr run wl over 1f out: styd on to go 3rd nr fin: nvr able to chal* **5/4**[1]
000 **4** *hd* **Indian Violet (IRE)**[9] 7925 6-9-7 60 .... (p) LiamKeniry 7 61
(Zoe Davison) *prom: rdn over 2f out: styd on same pce fnl f* **10/1**
4330 **5** *2 1/2* **Chandrayaan**[92] 6000 5-8-7 49 .... (v) NataliaGemelova(3) 1 44
(John E Long) *sn pushed along in rr: rdn over 2f out: styd on ins fnl f: nvr nrr* **5/1**[3]
0000 **6** *3/4* **Cuthbert (IRE)**[120] 5049 5-8-7 46 oh1 .... KirstyMilczarek 6 40
(Michael Attwater) *chsd wnr: rdn over 2f out: wknd ins fnl f* **14/1**
0000 **7** *3/4* **Diddums**[2] 8005 6-8-0 46 oh1 .... (e) CarolineKelly(7) 5 38
(John Ryan) *dwlt: a in rr* **25/1**
0000 **8** *4 1/2* **Sovento (GER)**[21] 7767 8-8-11 57 .... NoraLooby(7) 3 38
(Alan McCabe) *hld up: rdn and wknd over 2f out* **14/1**
5600 **9** *1/2* **Inquisitress**[2] 8004 8-8-7 46 oh1 .... KieranO'Neill 4 26
(John Bridger) *chsd ldrs: rdn over 2f out: wknd over 1f out* **25/1**

1m 36.44s (-1.76) **Going Correction** -0.125s/f (Stan)
WFA 3 from 4yo+ 1lb 9 Ran SP% 117.1
Speed ratings (Par 101): **103,99,98,97,95 94,93,89,88**
CSF £80.15 CT £140.32 TOTE £33.20: £5.30, £1.50, £1.10; EX 100.50 Trifecta £235.20 Pool: £1,132.57 - 3.61 winning units..
Owner B & B Hygiene Limited **Bred** H Bourchier **Trained** Saighton, Cheshire

FOCUS
Not form to dwell on for long as only a couple came into it in form. The winner got a pretty easy lead. It was the faster division.
Silly Billy(IRE) Official explanation: jockey said gelding was denied a clear run.
T/Plt: £101.60 to a £1 stake. Pool: £44,641.00 - 320.68 winning tickets. T/Qpdt: £17.30 to a £1 stake. Pool: £4,131.00 - 175.90 winning tickets. CR

1902 SHA TIN (R-H)
Sunday, December 9

OFFICIAL GOING: Turf: good

8040a LONGINES HONG KONG VASE (GROUP 1) (3YO+) (TURF) — 1m 4f
6:00 (12:00) 3-Y-0+
£710,723 (£274,314; £124,688; £71,072; £41,147; £24,937)

RPR
1 **Red Cadeaux**[14] 7872 6-9-0 0 .... GeraldMosse 7 118
(Ed Dunlop) *midfield early: sn prom: rdn on turn into st: r.o to chal over 1f out: led ins fnl f: drvn and hld on wl cl home* **10/1**
2 *shd* **Jaguar Mail (JPN)**[14] 7872 8-9-0 0 .... (b) DouglasWhyte 3 118
(Noriyuki Hori, Japan) *midfield: rdn on turn into st: hdwy to chal 1 1/2f out: wnt 2nd ins fnl f: styd on wl: jst denied* **25/1**
3 *1/2* **Meandre (FR)**[63] 6912 4-9-0 0 .... MaximeGuyon 9 117+
(A Fabre, France) *hld up in tch: hdwy into midfield over 5f out: rdn on turn into st: styd on to go 3rd cl home: fin wl but nt pce to chal* **9/2**[2]
4 *1/2* **Liberator (AUS)**[21] 5-9-0 0 .... (bt) WCMarwing 6 116
(D E Ferraris, Hong Kong) *trckd ldr on inner: rdn to chal on turn into st: led over 1f out: hdd ins fnl f: no ex and dropped to 4th cl home* **20/1**
5 *nk* **Dunaden (FR)**[33] 7621 6-9-0 0 .... CraigAWilliams 2 116+
(M Delzangles, France) *midfield on outer: rdn over 2f out: styd on to go 5th wl ins fnl f: fin wl but nt pce to chal* **5/2**[1]
6 *1 1/4* **Bayrir (FR)**[63] 6912 3-8-9 0 .... Christophe-PatriceLemaire 1 114
(A De Royer-Dupre, France) *prom on inner: rdn over 2f out: ev ch ent fnl f: sn outpcd: kpt on* **8/1**
7 *1/2* **Dandino**[56] 7094 5-9-0 0 .... JimCrowley 8 113+
(James Fanshawe) *midfield: rdn 3f out: towards rr and outpcd on turn into st: styd on to go 7th post but n.d* **14/1**
8 *nse* **Dancing Rain (IRE)**[50] 7237 4-8-10 0 .... JohnnyMurtagh 4 109
(William Haggas) *led: set stdy pce: rdn on turn into st: strly pressed and hdd over 1f out: no ex and fdd: dropped to 8th post* **6/1**[3]
9 *1* **Joshua Tree (IRE)**[56] 7094 5-9-0 0 .... (t) ChristopheSoumillon 5 111
(Marco Botti) *trckd ldr: rdn 2f out: outpcd ent fnl f: fdd* **12/1**
10 *3/4* **Scarlet Camellia (NZ)**[21] 5-9-0 0 .... (t) ZacPurton 12 110
(C S Shum, Hong Kong) *dropped in and hld up in last trio: rdn 2 1/2f out: plugged on but nvr a factor* **25/1**
11 *1 1/2* **Pagera (FR)**[56] 7093 4-8-10 0 .... OlivierPeslier 10 104
(H-A Pantall, France) *hld up in last pair: rdn on turn into st: plugged on but nvr a factor* **25/1**
12 *1 1/2* **Chinchon (IRE)**[49] 7284 7-9-0 0 .... ODoleuze 11 105
(C Laffon-Parias, France) *hld up in last: rdn over 2f out: plugged on but nvr a factor* **16/1**

2m 28.73s (0.53)
WFA 3 from 4yo+ 5lb 12 Ran SP% 117.8
PARI-MUTUEL (all including HK$10 stake): WIN 105.50; PLACE 29.00, 97.00, 22.00; DF 1,710.50.
Owner R J Arculli **Bred** Foursome Thoroughbreds **Trained** Newmarket, Suffolk

FOCUS
A race with plenty of depth and a good even gallop was set by Dancing Rain. Red Cadeaux did not need to match his very best form.

NOTEBOOK
Red Cadeaux has enjoyed a good season again and it was easy to ignore his last two outings in a falsely run affair at Flemington and on firm ground in Tokyo. Third here in 2011, he was nicely positioned turning in and showed plenty of heart to hold on when hitting the front, claiming a much deserved first Group 1 victory. The winner of a Wolverhampton handicap back in 2009 off an official rating of just 72, a trip to Dubai for the Sheema Classic could be next for him, and he will be aimed at the Melbourne Cup again next year as part of a farewell tour.
Jaguar Mail(JPN), who finished fourth in the 2009 and 2010 renewal of this and third back in 2008, was behind the winner in the Japan Cup recently and ran a cracker here even in defeat. Another who was in the right place throughout, he clearly enjoys the way races are run at Sha Tin.
Meandre(FR) moved stylishly into contention and, after facing a wall of horses about 1f out, stayed on gamely. All his victories have come in fields of seven or less, but he's surely capable of breaking that statistic if remaining in training.

Liberator(AUS), who won a decent-looking Group 1 here in May, had been well beaten since and was behind Scarlet Camellia last time, but comfortably reversed that form back up in distance under a prominent ride.
Dunaden(FR) was keen early, came a little wide in the home straight but basically had every chance. Perhaps his massive effort when winning the Caulfield Cup has taken its toll subsequently.
Bayrir(FR) had the statistics against him (3yo colts are now 0-18, with only one placed) in this, and may prefer 1m2f if seen again next year.
Dandino looked to have a bit to find on the figures and got outpaced in the home straight before keeping on. He ran as well as he was entitled to.
Dancing Rain(IRE) was able to control the fractions in front and ran fairly well as a result without being able to get away from her rivals late on.
Joshua Tree(IRE), under Christophe Soumillon for the first time, looked all set to get involved as the field came off the final bend but was another not to pick up.
Pagera(FR) never got involved (jockey said the going was too fast and she took too long to get going).
Chinchon(IRE)'s jockey said his mount was never travelling.

8041a LONGINES HONG KONG SPRINT (GROUP 1) (3YO+) (TURF) 6f
6:40 (12:00) 3-Y-0+

£710,723 (£274,314; £124,688; £71,072; £41,147; £24,937)

RPR
1 **Lord Kanaloa (JPN)**70 6724 4-9-0 0 Yasunarilwata 6 122+
(Takayuki Yasuda, Japan) *a.p: rdn on turn into st: r.o to ld ins fnl f and surged clr: drvn out: readily* **5/1**
2 2 1/2 **Cerise Cherry (SAF)**21 7-9-0 0 (bt) RFourie 5 114
(D Cruz, Hong Kong) *led: rdn 2f out: hdd ins fnl f: kpt on wl for 2nd but no rspnse to wnr* **16/1**
3 shd **Captain Sweet (AUS)**21 5-9-0 0 (p) JamesMcDonald 2 114
(J Moore, Hong Kong) *a.p: rdn in 2nd 2f out: dropped to 3rd ent fnl f and qckly outpcd by wnr: kpt on* **33/1**
4 3/4 **Joy And Fun (NZ)**173 3238 9-9-0 0 (tp) GeraldMosse 1 111+
(D Cruz, Hong Kong) *midfield on inner: rdn 2f out: wnt 4th 1 1/2f out: kpt on but nt pce to chal* **20/1**
5 shd **Lucky Nine (IRE)**21 5-9-0 0 BrettPrebble 12 111+
(C Fownes, Hong Kong) *hld up in last pair: rdn 3f out: last 2f out: r.o down wd outside to go 5th cl home: fin wl but n.d* **4/1**3
6 3/4 **Admiration (AUS)**21 5-9-0 0 (b) NeilCallan 9 109+
(J Moore, Hong Kong) *racd towards rr: rdn 3f out: sn outpcd: nt clr run briefly ins fnl f: swtchd out and r.o to take 6th fnl strides* **20/1**
7 nk **Curren Chan (JPN)**70 6724 5-8-10 0 Kenichilkezoe 8 104+
(Takayuki Yasuda, Japan) *racd towards rr: rdn 3f out: kpt on but nt pce to chal: dropped to 7th fnl strides* **9/1**
8 nk **Flying Blue (AUS)**21 6-9-0 0 (b) UmbertoRispoli 11 107+
(D Cruz, Hong Kong) *hld up in last: rdn on turn into st: r.o but n.d* **40/1**
9 1 **Sea Siren (AUS)**29 7695 4-8-10 0 (b) JimCassidy 7 99+
(J O'Shea, Australia) *midfield: rdn 2f out: no ex and btn ent fnl f: fdd* **3/1**1
10 1 1/2 **Super Easy (NZ)**21 4-9-0 0 (t) JoaoMoreira 10 99+
(M Freedman, Singapore) *midfield on outer: rdn on turn into st: sn outpcd and btn: fdd* **25/1**
11 nk **Leading City (AUS)**21 6-9-0 0 (t) MatthewChadwick 4 98
(J Moore, Hong Kong) *trckd ldr on outer: rdn on turn into st: sn outpcd and btn: fdd* **50/1**
12 1 1/4 **Time After Time (AUS)**21 5-9-0 0 (t) DouglasWhyte 3 94+
(J Moore, Hong Kong) *midfield: rdn over 2f out: sn outpcd and btn: fdd and dropped to last ent fnl f* **7/2**2

1m 8.5s (68.50) **12 Ran SP% 120.5**
PARI-MUTUEL (all including HK$10 stake): WIN 40.50; PLACE 18.00, 30.00, 93.50; DF 318.00.
Owner Lord Horse Club **Bred** K I Farm **Trained** Japan

FOCUS
Plenty of in-form and talented sprinters took their chance here. The gallop looked decent and not too many appeared to have a hard-luck story.

NOTEBOOK
Lord Kanaloa(JPN), now the winner of eight of his 13 career starts and placed in another four, had finished in front of a couple of these when taking the Sprinters Stakes last time at Nakayama, and comfortably confirmed the form. Gaining Japan's first success in this race, he is seemingly improving and is very much one to fear on the world stage.
Cerise Cherry(SAF) ran a cracker under a prominent ride and did best of those who ran in the Jockey Club Sprint here the previous month. He'd be okay over 5f judged on this.
Captain Sweet(AUS) may not be totally consistent but ran up to his best here.
Joy And Fun(NZ), twice placed in this race and with a tongue-tie added, hadn't been out since flopping in the King's Stand Stakes and just kept on in the final stages.
Lucky Nine(IRE) was the unlucky horse in the race. He was always going to find it hard from his draw, but kept on in game style down the home straight after being forced to make his challenge wide.
Curren Chan(JPN) started slowly but came home strongly. Her effort can be marked up a bit.
Sea Siren(AUS), who had shown good form in Australia at the top level, was keen early while chasing, and failed to land a blow. Jockey Jim Cassidy said afterwards that she wasn't herself for some reason.
Time After Time(AUS) could have been expected to do better after a good run of form coming into this.

8042a LONGINES HONG KONG MILE (GROUP 1) (3YO+) (TURF) 1m
7:50 (12:00) 3-Y-0+

£947,630 (£365,752; £166,251; £94,763; £54,862; £33,250)

RPR
1 **Ambitious Dragon (NZ)**21 6-9-0 0 (b) ZacPurton 11 122+
(A T Millard, Hong Kong) *stdd s and hld up in last trio: rdn over 1 1/2f out: edgd rt and twice bmpd rival: r.o to chal ins fnl f: led ins fnl 100yds: pushed out: cosily* **7/2**2
2 3/4 **Glorious Days (AUS)**21 5-9-0 0 (b) DouglasWhyte 3 120
(J Size, Hong Kong) *midfield on inner: swtchd out and hdwy on turn into st: rdn to chal 1 1/2f out: led ent fnl f: strly pressed and hdd ins fnl 100yds: kpt on but easily hld by wnr* **3/1**1
3 1 1/2 **Packing Ok (AUS)**21 6-9-0 0 WCMarwing 9 117
(J Moore, Hong Kong) *trckd ldr in 2nd: rdn to chal on turn into st: stl ev ch ent fnl f: sn outpcd by front pair ins fnl f: styd on to go 3rd fnl strides* **66/1**
4 shd **Gordon Lord Byron (IRE)**63 6913 4-9-0 0 WilliamBuick 6 116
(T Hogan, Ire) *a.p: rdn to chal 1 1/2f out: stl ev ch ent fnl f: sn outpcd by front pair ins fnl f: styd on but dropped to 4th fnl strides* **11/1**
5 3/4 **Packing Whiz (IRE)**21 4-9-0 0 BrettPrebble 10 115
(J Moore, Hong Kong) *hld up in last pair on inner: swtchd out and rdn on turn into st: styd on to go 5th ins fnl f: nvr able to chal* **7/1**3
6 nk **Sadamu Patek (JPN)**21 4-9-0 0 YutakaTake 2 114
(Masato Nishizono, Japan) *midfield on inner: t.k.h: rdn on turn into st: styd on but nvr gng pce to chal* **10/1**
7 nk **Xtension (IRE)**21 5-9-0 0 JamesMcDonald 4 113
(J Moore, Hong Kong) *midfield: rdn over 2f out: styd on but nvr gng pce to chal* **10/1**
8 shd **Pure Champion (IRE)**21 5-9-0 0 (t) MatthewChadwick 12 113
(A S Cruz, Hong Kong) *hld up in last: rdn on turn into st: styd on to go 8th cl home but n.d* **50/1**
9 2 1/2 **Don Bosco (FR)**38 7515 5-9-0 0 OlivierPeslier 5 107
(D Smaga, France) *led: rdn 2f out: strly pressed and hdd ent fnl f: sn no ex and btn: fdd* **33/1**
10 nk **Master Of Hounds (USA)**50 7239 4-9-0 0 ChristopheSoumillon 7 107
(William Haggas) *midfield: rdn 2 1/2f out: outpcd and btn over 1f out: fdd* **25/1**
11 1 1/2 **Siyouma (IRE)**56 7093 4-8-10 0 GeraldMosse 8 99
(F Doumen, France) *midfield on outer: rdn 2 1/2f out: outpcd and towards rr whn twice bmpd by eventual wnr over 1 1/2f out: sn no ex and btn* **7/1**3
12 shd **Grand Prix Boss (JPN)**21 4-9-0 0 HiroyukiUchida 1 103
(Yoshito Yahagi, Japan) *prom on inner: rdn on turn into st: no ex and btn 1 1/2f out: fdd and dropped to last* **11/1**

1m 34.12s (-0.58) **12 Ran SP% 117.3**
PARI-MUTUEL (all including HK$10 stake): WIN 41.50; PLACE 16.50, 12.00, 162.00; DF 53.50.
Owner Johnson Lam Pui Hung & Anderson Lam Him Yue **Bred** E P Lowry **Trained** Hong Kong

FOCUS
This didn't look an easy race to call with so many talented milers taking their chance, and the pace picked up significantly from the half mile mark to the finish.The first three home were all Hong Kong-trained.

NOTEBOOK
Ambitious Dragon(NZ), who had to pass the vet for a mild lameness issue before racing, is extremely good when at his best, and he delivered in style, coming home strongly when finding room. Hopefully he'll be seen in Meydan next spring in an attempt to improve on his poor showing in the Dubai Duty Free earlier this year.
Glorious Days(AUS) had blinkers on for the first time and was receiving 5lb when beating Ambitious Dragon over this C&D last time, but he wasn't able to confirm the placings on these terms despite moving stylishly throughout.
Packing Ok(AUS), a dual Group 3 winner, seemed to have every chance and ran well considering his starting price.
Gordon Lord Byron(IRE) put up a fine performance at the end of a long season, although William Buick was unsure whether his mount stayed the distance.
Packing Whiz(IRE) was expected to go well returned to this trip, but he didn't figure. The jockey reported afterwards that his mount lacked a bit of ping.
Don Bosco(FR) got to the front and set a reasonable gallop before weakening.
Master Of Hounds(USA), last seen being thrashed by Frankel, never really looked dangerous after chasing the leader.
Siyouma(IRE) was already held when bumped by the winner as he came past. She'd raced wide of her rivals for much of the contest.

8043a LONGINES HONG KONG CUP (GROUP 1) (3YO+) (TURF) 1m 2f
8:30 (12:00) 3-Y-0+

£1,042,394 (£402,327; £182,876; £104,239; £60,349; £36,575)

RPR
1 **California Memory (USA)**21 6-9-0 0 MatthewChadwick 1 121
(A S Cruz, Hong Kong) *sn settled in midfield on inner: rdn 2f out: swtchd out and r.o to ld ent fnl f: sn clr: pushed out: comf* **9/4**1
2 1 **Giofra**63 6911 4-8-10 0 (t) ChristopheSoumillon 9 115+
(A De Royer-Dupre, France) *hld up towards rr: rdn on turn into st: styd on to go 2nd wl ins fnl f: clsng at fin but n.d to wnr* **6/1**3
3 1 3/4 **Alcopop (AUS)**36 7562 8-9-0 0 CraigAWilliams 4 116+
(Jake Stephens, Australia) *slow to stride and hld up towards rr: last 4f out: rdn 2f out: styd on to go 3rd fnl strides: fin strly but nt pce to chal* **10/1**
4 1/2 **Dan Excel (IRE)**21 4-9-0 0 (t) NeilCallan 8 115
(J Moore, Hong Kong) *sn led: set slow pce: hdd 5f out: led again over 3f out: rdn on turn into st: hdd ent fnl f: sn outpcd by wnr: fdd and dropped to 4th fnl strides* **25/1**
5 1 1/4 **Military Attack (IRE)**21 4-9-0 0 BrettPrebble 11 112+
(J Moore, Hong Kong) *hld up towards rr: rdn 3f out: styd on down wd outside to go 5th fnl strides but n.d* **33/1**
6 nk **Carlton House (USA)**50 7238 4-9-0 0 RyanMoore 2 111
(Sir Michael Stoute) *hld up towards rr on inner: rdn 3f out: plugged on but nt pce to chal: dropped to 6th fnl strides* **13/2**
7 3/4 **Zaidan (USA)**21 4-9-0 0 JamesMcDonald 10 110
(J Moore, Hong Kong) *led v early stages: sn hdd and trckd ldr: rdn in 3rd 2f out: outpcd ent fnl f: fdd* **14/1**
8 3 1/4 **Irian (GER)**21 6-9-0 0 GeraldMosse 7 103
(J Moore, Hong Kong) *hld up towards rr on outer: hdwy into midfield over 4f out: rdn 2 1/2f out: sn outpcd and btn: fdd* **13/2**
9 shd **Autumn Gold (GER)**21 3-8-11 0 DouglasWhyte 3 103
(S Woods, Hong Kong) *prom: rdn 3f out: outpcd on turn into st: steadily fdd* **12/1**
10 3/4 **Saonois (FR)**63 6912 3-8-11 0 AntoineHamelin 6 102
(J-P Gauvin, France) *midfield: rdn 2f out: outpcd over 1f out: fdd* **9/2**2
11 3/4 **Feuerblitz (GER)**35 7586 3-8-11 0 MaximeGuyon 5 100
(M Figge, Germany) *midfield: t.k.h: rapid hdwy on outer to ld 5f out: hdd over 3f out: rdn in 2nd on turn into st: no ex and btn ent fnl f: fdd: eased and dropped to last cl home* **20/1**

2m 3.09s (1.69)
WFA 3 from 4yo+ 3lb **11 Ran SP% 124.9**
PARI-MUTUEL (all including HK$10 stake): WIN 27.50; PLACE 14.00, 61.50, 55.00; DF 310.00.
Owner Howard Liang Yum Shing **Bred** Fred Seitz **Trained** Hong Kong

FOCUS
This is far from strong form, as the fractions set by the leaders were uneven and the winner was best positioned of the fancied runners to take advantage of the situation. He's rated to his mark.

NOTEBOOK
California Memory(USA), who won this last year when also drawn in stall one, has been a model of consistency throughout his career and came here off the back of a victory in November. Never far away, Matthew Chadwick sent the likeable grey to the front in the final stages and was never going to be caught.
Giofra was settled out the back from her wide draw and had plenty to do turning in. She passed plenty of rivals to come home strongly, but the winner had gone beyond recall by the time she hit top gear. With more luck next year she'll win plenty of nice prizes.
Alcopop(AUS), back to his best in Australia this year, putting up three big performances in a row, started slowly and was another inconvenienced by the way the contest was run. He made giant strides up the inside rail late on, but it was all too late.

Dan Excel(IRE), better known to Europeans as Dunboyne Express, a Group-class performer when trained by Kevin Prendergast, had a tongue-tie added, an aid he wore once in Ireland, and ran his best race in Hong Kong. He mainly controlled things from the front, so whether his effort is believable or not is open to debate.
Carlton House(USA) could have been given a chance if reproducing his Prince Of Wales's Stakes second this year but he never really looked like winning. The colt heads off to Australia now to be trained by Gai Waterhouse, but will remain under the same ownership.
Saonois(FR) had some poor statistics to overcome (3yo colts are now 0-14 in this contest, with only three placing) and made no impression in the latter stages.
Feuerblitz(GER) soon helped to put some pace into the contest but was too keen and ended up being eased when his chance was gone.

8032 LINGFIELD (L-H)
Sunday, December 9

OFFICIAL GOING: Standard
Wind: fresh, across Weather: dry

8044 32REDPOKER.COM MEDIAN AUCTION MAIDEN STKS 5f (P)
11:50 (11:50) (Class 6) 2-Y-O £2,181 (£644; £322) Stalls High

Form RPR
03 **1** **Freddy With A Y (IRE)**[23] 7738 2-9-3 0 GeorgeBaker 6 76+
(Gary Moore) *w ldr tl led wl over 1f out: sn pushed along and readily asserted: eased towards fin: easily* **5/4**[1]
4 **2** 2¾ **Little Choosey**[56] 7078 2-8-12 0 JohnFahy 4 59
(Clive Cox) *led: rdn and hdd wl over 1f out: unable qck w wnr and btn 1f out: battled on gamely to hold 2nd* **7/4**[2]
042 **3** *hd* **Ada Lovelace**[15] 7855 2-8-12 64 JimmyQuinn 5 58
(Dean Ivory) *t.k.h: chsd ldrs: rdn and unable qck w wnr over 1f out: battling for 2nd and kpt on fnl f* **5/1**[3]
6 **4** ½ **La Luz Del Sol**[8] 7953 2-8-12 0 TonyHamilton 2 57+
(Richard Fahey) *chsd ldrs: rdn and outpcd by wnr over 1f out: kpt on same pce u.p fnl f* **14/1**
5 **5** 7 **Alfaisaliah (IRE)**[9] 7931 2-8-12 0 DavidProbert 7 31
(J S Moore) *chsd ldrs tl rdn and struggling 2f out: sn wknd: bhd and eased wl ins fnl f* **8/1**
40 **6** 3 **Lager Time (IRE)**[8] 7953 2-9-3 0 AdamKirby 1 26
(David Evans) *sn detached in last: hung rt and lost tch bnd 2f out* **33/1**

58.68s (-0.12) **Going Correction** -0.10s/f (Stan) 6 Ran SP% **118.2**
Speed ratings (Par 94): **96,91,91,90,79 74**
Tote Swingers 1&2 £1.40, 2&3 £1.10, 1&3 £1.20 CSF £4.01 TOTE £1.90: £1.70, £1.10; EX 4.50 Trifecta £10.80 Pool: £543.86 - 37.61 winning tickets..
Owner Mrs M J George **Bred** David McGuinness **Trained** Lower Beeding, W Sussex

FOCUS
A weak two-year-old maiden. The winner was always in command and the form could rate a little higher.

NOTEBOOK
Freddy With A Y(IRE) found this easy pickings. Third over course and distance on his second start in November, recording a RPR of 69, the second and fourth have won since. He always looked to have the measure of the runner-up and skipped clear to score with a fair bit in hand. He can expect a nursery mark in the low 70s. (op Evens)
Little Choosey, who appears to be well named, had shown promise when fourth over 6f in soft ground at Goodwood in October on her only previous start. She matched strides with the winner but had no answer when he moved up a gear. (op 5-2)
Ada Lovelace, runner-up over the C&D two weeks ago on her third start, has an official rating of 64. She is probably the best guide to the overall value of the form.
La Luz Del Sol, speedily bred, stepped up markedly on her debut effort at Wolverhampton a week earlier. There should be even better to come.
Lager Time(IRE) Official explanation: jockey said gelding hung right.

8045 32REDBET.COM H'CAP (DIV I) 5f (P)
12:20 (12:20) (Class 6) (0-55,55) 3-Y-0+ £2,181 (£644; £322) Stalls High

Form RPR
0462 **1** **Pharoh Jake**[10] 7929 4-8-9 48 SeanLevey 7 52
(John Bridger) *in tch in last trio: swtchd lft and hdwy ent fnl f: r.o strly fnl 100yds to ld cl home* **3/1**[2]
6030 **2** *hd* **Molly Jones**[30] 7673 3-9-0 53 WilliamCarson 5 56
(Derek Haydn Jones) *led: rdn wl over 1f out: kpt on wl u.p tl hdd and no ex cl home* **5/2**[1]
5000 **3** *nk* **Chateau Lola**[6] 7970 3-8-13 52 MartinDwyer 1 54
(Derek Shaw) *pressed ldr: rdn and ev ch wl over 1f out: hrd drvn and kpt on wl fnl f: no ex cl home* **25/1**
2001 **4** 1¼ **Brandywell Boy (IRE)**[25] 7703 9-9-0 53 SilvestreDeSousa 8 50
(Dominic Ffrench Davis) *rdn along leaving stalls: in tch in last trio: hdwy u.p 1f out: styd on but nvr gng pce to rch ldrs* **3/1**[2]
0040 **5** *nse* **Deveze (IRE)**[23] 7746 4-8-7 46 (b) RichardKingscote 9 43
(Milton Bradley) *t.k.h: rdn and unable qck over 1f out: styd on same pce and lost 2 pls fnl 100yds* **14/1**
0645 **6** 2 **Mr Hendrix**[40] 7471 3-8-12 51 JohnFahy 4 41
(Mark Hoad) *fly-jmpd and rdn along leaving stalls: sn chsng ldrs: rdn and unable qck over 1f out: wknd ins fnl f* **6/1**[3]
3400 **7** 4½ **College Doll**[11] 7914 3-8-8 47 JimmyQuinn 2 21
(Christine Dunnett) *chsd ldrs: rdn and struggling wl over 1f out: wknd 1f out* **8/1**
0-40 **8** 2 **Valdemar**[250] 1178 6-8-7 46 oh1 DavidProbert 6 13
(John Weymes) *taken down early: rdn along thrght: a in rr: lost tch over 2f out* **20/1**

58.47s (-0.33) **Going Correction** -0.10s/f (Stan) 8 Ran SP% **119.2**
Speed ratings (Par 101): **98,97,97,95,95 91,84,81**
Tote Swingers 1&2 £3.20, 2&3 £11.50, 1&3 £9.20 CSF £11.53 CT £159.52 TOTE £4.80: £1.60, £1.60, £6.10; EX 14.20 Trifecta £375.30 Pool: £720.72 - 1.44 winning tickets..
Owner The Hair & Haberdasher Partnership **Bred** J J Bridger **Trained** Liphook, Hants

FOCUS
Part one of a low-grade sprint handicap. It was 0.25sec slower than division II. The form is rated around the second and third.
College Doll Official explanation: vet said filly finished lame right-hind

8046 32REDBET.COM H'CAP (DIV II) 5f (P)
12:50 (12:50) (Class 6) (0-55,55) 3-Y-0+ £2,181 (£644; £322) Stalls High

Form RPR
0304 **1** **Monumental Man**[54] 7146 3-8-13 52 (p) DavidProbert 5 65
(James Unett) *sn led and mde rest: rdn and wnt clr over 1f out: in command 1f out: r.o wl: comf* **3/1**[1]
0420 **2** 2¾ **Kaylee**[10] 7929 3-8-5 51 NedCurtis(7) 4 54
(Gary Moore) *chsd ldng trio: rdn and outpcd by wnr over 1f out: styd on to chse clr wnr ins fnl f: kpt on but no threat* **6/1**[2]
0000 **3** 1¼ **Little Perisher**[83] 6321 5-8-2 46 (p) RachealKneller(5) 1 45
(Mark Brisbourne) *chsd ldrs: pushed along and hit rail over 2f out: kpt on same pce fr over 1f out* **8/1**[3]
1563 **4** *shd* **Lord Buffhead**[40] 7471 3-9-0 53 RobbieFitzpatrick 6 51
(Richard Guest) *chsd ldr: rdn and outpcd by wnr over 1f out: kpt on same pce after* **3/1**[1]
6-40 **5** 2½ **Brian Sprout**[25] 7703 4-8-9 48 JimmyQuinn 2 37
(John Weymes) *taken down early: hld up in last trio: rdn and no imp wl over 1f out: wl hld and swtchd rt ins fnl f* **10/1**
0242 **6** ¾ **Itum**[25] 7703 5-8-11 50 SebSanders 9 37
(Christine Dunnett) *in tch towards rr on outer: hdwy into midfield and rdn ent fnl 2f: sn struggling: wknd over 1f out* **3/1**[1]
0500 **7** 1¼ **Replicator**[11] 7901 7-8-7 46 oh1 (e) JamieMackay 7 28
(Patrick Gilligan) *hld up in last trio: rdn and no hdwy over 1f out: n.d* **25/1**
-000 **8** 2¼ **Silver Marizah (IRE)**[30] 7668 3-9-2 55 MartinLane 3 29
(Roger Ingram) *sn nudged along in rr: rdn and struggling over 2f out: bhd over 1f out* **10/1**

58.22s (-0.58) **Going Correction** -0.10s/f (Stan) 8 Ran SP% **122.4**
Speed ratings (Par 101): **100,95,93,93,89 88,86,82**
Tote Swingers 1&2 £4.00, 2&3 £10.50, 1&3 £8.00 CSF £23.66 CT £137.20 TOTE £3.30: £1.90, £1.90, £5.20; EX 31.60 Trifecta £290.90 Pool: £473.32 - 1.22 winning tickets..
Owner James Unett **Bred** Christopher Chell **Trained** Tedsmore Hall, Shropshire

FOCUS
Division two and more of the same, but the faster leg by 0.25sec. The winner is rated back to his 2yo best.

8047 32RED.COM CLASSIFIED CLAIMING STKS 1m (P)
1:20 (1:20) (Class 5) 3-Y-0+ £2,911 (£866; £432; £216) Stalls High

Form RPR
0200 **1** **Hurricane Spirit (IRE)**[33] 7618 8-7-13 70 NicoleNordblad(5) 10 74
(Hans Adielsson) *t.k.h early: hdwy to ld after 1f: mde rest: pushed along and qcknd clr over 1f out: in command 1f out: rdn out* **5/1**[3]
0226 **2** 2½ **One Way Or Another (AUS)**[23] 7743 9-8-4 66 (t) KirstyMilczarek 7 68+
(David Evans) *stdd s: hld up in rr: rdn and hdwy on inner jst over 1f out: r.o u.p to go 2nd wl ins fnl f: no ch w wnr* **3/1**[1]
2406 **3** ½ **Aciano (IRE)**[43] 7415 4-8-4 68 (p) ChrisCatlin 9 67
(Brendan Powell) *chsd ldrs: rdn and outpcd by wnr wl over 1f out: wnt 2nd but no ch w wnr 1f out: plugged on: lost 2nd wl ins fnl f* **9/2**[2]
2004 **4** ½ **Sir George (IRE)**[19] 7798 7-8-0 64 (p) JimmyQuinn 6 62
(Ollie Pears) *chsd wnr over 6f out: rdn and outpcd by wnr wl over 1f out: lost 2nd and styd on same pce fnl f* **6/1**
205 **5** *nk* **Conducting**[10] 7925 4-8-8 65 RobertWinston 1 69+
(Gay Kelleway) *hld up in last trio: nt clr run ent fnl 2f tl jst over 1f out: r.o fnl f but no ch w wnr* **5/1**[3]
106 **6** ¾ **Hierarch (IRE)**[127] 4812 5-8-4 65 (p) MartinLane 8 63+
(David Simcock) *hld up in last trio: rdn and effrt over 1f out: styd on ins fnl f: no ch w wnr* **7/1**
6305 **7** 5 **Irons On Fire (USA)**[18] 7816 4-8-6 53 ow1 (p) MarkCoumbe(3) 4 56
(Lee Carter) *dwlt and rdn along leaving stalls: in tch in midfield: drvn and wknd wl over 1f out* **33/1**
5454 **8** ½ **Faithful Ruler (USA)**[262] 999 8-8-4 68 (p) WilliamCarson 5 50
(Ronald Harris) *t.k.h: led for 1f: hld up wl in tch after: rdn and wknd wl over 1f out* **6/1**
10/0 **9** *nk* **Love Pegasus (USA)**[6] 7964 6-7-10 60 ow1 NatashaEaton(5) 3 46
(Paddy Butler) *hld up in tch towards rr: rdn and no hdwy 2f out: wknd over 1f out* **33/1**

1m 37.55s (-0.65) **Going Correction** -0.10s/f (Stan)
WFA 3 from 4yo+ 1lb 9 Ran SP% **123.5**
Speed ratings (Par 103): **99,96,96,95,95 94,89,88,88**
Tote Swingers 1&2 £5.90, 2&3 £5.20, 1&3 £5.20 CSF £21.99 TOTE £9.50: £1.90, £1.80, £1.20; EX 32.70 Trifecta £333.10 Pool: £635.26 - 1.43 winning tickets..There were no claims.
Owner Hans Adielsson A B **Bred** Knocktoran Stud **Trained** Kingston Lisle, Oxon

FOCUS
A competitive claimer but a clear-cut winner under a well-judged ride. He's rated around 10lb off his best form of the year.
Sir George(IRE) Official explanation: jockey said gelding hung right.

8048 32RED SUPPORTING BRITISH RACING H'CAP 1m 4f (P)
1:50 (1:50) (Class 6) (0-65,65) 3-Y-0 £2,181 (£644; £322) Stalls Low

Form RPR
1315 **1** **Norfolk Sky**[24] 7718 3-9-4 62 IanMongan 1 71
(Laura Mongan) *in tch in midfield: effrt and rdn over 2f out: drvn and ev ch over 1f out: styd on wl to ld wl ins fnl f: rdn out* **7/1**[2]
4514 **2** *nk* **Lady Bellatrix**[18] 7811 3-9-1 59 MartinDwyer 12 67
(Mark H Tompkins) *chsd ldrs tl wnt 2nd 8f out: rdn to ld over 1f out: kpt on u.p tl hdd and no ex wl ins fnl f* **8/1**[3]
-066 **3** 1¼ **Midnight Bahia (IRE)**[19] 7800 3-8-2 46 oh1 SilvestreDeSousa 5 52
(Dean Ivory) *chsd ldr tl 8f out: chsd ldrs after: rdn and effrt over 2f out: kpt on same pce ins fnl f* **10/1**
0603 **4** 2¾ **Guava**[11] 7921 3-8-2 46 oh1 JamieMackay 7 48
(Shaun Harris) *hld up in tch towards rr: hdwy over 4f out: chsd ldrs and rdn ent fnl 2f: styd on same pce and no imp fnl f* **14/1**
0322 **5** ¾ **Dewala**[11] 7921 3-8-12 56 AndrewMullen 2 57
(Michael Appleby) *led: rdn and hrd pressed jst over 2f out: hdd over 1f out: wknd ins fnl f* **4/1**[1]
0130 **6** 1 **Bramshill Lass**[11] 7893 3-9-7 65 (b) GrahamLee 13 64
(Amanda Perrett) *in tch in midfield on outer: effrt and unable qck u.p 2f out: styd on same pce and wl hld fr over 1f out* **8/1**[3]
0034 **7** ¾ **Guarda Pampa**[11] 7892 3-9-4 62 AdamBeschizza 8 60
(William Haggas) *hld up in tch in midfield: rdn and effrt ent fnl 2f: edgd lft and hdwy u.p over 1f out: kpt on but nvr trbld ldrs* **7/1**[2]
2100 **8** *nse* **Sir Dylan**[2] 8023 3-9-2 60 WilliamCarson 3 58
(Ronald Harris) *taken down early: stdd s: hld up in detached last: clsd 8f out: hdwy on outer 3f out: hung lft over 1f out: kpt on but no threat to ldrs* **12/1**
5443 **9** ½ **Neil's Pride**[19] 7800 3-8-8 52 TomEaves 9 49
(Richard Fahey) *hld up in tch in midfield: nt clr run jst over 3f out: drvn and effrt jst over 2f out: kpt on same pce u.p fr over 1f out* **7/1**[2]
10 2¼ **Nadia Naes (IRE)**[51] 7232 3-8-4 48 oh1 ow2 (e1) RichardThomas 4 42
(Roger Ingram) *hld up in tch in last quartet: rdn 4f out: racd awkwardly but sme hdwy 2f out: wknd 1f out* **33/1**

056 **11** *5* **Bada Bing**[66] 6810 3-8-3 47 .... NickyMackay 6 33
(Scott Dixon) *hld up in tch in midfield: rdn and lost pl 4f out: wknd u.p 2f out* **33/1**

0500 **12** *3 ½* **Ecechiera**[18] 7811 3-8-2 46 oh1 .... JimmyQuinn 11 26
(Dean Ivory) *hld up in tch towards rr: struggling and n.m.r over 2f out: rdn and wknd 2f out* **40/1**

4255 **13** *½* **Merchants Return**[32] 7632 3-8-6 50 ....(v) ChrisCatlin 14 29
(Lydia Pearce) *chsd ldrs: rdn and wkng jst over 2f out: bhd fnl f* **7/1**[2]

0-60 **14** *50* **Princeofperfection**[58] 7025 3-8-2 46 oh1 .... KieranO'Neill 10
(Richard Ford) *chsd ldrs tl 8f out: steadily lost pl: bhd 4f out: lost tch and t.o fnl 2f: eased* **50/1**

2m 31.04s (-1.96) **Going Correction** -0.10s/f (Stan) **14** Ran SP% **126.0**
Speed ratings (Par 98): **102,101,100,99,98 97,97,97,97,95 92,89,89,56**
Tote Swingers 1&2 £12.70, 2&3 £17.40, 1&3 £15.00 CSF £63.63 CT £578.11 TOTE £5.90: £1.80, £3.90, £4.10; EX 44.60 TRIFECTA Not won..
Owner Condover Racing **Bred** Farmers Hill Stud **Trained** Epsom, Surrey

FOCUS
It paid to race up with the pace, but the time was reasonable and the form seems sound enough.

8049 32RED MEDIAN AUCTION MAIDEN STKS 1m 2f (P)
2:20 (2:21) (Class 5) 3-4-Y-O **£2,911** (£866; £432; £216) **Stalls** Low

Form RPR

0522 **1** **Harry Buckle**[18] 7818 3-9-3 72 .... JimmyFortune 6 74
(Philip McBride) *led tl over 8f out: chsd ldr tl 7f out: styd handy: effrt to press ldrs 2f out: rdn to ld over 1f out: sn qckn clr: r.o wl: easily* **8/15**[1]

34 **2** *4 ½* **Syncopate**[44] 7384 3-9-3 0 .... LiamKeniry 10 65
(Pam Sly) *chsd ldrs tl wnt 2nd 7f out: rdn to ld 2f out: hdd over 1f out and sn outpcd by wnr: wl btn but kpt on for clr 2nd fnl f* **6/1**[3]

5436 **3** *3* **Princess Willow**[75] 6569 4-9-1 52 .... KirstyMilczarek 8 54
(John E Long) *chsd ldrs: rdn 4f out: stl wl in tch 2f out: outpcd over 1f out: 3rd and wl hld fnl f* **16/1**

6600 **4** *2 ¾* **Santadelacruze**[22] 7767 3-9-3 62 ....(p) GeorgeBaker 1 54
(Gary Moore) *hld up in tch in midfield: hdwy to trck ldrs 2f out: rdn and fnd little over 1f out: btn 1f out and wknd fnl f* **7/2**[2]

2206 **5** *1 ½* **Humungosaur**[8] 7954 3-9-3 65 .... GrahamLee 9 51
(Richard Ford) *t.k.h: chsd ldr tl led over 8f out: hdd and rdn 2f out: wknd ent fnl f* **8/1**

0004 **6** *1* **Corn Maiden**[32] 7632 3-8-12 45 ....(b) DominicFox 3 44
(Mark Rimmer) *hld up in tch towards rr: rdn and struggling over 2f out: wknd 2f out* **33/1**

/0-6 **7** *¾* **Educated Son**[24] 7474 4-9-6 60 .... JohnFahy 2 47
(Ben De Haan) *stdd s: hld up in detached last: clsd and in tch 4f out: rdn over 2f out: wknd 2f out* **12/1**

8 *5* **Nova Nimph**[16] 3-8-12 0 ....(t) ShaneKelly 5 32
(Mark Brisbourne) *s.i.s: in tch in rr of main gp: rdn 4f out: wknd over 2f out* **33/1**

06 **9** *22* **Dubai Emerald (USA)**[9] 7933 3-8-9 0 .... AshleyMorgan(3) 4
(Chris Dwyer) *in tch in midfield on outer: rdn and struggling 3f out: sn bhd: t.o over 1f out* **50/1**

2m 3.78s (-2.82) **Going Correction** -0.10s/f (Stan)
WFA 3 from 4yo 3lb **9** Ran SP% **134.3**
Speed ratings (Par 103): **107,103,101,98,97 96,96,92,74**
Tote Swingers 1&2 £2.00, 2&3 £8.40, 1&3 £3.20 CSF £5.99 TOTE £1.60: £1.02, £2.40, £3.60; EX 5.50 Trifecta £26.10 Pool: £857.79 - 24.60 winning tickets..
Owner Four Winds Racing Partnership **Bred** Wood Farm Stud (Waresley) **Trained** Newmarket, Suffolk

FOCUS
A one-sided maiden. Modest form set around the third and sixth, and the winner did not need to improve.

8050 £32 BONUS AT 32RED.COM H'CAP 1m 2f (P)
2:50 (2:52) (Class 6) (0-60,60) 3-Y-O **£2,181** (£644; £322) **Stalls** Low

Form RPR

050 **1** **Chella Thriller (SPA)**[9] 7417 3-9-2 55 ....(b) RichardKingscote 12 63
(Alastair Lidderdale) *taken down early: hld up in tch towards rr: rdn and hdwy over 1f out: edgd lft ins fnl f: r.o strly to ld cl home* **7/1**[3]

3316 **2** *hd* **Taro Tywod (IRE)**[11] 7921 3-9-4 57 .... ShaneKelly 11 65
(Mark Brisbourne) *t.k.h: chsd ldrs: wnt 2nd over 3f out tl led over 2f out: rdn and clr over 1f out: drvn ins fnl f: hdd cl home* **7/1**[3]

4230 **3** *¾* **Sweet Liberta (IRE)**[23] 7752 3-9-0 53 .... DavidProbert 6 59
(Andrew Balding) *chsd ldr: rdn and chsd ldr over 1f out: no imp tl kpt on u.p fnl 75yds* **14/1**

5642 **4** *¾* **Awesome Rock (IRE)**[32] 7632 3-8-12 51 .... SebSanders 3 56
(Louise Best) *t.k.h: hld up in tch towards rr: hdwy on inner over 1f out: edgd rt ins fnl f: kpt on same pce fnl 100yds* **12/1**

0413 **5** *½* **Tatting**[16] 7841 3-9-7 60 .... GrahamLee 2 64
(Chris Dwyer) *hld up in tch in midfield: rdn and effrt to chse ldrs over 1f out: styd on same pce ins fnl f* **7/4**[1]

530 **6** *2* **Transfix**[30] 7668 3-9-5 58 .... JimmyFortune 5 58
(Ed Vaughan) *stdd s: t.k.h: hld up in tch in rr: swtchd rt and hdwy 2f out: kpt on same pce ins fnl f* **14/1**

5460 **7** *nk* **Barnacle**[54] 7148 3-8-10 49 ....(b[1]) SeanLevey 8 48
(Pat Eddery) *hld up in tch in midfield: rdn and effrt wl over 1f out: kpt on ins fnl f but nvr gng pce to trble ldrs* **16/1**

5010 **8** *2* **Nurse Dominatrix (IRE)**[19] 7798 3-8-10 49 .... RobbieFitzpatrick 4 44
(Richard Guest) *hld up in tch in last pair: edgd lft and hdwy over 1f out: kpt on ins fnl f: nvr trbld ldrs* **20/1**

6-6 **9** *¾* **Egretta (IRE)**[1] 8038 3-9-6 59 ....(p) MartinDwyer 7 52
(Richard Brabazon, Ire) *t.k.h: hld up in tch in midfield: effrt to chal whn rn wd bnd 2f out: lost pl and sn drvn: no hdwy and wknd ins fnl f* **9/2**[2]

-650 **10** *1 ½* **Our Ivor**[202] 2333 3-8-11 50 .... AndrewMullen 1 40
(Michael Appleby) *led tl 7f out: chsd ldr tl over 3f out: sn rdn and unable qck: wknd over 1f out* **33/1**

450 **11** *¾* **Fushicho**[185] 2864 3-9-0 53 .... SilvestreDeSousa 14 42
(Michael Wigham) *chsd ldr tl led 7f out: rdn and hdd over 2f out: wkng whn short of room and sltly hmpd 1f out* **8/1**

0042 **12** *¾* **Hill Of Dreams (IRE)**[23] 7752 3-9-2 55 .... JimmyQuinn 13 42
(Dean Ivory) *t.k.h: hld up in tch in midfield: rdn and effrt whn nt clr run jst over 2f out: wknd over 1f out* **12/1**

060 **13** *4 ½* **Sherry Cherie (IRE)**[20] 7787 3-8-10 49 .... TonyHamilton 10 27
(Richard Fahey) *t.k.h: chsd ldrs: rdn and struggling over 2f out: wknd 2f out: bhd fnl f* **25/1**

2m 6.56s (-0.04) **Going Correction** -0.10s/f (Stan) **13** Ran SP% **136.8**
Speed ratings (Par 98): **96,95,95,94,94 92,92,90,90,89 88,87,84**
Tote Swingers 1&2 £7.30, 2&3 £16.10, 1&3 £12.00 CSF £62.69 CT £710.22 TOTE £9.50: £2.40, £2.50, £4.10; EX 63.60 Trifecta £470.70 Part won. Pool: £627.73 - 0.93 winning tickets..
Owner The Saucy Horse Partnership **Bred** John Patrick Duffy **Trained** Lambourn, Berks

FOCUS
The complexion changed late on this this very modest 1m2f handicap run at just a steady pace until the final half-mile. Muddling and ordinary form.

8051 32RED CASINO APPRENTICE H'CAP 1m 2f (P)
3:20 (3:21) (Class 6) (0-65,64) 3-Y-O+ **£2,181** (£644; £322) **Stalls** Low

Form RPR

456 **1** **Idol Deputy (FR)**[16] 7843 6-9-8 64 ....(p) RachealKneller 1 72
(Mark Usher) *t.k.h: hld up in tch in midfield: travelling wl but nt clr run wl 2f out: gap opened and hdwy ins fnl f: r.o wl to ld last strides* **10/1**

4130 **2** *shd* **Graylyn Valentino**[22] 7776 3-8-12 64 .... SemiraPashai(7) 8 72
(Robin Dickin) *s.i.s: hld up in tch in rr: hdwy on outer over 2f out: pressed ldrs and pushed along over 1f out: led wl ins fnl f: hdd last strides* **8/1**

0100 **3** *1* **Stylistickhill (IRE)**[16] 7844 4-9-2 63 ....(t) JordanUys(5) 5 69
(Scott Dixon) *stdd s: t.k.h: chsd ldrs: rdn and effrt over 1f out: swtchd rt and pressed ldrs ins fnl f: one pce towards fin* **20/1**

0502 **4** *½* **Resplendent Alpha**[11] 7905 8-9-1 62 .... JoeyHaynes(5) 2 67
(Jamie Osborne) *hld up in tch towards rr: rdn and hdwy 2f out: kpt on u.p ins fnl f* **5/1**[1]

4300 **5** *nk* **Derfenna Art (IRE)**[22] 7767 3-9-3 62 ....(t) WilliamTwiston-Davies 10 66
(Seamus Durack) *led: rdn wl over 1f out: hdd wl ins fnl f: wknd towards fin* **12/1**

4003 **6** *¾* **Athletic**[32] 6967 3-8-12 57 ....(p) NoraLooby 7 60
(Alan McCabe) *t.k.h: chsd ldrs: ducked rt bnd 9f out: pushed along to chse ldr 2f out tl ins fnl f: wknd towards fin* **16/1**

3100 **7** *¾* **Mount Abora (IRE)**[26] 7301 5-9-7 63 .... NicoleNordblad 3 64+
(Laura Mongan) *stdd s: hld up in tch in rr: stl last and swtchd rt wl over 1f out: styd on wl fnl f: nvr trbld ldrs* **7/1**[3]

3450 **8** *1* **Arkaim**[19] 3047 4-9-7 63 .... ThomasBrown 9 62
(Pam Sly) *t.k.h: hld up in tch in midfield: pushed wd bnd 9f out: rdn and effrt whn swtchd rt over 1f out: styd on same pce ins fnl f* **14/1**

6000 **9** *½* **Temuco (IRE)**[58] 7015 3-8-12 62 ....(v) EoinWalsh(5) 4 60+
(David Evans) *hld up in tch in rr: rdn and effrt wl over 1f out: styng on whn nt clr run and swtchd lft 1f out: kpt on: nvr trbld ldrs* **8/1**

0000 **10** *1 ¼* **City Of The Kings (IRE)**[43] 7413 7-9-7 63 ....(p) JacobButterfield 6 59
(Ollie Pears) *dwlt: sn rdn along and hdwy to chse ldrs after 1f: chsd ldr 7f out tl 2f out: wknd u.p ent fnl f* **6/1**[2]

434 **11** *nk* **Green Earth (IRE)**[6] 7964 5-9-4 60 ....(p) JakePayne 13 55
(Pat Phelan) *hld up in tch towards rr: pushed wd bnd 9f out: rdn and no real imp 3f out: one pce and btn over 1f out* **8/1**

6001 **12** *2 ½* **Daniel Thomas (IRE)**[16] 7841 10-9-7 63 ....(tp) JoshBaudains 11 53
(Violet M Jordan) *hld up wl in tch: rdn and unable qck over 2f out: wknd over 1f out* **5/1**[1]

0500 **13** *1 ¼* **Dzesmin (POL)**[26] 7495 10-8-1 50 oh5 ....(p) LisaTodd(7) 14 38
(Richard Guest) *t.k.h: hld up in tch towards rr: rdn and no hdwy jst over 2f out: wknd over 1f out* **50/1**

-114 **14** *9* **Meglio Ancora**[93] 5998 5-8-13 60 .... RyanTate(5) 12 30
(Richard Ford) *chsd ldr tl 7f out: rdn and lost pl 3f out: bhd fnl f* **12/1**

2m 4.91s (-1.69) **Going Correction** -0.10s/f (Stan)
WFA 3 from 4yo+ 3lb **14** Ran SP% **137.2**
Speed ratings (Par 101): **102,101,101,100,100 99,99,98,98,97 96,94,93,86**
Tote Swingers 1&2 £22.80, 2&3 £26.20, 1&3 £19.50 CSF £100.30 CT £1640.17 TOTE £9.50: £3.30, £4.00, £12.50; EX 134.50 TRIFECTA Not won..
Owner Miss J C Blackwell **Bred** Sheikh Sultan Bin Khalifa Al Nayan **Trained** Upper Lambourn, Berks

FOCUS
Again the winner played his cards very late. The form is sound enough at face value.
Athletic Official explanation: jockey said gelding hung right.
T/Plt: £63.20 to a £1 stake. Pool: £51,215.59 - 591.53 winning tickets. T/Qpdt: £14.60 to a £1 stake. Pool: £4,871.34 - 245.90 winning tickets. SP

8044 LINGFIELD (L-H)
Monday, December 10

OFFICIAL GOING: Standard
Wind: Light, against Weather: Fine, cold

8052 AT THE RACES SKY 415 MEDIAN AUCTION MAIDEN STKS 1m (P)
12:10 (12:11) (Class 6) 2-Y-O **£1,704** (£503; £251) **Stalls** High

Form RPR

03 **1** **Lion Beacon**[12] 7900 2-9-3 0 .... JimCrowley 6 71+
(Amanda Perrett) *trckd ldrs: shkn up 2f out: prog to chal fnl f: drvn and r.o to ld post* **11/4**[2]

3 **2** *nse* **Spillway**[26] 7707 2-9-3 0 .... LiamKeniry 4 71
(Eve Johnson Houghton) *cl up on inner gng wl: wnt 2nd 2f out: led ins fnl f: hrd rdn and hdd post* **2/1**[1]

0 **3** *¾* **Big Moza**[26] 7707 2-8-12 0 .... RobertWinston 2 64
(John Best) *led: rdn 2f out: hdd ins fnl f: kpt on* **100/1**

03 **4** *¾* **Mosman**[20] 7796 2-9-3 0 .... FergusSweeney 9 68
(Jamie Osborne) *trckd ldr: nt qckn and lost 2nd 2f out: styd on u.p over 1f out: a hld* **16/1**

6 **5** *1* **Exclusive Waters (IRE)**[12] 7900 2-9-3 0 .... AdamKirby 5 65
(William Knight) *hld up in 7th: prog on inner over 1f out: tried to chal ins fnl f: fdd last 100yds* **10/1**

0 **6** *shd* **Exclusion (USA)**[83] 6330 2-8-12 0 .... StevieDonohoe 8 60
(Noel Quinlan) *hld up in rr: pushed along 2f out: sme prog over 1f out: nvr rchd ldrs but kpt on steadily* **100/1**

60 **7** *1 ¼* **Halling's Wish**[33] 7628 2-9-3 0 .... GeorgeBaker 3 62
(John Best) *hld up and sn in last: pushed along 2f out: styd on fnl f wout being knocked abt* **50/1**

0 **8** *nk* **Rainford Glory (IRE)**[16] 7868 2-9-3 0 .... ShaneKelly 10 61
(Ed Dunlop) *wl in tch bhd ldrs: rdn 2f out: one pce and no imp fr over 1f out* **8/1**

6 **9** *4* **Marlborough House**[40] 7492 2-9-3 0 .... SilvestreDeSousa 11 52
(Mark Johnston) *racd wd: prom: rdn 3f out: wknd 2f out* **6/1**[3]

10 *1* **Endorsing (IRE)** 2-9-3 0 .... SeanLevey 7 50
(Richard Hannon) *s.s: sn in tch in rr: pushed along 2f out: no prog over 1f out: eased ins fnl f* **8/1**

11 *3 ¼* **Mercators View** 2-9-3 0 .... JimmyFortune 1 42
(Hughie Morrison) *wl in rr: pushed along 3f out: no prog 2f out: wknd fnl f* **33/1**

1m 38.46s (0.26) **Going Correction** -0.025s/f (Stan) **11** Ran SP% **118.4**
Speed ratings (Par 94): **97,96,96,95,94 94,93,92,88,87 84**
Tote swingers 1&2 £1.80, 1&3 £27.80, 2&3 £12.90 CSF £8.63 TOTE £4.20: £2.50, £1.60, £10.90; EX 11.10 TRIFECTA Not won..

The Form Book Flat, Raceform Ltd, Compton, RG20 6NL

Owner Mrs Alexandra J Chandris **Bred** The Late A M Jenkins & J Chandris **Trained** Pulborough, W Sussex

FOCUS

An ordinary maiden and it paid to race handily. The race is rated around those with previous form.

NOTEBOOK

Lion Beacon was only seventh when Spillway ran third on their respective debuts over 1m at Kempton, but today's winner had subsequently progressed again to himself finish third over this C&D and clearly he continues to go the right way. He should make a fair handicapper. (op 5-2)

Spillway confirmed his debut promise, even without confirming placings with Lion Beacon, but was just held. He can win a similar race. (op 7-4)

Big Moza, as her name suggests, is a sizeable type and she improved a good deal on the form she showed behind the front two when debuting in the same Kempton maiden. She ought to keep progressing.

Mosman is going the right way and now has the option of handicaps. (op 14-1)

Exclusive Waters(IRE) again showed ability and may do better in time. (op 16-1)

Exclusion(USA), absent for 83 days after a moderate debut, kept on and should do better.

Halling's Wish ◆, a stablemate of the third, is bred to want further and stayed on from well back in a race in which it proved hard to make up ground. He's now qualified for a handicap mark and is one to keep in mind when he goes up in trip. (op 66-1)

Marlborough House had a wide trip and looks the type to do much better in time. (op 8-1)

Endorsing(IRE) ◆, a 50,000gns half-brother to a couple of 7f winners, missed the break, ran green and did not receive anything like a hard ride. Sean Levey reported the colt ran green. Official explanation: jockey said colt ran green (op 12-1)

8053 £32 BONUS AT 32RED.COM (S) STKS — 6f (P)

12:40 (12:40) (Class 6) 2-Y-O — **£1,704** (£503; £251) **Stalls** Low

Form — RPR

5421 **1** — **Sofi's Spirit (IRE)**[6] 7977 2-8-11 60 ... LiamKeniry 3 — 60
(J S Moore) *pressed ldr: led 2f out: drvn and hrd pressed ins fnl f: hld on* **7/4**[1]

6132 **2** ½ **Divine Angel (IRE)**[4] 8003 2-8-6 65 ... LeonnaMayor(5) 4 — 59
(Phil McEntee) *sn hld up in last: pushed along and prog over 1f out: rdn to chse wnr jst ins fnl f: tried to chal but nt qckn last 100yds* **9/4**[2]

0565 **3** 2 **Proventi**[26] 7711 2-8-11 50 ... (v) SebSanders 1 — 53
(Alan McCabe) *trckd ldng pair: rdn to chse wnr over 1f out and threatened to chal: wandered bdly and fnd nil: lost 2nd and wl hld ins fnl f* **12/1**

54 **4** 2½ **Squawk**[16] 7865 2-8-6 0 ... AndrewMullen 2 — 40
(Bill Turner) *led to 2f out: steadily wknd* **16/1**

301P **5** 14 **Lexi The Princess (IRE)**[146] 4191 2-8-11 72 ... JamieSpencer 5 — 3
(Jamie Osborne) *racd on outer: chsd ldng pair: rdn and hanging 2f out: sn wknd: lame* **11/4**[3]

1m 12.84s (0.94) **Going Correction** -0.025s/f (Stan) — **5** Ran SP% **107.4**

Speed ratings (Par 94): **92,91,88,85,66**

CSF £5.64 TOTE £2.20: £1.20, £1.40; EX 4.50 Trifecta £19.90 Pool: £587.91 - 22.11 winning units..There was no bid for the winner.

Owner J S Moore **Bred** Yvonne & Gerard Kennedy **Trained** Upper Lambourn, Berks

FOCUS

A moderate juvenile seller and average form for the grade.

NOTEBOOK

Sofi's Spirit(IRE) scrambled home in a 7f Wolverhampton seller on her previous start, but she'd travelled well that day and had no problems coping with the drop in trip, finding enough after being well placed. She should be competitive in low-grade handicaps. (tchd 6-4 and 2-1)

Divine Angel(IRE), who would have been 5lb worse off with the winner in a handicap, may not have been ideally suited by this drop back from 1m. (op 5-2 tchd 11-4)

Proventi came into this rated only 50 and he limits the level. (op 20-1)

Squawk just wasn't good enough. (op 10-1)

Lexi The Princess(IRE) was the pick of the weighs, but she'd been absent since being pulled up lame at Southwell in July when with Kevin Ryan, and here she was again found to be lame (right fore). Official explanation: vet said filly returned lame right-fore (op 2-1)

8054 32RED CASINO H'CAP — 5f (P)

1:10 (1:10) (Class 5) (0-70,70) 3-Y-O+ — **£2,385** (£704; £352) **Stalls** High

Form — RPR

0020 **1** — **Roy's Legacy**[7] 7967 3-9-0 68 ... (t) MichaelJMMurphy(5) 7 — 76
(Shaun Harris) *trckd ldr: clsd fr 2f out: rdn to ld jst over 1f out: kpt on wl* **5/1**[1]

0055 **2** ½ **Desert Strike**[7] 7970 6-9-2 65 ... (p) AdamKirby 2 — 71
(Conor Dore) *chsd ldrs: prog on inner over 1f out: chsd wnr ins fnl f: styd on but a hld* **5/1**[1]

4006 **3** 1 **Billy Red**[24] 7742 8-9-5 68 ... (b) FergusSweeney 4 — 71
(J R Jenkins) *in tch in midfield: clsd fr 2f out: rdn and nt qckn over 1f out: styd on fnl f to take 3rd nr fin* **6/1**[2]

3020 **4** nk **Picansort**[48] 7308 5-9-3 66 ... ShaneKelly 8 — 68
(Peter Crate) *racd on outer: hld up wl in rr: gng wl enough but same pl over 1f out: reminder and r.o to take 4th last strides: nvr involved* **5/1**[1]

0565 **5** shd **Fathom Five (IRE)**[16] 7860 8-9-4 67 ... (p) GeorgeBaker 1 — 68
(Gary Moore) *fast away fr ins draw: led and gng easily: shkn up and hdd jst over 1f out: fdd* **6/1**[2]

00 **5** dht **Celtic Sixpence (IRE)**[143] 4300 4-9-7 70 ... AdamBeschizza 5 — 71
(Peter Salmon) *chsd ldrs: rdn over 1f out: styd on fnl f but nvr able to chal* **10/1**

4054 **7** ½ **Atlantic Beach**[7] 7970 7-9-2 65 ... (b) RobertWinston 10 — 64
(Milton Bradley) *chsd ldng pair: rdn and nt qckn over 1f out: fdd last 100yds* **10/1**

3002 **8** ¾ **Even Bolder**[70] 6737 9-8-8 64 ... JoeyHaynes(7) 9 — 61
(Eric Wheeler) *racd wdst of all and wl in rr: forfeited grnd bnd 2f out: no ch but kpt on u.p fnl f* **25/1**

5060 **9** ½ **Dancing Freddy (IRE)**[4] 8009 5-9-7 70 ... (tp) WilliamCarson 6 — 65
(Violet M Jordan) *sn shoved along in last pair: gng bttr fr 1/2-way but stl same pl: effrt over 1f out: no prog fnl f* **7/1**[3]

3060 **10** 3½ **Charming (IRE)**[23] 7775 3-9-2 65 ... SebSanders 3 — 47
(Olivia Maylam) *dwlt: wl in rr on inner: no prog over 1f out: sn wknd* **10/1**

58.68s (-0.12) **Going Correction** -0.025s/f (Stan) — **10** Ran SP% **122.2**

Speed ratings (Par 103): **99,98,96,96,95 95,95,93,93,87**

Tote swingers 1&2 £8.20, 1&3 £7.50, 2&3 £6.20 CSF £31.18 CT £161.34 TOTE £6.40: £2.00, £2.20, £1.80; EX 50.20 Trifecta £67.00 Pool: £555.43 - 6.21 winning units..

Owner Karl Blackwell Steve Mohammed S A Harris **Bred** A Christou **Trained** Carburton, Notts

FOCUS

An ordinary sprint handicap for the class with the runner-up rated to his best.

8055 32REDBET.COM CLAIMING STKS — 7f (P)

1:40 (1:40) (Class 6) 3-Y-O+ — **£1,704** (£503; £251) **Stalls** Low

Form — RPR

0013 **1** — **Brocklebank (IRE)**[12] 7901 3-9-0 75 ... (p) RobertWinston 8 — 85
(Kevin Ryan) *t.k.h: pressed ldr: led 2f out: drvn and styd on wl fnl f* **5/1**

1435 **2** 1 **Lockantanks**[10] 7934 5-9-0 89 ... MichaelJMMurphy(5) 2 — 87
(Michael Appleby) *trckd ldrs: pushed along and prog 2f out: chsd wnr jst over 1f out: rdn and styd on but no imp fnl f* **5/4**[1]

601 **3** 1¾ **Fathsta (IRE)**[2] 8036 7-8-12 77 ... JamieSpencer 4 — 76
(Ian Williams) *stdd s: t.k.h and hld up in last trio: prog on outer 3f out: rdn to dispute 2nd over 1f out: effrt petered out fnl f* **7/2**[2]

5000 **4** 2¼ **Decent Fella (IRE)**[72] 6676 6-9-4 89 ... (vt) JimmyFortune 3 — 76
(David Nicholls) *hld up in midfield: dropped to last trio over 2f out but stl gng wl: swtchd out v wd sn after and lost all ch: styd on fnl f* **4/1**[3]

6 **5** nse **Fairy Wing (IRE)**[7] 7961 5-9-1 81 ... (p) KirstyMilczarek 5 — 72
(Conor Dore) *chsd ldng pair to wl over 1f out: rdn and kpt on same pce after* **20/1**

4004 **6** ½ **Imprimis Tagula (IRE)**[7] 7961 8-8-9 74 ... (v) NatashaEaton(5) 9 — 70
(Alan Bailey) *t.k.h: led to 2f out: lost 2nd jst over 1f out: wknd* **25/1**

4015 **7** 3½ **Flying Pickets (IRE)**[20] 7799 3-8-13 70 ... (be) JohnFahy 6 — 60
(Alan McCabe) *s.s: mostly in last tl sme prog 2f out: no imp over 1f out: wknd* **25/1**

0000 **8** 5 **Ivan The Engine**[53] 7189 4-8-10 45 ... (t) SebSanders 7 — 43
(Paul Fitzsimons) *chsd ldrs on outer tl wknd qckly fr 2f out* **100/1**

50/0 **9** 1 **Bravo Belle (IRE)**[19] 7818 5-8-1 27 ... RyanPowell(3) 1 — 34
(Paddy Butler) *a in rr: wknd 2f out* **100/1**

1m 24.96s (0.16) **Going Correction** -0.025s/f (Stan) — **9** Ran SP% **117.8**

Speed ratings (Par 101): **98,96,94,92,92 91,87,81,80**

Tote swingers 1&2 £2.70, 1&3 £2.80, 2&3 £2.40 CSF £11.53 TOTE £6.00: £1.50, £1.70, £1.10; EX 16.30 Trifecta £47.10 Pool: £1,113.38 - 17.69 winning units..Brocklebank was claimed by Mr S. Dow for £10,000. Decent Fella was claimed by Mr S. Arnold for £14,000.

Owner Mrs Margaret Forsyth **Bred** Vincent Reen **Trained** Hambleton, N Yorks

FOCUS

The pace was ordinary and this is typically muddling claiming form. The race could be rated higher at face value.

Fathsta(IRE) Official explanation: jockey said gelding ran too free

Decent Fella(IRE) Official explanation: jockey said gelding hung badly right

8056 32RED H'CAP — 1m 2f (P)

2:10 (2:14) (Class 3) (0-95,94) 3-Y-O+ — **£6,663** (£1,982; £990; £495) **Stalls** Low

Form — RPR

102 **1** — **Viewpoint (IRE)**[5] 7986 3-8-8 84 ... SeanLevey 4 — 93
(Richard Hannon) *trckd ldng pair: wnt 2nd wl over 1f out: rdn to ld ins fnl f: styd on wl* **7/2**[2]

0004 **2** 1¼ **Mia's Boy**[10] 7934 8-9-7 94 ... GeorgeBaker 6 — 101
(Chris Dwyer) *stdd s: hld up in last pair: rdn and prog over 1f out: styd on to take 2nd nr fin: unable to chal* **20/1**

0010 **3** nse **Shamir**[39] 7502 5-9-0 87 ... IanMongan 3 — 93
(Jo Crowley) *trckd ldrs in 5th: shkn up over 2f out: prog on inner over 1f out: styd on to press for 2nd nr fin* **12/1**

0012 **4** nk **Robin Hoods Bay**[12] 7904 4-9-6 93 ... JimmyFortune 8 — 99
(Ed Vaughan) *led: kicked on over 2f out: hdd ins fnl f: one pce and lost 2 pls nr fin* **9/2**[3]

4046 **5** ¾ **Bancnuanaheireann (IRE)**[23] 7771 5-9-4 91 ... AndrewMullen 1 — 96+
(Michael Appleby) *t.k.h: hld up in last pair: pushed along over 2f out: hmpd over 1f out: swtchd rt and r.o fnl f: nrst fin* **7/1**

0415 **6** 1 **Layline (IRE)**[34] 7601 5-9-3 90 ... RobertWinston 2 — 92
(Gay Kelleway) *t.k.h: hld up in 6th: prog on outer over 2f out: chsd ldrs over 1f out: nt qckn and fdd ins fnl f* **16/1**

-001 **7** 3¼ **Trois Vallees (USA)**[17] 7843 3-8-5 81 ... SilvestreDeSousa 5 — 77
(James Tate) *trckd ldr: rdn over 2f out: lost 2nd wl over 1f out: sn wknd* **7/1**

421 **8** 1¼ **Hill Street (IRE)**[198] 2496 3-8-12 88 ... RobertHavlin 7 — 83
(John Gosden) *trckd ldng trio: losing pl and shkn up whn nt clr run wl over 1f out: no ch after* **5/2**[1]

2m 6.32s (-0.28) **Going Correction** -0.025s/f (Stan)

WFA 3 from 4yo+ 3lb — **8** Ran SP% **112.3**

Speed ratings (Par 107): **100,99,98,98,98 97,94,93**

Tote swingers 1&2 £14.10, 1&3 £9.00, 2&3 £17.70 CSF £64.89 CT £746.50 TOTE £4.20: £1.40, £6.10, £4.30; EX 73.70 Trifecta £1035.20 Part won. Pool: £1380.27 - 0.93 winning units..

Owner The Heffer Syndicate **Bred** F Dunne **Trained** East Everleigh, Wilts

FOCUS

A good handicap, but there wasn't much pace on. The race is rated around the third and fourth and fifth more or less to form.

NOTEBOOK

Viewpoint(IRE), helped by being forwardly placed, stayed on well to record a career best. This was only his ninth start and he can progress again. (op 9-2 tchd 3-1)

Mia's Boy was outpaced as the tempo lifted, but finished well. He had shaped as though on the way back at Wolverhampton last time and is one to keep in mind from this sort of mark. (op 14-1 tchd 25-1)

Shamir has never won beyond 1m, but this wasn't a proper stamina test and he ran well. (op 14-1 tchd 10-1)

Robin Hoods Bay looked to be well ridden from the front and this effort suggests he's now high enough in the weights. (op 7-2 tchd 5-1)

Bancnuanaheireann(IRE) ◆ was set a lot to do considering the lack of pace in the race and lost all chance when hampered early in the straight. His only win came first-time out when with Jim Bolger, but he's with a good yard and can do better. (tchd 6-1 and 8-1)

Trois Vallees(USA) impressed when a clear winner (from 6lb lower) in a slowly run race over the extended 1m at Wolverhampton on his recent debut for this yard, his first start since leaving Mahmood Al Zarooni. However, despite this race unfolding in similar fashion, he was in trouble a long way out and Godolphin presumably got rid of him for a reason. (op 6-1 tchd 5-1)

Hill Street(IRE) hadn't been seen since winning a 1m maiden here in May (Viewpoint behind) and this was a disappointing return. He looked in trouble when short of room in the straight. (op 11-4 tchd 3-1)

8057 32RED.COM H'CAP — 1m (P)

2:40 (2:42) (Class 4) (0-85,79) 3-Y-O+ — **£4,294** (£1,268; £634) **Stalls** High

Form — RPR

0462 **1** — **Aquilonius (IRE)**[17] 7844 3-9-1 74 ... (t) JamieSpencer 3 — 83
(Stuart Williams) *trckd ldng pair: led wl over 1f out: drvn and kpt on fnl f* **5/2**[1]

656 **2** ¾ **Jack Who's He (IRE)**[12] 7920 3-8-13 79 ... (v[1]) EoinWalsh(7) 11 — 86
(David Evans) *s.i.s: rcvrd on outer and sn trckd ldrs: rdn and wd bnd 2f out: rallied over 1f out: chsd wnr last 100yds: clsd but nvr able to chal* **7/1**[3]

3213 **3** 1 **Fabled City (USA)**[21] 7789 3-9-6 79 ... (t) AdamKirby 10 — 84
(Clive Cox) *hld up in last pair: prog jst over 2f out: rdn and styd on to dispute 2nd ins fnl f: one pce after* **11/4**[2]

0404 **4** nk **Patriotic (IRE)**[17] 7842 4-9-6 78 ... GeorgeBaker 1 — 82
(Chris Dwyer) *trckd ldrs: shkn up 2f out: styd on to dispute 2nd ins fnl f: one pce after* **7/1**[3]

10 **5** *1 3/4* **Wordismybond**[70] 6735 3-8-7 **66** SilvestreDeSousa 9 66
(Peter Makin) *trckd ldr: led over 2f out to wl over 1f out: wknd ins fnl f* **16/1**

2565 **6** *nk* **Follow The Flag (IRE)**[12] 7920 8-9-2 **74** (v) SebSanders 6 74
(Alan McCabe) *sn pushed along in last pair: rdn 3f out: kpt on one pce fnl 2f: n.d* **16/1**

6040 **7** *1 1/4* **Fantasy Gladiator**[7] 7966 6-9-2 **74** (p) JimCrowley 7 71
(Robert Cowell) *hld up in rr: dropped to last and rdn over 2f out: nvr on terms after* **14/1**

5005 **8** *1 3/4* **Miami Gator (IRE)**[77] 6526 5-9-2 **74** (v) RichardKingscote 2 67
(Mrs K Burke) *led to over 2f out: wknd over 1f out* **25/1**

03 **9** *4 1/2* **Morant Bay (IRE)**[17] 7843 3-8-13 **72** (p) StevieDonohoe 5 54
(Ian Williams) *chsd ldrs: rdn 3f out: lost pl and wknd 2f out* **20/1**

3000 **10** *4* **California English (IRE)**[110] 5480 3-9-3 **76** ChrisCatlin 8 49
(Marco Botti) *awkward s: rcvrd on wd outside to be in tch after 2f: wknd over 2f out and wd bnd sn after: sn bhd* **8/1**

1m 36.57s (-1.63) **Going Correction** -0.025s/f (Stan) **10** Ran SP% **118.4**
WFA 3 from 4yo+ 1lb
Speed ratings (Par 105): **107,106,105,104,103 102,101,99,95,91**
Tote swingers 1&2 £4.90, 1&3 £2.80, 2&3 £5.90 CSF £21.02 CT £52.97 TOTE £3.00: £2.20, £2.40, £1.10; EX 28.30 Trifecta £112.40 Pool: £1,013.11 - 6.76 winning units..
Owner T W Morley & Mrs J Morley **Bred** Redmondstown Stud **Trained** Newmarket, Suffolk

FOCUS
A fair handicap and the form looks solid rated around the placed horses.

8058 32RED SUPPORTING BRITISH RACING H'CAP (DIV I) 6f (P)
3:10 (3:11) (Class 5) (0-75,75) 3-Y-O+ **£2,385** (£704; £352) **Stalls** Low

Form RPR

050 **1** **Gabrial's Gift (IRE)**[10] 7936 3-9-2 **70** JamieSpencer 2 80
(Ian Williams) *hit stalls bef they opened: trckd ldrs: prog on inner 2f out: led over 1f out: hrd pressed fnl f: drvn out* **16/1**

2202 **2** *1* **Lastkingofscotland (IRE)**[7] 7967 6-8-12 **66** (b) KirstyMilczarek 4 73
(Conor Dore) *hld up in rr: prog on inner 2f out: rdn to chal fnl f: nt qckn last 100yds* **7/2**[1]

6005 **3** *1/2* **Key Ambition**[24] 7741 3-9-4 **72** (vt[1]) AdamKirby 9 77
(Garry Moss) *reminder after 100yds then settled in rr: stl 9th 2f out and taken to wd outside: prog jst over 1f out: r.o to take 3rd nr fin* **6/1**[3]

1040 **4** *1/2* **Divine Call**[21] 7789 5-9-7 **75** RichardKingscote 7 78
(Milton Bradley) *hld up in rr: prog on inner wl over 1f out: chsd ldng pair ins fnl f: one pce and lost 3rd nr fin* **8/1**

0011 **5** *3/4* **Gung Ho Jack**[16] 7864 3-9-1 **69** GeorgeBaker 10 70
(John Best) *trckd ldrs: rdn 2f out: one pce u.p over 1f out* **7/2**[1]

3103 **6** *nk* **Dark Lane**[2] 8036 6-8-5 **66** EoinWalsh(7) 8 66
(David Evans) *trckd ldrs: lost pl sltly 2f out: rdn and one pce over 1f out* **5/1**[2]

2360 **7** *1* **Commandingpresence (USA)**[24] 7741 6-8-8 **62** SeanLevey 6 59
(John Bridger) *chsd ldng pair to 2f out: steadily fdd* **33/1**

0000 **8** *3* **Midnight Feast**[18] 7827 4-9-1 **69** WilliamCarson 1 56
(Lee Carter) *pressed ldr at str pce: led 1/2-way: hdd over 1f out: wknd rapidly* **20/1**

3644 **9** *1 3/4* **Rambo Will**[25] 7730 4-9-3 **71** DavidProbert 3 53
(J R Jenkins) *led at gd pce to 1/2-way: wknd qckly wl over 1f out* **5/1**[2]

0023 **10** *2 3/4* **Shawkantango**[23] 7775 5-9-1 **69** (v) MartinDwyer 5 42
(Derek Shaw) *outpcd and a detached in last* **20/1**

1m 11.04s (-0.86) **Going Correction** -0.025s/f (Stan) **10** Ran SP% **121.5**
Speed ratings (Par 103): **104,102,102,101,100 99,98,94,92,88**
Tote swingers 1&2 £16.30, 1&3 £20.10, 2&3 £7.10 CSF £72.83 CT £397.22 TOTE £25.60: £7.30, £1.10, £2.60; EX 104.80 TRIFECTA Not won..
Owner Dr Marwan Koukash **Bred** Skymarc Farm **Trained** Portway, Worcs

FOCUS
The time was similar to the second division and the form looks straighforward rated around the third and fourth.
Gabrial's Gift(IRE) Official explanation: trainer said, regarding apparent improvement in form, that the gelding was better suited by the Polytrack surface.

8059 32RED SUPPORTING BRITISH RACING H'CAP (DIV II) 6f (P)
3:40 (3:43) (Class 5) (0-75,74) 3-Y-O+ **£2,385** (£704; £352) **Stalls** Low

Form RPR

3302 **1** **Hoover**[4] 8004 4-8-10 **63** (t) WilliamCarson 3 72
(Jim Boyle) *hld up in last pair: prog 2f out: urged along and r.o to ld ins fnl f: drvn and hld on nr fin* **5/2**[1]

6053 **2** *hd* **Parisian Pyramid (IRE)**[2] 8034 6-9-2 **69** JamieSpencer 4 77
(Ian Williams) *hld up in midfield: prog over 1f out: urged along to chal ins fnl f: jst hld* **3/1**[2]

0250 **3** *3/4* **Button Moon (IRE)**[12] 7902 4-9-0 **67** (p) SebSanders 1 73
(Paul Fitzsimons) *led at gd pce: drvn over 1f out: hdd and no ex ins fnl f* **20/1**

0513 **4** *1/2* **Half A Crown (IRE)**[31] 7666 7-9-2 **69** AdamBeschizza 2 73
(Peter Salmon) *prom: rdn to dispute 2nd over 1f out: one pce ins fnl f* **8/1**

6510 **5** *1/2* **Mother Jones**[4] 8009 4-9-0 **74** EoinWalsh(7) 7 76
(David Evans) *racd wd: prog and prom 1/2-way: 3rd whn hanging and wd bnd 2f out: rallied to dispute 2nd over 1f out: one pce after* **10/1**

0003 **6** *1 1/2* **Dancing Welcome**[12] 7902 6-9-6 **73** (b) RichardKingscote 6 71
(Milton Bradley) *chsd ldrs: rdn 2f out: lost pl over 1f out: n.d after* **8/1**

5500 **7** *1/2* **Dishy Guru**[44] 7412 3-9-3 **70** FergusSweeney 5 66
(Michael Blanshard) *hld up in rr: shkn up on wd outside over 1f out: kpt on fnl f: n.d* **6/1**[3]

5100 **8** *2* **Saskia's Dream**[18] 7827 4-9-3 **70** (p) RobertHavlin 8 60
(Jane Chapple-Hyam) *pressed ldr at gd pce to over 1f out: wknd* **10/1**

2430 **9** *1 1/2* **Prince Of Passion (CAN)**[67] 6811 4-8-13 **66** (v) SilvestreDeSousa 9 51
(Derek Shaw) *missed break: hld up in last: pushed along and no prog 2f out: no ch whn shkn up fnl f* **16/1**

1m 10.94s (-0.96) **Going Correction** -0.025s/f (Stan) **9** Ran SP% **118.9**
Speed ratings (Par 103): **105,104,103,103,102 100,99,97,95**
Tote swingers 1&2 £2.50, 1&3 £9.20, 2&3 £9.30 CSF £10.40 CT £122.68 TOTE £3.40: £1.10, £2.90, £5.60; EX 11.60 Trifecta £189.30 Pool: £1,075.48 - 4.26 winning units..
Owner The Clean Sweep Partnership **Bred** Paddock Space **Trained** Epsom, Surrey

FOCUS
The second division of an ordinary handicap run in a slightly faster time. The form looks reliable rated around the winner, third and fourth.
T/Plt: £23.00 to a £1 stake. Pool: £60,630.15 - 1924.10 winning tickets. T/Qpdt: £9.70 to a £1 stake. Pool: £5,391.04 - 407.16 winning tickets. JN

8052 LINGFIELD (L-H)
Tuesday, December 11

OFFICIAL GOING: Standard
Wind: Virtually nil Weather: Sunny but cold

8060 GREAT OFFERS AT LINGFIELDPARK.CO.UK H'CAP 1m 4f (P)
12:00 (12:00) (Class 6) (0-65,71) 3-Y-O+ **£1,704** (£503; £251) **Stalls** Low

Form RPR

0231 **1** **Thecornishcowboy**[4] 8023 3-9-11 71 6ex (t) AdamKirby 10 81
(John Ryan) *hld up in rr: hdwy on outer 4f out: effrt and qcknd on outer to ld 2f out: rdn over 1f out: kpt on wl* **5/4**[1]

3020 **2** *2* **Elegant Ophelia**[36] 7596 3-9-3 63 JimCrowley 8 69
(Dean Ivory) *hld up in rr: hdwy 4f out: trckd ldrs whn n.m.r 2f out: sn rdn and chsd wnr over 1f out: drvn and kpt on wl fnl f* **12/1**

3366 **3** *5* **Stanley Rigby**[35] 7603 6-9-10 65 (b) BarryMcHugh 6 63
(Richard Fahey) *in tch: hdwy on inner over 3f out: rdn 2f out: chsd ldng pair over 1f out: kpt on same pce* **20/1**

0546 **4** *1 3/4* **Astroscarlet**[34] 7629 3-8-11 57 MartinDwyer 4 52
(Mark H Tompkins) *led: rdn along over 3f out: drvn and hdd 2f out: grad wknd* **5/1**[2]

-463 **5** *2 3/4* **On The Feather**[7] 2735 6-9-8 63 (b[1]) JamieGoldstein 1 54
(Jim Best) *in rr: sme hdwy over 2f out: sn rdn along and n.d* **10/1**[3]

2426 **6** *7* **Mohair**[26] 7718 3-9-5 65 IanMongan 2 45
(Luke Dace) *in tch: effrt 4f out: rdn along 3f out: sn outpcd* **10/1**[3]

5600 **7** *1 3/4* **Minty Fox**[20] 7811 3-9-2 62 SebSanders 9 39
(Rae Guest) *prom on outer: pushed along 5f out: rdn wl over 3f out: edgd lft and wknd over 2f out* **14/1**

0000 **8** *8* **Shirataki (IRE)**[4] 8023 4-9-6 61 ChrisCatlin 7 25
(Peter Hiatt) *cl up: effrt to dispute ld 4f out: pushed along wl 3f out: rdn over 2f out and sn wknd* **5/1**[2]

0435 **9** *11* **Darsan (IRE)**[27] 7717 4-8-12 53 SilvestreDeSousa 3
(Phil McEntee) *chsd ldrs: rdn along over 3f out: sn wknd* **16/1**

2m 29.25s (-3.75) **Going Correction** -0.075s/f (Stan)
WFA 3 from 4yo+ 5lb **9** Ran SP% **121.0**
Speed ratings (Par 101): **109,107,104,103,101 96,95,90,82**
Tote swingers 1&2 £5.50, 1&3 £9.80, 2&3 £39.50 CSF £19.76 CT £220.93 TOTE £2.30: £1.10, £4.60, £5.00; EX 24.30 Trifecta £382.00 Part won. Pool: £509.39 - 0.30 winning tickets..
Owner C Letcher & J Ryan **Bred** Hadi Al Tajir **Trained** Newmarket, Suffolk

FOCUS
An uncompetitive handicap, and with the pace good by the usual standards of a Polytrack middle-distance, they finished strung out. The runner-up sets the level.

8061 STAY AT THE MARRIOTT HOTEL LINGFIELD PARK H'CAP (DIV I) 7f (P)
12:30 (12:30) (Class 6) (0-60,60) 3-Y-O+ **£1,704** (£503; £251) **Stalls** Low

Form RPR

0032 **1** **Mack's Sister**[25] 7748 5-9-2 55 (p) JimCrowley 6 63
(Dean Ivory) *trckd ldrs: hdwy over 2f out: rdn to ld wl over 1f out: drvn ins fnl f: hld on wl* **9/2**[3]

000 **2** *nk* **Jackie Love (IRE)**[13] 7898 4-8-7 46 (v) KirstyMilczarek 1 53
(Olivia Maylam) *trckd ldrs: hdwy over 2f out: effrt on inner wl over 1f out: sn chal and ev ch: drvn ins fnl f: no ex towards fin* **8/1**

2001 **3** *1 3/4* **Renoir's Lady**[47] 7362 4-9-0 53 GrahamLee 3 55
(Simon Dow) *hld up in rr: hdwy 3f out: trckd ldrs and n.m.r over 1f out: sn swtchd lft to inner and rdn: kpt on same pce fnl f* **3/1**[1]

466 **4** *1/2* **Jonnie Skull (IRE)**[5] 8005 6-9-0 53 (vt) SilvestreDeSousa 2 54
(Phil McEntee) *sn led: rdn along over 2f out: hdd wl over 1f out: sn drvn and one pce* **5/1**

3630 **5** *1 1/4* **Buxton**[6] 7992 8-9-7 60 (t) SebSanders 7 58
(Roger Ingram) *hld up and bhd: hdwy on outer over 2f out: rdn wl over 1f out: kpt on ins fnl f: nrst fin* **6/1**

0600 **6** *1/2* **Royal Envoy (IRE)**[69] 6771 9-8-10 49 ow2 (p) MichaelStainton 9 45
(Paul Howling) *prom: rdn along wl over 2f out: drvn 2f out and sn wknd* **25/1**

-060 **7** *3 3/4* **Witchry**[63] 6951 10-9-4 57 ChrisCatlin 4 43
(Tony Newcombe) *a towards rr* **12/1**

0000 **8** *3 1/2* **Desert Red (IRE)**[35] 7605 3-8-4 46 oh1 (b) RaulDaSilva(3) 5 23
(Phil McEntee) *chsd ldng pair on inner: rdn along wl over 2f out: sn wknd* **25/1**

0530 **9** *8* **Venetias Dream (IRE)**[18] 7837 3-8-12 51 (t) JamieSpencer 8 +
(Stuart Williams) *towards rr: niggled along after 2f: sme hdwy on outer 1/2-way: rdn along over 2f out: sn wknd and eased* **4/1**[2]

1m 23.86s (-0.94) **Going Correction** -0.075s/f (Stan) **9** Ran SP% **120.6**
Speed ratings (Par 101): **102,101,99,99,97 97,92,88,79**
Tote swingers 1&2 £12.60, 1&3 £2.40, 2&3 £7.70 CSF £42.20 CT £125.69 TOTE £4.80: £1.90, £2.90, £1.70; EX 43.70 Trifecta £131.00 Pool: £475.13 - 2.72 winning tickets.
Owner Recycled Products Limited **Bred** Mrs L R Burrage **Trained** Radlett, Herts
■ Stewards' Enquiry : Kirsty Milczarek two-day ban: use of whip (26, 27 Dec)

FOCUS
A moderate but competitive handicap run in a time 0.51 seconds quicker than the second leg. The form looks sound but ordinary.

8062 STAY AT THE MARRIOTT HOTEL LINGFIELD PARK H'CAP (DIV II) 7f (P)
1:00 (1:00) (Class 6) (0-60,59) 3-Y-O+ **£1,704** (£503; £251) **Stalls** Low

Form RPR

4056 **1** **Basle**[105] 5720 5-9-2 54 (t) RichardKingscote 8 61
(Michael Blake) *hld up towards rr: hdwy 2f out: swtchd lft to inner and rdn over 1f out: led jst ins fnl f: drvn out* **8/1**

5060 **2** *nk* **Putin (IRE)**[5] 8010 4-8-4 45 (bt) RaulDaSilva(3) 4 51
(Phil McEntee) *t.k.h: chsd ldr 2f: styd prom: effrt 2f out: rdn to chal over 1f out: led briefly ent fnl f: sn hdd: drvn and ev ch tl no ex last 50yds* **7/1**

6220 **3** *3/4* **Rogue Reporter (IRE)**[13] 7906 3-9-4 56 (v) JamieSpencer 7 60
(Stuart Williams) *led: rdn 2f out: drvn hdd ent fnl f: kpt on same pce* **6/4**[1]

0-05 **4** *1/2* **Back For Tea (IRE)**[4] 8021 4-8-0 45 (b) RyanTate(7) 1 48
(Phil McEntee) *hld up towards rr: hdwy over 2f out: rdn to chse ldrs appr fnl f: sn drvn and one pce* **33/1**

6000 **5** *3/4* **Great Charm (IRE)**[8] 7960 7-9-2 59 HarryPoulton(5) 3 60
(Sheena West) *trckd ldrs: hdwy over 2f out: rdn over 1f out: one pce* **14/1**

0026 **6** *2* **Mystical Witch**[13] 7896 3-8-10 48 (v) JimmyQuinn 5 43
(Christine Dunnett) *prom: chsd ldr after 2f: rdn along 2f out: drvn and wknd over 1f out* **25/1**

0000 **7** *3/4* **Not My Choice (IRE)**[40] 7504 7-8-11 49 (t) J-PGuillambert 6 42
(Paul Howling) *blindfold removed late and v.s.a: hdwy on outer and in tch 1/2-way: rdn to chse ldrs over 2f out: wknd over 1f out* **7/1**

The Form Book Flat, Raceform Ltd, Compton, RG20 6NL

0003 **8** *1* **Hawaiian Storm**[35] 7602 3-9-1 53..........................(p) SilvestreDeSousa 2 43
(Mrs K Burke) *trckd ldrs: rdn along 2f out: ch over 1f out: sn drvn and wknd* **6/1**[3]

0631 **9** *4* **Artful Lady (IRE)**[18] 7837 3-8-6 51.......................... JordanVaughan(7) 9 31
(George Margarson) *rdr lost iron sn after s: a in rr* **9/2**[2]

1m 24.37s (-0.43) **Going Correction** -0.075s/f (Stan) **9** Ran SP% **122.0**
Speed ratings (Par 101): **99,98,97,97,96 94,93,92,87**
Tote swingers 1&2 £9.80, 1&3 £3.50, 2&3 £3.10 CSF £66.33 CT £132.55 TOTE £11.10: £3.20, £2.10, £1.60; EX 74.60 Trifecta £215.30 Pool: £519.63 - 1.81 winning tickets.
Owner West Wilts Hockey Lads **Bred** W H R John And Partners **Trained** Trowbridge, Wilts

FOCUS
Hand times show they covered the first 5f in a similar time to the first division, but they stopped the clock 0.51 seconds slower overall. The winner is rated to this year's form backed up by the second and third.

8063 CYPRIUM RESTAURANT AT LINGFIELD PARK CLASSIFIED CLAIMING STKS 6f (P)
1:30 (1:32) (Class 6) 3-Y-0+ **£1,704** (£503; £251) **Stalls** Low

Form RPR

0004 **1** **Efistorm**[5] 8004 11-8-4 65.......................... KirstyMilczarek 2 71
(Joseph Tuite) *stmbld s: towards rr: hdwy wl over 1f out: rdn over 1f out: styd on wl to ld ins fnl f: edgd rt and kpt on gamely towards fin* **9/2**[3]

4434 **2** *nk* **Restless Bay (IRE)**[11] 7936 4-8-4 68..........................(v) SilvestreDeSousa 3 70
(Mrs K Burke) *dwlt and towards rr: pushed along and hdwy over 2f out: rdn wl over 1f out: styd on to chse ldrs whn edgd lft ins fnl f: kpt on* **6/4**[1]

1066 **3** *1* **Frognal (IRE)**[5] 8004 6-7-10 64..........................(bt) NoraLooby(7) 7 66
(Violet M Jordan) *hld up and bhd: gd hdwy on inner over 1f out: rdn and hung rt ins fnl f: kpt on* **8/1**

0604 **4** *nse* **For Shia And Lula (IRE)**[17] 7863 3-8-11 67.......................... ShaneKelly 6 74
(Daniel Mark Loughnane) *trckd ldng pair: hdwy to chse ldr wl over 1f out: sn rdn and kpt on same pce ins fnl f* **7/1**

0030 **5** *1* **Waabel**[17] 7857 5-8-5 65..........................(t) WilliamCarson 9 66
(Violet M Jordan) *set str pce: rdn clr 2f out: drvn and hdd ins fnl f: hld whn n.m.r and eased nr fin* **12/1**

055 **6** *1 1/2* **Lexington Spirit (IRE)**[114] 5388 3-8-7 62.......................... BarryMcHugh 11 62
(Richard Fahey) *dwlt: in rr whn hmpd sltly after 1f: rdn along and outpcd 3f out: wd st: styd on fnl f: nrst fin* **20/1**

5315 **7** *1* **Victorian Bounty**[32] 7666 7-8-5 69.......................... ChrisCatlin 8 57
(Tony Newcombe) *chsd ldrs on inner: rdn along over 2f out: grad wknd* **4/1**[2]

2005 **8** *7* **Waterloo Dock**[120] 5157 7-8-3 62..........................(v) AndreaAtzeni 4 32
(Michael Quinn) *chsd ldrs: rdn along over 2f out: sn wknd* **33/1**

3430 **9** *1* **Wreningham**[55] 7178 7-8-4 62.......................... KieranO'Neill 12 30
(Pat Eddery) *in tch: rdn along over 2f out: sn wknd* **20/1**

5500 **10** *8* **Thorpe Bay**[191] 2730 3-8-2 59..........................(b) DominicFox 1
(Conor Dore) *prom: rdn along over 2f out: sn wknd* **66/1**

1m 10.77s (-1.13) **Going Correction** -0.075s/f (Stan) **10** Ran SP% **123.4**
Speed ratings (Par 101): **104,103,102,102,100 98,97,88,86,76**
Tote swingers 1&2 £3.30, 1&3 £7.50, 2&3 £4.10 CSF £11.95 TOTE £6.50: £1.80, £1.10, £2.90; EX 20.20 Trifecta £62.70 Pool: £1,197.23 - 14.31 winning tickets.The winner was claimed by Mr C. R. Dore £7,000
Owner Andrew Liddiard **Bred** E Duggan And D Churchman **Trained** Great Shefford, Berks
■ Stewards' Enquiry : Kirsty Milczarek two-day ban: careless riding (28, 29 Dec)

FOCUS
The pace was overly quick in this modest claimer and the fourth is the best guide to the level.

8064 BREATHE SPA AT LINGFIELD PARK H'CAP 6f (P)
2:00 (2:00) (Class 6) (0-60,60) 3-Y-0+ **£1,704** (£503; £251) **Stalls** Low

Form RPR

045 **1** **Rich Again (IRE)**[18] 7838 3-9-7 60.......................... JamieSpencer 6 70
(James Bethell) *dwlt and in rr: gd hdwy on inner wl over 1f out: rdn to chal jst ins fnl f: kpt on to ld last 100yds: edgd rt towards fin* **5/1**[3]

0012 **2** *3/4* **Mey Blossom**[13] 7915 7-9-7 60..........................(p) RobertWinston 3 68
(Richard Whitaker) *chsd ldrs: hdwy over 1f out: rdn to ld ent fnl f: drvn and hdd last 100yds: kpt on* **8/1**

-002 **3** *3/4* **Spartic**[17] 7861 4-9-5 58.......................... SeanLevey 8 64
(Alan McCabe) *towards rr: hdwy on outer whn carried wd home turn: sn rdn and edgd lft over 1f out: drvn and styd on fnl f* **5/1**[3]

4252 **4** *shd* **Loyal Royal (IRE)**[6] 7990 9-9-6 59..........................(bt) GrahamLee 5 64
(Milton Bradley) *t.k.h: hld up towards rr: hdwy over 2f out: rdn and ev ch over 1f out: drvn and one pce ins fnl f: hld whn hmpd nr fin* **3/1**[1]

6222 **5** *3/4* **Miakora**[24] 7770 4-9-2 55.......................... AndreaAtzeni 2 58
(Michael Quinn) *chsd ldr on inner: rdn 2f out: styd on and ev ch appr fnl f: drvn and hld whn hmpd nr fin* **14/1**

0003 **6** *1/2* **Chjimes (IRE)**[17] 7861 8-9-5 58..........................(b) LiamKeniry 11 59
(Conor Dore) *hld up in tch: hdwy to chse ldrs 2f out: rdn and ch over 1f out: drvn and one pce fnl f* **7/1**

0031 **7** *1* **Ace Of Spies (IRE)**[26] 7733 7-9-6 59.......................... KirstyMilczarek 12 57
(Conor Dore) *led: rdn along wl over 1f out: drvn and hdd 1f out: sn wknd* **20/1**

0356 **8** *6* **Mary's Pet**[40] 7512 5-9-6 59..........................(p) WilliamCarson 10 38+
(Lee Carter) *chsd ldr: rdn along 2f out: drvn over 1f out: sn wknd* **4/1**[2]

0603 **9** *1* **Christopher Chua (IRE)**[13] 7903 3-9-4 57.......................... SebSanders 9 33+
(Simon Dow) *towards rr: effrt 2f out: rdn along and hung rt on outer ent fnl f: styng on u.p whn hmpd jst ins fnl f: nt rcvr* **8/1**

1m 11.58s (-0.32) **Going Correction** -0.075s/f (Stan) **9** Ran SP% **124.5**
Speed ratings (Par 101): **99,98,97,96,95 95,93,85,84**
Tote swingers 1&2 £6.90, 1&3 £6.70, 2&3 £8.50 CSF £48.26 CT £217.81 TOTE £5.80: £2.70, £2.60, £2.50; EX 47.40 Trifecta £225.30 Pool: £1,309.90 - 4.36 winning tickets.
Owner Richard T Vickers **Bred** Mrs Sandra Maye **Trained** Middleham Moor, N Yorks

FOCUS
A rough race, so form to treat with caution. The placed horses offer the best guides to the level.

8065 PLAY GOLF AT LINGFIELD PARK NURSERY 5f (P)
2:30 (2:31) (Class 5) (0-75,74) 2-Y-0 **£2,264** (£673; £336; £168) **Stalls** High

Form RPR

0000 **1** **Mossgo (IRE)**[25] 7745 2-9-0 67.......................... RobertWinston 1 68
(John Best) *t.k.h: in tch: hdwy 2f out: effrt on outer over 1f out: sn rdn and chal ins fnl f: kpt on wl to ld nr line* **20/1**

1223 **2** *shd* **Modern Lady**[11] 7930 2-8-11 64.......................... RobbieFitzpatrick 7 65
(Richard Guest) *trckd ldng pair: hdwy to chse ldr 2f out: rdn over 1f out: led ins fnl f: sn drvn: hdd and nt qckn nr line* **7/1**

0120 **3** *nk* **Work Ethic (IRE)**[34] 7635 2-9-6 73..........................(b[1]) NickyMackay 4 73
(Gerard Butler) *hld up towards rr: hdwy 2f out: rdn over 1f out and sn ev ch: drvn ins fnl f: no ex towards fin* **7/4**[1]

3014 **4** *1/2* **Layla's Oasis**[13] 7891 2-9-7 74.......................... JamieSpencer 6 72
(Jamie Osborne) *stdd s: hld up in rr: hdwy 2f out: sn rdn and styd on fnl f: no ex towards fin* **9/2**[3]

2255 **5** *1* **Spicy (IRE)**[17] 7866 2-9-3 70.......................... AdamKirby 2 64
(Marco Botti) *in tch: hdwy 2f out: rdn over 1f out: kpt on same pce* **9/2**[3]

0330 **6** *shd* **Con Leche**[11] 7930 2-8-7 60..........................(p) RichardKingscote 5 54
(Scott Dixon) *led: rdn over 1f out: drvn and hdd ins fnl f: wknd towards fin* **12/1**

61 **7** *3/4* **Tartan Blue**[13] 7891 2-8-4 57.......................... SilvestreDeSousa 3 48
(Robert Cowell) *cl up: rdn over 1f out: ev ch tl drvn and one pce ins fnl f* **4/1**[2]

58.91s (0.11) **Going Correction** -0.075s/f (Stan) **7** Ran SP% **117.7**
Speed ratings (Par 96): **96,95,95,94,92 92,91**
Tote swingers 1&2 £22.50, 1&3 £10.50, 2&3 £2.70 CSF £154.06 TOTE £34.50: £18.70, £4.40; EX 232.20 Trifecta £1192.20 Pool: £1,037.39 - 1.03 winning tickets.
Owner Hucking Horses V **Bred** Louis Robinson **Trained** Hucking, Kent

FOCUS
A modest nursery and messy form with the third looking the best guide.

NOTEBOOK
Mossgo(IRE) looked to have completely lost his way, but finally returned to the sort of form that saw him make a winning debut in April. Now that he's back on track he could defy a rise. Official explanation: trainer said, regarding the apparent improvement of form, that the gelding had benefitted from being held up today
Modern Lady is a game sort who continues to go the right way, finishing in the money for the fifth consecutive race.
Work Ethic(IRE) went okay in first-time blinkers and might do better returned to 6f. (op 5-2)
Layla's Oasis was never going well enough to get involved. (op 4-1)
Spicy(IRE) took an age to pick up and is proving difficult to win with. (op 5-1)
Tartan Blue, unable to dominate this time, was below the form she showed when winning a 5f claimer at Kempton last time. (op 3-1)

8066 ATTHERACES.COM EXCLUSIVE BARRY GERAGHTY BLOG H'CAP 5f (P)
3:00 (3:00) (Class 3) (0-95,100) 3-Y-0+ **£6,663** (£1,982; £990; £495) **Stalls** High

Form RPR

6505 **1** **Woolfall Sovereign (IRE)**[5] 8008 6-8-13 87.......................... IanMongan 6 96
(George Margarson) *in tch: hdwy wl over 1f out: rdn ent fnl f: kpt on to ld last 100yds* **7/1**[3]

0231 **2** *1* **Swiss Cross**[5] 8008 5-9-12 100 6ex.......................... DavidProbert 2 105
(Phil McEntee) *trckd ldng pair: hdwy to chse ldr 2f out: rdn to ld ent fnl f: drvn and hdd last 100yds* **7/2**[2]

3535 **3** *1 1/2* **Ajjaadd (USA)**[13] 7897 6-9-2 95..........................(p) WilliamTwiston-Davies(5) 1 95
(Ted Powell) *dwlt and in rr: hdwy wl over 1f out: swtchd rt and rdn ins fnl f: kpt on: nrst fin* **7/1**[3]

303 **4** *3/4* **Seeking Magic**[12] 7928 4-8-11 85..........................(t) GrahamLee 8 82
(Clive Cox) *hld up in rr: hdwy on outer over 2f out: pushed wd home turn: sn rdn and kpt on fnl f* **6/4**[1]

1624 **5** *1/2* **Last Sovereign**[13] 7918 8-8-6 87..........................(b) JacobButterfield(7) 5 82
(Ollie Pears) *trckd ldrs on inner: rdn along wl over 1f out: one pce fnl f* **8/1**

4425 **6** *1* **Six Wives**[5] 8009 5-8-8 82..........................(p) SilvestreDeSousa 9 74
(Scott Dixon) *chsd ldrs: rdn along wl over 1f out: edgd rt on home turn: one pce appr fnl f* **12/1**

0016 **7** *2* **Royal Bajan (USA)**[17] 7860 4-8-9 83..........................(b) J-PGuillambert 3 67
(James Given) *led: rdn along wl over 1f out: hdd ent fnl f: sn wknd* **20/1**

0300 **8** *nse* **Even Stevens**[5] 8008 4-9-7 95..........................(p) AdamKirby 4 79
(Scott Dixon) *cl up: rdn along 2f out: edgd rt home turn: sn wknd* **8/1**

57.51s (-1.29) **Going Correction** -0.075s/f (Stan) **8** Ran SP% **121.9**
Speed ratings (Par 107): **107,105,103,101,101 99,96,96**
Tote swingers 1&2 £8.00, 1&3 £11.60, 2&3 £3.70 CSF £33.96 CT £185.53 TOTE £13.00: £2.70, £1.50, £1.40; EX 48.70 Trifecta £191.20 Pool: £1,078.38 - 4.23 winning tickets.
Owner Wildcard Racing Syndicate **Bred** Saud Bin Saad **Trained** Newmarket, Suffolk

FOCUS
A good race, run in a time only 0.25 seconds outside the track record. The third looks the best guide to the level.

NOTEBOOK
Woolfall Sovereign(IRE) was returning from a break when fifth behind Swiss Cross over 6f here the previous week and clearly that run brought him on enough for him to reverse form over this shorter trip on 6lb better terms. He is relatively lightly raced for his age and this was a career best. (op 6-1)
Swiss Cross ran well, the 5yo just missing out under his penalty. (op 5-2)
Ajjaadd(USA) is also still on an upward curve and he kept on after a sluggish beginning. (op 6-1)
Seeking Magic didn't handle the track, going much too wide into the straight, and he did well to finish so close. (op 9-4)
Last Sovereign reversed recent Wolverhampton form with Six Wives, but both of them were well held. (op 10-1)

8067 FIND US ON TWITTER @LINGFIELDPARK H'CAP 1m 5f (P)
3:30 (3:31) (Class 6) (0-60,59) 3-Y-0+ **£1,704** (£503; £251) **Stalls** Low

Form RPR

003 **1** **Honest Strike (USA)**[21] 7793 5-9-1 50..........................(b) ShaneKelly 4 57
(Daniel Mark Loughnane) *trckd ldrs: hdwy 3f out: rdn over 1f out: styd on to ld jst ins fnl f: drvn out* **5/1**[3]

36-4 **2** *3/4* **Stetson**[17] 7869 6-9-7 56.......................... GrahamLee 10 62+
(Ian Williams) *hld up in midfield: hdwy to trck ldrs 1/2-way: effrt 2f out: rdn over 1f out: chsd wnr ins fnl f: no imp towards fin* **7/4**[1]

652P **3** *1* **Five Hearts**[21] 7793 4-9-2 51.......................... MartinDwyer 14 55
(Mark H Tompkins) *trckd ldrs: hdwy and cl up 1/2-way: led over 3f out: rdn wl over 1f out: drvn and hdd jst ins fnl f: kpt on same pce* **25/1**

6000 **4** *hd* **Bennelong**[4] 8023 6-9-9 58..........................(p) AmirQuinn 8 62
(Richard Rowe) *trckd ldrs: effrt over 2f out: rdn over 1f out: drvn and kpt on same pce fnl f* **8/1**

0000 **5** *nk* **Soweto Star (IRE)**[13] 7905 4-9-10 59.......................... GeorgeBaker 11 63
(John Best) *hld up towards rr: hdwy 4f out: in tch 2f out: sn rdn and styd on fnl f: nrst fin* **8/1**

5315 **6** *1* **Midnight Sequel**[180] 1726 3-8-8 49.......................... RichardKingscote 1 51
(Michael Blake) *midfield: hdwy over 4f out: rdn along to chse ldrs 2f out: drvn and no imp appr fnl f* **16/1**

0000 **7** *1 3/4* **Broughton Place**[46] 7385 4-8-10 45.......................... RobertWinston 2 45
(Willie Musson) *hld up and bhd: stdy hdwy 5f out: chsd ldrs on outer 2f out: sn rdn and no imp* **25/1**

0066 **8** *hd* **Glaze**[40] 7499 3-8-5 46.......................... ChrisCatlin 3 45
(Hughie Morrison) *chsd ldr: rdn along 3f out: drvn wl over 1f out and grad wknd* **20/1**

4130 **9** *nk* **Bold Adventure**[176] 3216 8-9-4 53.......................... JamieMackay 13 52
(Willie Musson) *hld up in rr: sme hdwy fnl 2f: n.d* **25/1**

2-50 **10** *1 1/2* **Red Current**[28] 566 8-9-8 57.......................... JamieGoldstein 6 54
(Michael Scudamore) *nvr bttr than midfield* **33/1**

0432 **11** ¾ **Barachiel**[8] 7960 4-9-4 58 NicoleNordblad(5) 5 53
(Luke Dace) *t.k.h: led: rdn along and hdd over 3f out: wknd fnl 2f* **3/1**[2]
3000 **U** **Crimson Monarch (USA)**[21] 7800 8-8-10 45 (b) WilliamCarson 12
(Peter Hiatt) *uns rdr s* **25/1**
2m 46.73s (0.73) **Going Correction** -0.075s/f (Stan)
WFA 3 from 4yo+ 6lb 12 Ran SP% **129.2**
Speed ratings (Par 101): **94,93,92,92,92 92,90,90,90,89 89,**
Tote swingers 1&2 £4.60, 1&3 £14.80, 2&3 £12.80 CSF £14.20 CT £220.15 TOTE £6.60: £2.40, £1.10, £7.00; EX 20.00 Trifecta £338.80 Pool: £1,305.70 - 2.89 winning tickets.
Owner K Kilbane, J O'Shea & S Hunt **Bred** Juddmonte Farms Inc **Trained** Baldwin's Gate, Staffs

FOCUS
A moderate staying contest which looks pretty sound but it is form that is hard to be positive about.
Barachiel Official explanation: vet said the trainer bled from the nose
T/Jkpt: Not won. T/Plt: £100.00 to a £1 stake. Pool: £60,567.33 - 441.97 winning tickets T/Qpdt: £39.60 to a £1 stake. Pool: £5,244.29 - 97.9 winning tickets JR

7986 KEMPTON (A.W) (R-H)
Wednesday, December 12

OFFICIAL GOING: Standard
Wind: Nil Weather: Low cloud, frozen

8068 WIN BIG WITH BETDAQ MULTIPLES MEDIAN AUCTION MAIDEN STKS 6f (P)
2:15 (2:17) (Class 6) 2-Y-O **£1,617** (£481; £240; £120) **Stalls** Low

Form RPR
0 **1** **Bobby Two Shoes**[156] 3916 2-9-3 0 EddieAhern 6 72+
(Brett Johnson) *prom on rail: drvn to ld over 1f out: rdn out* **33/1**
2 ¾ **Master Wizard** 2-9-3 0 RichardHughes 9 68
(Jane Chapple-Hyam) *towards rr: rdn and hdwy over 1f out: kpt on to take 2nd ins fnl f* **9/4**[2]
3 *nk* **Upavon** 2-9-3 0 WilliamBuick 1 68
(David Elsworth) *s.s and rdn early: bhd: gd hdwy over 1f out: kpt on fnl f* **6/1**[3]
2302 **4** 1 **Whipper Snapper (IRE)**[21] 7813 2-9-3 73 JimCrowley 7 65
(William Knight) *mid-div: hdwy to chse wnr over 1f out: lost 2nd and one pce ins fnl f* **1/1**[1]
U **5** 1 **Wishing Bridge**[32] 7686 2-9-3 0 JimmyFortune 12 62
(Pat Eddery) *chsd ldr: led over 2f out: hdd and no ex over 1f out* **33/1**
0 **6** 1 ½ **Indigo Moon**[21] 7813 2-8-12 0 ShaneKelly 3 52
(Denis Coakley) *dwlt: mid-div: hdwy over 2f out: wknd over 1f out* **16/1**
7 *nk* **Batchworth Lady** 2-8-12 0 JimmyQuinn 8 51
(Dean Ivory) *s.s: hld up and bhd: shkn up over 2f out: nvr in chalng position* **50/1**
00 **8** 5 **Suspension**[13] 7924 2-8-12 0 NickyMackay 4 36
(Hughie Morrison) *chsd ldrs tl wknd 2f out* **14/1**
5 **9** 2 ¼ **Blue Missile**[8] 7979 2-8-10 0 RyanWhile(7) 10 34
(Bill Turner) *led tl over 2f out: wknd qckly over 1f out* **33/1**
1m 13.65s (0.55) **Going Correction** -0.125s/f (Stan) 9 Ran SP% **118.4**
Speed ratings (Par 94): **91,90,89,88,86 84,84,77,74**
toteswingers 1&2 £9.20, 1&3 £23.40, 2&3 £2.80 CSF £107.88 TOTE £50.80: £8.80, £1.10, £3.10; EX 140.30 Trifecta £736.50 Pool: £1,590.89 - 1.62 winning tickets..
Owner Mrs A M Upsdell **Bred** Brian Liversage **Trained** Epsom, Surrey

FOCUS
Probably just a moderate maiden, run at a steady pace with plenty in contention at the furlong pole. The opening level is fluid but the winner can do better.

NOTEBOOK
Bobby Two Shoes, returning from a 156 day break, was always travelling well behind the pace, enjoyed a dream run up the inner and none of his rivals were good enough to go past him. This was a big improvement on his debut at Windsor (6f, soft), but this was a weak contest and he enjoyed the run of the race.
Master Wizard, a half-brother to a pair of useful 6f/7f performers in Take Cover and Arteus, was well fancied in the market on his debut and travelled nicely enough into the contest. He was outpaced when the winner kicked for home and could never quite reel him in. (op 3-1)
Upavon, a 10,000gns yearling, was not that well away but was doing his best work late. He's from a yard whose runners tend to improve with experience. (tchd 7-1)
Whipper Snapper(IRE) was the clear form choice coming into the contest after finishing a decent second at Lingfield last time, but he still looked a shade green throughout and showed disappointingly little when asked for his effort out wide. (op 10-11 tchd 11-10)
Wishing Bridge took up the running at the 2f pole but was outpaced when the gallop quickened a furlong out, although he was sticking on again late on and may need further in time.
Batchworth Lady was slowly away and had plenty on turning for home, but was keeping on well out wide, without reaching the leaders. This rates a fair debut. Official explanation: jockey said that the filly was slowly away (op 33-1)

8069 BACK AND LAY AT BETDAQ.COM MEDIAN AUCTION MAIDEN STKS 7f (P)
2:45 (2:47) (Class 6) 3-5-Y-O **£1,617** (£481; £240; £120) **Stalls** Low

Form RPR
2222 **1** **Kalokagathia (IRE)**[14] 7896 3-9-3 74 IanMongan 7 83
(Jo Crowley) *mde all: rdn over 2f out: clr fnl f: comf* **8/13**[1]
6205 **2** 4 **Excellent Jem**[7] 7998 3-9-3 70 RichardHughes 8 72
(Jane Chapple-Hyam) *chsd wnr: rdn over 3f out: no imp over 1f out* **2/1**[2]
5060 **3** 7 **Ishi**[7] 7988 3-8-13 48 ow1 JamesMillman 4 49
(Rod Millman) *chsd ldrs: outpcd over 2f out: sn btn* **20/1**
0 **4** 5 **Rosa Lockwood**[90] 6154 3-8-12 0 DavidProbert 3 35
(Tony Carroll) *stdd s: in tch: rdn 4f out: outpcd and no ch w ldrs fnl 3f* **20/1**
/00 **5** 3 ¾ **Island Express (IRE)**[11] 7952 5-8-12 46 (bt) AnnStokell(5) 5 30
(Ann Stokell) *stdd s: plld hrd towards rr: sme hdwy 3f out: sn wknd* **66/1**
6 ¾ **Sign Pro (IRE)**[45] 4-9-3 0 StevieDonohoe 9 28
(Peter Bowen) *s.s: outpcd and bhd: nvr nr ldrs* **16/1**
00 **7** ¾ **Twilight Legend (IRE)**[14] 7896 3-8-12 0 JimmyQuinn 1 21
(Seamus Mullins) *t.k.h: chsd ldrs tl wknd over 2f out* **50/1**
0360 **8** 2 ¼ **Batchworth Firefly**[7] 7993 4-8-12 60 JimCrowley 2 15
(Dean Ivory) *a bhd* **14/1**[3]
-000 **9** 5 **Aaranyow (IRE)**[26] 7739 4-9-3 33 FrankieMcDonald 6
(Terry Clement) *mid-div: rdn and struggling 3f out: sn bhd* **66/1**
1m 24.29s (-1.71) **Going Correction** -0.125s/f (Stan) 9 Ran SP% **122.3**
Speed ratings (Par 101): **104,99,91,85,81 80,79,77,71**
toteswingers 1&2 £1.10, 1&3 £4.70, 2&3 £7.90 CSF £2.07 TOTE £1.80: £1.02, £1.10, £6.10; EX 2.30 Trifecta £17.40 Pool: £2,099.97 - 90.33 winning tickets..
Owner Kilstone Limited **Bred** C Amerian **Trained** Whitcombe, Dorset

FOCUS
The market suggested this was a two horse race and they had the contest between themselves from a long way out. The winner is rated in line with the best of his previous form, backed up by the runner-up.
Island Express(IRE) Official explanation: jockey said that the gelding was slowly away, and ran keen early

8070 BETDAQ MOBILE APPS/BRITISH STALLION STUDS E B F MAIDEN STKS (DIV I) 1m (P)
3:15 (3:22) (Class 5) 2-Y-O **£3,169** (£943; £471; £235) **Stalls** Low

Form RPR
1 **Ajman Bridge** 2-9-0 0 PatrickHills(3) 3 79+
(Luca Cumani) *in tch: effrt over 2f out: led over 1f out: rdn clr: comf* **20/1**
552 **2** 2 ¾ **Rangi**[21] 7806 2-9-3 76 [1] WilliamBuick 4 73
(John Gosden) *pressed ldrs: drvn to chse wnr over 1f out: kpt on same pce* **6/4**[1]
3 1 **Double Discount (IRE)** 2-9-3 0 RichardKingscote 6 71+
(Tom Dascombe) *mid-div: rdn 4f out: styd on fnl 2f: nt rch first 2* **20/1**
30 **4** ½ **Kelvingrove (IRE)**[49] 7324 2-9-3 0 IanMongan 2 70
(Ed Vaughan) *pushed along early: towards rr: rdn and r.o fr over 1f out: nrest at fin* **20/1**
6 **5** *nk* **Little Buxted (USA)**[9] 7962 2-9-3 0 JimmyFortune 10 69
(Robert Mills) *mid-div: rdn 3f out: r.o fnl 2f: nt rch ldrs* **33/1**
024 **6** *nk* **Secret Rebel**[18] 7856 2-9-3 74 LiamKeniry 1 68
(Sylvester Kirk) *led: rdn over 2f out: hdd over 1f out: sn wknd* **11/2**[2]
7 2 **Pencombe (FR)** 2-9-3 0 ShaneKelly 9 64+
(David Simcock) *dwlt: bhd: rdn over 2f out: sme late hdwy* **33/1**
04 **8** 2 **Atlantis City (FR)**[13] 7926 2-9-3 0 RichardHughes 11 59
(Richard Hannon) *sn pressing ldr: hrd rdn 2f out: wknd over 1f out* **9/1**
0 **9** 2 **Lunette (IRE)**[27] 7721 2-8-12 0 JimCrowley 12 49
(Ralph Beckett) *prom on outer tl wknd jst over 2f out* **14/1**
00 **10** 4 ½ **Father And Son (IRE)**[25] 7780 2-9-3 0 AndreaAtzeni 7 44
(Marco Botti) *chsd ldrs tl wknd 2f out* **33/1**
0 **11** 2 ¼ **Dusky Lark**[14] 7899 2-9-3 0 GeorgeBaker 5 39
(Hughie Morrison) *prom early: sn stdd bk into midfield: rdn and wknd over 2f out* **12/1**
0 **12** 6 **Upper Echelon**[169] 3474 2-8-12 0 SilvestreDeSousa 8 20
(Mark Johnston) *dwlt: nvr gng wl: a bhd* **6/1**[3]
1m 38.46s (-1.34) **Going Correction** -0.125s/f (Stan) 12 Ran SP% **117.1**
Speed ratings (Par 96): **101,98,97,96,96 96,94,92,90,85 83,77**
toteswingers 1&2 £8.60, 1&3 £18.20, 2&3 £11.80 CSF £46.48 TOTE £37.40: £7.20, £1.50, £7.20; EX 83.80 Trifecta £461.40 Pool: £1,864.12 - 3.03 winning tickets..
Owner Sheikh Mohammed Obaid Al Maktoum **Bred** Rabbah Bloodstock Limited **Trained** Newmarket, Suffolk

FOCUS
Some powerful stables in opposition for this maiden. The pace was honest, with the winner scoring impressively on his debut and the second and fourth setting the level.

NOTEBOOK
Ajman Bridge, a 125,000gns yearling and second foal of a 1m2f winner from the family of Verglas and Cassandra Go, was always travelling well behind the strong pace and showed a willing attitude, as well as a decent turn-of-foot, to pull clear inside the final furlong. His trainer is more than capable of readying one first time but there should be plenty of improvement to come. (op 33-1)
Rangi had shown ability in three 7f maidens and travelled strongly into the contest in a first-time hood, but he did not see this longer trip out as well as the winner. (op 5-4)
Double Discount(IRE), a 70,000euros yearling and second foal of an unraced mare from an excellent family, did best of those coming from behind and one would expect this experience to bring him on a good deal. (op 33-1 tchd 16-1)
Kelvingrove(IRE), having his first run for Ed Vaughan, unseated his jockey before loading but still ran an eyecatching race once in. Settled near the rear, he was doing his best work late, suggesting he can step up on this over further. (op 25-1)
Little Buxted(USA) showed ability on his debut over C&D and again ran a promising race here, closing late out wide having been held up near the rear. One can expect him to come on again for this. (op 50-1)
Pencombe(FR) was slowly away and green through the early parts of the contest but was staying on strongly up the straight in what was an encouraging debut, over what might be an inadequate trip. (op 50-1)

8071 BETDAQ MOBILE APPS/BRITISH STALLION STUDS E B F MAIDEN STKS (DIV II) 1m (P)
3:45 (3:48) (Class 5) 2-Y-O **£3,169** (£943; £471; £235) **Stalls** Low

Form RPR
5 **1** **Ningara**[14] 7899 2-9-3 0 DavidProbert 5 77
(Andrew Balding) *led 1f: trckd ldr gng wl: qcknd and led jst over 1f out: rdn out* **7/2**[1]
00 **2** 1 ¾ **Mallory Heights (IRE)**[18] 7868 2-9-0 0 PatrickHills(3) 1 73
(Luca Cumani) *mid-div on rail: rdn and hdwy 2f out: r.o to take 2nd fnl 100yds* **8/1**
3 ½ **Quadriga (IRE)**[108] 5639 2-9-3 0 AndreaAtzeni 11 72
(Robert Eddery) *led after 1f tl jst over 1f out: kpt on same pce* **6/1**
4 *nk* **Thomas Hobson** 2-9-3 0 WilliamBuick 4 71+
(John Gosden) *s.s: rn green: bhd tl late gd hdwy: gng on wl at fin: should improve* **4/1**[2]
03 **5** 1 ¾ **Snoqualmie Chief**[70] 6796 2-9-3 0 LiamKeniry 7 67
(David Elsworth) *chsd ldrs: rdn over 2f out: no ex fnl f* **6/1**
426 **6** 1 ½ **Dolphin Village (IRE)**[26] 7750 2-9-3 72 TonyHamilton 9 64
(Richard Fahey) *prom: hrd rdn over 2f out: wknd over 1f out* **12/1**
7 *shd* **Autrisk (IRE)** 2-9-3 0 JimCrowley 8 63
(Marco Botti) *mid-div: rdn and no hdwy fnl 3f* **12/1**
0 **8** 1 ¾ **Handsome Stranger (IRE)**[4] 8033 2-9-3 0 WilliamCarson 3 59
(David Evans) *towards rr: rdn 3f out: nvr nr to chal* **50/1**
9 1 **Ray Ward (IRE)** 2-9-3 0 JamieSpencer 2 57
(David Simcock) *a in rr: rdn and struggling to get on terms fnl 3f* **11/2**[3]
0 **10** *nk* **Thought And Memory (IRE)**[47] 7373 2-9-3 0 GeorgeBaker 10 56
(Mick Channon) *bhd: sme hdwy 2f out: wknd over 1f out* **10/1**
0 **11** 16 **Putmeintheswindle**[35] 7628 2-9-3 0 IanMongan 6 20
(Peter Hedger) *chsd ldrs tl wknd over 2f out* **100/1**
1m 39.07s (-0.73) **Going Correction** -0.125s/f (Stan) 11 Ran SP% **124.7**
Speed ratings (Par 96): **98,96,95,95,93 92,92,90,89,89 73**
toteswingers 1&2 £15.60, 1&3 £5.10, 2&3 £22.50 CSF £34.41 TOTE £2.30: £1.70, £5.90, £2.00; EX 68.20 Trifecta £1162.10 Part won. Pool: £1,549.59 - 0.72 winning tickets..
Owner G B Russell **Bred** S R Hope **Trained** Kingsclere, Hants

FOCUS
This did not look a bad maiden, run at a fair pace with the winner perfectly positioned throughout. The opening level is fluid but the winner is an improver.

NOTEBOOK

Ningara, who showed promise on his debut from an unpromising position, was much better berthed here and showed a good turn-of-foot up the straight to win well. As was the case in two of the three previous races on the card, he came with his winning move up the far rail but was well on top at the line and he can go on from this. (op 4-1)

Mallory Heights(IRE) was doing his best work late, also up the far rail, and this was his best effort to date. He is now qualified for a mark and will be one to keep on the right side of.

Quadriga(IRE), who had shown his best form in three starts for Aidan O´Brien on his only try on the AW, when runner-up at Dundalk (6f), ran a promising race here on his first run for Robert Eddery. He travelled nicely in front but weakened late on, stepping up in trip, returning from a break. (op 11-2)

Thomas Hobson, a 35,000gns yearling and second foal of a Listed-placed AW winner, was driven near the rear 2f out but came with a fine late burst to snatch fourth. This Derby entrant looks more than capable of landing a similar contest. (op 9-2 tchd 7-2)

Snoqualmie Chief again showed promise on his first AW start but was outpaced inside the final furlong. He will be seen to better effect over further, given time to develop over the winter. (op 9-2)

Autrisk(IRE), a 22,000euros yearling and half-brother to a couple of winners, travelled like a nice type into the straight and, while he was a shade green once coming under pressure, was staying on well to the line. He can build on this. (op 14-1)

8072 BETDAQ CASINO GAMES NURSERY 1m (P)

4:15 (4:15) (Class 5) (0-75,78) 2-Y-O **£2,264** (£673; £336; £168) **Stalls** Low

Form RPR

6331 **1** **Jodies Jem**[19] 7840 2-9-7 **75** GrahamLee 5 80+
(William Jarvis) chsd ldrs on outer: led 1f out: rdn out **7/2**[2]

4261 **2** ¾ **Canadian Run (IRE)**[7] 7989 2-9-10 **78** 6ex JimmyFortune 2 81
(Robert Mills) prom: led briefly over 1f out: kpt on **4/1**[3]

0525 **3** 1 ¼ **Beau Select (IRE)**[7] 7989 2-8-11 **65** (v[1]) AndreaAtzeni 9 65
(Robert Eddery) towards rr: rdn and hdwy over 1f out: styd on fnl f **12/1**

6625 **4** nk **Makinson Lane (IRE)**[9] 7965 2-8-13 **67** TonyHamilton 4 66
(Richard Fahey) led tl over 1f out: one pce **33/1**

0102 **5** 1 ¼ **Run It Twice (IRE)**[7] 7994 2-8-13 **67** WilliamCarson 7 64
(David Evans) s.i.s and rdn early: bhd: sme hdwy 2f out: styd on same pce **7/1**

5464 **6** ½ **Abraq**[84] 6363 2-9-2 **70** WilliamBuick 1 65+
(Ed Dunlop) bhd: rdn over 2f out: styd on fnl f **14/1**

153 **7** 1 ¼ **Mick Duggan**[9] 7965 2-9-5 **73** DavidProbert 8 66
(Simon Hodgson) chsd ldr tl over 2f out: wknd over 1f out **10/1**

033 **8** ½ **Emulating (IRE)**[21] 7814 2-9-1 **69** RichardHughes 3 60
(Richard Hannon) in tch on rail: rdn 4f out: chsd ldrs 2f out: fdd out of the pls fr over 1f out **5/2**[1]

0532 **9** hd **Lambert Pen (USA)**[8] 7977 2-8-8 **62** ChrisCatlin 6 53
(Mick Channon) mid-div: mod effrt over 2f out: sn hrd rdn and wknd fnl f **12/1**

1m 40.03s (0.23) **Going Correction** -0.125s/f (Stan) **9** Ran SP% **117.4**

Speed ratings (Par 96): **93,92,91,90,89 88,87,87,87**

toteswingers 1&2 £3.80, 1&3 £10.10, 2&3 £10.10 CSF £18.31 CT £152.48 TOTE £4.30: £2.10, £1.20, £4.90; EX 16.00 Trifecta £168.40 Pool: £1,520.64 - 6.77 winning tickets..

Owner Mrs M C Banks **Bred** Wickfield Stud And Hartshill Stud **Trained** Newmarket, Suffolk

FOCUS

Plenty of in-form runners in this nursery. It was run at a steady pace, meaning plenty were in contention inside the final furlong. The form makes sense but cannot be trusted implicitly.

NOTEBOOK

Jodies Jem saw this longer trip out well to win on his handicap debut. He was always ideally positioned but showed a decent turn-of-foot at the furlong pole and was always holding the runner-up. (op 6-1)

Canadian Run(IRE) ran a solid race back in second, but would have been suited by a stronger pace and possibly found the 6lb penalty for a recent success just too much to overcome. (op 9-2 tchd 5-1)

Beau Select(IRE) was closing nicely on the leaders in a first-time visor, but is finding it tough to land a second career prize from his current mark. (op 14-1)

Makinson Lane(IRE) travelled well in front but was outpaced when the gallop quickened with a furlong to go, and is yet to find his optimum trip.

Run It Twice(IRE), on whom William Carson was a late replacement, struggled to go the early pace but was closing at the finish. This trip appears to be his minimum. (op 11-2)

Abraq was staying on strongly out wide down in trip, and this rates a fair enough effort. He looks capable of going close when things drop right. (tchd 12-1)

Emulating(IRE) was well-backed in the morning but his rider did not look happy a long way from home and this rates a slightly disappointing effort. (op 2-1)

8073 CALVERTS CARPETS YORK H'CAP 2m (P)

4:45 (4:48) (Class 4) (0-85,86) 3-Y-O+ **£4,075** (£1,212; £606; £303) **Stalls** Low

Form RPR

324 **1** **Fourth Generation (IRE)**[21] 7810 5-9-7 **78** RobertWinston 1 86
(Alan Swinbank) towards rr: hdwy over 2f out: led over 1f out: hld on wl fnl f **7/1**

5211 **2** nk **Thecornishcockney**[9] 7972 3-9-7 **86** 6ex (tp) AdamKirby 4 94
(John Ryan) hld up in midfield: effrt over 2f out: r.o fnl f: clsng at fin **5/1**[1]

0142 **3** ½ **Tartan Jura**[9] 7972 4-9-3 **74** (b[1]) SilvestreDeSousa 11 81
(Mark Johnston) led after 1f tl 10f out: w ldr: led over 2f out tl over 1f out: kpt on wl nr fin **11/2**[2]

4015 **4** ½ **Somemothersdohavem**[13] 7927 3-8-12 **77** (p) MichaelO'Connell 2 83
(John Ryan) sn towards rr: gd hdwy 2f out: pressed ldrs 1f out: kpt on **7/1**

205P **5** ¾ **Woolfall Treasure**[43] 7109 7-9-12 **83** (v) GeorgeBaker 3 89
(Gary Moore) led 1f: remained prom: one pce fnl f **20/1**

6363 **6** nse **Spensley (IRE)**[20] 7825 6-10-0 **85** EddieAhern 6 90
(James Fanshawe) hld up in midfield: smooth hdwy on rail over 3f out: pressed ldrs 2f out: no ex fnl f **5/1**[1]

5350 **7** 4 **Icebuster**[21] 7810 4-9-7 **78** JamesMillman 9 79
(Rod Millman) s.s: bhd: effrt on outer over 2f out: nt rch ldrs **7/1**

5121 **8** 2 ¼ **Gabrial's King (IRE)**[13] 7927 3-8-8 **73** (p) StevieDonohoe 12 71
(Ian Williams) in tch: lost pl over 4f out: no hdwy fnl 3f **6/1**[3]

0402 **9** 2 **Honourable Knight (IRE)**[13] 7927 4-8-12 **69** LiamKeniry 13 65
(Mark Usher) s.s: bhd: rdn 3f out: sme hdwy 2f out: n.d **20/1**

-040 **10** 8 **Tuscan Gold**[37] 6333 5-9-9 **80** IanMongan 7 66
(Laura Mongan) chsd ldrs: led 10f out tl over 2f out: sn wknd **20/1**

0434 **11** 11 **Big Time Billy (IRE)**[131] 4756 6-8-9 **66** oh4 (p) WilliamCarson 8 39
(Peter Bowen) chsd ldrs tl wknd 3f out **25/1**

13 **12** 7 **Reillys Daughter**[168] 3498 4-8-4 **66** oh4 NatashaEaton[(5)] 10 30
(Richard Mitchell) prom tl wknd 4f out **50/1**

550 **P** **Praxiteles (IRE)**[95] 4731 8-9-4 **75** (tp) FrankieMcDonald 5
(Nikki Evans) rdn early: towards rr: lost action over 4f out: sn wl bhd: p.u and dismntd 3f out **66/1**

3m 27.81s (-2.29) **Going Correction** -0.125s/f (Stan)

WFA 3 from 4yo+ 8lb **13** Ran SP% **122.1**

Speed ratings (Par 105): **100,99,99,99,98 98,96,95,94,90 85,81,**

toteswingers 1&2 £4.30, 1&3 £17.60, 2&3 £25.90 CSF £39.16 CT £212.98 TOTE £7.20: £2.20, £1.90, £3.80; EX 46.90 Trifecta £259.00 Pool: £1,844.56 - 5.34 winning tickets..

Owner B Boanson & M Wane **Bred** Mrs Christine Kelly **Trained** Melsonby, N Yorks

FOCUS

A wide-open staying handicap run at a messy pace, with little covering the front six home but the form makes sense with the sixth to summer course form. The visibility was poor up the home straight.

8074 TIME ORDERED CARDS IN RACING PLUS H'CAP 7f (P)

5:15 (5:18) (Class 6) (0-65,65) 3-Y-O **£1,617** (£481; £240; £120) **Stalls** Low

Form RPR

5602 **1** **Mr Knightley (IRE)**[6] 8005 3-9-6 **64** (b) JimCrowley 1 78
(Jim Boyle) prom: led over 1f out: rdn clr **5/2**[1]

0200 **2** 3 ¼ **Al's Memory (IRE)**[32] 7684 3-9-7 **65** AdamKirby 12 70
(David Evans) chsd ldrs: effrt over 2f out: kpt on to take 2nd ins fnl f **6/1**[3]

3000 **3** 1 ¼ **Compton Rainbow**[25] 7776 3-9-4 **62** (t) WilliamCarson 13 64
(Hans Adielsson) led tl over 1f out: no ex **25/1**

2231 **4** 1 ½ **Tidal's Baby**[25] 7770 3-9-7 **65** DavidProbert 7 63
(Tony Carroll) s.s: bhd: rdn and hdwy 2f out: styd on **9/1**

6044 **5** 1 ¼ **The Noble Ord**[6] 8005 3-9-5 **63** (t) LiamKeniry 5 57
(Sylvester Kirk) mid-div: rdn over 2f out: no imp **10/1**

5262 **6** hd **Darnathean**[41] 7512 3-8-11 **62** LouisSteward[(7)] 9 56
(Paul D'Arcy) chsd ldr tl over 2f out: sn outpcd **16/1**

2-40 **7** ½ **Compton Bird**[19] 7841 3-9-2 **60** [1] J-PGuillambert 2 53
(Hans Adielsson) in tch on rail: effrt over 2f out: btn over 1f out **33/1**

3651 **8** 1 **Percythepinto (IRE)**[21] 7815 3-9-3 **61** (t) RichardHughes 11 51
(George Baker) stdd s: mid-div after 2f: rdn and sme hdwy over 2f out: wknd over 1f out **6/1**[3]

-200 **9** 1 **Just Breathe (IRE)**[9] 7969 3-9-6 **64** KirstyMilczarek 6 51
(Olivia Maylam) stdd s: hld up in rr: rdn over 2f out: n.d **33/1**

62-0 **10** nk **Going Grey (IRE)**[237] 1479 3-9-7 **65** TonyHamilton 8 51
(Richard Fahey) t.k.h towards rr: rdn 3f out: sn struggling **20/1**

0000 **11** 1 **Minstrels Gallery (IRE)**[34] 7644 3-9-1 **59** GrahamLee 10 43
(J R Jenkins) prom on outer tl wknd over 2f out **9/2**[2]

4500 **12** 7 **Le King Beau (USA)**[9] 7961 3-9-4 **62** (v) SeanLevey 3 27
(John Bridger) towards rr: sme hdwy and hrd rdn 2f out: sn wknd **14/1**

1m 24.78s (-1.22) **Going Correction** -0.125s/f (Stan) **12** Ran SP% **121.5**

Speed ratings (Par 98): **101,97,95,94,92 92,91,90,89,89 88,80**

toteswingers 1&2 £4.30, 1&3 £17.60, 2&3 £25.90 CSF £16.96 CT £311.49 TOTE £4.00: £1.30, £2.70, £5.90; EX 21.50 Trifecta £934.50 Pool: £1,408.11 - 1.13 winning tickets..

Owner The 'In Recovery' Partnership **Bred** Miss Deirdre Cogan **Trained** Epsom, Surrey

FOCUS

Another open-looking contest, run at a fair pace with the winning pulling clear to win impressively. He built on his latest effort while the placed horses are rated a little below their best for now.

Tidal's Baby Official explanation: jockey said that the gelding fly-leapt leaving the stalls

8075 MPR SOLICITORS CLASSIFIED STKS 6f (P)

5:45 (5:48) (Class 6) 3-Y-O+ **£1,617** (£481; £240; £120) **Stalls** Low

Form RPR

5504 **1** **Temple Road (IRE)**[26] 7748 4-9-0 55 GrahamLee 2 66+
(Milton Bradley) hld up in midfield on rail: smooth hdwy over 2f out: led wl over 1f out: sn clr: comf **9/2**[3]

242 **2** 2 **Clapped**[7] 7988 3-9-0 54 RichardHughes 7 60
(Ed Vaughan) bhd: rdn and hdwy 2f out: r.o to take 2nd ins fnl f **3/1**[1]

236 **3** ¾ **Valdaw**[70] 6774 4-9-0 55 AdamKirby 6 58+
(Tony Carroll) bhd: rdn and hdwy over 1f out: styd on fnl f **3/1**[1]

5-63 **4** ½ **Littlecote Lady**[301] 564 3-9-0 55 DavidProbert 4 56
(Mark Usher) prom: rdn 2f out: one pce appr fnl f **25/1**

0500 **5** 1 ¾ **Hold The Star**[135] 4656 6-8-9 53 AnnStokell[(5)] 5 50
(Ann Stokell) led tl wl over 1f out: sn outpcd **25/1**

4630 **5** dht **Dixie Gwalia**[19] 7837 4-9-0 51 MartinLane 10 50
(David Simcock) bhd: rdn over 2f out: styd on wl fnl f: nrest at fin **20/1**

0331 **7** 2 ¼ **Quan (IRE)**[27] 7729 3-9-0 55 RobertWinston 1 43
(Alan Swinbank) chsd ldrs: rdn and btn 2f out **7/2**[2]

5206 **8** ½ **Lisselton Cross**[26] 7748 4-9-0 52 (v) StevieDonohoe 8 42
(Martin Bosley) chsd ldrs: outpcd over 2f out: sn btn **25/1**

054 **9** 3 ¼ **Outside Art**[14] 7903 3-9-0 52 JimCrowley 9 31
(Paul Fitzsimons) mid-div: rdn over 2f out: sn btn **16/1**

/0-0 **10** 3 ¼ **Fast Samurai (USA)**[34] 7654 4-8-7 54 JoeyHaynes[(7)] 12 21
(Tony Carroll) chsd ldr tl over 2f out: sn wknd **33/1**

3000 **11** 5 **Cappielow Park**[43] 7470 3-9-0 55 (p) WilliamCarson 11
(Fleur Hawes) s.s and rdn early: mid-div after 2f: rdn and wknd over 2f out **33/1**

0-60 **U** **Desert Spree**[11] 7952 3-9-0 44 SebSanders 3
(Jeremy Gask) mid-div tl stmbld and uns rdr over 4f out **66/1**

1m 12.51s (-0.59) **Going Correction** -0.125s/f (Stan) **12** Ran SP% **120.0**

Speed ratings (Par 101): **98,95,94,93,91 91,88,87,83,79 72,**

toteswingers 1&2 £3.30, 1&3 £4.20, 2&3 £3.60 CSF £17.09 TOTE £4.30: £1.20, £1.50, £1.40; EX 18.10 Trifecta £80.90 Pool: £1,155.58 - 10.71 winning tickets..

Owner Darren Hudson-Wood **Bred** Paul Monaghan **Trained** Sedbury, Gloucs

FOCUS

A weak classified stakes with all bar one of the runners rated within 4lb of each other. It was run at a sound pace, with the winner pulling clear inside the final furlong. The runner-up is rated close to recent C&D form and sets the standard.

Lisselton Cross Official explanation: trainer said that the gelding lost a front shoe

T/Plt: £105.60 to a £1 stake. Pool: £79,667.63 - 550.49 winning tickets T/Qpdt: £14.00 to a £1 stake. Pool: £8,043.12 - 424.40 winning tickets LM

8060 LINGFIELD (L-H)

Wednesday, December 12

OFFICIAL GOING: Standard

Wind: Nil Weather: Hard frost, very cold

8076 ATRVIRTUALOWNER.COM CLAIMING STKS 7f (P)

12:00 (12:00) (Class 6) 2-Y-O **£1,704** (£503; £251) **Stalls** Low

Form RPR

6322 **1** **Secret Symphony**[13] 7922 2-8-13 65 (t) RichardHughes 3 65
(Sylvester Kirk) cl up: shkn up over 2f out: rdn to ld appr fnl f: styd on **5/4**[1]

60 **2** 1 ¾ **Opus Cactus (USA)**[59] 7078 2-8-6 0 AndreaAtzeni 5 53
(Marco Botti) trckd ldng pair: hdwy 2f out: rdn to chal and hung lft over 1f out: kpt on u.p fnl f **6/1**

3 ¾ **Lady Lunchalot (USA)** 2-8-11 0 LiamKeniry 6 57+
(J S Moore) dwlt and in rr: green and pushed along 3f out: hdwy over 1f out: styd on wl fnl f: nrst fin **6/1**

6010 **4** *3 ¼* **Krupskaya (FR)**[45] 7700 2-8-13 70.........................(p) SilvestreDeSousa 1 50
(Mrs K Burke) *led: rdn along over 2f out: drvn and hdd appr fnl f: sn wknd* **5/1**[3]

0000 **5** *hd* **Sally Bruce**[26] 7738 2-8-1 47.................................. JenniferFerguson(7) 4 45
(Louise Best) *hld up: effrt and hdwy on inner 2f out: sn rdn and wknd appr fnl f* **100/1**

40 **6** *3 ½* **Ilsa Lund (IRE)**[65] 6936 2-8-11 0.................................... JamieSpencer 2 38
(Peter Chapple-Hyam) *trckd ldrs: effrt 2f out: sn rdn and wknd over 1f out* **4/1**[2]

1m 24.38s (-0.42) **Going Correction** -0.05s/f (Stan) **6** Ran SP% **110.7**
Speed ratings (Par 94): **100,98,97,93,93 89**
toteswingers 1&2 £2.60, 1&3 £2.70, 2&3 £4.50 CSF £9.07 TOTE £1.90: £2.40, £2.40; EX 11.10 Trifecta £61.60 Pool: £662.70 - 8.06 winning tickets..
Owner Verano Quartet I **Bred** Miss K J Keir **Trained** Upper Lambourn, Berks

FOCUS
A pretty weak claimer best rated around the first two.

NOTEBOOK
Secret Symphony, who'd finished runner-up in a couple of similar events over a little further on his most recent starts, won nicely. His win took his trainer off the cold list, having sent out 68 runners without success prior to this. (op 6-4)
Opus Cactus(USA) was open to improvement back on the AW, but there was no move for her in the market and, while the only one to give the winner a bit of a race, she was well held at the finish. Handicaps are now an option. (op 7-1)
Lady Lunchalot(USA), who never made the track for Ed Dunlop, has an encouraging pedigree for the AW. She finished well having run green and there should be improvement in her.
Krupskaya(FR), wearing cheekpieces for the first time, has shown her best form in soft/heavy ground. After making the early running, she just plugged on one-paced in the straight. Southwell should suit her better in due course. (op 3-1)
Ilsa Lund(IRE) didn't get home over this longer trip. A return to sprinting should be in her favour. (op 9-2)

8077 FOLLOW US ON TWITTER @LINGFIELDPARK (S) STKS 7f (P)
12:30 (12:33) (Class 6) 3-Y-O+ **£1,704** (£503; £251) **Stalls** Low

Form RPR

0032 **1** **Majuro (IRE)**[14] 7901 8-9-4 81......................................(t) RobertWinston 8 73
(Charles Smith) *t.k.h: cl up: led wl over 1f out: rdn ent fnl f: kpt on wl towards fin* **8/13**[1]

6000 **2** *nk* **Irish Heartbeat (IRE)**[9] 7966 7-8-12 82......................(p) TonyHamilton 7 66
(Richard Fahey) *t.k.h: trckd ldrs: effrt and edgd rt home turn: rdn over 1f out: styd on to chal ins fnl f: ev ch tl no ex towards fin* **7/2**[2]

0400 **3** *1 ½* **Abhaath (USA)**[12] 7935 3-9-4 67.................................... WilliamCarson 2 68
(Ronald Harris) *t.k.h: trckd ldrs: effrt 2f out: rdn along over 1f out: kpt on same pce* **7/1**[3]

0430 **4** *2 ¼* **El Dececy (USA)**[36] 7610 8-8-12 60.......................(tp) RobbieFitzpatrick 6 56
(Charles Smith) *t.k.h: led: rdn along 2f out: sn hdd and grad wknd* **16/1**

5503 **5** *2 ½* **Memphis Man**[13] 7929 9-8-11 47.. EoinWalsh(7) 3 55
(David Evans) *hld up in rr: hdwy over 1f out: n.d* **33/1**

502 **6** *1 ½* **Divine Rule (IRE)**[14] 7898 4-9-4 51.....................................(p) IanMongan 4 51
(Laura Mongan) *hld up: a towards rr* **12/1**

-000 **7** *4 ½* **Prophet In A Dream**[169] 3467 4-8-5 45.............................. JakePayne(7) 9 33
(Paddy Butler) *dwlt: t.k.h: hld up: a towards rr* **66/1**

2600 **8** *½* **The Dancing Lord**[4] 8036 3-8-12 64.................................. AndrewMullen 1 32
(Bill Turner) *trckd ldrs: pushed along 3f out: sn rdn and wknd 2f out* **20/1**

1m 24.2s (-0.60) **Going Correction** -0.05s/f (Stan) **8** Ran SP% **119.4**
Speed ratings (Par 101): **101,100,98,96,93 91,86,86**
toteswingers 1&2 £1.40, 1&3 £2.10, 2&3 £2.90 CSF £3.17 TOTE £1.60: £1.02, £1.70, £2.30; EX 3.40 Trifecta £9.70 Pool: £1,648.80 - 126.46 winning tickets..There was no bid for the winner. Irish Heartbeat was claimed by Jamie Osborne for £6,000.
Owner Willie McKay **Bred** Tally-Ho Stud **Trained** Temple Bruer, Lincs

FOCUS
There was a lack of pace early in this seller. The form is muddling and limited by the fifth and sixth.

8078 MARSH GREEN H'CAP (DIV I) 1m 2f (P)
1:00 (1:02) (Class 6) (0-65,77) 3-Y-O+ **£1,704** (£503; £251) **Stalls** Low

Form RPR

0405 **1** **Calypso Magic (IRE)**[9] 7960 4-8-10 **54**.....................(t) KirstyMilczarek 4 62
(Olivia Maylam) *hld up: stdy hdwy 3f out: chsd ldrs wl over 1f out: rdn to ld ins fnl f: drvn out* **16/1**

055 **2** *hd* **Conducting**[3] 8047 4-9-7 **65**.. RobertWinston 3 72
(Gay Kelleway) *trckd ldrs: hdwy 2f out: rdn over 1f out: styd on to chal ins fnl f: ev ch tl no ex towards fin* **9/2**[3]

40 **3** *1 ¼* **With Hindsight (IRE)**[189] 2809 4-9-7 **65**................. JamieGoldstein 10 70
(Michael Scudamore) *cl up: led over 7f out: pushed along and hdd 2f out: sn rdn and kpt on same pce fnl f* **8/1**

6633 **4** *nse* **Sail Home**[14] 7892 5-8-13 **64**.. ShelleyBirkett(7) 9 69
(Julia Feilden) *led 3f: cl up tl led again 2f out: sn rdn: drvn and hdd ins fnl f: kpt on same pce* **10/1**

1000 **5** *nk* **Mount Abora (IRE)**[3] 8051 5-9-5 **63**.................................. IanMongan 6 67
(Laura Mongan) *hld up and bhd: gd hdwy wl over 1f out: swtchd lft and rdn ins fnl f: styd on wl: nrst fin* **6/1**

0464 **6** *¾* **Lady Arabella (IRE)**[14] 7905 3-9-2 **63**............................ GrahamLee 7 66
(Alastair Lidderdale) *trckd ldrs on inner: effrt 2f out: sn rdn along and sltly outpcd: styd on fnl f* **4/1**[2]

2311 **7** *½* **Thecornishcowboy**[1] 8060 3-10-2 **77** 12ex.......................(t) AdamKirby 1 79
(John Ryan) *hld up towards rr: hdwy on wd outside over 2f out: rdn to chse ldrs over 1f out: drvn and one pce ent fnl f* **3/1**[1]

0066 **8** *1* **Mafi (IRE)**[14] 7905 4-9-3 **61**...(b) WilliamCarson 8 61
(Mark Hoad) *chsd ldrs: cl up 4f out: rdn along 2f out: grad wknd* **16/1**

3210 **9** *1 ¼* **Saint Irene**[51] 7302 3-9-2 **63**... LiamKeniry 2 60
(Michael Blanshard) *midfield: pushed along over 4f out: lost pl over 3f out: sn in rr* **16/1**

6500 **10** *8* **Byrd In Hand (IRE)**[25] 7768 5-8-7 **51**.............................. SeanLevey 5 32
(John Bridger) *hld up towards rr: hdwy 1/2-way: effrt on outer to chse ldrs 3f out: rdn along over 2f out: sn wknd and eased fnl f* **33/1**

2m 5.57s (-1.03) **Going Correction** -0.05s/f (Stan)
WFA 3 from 4yo+ 3lb **10** Ran SP% **118.3**
Speed ratings (Par 101): **102,101,100,100,100 99,99,98,97,91**
toteswingers 1&2 £12.40, 1&3 £18.10, 2&3 £9.20 CSF £87.90 CT £635.24 TOTE £17.20: £5.90, £1.20, £4.00; EX 68.60 Trifecta £484.30 Pool: £846.06 - 1.31 winning tickets..
Owner Christian Main **Bred** J Quigley **Trained** Epsom, Surrey

FOCUS
Just a modest handicap, but faster than division two. Ordinary form with the runner-up building slightly on recent form.

Lady Arabella(IRE) Official explanation: vet said that the filly had bled from the nose

8079 MARSH GREEN H'CAP (DIV II) 1m 2f (P)
1:30 (1:30) (Class 6) (0-65,65) 3-Y-O+ **£1,704** (£503; £251) **Stalls** Low

Form RPR

1036 **1** **Zenarinda**[5] 8020 5-9-7 **65**.. MartinDwyer 3 73
(Mark H Tompkins) *trckd ldrs: hdwy on outer wl over 1f out: rdn to ld ins fnl f: hung lft last 50yds: kpt on* **6/1**

5024 **2** *1 ¼* **Resplendent Alpha**[3] 8051 8-8-13 **62**........................ LeonnaMayor(5) 7 67
(Jamie Osborne) *hld up and bhd: pushed along and sltly outpcd wl over 2f out: str run on inner over 1f out: rdn and ev ch ins fnl f: one pce towards fin* **5/1**

3024 **3** *shd* **Hawaana (IRE)**[14] 7893 7-9-7 **65**................................ RobertWinston 4 70
(Gay Kelleway) *trckd ldrs: hdwy 3f out: rdn and ev ch ent fnl f: drvn and nt qckn towards fin* **4/1**[2]

4000 **4** *½* **Ellie In The Pink (IRE)**[26] 7743 4-9-2 **65**............... JemmaMarshall(5) 1 69
(Pat Phelan) *hld up in rr: stdy hdwy 3f out: rdn and ev ch ins fnl f: hld whn n.m.r nr fin* **12/1**

4055 **4** *dht* **Maz**[42] 7474 4-8-12 **61**...(p) NatashaEaton(5) 2 65
(Alan Bailey) *trckd ldrs on inner: hdwy wl over 1f out: rdn to chal and ev ch ent fnl f: sn edgd rt and kpt on same pce* **16/1**

0334 **6** *½* **Wordiness**[25] 7768 4-9-0 **63**.........................(t) WilliamTwiston-Davies(5) 9 67
(Seamus Durack) *hld up in rr: gd hdwy wl over 1f out: styng on whn nt clr run ins fnl f: swtchd rt and kpt on: nrst fin* **9/2**[3]

5040 **7** *nk* **Salient**[21] 7815 8-8-9 **53**.. SebSanders 10 55
(Michael Attwater) *trckd ldrs: hdwy on outer 3f out: rdn to ld over 1f out: drvn and hdd ins fnl f: wknd towards fin* **16/1**

1500 **8** *2* **Dolly Colman (IRE)**[42] 7479 4-8-4 **51** oh5.................... RyanPowell(3) 6 49
(Zoe Davison) *cl up: rdn along over 2f out: wknd over 1f out* **100/1**

0535 **9** *4 ½* **Landesherr (GER)**[14] 7905 5-9-2 **60**..........................(p) JamieSpencer 5 49
(Steve Gollings) *set stdy pce: qcknd over 3f out: rdn along over 2f out: drvn and hdd appr fnl f: sn wknd* **3/1**[1]

0/ **10** *1 ½* **Grace And Beauty (IRE)**[16] 6198 4-8-13 **57**..................... ChrisCatlin 8 43
(Paul Henderson) *a towards rr* **66/1**

2m 8.29s (1.69) **Going Correction** -0.05s/f (Stan) **10** Ran SP% **116.1**
Speed ratings (Par 101): **91,90,89,89,89 89,88,87,83,82**
toteswingers 1&2 £2.90, 1&3 £2.20, 2&3 £2.80 CSF £35.92 CT £134.99 TOTE £7.40: £2.40, £1.80, £1.90; EX 35.80 Trifecta £205.70 Pool: £957.19 - 3.49 winning tickets..
Owner Dullingham Park **Bred** Dullingham Park **Trained** Newmarket, Suffolk

FOCUS
They didn't go a great pace early and it turned into something of a burn-up from the run down the hill. The final time was 2.72sec slower than the first division. The winner recorded a personal best but not form to be confident about.

Wordiness Official explanation: jockey said that the colt was denied a clear run
Dolly Colman(IRE) Official explanation: jockey said that the filly hung right

8080 FELBRIDGE MEDIAN AUCTION MAIDEN STKS 1m 2f (P)
2:00 (2:00) (Class 6) 3-5-Y-O **£1,704** (£503; £251) **Stalls** Low

Form RPR

342 **1** **Syncopate**[3] 8049 3-9-3 0... AdamKirby 8 75
(Pam Sly) *trckd ldr: cl up 3f out: led 2f out: rdn over 1f out: kpt on* **11/8**[1]

5-20 **2** *1 ¼* **Grand Theft Equine**[322] 301 4-9-6 66............................... GrahamLee 4 72
(Jim Boyle) *trckd ldrs: hdwy on outer 2f out: sn chsng wnr: rdn appr fnl f and kpt on same pce* **6/1**[3]

U236 **3** *3 ¼* **Heezararity**[35] 7640 4-8-13 67...................................... EoinWalsh(7) 9 66
(David Evans) *in tch: hdwy over 2f out: rdn to chse ldng pair appr fnl f: sn edgd lft and no imp* **5/2**[2]

5 **4** *4 ½* **Handsome Molly**[20] 7822 3-8-12 0..................................... LiamKeniry 3 52
(David Elsworth) *trckd ldng pair on inner: effrt whn n.m.r wl over 1f out: sn rdn and one pce* **7/1**

0 **5** *5* **Sugar Lips**[20] 7822 3-8-12 0.. SebSanders 10 42
(Simon Dow) *hld up towards rr: hdwy over 3f out: rdn along over 2f out: n.d* **50/1**

0 **6** *1 ¼* **Tiny Thompson**[58] 7112 3-8-12 0................................ TomMcLaughlin 2 39
(Lydia Pearce) *in tch: hdwy on inner 3f out: rdn along 2f out: sn wknd* **100/1**

7 *3 ½* **Phantom Prince (IRE)**[15] 3-9-3 0.. ChrisCatlin 6 37
(Brendan Powell) *a towards rr* **8/1**

000- **8** *2* **Roe Valley (IRE)**[543] 3176 5-9-6 50............................ FergusSweeney 5 33
(Linda Jewell) *a towards rr* **100/1**

0-06 **9** *7* **Buckley Boy**[286] 742 3-9-3 0.. JamieMackay 1 19
(K F Clutterbuck) *set stdy pce: pushed along 3f out: hdd 2f out and sn wknd* **66/1**

10 *7* **Johns Porridge** 3-8-12 0.. WilliamCarson 7
(Peter Hiatt) *s.i.s: a in rr* **33/1**

2m 6.62s (0.02) **Going Correction** -0.05s/f (Stan)
WFA 3 from 4yo+ 3lb **10** Ran SP% **116.9**
Speed ratings (Par 101): **97,96,93,89,85 84,82,80,74,69**
toteswingers 1&2 £2.90, 1&3 £2.20, 2&3 £2.80 CSF £10.35 TOTE £2.20: £1.10, £1.10, £2.50; EX 9.50 Trifecta £13.60 Pool: £1,229.03 - 67.59 winning tickets..
Owner Pam's People **Bred** Meon Valley Stud **Trained** Thorney, Cambs

FOCUS
A steadily run maiden, and ordinary form. The runner-up is rated close to his best with the third to his mark.

8081 BRYAN ARTHUR CRAWFORD MEMORIAL H'CAP 7f (P)
2:30 (2:31) (Class 4) (0-85,83) 3-Y-O+ **£4,075** (£1,212; £606; £303) **Stalls** Low

Form RPR

2210 **1** **Stir Trader (IRE)**[65] 6934 3-8-12 **74**................................ TomEaves 1 82
(Philip Hide) *trckd ldng pair: effrt 2f out: rdn along over 1f out: styd on strly u.p ins fnl f to ld nr fin* **14/1**

5422 **2** *hd* **Roy The Boy (USA)**[9] 7966 4-8-13 **75**........................... JamieSpencer 3 82
(Alan Bailey) *stdd s: swtchd rt to outer and hdwy to go cl up after 2f: effrt to chal over 2f out: rdn wl over 1f out: drvn to ld ins fnl f: hdd and no ex nr fin* **6/4**[1]

3513 **3** *1* **Waking Warrior**[28] 7716 4-8-13 **78**...............................(tp) JulieBurke(3) 7 83
(Kevin Ryan) *led: pushed along wl over 2f out: rdn wl over 1f out: drvn and hdd ins fnl f: one pce* **7/1**

5003 **4** *2 ¾* **Avonrose**[9] 7975 5-8-11 **73**..(v) MartinDwyer 4 70
(Derek Shaw) *dwlt and in rr: hdwy on inner wl over 1f out: sn rdn and no imp fnl f* **16/1**

6562 **5** *2 ¼* **Jack Who's He (IRE)**[2] 8057 3-8-10 **79**.......................... EoinWalsh(7) 5 70
(David Evans) *trckd ldrs: effrt 3f out: sn rdn and one pce fnl 2f* **2/1**[2]

6144 **6** 2 1/4 **Prime Exhibit**[14] 7920 7 -9-682....................................(t) WilliamCarson 8 67
(Daniel Mark Loughnane) *trckd ldrs: rdn along over 2f out: sn wknd* **6/1**[3]

1m 24.04s (-0.76)**Going Correction** -0.05s/f (Stan) **6**Ran SP% **112.7**
Speed ratings (Par 105): **102,101,100,97,94 92**
toteswingers 1&2 £3.70, 1&3 £6.30, 2&3 £2.10 CSF £36.01 CT £165.27 TOTE £17.40 : £5.80, £1.10; EX 41.00 Trifecta £218.40 Pool: £1,479.42 - 5.08 winning tickets.
Owner A Long Furlong **Bred** Newlands House Stud **Trained** Findon, W Sussex
■ A first winner as a trainer for former jump jockey Philip Hide.

FOCUS
They didn't go that quick here and from the turn in the race looked between the leaders, but both were beaten. The form is worth taking at face value with the runner-up rated to form.

8082 BREATHE SPA AT LINGFIELD MARRIOTT H'CAP 1m 4f (P)
3:00 (3:00) (Class 5) (0-75,81) 3-Y-O+ **£2,385** (£704; £352) **Stalls** Low

Form RPR
1401 **1** **Stand Guard**[8] 7980 8 -10-281 6ex.. AdamKirby 8 91
(John Butler) *hld up towards rr: gd hdwy on outer 2f out: rdn over 1f out: str run to ld ins fnl f: sn clr* **6/1**[1]
4601 **2** 2 1/4 **Focail Maith**[7] 8000 4 -10-180 6ex............................(p) FergusSweeney 9 86
(John Ryan) *hld up towards rr: stdy hdwy on outer over 3f out: chsd ldrs wl over 1f out: rdn to ld briefly jst ins fnl f: sn hdd and kpt on same pce* **8/1**[3]
0003 **3** nse **Standpoint**[7] 8000 6 -9-1075.................................. KirstyMilczarek 6 81
(Conor Dore) *hld up and bhd: hdwy 2f out: rdn over 1f out: styd on wl fnl f: nrst fin* **8/1**[3]
6134 **4** nk **Any Given Dream (IRE)**[89] 6213 3 -8-1066...................... MartinLane 5 71
(David Simcock) *hld up in rr: hdwy 3f out: rdn along wl over 1f out: styd on fnl f: nrst fin* **12/1**
6406 **5** 2 **Port Charlotte**[67] 6891 3 -8-1167....................................... RobertHavlin 10 69
(Hughie Morrison) *hld up: hdwy and in tch over 4f out: chsd ldrs 3f out: rdn along 2f out: drvn appr fnl f: kpt on same pce* **14/1**
0042 **6** 1/2 **Sherman McCoy**[106] 5718 6 -9-070........... WilliamTwiston-Davies(5) 12 71
(Daniel Kubler) *led 2f: cl up: led again over 2f out and sn rdn clr: drvn over 1f out: hdd jst ins fnl f: wknd* **7/1**[2]
2060 **7** 3/4 **Flying Trader (USA)**[64] 6971 3 -8-1275............................ IanBurns(7) 11 75
(Jane Chapple-Hyam) *trckd ldrs: hdwy 3f out: rdn along wl over 1f out: drvn and wknd ent fnl f* **7/1**[2]
1630 **8** 3/4 **Beat Route**[7] 8000 5 -9-873... SebSanders 2 72+
(Michael Attwater) *hld up in midfield: hdwy over 2f out: effrt and nt clr run ent fnl f: no hdwy after* **6/1**[1]
00- **9** 1/2 **Ordensritter (GER)**[27] 4 -9-469.. ChrisCatlin 13 67
(Chris Down) *dwlt: sn trcking ldng pair on outer: effrt 3f out: rdn along 2f out: wknd over 1f out* **20/1**
42-0 **9** dht **Winning Spark (USA)**[41] 7511 5 -9-772.............................. SeanLevey 7 70
(Gary Moore) *trckd ldrs: effrt over 3f out: rdn along over 2f out: wknd over 1f out* **8/1**[3]
3064 **11** 1 1/2 **Miss Blink**[23] 7792 5 -9-166..(p) J-PGuillambert 3 62
(Robin Bastiman) *trckd ldrs on inner: effrt 3f out: rdn along 2f out: sn wknd* **20/1**
2100 **12** 24 **My Guardian Angel**[52] 5063 3 -9-272..........................(b[1]) MartinDwyer 4 29
(Mark H Tompkins) *cl up: slt ld after 2f: rdn along 3f out: sn hdd & wknd* **20/1**

2m 30.78s (-2.22)**Going Correction** -0.05s/f (Stan)
WFA 3 from 4yo+ 5lb **12**Ran SP% **115.5**
Speed ratings (Par 103): **105,103,103,103,101 101,101,100,100,100 99,83**
toteswingers 1&2 £3.80, 1&3 £7.10, 2&3 £9.10 CSF £49.83 CT £381.96 TOTE £3.90 : £1.20, £2.80, £3.50; EX 26.00 Trifecta £98.00 Pool: £849.59 - 6.50 winning tickets.
Owner J Butler **Bred** Juddmonte Farms Ltd **Trained** Newmarket, Suffolk

FOCUS
A competitive event according to the betting and the form looks sound.

8083 TANDRIDGE ALL-WEATHER "HANDS AND HEELS" APPRENTICE SERIES H'CAP (RACING EXCELLENCE INITIATIVE) 1m (P)
3:30 (3:30) (Class 6) (0-65,65) 3-Y-O+ **£1,704** (£503; £251) **Stalls** High

Form RPR
1322 **1** **Refresheststheparts (USA)**[81] 6502 3 -8-1163............. AaronJones(7) 6 72
(George Baker) *in tch: hdwy over 2f out: pushed along wl over 1f out: led ins fnl f: sn rdn and kpt on wl towards fin* **7/2**[2]
066 **2** 3/4 **Hierarch (IRE)**[3] 8047 5 -9-765..........................(p) AliceHaynes 1 72
(David Simcock) *in tch: sltly outpcd 3f out: hdwy 2f out: chsd ldrs over 1f out: swtchd lft ins fnl f: kpt on wl towards fin* **10/1**
5205 **3** nk **The New Black (IRE)**[7] 7993 3 -8-355..................(e) LaurenHunter(7) 10 61
(Gay Kelleway) *dwlt and towards rr: stdy hdwy on outer over 3f out: chsd ldrs wl over 1f out: sn ev ch tl nt qckn wl ins fnl f* **16/1**
5202 **4** nse **Exopuntia**[21] 7816 6 -8-352.. ShelleyBirkett(5) 8 58
(Julia Feilden) *in tch: hdwy 2f out: rdn over 1f out and ev ch tl one pce wl ins fnl f* **14/1**
0050 **5** nse **Bloodsweatandtears**[18] 7857 4 -9-563.............................. PatMillman 3 69
(William Knight) *prom: effrt over 2f out: rdn to ld over 1f out: hdd ins fnl f: kpt on same pce* **6/1**
3006 **6** 3 1/2 **Aquilifer (IRE)**[6] 8010 4 -9-765.......................................(v) ConorHarrison 7 63
(Mrs K Burke) *bhd: hdwy 2f out: rdn and kpt on fnl f: n.d* **8/1**
440- **7** 1 **West Side (IRE)**[476] 5394 4 -8-455 ow1..................... SiobhanMiller(7) 9 51
(Michael Quinn) *hld up in rr: sme hdwy over 2f out: n.d* **50/1**
5-23 **8** 1/2 **Captain Kendall (IRE)**[220] 1889 3 -8-1262...................... EoinWalsh(5) 5 57
(David Evans) *plld hrd: cl up: pushed along 2f out: sn wknd* **4/1**[3]
0500 **9** 5 **Schoolboy Champ**[7] 7993 5 -8-051 oh3..........(bt[1]) MatthewMcGhee(7) 2 34
(Lisa Williamson) *plld hrd: set str pce: pushed along 2f out: hdd over 1f out and sn wknd* **66/1**
0001 **10** 3 1/4 **Breakheart (IRE)**[14] 7898 5 -8-655.. JoeyHaynes(5) 4 31
(Andrew Balding) *s.i.s: a in rr* **3/1**[1]

1m 37.66s (-0.54)**Going Correction** -0.05s/f (Stan)
WFA 3 from 4yo+ 1lb **10**Ran SP% **117.7**
Speed ratings (Par 101): **100,99,98,98,98 95,94,93,88,85**
toteswingers 1&2 £9.40, 1&3 £12.90, 2&3 £13.60 CSF £38.96 CT £514.30 TOTE £4.60 : £1.90, £3.00, £3.40; EX 42.20 Trifecta £172.00 Pool: £1,077.90 - 4.70 winning tickets.
Owner Keith Jones & Family **Bred** Lazy Lane Farms Inc **Trained** Manton, Wilts

FOCUS
The leaders went too quick early here and things were set up nicely for the winner. The runner-up is rated pretty much to his best with the third and fourth fitting in with recent efforts, although the race is not entirely convincing.
T/Jkpt: Not won. T/Plt: £35.30 to a £1 stake. Pool: £78,245.80 - 1,615.64 winning tickets T/Qpdt: £13.90 to £1. Pool: £7,683.03 - 406.20 w. tckts JR 8084a - 8011a (Foreign Racing) See RI

8068 KEMPTON (A.W) (R-H)
Thursday, December 13

OFFICIAL GOING: Standard
Wind: Virtually nil Weather: Chilly

8092 32REDBINGO.COM CLAIMING STKS 6f (P)
4:00 (4:00) (Class 6) 2-Y-O **£1,617** (£481; £240; £120) **Stalls** Low

Form RPR
4211 **1** **Sofi's Spirit (IRE)**[9] 8053 2 -8-760 ow1................................ LiamKeniry 4 61
(J S Moore) *sn led: pushed along 2f out: styd on wl u.p fnl f: hld on all out* **9/2**
1062 **2** shd **Ishigunnaeatit**[64] 6076 2 -8-1260............................... SilvestreDeSousa 1 66
(Mrs K Burke) *chsd ldr over 3f out: rdn along fr over 2f out: kpt on strly clsng stages: jst failed* **3/1**[2]
0244 **3** 1/2 **Not Rigg (USA)**[2] 7953 2 -9-370.................................(t) JamieSpencer 2 70
(Andrew Balding) *hld up in rr: drvn and hdwy over 2f out: styd on u.p fnl f: kpt on clsng stages but nt quite pce of ldng duo* **2/1**[1]
6312 **4** 1/2 **Windforpower (IRE)**[13] 7932 2 -8-968........................(b) WilliamCarson 3 60
(Ronald Harris) *chsd ldr tl over 3f out: styd disputing 2nd: rdn fr 2f out: nt qckn ins fnl f* **6/1**
2360 **5** 1 1/4 **Imperial Spirit**[14] 7926 2 -8-1369.................................... RichardHughes 5 60
(Mick Channon) *in tch: pushed along over 2f out: styd on same pce fnl f* **7/2**[3]

1m 13.14s (0.04)**Going Correction** -0.20s/f (Stan) **5**Ran SP% **113.0**
Speed ratings (Par 94): **91,90,90,89,87**
CSF £18.50 TOTE £3.80 : £2.30, £1.30; EX 12.50 Trifecta £15.10 Pool: £1,541.17 - 76.42 winning tickets.
Owner J S Moore **Bred** Yvonne & Gerard Kennedy **Trained** Upper Lambourn, Berks
■ Stewards' Enquiry : Silvestre De Sousa seven-day ban: used whip above permitted level (Dec 27-31,Jan 1-2)
Liam Keniry four-day ban: used whip above permitted level (Dec 27-30)

FOCUS
A modest claimer and the form is limited.

NOTEBOOK
Sofi's Spirit (IRE) helped by being allowed her own way in front, completed a quick hat-trick, adding to a couple of selling victories. Her first win was gained over 7f, so it was a sensible decision to make plenty of use of her and she just did enough, despite carrying 1lb overweight. She ought to be competitive in ordinary handicaps. (tchd 4-1)
Ishigunnaeatit, much like when failing by a nose in a C&D claimer when last seen in October, just took too long to pick up. She has a bit of a knee action and doesn't look a natural on this surface. (op 7-4 tchd 7-2)
Not Rigg (USA) beaten at shortish prices on his last three starts, wasn't helped by being held up last of the five runners and could never quite muster the required pace. (op 11-4 tchd 7-4)
Windforpower(IRE) again didn't convince with his attitude. Official explanation: jockey said gelding hung left (op 11-2)
Imperial Spirit offered little on this drop in grade and trip. (op 6-1)

8093 32REDPOKER.COM NURSERY (DIV I) 1m (P)
4:30 (4:30) (Class 6) (0-60,60) 2-Y-O **£1,617** (£481; £240; £120) **Stalls** Low

Form RPR
000 **1** **Seaside Rock (IRE)**[29] 7706 2 -9-760.......................... RichardHughes 2 64+
(Richard Hannon) *trckd ldrs: pushed along to ld ins fnl f: comf* **7/2**[1]
0010 **2** 1/2 **Royal Caper**[15] 7919 2 -9-659.. AdamKirby 11 60
(John Ryan) *in rr: hdwy over 2f out: styd on to take 2nd clsng stages but no ch w wnr* **10/1**
4006 **3** 1 1/4 **Lincolnrose (IRE)**[37] 7606 2 -8-1251...............................(p) SebSanders 9 49
(Alan McCabe) *sn led: rdn along 2f out: hdd ins fnl 2f: styd on wl to take 3rd clsng stages but no ch w wnr* **50/1**
0551 **4** shd **Roland**[7] 8003 2 -9-659 6ex...(b) GrahamLee 12 57
(Kevin Ryan) *trckd ldrs: drvn to ld ins fnl 2f: hdd inaside fnl f: wknd and lost two pls clsng stages* **5/1**[2]
4466 **5** 2 **Subtle Difference**[10] 7974 2 -9-760.................................. DavidProbert 5 53
(Andrew Balding) *in tch: drvn along over 2f out: styd on fnl f but nvr gng pce to rch ldrs* **7/1**
0000 **6** hd **Lilly White (USA)**[21] 7821 2 -9-255..............................(tp) JamieSpencer 6 48
(Brian Meehan) *stdd in rr: swtchd lft to wd outside over 2f out: styd on fnl f: nt rch ldrs* **16/1**
0003 **7** 3/4 **Misty Secret (IRE)**[7] 7979 2 -8-1049..................... RichardKingscote 1 40
(Tom Dascombe) *chsd ldrs: rdn over 2f out: wknd fnl f* **8/1**
0006 **8** shd **Epsom Flyer**[5] 8032 2 -8-448..................................... JemmaMarshall(5) 7 39
(Pat Phelan) *disp 2nd: rdn over 2f out: wknd appr fnl f* **12/1**
5502 **9** nk **It's Only Business**[23] 7795 2 -8-1056................................ JakePayne(7) 10 46
(Bill Turner) *in rr: hdwy on outer and rdn ins fnl 3f: hung rt and no prog fnl 2f* **25/1**
4544 **10** 1 1/2 **Maypole Joe (IRE)**[7] 8003 2 -8-1251......................(v) SilvestreDeSousa 3 38
(David Evans) *s.i.s: sn in tch w main gp: along 3f out: wknd ins fnl 2f* **6/1**[3]
300 **11** 3/4 **Don Eduardo**[51] 7305 2 -9-659.. LiamKeniry 4 44
(J S Moore) *chsd ldrs: rdn over 2f out: wknd wl over 1f out* **14/1**
6530 **12** 14 **Caramel Sundae**[10] 7973 2 -9-558.................................... AndreaAtzeni 8 11
(Robert Eddery) *s.i.s: a in rr* **25/1**

1m 39.18s (-0.62)**Going Correction** -0.20s/f (Stan) **12**Ran SP% **115.8**
Speed ratings (Par 94): **95,94,93,93,91 90,90,90,89,88 87,73**
toteswingers 1&2 £8.50, 1&3 £51.80, 2&3 £70.30 CSF £37.40 CT £1497.51 TOTE £4.30 : £1.50, £3.60, £13.90; EX 48.10 Trifecta £632.00 Pool: £1,736.13 - 2.06 winning tickets.
Owner The Heffer Syndicate **Bred** Suroben Ltd **Trained** East Everleigh, Wilts

FOCUS
A moderate nursery but sound form rated around the second and fourth, although somewhat limited.

NOTEBOOK
Seaside Rock (IRE) never better than seventh in three maidens, showed himself well handicapped on this switch to nursery company, looking to win with something to spare. He can remain competitive off higher marks. Official explanation: trainer's rep said, regarding apparent improvement in form, that the colt was a late maturing sort, and benefited from a drop to lower class. (op 4-1 tchd 9-2)
Royal Caper was reported by his rider to have never been travelling at Wolverhampton last time, but prior to that he'd won a 7f nursery here and he returned to form, staying on from a long way back. (tchd 9-1)
Lincolnrose(IRE), upped to her furthest trip to date, stayed on better than expected after leading.
Roland was 3lb well-in under the penalty he picked up for winning a Lingfield seller the previous week, but he wasn't helped by a wide trip from the least favourable stall. (tchd 9-2)
Subtle Difference didn't offer much. (op 11-2)

Caramel Sundae Official explanation: jockey said filly never travelled

8094 32REDPOKER.COM NURSERY (DIV II) 1m (P)
5:00 (5:00) (Class 6) (0-60,60) 2-Y-O **£1,617** (£481; £240; £120) **Stalls** Low

Form RPR
0605 **1** **Pairumani Prince (IRE)**^{29} 7708 2-9-5 **58**........................ GrahamLee 4 63
(Ed Dunlop) *in tch: drvn to chse ldrs 2f out: led 1f out: hld on wl* **11/2**
0500 **2** *nk* **Day In Day Out**^{68} 6893 2-9-7 **60**.. JimCrowley 6 64
(Ralph Beckett) *in tch: bmpd over 4f out: hdwy on outside over 1f out: styd on to take 2nd fnl 100yds: fin wl: nt quite rch wnr* **5/1**^{3}
0600 **3** *1 ½* **Misleading Promise (IRE)**^{80} 6533 2-9-3 **56**.................... AdamKirby 1 57
(John Butler) *in tch: rdn and hdwy over 1f out: sn swtchd lft and one pce: rallied and kpt on wl to take 3rd clsng stages: no imp on ldng duo* **5/1**^{3}
0003 **4** *1 ¼* **Una Bella Cosa**^{28} 7728 2-8-13 **52**..................................(p) SebSanders 9 50
(Alan McCabe) *sn led: rdn over 2f out: hdd 1f out: one pce fnl f* **12/1**
562 **5** *½* **Elusive Thought (IRE)**^{22} 7812 2-9-7 **60**......................... JamieSpencer 12 57
(J S Moore) *in rr: hdwy on outside over 1f out: kpt on: nt rch ldrs* **9/2**^{2}
6606 **6** *nk* **She's Some Girl (IRE)**^{15} 7919 2-8-8 **47**........................... TomEaves 11 43
(Richard Fahey) *in rr: hdwy fr 2f out: styd on fr 2f out: kpt on same pce: nvr rchd ldrs* **20/1**
0054 **7** *hd* **Warrant Officer**^{44} 7467 2-9-6 **59**...................................... GeorgeBaker 2 55
(Mick Channon) *chsd ldrs: drvn and ev ch fr 2f out: wknd fnl f* **14/1**
4600 **8** *½* **Chelsea Grey (IRE)**^{68} 6893 2-8-10 **49**......................... WilliamCarson 8 44
(Ronald Harris) *in rr: hdwy ins fnl 2f: kpt on fnl f but n.m.r: nvr gng pce to rch ldrs* **16/1**
000 **9** *1 ¼* **Aphrodite Spirit (IRE)**^{15} 7894 2-8-11 **50**...................... JimmyQuinn 5 42
(Pat Eddery) *in rr and sn rdn along: hdwy on inner to chse ldrs 2f out: wknd 1f out* **33/1**
0006 **10** *11* **Elvin**^{22} 7808 2-8-12 **51**.. RichardHughes 10 17
(Amanda Perrett) *chsd ldr: rdn over 2f out: wknd wl over 1f out and no ch whn n.m.r appr fnl f* **4/1**^{1}
0006 **11** *7* **Mickstathetricksta**^{37} 7614 2-9-6 **59**................................. IanMongan 7 9
(Scott Dixon) *chsd ldrs: rdn 3f out: wknd ins fnl 2f: eased ins fnl f* **33/1**

1m 39.37s (-0.43) **Going Correction** -0.20s/f (Stan) **11** Ran SP% **117.8**
Speed ratings (Par 94): **94,93,92,90,90 90,89,89,88,77 70**
toteswingers 1&2 £8.90, 1&3 £7.60, 2&3 £7.40 CSF £32.49 CT £146.03 TOTE £6.00: £1.80, £2.00, £2.40; EX 37.40 Trifecta £205.80 Pool: £1,611.07 - 5.87 winning tickets..
Owner Anamoine Ltd **Bred** Windflower Overseas **Trained** Newmarket, Suffolk
■ Stewards' Enquiry : Adam Kirby two-day ban: careless riding (Dec 27-28)

FOCUS
A slightly slower time than the first division and the form is limited due to the proximity of such as the fourth.

NOTEBOOK
Pairumani Prince(IRE) found some improvement to get off the mark at the sixth attempt. Seeing as he's taken a little while to come good, he may go on from this. Official explanation: trainer's rep said, regarding apparent improvement in form, that he had no explanation other than the colt had been performing consistently in previous races, without winning. (op 5-1)
Day In Day Out, returning from a 68-day break, came off the bridle a fair way from the finish but kept plugging on. This might sharpen him up, otherwise headgear could help. (tchd 9-2)
Misleading Promise(IRE) ◆, a bit keen early, didn't have a great deal of room when first looking to challenge. His effort flattened out late on, but there was definite promise in this run, his first for 80 days. (op 8-1)
Una Bella Cosa, much like her stablemate in the first division, kept on after leading.
Elusive Thought(IRE) was making his handicap debut, yet he was already due to be eased 2lb. He plugged on from further back than those who finished in front of him, but this wasn't particularly encouraging. (op 7-2)
Elvindidn't build on the form he showed over 7f here on his recent return from a three-month break. (op 9-2)

8095 32RED H'CAP 1m (P)
5:30 (5:35) (Class 2) (0-100,97) 3-Y-0+ **£10,221** (£3,041; £1,519; £759) **Stalls** Low

Form RPR
0464 **1** **George Guru**^{26} 7774 5-8-12 **91**................................... MarkCoumbe$^{(3)}$ 2 100
(Michael Attwater) *in rr: hdwy 2f out: drvn to ld ins fnl f: readily* **10/1**
1425 **2** *¾* **True To Form (IRE)**^{26} 7771 5-9-6 **96**...........................(p) DavidProbert 7 103
(Martyn Meade) *chsd ldrs: drvn over 2f out: styd u.p and led briefly jst ins fnl f: sn hdd: kpt on* **6/1**
2021 **3** *nse* **Rakaan (IRE)**^{13} 7934 5-8-11 **87**.................................... FergusSweeney 3 94
(Jamie Osborne) *hld up in rr: drvn and hdwy over 1f out: styd on wl fnl f to dispute 2nd clsng stages but no ch w wnr* **14/1**
1442 **4** *½* **Storm King**^{26} 7774 3-9-3 **94**.. RichardHughes 5 100
(Jane Chapple-Hyam) *led 1f: styd chsng ldrs: rdn and kpt on fnl f: no ex clsng stages* **11/4**^{1}
0432 **5** *nk* **Bank On Me**^{21} 7824 3-8-4 **84**....................................... RaulDaSilva$^{(3)}$ 10 89
(Philip McBride) *chsd ldrs: rdn over 1f out: kpt on same pce* **12/1**
053 **6** *1* **Grey Mirage**^{27} 7751 3-8-9 **86**... AndreaAtzeni 9 89
(Marco Botti) *led after 1f: rdn over 2f out: hdd jst ins fnl f: wknd fnl 120yds* **9/2**^{3}
062 **7** *½* **Alfred Hutchinson**^{13} 7934 4-8-7 **83** oh2............................ TomEaves 1 85
(Geoffrey Oldroyd) *chsd ldrs: rdn over 2f out: styd on same pce fnl f* **25/1**
6004 **8** *13* **Nazreef**^{15} 7904 5-9-7 **97**..(t) RobertWinston 6 69
(Hughie Morrison) *chsd ldrs: wknd 2f out: eased fnl f* **8/1**
0000 **9** *2* **Docofthebay (IRE)**^{22} 7817 8-8-11 **87**................(p) SilvestreDeSousa 11 54
(Scott Dixon) *a in rr* **33/1**
011 **10** *5* **Embankment**^{21} 7823 3-8-8 **85**.. JimmyQuinn 8 41
(William Jarvis) *pushed along and wd into st: a in rr: eased whn no ch fnl f* **7/2**^{2}

1m 36.79s (-3.01) **Going Correction** -0.20s/f (Stan)
WFA 3 from 4yo+ 1lb **10** Ran SP% **122.7**
Speed ratings (Par 109): **107,106,106,105,105 104,103,90,88,83**
toteswingers 1&2 £9.00, 1&3 £13.10, 2&3 £9.70 CSF £72.55 CT £862.23 TOTE £13.40: £3.00, £2.10, £3.90; EX 78.90 Trifecta £1125.00 Part won. Pool: £1,500.03 - 0.50 winning tickets..
Owner T M Jones **Bred** T M Jones **Trained** Epsom, Surrey

FOCUS
A good handicap run at a decent pace. The third sets the level to his recent best, backed up by the favourite.

NOTEBOOK
George Guru, probably in front soon enough when only fourth at Lingfield on his previous start, tanked along for most of the way and found plenty for pressure. This was a career best and he can rate even higher whilst in this sort of mood.
True To Form(IRE), fifth in a Lingfield Listed race last time, put up a useful performance back in handicap company.
Rakaan(IRE), up 2lb for his recent Wolverhampton win (Alfred Hutchinson second), was produced with his chance but couldn't sustain his challenge and this is about as good as he is these days. (op 12-1)
Storm King couldn't match the form of his recent second at Lingfield, a race in which George Guru ran fourth, but perhaps paid for chasing the good gallop. (op 7-2 tchd 5-2)
Bank On Me, nudged up 2lb for a close second here last time, was another who raced close to the good pace and the impression is we may not have seen the best of him yet. (op 9-1 tchd 8-1)
Grey Mirage couldn't sustain his bid after setting a good gallop, but he's likely to be eased again for this and ought to be able to contest a Class 4 next time. (op 6-1)
Embankment had won his last two starts, including a C&D handicap off 6lb lower on his recent debut for this yard, but he missed the break this time and raced wide, giving him little hope. Official explanation: jockey said colt never travelled (op 9-2 tchd 11-2)

8096 32RED CASINO NURSERY 6f (P)
6:00 (6:02) (Class 4) (0-85,81) 2-Y-0 **£3,428** (£1,020; £509; £254) **Stalls** Low

Form RPR
2513 **1** **Equitania**^{19} 7856 2-9-7 **81**... RichardHughes 2 83
(Alan Bailey) *mde all: shkn up and qcknd 2f out: unchal* **4/7**^{1}
0160 **2** *2 ½* **Harrogate Fair**^{13} 7930 2-8-4 **64**....................................... JimmyQuinn 3 59
(Michael Squance) *trckd ldrs in 3rd: drvn to chse wnr 2f out: kpt on fnl f but no imp* **20/1**
6513 **3** *nk* **Hardy Red (IRE)**^{76} 6629 2-9-1 **75**.................................. FergusSweeney 1 69
(Jamie Osborne) *racd in 4th tl drvn and hdwy over 1f out: wnt 3rd ins fnl f and clsd on 2nd nr fin but no ch w wnr* **6/1**^{3}
0001 **4** *4* **Bay Laurel (IRE)**^{15} 7916 2-8-3 **63**............................ SilvestreDeSousa 4 45
(Mrs K Burke) *chsd ldr: rdn ins fnl 3f: lost 2nd 2f out: wknd into 4th fnl f* **3/1**^{2}

1m 12.13s (-0.97) **Going Correction** -0.20s/f (Stan) **4** Ran SP% **107.7**
Speed ratings (Par 98): **98,94,94,88**
CSF £11.22 TOTE £1.60; EX 15.60 Trifecta £61.00 Pool: £465.02 - 5.71 winning tickets..
Owner John Stocker **Bred** Longdon Stud **Trained** Newmarket, Suffolk

FOCUS
An uncompetitive nursery and straightforward form.

NOTEBOOK
Equitania found this easier than the 7f conditions race she tried to dominate at Lingfield last time. She's likely to face tougher assignments. (op 4-5)
Harrogate Fair remains unproven beyond 5f, just holding second from the never-dangerous Hardy Red. (op 12-1)
Hardy Red(IRE) might have needed this after 76 days off. (op 5-1)
Bay Laurel(IRE), who won a really weak maiden over 7f at Wolverhampton on her recent debut for this yard, offered nothing. (op 5-2)

8097 £32 FREE AT 32RED.COM MEDIAN AUCTION MAIDEN STKS 1m 4f (P)
6:30 (6:30) (Class 6) 3-5-Y-0 **£1,617** (£481; £240; £120) **Stalls** Centre

Form RPR
2522 **1** **Miss Blakeney**^{12} 7954 3-8-12 70....................................(v) GrahamLee 2 56+
(Marcus Tregoning) *trckd ldrs: smooth hdwy on bit to ld over 1f out: v easily* **1/8**^{1}
-000 **2** *6* **Highly Likely (IRE)**^{191} 2787 3-9-3 39........................... WilliamCarson 6 52
(Steve Woodman) *led 1f: styd chsng ldrs tl led again 3f out: hdd over 1f out and no ch w easy wnr* **25/1**
00 **3** *2 ¼* **Irene Kennet**^{62} 7016 5-8-12 0.................................... KatiaScallan$^{(5)}$ 1 43
(Paul Burgoyne) *t.k.h: trckd ldrs: disp 2nd 2f out: dropped to wl hld 3rd over 1f out* **16/1**^{3}
5050 **4** *5* **Litmus (USA)**^{9} 7982 3-8-12 52...^{1} JimCrowley 5 35
(Simon Dow) *in tch: rdn 3f out: sn btn* **10/1**^{2}
0006 **5** *3* **Ice Apple**^{27} 7739 4-9-0 35....................................... NataliaGemelova$^{(3)}$ 4 30
(John E Long) *in rr: hdwy 1/2-way and disp 2nd 4f out: wknd wl over 2f out* **66/1**
0-66 **6** *1* **Arbeejay**^{119} 2497 3-8-5 39..(t) JakePayne$^{(7)}$ 3 29
(Simon Hodgson) *in rr: effrt to cl over 3f out: sn btn* **33/1**
50/ **7** *16* **Fluter Phil**^{38} 5842 5-9-8 0.. RobertHavlin 7
(Roger Ingram) *led after 1f: hdd 3f out: wknd qckly* **16/1**^{3}

2m 34.48s (-0.02) **Going Correction** -0.20s/f (Stan)
WFA 3 from 4yo+ 5lb **7** Ran SP% **118.0**
Speed ratings (Par 101): **92,88,86,83,81 80,69**
toteswingers 1&2 £3.50, 1&3 £2.00, 2&3 £11.30 CSF £9.29 TOTE £1.10: £1.02, £8.70; EX 10.70 Trifecta £42.00 Pool: £2,079.31 - 37.13 winning tickets..
Owner Mr And Mrs A E Pakenham **Bred** Mr & Mrs A E Pakenham **Trained** Lambourn, Berks

FOCUS
A dire maiden run in a slow time and nothing solid about the form.

8098 32 BONUS H'CAP 7f (P)
7:00 (7:00) (Class 3) (0-95,95) 3-Y-0+ **£6,663** (£1,982; £990; £495) **Stalls** Low

Form RPR
2240 **1** **Chapter And Verse (IRE)**^{26} 7774 6-8-10 **84**.................... EddieAhern 9 93
(Mike Murphy) *in tch: chsd ldrs 2f out: styd on to ld fnl 120yds: kpt on wl* **7/1**^{3}
5552 **2** *½* **Webbow (IRE)**^{21} 7826 10-9-6 **94**.................................... GeorgeBaker 1 102
(Julie Camacho) *in rr: hdwy on ins over 2f out: slt ld u.p 1f out: hdd and outpcd fnl 120yds* **6/1**^{2}
0006 **3** *¾* **Valencha**^{22} 7809 5-9-5 **93**... RichardHughes 2 99
(Hughie Morrison) *in rr: hdwy over 1f out: styd on to take 3rd fnl 30yds: nt rch ldng duo* **5/1**^{1}
6406 **4** *1 ½* **Axiom**^{26} 7774 8-8-13 **87**...(b^{1}) JimCrowley 12 89
(Ed Walker) *chsd ldrs: drvn and chal over 1f out: wknd fnl 100yds* **16/1**
4065 **5** *nk* **Poetic Dancer**^{26} 7774 3-8-12 **86**.. JohnFahy 5 87
(Clive Cox) *chsd ldrs: rdn and slt advantge over 1f out: sn hdd: wknd fnl 120yds* **8/1**
0143 **6** *¾* **Kingscroft (IRE)**^{13} 7934 4-9-1 **89**........................... SilvestreDeSousa 6 88
(Mark Johnston) *s.i.s: in rr: hdwy fnl f: kpt on cl home* **6/1**^{2}
4343 **7** *1* **Roninski (IRE)**^{21} 7826 4-8-13 **87**...................................... JimmyQuinn 11 83
(Bryan Smart) *chsd ldrs: rdn and one pce fnl 2f* **9/1**
1000 **8** *nk* **Seek The Fair Land**^{22} 7817 6-8-13 **87**....................(b) FergusSweeney 3 82
(Jim Boyle) *towards rr: rdn over 2f out and no imp on ldrs* **12/1**
0166 **9** *nk* **Thunderball**^{22} 7817 6-9-0 **88**..(p) IanMongan 7 82
(Scott Dixon) *sn led: rdn over 2f out: hdd over 1f out: sn wknd* **16/1**
313 **10** *¾* **Corporal Maddox**^{7} 8008 5-8-12 **86**............................ WilliamCarson 4 78
(Ronald Harris) *s.i.s: in rr: hdwy on ins and in tch 2f out: hung rt and sn btn* **8/1**
0016 **11** *5* **Outpost (IRE)**^{15} 7897 4-8-8 **87**................................... NatashaEaton$^{(5)}$ 10 66
(Alan Bailey) *chsd ldrs: rdn and btn over 2f out* **33/1**
0046 **12** *hd* **Bajan Tryst (USA)**^{7} 8008 6-9-7 **95**................................(b) GrahamLee 8 73
(Kevin Ryan) *bhd most of way* **16/1**

1m 23.41s (-2.59) **Going Correction** -0.20s/f (Stan) **12** Ran SP% **118.2**
Speed ratings (Par 107): **106,105,104,102,102 101,100,100,99,98 93,93**
toteswingers 1&2 £5.60, 1&3 £9.40, 2&3 £7.90 CSF £48.54 CT £235.28 TOTE £7.90: £2.60, £2.30, £2.30; EX 61.10 Trifecta £368.20 Pool: £1,040.87 - 2.12 winning tickets..
Owner D J Ellis **Bred** Stuart Weld **Trained** Westoning, Beds

FOCUS
A good handicap run in a time only 0.12 seconds outside the track record. The winner is rated to this year's best backed up by the placed horses.

NOTEBOOK

Chapter And Verse(IRE) was only 2lb higher than when a clear winner over C&D in August and had been a bit better than he'd shown in recent starts. He did this well enough, but a rise in the weights will probably find him out. (tchd 6-1)

Webbow(IRE), up 1lb for finishing second over C&D last time, ran his race but was always just held. (op 11-2 tchd 5-1)

Valencha was given her usual waiting ride, but she didn't find a great deal off the bridle, only plugging on for third having looked to be going well. (tchd 11-2)

Axiom shaped okay in first-time blinkers from the widest stall. (op 14-1)

Poetic Dancer had no obvious excuse, but she failed to confirm recent 1m Lingfield form with Chapter And Verse and Axiom. (op 9-1)

Kingscroft(IRE) wasn't as well away as some and was soon hopelessly placed. He was going on at the finish. (tchd 7-1)

8099 32REDBET.COM H'CAP — 7f (P)

7:30 (7:30) (Class 7) (0-50,50) 3-Y-0+ — £1,455 (£433; £216; £108) Stalls Low

Form — RPR

0034 **1** **Bussa**[8] 7993 4-9-3 **50**....(t) AdamKirby 7 — 60
(David Evans) *chsd ldrs: wnt 2nd over 1f out: styd on wl u.p to ld clsng stages* **9/2**[1]

5000 **2** *hd* **Sandy Lane (IRE)**[37] 7615 3-9-3 **50**.... SilvestreDeSousa 6 — 59
(Amy Weaver) *chsd ldrs: wnt 2nd over 3f out: drvn to ld over 1f out: hdd and nt qckn clsng stages* **8/1**

0000 **3** *2 ½* **Vale Of Lingfield (IRE)**[22] 7815 3-9-2 **49**.... RobertWinston 4 — 52
(John Best) *led 1f: chsd ldrs: rdn over 2f out: styd on to take one pce 3rd fnl f* **12/1**

0003 **4** *1 ½* **Huzzah (IRE)**[8] 7993 7-9-3 **50**.... MichaelStainton 1 — 49
(Paul Howling) *chsd ldrs: rdn and one pce fnl 2f* **7/1**[3]

6400 **5** *3* **Northern Spy (USA)**[15] 7898 8-9-2 **49**.... GrahamLee 5 — 40+
(Simon Dow) *in rr: rdn over 2f out: styd on wl fnl f: nt rch ldrs* **7/1**[3]

051U **6** *1 ¼* **Coach Montana (IRE)**[20] 7837 3-9-3 **50**....(b) RichardHughes 14 — 37
(Jane Chapple-Hyam) *broke wl: led after 1f: rdn and hung rt 2f out: hdd over 1f out: sn btn* **11/2**[2]

4006 **7** *nk* **Do More Business (IRE)**[22] 7816 5-9-0 **50**.... RyanPowell(3) 12 — 36
(Alison Batchelor) *chsd ldrs: rdn: hung rt and btn 2f out* **16/1**

40 **8** *3 ¾* **The Kernigal (IRE)**[42] 7504 3-9-0 **50**....(t) AshleyMorgan(3) 3 — 26
(Paul Howling) *in rr: sme hdwy over 2f out: sn wknd* **9/1**

6140 **9** *1 ½* **Mucky Molly**[37] 7604 4-9-2 **49**.... SebSanders 8 — 21
(Alison Hutchinson) *t.k.h: chsd ldrs: wknd over 2f out* **16/1**

000 **10** *1* **Emma Jean (IRE)**[42] 7504 3-9-3 **50**....(bt) LiamKeniry 9 — 20
(Frank Sheridan) *in rr: rdn and sme hdwy over 2f out: sn wknd* **20/1**

6650 **11** *12* **Narapatisithu (FR)**[56] 7189 5-9-3 **50**.... JamieMackay 11
(K F Clutterbuck) *chsd ldrs to 1/2-way* **25/1**

50-0 **12** *31* **Treasure Act**[204] 2385 4-9-2 **49**.... JimCrowley 10
(Patrick Chamings) *a in rr: t.o fnl 2f* **25/1**

0000 **P** **Dichoh**[42] 7500 9-9-3 **50**....(v) GeorgeBaker 13
(Michael Madgwick) *in rr: p.u and dismntd ins fnl 3f* **8/1**

1m 24.87s (-1.13) **Going Correction** -0.20s/f (Stan) — **13** Ran SP% **122.7**

Speed ratings (Par 97): **98,97,94,93,89 88,88,83,82,80 67,31,**

toteswingers 1&2 £12.90, 1&3 £19.20, 2&3 £21.90 CSF £40.17 CT £410.03 TOTE £3.30: £1.50, £4.60, £4.60; EX 62.00 Trifecta £368.90 Pool: £1,032.92 - 2.10 winning tickets..

Owner Nick Shutts **Bred** Natton House Thoroughbreds & Mark Woodall **Trained** Pandy, Monmouths

FOCUS

A moderate handicap with the winner building on recent form.

Dichoh Official explanation: jockey said gelding lost its action

T/Plt: £291.40 to a £1 stake. Pool: £89,196.67 - 223.42 winning tickets T/Qpdt: £19.40 to a £1 stake. Pool: £8,219.73 - 312.00 winning tickets ST

1151 GULFSTREAM PARK (L-H)

Thursday, December 13

OFFICIAL GOING: Turf: firm

8100a ALLOWANCE OPTIONAL CLAIMING (CLAIMER) (3YO+) (TURF) — 5f

9:05 (12:00) 3-Y-0+ — £16,838 (£5,612; £3,235; £1,122; £280)

RPR

1 **Big Notion (USA)** 5-8-7 0.... JAGarcia 2
(Gary G Jackson, U.S.A) **116/10**

2 *2* **Tiz In Court (USA)** 5-8-7 0....(b) JZSantana 1
(Dennis Ward, U.S.A) **27/10**[2]

3 *nse* **Quiz Whiz (USA)** 4-8-7 0....(b) PLopez 11
(Kirk Ziadie, U.S.A) **21/10**[1]

4 *1 ¼* **Core Inflation (USA)** 3-8-5 0 ow1....(b) JRosario 3
(Teresa Pompay, U.S.A) **18/5**[3]

5 *2 ½* **Julius Geezer (IRE)**[35] 7651 4-8-7 0.... CLanerie 5
(Amy Weaver) **97/10**

5 *dht* **The Jackal (USA)** 6-8-7 0.... LPanici 9
(R L Wallace, U.S.A) **89/1**

7 *½* **Don't Put It Back (USA)**[1060] 5-8-8 0 ow1....(b) JASanchez 10
(D Paulus, U.S.A) **48/1**

8 *1* **Poppa Loves Mambo (USA)** 3-8-4 0.... EPrado 7
(Kathy Ritvo, U.S.A) **20/1**

9 *4* **The Chill Zone (USA)** 4-8-7 0....(b) JRoccoJr 4
(John E. Shaw, U.S.A) **123/10**

10 *1 ¼* **Gary D (USA)**[641] 5-8-2 0.... HSanchez(5) 8
(Ronald B Spatz, U.S.A) **164/10**

11 *¾* **Concorde Express (USA)** 4-8-7 0.... JCLeyva 6
(Douglas J Seyler, U.S.A) **79/1**

56.29s (56.29) — **11** Ran SP% **120.7**

PARI-MUTUEL (all including $2 stakes): WIN 25.20; PLACE (1-2) 10.00, 4.00; SHOW (1-2-3) 5.80, 3.20, 3.20; SF 94.20.

Owner Gary G. Jackson & M & G Stables LLC **Bred** VA Tech Foundation Inc **Trained** USA

8076 LINGFIELD (L-H)

Friday, December 14

OFFICIAL GOING: Standard

Wind: medium, half behind Weather: rain

8101 32RED CASINO CLAIMING STKS — 1m (P)

12:10 (12:11) (Class 6) 2-Y-0 — £1,704 (£503; £251) Stalls High

Form — RPR

5540 **1** **Club House (IRE)**[6] 8032 2-8-11 65.... GrahamLee 1 — 66
(Robert Mills) *hld up in tch in rr: effrt on inner over 1f out: chsd ldr and swtchd rt 1f out: qcknd to ld fnl 100yds: r.o wl* **6/4**[1]

0030 **2** *1* **Myzamour**[20] 7854 2-8-3 54 ow2....(b) AndreaAtzeni 2 — 56
(J S Moore) *chsd ldr over 5f out tl 2f out: drvn over 3f out: kpt on u.p and stl pressing ldrs 1f out: styd on same pce fnl 100yds* **16/1**

1322 **3** *1* **Divine Angel (IRE)**[4] 8053 2-8-2 65.... LukeMorris 6 — 52
(Phil McEntee) *led: rdn and qcknd wl over 1f out: sn drvn: hdd and no ex fnl 100yds* **2/1**[2]

5331 **4** *2* **Lucy Bee**[11] 7971 2-8-2 54.... JimmyQuinn 4 — 48
(Keith Dalgleish) *chsd ldr tl over 5f out: rdn to chse ldr again 2f out tl 1f out: styng on same pce whn short of room ins fnl f: wknd towards fin* **9/4**[3]

1m 38.84s (0.64) **Going Correction** 0.0s/f (Stan) — **4** Ran SP% **110.0**

Speed ratings (Par 94): **96,95,94,92**

CSF £18.32 TOTE £1.90; EX 16.40 Trifecta £56.60 Pool: £278.64 - 3.69 winning tickets..

Owner Trevor Jacobs & Mrs B B Mills **Bred** Val & Angela Leeson **Trained** Headley, Surrey

FOCUS

A moderate claimer reduced to just the four runners, but the market got it right and the form looks straightforward.

NOTEBOOK

Club House(IRE) came into this 0-11 and wasn't favoured by these weights, but he didn't stay 1m2f here last time and found this more suitable. Held up last, he managed to find the gap when switched off the rail over a furlong out and produced plenty when asked. This looks modest form, however. (op 2-1)

Myzamour, worst in at the weights even before the 2lb overweight, ran poorly in a C&D seller last month and looked the first cooked here when she came seriously off the bridle before halfway. However, she refused to go away and kept at it all the way to the line, but her proximity probably says more about her rivals. (op 12-1)

Divine Angel(IRE), narrowly beaten over 6f here four days earlier (winner has gone in again since), was the one to beat at the weights and she had the run of the race out in front, but she was done for speed in the run to the line. She will probably appreciate the return of Southwell in a couple of months' time. (op 6-4)

Lucy Bee had every chance turning in, but looked to be getting the worst of it when running out of room inside the last. She may appreciate a return to further. (tchd 2-1 and 5-2)

8102 BRITISH STALLION STUDS SUPPORTING BRITISH RACING EBF MAIDEN STKS — 7f (P)

12:40 (12:40) (Class 5) 2-Y-0 — £3,408 (£1,006; £503) Stalls Low

Form — RPR

53 **1** **Absolutely Right (IRE)**[29] 7720 2-8-12 0.... SeanLevey 10 — 71
(Richard Hannon) *chsd ldr: rdn and ev ch 2f out: drvn to ld ent fnl f: styd on wl u.p: rdn out* **11/4**[2]

3 **2** *¾* **Emerging**[11] 7962 2-9-3 0.... LiamKeniry 4 — 74
(David Elsworth) *led: rdn and hrd pressed 2f out: hdd and drvn ent fnl f: kpt on but a hld ins fnl f* **3/1**[3]

3 **3** *½* **Rome**[15] 7926 2-9-3 0.... IanMongan 3 — 73+
(Sir Henry Cecil) *chsd ldng pair: rdn and effrt jst over 2f out: no imp and swtchd rt jst ins fnl f: styd on towards fin but nvr looked like rching ldrs* **7/4**[1]

4 *5* **Testa Rossa (IRE)** 2-9-3 0.... SebSanders 7 — 60+
(J W Hills) *squeezed for room sn after s: towards rr: hdwy into midfield over 3f out: wnt modest 4th over 1f out: kpt on but no threat to ldrs* **16/1**

0 **5** *3 ½* **Prom Dress**[57] 7198 2-8-12 0.... JimCrowley 8 — 46
(Robert Cowell) *chsd ldng trio: rdn and struggling whn rn wd bnd 2f out: wl hld after and lost 4th over 1f out* **50/1**

0 **6** *1 ½* **Balatina**[15] 7926 2-8-12 0.... KirstyMilczarek 1 — 42+
(Chris Dwyer) *t.k.h: hld up in tch in midfield: rdn and outpcd over 2f out: no threat to ldrs fr over 1f out* **66/1**

0 **7** *1 ¼* **Hannahs Turn**[15] 7926 2-8-12 0.... MartinDwyer 2 — 39
(Chris Dwyer) *t.k.h: hld up in tch in midfield: rdn and struggling 3f out: wknd over 2f out* **100/1**

00 **8** *1* **Aloha**[15] 7926 2-8-12 0.... AndreaAtzeni 9 — 36+
(Roger Varian) *squeezed for room sn after s: racd off the pce in last pair: rdn and lost tch over 2f out* **33/1**

0 **9** *1 ¾* **Zhuba (IRE)**[183] 3074 2-9-3 0.... GeorgeBaker 5 — 36+
(John Best) *a bhd: lost tch over 2f out* **6/1**

10 *¾* **Carneades (IRE)** 2-9-3 0.... LukeMorris 6 — 34
(Ed Walker) *rn green: in tch towards rr: rdn and dropped to last 3f out: sn lost tch* **14/1**

1m 26.01s (1.21) **Going Correction** 0.0s/f (Stan) — **10** Ran SP% **122.2**

Speed ratings (Par 96): **93,92,91,85,81 80,78,77,75,74**

Tote swingers 1&2 £3.40, 1&3 £1.50, 2&3 £2.40 CSF £12.06 TOTE £3.40: £1.20, £1.50, £1.40; EX 14.40 Trifecta £16.70 Pool: £710.71 - 31.79 winning tickets..

Owner Hamed Rashed Bin Ghadayer **Bred** Round Hill Stud **Trained** East Everleigh, Wilts

FOCUS

Probably not the strongest of Lingfield maidens. They dawdled for the first couple of furlongs, but the three market leaders were up there from the start and dominated. The winner is rated to his mark.

NOTEBOOK

Absolutely Right(IRE) had shown plenty of ability in both previous outings, including when third at Kempton last month, and benefited from being in a good position throughout over this shorter trip. Getting a nice lead from the runner-up, she found plenty when produced over a furlong out and looks the type to progress again. (op 9-4)

Emerging ran a most promising debut at Kempton 11 days earlier, but looked to need every inch of the mile there so this drop in trip may not have been ideal for him either. He didn't set much of a pace and, sticking to the rail, couldn't hold off the winner in the straight, though he kept on to the line. A stiffer test should see him off the mark. (op 11-4)

Rome didn't quite get home after making the running on last month's Kempton debut, but still had three of these behind him. Getting a lead this time, he became momentarily outpaced on the home bend and, although he was closing down the font pair at the line, he was never getting there in time. A more strongly run race will also suit him. (op 2-1)

Testa Rossa(IRE), a 52,000GBP half-brother to four winners including the Listed winner Foodbroker Fancy, wasn't totally disgraced as he was off the bridle at halfway and was at a big disadvantage in trying to come from off the pace. (op 20-1)

8103 32RED NURSERY 7f (P)

1:10 (1:10) (Class 5) (0-75,70) 2-Y-O £2,264 (£673; £336; £168) Stalls Low

Form RPR

5433 **1** *shd* **Roman Order (IRE)**[32] 7699 2-9-5 68 MartinDwyer 5 70
(Brian Meehan) *sn bustled along to chse ldrs: pushed rt bnd wl over 1f out: rallied u.p 1f out: ev ch and bmpd wl ins fnl f: stl ev ch whn bmpd again and no ex last strides: fin 2nd: plcd 1st* **11/4**[1]

0020 **2** **Bubbly Bailey**[11] 7974 2-8-10 59 GrahamLee 6 61
(Alan Bailey) *in tch towards rr but pushed along: hdwy u.p 1f out: str run to chal whn edgd rt and bmpd rival wl ins fnl f: led and bmpd rival again towards fin: r.o: fin 1st: disqualified and plcd 2nd* **4/1**[3]

4202 **3** *3/4* **Girl Of Cadiz**[23] 7808 2-8-13 67 WilliamTwiston-Davies(5) 1 67
(Richard Hannon) *led: rdn and hrd pressed 2f out: hdd jst over 1f out: kpt on gamely to ld again ins fnl f: hdd and no ex wl ins fnl f* **8/1**

1005 **4** *nk* **Whitford (IRE)**[70] 6849 2-9-1 64 KirstyMilczarek 4 63
(Chris Dwyer) *chsd ldrs: effrt to chal wl over 1f out: rdn to ld jst over 1f out: hung lft and hdd ins fnl f: styd on same pce fnl 75yds* **25/1**

6200 **5** *1 1/4* **Man In The Arena**[122] 5202 2-8-13 62 LukeMorris 7 58
(Dr Jon Scargill) *in tch towards rr: effrt and rdn over 2f out: sme hdwy u.p over 1f out: styd on same pce ins fnl f* **50/1**

0004 **6** *1/2* **Derwentwater (IRE)**[23] 7808 2-8-13 62 NickyMackay 3 57
(John Gosden) *chsd ldrs: rdn and effrt on inner 2f out: unable qck u.p over 1f out: styd on same pce ins fnl f* **3/1**[2]

4155 **7** *3/4* **Pippy**[84] 6451 2-9-5 68 RichardKingscote 8 61
(Tom Dascombe) *stdd and swtchd lft s: in tch in last pair: rdn and effrt over 1f out: nt clr run and swtchd rt ins fnl f: nvr enough room and nvr trbld ldrs* **5/1**

0011 **8** *nk* **Seemenomore**[24] 7797 2-9-0 70 (v) ThomasBrown(7) 2 62
(Michael Bell) *pressed ldr tl hung rt and lost pl bnd wl over 1f out: wknd u.p 1f out* **7/1**

4063 **9** *11* **Forceful Flame**[36] 7653 2-9-5 68 (p) AndreaAtzeni 9 31
(Robert Eddery) *s.i.s: hld up in rr: lost tch 2f out: bhd and eased wl ins fnl f* **14/1**

1m 25.59s (0.79) **Going Correction** 0.0s/f (Stan) **9** Ran SP% **124.4**
Speed ratings (Par 96): **94,95,94,93,92 91,90,90,77**
Tote swingers 1&2 £2.40, 1&3 £7.00, 2&3 £5.90 CSF £15.45 CT £83.35 TOTE £4.30: £2.10, £2.20, £2.80; EX 13.70 Trifecta £287.70 Part won. Pool: £383.62 - 0.93 winning tickets..
Owner Decadent Racing **Bred** John Yarr **Trained** Manton, Wilts
■ Stewards' Enquiry : Graham Lee one-day ban: careless riding (Dec 28)

FOCUS
An ordinary nursery, but a controversial finish. Nevertheless, the form looks straightforward.

NOTEBOOK
Roman Order(IRE) had been gradually getting closer to winning in his recent starts and this was his nursery debut. Wide throughout, especially on the home bend, he hung about when first into the straight, but ran on well when straightened and may well have hit the line first had he not met the interference. (op 9-2)
Bubbly Bailey, narrowly beaten in a 1m seller here two starts back, was off the bridle before the home turn, but he responded to the pressure and appeared to have done just enough when forcing his head in front well inside the last furlong. However, he hung away to his right near the line, bumping Roman Order a couple of times, and with the margin so narrow the Stewards decided it was enough to alter the result and reversed the placings. He obviously likes it here and can gain compensation. (op 7-1)
Girl Of Cadiz had finished runner-up three times in five starts in nurseries, but found herself off her highest mark to date here. She ran another good race here, though, as she disputed the lead against the inside rail from the start and kept on gamely even after being headed. She deserves to win one of these. (op 7-1)
Whitford(IRE)'s romp in a C&D nursery in August stands head and shoulders above his other efforts and he is still 8lb higher, but he had every chance here and went down only narrowly. His rider reported that the colt hung left, but he is still another who looks different gear here. Official explanation: jockey said colt hung left
Man In The Arena, up a furlong on this return from 122 days off, kept on in the straight and should come on for it.
Derwentwater(IRE), over 3l behind Girl Of Cadiz at Kempton last month and 3lb better off, had every chance but was trying to make his effort tight against the rail and couldn't get on terms. (op 5-2)
Pippy also never landed a blow and has now disappointed three times since winning a four-runner Wolverhampton nursery. (op 4-1)
Seemenomore had been a revelation since fitted with a visor, winning two 6f Fibresand nurseries, but he was back up in trip on a different surface off an 11lb higher mark and was on the retreat well over a furlong out after disputing the running. (op 5-1)
Forceful Flame Official explanation: jockey said colt missed the break and lost its action

8104 32RED SUPPORTING BRITISH RACING H'CAP 2m (P)

1:45 (1:45) (Class 6) (0-60,60) 3-Y-O+ £1,704 (£503; £251) Stalls Low

Form RPR

6/00 **1** **Llamadas**[9] 7991 10-9-5 53 IanMongan 3 61
(Olivia Maylam) *hld up in midfield: clsd on ldrs 5f out: swtchd rt and effrt wl over 1f out: hdwy u.p 1f out: led fnl 75yds: sn in command: eased cl home* **33/1**

4651 **2** *1 3/4* **Roughlyn**[9] 8001 3-8-9 51 6ex (b) AndreaAtzeni 5 57
(Lisa Williamson) *chsd ldrs: wnt 2nd 12f out tl led 4f out: edgd rt u.p over 1f out: hdd and one pce fnl 75yds* **9/2**[3]

114/ **3** *nk* **If I Had Him (IRE)**[649] 6933 8-9-9 57 (v) LukeMorris 2 63
(George Baker) *chsd ldr for 3f: off the bridle after but styd chsng ldrs: hrd drvn to press ldr jst over 1f out: styd on same pce fnl 100yds* **7/2**[2]

0S32 **4** *1* **Red Mystique (IRE)**[9] 8001 3-8-9 51 (b) JimCrowley 4 55
(Philip Hide) *hld up in midfield: clsd on ldrs 5f out: effrt on inner to press ldrs 1f out: no ex and one pce ins fnl f* **11/4**[1]

2350 **5** *1 1/2* **Galiotto (IRE)**[9] 8001 6-9-12 60 (v) GeorgeBaker 11 63
(Gary Moore) *s.i.s: hld up off the pce towards rr: clsd on ldrs and hdwy into midfield 5f out: rdn to chse ldr over 2f out tl wl over 1f out: wknd ins fnl f* **8/1**

0356 **6** *3/4* **Waldsee (GER)**[9] 8001 7-9-2 50 AdamKirby 12 52
(Sean Curran) *hld up off the pce towards rr: clsd on ldrs 5f out: chsd ldrs and rdn 2f out: styd on same pce fnl f* **8/1**

3405 **7** *1* **Rollin 'n Tumblin**[6] 8035 8-8-12 46 oh1 JimmyQuinn 8 47
(Michael Attwater) *hld up off the pce in last quartet: pushed along and hdwy on inner 6f out: nt clr run over 3f out: rallied and hdwy 2f out: kpt on same pce fnl f: b.b.v* **12/1**

2000 **8** *2 1/2* **Delorain (IRE)**[287] 772 9-8-9 46 (tp) RyanClark(3) 10 44
(William Stone) *dropped to rr and rdn 12f out: struggling u.p 4f out: styd on fr 1f out but no threat to ldrs* **40/1**

4064 **9** *11* **Saloon (USA)**[44] 7479 8-8-6 47 JoshQuinn(7) 9 31
(Jane Chapple-Hyam) *hld up off the pce in rr: clsd 5f out: wknd 3f out: wl btn and hung lft 1f out* **16/1**

1205 **10** *10* **Omid**[104] 5811 4-9-12 60 (tp) GrahamLee 1 32
(Nicky Vaughan) *led tl 4f out: rdn and lost pl 3f out: bhd over 1f out: eaesd ins fnl f* **8/1**

0006 **11** *40* **Before Bruce**[11] 7968 5-9-7 55 (b) SebSanders 7
(Brendan Powell) *hld up in midfield: n.m.r 3f out: sn wknd: wl bhd and eased over 1f out: t.o* **33/1**

/45- **P** **Daylami Dreams**[577] 2183 8-9-9 57 RussKennemore 6
(John Holt) *chsd ldrs: wnt 2nd 13f out tl 12f out: styd chsng ldrs tl wknd over 3f out: t.o whn eased and p.u ins fnl f: dismntd* **16/1**

3m 25.49s (-0.21) **Going Correction** 0.0s/f (Stan)
WFA 3 from 4yo+ 8lb **12** Ran SP% **128.2**
Speed ratings (Par 101): **100,99,98,98,97 97,96,95,90,85 65,**
Tote swingers 1&2 £38.10, 1&3 £31.50, 2&3 £4.10 CSF £188.37 CT £684.71 TOTE £52.40: £10.00, £1.50, £1.90; EX 710.80 Trifecta £876.00 Part won. Pool: £1,168.05 - 0.10 winning tickets..
Owner K Tyre **Bred** Burton Agnes Stud Co Ltd **Trained** Epsom, Surrey

FOCUS
A moderate staying handicap and there were seven horses still in with a chance approaching the last furlong. A surprise winner with the runner-up confirming recent course form with the fourth.
Llamadas Official explanation: trainer said, regarding apparent improvement in form, that the gelding had benefited from a step up in trip and the strong pace.
Rollin 'n Tumblin Official explanation: trainer said gelding bled from the nose
Omid Official explanation: jockey said gelding lost its action
Before Bruce Official explanation: jockey said gelding hung right throughout

8105 32RED.COM H'CAP 1m (P)

2:20 (2:22) (Class 5) (0-75,75) 3-Y-O+ £2,264 (£673; £336; £168) Stalls High

Form RPR

0002 **1** **Lowther**[9] 7997 7-9-5 73 (b) WilliamCarson 1 82
(Lee Carter) *j. awkwardly: sn chsng ldrs: rdn and qcknd to ld over 1f out: edgd rt and r.o wl fnl f: rdn out* **10/11**[1]

6223 **2** *1 3/4* **Srinagar Girl**[9] 7996 3-9-3 72 IanMongan 6 77
(Sir Henry Cecil) *hld up in tch towards rr: gd hdwy on outer to chse ldrs 2f out: chsd wnr over 1f out: swtchd lft and styd on same pce ins fnl f* **9/2**[2]

6010 **3** *1 3/4* **Golden Desert (IRE)**[9] 7998 8-8-13 67 GrahamLee 7 68
(Simon Dow) *hld up in tch in last pair: rdn and hdwy 1f out: styd on ins fnl f: no threat to ldng pair* **8/1**[3]

6600 **4** *1 1/4* **Hereford Boy**[9] 7998 8-8-13 67 (v) JimCrowley 4 65
(Dean Ivory) *hld up in tch in midfield: rdn and hdwy on inner wl over 1f out: no imp fnl f* **12/1**

1/00 **5** *3* **Everybody Knows**[22] 7824 7-8-12 71 NathanSweeney(5) 2 62
(Jo Crowley) *led after 1f: rdn and hdd over 1f out: sn outpcd and btn: wknd 1f out* **20/1**

0000 **6** *1* **Spirit Of Xaar (IRE)**[25] 7171 6-8-10 64 ow1 (p) RobertHavlin 3 52
(Linda Jewell) *hld up in tch in midfield: nt clr run 3f out tl over 2f out: no hdwy u.p over 1f out: wknd fnl f* **50/1**

0010 **7** *1 1/2* **L'Hirondelle (IRE)**[28] 7743 8-9-3 71 SebSanders 5 56
(Michael Attwater) *led for 1f: chsd ldr after tl wl over 1f out: wknd over 1f out* **8/1**[3]

0000 **8** *hd* **Titan Triumph**[9] 7997 8-9-7 75 (t) AdamKirby 9 59
(William Knight) *stdd s: hld up in rr: rdn and no hdwy over 1f out: sn wknd* **8/1**[3]

0030 **9** *1/2* **Mishrif (USA)**[93] 6145 6-8-12 66 (b) SeanLevey 8 49
(J R Jenkins) *chsd ldrs: rdn over 2f out: wknd over 1f out* **14/1**

1m 36.41s (-1.79) **Going Correction** 0.0s/f (Stan)
WFA 3 from 6yo+ 1lb **9** Ran SP% **125.0**
Speed ratings (Par 103): **108,106,104,103,100 99,97,97,97**
Tote swingers 1&2 £2.00, 1&3 £2.80, 2&3 £3.70 CSF £5.92 CT £24.00 TOTE £2.00: £1.10, £1.80, £2.20; EX 5.90 Trifecta £18.50 Pool: £1,283.36 - 52.01 winning tickets..
Owner P G Marsh **Bred** L J Barratt **Trained** Epsom, Surrey

FOCUS
Just a fair handicap with the winner rated similar to his latest C&D mark.

8106 £32 BONUS AT 32RED.COM H'CAP 1m 4f (P)

2:55 (2:55) (Class 6) (0-65,77) 3-Y-O+ £1,704 (£503; £251) Stalls Low

Form RPR

0043 **1** **Cool Sky**[23] 7811 3-9-5 65 JimCrowley 8 73+
(William Knight) *chsd ldrs tl wnt 2nd 3f out: drvn to ld 1f out: kpt on wl u.p fnl f: hld on cl home* **2/1**[1]

112 **2** *nk* **Chookie Hamilton**[10] 7980 8-9-7 67 6ex JasonHart(5) 5 74+
(Keith Dalgleish) *hld up in tch in midfield: rdn and effrt over 2f out: chsd ldrs ent fnl f: chsd wnr wl ins fnl f: kpt on towards fin* **5/2**[2]

0003 **3** *1 1/4* **Jacobs Son**[50] 7353 4-9-7 62 GrahamLee 6 67
(Robert Mills) *led tl 8f out: pressed ldr tl led again over 3f out: drvn wl over 1f out: hdd 1f out: styd on same pce fnl 100yds* **4/1**[3]

0004 **4** *hd* **Eagle Nebula**[7] 8023 8-9-9 64 IanMongan 10 69
(Brett Johnson) *in tch in last pair: pushed along at times: rdn and hdwy on outer over 2f out: swtchd lft and styd on u.p ins fnl f* **16/1**

5442 **5** *1/2* **Kames Park (IRE)**[11] 7968 10-9-6 61 JimmyQuinn 9 65
(Richard Guest) *stdd s: hld up in tch in rr: hdwy to chse ldrs 2f out: swtchd lft and rdn 1f out: styd on same pce ins fnl f* **10/1**

12-4 **6** *1 1/2* **Ministry**[39] 1085 4-9-10 65 GeorgeBaker 4 67
(Gary Moore) *wl in tch in midfield: rdn and pressing ldrs but unable qck over 1f out: wknd ins fnl f* **20/1**

062 **7** *3* **Sweet Lavender (IRE)**[65] 6981 4-9-10 65 WilliamCarson 2 62
(Michael Wigham) *chsd ldrs: effrt u.p wl over 1f out: unable qck ent fnl f: wknd ins fnl f* **7/1**

0010 **8** *4* **Daniel Thomas (IRE)**[5] 8051 10-9-8 63 (tp) SeanLevey 7 54
(Violet M Jordan) *s.i.s: hld up in tch in last trio: dropped to rr and rdn over 2f out: wknd over 1f out* **20/1**

0/00 **9** *19* **Whiepa Snappa (IRE)**[7] 8023 5-8-6 52 JemmaMarshall(5) 1 12
(Pat Phelan) *t.k.h: w ldr tl led 8f out tl over 3f out: sn dropped out: bhd and eased ins fnl f* **25/1**

2m 33.35s (0.35) **Going Correction** 0.0s/f (Stan)
WFA 3 from 4yo+ 5lb **9** Ran SP% **122.7**
Speed ratings (Par 101): **98,97,96,96,96 95,93,90,78**
Tote Swingers 1&2 £1.90, 1&3 £2.70, 2&3 £3.30 CSF £7.47 CT £18.96 TOTE £3.40: £1.10, £2.00, £1.70; EX 11.30 Trifecta £31.80 Pool: £1,857.21 - 43.68 winning tickets..
Owner No Quarter Partnership **Bred** Miss K J Keir **Trained** Patching, W Sussex

FOCUS
A moderate middle-distance handicap and they didn't go much of a pace despite a disputed lead so it is difficult to be too positive, although the winner is rated close to his maiden form backed up by the second.

8107 AT THE RACES VIRGIN 534 APPRENTICE H'CAP — 5f (P)
3:30 (3:31) (Class 6) (0-60,58) 3-Y-O+ — £1,704 (£503; £251) Stalls High

Form — RPR
4621 **1** **Pharoh Jake**[5] 8045 4-9-0 54 6ex WilliamTwiston-Davies(3) 1 — 62
(John Bridger) *pressed ldrs on inner: drvn to chal over 1f out: kpt on u.p to ld wl ins fnl f* 4/1[2]
3433 **2** ½ **Baby Dottie**[9] 7990 5-9-2 56 (tp) JakePayne(3) 6 — 62
(Pat Phelan) *led: rdn wl over 1f out: kpt on wl u.p tl hdd and no ex wl ins fnl f* 7/2[1]
2350 **3** ¾ **Imaginary Diva**[74] 6737 6-9-2 58 JordanVaughan(5) 4 — 61
(George Margarson) *hld up in tch in last pair: hdwy on inner over 1f out: chsd ldrs but nt clr run ins fnl f: kpt on towards fin* 10/1
0014 **4** nk **Brandywell Boy (IRE)**[5] 8045 9-8-13 53 JoshBaudains(3) 2 — 56
(Dominic Ffrench Davis) *w ldr: rdn and ev ch over 1f out: unable qck ins fnl f: hld whn nt clr run and lost 3rd towards fin* 6/1[3]
0036 **5** hd **Chjimes (IRE)**[3] 8064 8-9-4 58 (b) ThomasBrown(3) 8 — 60
(Conor Dore) *hld up in tch on outer: effrt u.p ent fnl f: styd on u.p fnl 100yds* 7/2[1]
2100 **6** ½ **Miss Polly Plum**[39] 7590 5-9-3 57 (p) JackDuern(3) 9 — 57
(Chris Dwyer) *chsd ldrs on outer: rdn and unable qck over 1f out: styd on same pce ins fnl f* 10/1
0000 **7** 1 **Cut The Cackle (IRE)**[23] 7815 6-9-1 52 (bt) CharlesBishop 5 — 48
(Violet M Jordan) *hld up in tch in midfield: effrt and rdn over 1f out: styd on same pce ins fnl f* 7/1
0304 **8** hd **Miserere Mei (IRE)**[88] 6314 3-8-6 46 (e) JasonHart(3) 7 — 41
(Richard Guest) *hld up in last pair: rdn and styd on same pce fr jst over 1f out* 12/1
4006 **9** 8 **Bailadeira**[11] 7970 4-9-2 58 (b[1]) JoeyHaynes(5) 3 — 25
(Tim Etherington) *taken down early: unruly at s: hld up wl in tch in midfield: rdn and no hdwy wl over 1f out: wknd 1f out* 12/1

58.73s (-0.07) **Going Correction** 0.0s/f (Stan) 9 Ran SP% **124.8**
Speed ratings (Par 101): **100,99,98,97,97 96,94,94,81**
Tote Swingers 1&2 £3.00, 1&3 £8.20, 2&3 £10.10 CSF £20.17 CT £138.18 TOTE £3.90: £1.10, £1.90, £4.80; EX 16.20 Trifecta £205.90 Pool: £1,674.73 - 6.10 winning tickets..
Owner The Hair & Haberdasher Partnership **Bred** J J Bridger **Trained** Liphook, Hants

FOCUS
A moderate sprint handicap for apprentice riders. It paid to race handily with the winner recording a personal best and the second rated in line with this year's form.
Bailadeira Official explanation: jockey said filly would not face the blinkers
T/Plt: £21.40 to a £1 stake. Pool:£44,080.68 - 1,498.12 winning tickets T/Qpdt: £7.60 to a £1 stake. Pool:£4,546.93 - 439.86 winning tickets SP

7976 WOLVERHAMPTON (A.W) (L-H)
Friday, December 14

OFFICIAL GOING: Standard to slow changing to standard after race 1 (3.50)
Wind: Fresh, behind Weather: Raining

8108 32RED.COM NURSERY — 5f 20y(P)
3:50 (3:51) (Class 6) (0-65,62) 2-Y-O — £1,704 (£503; £251) Stalls Low

Form — RPR
312 **1** **Small Fury (IRE)**[8] 8007 2-9-7 62 J-PGuillambert 1 — 66
(Jo Hughes) *chsd ldrs: led over 1f out: rdn out* 4/5[1]
0005 **2** 2¼ **Fat Bottom Girl**[14] 7930 2-8-4 45 JamesSullivan 4 — 41
(Michael Easterby) *led early: chsd ldrs: rdn 1/2-way: r.o to go 2nd wl ins fnl f: no ch w wnr* 14/1
0500 **3** nk **Hats Off**[23] 7808 2-8-7 48 (b[1]) DavidProbert 2 — 43
(John Best) *hld up: swtchd rt 1/2-way: rdn over 1f out: r.o ins fnl f: nrst fin* 16/1
4656 **4** nk **Lexi's Beauty (IRE)**[14] 7930 2-8-4 45 (b[1]) SilvestreDeSousa 6 — 39
(Ian Williams) *sn led: rdn and hdd over 1f out: no ex ins fnl f* 9/1
6546 **5** ½ **Beacon Tarn**[27] 7777 2-9-4 59 GrahamGibbons 10 — 51
(Eric Alston) *chsd ldr: rdn over 1f out: styd on same pce fnl f* 7/1[3]
6000 **6** ½ **Cashel's Missile (IRE)**[58] 7156 2-9-2 57 TomEaves 5 — 47
(John Spearing) *hld up: hdwy u.p over 1f out: styd on same pce ins fnl f* 66/1
0005 **7** 1½ **Fit For A King (IRE)**[8] 8007 2-8-12 53 (b) RobertWinston 8 — 38
(John Best) *sn pushed along towards rr: hdwy 1/2-way: sn rdn: styng on same pce whn rdr dropped whip 1f out* 6/1[2]
0264 **8** 2 **Cymeriad**[28] 7745 2-9-0 55 AmyRyan 7 — 33
(Michael Easterby) *hld up: rdn over 1f out: n.d* 8/1

1m 2.27s (-0.03) **Going Correction** -0.025s/f (Stan) 8 Ran SP% **117.5**
Speed ratings (Par 94): **99,95,94,94,93 92,90,87**
Tote Swingers 1&2 £4.70, 1&3 £6.10, 2&3 £17.10 CSF £15.04 CT £113.79 TOTE £1.50: £1.10, £4.20, £6.10; EX 13.70 Trifecta £139.80 Pool: £1,815.64 - 9.74 winning units..
Owner Joseph Hearne, D Bird, H Downs, J Hughes **Bred** Tally-Ho Stud **Trained** Lambourn. Berks

FOCUS
The first meeting at the course for ten days, 40,000 gallons of binder had been applied to the track to prevent "balling" under the horses feet during freezing conditions. They went a decent pace in this sprint nursery. The favourite delivered in good style and there didn't seem to be much kickback. A low-grade nursery but straightforward form.

NOTEBOOK
Small Fury(IRE) won a Southwell maiden last month before going very close over 6f at Lingfield on her nursery debut last week. Racing off the same mark, she was always prominent from a good draw and surged clear in the final furlong to justify strong support and improve her strike-rate to 2-4. A tough filly who has scope for further improvement, she should be able to win again and is bred to stay quite a bit further than this. (tchd 10-11)
Fat Bottom Girl had not shown a great deal in six previous starts but she stayed on strongly to snatch second this time. This was a promising run from this Pastoral Pursuits half-sister to six Flat/jumps winners and she shaped like a step back up in trip will suit. (op 12-1)
Hats Off has a patchy seven-race profile but first-time blinkers and a drop back to 5f helped spark a better effort from this sprint-bred gelding. (op 20-1)
Lexi's Beauty(IRE) showed plenty of speed before fading in the closing stages. Her mark has bottomed out and she has already had three different trainers, but first-time blinkers seem to have ignited her and she could build on this. (op 11-1)
Beacon Tarn had every chance but lacked the finishing speed of some others on this switch back to 5f. (op 6-1 tchd 11-2)
Fit For A King(IRE) was laboured back at 5f. He has not progressed from a promising debut run and has form figures of 97757 in nurseries. (op 7-1)

8109 32RED CASINO MEDIAN AUCTION MAIDEN STKS — 5f 20y(P)
4:20 (4:20) (Class 6) 3-5-Y-O — £1,704 (£503; £251) Stalls Low

Form — RPR
05 **1** **Resonare**[13] 7952 3-9-3 0 DavidProbert 5 — 47+
(Stuart Williams) *a.p: rdn ins fnl f: r.o to ld towards fin* 15/8[2]
0644 **2** ¾ **Red Ramesses (IRE)**[9] 7988 3-9-3 62 RobertWinston 6 — 45
(John Best) *sn pushed along to chse ldr: rdn to ld ins fnl f: hdd towards fin* 4/6[1]
0065 **3** hd **Love Club**[28] 7746 4-9-3 44 GrahamGibbons 8 — 44
(Brian Baugh) *led: rdn and hdd ins fnl f: styd on* 12/1[3]
060 **4** 1¼ **Busy Bimbo (IRE)**[21] 7838 3-8-12 45 (b) TomEaves 3 — 35
(Alan Berry) *hld up: hdwy over 1f out: sn rdn: styd on same pce wl ins fnl f* 33/1
5500 **5** 2 **Colamandis**[27] 7782 5-8-5 40 (b) VictorSantos(7) 2 — 27
(Hugh McWilliams) *chsd ldrs: rdn over 1f out: no ex ins fnl f* 50/1
060 **6** 2 **Stoneacre Hull (IRE)**[35] 7667 3-8-12 46 DominicFox 7 — 20
(Peter Grayson) *s.i.s: nvr on terms* 16/1
050 **7** 2 **Bonbon Bonnie**[38] 7611 4-8-12 41 (v[1]) TomMcLaughlin 1 — 13
(Phil McEntee) *mid-div: pushed along 3f out: wknd 2f out* 40/1
50 **8** 13 **Dancing Ellie Mae**[291] 720 3-8-12 0 SilvestreDeSousa 4
(Derek Shaw) *hmpd sn after s: hdwy over 3f out: hung rt and wknd 1/2-way* 20/1

1m 2.36s (0.06) **Going Correction** -0.025s/f (Stan) 8 Ran SP% **120.4**
Speed ratings (Par 101): **98,96,96,94,91 88,84,64**
Tote Swingers 1&2 £1.30, 1&3 £3.30, 2&3 £2.50 CSF £3.55 TOTE £3.00: £1.10, £1.02, £2.30; EX 4.30 Trifecta £15.00 Pool: £2,029.76 - 100.84 winning units..
Owner G D Thompson **Bred** Old Mill Stud **Trained** Newmarket, Suffolk

FOCUS
A weak maiden, but it was won by an unexposed type who could continue to progress. The form is rated around the third.
Dancing Ellie Mae Official explanation: jockey said filly yung right-handed turning into straight

8110 32RED H'CAP — 1m 4f 50y(P)
4:50 (4:50) (Class 4) (0-85,85) 3-Y-O+ — £4,204 (£1,251; £625; £312) Stalls Low

Form — RPR
4331 **1** **Flying Power**[35] 7672 4-9-5 80 ow2 PaddyAspell 10 — 87
(John Norton) *trckd ldrs: rdn to ld ins fnl f: hung lft: r.o* 4/1[1]
1/50 **2** 1¼ **Ascendant**[279] 202 6-9-5 80 RobertWinston 2 — 85
(Alan McCabe) *chsd ldrs: rdn to ld over 1f out: hdd ins fnl f: styng on same pce whn hmpd towards fin* 11/1
0131 **3** ¾ **Desert Vision**[20] 7867 8-9-8 83 (vt) GrahamGibbons 6 — 87
(Michael Easterby) *a.p: rdn and ev ch whn hmpd ins fnl f: styd on* 5/1[3]
0135 **4** nk **The Lock Master (IRE)**[46] 7438 5-9-9 84 DominicFox 3 — 87
(Michael Appleby) *chsd ldr: rdn and ev ch fr over 1f out tl hmpd ins fnl f: styd on* 10/1
0004 **5** ½ **Musnad (USA)**[49] 7368 4-8-10 71 oh3 (b[1]) SilvestreDeSousa 4 — 73
(Brian Ellison) *s.s: hld up: hdwy over 1f out: styd on* 12/1
3000 **6** ¾ **Royal Peculiar**[22] 7825 4-9-8 83 AndrewMullen 12 — 84
(Michael Appleby) *hld up: pushed along and hdwy over 2f out: rdn over 1f out: styd on same pce fnl f* 16/1
310- **7** 1¼ **Lemon Drop Red (USA)**[34] 6666 4-9-5 80 EddieAhern 5 — 79
(Paul Webber) *hld up: rdn over 1f out: nvr trbld ldrs* 10/1
-214 **8** ½ **Epic Storm (IRE)**[9] 8000 4-9-1 76 JohnFahy 9 — 74
(Sean Curran) *hld up: rdn over 1f out: nvr on terms* 9/2[2]
2631 **9** 3½ **Saaboog**[50] 7353 3-9-2 82 MartinLane 11 — 75
(James Tate) *led: rdn over 2f out: hdd over 1f out: wknd ins fnl f* 9/2[2]
/00- **10** 7 **Blizzard Blues (USA)**[549] 3013 6-9-10 85 (b) ChrisCatlin 1 — 66
(Aytach Sadik) *hld up: a in rr: rdn over 2f out: sn wknd* 80/1

2m 40.07s (-1.03) **Going Correction** -0.025s/f (Stan)
WFA 3 from 4yo+ 5lb 10 Ran SP% **114.4**
Speed ratings (Par 105): **102,101,100,100,100 99,98,98,96,91**
Tote Swingers: 1&2 £6.70, 1&3 £5.10, 2&3 £13.20 CSF £47.57 CT £223.27 TOTE £5.60: £2.20, £2.50, £2.40; EX 63.00 Trifecta £497.50 Pool: £1,486.08 - 2.24 winning units..
Owner Jaffa Racing Syndicate **Bred** Rabbah Bloodstock Limited **Trained** High Hoyland, S Yorks
■ Stewards' Enquiry : Paddy Aspell five-day ban: careless riding (Dec 28-31,Jan 1)

FOCUS
A fair middle-distance handicap. It was run at a stop-start gallop and the winner scored with something in hand, despite some steering problems in the closing stages. The form is messy and looks ordinary for the grade.

8111 32RED SUPPORTING BRITISH RACING H'CAP — 1m 141y(P)
5:20 (5:21) (Class 7) (0-50,56) 3-Y-O+ — £1,704 (£503; £251) Stalls Low

Form — RPR
0044 **1** **Big Sylv (IRE)**[10] 7982 3-9-3 50 (p) DavidProbert 10 — 62
(James Unett) *trckd ldr tl led 3f out: rdn clr fr over 1f out* 5/1[2]
0050 **2** 3½ **Stamp Duty (IRE)**[120] 5259 4-9-2 47 TomEaves 5 — 51
(Suzzanne France) *s.i.s: hld up: rdn and r.o to go 2nd ins fnl f: no ch w wnr* 12/1
5466 **3** 1 **Avon Supreme**[50] 7362 4-9-2 47 (p) RobertWinston 1 — 49
(Gay Kelleway) *chsd ldrs: rdn over 2f out: styd on same pce fr over 1f out* 13/2[3]
0100 **4** hd **Nurse Dominatrix (IRE)**[5] 8050 3-9-2 49 RobbieFitzpatrick 6 — 51
(Richard Guest) *a.p: rdn to chse wnr over 2f out: styd on same pce fr over 1f out* 11/1
6541 **5** 1¼ **Angel Cake (IRE)**[10] 7983 3-9-9 56 6ex AndrewMullen 8 — 55
(Michael Appleby) *a.p: rdn over 2f out: no ex fnl f* 15/8[1]
6301 **6** 1 **Gay Gallivanter**[38] 7605 4-9-5 50 (p) SilvestreDeSousa 4 — 46
(Michael Quinn) *mid-div: nt clr run and lost pl over 2f out: styd on ins fnl f: nvr nrr* 11/1
1004 **7** 1½ **Compton Crofter**[16] 7898 3-9-2 49 (t) J-PGuillambert 9 — 42
(Hans Adielsson) *s.i.s: hld up: rdn over 1f out: nvr on terms* 20/1
4035 **8** ¾ **Winnetou**[16] 7898 3-9-2 49 LiamKeniry 11 — 40
(Frank Sheridan) *hld up: hdwy over 2f out: rdn and wknd over 1f out* 8/1
0506 **9** 3 **Crucis Abbey (IRE)**[35] 7671 4-9-5 50 (p) ShaneKelly 13 — 34
(Mark Brisbourne) *s.i.s: hld up: a in rr* 20/1
400 **10** 20 **The Kernigal (IRE)**[1] 8099 3-9-3 50 (t) JohnFahy 3
(Paul Howling) *sn pushed along to ld: hdd 3f out: rdn and wknd wl over 1f out: t.o* 14/1

1m 50.37s (-0.13) **Going Correction** -0.025s/f (Stan)
WFA 3 from 4yo+ 2lb 10 Ran SP% **116.4**
Speed ratings (Par 97): **99,95,95,94,93 92,91,90,88,70**
Tote Swingers: 1&2 £9.20, 1&3 £6.20, 2&3 £6.70 CSF £63.26 CT £400.47 TOTE £5.40: £1.90, £3.80, £1.80; EX 43.50 Trifecta £318.40 Pool: £1,129.39 - 2.66 winning units..
Owner Miss Ciara Doyle **Bred** John Doyle **Trained** Tedsmore Hall, Shropshire

FOCUS
There was an emphatic winner of this steadily run handicap. This was a clear personal best with the third setting the standard and close to recent marks.
The Kernigal(IRE) Official explanation: jockey said gelding hung right-handed

8112 £32 BONUS AT 32RED.COM NURSERY 1m 1f 103y(P)
5:50 (5:50) (Class 6) (0-60,60) 2-Y-O £1,704 (£503; £251) Stalls Low

Form RPR
000 1 **Good Speech (IRE)**[99] 5962 2-9-4 **57**........ JohnFahy 4 61
(Tom Tate) *s.i.s: drvn along to ld after 1f: hdd 7f out: chsd ldrs: led over 1f out: rdn clr fnl f* **10/1**
000 2 2 ½ **Great Ormond (IRE)**[30] 7706 2-8-13 **52**........ MartinLane 1 51
(David Simcock) *s.i.s: hld up: rdn over 1f out: edgd lft and r.o ins fnl f: no ch w wnr* **10/1**
2004 3 nse **Unidexter (IRE)**[15] 7922 2-8-11 **50**........ SilvestreDeSousa 9 49
(Mick Channon) *hld up: rdn over 2f out: r.o ins fnl f: nrst fin* **16/1**
3240 4 nk **Poetic Verse**[16] 7919 2-9-3 **56**........ JamesMillman 8 54
(Rod Millman) *chsd ldrs: led 5f out: rdn and hdd over 2f out: styd on same pce fnl f* **14/1**
0501 5 nk **Crystal Peaks**[16] 7919 2-9-7 **60**........ JamesSullivan 7 58
(James Given) *led 1f: led again 7f out: hdd 5f out: rdn to ld over 2f out: hung rt and hdd over 1f out: no ex ins fnl f* **7/4**[1]
500 6 1 ½ **Pacquiao (IRE)**[142] 4448 2-9-0 **53**........ MichaelO'Connell 2 48
(John Quinn) *hld up: hdwy u.p over 1f out: no ex ins fnl f* **9/2**[3]
000 7 3 ¼ **Lady Of Yue**[16] 7900 2-9-0 **53**........ ChrisCatlin 3 42
(Ed Dunlop) *in rr: pushed along 5f out: rdn over 1f out: wknd fnl f* **8/1**
060 8 2 ¾ **Orla's Rainbow (IRE)**[25] 7785 2-9-1 **54**........(b) TomMcLaughlin 6 38
(John Berry) *prom: rdn over 3f out: wknd fnl f* **22/1**
5625 9 4 **Elusive Thought (IRE)**[1] 8094 2-9-7 **60**........ DavidProbert 5 36
(J S Moore) *chsd ldrs: rdn over 2f out: wknd over 1f out* **3/1**[2]
2m 2.82s (1.12) **Going Correction** -0.025s/f (Stan) 9 Ran SP% **125.7**
Speed ratings (Par 94): **94,91,91,91,91 89,86,84,80**
Tote Swingers: 1&2 £13.10, 1&3 £18.00, 2&3 £26.90 CSF £113.65 CT £1618.90 TOTE £6.80: £1.60, £2.30, £3.80; EX 103.00 Trifecta £666.20 Pool: £1,101.55 - 1.24 winning units..
Owner T T Racing **Bred** D Veitch, E McEvoy & P Costigan **Trained** Tadcaster, N Yorks

FOCUS
A modest nursery but the pace was fair and an unexposed handicap debutante powered clear to get off the mark. The form is very ordinary.

NOTEBOOK
Good Speech(IRE) didn't show much in three 7f-1m maidens on turf during the summer but this well-related filly raced enthusiastically off the pace before surging to a comfortable victory on her nursery/AW debut back from 99 days off. She could face a sharp rise for this decisive win, but she has plenty of potential for further improvement at this trip and possibly a bit further. Official explanation: trainer's rep said, regarding apparent improvement in form, that the filly had benefited from a 99-day break in which time it had become physically stronger. (op 9-1 tchd 8-1)
Great Ormond(IRE) finished ahead of only three rivals in maidens, but he put in a better effort stepped up in trip on his nursery debut and has scope for further progress after just four runs. (op 12-1)
Unidexter(IRE) gave some problems in the stalls and looked in trouble around the final bend but he battled well to finish third. He is now 0-10 but is 18lb lower than his opening mark and shapes like another step up in trip could suit. (op 20-1)
Poetic Verse ran a fair race under a positive ride but she is exposed and has a record of 0-9. (op 16-1)
Crystal Peaks bounced back to form when off the mark with a 20-1 win in an 8.6f nursery here last month. She was a bit disappointing off 4lb higher here, but she may have paid the price for getting involved in a destructive battle up front and could resume her progress next time. (op 11-4 tchd 7-2)
Pacquiao(IRE) attracted some support on his nursery debut back from a break and gelding operation, but he hit a flat spot at a crucial stage and was never dangerous. (tchd 4-1)
Elusive Thought(IRE) shaped with some promise on his handicap debut over 1m at Kempton 24 hours earlier but he was lacklustre turned out quickly here. Official explanation: jockey said gelding ran flat (op 7-2)

8113 32REDBET.COM H'CAP 1m 1f 103y(P)
6:20 (6:20) (Class 6) (0-60,60) 3-Y-O+ £1,704 (£503; £251) Stalls Low

Form RPR
5- 1 **Reasons Unknown (IRE)**[56] 7231 4-8-8 **47**........ ShaneKelly 5 57
(Thomas McLaughlin, Ire) *hld up: hdwy 2f out: rdn to ld 1f out: drvn out* **11/1**
6106 2 nk **Chasin' Rainbows**[44] 7479 4-8-13 **52**........ LiamKeniry 2 61
(Sylvester Kirk) *hld up: hdwy over 1f out: sn rdn: r.o u.p* **6/1**[3]
0000 3 1 ¼ **Flying Applause**[37] 7640 7-9-2 **58**........(b) MarkCoumbe(3) 7 65
(Roy Bowring) *s.i.s: sn prom: led over 3f out: rdn and hdd 1f out: no ex towards fin* **10/1**
0146 4 hd **Sasheen**[20] 7867 5-9-0 **56**........(p) RaulDaSilva(3) 4 62
(Jeremy Gask) *trckd ldrs: racd keenly: rdn and ev ch 1f out: edgd rt: styd on same pce* **16/1**
0-60 5 1 **Kingarrick**[34] 7684 4-9-7 **60**........ RobertWinston 11 64
(Noel Wilson) *hld up: rdn and nt clr run over 1f out: r.o: nt trble ldrs* **9/1**
6430 6 hd **Bonnie Prince Blue**[50] 7347 9-9-4 **57**........(b) AmyRyan 6 61
(Ian McInnes) *s.i.s: hld up: rdn and r.o ins fnl f: nvr nrr* **33/1**
5001 7 shd **Dream Win**[10] 7976 6-9-7 **60**........ SilvestreDeSousa 1 64
(Brian Ellison) *chsd ldrs: rdn over 1f out: styd on same pce ins fnl f* **9/4**[1]
5000 8 nse **Baharat (IRE)**[22] 5809 4-8-10 **49**........(bt) RobbieFitzpatrick 10 52
(Richard Guest) *hld up: hdwy over 2f out: sn rdn: no ex ins fnl f* **33/1**
3043 9 2 ¼ **Essell**[10] 7982 3-8-10 **51**........ ChrisCatlin 9 50
(Mick Channon) *led: hdd over 3f out: sn rdn: no ex fnl f* **9/2**[2]
1140 10 1 ¼ **Meglio Ancora**[5] 8051 5-9-0 **60**........ VictorSantos(7) 3 56
(Richard Ford) *s.i.s: hld up: hdwy over 1f out: wknd ins fnl f* **20/1**
0020 11 11 **Macy Anne (IRE)**[123] 5156 3-9-1 **56**........ J-PGuillambert 12 29
(Jo Hughes) *hld up in tch: chsd ldr over 2f out: shkn up over 1f out: eased fnl f* **25/1**
12 18 **Reina De Luz (IRE)**[65] 6994 3-9-5 **60**........(p) JamesSullivan 13
(Lee Smyth, Ire) *chsd ldr tl rdn over 3f out: wknd over 2f out: t.o* **14/1**
2m 2.62s (0.92) **Going Correction** -0.025s/f (Stan)
WFA 3 from 4yo+ 2lb 12 Ran SP% **117.7**
Speed ratings (Par 101): **94,93,92,92,91 91,91,91,89,88 78,62**
Tote Swingers: 1&2 £10.50, 1&3 £7.90, 2&3 £10.00 CSF £71.85 CT £686.05 TOTE £14.20: £3.40, £1.80, £2.50; EX 89.60 Trifecta £555.80 Part won. Pool: £741.17 - 0.62 winning units..
Owner Andrew Stinchon **Bred** Martyn J McEnery **Trained** Rathmullan, Co Donegal

FOCUS
An ordinary handicap run at just a fair pace. The third and fourth set a modest standard.
Reina De Luz(IRE) Official explanation: jockey said filly lost its action

8114 32REDPOKER.COM H'CAP (DIV I) 7f 32y(P)
6:50 (6:52) (Class 6) (0-65,65) 3-Y-O+ £1,704 (£503; £251) Stalls High

Form RPR
4000 1 **Bang Tidy (IRE)**[16] 7915 3-8-8 **52**........(t) SilvestreDeSousa 10 63
(Brian Ellison) *hld up: pushed along 1/2-way: hdwy over 2f out: rdn to ld ins fnl f: r.o* **16/1**
1212 2 ½ **See The Storm**[9] 7992 4-8-11 **58**........ RyanPowell(3) 11 68
(Ian Williams) *s.i.s: hld up: hdwy over 2f out: nt clr run over 1f out: r.o* **5/1**[2]
2406 3 ½ **Sir Bruno (FR)**[15] 7925 5-9-5 **63**........(p) LukeMorris 1 71
(Bryn Palling) *chsd ldrs: led over 1f out: rdn and hdd ins fnl f: styd on* **8/1**
6051 4 2 ¾ **Honey Of A Kitten (USA)**[8] 8010 4-8-13 **64**........(v) EoinWalsh(7) 9 65
(David Evans) *a.p: rdn over 1f out: styd on same pce ins fnl f* **7/1**
4105 5 5 **Elegant Muse**[14] 7936 4-9-3 **61**........(t) AndrewMullen 6 48
(Michael Appleby) *led at str pce: rdn and hdd over 1f out: wknd ins fnl f* **12/1**
0606 6 1 **Mubtadi**[50] 7348 4-9-4 **62**........(t[1]) ShaneKelly 7 47
(Ismail Mohammed) *s.i.s: hld up: shkn up over 1f out: nvr on terms* **6/1**[3]
16 7 3 **Purley Queen (IRE)**[9] 7998 3-9-2 **65**........ LeeNewnes(5) 8 42
(Sylvester Kirk) *s.i.s: nvr nrr* **25/1**
0222 8 2 ¼ **Green Mitas (ITY)**[27] 7776 3-9-6 **64**........ LiamKeniry 2 35
(Frank Sheridan) *trckd ldrs: rdn over 1f out: wknd fnl f* **5/1**[2]
0000 9 5 **Fighter Boy (IRE)**[111] 5588 5-9-7 **65**........(b[1]) JamesSullivan 4 22
(Michael Easterby) *chsd ldr over 5f out: rdn over 2f out: wknd over 1f out* **7/2**[1]
6101 10 19 **North Central (USA)**[43] 7512 5-9-1 **59**........(p) TomEaves 5
(Ruth Carr) *chsd ldrs: pushed along 1/2-way: wknd over 2f out* **20/1**
0/00 11 7 **Muktasb (USA)**[295] 664 11-8-8 **52** oh6 ow1........(v) RobbieFitzpatrick 3
(Richard Guest) *hld up: rdn and wknd over 2f out* **100/1**
1m 28.66s (-0.94) **Going Correction** -0.025s/f (Stan) 11 Ran SP% **116.6**
Speed ratings (Par 101): **104,103,102,99,94 92,89,86,81,59 51**
Tote Swingers: 1&2 £14.10, 1&3 £11.90, 2&3 £4.30 CSF £91.88 CT £712.51 TOTE £15.80: £4.10, £1.90, £2.90; EX 76.40 Trifecta £162.20 Pool: £1,001.91 - 4.63 winning units..
Owner Koo's Racing Club **Bred** James And Sarah Mulcahy **Trained** Norton, N Yorks

FOCUS
They went a strong pace in this minor handicap which played into the hands of the hold-up horses. The third sets the level running close to his September C&D form.

8115 32REDPOKER.COM H'CAP (DIV II) 7f 32y(P)
7:20 (7:21) (Class 6) (0-65,65) 3-Y-O+ £1,704 (£503; £251) Stalls High

Form RPR
3260 1 **Strong Man**[46] 7446 4-9-5 **63**........(b) GrahamGibbons 3 72
(Michael Easterby) *mde all: rdn over 1f out: all out* **9/4**[1]
633 2 nk **Ifan (IRE)**[36] 7654 4-9-4 **62**........ LukeMorris 6 70
(Bryn Palling) *hld up: hdwy over 1f out: rdn to chse wnr and hung lft ins fnl f: r.o* **13/2**[3]
0266 3 1 ½ **Piccolo Express**[16] 7917 6-9-0 **58**........ J-PGuillambert 1 62
(Brian Baugh) *prom: nt clr run fr over 2f out tl jst over 1f out: r.o* **12/1**
4050 4 shd **Ace Master**[46] 7446 4-8-12 **59**........ MarkCoumbe(3) 2 63
(Roy Bowring) *chsd ldrs: rdn over 1f out: styd on same pce ins fnl f* **16/1**
0340 5 ½ **Hawk Moth (IRE)**[20] 7857 4-9-6 **64**........ ChrisCatlin 4 67
(John Spearing) *s.i.s: hld up: nt clr run over 1f out: rdn and r.o ins fnl f: nrst fin* **9/1**
3502 6 1 **Travis County (IRE)**[38] 7600 3-9-7 **65**........ SilvestreDeSousa 8 65
(Brian Ellison) *chsd wnr 6f out: rdn over 2f out: lost 2nd 1f out: no ex* **5/2**[2]
3043 7 2 **Eastern Hills**[24] 7798 7-8-11 **62**........(p) NoraLooby(7) 5 56
(Alan McCabe) *prom: rdn over 1f out: wknd fnl f* **8/1**
0006 8 2 **Madame Kintyre**[9] 7990 4-9-2 **60**........ JamesMillman 9 49
(Rod Millman) *hld up: rdn and wknd 2f out* **50/1**
0020 9 15 **Gracie's Gift (IRE)**[46] 7447 10-8-8 **52** ow1........(v) RobbieFitzpatrick 7
(Richard Guest) *mid-div: rdn 1/2-way: wknd 2f out* **25/1**
1m 29.14s (-0.46) **Going Correction** -0.025s/f (Stan) 9 Ran SP% **113.2**
Speed ratings (Par 101): **101,100,98,98,98 97,94,92,75**
Tote Swingers: 1&2 £3.70, 1&3 £6.10, 2&3 £7.20 CSF £17.04 CT £141.53 TOTE £3.00: £1.30, £1.60, £2.70; EX 16.00 Trifecta £73.30 Pool: £975.60 - 9.97 winning units..
Owner Mrs Jean Turpin **Bred** Mrs Jean Turpin **Trained** Sheriff Hutton, N Yorks
■ Stewards' Enquiry : Graham Gibbons two-day ban: used whip above permitted level (Dec 28-29)

FOCUS
There was a front-running winner in the second division of this low-grade handicap, but there were also eyecatching efforts from the placed horses. The winner is rated back to his best and sets the level.
T/Plt: £876.00 to a £1 stake. Pool: £68,016.27. 56.68 winning tickets. T/Qpdt: £270.40 to a £1 stake. Pool: £7,820.92. 21.40 winning tickets. CR

8116 - 8130a (Foreign Racing) - See Raceform Interactive

8108 WOLVERHAMPTON (A.W) (L-H)
Saturday, December 15

OFFICIAL GOING: Standard
A double-header as a result of Southwell's abandonment.
Wind: Light behind Weather: Cloudy turning to rain after the 7-50

8131 TRACK YOUR HORSES AT ATTHERACES.COM H'CAP 7f 32y(P)
2:05 (2:06) (Class 6) (0-55,56) 3-Y-O+ £2,070 (£616; £307; £153) Stalls High

Form RPR
402 1 **Nant Saeson (IRE)**[39] 7599 3-9-2 55........(p) MichaelO'Connell 4 63
(John Quinn) *trckd ldrs: hdwy 3f out: led 2f out: rdn over 1f out: drvn and kpt on wl towards fin* **10/3**[1]
0001 2 shd **Ensnare**[28] 7781 7-9-1 54........ StevieDonohoe 3 62
(Willie Musson) *dwlt and towards rr: hdwy on outer wl over 1f out: rdn and str run fnl f: jst failed* **7/2**[2]
4062 3 ¾ **Lindoro**[11] 7982 7-9-3 56........ AdamKirby 2 62
(Sean Curran) *in tch: hdwy to chse ldrs over 2f out: sn rdn and kpt on same pce fnl f* **7/2**[2]
4520 4 ¾ **Kai**[44] 7504 3-9-1 54........(v) LukeMorris 1 58
(Alan McCabe) *trckd ldr on inner: pushed along 3f out: rdn 2f out: drvn and one pce fnl f* **10/1**
044 5 1 ½ **White Flight**[10] 7992 3-8-7 53........ IanBurns(7) 8 53
(Jane Chapple-Hyam) *prom: hdwy 3f out: chsd wnr 2f out: sn rdn and wknd over 1f out* **9/1**
4500 6 1 ¼ **Cadmium Loch**[57] 7224 4-8-11 55........(p) JackDuern(5) 9 51
(Reg Hollinshead) *hld up in tch: hdwy to chse ldrs 2f out: sn rdn and no imp* **11/1**

The Form Book Flat, Raceform Ltd, Compton, RG20 6NL

0630 **7** 1 ½ **Dark Orchid**[72] 6829 3-9-1 54 .... JamieSpencer 6 46
(Peter Chapple-Hyam) *led: rdn along over 2f out: sn hdd & wknd* **17/2**[3]
0000 **8** 7 **Ryedale Dancer (IRE)**[17] 7917 4-9-2 55 .... RobbieFitzpatrick 5 28
(Richard Guest) *towards rr: pushed along 1/2-way: rdn along wl over 2f out: n.d* **16/1**
0000 **9** 2 ½ **Prohibition (IRE)**[50] 7385 6-9-0 53 .... ChrisCatlin 7 20
(John Butler) *s.i.s: a bhd* **28/1**
1m 29.02s (-0.58) **Going Correction** -0.025s/f (Stan) **9** Ran SP% **114.8**
Speed ratings (Par 101): **102,101,101,100,98 97,95,87,84**
toteswingers: 1&2 £7.80, 1&3 £3.50, 2&3 £2.80. CSF £15.09 CT £43.00 TOTE £5.70: £1.80, £1.50, £1.90; EX 17.30 Trifecta £59.60 Pool: £541.60 - 6.81 winning units..
Owner R A Kaye **Bred** Dr Myles Sweeney **Trained** Settrington, N Yorks
■ Stewards' Enquiry : Michael O'Connell four-day ban: used whip above permitted level (Dec 29-31,Jan 1)

FOCUS
The first of a marathon 14-race card with Southwell's original afternoon fixture moved to join the existing evening meeting here. A moderate handicap to start proceedings with little covering the principals at the line. The runner-up is rated to his recent run over further with the third close to his latest mark.

8132 32RED CASINO NURSERY 1m 141y(P)
2:40 (2:41) (Class 6) (0-65,68) 2-Y-0 **£2,070** (£616; £307; £153) **Stalls** Low

Form RPR
6520 **1** **Red Eight (USA)**[17] 7919 2-9-6 64 .... AdamKirby 4 73
(John Butler) *mde all: rdn clr wl over 1f out: clr whn edgd rt ins fnl f: kpt on strly* **13/2**[3]
0033 **2** 3 ¼ **Classy Trick (USA)**[7] 8032 2-8-13 57 .... JamieSpencer 5 59
(Richard Fahey) *trckd wnr: effrt and cl up 3f out: rdn 2f out: drvn and one pce ent fnl f* **2/1**[1]
5440 **3** 1 ¼ **Maypole Joe (IRE)**[2] 8093 2-8-11 55 ....(v) LukeMorris 1 55
(David Evans) *chsd ldrs: rdn along wl over 2f out: drvn and one pce appr fnl f* **12/1**
003 **4** nk **Mick Dundee (IRE)**[16] 7922 2-9-6 64 .... SebSanders 2 63
(J W Hills) *in tch: hdwy on inner 5f out: rdn and n.m.r over 2f out: drvn and kpt on same pce appr fnl f* **12/1**
3623 **5** ¾ **Holding Fast (IRE)**[24] 7808 2-8-9 53 .... MartinLane 3 50
(Tobias B P Coles) *dwlt and in rr: hdwy on outer 2f out: sn rdn and no imp* **15/2**
3610 **6** 4 ½ **Precision Strike**[53] 7313 2-8-12 56 .... RobbieFitzpatrick 7 44
(Richard Guest) *a in rr* **22/1**
0053 **7** nse **Hazard Warning (IRE)**[25] 7797 2-8-1 45 ....(b) PaulQuinn 6 33
(Tim Easterby) *hld up in tch: pushed along over 3f out: sn wknd* **14/1**
0532 **8** 2 **Sewn Up**[12] 7973 2-9-10 68 .... ShaneKelly 8 52
(Reg Hollinshead) *t.k.h: chsd ldrs on outer: rdn along wl over 2f out: sn wknd* **9/4**[2]
1m 49.72s (-0.78) **Going Correction** -0.025s/f (Stan) **8** Ran SP% **115.6**
Speed ratings (Par 94): **102,99,98,97,97 93,93,91**
toteswingers: 1&2 £3.30, 1&3 £11.90, 2&3 £6.40. CSF £20.18 CT £155.92 TOTE £13.60: £2.60, £1.50, £3.10; EX 46.60 Trifecta £466.30 Part won. Pool: £621.79 - 0.41 winning units..
Owner Maxilead Limited **Bred** Farfellow Farms Ltd & Mill Ridge Farmltd **Trained** Newmarket, Suffolk

FOCUS
A moderate nursery and the front pair held those positions throughout. The form stacks up through the placed horses.

NOTEBOOK
Red Eight(USA) had questions to answer after stopping quickly over C&D last time, having only been pipped on the line at Kempton previously, but he showed that last effort to be all wrong. Soon in front, he kept on finding for pressure and was in no danger inside the last furlong. He should be able to win one or two more this winter. (op 11-2 tchd 7-1)
Classy Trick(USA) had run two solid races since switched to nurseries this month and always had the winner in his sights, but despite maximum assistance he could never quite get on terms. He may be worth another try over further. (op 5-2)
Maypole Joe(IRE), who found himself off a 4lb higher mark after seeming to run above himself in a Lingfield seller two starts back, did well to keep on for third as he was off the bridle at halfway. He may need to drop back a few pounds, though. (op 10-1)
Mick Dundee(IRE), making his nursery debut after finishing well held in two turf maidens and a Polytrack claimer, burrowed his way up the inside rail to take a more handy position at halfway, but could never find enough off the bridle to be a threat to the leading pair. (op 11-1)
Holding Fast(IRE), up 3lb after placing in a Southwell seller and a Kempton nursery, missed the break and found himself last early, which was an inconvenience given the way the race was run. He stayed on late, but never had a prayer of landing a blow. (op 9-1 tchd 10-1)
Sewn Up, raised 3lb after finishing runner-up over C&D on his nursery debut earlier this month, raced far too freely on the wide outside early and that was always likely to tell later on. The Stewards considered his running and noted the trainer's representative could offer no explanation for the colt's performance. They ordered Sewn Up to be routine tested. Official explanation: trainer's rep had no explanation for the poor form shown (op 5-2 tchd 11-4)

8133 32RED SUPPORTING BRITISH RACING (S) STKS 1m 141y(P)
3:15 (3:15) (Class 6) 3-Y-0+ **£2,181** (£644; £322) **Stalls** Low

Form RPR
4525 **1** **Dozy Joe**[17] 7901 4-9-2 72 ....(v) SebSanders 1 68
(Paul Fitzsimons) *trckd ldng pair: effrt over 2f out: rdn over 1f out: drvn to chal ent fnl f: kpt on to ld on line* **9/4**[2]
0046 **2** nse **Imprimis Tagula (IRE)**[5] 8055 8-9-3 70 ....(v) NatashaEaton(5) 4 74
(Alan Bailey) *led: rdn along and jnd 2f out: drvn ent fnl f: kpt on gamely: hdd on line* **10/1**
4540 **3** ½ **Faithful Ruler (USA)**[6] 8047 8-9-8 68 ....(p) LukeMorris 7 73
(Ronald Harris) *in tch: hdwy over 2f out: rdn over 1f out: drvn and ev ch ins fnl f: one pce towards fin* **8/1**
2201 **4** 2 **Bold Marc (IRE)**[25] 7798 10-9-1 66 .... ConorHarrison(7) 6 68
(Mrs K Burke) *trckd ldr: cl up 3f out: rdn to chal 2f out and ev ch tl wknd appr fnl f* **4/1**[3]
6304 **5** 22 **Kimbali (IRE)**[68] 6923 3-9-0 75 ....(p) JamieSpencer 3
(Richard Fahey) *v.s.a and virtually ref to r in early stages: bhd: sme hdwy over 3f out: nvr a factor* **13/8**[1]
6000 **6** 3 **Ave Sofia**[17] 7915 3-8-10 42 ow1 .... GrahamGibbons 5
(John Holt) *trckd ldrs: rdn along over 3f out: wknd over 2f out* **100/1**
5-U **7** 1 ½ **Supastarqueen (USA)**[349] 1 4-8-11 0 .... WilliamCarson 2
(Brian Baugh) *sn outpcd and a bhd* **100/1**
/0-0 **8** 6 **Reach For The Sky (IRE)**[29] 7746 5-8-4 45 .... VictorSantos(7) 8
(Hugh McWilliams) *a towards rr* **100/1**
1m 50.81s (0.31) **Going Correction** -0.025s/f (Stan)
WFA 3 from 4yo+ 2lb **8** Ran SP% **112.0**
Speed ratings (Par 101): **97,96,96,94,75 72,71,65**
toteswingers: 1&2 £6.50, 1&3 £2.70, 2&3 £12.30. CSF £23.40 TOTE £2.60: £1.20, £4.10, £1.70; EX 24.90 Trifecta £101.30 Pool: £453.85 - 3.36 winning units..
Owner Paddy Barrett **Bred** John Morton **Trained** Upper Lambourn, Berks

FOCUS
Only five mattered in this modest seller and the form is rather fluid with the favourite being reluctant to race.

8134 STAN HILL MAIDEN STKS 1m 141y(P)
3:50 (3:50) (Class 5) 2-Y-0 **£2,911** (£866; £432; £216) **Stalls** Low

Form RPR
04 **1** **Magika**[17] 7899 2-8-12 0 .... AndreaAtzeni 7 65
(Marco Botti) *hld up in tch: hdwy on outer 2f out: rdn to chal over 1f out: styd on wl to ld fnl 100yds* **7/2**[3]
4 **2** ½ **Liliana (IRE)**[28] 7778 2-8-12 0 .... JamieSpencer 6 64
(Peter Chapple-Hyam) *trckd ldng pair: smooth hdwy on outer to ld 2f out: rdn over 1f out: drvn and edgd rt ins fnl f: hdd and one pce last 100yds* **11/4**[2]
00 **3** 1 **Candyman Can (IRE)**[16] 7923 2-9-3 0 .... LiamKeniry 3 67
(Dominic Ffrench Davis) *trckd ldrs: hdwy over 3f out: chsd ldrs over 2f out: sn rdn: kpt on fnl f to take 3rd nr fin* **100/1**
00 **4** ½ **Platinum Proof (USA)**[17] 7899 2-9-3 0 .... TomMcLaughlin 4 66
(John Berry) *cl up: led over 4f out: rdn along wl over 2f out: drvn and one pce appr fnl f: lost 3rd nr fin* **25/1**
5 5 **Ofcoursewecan (USA)** 2-9-3 0 .... SilvestreDeSousa 2 55
(Mark Johnston) *trckd ldrs on inner: pushed along after 2f: green and rdn along over 3f out: sn no hdwy* **2/1**[1]
6 4 ½ **Multilicious** 2-8-12 0 .... GrahamGibbons 9 41
(Tim Easterby) *dwlt: a in rr* **14/1**
60 **7** 1 ½ **Jebulani**[38] 7636 2-9-3 0 .... TomEaves 8 43
(David O'Meara) *t.k.h: sn led: hdd over 4f out: wknd 3f out* **16/1**
8 3 ¾ **Nelson's Muse** 2-8-12 0 .... MartinLane 5 30
(Tobias B P Coles) *hld up: a in rr* **33/1**
9 3 ½ **High Lightning** 2-8-12 0 .... LukeMorris 1 22
(Mrs K Burke) *dwlt and towards rr: sme hdwy 1/2-way: sn rdn along and nvr a factor* **7/1**
1m 52.19s (1.69) **Going Correction** -0.025s/f (Stan) **9** Ran SP% **115.0**
Speed ratings (Par 96): **91,90,89,89,84 80,79,76,73**
toteswingers: 1&2 £2.30, 1&3 £23.90, 2&3 £19.90. CSF £13.33 TOTE £4.20: £1.80, £1.30, £9.80; EX 8.10 Trifecta £46.20 Pool: £1,266.38 - 20.55 winning units..
Owner Marco & Sara Moretti & Partner **Bred** Immobiliare Casa Paola SRL **Trained** Newmarket, Suffolk

FOCUS
An ordinary maiden with the finish fought out between the two form horses, both of whom came closest to the stands' rail in the straight, and they set the level of the form.

NOTEBOOK
Magika improved from her debut when fourth (just ahead of a subsequent winner) stepped up to 1m at Lingfield on her second start and progressed again to break her duck here. She wasn't travelling as well as a few when making progress on the wide outside turning in, but stamina looks to be her forte and she maintained her effort to hit the front well inside the last. She has a future in handicaps over this trip or a bit further. (op 5-2 tchd 9-4)
Liliana(IRE), up in trip after finishing a staying-on fourth of seven on her debut over 7f here last month, travelled well enough up with the pace, but may have found herself in front soon enough as she couldn't hold off the winner late on. She should be able to win a similar event if held on to a bit longer. (op 2-1 tchd 3-1)
Candyman Can(IRE) showed nothing in his first two starts, but this was a lot better. He was travelling as well as anything when becoming short of room off the final bend, but kept on well once in the clear. He now gets a mark.
Platinum Proof(USA), who had beaten a total of one rival in his first two starts, was always up with the pace and wasn't shaken off until late. He too now becomes eligible for a mark. (op 50-1)
Ofcoursewecan(USA), a $55,000 brother to three winners (including a Group 3 winner in Dubai) and a half-brother to four other winners, was expected to do better according to the market, but he proved green from the start, needing to be niggled along at various stages. This was very much needed and he is surely capable of better. (op 3-1)

8135 32RED.COM MAIDEN STKS 1m 4f 50y(P)
4:20 (4:20) (Class 5) 3-4-Y-0 **£2,911** (£866; £432; £216) **Stalls** Low

Form RPR
0320 **1** **Stunning View (USA)**[55] 7269 3-8-12 69 .... RobertHavlin 9 73
(John Gosden) *sn led: rdn clr wl over 1f out: drvn and kpt on fnl f* **5/6**[1]
6020 **2** 2 **Easter Diva (IRE)**[37] 7644 3-8-12 68 .... NickyMackay 5 69
(Gerard Butler) *trckd ldrs gng wl: smooth hdwy over 2f out: chsd wnr over 1f out: rdn and edgd lft ins fnl f: kpt on* **9/2**[3]
5 **3** 2 ¾ **Nashville (IRE)**[14] 7954 3-9-3 66 .... JamieSpencer 6 71
(Ian Williams) *trckd ldng pair: pushed along after 4f: effrt 3f out and sn rdn along: styd on to chse wnr over 1f out: sn drvn and one pce* **3/1**[2]
0- **4** 3 ¼ **Watch The Birdie (IRE)**[33] 5334 4-9-3 60 .... LukeMorris 8 60
(Ronald Harris) *trckd wnr: rdn along over 3f out: drvn and wknd fnl 2f* **16/1**
4500 **5** 12 **Artistic Dawn (IRE)**[102] 5918 3-8-12 52 .... DavidProbert 4 41
(John Weymes) *trckd ldrs: rdn along 3f out: sn wknd* **20/1**
0 **6** 2 ¼ **Nova Nimph**[6] 8049 3-8-12 0 ....(t) ShaneKelly 3 37
(Mark Brisbourne) *in tch: rdn along 5f out: sn outpcd* **100/1**
0 **7** 28 **Primo Blanca**[15] 7933 3-9-3 0 .... TomEaves 2
(Michael Mullineaux) *a in rr: bhd fr 1/2-way* **50/1**
8 34 **Barlows Glance**[14] 3-8-12 0 .... ChrisCatlin 1
(Peter Hiatt) *a bhd: t.o fnl 4f* **40/1**
2m 40.99s (-0.11) **Going Correction** -0.025s/f (Stan)
WFA 3 from 4yo 5lb **8** Ran SP% **113.8**
Speed ratings (Par 103): **99,97,95,93,85 84,65,42**
toteswingers: 1&2 £1.80, 1&3 £1.50, 2&3 £2.70. CSF £4.82 TOTE £2.20: £1.10, £2.20, £1.10; EX 5.80 Trifecta £10.50 Pool: £1,173.80 - 83.84 winning units..
Owner George Strawbridge **Bred** Augustin Stable **Trained** Newmarket, Suffolk

FOCUS
An uncompetitive older-horse maiden in which they finished well spread out. The form is rated around the first two to their previous bests.

8136 32RED H'CAP 1m 4f 50y(P)
4:50 (4:50) (Class 5) (0-75,75) 3-Y-0+ **£2,911** (£866; £432; £216) **Stalls** Low

Form RPR
415 **1** **De Rigueur**[53] 7315 4-9-2 67 ....(t) AdamKirby 3 83+
(Marco Botti) *trckd ldrs: smooth hdwy 3f out: led wl over 1f out and sn rdn clr: styd on* **2/1**[1]
2624 **2** 2 **English Summer**[22] 7839 5-9-5 70 ....(t) JamieSpencer 7 79
(David Simcock) *hld up in rr: hdwy 1/2-way: effrt over 2f out: rdn to chse wnr over 1f out: no imp fnl f* **9/2**[2]
5030 **3** 1 **Sir Boss (IRE)**[14] 7954 7-9-4 69 .... TomEaves 4 76
(Michael Mullineaux) *hld up towards rr: n.m.r 4f out: hdwy 3f out: rdn to chse ldrs whn n.m.r wl over 1f out: styd on fnl f* **25/1**

0033 **4** 2 **Standpoint**[3] 8082 6-9-10 75 KirstyMilczarek 8 79
(Conor Dore) *hld up in rr: hdwy over 2f out: rdn over 1f out: kpt on fnl f: nrst fin* **6/1**

5403 **5** nk **Toughness Danon**[14] 7954 6-9-3 68 (t) SebSanders 10 72
(Brendan Powell) *hld up in rr: stdy hdwy 4f out: chsd ldrs 2f out: sn rdn and one pce* **5/1**[3]

1033 **6** 3/4 **Dazzling Valentine**[64] 7027 4-8-13 69 NatashaEaton(5) 2 72
(Alan Bailey) *in tch: effrt on inner over 2f out: rdn wl over 1f out: drvn and one pce fr wl over 1f out* **10/1**

6000 **7** 2 1/4 **Carter**[36] 7672 6-9-7 72 (v) StevieDonohoe 5 71
(Ian Williams) *in tch: hdwy 3f out: rdn to chse ldrs whn n.m.r wl over 1f out: sn no imp* **16/1**

1365 **8** 1 **Badea**[10] 8000 3-9-2 72 (v) TonyHamilton 12 69
(Richard Fahey) *led after 1f: rdn along over 2f out: hdd and drvn wl over 1f out: sn wknd* **10/1**

3064 **9** 7 **West End Lad**[38] 7639 9-9-5 70 (b) RussKennemore 1 56
(Roy Bowring) *trckd ldrs on inner: rdn along 3f out: sn wknd* **28/1**

3514 **10** 4 1/2 **Elizabeth Coffee (IRE)**[150] 4209 4-9-9 74 LukeMorris 9 53
(John Weymes) *hld up: a bhd* **25/1**

2006 **11** 21 **Jack Dawkins (USA)**[98] 6055 7-9-0 65 AdrianNicholls 6 10
(David Nicholls) *led 1f: prom: rdn along over 2f out: sn wknd* **33/1**

2010 **12** 1 1/2 **Boa**[14] 7954 7-9-7 72 GeorgeBaker 11 15
(Reg Hollinshead) *prom: rdn along over 3f out: sn wknd* **20/1**

2m 39.09s (-2.01) **Going Correction** -0.025s/f (Stan)
WFA 3 from 4yo+ 5lb **12** Ran SP% **125.4**
Speed ratings (Par 103): **105,103,103,101,101 100,99,98,94,91 77,76**
toteswingers: 1&2 £3.20, 1&3 £15.70, 2&3 £16.90. CSF £10.51 CT £185.42 TOTE £2.70: £1.60, £1.90, £9.10; EX 9.60 Trifecta £184.50 Pool: £1,114.96 - 4.53 winning units..
Owner K J P Gundlach **Bred** Cheveley Park Stud Ltd **Trained** Newmarket, Suffolk

FOCUS
A modest handicap, but the pace seemed solid enough and the second, backed up by the third, sets a sound standard.
De Rigueur ◆ Official explanation: trainer's rep said, regarding apparent improvement in form, that had benefited from being gelded.
Standpoint Official explanation: jockey said gelding was denied a clear run

8137 £32 BONUS AT 32RED.COM H'CAP 1m 141y(P)
5:20 (5:21) (Class 6) (0-65,65) 3-Y-0+ **£2,070** (£616; £307; £153) **Stalls** Low

Form RPR

4561 **1** **Idol Deputy (FR)**[6] 8051 6-9-0 64 (p) RachealKneller(5) 2 73
(Mark Usher) *hld up towards rr: smooth hdwy 3f out to trck ldrs wl over 1f out: swtchd lft and effrt to chal ins fnl f: rdn to ld last 75yds: kpt on* **3/1**[2]

0466 **2** hd **Caledonia Prince**[30] 7722 4-9-6 65 (b[1]) ShaneKelly 4 73
(Jo Hughes) *trckd ldr: hdwy to ld 2f out: sn rdn: drvn ins fnl f: hdd and nt qckn last 75yds* **7/1**

0060 **3** 1 1/2 **File And Paint (IRE)**[70] 6881 4-9-4 63 GrahamGibbons 8 68
(Lawrence Mullaney) *prom: hdwy 3f out: cl up 2f out: sn rdn and ev ch tl drvn and one pce wl ins fnl f* **20/1**

-000 **4** 1 1/2 **Casela Park (IRE)**[25] 7799 7-9-4 63 (bt) RobertWinston 9 65
(David O'Meara) *dwlt and in rr: hdwy 5f out and sn pushed along: rdn 2f out: styd on fnl f: nreest fin* **15/8**[1]

4030 **5** 4 **Striker Torres (IRE)**[16] 7925 6-9-3 62 (v) GeorgeBaker 6 54
(Ian McInnes) *trckd ldrs on inner: effrt 3f out: rdn along 2f out: sn drvn and no imp* **5/1**[3]

6403 **6** 3/4 **Poetic Power (IRE)**[6] 5018 3-9-4 65 StevieDonohoe 1 56
(Ian Williams) *dwlt: a towards rr* **12/1**

0660 **7** 4 **John Potts**[173] 3454 7-9-3 62 KellyHarrison 3 43
(Brian Baugh) *trckd ldrs: rdn along over 2f out: sn wknd* **14/1**

0440 **8** 1 1/2 **My Own Way Home**[7] 8034 4-9-3 62 AdamKirby 7 40
(David Evans) *led: rdn along 3f out: hdd 2f out and wknd qckly* **25/1**

0106 **9** 3 1/4 **Master Of Song**[51] 7347 5-8-13 61 (p) MarkCoumbe(3) 5 32
(Roy Bowring) *dwlt and in rr: hdwy on outer to chse ldrs 5f out: rdn along over 2f out: sn wknd* **25/1**

1m 49.46s (-1.04) **Going Correction** -0.025s/f (Stan)
WFA 3 from 4yo+ 2lb **9** Ran SP% **115.8**
Speed ratings (Par 101): **103,102,101,100,96 95,92,91,88**
toteswingers: 1&2 £2.70, 1&3 £23.00, 2&3 £24.30. CSF £23.59 CT £348.55 TOTE £3.40: £1.30, £2.20, £7.70; EX 12.00 Trifecta £743.50 Pool: £1,417.43 - 1.43 winning units..
Owner Miss J C Blackwell **Bred** Sheikh Sultan Bin Khalifa Al Nayan **Trained** Upper Lambourn, Berks

FOCUS
A moderate handicap, but a true pace. The winner ran close to his previous Lingfield form.

8138 32RED.COM MAIDEN STKS 5f 20y(P)
6:20 (6:21) (Class 5) 2-Y-0 **£2,911** (£866; £432; £216) **Stalls** Low

Form RPR

3 **1** **Saga Lout**[14] 7953 2-9-3 0 RichardKingscote 7 75
(Tom Dascombe) *disp ld tl wnt on over 1f out: rdn and edgd lft ins fnl f: styd on* **11/8**[1]

2 1/2 **Hand In Glove** 2-8-12 0 ShaneKelly 8 68
(Robert Cowell) *chsd ldrs: rdn ins fnl f: styd on* **16/1**

3 1 1/2 **Lead Role** 2-8-12 0 AndreaAtzeni 2 63
(James Tate) *chsd ldrs: pushed along 1/2-way: rdn over 1f out: styd on* **18/1**

323 **4** 1/2 **Quality Mark (USA)**[66] 6983 2-9-3 70 JimmyFortune 1 66
(Jeremy Noseda) *disp ld tl rdn over 1f out: no ex ins fnl f* **15/8**[2]

5 3 3/4 **Magic Ice** 2-8-12 0 TomMcLaughlin 5 48
(John Berry) *hld up: hdwy over 1f out: nt trble ldrs* **33/1**

00 **6** 1 **Elounta**[150] 4217 2-8-12 0 LukeMorris 3 44
(John Best) *prom: rdn over 1f out: wknd fnl f* **33/1**

06 **7** nk **Niknad**[30] 7728 2-8-12 0 TomEaves 4 43
(Brian Ellison) *stdd s: hld up: shkn up over 1f out: nvr nr to chal* **80/1**

04 **8** 1 1/4 **Seraphima**[167] 3669 2-8-7 0 NatashaEaton(5) 9 38
(Alan Bailey) *hld up: pushed along 1/2-way: wknd over 1f out* **7/1**[3]

64 **9** 1 1/4 **La Luz Del Sol**[6] 8044 2-8-12 0 TonyHamilton 6 34
(Richard Fahey) *sn pushed along in rr: wknd 1/2-way* **12/1**

1m 1.5s (-0.80) **Going Correction** -0.025s/f (Stan) **9** Ran SP% **115.3**
Speed ratings (Par 96): **105,104,101,101,95 93,92,90,88**
toteswingers: 1&2 £9.00, 1&3 £16.60, 2&3 £11.40. CSF £25.50 TOTE £2.60: £1.10, £4.00, £4.00; EX 48.00 Trifecta £204.80 Pool: £1,239.80 - 4.54 winning units..
Owner Laurence A Bellman **Bred** G E Amey **Trained** Malpas, Cheshire

FOCUS
Just a modest maiden and the bare form is fluid.

NOTEBOOK
Saga Lout was prominent throughout and made his previous experience count, seeing off a couple of newcomers to get off the mark second time out. His sire was at his best on fast ground on turf, and Tom Dascombe expects this fellow to be the same. (tchd 6-4)
Hand In Glove ◆, who refused to enter the stalls on her intended debut in October, went in fine this time and ran a promising race on her debut. She knew her job, showed speed to track the pace, and ought to be able to win one of these weak maidens this winter.
Lead Role, a 38,000gns half-sister to 6f 2yo winner Jolah, showed signs of greenness (reported to have hung left-handed) but was keeping on pleasingly along the inside rail at the end. She should step up on this next time. Official explanation: jockey said filly hung left-handed (op 20-1)
Quality Mark(USA) could be excused his disappointing effort on softish ground at Nottingham last time, but this is harder to forgive. He's becoming disappointing. (op 2-1)
Magic Ice is related to plenty of winners and can be expected to benefit from this debut effort.

8139 £32 BONUS AT 32RED.COM H'CAP 1m 4f 50y(P)
6:50 (6:50) (Class 6) (0-60,60) 3-Y-0+ **£2,070** (£616; £307; £153) **Stalls** Low

Form RPR

0420 **1** **Honoured (IRE)**[45] 7496 5-9-10 60 (t) AndrewMullen 7 71
(Michael Appleby) *a.p: chsd ldr 5f out: led 2f out: sn rdn clr: styd on* **9/2**[3]

-045 **2** 2 1/2 **Gabrial's Hope (FR)**[7] 8037 3-9-5 60 JamieSpencer 4 66
(Ian Williams) *stdd s: hld up: hmpd 2f out: hdwy over 1f out: sn rdn: styd on to go 2nd ins fnl f: no ch w wnr* **9/1**

0566 **3** nse **No Diamond**[22] 7841 5-9-3 53 (p) LukeMorris 8 59
(Michael Appleby) *prom: rdn 3f out: styd on u.p* **16/1**

6561 **4** 1 3/4 **Shamo Hill Theatre**[36] 7496 5-9-0 50 (p) MartinLane 9 53
(Lawrence Mullaney) *hld up: hdwy over 2f out: sn edgd lft: rdn over 1f out: styd on u.p* **33/1**

3332 **5** hd **White Deer (USA)**[21] 7869 8-9-6 56 (v) RobertWinston 6 59
(Geoffrey Harker) *hld up: nt clr run over 2f out: styd on ins fnl f: nvr nrr* **3/1**[2]

235- **6** shd **Amtired**[241] 5622 6-9-6 56 SilvestreDeSousa 1 59
(Brian Ellison) *chsd ldrs: rdn over 2f out: styd on same pce fnl f* **11/4**[1]

0643 **7** 2 **El Bravo**[21] 7869 6-9-7 57 RussKennemore 2 57
(Shaun Harris) *hld up: nt clr run over 2f out: hmpd sn after: rdn and swtchd lft over 1f out: n.d* **6/1**

5232 **8** 10 **Lakeman (IRE)**[30] 7731 6-9-4 57 PaulPickard(3) 5 41
(Brian Ellison) *chsd ldr 7f: rdn over 3f out: wknd over 1f out* **20/1**

5200 **9** 5 **Youm Jamil (USA)**[12] 7960 5-9-8 58 AdamKirby 3 34
(Tony Carroll) *led: clr 10f out tl over 4f out: rdn and hdd 2f out: wknd fnl f* **16/1**

2m 39.08s (-2.02) **Going Correction** -0.025s/f (Stan)
WFA 3 from 5yo+ 5lb **9** Ran SP% **113.6**
Speed ratings (Par 101): **105,103,103,102,102 101,100,93,90**
toteswingers: 1&2 £12.90, 1&3 £16.20, 2&3 £17.60. CSF £43.60 CT £589.14 TOTE £5.30: £2.30, £2.80, £2.90; EX 83.10 Trifecta £690.30 Part won. Pool: £920.53 - 0.91 winning units..
Owner Dallas Racing **Bred** Kilfrush Stud **Trained** Danethorpe, Notts

FOCUS
A moderate handicap but a gamble was landed here and the form is rated on the positive side.
Youm Jamil(USA) Official explanation: jockey said gelding had no more to give

8140 32REDBET.COM (S) STKS 1m 1f 103y(P)
7:20 (7:20) (Class 6) 2-Y-0 **£2,070** (£616; £307; £153) **Stalls** Low

Form RPR

3305 **1** **Woza Moya (USA)**[9] 8003 2-8-12 60 (b[1]) RobertWinston 1 61
(Gay Kelleway) *chsd ldrs: rdn over 2f out: led ins fnl f: r.o* **4/1**[3]

1422 **2** 3/4 **Rakticate (IRE)**[12] 7971 2-8-12 61 AndreaAtzeni 3 60
(J S Moore) *led: hdd 8f out: chsd ldr: rdn over 2f out: led 1f out: sn edgd lft and hdd: styd on* **2/1**[2]

00 **3** 3 3/4 **Rainford Glory (IRE)**[5] 8052 2-8-12 0 JamieSpencer 5 52
(Ed Dunlop) *plld hrd: led 8f out: rdn: hung lft and hdd 1f out: no ex whn n.m.r ins fnl f* **5/6**[1]

0005 **4** 1/2 **Honey Haven (IRE)**[12] 7971 2-8-7 40 LukeMorris 6 47
(Mark Brisbourne) *chsd ldrs: pushed along 5f out: outpcd 3f out: r.o ins fnl f* **50/1**

000 **5** 24 **Bryter Layter**[22] 7840 2-8-7 0 JackDuern(5) 2 6
(Christopher Kellett) *hld up: drvn along over 4f out: wknd 3f out* **200/1**

P **Yingymshoo** 2-8-8 0 ow1 TomEaves 4
(George Foster) *s.i.s: hld up: rdn over 4f out: wknd 3f out: p.u over 2f out* **20/1**

2m 3.3s (1.60) **Going Correction** -0.025s/f (Stan) **6** Ran SP% **115.1**
Speed ratings (Par 94): **91,90,87,86,65**
toteswingers: 1&2 £1.50, 1&3 £1.50, 2&3 £1.30. CSF £12.76 TOTE £4.70: £2.50, £1.80; EX 12.30 Trifecta £18.80 Pool: £870.21 - 34.64 winning units..
Owner Ivor Collier **Bred** Lemons Mill Farm **Trained** Exning, Suffolk

FOCUS
This looked quite a competitive heat on paper between the three market principals, with nothing much between them on ratings, but the market spoke heavily in favour of Rainford Glory, the least exposed of the trio, and he was supported in from 7-4 early to odds-on. He did not get home though and the form is moderate, with the fourth suggesting it could still be a little high.

NOTEBOOK
Woza Moya(USA) benefited from a combination of a longer trip and having blinkers fitted for the first time. He was under the pump on the turn but saw it out best of all. (op 9-2 tchd 5-1)
Rakticate(IRE) again found one too good, and didn't help his cause by hanging left under pressure in the closing stages. (op 6-4 tchd 9-4)
Rainford Glory(IRE) was well backed but, having raced keenly early and made most, he was eventually overhauled by both his closest rivals and had to be pushed out just to hold third place. He might do better if consenting to take a lead. (op 5-4)
Honey Haven(IRE), left behind by the leading trio leaving the back straight, kept on nicely late in the day to almost catch Rainford Glory for third. This was a good effort considering she had plenty to find at the weights with those who finished in front of her.

8141 32RED CASINO MAIDEN STKS 7f 32y(P)
7:50 (7:50) (Class 5) 3-Y-0+ **£2,911** (£866; £432; £216) **Stalls** High

Form RPR

6052 **1** **The Mongoose**[8] 8021 4-9-3 63 (t) AdamKirby 5 72
(David Evans) *led 1f: chsd ldrs: shkn up to ld over 1f out: edgd rt: rdn clr fnl f* **2/1**[2]

-460 **2** 3 **Abbraccio**[121] 5268 4-9-3 75 LukeMorris 4 64
(Ronald Harris) *a.p: pushed along 3f out: rdn to chse wnr fnl f: edgd lft and no imp* **5/4**[1]

3665 **3** 3 1/2 **Lieutenant Dan (IRE)**[10] 7992 5-9-3 57 AndrewMullen 6 54
(Michael Appleby) *led 6f out: rdn and hdd over 1f out: wknd ins fnl f* **10/1**

32 **4** 3 1/4 **Infortual (TUR)**[11] 7978 3-8-12 0 RobertWinston 7 41
(Charles Hills) *chsd ldr 6f out: ev ch 2f out: sn rdn: wknd fnl f* **8/1**[3]

5 1 3/4 **Ches Jicaro (IRE)** 4-9-3 0 DavidProbert 2 41
(James Unett) *s.i.s: hld up: hdwy over 2f out: sn rdn: wknd fnl f* **8/1**[3]

4 **6** 4 **Just River**[11] 7978 3-9-3 0 (t) ChrisCatlin 8 30
(Natalie Lloyd-Beavis) *s.i.s: outpcd* **25/1**

00 **7** 3 3/4 **Indian Moon**[228] 1723 3-8-12 0[1] MartinLane 3 15
(Tobias B P Coles) *s.i.s and wnt lft s: in rr: drvn along 1/2-way: wknd over 2f out* **40/1**
1m 28.74s (-0.86) **Going Correction** -0.025s/f (Stan) 7 Ran SP% **115.4**
Speed ratings (Par 103): **103,99,95,91,89 85,81**
toteswingers: 1&2 £3.60, 1&3 £7.50, 2&3 £5.60. CSF £4.96 TOTE £2.70: £1.90, £2.20; EX 8.00 Trifecta £28.80 Pool: £680.87 - 17.67 winning units..
Owner G Evans & P D Evans **Bred** Kincorth Investments Inc **Trained** Pandy, Monmouths
FOCUS
A weak maiden but the winner is getting back to his best with the third to his latest Kempton form.

8142 32RED SUPPORTING BRITISH RACING H'CAP 7f 32y(P)
8:20 (8:20) (Class 5) (0-75,76) 3-Y-0+ **£2,911** (£866; £432; £216) **Stalls** High

Form RPR
0061 **1** **On The Hoof**[22] 7844 3-8-12 **66** GrahamGibbons 6 76
(Michael Easterby) *a.p: rdn over 1f out: r.o u.p to ld wl ins fnl f* **13/2[3]**
2002 **2** *shd* **Al's Memory (IRE)**[3] 8074 3-8-11 **65** LukeMorris 10 74
(David Evans) *chsd ldrs: led 2f out: sn rdn: hdd wl ins fnl f* **9/2[2]**
4222 **3** 1 3/4 **Roy The Boy (USA)**[3] 8081 4-9-3 **76** (v) NatashaEaton(5) 5 81
(Alan Bailey) *chsd ldrs: n.m.r over 2f out: rdn over 1f out: styd on same pce ins fnl f* **2/1[1]**
1002 **4** 2 1/2 **Rossetti**[91] 6239 4-9-5 **73** StevieDonohoe 8 71
(Ian Williams) *s.i.s: hld up: hung lft and r.o ins fnl f: nvr nrr* **8/1**
5026 **5** 1 1/4 **Travis County (IRE)**[1] 8115 3-8-11 **65** SilvestreDeSousa 9 60
(Brian Ellison) *s.i.s: hld up: hdwy u.p and hung lft over 1f out: no imp fnl f* **15/2**
006 **6** 1 1/2 **April Fool**[17] 7901 8-9-6 **74** (b) DavidProbert 7 65
(Ronald Harris) *led: rdn and hdd 2f out: wknd ins fnl f* **11/1**
1005 **7** *1* **Fluctuation (IRE)**[235] 1578 4-8-13 **70** RyanPowell(3) 4 58
(Ian Williams) *hld up: nvr on terms* **50/1**
0216 **8** *1* **Buckland (IRE)**[10] 7997 4-9-0 **73** NicoleNordblad(5) 1 58+
(Hans Adielsson) *hld up: n.d* **8/1**
5420 **9** *6* **Orwellian**[39] 7600 3-8-13 **67** TomEaves 3 36
(Bryan Smart) *chsd ldrs: pushed along 3f out: rdn and wknd over 1f out* **28/1**
0010 **10** 2 3/4 **Intiqaal (IRE)**[9] 8004 5-8-9 **63** (t) MartinDwyer 2 25
(Derek Shaw) *hld up: a in rr: pushed along 3f out: sn wknd* **40/1**
-006 **11** *11* **Slewtoo**[12] 7975 3-8-9 **63** JamesSullivan 11
(Michael Easterby) *s.i.s: hdwy 4f out: wknd over 2f out* **66/1**
1m 27.45s (-2.15) **Going Correction** -0.025s/f (Stan) 11 Ran SP% **116.5**
Speed ratings (Par 103): **111,110,108,106,104 102,101,100,93,90 78**
toteswingers: 1&2 £5.40, 1&3 £3.50, 2&3 £2.10. CSF £34.76 CT £81.75 TOTE £8.20: £2.20, £1.10, £1.70; EX 37.50 Trifecta £102.20 Pool: £680.51 - 4.99 winning units..
Owner A Chandler & L Westwood **Bred** Whitsbury Manor Stud & Pigeon House Stud **Trained** Sheriff Hutton, N Yorks
FOCUS
Sound form for the grade, with in-form horses dominating the finish and the first two set the level.

8143 32RED H'CAP 5f 216y(P)
8:50 (8:51) (Class 4) (0-85,83) 3-Y-0+ **£5,175** (£1,540; £769; £384) **Stalls** Low

Form RPR
0131 **1** **Forest Edge (IRE)**[8] 8022 3-9-6 **82** (b) AdamKirby 10 95+
(David Evans) *mde all: pushed along early: rdn clr over 1f out: eased nr fin* **2/1[1]**
0450 **2** 1 1/4 **Clear Praise (USA)**[16] 7928 5-9-4 **80** SebSanders 5 87
(Simon Dow) *hld up: hdwy over 1f out: rdn to go 2nd ins fnl f: no ch w wnr* **5/1[2]**
013 **3** *1* **Fathsta (IRE)**[5] 8055 7-9-1 **77** JamieSpencer 12 81
(Ian Williams) *hld up: rdn: edgd lft and r.o wl ins fnl f: nt rch ldrs* **6/1[3]**
1002 **4** 1 3/4 **Mount Hollow**[46] 7464 7-8-13 **80** (p) JackDuern(5) 7 78
(Reg Hollinshead) *hld up in tch: rdn over 1f out: styd on* **9/1**
5306 **5** *nk* **Damika (IRE)**[16] 7928 9-9-6 **82** (b) MichaelStainton 3 79
(David Brown) *a.p: rdn over 2f out: styd on* **10/1**
0550 **6** 1 1/2 **Fred Willetts (IRE)**[22] 7842 4-9-2 **78** GrahamGibbons 8 70
(Mark Brisbourne) *pushed along in rr early: rdn and r.o ins fnl f: nvr nrr* **8/1**
6000 **7** 2 1/4 **Caldercruix (USA)**[12] 7966 5-9-2 **78** (p) LukeMorris 2 63
(James Evans) *chsd ldrs: rdn over 2f out: wknd fnl f* **16/1**
-000 **8** *hd* **Al Khan (IRE)**[37] 7651 3-9-6 **82** JamesSullivan 6 67
(Michael Easterby) *hld up: nt clr run over 1f out: nvr on terms* **20/1**
1063 **9** *nk* **Titus Gent**[9] 8009 7-9-7 **83** RobertWinston 13 67+
(Jeremy Gask) *hld up: nt clr run over 1f out: n.d* **14/1**
200 **10** 1/2 **Tango Sky (IRE)**[17] 7918 3-9-6 **82** AdrianNicholls 1 64
(David Nicholls) *chsd wnr: swtchd rt 5f out: rdn over 2f out: wknd fnl f* **33/1**
0150 **11** *nk* **Song Of Parkes**[9] 8008 5-9-3 **79** DominicFox 4 60
(Peter Grayson) *chsd ldrs: rdn over 2f out: hung lft and wknd over 1f out* **20/1**
1m 13.35s (-1.65) **Going Correction** -0.025s/f (Stan) 11 Ran SP% **119.5**
Speed ratings (Par 105): **110,108,107,104,104 102,99,99,98,97 97**
toteswingers: 1&2 £12.50, 1&3 £2.90, 2&3 £13.40. CSF £11.29 CT £53.71 TOTE £3.30: £1.50, £2.50, £2.60; EX 28.60 Trifecta £209.30 Pool: £854.32 - 3.06 winning units..
Owner Peter Swinnerton **Bred** Alberto Panetta **Trained** Pandy, Monmouths
FOCUS
They went a decent gallop in this sprint handicap. The winner is on a roll at present while the placed horses set the standard.

8144 32REDPOKER.COM H'CAP 5f 216y(P)
9:20 (9:20) (Class 6) (0-65,66) 3-Y-0+ **£2,070** (£616; £307; £153) **Stalls** Low

Form RPR
5535 **1** **Belle Bayardo (IRE)**[25] 7794 4-9-3 **64** LukeMorris 2 74
(Ronald Harris) *chsd ldrs: rdn to ld over 1f out: r.o* **12/1**
0060 **2** 1 3/4 **Master Of Disguise**[21] 7864 6-9-4 **65** (t) WilliamCarson 3 69
(Brian Baugh) *chsd ldrs: rdn over 2f out: styd on u.p* **13/2[3]**
2211 **3** *hd* **Angelo Poliziano**[12] 7970 6-9-5 **66** TomEaves 9 70
(George Foster) *broke wl: stdd and lost pl 5f out: hdwy over 1f out: styd on* **7/1**
5432 **4** 1/2 **Greenhead High**[12] 7969 4-9-4 **65** AdrianNicholls 8 67
(David Nicholls) *sn pushed along to ld: rdn and hdd over 1f out: no ex ins fnl f* **9/2[2]**
0206 **5** 1 1/4 **Sir Nod**[40] 7589 10-9-2 **63**[1] PaddyAspell 1 61
(Julie Camacho) *s.i.s: hld up: hdwy over 1f out: nt trble ldrs* **20/1**
0253 **6** 1 1/4 **Above The Stars**[10] 7995 4-8-11 **65** LauraBarry(7) 4 59
(Richard Fahey) *sn chsng ldr: rdn 2f out: wknd fnl f* **7/1**
0410 **7** 1 1/4 **Prince James**[21] 7863 5-9-4 **65** GrahamGibbons 5 55
(Michael Easterby) *s.i.s: outpcd: nvr nrr* **11/1**
2465 **8** *1* **Haadeeth**[10] 7995 5-9-4 **65** AdamKirby 6 52
(David Evans) *prom: rdn over 2f out: wknd fnl f* **7/2[1]**
0552 **9** 1 3/4 **Desert Strike**[5] 8054 6-9-3 **64** (p) KirstyMilczarek 7 45
(Conor Dore) *prom: racd keenly: rdn over 2f out: wknd fnl f* **7/2[1]**
1m 14.06s (-0.94) **Going Correction** -0.025s/f (Stan) 9 Ran SP% **121.7**
Speed ratings (Par 101): **105,102,102,101,100 98,96,95,93**
toteswingers: 1&2 £8.50, 1&3 £5.30, 2&3 £4.70. CSF £92.20 CT £606.29 TOTE £13.40: £4.00, £2.90, £2.00; EX 119.80 Trifecta £429.20 Part won. Pool: £572.36 - 0.60 winning units..
Owner William Jones Lisa Harrington **Bred** L Mulryan **Trained** Earlswood, Monmouths
FOCUS
Four of these could boast four previous course wins each, but they were all eclipsed by a first-timer at Wolverhampton. The form looks sound at face value with those in the frame behind the winner rated close to their marks.

8131 WOLVERHAMPTON (A.W) (L-H)
Monday, December 17
OFFICIAL GOING: Standard
Wind: Fresh behind Weather: Cloudy tuning to rain after race 3

8145 YOUR FAVOURITE POOL BETS AT TOTEPOOL.COM AMATEUR RIDERS' H'CAP (DIV I) 1m 1f 103y(P)
1:55 (1:55) (Class 5) (0-70,70) 3-Y-0+ **£2,183** (£677; £338; £169) **Stalls** Low

Form RPR
-005 **1** **Teide Peak (IRE)**[70] 6940 3-9-7 **58** MrsRWilson(7) 9 66
(Paul D'Arcy) *mid-div: hdwy 6f out: chsd ldr over 3f out: led over 1f out: r.o* **16/1**
3664 **2** *1* **Silver Alliance**[58] 7256 4-10-9 **65** MrPCollington 4 71
(Julia Feilden) *prom: lost pl 3f out: hdwy over 1f out: rdn to chse wnr ins fnl f: r.o* **4/1[2]**
2120 **3** 1/2 **Aragorn Rouge**[24] 7841 4-10-6 **62** MrSWalker 7 67+
(Keith Dalgleish) *hld up: hdwy 2f out: nt clr run over 1f out: rdn and r.o to go 3rd post: nt rch ldrs* **6/5[1]**
0630 **4** *nse* **Elijah Pepper (USA)**[10] 8020 7-10-12 **68** (p) MissEJJones 10 73
(Conor Dore) *chsd ldr over 4f: remained handy: rdn and ev ch over 1f out: styd on same pce ins fnl f* **10/1**
1200 **5** 3/4 **Cabal**[13] 7976 5-9-8 **57** (b) MrDarrenCostello(7) 2 60
(Andrew Crook) *s.s: hld up: hdwy 1/2-way: rdn and ev ch over 1f out: styd on same pce ins fnl f* **25/1**
0000 **6** *1* **Benandonner (USA)**[31] 7743 9-10-9 **70** MissMBryant(5) 8 71
(Paddy Butler) *led: racd keenly: hdd over 1f out: no ex ins fnl f* **25/1**
0-06 **7** 1/2 **Kerchak (USA)**[24] 7839 5-10-2 **63** MrWEasterby(5) 6 63
(Brian Ellison) *prom: chsd ldr 5f out tl over 3f out: sn rdn: hung lft and styd on same pce fnl f* **7/1[3]**
0060 **8** *nse* **King Of Windsor (IRE)**[27] 7798 5-10-3 **66** MrKWood(7) 1 66
(John Wainwright) *s.i.s: hld up: r.o towards fin: nvr on terms* **40/1**
4000 **9** *1* **Yourinthewill (USA)**[40] 7640 4-10-1 **64** MrSClarke(7) 3 62
(Daniel Mark Loughnane) *hld up: hdwy 2f out: no ex fnl f* **28/1**
0234 **10** 3 1/2 **Fonterutoli (IRE)**[9] 8038 5-9-7 **56** (e) MissRBIngram(7) 5 47
(Roger Ingram) *s.i.s: a in rr* **8/1**
2m 5.03s (3.33) **Going Correction** -0.10s/f (Stan)
WFA 3 from 4yo+ 2lb 10 Ran SP% **117.6**
Speed ratings (Par 103): **81,80,79,79,78 78,77,77,76,73**
Tote swingers 1&2 £11.50, 1&3 £5.00, 2&3 £2.20 CSF £76.89 CT £138.51 TOTE £21.60: £3.90, £1.40, £2.10; EX 123.60 Trifecta £351.30 Part won. Pool: £468.49 - .61 winning units..
Owner C M Wilson **Bred** Blue Bloodstock Ltd **Trained** Newmarket, Suffolk
■ Rachel Wilson's first winner.
FOCUS
They went a slow early pace (time over four seconds slower than the second division) and this form looks unreliable, with a bunch finish. The form is rated around the second and fourth to their recent marks.

8146 YOUR FAVOURITE POOL BETS AT TOTEPOOL.COM AMATEUR RIDERS' H'CAP (DIV II) 1m 1f 103y(P)
2:25 (2:25) (Class 5) (0-70,70) 3-Y-0+ **£2,183** (£677; £338; £169) **Stalls** Low

Form RPR
0655 **1** **Cheers For Thea (IRE)**[24] 7843 7-10-1 **62** (bt) MrWEasterby(5) 7 78
(Tim Easterby) *hld up: hdwy over 3f out: chsd ldr over 2f out: led over 1f out: r.o wl* **5/1[3]**
0065 **2** *6* **Knowe Head (NZ)**[13] 7976 5-10-9 **70** (v[1]) MissCHJones(5) 10 73
(James Unett) *s.i.s: hld up: hdwy over 5f out: led over 3f out: pushed along and hdd over 1f out: no ex ins fnl f* **11/4[1]**
0/00 **3** *1* **Love Pegasus (USA)**[8] 8047 6-9-11 **58** MissMBryant(5) 2 59
(Paddy Butler) *hld up: hdwy over 2f out: rdn to go 3rd over 1f out: nvr trbld ldrs* **50/1**
0000 **4** 3 1/4 **Flag Of Glory**[26] 7819 5-9-7 **56** MissMEdden(7) 1 50
(Peter Hiatt) *led 1f: remained w ldr tl pushed along 3f out: wknd over 1f out* **14/1**
3500 **5** 1/2 **Quiet Route (IRE)**[19] 7921 3-9-7 **56** (b) MrDLevey(5) 6 49
(Brian Ellison) *chsd ldrs: outpcd over 3f out: n.d after* **10/1**
3402 **6** *nk* **Daring Damsel (IRE)**[68] 6976 3-10-4 **62** (b) MissSBrotherton 5 54
(Brian Baugh) *chsd ldrs: pushed along over 3f out: wknd over 2f out* **6/1**
1000 **7** *1* **Cadgers Brig**[28] 7792 4-10-9 **65** (p) MrSWalker 8 55
(Keith Dalgleish) *led after 1f: pushed along and hdd over 3f out: rdn and wknd over 1f out* **9/2[2]**
426- **8** 1/2 **State Senator (USA)**[186] 6978 4-9-13 **62** MrTGreenwood(7) 3 51
(Richard Ford) *mid-div: lost pl over 4f out: sn bhd* **33/1**
4313 **9** 1/2 **Jordaura**[40] 7640 6-10-7 **66** MissJRRichards(3) 4 54
(Alan Berry) *hld up: pushed along over 2f out: a in rr* **11/2**
2200 **10** *6* **Bountiful Girl**[19] 7895 3-10-4 **69** MrAFrench(7) 9 45
(John Wainwright) *mid-div: rdn and wknd over 3f out* **25/1**
2m 0.9s (-0.80) **Going Correction** -0.10s/f (Stan)
WFA 3 from 4yo+ 2lb 10 Ran SP% **115.7**
Speed ratings (Par 103): **99,93,92,89,89 89,88,87,87,82**
Tote swingers 1&2 £3.70, 1&3 £50.70, 2&3 £47.90 CSF £18.67 CT £612.97 TOTE £4.90: £2.60, £1.60, £16.90; EX 21.70 Trifecta £407.30 Part won. Pool: £543.07 - 0.20 winning units..
Owner Ron George **Bred** Crone Stud Farms Ltd **Trained** Great Habton, N Yorks

FOCUS
The pace was much stronger than in the first division, with Flag Of Glory and Cadgers Brig taking each other on, and the time was more than four seconds quicker. The form has been given a bit of a chance.

8147 FOOTBALL BET IN PLAY AT TOTEPOOL.COM MEDIAN AUCTION MAIDEN STKS 1m 1f 103y(P)
2:55 (2:55) (Class 6) 2-Y-O £1,704 (£503; £251) Stalls Low

Form RPR
02 1 **Makin (IRE)**23 7868 2-9-3 0 (t) AdamKirby 3 74+
(Marco Botti) *led 1f: led again 7f out: shkn up over 1f out: edgd lft: r.o: eased nr fin* 3/1[2]
45 2 2 **Solace (USA)**104 5907 2-8-12 0 RobertHavlin 1 65
(John Gosden) *hld up in tch: rdn over 1f out: styd on same pce* 10/3[3]
034 3 ¾ **Mosman**7 8052 2-9-3 0 FergusSweeney 6 69
(Jamie Osborne) *led after 1f: hdd 7f out: chsd wnr tl rdn over 1f out: styd on same pce* 11/2
06 4 4½ **Exclusion (USA)**7 8052 2-8-12 0 StevieDonohoe 5 55
(Noel Quinlan) *prom tl rdn and wknd over 1f out* 20/1
5 9 **Colour My World** 2-9-3 0 RobertWinston 2 43+
(Ed McMahon) *s.s: rn green in rr: rdn and wknd over 2f out* 5/4[1]
00 6 2¼ **Sweet Force**14 7962 2-8-12 0 TobyAtkinson(5) 4 39
(Marco Botti) *chsd ldrs tl rdn: hung rt and wknd over 2f out* 66/1

2m 1.13s (-0.57) **Going Correction** -0.10s/f (Stan) 6 Ran SP% **114.2**
Speed ratings (Par 94): **98,96,95,91,83 81**
Tote swingers 1&2 £2.80, 1&3 £1.70, 2&3 £2.10 CSF £13.72 TOTE £4.00: £1.60, £1.20; EX 12.20 Trifecta £30.20 Pool: £1,016.28 - 25.16 winning units..
Owner Mubarak Al Naemi **Bred** Tom Claffey **Trained** Newmarket, Suffolk

FOCUS
An ordinary maiden run at a modest gallop.

NOTEBOOK
Makin(IRE) was up in trip after finishing runner-up over the extended 1m here last time. He might get even further and should make an okay handicapper. (op 7-2 tchd 4-1)
Solace(USA), debuting on Polytrack after 104 days off, was outpaced when the tempo increased and posed no threat to the winner. She might find a similarly weak maiden. (op 7-4 tchd 7-2)
Mosman is bred to stay but didn't offer much on this step up in distance. He might do better off a stronger pace in handicaps. (op 6-1 tchd 9-2)
Exclusion(USA) was unable to reverse recent Lingfield placings with the third, but can also now switch to handicaps. (op 16-1)
Colour My World, a half-brother to a 6f winner, out of a 1m4f winner, was well backed to make a winning debut but he proved far too green. Clearly he's thought capable of much better. (op 5-2)

8148 HOTEL & CONFERENCING AT WOLVERHAMPTON (S) STKS 1m 4f 50y(P)
3:25 (3:25) (Class 6) 3-Y-0+ £1,704 (£503; £251) Stalls Low

Form RPR
1111 1 **La Estrella (USA)**41 7608 9-9-8 89 AdamKirby 6 93
(Don Cantillon) *chsd ldr tl over 10f out: remained handy: wnt 2nd again over 4f out: led 3f out: sn pushed clr: comf* 4/7[1]
5334 2 4½ **Pass Muster**31 7751 5-9-4 79 TomEaves 4 82
(Ollie Pears) *hld up: hmpd after 1f: hdwy over 3f out: rdn to chse wnr over 2f out: styd on same pce fr over 1f out* 11/4[2]
5000 3 11 **Activate**52 7367 5-9-4 77 JamieSpencer 5 64
(David O'Meara) *hld up: hdwy over 3f out: rdn and wknd 2f out* 6/1[3]
/5 4 3¾ **Low Key (IRE)**41 7608 5-9-4 78 (p) MickyFenton 7 58
(John Butler) *led: rdn and hdd 3f out: wknd 2f out* 33/1
3000 5 19 **Turjuman (USA)**17 7819 7-8-13 57 (p) NatashaEaton(5) 2 28
(Alan Bailey) *s.i.s: sn prom: chsd ldr over 10 out tl pushed along 4f out: sn wknd: t.o* 80/1

2m 37.26s (-3.84) **Going Correction** -0.10s/f (Stan) 5 Ran SP% **108.8**
Speed ratings (Par 101): **108,105,97,95,82**
CSF £2.32 TOTE £2.00: £1.40, £1.10; EX 2.10 Trifecta £4.20 Pool: £1,003.49 - 178.85 winning units..There was no bid for the winner. Pass Muster was bought by Mrs K. Walton for £6,000.
Owner Don Cantillon **Bred** Five Horses Ltd And Theatrical Syndicate **Trained** Newmarket, Suffolk

FOCUS
An uncompetitive seller run at a decent pace. This is up with the winner's better efforts at face value.

8149 100% DEPOSIT BONUS AT TOTEPOOL.COM CASINO H'CAP 1m 5f 194y(P)
3:55 (3:56) (Class 5) (0-75,75) 3-Y-0+ £2,264 (£673; £336; £168) Stalls Low

Form RPR
1122 1 **Chookie Hamilton**3 8106 8-9-7 70 JoeFanning 2 81
(Keith Dalgleish) *chsd ldrs: led over 2f out: shkn up ins fnl f: styd on* 5/4[1]
1210 2 2 **Gabrial's King (IRE)**5 8073 3-9-3 73 (v[1]) JamieSpencer 8 80
(Ian Williams) *hld up: hdwy on outer 3f out: rdn over 1f out: edgd lft and chsd wnr ins fnl f: styd on* 13/8[2]
0010 3 8 **Jeer (IRE)**79 6691 8-9-4 67 GrahamGibbons 4 63
(Michael Easterby) *led: hdd over 2f out: wknd fnl f* 10/1
2-00 4 2½ **Raktiman (IRE)**28 7791 5-9-3 66 (b) LiamKeniry 1 58
(Chris Bealby) *chsd ldr 2f: remained handy: rdn over 2f out: wknd wl over 1f out* 12/1
0500 5 1¾ **Cape Safari (IRE)**12 7999 3-9-0 75 HarryPoulton(5) 3 65
(Tim Vaughan) *hld up: rdn over 2f out: sn wknd* 33/1
1-06 6 18 **Agglestone Rock**41 7610 7-9-2 65 AdamKirby 7 30
(Philip Kirby) *prom: chsd ldr 12f out tl rdn and wknd over 2f out: t.o* 8/1[3]
20- 7 3¼ **Kingston Tiger**422 7022 4-9-2 65 (p) FergusSweeney 6 25
(Jo Davis) *sn prom: rdn and wknd over 3f out: t.o* 33/1

3m 0.83s (-5.17) **Going Correction** -0.10s/f (Stan)
WFA 3 from 4yo+ 7lb 7 Ran SP% **116.3**
Speed ratings (Par 103): **110,108,104,102,101 91,89**
Tote swingers 1&2 £1.30, 1&3 £2.80, 2&3 £3.30 CSF £3.63 CT £10.74 TOTE £2.50: £1.90, £1.50; EX 4.70 Trifecta £19.60 Pool: £1,753.49 - 66.86 winning units..
Owner Straightline Construction Ltd **Bred** D And J Raeburn **Trained** Carluke, S Lanarks

FOCUS
A weak handicap run at a decent pace and won in straightforward fashion. The winner is rated to this year's best.
Agglestone Rock Official explanation: jockey said gelding hung badly left

8150 WOLVERHAMPTON-RACECOURSE.CO.UK CLAIMING STKS 1m 141y(P)
4:25 (4:26) (Class 6) 2-Y-O £1,704 (£503; £251) Stalls Low

Form RPR
0030 1 **Gabrial The Boss (USA)**28 7785 2-8-7 59 (t) AndreaAtzeni 6 63
(David Simcock) *hld up: hdwy over 3f out: rdn to ld over 1f out: sn hung lft: styd on* 11/4[2]
0302 2 ¾ **Myzamour**3 8101 2-8-0 54 (b) JimmyQuinn 1 55
(J S Moore) *chsd ldr 3f: remained handy: rdn over 3f out: cl up whn hmpd ins fnl f: swtchd rt: r.o* 8/1
2210 3 1¼ **Marmot Bay (IRE)**11 8007 2-8-6 64 MartinDwyer 3 58
(Alastair Lidderdale) *racd keenly: set stdy pce tl qcknd over 2f out: rdn and hdd over 1f out: styd on same pce ins fnl f* 8/1
0645 4 nse **Walter White (IRE)**9 8032 2-8-11 64 (p) DavidProbert 4 62
(Andrew Balding) *prom: chsd ldr over 5f out tl rdn over 2f out: styd on* 11/8[1]
0315 5 15 **Bix (IRE)**59 7209 2-8-13 71 TomEaves 2 31
(Alan Berry) *hld up: rdn and wknd over 2f out* 9/2[3]

1m 51.32s (0.82) **Going Correction** -0.10s/f (Stan) 5 Ran SP% **109.2**
Speed ratings (Par 94): **92,91,90,90,76**
CSF £22.03 TOTE £3.80: £1.60, £2.30; EX 26.30 Trifecta £63.50 Pool: £1,483.74 - 17.52 winning units..
Owner Dr Marwan Koukash **Bred** Hunter Valley Farm Et Al **Trained** Newmarket, Suffolk
■ Stewards' Enquiry : Andrea Atzeni two-day ban: careless riding (Dec 31,Jan 1)

FOCUS
Only 6lb separated this modest bunch on adjusted official figures and they went a steady pace.

NOTEBOOK
Gabrial The Boss(USA) was continually short of room and stuck on a slow rail when well down the field in a nursery here last time, and he was also reported by the vet to have suffered an injury to his left fore that day. However, this time he was taken wide to avoid trouble and was on top when hanging left in the straight, hampering the runner-up. He had to survive a stewards' enquiry, but looked the winner on merit and this was a creditable performance considering he was the worst off at the weights. (op 3-1)
Myzamour, runner-up in a Lingfield claimer just three days earlier, again ran respectably and can win one of these. (op 7-1 tchd 9-1)
Marmot Bay(IRE) was reported to have run too free and failed to handle the bend over 6f at Lingfield last time, and she didn't settle in front this time either on what was her first try beyond 7f. (op 5-1)
Walter White(IRE) was plugging on when his rider dropped his whip inside the final furlong and he just failed to get third. A more severe type of headgear looks worth a try. (op 2-1 tchd 9-4)
Bix(IRE) offered nothing at all after a two-month break. (op 7-2)

8151 TOTEPOOL.COM SPORTS, GAMES, BINGO & MORE MAIDEN STKS 1m 141y(P)
4:55 (4:55) (Class 5) 3-Y-0+ £2,264 (£673; £336; £168) Stalls Low

Form RPR
622 1 **Light Shine**47 7488 3-8-12 75 JamieSpencer 1 59+
(Peter Chapple-Hyam) *mde all: rdn over 1f out: styd on* 1/12[1]
2 1¼ **Dutch Mistress** 3-8-12 0 DavidProbert 3 56
(James Unett) *a.p: chsd wnr over 1f out: sn rdn: edgd lft and ev ch: unable qck towards fin* 25/1
3 2¾ **My Mum Mo**38 4-9-0 0 AmyRyan 4 50
(Simon West) *s.i.s: hld up: hdwy over 2f out: rdn over 1f out: styd on to go 3rd nr fin: nt trble ldrs* 22/1
0303 4 ¾ **American Lover (FR)**89 6361 5-8-9 45 AdamCarter(5) 8 48
(John Wainwright) *trckd ldrs: racd keenly: wnt 2nd 5f out tl rdn over 1f out: no ex fnl f* 14/1[3]
00 5 7 **Dr Victoria**32 7729 3-8-12 0 AndrewMullen 6 32
(John Norton) *chsd wnr over 3f: remained handy tl rdn and wknd over 1f out* 80/1
5 6 7 **Village Green**188 3012 3-9-3 0 TomEaves 5 21
(Ollie Pears) *hld up: rdn and wknd over 3f out* 12/1[2]

1m 50.51s (0.01) **Going Correction** -0.10s/f (Stan)
WFA 3 from 4yo+ 2lb 6 Ran SP% **116.1**
Speed ratings (Par 103): **95,93,91,90,84 78**
Tote swingers 1&2 £2.40, 1&3 £1.40, 2&3 £12.10 CSF £7.25 TOTE £1.10: £1.02, £6.60; EX 4.80 Trifecta £30.70 Pool: £1,767.36 - 43.10 winning units..
Owner P W Chapple-Hyam **Bred** George Strawbridge **Trained** Newmarket, Suffolk

FOCUS
The proximity of the 45-rated American Lover shows this wasn't much of a race, and the winner did not need get close to her turf form.

8152 JOAN HALL MEMORIAL CELEBRATION H'CAP 1m 141y(P)
5:25 (5:31) (Class 5) (0-75,75) 3-Y-0+ £2,264 (£673; £336; £168) Stalls Low

Form RPR
0611 1 **On The Hoof**2 8142 3-9-2 72 6ex GrahamGibbons 5 81
(Michael Easterby) *a.p: rdn to chse ldr over 1f out: led ins fnl f: edgd lft: styd on u.p* 6/5[1]
2610 2 ¾ **Silverware (USA)**24 7842 4-9-7 75 TomEaves 4 82
(Linda Stubbs) *plld hrd: led 2f: remained w ldr tl led again over 2f out: rdn and hdd ins fnl f: styd on* 11/2[3]
025 3 1 **McCool Bannanas**122 5322 4-9-0 68 DavidProbert 3 73
(James Unett) *hld up: hdwy over 2f out: rdn over 1f out: r.o* 16/1
5U35 4 2 **Rock Anthem (IRE)**24 7844 8-8-7 61 KieranO'Neill 9 61
(Mike Murphy) *chsd ldrs: rdn over 2f out: styd on same pce fnl f* 10/1
5433 5 nk **Handheld**62 7141 5-8-6 67 ShelleyBirkett(7) 8 66
(Julia Feilden) *mid-div: r.o ins fnl f: nt trble ldrs* 10/1
4000 6 ½ **Celtic Sultan (IRE)**12 7995 8-9-2 70 JamieSpencer 6 68
(Alastair Lidderdale) *s.i.s: hld up: rdn and r.o ins fnl f: nvr nrr* 22/1
0000 7 2½ **Final Drive (IRE)**10 8020 6-9-4 72 (tp) AdamKirby 2 65
(John Butler) *got loose prior to the s: dwlt: hld up: nt clr run ins fnl f: nvr nr to chal* 5/1[2]
1056 8 nk **Where's Reiley (USA)**12 7995 6-9-1 74 LeonnaMayor(5) 1 66
(Alastair Lidderdale) *chsd ldr tl led over 6f out: hdd over 2f out: wknd fnl f* 40/1
0010 9 5 **Perfect Mission**102 5983 4-9-0 75 JonathanWilletts(7) 7 55
(Andrew Balding) *prom: pushed along over 3f out: wknd over 2f out* 15/2

1m 48.06s (-2.44) **Going Correction** -0.10s/f (Stan)
WFA 3 from 4yo+ 2lb 9 Ran SP% **120.1**
Speed ratings (Par 103): **106,105,104,102,102 101,99,99,95**
Tote swingers 1&2 £2.80, 1&3 £4.40, 2&3 £13.00 CSF £8.56 CT £74.56 TOTE £2.20: £1.30, £1.70, £3.40; EX 10.90 Trifecta £53.80 Pool: £2,054.71 - 28.60 winning units..
Owner A Chandler & L Westwood **Bred** Whitsbury Manor Stud & Pigeon House Stud **Trained** Sheriff Hutton, N Yorks

FOCUS
The lead was disputed by Silverware and Where's Reiley, and the time was much quicker than a couple of lesser races at the same distance, but it still paid to be handy. The form is rated around the runner-up.
Celtic Sultan(IRE) Official explanation: vet said gelding returned lame left-fore
Final Drive(IRE) ◆ Official explanation: jockey said, regarding running and riding, that his orders were to get the gelding travelling and get it to finish, it fell out of the stalls and was never on the bridle throughout and finished very one-paced.
T/Jkpt: £3,606.00 to a £1 stake. Pool: £5,078.97 - 1.00 winning units. T/Plt: £10.30 to a £1 stake. Pool: £79,838.29 - 5,606.69 winning units. T/Qpdt: £3.40 to a £1 stake. Pool: £6,063.80 - 1,319.24 winning units. CR

[8101] LINGFIELD (L-H)

Tuesday, December 18

OFFICIAL GOING: Standard
Wind: Light against Weather: Overcast

8153 LINGFIELD PARK MARRIOTT HOTEL CLAIMING STKS 1m 4f (P)
11:50 (11:50) (Class 6) 3-Y-O+ £1,704 (£503; £251) Stalls Low

Form RPR

1000 **1** **Icelander (USA)**[20] 7920 3-9-1 74 (b[1]) JoeFanning 2 78
(Jo Hughes) *led over 1f: trckd ldrs: hdwy over 2f out: led over 1f out: sn rdn clr* **14/1**

2400 **2** *5* **Right Stuff (FR)**[12] 7051 9-9-12 93 (p) GeorgeBaker 7 77
(Gary Moore) *hld up: hdwy to trck ldrs over 4f out: effrt over 2f out: sn rdn and outpcd: drvn and kpt on to take 2nd ins fnl f* **4/7**[1]

0055 **3** *1* **If You Whisper (IRE)**[24] 7869 4-8-12 54 (b) EddieAhern 5 61
(Mike Murphy) *led after 11/2f: pushed along over 2f out: sn rdn and hdd over 1f out: one pce* **7/1**[3]

3050 **4** *3 1/4* **Irons On Fire (USA)**[9] 8047 4-9-0 53 (b[1]) WilliamCarson 4 58
(Lee Carter) *chsd ldrs: rdn along 3f out: drvn 2f out and sn wknd* **16/1**

2324 **5** *4* **Renegotiate**[17] 7954 3-9-1 66 (p) DavidProbert 3 58
(Andrew Balding) *awkward and reminders s: hld up in tch whn stmbld bdly over 5f out: rdn along over 3f out: n.d* **5/2**[2]

0000 **6** *3/4* **Diddums**[10] 8039 6-8-3 42 (e) CarolineKelly(7) 1 47
(John Ryan) *hld up towards rr: pushed along over 4f out: sn outpcd* **33/1**

00 **7** *40* **Naael (USA)**[28] 5796 3-8-4 60 (v[1]) RaulDaSilva(3) 6
(Luke Dace) *keen: trckd ldrs: cl up after 3f: rdn along 5f out: sn outpcd and bhd fnl 3f* **25/1**

2m 31.58s (-1.42) **Going Correction** +0.05s/f (Slow)
WFA 3 from 4yo+ 5lb 7 Ran SP% **124.1**
Speed ratings (Par 101): **106,102,102,99,97 96,70**
Tote swingers 1&2 £3.00, 1&3 £6.20, 2&3 £1.80 CSF £25.06 TOTE £22.90: £4.10, £1.10; EX 53.90 Trifecta £150.40 Pool: £656.01 - 3.27 winning units..
Owner Mrs Joanna Hughes **Bred** Darley **Trained** Lambourn, Berks

FOCUS
A moderate claimer with the seven runners officially rated between 42 and 93. The form has been rated negatively.

8154 BOOK HOSPITALITY AT LINGFIELD PARK MEDIAN AUCTION MAIDEN STKS 6f (P)
12:20 (12:20) (Class 6) 3-5-Y-O £1,704 (£503; £251) Stalls Low

Form RPR

0603 **1** **Ishi**[6] 8069 3-8-12 47 (b[1]) JamesMillman 1 49
(Rod Millman) *trckd ldrs on inner: hdwy 2f out: rdn to ld over 1f out: kpt on* **5/2**[2]

/005 **2** *1 1/4* **Island Express (IRE)**[6] 8069 5-8-12 46 (tp) AnnStokell(5) 4 51
(Ann Stokell) *trckd ldr: rdn along wl over 1f out: kpt on fnl f: tk 2nd nr line* **16/1**

3224 **3** *hd* **Summer Sun**[11] 8021 3-8-7 52 LeonnaMayor(5) 3 45
(Phil McEntee) *led: rdn along 2f out: hdd and drvn over 1f out: one pce: lost 2nd nr line* **4/6**[1]

-054 **4** *1 1/4* **Back For Tea (IRE)**[7] 8062 4-8-10 45 (b) RyanTate(7) 5 46
(Phil McEntee) *hld up in tch: hdwy to trck ldrs 1/2-way: effrt 2f out: sn rdn and one pce appr fnl f* **7/1**[3]

6 **5** *2 3/4* **Sign Pro (IRE)**[6] 8069 4-9-3 0 RobertWinston 2 38
(Peter Bowen) *dwlt and sn rdn along: a in rr* **8/1**

-000 **6** *8* **La Passionata**[20] 7903 3-8-12 41 LukeMorris 6 9
(Jeremy Gask) *trckd ldrs on outer: rdn along over 2f out: hung rt and wd home turn: sn wknd* **20/1**

1m 12.82s (0.92) **Going Correction** +0.05s/f (Slow) 6 Ran SP% **122.8**
Speed ratings (Par 101): **95,93,93,91,87 77**
Tote swingers 1&2 £4.00, 1&3 £1.70, 2&3 £3.70 CSF £41.00 TOTE £2.80: £1.80, £8.70; EX 61.60 Trifecta £100.60 Pool: £806.64 - 6.01 winning units..
Owner Kintyre Racing **Bred** Mrs L S Millman **Trained** Kentisbeare, Devon
■ A winner on his last ride for James Millman.

FOCUS
An awful maiden. The five holding official marks were rated between 41 and 52, which says it all.

8155 PLAY GOLF AT LINGFIELD PARK RACECOURSE NURSERY 6f (P)
12:50 (12:52) (Class 6) (0-60,57) 2-Y-O £1,704 (£503; £251) Stalls Low

Form RPR

6203 **1** **Katy Spirit (IRE)**[12] 8007 2-9-6 56 LiamKeniry 9 59
(Michael Blanshard) *cl up: rdn wl over 1f out: led ent fnl f: sn drvn and edgd lft: hld on gamely* **16/1**

000 **2** *nk* **Devout (IRE)**[190] 2983 2-9-0 50 FergusSweeney 2 52
(Jamie Osborne) *led: rdn 2 out: drvn and hdd ent fnl f: kpt on gamely u.p towards fin* **8/1**

0000 **3** *hd* **Black Truffle (FR)**[27] 7808 2-8-11 47 DavidProbert 4 48+
(Mark Usher) *hld up towards rr: hdwy on inner over 2f out: swtchd rt and rdn over 1f out: n.m.r and drvn ins fnl f: kpt on wl* **14/1**

0032 **4** *1/2* **Prince Of Prophets (IRE)**[62] 7156 2-9-0 50 (t) AndreaAtzeni 11 50
(Stuart Williams) *hld up in midfield: hdwy over 2f out: rdn to chse ldrs over 1f out: drvn and kpt on fnl f* **2/1**[1]

5565 **5** *nk* **Little Indian**[28] 7797 2-9-3 53 JoeFanning 3 53
(J R Jenkins) *trckd ldrs: effrt 2f out: sn rdn: ev ch on inner ins fnl f: drvn and one pce whn n.m.r and eased towards fin: one pce and hld* **16/1**

3442 **6** *1 1/2* **Frans Hals**[18] 7930 2-8-10 53 JoshBaudains(7) 8 48
(Dominic Ffrench Davis) *hld up towards rr: hdwy 2f out: rdn over 1f out: styd on fnl f: nrst fin* **4/1**[2]

6434 **7** *1 1/4* **Persian Marvel (IRE)**[12] 8007 2-9-1 51 (b) WilliamCarson 12 42
(Jim Boyle) *prom on outer: effrt 2f out: sn rdn: ev ch ent fnl f: sn edgd lft and one pce* **7/1**

5653 **8** *hd* **Proventi**[8] 8053 2-9-0 50 (b[1]) SebSanders 5 40
(Alan McCabe) *chsd ldrs: effrt 2f out: rdn and n.m.r over 1f out: kpt on same pce fnl f* **12/1**

0063 **9** *1/2* **Fiance Fiasco**[20] 7891 2-8-6 45 RaulDaSilva(3) 1 34
(Luke Dace) *chsd ldrs on inner: rdn along wl over 1f out: grad wknd* **25/1**

605 **10** *1 1/4* **Mont Signal**[20] 7894 2-9-3 53 (bt[1]) RichardKingscote 6 38
(Daniel Kubler) *s.i.s and sn swtchd lft to inner* **11/2**[3]

0003 **11** *2* **Kalahari Breeze (IRE)**[131] 4982 2-9-7 57 MartinDwyer 7 36
(William Muir) *keen: hld up: a towards rr* **25/1**

0656 **12** *1 1/4* **Hanga Roa (IRE)**[28] 7797 2-8-9 45 ChrisCatlin 10 20
(Gary Moore) *a rr* **33/1**

1m 13.03s (1.13) **Going Correction** +0.05s/f (Slow) 12 Ran SP% **129.1**
Speed ratings (Par 94): **94,93,93,92,92 90,88,88,87,86 83,81**
Tote swingers 1&2 £18.10, 1&3 £32.30, 2&3 £19.50 CSF £147.80 CT £1907.79 TOTE £22.50: £4.90, £1.40, £6.00; EX 190.30 TRIFECTA Not won..
Owner A D Jones **Bred** Allevamento Pian Di Neve Srl **Trained** Upper Lambourn, Berks

FOCUS
All 12 of these came into this as maidens with a combined record of 0-67. The front pair were on the pace throughout.

NOTEBOOK
Katy Spirit(IRE) had run well in a couple of Polytrack nurseries over this trip in her recent starts and finally got off the mark at the 11th attempt. She showed a willing attitude to force her head in front where it mattered, having been up with the pace from the start, but the form looks ordinary and she lacks scope (tchd 14-1)
Devout(IRE), making her Polytrack and nursery debut after an absence of 190 days, tried to make all the running and kept battling all the way to the line. She should come on for it and ought to be able to win a similar event. (op 6-1 tchd 11-2)
Black Truffle(FR), well held in his first four starts and having his second start for the yard, did much the best of those held up and he finished with a rare rattle. This was much better and offers hope for the future.
Prince Of Prophets(IRE) ◆, placed in 5f Kempton nurseries in his last two starts, was doing all his best work late on both occasions and promised to be suited by the return to this trip. However, he got upset in the stalls and endured a wide trip from his high draw throughout, but still wasn't beaten far and is worth another chance. (op 7-4 tchd 13-8)
Little Indian, unplaced in three maidens and a Fibresand nursery, ran much better here and was still in with a chance of a place when short of room on the inside close to the line. (op 20-1)
Frans Hals ran his best race so far when chasing home an unexposed rival at Wolverhampton last time but, after getting outpaced on the turn for home, his finishing effort was too little too late. (op 6-1)
Persian Marvel(IRE) had run well in similar events since the blinkers were applied, but he had a wide draw to overcome again and seemed to have run his race when hampered well inside the last furlong.
Mont Signal, wearing first-time blinkers for this nursery debut, never got into it following a slow start. (op 7-1 tchd 5-1)

8156 BOOK TICKETS ONLINE @ LINGFIELDPARK.CO.UK H'CAP 7f (P)
1:20 (1:20) (Class 6) (0-65,65) 3-Y-O+ £1,617 (£360; £360; £120) Stalls Low

Form RPR

2664 **1** **Patavium Prince (IRE)**[88] 6434 9-8-13 57 FergusSweeney 5 65
(Jo Crowley) *in tch: hdwy wl over 1f out: swtchd rt and rdn ins fnl f: styd on strly to ld nr fin* **10/1**

5004 **2** *hd* **Amosite**[20] 7917 6-9-4 62 (p) JoeFanning 7 69
(J R Jenkins) *bmpd s: sn led: rdn wl over 1f out: drvn ins fnl f: hdd and no ex nr line* **25/1**

3013 **2** *dht* **Glastonberry**[20] 7906 4-9-6 64 GeorgeBaker 12 71
(Geoffrey Deacon) *hld up towards rr: hdwy on outer over 2f out: rdn over 1f out: styd on strly fnl f: jst failed* **9/4**[1]

5205 **4** *1* **Paperetto**[92] 6306 4-9-4 62 RichardKingscote 13 67
(Robert Mills) *hld up in tch: hdwy to trck ldrs over 2f out: rdn and n.m.r ins fnl f: kpt on* **7/1**

0001 **5** *nse* **Blue Deer (IRE)**[69] 6982 4-9-4 62 (p) WilliamCarson 3 67
(Lee Carter) *hld up in midfield: hdwy on inner to chse ldrs 2f out: rdn over 1f out: drvn: edgd rt and nt qckn wl ins fnl f* **8/1**

6661 **6** *2 1/4* **Lucky Mark (IRE)**[12] 8004 3-9-2 60 JimmyQuinn 8 59
(Garry Moss) *bmpd s: keen: trckd ldrs: hdwy to chse ldr wl over 2f out: rdn over 1f out: wknd ins fnl f* **5/2**[2]

1006 **7** *hd* **Paphos**[10] 8034 5-9-2 65 (v) TobyAtkinson(5) 6 63+
(Stuart Williams) *bmpd and reminders s: towards rr and rdn along bef 1/2-way: sme hdwy on outer whn sltly hmpd over 1f out: n.d* **9/2**[3]

2-00 **8** *3 3/4* **Automotive**[274] 964 4-9-0 58 AdamBeschizza 1 47
(Julia Feilden) *bmpd s and in rr: hdwy 2f out: swtchd rt and rdn over 1f out: n.d* **25/1**

0000 **9** *3/4* **Da Ponte**[24] 7857 4-9-3 61 (v) JamieGoldstein 9 48
(Michael Scudamore) *chsd ldrs: hdwy 2f out: rdn over 1f out: wknd fnl f* **33/1**

005 **10** *1/2* **Silvee**[13] 7990 5-8-13 57 SeanLevey 4 42
(John Bridger) *prom on inner: rdn along wl over 2f out: sn wknd* **25/1**

0000 **11** *2 1/2* **Cornus**[24] 7857 10-9-5 63 (be) SebSanders 11 42
(Alan McCabe) *cl up on outer: rdn along 2f out: wknd over 1f out* **33/1**

0020 **12** *1 3/4* **Katmai River (IRE)**[13] 7993 5-9-2 60 (v) DavidProbert 14 34
(Mark Usher) *a rr: rdn along and outpcd fr over 2f out* **14/1**

1m 24.12s (-0.68) **Going Correction** +0.05s/f (Slow) 12 Ran SP% **134.3**
Speed ratings (Par 101): **105,104,104,103,103 101,100,96,95,95 92,90**
CSF £127.44 CT £393.83 TOTE £24.90: £5.00 Trifecta £316.20 Part won. Pool of £843.29 - 0.60 winning units..
Owner Mrs Liz Nelson **Bred** J P Hardiman **Trained** Whitcombe, Dorset

FOCUS
A typically tight, if modest, Lingfield handicap. Things got tight for a few after the start, with Lucky Mark and Paphos appearing the main sufferers. The bare form is ordinary.

8157 LINGFIELDPARK.CO.UK H'CAP 5f (P)
1:50 (1:51) (Class 5) (0-75,75) 3-Y-O+ £2,264 (£673; £336; £168) Stalls High

Form RPR

1106 **1** **Danzoo (IRE)**[24] 7864 5-8-13 67 TomMcLaughlin 5 76
(Christine Dunnett) *cl up: disp ld wl over 1f out: rdn ent fnl f: kpt on wl to ld last 40 yds* **11/1**

5333 **2** *nk* **Welease Bwian (IRE)**[15] 7967 3-8-11 65 RichardKingscote 4 73
(Stuart Williams) *slt ld: rdn along wl over 1f out: drvn ent fnl f: hdd and no ex last 40 yds* **10/11**[1]

0201 **3** *1 3/4* **Roy's Legacy**[8] 8054 3-9-6 74 6ex (t) RobertWinston 3 76
(Shaun Harris) *trckd ldrs: hdwy 2f out: rdn over 1f out: kpt on same pce fnl f* **11/2**[3]

0051 **4** *nse* **Speightowns Kid (USA)**[20] 7914 4-9-2 70 JoeFanning 9 72+
(Jo Hughes) *cl up on outer: rdn along wl over 1f out: ev ch tl drvn and one pce ins fnl f* **4/1**[2]

5105 **5** *hd* **Mother Jones**[8] 8059 4-9-6 74 LukeMorris 1 75
(David Evans) *hld up: hdwy on inner 2f out: rdn and kpt on fnl f: nrst fin* **8/1**

0000 **6** *1* **Golconde (IRE)**[24] 7863 3-8-9 63 (p) ShaneKelly 6 60
(Robert Cowell) *chsd ldrs: rdn along 2f out: wknd appr fnl f* **25/1**

0000 **7** *shd* **Khawatim**[24] 7859 4-9-7 75 StevieDonohoe 7 72
(Noel Quinlan) *towards rr: rdn along and hdwy wl over 1f out: kpt on ins fnl f: nt rch ldrs* **25/1**

0500 **8** *nk* **Yurituni**[13] 7995 5-8-10 69..........(v) AmyScott(5) 8 65
(Eve Johnson Houghton) *trckd ldrs: effrt 2f out: sn rdn and wknd over 1f out* **20/1**

0616 **9** *2 ¾* **Pucon**[92] 6307 3-8-6 63.......... MarkCoumbe(3) 2 49
(Roger Teal) *in rr: wd st: nvr a factor* **16/1**

58.71s (-0.09) **Going Correction** +0.05s/f (Slow) **9** Ran SP% **125.5**
Speed ratings (Par 103): **102,101,98,98,98 96,96,96,91**
Tote swingers 1&2 £4.40, 1&3 £9.60, 2&3 £2.40 CSF £22.99 CT £69.50 TOTE £14.50: £3.20, £1.20, £2.70; EX 36.40 Trifecta £194.30 Pool: £1,093.71 - 4.22 winning units..
Owner One For All **Bred** Miss Anne Ormsby **Trained** Hingham, Norfolk

FOCUS
An ordinary sprint handicap and another race dominated by the pace-setters. Straightforward form.

8158 AT THE RACES ON FACEBOOK FILLIES' H'CAP 1m (P)
2:20 (2:20) (Class 5) (0-75,73) 3-Y-0+ **£2,264** (£505; £505; £168) **Stalls** High

Form RPR

0222 **1** **Fairyinthewind (IRE)**[20] 7892 3-9-3 70..........(p) SebSanders 2 77
(Paul D'Arcy) *keen: hld up: hdwy on outer wl over 1f out: rdn ent fnl f: kpt on wl to ld last 50 yds* **5/4**[1]

0440 **2** *¾* **Russian Ice**[13] 7997 4-9-7 73..........(b) GeorgeBaker 6 79
(Dean Ivory) *hld up: hdwy on outer 2f out: rdn over 1f out: ev ch ent fnl f tl no ex last 50 yds* **6/1**[3]

012- **2** *dht* **Princess Icicle**[413] 7208 4-9-2 68.......... FergusSweeney 1 74
(Jo Crowley) *trckd ldrs on inner: hdwy over 1f out: rdn to ld jst ins fnl f: drvn: hdd and no ex last 50 yds* **3/1**[2]

0010 **4** *1 ¼* **Chrissycross (IRE)**[20] 7893 3-8-13 66..........(b) RobertWinston 3 68
(Roger Teal) *cl up: rdn to ld 2f out: drvn over 1f out: hdd jst ins fnl f: kpt on same pce* **9/1**

2053 **5** *hd* **The New Black (IRE)**[6] 8083 3-8-6 59 oh5..........(e) DavidProbert 7 61
(Gay Kelleway) *in rr and sn pushed along: rdn along 1/2-way: wd st: styd on u.p fnl f: nrst fin* **10/1**

030 **6** *1* **Morant Bay (IRE)**[8] 8057 3-9-5 72.......... StevieDonohoe 4 71
(Ian Williams) *sn led: rdn along and hdd 2f out: drvn and rallied ent fnl f: sn wknd* **20/1**

4003 **7** *6* **Chevise (IRE)**[13] 7998 4-9-0 66.......... WilliamCarson 5 53
(Steve Woodman) *cl up: rdn along 2f out: wknd over 1f out* **8/1**

1m 38.78s (0.58) **Going Correction** +0.05s/f (Slow)
WFA 3 from 4yo 1lb **7** Ran SP% **118.7**
Speed ratings (Par 100): **99,98,98,97,96 95,89**
CSF £2.75 TOTE £2.10: £1.10.
Owner Spittinginthewind Partnership **Bred** J Cullinan **Trained** Newmarket, Suffolk

FOCUS
A tight handicap with five of the seven fillies in a line across the track half a furlong from home. The form makes sense though.

8159 FOLLOW US ON TWITTER @LINGFIELDPARK H'CAP (DIV I) 6f (P)
2:50 (2:51) (Class 5) (0-70,70) 3-Y-0+ **£2,264** (£673; £336; £168) **Stalls** Low

Form RPR

0106 **1** **Belinsky (IRE)**[15] 7967 5-8-13 62.......... RichardKingscote 2 70
(Julie Camacho) *trckd ldrs: hdwy 2f out: rdn ent fnl f: drvn and edgd rt last 100 yds: kpt on to ld nr line* **10/1**

0532 **2** *hd* **Parisian Pyramid (IRE)**[8] 8059 6-9-5 68.......... JoeFanning 10 76
(Ian Williams) *chsd ldrs: hdwy 2f out: rdn to ld ent fnl f: sn drvn and edgd lft: hdd and no ex nr line* **11/4**[1]

0304 **3** *hd* **Speak The Truth (IRE)**[15] 7967 6-8-8 62..........(p) NathanAlison(5) 6 69
(Jim Boyle) *bmpd s: keen: hld up in rr: hdwy on inner wl over 1f out: rdn and str run to chal ins fnl f: ev ch tl drvn and no ex towards fin* **7/2**[2]

11 **4** *2 ¼* **George Fenton**[63] 7146 3-8-10 59..........(p) J-PGuillambert 1 59
(Richard Guest) *hld up: hdwy on inner 2f out: rdn to chse ldrs 1f out: kpt on fnl f: nrst fin* **8/1**

0241 **5** *¾* **Bull Bay**[13] 7988 3-8-9 65.......... IanBurns(7) 8 63
(Jane Chapple-Hyam) *bmpd s: trckd ldrs: hdwy 2f out: led 11/2f out: sn rdn and hdd ent fnl f: kpt on same pce* **7/1**[3]

1116 **6** *nk* **Alnoomaas (IRE)**[75] 6825 3-9-7 70.......... TomMcLaughlin 9 67
(Luke Dace) *wnt lft s: cl up: rdn and wd st: sn drvn and one pce* **7/1**[3]

0004 **7** *½* **Diamond Vine (IRE)**[20] 7902 4-9-4 67..........(p) LukeMorris 3 63
(Ronald Harris) *chsd ldrs: rdn along 2f out: no imp* **7/1**[3]

600 **8** *1 ½* **Hinton Admiral**[88] 6452 8-9-0 63..........(b[1]) KirstyMilczarek 7 54
(Conor Dore) *bmpd s: midfield: hdwy 2f out: rdn to chse ldrs over 1f out: sn no imp* **33/1**

5600 **9** *nk* **Dorothy's Dancing (IRE)**[15] 7967 4-8-13 62..........(p) ChrisCatlin 5 52
(Gary Moore) *led: rdn 2f out: wd st: sn hdd & wknd* **16/1**

0503 **10** *4 ½* **Duke Of Aricabeau (IRE)**[56] 7308 3-9-2 68.......... SimonPearce(3) 11 45
(Lydia Pearce) *a towards rr* **20/1**

3002 **11** *1 ½* **Homeward Strut**[188] 3041 3-9-4 67.......... LiamKeniry 4 39
(Zoe Davison) *a rr* **25/1**

6536 **12** *½* **Mambo Spirit (IRE)**[26] 7820 8-9-1 64.......... FergusSweeney 12 35
(Tony Newcombe) *a rr* **33/1**

1m 11.65s (-0.25) **Going Correction** +0.05s/f (Slow) **12** Ran SP% **127.0**
Speed ratings (Par 103): **103,102,102,99,98 98,97,95,95,89 87,86**
Tote Swingers 1&2 £10.80, 2&3 £3.70, 1&3 £12.70 CSF £38.92 CT £123.95 TOTE £17.50: £4.60, £1.10, £2.30; EX 75.50 Trifecta £545.50 Pool: £967.40 - 1.33 winning units..
Owner Wentdale Limited **Bred** Camogue Stud Ltd **Trained** Norton, N Yorks

FOCUS
A modest sprint handicap, but they went a decent pace. Fairly solid, if ordinary form.

8160 FOLLOW US ON TWITTER @LINGFIELDPARK H'CAP (DIV II) 6f (P)
3:20 (3:22) (Class 5) (0-70,69) 3-Y-0+ **£2,264** (£673; £336; £168) **Stalls** Low

Form RPR

-303 **1** **Stepturn**[13] 7988 3-9-0 62..........(p) ChrisCatlin 4 70
(Michael Wigham) *led: rdn along wl over 1f out: hdd jst ins fnl f: drvn and rallied gamely to ld again nr fin* **5/1**[3]

2022 **2** *nk* **Lastkingofscotland (IRE)**[8] 8058 6-9-6 68..........(b) KirstyMilczarek 11 75
(Conor Dore) *hld up in rr: gd hdwy wl over 1f out: sn rdn and str run ins fnl f: jst failed* **4/1**[2]

5236 **3** *nse* **Catalinas Diamond (IRE)**[20] 7915 4-9-1 63..........(t) FergusSweeney 1 70
(Pat Murphy) *trckd ldrs on inner: hdwy wl over 1f out: rdn to ld jst ins fnl f: drvn: hdd and no ex nr fin* **10/1**

2331 **4** *1 ½* **Fortrose Academy (IRE)**[15] 7967 3-9-4 66.......... DavidProbert 8 68
(Andrew Balding) *cl up: pushed along 2f out: sn rdn and ev ch tl rdn and one pce ins fnl f* **6/4**[1]

5000 **5** *nk* **Lady Mango (IRE)**[12] 8005 4-8-13 61.......... LukeMorris 2 62
(Ronald Harris) *chsd ldrs: rdn over 2f out: drvn wl over 1f out: kpt on same pce* **14/1**

2503 **6** *¾* **Button Moon (IRE)**[8] 8059 4-9-5 67..........(p) SebSanders 9 66
(Paul Fitzsimons) *dwlt: sn trcking ldrs on inner: hdwy wl over 1f out: sn rdn and no imp fnl f* **6/1**

3600 **7** *2* **Commandingpresence (USA)**[8] 8058 6-9-0 62.......... SeanLevey 10 55
(John Bridger) *keen and sn chsng ldrs: rdn along 2f out: sn wknd* **25/1**

2405 **8** *¾* **Dvinsky (USA)**[12] 8005 11-9-0 62..........(b) JimmyQuinn 6 53
(Paul Howling) *hld up: a towards rr* **6/1**

03-0 **9** *½* **Onceaponatime (IRE)**[13] 7990 7-8-10 58.......... AndreaAtzeni 12 47
(Michael Squance) *wnt rt s: a rr* **33/1**

1m 12.08s (0.18) **Going Correction** +0.05s/f (Slow) **9** Ran SP% **127.8**
Speed ratings (Par 103): **100,99,99,97,97 96,93,92,91**
Tote swingers 1&2 £6.20, 1&3 £9.20, 2&3 £6.30 CSF £28.35 CT £206.13 TOTE £7.00: £1.70, £1.30, £2.50; EX 29.80 Trifecta £307.70 Pool: £1,633.09 - 3.98 winning units..
Owner R J Lorenz **Bred** Cheveley Park Stud Ltd **Trained** Newmarket, Suffolk

FOCUS
The pace didn't look as strong as in the first division and the winning time was 0.43 seconds slower. The winner is on the upgrade.
T/Plt: £166.50 to a £1 stake. Pool: £41,471.33 - 181.75 winning units. T/Qpdt: £30.10 to a £1 stake. Pool: £6,696.87 - 164.26 winning units. JR

8092 KEMPTON (A.W) (R-H)
Wednesday, December 19

OFFICIAL GOING: Standard
Wind: Strong, half behind Weather: Very overcast, drizzly, rain from race 3

8161 WIN BIG WITH BETDAQ MULTIPLES NURSERY 5f (P)
3:55 (3:55) (Class 5) (0-75,74) 2-Y-O **£2,264** (£673; £336; £168) **Stalls** Low

Form RPR

0341 **1** **Ovett**[12] 8016 2-9-7 **74**..........(p) FergusSweeney 4 84
(Gary Moore) *mde all: shkn up and clr over 1f out: styd on strly* **7/4**[2]

416 **2** *3 ¼* **Multitask**[25] 7856 2-9-6 **73**.......... JamieGoldstein 3 71
(Michael Madgwick) *chsd wnr over 3f out: rdn and no imp over 1f out: one pce after* **14/1**

2232 **3** *1 ½* **Modern Lady**[8] 8065 2-8-11 **64**.......... RobbieFitzpatrick 2 57
(Richard Guest) *chsd wnr to over 3f out: sn rdn: one pce and no prog fnl 2f* **4/1**[3]

2103 **4** *nse* **Marmot Bay (IRE)**[2] 8150 2-8-6 **64**.......... AmyScott(5) 1 57
(Alastair Lidderdale) *stdd s: hld up in last pair: pushed along and no prog over 1f out: kpt on to press for modest 3rd nr fin: nvr involved* **14/1**

6621 **5** *6* **Midnight Dream (FR)**[18] 7953 2-9-7 **74**.......... TomEaves 5 45
(Linda Stubbs) *dwlt and awkward s: a in last pair: rdn and fnd nil over 1f out: wknd* **6/4**[1]

59.05s (-1.45) **Going Correction** -0.125s/f (Stan) **5** Ran SP% **109.7**
Speed ratings (Par 96): **106,100,98,98,88**
CSF £22.13 TOTE £2.60: £1.60, £9.60; EX 28.60 Trifecta £159.20 Pool: £1,231.41 - 5.80 winning units..
Owner 8 Wealth Management **Bred** Whatton Manor Stud **Trained** Lower Beeding, W Sussex

FOCUS
An uncompetitive nursery, but an improving winner and the time was fractionally quicker than the later Class 4 handicap for older horses.

NOTEBOOK
Ovett was a cut above this lot, but his task was made all the more straightforward by being allowed an uncontested lead and he readily defied a 4lb rise for his recent 6f Lingfield win. He was declared to run again quickly under a penalty. (op 2-1)
Multitask, who won his maiden over 5f at Lingfield, was too free when upped to 7f at the same venue next time and this trip is probably more suitable. He was no match for the winner, however.
Modern Lady had been holding her form well lately but she now looks to have had enough for the time being.
Marmot Bay(IRE), third in a weak claimer over the extended 1m at Wolverhampton two days earlier, needs a bit further than the minimum trip. (op 10-1)
Midnight Dream(FR) was nowhere near the form he showed when off the mark over 5f at Wolverhampton last time. Official explanation: jockey said gelding was never travelling. (tchd 7-4)

8162 BACK OR LAY AT BETDAQ.COM H'CAP 1m 2f (P)
4:25 (4:27) (Class 5) (0-70,70) 3-Y-0+ **£2,264** (£673; £336; £168) **Stalls** Low

Form RPR

6445 **1** **Whitby Jet (IRE)**[53] 7409 4-9-7 **70**.......... WilliamCarson 11 77
(Ed Vaughan) *hld up in 9th: prog 3f out: rdn 2f out: styd on wl fr over 1f out to ld last strides* **7/2**[1]

660 **2** *hd* **Sporting Gold (IRE)**[204] 2585 3-8-10 **62**.......... AndreaAtzeni 13 69
(Roger Varian) *prog to chse ldr after 2f: led wl over 2f out: sn rdn: hdd over 1f out: kpt on wl to ld again last 100yds: hdd fnl strides* **4/1**[2]

3616 **3** *2 ¼* **Having A Ball**[21] 7892 8-8-13 **62**.......... JohnFahy 7 64
(Peter Cundell) *trckd ldrs in 6th: prog 3f out: produced to ld over 1f out and looked sure to win: fnd little in front: hdd & wknd last 100yds* **8/1**

5536 **4** *1 ¼* **Silkee Supreme**[14] 7992 3-8-6 **58**.......... KieranO'Neill 8 58
(Richard Hannon) *t.k.h: hld up in midfield on inner: shkn up over 2f out: prog to go 4th 1f out: kpt on but no real imp* **14/1**

4004 **5** *1* **May's Boy**[13] 8010 4-8-7 **61**..........(p) RachealKneller(5) 5 59
(Mark Usher) *hld up in last quartet: nt clr run jst over 2f out: pushed along and styd on fr over 1f out: nvr involved* **16/1**

35-0 **6** *1 ¼* **Al Amaan**[12] 8020 7-9-3 **66**.......... GeorgeBaker 9 62
(Gary Moore) *stdd s: hld up in last trio: pushed along over 2f out: nt clr run v briefly wl over 1f out: styd on: nrst fin* **20/1**

4505 **7** *½* **Hydrant**[12] 8020 6-9-3 **66**.......... AdamBeschizza 6 61
(Peter Salmon) *chsd ldr 2f: styd prom: rdn over 2f out: fdd over 1f out* **9/2**[3]

0000 **8** *hd* **Simayill**[48] 7511 4-9-5 **68**..........(b[1]) TomMcLaughlin 10 62
(John Berry) *pressed ldrs on outer: rdn over 2f out: wknd over 1f out* **14/1**

0010 **9** *1 ¾* **Royal Etiquette (IRE)**[21] 7892 5-9-2 **65**..........(v) KirstyMilczarek 12 56
(Lawney Hill) *bmpd s: racd wd thrght: nvr bttr than midfield: rdn over 2f out: sn struggling* **16/1**

4104 **10** *4 ½* **Aviso (GER)**[12] 8019 8-9-2 **65**.......... AdamKirby 14 47
(David Evans) *nvr bttr than midfield: rdn and lost pl over 2f out: sn btn* **14/1**

000 **11** *2 ½* **Understory (USA)**[28] 7805 5-9-6 **69**.......... MartinLane 3 47
(Tim McCarthy) *led: drvn and hdd wl over 2f out: lost 2nd and wknd rapidly wl over 1f out* **25/1**

12 *shd* **Capellini**[22] 5-8-13 **67**..........(p) LeonnaMayor(5) 4 45
(Charles Egerton) *stdd s then s.i.s: hld up: a in last pair: shkn up and no prog 2f out* **33/1**

1500 **13** *10* **Trip Switch**[238] 1611 6-9-5 **68**.. LiamKeniry 2 27
(John Butler) *trckd ldrs on inner: rdn over 2f out: wknd rapidly over 1f out: t.o* **20/1**

2m 5.18s (-2.82) **Going Correction** -0.125s/f (Stan)
WFA 3 from 4yo+ 3lb **13** Ran SP% **119.6**
Speed ratings (Par 103): **106,105,104,103,102 101,100,100,99,95 93,93,85**
Tote swingers 1&2 £3.50, 1&3 £6.80, 2&3 £9.30 CSF £16.04 CT £106.63 TOTE £4.80: £1.30, £2.30, £3.40; EX 19.20 Trifecta £105.10 Pool: £1,141.58 - 8.14 winning units..
Owner A M Pickering **Bred** Rathasker Stud **Trained** Newmarket, Suffolk
■ Stewards' Enquiry : Andrea Atzeni two-day ban; used whip above permitted level (2nd,3rd Jan).

FOCUS
A modest handicap run at a fair pace.

8163 BETDAQ MOBILE APPS H'CAP 5f (P)
4:55 (4:56) (Class 4) (0-85,88) 3-Y-0+ **£4,075** (£1,212; £606; £303) **Stalls** Low

Form RPR
3000 **1** **Island Legend (IRE)**[25] 7860 6-9-1 **79**......................(p) RobertWinston 1 87
(Milton Bradley) *mde all fr inner draw: edgd lft over 1f out: drvn and pressed fnl f: hld on* **25/1**
0452 **2** *nk* **Moorhouse Lad**[13] 8009 9-9-7 **85**.. JimCrowley 6 92
(Garry Moss) *chsd wnr: rdn over 1f out: chal fnl f: kpt on but nt qckn last 100yds* **4/1**[2]
0003 **3** *½* **Italian Tom (IRE)**[12] 8022 5-8-13 **77**.................................... LukeMorris 2 82
(Ronald Harris) *chsd ldrs in 5th: drvn and no prog over 1f out: styd on to take 3rd ins fnl f: nvr quite able to chal* **12/1**
0016 **4** *hd* **Dorback**[25] 7859 5-9-2 **80**... MartinDwyer 3 84
(David Nicholls) *patiently rdn in 7th: prog on inner over 1f out: clsd on ldrs fnl f: kpt on same pce nr fin* **6/1**[3]
2412 **5** *1 ¼* **Ring For Baileys**[25] 7860 3-9-1 **79**...................................... JoeFanning 7 79
(Chris Dwyer) *chsd ldrs on outer: rdn over 1f out: one pce and no prog fnl f* **8/1**
4341 **6** *hd* **Bubbly Ballerina**[13] 8009 3-8-13 **77**................................. AndreaAtzeni 8 76
(Alan Bailey) *chsd ldrs in 6th: rdn over 2f out: no imp over 1f out: kpt on nr fin* **10/1**
5600 **7** *hd* **Little Garcon (USA)**[41] 7646 5-9-3 **81**................................. ShaneKelly 4 79
(Robert Cowell) *dwlt: hld up in last trio: rdn fnl f: styd on: nvr rchd ldrs* **14/1**
2013 **8** *shd* **Roy's Legacy**[1] 8157 3-8-10 **74** 6ex..............................(t) DavidProbert 5 72
(Shaun Harris) *chsd ldng pair: rdn 2f out: stl cl enough in 3rd 1f out: wknd last 100yds* **16/1**
6301 **9** *1 ¼* **Rocket Rob (IRE)**[91] 6370 6-8-12 **76**......................... StevieDonohoe 10 70
(Willie Musson) *s.i.s and dropped in last fr wdst draw: stl there and pushed along wl over 1f out: nvr involved but styd on fnl f* **14/1**
1311 **10** *12* **Forest Edge (IRE)**[4] 8143 3-9-10 **88** 6ex........................(b) AdamKirby 9 38
(David Evans) *a in rr on outer: wknd 2f out: t.o* **5/2**[1]

59.07s (-1.43) **Going Correction** -0.125s/f (Stan) **10** Ran SP% **113.8**
Speed ratings (Par 105): **106,105,104,104,102 102,101,101,99,80**
Tote swingers 1&2 £17.50, 1&3 £24.60, 2&3 £11.10 CSF £119.92 CT £1315.18 TOTE £36.90: £7.60, £1.60, £4.00; EX 157.70 Trifecta £1229.80 Part won. Pool: £1,639.74 - 0.41 winning units..
Owner J M Bradley **Bred** Jerome Casey **Trained** Sedbury, Gloucs

FOCUS
The winner and runner-up raced in the first two throughout.
Island Legend(IRE) Official explanation: trainers representative had no explanation for apparent improvement in form.
Forest Edge(IRE) Official explanation: trainers representative said regarding apparent poor run that the gelding was unsuited by a drop back to 5f and had a wide draw.

8164 BETDAQ CASINO GAMES (S) STKS 7f (P)
5:25 (5:26) (Class 6) 2-Y-O **£1,617** (£481; £240; £120) **Stalls** Low

Form RPR
602 **1** **Opus Cactus (USA)**[7] 8076 2-8-6 0.................................. AndreaAtzeni 1 56+
(Marco Botti) *t.k.h: trckd ldng pair: wnt 2nd 2f out: pushed into ld over 1f out: rdn and edgd lft fnl f: sn clr* **10/11**[1]
3000 **2** *2 ¼* **Don Eduardo**[6] 8093 2-8-11 59..(b[1]) LiamKeniry 3 55
(J S Moore) *racd freely: led: hrd rdn and hdd over 1f out: wl hld whn sltly impeded ins fnl f: clung on for 2nd* **9/2**[2]
4403 **3** *hd* **Maypole Joe (IRE)**[4] 8132 2-8-11 55..........................(v) WilliamCarson 2 55
(David Evans) *trckd ldng trio on outer: rdn over 2f out: kpt on same pce fr over 1f out* **6/1**[3]
3223 **4** *shd* **Divine Angel (IRE)**[5] 8101 2-8-11 60.................................. LukeMorris 7 54
(Phil McEntee) *chsd ldr to 2f out: wl hld whn sltly impeded ins fnl f: one pce* **9/2**[2]
06 **5** *5* **Ely Valley**[15] 7979 2-8-6 0... MartinDwyer 6 36
(William Muir) *hld up in last pair: shkn up and nt on terms fr over 2f out: no imp* **20/1**
5500 **6** *17* **Belle Voir**[15] 7979 2-7-13 40..[1] LaurenHunter(7) 4
(Gay Kelleway) *racd keenly and wd: hld up in last pair: wknd 2f out: t.o* **66/1**

1m 27.01s (1.01) **Going Correction** -0.125s/f (Stan) **6** Ran SP% **109.3**
Speed ratings (Par 94): **89,86,86,86,80 60**
Tote swingers 1&2 £1.40, 1&3 £2.10, 2&3 £2.30 CSF £5.02 TOTE £2.30: £1.40, £1.60; EX 6.70 Trifecta £17.40 Pool: £1,669.57 - 71.87 winning units..The winner was bought by Alastair Lidderdale for 6,600gns.
Owner Scuderia Vittadini Srl **Bred** Scuderia Vittadini S R L **Trained** Newmarket, Suffolk

FOCUS
Not form to be positive about.

NOTEBOOK
Opus Cactus(USA), who improved to finish runner-up in a Lingfield claimer on her previous start, was much too good for this moderate bunch despite racing keenly and not impressing with her head carriage. She was sold to Alastair Lidderdale for £6,600. (op 4-5)
Don Eduardo had his chance from the front in first-time blinkers. (op 10-1)
Maypole Joe(IRE) offered little, although he did reverse Lingfield form from December 6 with Divine Angel. (tchd 11-2)
Divine Angel(IRE) was well held under her penalty. (op 3-1)

8165 SPORTINGLIFE.COM MEDIAN AUCTION MAIDEN STKS 6f (P)
5:55 (5:57) (Class 6) 2-Y-O **£1,617** (£481; £240; £120) **Stalls** Low

Form RPR
3024 **1** **Whipper Snapper (IRE)**[7] 8068 2-9-3 73.......................... JimCrowley 6 72
(William Knight) *hld up in last trio: prog towards inner 2f out: hrd rdn to cl over 1f out and drifted lft: led ins fnl f: drvn out* **5/2**[1]
2 **2** *1 ¼* **Charter (IRE)**[50] 7466 2-9-3 0...................................... TomMcLaughlin 4 68
(Michael Wigham) *trckd ldng pair: rdn to chse ldr 2f out: led briefly jst ins fnl f: edgd lft and one pce last 100yds* **11/2**
4 **3** *¾* **Two In The Pink (IRE)**[14] 7987 2-8-12 0............................ MartinLane 3 61
(Hugo Palmer) *trckd ldr: lft in ld over 2f out: rn green in front: hdd and nt qckn jst ins fnl f* **4/1**[2]
43 **4** *3 ¼* **Groove On (IRE)**[13] 8006 2-9-0 0..........................(t) NataliaGemelova(3) 1 56
(Marco Botti) *led: hung bdly lft bnd 3f out: hdd over 2f out: fdd fnl f* **9/2**[3]
5 *hd* **Shenval** 2-9-3 0.. AdamKirby 7 56
(Noel Quinlan) *trckd ldrs in 5th: shkn up over 2f out: no imp over 1f out: fdd* **6/1**
0 **6** *4 ½* **Compton Albion (IRE)**[14] 7987 2-8-12 0.................... FergusSweeney 8 37
(Jeremy Gask) *hld up in detached last: shkn up and wl off the pce over 2f out: nvr in it* **33/1**
6 **7** *¾* **Al Sahraa**[28] 7807 2-8-12 0... LukeMorris 5 35
(John Butler) *chsd ldrs to 1/2-way: sn btn* **9/1**
8 *½* **Quelle Affaire** 2-8-12 0 KirstyMilczarek 9 33
(Brendan Powell) *rn green in last trio: pushed along after 2f: nvr on terms* **33/1**

1m 12.36s (-0.74) **Going Correction** -0.125s/f (Stan) **8** Ran SP% **112.3**
Speed ratings (Par 94): **99,97,96,92,91 85,84,84**
Tote swingers 1&2 £3.00, 1&3 £2.90, 2&3 £5.10 CSF £15.96 TOTE £2.60: £1.30, £1.20, £1.80; EX 13.90 Trifecta £41.00 Pool: £1,554.88 - 28.41 winning units..
Owner The Oil Merchants **Bred** Michael Mullins **Trained** Patching, W Sussex

FOCUS
The pace looked overly strong and this ordinary sprint maiden set up nicely for the patiently ridden Whipper Snapper.

NOTEBOOK
Whipper Snapper(IRE) got a good run towards the inside as his main rivals went left to varying degrees, and despite then edging in the same direction himself, he was nicely on top at the line. He was confirming earlier promise and should be competitive in handicaps. (op 11-4 tchd 3-1)
Charter(IRE) had been sold out of Michael Bell's yard for 18,000gns since finishing runner-up in a Yarmouth maiden (7f, heavy) on his debut in October. He paid for chasing the good pace but this was a pleasing enough performance. (op 7-2)
Two In The Pink(IRE), fourth over C&D on her debut, chased the good gallop and was further compromised by being carried slightly left off the home turn. She can yet do a bit better. (op 7-2)
Groove On(IRE) was too free in front and failed to handle the bend into the straight. He now has the option of handicaps and is open to improvement.
Shenval, a brother to the same stable's multiple 7f-1m winner (including here) Abriachan, showed plenty of zip on this racecourse debut and has ability. (op 9-1)

8166 RACING PLUS - THE BEST WEEKEND ACTION MEDIAN AUCTION MAIDEN FILLIES' STKS 7f (P)
6:25 (6:29) (Class 6) 2-Y-O **£1,617** (£481; £240; £120) **Stalls** Low

Form RPR
0 **1** **Byroness**[159] 4055 2-8-7 0.. RyanTate(7) 5 70+
(Heather Main) *hld up in 5th: nt clr run briefly 3f out: gd prog over 2f out to ld over 1f out: rdn and sn clr* **7/2**[3]
2 *3 ¼* **Ruff Luck** 2-9-0 0... LiamKeniry 6 61+
(Seamus Mullins) *dwlt: hld up in last: pushed along and prog on outer 2f out: styd on wl to take 2nd last 100yds: no ch w wnr* **11/4**[2]
00 **3** *1 ½* **Guru Baby**[28] 7813 2-9-0 0.. RichardThomas 2 57
(John E Long) *reluctant to enter stalls: led: rdn and hdd over 1f out: fdd* **100/1**
0005 **4** *4 ½* **Sally Bruce**[7] 8076 2-8-7 47................................... JenniferFerguson(7) 4 45
(Louise Best) *pressed ldr to wl over 1f out: wknd rapidly fnl f* **20/1**
00 **5** *¾* **Mariella**[21] 7916 2-9-0 0... LukeMorris 1 43
(Peter Chapple-Hyam) *chsd ldrs: pushed along 1/2-way: wknd 2f out* **8/1**
6 *1* **Bullseye Babe** 2-9-0 0... DavidProbert 3 40
(Mark Usher) *s.i.s: chsd ldng pair to 2f out: wknd qckly over 1f out* **12/1**
7 *2* **Beautiful Life** 2-9-0 0.. MartinLane 7 35
(David Simcock) *rn green: hld up in last pair: shkn up and no prog over 2f out: bhd after* **6/4**[1]

1m 27.13s (1.13) **Going Correction** -0.125s/f (Stan) **7** Ran SP% **113.4**
Speed ratings (Par 91): **88,84,82,77,76 75,73**
Tote swingers 1&2 £1.10, 1&3 £42.20, 2&3 £20.40 CSF £13.34 TOTE £3.60: £2.20, £2.10; EX 15.50 Trifecta £1247.30 Part won. Pool: £1,663.19 - 0.40 winning units..
Owner Les Chevaliers **Bred** J P M Main **Trained** Kingston Lisle, Oxon
■ Stewards' Enquiry : Ryan Tate caution; entered wrong stall.

FOCUS
Fourth-placed Sally Bruce came into this rated just 47, and the time was 0.12 seconds slower than the earlier juvenile seller.

NOTEBOOK
Byroness, who hinted at ability in a Newbury maiden (6f, soft) on her debut in July, travelled well before bounding clear, but she probably only had to run to a moderate level. (op 9-2)
Ruff Luck, out of a triple winner at around 1m on Fibresand and Polytrack, was no match at all for the winner. (op 4-1)
Guru Baby was well beaten in a couple of 6f maidens on her first two starts and probably didn't achieve much.
Bullseye Babe Official explanation: vet's said filly had been struck into.
Beautiful Life, a half-sister to, among others, a couple of winners over 7f-1m in Britain, showed nothing on this racecourse debut. (tchd 7-4)

8167 SPORTINGLIFE.COM RACING ALL WEATHER "HANDS AND HEELS" APPRENTICE SERIES H'CAP (RACING EXCELLENCE) 1m (P)
6:55 (6:56) (Class 6) (0-60,60) 4-Y-O+ **£1,617** (£481; £240; £120) **Stalls** Low

Form RPR
03-0 **1** **Lord Of The Dance (IRE)**[19] 7935 6-9-4 **60**.................... RobertTart(3) 5 70
(Michael Mullineaux) *hld up in rr and wl off the pce: prog jst over 2f out: chal fnl f: led last 100yds: styd on wl* **12/1**
0010 **2** *½* **Breakheart (IRE)**[7] 8083 5-8-13 **55**............................(p) JoeyHaynes(3) 7 64
(Andrew Balding) *hld up off the pce in midfield: prog 2f out: led jst ins fnl f: hdd last 100yds: styd on* **9/2**[2]
3141 **3** *2* **Pastoral Jet**[62] 7189 4-9-0 **56**.. AaronJones(3) 12 60+
(Richard Rowe) *trckd ldng pair at str pce and clr of rest: led over 2f out: hdd and no ex jst ins fnl f* **4/1**[1]
5000 **4** *1 ¼* **Michael's Nook**[51] 7446 5-8-7 **49**................................ ShelleyBirkett(3) 6 50
(Alastair Lidderdale) *t.k.h: hld up wl off the pce: clsd over 2f out: kpt on same pce to take 4th ins fnl f* **25/1**
0100 **5** *1 ¾* **Menadati (USA)**[12] 8020 4-9-4 **60**..................................... PaulBooth(3) 2 57
(Peter Hiatt) *reluctant to enter stalls: s.v.s: mostly in last and wl bhd: weaved through unenthusiastically fnl 2f: tk 5th nr fin* **4/1**[1]
0400 **6** *¾* **Arachnophobia (IRE)**[34] 7733 6-9-0 **58**....................(b) KirstenSmith(5) 4 53
(Martin Bosley) *chsd clr ldng trio: effrt to go 2nd 2f out to over 1f out: wknd* **33/1**
6646 **7** *1 ¼* **Delightful Sleep**[15] 7982 4-8-4 **46** oh1.............................. EoinWalsh(3) 3 39
(David Evans) *hld up off the pce: clsd over 2f out: no imp over 1f out: fdd* **6/1**[3]

0060 **8** *3* **Pytheas (USA)**[14] 7992 5-8-8 **52**............................(t[1]) SemiraPashai(5) 8 38
(Alastair Lidderdale) *chsd clr ldng quartet: tried to cl over 2f out: wknd over 1f out* **25/1**
4006 **9** *1 ¾* **Takitwo**[21] 7898 9-8-6 **48**.. RyanTate(3) 9 30
(Peter Cundell) *a wl in rr: no prog and btn over 2f out: modest late hdwy* **20/1**
2610 **10** *2 ½* **Rapid Water**[11] 8038 6-9-4 **57**..(p) GemmaTutty 1 33
(Pat Eddery) *mistimed s: a wl in rr: detached fr over 2f out* **8/1**
3000 **11** *5* **Spirit Of Gondree (IRE)**[49] 7486 4-9-4 **57**...................(b) PatMillman 13 21
(Milton Bradley) *led at str pce to wl over 2f out: wknd rapidly* **12/1**
0430 **12** *½* **Georgebernardshaw (IRE)**[93] 6313 7-9-0 **58**.............. LisaTodd(5) 10 21
(Richard Guest) *s.i.s: rapid prog to press ldr after 1f at str pce: led briefly wl over 2f out: sn wknd rapidly* **12/1**
0-00 **13** *20* **Femme D'Espere**[41] 7656 6-8-2 **46** oh1................... GemmaNellist(5) 11
(Christopher Kellett) *dwlt: racd wd: rcvrd into midfield after 3f: wknd rapidly 3f out: t.o* **100/1**

1m 39.66s (-0.14) **Going Correction** -0.125s/f (Stan) **13 Ran SP% 123.0**
Speed ratings (Par 101): **95,94,92,91,89 88,87,84,82,80 75,74,54**
Tote swingers 1&2 £17.00, 1&3 £14.70, 2&3 £2.90 CSF £63.87 CT £272.39 TOTE £18.70: £4.80, £2.60, £2.20; EX 66.70 Trifecta £426.30 Pool: £568.42 - 0.45 winning units..
Owner H Clewlow **Bred** Bridgewater Equine Ltd **Trained** Alpraham, Cheshire

FOCUS
The pace was overly strong, with the lead disputed by Spirit Of Gondree and Georgebernardshaw, and this is misleading form.
T/Plt: £238.60 to a £1 stake. Pool: £58,916.83 - 180.24 winning units T/Qpdt: £53.20 to a £1 stake. Pool: £8,559.91 - 119.01 winning units JN

8153 LINGFIELD (L-H)
Wednesday, December 19

OFFICIAL GOING: Standard
Wind: Modest; half behind Weather: Overcast; dry

8168 FOLLOW @ATTHERACES ON TWITTER H'CAP (DIV I) 6f (P)
12:00 (12:00) (Class 6) (0-55,61) 3-Y-0+ **£1,704** (£503; £251) **Stalls Low**

Form RPR
5041 **1** **Temple Road (IRE)**[7] 8075 4-9-13 **61** 6ex................... RobertWinston 2 74+
(Milton Bradley) *stdd s: t.k.h: hld up wl in tch in rr: nt clr run over 1f out: gap opened and qcknd to chal jst ins fnl f: led and edgd rt ins fnl f: sn in command: eased nr fin* **4/5[1]**
0060 **2** *1 ¼* **Do More Business (IRE)**[6] 8099 5-8-13 **50**..............(v) RyanPowell(3) 1 56
(Alison Batchelor) *chsd ldrs on inner: rdn and effrt over 1f out: kpt on ins fnl f* **14/1**
003 **3** *1 ½* **Kerfuffle (IRE)**[28] 7804 3-8-13 **47**.................................... SebSanders 10 49
(Simon Dow) *stdd and swtchd lft after s: hld up in tch in rr: hdwy on inner over 1f out: 3rd and running on whn nt clr run fnl 100yds: no imp and swtchd rt towards fin* **16/1**
0305 **4** *¾* **Adaeze (IRE)**[35] 7703 4-8-12 **46** oh1.................................(v) JohnFahy 5 45
(Jonathan Portman) *led: rdn over 1f out: hdd and pushed rt ins fnl f: wknd towards fin* **33/1**
664 **5** *½* **Jonnie Skull (IRE)**[8] 8061 6-8-10 **51**.............................(vt) RyanTate(7) 9 49
(Phil McEntee) *chsd ldrs on outer: rdn ent fnl 2f: styng on same pce whn pushed rt jst ins fnl f: wknd fnl 100yds* **12/1[3]**
6005 **6** *½* **Doctor Hilary**[48] 7504 10-9-4 **52**....................................(v) RobertHavlin 7 48
(Mark Hoad) *in tch in last quartet: rdn wl over 1f out: styd on ins fnl f: no threat to ldrs* **25/1**
5005 **7** *nk* **Hold The Star**[7] 8075 6-9-0 **53**....................................... AnnStokell(5) 12 48
(Ann Stokell) *in tch: rdn and unable qck over 1f out: styd on same pce fnl f* **33/1**
0003 **8** *nk* **Little Perisher**[10] 8046 5-8-7 **46**............................(p) RachealKneller(5) 4 40
(Mark Brisbourne) *chsd ldrs: rdn and unable qck wl over 1f out: wknd ent fnl f* **25/1**
6211 **9** *nk* **Pharoh Jake**[5] 8107 4-9-1 **54** 6ex.................. WilliamTwiston-Davies(5) 6 48+
(John Bridger) *hld up wl in tch: nt clr run over 1f out tl ins fnl f: nt rcvr and nvr able to mount a chal* **4/1[2]**
0400 **10** *hd* **Microlight**[71] 6951 4-8-12 **46** oh1............................(b) RichardThomas 11 39
(John E Long) *in tch in midfield on outer: rdn and unable qck over 1f out: wknd fnl f* **25/1**
2225 **11** *hd* **Miakora**[8] 8064 4-9-7 **55**... AndreaAtzeni 8 47
(Michael Quinn) *pressed ldr: rdn and unable qck over 1f out: wknd fnl f* **12/1[3]**

1m 12.45s (0.55) **Going Correction** +0.05s/f (Slow) **11 Ran SP% 120.9**
Speed ratings (Par 101): **98,96,94,93,92 92,91,91,90,90 90**
Tote swingers 1&2 £6.00, 1&3 £3.60, 2&3 £23.80 CSF £13.61 CT £116.72 TOTE £1.80: £1.10, £3.90, £3.40; EX 14.10 Trifecta £375.10 Part won. Pool: £500.25 - 0.61 winning units..
Owner Darren Hudson-Wood **Bred** Paul Monaghan **Trained** Sedbury, Gloucs

FOCUS
They didn't go that quick early on and they were well bunched running down the hill.
Hold The Star Official explanation: jockey said mare was slowly away.

8169 FOLLOW @ATTHERACES ON TWITTER H'CAP (DIV II) 6f (P)
12:30 (12:30) (Class 6) (0-55,55) 3-Y-0+ **£1,704** (£503; £251) **Stalls Low**

Form RPR
3140 **1** **Reginald Claude**[14] 7992 4-9-2 **55**........................... RachealKneller(5) 1 62
(Mark Usher) *hld up in tch in midfield: hdwy to join ldrs on bit jst ins fnl f: pushed along hands and heels fnl 100yds and fnd enough to ld cl home* **7/2[1]**
0602 **2** *shd* **Putin (IRE)**[8] 8062 4-8-7 **46**.................................(bt) LeonnaMayor(5) 6 53
(Phil McEntee) *hld up wl in tch: effrt on outer to press ldrs bnd 2f out: rdn to ld jst ins fnl f: edgd lft u.p and hdd cl home* **6/1[3]**
6305 **3** *1 ¼* **Dixie Gwalia**[7] 8075 4-8-10 **51**...................................... SiobhanMiller(7) 5 54
(David Simcock) *hld up in midfield: hdwy on inner over 1f out: rdn and ev ch jst ins fnl f: no ex and outpcd fnl 75yds* **8/1**
0500 **4** *1* **Athaakeel (IRE)**[20] 7929 6-9-0 **48**.................................... LukeMorris 11 48
(Ronald Harris) *hld up in midfield: rdn and hdwy over 1f out: styd on wl ins fnl f: nt rch ldrs* **14/1**
5600 **5** *1* **Sherjawy (IRE)**[20] 7929 8-8-13 **47**.............................. KirstyMilczarek 4 44
(Zoe Davison) *pressed ldr: ev ch and drvn over 1f out: unable qck 1f out: wknd ins fnl f* **14/1**
2602 **6** *hd* **Whiskey Junction**[33] 7747 8-9-7 **55**.............................. AndreaAtzeni 3 51
(Michael Quinn) *led: rdn wl over 1f out: hdd jst ins fnl f: wknd fnl 100yds* **6/1[3]**
4500 **7** *1* **Flying Kitty**[14] 7992 3-8-12 **46**.. KieranO'Neill 2 39
(John Bridger) *chsd ldrs: rdn over 2f out: no ex 1f out: wknd ins fnl f* **16/1**

5600 **8** *shd* **Mr Optimistic**[33] 7748 4-9-5 **53**....................................(t) DavidProbert 7 46
(Paul Howling) *taken down early: chsd ldrs: rdn and ev ch 2f out: unable qck over 1f out: wknd fnl f* **8/1**
0-00 **9** *¾* **Fast Samurai (USA)**[7] 8075 4-8-13 **54**....................... JoeyHaynes(7) 10 45
(Tony Carroll) *stdd and swtchd lft after s: hld up in rr: rdn and hdwy over 1f out: no ex 1f out: wknd ins fnl f* **40/1**
6456 **10** *3 ½* **Mr Hendrix**[10] 8045 3-9-3 **51**.. WilliamCarson 8 31
(Mark Hoad) *stdd and dropped in bhd after s: swtchd rt and effrt wl over 1f out: no prog: wknd 1f out* **25/1**
6000 **11** *5* **Kings 'n Dreams**[25] 7861 5-9-7 **55**................................(b) JimCrowley 9 20
(Dean Ivory) *stdd and swtchd lft after s: hld up in rr: rdn and effrt wd bnd 2f out: no hdwy and wknd jst over 1f out* **4/1[2]**

1m 12.13s (0.23) **Going Correction** +0.05s/f (Slow) **11 Ran SP% 118.5**
Speed ratings (Par 101): **100,99,98,96,95 95,93,93,92,88 81**
Tote swingers 1&2 £3.50, 1&3 £6.10, 2&3 £8.00 CSF £24.77 CT £162.18 TOTE £5.10: £1.50, £2.80, £2.70; EX 28.50 Trifecta £134.60 Pool: £739.90 - 4.12 winning units..
Owner High Five Racing **Bred** Whitsbury Manor Stud **Trained** Upper Lambourn, Berks

FOCUS
The quicker of the two divisions by 0.32sec.

8170 32RED SUPPORTING BRITISH RACING H'CAP 2m (P)
1:00 (1:00) (Class 5) (0-70,70) 3-Y-0+ **£2,385** (£704; £352) **Stalls Low**

Form RPR
53 **1** **Nashville (IRE)**[4] 8135 3-9-2 **66**.................................... JamieSpencer 2 73
(Ian Williams) *hld up in tch: rdn to chse ldr 3f out: led over 2f out: hld on u.p ins fnl f* **7/2[1]**
1264 **2** *½* **Squad**[20] 7927 6-10-0 **70**..(v) EddieAhern 10 76
(Simon Dow) *hld up in last quartet: hdwy 5f out: chsd ldng pair over 2f out: rdn and effrt over 1f out: ev ch ins fnl f: no ex towards fin* **5/1[2]**
664 **3** *nk* **Ginger Fizz**[19] 7933 5-9-12 **68**.. MartinDwyer 11 74
(Ben Case) *t.k.h: hld up in midfield: rdn to chse ldrs over 2f out: unable qck and looked hld 1f out: rallied ins fnl f: kpt on* **10/1**
2100 **4** *½* **The Absent Mare**[20] 7927 4-9-10 **66**................................ LukeMorris 9 71
(Robin Dickin) *hld up in last quartet: rdn and hdwy 3f out: chsd ldrs 2f out drvn over 1f out: kpt on towards fin* **6/1[3]**
-300 **5** *2 ¼* **Ninfea (IRE)**[12] 8023 4-9-9 **65**... LiamKeniry 3 67
(David Bridgwater) *chsd ldrs: wnt 2nd 6f out tl led over 3f out: rdn and hdd over 2f out: no ex 1f out: wknd ins fnl f* **8/1**
0426 **6** *4 ½* **Sherman McCoy**[7] 8082 6-9-9 **70**................ WilliamTwiston-Davies(5) 4 67
(Daniel Kubler) *chsd ldr tl 6f out: wkng whn short of room and hmpd over 2f out: plugged on but wl hld after* **5/1[2]**
- **7** *2 ¾* **Golan Guy (IRE)**[272] 6966 7-9-8 **67**.............................. RyanPowell(3) 6 61
(Alison Batchelor) *t.k.h: hld up in tch in midfield: rdn and outpcd over 2f out: wl btn over 1f out* **50/1**
0620 **8** *9* **Caunay**[28] 7819 5-9-3 **62**..(tp) AmyBaker(3) 1 45
(Neil Mulholland) *dwlt: hld up in last pair: rdn and no prog 4f out: wknd wl over 2f out* **25/1**
5545 **9** *4 ½* **Murphy (IRE)**[14] 8001 10-8-9 **56**........................(t) JemmaMarshall(5) 7 33
(Nick Gifford) *led: clr after 2f: rdn and hdd over 3f out: sn dropped out: bhd fnl 2f* **10/1**
0345 **10** *22* **Za'Lan (USA)**[35] 3891 3-8-13 **63**................................... FergusSweeney 5 14
(Chris Gordon) *a bhd: rdn and nvr gng fr 8f out: lost tch over 3f out: t.o* **12/1**
00-0 **11** *dist* **Brilliant Barca**[31] 521 4-9-9 **65**.. ChrisCatlin 8
(Sheena West) *in tch: lost pl and rdn w no rspnse 10f out: last and lost tch 9f out: sn eased and wl t.o fnl 7f* **25/1**

3m 23.6s (-2.10) **Going Correction** +0.05s/f (Slow)
WFA 3 from 4yo+ 8lb **11 Ran SP% 116.5**
Speed ratings (Par 103): **107,106,106,106,105 102,101,97,94,83**
Tote swingers 1&2 £3.60, 1&3 £8.80, 2&3 £8.00 CSF £19.88 CT £160.01 TOTE £3.10: £1.80, £2.50, £2.60; EX 17.40 Trifecta £215.60 Part won. Pool: £287.56 - 0.51 winning units..
Owner Dr Marwan Koukash **Bred** B L Harvey & Balmerino Bloodstock **Trained** Portway, Worcs

FOCUS
Recent winning form was thin on the ground here.
Brilliant Barca Official explanation: jockey said gelding moved badly throughout.

8171 BRITISH STALLION STUDS E.B.F./32RED.COM MAIDEN FILLIES' STKS 7f (P)
1:30 (1:31) (Class 5) 2-Y-0 **£3,340** (£986; £493) **Stalls Low**

Form RPR
045 **1** **Lucky Di**[54] 7371 2-9-0 68.. JimCrowley 2 74
(Peter Hedger) *chsd ldrs: rdn over 2f out: hdwy u.p on inner to ld jst ins fnl f: r.o wl* **10/1**
2 **2** *1 ½* **Iridescence**[48] 7506 2-9-0 0... ShaneKelly 4 70
(Jeremy Noseda) *chsd ldrs: rdn and effrt to chal 2f out: chsd wnr ins fnl f: kpt on but no real imp* **7/4[1]**
63 **3** *2* **Bouyrin (IRE)**[14] 7987 2-9-0 0.. JamieSpencer 5 65+
(Michael Bell) *hld up in tch: wdst of ldng gp bnd wl over 1f out: rdn over 1f out: kpt on ins fnl f to go 3rd towards fin: no threat to wnr* **8/1**
4224 **4** *nk* **Desert Sunrise**[12] 8016 2-9-0 70..................................... DavidProbert 3 64
(Sir Michael Stoute) *led: rdn and hrd pressed ent fnl 2f: hdd jst ins fnl f: no ex and lost 2 pls ins fnl f* **5/1[2]**
4 **5** *½* **Gebayl**[43] 7613 2-9-0 0... JoeFanning 11 63
(James Tate) *t.k.h: chsd ldr: rdn and ev ch 2f out: no ex over 1f out: wknd ins fnl f* **10/1**
6 **6** *nk* **Lucilla**[35] 7706 2-9-0 0... KieranO'Neill 12 62+
(Paul Howling) *stdd and swtchd lft after s: hld up in rr: stl plenty to do and effrt over 1f out: styd on ins fnl f: nvr trbld ldrs* **50/1**
5 **7** *1* **Last Hooray**[14] 7987 2-9-0 0... LiamKeniry 6 59
(David Elsworth) *in tch in midfield: rdn and no imp over 2f out: kpt on same pce u.p fr over 1f out* **5/1[2]**
8 *½* **Tammuz (IRE)** 2-9-0 0.. WilliamCarson 8 58+
(Tony Carroll) *stdd s: hld up in rr: rdn and effrt over 1f out: kpt on ins fnl f: nvr trbld ldrs* **50/1**
9 *shd* **Flirtini** 2-9-0 0..[1] RobertHavlin 1 58
(John Gosden) *dwlt: sn in tch in midfield: rdn and unable qck over 2f out: kpt on same pce and no imp fr over 1f out* **6/1[3]**
0 **10** *nk* **Woodland Fleur**[21] 7894 2-9-0 0...................................... LukeMorris 7 57
(Tony Carroll) *hld up in tch in midfield: rdn and outpcd over 2f out: plugged on same pce and no threat to ldrs fr over 1f out* **100/1**
11 *8* **Club Electra (IRE)** 2-9-0 0.. MartinLane 9 36
(Tobias B P Coles) *dwlt and swtchd lft after s: in tch towards rr: rdn over 3f out: wknd over 1f out* **50/1**

0 **12** 2 ½ **Nelson's Muse**[4] 8134 2-9-0 0 StevieDonohoe 10 30
(Tobias B P Coles) *dwlt: swtchd lft after s: in tch towards rr: rdn over 2f out: rn green and hung bdly rt bnd 2f out: bhd after* **100/1**

1m 25.31s (0.51) **Going Correction** +0.05s/f (Slow) 12 Ran SP% **121.1**
Speed ratings (Par 93): **99,97,95,94,94 93,92,92,91,91 82,79**
Tote swingers 1&2 £4.60, 1&3 £8.20, 2&3 £3.20 CSF £28.37 TOTE £13.90: £4.20, £1.30, £2.00; EX 40.10 Trifecta £277.00 Pool: £901.45 - 2.44 winning units..
Owner P C F Racing Ltd **Bred** Cranford Stud **Trained** Dogmersfield, Hampshire

FOCUS
Just a modest maiden.

NOTEBOOK
Lucky Di, who probably only had to run to a mark in the low-70s to win, picked up well from the turn in and clearly appreciated the return to Polytrack. Her trainer plans to bring her back here for a nursery under a penalty on New Year's Eve. (op 12-1)
Iridescence had her chance in the straight but still looked quite green and took her time to pick up. Judged on her first two efforts a mile should suit her. (op 6-4)
Bouyrin(IRE) was alongside the winner turning in but she swung widest of all off the bend while the winner saved ground, nipping through on the inside. She can go the handicap route now and might have more to offer in that sphere. (tchd 10-1)
Desert Sunrise is thoroughly exposed and not as good as her official mark of 70 would suggest. (op 7-2)
Gebayl improved on her debut effort. (op 12-1)
Lucilla ◆ shaped much better than the bare form suggests having been given plenty to do. (op 66-1)
Last Hooray didn't really improve for the extra furlong. (op 9-2 tchd 4-1 and 6-1)
Flirtini, who's a half-sister to four winners including Irish 2000 Guineas winner Power and Ribblesdale winner Thakafaat, didn't show a great deal, but is entitled to improve for the run. (op 8-1)

8172 BRITISH STALLION STUDS E.B.F./32RED CASINO MAIDEN STKS 7f (P)
2:00 (2:01) (Class 5) 2-Y-O £3,340 (£986; £493) **Stalls** Low

Form RPR
00 **1** **King Of The Danes**[42] 7627 2-9-0 0 JoeFanning 3 69+
(Mark Johnston) *sn led and mde rest: rdn 2f out: styd on wl u.p fnl f* **5/1**[3]
05 **2** ½ **Sabre Rock**[42] 7627 2-9-0 0 RobertWinston 6 68+
(John Best) *chsd wnr: rdn and ev ch 2f out: unable qck ent fnl f: kpt on again towards fin* **3/1**[2]
3 **3** 1 **You're The Boss**[216] 2193 2-9-0 0 JamieSpencer 2 65+
(Ed Walker) *chsd ldng pair: rdn and unable qck over 1f out: kpt on ins fnl f but nvr gng pce to chal* **4/6**[1]
0 **4** 4 **The Ginger Berry**[62] 7191 2-9-0 0 RobertHavlin 4 55
(Dr Jon Scargill) *hld up in tch in midfield: rdn and outpcd over 1f out: wknd 1f out* **100/1**
5 3 ¼ **Desert Donkey** 2-9-0 0 DavidProbert 5 47
(Andrew Balding) *hld up in tch in last pair: rdn and outpcd ent fnl 2f: wknd jst over 1f out* **10/1**
6 9 **Master Hamilton** 2-9-0 0 MartinLane 1 23
(Tobias B P Coles) *in tch in last pair: rdn 1/2-way: wknd 2f out: bhd fnl f* **33/1**

1m 25.77s (0.97) **Going Correction** +0.05s/f (Slow) 6 Ran SP% **114.7**
Speed ratings (Par 96): **96,95,94,89,86 75**
Tote swingers 1&2 £1.70, 1&3 £1.60, 2&3 £1.80 CSF £20.86 TOTE £6.70: £2.50, £1.40; EX 24.90 Trifecta £41.50 Pool: £1,072.35 - 19.36 winning units..
Owner Newsells Park Stud **Bred** Newsells Park Stud **Trained** Middleham Moor, N Yorks

FOCUS
With the favourite disappointing, this didn't take a lot of winning.

NOTEBOOK
King Of The Danes improved from his debut to his second start, and this was another step up. A half-brother to six winners including Group 1 Sun Chariot Stakes winner Spinning Queen, he can't be given too stiff a mark on the back of this and should have more to offer. (op 7-1)
Sabre Rock finished three lengths in front of King Of The Danes at Kempton last time, but couldn't confirm the form. Like the winner, handicaps are now open to him. (op 4-1 tchd 9-2)
You're The Boss has had his injury problems and simply didn't run to the level of his debut effort at Newmarket back in May. His trainer considered him a potential Royal Ascot type back then, and, while this run can be expected to bring him on, it might be worth being cautious as to what to expect next time. (op 4-7 tchd 1-2)
The Ginger Berry ran a lot better than on his debut and at least looks to be going the right way.

8173 32REDBET.COM CLASSIFIED (S) STKS 1m 2f (P)
2:35 (2:37) (Class 6) 3-Y-0+ £1,704 (£503; £251) **Stalls** Low

Form RPR
0242 **1** **Resplendent Alpha**[7] 8079 8-9-4 63 LeonnaMayor(5) 3 70
(Jamie Osborne) *hld up in tch in last: hdwy to chse ldrs 2f out: rdn and ev ch 1f out: kpt on fnl 100yds to ld last strides* **9/4**[2]
0140 **2** shd **Bert The Alert**[21] 7892 4-9-9 70 GeorgeBaker 5 70
(Gary Moore) *stdd after s: hld up in tch in last pair: hdwy to chse ldr jst over 2f out: ev ch and carried rt over 1f out: led ins fnl f: drvn fnl 100yds: hdd last stride* **4/6**[1]
5036 **3** 1 ¾ **Anychanceofabirdie (USA)**[12] 8019 3-9-0 58 MartinLane 2 60
(David Simcock) *led: rdn ent fnl 2f: edgd rt u.p over 1f: hdd ins fnl f: styd on same pce after* **5/1**[3]
0060 **4** 12 **Carlton Scroop (FR)**[14] 8001 9-8-10 44 (p) JakePayne(7) 4 38
(Paddy Butler) *chsd ldr: rdn over 3f out: lost pl 2f out: wknd over 1f out* **33/1**
0/00 **5** 5 **Bravo Belle (IRE)**[9] 8055 5-9-0 27 RyanPowell(3) 1 28
(Paddy Butler) *t.k.h: chsd ldng pair: rdn and struggling over 2f out: wknd wl over 1f out* **100/1**

2m 8.09s (1.49) **Going Correction** +0.05s/f (Slow)
WFA 3 from 4yo+ 3lb 5 Ran SP% **111.4**
Speed ratings (Par 101): **96,95,94,84,80**
CSF £4.18 TOTE £2.90: £1.20, £1.30; EX 4.20 Trifecta £8.30 Pool: £1,243.76 - 111.70 winning units..There was no bid for the winner.
Owner Leslie Marshall **Bred** Sunley Stud **Trained** Upper Lambourn, Berks

FOCUS
Not a strong race, but a good finish.

8174 32RED H'CAP 1m 2f (P)
3:10 (3:10) (Class 4) (0-85,82) 3-Y-0+ £4,075 (£1,212; £606; £303) **Stalls** Low

Form RPR
2430 **1** **Kaafel (IRE)**[91] 6376 3-9-4 82 JimCrowley 7 89
(Peter Hedger) *in tch: rdn and effrt to chse ldr wl over 1f out: hrd drvn and styd on wl ins fnl f to ld on post* **8/1**
-441 **2** shd **Cayuga**[119] 5482 3-9-3 81 DavidProbert 4 88
(Brett Johnson) *chsd ldrs tl wnt 2nd 5f out: rdn to ld on inner over 2f out: drvn over 1f out: kpt on wl whn hrd pressed ins fnl f: hdd on post* **10/1**
-355 **3** ¾ **Ajeeb (USA)**[14] 7999 4-9-5 80 AdamKirby 8 86
(David Simcock) *hld up in tch in last quartet: rdn and hdwy to chse ldrs wl over 1f out: kpt on u.p ins fnl f* **7/2**[1]
4046 **4** 2 ¼ **Tuscania**[14] 7986 4-9-6 81 LukeMorris 1 82
(Lucy Wadham) *chsd ldrs: rdn over 2f out: pressing ldrs and drvn over 1f out: no ex ins fnl f: wknd fnl 75yds* **6/1**[3]
2215 **5** ½ **Odin (IRE)**[68] 7034 4-9-5 80 JamieSpencer 3 80
(Don Cantillon) *hld up in tch towards rr: switching rt over 2f out: hdwy over 1f out: styd on ins fnl f: nvr looked like rching ldrs* **4/1**[2]
04-2 **6** ½ **Noguchi (IRE)**[12] 8019 7-9-3 78 TomMcLaughlin 9 77
(Michael Murphy) *dwlt and bustled along leaving stalls: in tch in last pair: rdn and effrt on outer ent fnl 2f: kpt on ins fnl f: nvr trbld ldrs* **6/1**[3]
1-05 **7** 4 **Parigino (FR)**[14] 7986 4-9-2 77 JoeFanning 12 69
(Nick Gifford) *hld up in tch in midfield: rdn and effrt ent fnl 2f: outpcd and swtchd rt over 1f out: no imp after* **8/1**
3-00 **8** ¾ **Wilfred Pickles (IRE)**[41] 7645 6-9-5 80 EddieAhern 13 70
(Jo Crowley) *stdd and dropped in bhd after s: hld up in rr: hmpd over 3f out: sme hdwy over 1f out: hung lft and no imp 1f out: n.d* **16/1**
3000 **9** ¾ **My Lord**[31] 7147 4-8-8 72 RaulDaSilva(3) 2 61
(Luke Dace) *led tl hdd and rdn over 2f out: wknd over 1f out* **33/1**
3-00 **10** 3 ½ **Six Silver Lane**[14] 7986 4-9-1 76 MartinDwyer 6 58
(Derek Shaw) *in tch in midfield: rdn and lost pl over 2f out: bhd over 1f out* **50/1**
5000 **11** 5 **Emma's Gift (IRE)**[21] 7904 4-9-0 82 ShelleyBirkett(7) 5 55
(Julia Feilden) *chsd ldr untl 5f out: styd chsng ldrs tl rdn and lost pl wl over 2f out: bhd over 1f out* **14/1**

2m 3.75s (-2.85) **Going Correction** +0.05s/f (Slow)
WFA 3 from 4yo+ 3lb 11 Ran SP% **119.6**
Speed ratings (Par 105): **113,112,112,110,110 109,106,105,105,102 98**
Tote swingers 1&2 £10.40, 1&3 £7.00, 2&3 £7.70 CSF £86.88 CT £335.38 TOTE £15.60: £4.40, £3.80, £1.40; EX 91.50 Trifecta £368.90 Part won. Pool: £491.88 - 0.30 winning units..
Owner P C F Racing Ltd **Bred** Shadwell Estate Company Limited **Trained** Dogmersfield, Hampshire
■ Stewards' Enquiry : David Probert two-day ban; used whip above permitted level (2nd,3rd Jan).

FOCUS
A good, competitive handicap, run at a fair gallop, and the two 3yos in the field came to the fore.

8175 £32 BONUS AT 32RED.COM APPRENTICE H'CAP 1m 4f (P)
3:40 (3:40) (Class 5) (0-70,70) 3-Y-0+ £2,385 (£704; £352) **Stalls** Low

Form RPR
6242 **1** **English Summer**[4] 8136 5-9-5 70 (t) AliceHaynes(5) 2 76
(David Simcock) *t.k.h: chsd ldrs tl wnt 2nd 9f out: rdn to ld on inner 2f out: edgd rt and kpt on u.p fnl f* **5/4**[1]
4323 **2** ¾ **Laser Blazer**[26] 7839 4-9-8 68 (p) RaulDaSilva 4 73
(Jeremy Gask) *led and set stdy gallop: hld and rdn 2f out: sltly outpcd over 1f out: rallied and carried rt ins fnl f: kpt on* **7/2**[2]
3605 **3** ½ **Foxhaven**[12] 8019 10-9-3 68 (v) ThomasBrown(5) 6 72
(Patrick Chamings) *t.k.h: chsd ldrs: wnt 2nd 10f out tl 9f out: rdn and ev ch 2f out: sltly outpcd over 1f out: rallied and carried rt ins fnl f: kpt on* **12/1**
5012 **4** ½ **Strike Force**[12] 8023 8-9-3 68 (t) NatashaEaton(5) 5 71
(Alison Hutchinson) *t.k.h: chsd ldr for 2f: stdd bk but stl wl in tch towards rr: rdn and effrt but wd bnd 2f out: kpt on ins fnl f* **8/1**
2225 **5** ¾ **Rowan Ridge**[106] 5908 4-9-3 68 (v) PatMillman(5) 7 70
(William Knight) *stdd s: hld up in tch in rr: effrt to press ldrs but wdst of ldng gp bnd 2f out: outpcd wl over 1f out: rallied and styd on ins fnl f* **10/1**
2160 **6** ½ **Shalambar (IRE)**[21] 7892 6-9-0 67 AidenBlakemore(7) 3 69
(Tony Carroll) *dwlt: hld up wl in tch in last pair: rdn and outpcd over 2f out: rallied and styd on ins fnl f* **25/1**
321 **7** ½ **The Wonga Coup (IRE)**[16] 7960 5-8-10 61 JakePayne(5) 8 62+
(Pat Phelan) *chsd ldrs: jnd ldrs 3f out: rdn and ev ch 2f out: outpcd over 1f out: no ex and hld whn nt clr run ins fnl f: eased towards fin* **6/1**[3]

2m 34.63s (1.63) **Going Correction** +0.05s/f (Slow)
WFA 3 from 4yo+ 5lb 7 Ran SP% **112.7**
Speed ratings (Par 103): **96,95,95,94,94 94,93**
Tote swingers 1&2 £1.80, 1&3 £4.70, 2&3 £8.40 CSF £5.50 CT £32.55 TOTE £2.90: £2.10, £3.90; EX 6.60 Trifecta £36.80 Pool: £1,023.30 - 20.83 winning units..
Owner Dr Marwan Koukash **Bred** Juddmonte Farms Ltd **Trained** Newmarket, Suffolk

FOCUS
They went no pace here and it developed into a sprint from the turn in.
T/Plt: £41.70 to a £1 stake. Pool: £51,194.05 - 895.68 winning units T/Qpdt: £10.60 to a £1 stake. Pool: £4,121.78 - 286.9 winning units SP

8130 DEAUVILLE (R-H)
Wednesday, December 19

OFFICIAL GOING: Fibresand: standard

8176a PRIX DE LA CHARENTONNE (MAIDEN) (2YO COLTS & GELDINGS) (FIBRESAND) 7f 110y
10:20 (12:00) 2-Y-O **£10,000** (£4,000; £3,000; £2,000; £1,000)

RPR
1 **Panama (FR)** 2-8-11 0 AntoineHamelin 11 74
(Mme Pia Brandt, France) **89/10**
2 2 ½ **Le Deluge (FR)**[44] 7597 2-9-2 0 JohanVictoire 16 73
(John Best) *broke wl to r 3rd on outside: sent into ld after 2f: established clr ld bef st: wnt wl clr 1 1/2f out: hdd 100yds out: styd on wl* **10/1**
3 nk **Algar (FR)** 2-9-2 0 JulienAuge 3 72
(C Ferland, France) **11/2**[2]
4 snk **Avanzini (USA)** 2-8-11 0 GregoryBenoist 9 67
(G Botti, Italy) **9/2**[1]
5 snk **Habeshia**[40] 7683 2-9-2 0 Pierre-CharlesBoudot 13 72
(John Best) *settled in 2nd: relegated to 3rd bef st: rdn 2f out: styd on u.p fnl f* **24/1**
6 1 ¼ **Hamatan (FR)**[29] 2-9-2 0 FabienLefebvre 4 69
(J E Hammond, France) **9/2**[1]
7 hd **Hubris (FR)**[14] 2-9-2 0 AnthonyCrastus 1 68
(J-L Pelletan, France) **48/1**
8 ½ **Rodion Raskolnikov (FR)**[37] 2-8-13 0 MarcLerner(3) 2 67
(C Lerner, France) **13/1**
9 ½ **Heartbreak City (FR)** 2-9-2 0 TheoBachelot 8 66
(S Wattel, France) **11/1**
10 7 **Tokum (FR)** 2-8-11 0 TonyPiccone 12 44
(N Bertran De Balanda, France) **42/1**

0			**Pangaea Prince (IRE)**[37] 2-9-2 0 ... MaximeGuyon 15 (A Fabre, France) **68/10**[3]
0			**El Negrito (FR)** 2-8-11 0 ... DavidMichaux 14 (J-L Pelletan, France) **60/1**
0			**Blacksou (FR)** 2-8-11 0 ... RonanThomas 10 (P Adda, France) **22/1**
0			**Big Jones (FR)** 2-8-11 0 ... ThomasMessina 7 (Mlle M-L Mortier, France) **41/1**
0			**Recurrens (FR)** 2-8-11 0 ... AnthonyClement 5 (A Clement, France) **63/1**

1m 31.4s (91.40) **15** Ran SP% **117.5**
WIN (incl. 1 euro stake): 9.90. PLACES: 3.00, 3.10, 2.30. DF: 53.30. SF: 133.00.
Owner Ecurie Des Monceaux **Bred** Ecurie Des Monceaux **Trained** France

8161 KEMPTON (A.W) (R-H)
Thursday, December 20

OFFICIAL GOING: Standard
Wind: Moderate across

8177 32REDBINGO.COM CLAIMING STKS 1m (P)
4:00 (4:00) (Class 6) 3-Y-O **£1,617** (£481; £240; £120) **Stalls** Low

Form				RPR
6021	1		**Mr Knightley (IRE)**[8] 8074 3-9-3 65 ...(b) JimCrowley 5 (Jim Boyle) *stdd and hld up in rr: stdy hdwy to ld on bridle appr fnl f: v easily* **4/5**[1]	78+
00	2	1 ½	**Balmoral Castle**[35] 7729 3-8-9 0 ... JohnFahy 7 (Jonathan Portman) *sn slt ld but jnd over 5f out tl def advantage wl over 2f out: hdd wl over 1f out and dropped to 4th: kpt on again for wl hld 2nd clsng stages* **50/1**	61?
0445	3	shd	**The Noble Ord**[8] 8074 3-8-8 62 ...(t) MartinDwyer 1 (Sylvester Kirk) *chsd ldrs: rdn to chal fr wl over 2f out to appr fnl f: kpt on same pce* **6/1**[3]	60
4	4	2 ¾	**Veyepea**[16] 7981 3-7-11 0 ow1 ... LouisSteward(7) 3 (Sylvester Kirk) *in rr but in tch: hdwy over 2f out to ld wl over 1f out tl appr fnl f: sn btn* **14/1**	49
0-00	5	2 ¼	**Electrician**[13] 8019 3-8-9 73 ...(p[1]) DavidProbert 2 (Tim Pitt) *chsd ldrs: rdn over 2f out: wknd appr fnl f* **5/1**[2]	49
6453	6	3 ½	**Amis Reunis**[15] 7992 3-8-0 60 ... RyanTate(7) 6 (Anthony Carson) *chsd ldrs: rdn over 2f out: wknd wl over 1f out* **8/1**	38
4600	7	9	**Barnacle**[11] 8050 3-8-10 49 ...(b) JimmyQuinn 4 (Pat Eddery) *drvn to press ldr over 5f out: rdn 3f out: wknd appr fnl 2f* **25/1**	20

1m 39.2s (-0.60) **Going Correction** -0.10s/f (Stan) **7** Ran SP% **110.1**
Speed ratings (Par 98): **99,97,97,94,92 88,79**
Tote swingers 1&2 £7.30, 1&3 £1.60, 2&3 £12.70 CSF £42.82 TOTE £1.70: £1.60, £11.90; EX 31.30 Trifecta £155.60 Pool: £2,426.46 - 11.69 winning units.
Owner The 'In Recovery' Partnership **Bred** Miss Deirdre Cogan **Trained** Epsom, Surrey

FOCUS
A moderate claimer.

8178 32REDPOKER.COM MEDIAN AUCTION MAIDEN STKS 1m (P)
4:30 (4:37) (Class 6) 2-Y-O **£1,617** (£481; £240; £120) **Stalls** Low

Form				RPR
0	1		**St Paul De Vence (IRE)**[180] 3368 2-9-3 0 ... ChrisCatlin 3 (Paul Cole) *chsd ldrs: pushed along 2f out: str run to chal 1f out and sn led: r.o strly* **4/1**[3]	77+
43	2	1 ¾	**Captain Starlight (IRE)**[21] 7924 2-9-3 0 ... EddieAhern 1 (Jo Crowley) *trckd ldrs: qcknd to trck ldr ins fnl 2f: chal 1f out but sn outpcd by wnr: kpt on wl for 2nd* **7/4**[1]	72
	3	2 ½	**Rouge Nuage (IRE)** 2-9-3 0 ... MartinDwyer 8 (Conrad Allen) *s.i.s: in rr tl styd on fr 2f out: shkn up and r.o strly to take 3rd clsng stages* **8/1**	66+
6	4	1	**Camachoice (IRE)**[17] 7963 2-9-3 0 ...(t) JimmyQuinn 11 (Marco Botti) *chsd ldrs: led over 2f out: hdd 1f out: sn btn* **10/1**	64
0022	5	4	**Marvelino**[109] 5854 2-9-3 68 ... RobertWinston 4 (Pat Eddery) *t.k.h: trckd ldrs: rdn and wknd fnl f* **3/1**[2]	55
	6	¾	**Gunning For Glory** 2-9-3 0 ... StevieDonohoe 10 (Martin Bosley) *s.i.s: in rr: pushed along 2f out and sme hdwy: sn one pce* **50/1**	53
00	7	¾	**Jd Rockefeller**[21] 7924 2-8-10 0 ... LouisSteward(7) 5 (Paul D'Arcy) *in rr: sme hdwy over 2f out: shkn up and no prog sn after* **33/1**	51
0	8	3	**Hail To Princess**[21] 7924 2-8-12 0 ... JimCrowley 7 (Patrick Chamings) *in rr: sme hdwy over 2f out: green: edgd rt and btn over 1f out* **14/1**	39
06	9	6	**Ocean Power (IRE)**[29] 7806 2-9-3 0 ... FergusSweeney 2 (Richard Phillips) *led tl hdd over 2f out: sn btn* **50/1**	31

1m 40.29s (0.49) **Going Correction** -0.10s/f (Stan) **9** Ran SP% **115.1**
Speed ratings (Par 94): **93,91,88,87,83 83,82,79,73**
Tote swingers 1&2 £2.70, 1&3 £5.90, 2&3 £4.00 CSF £11.26 TOTE £3.60: £1.40, £1.10, £2.20; EX 14.10 Trifecta £51.10 Pool: £2,789.36 - 40.86 winning units.
Owner Sir M Arbib, C Wright & PFI Cole Ltd **Bred** John Connaughton **Trained** Whatcombe, Oxon

FOCUS
The time was the slowest of five races at the trip.

NOTEBOOK
St Paul De Vence(IRE), who showed ability in the Chesham on his only previous start, was on and off the bridle but gradually got the idea and created quite a good impression. He can improve again. (op 5-2 tchd 9-2)
Captain Starlight(IRE), who was reluctant to enter the stalls and again carried his head high, got there soon enough yet wasn't asked for everything until late on and the winner swept by with all the momentum inside the final furlong. This wasn't a good ride, but he looks a tricky customer. Handicaps are now an option. (op 9-4)
Rouge Nuage(IRE), a 5,500euros gelded brother to 7f-1m winners Angelena Ballerina and Itzakindamagic (also half-brother to a few other winners), started sluggishly and ran green, but he finished nicely. He's open to plenty of improvement. (tchd 9-1)
Camachoice(IRE), well beaten over C&D on his debut, raced freely without cover early on and didn't see his race out. (tchd 9-1)
Marvelino spread a plate before he reached the start.Up in trip after 109 days off, he raced keenly and didn't stay. (op 7-2)
Jd Rockefeller finished up well beaten, but he travelled like he has ability and can now switch to handicaps. (tchd 25-1)

8179 32REDBET.COM H'CAP (DIV I) 1m (P)
5:00 (5:05) (Class 6) (0-55,55) 3-Y-O+ **£1,617** (£481; £240; £120) **Stalls** Low

Form				RPR
0020	1		**Bahri Sheen (IRE)**[29] 7816 4-9-5 53 ... GeorgeBaker 3 (John Best) *hld up in rr: stdy hdwy on ins to ld over 1f out: drvn out* **12/1**	65
31	2	½	**Norwegian Reward (IRE)**[12] 8038 4-9-4 52 ... MartinDwyer 6 (Michael Wigham) *in tch: hdwy over 2f out to chse wnr appr fnl f: kpt on u.p but a hld* **11/10**[1]	63
5000	3	5	**Petersboden**[30] 5037 3-8-12 47 ... FergusSweeney 9 (Michael Blanshard) *chsd ldrs: rdn over 2f out: styd on fnl f: no ch w ldng duo* **20/1**	46
0323	4	2 ¼	**Silly Billy (IRE)**[12] 8039 4-9-1 54 ...(v) JemmaMarshall(5) 13 (Pat Phelan) *pressed ldr tl led over 2f out: hdd wl over 1f out: wknd fnl f* **10/1**	48
006	5	1 ¼	**Carpentras**[91] 6396 4-9-3 51 ...(b) RobertHavlin 1 (Dr Jon Scargill) *chsd ldrs: rdn over 2f out: btn over 1f out* **25/1**	42
2003	6	½	**Querido (GER)**[29] 7816 8-8-13 52 ...(tp) WilliamTwiston-Davies(5) 2 (Paddy Butler) *in rr: hdwy over 2f out: no prog fr over 1f out* **16/1**	42
2024	7	2	**Exopuntia**[8] 8083 6-9-4 52 ... AdamBeschizza 5 (Julia Feilden) *in rr: styd on fr over 1f out: nvr a threat* **8/1**[3]	38
0066	8	3 ¼	**Snowy Valley**[17] 7960 3-9-2 54 ... RyanPowell(3) 7 (Simon Earle) *in rr: sme late prog* **12/1**	32
000P	9	hd	**Dichoh**[7] 8099 9-9-2 50 ...(v) JamieGoldstein 10 (Michael Madgwick) *chsd ldrs: rdn 3f out: wknd 2f out* **33/1**	28
0000	10	¾	**Not My Choice (IRE)**[9] 8062 7-9-1 49 ...(tp) J-PGuillambert 4 (Paul Howling) *sn slt ld: hdd over 2f out and sn btn* **33/1**	25
0450	11	1	**Trevose (IRE)**[48] 7527 3-9-5 54 ... TomEaves 8 (Roy Brotherton) *a towards rr* **66/1**	28
/450	12	2 ¾	**Mutanaker**[180] 3392 5-9-7 55 ...(p) LiamKeniry 12 (Ed de Giles) *sn towards rr* **25/1**	22
0012	13	17	**Ensnare**[5] 8131 7-9-6 54 ... StevieDonohoe 14 (Willie Musson) *unruly in stalls: sn wl bhd* **7/1**[2]	

1m 38.86s (-0.94) **Going Correction** -0.10s/f (Stan)
WFA 3 from 4yo+ 1lb **13** Ran SP% **121.4**
Speed ratings (Par 101): **100,99,94,92,91 90,88,85,85,84 83,80,63**
Tote swingers 1&2 £4.20, 1&3 £50.40, 2&3 £10.40 CSF £24.21 CT £303.72 TOTE £17.80: £4.00, £1.30, £8.10; EX 40.40 Trifecta £1478.30 Part won. Pool: £1,971.11 - 0.30 winning units..

Owner Kingsgate Racing 2 **Bred** J Cullinan **Trained** Hucking, Kent

FOCUS
The lead was disputed by Silly Billy and Not My Choice and this set up for the closers.
Bahri Sheen(IRE) Official explanation: trainer's rep said, regarding apparent improvement in form, that the gelding had settled better.
Snowy Valley Official explanation: jockey said gelding hung left
Ensnare Official explanation: jockey said gelding became upset in stalls and never travelled; trainer said gelding was found to have a cut above its eye following morning

8180 32REDBET.COM H'CAP (DIV II) 1m (P)
5:30 (5:33) (Class 6) (0-55,55) 3-Y-O+ **£1,617** (£481; £240; £120) **Stalls** Low

Form				RPR
/-00	1		**Aegean King**[15] 7992 6-9-1 49 ... JimCrowley 4 (Michael Wigham) *in rr: gd hdwy over 1f out: drvn and str run to ld fnl 110yds: kpt on wl* **8/1**	57
4000	2	nk	**Signora Frasi (IRE)**[63] 7200 7-9-5 53 ... FergusSweeney 12 (Tony Newcombe) *in rr: drvn and gd hdwy over 1f out: styd on wl fnl f to chse wnr clsng stages: nt quite get up* **12/1**	60+
-600	3	¾	**Teth**[22] 7906 3-8-11 53 ... RobertTart(7) 13 (Anthony Carson) *chsd ldrs: drvn to ld 1f out: hdd and outpcd fnl 110yds* **10/1**	58
0133	4	½	**Precision Five**[16] 7983 3-9-2 51 ...(p) LukeMorris 11 (Jeremy Gask) *in rr: drvn over 1f out: str run ins fnl f: fin wl* **11/2**[1]	55+
0000	5	1 ½	**Fleetwoodsands (IRE)**[22] 7906 5-9-5 53 ...(t) LiamKeniry 10 (Milton Bradley) *in rr: hdwy appr fnl f: styd on wl clsng stages* **8/1**	54
0034	6	2 ½	**Huzzah (IRE)**[7] 8099 7-9-2 50 ...(p) MichaelStainton 5 (Paul Howling) *pressed ldr after 2f tl over 2f out: wknd over 1f out* **7/1**[3]	45
0360	7	nse	**Play The Blues (IRE)**[17] 7964 5-8-11 52 ...(t) NedCurtis(7) 1 (Roger Curtis) *sn slt ld but hrd pressed tl pushed clr over 2f out: hdd 1f out and wknd qckly* **33/1**	47
4622	8	5	**Ermyn Flyer**[12] 8038 3-8-13 53 ... JemmaMarshall(5) 8 (Pat Phelan) *in rr: hdwy 3f out: wknd over 1f out* **6/1**[2]	36
0405	9	nk	**Pose (IRE)**[12] 8036 5-8-12 46 oh1 ...(t) AdamBeschizza 3 (Roger Ingram) *in rr: sme hdwy ins fnl 2f: nvr rchd ldrs* **33/1**	28
00-5	10	14	**Compton Bell**[29] 7815 3-9-5 54 ...(t) GeorgeBaker 9 (Hans Adielsson) *hld up in mid-div: fdd wl over 2f out* **6/1**[2]	
2600	11	5	**Gower Rules (IRE)**[168] 3782 4-9-0 53 ... WilliamTwiston-Davies(5) 7 (John Bridger) *a towards rr* **10/1**	
0060	12	¾	**Smirfy's Silver**[27] 7841 8-9-6 54 ... JoeFanning 2 (Michael Mullineaux) *chsd ldrs tl wknd qckly 3f out* **16/1**	
0005	13	1	**Great Charm (IRE)**[9] 8062 7-9-2 55 ... HarryPoulton(5) 14 (Sheena West) *chsd ldrs to 3f out* **33/1**	
000	14	15	**Cape Sky**[66] 7112 5-8-12 46 ... ChrisCatlin 6 (Roy Brotherton) *slowly away: sn t.o* **50/1**	

1m 39.12s (-0.68) **Going Correction** -0.10s/f (Stan)
WFA 3 from 4yo+ 1lb **14** Ran SP% **121.2**
Speed ratings (Par 101): **99,98,97,97,95 93,93,88,88,74 69,68,67,52**
Tote swingers 1&2 £21.40, 1&3 £21.80, 2&3 £35.40 CSF £98.39 CT £1009.09 TOTE £7.80: £2.40, £4.80, £6.40; EX 146.60 TRIFECTA Not won..
Owner D Hassan **Bred** Theobalds Stud **Trained** Newmarket, Suffolk
■ Stewards' Enquiry : Robert Tart two-day ban: used whip above permitted level (Jan 3-4)

FOCUS
Like in the first division, a couple of these took each other on, namely Huzzah and Play The Blues, and those ridden patiently were favoured.
Aegean King Official explanation: trainer said, regarding apparent improvement in form, that the gelding was better suited by being covered up.
Compton Bell Official explanation: jockey said gelding hung badly left
Smirfy's Silver Official explanation: jockey said gelding moved poorly

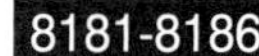

Cape Sky Official explanation: trainer said mare lost its action and was subsequently found to be lame behind

8181 32RED H'CAP 1m (P)
6:00 (6:01) (Class 4) (0-85,84) 3-Y-0+ **£4,075** (£1,212; £606; £303) **Stalls** Low

Form RPR
451 **1** **Guest Of Honour (IRE)**[33] 7782 3-9-1 **79**.......................... AdamKirby 7 91+
(Marco Botti) *trckd ldrs: drvn to ld 1f out: readily* **9/4**[1]
2102 **2** *2* **Multi Bene**[27] 7842 3-9-2 **80**.......................... GrahamGibbons 3 87+
(Ed McMahon) *chsd ldr: led over 2f out: sn rdn: hdd 1f out: kpt on but nt pce of wnr* **11/4**[3]
2160 **3** *1* **Buckland (IRE)**[5] 8142 4-8-5 **73**.......................... NicoleNordblad(5) 5 78
(Hans Adielsson) *in rr: swtchd lft ins fnl 2f: shkn up and hdwy on outside fnl f: kpt on to take 3rd cl home* **25/1**
1242 **4** *hd* **Light From Mars**[31] 7788 7-8-9 **77**.......................... WilliamTwiston-Davies(5) 8 81
(Ronald Harris) *in tch: pushed along over 2f out: kpt on to press for 3rd clsng stages but no ch w wnr* **16/1**
4325 **5** *nk* **Bank On Me**[7] 8095 3-9-3 **84**.......................... RaulDaSilva(3) 1 88
(Philip McBride) *sn led: rdn and hdd over 2f out: outpcd fnl f* **5/2**[2]
2126 **6** *1* **Saharia (IRE)**[28] 7823 5-9-3 **80**..........................(v) ShaneKelly 2 81
(Michael Attwater) *s.i.s: in rr: sme hdwy fr 2f out: styd on same pce fnl f* **16/1**
0414 **7** *18* **George Baker (IRE)**[17] 7966 5-8-9 **72**.......................... JimCrowley 6 32
(George Baker) *chsd ldrs: rdn 2f out: sn btn: eased whn no ch* **8/1**

1m 37.57s (-2.23) **Going Correction** -0.10s/f (Stan)
WFA 3 from 4yo+ 1lb **7 Ran SP% 112.7**
Speed ratings (Par 105): **107,105,104,103,103 102,84**
Tote swingers 1&2 £1.50, 1&3 £11.80, 2&3 £16.20 CSF £8.49 CT £112.97 TOTE £1.80: £1.50, £2.50; EX 9.20 Trifecta £194.00 Pool: £1,286.20 - 4.97 winning units.
Owner Giuliano Manfredini **Bred** Azienda Agricola Gennaro Stimola **Trained** Newmarket, Suffolk

FOCUS
A fair handicap.
George Baker(IRE) Official explanation: jockey said gelding never travelled

8182 CONSTANTINE FETTEL & LINDA EMERY MEMORIAL H'CAP 1m 4f (P)
6:30 (6:30) (Class 5) (0-75,75) 3-Y-0 **£2,264** (£673; £336; £168) **Stalls** Centre

Form RPR
-334 **1** **Honour**[13] 8020 3-9-3 **71**.......................... DavidProbert 6 82
(Sir Michael Stoute) *sn trcking ldr: led 2f out: narrowly hdd 1f out: styd chalng and rallied to ld again last strides* **7/2**[2]
1023 **2** *shd* **Brimstone Hill (IRE)**[29] 7805 3-9-7 **75**.......................... WilliamCarson 4 86
(Anthony Carson) *hld up in rr but in tch: hdwy 2f out: drvn to take slt ld 1f out: rdn and rdr dropped reins fnl 100yds: hdd last strides* **9/4**[1]
61 **3** *6* **Purple 'n Gold (IRE)**[36] 7702 3-8-13 **70**..........................(v) SimonPearce(3) 3 71
(David Pipe) *in tch: chsd 2f out: chsd ldng duo over 1f out: sn outpcd into wl-hld 3rd* **9/1**
1000 **4** *3 ½* **Sir Dylan**[11] 8048 3-8-5 **59**.......................... LukeMorris 1 55
(Ronald Harris) *in rr: rdn 2f out: chsd ldrs wl over 1f out: sn wknd* **16/1**
2220 **5** *1 ¼* **Elsie Bay**[33] 7768 3-8-1 **60**.......................... RachealKneller(5) 7 54
(Mark Usher) *in tch: chsd ldrs 1/2-way: wknd ins fnl 2f* **6/1**
6666 **6** *1* **Perfect Delight**[15] 8000 3-9-0 **75**.......................... RyanTate(7) 2 67
(Clive Cox) *chsd ldr: rdn over 2f out: sn wknd* **7/1**
3650 **7** *6* **Badea**[5] 8136 3-9-4 **72**..........................(v) JamieSpencer 5 55
(Richard Fahey) *led tl hdd 2f out sn wknd* **5/1**[3]

2m 32.23s (-2.27) **Going Correction** -0.10s/f (Stan) **7 Ran SP% 112.3**
Speed ratings (Par 102): **103,102,98,96,95 95,91**
Tote swingers 1&2 £3.30, 1&3 £3.40, 2&3 £4.00 CSF £11.37 TOTE £2.60: £2.30, £1.80; EX 10.90 Trifecta £35.90 Pool: £1,431.58 - 29.86 winning units.
Owner Cheveley Park Stud **Bred** Cheveley Park Stud Ltd **Trained** Newmarket, Suffolk

FOCUS
The pace was fair, thanks to the disappointing Badea, and the front two pulled clear, but this might not be form to get carried away with.

8183 32RED CASINO H'CAP 7f (P)
7:00 (7:01) (Class 5) (0-75,76) 3-Y-0 **£2,264** (£673; £336; £168) **Stalls** Low

Form RPR
1326 **1** **Atlantis Crossing (IRE)**[17] 7966 3-9-6 **73**.......................... JimCrowley 6 83
(Jim Boyle) *hld up in rr: pushed along and hdwy over 1f out: drvn and atrong run fnl f to ld fnl 100yds: won gng away* **6/1**[2]
11 **2** *2* **Haftohaf**[20] 7936 3-9-7 **74**.......................... AdamKirby 8 79
(Marco Botti) *chsd ldrs: rdn over 1f out: styd on fnl f to take 2nd nr fin but no ch w wnr* **4/6**[1]
4202 **3** *¾* **Exceedexpectations (IRE)**[15] 7998 3-9-1 **68**.......................... MartinLane 2 71
(Michael Bell) *chsd ldr tl drvn to ld over 2f out: kpt on fnl f tl hdd and outpcd fnl 100yds: lost 2nd nr fin* **14/1**
501 **4** *1 ¼* **Gabrial's Gift (IRE)**[10] 8058 3-9-9 **76** 6ex.......................... JamieSpencer 3 76
(Ian Williams) *chsd ldrs: drvn 2f out: outpcd fnl f* **10/1**[3]
31 **5** *nse* **Polar Venture**[22] 7903 3-9-0 **67**.......................... AdamBeschizza 5 66
(William Haggas) *chsd ldrs: rdn to dispute 3rd over 1f out: no ex ins fnl f* **10/1**[3]
0053 **6** *2* **Key Ambition**[10] 8058 3-9-5 **72**..........................(vt) SebSanders 4 66
(Garry Moss) *in rr: drvn and sme hdwy fr 2f out: no imp over 1f out* **20/1**
2302 **7** *1 ¼* **Travelling**[17] 7975 3-9-0 **67**.......................... WilliamCarson 1 58
(Tony Carroll) *in tch: and drvn over 2f out: no prog fr over 1f out* **25/1**
4003 **8** *11* **Abhaath (USA)**[8] 0077 3-9-0 **67**.......................... LukeMorris 9 28
(Ronald Harris) *rdn 3f out: a in rr* **25/1**
1130 **9** *1 ½* **Ziefhd**[50] 7483 3-9-5 **72**..........................(p) JoeFanning 7 29
(Tim McCarthy) *pressed ldr tl wknd over 2f out* **25/1**

1m 25.32s (-0.68) **Going Correction** -0.10s/f (Stan) **9 Ran SP% 115.4**
Speed ratings (Par 102): **99,96,95,94,94 92,90,78,76**
Tote swingers 1&2 £1.40, 1&3 £12.70, 2&3 £2.30 CSF £9.88 CT £51.69 TOTE £9.20: £1.60, £1.10, £3.50; EX 13.90 Trifecta £52.00 Pool: £1,416.65 - 20.41 winning units.
Owner The 'In Recovery' Partnership **Bred** J K Thoroughbreds & P Doyle Bloodstock **Trained** Epsom, Surrey

FOCUS
The pace looked modest.
Polar Venture Official explanation: jockey said gelding was struck into early stages and ran too freely

8184 32 BONUS H'CAP 6f (P)
7:30 (7:31) (Class 7) (0-50,54) 3-Y-0+ **£1,455** (£433; £216; £108) **Stalls** Low

Form RPR
2110 **1** **Pharoh Jake**[1] 8168 4-9-4 **54** 6ex.......................... WilliamTwiston-Davies(5) 5 64
(John Bridger) *towards rr: hdwy over 2f out: styd on appr fnl f: led fnl 110yds: drvn out* **7/2**[2]
1400 **2** *½* **Mucky Molly**[7] 8099 4-9-4 **49**..........................(v) SebSanders 2 57
(Alison Hutchinson) *chsd ldrs: drvn to ld 1f out: sn hrd pressed: hdd and no ex fnl 110yds* **16/1**
5604 **3** *hd* **Victorian Number (FR)**[56] 7362 4-9-4 **49**.......................... KirstyMilczarek 1 56
(Geoffrey Deacon) *sn led: rdn over 2f out: hdd 1f out: styd on same pce fnl 110yds* **3/1**[1]
0033 **4** *2* **Kerfuffle (IRE)**[1] 8168 3-8-13 **47**.......................... SimonPearce(3) 4 48
(Simon Dow) *in rr: rdn and hdwy fr 2f out: chsd ldrs fnl f but no imp* **4/1**[3]
0360 **5** *4* **Burnt Cream**[27] 7837 5-9-4 **49**..........................(t) StevieDonohoe 3 37
(Martin Bosley) *in tch: rdn over 2f out: wknd fnl f* **16/1**
3235 **6** *1 ¼* **Bobbyow**[243] 1516 4-9-4 **49**.......................... GeorgeBaker 7 33
(Terry Clement) *in rr: drvn and sme prog fr 2f out: no hdwy fnl f* **6/1**
3645 **7** *6* **Johnny Splash (IRE)**[15] 7988 3-9-4 **49**.......................... AdamKirby 6 14
(Roger Teal) *chsd ldr: rdn over 2f out: sn btn* **7/1**
000 **8** *nk* **Monty Fay (IRE)**[80] 0737 3-9-4 **49**..........................(tp) JohnFahy 0 13
(John Flint) *chsd ldrs: wknd over 2f out* **25/1**
5646 **9** *hd* **Blueberry Fizz (IRE)**[21] 7929 4-9-4 **49**..........................(v) JimCrowley 10 12
(John Ryan) *s.i.s: rdn: hung rt and no rspnse over 2f out* **12/1**
0000 **10** *1 ¾* **Smoky Cloud (IRE)**[15] 7993 5-9-5 **50**.......................... AdamBeschizza 9 8
(Dave Morris) *s.i.s: sn rcvrd to chse ldrs: wknd 2f out* **25/1**

1m 12.49s (-0.61) **Going Correction** -0.10s/f (Stan) **10 Ran SP% 121.2**
Speed ratings (Par 97): **100,99,99,96,91 89,81,81,80,78**
Tote swingers 1&2 £13.40, 1&3 £3.50, 2&3 £11.30 CSF £60.65 CT £188.50 TOTE £3.10: £1.90, £4.30, £1.80; EX 60.70 Trifecta £600.60 Part won. Pool: £800.80 - 0.41 winning units..
Owner The Hair & Haberdasher Partnership **Bred** J J Bridger **Trained** Liphook, Hants

FOCUS
A moderate sprint handicap.
Kerfuffle(IRE) Official explanation: jockey said filly was slowly away
Blueberry Fizz(IRE) Official explanation: vet said filly returned lame behind
T/Jkpt: Not won. T/Plt: £66.40 to a £1 stake. Pool: £70,659.19 - 776.55 winning units T/Qpdt: £41.40 to a £1 stake. Pool: £8,176.52 - 146.00 winning units ST

8168 LINGFIELD (L-H)
Thursday, December 20

OFFICIAL GOING: Standard
Wind: Moderate behind Weather: Havy cloud and raining

8185 32RED CASINO MAIDEN STKS 7f (P)
12:30 (12:30) (Class 5) 2-Y-0 **£2,264** (£673; £336; £168) **Stalls** Low

Form RPR
200 **1** **Intrepid (IRE)**[101] 6099 2-9-3 71.......................... JamieSpencer 7 76
(Jeremy Noseda) *sn led: shkn up and qcknd clr wl over 1f out: readily* **3/1**[2]
0 **2** *3 ¾* **Daring Dragon**[36] 7707 2-9-3 0..........................(b[1]) GeorgeBaker 2 66+
(Ed Walker) *hld up in rr: smooth hdwy 3f out: effrt on outer wl over 1f out: rdn and hung lft ins fnl f: kpt on to take 2nd nr line* **12/1**
02 **3** *nk* **Go Far**[14] 8006 2-9-3 0.......................... LukeMorris 6 65
(Alan Bailey) *trckd ldrs: hdwy over 2f out: sn rdn: kpt on to chse wnr ins fnl f: lost 2nd nr line* **5/1**
0 **4** *3 ¾* **Masaadr**[34] 7749 2-9-3 0.......................... JoeFanning 5 56
(James Tate) *dwlt and wnt lft s: reminders and sn trcking ldrs: trckd wnr over 4f out: cl up and rdn along 2f out: drvn and wknd over 1f out* **5/1**
0430 **5** *3* **Wallenberg**[22] 7899 2-9-3 72..........................(e) RobertHavlin 9 48
(John Gosden) *in tch: hdwy to trck ldrs over 4f out: effrt over 2f out: sn rdn along and wknd* **11/4**[1]
00 **6** *1 ¼* **Blackball (USA)**[34] 7749 2-9-3 0.......................... FrankieMcDonald 10 45
(David Lanigan) *in tch: pushed along over 4f out: rdn 3f out: sn outpcd* **25/1**
06 **7** *¾* **Balatina**[6] 8102 2-8-12 0.......................... KirstyMilczarek 11 38
(Chris Dwyer) *a towards rr* **66/1**
8 *1* **Maxi Dress (IRE)** 2-8-12 0.......................... NickyMackay 3 35+
(John Gosden) *midfield: rdn along 3f out: n.d* **7/2**[3]
00 **9** *3 ¼* **Hannahs Turn**[6] 8102 2-8-12 0.......................... MartinDwyer 4 27
(Chris Dwyer) *led early: cl up on inner: rdn along 3f out: sn wknd* **66/1**
0 **10** *nse* **Running Bull (IRE)**[21] 7926 2-9-3 0.......................... RobertWinston 8 32
(Linda Jewell) *towards rr: effrt and sme hdwy on outer 1/2-way: sn rdn along and outpcd* **66/1**

1m 24.32s (-0.48) **Going Correction** +0.025s/f (Slow) **10 Ran SP% 123.2**
Speed ratings (Par 96): **103,98,98,94,90 89,88,87,83,83**
Tote swingers 1&2 £10.30, 1&3 £3.50, 2&3 £10.00 CSF £40.08 TOTE £5.50: £2.20, £4.20, £1.70; EX 61.10 Trifecta £137.50 Pool: £1,300.29 - 7.09 winning units.
Owner Sanford R Robertson **Bred** Sanford Robertson **Trained** Newmarket, Suffolk

FOCUS
An ordinary maiden in which few got involved.

NOTEBOOK
Intrepid(IRE), officially rated 71, had twice disappointed on turf after a very promising debut, but he had been gelded since last seen 101 days ago and it appears to have made a difference. Soon in front, he was kicked into a clear lead off the home bend and was soon in no danger. The surface clearly suited and he can surely hold his own in handicap company. (tchd 7-2)
Daring Dragon, last of 14 when second-favourite for his Kempton debut last month, was tried in blinkers this time and this was much better, especially as he was the only one to make any impact from off the pace. The only note of caution is that he was inclined to hang about inside the last furlong, suggesting he may not be completely straightforward. (op 10-1 tchd 8-1)
Go Far improved plenty from his debut when runner-up over 6f here a fortnight earlier, and ran well again having held every chance. He didn't seem to lack for stamina and now gets a mark. (op 11-4)
Masaadr was well beaten on last month's Wolverhampton debut, but his price shortened considerably before the off here. He always had the winner in his sights, but found little off the bridle and appeared not to get home. (op 12-1)
Wallenberg, rated 72 after showing some ability in his first four starts, had run his race when hampered over a furlong out and looks exposed. (op 7-2)
Maxi Dress(IRE), an 80,000gns filly out of a half-sister to the Cheveley Park winner Prophecy and the only newcomer in the field, was too green to do herself justice, especially when failing to handle the home bend. (op 4-1)

8186 £32 BONUS AT 32RED.COM (S) STKS 1m (P)
1:00 (1:00) (Class 6) 2-Y-0 **£1,704** (£503; £251) **Stalls** High

Form RPR
0301 **1** **Gabrial The Boss (USA)**[3] 8150 2-9-2 59..........................(t) AndreaAtzeni 4 66
(David Simcock) *trckd ldrs: hdwy to chse ldr wl over 1f out: swtchd lft and rdn ent fnl f: drvn and styd on to ld last 100yds* **2/1**[2]
0343 **2** *¾* **Dream About You (IRE)**[14] 8003 2-8-7 60 ow1.......................... RobertHavlin 5 55
(Robert Mills) *sn led: rdn along 2f out: drvn and edgd rt ent fnl f: hdd and no ex last 100yds* **9/2**[3]

0002 **3** 3 1/4 **Don Eduardo**[1] 8164 2-8-11 59......(b) LiamKeniry 3 52
(J S Moore) *trckd ldng pair: effrt over 2f out: sn rdn along and one pce fr wl over 1f out* **12/1**

0416 **4** 1 3/4 **Amelia Hull**[14] 8003 2-8-6 55...... MatthewLawson(5) 2 48
(J S Moore) *trckd ldrs on inner: hdwy 3f out: rdn along 2f out: no imp fr over 1f out* **7/1**

5514 **5** nk **Roland**[7] 8093 2-9-2 62......(b) JamieSpencer 6 52
(Kevin Ryan) *hld up: a in rr* **7/4**[1]

4033 **6** 1 1/2 **Maypole Joe (IRE)**[1] 8164 2-8-11 55......(v) LukeMorris 1 44
(David Evans) *sn cl up: pushed along 3f out: rdn 2f out: sn wknd* **12/1**

1m 38.54s (0.34) **Going Correction** +0.025s/f (Slow) **6** Ran SP% **115.8**
Speed ratings (Par 94): **99,98,95,93,92 91**
Tote swingers 1&2 £1.70, 1&3 £7.70, 2&3 £8.00 CSF £11.93 TOTE £5.00: £3.40, £5.50; EX 12.80 Trifecta £77.40 Pool: £1,069.64 - 10.36 winning units.Winner bought in for 7,200gns.
Owner Dr Marwan Koukash **Bred** Hunter Valley Farm Et Al **Trained** Newmarket, Suffolk

FOCUS
A moderate seller and a few of these had met each other before. As in the opening race, the winner didn't seem to be inconvenienced by the usually unfavoured inside rail.

NOTEBOOK
Gabrial The Boss(USA) wasn't well treated at the weights but he came into this in form having won a Wolverhampton claimer three days earlier, and that counted for plenty. He produced a decent turn of speed to get himself into the race turning in and maintained it after being switched to the inside rail a furlong out. He has been placed a couple of times off similar marks in nurseries, but may go up a few pounds for this. He was bought in for 7,200gns. (op 11-4)
Dream About You(IRE), in the frame in races won by Amelia Hull and Roland over C&D in her last two starts, was nonetheless best in on adjusted official ratings, even with the 1lb overweight, and managed to turn the form around with both. She made a bold bid to make just about all and never stopped trying, but the winner produced a better turn of foot.
Don Eduardo, runner-up in a Kempton seller in first-time blinkers the previous evening, had every chance after taking a grip early, but was outpaced by the front pair inside the last.
Amelia Hull was having to be shoved along to stay in touch from some way out and could never get involved. (op 5-1)
Roland has looked an awkward ride on occasions in the past and never appeared to be travelling with much fluency. His rider reported that the gelding hung right throughout. Official explanation: jockey said gelding hung right throughout

8187 ATTHERACES.COM EXCLUSIVE HUGH TAYLOR TIPPING MAIDEN FILLIES' STKS 1m (P)
1:30 (1:30) (Class 5) 3-Y-O+ **£2,328** (£693; £346; £173) **Stalls** High

Form RPR

1 **Honky Tonk Queen (USA)**[84] 6618 3-9-0 0...... JimCrowley 4 62
(John Berry) *hld up in tch: hdwy 3f out: trckd ldrs 2f out: effrt and squeezed through to ld ent fnl f: kpt on* **7/1**

5535 **2** 1 1/4 **Bowstar**[15] 7996 3-9-0 65......(p) J-PGuillambert 7 59
(Michael Attwater) *dwlt and hld up in rr: hdwy 2f out: rdn over 1f out: styd on to chse wnr ins fnl f: sn drvn and one pce* **7/4**[1]

-004 **3** 1 **Tijuca (IRE)**[108] 5874 3-9-0 40...... EddieAhern 8 57
(Ed de Giles) *in tch: hdwy to chse ldrs on outer 2f out: rdn over 1f out and ev ch tl drvn and one pce ins fnl f* **12/1**

0- **4** 1/2 **Cape Crossing**[418] 7165 3-9-0 0...... LiamKeniry 2 56
(Andrew Balding) *dwlt and in rr: hdwy on inner over 2f out: rdn and ev ch whn n.m.r ent fnl f: kpt on same pce* **3/1**[2]

5 **5** nk **Zaminate**[22] 7896 3-9-0 0...... DavidProbert 6 55
(Andrew Balding) *cl up: rdn wl over 1f out and ev ch tl drvn and one pce ins fnl f* **5/1**[3]

6 **6** 1 **My Colleen (USA)**[33] 7770 3-9-0 0...... ChrisCatlin 10 52
(Rae Guest) *in rr: hdwy 2f out: sn rdn and styd on fnl f: nrst fin* **25/1**

3000 **7** nk **Sangrail**[147] 4490 3-9-0 59...... MartinDwyer 11 52
(William Muir) *chsd ldrs: rdn along wl over 1f out: sn one pce* **25/1**

0000 **8** nk **Silver Marizah (IRE)**[11] 8046 3-9-0 55...... RobertHavlin 5 51
(Roger Ingram) *in rr: hdwy 2f out: sn rdn and no imp fnl f* **33/1**

9 1 1/4 **Bestfootforward** 3-9-0 0...... KirstyMilczarek 1 48
(Olivia Maylam) *led: rdn along 2f out: drvn and hdd ent fnl f: wknd* **16/1**

5306 **10** hd **Transfix**[11] 8050 3-9-0 58......(p) JamieSpencer 3 48
(Ed Vaughan) *prom: rdn along 2f out: drvn over 1f out: wkng whn n.m.r ent fnl f: fin lame* **8/1**

5050 **11** 3 **Lea Valley**[90] 6442 3-8-7 45...... ShelleyBirkett(7) 9 40
(Julia Feilden) *towards rr: hdwy on outer to chse ldrs 3f out: rdn along 2f out: sn wknd* **66/1**

1m 39.32s (1.12) **Going Correction** +0.025s/f (Slow) **11** Ran SP% **127.3**
Speed ratings (Par 100): **95,93,92,92,91 90,90,90,89,88 85**
Tote swingers 1&2 £5.10, 1&3 £17.60, 2&3 £8.60 CSF £20.80 TOTE £8.90: £2.40, £1.90, £6.20; EX 30.40 Trifecta £368.20 Pool: £1,094.94 - 2.23 winning units.
Owner John Berry **Bred** Kingswood Farm **Trained** Newmarket, Suffolk

FOCUS
A modest older-horse fillies' maiden.
Transfix Official explanation: vet said filly finished lame

8188 32RED H'CAP 7f (P)
2:00 (2:00) (Class 4) (0-85,85) 3-Y-O+ **£4,075** (£1,212; £606; £303) **Stalls** Low

Form RPR

0400 **1** **Kickingthelilly**[175] 3542 3-9-2 80...... ChrisCatlin 5 90+
(Rae Guest) *hld up: hdwy over 2f out: effrt on outer over 1f out: sn rdn and styd on wl fnl f to ld nr fin* **20/1**

0453 **2** nk **Warfare**[15] 7997 3-8-10 74...... JamieSpencer 1 83
(Kevin Ryan) *trckd ldrs: effrt wl over 1f out: rdn and styng on wl whn n.m.r towards fin: jst hld* **4/1**[2]

0142 **3** hd **Cut Across (IRE)**[20] 7936 4-8-11 75...... SebSanders 2 84
(Nick Littmoden) *prom: effrt wl over 1f out: rdn to ld jst ins fnl f: sn drvn: hdd and no ex towards fin* **5/2**[1]

3604 **4** 1 1/4 **Crew Cut (IRE)**[78] 6800 4-9-0 78......(p) JimCrowley 4 83
(Jeremy Gask) *trckd ldrs: hdwy 3f out: rdn wl over 1f out: ev ch ent fnl f: sn drvn and kpt on same pce* **8/1**

421 **5** 3/4 **Ertikaan**[28] 7820 5-9-5 83......(tp) LukeMorris 11 86
(Brendan Powell) *chsd ldrs: rdn wl over 1f out: drvn ent fnl f: kpt on same pce* **8/1**

0000 **6** nk **Bayleyf (IRE)**[67] 7080 3-9-7 85......(t) GeorgeBaker 10 87
(John Best) *hld up in rr: hdwy wl over 1f out: sn rdn and kpt on fnl f: nrst fin* **14/1**

5600 **7** 1 **Prince Of Burma (IRE)**[17] 7966 4-9-4 82...... RobertWinston 8 82
(Jeremy Gask) *cl up: rdn along 2f out: drvn and wknd ent fnl f* **6/1**

0666 **8** 3/4 **Blue Jack**[42] 7651 7-8-6 75...... NannaHansen(5) 3 73
(Stuart Williams) *sn led: rdn along wl over 1f out: drvn ent fnl f: sn hdd & wknd* **20/1**

0450 **9** hd **Quasi Congaree (GER)**[153] 4286 6-9-2 80......(t) JoeFanning 6 77
(Paul Fitzsimons) *a towards rr* **33/1**

0533 **10** 10 **Shahzan (IRE)**[42] 7645 4-8-13 84...... JeanVanOvermeire(7) 7 54
(Roger Varian) *a in rr: rdn along over 3f out: sn bhd* **9/2**[3]

1m 24.53s (-0.27) **Going Correction** +0.025s/f (Slow) **10** Ran SP% **122.4**
Speed ratings (Par 105): **102,101,101,100,99 98,97,96,96,85**
Tote swingers 1&2 £14.50, 1&3 £15.40, 2&3 £2.70 CSF £101.16 CT £281.47 TOTE £39.00: £7.40, £1.90, £1.90; EX 178.40 Trifecta £483.80 Pool: £1,451.63 - 2.25 winning units.
Owner Hailstone Piper Scott Hirschfeld & Guest **Bred** Tony Hirschfeld & L K Piggott **Trained** Newmarket, Suffolk

FOCUS
Not a bad handicap at all and the form looks solid.

8189 32REDBET.COM H'CAP 1m 5f (P)
2:30 (2:30) (Class 6) (0-65,64) 3-Y-O+ **£1,704** (£503; £251) **Stalls** Low

Form RPR

0033 **1** **Jacobs Son**[6] 8106 4-9-5 62...... WilliamTwiston-Davies(5) 3 70
(Robert Mills) *trckd ldr: cl up 3f out: led 2f out and sn rdn clr: kpt on wl towards fin* **7/2**[1]

6543 **2** 1 1/4 **El Libertador (USA)**[15] 7991 6-8-9 54......(b) JoeyHaynes(7) 6 60
(Eric Wheeler) *trckd ldrs: effrt over 2f out: rdn to chse wnr ent fnl f: sn drvn and kpt on* **7/1**[3]

2226 **3** nk **Annelko**[26] 7869 5-9-7 59...... JamieSpencer 10 65
(Michael Blake) *stdd s and hld up in rr: hdwy 2f out: effrt on inner to chse ldrs over 1f out: sn rdn and kpt on same pce ins fnl f* **7/2**[1]

4310 **4** 1 3/4 **Kampai**[13] 8023 4-9-9 61...... AdamBeschizza 5 64
(Julia Feilden) *trckd ldrs: hdwy 3f out: rdn to chse wnr wl over 1f out: drvn ent fnl f: one pce* **5/1**[2]

2505 **5** nk **Coup De Grace (IRE)**[13] 5707 3-8-8 57...... JemmaMarshall(5) 8 59
(Pat Phelan) *in tch: pushed along and outpcd over 2f out: rdn wl over 1f out: styd on wl fnl f: nrst fin* **10/1**

0005 **6** 3 3/4 **Soweto Star (IRE)**[9] 8067 4-9-7 59...... GeorgeBaker 1 56
(John Best) *hld up: hdwy over 3f out: chsd ldrs 2f out: sn rdn and no imp* **7/1**[3]

0004 **7** 1 1/4 **Bennelong**[9] 8067 6-9-5 57......(p) AmirQuinn 2 52
(Richard Rowe) *trckd ldng pair: pushed along 3f out: rdn 2f out: drvn over 1f out and sn wknd* **10/1**

0020 **8** 4 1/2 **Novel Dancer**[12] 8035 4-9-1 53...... RobertHavlin 9 41
(Lydia Richards) *set stdy pce: pushed along and jnd 3f out: rdn and hdd 2f out: sn wknd* **10/1**

014 **9** 1 1/2 **Neighbourhood (USA)**[12] 8035 4-8-11 49...... ChrisCatlin 7 35
(James Evans) *chsd ldrs: rdn along 3f out: wknd over 2f out* **16/1**

210- **P** **Baileys Agincourt**[423] 7070 4-9-12 64...... TomEaves 11
(Michael Herrington) *a in rr: bhd whn p.u 2f out: fatally injured* **25/1**

2m 46.49s (0.49) **Going Correction** +0.025s/f (Slow)
WFA 3 from 4yo+ 6lb **10** Ran SP% **123.1**
Speed ratings (Par 101): **99,98,98,96,96 94,93,90,90,**
Tote swingers 1&2 £3.70, 1&3 £3.40, 2&3 £5.90 CSF £30.29 CT £95.29 TOTE £4.90: £2.30, £2.20, £1.50; EX 17.80 Trifecta £67.80 Pool: £1,240.52 - 13.72 winning units.
Owner Jacobs Construction (Holdings) Limited **Bred** Stowell Park Stud **Trained** Headley, Surrey

FOCUS
A moderate staying handicap, but an enterprisingly ridden winner.

8190 32RED SUPPORTING BRITISH RACING H'CAP 5f (P)
3:00 (3:06) (Class 6) (0-60,60) 3-Y-O+ **£1,704** (£503; £251) **Stalls** High

Form RPR

4556 **1** **Liberal Lady**[76] 6836 4-9-3 56......[1] JoeFanning 3 64
(Ralph Smith) *mde all: qcknd clr wl over 1f out: rdn ins fnl f: hld on wl* **8/1**

0040 **2** shd **Volcanic Dust (IRE)**[17] 7970 4-9-5 58......(b) RobertWinston 4 66
(Milton Bradley) *in tch: hdwy wl over 1f out: rdn ent fnl f: styd on wl towards fin: jst hld* **5/1**[3]

0365 **3** 2 **Chjimes (IRE)**[6] 8107 8-9-5 58......(b) LukeMorris 2 58
(Conor Dore) *trckd ldng pair: hdwy to chse wnr 2f out: rdn over 1f out: drvn and one pce ins fnl f* **9/4**[1]

0540 **4** 1/2 **Scommettitrice (IRE)**[82] 6685 4-8-13 57..(p) WilliamTwiston-Davies(5) 1 56
(David Evans) *trckd ldrs on inner: effrt 2f out: sn rdn and one pce fnl f* **16/1**

0302 **4** dht **Molly Jones**[11] 8045 3-9-0 53...... WilliamCarson 6 52
(Derek Haydn Jones) *dwlt and in rr: hdwy 2f out: rdn over 1f out: kpt on fnl f: nrst fin* **7/2**[2]

0006 **6** 1 1/2 **Colourbearer (IRE)**[17] 7969 5-9-7 60......(t) AdamKirby 9 53
(Milton Bradley) *hld up and bhd: hdwy wl over 1f out: sn rdn: kpt on fnl f: nrst fin* **7/2**[2]

3503 **7** 1/2 **Imaginary Diva**[6] 8107 6-8-12 58...... JordanVaughan(7) 5 49
(George Margarson) *prom: effrt 2f out: sn rdn and wknd appr fnl f* **6/1**

0000 **8** 7 **Exkaliber**[176] 3489 3-8-10 52......[1] RaulDaSilva(3) 7 18
(Jeremy Gask) *midfield: rdn along over 2f out: sn wknd* **25/1**

5000 **9** 5 **Thorpe Bay**[9] 8063 3-9-6 59......(b) KirstyMilczarek 8 7
(Conor Dore) *chsd ldrs: rdn along 2f out: sn wknd* **50/1**

1006 **10** 8 **Miss Polly Plum**[6] 8107 5-9-4 57......(p) AndreaAtzeni 10
(Chris Dwyer) *racd wd: chsd ldrs: rdn along over 2f out: sn wknd* **14/1**

59.27s (0.47) **Going Correction** +0.025s/f (Slow) **10** Ran SP% **135.6**
Speed ratings (Par 101): **97,96,93,92,92 90,89,78,70,57**
Tote swingers 1&2 £7.90, 1&3 £7.30, 2&3 £5.70 CSF £55.96 CT £126.39 TOTE £8.50: £2.20, £1.90, £2.00; EX 47.10 Trifecta £368.50 Pool: £1,960.58 - 4.86 winning units.
Owner N Tozer **Bred** Deepwood Farm Stud **Trained** Epsom, Surrey

FOCUS
A moderate sprint handicap.

8191 32RED.COM H'CAP 1m 4f (P)
3:30 (3:32) (Class 4) (0-85,82) 3-Y-O+ **£4,075** (£1,212; £606; £303) **Stalls** Low

Form RPR

406 **1** **Wildomar**[22] 7895 3-9-0 77...... AdamKirby 5 86
(John Ryan) *hld up towards rr: hdwy wl over 1f out: swtchd lft and rdn to chal ins fnl f: styd on wl to ld nr line* **3/1**[2]

3212 **2** shd **Noble Silk**[15] 8000 3-9-2 79...... LukeMorris 3 88
(Lucy Wadham) *trckd ldng pair: hdwy to chse ldr 2f out: rdn over 1f out: styd on to ld ins fnl f: jnd and drvn last 100yds: hdd on line* **9/4**[1]

5640 **3** 1 1/4 **Nave (USA)**[15] 8000 5-8-12 70...... MartinLane 8 77
(David Simcock) *cl up: led after 3f: rdn clr 2f out: drvn and hdd ins fnl f: kpt on same pce* **10/1**[3]

1423 **4** 2 **Tartan Jura**[8] 8073 4-9-2 74......(b) JoeFanning 2 78
(Mark Johnston) *led 3f: chsd ldr: rdn along over 4f out: drvn over 2f out: kpt on same pce* **3/1**[2]

6300 **5** hd **Beat Route**[8] 8082 5-9-1 73...... SebSanders 7 76
(Michael Attwater) *hld up in rr: hdwy on inner 2f out: rdn to chse ldrs over 1f out: drvn and kpt on same pce fnl f* **10/1**[3]

0334 **6** *nk* **Standpoint**[5] 8136 6-9-3 75 KirstyMilczarek 4 78
(Conor Dore) *hld up in rr: hdwy on outer 2f out: rdn wl over 1f out: no imp fnl f* **10/1**[3]

0003 **7** *½* **Silken Thoughts**[54] 6333 4-9-10 82 JamieSpencer 1 84
(John Berry) *trckd ldrs: effrt 3f out: rdn 2f out and sn wknd* **10/1**[3]

5656 **8** *3 ½* **Follow The Flag (IRE)**[10] 8057 8-9-2 74 (v) ShaneKelly 6 71
(Alan McCabe) *trckd ldrs: pushed along 2f out: rdn wl over 1f out and sn wknd* **20/1**

2m 31.44s (-1.56) **Going Correction** +0.025s/f (Slow)
WFA 3 from 4yo+ 5lb **8** Ran SP% **121.9**
Speed ratings (Par 105): **106,105,105,103,103 103,103,100**
Tote swingers 1&2 £2.80, 1&3 £6.50, 2&3 £6.10 CSF £11.02 CT £61.65 TOTE £4.00: £1.40, £1.50, £2.50; EX 13.70 Trifecta £151.00 Pool: £2,165.10 - 10.75 winning units.
Owner W McLuskey **Bred** Wood Hall Stud Limited **Trained** Newmarket, Suffolk

FOCUS
A fair handicap and a true test at the trip thanks to a contested lead.
T/Plt: £46.10 to a £1 stake. Pool: £61,620.91 - 974.27 winning units T/Qpdt: £5.70 to a £1 stake. Pool: £6,820.48 - 874.02 winning units JR

8176 DEAUVILLE (R-H)
Thursday, December 20

OFFICIAL GOING: Fibresand: standard

8192a PRIX HABITAT (CONDITIONS) (2YO COLTS & GELDINGS) (FIBRESAND) 7f 110y
9:30 (12:00) 2-Y-O **£12,083** (£4,833; £3,625; £2,416; £1,208)

RPR

1 **Intermix (IRE)**[50] 7492 2-8-13 0 JohanVictoire 10 82+
(Paul Cole) *broke wl on outside: racd in 2nd: rdn early in st: led 2f out: sn wnt clr: r.o wl fnl f: easily* **112/10**

2 *2 ½* **Pont Neuilly (FR)**[16] 7984 2-9-3 0 Pierre-CharlesBoudot 8 80
(Y De Nicolay, France) **9/10**[1]

3 *1 ¼* **Carletti (IRE)**[23] 2-8-13 0 GregoryBenoist 2 73
(G Botti, Italy) **20/1**

4 *1* **Aldo Bere (FR)**[5] 2-8-7 0 (b) JimmyTastayre(6) 6 71
(C Boutin, France) **8/1**[3]

5 *½* **Chene Boppe (FR)**[57] 2-8-13 0 AlexisBadel 7 70
(F-X De Chevigny, France) **20/1**

6 *2* **You're Golden (IRE)**[144] 4632 2-8-13 0 JulienAuge 4 65
(C Ferland, France) **4/1**[2]

7 *1* **Heintassin (FR)**[30] 2-8-5 0 StephaneLaurent(8) 3 62
(Mlle B Renk, France) **63/1**

8 *4* **Herve (IRE)** 2-8-13 0 StephanePasquier 5 53
(T Castanheira, France) **26/1**

9 *1 ½* **Leargas (IRE)**[60] 7276 2-8-13 0 MaximeGuyon 9 50
(F Vermeulen, France) **12/1**

10 *snk* **Echion (IRE)**[55] 7374 2-9-3 0 (p) AntoineHamelin 1 53
(F Vermeulen, France) **26/1**

1m 32.3s (92.30) **10** Ran SP% **118.1**
WIN (incl. 1 euro stake): 12.20. PLACES: 2.50, 1.20, 3.10. DF: 11.40. SF: 33.20.
Owner P F I Cole Ltd **Bred** D G Iceton **Trained** Whatcombe, Oxon

8193a PRIX DE CHEFFRETEAU (H'CAP) (2YO) (FIBRESAND) 7f 110y
11:00 (12:00) 2-Y-O **£10,416** (£4,166; £3,125; £2,083; £1,041)

RPR

1 **Zor (FR)**[165] 2-8-3 0 AlexisBadel 7 75
(T Larriviere, France) **207/10**

2 *nk* **Catushaba (IRE)**[45] 7597 2-8-6 0 MarcLerner 8 78
(C Lerner, France) **28/1**

3 *1 ½* **Liberty Dancer (FR)**[38] 2-8-9 0 GregoryBenoist 3 77
(Y Barberot, France) **14/5**[1]

4 *½* **Chalnetta (FR)**[170] 2-9-2 0 (b) JulienAuge 4 83
(C Ferland, France) **5/1**[2]

5 *shd* **Lewamy (IRE)**[41] 7682 2-8-11 0 JohanVictoire 5 78
(John Best) *broke fast to ld: u.p 2f out: hdd 250yds out: styd on one pce fnl f* **52/1**

6 *¾* **Shingueti (FR)**[90] 2-8-11 0 MaximeGuyon 2 76
(C Baillet, France) **11/2**[3]

7 *1 ¼* **Bahaa (FR)**[38] 2-8-10 0 AurelienLemaitre 9 72
(F Head, France) **11/1**

8 *1* **Melivea (FR)**[15] 2-8-8 0 RudyPimbonnet(2) 10 70
(C Laffon-Parias, France) **15/1**

9 *2 ½* **Sparks Fly (FR)**[164] 3928 2-8-10 0 ThomasHuet 6 64
(S Kobayashi, France) **44/1**

10 *¾* **Mesha Dream (FR)**[38] 2-8-13 0 (b) ThierryThulliez 14 65
(S Wattel, France) **16/1**

0 **Golden Dylan (FR)**[78] 2-8-9 0 FabriceVeron 12
(H-A Pantall, France) **11/1**

0 **L'Etoile Du Soir (FR)**[23] 2-8-13 0 ChristopherGrosbois(5) 13
(J Boisnard, France) **36/1**

0 **Battante (FR)**[38] 2-8-10 0 AnthonyCrastus 15
(L A Urbano-Grajales, France) **19/1**

0 **Sakura Mambo (FR)**[23] 2-8-9 0 AntoineHamelin 1
(S Kobayashi, France) **54/1**

0 **Huacachina** 2-8-10 0 StephanePasquier 16
(D Sepulchre, France) **19/1**

0 **Tucky Even (FR)** 2-8-2 0 JimmyTastayre(3) 11
(C Boutin, France) **27/1**

1m 31.5s (91.50) **16** Ran SP% **117.4**
WIN (incl. 1 euro stake): 21.70. PLACES: 5.50, 6.60, 1.80. DF: 134.50. SF: 562.80.
Owner Ecurie Kura **Bred** Ecurie Kura **Trained** France

8194 - 8198a (Foreign Racing) - See Raceform Interactive

8185 LINGFIELD (L-H)
Friday, December 21

OFFICIAL GOING: Standard
Wind: Light half behind Weather: Fine and DRY

8199 PLAY GOLF AT LINGFIELD PARK H'CAP 1m (P)
11:25 (11:25) (Class 6) (0-65,65) 3-Y-0+ **£1,617** (£481; £240; £120) **Stalls** High

Form RPR

6-52 **1** **Avertis**[22] 7925 7-9-2 65 AmyScott(5) 1 75
(Alastair Lidderdale) *trckd ldrs on inner: hdwy 2f out: rdn to ld ins fnl f: kpt on* **8/1**[3]

3005 **2** *¾* **Derfenna Art (IRE)**[12] 8051 3-9-3 62 (t) MickyFenton 3 70
(Seamus Durack) *led: jnd and rdn 2f out: drvn and hdd jst ins fnl f: kpt on wl u.p towards fin* **12/1**

0012 **3** *1 ¾* **Whinging Willie (IRE)**[42] 7671 3-9-3 62 GeorgeBaker 11 66+
(Gary Moore) *hld up and bhd: hdwy wl over 1f out: swtchd rt and rdn ent fnl f: styd on* **4/1**[1]

0505 **4** *½* **Bloodsweatandtears**[9] 8083 4-9-5 63 SebSanders 7 66
(William Knight) *cl up: rdn to chal 2f out: drvn and ev ch over 1f out: one pce fnl f* **5/1**[2]

0405 **5** *½* **Spin Again (IRE)**[15] 8004 7-9-6 64 AdamKirby 5 66
(John Ryan) *trckd ldrs: hdwy 2f out: rdn over 1f out: kpt on same pce fnl f* **14/1**

004 **6** *2 ¼* **Indian Violet (IRE)**[13] 8039 6-9-0 58 (p) LiamKeniry 12 55
(Zoe Davison) *hld up towards rr: hdwy 2f out: sn rdn: styd on fnl f: nrst fin* **25/1**

0006 **7** *2* **Spirit Of Xaar (IRE)**[7] 8105 6-9-5 63 (p) RobertHavlin 10 55
(Linda Jewell) *dwlt and stdd s: hld up in rr: sme hdwy 2f out: sn rdn and n.d* **25/1**

1045 **8** *¾* **Olney Lass**[34] 7781 5-8-12 59 SimonPearce(3) 4 49
(Lydia Pearce) *in tch: effrt over 2f out: sn rdn along and wknd over 1f out* **33/1**

2100 **9** *nk* **Saint Irene**[9] 8078 3-9-4 63 FergusSweeney 9 52
(Michael Blanshard) *a towards rr* **20/1**

3221 **10** *hd* **Refreshestheparts (USA)**[9] 8083 3-8-11 63 AaronJones(7) 6 52
(George Baker) *hld up: effrt and sme hdwy 2f out: rdn and wkng whn hmpd ent fnl f* **4/1**[1]

0000 **11** *2* **Rezwaan**[30] 7805 5-9-6 64 (be) ShaneKelly 2 48
(Murty McGrath) *chsd ldng pair on outer: rdn along over 2f out: sn drvn and wkng whn hmpd ent fnl f* **8/1**[3]

6614 **12** *3* **Bladewood Girl**[22] 7925 4-9-6 64 JoeFanning 8 42
(J R Jenkins) *chsd ldrs: rdn along over 2f out: sn wknd* **5/1**[2]

1m 36.85s (-1.35) **Going Correction** -0.15s/f (Stan)
WFA 3 from 4yo+ 1lb **12** Ran SP% **125.3**
Speed ratings (Par 101): **100,99,97,97,96 94,92,91,91,91 89,86**
Tote swingers 1&2 £21.90, 1&3 £3.90, 2&3 £15.90 CSF £100.61 CT £459.43 TOTE £10.40: £3.40, £5.90, £2.20; EX 166.40 Trifecta £338.40 Part won. Pool: £451.30 - 0.10 winning units..
Owner C S J Beek **Bred** Mrs Sally Doyle **Trained** Lambourn, Berks
■ Stewards' Enquiry : George Baker one-day ban: careless riding (Jan 4)

FOCUS
It paid to be handy in this moderate event and few were involved. The winner's best form since 2010.

8200 FOLLOW US ON TWITTER @LINGFIELDPARK FILLIES' MAIDEN STKS (DIV I) 1m (P)
11:55 (11:56) (Class 5) 2-Y-O **£2,264** (£673; £336; £168) **Stalls** High

Form RPR

1 **Ice Pie** 2-9-0 0 RichardKingscote 7 69+
(Tom Dascombe) *dwlt and in rr: hdwy on outer 2f out: rdn: rn green and edgd lft over 1f out: styd on strly fnl f to ld last 50yds* **5/2**[2]

05 **2** *1* **Fusion (IRE)**[34] 7777 2-9-0 0 JoeFanning 3 66
(Mark Johnston) *cl up: rdn over 1f out: slt ld jst ins fnl f: hdd and no ex last 50yds* **8/1**[3]

5 **3** *¾* **Gertrude Versed**[14] 8017 2-9-0 0 MarcHalford 1 64
(John Gosden) *slt ld: rdn along 2f out: drvn and hdd jst ins fnl f: kpt on same pce* **5/2**[2]

0 **4** *¾* **Pearla**[14] 8017 2-9-0 0 KellyHarrison 2 63
(William Haggas) *trckd ldrs on inner: hdwy 2f out: rdn and ch over 1f out: kpt on same pce fnl f* **33/1**

3 **5** *1* **Debdebdeb**[14] 8017 2-9-0 0 DavidProbert 8 60
(Andrew Balding) *trckd ldrs on outer: pushed along 3f out: swtchd lft to inner and rdn to chse ldrs over 1f out: sn no imp* **7/4**[1]

00 **6** *2 ¾* **Salute To Seville (IRE)**[14] 8018 2-9-0 0 LiamKeniry 6 54
(J S Moore) *in rr: hdwy wl over 1f out: sn rdn and no imp fnl f* **50/1**

7 *1 ¼* **Countess Lovelace** 2-8-9 0 JemmaMarshall(5) 9 51
(Pat Phelan) *dwlt and in rr: green and rdn along 1/2-way: sme late hdwy* **50/1**

4455 **8** *½* **Fair Comment**[73] 6946 2-9-0 67 FergusSweeney 4 50
(Michael Blanshard) *chsd ldrs: rdn along wl over 2f out: sn wknd* **12/1**

66 **9** *1 ¼* **Aegean Whispers**[22] 7923 2-9-0 0 SeanLevey 5 47
(Richard Hannon) *chsd ldrs: rdn along 3f out: drvn 2f out and sn wknd* **25/1**

1m 37.63s (-0.57) **Going Correction** -0.15s/f (Stan) **9** Ran SP% **123.0**
Speed ratings (Par 93): **96,95,94,93,92 89,88,88,86**
Tote swingers 1&2 £4.00, 1&3 £2.40, 2&3 £4.40 CSF £23.68 TOTE £2.90: £1.30, £2.20, £1.60; EX 32.30 Trifecta £180.10 Pool: £1,270.44 - 5.29 winning units.
Owner A Black & Owen Promotions Limited **Bred** Newsells Park Stud **Trained** Malpas, Cheshire

FOCUS
The form looks no better than fair, but there were some decent stables represented and this was quite an interesting fillies' maiden. The winner created a decent impression. The leader covered the first 6f around 1.80 seconds quicker than the pacesetter in the second division, and the final time was 1.09 seconds faster.

NOTEBOOK
Ice Pie ◆ looked plenty fit enough and had a bit of shine to her coat, unlike some of the others. She fetched 60,000euros last year and is a half-sister to a few winners, most notably smart 7f-1m2f winner (including Listed) St Moritz. This was a nice performance, the filly overhauling some more forwardly ridden rivals who had experience, and she's open to improvement. (op 7-2 tchd 4-1)
Fusion(IRE), a half-sister to Attraction, bettered the form she showed over 7f in her first two starts. She has a bit of size and ought to progress again. (tchd 10-1)
Gertrude Versed, a half-sister to Gertrude Bell (fourth in the Oaks, won Lancashire Oaks for these connections), showed ability, like her on her debut over C&D, but she needs more of a stamina test.

Pearla showed more than when behind a couple of these on her debut. She's another who is going to want further.
Debdebdeb didn't build on the form she showed when ahead of Gertrude Versed and Pearla over C&D on her debut, but she might be worth excusing. Wide without cover early, she rather raced in snatches, and although she went okay here first-time up, she's a long-striding filly who's probably going to be more effective on a galloping track. (op 6-4 tchd 11-8)
Countess Lovelace ◆ was not sold at £400 in February, but she's a half-sister to a couple of winners, namely Black Falcon (1m-1m4f) and Majestic Cheer (7f), and she showed ability. She was extremely green for much of the way, but made encouraging late progress.

8201 FOLLOW US ON TWITTER @LINGFIELDPARK FILLIES' MAIDEN STKS (DIV II) 1m (P)
12:25 (12:25) (Class 5) 2-Y-O **£2,264** (£673; £336; £168) **Stalls** High

Form RPR
1 **Keep The Secret** 2-9-0 0 .... AdamKirby 9 75+
(William Knight) *t.k.h early: hld up in rr: hdwy over 1f out: rdn and qcknd wl to ld ins fnl f: sn clr* **12/1**
04 2 3 **Easy Life**[14] 8018 2-9-0 0 .... MartinDwyer 2 65+
(Marcus Tregoning) *led: rdn along 2f out: drvn and hdd ins fnl f: kpt on same pce* **8/1**[3]
3 1 **Empowermentofwomen (IRE)** 2-9-0 0 .... LukeMorris 1 63+
(Michael Bell) *trckd ldng pair on inner: rdn over 1f out: ch whn n.m.r ent fnl f: kpt on* **20/1**
4 nk **Mistral Wind (IRE)** 2-9-0 0 .... TomMcLaughlin 3 63+
(Ed Dunlop) *t.k.h: trckd ldrs: pushed along wl over 1f out: effrt and ch whn hmpd ent fnl f: sn rdn and kpt on towards fin* **16/1**
02 5 nk **Give Me High Five**[14] 8018 2-9-0 0 .... SeanLevey 4 61
(Richard Hannon) *cl up: rdn wl over 1f out: edgd lft ent fnl f: sn drvn and one pce* **3/1**[2]
3 6 shd **Special Meaning**[14] 8018 2-9-0 0 .... JoeFanning 6 61
(Mark Johnston) *cl up on outer: pushed along 2f out: rdn wl over 1f out: sn drvn and wknd ent fnl f* **8/11**[1]
0 7 1 ¾ **Tebee's Oasis**[18] 7962 2-9-0 0 .... RobertHavlin 5 57
(John Gosden) *t.k.h early: in tch: rdn along 2f out: sn wknd* **8/1**[3]
00 8 5 **Veronica's Pursuit**[36] 7720 2-9-0 0 .... FergusSweeney 7 46
(Peter Hedger) *a in rr: outpcd fnl 2f* **50/1**

1m 38.72s (0.52) **Going Correction** -0.15s/f (Stan) **8** Ran SP% **125.4**
Speed ratings (Par 93): **91,88,87,86,86 86,84,79**
Tote swingers 1&2 £6.20, 1&3 £14.40, 2&3 £7.40 CSF £112.10 TOTE £28.30: £4.10, £1.20, £6.90; EX 119.10 TRIFECTA Not won..
Owner Mr & Mrs N Welby **Bred** Mrs N F M Sampson And C M Oakshott **Trained** Patching, W Sussex

FOCUS
This looked the weaker of the two divisions, but the winner created a good impression and can rate a lot higher. The pace was steadier than in the first leg - about 1.80 seconds slower for the first 6f - and the final time was 1.09 seconds slower.

NOTEBOOK
Keep The Secret ◆, a 19,000gns half-sister to US 1m Grade 2 winner Mr Napper Tandy, and 1m-1m2f scorer Wind Star, showed good speed to easily pick off her rivals, having been held up off the slow pace, and she looks a useful prospect.
Easy Life reversed recent placings with the disappointing pair Give Me High Five and Special Meaning, and she seems to be going the right way. (op 7-1 tchd 6-1)
Empowermentofwomen(IRE), the first foal of a 1m Polytrack winner for these connections, was a bit short of room around a furlong out but it made little difference. She showed ability and is entitled to come on for the run.
Mistral Wind(IRE), a 32,000gns half-sister to a couple of minor winners in Europe, was denied a clear run when staying on in the straight and looked third-best. (op 20-1)
Give Me High Five was below the form she showed when runner-up over C&D (Special Meaning and Easy Life third and fourth) on her previous start. (op 9-4)
Special Meaning didn't build on the form she showed when splitting Give Me High Five and Easy Life on her debut here, finding disappointingly little, even allowing for a wide trip. (op Evens)

8202 BOOK THE TRACKSIDE RESTAURANT AT LINGFIELD PARK CLAIMING STKS 6f (P)
1:00 (1:00) (Class 6) 3-Y-O+ **£1,103** (£1,103; £251) **Stalls** Low

Form RPR
0321 1 **Majuro (IRE)**[9] 8077 8-8-7 81 ....(t) LeonnaMayor(5) 4 84
(Charles Smith) *sn led: pushed clr 2f out: rdn ins fnl f: jnd on line* **5/1**[3]
5522 1 dht **Lujeanie**[14] 8022 6-9-0 79 ....(p) AdamKirby 1 86
(Dean Ivory) *hld up: hdwy wl over 1f out: rdn and styd on ins fnl f to join ldr on line* **3/1**[2]
0062 3 1 ¼ **Hamoody (USA)**[13] 8036 8-8-11 75 ow1 .... SebSanders 2 79
(David Nicholls) *trckd ldng pair: hdwy on inner wl over 1f out: rdn and kpt on fnl f* **12/1**
4101 4 1 **Noverre To Go (IRE)**[22] 7928 6-9-3 88 .... LukeMorris 5 82
(Ronald Harris) *trckd ldrs: hdwy 2f out: rdn to chse ldr wl over 1f out: drvn and wknd ins fnl f* **4/5**[1]
0006 5 1 **Amenable (IRE)**[13] 8036 5-8-9 77 .... SeanLevey 3 71
(Violet M Jordan) *cl up: pushed along over 2f out: rdn wl over 1f out: sn wknd* **33/1**
006 6 5 **Camache Queen (IRE)**[74] 6939 4-8-3 73 ....(v[1]) WilliamCarson 8 49
(Joseph Tuite) *in rr: rdn along over 2f out: sn outpcd* **10/1**

1m 10.55s (-1.35) **Going Correction** -0.15s/f (Stan) **6** Ran SP% **116.9**
TRIFECTA L/M/H £25.60, M/L/H £36.70 Pool of £1,742.34 - L/M/H 25.49 winning units,27 Owner.
Owner Willie McKay **Bred** Tally-Ho Stud **Trained** Temple Bruer, Lincs

FOCUS
A fair claimer in which the front-running Majuro was joined on the line by Luleanie. Majro did not need to match his best, and Lujeanie was close to recent form.

8203 FIND US ON FACEBOOK LINGFIELD PARK NURSERY 7f (P)
1:35 (1:36) (Class 6) (0-60,66) 2-Y-O **£1,704** (£503; £251) **Stalls** Low

Form RPR
0662 1 **Blazeofenchantment (USA)**[18] 7974 2-9-4 57 ....(p) AdamKirby 10 65+
(Noel Quinlan) *dwlt: hld up towards rr: hdwy wl over 2f out: effrt on outer over 1f out: rdn to ld jst ins fnl f: sn edgd lft: styd on* **3/1**[1]
0001 2 1 **Seaside Rock (IRE)**[8] 8093 2-9-8 66 6ex .... WilliamTwiston-Davies(5) 7 71+
(Richard Hannon) *trckd ldng pair: hdwy to chse ldr over 1f out: rdn to ld briefly ent fnl f: sn hdd and drvn: kpt on same pce* **3/1**[1]
0063 3 2 ¼ **Lincolnrose (IRE)**[8] 8093 2-8-12 51 ....(p) SebSanders 8 50
(Alan McCabe) *led: rdn clr over 2f out: drvn and hdd ent fnl f: kpt on same pce* **14/1**
2561 4 ½ **My Sweet Lord**[15] 8007 2-9-2 55 .... TomMcLaughlin 11 53
(Mark Usher) *hld up in rr: hdwy over 2f out: effrt on inner wl over 1f out: sn rdn and styd on fnl f: nrst fin* **6/1**[3]
6300 5 nk **Taxiformissbyron**[18] 7974 2-8-10 49 ow1 .... EddieAhern 5 46
(Michael Herrington) *hld up in rr: hdwy on outer wl over 1f out: sn rdn and sltly hmpd appr fnl f: kpt on wl: nrst fin* **20/1**
0053 6 ¾ **Darkest Night (IRE)**[18] 7974 2-9-2 55 .... FergusSweeney 2 50
(Jamie Osborne) *chsd ldr: rdn along 2f out: drvn wl over 1f out: grad wknd* **14/1**
00 7 ½ **Our Three Graces (IRE)**[30] 7808 2-9-4 57 .... GeorgeBaker 4 51
(Gary Moore) *chsd ldrs: pushed along and outpcd 3f out: rdn wl over 1f out: kpt on u.p fnl f* **20/1**
0102 8 nk **Royal Caper**[8] 8093 2-9-6 59 .... JohnFahy 6 52
(John Ryan) *hld up: hdwy on outer 3f out: rdn to chse ldrs wl over 1f out: drvn and wknd appr fnl f* **7/1**
0201 9 ¾ **Bubbly Bailey**[7] 8103 2-9-6 59 ....(p) LiamKeniry 12 50
(Alan Bailey) *chsd ldrs on outer: rdn along 3f out: drvn 2f out: sn wknd and towards rr whn edgd rt over 1f out* **9/2**[2]
6600 10 1 ½ **World Freight Girl**[15] 8007 2-8-13 52 .... JimmyQuinn 9 39
(Dean Ivory) *a in rr* **66/1**
6505 11 ½ **Our Sweet Art**[14] 8016 2-9-6 59 .... MartinDwyer 3 45
(John Best) *in tch: hdwy over 2f out: rdn wl over 1f out: sn wknd* **20/1**
005 12 ¾ **Armada Bay (IRE)**[73] 6970 2-8-6 45 .... MartinLane 1 29
(Bryan Smart) *in tch on inner: rdn along over 2f out: sn wknd* **25/1**

1m 24.55s (-0.25) **Going Correction** -0.15s/f (Stan) **12** Ran SP% **127.9**
Speed ratings (Par 94): **95,93,91,90,90 89,88,88,87,86 85,84**
Tote swingers 1&2 £3.40, 1&3 £9.20, 2&3 £9.80 CSF £11.66 CT £117.58 TOTE £3.20: £1.60, £2.00, £4.50; EX 14.70 Trifecta £79.00 Pool: £1,384.61 - 13.13 winning units.
Owner The Unique Partnership **Bred** Gulf Coast Farms LLC **Trained** Newmarket, Suffolk

FOCUS
The pace was fair, thanks to Lincolnrose, and the form looks solid for the grade with the right two horses pulling clear. The winner should go in again.

NOTEBOOK
Blazeofenchantment(USA) ◆ had caught the eye more than once prior to an improved performance when gambled on at Wolverhampton last time, when he found only one too good. Up just 1lb, there was again money for him and he showed himself a good deal better than his current mark, winning well despite not really travelling (hard to say whether the first-time cheekpieces helped) and being taken extremely wide into the straight. If he goes the right way mentally then he can rate a fair bit higher. (op 4-1 tchd 5-2)
Seaside Rock(IRE) was 1lb wrong under the penalty picked up for a clear win over 1m at Kempton on his recent handicap debut, but he improved again, not minding the drop in trip. (op 4-1)
Lincolnrose(IRE) posted another respectable performance following her third to Seaside Rock over 1m at Kempton last time.
My Sweet Lord, 4lb higher than when winning over 6f here last time, was never really involved after being set a lot to do. (op 5-1)
Taxiformissbyron, carrying 1lb overweight, got too far back to pose a meaningful threat. (op 16-1)
Royal Caper, who split Seaside Rock and Lincolnrose at Kempton last time, raced wide and couldn't match that form over this furlong shorter trip. (tchd 10-1)
Bubbly Bailey, disqualified after passing the post first over C&D on his previous start, was off the same mark but disappointed in first-time cheekpieces. (op 5-1 tchd 6-1)

8204 LINGFIELDPARK.CO.UK NURSERY 6f (P)
2:10 (2:12) (Class 5) (0-75,80) 2-Y-O **£2,264** (£673; £336; £168) **Stalls** Low

Form RPR
3135 1 **Archie Stevens**[16] 7994 2-9-4 72 .... GeorgeBaker 2 78
(Tom Dascombe) *trckd ldng pair: smooth hdwy and cl up whn carried wd home turn: rdn and styd on ins fnl f to ld last 75yds* **5/2**[2]
3121 2 nk **Small Fury (IRE)**[7] 8108 2-9-3 71 6ex .... J-PGuillambert 3 76
(Jo Hughes) *trckd ldr: pushed along on inner wl over 1f out: sn rdn and hdwy to take slt ld ent fnl f: sn drvn: hdd and no ex last 75yds* **7/1**
3411 3 ¾ **Ovett**[2] 8161 2-9-5 80 6ex ....(p) NedCurtis(7) 5 83
(Gary Moore) *qckly away: keen and sn clr: rdn and edgd rt home turn: hdd jst ins fnl f: kpt on* **11/10**[1]
2110 4 2 ¾ **Blazing Knight (IRE)**[41] 7687 2-9-7 75 .... SebSanders 4 70
(Ralph Beckett) *hld up in rr: pushed along and hdwy 2f out: rdn wl over 1f out: drvn and one pce ent fnl f* **4/1**[3]

1m 11.05s (-0.85) **Going Correction** -0.15s/f (Stan) **4** Ran SP% **108.7**
Speed ratings (Par 96): **99,98,97,93**
CSF £16.56 TOTE £2.90; EX 17.30 Trifecta £30.10 Pool: £1,255.87 - 31.27 winning units.
Owner L Bellman & Manor House Stables LLP **Bred** Howard Barton Stud **Trained** Malpas, Cheshire

FOCUS
Only four runners, but fair form.

NOTEBOOK
Archie Stevens proved suited by the drop in trip, his first try over 6f since winning at Wolverhampton off 9lb lower the previous month, and just did enough despite being forced a bit wide by the third. He has more to offer as a sprinter. (op 7-2)
Small Fury(IRE), 9lb higher than when winning over 5f at Wolverhampton last time, covered less ground than the winner and third, but was outstayed. It was a similar story to her penultimate start, when she was touched over C&D, and she looks better suited by the minimum trip. (op 5-1 tchd 4-1)
Ovett had won his last two starts, over 6f here and most recently going 5f at Kempton, but that latest victory was achieved in a really quick time and he probably found this race, off only a two-day break, coming soon enough. He was also free in front and may be best suited by the furlong shorter trip. (tchd Evens)
Blazing Knight(IRE) was never a threat after 41 days off. (op 7-2 tchd 9-2)

8205 BOOK HOSPITALITY AT LINGFIELD PARK CLASSIFIED STKS 7f (P)
2:45 (2:45) (Class 6) 3-Y-O+ **£1,617** (£481; £240; £120) **Stalls** Low

Form RPR
0002 1 **Sandy Lane (IRE)**[8] 8099 3-9-0 50 .... RobertHavlin 6 63
(Amy Weaver) *trckd ldrs: hdwy to chse ldr wl over 1f out: sn chal: rdn to ld ins fnl f: sn clr* **3/1**[1]
040 2 3 ½ **My Scat Daddy (USA)**[100] 6151 3-9-0 50 .... EddieAhern 11 53
(Brett Johnson) *trckd ldrs: pushed along over 2f out: rdn over 1f out: swtchd lft and drvn ins fnl f: kpt on: no ch w wnr* **3/1**[1]
0400 3 ½ **Greek Islands (IRE)**[31] 7794 4-9-0 52 .... LiamKeniry 10 52
(Ed de Giles) *prom: chsd ldr after 3f: effrt to ld over 2f out: rdn wl over 1f out: drvn and hdd ins fnl f: kpt on same pce* **12/1**
00-6 4 1 ½ **Future Impact (IRE)**[303] 653 4-9-0 45 .... AdamKirby 3 48
(John Butler) *hld up towards rr: hdwy 2f out: rdn over 1f out: kpt on fnl f: nrst fin* **9/2**[2]
0003 5 nse **Fairy Mist (IRE)**[45] 7612 5-8-9 44 .... WilliamTwiston-Davies(5) 2 48
(John Bridger) *trckd ldr: rdn along 2f out: drvn over 1f out: sn one pce* **16/1**
3305 6 nk **Chandrayaan**[13] 8039 5-8-11 48 ....(v) SimonPearce(3) 1 47
(John E Long) *hld up in rr: sme hdwy wl over 1f out: sn rdn and no imp fnl f* **12/1**

6310 **7** *1* **Artful Lady (IRE)**[10] 8062 3-8-7 51 JordanVaughan(7) 7 44
(George Margarson) *hld up in rr: sme hdwy wl over 1f out: sn rdn and n.d* **8/1**

-000 **8** *2* **Zammy**[175] 3555 3-9-0 55 ShaneKelly 5 39
(Michael Wigham) *trckd ldrs: effrt 2f out: sn rdn and wknd over 1f out* **6/1**[3]

00-0 **9** *10* **Imogen Louise (IRE)**[212] 2406 4-9-0 55 SeanLevey 9 12
(Violet M Jordan) *led: rdn along and hdd over 2f out: sn wknd* **33/1**

0465 **10** *3 ¼* **Loved To Bits**[22] 7929 4-8-7 48 JoeyHaynes(7) 8
(Eric Wheeler) *a towards rr* **20/1**

1m 23.81s (-0.99) **Going Correction** -0.15s/f (Stan) **10** Ran SP% **122.5**
Speed ratings (Par 101): **99,95,94,92,92 92,91,88,77,73**
Tote swingers 1&2 £2.90, 1&3 £10.10, 2&3 £8.90 CSF £12.27 TOTE £2.90: £1.90, £1.20, £3.40; EX 11.20 Trifecta £98.50 Pool: £1,788.27 - 13.61 winning units.
Owner Colm White **Bred** John Donegan **Trained** Newmarket, Suffolk
■ Stewards' Enquiry : Adam Kirby two-day ban: used whip above permitted level (Jan 4-5)

FOCUS
The pace seemed fair, but it proved difficult to make up significant ground in this moderate contest. The form is sound, and reasonable for the grade.

8206 AT THE RACES SKY 415 H'CAP 1m 4f (P)
3:20 (3:20) (Class 5) (0-70,74) 3-Y-O **£2,385** (£704; £352) **Stalls** Low

Form RPR

3600 **1** **Tingo In The Tale (IRE)**[100] 6146 3-9-2 69.. WilliamTwiston-Davies(5) 4 77
(David Arbuthnot) *trckd ldr: hdwy and cl up 3f out: led wl over 1f out: sn rdn: drvn and edgd lft ins fnl f: styd on* **7/1**[3]

6223 **2** *1* **Elysian**[13] 8037 3-9-4 66 SebSanders 1 73
(Sir Michael Stoute) *dwlt: hld up in rr: hdwy on inner 2f out: rdn and ev ch whn n.m.r ent fnl f: sn drvn and kpt on* **11/4**[2]

0452 **3** *½* **Gabrial's Hope (FR)**[6] 8139 3-8-12 60 JimmyQuinn 5 66
(Ian Williams) *set stdy pce: pushed along and jnd 3f out: rdn and hdd wl over 1f out: sn drvn and kpt on same pce fnl f* **11/4**[2]

3110 **4** *shd* **Thecornishcowboy**[9] 8078 3-9-12 74 6ex (t) AdamKirby 2 80
(John Ryan) *trckd ldng pair: effrt 2f out: rdn to chal wl over 1f out: sn drvn and one pce ins fnl f* **5/4**[1]

2m 36.16s (3.16) **Going Correction** -0.15s/f (Stan) **4** Ran SP% **110.3**
Speed ratings (Par 102): **83,82,82,81**
CSF £25.05 TOTE £8.20; EX 33.40 Trifecta £35.10 Pool: £443.05 - 9.46 winning units.
Owner George S Thompson **Bred** Brian Williamson **Trained** Beare Green, Surrey

FOCUS
The early pace was steady and there was a bunch finish, so this isn't strong form. The winner's bare form is close to his best.
T/Plt: £2,803.20 to a £1 stake. Pool: £50,112.29 - 13.05 winning units T/Qpdt: £168.00 to a £1 stake. Pool: £7,336.61- 32.30 winning units JR

8145 WOLVERHAMPTON (A.W) (L-H)
Friday, December 21

OFFICIAL GOING: Standard
Wind: Light behind Weather: Overcast

8207 32RED.COM MEDIAN AUCTION MAIDEN STKS 7f 32y(P)
3:15 (3:16) (Class 5) 2-Y-O **£2,385** (£704; £352) **Stalls** High

Form RPR

0364 **1** **Overrider**[30] 7813 2-9-3 72 RobertWinston 2 81+
(Charles Hills) *mde all: racd keenly: shkn up and c clr fr over 1f out: easily* **4/5**[1]

2 *7* **Rosie Rebel** 2-8-12 0 ChrisCatlin 5 56+
(Rae Guest) *prom: pushed along 1/2-way: outpcd over 2f out: styd on to go 2nd ins fnl f: no ch w wnr* **11/4**[2]

6 **3** *5* **Multilicious**[6] 8134 2-8-12 0 DuranFentiman 6 44
(Tim Easterby) *hld up: hdwy 1/2-way: chsd wnr over 2f out: sn rdn: wknd over 1f out* **10/1**

00 **4** *½* **Show More Faith**[66] 7143 2-8-10 0 ThomasBrown(7) 1 48
(Sylvester Kirk) *plld hrd and prom: lost pl 1/2-way: no ch whn hmpd over 1f out* **14/1**

5 *4 ½* **Arabougg** 2-9-3 0 FrankieMcDonald 4 37
(Nikki Evans) *s.s: a in rr: rdn over 2f out: sn wknd* **66/1**

4 **6** *hd* **Barbsiz (IRE)**[23] 7916 2-8-12 0 TomEaves 7 31
(Mark H Tompkins) *s.s: sn prom: chsd wnr over 5f out: rdn over 2f out: wknd over 1f out* **7/1**[3]

7 *2* **How You Fixed (IRE)** 2-8-10 0 TimClark(7) 3 32
(Denis P Quinn, Ire) *chsd ldrs: rdn over 2f out: wknd over 1f out* **25/1**

1m 30.12s (0.52) **Going Correction** -0.175s/f (Stan) **7** Ran SP% **115.8**
Speed ratings (Par 96): **90,82,76,75,70 70,68**
Tote swingers 1&2 £2.00, 1&3 £2.40, 2&3 £3.50 CSF £3.28 TOTE £1.80: £2.60, £1.30; EX 4.40 Trifecta £14.90 Pool: £1,482.07 - 74.34 winning tickets..
Owner Phil Cunningham & D Nightingale **Bred** P M Cunningham **Trained** Lambourn, Berks

FOCUS
A fair juvenile median auction maiden in which the early pace was modest, racing on standard Polytrack, with a reported tailwind up the home straight on a bright and breezy winter's afternoon. The easy winner was quite impressive but the race lacked depth.

NOTEBOOK
Overrider set a clear form standard here arriving with a BHA rating of 72 after five 6f starts on turf/Polytrack. He also looked likely to appreciate this extra furlong, and so it proved. He reportedly looked well beforehand, and broke well from the gates into an uncontested lead. He raced a tad freely early on but soon settled into his own rhythm. He won very easily after travelling all over this field rounding the bend for home. He looks a decent 1m prospect for next year. (op 5-6 tchd 10-11)
Rosie Rebel was a 9,000gns yearling who made it a one-two for her sire Cockney Rebel. She reportedly looked fit and well having attracted market support earlier in the day. This trip looked sharp enough on pedigree beforehand, and she performed as if a step up in distance will help in the future. (tchd 3-1)
Multilicious showed slightly more, dropping back in trip than when a moderate sixth over 8.6f here on debut six days previously. (op 12-1 tchd 14-1)
Show More Faith did marginally better here returning from a nine-week break since two moderate Polytrack displays over this trip in October. Lowly handicaps now beckon. (op 16-1)
Barbsiz(IRE) went the wrong way from her respectable C&D debut the previous month. (op 6-1)

8208 32RED CASINO MEDIAN AUCTION MAIDEN FILLIES' STKS 5f 216y(P)
3:50 (3:50) (Class 6) 2-Y-O **£1,704** (£503; £251) **Stalls** Low

Form RPR

422 **1** **Midnight Flower (IRE)**[66] 7143 2-9-0 75 JamieSpencer 7 74
(David Simcock) *chsd ldr 5f out: shkn up to ld over 1f out: r.o: readily* **4/6**[1]

20 **2** *2 ¼* **Sherinn**[16] 7987 2-9-0 0 [1] AndreaAtzeni 1 67
(Roger Varian) *a.p: chsd wnr over 1f out: styd on same pce ins fnl f* **3/1**[2]

56 **3** *1 ¼* **Clock Opera (IRE)**[206] 2587 2-9-0 0 MichaelO'Connell 3 64
(Mrs K Burke) *chsd ldr 1f: remained handy: rdn over 1f out: styd on same pce fnl f* **9/1**[3]

2 **4** *2 ¾* **Last Minute Lisa (IRE)**[28] 7840 2-9-0 0 RobertWinston 6 55
(S Donohoe, Ire) *led: rdn and hdd over 1f out: wknd ins fnl f* **14/1**

5 *2* **Spymistress** 2-9-0 0 RichardKingscote 2 49+
(Tom Dascombe) *sn pushed along in rr: rdn and wknd over 1f out* **9/1**[3]

6 *5* **Scarlet Strand** 2-8-9 0 JackDuern(5) 4 34
(Reg Hollinshead) *hld up: pushed along over 2f out: wknd over 1f out* **33/1**

000 **7** *15* **Equinox**[66] 7143 2-9-0 37 TomEaves 5
(Bryan Smart) *hld up: wknd over 2f out* **100/1**

1m 14.2s (-0.80) **Going Correction** 0.175s/f (Stan) **7** Ran SP% **115.6**
Speed ratings (Par 91): **98,95,93,89,87 80,60**
Tote swingers 1&2 £1.50, 1&3 £2.20, 2&3 £2.90 CSF £2.99 TOTE £1.50: £1.10, £1.80; EX 3.70 Trifecta £13.40 Pool: £2,179.22 - 121.25 winning tickets..
Owner Saeed Suhail **Bred** Rabbah Bloodstock Limited **Trained** Newmarket, Suffolk

FOCUS
A modest juvenile fillies' median auction maiden in which they went an honest gallop. Straightforward form, the winner to her best.

NOTEBOOK
Midnight Flower(IRE) was returning from a nine-week break since showing enough to warrant a BHA rating of 75 in three starts at up to 7f on turf/Polytrack. She travelled notably well round the bend for home, and won readily here dropping back to 6f. She should have no trouble going back up in trip next year on this evidence. (op Evens)
Sherinn showed the benefit of a first-time hood in returning to a level of form which is approaching her debut second over 6f at Newmarket in August (RPR 74). (op 5-2)
Clock Opera(IRE) was returning from a seven-month break and recorded a peak career display on this third start. She should prove competitive in sprint handicaps. (op 11-2)
Last Minute Lisa(IRE) is exposed with an official rating of 52 in Ireland. She would be better off in lowly handicap company at around this 6f trip. (op 10-1)
Spymistress cost 85,000euros as a yearling and is the first foal of a sister to Cornwallis/King's Stand winner Dominica. She reportedly looked the pick of these in the paddock, but struggled on this debut.. (op 10-1 tchd 11-1 and 15-2)

8209 32RED SUPPORTING BRITISH RACING H'CAP (DIV I) 5f 20y(P)
4:20 (4:20) (Class 6) (0-52,58) 3-Y-O+ **£1,704** (£503; £251) **Stalls** Low

Form RPR

3041 **1** **Monumental Man**[12] 8046 3-9-13 **58** 6ex (p) DavidProbert 7 70
(James Unett) *chsd ldr tl led 4f out: clr over 1f out: all out* **5/4**[1]

51 **2** *shd* **Rose Garnet (IRE)**[22] 7929 4-9-0 **52** RyanTate(7) 10 64
(Tony Carroll) *a.p: rdn to chse wnr over 1f out: r.o wl* **2/1**[2]

4000 **3** *5* **Divertimenti (IRE)**[44] 7634 8-8-12 **46** oh1 (b) MarkCoumbe(3) 6 40
(Roy Bowring) *chsd ldrs: rdn over 1f out: styd on same pce* **12/1**

0030 **4** *½* **Little Perisher**[2] 8168 5-9-1 **46** (p) MichaelStainton 8 38
(Mark Brisbourne) *sn pushed along and prom: outpcd 4f out: rallied over 1f out: r.o* **12/1**

6300 **5** *nk* **Rightcar**[35] 7746 5-9-4 **49** JamieSpencer 5 40
(Peter Grayson) *s.i.s: hld up: r.o ins fnl f: nvr nrr* **8/1**[3]

3040 **6** *2* **Miserere Mei (IRE)**[7] 8107 3-9-1 **46** (p) RobbieFitzpatrick 4 30
(Richard Guest) *hld up: hdwy over 1f out: wknd fnl f* **16/1**

-405 **7** *½* **Brian Sprout**[12] 8046 4-9-3 **48** (be[1]) DuranFentiman 3 30
(John Weymes) *led 1f: chsd wnr tl rdn and edgd lft over 1f out: wknd fnl f* **14/1**

0000 **8** *1 ¾* **Forever Janey**[52] 7457 3-9-1 **46** oh1 (bt[1]) JoeFanning 2 22
(Paul Green) *hld up in tch: rdn and wknd over 1f out* **28/1**

5005 **9** *nse* **Colamandis**[7] 8109 5-8-8 **46** oh1 (b) VictorSantos(7) 9 22
(Hugh McWilliams) *s.i.s: outpcd* **80/1**

1m 1.29s (-1.01) **Going Correction** -0.175s/f (Stan) **9** Ran SP% **121.5**
Speed ratings (Par 101): **101,100,92,92,91 88,87,84,84**
Tote swingers 1&2 £1.70, 1&3 £5.50, 2&3 £4.00 CSF £4.11 CT £20.20 TOTE £2.40: £1.30, £1.20, £2.90; EX 5.10 Trifecta £38.70 Pool: £2,144.22 - 41.46 winning tickets..
Owner James Unett **Bred** Christopher Chell **Trained** Tedsmore Hall, Shropshire

FOCUS
The first division of a moderate sprint handicap in which the early pace was contested producing a truly-run affair. it was the faster division and the first pair were clear, so the form is rated on the positive side.

8210 32RED SUPPORTING BRITISH RACING H'CAP (DIV II) 5f 20y(P)
4:50 (4:50) (Class 6) (0-52,52) 3-Y-O+ **£1,704** (£503; £251) **Stalls** Low

Form RPR

5634 **1** **Lord Buffhead**[12] 8046 3-9-7 **52** (v[1]) RobbieFitzpatrick 3 59
(Richard Guest) *chsd ldrs: rdn over 1f out: edgd rt and r.o to ld wl ins fnl f* **3/1**[1]

0003 **2** *nk* **Chateau Lola**[12] 8045 3-9-5 **50** JoeFanning 5 56
(Derek Shaw) *chsd ldr tl led over 1f out: rdn and hdd wl ins fnl f* **9/2**[3]

542 **3** *¾* **First Rebellion**[44] 7633 3-8-8 **46** RyanTate(7) 10 49
(Tony Carroll) *chsd ldrs: rdn over 1f out: styd on* **7/2**[2]

0405 **4** *¾* **Deveze (IRE)**[12] 8045 4-9-1 **46** (b) RichardKingscote 11 47
(Milton Bradley) *hld up: r.o ins fnl f: nt rch ldrs* **10/1**

0000 **5** *¾* **Bond Blade**[115] 5719 4-8-9 **47** JacobButterfield(7) 9 45
(Suzzanne France) *s.i.s: hdwy 2f out: rdn over 1f out: edgd rt: styd on* **9/1**

5000 **6** *1 ½* **Replicator**[12] 8046 7-9-1 **46** oh1 (e) JamieMackay 7 39
(Patrick Gilligan) *hld up: drvn along 1/2-way: styd on ins fnl f: nt trble ldrs* **25/1**

460 **7** *hd* **Cri Na Mara (IRE)**[18] 7969 4-9-3 **48** (t) AndreaAtzeni 2 40
(Mark Michael McNiff, Ire) *led: rdn and hdd over 1f out: nt clr run and no ex ins fnl f* **9/2**[3]

4600 **8** *½* **Vhujon (IRE)**[37] 7703 7-9-1 **46** oh1 JamieSpencer 8 36
(Peter Grayson) *s.i.s: hld up: nt clr run ins fnl f: nvr nr to chal* **8/1**

0000 **9** *½* **Spoken Words**[17] 7981 3-8-8 **46** oh1 (b[1]) VictorSantos(7) 4 34
(Hugh McWilliams) *s.i.s: hdwy 2f out: sn rdn: no ex fnl f* **33/1**

1m 2.03s (-0.27) **Going Correction** -0.175s/f (Stan) **9** Ran SP% **120.6**
Speed ratings (Par 101): **95,94,93,92,90 88,88,87,86**
Tote swingers 1&2 £2.20, 1&3 £3.00, 2&3 £3.30 CSF £17.65 CT £50.58 TOTE £3.90: £1.50, £1.80, £1.70; EX 10.40 Trifecta £19.20 Pool: £1,701.87 - 66.20 winning tickets..
Owner Future Racing (Notts) Limited **Bred** T K & Mrs P A Knox **Trained** Stainforth, S Yorks

FOCUS
The second division of a moderate sprint handicap. This looked the weaker of the two divisions with the top-weight rated 6lb lower, and a slower winning time appears to confirm as much. The form is not especially unconvincing.

Vhujon(IRE) Official explanation: jockey said, regarding running and riding, that he was given no orders but the gelding never travelled, he pushed it hard to catch the field and balanced it round the bend to prepare for an effort in the home straight, having picked up, it followed Bond Blade which kept moving off its line and he felt it was safer to take avoiding action and ease off.

8211 32RED NURSERY 7f 32y(P)
5:20 (5:21) (Class 4) (0-85,83) 2-Y-O £3,428 (£1,020; £509; £254) Stalls High

Form RPR
4231 1 **Lilac Lace (IRE)**[36] 7728 2-8-4 **66** DuranFentiman 5 71
(Tim Easterby) *trckd ldrs: rdn to ld ins fnl f: r.o* **4/1**[3]
51 2 1 ½ **Staffhoss**[13] 8033 2-9-2 **78** JoeFanning 4 79
(Mark Johnston) *sn led: rdn and hdd over 1f out: hung lft: styd on* **9/4**[2]
2301 3 ½ **Hipster**[82] 6699 2-9-7 **83** (v) JamieSpencer 6 83
(Ralph Beckett) *pushed along early: chsd ldr over 5f out: rdn to ld over 1f out: hdd and unable qck ins fnl f* **2/1**[1]
3046 4 1 ½ **Ocean Applause**[16] 7994 2-9-2 **81** RyanPowell(3) 1 77
(John Ryan) *hld up: rdn over 1f out: nvr trbld ldrs* **8/1**
1550 5 ½ **Pippy**[7] 8103 2-8-6 **68** (v[1]) RichardKingscote 3 63
(Tom Dascombe) *chsd ldrs: rdn over 1f out: no ex ins fnl f* **8/1**
510 6 ½ **Be On The Bell**[18] 7965 2-8-13 **75** FergusSweeney 2 69
(Jamie Osborne) *hld up: rdn over 1f out: n.d* **12/1**
1m 28.13s (-1.47) **Going Correction** -0.175s/f (Stan) 6 Ran SP% **114.0**
Speed ratings (Par 98): **101,99,98,97,96 95**
Tote Swingers 1&2 £1.90, 2&3 £1.50, 1&3 £1.10 CSF £13.77 TOTE £4.40: £2.10, £1.70; EX 13.50 Trifecta £25.10 Pool: £2,039.91 - 60.91 winning tickets..
Owner S A Heley **Bred** Robert Ryan, Brendan Quinn & Joan Quinn **Trained** Great Habton, N Yorks

FOCUS
A good nursery handicap in which they went a respectable gallop. Not surprisingly, the winner recorded the best comparative winning time on the card. The winner is improving with racing.

NOTEBOOK
Lilac Lace(IRE) was returning from a five-week break since getting off the mark over this 7f trip in a Southwell maiden the previous month. She did it well, and proved herself helpfully versatile in terms of surface in the process. She is entered to race under a penalty over 8.6f here on Boxing Day, and the longer trip shouldn't inconvenience her. (op 9-2 tchd 5-1)
Staffhoss got off the mark at the second attempt over 7f at Lingfield 13 days previously. He rallied well when headed here, and needs further already. A potential rematch with the winner, upped in trip on Boxing Day, would be a close call. (op 5-2)
Hipster ran respectably returning from a 12-week break, and this looks the right trip for him. (op 15-8 tchd 7-4)
Ocean Applause looked one-paced dropped to this trip. (op 12-1)
Pippy failed to find any benefit from a first-time visor. (op 7-1)

8212 £32 BONUS AT 32RED.COM H'CAP 1m 141y(P)
5:50 (5:57) (Class 7) (0-50,56) 3-Y-O+ £1,704 (£503; £251) Stalls Low

Form RPR
6000 1 **Brown Pete (IRE)**[28] 7841 4-9-5 **50** WilliamCarson 6 62
(Violet M Jordan) *a.p: rdn to ld over 1f out: hung rt: r.o* **5/2**[2]
4663 2 3 ¼ **Avon Supreme**[7] 8111 4-9-2 **47** (p) RobertWinston 5 52
(Gay Kelleway) *led: rdn and hdd over 1f out: edgd lft: styd on same pce ins fnl f* **2/1**[1]
0004 3 nk **Michael's Nook**[2] 8167 5-9-4 **49** KirstyMilczarek 1 53
(Alastair Lidderdale) *hld up: plld hrd: hdwy over 1f out: sn rdn: styd on same pce ins fnl f* **3/1**[3]
040 4 2 ¼ **Supa Seeker (USA)**[95] 6316 6-8-10 **48** AidenBlakemore(7) 8 47
(Tony Carroll) *hld up: hdwy over 1f out: no ex ins fnl f* **12/1**
0000 5 nk **Just Five (IRE)**[17] 7983 6-9-5 **50** (b[1]) LukeMorris 10 48
(John Weymes) *s.i.s: sn pushed along and prom: rdn over 2f out: wknd ins fnl f* **8/1**
0050 6 1 ¾ **General Tufto**[31] 7800 7-9-5 **50** (b) RobbieFitzpatrick 2 44
(Charles Smith) *hld up: drvn along over 3f out: nvr on terms* **28/1**
0056 7 ¾ **Perfect Outlook**[112] 5804 4-9-1 **49** [1] RaulDaSilva(3) 7 41
(Jeremy Gask) *sn chsng ldr: lost 2nd over 3f out: pushed along whn hmpd over 1f out: wknd fnl f* **9/1**
0000 8 4 ½ **Justcallmehandsome**[179] 3454 10-8-12 **50** (v) JoshBaudains(7) 11 32
(Dominic Ffrench Davis) *prom: chsd ldr over 3f out tl rdn over 1f out: wknd fnl f* **16/1**
1m 49.24s (-1.26) **Going Correction** -0.175s/f (Stan)
WFA 3 from 4yo+ 2lb 8 Ran SP% **125.0**
Speed ratings (Par 97): **98,95,94,92,92 91,90,86**
Tote Swingers 1&2 £2.80, 2&3 £3.00, 1&3 £3.30 CSF £8.88 CT £16.36 TOTE £3.80: £1.10, £1.60, £1.10; EX 11.90 Trifecta £34.80 Pool: £2,014.76 - 43.42 winning tickets..
Owner Rakebackmypoker.com **Bred** Jim Halligan **Trained** Moreton Morrell, Warwicks

FOCUS
A moderate handicap. The winner is rated back to last winter's Polytrack form.
Brown Pete(IRE) Official explanation: trainer's rep said, regarding apparent improvement in form, that the gelding had benefited from a change in tactics by being held up.

8213 32REDBET.COM H'CAP 1m 1f 103y(P)
6:20 (6:25) (Class 6) (0-65,64) 3-Y-O £1,704 (£503; £251) Stalls Low

Form RPR
1222 1 **Neige D'Antan**[17] 7976 3-9-5 **62** LukeMorris 1 71
(Sir Mark Prescott Bt) *a.p: nt clr run over 2f out: rdn to ld ins fnl f: edgd rt: jst hld on* **5/2**[1]
4 2 nse **Ferryview Place**[28] 7843 3-9-6 **63** (v[1]) StevieDonohoe 5 72
(Ian Williams) *hld up: hdwy over 3f out: rdn and ev ch wl ins fnl f: r.o* **11/2**[3]
61 3 nk **Alezanna**[17] 7981 3-8-11 **54** KirstyMilczarek 9 62
(James Toller) *led: rdn and hdd ins fnl f: styd on* **6/1**
0004 4 1 **Landown Littlerock**[23] 7921 3-8-4 **52** (p[1]) JackDuern(5) 2 58
(Reg Hollinshead) *chsd ldrs: wnt 2nd over 2f out: rdn and ev ch 1f out: no ex towards fin* **25/1**
0000 5 1 ¼ **Arabian Flight**[79] 6774 3-8-13 **56** AndrewMullen 7 60
(Michael Appleby) *hld up: hdwy over 2f out: rdn over 1f out: styd on* **33/1**
3162 6 1 ¾ **Taro Tywod (IRE)**[12] 8050 3-9-0 **57** ShaneKelly 10 57
(Mark Brisbourne) *hld up: hdwy 3f out: rdn over 1f out: no ex ins fnl f* **6/1**
1302 7 8 **Graylyn Valentino**[12] 8051 3-9-7 **64** JoeFanning 11 47
(Robin Dickin) *s.i.s: hld up: hdwy over 2f out: rdn and wknd over 1f out* **5/1**[2]
003 8 6 **Her Nibbs**[140] 4780 3-9-4 **61** TomEaves 12 32
(Micky Hammond) *hld up: bhd 1/2-way: nvr nrr* **25/1**
0024 9 3 ¾ **Gunner Will (IRE)**[50] 7499 3-9-6 **63** FergusSweeney 6 26
(Jamie Osborne) *chsd ldr tl rdn over 2f out: wknd over 1f out* **7/1**
0055 10 18 **Rockgoat (IRE)**[55] 7417 3-9-5 **62** RichardKingscote 8
(Ian McInnes) *prom tl wknd 3f out: t.o* **17/2**
0330 11 5 **Come Hither**[31] 7798 3-9-4 **61** PhillipMakin 13
(David O'Meara) *prom: rdn over 3f out: wknd over 2f out: t.o* **16/1**
1m 59.18s (-2.52) **Going Correction** -0.175s/f (Stan) 11 Ran SP% **128.7**
Speed ratings (Par 98): **104,103,103,102,101 100,93,87,84,68 63**
Tote Swingers 1&2 £5.80, 2&3 £11.80, 1&3 £4.60 CSF £17.76 CT £81.58 TOTE £2.80: £1.50, £2.70, £2.70; EX 24.70 Trifecta £237.00 Pool: £1,157.02 - 3.66 winning tickets..
Owner Miss K Rausing **Bred** Miss K Rausing **Trained** Newmarket, Suffolk
■ Stewards' Enquiry : Shane Kelly two-day ban: careless riding (Jan 4-5)
Luke Morris two-day ban: careless riding (Jan 4-5)

FOCUS
A modest 3-y-o handicap in which they went an honest gallop. Fair form for the grade.
Gunner Will(IRE) Official explanation: jockey said gelding lost its action

8214 32REDPOKER.COM H'CAP 1m 4f 50y(P)
6:50 (6:51) (Class 6) (0-65,69) 3-Y-O+ £1,704 (£503; £251) Stalls Low

Form RPR
6430 1 **El Bravo**[6] 8139 6-8-11 **57** ShirleyTeasdale(5) 9 63
(Shaun Harris) *mde all: set stdy pce tl qcknd 4f out: rdn and edgd rt ins fnl f: styd on* **5/1**[3]
0 2 nk **Cool Kid**[28] 7839 4-8-11 **52** StevieDonohoe 8 58
(Ian Williams) *a.p: chsd wnr 7f out: rdn over 1f out: styd on* **20/1**
5402 3 nk **Mcbirney (USA)**[62] 7251 5-9-3 **65** LouisSteward(7) 5 70+
(Paul D'Arcy) *hld up: hdwy over 1f out: edgd lft ins fnl f: r.o* **11/4**[1]
3346 4 nk **Wordiness**[9] 8079 4-9-8 **63** (t) JohnFahy 12 68
(Seamus Durack) *hld up in tch: rdn over 1f out: styd on* **4/1**[2]
6400 5 1 **Icy Quiet**[210] 2468 4-8-10 **51** oh2 TomEaves 6 54
(David O'Meara) *chsd ldr 5f: remained handy: rdn over 1f out: kpt on* **6/1**
0552 6 ¾ **Conducting**[9] 8078 4-9-10 **65** RobertWinston 1 67
(Gay Kelleway) *chsd ldrs: rdn over 2f out: no ex ins fnl f* **5/1**[3]
0100 7 1 **Daniel Thomas (IRE)**[7] 8106 10-9-8 **63** (tp) WilliamCarson 3 63
(Violet M Jordan) *hld up: hdwy u.p over 1f out: swtchd rt sn after: no imp ins fnl f* **14/1**
4600 8 nk **Eanans Bay (IRE)**[44] 7632 3-8-5 **51** oh2 (b[1]) JoeFanning 10 51
(Mark H Tompkins) *hld up: rdn over 3f out: r.o ins fnl f: nvr nrr* **14/1**
5004 9 10 **Life Of Laughter (USA)**[16] 7991 4-8-10 **51** JamieMackay 4 35
(Willie Musson) *s.i.s: hld up: bhd fnl 4f* **11/1**
5000 10 hd **Dzesmin (POL)**[12] 8051 10-8-10 **51** oh6 (p) RobbieFitzpatrick 7 34
(Richard Guest) *mid-div: hdwy 7f out: rdn and wknd over 2f out* **66/1**
4306 11 1 ½ **Bonnie Prince Blue**[7] 8113 9-9-2 **57** (b) AmyRyan 11 38
(Ian McInnes) *hld up: racd keenly: rdn over 3f out: sn lost tch* **33/1**
2m 47.39s (6.29) **Going Correction** -0.175s/f (Stan)
WFA 3 from 4yo+ 5lb 11 Ran SP% **125.1**
Speed ratings (Par 101): **72,71,71,71,70 70,69,69,62,62 61**
Tote Swingers 1&2 £31.00, 2&3 £16.20, 1&3 £6.20 CSF £106.49 CT £339.00 TOTE £5.00: £1.60, £14.70, £1.20; EX 133.70 Trifecta £985.50 Part won. Pool: £1,314.11 - 0.61 winning tickets..
Owner Nottinghamshire Racing **Bred** D J And Mrs Deer **Trained** Carburton, Notts
■ Stewards' Enquiry : John Fahy Caution: careless riding.
Louis Steward Caution: careless riding.

FOCUS
A modest middle-distance handicap for 3yos and up in which they went slowly until the tempo increased 4f out, and a winning time nearly 12 seconds slower than standard tells its own story. The form is rated around the third.
T/Jkpt: £805.30 to a £1 stake. Pool: £38,565.30 - 34.00 winning tickets. T/Plt: £3.90 to a £1 stake. Pool: £82,344.78 - 15345.12 winning tickets. T/Qpdt: £2.70 to a £1 stake. Pool: £8,112.86 - 2144.30 winning tickets. CR

8215 - 8222a (Foreign Racing) - See Raceform Interactive

8199 LINGFIELD (L-H)
Saturday, December 22

OFFICIAL GOING: Standard
Wind: medium, across Weather: rain

8223 TRACK YOUR HORSES AT ATTHERACES.COM NOVICE STKS 1m (P)
12:20 (12:20) (Class 5) 2-Y-O £3,067 (£905; £453) Stalls High

Form RPR
41 1 **El Buen Turista**[19] 7962 2-9-5 0 DavidProbert 6 91
(Andrew Balding) *chsd ldr: rdn to chal wl over 1f out: led ent fnl f: clr fnl 100yds: r.o wl: rdn out* **5/2**[2]
4311 2 2 **Yarroom (IRE)**[17] 7994 2-9-10 90 AndreaAtzeni 4 91
(Roger Varian) *hld up in tch in last pair: chsd ldng pair 3f out and sn rdn: styd on to chse wnr fnl 100yds: r.o but no threat to wnr* **4/5**[1]
3 1 ½ **King George River (IRE)**[134] 5069 2-9-5 0 AdamKirby 5 83
(Alan Bailey) *hld up in tch in rr: rdn and effrt over 2f out: styng on whn n.m.r ins fnl f: wnt 3rd towards fin: no threat to wnr* **6/1**[3]
1 4 1 **Plunder**[31] 7807 2-9-5 0 JamieSpencer 2 80
(Kevin Ryan) *t.k.h: led: drvn wl over 1f out: hdd ent fnl f: wknd and lost 2 pls fnl 100yds* **8/1**
0 5 14 **Hurry Home Poppa (IRE)**[14] 8033 2-9-0 0 RichardKingscote 3 43
(Tom Dascombe) *dwlt: sn rdn along and rcvrd to chse ldrs after 1f tl 3f out: sn struggling: lost tch 2f out* **33/1**
1m 36.6s (-1.60) **Going Correction** -0.075s/f (Stan) 5 Ran SP% **112.5**
Speed ratings (Par 96): **105,103,101,100,86**
CSF £5.04 TOTE £3.30: £1.50, £1.10; EX 5.90 Trifecta £13.30 Pool: £836.40 - 46.85 winning tickets..
Owner N M Watts **Bred** Newsells Park Stud **Trained** Kingsclere, Hants

FOCUS
Good form, which has been rated at face value.The winner built on his good Kempton win.

NOTEBOOK
El Buen Turista created a good impression when a clear winner of a Kempton maiden on his second start and readily followed up. He was getting 5lb from the runner-up and got first run on that rival, but there was much to like about how strongly he kept on and he's pretty decent. Now set for a break, he'll be worth his place in a good race when returning. (op 9-4 tchd 11-4)
Yarroom(IRE), the winner of his last two starts, most recently off 85 over C&D, was caught out when the winner committed for home and was always held. This was another useful performance, conceding weight all round, although it also exposed his limitations for now. (op Evens)
King George River(IRE) won on his debut for Aidan O'Brien but was a beaten favourite in Listed company next time and had since been sold for 34,000gns. Returning from 134 days off and trying Polytrack for the first time, he raced further back than the first two but was keeping on when slightly short of room late on. He can do better.
Plunder, who made all in a 7f Kempton maiden first time up, tried to repeat the trick but struggled over this extra furlong in better company. (op 10-1)

Hurry Home Poppa(IRE) looks like he needs more time and is a handicap prospect.

8224 MARSH GREEN CLAIMING STKS 6f (P)
12:50 (12:50) (Class 6) 2-Y-O **£2,181** (£644; £322) **Stalls** Low

Form RPR

2111 **1** **Sofi's Spirit (IRE)**[9] 8092 2-8-8 64 LiamKeniry 1 59
(J S Moore) *veered rt s: mde all: rdn 2f out: drvn ent fnl f: hld on wl and outbattled runner-up cl home* **5/2**[2]

3124 **2** *shd* **Windforpower (IRE)**[9] 8092 2-8-12 66 (b) LukeMorris 4 63
(Ronald Harris) *hld up in tch in midfield: trckd ldrs 2f out: pressed ldr and stl on bit jst ins fnl f: drvn hands and heels and chal fnl 75yds: nt go past and hld cl home* **4/1**[3]

6060 **3** *1 1/2* **Schottische**[130] 5206 2-8-4 40 (p) WilliamCarson 7 50
(Derek Haydn Jones) *off the pce in last trio: reminders and rdn 4f out: hdwy under pressre 1f out: styd on wl to go 3rd nr fin* **100/1**

1034 **4** *1/2* **Marmot Bay (IRE)**[3] 8161 2-8-8 61 KirstyMilczarek 5 53
(Alastair Lidderdale) *chsd wnr: rdn 2f out: lost 2nd jst ins fnl f and styd on same pce after* **6/1**

5133 **5** *hd* **Hardy Red (IRE)**[9] 8096 2-9-5 74 FergusSweeney 6 63
(Jamie Osborne) *chsd ldrs: rdn and no imp 2f out: plugged on ins fnl f but no threat to ldrs* **6/4**[1]

6530 **6** *5* **Proventi**[4] 8155 2-9-0 52 (v) SebSanders 3 43
(Alan McCabe) *short of room and dropped to rr after s: hld up off the pce in last trio: rdn and effrt wl over 1f out: no imp: wknd fnl f* **20/1**

00 **7** *1 1/2* **Copper Rag**[36] 7749 2-8-9 0 RachealKneller(5) 2 39
(Mark Usher) *racd off the pce in last trio: rdn and struggling 2f out: wknd over 1f out* **100/1**

1m 11.84s (-0.06) **Going Correction** -0.075s/f (Stan) **7 Ran SP% 109.6**
Speed ratings (Par 94): **97,96,94,94,93 87,85**
Tote Swingers: 1&2 £2.30, 1&3 £17.10, 2&3 £24.50 CSF £11.65 TOTE £3.10: £1.50, £2.40; EX 9.40 Trifecta £136.10 Pool: £1,151.11 - 6.34 winning tickets..Sofi's Spirit was the subject of a friendly claim for £7,000.
Owner J S Moore **Bred** Yvonne & Gerard Kennedy **Trained** Upper Lambourn, Berks
■ Stewards' Enquiry : Liam Keniry two-day ban: used whip above permitted level (Jan 5-6)

FOCUS
A very modest contest. The winner wanted it more than the second.

NOTEBOOK
Sofi's Spirit(IRE) showed a much better attitude than the runner-up to complete a four-timer (all gained in Polytrack sellers and claimers). She could get into a Class 6 handicap off her current mark and would surely be competitive. (op 7-4)
Windforpower(IRE) was given every chance by Luke Morris, cruising upsides the winner before being asked for his effort as late as possible, but he once again threw away a winning opportunity. (op 5-1)
Schottische, dropped in trip after 130 days off, was outpaced for most of the way but kept on and ran some way above his official mark of 40.
Marmot Bay(IRE) reportedly ran flat and hung right in the straight. Official explanation: jockey said filly ran flat and hung right in straight (op 9-2)
Hardy Red(IRE) was below the form he showed when third in a four-runner event off 75 at Kempton last time. (op 2-1)

8225 CWB CONTROLS H'CAP 5f (P)
1:20 (1:21) (Class 5) (0-70,70) 3-Y-O+ **£3,067** (£905; £453) **Stalls** High

Form RPR

0000 **1** **Hot Sugar (USA)**[79] 6825 3-9-1 **64** AndrewMullen 8 72
(Michael Appleby) *chsd ldr: rdn and ev ch over 1f out: drvn and led ins fnl f: r.o wl* **12/1**

0514 **2** *nk* **Speightowns Kid (USA)**[4] 8157 4-9-7 **70** J-PGuillambert 1 77
(Jo Hughes) *led: rdn wl over 1f out: drvn and hdd ins fnl f: kpt on but no ex cl home* **4/1**[2]

0204 **3** *nk* **Picansort**[12] 8054 5-9-3 **66** [1] ShaneKelly 3 72
(Peter Crate) *chsd ldrs: effrt on inner and rdn over 1f out: pressed ldrs ins fnl f: styd on same pce towards fin* **6/1**[3]

0020 **4** *1* **Even Bolder**[12] 8054 9-8-6 **62** (b) JoeyHaynes(7) 4 64
(Eric Wheeler) *chsd ldrs: drvn and unable qck over 1f out: styd on same pce ins fnl f* **25/1**

3332 **5** *nk* **Welease Bwian (IRE)**[4] 8157 3-9-2 **65** [1] RichardKingscote 9 66+
(Stuart Williams) *t.k.h: hld up in tch: rdn and effrt over 1f out: drvn and styd on ins fnl f: nvr trbld ldrs* **5/4**[1]

6610 **6** *hd* **Aubrietia**[52] 7489 3-9-6 **69** (b) LukeMorris 2 70+
(Alan McCabe) *s.i.s: hld up in tch towards rr: rdn and effrt over 1f out: kpt on ins fnl f: nvr trbld ldrs* **12/1**

5520 **7** *2 1/4* **Desert Strike**[7] 8144 6-9-4 **67** (p) AdamKirby 7 59
(Conor Dore) *hld up in tch in last pair: rdn and no imp over 1f out: nvr trbld ldrs* **10/1**

0063 **8** *1/2* **Billy Red**[12] 8054 8-9-5 **68** (b) FergusSweeney 6 59
(J R Jenkins) *stdd s: hld up towards rr: hdwy on outer 3f out: rdn and struggling wl over 1f out: wknd ins fnl f* **12/1**

0000 **9** *1 3/4* **Bookiesindexdotnet**[35] 7775 3-9-4 **67** EddieAhern 10 51
(J R Jenkins) *stdd after s: hld up wl in tch: rdn and unable qck over 1f out: wknd ins fnl f* **50/1**

4600 **10** *nk* **Rafaaf (IRE)**[19] 7967 4-9-4 **67** SeanQuinlan 5 50
(Richard Phillips) *hld up in tch in rr: rdn and no imp over 1f out: n.d* **20/1**

58.57s (-0.23) **Going Correction** -0.075s/f (Stan) **10 Ran SP% 121.5**
Speed ratings (Par 103): **98,97,97,95,94 94,91,90,87,86**
Tote Swingers: 1&2 £10.10, 1&3 £10.50, 2&3 £5.50 CSF £61.01 CT £334.29 TOTE £13.90: £2.70, £1.20, £1.80; EX 85.50 Trifecta £720.70 Pool: £1,249.30 - 1.30 winning tickets..
Owner Michael Appleby **Bred** Winchester Farm **Trained** Danethorpe, Notts

FOCUS
It proved hard to make up ground and not many became involved in this modest handicap. The runner-up helps set the standard.

8226 HAPPY CHRISTMAS FROM ALL AT LINGFIELD PARK CONDITIONS STKS 1m (P)
1:55 (1:55) (Class 3) 3-Y-O+ **£8,409** (£2,502; £1,250; £625) **Stalls** High

Form RPR

4352 **1** **Lockantanks**[12] 8055 5-8-12 88 LukeMorris 2 98
(Michael Appleby) *trckd ldrs: swtchd rt and bmpd rival wl over 1f out: drvn and ev ch over 1f out: led wl ins fnl f: r.o wl* **8/1**

30-1 **2** *1/2* **Anaconda (FR)**[269] 1068 3-9-2 90 RichardKingscote 5 102
(Tom Dascombe) *led: t.k.h tl 1/2-way: rdn wl over 1f out: kpt on wl tl hdd wl ins fnl f: one pce towards fin* **1/1**[1]

4226 **3** *nk* **Strictly Silver (IRE)**[101] 6143 3-8-11 92 LiamKeniry 4 96
(Alan Bailey) *chsd ldr: pressing ldr whn bmpd and pushed rt wl over 1f out: styd pressing ldrs: styd on same pce u.p fnl 100yds* **3/1**[2]

0042 **4** *1/2* **Mia's Boy**[12] 8056 8-8-12 94 AndreaAtzeni 3 95
(Chris Dwyer) *hld up in tch in rr: rdn and clsd on ldrs over 1f out: kpt on ins fnl f* **9/2**[3]

6300 **5** *3/4* **Spirit Of Sharjah (IRE)**[309] 616 7-8-12 95 RobertWinston 6 93
(Julia Feilden) *t.k.h: hld up in tch in last pair: swtchd rt and effrt over 1f out: styd on same pce ins fnl f* **12/1**

1m 36.58s (-1.62) **Going Correction** -0.075s/f (Stan)
WFA 3 from 5yo+ 1lb **5 Ran SP% 112.0**
Speed ratings (Par 107): **105,104,104,103,102**
CSF £17.08 TOTE £6.90: £3.20, £1.40; EX 17.90 Trifecta £63.10 Pool: £1,268.51 - 15.05 winning tickets..
Owner Dallas Racing **Bred** Jeremy Green And Sons **Trained** Danethorpe, Notts

FOCUS
The pace was ordinary and there was a bunch finish, but still useful enough form, rated around the winner.

NOTEBOOK
Lockantanks got a bit too far back off a modest gallop when runner-up in a decent 7f claimer here on his previous start, but this time he was ridden from some way out to hold his position and the extra furlong helped. He's another success story for Michael Appleby, who picked him up for just £500 in 2010. (op 7-1)
Anaconda(FR) ◆ had been absent since winning a 7f maiden here by 6l in March (bone chips reportedly found in a knee), but he's done really well physically and made an encouraging return. He was a bit free early, and that left him vulnerable, but he plugged on. While his connections apparently hoped to win here and earn an invite to Dubai, this big sort should have more to offer. (op 5-4)
Strictly Silver(IRE), better than he showed at Doncaster when last seen in September, shaped nicely enough and should better this form. He was bumped by the winner early in the straight but it didn't look to cost him. (tchd 4-1)
Mia's Boy, who was waited with, found this not setting up for him and he couldn't match his recent handicap form (tchd 4-1 and 5-1)
Spirit Of Sharjah(IRE) was entitled to need this after 309 days off. (op 10-1 tchd 14-1)

8227 QUEBEC STKS (LISTED RACE) 1m 2f (P)
2:25 (2:27) (Class 1) 3-Y-O+
£18,714 (£7,095; £3,550; £1,768; £887; £445) **Stalls** Low

Form RPR

4252 **1** **True To Form (IRE)**[9] 8095 5-9-3 96 (p) DavidProbert 9 99
(Martyn Meade) *hld up in tch in midfield: effrt whn sltly hmpd over 1f out: hdwy u.p ins fnl f: r.o wl to ld towards fin* **10/1**

0032 **2** *nk* **Emerald Wilderness (IRE)**[17] 7999 8-9-3 87 EddieAhern 10 98
(Mark Rimmer) *t.k.h: hld up in tch in last quartet: hdwy on outer over 1f out: str run u.p ins fnl f: wnt 2nd cl home* **16/1**

062 **3** *nk* **Be Perfect (USA)**[30] 7825 3-9-0 95 (t) AdamKirby 5 97
(Marco Botti) *t.k.h: sn led: rdn and wnt 2 l clr whn hung rt bnd wl over 1f out: edgd bk lft over 1f out: edgd rt u.p ins fnl f: hdd and lost 2 pls cl home* **5/2**[1]

3041 **4** *nse* **Tinshu (IRE)**[24] 7904 6-8-12 95 (p) WilliamCarson 1 92
(Derek Haydn Jones) *broke wl: stdd bk to chse ldrs: rdn and chsd ldr 2f out: swtchd rt over 1f out: ev ch wl ins fnl f: no ex last strides* **6/1**[3]

6001 **5** *1 1/2* **Mawaakef (IRE)**[17] 7986 4-9-3 88 ShaneKelly 3 94
(J R Jenkins) *in tch: rdn and effrt wl over 1f out: styd on same pce u.p ins fnl f* **25/1**

0201 **6** *1/2* **Chapter Seven**[70] 7064 3-9-0 98 JamieSpencer 4 93
(Stuart Williams) *awkward leaving stalls and slowly away: sn rcvrd and in tch in midfield: rdn and effrt wl over 1f out: styd on same pce ins fnl f* **5/1**[2]

3225 **7** *1 1/4* **Solfilia**[24] 7895 3-8-9 80 RobertHavlin 11 86
(Hughie Morrison) *dwlt: hld up in tch in last pair: edging out rt and hdwy u.p over 1f out: styd on but nvr threatened ldrs* **25/1**

15/ **8** *nk* **Shadow Gate (JPN)**[64] 7233 10-9-3 105 FMBerry 6 90
(Takashi Kodama, Ire) *t.k.h: sn chsng ldr: rdn over 3f out: unable qck u.p and sltly hmpd over 1f out: no threat to ldrs ins fnl f* **5/2**[1]

251 **9** *4* **Sheila's Buddy**[44] 7644 3-9-0 78 LiamKeniry 7 82
(J S Moore) *hld up in tch in midfield: rdn and unable qck over 2f out: wknd over 1f out: wl hld and eased wl ins fnl f* **33/1**

0004 **10** *3 1/4* **Decent Fella (IRE)**[12] 8055 6-9-3 89 (tp) SeanLevey 2 76
(Violet M Jordan) *t.k.h: hld up in tch in last quartet: rdn and effrt wl over 1f out: no prog 1f out: sn wknd and eased wl ins fnl f* **50/1**

4156 **11** *22* **Layline (IRE)**[12] 8056 5-9-3 88 RobertWinston 8 32
(Gay Kelleway) *hld up in tch in last pair: wknd jst over 2f out: eased fr wl over 1f out: t.o* **33/1**

2m 4.42s (-2.18) **Going Correction** -0.075s/f (Stan)
WFA 3 from 4yo+ 3lb **11 Ran SP% 118.6**
Speed ratings (Par 111): **105,104,104,104,103 102,101,101,98,95 78**
Tote Swingers: 1&2 £11.50, 1&3 £6.60, 2&3 £7.30 CSF £145.49 TOTE £10.20: £2.60, £3.90, £1.60; EX 89.20 Trifecta £727.80 Pool: £1,591.49 - 1.64 winning tickets..
Owner Ladyswood Stud **Bred** Sir E J Loder **Trained** Sherston, Wilts

FOCUS
This weak Listed race was run at a muddling gallop. The runner0up is perhaps the key to the form, but it's hard to be confident about the race.

NOTEBOOK
True To Form(IRE) came here off the back of a career-best when second in a 1m handicap at Kempton off 96 and he's at least as good at this trip. While the form is ordinary at best for the level, his profile suggests he may have more to offer. (op 8-1)
Emerald Wilderness(IRE) had been beaten off 85 the last twice, so had plenty to find at the weights, but he was formerly quite decent. He put up a good performance in defeat, despite going freely to post, but you wouldn't want to bank on him repeating this level next time. (op 12-1)
Be Perfect(USA) set the pace and the long-time leader would probably have won had he not conceded ground when failing to handle the bend into the straight. Marco Botti's runner held a clear lead going into the final turn, at which point he was already trading at long odds-on (touched a low of 1.12 on Betfair). Although run out of it, this trip suited him better than the 1m4f he faced at Kempton on his previous start. (op 3-1)
Tinshu(IRE), last year's winner and successful off 92 last time, might have preferred a stronger gallop. (op 9-2)
Mawaakef(IRE) found this tougher than the Kempton handicap he won from a mark of 83 on his previous start. (op 20-1)
Chapter Seven, last seen winning off 92 at York (1m1f, soft) in October, had since been sold out of Richard Fahey's yard for 95,000gns. This wasn't a particularly encouraging first start for new connections/Polytrack debut, but he may not be best judged on a muddling race like this. (op 6-1)
Shadow Gate(JPN), who formerly raced in Japan, had won a decent event at Dundalk on his Irish debut in October, but this was disappointing, the 10yo finding little despite being well placed. (op 7-2)

Layline(IRE) Official explanation: jockey saisd gelding lost its action

8228 LINGFIELDPARK.CO.UK H'CAP — 1m 4f (P)

3:00 (3:00) (Class 2) (0-100,90) 3-Y-O+ **£12,938** (£3,850; £1,924; £962) **Stalls** Low

Form				RPR
0006	1		**Royal Peculiar**[8] 8110 4-9-0 **80** ... AndrewMullen 5 (Michael Appleby) *chsd ldr: rdn and pressed ldr 3f out: led 2f out: hld on wl u.p fnl f* **5/1**[3]	88
0021	2	*nk*	**Super Say (IRE)**[15] 8019 6-9-10 **90** ... (t) JamieSpencer 7 (Mark Rimell) *chsd ldng pair: clsd to chal 2f out: sustained duel w wnr fr over 1f out: hld towards fin* **7/1**	97
2423	3	*1 1/2*	**Uphold**[17] 7999 5-8-10 **76** oh1 ... (e) RobertWinston 8 (Gay Kelleway) *led: clr 9f out tl over 3f out: hdd and rdn 2f out: styd on same pce u.p fnl f* **7/2**[2]	81
2112	4	*1*	**Thecornishcockney**[10] 8073 3-9-3 **88** ... (tp) StevieDonohoe 6 (John Ryan) *hld up in last pair: hdwy to chse ldrs over 2f out: hung lft whn asked for effrt over 1f out: continued to hang and one pce ins fnl f* **5/1**[3]	91
4011	5	*4 1/2*	**Stand Guard**[10] 8082 8-9-7 **87** ... AdamKirby 4 (John Butler) *in tch in midfield: pushed along 4f out: rdn and chsd ldr 2f out: no imp over 1f out: wknd and eased ins fnl f* **11/4**[1]	83
2203	6	*8*	**Tornado Force (IRE)**[15] 8019 4-9-2 **82** ... AndreaAtzeni 3 (Chris Dwyer) *hld up in tch in midfield: rdn and struggling over 2f out: wknd 2f out* **5/1**[3]	65
00-0	7	*4 1/2*	**Blizzard Blues (USA)**[8] 8110 6-8-11 **77** ... (b) EddieAhern 2 (Aytach Sadik) *hld up in last pair: rdn and struggling over 2f out: sn wknd* **66/1**	53

2m 29.95s (-3.05) **Going Correction** -0.075s/f (Stan)
WFA 3 from 4yo+ 5lb — 7 Ran SP% **112.9**
Speed ratings (Par 109): **107,106,105,105,102 96,93**
Tote Swingers: 1&2 £4.90, 1&3 £4.60, 2&3 £2.90 CSF £37.86 CT £136.48 TOTE £7.00: £3.10, £2.80; EX 44.20 Trifecta £216.80 Pool: £1,798.80 - 6.22 winning tickets..
Owner Terry Pryke **Bred** Newsells Park Stud **Trained** Danethorpe, Notts

FOCUS

The top-weight was rated 10lb below the race ceiling of 100, so not a strong race for the class. They went a good gallop and the third is the best guide.

NOTEBOOK

Royal Peculiar cost just 4,000gns out of Sir Henry Cecil's yard in October, but he improved on the form he showed on his first two starts for this trainer, who was completing a treble on the card. He showed a good attitude and may have more to offer. (op 4-1)

Super Say(IRE), claimed out of Jamie Osborne's yard for £10,000 after winning over 1m2f here last time, bettered that form despite finding a bit less than looked likely after travelling strongly. (op 8-1)

Uphold set the pace, but was a bit free and couldn't sustain his bid. (op 5-1 tchd 6-1)

Thecornishcockney, an awkward horse, didn't help his rider and is better over further. (tchd 6-1)

Stand Guard had won his last two, the most recent over C&D off 6lb lower, but this time he was reported by Adam Kirby to have run flat. Official explanation: jockey said gelding ran flat (tchd 5-2)

8229 HARRISONS LOFT CONVERSIONS H'CAP — 1m 4f (P)

3:35 (3:36) (Class 6) (0-65,69) 3-Y-O **£2,181** (£644; £322) **Stalls** Low

Form				RPR
0431	1		**Cool Sky**[8] 8106 3-9-11 **69** ... AdamKirby 13 (William Knight) *hld up in tch: qcknd to ld 3f out and sn clr: in command after: readily* **7/4**[1]	82+
0202	2	*3*	**Elegant Ophelia**[11] 8060 3-9-7 **65** ... AndreaAtzeni 6 (Dean Ivory) *hld up in tch in midfield: rdn and effrt over 2f out: chsd clr wnr wl over 1f out: r.o but no real imp* **5/1**[2]	72
2303	3	*1/2*	**Sweet Liberta (IRE)**[13] 8050 3-8-9 **53** ... DavidProbert 5 (Andrew Balding) *in tch in midfield: nt clr run and shuffled bk over 2f out: rallied and hdwy wl over 1f out: kpt on u.p ins fnl f: no threat to wnr* **14/1**	59+
3151	4	*1/2*	**Norfolk Sky**[13] 8048 3-9-1 **66** ... ThomasBrown(7) 3 (Laura Mongan) *chsd ldrs: nt clr run over 2f out: rdn and rallied wl over 1f out: kpt on u.p ins fnl f: no threat to wnr* **6/1**[3]	71
000	5	*1 1/2*	**Made Of More**[19] 7964 3-8-12 **56** ... RobertHavlin 16 (Roger Ingram) *t.k.h: hld up in tch towards rr: rdn and hdwy whyen rn wd bnd 2f out: styd on ins fnl f: nvr trbld ldrs* **33/1**	59
0000	6	*shd*	**Extremely Alert**[13] 7174 3-7-13 **46** oh1 ... SimonPearce(3) 12 (Michael Bell) *s.i.s: in rr: hdwy into midfield 7f out: rdn to chse ldrs ent fnl 2f: kpt on but no ch w wnr* **16/1**	49
1306	7	*shd*	**Bramshill Lass**[13] 8048 3-9-6 **64** ... (b) SeanLevey 11 (Amanda Perrett) *chsd ldrs: rdn to chse clr wnr jst over 2f out tl 2f out: no ex over 1f out: wknd ins fnl f* **20/1**	67
5603	8	*3 1/4*	**Tallevu (IRE)**[19] 7960 3-8-12 **56** ... RichardKingscote 9 (Noel Chance) *hld up in tch in midfield: rdn and effrt jst over 2f out: no imp over 1f out: wl hld fnl f* **14/1**	53
60-0	9	*2 1/2*	**Fromthestables Com (IRE)**[19] 7964 3-8-13 **57** ... SebSanders 7 (Brendan Powell) *stdd and awkward leaving stalls: hld up in rr: rdn and sme hdwy over 1f out: no real imp fnl f* **66/1**	50
6034	10	*3/4*	**Guava**[13] 8048 3-8-2 **46** oh1 ... JamieMackay 14 (Shaun Harris) *hld up in tch in rr: rdn and no imp ent fnl 2f: nvr trbld ldrs* **25/1**	38
0233	11	*hd*	**Masters Blazing**[14] 8035 3-9-5 **63** ... StevieDonohoe 8 (John Ryan) *hld up in tch towards rr: effrt and no imp jst over 2f out: wknd over 1f out* **8/1**	55
0000	12	*1 1/2*	**I'm Harry**[31] 7811 3-8-7 **58** ... (t) AaronJones(7) 4 (George Baker) *t.k.h: led tl 3f out: lost pl over 2f out: bhd fnl f* **10/1**	48
6304	13	*9*	**Hoonose**[17] 8001 3-8-2 **46** ... (b) LukeMorris 1 (Pat Eddery) *chsd ldr tl 3f out: sn lost pl: bhd and eased fnl f* **16/1**	21

2m 30.8s (-2.20) **Going Correction** -0.075s/f (Stan) — 13 Ran SP% **125.7**
Speed ratings (Par 98): **104,102,101,101,100 100,100,98,96,95 95,94,88**
Tote Swingers: 1&2 £5.00, 1&3 £6.10, 2&3 £10.20 CSF £10.05 CT £101.62 TOTE £2.90: £1.90, £1.70, £2.60; EX 14.00 Trifecta £204.40 Pool: £50,986.85 - 187.02 winning tickets..
Owner No Quarter Partnership **Bred** Miss K J Keir **Trained** Patching, W Sussex

FOCUS

A moderate handicap run at a fairly steady pace. Sound form, with a clear personal best from the winner.

T/Jkpt: Not won. T/Plt: £151.90 to a £1 stake. Pool: £64,379.25 - 309.33 winning tickets. T/Qpdt: £36.50 to a £1 stake. Pool: £5,029.66 - 101.72 winning tickets. SP

8207 WOLVERHAMPTON (A.W) (L-H)

Saturday, December 22

OFFICIAL GOING: Standard
Wind: Light across Weather: Raining

8230 HORSE RACING FREE BETS WITH BOOKMAKERS.CO.UK MAIDEN STKS — 5f 20y(P)

1:00 (1:05) (Class 5) 2-Y-O **£3,040** (£904; £452; £226) **Stalls** Low

Form				RPR
2	1		**Golden Flower**[21] 7953 2-8-12 0 ... TomEaves 3 (David O'Meara) *mde all: clr over 1f out: shkn up and r.o wl: easily* **1/4**[1]	71+
	2	*4 1/2*	**Black Rider (IRE)** 2-9-3 0 ... AmyRyan 2 (Kevin Ryan) *s.s: outpcd: hdwy over 1f out: wnt 2nd fnl f: edgd lft: no ch w wnr* **4/1**[2]	57+
0650	3	*3 1/2*	**Her Royal Empress**[117] 5682 2-8-12 45 ... GrahamGibbons 4 (James Unett) *chsd wnr: rdn 1/2-way: wkng whn lost 2nd 1f out* **16/1**[3]	39
0	4	*2*	**Copper Leyf**[22] 7931 2-9-0 0 ... RaulDaSilva(3) 5 (Jeremy Gask) *chsd ldrs: rdn and wknd over 1f out* **18/1**	37
	5	*3 3/4*	**Whiteflats** 2-9-3 0 ... MartinDwyer 1 (Derek Shaw) *s.s: effrt 1/2-way: wknd wl over 1f out* **25/1**	23

1m 1.75s (-0.55) **Going Correction** -0.10s/f (Stan) — 5 Ran SP% **115.0**
Speed ratings (Par 96): **100,92,87,84,78**
Tote Swinger 1&2 £2.40 CSF £1.87 TOTE £1.10: £1.02, £1.80; EX 1.90 Trifecta £5.50 Pool: £687.83 - 93.55 winning tickets..
Owner Middleham Park Racing XLII **Bred** Whitley Stud **Trained** Nawton, N Yorks

FOCUS

An uncompetitive maiden. The winner scored with something in hand but is rated only to form.

NOTEBOOK

Golden Flower had an excellent opportunity to finally break her duck and she had the race won after about 100yds, pinging out of the gate and securing an easy lead, whereas the runner-up, her main market rival, was slowly away and soon outpaced. The winner is effective at both 5f-6f and can pay her way in handicaps. (op 2-9)

Black Rider(IRE), whose dam was placed over 1m2f (half-sister to a 5f winner), was in trouble soon after the start but got nicely on top in the battle for second and shouldn't be long in going one better. (tchd 7-2)

Her Royal Empress, rated just 45, showed a bit more on this return from 117 days off and may find a poor handicap. (op 14-1)

Copper Leyf is bred for a bit further and may do better in time. (op 16-1 tchd 20-1)

Whiteflats, whose dam was placed up to 1m, was always struggling on debut. (op 16-1)

8231 BEST HORE RACING ODDS WITH BOOKMAKERS.CO.UK H'CAP — 5f 20y(P)

1:35 (1:40) (Class 6) (0-62,61) 3-Y-O+ **£2,102** (£625; £312; £156) **Stalls** Low

Form				RPR
010	1		**M J Woodward**[35] 7776 3-9-4 58 ... JamesSullivan 3 (Paul Green) *led to 1/2-way: rdn to ld ins fnl f: r.o* **4/1**[2]	65
0000	2	*hd*	**Ryedale Dancer (IRE)**[7] 8131 4-8-13 53 ... RobbieFitzpatrick 2 (Richard Guest) *hld up: hdwy over 1f out: r.o wl* **25/1**	59
5345	3	*nk*	**Trending (IRE)**[47] 7590 3-9-4 61 ... (b) RaulDaSilva(3) 1 (Jeremy Gask) *trckd ldrs: rdn over 1f out: r.o* **15/8**[1]	66
5404	4	*nk*	**Scommettitrice (IRE)**[2] 8190 4-8-12 57 ... (p) WilliamTwiston-Davies(5) 4 (David Evans) *w ldr tl led 1/2-way: rdn over 1f out: hdd ins fnl f: styd on* **11/1**	61
1200	5	*1 3/4*	**Athwaab**[17] 7990 5-9-6 60 ... GeorgeBaker 8 (Noel Chance) *chsd ldrs: rdn over 1f out: no ex ins fnl f* **11/2**[3]	58
2524	6	*nk*	**Loyal Royal (IRE)**[11] 8064 9-9-4 58 ... (bt) AmyRyan 6 (Milton Bradley) *hld up: plld hrd: effrt and n.m.r over 1f out: nvr trbld ldrs* **6/1**	55
0460	7	*3/4*	**Sophie's Beau (USA)**[53] 7456 5-8-2 49 ow2 ... (bt) RyanTate(7) 7 (Michael Chapman) *hld up: rdn over 1f out: styd on same pce ins fnl f* **14/1**	43
1005	8	*2 1/2*	**Sally's Swansong**[19] 7969 6-9-3 57 ... (b) GrahamGibbons 5 (Eric Alston) *s.s: a in rr* **7/1**	42

1m 1.77s (-0.53) **Going Correction** -0.10s/f (Stan) — 8 Ran SP% **115.8**
Speed ratings (Par 101): **100,99,99,98,95 95,94,90**
Tote Swingers 1&2 £25.80, 2&3 £24.80, 1&3 £3.30 CSF £92.38 CT £242.46 TOTE £3.70: £1.10, £11.80, £1.70; EX 90.60 Trifecta £377.40 Pool: £1,283.35 - 2.55 winning tickets..
Owner E Sciarrillo **Bred** Paul Green **Trained** Lydiate, Merseyside

FOCUS

Little got into this modest handicap, in which there was a bunch finish. The winner is rated to his Catterick win in October.

Sally's Swansong Official explanation: jockey said mare was slowly away

8232 NO DEPOSIT FREE BETS WITH BOOKMAKERS.CO.UK H'CAP — 5f 216y(P)

2:05 (2:10) (Class 5) (0-78,78) 3-Y-O+ **£3,040** (£904; £452; £226) **Stalls** Low

Form				RPR
133	1		**Fathsta (IRE)**[7] 8143 7-9-4 75 ... TonyHamilton 7 (Ian Williams) *broke wl: sn stdd and lost pl: hdwy over 1f out: r.o u.p to ld wl ins fnl f* **9/1**	85
0002	2	*nk*	**Irish Heartbeat (IRE)**[10] 8077 7-9-3 74 ... GeorgeBaker 5 (Jamie Osborne) *chsd ldrs: stdd and lost pl over 4f out: hdwy over 1f out: rdn and ev ch wl ins fnl f: r.o* **7/2**[1]	83
5133	3	*1 1/4*	**Waking Warrior**[10] 8081 4-9-7 78 ... (tp) AmyRyan 9 (Kevin Ryan) *a.p: led over 1f out: rdn and hdd wl ins fnl f* **4/1**[2]	83
0062	4	*1 1/4*	**Master Bond**[61] 7291 3-9-5 76 ... (t) TomEaves 2 (Bryan Smart) *dwlt: sn prom and racing keenly: rdn over 1f out: styd on u.p* **8/1**	77
400	5	*1/2*	**Summerinthecity (IRE)**[19] 7966 5-9-4 75 ... GrahamGibbons 6 (David Nicholls) *led 5f out: rdn and hdd over 1f out: styd on same pce ins fnl f* **6/1**	74
5322	6	*1/2*	**Parisian Pyramid (IRE)**[4] 8159 6-9-0 71 ... StephenCraine 3 (Ian Williams) *chsd ldrs: rdn over 2f out: styd on* **9/2**[3]	69
0036	7	*1*	**Dancing Welcome**[12] 8059 6-8-8 72 ... (b) RyanTate(7) 10 (Milton Bradley) *sn pushed along in rr: r.o towards fin: nvr nrr* **20/1**	67
5252	8	*nk*	**Red Cape (FR)**[28] 7863 9-8-13 70 ... (b) JamesSullivan 1 (Ruth Carr) *led 1f: chsd ldrs: rdn over 1f out: wknd ins fnl f* **12/1**	64
0404	9	*1 1/2*	**Divine Call**[12] 8058 5-9-4 75 ... MichaelO'Connell 13 (Milton Bradley) *hld up: rdn over 1f out: nvr on terms* **10/1**	64
4300	10	*3/4*	**Prince Of Passion (CAN)**[12] 8059 4-8-7 64 ... (v) MartinDwyer 12 (Derek Shaw) *chsd ldrs: rdn over 1f out: wknd fnl f* **33/1**	50

000 **11** *6* **Quality Art (USA)**106 6005 4-9-6 77 KellyHarrison 8 44
(Richard Guest) *hld up: rdn and wknd wl over 1f out* **20/1**
1m 13.45s (-1.55) **Going Correction** -0.10s/f (Stan) **11** Ran SP% **125.0**
Speed ratings (Par 103): **106,105,103,102,101 100,99,99,97,96 88**
Tote Swingers 1&2 £9.60, 2&3 £4.20, 1&3 £3.20 CSF £42.24 CT £153.58 TOTE £11.00: £2.70, £1.30, £2.50; EX 46.40 Trifecta £315.30 Pool: £773.58 - 1.84 winning tickets..
Owner Dr Marwan Koukash **Bred** Brian Miller **Trained** Portway, Worcs
FOCUS
A well-run, competitive handicap and the form looks fair for the grade, rated around the winner.

8233 BOOKIE FREE BETS WITH BOOKMAKERS.CO.UK MAIDEN STKS 5f 216y(P)
2:40 (2:46) (Class 5) 2-Y-O **£3,040** (£904; £452; £226) **Stalls** Low

Form RPR
0 **1** **Rene Mathis (GER)**107 5963 2-9-3 0 TonyHamilton 3 74+
(Richard Fahey) *plld hrd and prom: wnt 2nd 1/2-way: rdn to ld over 1f out: hung lft ins fnl f: r.o* **6/1**3
52 **2** *2* **Lady Malet**14 8033 2-8-12 0 AdamBeschizza 5 63
(William Haggas) *sn led: rdn and hdd over 1f out: no ex ins fnl f* **4/7**1
506 **3** *3 3/4* **Perfect Venture**17 7987 2-8-12 66 JohnFahy 4 52
(Clive Cox) *prom: rdn over 1f out: styd on same pce* **9/2**2
00 **4** *1 1/2* **Handsome Stranger (IRE)**10 8071 2-9-3 0 TomMcLaughlin 2 52
(David Evans) *s.i.s: hld up: shkn up over 1f out: nvr trbld ldrs* **12/1**
063 **5** *shd* **Twinwood Star (IRE)**130 5194 2-8-12 47 TomEaves 1 47
(John Weymes) *led early: chsd ldrs: rdn over 1f out: no ex* **33/1**
6 *2* **Polar Forest** 2-9-3 0 RobbieFitzpatrick 7 46
(Richard Guest) *s.s: in rr: nvr on terms* **20/1**
00 **7** *8* **Actonetaketwo**15 8018 2-8-7 0 ow2 RyanWhile(7) 6 19
(Ron Hodges) *prom: chsd ldr 5f out tl 1/2-way: rdn and wknd over 1f out* **100/1**
1m 14.84s (-0.16) **Going Correction** -0.10s/f (Stan) **7** Ran SP% **112.5**
Speed ratings (Par 96): **97,94,89,87,87 84,73**
Tote Swingers 1&2 £2.00, 2&3 £1.10, 1&3 £3.50 CSF £9.60 TOTE £4.00: £2.00, £1.10; EX 12.40 Trifecta £44.20 Pool: £1,464.56 - 24.81 winning tickets..
Owner Dr Marwan Koukash **Bred** Stall 5-Stars **Trained** Musley Bank, N Yorks
FOCUS
The front two pulled clear, but didn't finish in the order the market suggested they would. The fifth and time offer perspective.
NOTEBOOK
Rene Mathis(GER), well beaten in one previous turf run for Ed Dunlop in September, readily disposed of the short-priced favourite despite having taken a fierce hold early. He'd been gelded since that initial effort and showed plenty of pace in making his winning move rounding the final bend. On this evidence he could develop into quite a decent handicapper. (op 5-1 tchd 9-2)
Lady Malet showed fair form in defeat over 7f at Lingfield last time, but the drop to 6f didn't work out against a speedier rival, being readily outpaced despite having been gifted an easy lead. She can win a maiden back up in trip. (op 4-9)
Perfect Venture was no match for the front pair and will find low-grade handicaps more to her liking. (op 8-1)
Handsome Stranger(IRE) will be of interest once handicapping returned to a longer trip.

8234 MONEY BACK RACING SPECIALS AT BOOKMAKERS.CO.UK H'CAP 1m 1f 103y(P)
3:15 (3:20) (Class 5) (0-78,76) 3-Y-O+ **£3,040** (£904; £452; £226) **Stalls** Low

Form RPR
0652 **1** **Knowe Head (NZ)**5 8146 5-9-2 70 (v) AdamBeschizza 2 78
(James Unett) *s.i.s: sn chsng ldrs: rdn over 1f out: led wl ins fnl f: jst hld on* **6/4**1
0124 **2** *nse* **Strike Force**3 8175 8-8-9 68 (t) NatashaEaton(5) 5 76
(Alison Hutchinson) *chsd ldr: rdn over 1f out: led ins fnl f: sn hdd: r.o* **5/1**3
5140 **3** *2 1/4* **Elizabeth Coffee (IRE)**7 8136 4-9-2 70 TomEaves 6 73
(John Weymes) *led: rdn over 1f out: hdd and unable qck ins fnl f* **25/1**
0262 **4** *4* **Reflect (IRE)**88 6555 4-9-7 75 (t) MartinDwyer 7 70
(Derek Shaw) *hld up: plld hrd: pushed along over 2f out: nvr on terms* **7/1**
0521 **5** *14* **The Mongoose**7 8141 4-8-13 67 (t) TomMcLaughlin 1 32
(David Evans) *prom: rdn over 2f out: wknd over 1f out* **15/8**2
2m 0.4s (-1.30) **Going Correction** -0.10s/f (Stan)
WFA 3 from 4yo+ 2lb **5** Ran SP% **107.8**
Speed ratings (Par 103): **101,100,98,95,82**
Tote Swinger 1&2 £3.40 CSF £8.86 TOTE £3.00: £2.20, £1.10; EX 7.40 Trifecta £44.70 Pool: £1,113.57 - 18.67 winning tickets..
Owner Lord Stuart J Stone **Bred** Glazeley Farms Trust **Trained** Tedsmore Hall, Shropshire
FOCUS
The pace appeared reasonable despite the small field. Modest form, the third the key.

8235 HORSE RACING BEST BETS AT BOOKMAKERS.CO.UK H'CAP 2m 119y(P)
3:50 (3:50) (Class 4) (0-85,82) 3-Y-O+ **£5,336** (£1,588; £793; £396) **Stalls** Low

Form RPR
05P5 **1** **Woolfall Treasure**10 8073 7-10-0 82 (v) GeorgeBaker 6 84
(Gary Moore) *mde all: rdn over 1f out: all out* **4/1**2
-424 **2** *nk* **Zakatal**22 7522 6-9-11 79 DaleSwift 5 81
(Julie Camacho) *chsd wnr after 2f: rdn and ev ch fnl 2f: styd on* **14/1**
2102 **3** *3/4* **Gabrial's King (IRE)**5 8149 3-8-11 73 (v) TonyHamilton 4 74
(Ian Williams) *hld up: hdwy over 1f out: sn rdn: hung lft ins fnl f: r.o* **7/4**1
4 *2* **Adiynara (IRE)**37 4299 4-9-4 77 WilliamTwiston-Davies(5) 1 76
(Neil Mulholland) *chsd ldrs: rdn over 2f out: hung lft and styd on same pce ins fnl f* **20/1**
0003 **5** *5* **Activate**5 8148 5-9-9 77 TomEaves 3 70
(David O'Meara) *chsd ldrs: rdn over 2f out: wknd over 1f out* **12/1**3
3241 **P** **Fourth Generation (IRE)**10 8073 5-9-13 81 MartinDwyer 2
(Alan Swinbank) *hld up: hdwy over 2f out: gng wl whn wnt wrong over 1f out: sn p.u: fatally injured* **7/4**1
3m 42.7s (0.90) **Going Correction** -0.10s/f (Stan)
WFA 3 from 4yo+ 8lb **6** Ran SP% **111.8**
Speed ratings (Par 105): **93,92,92,91,89**
Tote Swingers 1&2 £6.00, 2&3 £2.70, 1&3 £1.20 CSF £51.15 TOTE £4.00: £1.10, £7.60; EX 28.20 Trifecta £154.70 Pool: £1,574.50 - 7.63 winning tickets..
Owner Andrew Bradmore **Bred** Serpentine Bloodstock Et Al **Trained** Lower Beeding, W Sussex
FOCUS
The pace, steady early, suddenly lifted 5f out. Messy form with joint favourite Fourth Generation going well when suffering a fatal injury.

8236 FREE SPORTS BETTING AT BOOKMAKERS.CO.UK H'CAP 7f 32y(P)
4:20 (4:20) (Class 5) (0-70,70) 3-Y-O+ **£3,040** (£904; £452; £226) **Stalls** High

Form RPR
0222 **1** **Lastkingofscotland (IRE)**4 8160 6-9-5 68 (b) GeorgeBaker 9 79
(Conor Dore) *mid-div: hdwy over 2f out: led on bit over 1f out: r.o wl: readily* **4/5**1
0450 **2** *2 3/4* **Colbyor**14 8034 3-9-1 64 TonyHamilton 10 68
(Richard Fahey) *chsd ldrs: rdn and ev ch over 1f out: styd on same pce ins fnl f* **7/2**2
0462 **3** *2 1/2* **Imprimis Tagula (IRE)**7 8133 8-9-2 70 (v) NatashaEaton(5) 3 67
(Alan Bailey) *prom: rdn over 1f out: styd on same pce* **5/1**3
4400 **4** *1/2* **My Own Way Home**7 8137 4-8-13 62 ow1 TomMcLaughlin 5 57
(David Evans) *led: rdn over 2f out: hdd over 1f out: no ex fnl f* **20/1**
003 **5** *1/2* **Mazovian (USA)**54 7436 4-9-7 70 RussKennemore 4 64
(Michael Chapman) *chsd ldrs: rdn over 3f out: wknd ins fnl f* **16/1**
5000 **6** *nk* **Mataajir (USA)**16 8005 4-8-9 58 MartinDwyer 11 51
(Derek Shaw) *hld up: rdn over 2f out: nvr trbld ldrs* **8/1**
006 **7** *3 1/4* **Sleepy Lucy**64 6000 3-8-7 56 oh11 (e) KellyHarrison 7 41
(Richard Guest) *hmpd s: hld up: rdn over 1f out: nvr on terms* **50/1**
1010 **8** *3 1/2* **North Central (USA)**8 8114 5-8-10 59 (p) JamesSullivan 8 34
(Ruth Carr) *chsd ldrs: rdn over 1f out: wknd fnl f* **16/1**
0040 **9** *3* **Upper Lambourn (IRE)**22 7937 4-9-6 69 DaleSwift 2 36
(Christopher Kellett) *hld up: rdn over 2f out: sn wknd* **66/1**
330- **10** *11* **Rubenstar (IRE)**445 6616 9-9-3 66 StephenCraine 1
(Daniel Mark Loughnane) *hld up: rdn and wknd over 2f out* **20/1**
1m 28.43s (-1.17) **Going Correction** -0.10s/f (Stan) **10** Ran SP% **130.3**
Speed ratings (Par 103): **102,98,96,95,94 94,90,86,83,70**
Tote Swingers 1&2 £1.90, 2&3 £7.00, 1&3 £2.20 CSF £4.34 CT £11.46 TOTE £2.30: £1.40, £1.02, £2.80; EX 7.70 Trifecta £18.40 Pool: £3,386.07 - 137.61 winning tickets..
Owner Mrs Jennifer Marsh **Bred** Baronrath Stud **Trained** Hubbert's Bridge, Lincs
FOCUS
An uncompetitive handicap won readily by the favourite, who is rated back to something like his best.
T/Plt: £110.00 to a £1 stake. Pool: £52,511.45 - 348.48 winning tickets. T/Qpdt: £25.80 to a £1 stake. Pool: £3,796.86 - 108.90 winning tickets. CR

8230 WOLVERHAMPTON (A.W) (L-H)
Wednesday, December 26

OFFICIAL GOING: Standard
Wind: Fresh behind Weather: Overcast turning to rain after race 1

8237 BRITISH STALLION STUDS SUPPORTING BRITISH RACING E B F MEDIAN AUCTION MAIDEN STKS 5f 20y(P)
1:40 (1:40) (Class 5) 2-Y-O **£3,137** (£933) **Stalls** Low

Form RPR
232 **1** **Boxing Shadows**26 7931 2-9-3 72 TomEaves 1 77+
(Bryan Smart) *mde all: clr fr over 1f out: easily* **1/10**1
0640 **2** *5* **Faffa**23 7974 2-9-3 58 DuranFentiman 4 59
(Tim Easterby) *chsd wnr: pushed along 1/2-way: sn outpcd* **7/1**2
1m 2.92s (0.62) **Going Correction** -0.15s/f (Stan) **2** Ran SP% **103.4**
Speed ratings (Par 96): **89,81**
CSF £1.11 TOTE £1.10.
Owner Clipper Logistics **Bred** Catridge Farm Stud Ltd **Trained** Hambleton, N Yorks
FOCUS
This was easy for Boxing Shadows, and the form is of little worth.
NOTEBOOK
Boxing Shadows, who had placed on his first three starts, most recently when returning from a break over 6f here, had 14lb in hand of his sole rival on official figures. We didn't learn anything new. (op 1-8)
Faffa, who finished last when blinkered over 7f here off a mark of 58 on his previous start, was totally outclassed. (op 11-2 tchd 5-1)

8238 THE HOLLY & THE IVY CLAIMING STKS 7f 32y(P)
2:10 (2:10) (Class 6) 3-Y-O+ **£1,704** (£503; £251) **Stalls** High

Form RPR
2424 **1** **Light From Mars**6 8181 7-8-12 77 WilliamTwiston-Davies(5) 2 83
(Ronald Harris) *w ldr: pushed along over 2f out: rdn over 1f out: hung rt ins fnl f: styd on u.p to ld towards fin* **85/40**2
3211 **2** *nse* **Majuro (IRE)**5 8202 8-9-3 81 (t) AdamKirby 1 83
(Charles Smith) *led: rdn over 1f out: hung rt ins fnl f: hdd towards fin* **1/1**1
6546 **3** *3 1/4* **Chambles**47 7666 3-8-10 67 MartinDwyer 6 67
(Alan McCabe) *s.i.s: outpcd: hdwy over 2f out: rdn over 1f out: no ex ins fnl f* **14/1**
0000 **4** *1 1/4* **Al Khan (IRE)**11 8143 3-9-3 77 GrahamGibbons 5 71
(Michael Easterby) *chsd ldrs: rdn over 1f out: styd on same pce* **9/1**3
5403 **5** *2 3/4* **Faithful Ruler (USA)**11 8133 8-8-9 69 (p) LukeMorris 7 55
(Ronald Harris) *sn pushed along and prom: rdn over 2f out: hung lft and wknd over 1f out* **16/1**
1055 **U** **Elegant Muse**12 8114 4-8-0 60 (t) DominicFox 4
(Michael Appleby) *stmbld and uns rdr sn after s* **10/1**
1m 27.72s (-1.88) **Going Correction** -0.15s/f (Stan) **6** Ran SP% **113.6**
Speed ratings (Par 101): **104,103,100,98,95**
toteswingers: 1&2 £1.70, 1&3 £3.20, 2&3 £3.40 CSF £4.71 TOTE £3.30: £1.70, £1.20; EX 4.80 Trifecta £22.60 Pool: £479.23 - 15.88 winning units..Al Khan was claimed by S. Arnold for £10,000
Owner Mrs N Macauley **Bred** Harts Farm And Stud **Trained** Earlswood, Monmouths
■ Stewards' Enquiry : William Twiston-Davies seven-day ban: use of whip (9-15 Jan)
FOCUS
The first two, fair sorts for the level, filled the front two positions more or less throughout. They've been rated around their recent best.

8239 MERRY CHRISTMAS MAIDEN STKS 1m 141y(P)
2:40 (2:40) (Class 5) 3-Y-O+ **£2,385** (£704; £352) **Stalls** Low

Form RPR
4602 **1** **Abbraccio**11 8141 4-9-5 72 LukeMorris 7 62
(Ronald Harris) *a.p: chsd ldr 7f out: pushed along over 4f out: led over 1f out: sn rdn: styd on* **11/10**1
2 *3/4* **Frontier Fighter** 4-9-5 0 TomEaves 8 61
(David O'Meara) *hld up: hdwy over 2f out: rdn over 1f out: r.o* **7/2**2
2 **3** *2* **Dutch Mistress**9 8151 3-8-12 0 DavidProbert 5 51
(James Unett) *led: rdn and hdd over 2f out: styd on same pce fnl f* **4/1**3
3034 **4** *nse* **American Lover (FR)**9 8151 5-8-9 45 AdamCarter(5) 1 51
(John Wainwright) *hld up: hdwy over 1f out: r.o: nt rch ldrs* **25/1**
0002 **5** *3 3/4* **Mistress Shy**22 7981 5-9-0 45 (t) GrahamGibbons 6 42
(Michael Appleby) *chsd ldrs tl rdn and wknd over 1f out* **12/1**
6 *5* **Dubai Story** 3-8-12 0 FergusSweeney 3 31
(Alastair Lidderdale) *s.i.s: hdwy 7f out: rdn and wknd over 2f out* **15/2**
000 **7** *6* **Kuraanda**41 7729 3-8-12 35 BarryMcHugh 4 17
(John Wainwright) *s.i.s: a in rr: drvn along over 3f out: sn wknd* **125/1**

000- 8 8 **Clouds Of Glory**[422] 7196 3-8-12 10 RobertWinston 2
(Jason Ward) *plld hrd and prom: rdn and wknd over 2f out: eased fnl f* 100/1

1m 49.65s (-0.85) **Going Correction** -0.15s/f (Stan)
WFA 3 from 4yo+ 2lb 8 Ran SP% 114.9
Speed ratings (Par 103): **97,96,94,94,91 86,81,74**
toteswingers: 1&2 £2.70, 1&3 £2.00, 2&3 £3.50 CSF £5.16 TOTE £2.30: £1.10, £2.60, £1.80; EX 8.60 Trifecta £23.50 Pool: £380.06 - 12.12 winning units..
Owner Ridge House Stables Ltd **Bred** Cheveley Park Stud Ltd **Trained** Earlswood, Monmouths

FOCUS
A weak maiden run at a muddling gallop. The form is limited by the fourth.

8240 GOOGLE "MFORTUNE" FOR £5 FREE BET NURSERY 1m 141y(P)
3:15 (3:17) (Class 4) (0-85,82) 2-Y-O £3,881 (£1,155; £577; £288) Stalls Low

Form				RPR
2621	1		**Glory City (IRE)**[57] 7460 2-9-3 78 (tp) AdamKirby 6 (Marco Botti) *chsd ldrs: rdn over 1f out: r.o to ld wl ins fnl f* 11/4[1]	80
214	2	½	**Infinite Magic (USA)**[55] 7501 2-9-7 82 SebSanders 3 (Jeremy Noseda) *sn pushed along and prom: rdn over 1f out: ev ch ins fnl f: r.o* 4/1[3]	83
0451	3	½	**Brownsea Brink**[35] 7806 2-8-11 77 WilliamTwiston-Davies(5) 1 (Richard Hannon) *chsd ldrs: led over 1f out: rdn and hdd wl ins fnl f* 3/1[2]	77
0351	4	½	**Tight Knit (USA)**[32] 7868 2-9-1 76 LukeMorris 7 (James Tate) *chsd ldr tl led wl over 1f out: sn rdn and hdd: edgd lft: styd on* 4/1[3]	75
5320	5	4 ½	**Sewn Up**[11] 8132 2-8-7 68 ChrisCatlin 2 (Reg Hollinshead) *n.m.r s: hld up: hdwy over 2f out: rdn over 1f out: hung lft and no ex fnl f* 20/1	57
5201	6	3	**Red Eight (USA)**[11] 8132 2-8-10 71 GrahamGibbons 4 (John Butler) *led: rdn and hdd wl over 1f out: wknd fnl f* 10/1	54
0504	7	2 ½	**Night's Watch**[27] 7924 2-8-7 68 MartinDwyer 5 (William Jarvis) *hld up: racd keenly: hdwy and hung rt over 2f out: wknd over 1f out* 12/1	46

1m 47.68s (-2.82) **Going Correction** -0.15s/f (Stan) 2y crse rec 7 Ran SP% 113.2
Speed ratings (Par 98): **106,105,105,104,100 98,95**
toteswingers: 1&2 £1.70, 1&3 £1.80, 2&3 £2.50 CSF £13.79 TOTE £4.10: £2.60, £1.10; EX 9.80 Trifecta £29.00 Pool: £618.70 - 15.96 winning units..
Owner Fung Lok Li **Bred** Eamon D Delany **Trained** Newmarket, Suffolk

FOCUS
This was run at a good gallop. The time was almost two seconds quicker than the earlier older-horse maiden and this was a fair race for the time of year.

NOTEBOOK
Glory City(IRE), off the mark in a C&D maiden when last seen in October, had cheekpieces added and found improvement to follow up. He may yet have more to offer. (op 5-2 tchd 2-1)
Infinite Magic(USA), returning from 55 days off, never really travelled but plugged on. He may yet do a bit better as he matures. (op 9-2)
Brownsea Brink couldn't follow up his 7f Kempton maiden win but this was a fair performance on his handicap debut. (op 4-1 tchd 5-1)
Tight Knit(USA) found this tougher than the C&D maiden in which he made all last time. Unable to dominate, he raced close enough to the strong pace and didn't really travel. (op 11-2)
Sewn Up wasn't good enough. (op 16-1 tchd 14-1)
Red Eight(USA), 7lb higher than when making all in a lesser race over C&D on his previous start, went off too fast. (op 11-2)
Night's Watch raced freely and went really wide into the straight. Martin Dwyer reported his mount hung right-handed. Official explanation: jockey said that the colt hung right-handed (op 9-1 tchd 8-1)

8241 FESTIVE SPIRIT H'CAP 1m 1f 103y(P)
3:45 (3:49) (Class 6) (0-60,60) 3-Y-O+ £1,704 (£503; £251) Stalls Low

Form				RPR
055	1		**Royal Sea (IRE)**[22] 7983 3-8-11 52 GrahamGibbons 11 (David O'Meara) *sn chsng ldr: led wl over 1f out: sn rdn and hung lft: styd on: eased nr fin* 11/4[1]	63+
0340	2	2	**Guava**[4] 8229 3-8-5 46 oh1 DavidProbert 3 (Shaun Harris) *chsd ldrs: rdn and ev ch 1f out: styd on same pce* 8/1	52
4603	3	3	**Corrib (IRE)**[50] 7620 9-8-7 46 oh1 (p) LukeMorris 6 (Bryn Palling) *sn pushed along and prom: rdn over 1f out: styd on same pce* 16/1	46
0654	4	nk	**May Boy**[40] 7752 6-8-8 47 ChrisCatlin 5 (Ron Hodges) *hld up: pushed along over 2f out: r.o ins fnl f: nrst fin* 16/1	46
0001	5	¾	**Count Ceprano (IRE)**[22] 7982 8-8-11 53 SimonPearce(3) 4 (Lydia Pearce) *mid-div: nt clr run over 1f out: r.o ins fnl f: nvr nrr* 8/1	51
4264	6	1 ¼	**My New Angel (IRE)**[100] 6316 3-8-5 46 NickyMackay 1 (Paul Green) *chsd ldrs: rdn over 1f out: wknd ins fnl f* 25/1	41
3-01	7	1 ¼	**Lord Of The Dance (IRE)**[7] 8167 6-9-7 60 TomEaves 12 (Michael Mullineaux) *hld up: nt clr run fr over 1f out: nvr able to chal* 9/2[3]	54+
6500	8	¾	**Our Ivor**[17] 8050 3-8-5 49 ow3 RyanPowell(3) 8 (Michael Appleby) *prom: rdn over 1f out: wknd ins fnl f* 12/1	40
-605	9	1 ¼	**Kingarrick**[12] 8113 4-9-6 59 RobertWinston 10 (Noel Wilson) *hld up: shkn up and hung lft fr over 1f out: n.d* 4/1[2]	47
030	10	½	**Bidable**[121] 5657 8-8-7 46 DuranFentiman 2 (Bryn Palling) *sn led: rdn and hdd wl over 1f out: wknd fnl f* 33/1	33
1400	11	1 ¼	**Meglio Ancora**[12] 8113 5-8-13 57 RachealKneller(5) 13 (Richard Ford) *s.s: hld up: nvr on terms* 28/1	41

2m 0.44s (-1.26) **Going Correction** -0.15s/f (Stan)
WFA 3 from 4yo+ 2lb 11 Ran SP% 116.8
Speed ratings (Par 101): **99,97,94,94,93 92,91,90,89,89 88**
toteswingers: 1&2 £4.20, 1&3 £7.40, 2&3 £10.60 CSF £24.60 CT £299.15 TOTE £3.80: £1.60, £3.50, £2.90; EX 29.80 Trifecta £338.40 Pool: £1,196.03 - 2.65 winning units..
Owner Direct Racing Partnership **Bred** Rabbah Bloodstock Limited **Trained** Nawton, N Yorks

FOCUS
A moderate handicap. The form is set around the second and third and the winner could do better.
Royal Sea(IRE) ◆ Official explanation: trainer said, regarding the apparent improvement of form, that the gelding had benefitted from the step up in trip
Count Ceprano(IRE) Official explanation: jockey said that the gelding was denied a clear run
Lord Of The Dance(IRE) Official explanation: jockey said that the gelding was denied a clear run
Meglio Ancora Official explanation: jockey said that the gelding hung left-handed

8242 WOLVERHAMPTON-RACECOURSE.CO.UK H'CAP 1m 1f 103y(P)
4:15 (4:17) (Class 2) (0-100,88) 3-Y-O+ £10,221 (£3,041; £1,519; £759)

Form				RPR
1021	1		**Viewpoint (IRE)**[16] 8056 3-9-4 87 KieranO'Neill 2 (Richard Hannon) *chsd ldrs: rdn to ld over 1f out: r.o* 2/1[1]	95
3000	2	nk	**Tepmokea (IRE)**[60] 7396 6-9-6 87 LukeMorris 4 (Mrs K Burke) *led: rdn and hdd over 1f out: r.o u.p* 11/2	93
1313	3	1 ½	**Desert Vision**[12] 8110 8-9-2 83 (vt) GrahamGibbons 8 (Michael Easterby) *chsd ldr: rdn and ev ch over 1f out: styd on same pce ins fnl f* 9/2[3]	86
0213	4	nk	**Rakaan (IRE)**[13] 8095 5-9-6 87 FergusSweeney 3 (Jamie Osborne) *hld up: hdwy over 1f out: sn rdn: r.o: nt rch ldrs* 3/1[2]	89
4001	5	3 ½	**Incendo**[83] 6828 6-9-4 88 RyanPowell(3) 7 (Ian Williams) *hld up in tch: rdn over 1f out: hung lft and no ex fnl f* 16/1	83
1110	6	8	**Boonga Roogeta**[18] 7688 3-8-4 80 HannahNunn(7) 5 (Peter Charalambous) *s.i.s: hdwy over 6f out: rdn and wknd over 1f out* 10/1	58
2231	7	24	**Kay Gee Be (IRE)**[50] 7601 8-9-2 83 RobertWinston 6 (Alan Berry) *prom tl rdn and wknd over 3f out: t.o* 10/1	11

1m 58.7s (-3.00) **Going Correction** -0.15s/f (Stan)
WFA 3 from 4yo+ 2lb 7 Ran SP% 116.0
Speed ratings (Par 109): **107,106,105,105,102 94,73**
toteswingers: wingers 1&2 £3.80, 1&3 £3.00, 2&3 £4.80 CSF £13.96 CT £44.31 TOTE £2.80: £2.50, £5.20; EX 16.50 Trifecta £84.90 Pool: £2,213.34 - 19.54 winning units..
Owner The Heffer Syndicate **Bred** F Dunne **Trained** East Everleigh, Wilts

FOCUS
No stalls for this race owing to a technical fault, so a flag start, and Tepmokea began best, taking the field along at a modest gallop. An ordinary race for the grade.

NOTEBOOK
Viewpoint(IRE), 3lb higher than when winning over 1m2f at Lingfield last time, was always well placed and saved ground for most of the way, notably into the straight where he nipped through towards the inside rail. He won with a bit more authority than the margin suggests and is progressing into a decent sort. (op 9-4 tchd 15-8)
Tepmokea(IRE) took the field along at a modest gallop before keeping on well. He shaped well after two months off, but plenty went his way. (op 9-1)
Desert Vision wasn't beaten far but he's high enough in the weights. (op 5-1 tchd 11-2)
Rakaan(IRE) didn't get the strong pace he needs and did well to get so close. (op 11-4 tchd 7-2)
Incendo, something of a bridle horse who was claimed out of James Fanshawe's yard for £10,000 after winning over 1m4f here in October, wasn't helped by a steadily run race at this shorter trip. (tchd 14-1)
Boonga Roogeta raced much too keenly without cover. (tchd 12-1)

8243 BOXING DAY H'CAP 1m 4f 50y(P)
4:45 (4:45) (Class 5) (0-75,74) 3-Y-O+ £2,264 (£673; £336; £168) Stalls Low

Form				RPR
0303	1		**Sir Boss (IRE)**[11] 8136 7-9-5 69 TomEaves 6 (Michael Mullineaux) *hld up: hdwy over 2f out: nt clr run over 1f out: r.o to ld wl ins fnl f* 7/1[3]	77
0000	2	¾	**Illustrious Forest**[37] 7792 4-9-7 71 DavidProbert 5 (John Mackie) *chsd ldr tl led over 2f out: rdn over 1f out: edgd lft: hdd wl ins fnl f* 9/1	78
5345	3	shd	**Cosmic Halo**[35] 7819 3-8-8 63 BarryMcHugh 3 (Richard Fahey) *hld up: hdwy and nt clr run 2f out: sn rdn: styd on* 12/1	70
0600	4	2 ½	**Flying Trader (USA)**[14] 8082 3-8-11 73 IanBurns(7) 4 (Jane Chapple-Hyam) *racd keenly: led at stdy pce tl qcknd over 3f out: hdd over 2f out: styd on same pce fnl f* 10/1	76
4201	5	hd	**Honoured (IRE)**[11] 8139 5-9-0 64 (t) LukeMorris 2 (Michael Appleby) *chsd ldrs: rdn over 2f out: styd on same pce fnl f* 5/2[1]	67
0000	6	¾	**Brunston**[21] 7986 6-9-10 74 FergusSweeney 8 (Anthony Middleton) *hld up: rdn over 2f out: styd on ins fnl f: nvr nrr* 10/1	75
2450	7	1 ½	**White Diamond**[16] 7839 5-8-12 65 RyanPowell(3) 9 (Michael Appleby) *mid-div: rdn over 2f out: nvr trbld ldrs* 16/1	64
0042	8	6	**Honest Deal**[37] 7792 4-9-7 71 RobertWinston 10 (Alan Swinbank) *prom: rdn over 2f out: wknd over 1f out* 11/4[2]	60
0100	9	¾	**Boa**[11] 8136 7-9-7 71 AdamKirby 1 (Reg Hollinshead) *hld up: rdn and hung lft over 1f out: a in rr* 25/1	59
0103	10	98	**Jeer (IRE)**[9] 8149 8-9-3 67 (t) GrahamGibbons 7 (Michael Easterby) *s.i.s: hdwy over 6f out: rdn over 3f out: wknd over 2f out: t.o* 9/1	

2m 36.42s (-4.68) **Going Correction** -0.15s/f (Stan)
WFA 3 from 4yo+ 5lb 10 Ran SP% 123.3
Speed ratings (Par 103): **109,108,108,106,106 106,105,101,100,35**
toteswingers: 1&2 £11.40, 1&3 £13.40, 2&3 £22.80 CSF £72.48 CT £761.40 TOTE £8.10: £2.40, £4.20, £4.20; EX 118.60 Trifecta £1466.50 Part won. Pool: £1,955.36 - 0.61 winning units..
Owner Miss M Mullineaux, P Lawton, I Ross **Bred** Mrs E R Cantillon **Trained** Alpraham, Cheshire

FOCUS
A modest handicap. The winner did not need to improve much on his recent form.
Jeer(IRE) Official explanation: jockey said that the gelding had stopped quickly
T/Jkpt: £550.80 to a £1 stake. Pool of £13,826.14 - 17.82 winning tickets. T/Plt: £10.90 to a £1 stake. Pool of £43,535.77 - 2,901.62 winning tickets. T/Qpdt: £9.20 to a £1 stake. Pool of £2,957.80 - 235.40 winning tickets. CR

8100 GULFSTREAM PARK (L-H)
Wednesday, December 26

OFFICIAL GOING: Turf: firm

8244a MAIDEN CLAIMING RACE (MAIDEN CLAIMER) (2YO) (TURF) 1m 1f
10:05 (12:00) 2-Y-O
£8,129 (£3,245; £1,219; £541; £135; £135)

			RPR
1		**Ricochet Court (USA)** 2-8-8 0 JVBridgmohan 3 (Nicholas Zito, U.S.A) 169/10	
2	1	**Rey Rocket (USA)** 2-8-6 0 (b[1]) LPanici 8 (Henry Collazo, U.S.A) 151/10	
3	½	**El Tuscano (USA)** 2-8-1 0 (b) EZayas(7) 6 (Manuel J Azpurua, U.S.A) 163/10	
4	1 ¼	**Mr Pumpermichael (USA)** 2-8-8 0 LSaez 9 (Philip A Gleaves, U.S.A) 73/10	
5	2 ¼	**Tango Kid (USA)** 2-8-8 0 (b[1]) LContreras 2 (Brian A Lynch, Canada) 21/10[1]	
6	¾	**Edson's Ridge (USA)** 2-8-8 0 (b[1]) ElvisTrujillo 4 (Philip A Gleaves, U.S.A) 189/10	
7	¾	**How About Peace (USA)** 2-8-8 0 (b) ENunez 7 (Kathleen O'Connell, U.S.A) 118/10	
8	1 ¾	**Big Boss Baby (USA)** 2-8-6 0 (b) JDelgado 1 (Luis Olivares, U.S.A) 96/1	
9	2 ¼	**Wardroom (USA)** 2-8-8 0 DiegoFGomez 10 (Manuel J Azpurua, U.S.A) 114/1	
10	½	**Marchwood**[83] 6826 2-8-6 0 JRoccoJr 5 (Amy Weaver) 23/5[3]	

11 1 1/4 **Sleeping Bull (USA)** 2-8-8 0........................(b) FJara 12
(R Posada, U.S.A) **67/1**
12 nse **Scandalo (USA)** 2-8-8 0........................(b) JLezcano 11
(Rodolfo Garcia, U.S.A) **29/10**[2]
1m 50.31s (110.31) **12** Ran SP% **121.6**
PARI-MUTUEL: WIN (all including $1 stakes): 35.80; PLACE (1-2): 15.00, 13.60; SHOW (1-2-3): 14.60, 9.60, 9.40; SF (including 2 ars stake) 816.10.
Owner Lucky Shamrock Stable **Bred** Lucky Shamrock Partners Llc **Trained** USA

8223 LINGFIELD (L-H)
Thursday, December 27
OFFICIAL GOING: Standard

8245 32RED CASINO NURSERY 5f (P)
11:45 (11:46) (Class 5) (0-75,71) 2-Y-O **£2,385** (£704; £352) **Stalls** High

Form RPR
31 **1** **Saga Lout**[12] 8138 2-9-7 71........................ RichardKingscote 3 75+
(Tom Dascombe) *chsd ldr towards outer: pushed along and briefly outpcd over 2f out: rdn and edgd lft over 1f out: r.o to ld fnl 75yds* **2/7**[1]
6104 **2** 3/4 **Pixilated**[141] 4936 2-9-5 69........................ DavidProbert 5 69
(Gay Kelleway) *led: rdn 2f out: kpt on: hdd fnl 75yds* **14/1**[3]
3040 **3** shd **Outbid**[21] 8007 2-8-5 60........................ LeonnaMayor(5) 1 60
(Jamie Osborne) *trckd ldr: rdn over 1f out: kpt on* **16/1**
610 **4** 1 1/4 **Tartan Blue**[16] 8065 2-8-0 57........................(p) HannahNunn(7) 4 52
(Robert Cowell) *trckd ldr: rdn 2f out: ev ch jst ins fnl f: no ex fnl 100yds* **20/1**
0001 **5** 6 **Mossgo (IRE)**[16] 8065 2-9-4 68........................ RobertWinston 2 42
(John Best) *sltly bmpd s: racd keenly hld up: rdn 2f out: sn btn* **6/1**[2]
59.12s (0.32) **Going Correction** -0.05s/f (Stan) **5** Ran SP% **109.4**
Speed ratings (Par 96): **95,93,93,91,82**
CSF £5.46 TOTE £1.10: £1.02, £5.90; EX 5.50 Trifecta £17.70 Pool: £676.93 - 28.65 winning tickets..
Owner Laurence A Bellman **Bred** G E Amey **Trained** Malpas, Cheshire

FOCUS
Just a handful of runners in a moderate nursery with an odds-on favourite. It's hard to ge excited about the bare form.

NOTEBOOK
Saga Lout, winner of a Wolverhampton maiden 12 days earlier, followed up with a snug victory. Not the fastest away, he needed to be driven to make ground in the home straight, but finally squeezed through between rivals to score with a bit in hand. He should handle a sixth furlong. (op 1-3)
Pixilated, a Yarmouth maiden winner in June and gelded since his last run, broke well and was soon in front. He responded gamely when the winner came past, but could not quicken sufficiently to make him work close home. (op 10-1)
Outbid, eighth in one of these on her latest start, fared a good deal better here. She was always close to the pace and battled on well in the closing stages. (op 14-1)
Tartan Blue, wearing first-time cheekpieces, was prominent until fading late on. (op 16-1)
Mossgo(IRE), up 1lb for his C&D victory last time out, never got into meaningful contention after an awkward start. Robert Winston reported that the gelding ran too free to post and in the early stages of the race. Official explanation: jockey said that the gelding ran too free to post and in the early stages of the race

8246 32REDBET.COM CLAIMING STKS 5f (P)
12:15 (12:15) (Class 6) 3-Y-O+ **£1,704** (£503; £251) **Stalls** High

Form RPR
2231 **1** **Drawnfromthepast (IRE)**[22] 7995 7-9-2 83........................ JimCrowley 5 68
(Jim Boyle) *trckd ldng pair: led appr fnl f: pushed out to assert: shade cosily* **4/6**[1]
5022 **2** 1 **Beauty Pageant (IRE)**[49] 7648 5-8-10 77........................ GrahamGibbons 1 59
(David Brown) *led narrowly: rdn whn hdd appr fnl f: kpt on but a hld by wnr* **2/1**[2]
0065 **3** 1/2 **Amenable (IRE)**[6] 8202 5-8-13 77........................(e[1]) WilliamCarson 6 60
(Violet M Jordan) *prom on outer: rdn 2f out: kpt on* **12/1**[3]
4650 **4** 2 **Haadeeth**[12] 8144 5-8-5 63........................ LukeMorris 4 45
(David Evans) *dwlt: sn in tch: pushed along 1/2-way: drvn over 1f out: sn no imp on ldrs* **12/1**[3]
6005 **5** 1/2 **Sherjawy (IRE)**[8] 8169 8-9-0 47........................ SimonPearce(3) 3 55
(Zoe Davison) *hld up: rdn 2f out: nvr threatened* **100/1**
000 **6** 11 **Bird Dog**[230] 2046 6-8-7 46........................(v) DavidProbert 2
(Phil McEntee) *in tch: pushed along 1/2-way: wknd over 1f out: eased* **100/1**
58.18s (-0.62) **Going Correction** -0.05s/f (Stan) **6** Ran SP% **110.7**
Speed ratings (Par 101): **102,100,99,96,95 78**
Tote swingers 1&2 £1.20, 1&3 £1.50, 2&3 £2.10 CSF £2.12 TOTE £1.60: £1.50, £1.10; EX 2.50 Trifecta £5.10 Pool: £880.95 - 127.43 winning tickets..Beauty Pageant was claimed by Mr P. D. Evans for £8,000. Drawnfromthepast was claimed by Mr J. A. Osborne for £8,500.
Owner M Khan X2 **Bred** D And Mrs D Veitch **Trained** Epsom, Surrey

FOCUS
A claimer featuring a wide range of abilities. The fifth probably sets the level.

8247 £32 BONUS AT 32RED.COM (S) STKS 5f (P)
12:45 (12:45) (Class 6) 2-Y-O **£1,704** (£503; £251) **Stalls** High

Form RPR
1242 **1** **Windforpower (IRE)**[5] 8224 2-9-3 66........................(be) LukeMorris 2 66
(Ronald Harris) *sn trckd ldr: chal on bit appr fnl f: upsides under hands and heels ins fnl f: drvn ahd nr fin* **7/4**[2]
6 **2** nk **Princess Cammie (IRE)**[78] 6975 2-8-7 0........................ KieranO'Neill 3 55
(Mike Murphy) *led: rdn over 1f out: sn strly pressed: kpt on: hdd nr fin* **14/1**[3]
3234 **3** 1 1/2 **Quality Mark (USA)**[12] 8138 2-8-12 65........................ JimCrowley 4 55
(Jeremy Noseda) *hld up in 4th: pushed along 2f out: rdn over 1f out: sn one pce and no threat to ldng pair* **4/7**[1]
50 **4** 5 **Blue Missile**[15] 8068 2-8-5 0........................ RyanWhile(7) 1 37
(Bill Turner) *chsd ldr: rdn 2f out: wknd fnl f* **33/1**
59.2s (0.40) **Going Correction** -0.05s/f (Stan) **4** Ran SP% **109.6**
Speed ratings (Par 94): **94,93,91,83**
CSF £18.35 TOTE £3.10; EX 11.70 Trifecta £43.00 Pool: £348.38 - 6.07 winning tickets..Quality Mark was bought by Gay Kelleway for £6,000.
Owner Anthony Cooke **Bred** Tally-Ho Stud **Trained** Earlswood, Monmouths

FOCUS
A modest juvenile seller and the level of the form is straightforward.

NOTEBOOK
Windforpower(IRE) was fitted with an eyeshield as well as his customary blinkers and travelled kindly in this new headgear combination. After racing in third, he cruised up to the pacesetting second at the 1f pole and edged to the front soon afterwards. He is far from straightforward, but was comfortably the best of these on the day. (tchd 2-1)
Princess Cammie(IRE), sixth of seven on her only previous outing, broke well and was soon in front. She proved no match for the winner in the closing stages, but has progressed from her debut effort and should find a little race. (op 6-1)
Quality Mark(USA), dropped to this level for the first time, was a disappointing odds-on favourite. Last until the turn for home, he produced much less than expected when asked to make ground. (op 4-6 tchd 4-5)
Blue Missile, dropped in both trip and grade on this third start, was prominent early, but faded tamely in the home straight.

8248 FOLLOW @ATTHERACES ON TWITTER H'CAP (DIV I) 1m (P)
1:15 (1:15) (Class 6) (0-60,60) 3-Y-O+ **£1,704** (£503; £251) **Stalls** High

Form RPR
0001 **1** **Brown Pete (IRE)**[6] 8212 4-9-3 56 6ex........................ WilliamCarson 1 64+
(Violet M Jordan) *trckd ldrs: rdn 2f out: drvn and kpt on fnl f: led fnl 50yds* **2/1**[1]
6022 **2** 3/4 **Putin (IRE)**[8] 8169 4-8-3 47........................(bt) LeonnaMayor(5) 7 53
(Phil McEntee) *prom on outer: rdn 2f out: kpt on* **5/1**[2]
4623 **3** 1/2 **Sudden Wish (IRE)**[19] 8038 3-9-1 55........................ LukeMorris 8 60
(David Evans) *w ldr: rdn to ld over 2f out: strly pressed ins fnl f: hdd and lost 2 pls fnl 50yds* **5/1**[2]
2220 **4** 1/2 **Songbird Blues**[24] 7964 3-9-3 57........................ DavidProbert 11 61
(Mark Usher) *hld up in midfield: pushed along 3f out: rdn and hdwy on outside over 1f out: kpt on fnl f* **20/1**
0503 **5** nse **Finlodex**[24] 7964 5-9-4 57........................ FrankieMcDonald 5 61
(Murty McGrath) *s.i.s and early reminder: hld up: rdn over 2f out: kpt on towards wd outside fr over 1f out: nrst fin* **11/2**[3]
0623 **6** 1/2 **Lindoro**[12] 8131 7-9-4 57........................ ChrisCatlin 12 60
(Sean Curran) *midfield: rdn to chse ldrs over 1f out: one pce and no further imp fnl f* **12/1**
40-0 **7** 3/4 **West Side (IRE)**[15] 8083 4-8-13 52........................ RichardKingscote 3 53
(Michael Quinn) *hld up: rdn over 1f out: kpt on: nvr threatened ldrs* **20/1**
0650 **8** shd **Archelao (IRE)**[29] 7905 4-9-7 60........................ AmirQuinn 6 61
(Richard Rowe) *trckd ldrs: rdn 2f out: sn one pce: no ex fnl f* **10/1**
5440 **9** hd **Shared Moment (IRE)**[182] 3544 6-9-7 60........................(v) TomMcLaughlin 9 60
(Luke Dace) *v.s.a: hld up in rr: rdn 2f out: nvr threatened* **12/1**
4050 **10** shd **Pose (IRE)**[7] 8180 5-8-9 48 oh1 ow2........................(t) RobertHavlin 2 48?
(Roger Ingram) *midfield: rdn 2f out: sn no imp* **40/1**
0046 **11** 15 **Indian Violet (IRE)**[6] 8199 6-9-2 58........................(p) SimonPearce(3) 4 24
(Zoe Davison) *led narrowly: hdd over 2f out: wknd* **20/1**
1m 37.64s (-0.56) **Going Correction** -0.05s/f (Stan)
WFA 3 from 4yo+ 1lb **11** Ran SP% **123.3**
Speed ratings (Par 101): **100,99,98,98,98 97,96,96,96,96 81**
Tote swingers 1&2 £3.90, 1&3 £3.30, 2&3 £5.80 CSF £11.70 CT £47.67 TOTE £2.80: £1.60, £1.90, £2.00; EX 18.60 Trifecta £33.90 Pool: £626.52 - 13.83 winning tickets..
Owner Rakebackmypoker.com **Bred** Jim Halligan **Trained** Moreton Morrell, Warwicks

FOCUS
Division one of a low-grade handicap, with the top weight rated only 60. It did look competitive, though. Slightly muddling with the runner-up to his latest 6f mark the best guide.

8249 FOLLOW @ATTHERACES ON TWITTER H'CAP (DIV II) 1m (P)
1:50 (1:50) (Class 6) (0-60,60) 3-Y-O+ **£1,704** (£503; £251) **Stalls** High

Form RPR
6152 **1** **Storm Runner (IRE)**[21] 8010 4-9-3 56........................ IanMongan 3 64
(George Margarson) *midfield: rdn and hdwy over 2f out: chsd ldr over 1f out: led ins fnl f: kpt on* **11/4**[1]
0435 **2** 1 **Community (USA)**[34] 7841 4-8-13 57........................ LeonnaMayor(5) 8 63
(Jamie Osborne) *trckd ldr: rdn over 2f out: kpt on* **12/1**
0601 **3** 1/2 **Bertie Blu Boy**[19] 8039 4-8-13 52........................(b) GrahamGibbons 9 57
(Lisa Williamson) *sn led: rdn over 2f out: hdd ins fnl f: no ex and lost 2nd towards fin* **4/1**[2]
1005 **4** hd **Menadati (USA)**[8] 8167 4-9-7 60........................ ChrisCatlin 4 64+
(Peter Hiatt) *hld up in rr: rdn over 2f out: stl last over 1f out: r.o wl fnl f: nrst fin* **8/1**
2340 **5** nk **Fonterutoli (IRE)**[10] 8145 5-9-3 56........................(e) RobertHavlin 11 60
(Roger Ingram) *hld up: rdn and hdwy over 2f out: chsd ldrs over 1f out: kpt on one pce* **7/1**
6 3/4 **Jumbo Prado (USA)**[98] 6419 3-9-4 58........................ RichardKingscote 10 60
(Daniel Mark Loughnane) *in tch towards outer: rdn over 2f out: kpt on one pce* **6/1**[3]
2434 **7** nse **Strategic Action (IRE)**[33] 7861 3-8-13 56........................(t) RyanClark(3) 6 58
(Linda Jewell) *hld up: rdn over 2f out: kpt on fnl f: nvr threatened ldrs* **16/1**
0051 **8** 2 **Gallantry**[22] 7992 10-9-4 57........................ TomMcLaughlin 7 54
(Paul Howling) *midfield: rdn over 2f out: one pce and nvr threatened ldrs* **14/1**
0544 **9** 3 3/4 **Back For Tea (IRE)**[9] 8154 4-8-7 46 oh1........................(b) DavidProbert 5 35
(Phil McEntee) *in tch: rdn over 2f out: wknd ins fnl f* **50/1**
0000 **10** 4 **Temuco (IRE)**[18] 8051 3-9-5 59........................(v) LukeMorris 1 38
(David Evans) *dwlt: hld up: rdn 3f out: sn btn* **12/1**
0200 **11** 9 **Macy Anne (IRE)**[13] 8113 3-9-0 54........................ JimCrowley 2 13
(Jo Hughes) *trckd ldr: wknd over 1f out* **20/1**
1m 38.1s (-0.10) **Going Correction** -0.05s/f (Stan)
WFA 3 from 4yo+ 1lb **11** Ran SP% **119.2**
Speed ratings (Par 101): **98,97,96,96,96 95,95,93,89,85 76**
Tote swingers 1&2 £6.90, 1&3 £2.70, 2&3 £10.90 CSF £38.34 CT £136.36 TOTE £2.90: £2.80, £4.00, £1.60; EX 31.80 Trifecta £333.80 Pool: £681.11 - 1.53 winning tickets..
Owner Pitfield Partnership **Bred** Kevin Foley **Trained** Newmarket, Suffolk

FOCUS
Division tTwo of this modest handicap looked tougher to predict than its predecessor. The third and fifth help set the standard.

8250 32RED H'CAP 1m (P)
2:25 (2:25) (Class 4) (0-85,81) 3-Y-O+ **£4,294** (£1,268; £634) **Stalls** High

Form RPR
4621 **1** **Aquilonius (IRE)**[17] 8057 3-9-3 78........................(t) GeorgeBaker 3 89+
(Stuart Williams) *mde all: rdn clr appr fnl f: kpt on* **1/1**[1]
2112 **2** 2 **Red Somerset (USA)**[218] 2398 9-9-3 77........................ KieranO'Neill 5 83
(Mike Murphy) *hld up in tch: rdn and hdwy over 2f out: kpt on to go 2nd ins fnl f: no threat wnr* **10/1**
5625 **3** 2 1/4 **Jack Who's He (IRE)**[15] 8081 3-9-5 80........................(v) RichardKingscote 6 81
(David Evans) *prom towards outer: rdn over 2f out: sn one pce* **11/4**[2]

0464 **4** *1* **Tuscania**[8] 8174 4-9-7 81 .... LukeMorris 1 80
(Lucy Wadham) *in tch: rdn to chse wnr over 1f out: wknd ins fnl f* **4/1**[3]
0006 **5** *4 ½* **Benandonner (USA)**[10] 8145 9-8-3 70 .... JakePayne(7) 7 58
(Paddy Butler) *in tch: pushed along and outpcd 4f out: no threat after* **25/1**
65 **6** *4 ½* **Fairy Wing (IRE)**[17] 8055 5-8-12 75 .... (p) SimonPearce(3) 4 53
(Conor Dore) *w ldr: pushed along and lost pl over 3f out: wknd over 1f out* **20/1**

1m 36.67s (-1.53) **Going Correction** -0.05s/f (Stan)
WFA 3 from 4yo+ 1lb **6** Ran SP% **114.4**
Speed ratings (Par 105): **105,103,100,99,95 90**
Tote swingers 1&2 £2.30, 1&3 £1.50, 2&3 £2.50 CSF £12.88 TOTE £1.90: £1.50, £2.90; EX 7.20 Trifecta £19.20 Pool: £980.20 - 38.21 winning tickets..
Owner T W Morley & Mrs J Morley **Bred** Redmondstown Stud **Trained** Newmarket, Suffolk

FOCUS
A decent handicap, with the top weight rated 81. The runner-up is rated to his spring claimer form but overall not a strong race.

8251 32RED SUPPORTING BRITISH RACING MAIDEN STKS 6f (P)
3:00 (3:00) (Class 5) 3-Y-O+ **£2,385** (£704; £352) **Stalls** Low

Form RPR
-230 **1** **Captain Kendall (IRE)**[15] 8083 3-9-3 61 .... LukeMorris 1 63
(David Evans) *trckd ldr: rdn to ld appr fnl f: sn clr* **4/5**[1]
2243 **2** *3 ½* **Summer Sun**[9] 8154 3-8-12 52 .... RichardKingscote 4 47
(Phil McEntee) *sltly awkward s: in tch: rdn over 2f out: kpt on one pce: wnt 2nd nr fin: no ch w wnr* **9/2**[3]
0052 **3** *hd* **Island Express (IRE)**[9] 8154 5-8-12 42 .... (tp) AnnStokell(5) 3 51
(Ann Stokell) *hld up in tch: rdn over 2f out: hdwy to chse wnr jst ins fnl f: one pce and lost 2nd nr fin* **14/1**
2250 **4** *1* **Miakora**[8] 8168 4-8-12 54 .... WilliamCarson 6 43
(Michael Quinn) *trckd ldr: rdn over 2f out: sn one pce* **3/1**[2]
0000 **5** *4* **Desert Red (IRE)**[16] 8061 3-8-12 40 .... (vt[1]) DavidProbert 5 30
(Phil McEntee) *led: rdn whn hdd appr fnl f: wknd* **20/1**
65 **6** *3 ½* **Sign Pro (IRE)**[9] 8154 4-8-10 0 .... DanielMuscutt(7) 2 24
(Peter Bowen) *hld up: rdn and outpcd over 3f out: a in rr* **25/1**

1m 12.18s (0.28) **Going Correction** -0.05s/f (Stan) **6** Ran SP% **114.0**
Speed ratings (Par 103): **96,91,91,89,84 79**
Tote swingers 1&2 £1.50, 1&3 £2.90, 2&3 £2.60 CSF £5.06 TOTE £2.10: £1.20, £1.90; EX 5.10 Trifecta £20.30 Pool: £1,363.98 - 50.30 winning tickets..
Owner J G White **Bred** Pier House Stud **Trained** Pandy, Monmouths

FOCUS
A weak maiden best rated around the placed horses to the previous week's C&D form.

8252 32RED.COM H'CAP 1m 2f (P)
3:35 (3:37) (Class 5) (0-75,80) 3-Y-O+ **£2,385** (£704; £352) **Stalls** Low

Form RPR
303 **1** **Saoi (USA)**[20] 8020 5-9-7 75 .... JimCrowley 5 85
(William Knight) *hld up: smooth hdwy over 2f out: rdn to ld ins fnl f: kpt on wl* **9/2**
3042 **2** *1* **Sakhee's Pearl**[20] 8020 6-9-7 75 .... IanMongan 1 83
(Jo Crowley) *hld up: hdwy over 2f out: rdn to ld jst ins fnl f: sn hdd: kpt on but a hld by wnr* **7/2**[2]
3500 **3** *5* **Abigails Angel**[64] 7328 5-9-5 73 .... DavidProbert 8 71
(Brett Johnson) *hld up in midfield: rdn and hdwy to chse ldr 2f out: ev ch 1f out: no ex* **20/1**
5641 **4** *hd* **Daffydowndilly**[29] 7892 4-9-3 71 .... (bt) RobertHavlin 6 69
(Hughie Morrison) *midfield: rdn and outpcd over 2f out: kpt on fnl f: nvr threatened* **5/2**[1]
000 **5** *1 ½* **Understory (USA)**[8] 8162 5-9-1 69 .... LukeMorris 2 64
(Tim McCarthy) *led: hdd over 6f out: trckd ldr: rdn to ld again over 2f out: hdd jst ins fnl f: wknd* **33/1**
0001 **6** *2 ¾* **Icelander (USA)**[9] 8153 3-9-4 80 6ex .... (b) JemmaMarshall(5) 4 69
(Jo Hughes) *trckd ldrs: led over 6f out: rdn whn hdd over 2f out: wknd appr fnl f* **14/1**
3300 **7** *nk* **Poetic Lord**[36] 7805 3-9-1 72 .... (b) KieranO'Neill 7 61
(Richard Hannon) *trckd ldrs: rdn over 2f out: wknd over 1f out* **4/1**[3]
0463 **8** *6* **Adorable Choice (IRE)**[33] 7858 4-9-0 68 .... (v) RichardKingscote 3 45
(Tom Dascombe) *midfield: rdn over 2f out: sn wknd* **8/1**

2m 4.22s (-2.38) **Going Correction** -0.05s/f (Stan)
WFA 3 from 4yo+ 3lb **8** Ran SP% **114.5**
Speed ratings (Par 103): **107,106,102,102,100 98,98,93**
Tote swingers 1&2 £3.10, 1&3 £11.40, 2&3 £9.40 CSF £20.67 CT £282.58 TOTE £4.10: £1.10, £1.90, £4.40; EX 19.90 Trifecta £183.60 Pool: £1,444.90 - 5.90 winning tickets..
Owner Surrey Horseracing Limited **Bred** Kilboy Estate Inc **Trained** Patching, W Sussex

FOCUS
A competitive finale, with three runners disputing favouritism. The form is rated around the principals.
T/Plt: £10.60 to a £1 stake. Pool: £38,649.36 - 2,644.37 winning units T/Qpdt: £6.90 to a £1 stake. Pool: £3,144.98 - 333.98 winning units AS

8237 WOLVERHAMPTON (A.W) (L-H)
Thursday, December 27
OFFICIAL GOING: Standard changing to standard to fast after race 1 (4:00)
Wind: Fresh behind Weather: Light rain

8253 32RED.COM H'CAP 5f 20y(P)
4:00 (4:01) (Class 6) (0-60,60) 3-Y-O+ **£1,704** (£503; £251) **Stalls** Low

Form RPR
0000 **1** **Sunrise Dance**[55] 7524 3-9-4 57 .... (p) AndrewMullen 2 67
(Robert Johnson) *mde all: hung lft fr over 1f out: rdn out* **6/1**[3]
051 **2** *2* **Miss Bunter**[26] 7952 3-9-5 58 .... AmyRyan 3 68+
(David O'Meara) *hld up: hdwy 2f out: rdn to chse wnr ins fnl f: hmpd sn after: nt rcvr* **7/2**[1]
4300 **3** *1 ½* **Wreningham**[16] 8063 7-9-2 60 .... (p) CharlesBishop(5) 11 57
(Pat Eddery) *chsd wnr: rdn over 1f out: no ex ins fnl f* **20/1**
0032 **4** *1* **Chateau Lola**[6] 8210 3-8-13 52 .... MartinDwyer 5 46
(Derek Shaw) *chsd ldrs: rdn over 1f out: styd on same pce* **16/1**
423 **5** *1 ½* **First Rebellion**[6] 8210 3-8-0 46 .... RyanTate(7) 6 34
(Tony Carroll) *chsd ldrs: rdn 1/2-way: styng on same pce whn hung lft fnl f* **8/1**
6406 **6** *shd* **Russian Bullet**[103] 6249 3-9-3 56 .... FergusSweeney 7 44
(Jamie Osborne) *prom: racd keenly: rdn over 1f out: hung lft and styd on same pce fnl f* **13/2**
0044 **7** *2 ¼* **Liberty Ship**[137] 5131 7-9-7 60 .... ShaneKelly 8 40
(Mark Buckley) *hld up: rdn over 1f out: nvr on terms* **50/1**
0050 **8** *½* **Sally's Swansong**[5] 8231 6-8-13 57 ....[1] JasonHart(5) 1 35
(Eric Alston) *sn pushed along towards rr: rdn over 1f out: n.d* **16/1**
0002 **9** *¾* **Ryedale Dancer (IRE)**[5] 8231 4-9-0 53 .... RobbieFitzpatrick 4 28
(Richard Guest) *hld up: sddled slipped and rdr lost irons wl over 3f out: n.d* **7/1**
0000 **10** *1* **Thorpe Bay**[7] 8190 3-9-4 57 .... (b) DaleSwift 12 29
(Conor Dore) *prom: pushed along early: rdn and wknd over 1f out* **100/1**
0402 **11** *nk* **Volcanic Dust (IRE)**[7] 8190 4-9-0 58 ...... (b) WilliamTwiston-Davies(5) 10 29
(Milton Bradley) *dwlt: a in rr* **4/1**[2]
0600 **12** *nk* **Sherry Cherie (IRE)**[18] 8050 3-8-7 46 oh1 .... PatrickMathers 9 16
(Richard Fahey) *dwlt: sn pushed along in rr: wknd 2f out* **40/1**

1m 0.84s (-1.46) **Going Correction** -0.275s/f (Stan) **12** Ran SP% **115.4**
Speed ratings (Par 101): **100,96,94,92,90 90,86,85,84,83 82,82**
toteswingers 1&2 £6.20, 1&3 £24.40, 2&3 £18.00 CSF £25.77 CT £400.71 TOTE £9.40: £2.50, £1.20, £6.40; EX 41.00 Trifecta £1116.00 Part won. Pool: £1,488.11 - 0.30 winning tickets..
Owner M Saunders **Bred** Mrs Ann Jarvis **Trained** Newburn, Tyne & Wear
■ Stewards' Enquiry : Andrew Mullen two-day ban: careless riding (10-11 Jan)

FOCUS
Mainly exposed performers in a moderate handicap. The gallop was a reasonable one and the winner raced close to the inside rail throughout. He posted his best effort of the year.
Ryedale Dancer(IRE) Official explanation: jockey said that his stirrup leather broke

8254 32RED CASINO MAIDEN AUCTION STKS 5f 216y(P)
4:30 (4:30) (Class 6) 2-Y-O **£1,704** (£503; £251) **Stalls** Low

Form RPR
0 **1** **Al Gharrafa**[22] 7987 2-8-7 0 .... JimmyQuinn 2 62
(Marco Botti) *s.i.s: sn prom: chsd ldr 2f out: rdn over 1f out: r.o to ld towards fin* **9/2**[2]
522 **2** *½* **Lady Malet**[5] 8233 2-8-10 0 .... AdamBeschizza 3 63
(William Haggas) *led: edgd rt over 1f out: sn rdn: hdd towards fin* **1/4**[1]
06 **3** *3* **Duchess Of Dreams**[49] 7653 2-8-7 0 ow1 .... RobbieFitzpatrick 1 51
(Richard Guest) *hld up: hdwy over 2f out: rdn over 1f out: styd on same pce fnl f* **28/1**
6 **4** *hd* **Polar Forest**[5] 8233 2-9-0 0 .... J-PGuillambert 4 57
(Richard Guest) *edgd rt s: sn pushed along to chse ldr: rdn over 2f out: styd on same pce fnl f* **12/1**[3]
000 **5** *7* **Shesthecaptain (IRE)**[55] 7525 2-8-1 47 .... NeilFarley(3) 6 26
(John Weymes) *prom: rdn over 3f out: wknd over 2f out* **100/1**
0 **6** *1* **Firey Sally (IRE)**[78] 6992 2-8-4 0 .... AndrewMullen 5 23
(Frank Sheridan) *s.i.s and hmpd s: nvr on terms* **50/1**

1m 14.11s (-0.89) **Going Correction** -0.275s/f (Stan) **6** Ran SP% **112.3**
Speed ratings (Par 94): **94,93,89,89,79 78**
toteswingers 1&2 £1.10, 1&3 £4.40, 2&3 £2.80 CSF £6.12 TOTE £3.10: £1.50, £1.10; EX 7.40 Trifecta £31.30 Pool: £3,175.88 - 75.98 winning tickets..
Owner Mubarak Al Naemi **Bred** A C M Spalding **Trained** Newmarket, Suffolk

FOCUS
A most uncompetitive maiden in which an ordinary gallop only picked up turning for home on a surface that was changed to "standard-to-fast" after the opener. The two market leaders, who pulled clear, raced in the centre in the straight. The winner improved from her debut.

NOTEBOOK
Al Gharrafa still looked green but she stepped up a fair way on her debut effort and showed a good attitude to nail the market leader in the closing stages. She'll be suited by the step up to 7f when she switches to handicaps and, given her dam was a multiple Fibresand winner, she'll be of interest on that surface when Southwell reopens early next year. (op 5-1)
Lady Malet was allowed to do her own thing in front and ran as well as she ever has done, despite racing with the choke out. This again underlined her vulnerability in this type of event but she'll be suited by the return to 7f and she remains capable of winning a minor event on this surface this winter. (tchd 2-7)
Duchess Of Dreams posted her best effort yet but, while flattered by the proximity to the first two in this moderately run race, she may do better granted a stiffer test of stamina in run-of-the-mill handicaps. (op 33-1)
Polar Forest also looks flattered by these bare facts and is another who is likely to find things tough in this type of event.
Firey Sally(IRE) Official explanation: jockey said that the filly suffered interference at the start

8255 32RED SUPPORTING BRITISH RACING H'CAP (DIV I) 5f 216y(P)
5:00 (5:01) (Class 6) (0-60,60) 3-Y-O+ **£1,704** (£503; £251) **Stalls** Low

Form RPR
1341 **1** **Invigilator**[50] 7634 4-9-6 59 .... (t) MartinDwyer 2 69+
(Derek Shaw) *hld up: swtchd rt and hdwy over 1f out: r.o u.p to ld post* **9/4**[1]
0066 **2** *nk* **Colourbearer (IRE)**[7] 8190 5-9-7 60 .... (t) SebSanders 9 69
(Milton Bradley) *a.p: chsd ldr over 2f out: rdn to ld over 1f out: hdd post* **3/1**[2]
5006 **3** *½* **Bitaphon (IRE)**[22] 7993 3-9-5 58 .... AndrewMullen 6 65
(Michael Appleby) *led: rdn and hdd over 1f out: r.o* **6/1**[3]
2060 **4** *¾* **Lisselton Cross**[15] 8075 4-8-11 50 .... (b) AmyRyan 10 55
(Martin Bosley) *hld up: hdwy over 2f out: rdn and ev ch fr over 1f out tl no ex nr fin* **17/2**
4200 **5** *½* **Imjin River (IRE)**[79] 6951 5-9-0 58 .... (t) NatashaEaton(5) 11 61
(William Stone) *chsd ldrs: rdn over 1f out: styd on same pce ins fnl f* **16/1**
00 **6** *1 ¼* **Romanticize**[96] 6480 6-9-4 57 ....[1] DaleSwift 4 56
(Jason Ward) *a.p: rdn over 1f out: styd on same pce fnl f* **33/1**
6341 **7** *1* **Lord Buffhead**[6] 8210 3-9-0 58 6ex .... (v) JasonHart(5) 12 54
(Richard Guest) *s.i.s: sn pushed along in rr: r.o ins fnl f: nvr nrr* **15/2**
5000 **8** *1 ¾* **Ishetoo**[37] 7794 8-9-2 55 .... FergusSweeney 3 45
(Peter Grayson) *hld up: nvr on terms* **20/1**
0304 **9** *1* **Little Perisher**[6] 8209 5-8-7 46 oh1 .... (p) AdamBeschizza 13 33
(Mark Brisbourne) *s.i.s: a in rr* **16/1**
000 **10** *hd* **Prigsnov Dancer (IRE)**[105] 6180 7-8-9 51 ow3 .... MarkCoumbe(3) 5 37
(Frank Sheridan) *chsd ldr over 3f: sn rdn: wknd fnl f* **40/1**
3600 **11** *¾* **Chester'Slittlegem (IRE)**[19] 8036 3-9-7 60 .... TomEaves 8 44
(Lisa Williamson) *prom: rdn over 2f out: wknd over 1f out* **22/1**

1m 13.99s (-1.01) **Going Correction** -0.275s/f (Stan) **11** Ran SP% **118.6**
Speed ratings (Par 101): **95,94,93,92,92 90,89,86,85,85 84**
toteswingers 1&2 £2.70, 1&3 £4.10, 2&3 £4.60 CSF £8.45 CT £36.40 TOTE £3.10: £2.00, £1.30, £3.00; EX 9.10 Trifecta £31.90 Pool: £2,670.95 - 62.65 winning tickets..
Owner The Warren Partnership **Bred** Granham Farm And P Hearson Bloodstock **Trained** Sproxton, Leics

FOCUS
A moderate handicap but a race that could throw up a winner or two. The gallop was sound throughout and the winner came down the centre in the straight. The winner built on his autumn form.

8256 32RED SUPPORTING BRITISH RACING H'CAP (DIV II) 5f 216y(P)
5:30 (5:31) (Class 6) (0-60,60) 3-Y-0+ £1,704 (£503; £251) Stalls Low

Form RPR
0205 1 **Methaaly (IRE)**[75] 7055 9-8-10 **56**..............................(be) RobertTart[(7)] 13 65
(Michael Mullineaux) *hld up: hdwy over 2f out: rdn and edgd lft ins fnl f: r.o to ld nr fin* **28/1**

512 2 ½ **Rose Garnet (IRE)**[6] 8209 4-8-7 **53**.................................... RyanTate[(7)] 8 60
(Tony Carroll) *chsd ldr tl led ins fnl f: sn rdn and edgd rt: hdd nr fin* **8/13**[1]

0000 3 ½ **Climaxfortackle (IRE)**[65] 7314 4-9-7 **60**...................... MartinDwyer 6 67
(Derek Shaw) *s.i.s: hld up: hdwy over 1f out: sn rdn: running on whn hmpd wl ins fnl f: nvr quite able to chal* **16/1**

0503 4 1 ½ **Silver Wind**[29] 7914 7-9-1 **59**........................(b) WilliamTwiston-Davies[(5)] 12 60
(Alan McCabe) *chsd ldrs: rdn over 1f out: styd on same pce ins fnl f* **5/1**[2]

2050 5 3 **Whipphound**[29] 7915 4-9-0 **58**.................................... RachealKneller[(5)] 1 49
(Mark Brisbourne) *prom: n.m.r over 4f out: nt clr run and lost pl over 2f out: rallied over 1f out: styd on same pce ins fnl f* **10/1**

5634 6 3 ¼ **Ridgeway Hawk**[268] 1178 4-9-0 **58**..............................(v) LeeNewnes[(5)] 9 39
(Mark Usher) *s.i.s: sn drvn along in rr: nvr nrr* **20/1**

4004 7 ¾ **Bachelor Knight (IRE)**[294] 837 4-8-8 **47**.................. AndrewMullen 11 26
(Suzzanne France) *hld up: rdn over 1f out: nt clr run and wknd ins fnl f* **50/1**

6535 8 hd **Hab Reeh**[29] 7915 4-8-11 **50**..(bt) AmyRyan 10 28
(Ruth Carr) *led: clr 4f out tl shkn up over 1f out: hdd & wknd ins fnl f* **8/1**[3]

-60U 9 ½ **Desert Spree**[15] 8075 3-8-7 **46** oh1.................................... JimmyQuinn 4 22
(Jeremy Gask) *hld up: pushed along 1/2-way: wknd over 2f out* **66/1**

3200 10 2 ¾ **Chester Deelyte (IRE)**[24] 7969 4-8-13 **57**............(v) ShirleyTeasdale[(5)] 2 25
(Lisa Williamson) *chsd ldrs tl wknd over 1f out* **25/1**

1m 13.57s (-1.43) **Going Correction** -0.275s/f (Stan) 10 Ran SP% **120.2**
Speed ratings (Par 101): **98,97,96,94,90 86,85,85,84,80**
toteswingers 1&2 £10.10, 1&3 £10.40, 2&3 £1.90 CSF £46.16 CT £365.21 TOTE £23.40: £8.20, £2.00, £6.70; EX 66.70 Trifecta £329.20 Pool: £1,615.50 - 3.68 winning tickets..
Owner S A Pritchard **Bred** Scuderia Golden Horse S R L **Trained** Alpraham, Cheshire
■ Stewards' Enquiry : Ryan Tate three-day ban: careless riding (10-12 Jan)

FOCUS
Division two of a moderate handicap. The gallop was a strong one and the winner came down the centre in the straight. He's rated to his summer form.

8257 £32 BONUS AT 32RED.COM H'CAP 7f 32y(P)
6:00 (6:00) (Class 7) (0-50,50) 3-Y-0+ £1,704 (£503; £125; £125) Stalls High

Form RPR
1 **Hittin'The Skids (IRE)**[74] 7088 4-9-4 **50**..........................[1] PaddyAspell 4 58
(Kevin Ryan) *a.p: rdn and edgd rt over 1f out: r.o to ld towards fin* **5/2**[1]

0000 2 ½ **Lord Paget**[40] 7671 3-8-12 **49**..................................(p) ShirleyTeasdale[(5)] 5 56
(Reg Hollinshead) *hld up: hdwy over 2f out: rdn and ev ch wl ins fnl f: r.o* **16/1**

3500 3 1 **Dhhamaan (IRE)**[23] 7983 7-9-2 **48**......................................(b) DaleSwift 1 52
(Ruth Carr) *led: racd keenly: rdn over 1f out: hdd towards fin* **11/2**[3]

0043 3 dht **Michael's Nook**[6] 8212 5-9-3 **49**.................................. FergusSweeney 11 53
(Alastair Lidderdale) *hld up: hdwy over 2f out: rdn and edgd lft over 1f out: r.o* **7/2**[2]

6063 5 1 **Give Us A Belle (IRE)**[23] 7981 3-9-3 **49**........................(t) JimmyQuinn 7 50
(Christine Dunnett) *chsd ldr: pushed along 3f out: styd on same pce ins fnl f* **16/1**

000 6 ½ **Autumnus (IRE)**[120] 5753 3-9-4 **50**......................................(t) ShaneKelly 3 50+
(Ismail Mohammed) *hld up: pushed along 3f out: rdn over 1f out: r.o towards fin: nt rch ldrs* **7/1**

51U6 7 1 **Coach Montana (IRE)**[14] 8099 3-9-4 **50**.....................(b) MartinDwyer 12 47
(Jane Chapple-Hyam) *mid-div: hdwy over 2f out: rdn over 1f out: styd on same pce fnl f* **9/1**

6030 8 1 ¼ **Under Par**[24] 7970 4-9-3 **49**..(t) TomEaves 2 43
(Michael Easterby) *chsd ldrs: rdn over 1f out: no ex fnl f* **8/1**

6006 9 8 **Artillery Train (IRE)**[22] 7988 3-8-9 **48**.........................(b) JoeyHaynes[(7)] 10 20
(Tim Etherington) *hld up: a in rr* **50/1**

0000 10 ¾ **Emma Jean (IRE)**[14] 8099 3-8-13 **48**.......................(bt) MarkCoumbe[(3)] 8 18
(Frank Sheridan) *s.s: outpcd* **40/1**

0540 11 9 **Outside Art**[15] 8075 3-9-3 **49**.. SebSanders 6
(Paul Fitzsimons) *chsd ldrs: rdn 1/2-way: wknd over 2f out* **22/1**

1m 28.31s (-1.29) **Going Correction** -0.275s/f (Stan) 11 Ran SP% **120.3**
Speed ratings (Par 97): **96,95,94,94,93 92,91,90,80,80 69**
PL: Michael's Nook £0.60, Dhhamaan £2.20. T/C: HS&LP& MN £73.75, HS&LP&D £105.14 CSF £46.33 TOTE £3.60: £2.80, £6.70; EX 61.40 TRIFECTA Trifecta: HS&LP&MN £582.70, HS&LP&D £265.30.
Owner D J Emsley **Bred** Michael Woodlock & Seamus Kennedy **Trained** Hambleton, N Yorks

FOCUS
A very moderate handicap in which the pace soon steadied. The winner came down the centre in the straight and the form seems sound enough.
Hittin'The Skids(IRE) Official explanation: trainer's representative said, regarding the apparent improvement of form, that the filly was having her first run for the yard and had benefitted from the drop back in trip and first time application of a hood
Artillery Train(IRE) Official explanation: jockey said that the gelding hung right-handed throughout
Outside Art Official explanation: jockey said that the filly had no more to give

8258 32REDBET.COM CLAIMING STKS 7f 32y(P)
6:30 (6:31) (Class 5) 2-Y-0 £2,749 (£818; £408; £204) Stalls High

Form RPR
5020 1 **It's Only Business**[14] 8093 2-8-7 52..............................(p) JimmyQuinn 3 60
(Bill Turner) *hld up: hdwy over 1f out: sn rdn: edgd lft and styd on to ld nr fin* **16/1**

1335 2 ½ **Hardy Red (IRE)**[5] 8224 2-9-5 74.................................. FergusSweeney 5 71
(Jamie Osborne) *chsd ldr tl rdn to ld over 1f out: hdd nr fin* **9/4**[1]

3605 3 4 **Imperial Spirit**[14] 8092 2-8-6 66.................................... CharlesBishop[(5)] 1 53
(Mick Channon) *chsd ldrs: rdn and ev ch over 1f out: no ex ins fnl f* **4/1**[2]

0344 4 3 ¼ **Marmot Bay (IRE)**[5] 8224 2-8-0 61 ow1........................ NatashaEaton[(5)] 2 39
(Alastair Lidderdale) *led: rdn and hdd over 1f out: wknd ins fnl f* **4/1**[2]

0023 5 7 **Don Eduardo**[7] 8186 2-8-7 57..(b) MartinDwyer 6 24
(J S Moore) *chsd ldrs: rdn over 2f out: wknd over 1f out* **9/2**[3]

3155 6 6 **Bix (IRE)**[10] 8150 2-8-9 71..(b) RobertWinston 4 11
(Alan Berry) *s.i.s: sn pushed along in rr: wknd over 2f out* **9/2**[3]

1m 28.16s (-1.44) **Going Correction** -0.275s/f (Stan) 6 Ran SP% **113.0**
Speed ratings (Par 96): **97,96,91,88,80 73**
toteswingers 1&2 £10.10, 1&3 £10.40, 2&3 £1.90 CSF £52.81 TOTE £35.30: £21.40, £4.70; EX 61.10 Trifecta £668.50 Pool: £1,176.73 - 1.32 winning tickets..
Owner Ansells Of Watford **Bred** South Wind Bloodstock **Trained** Sigwells, Somerset

FOCUS
An ordinary claimer run at a modest gallop to the home turn. The principals raced towards the far rail in the straight. Not form to place great stock in.

NOTEBOOK
It's Only Business looked to have plenty to find at the weights but he returned to his best in first-time cheekpieces to get off the mark at the 10th attempt. A stronger pace would have suited but his record suggests he wouldn't be sure to reproduce this next time. (op 14-1 tchd 12-1)
Hardy Red(IRE), up in trip, is a fairly reliable yardstick who seemed to give his running conceding weight all round, despite racing with the choke out early on. He finished clear of the rest and is capable of winning a similar event. (tchd 11-4)
Imperial Spirit, whose last run has thrown up winners, wasn't totally disgraced but didn't really improve for the return to this trip. A strongly run 6f may suit better but he has something to prove at present. (op 5-1)
Marmot Bay(IRE), a triple 6f course winner, had a good chance at the weights and an easy lead back up in trip so this run has to go down as disappointing. She may have had enough for the time being. (op 3-1 tchd 11-4)
Don Eduardo failed to match the form of his two previous efforts in blinkers. He isn't fully exposed but looks on to tread carefully with. (op 6-1)
Bix(IRE) had a good chance at the weights but was again a long way below the form of his Hamilton maiden win in autumn. He's best avoided at present. (op 6-1 tchd 4-1)

8259 32RED H'CAP 1m 1f 103y(P)
7:00 (7:00) (Class 4) (0-85,85) 3-Y-0+ £4,075 (£1,212; £606; £303) Stalls Low

Form RPR
0620 1 **Alfred Hutchinson**[14] 8095 4-9-3 **81**.................................... TomEaves 2 90
(Geoffrey Oldroyd) *racd keenly: trckd ldr over 2f: remained handy: wnt 2nd again 4f out: led 2f out: drvn out* **15/8**[1]

5040 2 ¾ **Dakota Canyon (IRE)**[22] 7986 3-8-5 **71** oh1...........(b[1]) PatrickMathers 5 78
(Richard Fahey) *sn pushed along and prom: drvn along fr over 3f out: styd on u.p* **7/1**

6406 3 ½ **Spifer (IRE)**[29] 7904 4-9-7 **85**..(p) SebSanders 1 91
(Marco Botti) *a.p: chsd ldr 7f out tl 4f out: rdn and ev ch fr over 1f out tl no ex nr fin* **4/1**[2]

6560 4 3 ½ **Follow The Flag (IRE)**[7] 8191 8-8-9 **73** ow1.................(be) ShaneKelly 7 72
(Alan McCabe) *hld up: hdwy over 3f out: rdn over 2f out: styd on same pce fr over 1f out* **18/1**

0024 5 nk **Rossetti**[12] 8142 4-8-9 **73**.. TonyHamilton 8 71
(Ian Williams) *hld up: hdwy over 1f out: sn rdn and edgd lft: styd on same pce fnl f* **11/2**[3]

0204 6 3 **Classic Colori (IRE)**[33] 7867 5-9-5 **83**....................(vt) GrahamGibbons 3 75
(David O'Meara) *led: rdn and hdd 2f out: wknd ins fnl f* **4/1**[2]

1000 7 8 **Oneofapear (IRE)**[82] 6884 6-9-0 **78**...................................... DaleSwift 6 53
(Ian McInnes) *hld up: rdn over 3f out: wknd over 2f out* **25/1**

1m 57.52s (-4.18) **Going Correction** -0.275s/f (Stan)
WFA 3 from 4yo+ 2lb 7 Ran SP% **111.8**
Speed ratings (Par 105): **107,106,105,102,102 99,92**
toteswingers 1&2 £6.30, 1&3 £2.50, 2&3 £8.00 CSF £15.01 CT £45.43 TOTE £3.80: £2.50, £9.10; EX 13.60 Trifecta £117.60 Pool: £1,245.66 - 7.94 winning tickets..
Owner R C Bond **Bred** R C Bond **Trained** Brawby, N Yorks
■ Stewards' Enquiry : Patrick Mathers two-day ban: use of whip (10-11 Jan)

FOCUS
Exposed performers in a useful handicap, and it may not have taken too much winning. The gallop was just a modest one to the straight and the winner came down the centre.

8260 32REDPOKER.COM H'CAP 1m 4f 50y(P)
7:30 (7:30) (Class 6) (0-60,60) 3-Y-0+ £1,704 (£503; £251) Stalls Low

Form RPR
0005 1 **Scribe (IRE)**[135] 5196 4-8-10 **46**.................................(t) GrahamGibbons 8 54
(David Evans) *hld up: hdwy u.p over 2f out: led ins fnl f: jst hld on* **9/1**

03-2 2 nk **Easydoesit (IRE)**[14] 602 4-8-11 **47**.................................... JimmyQuinn 7 55
(Tony Carroll) *hld up: hdwy over 2f out: rdn and ev ch ins fnl f: styd on* **18/1**

3325 3 1 ½ **White Deer (USA)**[12] 8139 8-9-6 **56**...........................(v) PaddyAspell 11 61
(Geoffrey Harker) *hld up: hdwy over 3f out: ev ch ins fnl f: sn rdn: hung lft and nt run on* **8/1**

0434 4 1 ½ **Layla's Boy**[42] 7731 5-9-7 **60**...(bt) RyanClark[(3)] 12 63
(John Mackie) *s.i.s: sn prom: led over 2f out: rdn: hdd and no ex ins fnl f* **7/1**

0640 5 1 ¼ **Saloon (USA)**[13] 8104 8-8-3 **46**...(p) IanBurns[(7)] 9 47
(Jane Chapple-Hyam) *s.i.s: hld up and bhd: pushed along over 3f out: styd on fr over 1f out: nrst fin* **16/1**

5663 6 1 ¾ **No Diamond**[12] 8139 5-9-3 **53**.................................(p) AndrewMullen 10 51
(Michael Appleby) *hdwy over 10f out: chsd ldr over 7f out: rdn to ld wl over 2f out: sn hdd: wknd ins fnl f* **9/4**[1]

4605 7 1 ¾ **Sacco D'Oro**[13] 6190 6-8-3 **46** oh1................................(v) RobertTart[(7)] 2 41
(Michael Mullineaux) *chsd ldrs: rdn over 2f out: wknd fnl f* **28/1**

6424 8 13 **Awesome Rock (IRE)**[18] 8050 3-8-10 **51** ow1................. SebSanders 3 26
(Louise Best) *hld up: plld hrd: nt clr run over 2f out: wknd over 1f out* **13/2**[3]

52P3 9 14 **Five Hearts**[16] 8067 4-9-1 **51**.. MartinDwyer 6
(Mark H Tompkins) *chsd ldr tl led over 9f out: rdn and hdd wl over 2f out: hmpd sn after: hung lft and wknd over 1f out: t.o* **12/1**

0320 10 8 **Missionaire (USA)**[41] 7744 5-9-5 **55**............................ RobertWinston 1
(Tony Carroll) *set stdy pce tl hdd over 9f out: remained handy: rdn over 3f out: sn wknd: t.o* **18/1**

10/2 11 10 **Dream Risk (FR)**[17] 4594 6-9-3 **53**......................................(t) TomEaves 4
(Brian Ellison) *prom: rdn over 4f out: wknd over 3f out: t.o* **3/1**[2]

0-60 12 14 **Crabbies Gold (IRE)**[190] 3277 4-8-10 **46** oh1................(b[1]) AmyRyan 5
(Lisa Williamson) *hld up: hdwy over 4f out: sn rdn and wknd: t.o* **66/1**

2m 38.74s (-2.36) **Going Correction** -0.275s/f (Stan)
WFA 3 from 4yo+ 5lb 12 Ran SP% **131.8**
Speed ratings (Par 101): **96,95,94,93,92 91,90,81,72,67 60,51**
toteswingers 1&2 £51.90, 1&3 £26.80, 2&3 £11.20 CSF £177.22 CT £1386.94 TOTE £13.90: £5.90, £7.00, £1.80; EX 115.40 TRIFECTA Not won..
Owner Shropshire Wolves/John Wilcox **Bred** Lynch Bages Ltd & Samac Ltd **Trained** Pandy, Monmouths
■ Stewards' Enquiry : Graham Gibbons six-day ban: weighed in 2lb heavy (10-15 Jan)
Andrew Mullen three-day ban: use of whip (12-14 Jan)

FOCUS
A moderate handicap in which the two market leaders disappointed to varying degrees. The pace was a moderate one and the winner came down the centre in the straight. The form is rated around the third and fourth.
Awesome Rock(IRE) Official explanation: jockey said that the gelding ran too free.
Dream Risk(FR) Official explanation: jockey said that the mare hung left-handed
Crabbies Gold(IRE) Official explanation: jockey said that the gelding hung right-handed

T/Jkpt: Not won. T/Plt: £9.70 to a £1 stake. Pool: £87,839.93 - 6552.07 winning tickets T/Qpdt: £4.70 to a £1 stake. Pool: £11,670.06 - 1,800.19 winning tickets CR

8245 LINGFIELD (L-H)

Friday, December 28

OFFICIAL GOING: Standard

Wind: Fresh, behind Weather: Very overcast, drizzly

8261 AT THE RACES ON FACEBOOK APPRENTICE (S) STKS — 1m (P)

12:00 (12:00) (Class 6) 3-Y-O+ — **£1,704** (£503; £251) **Stalls** High

Form — RPR

1000 **1** **Daniel Thomas (IRE)**[7] 8214 10-9-7 62...................(tp) JoshBaudains 10 63
(Violet M Jordan) *hld up in 6th in fast run r: prog to trck ldrs wl over 1f out: rdn and r.o to ld ins fnl f: sn clr* **6/1**

026 **2** 1 ¾ **Divine Rule (IRE)**[16] 8077 4-9-7 51...........................(v) ThomasBrown 5 59
(Laura Mongan) *trckd ldrs: gng wl in 3rd wl over 1f out: brought to chal fnl f: nt qckn and sn outpcd by wnr* **8/1**

2014 **3** ½ **Bold Marc (IRE)**[13] 8133 10-9-4 66........................... ConorHarrison(3) 4 58
(Mrs K Burke) *trckd ldr at str pce: clsd over 2f out: rdn to ld over 1f out: hdd and no ex ins fnl f* **3/1**[2]

0554 **4** 2 ¼ **Maz**[16] 8079 4-8-11 60..(b¹) RobertTart(5) 6 48
(Alan Bailey) *chsd ldrs: lost pl 1/2-way: no prog 2f out: kpt on one pce fnl f* **11/4**[1]

4056 **5** ¾ **King's Future**[21] 8021 3-8-9 50.................................(b¹) AaronJones(5) 3 45
(Lee Carter) *pushed up to ld and set str pce: hdd over 1f out: wknd fnl f* **16/1**

6046 **6** 1 ¾ **Connishka**[59] 7470 3-8-4 45... ShelleyBirkett(5) 7 36
(Alan Bailey) *sn pushed along in last pair: nvr a factor: plugged on fnl f* **12/1**

0006 **7** 6 **Bubbly Bounty**[70] 7222 3-8-6 46.............................(b) DanielMuscutt(3) 8 22
(Alan Bailey) *t.k.h: racd wd: chsd ldrs: wknd 2f out* **16/1**

4055 **F** **Spin Again (IRE)**[7] 8199 7-9-7 64............................... NatashaEaton 1 61
(John Ryan) *hld up in last in fast run r: stdy prog 2f out: gng wl whn nt clr run on inner 1f out and swtchd rt: styng on to press for a pl whn stmbld and fell 50yds out* **4/1**[3]

1m 38.24s (0.04) **Going Correction** +0.025s/f (Slow)
WFA 3 from 4yo+ 1lb — **8** Ran SP% **116.5**
Speed ratings (Par 101): **100,98,97,95,94 93,87,**
toteswingers 1&2 £5.70, 1&3 £3.80, 2&3 £3.60 CSF £53.56 TOTE £9.10: £2.30, £2.60, £1.20; EX 51.00 Trifecta £376.00 Pool: £972.84 - 1.94 winning tickets..There was no bid for the winner.
Owner Rakebackmypoker.com **Bred** Lawn Stud **Trained** Moreton Morrell, Warwicks

FOCUS

The opening seller was run at a strong pace and the winner was ridden with restraint in the early stages. The form is rated around the second.

8262 BRITISH STALLION STUDS E.B.F./32RED.COM MAIDEN STKS — 7f (P)

12:30 (12:36) (Class 5) 2-Y-O — **£3,169** (£943; £471; £235) **Stalls** Low

Form — RPR

53 **1** **Consign**[20] 8033 2-9-3 0.. GeorgeBaker 7 77+
(Jeremy Noseda) *mostly trckd ldr: led bnd 2f out but hung rt: edgd rt and rdn over 1f out: in command fnl f: eased nr fin* **4/7**[1]

04 **2** 1 ¼ **Dark Templar**[130] 5407 2-9-3 0.. IanMongan 13 72+
(Ed Vaughan) *free to post: racd v wd but led: forfeited ld bnd 2f out and almost against nr side rail in st: styd on wl and clr in 2nd: eased nr fin but clsd on wnr* **16/1**

3 **3** 3 ¼ **Lady Lunchalot (USA)**[16] 8076 2-8-12 0.................. WilliamCarson 10 57
(J S Moore) *pushed along in midfield: prog to chse ldrs over 2f out: kpt on one pce over 1f out* **6/1**[2]

0 **4** 1 **Tammuz (IRE)**[9] 8171 2-8-12 0.. DavidProbert 1 55
(Tony Carroll) *chsd ldrs: outpcd by ldng pair over 2f out: one pce after* **20/1**

5 2 ½ **Mastered (IRE)** 2-9-3 0... EddieAhern 2 53
(John Best) *dwlt: sn in midfield: shkn up over 2f out and wl outpcd in 5th: no hdwy after* **33/1**

6 2 **Happy Families** 2-8-12 0... ChrisCatlin 6 43
(Heather Main) *wl in rr: pushed along over 4f out: sme prog to take 6th over 2f out but nt on terms: no hdwy after* **33/1**

7 1 ½ **Switcharooney (IRE)** 2-9-3 0............................... RichardKingscote 11 44
(Tom Dascombe) *nvr bttr than midfield: pushed along and green over 4f out: wl off the pce over 2f out* **10/1**

8 nk **Alshan Fajer** 2-9-3 0... JimmyQuinn 12 43
(Paul Howling) *slowly away: rn green and hld up in last: pushed along 3f out: modest late prog* **66/1**

9 2 ½ **So Vain (IRE)** 2-9-3 0.. JimCrowley 8 37
(David Brown) *dwlt: a wl in rr: pushed along 4f out: modest prog over 2f out: wknd over 1f out* **7/1**[3]

6 **10** 3 **Master Hamilton**[9] 8172 2-9-3 0.................................. TomMcLaughlin 3 29
(Tobias B P Coles) *a in rr: pushed along over 4f out: wl bhd fnl 2f* **100/1**

00 **11** 2 **Nelson's Muse**[9] 8171 2-8-12 0.................................... J-PGuillambert 4 19
(Tobias B P Coles) *chsd ldrs 3f: sn wknd and bhd* **150/1**

1m 25.66s (0.86) **Going Correction** +0.025s/f (Slow) — **11** Ran SP% **119.2**
Speed ratings (Par 96): **96,94,90,89,86 84,82,82,79,76 73**
toteswingers 1&2 £4.00, 2&3 £8.30, 1&3 £2.00 CSF £11.74 TOTE £1.70: £1.10, £2.80, £1.40; EX 12.30 Trifecta £26.50 Pool: £1,243.09 - 35.16 winning tickets..
Owner Miss Yvonne Jacques **Bred** Natton House Thoroughbreds & Mark Woodall **Trained** Newmarket, Suffolk

FOCUS

The three non-runners meant there was little depth to this maiden, which went to the well-backed favourite. The first two are both a bit better than the facts.

NOTEBOOK

Consign set the standard on his improved run over C&D last time and opened his account at the third attempt. After breaking well, he was happy sit behind the leader and despite running wide into the straight and, showing signs of greenness, he found a good turn of foot to win readily. He can make his mark in handicaps and may be suited by a stiffer test. (op 4-5)

Dark Templar, back down in trip on his return from 130 days off, was drawn widest of all but made a bright start and had grabbed the lead approaching the first bend. He wasn't helped by racing keenly and also lost ground by running wide entering the straight, only to finish strongly again on the heels of the winner. He looks capable of winning a maiden and shapes as though he will relish a step back up in trip. His jockey reported that he hung right throughout and the stewards ordered him to be routine tested. Official explanation: jockey said gelding hung right throughout (tchd 14-1)

Lady Lunchalot(USA) finished third in a claimer over C&D on her debut and bettered that form on this second start. She showed a willing attitude and found for pressure without ever looking a threat to the front two. (op 9-2)

Tammuz(IRE), made some late progress on her debut over C&D and again was keeping on well at the finish. She looks capable of further improvement. (op 16-1)

Mastered(IRE), a half-brother to three winners at up to 7f, fared best of the newcomers but only showed moderate promise. (op 16-1)

Switcharooney(IRE), a 60,000gns third foal of a dam who won over 1m (at 2) and 5.5f, was weak in the market on this debut and ran as though he would improve significantly for the experience. (op 7-1)

So Vain(IRE), a 38,000GBP yearling and half-brother to two winners, never got into it after a tardy start and should know more next time. (op 10-1)

8263 32REDBET.COM CASINO H'CAP — 1m (P)

1:00 (1:00) (Class 6) (0-65,63) 3-Y-O — **£1,704** (£503; £251) **Stalls** High

Form — RPR

4-06 **1** **Whispering Warrior (IRE)**[223] 2280 3-9-4 60.................. JimCrowley 1 72+
(David Simcock) *trckd ldrs: clsd on inner 2f out: rdn over 1f out: styd on to ld last 100yds: edgd rt and pushed out* **7/4**[1]

0052 **2** ½ **Derfenna Art (IRE)**[7] 8199 3-9-5 61...............................(t) MickyFenton 5 72
(Seamus Durack) *trckd ldr 2f and again over 3f out: rdn to ld over 2f out: hdd last 100yds: styd on* **6/1**

401 **3** 2 **Duke Of Destiny (IRE)**[140] 5049 3-9-7 63......................... LukeMorris 2 69
(Ed Walker) *trckd ldrs: cl up 2f out: drvn to try to chal jst over 1f out: one pce* **4/1**[3]

0123 **4** ¾ **Whinging Willie (IRE)**[7] 8199 3-9-6 62........................... GeorgeBaker 6 67+
(Gary Moore) *stdd s: hld up in last pair: prog 2f out: tk 4th and drvn 1f out: styd on but no ch to chal* **3/1**[2]

0535 **5** 1 ¼ **The New Black (IRE)**[10] 8158 3-8-13 55......................(e) DavidProbert 7 57
(Gay Kelleway) *hld up in last: brought wd bnd 2f out: drvn over 1f out: styd on after but no ch* **14/1**

5050 **6** 3 ½ **Holy Roman Warrior (IRE)**[98] 6429 3-9-6 62..........(t) RobertWinston 8 56
(Kevin Ryan) *hld up in 6th: prog on outer 3f out to chse ldrs 2f out: sn rdn and nt qckn: wknd over 1f out* **12/1**

0266 **7** 6 **Mystical Witch**[17] 8062 3-8-7 49 oh4...............................(v) JimmyQuinn 4 29
(Christine Dunnett) *trckd ldr after 2f: led 1/2-way: rdn and hdd over 2f out: wknd qckly* **100/1**

2626 **8** 19 **Darnathean**[16] 8074 3-9-5 61... SebSanders 3
(Paul D'Arcy) *led to 1/2-way: losing pl qckly whn squeezed out over 2f out: wknd rapidly: t.o* **20/1**

1m 37.78s (-0.42) **Going Correction** +0.025s/f (Slow) — **8** Ran SP% **115.8**
Speed ratings (Par 98): **103,102,100,99,98 95,89,70**
toteswingers 1&2 £4.00, 2&3 £3.90, 1&3 £2.50 CSF £13.21 CT £37.29 TOTE £3.50: £1.60, £1.60, £1.60; EX 15.40 Trifecta £58.30 Pool: £613.81 - 7.89 winning tickets..
Owner Daniel Pittack **Bred** Epona Bloodstock Ltd **Trained** Newmarket, Suffolk

FOCUS

An open 3-y-o handicap in which those racing close to the pace were at an advantage. Decent form for the grade, rated around the runner-up.

Darnathean Official explanation: jockey said gelding never travelled

8264 32RED SUPPORTING BRITISH RACING H'CAP (DIV I) — 1m 2f (P)

1:30 (1:31) (Class 6) (0-55,62) 3-Y-O+ — **£1,704** (£503; £251) **Stalls** Low

Form — RPR

0011 **1** **Brown Pete (IRE)**[1] 8248 4-10-0 62 12ex..................... WilliamCarson 6 73
(Violet M Jordan) *hld up towards rr: prog to chse ldrs over 2f out: swtchd to outer and drvn over 1f out: gd run to ld ins fnl f: styd on wl* **5/2**[1]

000 **2** ¾ **Peace In Our Time**[89] 6704 3-8-2 46 oh1......................... RyanTate(7) 1 55
(Anthony Carson) *trckd ldrs: gng wl 3f out: prog 2f out: rdn to chal fnl f: styd on but jst outpcd by wnr* **4/1**[3]

2000 **3** 1 ½ **Youm Jamil (USA)**[13] 8139 5-9-7 55.................................... JimCrowley 2 61
(Tony Carroll) *hld up in midfield: prog on inner fr 3f out gng strly: rdn to chal and upsides fnl f: fin weakly* **7/1**

-265 **4** nk **Raise The Rafters (IRE)**[106] 6184 7-9-5 53.................. GeorgeBaker 12 58+
(John Butler) *led to over 6f out: trckd ldr gng easily: led again over 2f out: drvn over 1f out: hdd & wknd ins fnl f* **3/1**[2]

0600 **5** 3 **Sommersturm (GER)**[59] 7472 8-9-5 53.............................. LukeMorris 11 52
(David Evans) *slowly away and drvn: rapid prog fr rr to ld over 6f out: hdd over 2f out: wknd fnl f* **20/1**

3000 **6** 2 ¾ **Prince Of Thebes (IRE)**[132] 5351 11-8-12 46 oh1......(v) SebSanders 10 40
(Michael Attwater) *s.s and urged along: gd prog fr rr on outer 4f out to press ldrs 2f out: sn wknd* **20/1**

0000 **7** ½ **Tidy Affair (IRE)**[58] 7482 3-9-4 55...................................... ChrisCatlin 5 48
(Gary Moore) *hld up in rr: pushed along over 4f out: sme prog on inner over 2f out but nt on terms: nvr threatened* **10/1**

0000 **8** ½ **Boris The Bold**[30] 7898 3-8-11 48................................. RobertWinston 13 40
(John Best) *wl in tch: chsd ldrs and drvn over 2f out: wkng whn briefly short of room wl over 1f out* **12/1**

0006 **9** nk **Diddums**[10] 8153 6-8-7 46 oh1...............................(e) ShirleyTeasdale(5) 7 37
(John Ryan) *s.s: hld up in last: pushed along and stdy prog fr 3f out: nvr remotely involved* **33/1**

0504 **10** ¾ **Litmus (USA)**[15] 8097 3-8-9 46.. EddieAhern 3 36
(Simon Dow) *chsd ldrs tl wknd 3f out* **25/1**

2200 **11** 11 **Emperors Waltz (IRE)**[38] 7793 3-9-1 52.......................[1] DavidProbert 4 20
(Ralph Smith) *prom tl wknd qckly 4f out: t.o* **25/1**

-600 **12** 12 **Bellinda**[280] 1012 3-8-6 46 oh1....................................... SimonPearce(3) 14
(Martin Bosley) *racd wd in rr: wknd 4f out: wl t.o* **66/1**

00-0 **13** ½ **Roe Valley (IRE)**[16] 8080 5-8-12 46 oh1.................... FrankieMcDonald 9
(Linda Jewell) *hld up: a wl in rr: rdn and no prog 4f out: wl t.o* **66/1**

-060 **14** 6 **Buckley Boy**[16] 8080 3-8-12 49...................................... JamieMackay 8
(K F Clutterbuck) *t.k.h: chsd ldrs 6f: wknd rapidly: wl t.o* **66/1**

2m 5.96s (-0.64) **Going Correction** +0.025s/f (Slow)
WFA 3 from 4yo+ 3lb — **14** Ran SP% **127.5**
Speed ratings (Par 101): **103,102,101,100,98 96,95,95,95,94 85,76,75,71**
toteswingers 1&2 £4.30, 2&3 £7.30, 1&3 £4.10 CSF £12.24 CT £65.78 TOTE £4.20: £1.50, £1.50, £2.90; EX 14.30 Trifecta £92.90 Pool: £841.45 - 6.79 winning tickets..
Owner Rakebackmypoker.com **Bred** Jim Halligan **Trained** Moreton Morrell, Warwicks

FOCUS

A moderate handicap but at least the pace was strong. The winning time was 2.05 seconds faster than the second division. The right horses were involved and the form seems sound enough.

8265 32RED SUPPORTING BRITISH RACING H'CAP (DIV II) — 1m 2f (P)

2:00 (2:03) (Class 6) (0-55,55) 3-Y-O+ — **£1,704** (£503; £251) **Stalls** Low

Form — RPR

312 **1** **Norwegian Reward (IRE)**[8] 8179 4-9-4 52......................... JimCrowley 1 62+
(Michael Wigham) *trckd ldrs on inner: prog 3f out: led wl over 1f out and sn in command: rdn out nr fin* **1/1**[1]

6601 **2** 1 1/4 **Bridge That Gap**[65] 7321 4-9-5 **53** .... EddieAhern 8 58+
(Roger Ingram) *hld up in midfield: pushed along in 6th over 2f out and outpcd by ldrs: prog 1f out: rdn and r.o to take 2nd last 50yds: no ch to chal* **3/1**[2]

000 **3** 1/2 **Asia Minor (IRE)**[74] 7112 3-9-1 **52** .... JimmyQuinn 5 56
(Dr Jon Scargill) *s.i.s but sn prom on outer: awkward bnd 4f out: prog to press ldr 3f out to 2f out: hrd rdn over 1f out: styd on same pce and 2nd briefly last 100yds* **10/1**

1062 **4** 1 1/4 **Chasin' Rainbows**[14] 8113 4-9-7 **55** .... GeorgeBaker 4 57+
(Sylvester Kirk) *hld up in last trio: nt clr run on inner over 2f out: prog wl over 1f out: styd on to take 4th last strides: nrst fin* **6/1**[3]

44-1 **5** hd **Brave Decision**[358] 45 5-9-0 **48** .... LukeMorris 11 49
(Suzy Smith) *led over 8f out and maintained mod pce: hdd wl over 1f out: fdd last 100yds* **16/1**

/003 **6** 3/4 **Love Pegasus (USA)**[11] 8146 6-9-0 **55** .... JakePayne(7) 2 55
(Paddy Butler) *hld up towards rr: effrt over 2f out: styd on fr over 1f out: nvr able to threaten* **20/1**

-050 **7** 2 1/2 **Tymismoni (IRE)**[42] 7739 4-8-12 **46** oh1 .... SebSanders 6 41
(Michael Attwater) *towards rr: pushed along 4f out: outpcd fr 3f out: nvr on terms after* **20/1**

0660 **8** 1/2 **Amber Moon**[141] 5015 7-8-9 **48** oh1 ow2 .... AnnStokell(5) 3 42
(Ann Stokell) *t.k.h early: led to over 8f out: styd prom: wknd 2f out* **66/1**

-000 **9** shd **Saffron Park**[30] 7898 3-8-10 **47** ow1 .... RobertWinston 9 40
(John Best) *dwlt: hld up and sn in last: stl there over 2f out: nudged along and kpt on same pce fr over 1f out: nvr involved* **33/1**

000- **10** 3/4 **Richo**[467] 5944 6-8-7 **46** oh1 .... ShirleyTeasdale(5) 13 38
(Shaun Harris) *dwlt: rchd midfield 4f out: rdn and wknd 2f out* **33/1**

00-0 **11** 1/2 **Cossack Prince**[32] 6255 7-8-9 **46** oh1 .... (p) SimonPearce(3) 12 37
(Laura Mongan) *hld up and sn in last trio: brought wd and rdn wl over 1f out: no prog* **33/1**

-666 **12** 1 **Arbeejay**[15] 8097 3-8-9 **46** oh1 .... (t) WilliamCarson 7 35
(Simon Hodgson) *prom tl wknd over 2f out* **50/1**

000 **13** 12 **Twilight Legend (IRE)**[16] 8069 3-8-9 **46** oh1 .... ChrisCatlin 10 11
(Seamus Mullins) *prom on outer: trckd ldr after 2f to 3f out: wknd rapidly: t.o* **33/1**

2m 8.01s (1.41) **Going Correction** +0.025s/f (Slow)
WFA 3 from 4yo+ 3lb 13 Ran SP% 129.0
Speed ratings (Par 101): **95,94,93,92,92 91,89,89,89,88 88,87,77**
toteswingers 1&2 £1.80, 2&3 £4.20, 1&3 £4.00 CSF £3.84 CT £22.56 TOTE £1.90: £1.10, £1.80, £3.20; EX 6.30 Trifecta £27.50 Pool: £1,700.27 - 46.26 winning tickets..
Owner Tapas Partnership **Bred** Sean O'Sullivan **Trained** Newmarket, Suffolk

FOCUS
A moderate handicap. The winning time was 2.05 seconds slower than the first division and the form is similarly weak.
Chasin' Rainbows Official explanation: jockey said filly was denied a clear run.
Amber Moon Official explanation: jockey said mare hung right final furlong.

8266 32RED H'CAP 6f (P)
2:30 (2:31) (Class 4) (0-85,82) 3-Y-O+ **£4,294** (£1,268; £634) **Stalls** Low

Form RPR
0300 **1** **Kakatosi**[39] 7790 5-9-5 **80** .... EddieAhern 1 89
(Mike Murphy) *prom in chsng gp: clsd 2f out: rdn to ld over 1f out: hld chalr last 100yds* **4/1**[2]

4502 **2** 1/2 **Clear Praise (USA)**[13] 8143 5-9-4 **79** .... SebSanders 3 86
(Simon Dow) *s.s: hld up in last pair: prog on inner wl over 1f out: pressed wnr ins fnl f: hld nr fin* **5/2**[1]

4342 **3** 1 1/4 **Restless Bay (IRE)**[17] 8063 4-8-7 **68** .... (v) ChrisCatlin 7 71
(Mrs K Burke) *prom on outer in chsng gp: clsd 2f out: nt qckn over 1f out: styd on same pce fnl f* **7/1**

0600 **4** 1 1/2 **Dancing Freddy (IRE)**[18] 8054 5-8-7 **68** .... (tp) WilliamCarson 2 67
(Violet M Jordan) *led and sn 5 l clr: c bk 2f out: hdd over 1f out: fdd fnl f* **25/1**

0124 **5** 1/2 **Millibar (IRE)**[21] 8022 3-9-7 **82** .... (b) TomMcLaughlin 4 79
(Nick Littmoden) *s.v.s: sn in tch in last pair: rdn on outer 2f out: no real prog* **8/1**

0033 **6** nk **Italian Tom (IRE)**[9] 8163 5-9-2 **77** .... LukeMorris 6 73
(Ronald Harris) *sn pushed along in chsng gp: no prog 2f out: lost pl and btn over 1f out* **5/1**[3]

540 **7** hd **Proper Charlie**[115] 5915 4-8-12 **73** .... JimCrowley 5 68
(William Knight) *mostly chsd clr ldr: clsd w others 2f out: lost 2nd and fdd over 1f out* **4/1**[2]

1m 11.11s (-0.79) **Going Correction** +0.025s/f (Slow) 7 Ran SP% 112.7
Speed ratings (Par 105): **106,105,103,101,101 100,100**
toteswingers 1&2 £2.70, 2&3 £5.50, 1&3 £3.70 CSF £14.00 TOTE £4.10: £2.70, £1.80; EX 16.90 Trifecta £132.40 Pool: £1,073.50 - 6.08 winning tickets..
Owner Robert E Tillett **Bred** T E Pocock **Trained** Westoning, Beds

FOCUS
A fair handicap, run at a strong gallop which provided a stiff test. The winner is rated to this year's turf form.
Millibar(IRE) Official explanation: jockey said filly was slowly away.

8267 32RED CASINO MAIDEN STKS 1m (P)
3:00 (3:01) (Class 5) 3-Y-O+ **£2,385** (£704; £352) **Stalls** High

Form RPR
000 **1** **Garrisson (IRE)**[126] 5555 3-9-3 53 .... RobertWinston 7 70+
(Charles Hills) *hld up disputing 5th: quick move on outer to ld over 2f out and sn clr: rdn and edgd rt over 1f out: pushed out and wl in command after* **2/1**[1]

0 **2** 3 **Fly Haaf (IRE)**[163] 4212 3-9-3 0 .... JimCrowley 9 63+
(William Knight) *stdd s: hld up in last pair: prog to chse wnr over 1f out: no imp but hld on for 2nd* **2/1**[1]

5352 **3** 1/2 **Bowstar**[8] 8187 3-8-12 65 .... (p) J-PGuillambert 5 57
(Michael Attwater) *trckd ldng pair: outpcd whn wnr kicked on over 2f out: pressed for 2nd over 1f out: kpt on one pce* **9/4**[2]

06-3 **4** 4 **Marshall Art**[21] 8021 3-9-3 58 .... LukeMorris 6 52
(David Evans) *trckd ldng pair: rdn to press for 2nd wl over 1f out: fdd fnl f* **5/1**[3]

0660 **5** 1 **Willow Beauty**[139] 5095 3-8-12 42 .... EddieAhern 2 45
(J R Jenkins) *hld up disputing 5th: outpcd over 2f out: pushed along and no imp over 1f out* **33/1**

06 **6** 3 **Tiny Thompson**[16] 8080 3-8-9 0 .... SimonPearce(3) 8 38
(Lydia Pearce) *hld up in last pair: outpcd over 2f out: wknd over 1f out* **66/1**

0000 **7** 2 1/2 **Doyle's Dream**[23] 7996 3-8-12 29 .... FrankieMcDonald 3 32
(Michael Madgwick) *t.k.h: pressed ldr to over 2f out: wknd qckly over 1f out* **100/1**

0/0 **8** 1 **Artful Dodger**[24] 7739 5-9-4 0 .... SebSanders 1 34
(Olivia Maylam) *led to over 2f out: wknd rapidly over 1f out* **40/1**

1m 38.34s (0.14) **Going Correction** +0.025s/f (Slow)
WFA 3 from 4yo+ 1lb 8 Ran SP% 122.0
Speed ratings (Par 103): **100,97,96,92,91 88,86,85**
toteswingers 1&2 £1.90, 2&3 £1.80, 1&3 £2.50 CSF £6.85 TOTE £2.50: £1.10, £1.20, £1.50; EX 9.60 Trifecta £18.90 Pool: £2,647.27 - 104.85 winning tickets..
Owner Mrs J K Powell **Bred** Mrs C Regalado-Gonzalez **Trained** Lambourn, Berks

FOCUS
An ordinary maiden in which only four runners mattered and the market leaders came to the fore. Obviously limited form, but the first two can rate higher.

8268 £32 BONUS AT 32RED.COM H'CAP 7f (P)
3:30 (3:31) (Class 6) (0-65,65) 3-Y-O+ **£1,704** (£503; £251) **Stalls** Low

Form RPR
0132 **1** **Glastonberry**[10] 8156 4-9-6 **64** .... GeorgeBaker 3 75+
(Geoffrey Deacon) *hld up in 5th and a gng wl: smooth prog on inner 2f out: led 1f out: shkn up and styd on wl* **5/4**[1]

2054 **2** 1 1/4 **Paperetto**[10] 8156 4-8-11 **62** .... RyanTate(7) 9 69
(Robert Mills) *prom: drvn to chal for 2nd 2f out: styd on to chse wnr ins fnl f: unable to chal* **9/2**[2]

4530 **3** 1/2 **Comadoir (IRE)**[23] 7992 6-8-9 **58** .... (p) NathanSweeney(5) 13 64
(Jo Crowley) *rousted along fr wd draw to ld and sn clr: stl 3 l ahd 2f out: hdd 1f out: kpt on* **33/1**

0522 **4** nk **Warbond**[23] 7993 4-9-2 **60** .... JamieGoldstein 1 65
(Michael Madgwick) *hld up in midfield and off the pce: prog over 2f out: drvn to cl on ldrs 1f out: styd on same pce* **10/1**[3]

303 **5** 3/4 **West Leake (IRE)**[106] 6157 6-9-0 **58** ow1 .... TomMcLaughlin 2 62
(Paul Burgoyne) *t.k.h and hld up in last trio: stdy prog on inner over 2f out: pushed along and styd on fr over 1f out: nvr chal* **20/1**

0041 **6** 3/4 **Efistorm**[17] 8063 11-9-4 **65** .... SimonPearce(3) 10 66
(Conor Dore) *racd off the pce in midfield: rdn and tried to cl 2f out: kpt on same pce after* **16/1**

6004 **7** 2 **Hereford Boy**[14] 8105 8-9-3 **64** .... (p) PatrickHills(3) 4 60
(Dean Ivory) *hld up wl in rr and wl off the pce: no ch fr 2f out: kpt on fnl f* **12/1**

6305 **8** nk **Buxton**[17] 8061 8-9-1 **59** .... (t) SebSanders 7 54
(Roger Ingram) *hld up in last and wl off the pce: sme prog on inner over 1f out: nvr rchd ldrs* **20/1**

0300 **9** 1 **Mishrif (USA)**[14] 8105 6-9-7 **65** .... (b) EddieAhern 6 57
(J R Jenkins) *hld up in rr and wl off the pce: brought wd bnd 2f out: pushed along and modest late hdwy* **16/1**

0321 **10** 3/4 **Mack's Sister**[17] 8061 5-9-1 **59** .... (p) JimCrowley 14 49
(Dean Ivory) *racd wd: hld up and off the pce: nvr involved* **10/1**[3]

0000 **11** 1/2 **Midnight Feast**[18] 8058 4-9-7 **65** .... J-PGuillambert 8 54
(Lee Carter) *dwlt but sn rcvrd and prom: rdn to chal for 2nd 2f out: wknd rapidly over 1f out* **20/1**

0310 **12** 3/4 **Ace Of Spies (IRE)**[17] 8064 7-8-12 **59** .... RyanPowell(3) 12 46
(Conor Dore) *chsd clr ldr to wl over 1f out: wknd qckly* **50/1**

0556 **13** 12 **Lexington Spirit (IRE)**[17] 8063 3-9-2 **60** .... JimmyQuinn 11 14
(Richard Fahey) *t.k.h: hld up off the pce: wknd 2f out: t.o* **25/1**

3560 **14** 10 **Mary's Pet**[17] 8064 5-8-13 **57** .... MickyFenton 5
(Lee Carter) *t.k.h: hld up wl in rr: wknd over 2f out: wl t.o* **33/1**

1m 24.48s (-0.32) **Going Correction** +0.025s/f (Slow) 14 Ran SP% 126.2
Speed ratings (Par 101): **102,100,100,99,98 97,95,95,94,93 92,91,78,66**
toteswingers 1&2 £3.50, 2&3 £53.50, 1&3 £26.10 CSF £5.94 CT £140.61 TOTE £2.00: £1.20, £1.60, £14.70; EX 8.40 Trifecta £414.40 Pool: £2,215.86 - 4.01 winning tickets..
Owner Jim Kelly **Bred** Geoffrey Deacon **Trained** Upper Basildon, Berks
■ Stewards' Enquiry : Nathan Sweeney three-day ban; careless riding (11th-13th Jan).

FOCUS
Just a modest handicap run at a solid pace. The runner-up helps set the standard.
Lexington Spirit(IRE) Official explanation: jockey said filly stopped quickly.
T/Plt: £22.50 to a £1 stake. Pool: £61,012.71 - 1979.3 winning tickets. T/Qpdt: £5.30 to a £1 stake. Pool: £4,987.04 - 694.8 winning tickets. JN

8253 WOLVERHAMPTON (A.W) (L-H)
Friday, December 28

OFFICIAL GOING: Standard
Wind: fresh, behind Weather: overcast

8269 CONNOLLY'S RED MILLS HORSE FEEDS H'CAP 7f 32y(P)
3:50 (3:50) (Class 5) (0-75,75) 3-Y-O+ **£2,587** (£770; £384; £192) **Stalls** High

Form RPR
6102 **1** **Silverware (USA)**[11] 8152 4-9-7 **75** .... PatrickMathers 10 84
(Linda Stubbs) *mde all: rdn and fnd ex over 1f out: styd on wl ins fnl f: rdn out* **4/1**[2]

0065 **2** 1 1/2 **Azrael**[20] 8034 4-8-11 **72** .... (p) NoraLooby(7) 9 77
(Alan McCabe) *chsd ldrs: chsd wnr 4f out: pressed wnr 2f out: rdn and unable qck over 1f out: styd on same pce ins fnl f* **10/1**

0002 **3** shd **Pelmanism**[30] 7914 5-8-10 **64** .... (b) TomEaves 12 69
(Brian Ellison) *in tch in last quartet: rdn ent fnl 2f: no imp tl styd on strly u.p ins fnl f: no real threat to wnr* **17/2**

2100 **4** 1/2 **Availed Speaker (IRE)**[85] 6812 3-8-7 **68** .... GeorgeChaloner(7) 5 71
(Richard Fahey) *chsd ldrs: rdn 3f out: styd on same pce u.p fr over 1f out* **20/1**

6044 **5** 1 **For Shia And Lula (IRE)**[17] 8063 3-9-0 **68** .... ShaneKelly 2 69
(Daniel Mark Loughnane) *hld up in tch in midfield: rdn and effrt over 1f out: drvn 1f out: kpt on but nvr gng pce to threaten ldrs* **16/1**

0022 **6** 1/2 **Irish Heartbeat (IRE)**[6] 8232 7-9-6 **74** .... FergusSweeney 4 73
(Jamie Osborne) *t.k.h: chsd wnr tl 4f out: styd chsng ldrs: rdn and effrt wl over 1f out: no ex ins fnl f: one pce* **2/1**[1]

2-00 **7** 3/4 **Going Grey (IRE)**[16] 8074 3-8-8 **62** .... BarryMcHugh 3 59
(Richard Fahey) *t.k.h: hld up wl in tch: rdn and effrt on inner over 1f out: styd on same pce fnl f: eased towards fin* **20/1**

5643 **8** shd **Jack My Boy (IRE)**[137] 5150 5-8-12 **66** .... (b) AndrewMullen 1 63
(David Evans) *in tch in last quartet: rdn and effrt over 1f out: kpt on but nvr gng pce to threaten ldrs* **11/2**[3]

0034 **9** nk **Avonrose**[16] 8081 5-9-2 **70** .... (v) DaleSwift 11 66
(Derek Shaw) *in tch in midfield on outer: hdwy 2f out: drvn and no imp over 1f out: wknd ins fnl f* **16/1**

060 **10** 6 **Saucy Brown (IRE)**[20] 8034 6-8-8 **62** .... (bt[1]) AmyRyan 8 42
(Kevin Ryan) *taken down early: t.k.h: hld up in last pair: rdn and no hdwy 2f out: sn wknd* **14/1**

4625 **11** *6* **Unlimited**[116] 5892 10 -8-5**66**.................................... AidenBlakemore(7) 6 30
(Tony Carroll) *awkward leaving stalls: a bhd: lost tch over 1f out* **33/1**
1m 28.15s (-1.45)**Going Correction** -0.15s/f (Stan) 11Ran SP% 119.2
Speed ratings (Par 103): **102,100,100,99,98 97,97,96,96,89 82**
toteswingers 1&2 £10.40, 2&3 £14.60, 1&3 £6.90 CSF £43.15 CT £266.76 TOTE £5.40 : £3.10, £4.00, £2.70 ; EX 66.60 Trifecta £380.90 Pool: £1,239.43 - 2.44 winning tickets.
Owner Paul & Linda Dixon **Bred** Alliand Equine **Trained** Norton, N Yorks

FOCUS
Few progressive sorts in just a fair handicap. An ordinary gallop suited the prominent-racers and the winner raced close to the inside rail throughout.

8270 32RED SUPPORTING BRITISH RACING MEDIAN AUCTION MAIDEN STKS 1m 141y (P)
4:20 (4:20) (Class 6) 2-Y-O £1,704 (£503; £251) **Stalls** Low

Form RPR
422 **1** **Magique (IRE)**[56] 7525 2 -8-12**73**.. ShaneKelly 4 71+
(Jeremy Noseda) *stdd s: trckd ldrs: swtchd out rt and jnd ldr on bit over 1f out: nudged into ld ins fnl f: comf* **4/7**[1]
0343 **2** *1 1/4* **Mosman**[11] 8147 2 -9-3**66**.. FergusSweeney 1 69
(Jamie Osborne) *led: drvn 2f out: hdd fnl f: sn brushed aside and styd on same pce* **13/2**[3]
3 *3 1/2* **Taming The Tweet** 2 -8-12**0**.. MartinDwyer 5 57
(Alan McCabe) *wnt rt s: rn green and sn pushed along: chsd ldrs: rdn over 3f out: outpcd 2f out: plugged on to go 3rd jst ins fnl f* **33/1**
4 *3 3/4* **Evan Elpus (IRE)** 2 -9-3**0**.. RichardKingscote 3 54
(Tom Dascombe) *dwlt: sn chsd ldr: drvn and unable qck whn rdr dropped reins ent fnl 2f: wknd jst over 1f out* **11/4**[2]
0 **5** *11* **Striking Echo**[20] 8033 2 -9-3**0**.. TomEaves 2 31
(Reg Hollinshead) *sn detached in last and nudged along: sme hdwy and clsd on ldrs 3f out: wknd 2f out* **50/1**
1m 49.94s (-0.56)**Going Correction** -0.15s/f (Stan) 5Ran SP% 108.6
Speed ratings (Par 94): **96,94,91,88,78**
CSF £4.81 TOTE £1.50 : £1.10 , £2.30 ; EX 3.10 Trifecta £11.60 Pool: £2,847.08 - 183.43 winning tickets..
Owner Miss Yvonne Jacques **Bred** Mrs Cherry Faeste **Trained** Newmarket, Suffolk

FOCUS
An uncompetitive maiden in which the gallop was no more than fair. The winner came down the centre in the straight.

NOTEBOOK
Magique(IRE) raced with the choke out in this muddling event over this longer trip but didn't have to improve to get off the mark in comfortable fashion. Life will be tougher from here but she is in good hands and may do better. (op 1-2 tchd 4-6)

Mosman had a bit to find at the weights with the winner but he's a reliable yardstick who was allowed an easy lead and he gave it his best shot. He should be able to pick up a race this winter. (op 6-1 tchd 5-1)

Taming The Tweet, a half-sister to fair 5f-7f turf and AW winner Little Knickers and modest 6f-7f Polytrack winner Chambles, was noticeably green but showed ability at an ordinary level on this debut. She's entitled to improve. (tchd 40-1)

Evan Elpus (IRE) a 24,000GBP half-brother to several winners, including very useful 1m-1m3f turf/Polytrack winner Charles Camoin, attracted support but dropped out tamely after racing with the choke out on this racecourse debut. He has a bit to recommend him on looks and he's presumably capable of a fair bit better. (op 3-1 tchd 10-3 and 9-4)

Striking Echo was again well beaten and is likely to remain vulnerable in this type of event.

8271 32RED CASINO H'CAP 1m 141y (P)
4:50 (4:50) (Class 6) (0-65,68) 3-Y-O+ £2,045 (£603; £302) **Stalls** Low

Form RPR
2131 **1** **Outlaw Torn (IRE)**[6] 7529 3 -9-2**62**.....................(e) RobbieFitzpatrick 10 70
(Richard Guest) *t.k.h: sn pressing ldr: rdn and sustained duel w rival fr over 1f out: kpt on wl: edgd rt ins fnl f: led last stride* **4/1**[2]
0211 **2** *shd* **Royal Holiday (IRE)**[8] 7799 5 -9-6**64**.........................(p) BarryMcHugh 1 72
(Marjorie Fife) *sn led: rdn 2f out: sustained duel w wnr fr over 1f out: edgd rt ins fnl f but kpt on wl tl hdd last stride* **8/1**
0600 **3** *1 1/4* **Apache Glory (USA)**[30] 7905 4 -9-4**62**.............................. IanMongan 4 67
(John Stimpson) *hld up in tch in midfield: hdwy u.p over 1f out: chsd ldng and swtchd lft fnl 100yds: no imp towards fin* **28/1**
021 **4** *3/4* **Nant Saeson (IRE)**[3] 8131 3 -8-12**58**.................(p) MichaelO'Connell 12 61
(John Quinn) *t.k.h: hld up in tch in midfield: swtchd rt and hdwy u.p jst over 1f out: styd on: nt rch ldrs* **4/1**[2]
3030 **5** *2 1/4* **Glass Mountain (IRE)**[35] 7844 4 -9-4**65**.......................(v) RyanClark(3) 6 63
(John Mackie) *hld up in tch in midfield: rdn and effrt over 1f out: styd on same pce and no imp fnl f* **14/1**
0400 **6** *3/4* **Moral Issue**[137] 5171 4 -9-6**64**.. DaleSwift 8 61
(Ian McInnes) *t.k.h: chsd ldrs: rdn and unable qck wl over 1f out: drvn and no imp 1f out: wknd towards fin* **25/1**
6551 **7** *1/2* **Cheers For Thea (IRE)**[1] 8146 7 -9-10**68** 6ex.....(bt) DuranFentiman 13 63
(Tim Easterby) *s.i.s: hld up in tch in last quartet: rdn and effrt on outer 2f out: no imp ins fnl f* **10/3**[1]
06-0 **8** *shd* **Shelovestobougie**[52] 7618 4 -9-1**59**...........................(t) ShaneKelly 5 54
(Mark Brisbourne) *stall opened sltly late: hld up in rr: hdwy over 1f out: no imp u.p 1f out* **50/1**
2220 **9** *nk* **Green Mitas (ITY)**[14] 8114 3 -9-1**64**............................ MarkCoumbe(3) 3 58
(Frank Sheridan) *t.k.h: hld up in tch in last quartet: rdn and effrt over 1f out: no real imp: nvr trbld ldrs* **11/1**
0006 **10** *shd* **Mataajir (USA)**[6] 8236 4 -9-0**58**.. MartinDwyer 2 52
(Derek Shaw) *broke wl but sn stdd bk: t.k.h: hld up wl in tch: rdn and unable qck over 1f out: wknd ins fnl f* **15/2**[3]
1464 **11** *7* **Sasheen**[14] 8113 5 -8-12**56**.......................................(p) FergusSweeney 9 34
(Jeremy Gask) *chsd ldrs: lost pl u.p 2f out: bhd and eased wl ins fnl f* **14/1**
1m 49.13s (-1.37)**Going Correction** -0.15s/f (Stan)
WFA 3 from 4yo+ 2lb 11Ran SP% 116.9
Speed ratings (Par 101): **100,99,98,98,96 95,95,94,94,94 88**
toteswingers 1&2 £8.10, 2&3 £52.60, 1&3 £31.70 CSF £35.17 CT £801.55 TOTE £5.50 : £1.80, £2.40, £8.00 ; EX 35.70 Trifecta £1708.00 Part won. Pool: £2,277.41 - 0.82 winning tickets.
Owner James S Kennerley **Bred** Derek Veitch & Rory O'Brien **Trained** Stainforth, S Yorks

FOCUS
Several previous winners in a modest handicap but the moderate gallop that saw very few get involved means this bare form isn't entirely reliable. The winner raced in the centre in the straight.

Shelovestobougie Official explanation: jockey said filly was slowly away.

8272 32RED H'CAP 5f 216y (P)
5:20 (5:20) (Class 2) (0-100,103) 3-Y-O+ £9,955 (£2,979; £1,489; £745; £371) Stalls Low

Form RPR
100 **1** **Piscean (USA)**[100] 6382 7 -8-13**95**.................................... RyanClark(3) 1 104
(Tom Keddy) *hld up in tch in rr: short of room and hmpd over 2f out: hdwy u.p over 1f out: running on and swtchd lft ins fnl f: r.o wl to ld last strides* **20/1**
5051 **2** *hd* **Woolfall Sovereign (IRE)**[7] 8066 6 -9-0**93**..................... IanMongan 4 101
(George Margarson) *chsd ldrs: rdn to chal and edgd lft u.p 1f out: led ins fnl f: kpt on wl tl hdd and no ex last strides* **9/2**[3]
4304 **3** *3/4* **Sulis Minerva (IRE)**[22] 8008 5 -8-4**86** oh1................. RaulDaSilva(3) 2 92
(Jeremy Gask) *in tch in last pair: hdwy 2f out: chsd ldrs and swtchd rt jst ins fnl f: kpt on towards fin* **16/1**
2312 **4** *3* **Swiss Cross**[17] 8066 5 -9-10**103**...................................(t) DavidProbert 7 99
(Phil McEntee) *pressed ldr tl rdn to ld 2f out: hdd ins fnl f: no ex and wknd wl ins fnl f* **11/2**
0210 **5** *shd* **Mezzotint (IRE)**[22] 8008 3 -8-10**89**........................ RichardKingscote 3 85
(Marco Botti) *led: hdd and rdn 2f out: stl pressing ldrs but no ex jst ins fnl f: wknd wl ins fnl f* **13/8**[1]
0051 **6** *5* **Doctor Parkes**[90] 6688 6 -8-10**89**................................ AdamBeschizza 5 69
(Stuart Williams) *hld up in last trio: swtchd rt and effrt 2f out: no prog and wknd 1f out* **12/1**
1361 **7** *6* **All Or Nothin (IRE)**[90] 6663 3 -8-9**88** ow1................ MichaelO'Connell 6 49
(John Quinn) *chsd ldrs: drvn and struggling over 2f out: wknd over 1f out* **7/2**[2]
0624 **8** *6* **Master Bond**[6] 8232 3 -8-7**86** oh10....................................(t) TomEaves 8 28
(Bryan Smart) *t.k.h: chsd ldrs on outer: rdn and wknd 2f out: bhd and eased wl ins fnl f* **25/1**
1m 13.31s (-1.69)**Going Correction** -0.15s/f (Stan) 8Ran SP% 116.1
Speed ratings (Par 109): **105,104,103,99,99 92,84,76**
toteswingers 1&2 £16.10, 2&3 £7.40, 1&3 £20.60 CSF £108.86 CT £1500.84 TOTE £18.60 : £5.00, £1.40 , £5.40 ; EX 137.60 Trifecta £1433.20 Pool: £2,331.42 - 1.22 winning tickets.
Owner Andrew Duffield **Bred** Connie And John Iacuone **Trained** Newmarket, Suffolk

FOCUS
A very useful handicap in which the gallop was fair. The first three pulled clear and the winner raced close to the inside rail the in the straight.

NOTEBOOK
Piscean(USA), a multiple winner on turf and Polytack, put a couple of below-par efforts behind and overcame trouble in running to confirm himself a very useful performer on Polytrack on this first run after a short break. An even stronger gallop would have suited better and he should continue to go well in this type of event. (op 14-1)
Woolfall Sovereign (IRE)has a fine strike-rate on Polytrack and, although nailed close home after getting the perfect tow into the race, ran as well as he ever has. He's effective over 5f and on Fibresand and can win again this winter. (tchd 4-1)
Sulis Minerva (IRE)confirmed he's at the very top of his game to pull clear of the remainder and this keen-going sort, who would be ideally suited by a really strong pace, is capable of going in again when things pan out in the coming months. (tchd 14-1)
Swiss Cross has developed into a smart sprinter but he couldn't confirm latest 5f placings with the runner-up over this longer trip. However he's a fairly reliable sort who should continue to go well over either sprint distance. (op 6-1 tchd 13-2)
Mezzotint(IRE), with the hood left off for this return to 6f, attracted plenty of support but was a shade disappointing for a stable that has been in good form of late. He's a useful sort with a reasonable strike-rate and he be better suited by getting a lead. (op 7-4 tchd 2-1)
Doctor Parkes, who scored on his AW debut over 5f at this course on his previous start, failed by some way to confirm that promise over this longer trip from this higher mark in this stronger grade on this first run for his new trainer. He's probably worth another chance. (op 11-1)
All Or Nothin (IRE)attracted a bit of support but proved disappointing on this AW debut and first run since September. However he's in good hands, he isn't fully exposed and will be worth another chance at some point. (op 9-2)

8273 £32 BONUS AT 32RED.COM H'CAP 1m 5f 194y (P)
5:50 (5:51) (Class 6) (0-65,65) 3-Y-O+ £1,704 (£503; £251) **Stalls** Low

Form RPR
0606 **1** **Tram Express (FR)**[20] 8035 8 -8-12**54**.......(t) WilliamTwiston-Davies(5) 4 61
(Shaun Lycett) *dwlt and rdn along leaving stalls: hld up in tch in last pair: swtchd rt and hdwy wl over 1f out: chsd ldrs u.p 1f out: styd on wl to ld last strides* **25/1**
3506 **2** *nk* **Reaction**[26] 5950 6 -9-9**60**..(v) AndrewMullen 5 67
(Michael Appleby) *hld up in tch in midfield: rdn and effrt 2f out: drvn and chsd ldrs 1f out: pressing ldrs and styd on wl fnl 100yds: wnt 2nd last strides* **9/1**
5/3 **3** *nk* **Day Of Destiny (IRE)**[1] 7638 7 -9-11**62**..................... JamesSullivan 10 68
(James Given) *t.k.h: chsd ldrs tl hdwy to chse ldr 10f out: led over 2f out: sn rdn: kpt on wl u.p tl hdd and lost 2 pls last strides* **4/1**[2]
6-42 **4** *nk* **Stetson**[17] 8067 6 -9-7**58**.. TonyHamilton 9 64
(Ian Williams) *t.k.h: chsd ldrs: rdn to chse ldr wl over 1f out: pressed ldr ins fnl f: kpt on* **9/2**[3]
4425 **5** *3/4* **Kames Park (IRE)**[14] 8106 10 -9-6**62**............................ JasonHart(5) 11 67
(Richard Guest) *stdd and dropped in bhd after s: hld up in rr: hdwy over 1f out: swtchd lft ins fnl f: styd on but nt rch ldrs* **11/2**
4430 **6** *3/4* **Neil's Pride**[19] 8048 3 -8-8**52**.. BarryMcHugh 8 56
(Richard Fahey) *led for 2f: chsd ldr tl 10f out: styd prom: chsd ldng pair and edgd lft u.p 1f out: one pce fnl f* **10/1**
4065 **7** *1 1/2* **Port Charlotte**[16] 8082 3 -9-7**65**.. RobertHavlin 2 67
(Hughie Morrison) *hld up in tch in midfield: rdn and unable qck 2f out: wknd ins fnl f* **10/3**[1]
0500 **8** *3 1/2* **Souter Point (USA)**[89] 7791 6 -9-1**263**........................ AdamBeschizza 6 60
(Peter Salmon) *hld up in tch in last trio: rdn and effrt wl over 1f out: no real imp: wknd 1f out* **12/1**
2034 **9** *4 1/2* **Holden Eagle**[25] 7968 7 -9-4**62**.. IanBurns(7) 12 53
(Tony Newcombe) *chsd ldr tl led after 2f: rdn and hdd over 2f out: wknd u.p over 1f out* **10/1**
5044 **10** *6* **David's Folly (IRE)**[98] 7793 3 -8-2**46** oh1........................ NickyMackay 1 28
(Bryn Palling) *in tch in midfield: rdn and no prog 3f out: wknd 2f out: bhd fnl f* **25/1**
3m 3.46s (-2.54)**Going Correction** -0.15s/f (Stan)
WFA 3 from 4yo+ 7lb 10Ran SP% 120.2
Speed ratings (Par 101): **101,100,100,100,100 99,98,96,94,90**
toteswingers 1&2 £31.60, 2&3 £4.70, 1&3 £22.80 CSF £240.13 CT £1102.42 TOTE £42.50 : £9.90, £4.00 , £1.50 ; EX 324.50 Trifecta £1114.00 Pool: £1,841.93 - 1.24 winning tickets.
Owner Shaun Lycett **Bred** Jean Francois Delbart And Pascale Menard **Trained** Clapton-on-the-Hill, Gloucs
■ Stewards' Enquiry : William Twiston-Davies two-day ban: used whip above permitted level (Jan 16-17)
Andrew Mullen two-day ban: used whip above permitted level (Jan 15-16)

FOCUS
A modest handicap run at just an ordinary gallop and saw the first six home finish in a heap. The winner came down the centre in the straight.
Tram Express(FR) Official explanation: trainer said, regarding apparent improvement in form, that the gelding had matured and benefited from runing on the all-weather surface again.

8274 32REDBET.COM NURSERY 5f 216y(P)
6:20 (6:22) (Class 6) (0-65,62) 2-Y-O **£1,704** (£503; £251) **Stalls** Low

Form RPR
000 **1** **Hazza The Jazza**[56] 7525 2-9-0 **55**........................(b[1]) RobbieFitzpatrick 8 59
(Richard Guest) *awkward leaving stalls and slowly away: in tch in rr: pushed rt after 1f: swtchd rt and effrt over 1f out: stl plenty to do but hdwy ins fnl f: hrd drvn and str run fnl 100yds to ld on post* **9/1**
0530 **2** *nse* **Hazard Warning (IRE)**[13] 8132 2-8-4 **45**..................(b) DuranFentiman 9 49
(Tim Easterby) *in tch in midfield: effrt u.p over 1f out: drvn and str run ins fnl f: led last strides: hdd on post* **20/1**
064 **3** *hd* **Loulou Vuitton**[28] 7931 2-9-3 **58**....................................[1] WilliamCarson 2 61
(Brian Baugh) *in tch in midfield: hmpd after 1f: rdn and effrt to chal 1f out: drvn to ld wl ins fnl f: hdd last strides* **10/1**
0002 **4** *3/4* **Devout (IRE)**[10] 8155 2-8-9 **50**.................................... FergusSweeney 11 51
(Jamie Osborne) *chsd ldr: rdn and ev ch ent fnl f: unable qck u.p fnl 100yds* **11/2[2]**
435 **5** *1/2* **Miako (USA)**[102] 6320 2-9-7 **62**.. AndrewMullen 3 62
(Michael Appleby) *chsd ldrs: rdn and effrt to ld over 1f out: drvn 1f out: hdd wl ins fnl f: no ex* **15/2**
0003 **6** *hd* **Black Truffle (FR)**[10] 8155 2-8-6 **47**...............................[1] DavidProbert 5 46
(Mark Usher) *dwlt: in tch in rr: swtchd rt after 1f: effrt u.p over 1f out: styd on ins fnl f* **9/4[1]**
4020 **7** *3* **Little Miss Zuri (IRE)**[28] 7930 2-8-8 **49**........................... NickyMackay 4 39
(Sylvester Kirk) *led: rdn and hdd over 1f out: wknd ins fnl f* **12/1**
4426 **8** *1/2* **Frans Hals**[10] 8155 2-8-12 **53**.................................... AdamBeschizza 10 41+
(Dominic Ffrench Davis) *dwlt: sn in tch: hmpd after 1f out: rdn and unable qck over 1f out: wknd ins fnl f* **6/1[3]**
506 **9** *3/4* **Exit Clause**[22] 8006 2-9-7 **62**.. RobertWinston 7 48
(Tony Carroll) *in tch: rdn and unable qck over 1f out: wknd ins fnl f* **10/1**
0405 **10** *1/2* **Eyeline**[25] 7974 2-8-10 **56**... JackDuern(5) 1 41+
(Reg Hollinshead) *hld up in tch towards rr: hmpd after 1f: rdn and effrt over 1f out: no prog 1f out: wknd ins fnl f* **18/1**
0635 **11** *1* **Twinwood Star (IRE)**[6] 8233 2-8-6 **47**.......................... JamesSullivan 6 29
(John Weymes) *t.k.h: hld up in tch towards rr: wknd u.p over 1f out* **33/1**
1m 15.2s (0.20) **Going Correction** -0.15s/f (Stan) **11** Ran SP% **121.0**
Speed ratings (Par 94): **92,91,91,90,90 89,85,85,84,83 82**
toteswingers 1&2 £36.60, 2&3 £36.50, 1&3 £26.30 CSF £178.55 CT £1879.01 TOTE £14.60: £4.50, £5.30, £2.70; EX 188.40 TRIFECTA Not won..
Owner Maze Rattan Limited **Bred** Aiden Murphy **Trained** Stainforth, S Yorks
■ Stewards' Enquiry : Robbie Fitzpatrick trainer's rep said, regarding apparent improvement in form, that the gelding had benefited from the application of first-time blinkers.

FOCUS
A moderate handicap run at a reasonable gallop and another in which several finished in a heap. The winner came down the centre in the straight.

NOTEBOOK
Hazza The Jazza ◆attracted support and turned in a much-improved effort on this handicap debut in the first-time blinkers. He deserves plenty of credit for making up a good deal of ground in the straight, he should be at least as good over 7f and, given he won't be going up much for this, appeals strongly as the type to win again. (op 22-1)
Hazard Warning(IRE) didn't get home over 1m at this course on his previous start but fared much better returned to sprinting. This wasn't much of a race but he isn't fully exposed and should be able to win for this yard. (op 25-1)
Loulou Vuitton improved with every run in maidens and stepped up again on this handicap debut in the first-time hood. (op 9-1 tchd 8-1)
Devout(IRE), who showed improved form on her handicap/AW debut at Lingfield, wasn't far off that level from this double-figure draw. She remains capable of picking up a race. (op 6-1 tchd 7-1 and 5-1)
Miako(USA), gelded since his last run and having his first start for a new yard, was far from disgraced back up in trip after racing with the choke out. He may do better. (op 13-2)
Black Truffle(FR) was far from disgraced with the first-time hood fitted and he could benefit from the step up to 7f. (op 7-4)

8275 32RED.COM H'CAP 1m 4f 50y(P)
6:50 (6:51) (Class 4) (0-85,85) 3-Y-O+ **£4,075** (£1,212; £606; £303) **Stalls** Low

Form RPR
4556 **1** **Mica Mika (IRE)**[37] 7810 4-9-2 **77**.................................... TonyHamilton 3 85
(Richard Fahey) *chsd ldr: rdn and effrt 2f out: styd on u.p to ld wl ins fnl f: rdn out* **6/1[3]**
0-01 **2** *3/4* **Alazan (IRE)**[23] 7999 6-8-11 **77**...................... WilliamTwiston-Davies(5) 7 84
(Philip Hobbs) *sn led: rdn and 2 l clr 2f out: drvn 1f out: hdd and no ex wl ins fnl f* **3/1[2]**
/502 **3** *1* **Ascendant**[14] 8110 6-9-7 **82**... RobertWinston 2 87
(Alan McCabe) *in tch in midfield: effrt u.p and chsd clr ldng pair over 1f out: kpt on ins fnl f: nt rch ldrs* **6/1[3]**
0232 **4** *1* **Brimstone Hill (IRE)**[8] 8182 3-8-9 **75**........................ WilliamCarson 10 79
(Anthony Carson) *stdd s: t.k.h: hld up in tch in last trio: hdwy and swtchd lft over 1f out: styd on fnl f but nvr trbld ldrs* **11/4[1]**
5 *1* **Private Equity (FR)**[207] 4-9-10 **85**.............................. FergusSweeney 5 87
(Nicky Henderson) *chsd ldrs: rdn and unable qck ent fnl 2f: styd on same pce fr over 1f out* **14/1**
0620 **6** *1* **Change The Subject (USA)**[63] 7368 4-9-3 **78**......(bt) AdamBeschizza 9 79
(Peter Salmon) *t.k.h: hld up in tch in midfield: effrt and swtchd lft over 1f out: no imp fnl f* **25/1**
0045 **7** *1 1/4* **Musnad (USA)**[14] 8110 4-8-10 **71** oh2..............................(b) TomEaves 11 70
(Brian Ellison) *hld up in tch: lost pl 4f out: rdn and styd on same pce fnl 2f* **22/1**
4600 **8** *nk* **All The Winds (GER)**[142] 4962 7-9-0 **80**.................... LeonnaMayor(5) 6 78
(Shaun Lycett) *s.i.s: hld up in rr: sme hdwy whn hmpd 3f out: kpt on ins fnl f: nvr trbld ldrs* **20/1**
6000 **9** *5* **Admirable Duque (IRE)**[23] 8000 6-8-8 **76**............... JoshBaudains(7) 8 66
(Dominic Ffrench Davis) *in tch on outer: hdwy 5f out: rdn and hmpd 3f out: no imp 2f out: wknd over 1f out* **20/1**
10-0 **10** *3/4* **Lemon Drop Red (USA)**[14] 8110 4-9-2 **77**...................... MartinDwyer 1 66
(Paul Webber) *chsd ldrs: rdn and unable qck ent fnl 2f: wknd over 1f out* **20/1**
1354 **11** *8* **The Lock Master (IRE)**[14] 8110 5-9-8 **83**...................... AndrewMullen 4 59
(Michael Appleby) *hld up in tch in midfield: hdwy to chse ldrs 5f out: veered rt u.p 3f out: sn wknd* **17/2**
2m 37.72s (-3.38) **Going Correction** -0.15s/f (Stan)
WFA 3 from 4yo+ 5lb **11** Ran SP% **119.9**
Speed ratings (Par 105): **105,104,103,103,102 101,101,100,97,96 91**
toteswingers 1&2 £5.10, 2&3 £3.90, 1&3 £6.70 CSF £22.63 CT £116.04 TOTE £6.90: £2.70, £1.60, £2.00; EX 36.20 Trifecta £246.10 Pool: £1,611.70 - 4.91 winning tickets..
Owner Mrs Una Towell **Bred** Yeomanstown Stud **Trained** Musley Bank, N Yorks

FOCUS
A useful handicap but one in which an ordinary gallop saw those held up at a disadvantage. The winner raced centre-to-far-side in the straight.
T/Plt: £1,901.40 to a £1 stake. Pool: £82,700.23 - 31.75 winning tickets. T/Qpdt: £239.80 to a £1 stake. Pool: £13,839.78 - 42.70 winning tickets. SP

8192 DEAUVILLE (R-H)
Friday, December 28

OFFICIAL GOING: Fibresand: standard

8276a PRIX DU PHARE (CLAIMER) (2YO) (FIBRESAND) 6f 110y
12:00 (12:01) 2-Y-O **£8,333** (£3,333; £2,500; £1,666; £833)

RPR
1 *snk* **Dance With Dragons (IRE)**[125] 5591 2-9-4 0(b[1]) ChristopheSoumillon 13
(Paul Cole) *sn led on outside: clr ld ent st: hdd 350yds out: rallied and r.o wl u.p fnl f: suffered interference fr wnr ins fnl 100yds: fin 2nd: awrdd the r* **11/10[1]**
2 **Snow Bell (FR)**[24] 2-9-2 0.. GregoryBenoist 14
(N Clement, France) *fin 1st: disqualified and plcd 2nd* **5/1[2]**
3 *1 1/4* **Princesse Leila (FR)**[14] 2-9-2 0.........................(b) MorganDelalande 6
(Y Barberot, France) **15/1**
4 *1/2* **Tita Caty (FR)**[150] 4696 2-8-11 0................................ SebastienMaillot 3
(M Boutin, France) **28/1**
5 *1/2* **Halloween Chope (FR)**[31] 2-9-1 0............................. MaximeGuyon 10
(D Prod'Homme, France) **11/1**
6 *shd* **Antonius Lady (FR)**[60] 2-8-11 0...................................... JeromeCabre 5
(E Danel, France) **24/1**
7 *3/4* **Maderienne (FR)**[8] 2-8-11 0.. AdrienFouassier 9
(L Baudron, France) **28/1**
8 *2* **Starki (FR)**[14] 2-9-1 0... FabriceVeron 15
(H-A Pantall, France) **15/2[3]**
9 *1 1/2* **Encore Un Matin (FR)**[9] 2-8-6 0................(p) ChristopherGrosbois(5) 12
(Y Barberot, France) **27/1**
10 *3/4* **Rock With Me (FR)**[46] 7699 2-9-1 0........................... AnthonyCrastus 11
(F Chappet, France) **28/1**
0 **Woodland Mill (IRE)**[8] 2-8-8 0................................... AntoineHamelin 8
(F Vermeulen, France) **31/1**
0 **La Vermandoise (FR)**[9] 2-8-13 0.................................. TheoBachelot 1
(Y Barberot, France) **37/1**
0 **Super (FR)**[13] 2-8-11 0..(p) AnthonyClement 7
(A Clement, France) **79/1**
0 **Victoria Bay (FR)** 2-8-11 0... KarlMartin 4
(Alex Fracas, France) **64/1**
1m 20.7s (80.70) **14** Ran SP% **117.1**
WIN (incl. 1 euro stake): 2.10. PLACES: 1.40, 1.70, 2.80. DF: 6.30. SF: 10.90.
Owner P F I Cole Ltd **Bred** Oak Lodge Bloodstock **Trained** Whatcombe, Oxon

8277a PRIX DE LA PLAGE (H'CAP) (3YO) (FIBRESAND) 6f 110y
3:10 (3:09) 3-Y-O **£10,000** (£4,000; £3,000; £2,000; £1,000)

RPR
1 **Mon Choix (FR)**[14] 3-9-1 **0**... GregoryBenoist 8 90
(Y Barberot, France) **19/5[2]**
2 *1* **Activiste (IRE)**[23] 3-8-9 **0**.. FlavienPrat 9 81
(C Laffon-Parias, France) **4/1[3]**
3 *2 1/2* **Silverheels (IRE)**[38] 7803 3-9-11 **0**........................... JohanVictoire 1 90
(Paul Cole) *broke wl on ins to r 3rd: wnt 2nd bef st: relegated to 3rd 1f out: styd on u.p fnl f* **5/2[1]**
4 *snk* **Paraggi**[14] 3-9-10 **0**.. MaximeGuyon 2 88
(Mme Pia Brandt, France) **11/2**
5 *hd* **Pat And Go (FR)**[14] 3-8-2 **0** ow2............................... AnthonyCrastus 7 66
(A Bonin, France) **13/1**
6 *1 3/4* **Turcoman's (FR)**[24] 3-8-10 **0**.. AlexisBadel 5 69
(A Junk, France) **13/2**
7 *2 1/2* **Cruel Summer (FR)**[14] 3-8-9 **0**................................... AntoineHamelin 4 61
(F Vermeulen, France) **28/1**
8 *2* **Fauvelinx (FR)**[49] 3-8-2 **0**... FabriceVeron 3 48
(H-A Pantall, France) **15/1**
9 *1 3/4* **Dr Thibault (FR)**[24] 3-8-13 **0**.......................................(b) FilipMinarik 6 54
(U Suter, France) **39/1**
1m 18.1s (78.10) **9** Ran SP% **117.5**
WIN (incl. 1 euro stake): 4.80. PLACES: 1.40, 1.60, 1.50. DF: 8.60. SF: 24.20.
Owner Gerard Augustin-Normand **Bred** M Andree **Trained** France

8244 GULFSTREAM PARK (L-H)
Friday, December 28

OFFICIAL GOING: Turf: firm

8278a CLAIMING RACE (CLAIMER) (3YO+) (TURF) 5f
6:41 (12:00) 3-Y-O+
£10,064 (£4,193; £2,096; £670; £167; £167)

RPR
1 **Don't Say No (CAN)** 5-8-7 0...(b) FTorres 5
(Luis M Ramirez, U.S.A) **48/10[2]**
2 *1/2* **Starship Sulu (USA)** 3-8-4 0..(b) LSaez 6
(Jose Pinchin, U.S.A) **192/10**
3 *nk* **Gibson (USA)**[27] 4-8-7 0...(b[1]) JJCastellano 10
(Michael J Maker, U.S.A) **7/5[1]**

4 1 1/4 **Longhunter**[174] 4-8-7 0 .... RAlbarado 7
(Darrin Miller, U.S.A) 5/1[3]
5 1/2 **Rob The Cradle (CAN)** 4-8-7 0 .... (b) LContreras 4
(Michael P De Paulo, Canada) 93/10
6 3/4 **Lady Rizzi (USA)**[825] 9-8-4 0 .... (b) JRoccoJr 8
(Linda Rice, U.S.A) 59/10
7 1/2 **Lawnswood (USA)** 5-8-7 0 .... JDelgado 2
(Barry Croft, U.S.A) 73/1
8 5 **Omar's Tiger (USA)** 5-8-7 0 .... (b) JCLeyva 9
(Michael Yates, U.S.A) 106/10
9 1/2 **Julius Geezer (IRE)**[15] 8100 4-8-7 0 .... CLanerie 3
(Amy Weaver) *a towards rr: rdn on turn into st: sn outpcd and btn: nvr a factor* 23/1
10 3 1/2 **Crockefeller (USA)** 4-8-7 0 .... (b) OBocachica 1
(Patricia Farro, U.S.A) 37/1

56.29s (56.29) **10** Ran SP% **121.5**
PARI-MUTUEL (all including $2 stakes): WIN 11.60; PLACE (1-2) 6.00, 13.60; SHOW (1-2-3) 4.00, 6.40, 2.60; SF 184.60.
Owner Frank Carl Calabrese **Bred** Hal Snowden Jr **Trained** North America

8279a ALLOWANCE RACE (CONDITIONS) (3YO+) (TURF) 1m (T)
9:35 (12:00) 3-Y-0+
£16,838 (£7,032; £2,806; £1,403; £280; £280)

RPR
1 **Batter Up (USA)** 4-8-7 0 .... JBravo 7
(Allen Iwinski, U.S.A) 15/2
2 hd **Rapacious (USA)**[412] 3-8-4 0 .... (b) JRoccoJr 9
(George R Arnold II, U.S.A) 18/5[3]
3 1/2 **Fact (USA)** 4-8-9 0 .... (b) DCohen 1
(Marcus J Vitali, U.S.A) 132/10
4 1/2 **Van Citra (USA)** 3-8-4 0 .... (b) LSaez 5
(Dubis Chaparro, U.S.A) 237/10
5 1 **Gaelico (USA)** 3-8-4 0 .... JLezcano 6
(Dale Romans, U.S.A) 11/5[1]
6 1 1/4 **Wharton (USA)** 3-8-4 0 .... (b) JJCastellano 2
(Chad C Brown, U.S.A) 23/10[2]
7 6 1/4 **Marford Missile (IRE)**[72] 7158 3-8-4 0 .... GSaez 3
(Amy Weaver) 201/10
8 1 1/2 **Haunted (USA)** 3-8-5 0 ow1 .... CLanerie 8
(Elizabeth Gray, U.S.A) 19/1
9 11 1/4 **Launch Commander (USA)** 3-8-5 0 ow1 .... JRosario 4
(David Fawkes, U.S.A) 153/10

1m 37.35s (97.35)
WFA 3 from 4yo+ 1lb **9** Ran SP% **122.0**
PARI-MUTUEL (all including $2 stakes): WIN 17.00; PLACE (1-2) 6.80, 5.40; SHOW (1-2-3) 4.60, 5.60; SF 87.00.
Owner Peter E Blum Thoroughbreds Llc **Bred** Peter E Blum **Trained** USA

8280 - 8284a (Foreign Racing) - See Raceform Interactive

[8269]WOLVERHAMPTON (A.W) (L-H)
Saturday, December 29

OFFICIAL GOING: Standard
Wind: Moderate behind Weather: Heavy cloud and rain

8285 32RED CASINO H'CAP 5f 20y(P)
2:05 (2:05) (Class 5) (0-75,75) 3-Y-0+ **£2,911** (£866; £432; £216) **Stalls** Low

Form RPR
0623 1 **Hamoody (USA)**[8] 8202 8-9-7 75 .... SebSanders 8 85
(David Nicholls) *hld up: hdwy on outer wl over 1f out: rdn and styd on wl to ld ins fnl f* 9/2[2]
2221 2 1 1/4 **Another Citizen (IRE)**[29] 7937 4-9-2 75 .... (b) AdamCarter(5) 12 81
(Tim Easterby) *trckd ldrs on outer: hdwy 2f out: rdn to chal over 1f out: led briefly ent fnl f: sn hdd and drvn: kpt on same pce* 9/4[1]
2536 3 3/4 **Above The Stars**[14] 8144 4-8-10 64 .... BarryMcHugh 11 67
(Richard Fahey) *hld up in rr: gd hdwy wl over 1f out: rdn and kpt on fnl f: nrst fin* 14/1
0560 4 1 **Where's Reiley (USA)**[12] 8152 6-9-6 74 .... (p) LukeMorris 6 73
(Alastair Lidderdale) *towards rr: hdwy wl over 1f out: rdn and styd on fnl f: nrst fin* 12/1
4324 5 1 1/4 **Greenhead High**[14] 8144 4-8-6 65 .... ShirleyTeasdale(5) 4 60
(David Nicholls) *trckd ldrs: effrt and n.m.r over 1f out: sn one pce* 5/1[3]
1633 6 1/2 **Ivestar (IRE)**[26] 7969 7-8-1 62 .... (v) MatthewHopkins(7) 5 55
(Michael Easterby) *towards rr: hdwy on inner 2f out: sn rdn and kpt on same pce* 12/1
6500 7 hd **No Mean Trick (USA)**[39] 7794 6-8-9 63 .... JamesSullivan 10 55
(Paul Midgley) *nvr bttr than midfield* 10/1
0002 8 1 1/2 **Steelcut**[29] 7937 8-8-12 66 .... (p) JimmyQuinn 2 53
(Mark Buckley) *trckd ldrs: hdwy 2f out: rdn to ld over 1f out: hdd ent fnl f and sn wknd* 16/1
1200 9 1 1/4 **Crimson Queen**[105] 6226 5-9-4 72 .... (b) ChrisCatlin 3 54
(Roy Brotherton) *cl up: rdn along 2f out: sn wknd* 33/1
0603 10 4 1/2 **Amadeus Denton (IRE)**[29] 7937 3-8-13 67 .... TomEaves 7 33
(Michael Dods) *prom: rdn along wl over 1f out: sn wknd* 16/1
0000 11 1/2 **Alive And Kicking**[63] 7411 4-8-13 67 .... TonyHamilton 1 31
(Richard Fahey) *led: rdn along 2f out: drvn and hdd over 1f out: wknd qckly* 16/1

1m 0.84s (-1.46) **Going Correction** -0.125s/f (Stan) **11** Ran SP% **117.3**
Speed ratings (Par 103): **106,104,102,101,99 98,98,95,93,86 85**
toteswingers: 1&2 £4.00, 1&3 £23.70, 2&3 £11.10 CSF £14.92 CT £126.69 TOTE £5.80: £2.00, £1.20, £6.30; EX 17.20 Trifecta £565.60 Part won Pool: £754.15 - 0.40 winning tickets..
Owner Hart Inn I **Bred** Ragged Mountain Farm **Trained** Sessay, N Yorks

FOCUS
A routine sprint in which the action developed towards the stand side in the straight, with both the winner and the runner-up arriving wide.
Alive And Kicking Official explanation: jockey said gelding had a breathing problem

8286 32RED SUPPORTING BRITISH RACING MAIDEN AUCTION STKS 5f 20y(P)
2:40 (2:40) (Class 6) 2-Y-0 **£2,181** (£644; £322) **Stalls** Low

Form RPR
6402 1 **Faffa**[3] 8237 2-8-7 58 .... AdamCarter(5) 4 60
(Tim Easterby) *cl up: led after 1f: rdn over 1f out: kpt on wl fnl f* 9/4[2]
5 2 1/2 **Magic Ice**[14] 8138 2-8-7 0 .... LukeMorris 1 53
(John Berry) *trckd ldng pair: swtchd lft to inner and effrt wl over 1f out: rdn to chal appr fnl f: ev ch tl drvn and one pce last 75yds* 5/6[1]
55 3 3 1/4 **Alfaisaliah (IRE)**[20] 8044 2-8-7 0 .... (b[1]) DavidProbert 2 44
(J S Moore) *slt ld: hdd after 1f: chsd wnr: rdn along wl over 1f out: wkng whn rdr dropped whip appr fnl f* 7/2[3]

1m 2.71s (0.41) **Going Correction** -0.125s/f (Stan) **3** Ran SP% **107.5**
Speed ratings (Par 94): **91,90,85**
CSF £4.56 TOTE £1.80; EX 3.20 Trifecta £2.10 Pool: £259.60 - 92.41 winning tickets..
Owner Habton Farms **Bred** P And Mrs A G Venner **Trained** Great Habton, N Yorks

FOCUS
A surprising lack of runners, combined with the moderate form of the three that did take part, made this easy to win. The pace was fair enough in the circumstances.

NOTEBOOK
Faffa battled creditably to hold off the challenge of the runner-up, but previous form suggests he is modest. 5f has been his best trip to date. (tchd 2-1)
Magic Ice would have to find a similarly weak maiden to have a chance of winning one, so she may have to wait for a handicap mark. (op 10-11 tchd 4-5)
Alfaisaliah(IRE) didn't travel in the first-time blinkers and the fact that her jockey dropped his whip in the straight made no difference. She needs at least 6f and a switch to low-grade handicaps. (tchd 4-1)

8287 32REDBET.COM CLASSIFIED STKS 5f 216y(P)
3:10 (3:11) (Class 6) 3-Y-0+ **£2,181** (£644; £322) **Stalls** Low

Form RPR
0021 1 **Sandy Lane (IRE)**[8] 8205 3-9-6 52 .... RobertHavlin 3 69
(Amy Weaver) *trckd ldrs: hdwy wl over 1f out: rdn to ld jst ins fnl f: styd on wl towards fin* 13/8[1]
363 2 nk **Valdaw**[17] 8075 4-9-0 55 .... AdamKirby 7 62
(Tony Carroll) *hld up towards rr: hdwy 2f out: swtchd rt to outer and rdn to chal ins fnl f: ev ch and kpt on wl towards fin* 11/4[2]
6030 3 2 1/4 **Christopher Chua (IRE)**[18] 8064 3-9-0 55 .... SebSanders 2 55
(Simon Dow) *trckd ldrs on inner: hdwy 2f out: rdn and n.m.r jst over 1f out: kpt on same pce* 17/2
-634 4 nk **Littlecote Lady**[17] 8075 3-9-0 54 .... DavidProbert 4 54
(Mark Usher) *slt ld: rdn wl over 1f out: drvn and hdd jst ins fnl f: sn one pce* 14/1
5204 5 1 1/2 **Kai**[14] 8131 3-9-0 54 .... (v) LukeMorris 1 49
(Alan McCabe) *cl up on inner: effrt and ev ch 2f out: rdn and edgd lft appr fnl f: sn wknd* 8/1
3053 6 3 3/4 **Dixie Gwalia**[10] 8169 4-8-7 51 .... SiobhanMiller(7) 5 37
(David Simcock) *a in rr* 20/1
4434 7 3/4 **Bridge Valley**[98] 6479 5-8-7 48 .... KieranSchofield(7) 8 35
(Jason Ward) *dwlt: a in rr* 33/1
2541 8 hd **Dazzlin Bluebell (IRE)**[53] 7611 3-9-0 55 .... (b) DuranFentiman 6 34
(Tim Easterby) *t.k.h: chsd ldrs: rdn along over 2f out: sn wknd* 7/1[3]

1m 14.31s (-0.69) **Going Correction** -0.125s/f (Stan) **8** Ran SP% **113.3**
Speed ratings (Par 101): **99,98,95,95,93 88,87,86**
toteswingers: 1&2 £1.30, 1&3 £5.90, 2&3 £7.70 CSF £5.95 TOTE £2.60: £1.10, £1.90, £2.70; EX 9.80 Trifecta £56.80 Pool: £729.52 - 9.63 winning tickets..
Owner Colm White **Bred** John Donegan **Trained** Newmarket, Suffolk

FOCUS
This was a low-grade race lacking prolific winners, but the winner has the scope to improve a little.

8288 CONNOLLY'S REDMILLS PURE NUTRITION (S) H'CAP 1m 1f 103y(P)
3:40 (3:40) (Class 6) (0-60,58) 3-Y-0+ **£2,181** (£644; £322) **Stalls** Low

Form RPR
6515 1 **Safwaan**[25] 7982 5-9-0 51 .... StevieDonohoe 7 61
(Willie Musson) *hld up in rr: hdwy on outer wl over 2f out: str run on wd outside fr over 1f out: led last 75yds* 5/1[2]
0551 2 1/2 **Royal Sea (IRE)**[3] 8241 3-9-5 58 6ex .... GeorgeBaker 8 67
(David O'Meara) *trckd ldrs: pushed along over 3f out: rdn to chse ldr over 1f out: hung lft ins fnl f: drvn and kpt on wl towards fin* 5/6[1]
0005 3 shd **Arabian Flight**[8] 8213 3-9-3 56 .... AndrewMullen 5 65
(Michael Appleby) *trckd ldng pair: hdwy to chse ldr 4f out: led 2f out and sn rdn clr: drvn ins fnl f: hdd and no ex last 75yds* 8/1[3]
0363 4 5 **Anychanceofabirdie (USA)**[10] 8173 3-9-5 58 .... AdamKirby 2 57
(David Simcock) *trckd ldrs: hdwy 3f out: rdn wl over 1f out: drvn and one pce fnl f* 12/1
3402 5 3/4 **Guava**[3] 8241 3-8-1 45 .... ShirleyTeasdale(5) 1 42
(Shaun Harris) *trckd ldrs on inner: hdwy 3f out: rdn to chse ldrs wl over 1f out: drvn and no imp ent fnl f* 12/1
060- 6 3/4 **Indian Emperor (IRE)**[293] 7859 4-9-0 51 .... TomEaves 3 46
(Peter Niven) *nvr bttr than midfield* 25/1
6545 7 1 **Lytham (IRE)**[114] 5974 11-8-11 48 .... FergusSweeney 10 41
(Tony Carroll) *a towards rr* 33/1
4056 8 hd **The Which Doctor**[194] 3236 7-9-2 53 .... (b) WilliamCarson 4 46
(Violet M Jordan) *hld up: a towards rr* 16/1
0400 9 1 1/4 **Nolecce**[59] 7496 5-8-12 54 .... (p) JasonHart(5) 9 44
(Richard Guest) *chsd ldr: pushed along 4f out: rdn over 2f out: wknd wl over 1f out* 16/1
0355 10 2 **Meydan Style (USA)**[21] 8038 6-8-3 45 .... RachealKneller(5) 6 31
(Richard Ford) *hld up: a towards rr* 50/1
4300 11 4 1/2 **Georgebernardshaw (IRE)**[10] 8167 7-9-7 58 ....(p) RobbieFitzpatrick 12 35
(Richard Guest) *led: rdn along 3f out: hdd 2f out and sn wknd* 33/1

1m 59.75s (-1.95) **Going Correction** -0.125s/f (Stan)
WFA 3 from 4yo+ 2lb **11** Ran SP% **121.2**
Speed ratings (Par 101): **103,102,102,98,97 96,95,95,94,92 88**
toteswingers: 1&2 £1.10, 1&3 £10.50, 2&3 £8.00 CSF £9.50 CT £35.20 TOTE £6.50: £1.80, £1.10, £3.00; EX 13.10 Trifecta £118.20 Pool: £701.89 - 4.45 winning tickets..There was no bid for the winner. Anychanceofabirdie was bought by A Weaver for £5,000. Royal Sea was bought by M Mullineaux for £5000.
Owner W J Musson **Bred** Shadwell Estate Company Limited **Trained** Newmarket, Suffolk

FOCUS
A moderate seller run at just a medium pace, but the tempo was good enough for the hold-up tactics employed on the winner.

8289 £32 BONUS AT 32RED.COM NURSERY 1m 141y(P)
4:10 (4:10) (Class 6) (0-65,65) 2-Y-O **£2,181** (£644; £322) **Stalls** Low

Form RPR
6051 1 **Pairumani Prince (IRE)**[16] 8094 2-9-5 63 .... GeorgeBaker 9 71+
(Ed Dunlop) *trckd ldrs: hdwy 3f out: rdn to chse clr ldr over 1f out: styd on strly fnl f to ld nr fin* 4/1[1]
6003 2 nk **Misleading Promise (IRE)**[16] 8094 2-9-0 58 ow1 .... AdamKirby 10 65+
(John Butler) *trckd ldr: led wl over 2f out: rdn clr over 1f out: edgd lft ins fnl f: hdd and no ex nr fin* 5/1[3]

5015 **3** 3 ¾ **Crystal Peaks**15 8112 2-9-2 60 DaleSwift 6 59
(James Given) *hld up in tch: pushed along on inner 3f out: effrt and n.m.r 2f out: sn rdn and kpt on fnl f* **9/2**2

6066 **4** 1 ½ **She's Some Girl (IRE)**16 8094 2-7-12 45 NeilFarley(3) 8 41
(Richard Fahey) *hld up in tch: hdwy on outer 1/2-way: rdn to chse ldr wl over 1f out: one pce ent fnl f* **20/1**

4222 **5** 2 ¼ **Rakticate (IRE)**14 8140 2-9-3 61 FergusSweeney 1 53
(J S Moore) *chsd ldrs on inner: rdn along over 2f out: sn no imp* **8/1**

0053 **6** 2 ¼ **Flywheel (IRE)**31 7919 2-8-8 52 LukeMorris 7 39
(Peter Chapple-Hyam) *chsd ldrs: rdn along 4f out: sn wknd* **9/2**2

000 **7** 1 ½ **Last Chance Ranch**84 6889 2-8-6 50 MartinDwyer 2 34
(Derek Shaw) *a towards rr* **50/1**

3051 **8** 1 **Woza Moya (USA)**14 8140 2-9-5 63 (b) DavidProbert 3 45
(Gay Kelleway) *hld up: a towards rr* **5/1**3

6106 **9** 1 ¾ **Precision Strike**14 8132 2-8-8 52 RobbieFitzpatrick 4 30
(Richard Guest) *hld up: a in rr* **25/1**

6040 **10** 7 **Reveille**26 7965 2-9-7 65 RobertHavlin 5 28
(Hughie Morrison) *led: rdn along 3f out: sn hdd & wknd* **25/1**

3600 **11** 2 ½ **Sylvia's Diamond**81 6953 2-8-1 45 AndrewMullen 11
(Richard Guest) *a in rr* **66/1**

1m 49.74s (-0.76) **Going Correction** -0.125s/f (Stan) **11** Ran SP% **116.7**
Speed ratings (Par 94): **98,97,94,93,91 89,87,86,85,79 76**
toteswingers: 1&2 £5.50, 1&3 £5.50, 2&3 £7.20 CSF £22.47 CT £93.75 TOTE £5.30: £2.00, £2.10, £1.40; EX 30.00 Trifecta £139.20 Pool: £2,505.44 - 13.49 winning tickets..
Owner Anamoine Ltd **Bred** Windflower Overseas **Trained** Newmarket, Suffolk

FOCUS
The first two home are improving with experience, but the others look modest.

NOTEBOOK
Pairumani Prince(IRE) stays this trip really well now he is maturing, and he should get at least 1m2f next year. However, he was slightly fortunate here, as it looked more a case of the runner-up losing the race than him winning it. (tchd 9-2)
Misleading Promise(IRE) ◆ showed last time that he had arrived in handicaps on a sporting mark and for most of the last 3f he looked set for victory despite carrying a pound overweight. Unbalanced in front, and with his rider presumably therefore not being as hard on him as he might have been, he was caught near the finish. He would be hard to beat with a small change in tactics if able to race again before being re-handicapped. (op 7-2 tchd 6-1)
Crystal Peaks hasn't been up to defying a 4lb higher mark since winning here two outings earlier, so that performance may have flattered her. (op 5-1)
She's Some Girl(IRE) is still falling short but without being disgraced, so she may find a little race eventually given a bit more time. (tchd 16-1)
Rakticate(IRE) is consistent enough in moderate company, but the first two home are more progressive. (op 9-1)
Flywheel(IRE), who has changed stables, didn't build on her previous outing. (tchd 4-1)

8290 32RED.COM H'CAP 2m 119y(P)
4:40 (4:40) (Class 5) (0-75,75) 3-Y-O+ £2,911 (£866; £432; £216) Stalls Low

Form RPR

0151 **1** **Six Of Clubs**21 8035 6-9-7 68 (b) SebSanders 7 75
(Bill Turner) *dwlt and hld up in rr: hdwy on outer over 5f out: led wl over 2f out: rdn clr wl over 1f out: drvn ins fnl f: jst hld on* **3/1**1

5-02 **2** shd **Vimiero (USA)**29 7933 5-10-0 75 GeorgeBaker 1 82
(Jonjo O'Neill) *trckd ldng pair: effrt whn n.m.r over 2f out: rdn to chse wnr appr fnl f: sn drvn and kpt on: jst hld* **3/1**1

0050 **3** 2 ¼ **Call It On (IRE)**51 7098 6-10-0 75 AdamKirby 4 79
(Philip Kirby) *trckd ldr: cl up 3f out: rdn wl over 1f out: sn drvn and kpt on same pce fnl f* **4/1**3

1004 **4** nse **The Absent Mare**10 8170 4-9-5 66 (p) LukeMorris 6 70
(Robin Dickin) *hld up in rr: hdwy over 4f out: rdn to chse ldr 3f out: drvn and one pce fr over 1f out* **7/2**2

2540 **5** 7 **Rosewood Lad**253 1496 5-9-9 70 FergusSweeney 3 66
(J S Moore) *set stdy pce: pushed along 4f out: hdd wl over 2f out: sn wknd* **13/2**

0400 **6** ½ **Golden Future**50 6706 9-9-0 61 TomEaves 5 56
(Peter Niven) *chsd ldrs: rdn along 4f out: sn outpcd* **20/1**

3m 42.89s (1.09) **Going Correction** -0.125s/f (Stan) **6** Ran SP% **110.3**
Speed ratings (Par 103): **92,91,90,90,87 87**
toteswingers 1&2 £1.20, 1&3 £2.80, 2&3 £2.60 CSF £11.78 TOTE £3.60: £1.60, £1.50; EX 7.50 Trifecta £33.00 Pool: £3,086.55 - 70.01 winning tickets..
Owner Gongolfin **Bred** R V Young **Trained** Sigwells, Somerset

FOCUS
This wasn't a bad staying race for the surface, but the pace was moderate until the winner made his move 5f out.

8291 32RED MAIDEN STKS 7f 32y(P)
5:10 (5:10) (Class 5) 3-Y-O+ £2,911 (£866; £432; £216) Stalls High

Form RPR

06 **1** **Ioannou**36 7838 3-9-3 0 StevieDonohoe 10 61+
(Noel Quinlan) *trckd ldrs: smooth hdwy 3f out: led wl over 1f out: rdn out* **1/1**1

4000 **2** 2 ½ **Coastal Passage**53 7611 4-9-3 46 AdamKirby 9 55
(Charles Smith) *led: rdn along over 2f out: hdd wl over 1f out: sn drvn and kpt on* **14/1**

6653 **3** 3 ¼ **Lieutenant Dan (IRE)**14 8141 5-9-3 55 AndrewMullen 4 46
(Michael Appleby) *cl up: rdn along over 2f out: drvn wl over 1f out: sn one pce* **2/1**2

5060 **4** nk **Crucis Abbey (IRE)**15 8111 4-9-3 46 (p) WilliamCarson 5 45
(Mark Brisbourne) *towards rr: hdwy over 2f out: rdn wl over 1f out: styd on fnl f: nrst fin* **12/1**

04 **5** ¾ **Rosa Lockwood**17 8069 3-8-12 0 DavidProbert 1 38
(Tony Carroll) *hld up: hdwy 4f out: rdn to chse ldrs 2f out: sn drvn and no impression fnl f* **20/1**

0 **6** 1 ¼ **Bestfootforward**9 8187 3-8-12 0 ChrisCatlin 2 35
(Olivia Maylam) *chsd ldrs on inner: rdn along over 2f out: sn no imp* **10/1**3

65-5 **7** ½ **Our Princess Ellie (USA)**358 66 4-8-12 43 MartinDwyer 6 33
(Derek Shaw) *hld up: a towards rr* **33/1**

05 **8** 1 ¼ **Acton Jenson**25 7978 3-9-3 0 J-PGuillambert 3 35
(Brian Baugh) *dwlt and in rr: sme hdwy fnl 2f: nvr a factor* **33/1**

0-00 **9** 4 **Prana (USA)**196 3137 4-8-12 36 FergusSweeney 8 19
(Jeremy Gask) *dwlt: a in rr* **100/1**

0200 **10** 17 **Morna's Glory**61 7446 3-8-12 59 TonyHamilton 11
(Jason Ward) *chsd ldrs: rdn along over 3f out: sn wknd and bhd* **10/1**3

1m 28.89s (-0.71) **Going Correction** -0.125s/f (Stan) **10** Ran SP% **127.5**
Speed ratings (Par 103): **99,96,92,92,91 89,89,87,83,63**
toteswingers 1&2 £5.20, 1&3 £1.90, 2&3 £8.40 CSF £19.99 TOTE £2.30: £1.10, £2.60, £1.70; EX 32.60 Trifecta £155.80 Pool: £2,974.15 - 14.31 winning tickets..
Owner A & P Skips Limited **Bred** Biddestone Stud **Trained** Newmarket, Suffolk

FOCUS
Many of these were well-exposed, and the winner hadn't been placed in two previous attempts, so this was a poor maiden. The pace was medium.
T/Plt: £21.90 to a £1 stake. Pool of £65,866.41 - 2,192.71 winning units. T/Qpdt: £3.60 to a £1 stake. Pool of £7,005 - 1,423.50 winning units. JR

8261 LINGFIELD (L-H)
Sunday, December 30

OFFICIAL GOING: Standard
Wind: fresh, half behind Weather: dry, breezy

8292 AT THE RACES ON FACEBOOK CLAIMING STKS 1m 2f (P)
12:00 (12:00) (Class 6) 3-4-Y-O £2,181 (£644; £322) Stalls Low

Form RPR

1402 **1** **Bert The Alert**11 8173 4-8-12 68 FergusSweeney 1 74
(Gary Moore) *trckd rivals: rdn and effrt over 1f out: led ins fnl f: styd on wl* **2/1**2

0514 **2** 1 **Honey Of A Kitten (USA)**16 8114 4-8-12 68 (v) WilliamCarson 2 72
(David Evans) *trckd ldr: qcknd to ld and drvn wl over 1f out: edgd lft and hdd ins fnl f: no ex towards fin* **7/2**3

5321 **3** 1 ¼ **Arley Hall**22 7602 3-8-7 72 LukeMorris 4 68
(Brian Ellison) *led and set stdy gallop: hdd and drvn wl over 1f out: edgd rt and one pce ins fnl f* **4/5**1

2m 11.21s (4.61) **Going Correction** 0.0s/f (Stan)
WFA 3 from 4yo 3lb **3** Ran SP% **111.1**
Speed ratings (Par 101): **81,80,79**
CSF £7.70 TOTE £2.50; EX 6.10 Trifecta £5.40 Pool: £325.96 - 44.77 winning tickets..Arley Hall was claimed by Mr Noel P. Quinlan for £13,000.
Owner Herbert Curwen Hinds & Waddingham **Bred** Pleasure Palace Racing **Trained** Lower Beeding, W Sussex

FOCUS
A Class 6 claimer run at a very steady pace until the final half-mile. Three almost in a line a furlong out.

8293 32RED.COM NURSERY 6f (P)
12:30 (12:31) (Class 4) (0-85,79) 2-Y-O £4,398 (£1,309; £654; £327) Stalls Low

Form RPR

1 **1** **Foxtrot Jubilee (IRE)**59 7497 2-9-7 79 JimCrowley 4 86+
(Ralph Beckett) *hld up trcking ldrs: effrt and rdn to chal 1f out: r.o wl under hands and heels fnl 100yds to ld cl home* **4/9**1

0412 **2** hd **Fortinbrass (IRE)**198 3097 2-9-6 78 SebSanders 6 84
(Ralph Beckett) *chsd ldrs: wnt 2nd jst over 2f out: drvn to ld 1f out: sustained duel w wnr ins fnl f: r.o wl tl hdd and no ex cl home* **6/1**2

1111 **3** 3 ½ **Sofi's Spirit (IRE)**8 8224 2-8-6 64 LukeMorris 3 60
(J S Moore) *w ldr tl led over 2f out: edgd lft bnd 2f out: drvn and hdd 1f out: wknd ins fnl f* **8/1**3

1602 **4** shd **Harrogate Fair**17 8096 2-8-5 63 JimmyQuinn 5 58
(Michael Squance) *s.i.s: in tch in rr: rdn 3f out: outpcd u.p wl over 1f out: edgd lft and rallied ins fnl f: styd on but no threat to ldng pair* **20/1**

01 **5** 2 ¼ **Bobby Two Shoes**18 8068 2-9-5 77 EddieAhern 2 65
(Brett Johnson) *t.k.h: led tl hdd and rdn over 2f out: sn hmpd and lost pl: wknd over 1f out* **12/1**

2234 **6** shd **Divine Angel (IRE)**11 8164 2-8-0 57 ow1 NickyMackay 1 46
(Phil McEntee) *chsd ldrs: rdn and outpcd wl over 1f out: wknd over 1f out* **25/1**

1m 11.77s (-0.13) **Going Correction** 0.0s/f (Stan) **6** Ran SP% **110.9**
Speed ratings (Par 98): **100,99,95,94,91 91**
toteswingers 1&2 £1.60, 1&3 £1.10, 2&3 £1.80 CSF £3.49 TOTE £1.40: £1.10, £2.80; EX 4.20 Trifecta £13.40 Pool: £1,429.44 - 79.61 winning tickets..
Owner Foxtrot Racing Partnership IV **Bred** Patrick Roche **Trained** Kimpton, Hants

FOCUS
The two at the head of the weights fought out the finish of this nursery, the pair clear.

NOTEBOOK
Foxtrot Jubilee(IRE) ◆, who made all from the plum draw on his debut at Kempton in November, made it 2-2 from an official mark of 79. Happy to accept a lead and switched inside once in line for home he showed his inexperience drifting right inside the final furlong. His rider was not hard on him and scored in slightly cosy fashion in the end. He should be able to be competitive from his revised mark in the mid-80s. (op 4-7)
Fortinbrass(IRE) had been absent since chasing home Birdman in a conditions event at Chepstow in June. That winner is now rated 105 so he looked potentially well treated off just 78. Racing wide he took it up once in line for home and battled all the way to the line. He should soon go one better. (op 9-2)
Sofi's Spirit(IRE), who came into this on the back of four wins in claiming and selling company this month, made her nursery debut from a mark of 64 and in the end found the first two much too good. (op 6-1)
Harrogate Fair, whose two wins were over 5f, was surprisingly the first of the runners to come under serious pressure. (op 16-1)
Bobby Two Shoes, 33-1 winner of a maiden at Kempton two weeks earlier on his second start, found a mark of 77 too stiff. (tchd 14-1)

8294 32REDBET.COM (S) STKS 6f (P)
1:00 (1:00) (Class 6) 3-Y-O+ £2,181 (£644; £322) Stalls Low

Form RPR

1036 **1** **Dark Lane**20 8058 6-9-6 66 AdamKirby 3 73
(David Evans) *hld up in tch in rr: hdwy over 2f out: rdn to chal ent fnl f: led ins fnl f: r.o wl: rdn out* **11/4**3

1024 **2** hd **Beat The Bell**22 8036 7-9-6 73 (p) MartinDwyer 2 72
(Jamie Osborne) *trckd ldrs: gap opened and rdn to chal over 1f out: ev ch and wnt clr w wnr ins fnl f: r.o wl but a jst hld* **5/4**1

0653 **3** 4 **Amenable (IRE)**3 8246 5-9-6 74 (e) WilliamCarson 4 60
(Violet M Jordan) *taken down early and led to post: sn led: rdn 2f out: hdd ins fnl f: wknd fnl 100yds* **9/4**2

6100 **4** ¾ **Ishiamiracle**24 8005 3-8-10 63 (p) LeonnaMayor(5) 1 52
(Phil McEntee) *chsd ldr tl over 4f out: lost pl and dropped to rr over 2f out: tried to rally on inner over 1f out: wknd ins fnl f* **20/1**

5000 **5** nk **Le King Beau (USA)**18 8074 3-9-0 57 (v) KieranO'Neill 5 50
(John Bridger) *chsd ldrs: wnt 2nd over 4f out tl over 1f out: wknd ins fnl f* **33/1**

1m 11.56s (-0.34) **Going Correction** 0.0s/f (Stan) **5** Ran SP% **109.6**
Speed ratings (Par 101): **102,101,96,95,95**
CSF £6.56 TOTE £3.30: £1.10, £1.60; EX 7.60 Trifecta £10.20 Pool: £1,091.91 - 80.08 winning tickets..There was no bid for the winner.
Owner Jason Tucker **Bred** David Jamison Bloodstock **Trained** Pandy, Monmouths

FOCUS
A fair contest of its type judged on the ratings.

8295 £32 BONUS AT 32RED.COM MAIDEN STKS 1m 2f (P)
1:35 (1:36) (Class 5) 3-Y-0 **£3,067** (£905; £453) **Stalls** Low

Form RPR
0340 **1** **Guarda Pampa**[21] 8048 3-8-12 60.........................(b[1]) AdamBeschizza 10 64
(William Haggas) *racd freely: mde all and sn clr: 8 l clr and rdn 2f out: kpt on: unchal* **7/1**[3]

05 **2** *4* **Sugar Lips**[18] 8080 3-8-12 0.. SebSanders 2 56
(Simon Dow) *prom in main gp: rdn and effrt in 4th over 2f out: styd on to chse wnr ins fnl f: no imp* **50/1**

5 **3** *1 ½* **Notabadgirl**[39] 7010 3-9-12 0.. NickyMackay 9 53
(Simon Dow) *led main gp: chsd clr wnr over 3f out tl over 2f out: kpt on steadily and chsd wnr again 1f out: no imp and lost 2nd ins fnl f* **66/1**

6 **4** *nk* **Morinda**[52] 7647 3-8-12 0.. LukeMorris 5 52
(Ed Walker) *prom in main gp: effrt to chse clr wnr over 2f out: plugged on u.p: lost 2nd and no ex fnl f* **10/1**

5 *5* **Golden Share (USA)** 3-9-3 0... AdamKirby 6 47
(Marco Botti) *s.i.s: racd wl off the pce in midfield: effrt and rdn over 2f out: no imp: 5th and wl hld fnl 2f* **5/4**[1]

0-4 **6** *3 ¼* **Dusty Red**[206] 2849 3-8-12 0... JimCrowley 8 36
(William Knight) *stdd s: hld up wl off the in last trio: rdn over 2f out: no imp: n.d* **9/4**[2]

7 *6* **Lenny The Great** 3-8-12 0.. HarryPoulton[(5)] 4 29
(Terry Clement) *racd wl off the pce in last quartet: rdn and no prog over 2f out: n.d* **100/1**

8 *5* **Rahy's Promise (USA)** 3-9-3 0.................................... DavidProbert 3 19
(Andrew Balding) *s.i.s: sn rdn along and rn green in rr: nvr on terms* **10/1**

6000 **9** *hd* **Kiss My Heart**[67] 7326 3-8-5 24...................................... JoeyHaynes[(7)] 7 14
(Eric Wheeler) *chsd clr wnr and clr of field tl rdn and lost pl over 3f out: bhd fnl f* **200/1**

10 *39* **Bryant Park (USA)** 3-9-3 0... GeorgeBaker 1
(Michael Wigham) *s.i.s: a in rr and nvr on terms: t.o fnl 2f: eased ins fnl f* **20/1**

2m 6.19s (-0.41) **Going Correction** 0.0s/f (Stan) **10** Ran SP% **115.6**
Speed ratings (Par 102): **101,97,96,96,92 89,84,80,80,49**
toteswingers 1&2 £15.70, 1&3 £36.40, 2&3 £35.70 CSF £291.97 TOTE £5.50: £1.80, £6.30, £12.90; EX 204.60 Trifecta £1429.40 Part won. Pool: £1,905.96 - 0.82 winning tickets..
Owner Mrs Melba Bryce **Bred** London Thoroughbred Services Ltd **Trained** Newmarket, Suffolk

FOCUS
The winner went off very strong and soon had the field strung out.
Dusty Red Official explanation: jockey said filly never travelled

8296 32RED H'CAP 1m (P)
2:10 (2:11) (Class 3) (0-95,95) 3-Y-0+ **£8,409** (£2,502; £1,250; £625) **Stalls** High

Form RPR
0536 **1** **Grey Mirage**[17] 8095 3-8-9 84...(p) JimmyQuinn 4 91
(Marco Botti) *sn led and mde rest: rdn 2f out: hrd pressed and drvn 1f out: kpt on gamely: drvn out* **11/4**[1]

5522 **2** *½* **Webbow (IRE)**[17] 8098 10-9-7 95..................................... GeorgeBaker 3 101
(Julie Camacho) *led briefly: chsd wnr after: rdn and pressed wnr over 1f out: styd on same pce and hld fnl 100yds* **9/2**

3521 **3** *½* **Lockantanks**[8] 8226 5-9-5 93... LukeMorris 1 98
(Michael Appleby) *chsd ldng pair: rdn 2f out: styd on same pce u.p fnl f* **8/1**

3021 **4** *½* **Hometown Glory**[25] 7997 3-8-7 82...............................(t) JamieMackay 6 86
(Brian Meehan) *t.k.h: chsd ldrs: hdwy to press ldrs whn hung rt bnd 2f out: kpt on same pce u.p fnl f* **7/2**[3]

4641 **5** *1 ¼* **George Guru**[17] 8095 5-9-3 94.................................... MarkCoumbe[(3)] 2 95
(Michael Attwater) *stdd s: hld up in tch in last pair: swtchd rt over 2f out: rdn wl over 1f out: nt clr run 1f out: styd on same pce ins fnl f* **3/1**[2]

0110 **6** *4* **Embankment**[17] 8095 3-8-10 85.. SebSanders 5 77
(William Jarvis) *stdd s: hld up in tch in last pair: hdwy to chse ldrs whn pushed rt and lost pl bnd 2f out: no imp over 1f out: wknd ins fnl f* **8/1**

1m 36.37s (-1.83) **Going Correction** 0.0s/f (Stan)
WFA 3 from 5yo+ 1lb **6** Ran SP% **114.3**
Speed ratings (Par 107): **109,108,108,107,106 102**
toteswingers 1&2 £2.80, 1&3 £3.60, 2&3 £3.50 CSF £15.79 TOTE £3.10: £1.80, £2.60; EX 18.30 Trifecta £98.60 Pool: £1,775.03 - 13.49 winning tickets..
Owner Scuderia Vittadini SRL 1 **Bred** Grundy Bloodstock Srl **Trained** Newmarket, Suffolk

FOCUS
An open look to this 82-95 handicap beforehand but the market support for the winner was justified.

NOTEBOOK
Grey Mirage, 5lb better off with George Guru after finishing about 2l behind him at Kempton two weeks earlier, again made the running. Sporting cheekpieces for the first time, Jimmy Quinn had the fractions worked out to a tee and they always looked like holding on. (op 5-1 tchd 5-2)
Webbow(IRE), who enters his 12th year on January 1, continues in fine form, but that seventh career success is proving elusive. (op 4-1)
Lockantanks, winner of a conditions event at Lingfield, returned to handicap company from a 4lb higher mark and was 4lb higher than when taking this a year ago. (op 7-1)
Hometown Glory, 7lb higher than for his win here, took a keen hold and had to make his effort wide. (tchd 4-1)
George Guru, who recorded a career-best effort when scoring at Kempton, had a 3lb higher mark to overcome. He was another to race with the choke out. (tchd 7-2)
Embankment, the least experienced in the line-up, had finished well beaten after never travelling in the race George Guru and Grey Mirage tackled at Kempton. It was a similar story here. (op 5-1)

8297 32RED CASINO H'CAP 1m 4f (P)
2:45 (2:45) (Class 5) (0-70,70) 3-Y-0+ **£3,067** (£905; £453) **Stalls** Low

Form RPR
5221 **1** **Miss Blakeney**[17] 8097 3-9-5 70.....................................(v) GeorgeBaker 4 84+
(Marcus Tregoning) *trckd ldrs: swtchd rt and effrt wl over 1f out: rdn and qcknd to ld 1f out: sn in command: easily* **4/5**[1]

2421 **2** *4 ½* **Resplendent Alpha**[11] 8173 8-8-12 63......................... LeonnaMayor[(5)] 8 67
(Jamie Osborne) *hld up in tch in last pair: rdn and effrt 2f out: chsd clr wnr ins fnl f: kpt on but no imp* **7/1**[3]

1242 **3** *hd* **Strike Force**[8] 8234 8-9-2 69.................................(t) RobertTart[(7)] 3 73
(Alison Hutchinson) *hld up wl in tch: rdn and effrt over 1f out: styd on and pressing for 2nd ins fnl f: kpt on but no ch w wnr* **9/2**[2]

0004 **4** *2* **Let's Confer**[22] 8037 3-8-9 60..(p) JimmyQuinn 7 60
(Michael Attwater) *chsd ldrs: hdwy to press ldr 3f out: rdn to ld 2f out: hdd and no ex 1f out: wknd ins fnl f* **33/1**

0-00 **5** *3 ¼* **Strewth (IRE)**[23] 8023 4-9-2 62.. JimCrowley 9 57
(John Best) *chsd ldr tl led 3f out: rdn and hdd 2f out: btn 1f out: fdd ins fnl f* **9/2**[2]

5005 **6** *1 ½* **Cape Safari (IRE)**[13] 8149 3-9-0 70............................. HarryPoulton[(5)] 2 63
(Tim Vaughan) *hld up in tch in last pair: outpcd over 2f out: bhd and rdn 2f out: no imp* **20/1**

3450 **7** *3 ¼* **Za'Lan (USA)**[11] 8170 3-8-9 60.................................(v[1]) FergusSweeney 6 48
(Chris Gordon) *led tl hdd and rdn 3f out: wknd 2f out: bhd fnl f* **25/1**

2m 34.29s (1.29) **Going Correction** 0.0s/f (Stan)
WFA 3 from 4yo+ 5lb **7** Ran SP% **116.0**
Speed ratings (Par 103): **95,92,91,90,88 87,85**
toteswingers 1&2 £1.60, 1&3 £1.40, 2&3 £2.20 CSF £7.26 CT £17.05 TOTE £1.90: £1.10, £2.40; EX 7.30 Trifecta £11.30 Pool: £2,290.57 - 150.70 winning tickets..
Owner Mr And Mrs A E Pakenham **Bred** Mr & Mrs A E Pakenham **Trained** Lambourn, Berks

Strewth(IRE) Official explanation: jockey said gelding pulled up lame

8298 32RED SUPPORTING BRITISH RACING H'CAP (DIV I) 7f (P)
3:20 (3:20) (Class 6) (0-55,55) 3-Y-0+ **£2,181** (£644; £322) **Stalls** Low

Form RPR
0341 **1** **Bussa**[17] 8099 4-9-5 53...(t) AdamKirby 6 67
(David Evans) *led: sn hdd and trckd ldrs: effrt to chal 2f out: led over 1f out: r.o strly and clr ins fnl f: readily* **6/4**[1]

402 **2** *4* **My Scat Daddy (USA)**[9] 8205 3-9-2 50............................. EddieAhern 2 53
(Brett Johnson) *chsd ldrs: rdn and effrt wl over 1f out: no threat to wnr but kpt on u.p ins fnl f: wnt 2nd last stride* **11/4**[2]

645 **3** *shd* **Jonnie Skull (IRE)**[11] 8168 6-8-10 51..............................(vt) RyanTate[(7)] 7 54
(Phil McEntee) *sn led: rdn and hdd over 1f out: outpcd and no threat to wnr ins fnl f: kpt on but lost 2nd last stride* **14/1**

0035 **4** *hd* **Fairy Mist (IRE)**[9] 8205 5-8-12 46 oh1.......................... KieranO'Neill 12 48
(John Bridger) *stdd s: bhd: rdn and hdwy on inner jst over 1f out: styd on wl ins fnl f: no threat to wnr* **25/1**

0003 **5** *1 ¼* **Vale Of Lingfield (IRE)**[17] 8099 3-8-13 47............... FergusSweeney 11 46
(John Best) *in tch in midfield: rdn and unable qck 2f out: styd on same pce u.p fr over 1f out* **6/1**[3]

0036 **6** *nse* **Querido (GER)**[10] 8179 8-8-12 51............(tp) WilliamTwiston-Davies[(5)] 9 50
(Paddy Butler) *hld up in last pair: rdn and hdwy over 1f out: swtchd rt and styd on ins fnl f: no threat to wnr* **16/1**

0050 **7** *hd* **Great Charm (IRE)**[10] 8180 7-9-2 55........................... HarryPoulton[(5)] 4 53
(Sheena West) *short of room sn after s: in tch in midfield: rdn and unable qck over 1f out: drvn and styd on same pce fnl f* **33/1**

0000 **8** *½* **Not My Choice (IRE)**[10] 8179 7-8-12 46....................(t) J-PGuillambert 5 43
(Paul Howling) *hld up in tch towards rr: swtchd lft and effrt over 1f out: styd on same pce ins fnl f* **20/1**

4202 **9** *1 ½* **Kaylee**[21] 8046 3-8-9 50.. NedCurtis[(7)] 10 43
(Gary Moore) *taken down early: restless in stalls: hld up in tch towards rr: swtchd rt and hdwy jst over 2f out: edgd lft and no imp over 1f out* **10/1**

2545 **10** *4 ½* **Steel City Boy (IRE)**[32] 7914 9-9-2 55............................ AnnStokell[(5)] 13 36
(Ann Stokell) *taken down early: in tch in midfield on outer: lost pl and bhd 2f out: n.d but kpt on again ins fnl f* **33/1**

0006 **11** *½* **Cuthbert (IRE)**[22] 8039 5-8-12 46 oh1............................(b) JimmyQuinn 1 25
(Michael Attwater) *pressed ldr: rdn and ev ch ent fnl 2f: no ex and btn jst over 1f out: wknd ins fnl f* **25/1**

1m 23.86s (-0.94) **Going Correction** 0.0s/f (Stan) **11** Ran SP% **120.9**
Speed ratings (Par 101): **105,100,100,100,98 98,98,97,96,90 90**
toteswingers 1&2 £2.30, 1&3 £6.80, 2&3 £6.30 CSF £5.20 CT £40.43 TOTE £2.70: £1.20, £1.50, £3.20; EX 7.30 Trifecta £36.50 Pool: £1,786.19 - 36.70 winning tickets..
Owner Nick Shutts **Bred** Natton House Thoroughbreds & Mark Woodall **Trained** Pandy, Monmouths

FOCUS
Division 1 of a low-grade 7f handicap.

8299 32RED SUPPORTING BRITISH RACING H'CAP (DIV II) 7f (P)
3:50 (3:50) (Class 6) (0-55,55) 3-Y-0+ **£2,181** (£644; £322) **Stalls** Low

Form RPR
0002 **1** **Jackie Love (IRE)**[19] 8061 4-8-10 49........................(v) NathanAlison[(5)] 3 57
(Olivia Maylam) *hld up in tch in midfield: rdn and chsd clr ldng trio over 1f out: styd on strly ins fnl f to ld towards fin* **10/1**

3234 **2** *½* **Silly Billy (IRE)**[10] 8179 4-9-5 53......................................(v) IanMongan 13 60
(Pat Phelan) *chsd ldrs: rdn and ev ch 2f out: drvn to ld narrowly 1f out: kpt on tl hdd and no ex towards fin* **11/4**[1]

0222 **3** *nk* **Putin (IRE)**[3] 8248 4-8-9 48.............................(bt) LeonnaMayor[(5)] 11 54
(Phil McEntee) *chsd ldr tl led after 1f: rdn and hrd pressed 2f out: kpt on and ev ch after tl no ex cl home* **9/2**[3]

0013 **4** *1* **Renoir's Lady**[19] 8061 4-9-7 55.. JimCrowley 10 58+
(Simon Dow) *hld up in tch towards rr: rdn and effrt over 1f out: styd on ins fnl f: nt rch ldrs* **3/1**[2]

3600 **5** *½* **Play The Blues (IRE)**[10] 8180 5-8-9 50............................(t) NedCurtis[(7)] 12 52
(Roger Curtis) *chsd ldrs: effrt to join ldrs 2f out: rdn and nt qckn over 1f out: btn ins fnl f and one pce fnl 100yds* **25/1**

5000 **6** *1 ½* **Schoolboy Champ**[18] 8083 5-8-10 47 oh1 ow1.....(bt) MarkCoumbe[(3)] 6 45
(Lisa Williamson) *chsd ldrs: rdn and outpcd wl over 1f out: kpt on same pce u.p fnl f* **50/1**

0300 **7** *nk* **Bedibyes**[59] 7512 4-8-13 47.. LukeMorris 2 44
(Richard Mitchell) *in tch in midfield: rdn and unable qck 3f out: kpt on same pce fr over 1f out* **8/1**

0050 **8** *nk* **Hold The Star**[11] 8168 6-8-11 50..................................... AnnStokell[(5)] 4 46
(Ann Stokell) *led for 1f: chsd ldrs tl rdn and outpcd wl over 1f out: wknd ins fnl f* **33/1**

5000 **9** *3 ¼* **Flying Kitty**[11] 8169 3-8-12 46 oh1.......................................[1] KieranO'Neill 8 33
(John Bridger) *s.i.s: in tch in rr: effrt on inner 2f out: no prog over 1f out: wknd ins fnl f* **33/1**

3056 **10** *2 ¾* **Chandrayaan**[9] 8205 5-8-9 46......................................(v) SimonPearce[(3)] 5 26
(John E Long) *hld up in tch in rr: rdn and no hdwy over 1f out: wknd ins fnl f* **25/1**

0056 **11** *1 ¾* **Doctor Hilary**[11] 8168 10-9-3 51................................(v) FergusSweeney 9 26
(Mark Hoad) *hld up in tch in last trio: rdn and no hdwy over 2f out: wl hld over 1f out* **8/1**

3-00 **12** *11* **Onceaponatime (IRE)**[12] 8160 7-9-5 53..............................(b) JimmyQuinn 7
(Michael Squance) *t.k.h: hld up in midfield on outer: wknd 2f out: bhd and eased ins fnl f* **25/1**

1m 24.69s (-0.11) **Going Correction** 0.0s/f (Stan) **12** Ran SP% **120.5**
Speed ratings (Par 101): **100,99,99,97,97 95,95,94,91,88 86,73**
toteswingers 1&2 £6.40, 1&3 £5.20, 2&3 £3.20 CSF £35.80 CT £149.02 TOTE £10.20: £3.10, £1.60, £1.90; EX 49.70 Trifecta £109.20 Pool: £2,296.58 - 15.76 winning tickets..
Owner Miss Olivia Maylam **Bred** Bigwigs Bloodstock **Trained** Epsom, Surrey

FOCUS
Part two and more of the same. The pace was generous and the winner and fourth came from off the pace.
Onceaponatime(IRE) Official explanation: jockey said gelding hung right throughout
T/Plt: £235.40 to a £1 stake. Pool: £69,346.50 - 215.02 winning tickets T/Qpdt: £67.70 to a £1 stake. Pool: £7,068.36 - 77.20 winning tickets SP

8276 DEAUVILLE (R-H)
Sunday, December 30

OFFICIAL GOING: Fibresand: standard

8300a PRIX MISS SATAMIXA (LISTED RACE) (3YO+ FILLIES & MARES) (FIBRESAND) 7f 110y
1:50 (1:51) 3-Y-O+ **£21,666** (£8,666; £6,500; £4,333; £2,166)

RPR
1 **Rhenania (IRE)**[26] 7985 5-8-11 0 FlavienPrat 6 97
(M Nigge, France) **146/10**
2 snk **Elenya (IRE)**[55] 3-8-11 0 AnthonyCrastus 7 98
(M Cesandri, France) **23/1**
3 hd **Baheeja**[59] 7509 3-8-11 0 AndreaAtzeni 12 97
(Roger Varian) *racd in midfield: rdn bef st: picked up wl: mde gd prog ent fnl f: r.o wl fnl 100yds: jst missed 2nd* **10/1**
4 1 **Sargasses (FR)**[26] 7985 6-8-11 0 AlexisBadel 5 94
(Mlle V Dissaux, France) **18/1**
5 ¾ **Casa Ingrid (FR)**[69] 5-8-11 0 StephanePasquier 9 92
(Y De Nicolay, France) **17/2**[3]
6 ¾ **Zayade (FR)**[38] 7830 3-8-11 0 AdrienFouassier 13 91
(J Boisnard, France) **12/1**
7 1 ¼ **Influence (FR)**[25] 3-8-11 0 AntoineHamelin 16 88
(G Henrot, France) **17/1**
8 ¾ **Shana Doyenne (GER)**[56] 5-8-11 0 TheoBachelot 15 85
(W Mongil, Germany) **49/1**
9 hd **Corsage (USA)**[25] 8002 3-8-11 0 ThierryThulliez 11 85
(N Clement, France) **63/10**[2]
10 shd **Hail Holy Queen (IRE)**[11] 4-8-11 0 FabienLefebvre 8 84
(J E Hammond, France) **14/1**
0 **So Long Malpic (FR)**[16] 8130 5-8-11 0 MaximeGuyon 2
(T Lemer, France) **33/10**[1]
0 **Cerveza**[40] 4-8-11 0 LouisBeuzelin 4
(F Poulsen, France) **82/1**
0 **Flash Mash (USA)**[38] 7829 4-9-2 0 ThomasMessina 1
(X Nakkachdji, France) **11/1**
0 **Sunday Nectar (IRE)**[91] 6726 4-9-2 0 Roberto-CarlosMontenegro 3
(X Thomas-Demeaulte, France) **20/1**
0 **Cashmere Cat (IRE)**[38] 7830 3-8-11 0 RonanThomas 14
(T Lemer, France) **24/1**
0 **Dyctynna (FR)**[40] 3-8-11 0 FabriceVeron 10
(H-A Pantall, France) **26/1**

1m 31.7s (91.70) **16** Ran SP% **116.3**
WIN (incl. 1 euro stake): 15.60. PLACES: 4.70, 7.60, 3.60. DF: 118.20. SF: 312.50.
Owner Mme Christa Zass **Bred** E Nuzum **Trained** France

8292 LINGFIELD (L-H)
Monday, December 31

OFFICIAL GOING: Standard
Wind: strong, half behind Weather: light rain, windy

8301 TRACK YOUR HORSES AT ATTHERACES.COM (S) STKS 1m 4f (P)
12:00 (12:00) (Class 6) 3-Y-O+ **£1,704** (£503; £251) **Stalls** Low

Form RPR
6422 1 **Priestley's Reward (IRE)**[55] 7602 3-9-3 67 (p) LukeMorris 3 68
(Mrs K Burke) *racd lazily: chsd ldr and rdn along at times: rdn to ld 3f out: hrd pressed after but kpt finding ex: a doing enough fnl f: rdn out* **11/4**[3]
/200 2 nk **High 'n Dry (IRE)**[28] 7960 8-8-6 51 NedCurtis(7) 2 59
(Roger Curtis) *t.k.h: hld up in tch: effrt to join ldrs 3f out: ev ch after: styd on ins fnl f but a jst hld* **33/1**
0005 3 ¾ **Mount Abora (IRE)**[19] 8078 5-9-3 62 IanMongan 1 62
(Laura Mongan) *chsd ldrs: pressed ldrs 3f out: sltly outpcd and swtchd lft over 1f out: styd on same pce ins fnl f* **9/4**[2]
0044 4 5 **Eagle Nebula**[17] 8106 8-9-8 65 (p) AdamKirby 5 59
(Brett Johnson) *in tch in rr: nvr travelling wl and pushed along at times: rdn and no prog 3f out: one pce and wl hld after* **1/1**[1]
0-00 5 8 **Cossack Prince**[3] 8265 7-9-4 45 (p) AmirQuinn 4 42
(Laura Mongan) *led tl 3f out: sn dropped out: bhd over 1f out* **66/1**

2m 33.77s (0.77) **Going Correction** +0.025s/f (Slow)
WFA 3 from 5yo+ 5lb **5** Ran SP% **111.9**
Speed ratings (Par 101): **98,97,97,93,88**
CSF £54.36 TOTE £2.90: £1.60, £4.50; EX 28.90 Trifecta £76.40 Pool: £1,018.89 - 9.99 winning tickets..Priestley's Reward was bought in for £6,000.
Owner P Dean & Mrs E Burke **Bred** Michael Mullins **Trained** Middleham Moor, N Yorks

FOCUS
Weak form.
Eagle Nebula Official explanation: jockey said gelding was never travelling.
Cossack Prince Official explanation: jockey said gelding hung right.

8302 32RED CASINO NURSERY 7f (P)
12:30 (12:30) (Class 5) (0-75,74) 2-Y-O **£2,385** (£704; £352) **Stalls** Low

Form RPR
265 1 **Ashamaly**[28] 7962 2-9-2 69 AdamKirby 6 84+
(James Tate) *chsd ldr after 1f: rdn to ld ent fnl 2f and sn qcknd clr: r.o strly and in n.d after: readily* **4/1**[2]
0451 2 5 **Lucky Di**[12] 8171 2-9-7 74 JimCrowley 8 75
(Peter Hedger) *chsd ldrs: rdn and outpcd by wnr ent fnl 2f: kpt on u.p to go 2nd ins fnl f: no ch w wnr* **7/4**[1]
0544 3 nk **Lyric Ballad**[28] 7973 2-8-9 62 RobertWinston 5 62
(Hughie Morrison) *led for 1f: chsd ldrs after: swtchd rt and rdn 2f out: sn outpcd by wnr: wnt 2nd over 1f out: no imp and lost 2nd ins fnl f* **6/1**[3]
5401 4 1 **Club House (IRE)**[17] 8101 2-8-9 67 WilliamTwiston-Davies(5) 7 65
(Robert Mills) *hld up in rr: rdn and hdwy on outer over 1f out: styd on ins fnl f: no ch w wnr* **7/1**
4332 5 1 **Roman Order (IRE)**[17] 8103 2-9-4 71 MartinDwyer 1 66
(Brian Meehan) *hld up in last trio: sme hdwy u.p over 1f out: styd on same pce fnl f: no ch w wnr* **4/1**[2]
064 6 hd **Malaysian Boleh**[33] 7894 2-8-12 65 LukeMorris 2 60
(Simon Dow) *hld up towards rr: rdn and effrt 2f out: no ch w wnr and styd on same pce fr over 1f out* **10/1**
0054 7 ½ **Whitford (IRE)**[17] 8103 2-8-11 64 KirstyMilczarek 4 57
(Chris Dwyer) *in tch in midfield: rdn and outpcd over 2f out: plugged on same pce and n.d after* **16/1**
2346 8 8 **Divine Angel (IRE)**[1] 8293 2-8-4 57 NickyMackay 3 29
(Phil McEntee) *in tch in midfield: rdn and struggling over 2f out: wknd 2f out* **33/1**
310 9 4 **Firstkissoflove**[95] 6597 2-9-5 72 DavidProbert 9 34
(David C Griffiths) *rdn along leaving stalls: hdwy to ld after 1f: rdn and hdd ent fnl 2f: sn outpcd and btn: wknd over 1f out: bhd and eased ins fnl f* **25/1**

1m 25.16s (0.36) **Going Correction** +0.025s/f (Slow) **9** Ran SP% **124.9**
Speed ratings (Par 96): **98,92,91,90,89 89,88,79,75**
toteswingers: 1&2 £3.00, 1&3 £6.20, 2&3 £3.90 CSF £12.48 CT £44.36 TOTE £3.50: £1.70, £1.10, £2.40; EX 14.70 Trifecta £109.60 Pool: £1,451.31 - 9.93 winning tickets..
Owner Saif Ali **Bred** Hascombe And Valiant Studs **Trained** Newmarket, Suffolk

FOCUS
This looked quite competitive on paper, but the race was taken apart by the winner.

NOTEBOOK
Ashamaly was sent for home heading to the turn into the straight and, with a strong wind behind him, soon shot clear. He's going to take a hammering from the handicapper for this, so a quick reappearance under a penalty might be on the cards. (op 5-1 tchd 7-2)
Lucky Di, who took an ordinary maiden here last time, won the separate race for second. She's clearly on a competitive mark, and was simply unlucky to bump into a very well treated rival. (tchd 11-4)
Lyric Ballad wasn't necessarily helped by the drop back to 7f. (op 4-1)
Club House(IRE) ran a respectable race back in handicap company, but he too probably found the trip on the short side. (op 14-1)
Roman Order(IRE) was a little tight for room early in the straight and struggled to get involved from the back of the field. (op 9-2)
Firstkissoflove Official explanation: jockey said filly hung right.

8303 32RED SUPPORTING BRITISH RACING MEDIAN AUCTION MAIDEN STKS 7f (P)
1:00 (1:00) (Class 5) 2-Y-O **£2,385** (£704; £352) **Stalls** Low

Form RPR
202 1 **Sherinn**[10] 8208 2-8-12 74 JimCrowley 5 70
(Roger Varian) *t.k.h: chsd ldr tl led 2f out: rdn and clr over 1f out: styd on wl* **4/6**[1]
42 2 2 ¼ **Liliana (IRE)**[16] 8134 2-8-12 0 LukeMorris 1 64
(Peter Chapple-Hyam) *chsd ldng pair: chsd wnr wl over 1f out: no imp fnl f but kpt on for clr 2nd* **7/4**[2]
0 3 6 **Star Sequence (IRE)**[160] 4433 2-8-12 0 MartinDwyer 6 49
(Hugo Palmer) *chsd ldng trio: rdn over 3f out: outpcd and btn over 1f out: wl hld but battled on for 3rd fnl f* **16/1**[3]
4 shd **Roaring Rocks (FR)** 2-8-10 0 RyanTate(7) 4 53+
(Heather Main) *s.i.s: rn v green thrght: outpcd in last pair: hdwy over 2f out: outpcd and btn over 1f out: styd on same pce fnl f* **33/1**
5 2 **Hammer Shaft (IRE)** 2-9-3 0 GeorgeBaker 3 48
(Amy Weaver) *s.i.s: outpcd in rr: sme hdwy over 2f out: no hdwy over 1f out: wknd ins fnl f* **20/1**
0000 6 8 **I'Ve No Money (IRE)**[41] 7795 2-8-10 45 (bt[1]) EmilyMelbourn(7) 2 27
(David C Griffiths) *led tl 2f out: wknd over 1f out: fdd ins fnl f* **100/1**

1m 26.79s (1.99) **Going Correction** +0.025s/f (Slow) **6** Ran SP% **110.9**
Speed ratings (Par 96): **89,86,79,79,77 68**
toteswingers 1&2 £1.20, 1&3 £2.10, 2&3 £1.40 CSF £1.95 TOTE £2.30: £1.10, £1.20; EX 2.10 Trifecta £6.20 Pool: £1,550.73 - 185.05 winning tickets..
Owner Sheikh Ahmed Al Maktoum **Bred** Darley **Trained** Newmarket, Suffolk

FOCUS
There wasn't much pace on early here, and a few of them wouldn't settle.

NOTEBOOK
Sherinn was keen herself, but was well placed heading down the hill and got first run on the runner-up. She comfortably held off her only serious rival and hopefully she can now build on this.
Liliana(IRE) lost a couple of lengths to the winner when that one kicked off the turn, and she was unable to close that gap. She might still be able to find a weak AW maiden. (op 6-4)
Star Sequence(IRE) showed more than on her debut back in the summer, and the step up in trip was certainly in her favour. (op 20-1)
Roaring Rocks(FR), who has plenty of size about him, was very green early but showed ability.
Hammer Shaft(IRE), who was slowly away, is a half-brother to a 1m6f winner, so should come into his own over a good deal further in time. (tchd 16-1)

8304 £32 BONUS AT 32RED.COM H'CAP (DIV I) 6f (P)
1:30 (1:30) (Class 6) (0-65,65) 3-Y-O+ **£1,704** (£503; £251) **Stalls** Low

Form RPR
0001 1 **Commanche**[26] 7990 3-9-6 64 AdamKirby 3 71
(Patrick Chamings) *in tch in last trio: drvn over 1f out: hdwy and edgd rt 1f out: styd on strly fnl 100yds to ld last stride* **4/5**[1]
2363 2 shd **Catalinas Diamond (IRE)**[13] 8160 4-9-7 65 (t) SebSanders 4 72
(Pat Murphy) *hld up in tch: shkn up and hdwy to join ldrs 1f out: delayed effrt tl rdn to ld wl ins fnl f: hdd last stride* **8/1**[3]
2415 3 ½ **Bull Bay**[13] 8159 3-8-12 63 IanBurns(7) 10 68
(Jane Chapple-Hyam) *chsd ldrs: rdn to jst ins fnl f: hdd and no ex wl ins fnl f* **8/1**[3]
0015 4 ¾ **Blue Deer (IRE)**[13] 8156 4-9-4 62 (p) MickyFenton 2 65
(Lee Carter) *squeezed for room and dropped to rr sn after s: hdwy u.p and swtchd rt bnd 2f out: styd on wl u.p ins fnl f: nt rch ldrs* **8/1**[3]
2223 5 hd **Putin (IRE)**[1] 8299 4-8-7 51 oh3 (bt) DavidProbert 7 53
(Phil McEntee) *chsd ldr tl led 5f out tl 4f out: rdn over 2f out: styd on same pce ins fnl f* **10/1**
0453 6 1 **Foot Tapper**[38] 7838 3-9-4 62 GeorgeBaker 6 61
(Chris Wall) *led for 1f: chsd ldrs after: rdn and stl pressing ldrs over 1f out: wknd fnl 100yds* **6/1**[2]
6000 7 2 ½ **Sextons House (IRE)**[28] 7970 4-8-10 54 WilliamCarson 8 45
(Alan McCabe) *taken down early: dwlt: steadily rcvrd to ld 4f out: rdn over 1f out: hdd jst ins fnl f: wknd ins fnl f* **8/1**[3]
4016 8 3 ¾ **Yungaburra (IRE)**[62] 7465 8-8-7 51 (tp) LukeMorris 1 30
(David C Griffiths) *led to s: in tch: rdn and lost pl 2f out: wl hld 1f out* **33/1**
00 9 2 ½ **Sweet Ovation**[141] 5122 3-9-1 64 LeeNewnes(5) 9 35
(Mark Usher) *swtchd lft and dropped in bhd after s: a in rr: wd bnd: rdn and no hdwy 2f out* **50/1**

2000 **10** *4* **Just Breathe (IRE)**[19] 8074 3-9-2 **60**........................(v[1]) KirstyMilczarek 5 18
(Olivia Maylam) *in tch in midfield: rdn 3f out: lost pl 2f out: bhd over 1f out* **20/1**

1m 12.02s (0.12) **Going Correction** +0.025s/f (Slow) **10** Ran SP% **133.0**
Speed ratings (Par 101): **100,99,99,98,97 96,93,88,84,79**
toteswingers: 1&2 £3.10, 1&3 £3.60, 2&3 £8.40 CSF £10.06 CT £43.19 TOTE £1.60: £1.10, £1.80, £2.30; EX 10.70 Trifecta £28.10 Pool: £1,906.07 - 50.78 winning tickets..
Owner K W Tyrrell **Bred** Paramount Bloodstock **Trained** Baughurst, Hants

8305 £32 BONUS AT 32RED.COM H'CAP (DIV II) 6f (P)
2:00 (2:00) (Class 6) (0-65,65) 3-Y-0+ **£1,704** (£503; £251) **Stalls** Low

Form RPR
6453 **1** **Jonnie Skull (IRE)**[1] 8298 6-8-0 **51**..................................(vt) RyanTate(7) 4 60
(Phil McEntee) *w ldrs tl led 2f out: hrd pressed but hld on wl u.p ins fnl f* **8/1**

0051 **2** *nk* **Welsh Inlet (IRE)**[26] 7993 4-8-12 **56**.................................. KieranO'Neill 7 64
(John Bridger) *stdd and dropped in bhd after s: clsng whn nt clr run 2f out tl swtchd rt and hdwy jst over 1f out: r.o to chal wl ins fnl f: hld cl home* **6/1**[3]

0602 **3** *3/4* **Do More Business (IRE)**[12] 8168 5-8-4 **51** oh1........(v) RyanPowell(3) 3 57
(Alison Batchelor) *chsd ldrs: rdn and effrt to press ldrs 1f out: unable qck and styd on same pce wl ins fnl f* **7/1**

0000 **4** *shd* **Cornus**[13] 8156 10-8-11 **60**.........................(be) WilliamTwiston-Davies(5) 2 65
(Alan McCabe) *trckd ldrs: rdn and effrt jst over 1f out: unable qck u.p 1f out: styng on same pce and hld whn edgd rt wl ins fnl f* **20/1**

0042 **5** *1* **Amosite**[13] 8156 6-9-6 **64**..(p) RobertWinston 6 66
(J R Jenkins) *led on outer of ldng trio: rdn and hdd 2f out: unable qck over 1f out: styd on same pce ins fnl f* **7/2**[2]

0040 **6** *3/4* **Diamond Vine (IRE)**[13] 8159 4-9-7 **65**.............................(p) LukeMorris 5 65
(Ronald Harris) *sn rdn along in last trio: drvn and kpt on fr over 1f out: nvr gng pce to threaten ldrs* **9/4**[1]

-000 **7** *nse* **Johnstown Lad (IRE)**[37] 7864 8-9-4 **62**.........................(bt) ShaneKelly 9 62
(Daniel Mark Loughnane) *dwlt: outpcd in last pair: hdwy u.p 1f out: keeping on but hld whn nt clr run and eased towards fin* **7/1**

1004 **8** *1 1/4* **Ishiamiracle**[1] 8294 3-9-5 **63**...(p) AdamKirby 8 59
(Phil McEntee) *sn niggled along in last quartet: drvn and no imp fr over 1f out* **20/1**

1010 **9** *6* **Demoiselle Bond**[25] 8004 4-9-4 **62**.................................... JimCrowley 1 38
(Lydia Richards) *w ldrs tl 2f out: wknd over 1f out: fdd fnl f* **14/1**

1m 11.58s (-0.32) **Going Correction** +0.025s/f (Slow) **9** Ran SP% **119.6**
Speed ratings (Par 101): **103,102,101,101,100 99,99,97,89**
totewingers 1&2 £9.80, 1&3 £6.20, 2&3 £4.00 CSF £57.27 CT £357.14 TOTE £9.60: £2.40, £1.90, £2.30; EX 56.30 Trifecta £244.00 Pool: £1,731.28 - 5.32 winning tickets..
Owner Eventmaker Racehorses **Bred** Canice Farrell Jnr **Trained** Newmarket, Suffolk

FOCUS
The quicker of the two divisions by 0.44sec.

8306 32RED H'CAP 7f (P)
2:30 (2:30) (Class 4) (0-85,85) 3-Y-0+ **£4,075** (£1,212; £606; £303) **Stalls** Low

Form RPR
1423 **1** **Cut Across (IRE)**[11] 8188 4-8-13 **77**..............................(b[1]) SebSanders 8 87
(Nick Littmoden) *t.k.h: hld up in tch in midfield: rdn and effrt to chal over 1f out: led ins fnl f: r.o wl* **5/2**[2]

0031 **2** *1 3/4* **Sunshine Always (IRE)**[26] 7998 6-8-7 **71** oh1............ KirstyMilczarek 1 76
(Michael Attwater) *in tch in midfield: nt clr run 2f out: rdn and hdwy over 1f out: styd on wl ins fnl f to go 2nd cl home* **8/1**

0200 **3** *nk* **Beautiful Day**[33] 7920 4-8-10 **74**.. MartinDwyer 7 78
(Kevin Ryan) *led: rdn wl over 1f out: hdd 1f out: kpt on same pce ins fnl f* **25/1**

1266 **4** *nk* **Saharia (IRE)**[11] 8181 5-9-1 **79**...(v) ShaneKelly 2 82
(Michael Attwater) *hld up in last pair: rdn and hdwy over 1f out: chsd ldrs but hanging lft and swtchd out rt ins fnl f: drvn and styd on wl towards fin* **16/1**

0040 **5** *shd* **Decent Fella (IRE)**[9] 8227 6-9-7 **85**...........................(tp) WilliamCarson 3 88
(Violet M Jordan) *chsd ldr: ev ch over 2f out: rdn to ld 1f out sn hdd and no ex: lost 3 pls towards fin* **10/1**

0051 **6** *1/2* **Kung Hei Fat Choy (USA)**[23] 8034 3-9-0 **78**................(b) JimCrowley 4 80
(James Given) *chsd ldrs: drvn and effrt to press ldrs over 1f out: unable qck ins fnl f: one pce towards fin* **5/4**[1]

0131 **7** *4 1/2* **Brocklebank (IRE)**[21] 8055 3-9-1 **79**..........................(p) RobertWinston 6 69
(Simon Dow) *s.i.s: hld up in last pair: rdn and no hdwy over 1f out: wl hld and eased towards fin* **5/1**[3]

4500 **8** *6* **Quasi Congaree (GER)**[11] 8188 6-9-0 **78**.......................(t) LukeMorris 5 51
(Paul Fitzsimons) *chsd ldrs: rdn and struggling over 2f out: wknd over 1f out* **33/1**

1m 24.03s (-0.77) **Going Correction** +0.025s/f (Slow) **8** Ran SP% **122.6**
Speed ratings (Par 105): **105,103,102,102,102 101,96,89**
toteswingers 1&2 £4.90, 1&3 £13.50, 2&3 £15.60 CSF £24.88 CT £428.07 TOTE £3.50: £1.10, £2.60, £6.40; EX 25.80 Trifecta £629.20 Pool: £2,147.77 - 2.56 winning tickets..
Owner Nigel Shields **Bred** D J And Mrs Brown **Trained** Newmarket, Suffolk

FOCUS
This looked a fair handicap.

8307 32REDBET.COM H'CAP 5f (P)
3:00 (3:00) (Class 6) (0-65,65) 3-Y-0+ **£1,704** (£503; £251) **Stalls** High

Form RPR
0134 **1** **Novabridge**[28] 7969 4-9-6 **64**..(b) AdamKirby 3 73
(Neil Mulholland) *in tch in midfield: rdn and hdwy to ld over 1f out: in command fnl 100yds: eased cl home* **4/1**[1]

0600 **2** *1 1/4* **Charming (IRE)**[21] 8054 3-9-4 **62**................................(e[1]) SebSanders 9 67
(Olivia Maylam) *in tch in midfield: effrt and wd bnd wl over 1f out: kpt on u.p ins fnl f to go 2nd towards fin* **12/1**

4332 **3** *1/2* **Baby Dottie**[17] 8107 5-8-8 **57**...............................(t) JemmaMarshall(5) 6 60
(Pat Phelan) *in tch: effrt to chse ldrs 1f out: chsd wnr and styd on same pce u.p ins fnl f: lost 2nd ins fnl f* **4/1**[1]

5200 **4** *nse* **Desert Strike**[9] 8225 6-9-7 **65**..(p) JimCrowley 8 68
(Conor Dore) *hld up in tch: rdn over 1f out: styd on u.p ins fnl f: no threat to wnr* **7/1**[3]

3024 **5** *1 3/4* **Molly Jones**[11] 8190 3-8-10 **54**.. WilliamCarson 10 50
(Derek Haydn Jones) *chsd ldr: ev ch 2f out: rdn and unable qck over 1f out: wknd wl ins fnl f* **8/1**

3653 **6** *1 1/4* **Chjimes (IRE)**[11] 8190 8-8-12 **56**.......................................(b) LukeMorris 2 48
(Conor Dore) *sn bustled along: in tch in midfield: effrt and drvn over 1f out: no imp 1f out: wknd fnl 100yds* **5/1**[2]

60 **7** *2 1/4* **Beach Candy (IRE)**[25] 8004 3-8-7 **51** oh1..................(vt[1]) DavidProbert 4 35
(Phil McEntee) *awkward leaving stalls: hld up in last pair: rdn and sme hdwy over 1f out: no imp fnl f* **25/1**

0540 **8** *1* **Atlantic Beach**[21] 8054 7-9-6 **64**...................................(p) RobertWinston 5 44
(Milton Bradley) *chsd ldrs: rdn and unable qck over 1f out: wknd fnl f* **5/1**[2]

0000 **9** *1 1/4* **Bookiesindexdotnet**[9] 8225 3-9-5 **63**.................................... EddieAhern 1 39
(J R Jenkins) *led: rdn and hdd over 1f out: wknd fnl f* **33/1**

0006 **10** *1 1/4* **Golconde (IRE)**[13] 8157 3-9-1 **59**.......................................(p) ShaneKelly 7 30
(Robert Cowell) *sn outpcd in last pair: rdn 1/2-way: no imp tl styd on ins fnl f: n.d* **14/1**

58.27s (-0.53) **Going Correction** +0.025s/f (Slow) **10** Ran SP% **118.1**
Speed ratings (Par 101): **105,103,102,102,99 97,93,92,90,88**
toteswingers: 1&2 £12.40, 1&3 £4.40, 2&3 £11.00 CSF £54.23 CT £211.98 TOTE £6.10: £2.80, £4.40, £1.40; EX 76.40 Trifecta £414.00 Pool: £2,152.93 - 3.90 winning tickets..
Owner Dajam Ltd **Bred** Bishopswood Bloodstock & Trickledown Stud **Trained** Limpley Stoke, Wilts

FOCUS
Modest stuff.
Molly Jones Official explanation: jockey said filly hung left.
Bookiesindexdotnet Official explanation: jockey said filly lost her action.

8308 32RED.COM H'CAP 1m (P)
3:30 (3:31) (Class 5) (0-75,75) 3-Y-0+ **£2,385** (£704; £352) **Stalls** High

Form RPR
1521 **1** **Storm Runner (IRE)**[4] 8249 4-8-5 **62** 6ex........................ RyanPowell(3) 6 69
(George Margarson) *niggled along early: in tch in last pair: hdwy to chse ldrs 2f out: led ins fnl f: r.o wl* **4/5**[1]

0104 **2** *2 1/4* **Chrissycross (IRE)**[13] 8158 3-8-10 **65**........................(b) RobertWinston 9 67
(Roger Teal) *chsd ldrs: wnt 2nd and ev ch 2f out: unable qck w wnr and styd on same pce fnl 100yds* **6/1**[3]

5060 **3** *shd* **Cyflymder (IRE)**[62] 7464 6-9-1 **69**................................. KirstyMilczarek 7 71
(David C Griffiths) *chsd ldr tl led over 2f out: sn hrd pressed and rdn: kpt on u.p tl hdd and outpcd by wnr ins fnl f* **9/2**[2]

304 **4** *3/4* **Yankee Storm**[100] 6497 7-9-1 **69**.......................................(b) JimCrowley 1 69
(Michael Wigham) *stdd s: hld up in rr: hdwy 2f out: chsd ldng trio over 1f out: kpt on but no threat to wnr* **8/1**

656 **5** *7* **Fairy Wing (IRE)**[4] 8250 5-9-7 **75**......................................(p) LukeMorris 8 59
(Conor Dore) *t.k.h: hld up in tch in last trio: rdn and no hdwy 2f out: sn wknd* **20/1**

0100 **6** *2* **L'Hirondelle (IRE)**[17] 8105 8-9-1 **69**.................................. SebSanders 3 48
(Michael Attwater) *led tl 2f out: sn rdn and btn: wknd over 1f out* **14/1**

3-40 **7** *8* **Confirmed**[117] 5942 3-8-13 **68**... RenatoSouza 5 29
(Alison Batchelor) *t.k.h: chsd ldrs tl lost pl qckly over 2f out: bhd fnl 2f* **25/1**

1m 38.33s (0.13) **Going Correction** +0.025s/f (Slow)
WFA 3 from 4yo+ 1lb **7** Ran SP% **114.4**
Speed ratings (Par 103): **100,97,97,96,89 87,79**
toteswingers 1&2 £1.80, 1&3 £2.30, 2&3 £3.50 CSF £6.20 CT £13.89 TOTE £1.80: £1.10, £2.90; EX 6.70 Trifecta £21.70 Pool: £2,296.16 - 79.31 winning tickets..
Owner Pitfield Partnership **Bred** Kevin Foley **Trained** Newmarket, Suffolk

FOCUS
They didn't go that quick early, but the pace picked up running down the hill.
T/Jkpt: £10,657.10 to a £1 stake. Pool: £22,515.02 - 1.50 winning tickets. T/Plt: £69.10 to a £1 stake. Pool: £88,620.49 - 936.00 winning tickets. T/Qpdt: £11.00 to a £1 stake. Pool: £9,844.21 - 660.91 winning tickets. SP

INDEX TO FLAT RACING

Horses are shown in alphabetical order; the trainer's name follows the name of the horse. The figures to the right are current master ratings for all-weather and turf; the all-weather rating is preceded by the letter 'a'.Underneath the horse's name is its age, colour and sex in abbreviated format e.g. 6 b g indicates the horse is six-years-old, bay in colour, and a gelding.The descriptive details are followed by the race numbers of the races in which it has taken part in chronological order; a superscript figure indicates its finishing position in that race (brackets indicate it was the winner of the race).

Aaim To Prosper (IRE) *Brian Meehan* a79 116
8 br g Val Royal(FR) Bint Al Balad (IRE) (Ahonoora)
2639[7] 3367a[4] 3881[2] 4737[10] 6198[9] 6600[6] ◆ (7051)

Aaman (IRE) *Bernard Llewellyn* a78 73
6 gr g Dubai Destination(USA) Amellnaa (IRE) (Sadler's Wells (USA))
366[2] 673[2]

Aaraas *Kevin Prendergast* a83 102
3 b f Haafhd Adaala (USA) (Sahm (USA))
1041a[6] 2187a[2] 6080a[7] 7680a[6]

Aaranyow (IRE) *Terry Clement* 54
4 ch g Compton Place Cutpurse Moll (Green Desert (USA))
1907[10] 2386[8] 7739[11] 8069[9]

Aarti (IRE) *William Haggas* a66 63
3 b f Oasis Dream Sewards Folly (Rudimentary (USA))
1472[6] 1736[4] ◆ 2344[7] 3312[7] 5949[3] 6500[3] 7314[11]

Aazif (IRE) *John Dunlop* a82 89
3 ch g Nayef(USA) Ayun (USA) (Swain (IRE))
1473[4] ◆ 2281[5] 4601[2] 5044[2] 6033[6] 7194[7]

Abadejo *J R Jenkins* a40 62
4 b g Acclamation Silvereine (FR) (Bering)
2611[3] 3151[14] 4438[12] 5850[10] 6362[5] 6771[9]

Abated *Roger Charlton* a76 76
2 b f Dansili Tantina (USA) (Distant View (USA))
5352[6] ◆ 7161[2]

Abayo (USA) *C Boutin* a72 78
3 b c Arch(USA) Sashimi (USA) (Mt. Livermore (USA))
5074a[5]

Abbraccio *Ronald Harris* a75 70
4 b g Pivotal Embraced (Pursuit Of Love)
2496[4] 4516[6] 5268[8] 8141[2] (8239)

A B Celebration *John Bridger* a39 44
4 ch m Sleeping Indian Silver Louie (IRE) (Titus Livius (FR))
2586[9] 2886[12] 3389[10]

Abdel (FR) *C Laffon-Parias* 107
4 b h Dyhim Diamond(IRE) Leonor De Guzman (SPA) (Glauco (SPA))
2989a[5] 4316a[3] 5117a[4] 7234a[5]

Abdul Malik *Kate Walton* a67 40
3 b g Bertolini(USA) Muwasim (USA) (Meadowlake (USA))
2449[13] 2589[8] 3066[11] 3713[8] 4406[7]

Abernethy (IRE) *Linda Perratt* a33 53
4 b g Hernando(FR) Marsh Harrier (USA) (Woodman (USA))
1240[7] 1801[5] 2034[3] 2225[10] 2600[7] 2621[11]

Abhaath (USA) *Ronald Harris* a74 74
3 b g Hard Spun(USA) Above Perfection (USA) (In Excess)
2150[8] 2689[14] 5229[4] (5427) 5501[9] 7142[4] 7725[14] 7935[7] 8077[3] 8183[8]

Abidhabidubai *John Quinn* 82
4 b m Dubai Destination(USA) Madamoiselle Jones (Emperor Jones (USA))
(1249) ◆ 2142[7] 2636[5] 3311[2] 3810[3] 4620[2] 5220[4]

Abigails Angel *Brett Johnson* a80 74
5 br m Olden Times Make Ready (Beveled (USA))
148[2] 276[2] (559) (826) (919) 2431[4] 2988[2] 4255[3] 5120[5] 5592[8] 7328[12] 8252[3]

Ability N Delivery *Michael J Browne* a76 70
7 gr g Kyllachy Tryptonic (FR) (Baryshnikov (AUS))
(763) 1073[2]

Abi Scarlet (IRE) *Hughie Morrison* a90
3 b f Baltic King Petarga (Petong)
121[10] (283) 482[2] 659[5] (1176) (2400) 3342[7] 4062[11] 6041[9] 6367[9]

Abishena (IRE) *Mark Johnston* a67 94
3 ch f Pivotal Massomah (USA) (Seeking The Gold (USA))
2022[5] 2485[13] 3376[10] 3636[5] 4091[7] 4505[8] 4984[5] 5405[4]

Abjer (FR) *Ismail Mohammed* a87 93
4 b h Singspiel(IRE) Fine And Mellow (FR) (Lando (GER))
53a[16] 260a[11] 319a[8] 618a[10]

Able Mabel *Charlie Longsdon*
4 b m Zafeen(FR) Charleigh Keary (Sulaafah (USA))
4888[11]

Able Master (IRE) *David O'Meara* a62 97
6 b g Elusive City(USA) Foresta Verde (USA) (Green Forest (USA))
1168[6] 1476[11] 2264[18] 2487[5] ◆ 2896[4] (3334) ◆ 3524[3] 4609[10] (5057) 5314[2] 6011[2] 7030[6]

Able One (NZ) *J Moore* 123
10 b g Cape Cross(IRE) Gardenia (NZ) (Danehill (USA))
1902a[5]

Abonito (GER) *J-P Carvalho* 72
2 ch c Lord Of England(GER) Amouage (GER) (Tiger Hill (IRE))
3714a[4]

Above Standard (IRE) *Michael Easterby* a86 81
4 ch g Shamardal(USA) Prealpina (IRE) (Indian Ridge)
5225[10] 5618[8] (7218) 7411[3]

Above The Stars *Richard Fahey* a76 77
4 b m Piccolo Swindling (Bahamian Bounty)
4631[6] ◆ (5389) 6427[6] 6886[5] 7411[8] 7775[2] 7937[5] 7995[3] 8144[6] 8285[3]

A Boy Named Suzi *James Eustace* a85 103
4 b g Medecis Classic Coral (USA) (Seattle Dancer (USA))
2706[2] 3642[3] 4072[2] 4800[2] 5580[3]

Abraham Monro *Kate Walton* 60
2 gr g Kyllachy Pendulum (Pursuit Of Love)
4545[14] 4877[5] 5367[9] 6121[15]

Abraq *Ed Dunlop* a70 69
2 b c Danehill Dancer(IRE) Nordhock (USA) (Luhuk (USA))
4066[17] 4340[5] 4917[4] 5890[6] 6363[4] 8072[6]

Abrasivo (ITY) *P Caravati* a81
3 ch c Munir Medullia (IRE) (Turtle Island (IRE))
290a[6] 476a[9] 661a[10]

Abriachan *Noel Quinlan* a71 72
5 b g Celtic Swing Cape Finisterre (IRE) (Cape Cross (IRE))
1761[2] 1051[5] 1729[9] 3053[6] 3497[5] (3964) 4950[6]

Absa Lutte (IRE) *Michael Mullineaux* a76 75
9 b m Darnay Zenana (IRE) (Lucky Guest)
272[7] 406[4] 461[4] (576) 1049[5] 1828[10] 2084[5] 2475[7] 3211[3] 3382[8] 3944[10]

Absent Amy (IRE) *Willie Musson* a64 66
3 b f Redback Twitcher's Delight (Polar Falcon (USA))
524[2] 1529[6] ◆ 3044[10] 5625[3]

Abshir Zain (IRE) *Clive Brittain* a63 66
3 b c Green Desert(USA) O Fourlunda (Halling (USA))
112[7]

Absinthe (IRE) *Donald McCain* a81 99
6 b g King's Best(USA) Triple Try (IRE) (Sadler's Wells (USA))
(1993)

Absinthe Minded (USA) *D Wayne Lukas* a112 95
5 b m Quiet American(USA) Rockford Peach (USA) (Great Above (USA))
1839a[4]

Absolute Bearing (IRE) *Tim Etherington* a38 30
3 b g Majestic Missile(IRE) Garnock Academy (USA) (Royal Academy (USA))
2262[18] 2695[5] 4798[11] 7361[9]

Absolute Crackers (IRE) *Mrs John Harrington* 92
3 ch f Giant's Causeway(USA) El Laoob (USA) (Red Ransom (USA))
1973[7] 2524a[5]

Absolute Fun (IRE) *Tim Easterby* a27 60
3 b f Lawman(FR) Jallaissine (IRE) (College Chapel)
4713[6] 5312[8] 5823[2] 6959[4] 7099[12]

Absolutely Me (IRE) *Dominic Ffrench Davis* a37 31
3 ch f Barathea(IRE) Attymon Lill (IRE) (Marju (IRE))
1257[8] 1737[7] 2578[9]

Absolutely Right (IRE) *Richard Hannon* a71 53
2 b f Teofilo(IRE) Dabawiyah (IRE) (Intikhab (USA))
7403[5] 7720[3] (8102)

Absolutely So (IRE) *Andrew Balding* a78 82
2 b c Acclamation Week End (Selkirk (USA))
7371[3] ◆ (7813)

Absolute Princess *Scott Dixon* a66 55
4 b m Avonbridge Park Ave Princess (IRE) (Titus Livius (FR))
381[2] 672[6] 906[4] 1002[5] 1135[15]

Absolute Soul (IRE) *Francisco Castro*
3 ch g Perfect Soul(IRE) Walklikeanegyptian (IRE) (Danehill (USA))
5144a[11]

Absolutly Me (FR) *H-A Pantall* 95
3 b f Anabaa Blue Tadawul (USA) (Diesis)
2107a[6]

Abtaal (USA) *J-C Rouget* 115
3 b c Rock Hard Ten(USA) Appealing Storm (USA) (Valid Appeal (USA))
1208a[2] 1856[8] 3656a[3]

Abundantly *Hughie Morrison* a34 78
3 b f Sakhee(USA) Composing (IRE) (Noverre (USA))
(2578) 3212[4] 4536[2] 5280[2] 5789[7] (6924) 7519[7]

Abu Sidra (FR) *J-F Bernard* a89 106
3 gr c Shirocco(GER) Mary Doun (FR) (Smadoun (FR))
6088a[8] 7829a[5]

Acacalia (GER) *C Sprengel* 104
4 b m Ransom O'War(USA) Adorea (GER) (Dashing Blade)
4386a[10]

Acappello (GER) *W Mongil* a90 67
3 b c Lateral Alphabetique (FR) (Zieten (USA))
7345a[10]

Accelerant (IRE) *Kevin Ryan* 54
2 gr c Dark Angel(IRE) Tarellia (Pivotal)
6360[8] 7031[5] 7290[12]

Accession (IRE) *Clive Cox* a94 97
3 b g Acclamation Pivotal's Princess (IRE) (Pivotal)
(1356) 1751[10] 2276[6] 4063[9] 4598[8] 5080[7] 6143[5] 6676[15]

Accord Secret (FR) *C Lerner* a81 77
6 b h Okawango(USA) Super Vite (USA) (Septieme Ciel (USA))
7701a[0]

Accumulate *Bill Moore* a81 78
9 b g Second Empire(IRE) Bee-Bee-Gee (IRE) (Lake Coniston (IRE))
(500) 6014

Ace Master *Roy Bowring* a68 52
4 ch g Ballet Master(USA) Ace Maite (Komaite (USA))
96[3] 478[6] 670[4] 2046[8] 6967[5] 7446[8] 8115[4]

Ace Of Spies (IRE) *Conor Dore* a73 61
7 br g Machiavellian(USA) Nadia (Nashwan (USA))
13[8] 100[3] 139[4] 284[4] 385[3] 580[6] 670[2] 752[3] 884[4] 1178[2] (1280) 1430[3] 1601[6] 1958[10] 2581[8] 3006[9] 3738[11] 3941[7] 4192[9] 4653[8] 5179[8] 5720[2] 6178[12] 6586[6] 6937[8] 7157[8] 7354[3] (7733) 8064[7] 8268[12]

Ace Of Valhalla *Sir Henry Cecil* a71 87
3 b c Authorized(IRE) Trick Of Ace (USA) (Clever Trick (USA))
1414[2] 4224[2] (4882)

Ace Pearl (USA) *David Brown* a55 19
2 b g Bernstein(USA) Pulpitina (USA) (Pulpit (USA))
1955[3] 2370[4] 5010[3] 6156[14]

Acer Diamonds (IRE) *Julia Feilden* 68
3 b g Red Clubs(IRE) Tree House (USA) (Woodman (USA))
1937[3] 2898[7] 3671[7] 4411[14]

A Certain Romance *Peter Chapple-Hyam* 81
2 b c Invincible Spirit(IRE) Tiger's Gene (GER) (Perugino (USA))
3545[2] (3989) 4763[13] 6344[3]

Ace Serve *Oliver Sherwood* a59 63
4 b m King's Best(USA) Match Point (Unfuwain (USA))
581[2] 810[7]

Achalas (IRE) *Heather Main* a84 83
4 b g Statue Of Liberty(USA) Princess Of Iona (IRE) (Fasliyev (USA))
1566[4] 1940[6] 2887[5] (3015) 3316[5] 4460[8] 5030a[5] 5546[3] ◆ 6584[10] 6703[2] 6933[7]

Achtung (SPA) *R Lopez Gallego* 84
4 ch g Sulamani(IRE) Aurea (GER) (Silvano (GER))
5252a[7] 6089a[3]

Aciano (IRE) *Brendan Powell* a79 85
4 b g Kheleyf(USA) Blue Crystal (IRE) (Lure (USA))
1416[14] 2151[11] 2576[3] 2623[5] 3703[13] (3947) 4334[2] 4603[3] 5440[2] 5993[4] 6894[7] 7415[6] 8047[3]

Acknowledgement *Philip Kirby* a52 63
10 b g Josr Algarhoud(IRE) On Request (IRE) (Be My Guest (USA))
3440[8] (3904)

Across The Galaxy *Hughie Morrison* 49
3 b f Cape Cross(IRE) Galaxy Highflyer (Galileo (IRE))
2200[8] 3100[7]

Across The Straits (FR) *Jonathan Geake*
8 b g Dansili Skipnight (Ashkalani (IRE))
2393[13]

Action Chope (FR) *D Guillemin* a91 102
4 b m Muhaymin(USA) Free Track (FR) (Solid Illusion (USA))
5118a[10] 7123a[5]

Action Front (USA) *Derek Shaw* a74 83
4 bb g Aptitude(USA) Palisade (USA) (Gone West (USA))
872[8] 1446[4] 2378[5] 2936[6] ◆ 3961[7] 6891[11]

Activate *David O'Meara* a71 99
5 b g Motivator Princess Manila (CAN) (Manila (USA))
1214[11] 2278[11] 3114[5] 3564[11] 3953[7] 7367[13] 8148[3] 8235[5]

Activiste (IRE) *C Laffon-Parias* a81 80
3 b c Giant's Causeway(USA) Occupandiste (IRE) (Kaldoun (FR))
8277a[2]

Actonetaketwo *Ron Hodges* a19
2 b f Act One Temple Dancer (Magic Ring (IRE))
3959[9] 8018[9] 8233[7]

Acton Jenson *Brian Baugh* a38
3 gr g Proclamation(IRE) Crystal Attraction (Mon Tresor)
7867[7] 7978[5] 8291[8]

Actor (IRE) *John Weymes*
3 b g Montjeu(IRE) Original (Caerleon (USA))
1250[12] 1597[5] 2340[13]

Act Your Shoe Size *Keith Dalgleish* 85
3 b f Librettist(USA) Howards Heroine (IRE) (Danehill Dancer (IRE))
1440[4] 1819[4] 2076[4] (2539) (3252) 4261[6] 5110[14] 6526[2] 6710[5] 6757[2] 7002[4]

Adaeze (IRE) *Jonathan Portman* a45 57
4 b m Footstepsinthesand Ringmoor Down (Pivotal)
3477[10] 3791[7] 4815[8] 5217[7] 5504[8] 6233[3] 6771[10] 7703[5] 8168[4]

Ada Lovelace *Dean Ivory* a64
2 br f Byron Satin Braid (Diktat)
7219[7] 7653[4] 7855[2] 8044[3]

Adamantina *E Botti* 103
4 b m Diktat Royal Hawk (IRE) (Wolfhound (USA))
1409a[3]

Adam De Beaulieu (USA) *Ben Haslam* a51 44
5 b g Broken Vow(USA) Gambling Champ (USA) (Fabulous Champ (USA))
1584[5] 2401[8] 2823[9]

Adam's Ale *Paul Midgley* 16
3 b g Ishiguru(USA) Aqua (Mister Baileys)
7445[9] 7729[12]

Adatara (IRE) *M M Lynch* a62 68
7 b m Celtic Swing Adalya (IRE) (Darshaan)
7381[6]

Addazero *Alastair Lidderdale* a75 72
3 b g Putra Sas(IRE) Poker Queen (Karinga Bay)
4410[11] 5048[6] 5901[5] ◆ 6615[6] 7655[4]

Addictive Dream (IRE) *David Nicholls* a104 111
5 ch g Kheleyf(USA) Nottambula (IRE) (Thatching)
(50a) ◆ (141a) 874a[5] 1146a[15] 1977[5] 2602[2]

Addictive Nature (IRE) *Clive Cox* 21
2 b g Acclamation Movie Queen (Danehill (USA))
4688[16]

Addikt (IRE) *Michael Scudamore* a73 74
7 b h Diktat Frond (Alzao (USA))
110[8] (1299) 2354[8] 3039[9]

Address Unknown *Ian Williams* a92 102
5 b g Oasis Dream Return (USA) (Sadler's Wells (USA))
1318[9] 1672[4] 1974[12] 3125[8] 4575[2] (5076) 5333[3] 6031[13]

Adeem (USA) *John Dunlop* 53
2 b c Invasor(ARG) Thawakib (IRE) (Sadler's Wells (USA))
6204[11] 6481[16] 7333[10]

Adelar (GER) *Venetia Williams* 44
7 b g Samum(GER) Arpista (GER) (Chief Singer)
4363[10]

Adelindus *Ed Vaughan* a44 43
3 b f King's Best(USA) Possessive Artiste (Shareef Dancer (USA))
892[9] 1303[11]

Adeste *Noel Quinlan* a57 75
3 b f Dansili Tu Eres Mi Amore (IRE) (Sadler's Wells (USA))
2249[5] 3352[2] (4182) 5277[5] 6383[4] 7024[9]

Adili (IRE) *Brian Ellison* a74 44
3 ch g Dubai Destination(USA) Adirika (IRE) (Miswaki (USA))
283[7] 383[4] ◆ 1173[5] 2118[6] 3938[3] (4188)

Adira (GER) *J-P Carvalho* a78 53
2 b f Lomitas Aberdeen (GER) (Polish Precedent (USA))
4476a[4]

Adiynara (IRE) *Neil Mulholland* a76 81
4 b m Halling(USA) Adirika (IRE) (Miswaki (USA))
8235[4]

Admirable Art (IRE) *Marco Botti* a45
2 b c Excellent Art Demi Voix (Halling (USA))
5162[8]

Admirable Duque (IRE) *Dominic Ffrench Davis* a94 73
6 b g Selkirk(USA) Stunning (USA) (Nureyev (USA))
213[3] (285) (751) 1056[8] 2561[8] 3400[11] 4061[12] 4944[6] 5359[9] 5936[7] 8000[7] 8275[9]

Admiral Barry (IRE) *Eoin Griffin* a72 93
7 b g Kalanisi(IRE) Kart Star (IRE) (Soviet Star (USA))
6066a[8] 7584a[16] 7852a[12]

Admiralofthesea (USA) *Robert Eddery* 67
2 b c Henrythenavigator(USA) Duchess Royale (IRE) (Danehill (USA))
2797[6] 7330[8] 7636[10]

Admirals Walk (IRE) *Sylvester Kirk* a63
2 b g Tagula(IRE) Very Racy (USA) (Sri Pekan (USA))
4604[13] 5765[8] 6015[7] 7060[11] 7592[4]

Admiralty *Ismail Mohammed* a78 57
3 b c Iffraaj Camp Riverside (USA) (Forest Camp (USA))
2543[3] 2865[4] 3447[7] 4211[3] 4874[2] 5428[4] 6152[7] 6813[2] (7022)

Admiration (AUS) *J Moore* 120
5 b h Encosta De Lago(AUS) Provence (AUS) (Redoute's Choice (AUS))
1902a[8] 8041a[6]

Admire Fuji (IRE) *S Kobayashi* a79
2 b c Oasis Dream Sun Bittern (USA) (Seeking The Gold (USA))
7984a[5]

Adorabella (IRE) *Paul Rich* a39 43
9 b m Revoque(IRE) Febrile (USA) (Trempolino (USA))
2851[10] 3216[3] 4145[7]

Adorable Choice (IRE) *Tom Dascombe* a72 76
4 bb m Choisir(AUS) Burnin' Memories (USA) (Lit De Justice (USA))
2539[8] 6895[8] 7356[4] 7618[6] 7858[3] 8252[8]

Adranian (IRE) *David C Griffiths* a81 62
3 gr g Dark Angel(IRE) Make Me Blush (USA) (Blushing John (USA))
(42) (230) 471[3] 659[3] 867[4] 897[2] 1721[12] 1983[5] 2400[5] 3762[10] 4081[7] 4644[2] 5099[5] 5298[2] 6051[4]

Adriana (GER) *M Rulec* 95
4 b m Poliglote An Angel (GER) (Trempolino (USA))
5844a[11]

Ad Value (IRE) *Alan Swinbank* a48 67
4 b g Ad Valorem(USA) Sopran Marida (IRE) (Darshaan)
(1240) 1822[8] 2635[6] 4955[11] 7454[3] 7603[11]

Advanced *Kevin Ryan* a88 100
9 b g Night Shift(USA) Wonderful World (GER) (Dashing Blade)
1157[2] 1865[8] 2068[17] 2825[3] 3331[17] 4086[8] 4609[4] 4802[11] 6466[8] 6659[7] 7366[17] 7645[4] 7934[6]

Adventure Story *Tony Carroll* a66 71
5 ch m Bold Edge Birthday Venture (Soviet Star (USA))
4235[9] ◆ 4793[8] 5327[7] 6737[6] 7634[6]

Adverse (IRE) *Michael Bell* a55 55
3 b f Refuse To Bend(IRE) Shadow Roll (IRE) (Mark Of Esteem (IRE))
1278[8] 1560[5] 2374[3] 2802[3]

Ad Vitam (IRE) *Micky Hammond* a64 62
4 ch g Ad Valorem(USA) Love Sonnet (Singspiel (IRE))
232[11] 390[8] 483[10] 837[2] 929[5] 1179[10] 1583[8]

Advocacy (USA) *Roy Brotherton*
7 br g Singspiel(IRE) Kiss The Devil (USA) (Kris S (USA))
3384[P]

Aednat *S Slevin* a44 42
2 ch f Sir Percy Moi Aussi (USA) (Mt. Livermore (USA))
5858a[9]

Aegaeus *Ed Dunlop* a81 76
3 b g Monsun(GER) Ouija Board (Cape Cross (IRE))
1414[8] 1866[6] 2430[6] ◆ 6574[4] 7368[2] 7644[3] (7818)

Aegean Destiny *John Mackie* a56 70
5 b m Beat Hollow Starlist (Observatory (USA))
2167[6] 3061[4] 3307[2] 6957[6] 7018[3]

Aegean King *Michael Wigham* a57 55
6 b g Falbrav(IRE) Aegean Dream (IRE) (Royal Academy (USA))
6361[0] 7992[12] (8180)

Aegean Pride *Barry Murtagh* a62 49
7 b m Sakhee(USA) Aegean Dream (IRE) (Royal Academy (USA))
453[13]

Aegean Whispers *Richard Hannon* a47
2 ch f Piccolo Aegean Dream (IRE) (Royal Academy (USA))
7642[6] 7923[6] 8200[9]

Aerodynamic (IRE) *Michael Easterby* a81 84
5 b g Oratorio(IRE) Willowbridge (IRE) (Entrepreneur)
36[3] 1156[6] 2119[7] 3167[14] 3403[3] 3994[2] (4747) 5492[15] 5888[9]

Aeronwyn Bryn (IRE) *Michael Dods* a65 63
2 b f Dylan Thomas(IRE) Hecuba (Hector Protector (USA))
4246[8] 4494[8] 4921[4] 5786[4] (6318)

Aeroplane *Richard Price* a107 64
9 b h Danehill Dancer(IRE) Anita At Dawn (IRE) (Anita's Prince)
6932[11]

Aesop's Fables (USA) *A Fabre* 118
3 b c Distorted Humor(USA) Abhisheka (IRE) (Sadler's Wells (USA))
2728a[3] (3681a) 5250a[2]

Afaal (USA) *William Haggas* 79
3 b g Hard Spun(USA) Alattrah (USA) (Shadeed (USA))
2490[13] 3393[12]

Affaire D'Etat (FR) *P Demercastel* 97
4 gr h Chichicastenango(FR) Uberaba (FR) (Garde Royale)
3367a[6]

Aficionado *Ed Dunlop* a66
2 ch g Halling(USA) Prithee (Barathea (IRE))
7641[2] ◆

Afkar (IRE) *Clive Brittain* a82 85
4 b g Invincible Spirit(IRE) Indienne (IRE) (Indian Ridge)
967[3] 1262[8] 5234[2] (5457) 5768[3] 6041[2] 6705[9] 7113[4]

Afleeting Lady (USA) *Dale Romans* a110 90
5 b m Afleet Alex(USA) Oatsee (USA) (Unbridled (USA))
1839a[5]

Afnoon (USA) *John Dunlop* 74
3 b f Street Cry(IRE) Tashawak (IRE) (Night Shift (USA))
2194[7] 3347[3] 4544[3] 5107[8] 6375[12]

Afonso De Sousa (USA) *A P O'Brien* 108
2 b c Henrythenavigator(USA) Mien (USA) (Nureyev (USA))
4066[4] 5488[3]

Afraah (USA) *Roger Varian* a88 77
3 b f Hard Spun(USA) Sarayir (USA) (Mr Prospector (USA))
3399[4] 4516[3] 5901[4] (6457) (7461) 7740[3]

African Art (USA) *P Schaerer* a89 89
6 ch g Johannesburg(USA) Perovskia (USA) (Stravinsky (USA))
443a[5] (630a)

African Oil (FR) *Charles Hills* 81
2 b c Royal Applause Ahdaaf (USA) (Bahri (USA))
4688[14] 5418[2] ◆ (5948) 6487[4] 6815[5]

African Story *Saeed Bin Suroor* a121 115
5 ch g Pivotal Blixen (USA) (Gone West (USA))
(315a) 487a[3] (876a) ◆ (1143a) 1902a[6]

Afro *Peter Hedger* a56 56
2 b f Araafa(IRE) Largo (IRE) (Selkirk (USA))
4946[8] 6017[5] 6572[5] 7205[3]

Afsare *Luca Cumani* a91 117
5 b g Dubawi(IRE) Jumaireyah (Fairy King (USA))
1471[4] 2106a[2] (3825) 4610[2] 5377a[2]

After (IRE) *A P O'Brien* 108
3 b f Danehill Dancer(IRE) Noahs Ark (IRE) (Charnwood Forest (IRE))
1403a[5] 2109a[4] 2527a[5] 3092a[2] 3983a[3] 4482a[3] 5067a[5] 5523a[6] 6061a[11]

After The Storm *Rebecca Curtis* a57 66
3 b g Dylan Thomas(IRE) Inchiri (Sadler's Wells (USA))
2266[6]

After Timer (IRE) *Julie Camacho* a40 44
3 b f Kheleyf(USA) Rustle In The Wind (Barathea (IRE))
583[5] 845[6] 1010[6] 2595[9]

Agadir Summer *David Simcock* a75 72
4 b m Cape Cross(IRE) Easy To Love (USA) (Diesis)
1380[2] 2755[7]

Agama (GER) *C Sprengel* 50
2 ch f Sholokhov(IRE) Ariana (GER) (Dashing Blade)
7588a[6]

Agapanthus (GER) *Neil Mulholland* a40 57
7 b g Tiger Hill(IRE) Astilbe (GER) (Monsun (GER))
651[8]

Agence Belge (FR) *Y Barberot* a79 80
2 b f Librettist(USA) Celere (FR) (Kabool)
5288a[2]

Agent Allison *Peter Chapple-Hyam* 97
2 b f Dutch Art Loquacity (Diktat)
(2977) 3326[2] 6909a[7]

Age Of Bronze *Richard Hannon* a62 18
2 ch c Byron Beechnut (IRE) (Mujadil (USA))
3569[8] 4462[3] 5478[4] 5806[8] 6115[12] 7008[2] 7305[6] 7724[10] 7795[4] 7854[6]

Agerzam *Roger Varian* a86 62
2 br c Holy Roman Emperor(IRE) Epiphany (Zafonic (USA))
6411[5] (6772) ◆ 7193[2] ◆

Aggbag *Michael Appleby* a54 53
8 b g Fath(USA) Emaura (Dominion)
7[7] 109[6] 390[4] 531[5] 1095[5] 1360[6] 1634[4] 2365[7] 2555[14]

Agglestone Rock *Philip Kirby* a37 83
7 b g Josr Algarhoud(IRE) Royalty (IRE) (Fairy King (USA))
7353[11] 7610[6] 8149[6]

Aggravation *Chris Grant* a72 51
10 b g Sure Blade(USA) Confection (Formidable (USA))
3213[11] 3753[5] 4766[7] 5735[P]

Aghareed (USA) *J E Hammond* 101
3 b f Kingmambo(USA) Lahudood (Singspiel (IRE))
4616a[8] 7449a[7]

Aglaja *Frank Sheridan* a47
3 b f Tiger Cafe(JPN) Undovica (Primo Dominie)
270[7] 466[5] 1530[6] 5127[8]

Aglaophonos *Roger Varian* a55
2 ch g Dutch Art Lasting Image (Zilzal (USA))
7006[5]

Agripin (IRE) *David Barron* 56
2 ch c Sakhee's Secret Candela Bay (IRE) (Captain Rio)
4825[8] 5586[9]

Ahaaly *Kevin Prendergast* a86 87
3 b f Exceed And Excel(AUS) Alshakr (Bahri (USA))
2777a[9]

Ahern *David Barron* 104
2 ch c Dutch Art Petra Nova (First Trump)
(2715) ◆ 3291[5] ◆ 4008[3] 4736[7]

Ahlaain (USA) *A Al Raihe* a99 93
4 b h Bernstein(USA) Brocatelle (Green Desert (USA))
48a[7] 618a[2]

Ahlawy (IRE) *Frank Sheridan* a87 54
9 gr g Green Desert(USA) On Call (Alleged (USA))
229[6] 330[8] 449[2] 634[2] 695[3] 944[3] 999[2] 1360[3] 1530[3] 1632[3] 1718[4] 2348[5] 2414[14]

Ahtoug *Mahmood Al Zarooni* a103 104
4 b h Byron Cherokee Rose (IRE) (Dancing Brave (USA))
2446[5] 5077[3]

Ahuqd (IRE) *Clive Brittain* a59 32
3 ch f Manduro(GER) Daruliyya (IRE) (Highest Honor (FR))
4464[5] 5510[7] 6598[14]

Ahzeemah (IRE) *Saeed Bin Suroor* a84 106
3 b g Dubawi(IRE) Swiss Roll (IRE) (Entrepreneur)
1473[2] 1641[4] 3124[3] (4365) 5078[2] (6025)

Aiaam Al Wafa (IRE) *Phil McEntee* a62 62
3 b f Authorized(IRE) State Secret (Green Desert (USA))
206[7] 495[6] 556[6] 840[3] 923[7] 998[3] 1093[6] (1413) 1591[2] 2577[7] 2624[7] 3048[4] 3391[3] 3592[11] 5152[5] 5632[7]

Aidan (IRE) *John Geoghegan* a64 65
3 b g Mountain High(IRE) Zuleika (IRE) (Lucky Guest)
1834a[4]

Aigue Marine *N Clement* 109
3 b f Galileo(IRE) Aiglonne (USA) (Silver Hawk (USA))
2532a[7] 6595a[2]

Aiken *John Gosden* 116
4 b h Selkirk(USA) Las Flores (IRE) (Sadler's Wells (USA))
(1603) (2066) (2744a) 3369[4] 6271a[4] 7235[2] ◆

Ailsa Craig (IRE) *Edwin Tuer* a66 83
6 b m Chevalier(IRE) Sharplaw Destiny (IRE) (Petardia)
1133[15] 1381[2] 1913[7] 2241[4] 2687[8] 3693[8] 4249[7] 4682[4] 5225[8] 6103[11]

Aine's Delight (IRE) *Andy Turnell* a61 58
6 b m King's Best(USA) Gentle Thoughts (Darshaan)
2394[7]

Aint Got A Scooby (IRE) *Clive Cox* 66
2 br c Red Clubs(IRE) La Bataille (USA) (Out Of Place (USA))
3444[9] 3996[3] 4813[6] (5236) 5786[8] 7079[2] 7365[3]

Ain't Talkin' *Michael Attwater* a42 27
6 ch g Zaha(CAN) Royal Ivy (Mujtahid (USA))
293[7] 3791[0]

Airborne Again (IRE) *Harry Dunlop* a62 84
3 gr g Acclamation Bunditten (IRE) (Soviet Star (USA))
1317[12] 1921[6] 4496[9] 5234[6] 6935[3]

Airmyles *Tracy Waggott* 51
4 br g Diktat Dance In The Sun (Halling (USA))
2339[9] 2794[3] 3352[6] 4349[14] 4715[10] 5171[13] 5708[6]

Airspace (IRE) *Riccardo Barontini* a74 85
6 bb g Kheleyf(USA) Peace In The Park (IRE) (Ahonoora)
2325a[U]

Air Support (USA) *Claude McGaughey III* 116
4 b h Smart Strike(CAN) Gaze (USA) (Danzig (USA))
7094a[5]

Aizavoski (IRE) *E Lellouche* 114
6 b h Monsun(GER) Arlesienne (IRE) (Alzao (USA))
4229a[5] 7320a[11]

Ajaan *Sir Henry Cecil* 102
8 br g Machiavellian(USA) Alakananda (Hernando (FR))
1974[15]

A J Cook (IRE) *David Barron* 62
2 b g Mujadil(USA) Undertone (IRE) (Noverre (USA))
5711[4] 6071[7]

Ajdaad (USA) *Alan McCabe* a76 80
5 b g Horse Chestnut(SAF) Hasene (FR) (Akarad (FR))
85[3] 175[5] 248[3] 330[5]

A Jealous Woman (USA) *Francis Meza* a85 98
6 ch m Muqtarib(USA) Miss Free Bird (USA) (Fly So Free (USA))
7577a[2]

Ajeeb (USA) *David Simcock* a86 72
4 b g Harlan's Holiday(USA) Fair Settlement (USA) (Easy Goer (USA))
5888[3] 7842[5] 7999[5] 8174[3]

Ajjaadd (USA) *Ted Powell* a99 98
6 b g Elusive Quality(USA) Millstream (USA) (Dayjur (USA))
3641[16] 4367[10] 4576[10] 5832[4] ◆ (6543) 7080[3] 7397[5] 7704[3] 7897[5] 8066[3]

Ajman Bridge *Luca Cumani* a79
2 ch c Dubawi(IRE) Rice Mother (IRE) (Indian Ridge)
(8070)

Ajmany (IRE) *Luca Cumani* 86
2 b c Kheleyf(USA) Passarelle (USA) (In The Wings)
3242[14] 3788[2] 4612[4] (5319) 6247[3]

A'Juba *Saeed Bin Suroor* a68 84
3 b g Kingmambo(USA) Arlette (IRE) (King Of Kings (IRE))
4948[5] 5555[2] ◆ 6102[2] (6925) 7493[10]

Akarana (IRE) *Willie Musson* a51
5 b g Danehill Dancer(IRE) Castle Quest (IRE) (Grand Lodge (USA))
578[9]

Akarshan (IRE) *Evan Williams* a50 55
7 b g Intikhab(USA) Akdara (IRE) (Sadler's Wells (USA))
546[3] 1272[10]

Akasaka (IRE) *Edward Lynam* a91 82
5 b g King's Best(USA) Daganya (IRE) (Danehill Dancer (IRE))
337a[3] 3647a[8] 5397a[13]

Akbabend *Chris Gordon* a55 36
6 b g Refuse To Bend(IRE) Akdariya (IRE) (Shirley Heights)
4697[16] 5158[5]

Akeed Mofeed *John M Oxx* 114
3 b c Dubawi(IRE) Wonder Why (GER) (Tiger Hill (IRE))
3651a[4]

Akeed Wafi (IRE) *John M Oxx* 101
3 b c Street Cry(IRE) Shy Lady (FR) (Kaldoun (FR))
1401a[2] 3322a[5]

Aklan (IRE) *John M Oxx* 108
3 gr g Dalakhani(IRE) Akdara (IRE) (Sadler's Wells (USA))
3361a[6] 5606a[4]

Aksil (FR) *M Boutin* 88
2 b f Spirit One(FR) Nera Zilzal (IRE) (Zilzal (USA))
5379a[0] 6128a[3] 7122a[7]

Akua'Da (GER) *A Wohler* 99
2 bb f Shamardal(USA) Akua'Ba (IRE) (Sadler's Wells (USA))
7281a[2]

Akula (IRE) *Mark H Tompkins* a55 63
5 ch g Soviet Star(USA) Danielli (IRE) (Danehill (USA))
452[7] 5022[2] ◆ 5637[2] 6478[2] 8035[10]

Akzar (IRE) *Rob Blacker* 91
5 ch g Selkirk(USA) Alaiyda (USA) (Shahrastani (USA))
7783a[10]

Al Aasifh (IRE) *Saeed Bin Suroor* a82 101
4 b g Invincible Spirit(IRE) Urgele (FR) (Zafonic (USA))
80a[4] 261a[9] 616a[14] 6676[3]

Alabanda (IRE) *Tim Easterby* a39 75
3 b f Camacho Alinda (IRE) (Revoque (IRE))
1441[6] 2824[8] 3214[5] 3555[8] 4192[10] 4397[8] 4830[5] 5803[3] 6258[10]

Aladdins Cave *C A Murphy* a91 83
8 b g Rainbow Quest(USA) Flight Of Fancy (Sadler's Wells (USA))
(7852a)

A Ladies Man (IRE) *Richard Hannon* 73
2 b c Kyllachy Ego (Green Desert (USA))
5303[10] 6491[6] 7081[10]

Alaghiraar (IRE) *Richard Ford* a69 84
8 b g Act One Tarsheeh (USA) (Mr Prospector (USA))
367[10] 2137[8]

Alakhan (IRE) *Ian Williams* a91 91
6 gr g Dalakhani(IRE) Alte Kunst (IRE) (Royal Academy (USA))
3036[3] 3779[7] 5111[5] 6380[8]

Al Amaan *Gary Moore* a68 72
7 b g Nayef(USA) Siobhan (Generous (IRE))
8020[9] 8162[6] ◆

Alandi (IRE) *P J Prendergast* 84
7 b h Galileo(IRE) Aliya (IRE) (Darshaan)
5575[5]

Alanlad (FR) *P Demercastel* a62
2 b c Hannouma(IRE) Marie Vison (IRE) (Entrepreneur)
3714a[0]

Alanza (IRE) *John M Oxx* 112
4 ch m Dubai Destination(USA) Alasha (IRE) (Barathea (IRE))
2515a[3] (3091a) 4065[7] 5355[3] 6061a[6]

Al Aqabah (IRE) *Brian Gubby* a79 70
7 ch m Redback Snow Eagle (IRE) (Polar Falcon (USA))
33[8] 378[9] 1729[5] 2044[6] 3154[4] 3443[8] 6801[12] (7166) 7484[13] 7901[10]

Alaskan Bullet (IRE) *Brian Ellison* a85 88
3 b g Kodiac Czars Princess (IRE) (Soviet Star (USA))
2509[4] 5363[12] 6026[10] 6837[4] (7591) 7918[3] 8009[6]

Alaskan Prince (IRE) *Peter Salmon* a40
7 b g Exit To Nowhere(USA) Alaskan Princess (IRE) (Prince Rupert (FR))
2095[12] 3024[6] 6215[10] 7793[11]

Alatasarai (IRE) *Alex Fracas* a35 54
3 ch f Giant's Causeway(USA) May (Montjeu (IRE))
5074a[10] 7267a[2]

Alazan (IRE) *Philip Hobbs* a84 90
6 ch g Dubai Destination(USA) Marion Haste (IRE) (Ali-Royal (IRE))
5665[7] (7999) 8275[2]

Alazeyab (USA) *A Al Raihe* a107 107
6 b g El Prado(IRE) Itnab (Green Desert (USA))
244a[8] 416a[2] 487a[9] 874a[7]

Albaasil (IRE) *Doug Watson* 115
4 b h Dansili Wrong Key (IRE) (Key Of Luck (USA))
316a[2] ◆ 590a[2] 879a[7]

Al Baidaa *Roger Varian* a89 91
3 b f Exceed And Excel(AUS) Intrum Morshaan (IRE) (Darshaan)
1704[3] 2344[3] (3556) 5752[2] 5951[2] 6333[4]

Albamara *Sir Mark Prescott Bt* a92 104
3 bb f Galileo(IRE) Albanova (Alzao (USA))
3069[3] 4261[3] 4848[4] 6598[2] 7510[7]

Albanka (USA) *Sir Michael Stoute* 45
3 ch f Giant's Causeway(USA) Alidiva (Chief Singer)
3189[9]

Albany Rose (IRE) *Rae Guest* a66 91
4 br m Noverre(USA) Teide Lady (Nashwan (USA))
2507[5] 3375[8] 5663[7] ◆

Albaqaa *P J O'Gorman* a91 103
7 ch g Medicean Basbousate Nadia (Wolfhound (USA))
1471[8] 2127[5] 3268[13] 3878[5] 4761[14] 5746[7] 6119[6] 6494[9] 7502[10] 8022[6]

Albaraka *Sir Mark Prescott Bt* a64 90
4 gr m Selkirk(USA) Alborada (Alzao (USA))
3652a[7] 4216[10]

Albasharah (USA) *Saeed Bin Suroor* a90 81
3 b f Arch(USA) Desert Gold (USA) (Seeking The Gold (USA))
(7174) (7475)

Albaspina (IRE) *Sir Mark Prescott Bt* a86 84
3 gr f Selkirk(USA) Alabastrine (Green Desert (USA))
4968[3] 5480[2] 5856[5]

Alben Star (IRE) *Richard Fahey* a104 101
4 b g Clodovil(IRE) Secret Circle (Magic Ring (IRE))
(64) ◆ 253[2] ◆ 405[2] (871) ◆ 1140[3] 1885[5] 3371[9] (3860) 4802[5] ◆ 5370[8] 6468[17]

Albert Bridge *Ralph Beckett* a75 94
4 gr g Hernando(FR) Alvarita (Selkirk (USA))
1890[2] 5944[10] (6472) 7051[7] ◆ 7584a[2]

Albert Tatlock (IRE) *David Nicholls* 73
3 b g Antonius Pius(USA) Double Precedent (Polish Precedent (USA))
4780[6] 5679[4] (6125) 7395[7]

Albillanbaz (IRE) *John Quinn* 52
3 b c One Cool Cat(USA) Toy Show (IRE) (Danehill (USA))
3352[4]

Albion *A Fabre* 110
3 b c With Approval(CAN) Alborada (Alzao (USA))
1869a[2] 2743a[12] 4121a[7] 6508a[3] 7284a[7]

Albonny (IRE) *Alan Jarvis* a72 56
3 b g Aussie Rules(USA) Silk Law (IRE) (Barathea (IRE))
1703[14] 2941[10] 4410[7] 5219[6] 5744[3] (6255)

Alborz (IRE) *Tim Vaughan* a61 77
3 b g Dubai Destination(USA) Mount Elbrus (Barathea (IRE))
3483[2] (5152) 5528[3]

Alcaeus *Sir Mark Prescott Bt* a46
2 b c Hernando(FR) Alvarita (Selkirk (USA))
4917[8] 5476[4] 5765[11]

Alcando (IRE) *Denis Coakley* a78 84
2 ch c Alhaarth(IRE) Cantando (IRE) (Hamas (IRE))
(5192) 5969[3] (6227) 6799[4] 7164[3] 7374[2]

Alchimia (FR) *P Bary* a98 104
4 gr m Trade Fair Alchimiste (FR) (Linamix (FR))
83a[3]

Alcohuaz (CHI) *Lennart Reuterskiold Jr* a112 103
7 b g Merchant Of Venice(USA) Giverny (CHI) (Hussonet (USA))
(2159a)

Alcopop (AUS) *Jake Stephens* 117
8 b g Jeune Iota Of Luck (AUS) (Blevic (AUS))
7264a[2] 8043a[3]

Al Dain (IRE) *Kevin Ryan* 21
3 b f Diamond Green(FR) Mitchella (IRE) (Persian Bold)
1274[12]

Aldedash (USA) *James Fanshawe* a78 75
4 b g Aldebaran(USA) Hawzah (Green Desert (USA))
(1391) 1633[3] 2199[10]

Aldermoor (USA) *Stuart Williams* a83 79
6 b g Tale Of The Cat(USA) Notting Hill (BRZ) (Jules (USA))
179[3] (252) 560[9] (710) 1708[8] 2083[3] 2545[12] 4503[4] 5269[9] 5457[4] 5703[6] 6172[5] 7485[2] (7741)

Alderton (IRE) *Martyn Meade* a44 31
3 b f Red Clubs(IRE) Chantilly Beauty (FR) (Josr Algarhoud (IRE))
5448[4] 5949[7] 6254[4] 7275[10] 7322[8]

Aldo *Alastair Lidderdale* a70 69
5 b h Lucky Owners(NZ) Chaperone (Shaamit (IRE))
(847)

Aldo Bere (FR) *C Boutin* a77 88
2 b c Hurricane Cat(USA) Relicia Bere (FR) (Until Sundown (USA))
8192a[4]

Al Doha *Kevin Ryan* a19 52
3 ch f Iffraaj Lobby Card (USA) (Saint Ballado (CAN))
38[11] 270[11] 3275[5]

Aldwick Bay (IRE) *Richard Hannon* a82 90
4 b g Danehill Dancer(IRE) Josie Doocey (IRE) (Sadler's Wells (USA))
(1939) 2180[5] 3121[4] 4060[5] 4823[8] 6039[6] 6450[5] 6933[2] (7300) 7487[8]

Alejandro (IRE) *Richard Fahey* 94
3 b g Dark Angel(IRE) Carallia (IRE) (Common Grounds)
1457^{5} 1858^{12} 2276^{12} 2660^{5} 3626^{7} 4740^{14} 5334^{3} ◆ 5827^{4} 6143^{4} 6471^{6}

Aleksandar *Luca Cumani* a75 76
3 ch g Medicean Alexander Celebre (IRE) (Peintre Celebre (USA))
1486^{5} 2716^{6} ◆ 3345^{10} 5219^{2} ◆ 6098^{2} 6971^{5} (7380)

Al Emirati (IRE) *David Simcock* 72
2 b c Tamayuz Corrine (IRE) (Spectrum (IRE))
2571^{4} (6431)

Al Enbess (IRE) *David Simcock* 41
2 b c Kyllachy Taghreed (IRE) (Zamindar (USA))
7127^{8}

Alerted (USA) *Roger Charlton* a72 62
2 b f First Defence(USA) Alvernia (USA) (Alydar (USA))
5684^{5} ◆ 6366^{4}

Alexandrakollontai (IRE) *Alistair Whillans* a55 65
2 b f Amadeus Wolf Story (Observatory (USA))
2164^{6} 2609^{2} 3339^{11} 3858^{8} 4195^{5} 4462^{4} (5046) 5424^{2} 6121^{14} (6511) 6753^{10} 7242^{4}

Alexandre D'Or (FR) *Mme C Head-Maarek* a89 49
3 ch c Gold Away(IRE) Reine Annicka (FR) (Lord Of Men)
7803a^{0}

Alexs Rainbow (USA) *Luke Dace* a57 55
4 b m Silver Deputy(CAN) Swirling Sky (USA) (Sky Classic (CAN))
1702^{5} ◆ 2170^{14} 2555^{10} 3318^{7} 5974^{7} 6399^{10}

Alex Zara *Jim Goldie* 41
2 b f Moss Vale(IRE) Mysterious Plans (IRE) (Last Tycoon)
4132^{5} 4494^{13}

Alezanna *James Toller* a62
3 ch f Halling(USA) Denica (IRE) (Night Shift (USA))
7656^{6} (7981) 8213^{3}

Alfaisaliah (IRE) *J S Moore* a61
2 b f Red Clubs(IRE) Falcolnry (IRE) (Hawk Wing (USA))
7931^{5} 8044^{5} 8286^{3}

Al Faylasoof (USA) *David Simcock* a41 13
3 b c Lemon Drop Kid(USA) Mahhdooda (USA) (Forty Niner (USA))
1484^{6} 2393^{10}

Alfie Joe *Ron Hodges* a35 49
3 b g Bandmaster(USA) The Grey Bam Bam (Baryshnikov (AUS))
3005^{6} 3663^{8} 4154^{9} 4900^{6} 5261^{3} 6157^{9} 6274^{8}

Alfie's Rose *William Haggas* a51 51
2 b g Royal Applause Take The Plunge (Benny The Dip (USA))
5325^{8} 5684^{9} 6845^{8} 7414^{9}

Alfkona (GER) *Jozef Roszival* 90
4 b m Areion(GER) Ariana (GER) (Dashing Blade)
7697a^{7}

Alfraamsey *Sheena West* a78 75
4 b g Fraam Evanesce (Lujain (USA))
(2175) (2396) 3283^{2} (3572) 4215^{3} 4606^{6}

Alfred Hutchinson *Geoffrey Oldroyd* a99 85
4 ch g Monsieur Bond(IRE) Chez Cherie (Wolfhound (USA))
(273) 1134^{3} ◆ (2510) 6073^{13} 6405^{6} 7934^{2} 8095^{7} (8259)

Al Freej (IRE) *Roger Varian* a76
3 b f Iffraaj Why Now (Dansili)
181^{2} ◆ (481) 637^{4} 1331^{11}

Alfresco *John Best* a63 81
8 b g Mtoto Maureena (IRE) (Grand Lodge (USA))
669^{6} 893^{8} 2482^{11} 3660^{9} 4468^{9}

Al Furat (USA) *Ron Barr* a40 71
4 b g El Prado(IRE) No Frills (IRE) (Darshaan)
2260^{4} (2792) 3353^{5} 4499^{7} 4714^{9} 5290^{5} 6126^{10} 6478^{5} 7496^{12}

Algar (FR) *C Ferland* a72
2 gr c Slickly(FR) Vivartic (FR) (Verglas (IRE))
8176a^{3}

Al Gharrafa *Marco Botti* a62
2 b f Dutch Art Smart Ass (IRE) (Shinko Forest (IRE))
7987^{9} (8254)

Algorithmic (IRE) *Michael Bell* 58
2 b c Danehill Dancer(IRE) Tanami Desert (Lycius (USA))
7363^{5}

Alhaarth Beauty (IRE) *Ismail Mohammed* a67 71
2 b f Alhaarth(IRE) Endis (IRE) (Distant Relative)
4282^{6} 4701^{4} 5153^{4} 5511^{2} 6541^{6} 7410^{3} 7669^{2}

Alhaban (IRE) *Ronald Harris* a80 77
6 gr g Verglas(IRE) Anne Tudor (IRE) (Anabaa (USA))
146^{2} (225) 403^{6} (567) 655^{6} 760^{2} 909^{2} (967) 1087^{4} 1416^{12} 2510^{11} 4233^{4} 4889^{8} 5751^{6} 6141^{13}

Alhebayeb (IRE) *Richard Hannon* 105
2 gr c Dark Angel(IRE) Miss Indigo (Indian Ridge)
(2729) 3242^{2} ◆ (4008) 5398a^{11} 7404^{2}

Alhellal (IRE) *M Phelan* a83 89
6 b g Kalanisi(IRE) Zafayana (IRE) (Mark Of Esteem (IRE))
7051^{22}

Aliante *Mark Johnston* a71 76
3 ch f Sir Percy Alexandrine (IRE) (Nashwan (USA))
1055^{2} 2148^{3} 2425^{4} 2885^{6} 4294^{5} 4971^{2} (5226)

Alianthus (GER) *W Giedt* 117
7 b h Hernando(FR) Allure (GER) (Konigsstuhl (GER))
(1410a) 2521a^{2} 3425a^{6} 6291a^{5} 6906a^{2} 7515a^{11}

Alice Neney (IRE) *C Lerner* 66
2 b f Orpen(USA) Gulsenim (TUR) (Abrek (TUR))
6751a^{9} 7265a^{7} 7699a^{0}

Alice Rose (IRE) *Rae Guest* 73
3 ch f Manduro(GER) Bold Assumption (Observatory (USA))
3719^{3} 4436^{5} 4711^{9} 7600^{12}

Alice's Dancer (IRE) *William Muir* 86
3 br f Clodovil(IRE) Islandagore (IRE) (Indian Ridge)
1894^{6} 2503^{13} (3343) 4234^{2} 4723^{2} (5324) 5980^{6} 6375^{10} 6870^{12}

Alioonagh (USA) *Peter Makin* a41 48
5 ch m Giant's Causeway(USA) Alidiva (Chief Singer)
666^{12}

A Little Bit Dusty *Conor Dore* a84 83
4 ch g Needwood Blade Dusty Dazzler (IRE) (Titus Livius (FR))
2580^{2} 3231^{6} 3775^{15} (4959) 5809^{8} (5967) (7413) 7617^{7}

Alive And Kicking *Richard Fahey* a31 83
4 b g Compton Place Strawberry Dale (IRE) (Bering)
(1290) (1675) 2264^{4} 2825^{13} 3612^{10} 5021^{7} 6044^{17} 7411^{11} 8285^{11}

Al Jabreiah *William Haggas* a75 72
3 b f Bertolini(USA) Nihal (IRE) (Singspiel (IRE))
1322^{4} (1531) ◆ 2379^{5} 3643^{5}

Aljamaaheer (IRE) *Roger Varian* 114
3 ch c Dubawi(IRE) Kelly Nicole (IRE) (Rainbow Quest (USA))
1500^{4} (2277) 3265^{3} 4760^{3} ◆ 5573^{3}

Al Jamal *Saeed Bin Suroor* a75
2 b f Authorized(IRE) Kydd Gloves (USA) (Dubai Millennium)
(7720)

Al Janadeirya *Peter Chapple-Hyam* a74 76
4 b m Oasis Dream Elegant Times (IRE) (Dansili)
1824^{3} 2251^{7} 3568^{2} 5096^{2} (5448) 6378^{10}

Al Jasrah (IRE) *Kevin Ryan* 21
2 b f Shirocco(GER) Ultra Finesse (USA) (Rahy (USA))
6790^{12}

Aljosan *David Evans* 48
3 b f Compton Place Little Caroline (IRE) (Great Commotion (USA))
1413^{6}

Alkadi (IRE) *Mark Johnston* a74 77
3 b f Oasis Dream Vista Bella (Diktat)
(730) 1241^{2} 1392^{7} 1798^{2} 2331^{8} 2898^{6} 3230^{4} 3619^{6} 4256^{6} 4675^{5} (4961) 5338^{3} 5942^{2} 6176^{3} 6560^{4} 6973^{13} 7356^{11} 7618^{8}

Al Karlovyyh (IRE) *Clive Brittain* a44 58
3 b f Authorized(IRE) Karlovy (Halling (USA))
2249^{11} 2585^{7} (3978) 4198^{11} 4971^{5} 5974^{11}

Al Kazeem *Roger Charlton* 121
4 b h Dubawi(IRE) Kazeem (Darshaan)
(1855)

Alkazim (IRE) *David Wachman* a85 105
3 b c Holy Roman Emperor(IRE) Tumbleweed Pearl (Aragon)
1468^{6} 2514a^{8}

Alkcama (IRE) *John Weymes* 56
2 b g Camacho Alkifaf (USA) (Mtoto)
4587^{5} 6134^{8} 6708^{6}

Al Khaleej (IRE) *David Simcock* a101 97
8 b g Sakhee(USA) Mood Swings (IRE) (Shirley Heights)
1741^{3}

Al Khali (USA) *William Mott* a57 111
6 b r Medaglia d'Oro(USA) Maya (USA) (Capote (USA))
6299a^{2}

Al Khan (IRE) *Michael Easterby* a71 93
3 b g Elnadim(USA) Popolo (IRE) (Fasliyev (USA))
1858^{18} 3348^{11} 7651^{8} 8143^{8} 8238^{4} ◆

Al Khawaneej *David Simcock* a88 95
4 br h Arch(USA) Fraulein (Acatenango (GER))
(1421) (2411) 3241^{2}

Al Khisa (IRE) *Kevin Ryan* a22 63
2 b f Diamond Green(FR) Rectify (IRE) (Mujadil (USA))
1437^{6} 2450^{11} 3490^{4} 6952^{7} 7223^{8}

Alkimos (IRE) *Saeed Bin Suroor* a89 108
4 b g High Chaparral(IRE) Bali Breeze (IRE) (Common Grounds)
145a^{6} 486a^{3} 755a^{9} 3372^{4} 4112^{7} 5600^{15} 6576^{4}

Alkmaar *J Reynier* a77 82
5 b h Marchand De Sable(USA) Sarmatie (IRE) (Lyphard (USA))
18a^{0}

All About You (IRE) *John Butler* a74 84
6 b g Mind Games Expectation (IRE) (Night Shift (USA))
297^{5} (572) (926)

Allanit (GER) *Barney Curley* a72 72
8 b g Tiger Hill(IRE) Astilbe (GER) (Monsun (GER))
276^{3} 3594^{14} 3976^{5} 4405^{8}

All Annalena (IRE) *Lucy Wadham* 88
6 b m Dubai Destination(USA) Alla Prima (IRE) (In The Wings)
6848^{6} 7034^{2} 7375^{5}

Alla Speranza *J S Bolger* 109
3 gr f Sir Percy Alvarita (Selkirk (USA))
1884^{6} 2101a^{7} (6062a) 6518a^{10} 7423a^{8}

All By Myself *Robert Collet* a50 83
4 b h Galileo(IRE) Pride (FR) (Peintre Celebre (USA))
1172a^{0}

Allegra Byron *Jonathan Portman* a49 49
3 ch f Byron Colourflash (IRE) (College Chapel)
1492^{4} 1705^{7} 4506^{10} 5095^{14}

Allegra Tak (ITY) *H Rogers* a50 87
6 b m Invincible Spirit(IRE) No Tiktak (IRE) (Diktat)
4380a^{8} 6716a^{5}

Allez (FR) *A Lamotte D'Argy* a67
2 b c Hurricane Run(IRE) Aliyeska (IRE) (Fasliyev (USA))
5378a^{0}

All For You (GER) *P Harley* 93
3 b f Shirocco(GER) All About Love (GER) (Winged Love (IRE))
2531a^{5} 4862a^{12}

All For You (IRE) *Jim Goldie* a68 72
6 b m High Chaparral(IRE) Quatre Saisons (FR) (Homme De Loi (IRE))
2598^{3} 2840^{6} 4641^{8}

All Fur Coat *Jo Hughes* 84
2 b f Multiplex Elegant Lady (Selkirk (USA))
1164^{2} 1466^{2} (1972) 3269^{19} 5516^{9} 6424^{8} 6658^{8}

Allied Answer *Steve Gollings* 90
4 gr g Danehill Dancer(IRE) Hotelgenie Dot Com (Selkirk (USA))
7034^{U} 7109^{10} 7294^{3}

Allied Powers (IRE) *Michael Bell* a70 112
7 b g Invincible Spirit(IRE) Always Friendly (High Line)
1507^{2} (1971a) 2744a^{5} 3369^{8} 3857^{9} 5650a^{10} 6866^{5}

All My Heart *Sir Mark Prescott Bt* a91 96
4 gr m Sadler's Wells(USA) Alba Stella (Nashwan (USA))
2965a^{4} 3768a^{5}

Allnecessaryforce (FR) *Richard Fahey* 84
2 gr c Verglas(IRE) Kosmic View (USA) (Distant View (USA))
6133^{6} (6779) 7209^{4} 7292^{4}

All Nighter (IRE) *Jamie Snowden* a73 71
3 b g Bertolini(USA) Symbol Of Peace (IRE) (Desert Sun)
(182) 3767^{12}

All On Black *James Eustace* 65
3 b g Pastoral Pursuits Ishona (Selkirk (USA))
5555^{7}

All On Red (IRE) *Tobias B P Coles* 84
2 b f Red Clubs(IRE) Champion Tipster (Pursuit Of Love)
(1623) 1891^{2} (2238) 2715^{3} 3326^{13} 4058^{3} 4820^{17} 5828^{6} 6632^{9}

All Or Nothin (IRE) *John Quinn* a49 92
3 b g Majestic Missile(IRE) Lady Peculiar (CAN) (Sunshine Forever (USA))
1864^{3} (2470) (2979) 3607^{3} 4588^{6} (6663) 8272^{7}

All Right Now *Derek Haydn Jones* a83 64
5 b g Night Shift(USA) Cookie Cutter (IRE) (Fasliyev (USA))
131^{8} 351^{9} 1117^{6} ◆ 1342^{7} 1431^{4} 1587^{5} 2207^{9} 2405^{8} 6812^{5} 7142^{7}

All Shamar *W Hickst* 114
3 b c Shamardal(USA) All Glory (Alzao (USA))
1900a^{2} (3206a)

All Squared Away (USA) *Peter Miller* a106 106
3 bb g Bellamy Road(USA) Squared (USA) (Posse (USA))
7566a^{4} 7882a^{8}

All Star Heart (CAN) *Ronald McAnally* a94 109
5 b m Arch(USA) Gift Of The Heart (CAN) (Ascot Knight (CAN))
6298a^{2} 7093a^{8}

All Stormy (USA) *Greg Geier* 101
3 bb c Stormy Atlantic(USA) Allspice (USA) (Coronado's Quest (USA))
5375a^{7}

All That Remains (IRE) *Brian Ellison* a59
7 b g King's Theatre(IRE) Morning Breeze (IRE) (Bigstone (IRE))
6614^{4} 6839^{7} 7352^{5}

All That Rules *Thomas Carmody* a74 89
3 b c Galileo(IRE) Alba Stella (Nashwan (USA))
1456^{7} 6066a^{7}

All The Winds (GER) *Shaun Lycett* a88 83
7 ch g Samum(GER) All Our Luck (GER) (Spectrum (IRE))
187^{6} 2346^{4} 2921^{6} 3766^{8} 4962^{8} 8275^{8}

All Time *Sir Henry Cecil* a71 71
4 b m Dansili Clepsydra (Sadler's Wells (USA))
2891^{4} 3918^{4} 4780^{2} 5387^{3} (6215)

All Too Hard (AUS) *Michael, Wayne & John Hawkes* 119
3 b c Casino Prince(AUS) Helsinge (AUS) (Desert Sun)
7426a^{2}

Alluring Star *Michael Easterby* a59 73
4 b m Gentleman's Deal(IRE) Alustar (Emarati (USA))
1384^{10} 1823^{4} 2090^{2} 5671^{9} 6057^{6} 6455^{4} 6782^{9}

All Ways To Rome (FR) *H P Rosport* a80 55
8 b g Slickly(FR) Always On Time (Lead On Time (USA))
7701a^{0}

Almaas (USA) *Saeed Bin Suroor* a81 81
3 ch g Hard Spun(USA) Summer Dream Girl (USA) (Unbridled (USA))
2313^{14} 3606^{4} 4548^{6} 5329^{2} 6401^{10}

Almadaa *David Marnane* a80 60
5 b g Exceed And Excel(AUS) Masaader (USA) (Wild Again (USA))
335a^{3}

Almagest *John Gosden* 93
4 br g Galileo(IRE) Arabesque (Zafonic (USA))
4821^{4}

Al Mahmeyah *Richard Hannon* a76 76
3 b f Teofilo(IRE) Aguilas Perla (IRE) (Indian Ridge)
2820^{4} 6375^{9}

Almail (USA) *Jamie Osborne* a84 76
6 b g Swain(IRE) Khassah (Green Desert (USA))
846^{7} 1008^{3} 1374^{8} 2447^{7} 5359^{5} 5772^{8} 7380^{9}

Al Malek (FR) *Mario Hofer* a90 107
3 b c Anabaa(USA) Rouge (FR) (Red Ransom (USA))
1208a^{5} 2568a^{9} 7345a^{5}

Almalekiah (IRE) *J S Moore* a75 73
2 gr f Clodovil(IRE) Majestic Night (IRE) (Mujadil (USA))
4532^{2} ◆ 5146^{7} 5784^{2} 6330^{3} 6853a^{2} (7410)

Al Mamzar (IRE) *David Simcock* a76 65
3 b c Teofilo(IRE) Avila (Ajdal (USA))
2418^{2} 4464^{4} 5293^{DSQ}

Al Manaal *Saeed Bin Suroor* a69
2 b f Echo Of Light Mall Queen (USA) (Sheikh Albadou)
6533^{9} 7143^{3}

Almanack *T Stack* a91 74
2 b c Haatef(USA) Openness (Grand Lodge (USA))
1832a^{3} 3649a^{6}

Almaty Express *John Weymes* a67 54
10 b g Almaty(IRE) Express Girl (Sylvan Express)
498^{4} 664^{8} (939) 1387^{5} 1483^{2} (2352) 3943^{5} 4653^{11} 4928^{3} 5191^{5} 5808^{11} 6178^{10} 6836^{8}

Al Mayasah (IRE) *David Simcock* a87 86
4 b m Shamardal(USA) Mia Mambo (USA) (Affirmed (USA))
3085^{8} 4336^{9} 4933^{2} 5769^{2} 6367^{8}

Almirah *David Evans* a15 22
3 ch f Ishiguru(USA) Brogue Lanterns (IRE) (Dr Devious (IRE))
6001^{8} 6582^{12}

Almond Branches *George Moore* 82
3 ch f Dutch Art Queens Jubilee (Cayman Kai (IRE))
2824^{10} 3613^{7} (4208) 4451^{3} 4558^{3} 5603^{10} 6357^{4}

Almost An Angel (USA) *Wesley A Ward* a95 88
2 b f Artie Schiller(USA) Earthly Angel (USA) (Crafty Prospector (USA))
7548a^{8}

Almost Gemini (IRE) *Roger Varian* 52
3 gr g Dylan Thomas(IRE) Streetcar (IRE) (In The Wings)
1567^{8} 1976^{10} 2453^{5} 6101^{8}

Almudena (PER) *J Suarez Villarroel* a107 103
5 ch m Silver Planet(ARG) Fire Legend (ARG) (Engrillado (ARG))
7546a^{10}

Almuftarris (USA) *Ed Dunlop* a81 81
3 b g Smart Strike(CAN) Ranin (Unfuwain (USA))
(1312) 2269^{10} 2484^{4} 4601^{5} 5312^{4} 5990^{3} 6430^{7} (6988)

Al Muheer (IRE) *Ruth Carr* a79 96
7 b g Diktat Dominion Rose (USA) (Spinning World (USA))
1156^{16} 1587^{9} (1917) 2029^{5} (2285) 2489^{11} 3534^{10} 3626^{6} 3855^{2} 3911^{3} 4321^{13} ◆ 4589^{7} 4828^{2} 5057^{8} 5369^{5} 5517^{14} 6235^{7} 6426^{4} 6670^{4} 7210^{5}

Al Mukhdam *Peter Chapple-Hyam* 75
2 b c Exceed And Excel(AUS) Sakhya (IRE) (Barathea (IRE))
4595^{4} (5311) 6414^{5}

Al Muntazah (IRE) *Ronald Harris* 67
2 b c Dark Angel(IRE) Rihana (IRE) (Priolo (USA))
3074^{7} 3824^{4} 4532^{4} 7111^{8}

Almutaham (USA) *Martin Todhunter* 40
5 bb g Dynaformer(USA) Forest Lady (USA) (Woodman (USA))
4431^{6}

Alnair (IRE) *Declan Carroll* a59 64
3 b g Red Clubs(IRE) Danccini (IRE) (Dancing Dissident (USA))
905^{7} (4428) 4798^{9} 5923^{5} 6264^{8} 6713^{3} 7001^{7} 7146^{12}

Alnawiyah *John Dunlop* 77
2 b f Dalakhani(IRE) Mokaraba (Unfuwain (USA))
5104^{3} ◆ 5947^{5} 6790^{8}

Al Nawras *F Head* a71 95
3 ch c Monsun(GER) Thamarat (Anabaa (USA))
1171a^{6}

Alnitak (USA) *Bent Olsen* 85
11 br g Nureyev(USA) Very True (USA) (Proud Truth (USA))
3886a^{7} 4863a^{7}

Alnoomaas (IRE) *Luke Dace* a75 53
3 b g Oasis Dream Remarkable Story (Mark Of Esteem (IRE))
2542^{9} 3079^{10} 4232^{7} 5479^{7} 5625^{6} (5972) (6178) (6402) 6825^{6} 8159^{6} ◆

Aloha *Roger Varian* a56
2 b f With Approval(CAN) Almamia (Hernando (FR))
7506^{9} 7926^{8} 8102^{8}

Along Came Casey (IRE) *D K Weld* a100 92
4 b m Oratorio(IRE) Secretariat's Tap (USA) (Pleasant Tap (USA))
5609a^{5} 6855a^{2}

Aloof (IRE) *David Wachman* a97 107
3 b f Galileo(IRE) Airwave (Air Express (IRE))
2187a^{6} 5286a^{4} 5643a^{2} 6079a^{3} (6518a) 6855a^{3}

Alo Pura *D Selvaratnam* a103 97
8 b m Anabaa(USA) Rubies From Burma (USA) (Forty Niner (USA))
244a^{6} 420a^{3}

Aloysia *Sylvester Kirk* a40
3 b f Amadeus Wolf Anthea (Tobougg (IRE))
196^{6}

Alpha (USA) *Kiaran McLaughlin* a119
3 b c Bernardini(USA) Munnaya (USA) (Nijinsky (CAN))
1872a^{12} 7576a^{12}

Alpha Arion (IRE) *Tim Easterby* 53
3 ch g Cadeaux Genereux Sancia (IRE) (Docksider (USA))
2143^{9} 2592^{5} 2881^{4} 3939^{11} 4263^{7} 5000^{8} 5680^{5} 6103^{15}

Alpha Delta Whisky *John Gallagher* a71 78
4 ch g Intikhab(USA) Chispa (Imperial Frontier (USA))
1417^{11} 1773^{3} 2853^{6} 3541^{11} 4743^{2} 5123^{4} 5681^{11} 5971^{5} 6370^{5}

Alpha Tauri (USA) *Charles Smith* a84 56
6 b g Aldebaran(USA) Seven Moons (JPN) (Sunday Silence (USA))
286^{7} 560^{8} 585^{6} 722^{5} 884^{2} 1768^{6} (1958) 2405^{2} 2617^{9} 3731^{2} 4190^{2} 4262^{3} 4401^{6} 6233^{12} 7634^{10} 7732^{7}

Alphorn (FR) *Y Barberot* a83 73
4 b g Vatori(FR) Vallee De Joux (FR) (Welkin (CAN))
1172a^{2}

Alpine Jerry (IRE) *J S Moore* a46 53
2 b f Jeremy(USA) Champoluc (IRE) (Indian Ridge)
5061^{5} 5574^{8} 5968^{5} 6435^{3} 6893^{6}

Alpine Mysteries (IRE) *John Dunlop* a59
2 b f Elusive City(USA) Alpine Gold (IRE) (Montjeu (IRE))
3282^{11} 3764^{7} 4463^{6} 5206^{2} 5763^{6} 6363^{2}

Al Qatari (USA) *William Haggas* a47 57
3 bb g Dynaformer(USA) Where's The Church (USA) (Deputy Minister (CAN))
2196^{12} 3349^{12} 5329^{9} 5945^{9} 6399^{9}

Alraased (USA) *John Dunlop* a96 90
3 bb c Exchange Rate(USA) Alabaq (USA) (Riverman (USA))
3399[3] 4301[2] 5387[2] *(5970)* 6381[2] *(6979)* ◆ *7163[3]*

Alrasm (IRE) *E Charpy* a104 95
5 b g Acclamation New Deal (Rainbow Quest (USA))
243a[3] 591a[10]

Alsadaa (USA) *Laura Mongan* a89 87
9 b g Kingmambo(USA) Aljawza (USA) (Riverman (USA))
4216[6] 5158[6]

Al Saham *Saeed Bin Suroor* a94 94
3 b c Authorized(IRE) Local Spirit (USA) (Lion Cavern (USA))
2269[12] *3042[2]* 3509[4] (4796)

Alsahil (USA) *Micky Hammond* a91 80
6 ch g Diesis Tayibah (IRE) (Sadler's Wells (USA))
1525[3] 2214[14] 2676[4] (3728) 5383[7]

Al Sahraa *John Butler* a50
2 ch f Piccolo Desert Daisy (IRE) (Desert Prince (IRE))
7807[6] 8165[7]

Al Shababiya (IRE) *Alison Thorpe* a48 25
5 b m Dubawi(IRE) Multaka (USA) (Gone West (USA))
1433[6] 1559[7]

Alshan Fajer *Paul Howling* a43
2 ch g Lemon Drop Kid(USA) Illuminise (IRE) (Grand Lodge (USA))
8262[8]

Al Shaqab (IRE) *Kevin Ryan* a67 77
3 b g Amadeus Wolf Common Rumpus (IRE) (Common Grounds)
1176[6] 1758[8] 2459[6] 2795[14]

Al Sharood *Doug Watson* a99 102
4 b m Shamardal(USA) Massomah (USA) (Seeking The Gold (USA))
245a[5] 617a[4] 756a[3] 875a[6]

Alshazah *Rod Millman* a83 77
4 b g Haafhd Mountain Law (USA) (Mountain Cat (USA))
2447[8] 3187[10] 3920[11] 4706[7] 5239[5] (5983) 6544[5] 6801[2] *6976[7]*

Al Shemali *A Al Raihe* a100 105
8 ch h Medicean Bathilde (IRE) (Generous (IRE))
319a[3] ◆ 591a[3] *878a[9]*

Alsindi (IRE) *Clive Brittain* a98 105
3 b f Acclamation Needles And Pins (IRE) (Fasliyev (USA))
77a[2] 418a[3] 680a[3] 1699a[8] 6161[9]

Al Sirat *Michael Appleby* 53
6 b g Josr Algarhoud(IRE) Toleration (Petong)
1261[6] 2799[10]

Alsium (IRE) *P D Deegan* a66 73
3 b f Invincible Spirit(IRE) Sweet Firebird (IRE) (Sadler's Wells (USA))
7680a[11]

Al's Memory (IRE) *David Evans* a74 76
3 b g Red Clubs(IRE) Consensus (IRE) (Common Grounds)
1721[4] 2265[5] 2733[5] 3555[10] 4583[2] 5036[4] *5099[4] 5892[2] 6052[5]* 6488[11] 7395[2] 7436[10] 7684[7] *8074[2]* 8142[2]

Al Sulaimi (IRE) *Ronald Harris* a20
2 b c Jeremy(USA) Capital Gain (FR) (Bluebird (USA))
7199[10]

Alta Lilea (IRE) *Mark Johnston* 84
2 b f Galileo(IRE) In My Life (IRE) (Rainbow Quest (USA))
(6960) 7319a[3]

Altalus (SWE) *Christer Hederud*
3 bb c Singspiel(IRE) Veronese (USA) (Bianconi (USA))
3655a[5]

Altano (GER) *A Wohler* 114
6 b g Galileo(IRE) Alanda (GER) (Lando (GER))
(1901a) 2534a[8] 3768a[4] (6290a) 7427a[2]

Altaria *Amanda Perrett* a81
3 b f Rail Link Costa Rica (IRE) (Sadler's Wells (USA))
3622[2] 5154[2] 5477[2] 6839[5]

Alterite (FR) *J-C Rouget* 106
2 b f Literato(FR) Ana Luna (Dream Well (FR))
(5899a) 6909a[3] ◆

Altharoos (IRE) *Sir Michael Stoute* 79
2 br g Sakhee(USA) Thamara (USA) (Street Cry (IRE))
5303[3] ◆ 5992[2] (6558)

Al Thumama *Kevin Ryan* 60
2 b f Byron Tanwir (Unfuwain (USA))
5184[6] 6132[3] 6997[4]

Altnaharra *Jim Goldie* a37 53
3 b g Halling(USA) Gargoyle Girl (Be My Chief (USA))
1591[6] 2141[9] 3729[5] 4744[8] 7102[5]

Altona (IRE) *Mick Channon* a69 70
3 b f Redback Flawless (Warning)
920[3] 1190[9] 1906[5] 2431[7] 2999[5] 6814[6]

Altruism (IRE) *Mahmood Al Zarooni* 83
2 b c Authorized(IRE) Bold Assumption (Observatory (USA))
4472[13] (5321)

Alubari *Adrian McGuinness* a72 71
5 b g Tiger Hill(IRE) Why So Silent (Mill Reef (USA))
6184a[9] 6838[7]

Al Udeid (IRE) *Kevin Ryan* a80
2 gr g Verglas(IRE) Gold Strike (IRE) (Rainbow Quest (USA))
6609[4] (7198) 7614[5]

Alvar (USA) *M Halford* a59 20
4 ch g Forest Danger(USA) Diameter (USA) (Boundary (USA))
335a[7] 775a[8]

Alvitude (USA) *Roger Charlton* a66 71
3 b g Aptitude(USA) Alvernia (USA) (Alydar (USA))
1922[9] 2560[3] 3448[10] 4755[6] *6364[5]*

Al Waab (IRE) *Sir Henry Cecil* 103
2 ch c Danehill Dancer(IRE) Aunt Julia (In The Wings)
(4340) (5270) 6027[2] 6671[3]

Al Wajba (USA) *William Haggas* a64 86
3 ch f Ghostzapper(USA) Crystal Symphony (USA) (Red Ransom (USA))
1937[2] (2672) 4298[7] 4713[2] 5556[3] 6376[4]

Always Certain (AUS) *M Freedman* 107
6 b g Not A Single Doubt(AUS) Akarana (AUS) (Akaaber (USA))
590a[10] 758a[9]

Always De One *K F Clutterbuck* a48 49
5 b m Fruits Of Love(USA) Yes Virginia (USA) (Roanoke (USA))
741[8]

Always Dixie (IRE) *Andrew Crook* a40 57
5 b m Lucky Story(USA) Jerre Jo Glanville (USA) (Skywalker (USA))
111[5] 1092[9]

Always Eager *Mark Johnston* a66 62
3 b g With Approval(CAN) Slew The Moon (ARG) (Kitwood (USA))
726[4] 973[4] (1424) 3727[7] *4586[8] 5052[10]* 5991[12] 6304[2] *6690[6] 7062[4] 7417[9]*

Always Ends Well (IRE) *Mark Johnston* a64 65
3 b f Tiger Hill(IRE) Awwal Malika (USA) (Kingmambo (USA))
1303[2] 1486[8] 1982[14] 2283[9] *2497[2] 2850[10]* 3275[8] *3620[10] 3938[10]*

Always The Lady *Clive Cox* a57 88
4 ch m Halling(USA) Hector's Girl (Hector Protector (USA))
1513[2] ◆ 2180[12] 4879[9] 6667[7] 7519[6] *7810[12]*

Alwilda *Sir Mark Prescott Bt* a73 56
2 gr f Hernando(FR) Albanova (Alzao (USA))
4946[4] 5184[5] *(7349)*

Alzavola *Sir Mark Prescott Bt* a58 15
2 gr f With Approval(CAN) Alizadora (Zilzal (USA))
6132[7] *7460[6] 7796[4]*

Al Zein *Richard Hannon* a53 12
2 b c Notnowcato Luminda (IRE) (Danehill (USA))
4846[9] *6533[8]*

Amaan (USA) *J-C Rouget* a84 100
3 ch c Nayef(USA) Saleela (USA) (Nureyev (USA))
1208a[10]

Amadeus Denton (IRE) *Michael Dods* a63 84
3 b g Amadeus Wolf Wood Sorrel (IRE) (Woodman (USA))
1524[6] 2509[8] 2824[12] 5167[7] 6357[6] *7775[10] 7937[3] 8285[10]*

Amadeus Wolfe Tone (IRE) *Jamie Osborne* a100 99
3 b g Amadeus Wolf Slieve (Selkirk (USA))
2785[4] 3063[4] 3393[2] 4298[4] (4607) 5363[4] ◆ (6165) 6466[13] *7503[2]*

Amana (USA) *Mark Brisbourne* a53 76
8 b m Diesis Ma-Arif (IRE) (Alzao (USA))
1485[7] 2454[2]

Amancaya (GER) *W Hickst* a83
5 b m Dai Jin Autriche (IRE) (Acatenango (GER))
94a[7]

Amandara (USA) *D Prod'Homme* a90 97
4 ch m Aragorn(IRE) Dixie Linedancer (USA) (Dixieland Band (USA))
83a[0]

Amantius *John Spearing* 39
3 b g Multiplex Ghana (GER) (Bigstone (IRE))
6965[7] *7249[8] 7654[11]*

Amaraja (GER) *Sir Henry Cecil* a75 93
3 b f Galileo(IRE) Apsara (FR) (Darshaan)
1502[8] 2008[3] *3279[4]* (3773) 4738[8] 6677[13]

Amare *P Harley* 100
5 b m Hernando(FR) Amore (GER) (Lando (GER))
2805a[2] 4386a[6] 6723a[5]

Amarillo (IRE) *P Schiergen* 111
3 b c Holy Roman Emperor(IRE) Alte Kunst (IRE) (Royal Academy (USA))
2568a[2] 3425a[2] 4130a[3] 5782a[4] 6727a[2]

Amaron *Andreas Lowe* 113
3 ch c Shamardal(USA) Amandalini (Bertolini (USA))
(1553a) 2110a[4] 2743a[17] 5782a[5] (6727a)

Amaroni *John E Long* a19 29
4 b g Sulamani(IRE) Fortunes Favourite (Barathea (IRE))
3227[14]

Amaze *Brian Ellison* 88
4 ch g Pivotal Dazzle (Gone West (USA))
(2826) 3493[14] 6630[2] (7002)

Amazing Amoray (IRE) *David Barron* 85
4 b g Tagula(IRE) Amistad (GER) (Winged Love (IRE))
1156[10] 2274[3] 2597[7] 5910[4] ◆ (6119)

Amazing Beauty (GER) *M Figge* a96 99
5 ch m Bahamian Bounty Amidala (GER) (Monsagem (USA))
953a[8]

Amazing Blue Sky *Ruth Carr* a71 84
6 b g Barathea(IRE) Azure Lake (USA) (Lac Ouimet (USA))
1134[13] 1275[16] 1525[2] 1657[5] (1913) 2241[5] 2419[10] 2921[7] 3253[4] (3386) 3628[3] 3906[3] 4249[6] 4745[7] 5224[8] 6073[17] 6884[12] 7131[8]

Amazing King (IRE) *Philip Kirby* a68 86
8 b g King Charlemagne(USA) Kraemer (USA) (Lyphard (USA))
(2457) 3377[6]

Amazing Star (IRE) *Declan Carroll* a84 85
7 b g Soviet Star(USA) Sadika (IRE) (Bahhare (USA))
(1117) 1354[6] *1587[7]* 1670[8] 1863[4] 2536[7] 2913[2] 3609[6] 4345[14] 6410[9] 7003[7] 7246[6]

Amazing Storm (IRE) *Jo Hughes* a92 92
3 b g Clodovil(IRE) Forest Storm (USA) (Woodman (USA))
1217[2] 1457[6] 4740[16] 5080[6]

Amazing Tiger (GER) *Peter Jardby* a87 64
6 b g Tiger Hill(IRE) Allure (GER) (Konigsstuhl (GER))
(3654a)

Amazing Win (IRE) *Mick Channon* a68 68
4 b m Marju(IRE) Aqaba (Lake Coniston (IRE))
474[9] 665[2] 781[6] (819) 970[3] 1049[3] 1306[2] 1497[4] 1910[5] 2244[6] (2413) 2538[2] 2618[2] (2647) 2994[3] 3103[4] (3210) 3724[9]

Amazombie (USA) *Bill Spawr* a125 108
6 b g Northern Afleet(USA) Wilshe Amaze (USA) (In Excess)
7574a[8]

Amazonas (IRE) *Ed Dunlop* 100
2 b f Cape Cross(IRE) Francesca D'Gorgio (USA) (Proud Citizen (USA))
(2797) 3326[4] 4514[5] 5571[3] 6635[3]

Amazon Twilight *Brett Johnson* a77 76
4 b m Librettist(USA) My Way (IRE) (Marju (IRE))
746[3] 991[11] 1300[2] 1614[11] 4300[5] 5122[2] *5791[7] 6934[11] 7308[5]*

Amba *Violet M Jordan* a73 77
6 ch m Hold That Tiger(USA) Gal Gloria (PR) (Tralos (USA))
1358[11] 2466[6] 3467[2] *3738[6] 4468[5]* (4584) (4812) *7356[5]*

Ambala *Chris Wall* a73 77
4 b m Intikhab(USA) Mighty Splash (Cape Cross (IRE))
2233[4] ◆ 2915[4] (4411)

Amber Heights *Henry Candy* a65 65
4 b m Kyllachy Jumairah Sun (IRE) (Scenic)
878 1734[2] 2170[9] 3466[8] 5279[4] (6233) 6788[5] 7179[8]

Amberley (FR) *Mlle S-V Tarrou* a74 49
3 b g Anabaa(USA) Desert Jewel (USA) (Caerleon (USA))
7803a[9]

Amberley Heights (IRE) *Richard Hannon* 76
2 b f Elnadim(USA) Fawaayid (USA) (Vaguely Noble)
(4055)

Amber Moon *Ann Stokell* a50 49
7 ch m Singspiel(IRE) Merewood (USA) (Woodman (USA))
1961[4] 2401[9] 2859[6] 3941[9] 4142[6] 4406[6] 5015[10] 8265[8]

Amber Silk (IRE) *Charles Hills* a67 84
3 b f Lawman(FR) Faraday Light (IRE) (Rainbow Quest (USA))
(2448) 3476[8] 4702[8] 5420[6] 6375[7] 7520[7]

Ambitious Boy *Reg Hollinshead* a73 73
3 bl g Striking Ambition Cherished Love (IRE) (Tomba)
41[4] 231[8] 2470[9] *2862[2]* 3218[7] 4965[3] (5454) (5831) *6211[3]* 6488[10]

Ambitious Dragon (NZ) *A T Millard* 125
6 b g Pins(AUS) Golden Gamble (NZ) (Oregon (USA))
1148a[7] 1902a[4] (8042a)

Ambitious Icarus *Richard Guest* a63 74
3 b g Striking Ambition Nesting Box (Grand Lodge (USA))
491[5] 769[10] 1758[6] 2595[2] 3050[8] 3357[2] 3566[5] 4348[2] 5000[4] 5538[5] 6264[3] 6529[2] (6788) 7100[4] ◆ 7489[8]

Ambivalent (IRE) *Roger Varian* a69 106
3 b f Authorized(IRE) Darrery (Darshaan)
(3080) 4338[3] (4848) 6163[5] 6911a[12]

Ambrose Princess (IRE) *Michael Scudamore* a45 80
7 b m Chevalier(IRE) Mark One (Mark Of Esteem (IRE))
1272[2] *1925[6]*

Amelia Hull *J S Moore* a54 10
2 b f Byron Sweetypie (IRE) (Golan (IRE))
7491[9] *7786[4] (7854) 8003[6] 8186[4]*

Amelia Jay *Danielle McCormick* a21 55
2 b f Avonbridge Rainbow Spectrum (FR) (Spectrum (IRE))
2450[12] 2837[7] 3520[2] 3776[9] 4637[7] 5041[5] *5716[8]* 6283[5] 6524[3] 6952[4] 7432[6]

Amelia May *Ed Vaughan* a78 80
3 b f Dansili Rebecca Sharp (Machiavellian (USA))
5322[2] 5837[11] *6613[4] 7416[3] 7656[4]*

Amelia's Surprise *M Delzangles* a96 58
4 b m Ad Valorem(USA) Salagama (IRE) (Alzao (USA))
83a[6]

Amelkis (FR) *J-V Toux* a72 70
7 gr m Take Risks(FR) Island Lady (FR) (Cardoun (FR))
92a[4]

Amen (IRE) *Gary Moore* a51 73
4 b g Galileo(IRE) Kitza (IRE) (Danehill (USA))
4504[12]

Amenable (IRE) *Violet M Jordan* a71 90
5 b g Bertolini(USA) Graceful Air (IRE) (Danzero (AUS))
1220[11] 2284[10] 2707[13] 3496[8] 4133[8] (5539) 6465[20] 7295[9] *7716[7] 8036[6] 8202[5] 8246[3] 8294[3]*

Americain (USA) *A De Royer-Dupre* 127
7 bb h Dynaformer(USA) America (IRE) (Arazi (USA))
5400a[6] 7264a[4] 7621a[11]

American Bling (USA) *Gary Moore* a31
3 b g Johannesburg(USA) American Jewel (USA) (Quiet American (USA))
1704[11] 2496[10]

American Devil (FR) *J Van Handenhove* 111
3 b c American Post Alcestes Selection (Selkirk (USA))
2064a[6] 3657a[4] 4861a[4] 6088a[10]

American Folie (FR) *K Borgel* a58
3 b f Gentlewave(IRE) Folle Envie (FR) (Un Desperado (FR))
475a[11]

American Impact (USA) *Tony Coyle* 67
2 bb c Rock Hard Ten(USA) Flip Side (USA) (Devil His Due (USA))
4433[3] (5053) 5488[5] 5920[8]

American Lover (FR) *John Wainwright* a54 63
5 b m American Post Lovarisk (FR) (Take Risks (FR))
46[5] 66[F] 1439[9] *1717[4]* 2091[6] 3416[8] *3712[2] 4890[4]* 5171[10] *5804[3] 6174[9]* 6361[3] *8151[4]* 8239[4]

American Saga (FR) *M Delzangles* a81 81
3 gr f American Post Saga D'Or (FR) (Sagacity (FR))
4477a[4] *7803a[3]*

American Spin *Luke Dace* a74 70
8 ch g Groom Dancer(USA) Sea Vixen (Machiavellian (USA))
521[3]

American Trilogy (IRE) *Paul Nicholls* 30
8 gr g Sendawar(IRE) Affaire Classee (FR) (Anabaa (USA))
3373[14]

Amethyst Dawn (IRE) *Alan McCabe* a69 91
6 gr m Act One A L'Aube (IRE) (Selkirk (USA))
1987 3781[1] 753[5] 3192[5] 3388[4] 3581[5] 4150[8] 5547[4] *6217[2] 6456[2] (7055)*

Ami Ami Chair *D Ducci* 61
4 b m Trade Fair Belle De Nuit (IRE) (Statoblest)
1409a[12]

Amicale (FR) *M Pimbonnet* 48
2 bb f American Post Conical (Zafonic (USA))
4205a[10]

Amico Fritz (GER) *H-A Pantall* a89 109
6 b h Fasliyev(USA) Arctic Appeal (IRE) (Ahonoora)
2325a[4] 3603a[6] *7123a[2]* 7551a[4]

Amiens *A Fabre* 103
3 b c Galileo(IRE) Dordogne (USA) (Thunder Gulch (USA))
6087a[4]

Amigo Tonio (FR) *Robert Collet* a70 85
2 b c Falco(USA) Veliana (FR) (Vettori (IRE))
7283a[7]

Amirah (IRE) *Tony Carroll* a61 64
2 b f Holy Roman Emperor(IRE) Nadwah (USA) (Shadeed (USA))
4494[6] 4960[9] *5943[8]* 6438[5] *7650[9]*

Amira's Prince (IRE) *David Wachman* 101
3 br c Teofilo(IRE) Twice The Ease (Green Desert (USA))
1468[4]

Amir Pasha (UAE) *Micky Hammond* a42 71
7 br g Halling(USA) Clarinda (IRE) (Lomond (USA))
600[7] 1297[10] 1562[8] 3061[6] 3437[4] 3752[3] 4455[8] 5039[3] 5735[5] 6956[10]

Amis Reunis *Anthony Carson* a61 78
3 b f Bahamian Bounty Spring Clean (FR) (Danehill (USA))
1331[8] 2194[11] 2846[8] 3547[5] (5203) 5681[4] *5975[6]* 7314[4] *7776[5] 7992[3] 8177[6]*

Amistress *Eve Johnson Houghton* a35 80
4 b m Kalanisi(IRE) Atwirl (Pivotal)
1418[12] 2414[6] 3793[5] 4470[6] 5197[3] 5441[5] 6229[7]

Amitola (IRE) *David Barron* a95 88
5 ch m Choisir(AUS) Emly Express (IRE) (High Estate)
29[7] (426) 785[4] 868[6] 1130[17] *1373[9]*

Amno Dancer (IRE) *Ian Semple* a53 62
5 b g Namid Special Dancer (Shareef Dancer (USA))
752[8] 927[8] 1387[4] 1801[9] 1876[7] 2037[5] 2458[5] 2618[3] 2839[6] 3893[8] 4392[2] 4593[3] 5087[9] 5919[3] *6179[5]*

A Moment With You (IRE) *F-X De Chevigny* a80 81
4 b m Redback Alexander Capetown (IRE) (Fasliyev (USA))
15a[9]

Among Equals *A P O'Brien* a87 98
3 b c Oasis Dream First (Highest Honor (FR))
4354a[3] 6917a[4]

Amoralist *Ed Dunlop* a74 78
3 b g Tobougg(IRE) Ellablue (Bahamian Bounty)
1557[7] 2898[3] *3736[11]* 4544[7]

Amosite *J R Jenkins* a69 69
6 b m Central Park(IRE) Waterline Dancer (IRE) (Danehill Dancer (IRE))
881[1] 2493[2] (3546) 4969[5] 5915[12] *7589[9] 7917[4] 8156[2] 8305[5]*

Amoure Medici *Ann Duffield* a91 75
3 b g Medicean Lifetime Romance (IRE) (Mozart (IRE))
2331[9] *3284[5]* 4624[2] ◆ 4954[8] *(5893)* ◆ *6319[3] (6610) 7145[2]*

Amour Fou (IRE) *W T Farrell* a56 72
4 b m Piccolo Elm Dust (Elmaamul (USA))
6270a[8] *7742[9]*

Amourous (IRE) *Tim Easterby* 24
2 b f Captain Marvelous(IRE) Amorous Pursuits (Pursuit Of Love)
1164[8] 1594[7]

Amour Propre *Henry Candy* 114
6 ch g Paris House Miss Prim (Case Law)
2664[4] 3238[22] 4762[10] 6116[4]

Amoya (GER) *Philip McBride* a82 87
5 b m Royal Dragon(USA) Arkona (GER) (Aspros (GER))
1652[9] 2199[14] (2465) 2801[6] 3594[5] 4199[6] (4578) 4822[5] 5218[2] 5856[6] 6236[7]

Amphora *Andrew Balding* a67 71
3 b f Oasis Dream Carafe (Selkirk (USA))
1449[4] 1730[5] 2503[5] 3343[4] 3488[3]

Ampleforth *Ian Williams* a76 79
4 ch g Pivotal Anna Amalia (IRE) (In The Wings)
361[3] 1923 ◆ 3386[3] 3997[5] 4475[2] 4731[3] 5798[3] *7744[10]*

Amralah (IRE) *Mick Channon* 83
2 b c Teofilo(IRE) Sharp Mode (USA) (Diesis)
4362[5] (7517)

Amtired *Brian Ellison* a65 58
6 gr g Beauchamp King Rising Talisker (Primitive Rising (USA))
8139[6]

Amulet *David Simcock* a57 65
2 gr f Ishiguru(USA) Loveofmylife (Dr Fong (USA))
6301[4] *6978[5]* 7329[4]

Amy Dorrit *John Gosden* a67 78
3 b f Pivotal Fascination Street (IRE) (Mujadil (USA))
1985[4] 2194[16] 2846[9] 3643[4]

Anabaa Stone (FR) *T Clout* a66 74
3 b f Anabaa(USA) Fancy Stone (IRE) (Rainbow Quest (USA))
17a[9]
Anabedweyah (IRE) *Clive Brittain* a75 60
3 b f Authorized(IRE) Al Kamah (USA) (Kingmambo (USA))
2079[7]
Anaconda (FR) *Tom Dascombe* a102 71
3 b c Anabaa(USA) Porretta (IRE) (Indian Ridge)
(1068) 8226[2] ◆
Ana Emaratiya *Kevin Ryan* a72 80
2 b f Sleeping Indian Vale Of Belvoir (IRE) (Mull Of Kintyre (USA))
2252[10] 2631[4] 3326[7] 4637[6]
Anaerobio (ARG) *M F De Kock* a81 108
5 b h Catcher In The Rye(IRE) Potra Anaia (ARG) (Potrillon (ARG))
51a[9] 246a[5] 489a[2] *587a[10]* 792a[3]
Anakin Skywalker (GER) *P Vovcenko* 101
3 b c Soldier Hollow Aughamore Beauty (IRE) (Dara Monarch)
3683a[9] 5250a[8]
Anam Allta (IRE) *D K Weld* 113
4 b m Invincible Spirit(IRE) Kiltubber (IRE) (Sadler's Wells (USA))
1041a[11]
Ana Shababiya (IRE) *Ismail Mohammed* a46 51
2 ch f Teofilo(IRE) Call Later (USA) (Gone West (USA))
2492[4] 2929[9] 4507[7] *5161[4]* *5763[9]*
Anatol Artist (GER) *Uwe Ostmann* 97
2 b c Doyen(IRE) Anna Spectra (IRE) (Spectrum (IRE))
7091a[2] 7698a[6]
Anatolian *Mahmood Al Zarooni* 108
4 ch g Pivotal Poseidon's Bride (USA) (Seeking The Gold (USA))
1882[8] 2933[2] 3372[13]
Anatolien (FR) *J-L Gay*
2 b c Anatoly(USA) Hollandia (FR) (Saumarez)
5378a[0]
Anaxis (FR) *S Wattel* a101 103
5 ch g Muhtathir Monadis (USA) (Miswaki (USA))
7985a[10]
An Cat Dubh (IRE) *Ian Williams* a80 83
3 b g One Cool Cat(USA) Bella Estella (GER) (Sternkoenig (IRE))
(5335) 6488[6]
Ancient Cross *Michael Easterby* a73 107
8 b g Machiavellian(USA) Magna Graecia (IRE) (Warning)
1157[9] 2208[10] 2507[8] 4073[8] 5487[6] 6244[5] 6466[10] 7063[6] 7243[2] 7366[2]
Ancient Greece *George Baker* a83 80
5 b g Pivotal Classicism (USA) (A.P. Indy (USA))
1087[7] 1680[12] 6545[2] 6931[6] *(7805)* *7986[3]*
Andalieb *David Simcock* a76 83
3 b c Zamindar(USA) Sakhya (IRE) (Barathea (IRE))
2246[5] (2883) 4097[6] 4997[4] 6931[5]
Anderiego (IRE) *David O'Meara* 98
4 b g Invincible Spirit(IRE) Anna Frid (GER) (Big Shuffle (USA))
2243[4] 2488[7] 2632[2] 3169[5] 3615[2] (4110) (4557) 5517[8] 6242[2] 6674[16] 7030[7] 7240[17]
Anderton (IRE) *Richard Fahey* 75
2 b g Invincible Spirit(IRE) Alarme Belle (Warning)
5410[4] 6360[3] 7031[2]
Andiamo Via *Michael Smith* a72 65
5 b g Mujahid(USA) Efizia (Efisio)
115[3] *(371)* ◆ *585[3]* *834[7]* 2924[11]
Andolini (GER) *A Wohler* 104
3 bb c Kallisto(GER) Auenpracht (GER) (General Assembly (USA))
2966a[6] 3683a[6] (5402a) 7282a[8]
Andorn (GER) *Philip Kirby* a70 71
8 b h Monsun(GER) Anthyllis (GER) (Lycius (USA))
2775[10] 5114[6]
Andrasta *Alan Berry* a45 55
7 b m Bertolini(USA) Real Popcorn (IRE) (Jareer (USA))
1601[7] 2032[5] 2120[6] 2839[7] 3026[12] 3523[6] 3893[10] 6530[7] 6958[15]
Andreas (GER) *Markus Klug* 86
3 ch c Dr Fong(USA) Annouche (GER) (Unfuwain (USA))
2966a[7]
Andromeda Galaxy (FR) *Sir Henry Cecil* 109
4 b m Peintre Celebre(USA) Arlesienne (IRE) (Alzao (USA))
1766a[8] 2570a[4] 6518a[6] 7449a[5]
Aneedh *William Haggas* a72 42
2 b g Lucky Story(USA) Seed Al Maha (USA) (Seeking The Gold (USA))
6636[13] *7199[2]*
Anegreen (ITY) *S Botti* 102
3 ch f Ekraar(USA) Sopran Danzas (ITY) (Astronef)
2522a[2]
Angela's Dream (IRE) *G M Lyons* a75 83
2 b f Chineur(FR) Church Mice (IRE) (Petardia)
1118a[2]
Angel Bright (IRE) *D K Weld* 81
3 b f Dark Angel(IRE) Cover Girl (IRE) (Common Grounds)
3645a[7]
Angel Cake (IRE) *Michael Appleby* a59 54
3 b f Dark Angel(IRE) Royal Jelly (King's Best (USA))
114[6] *204[3]* *288[5]* *619[3]* *923[9]* 1740[5] *2495[3]* 2788[7] *3233[3]* *3710[3]* *4214[3]* 4538[6] 4744[6] 5208[3] 7314[6] 7470[5] 7615[4] (7983) ◆ 8111[5]
Angelena Ballerina (IRE) *Dai Williams* a68 70
5 ch m Indian Haven Nom Francais (First Trump)
480[10] *600[6]* *721[5]* *929[10]* *1092[4]* 1154[13] 1496[6] *2348[12]*
Angel Gabrial (IRE) *Ian Williams* a77 94
3 b g Hurricane Run(IRE) Causeway Song (USA) (Giant's Causeway (USA))
107[3] *195[3]* *362[2]* 2866[4] 3558[2] (4515) 5006[4] (5273) 6025[6] 6677[9] ◆

Angel Grigio *Bryan Smart* a49 36
2 gr f Dark Angel(IRE) Owdbetts (IRE) (High Estate)
2537[6] 6335[8] 6627[8] 7441[6] *7609[6]* *7797[4]*
Angelic Note (IRE) *Brian Meehan* a63 54
3 b f Excellent Art Evangeline (Sadler's Wells (USA))
2849[6] 3345[11] *4153[8]*
Angelic Upstart (IRE) *Andrew Balding* a87 77
4 b g Singspiel(IRE) Rada (IRE) (Danehill (USA))
1342[2] ◆ *1633[2]* 2274[5] 4317[11] *(4889)* *5480[3]* *6013[2]* *7163[8]* *7751[5]* *7920[3]*
Angelito *Ed McMahon* a82 78
3 ch g Primo Valentino(IRE) Supreme Angel (Beveled (USA))
3702[3] 4456[2] (5505) (5934) *6689[3]*
Angel Kiss (IRE) *Colin Teague* 50
3 b f Dark Angel(IRE) Sharplaw Destiny (IRE) (Petardia)
1817[9] 2595[6] 3275[13] *3706[10]*
Angel Of Harlem (FR) *H-A Pantall* a89 94
4 b m Holy Roman Emperor(IRE) Music Express (FR) (Compton Place)
83a[0]
Angel Of Mercy *Julia Feilden*
4 b m Green Tune(USA) Hula Queen (USA) (Irish River (FR))
2800[7]
Angelo Poliziano *George Foster* a70 83
6 ch g Medicean Helen Sharp (Pivotal)
62[2] *870[4]* *1187[4]* 2122[2] 2230[6] 2841[10] 3109[5] 3276[4] 3523[4] 4430[6] 5190[6] 5923[12] 6264[9] 6713[4] 6958[2] 7099[2] 7456[2] (7673) (7970) 8144[3]
Angels Calling *Mrs K Burke* a33 60
2 b f Multiplex Angel Voices (IRE) (Tagula (IRE))
3533[3] 4778[4] *5424[12]* (6283) 6629[6]
Angel's Pursuit (IRE) *David Marnane* a113 100
5 ch g Pastoral Pursuits Midnight Angel (Machiavellian (USA))
80a[2] *420a[8]*
Angels Will Fall (IRE) *Charles Hills* 107
3 b f Acclamation Coconut Squeak (Bahamian Bounty)
2559[3] (3375) ◆ 4762[5] 5561[13] 6485[8] ◆ 6878[3]
Angel Warrior (IRE) *Ben Haslam* a40 59
3 b g Dark Angel(IRE) Red Slipper (IRE) (Alzao (USA))
407[6] *641[6]* 2668[5]
Angel Way (IRE) *Denis W Cullen* 77
3 b f Trans Island Zilayah (USA) (Zilzal (USA))
(5878)
An Ghalanta (IRE) *J S Bolger* a88 95
3 b f Holy Roman Emperor(IRE) Alamanta (IRE) (Ali-Royal (IRE))
1944a[4]
Angilina *Kevin Ryan* a42 52
2 b f Teofilo(IRE) Finnmark (Halling (USA))
5339[10] 7205[4] *7780[10]*
Anginola (IRE) *David Evans* a68 63
3 b f Kodiac Lady Montekin (Montekin)
(194) *362[4]* *547[5]* *727[4]* 3246[5] 3469[7] (4147) 5152[6] 5419[5] *6323[9]*
Angus Og *Mrs K Burke* 79
2 b g Pastoral Pursuits Winter Moon (Mujadil (USA))
(6122) 6984[5]
Animal Kingdom (USA) *H Graham Motion* a126 123
4 ch h Leroidesanimaux(BRZ) Dalicia (GER) (Acatenango (GER))
7575a[2]
Aniseed (IRE) *William Haggas* a99 99
3 gr f Dalakhani(IRE) Anna Karenina (USA) (Atticus (USA))
1532[3] 2178[5] *(4648)* 5519[5] 6379[2] 6877[4] *7510[3]*
Anjaz (USA) *Saeed Bin Suroor* a103 96
3 b f Street Cry(IRE) Playful Act (IRE) (Sadler's Wells (USA))
4608[6] 5089[4] 6380[3] *7168[5]* *(7751)*
Anjomarba (IRE) *Conor Dore* a67 75
5 b m Tillerman Golden Charm (IRE) (Common Grounds)
102[8] *154[5]* *687[6]* *828[4]* *926[6]* *1387[2]* *1788[4]* *2170[12]* 2973[3] 3181[5] 3442[7] 3701[3] 3943[10] 4196[3] 4436[7]
Anjuna Beach (USA) *Gary Moore* a71 68
2 b c Artie Schiller(USA) Hidden Temper (USA) (Miswaki (USA))
4803[9] *5478[2]* *7507[5]* *7796[2]*
Annabella Milbanke *John Holt* a6 29
2 ch f Byron Sophie'Jo (Agnes World (USA))
5291[6] 6115[14] *6826[8]*
Anna Isabella *Derek Shaw* a5
2 b f Byron Florentine Lady (Medicean)
4651[9] *4886[6]* *5242[10]*
Anna Law (IRE) *Charles Hills* 41
2 b f Lawman(FR) Portelet (Night Shift (USA))
4011[16] 4825[13] 6443[11] 6850[7]
Annaley My Darling (IRE) *Jo Hughes* a68
2 b f Shamardal(USA) Unreal (Dansili)
1629[2] 1997[8] *5748[2]*
Annalova *Richard Fahey* a41 23
2 b f Araafa(IRE) Danalova (Groom Dancer (USA))
4625[7] *5176[4]* 5727[5] 6335[11]
Annaluna (IRE) *David Evans* a57 61
3 b f Whipper(USA) Annaletta (Belmez (USA))
6280[2] 7271[3] *7862[4]*
Anna's Arch (IRE) *Alan Swinbank* 72
5 b g Arch(USA) Lady Angharad (IRE) (Tenby)
2288[6] 2877[2] 3181[5] 3750[3] 4626[4] 4925[3]
Anna's Pearl *Ralph Beckett* 110
2 ch c Pivotal Mi Anna (GER) (Lake Coniston (IRE))
5578[2] ◆ 6423[2] 6874[4] 7514a[2]
Annecdote *Jonathan Portman* 84
2 b f Lucky Story(USA) May Fox (Zilzal (USA))
2499[4] ◆ 3473[2] (5274) 6160[4] ◆ (6675)
Annelko *Michael Blake* a65 64
5 b g Sulamani(IRE) Creeking (Persian Bold)
5196[7] 5817[4] 6097[4] *6616[2]* *7252[2]* ◆ *7528[2]* *7869[6]* *8189[3]*

Annes Rocket (IRE) *Jimmy Fox* a67 76
7 b h Fasliyev(USA) Aguilas Perla (IRE) (Indian Ridge)
1447[4] 2421[3] 3511[13] (4517) 5120[3] 5993[5] (6277)
Annia Galeria (IRE) *T Le Brocq* a54 35
5 b m Antonius Pius(USA) Jay Gee (IRE) (Second Set (IRE))
2114a[6]
Annie Beach (IRE) *David Barron* 95
3 ch f Redback Kiva (Indian Ridge)
2256[2] ◆ (3396)
Annie Besant *David C Griffiths* a49 50
2 ch f Sir Percy Caribana (Hernando (FR))
2402[6] 4045[4] 4433[9] 4792[10] *5160[3]* 5485[4] *5806[4]* 6237[6]
Annie Gogh *Tim Easterby* a57 67
2 b f Dutch Art Spunger (Fraam)
1474[4] 2437[5] 2770[2] 3110[7] 4710[3] 5169[3] *5887[5]* 6121[9]
Annie's Fortune (IRE) *Alan Jarvis* 100
2 b f Montjeu(IRE) Semaphore (Zamindar (USA))
2450[5] 2892[5] 4408[2] (4739) 5571[4] 6632[3] 7052[10]
Anniesuella (IRE) *Martin Bosley* a13
3 b f Whipper(USA) Viking Fair (Zamindar (USA))
1736[14] *2865[10]* *5350[5]*
Annie Walker (IRE) *David Nicholls* a67 78
3 b f Bertolini(USA) Pantoufle (Bering)
1419[3] (2689) 3214[3] 3383[4] *3940[3]* (4713) 5112[3]
Annina (IRE) *John Dunlop* 84
2 b f Singspiel(IRE) Lysandra (IRE) (Danehill (USA))
(6437) ◆
Annunciation *Richard Hannon* 97
2 b c Proclamation(IRE) Rockburst (Xaar)
2073[2] 2261[2] (2556) 3291[10] (3604) 5515[19] 6883[3]
Anomaly *Mahmood Al Zarooni* 99
3 ch c Pivotal Anna Palariva (IRE) (Caerleon (USA))
(2196) 3296[4]
Another Citizen (IRE) *Tim Easterby* a81 86
4 b g Byron Royal Rival (IRE) (Marju (IRE))
1168[13] 1478[13] 2096[13] 2750[6] 3211[5] (3285) 3730[4] *3944[2]* 4245[4] 4393[4] (4784) *4887[2]* 5035[7] 5674[9] 6195[3] 6403[13] *6825[2]* 7666[2] 7864[2] (7937) 8285[2]
Another Claret *Richard Fahey* 72
2 b g Avonbridge Sylvan (IRE) (Shinko Forest (IRE))
5586[3] 6042[4] 6404[5] 6815[13]
Another Cocktail *Hughie Morrison* 81
2 b c Dalakhani(IRE) Yummy Mummy (Montjeu (IRE))
5303[9] ◆ 5962[3] 6447[3] 7081[3]
Another For Joe *Jim Goldie* 80
4 b g Lomitas Anna Kalinka (GER) (Lion Cavern (USA))
2619[4] (3031) 3906[2] 4745[4] 5345[2] (5759) 6638[23]
Another Ponty *Tim Easterby* 51
2 b f Sleeping Indian Camp Fire (IRE) (Lahib (USA))
1671[8] 2508[9] 2790[5] 4450[9] 5799[4] 7173[10]
Another Squeeze *Peter Hiatt* a46 58
4 gr m Proclamation(IRE) Tight Squeeze (Petoski)
4992[3] 5687[7] 6792[12] *7383[9]*
Another Try (IRE) *Alan Jarvis* a88 90
7 b g Spinning World(USA) Mad Annie (USA) (Anabaa (USA))
(1007) 1255[4] *1373[8]* 2488[6] 3128[13] 4554[10] (4999) 6165[4] 6800[5] *7646[6]*
Another Wise Kid (IRE) *Paul Midgley* 90
4 b g Whipper(USA) Romancing (Dr Devious (IRE))
1643[9] 2337[3] 3845[5] 4629[14] 4880[7] 4998[8] 6005[2] 6347[3] (6755)
Anoumane (FR) *J-C Rouget* 68
3 b c Le Vie Dei Colori Anoush (USA) (Giant's Causeway (USA))
247a[0]
Anqooda (USA) *Marcus Tregoning* 53
3 b f Oasis Dream Atayeb (USA) (Rahy (USA))
6408[4] 6925[11]
Ansaab *Kevin Prendergast* a89 98
4 b g Cape Cross(IRE) Dawn Raid (IRE) (Dockside (USA))
1043a[2]
An Saighdiur (IRE) *Andrew Slattery* a85 101
5 b g Acclamation Brief Sentiment (IRE) (Brief Truce (USA))
(335a) (3648a) 4380a[3] 6466[3]
An Saincheann (IRE) *J S Bolger* 97
3 b f Dylan Thomas(IRE) Uimhir A Haon (IRE) (Montjeu (IRE))
7423a[3]
Ansells Pride (IRE) *Bill Turner* a63 72
9 b g King Charlemagne(USA) Accounting (Sillery (USA))
(2366) 2652[7] *3709[5]* 4332[2] 4783[5] (5347) 5801[2] *6150[7]* *6837[9]*
Antalia (FR) *J-C Rouget* a93 91
3 b f Indian Rocket Gooseley Lane (Pyramus (USA))
1125a[7] *5473a[0]* 6752a[10]
Antarctic (IRE) *John Gosden* a77 76
4 ch g Alhaarth(IRE) Holda (IRE) (Docksider (USA))
2857[7] 3594[4] 4199[7]
Antigua Sunrise (IRE) *Richard Fahey* a58 88
6 b m Noverre(USA) Staff Approved (Teenoso (USA))
1756[7] 2504[5] ◆ 3163[5] 3556[5] 4088[4]
Antiquus (IRE) *Ms Joanna Morgan* 72
3 bb f Footstepsinthesand Antiguan Wells (IRE) (Sadler's Wells (USA))
6352a[5]
Antoella (IRE) *Philip Kirby* a42 47
5 gr m Antonius Pius(USA) Bella Estella (GER) (Sternkoenig (IRE))
493[6]

Anton Chigurh *Tom Dascombe* a87 94
3 b g Oasis Dream Barathiki (Barathea (IRE))
2273[12] 3421[3] 3790[6] (3994) ◆ *4401[2]* 4675[2] (6135) (6670)
Anton Dolin (IRE) *John Dunlop* a85 87
4 ch g Danehill Dancer(IRE) Ski For Gold (Shirley Heights)
1258[5] 2561[3] 3661[4] *6039[7]* *7147[8]*
Antonio Gramsci *David Barron* 78
2 b g Misu Bond(IRE) La Corujera (Case Law)
3286[2] ◆
Antonius *Linda Stubbs* a41 58
2 b g Antonius Pius(USA) Queen Of Poland (FR) (Polish Precedent (USA))
6099[7] 6603[4] 7363[11] *7649[8]*
Antonius Lady (FR) *E Danel* 65
2 b f Antonius Pius(USA) Askhada (IRE) (Alhaarth (IRE))
8276a[6]
Anya *Ed Walker* 82
3 b f Monsieur Bond(IRE) Dyanita (Singspiel (IRE))
1472[4] 1852[4] (3001) 4057[5] 5372[3] 6375[3] (7376)
Anychanceofabirdie (USA) *David Simcock* a64 62
3 b g Proud Citizen(USA) Quiet Strike (USA) (Quiet American (USA))
2339[3] *4916[5]* *7011[9]* *7702[3]* *8019[6]* *8173[3]* *8288[4]*
Any Given Dream (IRE) *David Simcock* a72
3 b g Bahri(USA) Anazara (USA) (Trempolino (USA))
2368[11] *3622[6]* *(5208)* *5809[3]* *6213[4]* *8082[4]*
Any Other Day *William Knight* a65 68
3 b f Royal Applause A Days Grace (Daylami (IRE))
4213[5] *4931[3]* 5795[4] ◆ *6364[6]* 7108[5]
Apache Crown (AUS) *S Burridge* a99 103
7 b g Beautiful Crown(USA) Genoese (AUS) (Luskin Star (AUS))
141a[4]
Apache Dawn *Aytach Sadik* a31 51
8 ch g Pursuit Of Love Taza (Persian Bold)
1956[5]
Apache Glory (USA) *John Stimpson* a67 86
4 bb m Cherokee Run(USA) Jumeirah Glory (USA) (Deputy Minister (CAN))
4608[11] *5429[9]* *7310[6]* *7416[12]* *7905[12]* *8271[3]*
Apache Moon *Alastair Lidderdale* a39
6 ch g Monsieur Bond(IRE) Mighty Squaw (Indian Ridge)
7671[9] *7793[10]*
Apache Rising *Bryan Smart* a59 53
2 ch c Sleeping Indian Distant Music (Darshaan)
5311[8] 6043[6] 6558[7] *(7606)*
Apache Warrior *David O'Meara* 66
5 b g Westerner Aldevonie (Green Desert (USA))
4541[4]
Apassionforfashion *Mark Rimell* a30
4 b m Beat Hollow Trinny (Rainbow Quest (USA))
284[7] *369[12]* *381[6]* *1105[5]* *1341[5]* *1423[RR]*
Aphrodite's Dream *Derek Shaw* a10
2 b f Manduro(GER) Trick Of Ace (USA) (Clever Trick (USA))
5476[9] *5765[14]* *6320[8]*
Aphrodite Spirit (IRE) *Pat Eddery* a42
2 b f Key Of Luck(USA) Rosewater (GER) (Winged Love (IRE))
6534[10] *6772[11]* *7894[7]* *8094[9]*
A Pocketful Of Rye (IRE) *Paul Howling* a54 55
5 b m Acclamation Rye (IRE) (Charnwood Forest (IRE))
126[9]
Apollo D'Negro (IRE) *Clive Cox* a75 85
4 br g Fasliyev(USA) Special One (Aragon)
1161[9] 2071[3] 2870[2] 4286[8] 4824[4] 5906[8] 6008[8] 7114[12]
Apostle (IRE) *Michael Bell* 95
3 gr g Dark Angel(IRE) Rosy Dudley (IRE) (Grand Lodge (USA))
(1894) 2485[8] 2930[9] 3294[23] 4317[2] 4740[10] 5271[7] 6831[5]
Apothecary *John Gosden* a89 82
3 br f Manduro(GER) Sister Maria (USA) (Kingmambo (USA))
1013[2] *(1190)* *2079[4]* 3069[4]
Apparition (FR) *S Wattel* a60 79
2 bb f Country Reel(USA) Apparence (IRE) (Sinndar (IRE))
5570a[2]
Appeal (IRE) *Sir Mark Prescott Bt* a83 62
4 gr m Selkirk(USA) Amenixa (FR) (Linamix (FR))
(63)
Appealing (IRE) *Marco Botti* a93 95
3 b f Bertolini(USA) Radiant Energy (IRE) (Spectrum (IRE))
(61) *1215[8]* (3085) 3542[4] 4764[3] 6161[6] *7509[7]*
Appease *Dean Ivory* a72
3 b g Oasis Dream Penchee (Grand Lodge (USA))
7838[2] ◆
Applaude *Chris Bealby* a55 50
7 b g Royal Applause Flossy (Efisio)
2048[11] *2348[7]* *(4405)* *5015[7]* 5259[6] *6690[5]* *7250[12]* *7605[4]* *7983[12]*
Applaudere *Jamie Osborne* a42 29
3 b f Royal Applause Let Alone (Warning)
1259[10] *1608[9]* *2130[8]* *2351[6]* *2862[11]*
Apple Blossom Time (IRE) *Derek Haydn Jones* a54 62
5 b m Invincible Spirit(IRE) Strina (IRE) (Indian Ridge)
274[4] *995[10]* *1179[14]*
Appointment *Zoe Davison* a52 51
7 ch m Where Or When(IRE) Shoshone (Be My Chief (USA))
2348[9] 4004[8]
Apricot Sky *Henry Candy* a65 58
2 ch g Pastoral Pursuits Miss Apricot (Indian Ridge)
7078[6] *7498[4]*
April Ciel *Ronald Harris* a63 73
3 b g Septieme Ciel(USA) By Definition (IRE) (Definite Article)
2548[6] *2860[6]* (3142) (3543) 4225[7] 4906[2] 5451[5] 5816[2] 6004[5] 6735[3] 7018[5] *7358[9]*

April Fool *Ronald Harris* a87 87
8 ch g Pivotal Palace Affair (Pursuit Of Love)
(128) 199^10 351^6 470^3 (989) 1117^2 (1627) 2029^4 2545^10 3772^5 4689^20 6051^8 7901^6 8142^6

April Leyf (IRE) *Mark Brisbourne* a31 42
3 b f Kheleyf(USA) Maroussies Rock (Rock Of Gibraltar (IRE))
1287^4 1673^4 2601^5 3048^7

April Love Song (USA) *S Kobayashi* a73
4 b m Bernstein(USA) April Green (FR) (Green Tune (USA))
15a^0

Aqua Ardens (GER) *George Baker* a73 64
4 b g Nayef(USA) Arduinna (GER) (Winged Love (IRE))
(457) 765^5 1935^8 2758^5 4300^8 6577^11

Aquamarine (JPN) *M Delzangles* 108
4 b m Deep Impact(JPN) Angelita (IRE) (Alzao (USA))
(1766a) 2570a^8 3856^9 6554a^3 7429a^10

Aquarian Spirit *Richard Fahey* a81 84
5 b g Fantastic Light(USA) Notable Lady (IRE) (Victory Note (USA))
(54) (302) 432^5 674^7 1249^9 2119^4 2510^8 3167^17 5111^7 5588^9 6124^5 6881^11

Aquasulis (IRE) *David Evans* a72 67
3 ch f Titus Livius(FR) Christoph's Girl (Efisio)
2503^15 2759^5 3188^8 3451^6 3670^4 4154^4 6195^7

Aquatinta (GER) *H-A Pantall* 104
2 b f Samum(GER) Arpista (GER) (Chief Singer)
(7622a)

Aquila Carina *James Given* a44
2 b f Cockney Rebel(IRE) Galaxy Of Stars (Observatory (USA))
5887^10

Aquila D'Oriente (ITY) *S Botti* 99
3 b f Dubawi(IRE) Fanofadiga (IRE) (Alzao (USA))
2522a^5 3426a^3 7075a^6

Aquilifer (IRE) *Mrs K Burke* a79 56
4 b g Holy Roman Emperor(IRE) Sassy Bird (USA) (Storm Bird (CAN))
16a^4 54^6 351^4 989^4 2168^3 2398^3 2581^3 7415^13 7901^9 8010^6 8083^6

Aquilonius (IRE) *Stuart Williams* a91 88
3 b c Soviet Star(USA) Via Verbano (IRE) (Caerleon (USA))
4600^10 5268^6 5666^7 6206^4 7644^6 7844^2 (8057) (8250)

Arabian Falcon *A Kleinkorres* a95 103
3 ch g Dutch Art Castilian Queen (USA) (Diesis)
1426a^0

Arabian Flight *Michael Appleby* a65 44
3 b f Exceed And Excel(AUS) Emirates First (IRE) (In The Wings)
38^5 322^10 394^4 518^7 621^3 801^U (916) 1046^8 1082^3 1307^3 1444^2 1622^7 1725^8 2397^9 6774^12 8213^5 8288^3

Arabian Heights *Alan King* a78 89
4 gr g Araafa(IRE) Makhsusah (IRE) (Darshaan)
2248^18

Arabian Skies (IRE) *Saeed Bin Suroor* 74
2 b c Authorized(IRE) Chaturanga (Night Shift (USA))
7636^2

Arabian Spirit *Richard Fahey* a63 97
7 b g Oasis Dream Royal Flame (IRE) (Royal Academy (USA))
1043a^17 1128^17 1578^2 1914^7 2754^6 3030^4

Arabian Star (IRE) *Andrew Balding* 97
4 b g Green Desert(USA) Kassiopeia (IRE) (Galileo (IRE))
(2250) 3268^26 5075^9 6674^23

Arabic *James Fanshawe* a70 63
3 b g Dubai Destination(USA) Artifice (Green Desert (USA))
1728^10 2624^8 5216^4 5764^2 6458^4 6968^2 7249^2

Arab League (IRE) *David Pipe* 83
7 b g Dubai Destination(USA) Johnny And Clyde (USA) (Sky Classic (CAN))
2936^4

Arabougg *Nikki Evans* a37
2 b g Tobougg(IRE) Arabellas Homer (Mark Of Esteem (IRE))
8207^5

Arachnophobia (IRE) *Martin Bosley* a64 51
6 b g Redback La Mata (IRE) (Danehill Dancer (IRE))
386^2 670^8 1934^4 3511^7 3943^4 5179^11 7733^9 8167^6

Aragorn Icon (IRE) *David Marnane* a69 68
5 b g Tagula(IRE) Greek Icon (Thatching)
337a^4

Aragorn Rouge *Keith Dalgleish* a80 75
4 b g Aragorn(IRE) Red Top (IRE) (Fasliyev (USA))
2403^4 3230^11 3947^8 4657^11 6829^3 7500^2 ◆ (7593) ◆ 7781^2 7841^9 ◆ 8145^3

Araldo *P Harley* 113
4 b h High Chaparral(IRE) Alanda (GER) (Lando (GER))
6523a^3 7287a^4

Arashi *Derek Shaw* a47 70
6 b g Fantastic Light(USA) Arriving (Most Welcome)
1533^11 2134^8 2767^5 4396^2 (4504) 4722^2 5226^2 5665^6

Arbaah (USA) *John Dunlop* 58
2 b f Invasor(ARG) Alshadiyah (USA) (Danzig (USA))
4701^7

Arbeejay *Simon Hodgson* a37 36
3 b f Iceman Diliza (Dilum (USA))
1625^6 2497^6 8097^6 8265^12

Arbeel *Peter Chapple-Hyam* 80
2 b f Royal Applause Waafiah (Anabaa (USA))
4739^3 ◆ 5571^8

Arbisselle (FR) *Y Barberot* a82 59
2 b f Panis(USA) Sukarita (IRE) (Priolo (USA))
5570a^10

Arbitrageur (IRE) *Donal Kinsella* a86 75
3 b g Elusive City(USA) Mother's Hope (IRE) (Idris (IRE))
1032^8 6716a^6 7229a^7

Archbishop (USA) *Brian Meehan* 111
3 b c Arch(USA) Avaricity (USA) (Carson City (USA))
1860^2 2951a^2 (4760) 5869a^2

Arch Ebony (USA) *David O'Meara*
2 bb g Arch(USA) Dot C C (USA) (Cozzene (USA))
4792^16

Archelao (IRE) *Richard Rowe* a73 43
4 br g Cape Cross(IRE) Brindisi (Dr Fong (USA))
248^5 570^8 746^5 894^3 989^3 (1105) 1566^5 1706^11 2173^9 2546^6 3154^5 7905^13 8248^8

Archers Road (IRE) *Mark Michael McNiff* a56 73
5 b g Titus Livius(FR) Somoushe (IRE) (Black Minnaloushe (USA))
4591^8

Arch Event *Bernard Llewellyn* a44 57
7 ch m Umistim Arch Angel (IRE) (Archway (IRE))
4988^9 5198^3 5483^3 (5817) 6232^9 6821^3 7377^3

Archie Rice (USA) *Tom Keddy* a85 61
6 b g Arch(USA) Gold Bowl (USA) (Seeking The Gold (USA))
36^11 (216) 432^6 529^6

Archie Stevens *Tom Dascombe* a83 69
2 b g Pastoral Pursuits Miss Wells (IRE) (Sadler's Wells (USA))
2822^8 3286^6 3604^4 6609^7 7379^3 (7650) 7737^3 7994^5 (8204)

Archina (IRE) *Chris Wall* a66 61
3 b f Arch(USA) Cross Your Fingers (USA) (Woodman (USA))
34^4 1357^18 (2386) 2802^5 (3665) 5459^5 6941^6 (7250) 7527^7 7841^4 8023^6

Arch Of Colours *Mark Johnston* a73 41
3 b f Monsun(GER) Sunray Superstar (Nashwan (USA))
(331) 1647^7 2038^8 3080^7

Arch Villain (IRE) *Amanda Perrett* a89 82
3 b g Arch(USA) Barzah (IRE) (Darshaan)
(2372) ◆ 3104^3 (4649) 5366^5 6037^2 6383^3 (7194)

Arch Walker (IRE) *John Weymes* a48 68
5 ch g Choisir(AUS) Clunie (Inchinor)
1481^13 2815^6 3256^7 3791^8 4438^2 4631^2 4969^4 5327^2 5504^3 7673^12

Archwarrior (USA) *Todd Pletcher* a101
2 bb c Arch(USA) Winner's Edge (USA) (Seeking The Gold (USA))
6901a^4

Arctic (IRE) *Tracey Collins* 107
5 gr g Shamardal(USA) Shawanni (Shareef Dancer (USA))
3648a^2 5067a^7 6268a^11

Arctic Admiral (IRE) *Richard Hannon* a71 68
2 gr c Verglas(IRE) Fag End (IRE) (Treasure Kay)
4813^5 5407^2 5655^4 6946^9 7190^2 7737^5

Arctic Cosmos (USA) *John Gosden* a113 113
5 b h North Light(IRE) Fifth Avenue Doll (USA) (Marquetry (USA))
(1137) 1507^5 2254^8 6637^7

Arctic Feeling (IRE) *Richard Fahey* a92 102
4 ch g Camacho Polar Lady (Polar Falcon (USA))
1141^7 (1362) 1975^3 2286^11 2704^20 3624^8 4077^3 4690^6 5343^7 6427^2 6465^17 6755^2 7243^13

Arctic Galaxy (CAN) *John Gosden* a66 63
3 bb c North Light(IRE) Minnie's Meadow (USA) (Affirmed (USA))
1031^8 1265^6 1567^6 1982^12 3088^5 3946^4 6962^2 7200^2 7383^8

Arctic Lynx (IRE) *Robert Cowell* a88 90
5 b g One Cool Cat(USA) Baldemara (FR) (Sanglamore (USA))
304^3 652^2 2195^2 ◆ 3571^6 4530^4 4799^24 5832^6 6938^3 (7145) 7646^7 7928^4

Arctic Mirage *Michael Blanshard* a63 69
4 b g Iceman Marysienka (Primo Dominie)
967^6 1305^7 1769^5 1895^4 2171^8 2758^6 3153^8 3392^6 3659^11

Arctic Stryker *John Best* a70 67
3 b c Iceman Khafayif (USA) (Swain (IRE))
1790^7 2045^4 4583^8 6565^3 6827^5 7201^7

Arctic Wings (IRE) *Tony Carroll* a52 48
8 b g In The Wings Arctic Hunt (IRE) (Bering)
465^3 5173^3 5683^8

Ardlui (IRE) *Alan King* 97
4 b g Galileo(IRE) Epping (Charnwood Forest (IRE))
5306^12 6191^2 ◆ 6834^2 ◆ (7522)

Ardmay (IRE) *Kevin Ryan* 92
3 b g Strategic Prince Right After Moyne (IRE) (Imperial Ballet (IRE))
(1441) 2182^15 (3063) ◆ (3376) 4097^5 4600^9 5386^7 6921^2

Area Fifty One *Richard Fahey* a87 105
4 b g Green Desert(USA) Secret History (USA) (Bahri (USA))
2176^8 3164^2 (3635) 4112^5 5600^5 5826^6 6236^5 6484^14

Arena Sempione (FR) *J Heloury* a56 81
2 b f Desert Style(IRE) Ambrosianella` (FR) (Take Risks (FR))
4696a^2

Are You Mine (IRE) *Ralph Beckett* 54
2 b f Nayef(USA) Celtic Slipper (IRE) (Anabaa (USA))
6796^7

Argaki (IRE) *Sir Michael Stoute* 61
2 ch g Strategic Prince Amathusia (Selkirk (USA))
6377^5 6795^7

Arganil (USA) *Kevin Ryan* a105 96
7 ch g Langfuhr(CAN) Sherona (USA) (Mr Greeley (USA))
(1168) 1236^U 1844^15 2133^5 (2284) 2825^8 3128^8 3304^2 3624^15 4077^4 4629^13 4880^8 5758^2 6465^21

Argentine (IRE) *Ian Semple* a70 70
8 b g Fasliyev(USA) Teller (ARG) (Southern Halo (USA))
(8) 445^2 456^2 887^2 1237^6 1875^6 (2617) 2748^5 3276^5 4393^6 4631^7 5013^3 (5082)

Argent Knight *William Jarvis* a61 51
2 gr g Sir Percy Tussah (Daylami (IRE))
7172^9 7780^4 7963^4

Ariete Arrollador *G Arizkorreta Elosegui* a106 90
5 b h Kingsalsa(USA) Proud Douna (FR) (Kaldoun (FR))
140a^2 314a^2 ◆ 589a^12

Arisea (IRE) *James Moffatt* a48 41
9 b m Cape Cross(IRE) Castelfranca (IRE) (Scenic)
105^5 632^5

Aristocrata (GER) *R Rohne* 84
3 b f Areion(GER) Arenea Diadema (IRE) (Digamist (USA))
7288a^6

Ariyfa (IRE) *Noel Quinlan* a84 88
4 br m Cape Cross(IRE) Arameen (IRE) (Halling (USA))
36^2 3395^2 4068^3 4702^5 5043^6 6352a^9 7163^12

Arizona High *Andrew Crook* a60 41
4 ch g Phoenix Reach(IRE) Floriana (Selkirk (USA))
1^2 97^7 2823^7 3752^4 4455^12 6056^6 6126^8

Arizona John (IRE) *John Mackie* a87 84
7 b g Rahy(USA) Preseli (IRE) (Caerleon (USA))
872^6 (1154) 1295^2 2419^3 2676^3 4499^2 4823^6 5383^2 6076^10

Arkaim *Pam Sly* a73 49
4 b g Oasis Dream Habariya (IRE) (Perugino (USA))
96^2 225^2 384^3 672^4 818^4 3047^10 8051^8

Arlecchino (IRE) *Ed McMahon* 78
2 b c Hernando(FR) Trullitti (IRE) (Bahri (USA))
4327^3 4837^5 5962^4 6597^12

Arley Hall *Brian Ellison* a68 78
3 ch f Excellent Art Gee Kel (IRE) (Danehill Dancer (IRE))
1363^7 2333^4 2885^5 3605^3 3910^4 4642^2 (5054) 5373^5 6263^5 6359^5 6957^3 7245^2 (7602) 8292^3

Armada Bay (IRE) *Bryan Smart* a41 24
2 b g Tamayuz Yara (IRE) (Sri Pekan (USA))
3844^9 4618^11 6970^5 8203^12

Armiger *William Muir* a51 66
3 b g Araafa(IRE) Welsh Valley (USA) (Irish River (FR))
734^3 845^13 1260^11 1826^6 2367^13 2845^4 3391^5 4457^5 5198^7

Armoise *Marco Botti* a64 81
4 b m Sadler's Wells(USA) Di Moi Oui (Warning)
2637^4 3400^14

Arms (IRE) *J W Hills* 63
2 b c Excellent Art Enchanting Way (Linamix (FR))
6481^10

Arnold Lane (IRE) *Mick Channon* 105
3 b c Footstepsinthesand Capriole (Noverre (USA))
(1996) 3239^15 3681a^8 4095^3 4319^6 4740^2 5572^2 6024^5 6868^3 7048^3

Arrigo (GER) *Ibrahim Saeed Al Malki* a105 114
4 b h Shirocco(GER) Aiyana (GER) (Last Tycoon)
5354^6 6035^5 6470^4 6866^6

Arrivaderci *Richard Guest* a64 66
4 b m Kyllachy Arrivato (Efisio)
20^2 154^11

Arriva La Diva *Linda Perratt* 68
6 ch m Needwood Blade Hillside Girl (IRE) (Tagula (IRE))
3113^6 3276^3 5058^DSQ 5923^9

Arrivederla (IRE) *C Boutin* a76 63
6 b m Acclamation Alwiyda (USA) (Trempolino (USA))
815a^9

Arrow Lake (FR) *Noel Quinlan* a46 60
3 b f Refuse To Bend(IRE) Lake Nipigon (Selkirk (USA))
2014^5 2846^5 3694^9 4506^3 5215^4 5590^11

Arry's Orse *David Nicholls* a89 81
5 b g Exceed And Excel(AUS) Georgianna (IRE) (Petardia)
1168^15 1480^F

Arsaadi (IRE) *William Haggas* a87 102
3 b f Dubawi(IRE) Arsad (IRE) (Cape Cross (IRE))
1215^5 1468^3 1887^8 3270^2 3879^6 5249a^6 5849a^3

Ars d'Ortige (FR) *Mme P Butel* a68 68
2 ch c Satri(IRE) Desert Show (IRE) (Desert Style (IRE))
7597a^10

Art Dzeko *Tim Easterby* a72 65
3 b g Acclamation Delitme (IRE) (Val Royal (FR))
1337^3 (1596) (1960) ◆ 2459^5 4496^14

Arte Del Calcio *Tony Carroll* a65 66
3 b g Manduro(GER) Movie Queen (Danehill (USA))
358^3 620^4 787^4 1353^6 2787^11 3315^3 (3965) 4906^5 5810^6

Arteus *Jane Chapple-Hyam* a96 94
6 b g Fantastic Light(USA) Enchanted (Magic Ring (IRE))
253^10 ◆ 431^10 563^5

Art Form *Alan McCabe* a59 76
3 br f Excellent Art Ballroom Dancer (IRE) (Danehill Dancer (IRE))
1843^4 2332^3 2864^4 3561^2 4348^4 4552^3 4793^5 5681^5 6806^10 7253^3

Artful Dodger *Olivia Maylam* a34
5 b g Josr Algarhoud(IRE) Artistic Belle (IRE) (Orpen (USA))
7739^9 8267^8

Artful Lady (IRE) *George Margarson* a57 41
3 br f Excellent Art Fear And Greed (IRE) (Brief Truce (USA))
1259^9 2130^2 2548^8 3547^9 5095^4 5991^7 7307^6 7512^3 (7837) 8062^9 8205^7

Artful Prince *James Given* 46
2 ch c Dutch Art Royal Nashkova (Mujahid (USA))
4710^16 5325^10 6880^9

Art History (IRE) *David O'Meara* a90 96
4 gr g Dalakhani(IRE) What A Picture (FR) (Peintre Celebre (USA))
7396^18 7689^23

Arthur's Edge *Christopher Mason* a104 45
8 b g Diktat Bright Edge (Danehill Dancer (IRE))
6286^6 6800^16

Arthurs Secret *John Quinn* a75 80
2 ch g Sakhee's Secret Angry Bark (USA) (Woodman (USA))
(3457) 4318^5 5969^2 7209^3

Artic Fern (CAN) *Michael Keogh* a111 107
5 bb g Langfuhr(CAN) Wood Fern (CAN) (Woodman (USA))
6300a^9 7092a^11

Artigiano (USA) *Mahmood Al Zarooni* 111
2 ch c Distorted Humor(USA) Angel Craft (USA) (A.P. Indy (USA))
2213^3 (2550) ◆ 3240^5 4098^4 4698^2 6671^2 7568a^6

Artillery Train (IRE) *Tim Etherington* a50 52
3 b g Amadeus Wolf Another Valentine (FR) (Bering)
3406^7 3561^5 4144^5 4671^4 5545^4 6136^7 7378^6 7446^13 7600^10 7988^6 8257^9

Artisan *Brian Ellison* a75 75
4 ch g Medicean Artisia (IRE) (Peintre Celebre (USA))
(642) 3129^15 4499^5 4626^6 5056^6 5967^2 (6478)

Artistic Dawn (IRE) *John Weymes* a41 66
3 b f Excellent Art Midnight Mist (IRE) (Green Desert (USA))
2313^8 2633^4 3521^4 4622^5 5312^9 5918^10 8135^5

Artistic Jewel (IRE) *Ed McMahon* a97 103
3 ch f Excellent Art Danish Gem (Danehill (USA))
2087^5 2713^2 3190^7 (4794) 5385^3 6346^2 7772^6

Artlana *Julie Camacho* a38 58
3 b f Dutch Art Latanazul (Sakhee (USA))
4623^7 5547^12

Art Mistress (IRE) *Tim Easterby* 68
2 b f Excellent Art Hammrah (Danehill (USA))
2508^6 2917^4 ◆ 3415^4 4178^6

Art News (IRE) *Gary Moore* a57 22
3 b g Dansili Lucky (IRE) (Sadler's Wells (USA))
737^6 1031^9 1312^9 2382^11 3002^8

Art Of Dreams (FR) *B Grizzetti* 93
3 b c Dutch Art Giant Dream (Giant's Causeway (USA))
1698a^5

Art Of Gold *Amy Weaver* a27 45
3 br f Excellent Art Siena Gold (Key Of Luck (USA))
1357^11 2341^9 2771^5

Art Scholar (IRE) *Michael Appleby* a89 102
5 b g Pyrus(USA) Marigold (FR) (Marju (IRE))
(187) 427^5 3502^5 3766^3 (4249) 4795^6 5091^4 5344^4 5944^5 6476^7 6776^5 (6987) 7175^2 7396^2 (7689) 7895^8

Art Show *Ed Dunlop* a64 59
3 b f Dutch Art Regina (Green Desert (USA))
135^3 352^3

Art Storm (IRE) *Richard Fahey* a31 5
2 ch c Excellent Art Tohama (In The Wings)
7290^11 7795^5

Art Thief *Michael Appleby* a59 54
4 b g Catcher In The Rye(IRE) Eurolink Sundance (Night Shift (USA))
156^6 389^8

Aruna (USA) *H Graham Motion* a113 114
5 bb m Mr Greeley(USA) Surya (USA) (Unbridled (USA))
5376a^10

Asatir (USA) *Saeed Bin Suroor* a94 98
3 b g Elusive Quality(USA) Valid Warning (USA) (Valid Appeal (USA))
(3667) 4735^14 5386^3 6580^6 6921^9

Ascalon *Pat Eddery* a74 45
8 ch h Galileo(IRE) Leaping Flame (USA) (Trempolino (USA))
3163^15 3766^9 6933^16 7927^3

Ascendant *Alan McCabe* a87 96
6 ch g Medicean Ascendancy (Sadler's Wells (USA))
44^5 202^11 8110^2 8275^3

Ascription (IRE) *Ed Dunlop* 85
3 b c Dansili Lady Elgar (IRE) (Sadler's Wells (USA))
2273^14 2799^3 3079^4 (4329) ◆ 6789^9

As De Trebol (USA) *M Delcher-Sanchez* a100 98
6 rg h Tapit(USA) Adelphi (USA) (Danzig (USA))
53a^4 ◆ 315a^5 589a^11 7092a^6

Aseela (IRE) *Clive Brittain* a62 72
2 b f Teofilo(IRE) Valse Mystique (IRE) (Grand Lodge (USA))
2784^4 3708^3 4494^9 5763^2 (6413) 6873^11

Asgardella (IRE) *Richard Fahey* 81
2 b f Duke Of Marmalade(IRE) Peaceful Kingdom (USA) (King Of Kings (IRE))
(5184) 6070^2 6490^5 6873^9

Ashaadd (IRE) *Roger Varian* a84 91
2 b g Dansili Vital Statistics (Indian Ridge)
3505^2 ◆ (4149) ◆ 5371^2 6038^7 6491^4 6883^19

Ashamaly *James Tate* a84
2 b c Shamardal(USA) Tullynally (Dansili)
7304^2 ◆ 7749^6 7962^5 (8302)

Ashbrittle *David Pipe* 99
5 b g Rainbow Quest(USA) Caesarea (GER) (Generous (IRE))
3241^8 5491^15 7051^24

Ashdan *John Gosden* 106
2 b c Dansili Bonash (Rainbow Quest (USA))
(5062) ◆ (6200) 7050^4

Ashdown Lad *William Jarvis* a70 79
3 ch g Sir Percy Antibes (IRE) (Grand Lodge (USA))
147^2 308^3 (6206) 6574^5 6964^4

Ashgrove Nell (IRE) *Daniel Mark Loughnane* a63 57
4 b m Ad Valorem(USA) Pennycairn (Last Tycoon)
477^6 633^11

A Shin Virgo (JPN) *Ken Kozaki* 114
5 ch m Falbrav(IRE) Kansas Girl (USA) (Thunder Gulch (USA))
1146a^12

Ashiri (IRE) *David Simcock* 90
4 ch h Hurricane Run(IRE) Gorband (USA) (Woodman (USA))
1513[4] ◆ 2312[4] 3992[5] 5002[8]
Ashkalara *Stuart Howe* a67 69
5 b m Footstepsinthesand Asheyana (IRE) (Soviet Star (USA))
1980[3] 2389[7] 2915[10] 4989[3] 5405[3] 7270[12] 7473[3]
Ashkiyr (FR) *A De Royer-Dupre* 112
3 b c Rock Of Gibraltar(IRE) Asharna (IRE) (Darshaan)
3204a[3] 5250a[3]
Ashmolian (IRE) *Zoe Davison* a52 55
9 b g Grand Lodge(USA) Animatrice (USA) (Alleged (USA))
3969[10]
Ashpan Sam *John Spearing* 87
3 b g Firebreak Sweet Patoopie (Indian Ridge)
1317[10] 1912[2] 2206[2] ◆ 2649[3] 2853[8] 3486[3] 4757[3] 4985[3] 5821[3] 6285[2] 6358[8] 6577[7] (7274) 7451[2]
Ashva (USA) *Michael Dods* a90 95
4 b g Quiet American(USA) Pondicherry (USA) (Sir Wimborne (USA))
(1087) 1924[12] 2882[7] 3767[9] 5314[8]
Asia Minor (IRE) *Dr Jon Scargill* a56 54
3 ch f Pivotal Anka Britannia (USA) (Irish River (FR))
3398[7] 6792[10] 7112[8] 8265[3]
Asian Trader *William Haggas* a67 65
3 b g Acclamation Tiger Waltz (Pivotal)
2262[3] 2470[7] 3809[6] 4644[4] 5177[2] 5505[2]
Asifa (IRE) *Saeed Bin Suroor* a89 74
3 b g Green Desert(USA) Agata (FR) (Poliglote)
1653[8] 2930[13] 4949[2] 5429[5] 5747[10]
Askar Tau (FR) *Marcus Tregoning* a106 115
7 b g Montjeu(IRE) Autriche (IRE) (Acatenango (GER))
2639[6] 3293[5] 3881[4] 4737[2] 5599[6] 6198[6] 7235[3]
Askaud (IRE) *Scott Dixon* a31 97
4 b m Iffraaj Tarabaya (IRE) (Warning)
1130[6] 1605[12] 1854[12] 2590[7] 2884[4] 4072[10] 4557[2] 4689[7] 5980[9] 6471[8] 6638[17]
Ask Dad *Richard Hannon* 97
2 b c Intikhab(USA) Don't Tell Mum (IRE) (Dansili)
2929[2] ◆ 3242[6] (3505) 5270[2] (5591)
Askell Gwen (FR) *G Collet* a61
3 b f Sandwaki(USA) Dolly Wice (FR) (Dolpour (IRE))
476a[0]
Asker (IRE) *Marcus Tregoning* 91
4 b g High Chaparral(IRE) Pay The Bank (High Top)
(3430) (4184) 5306[14] 6428[3]
Ask Jack (USA) *Joseph G Murphy* a44 106
8 ch g Mt. Livermore(USA) Moll (USA) (Criminal Type (USA))
2100a[4]
Ask The Guru *Ralph Beckett* a88 89
2 b c Ishiguru(USA) Tharwa (IRE) (Last Tycoon)
(2202) 2688[4] 3662[2] 4045[2] 5045[2]
Aslana (IRE) *P Schiergen* 104
5 b m Rock Of Gibraltar(IRE) Alte Kunst (IRE) (Royal Academy (USA))
1745a[6]
A Southside Boy (GER) *Jim Goldie* 56
4 b g Samum(GER) Anthurium (GER) (Hector Protector (USA))
3891[4] 4429[3] 4768[7] (5761) 6956[12]
Asparella *Raymond York* a9
3 b f Equerry(USA) Aspra (FR) (Green Tune (USA))
6398[9]
Aspasia De Mileto *C Laffon-Parias* 103
4 b m Hurricane Run(IRE) Fabulous Speed (USA) (Silver Hawk (USA))
4386a[0] 5030a[6]
Assertive Agent *David Lanigan* a35
2 b f Assertive Agent Kensington (Mujahid (USA))
2812[10]
Assizes *Mark Johnston* a93 96
3 gr c Teofilo(IRE) Requesting (Rainbow Quest (USA))
2076[6] 2916[7] 3376[5] 3779[3] 4110[9] 4347[2] 4741[2] 5101[3] 5540[9] 6018[4] 6348[5] 6875[9]
A Star In My Eye (IRE) *Kevin Ryan* 59
2 b f Authorized(IRE) Vyatka (Lion Cavern (USA))
6257[2]
Asterales *Jo Hughes* a57 64
5 b m Royal Applause Shalimar (IRE) (Indian Ridge)
200[7] 395[2] (575) 961[2] 1631[7] 2391[3] 2823[3] 3143[3] (3440) 3519[5] 4905[4] 5811[9] 7819[8] 7968[10]
Asteria (FR) *J E Pease* a80 82
2 b f Orpen(USA) Latona (FR) (Kendor (FR))
7682a[5]
Asteroid Belt (IRE) *Chris Grant* a67 66
3 ch g Heliostatic(IRE) Affaire Royale (IRE) (Royal Academy (USA))
336a[4] 4594[5] 4955[7] 5589[3] 6101[3]
Astonished Harry (GER) *Reg Hollinshead* a50 56
3 b g Dubai Destination(USA) Aijala (FR) (Night Shift (USA))
3023[6] 3697[11] 4399[5] 4744[4] 5330[2] 5683[3]
Astonishing (IRE) *Sir Michael Stoute* 65
2 b f Galileo(IRE) Amazing Krisken (USA) (Kris S (USA))
5978[6]
Astragal *Shaun Lycett* a44 57
4 b m Shamardal(USA) Landinium (ITY) (Lando (GER))
2755[6] 3942[3] 4988[5] 5481[5]
Astra Hall *Ralph Beckett* a49 73
3 ch f Halling(USA) Star Precision (Shavian)
2125[7] 2856[8] (3968) (4181) 5151[3] ◆ 5789[6] 6933[3] 7640[2]
Astral Thunder (ARG) *Marco Botti* a98 105
5 b h Thunder Gulch(USA) Potra Venus (ARG) (Potrillon (ARG))
421a[13] 4072[8] 5076[7] 6668[7] 7051[29]

Astrogold *Mark H Tompkins* 54
3 ch f Motivator Mega (IRE) (Petardia)
2418[4] 2668[6]
Astroleo *Mark H Tompkins* a50 55
6 ch g Groom Dancer(USA) Astrolove (IRE) (Bigstone (IRE))
4491[10] 5038[7]
Astrolibra *Mark H Tompkins* a49 58
8 b m Sakhee(USA) Optimistic (Reprimand)
530[8]
Astrology (IRE) *A P O'Brien* 117
3 b c Galileo(IRE) Ask For The Moon (FR) (Dr Fong (USA))
(2026) 2705[3] 3327[4] 3651a[5]
Astromagick *Mark H Tompkins* 81
4 b m Rainbow Quest(USA) Astrocharm (IRE) (Charnwood Forest (IRE))
(2412) 6600[12]
Astrophysical Jet *Ed McMahon* 98
5 b m Dubawi(IRE) Common Knowledge (Rainbow Quest (USA))
1494[U] 1857[11] 2602[4] 3375[5]
Astrosapphire *Mark H Tompkins* a69 72
2 b f Manduro(GER) Astromancer (USA) (Silver Hawk (USA))
3590[11] 5098[3] 5534[2] 6344[2] 6972[7]
Astroscarlet *Mark H Tompkins* a66 47
3 ch f Carnival Dancer Astrolove (IRE) (Bigstone (IRE))
217[2] 472[4] (2850) 3621[3] 4153[3] 4971[8] 6323[5] 6807[4] 7629[6] 8060[4]
Astrum *Rod Millman* a47 54
2 gr g Haafhd Vax Star (Petong)
5235[12] 5785[7] 6114[11] 6822[9] 7026[10]
Atalanta Bay (IRE) *Marcus Tregoning* a36 54
2 b f Strategic Prince Wood Sprite (Mister Baileys)
5476[5] 5902[7] 6366[12]
Atempo (GER) *J Hirschberger* 113
4 ch h Monsun(GER) Anatola (GER) (Tiger Hill (IRE))
(1700a) 3746a[3] 5145a[P]
Athaakeel (IRE) *Ronald Harris* a69 63
6 b m Almutawakel Asaafeer (USA) (Dayjur (USA))
106[8] 210[4] 498[6] 3718[3] 3943[9] 5447[6] (5660) 5874[7] 6640[9] 6951[6] 7224[10] 7465[7] 7747[5] 7837[7] 7929[8] 8169[4]
Athaar (USA) *J-C Rouget* a33
3 ch f Lawyer Ron(USA) The Hess Express (USA) (Lord Carson (USA))
211a[9]
Athenian (IRE) *Sir Mark Prescott Bt* a85 89
3 b f Acclamation Ziria (IRE) (Danehill Dancer (IRE))
(2547) (2759) 2893[2] (3500) (3912) ◆
Athenian Garden (USA) *Richard Guest* a41 70
5 b m Royal Academy(USA) Webee (USA) (Kingmambo (USA))
148[8] 289[10] 725[9]
Athens (IRE) *A P O'Brien* 106
3 b c Dylan Thomas(IRE) Rafina (USA) (Mr Prospector (USA))
1404a[4] 2108a[5] 2524a[3] 3330[2]
Athletic *Alan McCabe* a61 55
3 b g Doyen(IRE) Gentle Irony (Mazilier (USA))
56[2] 209[2] 1046[11] 1288[7] 2162[4] 3575[4] 4490[9] 5175[10] 6967[3] 8051[6]
Athman (IRE) *Mahmood Al Zarooni* 77
2 b c Haatef(USA) Ikan (IRE) (Sri Pekan (USA))
3182[5] 3770[4] 5221[2]
Athwaab *Noel Chance* a65 73
5 b m Cadeaux Genereux Ahdaaf (USA) (Bahri (USA))
473[7] 576[4] 763[8] 1061[3] 1305[11] (6585) 7382[2] 7590[8] 7990[9] 8231[5]
Atigun (USA) *Kenneth McPeek* a119 102
3 b c Istan(USA) Rimini Road (USA) (Dynaformer (USA))
2954a[3] 7546a[3]
Atilia *George Baker* a31
2 ch f Notnowcato Gib (IRE) (Rock Of Gibraltar (IRE))
6153[11] 6533[12]
Atlantic Beach *Milton Bradley* a75 82
7 ch g Kyllachy Amused (Prince Sabo)
272[5] 763[4] 844[8] 1069[5] 7970[4] 8054[7] 8307[8]
Atlantic Brave *M Al Muhairi* a106 54
6 b h Piccolo Princess Anabaa (FR) (Anabaa (USA))
587a[8]
Atlantic Cycle (IRE) *Milton Bradley* a71 75
5 ch m Stormy Atlantic(USA) Cycle Of Life (USA) (Spinning World (USA))
2377[6] 2647[7] 2943[7] 3464[4] 3791[13] 4236[11]
Atlantic Sport (USA) *Mick Channon* a105 106
7 b h Machiavellian(USA) Shy Lady (FR) (Kaldoun (FR))
2896[8] 3331[3] (3855) 4099[11] 4609[7] 4802[12] 5342[5] 5686[2] 6024[13] 6513[2] 6879[7] 7240[10] 7435[5]
Atlantic Story (USA) *Michael Easterby* a81 79
10 bb g Stormy Atlantic(USA) Story Book Girl (USA) (Siberian Express (USA))
3709[9]
Atlantic Tiger (IRE) *Anthony Honeyball* a87 58
5 b g Tiger Hill(IRE) Summertime Legacy (Darshaan)
6012[6]
Atlantis City (FR) *Richard Hannon* a59
2 b c Elusive City(USA) Feld Marechale (FR) (Deputy Minister (CAN))
7627[9] 7926[4] 8070[8]
Atlantis Crossing (IRE) *Jim Boyle* a83 60
3 b g Elusive City(USA) Back At De Front (IRE) (Cape Cross (IRE))
(1725) 2206[5] 3547[7] 4506[7] 5975[4] (6455) 7484[3] 7725[2] 7966[6] (8183) ◆
Atlantis Star *James Tate* a88 95
5 b h Cape Cross(IRE) Ladeena (IRE) (Dubai Millennium)
4703[12] 5768[4] 6036[9] 6705[7] 7452[4]
Atmanna *Clive Brittain* a48 53
3 br f Manduro(GER) Samdaniya (Machiavellian (USA))
2361[3] 6345[4]

Ato (SAF) *Patrick Shaw* 116
5 b h Royal Academy(USA) Another Legend (USA) (Lyphard's Wish (FR))
(2326a)
Atora Bere (FR) *M Boutin* a76 87
2 b f Della Francesca(USA) Monatora (FR) (Hector Protector (USA))
5697a[2] 6463a[5] 7122a[9] 7699a[0]
A Touch Of Fashion (USA) *Gerard Butler* a63
2 b f Elusive Quality(USA) Fashion Rocks (IRE) (Rock Of Gibraltar (IRE))
6534[3] 7505[12]
Attain *Julia Feilden* a74 73
3 b g Dansili Achieve (Rainbow Quest (USA))
249[4] 523[2] 869[3] 1312[10] 1607[3] 2626[3] 3338[7] 4256[7] 5810[8] 6365[6] 7470[13]
Attansky (IRE) *Tim Easterby* 62
2 b g Ivan Denisovich(IRE) Attanagh (IRE) (Darnay)
4792[11] 5169[4] 5619[6] 6337[4] ◆ 6793[7]
Attenborough (USA) *Jeremy Noseda* 79
3 b g Medaglia d'Oro(USA) Julie's Prospect (USA) (Allen's Prospect (USA))
1160[9] 2408[6] 4745[3] 5837[8]
Attenshun (IRE) *Tom Dascombe* a72 51
2 ch g Salute The Sarge(USA) Southern House (IRE) (Paris House)
2844[8] 6177[4] 6889[2] 7176[5] 7462[4]
Attention Baileys (FR) *E J O'Neill* a70 70
2 b c Dubai Destination(USA) Baileys Outshine (Inchinor)
7984a[10]
Atticus Finch (IRE) *Edward Lynam* a79 60
3 b g Kodiac Hayley's Affair (IRE) (Night Shift (USA))
336a[2] 7229a[11]
Attila (SWE) *Christer Andersson*
3 b c Mr Wells(USA) Goofy Cat (SWE) (Leader Of The Pack)
3655a[8]
Attraction Ticket *David Simcock* a72 64
3 b g Selkirk(USA) Trick (IRE) (Shirley Heights)
2197[11] 3122[6] 4440[2] (4870) (5164) 6146[8] 7117[6]
Attwaal (IRE) *Roger Varian* 63
3 b g Teofilo(IRE) Qasirah (IRE) (Machiavellian (USA))
1567[7] 2095[6] 3345[7]
Aubrietia *Alan McCabe* a70 74
3 b f Dutch Art Petong's Pet (Petong)
1376[9] 2131[7] 2862[7] (3451) 3548[6] 4653[12] 4937[2] (5327) (5446) (5624) 5808[3] 6173[6] 6961[6] (7178) 7489[13] 8225[6]
Auction (IRE) *Ed Dunlop* 75
2 b f Mr Greeley(USA) Exhibit One (USA) (Silver Hawk (USA))
5902[5] ◆ 6790[3] 7364[3]
Audacia (IRE) *Hugo Palmer* a67 67
2 b f Sixties Icon Indiannie Moon (Fraam)
6791[6] 7306[2] ◆
Audacious *Michael Quinn* a44 85
4 b g Motivator Flash Of Gold (Darshaan)
1134[16] 2328[4] 2801[8] 3574[7] 4199[9] 4915[8] 5323[2] 6250[11]
Audeamus (IRE) *Tobias B P Coles* a30 37
3 b f Azamour(IRE) Nouveau Riche (IRE) (Entrepreneur)
5244[5] 5555[9] 5687[8] 6210[11] 6442[10]
Augustinian *Richard Hannon* a64
2 b c Holy Roman Emperor(IRE) Aurore (IRE) (Fasliyev (USA))
2039[4] 2808[6] 4462[2]
August Rush (SAF) *P Bary* a108 112
6 ch g Var(USA) Bushgirl (ZIM) (Huntingdale (IRE))
874a[3] 1146a[5] 4790a[3] 5647a[8] 6292a[6]
Augustus John (IRE) *Roy Brotherton* a53 73
9 gr g Danehill(USA) Rizerie (FR) (Highest Honor (FR))
7792[12] 7968[8]
Aujourd'Hui *Richard Hannon* a51 48
3 ch f Tobougg(IRE) Evening (Mark Of Esteem (IRE))
6154[10] 6433[5] 6765[6] 7106[9]
Auld Alliance (IRE) *Sir Michael Stoute* a72
2 b f Montjeu(IRE) Highland Gift (IRE) (Generous (IRE))
7720[2]
Auld Burns *David Hayes* 109
4 gr g Pastoral Pursuits Crackle (Anshan)
7073a[16]
Aultcharn (FR) *Hans Adielsson* a81 65
5 b g Kyllachy Nuit Sans Fin (FR) (Lead On Time (USA))
3958[12]
Aunt Ger (IRE) *Hugo Palmer* a32
3 gr f Bertolini(USA) Nuit Chaud (USA) (Woodman (USA))
5477[4]
Auntie Joy *Michael Easterby* a61 64
3 b f Pursuit Of Love Aunt Hilda (Distant Relative)
693[4] 943[7] 1013[6] 1441[7] 2130[10]
Auntie Kathryn (IRE) *Peter Chapple-Hyam* a50 62
3 b f Acclamation Congress (IRE) (Dancing Brave (USA))
40[4] 191[6] 294[5] 743[4] 1012[4] 1067[3] 2010[2] 2628[2] 2862[3] 3098[5] 6968[7] (7471) 7633[4]
Auntie Mabel *Andrew Balding* a67 59
3 b f Tagula(IRE) Vive La Chasse (IRE) (Mull Of Kintyre (USA))
684[5] 892[5] 1201[2] 1445[2] ◆ 4493[5] (4920) 5446[6] 7307[7] 7591[10]
Aureate *Brian Forsey* a60 30
8 ch g Jade Robbery(USA) Anne D'Autriche (IRE) (Rainbow Quest (USA))
2391[12]
Aurens (IRE) *Gary Moore* a72 64
3 b g One Cool Cat(USA) Al Aqabah (IRE) (Redback)
1048[U] 1492[RR] 3155[8] 3389[5] 4582[14]
Aureolin Gulf *Reg Hollinshead* a55 61
3 b g Proclamation(IRE) Vermilion Creek (Makbul)
499[8] 3539[3] 4992[6] 6052[8] 6500[9] 7782[6]

Aurora Lights *Richard Fahey* a50
5 ch m Fantastic Light(USA) Sweet Revival (Claude Monet (USA))
45[4]
Aurore Bere (FR) *Mme C Head-Maarek* a67 41
2 gr f Peer Gynt(JPN) Mysterious Land (IRE) (Kaldoun (FR))
7683a[8]
Aurorian (IRE) *Lawney Hill* a59 92
6 b g Fantastic Light(USA) Aurelia (Rainbow Quest (USA))
4216[12]
Aussie Blue (IRE) *Charles Pogson* a75 65
8 b g Bahamian Bounty Luanshya (First Trump)
2329[3] 2675[8] 5203[2]
Aussie Lyrics (FR) *George Baker* a77 67
2 gr c Aussie Rules(USA) Operam (Kris)
7127[4] ◆ (7642) ◆
Aussie Reigns (IRE) *William Knight* a72 74
2 b c Aussie Rules(USA) Rohain (IRE) (Singspiel (IRE))
2888[6] 3346[6] 4253[4] (4763) 5552[4] 5836[4] 6597[6] 7190[4] 7478[3]
Austerity (FR) *Mme J Bidgood*
2 ch f Falco(USA) Life Is Beautiful (IRE) (Septieme Ciel (USA))
5697a[0]
Austerity Boy *Des Donovan* a38 24
3 ch g Three Valleys(USA) Crossed Wire (Lycius (USA))
2881[10] 3453[5]
Australia Day (IRE) *Paul Webber* a93 93
9 gr g Key Of Luck(USA) Atalina (FR) (Linamix (FR))
2346[10] 3502[2] 5252a[3] (6089a)
Australia Fair *Charles Hills* a19
3 ch f Pivotal Australian Dreams (Magic Ring (IRE))
565[7]
Autarch (USA) *Amanda Perrett* a35 73
3 ch g Gone West(USA) Vargas Girl (USA) (Deputy Minister (CAN))
1853[12] 2281[10] (2624) 3621[7] 4504[14] 5038[9] 5506[10]
Authentication *Mark Johnston* a66 70
3 b c Authorized(IRE) Valley Of Gold (FR) (Shirley Heights)
195[5] 642[4] 3720[5] 4200[4] 4399[10] 4883[5] 5456[4] 6103[10] (6474) (6567) 6957[2] 7271[6] 7380[7]
Authora (IRE) *Peter Chapple-Hyam* a40 67
3 b f Authorized(IRE) Danseuse Du Soir (IRE) (Thatching)
(4971) 5413[3] 6626[7]
Authoritarian *Richard Hannon* a52 81
3 b f Authorized(IRE) Favourita (Diktat)
2042[10] 2628[3] 2802[12] 3665[6] 3966[2] 4490[2] (4754) 5998[2] 6275[3] 6801[3] (7015) (7302)
Authorship (IRE) *Mahmood Al Zarooni* 74
2 b g Authorized(IRE) Desert Frolic (IRE) (Persian Bold)
(4995) 6597[7] ◆
Autocracy *Daniel Kubler* a58 68
5 b g Green Desert(USA) Imperial Bailiwick (IRE) (Imperial Frontier (USA))
910[5] (3008) 3243[2] 3791[3] 4439[2] 4758[6] 5445[6] 6439[10]
Auto Mac *Neville Bycroft* a61 70
4 b g Auction House(USA) Charlottevalentina (IRE) (Perugino (USA))
4398[10] 4879[7] 5171[5] 6127[4] 6258[3] 7347[5] 7799[13]
Automotive *Julia Feilden* a63 53
4 b g Beat Hollow Bina Ridge (Indian Ridge)
574[9] 964[10] 8156[8]
Autrisk (IRE) *Marco Botti* a63
2 b c Authorized(IRE) Maid To Order (IRE) (Zafonic (USA))
8071[7]
Autumn Blades (IRE) *Ruth Carr* a83 79
7 ch g Daggers Drawn(USA) September Tide (IRE) (Thatching)
103[3]
Autumn Fire *Andrew Balding* a54 65
3 b f Avonbridge Brand (Shareef Dancer (USA))
1737[5] (2387) 3193[4] 4914[6] 5262[2] 5998[7]
Autumn Gold (GER) *S Woods* 112
3 b c Ransom O'War(USA) Auenglocke (GER) (Surumu (GER))
1553a[3] 8043a[9]
Autumn Shadow (IRE) *Richard Fahey* a57 58
2 gr f Dark Angel(IRE) Fall Habit (IRE) (Hamas (IRE))
2450[10] 3776[5] 4395[2] 5411[4] 6016[3] 6318[9] 7059[9]
Autumnus (IRE) *Ismail Mohammed* a50 48
3 b c Manduro(GER) Turning Light (GER) (Fantastic Light (USA))
3763[9] 4542[9] 5753[10] 8257[6]
Autun (USA) *Sir Henry Cecil* 80
2 b c Empire Maker(USA) Sense Of Joy (Dansili)
6596[8] (6985)
Available (IRE) *John Mackie* a70 78
3 b f Moss Vale(IRE) Divert (IRE) (Averti (IRE))
(621) 768[2] 940[4] 1110[3] 1482[2] (2375) 2824[11] 3613[9] 4496[7] 5388[2] 6052[6] 6497[9] 6824[5] 7411[9]
Availed Speaker (IRE) *Richard Fahey* a71 43
3 ch g Iffraaj Privileged Speech (USA) (General Assembly (USA))
184[3] (362) 547[3] 747[2] (1013) 6342[11] 6812[8] 8269[4]
Avalanche *Luca Cumani* 75
3 gr c Three Valleys(USA) Silent Waters (Polish Precedent (USA))
2461[5] 3389[3] ◆ 4001[2]
Avalon Bay *Pat Eddery* a61 67
4 b g Avonbridge Feeling Blue (Missed Flight)
214[7] 744[10] 829[4] 988[6] 4193[10] 4914[12] 5908[11] 6304[9]
Avantage (FR) *Mme Pia Brandt* 107
2 ch c Layman(USA) Territorial (Selkirk (USA))
5140a[3] 6086a[2] 6910a[7]
Avanzare *Charles Hills* a37 47
2 b f Kyllachy Never Away (Royal Applause)
4701[13] 6444[10] 6817[8] 7379[8]

Avanzini (USA) *G Botti* a67
2 b c Mr Greeley(USA) Spira (IRE) (Sadler's Wells (USA))
8176a[4]

Ava Schmetterling *Dr Jon Scargill* 12
2 b f Avonbridge Manila Selection (USA) (Manila (USA))
6871[13]

Avatar Star (IRE) *Marco Botti* a72 67
2 b c Peintre Celebre(USA) Homegrown (IRE) (Mujadil (USA))
6175[6] 6818[5] 7806[3] 7989[7]

Avec Moi *Christine Dunnett* a53 51
5 b m Reset(AUS) Pardon Moi (First Trump)
1987[10] 2406[7] 2973[9] 3721[14] 4406[11]

Avec Rose *Richard Fahey* a75 77
2 b f Tagula(IRE) Rose Siog (Bahamian Bounty)
3217[3] 4545[2] 5255[2] (5886) 6883[8]

Aventino (JPN) *Yasutoshi Ikee* 101
8 b h Jungle Pocket(JPN) Assam Hill (JPN) (Sunday Silence (USA))
6293a[5] 6912a[17]

Averroes (IRE) *Ernst Oertel* a107 114
5 ch h Galileo(IRE) Shapely (USA) (Alleged (USA))
421a[2] 759a[10] 1144a[4]

Avertis *Alastair Lidderdale* a75 75
7 b g Averti(IRE) Double Stake (USA) (Kokand (USA))
7256[5] 7925[2] (8199)

Ave Sofia *John Holt* a43 52
3 b f Byron Snoozy (Cadeaux Genereux)
5447[5] 6178[6] 7437[9] 7748[9] 7915[10] 8133[6]

Aviator (FR) *Mme M Bollack-Badel* a90 101
3 b c Motivator Summer Wave (IRE) (King's Best (USA))
1426a[8]

Aviator (GER) *P Harley* 103
4 b h Motivator Amore (GER) (Lando (GER))
1901a[9] 2965a[5] 6864a[2]

Aviso (GER) *David Evans* a71 68
8 b g Tertullian(USA) Akasma (GER) (Windwurf (GER))
85[5] (104) (175) 349[6] 570[3] 636[2] 960[8] 1341[4] (2117a) 2498[13] 8019[4] 8162[10]

Avison (IRE) *Richard Fahey* a58 67
4 b g Diamond Green(FR) Actoris (USA) (Diesis)
1879[8] 2670[3] 3029[6] 4048[7] 5175[4] 5708[4] 6102[4] 6262[4] 6885[9] 7490[10]

Avon Breeze *Richard Whitaker* a71 70
3 b f Avonbridge African Breeze (Atraf)
5340[4] (5823) 6211[2] 7775[13]

Avoncreek *Brian Baugh* a56 54
8 b g Tipsy Creek(USA) Avondale Girl (IRE) (Case Law)
(356) 690[8] 2046[5] 3026[11] 4865[12] 6178[11]

Avon Light *Milton Bradley* a46 55
4 ch g Avonbridge Veronese (USA) (Bianconi (USA))
837[9] 938[7] 1768[8] 1907[8]

Avonlini *Brian Baugh* a59 54
6 b m Bertolini(USA) Avondale Girl (IRE) (Case Law)
356[9] 665[4] 938[4] (1387) 2350[10] 6322[2] 6937[7] 7465[10]

Avonmore Star *Richard Hannon* a87 91
4 b g Avonbridge Pooka's Daughter (IRE) (Eagle Eyed (USA))
1417[8] (2629) 3960[2] 4530[8] 4824[10] 5035[6] 5703[3] 6041[7] 6256[8] 6705[3]

Avon River *Dean Ivory* a70 92
5 ch g Avonbridge Night Kiss (FR) (Night Shift (USA))
7300[11] 7843[9] 7997[11]

Avonrose *Derek Shaw* a81 78
5 b m Avonbridge Loveleaves (Polar Falcon (USA))
100[8] (134) 269[2] 371[4] 458[10] 834[5] 997[4] 1609[6] (2503) 3221[3] 3696[7] 4317[20] (4726) 5326[5] 6172[7] 7607[8] 7975[3] 8081[4] 8269[9]

Avon Supreme *Gay Kelleway* a61 57
4 ch m Avonbridge Fredora (Inchinor)
151[6] 265[6] 530[5] 848[2] 1095[12] 1831[4] 2013[4] 2804[3] 3051[3] 3470[6] (5212) 5938[5] 6646[4] 6829[6] 7362[6] 8111[3] 8212[2]

Avonvalley *Peter Grayson* a72 65
5 b m Avonbridge Piper's Ash (USA) (Royal Academy (USA))
118[8] (227) 297[3] 396[7] 576[6] 986[2] 1070[3] 1387[9] 1735[3] 2377[3] (2971) 3382[4] 4495[10] (4885) 6497[2] 6666[12] 6824[2] 7411[2] 7937[7] ◆

Await The Dawn (USA) *A P O'Brien* 125
5 b h Giant's Causeway(USA) Valentine Band (USA) (Dixieland Band (USA))
1148a[15]

Awake My Soul (IRE) *Luca Cumani* 86
3 ch g Teofilo(IRE) Field Of Hope (IRE) (Selkirk (USA))
3349[2] 4067[5] ◆ 7016[5]

Awakened Spirit (IRE) *David Wachman* 85
2 ch f Fracas(IRE) Rajani (IRE) (Johannesburg (USA))
2977[5]

Awaywithefairies *Richard Ford*
3 b f Courteous Shahadah (IRE) (Daylami (IRE))
2335[14] 3606[8]

Awesome Feather (USA) *Chad C Brown* a120
4 b m Awesome Of Course(USA) Precious Feather (USA) (Gone West (USA))
7550a[6]

Awesome Pearl (USA) *Sir Mark Prescott Bt* a83 60
3 bb g Awesome Again(CAN) Gottcha Last (USA) (Pleasant Tap (USA))
2038[5] 2372[3] (4918) 6037[4] 6383[5] 7098[8]

Awesome Rock (IRE) *Louise Best* a56 46
3 ch g Rock Of Gibraltar(IRE) Dangerous Diva (IRE) (Royal Academy (USA))
3548[9] 5037[5] 5198[6] 7488[4] 7632[2] 8050[4] 8260[8]

Axiom *Ed Walker* a104 104
8 ch g Pivotal Exhibitor (USA) (Royal Academy (USA))
1035[2] 1212[12] 2409[10] 2657[16] 6494[6] 6879[4] 7240[16] 7774[6] 8098[4]

Axiom (GER) *J Hirschberger* 104
3 b c Tertullian(USA) Akasma (GER) (Windwurf (GER))
2568a[5]

Ayaar (IRE) *Mick Channon* 97
2 bb c Rock Of Gibraltar(IRE) Teide Lady (Nashwan (USA))
2662[4] 3067[3] 3649a[4] 4056[4] (4507) (5348) (5755a) 6272a[5]

Ayaarah (IRE) *William Knight* a68 27
4 b m Cape Cross(IRE) La Jwaab (Alhaarth (IRE))
150[8] 296[10] 3318[8] 4242[8] 5021[7]

Ayasha *Bryan Smart* a65 69
2 b f Indesatchel(IRE) Nizhoni (USA) (Mineshaft (USA))
2790[8] (4710) 5537[4] 6541[4] 7463[3] 7713[2]

Aye Aye Digby (IRE) *Patrick Chamings* a91 85
7 b g Captain Rio Jane Digby (IRE) (Magical Strike (USA))
(1789) 2482[3] 3570[2] 4000[3] 5035[11] 5486[2] 5906[4] 6370[4] 6578[6]

Aye Aye Skipper (IRE) *Dean Ivory* a76 45
2 b g Captain Marvelous(IRE) Queenfisher (Scottish Reel)
5911[6] 6533[4] 6977[2] (7525) 7737[4]

Ayla's Emperor *Mick Channon* 54
3 b f Holy Roman Emperor(IRE) Ayla (IRE) (Daylami (IRE))
1518[8]

Aylin (FR) *N Clement* 86
2 ch f Gold Away(IRE) Street Lightning (FR) (Best Of The Bests (IRE))
5288a[6]

Ayr Missile *Kevin Ryan* 74
2 b f Cadeaux Genereux Venoge (IRE) (Green Desert (USA))
2450[2] ◆ 2917[5] 4173[3]

Ay Tay Tate (IRE) *David C Griffiths* a72 72
6 b g Catcher In The Rye(IRE) Vintage Belle (IRE) (Waajib)
98[3] (222) 452[9] (592) (825) 1071[3] 1275[2] 1525[10]

Azamara Star *Derek Shaw* a30 30
3 ch f Three Valleys(USA) Sunrise Girl (King's Signet (USA))
1739[7] 1986[8]

Azelle *Richard Hannon* 68
2 b f Starcraft(NZ) Zola (NZ) (Volksraad)
5551[7] 5907[9] 6444[3]

Azerodegree (IRE) *Marco Botti* a66 69
3 b g Azamour(IRE) Fairy (USA) (Gulch (USA))
2280[14] 2800[3] 3079[8] 4499[10] 5159[6]

Azeville (GER) *F Rohaut* a97 104
3 rg f Shamardal(USA) At Once (GER) (Kendor (FR))
2109a[6]

Azma (USA) *Conrad Allen* a72
2 b f Bernardini(USA) Dyna's Destiny (USA) (Dynaformer (USA))
(8017)

Azrael *Alan McCabe* a88 94
4 b g Makbul Fontaine Lady (Millfontaine)
1161[4] 1373[4] 1844[4] 2487[12] 3128[18] 3348[12] 4580[8] 7790[6] 8034[5] 8269[2]

Azrag (USA) *Gerard Butler* a73 76
4 rg g Mizzen Mast(USA) Call Account (USA) (Private Account (USA))
4712[3] (6323) 6399[2] (6616) 6691[7] 7455[3]

Azrur (IRE) *Michael Bell* 82
2 b c Sir Percy Tiger Spice (Royal Applause)
(3611) ◆ 6027[6]

Azzurra Du Caprio (IRE) *Ben Haslam* 93
4 ch m Captain Rio Dunbrody (FR) (Jeune Homme (USA))
2337[6] 3612[8] 4829[12] 6044[14]

Azzurra Leonessa (IRE) *Ben Haslam* 18
2 b f Bachelor Duke(USA) Dunbrody (FR) (Jeune Homme (USA))
3611[15]

Baan (USA) *James Eustace* a66 66
9 ch g Diesis Madaen (USA) (Nureyev (USA))
1559[8] 4722[7] 5706[5] 6255[5] 6821[7] 7472[2] 8001[3]

Babich Bay (IRE) *Jo Hughes* a59 72
4 b g Captain Rio Ibtihal (IRE) (Hamas (IRE))
100[9] 328[6]

Baby Cross *J-C Rouget* a93 93
3 b c Cape Cross(IRE) Priere (Machiavellian (USA))
(247a) 628a[2] 7345a[4]

Baby Dottie *Pat Phelan* a62 76
5 ch m Dr Fong(USA) Auntie Dot Com (Tagula (IRE))
252[10] 474[7] 647[7] 1185[7] 1734[3] 2943[12] 5444[3] 5972[4] 6307[3] 7990[3] 8107[2] 8307[3]

Baby Driver *David Evans* a55 69
4 gr g Proclamation(IRE) Renee (Wolfhound (USA))
45[8] 744[2] 822[5] 848[3] 988[3] 4241[2] 4981[12] 5804[7] 5996[10]

Babylon Candle *Lisa Williamson* 8
2 ch g Auction House(USA) Dazzling Quintet (Superlative)
1164[9]

Babylone (IRE) *Mlle S-V Tarrou* a80 85
5 ch g Dubai Destination(USA) Abime (USA) (Woodman (USA))
815a[8]

Baby Queen (IRE) *Brian Baugh* a66 80
6 b m Royal Applause Kissing Time (Lugana Beach)
1828[8] 2369[11] 2789[8]

Baby Strange *Derek Shaw* a89 95
8 gr g Superior Premium The Manx Touch (IRE) (Petardia)
715[5] 835[8] 1007[5] 1362[5] 1438[3] 1844[6] ◆ 2177[2] 2707[5] 3004[8] 3624[10] 4286[4] 4799[8] 6192[8] 6495[6] 6705[6] 6939[7] (7291) 7595[7] 7730[10]

Baccarat (IRE) *Richard Fahey* a74 88
3 ch c Dutch Art Zut Alors (IRE) (Pivotal)
(2182) 3376[9]

Bachelor Knight (IRE) *Suzzanne France* a56 53
4 b g Bachelor Duke(USA) Labetera (Lujain (USA))
101[10] 155[8] 356[4] 483[11] 690[7] 837[4] 8256[7]

Bachotheque (IRE) *Tim Easterby* 82
2 b g Chineur(FR) Bacchanalia (IRE) (Blues Traveller (IRE))
3491[4] 4114[2] 4344[2] 4612[5] 5367[4] (5727) (6425) 7028[9]

Backbench Blues (IRE) *Mrs John Harrington* a80 107
3 b g Big Bad Bob(IRE) Heroine (Sadler's Wells (USA))
3361a[2]

Back Burner (IRE) *Mrs John Harrington* a95 95
4 br g Big Bad Bob(IRE) Marl (Lycius (USA))
5397a[5]

Back For Tea (IRE) *Phil McEntee* a48 51
4 b g Redback Jasmine Pearl (IRE) (King Of Kings (IRE))
7822[8] 8021[5] 8062[4] 8154[4] 8249[9]

Back In Black (NZ) *John Steffert* 112
7 bl g Storm Creek(USA) Shutricia (NZ) (Grosvenor (NZ))
7346a[4] 7783a[12]

Back In The Frame *Tom Dascombe* a64 65
2 b f Dutch Art Ile Deserte (Green Desert (USA))
1388[2] ◆ 1556[2] 2812[6] 6920[14]

Backstage Tour *Mahmood Al Zarooni* 69
2 ch c Manduro(GER) Welsh Diva (Selkirk (USA))
6572[3] ◆ 6947[3] 7442[4]

Back To Capri (IRE) *G Collet* a75 55
2 b c Holy Roman Emperor(IRE) Prairie Moon (Halling (USA))
3714a[0] 5378a[6]

Backtrade (IRE) *Andrew Balding* a75 68
3 b g Holy Roman Emperor(IRE) Braari (USA) (Gulch (USA))
1723[4] 2611[4] 3284[8]

Bada Bing *Scott Dixon* a42 58
3 ch f Beat Hollow Trustthunder (Selkirk (USA))
3025[2] ◆ 4172[9] 5764[9] 6216[5] 6810[6] 8048[11]

Baddilini *Alan Bailey* a85 90
2 b g Bertolini(USA) Baddi Heights (FR) (Shirley Heights)
(1411) 1747[3] 1972[3] 3240[13] 4774[5] 5515[13] (6032) 6883[4]

Badea *Richard Fahey* a77 76
3 b g Cockney Rebel(IRE) Gibraltar Bay (IRE) (Cape Cross (IRE))
1976[12] 3035[4] 3614[4] 4188[3] 6240[7] 6631[2] 6842[6] (7596) 7655[3] 7792[6] 8000[5] 8136[8] 8182[7]

Badr Al Badoor (IRE) *James Fanshawe* 83
2 b f Acclamation Dani Ridge (IRE) (Indian Ridge)
(3560) 5516[8] 6490[2] 6873[5]

Bahaa (FR) *F Head* a75 72
2 b f Kentucky Dynamite(USA) La Bahamienne (IRE) (Fasliyev (USA))
8193a[7]

Bahamamay *Richard Fahey* 69
2 ch g Bahamian Bounty May West (Act One)
5221[3] ◆ 6423[4]

Bahama Spirit (IRE) *Jeremy Gask* 82
3 b f Invincible Spirit(IRE) Braziliz (USA) (Kingmambo (USA))
2893[7] 3613[11] 4903[4] 5502[13]

Bahamian Lad *Reg Hollinshead* a73 82
7 b g Bahamian Bounty Danehill Princess (IRE) (Danehill (USA))
359[7] (639) 1117[5]

Bahamian Music (IRE) *Ed Vaughan* a60 87
5 b m Bahamian Bounty Strings (Unfuwain (USA))
1186[8]

Baharat (IRE) *Richard Guest* a65 77
4 b g Iffraaj Gharam (USA) (Green Dancer (USA))
714[5] 826[5] 1083[7] 2260[17] 5809[11] 8113[8]

Baheeja *Roger Varian* a97 97
3 b f Dubawi(IRE) Hasty Words (IRE) (Polish Patriot (USA))
2891[3] 3785[6] (4782) (5099) (5512) (5980) 6878[4] 7509[4] 8300a[3]

Bahrain Storm (IRE) *Noel Quinlan* a73 89
9 b g Bahhare(USA) Dance Up A Storm (USA) (Storm Bird (CAN))
7367[15]

Bahri Beat (IRE) *John Norton* a31
4 b g Bahri(USA) Optimal Quest (IRE) (Septieme Ciel (USA))
113[13]

Bahri Sheen (IRE) *John Best* a65 40
4 b g Bahri(USA) Kama's Wheel (Magic Ring (IRE))
896[7] 3972[4] 4438[8] 5047[4] 6455[10] 6778[11] 7504[2] 7816[10] (8179)

Bailadeira *Tim Etherington* a68 62
4 bb m Intikhab(USA) Sainte Gig (FR) (Saint Cyrien (FR))
1246[2] 1383[10] 1638[5] 1990[4] 7456[11] 7861[12] 7970[6] 8107[9]

Baile Atha Cliath (IRE) *Declan Carroll* a44
3 b g Barathea(IRE) Danielli (IRE) (Danehill (USA))
7981[5]

Baileys Agincourt *Michael Herrington* a60
4 ch g Beat Hollow Numberonedance (USA) (Trempolino (USA))
8189[P]

Baileys Bigishu *James Given*
3 ch g Ishiguru(USA) Jane Jubilee (IRE) (Mister Baileys)
1560[12] 2542[14]

Baileys Dutch *Mark Johnston*
3 gr g Dutch Art Southern Psychic (USA) (Alwasmi (USA))
382[6]

Baileys Jubilee *Mark Johnston* a84 105
2 b f Bahamian Bounty Missisipi Star (IRE) (Mujahid (USA))
(1211) (1451) 2252[6] 2638[7] 3269[13] 3631[3] (4205a) 4632a[2] 5516[2] 6128a[2] 6672[3]

Baileys Over Ice *James Given* a33 62
3 b f Iceman Exhibitor (USA) (Royal Academy (USA))
3184[7] 3847[4] 4549[9] 4826[5] 5589[10] 6210[12]

Baileys Strider *Mark Johnston* a71
3 b c Aragorn(IRE) Missisipi Star (IRE) (Mujahid (USA))
231[5] (350)

Baino Rock (FR) *J-C Rouget* 105
3 b f Rock Of Gibraltar(IRE) Baino Ridge (FR) (Highest Honor (FR))
7665a[2]

Bain's Pass (IRE) *Kevin Ryan* 60
2 ch g Johannesburg(USA) Rose Bourbon (USA) (Woodman (USA))
3182[10] 4587[10]

Bairam *Brian Meehan* 79
2 gr g Haatef(USA) Intishaar (IRE) (Dubai Millennium)
2202[2] ◆ 2763[4] 3506[3] (4047) (Dead)

Baisse *R Dzubasz* a73 99
4 b m High Chaparral(IRE) Best Side (IRE) (King's Best (USA))
3652a[8]

Baitsileir (IRE) *J S Bolger* a85 87
4 b g Bachelor Duke(USA) Alamanta (IRE) (Ali-Royal (IRE))
341a[4]

Bajan Bear *Michael Blanshard* a76 79
4 ch g Compton Place Bajan Rose (Dashing Blade)
3388[5] 4517[3] 5004[5] 5341[6] 5915[2] 6277[4] 6495[4] 7142[2] 7485[5] 7743[10] ◆ 7843[7]

Bajan Hero *David Evans* a44 68
3 b g Haafhd Maid To Dance (Pyramus (USA))
1319[10] 3014[7] 3433[2] 4185[5] 4705[7] 5095[6] 5127[6]

Bajan Story *Michael Blanshard* a64 66
3 b g Lucky Story(USA) Bajan Rose (Dashing Blade)
1737[4] 3012[4] 4605[3] 4876[5] 5501[8] 6275[9]

Bajan Tryst (USA) *Kevin Ryan* a104 105
6 bb g Speightstown(USA) Garden Secrets (USA) (Time For A Change (USA))
1033[3] (2717) 3648a[12] 4576[17] 4802[10] 6244[14] 6854a[11] 7897[4] 8008[6] 8098[12]

Baker's Pursuit *Jim Goldie* 67
2 b f Pastoral Pursuits Little Caroline (IRE) (Great Commotion (USA))
1818[5] ◆ 2261[14] 2614[6] 6130[10]

Balada Sale (ARG) *P Bary* a112 98
4 b m Not For Sale(ARG) La Balada (ARG) (Confidental Talk (USA))
1145a[6] 7124a[8]

Balady (IRE) *John Dunlop* a78 81
3 b f Zamindar(USA) Faydah (USA) (Bahri (USA))
(1852) 2820[6] 4647[5] 5747[4] ◆ 6169[2] 6986[3]

Balance The Books (USA) *Chad C Brown* 113
2 b c Lemon Drop Kid(USA) Kreisleriana (USA) (Seeking The Gold (USA))
7568a[3]

Balatina *Chris Dwyer* a42
2 ch f Byron Primavera (Anshan)
7926[10] 8102[6] 8185[7]

Balaton *Brian Meehan* 23
3 br f Singspiel(IRE) Traverse City (USA) (Halo (USA))
2848[12]

Balaythous (FR) *Mlle B Renk* a98 109
6 ch g Bahhare(USA) Silirisa (FR) (Sillery (USA))
1697a[8] 7985a[0]

Balcary Bay *James Eustace* a46 62
3 ch g Zamindar(USA) Chantress (Peintre Celebre (USA))
3975[4] 5404[5] 6792[11] 7315[6]

Baldemar *Richard Fahey* a93 90
7 b g Namid Keen Melody (USA) (Sharpen Up)
1236[6] 2707[3] 3771[7] 4077[7] 4554[11] 6465[11] 6705[11]

Balducci *David Simcock* a89 107
5 b g Dansili Miss Meltemi (IRE) (Miswaki Tern (USA))
246a[11] 416a[10] 587a[13] 4822[2] 5686[4] 6494[10]

Balerina (FR) *Alan King* 78
5 b m Della Francesca(USA) Santa Marina (FR) (Kendor (FR))
1940[10] 3661[9]

Balesteem *Clifford Lines*
5 ch g Mark Of Esteem(IRE) Ball Gown (Jalmood (USA))
1981[P]

Balinka *Mel Brittain* 70
2 b f Bahamian Bounty Eurolinka (IRE) (Tirol)
3126[3] 3415[8] 4178[2] 4344[4] 5367[2] (5709) 6984[3] 7635[7]

Ballade De La Mer *George Foster* a51 40
6 b m Ishiguru(USA) Riviere Rouge (Forzando)
2599[8] 3579[5]

Balladiene (IRE) *Jarlath P Fahey* a68 91
6 b m Noverre(USA) Kinnego (IRE) (Sri Pekan (USA))
6352a[7]

Balladry (USA) *Eoin Harty* a102
4 rg h Unbridled's Song(USA) Storm Song (USA) (Summer Squall (USA))
7546a[6]

Ballarina *Eric Alston* a61 68
6 b m Compton Place Miss Uluwatu (IRE) (Night Shift (USA))
1298[10] 2749[3] 3109[4] ◆ 3382[6] 4592[2] 5294[10] 6264[4] 6836[7] 7673[9] (7746)

Ballesteros *Brian Meehan* 109
3 ch g Tomba Flamenco Dancer (Mark Of Esteem (IRE))
1457[12] (1644) (2028) ◆ 2691[3] 5814[6] ◆ 6908a[4] 7624a[7]

Ballinargh Boy *Robert Wylie* a48 51
4 b g Royal Applause Can Can Lady (Anshan)
66[3]

Ballinargh Girl (IRE) *Danielle McCormick* a61 79
4 b m Footstepsinthesand Rack And Ruin (IRE) (King's Best (USA))
2094[14] 2476[7] 2841[3] 3524[6] 4638[10] 5548[8] 6179[6] 6836[3] 7275[15] 7604[15]

Ballinderry Boy *Andrew Balding* a45 18
2 b g Kayf Tara Spring Dream (IRE) (Kalanisi (IRE))
7492[11] 7750[9]

Ballista (IRE) *Tom Dascombe* a113 109
4 b g Majestic Missile(IRE) Ancient Secret (Warrshan (USA))
1844[17] (2438) 2697[6] 3304[3] 3557[3] (4640) 5368[7] (5829) (6116) 7397[18] (7772)

Ballivor (IRE) *W T Farrell* a76 88
9 b g Marju(IRE) Delphinus (Soviet Star (USA))
5609a[18]

Ball Prince (IRE) *T Clout* 104
5 gr h Slickly(FR) Queen's Ball (King's Theatre (IRE))
4316a[2] 7124a[6]

Ballroom Blitz *Doug Watson* a75 36
3 b f Ishiguru(USA) Twilight Time (Aragon)
77a[5]

Ballybacka Lady (IRE) *Mrs John Harrington* a81 109
4 b m Hurricane Run(IRE) Southern Queen (Anabaa (USA))
4521a[2] 5286a[2] 5643a[3] 6061a[10]

Ballyheigue (IRE) *Gary Moore* a78 68
3 b g High Chaparral(IRE) Lyphardess (IRE) (Lyphard's Special (USA))
1518[5] (1981) 2427[5] 3737[8] 3962[4] 6976[5]

Balmont Mast (IRE) *Edward Lynam* a110 103
4 b g Balmont(USA) Corn Futures (Nomination)
1538a[5] (6854a) (7390a)

Balmoral Castle *Jonathan Portman* a61
3 b g Royal Applause Mimiteh (USA) (Maria's Mon (USA))
7477[8] 7729[7] 8177[2]

Balrath Hope (IRE) *Gavin Cromwell* a76 91
3 b f Intikhab(USA) Best Shift (IRE) (King's Best (USA))
6352a[3]

Baltic Bomber (IRE) *John Quinn* 66
3 b g Baltic King Dieci Anno (IRE) (Classic Music (USA))
1441[11] (3357) 3954[5] 4174[11] (4593) 4953[5] 5831[5] 7395[9]

Baltic Fizz (IRE) *Mrs K Burke* a61 72
3 b f Baltic King Holly Springs (Efisio)
180[6] 2336[4] 2672[5] 4623[3]

Baltic Flyer (IRE) *Robert Eddery* a64 61
3 b f Baltic King Negria (IRE) (Al Hareb (USA))
2045[12] 3118[7] 3701[9] 4438[13]

Baltic Gin (IRE) *Malcolm Saunders* a49 64
2 b f Baltic King Deeday Bay (IRE) (Brave Act)
1495[7] 2163[5] 2384[2] 3009[8] 4331[4] 5424[4] 5654[7] 7272[2]

Baltic Knight (IRE) *Richard Hannon* a81 92
2 b c Baltic King Night Of Joy (IRE) (King's Best (USA))
4845[5] (5765) 6372[2] (6797)

Baltic Prince (IRE) *Paul Green* a51 50
2 b c Baltic King Brunswick (Warning)
2662[10] 3217[4] 3491[7] 5423[7] 5749[9] 6354[4] 6451[3] 7060[12] 7491[4] 7974[10]

Baltic Rock (IRE) *J D Hillis* 110
3 b c Rock Of Gibraltar(IRE) Born Wild (GER) (Sadler's Wells (USA))
1900a[6] 3683a[4] 5145a[5]

Baltic Rose (IRE) *Ian McInnes* 25
2 b f Baltic King Rosy Scintilla (IRE) (Thatching)
2686[12]

Baltic Sea (IRE) *David Evans* a39 45
2 b f Baltic King Lady Redera (IRE) (Inzar (USA))
4990[5] 5325[11] 5807[8] 7156[9] 7357[7]

Balti's Sister (IRE) *Terry Clement* a82 67
3 b f Tiger Hill(IRE) Itsibitsi (IRE) (Brief Truce (USA))
1798[9] 1916[4] 2879[2] 3184[4] 3462[7] (3892) 3908[5] 5775[2] 6216[2] (6456) 7469[6] (7776) ◆ (7975)

Balty Boys (IRE) *Charles Hills* 109
3 b c Cape Cross(IRE) Chatham Islands (USA) (Elusive Quality (USA))
1452[7] 2277[3] 2659[5] 4598[7] 5342[8] 6143[8] 6676[20]

Bamurru (IRE) *Peter Makin* a26 70
2 ch g Kheleyf(USA) Pearl Trader (IRE) (Dubai Destination (USA))
2571[2] 3140[10] 5260[5] 5786[10] 7355[6]

Bana Wu *Andrew Balding* a85 101
3 ch f Shirocco(GER) My Way (IRE) (Marju (IRE))
1215[7] 3879[3] (5309) 6598[8]

Bancnuanaheireann (IRE) *Michael Appleby* a96 97
5 b g Chevalier(IRE) Alamanta (IRE) (Ali-Royal (IRE))
3647a[14] 4689[2] 5075[6] 5301[9] 6242[6] 6674[4] 7030[10] 7556[4] 7771[6] 8056[5] ◆

Bandanaman (IRE) *Alan Swinbank* a16 68
6 b g Danehill Dancer(IRE) Band Of Angels (IRE) (Alzao (USA))
366[10] 2599[3] (4867) 5086[5] 6784[7]

Bandidazo (USA) *A Fabre* 91
3 ch c Van Nistelrooy(USA) Bailonguera (ARG) (Southern Halo (USA))
1125a[6]

Bandstand *Bryan Smart* a85 78
6 b g Royal Applause Incise (Dr Fong (USA))
(100) 311[7] (458) 2841[5] 3255[8] 4784[5] 6260[2] 7464[10]

Bandy Bob *Iain Jardine* a46 34
3 b g Distant Music(USA) Angelic Girl (USA) (Swain (IRE))
3273[7] 4211[7] 4807[4] 7620[5]

Bang Tidy (IRE) *Brian Ellison* a63 60
3 b g Moss Vale(IRE) Bound To Glitter (USA) (Boundary (USA))
5923[8] 6100[5] 6806[4] 7055[7] 7201[10] 7915[8] (8114)

Bank Bonus *Andrew Balding* a82 89
3 b g Motivator Small Fortune (Anabaa (USA))
2125[2] 3106[2] 3786[3] 4323[5] 5048[3] (6662)

Bank Of Burden (USA) *Niels Petersen* a76 104
5 ch g Hawk Wing(USA) Wewantitall (Pivotal)
319a[12] 486a[8] 2807a[3] 3886a[3] (4863a) (5651a) (6091a)

Bank On Me *Philip McBride* a90 82
3 ch c Medicean Red Garland (Selkirk (USA))
1304[2] 1653[5] 2263[10] 2678[4] 6381[3] 7824[2] 8095[5] 8181[5]

Banna Boirche (IRE) *M Halford* a107 107
6 b g Lucky Owners(NZ) Ziet D'Alsace (FR) (Zieten (USA))
51a[7] ◆ 243a[5] 416a[6] 586a[7] 2777a[7] 5286a[7] 6079a[5] 6855a[6]

Bannock (IRE) *Mark Johnston* a109 113
3 b c Bertolini(USA) Laoub (USA) (Red Ransom (USA))
1032[3] 1129[14] 1453[2] 1751[2] 2179[11] 3265[15] 3633[4] 4321[11] 4628[4] 4761[12] 5597[2] 5827[3] 6024[12] 6868[12]

Banovallum *Sylvester Kirk* 81
2 b c Invincible Spirit(IRE) Sinduda (Anabaa (USA))
4056[10] 5851[2] (6330) 6874[10]

Banreenahreenkah (IRE) *Denis Coakley* 62
2 b f Steppe Dancer(IRE) Carmencita (Rock Of Gibraltar (IRE))
5911[3] 6431[2]

Banu (GER) *J-P Carvalho* a75 75
2 b f Lateral Barbea (GER) (Kallisto (GER))
7600a[?]

Bapak Bangsawan *Kevin Ryan* a66 69
2 b c Pastoral Pursuits Nsx (Roi Danzig (USA))
1515[3] 2308[9] 4952[3] 5242[2] 6071[4] 6320[3]

Bapak Besar (CAN) *Kevin Ryan* a54 40
2 ch c Speightstown(USA) Valid Move (USA) (Valid Expectations (USA))
2594[8] 6015[11] 7497[8]

Bapak Chinta (USA) *Kevin Ryan* 106
3 rg c Speightstown(USA) Suena Cay (USA) (Maria's Mon (USA))
2486[9] 3238[17]

Bapak Muda (USA) *Kevin Ryan* a62 47
2 ch c Distorted Humor(USA) Shiva (JPN) (Hector Protector (USA))
7458[7] 7686[6]

Bapak Pesta (IRE) *Kevin Ryan* 66
2 b c Haatef(USA) Penny Fan (Nomination)
4545[5] 4960[5] 6404[6]

Bapak Pintar *Kevin Ryan* a62 68
3 gr c Royal Applause Victory Spirit (USA) (Alphabet Soup (USA))
32[4] 747[5] 1167[4] 1519[3] 1757[4] 2382[4] 2788[5] 2843[2]

Bapak Sayang (USA) *Kevin Ryan* a66 79
2 b c Medaglia d'Oro(USA) Emily Ring (USA) (Fit To Fight (USA))
5176[5] (5963) 7773[5]

Baraamej (IRE) *C Boutin* a64 63
3 b f Marju(IRE) Ballyvarra (IRE) (Sadler's Wells (USA))
476a[10]

Baraboy (IRE) *Barry Murtagh* a22 54
2 b c Barathea(IRE) Irina (IRE) (Polar Falcon (USA))
1955[4] 4677[7] 5291[3] 6130[3] 6753[4]

Barachiel *Luke Dace* a67 67
4 b g Pivotal Coveted (Sinndar (IRE))
2576[6] 2821[3] 3081[2] ◆ 4181[3] 5596[4] 5908[7] 6976[4] 7486[3] 7960[2] 8067[11]

Barack (IRE) *W McCreery* a90 107
6 b g Pyrus(USA) Morna's Fan (FR) (Lear Fan (USA))
2100a[3] 2777a[8] 3647a[10] 4521a[6] 5609a[12] 6855a[9] 7423a[7]

Barathea Dancer (IRE) *Gay Kelleway* a73 81
4 b m Barathea(IRE) Showering (Danehill (USA))
2161[2] 2637[10] 3643[12] 3940[7] 4722[9] 5008[10] 5625[9] 7221[4] (7443) 7599[5]

Barbarella Blue (IRE) *Alan Berry* a65 38
3 b f Iffraaj Ditton Dancer (Danehill Dancer (IRE))
291[3] ◆ 784[4] 1363[10] 2203[5] 2840[7] 3214[8] 3451[10] 3727[6] 4258[5]

Barbayam *F Head* a84 109
3 gr f Stormy River(FR) Senkaya (FR) (Valanour (IRE))
1125a[3] 2728a[11] (3987a) 5648a[10] 7624a[13]

Barbecue Eddie (USA) *Doug Watson* a110 110
8 br g Stormy Atlantic(USA) The Green Owl (USA) (Carson City (USA))
(140a) 315a[2] 487a[6] 588a[13] (757a)

Barberton (USA) *Jeremy Noseda* 38
3 ch g Johannesburg(USA) Mythical Echo (USA) (Stravinsky (USA))
3155[P]

Barbican *Alan Bailey* a114 111
4 b g Hurricane Run(IRE) The Faraway Tree (Suave Dancer (USA))
1144a[7] 1750[4] 1974[10] 2506[4] 3632[3] 4363[4]

Barbirolli *William Stone* a53 52
10 b g Machiavellian(USA) Blushing Barada (USA) (Blushing Groom (FR))
1047[7] 1770[5] 2395[5] 2651[3] 2997[4] 3573[5] 4244[4] 5022[5] 5509[6] 6255[9]

Barbsiz (IRE) *Mark H Tompkins* a56
2 ch f Elnadim(USA) Bianca Cappello (IRE) (Glenstal (USA))
7916[4] 8207[6]

Barbs Princess *Charles Hills* 70
2 ch f Bahamian Bounty Halland Park Girl (IRE) (Primo Dominie)
2426[7] (7434)

Bareback (IRE) *John Best* a74 53
3 b g Redback Lady Lucia (IRE) (Royal Applause)
127[6] (667) ◆ 841[5] 920[7] 7170[11] 7480[11]

Barefoot Lady (IRE) *Richard Fahey* 110
4 b m Footstepsinthesand Lady Angharad (IRE) (Tenby)
1851[4] 2209[4] 2654[3] 3266[4] 4065[6] (4556) 5560[4] (6298a) 7093a[6]

Barefoot Sandy *Tony Coyle* a36 65
2 b f Sixties Icon Jollyhockeysticks (Fantastic Light (USA))
4813[10] 5300[10] 6355[3] 6607[3]

Bares Tripper (USA) *Peter Miller* a101 74
2 ch f Sky Mesa(USA) Bare Dancer (USA) (Cherokee Run (USA))
5031a[8]

Barista (IRE) *Brian Forsey* a66 79
4 b g Titus Livius(FR) Cappuccino (IRE) (Mujadil (USA))
359[10] 574[7] 736[9] 4988[8] 5127[2] 5658[4] 6001[3] 6275[8] 7126[2] 7437[4]

Barkis *Luca Cumani* 78
3 ch c Selkirk(USA) Batik (IRE) (Peintre Celebre (USA))
2800[2] 3447[3] 4706[8]

Barkston Ash *Eric Alston* 86
4 b g Kyllachy Ae Kae Ae (USA) (King Of Kings (IRE))
1156[21] 2264[13] 2488[11] 2841[2] 3027[3] (3272) 3778[7] 4554[9] 4998[7] 5539[2] 6009[6] 6260[4] 6820[8] (6999)

Barlows Glance *Peter Hiatt*
3 b f Passing Glance Mud Pie (Clantime)
8135[8]

Barnaby Brook (CAN) *Nick Littmoden* a66 37
2 b c North Light(IRE) Mascara (USA) (Milwaukee Brew (USA))
7330[13] 7641[3]

Barnacle *Pat Eddery* a51 56
3 b g Compton Place Bombalarina (IRE) (Barathea (IRE))
3389[11] 3702[13] 4456[6] 5659[5] 6279[4] 6892[6] 7148[8] 8050[7] 8177[7]

Barnacre *Richard Ford* a40
3 b g Tobougg(IRE) No Comebacks (Last Tycoon)
3232[8] 3710[P]

Barnet Fair *Richard Guest* a100 98
4 br g Iceman Pavement Gates (Bishop Of Cashel)
2177[12] 2717[7] 3641[9] 4367[6] ◆ (4576) 5370[7] 6244[4] 7503[4]

Barney McGrew (IRE) *Michael Dods* a80 97
9 b g Mark Of Esteem(IRE) Success Story (Sharrood (USA))
2284[9] 2487[6] 3049[6] 3336[4] 3960[6] 4554[4] 4770[2] 5412[10]

Barolo Top (IRE) *K F Clutterbuck* a62 79
3 b g Amadeus Wolf Princess Mood (GER) (Muhtarram (USA))
1181[3] 1721[11]

Baroness (FR) *F Monnier* a98 96
5 b m Okawango(USA) Danira (IRE) (Danehill (USA))
83a[2]

Baron Run *Mrs K Burke* 72
2 ch g Bertolini(USA) Bhima (Polar Falcon (USA))
4512[2] 5367[7]

Barons Spy (IRE) *Richard Price* a84 93
11 b g Danzero(AUS) Princess Accord (USA) (D'Accord (USA))
2029[11] 2870[3] (3221) 4286[18] 4998[9] (5812) 7107[4]

Barracuda Boy (IRE) *Tom Dascombe* 86
2 b c Bahamian Bounty Madame Boulangere (Royal Applause)
1651[2] 2073[5] 2763[3] (4230) (5088) 5515[7]

Barren Brook *Michael Easterby* 95
5 b g Beat Hollow Carinthia (IRE) (Tirol)
1130[7] 2257[5] 3164[10] 4828[9] 5091[6] 5712[2] 6630[8] 6884[7] 7175[8]

Barristers Brief *Eve Johnson Houghton* a37
4 b g Diktat Ski Run (Petoski)
428[6]

Barrow Island (IRE) *M Halford* a91 88
5 b g Chevalier(IRE) Shelini (Robellino (USA))
5397a[4]

Bartack (IRE) *Luca Cumani* a74 71
2 b g Acclamation Bentley's Bush (IRE) (Barathea (IRE))
3545[4] 5325[4] 5851[4] 6344[6] 7458[3]

Bartley *Bryan Smart* a67 76
3 ch g Monsieur Bond(IRE) Annie Harvey (Fleetwood (IRE))
975[5] 1441[12] 3075[3] 3210[2] 3994[8] 4957[4] 5317[2] 5538[4] 6403[9] 7604[14]

Bartolomeu *Marco Botti* a92 95
3 b g Footstepsinthesand Catch Us (FR) (Selkirk (USA))
1138[2] (1377) (1721) ◆ 2276[2] ◆ 3396[5] 4598[12]

Barton Bounty *Peter Niven* a65 57
5 b g Bahamian Bounty Tenebrae (IRE) (In The Wings)
2455[3] 2600[2] 2692[4] 4594[4] (7200) 7473[2] 7619[3] 7869[7]

Barwick *Mark H Tompkins* a68 87
4 b g Beat Hollow Tenpence (Bob Back (USA))
(1262) 1680[2] (2801) 3493[5] 4068[9] 5634[3] 5794[4] 6381[6]

Barzini (GER) *J Phelippon* a89 80
5 b g Lando(GER) Bella Flora (GER) (Slip Anchor)
815a[3] 965a[6]

Basantee *Tom Dascombe* a78 82
3 ch f Lucky Story(USA) Soft Touch (IRE) (Petorius)
1217[11] 1653[10] 2846[6] 3252[6] 3940[6] 5262[6]

Baschar *M G Mintchev* 115
5 b h Starcraft(NZ) Belle Et Deluree (USA) (The Minstrel (CAN))
3746a[4] 4383a[3] 6523a[6]

Bashaash (USA) *Ed Dunlop* a24 20
3 b f Dixie Union(USA) Destination (USA) (Seattle Slew (USA))
1532[12] 3349[14]

Bashama *Nikki Evans* a57 58
4 ch m Dubai Destination(USA) My Amalie (IRE) (Galileo (IRE))
981[6] 1191[10] 1423[4] 1984[9] 2872[6] 3430[5] 4993[2] 6000[7] 6158[9] 7362[10] 7612[7]

Basilica *Bill Turner* 78
4 ch g Zafeen(FR) Thicket (Wolfhound (USA))
(5447) 5852[6]

Basingstoke (IRE) *Andrew Balding* 68
3 b g Elusive City(USA) Ryninch (IRE) (Dr Devious (IRE))
2273[10] 6965[3] 7494[5]

Basle *Michael Blake* a63 78
5 b m Trade Fair Gibaltarik (IRE) (Jareer (USA))
212[7] ◆ 372[8] 687[2] 806[6] 1428[4] 1628[4] 2012[3] 2551[3] 2845[2] 3455[3] 3949[5] 4196[4] 4981[11] 5050[5] 5720[6] (8062)

Bassamba (FR) *F Rohaut* 104
3 b f American Post Benzolina (IRE) (Second Empire (IRE))
3423a[4] 6595a[4] 7234a[3] 7665a[7]

Bassara (IRE) *Chris Wall* 79
3 b f Oasis Dream Sauvage (FR) (Sri Pekan (USA))
1472[12] (3398)

Basseterre (IRE) *Charles Hills* a92 90
3 b c Cape Cross(IRE) Higher Love (IRE) (Sadler's Wells (USA))
(249) ◆ 1565[7] 2150[2] ◆ (2452) ◆ 3376[3] 6205[7] (6601) 7502[2]

Bassett Road (IRE) *Keith Dalgleish* a71 85
4 ch g Byron Topiary (IRE) (Selkirk (USA))
1936[10] 3589[11] 4302[8] 4872[6] 6145[10] 6774[6] (7105) 7857[3] ◆

Bastion (USA) *Roger Varian* a65
2 b c Giant's Causeway(USA) Marital Spook (USA) (Silver Ghost (USA))
7497[7]

Batchelors Star (IRE) *Jim Boyle* a74 89
4 ch g Fath(USA) Batchelor's Button (FR) (Kenmare (FR))
1602[11] 2024[4] 3105[6] 4503[9]

Batchworth Blaise *Eric Wheeler* a63 50
9 b g Little Jim Batchworth Dancer (Ballacashtal (CAN))
197[7] 422[8] 5240[4]

Batchworth Firefly *Dean Ivory* a57 30
4 b m Piccolo Batchworth Belle (Interrex (CAN))
6930[14] 7322[3] 7719[6] 7993[9] 8069[8]

Batchworth Lady *Dean Ivory* a51
2 b f Pastoral Pursuits Batchworth Belle (Interrex (CAN))
8068[7]

Bated Breath *Roger Charlton* 122
5 b h Dansili Tantina (USA) (Distant View (USA))
(2486) 3238[2] 5561[6] 6030[3]

Bateleur *Mick Channon* a64 66
8 b g Fraam Search Party (Rainbow Quest (USA))
2572[5] 3008[6] 3245[9] 3660[4] 4003[5] 4236[5] 4492[6] 4758[7]

Batgirl *John Berry* a65 81
5 ch m Mark Of Esteem(IRE) Serriera (FR) (Highest Honor (FR))
1262[2] 2011[3] 2465[5] 3192[3] 3615[5] 4517[10] 4966[2] 6687[7] 7314[7]

Bathwick Bear (IRE) *David Evans* a96 97
4 b g Kodiac Bayleaf (Efisio)
1255[2] 1885[18] 1975[9] 2286[10] 2507[3] 2558[2] 3127[11] 4367[16] 5530[9] 5829[7] ◆ 6286[3] 6543[4] 6663[4] 7113[3] 7295[11]

Bathwick Street *David Evans* 75
3 ch g Compton Place Bahawir Pour (USA) (Green Dancer (USA))
1519[7] 2049[2] 2424[2] (2818) 3592[3] 4225[2] 4606[5] 5366[6]

Battante (FR) *L A Urbano-Grajales* a69
2 b f Muhtathir Bahama Love (USA) (Hennessy (USA))
8193a[0]

Batter Up (USA) *Allen Iwinski*
4 bb g Johannesburg(USA) Ninth Inning (USA) (Meadowlake (USA))
(8279a)

Battery Power *Mark H Tompkins* a79 86
4 b m Royal Applause Missouri (Charnwood Forest (IRE))
1656[2] ◆ 2419[9] 2921[2] 3129[2]

Battle Of Marengo (IRE) *A P O'Brien* 110
2 b c Galileo(IRE) Anna Karenina (IRE) (Green Desert (USA))
(6060a) ◆ (6718a) ◆

Battleoftrafalgar *Michael Attwater* a88 72
5 b g Galileo(IRE) Pink Stone (FR) (Bigstone (IRE))
577[8] 625[2] 745[6] 2412[8] 3015[3] 3997[8] 6802[7]

Battleroftheboyne (IRE) *Michael Mulvany* a71 94
3 b c Majestic Missile(IRE) Khaytada (IRE) (Doyoun)
3648a[10] 4833a[2] 6270a[3] 6716a[16]

Bavarian Nordic (USA) *Richard Whitaker* a79 65
7 b g Barathea(IRE) Dubai Diamond (Octagonal (NZ))
1297[11] 1598[4] 2260[3] 3290[10] 3440[3] 3891[3] (4869) 5714[3] 6517[5] 6957[8]

Bavarian Princess (USA) *Mrs K Burke* a78 81
4 b m Invincible Spirit(IRE) Lileagh (IRE) (Sadler's Wells (USA))
359[9] (537) 686[4] (4655) 4933[8] 5548[2] 5853[4]

Bawaardi (IRE) *David Evans* a88 95
6 b g Acclamation Global Trend (Bluebird (USA))
90[9] (190) 378[7] 431[4] 785[11] 941[4] 1156[8] (1586) 2489[7] 2597[8] 3709[2] 5305[6]

Bayan (IRE) *Brian Meehan* 88
3 b g Danehill Dancer(IRE) Kindling (Dr Fong (USA))
2197[3] ◆ 2708[2] 3592[5] 3910[2] 4243[2] 4732[3]

Bayan Kasirga (IRE) *Richard Fahey* a68 69
2 b f Aussie Rules(USA) Gwyllion (USA) (Red Ransom (USA))
2450[9] 2837[3] 3282[6] 3858[4] 4574[3] 5254[7] 6121[12]

Bayargal (USA) *A Fabre* a85
2 b f Bernstein(USA) Bailonguera (ARG) (Southern Halo (USA))
7682a[4]

Baybshambles (IRE) *Ron Barr* 63
8 b g Compton Admiral Payvashooz (Ballacashtal (CAN))
1294[8] 1480[6] 2120[3] 2314[5] 4174[6] 4452[3] 4717[3] 5416[8] 6958[3] 7456[9]

Bay Knight (IRE) *Sean Curran* a82 104
6 b g Johannesburg(USA) Sabeline (IRE) (Caerleon (USA))
416a[14] 589a[14] 756a[10] 2268[8] 2819[4] 2919[10] 5301[14] 5746[9] 6800[8] 7559[9]

Bay Laurel (IRE) *Mrs K Burke* a68 38
2 b f Baltic King Bayleaf (Efisio)
3040[3] 3971[5] 4463[5] 6016[9] 6332[7] 7056[8] (7916) 8096[4]

Bayleyf (IRE) *John Best* a101 96
3 b g Kheleyf(USA) Hi Katriona (IRE) (Second Empire (IRE))
1751[7] 2236[9] 3158[4] 4063[16] 4740[15] 4802[26] 7080[16] 8188[6] ◆

Bay Of Fires (IRE) *David O'Meara* 76
4 b m Iffraaj No Tippling (IRE) (Unblest)
2538[12] 2878[2] 3115[8] 3749[9] 4207[3] 4547[4] 4717[6] 4909[10]

Bayrir (FR) *A De Royer-Dupre* 114
3 b c Medicean Balankiya (IRE) (Darshaan)
(4385a) (5375a) ◆ 6294a[2] 6912a[10] 8040a[6]

Bay Shore (IRE) *J-C Rouget* 92
3 b f Kheleyf(USA) Marillen (IRE) (Daylami (IRE))
1125a[4]

Bay Vatoria (GER) *H Zappe* 100
3 b f Vatori(FR) Bebe Kamira (GER) (Kamiros (IRE))
2522a[4]

Bazart *Bernard Llewellyn* a76 62
10 b g Highest Honor(FR) Summer Exhibition (Royal Academy (USA))
4181[4] 4536[6] 4994[3] 5265[3] 6232[10]

Bazron (IRE) *Des Donovan* a26 51
4 b m Byron Bazelle (Ashkalani (IRE))
2974[5] 3568[7] 5299[5]

Beach Candy (IRE) *Phil McEntee* a61 78
3 ch f Footstepsinthesand Endure (IRE) (Green Desert (USA))
1790[9] 1921[8] 4299[4] 4437[5] 5150[7] 5737[6] 5995[10] 6961[12] 7316[15] 7471[6] 8004[10] 8307[7]

Beach Club *David Brown* 80
2 b c Footstepsinthesand Dunya (Unfuwain (USA))
(5410) 6162[19]

Beachfire *John Gosden* a80 110
5 ch g Indian Haven Maine Lobster (USA) (Woodman (USA))
2081[7] 3329[12]

Beach Rhythm (USA) *Jim Allen* a51 33
5 ch g Footstepsinthesand Queen's Music (USA) (Dixieland Band (USA))
2042[11] 2496[8] 3012[7]

Beachwood Bay *Jo Hughes* a71 53
4 b g Tobougg(IRE) The Terrier (Foxhound (USA))
(101) 139[7] 372[4] (670) 899[3] 1384[12] 1958[2] 2760[7] 3442[11] 3941[6] 4406[2]

Beacon Lady *William Knight* a29 60
3 ch f Haafhd Oriental Lady (IRE) (King's Best (USA))
2850[8] 3621[11] (5991) 6442[4] 6948[2]

Beacon Lodge (IRE) *David Nicholls* 114
7 b g Clodovil(IRE) Royal House (FR) (Royal Academy (USA))
1549a[6] 2075[6] 5597[8] 6244[17] 6468[23] 6670[3] 6879[2]

Beacon Tarn *Eric Alston* a57 61
2 b f Shamardal(USA) Baize (Efisio)
5828[8] 6490[6] 6787[5] 7441[4] 7777[6] 8108[5]

Beadle *Richard Fahey* 57
2 b c Jeremy(USA) Twilight Belle (IRE) (Fasliyev (USA))
2537[7] 2837[8] 4083[4] 4672[7]

Beam Of Light *Jamie Osborne* 73
2 b f Bertolini(USA) Lighted Way (Kris)
5192[5] (5511)

Bear Behind (IRE) *Tom Dascombe* 107
3 b g Kodiac Gerobies Girl (USA) (Deposit Ticket (USA))
1219[2] 1644[2] 2704[19]

Bearheart (IRE) *P Monfort* a79 79
4 b h Aragorn(IRE) Guana (FR) (Sillery (USA))
16a[3] 1172a[3]

Bear Totem (IRE) *Jo Hughes* a35 59
2 b c Kodiac Sign Of Luck (IRE) (Daylami (IRE))
4152[7] (4449) 5009[5]

Bear Tough Tiger (USA) *Reade Baker* a104 105
4 ch g Roar Of The Tiger(USA) Dazzling Deelite (USA) (Afternoon Deelites (USA))
7092a[3]

Beat Black (JPN) *Hitoshi Nakamura* 120
5 bl h Miscast(JPN) Alarm Call (JPN) (Brian's Time (USA))
7872a[7]

Beaten Up *William Haggas* 120
4 b g Beat Hollow Frog (Akarad (FR))
1149a[6] 2703[5] 6142[4] 7029[3]

Beating Harmony *Michael Appleby* a60 53
4 b g Beat Hollow Heart's Harmony (Blushing Groom (FR))
66[10]

Beat Of The Blues *Michael Appleby* a79 60
4 b g Beat Hollow Skies Are Blue (Unfuwain (USA))
1133[13] 1266[7]

Beat Of The Drum (IRE) *Richard Hannon* 69
2 b f Duke Of Marmalade(IRE) Square Pants (USA) (King Of Kings (IRE))
6489[6] 6791[8]

Beatrice *H-A Pantall* a82 96
2 b f Dr Fong(USA) Brangane (IRE) (Anita's Prince)
7319a[2] 7698a[3]

Beatrice Aurore (IRE) *John Dunlop* 112
4 b m Danehill Dancer(IRE) Mondschein (Rainbow Quest (USA))
1471[3] 2209[5] ◆ 3266[5] 4527[6] 5849a[2] 6518a[2]

Beat Route *Michael Attwater* a78 69
5 ch g Beat Hollow Steppin Out (First Trump)
1418[7] 1706[8] (3472) 3782[7] 4944[2] 6703[8] (6981) 7301[6] 7810[3] 8000[9] 8082[8] 8191[5]

Beat The Ballot (IRE) *Tracey Collins* a79 79
3 br g Big Bad Bob(IRE) Cosmic Speed Queen (USA) (On To Glory (USA))
7229a[6]

Beat The Bell *Jamie Osborne* a80 95
7 b g Beat All(USA) Bella Beguine (Komaite (USA))
1279[4] 1430[5] 1935[5] (2482) 2629[5] 3045[8] 3570[3] 4660[3] 5347[2] 5852[3] 6150[8] 6837[3] 7308[2] ◆ (7464) 7716[9] 7820[2] 8036[4] 8294[2]

Beat The Ground (IRE) *Robert Collet* a69 73
4 b h Cape Cross(IRE) Nipping (IRE) (Night Shift (USA))
16a[2]

Beat The Ref *Ronald Harris*
4 b g Beat Hollow Bel (Darshaan)
1632[6]

Beat The Shower *Peter Niven* a46 83
6 b g Beat Hollow Crimson Shower (Dowsing (USA))
2093[8] 3253[5] 3953[3] 6712[4]

Beat The Tide *Michael Dods* 70
2 b c Black Sam Bellamy(IRE) Sablonne (USA) (Silver Hawk (USA))
3401[3] (4587) 5670[8]

Beat Up *Patrick Chamings* a60 26
6 b g Beat Hollow Whitgift Rose (Polar Falcon (USA))
4219[8] 4817[8] 6252[9]

Beauchamp Astra *Hans Adielsson* a38
2 b f Observatory(USA) Ashford Castle (USA) (Bates Motel (USA))
7669[5] 7855[6] ◆ 8006[8]

Beauchamp Castle *Hans Adielsson* a72 64
3 b f Motivator Ashford Castle (USA) (Bates Motel (USA))
(743) 920[2] 1190[3] 1707[6] 2372[9] 3068[3] 3968[6] 4359a[3]

Beauchamp Sunset *Hans Adielsson* a46
2 b g Tiger Hill(IRE) Orange Sunset (IRE) (Roanoke (USA))
7669[4] 7855[7] ◆ 8006[7]

Beauchamp Viking *Simon Burrough* a35 42
8 b g Compton Admiral Beauchamp Jade (Kalaglow)
2175[9]

Beauchamp Xerxes *Hans Adielsson* a57 81
6 ch g Compton Admiral Compton Astoria (USA) (Lion Cavern (USA))
7163[13] 7824[9] 7997[10]

Beauchamp Zorro *Henry Candy* 63
4 ch g Zamindar(USA) Aquarelle (Kenmare (FR))
3344[4] 4584[5] 5008[8] 5658[8]

Beau Duke (IRE) *Andrew Balding* a73 73
3 b g Bachelor Duke(USA) Xema (Danehill (USA))
959[2] 1422[3] 2021[7] 2557[8] 4607[7] 5705[4] 6172[6] (6643)

Beau Fighter *Gary Moore* a79 80
7 b g Tobougg(IRE) Belle De Jour (Exit To Nowhere (USA))
625[5] 751[10]

Beaufort Twelve *William Jarvis* 97
3 b g Hurricane Run(IRE) Violette (Observatory (USA))
1470[9] (2408) 3124[5] 3668[2] 4735[15] 5273[6] 6010[3] 6677[14]

Beau Michael *Adrian McGuinness* a74 87
8 b g Medicean Tender Moment (IRE) (Caerleon (USA))
7584a[8] 7852a[10]

Beau Mistral (IRE) *Paul Green* a80 89
3 ch f Windsor Knot(IRE) Carpet Lover (IRE) (Fayruz)
905[3] 1322[8] 1658[4] 1960[2] 2400[4] (2914) 3234[3] 3608[U] (4044) 4765[11] 5337[3] 6006[3] 6234[3] 6666[7] 7177[10]

Beaumont Cooper *Tony Carroll* 67
3 b g Invincible Spirit(IRE) Atlantide (USA) (Southern Halo (USA))
5687[2] 6792[6] 7108[9]

Beaumont's Party (IRE) *Chris Grant* a71 100
5 b g High Chaparral(IRE) Miss Champagne (FR) (Bering)
1273[6] 1654[10] 3911[8] 4879[11]

Beaurepaire Kid *David Barron* a43
3 b g Moss Vale(IRE) Drastic Measure (Pivotal)
1560[11] 1986[7]

Beau Select (IRE) *Robert Eddery* a65 65
2 b g Lucky Story(USA) Practicallyperfect (IRE) (King Charlemagne (USA))
2852[5] (3387) 5202[5] 5946[11] 7173[13] 7501[5] 7724[2] 7989[5] 8072[3]

Beautiful Day *Kevin Ryan* a89 69
4 b g Piccolo Evening (Mark Of Esteem (IRE))
812[2] 1520[6] 2033[7] 2455[5] 2922[11] 6785[10] 7317[2] 7715[10] 7920[9] 8306[3]

Beautiful Lando (FR) *Heather Main* a70 59
4 b g Lando(GER) Beautiful Baroness (USA) (Fortunate Prospect (USA))
353[10] 2373[13] 2811[2] 3229[9] 3958[10] 6145[8] 6458[11] 6804a[10] 7383[5]

Beautiful Life *David Simcock* a35
2 b f Footstepsinthesand My Heart's Deelite (USA) (Afternoon Deelites (USA))
8166[7]

Beautiful Story (IRE) *Mick Channon* 63
2 gr f Verglas(IRE) To The Skies (USA) (Sky Classic (CAN))
5574[3] 5907[8]

Beautiful View *Richard Hannon* 86
2 ch f Dubawi(IRE) Flamenco Dancer (Mark Of Esteem (IRE))
7372[2] ◆ (7553)

Beautifulwildthing *Peter Salmon* 60
2 b f Mount Nelson Euro Empire (USA) (Bartok (IRE))
5311[10] 6132[5] 6355[4] 7432[4] 7636[13]

Beauty Flash (NZ) *A S Cruz* 119
7 ch g Golan(IRE) Wychwood Rose (NZ) (Volksraad)
1902a[12]

Beauty Pageant (IRE) *David Brown* a82 87
5 ch m Bahamian Bounty My American Beauty (Wolfhound (USA))
1828[6] 2289[10] 2793[7] 3815[5] 5412[9] 6226[2] 7648[2] 8246[2]

Beauty Parlour *Sir Henry Cecil* 119
3 b f Deep Impact(JPN) Bastet (IRE) (Giant's Causeway (USA))
(1407a) (2109a) 3203a[2] 6673[7]

Beauvoir (IRE) *J-C Rouget* a109 109
3 gr c Footstepsinthesand Tipperary Honor (FR) (Highest Honor (FR))
1244a[3] 2110a[8]

Beaux Yeux *Ann Stokell* a22 39
6 b m Cadeaux Genereux Cloud Hill (Danehill (USA))
1662[8] 1957[3] 3235[8] 3848[11]

Be Calm *Michael Easterby* a56 59
3 b f Gentleman's Deal(IRE) Flower O'Cannie (IRE) (Mujadil (USA))
1918[4] 2118[11]

Becausewecan (USA) *Mark Johnston* a94 97
6 b g Giant's Causeway(USA) Belle Sultane (USA) (Seattle Slew (USA))
3241[7] 3642[9] 3857[13] 4575[6] 4925[4] 5076[5] 5540[12] 6031[7] 6472[7] 7068[7] 7377[4]

Beckermet (IRE) *Ruth Carr* a78 93
10 b g Second Empire(IRE) Razida (IRE) (Last Tycoon)
1161[17] 1478[11] 1844[3] 2119[3] 2284[3] 2597[5] 2825[2] 3128[7] 3557[4] (3812) 4286[6] 4629[5] 4880[3] 5186[6] 5368[6] 6011[12] 6471[5] 6663[3] 6888[3] 7000[6] 7453[6]

Beckfield Point *Stuart Williams* a54 4
3 b g Shirocco(GER) Platinum Princess (Diktat)
918[8] 1068[5] 2624[9]

Becksies *Paul Midgley* 46
3 b f Danbird(AUS) Cut Back (Factual (USA))
1596[3] 2336[16] 2438[4] 4913[9] 5246[12]

Becky Lou (USA) *Jeremy Noseda* 87
2 bb f Johannesburg(USA) Elle Nicole (USA) (El Corredor (USA))
2193[5] ◆ 3326[6] ◆ 4494[3] (5825) 7555[8]

Becqualink (FR) *M Gentile*
3 b c Rail Link Khayriya (FR) (Valanour (IRE))
290a[0]

Bedazzled *James Fanshawe* a93 90
3 b f Authorized(IRE) Dazzle (Gone West (USA))
1923[8] 2430[3] 4791[2] 5474[2] ◆ (6148) 6667[3] 7519[8]

Bedecked (IRE) *J S Bolger* a62 68
2 b f Holy Roman Emperor(IRE) Fainne (IRE) (Peintre Celebre (USA))
2958a[6]

Bedibyes *Richard Mitchell* a61 59
4 b m Sleeping Indian Aunt Sadie (Pursuit Of Love)
1009[2] 1626[8] 2170[13] 3006[4] 3485[10] 4942[11] 5049[3] 6646[9] 7512[9] 8299[7]

Bedlam *Tim Easterby* 69
3 b f Auction House(USA) Frantic (Fraam)
2118[7] 3781[9] 4549[5] 4958[8]

Bedloe's Island (IRE) *Neville Bycroft* a34 87
7 b g Statue Of Liberty(USA) Scenaria (IRE) (Scenic)
1642[3] 2208[6] (2337) 2793[11] 3127[8]

Bedouin Bay *Alan McCabe* a83 77
5 b g Dubai Destination(USA) Sahara Sonnet (USA) (Stravinsky (USA))
285[4] 1056[4] 1282[3] 1640[4] 2214[8]

Bedouin Invader (IRE) *Sir Michael Stoute* 48
2 b g Oasis Dream Hovering (IRE) (In The Wings)
7130[7]

Bee Brave *Sharon Watt* 68
2 b f Rail Link Swynford Pleasure (Reprimand)
(5083)

Beedee *Richard Hannon* a87 88
2 b c Beat Hollow Dawnus (IRE) (Night Shift (USA))
(2384) 2797[3] 3097[3] 4540[3] (5969) 6699[2] 7009[5] 7374[3]

Bee Sting *Lisa Williamson* a52 27
8 b g Selkirk(USA) Desert Lynx (IRE) (Green Desert (USA))
582[5] 695[5] 889[7] 1361[8]

Beetuna (IRE) *Daniel Mark Loughnane* a75 63
7 b g Statue Of Liberty(USA) High Atlas (Shirley Heights)
67[3] 574[2] 736[5] 1636[8] 1988[8] 2858[6] 3081[8]

Be Fabulous (GER) *Mahmood Al Zarooni* 111
5 b m Samum(GER) Bandeira (GER) (Law Society (USA))
2254[7]

Before Bruce *Brendan Powell* a51 67
5 b g Danbird(AUS) Bisque (Inchinor)
3311[4] 3431[2] 3969[7] (4536) 5038[4] 5908[4] 6159[10] 6981[11] 7596[9] 7819[12] 7862[8] 7968[6] 8104[11]

Befortyfour *Charles Smith* a78 99
7 b g Kyllachy Ivania (First Trump)
1073[5] 2369[2] ◆ 2693[2] ◆ 3993[11] 4660[8] 6226[13] 7666[10] 7970[9]

Beggar's Banquet (IRE) *Ed Vaughan* a71 62
3 b g Dubawi(IRE) Colour Splash (Rainbow Quest (USA))
147[4] 1031[5] 5316[6] 6570[5] 6965[4]

Beggar's Opera (IRE) *Jim Best* a19 59
5 b g Singspiel(IRE) Hannda (IRE) (Dr Devious (IRE))
3620[7] 5038[6] 5483[5] 5771[3]

Beggers Belief *Eric Wheeler* a71 62
4 ch g Bertolini(USA) Dropitlikeit's Hot (IRE) (Tagula (IRE))
60[4] 296[2] 818[DSQ] 1083[8] 2237[10] 2867[9] 3659[6] 7409[10] 7960[4]

Begonia (FR) *M Nigge* a67 69
3 b f Sakhee(USA) Queen Sceptre (IRE) (Fairy King (USA))
4477a[8]

Beholder (USA) *Richard E Mandella* a116
2 b f Henny Hughes(USA) Leslie's Lady (USA) (Tricky Creek (USA))
(7548a)

Behtarini (IRE) *Evan Williams* a87 17
5 b g Dalakhani(IRE) Behkiyra (IRE) (Entrepreneur)
4908[6]

Beidh Tine Anseo (IRE) *Lucinda Russell* 81
6 b g Rock Of Gibraltar(IRE) Siamsa (USA) (Quest For Fame)
3377[7]

Belatorio (IRE) *James Given* a19 37
2 b f Oratorio(IRE) Tarbela (IRE) (Grand Lodge (USA))
6985[7] 7592[9]

Belgian Bill *George Baker* a110 104
4 b h Exceed And Excel(AUS) Gay Romance (Singspiel (IRE))
145a[2] 317a[6] 591a[8] 866[2] 3268[12] 3331[7] 4099[12] 4761[8] 5848a[4] (7010) (7709) 7809[2]

Believe In Me *Julia Feilden* a42 42
2 b f Bertolini(USA) Zephrina (Zafonic (USA))
2193[13] 3084[4] 4658[6] 5886[8] 7008[4]

Belinsky (IRE) *Julie Camacho* a70 68
5 b g Compton Place Westwood (FR) (Anabaa (USA))
(122) 267[7] 473[3] 819[4] 1305[3] 2690[4] 4245[3] 4631[3] 5223[9] (5971) 7590[7] 7967[6] (8159)

Bella Bijou *Owen Brennan* a16 24
2 br f Multiplex Madam Bijou (Atraf)
6453[9] 6960[11]

Bella Michelle *William Muir*
2 b f Sakhee's Secret Michelle Ma Belle (IRE) (Shareef Dancer (USA))
6153[14]

Bella Noir *Mrs K Burke* a70 81
5 b m Kyllachy Lady Broughton (IRE) (Grand Lodge (USA))
1520[8] 1652[2] 3030[2] 3780[2] 4150[5]

Bella Ophelia (IRE) *Hughie Morrison* a82 80
3 b f Baltic King Banco Solo (Distant Relative)
(135) (645) (749) 977[3] 2347[6] 2894[2] 3639[8] 4081[5] 5233[8] 5877[8] 6811[12]

Bellapais Abbey (IRE) *David Brown* a29
6 b g Shernazar Wealthy And Wise (IRE) (Camden Town)
137[7]

Bell'Arte (IRE) *Mark Johnston* 65
2 b f Zamindar(USA) Art Eyes (USA) (Halling (USA))
5668[3] 6007[10] 6997[3] 7439[4]

Belleau (IRE) *Matt Sheppard* a71 73
4 b m Big Bad Bob(IRE) Fantasy Wood (IRE) (Charnwood Forest (IRE))
2755[5] 4061[9] 4491[6] 5508[7] 6000[11]

Belle Bayardo (IRE) *Ronald Harris* a74 74
4 b g Le Vie Dei Colori Heres The Plan (IRE) (Revoque (IRE))
2572[6] 4146[3] ◆ 4535[6] 5097[8] 5150[5] 5774[7] (6094) 6277[7] 6578[5] 7114[5] 7274[3] 7794[5] (8144)

Belle De Crecy (IRE) *Richard Hannon* 80
3 b f Rock Of Gibraltar(IRE) Bloemfontain (IRE) (Cape Cross (IRE))
2344[2]

Belle De Lune (FR) *J-L Pelletan* a91 108
3 b f Ski Chief(USA) Oppamattox (FR) (Munir)
1209a[2]

Belle Echappee (FR) *A Lyon* a68 30
3 b f Lando(GER) Shining Molly (FR) (Shining Steel)
117a[0]

Belle Intrigue *Amanda Perrett* 64
2 ch f Sakhee's Secret Belle Bellino (FR) (Robellino (USA))
(2995) 3269[25] 4230[6] 5532[4] 5903[7] 6332[8]

Belle Josephine *Mark Johnston* a77
4 b m Dubawi(IRE) Bella Lambada (Lammtarra (USA))
(451) ◆ 625[3] (728)

Belle Noverre (IRE) *John Butler* a68 83
8 b m Noverre(USA) Belle Etoile (FR) (Lead On Time (USA))
1310[7]

Belle Of The Hall (USA) *Thomas Albertrani* a104
5 ch m Graeme Hall(USA) Vines Of Justice (USA) (Judge T C (USA))
7569a[4]

Belle Park *Karen George* a60 60
5 b m Hamairi(IRE) Cape Siren (Warning)
1908[9] 2574[7] 3137[7] 4536[7] (5506) 6157[2] 7015[4] 7643[4] 7841[11]

Belle Voir *Gay Kelleway* a26 40
2 b f Phoenix Reach(IRE) Cow Girl (IRE) (King's Best (USA))
2622[5] 3150[5] 6844[7] 7979[7] 8164[6]

Belleza (FR) *S Smrczek* a68 71
5 ch m Muhtathir Rainbird (Rainbow Quest (USA))
93a[9]

Bellinda *Martin Bosley* a41
3 b f Aussie Rules(USA) Bonnie Belle (Imperial Ballet (IRE))
56[6] 294[7] 1012[10] 8264[12]

Bellitudo (IRE) *Marco Botti* a69
2 ch f Shamardal(USA) Night Life (IRE) (Night Shift (USA))
7160[6] 7505[3] 7987[2]

Bells Of Berlin *Alan McCabe* a52 17
3 ch g Pivotal Choirgirl (Unfuwain (USA))
1113[5] 3233[9] 3781[8] 4350[13]

Belly To Belly (IRE) *S Botti* 85
3 b f Dubawi(IRE) Penfection (IRE) (Orpen (USA))
1409a[9]

Beluckyformammy (IRE) *S Donohoe* a61 31
2 b f Key Of Luck(USA) Red Spinel (Fantastic Light (USA))
4161a[5] 5424[11]

Be My Rock *Rae Guest* a71 79
3 b f Rock Of Gibraltar(IRE) Supa Sal (King's Best (USA))
5166[2] 5529[2] 6792[2] 7395[3]

Benandonner (USA) *Paddy Butler* a97 97
9 ch g Giant's Causeway(USA) Cape Verdi (IRE) (Caerleon (USA))
1416[9] 1752[2] 2068[15] (2329) (2536) 2845[3] 4317[16] 4864[10] 5359[4] 5783[8] 6434[7] 7409[9] 7743[12] 8145[6] 8250[5]

Benartic (IRE) *Harry Dunlop* a71 66
8 b g Beneficial Glacial Queen (IRE) (Glacial Storm (USA))
3484[5] 4464[6] 4648[6] 6255[2] 7610[4]

Benbecula *Richard Hannon* a82 60
3 b g Motivator Isle Of Flame (Shirley Heights)
723[4] ◆ 921[2] 1031[2] 1468[10]

Ben Croy *Brian Meehan* a57 51
3 b g Nayef(USA) Chrysalis (Soviet Star (USA))
1303[12] 2495[6] 3246[9] 3469[3]

Bendzoldan (IRE) *Mrs John Harrington* a71 78
4 b m Refuse To Bend(IRE) Zoldan (Deploy)
4833a[9]

Beneath *Neil Mulholland* a64 69
5 b g Dansili Neath (Rainbow Quest (USA))
333[3] 389[3] 477[4] 651[12] 961[6] 2137[2] 4491[4] 5164[6] (6232)

Benefit Of Porter (IRE) *Patrick Sinnott* a69 84
8 b m Beneficial Porter Tastes Nice (IRE) (Dry Dock)
5580[5]

Bengaline *Scott Dixon* a69 48
3 b g Bahamian Bounty Indian Silk (IRE) (Dolphin Street (FR))
462[3] 748[4] 7055[8] 7402[9] 7914[6] 8005[7]

Bengal Tiger *Tony Carroll* a55 59
6 ch g Tagula(IRE) Floriana (Selkirk (USA))
119[9] 276[11] 895[3] 968[4] 2371[3] 3498[6] (4941) 5817[3]

Benidorm *John Wainwright* a47 56
4 b g Bahamian Bounty Famcred (Inchinor)
1755[9] 2441[8] 2796[7] 3356[8] 4551[4] 5113[4] 5259[10] 5549[4] 5823[6] 6477[3] 6643[6] 7361[10]

Benjamin (FR) *I A Urbano-Grajales* a90 90
7 b g Highest Honor(FR) Mia's Baby (USA) (Rahy (USA))
(2685a)

Bennelong *Richard Rowe* a76 71
6 b g Bahamian Bounty Bundle Up (USA) (Miner's Mark (USA))
263[4] 310[6] 577[7] 672[7] 1984[2] ◆ 2174[4] 2623[3] (2997) 3659[4] 4585[9] 5159[7] 6251[8] 6949[6] 7169[11] 7596[12] 8023[10] 8067[4] 8189[7]

Benoni *Henry Candy* 73
2 b g Bertolini(USA) Ladykirk (Slip Anchor)
4222[7] 4792[6] 5911[4] (6629)

Benozzo Gozzoli *Seamus Mullins* a46 62
6 ch g Medicean Star Precision (Shavian)
395[8] 632[8]

Bensoon *M Halford* a76 60
3 b g Refuse To Bend(IRE) Monsoon Wedding (Monsun (GER))
1834a[6]

Bentley *Brian Baugh* a77 62
8 b g Piccolo April Lee (Superpower)
7[9] 96[4] 274[2] 450[9] 532[4]

Bentleysoysterboy (IRE) *David Elsworth* a59 71
2 b g Kheleyf(USA) Morality (Elusive Quality (USA))
1886[6] ◆ 2193[7] 2817[3] 4324[3] 4873[5] 5790[4] 6983[2] 7176[3]

Benzanno (IRE) *Andrew Balding* a72 93
3 b g Refuse To Bend(IRE) Crossanza (IRE) (Cape Cross (IRE))
1192[2] 1606[4] 3999[2] (4256) 4603[9] 6374[3] 6701[2] (7210) ◆

Be On The Bell *Jamie Osborne* a74
2 br f Byron Bella Beguine (Komaite (USA))
7219[5] (7777) 7965[9] 8211[6]

Be Perfect (USA) *Marco Botti* a99 96
3 b c Street Cry(IRE) Binya (GER) (Royal Solo (IRE))
6446[8] 6879[6] 7825[2] 8227[3]

Berabani (FR) *M Delzangles* a66 84
3 gr c Lawman(FR) Bernimixa (FR) (Linamix (FR))
1171a[9]

Berberana (IRE) *Jeremy Gask* a68 85
4 b m Acclamation Barbera (GER) (Night Shift (USA))
715[8] 3496[9] 4423[4] 4849[6] 5514[4] 5815[5] 6370[3] 6578[7] 7197[11] 7489[11]

Berbice (IRE) *Linda Perratt* a72 74
7 gr g Acclamation Pearl Bright (FR) (Kaldoun (FR))
3115[9] 3888[8] 4134[9] 4432[3] 4769[5] 5058[4] 5362[11] 5918[2] 6309[3] 6479[6] 6711[9] 7788[3]

Berengar (IRE) *Brian Meehan* a76 62
3 b g Holy Roman Emperor(IRE) Double Fantasy (GER) (Indian Ridge)
1506[14] 6450[9] 6973[6] 7302[14] 7415[10]

Beringson (FR) *Mlle H Mennessier* 80
6 ch g Bering Winter Ice (Wolfhound (USA))
7701a[9]

Berkeley Street (USA) *Sir Michael Stoute* 61
2 b g Street Cry(IRE) Dream Ticket (USA) (Danzig (USA))
6985[3]

Berlin Berlin *Markus Klug* 103
3 b f Dubai Destination(USA) Bombazine (IRE) (Generous (IRE))
6723a[2] 7282a[9]

Berling (IRE) *John Dunlop* 106
5 gr h Montjeu(IRE) Danaskaya (IRE) (Danehill (USA))
2481[3] ◆ 3632[4] 4759[7] 5575[3] 6091a[4] 6600[8]

Berlusca (IRE) *Mark Brisbourne* a73 73
3 b g Holy Roman Emperor(IRE) Shemanikha (FR) (Sendawar (IRE))
201[4] 377[3] (549) 667[4] 841[2] 3063[5] 3736[8] 4082[3] 4830[11] 5336[4] 7141[6] 7529[8] 7925[8]

Bermondsey Bob (IRE) *John Spearing* a14 75
6 b g Trans Island Tread Softly (IRE) (Roi Danzig (USA))
1254[16] 2421[9] 2572[4] 2815[5] 3245[2] 3434[3] 4238[2] 4332[4] (4492) 4708[6] 5093[11] 5915[15] 5933[7] 6094[11]

Bernando (FR) *J Phelippon* a88 62
8 b h Hernando(FR) Beggars Belief (IRE) (Common Grounds)
965a[2]

Bernardino *David Barron* 55
2 b g Bertolini(USA) Moon Royale (Royal Abjar (USA))
2837[6] 3208[7] 6556[3]

Bernie The Bolt (IRE) *Andrew Balding* a50 93
6 br g Milan Chaparral Lady (IRE) (Broken Hearted)
1882[7] 2278[9] 3373[9] 5076[6] 6493[5] 7051[23]

Bernisdale *John Flint* a55 73
4 ch m Bertolini(USA) Carradale (Pursuit Of Love)
2389[12] 3443[2] (3704) 4411[10] (6927) 7129[3] 7301[11]

Be Royale *Bryn Palling* 42
2 b f Byron Sofia Royale (Royal Applause)
4813[11] 5656[7] 6571[8]

Berrymead *Ann Stokell* a52 18
7 br m Killer Instinct Mill End Quest (King's Signet (USA))
3076[10] 3243[10] 5013[11]

Bertbrand *Ian McInnes* a36 51
7 b g Bertolini(USA) Mi Amor (IRE) (Alzao (USA))
14[9] 101[7] 226[9] 368[6]

Bertie Blu Boy *Lisa Williamson* a59 63
4 b g Central Park(IRE) Shaymee's Girl (Wizard King)
929[9] 1179[5] 1634[9] 1961[7] 3317[8] 3454[9] 3914[10] 7443[6] 7619[8] (8039) 8249[3]

Bertie Moon *Geoffrey Deacon* a31 17
2 b c Bertolini(USA) Fleeting Moon (Fleetwood (IRE))
7103[9] 7324[13]

Bertie Royale *J S Moore* 79
2 b g Bertolini(USA) Riva Royale (Royal Applause)
(4730)

Bertie Southstreet *Paul Midgley* a66 64
9 bb g Bertolini(USA) Salvezza (IRE) (Superpower)
719[6] (839) 1483[5] 2092[5] 2377[7]

Bertiewhittle *David Barron* a65 99
4 ch g Bahamian Bounty Minette (Bishop Of Cashel)
1885[15] 2268[7] 3183[4] 3648a[11] 4321[3] 5370[12] 5572[4] 6024[7] 6676[4] ◆ 7240[6]

Bertimont (FR) *C Lerner* a81 75
2 gr c Slickly(FR) Bocanegra (FR) (Night Shift (USA))
3714a[2]

Bertoliver *Stuart Williams* a85 84
8 b g Bertolini(USA) Calcavella (Pursuit Of Love)
2195[10] 2439[8] 3595[5] 4013[15] 4501[6] 4690[22] 6234[14] 6347[7]

Bert The Alert *Gary Moore* a77 67
4 b g Proclamation(IRE) Megalex (Karinga Bay)
(149) 625[4] 2115a[2] 2886[11] (7310) ◆ 7473[4] 7892[9] 8173[2] (8292)

Berwaaz (GER) *Andrew Crook*
4 b g Tertullian(USA) Birthday Night (USA) (Southern Halo (USA))
1055[5]

Berwin (IRE) *Sylvester Kirk* a74 73
3 b f Lawman(FR) Topiary (IRE) (Selkirk (USA))
2200[2] 2866[7] 5592[7] 5931[3] ◆ 6613[5] 6981[6] 7644[7] 7954[11]

Besito (IRE) *William Jarvis* a55 79
3 b f Kodiac Christmas Kiss (Taufan (USA))
2893[6] 4497[9] 5837[7] 6209[6] 6973[10]

Bessichka *Simon Dow* 63
3 b f Exceed And Excel(AUS) Jouet (Reprimand)
1274[2]

Best Be Careful (IRE) *Mark Usher* a64 81
4 b m Exceed And Excel(AUS) Precautionary (Green Desert (USA))
2040[5] 2494[3] (4530) 4849[9] 5272[8] 6226[10] 7483[9]

Bestfootforward *Olivia Maylam* a48
3 ch f Motivator Best Side (IRE) (King's Best (USA))
8187[9] 8291[6]

Best In Show *Roger Curtis* a53 53
3 b g Exceed And Excel(AUS) Alashaan (Darshaan)
2131[11] 2862[12] 6396[7] 7189[7] 7362[8]

Best Of All (GER) *E Lellouche* 84
3 b f Dylan Thomas(IRE) Bright Sky (IRE) (Wolfhound (USA))
2741a[7] 3203a[12]

Best Of Order (IRE) *E J O'Neill* a89 93
5 ch h Pivotal Groom Order (Groom Dancer (USA))
5648a[9] 7829a[8]

Best Present Ever (USA) *J Eric Kruljac* 102
3 bb f Unusual Heat(USA) Centerofattention (USA) (Beau Genius (CAN))
4131a[3]

Best Tango (ITY) *Gianluca Bietolini* 97
2 b c Mujahid(USA) Nikita Tango (FR) (Sicyos (USA))
7076a[6] 7513a[4]

Best Terms *Richard Hannon* a87 114
3 b f Exceed And Excel(AUS) Sharp Terms (Kris)
1508[5] 2078[10] 2486[10]

Best To Better (IRE) *Marco Botti* a61 55
2 b f Acclamation Searching Blaze (IRE) (Desert Prince (IRE))
4742[5] 5887[4] 6581[4] 7223[3]

Best Trip (IRE) *Brian Ellison* a89 86
5 b g Whipper(USA) Tereed Elhawa (Cadeaux Genereux)
120[10] 282[6] 560[7] 649[4] 735[7] 1823[5] (2538) (3314) (3496) 3778[10] 4367[17] 4924[6] 5539[3] 6465[3] 6820[2] 7690[15]

Besty *Paul Midgley* a25 63
5 ch g Compton Place Petrovna (IRE) (Petardia)
1526[2] 3256[3] 3442[3] 3730[6] 4452[11] 4717[5] 5203[12] 5416[14] 6104[5] 7099[3] 7457[6] 7747[13]

Bet Noir (IRE) *Tony Carroll* a62 64
7 b m King's Best(USA) Ivowen (USA) (Theatrical (IRE))
5935[12]

Betteras Bertie *Tony Coyle* a62 67
9 gr g Paris House Suffolk Girl (Statoblest)
1755[5] 2094[8] 2593[8] 4627[9] 4959[4]

Better Be Mine (IRE) *John Dunlop* a63 52
3 br f Big Bad Bob(IRE) Cara Fantasy (IRE) (Sadler's Wells (USA))
1303[2] ◆ 1726[3] 2850[2] 6365[7] 7062[10]

Better Be The One (AUS) *M Freedman* a110 115
6 b g More Than Ready(USA) Common Smytzer (AUS) (Snippets (AUS))
681a[7] 1146a[9] 2326a[6]

Betterbetterbetter (IRE) *A P O'Brien* a76 105
3 b f Galileo(IRE) Jude (Darshaan)
1973[2] 2658[8] 3197a[2]

Better Lucky (USA) *Thomas Albertrani* 108
3 b f Ghostzapper(USA) Sahara Gold (USA) (Seeking The Gold (USA))
4478a[2]

Bettolle (ITY) *P Cadeddu* 100
3 b f Blu Air Force(IRE) Happy Sue (IRE) (City On A Hill (USA))
1409a[4]

Betty Boo (IRE) *Shaun Harris* 55
2 ch f Thousand Words Poker Dice (Primo Dominie)
2047[4] 2376[10] 3286[9] 4545[16] 5313[4] 5733[6] 6283[7]

Betty Brook (IRE) *Nick Littmoden* a65 46
3 b f Refuse To Bend(IRE) Ikan (IRE) (Sri Pekan (USA))
524[7] 802[2] ◆ (1585)

Between Us *Sir Mark Prescott Bt* a66 88
3 b f Galileo(IRE) Confidante (USA) (Dayjur (USA))
2287[5] 2877[7] 4466[7] (5219) (5442) 6033[10] 6416[3]

Betzyoucan *Mark Johnston* a58 63
2 b f Royal Applause Mint Royale (IRE) (Cadeaux Genereux)
4512[6] 4877[9] 7434[3] 7713[3] 8016[6]

Be Very Careful *Richard Hannon* a13 13
2 b f Misu Bond(IRE) Lady In The Bath (Forzando)
4408[13] 5153[6] 6366[13]

Bevis Marks (USA) *Mark Johnston* a59 50
3 b c Street Cry(IRE) Blue Duster (USA) (Danzig (USA))
1036[4] 1320[10] 2353[12]

Beyeh (IRE) *Michael Appleby* a49 72
4 b m King's Best(USA) Cradle Rock (IRE) (Desert Sun)
(7472)

Beyond (IRE) *David Pipe* a81 91
5 ch g Galileo(IRE) Run To Jane (IRE) (Doyoun)
4697[4] 7051[19]

Beyond Conceit (IRE) *Tom Tate* 92
3 b g Galileo(IRE) Baraka (IRE) (Danehill (USA))
1641[2] 2484[3] 3614[2] 5598[7] ◆ 6033[7]

Beyond Desire *Roger Varian* 112
5 b m Invincible Spirit(IRE) Compradore (Mujtahid (USA))
(1494) (2112a) 2745a[10] 4762[11] 5561[5] 6908a[14]

Beyond Thankful (IRE) *J S Bolger* 96
2 b c Whipper(USA) Beyond Compare (IRE) (Galileo (IRE))
7419a[2]

Bez *Nicky Vaughan*
4 b g Green Card(USA) Dakisi Royale (King's Signet (USA))
2765[8] 4550[11]

Bezique *Luca Cumani* 101
4 gr m Cape Cross(IRE) Batik (IRE) (Peintre Celebre (USA))
2211[9] 2554[2]

B Fifty Two (IRE) *J W Hills* a101 107
3 br c Dark Angel(IRE) Petite Maxine (Sharpo)
1453[7] 1751[5] 4367[12] 4790a[6] 5077[10] 6075[19]

Bheleyf (IRE) *Joseph Tuite* a76 72
2 b f Kheleyf(USA) Carraigoona (IRE) (Rock Of Gibraltar (IRE))
1136[5] 1563[5] (2622) 3970[2] 4526[7] 4936[5]

Bianca De Medici *Hughie Morrison* a82 79
5 b m Medicean Tremiere (FR) (Anabaa (USA))
115[2] 378[3]

Bianmick (AUS) *Michael Brady* 106
6 b g Bianconi(USA) Cross Dancer (AUS) (Citidancer (IRE))
7073a[11]

Biba Diva (IRE) *Jeremy Noseda* a74 75
3 b f Danehill Dancer(IRE) Mowaadah (IRE) (Alzao (USA))
32[2] 398[5] 667[9]

Bible Belt (IRE) *Mrs John Harrington* 114
4 br m Big Bad Bob(IRE) Shine Silently (IRE) (Bering)
2525a[4] 5027a[3] 5518[5]

Bible Black (IRE) *G M Lyons* a99 96
3 br g Big Bad Bob(IRE) Convent Girl (IRE) (Bishop Of Cashel)
142a[13] 417a[6] 2524a[8] 3322a[3] 5334[7]

Bidable *Bryn Palling* a56 74
8 b m Auction House(USA) Dubitable (Formidable (USA))
2574[10] 3485[12] 4533[8] 5193[3] 5657[9] 8241[10]

Bid For Gold *Jedd O'Keeffe* a36 67
8 b g Auction House(USA) Gold And Blue (IRE) (Bluebird (USA))
3026[2] 3731[5] 4315[2] 4866[4]

Big Bad Lily (IRE) *Augustine Leahy* a74 70
4 br m Big Bad Bob(IRE) Ginger Lily (IRE) (Lucky Guest)
6226[5]

Big Band Sound (USA) *Daniel J Vella* a102 112
5 b h Bernstein(USA) Ensnare (USA) (Seeking The Gold (USA))
6300a[6] 7092a[4]

Big Bane Theory (USA) *Carla Gaines* 96
3 b c Artie Schiller(USA) Shebane (USA) (Alysheba (USA))
7882a[9]

Big Bay (USA) *Jane Chapple-Hyam* a81 53
6 b g Horse Chestnut(SAF) Takipy (USA) (Persian Bold)
199[3] ◆ 517[7] 991[5] 2463[4] 3544[11] 5741[8] 7722[10]

Big Blue Kitten (USA) *Chad C Brown* a101 107
4 b h Kitten's Joy(USA) Spent Gold (USA) (Unaccounted For (USA))
3267[10]

Big Boss Baby (USA) *Luis Olivares*
2 bb g Montbrook(USA) Candlelightdinner (USA) (Slew Gin Fizz (USA))
8244a[8]

Big Break *D K Weld* 104
2 b f Dansili Fame At Last (USA) (Quest For Fame)
(7419a)

Big Creek (IRE) *Jeremy Noseda* a85 83
5 b h Galileo(IRE) Baranja (USA) (St Jovite (USA))
36[5] ◆ 187[2] 751[3] 1186[3] 1939[4] 3766[11]

Big Johnny D (IRE) *John Dunlop* 84
3 ch g Alhaarth(IRE) Bakiya (USA) (Trempolino (USA))
4067[3] 6677[11] 7174[6]

Big Jones (FR) *Mlle M-L Mortier*
2 gr c Nombre Premier Cardamome (FR) (Cardoun (FR))
8176a[0]

Big Memory (FR) *J-P Carvalho* 96
2 b c Duke Of Marmalade(IRE) Nicara (GER) (Nebos (GER))
7698a[4]

Big Moza *John Best* a64
2 b f Pastoral Pursuits Zaynah (IRE) (Kahyasi)
7707[12] 8052[3]

Big Note (IRE) *Andrew Balding* a94 102
3 b c Amadeus Wolf Double Vie (IRE) (Tagula (IRE))
1032[9] 1356[2] 1751[9] 2659[6] 4063[4] 5080[5] (6659)

Big Notion (USA) *Gary G Jackson*
5 b g Great Notion(USA) Empress Kell (USA) (Wavering Monarch (USA))
(8100a)

Big Old Unit *Tom Dascombe*
3 b f Byron Veiled Beauty (USA) (Royal Academy (USA))
1501[18]

Big Spender (IRE) *Ian McInnes* 28
2 b g Jeremy(USA) Truly Generous (IRE) (Generous (IRE))
5108[5] 5291[7] 6099[14]

Big Storm Coming *Brian Ellison* 27
2 b g Indesatchel(IRE) Amber Valley (Foxhound (USA))
7598[9]

Big Sur *Tom Keddy* a64 61
6 ch g Selkirk(USA) Bombazine (IRE) (Generous (IRE))
6773[12]

Big Sylv (IRE) *James Unett* a62 49
3 gr f Clodovil(IRE) Casual Remark (IRE) (Trans Island)
838[6] 1016[8] 1420[7] 2130[5] 3218[3] 3455[7] 4185[2] 5014[7] 5446[8] 7787[4] 7982[4] (8111)

Big Thunder *Sir Mark Prescott Bt* a51 49
2 gr g Dalakhani(IRE) Charlotte O Fraise (IRE) (Beat Hollow)
4917[7] 5162[6] 5825[7] 6133[8]

Big Time Billy (IRE) *Peter Bowen* a39 66
6 b m Definite Article Zaratu (IRE) (Key Of Luck (USA))
2418[5] 2708[9] 3100[4] 4004[3] 4756[4] 8073[11]

Big Wave (IRE) *Alison Hutchinson* a73 76
4 b m Choisir(AUS) Mystery Solved (USA) (Royal Academy (USA))
533[4] 892[3] (1285) 1788[2] (3076) 3724[4] 4003[10] (4969) 5548[6] 5995[9] 6378[9] 6934[3] 7485[12] 7827[12]

Bijou Dan *George Moore* a49 66
11 ch g Bijou D'Inde Cal Norma's Lady (IRE) (Lyphard's Special (USA))
2874[3] 3437[2] 3750[2] 5172[2] 5735[3] 6956[13]

Bilash *Reg Hollinshead* 72
5 gr g Choisir(AUS) Goldeva (Makbul)
(2377) 2982[9] 4743[3] 5205[6] 6094[12]

Bilge Kagan (IRE) *A Savujev* 87
2 br c Whipper(USA) Privet (IRE) (Cape Cross (IRE))
6463a[7]

Bilidn *Noel Quinlan* a64 94
4 b m Tiger Hill(IRE) Brightest Star (Unfuwain (USA))
97[9] 281[8] 433[5] 575[4] 968[2] (1112) (2468) (2635) (2925) (3077) 4184[2] 4528[5] 7522[14]

Bilko Pak (IRE) *Brendan Powell* a77 86
4 b g Barathea(IRE) Vale View (FR) (Anabaa (USA))
1306[9] 1722[10] 1789[5]

Billion Dollar Kid *Jo Davis* a72 77
7 br g Averti(IRE) Fredora (Inchinor)
5035[9] 5783[2] 5998[3]

Billy Budd (IRE) *S Botti* 98
4 b h Shamardal(USA) Baranja (USA) (St Jovite (USA))
2521a[6]

Billy Buttons *Andrew Balding* a79 90
4 gr g Act One Dolce Thundera (USA) (Thunder Gulch (USA))
(983)

Billy Cadiz *Julie Camacho* a58 58
7 b g Zilzal(USA) Faraway Moon (Distant Relative)
7[3]

Billy Dane (IRE) *Barry Murtagh* a77 92
8 b g Fayruz Lomalou (IRE) (Lightning Dealer)
2535[P]

Billyford (IRE) *Liam Roche* a96 98
7 b g Lil's Boy(USA) Alamanta (IRE) (Ali-Royal (IRE))
1549a[4] 2777a[4]

Billyrayvalentine (CAN) *George Baker* a63 86
3 b g Elusive Quality(USA) Sweet And Careless (USA) (Hennessy (USA))
2509[11] 4723[4]

Billy Red *J R Jenkins* a81 80
8 ch g Dr Fong(USA) Liberty Bound (Primo Dominie)
525[10] 647[5] 911[8] (1073) 2494[8] (2994) 3618[3] 3919[6] 4980[4] 7309[9] 7648[7] 7742[6] 8054[3] 8225[8]

Billy Redpath *Frederick Watson* 22
4 b g Distant Music(USA) Shardda (Barathea (IRE))
5679[11] 6102[9]

Bin End *Barry Brennan* a64 28
6 b g King's Best(USA) Overboard (IRE) (Rainbow Quest (USA))
296[9]

Bin Manduro *James Tate* a60
2 b c Manduro(GER) Dust Dancer (Suave Dancer (USA))
7963[5]

Bin Singspiel *James Tate* a69
2 br c Singspiel(IRE) Mexican Hawk (USA) (Silver Hawk (USA))
7057[3] 7780[2]

Bint Alakaaber (IRE) *J R Jenkins* a46
4 b m Elusive City(USA) Lady Of Pleasure (IRE) (Marju (IRE))
373[6]

Bint Alzain (IRE) *Gerard Butler* a78 55
3 b f Marju(IRE) Barconey (IRE) (Danehill Dancer (IRE))
279[3] (724) 917[3] 1392[6] 2136[2] 2503[7] (3044) 3762[4] 4218[6] 4647[3] 4933[6] (5298) 5769[7] 6150[2] 6367[5] 6840[6] 7415[9] 7769[2]
Bint Elnadim (IRE) *Derek Shaw* a54
4 b m Elnadim(USA) Redrightreturning (Diktat)
5031[1] 550[8] 690[3]
Bintisultan (FR) *T Clout* a68 70
2 b f King's Best(USA) Babola (IRE) (Grand Lodge (USA))
5288a[5]
Bint Youmzain (IRE) *Mick Channon* 56
2 b f Exceed And Excel(AUS) Chaussons (IRE) (Indian Ridge)
4002[6] 4701[15] 6355[6]
Biographer *David Lanigan* a91 106
3 b c Montjeu(IRE) Reflective (USA) (Seeking The Gold (USA))
1567[2] (3181) 4216[2] (4732) 5598[2] (6833)
Biondetti (USA) *Mahmood Al Zarooni* a109 105
4 b h Bernardini(USA) Lyphard's Delta (USA) (Lyphard (USA))
488a[4] 878a[13] 3825[6]
Bircham (IRE) *Mahmood Al Zarooni* 85
2 ch c Dubawi(IRE) Royale Danehill (IRE) (Danehill (USA))
2822[2] ◆ (3303) 4101[2] 4763[10] 6032[10] 7028[7]
Bird Dog *Phil McEntee* a56
6 ch g Compton Place Form At Last (Formidable (USA))
(95) 289[7] 372[6] 551[5] 580[7] 910[10] 1987[12] 2046[12] 8246[6]
Birdie King *John Best* a59
2 b g Dutch Art Daughters World (Agnes World (USA))
7498[7] 7813[5] 7894[6]
Birdie Queen *John Best* a54
2 b f Pastoral Pursuits Silver Miss (FR) (Numerous (USA))
2039[6]
Birdlover *Ralph Beckett* a72 90
2 ch f Byron Bird Over (Bold Edge)
5418[6] 6871[2] (7191)
Birdman (IRE) *David Simcock* 108
2 b g Danehill Dancer(IRE) Gilded Vanity (IRE) (Indian Ridge)
2247[3] (2648) (3097) 4098[2] 4698[7] 5642a[3] 6243[5] 6671[4] 7398[7]
Birdy Boy (USA) *Mark Johnston* a38 33
2 ch g Elusive Quality(USA) Flip Flop (FR) (Zieten (USA))
2213[9] 3491[9] 4502[6] 5161[7] 7606[4] 7650[7]
Birthday Lion (GER) *U Stoltefuss* a86 100
7 ch g Areion(GER) Boucheron (GER) (Turfkonig (GER))
1745a[5]
Birthday Sun (GER) *W Hickst* a86 80
4 b m Areion(GER) Boucheron (GER) (Turfkonig (GER))
18a[2]
Birzali (FR) *John Joseph Hanlon* a60 71
5 gr g Kalanisi(IRE) Bernimixa (FR) (Linamix (FR))
7852a[14]
Biscaya Bay *A Fabre* a81 99
3 b f Dansili Borgia (GER) (Acatenango (GER))
5142a[4]
Bishopbriggs (USA) *John Butler* a68 46
7 ch g Victory Gallop(CAN) Inny River (USA) (Seattle Slew (USA))
2401[2] 6585[9]
Bishop Roko *Roger Charlton* 97
3 b g Rock Of Gibraltar(IRE) Kirk (Selkirk (USA))
(2266)
Bishop's Castle (USA) *Mark Johnston* 82
3 bb c Distorted Humor(USA) Miss Caerleona (FR) (Caerleon (USA))
6792[4] 6925[2] 7112[3]
Bispham Green *Richard Fahey* 78
2 b c Green Desert(USA) Royal Grace (Royal Applause)
1842[6] 2213[6] 2880[5] 4071[4] 4614[2] 5332[2] 6022[2] 6312[2]
Bitaphon (IRE) *Michael Appleby* a70 73
3 br g Acclamation Pitrizzia (Lando (GER))
112[5] (2382) 2883[5] 4329[11] 4830[10] 6048[5] 6810[8] 7964[9] 7993[6] 8255[3]
Bit By Bit *D Smaga* a82 101
3 gr f Rail Link Lixian (Linamix (FR))
5142a[9]
Bite Of The Cherry *Michael Bell* a60 101
3 br f Dalakhani(IRE) Bianca Nera (Salse (USA))
1532[7] 2249[7] 3773[2] (4601) 5519[4] 6163[6]
Bit Of A Gift (FR) *Roger Varian* 76
2 b c Dark Angel(IRE) Dilag (IRE) (Almutawakel)
6481[13] (6880)
Bitter Ale *Alan McCabe* a7
2 b g Auction House(USA) Pesse (IRE) (Eagle Eyed (USA))
3708[6]
Bitter Harvest *Michael Bell* a59 63
3 b g Singspiel(IRE) Bijou A Moi (Rainbow Quest (USA))
1512[9] 1922[6] 2143[10] 2671[6]
Bitter Lemon *Tony Newcombe* a55 56
3 b f Indesatchel(IRE) Citron (Reel Buddy (USA))
40[6] 845[3] 1337[9] 2762[4] 3489[4] 4237[5] 5263[7] (5875) 7633[9]
Bittersweet (SWE) *Pal Jorgen Nordbye* a15
5 b m Academy Award(IRE) Sweet Chili (SWE) (Diaghlyphard (USA))
5143a[9]
Bitusa (USA) *Alan Swinbank* 67
2 b g Roman Ruler(USA) Richen (USA) (Well Decorated (USA))
5382[9] 6780[4] 7067[4]
Bivouac (UAE) *Alan Swinbank* a75 65
8 b g Jade Robbery(USA) Tentpole (USA) (Rainbow Quest (USA))
44[6] 285[9]
Bix (IRE) *Alan Berry* a71 71
2 b c Holy Roman Emperor(IRE) Belle Rebelle (IRE) (In The Wings)
2231[15] 2609[4] 3387[3] 4140[2] 5155[7] 6188[3] (6512) 7209[5] 8150[5] 8258[6]
Biz The Nurse (IRE) *S Botti* 91
2 b c Oratorio(IRE) Biz Bar (Tobougg (IRE))
7513a[5]
Bizzy Caroline (USA) *Kenneth McPeek* 108
4 bb m Afleet Alex(USA) Sacre Coeur (USA) (Saint Ballado (CAN))
6695a[6]
Blackamoor Harry *Richard Ford* a34 47
3 b g Indesatchel(IRE) Libretta (Highest Honor (FR))
5208[6] 5805[5] 6001[9] 6758[5] 7106[3] 7470[4]
Blackamoor Zara *Richard Ford* a18 34
3 b f Haafhd Sara Mana Mou (Medicean)
5212[10]
Black Annis Bower *Michael Easterby* 75
4 gr m Proclamation(IRE) Bow Bridge (Bertolini (USA))
2084[7] 2439[9] 2875[3] 3993[12] 4400[14] 4866[5] 5257[7]
Black Arrow (IRE) *A Wohler* 108
3 b c Teofilo(IRE) Fann (USA) (Diesis)
2569a[2] 3683a[5]
Black Baccara *Phil McEntee* a74 68
5 b m Superior Premium Areish (IRE) (Keen)
208[4] 560[6] 576[7] 763[7] 890[4] (958) 996[2] 1187[8] 1720[3] 2809[2] 3500[8]
Blackball (USA) *David Lanigan* a56 23
2 bb c Speightstown(USA) Wild Decision (USA) (Wild Again (USA))
7330[16] 7749[7] 8185[6]
Blackboard (FR) *A Sagot*
5 b g Crillon(FR) La Pelaude (FR) (Marignan (USA))
94a[0]
Black Cadillac (IRE) *Andrew Balding* a80 66
4 bl g Kheleyf(USA) Desert Design (Desert King (IRE))
893[2] 958[4] ◆ (1306) 1481[2] 2369[7] 3960[10]
Black Caviar (AUS) *Peter G Moody* 133
6 br m Bel Esprit(AUS) Helsinge (AUS) (Desert Sun)
(3370)
Black Coffee *Mark Brisbourne* a79 72
7 br g Vettori(IRE) In The Woods (You And I (USA))
480[5] 648[9] 722[3] 922[11] 1000[5] 1094[2] 1391[5] 1533[10] 3782[11] 4183[2] 4843[8] 5199[8]
Black Dave (IRE) *David Evans* a57 57
2 b c Excellent Art Miss Latina (IRE) (Mozart (IRE))
2384[6] 4846[8] 5121[5] 5503[4] 6147[4] 6318[3] ◆ 7059[11] 7708[4]
Black Douglas *William Jarvis* a42 63
3 b g Kyllachy Penmayne (Inchinor)
3990[6] 4456[5] 5454[7] 5919[5] 6455[11] 6565[4] 7316[10]
Blackdown Fair *Rod Millman* a78 78
3 b f Trade Fair Shielaligh (Aragon)
4919[4] 5422[6] 5877[6] 6367[4] ◆ 6840[5] 7356[8]
Blackdown Spirit *Rod Millman* 87
2 b g Ishiguru(USA) Shielaligh (Aragon)
3444[5] (4180) 4488[3] 5088[10] 5903[6] 6871[3]
Black Dragon *Mark Rimmer* a48
4 b g Iceman My Valentina (Royal Academy (USA))
833[5] 6215[9] 6398[7]
Black Eider *John Spearing* a41 45
2 b f Piccolo The Dark Eider (Superlative)
1253[4] 1629[6] 3465[4]
Black Eyed Girl (IRE) *J S Moore* a57 50
2 br f Jeremy(USA) Holda (IRE) (Docksider (USA))
5478[7] 5656[4] 6936[8]
Black Iceman *Lydia Pearce* a63 44
4 bl g Iceman Slite (Mind Games)
105[2] (160) (389) 575[5] 850[11] 1534[4] 1631[6]
Black Jewel (FR) *Mlle S-V Tarrou* a92 83
3 b g Layman(USA) Belle Alicia (FR) (Smadoun (FR))
211a[5]
Black Mascara (IRE) *Richard Hannon* a58 77
3 br f Authorized(IRE) Pina Colada (Sabrehill (USA))
1256[4] 1610[7] 2249[6] 2895[3] 3786[4] 4323[10]
Black Minstrel (IRE) *Amanda Perrett* a51 66
3 b g Dylan Thomas(IRE) Overlook (Generous (IRE))
6397[9] 6792[13]
Black Monk (IRE) *Richard Hannon* a69 77
2 b c Dark Angel(IRE) Double Eight (IRE) (Common Grounds)
1315[2] 2420[4] 4502[2] (4837) 5236[4] 6414[2] 7193[6]
Blackmore *Julia Feilden* a81 76
5 b g Rainbow Quest(USA) Waki Music (USA) (Miswaki (USA))
309[2] 555[2] ◆ (673) 849[2] 1003[5] 1282[7]
Black Motive *Michael Bell* a52 46
3 b g Motivator Queen Of Norway (USA) (Woodman (USA))
1981[10] 2368[8] 2560[10] 3233[5]
Black Rider (IRE) *Kevin Ryan* a57
2 b c Elnadim(USA) Barracade (IRE) (Barathea (IRE))
8230[2]
Blacksou (FR) *P Adda*
2 b g Blackdoun(FR) Cadline (FR) (Cardoun (FR))
8176a[0]
Black Spirit (USA) *Clive Cox* a104 112
5 b g Black Minnaloushe(USA) L'Extra Honor (USA) (Hero's Honor (USA))
1034[4] 1475[4] 2655[4] 3329[2] (6166) (6482) 6855a[8]
Blackstone Vegas *Derek Shaw* a64 72
6 ch g Nayef(USA) Waqood (USA) (Riverman (USA))
452[8] 500[7] 772[8] 963[3] 1272[4] (2371) (2978) 3419[3] 4176[7] 5384[9] 6407[13] 7293[7]
Blackthorn Stick (IRE) *John Butler* a67 10
3 b g Elusive City(USA) Hi Lyla (IRE) (Lahib (USA))
2865[11] 3155[11] 3539[8] 5212[9] 7189[2] (7615)
Black Truffle (FR) *Mark Usher* a48 33
2 b c Kyllachy Some Diva (Dr Fong (USA))
4625[10] 4921[7] 5424[8] 7808[7] 8155[3] 8274[6]
Black Whip (IRE) *Mlle M Henry* a60 70
2 b f Whipper(USA) Southern Queen (Anabaa (USA))
5248a[10] 5697a[7]
Blades Lad *Richard Fahey* 75
3 ch g Haafhd Blades Girl (Bertolini (USA))
(1676) 2258[9] 2701[6] 3417[6] 4199[8]
Blades Rose *Richard Fahey* 56
2 b f Vita Rosa(JPN) Blades Baby (Bertolini (USA))
2338[6] 2790[7] 3251[2] 4195[2] 4778[P]
Bladewood Girl *J R Jenkins* a69 62
4 b m Needwood Blade Willmar (IRE) (Zafonic (USA))
5970[5] ◆ 6582[6] 7112[6] (7486) 7925[4] 8199[12]
Blaine *Kevin Ryan* 108
2 ch c Avonbridge Lauren Louise (Tagula (IRE))
(4114) ◆ (5559) 7049[9]
Blanc De Chine (IRE) *Peter Makin* a86 82
3 gr f Dark Angel(IRE) Nullarbor (Green Desert (USA))
(2443) ◆ 3486[6] 4500[6] (5422) 6226[14] (6767)
Blanche Dubawi (IRE) *Noel Quinlan* a73 106
4 b m Dubawi(IRE) Dixie Belle (Diktat)
5581[6] ◆ 6072[6]
Blank Czech (IRE) *Amanda Perrett* a77 79
3 b g Clodovil(IRE) Shambodia (IRE) (Petardia)
2942[9] 7083[9] 7511[5] 7625[2] 7896[3] 7996[4]
Blaugrana (IRE) *John Gosden* a72
3 ch f Exceed And Excel(AUS) Acts Of Grace (USA) (Bahri (USA))
(20)
Blazeofenchantment (USA) *Noel Quinlan* a65 51
2 b c Officer(USA) Willow Rush (USA) (Wild Rush (USA))
4114[12] 4792[9] ◆ 5371[6] 6822[6] 7974[2] ◆ (8203) ◆
Blazing Apostle (IRE) *Christine Dunnett* a48 43
4 ch m Redback Salonika Sky (Pursuit Of Love)
1131[1] 2641[3] 3079
Blazing Field *Clive Cox* 83
4 ch m Halling(USA) Autumn Wealth (IRE) (Cadeaux Genereux)
1505[3] 2412[5] 4096[4] 5002[4] 6012[5] 6493[14]
Blazing Knight (IRE) *Ralph Beckett* a76 69
2 b c Red Clubs(IRE) Johar Jamal (IRE) (Chevalier (IRE))
2261[12] 3638[3] 4502[3] 4947[3] 5940[3] 6155[6] 6438[2] (6611) (7463) ◆ 7687[11] 8204[4]
Blazing Speed *James Fanshawe* 105
3 b g Dylan Thomas(IRE) Leukippids (IRE) (Sadler's Wells (USA))
3349[4] (4797) (6875)
Blazon (FR) *P Van De Poele* a85 100
5 gr h Verglas(IRE) Hidden Silver (Anabaa (USA))
(92a) 7551a[3]
Blessing Box *Chris Wall* a60 57
2 b f Bahamian Bounty Bible Box (IRE) (Bin Ajwaad (IRE))
6203[8] 7007[7] 7481[2]
Blessington (IRE) *John Gosden* 88
2 b c Kheleyf(USA) Madam Ninette (Mark Of Esteem (IRE))
3637[6] (4688)
Bless You *Henry Candy* a68 87
4 b m Bahamian Bounty Follow Flanders (Pursuit Of Love)
1602[6] 2890[8] 3571[8] 4824[18]
Blimey O'Riley (IRE) *Mark H Tompkins* 79
7 b g Kalanisi(IRE) Kafayef (USA) (Secreto (USA))
2423[7] 2978[5] 4103[8] 6349[8]
Bling King *F Vermeulen* a89 94
3 b c Haafhd Bling Bling (IRE) (Indian Ridge)
364a[4]
Blissamore *Hughie Morrison* a40 32
3 b f Kyllachy Tremiere (FR) (Anabaa (USA))
1501[10] 2483[8] 2865[5] 5479[11] 5999[8]
Blissful Thinking *F-H Graffard* a81 80
2 b c Oasis Dream Sky Wonder (Observatory (USA))
4118a[5]
Blizzard Blues (USA) *Aytach Sadik* a67 104
6 ch g Mr Greeley(USA) Blush Damask (USA) (Green Dancer (USA))
8110[10] 8228[7]
Blodwen Abbey *James Unett* a75 60
3 b f Firebreak Miss Mirasol (Sheikh Albadou)
1063[6] 1721[10] 2136[7] 4081[RR]
Blonde Maite *Roy Bowring* a35
6 ch g Ballet Master(USA) Ace Maite (Komaite (USA))
109[9] 367[7] 477[10]
Bloodsweatandtears *William Knight* a76 79
4 b g Barathea(IRE) Celestial Princess (Observatory (USA))
1358[6] (1772) 2399[4] 2857[5] 3774[5] 4287[7] 4805[9] 5667[7] 6703[15] 7302[5] 7857[10] 8083[5] 8199[4]
Blown It (USA) *Keith Dalgleish* a76 74
6 bb g More Than Ready(USA) Short Shadow (USA) (Out Of Place (USA))
152[2] (272) 387[5] 406[5] 844[3] 912[4] 1116[2] 1187[3] 1237[7] 2476[6] 2719[8] 2750[8] 3578[6] (4392) 4638[9] 4770[7] 5082[7] 6314[8] 7101[7] 7412[11] 7863[12] 7970[3]
Blu Constellation (ITY) *R Biondi* 109
4 b h Orpen(USA) Stella Celtica (ITY) (Celtic Swing)
(7697a)
Blue Bajan (IRE) *David O'Meara* a98 115
10 b g Montjeu(IRE) Gentle Thoughts (Darshaan)
1318[4] 1855[5] 2254[6] 2639[9] 4111[4] 5600[13] 6031[4] 6197[9] 7051[6]
Blueberry Fizz (IRE) *John Ryan* a62 42
4 b m Kheleyf(USA) Miss Poppets (Polar Falcon (USA))
46[2] 125[2] 379[6] 578[2] 662[4] 781[2] (985) 1070[8] 1601[8] 2406[4] 2815[8] 2973[6] 3761[3] 3943[2] 4467[5] 6585[11] 7157[6] 7204[11] 7378[4] 7774[8] 7837[6] ◆ 7914[4] 7929[6] 8184[9]
Blue Bullet (IRE) *W P Mullins* a87 89
2 b c Red Clubs(IRE) Blue Holly (IRE) (Blues Traveller (IRE))
7038a[9]
Blue Charm *Ian McInnes* a56 68
8 b g Averti(IRE) Exotic Forest (Dominion)
1283[5]
Blue Clumber *Shaun Harris* 82
2 b f Sleeping Indian Blue Nile (IRE) (Bluebird (USA))
1651[3] 1972[5] 2450[7] 2603[2] 3844[5] 4546[8] 4836[7] 5255[5]
Blue Corner (IRE) *M Halford* 101
3 b c Teofilo(IRE) Indian Belle (IRE) (Indian Ridge)
5027a[5]
Blue Cossack (IRE) *Neil King* a66 38
4 b g Ivan Denisovich(IRE) Biasca (Erhaab (USA))
129[9] 392[2] 566[3] (772) 963[4] 3102[6] 3283[9] 3734[7] 4652[5] 5241[8] 7012[7]
Bluecrop Boy *Dominic Ffrench Davis* a29 44
8 b g Zaha(CAN) Pearl Dawn (IRE) (Jareer (USA))
446[6] 811[9]
Blue Deer (IRE) *Lee Carter* a69 72
4 b g Bahamian Bounty Jaywick (UAE) (Jade Robbery (USA))
1378[12] 2173[8] 2546[9] 3153[3] 3497[2] 3995[3] 4413[12] 4950[10] 5239[7] 5990[9] 6334[10] (6982) 8156[5] 8304[4]
Blue Destination *John Quinn* 87
4 b g Dubai Destination(USA) Bluebelle (Generous (IRE))
1381[10] (3114) 3377[3]
Blue Dune *Mark Johnston* a67 69
3 b f Invincible Spirit(IRE) Scatina (IRE) (Samum (GER))
4341[9] 4630[7] 4931[7] 5454[10] 5892[6] 6305[2] 6691[2] 6769[2] (6956) 7248[4]
Blue Eyed Grey (IRE) *Karen George*
4 gr g Desert Style(IRE) Thistle Hill (IRE) (Danehill (USA))
7112[12]
Bluefields (FR) *D Chenu* a74 84
11 b g Anabaa(USA) Providenc Mill (FR) (French Stress (USA))
2685a[6]
Bluegrass Blues (IRE) *Paul Cole* 70
2 b c Dark Angel(IRE) Dear Catch (IRE) (Bluebird (USA))
6443[6] 7031[3]
Blue Jack *Stuart Williams* a98 98
7 b g Cadeaux Genereux Fairy Flight (IRE) (Fairy King (USA))
1033[4] 1498[2] 1975[12] 3127[7] 4312[8] 5447[2] 6028[11] 6689[6] 7297[6] 7651[6] 8188[8]
Blue Lotus (IRE) *Tim Easterby* 77
2 ch c Elnadim(USA) Saffa Garden (IRE) (King's Best (USA))
1818[4] ◆ 2261[7] (3490) 4071[2] 4614[7] 5041[7] 5602[8] 6032[2] 6883[11] 7206[2] 7635[6]
Blue Maisey *Peter Makin* a69 73
4 b m Monsieur Bond(IRE) Blue Nile (IRE) (Bluebird (USA))
2503[8] 2847[12] 3485[4] 4413[5] 5310[15]
Blue Missile *Bill Turner* a41
2 b g Majestic Missile(IRE) Secret Combe (IRE) (Mujadil (USA))
7979[5] 8068[9] 8247[4]
Blue Moon *Kevin Ryan* a101 83
5 gr m Trade Fair Sunningdale (IRE) (Indian Ridge)
5[4]
Blue Noodles *John Wainwright* a59 56
6 b g Reset(AUS) Gleam Of Light (IRE) (Danehill (USA))
101[12] 356[3] 430[5] 532[5] 666[8] 3026[10] 3463[3] 3893[5] 4717[10] 4865[11] 5543[11] 6958[8]
Blue Nova *Jeremy Noseda* a75 74
2 b f Nayef(USA) Blue Rhapsody (Cape Cross (IRE))
2245[7] 3764[2] 4792[5] 5300[4] 6253[3] 7059[4] (7814)
Blue Panis (FR) *X Thomas-Demeaulte* a97 113
5 b h Panis(USA) Rhapsody In Blue (FR) (Bering)
(246a)
Blue Pencil *Roger Curtis* a45 36
3 b g Ishiguru(USA) Gold And Blue (IRE) (Bluebird (USA))
993[6] 1448[3] 2049[6] 4214[10] 4537[6] 5508[10]
Blue Saphire (DEN) *Bettina Wilson* 53
3 b f Academy Award(IRE) Blue Magic (NOR) (Diaghlyphard (USA))
4359a[2]
Blue Shoes (IRE) *Tim Easterby* 75
3 b f Kodiac Alexander Capetown (IRE) (Fasliyev (USA))
1441[5] 1912[6] 2591[3] 3954[2] 4208[2] 4547[15] 4909[2] 5538[2] (5728) 6514[7] 7451[3]
Blues Jazz *Ian Semple* a69 86
6 b g Josr Algarhoud(IRE) Belle Of The Blues (IRE) (Blues Traveller (IRE))
1249[3] 1863[8] 2488[8] 2597[6] 3027[6] 3334[2] 3890[6] 4868[4] 5186[8] 6513[4] 6881[9]
Blue Soave (FR) *F Chappet* a100 114
4 ch g Soave(GER) Rhapsody In Blue (FR) (Bering)
1746a[6] 3205a[7] (6088a) 6913a[6] 7697a[6]
Blue Surf *Amanda Perrett* 104
3 ch g Excellent Art Wavy Up (IRE) (Brustolon)
(3703) 4735[3] (5626) 6025[11] 6484[3] (7407) 7689[11]
Blue Tiger *Saeed Bin Suroor* a55 72
3 b g Pivotal Poised (USA) (Rahy (USA))
1824[7] 3702[2] 4729[2] 5096[4] 6100[11]
Blue Top *Tim Walford* 63
3 b g Millkom Pompey Blue (Abou Zouz (USA))
2144[10] 2673[9] 4397[5] 4830[4] 5170[3] 6361[10]
Blue Twister *Andrew Balding* 48
2 ch c Pivotal Blue Siren (Bluebird (USA))
5235[9] 7110[7]
Blue Wave (IRE) *Mahmood Al Zarooni* a80 81
2 b c Raven's Pass(USA) Million Waves (IRE) (Mull Of Kintyre (USA))
3634[8] 4595[2] (5098) 5890[4]

Blue Zealot (IRE) *Anthony Honeyball* a63 51
5 b m Galileo(IRE) Massada (Most Welcome)
3143[2] 5771[2] (7255) 7528[4] 7862[6]

Boa *Reg Hollinshead* a78 70
7 b m Mtoto Maradata (IRE) (Shardari)
192[2] (363) 535[3] 601[3] 721[3] 1011[4] 7413[2] 7672[9] (7792) 7954[8] 8136[12] 8243[9]

Boarding Pass (FR) *A Lyon* a78 82
4 gr h One Cool Cat(USA) Aifa (Johann Quatz (FR))
7701a[8]

Boastful (IRE) *Mrs K Burke* a81 104
4 gr m Clodovil(IRE) Vanity (IRE) (Thatching)
(1851) ◆ 2654[8] 3623[2] 4070[4] 5523a[3] 5641a[6] 6468[20]

Bobbyow *Terry Clement* a56 59
4 b g Bertolini(USA) Brooklyn's Sky (Septieme Ciel (USA))
373[3] 396[4] 467[3] 572[2] 740[3] 1516[5] 8184[6]

Bobbyscot (IRE) *Gary Moore* a76 47
5 b g Alhaarth(IRE) Sogno Verde (IRE) (Green Desert (USA))
3372[18] 3766[10] 7774[11] 7986[7]

Bobby's Doll *Terry Clement* a73 73
5 ch m Needwood Blade Nine To Five (Imp Society (USA))
1428[3] 1788[6] 2360[8] 3085[9] 3390[9] 4663[5] 4903[5] 5995[12] 6982[10]

Bobby Two Shoes *Brett Johnson* a72 42
2 b g Byron Taminoula (IRE) (Tagula (IRE))
3916[9] (8068) 8293[5]

Bob Le Beau (IRE) *Mrs John Harrington* a103 110
5 br g Big Bad Bob(IRE) Shine Silently (IRE) (Bering)
1946a[6] 5027a[8] 5134a[4] 5600[12]

Bobs Her Uncle *James Bethell* a68 63
3 b f Fair Mix(IRE) Shazana (Key Of Luck (USA))
2826[5] 3565[7] 4542[8] 6364[2] 7417[3]

Bob's World *Jennie Candlish* a79 79
3 b g Multiplex Vocation (IRE) (Royal Academy (USA))
(1113) 1978[7] ◆ 2484[5] 3711[6] 5373[8]

Bocamix (FR) *Andrew Crook* a69 69
6 gr g Linamix(FR) Bocanegra (FR) (Night Shift (USA))
500[9] 1282[4] 2698[4] 2978[10] 3437[6] 4831[8] 5241[3] 6956[15] (7793)

Boccalino (GER) *P Schaerer* a95 98
4 b h Iron Mask(USA) Bella Monica (GER) (Big Shuffle (USA))
629a[11]

Bocciani (GER) *Brian Ellison* 73
7 b g Banyumanik(IRE) Baila (Lando (GER))
6137[2]

Bodemeister (USA) *Bob Baffert* a126
3 b c Empire Maker(USA) Untouched Talent (USA) (Storm Cat (USA))
1872a[2] 2299a[2]

Body And Soul (IRE) *Tim Easterby* 95
2 b f Captain Rio Goodwood March (Foxhound (USA))
2047[6] ◆ (2587) (3250) (4093) 5515[3] (6883)

Body Language (IRE) *Ian Williams* a82 83
4 b m Beat Hollow Banco Suivi (IRE) (Nashwan (USA))
4326[12] (4925) 6493[18]

Boga (IRE) *Karen Tutty* a46 55
5 b m Invincible Spirit(IRE) Miznapp (Pennekamp (USA))
1095[9] 1294[6] 2791[6] 3462[U] 4134[6] 4717[14] 5739[8]

Bogart *Kevin Ryan* 111
3 ch c Bahamian Bounty Lauren Louise (Tagula (IRE))
2179[4] ◆ 2712[4] 3370[14] 4794[4] 5561[18]

Bogini (IRE) *M D O'Callaghan* a76 93
3 b f Holy Roman Emperor(IRE) Alexander Queen (IRE) (King's Best (USA))
2256[7] 2615[3] (2869) (3118) 4380a[4] 4838[8] 5067a[6]

Bogsnog (IRE) *Linda Stubbs* 76
2 b g Moss Vale(IRE) Lovers Kiss (Night Shift (USA))
2370[10] 4173[2] 4670[2] 5222[2] 5586[2] (5932)

Bohemian Melody *Marco Botti* a100 108
5 b g Desert Sun Chamonis (USA) (Affirmed (USA))
141a[5] 419a[3]

Bohemian Rhapsody (IRE) *J W Hills* a69 78
3 b c Galileo(IRE) Quiet Mouse (USA) (Quiet American (USA))
2273[9] 2942[5] 3305[5] 3945[6] 4648[5] 5456[2] 6098[7] 6971[9]

Boisterous (USA) *Claude McGaughey III* 115
5 bb h Distorted Humor(USA) Emanating (USA) (Cox's Ridge (USA))
5377a[9]

Boite (IRE) *Peter Chapple-Hyam* 69
2 b c Authorized(IRE) Albiatra (USA) (Dixieland Band (USA))
7637[4]

Bojangle (IRE) *Dominic Ffrench Davis* a45 48
3 b f Namid Fine Detail (IRE) (Shirley Heights)
556[5] 726[6]

Bolanderi (USA) *Andy Turnell* a64 70
7 ch g Seeking The Gold(USA) Lilium (Nashwan (USA))
6734[11] 7473[6] 7905[11] 8019[9]

Bold Adventure *Willie Musson* a59 65
8 ch g Arkadian Hero(USA) Impatiente (USA) (Vaguely Noble)
23[2] 129[2] 278[4] (465) 1011[3] 3216[9] 8067[9]

Bold And Free *David Elsworth* a55 69
2 b g Bertolini(USA) Lady Broughton (IRE) (Grand Lodge (USA))
6876[11] 7330[5] 7806[5]

Bold Cross (IRE) *Edward Bevan* a71 73
9 b g Cape Cross(IRE) Machikane Akaiito (IRE) (Persian Bold)
1830[6] (2389) 2767[4] 3485[5] 4722[8] (5199) 5688[7] 6120[3] 6458[3] 6842[4] 7250[2]

Bold Cuffs *Sir Mark Prescott Bt* a73 87
3 b g Dutch Art Chambray (IRE) (Barathea (IRE))
(3622) 4289[5] 4945[4] 5528[2] 6340[4] 6662[3] (6957)

Bold Diva *Tony Carroll* a63 10
7 ch m Bold Edge Trina's Pet (Efisio)
964[6] 1178[5] 1583[6] 1722[7] 2350[8] 3456[2] 4240[8] 4928[8]

Bold Duke *Edward Bevan* a24 73
4 b g Sulamani(IRE) Dominant Duchess (Old Vic)
546[9] 3035[9] 3430[4] 5817[9] 6097[10] 7129[2] 7409[2] (7640)

Bold Identity (IRE) *Richard Phillips* 71
6 b g Tagula(IRE) Identify (IRE) (Persian Bold)
3316[9] 5264[P] 6616[P] 6821[14]

Bold Marc (IRE) *Mrs K Burke* a74 81
10 b g Bold Fact(USA) Zara's Birthday (IRE) (Waajib)
18a[9] 92a[3] 815a[7] 965a[4] (1578) 1659[9] 2405[6] 4141[7] 4864[11] 6313[6] 7095[2] 7347[2] 7701a[7] (7798) 8133[4] 8261[3]

Bold Prediction (IRE) *Richard Hannon* a71 82
2 b c Kodiac Alexander Eliott (IRE) (Night Shift (USA))
3191[3] 3637[2] 4604[2] 4707[3] 5602[11] 6114[5] 6579[2] 7311[6]

Bold Ring *Eric Wheeler* a71 64
6 ch m Bold Edge Floppie Disk (Magic Ring (IRE))
124[2] 262[8] 323[4] 919[5] 1311[6] 1626[6] 3388[10] 3511[4] 3915[4] 4469[6] 4872[8] 5592[3] 6396[4] 6778[4] 7105[8]

Bold Silvano (SAF) *M F De Kock* a119 117
6 b h Silvano(GER) Bold Saffron (SAF) (Al Mufti (USA))
487a[5] 878a[12] 1149a[10]

Bold Thady Quill (IRE) *K J Condon* a72 97
5 ch g Tale Of The Cat(USA) Jazzie (FR) (Zilzal (USA))
(3647a) 4692a[5] 4833a[7] 5609a[2]

Boleyn *Richard Hannon* a67 67
2 b f Sir Percy Moody Margaret (Bahamian Bounty)
2622[2] ◆ 3009[3] 3444[2] 3970[3] 4752[5] 5032[4]

Bolingbroke (IRE) *A Fabre* a83 97
3 b c King's Best(USA) Noble Rose (IRE) (Caerleon (USA))
1171a[3]

Bolivia (GER) *Lucy Wadham* a88 92
6 ch m Monsun(GER) Be My Lady (GER) (Be My Guest (USA))
1654[6] 1848[5] 2884[5] (3162) 4338[4] 4738[11] 5826[13] 6428[9]

Bollin Billy *Tim Easterby* 35
2 b g Lucky Story(USA) Bollin Jeannie (Royal Applause)
2334[9] 2822[9] 3401[12] 4921[6] 5254[10]

Bollin Dolly *James Moffatt* 78
9 ch m Bien Bien(USA) Bollin Roberta (Bob's Return (IRE))
(2034) 6229[6]

Bollin Felix *Tim Easterby* 83
8 br g Generous(IRE) Bollin Magdalene (Teenoso (USA))
2180[14] 2921[5] 3129[6] 3535[3] 3953[5] 5344[8] (5673) 5798[7]

Bollin Greta *Tim Easterby* a47 92
7 bb m Mtoto Bollin Zola (Alzao (USA))
3036[8] 3377[5] 3494[8] (4072) 4338[5] 4962[6] 7175[12] 7689[22]

Bollin Judith *Jim Best* a51 88
6 br m Bollin Eric Bollin Nellie (Rock Hopper)
3661[10]

Bollin Julie *Donald Whillans* 39
5 b m Bollin Eric Bollin Nellie (Rock Hopper)
2635[8]

Bollin Nancy *Tim Easterby* 37
3 b f Bollin Eric Bollin Nellie (Rock Hopper)
1250[7] 1595[8] 1864[12] 2771[10] 3023[8] 4678[7]

Bollin Tommy *Tim Easterby* 65
3 ch g Carnival Dancer Bollin Ann (Anshan)
1757[6] 2336[6] 2689[12] 3111[6] 5623[9] 6125[7]

Bollistick *Michael Mullineaux* a53 56
6 b g Bollin Eric Slip Killick (Cosmonaut)
1484[4] 2418[7] 3061[7] 3988[12]

Bolt (FR) *M Boutin* a66 66
4 b g Night Tango(GER) Roannaise (FR) (Octagonal (NZ))
16a[0]

Bomar (IRE) *Wido Neuroth* a100 78
3 b c Sir Percy Rubileo (Galileo (IRE))
(3655a)

Bon Allumage *Sir Henry Cecil* a78 36
3 b f Nayef(USA) Brisk Breeze (GER) (Monsun (GER))
(1363) 1887[9]

Bonbon Bonnie *Phil McEntee* a35 22
4 b m Storming Home Form At Last (Formidable (USA))
2461[7] 2865[8] 3622[10] 3946[9] 4296[15] 6254[5] 7611[12] 8109[7]

Bondage (IRE) *Gordon Elliott* a67 93
5 b g Whipper(USA) Shamah (Unfuwain (USA))
7584a[5]

Bond Blade *Suzzanne France* a65 65
4 ch g Needwood Blade Bond Cat (IRE) (Raise A Grand (IRE))
372[3] ◆ 813[4] 3442[19] 4193[11] 5246[11] 5719[7] 8210[5]

Bond Club *Geoffrey Oldroyd* 70
2 b c Misu Bond(IRE) Bond Platinum Club (Pivotal)
3989[4] 5410[3] 6099[4] (6628) 7028[8] 7687[9]

Bondesire *David O'Meara* 69
2 b f Misu Bond(IRE) Lawless Bridget (Alnasr Alwasheek)
3415[3] ◆ 3909[2] 4618[6]

Bond Fastrac *Geoffrey Oldroyd* a82 90
5 b g Monsieur Bond(IRE) Kanisfluh (Pivotal)
282[3] 893[4] 1177[6] 1827[2] 2096[4] (2690) 3169[10] 3845[2] 4629[9] (7000) 7559[7]

Bondi Beach Boy *James Turner* 16
3 b g Misu Bond(IRE) Nice One (Almaty (IRE))
6341[9] 6792[15] 7445[10]

Bondi Mist (IRE) *Jonathan Portman* 68
3 gr f Aussie Rules(USA) Akoya (IRE) (Anabaa (USA))
1649[5] 1937[4] 2431[3] 3228[9] 3671[9] 4510[5] 4940[3] (5266) 5653[3]

Bond Style *Bryan Smart* a62 46
3 ch c Monsieur Bond(IRE) In Some Style (IRE) (Grand Lodge (USA))
383[2] 462[2] 536[3] 3184[11] 5113[5] 5708[8]

Bonfire *Andrew Balding* 117
3 b g Manduro(GER) Night Frolic (Night Shift (USA))
(2210) ◆ 2705[6] 3880[6]

Bonne Amie (FR) *Tom Dascombe*
2 b f Elusive City(USA) Sintra (IRE) (Kris)
5570a[0] 6512[7]

Bonne Idee (FR) *E Charpy* a83 86
3 b f Choisir(AUS) Balsannda (USA) (Rahy (USA))
754a[7]

Bonnet De Douche (IRE) *Peter Chapple-Hyam* 63
3 ch f Modigliani(USA) Isadora Duncan (IRE) (Sadler's Wells (USA))
1265[5] 1443[9]

Bonnie Blade *James Unett* a41
3 b f Needwood Blade Kyrhena (Desert Prince (IRE))
845[12]

Bonnie Brae *David Elsworth* a59 108
5 b m Mujahid(USA) Skara Brae (Inchinor)
2068[2] ◆ 2409[6] 3268[20] (4099) 4321[8] 6161[13] 6870[9]

Bonnie Charlie *David Nicholls* a76 86
6 ch g Intikhab(USA) Scottish Exile (IRE) (Ashkalani (IRE))
3255[9] 4133[5] 4924[12] 5557[10] (6044) 6465[14]

Bonnie Lesley (IRE) *Keith Dalgleish* 79
2 b f Iffraaj Hazium (IRE) (In The Wings)
2587[9] 3110[2] ◆ 3378[4] (4672) (4806) 5602[4] 6469[3]

Bonnie Prince Blue *Ian McInnes* a73 65
9 ch g Tipsy Creek(USA) Heart So Blue (Dilum (USA))
372[7] 551[6] 670[7] 807[2] 831[3] 938[5] 1179[3] (1283) 1584[2] 1961[2] 3021[7] 3460[5] 4192[6] 4405[4] 6530[3] 7347[7] 8113[6] 8214[11]

Bontoni (FR) *H-A Pantall* a82 80
2 ro c Silvano(GER) Brictop (USA) (Mizzen Mast (USA))
(3928a)

Boogie Dancer *Stuart Howe* a59 34
8 b m Tobougg(IRE) Bolero (Rainbow Quest (USA))
4994[8]

Boogie De Bispo *Stuart Kittow* 45
2 b f Tobougg(IRE) Mellifluous (IRE) (Noverre (USA))
6153[13] 7130[5] 7364[14]

Boogie Shoes *Roger Varian* a75 101
4 b g Bertolini(USA) Space Time (FR) (Bering)
2250[2] 2657[15] 3268[24] 5075[3] 6010[7] 6601[2] 7240[11]

Bookiesindex Boy *J R Jenkins* a68 55
8 bb g Piccolo United Passion (Emarati (USA))
24[6] 133[3] 380[4] 580[5] 904[6] 964[7] 1054[3] 1300[6] 1987[3] 2406[2] 2971[2] 3435[9]

Bookiesindexdotnet *J R Jenkins* a76 70
3 b f Piccolo United Passion (Emarati (USA))
86[4] 977[2] (1063) 2443[6] 2816[5] 3234[7] 3450[7] 6439[9] 7197[12] 7775[12] 8225[9] 8307[9]

Booktheband (IRE) *Clive Brittain* a49 19
2 ch c Dubawi(IRE) Songbook (Singspiel (IRE))
6204[13] 7642[5]

Boom And Bloom (IRE) *Richard Fahey* 78
2 b f Lawman(FR) Mamela (GER) (Protektor (GER))
2631[2] 3490[2] (4076) 4763[12] 5361[11]

Boom And Bust (IRE) *Marcus Tregoning* a69 111
5 b g Footstepsinthesand Forest Call (Wolfhound (USA))
3268[16] 4761[4] (5075) 6029[3] 6446[2] 6674[3]

Boomerang Bob (IRE) *J W Hills* a73 107
3 b c Aussie Rules(USA) Cozzene's Pride (USA) (Cozzene (USA))
1509[2] 1856[13] 2505[2] 3265[7] 3901a[4] 4794[3] 5647a[3]

Boomshackerlacker (IRE) *George Baker* a46 105
2 gr c Dark Angel(IRE) Allegrina (IRE) (Barathea (IRE))
2648[3] (3346) 4058[2] 6038[11] (6463a) 7404[3] 7623a[3]

Boomtown *Claire Dyson* a80 11
7 b g Fantastic Light(USA) Ville D'Amore (USA) (Irish River (FR))
4988[11]

Boonga Roogeta *Peter Charalambous* a78 81
3 b f Tobougg(IRE) Aberlady Bay (IRE) (Selkirk (USA))
4931[6] 5555[6] 6704[5] (6962) 7201[2] (7270) (7470) (7520) (7619) 7688[7] 8242[6]

Boots And Spurs *Mrs K Burke* a81 84
3 b g Oasis Dream Arctic Char (Polar Falcon (USA))
117a[0] 350[5] (565) 704[1] 2416[3] 3052[3] 5173a[6] 5732[3] (6136) 6921[6] 7556[5]

Bop It *Bryan Smart* a80 85
3 b g Misu Bond(IRE) Forever Bond (Danetime (IRE))
1271[14] 2229[7] (3065) ◆ 3613[8] 5603[8] 6005[3] 7145[6]

Boragh Waters (IRE) *Brian Meehan* 40
3 ch f Araafa(IRE) Pelican Waters (IRE) (Key Of Luck (USA))
2145[11] 2483[10] 2935[12] 4424[7] 4734[5] 5458[5] 6157[8]

Border Abby *Rae Guest* a41 62
4 ch m Selkirk(USA) Perfect Solution (IRE) (Entrepreneur)
1624[8] 2386[3] 3137[3] 3469[8] 4715[11]

Border Bandit (USA) *Tracy Waggott* 66
4 b g Selkirk(USA) Coretta (IRE) (Caerleon (USA))
1250[4] 1878[4] 2287[8] 3353[9] 4349[2] 4627[6] 5054[8] 5345[5] 5672[10] 6262[15]

Border Hill Jack *Robin Bastiman* 31
3 b g Danbird(AUS) Edge Of Darkness (Vaigly Great)
1676[6] 2313[7]

Border Legend *Roger Charlton* 92
3 ch g Selkirk(USA) Bonnie Doon (IRE) (Grand Lodge (USA))
1512[3] 2271[6] (2941) ◆ 6205[3] 6789[2]

Borderlescott *Robin Bastiman* a90 113
10 b g Compton Place Jeewan (Touching Wood (USA))
1033[8] 1219[5] 1977[2] 2486[4] 3196a[6] 3441[2] 4802[9] (5822) 6468[14] 6908a[9] 7390a[10]

Border Revia (IRE) *Richard Fahey* 82
3 b g Celtic Swing Maraami (Selkirk (USA))
1819[6] 3064[3] 3274[8] 4082[10]

Border Tale *James Moffatt* a44 41
12 b g Selkirk(USA) Likely Story (IRE) (Night Shift (USA))
3988[7] 4867[14]

Bordoni (USA) *Mark Johnston* a92 94
3 b g Bernardini(USA) Argentina (IRE) (Sadler's Wells (USA))
523[7] (921) 1302[2] ◆ 1597[2] 1978[10] 2718[7] (6383) ◆

Boris Grigoriev (IRE) *Michael Easterby* a81 97
3 bb g Excellent Art Strategy (Machiavellian (USA))
1032[10] 1129[6] 1271[10] 1996[6] 2714[9] 3165[4] ◆ 4075[8] 5110[5] ◆ 6046[7] 6789[11] 7247[8] 7452[10]

Boris The Bold *John Best* a61
3 b g Librettist(USA) Santiburi Girl (Casteddu)
7005[9] 7321[8] 7500[11] 7898[8] 8264[8]

Bornean (IRE) *Mahmood Al Zarooni* 74
2 ch g Street Cry(IRE) Calando (USA) (Storm Cat (USA))
2648[2] 3611[4] 5032[3] 5946[12]

Born To Be Achamp (BRZ) *Geoffrey Harker* a48 62
6 ch g Redattore(BRZ) Small High Plain (BRZ) (Spring Halo (ARG))
153[8] 4656[10] 5187[8]

Born To Run *Hugo Palmer* a26
2 b f Ishiguru(USA) Maid For Running (Namaqualand (USA))
6533[13]

Born To Sea (IRE) *John M Oxx* 116
3 b c Invincible Spirit(IRE) Urban Sea (USA) (Miswaki (USA))
1856[12] 2514a[5] 3239[4] 3651a[2] 5134a[2] 6063a[5]

Born To Surprise *Michael Bell* 101
3 b g Exceed And Excel(AUS) Dubai Surprise (IRE) (King's Best (USA))
(1155) 1470[8] 3294[7] 3977[2] ◆ 4760[13] (6143) 6835[11]

Borodino (IRE) *Richard Fahey* a65 58
2 b g Strategic Prince Silk Meadow (IRE) (Barathea (IRE))
6780[8] 7021[4] 7442[3]

Borough Boy (IRE) *Derek Shaw* a62 44
2 b c Jeremy(USA) Ostrusa (AUT) (Rustan (HUN))
3452[7] 4148[5] 4816[8] 5160[5] 5544[7] 6054[4]

Borug (USA) *James Tate* a89 95
4 b g Kingmambo(USA) Marienbad (FR) (Darshaan)
1416[3] 1820[5] 2248[6] 2655[3] 3502[8] 3642[5] 4068[5] 4805[4] 5101[9] 5888[2] ◆ 6207[7] (6702) 7147[5] 7407[2]

Bosonic *Alan McCabe*
3 b g Phoenix Reach(IRE) Antigoni (IRE) (Grand Lodge (USA))
2553[12]

Boss's Destination *Alan Swinbank* a89 85
5 b g Dubai Destination(USA) Blushing Sunrise (USA) (Cox's Ridge (USA))
1056[2] (1282) 1640[6] 2936[7] 3535[7] 4176[8] 5673[8]

Boston Blue *Tony Carroll* a75 81
5 b g Halling(USA) City Of Gold (IRE) (Sadler's Wells (USA))
521[5] (2623) 3535[6] 7927[12]

Boston Rocker (IRE) *Edward Lynam* 98
2 b f Acclamation Rocking (Oasis Dream)
3674a[5] 6424[3]

Bosun Breese *David Barron* a61 98
7 b g Bahamian Bounty Nellie Melba (Hurricane Sky (AUS))
(2314) 2596[2] (2719) (2793) (3374) 4576[13] 4924[3] 5370[19] 6028[13] 6755[8] 7063[9] 7243[11]

Botanica (IRE) *Richard Hannon* 82
2 b f Clodovil(IRE) Bent Al Fala (IRE) (Green Desert (USA))
2938[2] 3339[3] 4739[2] 5274[2] (5574) 6675[5]

Botanic Garden *William Haggas* 90
2 b c Royal Applause Rock Lily (Rock Of Gibraltar (IRE))
1474[2] 2181[6] 2587[4] (2912) 3823[3] 5088[7] 5678[3]

Botanist *Milton Bradley* a74 69
5 b g Selkirk(USA) Red Camellia (Polar Falcon (USA))
2421[15] 2761[9] 3153[11] 3717[7] 4929[3] 5191[2] 5504[7] 5659[2] 6002[11] 6321[8] 6771[7]

Botham (USA) *Jim Goldie* a58 75
8 bb g Cryptoclearance(USA) Oval (USA) (Kris S (USA))
1820[10] 2227[4] 2619[7] 3213[6] 3525[2] 4260[6]

Bothy *Brian Ellison* a35 83
6 ch g Pivotal Villa Carlotta (Rainbow Quest (USA))
6642[12]

Bottle Blonde *Ed McMahon* a78 76
2 b f Indesatchel(IRE) Sukuma (IRE) (Highest Honor (FR))
(5425) 5909[4] 6920[7] 7523[2]

Bottoms Up (IRE) *Robert Collet* 94
2 b c Whipper(USA) Graten (IRE) (Zieten (USA))
5471a[7]

Boucher Garcon (IRE) *Declan Carroll* a51 69
4 b g Spartacus(IRE) Valamander (IRE) (Val Royal (FR))
(1242) (1298) ◆ 1383[2] 1516[6] 1675[2] 1800[4] 2084[2] 2377[8] 3211[4] 4187[6] 4245[8] 5739[11]

Boudicca (IRE) *Daniel Mark Loughnane* 27
3 b f Majestic Missile(IRE) Laoise Beag (IRE) (Woodborough (USA))
4422[7]

Boudoir (IRE) *Ian Williams* a77 63
3 gr f Clodovil(IRE) Adultress (IRE) (Ela-Mana-Mou)
(185) 1531^{6} (1733) 2272^{14} 3041^{6} 3619^{7} 4218^{3} 6194^{8} 6641^{5} 7166^{5} (7307)

Bougaloo *Alan McCabe* a67 48
2 b g Tobougg(IRE) Benjarong (Sharpo)
4140^{5} 5912^{7} 6164^{13} 6822^{8} 7350^{2} 7432^{10} 7713^{7}

Bouggatti *Lady Herries* a71 78
4 b g Tobougg(IRE) Western Sal (Salse (USA))
2857^{6} (3468) 4504^{3} (5509) 5913^{7}

Bouncy Bouncy (IRE) *Michael Bell* a83 83
5 ch m Chineur(FR) Wunderbra (IRE) (Second Empire (IRE))
(1290) 1642^{5} 1990^{2} 2230^{8} 2853^{3} 3159^{4} 3696^{2} 4336^{7} 4655^{9} 5877^{3} 6788^{3} 7295^{12}

Boundaries *Tim Easterby* a53 84
4 b g Indesatchel(IRE) On The Brink (Mind Games)
1236^{7} 1675^{3} 2476^{10} 2719^{6} 3749^{8} 3944^{7}

Bountiful Bess *Pam Sly* a51 66
2 ch f Bahamian Bounty Saida Lenasera (FR) (Fasliyev (USA))
5407^{5} 6117^{7} 6790^{10} 7965^{8}

Bountiful Catch *Pam Sly* a54 54
3 ch g Bahamian Bounty Saida Lenasera (FR) (Fasliyev (USA))
832^{2} 1062^{8} 1517^{5} 2085^{5}

Bountiful Girl *John Wainwright* a67 79
3 b f Bahamian Bounty Cheeky Girl (College Chapel)
1477^{5} 2076^{5} 2539^{9} 3383^{7} 3906^{5} (4623) 4850^{5} 5227^{2} 5336^{2} 7640^{8} 7895^{9} 8146^{10}

Bountybeamadam *George Baker* a35 75
2 b f Bahamian Bounty Madamoiselle Jones (Emperor Jones (USA))
2370^{7} 3010^{4} 3783^{2} 4574^{12}

Bounty Rock *Rebecca Curtis* 22
2 b c Bahamian Bounty Absoluta (IRE) (Royal Academy (USA))
4180^{5}

Bounty Seeker (USA) *Mark Johnston* a79 78
3 b g A.P. Indy(USA) Plenty Of Light (USA) (Colony Light (USA))
1093^{3} 1707^{11} 2613^{2} 3827^{8}

Bourbon (IRE) *Mahmood Al Zarooni* 75
2 b c Raven's Pass(USA) Traou Mad (IRE) (Barathea (IRE))
2929^{4}

Bousatet (FR) *Kevin Ryan* 64
2 b f Muhtathir Miss Mission (IRE) (Second Empire (IRE))
6751a^{8}

Bouyrin (IRE) *Michael Bell* a65
2 b f Invincible Spirit(IRE) Needles And Pins (IRE) (Fasliyev (USA))
7778^{6} 7987^{3} 8171^{3}

Bov La Raconteuse *Carroll Gray* 59
3 b f Lucky Story(USA) Richenda (Mister Baileys)
4992^{8} 6001^{6} 6736^{7} 6962^{7} 7270^{11}

Bowdler's Magic *Mark Johnston* a92 92
5 b g Hernando(FR) Slew The Moon (ARG) (Kitwood (USA))
2278^{7} 2936^{9} 3377^{9} 3766^{5} 4326^{5} (4831) (5051)

Bowland Princess *Ed Dunlop* a53 63
2 b f Tiger Hill(IRE) Kozmina (IRE) (Sadler's Wells (USA))
6117^{9} 6791^{9} 7199^{5}

Bowmans Well (IRE) *Peter Purdy* a10
7 b m Cadeaux Genereux Guignol (IRE) (Anita's Prince)
273^{8}

Bow River Arch (USA) *Peter Hiatt* a76 79
4 b m Arch(USA) Bow River Gold (Rainbow Quest (USA))
4^{2} ◆ 271^{4} 355^{9} 582^{7}

Bowstar *Michael Attwater* a71 65
3 b f Oasis Dream Bold Empress (USA) (Diesis)
2542^{11} 3107^{5} 7477^{5} 7925^{3} 7996^{5} 8187^{2} 8267^{3}

Boxeur Des Rues (USA) *Doug O'Neill* a107 99
4 b h Smart Strike(CAN) Marseille Express (USA) (Caerleon (USA))
7574a^{13}

Boxing Day *Bent Olsen* 95
5 b h Galileo(IRE) Special Oasis (Green Desert (USA))
2807a^{8} 3886a^{5}

Boxing Shadows *Bryan Smart* a77 77
2 b g Camacho Prima Ballerina (Pivotal)
1818^{2} 2686^{3} 7931^{2} (8237)

Boy The Bell *Ollie Pears* a78 76
5 b g Choisir(AUS) Bella Beguine (Komaite (USA))
329^{7} 3460^{10} 4192^{4} 4452^{5} 5171^{6} 5295^{8} 6403^{3} 6967^{10} 7733^{7} 7917^{7}

Boyzee *Linda Jewell* a16
4 b g Resplendent Glory(IRE) Busy (IRE) (In The Wings)
7477^{10} 7988^{8}

Brabazon (IRE) *Shaun Harley* a69 70
9 b g In The Wings Azure Lake (USA) (Lac Ouimet (USA))
7791^{12}

Brackendale *John Weymes* a43 40
3 gr g Three Valleys(USA) Heather Mix (Linamix (FR))
534^{7}

Bradbury (IRE) *James Bethell* a67 74
4 ch g Redback Simonaventura (IRE) (Dr Devious (IRE))
(1797) 2457^{4} 2827^{6} 3564^{8} 4590^{3} 5056^{3} 5830^{2} 6493^{6}

Brae Hill (IRE) *Richard Fahey* a74 104
6 b g Fath(USA) Auriga (Belmez (USA))
(1130) 2068^{4} 2505^{4} 3268^{15} 3626^{2} 4321^{15} 5827^{15} 6468^{6} 6868^{13} 7066^{13}

Brailsford (IRE) *Ismail Mohammed* a54 73
3 b c Dubawi(IRE) Meynell (Sakhee (USA))
1322^{12} 2336^{11} 3229^{12} 3548^{11} 4192^{5} 4506^{8} 5014^{3} 6321^{4}

Bramante Di Parma (ITY) *D Grilli* a75
3 b c Mujahid(USA) Luna D'Irlanda (IRE) (Up And At 'Em)
365a^{7}

Bramshaw (USA) *Amanda Perrett* a50 90
5 rg g Langfuhr(CAN) Milagra (USA) (Maria's Mon (USA))
1087^{9} 3039^{13}

Bramshill Lass *Amanda Perrett* a72 54
3 ch f Notnowcato Disco Ball (Fantastic Light (USA))
182^{3} (324) 656^{4} 1707^{9} 2425^{5} 3003^{5} 4335^{7} 5037^{7} 5483^{7} (5945) 6365^{3} 7893^{8} 8048^{6} 8229^{7}

Branderburgo (IRE) *M Grassi* 109
5 b h High Chaparral(IRE) Farhad (Red Ransom (USA))
2323a^{3} 6554a^{2} 7287a^{3} 7586a^{5}

Brandy Snapping *Mark Brisbourne* a52
3 ch f Needwood Blade Sunisa (IRE) (Daggers Drawn (USA))
358^{8} 533^{6} 816^{3} 7527^{9} 7921^{7}

Brandywell Boy (IRE) *Dominic Ffrench Davis* a65 75
9 b g Danetime(IRE) Alexander Eliott (IRE) (Night Shift (USA))
1497^{13} 2572^{11} 3008^{7} 3477^{7} 4467^{2} 4492^{5} 5191^{7} 5937^{4} 6233^{2} 6496^{12} 6640^{8} (7703) 8045^{4} 8107^{4}

Branson (IRE) *Richard Hannon* a66 72
2 b c Mujadil(USA) Rorkes Drift (IRE) (Royal Abjar (USA))
3010^{7} 3444^{3} 4152^{3} 5439^{2} 6978^{4}

Branston Jubilee *Geoffrey Harker* 32
2 ch f Assertive Branston Jewel (IRE) (Prince Sabo)
6335^{10} 6627^{7}

Brasileira *J-M Beguigne* 104
4 b m Dubai Destination(USA) Shifting Sands (FR) (Hernando (FR))
(2805a) 5116a^{9} (6595a) 7665a^{3}

Brasingaman Espee *George Moore* 58
3 b c Silver Patriarch(IRE) Serene Pearl (IRE) (Night Shift (USA))
1600^{7} 2340^{10} 3023^{7} 3697^{4} 4399^{9} 5115^{7} (5738) 6103^{14}

Brave Battle *Ron Barr* a68 67
4 b g Compton Place War Shanty (Warrshan (USA))
2924^{3} 3254^{5} 3843^{5} 4042^{7} 4495^{12} 4957^{3} 5543^{9} 6105^{10}

Brave Command (USA) *Mahmood Al Zarooni* a80 83
2 bb c Hard Spun(USA) Lucky Lavender Gal (USA) (Carson City (USA))
4507^{2} 4917^{2} 5562^{U} (Dead)

Brave Decision *Suzy Smith* a51 53
5 gr g With Approval(CAN) Brave Vanessa (USA) (Private Account (USA))
(45) 8265^{5}

Brave Dream *Kevin Ryan* a76 72
4 b g Sleeping Indian Aimee's Delight (Robellino (USA))
1254^{10} 1875^{7}

Brave Enough (USA) *Roger Curtis* a44 45
5 b g Yes It's True(USA) Courageous (USA) (Kingmambo (USA))
809^{6}

Braveheart Move (IRE) *Geoffrey Harker* a78 86
6 b g Cape Cross(IRE) Token Gesture (IRE) (Alzao (USA))
2077^{5} 2419^{8} (4823)

Brave Kiss *Mark Gillard* 32
3 b f Manipulator(IRE) Brave Vanessa (USA) (Private Account (USA))
620^{9} 1415^{8} 1893^{11} 2578^{10}

Brave One (IRE) *David Nicholls* a24 32
3 b f Moss Vale(IRE) Smart Pet (Petong)
901^{6}

Bravestofthebrave (USA) *John Gosden* a76 57
4 b g Elusive Quality(USA) Victoria Cross (IRE) (Mark Of Esteem (IRE))
10^{4} (137)

Bravo Belle (IRE) *Paddy Butler* a34
5 b m Bertolini(USA) Dazilyn Lady (USA) (Zilzal (USA))
7818^{8} 8055^{9} 8173^{5}

Bravo Echo *Michael Attwater* a103 89
6 b g Oasis Dream Bold Empress (USA) (Diesis)
51a^{11} 261a^{8} ◆ 616a^{9} 962^{2} ◆ 1140^{5} 1354^{13} 3004^{9} 4286^{11} 4824^{11} (5630) (5906) 6235^{12} 7123a^{4} 7503^{9} 7826^{8}

Bravo King (IRE) *Richard Guest* a83 86
4 b g Sakhee(USA) Ashbilya (USA) (Nureyev (USA))
19^{6} 371^{10} 2360^{6}

Bravo Ragazzo (IRE) *Mark Johnston* 57
2 b c Pivotal Kitza (IRE) (Danehill (USA))
6134^{3} 6779^{3}

Bravo Youmzain (IRE) *Marco Botti* 89
2 b c Invincible Spirit(IRE) Grizel (Lion Cavern (USA))
3346^{3} ◆ 4604^{3} 5325^{2} 6540^{2} 7207^{2}

Brazen *David Simcock* 82
2 b c Kyllachy Molly Brown (Rudimentary (USA))
2934^{5} (5121) 6487^{3}

Brazilian Clown (IRE) *Tom Dascombe* a80 65
2 ch g Captain Rio Chaukao (IRE) (Inchinor)
1861^{6} 1972^{6} 2334^{12} 4140^{3} 5009^{2} 5254^{2} 6337^{3} (6612)

Bread Loft (FR) *Mlle M Henry* a81 85
4 ch g Touch Of The Blues(FR) Jamouna (FR) (Trempolino (USA))
7701a^{6}

Breakheart (IRE) *Andrew Balding* a64 96
5 b g Sakhee(USA) Exorcet (FR) (Selkirk (USA))
1633^{6} 2274^{15} 2637^{15} 3039^{12} 3454^{12} 4219^{7} 4652^{9} 5164^{9} (7898) 8083^{10} 8167^{2}

Breaking The Bank *William Muir* a68 73
3 ch g Medicean Russian Dance (USA) (Nureyev (USA))
4233^{3} 5231^{5} 6502^{6} 6798^{2} 7129^{4}

Break Rank (USA) *Ed de Giles* a79 79
3 b c Broken Vow(USA) Divert (USA) (Chester House (USA))
6704^{3}

Breathless Kiss (USA) *Kevin Ryan* a99 101
5 b m Roman Ruler(USA) Crusading Miss Cox (USA) (Crusader Sword (USA))
2931^{9} 4113^{10} 4611^{11} 4802^{24}

Breden (IRE) *John Gosden* 65
2 b c Shamardal(USA) Perfect Touch (USA) (Miswaki (USA))
7127^{5} 7363^{3}

Breezily (USA) *Mahmood Al Zarooni* a8 28
2 bb f Hard Spun(USA) Offshore Breeze (USA) (Thunder Gulch (USA))
4002^{9} 6535^{10}

Breezolini *Geoffrey Harker* a51 80
4 b m Bertolini(USA) African Breeze (Atraf)
1875^{2} (2230) 3027^{7} (3815) 5539^{6} 6515^{3} 7000^{2} 7291^{9}

Brendan Brackan (IRE) *G M Lyons* a98 106
3 b g Big Bad Bob(IRE) Abeyr (Unfuwain (USA))
5397a^{6} 6855a^{4}

Brenin Taran *David Simcock* a86 94
6 gr g Lujain(USA) Silver Chime (Robellino (USA))
253^{3} ◆ (654) 1015^{2} 1720^{5}

Brenkley Melani *Tim Fitzgerald*
4 b m Jelani(IRE) Meltonby (Sayf El Arab (USA))
5316^{9} 6341^{11}

Brent Pelham *Tobias B P Coles* a49
5 b g Royal Applause Little Firefly (IRE) (Danehill (USA))
468^{11}

Breton Rock (IRE) *David Simcock* 84
2 b c Bahamian Bounty Anna's Rock (IRE) (Rock Of Gibraltar (IRE))
(5785) (6799)

Brett Vale (IRE) *Peter Hedger* a91 43
6 br g Sinndar(IRE) Pinta (IRE) (Ahonoora)
2423^{10}

Brian's Best *Richard Ford* a34
3 ch g Tobougg(IRE) Approved Quality (IRE) (Persian Heights)
455^{7} 845^{10} 1090^{5} 1292^{8}

Brian Sprout *John Weymes* a57 57
4 ch g Zafeen(FR) Ducal Diva (Bahamian Bounty)
118^{4} 7703^{7} 8046^{5} 8209^{7}

Brick Rising *Andrew Balding* a48 65
2 ch c Phoenix Reach(IRE) Comtesse Noire (CAN) (Woodman (USA))
5207^{6} 5574^{6} 5997^{2}

Brick Tops *David Simcock* 76
3 br f Danehill Dancer(IRE) Rag Top (IRE) (Barathea (IRE))
1508^{6} 2310^{4} 2893^{5} 7521^{3}

Bridal Medic *Barry Leavy* a40 48
3 ch g Medicean Bridal Path (Groom Dancer (USA))
1001^{6} 1270^{6} 2380^{9} 3066^{10} 3543^{10} 4406^{8} 5261^{7} 7620^{10} 7933^{10}

Bridgefield (USA) *Mahmood Al Zarooni* a102 105
4 ch g Speightstown(USA) Treysta (USA) (Belong To Me (USA))
51a^{2} 261a^{7} 2211^{4} 3268^{30} 4248^{2} 4822^{4}

Bridgehampton *Michael Bell* a82 77
3 b g Lando(GER) Gaze (Galileo (IRE))
1427^{4} 1716^{4} ◆ (2141) (2333) 3621^{2} (4513) 4930^{3}

Bridge Night *Eve Johnson Houghton* a78 87
2 b f Avonbridge Midnight Fling (Groom Dancer (USA))
2343^{3} (2579) (3138) 3631^{7} 4687^{9} 5307^{9} 6284^{4} 6929^{2}

Bridge Of Gold (USA) *Mikael Magnusson* a109 111
6 bb h Giant's Causeway(USA) Lady Doc (USA) (Doc's Leader (USA))
1507^{3} 2228^{5} 3293^{9} 5374a^{9}

Bridge That Gap *Roger Ingram* a59
4 b h Avonbridge Figura (Rudimentary (USA))
1724^{6} 6398^{6} 6770^{9} (7321) 8265^{2}

Bridgetown (USA) *Todd Pletcher* 115
5 ch h Speightstown(USA) Ellesmere (USA) (Tabasco Cat (USA))
7571a^{14}

Bridge Valley *Jason Ward* a53 53
5 ch g Avonbridge Go Between (Daggers Drawn (USA))
2791^{3} 3332^{5} 4262^{4} 4865^{4} 5720^{3} 6479^{4} 8287^{7}

Bridle Belle *Richard Fahey* a73 95
4 b m Dansili River Belle (Lahib (USA))
1374^{10} 1882^{10} 2253^{6} ◆ 3125^{2} 4072^{12} 4608^{5} 5558^{6} 6012^{3} 6476^{8} (7069) (7519) 7689^{18}

Brief Chat (USA) *Amanda Perrett* a66 55
3 bb f Pleasant Tap(USA) Sambac (USA) (Mr Prospector (USA))
3340^{13} 6092^{5}

Brigadoon *William Jarvis* a82 82
5 b g Compton Place Briggsmaid (Elegant Air)
3278^{6} 4243^{5} 4657^{5} ◆ (5159) 5838^{3} 6039^{5} 6584^{6}

Brigantin (USA) *A Fabre* a65 114
5 ch g Cozzene(USA) Banyu Dewi (GER) (Poliglote)
1697a^{4} 4120a^{6} 5400a^{2} 7346a^{3}

Brigh (IRE) *David Simcock* 54
2 ch f Galileo(IRE) La Vida Loca (IRE) (Caerleon (USA))
5902^{9} 6257^{3}

Bright Abbey *Philip Hobbs* a73 80
4 ch g Halling(USA) Bright Hope (IRE) (Danehill (USA))
(5596) 6933^{10}

Bright Applause *Tracy Waggott* a57 76
4 b g Royal Applause Sadaka (USA) (Kingmambo (USA))
(2593) (3290) 4080^{2} 4621^{7} 5345^{6} 5546^{9} 6076^{8} 7245^{4}

Bright Girl (IRE) *Mark Rimmer* a35
4 b m Invincible Spirit(IRE) Honour Bright (IRE) (Danehill (USA))
784^{10} 1004^{5} 1532^{11} 1742^{6}

Bright Glow *David Lanigan* a68 57
2 ch f Exceed And Excel(AUS) Lighthouse (Warning)
6343^{8} 7458^{4} 7778^{2} ◆

Bright Strike (USA) *John Gosden* 82
2 b c Smart Strike(CAN) Seebe (USA) (Danzig (USA))
4595^{3} ◆ 5562^{3} 6486^{2}

Brillante Etoile (FR) *Y Durepaire* 99
3 b f American Post Black Dalhia (FR) (Sanglamore (USA))
7803a^{0}

Brilliant Barca *Sheena West* a51 57
4 b g Imperial Dancer Fading Away (Fraam)
521^{11} 8170^{11}

Brilliant Speed (USA) *Thomas Albertrani* a120 121
4 bb h Dynaformer(USA) Speed Succeeds (USA) (Gone West (USA))
7576a^{11}

Brimstone Hill (IRE) *Anthony Carson* a86 79
3 b c Royal Applause Right As Rain (Rainbow Quest (USA))
1612^{13} 2331^{5} 3347^{8} 3790^{14} 5892^{4} 6169^{3} (6647) 6973^{7} 7359^{2} 7805^{3} 8182^{2} 8275^{4}

Bring It On Home *Brendan Powell* a48 31
8 b g Beat Hollow Dernier Cri (Slip Anchor)
9^{5}

Bring Sweets (IRE) *Brian Ellison* a62 56
5 b g Firebreak Missperon (IRE) (Orpen (USA))
1052^{4} 1580^{3} 2926^{8} 4189^{2} 4402^{4} 5012^{3}

Broadway Babe (IRE) *Harry Dunlop* a66 52
3 br f Big Bad Bob(IRE) Lady Sharp Shot (IRE) (Son Of Sharp Shot (IRE))
1793^{5} 2368^{2} ◆ 3551^{5} 5154^{4} 6004^{11}

Broadway Duchess (IRE) *Richard Hannon* 68
2 ch f New Approach(IRE) Annee Lumiere (IRE) (Giant's Causeway (USA))
6873^{13}

Brockfield *Mel Brittain* a73 79
6 ch g Falbrav(IRE) Irish Light (USA) (Irish River (FR))
1275^{5} 1561^{9} 1913^{2} 2093^{9} 2588^{2} 2687^{2} 2926^{4} (3287) 4080^{6} 4396^{9} 4879^{8} 5224^{7} 5345^{11} 6638^{20} 7003^{2} (7369)

Brocklebank (IRE) *Simon Dow* a85 89
3 b g Diamond Green(FR) La Stellina (IRE) (Marju (IRE))
2490^{11} 3417^{8} 4347^{8} 5220^{2} 5618^{11} 6173^{2} 6752a^{3} 7415^{8} 7732^{11} (7769) 7901^{3} (8055) 8306^{7}

Brockwell *Tom Dascombe* 95
3 b g Singspiel(IRE) Noble Plum (IRE) (King's Best (USA))
1606^{5} ◆ 2336^{5} 2552^{2} 3066^{2} (3775) (5044) (5966) 6677^{3}

Brocottes (FR) *N Clement* 105
3 b f Lando(GER) Macotte (FR) (Nicolotte)
1434a^{4} 2156a^{5}

Broctune Papa Gio *Keith Reveley* 76
5 b g Tobougg(IRE) Fairlie (Halling (USA))
1251^{2} 2535^{3} 3356^{3} 4715^{2} 5111^{9} 5588^{3} (6127) 6881^{15}

Broken Spell (USA) *D Wayne Lukas* a108 93
2 ch f Broken Vow(USA) Rich Find (USA) (Exploit (USA))
7548a^{6}

Bronte *David Wachman* a83 81
2 b f Oasis Dream Interchange (IRE) (Montjeu (IRE))
4276a^{7}

Bronte Belle *Jedd O'Keeffe* a25 44
2 b f Pastoral Pursuits Katy O'Hara (Komaite (USA))
1842^{10} 2686^{13} 3286^{10} 7713^{8}

Bronterre *Richard Hannon* 115
3 b c Oasis Dream Wondrous Story (USA) (Royal Academy (USA))
1509^{3} ◆ 1856^{15} 3784^{4} 7401^{6}

Bronze Angel (IRE) *Marcus Tregoning* a89 106
3 b c Dark Angel(IRE) Rihana (IRE) (Priolo (USA))
(180) 1221^{6} (2263) 3294^{3} ◆ (6674) 7054^{5}

Bronze Beau *Linda Stubbs* a64 88
5 ch g Compton Place Bella Cantata (Singspiel (IRE))
1237^{5} 1868^{4} 2195^{4} 2439^{2} 2674^{7} 3065^{2} 3374^{8} 3845^{6} 4292^{5} 4430^{5} 5412^{6} 6358^{2} 6605^{8} 6886^{4}

Bronze Cannon (USA) *H J Brown* a109 86
7 br h Lemon Drop Kid(USA) Victoria Cross (IRE) (Mark Of Esteem (IRE))
242a^{10} 484a^{4} (755a) 877a^{13} 1144a^{F}

Bronze Prince *Michael Attwater* a102 100
5 b g Oasis Dream Sweet Pea (Persian Bold)
1373^{11} 1679^{4} (2082) 2409^{5} 3331^{13} 4321^{12} 5356^{14} 5572^{16}

Brooke's Bounty *Richard Fahey* 70
2 ch g Bahamian Bounty Choysia (Pivotal)
6754^{2} 7450^{2}

Brooklyn Thomas (IRE) *F Rohaut* a78
3 b c Dylan Thomas(IRE) Brooklyn Academy (USA) (Royal Academy (USA))
365a^{5}

Brook Star (IRE) *Michael Dods* 56
4 b m Refuse To Bend(IRE) Star Of Cayman (IRE) (Unfuwain (USA))
2775^{9} 3081^{5} 3402^{6} 4138^{6} 5672^{6}

Broox (IRE) *E J O'Neill* a77 94
4 b h Xaar Miss Brooks (Bishop Of Cashel)
2728a^{13}

Brother Superior *Tim Easterby* 44
3 b g Vital Equine(IRE) Amber Mill (Doulab (USA))
1166^{4} 1953^{6} 2262^{17}

Broughton (GER) *Mahmood Al Zarooni* 59
2 b c Teofilo(IRE) Boccassini (GER) (Artan (IRE))
4677^{5} 6412^{7}

Broughton Place *Willie Musson* a54
4 b m Compton Place Classic Millennium (Midyan (USA))
175^{7} 399^{4} 689^{6} 966^{7} 1379^{10} 6690^{11} 7385^{10} 8067^{7} ◆

Broughton Sands *Willie Musson* a69 72
4 b m Nayef(USA) Pachanga (Inchinor)
149^{2} 355^{2} (688) 1418^{4} 1566^{3} 2233^{9} 3222^{4} 3979^{5} 4875^{8}

Broughtons Bandit *Willie Musson* a59 44
5 b g Kyllachy Broughton Bounty (Bahamian Bounty)
303^{2} 493^{2} (968) 1361^{2} ◆ 2175^{4} 2371^{7}

Broughtons Charm (IRE) *Willie Musson* a74 72
2 b f Invincible Spirit(IRE) Parisian Elegance (Zilzal (USA))
5943[3] (6936) 7298[3] ◆

Broughtons Maxim *Willie Musson* a42 34
3 b g Araafa(IRE) Broughtons Motto (Mtoto)
4410[13] 5297[9] 5717[6]

Broughtons Paradis (IRE) *Willie Musson* a73 78
6 b m Royal Applause Amankila (IRE) (Revoque (IRE))
58[2] 281[3] 786[4] 2199[P]

Broughtons Pearl *Willie Musson* a58
3 b f Iceman Broughton Bounty (Bahamian Bounty)
4157[6]

Broughtons Swinger *Willie Musson* a66 73
5 b m Celtic Swing Pachanga (Inchinor)
150[6] 3220[6] 3968[8] 4652[4] 7270[3]

Brouhaha *Tom Dascombe* a87 87
8 b g Bahhare(USA) Top Of The Morning (Keen)
501[6] 745[4] 1258[7] 1706[6] 2077[4] 2454[6] 3552[2] 4251[5] 4639[5] 6838[6] 7380[2]

Brown Almighty (USA) *Tim Ice* 102
2 ch c Big Brown(USA) Gone Goodbye (USA) (Gone For Real (USA))
7568a[9]

Brown Butterfly *Kevin Prendergast* a85 86
4 b m Medicean Auspicious (Shirley Heights)
3647a[9] 7230a[2]

Brown Colt (IRE) *Mme I T Oakes-Cottin* a62 60
7 b g Statue Of Liberty(USA) Olivia Jane (IRE) (Ela-Mana-Mou)
7123a[0]

Brown Panther *Tom Dascombe* a75 120
4 b h Shirocco(GER) Treble Heights (IRE) (Unfuwain (USA))
2027[4] (3418) 4322[7] 5354[2] 6271a[3] 7431a[8]

Brown Pete (IRE) *Violet M Jordan* a73 72
4 bb g Aussie Rules(USA) Banba (IRE) (Docksider (USA))
676[9] 900[5] 1179[2] 1772[2] 2365[3] (2464) 2652[5] 2937[3] 3247[4] 4089[6] 4405[9] (4662) 5628[4] 6334[7] 7200[5] 7486[6] 7619[7] 7816[7] 7841[8] (8212) (8248) (8264)

Brownsea Brink *Richard Hannon* a77 68
2 b c Cadeaux Genereux Valiantly (Anabaa (USA))
6481[7] ◆ 6795[4] 7078[5] (7806) 8240[3]

Brown Volcano (IRE) *John O'Shea* a39 63
3 b c Waky Nao Lavish Spirit (USA) (Southern Halo (USA))
4992[5] 5505[3] 6095[4] 6287[4] 7667[8]

Broxbourne (IRE) *Mark Johnston* a59 69
3 b f Refuse To Bend(IRE) Rafting (IRE) (Darshaan)
4544[8] 6545[7] 6968[6] 7303[8]

Brundon *Henry Candy* a44 59
3 ch f Refuse To Bend(IRE) Anna Of Brunswick (Rainbow Quest (USA))
1414[7] 1726[10] 3142[5]

Brunello *David O'Meara* a71 40
4 b g Leporello(IRE) Lydia Maria (Dancing Brave (USA))
4[3] 110[2] 366[3] (557) 644[7]

Brunston *Anthony Middleton* a91 36
6 gr g High Chaparral(IRE) Molly Mello (GER) (Big Shuffle (USA))
175[3] 427[4] (601) 846[3] 1139[7] 6702[9] 7175[15] 7672[12] 7824[8] 7986[9] 8243[6] ◆

Brunswick Vale (IRE) *Paul Midgley* a47 55
3 b f Moss Vale(IRE) Brunswick (Warning)
1169[4] 2139[3] 2595[10] 3463[2] 3848[5] 4348[12] 5013[7] 5247[5] 5728[6] 6477[9]

Bruslini (FR) *Brian Ellison* 83
7 gr g Linamix(FR) Brusca (USA) (Grindstone (USA))
2214[3] 4115[10]

Bryant Park (USA) *Michael Wigham*
3 ch g Street Cry(IRE) Cala (FR) (Desert Prince (IRE))
8295[10]

Bryer (IRE) *Mark Johnston* a48
3 b c Street Cry(IRE) Meiosis (USA) (Danzig (USA))
1704[8] 2226[5] 3763[8]

Brynfa Boy *Daniel Mark Loughnane* a79 83
6 b g Namid Funny Girl (IRE) (Darshaan)
371[12] 623[7] 696[11]

Brynford *Chris Dwyer* 47
2 b f Sir Percy Bull's Crown (USA) (Holy Bull (USA))
5631[7] 5932[8]

Bryter Layter *Christopher Kellett* a20
2 b g Deportivo Bahhmirage (IRE) (Bahhare (USA))
6890[8] 7379[11] 7840[10] 8140[5]

Buachaill Tapa (IRE) *H Rogers* a61 10
3 b g Windsor Knot(IRE) Hamsah (IRE) (Green Desert (USA))
336a[6]

Buaiteoir (FR) *Amy Weaver* a67 79
6 b g Mineshaft(USA) Witching Hour (FR) (Fairy King (USA))
3709[6] 3947[3] 5322[10] 6184a[6] 6452[8]

Bubblina *Alastair Lidderdale* a47
5 b m Pastoral Pursuits Streccia (Old Vic)
7896[4] 7996[8]

Bubbly Bailey *Alan Bailey* a61 40
2 b g Byron Night Gypsy (Mind Games)
7057[7] 7686[9] 7854[2] 7974[8] 8103[2] 8203[9]

Bubbly Ballerina *Alan Bailey* a82 86
3 ch f Footstepsinthesand Pain Perdu (IRE) (Waajib)
645[4] 1977[6] 2028[7] 2347[11] 2914[4] 5584[8] 6234[2] 6347[2] 6689[5] 6767[4] 7177[4] 7726[3] 7859[4] (8009) 8163[6]

Bubbly Bellini (IRE) *Adrian McGuinness* a65 96
5 b g Mull Of Kintyre(USA) Gwapa (IRE) (Imperial Frontier (USA))
3648a[4] (4380a) 4833a[11] (6716a) 7066[7]

Bubbly Bounty *Alan Bailey* a37 47
3 b f Bahamian Bounty Eljariha (Unfuwain (USA))
2799[6] 3666[12] 4067[10] 5175[8] 7222[6] 8261[7]

Bubbly Braveheart (IRE) *Pat Phelan* a67 70
5 b g Cape Cross(IRE) Infinity (FR) (Bering)
31[10] 225[7] 568[7] 736[10] 1379[11]

Buckland (IRE) *Hans Adielsson* a79 79
4 b g Oratorio(IRE) Dollar Bird (IRE) (Kris)
3963[11] 4155[2] 4517[2] 6545[4] 6934[9] 7115[7] 7743[2] (7838) 7997[6] 8142[8] 8181[3]

Buckley Boy *K F Clutterbuck* a48 12
3 b g Araafa(IRE) Waseyla (IRE) (Sri Pekan (USA))
399[7] 742[6] 8080[9] 8264[14]

Buckshee *Tim Easterby* 42
4 b g Sulamani(IRE) Cumbrian Rhapsody (Sharrood (USA))
3035[13]

Buckstay (IRE) *Peter Chapple-Hyam* a75
2 b g Lawman(FR) Stella Del Mattino (USA) (Golden Gear (USA))
5207[3] (6214) ◆

Budai (GER) *David Hayes* 84
6 b g Dai Jin Bejaria (GER) (Konigsstuhl (GER))
7073a[14]

Buddhist Monk *Dagmar Geissmann* a42 91
7 b g Dr Fong(USA) Circle Of Light (Anshan)
444a[4]

Budley *Bill Turner* a55 66
4 b g Avonbridge Icecap (Polar Falcon (USA))
1772[4] 2574[8]

Buds Bruvver *Brian Baugh*
3 ch g Reel Buddy(USA) Spectrum Queen (IRE) (Spectrum (IRE))
1257[10] 1824[10]

Budva *Bernard Llewellyn* a74 59
5 b g Kylian(USA) Danlu (USA) (Danzig (USA))
557[6]

Buenos Aires (TUR) *S Karagoz* a95
5 ch h Unaccounted For(USA) Angelica (TUR) (Spectrum (IRE))
5848a[8]

Bugie D'Amore *A De Royer-Dupre* 106
3 b f Rail Link Asmita (Efisio)
2742a[4] 3328[5] 4616a[3] 5249a[8] 7234a[8]

Bugsy *Richard Hannon* a29 48
2 b g Dansili Maroussie (FR) (Saumarez)
6796[14] 7172[11] 7786[6]

Bugsy's Babe *George Baker* a23 34
2 ch f Tobougg(IRE) Oak Tree Miss (USA) (Woodman (USA))
3959[8] 5685[9] 6276[9]

Bugsy's Boy *George Baker* a64 77
8 b g Double Trigger(IRE) Bugsy's Sister (Aragon)
5051[3]

Bulbul (IRE) *Kevin Prendergast* 98
3 b f Shamardal(USA) Oriental Fashion (IRE) (Marju (IRE))
1403a[8] 1944a[2] 2513a[7] 3983a[4] 6268a[9]

Bull Bay *Jane Chapple-Hyam* a70 60
3 b g Bahamian Bounty Buffy Boo (Agnes World (USA))
4456[4] 5453[3] 6965[10] 7667[2] 7864[4] (7988) 8159[5] 8304[3]

Bulldog Beasley (USA) *Brian Meehan* a61 48
3 b g Van Nistelrooy(USA) Dixie Eyes Blazing (USA) (Gone West (USA))
194[3] 360[4]

Bullet Train *Sir Henry Cecil* 113
5 b h Sadler's Wells(USA) Kind (IRE) (Danehill (USA))
2270[4] 3237[6] 4699[4] 5490[5] 7239[6]

Bull Five *Nick Littmoden* a62
5 b g Intikhab(USA) Digamist Girl (IRE) (Digamist (USA))
65[3] 176[6] 224[11] 1299[8]

Bull Market (IRE) *Alan Jones* a24 36
9 b g Danehill(USA) Paper Moon (IRE) (Lake Coniston (IRE))
5265[10] 6323[11]

Bullseye Babe *Mark Usher* a40
2 ch f Notnowcato Mary Sea (FR) (Selkirk (USA))
8166[6]

Bunce (IRE) *David O'Meara* a73 80
4 b g Good Reward(USA) Bold Desire (Cadeaux Genereux)
1769[2] 2071[8] 2444[12] (2939) 3011[4] 5674[5] 5737[5] 6044[4] 6811[4] 7246[7]

Bungle Inthejungle *Mick Channon* 108
2 b c Exceed And Excel(AUS) Licence To Thrill (Wolfhound (USA))
1499[10] (2420) ◆ (2688) 3242[4] 3680a[5] (4687) 5136a[5] 6196[2] (6865)

Bunkered Again *Jeremy Gask* a49 38
5 b m Footstepsinthesand Cragreen (Green Desert (USA))
307[6] 450[11]

Bunraku *Charles Hills* 82
3 b f Cacique(IRE) Wooden Doll (USA) (Woodman (USA))
1467[4] ◆ 2030[6] 3507[3] (3811) 4150[4] 5520[11] 7559[12]

Buona Fortuna *Andrew Balding* a42 69
2 b f Oasis Dream Sadie Thompson (IRE) (King's Best (USA))
7552[5] 7780[9] 8003[7]

Burano (IRE) *Brian Meehan* a86 107
3 ch c Dalakhani(IRE) Kalimanta (IRE) (Lake Coniston (IRE))
417a[5] 485a[8] (679a) 1145a[8] 6446[4] 6674[21] 7054[6] 7557[6]

Burdlaz (IRE) *S Seemar* a98 19
7 ch g Indian Ridge Babalu (IRE) (Doyoun)
260a[12] 678a[11]

Burj Alzain (IRE) *Gerard Butler* a107
4 b h Marju(IRE) Bahareeya (USA) (Riverman (USA))
5118a[5] 6400[3] 6854a[4] 7010[4] 7709[3] 7772[5]

Burke's Rock *Jeremy Noseda* a99 97
3 b f Cape Cross(IRE) Miss Lacey (IRE) (Diktat)
206[4] (523) (2194) 2772[6] 4474[2] 5043[2] (5420) 5834[15] 6875[10] 7509[2]

Burlesque Star (IRE) *Harry Dunlop* a15 50
2 b f Thousand Words Es Que (Inchinor)
3783[8] 4813[4] 5485[7] 6253[7]

Burma Days (USA) *Sylvester Kirk* a36 50
2 b g Medaglia d'Oro(USA) Becky In Pink (USA) (Formal Gold (CAN))
6014[12] 6796[13] 7705[9]

Burnbrake *Richard Rowe* a45 52
7 b g Mujahid(USA) Duena (Grand Lodge (USA))
6399[7] 7629[12] 8035[8]

Burnham *Hughie Morrison* 83
3 b g Nayef(USA) Salim Toto (Mtoto)
2126[2] 2424[7] (3228) 3448[4] 4323[3] 5789[2] 6964[2] 7269[6]

Burnhope *Scott Dixon* a75
3 b g Choisir(AUS) Isengard (USA) (Cobra King (USA))
231[4] (429) 982[6] 7023[8] 7411[7]

Burning Blaze *Kevin Ryan* 87
2 b c Danroad(AUS) Demeter (USA) (Diesis)
3887[3] ◆ (4612) 5563[12] 7028[3]

Burning Dawn (USA) *David Brown* 69
2 b f Bernstein(USA) Winter Morning (USA) (Rahy (USA))
3989[2] ◆ 4742[4] 6335[4]

Burning Passion *Michael Easterby* a54
3 b g Gentleman's Deal(IRE) Search For Love (FR) (Groom Dancer (USA))
195[7] 369[9] 638[4] 1590[6] 2118[10] 2341[14]

Burning Thread (IRE) *Tim Etherington* a43 102
5 b g Captain Rio Desert Rose (Green Desert (USA))
2717[3] 4367[14] 4576[7] 5343[6] 5487[16] 6026[14] 6557[4] 7243[12] 7704[12]

Burns Night *Ollie Pears* a66 79
6 ch g Selkirk(USA) Night Frolic (Night Shift (USA))
1598[10] 6259[3] ◆ 7347[8] 7768[5]

Burnt Cream *Martin Bosley* a48 63
5 b m Exceed And Excel(AUS) Basbousate Nadia (Wolfhound (USA))
6640[10] 7157[3] 7746[6] 7837[10] ◆ 8184[5]

Burnt Fingers (IRE) *Rod Millman* 15
2 b f Kheleyf(USA) Play With Fire (FR) (Priolo (USA))
7371[10]

Burnt Sienna (IRE) *John Joseph Murphy* 65
2 ch f Papal Bull Lucky Achievement (USA) (St Jovite (USA))
6266a[7]

Burnwynd Boy *Ian Semple* a55 68
7 b g Tobougg(IRE) Cadeau Speciale (Cadeaux Genereux)
(2621) 4388[6] (5084) 6106[5]

Burnwynd Spirit (IRE) *Ian Semple* a51 48
3 b g Kodiac Bluebird Spirit (Bluebird (USA))
25[3] 459[7] 1241[11] 1482[4]

Bursledon (IRE) *Richard Hannon* 63
2 b c Jeremy(USA) Desert Drama (IRE) (Green Desert (USA))
6020[12] 7332[5]

Bursting Bubbles (IRE) *Ed Dunlop* a57 44
3 br f Big Bad Bob(IRE) Ski For Gold (Shirley Heights)
1424[11] 2141[4]

Burwaaz *Ed Dunlop* a104 109
3 b c Exceed And Excel(AUS) Nidhaal (IRE) (Observatory (USA))
1751[3] ◆ 2236[4]

Burza *Pat Murphy* a43 67
6 ch m Bold Edge Welcome Star (IRE) (Most Welcome)
2767[6] 3236[8]

Bussa *David Evans* a67 74
4 b g Iceman Maid To Dance (Pyramus (USA))
1205[5] 4147[5] 6798[4] 7015[9] 7200[11] 7437[12] 7898[3] 7993[4] (8099) (8298)

Buster Brown (IRE) *James Given* a74 75
3 ch c Singspiel(IRE) Gold Dodger (USA) (Slew O'Gold (USA))
2126[6] 3186[3] 4250[5] (5312) 6240[4] 7032[15] 7359[5]

Busy Bimbo (IRE) *Alan Berry* a43 60
3 b f Red Clubs(IRE) Unfortunate (Komaite (USA))
1296[9] 2460[7] 2615[9] 3462[9] 4348[14] 4547[16] 5087[8] 5542[7] 5823[5] 6100[9] 7253[6] 7838[8] 8109[4]

Bute Hall *Mark Johnston* a78 86
3 ch c Halling(USA) Les Hurlants (IRE) (Barathea (IRE))
2271[7] (2668) 3614[3] 3859[4] 4216[5] (4910) ◆

Bute Street *Ron Hodges* a59 67
7 b g Superior Premium Hard To Follow (Dilum (USA))
594[6] 968[7] 1184[5] (1338) 1496[3] 2396[6] (2872) (3143) 4061[3] 7968[11]

Buthelezi (USA) *John Gosden* a102 105
4 bb g Dynaformer(USA) Ntombi (USA) (Quiet American (USA))
1374[5] 2278[10]

Butterfly Dream *William Haggas* a57 53
2 ch f Kyllachy Dream Again (Medicean)
5631[5] 6645[4] 7312[6]

Butterfly McQueen (USA) *Andrew Balding* 71
2 b f Curlin(USA) Distant Roar (CAN) (Storm Cat (USA))
7208[2]

Button Moon (IRE) *Paul Fitzsimons* a74 90
4 ch m Compton Place Portelet (Night Shift (USA))
1141[12] 1494[7] 1727[11] 2195[7] 3049[10] 3394[2] ◆ 3960[8] 4336[5] 4824[16] 4920[5] 5812[7] (5995) 6094[2] 6577[8] 6825[3] 7144[7] 7483[2] 7742[5] 7902[9] 8059[3] 8160[6]

Buxfizz (USA) *George Prodromou* a82 77
4 b g Elusive Quality(USA) Argentina (USA) (Storm Cat (USA))
(248) 351[7] ◆ 374[8] 570[7]

Buxted's Choice (IRE) *Robert Mills* a56
2 ch c Footstepsinthesand Choose Me Please (IRE) (Choisir (AUS))
3499[5] 4056[12] 4404[4]

Buxton *Roger Ingram* a64 79
8 b g Auction House(USA) Dam Certain (IRE) (Damister (USA))
(729) 828[3] 972[6] 7917[3] 7992[8] 8061[5] 8268[8]

Buy Art *Gary Moore* 71
2 b g Acclamation Kondakova (IRE) (Soviet Star (USA))
2868[6] (3244)

Buzkashi (IRE) *David Lanigan* a74 73
3 b f Nayef(USA) Min Alhawa (USA) (Riverman (USA))
2431[5] ◆ 4335[4] 5154[6]

Buzz Law (IRE) *Mrs K Burke* a75 82
4 b g Fasliyev(USA) Buzz Two (IRE) (Case Law)
2792[8] 4295[4] 5322[4]

Bwana Go Fast (USA) *Nathan Squires* a79 40
2 bb f Bwana Charlie(USA) Pleasant Thunder (USA) (Thunder Gulch (USA))
6289a[14]

By A Wiska *Ann Duffield* a44 53
2 b g Kheleyf(USA) Tropical Breeze (IRE) (Kris)
3842[6] 4618[9] 4907[6] 7973[10]

Bygones For Coins (IRE) *Robert Johnson* a55 56
4 ch m Danroad(AUS) Reservation (IRE) (Common Grounds)
135[4] 214[7] 691[4] 979[4] 1089[2] 1242[7] 1635[3] 1831[8] 2239[3] 2669[3] 2925[6] 4594[9] 5543[2] 6106[13] 6783[7]

By Implication *Ed de Giles* a51
4 br g Cacique(IRE) Insinuate (USA) (Mr Prospector (USA))
375[8] 561[4] 653[11] 773[2] 1425[12]

By Invitation (USA) *Ralph Beckett* a72 69
3 b f Van Nistelrooy(USA) Sahara Star (Green Desert (USA))
(26) ◆ 2503[12] 4496[15] 4920[7]

By Popular Demand (IRE) *Lisa Williamson* a50
4 b g Indian Haven Green Belt (FR) (Tirol)
502[6]

Byrd In Hand (IRE) *John Bridger* a62 68
5 b g Fasliyev(USA) Military Tune (IRE) (Nashwan (USA))
1009[3] 1310[2] 1624[2] (1771) 2363[7] 2886[4] 3073[7] 3705[9] 6950[2] 7302[6] 7486[5] 7643[11] 7768[13] 8078[10]

Byron Bear (IRE) *Paul Midgley* a37 58
4 b g Byron Paulas Pride (Pivotal)
1831[7] 2455[10] 2692[3] 5059[4] 5171[11] 6361[11]

Byron Blue (IRE) *Jamie Osborne* a77 76
3 br c Dylan Thomas(IRE) High Society (IRE) (Key Of Luck (USA))
1853[5] 2605[6] 3087[6] (3781) 4225[3] 4918[2] 5798[6] 6407[3] 6784[9]

Byroness *Heather Main* a70 51
2 b f Byron Parting Gift (Cadeaux Genereux)
4055[7] (8166)

Byron Get One Free *Richard Ford*
3 b g Byron Ishela (IRE) (Barathea (IRE))
2418[9]

Byronic Hero *Jedd O'Keeffe* 84
3 b g Byron Starbeck (IRE) (Spectrum (IRE))
1271[6] 2182[16] 2785[11] (3421) 3778[14] 4629[16] 5618[9] 6405[12] 6885[8]

Byron's Dream *Jedd O'Keeffe* a51 60
2 b g Byron Fresher (Fabulous Dancer (USA))
3611[9] 4618[4] 5169[6] 7223[4]

Byron's Gem *J R Jenkins*
3 b f Byron Maddie's A Jem (Emperor Jones (USA))
4144[10]

Byrony (IRE) *John W Sadler* a90 94
4 ch m Byron Saphire (College Chapel)
7577a[6]

Byton *Henry Candy* a71 79
3 b f Byron Arculinge (Paris House)
2042[5] (3568) 5308[6] 5995[6] 6378[5] 6705[12]

Cabal *Andrew Crook* a65 63
5 br m Kyllachy Secret Flame (Machiavellian (USA))
477[3] (773) (1096) 1222[2] 1439[8] 7976[7] 8145[5]

Caboodle *Tom Dascombe* a37 21
3 b f Bahamian Bounty Bowness (Efisio)
925[7] 1274[11] 7804[5]

Cactus Valley (IRE) *Roger Charlton* a71 90
3 b g Lawman(FR) Beech Gardens (Sadler's Wells (USA))
1703[4] 2856[5] 3227[4] 4548[3] (5007) ◆ 5451[3] 6987[2]

Cadeaux Pearl *Scott Dixon* a88 92
4 b g Acclamation Anneliina (Cadeaux Genereux)
(120) 286[6] 835[2] 1015[7] 1417[14] (1602) 4690[21] 5343[11] 5663[12] 6466[22] 7019[14] 7859[9]

Cades Reef (IRE) *Linda Perratt* a52 72
3 gr g Dalakhani(IRE) Just Special (Cadeaux Genereux)
1892[3] 2129[5] (2495) 2716[P]

Cadgers Brig *Keith Dalgleish* a74 68
4 ch g Halling(USA) Burghmuir (IRE) (Cadeaux Genereux)
63[7] 271[3] 500[5] 2842[3] 3577[3] 4138[3] 4391[2] 4766[8] 5672[12] (6262) 6711[13] 7003[8] 7792[9] 8146[7]

Cadmium Loch *Reg Hollinshead* a69 66
4 b g Needwood Blade Vermilion Creek (Makbul)
1487[2] 2555[3] 2981[7] 3950[12] 4993[4] 5427[5] 7106[10] 7224[8] 8131[6]

Cadore (IRE) *Lucinda Russell* 78
4 b g Hurricane Run(IRE) Mansiya (Vettori (IRE))
1797[6] 3031[7] 4429[4]

Cafe Express (IRE) *Linda Perratt* a45 71
3 ch f Bertolini(USA) Cafe Creme (IRE) (Catrail (USA))
7356[12]

Cafe Society (FR) *David Simcock* a71
2 b c Motivator Mishina (FR) (Highest Honor (FR))
(7057) ◆

Caffea (FR) *Y-M Porzier* 75
3 ch f Satri(IRE) Capuccina (FR) (Lavirco (GER))
5726a[0]

Cahala Dancer (IRE) *Roger Teal* a65 66
4 ch m Elnadim(USA) Ranma (In The Wings)
1084[5] 1379[7] 1625[2] 1907[2] 2364[6] 3152[3] 3392[12]

Cailin Coillteach *W McCreery* a68 65
4 b m Woodman(USA) Kathy's Rocket (USA) (Gold Legend (USA))
775a[3]

Cairanne *Tom Keddy* a57 64
4 b m High Chaparral(IRE) Celestial Choir (Celestial Storm (USA))
125^{13} 218^{2} 375^{2} 503^{2} 578^{4} 773^{12} 1014^{2} 1096^{3} 1379^{8} 1423^{2} 1634^{6} (2013) 2233^{2} 2899^{6} 3047^{5} 3920^{8} 4296^{10} 6569^{5} 7321^{9} 7620^{8}

Cai Shen (IRE) *Richard Hannon* a109 112
4 ch h Iffraaj Collada (IRE) (Desert Prince (IRE))
1034^{2} ◆ 2081^{3} 3268^{6} 3825^{3} 4320^{4} 4684^{12} 6142^{2} 6446^{6}

Caitania (IRE) *U Stoltefuss* 99
3 gr f Aussie Rules(USA) Celestia (Anabaa (USA))
$2531a^{7}$ $3802a^{2}$ $5145a^{4}$ $5844a^{8}$ $6911a^{11}$

Caitlin *Andrew Balding* a22 73
3 b f Dylan Thomas(IRE) Kassiopeia (IRE) (Galileo (IRE))
1649^{4} 5555^{11} 7644^{11}

Calaf *Brian Ellison* a53 89
4 b g Dubai Destination(USA) Tarandot (IRE) (Singspiel (IRE))
907^{13} 1134^{2} 1381^{9} (1841) 1999^{3} 2473^{4} 2911^{8} 3417^{4} 4795^{7} 5540^{5} (5965) (6757) 7069^{4}

Calahorra (FR) *C Baillet* 104
3 ch f Soave(GER) Kendorya (FR) (Kendor (FR))
$1426a^{9}$ $2112a^{3}$ $2745a^{6}$ $4790a^{8}$

Cala Santanyi *Gerard Butler* a81 82
4 b m Green Desert(USA) Fantastic Santanyi (Fantastic Light (USA))
(1314) 1756^{8} 2539^{5} 3278^{11}

Calculaite *Richard Ford* 51
11 b g Komaite(USA) Miss Calculate (Mummy's Game)
1794^{10}

Calculated (USA) *Mahmood Al Zarooni* 53
2 bb c Tiznow(USA) Contrive (USA) (Storm Cat (USA))
6636^{8}

Calculated Risk *Willie Musson* a61 71
3 ch g Motivator Glen Rosie (IRE) (Mujtahid (USA))
2246^{9} 3228^{6} (4250) 5323^{3} 7108^{3}

Caldercruix (USA) *James Evans* a90 86
5 ch g Rahy(USA) Al Theraab (USA) (Roberto (USA))
64^{4} 458^{3} 765^{3} (883) 1161^{6} 3004^{5} 3394^{6} 4286^{12} 5557^{8} 7966^{13} 8143^{7}

Caldermud (IRE) *Olivia Maylam* a59 75
5 ch g Chineur(FR) Dalal (Cadeaux Genereux)
(1263) 1650^{9}

Caledonia Lady *Jo Hughes* 105
3 b f Firebreak Granuaile O'Malley (IRE) (Mark Of Esteem (IRE))
1494^{2} 1857^{6} 2212^{3} 3238^{7} ◆ (3877) 4113^{8}

Caledonian Lad *Hughie Morrison* a39 50
3 ch g Pastoral Pursuits Jasmick (IRE) (Definite Article)
2543^{9} 2941^{12} 4189^{5} 4870^{11} 6210^{6}

Caledonia Prince *Jo Hughes* a77 52
4 b g Needwood Blade Granuaile O'Malley (IRE) (Mark Of Esteem (IRE))
370^{2} (490) 676^{2} 900^{3} (1052) 1251^{7} 2090^{8} 5752^{9} 6812^{4} 7436^{6} 7722^{6} 8137^{2}

Caledonia Princess *Stuart Williams* a79 78
6 b m Kyllachy Granuaile O'Malley (IRE) (Mark Of Esteem (IRE))
325^{4} 528^{10} 1049^{4}

Calgacus (IRE) *Tracey Collins* a71 89
3 ch c Galileo(IRE) Katdogawn (Bahhare (USA))
$2102a^{4}$

Calico Cat *Alastair Lidderdale* 106
4 b g Tiger Hill(IRE) Gossamer (Sadler's Wells (USA))
2027^{3} (2287) 2506^{2} 3369^{9}

Calidoscopio (ARG) *Guillermo J Frenkel Santillan* a111 104
9 b h Luhuk(USA) Calderona (ARG) (Lefty (USA))
(7546a)

Califante *Richard Hannon* 98
2 b f Kyllachy Call Mariah (USA) (Dixie Union (USA))
3182^{4} ◆ 3474^{3} (4408) 4820^{2} $5379a^{5}$ 5787^{2} 6632^{7}

California English (IRE) *Marco Botti* a81 69
3 b g Oasis Dream Muwali (USA) (Kingmambo (USA))
1304^{3} 2408^{9} 2813^{3} 3792^{11} 4889^{9} 5480^{9} 8057^{10}

California Flag (USA) *Brian Koriner* a93 116
8 rg g Avenue Of Flags(USA) Ultrafleet (USA) (Afleet (CAN))
$7571a^{13}$

California Memory (USA) *A S Cruz* 122
6 gr g Highest Honor(FR) Kalpita (USA) (Spinning World (USA))
$1148a^{12}$ (8043a)

Calipatria *H-A Pantall* a74 107
5 ch m Shamardal(USA) Golden Silca (Inchinor)
$2805a^{5}$ (6723a) $7784a^{5}$ $7985a^{0}$

Calissa (IRE) *Mrs John Harrington* a36 70
2 b f Danehill Dancer(IRE) Mauralakana (FR) (Muhtathir)
$3674a^{7}$

Callisto Moon *Jo Hughes* a29 82
8 b g Mujahid(USA) Nursling (IRE) (Kahyasi)
1925^{7} (2698) (3337) (4475) 4756^{2}

Call It On (IRE) *Philip Kirby* a79 84
6 ch g Raise A Grand(IRE) Birthday Present (Cadeaux Genereux)
3241^{11} 4284^{7} 6415^{5} 7098^{10} 8290^{3}

Call It Out *Alan Kirtley*
5 ch g Rock City Phisus (Henbit (USA))
6885^{13}

Callmeakhab (IRE) *Charles Hills* 61
2 b f Intikhab(USA) Viola Royale (IRE) (Royal Academy (USA))
6966^{6}

Call Me April *Karen George* a46 51
4 b m Generous(IRE) Anyhow (IRE) (Distant Relative)
1301^{6} 1724^{7} 2387^{5} 3485^{13} 5280^{5} 5789^{10}

Call Me Bubbles (FR) *W P Mullins* a59 89
3 gr g Stormy River(FR) Tempete Tropicale (FR) (Kaldoun (FR))
$6066a^{2}$

Call Me Marilyn (USA) *Michael Bell* a24
2 ch f Henny Hughes(USA) Ball Gown (USA) (Silver Hawk (USA))
7525^{10}

Call Of Duty (IRE) *Dianne Sayer* a49 75
7 br g Storming Home Blushing Barada (USA) (Blushing Groom (FR))
2134^{6} (2454) 2661^{3} 3213^{5} 3492^{9} (4594) ◆ 4768^{2} 4864^{4} (5039) 5290^{6} 5730^{7} 6131^{10}

Call To Battle (IRE) *John M Oxx* 109
3 b c King's Best(USA) Dance The Classics (IRE) (Sadler's Wells (USA))
$1404a^{2}$ 1995^{3}

Call To Reason (IRE) *Ian Williams* a91 91
5 ch m Pivotal Venturi (Danehill Dancer (IRE))
5^{3} ◆ (584) ◆ 1321^{12} 1993^{6} 2984^{4}

Calmer Waters (USA) *David Elsworth* a57
2 b f Henrythenavigator(USA) Passified (Compton Place)
8006^{5}

Calrissian (GER) *Fredrik Reuterskiold* a96 109
8 ch g Efisio Centaine (Royal Academy (USA))
$3603a^{8}$

Calvados Blues (FR) *Mahmood Al Zarooni* a100 117
6 ch h Lando(GER) Persian Belle (Machiavellian (USA))
5364^{2} 6035^{9}

Calypso Cay *Peter Salmon* a67 65
4 b g Tiger Hill(IRE) Tessa Reef (IRE) (Mark Of Esteem (IRE))
176^{10} 1527^{3} 2096^{10} 2314^{10} 2926^{7} 3388^{2} 6439^{6} 6967^{13} 7593^{6} 7733^{8}

Calypso Magic (IRE) *Olivia Maylam* a86 92
4 gr g Aussie Rules(USA) Calypso Dancer (FR) (Celtic Swing)
131^{9} $443a^{12}$ $630a^{15}$ 907^{7} 1181^{4} 2199^{15} 2847^{11} 3705^{3} 4413^{11} 5008^{9} 5804^{9} 6250^{4} 6690^{10} 7960^{5} (8078)

Calzaghe (IRE) *Martin Hill* a52 75
8 ch g Galileo(IRE) Novelette (Darshaan)
825^{7} 968^{5}

Camache Queen (IRE) *Joseph Tuite* a85 85
4 b m Camacho Alinda (IRE) (Revoque (IRE))
1926^{2} 2558^{6} 3342^{4} 3696^{6} 4655^{3} 5906^{7} 6406^{7} 6939^{6} 8202^{6}

Camachoice (IRE) *Marco Botti* a64
2 b c Camacho Nouvelle Reve (GER) (Acatenango (GER))
7963^{6} 8178^{4}

Camberley Two *Roger Charlton* a84 90
4 bg g Invincible Spirit(IRE) Diamond Line (FR) (Linamix (FR))
1924^{9} 2932^{8} 3963^{6}

Camborne *John Gosden* a92 111
4 b g Doyen(IRE) Dumnoni (Titus Livius (FR))
(1186) 1381^{13} 2257^{6} (2921) (3372) 5600^{7} 6866^{2} 7405^{5}

Cambridge Duchess *Stuart Williams* a55 51
3 br f Singspiel(IRE) Roseum (Lahib (USA))
181^{7} 219^{5} 2610^{5} 3548^{5}

Camelopardalis *Tobias B P Coles* 54
3 b f Tobougg(IRE) Bonne Etoile (Diesis)
4908^{3}

Camelot *A P O'Brien* 127
3 b c Montjeu(IRE) Tarfah (USA) (Kingmambo (USA))
(1856) ◆ (2705) (3651a) 6245^{2} $6912a^{7}$

Camera Shy (IRE) *Kevin Morgan* a61 60
8 ch g Pivotal Shy Danceuse (FR) (Groom Dancer (USA))
1984^{11} 2804^{2} 3392^{3} 3794^{4}

Cameron Highland (IRE) *Roger Varian* 114
3 b c Galileo(IRE) Landmark (USA) (Arch (USA))
(1250) ◆ 1604^{3} 3630^{2} (4725) (5593) 6482^{4}

Camerooney *Brian Ellison* a64 92
9 b g Sugarfoot Enkindle (Relkino)
1275^{11} 1561^{13}

Camilla De Rossi *Rae Guest* 23
2 b f Oratorio(IRE) Supa Sal (King's Best (USA))
7433^{7}

Campanologist (USA) *Saeed Bin Suroor* a102 117
7 b h Kingmambo(USA) Ring Of Music (Sadler's Wells (USA))
$877a^{3}$

Campanology *Richard Hannon* 96
3 b c Royal Applause Savannah Belle (Green Desert (USA))
1470^{6} 1860^{6} 2930^{8} (3393) 4740^{12} 5556^{2} 6701^{6}

Camp Floyd (USA) *Mahmood Al Zarooni* a68 60
2 ch c Street Cry(IRE) Love Dancing (ARG) (Salt Lake (USA))
5062^{10} 5742^{5} 5962^{10} 6451^{2}

Camp Victory (USA) *Mike Mitchell* a124 112
5 bb g Forest Camp(USA) Victory Trick (CAN) (Clever Trick (USA))
$7571a^{11}$

Camrock Star (IRE) *Alastair Lidderdale* a54 63
3 b f Rock Of Gibraltar(IRE) Night Cam (IRE) (Night Shift (USA))
1322^{7} 1517^{6} 2787^{4} 4510^{6} 4844^{4} (5148) 5998^{5} 6275^{7} 6814^{7} 7148^{7}

Canadian (IRE) *M bin Shafya* a74 89
4 b g Tiger Hill(IRE) Vimy Ridge (FR) (Indian Ridge)
$317a^{11}$ $587a^{14}$

Canadian Danehill (IRE) *Robert Cowell* a65 53
10 b g Indian Danehill(IRE) San Jovita (CAN) (St Jovite (USA))
95^{2} 227^{2} 445^{4} (544) (580) 691^{6} 844^{10} 887^{7} 3791^{9} 5327^{8}

Canadian Red *Tom Dascombe* a33 57
2 b g Sleeping Indian Pontressina (USA) (St Jovite (USA))
5207^{8} 5685^{5} 5963^{12} 7432^{8}

Canadian Run (IRE) *Robert Mills* a81 75
2 ch g Hurricane Run(IRE) Vale View (FR) (Anabaa (USA))
4463^{4} 4938^{2} 5765^{6} (7989) 8072^{2}

Canary Row (IRE) *P J Prendergast* 93
2 b c Holy Roman Emperor(IRE) Fresh Mint (IRE) (Sadler's Wells (USA))
$2184a^{2}$ $6060a^{4}$ 6599^{6} $7419a^{4}$

Canary Wharf (IRE) *Marco Botti* a81 81
3 b c Danehill Dancer(IRE) Wedding Morn (IRE) (Sadler's Wells (USA))
(195) 6964^{11} 7999^{7}

Candelita *Jo Hughes* a68
5 b m Trade Fair Gramada (IRE) (Cape Cross (IRE))
137^{4} 300^{3} (581) 7792^{5} 7968^{5}

Can Do Les (IRE) *Richard Phillips* a57 57
3 b g Modigliani(USA) Yulara (IRE) (Night Shift (USA))
132^{9} 294^{8} 407^{7} 3543^{11} 4900^{9} 5212^{8} 5452^{9} 5751^{8}

Candoluminescence *Roger Charlton* 67
2 bb f Dansili Flash Of Gold (Darshaan)
6795^{11} 7552^{6}

Candycakes (IRE) *Michael Bell* a70 82
3 b f Cape Cross(IRE) Charita (IRE) (Lycius (USA))
1363^{2} ◆ 2201^{10} 2820^{5} 3643^{7} 3978^{3} (4538) 5328^{5} 5856^{3} 6416^{10} 6667^{12}

Candyman Can (IRE) *Dominic Ffrench Davis* a67
2 b g Holy Roman Emperor(IRE) Palwina (FR) (Unfuwain (USA))
7642^{8} 7923^{8} 8134^{3}

Cane Cat (IRE) *Tony Carroll* a67 69
5 bb m One Cool Cat(USA) Seven Wonders (USA) (Rahy (USA))
276^{4} 559^{2} 818^{2} ◆ 891^{5} 1533^{6} (2767) 3081^{11} 3220^{4} 5310^{8} 6120^{11}

Canning Vale *Julia Feilden* a55 25
3 ch f Araafa(IRE) Elegant Beauty (Olden Times)
255^{8} 641^{5} 743^{12} 1062^{6} 2625^{8} 3548^{8} 5215^{13}

Cannizaro House (IRE) *Terry Clement* a59 83
3 ch g Dutch Art Travel On (USA) (Joyeux Danseur (USA))
2585^{5} (3447)

Cannon Bolt (IRE) *Robin Bastiman* a21 63
4 b g Chineur(FR) Prime Time Girl (Primo Dominie)
(1799) 2091^{12} 3115^{6} 4432^{6} 5059^{3} 5918^{8} 6309^{5} 7446^{15}

Cantabilly (IRE) *Ron Hodges* a47 54
9 b g Distant Music(USA) Cantaloupe (Priolo (USA))
592^{5}

Cantal *Sir Michael Stoute* a82 83
3 ch f Pivotal Canda (USA) (Storm Cat (USA))
2448^{3} ◆ 3085^{2} 6040^{3} 6768^{4}

Canticum *D Smaga* 111
3 b c Cacique(IRE) Allegro Viva (USA) (Distant View (USA))
$6087a^{2}$ (6896a)

Cantor *Giles Bravery* a61 69
4 b g Iceman Choir Mistress (Chief Singer)
28^{4} 188^{6} 389^{2} (519) 1106^{7} 1613^{6} 2394^{3} 2814^{5} 3721^{2} (3995) 4296^{8}

Canwinn (IRE) *D Selvaratnam* a102 93
6 b g Refuse To Bend(IRE) Born To Glamour (Ajdal (USA))
$51a^{5}$ $261a^{5}$ $586a^{3}$ $757a^{4}$

Capacious *James Fanshawe* a71 58
3 b f Nayef(USA) Palatial (Green Desert (USA))
4746^{7} 5555^{8} 6457^{2} 6973^{8}

Capaill Liath (IRE) *Kevin Ryan* a73 97
4 gr g Iffraaj Bethesda (Distant Relative)
1212^{14} 1510^{6} 1821^{3} (2243) ◆ 2657^{14} 3268^{9} 4321^{17} 4611^{9} 5368^{10} 5827^{6} 6471^{DSQ} 6659^{2} 7097^{3} 7435^{7}

Cape Alex *Clive Brittain* a58 56
3 b f Cape Cross(IRE) Alexander Three D (IRE) (Pennekamp (USA))
1503^{9} 2665^{3} 5297^{7} 5744^{7} 5945^{8} 6807^{7}

Cape Classic (IRE) *William Haggas* a71 103
4 b h Cape Cross(IRE) Politesse (USA) (Barathea (IRE))
2264^{2} ◆ (2558) ◆ 4824^{13} 5102^{10} 6011^{3} (6201) 6676^{9} 6868^{6}

Cape Crossing *Andrew Balding* a56 49
3 br f Cape Cross(IRE) Dame Hester (IRE) (Diktat)
8187^{4}

Cape Explorer *James Tate* a66 79
3 b g Cape Cross(IRE) Eve (Rainbow Quest (USA))
1867^{5} 2196^{13} 2553^{5} (4709) (5129) 5838^{4} ◆ 6359^{2} 7131^{3} 7353^{5}

Cape Express (IRE) *Nicky Henderson* a102 89
7 b g Cape Cross(IRE) Lilissa (IRE) (Doyoun)
2474^{3} 4697^{5} 5491^{8}

Cape Joy (IRE) *Richard Hannon* a31 73
3 b f Cape Cross(IRE) Perils Of Joy (IRE) (Rainbow Quest (USA))
2553^{7} 3663^{4} 4486^{4} (5125) 5351^{11} 5942^{10}

Capella's Song (IRE) *Michael Bell* 74
2 b f Oratorio(IRE) Bright Bank (IRE) (Sadler's Wells (USA))
6791^{3} 7329^{3}

Capellini *Charles Egerton* a45 84
5 b g Cape Cross(IRE) Red Stella (FR) (Rainbow Quest (USA))
8162^{12}

Cape Of Approval (IRE) *T Stack* 96
3 b g Cape Cross(IRE) Wyola (USA) (Sadler's Wells (USA))
(6270a) ◆

Cape Of Hope (IRE) *Peter Chapple-Hyam* 70
2 b c Cape Cross(IRE) Bright Hope (IRE) (Danehill (USA))
6164^{9} 6818^{4} 7311^{4}

Cape Of Storms *Roy Brotherton* a71 24
9 b g Cape Cross(IRE) Lloc (Absalom)
(215) 640^{4} 719^{3} 1116^{7} 1481^{8} 1910^{11} 7589^{8} 7794^{12}

Cape Peron *Henry Candy* 72
2 b g Beat Hollow Free Offer (Generous (IRE))
7686^{3} ◆

Cape Rainbow *Mark Usher* a62 75
3 b g Cape Cross(IRE) Mambo Halo (USA) (Southern Halo (USA))
1607^{8} 2428^{12} 4288^{6} 4776^{9} 6365^{2} ◆ 6691^{10} 7062^{6}

Cape Rising (IRE) *Alan Swinbank* 84
5 b m Cape Cross(IRE) Woodrising (Nomination)
1295^{9} 2312^{2} 2751^{3} 3377^{2} (4326) 5002^{3} 5540^{8} 6492^{9} 7098^{11}

Cape Rock *William Knight* a87 65
7 b g Cape Cross(IRE) Wildwood Flower (Distant Relative)
1708^{3} 2545^{13} 3348^{7}

Cape Royal *Milton Bradley* a68 79
12 b g Prince Sabo Indigo (Primo Dominie)
2084^{8} 2494^{12} 3464^{3} 3724^{3} 4059^{6} 4535^{7} 5149^{5} 6288^{3}

Cape Safari (IRE) *Tim Vaughan* a84 84
3 b f Cape Cross(IRE) Finnmark (Halling (USA))
84^{6} 369^{2} (675) 994^{3} (1281) (1355) 1442^{2} 1756^{2} 2281^{7} 3042^{7} 3163^{14} 3630^{9} 4601^{7} 4884^{2} 5211^{5} (5718) 6033^{8} 6416^{5} 6667^{8} 6964^{6} 7147^{7} 7413^{5} 7655^{8} 7999^{9} 8149^{5} 8297^{6}

Cape Samba *Ismail Mohammed* a73 75
3 b c Cape Cross(IRE) Dancing Feather (Suave Dancer (USA))
1001^{2} 1567^{5} 2544^{9} 3711^{7}

Cape Savannah *David Simcock* a86 87
3 b c Cape Cross(IRE) Lady High Havens (IRE) (Bluebird (USA))
249^{3} (635) 3042^{4} 3592^{6} 4930^{2} 5788^{2} 6625^{6} 7194^{6}

Cape's Best *James Tate* 58
2 b c Cape Cross(IRE) Queen's Best (King's Best (USA))
4677^{6} 5704^{7} 6607^{8}

Cape Schanck *Alan Coogan* a31 74
8 b g Observatory(USA) Sally Gardens (Alzao (USA))
1014^{12}

Cape Sky *Roy Brotherton* 41
5 gr m Cape Town(IRE) Herecomespapin (IRE) (Naheez (USA))
6215^{11} 6736^{9} 7112^{9} 8180^{14}

Cape Tribulation *Malcolm Jefferson* 90
8 b g Hernando(FR) Gay Fantastic (Ela-Mana-Mou)
2214^{6} 7068^{2}

Cape Velvet (IRE) *Mme J Bidgood* a67 81
8 b m Cape Cross(IRE) Material Lady (IRE) (Barathea (IRE))
$965a^{8}$

Caphene *John Dunlop* 73
3 b f Sakhee(USA) Claxon (Caerleon (USA))
1503^{5} 1893^{9} 5309^{6} 6033^{9} 7271^{7}

Caphira *William Knight* a84 68
3 ch f Singspiel(IRE) Dream Quest (Rainbow Quest (USA))
2585^{4} 3279^{8} 4648^{2} (5154) 6025^{17} 6537^{4}

Capital Account (USA) *Bob Baffert* a120
5 b h Closing Argument(USA) Accountess (USA) (Private Account (USA))
$7574a^{12}$

Capital Attraction (USA) *Ernst Oertel* a100 102
5 ch g Speightstown(USA) Cecilia's Crown (USA) (Chief's Crown (USA))
$242a^{7}$ (616a)

Capital Market (USA) *Ismail Mohammed* a79 90
5 b h Indian Charlie(USA) Near Mint (USA) (Dehere (USA))
$51a^{12}$ $246a^{15}$

Capitol Gain (IRE) *Brian Meehan* a45 76
3 b g Bahamian Bounty Emmas Princess (IRE) (Bahhare (USA))
1467^{7} 1923^{12} 2553^{8} 3228^{4} 3621^{8} 4172^{8} 4709^{7} (5018) 5349^{3} 5783^{7} (6275) (6931) 7376^{6}

Capitol Hill (IRE) *John Joseph Murphy* a59 63
2 b c Papal Bull Florencia (GER) (Indian Ridge)
7130^{4}

Capo Bastone (USA) *John W Sadler* a108
2 ch c Street Boss(USA) Fight To Love (USA) (Fit To Fight (USA))
$7572a^{3}$

Caponata (USA) *D K Weld* 113
3 b f Selkirk(USA) Daring Diva (Dansili)
$4376a^{2}$ $6080a^{2}$ $6518a^{8}$

Capone (IRE) *Garry Moss* a106 91
7 b g Daggers Drawn(USA) Order Of The Day (USA) (Dayjur (USA))
89^{3} (405) 711^{3} 866^{6} 6165^{7} ◆ 7243^{4} (7503) 7772^{9}

Capo Rosso (IRE) *Tom Dascombe* a81 84
2 b g Red Clubs(IRE) Satin Cape (IRE) (Cape Cross (IRE))
1818^{8} 2912^{3} 3271^{3} 3777^{4} (4152) (5041) 6032^{3} 6487^{8}

Cap O'Rushes *Mahmood Al Zarooni* a85 95
2 b c New Approach(IRE) Valley Of Gold (FR) (Shirley Heights)
(5407) (5976) 7053^{6} 7554^{2}

Cappadocia (IRE) *Mick Channon* a76 70
2 b c Mujadil(USA) Green Vision (IRE) (Green Desert (USA))
2231^{8} 2594^{2} 2852^{6} 3996^{4} 4502^{P} 5041^{4} 5484^{2} (6016) 6247^{8} 7059^{2} (7193) 7478^{5}

Cappielow Park *Fleur Hawes* a73 71
3 b g Exceed And Excel(AUS) Barakat (Bustino)
1506^{10} 2246^{15} 2605^{5} ◆ 3448^{9} 3974^{3} 6349^{11} 7117^{7} 7470^{12} 8075^{11}

Capponi (IRE) *Mahmood Al Zarooni* a120 110
5 ch h Medicean Nawaiet (USA) (Zilzal (USA))
$47a^{2}$ $317a^{DSQ}$ (677a) (878a) $1150a^{2}$

Caprella *P D Deegan* a87 101
3 b f Kheleyf(USA) Angie And Liz (IRE) (Spectrum (IRE))
$3196a^{7}$ $3983a^{2}$ $4482a^{2}$ ◆ $5523a^{9}$

Capriska *Willie Musson* a48 55
3 b f Bahri(USA) Guignol (IRE) (Anita's Prince)
2340^{3} 3483^{5} 4932^{12} 6152^{8}

Captain Baldwin *Jim Goldie* a39 37
3 b g Dubai Destination(USA) Tripti (IRE) (Sesaro (USA))
2595^{8} 3111^{11} 3575^{5} 3727^{4} 4771^{8} 5187^{5} 5589^{7}

Captain Bellamy (USA) *Hughie Morrison* a84 15
4 ch g Bellamy Road(USA) Thesky'sthelimit (USA) (Northern Prospect (USA))
(9) (555) 1056^{3} 1282^{6} 7377^{8}

Captain Bertie (IRE) *Charles Hills* 98
4 ch g Captain Rio Sadika (IRE) (Bahhare (USA))
1128^{4} ◆ (1510) 3268^{11} 3878^{8} 4099^{2} 4761^{13} 6868^{5}

Captain Blue *Bill Turner* 61
2 b g Captain Marvelous(IRE) Amoras (IRE) (Hamas (IRE))
1767^{6} 1904^{3} (2309) 2797^{8} 4331^{7} 4778^{6}

Captain Cardington (IRE) *Sheena West* a66 73
3 b g Strategic Prince Alkaffeyeh (IRE) (Sadler's Wells (USA))
398^{6} (720) 803^{8} 1320^{6} 1863^{7} 2283^{7} (7301) 7490^{5}

Captain Caroline *Mike Murphy* a44
2 b f Multiplex Nut (IRE) (Fasliyev (USA))
7627^{10}

Captain Cat (IRE) *Roger Charlton* 96
3 bb g Dylan Thomas(IRE) Mother Of Pearl (IRE) (Sadler's Wells (USA))
1506^{3} (2279) ◆ 6831^{2} ◆

Captain Cavallo *Nicky Vaughan* a42 34
5 b g Pastoral Pursuits Nopalea (Warrshan (USA))
1422^{11} 2387^{8} 2665^{10} 6930^{13} 7978^{3}

Captain Chop (FR) *D Guillemin* a102 104
4 b h Indian Rocket Hatane Chope (FR) (Sin Kiang (FR))
2112a^{10}

Captain Cruz (IRE) *Ronald Harris* a32 51
2 b c Captain Marvelous(IRE) Danetime Out (IRE) (Danetime (IRE))
6983^{4} 7296^{3} 7481^{7}

Captain Dimitrios *Alastair Lidderdale* a84 84
4 b g Dubai Destination(USA) Tripti (IRE) (Sesaro (USA))
(88) 179^{2} 252^{5} 424^{4} 528^{3} 624^{2} 710^{7} (912) (1005) (1116) 1220^{2} (1236) 1522^{8} (Dead)

Captain Dunne (IRE) *Tim Easterby* a107 111
7 b g Captain Rio Queen Bodicea (IRE) (Revoque (IRE))
1219^{6} 1498^{5} 2704^{9} 5487^{14} 6244^{18} 6666^{14} 7063^{2} 7397^{11}

Captain Hero (IRE) *Laura Mongan* 30
5 b g Captain Rio Fairy Free (Rousillon (USA))
4582^{12} 5305^{10} 7297^{8}

Captain Joy (IRE) *Tracey Collins* a93 86
3 gr g Dark Angel(IRE) Ardea Brave (IRE) (Chester House (USA))
7229a^{2}

Captain Kendall (IRE) *David Evans* a63 61
3 b g Clodovil(IRE) Queen's Lace (IRE) (King's Best (USA))
1492^{2} 1889^{3} 8083^{8} (8251)

Captain Loui (IRE) *Dai Burchell* a65 59
4 gr g Verglas(IRE) Miss Corinne (Mark Of Esteem (IRE))
480^{7}

Captain McCaw *Brian Meehan* a69 72
2 ch g Exceed And Excel(AUS) Our Sheila (Bahamian Bounty)
4507^{6} 5274^{8} 6177^{6} 6611^{2} 7059^{8}

Captain Oats (IRE) *Pam Ford* a54 59
9 b g Bahhare(USA) Adarika (Kings Lake (USA))
2391^{10} 2872^{2} 4994^{2} 5508^{4} 6821^{9} 7496^{4}

Captain Obvious (AUS) *S Burridge* a115 113
7 gr g Verglas(IRE) Shathor (AUS) (Tirol)
(244a) 420a^{4} 588a^{6} 2326a^{4}

Captain Ramius (IRE) *Kevin Ryan* a89 114
6 b g Kheleyf(USA) Princess Mood (GER) (Muhtarram (USA))
140a^{7} 315a^{8} 4099^{3} 5370^{4} (6468) 6868^{4} (7401) 7809^{12}

Captainrisk (IRE) *Christine Dunnett* a64 65
6 b g Captain Rio Helderberg (USA) (Diesis)
87^{12} 353^{4} ◆ 424^{8} 598^{7} 828^{5} 1263^{5} 1702^{12} 2171^{7} 3152^{8} 3717^{2} 4241^{6} 5050^{9} 5632^{5}

Captain Royale (IRE) *Tracy Waggott* a46 82
7 ch g Captain Rio Paix Royale (Royal Academy (USA))
5821^{10} 6144^{16} 6260^{8} 6605^{7} 6887^{7} 7099^{7} 7457^{5} 7604^{2} 7794^{10}

Captain Scooby *Richard Guest* a83 86
6 b g Captain Rio Scooby Dooby Do (Atraf)
3^{4} 64^{7} 252^{12} 528^{8} 560^{3} 647^{8} (735) 870^{2} 896^{2} 1015^{5} 1091^{7} 1289^{7} 1478^{6} 1643^{6} 2337^{4} 2940^{11} 3159^{5} 3308^{3} (3845) 4292^{6} 4999^{8} 6144^{12} 6525^{3} 7114^{10} 7295^{4} 7489^{14}

Captain's Dream (IRE) *Jedd O'Keeffe* 60
2 b g Kheleyf(USA) Somaggia (IRE) (Desert King (IRE))
3611^{16} 4587^{4} 5311^{11} 7173^{14}

Captain Sharpe *Bernard Llewellyn* a63 68
4 ch g Tobougg(IRE) Helen Sharp (Pivotal)
557^{3} 968^{3} 1905^{4} 6769^{5}

Captain Starlight (IRE) *Jo Crowley* a72
2 b c Captain Marvelous(IRE) Jewell In The Sky (IRE) (Sinndar (IRE))
7705^{4} 7924^{3} 8178^{2}

Captain Sweet (AUS) *J Moore* 116
5 b g Fastnet Rock(AUS) Strega (AUS) (Lake Coniston (IRE))
8041a^{3}

Caption *Sir Michael Stoute* 70
3 b f Motivator Razzle (USA) (Danzig (USA))
3399^{6} 4458^{3} 5952^{3}

Captivator *James Fanshawe* a104 104
5 gr m Motivator Cashew (Sharrood (USA))
(1213) 1883^{2} ◆ 3266^{13} 5834^{16}

Captivity *Mark Johnston* a77 77
3 b c Echo Of Light Tee Cee (Lion Cavern (USA))
404^{2} (502) 1440^{9} 2604^{2} 2860^{7} 3846^{2}

Cara Carmela *Stuart Williams* a46 50
4 gr m Compton Place Carmela Owen (Owington)
118^{6} 297^{9}

Cara Gina *William Haggas* 19
2 b f Bahamian Bounty Princess Georgina (Royal Applause)
6983^{5}

Caramack *Richard Hannon* 80
2 ch c Danehill Dancer(IRE) Oshiponga (Barathea (IRE))
3824^{8} 5040^{3} 5948^{2} 6443^{3}

Caramelita *J R Jenkins* a71 73
5 b m Deportivo Apple Of My Eye (Fraam)
139^{9} 813^{3} 1193^{2} 1742^{2} 2012^{2} (2973) 3434^{7} 4300^{9} 6961^{5} (7314) 7524^{6} 7858^{5}

Caramel Sundae *Robert Eddery* a45 58
2 b f Oratorio(IRE) Sundae Girl (USA) (Green Dancer (USA))
3948^{7} 5230^{6} 6437^{5} 7313^{3} 7973^{9} 8093^{12}

Caranbola *Mel Brittain* a65 88
6 br m Lucky Story(USA) Ladywell Blaise (IRE) (Turtle Island (IRE))
1168^{9} 1476^{5} (2693) 3169^{9} 3845^{4} 4312^{3} 4829^{4} (4880) 5368^{8} 6008^{9} 6165^{13}

Cara's Delight (AUS) *Frederick Watson* 24
5 b m Fusaichi Pegasus(USA) Carahill (AUS) (Danehill (USA))
1250^{13} 4780^{9} 5317^{8} 6125^{12}

Caraside (FR) *S Wattel* a83 80
3 b f Fol Parade(ARG) Carabiola (FR) (Grape Tree Road)
17a^{8}

Cara's Request (AUS) *David Nicholls* a55 81
7 gr g Urgent Request(IRE) Carahill (AUS) (Danehill (USA))
1269^{11} 1659^{13} 2879^{9} 4134^{13} 6309^{8} 7447^{8}

Caratteraccio (IRE) *Marco Botti* 89
4 b h Oasis Dream Caractere (IRE) (Indian Ridge)
2325a^{10} 6346^{5} 7080^{15}

Caravan Rolls On *Peter Chapple-Hyam* a84 101
4 b h Hernando(FR) Grain Only (Machiavellian (USA))
(5580) 6197^{5} ◆

Caraziyan (FR) *M Boutin* a90 96
6 b g Slickly(FR) Carlitta (USA) (Olympio (USA))
18a^{6}

Cardigan (IRE) *William Haggas* 91
3 ch f Barathea(IRE) Precipitous (IRE) (Indian Ridge)
3328^{10} 4062^{9} 7408^{9}

Cardi King *Ian Wood* a56 56
4 b g Fasliyev(USA) Tinsel (Lion Cavern (USA))
2395^{4} 2851^{4} 3043^{11} 3988^{9}

Cardinal *Robert Cowell* a69 80
7 ch h Pivotal Fictitious (Machiavellian (USA))
1935^{4} (2940) (3159) 3541^{6} 4013^{9} 6577^{3} 7113^{7} 7489^{10} 7741^{11}

Cardinal Walter (IRE) *David Simcock* 96
3 bb g Cape Cross(IRE) Sheer Spirit (IRE) (Caerleon (USA))
2196^{3} (3035) ◆ 4072^{9} 4700^{3} ◆ 5598^{3} 6576^{3}

Cardmaster (IRE) *Eve Johnson Houghton* 71
2 gb g Red Clubs(IRE) El Morocco (USA) (El Prado (IRE))
2983^{13} (5485) 5903^{5}

Card Sweep *Ismail Mohammed* a44 56
3 b c Echo Of Light Sharp Secret (IRE) (College Chapel)
2380^{7} 2895^{6} 3710^{2}

Carina Palace *Jamie Osborne* a66
2 b f Dutch Art Ellcon (IRE) (Royal Applause)
5943^{5} 6177^{3} 6645^{3} 7713^{5}

Carinya (IRE) *Amy Weaver* a64 85
4 br m Iffraaj Ma N'Ieme Biche (USA) (Key To The Kingdom (USA))
1491^{5}

Carla Allegra *Jim Goldie* 32
3 ch f Byron Big Mystery (IRE) (Grand Lodge (USA))
5549^{9} 5919^{6}

Carlarajah *Michael Bell* a63 65
2 ch g Sleeping Indian Carla (FR) (Cardoun (FR))
5319^{7} 6020^{8} 7020^{5}

Carletti (IRE) *G Botti* a73
2 b c Zamindar(USA) Alsace (King's Best (USA))
8192a^{3}

Carlitos Spirit (IRE) *Ian McInnes* a48 58
8 ch g Redback Negria (IRE) (Al Hareb (USA))
4350^{4}

Carlton Blue (IRE) *Paul Cole* a81 81
2 gr c Aussie Rules(USA) Nurama (Daylami (IRE))
1499^{9} 2784^{2} 3638^{4} (4526) 5515^{15} 6162^{16} 6777^{3} 6980^{12} (7699a)

Carlton House (USA) *Sir Michael Stoute* 122
4 b h Street Cry(IRE) Talented (Bustino)
(2640) 3267^{2} 4320^{4} 7238^{4} 8043a^{6}

Carlton Mac *Simon Griffiths* a26 58
7 ch g Timeless Times(USA) Julie's Gift (Presidium)
1247^{9}

Carlton Scroop (FR) *Paddy Butler* a70 57
9 ch g Priolo(USA) Elms Schooldays (Emarati (USA))
9^{9} 130^{4} 453^{2} 632^{7} 984^{7} 2348^{11} 2653^{6} 8001^{11} 8173^{4}

Carmel Beauty (USA) *Barbara J Minshall* 91
2 bb f Arch(USA) Kalosca (FR) (Kaldoun (FR))
6289a^{7}

Carmen's Concerto *Andrew Balding* a58 61
3 b f Singspiel(IRE) Lady McNair (Sheikh Albadou)
2430^{11} 2849^{8} 3664^{4} 4536^{13}

Carmen Tango (IRE) *James Halpin* a48 49
5 b m Shinko Forest(IRE) Moon Tango (IRE) (Last Tycoon)
5937^{3}

Carnac (IRE) *Alan McCabe* a68 56
6 gr g Dalakhani(IRE) Traou Mad (IRE) (Barathea (IRE))
366^{7} 555^{7} (1057) 1175^{5} (1433) 1631^{10} 1991^{3} 3180^{6} 3942^{5} 4145^{6} 7610^{7}

Carneades (IRE) *Ed Walker* a34
2 b c Exceed And Excel(AUS) Ivy League Star (IRE) (Sadler's Wells (USA))
8102^{10}

Carnelian (IRE) *Ian Semple* a40 36
5 b g Singspiel(IRE) Red Zinger (USA) (Red Ransom (USA))
937^{7} 1222^{9}

Carnival Dream *Hugh McWilliams* a52 52
7 b m Carnival Dancer Reach The Wind (USA) (Relaunch (USA))
1248^{2} 2536^{4} 3460^{12} 5185^{10} 6756^{10}

Carnoustie (FR) *N Clement* a94 101
3 b f Acclamation Matin De Tempete (FR) (Cardoun (FR))
1426a^{2} 3987a^{2}

Carols Blizzard (USA) *G Botti* a74 45
3 gr c Flashy Bull(USA) Nifty Slew (USA) (Slewdledo (USA))
865a^{0}

Carpentras *Dr Jon Scargill* a49 57
4 b m Val Royal(FR) Molly Brown (Rudimentary (USA))
(2463) 3497^{8} 4436^{8} 6396^{6} 8179^{5}

Carragold *Mel Brittain* a54 82
6 b g Diktat Shadow Roll (IRE) (Mark Of Esteem (IRE))
1914^{2} (2142) 2606^{3} 3167^{4} 3459^{5} 4347^{3} 4821^{5} (5227) 5622^{5} 6073^{9} 6638^{11} 6884^{5} 7069^{5} 7294^{4}

Carrera *J W Hills* a62
2 b c Sixties Icon Aileen's Gift (IRE) (Rainbow Quest (USA))
7192^{7} 7525^{5}

Carr Hall (IRE) *Tony Carroll* a62 60
9 b g Rossini(USA) Pidgeon Bay (IRE) (Perugino (USA))
265^{14} 450^{7} 632^{11} 1014^{6} 1299^{4} 2391^{16}

Carrie's Magic *Alistair Whillans* a67 72
5 b m Kyllachy Carrie Pooter (Tragic Role (USA))
3731^{8} 4592^{9} 5084^{2} 5671^{4} 5917^{4} 6105^{7} 7221^{5} 7251^{11}

Carrowbeg (IRE) *Lawney Hill* a73 73
4 b g Cape Cross(IRE) Love And Affection (USA) (Exclusive Era (USA))
4251^{8}

Carry On Clapping (IRE) *Richard Hannon* 62
2 b f Acclamation Embassy Belle (IRE) (Marju (IRE))
6443^{5} 7104^{3}

Carry On Sydney *Richard Hannon* 84
2 ch c Notnowcato River Fantasy (USA) (Irish River (FR))
7078^{7} (7371)

Cartaya *M Rulec* a87 103
4 b m Singspiel(IRE) Benalmadena (FR) (Nashwan (USA))
(7075a) 7429a^{6}

Cartel (IRE) *M bin Shafya* a79 95
6 b h Cape Cross(IRE) Nadia (Nashwan (USA))
80a^{7}

Carter *Ian Williams* a72 81
6 b g Reset(AUS) Cameo Role (GER) (Acatenango (GER))
1258^{6} 5789^{9} 6642^{9} 7672^{7} 8136^{7}

Cartesien *Robert Collet* 86
5 b g Danehill Dancer(IRE) Chiang Mai (IRE) (Sadler's Wells (USA))
2685a^{4}

Carthaginian (IRE) *Ed Dunlop* a54
3 b c Azamour(IRE) Khayrat (IRE) (Polar Falcon (USA))
1703^{9}

Casa Bex *Philip McBride* a69 69
3 b g Auction House(USA) Feather Game (Hernando (FR))
121^{4} 322^{6} 518^{4} 1365^{2} 3048^{3} 3347^{9} 4709^{2} 4950^{2} 5229^{9} 6152^{3} 6317^{2}

Casaca *J-M Osorio* 106
6 ch m Medicean Priena (IRE) (Priolo (USA))
(7665a)

Casa Ingrid (FR) *Y De Nicolay* a92 88
5 b m Singspiel(IRE) Nigrita (GER) (Lichine (USA))
5118a^{3} 8300a^{5}

Casar (IRE) *M Delcher-Sanchez* 86
4 ch g Hurricane Run(IRE) Thoroughly (IRE) (Woodman (USA))
6089a^{2}

Casela Park (IRE) *David O'Meara* a73 89
7 ch g Elnadim(USA) Taormina (IRE) (Ela-Mana-Mou)
337a^{10} 7684^{12} 7799^{7} 8137^{4}

Cash Des Aigles (FR) *C Plisson* a68 57
4 gr h Enrique Passion Des Aigles (IRE) (Vettori (IRE))
16a^{0}

Cashelgar (IRE) *Richard Guest* a97 96
6 b g Anabaa(USA) Tropical Barth (IRE) (Peintre Celebre (USA))
177^{6} 427^{7} 2984^{5}

Cashel's Missile (IRE) *John Spearing* a52 55
2 b g Majestic Missile(IRE) Cashel Mead (Bishop Of Cashel)
4180^{3} 5192^{6} 5932^{10} 6579^{7} 7156^{10} 8108^{6}

Cash Injection *Karen George* a46 53
3 b g Halling(USA) Cape Siren (Warning)
2578^{7} 3142^{4} 3483^{10} 5508^{12} 6231^{6}

Cash Is King *Richard Fahey* 74
2 b g Bahamian Bounty Age Of Chivalry (IRE) (Invincible Spirit (IRE))
3168^{7} 4555^{3} 5668^{4}

Cash Luck (AUS) *M Freedman* a94 101
4 b g Bradbury's Luck(AUS) Blue Celeste (AUS) (Geiger Counter (USA))
679a^{6} 873a^{6}

Cashmere Cat (IRE) *T Lemer* a91 98
3 b f One Cool Cat(USA) Pink Cashmere (IRE) (Polar Falcon (USA))
542a^{4} 8300a^{0}

Cashpoint *Ian Williams* a89 88
7 b g Fantastic Light(USA) Cashew (Sharrood (USA))
2857^{3}

Cash Rich *Jamie Osborne* a21
2 ch g Assertive Dahshah (Mujtahid (USA))
6533^{14} 7219^{9} 7459^{8}

Caskelena (IRE) *Sir Michael Stoute* a67 84
3 b f Galileo(IRE) Clara Bow (FR) (Top Ville)
2496^{5} 4791^{4} (5316) 6416^{2}

Caspar Netscher *Alan McCabe* 119
3 b c Dutch Art Bella Cantata (Singspiel (IRE))
(1509) 1856^{9} (2568a) 3681a^{6} 5141a^{5} 6296a^{4}

Casquito (IRE) *U Suter* a78 96
4 b g Blue Canari(FR) Copacabana (IRE) (Entrepreneur)
1172a^{6}

Cassano (DEN) *Wido Neuroth*
3 bb g Kheleyf(USA) Chiquette (Selkirk (USA))
5144a^{4}

Cassiopee (FR) *Y Barberot* a79 87
2 ch f Kentucky Dynamite(USA) Teatime (FR) (Loup Solitaire (USA))
5899a^{3} 6225a^{3} 7343a^{5} 7693a^{6}

Casta Diamante *Ralph Beckett* 30
2 ch f Dutch Art Casterossa (Rossini (USA))
3783^{10} 4149^{7} 4581^{6} 5046^{7}

Casta Diva (FR) *F-X De Chevigny* a78 80
5 gr m Linamix(FR) Street Maya (FR) (Mtoto)
93a^{7}

Castalian Spring (IRE) *Terry Clement* a52 45
3 b f Oasis Dream Lady Lafitte (USA) (Stravinsky (USA))
30^{4} 196^{8} 556^{7} 619^{7} 3968^{10} 4333^{5} 4870^{8} 5164^{8}

Cast A Vision (USA) *Amanda Perrett* a57 64
2 b c E Dubai(USA) Shoogle (USA) (A.P. Indy (USA))
6014^{5} 6572^{4}

Castello Aragonese *R Biondi* 102
2 b c Authorized(IRE) Bronwen (IRE) (King's Best (USA))
7076a^{10} 7513a^{2}

Casternova *Hughie Morrison* a24 47
4 ch m Avonbridge Casterossa (Rossini (USA))
124^{7} 372^{11}

Castilo Del Diablo (IRE) *David Simcock* a93 89
3 br c Teofilo(IRE) Hundred Year Flood (USA) (Giant's Causeway (USA))
2584^{5} 4410^{4} (5105) 6025^{12} (7195) ◆

Castle Bar Sling (USA) *T J O'Mara* a80 95
7 b g Diesis Lady Of The Woods (USA) (Woodman (USA))
3647a^{7} 4692a^{7} 5609a^{16}

Castle Legend *David Lewis*
7 ch g Midnight Legend Morstoncastle Rose (Carlingford Castle)
3484^{12}

Castlemorris King *Michael Attwater* a75 70
4 br g And Beyond(IRE) Brookshield Baby (IRE) (Sadler's Wells (USA))
2502^{9} 3400^{5} 5507^{3}

Castles In The Air *Richard Fahey* a95 100
7 b g Oasis Dream Dance Parade (USA) (Gone West (USA))
1220^{8} 3331^{14} 4321^{14} 5102^{5} 6024^{18}

Casual Glimpse *M F De Kock* a96 108
4 b h Compton Place Glimpse (Night Shift (USA))
589a^{4} 757a^{10}

Casual Mover (IRE) *John Best* a81 60
4 b g Diamond Green(FR) Baileys On Line (Shareef Dancer (USA))
301^{6} (570) 960^{3} ◆ 1513^{10} 2199^{11} 7626^{10} 7805^{13} (8020)

Catalinas Diamond (IRE) *Pat Murphy* a72 65
4 b m One Cool Cat(USA) Diamondiferous (USA) (Danzig (USA))
658^{4} 806^{2} 970^{2} 1305^{9} 1734^{5} 2421^{8} (3006) 4059^{5} 4493^{2} 7590^{3} 7915^{6} 8160^{3} 8304^{2}

Catallout (IRE) *Declan Carroll* a54 71
4 b m One Cool Cat(USA) America Lontana (FR) (King's Theatre (IRE))
1002^{10}

Catalyze *Charles Smith* a70 83
4 b g Tumblebrutus(USA) Clarita Dear (CHI) (Hussonet (USA))
115^{10} 371^{7} 526^{6} 623^{4} 718^{6} (1069) 2173^{11} 4663^{6} 6195^{8} 6456^{10} 6530^{8} 6982^{11} 7354^{4} 7612^{5}

Cataract *John Weymes* a46 48
3 ch f Avonbridge Catspraddle (USA) (High Yield (USA))
1585^{10} 2730^{3} 4593^{4} 5317^{6} 5624^{5} 6100^{6} 6362^{6} 6959^{3} 7457^{14}

Catboss (USA) *R Menichetti* a88 84
2 bb f Street Boss(USA) Glorious Cat (USA) (Tabasco Cat (USA))
6090a^{4}

Catchanova (IRE) *Eve Johnson Houghton* a81 76
5 b g Catcher In The Rye(IRE) Head For The Stars (IRE) (Head For Heights)
1611^{7} 2399^{3} 2801^{3} 3039^{10} 3485^{6} 4333^{4} 5349^{7} (5628) 5983^{7} 6801^{9} 7115^{6}

Catcher Of Dreams (IRE) *George Foster* a17 48
6 b g Catcher In The Rye(IRE) No Islands (Lomond (USA))
884^{6} 3889^{6} 4350^{9} 4643^{9}

Catch The Cider *Hans Adielsson* a67
2 b g Medicean Zanna (FR) (Soviet Star (USA))
7613^{2}

Catchy Tune (IRE) *Graeme McPherson* a50 50
3 ch g Redback Magic Melody (Petong)
472^{5} 4156^{6}

Categorical *Keith Reveley* a69 77
9 b g Diktat Zibet (Kris)
1822^{2} (7603)

Caterina *Richard Hannon* a75 76
3 b f Medicean Senta's Dream (Danehill (USA))
2846^{12} 3343^{7} 3732^{3} 4531^{6} 5305^{4} (6334) 6734^{13} 7310^{4}

Catfish (IRE) *Brian Meehan* 94
4 bb m One Cool Cat(USA) Castellane (FR) (Danehill (USA))
2507^{2} 2704^{3} 3593^{6} 4576^{11} 4799^{22} 5832^{13}

Catflap (IRE) *Derek Haydn Jones* a65 38
3 b f One Cool Cat(USA) Consignia (IRE) (Definite Article)
1016^{4} 1376^{2} 1705^{3} 3510^{12} 4655^{5} 4885^{5} 5774^{6}

Catfromtherock (IRE) *David Marnane* a77 77
3 b g One Cool Cat(USA) Campbellite (Desert Prince (IRE))
7229a^{8}

Cathcart Castle *Simon West* a60 60
4 b g Imperial Dancer Stephanie's Mind (Mind Games)
2438[2] 2692[14] 3309[4] 3751[6] 4158[7] 4912[7] 5054[9] 5708[9] 6403[11] 6969[9] 7437[7] 7612[4]

Cathedral *Michael Wigham* a51 82
3 b c Invincible Spirit(IRE) Capades Dancer (USA) (Gate Dancer (USA))
2271[3] 2856[6] 3913[2] 4341[3] 5008[6] 7997[12]

Catherine Laboure (IRE) *Eve Johnson Houghton* a65 75
3 br f Kheleyf(USA) Caro Mio (IRE) (Danehill Dancer (IRE))
3507[5] ◆ (4582) 5302[6] 6023[14]

Catherines Call (IRE) *Des Donovan* a81 75
5 b m Captain Rio It's Academic (Royal Academy (USA))
593[2] 839[2] (1050)

Cat Island *Mark H Tompkins* 40
4 b m Bahamian Bounty Dolls House (Dancing Spree (USA))
2329[5]

Cativo Cavallino *John E Long* a70 74
9 ch g Bertolini(USA) Sea Isle (Selkirk (USA))
91[5] 301[9] 685[2] 894[5] 1108[5] 1378[11] 2173[7] 3388[8] 6773[9] 7643[3] 7815[4]

Cato Minor *Amanda Perrett* a50 58
3 b g Notnowcato Violet (IRE) (Mukaddamah (USA))
1726[12] 2424[13] 3142[12] 3391[8]

Cat O'Mountain (USA) *Mahmood Al Zarooni* a87 70
2 bb c Street Cry(IRE) Thunder Kitten (USA) (Storm Cat (USA))
5321[4] (5742) (7325)

Cat O' Nine Tails *Brian Rothwell* 80
5 b m Motivator Purring (USA) (Mountain Cat (USA))
4311[8] 4955[12]

Cat Queen *Gay Kelleway* a55 58
3 b f One Cool Cat(USA) Oatey (Master Willie)
108[6] 288[4] 534[5] 619[5]

Catramis *Geoffrey Oldroyd* 54
3 b g Misu Bond(IRE) Bond Cat (IRE) (Raise A Grand (IRE))
3025[7] ◆ 3727[5] 4349[11] 4826[7]

Cats Eyes *Robert Cowell* a61 81
3 b f Echo Of Light Desert Lynx (IRE) (Green Desert (USA))
121[5] (373) 637[7] 1709[5] (2166) (2816) 3350[6] 4558[8] (5195) 5815[6]

Cat Spirit (FR) *C Boutin* 89
4 ch g Bachir(IRE) The Cat Eater (FR) (Tagel (USA))
7701a[0]

Catushaba (IRE) *C Lerner* a78
2 gr f Aussie Rules(USA) Allegro Vivace (FR) (Muhtathir)
7597a[6] 8193a[2]

Catwalk (IRE) *James Fanshawe* a79 87
3 ch f Pivotal Mona Em (IRE) (Catrail (USA))
1637[3] 2332[4] 3811[2] 4876[3] (5800) 6515[6] 6878[11]

Caucus *John Gosden* 108
5 b g Cape Cross(IRE) Maid To Perfection (Sadler's Wells (USA))
1882[3] 2253[12] 3293[8] (6600)

Caudillo (GER) *Dr A Bolte* 108
9 b h Acatenango(GER) Corsita (Top Ville)
1901a[8] 4634a[10] 7427a[8]

Caught Napping *Bill Turner* a66 94
2 b c Sleeping Indian Seagreen (IRE) (Green Desert (USA))
1164[5] (1308) (2132)

Caunay *Neil Mulholland* a65 60
5 ch g Generous(IRE) Chantilly Lady (Rising)
6228[10] 6770[11] 7016[6] 7717[2] 7819[13] 8170[8]

Causeway Foot (USA) *Jedd O'Keeffe* a54 68
2 ch c Giant's Causeway(USA) Flat Fleet Feet (USA) (Afleet (CAN))
4387[5] 5083[3] 6043[5] 7325[7]

Causeway King (USA) *Alex Hales* a52 68
6 ch g Giant's Causeway(USA) A P Petal (USA) (A.P. Indy (USA))
6399[6]

Cause You're Mine (FR) *C Lerner*
3 b f Bad As I Wanna Be(IRE) Iputaspellonyou (Highest Honor (FR))
5726a[0]

Cavaleiro (IRE) *Marcus Tregoning* a101 104
3 ch g Sir Percy Khibraat (Alhaarth (IRE))
2080[3] ◆ 2705[9] 3295[8] 6445[2] ◆ 6833[3]

Cavalry Guard (USA) *Tim McCarthy* a50 57
8 ch g Officer(USA) Leeward City (USA) (Carson City (USA))
264[12] 379[4] 662[6]

Cavalryman *Saeed Bin Suroor* a114 117
6 b h Halling(USA) Silversword (FR) (Highest Honor (FR))
877a[2] ◆ 1149a[7] (2506) (3881) 5599[4] 6600[2] 7621a[12]

Cavenaco (ITY) *A Marcialis* 99
5 b h Gold Sphinx(USA) Cadenza (USA) (Machiavellian (USA))
7565a[6]

Cavendish Road (IRE) *Nicky Vaughan* a57 31
6 b g Bachelor Duke(USA) Gronchi Rosa (IRE) (Nashwan (USA))
3344[10]

Cayman Fox *Linda Perratt* a57 66
7 ch m Cayman Kai(IRE) Kalarram (Muhtarram (USA))
1881[11] 2230[5] 2458[9] 2839[9] 3113[4] 3730[9]

Cayuga *Brett Johnson* a88 87
3 b c Montjeu(IRE) Ithaca (USA) (Distant View (USA))
1754[4] 3447[4] (5482) 8174[2]

Cay Verde *Mick Channon* 112
2 b g Bahamian Bounty All Quiet (Piccolo)
1499[5] (2069) ◆ (2512a) ◆ 3291[6] 4736[3] 5559[3] (6128a) 6483[4]

Cazza *David Nicholls* 9
2 b f Indesatchel(IRE) Yanomami (USA) (Slew O'Gold (USA))
4921[9] 5108[8] 6336[6]

Ceekay's Girl *Mrs K Burke* a50 48
2 ch f Medicean Duena (Grand Lodge (USA))
3776[7] 4494[11] 4886[5] 6893[9]

Ceelo *Richard Hannon* a68 79
2 b c Green Desert(USA) Mindsharp (USA) (Gone West (USA))
2330[3] 4093[16] (4846) 5743[5] 6491[5]

Ceiling Kitty *Tom Dascombe* a75 104
2 b f Red Clubs(IRE) Baldovina (Tale Of The Cat (USA))
1136[2] ◆ 1435[4] (1920) (2252) (3269) 6196[4] 6672[7] 7545a[5]

Celebrated Talent (USA) *Mahmood Al Zarooni* a55 71
2 b c Bernardini(USA) Lauren's Tizzy (USA) (Tiznow (USA))
6796[5] 7323[8]

Celebrian *George Baker* a64 19
5 b m Fasliyev(USA) Triplemoon (USA) (Trempolino (USA))
3721[11]

Celebrissime (IRE) *F Head* a105 113
7 ch g Peintre Celebre(USA) Ring Beaune (USA) (Bering)
1163a[5] 5649a[0] 7124a[3]

Celebrity Choice (IRE) *M Gentile* a73 81
5 b h Choisir(AUS) Femme Celebre (IRE) (Peintre Celebre (USA))
815a[6]

Celerina (IRE) *T Stack* a90 103
5 ch m Choisir(AUS) Chantarella (IRE) (Royal Academy (USA))
2507[4] 3375[10]

Celestial Dawn *John Weymes* a51 69
3 b f Echo Of Light Celestial Welcome (Most Welcome)
845[7] 1173[3] 1278[3] 1599[3] 1960[4] 2928[2] (3141) 3540[3] 3954[4] 4461[6] 4957[7] (5538) 5757[3] 6514[5] 7446[5]

Celia (IRE) *H-A Pantall*
2 b f Hurricane Run(IRE) Cloudy Bay (GER) (Zilzal (USA))
5612a[3]

Cellist *William Haggas* a76 77
3 b g Halling(USA) Ae Kae Ae (USA) (King Of Kings (IRE))
2856[12] 3551[4] (3710) 4225[4] 5373[4] 6037[3] 6802[4] 7194[9]

Celtic Charlie (FR) *Pat Phelan* a61 43
7 ch g Until Sundown(USA) India Regalona (USA) (Dehere (USA))
200[2] (303) (530) 1047[3] 1184[7] 1631[3] 2364[10] 2937[6] 5164[3] 5771[4] 7012[3] 7629[2] 7744[3] 7927[6]

Celtic Conviction (CAN) *Michael J Doyle* 97
4 ch g Strut The Stage(USA) All My Lovin' (USA) (Cat's Career (USA))
6299a[8]

Celtic Sixpence (IRE) *Peter Salmon* a71 84
4 b m Celtic Swing Penny Ha'Penny (Bishop Of Cashel)
2310[8] 3500[7] 4300[10] 8054[5]

Celtic Step *Peter Niven* a66 59
8 br g Selkirk(USA) Inchiri (Sadler's Wells (USA))
2239[5] 3236[2] (4350) 5824[4] 6690[2] 7251[8]

Celtic Sultan (IRE) *Alastair Lidderdale* a90 90
8 b g Celtic Swing Farjah (IRE) (Charnwood Forest (IRE))
866[7] 1156[2] 1821[5] 2597[3] 3334[12] 4252[3] 4703[15] 5110[6] 5852[4] 7646[10] 7902[10] 7995[10] 8152[6]

Central Line (USA) *Mahmood Al Zarooni* a46 54
3 b f Redoute's Choice(AUS) Causeway Lass (AUS) (Giant's Causeway (USA))
1472[11] 1736[12]

Centre Court (USA) *George R Arnold II* 107
3 bb f Smart Strike(CAN) Let (USA) (A.P. Indy (USA))
(4478a)

Centred (IRE) *Sir Michael Stoute* a73 72
2 gr f Dalakhani(IRE) Drama Class (IRE) (Caerleon (USA))
5300[3] ◆ 6117[6] 7721[2]

Centre Stage *Michael Appleby* 39
4 b g Fasliyev(USA) Purple Rain (IRE) (Celtic Swing)
1429[7] 2090[6] 2329[6]

Centrifugal (IRE) *Mark Johnston* a77 89
3 ch g Pivotal Tempting Fate (IRE) (Persian Bold)
3521[5] 3913[10] 4213[2] 4679[3] 4889[11] 5717[2] (5919) (6331) 6566[4] 6979[13] 7229a[10] 7520[6]

Cerejeira (IRE) *Eric Alston* a57 59
4 b m Exceed And Excel(AUS) Camassina (IRE) (Taufan (USA))
231[7] 720[5] 1242[3] 2032[3] 2538[9]

Ceremonial Jade (UAE) *Marco Botti* a94 82
9 b g Jade Robbery(USA) Talah (Danehill (USA))
5634[5] ◆ 7508[11]

Cerise Cherry (SAF) *D Cruz* 114
7 ch g Goldkeeper(USA) Cherry Girl (ZIM) (Pochard (ARG))
8041a[2]

Cernanova (IRE) *Hugo Palmer* a30 39
2 b f Strategic Prince Ellanova (Kyllachy)
1466[8] 2579[6] 3465[5] 4659[5] 5161[9]

Certainly Elusive (IRE) *Alan Swinbank* 50
3 gr g Elusive City(USA) Certainlei (IRE) (Definite Article)
2095[10] 2339[6] 2826[7] 3275[9] 5623[7]

Certavi (IRE) *Seamus Durack* a54 61
3 b g Antonius Pius(USA) The Quiet Woman (IRE) (Barathea (IRE))
3155[4]

Certerach (IRE) *M Halford* a96 95
4 b g Halling(USA) Chartres (IRE) (Danehill (USA))
5397a[12] 6066a[6]

Certify (USA) *Mahmood Al Zarooni* 112
2 b f Elusive Quality(USA) Please Sign In (USA) (Doc's Leader (USA))
(4011) (5103) (6199) (6635)

Certral *Brian Ellison* a81 86
4 b m Iffraaj Craigmill (Slip Anchor)
1321[2] 2067[6] 2504[4] 4407[2] 4608[8] 5224[6]

Cerveza *F Poulsen* a85 102
4 ch m Medicean Kalindi (Efisio)
2728a[15] 3653a[4] 6088a[0] 8300a[0]

Cerys *Derek Haydn Jones* a38 38
2 ch f Three Valleys(USA) Tenebrae (IRE) (In The Wings)
4152[10] 4487[13] 5997[6] 6645[9] 7714[3] 7971[7]

C'Est Moi (IRE) *R Biondi* 86
4 b m Intikhab(USA) Swinging Secret (IRE) (Classic Secret (USA))
7075a[8]

Ceto *Phil McEntee* a29 29
5 b m Tobougg(IRE) Natural Grace (Zamindar (USA))
5148[9] 7314[15] 7619[10] 7800[9]

Chabada (JPN) *Ian Williams* a89 78
4 b m Bago(FR) Taygete (USA) (Miswaki (USA))
(10) (271) (872) ◆ 2474[5] 3341[8] 3765[3]

Chachamaidee (IRE) *Sir Henry Cecil* a104 116
5 b m Footstepsinthesand Canterbury Lace (USA) (Danehill (USA))
(2078) ◆ 3266[2] (4686) 5573[4] (6061a) 6673[5]

Cha Ching (IRE) *J W Hills* a56 64
3 b f Elnadim(USA) Sudden Interest (FR) (Highest Honor (FR))
2145[9] 3507[8] 3950[11] (4490) 4986[8] 5983[14] 6092[6] 7200[13]

Chahimanga (FR) *C Baillet* a72 81
3 ch f Indian Rocket Dette D'Honneur (FR) (Septieme Ciel (USA))
117a[9]

Chain Of Events *Sarah Humphrey* a76 86
5 ch g Nayef(USA) Ermine (IRE) (Cadeaux Genereux)
1939[3] 2199[6] (2637) (3121) ◆ 3826[8] 5835[9] 6380[7] 6819[15]

Chalk And Cheese (USA) *Stuart Williams* a76 67
3 ch g Rahy(USA) Escoltada (ARG) (Political Ambition (USA))
2975[9] 3589[13] 4043[11] 4218[8] 4644[5] 4871[2]

Chalnetta (FR) *C Ferland* a83 82
2 gr f Oratorio(IRE) Aifa (Johann Quatz (FR))
8193a[4]

Chambers (IRE) *Richard Ford* a27 61
6 b g Green Desert(USA) Court Lane (USA) (Machiavellian (USA))
46[10] 1799[9] 2618[8] 4452[12]

Chambles *Alan McCabe* a74 61
3 b f Shamardal(USA) Pants (Pivotal)
127[3] 322[9] 739[2] 982[7] (3230) 4779[6] 5893[5] 7412[4] 7666[6] 8238[3]

Champagne Reefing (USA) *Jane Chapple-Hyam* a67 43
3 ch c Van Nistelrooy(USA) Wewantitall (Pivotal)
3398[11]

Champagne Valley *Sharon Watt* a28 49
3 ch f Three Valleys(USA) Volitant (Ashkalani (IRE))
1386[7] 2131[9] 3456[10] 4390[10] 5081[9] 5623[12]

Chamtille (IRE) *Derek Haydn Jones* a40
2 gr f Verglas(IRE) Tahtheeb (IRE) (Muhtarram (USA))
3948[9] 5011[2] 6535[12]

Chancery (USA) *David O'Meara* a85 85
4 bb g Street Cry(IRE) Follow That Dream (Darshaan)
4882[2] ◆ 6770[2] ◆

Chandelle Celeste *Daniel Kubler* a50 17
2 ch f Septieme Ciel(USA) First Candlelight (First Trump)
7371[9] 7738[8] 7987[8]

Chandigarh (IRE) *Paul Fitzsimons* 76
3 b f Moss Vale(IRE) Secret Justice (USA) (Lit De Justice (USA))
2331[10] 2972[3] 3304[6]

Chandrayaan *John E Long* a54 55
5 ch g Bertolini(USA) Muffled (USA) (Mizaaya)
203[9] 375[7] 662[3] 828[2] 1074[2] 1310[4] 2366[3] 5050[3] 6000[8] 8039[5] 8205[6] 8299[10]

Change The Subject (USA) *Peter Salmon* a84 78
4 rg g Maria's Mon(USA) Victory Lap (USA) (Touch Gold (USA))
1321[13] 2142[5] 3699[3] 4175[7] 4499[6] 5001[2] 7368[9] 8275[6]

Chaninbar (FR) *Brendan Powell* a24
9 b g Milford Track(IRE) Logicia (FR) (Homme De Loi (IRE))
600[9] 963[10]

Chankillo *Mark H Tompkins* a61 64
3 ch g Observatory(USA) Seasonal Blossom (IRE) (Fairy King (USA))
182[7] 571[6] 726[3] 1267[2] 1982[11] 2818[3] 4200[5] 6474[12] 7921[9]

Chant (IRE) *Ann Duffield* a68 65
2 b g Oratorio(IRE) Akarita (IRE) (Akarad (FR))
3351[6] 3948[3] 4427[4] 4778[7] 4907[3] 5619[4] 5920[7] 7357[2]

Chaparral Ridge (FR) *F Chappet* a75 69
2 b c Panis(USA) Chaussette (FR) (High Chaparral (IRE))
3928a[4]

Chapelle du Roi (USA) *David Lanigan* a56 70
3 ch g Danehill Dancer(IRE) Capilla Bonita (USA) (Pleasant Colony (USA))
1567[9] 2197[5] 3349[9] 5297[8] 6118[6]

Chapellerie (IRE) *Richard Guest* a68 70
3 b f Acclamation Castellane (FR) (Danehill (USA))
127[4] (250) 536[2] 659[6] 749[5] 867[8] 1058[5] 1241[8] 4394[5]

Chapter And Verse (IRE) *Mike Murphy* a96 91
6 gr g One Cool Cat(USA) Beautiful Hill (IRE) (Danehill (USA))
1212[5] 1924[13] 2642[11] 3667[4] 4772[9] 5301[4] (5746) 6036[11] 6601[7] 7163[2] 7327[2] 7631[4] 7774[8] (8098)

Chapter Nine (IRE) *Mike Hammond* a54 61
6 b g Expelled(USA) Abbey Ever After (Glenstal (USA))
4941[3] (5198) 5508[6] 5938[6] 6305[6] 7629[14]

Chapter Seven *Stuart Williams* a93 103
3 ch g Excellent Art My First Romance (Danehill (USA))
(1221) 1468[7] 2485[10] (2916) 3294[20] 4097[4] 4735[7] 5820[2] 6484[8] (7064) 8227[6]

Charismas Birthday (IRE) *Philip M Byrne* a59 56
4 b m Choisir(AUS) Paradise Blue (IRE) (Bluebird (USA))
(775a)

Charitable Act (FR) *William Muir* a81 88
3 b g Cadeaux Genereux Acatama (USA) (Efisio)
1217[8] 2265[13] 4412[9] 4876[6] (5501) 6046[4] 6376[10] 6842[2] 7359[9]

Charity Box *Chris Wall* a63 76
3 b f Haafhd Bible Box (IRE) (Bin Ajwaad (IRE))
1705[8] 2145[4] 3082[3] (3547) ◆ 4965[6]

Charity Fair *Ron Barr* a15 38
5 ch m Bahamian Bounty Be Most Welcome (Most Welcome)
7443[5]

Charity Rainbow *Brendan Powell* 11
5 b m Lucky Owners(NZ) America Star (Norwick (USA))
2757[9] 3100[8]

Charlcot *James Bethell* a71
4 ch g Monsieur Bond(IRE) Miss Apricot (Indian Ridge)
231[9] 638[3] 1278[2] 2354[6] 6456[3] 7256[2] 7799[9]

Charlemagne Diva *Ann Duffield* a48 61
2 b f Holy Roman Emperor(IRE) Opera Ridge (FR) (Indian Ridge)
2631[9] 3110[9] 3951[2] 4806[3] (5411) 5682[6] 5916[3] 6212[4] 6707[6]

Charles Camoin (IRE) *Sylvester Kirk* a98 95
4 b g Peintre Celebre(USA) Birthday (IRE) (Singspiel (IRE))
(1139) ◆ 1882[15]

Charles De Mille *George Moore* 68
4 b g Tiger Hill(IRE) Apple Town (Warning)
1523[7] 2441[4] 2879[3] ◆ 3254[7]

Charles Parnell (IRE) *Simon Griffiths* a62 51
9 b g Elnadim(USA) Titania (Fairy King (USA))
1280[8] 1430[6] 1987[5] 3442[6] 7604[7]

Charles Tyrwhitt *George Baker* 65
3 b g Iffraaj Riverside Dancer (USA) (Stravinsky (USA))
1256[3] 1852[7] 2626[5] 4709[13]

Charlie Em *Brendan Powell* a61 86
2 b f Kheleyf(USA) Miss Meggy (Pivotal)
3110[8] 3381[6] 3909[4] (4450) ◆ 4951[2] (5806) (7289) 7588a[3]

Charlotte Rosina *Roger Teal* a93 92
3 b f Choisir(AUS) Intriguing Glimpse (Piccolo)
(1412) 1921[3] (2893) 3542[5] 4336[3] 6075[12] 6536[3] 6835[8]

Charm Cry (USA) *Mark Johnston* a65
2 b f Street Cry(IRE) Nasheej (USA) (Swain (IRE))
6366[6] 6644[4] 7167[11] 7476[11] 7866[6]

Charmel's Delight *Geoffrey Oldroyd* a38 49
3 b f Monsieur Bond(IRE) Jane's Delight (IRE) (Namid)
3561[4] 3848[7] 4550[7] 5014[8]

Charming (IRE) *Olivia Maylam* a69 74
3 b f Invincible Spirit(IRE) Nofa's Magic (IRE) (Rainbow Quest (USA))
2543[5] 3235[3] 3568[5] (4003) 4423[3] 7019[15] 7483[6] 7775[9] 8054[10] 8307[2]

Charming Touch (USA) *F Head* 85
2 b f Elusive Quality(USA) Charmgoer (USA) (Nureyev (USA))
6463a[4]

Charpoy (USA) *Ian Semple* a84 84
4 b g Street Cry(IRE) Honolua Bay (USA) (Storm Bird (CAN))
2720[3] 3380[5] 4674[8] 5429[11]

Chart *William Jarvis* a58 54
3 b g Dutch Art Masandra (IRE) (Desert Prince (IRE))
201[9] 376[2] 1072[4] 1600[9] 3548[10]

Charter (IRE) *Michael Wigham* a68 68
2 b c Elusive City(USA) Lucky Norwegian (IRE) (Almutawakel)
7466[2] 8165[2]

Chasing Dreams *Kevin Ryan* 76
2 ch f Pastoral Pursuits Welanga (Dansili)
5003[4] (5733) 6312[4] 6658[4] 7028[5]

Chasin' Rainbows *Sylvester Kirk* a61 57
4 b m Piccolo Tamara (Marju (IRE))
225[8] 3497[7] 3721[5] 4817[3] (4940) 5481[4] 5974[6] (6690) 6948[8] 7479[6] 8113[2] 8265[4]

Chat (USA) *John Gosden* 82
2 bb f Dynaformer(USA) Verbal (USA) (Kingmambo (USA))
(3034)

Chateau Lola *Derek Shaw* a56 29
3 b f Byron Glensara (Petoski)
455[5] 599[2] 734[8] (898) 1393[5] 1514[8] 2730[11] 7970[11] 8045[3] 8210[2] 8253[4]

Chateau Margaux (AUS) *Peter G Moody* 106
4 bb m Redoute's Choice(AUS) Kylikwong (AUS) (Red Ransom (USA))
7346a[2]

Chater Garden (IRE) *Alan Jarvis* a56 26
3 b g Kheleyf(USA) Laraissa (Machiavellian (USA))
1260[12] 2367[11] 2845[7] 3622[9]

Chatterati (USA) *Mark Johnston* a79 65
3 b f Street Cry(IRE) Melhor Ainda (USA) (Pulpit (USA))
291[2] (747) 2067[11] 2672[6] 3031[6] 3503[12] 3847[5] 4391[3] 4714[3] 4945[7] 5441[8] 5921[7] 6334[3] 6569[2] 7003[14] 7250[5]

Chatterer (IRE) *Marcus Tregoning* a83 80
4 b m Alhaarth(IRE) Miss Bellbird (IRE) (Danehill (USA))
1314[2] 2199[2] 3290[7] 7131[5] (7416)

Chattleya (FR) *S Smrczek* a75 78
3 b f Desert King(IRE) Cinecitta (USA) (Diesis)
364a[8] 1900a[5]

Checkpoint *Sir Henry Cecil* 85
3 ch g Zamindar(USA) Kalima (Kahyasi)
3161[9] 3664[2] 4797[9]

Cheddar George *Peter Chapple-Hyam* a68 73
6 ch g Pivotal Grandalea (Grand Lodge (USA))
2233[12]

Cheektocheek (IRE) *Marco Botti* a76 70
2 b g Chineur(FR) Diamond Soles (IRE) (Danetime (IRE))
(4658) 5890[3] 7111[5] 7922[6]

Cheeky Wee Red *Richard Fahey* a47 64
4 ch m Pastoral Pursuits Swynford Elegance (Charmer)
2225[3] 2621[3] (3332) (3581) 4389[4] (4643) 5081[2]

Cheers *Oliver Sherwood* a68 69
4 b m Haafhd Ziggy Zaggy (Diktat)
(154) 574[4] 2165[2] 2421[4] 3485[11] 4468[4] 4942[10]

Cheers Big Ears (IRE) *Richard Price* a56 41
6 gr g Kheleyf(USA) Grey Galava (Generous (IRE))
3544[13] 4708[12] 5261[6] 5658[7] 6000[4] 7105[12]

Cheers Buddy (IRE) *Ian Semple* a66 84
4 b g Acclamation Victorian Dancer (IRE) (Groom Dancer (USA))
449[4] 655[5] 804[6] 1269[4] 2735[4] 4389[10] 5081[6] 5428[6] 5918[4] 6646[3]

Cheers For Thea (IRE) *Tim Easterby* a78 92
7 gr m Distant Music(USA) Popiplu (USA) (Cozzene (USA))
4933[7] 5372[6] 6176[8] 6613[6] 7416[5] 7843[5] (8146) 8271[7]

Cheery Cat (USA) *Richard Ford* a55 51
8 bb g Catienus(USA) Olinka (USA) (Wolfhound (USA))
100[10] 267[6] 664[4] 985[3] 1387[6] 1487[9] (5937) 6322[10] 6529[7] 6958[13]

Chef Oui Chef (FR) *Y De Nicolay* a89 96
2 b c Medecis Romantic Pearl (FR) (Kahyasi)
6463a[2] 7122a[3] 7623a[7] 7828a[8]

Chellalla *L Polito* 82
3 b f Elnadim(USA) Cheloca (Selkirk (USA))
1699a[7]

Chella Thriller (SPA) *Alastair Lidderdale* a63 37
3 b f Chevalier(IRE) Arundhati (IRE) (Royal Academy (USA))
2849[7] 3292[13] 4465[4] 5280[8] 7062[5] 7417[7] (8050)

Chelsea Grey (IRE) *Ronald Harris* a49 44
2 gr f Verglas(IRE) Kapera (FR) (Linamix (FR))
4654[4] 4990[6] 6153[9] 6893[7] 8094[8]

Chelsea Mick *John Mackie* a75 72
3 b g Hawk Wing(USA) Chelsey Jayne (IRE) (Galileo (IRE))
193[3] 1320[9] 2449[3] 2980[5] 3558[5] 4498[12] 5129[7] 5810[7] 6647[10]

Chelwood Gate (IRE) *Roger Varian* 81
2 gb c Aussie Rules(USA) Jusoor (USA) (El Prado (IRE))
(2667) ◆

Chemistry Master *Jeremy Gask* a67 67
4 b g Doyen(IRE) Elemental (Rudimentary (USA))
3079[6] 3664[7] 4157[7] 4915[4] 5706[10] 6503[7]

Chene Boppe (FR) *F-X De Chevigny* a70 72
2 ch c Turtle Bowl(IRE) Beggars Belief (IRE) (Common Grounds)
8192a[5]

Chengho (USA) *Sir Michael Stoute* a79
2 b g Henrythenavigator(USA) Christmas In Aiken (USA) (Affirmed (USA))
(7507)

Cheriearch (USA) *L A Urbano-Grajales* a107 101
3 gr f Arch(USA) Cherish Destiny (USA) (Grand Slam (USA))
2109a[10]

Cherokee Lord (USA) *Charlie Livesay* a54 106
5 b g Sir Cherokee(USA) Sequins N'Lace (USA) (Mari's Book (USA))
5377a[10]

Cherry Collect (IRE) *S Botti* 106
3 b f Oratorio(IRE) Holy Moon (IRE) (Hernando (FR))
(1699a) (2522a) 7429a[2]

Cherry Danon (IRE) *P Schiergen* 106
3 br f Rock Of Gibraltar(IRE) Sherifa (GER) (Monsun (GER))
2746a[2] (3653a) 5249a[9] 6726a[2]

Cherry Malotte *John Gosden* a36 54
2 b f Pivotal Shanghai Lily (IRE) (King's Best (USA))
7159[12] 7403[4] 7720[12]

Cherryred Girl (IRE) *J S Moore* a45 39
2 b f Redback Gypsy Royal (IRE) (Desert Prince (IRE))
1136[9] 1165[4] 1891[6] 2309[6] 2462[3] 2798[5] (Dead)

Cherry Street *Andrew Balding* a88 88
3 b g Alhaarth(IRE) Weqaar (USA) (Red Ransom (USA))
1302[3] 1978[9] 3509[6] 6537[9] 7195[10]

Cherry Tiger *James Toller* a44
2 b c Tiger Hill(IRE) Lolla's Spirit (IRE) (Montjeu (IRE))
7707[11]

Cherry Tree Hill (IRE) *Alan Swinbank* 20
4 b g Ivan Denisovich(IRE) Ring Pink (USA) (Bering)
6409[7]

Cheshire Lady (IRE) *David Barron* a31 41
5 b m Marju(IRE) Kiris World (Distant Relative)
226[7]

Ches Jicaro (IRE) *James Unett* a41
4 ch g Majestic Missile(IRE) Kelso Magic (USA) (Distant View (USA))
8141[5]

Chester Aristocrat *Eric Alston* a76 74
3 ch g Sakhee(USA) New Light (Generous (IRE))
1155[4] 1661[3] 2118[4] 2689[5] 3111[3] 3555[4] 4082[P] 4329[8] 4675[4] (5000) 5728[3] 7141[4]

Chester Deelyte (IRE) *Lisa Williamson* a64 57
4 b m Desert Style(IRE) Bakewell Tart (IRE) (Tagula (IRE))
106[2] 212[3] 550[2] 7382[12] 7969[7] 8256[10]

Chesterfield (IRE) *Mahmood Al Zarooni* 83
2 ch c Pivotal Antique (IRE) (Dubai Millennium)
(3397)

Chester'Slittlegem (IRE) *Lisa Williamson* a66
3 b f Atraf Ceylon Round (FR) (Royal Applause)
189[4] 749[6] 970[4] 1115[3] 1313[5] 2397[3] 3044[6] 7218[10] 8036[8] 8255[11]

Chevalgris *Alan Swinbank* 65
2 gr g Verglas(IRE) Danzelline (Danzero (AUS))
7598[3]

Cheval Rouge (IRE) *H Rogers* a53 83
5 ch m Tagula(IRE) Izibi (FR) (Saint Cyrien (FR))
6352a[2]

Cheveton *Richard Price* a106 99
8 ch g Most Welcome Attribute (Warning)
1498[4] 1885[14] 2286[7] 2717[12] 3078[6] 3624[6] 4824[7] 5530[6] 6286[2] ◆ 6465[2] 6666[6] (7295) 7366[9]

Cheviot (USA) *Ian Semple* a70 111
6 b g Rahy(USA) Camlet (Green Desert (USA))
1409[1] 2074[6] (2602) 5022[14] (6020) 6468[26] 7397[14]

Cheviot Quest (IRE) *William Jarvis* a55 71
3 ch g Sir Percy Cushat Law (IRE) (Montjeu (IRE))
1519[5] 2141[2] 2424[3] 3087[2] 3592[2]

Chevise (IRE) *Steve Woodman* a83 81
4 b m Holy Roman Emperor(IRE) Lipica (IRE) (Night Shift (USA))
280[10] 563[10] 686[5] 1049[6] 3761[5] 5298[4] 5972[7] 6434[10] 7998[3] 8158[7]

Cheworee *David Elsworth* a69 90
3 b f Milk It Mick Jodrell Bank (IRE) (Observatory (USA))
1357[10] 2147[3] (2501) 2894[4] 5065[5] 6144[3] 6495[2]

Cheyenne Red (IRE) *Michael Herrington* a58 56
6 br g Namid Red Leggings (Shareef Dancer (USA))
(226) 356[7] 551[3] 938[10] 1383[7] 1987[9] 5590[16] 6530[5]

Cheylesmore (IRE) *Michael Wigham* a72 80
4 b g Kodiac Hemaca (Distinctly North (USA))
119[8] 1064[4] 1561[14] 2629[3] (3000) 3245[4] 3471[3]

Chez Laurent (IRE) *Robert Collet* a88 88
3 b g Acclamation Lorientaise (IRE) (Xaar)
247a[0]

Chez Vrony *Dave Morris* a51 44
6 b g Lujain(USA) Polish Abbey (Polish Precedent (USA))
822[2] 2464[8] 5246[3] 5939[6] 6396[3] 7605[3]

Chhota Naa *Harry Dunlop* a52
4 b g Calcutta Ceilidh Band (Celtic Swing)
149[5] 355[8] 546[7] 968[9]

Chiara Wells (IRE) *A Floris* 93
3 gr f Refuse To Bend(IRE) Docklands Grace (USA) (Honour And Glory (USA))
7697a[4]

Chiberta King *Andrew Balding* 111
6 b g King's Best(USA) Glam Rock (Nashwan (USA))
2639[3] 3881[3] 4737[5] 5981[2] 6600[5]

Chica Loca (FR) *M Figge* 104
3 ch f American Post Comete (FR) (Jeune Homme (USA))
2109a[7] 3653a[11]

Chicamia *Michael Mullineaux* a34 51
8 b m Kyllachy Inflation (Primo Dominie)
5996[7] 6157[12]

Chicarito *John Gallagher* a62 59
3 b g Striking Ambition Mary Jane (Tina's Pet)
802[4] 1006[2] 1492[3] 1941[3] 2166[8] 3540[5] 5033[6] 5505[4] 6180[12]

Chief Executive (IRE) *Mikael Magnusson* a62
2 gr c Dalakhani(IRE) Lucky (IRE) (Sadler's Wells (USA))
7868[4] ◆

Chief Havoc (USA) *Jeremy Noseda* a91 84
2 ch c Giant's Causeway(USA) La Reina (USA) (A.P. Indy (USA))
5742[3] ◆ 6447[2] 6901a[6]

Chief Hawkeye (IRE) *J-V Toux* a65 66
3 b g Hawk Wing(USA) Pacy's Ridge (IRE) (Indian Ridge)
1127a[6] 4477a[9]

Chief Inspector (IRE) *Brian Meehan* 72
2 b g Kheleyf(USA) Catching Stars (IRE) (Halling (USA))
(4773)

Chief Of Men *Denis Coakley* a72 63
4 b g Sleeping Indian Hidden Meaning (Cadeaux Genereux)
2274[11] 2580[3]

Chignon (IRE) *Sir Henry Cecil* a59 69
3 b f Dalakhani(IRE) Fringe (In The Wings)
2050[5] (2625) ◆ 2999[4] 4538[9] 6647[8]

Chigun *Sir Henry Cecil* a68 107
3 b f Oasis Dream Stormy Weather (Nashwan (USA))
1923[4] 2344[5] 2734[2] (3189) 4702[6] (6023) ◆ (6633)

Chika Dream (FR) *Y Barberot* a73
2 ch c Danehill Dancer(IRE) Smala Tica (FR) (Loup Solitaire (USA))
7984a[4]

Chik's Dream *Derek Haydn Jones* a51 57
5 ch g Dreams End Chik's Secret (Nalchik (USA))
6616[8] 7620[7] 8038[8]

Childa (IRE) *S Wattel*
2 gr f Duke Of Marmalade(IRE) Chill (FR) (Verglas (IRE))
5570a[0]

Chillianwallah *James Unett* a42
4 ch g Primo Valentino(IRE) Spark Up (Lahib (USA))
532[9]

Chilli Green *Lee Carter* a93 92
5 b m Desert Sun Jade Pet (Petong)
90[5] 304[2] (563) 622[8] 962[3] ◆ 2024[2] (2446) 3190[9] 4799[28]

Chilly Filly (IRE) *Brian Ellison* a69 89
6 b m Montjeu(IRE) Chill Seeking (USA) (Theatrical (IRE))
(1295)

Chiltern Secret *Martin Bosley* a32
2 ch f Sakhee's Secret Regal Curtsy (Royal Applause)
6534[12]

Chil The Kite *Hughie Morrison* 108
3 b c Notnowcato Copy-Cat (Lion Cavern (USA))
2930[6] (3563) (4319) ◆ 6029[4] ◆ 6674[6] (7124a) 7515a[8]

Chilworth Icon *Mick Channon* a87 101
2 b c Sixties Icon Tamara Moon (IRE) (Acclamation)
1211[7] (1495) 1747[2] (2702) 3368[5] (3684a) 4008[5] 4698[9] 5833[5] 6599[5]

Chiming Hart *Tim Easterby* 47
2 b f Pastoral Pursuits Elsie Hart (IRE) (Revoque (IRE))
2138[7] 2631[11] 3844[11]

China Excels *Sue Smith* 59
5 b g Exceed And Excel(AUS) China Beauty (Slip Anchor)
3561[7] 4207[4] 4550[6] 5314[10] 5737[9] 6479[11]

Chinchon (IRE) *C Laffon-Parias* 118
7 b h Marju(IRE) Jarama (IRE) (Hector Protector (USA))
(953a) 7284a[5] 8040a[12]

Chips Are Down (IRE) *Michael Mulvany* 75
2 b c Ad Valorem(USA) Missperon (IRE) (Orpen (USA))
6550a[8]

Chiquitita (IRE) *J Heloury* a66 66
3 b f Oratorio(IRE) Sweeten Up (Shirley Heights)
5726a[6]

Chiswick Bey (IRE) *Ollie Pears* a66 95
4 b g Elusive City(USA) Victoria Lodge (IRE) (Grand Lodge (USA))
1321[10] 2243[7] 2882[6] 3385[5] 3890[7] (4998) 6009[12] 7144[8]

Chittenden (USA) *Mahmood Al Zarooni* a68 74
2 b f Raven's Pass(USA) Port Roberto (USA) (Dynaformer (USA))
6117[4] 6534[6] 7720[4]

Chjimes (IRE) *Conor Dore* a71 79
8 b g Fath(USA) Radiance (IRE) (Thatching)
88[5] 179[5] 210[3] (320) 425[4] 522[8] 687[5] 763[6] (823) 958[6] 996[9] 1185[5] 1307[2] 1630[4] (1735) 2169[3] 2581[5] 3008[2] 3944[12] 4468[6] 6053[8] 7218[11] 7589[11] 7861[3] 8064[6] 8107[5] 8190[3] 8307[6]

Chlodan *Michael Easterby* a36 50
5 b g Mark Of Esteem(IRE) Latch Key Lady (USA) (Tejano (USA))
3236[11] 3458[4]

Chloe's Dream (IRE) *Ann Duffield* a59 65
2 gr f Clodovil(IRE) Extravagance (IRE) (King's Best (USA))
3415[10] 4173[10] 5807[2] (6354) 6611[6] 7355[4]

Chloe's Image *Philip Kirby* 48
2 b f Lucky Story(USA) Iwunder (IRE) (King's Best (USA))
4494[14] 4952[5] 5619[9]

Chocala (IRE) *Alan King* 67
2 b g Rock Of Gibraltar(IRE) Arbella (Primo Dominie)
5684[8] 6114[15] 7492[2]

Choc'A'Moca (IRE) *Paul Midgley* a29 71
5 b g Camacho Dear Catch (IRE) (Bluebird (USA))
1177[9] 1526[10] 2314[3] (2748) (2878) 4400[9] 4495[14] 4829[14] 5223[11] 5821[9] 6264[6] 7055[13] 7457[13]

Choccywoccydoodah *James Given* a64 47
3 b f Dr Fong(USA) Galaxy Of Stars (Observatory (USA))
2136[10] 2628[6] 3044[13]

Chocolat Chaud (IRE) *J W Hills* a55 58
3 b f Excellent Art Thaidah (CAN) (Vice Regent (CAN))
1424[7] 2424[12] 3122[5] 4650[11]

Chocolate Block (IRE) *William Haggas* 37
2 br f Singspiel(IRE) Pingus (Polish Precedent (USA))
6603[6] 7244[5] 7553[8]

Chocolate Pursuits *Tom Dascombe* a22
3 ch f Pastoral Pursuits Yes Dear (Fantastic Light (USA))
604[5] 838[9]

Choice Pearl (USA) *Tobias B P Coles* a61 46
3 bb f Any Given Saturday(USA) Horns Gray (USA) (Pass The Tab (USA))
3990[7] 4434[10] 5014[2] 5246[4] 5479[6] 6180[2] 6249[4] 6806[9] 6937[2]

Choice Words (USA) *Natalie Lloyd-Beavis* a70 54
4 b g Redoute's Choice(AUS) Alizes (NZ) (Rory's Jester (AUS))
969[3] ◆ 1138[5] 1889[6] 2421[11] 2809[3] 5017[7] 5298[7] 6926[8] 7218[6] 7591[12]

Choisan (IRE) *Tim Easterby* 82
3 b g Choisir(AUS) Attanagh (IRE) (Darnay)
1477[9] 1653[9] 2258[6] 2716[4] (3305) 3859[3] 4346[2] 4925[5] 5598[8] 6045[3]

Choisirez (IRE) *David Evans* 55
3 b f Choisir(AUS) Filimeala (IRE) (Pennekamp (USA))
1278[7] 2353[11] 2578[8] 3246[6] 3470[15] 6305[8]

Choisir Shadow (IRE) *B Grizzetti* 104
3 ch f Choisir(AUS) Mujadil Shadow (IRE) (Mujadil (USA))
2325a[6] 7288a[4] 7565a[5]

Chokidar (IRE) *Scott Dixon* a80 78
4 b g Sleeping Indian Lola Sapola (IRE) (Benny The Dip (USA))
5630[3] 6934[4]

Chookie Avon *Keith Dalgleish* a83 75
5 ch g Avonbridge Lady Of Windsor (IRE) (Woods Of Windsor (USA))
115[8] 134[3] 199[9] 639[6] (942) 1293[11] 2355[6] 2535[9] 2753[6] 2924[6] 3581[7] 4134[8] 4388[2] 4769[4] (5185) 6141[9] 6709[3] (6934) 7202[5] 7360[2] 7901[4]

Chookie Hamilton *Keith Dalgleish* a81 83
8 ch g Compton Place Lady Of Windsor (IRE) (Woods Of Windsor (USA))
202[6] ◆ 285[7] 500[3] 643[3] (1003) 1114[2] 1797[7] 2666[4] 3114[7] 3337[6] 4639[6] 4912[3] 5174[3] 5921[10] 6712[10] (7869) (7968) 7980[2] 8106[2] (8149)

Chookie Royale *Keith Dalgleish* a91 82
4 ch g Monsieur Bond(IRE) Lady Of Windsor (IRE) (Woods Of Windsor (USA))
1951[9] 2632[5] 3027[4] 3492[8] 3905[6] 4393[3] 5084[3] (5341) 5802[2] 7246[3] (7685) (7920)

Chooseday (IRE) *Kevin Ryan* 89
3 b g Choisir(AUS) Break Of Day (USA) (Favorite Trick (USA))
1658[3] 2256[11] 2824[2] 2979[4] 3912[5] 4881[2] (5337)

Chopouest (FR) *T Castanheira* a100 103
5 b g Indian Rocket Free Track (FR) (Solid Illusion (USA))
814a[7] 3901a[6] 4790a[7] 6943a[0]

Chopsoave (FR) *Mme C Dufreche* 94
4 ch h Soave(GER) Moon Serenade (Key Of Luck (USA))
7701a[0]

Choral *Richard Hannon* a84 90
4 b m Oratorio(IRE) Sierra (Dr Fong (USA))
33[2] (1609) 2083[9] 2766[2] 3045[2] 4336[6] 4775[3] 5769[3] (6800)

Choral Bee *Henry Candy* a61 60
3 b f Oratorio(IRE) Chief Bee (Chief's Crown (USA))
1518[6] 2162[3] 3483[7] 4458[4] 5351[10] (5974) 6210[3] 6631[8]

Choral Festival *John Bridger* a77 83
6 b m Pivotal Choirgirl (Unfuwain (USA))
36[6] 349[7] 2233[8] (2857) 3226[2] 3643[3] 3703[3] 4150[2] 4474[11] 5007[6] 5417[2] 5592[2] 6207[4] 6819[6] 7300[3] 7375[7]

Choral Prince (IRE) *Mike Murphy* a63 72
2 b g Oratorio(IRE) Princess Of Iona (IRE) (Fasliyev (USA))
3387[5] 4658[2] 5478[5] 6372[4] 7057[4] 7501[6]

Choral Rhythm (IRE) *Richard Hannon* a25 26
2 b f Oratorio(IRE) Sierra (Dr Fong (USA))
4217[9] 4704[7] 5267[8]

Chorister Choir (IRE) *David Elsworth* 60
2 b f Choisir(AUS) Cape Jasmine (IRE) (Danehill (USA))
5003[5] 5267[10]

Chorister Girl *Richard Ford* a25 51
3 b f Acclamation Hazelhurst (IRE) (Night Shift (USA))
7993[12]

Chorister Sport (IRE) *N Caullery* a65 61
3 b c Diamond Green(FR) Spend A Rubble (USA) (Spend A Buck (USA))
214[3] 1731[5] 2331[7] 6752a[0]

Chosen Character (IRE) *Tom Dascombe* 96
4 b g Choisir(AUS) Out Of Thanks (IRE) (Sadler's Wells (USA))
1293[5] 1561[3] 2096[7] 2696[6] 3559[3] (4295) (4388) (4531) 4939[2] 5269[4] 5914[2] (6235) (6630) 7210[2]

Chosen Forever *Geoffrey Oldroyd* a86 79
7 b g Choisir(AUS) Forever Bond (Danetime (IRE))
216[11] 907[5] 7842[13]

Chosen Miracle (USA) *Jerry Hollendorfer* a72 104
4 b h Ghostzapper(USA) Royally Chosen (USA) (In Excess)
7571a[12]

Chosen One (IRE) *Ruth Carr* a49 71
7 ch g Choisir(AUS) Copious (IRE) (Generous (IRE))
887[11] 1054[6] 1298[7] 1516[8] 2032[6] (2436) 2617[8] 2875[2] 3109[6] 3308[5] 4174[12] 4452[2] (4631) 4784[4] 5294[8] 5739[7] 5923[13] 6314[10]

Chrissycross (IRE) *Roger Teal* a70 63
3 b f Cape Cross(IRE) Penang (IRE) (Xaar)
1906[7] 2624[4] 3122[3] 3443[9] 3998[5] 4776[7] 6949[7] (7643) 7893[9] 8158[4] 8308[2]

Christingle *William Haggas* a71 61
3 b f Iceman Pious (Bishop Of Cashel)
2387[3] 3946[3] 4888[2] 6736[5] (7025) 7376[8]

Christmas Carnival *Michael Easterby* a79 74
5 ch g Cadeaux Genereux Ellebanna (Tina's Pet)
136[8]

Christmas Light *Brian Ellison* a79 78
5 b m Zafeen(FR) Arabian Dancer (Dansili)
4089[5] 4175[2] 4426[3] 4768[4] 6073[2] 6410[2] 6638[4] 7530[2]

Christopher Chua (IRE) *Simon Dow* a63 56
3 gr g Clodovil(IRE) Pearls Of Wisdom (Kyllachy)
1072[2] 1622[5] 2443[7] 3350[7] 3732[6] 4467[7] 7903[3] 8064[9] ◆ 8287[3]

Chronic Flame (TUR) *Marcus Tregoning* a62 56
3 ch g Dubai Destination(USA) All Grain (Polish Precedent (USA))
350[6] 523[9] 595[4] 6364[11] 6949[4] 7348[9]

Chrysanthemum (IRE) *David Wachman* 110
4 b m Danehill Dancer(IRE) Well Spoken (IRE) (Sadler's Wells (USA))
(1041a) 6080a[6] 7423a[5]

Ch'Tio Bilote (FR) *J-P Gallorini* a88 112
4 b h Ultimately Lucky(IRE) Neicha (FR) (Neverneyev (USA))
1746a[5] 3205a[10] 3657a[8] 4316a[7]

Chuckle *Rae Guest* a52 47
3 b f Pivotal Enrapture (USA) (Lear Fan (USA))
838[5] 4341[14] 5687[5]

Chunky Diamond (IRE) *Peter Chapple-Hyam* 101
3 b g Diamond Green(FR) Balance The Books (Elmaamul (USA))
2664[7] 3158[6] 4611[15] 5487[12] 6075[17]

Church Music (IRE) *Michael Scudamore* a89 85
3 b c Amadeus Wolf Cappella (IRE) (College Chapel)
1217[7] 1644[3] 2028[3] 2276[11] 2853[2] 3608[4] 3861[2] 4364[7] 6427[11] (7595)

Chutney Flight (FR) *N Leenders* a77 107
3 ch f Dylan Thomas(IRE) Karly Flight (FR) (Mansonnien (FR))
5472a[6]

Ciel De Jade (FR) *B Goudot* a77
4 ch h Vatori(FR) Abedissa (FR) (Bishop Of Cashel)
16a[5]

Cielo Canarias (IRE) *E Leon Penate* 91
4 b g Exceed And Excel(AUS) Summer Dance (Sadler's Wells (USA))
7587a[6]

Cielo Rojo (IRE) *Richard Fahey* a42 42
2 b g Red Clubs(IRE) Roses From Ridey (IRE) (Petorius)
3062[9] 3457[5] 4327[7] 5716[7] 6147[10] 7728[5]

Cill Rialaig *Hughie Morrison* a98 108
7 gr m Environment Friend Pang Valley Girl (Rock Hopper)
2481[4] 3372[5] 3825[4] 4363[2]

Cima De Pluie *B Grizzetti* 104
5 b g Singspiel(IRE) Grey Way (USA) (Cozzene (USA))
2323a[6]

Cincinnati Kit *Stuart Williams* a53 58
3 br f Cape Cross(IRE) Princess Georgina (Royal Applause)
4467[4] 4757[7] 5635[5] 6249[5]

Cinderkamp *Doug Watson* a96 100
4 b h Kyllachy Topkamp (Pennekamp (USA))
616a[3]

Cinderslipper (IRE) *Ann Duffield* 66
2 b f Jeremy(USA) Love City (IRE) (Spectrum (IRE))
(7598)

Cio Cio San (IRE) *Richard Hannon* 66
2 ch f Dalakhani(IRE) Unreachable Star (Halling (USA))
2384[3] 2499[7] 3487[3] 4574[8] 5532[6]

Circle Of Angels *Ian Williams* a54 75
4 b m Royal Applause City Of Angels (Woodman (USA))
2389[3] 3220[2] 3616[DSQ] 4627[3] ◆ 5151[9] 5913[6] 6734[7]

Circuitous *Keith Dalgleish* a61 71
4 b g Fasliyev(USA) Seren Devious (Dr Devious (IRE))
1801[2] 2225[5] 2350[11] 2538[4] (2618) 3115[7] (4956) 5427[6] 6123[10] 6937[10] 7224[2] (7504) 7906[13]

Circumvent *Paul Cole* a109 105
5 ch g Tobougg(IRE) Seren Devious (Dr Devious (IRE))
1034[3] 1854[14] 2081[2] 6035[6] 6470[2] 7771[3] 7985a[0]

Circus Mondao (USA) *Mahmood Al Zarooni* a70 88
3 b g Hard Spun(USA) Dominique's Show (USA) (Theatrical (IRE))
(2197)

Cirrus Des Aigles (FR) *Mme C Barande-Barbe* a112 132
6 b g Even Top(IRE) Taille De Guepe (FR) (Septieme Ciel (USA))
(1149a) (1696a) 2533a[DSQ] (6898a) 7239[2]

Citius (IRE) *Richard Hannon* a78 70
2 b g Iffraaj Brave Madam (IRE) (Invincible Spirit (IRE))
1495[3] ◆ 1920[2] 2181[7]

Citizenship *Mrs John Harrington* a49 78
6 b g Beat Hollow Three More (USA) (Sanglamore (USA))
7584a[17]

Citizen Smith (IRE) *Alan Bailey* a67
3 b g Amadeus Wolf Queen Al Andalous (IRE) (King's Best (USA))
2864[3] 3235[12]

Citrus Star (USA) *Chris Wall* a105 98
5 b g Broken Vow(USA) Twist A Lime (USA) (Copelan (USA))
1558[16] 2409[3] 4099[14] 4609[5] ◆ 5102[4] 5572[9] 6192[3] 6676[18] 7240[23]

Cityar (FR) *John O'Shea* a42 51
8 b g Sagacity(FR) Starry Dust (FR) (Zino)
4992[10] 5419[6] 6098[7] 6232[5]

Citybell (IRE) *Richard Fahey* a57 60
3 b f Elusive City(USA) Bella Vie (IRE) (Sadler's Wells (USA))
1758[5] 2540[8] 3050[10] (Dead)

City Chope (FR) *C Boutin* a67 72
2 b f Sagacity(FR) Grenoble (FR) (Marignan (USA))
5697a[6] 7700a[3]

City Dazzler (IRE) *Richard Hannon* a63 64
3 b f Elusive City(USA) Shady Nook (IRE) (Key Of Luck (USA))
1733[4] 1906[4] 2382[8] 2583[8] 2846[10] 3014[9]

City Girl (IRE) *Ralph Beckett* a77 95
2 b f Elusive City(USA) Lochridge (Indian Ridge)
3504[2] ◆ 4180[2] (4645) 5516[4] 6467[4]

City Ground (USA) *Michael Easterby* a83 32
5 bb g Orientate(USA) Magnet (USA) (Seeking The Gold (USA))
501[4] 1133[14] 6885[10] 7245[7]

City Image (IRE) *Richard Hannon* 99
2 gr f Elusive City(USA) Photophore (IRE) (Clodovil (IRE))
(2938) (3631) 4064[6] 5379a[4] 7518[4]

City Legend *Alan McCabe* a80 80
4 b g Lucky Story(USA) Urban Calm (Cadeaux Genereux)
33[4] (91) (269) 301[7]

City Of Canton (IRE) *Luca Cumani* a74 74
3 b c Monsun(GER) Snow Crystal (IRE) (Kingmambo (USA))
3349[7] 4465[2] 5048[7]

City Of The Kings (IRE) *Ollie Pears* a65 92
7 b g Cape Cross(IRE) Prima Volta (Primo Dominie)
1670[14] 2590[8] 3287[8] 4620[3] 5111[13] 5819[12] 6313[9] 7027[9] 7413[9] 8051[10]

Cityscape *Roger Charlton* 126
6 ch h Selkirk(USA) Tantina (USA) (Distant View (USA))
(1148a) 1902a[10] 3880[4] 5141a[2] 6300a[3] 7238[2]

City Style (USA) *Mahmood Al Zarooni* a107 119
6 ch g City Zip(USA) Brattothecore (CAN) (Katahaula County (CAN))
(51a) 318a[2] (682a) 879a[2] 1148a[3] 3267[6] 3880[9]

Claim (IRE) *Sir Michael Stoute* 78
2 b c Acclamation Raysiza (IRE) (Alzao (USA))
4595[6] (5221) 6344[4]

Claimant (IRE) *Michael Appleby* a52 46
5 b g Acclamation Between The Winds (USA) (Diesis)
843[12] 1092[7]

Clanachy *George Foster* a30 28
6 b m Kyllachy Antonia's Dream (Clantime)
95[5] 492[6]

Clancy Avenue (USA) *T Stack* a78 90
2 b c Henrythenavigator(USA) Saintly Speech (USA) (Southern Halo (USA))
6874[6]

Clapped *Ed Vaughan* a63 41
3 b g Royal Applause Susun Kelapa (USA) (St Jovite (USA))
2147[8] 4583[4] 7326[2] 7671[4] 7988[2] 8075[2]

Clarach (IRE) *Anthony Mullins* 78
7 b m Beneficial Claramanda (IRE) (Mandalus)
6066a[13]

Clara Zetkin *James J Hartnett* a67 75
4 b m Elusive City(USA) Pantita (Polish Precedent (USA))
809[4] 960[6] 3645a[15]

Clare Glen (IRE) *A Oliver* a89 96
6 b m Sakhee(USA) Desert Grouse (USA) (Gulch (USA))
4738[12] 7584a[15]

Clare Island Boy (IRE) *Richard Hannon* 91
3 ch c Strategic Prince Tea Chest (IRE) (In The Wings)
1473[3] 1647[4] 2076[7] (3106) 4529[4] 5064[3] 6661[10] 7017[4]

Clarendale (IRE) *Alan Swinbank* 44
2 b g Holy Roman Emperor(IRE) Fafinta (IRE) (Indian Ridge)
5727[6] 6134[7]

Claretintheblood (IRE) *Richard Fahey* a58 57
3 b c Elusive City(USA) River Abouali (Bluebird (USA))
86[5] 455[3]

Clarkson (IRE) *Jamie Osborne* a54 65
3 b g Jeremy(USA) Gold Marie (IRE) (Green Desert (USA))
132[RR] 270[5] 459[5]

Clasp *Doug Watson* a95 98
10 ch g Singspiel(IRE) Embrace Me (Nashwan (USA))
618a[7]

Classically (IRE) *Peter Hedger* a80 71
6 b g Indian Haven Specifically (USA) (Sky Classic (CAN))
85[7]

Classic Art *Roger Teal* a21 64
2 ch g Excellent Art Sensibility (Halling (USA))
2069[6] 3117[3] 3733[9] 5946[10]

Classic Blade (IRE) *Doug Watson* a87 94
6 b h Daggers Drawn(USA) Queen Bodicea (IRE) (Revoque (IRE))
80a[9]

Classic Colori (IRE) *David O'Meara* a90 98
5 b g Le Vie Dei Colori Beryl (Bering)
2257[8] 2882[2] 3164[7] 3878[10] 4828[6] 5079[10] 6638[2] 7556[8] 7867[4] 8259[6]

Classic Falcon (IRE) *William Haggas* a60 74
3 ch f Dubawi(IRE) Livius Lady (IRE) (Titus Livius (FR))
1529[10] 4506[4] (5095) (5592) 6169[7]

Classic Punch (IRE) *David Elsworth* a109 105
9 b g Mozart(IRE) Rum Cay (USA) (Our Native (USA))
2933[11] 3635[9] 4596[5] 5101[10] 5554[6] 6202[6]

Classic Vintage (USA) *Amanda Perrett* 98
6 b g El Prado(IRE) Cellars Shiraz (USA) (Kissin Kris (USA))
2933[10] 3372[16] 4284[P] 6576[7] 7109[6] 7396[P]

Class Included (USA) *Jim Penney* a100
4 b m Include(USA) A Classic Life (USA) (Sky Classic (CAN))
7550a[7]

Class Monitor *Mrs K Burke* a78 67
3 b f Indesatchel(IRE) First Tarf (Primo Dominie)
17a[2] 865a[6]

Class Win *Sir Michael Stoute* a59 47
3 ch c Notnowcato Prithee (Barathea (IRE))
1704[7] 1937[8]

Classy Anne *Jim Goldie* 32
2 ch f Orientor Class Wan (Safawan)
2614[5]

Classy Lass *Derek Shaw* a19
3 b f Trade Fair Kythia (IRE) (Kahyasi)
382[5] 1062[9]

Classy Trick (USA) *Richard Fahey* a59
2 b c Hat Trick(JPN) Classiest Gem (CAN) (Dehere (USA))
7198[6] 7749[9] 7807[8] 7973[3] 8032[3] 8132[2]

Claude Greenwood *Jamie Osborne* a75 74
2 b c Lucky Story(USA) Greenmeadow (Sure Blade (USA))
2844[9] (3452) 4318[6] 5232[4] 6138[8] 6815[6] 7325[8] 7786[5] 7932[5]

Claude Monet (BRZ) *Jeremy Noseda* a66 67
3 ch g Vettori(IRE) Femme Fatale (BRZ) (Clackson (BRZ))
4948[3] 5901[2] 6409[3] 7174[8]

Clayton *Kevin Ryan* a87 102
3 b g Peintre Celebre(USA) Blossom (Warning)
(974) 1819[3] 2269[3] 2718[2] 6875[6] 7689[9]

Clean Blow (USA) *David Brown* a54 69
2 bb f Street Boss(USA) Strike Hard (IRE) (Green Desert (USA))
3700[3] 4651[4] 5449[2] 6284[5]

Clean Bowled (IRE) *Roger Curtis* a87 56
3 b g Footstepsinthesand Miznapp (Pennekamp (USA))
108[3] 196[4] (479) (619) (683) (840) (920) 1142[2] 1302[5]

Clear Ice (IRE) *Gay Kelleway* a73 79
5 gr g Verglas(IRE) Mynu Girl (IRE) (Charnwood Forest (IRE))
24[8] 100[6] 325[5] 624[5] 2251[11]

Clearing *Jim Boyle* a57
2 br f Sleeping Indian Spring Clean (FR) (Danehill (USA))
7161[5]

Clearing House *John Ryan* a66 59
7 ch g Zamindar(USA) Easy Option (IRE) (Prince Sabo)
3709[7] 4158[12] 4541[10] 5234[7] 6316[10] 6395[8]

Clear Loch *John Spearing* a67 67
2 gr g Proclamation(IRE) Loch Shiel (IRE) (Selkirk (USA))
4752[2] 5911[8] 7931[3]

Clear Pearl (USA) *Ed Vaughan* a60
2 ch f Giant's Causeway(USA) Clear In The West (USA) (Gone West (USA))
6534[4] ◆

Clear Praise (USA) *Simon Dow* a88 83
5 b g Songandaprayer(USA) Pretty Clear (USA) (Mr Prospector (USA))
311[10] 525[3] (652) 1204[2] 2994[6] 3618[2] 4530[9] (5123) 5703[5] 6303[5] 6688[2] 6767[8] 7595[4] 7704[5] 7928[7] 8143[2] 8266[2]

Clear Spring (IRE) *John Spearing* a69 83
4 b h Chineur(FR) Holly Springs (Efisio)
773[8] 988[9] 1625[3] (2401) (3152) 3249[4] (3466) 3941[3] (5681) (6303) 7114[3]

Clearwater Bay (IRE) *Gary Moore* a19 60
5 b g Sadler's Wells(USA) Shouk (Shirley Heights)
3372[17] 3765[9]

Clear Wonder *Giles Bravery*
3 gr f Verglas(IRE) Pure Wonder (IRE) (Hernando (FR))
6965[14]

Clement (IRE) *Eve Johnson Houghton* a65 68
2 b c Clodovil(IRE) Winnifred (Green Desert (USA))
3191[3] 4502[5] 5784[4] 6451[4]

Cleofila (IRE) *J S Bolger* 98
3 b f Teofilo(IRE) Altarejos (IRE) (Vettori (IRE))
2187a[4] 2524a[7]

Clerical (USA) *Robert Cowell* a61 52
6 b g Yes It's True(USA) Clerical Etoile (ARG) (The Watcher (USA))
(46) 126[10] 503[8] 837[8]

Clerk's Choice (IRE) *Oliver Sherwood* a74 25
6 b g Bachelor Duke(USA) Credit Crunch (IRE) (Caerleon (USA))
3610[9]

Clever Man *P Vovcenko* a75 67
4 b g Librettist(USA) Lindesberg (Doyoun)
5118a[9]

Cliffords Reprieve *Eric Wheeler* a67 55
4 b g Kheleyf(USA) Bijan (IRE) (Mukaddamah (USA))
152[3] 277[3] 320[2] 623[2] 763[2] 912[6] 2809[8] 4468[10] 5349[11] 6586[5] 6823[13]

Climaxfortackle (IRE) *Derek Shaw* a71 71
4 b m Refuse To Bend(IRE) Miss Asia Quest (Rainbow Quest (USA))
1191[11] 1311[3] 1439[4] 1652[5] 2546[7] 2859[4] 3220[3] 3589[3] 4325[7] (4890) 5428[5] 5547[5] 6057[5] 6455[7] 6824[7] 6961[7] 7314[9] 8256[3]

Clinical *Sir Mark Prescott Bt* a105 110
4 gr m Motivator Doctor's Glory (USA) (Elmaamul (USA))
(2654) 3266[10] 4801[7] 5834[5] 6379[11]

Clockmaker (IRE) *Tim Easterby* a101 95
6 b g Danetime(IRE) Lady Ingabelle (IRE) (Catrail (USA))
29[2] 254[3] 866[3] 1130[16] 1558[12] 1865[9] 2697[3] 2910[3] 3128[14] 3855[8] 5057[6] 5342[16] (6192) 6659[6] 7097[9]

Clock On Tom *Michael Easterby* a44 49
2 b g Trade Fair Night Owl (Night Shift (USA))
1911[10] 2138[10] 2880[9] 4450[5] 5254[8] 5920[2] 6893[8]

Clock Opera (IRE) *Mrs K Burke* a64 60
2 b f Excellent Art Moving Diamonds (Lomitas)
2019[5] 2587[6] 8208[3]

Clodhopper (IRE) *Jamie Osborne* a67 39
3 gr f Clodovil(IRE) Clochette (IRE) (Namaqualand (USA))
(376) 491[4] (564) (739)

Clon Brulee (IRE) *David Barron* a36 87
3 ch g Modigliani(USA) Cloneden (IRE) (Definite Article)
(3066) ◆ (3558) 4741[8] 6193[3]

Clone Devil (IRE) *Alastair Lidderdale* a48
3 gr g Clodovil(IRE) Mrs Willy Nilly (Timeless Times (USA))
407[8] 466[6] 649[6]

Close At Hand *John Gosden* 62
2 b f Exceed And Excel(AUS) Classic Remark (IRE) (Dr Fong (USA))
4525[4]

Close Together (IRE) *Robert Mills* a63 47
2 b f Dylan Thomas(IRE) Maritana (USA) (Rahy (USA))
1563[8] 6816[4] (7165)

Close To Heaven (GER) *A Trybuhl* a88 84
5 gr g Diktat Caronment (Environment Friend)
443a[7]

Close To The Edge (IRE) *Alan McCabe* a87 87
4 b m Iffraaj Iktidar (Green Desert (USA))
286[5] 458[4] 554[4] 883[3] 2264[9] (2636) 3571[4] 3960[7] 4629[8] 6144[17]

Cloture (USA) *Claude McGaughey III*
2 b f Political Force(USA) Impressionism (USA) (Broad Brush (USA))
6944a[5]

Cloud (IRE) *L Riccardi* 96
2 bb c Clodovil(IRE) Noble Indiana (ITY) (Indian Ridge)
3684a[3]

Clouded Vision (IRE) *Noel Quinlan* 19
2 gr c Dark Angel(IRE) Western Sky (Barathea (IRE))
6779[4]

Cloud Illusions (USA) *Heather Main* a77 83
4 rg m Smarty Jones(USA) Ilusoria (USA) (Maria's Mon (USA))
1652[13] 2161[4] 3443[14] 3785[12]

Clouds Of Glory *Jason Ward*
3 b f Resplendent Glory(IRE) Rosewings (In The Wings)
8239[8]

Cloudwalker (USA) *Ed Vaughan* a70 77
2 bb f Tale Of The Cat(USA) Angel Flying (USA) (Saint Ballado (CAN))
7159[4] ◆ 7555[5]

Cloudy Spirit *Reg Hollinshead* a69 84
7 gr m Silver Patriarch(IRE) Miss Lacroix (Picea)
1113[3] (1272) (2214) ◆ 3373[13] 4697[12]

Cloudy Start *Jamie Osborne* a80 81
6 b g Oasis Dream Set Fair (USA) (Alleged (USA))
85[6] 276[6] 446[3] (493) 644[4] 738[7] 850[5] 889[5] 1184[3] (1361) 1588[4] 2134[4] 3283[8] 4664[5] 5683[5]

Clowance Estate (IRE) *Roger Charlton* 81
3 b g Teofilo(IRE) Whirly Bird (Nashwan (USA))
(2393) ◆

Clowance House *Barry Brennan* 70
6 ch g Galileo(IRE) Corsican Sunset (USA) (Thunder Gulch (USA))
3572[4]

Clowance Keys *Rod Millman* a40 56
3 b g High Chaparral(IRE) Seasons Parks (Desert Prince (IRE))
1256[5] 4213[8] 4457[6] 4705[5] 5127[7]

Clu Agus Cail (IRE) *Alison Batchelor* a15
7 b m Rock Of Gibraltar(IRE) Political Society (IRE) (Law Society (USA))
3763[10]

Cluaindubhloch (IRE) *Tony Carroll* a46
4 b g Danroad(AUS) Kealbra Lady (Petong)
4212[11] 4874[U] 5208[5] 5805[4] 6396[13] 6927[7]

Club Electra (IRE) *Tobias B P Coles* a36
2 br f Red Clubs(IRE) Princess Electra (IRE) (Lake Coniston (IRE))
8171[11]

Club House (IRE) *Robert Mills* a71 75
2 b g Marju(IRE) Idesia (IRE) (Green Desert (USA))
2480[5] 2934[4] 3452[2] 4804[4] 5242[3] 5946[7] 6572[6] 7079[5] 7325[5] 7814[4] 8032[7] (8101) 8302[4]

Clubland (IRE) *Kevin Ryan* a71 71
3 b g Red Clubs(IRE) Racjilanemm (Kyllachy)
5621[6] (5719) 5923[10] 6786[10] (6935) 7197[9] 7254[5]

Club Oceanic *Saeed Bin Suroor* a89 107
4 b g Cape Cross(IRE) My Lass (Elmaamul (USA))
241a[5] 489a[5] 677a[7]

Clumber Place *James Given* a45 77
6 ch m Compton Place Inquirendo (USA) (Roberto (USA))
2012[5] 2546[10] 3257[4] 3559[5] 3749[5] 4624[4] 5671[2] 5999[2] 6546[5] (6782) 7314[2] 7685[15]

Clunia (IRE) *C Laffon-Parias* 97
4 ch m Silent Times(IRE) Doohulla (USA) (Stravinsky (USA))
7665a[6]

C'Mon You Irons (IRE) *Mark Hoad* a80 68
7 b g Orpen(USA) Laissez Faire (IRE) (Tagula (IRE))
39[8] 312[10] 6002[13]

Cnocan Diva (IRE) *T Stack* a75 85
4 b m Danehill Dancer(IRE) Dancing Diva (FR) (Sadler's Wells (USA))
7680a[9]

Coach Montana (IRE) *Jane Chapple-Hyam* a56 56
3 b g Proud Citizen(USA) Market Day (Tobougg (IRE))
1260[3] 1740[10] 2802[6] 5215[9] 6396[5] (7616) 7837[U] 8099[6] 8257[7]

Coastal Passage *Charles Smith* a61 43
4 b g Ishiguru(USA) Ellcon (IRE) (Royal Applause)
1722[3] 1961[5] 2225[4] 5246[10] 7221[7] 7611[10] 8291[2]

Coax *Patrick Holmes* a55 75
4 b g Red Ransom(USA) True Glory (IRE) (In The Wings)
692[7] 1796[10] 2593[3] 2669[2] 3307[11] 3753[4] 4626[8] 5054[2] 5622[3]

Cobbs Quay *Daniel Kubler* a61 76
4 b g Danehill Dancer(IRE) Rave Reviews (IRE) (Sadler's Wells (USA))
2051[10] 2886[8] 3485[7] 6262[12] 6773[2] 7058[5] 7252[7]

Cochabamba (IRE) *Roger Teal* a98 98
4 ch m Hurricane Run(IRE) Bolivia (USA) (Distant View (USA))
866[9] 1140[6] 1213[6] 1646[6] 2067[7] 2890[6] 4984[2] 5856[2] 6667[10] (7128)

Cockney Class (USA) *Brian Meehan* a96 73
5 rg g Speightstown(USA) Snappy Little Cat (USA) (Tactical Cat (USA))
2250[10]

Cockney Dancer *Charles Hills* a88 83
3 ch f Cockney Rebel(IRE) Roo (Rudimentary (USA))
3446[8] 4068[11] (6176) 6488[8] (7789)

Cockney Fire *David Evans* 79
3 ch f Cockney Rebel(IRE) Camp Fire (IRE) (Lahib (USA))
1639[5] 2616[7] 2986[4] 3613[10] 4420[5] (4903) 5195[3] 5502[7] 6094[8]

Cockney Rhyme *Heather Main* a71 73
3 b f Cockney Rebel(IRE) Regent's Park (Green Desert (USA))
2448[11] 2813[10] 3120[5] 3643[13] 4901[2] 5231[6]

Cockney Sparrow *Peter Chapple-Hyam* a72 86
3 b f Cockney Rebel(IRE) Compose (Anabaa (USA))
784[3] (959) (1442) 1973[6] 5598[9] 6349[5] 6964[3]

Cocktail Charlie *Tim Easterby* 97
4 b g Danbird(AUS) Royal Punch (Royal Applause)
1438[8] 2208[13] 2825[9] 3127[16] 4292[3] 4554[6] 4829[6] 5223[4] 6044[3] 7100[5]

Cocktail Hour (IRE) *D K Weld* a65 82
2 b f Notnowcato Out Of Thanks (IRE) (Sadler's Wells (USA))
6853a[7]

Cocktail Queen (IRE) *David Elsworth* 101
2 b f Motivator Premier Prize (Selkirk (USA))
5977[5] 6489[11] (6790) 7343a[2]

Cocohatchee *Pat Phelan* a60 77
4 b g Avonbridge Chilly Cracker (Largesse)
987[10] 1680[7] 1935[3] 2207[2] (3016) 3225[4] 4000[6] 5531[10] 6932[9]

Coconut Kisses *Bill Turner* a67 67
2 ch f Bahamian Bounty Royal Mistress (Fasliyev (USA))
1211[5] ◆ (1388) 5045[3] 5411[2] 5807[5] (6336) 6707[8] 7355[5]

Coconut Shrimp (USA) *Todd Pletcher* 96
2 ch f Giant's Causeway(USA) Weekend Whim (USA) (Distorted Humor (USA))
6289a[5]

Coco Rouge (IRE) *James Fanshawe* a73 70
4 ch m Shamardal(USA) Coquette Rouge (IRE) (Croco Rouge (IRE))
(3735) 5218[4]

Cocozza (USA) *Marco Botti* a94 103
4 b g Elusive Quality(USA) Watership Crystal (IRE) (Sadler's Wells (USA))
1130[20] 1212[7]

Codebreaker *Hughie Morrison* a68 63
2 ch g Sakhee's Secret Folly Lodge (Grand Lodge (USA))
5304[9] 6571[5] 7349[2]

Code Of Honor *Henry Candy* 89
2 b c Zafeen(FR) Verbal Intrigue (USA) (Dahar (USA))
5303[8] (6481) (7399)

Code Six (IRE) *Bryan Smart* a68 68
3 gr f Kodiac Grey Pursuit (IRE) (Pursuit Of Love)
637[3] ◆ 749[3] 905[8] 4547[10] 4793[3] 5548[5] 5923[7] 6211[9]

Cody Maverick (IRE) *A Al Raihe* a66 86
3 b c Diamond Green(FR) Miss Dilletante (Primo Dominie)
417a[9] 679a[11]

Coeur A Coeur (FR) *W Walton* a77 96
3 b c Carlotamix(FR) Zanicoeur (FR) (Zayyani)
475a[4]

Cogito (USA) *Doug O'Neill* 115
3 b c Giant's Causeway(USA) Ladies Cruise (USA) (Fappiano (USA))
(1450) (2641) 3239[8] 4385a[2] 6902a[4] 7573a[7]

Coil (USA) *Bob Baffert* a123
4 ch h Point Given(USA) Eversmile (USA) (Theatrical (IRE))
7574a[7]

Coincidently *Alan Bailey* a74 72
2 b f Acclamation Miss Chaussini (IRE) (Rossini (USA))
5360[2] 5828[3] (7160)

Colamandis *Hugh McWilliams* a40 44
5 b m Lucky Story(USA) Merry Mary (Magic Ring (IRE))
690[9] 2617[5] 2838[5] 6179[9] 7782[8] 8109[5] 8209[9]

Colbyor *Richard Fahey* a68 77
3 ch g Orientor College Maid (IRE) (College Chapel)
1241[4] (2085) 2616[4] 4393[2] 5676[3] 6514[9] 7001[4] 7684[5] 8034[8] 8236[2]

Colima (IRE) *Ralph Beckett* a98 100
3 b f Authorized(IRE) Coyote (Indian Ridge)
2079[2] ◆ 2658[9] 3292[10]

Colinca's Lad (IRE) *Peter Charalambous* a65 82
10 b g Lahib(USA) Real Flame (Cyrano De Bergerac)
(1286) 1566[2] 1882[13] (3769) 3995[4]

Collateral Damage (IRE) *Tim Easterby* a92 86
9 b g Orpen(USA) Jay Gee (IRE) (Second Set (IRE))
1161[14] 1249[8] 1820[9] 1914[4] 2142[4] 2754[7] 3185[9] 3914[8] ◆ (4089) 4398[9] 5059[5] 5414[5] 5547[7] 6528[5] 6881[7]

Collectable *Jonathan Portman* a54 57
3 b f Excellent Art Tiriana (Common Grounds)
1182[7] 2131[4] 2367[2] 2802[7] 4533[4] 5095[2] 5633[3] 6158[4] 6442[3] 7117[5]

College Doll *Christine Dunnett* a50 51
3 ch f Piccolo Southwarknewsflash (Danetime (IRE))
1843[9] 2332[8] 3082[5] 6496[11] 6771[3] 7611[4] 7703[8] 7914[7] 8045[7]

Colliding Worlds (IRE) *John Patrick Shanahan* 105
3 b f High Chaparral(IRE) Wee Mad Snout (IRE) (Soviet Star (USA))
4378a[6] 7423a[6]

Colliers Castle (IRE) *Lisa Williamson* a59 44
6 b m Karinga Bay Aneeza (IRE) (Charnwood Forest (IRE))
767[4] 889[U] 1112[5] 1361[4] 1794[8]

Collingbourneducis (IRE) *Richard Hannon* a62 68
2 b c Bahamian Bounty Quickstyx (Night Shift (USA))
7371[4]

Colloquial *Henry Candy* a90 98
11 b g Classic Cliche(IRE) Celia Brady (Last Tycoon)
3341[9]

Colmar Kid (IRE) *Richard Hannon* 81
2 b c Choisir(AUS) Roselyn (Efisio)
4056[6] 4472[5] 4803[5] (5418) 6162[15] 7079[6]

Colombian (IRE) *John Gosden* 117
4 b h Azamour(IRE) Clodora (FR) (Linamix (FR))
(1677) 2640[5] 3267[8] 5377a[3] 6898a[4]

Colonel Flay *Nerys Dutfield* a66 63
8 ch g Danehill Dancer(IRE) Bobbie Dee (Blakeney)
4491[5]

Colonel Mak *David Barron* a86 111
5 br g Makbul Colonel's Daughter (Colonel Collins (USA))
89[9] 286[9] 871[12] (1157) 1885[3] 3371[27] 4086[7] (4258) 4611[5] 5370[15] 6468[5] 7066[11] 7366[7] 7691[11]

Colonial (IRE) *Saeed Bin Suroor* a110 112
5 b h Cape Cross(IRE) Elizabeth Bay (USA) (Mr Prospector (USA))
53a[11] 588a[16] 6886[8] 7638[4]

Colonial Flag (USA) *Michael Matz* 96
3 bb f Pleasant Tap(USA) Silk N' Sapphire (USA) (Smart Strike (CAN))
4131a[8]

Colony (IRE) *M bin Shafya* a91 92
7 b h Statue Of Liberty(USA) Funoon (IRE) (Kris)
52a[8]

Colorful Notion (IRE) *Marco Botti* a89 85
3 b f Danehill Dancer(IRE) Red Yellow Blue (USA) (Sky Classic (CAN))
418a[5] 680a[6] 754a[3] 4497[4] 5385[10] 6367[2] 7680a[7]

Color Shades *Clive Cox* 71
2 ch f Galileo(IRE) Red Yellow Blue (USA) (Sky Classic (CAN))
3474[5] 5339[8] 5907[6] ◆

Colourbearer (IRE) *Milton Bradley* a79 68
5 ch g Pivotal Centifolia (FR) (Kendor (FR))
1773[5] 2165[8] 2572[15] 2973[7] 3243[3] 3467[6] 4059[10] 4187[11] 7864[9] 7969[6] 8190[6] ◆ 8255[2] ◆

Colour Guard *Mark Johnston* a95 92
4 b g Shamardal(USA) Colorvista (Shirley Heights)
(495) 674[4] (753) (812) 1008[2] 1087[8] 3164[5] 3306[4] 3534[7] 4136[10] 4578[3] 4689[6] 5397a[9] 5835[4] 6380[5] 6638[22]

Colourist *Gary Moore* a1 60
2 b c Dutch Art Zagala (Polar Falcon (USA))
4220[6] 4604[6] 4816[10] 5654[2] 6564[2] 6850[4]

Colour My World *Ed McMahon* a43
2 gr c With Approval(CAN) Nadeszhda (Nashwan (USA))
8147[5]

Colour Of Love (IRE) *W McCreery* a88 102
4 ch m Le Vie Dei Colori Priceoflove (IRE) (Inchinor)
1040a[8] 3645a[6] 4482a[4] 6072[2] (Dead)

Colours Of Nature *Eric Alston* 57
2 b g Lucky Story(USA) Sweetly Sharp (IRE) (Daggers Drawn (USA))
2415[12] 2912[4] 3286[8] 4625[6]

Colour Vision (FR) *Saeed Bin Suroor* a121 118
4 gr g Rainbow Quest(USA) Give Me Five (GER) (Monsun (GER))
(1750) ◆ (3293) 4737[3] 6198[7] 6914a[3] 7235[9]

Columella *William Haggas* a66 74
2 b f Kyllachy Nausicaa (USA) (Diesis)
(3313) 3669[5] 5361[10] 5886[5] (6815) 7242[5]

Comadoir (IRE) *Jo Crowley* a67 69
6 ch g Medecis Hymn Of The Dawn (USA) (Phone Trick (USA))
262[4] 574[5] 818[7] 995[8] 2847[13] (3249) 4584[4] 5440[5] 6306[3] 7992[10] 8268[3]

Combat Zone (IRE) *Mario Hofer* 107
6 b g Refuse To Bend(IRE) Zeiting (IRE) (Zieten (USA))
(6291a) 6906a[4] 7286a[2] 7587a[9]

Comedy Award (USA) *A Fabre* a52 73
3 b g Distorted Humor(USA) Composure (USA) (Touch Gold (USA))
1171a[0]

Comedy House *Michael Madgwick* a64 56
4 b g Auction House(USA) Kyle Akin (Vettori (IRE))
3622[7] 4410[5] 5100[3] 5936[6] 6232[4] 7303[7] 7629[5] 7991[2]

Come Here Yew (IRE) *Declan Carroll* 83
4 ch g Refuse To Bend(IRE) Red Zinger (USA) (Red Ransom (USA))
2339[2] 2792[6] 3290[5] (4590) 4831[5] 5188[7] 5730[2] 6884[4] 7098[2] 7367[10]

Come Hither *David O'Meara* a43 67
3 b f Pastoral Pursuits Stolen Glance (Mujahid (USA))
(4913) 5130[5] 6127[13] 6479[7] 6783[3] 7600[3] 7798[8] 8213[11]

Come On Blue Chip (IRE) *Paul D'Arcy* a100 89
3 b g Holy Roman Emperor(IRE) Rapid Action (USA) (Quest For Fame)
398[2] (841) 3294[25] 4600[5] 5006[8] 5768[5] 6036[2] 6374[5] 6580[3] 7168[6] 7751[2] 7904[7]

Come On Dave (IRE) *David Nicholls* a69 84
3 b g Red Clubs(IRE) Desert Sprite (IRE) (Tagula (IRE))
1089[3] 1169[2] 1317[8] 2256[9] 2875[4] 3578[3] 4558[9] 4878[3] (5013) (5739) 6427[3] (6886)

Come On Mate (FR) *E J O'Neill* a74 67
4 gr m Chichicastenango(FR) Sendback Lady (USA) (Elusive Quality (USA))
3207a[4]

Cometography (IRE) *Ismail Mohammed* a65 55
3 b c Teofilo(IRE) Halle Bop (Dubai Millennium)
3349[13] 4464[8] 5753[6] 6334[11]

Come To Mind *Alan Berry* 46
3 b g Mind Games Hillside Heather (IRE) (Tagula (IRE))
4087[10] 4549[15] 4913[10] 5757[10]

Comical *Mark Johnston* a52 79
3 b g Dubai Destination(USA) Amusing Time (IRE) (Sadler's Wells (USA))
2440[10] 4504[13] 4914[7]

Commanche *Patrick Chamings* a72 74
3 ch g Sleeping Indian Happy Memories (IRE) (Thatching)
3063[8] 3421[4] 3912[4] 5728[7] 7001[9] 7178[11] (7990) (8304)

Commanche Raider (IRE) *Michael Dods* a57 78
5 b g Tale Of The Cat(USA) Alsharq (IRE) (Machiavellian (USA))
1526[12] 2674[2] (2982) 4638[11] 4963[4] 5389[7] 6044[2] 6887[3] 7023[11]

Commander (USA) *Troy Taylor* a106
4 b g Broken Vow(USA) Pout (USA) (Deputy Minister (CAN))
7546a[9]

Commander Veejay *Brian Rothwell* 53
4 ch g Piccolo Poly Blue (IRE) (Thatching)
2823[2] 3029[5] 3402[8] 3988[8] 4209[3] 4908[4] 5253[9]

Commandingpresence (USA) *John Bridger* a60 75
6 bb m Thunder Gulch(USA) Sehra (USA) (Silver Hawk (USA))
4238[6] 4815[4] 5035[4] (5346) 6303[7] 6439[2] 6578[3] 7299[6] 7741[12] 8058[7] 8160[7]

Commend *Sir Michael Stoute* a80 93
3 ch g Pivotal Reputable (Medicean)
1312[2] 2313[2] (4622) 5358[2] 5626[3] ◆ 6193[5] 7017[6]

Commerce *Dai Burchell* a61 70
5 b m Trade Fair Well Away (IRE) (Sadler's Wells (USA))
2137[9]

Commissar *Mahmood Al Zarooni* 92
3 b g Soviet Star(USA) Sari (Faustus (USA))
1477[12]

Commitment *Luca Cumani* 92
3 b g Motivator Courting (Pursuit Of Love)
(1754) 2235[2] 2718[8] 3296[14] 6380[6] 7082[9]

Common Cents *Ronald Harris* 63
3 ch g Pivotal Small Change (IRE) (Danzig (USA))
1155[13] 2065[5] 3389[6]

Common Courtesy *Michael Bell* a57
2 b f Motivator Crystal Swan (IRE) (Dalakhani (IRE))
7460[5] 7780[5]

Common Touch (IRE) *Richard Fahey* 101
4 ch g Compton Place Flying Finish (FR) (Priolo (USA))
2211[8] 3268[25] 4110[7] 4703[13] (5269) 6119[4] (6471) 7097[6]

Communicator *Andrew Balding* a95 102
4 b g Motivator Goodie Twosues (Fraam)
1603[3] 2706[4] ◆ 3502[4] 4103[3] (5333) 5826[2] ◆ 7689[2] 7895[4]

Community (USA) *Jamie Osborne* a67 59
4 b m Proud Citizen(USA) Rimini Road (USA) (Dynaformer (USA))
136[4] 199[12] 494[3] 584[8] 836[4] 922[9] 1052[10] 1625[5] (4981) (5720) 6157[10] 7225[4] 7593[3] 7841[5] 8249[2]

Complex *David Evans* a57 56
3 b f Multiplex Dockside Strike (Docksider (USA))
(108) 255[3] 360[3] 466[3] 726[7]

Complexity *Charles Hills* 78
2 b c Multiplex Asinara (GER) (Big Shuffle (USA))
4487[10] (5119) 6469[8]

Complicator *Alan McCabe* 53
2 br c Pastoral Pursuits Thara'A (IRE) (Desert Prince (IRE))
3168[4] 3611[12]

Complimentor (IRE) *X Thomas-Demeaulte* a92 92
2 ch c Acclamation Lovely Blossom (FR) (Spinning World (USA))
6128a[4] (7682a)

Composed *Paul Cole* a80 68
2 b c Sakhee's Secret Cheeky Girl (College Chapel)
1920[4] 2550[4] 2983[8] 4540[6] 4778[2] (5378a)

Compton *Ralph Beckett* a60 102
3 ch g Compton Place Look So (Efisio)
3294[4] 4097[7] 4997[3] 5677[4] 6143[10] (6830) 7240[4]

Compton Albion (IRE) *Jeremy Gask* a46
2 ch f Compton Place Yomalo (IRE) (Woodborough (USA))
7987[10] 8165[6]

Compton Ashdown *Hans Adielsson* a64
3 b g Proclamation(IRE) Ashlinn (IRE) (Ashkalani (IRE))
3706[6]

Compton Bell *Hans Adielsson* a53 47
3 b g Shirocco(GER) Bela-M (IRE) (Ela-Mana-Mou)
7815[5] 8180[10]

Compton Bird *Hans Adielsson* a62 34
3 b f Motivator Noble Peregrine (Lomond (USA))
4186[4] 7841[10] 8074[7]

Compton Blue *Alan King* a63 81
6 b g Compton Place Blue Goddess (IRE) (Blues Traveller (IRE))
6170[10]

Compton Crofter *Hans Adielsson* a52 52
3 ch g Sleeping Indian Crofters Ceilidh (Scottish Reel)
2147[10] 2542[12] 2864[9] 3706[7] 4185[4] 4734[6] 5229[10] (5443) 5770[11] 7615[11] 7898[4] 8111[7]

Compton Monarch *Hans Adielsson* a18 40
3 b g Red Ransom(USA) Monaiya (Shareef Dancer (USA))
832[5]

Compton Prince *Clive Cox* a73 69
3 ch c Compton Place Malelane (IRE) (Prince Sabo)
770[3] 969[4] ◆ 1723[5] 3566[8] 4876[7] 5302[4] 5837[6] 6401[4] 7203[6]

Compton Rainbow *Hans Adielsson* a67 60
3 b f Exceed And Excel(AUS) Rainbow Goddess (Rainbow Quest (USA))
5975[2] 6402[3] 6801[11] 7308[9] 7776[8] 8074[3]

Compton Silver *Hans Adielsson* a60
2 ch g Haafhd Anna Oleanda (IRE) (Old Vic)
3499[9] 6054[2] 6609[5] 7476[10] 7821[10]

Comptonspirit *Brian Baugh* a29 83
8 ch m Compton Place Croeso Cynnes (Most Welcome)
1827[11] 2264[17] 2693[3] 3496[6] 4680[4] 4963[9] 5223[10] 6094[3] 6277[3] 6788[6]

Compton Target (IRE) *Milton Bradley* a72 68
3 b g Strategic Prince Tarakana (USA) (Shahrastani (USA))
982[5] 1445[3] 1979[5] (2786) 3193[8] 3950[5] 4438[9] 4932[13] 5660[4] 6000[9]

Compton Time *Michael Dods* 67
3 b g Compton Place Surrealist (ITY) (Night Shift (USA))
1560[7] 2774[2] 3289[6] 4552[10]

Comrade Bond *Mark H Tompkins* a74 82
4 ch g Monsieur Bond(IRE) Eurolink Cafe (Grand Lodge (USA))
1289[8] 2043[3] 2207[7] 2815[3] (3549) (3977) 6338[3] 7559[14]

Comradeship (IRE) *R Bouresly* a95 82
5 ch h Dubawi(IRE) Friendlier (Zafonic (USA))
314a[13]

Con Artist (IRE) *Saeed Bin Suroor* a83 108
5 b h Invincible Spirit(IRE) Hoodwink (IRE) (Selkirk (USA))
2773[3] 3329[10] 3878[4]

Concise *Ed Dunlop* a81 75
2 b f Lemon Drop Kid(USA) Cut Short (USA) (Diesis)
5162[3] ◆ (6014) 6873[8]

Concordat *S Seemar* a99 100
4 ch g Selkirk(USA) African Peace (USA) (Roberto (USA))
260a[9]

Concorde Express (USA) *Douglas J Seyler*
4 rg g Concorde's Tune(USA) Express Fashion (USA) (Private Express (USA))
8100a[11]

Concrete Jungle (IRE) *Bill Turner* a44 62
4 b g Chineur(FR) Finty (IRE) (Entrepreneur)
5021[8] 5653[7] 7733[14]

Conduct (IRE) *Sir Michael Stoute* 100
5 gr g Selkirk(USA) Coventina (IRE) (Daylami (IRE))
4795[2]

Conducting *Gay Kelleway* a74 72
4 b g Oratorio(IRE) Aiming (Highest Honor (FR))
349[3] 826[2] 960[5] 1051[2] 1266[6] 1755[6] 2011[5] 4333[2] 4662[3] 4914[2] 6302[7] 7925[5] 8047[5] 8078[2] 8214[6]

Cone Donkey (IRE) *Bryan Smart* a59 67
3 b f Medicean Nan Scurry (FR) (Danehill (USA))
1296[2] 1599[10] 1960[5] (5734) 6179[7]

Confessional *Tim Easterby* a92 110
5 b g Dubawi(IRE) Golden Nun (Bishop Of Cashel)
1157[10] 1498[6] (1975) 2486[5] 2704[5] 3623[8] 3877[2] 4113[9] 4762[4] 5561[15] 5822[3] 6140[4] 6867[4]

Confide In Me *Mark Hoad* a13 66
8 b g Medicean Confidante (USA) (Dayjur (USA))
151[11]

Confidence (USA) *Luke Comer* a90 76
5 b g More Than Ready(USA) Caramel Custard (USA) (Chief Honcho (USA))
342a[3]

Confidential Creek *Ollie Pears* a56 64
2 b g Sakhee's Secret Upstream (Prince Sabo)
2686[4] 3110[10] 4545[10] 5940[4] 6809[2]

Confirmed *Alison Batchelor* a67 70
3 b g Authorized(IRE) Vas Y Carla (USA) (Gone West (USA))
4901[4] 5942[9] 8308[7]

Confluence *Clifford Lines* a57 57
3 ch f Milk It Mick Skimra (Hernando (FR))
2280[8] 2848[9] 3349[11] 3975[3] 5019[6] 5454[8] 6965[8]

Conjuror's Bluff *Frederick Watson* 66
4 b h Tiger Hill(IRE) Portmeirion (Polish Precedent (USA))
5585[12]

Con Leche *Scott Dixon* a60 12
2 b c Milk It Mick Capital Lass (Forzando)
2442[6] 6808[9] 7669[3] 7855[3] 7930[9] 8065[6]

Connie Carlton *David Thompson*
3 b f Distant Music(USA) Transylvania (Wolfhound (USA))
3565[11] 3913[11] 4211[8] 4826[13]

Connishka *Alan Bailey* a50 46
3 gr f Verglas(IRE) Profit Alert (IRE) (Alzao (USA))
2935[10] 3454[6] 4198[7] 6810[4] 7470[6] 8261[6]

Conowen *William Jarvis* a58 68
3 ch g Ishiguru(USA) Velma Kelly (Vettori (IRE))
597[3] 1622[3] 3567[6] 4509[5] 5017[8] 5443[11] 5991[13]

Cono Zur (FR) *Ruth Carr* a74 81
5 b g Anabaa(USA) Alaskan Idol (USA) (Carson City (USA))
1276[7] (1830) (2491) 3335[3] 4398[8] 4747[10] 5111[2] 5429[10] 6047[7] 6342[13]

Conry (IRE) *Ian Williams* a68 88
6 ch g Captain Rio Altizaf (Zafonic (USA))
1958[11] 2355[10] (3455) 3843[3] 5750[4] 5892[3] 6338[11] (7247) (7452)

Consenting *Roger Charlton* a2 30
3 ch f Refuse To Bend(IRE) Perfect Night (Danzig Connection (USA))
3312[9] 3972[12]

Conserve (IRE) *Sir Henry Cecil* 52
2 b f Duke Of Marmalade(IRE) Minor Point (Selkirk (USA))
6966[7]

Consider Yourself (USA) *Anthony Carson* a85 85
5 rg m Afleet Alex(USA) Champagne Royale (USA) (French Deputy (USA))
374[9] 3914[5] (4242) (4435) 5218[3] 5688[2] (6819) 7375[11]

Consign *Jeremy Noseda* a77
2 b c Dutch Art Maid To Dance (Pyramus (USA))
7498[5] 8033[3] (8262)

Consistant *Brian Baugh* a66 71
4 b g Reel Buddy(USA) Compact Disc (IRE) (Royal Academy (USA))
(155) (498) 912[10] 1481[5] 2538[3] 2981[2] 4495[7] 5389[2] 6403[7]

Constans (IRE) *Clive Cox* a12 67
2 gr c Holy Roman Emperor(IRE) Rosamixa (FR) (Linamix (FR))
3611[5] ◆ 5005[5] 5655[5]

Constant Contact *Donald McCain* a100 99
5 b g Passing Glance Floriana (Selkirk (USA))
2228[4] 3125[11]

Constant Dream *James Given* a62 45
2 br f Kheleyf(USA) Pizzicato (Statoblest)
2783[11] 3217[5] 4742[8] 7156[6] (7609)

Contender (FR) *X Nakkachdji* a78 75
3 b c Exceed And Excel(AUS) Nikolenka (IRE) (Indian Ridge)
4477a[2]

Contesurmoi (FR) *A Bonin* a58 75
2 b c One Cool Cat(USA) Ymlaen (IRE) (Desert Prince (IRE))
5378a[8] 7699a[4]

Contradict *Sir Michael Stoute* a72 71
2 b f Raven's Pass(USA) Acts Of Grace (USA) (Bahri (USA))
3504[3] 4886[2] 5742[7]

Contributer (IRE) *Ed Dunlop* a81 75
2 b c High Chaparral(IRE) Serisia (FR) (Exit To Nowhere (USA))
4066[6] ◆ (7750) ◆

Conversing (USA) *Mahmood Al Zarooni* a44 33
2 ch c Raven's Pass(USA) Mini Chat (USA) (Deputy Minister (CAN))
6501[10] 6795[15]

Cookie Crumbles (IRE) *Adrian McGuinness* a54 54
5 ch m Bahamian Bounty Diaspora (IRE) (Kris)
7837[5]

Cookieshake *Peter Hiatt* a67 67
4 b g Cadeaux Genereux Hawait Al Barr (Green Desert (USA))
2502[12] 2937[7] 3939[8] 4664[3] 5196[9] 5264[4] 5683[7]

Cool And Clear (IRE) *Tim Easterby* 50
2 b g One Cool Cat(USA) Manon's Song (IRE) (Sadler's Wells (USA))
6360[7] 6556[6] 7290[5] 7606[8]

Cool As Cash *Paul D'Arcy* a57 64
3 ch g Notnowcato Coconut Queen (IRE) (Alhaarth (IRE))
3735[10] 4301[5] 4746[6] 5428[9]

Cool Baranca (GER) *Dianne Sayer* 56
6 b m Beat Hollow Cool Storm (IRE) (Rainbow Quest (USA))
2137[12] 3116[3] 3307[9] 4867[2] (7102)

Cooler Climes *Pat Eddery* a77 38
3 ch c Three Valleys(USA) Balmy (Zafonic (USA))
969[5] 1182[2] 2145[2] 3068[8] 5970[6] 7116[8]

Cool Fantasy (IRE) *Paul D'Arcy* a53 9
3 b g One Cool Cat(USA) Regal Fantasy (IRE) (King's Theatre (IRE))
923[3] 1267[5] 1591[4]

Cool Hand Jake *Jamie Osborne* a77 58
6 b g Storming Home Monawara (IRE) (Namaqualand (USA))
3039[3] 3485[9] 4411[9]

Cool Hand Luke (IRE) *Ian Williams* a71 68
3 br g Le Vie Dei Colori Thelma Louise (IRE) (Desert Style (IRE))
159[3] (464) 1013[4] 1319[7] 2788[8] 3711[5] 5197[4]

Coolibah (IRE) *Charles O'Brien* 91
2 b f Peintre Celebre(USA) Honour Bright (IRE) (Danehill (USA))
7419a[3]

Cool In The Shade *Paul Midgley* 76
4 b m Pastoral Pursuits Captain Margaret (Royal Applause)
2793[12] 3382[9]

Coolita (FR) *D Allard* a66 62
3 b f One Cool Cat(USA) Italienne (USA) (Distant View (USA))
475a[6]

Cool Kid *Ian Williams* a58 60
4 b g Iceman Clashfern (Smackover)
7839[9] 8214[2]

Cool Macavity (IRE) *Charles Hills* a75 91
4 b g One Cool Cat(USA) Cause Celebre (IRE) (Peintre Celebre (USA))
1999[7] 2642[7] (3380) 3826[7] 4365[4] 4795[4] 5492[11] 6202[3] 7017[2] 7407[6]

Cool Marble (IRE) *Jeremy Gask* a36 96
5 b h Oasis Dream Nini Princesse (IRE) (Niniski (USA))
2068[10] 2642[9] 3167[12] 3492[7] 4317[10] 5674[6] 7936[7]

Cool Metallic (IRE) *D K Weld* 78
2 b g Medicean Polite Reply (IRE) (Be My Guest (USA))
2958a[7]

Coolminx (IRE) *Richard Fahey* a84 94
5 b m One Cool Cat(USA) Greta D'Argent (IRE) (Great Commotion (USA))
1558[6] 2177[6] 2825[7] 3183[15] 3696[4] 4336[4] 4998[4] 6008[15] 6465[5] (6515) 7080[13]

Coolnagree (IRE) *W McCreery* 101
3 gr f Dark Angel(IRE) Win Cash (IRE) (Alhaarth (IRE))
1943a[2] 5523a[4] 6161[12] 6917a[3]

Cool Rhythm *Ralph Beckett* a68 81
4 b g Iceman With Music In Mind (Mind Games)
(3012) 3503[13] 4252[8]

Cool Runnings (IRE) *Tom Dascombe* 57
2 gr c Dalakhani(IRE) Aguinaga (IRE) (Machiavellian (USA))
7208[3]

Cool Sea (IRE) *Nigel Tinkler* 38
2 br f Kheleyf(USA) Creekhaven (IRE) (Definite Article)
4173[8] 4681[4] 5169[7] 5799[10] 6164[15] 6556[7]

Cool Sky *William Knight* a82 74
3 b g Millkom Intersky High (USA) (Royal Anthem (USA))
1923[6] ◆ 2584[8] 3447[2] 4516[7] 5387[4] 6146[10] 6647[7] 7301[4] 7811[3] ◆ (8106) (8229)

Cool Wave *B Grizzetti* 99
3 bb f One Cool Cat(USA) Onda Chiara (ITY) (Dane Friendly)
1699a[6] 6726a[7]

Coplow *Richard Hannon* a62 82
3 ch f Manduro(GER) Anna Oleanda (IRE) (Old Vic)
2201[7] 3070[2] 3565[8] 4542[4] 5048[8]

Copper Canyon *J S Moore* a83 88
4 ch g Haafhd Deep Ravine (USA) (Gulch (USA))
(480) 570[4] ◆ 820[3] (1071) 1239[11] 1939[2]

Copper Dock (IRE) *T G McCourt* a84 76
8 b g Docksider(USA) Sundown (Polish Precedent (USA))
6270a[10]

Copper Falls *Brendan Powell* a56 64
3 b f Trade Fair Strat's Quest (Nicholas (USA))
1514[6] 2547[2] 3141[4] 3489[8] 4937[3] 5191[11] (5701a) 6003[10] 6585[RR] 7378[R]

Copper Leyf *Jeremy Gask* a37
2 ch c Kheleyf(USA) Silver Quest (Rainbow Quest (USA))
7931[7] 8230[4]

Copper Rag *Mark Usher* a39 18
2 ch c Kirkwall Pajada (Bertolini (USA))
7373[12] 7749[10] 8224[7]

Copper To Gold *Robin Bastiman* a29 13
3 ch f Avonbridge Faithful Beauty (IRE) (Last Tycoon)
7445[7] 7787[6]

Copperwood *Mark Johnston* a84 80
7 ch g Bahamian Bounty Sophielu (Rudimentary (USA))
205[6] (713) (900) 991[6] 1293[9] 1796[5] 1879[3] 2083[2] (2227) 2549[3] 2754[4] 2879[5] (3215) 3699[7] (4541) 5057[3] 5243[5] 5667[3] 5819[6] (6241) 6538[4] 6932[3] 7083[16]

Copp The Lot (USA) *Dean Ivory* 61
3 gr g Exchange Rate(USA) Argentum (USA) (Silver Deputy (CAN))
3732[10]

Coquet *Hughie Morrison* a79 110
3 b f Sir Percy One So Marvellous (Nashwan (USA))
(2410) 2658[6] 5518[6] 6482[3] 6899a[8]

Coral Sands (IRE) *Alan Swinbank* a49 58
4 b g Footstepsinthesand Daziyra (IRE) (Doyoun)
283[3] 457[3] 2227[3] 2593[7] 3353[7] 3939[6]

Coral Wave (IRE) *P J Prendergast* 105
3 b f Rock Of Gibraltar(IRE) Common Knowledge (Rainbow Quest (USA))
2101a[3]

Cordillera *Donald McCain* a56 56
4 ch m Araafa(IRE) Alexander Celebre (IRE) (Peintre Celebre (USA))
3449[3]

Core Element (IRE) *S Buggy* a84 84
5 b m Consolidator(USA) Millstream (USA) (Dayjur (USA))
6716a[13] 6854a[12] 7230a[5] 7680a[10]

Core Inflation (USA) *Teresa Pompay*
3 ch c Closing Argument(USA) J's Crafty Cat (USA) (Tabasco Cat (USA))
8100a[4]

Corlough Mountain *Paddy Butler* a37 46
8 ch g Inchinor Two Step (Mujtahid (USA))
200[10] 531[7]

Corn Maiden *Mark Rimmer* a49 50
3 b f Refuse To Bend(IRE) Namat (IRE) (Daylami (IRE))
195[8] 816[5] 1267[3] 1982[6] 2341[7] 6210[10] 6948[7] 7196[9] 7632[4] 8049[6]

Corn Snow (USA) *Mahmood Al Zarooni* 55
2 b c Raven's Pass(USA) Zofzig (USA) (Danzig (USA))
3074[8] 4938[5]

Cornucopia (FR) *E J O'Neill* a90 101
4 gr m Kaldounevees(FR) Cospicua (IRE) (High Estate)
83a[0]

Cornus *Alan McCabe* a66 83
10 ch g Inchinor Demerger (USA) (Distant View (USA))
5388[4] 5819[11] 6260[9] 7295[13] 7857[8] 8156[11] 8305[4]

Corporal Maddox *Ronald Harris* a91 96
5 b g Royal Applause Noble View (USA) (Distant View (USA))
1373[5] 2029[6] 2444[3] 3004[2] 3105[4] 3281[4] 3772[4] 4077[2] (4580) 4828[14] 5342[4] 6235[13] 6659[13] 7732[3] (7901) 8008[3] 8098[10]

Corporate Jungle (USA) *Chad C Brown* 111
4 bb h Giant's Causeway(USA) Lady Carson (USA) (Carson City (USA))
7571a[6]

Correct *K Borgel* a67 91
3 b f Oasis Dream Dusty Answer (Zafonic (USA))
716a[8]

Correggio *Richard Hannon* 79
2 ch c Bertolini(USA) Arian Da (Superlative)
4773[7] 5792[3] 6486[5]

Correspondent *Brian Meehan* a89 59
2 ch c Exceed And Excel(AUS) Indian Love Bird (Efisio)
6443[7] (7167) ◆ (7523)

Corrib (IRE) *Bryn Palling* a59 60
9 b m Lahib(USA) Montana Miss (IRE) (Earl Of Barking (IRE))
1908[5] 2364[9] 3137[4] 4817[12] 5266[2] 5935[4] 7015[6] 7496[11] 7620[3] 8241[3]

Corsage (USA) *N Clement* a97
3 gr f Exchange Rate(USA) Gingivere (USA) (Chester House (USA))
8300a[9]

Corsetry (USA) *Sir Henry Cecil* a80 78
3 b f Distorted Humor(USA) Lingerie (Shirley Heights)
1893[4] 2379[3] 2980[3] 3737[6] 5163[2] 5856[4]

Corton Lad *Keith Dalgleish* a62 55
2 b g Refuse To Bend(IRE) Kelucia (IRE) (Grand Lodge (USA))
3378[6] 3725[3] 6133[5] 6753[6] 6998[3] 7779[5] 7919[2] (7973)

Corvette *Michael Appleby* a68 62
4 b m Araafa(IRE) Clipper (Salse (USA))
97[5] 271[6] 446[2] 767[2] (937) 1338[4] 1588[7] 4831[4] (5173) 5637[8] 5891[5] 6838[11]

Cos I Can *Derek Shaw* a25 24
2 ch f Compton Place Blushing Sunrise (USA) (Cox's Ridge (USA))
4178[8] 4654[10] 5449[7] 6850[6] 7526[9]

Cos Im Cool *Robert Johnson*
2 ch f Three Valleys(USA) Evening Guest (FR) (Be My Guest (USA))
2631[13]

Cosimo de Medici *Hughie Morrison* a95 93
5 b g Medicean Wish (Danehill (USA))
2479[4] 3241[20] 6428[4] 7051[18] 7367[8]

Cosmic Chatter *David Barron* 98
2 b g Paris House Paradise Eve (Bahamian Bounty)
(2663) 3242[11] (5055) ◆ 5601[5]

Cosmic Dream *Garry Moss* 31
2 b g Refuse To Bend(IRE) Cosmic Case (Casteddu)
1911[9] 2667[6] 6473[7]

Cosmic Halo *Richard Fahey* a70 66
3 ch f Halling(USA) Cosmic Case (Casteddu)
1250[6] (2592) 3031[5] 4046[3] 6118[4] 7819[5] 8243[3]

Cosmic Moon *Richard Fahey* 72
4 b m Doyen(IRE) Cosmic Case (Casteddu)
1439[10] 1823[10] 2588[6] (2926) 3692[4] 4325[4] ◆ 4641[10] 5824[3] 6528[4] 7003[12]

Cosmic Sun *Richard Fahey* a68 67
6 b g Helissio(FR) Cosmic Case (Casteddu)
6018[12] 6668[9] 7396[17] 7672[11]

Cossack Prince *Laura Mongan* a42 26
7 b g Dubai Destination(USA) Danemere (IRE) (Danehill (USA))
6255[10] 8265[11] 8301[5]

Cote Reveur *David C Griffiths*
2 b f Croco Rouge(IRE) Reveur (Rossini (USA))
6237[9]

Cotes Du Rhone (IRE) *David Evans* a49 20
3 b g Catcher In The Rye(IRE) La Vie En Rouge (IRE) (College Chapel)
30[2] 217[3] 472[7] 998[5] 2113a[3]

Cotillion *Ian Williams* a81 94
6 b g Sadler's Wells(USA) Riberac (Efisio)
3502[10]

Cottam Donny *Mel Brittain* 71
4 ch g Doyen(IRE) Northern Bird (Interrex (CAN))
1135[3] 1917[2] ◆ 2692[2] 3021[5] 4714[5] 5226[8] 5547[6] 6258[5] (6561) 6638[16] 6785[4]

Cottam Stella *Mel Brittain* a39 54
4 br m Diktat Flower Breeze (USA) (Rahy (USA))
1383[13] 2046[6] 2981[12] 4348[8]

Cottesmore (USA) *Mark Johnston* a83 83
3 bb g Medaglia d'Oro(USA) Racing Heart (USA) (Fusaichi Pegasus (USA))
4259[7] 4464[2] 4882[6] 5293[2] (5541) 6193[4]

Cotton Dancer (IRE) *David Peter Nagle* 40
2 b f Kheleyf(USA) Dancing Guest (IRE) (Danehill Dancer (IRE))
3789[4]

Cottonfields (USA) *Heather Main* a58 32
6 rg g Maria's Mon(USA) Known Romance (USA) (Known Fact (USA))
2586[4] 3153[12] 3721[7] 3782[10]

Cotton Grass *Mark H Tompkins* a65 65
4 b m Medicean Astromancer (USA) (Silver Hawk (USA))
728[4] 1272[14] 2468[2] 3086[6] 3552[4] 3794[5]

Cotton King *Lady Herries* a84 78
5 b g Dubawi(IRE) Spinning The Yarn (Barathea (IRE))
810[6] (849) 872[4] 1421[5] 3162[6]

Cotton Trader (USA) *John Gosden* a81 55
3 b c Hard Spun(USA) Saytarra (USA) (Seeking The Gold (USA))
195[2] 324 [2] 642[2] 1001[3] 1206[6] (Dead)

Cougar Ridge (USA) *David Wachman* a88 101
2 bb c Johannesburg(USA) Wild As Elle (USA) (Elnadim (USA))
6078a[2] 6483[6] 7038a[5]

Could It Be Magic *Olivia Maylam* a77 76
5 b g Dubai Destination(USA) Lomapamar (Nashwan (USA))
329[4]

Couloir Extreme (IRE) *Gary Moore* a66 58
2 gr c Verglas(IRE) Chica Roca (USA) (Woodman (USA))
6572[9] 6947[4] 7707[4]

Counsel (IRE) *Sir Michael Stoute* a87 76
3 b g Dansili Kitty O'Shea (Sadler's Wells (USA))
1641[9] 2429[4] ◆ 2898[2] (3280)

Count Bertoni (IRE) *David O'Meara* a77 85
5 b g Bertolini(USA) Queen Sceptre (IRE) (Fairy King (USA))
1156[19] 1913[6] 2510[19] 2792[4] 3459[3] 3699[9] 5225[5] 5713[9] 6410[3]

Count Ceprano (IRE) *Lydia Pearce* a62 74
8 b g Desert Prince(IRE) Camerlata (Common Grounds)
843[3] 1000[2] 1106[4] 1533[3] 4722[12] 5323[9] 5636[7] 6690[8] 7058[7] (7982) 8241[5]

Count Curlin (USA) *Gerard Butler* a49
2 bb c Curlin(USA) Zappeuse (USA) (Kingmambo (USA))
7323[10]

Counterglow (IRE) *Mahmood Al Zarooni* a103 92
3 b g Echo Of Light Quintellina (Robellino (USA))
(754a) 873a[3] 2920[4] 6400[10]

Counterparty *Alan King* a41 56
4 b m Nayef(USA) Mistress Bankes (IRE) (Petardia)
546[4] 961[4]

Countess Comet (IRE) *Chris Bealby* a84 82
5 b m Medicean Countess Sybil (IRE) (Dr Devious (IRE))
501[7]

Countess Ferrama *William Haggas* 77
3 b f Authorized(IRE) Madame Dubois (Legend Of France (USA))
(1866) 3033[6]

Countess Lovelace *Pat Phelan* a51
2 b f Byron Muwasim (USA) (Meadowlake (USA))
8200[7] ◆

Counting House (IRE) *Jim Old* a68 56
9 ch g King's Best(USA) Inforapenny (Deploy)
7377[5]

Count Of Limonade (IRE) *A P O'Brien* 91
2 b c Duke Of Marmalade(IRE) Hoity Toity (Darshaan)
4377a[3]

Countrycraft *Sally Hall* a19 32
5 b g Pastoral Pursuits Turn Back (Pivotal)
284[6]

Country Love (FR) *Anar Balahuseynov* a84 60
5 b m Country Reel(USA) White Love (FR) (Northern Crystal)
5849a[9]

Countryman *Hughie Morrison* a74 58
2 b c Pastoral Pursuits Baileys Silver (USA) (Marlin (USA))
6444[7] 6977[4] (7304)

Country Music (FR) *P Van De Poele* a79 86
5 b h Country Reel(USA) Song Of Lark (GER) (Platini (GER))
93a[8]

Country Road (IRE) *Michael Appleby* a82 71
6 b g Montjeu(IRE) Souffle (Zafonic (USA))
213[2] 402[3] (721) 824[2] (1632)

Country Western *Charles Hills* 77
2 b c Oasis Dream Musical Horizon (USA) (Distant View (USA))
4340[3] 4803[11] 6330[6]

Countrywide Flame *John Quinn* a63 96
4 b g Haafhd Third Party (Terimon)
(6191) 7051[2]

Coup De Grace (IRE) *Pat Phelan* a59 63
3 b g Elusive City(USA) No Way (IRE) (Rainbows For Life (CAN))
1852[5] 2802[9] 3068[2] ◆ 3966[5] 4504[8] 5707[5] 8189[5]

Coup De Theatre (FR) *P Van De Poele* a105 112
3 ch c Gold Away(IRE) Storma (FR) (Starborough)
1408a[6] 2951a[6] 3681a[3]

Coupe De Ville (IRE) *Richard Hannon* 111
3 b c Clodovil(IRE) Fantastic Account (Fantastic Light (USA))
1468[5] 1856[5] 2110a[7] 2951a[3] 3640[2] 4760[9] (5064) 5594[6]

Coupland Lass (IRE) *Willie Musson* a62 59
4 b m Chineur(FR) Negria (IRE) (Al Hareb (USA))
838[8] 1004[4] 2467[4] 2804[10]

Courage (IRE) *Sir Michael Stoute* 87
3 b g Invincible Spirit(IRE) Mamonta (Fantastic Light (USA))
1450[6] 2143[2] 4410[2] 5006[6] 7016[2]

Courageous (IRE) *Milton Bradley* a92 95
6 ch g Refuse To Bend(IRE) Bella Bella (IRE) (Sri Pekan (USA))
871[3] ◆ 1141[5] 1438[5] 1828[5] 2289[5] 2488[16] 2704[15] 3612[5] 3822[13] 4231[5] 4367[9] 5035[3] 5486[7] 6005[4] 6226[8] 6303[4] 6610[3] 6837[7]

Courcy (FR) *J-C Rouget* a85
2 b c Mizzen Mast(USA) Insan Mala (IRE) (Bahhare (USA))
5471a[11]

Court Applause (IRE) *William Muir* a71 64
4 b g Royal Applause Forever Blue (Spectrum (IRE))
425[6] 497[2] (696) 1073[4] 2360[5] 2789[9] 4003[11] 4439[7] 6053[4]

Court Circle *Rune Haugen* 101
5 ch g Pivotal Noble Lady (Primo Dominie)
6091a[2]

Courtesy Call (IRE) *Mark Johnston* a88 93
3 br g Manduro(GER) Three Wrens (IRE) (Second Empire (IRE))
993[2] 1062[5] 1726[9] 2141[3] (2577) (2843) 3605[2] (4215) ◆ (4930) 5598[14] (6033) 6493[2]

Courtland Avenue (IRE) *Jonathan Portman* 70
3 b g Kodiac Chingford (IRE) (Redback)
1941[2] 3488[2] 4777[9] 5775[9] 7299[9]

Courtland King (IRE) *David Evans* a70 76
3 b g Baltic King Red Rabbit (Suave Dancer (USA))
1529[11] 2573[4] 3005[8] 3243[7]

Court Wing (IRE) *Richard Price* a52 58
6 b m Hawk Wing(USA) Nicely (IRE) (Bustino)
493[9]

Cour Valant *Noel Quinlan* 98
2 b c Bahamian Bounty Gee Kel (IRE) (Danehill Dancer (IRE))
4612[2] (5325) (6139)

Cousin Melchior (IRE) *John Gosden* a65 68
2 b c Kodiac Poetry Aloud (IRE) (Kheleyf (USA))
7306[6] 7517[4]

Covert Decree *Clive Cox* a71 88
4 ch m Proclamation(IRE) Armada Grove (Fleetwood (IRE))
1421[8] 3766[12] 6450[8] 6987[9]

Cowslip *Richard Hannon* a14 35
3 b f Tobougg(IRE) Forsythia (Most Welcome)
5299[8] 5795[13] 6582[13] 6930[8]

Coya (GER) *U Stoltefuss*
2 ch f Doyen(IRE) Cominales (IRE) (Primo Dominie)
5612a[9]

Cozy Tiger (USA) *Willie Musson* a70 48
7 gr g Hold That Tiger(USA) Cozelia (USA) (Cozzene (USA))
714[7] 2863[8] 3162[7] 3942[6]

Cozzetti (USA) *Dale Romans* a105 105
3 rg c Cozzene(USA) Lemon Drop Cello (USA) (Lemon Drop Kid (USA))
2299a[7] 5375a[6]

C P Joe (IRE) *Paul Green* a73 68
4 br g One Cool Cat(USA) Trinity Fair (Polish Precedent (USA))
332[4] 673[7]

Crabbies Ginger *Lisa Williamson* 49
4 ch g Needwood Blade Dazzling Quintet (Superlative)
2225[8] 2617[7] 3791[6] 4493[8] 6233[13]

Crabbies Gold (IRE) *Lisa Williamson* 53
4 ch g Sleeping Indian Sharpe's Lady (Prince Des Coeurs (USA))
2013[6] 3277[8] 8260[12]

Crackentorp *Tim Easterby* a91 103
7 b g Generous(IRE) Raspberry Sauce (Niniski (USA))
2253[3] (3163) 3625[2] 4111[9] 5600[17] 6031[8] 7396[20]

Crackerjack King (IRE) *Marco Botti* 118
4 rg h Shamardal(USA) Claba Di San Jore (IRE) (Barathea (IRE))
(2106a) 3880[5] 5377a[5]

Cracking Choice (IRE) *Michael Dods* a64 67
2 ch c Choisir(AUS) Champagne Cracker (Up And At 'Em)
2456[2] 3490[6] 4670[4] 5313[2] 5544[3] 6049[4] 6336[3] 7379[2]

Cracking Lass (IRE) *Richard Fahey* 104
5 b m Whipper(USA) Lady From Limerick (IRE) (Rainbows For Life (CAN))
5519[3] 6163[8] 6600[11] (7438)

Crackos (FR) *F Belmont* 65
2 gr g Sunday Break(JPN) Jenauraisjamaiscru (FR) (Kendor (FR))
3714a[6]

Crafty Cruiser (AUS) *Bryce Stanaway* 92
5 ch g Good Journey(USA) Sly One (NZ) (O'Reilly (NZ))
7783a[9]

Crafty Roberto *Noel Quinlan* a76 68
4 ch g Intikhab(USA) Mowazana (IRE) (Galileo (IRE))
2447[6]

Crafty Wonder (IRE) *David Evans* a43 28
2 b g Refuse To Bend(IRE) Crafty Fancy (IRE) (Intikhab (USA))
3506[11] 6188[5] 6501[11]

Cragganmore Creek *Dave Morris* a47 13
9 b g Tipsy Creek(USA) Polish Abbey (Polish Precedent (USA))
200[11] 2468[P]

Craniac *Frank Sheridan* a14 27
5 b g Iron Mask(USA) Ave Atque Vale (FR) (Most Welcome)
1420[10] 1716[10] 3079[12] 3544[12]

Crassula *Terry Clement* a77 89
4 b m Cacique(IRE) Neath (Rainbow Quest (USA))
2706[13]

Cravat *Ed de Giles* 92
3 b c Dubai Destination(USA) Crinolette (IRE) (Sadler's Wells (USA))
1221[9] 1604[5] 1888[10] 2490[6] 2910[8] 3160[4] 3393[14] 3977[9] 4517[4] 4819[10] 6171[6]

Crazy Beloved (IRE) *Robert Collet* 36
2 b c Acclamation Tender Is Thenight (IRE) (Barathea (IRE))
3928a[7]

Crazy Chris *Milton Bradley* a52 53
7 b m Ishiguru(USA) Ellopassoff (Librate)
669[8] 842[8] 1002[11] 2607[6] 3137[12] 4536[12]

Crazy Too (IRE) *David Simcock* a65 67
3 b f Invincible Spirit(IRE) Reform Act (USA) (Lemon Drop Kid (USA))
4425[4] 6095[2] 6765[4] 7061[3] 7667[4]

Creative Cause (USA) *Mike Harrington* a120
3 rg c Giant's Causeway(USA) Dream Of Summer (USA) (Siberian Summer (USA))
1872a[5] 2299a[3]

Crecy *Y Fouin* 105
3 b f Refuse To Bend(IRE) In A Silent Way (IRE) (Desert Prince (IRE))
1434a[2] 2532a[5] 3682a[8]

Creditas *Jedd O'Keeffe* 20
2 b f Avonbridge Jade Pet (Petong)
2631[12]

Credit Swap *Michael Wigham* a84 98
7 b g Diktat Locharia (Wolfhound (USA))
6674[13] 7030[2] 7407[9] 7556[2]

Creme Anglaise *Michael Bell* 97
4 b m Motivator Reading Habit (USA) (Half A Year (USA))
1848[3] 2228[3] 2655[11] 6595a[7]

Cresta Star *Richard Hannon* a77 84
3 b f Teofilo(IRE) Fleet Hill (IRE) (Warrshan (USA))
2194[4] 2431[2] (2942) 4543[2] 4741[15] 5451[S] 5973[6] 6492[7] 6933[4]

Crew Cut (IRE) *Jeremy Gask* a83 85
4 gb g Acclamation Carabine (USA) (Dehere (USA))
1827[4] (2870) 3394[3] ◆ 4300[3] 4775[6] 5362[7] 6800[4] 8188[4]

Cried For You (IRE) *Tim Easterby* 58
3 b f Moss Vale(IRE) Baywood (Emarati (USA))
1521[11] 1843[17] 3357[9]

Crimea (IRE) *David Nicholls* a83 91
6 b g Kheleyf(USA) Russian Countess (USA) (Nureyev (USA))
1237[8] 2674[8] 2861[3] 3608[11] 3707[2] 4454[8] 4680[7] 5058[3] 6685[6]

Crimson Cheer (USA) *Brian Meehan*
3 b f Van Nistelrooy(USA) Yousefia (USA) (Danzig (USA))
2145[12] 2665[9]

Crimson Knot (IRE) *Alan Berry* 86
4 b m Red Ransom(USA) Green Minstrel (FR) (Green Tune (USA))
1236[5] 1875[3] (2037) 2230[3] 2596[9] 3027[2] 3336[2] 3524[5] 3903[3] 4133[3] (4430) 5539[7] 6234[4] 6525[7] 6755[7]

Crimson Monarch (USA) *Peter Hiatt* a51 51
8 b g Red Ransom(USA) Tolltally Light (USA) (Majestic Light (USA))
1792[9] 2391[9] 2769[2] 2851[2] 3143[5] 3468[4] 4156[3] 4244[7] 7528[8] 7800[7] 8067[U]

Crimson Queen *Roy Brotherton* a67 80
5 ch m Red Ransom(USA) Rainbow Queen (Rainbow Quest (USA))
445[6] 3435[4] (4493) (4758) 4903[2] 5502[16] 6226[15] 8285[9]

Cri Na Mara (IRE) *Mark Michael McNiff* a59 32
4 b m Tagula(IRE) Northweststar (IRE) (Revoque (IRE))
544[4] 4592[6] 7969[8] 8210[7]

Cristal Gem *Alan McCabe* a72 67
3 ch f Cadeaux Genereux Desert Cristal (IRE) (Desert King (IRE))
2846[13] 5132[6] 5426[8]

Cristaliyev *John Flint* a65 59
4 b g Fasliyev(USA) Desert Cristal (IRE) (Desert King (IRE))
205[4] 361[5] 422[5] 598[3] 732[7] 818[10] 1628[3] 1768[4] 2366[10] 4890[11] 5660[7] (6737) 6926[4]

Cristoforo Colombo (USA) *A P O'Brien* 111
2 b c Henrythenavigator(USA) La Traviata (USA) (Johannesburg (USA))
3240[3] 3649a[2] 5136a[S] 7049[4]

Critical Moment (USA) *F Nass* a87 107
5 b g Aptitude(USA) Rouwaki (USA) (Miswaki (USA))
420a[12] 587a[12]

Critical Point *Sir Mark Prescott Bt* a73 64
3 ch g Pivotal Finlaggan (Be My Chief (USA))
2802[10] 3275[3] 3907[9] (5021) 5266[6] 5989[4] (6305) (7062) ◆

Crius (IRE) *Richard Hannon* 110
3 b c Heliostatic(IRE) Fearless Flyer (IRE) (Brave Act)
1470[2] 2524a[6] 3295[10] 4012[6]

Crockefeller (USA) *Patricia Farro*
4 bb g Outflanker(USA) Ritzy Affair (USA) (Sword Dance)
8278a[10]

Crocodile Bay (IRE) *Richard Guest* a59 57
9 b g Spectrum(IRE) Shenkara (IRE) (Night Shift (USA))
14[6] 113[2] 153[2] (305) 370[8] (422) 550[9] 729[7] 926[10] 1074[4] 1178[9] 1283[9] 1801[3] 2090[5] 3053[5] 3332[6] 3455[4] 4406[9] 4783[9] 5015[11] 5459[8] 5917[11] 6308[9]

Croeso Mawr *John Spearing* 77
6 ch m Bertolini(USA) Croeso-I-Cymru (Welsh Captain)
2385[5] ◆ 3096[2] 5148[2] (5262) (5657) (5998)

Croftamie *Tracy Waggott* a71 71
3 b f Selkirk(USA) Embraced (Pursuit Of Love)
635[2] 2848[6] 3728[5] (4912) 6263[7] 6885[2]

Croisultan (IRE) *D K Weld* a83 108
6 ch g Refuse To Bend(IRE) Zoudie (Ezzoud (IRE))
(1040a) 1640a[2] 2777a[10] 6268a[10]

Croix Rouge (USA) *Ralph Smith* a57 60
10 b g Chester House(USA) Rougeur (USA) (Blushing Groom (FR))
5509[7]

Cromwell Rose (IRE) *John Weymes* 50
2 ch f Haafhd Bonny Rose (Zaha (CAN))
3208[11] 3490[8] 4344[13] 4767[9] 5799[9] 6115[2] 6435[4]

Crop Report (USA) *William Haggas* 84
2 bb c Medaglia d'Oro(USA) Amarillo (USA) (Crafty Prospector (USA))
6872[7] (7333)

Croquembouche (IRE) *Ed de Giles* 83
3 b g Acclamation Wedding Cake (IRE) (Groom Dancer (USA))
2428[10] 3347[7] (4511) 5197[5] 5386[2] 5796[2] 6376[8] 6819[14]

Crossley *Geoffrey Oldroyd* 65
3 ch g Monsieur Bond(IRE) Dispol Diamond (Sharpo)
2095[8] 2689[10] 6925[6] 7600[4]

Cross My Heart *William Haggas* 71
2 b f Sakhee's Secret Sacre Coeur (Compton Place)
5449[5] 6071[3] (6404)

Cross Of Lorraine (IRE) *Chris Grant* a38 72
9 b g Pivotal My-Lorraine (IRE) (Mac's Imp (USA))
1298[12] 1954[9] 2538[14] 3209[4] 3442[9] 4085[6] 4593[2] 4956[9] 5740[6] 6106[10] 6786[11]

Cross Pattee (IRE) *John Gosden* a74 53
2 b f Oasis Dream Victoria Cross (IRE) (Mark Of Esteem (IRE))
2938[6] 3282[3] 4701[14] 5425[4] 6541[8]

Cross The Boss (IRE) *Ben Haslam* a63 60
5 b g Cape Cross(IRE) Lady Salsa (IRE) (Gone West (USA))
4715[6] 5824[10] (6106) 6941[5] 7256[8]

Crown Choice *Paul Midgley* a86 102
7 b g King's Best(USA) Belle Allemande (CAN) (Royal Academy (USA))
871[10] 1157[18] 1523[6] 1558[15] 2697[9] 3336[8] 4690[13] 6495[12] 6939[10] 7202[4] 7484[8]

Crown Counsel (IRE) *Mark Johnston* a88 98
4 b h Invincible Spirit(IRE) Virgin Hawk (USA) (Silver Hawk (USA))
962[5] 1128[21] 3306[5] 3667[3] 4557[8] 4689[11] 4828[7] ◆ 5186[2] 5517[5] 5914[3] 6494[4] 6601[5] 7069[2] 7210[4] 7493[3]

Crown Dependency (IRE) *David Evans* a98 99
3 b g Acclamation Top Row (Observatory (USA))
1032[6] 2022[8] 2660[11] 3311[6] 4705[4] 5034[5] 5347[5] 5975[11] 6500[8] 7015[12] 7703[3] 7748[F]

Crowning Star (IRE) *Gay Kelleway* a74 75
3 b g Royal Applause Dossier (Octagonal (NZ))
230[3] 479[2] 619[2] 683[2] (766) (1365) 1582[3]

Cruachan (IRE) *Ian Semple* a23 54
3 b g Authorized(IRE) Calico Moon (USA) (Seeking The Gold (USA))
1385[6] 1867[8] 6527[3] 7062[11]

Crucis Abbey (IRE) *Mark Brisbourne* a70 62
4 b g Acclamation Golden Ribes (USA) (Charismatic (USA))
3559[14] 4240[4] 4993[13] 7222[5] 7385[9] 7671[6] 8111[9] 8291[4]

Cruck Realta *Mick Channon* 88
2 b f Sixties Icon Wansdyke Lass (Josr Algarhoud (IRE))
2407[2] 2917[3] (3010) 3368[2] (3662)

Cruel Summer (FR) *F Vermeulen* a69 83
3 gr f Nombre Premier Cruelle (USA) (Irish River (FR))
17a[6] 6752a[0] 8277a[7]

Cruiser *William Muir* a90 91
4 b g Oasis Dream Good Girl (IRE) (College Chapel)
1510[17] (1924) 2500[12] 3348[10] 3767[3] 4689[19] 5914[6] 6036[5] 6538[5] 7163[6]

Cruise Tothelimit (IRE) *Ian Williams* a60 84
4 b g Le Vie Dei Colori Kiva (Indian Ridge)
2084[4] 2748[2] 2789[5] (3477) 4146[2] (4292) 4690[5] 4999[2] (6234) 6820[10]

Crunched *Tim Pitt* a84 38
5 b g Dubai Destination(USA) Amica (Averti (IRE))
207[2] 332[3] (625) 2180[17] 2936[11] 3355[5]

Crusade (USA) *A P O'Brien* a103 113
3 bb c Mr Greeley(USA) La Traviata (USA) (Johannesburg (USA))
2513a[11]

Cry For The Moon (USA) *J H Culloty* a70 87
6 b g Street Cry(IRE) Kafaf (USA) (Zilzal (USA))
6066a[12] 7051[15] 7584a[12]

Cry Fury *Roger Charlton* a86 101
4 b g Beat Hollow Cantanta (Top Ville)
2655[8]

Cryptic Choice (IRE) *Charles Hills* a70 74
3 b g Johannesburg(USA) Royal Fupeg (USA) (Fusaichi Pegasus (USA))
1068[2]

Crystal Cove *Tim Easterby* a64 56
2 gr c Dubawi(IRE) Cristal Clear (IRE) (Clodovil (IRE))
1277[3] 2138[5] 2456[4] 2873[4] 3936[4]

Crystal Gal (IRE) *Lucy Wadham* a94 103
5 b m Galileo(IRE) Park Crystal (IRE) (Danehill (USA))
622[9] 1041a[7] 6877[12] 7128[5] 7689[14]

Crystal High *Mme J Bidgood* 75
4 b m High Chaparral(IRE) Park Crystal (IRE) (Danehill (USA))
5118a[0]

Crystal Mist *Harry Dunlop* 67
2 bg f Dalakhani(IRE) Snow Crystal (IRE) (Kingmambo (USA))
6873[14]

Crystal Monarch (IRE) *Sir Henry Cecil* a23 59
3 b g Dalakhani(IRE) Top Crystal (IRE) (Sadler's Wells (USA))
3420[4] 3786[8] 4465[7]

Crystal Peaks *James Given* a60 60
2 b f Intikhab(USA) Crozon (Peintre Celebre (USA))
5977[9] 6790[11] 7191[5] 7708[7] (7919) 8112[5] 8289[3]

Crystal Rock (IRE) *Tony Coyle* a24 76
7 br g Rock Of Gibraltar(IRE) State Crystal (IRE) (High Estate)
6045[6] 6340[5] 7353[9]

Crystal Sky (IRE) *Natalie Lloyd-Beavis* a63 63
4 b m Bachelor Duke(USA) Fen Style (IRE) (Desert Style (IRE))
3713[7] 4158[13] 4817[7] 5657[14] 6434[9]

Crystifou (FR) *Mme V Seignoux* a70 81
5 ch g Le Fou(IRE) Crystivoli (FR) (Northern Crystal)
7320a[8]

Ctappers *Mick Channon* a65 70
3 b g Imperial Dancer Stride Home (Absalom)
472[2] 709[3] 847[3] 983[2] 1591[5] 2424[9] 3087[9] 4918[5] (5264) 6474[4] 6738[4] 7454[2] 7972[5]

Cubanita *Ralph Beckett* 105
3 ch f Selkirk(USA) Caribana (Hernando (FR))
1973[3] 2522a[9] 6576[2] ◆ (7688)

Cuban Tash *Tom Dascombe* a31
2 b c Exceed And Excel(AUS) Crinkle (IRE) (Distant Relative)
6175[11] 7198[8]

Cubism *Anthony Middleton* a47 47
6 b g Sulamani(IRE) Diagonale (IRE) (Darshaan)
3077[6] 4004[6] 7381[9] 7629[9]

Cuckoo Rock (IRE) *Jonathan Portman* a54 67
5 b g Refuse To Bend(IRE) Ringmoor Down (Pivotal)
2009[2] 2389[4] 3073[2] (3220) 4843[7] 7301[5]

Cucuma (FR) *P Bary* 89
2 b f Invincible Spirit(IRE) Cumin (USA) (Fusaichi Pegasus (USA))
4118a[4] 4632a[5] 7430a[6]

Cufflink *Rae Guest* a75 78
3 b f Rail Link Fred's Dream (Cadeaux Genereux)
2050[2] 2941[7] 3461[2] (5805) (6798)

Cuisine (IRE) *Andrew Balding* a72 74
2 b g Holy Roman Emperor(IRE) Samorra (IRE) (In The Wings)
1886[10] 2376[8] (2868) 3138[6] 4804[10] 5236[6] 5886[2] 6487[16] 7220[5] 7462[5]

Cul Baire (IRE) *J S Bolger* a85 76
4 ch g King's Best(USA) Voronova (IRE) (Sadler's Wells (USA))
7852a[4]

Cumbrian Craic *Tim Easterby* 76
2 b g Pastoral Pursuits Bollin Janet (Sheikh Albadou)
(1651) 2181[8] 2688[5] 4951[8] 5544[4] 6130[8]

Cuore (IRE) *Jamie Osborne* a59
3 b g Singspiel(IRE) Miss Trish (IRE) (Danetime (IRE))
324[6] 464[3] 683[4] 727[3]

Curacao *Amanda Perrett* a21 32
6 br g Sakhee(USA) Bourbonella (Rainbow Quest (USA))
3962[12] 4606[10] 5051[4]

Curia Regis *David Marnane* a78 73
3 b c Exceed And Excel(AUS) Court Lane (USA) (Machiavellian (USA))
7229a[4]

Curl (IRE) *Richard Hannon* 69
2 b f Duke Of Marmalade(IRE) Fringe (In The Wings)
2234[5] 2450[3] 2917[6] 5484[6] 7364[5]

Curl Cat (USA) *Thomas Cleary* a71 73
6 b g Tale Of The Cat(USA) Charade Queen (USA) (A.P. Indy (USA))
775a[12]

Curlew (IRE) *Chris Down* a38 60
6 b g Cape Cross(IRE) Billbill (USA) (Storm Cat (USA))
961[5] 1310[12]

Curly Come Home *Chris Wall* 73
3 b f Notnowcato Cuyamaca (IRE) (Desert King (IRE))
1414[5] 2424[6] (3088) 3543[7] 4005[3] 5219[3]

Curly Wee (IRE) *David Wachman* 81
2 b f Excellent Art Pietra Dura (Cadeaux Genereux)
6078a[8]

Curren Chan (JPN) *Takayuki Yasuda* 120
5 gr m Kurofune(USA) Spring Ticket (JPN) (Tony Bin)
8041a[7]

Curro Perote (FR) *L A Urbano-Grajales* a95 86
5 gr g Smadoun(FR) First Choice (FR) (Exit To Nowhere (USA))
5118a[2] 7985a[5]

Curzon Line *Mahmood Al Zarooni* a92 73
3 b g Dubawi(IRE) Polska (USA) (Danzig (USA))
1825[2] (2150) (2813)

Cushion *John Gosden* 80
2 b f Galileo(IRE) Attraction (Efisio)
4818[7] 5902[3] 6790[2]

Custom Cut (IRE) *George J Kent* a68 107
3 b g Notnowcato Polished Gem (IRE) (Danehill (USA))
4692a[3] 4833a[5] 6917a[5]

Custom House (IRE) *John E Long* a70 67
4 b g Tale Of The Cat(USA) L'Acajou (CAN) (Gulch (USA))
88[12] 353[6] 425[9] 972[10] 1070[5] 1608[4] (1768) 2466[8] 2847[2] 6585[10] 6982[13] 7106[6] 7504[6] 7816[9]

Cut Across (IRE) *Nick Littmoden* a87 77
4 b g Cape Cross(IRE) Incise (Dr Fong (USA))
(524) 2360[2] ◆ 4530[6] 6824[6] (7360) 7742[4] 7936[2] 8188[3] (8306) ◆

Cut And Thrust (IRE) *Mark Wellings* a73 62
6 b g Haafhd Ego (Green Desert (USA))
(39) 262[5] 713[7] 1050[8] ◆

Cuthbert (IRE) *Michael Attwater* a56 75
5 ch g Bertolini(USA) Tequise (IRE) (Victory Note (USA))
765[8] 1050[14] 1628[9] 2365[9] 3152[14] 4240[7] 5049[9] 8039[6] 8298[11]

Cut No Ice (IRE) *Paul Cole* a75 74
2 gr f Verglas(IRE) Limpopo (Green Desert (USA))
2783[7] ◆ 3783[3] 4701[11] 5267[3] (5854) 7164[4]

Cut The Cackle (IRE) *Violet M Jordan* a69 70
6 b m Danetime(IRE) Alexander Anapolis (IRE) (Spectrum (IRE))
312[2] (424) 526[11] 904[7] 970[5] 1084[3] ◆ 1193[4] 1609[8] 1638[8] 2171[2] 2362[4] (2466) 2750[5] 2840[3] (3026) 3249[2] 3495[7] 4085[5] 4407[8] 6961[17] 7486[9] 7670[12] 7815[9] 8107[7]

Cutting It Fine (IRE) *Jeremy Noseda* a66 17
3 b g Iffraaj Limit (IRE) (Barathea (IRE))
182[8] 350[4] ◆ 737[9] 3347[11]

Cwmni *Bryn Palling* a65 66
6 b m Auction House(USA) Sontime (Son Pardo)
45[6] (334) 633[4] 929[3] 1425[10] 1634[11]

Cyclone *Richard Hannon* 53
2 b c Teofilo(IRE) Ascot Cyclone (USA) (Rahy (USA))
6204[9]

Cyflymder (IRE) *David C Griffiths* a74 78
6 b g Mujadil(USA) Nashwan Star (IRE) (Nashwan (USA))
13[10] 115[7] 447[2] 550[3] (593) (761) 1108[4] 1384[4] 1796[4] 1823[2] 2173[2] 3559[4] (4042) 4469[2] (4769) 4868[5] 6239[5] 6934[7] 7247[6] 7464[8] 8308[3]

Cymeriad *Michael Easterby* a56 41
2 ch f Choisir(AUS) Danifah (IRE) (Perugino (USA))
2135[2] 2873[6] 3747[8] 4545[15] 4651[6] 5108[3] 5424[9] 5806[2] 6644[7] 7056[2] 7463[6] 7745[4] 8108[8]

Cynthia Calhoun *Clive Cox* a65 69
3 b f Exceed And Excel(AUS) The Jotter (Night Shift (USA))
1705[4] 2422[3] 3044[5] 4647[8] 5130[2] 6402[4] 7395[8]

Cyril The Squirrel *Karen George* a71 66
8 b g Cyrano De Bergerac All Done (Northern State (USA))
3659[8] 4295[7] (5193) 5657[2] 6275[2] 6801[5] 7115[4] 7495[4]

Cyrus Sod *Ed Dunlop* a76 78
3 b g Nayef(USA) Tahirah (Green Desert (USA))
1182[4] 1606[2] 2126[4] 3003[2] 3430[3] 4254[6] 6843[5] 7269[4]

Daaree (IRE) *Saeed Bin Suroor* a77 72
2 b c Teofilo(IRE) Mawaakeb (USA) (Diesis)
4773[9] (6188) (6972)

Dabirsim (FR) *C Ferland* 120
3 b c Hat Trick(JPN) Rumored (USA) (Royal Academy (USA))
1408a[2] 2110a[6]

Daddy Long Legs (USA) *A P O'Brien* a115 114
3 ch c Scat Daddy(USA) Dreamy Maiden (USA) (Meadowlake (USA))
(1145a) 1872a[P] 2514a[4] 5375a[8] 6063a[6]

Daddy Nose Best (USA) *Steven Asmussen* a112 106
3 b c Scat Daddy(USA) Follow Your Bliss (USA) (Thunder Gulch (USA))
1872a[10] 2299a[9]

Daddyow *Terry Clement* a70 25
4 b g Indesatchel(IRE) Generous Share (Cadeaux Genereux)
1278[6] 1722[11] 3392[9] 3620[8]

Daddy Warbucks (IRE) *David Nicholls* a75 81
3 b g Multiplex Skerries (IRE) (Dr Fong (USA))
(1058) 1241[6] 2336[8] 2689[6] 3575[2] (3938) (4397) 4830[2] (5170) 5736[4] 6240[2] 7032[5]

Dado Mush *Terry Clement* a37 42
9 b g Almushtarak(IRE) Princess Of Spain (King Of Spain)
7[11] 109[5]

Da Do Run Run *Brian Meehan* 78
2 b g Sixties Icon Fascinatin Rhythm (Fantastic Light (USA))
5976[3] ◆ 6872[13]

Dafeef *Doug Watson* a96 112
5 b g Medicean Almahab (USA) (Danzig (USA))
419a[8]

Daffyd *Kevin Ryan* 62
3 b g Green Desert(USA) Ffestiniog (IRE) (Efisio)
2501[12] 4293[7] 4715[12]

Daffydowndilly *Hughie Morrison* a77 71
4 b m Oasis Dream Art Eyes (USA) (Halling (USA))
2555[3] 3247[2] 4533[7] (4986) 5983[5] 6302[6] 6950[4] (7892) 8252[4]

Dagda Mor (ITY) *S Botti* 113
5 b h Martino Alonso(IRE) Bagnolese (ITY) (Cape Cross (IRE))
7288a[2] 7697a[5]

Daghash *Clive Brittain* 83
3 b c Tiger Hill(IRE) Zibet (Kris)
1468[9] 5101[6] 5451[2] 5820[4] (6348) 6677[4]

Daghashah *Clive Brittain*
3 b f Authorized(IRE) Bunting (Shaadi (USA))
2768[12] 6409[6]

Dahab Gold (IRE) *Jane Chapple-Hyam* a64 31
3 gr f Clodovil(IRE) Desert Alchemy (IRE) (Green Desert (USA))
3312[8] 3732[9]

Dairam (USA) *John Dunlop* 53
2 b c Jazil(USA) Tarteel (USA) (Bahri (USA))
7330[11]

Daisie Cutter *Lydia Pearce* a53 56
2 b f Tobougg(IRE) Bowled Out (GER) (Dansili)
4433[6] 5485[3] 5912[3] 6583[6] 7410[5]

Daisy Daze *David Evans* a16
4 ch m Dr Fong(USA) Halcyon Daze (Halling (USA))
1340[4]

Daisy Mountain (IRE) *J A Nash* a66 66
5 gr m Chineur(FR) Whitershadeofpale (IRE) (Definite Article)
7732[5]

Daivika (USA) *P Bary* 73
2 b f Dynaformer(USA) Divine Proportions (USA) (Kingmambo (USA))
6751a[3]

Dakota Canyon (IRE) *Richard Fahey* a78 76
3 b g Rock Of Gibraltar(IRE) Dakota Sioux (IRE) (College Chapel)
4075[5] 5802[7] 7520[4] 7986[8] 8259[2] ◆

Daktani *Markus Klug* 96
2 ch c Kallisto(GER) Diacada (GER) (Cadeaux Genereux)
7091a[6]

Dalarna (GER) *W Hickst* 102
4 b m Dashing Blade Daily Mail (GER) (Konigsstuhl (GER))
3653a[9]

Dalaway (IRE) *Mick Channon* 50
2 gr f Dalakhani(IRE) In The Limelight (IRE) (Sadler's Wells (USA))
6117[11] 6791[11]

Dalayir (FR) *Gary Moore* 15
5 gr g Tiger Hill(IRE) Dalataya (IRE) (Sadler's Wells (USA))
2393[12] 2997[7]

Dalgig *Henry Candy* 75
2 b c New Approach(IRE) Bright Halo (IRE) (Bigstone (IRE))
6486[3] ◆

Dalhaan (USA) *Luke Dace* a78 42
7 b g Fusaichi Pegasus(USA) Khazayin (USA) (Bahri (USA))
963[5] 3373[18]

Dalhousie Lassie *James Unett* 33
2 b f Indesatchel(IRE) Miss Mirasol (Sheikh Albadou)
2047[8] 7433[8]

Daliamoon (FR) *F Lemercier* 82
5 b g Daliapour(IRE) Flying To The Moon (FR) (Sicyos (USA))
7701a[0]

Daliance (IRE) *Tom Dascombe* a90 83
3 ch g Dalakhani(IRE) Everlasting Love (Pursuit Of Love)
1250[5] 1703[2] 2428[9] 3736[4] 4254[5] 4714[2] ◆ (6181) ◆ 6441[5] 7195[3] 7487[4]

Dali's Lover (IRE) *Charles Hills* 66
2 b f Excellent Art Hendrina (IRE) (Daylami (IRE))
3783[7] 5550[4] 6607[2]

Dalkala (USA) *A De Royer-Dupre* 112
3 b f Giant's Causeway(USA) Daltaya (FR) (Anabaa (USA))
(2156a) 3203a[5] 5116a[3] (6899a) 7431a[5]

Dalkova *Richard Hannon* a32 95
3 b f Galileo(IRE) Dalasyla (IRE) (Marju (IRE))
2734[4] 3507[2] (4366) 5834[11] 6379[7]

Dalmo *Gary Moore* a59 64
3 b g Dalakhani(IRE) Morina (USA) (Lyphard (USA))
84[12] 709[5] 762[2] 1267[4] 2625[5] 3088[4] 3621[9] 5577[4] 5989[9]

Damascus Symphony *James Bethell* a21 70
4 b m Pastoral Pursuits Syrian Queen (Slip Anchor)
1640[8] 1952[7] 2842[5] 3310[6] 3728[4] 6626[12]

Dam Beautiful *Kevin Ryan* 99
3 b f Sleeping Indian Nellie Melba (Hurricane Sky (AUS))
1457[10] (1877) 2028[5] 2691[2] 3165[15] 4063[13]

Dame Claire (NZ) *Pat Carey* 102
5 b m Danehill Dancer(IRE) Lovely Actress (FR) (Kaldoun (FR))
7560a[5]

Dame Nellie Melba *Mark Johnston* 43
2 gr f Aussie Rules(USA) Scandalette (Niniski (USA))
7329[11] 7636[5]

Dame Shirley *J W Hills* 48
3 ch f Haafhd Welsh Diva (Selkirk (USA))
2273[13] 4001[8]

Damian One *Joseph Tuite* a55 52
2 ch g Indian Haven Emerald Storm (USA) (Diesis)
5303[13] 6796[12] 7592[7]

Damika (IRE) *David Brown* a87 94
9 ch g Namid Emly Express (IRE) (High Estate)
1157[13] 1885[20] 2488[14] (3078) ◆ 3183[6] 4086[10] 4337[5] 4629[4] 5368[4] 5663[10] 6767[5] 7295[5] 7595[3] 7730[9] 7928[6] 8143[5]

Dampierre *A De Mieulle* a87 82
3 b c Dubawi(IRE) Legend House (FR) (Grand Lodge (USA))
5473a[4]

Danadana (IRE) *Luca Cumani* a73 113
4 b h Dubawi(IRE) Zeeba (IRE) (Barathea (IRE))
1854[8] (2248) (2773) 4684[9] (5492)

Danafisiak (IRE) *Frank Sheridan* a32
3 b c Stardan(IRE) Afisiak (Efisio)
107[7]

Danaher *George Margarson* a45
5 ch g Where Or When(IRE) Quirkie (IRE) (Revoque (IRE))
65[4] 300[4]

Dana's Present *George Baker* a77 59
3 ch g Osorio(GER) Euro Empire (USA) (Bartok (IRE))
1725[6] 2374[5] 4490[4] 4981[2] 5764[3] (6152) 6690[3] ◆ (6774) ◆ (6968)

Danat Al Atheer *William Haggas* 70
2 ch f Shamardal(USA) Height Of Vanity (IRE) (Erhaab (USA))
6153[4] (6781)

Danbrook (IRE) *George Moore*
4 ch g Danroad(AUS) Pip'n Judy (IRE) (Pips Pride)
581[8]

Dance And Dance (IRE) *Ed Vaughan* a108 116
6 b g Royal Applause Caldy Dancer (IRE) (Soviet Star (USA))
144a[6] 591a[11] 2656[2] 3166[3] (4248) 4822[3] 6300a[5] 6882[4] 7558[7]

Dance Company *William Knight* a93 81
3 b f Aussie Rules(USA) Corps De Ballet (IRE) (Fasliyev (USA))
(1736) ◆ 2272[13] 3085[4] (4647) (4933) 5980[12] 6375[6] 7502[3] 7809[11]

Dance Express (IRE) *Clive Cox* a79
3 b f Rail Link Swingsky (IRE) (Indian Ridge)
(7719)

Dance For Georgie *Ben Haslam* a35 70
3 ch f Motivator Chetwynd (IRE) (Exit To Nowhere (USA))
358[9] 2673[2] (4771) ◆ (5036)

Dance For Livvy (IRE) *Robin Dickin* a70 63
4 br m Kodiac Dancing Steps (Zafonic (USA))
521[2] 6691[12] 7077[13]

Danceintothelight *Micky Hammond* a60 69
5 gr g Dansili Kali (Linamix (FR))
1297[4] 1598[5]

Dance King *David Lanigan* 67
2 ch c Danehill Dancer(IRE) One So Wonderful (Nashwan (USA))
7333[5]

Dance Moves *A Fabre* 109
4 b h Dansili Dance Routine (Sadler's Wells (USA))
1971a[4] 2744a[4] 7284a[4]

Dance Off (IRE) *Richard Fahey* 59
2 b f Tagula(IRE) Glamorous Lady (IRE) (Galileo (IRE))
4173[6] 4825[9] 5168[2] 6156[9]

Dance The Rain *Bryan Smart* a81 84
3 b f Rock Of Gibraltar(IRE) Antediluvian (Air Express (IRE))
1477[2] ◆ 2076[2] 2452[6] 3064[7] 4135[6] 5314[6] 7203[3]

Dance To Destiny *K F Clutterbuck* a23
4 ch m Carnival Dancer Java Dawn (IRE) (Fleetwood (IRE))
2858[12]

Dance With Dragons (IRE) *Paul Cole* 77
2 b c Namid Duck Over (Warning)
3916[4] 4222[3] (4792) 5591[2] (8276a)

Dance With Her (AUS) *David Brideoake & Bahri Feek* 105
6 b m Al Maher(AUS) Dance Hit (NZ) (Tights (USA))
7073a[10]

Dance With Me (IRE) *Jonathan Geake* 73
3 b g Danehill Dancer(IRE) Perpetual Time (Sadler's Wells (USA))
1138[10] 2941[3] 3630[7] 5237[8] 5796[13]

Danceyourselfdizzy (IRE) *Phil McEntee* a58 63
4 b g Danehill Dancer(IRE) Gamra (IRE) (Green Desert (USA))
1095[6] 1310[10] 1628[7] 2013[7] 2627[7] 2845[8] 3051[2] 3712[9] 5216[8] 5459[9]

Danchai *William Haggas* 90
3 gr g Authorized(IRE) Scarlet Empire (IRE) (Red Ransom (USA))
(6527) 7082[5] ◆

Dancheur (IRE) *Mrs K Burke* a66 82
3 ch f Chineur(FR) Daneville (IRE) (Danetime (IRE))
1252[5] 1709[2] 2375[2] (2795) 3762[7] 4497[2] 5326[3] 6406[6]

Dancing All Night *Mme J Hendriks* 53
4 b m Iceman Sociable (Danehill (USA))
15a[0]

Dancing Chief (IRE) *Alan Jarvis* a43
2 ch c Fracas(IRE) Dance Fontaine (IRE) (Danehill Dancer (IRE))
3733[10] 5742[10] 7008[6]

Dancing Dynamite (GER) *S Cerulis* 86
4 b h Auenadler(GER) Donatio (IRE) (Royal Academy (USA))
7551a[6]

Dancing Ellie Mae *Derek Shaw* a32
3 b f Proclamation(IRE) Park Star (Gothenberg (IRE))
462[5] 720[8] 8109[8]

Dancing For Glory (USA) *Chad C Brown* 87
2 rg f Exchange Rate(USA) Hard Evidence (USA) (Alleged (USA))
6289a[9]

Dancing Freddy (IRE) *Violet M Jordan* a81 95
5 b g Chineur(FR) Majesty's Dancer (IRE) (Danehill Dancer (IRE))
24[3] 100[2] 251[7] 406[3] 458[8] 718[3] (808) 1581[8] (2195) (2507) 2717[11] 3374[7] 4013[4] 4367[15] 4576[15] 6382[6] 6666[15] 7197[5] 7648[5] 7730[8] 7902[6] 8009[10] 8054[9] 8266[4]

Dancing Maite *Roy Bowring* a76 77
7 ch g Ballet Master(USA) Ace Maite (Komaite (USA))
388[3] 492[4] 639[4] 2084[6] 2549[10] 2815[11] 3075[6] 3994[12] 5203[8] 6106[11] (6498) 6687[12] 7178[8] 7254[4] 7633[3]

Dancing Paddy (IRE) *Alan Swinbank* a49 39
4 b g Azamour(IRE) Moucha (FR) (Fabulous Dancer (USA))
4622[8] 4864[12] 5679[10] 7443[3] 7710[3]

Dancing Primo *Mark Brisbourne* a41 87
6 b m Primo Valentino(IRE) Tycoon's Last (Nalchik (USA))
4061[2] 4733[3] 5039[2] (6076) (6229) 6667[9]

Dancing Rain (IRE) *William Haggas* 118
4 ch m Danehill Dancer(IRE) Rain Flower (IRE) (Indian Ridge)
7237[3] 8040a[8]

Dancing Shuffle (GER) *S Smrczek* 87
2 b f Big Shuffle(USA) Donatio (IRE) (Royal Academy (USA))
(7588a)

Dancing Solo (USA) *Todd Pletcher* a90 107
3 ch f Giant's Causeway(USA) Dancing Alone (USA) (Kingmambo (USA))
4478a[7]

Dancing Wave *Michael Chapman* a50 65
6 b m Baryshnikov(AUS) Wavet (Pursuit Of Love)
289[12]

Dancing Welcome *Milton Bradley* a80 74
6 b m Kyllachy Highland Gait (Most Welcome)
(106) (212) 387[3] 537[3] 735[4] 806[4] 1497[2] (1638) 1934[2] 2207[6] 2493[5] 2973[5] (3075) 3434[8] 4235[8] 4533[10] 7483[8] 7902[3] 8059[6] 8232[7]

Dandarrell *Julie Camacho* a63 59
5 b g Makbul Dress Design (IRE) (Brief Truce (USA))
3914[7] ◆ 4349[7] 5021[2] 5730[3] (6258) (7620) 7841[7]

Dandino *James Fanshawe* a113 115
5 br h Dansili Generous Diana (Generous (IRE))
1318[3] 2481[2] 3632[2] 4010[7] 4759[2] (6035) 7094a[2] 8040a[7]

Dandy (GER) *Andrew Balding* a41 81
3 b c Nayef(USA) Diacada (GER) (Cadeaux Genereux)
3882[6] 4529[7] 6574[6] 7194[11]

Dandy Boy (ITY) *David Marnane* a92 117
6 b h Danetime(IRE) Fleet Of Light (Spectrum (IRE))
53a[5] 416a[9] 590a[9] (3371) 4100[9] 5561[11] 6030[4] 7772[11]

Dane Cottage *Richard Ford* a52 68
5 ch m Beat Hollow Lady Soleas (Be My Guest (USA))
7991[7]

Danedream (GER) *P Schiergen* 128
4 b m Lomitas Danedrop (IRE) (Danehill (USA))
(2322a) 3424a[4] (4322) (5865a)

Daneglow (IRE) *Mike Murphy* a9
2 ch f Thousand Words Valluga (IRE) (Ashkalani (IRE))
4946[10]

Danehill Dante (IRE) *Alan King* a80 82
4 ch g Danehill Dancer(IRE) En Garde (USA) (Irish River (FR))
1706[10] 3484[4] 4843[6] 5507[5]

Danehill Flyer (IRE) *Philip Kirby* 62
2 b c Danehill Dancer(IRE) Zagreb Flyer (Old Vic)
4710[17] 5221[4] 5727[3] 6121[6] 6753[3]

Danehillsundance (IRE) *Philip Kirby* a91 37
8 b g Danehill Dancer(IRE) Rosie's Guest (IRE) (Be My Guest (USA))
4712[8]

Daneking *John Gosden* a84 93
3 b c Dylan Thomas(IRE) Sadie Thompson (IRE) (King's Best (USA))
1647[3] 2258[2] 4513[3] 5228[3] 5598[10] 6037[8] 6662[2] 7082[3] (7367)

Daneside (IRE) *Gary Harrison* a64 77
5 b g Danehill Dancer(IRE) Sidecar (IRE) (Spectrum (IRE))
2574[2] 2855[6]

Dane Street (USA) *Mrs John Harrington* 83
3 br f Street Cry(IRE) Daneleta (IRE) (Danehill (USA))
5519[7]

Dan Excel (IRE) *J Moore* 115
4 b g Shamardal(USA) Love Excelling (FR) (Polish Precedent (USA))
8043a[4]

Dangerous Midge (USA) *Brian Meehan* 94
6 b h Lion Heart(USA) Adored Slew (USA) (Seattle Slew (USA))
3178a[9] 3635[7]

Dangerous To Know *Hughie Morrison* a35 55
3 b f Byron Bogus Mix (IRE) (Linamix (FR))
2734[8] 3543[3] 4214[9] 4994[9] 6569[3] 7499[8]

Daniel Thomas (IRE) *Violet M Jordan* a76 67
10 b g Dansili Last Look (Rainbow Quest (USA))
(151) (293) (403) 626[9] (655) 760[3] (824) 915[2] 1105[4] 1718[2] 2199[8] 5585[11] 6250[6] 7250[6] 7310[12] 7473[9] (7841) 8051[12] 8106[8] 8214[7] (8261)

Dank *Sir Michael Stoute* a87 105
3 b f Dansili Masskana (IRE) (Darshaan)
(1610) 2263[9] (4579) 5092[2] ◆ (5834) 6633[5]

Dan Loose Daughter *B Grizzetti* 98
3 b f Sakhee(USA) Dan Loose (IRE) (Danehill (USA))
2522a[11]

Dannios *Ed Walker* a41 79
6 b g Tobougg(IRE) Fleuve D'Or (IRE) (Last Tycoon)
(4966) (5214) 6381[7]

Dan's Heir *Wilf Storey* a56 57
10 b g Dansili Million Heiress (Auction Ring (USA))
1247[2] 1952[5] 2925[7] 3437[3] 3750[4] 3988[11] 5735[6] 6956[3]

Dansico *J M Borrego* 109
5 b g Dansili Chicodove (In The Wings)
6089a[9]

Dansili Dual (IRE) *Richard Hannon* 78
2 b g Dansili Jewel In The Sand (IRE) (Bluebird (USA))
2663[3] ◆ 2868[2] (3223) 4526[3] 4804[8] 6929[6]

Dansili Dutch (IRE) *Andrew Crook* a64 73
3 gr f Dutch Art Joyful Leap (Dansili)
491[2] 1058[4] 1826[4] 2540[7] (3416) (3616) 4553[10] 4961[7] 5680[9] 6480[8] 6813[9] 7781[6] 7982[7]

Dan's Martha *Robin Dickin* a64 60
4 b m Tagula(IRE) Piedmont (UAE) (Jade Robbery (USA))
8010[11]

Danube River *Mark Johnston* a80 84
3 ch f Teofilo(IRE) Last Rhapsody (IRE) (Kris)
918[5] (1107) 1757[3] 2201[11] 2589[5] 3556[6] 4137[4] (6735) 6988[9] 7132[2] 7353[8] 7626[6]

Danvilla *Paul Webber* a76 88
5 b m Dansili Newtown Villa (Spectrum (IRE))
2423[P] 2936[2] 3241[19]

Danz Choice (IRE) *Richard Hannon* a77 75
2 b c Kheleyf(USA) Aphorism (Halling (USA))
2202[7] 2648[4] 3138[7] (4471) (4936) 5450[3] 5946[3] 6815[2] 7501[7] 7856[2]

Danzoe (IRE) *Christine Dunnett* a76 71
5 br g Kheleyf(USA) Fiaba (Precocious)
1290[4] 1735[3] 2377[5] (3151) 3546[7] 4000[2] 4332[11] 4663[3] 4969[6] 5557[11] 5774[3] 5972[9] (6563) (7179) 7489[7] 7864[6] (8157)

Da Paolino (FR) *D Prod'Homme* a66 104
5 b g Enrique Tora Tune (FR) (Green Tune (USA))
5117a[7]

Daphne Joy *Peter Hedger* a7
3 ch f Reel Buddy(USA) Elegia Prima (Mon Tresor)
185[6]

Da Ponte *Michael Scudamore* a59 79
4 b g Librettist(USA) Naharnook (Fantastic Light (USA))
1117[9] 1680[9] 2413[10] 7857[13] 8156[9]

Da'Quonde (IRE) *Bryan Smart* a69 84
4 br m Pivotal Bobcat Greeley (USA) (Mr Greeley (USA))
101[9] (497) 696[3] (1246) 1428[2] 2032[2] 2750[4] (3113) 3578[7] 7295[6]

Daraa (IRE) *Clive Brittain* a69 71
3 b f Cape Cross(IRE) Guarantia (Selkirk (USA))
867[5] 1331[10] 2785[13]

Darabani (FR) *P Monfort* a79 78
7 b g Fantastic Light(USA) Darakiyla (IRE) (Last Tycoon)
94a[8]

Darakti (IRE) *Alan McCabe* a37 37
2 b g Rakti Mitawa (IRE) (Alhaarth (IRE))
6164[14] 7172[10] 7728[4] 7796[7]

Darat Al Ayam (FR) *R Pritchard-Gordon* 64
2 b f King's Best(USA) Take Blood (FR) (Take Risks (FR))
5697a[0]

Darayya (IRE) *A De Royer-Dupre* a81 72
3 b f Zamindar(USA) Darakiyla (IRE) (Last Tycoon)
3423a[6] 5142a[11]

Darcey *Amy Weaver* a80 77
6 ch m Noverre(USA) Firozi (Forzando)
2251[12] 2801[7] 3344[11] 4302[11]

Darcy May *Garry Woodward* a14
4 b m Danbird(AUS) Oakwell Ace (Clantime)
20[5] 135[9]

Dare To Achieve *William Haggas* 63
2 b c Galileo(IRE) Mussoorie (FR) (Linamix (FR))
6636[6]

Dare To Dream *Richard Hannon* 87
3 b f Exceed And Excel(AUS) Secret History (USA) (Bahri (USA))
2272[2] ◆ 5237[9] 6023[8] 6488[3] 7408[8]

Dare To Dream (IRE) *Bart Cummings* a81 111
4 b h Danehill Dancer(IRE) Beneventa (Most Welcome)
7560a[2] 7696a[4]

Daring Damsel (IRE) *Brian Baugh* a68 59
3 b f Van Nistelrooy(USA) Serengeti Day (USA) (Alleged (USA))
1303[8] (1443) 1982[2] 2544[11] 3621[6] 5629[3] 5945[4] 6814[12] 6976[2] 8146[6]

Daring Dragon *Ed Walker* a66
2 gr g Intikhab(USA) The Manx Touch (IRE) (Petardia)
7707[14] 8185[2]

Daring Dream (GER) *Jim Goldie* a52 86
7 ch g Big Shuffle(USA) Daring Action (Arazi (USA))
1670[12] 2035[5] 2924[4] 3335[5] 4135[5] 4673[3] 5414[11] 7142[9]

Daring Indian *Tom Dascombe* a79 79
4 ch g Zamindar(USA) Anasazi (IRE) (Sadler's Wells (USA))
971[7] 1275[9] 1513[11] 3594[2] ◆ 4088[2] 4460[2] (5002) 5344[6] 6012[7]

Daring Man (IRE) *Denis W Cullen* a62 80
7 b g Talkin Man(CAN) Emotions High (IRE) (Mujadil (USA))
775a[7]

Dark Ages (IRE) *Paul Burgoyne* a73 77
3 bl f Dark Angel(IRE) Prosaic Star (IRE) (Common Grounds)
1731[3] 2351[3] (2573) (3005) (3510) 4081[3] 4412[4] 4726[4] 5308[7]

Dark Ambition (IRE) *N Minner* a73 76
3 b c Dark Angel(IRE) Date Mate (USA) (Thorn Dance (USA))
7266a[5]

Dark And Dangerous (IRE) *Brendan Powell* a55 63
4 b g Cacique(IRE) Gilah (IRE) (Saddlers' Hall (IRE))
6567[3]

Dark Castle *Sylvester Kirk* a89 77
3 b g Dark Angel(IRE) True Magic (Magic Ring (IRE))
(121) ◆ 295[2] (1449) 2276[10] 6008[11] 6369[2] 6536[4]

Dark Celt (IRE) *Michael Madgwick* a47 38
3 b g Lawman(FR) Dark Raider (IRE) (Definite Article)
620[8] 1303[5] 1726[7] 5037[12] 5817[10]

Dark Danger (IRE) *David Peter Nagle* a48 66
3 br f Amadeus Wolf Danzelline (Danzero (AUS))
5263[3]

Dark Diamond (IRE) *Robert Cowell*
2 b c Dark Angel(IRE) Moon Diamond (Unfuwain (USA))
7963[9]

Dark Don (IRE) *Charles Hills* a66 73
3 b c Dark Angel(IRE) Bint Al Hammour (IRE) (Grand Lodge (USA))
2542[5] 3702[8] 4509[7]

Dark Dune (IRE) *Tim Easterby* a83 85
4 b g Diamond Green(FR) Panpipes (USA) (Woodman (USA))
1295[8] (2676) 3494[7] 4326[2] ◆ 4621[11] 5383[4] 6476[2] 7147[9]

Dark Emerald (IRE) *Brendan Powell* 83
2 gr c Dark Angel(IRE) Xema (Danehill (USA))
2480[8] 2888[2] 3240[12] (5912) 6447[6] 7125[3]

Darkening (IRE) *Mahmood Al Zarooni* 89
2 b g Shamardal(USA) Dama'A (IRE) (Green Desert (USA))
3346[4] 4921[3] 5684[2] ◆ (6414) 6597[2] 7365[5]

Dark Eros (IRE) *Tim Easterby* 41
2 b f Dark Angel(IRE) Capetown Girl (Danzero (AUS))
2282[8] 2977[9]

Darkest Night (IRE) *Jamie Osborne* a53 47
2 b g Dark Angel(IRE) Vadarousse (GER) (Numerous (USA))
5851[9] 6214[11] 6501[12] 6822[7] 7808[5] 7974[3] 8203[6]

Dark Falcon (IRE) *James Tate* a76 54
3 bb g Dark Angel(IRE) Absolute Pleasure (Polar Falcon (USA))
1862[4] 2583[4] 2785[12] 4401[8] 5545[6] 5915[16] 7202[6]

Dark Justice (IRE) *Tim Pitt* a31 54
2 b f Lawman(FR) Dark Raider (IRE) (Definite Article)
4525[6] 5476[7] 6168[5]

Dark Lane *David Evans* a80 83
6 b g Namid Corps De Ballet (IRE) (Fasliyev (USA))
4014[8] 5120[7] 5681[6] 6033[4] 6071[4] 6053[3] 7141[7] 7218[3] (7590) 7864[7] 8036[3] 8058[6] (8294)

Dark Marvel (IRE) *Alan Berry*
2 b f Captain Marvelous(IRE) Starisa (IRE) (College Chapel)
5756[4] 6336[7] 7096[8]

Dark Matter (AUS) *S Burridge* a103 111
4 b h Stratum(AUS) Loving New (BRZ) (Choctaw Ridge (USA))
(142a) (316a) 485a[5] 758a[6]

Dark Ocean (IRE) *Jedd O'Keeffe* 74
2 b g Dylan Thomas(IRE) Neutral (Beat Hollow)
3401[5] 4387[2] 5311[7] 6780[3]

Dark Opal (IRE) *John Weymes* 75
2 b f Camacho Dark Albatross (USA) (Sheikh Albadou)
2747[3] 3491[3] 4612[8] (5544)

Dark Orchid *Peter Chapple-Hyam* a46 55
3 br f Shamardal(USA) Misty Waters (IRE) (Caerleon (USA))
2935[11] 3539[6] 5215[3] 6829[9] 8131[7]

Dark Orchid (USA) *A Fabre* 106
3 b f Dansili Pleione (FR) (Sadler's Wells (USA))
2742a[8] 3682a[4] 4616a[5] 5472a[4]

Dark Pulse (USA) *M D O'Callaghan* a80 60
2 b c Midnight Lute(USA) Top Time (USA) (Marquetry (USA))
7038a[8]

Dark Ranger *Tim Pitt* a85 91
6 br g Where Or When(IRE) Dark Raider (IRE) (Definite Article)
202[2] 577[2] 2214[2] 3241[9] 4528[6] 6493[4] 7051[8] 7522[12]

Dark Ray (IRE) *L Riccardi* 91
3 b f Dark Angel(IRE) Magiustrina (IRE) (Indian Ridge)
1699a[11]

Dark Ruler (IRE) *Alan Swinbank* 74
3 b g Dark Angel(IRE) Gino Lady (IRE) (Perugino (USA))
4926[4] 5541[2] 6136[4] 6477[2] (6711)

Dark Shadow (JPN) *Noriyuki Hori* 125
5 ch h Dance In The Dark(JPN) Matikanehatusimada (USA) (Private Account (USA))
1148a[9] 7872a[4]

Darkside *Tracy Waggott* 54
2 b c Indesatchel(IRE) Romantic Destiny (Dubai Destination (USA))
4778[5] 5586[12] 5799[2] 6780[6]

Dark Stranger (USA) *John Gosden* a82 93
3 b c Stormy Atlantic(USA) Vivacious Vivian (USA) (Distorted Humor (USA))
(1031) 3156[4] 4342[2]

Dark Templar *Ed Vaughan* a72 49
2 ch g Starcraft(NZ) Shuaily (PER) (Shuailaan (USA))
4595[12] 5407[4] 8262[2]

Darley Sun (IRE) *Saeed Bin Suroor* a61 104
6 b g Tiger Hill(IRE) Sagamartha (Rainbow Quest (USA))
6600[10] 6922[4] 7689[15]

Darling Grace *William Haggas* a44 67
3 b f Nayef(USA) Lady Grace (IRE) (Orpen (USA))
2143[8] 3083[3] 3978[5] (4436) 4914[9]

Darling Lexi (IRE) *Richard Fahey* a62 67
3 gr f Dylan Thomas(IRE) My Girl Lisa (USA) (With Approval (CAN))
3616[3] ◆ 4057[4] 4676[5] (5336) 6240[6] 6364[4] 6626[4] 6971[8]

Darnathean *Paul D'Arcy* a75 67
3 b g Librettist(USA) Meddle (Diktat)
377[6] 637[9] 865a[4] 1730[6] 3002[6] 3475[2] 5323[15] 5721[8] 6057[8] 6402[5] 6982[2] 7224[6] 7512[2] 8074[6] 8263[8]

Darnetal (IRE) *F Rohaut* a75
3 b c Invincible Spirit(IRE) Larme (IRE) (Soviet Star (USA))
211a[3]

Darrow (IRE) *Wilf Storey* a72 68
3 b g Lawman(FR) Azolla (Cadeaux Genereux)
1288[5] 1728[3] 2045[9] 2733[9] 3952[9] 4334[8] 5295[7] 5738[9] 7382[11] 7602[5] 7798[13]

Darsan (IRE) *Phil McEntee* a67 66
4 ch m Iffraaj Coolrain Lady (IRE) (Common Grounds)
495[2] 552[3] 573[6] 842[5] 974[7] 1624[6] 1791[5] (2009) 2237[9] 2623[6] 2937[5] 4296[7] 4402[9] 7015[11] 7315[4] 7472[3] 7717[5] 8060[9]

Dart *John Mackie* a75 49
8 br m Diktat Eilean Shona (Suave Dancer (USA))
63[3] 271[7]

Dartford (USA) *John Gosden* a78 88
3 ch c Giant's Causeway(USA) Apple Of Kent (USA) (Kris S (USA))
827[3] 1086[2] 1312[5] 1707[3] 2372[7] 5354[5] 6245[9] 7024[8]

Dartrix *Michael Dods* a44 64
3 b f Dutch Art Shrink (Mind Games)
1173[6] 1274[3] 2262[12] 3407[4] ◆ 3892[4] 4348[9] 4798[2] 5318[4] 5624[6] 6806[11]

Daruband *Michael Bell* a85 83
4 ch g Singspiel(IRE) Gagajulu (Al Hareb (USA))
2549[2] (3589) 4345[10] 4772[6] 5414[12] 6545[5] 7171[2] (7328)

Darwinian *Dave Morris* a38 18
3 b f Three Valleys(USA) Force Of Nature (USA) (Sadler's Wells (USA))
1261[10] 6398[8] 7158[8] 7769[7]

Darwin Star *Dean Ivory* a62 66
4 gr m Aussie Rules(USA) Fine Lady (Selkirk (USA))
122[7] 152[8] 313[4]

Dashing David (IRE) *Richard Hannon* a93 85
2 b c Lemon Drop Kid(USA) Nyarhini (Fantastic Light (USA))
(2817) 3562[3] 7009[4] 7400[6] 7478[2]

Dashing Eddie (IRE) *Kevin Ryan* a70 65
4 b h Dubawi(IRE) Step Too Far (USA) (Cozzene (USA))
(14) (136) 154[4] 384[4] 1659[7] 1879[5]

Dashing Star *David Elsworth* 84
2 b c Teofilo(IRE) Dashiba (Dashing Blade)
6876[10] 7332[3] (7636)

Dashing Storm *Jeremy Gask* a50
2 b f Milk It Mick Salalah (Lion Cavern (USA))
3733[5] 4651[7] 5423[6] 6822[13]

Dasho *Gay Kelleway* a86 77
4 ch g Dubawi(IRE) New Choice (IRE) (Barathea (IRE))
311[3] 711[10] 2545[4] 3557[12] 5035[12]

Dashwood *Anthony Carson* a79 81
5 b g Pivotal Most Charming (FR) (Darshaan)
4302[9] 4772[12] 5320[12] 6926[9] 7589[7]

Dastarhon (IRE) *Mme Pia Brandt* a83
2 gr c Dansili Top Toss (IRE) (Linamix (FR))
(7683a)

Daunt (IRE) *John Quinn* a41 74
3 ch g Namid Pearl Egg (IRE) (Mukaddamah (USA))
1985[9] (2203) 3248[8] 4588[10] 5093[10] 5713[10] 6261[7]

Dauphine Russe (FR) *F Doumen* 95
2 b f Russian Blue(IRE) Dauphine (SAF) (Rich Man's Gold (USA))
5288a[3] 7622a[5]

Davana *Colin Teague* a57 42
6 b m Primo Valentino(IRE) Bombay Sapphire (Be My Chief (USA))
830[4] 976[5]

Davanti (FR) *Mlle B Renk* a82 43
2 b c Turtle Bowl(IRE) Daisy Town (Doyoun)
7683a[6]

David Jack *Brian Meehan* a70 67
2 ch c Exceed And Excel(AUS) Psychic (IRE) (Alhaarth (IRE))
2202[4] 5963[9] 7192[4]

David Livingston (IRE) *A P O'Brien* 115
3 b c Galileo(IRE) Mora Bai (IRE) (Indian Ridge)
1404a[5] 1995[4] 5606a[3]

David's Folly (IRE) *Bryn Palling* a47 57
3 b f Asian Heights Dolphin Stamp (IRE) (Dolphin Street (FR))
908[8] 1113[9] 3100[5] 4181[8] 4537[9] 5265[4] 5817[5] 7169[10] 7490[4] 7793[4] 8273[10]

David's Secret *Hughie Morrison* a68 53
2 ch c Sakhee's Secret Mozie Cat (IRE) (Mozart (IRE))
6486[9] 6945[3] 7305[3] 7642[3]

Dawn Approach (IRE) *J S Bolger* 123
2 ch c New Approach(IRE) Hymn Of The Dawn (USA) (Phone Trick (USA))
(2184a) ◆ (2779a) ◆ (3240) ◆ (6272a) ◆ (7050)

Dawn Catcher *Tony Carroll* a39 65
2 ch f Bertolini(USA) First Dawn (Dr Fong (USA))
4487[3] 4990[3] 5503[2] 5940[8]

Dawn Gale (IRE) *Hughie Morrison* a37 86
4 b m Hurricane Run(IRE) Latest Chapter (IRE) (Ahonoora)
2708[4] 3400[2] ◆ 4326[7] 4905[5] 6416[13]

Dawn Glory *Roger Charlton* 72
3 b f Oasis Dream Fairy Godmother (Fairy King (USA))
4341[5] 5096[3]

Dawn Lightning *Alan McCabe* a66 66
3 gr f Dark Angel(IRE) River Crossing (Zafonic (USA))
86[6] 189[2] 352[7] 469[5] 749[7] 1912[10] 2547[7]

Dawn Mystery *Alan Berry* a48 54
8 gr m Daylami(IRE) Frustration (Salse (USA))
632[12] 830[5]

Dawn Rock *Simon Dow* 45
2 b f Rock Of Gibraltar(IRE) Ommadawn (IRE) (Montjeu (IRE))
4282[9] 4845[11] 5661[6]

Dawn Salute (FR) *H-A Pantall* 84
2 b c Royal Applause Nice Matin (USA) (Tiznow (USA))
5899a[6]

Dawn Twister (GER) *Lucy Wadham* 107
5 br g Monsun(GER) Dawn Side (CAN) (Bold Forbes (USA))
(1674) 2066[3] 3373[16]

Day In Day Out *Ralph Beckett* a64 54
2 b g Notnowcato Cockatrice (Petong)
4066[14] 4646[5] 5274[9] 6893[10] 8094[2]

Daylami Dreams *John Holt* a60 72
8 gr g Daylami(IRE) Kite Mark (Mark Of Esteem (IRE))
8104[P]

Daylight *Andrew Balding* 79
2 ch g Firebreak Dayville (USA) (Dayjur (USA))
4688[5]

Day Of Destiny (IRE) *James Given* a68 68
7 gr g Clodovil(IRE) El Corazon (IRE) (Mujadil (USA))
7638[3] 8273[3]

Day Of The Eagle (IRE) *Michael Easterby* 76
6 b g Danehill Dancer(IRE) Puck's Castle (Shirley Heights)
1863[14] 2285[8] 2882[10] 3167[15] 3439[4] (4043) 4317[3]

Dazakhee *Jo Hughes* a71 71
5 ch m Sakhee(USA) Ziya (IRE) (Lion Cavern (USA))
449[6]

Dazinski *Mark H Tompkins* 96
6 ch g Sulamani(IRE) Shuheb (Nashwan (USA))
1974[7] 2709[2] 4613[7] 5106[4] 5491[3] 6493[17]

Dazzlin Bluebell (IRE) *Tim Easterby* a58 54
3 b f Strategic Prince Sharamaine (IRE) (King Charlemagne (USA))
2130[9] 2795[6] 3256[9] 3407[5] 4878[2] 5247[3] 5719[2] 6958[5] 7457[4] (7611) 8287[8]

Dazzling Begum *Lydia Pearce* a45 22
7 b m Okawango(USA) Dream On Me (Prince Sabo)
160[3] 6566[7] 6948[9] 7255[9]

Dazzling Valentine *Alan Bailey* a80 78
4 b m Oratorio(IRE) Bedazzling (IRE) (Darshaan)
119[4] 275[2] 548[4] 582[4] 771[5] 804[2] 906[2] (1485) 1719[8] 2392[2] 2679[3] 2915[6] 3775[6] 4325[2] 4538[3] 4641[6] 5754[2] (5990) 6631[9] 6988[3] 7027[3] 8136[6]

Deacon Blue (FR) *C Boutin* a55 67
7 ch g Anabaa Blue Kansas (Kahyasi)
7701a[0]

Dead Cool *Robert Cowell* a69 72
4 ch m Kyllachy Dead Certain (Absalom)
179[6]

Dean Iarracht (IRE) *Tracy Waggott* a60 65
6 b g Danetime(IRE) Sirdhana (Selkirk (USA))
2239[14] 2670[5] 4396[5] 4594[7] 4683[2] (5114) 5253[2] 5585[13] 6103[7] 6126[12] 6562[6]

Dear Ben *Brian Baugh* a50 35
3 b g Echo Of Light Miss Up N Go (Gorytus (USA))
107[6] 720[7] 1111[5] 2351[2] 2862[9] 5000[6]

Dear Maurice *Tobias B P Coles* a77 76
8 b g Indian Ridge Shamaiel (IRE) (Lycius (USA))
1050[5] 3464[2] 4003[2] (4238)

Dear Nofa (IRE) *A Fabre* a67 70
2 b f Galileo(IRE) Classira (IRE) (Danehill (USA))
6751a[6] 7683a[7]

Deauville Flyer *Tim Easterby* 99
6 b g Dubai Destination(USA) Reaf (In The Wings)
(1273) 2253[11] 3125[6] 3857[11] 4613[5] 5491[11] 6191[6]

Deauville Prince (FR) *Tom Dascombe* 104
2 b c Holy Roman Emperor(IRE) Queen Of Deauville (FR) (Diableneyev (USA))
1972[7] 2662[2] ◆ (4327) 5140a[4] (5678) 6507a[4] 7076a[4]

Debating Society (IRE) *Sir Michael Stoute* a82 92
3 b c Invincible Spirit(IRE) Drama Class (IRE) (Caerleon (USA))
1261[2] 1938[4] 3737[3] 4224[6] (5707) (5951) 6819[13]

Debbie Doo *Anthony Carson* a47
4 b m Beat Hollow Pleasing (Dr Fong (USA))
248[6]

Debdebdeb *Andrew Balding* a66
2 b f Teofilo(IRE) Windmill (Ezzoud (IRE))
8017[3] 8200[5]

Decadence *Nigel Tinkler* a20 56
4 b m Singspiel(IRE) Penny Cross (Efisio)
2287[9] 2669[9] 2823[5] 3577[8] 4350[8] 4711[5] 5317[5] 6125[6] 7126[5]

Decana *Hughie Morrison* a71 62
4 ch m Doyen(IRE) Sahara Belle (USA) (Sanglamore (USA))
2814[3] 3102[4] 3961[8] 5241[4] 5908[3]

December Draw (IRE) *Mark Kavanagh* a105 117
6 br g Medecis New York (IRE) (Danzero (AUS))
7264a[17]

Decent Fella (IRE) *Violet M Jordan* a88 101
6 b g Marju(IRE) Mac Melody (IRE) (Entrepreneur)
3331[5] 4099[5] 4761[16] 5572[17] 6676[19] 8055[4] 8227[10] 8306[5]

Deceptive *Paul Webber* a77 65
4 b m Red Ransom(USA) Fleeting Memory (Danehill (USA))
4875[4]

Dechiper (IRE) *Robert Johnson* a35 54
10 bb g Almutawakel Safiya (USA) (Riverman (USA))
1247[4] 1794[3] 2242[5] 2635[4]

Decider (USA) *Ronald Harris* a68 61
9 ch g High Yield(USA) Nikita Moon (USA) (Secret Hello (USA))
152[5] 277[4] 445[9] 497[4] 654[5] (782) 870[5] 996[4] 1343[3] 1497[15] 1910[8] 2352[6] 3008[4] 4236[9] 4422[6] 4885[4] 5191[8]

Decimate *Alan McCabe* a72 64
4 br g Teofilio(IRE) Kirriemuir (Lochnager)
746[11] 896[9] 1306[7] 2761[8] (5246) 5750[2]

Decision By One *Tom Dascombe* a87 88
3 ch g Bahamian Bounty Intellibet One (Compton Place)
1998[7] (2451) 3607[9] 4496[2] (4671) 5128[7] 6009[7] 6939[4] 7595[12]

Declamation (IRE) *Mark Johnston* a65
2 ch c Shamardal(USA) Dignify (IRE) (Rainbow Quest (USA))
7459[2]

Declaration Of War (USA) *A P O'Brien* a105 103
3 b c War Front(USA) Tempo West (USA) (Rahy (USA))
6079a[4] (6855a)

Decoy (FR) *David Pipe* a83 10
6 b g Della Francesca(USA) Vagualame (FR) (Saint Estephe (FR))
7051[25]

Dedication *Roger Charlton* a79 56
3 b f Beat Hollow Total Devotion (Desert Prince (IRE))
(2148) 6537[8] 7194[5]

Deduction (IRE) *Nigel Tinkler* a25 58
3 b f Holy Roman Emperor(IRE) Briery (IRE) (Salse (USA))
132[12] 382[4]

Dee Aitch Dove *George Baker* a44
2 gr f Sakhee's Secret Fluttering Rose (Compton Place)
7498[6]

Dee Ee Williams (IRE) *Nick Gifford* a44 35
9 b g Dushyantor(USA) Fainne Oir (IRE) (Montelimar (USA))
3227[11] 3763[6] 4464[7]

Deep Applause *Michael Dods* a28 68
4 b g Royal Applause Deep Deep Blue (Hernando (FR))
1276[10] 1598[7] 2033[4] 2600[6] 3032[6] 3907[7] 4389[5] 4683[8] 5114[4] 5708[5] 5762[3] 6316[8]

Deep Brillante (JPN) *Yoshito Yahagi* 118
3 b c Deep Impact(JPN) Love And Bubbles (USA) (Loup Sauvage (USA))
4322[8]

Deepest Blue *Jamie Osborne* a69 69
2 b g Sakhee's Secret Midnight Sky (Desert Prince (IRE))
1131[12] 2420[5] 3303[2] 3638[2] 3748[3] 6016[3] 6511[8]

Deepsand (IRE) *Tim Easterby* 89
3 br g Footstepsinthesand Sinamay (USA) (Saint Ballado (CAN))
1440[6] 2182[6] 2678[2] 3064[4] 4046[2] 5044[3] 5540[3] 6190[6] 6661[11] 7032[7]

Defence Council (IRE) *Mel Brittain* a84 88
4 b g Kheleyf(USA) Miss Gally (IRE) (Galileo (IRE))
1161[3] 1863[5] 3169[4] 3439[6] 3612[2] 3778[11] 4077[5] 4554[17] 4924[5] 5412[4] 5674[2] 6044[5] 6338[9] 6665[2] 6999[5]

Defence Of Duress (IRE) *T J Taaffe* 86
4 b g Motivator Ultra Finesse (USA) (Rahy (USA))
4697[2]

Deferto Delphi *Barry Murtagh* a45 51
5 ch g Mark Of Esteem(IRE) Delphic Way (Warning)
390[5] 767[F]

Deficit (IRE) *Michael Bell* 59
2 gr c Dalakhani(IRE) Venturi (Danehill Dancer (IRE))
6876[7] 7130[6] 7466[4]

Definightly *Roger Charlton* 111
6 bb g Diktat Perfect Night (Danzig Connection (USA))
1857[2] 3190[3] (3650a) 4092[7] 5137a[3] 6908a[15]

Defining Year (IRE) *M Halford* 106
4 b g Hawk Wing(USA) Tajaathub (USA) (Aljabr (USA))
1043a[8] 3361a[3] 3675a[2] 4521a[4] 6062a[4]

Deflection (IRE) *S Botti* 94
2 ch f Dylan Thomas(IRE) Crumpetsfortea (IRE) (Henbit (USA))
6725a[5] 7285a[5]

Dei Amore (IRE) *Jonathan Portman* a28 49
3 b f Catcher In The Rye(IRE) Baby Loves (Sadler's Wells (USA))
3663[6] 5745[6] 6228[9]

Deia Sunrise (IRE) *John Gosden* 102
3 gr g Clodovil(IRE) Hedera (USA) (Woodman (USA))
1888[2] ◆ 2235[7] 2930[4] (4459) 5006[5] 6193[2] (6661)

Deire Na Sli (IRE) *Martyn Meade* a76 95
4 b m Aussie Rules(USA) Malignia (IRE) (Pursuit Of Love)
1670[11] 2657[4] 3878[11] 4321[23] 5980[10] 6702[6] 7858[4]

Delagoa Bay (IRE) *Sylvester Kirk* a60 52
4 b m Encosta De Lago(AUS) Amory (GER) (Goofalik (USA))
468[9] 850[6] 924[6] 1189[2] 1631[4] (2134) 2371[4] 2872[5] 3498[5] 5265[9] 5430[9]

Delegation (FR) *M Rulec* 74
2 b f Mount Nelson Delta Diva (USA) (Victory Gallop (CAN))
7343a[6]

Delegation (USA) *Mark Casse* a111 105
3 b g Speightstown(USA) Cindy's Hero (USA) (Sea Hero (USA))
7570a[3]

Delegator *Saeed Bin Suroor* 117
6 b h Dansili Indian Love Bird (Efisio)
(588a) 1148a[8]

De Lesseps (USA) *Alan Berry* a60 37
4 ch g Selkirk(USA) Suez (Green Desert (USA))
3215[10] 4295[8] 4328[4] 4911[11] 5185[11]

Delft *Jeremy Noseda* a87 84
3 b f Dutch Art Plucky (Kyllachy)
(2583) 3342[5] 4300[3] 5308[4] (6369) 6939[3] 7645[2] 7966[9]

Deliberation (IRE) *Mark Buckley* a61 78
4 b g Antonius Pius(USA) Pursuit Of Truth (USA) (Irish River (FR))
1643[13] 2264[15] 2475[8] 4495[15]

Delicatezza *E Botti* 98
3 b f Danehill Dancer(IRE) Wickwing (In The Wings)
3426a[2]

Delightful Sleep *David Evans* a49
4 b g Sulamani(IRE) Naemi (GER) (Tannenkonig (IRE))
569[8] 635[6] 724[6] 7512[4] 7982[6] 8167[7]

Delishuss *Dominic Ffrench Davis* a37 40
3 gr f Aussie Rules(USA) Effie (Royal Academy (USA))
1415[9] 2787[13] 3391[6] 4744[14] 4941[10]

Dellbuoy *Pat Phelan* a83 83
3 b c Acclamation Ruthie (Pursuit Of Love)
(981) (2898) 3446[9] 3963[5]

Dells Breezer *Pat Phelan* a54 60
4 ch g Kheleyf(USA) Here To Me (Muhtarram (USA))
320[9] 578[11] 986[9]

Delorain (IRE) *William Stone* a55 49
9 b g Kalanisi(IRE) Lady Nasrana (FR) (Al Nasr (FR))
9[3] 111[2] 278[11] 566[10] 772[11] 8104[8]

Delores Rocket *Kevin Ryan* a62 87
2 b f Firebreak Artistic (IRE) (Noverre (USA))
2261[10] 2770[7] 3034[7] 3858[7] 4450[4] 4672[5] (6130) 6451[6] (6920) (6998) 7242[3]

Delphica (IRE) *Gary Moore* a34 47
2 b f Acclamation Expectation (IRE) (Night Shift (USA))
3269[27] 4701[9] 5948[6] 7156[7]

Delwyn *Marcus Tregoning* a23
2 b f Bahamian Bounty Acquifer (Oasis Dream)
5785[8] 6826[7]

Demeteor (ITY) *R Menichetti* 92
2 b c Mujahid(USA) Eros Love (ITY) (Love The Groom (USA))
7076a[9] 7513a[6]

Democretes *Richard Hannon* a77 89
3 ch c Cadeaux Genereux Petite Epaulette (Night Shift (USA))
1858[3] 2276[8] 3294[14] 5102[7] 6119[3]

Demoiselle Bond *Lydia Richards* a67 22
4 ch m Monsieur Bond(IRE) Baytown Flyer (Whittingham (IRE))
123[7] 312[6] 665[5] 3006[3] 3152[11] 4920[2] 5625[12] (6586) 6982[12] (7482) 8004[9] 8305[9]

Demolition *Noel Wilson* a75 99
8 ch g Starborough Movie Star (IRE) (Barathea (IRE))
2773[8] 3163[12] 4072[7] 4596[6] 4879[2] 7415[7]

Demonic *Sir Henry Cecil* a72
2 b c Dansili Bionic (Zafonic (USA))
7900[4]

Demora *Michael Appleby* a63 85
3 b f Deportivo Danzanora (Groom Dancer (USA))
214[5] 720[6] 1389[6] 1986[2] (2730) 2816[2] 4208[3] 4793[6] 5167[3] (6226) (7177)

Demurely (IRE) *A P O'Brien* a31 98
3 ch f Galileo(IRE) Solo De Lune (IRE) (Law Society (USA))
3197a[5] 7423a[2]

Denbigh Raur (IRE) *Ann Duffield* 56
2 bb f Footstepsinthesand Gate Lodge (IRE) (Grand Lodge (USA))
2437[3] 2747[5]

Denison Flyer *Lawrence Mullaney* a42 53
5 b g Tobougg(IRE) Bollin Victoria (Jalmood (USA))
6821[12] 7603[4]

Den Maschine *Sean Curran* a88 57
7 b g Sakhee(USA) Flamingo Flower (USA) (Diesis)
(602) (1092) 1112[2] (5809) 6019[2] 6642[2] 7147[2]

Denny Crane *Edward Lynam* a92 86
6 b g Red Ransom(USA) Fleeting Rainbow (Rainbow Quest (USA))
7852a[5]

Den's Gift (IRE) *Clive Cox* a87 86
8 rg g City On A Hill(USA) Romanylei (IRE) (Blues Traveller (IRE))
90[3] 520[5] 1087[3] 2151[5] 3039[7]

Den's Legacy (USA) *Bob Baffert* a109 100
2 b c Medaglia d'Oro(USA) Sunshine Song (USA) (War Chant (USA))
7567a[2]

Denton Dancer *James Eustace* a52 61
3 bb g Halling(USA) Rapid Revalation (USA) (Bianconi (USA))
1288[9] 2548[13] 2803[13] 4440[5] 5037[10] 6304[3] 6976[8] 7303[6]

Denton Skyline (IRE) *Michael Dods* 48
2 b g Celtic Swing Fayr Sky (IRE) (Fayruz)
4587[11] 5668[8] 6133[7]

Deodora (FR) *Mario Hofer* a65 69
2 b f Dai Jin Denissa (GER) (Second Set (IRE))
5612a[10]

Depden (IRE) *Richard Price* a6 50
4 ch g Captain Rio Attribute (Warning)
3076[9] 3435[8] 4237[4] 4943[5] 5659[4] 5937[2] 6233[11]

Depict *Charles Hills* 35
2 gr c Smoke Glacken(USA) Zaghruta (USA) (Gone West (USA))
5319[10] 5792[11] (Dead)

Derbaas (USA) *A Al Raihe* a108 112
6 b h Seeking The Gold(USA) Sultana (USA) (Storm Cat (USA))
52a[3] 144a[5] 487a[4] 590a[4] 758a[2] 879a[5] 1143a[9]

Derek The Diamond *Michael Appleby* a39 47
3 b g Araafa(IRE) West One (Gone West (USA))
1270[7] 1590[7] 3024[4] 5247[7]

Derfenna Art (IRE) *Seamus Durack* a72 74
3 b g Excellent Art Cordelia (Green Desert (USA))
2128[3] (2756) 3068[4] 4531[4] 5657[3] 6932[7] 7767[13] 8051[5] 8199[2] 8263[2]

De Rigueur *Marco Botti* a83 75
4 b g Montjeu(IRE) Exclusive (Polar Falcon (USA))
5809[4] (6626) 7315[5] (8136) ◆

Derivatives (IRE) *H-A Pantall* a75 82
3 b f Dansili Favourable Terms (Selkirk (USA))
283[2] 457[2] 597[2] 720[3] 925[2] 1115[2] 1313[10] (4477a)

Derrochadora (IRE) *Robert Cowell* 43
2 b f Camacho Garnock Academy (USA) (Royal Academy (USA))
3313[3] 3748[6] 5799[8]

Dervis Aga (TUR) *S Mutlu* a99
7 b h Unaccounted For(USA) Mesitas (GER) (Surumu (GER))
5848a[6]

Derwent (USA) *Roger Charlton* 82
2 b g Mizzen Mast(USA) Skiable (IRE) (Niniski (USA))
3916[6] (4845) 5527[2] 6032[8] 6487[11]

Derwentwater (IRE) *John Gosden* a57 57
2 ch g Raven's Pass(USA) Waterways (IRE) (Alhaarth (IRE))
4917[10] 5948[7] 6411[8] 7808[4] 8103[6]

Descaro (USA) *David O'Meara* a64 77
6 gr g Dr Fong(USA) Miarixa (FR) (Linamix (FR))
1272[9] 1559[3] 2378[7] 2978[6] 3419[5] 3750[5] 4590[8] 5172[3] 5384[4] 6101[5] 6407[9] 6956[4] 7102[3]

Desert Al (IRE) *Owen Weldon* a53 24
9 b g Desert Style(IRE) Glass Lady (Muhtarram (USA))
775a[10]

Desert Berry *Chris Wall* a71 71
3 b f Green Desert(USA) Foreign Language (USA) (Distant View (USA))
6215[5] 6792[3] (7996)

Desert Blossom (IRE) *Mahmood Al Zarooni* 101
2 ch f Shamardal(USA) Elshamms (Zafonic (USA))
(5550) ◆ 6021[3] 7052[3] ◆

Desert Command *Andrew Balding* a66 56
2 b g Oasis Dream Speed Cop (Cadeaux Genereux)
5235[7] 6015[6] 6443[8]

Desertcougar (IRE) *Daniel Mark Loughnane* a68 69
3 b f Tagula(IRE) Krasotka (IRE) (Soviet Star (USA))
6050[5] 6217[5] 6774[9] 7158[5] 7382[6]

Desert Creek (IRE) *David Nicholls* a86 86
6 ch g Refuse To Bend(IRE) Flagship (Rainbow Quest (USA))
3749[10] 4864[5] 5669[4] 6127[3] 6342[4] ◆ 7247[3] (7436) (7684) (7715) 7920[7]

Desert Donkey *Andrew Balding* a47
2 b g Acclamation Honky Tonk Sally (Dansili)
8172[5]

Deserted *Luca Cumani* 67
2 b f Oasis Dream Tentpole (USA) (Rainbow Quest (USA))
4246[5]

Desert Hunter (IRE) *Micky Hammond* a53 61
9 b g Desert Story(IRE) She-Wolff (IRE) (Pips Pride)
153[5] 401[8] 531[4] 2535[14] 5258[11]

Desert Image *Charles Hills* 96
2 b f Beat Hollow Western Appeal (USA) (Gone West (USA))
6448[2] ◆ 6966[3] (7329) 7555[2]

Desert Law (IRE) *Andrew Balding* a76 110
4 b g Oasis Dream Speed Cop (Cadeaux Genereux)
1157[17] 2704[2] 3371[22] 4576[8] (5077) 5581[7] 6485[6]

Desert Phantom (USA) *David Simcock* 88
6 b g Arch(USA) Junkinthetrunk (USA) (Top Account (USA))
1602[7] 1849[7]

Desert Philosopher *Kevin Ryan* a95 82
3 b c Pastoral Pursuits Tembladora (IRE) (Docksider (USA))
1457[8] 2229[4] 2451[6] (3284) 4723[6]

Desert Recluse (IRE) *Pat Eddery* a64 98
5 ch g Redback Desert Design (Desert King (IRE))
7825[7]

Desert Red (IRE) *Phil McEntee* a52 50
3 b f Green Desert(USA) Penicuik (Hernando (FR))
1261[8] 1736[9] 2353[5] 3965[6] 4232[9] 4436[6] 4744[12] 5216[3] 5458[8] 5734[3] 5994[8] 7158[7] 7307[10] 7605[7] 8061[8] 8251[5]

Desert Romance (IRE) *David O'Meara* a71 95
6 b g Green Desert(USA) Springtime Romance (USA) (Kris S (USA))
2417[3] 2720[5] 3287[4] 3493[11] 4679[5] 4964[6] 5712[5] 6073[11] 6313[3] 6405[3] 6559[9]

Desert Spree *Jeremy Gask* a40 42
3 ch f Byron Babaraja (Dancing Spree (USA))
5878[6] 7952[8] 8075[U] 8256[9]

Desert Strike *Conor Dore* a86 79
6 b g Bertolini(USA) Mary Jane (Tina's Pet)
(62) 120[5] 186[2] (208) 251[4] 629a[3] 715[2] 1007[7] 1417[6] 1564[7] ◆ 1828[2] 2040[2] 2195[6] 2494[9] 2647[3] (4508) 4690[9] 4999[6] 5097[5] 5447[3] 5853[5] 6369[9] 6689[8] 7023[13] 7309[10] 7648[10] 7864[5] 7970[5] 8054[2] 8144[9] 8225[7] 8307[4]

Desert Sunrise *Sir Michael Stoute* a71 65
2 b f Green Desert(USA) Dorothea Brooke (IRE) (Dancing Brave (USA))
2492[2] ◆ 3560[12] 7497[4] 7777[2] 7866[2] 8016[4] 8171[4]

Desert Version *S Botti* 86
4 b m Green Desert(USA) Anita Via (IRE) (Anita's Prince)
1409a[10]

Desert Vision *Michael Easterby* a87 80
8 b g Alhaarth(IRE) Fragrant Oasis (USA) (Rahy (USA))
2094[11] 2510[7] 4325[9] 4768[8] 6131[8] (6969) 7415[3] (7867) 8110[3] 8242[3]

Designs On Rome (IRE) *Patrick J Flynn* 111
2 b c Holy Roman Emperor(IRE) Summer Trysting (USA) (Alleged (USA))
6272a[2]

Deslaya (IRE) *Linda Stubbs* a58 57
4 b m Green Desert(USA) Behlaya (IRE) (Kahyasi)
274[10] 1717[8] 2796[11]

Despatch *Ralph Beckett* a26 51
3 b f Nayef(USA) Time Saved (Green Desert (USA))
1503[8] 2204[9] 4214[11]

Dessau (GER) *W Hickst* 95
3 b f Soldier Hollow Desabina (GER) (Big Shuffle (USA))
2746a[7] 3653a[8]

Destination Aim *Frederick Watson* 2
5 b g Dubai Destination(USA) Tessa Reef (IRE) (Mark Of Esteem (IRE))
7369[10]

Destined For Glory (IRE) *J Moore* a104 117
5 b g Azamour(IRE) Tekindia (FR) (Indian Ridge)
1902a[14]

Destiny Awaits (IRE) *George Foster* a61 19
3 b g Dubai Destination(USA) Mellow Jazz (Lycius (USA))
3333[9] 4157[9] 4630[11] 6429[9] 6646[8] 7025[4] 7527[5] 7800[4]

Destiny Highway (FR) *Gay Kelleway* 47
2 b c Sir Percy Grace Bankes (Efisio)
7332[10]

Destiny Of Dreams *Jo Crowley* a72 86
4 b m Dubai Destination(USA) Valjarv (IRE) (Bluebird (USA))
1491[4] 3703[2] 4515[7] 6847[7] 7986[10]

Desuetude (AUS) *S Seemar* a86 86
7 gr g Strategic(AUS) Martella (AUS) (Unbridled's Song (USA))
261a[12]

Deutschland (USA) *W P Mullins* a81 83
9 b g Red Ransom(USA) Rhine Valley (USA) (Danzig (USA))
7584a[14]

Devdas (IRE) *Clive Cox* a74 85
3 b c Dylan Thomas(IRE) Drifting (IRE) (Sadler's Wells (USA))
1860[8] 2452[2] ◆ 4600[4] 5794[3]

Deveze (IRE) *Milton Bradley* a54 39
4 b m Kyllachy La Caprice (USA) (Housebuster (USA))
(118) 227[7] 467[9] 691[2] 783[4] 910[4] 2760[10] 7591[10] 7703[4] 7746[9] 8045[5] 8210[4]

Devine Guest (IRE) *Mick Channon* 83
3 b f Holy Roman Emperor(IRE) Mandavilla (IRE) (Sadler's Wells (USA))
1502[3] ◆ 3069[5] 3606[3] 4735[5] ◆ 5358[4] 5510[5]

Devineur (FR) *A Schaerer* a70 77
4 b g Panis(USA) Dives (FR) (Anabaa (USA))
444a[2]

Devon Diva *David Bridgwater* a51 51
6 b m Systematic General Jane (Be My Chief (USA))
2998[2] 3721[8] 4940[12] 5935[13]

Devonelli (IRE) *John Wainwright* a79 74
4 b m Mujadil(USA) Ann's Annie (IRE) (Alzao (USA))
692[6] 2675[11]

Devoted (IRE) *Ralph Beckett* 83
4 gr m Dalakhani(IRE) Wavertree Girl (IRE) (Marju (IRE))
1940[7] 2755[3] 3316[7]

Devote Myself (IRE) *David Evans* a71 68
3 b f Kodiac Hazarama (IRE) (Kahyasi)
360[2] 523[4] 620[2] 784[2] 869[2] 1031[4] 1976[8] (2425) 3186[5] 3432[4]

Devotion (IRE) *A P O'Brien* a88 107
3 b f Dylan Thomas(IRE) Bright Bank (IRE) (Sadler's Wells (USA))
2101a[2] 2658[10] 3270[17] 4378a[5] 5643a[7] 6518a[9] 7680a[12]

Devout (IRE) *Jamie Osborne* a52 40
2 b f Holy Roman Emperor(IRE) Raphimix (FR) (Linamix (FR))
2163[8] 2499[12] 2983[9] 8155[2] 8274[4]

Dewala *Michael Appleby* a62
3 b f Deportivo Fuwala (Unfuwain (USA))
369[5] 552[8] 642[3] 973[2] 6807[10] 7117[8] 7712[3] 7800[2] 7921[2] 8048[5]

Dewi Chinta (IRE) *Kevin Ryan* 59
2 b f Tagula(IRE) Damjanich (IRE) (Mull Of Kintyre (USA))
6335[9] 7290[3] 7433[5]

Dew Reward (IRE) *Bill Turner* a65 67
4 b g Aussie Rules(USA) Shariyfa (FR) (Zayyani)
(395) 465[DSQ] 2874[5] 3449[8] 3620[3] (3969)

Dha Chara (IRE) *Reg Hollinshead* a53 19
2 b g Ramonti(FR) Campiglia (IRE) (Fairy King (USA))
1437[9] 2261[15] 2663[6] 7840[3]

Dhaular Dhar (IRE) *Jim Goldie* a87 92
10 b g Indian Ridge Pescara (IRE) (Common Grounds)
2068[23] 2473[6] 4136[7] 4795[11] 5186[11] 5588[6] ◆ 6124[6] 6313[5] 6638[19] 6881[10] 7202[10] 7529[6]

Dhhamaan (IRE) *Ruth Carr* a68 76
7 b g Dilshaan Safe Care (IRE) (Caerleon (USA))
1951[10] 2355[9] 2696[11] 2924[8] 3254[4] 3455[11] 4388[3] 4779[5] 7781[7] 7983[8] 8257[3]

Diablo Dancer *Tim Walford* 77
4 b m Zafeen(FR) Faithful Beauty (IRE) (Last Tycoon)
1561[12]

Diala (IRE) *William Haggas* 92
3 b f Iffraaj Quaich (Danehill (USA))
1884[11] 3542[6] 4579[4] 5271[5] 6023[4]

Dialogue *David Nicholls* a89 74
6 b g Singspiel(IRE) Zonda (Fabulous Dancer (USA))
941[2] 1135[13]

Diaminda (IRE) *Alan Jarvis* 94
2 b f Diamond Green(FR) Lominda (IRE) (Lomond (USA))
3560[2] (4282) ◆ 5979[4]

Diamond Belle *Noel Quinlan* a83 81
3 b f Rock Of Gibraltar(IRE) Dixie Belle (Diktat)
(4711) 5409[2] 6331[4]

Diamond Blue *Richard Whitaker* a68 76
4 ch m Namid Petra Nova (First Trump)
1954[3] 2140[3] 2674[5] 4770[9] (5257) 5821[5] 6044[7] 6357[3] 7483[4]

Diamond Charlie (IRE) *Simon Dow* a87 86
4 br g Diamond Green(FR) Rosy Lydgate (Last Tycoon)
715[6] 1602[14] 2040[3] 2704[14] 3771[10] 4501[7] 5233[6] 5832[11]

Diamond Dame (IRE) *Sir Michael Stoute* a69
3 b f King's Best(USA) Arabian Treasure (USA) (Danzig (USA))
(1589) 2038[7]

Diamond Finesse (IRE) *Ed Dunlop* a55 74
3 b f Red Clubs(IRE) Birthday Present (Cadeaux Genereux)
20[3]

Diamond Fire (IRE) *Adrian McGuinness* a51 33
8 b g King Charlemagne(USA) Diamond Sun (Primo Dominie)
67[11] 483[6] 503[4] 939[4]

Diamondhead (IRE) *Brian Meehan* a41 91
3 b c Kyllachy Hammrah (Danehill (USA))
4063[12] 4740[11] 5517[13] 6075[8] ◆ 6768[9]

Diamond Marks (IRE) *John Gallagher* a65 59
3 b g Diamond Green(FR) Miss Megs (IRE) (Croco Rouge (IRE))
565[5] 663[2] 982[3] 1331[7] 1622[4] 2361[5] 3005[3] 3248[7]

Diamond Penny (IRE) *Seamus Durack* a68 87
4 b g Diamond Green(FR) Penny Fan (Nomination)
7715[8]

Diamondsinhereyes (IRE) *Ed Vaughan* a55
3 b f Diamond Green(FR) Glencoagh Order (IRE) (Danehill (USA))
499[4] ◆ 2030[7]

Diamond Sky (IRE) *J S Bolger* 98
2 gr f Montjeu(IRE) Danaskaya (IRE) (Danehill (USA))
5135a[3] 6081a[8]

Diamond Sunrise (IRE) *Noel Wilson* a24 54
4 b m Diamond Green(FR) Sunrise (IRE) (Sri Pekan (USA))
2600[11] 4158[9] 5720[11]

Diamond Twister (USA) *Lisa Williamson* a65 62
6 b g Omega Code(USA) King's Pact (USA) (Slewacide (USA))
395[7] 558[2] 741[6] 1106[8] 1299[5] 1831[2] 3392[7] 3907[8] 4594[10] 5052[8]

Diamond Vine (IRE) *Ronald Harris* a76 74
4 b h Diamond Green(FR) Glasnas Giant (Giant's Causeway (USA))
88[4] 178[2] (353) 425[3] (658) 710[4] 1187[7] 1254[8] 1789[2] 2165[4] 2572[14] 2972[2] 3139[6] 4708[10] 5150[6] 5502[5] 5775[4] 5933[2] 6094[10] 7273[8] 7864[10] 7902[4] 8159[7] 8305[6]

Diamond Vision (IRE) *Carroll Gray* a56 80
4 b g Diamond Green(FR) Tranquil Sky (Intikhab (USA))
4884[11]

Dibajj (FR) *C Ferland* a87 91
2 ch f Iffraaj Goleta (IRE) (Royal Applause)
6942a[7]

Dibayani (IRE) *M Halford* 98
2 b c Shamardal(USA) Dibiya (IRE) (Caerleon (USA))
6060a[3]

Dibella (IRE) *Ms Joanna Morgan* 81
5 b m Observatory(USA) Dibiya (IRE) (Caerleon (USA))
7584a[6]

Dicey Vows (USA) *Alan Jarvis* a64 50
4 b g Broken Vow(USA) Pretty Dicey (USA) (Cherokee Run (USA))
1065[4] 5001[7] 7473[12]

Dichoh *Michael Madgwick* a66 54
9 b g Diktat Hoh Dancer (Indian Ridge)
554 306[6] 732[5] 995[6] 1309[7] 2364[11] 5349[12] 7500[7] 8099[P] 8179[9]

Dick Bos *Peter Chapple-Hyam* a71 83
3 ch g Dutch Art Cosmic Countess (IRE) (Lahib (USA))
1506[7] 6643[2] (6930) ◆

Dick Doughtywylie *John Gosden* 94
4 b g Oasis Dream Sugar Mill (FR) (Polar Falcon (USA))
1605[11] 1854[10] 2248[19] (6202)

Dickens Rules (IRE) *David Bridgwater* a67 68
3 gr g Aussie Rules(USA) Lisfannon (Bahamian Bounty)
6000[12]

Dickie Le Davoir *Richard Guest* a74 81
8 b g Kyllachy Downeaster Alexa (USA) (Red Ryder (USA))
(19) 122[9] 178[10] 325[7] 385[2] 473[10] 670[3] 746[6] 834[9] 1168[4] 1289[5] 1476[4] 1650[10] 4315[9] 4591[4] 4998[6] 5774[2] 5915[10] 6044[8] (6260) 6403[12] 7273[9] 7589[4] 7684[6] (7915)

Dickie's Lad (IRE) *Kevin Ryan* a100 97
4 b g Diamond Green(FR) Shadow Mountain (Selkirk (USA))
1975[10] 2177[5] ◆ 2704[18] 3374[10] 4799[26] 5487[13] 6165[14] 6685[3] 7000[4] 7291[4] 7651[10]

Dicky Mint *Michael Easterby* a57 68
3 ch g Osorio(GER) Oh Bej Oh Bej (IRE) (Distinctly North (USA))
191[3] 270[3]

Diddums *John Ryan* a47 65
6 b g Royal Applause Sahara Shade (USA) (Shadeed (USA))
2988[3] 3006[5] 3318[5] 3470[10] 3721[9] 4061[8] 7915[11] 8005[8] 8039[7] 8153[6] 8264[9]

Diddy Eric *Micky Hammond* 40
2 b c Oratorio(IRE) Amber Queen (IRE) (Cadeaux Genereux)
6473[6] 6954[9] 7450[4]

Didnt I Do Well *Julia Feilden* a45
2 b g Byron Sovereign Seal (Royal Applause)
6034[3] 7008[8] 7714[7]

Diescentric (USA) *Julie Camacho* a97 97
5 b g Diesis Hawzah (Green Desert (USA))
5342[15] 6201[4] ◆ 6676[12] 7097[11] (7826)

Different *Bryan Smart* 60
2 ch f Bahamian Bounty Hill Welcome (Most Welcome)
4545[6]

Diggers Daydream (IRE) *Lisa Williamson* 6
4 b g Refuse To Bend(IRE) Enlightened Way (FR) (Indian Ridge)
1001[8] 1173[7] 1422[10] 1881[14]

Diggory Delvet *Richard Fahey* 75
2 b g Pastoral Pursuits Digger Girl (USA) (Black Minnaloushe (USA))
(3844) ◆ 5109[3] 5563[10] 6920[6] 7399[5]

Digress *Sir Michael Stoute* 74
2 b c Oasis Dream Change Course (Sadler's Wells (USA))
3505[10] 4330[3] 5235[3] ◆ 5948[3]

Dikanta *Robert Cowell* a47 8
4 b g Diktat Frascati (Emarati (USA))
925[5] 1111[4] 1343[9] 2046[10]

Dilady *Kevin Ryan* 43
2 b f Bertolini(USA) Flying Highest (Spectrum (IRE))
6627[6] 7290[10]

Diletta Tommasa (IRE) *Marco Botti* a61 35
2 ch f Dylan Thomas(IRE) Chronicle (Observatory (USA))
6816[5] (7786)

Dilizan (IRE) *Brian Ellison* a59 62
3 b g Dubai Destination(USA) Dibiya (IRE) (Caerleon (USA))
231[6] 383[5] 903[3] 1322[6] 1915[4]

Dil Laney (IRE) *David O'Meara* a16 63
2 b g Mujadil(USA) Maddie's Pearl (IRE) (Clodovil (IRE))
1795[2] ◆ 2261[11] 2770[5] 3019[3] 3251[3] 3936[5] 5108[2] 5675[5] 6310[5]

Diman Waters (IRE) *Eric Alston* a78 83
5 br g Namid Phantom Waters (Pharly (FR))
1293[7] 2119[5] (2596) 2690[2] 3065[5] 3608[3] 4770[5] 5272[7] 6005[9] 6123[3] 6234[12] 6665[14] 7145[9] 7464[5] (7666)

Dimashq *Paul Midgley* a33 54
10 b m Mtoto Agwaas (IRE) (Rainbow Quest (USA))
1950[4] 2670[8] 3116[7] 4766[11] 4912[4] 6315[9] 6956[6]

Dimension *James Fanshawe* a102 111
4 b g Medicean Palatial (Green Desert (USA))
2082[2] 3268[8] (4609) ◆

Dinas Lane *Paul Green*
2 b c Indian Haven Foolish Optimist (Cadeaux Genereux)
6787[15] 7357[12]

Dine Out *Mark H Tompkins* a40 60
3 b f Piccolo Sosumi (Be My Chief (USA))
2548[10] 3048[10] 5018[5]

Dingaan (IRE) *Peter Grayson* a60 30
9 b g Tagula(IRE) Boughtbyphone (Warning)
122[8] 203[6] 313[2] 473[8] 578[6] 823[3] 985[7] 1061[9] 2350[9] 2973[8] 4929[2] 6179[8] 6321[5]

Dingle View (IRE) *Bent Olsen* 94
4 b m Mujadil(USA) Livius Lady (IRE) (Titus Livius (FR))
4751a[6]

Dinkie *Ollie Pears* 33
2 b f Misu Bond(IRE) Chez Cherie (Wolfhound (USA))
2437[8] 4448[10]

Dinkum Diamond (IRE) *Henry Candy* 110
4 b h Aussie Rules(USA) Moving Diamonds (Lomitas)
1316[6] 3238[20] 3877[5] 4299[3] (5204) 5822[7]

Dinnar (FR) *Mario Hofer* a73 73
3 b c Sinndar(IRE) Dunnellon (Shareef Dancer (USA))
247a[6] 1127a[5]

Dinner Date *Tom Keddy* a63 64
10 ch g Groom Dancer(USA) Misleading Lady (Warning)
821[12] 967[7] 1611[5] 1919[7] 3497[9]

Dinvar Diva *John Gosden* a77 96
3 gr f Dalakhani(IRE) Musique Magique (IRE) (Mozart (IRE))
2079[6] (2633) ◆ 3292[14] 6877[5] 7688[12]

Diplomasi *Clive Brittain* a70 72
4 b g Iceman Piper's Ash (USA) (Royal Academy (USA))
1045[6]

Diplomatic (IRE) *Michael Squance* a75
7 b g Cape Cross(IRE) Embassy (Cadeaux Genereux)
(264) (578) 972[2] 1088[2] (2373) 3045[11] 4068[12] 4469[8] (7480) 7722[2] 7893[5]

Director's Dream (IRE) *Mark Rimmer* a56 58
4 gr m Act One Najayeb (USA) (Silver Hawk (USA))
770[6] 974[5] 1263[9] 2013[7] 2467[5] 2851[9] 3470[3] 3978[4] 4435[7] 4538[10]

Directorship *Patrick Chamings* a94 98
6 br g Diktat Away To Me (Exit To Nowhere (USA))
1924[5] ◆ 2642[2] 3331[6] 3878[14] 6601[3] 7556[10]

Direct Trade *Mark Usher* a48 19
2 ch f Trade Fair Bold Love (Bold Edge)
6772[10] 7296[5] 7813[9] 8007[6]

Disa Leader (SAF) *M F De Kock* a107 107
7 b g Parade Leader(USA) Plumosa (SAF) (Sapieha (IRE))
246a[9] 416a[4] 677a[2] 755a[10]

Discay *Mark Johnston* 72
3 b g Distant Music(USA) Caysue (Cayman Kai (IRE))
5679[5] 6102[7] 6408[3] 6924[10]

Discernable *Mark Johnston* a79 99
2 ch f Elusive Quality(USA) Louve Mysterieuse (USA) (Seeking The Gold (USA))
(3282) 4283[2] (4615a) 5379a[0] 6635[5] 6874[9]

Disclaimer *Sir Henry Cecil* 76
2 b g Dansili Novellara (Sadler's Wells (USA))
3634[5] 4194[3] 4995[2] 5992[3] 6880[2] (7442)

Discourse (USA) *Mahmood Al Zarooni* 113
3 bb f Street Cry(IRE) Divine Dixie (USA) (Dixieland Band (USA))
1884[16]

Discoverer (IRE) *John Gosden* a91 89
3 b c Bernardini(USA) Danuta (USA) (Sunday Silence (USA))
(147) (471) ◆ 5237[3] 5768[8]

Discovery Bay *C F Swan* a82 82
4 b g Dansili Rainbow's Edge (Rainbow Quest (USA))
7852a[6]

Discression *Kevin Ryan* a73 96
3 b c Indesatchel(IRE) Night Gypsy (Mind Games)
1257[5] 1824[4] 2616[6] 3379[2] 4496[3] (4954) (5314) 6143[12]

Dishy Guru *Michael Blanshard* a81 82
3 ch g Ishiguru(USA) Pick A Nice Name (Polar Falcon (USA))
(1110) (1331) 2276[16] 2714[7] 3445[10] 5128[5] 5662[5] 5906[5] 6173[9] 7412[9] 8059[7]

Disko Dasko (FR) *Mrs K Burke* 95
2 b f Country Reel(USA) Rosalita (FR) (Nashamaa)
2977[4] 6627[4] 7265a[3] (7430a)

Dispol Diva *Paul Midgley* a28 66
6 b m Deportivo Kingston Rose (GER) (Robellino (USA))
3222[3] (3577) 4639[7] 5012[9] 6608[7]

Dispol Grand (IRE) *Paul Midgley* a65 79
6 b g Raise A Grand(IRE) Hever Rosina (Efisio)
844[6] 996[5] 1298[2] (1516) 1868[7] (2084) 5412[11] 6006[8] 6234[11] 6886[8] 7299[5] 7489[12]

Disposition *John Gosden* a81 79
3 ch f Selkirk(USA) Far Shores (USA) (Distant View (USA))
1610[3] 2344[4] 3070[6] 3792[3] 4648[3]

Dissent (IRE) *David C Griffiths* a81 56
3 b c Dansili Centifolia (FR) (Kendor (FR))
2265[12] 2660[12] 3049[13] 6641[3]

Distant Love (IRE) *Andrew Balding* a59 62
3 b f Halling(USA) Conference (IRE) (Montjeu (IRE))
816[2] 1443[10]

Distant Sun (USA) *Linda Perratt* a50 63
8 b g Distant View(USA) The Great Flora (USA) (Unaccounted For (USA))
1800[9] 2458[7] 2719[7] 2839[2] 3109[9] 3523[2] 3730[3] 3893[3] 3905[7] 4262[5] 4392[3] 4865[2] 5087[4] 5190[4] 5542[6] 5758[4] 5923[3] 6264[11] 6531[4] (6713) 7099[5] 7447[13]

Distant Sunrise *Ann Duffield* 21
2 b f Tobougg(IRE) Prairie Sun (GER) (Law Society (USA))
6985[9] 7442[6]

Distinctive Image (USA) *C Von Der Recke* a96 75
7 b g Mineshaft(USA) Dock Leaf (USA) (Woodman (USA))
631a[9]

District Attorney (IRE) *William Haggas* a70 70
3 b c Lawman(FR) Mood Indigo (IRE) (Indian Ridge)
1703[5] 3031[4] 3558[4] 4466[3] 6364[9] 7417[8]

Disturbia (IRE) *Olivia Maylam* a50 51
4 b m Dubai Destination(USA) Eoz (IRE) (Sadler's Wells (USA))
1534[11] 1771[7] 3137[10] 3573[8]

Diva Cavallina *Alan McCabe* a22
2 b f Auction House(USA) Vida (IRE) (Wolfhound (USA))
3282[13] 3569[7] 4246[10]

Diva Donkey (IRE) *Bryan Smart* a48 34
3 b f Acclamation Lupulina (CAN) (Saratoga Six (USA))
495[3] 1012[11] 5801[6]

Divea *Charles Hills* 63
3 b f Dylan Thomas(IRE) Cumin (USA) (Fusaichi Pegasus (USA))
3918[8] 4366[7] 5309[7]

Divergence (IRE) *Michael Bell* 73
2 b f Teofilo(IRE) Min Alhawa (USA) (Riverman (USA))
5551[6] 6117[5]

Divertimenti (IRE) *Roy Bowring* a61 70
8 b g Green Desert(USA) Ballet Shoes (IRE) (Ela-Mana-Mou)
8[5] 139[12] 370[10] 544[8] 2314[8] 2377[2] 2549[7] 2981[6] 3018[7] 4631[9] 4743[5] 5131[6] 5205[3] 5681[13] 6105[12] 6321[10] 6496[4] 7179[7] 7447[10] 7634[7] 8209[3]

Diverting *William Jarvis* a75 94
4 b m Nayef(USA) Tawny Way (Polar Falcon (USA))
2067[8] 2642[5] 3636[7] 4579[8] 7334[5] 7558[4] 7809[13]

Dividend Dan (IRE) *Mike Murphy* a50
2 ch g Danroad(AUS) Pip'n Judy (IRE) (Pips Pride)
6978[9] 7191[7]

Divine Angel (IRE) *Phil McEntee* a59 65
2 gr f Dark Angel(IRE) Downland (USA) (El Prado (IRE))
4433[13] 6844[4] (6928) 7335[6] (7714) 7971[3] 8003[2] 8053[2] 8101[3] 8164[4] 8293[6] 8302[8]

Divine Call *Milton Bradley* a78 85
5 b g Pivotal Pious (Bishop Of Cashel)
(1254) 1520[11] 2071[6] 2870[12] 3281[8] 3778[15] (5502) 5933[8] 7274[4] 7789[11] 8058[4] 8232[9]

Divine Music (IRE) *P Van De Poele* a96 109
5 b m Gold Away(IRE) Divine Island (FR) (Anabaa (USA))
2570a[10] 4386a[5] 7985a[0]

Divine Pamina (IRE) *Jim Boyle* a69 62
3 br f Dark Angel(IRE) Greek Symphony (IRE) (Mozart (IRE))
1501[6] 2891[6] 3630[8] 4435[5] 4914[3] 6152[5]

Divine Reward (USA) *Reg Hollinshead* 72
2 b g Divine Park(USA) World Of Thanks (USA) (Wild Again (USA))
6799[3] ◆ 7290[4]

Divine Rule (IRE) *Laura Mongan* a59 58
4 br g Cacique(IRE) Island Destiny (Kris)
(55) 146[6] 198[8] 422[4] 593[3] 781[9] 2845[6] 3701[8] 4817[9] 5996[9] 6329[6] 6396[2] 6778[5] 7500[9] 7898[2] 8077[6] 8261[2]

Divine Success (IRE) *Richard Fahey* a38 56
3 b g Amadeus Wolf Divine Pursuit (Kris)
1259[4] 1918[5] 2340[11] 3575[3] 4397[12] 4771[10] 6316[6]

Divin Honor (FR) *A Schaerer* a86 90
5 b g Highest Honor(FR) Dives (FR) (Anabaa (USA))
629a[9]

Divin Leon (FR) *M Boutin* a86 100
4 b h Divine Light(JPN) Nera Zilzal (IRE) (Zilzal (USA))
(1172a)

Dixie Gwalia *David Simcock* a56 60
4 b m Tobougg(IRE) Dixieanna (Night Shift (USA))
1742[3] 1934[6] 4237[3] 4422[3] 7204[4] 7316[6] 7748[3] 7837[8] 8075[5] 8169[3] 8287[6]

Dixie's Dream (IRE) *Richard Hannon* a83 88
3 b c Hawk Wing(USA) Hams (USA) (Dixie Union (USA))
1612[4] (2331) 2930[12] 3446[4] 4772[2] 5269[3] 5747[5] 6205[4] 6789[4]

Dixie Sky (USA) *Noel Quinlan* 66
2 bb f Dixie Union(USA) Mona Quita (USA) (El Corredor (USA))
3560[5] 4246[6] 6664[5]

Doc Hay (USA) *David O'Meara* a74 111
5 bb g Elusive Quality(USA) Coherent (USA) (Danzig (USA))
1438[2] 1885[16] 2286[3] 2602[3] 3078[7] 6028[4] (6244) 6468[7] (6869) 7397[7] ◆ 7690[13]

Doc Hill *Michael Blanshard* a51 47
3 ch g Dr Fong(USA) Cultural Role (Night Shift (USA))
1260[4] 2548[7] 2862[8] 3433[4] 4900[3] 5443[9] 5998[12] 6442[5] 7619[9] 7811[12]

Docofthebay (IRE) *Scott Dixon* a106 101
8 ch g Docksider(USA) Baize (Efisio)
711[4] 866[5] 1157[4] 1558[10] 3078[3] 3331[18] 4086[13] 7010[11] 7691[19] 7817[8] 8095[9]

Docs Legacy (IRE) *Richard Fahey* a76 84
3 b g Ad Valorem(USA) Lunamixa (GER) (Linamix (FR))
4623[2] 5358[7] 6884[2] 7032[3] 7842[6]

Doctor Hilary *Mark Hoad* a67 60
10 b g Mujahid(USA) Agony Aunt (Formidable (USA))
819[6] 964[9] 1263[6] 1768[7] 2373[11] 7504[5] 8168[6] 8299[11]

Doctor Parkes *Stuart Williams* a94 102
6 b g Diktat Lucky Parkes (Full Extent (USA))
1975[5] 2208[5] ◆ 3374[6] 5204[3] 5487[8] 5829[12] 6028[5] (6688) 8272[6]

Doctor's Gift *Andrew Balding* a46 33
2 b g Motivator Josie May (USA) (Aljabr (USA))
7517[8] 7922[5]

Doctor Zhivago *Ian McInnes* a54 89
5 b g Shamardal(USA) Balalaika (Sadler's Wells (USA))
1275[3] 1429[3] 1913[5] 2593[9] 5012[5]

Dohasa (IRE) *Ismail Mohammed* a108 108
7 b g Bold Fact(USA) Zara's Birthday (IRE) (Waajib)
420a[10] 588a[7] 756a[5]

Do It All (USA) *Saeed Bin Suroor* a108 110
5 bb h Distorted Humor(USA) Stupendous Miss (USA) (Dynaformer (USA))
246a[14] 590a[11] (758a) 1143a[12]

Doku (TUR) *D Ergin* a48
6 b m Ocean Crest(USA) Irish Victory (IRE) (Danehill (USA))
5848a[9]

Dollar Bill *Andrew Balding* a67 73
3 ch g Medicean Jardin (Sinndar (IRE))
1707[8] 2427[3] 3592[7]

Dollar King (GER) *Exors Of W Baltromei* a60
3 b g Kahyasi Dora Bella (GER) (Johan Cruyff)
247a[0] 661a[5]

Dolly Bantry *Alan McCabe*
2 ch f Pastoral Pursuits Seeker (Rainbow Quest (USA))
3282[14]

Dolly Bay *Julia Feilden* a50 43
4 ch m Kyllachy Loblolly Bay (Halling (USA))
910[9]

Dolly Colman (IRE) *Zoe Davison* a54 53
4 bg m Diamond Green(FR) Absolutely Cool (IRE) (Indian Ridge)
200[8] 454[9] (741) 895[5] 7303[14] 7479[14] 8079[8]

Dolly Diva *Paul Midgley* 62
3 b f Iffraaj Charlie Girl (Puissance)
2121[6] 2335[4] 2680[3] 3421[8] 4793[11] 5545[2] 6106[4]

Dolly Royal (IRE) *Robert Johnson* a25 46
7 b m Val Royal(FR) Roos Rose (IRE) (Grand Lodge (USA))
1178[10] 1384[7] 2239[6] 2670[11] 2922[10] 3209[2] 3495[6] 3731[6] 6258[14] 6959[10]

Dolphin Rock *Brian Ellison* a77 91
5 b g Mark Of Esteem(IRE) Lark In The Park (IRE) (Grand Lodge (USA))
1249[6] 1670[16] 2285[6] 2510[9] 3167[3] 3385[4] 4345[7] 4889[7] 5588[7] (6047) 6342[3] 6881[2] 7083[15] 7715[4]

Dolphin Village (IRE) *Richard Fahey* a64 74
2 b c Cape Cross(IRE) Reform Act (USA) (Lemon Drop Kid (USA))
6512[4] 7096[2] 7750[6] 8071[6]

Dominate *Richard Hannon* 91
2 b c Assertive Blue Goddess (IRE) (Blues Traveller (IRE))
3916[2] (4220) 4687[6] 4804[6] 6022[3] 6487[5] 7374[9]

Domination *C Byrnes* a82 89
5 b g Motivator Soliza (IRE) (Intikhab (USA))
6066a[10] (6493)

Dominium (USA) *Jeremy Gask* a82 82
5 b g E Dubai(USA) Sudenlylastsummer (USA) (Rinka Das (USA))
4554[13] 5269[8] 6495[8]

Domino Rock (FR) *C Boutin* a83 91
4 b h Indian Rocket Lady Domino (FR) (Second Empire (IRE))
16a[0]

Do More Business (IRE) *Alison Batchelor* a60 60
5 b g Dubai Destination(USA) Tokyo Song (USA) (Stravinsky (USA))
126[3] 210[2] (396) 522[4] 598[2] 972[7] 1787[4] 2171[3] 2365[2] 3497[6] 3723[3] 3964[4] 4241[7] 6778[9] 7816[6] 8099[7] 8168[2] 8305[3]

Donatia *David Nicholls* 40
3 b f Shamardal(USA) Donna Anna (Be My Chief (USA))
5541[4] 6190[6] 6925[7] 7527[13]

Don Bosco (FR) *D Smaga* a106 112
5 ch h Barathea(IRE) Perfidie (IRE) (Monsun (GER))
953a[7] 4229a[3] (5117a) 5650a[6] 6898a[5] (7515a) 8042a[9]

Doncaster Rover (USA) *Richard Fahey* a90 113
6 b h War Chant(USA) Rebridled Dreams (USA) (Unbridled's Song (USA))
2179[8] 2710[3] 3166[2] 3623[7] 4078[4] 5597[5] 5964[5]

Done Dreaming (IRE) *Richard Fahey* a64 72
2 b g Diamond Green(FR) Wishing Chair (USA) (Giant's Causeway (USA))
4344[9] (4670) 5411[5] (5916) 6312[5] 6499[3]

Don Eduardo *J S Moore* a55 59
2 b c Byron Angie And Liz (IRE) (Spectrum (IRE))
6431[3] 6871[12] 7305[9] 8093[11] 8164[2] 8186[3] 8258[5]

Done Talking (USA) *Hamilton Smith* a110 90
3 b c Broken Vow(USA) Dixie Talking (USA) (Dixieland Band (USA))
1872a[14]

Don Juan *Eric Alston* 55
2 b g Byron Zell (IRE) (Lend A Hand)
5586[10] 5963[8] 7020[10]

Don Libre *Paul Cole* a87 61
3 b c Librettist(USA) Darwinia (GER) (Acatenango (GER))
(3155) 4298[9] 4607[6] 4876[2] 5302[2] (6256) ◆

Don Marco *Roger Charlton* 85
2 b g Choisir(AUS) Dolma (FR) (Marchand De Sable (USA))
6443[4] ◆ (7078)

Donna Elvira *Edwin Tuer* a38 62
5 b m Doyen(IRE) Impatiente (USA) (Vaguely Noble)
2670[7] 3310[9] 5114[5]

Donn Halling (IRE) *V Luka Jr* 107
4 b g Halling(USA) Papering (IRE) (Shaadi (USA))
6290a[8] (7427a)

Donnywardsbird *Eric Alston* 5
4 b g Danbird(AUS) Sweetly Sharp (IRE) (Daggers Drawn (USA))
6125[10] 7025[9]

Don Padeja *Luca Cumani* a65
2 b c Dansili La Leuze (IRE) (Caerleon (USA))
7899[6]

Don't Be *F-H Graffard* a75
2 b f Cape Cross(IRE) Faslen (USA) (Fasliyev (USA))
7683a[3]

Dont Bother Me (IRE) *Niall Moran* 95
2 br c Dark Angel(IRE) Faleh (USA) (Silver Hawk (USA))
5833[6] 7419a[5]

Don't Call Me (IRE) *David Nicholls* a70 109
5 ch g Haafhd Just Call Me (NZ) (Blues Traveller (IRE))
1130[12] 1865[15] 2311[6] 2657[12] 3268[3] (3779) 4684[18] 5677[6] (6024) 6868[2]

Don't Call Me Tiny (IRE) *Don Cantillon* a34 37
4 b m Acclamation Holly Rose (Charnwood Forest (IRE))
188[11] 334[9]

Don't Look Bach (IRE) *Brian Barr*
7 b g Bach(IRE) Buckalong (IRE) (Buckskin (FR))
(2113a)

Dontpaytheferryman (USA) *Brian Ellison* a86 72
7 ch g Wiseman's Ferry(USA) Expletive Deleted (USA) (Dr Blum (USA))
1950[3]

Don't Put It Back (USA) *D Paulus* a79
5 b h Put It Back(USA) Lac Dawat (USA) (Lac Ouimet (USA))
8100a[7]

Don't Say No (CAN) *Luis M Ramirez*
5 rg g Margie's Wildcat(USA) Liquid Fill (USA) (Relaunch (USA))
(8278a)

Dont Take Me Alive *Clive Cox* a73 73
3 b g Araafa(IRE) Up At Dawn (Inchinor)
1853[9] 3142[9] (4005) 4649[4] 5442[2]

Don't Tell *George Moore* 27
2 ch f Sakhee's Secret Starry Sky (Oasis Dream)
4618[10] 6042[10] 7450[8]

Dont Teutch (FR) *D Smaga* a70 99
3 b f Country Reel(USA) Simonkikou (FR) (Panis (USA))
1426a[0]

Doodles *David Nicholls* a44 31
2 b f Pastoral Pursuits Burton Ash (Diktat)
7440[3] 7932[4]

Dorade Rose (FR) *D Smaga* a79 77
4 b m Marchand De Sable(USA) Shadai Stone (JPN) (Real Shadai (USA))
1172a[8]

Dora's Gift *Hughie Morrison* a77 72
3 b f Cadeaux Genereux Conquestadora (Hernando (FR))
3142[2] ◆ 4606[7] 4875[3] 6037[6]

Dora's Sister (IRE) *John Quinn* a38 68
3 b f Dark Angel(IRE) Teodora (IRE) (Fairy King (USA))
1758[2] 2375[5] 3111[4] (3751) 5548[7]

Dorback *David Nicholls* a88 86
5 ch g Kyllachy Pink Supreme (Night Shift (USA))
6465[22] 7291[10] (7730) 7859[6] 8163[4]

Dorcas Lane *David Lanigan* a87 107
4 ch m Norse Dancer(IRE) Waqood (USA) (Riverman (USA))
2711[6] ◆ 4338[2] 6877[2] 7688[9]

Dorothy's Dancing (IRE) *Gary Moore* a75 59
4 b m Acclamation Segoria (IRE) (Shinko Forest (IRE))
320[6] 445[3] (665) ◆ 783[2] (1070) (1185) 1614[3] 2114a[5] 7308[6] 7742[10] 7967[7] 8159[9]

Dorry K (IRE) *David Barron* 78
3 b f Ad Valorem(USA) Ashtaroute (USA) (Holy Bull (USA))
(1320) 2144[11] 2885[2] 3212[5] 4250[4] 4781[4] (5413) 7032[9] (7444)

Dorset Square (IRE) *Sarah Humphrey* a65 73
8 b g Fantastic Light(USA) Albula (FR) (Anabaa (USA))
1991[2] 2214[13] 2698[9]

Dos Amigos (IRE) *Michael Dods* 86
3 b c Clodovil(IRE) Ide Say (IRE) (Grand Lodge (USA))
(1864) 3063[3] ◆

Dotada (IRE) *Peter Casey* a74 88
7 gr m Noverre(USA) Nichodoula (Doulab (USA))
7230a[6]

Doting *Peter Salmon* 14
3 b g Pursuit Of Love Star Sign (Robellino (USA))
3809[9] 4791[10] 6408[8]

Dot's Delight *Mark Rimell* a53 51
8 b m Golden Snake(USA) Hotel California (IRE) (Last Tycoon)
213[4]

Dotty Darroch *Robin Bastiman* a30 58
4 b m Ad Valorem(USA) Sensible Idea (Dr Fong (USA))
1383[8] (1881) 2436[7] 3018[2] 3462[3] 4453[8] 5082[6] 5590[8] 6003[3] 6958[6]

Doublebarreljimmy (IRE) *John Butler* a42 56
3 b g Modigliani(USA) Petitesse (Petong)
7616[9] 7752[7]

Double Carpet (IRE) *Garry Woodward* a65 2
9 b g Lahib(USA) Cupid Miss (Anita's Prince)
102[5] 328[3] 359[11] 2091[14] 7446[19]

Double Cee *Richard Fahey* a18 80
3 ch g Haafhd Razzle (IRE) (Green Desert (USA))
2089[4] 2336[3] 2604[5] (3275) 3555[11] (4260) (4768) 6073[15] 6701[8] 7032[6]

Double Dealer *Mahmood Al Zarooni* a101 101
4 b g Dubawi(IRE) Infiel (Luge)
1212[2] 2082[4] 5301[3] 6036[15] 6674[9]

Double Discount (IRE) *Tom Dascombe* a71
2 b g Invincible Spirit(IRE) Bryanstown Girl (IRE) (Kalanisi (IRE))
8070^{3}

Double Double (FR) *Charles O'Brien* 82
6 b g Sakhee(USA) Queen Sceptre (IRE) (Fairy King (USA))
7584a^{7}

Double Happiness *Brian Rothwell* 22
2 ch f Sakhee(USA) Fu Wa (USA) (Distant View (USA))
2790^{9} 3457^{8} 4778^{8}

Double Jeopardy *Dr Jon Scargill* a14 32
2 b g Tobougg(IRE) Four-Legged Friend (Aragon)
3569^{5} 3948^{12} 5511^{6} 6016^{12}

Double Proposition *Bryan Smart* 36
3 b f Iceman Double Fantasy (Mind Games)
2335^{11} 4551^{5}

Double Star *Jonathan Portman* a39 20
2 b f Elusive City(USA) Tease (IRE) (Green Desert (USA))
6817^{9} 7165^{10}

Double Trouble *Marco Botti* a65 61
4 b m Royal Applause Requiem (USA) (Royal Anthem (USA))
1743^{6}

Double Trouble (GER) *Boze Majic*
2 b f Liquido(GER) Double Dagger Lady (USA) (Diesis)
5612a^{12}

Double Your Money (IRE) *Mark Johnston* a81 69
2 b g Shamardal(USA) Zeiting (IRE) (Zieten (USA))
5325^{5} (5715) 6189^{5} 6980^{6} ◆ 7350^{3}

Douce Vie (IRE) *S Botti* 109
6 b h Desert Prince(IRE) Ellendellendoo (IRE) (Ela-Mana-Mou)
(7286a) 7587a^{3}

Dougie Boy *Bill Turner* a55 61
3 b g Trade Fair Wavet (Pursuit Of Love)
3947^{9}

Douglas Pasha (IRE) *Richard Hannon* a22
2 b g Compton Place Lake Nayasa (Nayef (USA))
7057^{8}

Douro *Roger Charlton* a54 17
3 b f Manduro(GER) Tamso (USA) (Seeking The Gold (USA))
3279^{10} 4410^{14}

Douze Points (IRE) *John Butler* a83 94
6 b g Redback Grade A Star (IRE) (Alzao (USA))
(848) ◆ 1191^{2} 1830^{2} 3099^{2} 3344^{3} 3958^{5} 4950^{5}

Dove Cottage (IRE) *Stuart Kittow* a41 67
10 b g Great Commotion(USA) Pooka (Dominion)
(1205) 2732^{5} 4491^{11} 6004^{7}

Dovils Date *Rod Millman* a64 78
3 gr g Clodovil(IRE) Lucky Date (IRE) (Halling (USA))
1568^{7} 1982^{4} (2424) 3072^{2} (3345) 4225^{6} 5044^{6} 5789^{3}

Downhill Dancer (IRE) *Brian Meehan* a39 64
2 b f Montjeu(IRE) Wiener Wald (USA) (Woodman (USA))
5104^{9} 6366^{8} 6790^{13}

Downhiller (IRE) *John Dunlop* a99 94
7 ch g Alhaarth(IRE) Ski For Gold (Shirley Heights)
4575^{7} 5491^{16} 6012^{9}

Downhill Skier (IRE) *Mark Brisbourne* a70 74
8 ch g Danehill Dancer(IRE) Duchy Of Cornwall (USA) (The Minstrel (CAN))
102^{11} 478^{3}

Downright Dizzie *Tom Keddy* 63
2 ch f Notnowcato Italian Goddess (Medicean)
3368^{11} 4056^{11} 6114^{14} 7313^{8} 7686^{10}

Downton Abbey (IRE) *Richard Hannon* a61 58
3 b f Dubai Destination(USA) Morality (Elusive Quality (USA))
1443^{6}

Downtown Boy (IRE) *Ray Craggs* a50 55
4 br g Kheleyf(USA) Uptown (IRE) (Be My Guest (USA))
1096^{5} 1179^{11} 1635^{5} 3029^{7} 3353^{8} 4453^{9} 4958^{3} 7248^{7}

Doyle's Dream *Michael Madgwick* a33
3 gr f Cape Town(IRE) Think It Over (IRE) (Bijou D'Inde)
1501^{16} 2422^{7} 3340^{14} 4214^{14} 7996^{7} 8267^{7}

Doyouknowwhoiam *Geoffrey Oldroyd* a58 57
3 ch g Monsieur Bond(IRE) Tibesti (Machiavellian (USA))
6892^{12} 7837^{11}

Dozy Joe *Paul Fitzsimons* a87 83
4 b g Sleeping Indian Surrey Down (USA) (Forest Wildcat (USA))
29^{5} 304^{8} 563^{4} 765^{2} 962^{12} 1066^{8} 2083^{5} 2500^{8} 3439^{10} 3767^{6} 3963^{7} 4661^{8} 5234^{5} 6041^{6} 6256^{3} 6687^{2} 7170^{4} 7328^{5} 7484^{2} 7901^{5} (8133)

Dragon City *Harry Dunlop* 57
2 b c Elusive City(USA) Oulianovsk (IRE) (Peintre Celebre (USA))
7373^{6}

Dragonera *Ed Dunlop* a85 98
4 b m Doyen(IRE) Time Will Show (FR) (Exit To Nowhere (USA))
(1656) 2072^{3} 2884^{2} 3219^{2} 4556^{8} 6674^{26} 6877^{10}

Dragon Pulse (IRE) *M Delzangles* 116
3 ch c Kyllachy Poetical (IRE) (Croco Rouge (IRE))
(1408a) 2110a^{9} 3239^{11}

Dragon Spirit (IRE) *Linda Perratt* 40
3 b g Whipper(USA) Rustic Princess (IRE) (Daggers Drawn (USA))
2262^{20} 2438^{9} 2927^{F} 3333^{10} 3580^{5} 4084^{6} 4807^{3} 5087^{11} 5542^{8} 5760^{6} 6314^{9} 6530^{9}

Drakes Drum *Clive Cox* a73 72
4 b g Dansili Perfect Echo (Lycius (USA))
1650^{7} 2043^{5} 2413^{5}

Dr Albert *Frank Sheridan* a55
3 b c Son And Heir(IRE) Tyne Goddess (Warningford)
1360^{5}

Dramatic Act *Arne O Karlsen* 75
4 b g Dansili Winter Solstice (Unfuwain (USA))
3886a^{9}

Drawnfromthepast (IRE) *Jim Boyle* a94 95
7 ch g Tagula(IRE) Ball Cat (FR) (Cricket Ball (USA))
62^{3} (220) (456) 654^{2} (800) 1005^{4} 1204^{7} 5035^{13} 5502^{15} (5853) 6150^{6} 6497^{5} 6824^{12} (7197) 7309^{2} 7595^{2} 7726^{2} 7859^{3} (7995) (8246)

Dream About You (IRE) *Robert Mills* a67
2 br f Amadeus Wolf Peshawar (Persian Bold)
7191^{14} 7553^{9} 7721^{3} 7854^{4} 8003^{3} 8186^{2}

Dream Ally (IRE) *Jedd O'Keeffe* a72 70
2 b c Oasis Dream Alexander Alliance (IRE) (Danetime (IRE))
2330^{8} 5382^{4} 6203^{10} (7462)

Dream Applause (IRE) *K J Condon* a70 72
4 b m Royal Applause Rainbow Dream (Rainbow Quest (USA))
7230a^{12}

Dream Cast (IRE) *David Simcock* 77
2 b c Refuse To Bend(IRE) Star Studded (Cadeaux Genereux)
4239^{4} 4730^{2} 5260^{4}

Dream Catcher (FR) *Henry Candy* a79 80
4 gr g Della Francesca(USA) Gallopade (FR) (Kendor (FR))
2421^{5} 3546^{6} (3915) (4315) 5362^{3} 6368^{5} 6577^{4} 7274^{2}

Dream Catcher (SWE) *Jonjo O'Neill* a69 64
9 b g Songline(SWE) Queen Ida (SWE) (Diligo (FR))
129^{7} 600^{3} 849^{5} 2396^{4} 3283^{3} 4145^{5} 5196^{6} 6280^{9}

Dream Clover *F Head* 109
3 b f Oasis Dream In Clover (Inchinor)
5249a^{3}

Dreamily (IRE) *Mark Johnston* 62
2 bb f New Approach(IRE) Idilic Calm (IRE) (Indian Ridge)
2662^{6} 3034^{6}

Dreaming Of Julia (USA) *Todd Pletcher* a113
2 b f A.P. Indy(USA) Dream Rush (USA) (Wild Rush (USA))
7548a^{3}

Dreaming Of Rubies *Ben Haslam* a71 80
3 b f Oasis Dream Rubies From Burma (USA) (Forty Niner (USA))
(1016) 2256^{3} 2928^{6} 5167^{2} 6358^{10}

Dream Lodge (IRE) *Scott Dixon* a96 83
8 ch g Grand Lodge(USA) Secret Dream (IRE) (Zafonic (USA))
275^{9}

Dream Maker (IRE) *Tom Dascombe* 88
2 ch f Bahamian Bounty Pointed Arch (IRE) (Rock Of Gibraltar (IRE))
2469^{3} 2770^{3} 3747^{3} 4471^{2} (4752) (4836) 5103^{7} 5515^{5} 5979^{8}

Dream Of Fortune (IRE) *David Evans* a74 68
8 b g Danehill Dancer(IRE) Tootling (IRE) (Pennine Walk)
330^{3} 402^{4}

Dream On Paddy *Ian McInnes* 48
3 ch g Hawk Wing(USA) Thumpers Dream (Cape Cross (IRE))
2881^{7} 3384^{4} 5113^{10}

Dream Peace (IRE) *Chad C Brown* a82 114
4 b m Dansili Truly A Dream (IRE) (Darshaan)
1766a^{4} 4617a^{2} 6695a^{3} 7093a^{3}

Dream Prospector *James Tate* a67 49
3 b g Oasis Dream Prospectress (USA) (Mining (USA))
552^{7} 737^{3} 1864^{11} 2689^{11} 3083^{10}

Dream Risk (FR) *Brian Ellison* 56
6 b m Dream Well(FR) Lovarisk (FR) (Take Risks (FR))
4594^{2} ◆ 8260^{11}

Dream Scenario *Mel Brittain* 76
2 b f Araafa(IRE) Notjustaprettyface (USA) (Red Ransom (USA))
2587^{3} ◆ (2686) ◆ 4116^{3} 4820^{19}

Dreams Of Fire (USA) *Sir Michael Stoute* a81 73
3 b f Dynaformer(USA) Angel In My Heart (FR) (Rainbow Quest (USA))
1973^{9} 4755^{5} 5218^{6}

Dreams Of Glory *Ron Hodges* a64 65
4 ch h Resplendent Glory(IRE) Pip's Dream (Glint Of Gold)
624^{11} 844^{7} 958^{5} 1185^{6} 2421^{6} 3139^{10} 3618^{5} 6277^{9} 6737^{3} 7275^{3}

Dreamspeed (IRE) *Andrew Balding* a97 103
5 b g Barathea(IRE) Kapria (FR) (Simon Du Desert (FR))
2267^{5} 3857^{4} 5600^{9} 6248^{7} 6637^{6}

Dream Tune *Clive Cox* 97
3 b c Oasis Dream Play Bouzouki (Halling (USA))
1506^{2} 2210^{4} 2856^{7} 4516^{2} (5276) 6235^{2} 6830^{5}

Dream Vale (IRE) *Tim Easterby* 73
2 b f Moss Vale(IRE) Dream State (IRE) (Machiavellian (USA))
1435^{8} (1949) 2252^{7} 2603^{4} 4820^{15} 5332^{7} 5411^{3} 6160^{11} 6629^{4} 6952^{2} (7441)

Dream Walker (FR) *Ian McInnes* a49 69
3 gr g Gold Away(IRE) Minnie's Mystery (FR) (Highest Honor (FR))
(2010) 3050^{3} 3421^{2} 3567^{2} 4397^{2} 4830^{7} 6514^{10} 7318 ^{2} 7600^{8} 7776^{9}

Dream Wedding *Mario Hofer* 92
2 ch f Medicean Wedding Party (Groom Dancer (USA))
5781a^{2} 6522a^{7}

Dream Whisperer *Dominic Ffrench Davis* a48 70
3 b f Piccolo Sweet Whisper (Petong)
4798^{8} 5296^{8}

Dream Win *Brian Ellison* a72 76
6 b h Oasis Dream Wince (Selkirk (USA))
899^{5} 2632^{8} 4142^{8} 4627^{5} 4715^{7} 7799^{12} (7976) 8113^{7}

Dreamwriter (USA) *Jim Boyle* a70 88
3 ch f Tale Of The Cat(USA) Rebridled Dreams (USA) (Unbridled's Song (USA))
1215^{10} 2890^{5} 3636^{8} 6705^{8} 7408^{10} 7646^{8}

Dreamy Ciara *David Evans* a71 75
2 b f Multiplex Billie Holiday (Fairy King (USA))
1136^{7} (1188) (1315) 1451^{3} 1891^{4}

Dressed In Lace *Jo Crowley* a74 68
3 b f Dark Angel(IRE) Pure Speculation (Salse (USA))
27^{2} 201^{7} (970) 3041^{3} 3762^{6} 7483^{11} 7967^{11}

Dr Faustus (IRE) *Doug Watson* a97 92
7 gr g Sadler's Wells(USA) Requesting (Rainbow Quest (USA))
48a^{6} 143a^{7} 317a^{5} 618a^{5}

Dr Finley (IRE) *Lydia Pearce* a69 74
5 ch g Dr Fong(USA) Farrfesheena (USA) (Rahy (USA))
3572^{5} 4590^{2} (5172) 5772^{7} 6407^{8}

Dr Houseman *Amanda Perrett* a71
3 b g Motivator Photogenic (Midyan (USA))
(5100) 6364^{3} ◆

Drift And Dream *Chris Wall* a59 82
5 b m Exceed And Excel(AUS) Sea Drift (FR) (Warning)
2195^{12} 2494^{6} 3500^{6} 4495^{4} 4793^{2} (5486) 6144^{7} 6495^{10}

Drinmoy Lad (IRE) *Michael McElhone* a60 65
3 b g Kheleyf(USA) Dafalia (IRE) (Mark Of Esteem (IRE))
(138) 660^{8} 6249^{3} 6288^{2}

Dr Irv *Kate Walton* 69
3 ch g Dr Fong(USA) Grateful (Generous (IRE))
2144^{9} 2589^{6} 3212^{3} 4210^{4} 4399^{3} (5115) 5330^{4} 6126^{2} 6474^{3}

Drive Home (USA) *Noel Wilson* a70 65
5 bb g Mr Greeley(USA) Unique Pose (IRE) (Sadler's Wells (USA))
(153) 478^{2} 2696^{7} 3257^{6} 4783^{6} 5918^{7} 6308^{3} (6479) 7412^{7} 7670^{7}

Drombeg Dawn (IRE) *A J McNamara* 91
6 b m Orpen(USA) Dawn's Sharp Shot (IRE) (Son Of Sharp Shot (IRE))
1043a^{9}

Dropzone (USA) *Marco Botti* a70 66
3 b g Smart Strike(CAN) Dalisay (IRE) (Sadler's Wells (USA))
869^{7} 1001^{4} 1250^{3} 3186^{4} 3781^{10} 4440^{6}

Dr Phibes (IRE) *Alan Swinbank* 79
2 ch g Dr Fong(USA) Garra Molly (IRE) (Nayef (USA))
3436^{7} 4257^{2} 4618^{2} 5169^{2} 6070^{4} 6337^{2} (6708) 7209^{2}

Dr Red Eye *Scott Dixon* a85 88
4 ch g Dr Fong(USA) Camp Fire (IRE) (Lahib (USA))
987^{3} 1134^{10} 1358^{7} 1659^{6} 2151^{6} 2696^{4} (3749) 3994^{6} (4255) 4503^{3} 5314^{7} 5827^{7} 6192^{2} 6659^{4} 7453^{3}

Dr Thibault (FR) *U Suter* a94 87
3 b g American Post Shashamene (FR) (Anabaa Blue)
8277a^{9}

Drummanmoremaster (IRE) *Niall Moran* 33
5 ch g Masterful(USA) Roguery (IRE) (Desert Prince (IRE))
23^{7}

Drummond *Clive Cox* 78
3 b g Zamindar(USA) Alrisha (IRE) (Persian Bold)
1322^{5} 2126^{3} 3703^{6} 4755^{2} 5358^{8} 6440^{5}

Drumpellier (IRE) *Simon West* a26 54
5 ch m Rakti Early Memory (USA) (Devil's Bag (USA))
1383^{6} 1584^{6} 1881^{8} 2458^{4} 2749^{4} 3020^{2} 3209^{8} 3462^{2} 4453^{7}

Dr Victoria *John Norton* a32
3 ch f Three Valleys(USA) Spielbound (Singspiel (IRE))
6827^{9} 7729^{8} 8151^{5}

Dr Yes (FR) *Sir Henry Cecil* a106 93
3 b c Dansili Light Shift (USA) (Kingmambo (USA))
2856^{4} ◆ 3349^{5} ◆ 4542^{2} 5048^{2} (6228) (7168) ◆

Dry Summer (USA) *Jeff Mullins* a92 96
2 ch r Any Given Saturday(USA) Greenstreet (USA) (Street Cry (IRE))
7568a^{11}

Dschahan (GER) *F Vermeulen* a99 98
4 b h Oasis Dream Desca (GER) (Cadeaux Genereux)
(7123a)

Dualagi *Martin Bosley* a66 68
8 b m Royal Applause Lady Melbourne (IRE) (Indian Ridge)
2421^{10} 2760^{8} 3016^{7}

Dubaianswer *Tony Coyle* a91 72
4 b m Dubawi(IRE) Answered Prayer (Green Desert (USA))
(22) 584^{4} (674) 866^{12} 1158^{8} 7294^{8} 7715^{12}

Dubai Applause *Charles Hills* a25
2 b f Royal Applause Maimoona (IRE) (Pivotal)
7894^{9}

Dubai Bay (FR) *Paul Midgley* a72 72
4 b m Zafeen(FR) Yemen Desert (IRE) (Sadler's Wells (USA))
907^{12} 1249^{16} 3615^{6} 4134^{10} 4779^{11} 6456^{4} 6823^{9}

Dubai Bounty *Gerard Butler* a84 87
5 ch m Dubai Destination(USA) Mary Read (Bahamian Bounty)
(275) 548^{5}

Dubai Celebration *Julie Camacho* a55 71
4 b g Dubai Destination(USA) Pretty Poppy (Song)
2750^{7} 4495^{5} 4783^{4} ◆ 5341^{3} (5917) 6711^{4} 7593^{8}

Dubai Dynamo *Ruth Carr* a91 101
7 b g Kyllachy Miss Mercy (IRE) (Law Society (USA))
871^{5} ◆ 1035^{4} 1130^{9} 1522^{3} 1670^{5} 1865^{3} 2025^{5} (2311) 2590^{5} 2819^{3} 2910^{4} 3164^{4} 3534^{5} 3855^{7} 3911^{2} (4136) 4287^{2} 4557^{5} 5075^{5} 5342^{12} 5827^{12} 6135^{6}

Dubai Emerald (USA) *Chris Dwyer* a51
3 bb f Henny Hughes(USA) Zanoubia (USA) (Our Emblem (USA))
2849^{11} 7933^{6} 8049^{9}

Dubai Glory *Sheena West* a73 84
4 b m Dubai Destination(USA) Rosse (Kris)
2174^{10} 2623^{2} 3187^{2} 3400^{7} 4983^{11} 5772^{9}

Dubai Hills *Bryan Smart* a90 96
6 b g Dubai Destination(USA) Hill Welcome (Most Welcome)
2505^{3} 3128^{4} (3403) 3626^{9} 4321^{20} 4828^{11} 5746^{6} 6192^{9} 6882^{9} 7370^{2} 7453^{9} 7639^{7} 7789^{10}

Dubai Prince (IRE) *Mahmood Al Zarooni* a96 115
4 b h Shamardal(USA) Desert Frolic (IRE) (Persian Bold)
488a^{7} 877a^{12} (4074) 4759^{6} (5560)

Dubai Rythm *Michael Appleby* a51 43
3 b g Echo Of Light Slave To The Rythm (IRE) (Hamas (IRE))
3005^{5} 4461^{8} 6806^{8} 7204^{13} 7316^{7}

Dubai Story *Alastair Lidderdale* a31
3 b f Dubai Destination(USA) Madrigale (Averti (IRE))
8239^{6}

Dubai Sunshine (IRE) *Michael Bell* a94 91
3 b g Dubawi(IRE) Star Express (Sadler's Wells (USA))
(369) ◆ 596^{5} 1264^{6} 1721^{7} 2229^{3} 3379^{7} 4291^{6} 5302^{7} (5721) 5942^{6} (6701) 7064^{7}

Dubara Reef (IRE) *Paul Green* a48 76
5 ch g Dubawi(IRE) Mamara Reef (Salse (USA))
767^{10} 1272^{5} 1631^{8} 1952^{3} 2775^{3} 3061^{5} 4455^{5}

Dubarshi *Jo Crowley* a92 32
4 gr g Dubawi(IRE) Asheyana (IRE) (Soviet Star (USA))
1066^{2} 1708^{9}

Dubawi Cheetah (IRE) *Richard Fahey* a74 38
3 b f Dubawi(IRE) Magical Cliche (USA) (Affirmed (USA))
107^{2} ◆ 5919^{4}

Dubawi Dancer *J S Moore* a38 84
4 ch m Dubawi(IRE) Adees Dancer (Danehill Dancer (IRE))
6207^{12}

Dubawi Gold *Richard Hannon* a105 120
4 b h Dubawi(IRE) Savannah Belle (Green Desert (USA))
879a^{10} 1646^{4} 2270^{3}

Dubawi Island (FR) *James Tate* a95 84
3 b g Dubawi(IRE) Housa Dancer (FR) (Fabulous Dancer (USA))
3913^{5} 4948^{2} (5717) 6539^{3} 6921^{8} 7715^{3} 7920^{2} 7986^{4}

Dubawi Sound *David Brown* 105
4 b g Dubawi(IRE) Hannah's Music (Music Boy)
1510^{18} (4589) ◆ 4703^{8} 5597^{3}

Dubawi Star *John M Oxx* a92 98
4 b g Dubawi(IRE) Cloud Hill (Danehill (USA))
246a^{12} 489a^{6} 587a^{9}

Dubaya *A Oliver* 87
2 b f Dubawi(IRE) Charlecote (IRE) (Caerleon (USA))
7419a^{6}

Dubious Escapade (IRE) *Ann Duffield* a70 76
3 b f Dubawi(IRE) Brief Escapade (IRE) (Brief Truce (USA))
1364^{4} (1918) 2283^{2} 2785^{6} 3495^{4} 3952^{5} 4624^{5} 7402^{2} 7975^{4}

Dubonny *Frank Sheridan* a49
5 b m Dubawi(IRE) Ravishing (IRE) (Bigstone (IRE))
226^{8} 450^{5} 848^{5} 1014^{11} 1096^{8}

Ducal *Mike Murphy* a94 96
4 b g Iceman Noble Lady (Primo Dominie)
(746) (1066) 1708^{4} 2545^{2} (3004) 4321^{19} 4703^{3} 5572^{6} 6119^{7}

Duchess Dora (IRE) *David Simcock* a98 106
5 b m Tagula(IRE) Teodora (IRE) (Fairy King (USA))
(1977) 2664^{5} 3375^{4} 3877^{9} 4113^{12} 6602^{5} ◆ 7772^{4}

Duchess Of Dreams *Richard Guest* a51 8
2 br f Royal Applause Wood Chorus (Singspiel (IRE))
7290^{9} 7653^{6} 8254^{3}

Duchess Of Foxland (IRE) *Mark L Fagan* a95 98
5 br m Medecis Itsanothergirl (Reprimand)
3645a^{5}

Duchess Of Gazeley (IRE) *Lydia Pearce* a49 54
2 ch f Halling(USA) Flying Finish (FR) (Priolo (USA))
4297^{8} 5300^{7} 6644^{8}

Dude Alert (IRE) *Peter Chapple-Hyam* a60 64
2 b c Windsor Knot(IRE) Policy (Nashwan (USA))
6844^{3} 7349^{4} 7812^{5}

Duke Liam (IRE) *David Nicholls* a63 43
3 b g Bachelor Duke(USA) Petite Arvine (USA) (Gulch (USA))
2^{4}

Duke Of Aricabeau (IRE) *Lydia Pearce* a71 76
3 ch g Modigliani(USA) Essential Fear (IRE) (Pivotal)
3184^{3} (3566) 3912^{6} 4496^{5} 5000^{2} 5536^{4} 6285^{7} 6824^{4} 7141^{10} 7308^{3} 8159^{10}

Duke Of Clarence (IRE) *Richard Hannon* a74 85
3 gr c Verglas(IRE) Special Lady (FR) (Kaldoun (FR))
724^{2} (816) (6734) (7116)

Duke Of Destiny (IRE) *Ed Walker* a69 53
3 br g Bachelor Duke(USA) Marghelan (FR) (Soviet Star (USA))
2332^{6} 2974^{4} 3539^{7} (5049) 8263^{3}

Duke Of Firenze *Sir Michael Stoute* 100
3 ch c Pivotal Nannina (Medicean)
1565^{12} (3445) ◆ 4598^{2} ◆ 6201^{6} 6835^{5}

Duke Of Orange (IRE) *Mick Channon* 68
2 br c Duke Of Marmalade(IRE) High Society (IRE) (Key Of Luck (USA))
4707^{8} 4960^{4} ◆

Duke Of Perth *Luca Cumani* 69
2 b g Danehill Dancer(IRE) Frangy (Sadler's Wells (USA))
6872^{5} ◆ 7333^{4}

Duke Of Rainford *Michael Herrington* a41 56
5 gr g Bahamian Bounty Night Haven (Night Shift (USA))
1383^{9} 2377^{12} 3256^{4} 4592^{5} 4911^{6} 5327^{3} 5740^{7} 7179^{9} 7633^{7} 7703^{9}

Duke Of Yorkshire *Declan Carroll* 72
2 b c Duke Of Marmalade(IRE) Dame Edith (FR) (Top Ville)
5797[4] 6669[3] 6997[2]

Dulkashe (IRE) *Luca Cumani* a80 84
3 br f Pivotal Saik (USA) (Riverman (USA))
(2379) 6376[6] 6987[3] 7375[10]

Dullahan (USA) *Dale Romans* a127 111
3 ch c Even The Score(USA) Mining My Own (USA) (Smart Strike (CAN))
1872a[3] 2954a[7] 6902a[5] 7573a[9]

Dumbarton Rock *William Jarvis* a56 69
2 b c Kyllachy Ellablue (Bahamian Bounty)
5360[9] 5715[3] 6411[4] 6849[2] 7298[5] 8016[8]

Dummy Traou Land (FR) *P Costes* a59 58
2 b f Apsis Peldrine (FR) (Pelder (IRE))
6751a[0]

Dunaden (FR) *M Delzangles* a75 124
6 b h Nicobar La Marlia (FR) (Kaldounevees (FR))
1855[3] 2744a[3] 3369[2] 4322[6] (7264a) 7621a[14] 8040a[5]

Dunaskin (IRE) *Richard Guest* a53 52
12 b g Bahhare(USA) Mirwara (IRE) (Darshaan)
367[8] 454[5] 493[5] 579[5] 672[5] 1174[2] 1240[4] 1433[2] (1580) 1744[2] 2348[10] 6056[10] 6956[14] 7472[7] 7490[8] 7717[4] 7793[2]

Dundonnell (USA) *Roger Charlton* 112
2 b c First Defence(USA) Family (USA) (Danzig (USA))
4066[3] ◆ (4813) ◆ (5488) 6243[2] ◆ 7568a[4]

Dundrum Dancer (IRE) *Alex Hales* a66 70
5 b m Refuse To Bend(IRE) Sincere (IRE) (Bahhare (USA))
3207a[5] 4242[3] 4942[3] 7684[16]

Duneen Dream (USA) *Nikki Evans* a50 64
7 ch g Hennessy(USA) T N T Red (USA) (Explosive Red (CAN))
848[9] 1014[5] 3713[11] 5198[4] 5935[7] 6231[3]

Dune Island *John Bridger* a49
4 b m Compton Admiral Desert Island Disc (Turtle Island (IRE))
653[8] 818[11] 995[11]

Dungannon *Andrew Balding* a90 105
5 b g Monsieur Bond(IRE) May Light (Midyan (USA))
1885[23] 3371[5] 4367[5] 4802[17] 7066[6] 7397[16] ◆ 7817[5]

Dunhoy (IRE) *Tony Newcombe* a87 87
4 ch g Goodricke Belle Of The Blues (IRE) (Blues Traveller (IRE))
520[2] ◆ (733) 1134[5] 1513[3] 2257[11] 2810[7] 3827[2] 5306[10] 7109[3]

Dunmore Boy (IRE) *Richard Fahey* a68 57
4 ch g Iffraaj Night Club (Mozart (IRE))
21[2] 329[5] 498[2] 639[5] 735[10] 1251[9] 2538[8] 4143[2] 4453[6]

Dunnboinee (IRE) *Mlle A Imaz-Ceca* a92
4 ch h King's Best(USA) For Starters (IRE) (In The Wings)
5252a[8]

Dunn'o (IRE) *David Nicholls* a65 102
7 b g Cape Cross(IRE) Indian Express (Indian Ridge)
2311[5] 2657[17] 6192[11] 6471[10] 7715[9]

Dunseverick (IRE) *Jo Hughes* a77 70
4 ch g Footstepsinthesand Theatrale (USA) (Theatrical (IRE))
269[7] 1052[8] 2546[3] 2791[8]

Duntle (IRE) *David Wachman* a97 115
3 ch f Danehill Dancer(IRE) Lady Angola (USA) (Lord At War (ARG))
2101a[4] (3270) (5286a) ◆ 6061a[2]

Durban Thunder (GER) *P Harley* a95 117
6 ch h Samum(GER) Donna Alicia (GER) (Highland Chieftain)
4636a[2] 5613a[6] 6805a[2] 7586a[6] 7784a[7]

D'Urberville *J R Jenkins* a74 24
5 b g Auction House(USA) Laser Crystal (IRE) (King's Theatre (IRE))
136[3] 384[5] 646[2] 900[2] 1358[9] 3154[6] 4142[10] 5052[7] 5941[10] 6774[8]

Durgan *Linda Jewell* a63 58
6 b g Dansili Peryllys (Warning)
2342[7]

During The War (USA) *Chris Dwyer* a45 67
5 b g Lion Heart(USA) Carson's Star (USA) (Carson City (USA))
389[12] 653[13]

Duroble Man *Roger Varian* a70 71
2 b g Manduro(GER) Jalousie (IRE) (Barathea (IRE))
6204[12] 6845[3] 7637[3] ◆ 7989[3]

Dusky Lark *Hughie Morrison* a61
2 b c Nayef(USA) Snow Goose (Polar Falcon (USA))
7899[8] 8070[11]

Dusky Queen (IRE) *Richard Fahey* 80
2 b f Shamardal(USA) Sanna Bay (IRE) (Refuse To Bend (IRE))
3560[7] (4246) 5361[2] 5836[2] 6469[4]

Dust And Diamonds (USA) *Steven Asmussen* a112
4 bb m Vindication(USA) Majestically (USA) (Gone West (USA))
7569a[2]

Duster *Hughie Morrison* a90 93
5 b g Pastoral Pursuits Spring Clean (FR) (Danehill (USA))
1416[6] 2250[7] (2975) 3812[4] 4703[14] 5305[3] (6566) 7083[6] 7370[8]

Dustland Fairytale (IRE) *Sean Curran* a55 59
4 b m Noverre(USA) Subtle Affair (IRE) (Barathea (IRE))
5850[2]

Dust Whirl *Richard Hannon* a64 79
2 b c Bahamian Bounty Dust (Green Desert (USA))
1499[3] 1842[2] 2213[13] 4148[3] 5032[5] 5886[7] 7220[9]

Dusty Red *William Knight* a66 53
3 ch f Teofilo(IRE) Dust Dancer (Suave Dancer (USA))
2849[4] 8295[6]

Dusty Storm (IRE) *Ed McMahon* a79 77
2 ch f Kyllachy Halliwell House (Selkirk (USA))
2282[5] 3700[2] 4344[3] (4922) 5450[2] 6227[5] 7220[2]

Dutch Diamond *John Gosden* a73 80
3 ch f Dutch Art Treasure Trove (USA) (The Minstrel (CAN))
990[3] (1192) 2201[3] 3080[2] 3476[4] 4505[4] 5931[2] 6416[7]

Dutch Gal *John Holt* 69
2 b f Dutch Art Spangle (Galileo (IRE))
6880[8] 7552[4]

Dutch Heritage *Richard Fahey* 78
3 bb g Dutch Art Starstone (Diktat)
3379[3] 3912[7] (4638) 5545[3] 6665[6]

Dutch Master *Andrew Balding* a70 73
3 ch g Dutch Art Duena (Grand Lodge (USA))
1565[5] 2089[5] 3338[5]

Dutch Masterpiece *Gary Moore* a80 90
2 b g Dutch Art The Terrier (Foxhound (USA))
(3937) ◆ 4804[7] (6929) (7206)

Dutch Mistress *James Unett* a56
3 b f Dutch Art Royal Mistress (Fasliyev (USA))
8151[2] 8239[3]

Dutch Old Master *Gary Moore* a80 84
3 b g Jeremy(USA) Wicken Wonder (IRE) (Distant Relative)
(2042) 2660[7] 3393[5] 4288[7]

Dutch Rose (IRE) *David O'Meara* 96
3 ch f Dutch Art Eloquent Rose (IRE) (Elnadim (USA))
(2441) (2591) 2795[3] (3214) (4075) 4740[7] (5520)

Dutch Supreme *David Lanigan* a96 95
3 ch g Dutch Art Barnacla (IRE) (Bluebird (USA))
1825[4] ◆ (2147) 3281[2] 3876[3] 4473[2] 5271[3]

Dutiful Son (IRE) *Jeremy Noseda* 64
2 b c Invincible Spirit(IRE) Grecian Dancer (Dansili)
5040[5]

Dutyfree (TUR) *S Karagoz* 101
4 b h Luxor(TUR) Freezone (TUR) (Wolf (CHI))
5869a[6]

Dux Scholar *A Savujev* a101 115
4 b h Oasis Dream Alumni (Selkirk (USA))
588a[11] ◆ 758a[3] 876a[14] 1143a[10] 5782a[2] 6897a[2] 7515a[10]

Dvinsky (USA) *Paul Howling* a71 55
11 b g Stravinsky(USA) Festive Season (USA) (Lypheor)
87[5] 122[3] 267[3] 474[4] (522) 658[5] 819[5] 991[7] 1306[5] 1734[7] 2170[2] 2373[2] (2546) 3006[2] 3738[4] 3958[8] 4469[4] 4872[7] 5750[3] 5972[2] 6145[4] 6456[9] 8005[5] 8160[8]

Dyctynna (FR) *H-A Pantall* a86 82
3 bb f Stormy River(FR) Dentelle (FR) (Apeldoorn (FR))
8300a[0]

Dylanbaru (IRE) *T Stack* a92 97
2 b c Footstepsinthesand Nubar Lady (IRE) (Danetime (IRE))
2512a[2] 3242[3] 4687[5] 6078a[7]

Dylan George *George Moore*
3 b g Sakhee(USA) Movie Star (IRE) (Barathea (IRE))
6341[10]

Dylan's Dream (IRE) *Tim Easterby* 53
3 b f Dark Angel(IRE) Catherinofaragon (USA) (Chief's Crown (USA))
1359[12] 3210[6] 3892[5]

Dylans Verse (IRE) *P Monfort* a84 84
3 b g Dylan Thomas(IRE) In My Dreams (IRE) (Sadler's Wells (USA))
290a[3] 476a[2] 1127a[2]

Dynamic Drive (IRE) *Linda Perratt* a71 84
5 b g Motivator Biriyani (IRE) (Danehill (USA))
2440[9] 2842[4] 3277[7] 3907[10] 4137[8] 5762[4] 6315[4] 6758[10]

Dynamic Duo (IRE) *Richard Hannon* a82 76
3 ch c Iffraaj Collada (IRE) (Desert Prince (IRE))
2150[3] 2429[6] 2941[6] 4474[7] 4746[2] 5297[3] (5404) 5837[2]

Dynamic Idol (USA) *Gary Moore* a78 70
5 bb g Dynaformer(USA) El Nafis (USA) (Kingmambo (USA))
569[4]

Dynamic Sky (CAN) *Mark Casse* a103
2 bb c Sky Mesa(USA) Murani (USA) (Distorted Humor (USA))
7572a[6]

Dynastic *Richard Hannon* a77 76
3 b c Dynaformer(USA) Demure (Machiavellian (USA))
918[4] 1065[3] 1707[4] 2038[6] 3072[7] 3664[3] (4901) 7376[9]

Dysphonia (AUS) *Saeed Bin Suroor* a98 108
6 b m Lonhro(AUS) Stutter (AUS) (Night Shift (USA))
617a[8] 876a[8] 2078[3] (2554) 3266[8] 4764[7]

Dzesmin (POL) *Richard Guest* a38 69
10 b g Professional(IRE) Dzakarta (POL) (Aprizzo (IRE))
1382[5] 2009[5] 2669[7] 3216[5] 6562[10] 7495[9] 8051[13] 8214[10]

Eager To Bow (IRE) *Patrick Chamings* a79 75
6 b g Acclamation Tullawadgeen (IRE) (Sinndar (IRE))
(91) (3738) 4814[11] (5440) 5993[2] 7484[12] (7827)

Eagle Nebula *Brett Johnson* a75 76
8 ch g Observatory(USA) Tarocchi (USA) (Affirmed (USA))
(57) 592[2] 786[2] 824[3] (1732) 2199[4] 2502[5] (2984) 3472[2] 3782[5] 5323[5] 5838[14] 7301[8] 7511[10] 7744[9] 8023[4] 8106[4] 8301[4]

Eagle Power (IRE) *James Fanshawe* a77 78
3 b g Teofilo(IRE) Changeable (Dansili)
1704[2] 2941[2]

Eagle Rock (IRE) *Tom Tate* 87
4 b g High Chaparral(IRE) Silk Fan (IRE) (Unfuwain (USA))
2180[3] ◆ 3163[4] 4613[2] 5491[6] 6493[3]

Eagles Peak *Sir Michael Stoute* 104
4 b h Galileo(IRE) High Praise (USA) (Quest For Fame)
(6576) ◆

Eamaadd *Roger Varian* a72 67
3 b g Medicean Emanant (Emarati (USA))
4213[6] 4780[4] 5387[5] 6968[3]

Eanans Bay (IRE) *Mark H Tompkins* a53 56
3 b g Tiger Hill(IRE) Gold Hush (USA) (Seeking The Gold (USA))
1270[11] 1724[4] 1981[7] 3781[4] 4399[6] 6838[10] 7632[11] 8214[8]

Earl Of Tinsdal (GER) *A Wohler* 116
4 b h Black Sam Bellamy(IRE) Earthly Paradise (GER) (Dashing Blade)
1700a[4] (2968a) 4383a[2] 5145a[3] 6523a[5]

Earl Of Winds (GER) *P Schaerer* a88
7 b g Samum(GER) Earthly Paradise (GER) (Dashing Blade)
(443a) 630a[12]

Earlsalsa (GER) *C Von Der Recke* 106
8 bb g Kingsalsa(USA) Earthly Paradise (GER) (Dashing Blade)
1901a[3] 6290a[6] 7427a[4]

Earlsmedic *Stuart Williams* a83 77
7 ch g Dr Fong(USA) Area Girl (Jareer (USA))
64[2] 120[7] 311[2] 652[3] 1564[9] 2070[11] 2940[13]

Early Applause *Charles Hills* 83
4 b g Royal Applause Early Evening (Daylami (IRE))
1999[6] 2473[7] 4772[5] 5322[3] 6239[11]

Early Emperor *Carmen Bocskai* a72
2 b c Araafa(IRE) Early Evening (Daylami (IRE))
7984a[9]

Early Shirley *Kevin Ryan* 18
3 b f Piccolo Ailsa (Bishop Of Cashel)
2036[8]

Easter Chorus *Clive Cox* 23
3 b f Oasis Dream Almatinka (IRE) (Indian Ridge)
5776[7]

Easter Diva (IRE) *Gerard Butler* a74 63
3 b f Dansili Easter Fairy (USA) (Fusaichi Pegasus (USA))
2200[6] 3070[8] 7416[2] 7644[12] 8135[2]

Eastern Amour (IRE) *Marco Botti* a60
3 b g Azamour(IRE) Eastern Appeal (IRE) (Shinko Forest (IRE))
523[10] 693[3] 908[6] 1365[7]

Eastern Destiny *Richard Fahey* 86
3 gr f Dubai Destination(USA) Night Haven (Night Shift (USA))
2118[2] (2589) ◆ 3124[4] (6193) 6661[9]

Eastern Dragon (IRE) *Michael Scudamore* a63 61
2 b c Elnadim(USA) Shulammite Woman (IRE) (Desert Sun)
2334[5] 2667[5] 3168[3] 5155[6] 5763[4] 6318[5] 6583[3] 7476[2] 7713[9] 7965[7]

Eastern Gift *Gay Kelleway* a74 76
7 ch g Cadeaux Genereux Dahshah (Mujtahid (USA))
21[3] 146[3]

Eastern Hills *Alan McCabe* a87 81
7 b g Dubai Destination(USA) Rainbow Mountain (Rainbow Quest (USA))
1581[7] 1650[3] 2243[9] 2405[9] 3779[6] 4190[5] 5751[7] 6452[4] 7347[3] 7436[11] 7732[4] 7798[3] 8115[7]

Eastern Magic *Reg Hollinshead* a58 68
5 b g Observatory(USA) Inchtina (Inchinor)
2237[5] 4491[7] (4904) 5811[4] 6821[6] 7490[3] 7791[8]

Eastern Seel *Tim Easterby* 39
3 b g Dubai Destination(USA) Maraseel (USA) (Machiavellian (USA))
3023[11]

Eastern Sun (IRE) *John Gosden* a103 103
3 b c Kodiac Always Friendly (High Line)
(1216) 1470[3] ◆ 2641[9] 3265[14] 4012[4] 5271[6] 6835[12]

Eastlands Lad (IRE) *Micky Hammond* a61 67
3 bb c Strategic Prince Uisce Tine (IRE) (Bluebird (USA))
1757[7] 3751[2] 4211[2] 4553[5] 4913[3] 5736[5] 6562[3]

East Meets West (IRE) *Bent Olsen* a94 95
3 b c Dansili Minkova (IRE) (Sadler's Wells (USA))
4863a[10]

East Texas Red (IRE) *Richard Hannon* a55 68
2 ch c Danehill Dancer(IRE) Evangeline (Sadler's Wells (USA))
5321[7] 5793[6] 6015[10] 6413[3] ◆ 6793[4] (7111)

Eastward Ho *Jason Ward* a67 78
4 ch g Resplendent Glory(IRE) Mofeyda (IRE) (Mtoto)
1269[5] 3021[2] (3309) (3615) 4345[3] 4954[5] 5186[7] 6410[10] 6785[5]

Easydoesit (IRE) *Tony Carroll* a55 48
4 b g Iffraaj Fawaayid (USA) (Vaguely Noble)
602[2] 8260[2]

Easy Life *Marcus Tregoning* a65
2 b f Sir Percy Eternelle (Green Desert (USA))
7721[9] 8018[4] 8201[2]

Easy Over (IRE) *Ed McMahon* a67 76
4 ch g Dr Fong(USA) Desert Alchemy (IRE) (Green Desert (USA))
2274[9] 3229[8]

Easy Terms *Edwin Tuer* 100
5 b m Trade Fair Effie (Royal Academy (USA))
(1756) ◆ (2253) 3857[15]

Ebalviyra (IRE) *John M Oxx* 92
3 b f Anabaa(USA) Ebareva (IRE) (Machiavellian (USA))
3197a[8]

Ebble *John Gosden* a67 73
3 b f Oasis Dream Sulk (IRE) (Selkirk (USA))
4782[3] 5276[2] 6154[3] (6765) 7975[5]

Ebn Arab (USA) *Charles Hills* 99
2 b c Dixie Union(USA) Daffaash (USA) (Mr Greeley (USA))
(4555) 5488[4] 6599[4]

Ebony Clarets *Linda Perratt* a57 69
3 b f Kyllachy Pachanga (Inchinor)
2331[3] 3063[9] 3952[8] (4705) (5112) 6048[11] 6308[2] 6429[3] 6711[2] 7003[11] 7256[10]

Ebony Express *Alan Swinbank* 18
3 br g Superior Premium Coffee Ice (Primo Dominie)
7445[8]

Ebony Roc (IRE) *Amanda Perrett* a45 47
2 br g Shirocco(GER) Chia Laguna (IRE) (Ela-Mana-Mou)
6486[13] 6818[10] 7627[11]

Ebony Song (USA) *Jo Crowley* a66 72
4 bb g Songandaprayer(USA) Thiscatsforcaryl (USA) (Storm Cat (USA))
4586[11]

Ebraam (USA) *Ronald Harris* a95 82
9 b g Red Ransom(USA) Futuh (USA) (Diesis)
215[4] 327[4]

Ebtisama (USA) *Marcus Tregoning* 44
3 b f Kingmambo(USA) Misterah (Alhaarth (IRE))
2483[9] 2891[9] 3340[15] 5215[14]

Ececheira *Dean Ivory* a44 47
3 ch f Three Valleys(USA) Evening Guest (FR) (Be My Guest (USA))
1610[10] 2560[13] 3189[12] 3985[6] 7032[7] 7011[11] 8048[12]

Echappee Belle *F Vermeulen* 87
4 b m Cape Cross(IRE) Elodie Des Charmes (FR) (Diesis)
15a[0]

Echion (IRE) *F Vermeulen* a80 77
2 b c Ishiguru(USA) Glittering Prize (UAE) (Cadeaux Genereux)
2202[3] 2763[2] 3506[2] 4102[4] 4526[8] (5202) 6227[4] 7374[6] 8192a[10]

Echo Brava *John Gallagher* a40 68
2 rg c Proclamation(IRE) Snake Skin (Golden Snake (USA))
4917[9] 5685[4] 6114[7] ◆

Echo Dancer *Trevor Wall* a56 62
6 br g Danehill Dancer(IRE) Entail (USA) (Riverman (USA))
7383[12]

Echo Knight (IRE) *C Moore* a59 65
3 b g Echo Of Light Saoodah (IRE) (Green Desert (USA))
38[10] 5212[7]

Echo Of Dream *Ismail Mohammed* a73 41
3 br g Echo Of Light Rahcak (IRE) (Generous (IRE))
4188[2] 4972[6]

Echo Of Footsteps *Michael Herrington* 67
3 b f Authorized(IRE) Opening Ceremony (USA) (Quest For Fame)
2633[5] 3352[3] 4259[4] 4781[8] 5413[6] 6262[2] ◆ 6516[4]

Echo Of Silence (FR) *Marco Botti* a60 70
2 bb c Sandwaki(USA) Statia (FR) (Anabaa (USA))
3545[3] 4539[9] 6015[8] 6611[8]

Echo Of Thunder (IRE) *Nick Littmoden* a40 58
3 b f Echo Of Light Aquatic Warrior (USA) (Fantastic Light (USA))
204[5] 743[11] 1608[10]

Echos Of Motivator *Ronald Harris* a75 75
4 ch g Motivator Echo River (USA) (Irish River (FR))
192[8] 355[4] 381[5]

Ecliptic (USA) *Mahmood Al Zarooni* a87 109
4 ch h Kingmambo(USA) Indy Five Hundred (USA) (A.P. Indy (USA))
487a[7]

Economic Crisis (IRE) *Alan Berry* a58 78
3 ch f Excellent Art Try The Air (IRE) (Foxhound (USA))
925[3] 1292[5] 1599[4] 1986[5] 2470[3] 3028[4] 3276[2] 3450[3] 3848[2] (4084) (4262) 5337[4] 5831[3] 6514[3] 7001[2] 7100[2] 7451[11]

Ecossaise *Mark Johnston* a76 78
4 ch m Selkirk(USA) Diablerette (Green Desert (USA))
(114) 337a[11]

Edas *Thomas Cuthbert* a74 66
10 b g Celtic Swing Eden (IRE) (Polish Precedent (USA))
2239[2] 2455[9] 3116[6] 3213[4] 4179[5] (5730) 6131[4] 6711[3]

Ed De Gas *Rae Guest* a92 101
3 b g Peintre Celebre(USA) Sambala (IRE) (Danehill Dancer (IRE))
(595) (1093) ◆ (1597) ◆ 2080[7] 3330[3] 4685[7] 6087a[8]

Eddie Jock (IRE) *S Seemar* a92 92
8 ch g Almutawakel Al Euro (FR) (Mujtahid (USA))
317a[10]

Edge Closer *Tony Carroll* a111 100
8 b g Bold Edge Blue Goddess (IRE) (Blues Traveller (IRE))
2268[5] 4013[3] (5832) 6244[15]

Edged Out *Christopher Mason* 70
2 b f Piccolo Edge Of Light (Xaar)
1499[6] 2124[5] 3138[3] 7272[7]

Edge Of Glory *Richard Hannon* a25 41
2 b f Pastoral Pursuits Bronze Star (Mark Of Esteem (IRE))
5978[9] 7078[9] 7329[9] 7797[7]

Edgewater (IRE) *Lee Carter* a77 83
5 b g Bahamian Bounty Esteemed Lady (IRE) (Mark Of Esteem (IRE))
280[7] 648[4] 1071[6] 1186[5] 1729[7] 2168[4] 2637[5] 5052[9] 5310[2] 5983[9]

Edgeworth (IRE) *David Bridgwater* a73 77
6 b g Pyrus(USA) Credibility (Komaite (USA))
374[5] 570[2] 1000[4] 1154[2] 1719[4] 2498[0] (2867) 3154[9] 5417[3] 6207[10] 6734[10] 7132[8] 7480[8] 7767[4] ◆ 7819[6]

Edgware Road *Sean Curran* a73 65
4 ch g Selkirk(USA) Bayswater (Caerleon (USA))
224[7] 818[6] 1984[7] 6159[5] 6616[4] 7383[2] 7496[2] 7620[2] 7819[14] 7960[8]

Edinburgh Knight (IRE) *Paul D'Arcy* a106 113
5 b g Selkirk(USA) Pippas Song (Reference Point)
1130[4] 3268[17] 3633[2] 4321[2] 4686[7] 5355[8] 6449[8] 7048[8]

Edith Anne *Paul Midgley* 54
2 b f Sakhee's Secret Accusation (IRE) (Barathea (IRE))
3126[8] 3844[3] 4395[3]

Edith Cowan (IRE) *Charles O'Brien* a77 77
3 b f Galileo(IRE) Mount Eliza (IRE) (Danehill (USA))
6352a[8]

Edmaaj (IRE) *David O'Meara* 98
4 ch g Intikhab(USA) Lady Angola (USA) (Lord At War (ARG))
1561[2] 1755[2] ◆ 2312[10] (3167) (3417) ◆ 4072[5] 4962[2] (5540)

Edraaq *Brian Meehan* a68 56
3 b g Dubai Destination(USA) Shatarah (Gulch (USA))
1793[3] 2895[8] 4157[4] 5100[6] 5810[10]

Edson's Ridge (USA) *Philip A Gleaves*
2 b c Thunder Gulch(USA) Just In Passing (USA) (Smoke Glacken (USA))
8244a[6]

Educate *Ismail Mohammed* 93
3 b g Echo Of Light Pasithea (IRE) (Celtic Swing)
3161[7] ◆ (3551) 4103[5] 4342[5] 5006[10] (6209) (7032)

Educated Son *Ben De Haan* a56 61
4 br g Diktat Spring Sunrise (Robellino (USA))
7474[6] 8049[7]

Eeny Mac (IRE) *Neville Bycroft* a47 73
5 ch g Redback Sally Green (IRE) (Common Grounds)
(2692) (3460) (4177) 4679[10] 5618[3] 6127[10] 6559[5]

Effervesce (IRE) *David Pipe* a67 61
5 ch m Galileo(IRE) Royal Fizz (IRE) (Royal Academy (USA))
43[6] 644[2]

Effie B *Mick Channon* a70 88
2 ch f Sixties Icon Blakeshall Rose (Tobougg (IRE))
1352[2] (1515) 1891[5] 2252[3] 2638[3] 3368[14] 4820[4] 5178[4] 5527[3] (5790) 5909[6] 6238[2] 7028[4] 7206[3] (7374) 7518[2] 7828a[7]

Effigy *Henry Candy* a80 79
8 b g Efisio Hymne D'Amour (USA) (Dixieland Band (USA))
2051[12] 4722[6] 5063[4] 5310[9]

Efisio Princess *John E Long* a59 37
9 br m Efisio Hardiprincess (Keen)
124[6] 687[3] 1070[11] 2406[5] 3151[8] 7275[8]

Efistorm *Conor Dore* a72 81
11 b g Efisio Abundance (Cadeaux Genereux)
39[5] 87[2] 178[6] 251[6] 353[9] 424[6] 550[4] (598) 713[2] 1050[6] 1614[10] (2146) (2342) 2581[2] 2939[2] 3139[7] ◆ 3660[6] 3915[6] 3944[8] 4508[2] 4887[6] (5034) 5440[4] 5853[9] 5993[6] (6577) 6837[6] 7113[9] 7297[7] 7967[9] 8004[4] ◆ (8063) 8268[6]

Eghnaa *Ed Dunlop* 54
2 bb f Cape Cross(IRE) Alzaroof (USA) (Kingmambo (USA))
2917[9]

Egretta (IRE) *Richard Brabazon* a62 67
3 b f Motivator Firecrest (IRE) (Darshaan)
8038[6] 8050[9]

Egyptian Lord *Peter Grayson* a40 57
9 ch g Bold Edge Calypso Lady (IRE) (Priolo (USA))
8[12] 979[6]

Ehkam (USA) *Saeed Bin Suroor* a70
3 ch c Seeking The Gold(USA) Ishtak (Nashwan (USA))
6614[5] 7011[3]

Ehtedaam (USA) *Saeed Bin Suroor* a84
3 bb c Arch(USA) Bow River Gold (Rainbow Quest (USA))
6397[6] (7488)

Eigelstein *P Schiergen* 103
4 b h Dubawi(IRE) Estefania (GER) (Acatenango (GER))
1410a[7] 2222a[6]

Eightfold *Seamus Durack* a66 70
3 b g Cadeaux Genereux Nirvana (Marju (IRE))
1109[6] 1313[7] 1517[3] ◆ 2283[4] 2544[8] (3966) 4440[3] 6004[3] 6626[5]

Eightfold Path (USA) *P Bary* 106
5 b h Giant's Causeway(USA) Divine Proportions (USA) (Kingmambo (USA))
6088a[5]

Eight Keys *Rod Millman* a52
4 b g Sakhee(USA) Summertime Parkes (Silver Patriarch (IRE))
137[5]

Eight Letters (USA) *Michael Bell* 21
3 bb f Mr Greeley(USA) Thara (USA) (Hennessy (USA))
1502[11] 3048[9]

Eighty Eight Red *Ed Walker* a90 82
4 ch g Dubawi(IRE) Half Past Twelve (USA) (Cozzene (USA))
7631[10]

Eijaaz (IRE) *Geoffrey Harker* a40 65
11 b g Green Desert(USA) Kismah (Machiavellian (USA))
1950[2] 2260[16] 2694[2] 2874[2] 3355[4] 3753[2] (4209) 4912[2] 6478[6] 7245[11]

Eilean Mor *R Mike Smith* a46 52
4 ch g Ishiguru(USA) Cheviot Heights (Intikhab (USA))
4640[6] 5189[7] 6309[4] 6941[8] 7095[5] 7385[11]

Einsteins Folly (IRE) *J S Bolger* a71 90
2 b c Whipper(USA) Azra (IRE) (Danehill (USA))
1832a[7]

Eishin Flash (JPN) *Hideaki Fujiwara* a112 124
5 bb h King's Best(USA) Moonlady (GER) (Platini (GER))
1150a[6] 7872a[9]

Ejeed (USA) *Zoe Davison* a50 60
7 b g Rahy(USA) Lahan (Unfuwain (USA))
562[6]

Ektihaam (IRE) *Roger Varian* 116
3 b g Invincible Spirit(IRE) Liscune (IRE) (King's Best (USA))
(1504) 2210[2] 2743a[15] 6575[2]

Elaala (USA) *Trevor Wall* a57 51
10 ch m Aljabr(USA) Nufuth (USA) (Nureyev (USA))
4156[9]

Ela Gonda Mou *Peter Charalambous* a58 74
5 ch m Where Or When(IRE) Real Flame (Cyrano De Bergerac)
1314[5] 1533[7] 2465[7] (3081) 3309[3] 4823[9] 5636[3] 6703[10] 6988[4] 7200[8]

Elammato (IRE) *Lisa Williamson* a25
3 b g Strategic Prince Boadicea (Celtic Swing)
4214[13]

Eland Ally *Tom Tate* 88
4 b g Striking Ambition Dream Rose (IRE) (Anabaa (USA))
2793[13] 4554[16]

Elas Diamond *Jeremy Noseda* 93
4 gb m Danehill Dancer(IRE) Ela Athena (Ezzoud (IRE))
4556[6] 6598[13]

Elasyaaf (FR) *J E Hammond* a97 88
3 b c Shamardal(USA) Policalle (FR) (Poliglote)
1171a[4]

Elavssom (IRE) *Jo Hughes* a49 40
3 b g Moss Vale(IRE) Noble Rocket (Reprimand)
597[7] 1053[12]

Elbe *Sir Henry Cecil* a70 81
3 b f Dansili Imroz (USA) (Nureyev (USA))
4336[8] 4919[7]

Elbow Beach *Rod Millman* a71 73
3 gr f Choisir(AUS) Impulsive Decision (IRE) (Nomination)
3780[4] 4329[5] 4753[3] (5528) 5931[6] 6794[11]

El Bravo *Shaun Harris* a63 86
6 ch g Falbrav(IRE) Alessandra (Generous (IRE))
5243[8] 6073[16] 6405[8] 6631[10] 7369[6] 7619[4] 7869[3] 8139[7] (8214)

El Buen Turista *Andrew Balding* a91
2 b c Cape Cross(IRE) Summer Sunset (IRE) (Grand Lodge (USA))
7806[4] ◆ (7962) (8223)

El Bulli (USA) *F Chappet* a74 63
5 b g Saint Liam(USA) Out With The Old (USA) (Time For A Change (USA))
94a[9]

El Calafate (USA) *John Best*
3 ch g Mr Greeley(USA) Jive Talk (USA) (Kingmambo (USA))
7647[8] 7818[9]

El Camino Real (IRE) *Charlie Longsdon* 64
4 b g Dansili Soviet Artic (FR) (Bering)
4410[9]

El Casco (FR) *S Cerulis* a76
3 b c Sabiango(GER) Red Kiss (IRE) (Fasliyev (USA))
5074a[8]

Eldaafer (USA) *Diane Alvarado* a106 106
7 bb g A.P. Indy(USA) Habibti (USA) (Tabasco Cat (USA))
7546a[7]

Eldandy (IRE) *C Laffon-Parias* 109
3 b c Danehill Dancer(IRE) Spinola (FR) (Spinning World (USA))
1869a[3]

El Dececy (USA) *Charles Smith* a76 64
8 b g Seeking The Gold(USA) Ashraakat (USA) (Danzig (USA))
13[5] 115[6] 562[3] 4715[9] 4872[12] 6230[4] 7348[3] 7610[9] 8077[4]

El Diamante (FR) *Richard Hannon* 64
3 b f Royal Applause Lumiere Rouge (FR) (Indian Ridge)
1472[P]

Electrelane *Ralph Beckett* 108
3 ch f Dubawi(IRE) Imperialistic (IRE) (Imperial Ballet (IRE))
1508[3] 2255[2] (2746a) 3270[16]

Electrician *Tim Pitt* a63 87
3 b g Echo Of Light Primrose Lane (JPN) (Sunday Silence (USA))
6768[8] 8019[7] 8177[5]

Electrickery *Mark Buckley* a24 57
3 b f Excellent Art Exultate Jubilate (USA) (With Approval (CAN))
5000[9]

Electric Qatar *Tom Dascombe* a84 87
3 b g Pastoral Pursuits Valandraud (IRE) (College Chapel)
892[4] 1639[4] 1921[7] 2028[6] 2337[5] 2816[3] (3234) (3450) 3608[5] 4234[7] 7704[7]

Electric Tiger (GER) *David Bridgwater* 55
5 b g Konigstiger(GER) Elle Plate (GER) (Platini (GER))
7077[5]

Electrolyser (IRE) *Clive Cox* a99 113
7 gr g Daylami(IRE) Iviza (IRE) (Sadler's Wells (USA))
421a[6] 759a[7] (1318) 1750[5] 2254[5] 3881[7] 4737[4] 5575[2] 7235[4]

Elegant Flight *Alan Jarvis* a68 74
3 ch f Deportivo On The Wing (Pivotal)
1733[11] 3475[3] (4553) 4996[5] 5705[2] 6488[12] 7356[9]

Elegant Girl (IRE) *Tim Easterby* a48 68
3 b f Amadeus Wolf Zuccini Wind (IRE) (Revoque (IRE))
1274[5] 1521[6] 2121[2] 2470[5] 2928[3] 3438[2] 3848[4] 4428[2] 4807[6] 5823[3] 6125[2] 6806[7] 7178[10] 7456[4]

Elegant In Silk (USA) *William Haggas* 73
2 bb f Hard Spun(USA) Jena Jena (USA) (Dixieland Band (USA))
4055[3] 4742[3] 5184[3] 5836[5] 6604[2] 7399[3]

Elegant Muse *Michael Appleby* a66 61
4 b m Fraam Georgianna (IRE) (Petardia)
(4653) 5326[9] 6053[5] 6641[4] (7382) 7670[10] 7936[5] 8114[5] 8238[U]

Elegant Ophelia *Dean Ivory* a72 66
3 ch f Osorio(GER) Ela's Giant (Giant's Causeway (USA))
2368[6] 3048[2] 3622[3] 6365[9] 7108[2] 7596[10] 8060[2] 8229[2]

Elenya (IRE) *M Cesandri* a98 92
3 b f Lawman(FR) Edwina (IRE) (Caerleon (USA))
8300a[2]

Eleona (GER) *Frau E Mader* 87
5 b m Areion(GER) Evry (GER) (Torgos)
6085a[8]

Elhaame (IRE) *Luca Cumani* a28 81
2 b g Acclamation Gold Hush (USA) (Seeking The Gold (USA))
4066[8] 4917[11] 5962[2]

Elhamri *Conor Dore* a74 71
8 bb g Noverre(USA) Seamstress (IRE) (Barathea (IRE))
13[4] 100[7] 115[5] 287[9] 696[9] (813) 904[2] 1177[3] 1279[5] 1430[2] 1581[4] 1958[9] 2581[6] 3008[10] 3761[8] 3941[8] 4468[8] 5245[7]

Elidor *Mick Channon* 75
2 b c Cape Cross(IRE) Honorine (IRE) (Mark Of Esteem (IRE))
6371[8] 7081[2] 7492[4]

Elijah Pepper (USA) *Conor Dore* a85 83
7 ch g Crafty Prospector(USA) Dovie Dee (USA) (Housebuster (USA))
158[3] 391[5] 1249[7] 1636[4] 2675[7] 3335[2] 4313[2] 4889[6] 6141[2] 6410[12] 6881[6] (7415) 7684[11] 7844[6] 7976[3] 8020[7] 8145[4]

Elik (IRE) *Sir Michael Stoute* 74
2 b f Dalakhani(IRE) Elopa (GER) (Tiger Hill (IRE))
6790[7] 7312[3]

Elite *Mick Channon* a66 64
3 b f Invincible Spirit(IRE) Garah (Ajdal (USA))
827[6] 5017[4] 5263[9]

Eliya *Jo Hughes* a37
2 b f Ishiguru(USA) Riff Raff (Daylami (IRE))
3084[7] 3948[6]

Elizabeth Coffee (IRE) *John Weymes* a81 77
4 b m Byron Queens Wharf (IRE) (Ela-Mana-Mou)
1999[4] 2473[3] ◆ 2909[5] (3355) 4209[4] 8136[10] 8234[3]

Eliza Snow (IRE) *Amy Weaver* a28
2 b f Majestic Missile(IRE) Windomen (IRE) (Forest Wind (USA))
5765[12] 6343[13]

Elkaayed (USA) *Roger Varian* 79
2 ch c Distorted Humor(USA) Habibti (USA) (Tabasco Cat (USA))
6020[4] ◆ 6596[2] ◆

Elkhart (IRE) *Michael Wigham* a70 97
3 b c Refuse To Bend(IRE) Princess Taise (USA) (Cozzene (USA))
1860[10] 2263[13] 2678[3] 3280[5] 4289[4] (4600) 5322[12] 6692[8]

Ellaal *Charles Hills* 89
3 b g Oasis Dream Capistrano Day (USA) (Diesis)
1468[12] 4997[8] 6789[8]

Ella Fitzgerald (IRE) *Rae Guest* a44 61
3 b f Moss Vale(IRE) Grand Slam Maria (FR) (Anabaa (USA))
6362[3] 6930[3] 7611[6]

Ella Motiva (IRE) *Mark Brisbourne* a58 67
2 b f Motivator Stormy View (USA) (Cozzene (USA))
4546[4] 5331[9] 7525[4] 7779[8] 7919[10]

Ella's Kitten (USA) *D K Weld* a55 74
2 b c Kitten's Joy(USA) Anura (IRE) (Giant's Causeway (USA))
4519a[5]

Ellastina (IRE) *Richard Fahey* a44 62
3 b f Zafeen(FR) Elle's Angel (IRE) (Tobougg (IRE))
2336[15] 2803[14]

Ellemujie *Dean Ivory* a91 91
7 b g Mujahid(USA) Jennelle (Nomination)
187[4] 3502[11] 4596[3] 5268[4] 7175[11] 7626[5] 7810[10]

Ellen Dean *Eve Johnson Houghton*
4 b m Pursuit Of Love Cressex Katie (Komaite (USA))
3539[11]

Elle Rebelle *Mark Brisbourne* 66
2 b f Cockney Rebel(IRE) Lille Ida (Hawk Wing (USA))
(3208)

Elle Woods (IRE) *Michael Dods* 82
2 b f Lawman(FR) Lady Livius (IRE) (Titus Livius (FR))
(2631) ◆ 4247[3] 5361[5] 6160[6] 6873[10]

El Libertador (USA) *Eric Wheeler* a68 57
6 bb g Giant's Causeway(USA) Istikbal (USA) (Kingmambo (USA))
28[10] 151[4] 265[8] (530) (594) 825[2] 963[9] 2396[7] 3573[2] 4504[7] 4844[11] 5351[8] 6616[5] 6838[4] 7169[6] 7652[5] 7744[4] 7991[3] 8189[2]

Ellie In The Pink (IRE) *Pat Phelan* a69 82
4 ch m Johannesburg(USA) Stravinia (USA) (Stravinsky (USA))
987[9] 1156[5] 3772[9] 4287[8] 5218[8] 5667[4] 6207[13] 7310[11] 7743[8] 8079[4]

Ellielusive (IRE) *Mark Brisbourne* a43 46
5 b m Elusive City(USA) Danzolin (Danzero (AUS))
503[9] 653[3] 822[7] 2161[5] 2601[6] 2915[11] 3318[9]

Ellies Girl (IRE) *Ronald Harris* 12
4 b m Clodovil(IRE) Miss Toto (Mtoto)
2200[10] 3143[11]

Ellies Image *Brian Baugh* a67 68
5 b m Lucky Story(USA) Crown City (USA) (Coronado's Quest (USA))
2355[11] 2549[6] 3215[8] 3549[9] 5338[11] 6941[11]

El Manati (IRE) *James Tate* 99
2 b f Iffraaj Limit (IRE) (Barathea (IRE))
3590[4] ◆ (4704) ◆ 5979[5] 6865[3]

El McGlynn (IRE) *Peter Salmon* a63 81
3 b f Elnadim(USA) Evelyn One (Alhaarth (IRE))
481[2] 621[2] 742[3] 1090[2] (1389) 1482[3] 2139[4] 2691[4] (3308) (3778) 4046[4] 4558[5] (4881) 6116[8] 6525[2] 6887[4] 7177[2] 7489[15]

El Mirage (IRE) *Dean Ivory* a72 64
2 b f Elusive Quality(USA) Hucking Hot (Desert Prince (IRE))
3590[10] 5304[8] 6343[9] 7007[5] (7223) 7523[4]

El Molino Blanco *Michael Easterby* 52
2 b f Royal Applause Forest Prize (Charnwood Forest (IRE))
2138[9] 2456[5] 3123[10] 4448[9] 5668[6]

Elmora *Sylvester Kirk* a51
3 ch f Elnadim(USA) Ringarooma (Erhaab (USA))
1793[8] 4001[11]

Elna Bright *Peter Crate* a99 92
7 b g Elnadim(USA) Acicula (IRE) (Night Shift (USA))
89[11] 266[2] 405[5] 2558[9] 2707[9] 3822[7] ◆ 4285[8] 5004[11] 6026[8] 7503[7] 7774[12] 8008[2]

Elnadancer (IRE) *Alan Swinbank* 84
2 b g Elnadim(USA) Freedom (GER) (Second Empire (IRE))
3378[2] (3887)

Elnadwa (USA) *Saeed Bin Suroor* a75 66
2 b f Daaher(CAN) Magical Allure (USA) (General Meeting (USA))
6168[3] (7020)

Elnawin *Richard Hannon* a106 113
6 b g Elnadim(USA) Acicula (IRE) (Night Shift (USA))
2179[9] 2559[2] 3877[6] 4092[5] 4299[2] 5077[7]

El Negrito (FR) *J-L Pelletan*
2 b c Hannouma(IRE) Dinger De L'Orme (FR) (Celtic Arms (FR))
8176a[0]

Eloquent Star (IRE) *David Evans* 56
2 ch g Thousand Words Autumn Star (IRE) (Mujadil (USA))
1284[4] ◆ 3224[10]

Elounta *John Best* a44 47
2 b f Dubawi(IRE) Santiburi Girl (Casteddu)
3506[7] 4217[10] 8138[6]

El Padrino (NZ) *S Burridge* a114 58
4 b g Mr Nancho(ARG) Crownie (AUS) (Luskin Star (AUS))
(261a) 417a[13] 757a[9]

El Padrino (USA) *Todd Pletcher* a111
3 ch c Pulpit(USA) Enchanted Rock (USA) (Giant's Causeway (USA))
1872a[13]

El Pib D'Oro (IRE) *C Schiff* a81 85
6 b g Oasis Dream Trinity Joy (Vettori (IRE))
6804a[0]

Elshabakiya (IRE) *Clive Brittain* a97 100
4 b m Diktat Amalie (IRE) (Fasliyev (USA))
866[8] (1111) 1213[7]

Elsie Bay *Mark Usher* a62 66
3 b f Sakhee(USA) Mary Sea (FR) (Selkirk (USA))
4366[8] 5100[5] 5795[8] 6231[2] 7270[2] 7470[2] 7768[10] 8182[5]

Elsie's Orphan *Patrick Chamings* a78 76
5 br m Pastoral Pursuits Elsie Plunkett (Mind Games)
6256[12] 6934[10] 7485[11] 7857[12]

Elspeth's Boy (USA) *Philip Kirby* a53 82
5 bb g Tiznow(USA) Miss Waki Club (USA) (Miswaki (USA))
2094[3] (2414) 2661[4] 7370[9] 7607[11]

Eltheeb *David O'Meara* a75 88
5 gr g Red Ransom(USA) Snowdrops (Gulch (USA))
2093[3] 2504[2] 2773[10] 3494[6] 4621[3]

Eltifaat (IRE) *Sir Michael Stoute* a77 50
3 ch c Medicean Dhelaal (Green Desert (USA))
3735[2] ◆ 4630[6] 6215[4] 7782[2]

Eltiqaa (IRE) *John Gosden* a63 68
3 b f Oasis Dream Dream Valley (IRE) (Sadler's Wells (USA))
1472[15] 4782[5] 5901[3] 6364[8]

El Torbellino (IRE) *David O'Meara* 88
4 b m Chineur(FR) Deeday Bay (IRE) (Brave Act)
1756[5] 2180[6] ◆ 2884[6] 3556[3]

El Trastolillo (IRE) *P Bary* 99
2 b c Oratorio(IRE) Etaaq (IRE) (Sadler's Wells (USA))
3680a[4] 5140a[7]

El Tuscano (USA) *Manuel J Azpurua*
2 b c Forestry(USA) Bella Bella Bella (USA) (Soft Gold (BRZ))
8244a[3]

Eluding *Mahmood Al Zarooni* a80 83
3 b f Street Cry(IRE) Without A Trace (IRE) (Darshaan)
2379[2] 2848[4]

Elusive Bonus (IRE) *David O'Meara* 79
3 b f Elusive City(USA) Over Rating (Desert King (IRE))
1252[7] 1599[9] 2540[13] (3407) (3463) 4798[5] (4878) 5167[6] 5831[11] 6357[10] 6887[2] (7001)

Elusive Flame *David Elsworth* a94 92
3 b f Elusive City(USA) Dimelight (Fantastic Light (USA))
1500[9] 2490[7] 3393[6] 4298[3] 4597[3] (4819) 5324[2] 5980[8] 6165[6] 7508[2]

Elusive Gold (IRE) *J W Hills* a59 59
2 b f Elusive City(USA) Lady Angola (USA) (Lord At War (ARG))
5003[6] 5932[5] 7506[8]

Elusive Hawk (IRE) *Barney Curley* a83 73
8 b g Noverre(USA) Two Clubs (First Trump)
3546[11] 3994[11] (4438) 4969[2] 7436[7]

Elusive Heir (IRE) *Bryan Smart* 71
2 b g Elusive City(USA) Princess Nala (IRE) (In The Wings)
3208[4] ◆ 4257[P]

Elusive Island (USA) *Ann Duffield* a47 59
3 b g Elusive Quality(USA) Quiet Word (USA) (Quiet American (USA))
1067[7] 3028[6] 3315[4] 4087[7] 4452[8] 5014[9]

Elusive Kate (USA) *John Gosden* a80 118
3 b f Elusive Quality(USA) Gout De Terroir (USA) (Lemon Drop Kid (USA))
4065[2] ◆ (4633a) 5141a[3] 6673[2] 7238[3]

Elusive Prince *David Barron* a80 101
4 b g Storming Home Ewenny (Warrshan (USA))
1157[19] 1821[8] 2284[P] (4077) 4802[23] 5370[18]

Elusive Pursuit *Clive Cox* a42 25
4 b m Pastoral Pursuits Elusive Maid (USA) (Elusive Quality (USA))
4874[5] 5687[9] 6362[4] 7322[9] 7746[7] 7914[9]

Elusive Ridge (IRE) *H Rogers* a102 104
6 b g Elusive City(USA) Woodwing (USA) (Indian Ridge)
1946a[7] 2525a[5] 6854a[3]

Elusive Rumour (USA) *Thomas Albertrani* 93
3 b f Elusive Quality(USA) Quiet Rumour (USA) (Alleged (USA))
4478a[8]

Elusive Shadow *Alan Brown* 33
2 ch f Avonbridge Cocabana (Captain Rio)
1861[8] 4395[8] 4952[7] 5255[3] 6122[8]

Elusive Storm (FR) *F Rohaut* a68
3 b f Elusive City(USA) Queen Of Fairies (IRE) (Fairy King (USA))
865a[5]

Elusive Thought (IRE) *J S Moore* a59 52
2 b g Elusive City(USA) Thought Is Free (Cadeaux Genereux)
4921[5] 6134[6] 7812[2] 8094[5] 8112[9]

Elusive Warrior (USA) *Alan McCabe* a65 46
9 b g Elusive Quality(USA) Love To Fight (CAN) (Fit To Fight (USA))
4141[2] 4406[4] 7348[8] 7733[2]

Elusivity (IRE) *Brian Meehan* a74 111
4 b g Elusive City(USA) Tough Chic (IRE) (Indian Ridge)
1469[6] 1857[3] 2486[6] 3371[11] 3877[7] (4299) 4762[17] 5822[5] 6030[10] 6666[9] 7236[9]

El Viento (FR) *Richard Fahey* 98
4 ch g Compton Place Blue Sirocco (Bluebird (USA))
1157[6] 2208[14] 2931[5] 4611[16] 4799[5] (5368) 6466[20] 7066[12] 7691[13]

Elvin *Amanda Perrett* a47 46
2 br c Rock Of Gibraltar(IRE) Petite Nymphe (Golan (IRE))
3506[10] 4463[8] 5235[8] 7808[6] 8094[10]

Elwazeer (USA) *David Peter Nagle* a81 11
4 b g Oasis Dream Hazimah (USA) (Gone West (USA))
3767[5]

Elyaadi *John Queally* a96 98
8 b m Singspiel(IRE) Abyaan (IRE) (Ela-Mana-Mou)
3241[14] 3373[5]

Elysian *Sir Michael Stoute* a73 67
3 b f Galileo(IRE) Echelon (Danehill (USA))
2553[6] 6704[2] 7739[2] 8037[3] 8206[2]

Elysian Heights (IRE) *Nigel Twiston-Davies* a18 51
4 b g Galileo(IRE) Ziffany (Taufan (USA))
7490[6] 7862[7]

Ely Valley *William Muir* a43
2 b f Haafhd Welsh Valley (USA) (Irish River (FR))
7721[12] 7979[6] 8164[5]

Embankment *William Jarvis* a91 82
3 b c Zamindar(USA) Esplanade (Danehill (USA))
6397[7] (7112) (7023) 8095[10] 8206[6]

Emboss (IRE) *H-A Pantall* 100
4 b m Cape Cross(IRE) Eilean Ban (USA) (Silver Hawk (USA))
6088a[0]

Embsay Crag *Kate Walton* 83
6 b g Elmaamul(USA) Wigman Lady (IRE) (Tenby)
1133[4] 1295[3] 1525[4] 2260[9] 2751[6] 3564[9]

Emcee (USA) *Kiaran McLaughlin* a123
4 bb h Unbridled's Song(USA) Surf Club (USA) (Ocean Crest (USA))
7570a[6]

Emell *Richard Hannon* 99
2 ch c Medicean Londonnetdotcom (IRE) (Night Shift (USA))
4149[4] 4982[2] (5784) 7400[2]

Emerald Commander (IRE) *Saeed Bin Suroor* 115
5 b g Pivotal Brigitta (IRE) (Sadler's Wells (USA))
243a[7]

Emerald Invader *David Elsworth* a76 72
3 b g Dr Fong(USA) Odabella's Charm (Cadeaux Genereux)
2196[6] (4916) 5788[7] 6206[6] 6544[4] 6798[6]

Emerald Royal *Eric Wheeler* a56 41
4 b g Royal Applause Bakhtawar (IRE) (Lomitas)
293[2] (375) 561[2] 662[5] ◆ 744[3] 995[3] 1310[9] 1625[7]

Emerald Sea *Chris Wall* 67
2 b f Green Desert(USA) Wind Surf (USA) (Lil's Lad (USA))
4011[9] 5016[5]

Emeralds Spirit (IRE) *John Weymes* a51 71
5 b m Rock Of Gibraltar(IRE) Spiritual Air (Royal Applause)
2598[4] (3254) 3495[5] 3888[3] 4640[3] 4676[2]

Emerald Wilderness (IRE) *Mark Rimmer* a100 90
8 b g Green Desert(USA) Simla Bibi (Indian Ridge)
(177) (354) 618a[13] 755a[12] 1034[8] 5751[4] (6380) 6848[8] 7487[9] 7771[10] 7904[3] ◆ 7999[2] 8227[2]

Emerging *David Elsworth* a74
2 b c Mount Nelson Pan Galactic (USA) (Lear Fan (USA))
7962[3] 8102[2]

Emilio Largo *Sir Henry Cecil* a82 98
4 b g Cadeaux Genereux Gloved Hand (Royal Applause)
1510[5] 2082[8] (2590) 3331[9] 4339[4] (5356)

Emily Carr (IRE) *Mark Johnston* 68
3 b f Teofilo(IRE) Vimy Ridge (FR) (Indian Ridge)
1660[2] ◆ 1878[5] 2381[5]

Emily Hall *Bryan Smart* 54
3 ch f Paris House Raven (IRE) (Alzao (USA))
2749[8] 3028[7] 4717[2] 4956[5] 5621[5]

Eminently *Richard Hannon* a61 73
2 b f Exceed And Excel(AUS) Imperial Bailiwick (IRE) (Imperial Frontier (USA))
5943[9] (6627) 7518[10] 7723[6]

Emirates Champion *Saeed Bin Suroor* a110 100
6 b g Haafhd Janaat (Kris)
143a[3]

Emiratesdotcom *Milton Bradley* a84 82
6 b g Pivotal Teggiano (IRE) (Mujtahid (USA))
1564[6] ◆ 1935[2] 2070[4] ◆ 2482[7] 2940[5] 3139[5] 3778[2] 4503[6] 5120[4] 5502[10] 5812[3] ◆ 6094[4] 6368[4] 6577[5] 7273[6]

Emirates Echo *David Simcock* a16 73
2 ch c Pivotal Kotsi (IRE) (Nayef (USA))
1886[2] 2556[2] 3244[4] 7198[10]

Emirates Jack (IRE) *David Simcock* a52 45
3 b g Red Clubs(IRE) Lady Windley (Baillamont (USA))
459[4] 660[6] 923[8]

Emirates Queen *Luca Cumani* 109
3 b f Street Cry(IRE) Zomaradah (Deploy)
2344[6] (3565) 4556[2] 5238[7] 6379[5]

Emir De La Vis (FR) *D Windrif* a75 75
2 ch c Touch Of The Blues(FR) Red Siel (FR) (Septieme Ciel (USA))
5378a[7]

Emkanaat *Roger Varian* a91 85
4 b g Green Desert(USA) Miss Anabaa (Anabaa (USA))
1935[7] 3045[6] 3503[5] (4155) 4775[3] 5630[2] 6041[4] (6454) 6979[6]

Emley Moor *Chris Fairhurst* a33 54
3 b f Misu Bond(IRE) Royal Curtsy (Pivotal)
7712[7]

Emma Jean (IRE) *Frank Sheridan* a58 59
3 b f Jeremy(USA) Second Prayer (IRE) (Singspiel (IRE))
40[5] 191[11] 766[2] 923[4] 1012[2] 1359[5] 1585[3] 1826[2] (2130) 2351[9] 6001[7] 6500[11] 6836[11] 7504[7] 8099[10] 8257[10]

Emman Bee (IRE) *John Gallagher* a71 81
3 gr f Dark Angel(IRE) Two Sets To Love (IRE) (Cadeaux Genereux)
827[4] 981[2] (1046) 1517[2] 1906[3] (2272) 2503[9] 3542[11] 5004[9] 5362[2] 6789[6] 7246[9] 7741[9] 7858[6]

Emma's Gift (IRE) *Julia Feilden* a96 91
4 gr m Aussie Rules(USA) Rose Of Mooncoin (IRE) (Brief Truce (USA))
354[U] (432) (529) 712[9] 1008[4] 1213[11] 5664[5] 6379[10] 7487[7] 7904[8] 8174[11]

Emmuska *Richard Hannon* a81 75
3 b f Sir Percy Tintac (Intikhab (USA))
2272[10] 3120[4] 4091[4] 4505[6] 5592[4] 5983[10]

Emotionalblackmail (IRE) *Joseph Tuite* a59 82
2 b f Azamour(IRE) Uva Fragola (Nashwan (USA))
4946[6] 5288a[4]

Emperatriz *John Holt* 67
2 b f Holy Roman Emperor(IRE) Fairmont (IRE) (Kingmambo (USA))
3346[5] 3776[2] 5083[5] (5668) 6597[11]

Emperical *Sir Henry Cecil* a74
2 b c Oasis Dream Kalima (Kahyasi)
7507[3]

Emperor Julius (IRE) *Jo Crowley* a71
2 b g Antonius Pius(USA) Queen's Victory (Mujadil (USA))
7191[4] 7707[2]

Emperor Of Rome (IRE) *Tim Fitzgerald* a13 75
4 b g Antonius Pius(USA) Fire Flower (Sri Pekan (USA))
1919[14] 2735[13]

Emperor's Daughter *Tim Pitt* a55 55
2 b f Bahamian Bounty Hatun Suyay (USA) (Strong Hope (USA))
1131[9] 2135[3] 2442[5] 4659[2] 4927[4] 5194[4] 5403[5] 5799[3] 6212[8]

Emperors Waltz (IRE) *Ralph Smith* a48 59
3 b f Antonius Pius(USA) Gavotte (Sadler's Wells (USA))
1989[4] 2548[9] 3023[5] (3974) 4147[2] 4678[2] 4941[7] 7793[9] 8264[11]

Emperor Vespasian *Andrew Balding* 83
3 b g Royal Applause Flavian (Catrail (USA))
1492[5] 1894[4] 2756[2] 3002[4] 3574[4]

Empire Hurricane (GER) *A Wohler* 91
2 bb c Hurricane Run(IRE) Emy Coasting (USA) (El Gran Senor (USA))
7091a[4]

Empire Storm (GER) *A Wohler* a106 109
5 b h Storming Home Emy Coasting (USA) (El Gran Senor (USA))
1410a[3] 2160a[3] (3425a) 4130a[6] 5651a[6]

Empiricist (IRE) *Amanda Perrett* 80
2 b g Holy Roman Emperor(IRE) Charaig (Rainbow Quest (USA))
4803[14] 5304[4] 6020[9] 6204[4] (7079)

Empirico (FR) *David Marnane* a81 87
6 b g Oasis Dream Esprit Libre (Daylami (IRE))
4380a[10] (Dead)

Empowering (IRE) *A P O'Brien* a84 104
4 b m Encosta De Lago(AUS) Blue Cloud (IRE) (Nashwan (USA))
3091a[6] 3650a[8] (4482a) 5523a[7]

Empowerment (IRE) *Richard Hannon* a66 80
2 b c Elusive City(USA) Maimana (IRE) (Desert King (IRE))
4845[6] 5162[5] 5704[3] (6332) 6629[2]

Empowermentofwomen (IRE) *Michael Bell* a63
2 b f Manduro(GER) Miss Brown To You (IRE) (Fasliyev (USA))
8201[3]

Empyrean (USA) *Sir Mark Prescott Bt* a33
4 b m Aptitude(USA) Eternity (Suave Dancer (USA))
23[6]

Emrani (USA) *Donald McCain* a75 79
5 b g Rahy(USA) Ebaza (IRE) (Sinndar (IRE))
2666[2] 2978[9] 3961[4]

Emulating (IRE) *Richard Hannon* a70 68
2 ch c Duke Of Marmalade(IRE) Ascendancy (Sadler's Wells (USA))
4595[5] ◆ 6164[8] 6571[3] 7814[3] 8072[8]

Emulous *D K Weld* 120
5 b m Dansili Aspiring Diva (USA) (Distant View (USA))
(2515a) 3266[7] 6061a[3]

Enaitch (IRE) *Mick Channon* 76
2 gr f New Approach(IRE) Hotelgenie Dot Com (Selkirk (USA))
7403[3] ◆

Ena Sharples *David Nicholls* 67
2 b f Firebreak Myths And Verses (Primo Valentino (IRE))
2587[10] 3747[5] 4344[7] (5675) 6130[4] (6707) 6920[3]

Enchanting Smile (FR) *Mark Gillard* a2 70
5 b m Rakti A Thousand Smiles (IRE) (Sadler's Wells (USA))
4844[12] 5657[11] 6097[12]

Encircled *J R Jenkins* a63 92
8 b m In The Wings Ring Of Esteem (Mark Of Esteem (IRE))
4251[9] 5767[9]

Encke (USA) *Mahmood Al Zarooni* 121
3 b c Kingmambo(USA) Shawanda (IRE) (Sinndar (IRE))
(3826) 4685[2] 5489[3] (6245)

Encompassing (IRE) *Sophie Leech* a72 41
5 b g Montjeu(IRE) Sophisticat (USA) (Storm Cat (USA))
3703[12] 3947[2] 4657[9] 5751[10]

Encore Un Matin (FR) *Y Barberot* a62 47
2 bl c Early March Ballade Viennoise (FR) (Cricket Ball (USA))
8276a[9]

Encouraging (IRE) *David Elsworth* 54
3 ch g Rock Of Gibraltar(IRE) Unreachable Star (Halling (USA))
1467[14] 2393[5] 2895[7]

Endaxi Mana Mou *Peter Charalambous* a54 44
4 bb m Araafa(IRE) Lake Nyasa (IRE) (Lake Coniston (IRE))
966[5] 1534[10] 1742[5]

Endeavor *Dianne Sayer* 36
7 ch g Selkirk(USA) Midnight Mambo (USA) (Kingmambo (USA))
3307[4]

Endless Applause *Richard Whitaker* 59
3 b f Royal Applause Petra Nova (First Trump)
2591[5] 3184[10] 4348[11] 4711[8] 5170[4]

End Of May (IRE) *Peter Bowen* 46
3 b f Iffraaj Lucky Bet (IRE) (Lucky Guest)
4182[3] 4542[10] 4900[8] 5148[6]

Endorsing (IRE) *Richard Hannon* a50
2 b c Dylan Thomas(IRE) Gently (IRE) (Darshaan)
8052[10] ◆

Endura *John Dunlop* 31
2 b f Manduro(GER) Special Moment (IRE) (Sadler's Wells (USA))
7552[10]

Energia Carioca (BRZ) *Fabricio Borges* a81 76
5 bb h Thignon Lafre(BRZ) Bear Hunter (BRZ) (Infamous Deed (USA))
80a[11] 3654a[3]

Energia Central (BRZ) *Fabricio Borges* a70 67
5 bb g Fahim Dona Thereza (BRZ) (Hibernian Rhapsody (IRE))
2807a[9]

Energia Colonial (BRZ) *Fabricio Borges* a104 64
5 bb g Giant Gentleman(USA) Karla Dora (BRZ) (Nugget Point (IRE))
586a[12]

Energia Cosmica (BRZ) *Fabricio Borges* 97
5 b h Thignon Lafre(BRZ) Chapelais (BRZ) (Hostage (USA))
52a[9]

Energia Davos (BRZ) *Fabricio Borges* 113
4 rg h Torrential(USA) Star Brisingamen (USA) (Maria's Mon (USA))
5865a[6] 7282a[6]

Energia Dust (BRZ) *Fabricio Borges* a82 101
4 ch h Amigoni(IRE) Key Largo (BRZ) (Roi Normand (USA))
417a[7] 679a[8] 873a[9] 4130a[5] 5782a[6]

Energize (FR) *Richard Hannon* a71 84
3 ch c Pivotal Breathe (FR) (Ocean Of Wisdom (USA))
1512[10] 2585[3] 3107[4] 3606[2] 3998[6]

Energizer (GER) *Mahmood Al Zarooni* 113
3 b c Monsun(GER) Erytheis (USA) (Theatrical (IRE))
1553a[2] 2568a[4] (3295) 5489[6]

Enery (IRE) *Mark Johnston* a90 89
3 b c Teofilo(IRE) Annee Lumiere (IRE) (Giant's Causeway (USA))
(547) ◆ 1661[6] 2471[6] 3736[2] (3945) 4396[4] 4796[5] 5211[3] (5706) (6039) (6333) 6677[8] 7168[3] 7487[3]

En Ete *Ralph Beckett* a35 46
3 b f Three Valleys(USA) Summer Lightning (IRE) (Tamure (IRE))
7322[10]

Enfant De Lune (FR) *David Pipe* a83 68
8 ch g Inchinor Ombre De Lune (IRE) (Polish Precedent (USA))
1890[7]

En Fuego *Geoffrey Harker* 76
5 b g Firebreak Yanomami (USA) (Slew O'Gold (USA))
1248[7]

Engai (GER) *David Bridgwater* a49
6 b g Noroit(GER) Enigma (GER) (Sharp Victor (USA))
67[12]

Englishman *Charles Hills* 86
2 b c Royal Applause Tesary (Danehill (USA))
(1499) ◆ 3240[15]

English Summer *David Simcock* a90 97
5 b g Montjeu(IRE) Hunt The Sun (Rainbow Quest (USA))
928[3] 1037[3] 1214[12] 2031[6] 2474[6] 2709[10] 3253[8] 4326[8] 5002[9] 5430[8] 6159[2] (6441) 6891[2] 7024[2] 7380[6] 7744[2] 7839[4] 8136[2] (8175)

Engrossing *Richard Hannon* a82 78
3 b g Tiger Hill(IRE) Pan Galactic (USA) (Lear Fan (USA))
1257[4] 2246[4] 3012[3] 4001[3] 4544[3] 5421[2] (5942)

Enjoy Dubai (ARG) *M F De Kock* a102 77
4 b h Seeker's Reward(CAN) Enjoying (ARG) (Candy Stripes (USA))
142a[10] 314a[14]

Enjoying (IRE) *David Evans* a60 62
3 b g Marju(IRE) Jazzy Jan (IRE) (Royal Academy (USA))
1568[8]

Enjoyment *Alan McCabe* a72 10
5 b m Dansili Have Fun (Indian Ridge)
(1528) 1827[8] 1990[7]

Enjoy The Life *Mario Hofer* a82 100
3 b f Medicean Accusation (IRE) (Barathea (IRE))
2107a[8]

Ennistown *Mahmood Al Zarooni* 88
2 b g Authorized(IRE) Saoirse Abu (USA) (Mr Greeley (USA))
5321[5] 6164[6] (6669) 6963[2]

Enobled *Sir Michael Stoute* a76
2 b c Dansili Peeress (Pivotal)
7324[3]

Enriching (USA) *Lydia Pearce* a61 65
4 ch g Lemon Drop Kid(USA) Popozinha (USA) (Rahy (USA))
655[2] 3589[7] 4296[6] (5216) (5632) (6231) 6819[10]

Enrol *Sir Michael Stoute* a91 80
3 b f Pivotal Constitute (USA) (Gone West (USA))
3507[6] 5340[3] (5776) (7023)

Enroller (IRE) *William Muir* a69 81
7 b g Marju(IRE) Walk On Quest (FR) (Rainbow Quest (USA))
1214[10] 2403[3]

Ensejaam (CAN) *Charles Hills* 77
3 bb f Dynaformer(USA) Catch The Ring (CAN) (Seeking The Gold (USA))
1501[2] 2483[2] 3189[3]

Ensnare *Willie Musson* a70 71
7 b g Pivotal Entrap (USA) (Phone Trick (USA))
328[7] 574[10] 761[2] 967[9] 1378[14] 2354[10] 2546[11] 3006[10] 3388[13] 3712[11] 6252[12] (7781) 8131[2] ◆ 8179[13]

Entangle *Rune Haugen* a82 103
6 b m Pivotal Entwine (Primo Dominie)
5651a[3] 7558[5]

Enthrall (IRE) *Phil McEntee* a45 52
3 b f Holy Roman Emperor(IRE) Intriguing (IRE) (Fasliyev (USA))
2010[5] 2582[8] 2786[3] 3489[9] 5095[12] 5406[6] 5949[4] 6345[2] 6565[5] 7322[7]

Enthusiastic *Michael Murphy* a91 85
4 b h Galileo(IRE) Que Puntual (ARG) (Contested Bid (USA))
5105[2] (5753) (6584)

Entifaadha *William Haggas* a98 107
3 b g Dansili Model Queen (USA) (Kingmambo (USA))
679a[2] 1145a[13] 1468[13] 2701[9]

Entihaa *Alan Swinbank* 84
4 b g Tiger Hill(IRE) Magic Tree (UAE) (Timber Country (USA))
1385[7] 1866[4] 2095[2] 2661[2] (3253) 3494[17] 4621[8]

Entitlement *James Fanshawe* a65 58
3 b f Authorized(IRE) Applecross (Glint Of Gold)
5309[4] 5753[9] 7594[4] 7862[3]

Entrance *Julia Feilden* a63 64
4 ch m Iceman Enrapture (USA) (Lear Fan (USA))
1314[3] 1613[7] 2653[2] 3693[2] 4843[10] 5638[4] 6097[5] 6562[7] 7303[10] 7898[9]

Entrapping *Richard Hannon* a61 58
2 b c Tiger Hill(IRE) Meddle (Diktat)
5478[3] 5997[4] 6532[5] 7103[6] 7989[6]

Entre Copas *J-M Osorio* 76
8 ch g Sakhee(USA) Priena (IRE) (Priolo (USA))
5252a[5] 6089a[5]

Entwined (IRE) *Clive Cox* 72
2 b f Elusive City(USA) Corryvreckan (IRE) (Night Shift (USA))
4408[10] (4899) 5836[3] 6675[9]

Enzaal (USA) *Mark Johnston* a72
2 b c Invasor(ARG) Ekleel (IRE) (Danehill (USA))
6177[7] 7021[2]

Epernay *Ian Williams* a78 85
5 b m Tiger Hill(IRE) Riberac (Efisio)
3385[2] 4091[3] 4702[4] ◆ 5238[4] 5834[14] 6470[5] 7128[4] 7334[9] 7858[7]

Epic Battle (IRE) *William Haggas* 77
2 b c Acclamation Wrong Key (IRE) (Key Of Luck (USA))
4773[11] 5685[3] (6043)

Epic Charm *Mick Channon* 58
2 b f Kodiac Gayala (IRE) (Iron Mask (USA))
6486[7] 6817[4]

Epic Storm (IRE) *Sean Curran* a81 68
4 b g Montjeu(IRE) Jaya (USA) (Ela-Mana-Mou)
6614[2] (7594) 8000[4] 8110[8]

Eponastone (IRE) *Gerard Butler* a69 68
3 ch f Footstepsinthesand Thermopylae (Tenby)
3666[4] 4366[4] 4888[5] 6207[9] 6842[5] 7270[8]

Epoque (USA) *Sir Henry Cecil* a73 75
3 b f Empire Maker(USA) Dock Leaf (USA) (Woodman (USA))
1532[5] (4551)

Epsom Flyer *Pat Phelan* a49 51
2 ch g Haafhd River Cara (USA) (Irish River (FR))
2039[7] 3009[6] 3996[9] 5702[6] 7814[7] 8032[6] 8093[8]

Epsom Salts *Pat Phelan* a81 79
7 b g Josr Algarhoud(IRE) Captive Heart (Conquistador Cielo (USA))
202[8] 1186[7] 1446[7] 1939[7] 2855[7] 3278[10] (4251) 5665[9] 6170[8] 6493[10] 7522[8]

Eqtiraab (IRE) *Tony Coyle* a41 61
4 b g Dalakhani(IRE) Mayara (IRE) (Ashkalani (IRE))
903[5]

Equalizer *Tom Dascombe* a73
3 b c Authorized(IRE) Octaluna (Octagonal (NZ))
6615[5]

Equation Of Time *Willie Musson* a78 68
3 gr g Proclamation(IRE) Winter Ice (Wolfhound (USA))
(597) 1032[11] 3393[10] 5747[7] 6789[12]

Equine Science *Jane Chapple-Hyam* a48 31
5 b g Lucky Owners(NZ) Miles (Selkirk (USA))
151[8]

Equinox *Bryan Smart* a21 27
2 b f Medicean Plucky (Kyllachy)
5255[7] 6355[7] 7143[9] 8208[7]

Equitania *Alan Bailey* a83 83
2 b f Pastoral Pursuits Clarice Orsini (Common Grounds)
2019[2] 3326[11] 3783[4] (4331) 5088[6] 5790[2] 6929[5] (7727) 7856[3] (8096)

Equitissa (IRE) *Richard Hannon* 63
2 b f Chevalier(IRE) Westcote (USA) (Gone West (USA))
3474^{9} 5352^{9} 5978^{8} 7432^{2}

Equity Card (FR) *Mark Johnston* a77 67
3 bb f Dubai Destination(USA) Snow Ballerina (Sadler's Wells (USA))
1190^{7} 2089^{7} 3002^{10} 3775^{3} 3910^{5}

Equity Risk (USA) *Kevin Ryan* a74
2 b c Henrythenavigator(USA) Moon's Tune (USA) (Dixieland Band (USA))
(7613)

Eraada *Mark Johnston* a64 72
3 ch f Medicean Elfaslah (IRE) (Green Desert (USA))
1612^{9} 6405^{11} 6981^{9}

Erdeli (IRE) *Tim Vaughan* a48 62
8 b g Desert Prince(IRE) Edabiya (IRE) (Rainbow Quest (USA))
6691^{11}

Ereka (IRE) *John Best* a61 52
4 ch m Tau Ceti Most-Saucy (Most Welcome)
(662) 972^{8} 1608^{3} (2170) 2607^{2} 5049^{7} 5444^{2} 5850^{5} 6585^{3} 6778^{13} 7225^{7} 7482^{11}

Ergiyas (USA) *H J Brown* a98
6 br h War Chant(USA) Southern Fiction (USA) (Brocco (USA))
874a^{12}

Ergo (FR) *James Moffatt* a55 55
8 b g Grand Lodge(USA) Erhawah (Mark Of Esteem (IRE))
104^{7} 333^{4} 725^{11}

Ergoz (TUR) *T Sit* 90
4 b h Iffraaj Midnight Mambo (USA) (Kingmambo (USA))
5869a^{9}

Erica Starprincess *George Moore* 25
2 b f Bollin Eric Presidium Star (Presidium)
6099^{12} 6335^{14}

Eric The Grey (IRE) *Richard Fahey* 66
2 gr g Verglas(IRE) Queens Wharf (IRE) (Ela-Mana-Mou)
5963^{11} 6708^{3}

Ermyn Flyer *Pat Phelan* a57 64
3 b f Sakhee(USA) Famcred (Inchinor)
920^{6} (1625) 1853^{6} 2846^{4} 3998^{4} 4726^{6} 6302^{2} 8038^{2} 8180^{8}

Ermyn Lodge *Pat Phelan* a82 99
6 br g Singspiel(IRE) Rosewood Belle (USA) (Woodman (USA))
2933^{14} 5076^{10} 7051^{32}

Ermyntrude *Pat Phelan* a64 63
5 bb m Rock Of Gibraltar(IRE) Ruthie (Pursuit Of Love)
122^{5} 305^{4} 966^{6} 1299^{6} 3043^{2} 4505^{9} 4940^{5} 5441^{7} (6252) 7500^{4}

Ernest Hemingway (IRE) *A P O'Brien* a98 91
3 br c Galileo(IRE) Cassydora (Darshaan)
2210^{7} ◆ 6912a^{16}

Erodium *Richard Hannon* 77
2 b c Kyllachy Alovera (IRE) (King's Best (USA))
4472^{7} 5304^{3} 5963^{4}

Eros De La Luna (FR) *C Boutin* a80 85
4 b g Johann Quatz(FR) Luna De Miel (Shareef Dancer (USA))
1172a^{5}

Errigal Lad *Garry Woodward* a60 64
7 ch g Bertolini(USA) La Belle Vie (Indian King (USA))
2549^{11} (2815) 3076^{2} 4174^{5} 4245^{10} 4438^{7} 5915^{14} 6403^{10} 7447^{11} 7634^{3}

Ersaal *Roger Varian* a66 66
2 b c Dubawi(IRE) Makaaseb (USA) (Pulpit (USA))
4595^{8} 5304^{6} 7750^{3}

Ertikaan *Brendan Powell* a89 88
5 b g Oasis Dream Aunty Mary (Common Grounds)
1476^{7} 1643^{8} 2289^{2} 2487^{11} 2870^{10} 3822^{9} 5812^{2} 6369^{5} 6800^{3} 7019^{4} 7297^{2} (7820) 8188^{5}

Erycina (IRE) *Noel Wilson* a17 47
4 gr m Aussie Rules(USA) Golden (FR) (Sanglamore (USA))
3753^{9} 5115^{5} 5922^{3}

Escape Artist *David Thompson* a54 63
5 gr g Act One Free At Last (Shirley Heights)
558^{3} 666^{5} 741^{7} 891^{2} 984^{4} 1051^{4} 1309^{10} 2635^{9} 3277^{4} 4209^{7}

Escape Route (USA) *S Seemar* a106 105
8 b g Elusive Quality(USA) Away (USA) (Dixieland Band (USA))
144a^{8} 315a^{6} ◆

Escape To Glory (USA) *Mikael Magnusson* a85 93
4 b g Bernstein(USA) Escape To Victory (Salse (USA))
1091^{8} 1289^{3} 1417^{2} 1885^{19} 2177^{8} (2608) 2896^{6} 4321^{25} 4703^{11} 5557^{3} (6008) 6432^{4}

Escardo (GER) *David Bridgwater* a52 51
9 b g Silvano(GER) Epik (GER) (Selkirk (USA))
634^{7}

Eseej (USA) *Geoffrey Deacon* a84 49
7 ch g Aljabr(USA) Jinaan (USA) (Mr Prospector (USA))
4470^{8} 6802^{12}

Esentepe (IRE) *David Wachman* a89 102
3 b f Oratorio(IRE) Mythie (FR) (Octagonal (NZ))
1215^{3} (1454) 1851^{6} 2178^{3} 3270^{13} 6079a^{6} 6518a^{4}

Eshaab (USA) *Ed Dunlop* a75 81
3 bb c Dynaformer(USA) Jaish (USA) (Seeking The Gold (USA))
908^{3} 1113^{2} 1484^{3} (1757) 2235^{3} 2980^{10} 3774^{7}

Eshtiaal (USA) *Brian Meehan* 73
2 b c Dynaformer(USA) Enfiraaj (USA) (Kingmambo (USA))
7333^{2} ◆

Eshtibaak (IRE) *John Gosden* a98 93
4 b h Dalakhani(IRE) Nanabanana (IRE) (Anabaa (USA))
(1008) 1139^{12} 4365^{9}

Esles (FR) *C Laffon-Parias* 106
4 b h Motivator Resquilleuse (USA) (Dehere (USA))
5252a^{P}

Especially Red (IRE) *Lisa Williamson* 72
3 b f Red Clubs(IRE) Midnight Special (IRE) (Danetime (IRE))
2451^{8} 3118^{6} 3567^{8}

Esperance (FR) *S Wattel* a76 76
3 b f Muhtathir Carmelixia (IRE) (Linamix (FR))
7267a^{5}

Espero (FR) *J-C Rouget* a104 104
3 gr c Verglas(IRE) Queen's Conquer (King's Best (USA))
716a^{2}

Espiritu (FR) *G Al Marri* a87 27
6 b g Dansili Red Bravo (USA) (Red Ransom (USA))
618a^{14}

Esprit Danseur *Jim Boyle* a66 65
3 b f Invincible Spirit(IRE) Oulianovsk (IRE) (Peintre Celebre (USA))
1445^{4} 1733^{6} (2367) 2610^{3} 3719^{7} 4726^{8} 4939^{14} 5440^{7} 5662^{7} 6171^{9}

Esprit De Midas *Dean Ivory* a92 98
6 b g Namid Spritzeria (Bigstone (IRE))
(1708) 2268^{10} 2545^{3} 3128^{2} 3855^{4} 4321^{22} 4802^{21} 5746^{5} (6041) 6676^{13}

Es Que Love (IRE) *Mark Johnston* 109
3 br c Clodovil(IRE) Es Que (Inchinor)
(1271) (1457) 2212^{4} 2712^{2} 2931^{2} 3370^{9} 4576^{14} 4802^{7} 5370^{20} 5581^{4} 6030^{13} 6557^{6}

Essell *Mick Channon* a57 62
3 ch f Singspiel(IRE) Londonnetdotcom (IRE) (Night Shift (USA))
1506^{8} 2266^{10} 2941^{8} 3248^{6} 4232^{3} 4490^{5} 5037^{8} 5501^{6} 5770^{3} 6948^{5} 7222^{3} 7321^{7} 7616^{4} 7982^{3} 8113^{9}

Essexbridge *David O'Meara* a35 68
5 b g Avonbridge Aonach Mor (Anabaa (USA))
7603^{12} 7731^{8}

Essexvale (IRE) *Robert Johnson* a58 66
3 b f Moss Vale(IRE) Danccalli (IRE) (Traditionally (USA))
138^{5} 462^{4} 975^{7} 1090^{6} 1252^{8} 2673^{12} 3028^{8} 3289^{5} 4084^{3} 5624^{8} 5757^{6} 6477^{7} 6958^{12}

Esteaming *Mick Channon* 76
2 b c Sir Percy Night Over Day (Most Welcome)
6481^{9} 6733^{2} 7033^{2} 7205^{2} 7292^{6}

Estebsaal (IRE) *John Dunlop* 90
3 b c Dansili Bunood (IRE) (Sadler's Wells (USA))
3398^{2} 4516^{4} (5329) 5951^{5} 7083^{2}

Estedaama (IRE) *Marcus Tregoning* a91 82
3 b f Marju(IRE) Mohafazaat (IRE) (Sadler's Wells (USA))
918^{3} (1206) (2258) (7487) ◆ 7825^{5}

Esteem Lord *Zoe Davison* a21 69
6 ch g Mark Of Esteem(IRE) Milady Lillie (IRE) (Distinctly North (USA))
6774^{13} 7815^{11}

Estee Will *John E Long* a40
5 ch m Mark Of Esteem(IRE) Irja (Minshaanshu Amad (USA))
399^{9} 1031^{11} 1379^{12}

Estejo (GER) *R Rohne* 112
8 b h Johan Cruyff Este (GER) (The Noble Player (USA))
1554a^{2} 2106a^{8}

Estemaala (IRE) *Marcus Tregoning* 77
3 b f Cape Cross(IRE) Elutrah (Darshaan)
(6408)

Estibdaad (IRE) *Charles Hills* 54
2 b c Haatef(USA) Star Of Siligo (USA) (Saratoga Six (USA))
7330^{10}

Estifzaaz (IRE) *Charles Hills* 81
2 b c Invincible Spirit(IRE) Lulua (USA) (Bahri (USA))
3634^{6} 5793^{2} 6237^{4}

Estimate (IRE) *Sir Michael Stoute* 108
3 b f Monsun(GER) Ebaziya (IRE) (Darshaan)
(1893) (3330) ◆ 4738^{3} 6163^{3}

Estinaad (USA) *Kevin Prendergast* a62 73
2 b f Street Sense(USA) Dawla (Alhaarth (IRE))
4161a^{4}

Estiqaama (USA) *William Haggas* 75
2 b f Nayef(USA) Ethaara (Green Desert (USA))
6489^{12} 7104^{2} 7403^{9}

Estonia *Michael Squance* a82 74
5 b m Exceed And Excel(AUS) Global Trend (Bluebird (USA))
208^{3} 560^{5} 647^{2} 715^{4} 1073^{3} 2195^{5} 2369^{5} 3595^{4} 4337^{9} 4849^{8}

Estrela *Roger Charlton* a90 87
3 b f Authorized(IRE) Wannabe Grand (IRE) (Danehill (USA))
2079^{3} 2410^{6} 4579^{6} 5094^{8} 5856^{9}

Estrelja (GER) *D Moser* 36
2 b f Desert Prince(IRE) Expensive Angel (GER) (Tannenkonig (IRE))
5781a^{7}

Esytopolishadimond (IRE) *Michael J Browne* a54 30
5 b g Starcraft(NZ) Scarlett Rose (Royal Applause)
218^{4} (744) 1096^{12}

Eternal Bounty (IRE) *David Wachman* 96
3 b f Galileo(IRE) Moments Of Joy (Darshaan)
3197a^{6} 5606a^{5}

Eternal Gift (FR) *Rae Guest* a86 73
3 b c Layman(USA) Get The Ring (FR) (Linamix (FR))
4082^{9} 6169^{4} 6840^{8} 7158^{2} 7437^{3}

Eternal Heart (IRE) *Mark Johnston* 106
4 b h Alhaarth(IRE) Lady In Pace (Burslem)
(1159) 1318^{6} 1974^{4} 2903a^{4} 3372^{7}

Ethics Girl (IRE) *John Berry* a89 87
6 b m Hernando(FR) Palinisa (FR) (Night Shift (USA))
3774^{4} (4983) 5830^{4} 6349^{3}

Ethiopia (AUS) *Pat Carey* 113
4 b g Helenus(AUS) Shona (AUS) (Spectrum (IRE))
7426a^{4} 7621a^{24}

Etijaah (USA) *Brian Meehan* 83
2 b c Daaher(CAN) Hasheema (IRE) (Darshaan)
5062^{6} (5792) 6447^{4}

Etoile D'Argent (ITY) *G Mosconi* 98
3 ch f Docksider(USA) Candy Candy (IRE) (Sikeston (USA))
1699a^{4} 3426a^{4} 7429a^{8}

Eton Forever (IRE) *Roger Varian* a96 115
5 b g Oratorio(IRE) True Joy (IRE) (Zilzal (USA))
1130^{5} 2472^{8} (3331) ◆ 4321^{16} 5597^{7} (6882)

Eton Miss (IRE) *Mike Murphy* a28
2 ch f Windsor Knot(IRE) Miss Barcelona (IRE) (Mac's Imp (USA))
7305^{11} 7653^{9}

Eton Rambler (USA) *George Baker* 67
2 bb c Hard Spun(USA) Brightbraveandgood (USA) (Smart Strike (CAN))
3506^{8} 4472^{9} 6928^{3}

Eton Rifles (IRE) *Stuart Williams* 113
7 b g Pivotal Maritsa (IRE) (Danehill (USA))
1857^{7} 2745a^{4} 3190^{4} ◆ 3623^{4} 5641a^{7} 6867^{3} (7690) (7829a)

Eurhythmic (IRE) *Jim Old* a55 55
5 b g Danehill Dancer(IRE) Russian Ballet (USA) (Nijinsky (CAN))
355^{7} 786^{7} 1771^{3} 2395^{6}

European Dream (IRE) *Richard Guest* a72 87
9 br g Kalanisi(IRE) Tereed Elhawa (Cadeaux Genereux)
1249^{10} 1680^{5} 1914^{8} 2011^{2} 2241^{2} 2720^{9} 3037^{7} 3167^{8}

Euroquip Boy (IRE) *Michael Scudamore* a64 69
5 b g Antonius Pius(USA) La Shalak (IRE) (Shalford (IRE))
4708^{3} ◆ 5681^{10} 5874^{9}

Euroquip Rose *Michael Scudamore*
3 b f Orientor Madrasee (Beveled (USA))
4456^{8}

Eurystheus (IRE) *Richard Hannon* a86 85
3 b g Acclamation Dust Flicker (Suave Dancer (USA))
2408^{4} 3503^{2} 3917^{5}

Euston Square *Alistair Whillans* a83 86
6 b g Oasis Dream Krisia (Kris)
1820^{11} 2417^{8} 3038^{2} 3906^{6} 4674^{4} 5085^{3} 5546^{7} 6073^{14} 7003^{5} 7455^{7}

Eutropius (IRE) *Alan Swinbank* a40
3 b g Ad Valorem(USA) Peps (IRE) (Val Royal (FR))
5753^{8}

Euxton Hall (IRE) *Richard Fahey* 99
2 b c Acclamation Medina (IRE) (Pennekamp (USA))
(2073) ◆ 2702^{4} (3695) 4058^{4} 4736^{5} 5559^{6}

Eva Luna (FR) *J-C Rouget* 66
2 ch f Peintre Celebre(USA) Honorable Love (Highest Honor (FR))
5570a^{6}

Evan Elpus (IRE) *Tom Dascombe* a54
2 br c Footstepsinthesand Birthday (IRE) (Singspiel (IRE))
8270^{4}

Evanescent (IRE) *Alan McCabe* a40 72
3 b g Elusive City(USA) Itsanothergirl (Reprimand)
1377^{4} 3990^{4} (4550) 5415^{4}

Evangelist *Sir Michael Stoute* 72
2 b c Oasis Dream Hi Calypso (IRE) (In The Wings)
4066^{10} 5005^{3}

Evaporation (FR) *C Laffon-Parias* a93 109
5 b m Red Ransom(USA) Polygreen (FR) (Green Tune (USA))
1163a^{2} 1746a^{3} 3205a^{3} 6897a^{3} 7515a^{2}

Evelyn May (IRE) *Charles Hills* a75 72
6 b m Acclamation Lady Eberspacher (IRE) (Royal Abjar (USA))
311^{11}

Even Bolder *Eric Wheeler* a73 78
9 ch g Bold Edge Level Pegging (IRE) (Common Grounds)
59^{6} 353^{5} ◆ 473^{4} 658^{3} 2413^{8} 3008^{3} 3477^{4} 4003^{3} 4146^{4} 4758^{3} 5346^{3} 5531^{9} 6233^{7} 6737^{2} 8054^{8} 8225^{4}

Evening Pinot *Simon Dow* a53 12
4 ch m Auction House(USA) Lady Of Limerick (IRE) (Thatching)
125^{5}

Even Stevens *Scott Dixon* a104 89
4 br g Ishiguru(USA) Promised (IRE) (Petardia)
(3) 286^{3} 1033^{9} 1643^{2} 2264^{10} 3065^{9} 4591^{3} 4770^{6} (6144) 6427^{9} 7019^{10} 7243^{3} 7690^{9} 8008^{8} 8066^{8}

Ever Fortune (USA) *Rae Guest* 78
3 ch g El Corredor(USA) Beyond Price (USA) (King Of Kings (IRE))
4582^{6} (5113) 7115^{3} (7469)

Evergreen Forest (IRE) *Tom Keddy* a72 73
4 ch g Haafhd Inaaq (Lammtarra (USA))
6891^{7} 7474^{10} 7768^{14} 7905^{9}

Everlasting Light *Luca Cumani* a68
2 b f Authorized(IRE) Blue Rocket (IRE) (Rock Of Gibraltar (IRE))
7720^{6} ◆

Everleigh *Richard Hannon* a76 79
2 b f Bahamian Bounty Blur (Oasis Dream)
3504^{5} 3959^{4} (4818) 5361^{9} 6980^{4} 7325^{4}

Everlong *Peter Chapple-Hyam* 89
3 b f Authorized(IRE) Crooked Wood (USA) (Woodman (USA))
1502^{2} 1973^{4} 2633^{3} (6190) 6877^{13}

Everreadyneddy *J S Moore* a47 42
2 ch g Ad Valorem(USA) Maugwenna (Danehill (USA))
4792^{15} 5784^{6} 7191^{8}

Ever Roses *Paul Midgley* a56 63
4 br m Pastoral Pursuits Eljariha (Unfuwain (USA))
1054^{8} 1298^{4} 1954^{4} 2244^{7} 3308^{7} 4174^{10} 5740^{4} 6786^{3} 7179^{4} 7456^{10}

Everstone (FR) *D Allard* a73 62
3 b g Vatori(FR) Emystone (FR) (L'Emigrant (USA))
247a^{0} 365a^{9}

Ever The Optimist (IRE) *Tony Newcombe* a61 60
4 b g Cape Cross(IRE) Have Faith (IRE) (Machiavellian (USA))
1614^{7} 2421^{14} 3076^{5} 4943^{3} 5660^{10}

Evervescent (IRE) *J S Moore* a66 88
3 b g Elnadim(USA) Purepleasureseeker (IRE) (Grand Lodge (USA))
1221^{2} 1996^{7} 3294^{26} 7163^{10} 7790^{9}

Everybody Knows *Jo Crowley* a62 96
7 b g King's Best(USA) Logic (Slip Anchor)
5768^{9} 7824^{7} 8105^{5}

Evoke (IRE) *Jeremy Noseda* a68 74
2 gr f Dark Angel(IRE) Happy Talk (IRE) (Hamas (IRE))
5352^{5} 5631^{3} 6411^{9} (6849) 7164^{7}

Ewans Princess *George Charlton* 39
5 b m Beat All(USA) Queens Stroller (IRE) (Pennine Walk)
3035^{12}

Ewell Place (IRE) *David Nicholls* a80 98
3 br g Namid Miss Gibraltar (Rock Of Gibraltar (IRE))
3265^{16} (4095) 4760^{10} 6143^{13} 6536^{7} 6835^{13} 7769^{8}

Ewenny Star *Bryn Palling* a26 9
3 b f Indesatchel(IRE) My Bonus (Cyrano De Bergerac)
1111^{6} 2762^{7}

Exactement (IRE) *Mrs K Burke* a78 83
2 ch f Speightstown(USA) Rakiza (IRE) (Elnadim (USA))
2630^{2} (7007) 7518^{4}

Exceedance *Bryan Smart* a97 77
3 ch c Exceed And Excel(AUS) Hill Welcome (Most Welcome)
(1921) ◆ 2509^{7}

Exceedexpectations (IRE) *Michael Bell* a74 63
3 b g Intikhab(USA) Jazan (IRE) (Danehill (USA))
2974^{3} 3702^{9} 3972^{5} 4506^{11} (4932) 5216^{6} 5810^{4} 6500^{2} 7317^{10} 7998^{2} 8183^{3}

Excel Bolt *Bryan Smart* 94
4 ch g Exceed And Excel(AUS) Dearest Daisy (Forzando)
1219^{3} 2286^{9} 2717^{16} 4576^{9} 4924^{8} 5829^{8} 6144^{13} 7295^{2}

Excelebration (IRE) *A P O'Brien* 131
4 b h Exceed And Excel(AUS) Sun Shower (IRE) (Indian Ridge)
(1549a) 2270^{2} 3237^{2} (5141a) (7238) 7575a^{4}

Excelette (IRE) *Bryan Smart* 106
3 b f Exceed And Excel(AUS) Madam Ninette (Mark Of Esteem (IRE))
1454^{13} (2664) 3375^{3} 4762^{12} 6140^{3} 6485^{4}

Excellent Aim *George Margarson* a69 60
5 b g Exceed And Excel(AUS) Snugfit Annie (Midyan (USA))
3546^{13} 4438^{4} 5217^{3} 5416^{13}

Excellent Guest *George Margarson* 103
5 b g Exceed And Excel(AUS) Princess Speedfit (FR) (Desert Prince (IRE))
2068^{14} 3268^{2} 4321^{18} 4761^{5} 5517^{9} 6024^{11} 6674^{33}

Excellent Jem *Jane Chapple-Hyam* a74 74
3 b g Exceed And Excel(AUS) Polar Jem (Polar Falcon (USA))
3347^{6} 3790^{2} 5454^{9} 7998^{5} 8069^{2}

Excellent Mariner (IRE) *Mark Johnston* a20 69
2 b f Henrythenavigator(USA) Castara Beach (IRE) (Danehill (USA))
4427^{3} 4677^{2} 4907^{2} 5670^{9} 6247^{9} 7414^{12}

Excellent News (IRE) *J W Hills* a65 59
3 ch f Excellent Art Subito (Darshaan)
549^{6} 726^{2} (998) 1390^{4} 2129^{6} 2578^{6} 4510^{10} 4850^{8} 5408^{8}

Excellent Result (IRE) *Saeed Bin Suroor* 78
2 b c Shamardal(USA) Line Ahead (IRE) (Sadler's Wells (USA))
6596^{3} 7081^{4}

Excellent Touch (IRE) *C Lerner* a71 69
2 b c Excellent Art Bold Bold (IRE) (Sadler's Wells (USA))
7700a^{5}

Excellent Vision *Milton Bradley* a61 54
5 b g Exceed And Excel(AUS) Classic Vision (Classic Cliche (IRE))
104^{5} 1908^{11} 2137^{10}

Excel Yourself (IRE) *James Tate* a78 81
2 b f Exceed And Excel(AUS) Purple Tiger (IRE) (Rainbow Quest (USA))
1556^{4} 2193^{4} 3269^{11} 3669^{6} (4651) 5307^{8} (5909) 7193^{5}

Exceptionally (NZ) *Terry & Karina O'Sullivan* 106
6 bb m Ekraar(USA) Sahayb (NZ) (Zabeel (NZ))
7073a^{3} 7346a^{7} 7560a^{3}

Exceptionelle *Roger Varian* a84 84
2 br f Exceed And Excel(AUS) Turning Leaf (IRE) (Last Tycoon)
(2812) ◆ 5201^{4} 5743^{3}

Excess Knowledge *John Gosden* 102
2 br c Monsun(GER) Quenched (Dansili)
(5005) ◆ 5353^{2} ◆ 6671^{7}

Exchange *A Schennach* a70 73
4 b g Kheleyf(USA) Quantum Lady (Mujadil (USA))
629a^{2}

Exciting Life (IRE) *P Schiergen* 104
4 b h Titus Livius(FR) Puerto Oro (IRE) (Entrepreneur)
1745a^{3} 3603a^{9}

Excluded (NZ) *Robert Hickmott* 101
5 br g High Chaparral(IRE) Cruzeiro (NZ) (Kaapstad (NZ))
7073a^{2} 7560a^{13} 7696a^{13}

Exclusion (USA) *Noel Quinlan* a60 15
2 bb f Include(USA) Long Silence (USA) (Alleged (USA))
6330^{10} 8052^{6} 8147^{4}

Exclusive Dancer *George Moore* 68
3 ch f Notnowcato Exclusive Approval (USA) (With Approval (CAN))
(2095) 2772^{5} 3616^{6} 4329^{3} 4868^{7} 7369^{9}

Exclusive Predator *Geoffrey Oldroyd* a37
3 b g Misu Bond(IRE) Triple Tricks (IRE) (Royal Academy (USA))
7981^{6}

Exclusive Waters (IRE) *William Knight* a65
2 b g Elusive City(USA) Pelican Waters (IRE) (Key Of Luck (USA))
7900[6] 8052[5]

Excuse Me *Kevin Ryan* a58
4 b g Diktat After You (Pursuit Of Love)
900[7]

Excuse To Linger *Jeremy Noseda* a80 71
2 ch c Compton Place Lady Le Quesne (IRE) (Alhaarth (IRE))
4362[7] 5176[2] (6177)

Execution (IRE) *Mme N Verheyen* a75 94
5 b h Alhaarth(IRE) Headrest (Habitat)
7985a[0]

Executiveprivilege (USA) *Bob Baffert* a114
2 b f First Samurai(USA) Refugee (USA) (Unaccounted For (USA))
(5031a) 7548a[2]

Exemplary *Mark Johnston* a96 92
5 b g Sulamani(IRE) Epitome (IRE) (Nashwan (USA))
44[2] ◆ (207) 427[3] (577)

Exempt *Jeremy Noseda* 65
2 gr f Exceed And Excel(AUS) Miss University (USA) (Beau Genius (CAN))
6444[5]

Exeptional Girl *Frank Sheridan*
6 b m Medicean Crimson Rosella (Polar Falcon (USA))
213[7]

Exhibition (IRE) *Francisco Castro* a97 94
7 b g Invincible Spirit(IRE) Moonbi Ridge (IRE) (Definite Article)
3603a[5]

Exit Clause *Tony Carroll* a57
2 b c Manipulator(IRE) Claws (Marju (IRE))
6581[5] 6978[7] 8006[6] 8274[9]

Exkaliber *Jeremy Gask* a50 30
3 b g Exceed And Excel(AUS) Kalindi (Efisio)
1048[4] 1376[7] 1723[10] 2388[12] 2730[10] 3489[17] 8190[8]

Exning Halt *James Fanshawe* a74 81
3 b g Rail Link Phi Phi (IRE) (Fasliyev (USA))
1737[3] ◆ 2883[4] 3622[4] 4224[3] 4945[3] 5680[2] 6639[2] 7131[4]

Exopuntia *Julia Feilden* a58 61
6 b m Sure Blade(USA) Opuntia (Rousillon (USA))
96[7] 676[6] 3978[6] 4435[3] 5216[5] 5633[5] 6395[2] 7500[8] 7816[2] 8083[4] 8179[7]

Ex Oriente (IRE) *John Gosden* a89 94
3 b g Azamour(IRE) Little Whisper (IRE) (Be My Guest (USA))
(84) 1160[4] 1468[14] 2429[3] 3042[3] 4323[4] 4796[4] (5366) 6033[4]

Exotic Guest *George Margarson* 78
2 ch g Bahamian Bounty Mamoura (IRE) (Lomond (USA))
4362[4] 5016[4] 5553[2] 6414[4] 7434[5]

Exotic Isle *Ralph Beckett* a68 56
2 ch f Exceed And Excel(AUS) Paradise Isle (Bahamian Bounty)
2426[5] (6579)

Expense Claim (IRE) *Andrew Balding* a79 105
3 b g Intikhab(USA) Indolente (IRE) (Diesis)
(1301) (1892) (2269) ◆ 2445[2] 2920[3] 4094[4] 6484[9] 7029[4]

Expensive Legacy *Tor Sturgis* a40 56
5 ch m Piccolo American Rouge (IRE) (Grand Lodge (USA))
334[7] 891[11]

Experience (IRE) *David Wachman* a87 105
3 b f Excellent Art Kloonlara (IRE) (Green Desert (USA))
2513a[8] 6268a[6] 6854a[5] 7390a[13]

Expert Fighter (USA) *Saeed Bin Suroor* a89 92
3 ch g Dubai Destination(USA) Porto Roca (AUS) (Barathea (IRE))
2235[9] 3280[2] (4543) 5558[13] 6348[4]

Expose *William Haggas* a80 89
4 ch g Compton Place Show Off (Efisio)
2853[9] 3394[7] 4367[21] 4824[8] 5165[4] 5486[5] 6044[15] 6347[4] 6824[11]

Extol *Colin Teague*
3 b g Exceed And Excel(AUS) Dance Of Light (USA) (Sadler's Wells (USA))
7445[15]

Extra (ITY) *L Riccardi* 93
4 b m Oasis Dream Egesia (Kaldoun (FR))
1409a[5]

Extrasolar *Amanda Perrett* a75 75
2 b g Exceed And Excel(AUS) Amicable Terms (Royal Applause)
4688[15] 5418[8] 6203[2] 6581[2] 7164[6]

Extraterrestrial *Richard Fahey* a89 96
8 b g Mind Games Expectation (IRE) (Night Shift (USA))
1212[6] ◆ 1865[6] 2590[3] 3164[6] 3534[4] 4136[8] 4828[15] 5094[6] 6426[2] 6630[6] 7210[7] 7493[9]

Extremely Alert *Michael Bell* a49 23
3 ch g Nayef(USA) Megdale (IRE) (Waajib)
1261[11] 2042[13] 2585[10] 7174[7] 8229[6]

Extremely So *Philip McBride* a55 68
6 ch m Kyllachy Antigua (Selkirk (USA))
110[5] 566[8]

Exzachary *Jo Hughes* a49 76
2 b g Multiplex Icky Woo (Mark Of Esteem (IRE))
3067[10] 5715[4] (6524) 7207[4]

Eyedoro (USA) *Mark Johnston* a76 76
4 bb g Medaglia d'Oro(USA) Critical Eye (USA) (Dynaformer (USA))
10[3] 137[2] 192[10]

Eye For The Girls *William Knight* 6
6 ch g Bertolini(USA) Aunt Ruby (USA) (Rubiano (USA))
4192[11] 4584[9] 5240[9] 5625[13]

Eyeline *Reg Hollinshead* a56 60
2 b g Needwood Blade Waterline Twenty (IRE) (Indian Danehill (IRE))
3182[9] 4076[4] 4654[5] 5716[9] 6451[8] 6975[4] 7650[8] 7974[5] 8274[10]

Eye Of The Storm (IRE) *A P O'Brien* 99
2 ch c Galileo(IRE) Mohican Princess (Shirley Heights)
7053[3] ◆

Eye Of The Tiger (GER) *Barney Curley* 46
7 b g Tiger Hill(IRE) Evening Breeze (GER) (Surumu (GER))
1507[4] 1882[14] 3036[10] 4103[10] 5306[15] 6626[13]

Eyes On *Frank Sheridan* a57 44
4 b m Diktat Almost Amber (USA) (Mt. Livermore (USA))
927[7] 1095[11] 1283[7] 1586[5] 1907[7]

Ezdeyaad (USA) *Ed Walker* a82 91
8 b g Lemon Drop Kid(USA) August Storm (USA) (Storm Creek (USA))
1416[11] 3045[3] 3503[7] 4775[7] 5305[2]

Ezra Church (IRE) *David Barron* a84 70
5 br g Viking Ruler(AUS) Redrightreturning (Diktat)
33[9] 190[4] (386) 496[4] 834[3]

Fabbiaano (IRE) *James Bernard McCabe* a56 68
4 ch g Kheleyf(USA) Lomond Heights (IRE) (Lomond (USA))
6184a[4]

Fabled City (USA) *Clive Cox* a84 84
3 ch g Johannesburg(USA) Fabulous Fairy (USA) (Alydar (USA))
2331[4] 2785[3] 4233[7] 4814[3] 5512[2] (6705) 7789[3] 8057[3]

Fab Lolly (IRE) *James Bethell*
2 b f Rock Of Gibraltar(IRE) Violet Ballerina (IRE) (Namid)
7364[15]

Fabulous Siam (FR) *P Boisgontier* a83 91
6 ch g Le Triton(USA) Queen Of Siam (FR) (Siam (USA))
2685a[2]

Face East (USA) *Alan Berry* 51
4 b g Orientate(USA) Yes Honey (USA) (Royal Academy (USA))
1881[10] 2618[5] 3333[7] 3889[10] 4087[2] 4807[11] 4865[16] 5760[4] 6100[13]

Face The Problem (IRE) *Jamie Osborne* 111
4 b g Johannesburg(USA) Foofaraw (USA) (Cherokee Run (USA))
(5343) 5832[2] 6028[2] 6244[2] (6666) 6869[5]

Face Value *Adrian McGuinness* a73 80
4 b g Tobougg(IRE) Zia (GER) (Grand Lodge (USA))
(433) 452[4] (7584a)

Faciascura *S Botti* 100
3 b f Oratorio(IRE) Sunsemperchi (Montjeu (IRE))
(3426a) 7075a[7]

Facoltoso *R Biondi* 96
3 b c Refuse To Bend(IRE) Fabulous Speed (USA) (Silver Hawk (USA))
1698a[6]

Fact (USA) *Marcus J Vitali*
4 ch g A.P. Indy(USA) Sharp Cat (USA) (Storm Cat (USA))
8279a[3]

Factory Time (IRE) *A Al Raihe* a91 107
3 b c Baltic King Mark One (Mark Of Esteem (IRE))
142a[8] (417a) 679a[7] 754a[4]

Fadeintoinfinity *Mick Channon* 74
2 b f Sixties Icon Fading Away (Fraam)
2234[6] 2450[4] 2790[2] ◆ (3126)

Fade To Grey (IRE) *Shaun Lycett* a70 34
8 gr g Aljabr(USA) Aly McBear (USA) (Alydeed (CAN))
(1588) (1925) 3283[10]

Fadhaa (IRE) *Charles Hills* a82 89
4 b g Bahri(USA) Weqaar (USA) (Red Ransom (USA))
2248[13] 3635[10] 4515[3] 5129[3] 5835[12]

Fading Sky (FR) *Mlle A Imaz-Ceca* 39
4 b m Lando(GER) Tramonto (Sri Pekan (USA))
6089a[7]

Faffa *Tim Easterby* a60 57
2 ch g Araafa(IRE) Forever Fine (USA) (Sunshine Forever (USA))
7031[4] 7290[8] 7450[6] 7711[4] 7974[12] 8237[2] (8286)

Fair Boss (IRE) *W Hickst* 111
4 ch h Mamool(IRE) Fair Dream (GER) (Dashing Blade)
1700a[8] (5030a)

Fair Bunny *Alan Brown* a54 56
5 b m Trade Fair Coney Hills (Beverley Boy)
1383[4] 2091[16] 3018[6] 4547[7]

Fair Comment *Michael Blanshard* a67 68
2 b f Tamayuz Cliche (IRE) (Diktat)
4408[9] 5098[4] 5907[4] 6253[5] 6946[5] 8200[8]

Fairest (IRE) *Jeremy Noseda* a56 64
3 ch f Elusive Quality(USA) Joan Joan Joan (USA) (Touch Gold (USA))
3082[4] 4782[4] 5776[5] 6455[9]

Fairlie Dinkum *Andrew Crook* a39 78
4 b m Tobougg(IRE) Fairlie (Halling (USA))
3615[11] 4996[8] 6709[10] 7935[10]

Fairmile *C Moore* a73 107
10 b g Spectrum(IRE) Juno Marlowe (IRE) (Danehill (USA))
7980[4]

Fair Moon (FR) *S Wattel* a76 82
2 b f Gold Away(IRE) La Fee De Breizh (FR) (Verglas (IRE))
5570a[8]

Fair Passion *Derek Shaw* a84 77
5 b m Trade Fair United Passion (Emarati (USA))
492[3] (647) 718[8] 835[4] 1015[9] 1362[2] 1643[4] 1868[13] 1990[3] 2369[6] 2861[5] 3382[2]

Fair Trade (AUS) *C Fownes* 116
7 b g Danewin(AUS) Villa Igea (AUS) (Papal Power (USA))
1902a[13]

Fair Trade *Hughie Morrison* a79 85
5 ch g Trade Fair Ballet (Sharrood (USA))
1137[5] 3268[23] 3855[6] 4112[17] 6638[28] 6987[8]

Fair Value (IRE) *Simon Dow* a92 96
4 b m Compton Place Intriguing Glimpse (Piccolo)
1926[5] 2558[7] 3571[2] 3822[10] (4501) 4799[6] 5663[2] 6026[12] 6602[8]

Fairview Sue *Graeme McPherson* a40
8 gr m Alflora(IRE) Tall Story (Arzanni)
5048[10]

Fairway To Heaven (IRE) *Michael Wigham* a75 89
3 b c Jeremy(USA) Luggala (IRE) (Kahyasi)
(308) 471[6] (1862)

Fairyinthewind (IRE) *Paul D'Arcy* a77 73
3 ch f Indian Haven Blue Daze (Danzero (AUS))
2557[12] 5837[4] 6375[4] 6613[13] 7359[8] 7644[2] 7805[2] 7892[2] (8158)

Fairy Mist (IRE) *John Bridger* a50 57
5 b g Oratorio(IRE) Prealpina (IRE) (Indian Ridge)
2091[4] 2735[8] 3032[7] 3442[15] 7612[3] 8205[5] 8298[4]

Fairy Path (IRE) *P J Prendergast* a63 48
2 b f Indian Haven So Glam So Hip (IRE) (Spectrum (IRE))
1832a[5]

Fairy Trader (IRE) *Keith Goldsworthy* 37
5 b m Hawk Wing(USA) Magic Touch (Fairy King (USA))
5529[4]

Fairy Wing (IRE) *Conor Dore* a74 85
5 b g Hawk Wing(USA) Mintaka (IRE) (Fairy King (USA))
7961[6] 8055[5] 8250[6] 8308[5]

Faither *Keith Dalgleish* a54
2 b c Bertolini(USA) Hawait Al Barr (Green Desert (USA))
5410[14] 7780[8] 7900[9]

Faithfilly (IRE) *Ed Walker* a73 97
2 b f Red Clubs(IRE) Bauci (IRE) (Desert King (IRE))
1911[3] 2499[3] 2631[3] (3117) 3604[3] 4205a[2] (5248a) 6038[9] 6424[6] 7518[14]

Faithful One (IRE) *F Doumen* a93 87
5 b m Dubawi(IRE) Have Faith (IRE) (Machiavellian (USA))
83a[8]

Faithful Ruler (USA) *Ronald Harris* a79 90
8 bb g Elusive Quality(USA) Fancy Ruler (USA) (Half A Year (USA))
(103) 268[2] 402[5] (447) 553[5] 634[4] 906[5] 999[4] 8047[8] 8133[3] 8238[5]

Faizeh (GER) *Andreas Lowe* 82
3 b f Soldier Hollow Flamingo Road (GER) (Acatenango (GER))
2531a[8]

Fake Or Fortune (IRE) *Tim Walford* 30
2 b g Antonius Pius(USA) Fancy Theory (USA) (Quest For Fame)
5169[8] 5410[12] 6708[5]

Fakhuur *Clive Brittain* a83 56
4 b m Dansili Halska (Unfuwain (USA))
177[9]

Falasteen (IRE) *Milton Bradley* a83 100
5 ch g Titus Livius(FR) Law Review (IRE) (Case Law)
3[8] 272[2] 325 [2] 525[9] 1975[14] 2838[2] 3707[3] 4231[4] 4501[4] 4690[13] 5165[3] 5812[6] 6226[12] 6788[4] 7023[9] 7254[3] 7309[8]

Falcativ *Ismail Mohammed* a86 86
7 b g Falbrav(IRE) Frottola (Muhtarram (USA))
48a[5]

Falcolina (IRE) *F Head* 59
2 b f Falco(USA) Flamenba (USA) (Kingmambo (USA))
5288a[8]

Falcon In Flight *Jeremy Noseda* 86
3 b f Shamardal(USA) Marine City (JPN) (Carnegie (IRE))
(1261) ◆ 1938[5] 5365[8] 6381[9]

Falcon's Reign (FR) *Michael Appleby* a71 72
3 ch g Haafhd Al Badeya (IRE) (Pivotal)
231[3] 428[2] 684[3] 827[7] 2416[6] (3002) 3692[6] 4094[6] 4498[16] 5451[4] 5942[8] 6136[2] 6560[3]

Falcun *Micky Hammond* a30 65
5 b g Danehill Dancer(IRE) Fanofadiga (IRE) (Alzao (USA))
2635[2] 3402[2] 4626[11] 4908[7]

Faleena (IRE) *Patrick J Flynn* a71 85
3 gr f Verglas(IRE) Dhairkana (IRE) (Soviet Star (USA))
6270a[11]

Falkland (IRE) *John Gosden* a71 70
3 b c Rock Of Gibraltar(IRE) Evita (Selkirk (USA))
1132[7] 1415[2] 1655[4] 5766[4] 7116[6]

Fallen For You *John Gosden* a94 118
3 b f Dansili Fallen Star (Brief Truce (USA))
(1748) 2078[6] (3328) 5141a[10]

Fallen Idol *Saeed Bin Suroor* a82 113
5 b h Pivotal Fallen Star (Brief Truce (USA))
319a[2] 591a[2]

Falls Of Lora (IRE) *Mahmood Al Zarooni* a104 108
3 b f Street Cry(IRE) Firth Of Lorne (IRE) (Danehill (USA))
(680a) 1145a[10] 3270[7] (3879) 4616a[6] 5834[8] 6633[7]

Falmouth Bay (USA) *Catharina Vang* a85 64
4 rg h Elusive Quality(USA) Halo America (USA) (Waquoit (USA))
2807a[10]

Faluka (IRE) *Paul Cole* 47
2 rg f Iffraaj Tortue (IRE) (Turtle Island (IRE))
2124[6]

Falun (GER) *M Nigge* a97 106
6 ch h Pentire Fortunata (GER) (Daun (GER))
93a[2]

Famagusta *Peter Charalambous* a46 52
5 b m Sakhee(USA) Gitane (FR) (Grand Lodge (USA))
1112[6] 1744[5] 4664[6]

Fama Mac *Neville Bycroft* a58 74
5 b g Fraam Umbrian Gold (IRE) (Perugino (USA))
1251[10] 1526[3] 2091[2] 2314[2] 3211[2] 3442[10] 4348[6] (6958) 7179[2] 7351[4] (7446) 7456[3] 7684[10]

Fame Again *Michael Easterby* a75 75
4 b g Gentleman's Deal(IRE) Ballet Fame (USA) (Quest For Fame)
1953[4] 2095[5] 2262[6] ◆ 4175[5] 4779[4] ◆ 4889[10] (6057) 6559[2] (6894) 7685[3]

Fame And Glory *A P O'Brien* 121
6 b h Montjeu(IRE) Gryada (Shirley Heights)
(2318a) 3293[7] 6271a[6] 7235[5] 7546a[P]

Familliarity *Roger Varian* a57
2 ch f Nayef(USA) Millistar (Galileo (IRE))
8018[5]

Famous Lilly (USA) *A De Royer-Dupre* 92
4 b m Rahy(USA) Famously (IRE) (Sadler's Wells (USA))
6595a[9]

Famous Name *D K Weld* 123
7 b h Dansili Fame At Last (USA) (Quest For Fame)
1646[3] (2100a) 2525a[2] (3675a) (4521a) (5134a) (6079a) (7423a)

Famous Poet (IRE) *Saeed Bin Suroor* a95 101
3 b c Exceed And Excel(AUS) Asfurah (USA) (Dayjur (USA))
(1612) 2265[2] 2660[4] (3963) 5094[3]

Famous Warrior (IRE) *Doug Watson* a101 101
5 b g Alhaarth(IRE) Oriental Fashion (IRE) (Marju (IRE))
51a[4] 261a[10]

Famusa *Marco Botti* a101 101
5 b m Medicean Step Danzer (IRE) (Desert Prince (IRE))
242a[6] 319a[11] 618a[4]

Fanditha (IRE) *Mick Channon* a99 100
6 ch m Danehill Dancer(IRE) Splendid (IRE) (Mujtahid (USA))
242a[8] 617a[7] 817[3]

Fani (FR) *N Bertran De Balanda* a66 69
3 b f Layman(USA) Smart Bomb (GR) (Ahalinotos (GR))
5074a[4]

Fannon Blue (ITY) *Mme C Barande-Barbe* a80 96
5 b h Denon(USA) Fantastic Fire (GER) (Platini (GER))
1971a[7]

Fanny May *Denis Coakley* a64 92
4 b m Nayef(USA) Sweet Wilhelmina (Indian Ridge)
1513[6] 2248[4]

Fanrouge (IRE) *Malcolm Saunders* a67 92
3 b f Red Clubs(IRE) Silk Fan (IRE) (Unfuwain (USA))
(1493) 2236[5] 2446[6] 2712[6] 3639[4] 4234[4] 5080[10] 5812[4] 6685[4]

Fantacise *Brian Meehan* 90
2 ch f Pivotal My First Romance (Danehill (USA))
2124[3] 2662[7] 3034[3] (3415) 4064[5] 5103[8] 6873[18]

Fantastic Indian *Roy Brotherton* a20 16
3 b f Sleeping Indian Quite Fantastic (IRE) (Fantastic Light (USA))
6154[9] 6827[10] 7249[6]

Fantastic Moon *Jeremy Noseda* 107
2 ch c Dalakhani(IRE) Rhadegunda (Pivotal)
(4774) (5833) 6671[5] ◆ 7568a[10]

Fantastic Storm *Robin Bastiman* 45
5 b g Fantastic Light(USA) Answered Prayer (Green Desert (USA))
453[14]

Fantasy Fighter (IRE) *John E Long* a64 50
7 b g Danetime(IRE) Lady Montekin (Montekin)
87[4] 178[5] 424[7] 624[8] 687[4] 5217[4] 5808[10] 7929[4]

Fantasy Fry *David Evans* a77 68
4 b g Avonbridge Footlight Fantasy (USA) (Nureyev (USA))
139[10] 284[2] 370[6] 386[4] 926[5] 1178[6] 1283[8] 1387[12]

Fantasy Gladiator *Robert Cowell* a92 89
6 b g Ishiguru(USA) Fancier Bit (Lion Cavern (USA))
1212[11] 2068[13] 3157[6] 3508[8] 4287[4] 4580[10] 5480[5] 5768[6] 7626[11] 7823[4] 7966[14] 8057[7]

Fantasy Hero *Ronald Harris* a14 42
3 br g Notnowcato Pearly River (Elegant Air)
638[6]

Fantasy Invader (IRE) *John Quinn* 66
2 b g Captain Marvelous(IRE) Fields Of Joy (GER) (Waky Nao)
4178[4] 4877[6] 4960[8] 5620[U] 6438[6]

Fantino *Pat Murphy* a68 52
6 b g Shinko Forest(IRE) Illustre Inconnue (USA) (Septieme Ciel (USA))
156[8] (392) 849[8]

Fanunalter *Michael Wigham* a98 118
6 b g Falbrav(IRE) Step Danzer (IRE) (Desert Prince (IRE))
144a[10] 682a[8] 758a[10] (4320) 5651a[8] 6634[9]

Fanzine *Hughie Morrison* 26
2 ch f Medicean Dash To The Front (Diktat)
7403[11]

Farang Kondiew *Declan Carroll* 85
3 ch c Selkirk(USA) Passiflora (Night Shift (USA))
1653[3] ◆ 2452[5] (3064) ◆

Faraway *Ronald Harris* a70 66
3 b c Royal Applause Somersault (Pivotal)
42[3] 250[4] 357[3] 583[3] 801[3] 2547[6] 3451[9] 4154[6]

Faraway Land (USA) *Julia Feilden* a51 43
4 b m Empire Maker(USA) Out Of Reach (Warning)
762[3] 1655[8]

Faraway Run (IRE) *P Khozian* a80 102
3 b c Hurricane Run(IRE) Melatonina (IRE) (King Charlemagne (USA))
247a[2] 475a[2]

Far East *Clive Cox* a63 61
3 b f Cape Cross(IRE) Hollow Dynasty (USA) (Deputy Commander (USA))
5949[2] 7005[4] 7668[2]

Farhaan (USA) *John Dunlop* 105
3 b c Jazil(USA) Alshadiyah (USA) (Danzig (USA))
2275[4] 4685[6] 5364[4]

Farhh *Saeed Bin Suroor* 126
4 b h Pivotal Gonbarda (GER) (Lando (GER))
(1865) ◆ 3267[3] ◆ 3880[2] 4699[2] 5490[2] 6296a[2]

Farleaze *Martyn Meade* a39 73
3 b f Rail Link Monkshill (Fraam)
4288[10] 4753[5] 5408[7] 5855[7]

Farleigh House (USA) *Neil King* a39 34
8 b g Lear Fan(USA) Verasina (USA) (Woodman (USA))
3962[11]

Farlow (IRE) *Ralph Beckett* a82 94
4 ch g Exceed And Excel(AUS) Emly Express (IRE) (High Estate)
1141^{6} (1844) 2489^{2} 4285^{5} 4611^{20} 7080^{11} 7366^{5} ◆

Farmers Dream (IRE) *Richard Price* a53 60
5 b m Antonius Pius(USA) Beucaire (IRE) (Entrepreneur)
46^{9} 483^{7} 744^{12}

Farmers Hill *Mark Hoad* a47 44
4 ch g Dalakhani(IRE) Wemyss Bight (Dancing Brave (USA))
200^{3} 303^{7} 741^{9} 895^{7}

Farmleigh House (IRE) *W J Martin* a96 81
5 ch g Medecis Tabessa (USA) (Shahrastani (USA))
$3648a^{8}$

Farraaj (IRE) *Roger Varian* a107 110
3 b g Dubai Destination(USA) Pastorale (Nureyev (USA))
$1698a^{3}$ (7771)

Fashion Flow *Michael Wigham* a47 57
5 ch m Danehill Dancer(IRE) Verasina (USA) (Woodman (USA))
7656^{7} 7782^{7} 7991^{13}

Fashion Icon (USA) *David O'Meara* a72 67
6 ch m Van Nistelrooy(USA) Los Altos (USA) (Robin Des Pins (USA))
380^{9} 887^{8} 1054^{7} 1246^{8} 1298^{15}

Fa'Side Castle (IRE) *Keith Dalgleish* a13
3 b g Dylan Thomas(IRE) Keyaki (IRE) (Shinko Forest (IRE))
723^{7} 908^{12}

Fast Bullet (USA) *Bob Baffert* a111
4 ch h Speightstown(USA) Renfro Valley Star (USA) (Dayjur (USA))
$7574a^{6}$

Fast Finian (IRE) *Paul D'Arcy* a92 75
3 gr g Clodovil(IRE) Delphie Queen (IRE) (Desert Sun)
(3041) 3445^{3} 4364^{8} 4919^{5} (5302) (6050) 6454^{2} 6768^{2}

Fast Freddie *Mrs A Corson* a76 55
8 b g Agnes World(USA) Bella Chica (IRE) (Bigstone (IRE))
$2114a^{2}$ $5701a^{6}$

Fastnet Storm (IRE) *David Barron* a78 89
6 br g Rock Of Gibraltar(IRE) Dreams (Rainbow Quest (USA))
480^{4} 2491^{7} (2754) 4679^{8} 4964^{10} 6405^{2} 6895^{4}

Fast Or Free *William Haggas* a85 103
3 ch g Notnowcato Ewenny (Warrshan (USA))
(2542) (2930) (3294) ◆

Fast Pace *Amanda Perrett* a66
2 ch f Observatory(USA) Market Forces (Lomitas)
7721^{5} ◆ 8017^{4}

Fast Samurai (USA) *Tony Carroll* a45 54
4 ch h First Samurai(USA) Lady Blockbuster (USA) (Silent Screen (USA))
7654^{10} 8075^{10} 8169^{9}

Fast Shot *Tim Easterby* a51 95
4 b g Fasliyev(USA) Final Pursuit (Pursuit Of Love)
1168^{12} (1478) ◆ 1844^{12} 2177^{3} 2825^{9} 3128^{11} (3624) 4086^{6} 4611^{8} 4880^{5} 5368^{12} 6466^{14}

Fast Stars Line (TUR) *N Kocken* 103
3 b c Ajmera Free Fighter (TUR) (Mujtahid (USA))
$5869a^{4}$

Fatara Froto (FR) *Y-M Porzier* a73 52
4 b m Layman(USA) My Pearly (FR) (Sagamix (FR))
$15a^{10}$

Fata Romana (IRE) *L Riccardi* 84
3 gr f Verglas(IRE) Silk Feather (USA) (Silver Hawk (USA))
$1699a^{5}$

Fat Bottom Girl *Michael Easterby* a48 3
2 b f Pastoral Pursuits Answered Prayer (Green Desert (USA))
5807^{12} 5887^{8} 6335^{13} 7462^{7} 7797^{10} 7930^{5} 8108^{2}

Fat Gary *Tom Dascombe* a79 86
2 ch c Dutch Art Suzuki (IRE) (Barathea (IRE))
1753^{9} (1997) 7125^{4} 7365^{2} 7773^{3} 7856^{5}

Father And Son (IRE) *Marco Botti* a56 3
2 b c Duke Of Marmalade(IRE) Slap Shot (IRE) (Lycius (USA))
7172^{12} 7780^{7} 8070^{10}

Father Of Science (IRE) *A P O'Brien* 100
3 b c Galileo(IRE) Kasora (IRE) (Darshaan)
(1976) ◆ $3678a^{4}$

Father Shine (IRE) *Shaun Harris* a43
9 bb g Supreme Leader Shean Hill (IRE) (Bar Dexter (USA))
5293^{6} 6055^{7}

Fathey (IRE) *Charles Smith* a43 55
6 ch g Fath(USA) Christoph's Girl (Efisio)
14^{5} 113^{10} 2401^{12} 2555^{8} 5013^{9}

Fathom Five (IRE) *Gary Moore* a76 95
8 b g Fath(USA) Ambria (ITY) (Final Straw)
1602^{9} 2040^{4} 5663^{11} 6026^{15} 7309^{5} ◆ 7648^{6} 7860^{5} 8054^{5}

Fathsta (IRE) *Ian Williams* a85 99
7 b g Fath(USA) Kilbride Lass (IRE) (Lahib (USA))
1885^{13} 2068^{19} 2446^{4} 2919^{6} 3049^{7} 3304^{5} (4252) 4589^{6} 4775^{11} (5618) 6192^{4} 6471^{4} 6888^{5} 6969^{7} 7297^{4} 7464^{6} 7789^{8} (8036) 8055^{3} 8143^{3} (8232)

Fatima's Gift *David Simcock* 69
2 b f Dalakhani(IRE) Heavenly Whisper (IRE) (Halling (USA))
6489^{5}

Fattsota *Marco Botti* a94 111
4 b g Oasis Dream Gift Of The Night (USA) (Slewpy (USA))
1139^{9} 1854^{4} 2346^{2} 3826^{4} (4363) 6248^{2} ◆ (6832) 7405^{6}

Fatty Foulkes *Alan Swinbank*
4 gr g Act One Etoile Volant (USA) (Silver Hawk (USA))
6408^{F}

Fault *Alastair Lidderdale* a67 73
6 b g Bahamian Bounty Trundley Wood (Wassl)
666^{7} 927^{4} 1074^{3} 1224^{8} (1310) 1635^{9} 2046^{2} 2170^{11} 2366^{9}

Fauran (IRE) *Clive Brittain* a38
3 b f Shamardal(USA) Zamhrear (Singspiel (IRE))
1182^{10} 2800^{9} 5244^{4} 5938^{10} 6810^{7}

Fauvelinx (FR) *H-A Pantall* a70 74
3 b f Invincible Spirit(IRE) Fauvelia (FR) (Polish Precedent (USA))
$117a^{8}$ $8277a^{8}$

Favorite Girl (GER) *Michael Appleby* a70 76
4 b m Shirocco(GER) Favorite (GER) (Montjeu (IRE))
148^{4} 401^{3} (579) 836^{2} 978^{3} 2915^{2} 3180^{2} 3564^{6} 3992^{7} 5012^{8}

Fayre Bella *John Gallagher* a56 71
5 ch m Zafeen(FR) Hollybell (Beveled (USA))
126^{7} 289^{8}

Fayr Fall (IRE) *Tim Easterby* a78 78
3 b g Fayruz Keshena Falls (IRE) (Desert Prince (IRE))
1241^{10} 2256^{13} 3285^{3} 3451^{5} (3950) 4779^{2} 5415^{2} 6052^{3} 6261^{3} 7142^{3} (7607) ◆ 7936^{3}

Fazza *Edwin Tuer* a74 89
5 ch g Sulamani(IRE) Markievicz (IRE) (Doyoun)
1249^{12} 1755^{3} (2094) 2473^{10} 3493^{6} 7069^{10} 7370^{7}

Fearless Dream *John Gosden* a77 75
3 b f Oasis Dream Fearless Spirit (USA) (Spinning World (USA))
1567^{3} 2584^{4} 6847^{8}

Fearless Jacq (IRE) *David Simcock* 81
2 b f Soviet Star(USA) Gravieres (FR) (Saint Estephe (FR))
(5267) $6289a^{12}$

Fearless Poet (IRE) *Bryan Smart* a58 36
4 b g Byron Fear Not (IRE) (Alzao (USA))
109^{4} (307) 561^{8} 729^{4} 807^{5}

Fear Nothing *David O'Meara* a78 81
5 ch g Exceed And Excel(AUS) Galatrix (Be My Guest (USA))
8^{2} ◆ 139^{6} 380^{6} (4245) (4592) ◆ (4680) 5223^{5} 5412^{5} 5821^{2} 6358^{3} 6767^{3} 7101^{4}

Feb Thirtyfirst *Sheena West* a36 51
3 ch g Shirocco(GER) My Mariam (Salse (USA))
3447^{8} 3965^{8} 4510^{11}

Fed Biz (USA) *Bob Baffert* a112
3 b c Giant's Causeway(USA) Spunoutacontrol (USA) (Wild Again (USA))
$7570a^{8}$

Fedora (IRE) *Olivia Maylam* a66 65
6 b m Cape Cross(IRE) Mahamuni (IRE) (Sadler's Wells (USA))
(124) 262^{12} 537^{4} $815a^{0}$

Feeling Good *Brian Ellison* a77 62
3 b g Shamardal(USA) Lady Golan (IRE) (Golan (IRE))
693^{7} 1053^{2} 1479^{7} 1959^{2} 2400^{3} 2689^{9} 5717^{4} 6502^{8} 6711^{5}

Feeling Peckish (USA) *Michael Chapman* a31 16
8 ch g Point Given(USA) Sunday Bazaar (USA) (Nureyev (USA))
5173^{5} 6922^{6}

Feelthedifference *Sir Henry Cecil* a74 78
3 b f Iceman Miss McGuire (Averti (IRE))
2246^{14} 3643^{6} 4288^{3} 5019^{2} 5592^{5} ◆ 6401^{6} 7171^{3} 7356^{7}

Feel The Heat *Bryan Smart* 78
5 ch g Firebreak Spindara (IRE) (Spinning World (USA))
4552^{6} 4866^{10} 5416^{5} 7446^{17}

Fehaydi *William Haggas* a48 83
2 b c Nayef(USA) Red Camellia (Polar Falcon (USA))
4330^{4} 7324^{11} 7517^{2}

Feisty Champion (IRE) *J W Hills* a69 77
3 b c Captain Rio Deylviyna (IRE) (Doyoun)
2246^{3} 2733^{3} 3338^{3} 3774^{6} 4250^{3} 5809^{5} 6924^{6}

Felician (GER) *F J Leve* 101
4 b g Motivator Felicity (GER) (Inchinor)
$6291a^{4}$ $6906a^{5}$

Felix Fabulla *Hughie Morrison* 77
2 b c Lucky Story(USA) Laser Crystal (IRE) (King's Theatre (IRE))
4472^{10} 5274^{7} 5704^{4} ◆ (6096) 6597^{10} (6732)

Fellini (GER) *N Leenders* a86 95
5 b g Hernando(FR) Fancy Lady (Cadeaux Genereux)
$93a^{5}$

Felona E Serona *Laura Young* a18
3 ch f Compton Place Felona (Caerleon (USA))
1357^{17} 1826^{8} 2148^{7}

Femme D'Espere *Christopher Kellett*
6 b m Celts Espere Drummer's Dream (IRE) (Drumalis)
7612^{9} 7656^{9} 8167^{13}

Femme Royale *Richard Price* a26 51
4 b m Val Royal(FR) Charmante Femme (Bin Ajwaad (IRE))
2090^{7} 2735^{9} 3137^{8} 3220^{7} 4181^{2} 4994^{6} 5198^{10} 6948^{14}

Fencing (USA) *John Gosden* 111
3 ch g Street Cry(IRE) Latice (IRE) (Inchinor)
1856^{6} 2210^{3} 3239^{13} 7048^{4}

Fenella Fudge *Derek Shaw* a72 74
4 b m Rock Hard Ten(USA) Rahcak (IRE) (Generous (IRE))
2373^{10} 2766^{3} (3021) 3395^{4} 3780^{3} 4655^{2} 4933^{4} ◆ 5320^{11} 5548^{4} 6176^{7} 7590^{6}

Fen Flyer *Chris Dwyer* 35
3 ch g Piccolo Maraffi (IRE) (Halling (USA))
1740^{6} 2802^{15} 3050^{12} 3591^{6}

Fennell Bay (IRE) *Mark Johnston* a79 97
3 b c Dubawi(IRE) Woodrising (Nomination)
1142^{6} (1582) 2021^{3} (2246) 2449^{2} 2701^{5} 2897^{5} (3157) (3296) 4009^{11} 4261^{5} 4735^{4} 5078^{8} 5558^{19} 6025^{9} 6484^{10} 6819^{5} 7168^{9}

Fenomeno (JPN) *Hirofumi Toda* 123
3 bb c Stay Gold(JPN) De Laroche (IRE) (Danehill (USA))
$7872a^{5}$

Fenwick Gale (IRE) *Kevin Ryan* 29
2 ch f Kyllachy Carranza (IRE) (Lead On Time (USA))
2977^{U} 4618^{P} 6099^{11} 6754^{5}

Ferdy (IRE) *Paul Green* a64 68
3 b c Antonius Pius(USA) Trinity Fair (Polish Precedent (USA))
108^{4} 973^{5} 2353^{7} 2843^{3} 3555^{2} 4043^{5} (4452) 4909^{6} 5093^{3} 5736^{6} 5831^{2} (6194) 6497^{7}

Ferjaan *John Gosden* a75 75
2 b c Oasis Dream Bahja (USA) (Seeking The Gold (USA))
2934^{6} 3505^{4} 6772^{2} (7006)

Ferney Boy *Chris Fairhurst* a44 57
6 b g Courteous Jendorcet (Grey Ghost)
2260^{13} 2775^{5} 3440^{6} 4145^{4} 4869^{11} 5672^{9} 6126^{5} 6784^{6} 7454^{4}

Ferro Sensation (GER) *J Pubben* 107
6 b g Paolini(GER) Fit To Ski (Niniski (USA))
$2222a^{8}$ $3603a^{3}$ (5647a) $7624a^{5}$

Ferryview Place *Ian Williams* a72 62
3 b g Compton Place Songsheet (Dominion)
7843^{4} 8213^{2}

Festival Dance *Ron Hodges* 71
4 b m Captain Rio Temple Dancer (Magic Ring (IRE))
1910^{7} 2572^{10} 2943^{3} (3243) (4059) 4535^{11}

Feuerblitz (GER) *M Figge* 114
3 b c Big Shuffle(USA) Flamingo Island (GER) (Acatenango (GER))
(2324a) $3683a^{10}$ $4636a^{5}$ $5145a^{2}$ $6523a^{2}$ $7586a^{2}$ $8043a^{11}$

Fever Few *Jane Chapple-Hyam* a73 24
3 b f Pastoral Pursuits Prairie Oyster (Emperor Jones (USA))
4366^{13} (5299) 6931^{11} 7170^{7} 7484^{4}

Fiance Fiasco *Luke Dace* a43 24
2 b f Motivator Wise Little Girl (Singspiel (IRE))
6453^{8} 6816^{7} 7349^{6} 7891^{3} 8155^{9}

Fibs And Flannel *Willie Musson* a69 76
5 ch g Tobougg(IRE) Queens Jubilee (Cayman Kai (IRE))
(21) 386^{3} 574^{6} 761^{5} 884^{3} 1108^{3} 1391^{4} 1533^{8}

Ficelle (IRE) *Ronald Harris* a46 68
3 b f Chineur(FR) Petite Boulangere (IRE) (Namid)
(1353) 1622^{6} 2166^{3} 2573^{5} 2759^{2} 2869^{4} 4235^{5} 4777^{5} 5149^{2} 5446^{7} 5876^{3} 6641^{6} 6739^{6} 7275^{2} 7437^{5}

Fictional Account (IRE) *David Hayes* a90 106
7 ch m Stravinsky(USA) Romantic Venture (IRE) (Indian Ridge)
$7560a^{9}$ $7783a^{11}$

Fidget *David Brown* 59
2 ch f Bertolini(USA) Record Time (Clantime)
3381^{7} 5168^{3} 5733^{4}

Fiducia *Simon Dow* a56 60
2 b f Lawman(FR) Silca Key (Inchinor)
1308^{3} 1767^{3} 2442^{3}

Field Finner *Scott Dixon* a51
4 ch m Goodricke Princess Carranita (IRE) (Desert Sun)
214^{6} 478^{9} 2796^{14}

Fieldgunner Kirkup (GER) *David Barron* 88
4 b g Acclamation Fire Finch (Halling (USA))
1917^{4} 2619^{3} (2924) 3334^{6} 3626^{4} 4135^{3} 5314^{9} (5802) (6338) 7000^{7} 7452^{5}

Field Of Dream *Jamie Osborne* 109
5 b g Oasis Dream Field Of Hope (IRE) (Selkirk (USA))
$246a^{6}$ 1130^{15} 2657^{13} 3268^{4} 3878^{7} (4321) 4761^{11} 5572^{18} 6024^{4} 6868^{8}

Fierecilla *Tom Keddy*
3 b f Firebreak Lizzie Simmonds (IRE) (Common Grounds)
3279^{14} 5453^{5}

Fiery Lad (IRE) *Luca Cumani* a98 105
7 b g Mull Of Kintyre(USA) Forget Paris (IRE) (Broken Hearted)
$143a^{11}$ $484a^{9}$ $678a^{5}$ 1605^{13} (2706) 4575^{4}

Fife Jo *Jim Goldie* 63
2 b c Misu Bond(IRE) Musical Refrain (IRE) (Dancing Dissident (USA))
3112^{4} 4637^{4} 5083^{10} 7687^{8}

Fifteentwo *David Nicholls* a48 71
3 b g Piccolo Turkish Delight (Prince Sabo)
2795^{11} 3451^{8} 6053^{9} 6641^{10}

Fifth Auntie *J R Jenkins* a21
5 ch m Nayef(USA) Subtle One (IRE) (Polish Patriot (USA))
37^{6} 312^{8}

Figaro *William Haggas* 97
4 ch g Medicean Chorist (Pivotal)
1841^{2} (2447) 3625^{16}

Fight (IRE) *John Best* 64
3 b g Danehill Dancer(IRE) Pretty Sharp (Interrex (CAN))
2206^{8} 2733^{11} 3719^{8} 4232^{6} 4754^{11} 6305^{5} 6567^{7}

Fighter Boy (IRE) *Michael Easterby* a22 69
5 b g Rock Of Gibraltar(IRE) In My Life (IRE) (Rainbow Quest (USA))
3164^{9} 3534^{9} 4110^{12} 4557^{7} ◆ 5085^{9} 5588^{13} 8114^{9}

Filatore (IRE) *Bernard Llewellyn* a64 71
3 ch g Teofilo(IRE) Dragnet (IRE) (Rainbow Quest (USA))
5152^{2} 5577^{5} (6738) 7271^{5}

File And Paint (IRE) *Lawrence Mullaney* a68 81
4 b m Chevalier(IRE) Have A Heart (IRE) (Daggers Drawn (USA))
1249^{15} 6141^{15} 6782^{6} 6881^{14} 8137^{3}

Filfil (USA) *Mahmood Al Zarooni* a86 67
2 b c Hard Spun(USA) Dixietwostepper (USA) (More Than Ready (USA))
(4917) 6149^{5} 6372^{5} 6775^{3} 7325^{3} (7614)

Filiatra (FR) *F Head* 70
3 b f Kentucky Dynamite(USA) Rosinda (FR) (Danehill (USA))
$1127a^{11}$

Fille D'Avril (FR) *E Leenders* a77 77
4 b m Zero Problemo(IRE) Taraison (FR) (The Quiet Bidder (IRE))
$15a^{3}$

Fillionaire *Mick Channon* a59 92
3 b f Kyllachy Autumn Pearl (Orpen (USA))
1508^{9} 2078^{12} 3270^{11} 3879^{5} 4497^{7} 5043^{7} 5365^{6} 5576^{3} (5877) 5980^{11} 6285^{3} 6602^{7} 7080^{6}

Filona (IRE) *B Grizzetti* 90
2 b f Motivator Furbeseta (Danehill Dancer (IRE))
$6090a^{6}$

Fils Anges (IRE) *Michael Bell* 85
2 gr c Dark Angel(IRE) La Piaf (FR) (Fabulous Dancer (USA))
1499^{11} 3637^{4} (6983)

Filun *Anthony Middleton* a59 76
7 b g Montjeu(IRE) Sispre (FR) (Master Willie)
1418^{11} 2363^{2} 2623^{4} 3722^{5} 4983^{8} 5908^{2} 6441^{7}

Final Delivery *Jim Boyle* a74 70
3 b g Three Valleys(USA) Bowled Out (GER) (Dansili)
209^{5} (1287) 3248^{4} 3938^{5} 4457^{3} 4727^{4} 6949^{9} 7301^{12} 7892^{5}

Final Destination (FR) *Mario Hofer* a96 96
3 b g Way Of Light(USA) Schicky Micky (FR) (Testa Rossa (AUS))
$542a^{3}$ $3425a^{5}$

Final Drive (IRE) *John Butler* a90 56
6 b g Viking Ruler(AUS) Forest Delight (IRE) (Shinko Forest (IRE))
868^{11} 1035^{8} 1212^{13} 1513^{13} 1755^{8} 2899^{10} 3344^{13} 4716^{5} 5301^{11} 5752^{3} 6013^{4} 6538^{8} 7461^{8} 7790^{11} 8020^{13} 8152^{7} ◆

Finalist *Dean Ivory* a60 46
3 b f Avonbridge High Finale (Sure Blade (USA))
250^{7} 397^{3} 660^{13}

Finalize *Bryan Smart*
2 b f Firebreak Choisette (Choisir (AUS))
2224^{F}

Final Tune (IRE) *Mandy Rowland* a58 79
9 ch g Grand Lodge(USA) Jackie's Opera (FR) (Indian Ridge)
333^{10} 493^{4} 644^{8} 889^{6}

Finaz *Noel Quinlan* a39 72
2 b c Bertolini(USA) Newkeylets (Diktat)
1818^{6} 2508^{3} 3168^{2} 3401^{6} 7931^{6}

Finbar *James Given* a77 76
3 b g Nayef(USA) Baralinka (IRE) (Barathea (IRE))
1473^{5} 2088^{7} 2813^{8} 4498^{8} 5373^{7} 6410^{4}

Finch Flyer (IRE) *Aytach Sadik* a48 57
5 ch g Indian Ridge Imelda (USA) (Manila (USA))
1624^{4} 3220^{5} 5199^{3} 5508^{3} 6278^{3}

Findeln *Eve Johnson Houghton* a50 60
3 b f Dubai Destination(USA) Alpenrot (IRE) (Barathea (IRE))
816^{4} 1107^{5} 1502^{7} 2379^{8} 3083^{11} 3966^{9} 4490^{10} 4942^{6} 5263^{5}

Findhornbay *Keith Dalgleish* a47 64
3 b f Ishiguru(USA) Sweet Cando (IRE) (Royal Applause)
3731^{10} 4394^{4} 5087^{14} 6104^{11} 7615^{5}

Findog *Linda Perratt* 71
2 b g Pastoral Pursuits Night Home (ITY) (Night Shift (USA))
3286^{3} (4395) 5055^{3}

Fine Altomis *Michael Dods* 74
3 b g Lomitas Mi Anna (GER) (Lake Coniston (IRE))
1320^{4} (2341) 2843^{4} (3575) 3727^{3} 4623^{4} 5415^{3} 6429^{4} 6988^{7}

Fine Finale *Michael Squance* a41
3 b g Lucky Story(USA) Lamees (USA) (Lomond (USA))
3002^{11} 3551^{8}

Finefrenzyrolling (IRE) *Mrs K Burke* a66 68
4 ch m Refuse To Bend(IRE) Oasis Star (IRE) (Desert King (IRE))
$15a^{4}$ $116a^{7}$ 1064^{5} 1248^{6} 1586^{4} 2169^{2} 2551^{4} 3285^{4} 7611^{7}

Fine Kingdom *Brian Ellison* 59
3 b g King's Best(USA) Eurolink Sundance (Night Shift (USA))
1319^{8} 1915^{7} 2141^{10} 2404^{4} 3914^{14} 4172^{5} (4678) 5054^{7}

Finellas Fortune *George Moore* 63
7 b m Elmaamul(USA) Fortune's Filly (Nomination)
2698^{2} 3988^{3} 4831^{7} 5735^{2} 6126^{13} 6956^{9}

Fine Painting (IRE) *Gary Moore* a72 55
3 ch f Iffraaj Just One Look (Barathea (IRE))
1733^{3} 2045^{6} 2397^{4} 2846^{7} 3619^{8}

Fine Resolve *Andrew Balding* a65 70
3 b g Refuse To Bend(IRE) Papillon De Bronze (IRE) (Marju (IRE))
56^{4} 1355^{6}

Finesse *Ralph Beckett* a78 78
3 ch f Shamardal(USA) Clare Hills (IRE) (Orpen (USA))
969^{6} 1274^{4} 5776^{2} (6287) 6961^{14} (7524)

Fine The World *T Le Brocq*
8 b m Agnes World(USA) Fine Honor (FR) (Highest Honor (FR))
$2117a^{4}$

Finity Run (GER) *Mark Johnston* a61 74
3 b f Hurricane Run(IRE) Finity (USA) (Diesis)
1754^{2} 1976^{13} 2204^{8} 2679^{2} 2877^{5} 3813^{3} 5456^{7} 5761^{2} 6118^{8} (6555) 6891^{10} 7129^{5}

Finjaan *Doug Watson* a102 102
6 b h Royal Applause Alhufoof (USA) (Dayjur (USA))
$80a^{3}$ $246a^{7}$ $586a^{6}$ $757a^{2}$

Finlodex *Murty McGrath* a62 63
5 ch g Pastoral Pursuits Ela Aphrodite (Halling (USA))
292^{7} 2387^{2} 6172^{9} 6949^{5} 7474^{8} 7964^{3} 8248^{5}

Finnegans Wake (USA) *Dale Romans* a90 109
3 b c Powerscourt Boat's Ghost (USA) (Silver Ghost (USA))
$5375a^{2}$

Finn Mac *John Norton* 37
2 ch g Norse Dancer(IRE) Strictly Elsie (IRE) (No Excuse Needed)
7363^{13}

Finn's Rainbow *John Weymes* a76 25
4 ch g Iffraaj Aptina (USA) (Aptitude (USA))
139^{13} 985^{9} 1987^{13}

Fiona's Spirit (IRE) *Daniel Mark Loughnane* a28 29
5 b m Invincible Spirit(IRE) Assigh Lady (IRE) (Great Commotion (USA))
5504[6] 5719[13] 6003[5] 6496[9] 6737[12] 7471[8]

Fiorente (IRE) *Gai Waterhouse* 120
4 br h Monsun(GER) Desert Bloom (IRE) (Pilsudski (IRE))
1855[6] 2478[2] 3369[6] (4010) 6293a[4] 7621a[2]

Firdaws (USA) *Roger Varian* 98
3 b f Mr Greeley(USA) Eswarah (Unfuwain (USA))
2232[7] 4556[5] 5519[6] 6379[13] 7334[7]

Fireback *Daniel Kubler* a39 95
5 b g Firebreak So Discreet (Tragic Role (USA))
2707[16] 3557[7] 4334[7]

Fireball Express *Brian Baugh*
4 ch g Firebreak Ashfield (Zilzal (USA))
41[8] 1825[10]

Firebeam *William Haggas* a64 112
4 b g Cadeaux Genereux Firebelly (Nicolotte)
2075[2] 2728a[8] 4092[2] 4686[4] 6268a[4] 6882[2]

Firebet (IRE) *A bin Huzaim* a64 95
6 b h Dubai Destination(USA) Dancing Prize (IRE) (Sadler's Wells (USA))
319a[9] 488a[10]

Fire Eyes *David Brown* 101
2 b c Exceed And Excel(AUS) Wunders Dream (IRE) (Averti (IRE))
(4545) 5601[2] 6196[7]

Fire Fairy (USA) *Charles Hills* a18
2 bb f Henrythenavigator(USA) Fabulous Fairy (USA) (Alydar (USA))
7894[10]

Firefly *John Weymes* a15 59
3 b g Firebreak Quick Flight (Polar Falcon (USA))
2604[6] 3233[11] 4172[6] 4642[5] 5917[9]

Fire In Babylon (IRE) *Noel Quinlan* a62 52
4 b g Montjeu(IRE) Three Owls (IRE) (Warning)
(188) ◆ 265[2] 651[4] 1092[8] 6949[11] 7252[9] 7479[5] 7991[12]

Fire King *Barry Brennan* a61 72
6 b g Falbrav(IRE) Dancing Fire (USA) (Dayjur (USA))
3485[15] (4602) 5193[5] 6275[10]

Fire Lily (IRE) *David Wachman* 113
3 b f Dansili Beauty Is Truth (IRE) (Pivotal)
1403a[2] 2109a[5] 2513a[6] (3092a) 4100[7] (5137a) 5641a[2] 6268a[3] 7092a[10]

Fire Ship *William Knight* a56 101
3 b g Firebreak Mays Dream (Josr Algarhoud (IRE))
1938[2] 2660[10] (2854) 3629[2] 4097[2] 4319[5] (5595) (6921) 7558[3]

Firestreak *M Al Muhairi* a96 96
7 b g Green Desert(USA) Flash Of Gold (Darshaan) (80a) 260a[8] 616a[7]

Firey Sally (IRE) *Frank Sheridan* a35 6
2 b f Strategic Prince Serious Rock (IRE) (Rock Of Gibraltar (IRE))
5858a[10] 8254[6]

Firmdecisions (IRE) *Brett Johnson* 34
2 b c Captain Rio Luna Crescente (IRE) (Danehill (USA))
3824[10] 4149[8]

First Avenue *Laura Mongan* a85 91
7 b g Montjeu(IRE) Marciala (IRE) (Machiavellian (USA))
(202) 427[6] 1214[7] 1505[2] 1603[2] 2346[8] 5666[2] 6493[8] 6834[3]

First Battalion (IRE) *Paul Rich* a55 76
4 b g Sadler's Wells(USA) Mubkera (IRE) (Nashwan (USA))
2174[13] 2502[13]

First Bid *James Given* a72 71
3 b c Kyllachy Toucantini (Inchinor)
132[3] 288[3] 556[2] 660[3] 748[3] 1353[3] (1826) (2045) 2375[3] 3041[5] 3555[13] 6052[7] 6436[5] 6888[8] 7166[4] 7307[8] 7604[10]

First City *A Al Raihe* a99 112
6 b m Diktat City Maiden (USA) (Carson City (USA))
(245a) 617a[2] 879a[11] 1143a[6]

First Class *Rae Guest* a67 68
4 b g Oasis Dream Break Point (Reference Point)
(126) ◆ 226[3] (664) ◆ 2466[3] 3549[2] 3790[3] 4302[6] (5338) 5910[9] 7484[5]

First Class Favour (IRE) *Tim Easterby* a52 78
4 b m Exceed And Excel(AUS) Lamh Eile (IRE) (Lend A Hand)
1269[2] 1561[8] 3254[3] 3544[8] (3843) 4177[3] 4676[4] 5372[7] (5731) 6241[6] 6710[9] 7246[11]

First Cornerstone (IRE) *A Oliver* 112
2 ch c Hurricane Run(IRE) Bintalreef (USA) (Diesis)
(5642a) 7398[4]

First Date *P Bary* 106
3 b c Selkirk(USA) Valentine Girl (Alzao (USA))
1869a[5]

First Fast Now (IRE) *Nigel Tinkler* a48 67
3 b f Kheleyf(USA) Montana Lady (IRE) (Be My Guest (USA))
1514[2] 1912[8] 2375[10] 2795[7] 3218[5] 3407[10] 4394[6] 4878[7] 5318[7] 5624[3] 5831[9] 6249[2] 6771[6] 6935[4] 7591[5]

First Glance *Michael Appleby* a50 52
3 br g Passing Glance Lady Santana (IRE) (Doyoun)
249[6] 620[5] 4250[10] 4830[8] (6281) 7148[12] 7222[9]

First In Command (IRE) *Daniel Mark Loughnane* a76 86
7 b g Captain Rio Queen Sigi (IRE) (Fairy King (USA))
123[4] 289[4] 380[3] 551[7] 580[2] (887) (979) (1054) 1954[2] 2230[2] 3065[3] 3308[2] (3382) 4380a[2] 5530[8] 6270a[2] 6716a[11]

Firstkissoflove *David C Griffiths* a34 71
2 br f Byron Jolies Dee (Diktat)
5511[3] (5911) 6597[14] 8302[9]

First Mohican *Sir Henry Cecil* 105
4 ch g Tobougg(IRE) Mohican Girl (Dancing Brave (USA))
(6884) (7175) ◆ 7689[12]

First Order *Ann Stokell* a90 87
11 b g Primo Dominie Unconditional Love (IRE) (Polish Patriot (USA))
1787[P]

First Phase *Mel Brittain* 63
3 b f First Trump Melandre (Lujain (USA))
6783[5]

First Post (IRE) *Derek Haydn Jones* a90 93
5 b g Celtic Swing Consignia (IRE) (Definite Article)
785[9] 907[3] 1128[8] 1752[11] 2500[6] 2642[4] 3037[3] 3508[10] 4474[5] 5094[11] 5794 [2] 6209[2] 6484[11] (7083) 7493[5] 7751[7]

First Rebellion *Tony Carroll* a49 50
3 ch g Cockney Rebel(IRE) First Dawn (Dr Fong (USA))
564[7] 734[4] 802[5] 1585[6] 2388[5] 2762[2] 3141[2] 3218[6] 3489[6] 4185[6] 4937[5] 5446[4] 7633[2] 8210[3] 8253[5]

First Rock (IRE) *Alan Swinbank* a73 66
6 b g Rock Of Gibraltar(IRE) Sakkara (IRE) (Sadler's Wells (USA))
(4) 3097 555[5] 810[3]

First Sargeant *Marco Botti* a65 62
2 gr c Dutch Art Princess Raya (Act One)
7311[3] 7706[7] 8033[7]

First Secretary *Roger Charlton* a54
2 b f Nayef(USA) Spinning Queen (Spinning World (USA))
7505[10]

First Serve (IRE) *David Barron* a48 61
2 b f Bachelor Duke(USA) Mauresmo (IRE) (Marju (IRE))
4344[6] 5242[5]

First Voice (IRE) *James Given* a46 55
3 ch g Dylan Thomas(IRE) Prealpina (IRE) (Indian Ridge)
2381[9] 3561[3] 3809[8] 5203[11] 5764[8] 7189[12]

Fiscal *M Al Jahouri* a22 98
3 b c Cape Cross(IRE) Fibou (USA) (Seeking The Gold (USA))
417a[3] 679a[4] 754a[6] 873a[13]

Fisher *David Nicholls* a68 70
3 br g Jeremy(USA) Elfin Laughter (Alzao (USA))
1053[5] 1270[3] (2144) 2449[7] 2716[10] 4210[6]

Fishforcompliments *Richard Fahey* a75 83
8 b g Royal Applause Flyfisher (USA) (Riverman (USA))
284[3] 323 [2] 4673[2] 5305[9] 5669[2] 6051[5] 6888[4] 7022[4] 7251[7] 7529[2] 7799[3] 7998[4]

Fishlake Rebel *Ruth Carr* 11
2 b g Cockney Rebel(IRE) Fishlake Flyer (IRE) (Desert Style (IRE))
6099[16] 6360[10]

Fistful Of Dollars (IRE) *David Nicholls* a69
3 b g Holy Roman Emperor(IRE) Taking Liberties (IRE) (Royal Academy (USA))
184[2] 362[6] 518[8] 7436[17]

Fit For A King (IRE) *John Best* a47 63
2 b g Royal Applause Sancia (IRE) (Docksider (USA))
3444[6] 3996[8] 4433[7] 6583[9] 7649[7] 7821[7] 8007[5] 8108[7]

Fityaan *M Al Muhairi* a102 96
4 b g Haafhd Welsh Diva (Selkirk (USA))
616a[5]

Fitz *Matthew Salaman* a66 65
6 b g Mind Games Timoko (Dancing Spree (USA))
1702[9] 2586[7]

Fitz Flyer (IRE) *David Nicholls* a104 100
6 b g Acclamation Starry Night (Sheikh Albadou)
1157[5] 1975[7] 2208[11] 2704[10] 4576[6] ◆ 4690[8] 4924[4] 5368[18] 5487[3] 6026[3] 7063[5] 7366[18]

Fitzwarren *Alan Brown* a30 28
11 b g Presidium Coney Hills (Beverley Boy)
160[9]

Fiulin *David Pipe* a94 71
7 ch g Galileo(IRE) Fafinta (IRE) (Indian Ridge)
3241[16]

Five Cents *A Al Raihe* a103 83
5 b h Exceed And Excel(AUS) Native Nickel (IRE) (Be My Native (USA))
588a[12]

Five Cool Kats (IRE) *Bill Turner* a46 14
4 b g One Cool Cat(USA) Katavi (USA) (Stravinsky (USA))
375[12]

Five Hearts *Mark H Tompkins* a57 57
4 b m Bertolini(USA) Light Hand (Star Appeal)
1269[14] 1742[4] 2171[11] (3047) 3793[6] 5638[5] 7479[2] 7793[P] 8067[3] 8260[9]

Five Sixteen (USA) *Dominick A Schettino* a107
3 b g Invasor(ARG) Third Street (USA) (Salt Lake (USA))
2954a[5]

Five Star Junior (USA) *Linda Stubbs* a103 99
6 b g Five Star Day(USA) Sir Harriett (USA) (Sir Harry Lewis (USA))
89[10] 253[6] 527[3] 871[7] 962[13] 3336[9] 4437[3] 4600[5] 4999[9]

Flag Is Up *Brett Johnson*
3 b g Dr Fong(USA) Rainbow Sky (Rainbow Quest (USA))
1737[11] 2041[14] 3012[9]

Flag Officer *Saeed Bin Suroor* a87 101
4 b g Dubai Destination(USA) Dusty Answer (Zafonic (USA))
2176[P]

Flag Of Glory *Peter Hiatt* a67 69
5 b g Trade Fair Rainbow Sky (Rainbow Quest (USA))
366[12] (891) 1106[2] 1207[4] 1650[8] 2043[7] 3692[3] 4179[3] 4844[10] 7495[10] 7819[9] 8146[4]

Flamborough Breeze *Ed Vaughan* a66 74
3 ro f Ad Valorem(USA) Lothian Lass (IRE) (Daylami (IRE))
2045[8] 2583[12] 3044[9] 3622[5] 4214[6] 4650[5] 5212[3] (7465) 7906[10] 8039[2]

Flameoftheforest (IRE) *Ed de Giles* a80 87
5 b g Danehill Dancer(IRE) Coralita (IRE) (Night Shift (USA))
1627[4] 2545[6] (2913) 3648a[6] 4833a[12] 5530[10] 6256[4] 6610[5] 7247[2]

Flaming Ferrari (IRE) *Peter Chapple-Hyam* a53 58
3 b f Authorized(IRE) Spirit Of Pearl (IRE) (Invincible Spirit (IRE))
191[4] 321 [3]

Flamingo Fantasy (GER) *S Smrczek* 108
7 ch h Fantastic Light(USA) Flamingo Road (GER) (Acatenango (GER))
1901a[5] 3768a[3] 4634a[2] 5400a[5] 6297a[12] 7282a[5]

Flamingo Star (GER) *R Dzubasz* 98
2 b c Areion(GER) Flamingo Island (GER) (Acatenango (GER))
(7698a)

Flaming Telepath *Christine Dunnett*
4 ch m Storming Home Possessive Lady (Dara Monarch)
1866[10] 3710[5] 4157[12] 5022[7] 5637[9]

Flashbang *Paul Cole* a78 72
4 ch m Dubawi(IRE) Colourflash (IRE) (College Chapel)
1305[4] 1614[8] (1788) 2012[6] 2493[6] 3477[6] (3761) 4933[3] 5233[4] 5971[8] 6369[7] 7308[8]

Flash City (ITY) *Bryan Smart* a80 89
4 b g Elusive City(USA) Furnish (Green Desert (USA))
1643[3] 2289[8] 2717[2] 3127[4] 4501[3] 5584[2] 6144[U] 6689[7] 7243[9]

Flash Crash *Robert Cowell* a68 70
3 b g Val Royal(FR) Tessara (GER) (Big Shuffle (USA))
(56) 596[7] 1288[8] 6639[3] ◆

Flash Dance (GER) *A Wohler* a93 100
5 b g Monsun(GER) Flashing Green (Green Desert (USA))
630a[2]

Flash Fox (GER) *Brian Ellison*
5 ch g Pentire Fleurie (GER) (Dashing Blade)
6940[12]

Flashheart (IRE) *Marcus Tregoning* 79
2 b c Nayef(USA) Emerald Peace (IRE) (Green Desert (USA))
6447[5] ◆ 6872[9]

Flashlight (IRE) *Mark Johnston* 78
2 b c Shamardal(USA) Jazzy Jan (IRE) (Royal Academy (USA))
6558[3] 6846[2] 7127[2] 7686[2]

Flashman *Richard Fahey* a61 84
3 ch g Doyen(IRE) Si Si Si (Lomitas)
1355[5] 2141[5] (2771) 3697[3] (4294) 4796[3] 5598[6] 6033[5] 6834[7]

Flash Mash (USA) *X Nakkachdji* a55 100
4 ch m Smarty Jones(USA) Magical Flash (USA) (Miswaki (USA))
4790a[4] 6292a[3] 6943a[4] 7829a[4] 8300a[0]

Flashy Star *Mick Channon* 62
3 ch f Mr Greeley(USA) Galileo's Star (IRE) (Galileo (IRE))
2344[10] 3227[7] 4516[8] 4906[4] 5219[4] 5577[6] 5989[7]

Flashy Ways (USA) *Richard Baltas* a88 95
2 ch f Catienus(USA) Golden Kitty (USA) (Carson City (USA))
7547a[11]

Flat Out (USA) *William Mott* a125 90
6 b h Flatter(USA) Cresta Lil (USA) (Cresta Rider (USA))
7576a[3]

Flavia Tatiana (IRE) *A P O'Brien* a86 75
4 b m Holy Roman Emperor(IRE) Sanctify (IRE) (Sadler's Wells (USA))
341a[5] ◆

Flavio Forte (GER) *U Stoltefuss*
3 b c Proclamation(IRE) Freixenet (GER) (Big Shuffle (USA))
6943a[0]

Flavius Victor (IRE) *Patrick Chamings* a70 67
3 b g Holy Roman Emperor(IRE) Teslemi (USA) (Ogygian (USA))
2583[7] 3184[5] 3671[3] 4517[7] 6582[5] (8021)

Flawless Beauty *Hugo Palmer* a77 76
2 b f Excellent Art Desert Classic (Green Desert (USA))
4525[2] ◆ 5551[4] 6603[3] (7161) 7518[8]

Flaxen Flare (IRE) *Andrew Balding* 91
3 ch g Windsor Knot(IRE) Golden Angel (USA) (Slew O'Gold (USA))
1450[9] (1937) 2428[8] 4319[3] 5101[7] 6638[14] (6986)

Flaxen Lake *Milton Bradley* a57 61
5 b g Sampower Star Cloudy Reef (Cragador)
232[8] 664[10] 837[7] 939[5] 1070[2] 1497[8] 2761[2] 3151[7] 3466[9] 4438[11] (4928) 5504[11] 5660[3] 6002[10] 6322[11]

Fleeting Fashion *Michael Appleby* a50 62
3 b f Alhaarth(IRE) Sempre Sorriso (Fleetwood (IRE))
195[6] 2418[6] (3023) 4210[3] 4626[9]

Fleeting Image *Alan Bailey* a94 85
3 ch f Sir Percy Fleeting Rainbow (Rainbow Quest (USA))
908[4] 1363[3] 1532[2] 1976[3] ◆ (2708) 3859[5] 4294[4] 4983[2] (5554) ◆ 7168[2] 7487[2]

Fleeting Indian (IRE) *Linda Jewell* a46 31
3 b g Sleeping Indian Glebe Garden (Soviet Star (USA))
182[9] 308[7] 523[11] 3966[10] 4510[8] 5989[11]

Fleeting Moment (IRE) *Patrick Martin* a69 67
7 b g Oasis Dream Snippets (IRE) (Be My Guest (USA))
6184a[3]

Fleeting Smile (USA) *Richard Hannon* 90
2 b f Distorted Humor(USA) Fleet Indian (USA) (Indian Charlie (USA))
2892[2] (4525) 5361[3] 6021[7] 6675[2]

Fleetwoodmaxi (USA) *Keith Dalgleish* a34 59
5 bb g Afleet Alex(USA) Swain's Gold (USA) (Swain (IRE))
262[11] 828[9] 3052[6] 5081[11]

Fleetwoodsands (IRE) *Milton Bradley* a77 62
5 b g Footstepsinthesand Litchfield Hills (USA) (Relaunch (USA))
67[10] (328) 528[5] 639[3] 896[5] 1117[8] 2758[7] 3229[10] 4758[5] 4993[10] 5179[10] 5750[7] 7224[11] 7382[8] 7906[8] 8180[5]

Flemish School *Gerard Butler* 73
2 ch f Dutch Art Rosewood Belle (USA) (Woodman (USA))
6164[7] 6791[5] 7081[6]

Fletcher Christian *John Gallagher* 73
2 b g Bahamian Bounty Lady Dominatrix (IRE) (Danehill Dancer (IRE))
1411[9] 1847[2] 2852[2] 3242[16] 3916[5] (5449)

Fleur De Cactus (IRE) *Sir Michael Stoute* a89 52
3 b f Montjeu(IRE) Desert Beauty (IRE) (Green Desert (USA))
3279[5] (5048) ◆

Fleur De La Vie (IRE) *Ralph Beckett* a81 64
3 ch f Primary(USA) Francophilia (Lomitas)
1319[5] 1726[2] 2424[4] 3087[3] (3621) (4875) (5430)

Fleur Enchantee (FR) *P Van De Poele* a53 107
8 b m Marchand De Sable(USA) Mademoiselle Fleur (FR) (River Mist (USA))
2805a[8]

Fleurtille *Ray Craggs* 59
3 b f Tillerman Miss Fleurie (Alzao (USA))
1953[3]

Flexible Flyer *Hughie Morrison* 77
3 b g Exceed And Excel(AUS) Windermere Island (Cadeaux Genereux)
(1256) ◆ 2785[5]

Flicka (FR) *J Van Handenhove* 65
2 b f Pyramus(USA) Gabrielle (GER) (Big Shuffle (USA))
7699a[0]

Flighty Clarets (IRE) *Richard Fahey* a65 66
2 ch f Bahamian Bounty Flying Clarets (IRE) (Titus Livius (FR))
2822[6] 3725[4] (4448) 5537[6] 6611[4]

Flipou (FR) *J-C Rouget* a69
3 b c Dr Fong(USA) Algoa (FR) (Common Grounds)
290a[4] 661a[3]

Flipping *Eric Alston* a61 80
5 br g Kheleyf(USA) Felona (Caerleon (USA))
1680[6] 2094[13] 2754[8] 3257[5] 3559[7] 4295[6] 5713[6] 6758[7] 7385[4] 7593[2] ◆ 7781[10]

Flirtinaskirt *Ed McMahon* 71
2 b f Avonbridge Talampaya (USA) (Elusive Quality (USA))
2783[2]

Flirtini *John Gosden* a58
2 b f Nayef(USA) Frappe (IRE) (Inchinor)
8171[9]

Floating Along (IRE) *William Haggas* a71 68
2 b f Oasis Dream Politesse (USA) (Barathea (IRE))
5357[4] ◆ 7497[2]

Floral Art (IRE) *D Camuffo* 67
3 br f Excellent Art Mrs Seek (Unfuwain (USA))
1699a[13]

Florentiner (GER) *A Trybuhl* a75 98
9 bl g Waky Nao Fatagiro (GER) (Mandelbaum (GER))
629a[8]

Floribundus (GER) *M Munch* a73 48
7 b g Monsun(GER) Flashing Green (Green Desert (USA))
94a[5]

Florio Vincitore (IRE) *Brian Ellison* a74 79
5 b g High Chaparral(IRE) Salome's Attack (Anabaa (USA))
997[6] 1384[5] 2621[8] (3231) (4432) (4716)

Flotation (USA) *Roy Brotherton* a37 74
5 bb m Chapel Royal(USA) Storm Dove (USA) (Storm Bird (CAN))
2741[2] 333[13] 468[12]

Flotilla (FR) *M Delzangles* 110
2 b f Mizzen Mast(USA) Louvain (IRE) (Sinndar (IRE))
6129a[5] 6909a[4] (7547a)

Flow (USA) *Sir Henry Cecil* 78
2 bb c Medaglia d'Oro(USA) Enthused (USA) (Seeking The Gold (USA))
4724[4] ◆ 5126[2] (6412)

Flow Chart (IRE) *Peter Grayson* a54 47
5 b g Acclamation Free Flow (Mujahid (USA))
8[8] 113[4] 289[2] 483[3] 572[7] 831[2] 939[3] 1178[7] 1283[2] 1987[4] 2225[2]

Flow Jo (IRE) *Karen George*
4 b m Intikhab(USA) Pespita (IRE) (Desert King (IRE))
6827[11] 7488[10]

Fluctuate (USA) *John Gosden* a90 93
3 ch c Exchange Rate(USA) Cut Short (USA) (Diesis)
1467[2] (1716) ◆ 4287[5] 5273[3]

Fluctuation (IRE) *Ian Williams* a77 49
4 b g Street Cry(IRE) Rise And Fall (USA) (Quiet American (USA))
14[3] (287) (370) 585[2] (899) 1161[18] 1354[15] 1578[5] 8142[7]

Flumps *John Stimpson* a45
3 ch f Auction House(USA) Demolition Jo (Petong)
7667[5] 7903[7] 7952[11]

Fluter Phil *Roger Ingram*
5 b g Piccolo Figura (Rudimentary (USA))
8097[7]

Fly By White (IRE) *Barry Murtagh* a72 73
4 ch m Hawk Wing(USA) Le Montrachet (Nashwan (USA))
676[13]

Fly Down (USA) *B Al Subaie* a124
5 ch h Mineshaft(USA) Queen Randi (USA) (Fly So Free (USA))
878a[6]

Fly Fisher (IRE) *Ian Semple* a58 70
2 ch g Camacho Kelsey Rose (Most Welcome)
1474[3] 1911[2] 2138[4] 3126[10] 3951[3] 4191[2] 6177[10] 6707[5] 7056[5] 7649[3]

Fly Haaf (IRE) *William Knight* a63
3 b g Haafhd Rose Indien (FR) (Crystal Glitters (USA))
4212[9] 8267[2]

Flying Applause *Roy Bowring* a65 83
7 b g Royal Applause Mrs Gray (Red Sunset)
98[4] 367[5] (477) 633[7] (1358) (1561) 1755[7] (1950) 2328[7] 2606[10] 5129[10] 7256[7] 7493[7] 7640[12] 8113[3]

Flying Blue (AUS) *D Cruz* 116
6 br g Piccolo Bright Blue (AUS) (Scenic)
8041a[8]

Flying Doha (IRE) *David Wachman* a71 71
3 b c Danehill Dancer(IRE) Royal Fizz (IRE) (Royal Academy (USA))
1834a[3]

Flying Kitty *John Bridger* a53 52
3 b f One Cool Cat(USA) Flying Millie (IRE) (Flying Spur (AUS))
185[5] 376[3] 564[4] 657[2] (734) 1067[8] 1608[5] 2582[10] 3670[9] 4920[4] 5513[5] 6152[10] 7992[9] 8169[7] 8299[9]

Flying Nellie *Tom Tate* 47
2 b f Mount Nelson Ares Vallis (IRE) (Caerleon (USA))
5962[14] 6607[5] 7208[6]

Flying Officer (USA) *John Gosden* 88
2 b c Dynaformer(USA) Vignette (USA) (Diesis)
(6204) 7053[7]

Flying Phoenix *Dai Burchell* a56 70
4 b m Phoenix Reach(IRE) Rasmalai (Sadler's Wells (USA))
1189[6] 1635[6] 1907[6] 8010[8]

Flying Pickets (IRE) *Alan McCabe* a76 56
3 b g Piccolo Burn (Selkirk (USA))
6[4] 619[4] (748) 840[2] 916[2] 1058[2] 1641[10] 2400[6] 3229[7] (4141) 4401[4] 5243[11] (7732) 7799[5] 8055[7]

Flying Power *John Norton* a87 81
4 b g Dubai Destination(USA) Rah Wa (USA) (Rahy (USA))
2093[7] 2419[6] 3253[2] ◆ 3945[4] 6642[3] 7147[3] (7672) ◆ (8110)

Flying Tempo *Ed Dunlop* a49 50
2 b c Royal Applause Bel Tempo (Petong)
5476[6] 5962[13] 6330[12] 6793[2] 7785[4]

Flying The Flag (IRE) *A P O'Brien* 108
2 ch c Galileo(IRE) Halfway To Heaven (IRE) (Pivotal)
5642a[2] 6272a[7]

Flying Trader (USA) *Jane Chapple-Hyam* a81 81
3 rg g Mizzen Mast(USA) Remediate (USA) (Miswaki (USA))
1302[4] (1707) 2427[2] 3330[10] 6537[6] 6971[10] 8082[7] 8243[4]

Flyman *Richard Fahey* 97
2 b c Pastoral Pursuits Satin Bell (Midyan (USA))
(3123) (5201) 6162[11]

Flynn's Boy *Rae Guest* a70 83
4 ch g Tobougg(IRE) Bukhoor (IRE) (Danehill (USA))
1354[14] 2083[11] 3049[5] 3571[3] ◆ 3790[4] 4661[3]

Flynn's Island (IRE) *Richard Ford* 50
6 b g Trans Island Cappuccino (IRE) (Mujadil (USA))
454[12]

Fly On By *Henry Candy* a59 56
3 b g Byron High Bird (IRE) (Polar Falcon (USA))
1506[9] 1937[7] 5421[6] 5998[8] 6582[7]

Fly Solo *Alan Swinbank* a73 76
3 b g Soviet Star(USA) Vino (Efisio)
4157[2] 5316[3] 6409[2] 7384[3]

Flywheel (IRE) *Peter Chapple-Hyam* a52 40
2 ch f Teofilo(IRE) Scarlett Rose (Royal Applause)
4217[6] 4701[12] 5550[9] 6583[5] 7919[3] 8289[6]

Focail Eile *John Ryan* a84 84
7 b g Noverre(USA) Glittering Image (IRE) (Sadler's Wells (USA))
90[8] 199[5] 280[9] 4068[10] 4662[8] 5990[10] 7250[7] 7469[4] 7638[2] 7781[3] (7925)

Focail Maith *John Ryan* a88 77
4 b g Oratorio(IRE) Glittering Image (IRE) (Sadler's Wells (USA))
36[4] 119[2] (263) 374[2] 3953[10] 4596[7] 5004[8] 5993[3] 6735[4] 7455[6] 7640[4] 7751[6] 7842[7] (8000) 8082[2]

Foie Gras *William Muir* a22 51
2 b g Kyllachy Bint Zamayem (IRE) (Rainbow Quest (USA))
3505[7] 4149[6] 6114[13] 6583[11]

Folding Gear (NZ) *Lee & Shannon Hope* 106
5 b g Johar(USA) Royal Show (NZ) (Deputy Governor (USA))
7264a[7] 7696a[9]

Fol Hollow (IRE) *David Nicholls* a69 86
7 b g Monashee Mountain(USA) Constance Do (Risk Me (FR))
(2122) 3255[5] (3523) 3993[10] 4207[5] 4454[5] 5013[2] 5758[5]

Folk Tune (IRE) *John Quinn* 65
9 b g Danehill(USA) Musk Lime (USA) (Private Account (USA))
3290[11]

Folle De Toi (FR) *T Trapenard* a53 75
2 bb f Sageburg(IRE) Folie Lointaine (FR) (Poliglote)
4696a[3]

Followeveryrainbow *Richard Hannon* 69
2 b f Oasis Dream Absolute Precision (USA) (Irish River (FR))
5104[12] 6204[5]

Follow The Flag (IRE) *Alan McCabe* a88 77
8 ch g Traditionally(USA) Iktidar (Green Desert (USA))
36[12] 177[2] 332[7] 501[3] 554[3] 674[5] 751[5] 812[3] 1135[2] 1258[2] 1513[8] 1657[7] 1841[4] 2051[13] 4401[3] 5243[6] 5345[9] 6405[7] (6794) 6988[2] 7294[6] 7369[2] 7640[5] 7715[6] 7920[5] 8057[6] 8191[8] 8259[4]

Font *Lawney Hill* 87
9 b g Sadler's Wells(USA) River Saint (USA) (Irish River (FR))
4697[18]

Fonterutoli (IRE) *Roger Ingram* a61 61
5 gr g Verglas(IRE) Goldendale (IRE) (Ali-Royal (IRE))
1771[6] 2365[5] 2627[2] 3053[3] 3099[4] 3471[6] 4196[13] 5444[8] 5659[6] 6302[4] 6774[4] 7495[7] 7643[2] 8010[3] 8038[4] 8145[10] 8249[5]

Font Of Wisdom (IRE) *D K Weld* 95
4 b g Marju(IRE) Fernanda (Be My Chief (USA))
1043a[18]

Foolbythepool *Keith Dalgleish* 65
2 b c Refuse To Bend(IRE) Rapsgate (IRE) (Mozart (IRE))
4132[8] 4387[4] 5083[7] 5670[7] 6121[3]

Fool's Wildcat (USA) *Miss Louise Allan* a47 15
7 b g Forest Wildcat(USA) Nine Flags (USA) (Forty Niner (USA))
4843[12]

Footprint (IRE) *Patrick Martin* a76 85
5 ch g Footstepsinthesand Ring The Relatives (Bering)
4833a[10]

Footsteppy (IRE) *J E Hammond* a95 95
4 b m Footstepsinthesand Final Opinion (IRE) (King's Theatre (IRE))
2805a[7]

Footstepsintherain (IRE) *David Lanigan* a75
2 b g Footstepsinthesand Champagne Toni (IRE) (Second Empire (IRE))
(7143) 7501[8]

Footstepsofspring (FR) *Willie Musson* a71 89
5 b g Footstepsinthesand Moon West (USA) (Gone West (USA))
551[10] (1717) 2586[3] (3713) 4158[2] 6456[7]

Foot Tapper *Chris Wall* a67 70
3 b c Invincible Spirit(IRE) Jazz Princess (IRE) (Bahhare (USA))
1331[9] 2045[2] 4914[10] 5427[4] 7668[5] 7838[3] 8304[6]

Forbidden (IRE) *Ian McInnes* a60 68
9 ch g Singspiel(IRE) Fragrant Oasis (USA) (Rahy (USA))
151[7] 468[6] 773[9] 848[11]

Forbidden Fruit (IRE) *Brian Meehan* a67 70
2 b g Acclamation Perils Of Joy (IRE) (Rainbow Quest (USA))
2069[7] 2550[10] 6444[8] 7198[4] 7516[2]

Forced Family Fun *Michael Bell* 68
2 b g Refuse To Bend(IRE) Juniper Girl (IRE) (Revoque (IRE))
4792[7] 5574[7] 5911[9] (6793)

Forceful Appeal (USA) *Simon Dow* a92 85
4 bb g Successful Appeal(USA) Kinetic Force (USA) (Holy Bull (USA))
(34) (351) (785) ◆ 1924[4] 2657[7] 3348[6] 4703[7] 7508[7] 7826[12]

Forceful Flame *Robert Eddery* a66 69
2 ch c Assertive Noor El Houdah (IRE) (Fayruz)
4658[8] 5319[4] 5765[9] 7298[6] 7653[3] 8103[9]

Forces Of Darkness (IRE) *F Vermeulen* a93 109
3 b f Lawman(FR) Miss Childrey (IRE) (Dr Fong (USA))
542a[6] 2532a[3] 3203a[4] (5142a) 6899a[4]

Foreign Rhythm (IRE) *Ron Barr* a69 71
7 ch m Distant Music(USA) Happy Talk (IRE) (Hamas (IRE))
1528[2] 2244[5] 2538[7] 3893[4] 4174[4] 4547[9] 4865[6] 5416[3] 5671[5] 6786[2] 7099[6] 7447[9]

Foreign Tune *C Laffon-Parias* a92 107
3 b f Invincible Spirit(IRE) Gwenseb (FR) (Green Tune (USA))
5249a[2]

Forest Edge (IRE) *David Evans* a95 87
3 b g Amadeus Wolf Compass Light (USA) (Lear Fan (USA))
867[9] 1412[2] 2557[13] 3541[8] 4814[12] (5130) 6008[10] (6285) 7114[7] (7273) 7860[3] (8022) (8143) ◆ 8163[10]

Forest Row *Clive Cox* 91
3 b g Cockney Rebel(IRE) Forest Fire (SWE) (Never So Bold)
(1512) 3294[17] 3630[11] 5626[7]

Forever Beauty (GER) *Mario Hofer* 90
2 ch f Dashing Blade Forever Nice (GER) (Greinton)
7281a[5] 7698a[9]

Forever Hope *Tony Coyle* a60 68
5 b m Mark Of Esteem(IRE) Polar Dancer (Polar Falcon (USA))
929[2] 1173[4] 1487[5]

Forever Janey *Paul Green* a49 37
3 b f Indesatchel(IRE) Nee Lemon Left (Puissance)
228[4] 769[11] 1585[9] 3025[13] 4911[8] 5247[11] 7457[15] 8209[8]

Forever's Girl *Geoffrey Oldroyd* a85 79
6 b m Monsieur Bond(IRE) Forever Bond (Danetime (IRE))
64[9]

Forget Me Not Lane (IRE) *Kevin Ryan* 81
3 b g Holy Roman Emperor(IRE) Mrs Arkada (FR) (Akarad (FR))
1238[3] (2336) (2671) (2980)

Forging The Path (USA) *Richard Fahey* a62 46
2 b c Henrythenavigator(USA) Atitudeofgratitude (IRE) (Deputy Minister (CAN))
5562[9] 7167[8] ◆

Forgive *Richard Hannon* a91 93
3 b f Pivotal Amira (Efisio)
2448[6] 3080[8] (3643) 4579[3] 4984[3] 5420[2] (6013) (6375) 7509[8]

Forgotten Hero (IRE) *Charles Hills* a91 89
3 bb g High Chaparral(IRE) Sundown (Polish Precedent (USA))
(1036) 1470[12] 7240[12]

Forjatt (IRE) *D Selvaratnam* a110 105
4 b g Iffraaj Graceful Air (IRE) (Danzero (AUS))
141a[6]

Fork Handles *Mick Channon* a98 90
4 b m Doyen(IRE) Natalie Jay (Ballacashtal (CAN))
1139[2] 2067[10] 2773[11] 3556[4] (4080) 4608[10] 5091[2] 5492[13] 5666[6] 6202[9] 6667[6] 7068[9] 7367[6]

Forks *Jane Chapple-Hyam* a80 77
5 ch g Fraam Balinsky (IRE) (Skyliner)
3549[3] (4302) 4775[5] 5457[6] 6256[2] 7113[8]

For Life (IRE) *John E Long* a66 79
10 b g Bachir(IRE) Zest (USA) (Zilzal (USA))
2171[6] (5047)

Formal Bid (IRE) *Gordon Elliott* a70 65
5 bb g Oratorio(IRE) Sharamaine (IRE) (King Charlemagne (USA))
7791[3]

Formidable Guest *Jamie Poulton* a64 60
8 b m Dilshaan Fizzy Treat (Efisio)
2371[8] 3392[5] 3704[9] 4219[3] 4817[4] 5351[9] 5974[10]

Forray *Ed McMahon* 84
2 ch c Choisir(AUS) Selique (Selkirk (USA))
1753[5] 2330[2] (2763) 3250[2] 4071[6] 5332[3] 6022[7] 6984[6]

Forrest Flyer (IRE) *Jim Goldie* 75
8 b g Daylami(IRE) Gerante (USA) (Private Account (USA))
2457[6] 3337[4] ◆ 3904[6] 4639[4] (5086) 6074[9] 7102[8]

For Shia And Lula (IRE) *Daniel Mark Loughnane* a74 60
3 b g Majestic Missile(IRE) Jack-N-Jilly (IRE) (Anita's Prince)
1477[11] 2459[7] 4777[4] 5130[7] 6498[2] 6610[4] 7197[8] 7309[6] 7666[11] 7863[4] 8063[4] ◆ 8269[5]

Forster Street (IRE) *Tim Easterby* 67
3 b g Acclamation Easy To Thrill (Soviet Star (USA))
(4172) 4623[6] 5225[6] 5680[6]

Fort Bastion (IRE) *Richard Hannon* 109
3 b c Lawman(FR) French Fern (IRE) (Royal Applause)
(1889) (2198)

Forte Dei Marmi *Roger L Attfield* a64 114
6 b g Selkirk(USA) Frangy (Sadler's Wells (USA))
6299a[3] 7094a[3]

Fortieth And Fifth (IRE) *Michael Bell* a71 87
3 b g Lemon Drop Kid(USA) Maugusta (USA) (Saint Ballado (CAN))
1676[2] (2226) 2589[3] 3882[9] 4741[4]

Fortify (USA) *Kiaran McLaughlin* a108
2 b c Distorted Humor(USA) Kotuku (A.P. Indy (USA))
6901a[3] 7572a[4]

Fortinbrass (IRE) *Ralph Beckett* a84 78
2 b c Baltic King Greta D'Argent (IRE) (Great Commotion (USA))
1211[9] 1411[4] (2193) 3097[2] 8293[2]

Fort Knox *Richard Hannon* a44 83
2 b c Dubawi(IRE) Savannah Belle (Green Desert (USA))
6772[7] (7372) ◆

Fort Larned (USA) *Ian Wilkes* a128 85
4 b h E Dubai(USA) Arlucea (USA) (Broad Brush (USA))
(7576a)

Fortrose Academy (IRE) *Andrew Balding* a77 71
3 b g Iceman Auspicious (Shirley Heights)
1862[7] 2246[6] 2583[10] 3071[10] 7022[2] 7402[3] 7776[3] (7967) 8160[4]

Fortun (IRE) *J L Maroto*
3 b c Bachelor Duke(USA) Duckmore Bay (IRE) (Titus Livius (FR))
5252a[4]

Fortunate Bid (IRE) *Linda Stubbs* a67 65
6 ch g Modigliani(USA) Mystery Bid (Auction Ring (USA))
972[3] 1224[9] 1487[3] 1722[5] 2170[10] 3456[6] 3712[7] 5171[4] 6316[3] 6646[2] 6829[4] 7385[3] 7983[4]

Fortunelini *Frank Sheridan* a48
7 b m Bertolini(USA) River Of Fortune (IRE) (Lahib (USA))
153[9] 328[8] 848[10]

Forty One Phases (IRE) *David Wachman* a64 41
2 b c Shirocco(GER) Shuhrah (USA) (Danzig (USA))
4161a[6]

Forty Proof (IRE) *David Evans* a74 72
4 b g Invincible Spirit(IRE) Cefira (USA) (Distant View (USA))
13[11] 62[7] 179[8] 205[9] 424[5] 498[7] 624[7] 654[4] 964[5] 1061[7] 1343[8] 1528[9] 1601[5] 2114a[4] 2551[5] 3511[9] 3791[11] 4422[4] 5660[8] 5937[10] 6002[5] 6233[4] 6322[5] 6546[4] 7362[11] 7747[12]

Forward Feline (IRE) *Bryn Palling* a73 54
6 b m One Cool Cat(USA) Ymlaen (IRE) (Desert Prince (IRE))
692[3] 842[4] 1191[9] 1635[10]

Forward March *Roger Charlton* a57 58
2 b g Beat Hollow Cantanta (Top Ville)
6796[9] 7143[6]

For What (USA) *David Lanigan* a87 71
4 ch h Mingun(USA) Cuanto Es (USA) (Exbourne (USA))
2044[3] (4142) 4584[2] 6801[10]

Forzarzi (IRE) *Hugh McWilliams* a59 44
8 b g Forzando Zarzi (IRE) (Suave Dancer (USA))
3456[3] 6178[2] 6640[2] 7225[8]

Fossa *Dean Ivory* a43 47
2 b g Dubai Destination(USA) Gayanula (USA) (Yonaguska (USA))
3444[13] 5230[7] 5912[9] 6332[4]

Fossgate *James Bethell* a60 81
11 ch g Halling(USA) Peryllys (Warning)
2093[11] 2751[8] 3290[2] 3814[2] 3992[4] (4883) 5546[14]

Foster's Road *Mick Channon* a74 71
3 b g Imperial Dancer Search Party (Rainbow Quest (USA))
255[4] 571[10] 709[4] 803[4] (1062) 1982[10] 4511[4] (5330) 5637[5] (7617) 7927[7]

Fountain Girl *Edward Bevan*
3 b f Green Card(USA) Ballydoyle Counsel (IRE) (Leading Counsel (USA))
7978[8]

Four Better *Jamie Osborne* a80 72
3 b f Holy Roman Emperor(IRE) Moonshadow (Diesis)
(377) 667[7] (1109)

Four Leaves (IRE) *Marco Botti* a87 80
3 ch f Singspiel(IRE) My Heart's Deelite (USA) (Afternoon Deelites (USA))
1502[13] 3279[3] 3666[2] 5107[2] 5747[9] (7656) 7740[2]

Four Nations (USA) *Amanda Perrett* a65 88
4 ch g Langfuhr(CAN) Kiswahili (Selkirk (USA))
1850[7] 2423[9] 4823[5] 5344[7] 6776[9] 7409[6]

Four Richer *Jamie Osborne* a77 41
3 b c Ishiguru(USA) To The Woods (IRE) (Woodborough (USA))
2987[5] 3230[3] 3471[9] 3938[8] 4603[8]

Foursquare Funtime *Reg Hollinshead* a69 68
3 b g Common World(USA) Farina (IRE) (Golan (IRE))
193[5] 549[5] 2787[9] (3846) 4398[13] 5132[4] 5721[6] 6240[10] 6502[7] 7126[3]

Four Steps Back *Mark Usher* a55 16
5 ch g Royal Academy(USA) Runaway Queen (USA) (Runaway Groom (CAN))
130[3] 575[6] 895[6] 1112[10] 1534[5] 2769[6]

Fourth Generation (IRE) *Alan Swinbank* a86 81
5 ch g Kris Kin(USA) Merewood Lodge (IRE) (Grand Lodge (USA))
1657[6] (2035) 2419[7] 3337[2] 4674[5] 5188[5] 7380[3] 7672[2] ◆ 7810[4] (8073) 8235[P]

Fourth Of June (IRE) *Ed Dunlop* a61 83
3 b c Amadeus Wolf Our Joia (Dansili)
(1264) 1860[9] 2331[6] 2975[6] 3917[4]

Foxhaven *Patrick Chamings* a78 84
10 ch g Unfuwain(USA) Dancing Mirage (IRE) (Machiavellian (USA))
2984[3] 3574[6] 4061[10] 8019[5] 8175[3]

Fox Hunt (IRE) *Mahmood Al Zarooni* a101 118
5 ch g Dubawi(IRE) Kiltubber (IRE) (Sadler's Wells (USA))
(421a) ◆ (759a)

Foxtrot India (IRE) *Jeremy Gask* 83
3 b g Tagula(IRE) Mayfair (Green Desert (USA))
3822[12] 4530[11] 5097[10]

Foxtrot Jubilee (IRE) *Ralph Beckett* a86
2 b g Captain Marvelous(IRE) Cool Cousin (IRE) (Distant Relative)
(7497) (8293) ◆

Foxtrot Romeo (IRE) *Bryan Smart* 113
3 b c Danehill Dancer(IRE) Hawala (IRE) (Warning)
2514a[2] 3239[6] 4686[5] 6246[7]

Foxy Dancer (IRE) *Richard Hannon* a30 40
2 b f Jeremy(USA) Date Mate (USA) (Thorn Dance (USA))
6153[7] 6572[8] 7306[12]

Foxy Forever (IRE) *Michael Wigham* a78 61
2 b g Kodiac Northern Tara (IRE) (Fayruz)
(5748) 6022[9]

Foxy Music *Eric Alston* a58 97
8 b g Foxhound(USA) Primum Tempus (Primo Dominie)
1316[2] 1857[14] 1975[2] 2286[4] 2717[5] 3127[10] 3903[5] 4454[7] 5829[13] 6666[11] 7291[6] 7726[8]

Fractional (IRE) *A Fabre* 111
3 b g Manduro(GER) Sharp Point (IRE) (Royal Academy (USA))
4385a[3] (5649a)

Francis Albert *Michael Mullineaux* a65 61
6 b g Mind Games Via Dolorosa (Chaddleworth (IRE))
1483[6] 5294[9] 6194[9]

Franciscan *Luca Cumani* a56 95
4 b g Medicean Frangy (Sadler's Wells (USA))
1882[5] (2504) 3857[12] 4800[12] 6445[7]

Franco Is My Name *Peter Hedger* a92 85
6 b g Namid Veronica Franco (Darshaan)
427[2] 745[2] 1139[13] 1374[7] (3574) 4249[8] 5007[11] 5595[6] 7626[3]

Frankel *Sir Henry Cecil* 143
4 b h Galileo(IRE) Kind (IRE) (Danehill (USA))
(2270) ◆ (3237) (4699) (5490) (7239)

Frankenstein *B Grizzetti* 111
5 b g Dubawi(IRE) Lifting (IRE) (Nordance (USA))
1554a[3] 2323a[2] 2968a[6] 6554a[4]

Frank's Folly (IRE) *Tim Walford* 71
3 b g Tiger Hill(IRE) Pocket Book (IRE) (Reference Point)
6409[5]

Frans Hals *Dominic Ffrench Davis* a52 61
2 b g Dutch Art Glory Oatway (IRE) (Desert Prince (IRE))
3140[9] 3996[5] 4532[6] 6611[10] 7268[3] 7526[4] 7713[4] 7930[2] 8155[6] 8274[8]

Fraserburgh (IRE) *Mark Johnston* a70 81
2 b g Shamardal(USA) Nova Cyngi (USA) (Kris S (USA))
2138[3] 2415[2] 2929[7] 6524[2] 7007[3]

Fratellino *Alan McCabe* a105 97
5 ch h Auction House(USA) Vida (IRE) (Wolfhound (USA))
89[2] ◆ 253[7] 711[2] 871[8] (1033) 1129[12] 2159a[4] 2507[16] 2664[6] 4367[3] ◆ 4576[5] 5065[3] 5343[17] 5487[4] 6072[11] 6244[13] 7772[8]

Freda's Rose (IRE) *Owen Brennan* a43 55
8 b m Rossini(USA) African Scene (IRE) (Scenic)
5618[12]

Freddy Q (IRE) *Roger Teal* a43 89
3 ch g Iffraaj Barnabas (ITY) (Slip Anchor)
(2429) 3106[5] 3668[7] 4515[8] 5358[6] 5794[10] 6574[2] 7082[6] 7300[7]

Freddy With A Y (IRE) *Gary Moore* a76 33
2 b g Amadeus Wolf Mataji (IRE) (Desert Prince (IRE))
7371[8] 7738[3] (8044)

Frederick Alfred *Mark H Tompkins* 32
2 ch c Halling(USA) Trew Class (Inchinor)
6412[10] 7323[14]

Frederickthegreat *David O'Meara* a67 62
3 b g Exceed And Excel(AUS) Torgau (IRE) (Zieten (USA))
1486[7] 3433[5] 3938[4] 4602[8] 6813[4] 7443[7] 7712[2]

Frederick William *Chris Gordon* a73 72
4 b g Tobougg(IRE) Bisaat (USA) (Bahri (USA))
221[4] 569[6] (963) 2396[8] 3961[3] 4215[4] 5158[7]

Fred Lalloupet *D Smaga* 114
5 b h Elusive City(USA) Firm Friend (IRE) (Affirmed (USA))
2112a[7] 2728a[6] 3901a[7] 6943a[9] 7624a[4] 7829a[3]

Fred Willetts (IRE) *Mark Brisbourne* a78 94
4 b g Noverre(USA) Intaglia (GER) (Lomitas)
1558[17] 2284[11] 2487[2] 4077[8] 4629[7] 5110[8] 5557[12] 6820[13] 7144[5] 7789[5] 7842[11] 8143[6]

Free Art *Geoffrey Harker* a83 74
4 b g Iffraaj Possessive Artiste (Shareef Dancer (USA))
1251[3] 2227[2] 2588[4] 3031[3] 3353[6] 4391[6] 4747[5] 6131[5] 6885[6]

Free Island *James Tate* a65 63
2 b f Kheleyf(USA) Island Race (Common Grounds)
6556[2] 6970[2] 7481[4]

Freemason (GER) *R Dzubasz* 86
4 bb g Second Set(IRE) Fortezza (GER) (Law Society (USA))
6805a[7]

Freeport *Brian Meehan* 72
2 b c Bahamian Bounty Perdicula (IRE) (Persian Heights)
2231[7] 2822[3] 3658[3] 5060[3]

Free Spin (IRE) *M Halford* a83 57
3 ch c Iffraaj Romea (Muhtarram (USA))
7229a[3] ◆

Freestyler (FR) *C Boutin* a72 85
2 b g Meshaheer(USA) Metaline (FR) (Dr Fong (USA))
5378a[2] 5698a[3]

Freetown (USA) *S Botti* 97
2 bb c Speightstown(USA) Fresnay (Rainbow Quest (USA))
3684a[5]

Free Verse *Richard Hannon* 102
3 b f Danehill Dancer(IRE) Fictitious (Machiavellian (USA))
2067[5] 2890[3] 3542[8] (4062) 4527[4] 5980[3] 6870[11]

Free Zone *Bryan Smart* 110
3 b g Kyllachy Aldora (Magic Ring (IRE))
(1524) 1877[3] (2691) 3158[2] 3877[3] ◆ 5067a[9] 5822[6] 6072[3] 6557[5] 6869[2]

Freezy (IRE) *S Botti* 90
3 gr f Dalakhani(IRE) Claba Di San Jore (IRE) (Barathea (IRE))
2522a[10] 3426a[7]

Frege (USA) *Brian Meehan* a74 74
2 ch f Johar(USA) Silent Cat (USA) (Rahy (USA))
2844[4] 3368[7] 4646[3] 5267[4] 5946[6] 6944a[3]

Fremen (USA) *David Nicholls* a78 82
12 ch g Rahy(USA) Northern Trick (USA) (Northern Dancer (CAN))
4864[14] 5618[6] 6313[10]

Fremont (IRE) *Hugo Palmer* a82 81
5 b g Marju(IRE) Snow Peak (Arazi (USA))
3594[13] 4334[5]

French Fifteen (FR) *N Clement* 120
3 ch c Turtle Bowl(IRE) Spring Morning (FR) (Ashkalani (IRE))
(1208a) 1856[2] 2743a[10] 3681a[7]

French Hollow *Tim Fitzgerald* a77 86
7 b g Beat Hollow Campaspe (Dominion)
3419[2] 3625[4] 4613[13] 5491[12] 6074[5] 6428[2] 7068[4]

French Navy *Mahmood Al Zarooni* 113
4 b h Shamardal(USA) First Fleet (USA) (Woodman (USA))
3329[11] 4094[2] 7054[9] (7558)

French Press (IRE) *David Brown* 75
2 ch c Kheleyf(USA) Coffee Cream (Common Grounds)
3611[2] 4327[5] 5319[5] 5946[2] 6414[6] 6880[5] (7272)

French Quebec (IRE) *Cestmir Olehla* 98
3 b f Excellent Art Soul Mountain (IRE) (Rock Of Gibraltar (IRE))
7075a[2]

French Revolution *Jedd O'Keeffe* 53
2 gr g Paris House Hula Ballew (Weldnaas (USA))
3842[7] 4587[9] 5311[13] 6134[5] 6793[12]

French Seventyfive *Tim Walford* 47
5 b g Pursuit Of Love Miss Tun (Komaite (USA))
3402[4] 3988[4]

Frenesia *C Lerner* a75 78
4 gr m Dansili Fantastic Filly (FR) (Myrakalu (FR))
18a[0]

Frequency *Keith Dalgleish* a86 84
5 br g Starcraft(NZ) Soundwave (Prince Sabo)
64[12] 157[6] 304[7] 765[7] 997[9] 1007[8] 1876[2] (2838) 3334[10] 3726[3] 4640[2] (5189) 6465[13] 7000[10] 7790[10] 7961[3]

Fresa *Sir Mark Prescott Bt* a69 79
3 b f Selkirk(USA) Flor Y Nata (USA) (Fusaichi Pegasus (USA))
3736[6] 4256[2] (4505) ◆

Fresque (FR) *G Guillermo*
3 b f Della Francesca(USA) Olea Bere (FR) (Rajpoute (FR))
6752a[0]

Friday Night Lad (IRE) *Dianne Sayer* 46
5 b g Redback Social Butterfly (USA) (Sir Ivor (USA))
4455[13]

Friendsinlowplaces *Evan Williams* 64
3 b g Common World(USA) Dont Look Sideways (Singspiel (IRE))
1479[3] 6814[9]

Friends Of Ama Gi *Mark Hoad* a43
3 b g Reel Buddy(USA) Skovshoved (IRE) (Danetime (IRE))
56[5] 4213[10]

Fritz The Cat (FR) *J Rossi* a79
3 b c Poliglote Cayenne Cat (USA) (Tabasco Cat (USA))
365a[3]

Frock (IRE) *Sylvester Kirk* a63
3 b f Excellent Art Maimana (IRE) (Desert King (IRE))
84[9] 377[7] 518[5] 743[10] 7861[8]

Frog Hollow *Ralph Beckett* a93 96
3 gr g Intikhab(USA) The Manx Touch (IRE) (Petardia)
1860[3] 2485[4] 3294[19] 4819[4] 5914[4]

Frognal (IRE) *Violet M Jordan* a70 82
6 b g Kheleyf(USA) Shannon Dore (IRE) (Turtle Island (IRE))
3334[5] 4661[4] 6329[5] 7202[3] (7670) 7725[8] 7857[6] 8004[6] 8063[3]

Fromthestables Com (IRE) *Brendan Powell* a50 65
3 b c Strategic Prince Kathy Tolfa (IRE) (Sri Pekan (USA))
7964[13] 8229[9]

Frontier (GER) *A P O'Brien* 86
3 b c Galileo(IRE) Four Roses (IRE) (Darshaan)
3361a[8]

Frontier Fighter *David O'Meara* a61
4 b g Invincible Spirit(IRE) Rawabi (Sadler's Wells (USA))
8239[2]

Front Page News *Robert Eddery* 73
2 ch f Assertive Branston Berry (IRE) (Mukaddamah (USA))
2499[6] (3444) 4526[6] 4847[2] 7298[4] 7687[14]

Front Rank (IRE) *Dianne Sayer* a52 12
12 b g Sadler's Wells(USA) Alignment (IRE) (Alzao (USA))
3310[11] 3519[7] 4867[11]

Frosted Off *John Spearing* a51 58
2 gr g Verglas(IRE) Dispol Veleta (Makbul)
1315[4] 2844[13] 3387[6] 4331[2] 4728[5] 5654[5] 6283[2] 6611[11] 7649[4]

Frosty Berry *John Wainwright* a70 75
3 gr f Proclamation(IRE) Star Entry (In The Wings)
(159) 1531[2] 2194[14] 3694[2] 4602[9] 5731[5]

Frosty Friday *J R Jenkins* a62
4 b m Storming Home Seasonal Blossom (IRE) (Fairy King (USA))
137[3] 974[2] 1423[6] 7469[8] 7712[5]

Frosty Secret *Jane Chapple-Hyam* a58 68
3 b f Echo Of Light Raze (Halling (USA))
2734[7] 3543[12] 5037[3] 5990[11] 6647[11] 7473[10]

Frozen Ardour (IRE) *P Bary* a75 100
5 b m Dr Fong(USA) Freezing Love (USA) (Danzig (USA))
92a[8]

Frozen Over *Stuart Kittow* a26 75
4 b g Iceman Pearly River (Elegant Air)
2207[10] 2847[5] 3485[8] 4302[2] (4939) 5910[11] (6239) 7302[4] 7559[3]

Fruity Bun *Matthew Salaman* 54
2 b f Dr Fong(USA) Little Conker (Red Ransom (USA))
3224[3] 4239[5] 4704[9] 6583[12] 7491[5]

Fu Fic Fas *Paul Fitzsimons* a41 61
3 b f Multiplex Sarcila (Primo Dominic)
1436[3] 2353[10] 3048[5] 3311[3]

Fugitive Motel (IRE) *Hans Adielsson* a71 66
3 b g Holy Roman Emperor(IRE) Zing Ping (IRE) (Thatching)
182[4] 298[3] 565[3] (731) 916[3] 1063[7] 1419[5] 2583[11]

Fularmada *B Grizzetti* 82
3 b f Manduro(GER) Step Danzer (IRE) (Desert Prince (IRE))
2522a[12]

Fulbright *Mark Johnston* 115
3 b c Exceed And Excel(AUS) Lindfield Belle (IRE) (Fairy King (USA))
1858[14] (3348) 3626[10] 3878[6] (4063) (4598) (4761) 5572[13] 6029[2] (6373) 6882[6] (7048)

Fulgur *Luca Cumani* 104
4 b h High Chaparral(IRE) Selebela (Grand Lodge (USA))
4795[9] ◆ 5580[9] 5835[8] 6848[3] 7396[3]

Full Bloom *Gerard Butler* a80 76
4 ch m Camacho Bint Alhabib (Nashwan (USA))
301[10]

Full Shilling (IRE) *John Spearing* a71 75
4 b m Intikhab(USA) Full Cream (USA) (Hennessy (USA))
1481[7] (2761) 3075[2] (3434) 4420[6] 4887[5] 5279[6] 6687[8] 6961[9] 7411[4] 7864[13]

Full Speed (GER) *Philip Kirby* a95 86
7 b g Sholokhov(IRE) Flagny (FR) (Kaldoun (FR))
5712[9] 6045[13] 6339[10] 6712[8] 7353[13]

Full Toss *Jim Goldie* a80 85
6 b g Nayef(USA) Spinning Top (Alzao (USA))
216[9] (2620) 3380[6] (5546) 6010[10] 6638[6]

Fulney *James Eustace* 85
3 b f Dr Fong(USA) Postage Stampe (Singspiel (IRE))
2734[3] 3792[4] 5019[3] (5795) 6375[2]

Funcheon Vale (IRE) *Hughie Morrison* a56 63
3 b f Acclamation Dwingeloo (IRE) (Dancing Dissident (USA))
2871[4] 3312[3] 3702[6] 4489[2] 5033[2] 5445[7] 6836[12] 7591[3] 7952[6]

Funding Deficit (IRE) *David Barron* 75
2 ch g Rakti Bukat Timah (Inchinor)
4257[6] 5083[8] 5797[3] 6356[2] 6708[4]

Funinthesand (IRE) *Wido Neuroth* a99 79
3 b g Footstepsinthesand Funny Legend (NOR) (Funambule (USA))
3655a[3]

Funk Soul Brother *Charles Hills* 86
2 b c Cockney Rebel(IRE) Sweet Afton (IRE) (Mujadil (USA))
(2213) 3240[19] 6483[8] 7050[6]

Funky Cold Medina *Peter Chapple-Hyam* 67
2 b f Cockney Rebel(IRE) Monica Campbell (Sakhee (USA))
5550[7] 6117[10] 6489[7]

Funky Munky *Alistair Whillans* a36 56
7 b g Talaash(IRE) Chilibang Bang (Chilibang)
1052[9]

Fun Victoire (FR) *B Barbier* a77 68
3 b f Victory Note(USA) Joie De Mai (FR) (Marignan (USA))
5726a[9]

Furbelow *Jeremy Noseda* a78 61
3 b f Pivotal Red Tiara (USA) (Mr Prospector (USA))
1472[7] (1705) 3284[9]

Furibondo *David Lanigan* 61
2 br g Monsun(GER) Geminiani (IRE) (King Of Kings (IRE))
7332[9] 7637[6] ◆

Furner's Green (IRE) *A P O'Brien* 113
3 b c Dylan Thomas(IRE) Lady Icarus (Rainbow Quest (USA))
(1401a) 2110a[3] (Dead)

Fury *William Haggas* 113
4 gr g Invincible Spirit(IRE) Courting (Pursuit Of Love)
1130[3] 1510[2] 1854[3] (2211) 3205a[5] 4074[2] 5560[7] 6446[5] 6674[10]

Furzanah *Luca Cumani* a56 63
3 b f Dubawi(IRE) Latent Lover (IRE) (In The Wings)
5795[7] 6364[10]

Fuscano (GER) *W Hickst* 80
3 ch c Dubai Destination(USA) Fusca (GER) (Lando (GER))
5473a[0]

Fushicho *Michael Wigham* a46
3 ch g Phoenix Reach(IRE) Rasmalai (Sadler's Wells (USA))
730[4] 1278[5] 2864[10] 8050[11]

Fusion (IRE) *Mark Johnston* a66
2 b f Cape Cross(IRE) Flirtation (Pursuit Of Love)
7505[9] 7777[5] 8200[2]

Future Impact (IRE) *John Butler* a49 74
4 b g Kheleyf(USA) Daring Imp (IRE) (Mac's Imp (USA))
653[6] 8205[4]

Future Reference (IRE) *Saeed Bin Suroor* a74 69
2 ch g Raven's Pass(USA) Mike's Wildcat (USA) (Forest Wildcat (USA))
6772[3] ◆ 7507[4] 7686[4]

Future Security (IRE) *Saeed Bin Suroor* 85
3 ch g Dalakhani(IRE) Schust Madame (IRE) (Second Set (IRE))
(4755) 5598[12] 6333[7] 6986[4]

Future Wonder (IRE) *Brian Ellison* a48 62
3 b f Whipper(USA) Savage (IRE) (Polish Patriot (USA))
4211[4] (4457) 5018[4] (5708) 6555[4] 6814[3] 7095[10] 7383[11]

Fuzzy Logic (IRE) *William Muir* a58 62
3 b g Dylan Thomas(IRE) Gates Of Eden (USA) (Kingmambo (USA))
1512[12] 2266[11] 3079[7] 4250[8] 4586[5] 4870[7] 5817[7] 5989[5] 6567[6]

Gaazaal (IRE) *F Head* 99
3 b f Iffraaj Safqa (Singspiel (IRE))
1126a[0]

Gabbiano *Jeremy Gask* a83 76
3 b g Zafeen(FR) Hollybell (Beveled (USA))
1493[5] 1983[9] 2451[5] 3041[4] 3284[6]

Gabrial (IRE) *Richard Fahey* 110
3 b g Dark Angel(IRE) Guajira (FR) (Mtoto)
1221[7] 1996[2] (2485) 3239[5] 4699[3] 5090[3] 6373[3]

Gabrial's Bounty (IRE) *Mick Channon* a80 87
3 ch g Bahamian Bounty Social Storm (USA) (Future Storm (USA))
121[2] ◆ (201) (482) 867[2] 1109[2] (1758) 1998[2] 3063[7]

Gabrial's Gift (IRE) *Ian Williams* a85 70
3 gr g Verglas(IRE) Sahara Lady (IRE) (Lomitas)
1142[3] 1894[7] 2490[8] 3790[7] 4329[6] 5000[10] 6768[7] 7412[5] 7936[8] (8058) 8183[4]

Gabrial's Hope (FR) *Ian Williams* a66
3 b g Teofilo(IRE) Wedding Night (FR) (Valanour (IRE))
5753[11] 6660[4] 8037[5] 8139[2] 8206[3]

Gabrial's Kaka (IRE) *Richard Fahey* 93
2 b g Jeremy(USA) Love In May (IRE) (City On A Hill (USA))
(6237) (6700)

Gabrial's King (IRE) *Ian Williams* a80 74
3 b g Hurricane Run(IRE) Danella (IRE) (Platini (GER))
108[2] (196) ◆ 393[2] (466) (1390) 1557[6] 2471[2] 2716[5] 3448[6] 6240[3] 6662[4] 7195[5] (7652) 7791[2] (7927) 8073[8] 8149[2] 8235[3]

Gabrial's Layla (IRE) *Mark Johnston* a49 44
3 b f Dylan Thomas(IRE) Marlene-D (Selkirk (USA))
1424[12] 1915[9] 2340[9]

Gabrial's Lexi (IRE) *Ian Williams* a67 56
3 b f Dubawi(IRE) Lady Causeway (USA) (Giant's Causeway (USA))
358[6] 533[5] 675[3] 803[2] ◆ 998[6] 1364[6] 3443[5] 3775[10] 4153[4] 5754[7] 6174[6] 6892[9]

Gabrial's Princess (IRE) *Bryan Smart* a52 61
3 b f Royal Applause Happy Go Lily (In The Wings)
191[2]

Gabrial's Star *Bryan Smart* 89
3 b c Hernando(FR) Grain Only (Machiavellian (USA))
1440[5] 2980[8] 4548[2] 4925[2] ◆ 5598[5] 6074[4] 6625[5]

Gabrial's Wawa *Richard Fahey* a70 71
2 b g Dubai Destination(USA) Celestial Welcome (Most Welcome)
6237[3] 6708[2] 7020[3]

Gabrial The Boss (USA) *David Simcock* a66 59
2 ch g Street Boss(USA) Bacinella (USA) (El Gran Senor (USA))
3499[8] 4327[6] 4595[10] 6156[4] 6435[6] 6893[2] 7026[8] 7414[10] 7708[3] 7785[11] (8150) (8186)

Gabrial The Duke (IRE) *Ian Williams* a60 59
2 ch g Duke Of Marmalade(IRE) Literacy (USA) (Diesis)
5962[12] 6412[9] 6644[5] 7111[6] 7414[6] 7785[5] 7919[8]

Gabrial The Great (IRE) *Michael Bell* 94
3 b c Montjeu(IRE) Bayourida (USA) (Slew O'Gold (USA))
(1385) 1978[2] ◆ 3296[11] (3859) 5089[6] 5598[11] 6661[7] 6875[8]

Gabrial The Hero (USA) *David Simcock* a69 88
3 b c War Front(USA) Ball Gown (USA) (Silver Hawk (USA))
399[2] 595[2] 1662[3] (2418) 3033[2] 3605[4] 5366[7]

Gabrial The Master (IRE) *Richard Fahey* a55 70
2 ch g Strategic Prince Kualke (IRE) (Celtic Swing)
6188[2] 6669[5] 7057[6]

Gabrial The Prince (IRE) *David Simcock* a46 43
3 b g Motivator Set Fire (IRE) (Bertolini (USA))
132[8] 294[10]

Gabrial The Thug (FR) *Richard Fahey* 73
2 b g Azamour(IRE) Baliyna (USA) (Woodman (USA))
6237[2] 7033[6]

Gabrial The Tyrant (IRE) *Mark Johnston* a26 7
2 b g Authorized(IRE) Kaaba (Darshaan)
6607[10] 7165[12] 7491[10]

Gabriel Charles (USA) *Jeff Mullins* a95 105
2 b c Street Hero(USA) Star Of Atticus (USA) (Atticus (USA))
(7567a)

Gabrielle Da Vinci *Andrew Price* a44
6 b m Erhaab(USA) Gulshan (Batshoof)
2391[15]

Gabriel's Lad (IRE) *Denis Coakley* a87 100
3 b g Dark Angel(IRE) Catherine Wheel (Primo Dominie)
(1723) 3165[2] 4234[6] 5363[2] 6075[3] (6835)

Gadobout Dancer *Tony Coyle* a42 59
5 b m Tobougg(IRE) Delta Tempo (IRE) (Bluebird (USA))
2091[9] 3021[3] ◆ 3356[2] 3694[6] 4715[5] 5015[4] 5258[3] 5762[5] (5824) 6561[5]

Gadreel (IRE) *Anthony Middleton* a46 54
3 b g Dark Angel(IRE) Borsalino (USA) (Trempolino (USA))
191[9] 1259[5] 2393[9] 3193[9] 4457[7]

Gaelic Ice *Rod Millman* a58 30
3 b f Iceman Gaelic Lime (Lomitas)
6930[11] 7322[2] 7719[5]

Gaelico (USA) *Dale Romans*
3 b c War Front(USA) Global Gold (USA) (Pleasant Tap (USA))
8279a[5]

Gaelic Style (FR) *J Bertran De Balanda* 52
2 b c Desert Style(IRE) Gaelic Dream (FR) (Shining Steel)
3714a[9]

Gaelic Wizard (IRE) *Dominic Ffrench Davis* a70 71
4 b h Fasliyev(USA) Fife (IRE) (Lomond (USA))
5878[3] 6287[2] 7061[2] 7253[2] 7611[5] 7719[4]

Gag (FR) *M Nigge* a74 81
3 b c Layman(USA) Woven Silk (USA) (Danzig (USA))
865a[9]

Gaiete (FR) *C Laffon-Parias* a73 89
2 ch f Kentucky Dynamite(USA) Grenade (FR) (Bering)
6463a[3]

Gala Casino Star (IRE) *Geoffrey Harker* a88 93
7 ch g Dr Fong(USA) Abir (Soviet Star (USA))
1275[7] 1951[8] 2414[8] (3353) (3906) (4745) 4879[6] 6010[9] 6757[3] 7002[3] 7601[7]

Gala Sakhee *B Grizzetti* 96
3 b f Sakhee(USA) Tenuta Di Gala (IRE) (Nashwan (USA))
3426a[5]

Gala Spirit (IRE) *Michael Wigham* a61 51
5 b m Invincible Spirit(IRE) Luggala (IRE) (Kahyasi)
203[3] 430[2] 550[6] 775a[4] 4656[3] 5191[4]

Galatian *Rod Millman* a83 88
5 ch g Traditionally(USA) Easy To Imagine (USA) (Cozzene (USA))
1354[12] 4998[5] 5486[9] 5630[6] 6256[5] ◆ (6824) 7114[9] 7485[13]

Gale Force Ten *A P O'Brien* a76 117
2 b c Oasis Dream Ronaldsay (Kirkwall)
(2958a) 3291[2] 4008[4] 7049[3]

Galenus (IRE) *F Vermeulen* a77 77
3 b c Montjeu(IRE) Inkling (USA) (Seeking The Gold (USA))
7266a[3]

Galician *Mark Johnston* a84 97
3 gr f Redoute's Choice(AUS) Gweneira (Machiavellian (USA))
1109[3] 1217[6] 1983[2] (2229) (2616) 2824[5] 4703[4] 5080[2] 5363[5] 5827[10] 6201[12] 7408[2]

Galikova (FR) *F Head* 121
4 b m Galileo(IRE) Born Gold (USA) (Blushing Groom (FR))
3424a[3] 5399a[2] 6295a[5] 6911a[6]

Galileano (USA) *F Vermeulen* a73 30
3 rg c Mizzen Mast(USA) Western Wind (USA) (Gone West (USA))
7266a[9]

Galilee Chapel (IRE) *Alistair Whillans* a66 62
3 b g Baltic King Triple Zero (IRE) (Raise A Grand (IRE))
4133[12] 4771[11] 6259[5] 7358[10] 7869[9]

Galileo Rock (IRE) *David Wachman* 95
2 ch c Galileo(IRE) Grecian Bride (IRE) (Groom Dancer (USA))
7053[5]

Galileo's Choice (IRE) *D K Weld* 111
6 b g Galileo(IRE) Sevi's Choice (USA) (Sir Ivor (USA))
(5027a) 7621a[20]

Galiotto (IRE) *Gary Moore* a65 66
6 b g Galileo(IRE) Welsh Motto (USA) (Mtoto)
129[5] 566[7] 1184[4] 1791[2] 3734[2] 5196[3] 7169[5] 8001[7] 8104[5]

Gallagher *Ruth Carr* a53 81
6 ch g Bahamian Bounty Roo (Rudimentary (USA))
883[6] 1091[9]

Gallantry *Paul Howling* a65 43
10 b g Green Desert(USA) Gay Gallanta (USA) (Woodman (USA))
130[8] 306[2] 732[3] 891[10] 995[2] 1154[15] 1447[9] (1702) 2373[7] 2811[3] 3154[10] 3738[8] 4219[11] 4950[9] 6252[10] 7500[5] (7992) 8249[8]

Gallego *Richard Price* a49 70
10 br g Danzero(AUS) Shafir (IRE) (Shaadi (USA))
2867[11] 3511[6] 4602[3] 4843[9] 5197[8] 5452[7] 5783[5] 6120[9] 6231[7]

Gallena *William Haggas* 70
2 b f Invincible Spirit(IRE) Emily Blake (IRE) (Lend A Hand)
6360[4] 6787[2] (7014) 7241[3]
Galleon *Sir Michael Stoute* a88 92
3 b c Galileo(IRE) Tempting Prospect (Shirley Heights)
2266[9] 3763[2] (5293) 5966[4] 6537[7]
Galletto (IRE) *Terry Clement* 40
3 b g Azamour(IRE) Galleta (Hernando (FR))
2279[11] 4341[11] 5063[6] 5738[3]
Gallipot *John Gosden* a100 108
3 b f Galileo(IRE) Spinning Queen (Spinning World (USA))
1502[9] 2848[7] 3345[3] ◆ 3968[2] (4945) (5474) 6163[4] (6598) ◆
Galloping Minister (IRE) *Pat Phelan* a62 53
4 b g Ad Valorem(USA) Gladstone Street (IRE) (Waajib)
67[6] 559[5]
Galloping Queen (IRE) *Sheena West* a57 71
4 b m Refuse To Bend(IRE) Rouge Noir (USA) (Saint Ballado (CAN))
3468[9] 4817[11]
Gambatte *Tony Carroll* a42 50
5 b m One Cool Cat(USA) Dahshah (Mujtahid (USA))
503[7] 653[4] 822[8] 1088[10] 1634[3] 2555[12] 2821[5] 3137[11]
Gambino (IRE) *Hugh McWilliams* a38 23
2 b c Red Clubs(IRE) Temptation Island (IRE) (Spectrum (IRE))
3491[8] 4654[9] 5040[10] 6134[P] 6753[8]
Gamble *Michael Bell* a55
2 ch f Galileo(IRE) Pretty Face (Rainbow Quest (USA))
7721[8]
Game All (IRE) *Hugo Palmer* a56 49
3 b f Acclamation Love Thirty (Mister Baileys)
1736[6] ◆ 6345[3] 7668[4]
Game On Dude (USA) *Bob Baffert* a125
5 bb g Awesome Again(CAN) Worldly Pleasure (USA) (Devil His Due (USA))
1150a[12] 7576a[7]
Gamilati *Mahmood Al Zarooni* a111 108
3 b f Bernardini(USA) Illustrious Miss (USA) (Kingmambo (USA))
(77a) (418a) ◆ 4764[10] 6161[2] 6673[8]
Gammarth (FR) *H-A Pantall* a98 109
4 ch h Layman(USA) Emouna Queen (IRE) (Indian Ridge)
2728a[12] 3901a[2] 4790a[2] 5648a[2] 6943a[5] 7624a[12]
Ganas (IRE) *Clive Cox* a94 88
4 b g Oasis Dream Hollow Dynasty (USA) (Deputy Commander (USA))
1727[12] 2558[4] 3225[6] 3822[4] 4690[7] 5343[5]
Gandolfini (IRE) *H Rogers* a52 75
9 b g Rossini(USA) Persian Myth (Persian Bold)
335a[10]
Gangsterbanksters (FR) *Mrs K Burke* a27 65
3 b g High Chaparral(IRE) Pantelleria (GER) (Monsun (GER))
1171a[0] 1518[4] 2240[2] 3212[6] 4172[7] 6474[11] 6976[9] 7443[4]
Ganimed *M G Mintchev* 99
4 ch h Cadeaux Genereux Chance For Romance (Entrepreneur)
3425a[4] 4130a[8]
Gantry (USA) *Ron Faucheux* a112 97
5 bb g Pulpit(USA) Rhum (USA) (Go For Gin (USA))
7574a[11]
Gap Of Dunloe (IRE) *Evan Williams* a59 55
4 b g Hurricane Run(IRE) Karri Valley (USA) (Storm Bird (CAN))
767[8]
Gap Princess (IRE) *Geoffrey Harker* a81 87
8 b m Noverre(USA) Safe Care (IRE) (Caerleon (USA))
3272[6] 4655[4] (4909) 5557[13] 6123[12] 6934[8] 7412[10]
Garajonay (FR) *F Rodriguez Puertas* a74
3 bb c First Samurai(USA) Hapster (USA) (Awesome Again (CAN))
5473a[0]
Garde Cotiere (USA) *Jeremy Noseda* a94 36
4 b h Giant's Causeway(USA) Amonita (Anabaa (USA))
2250[12]
Garde Slickly (FR) *Mlle Valerie Boussin* a91 99
4 b h Slickly(FR) Royal Bride (FR) (Garde Royale)
6804a[3]
Garmelow Girl *Stuart Kittow* a49 52
2 b f Piccolo Juncea (Elnadim (USA))
3436[6] 4310[11] 4742[10] 5161[6] 6793[6] 7313[6] 7592[6] 7785[6] 8003[9]
Garrisson (IRE) *Charles Hills* a70 47
3 b g Cape Cross(IRE) Desertion (IRE) (Danehill (USA))
4341[8] 5276[8] 5555[10] (8267)
Garstang *Richard Ford* a84 66
9 ch g Atraf Approved Quality (IRE) (Persian Heights)
(262) 328[2] (669) 987[11] (1801)
Garswood *Richard Fahey* 103
2 b c Dutch Art Penchant (Kyllachy)
4114[3] 4688[4] (6424) 6865[2]
Gary D (USA) *Ronald B Spatz* a73 80
5 rg h Successful Appeal(USA) Harford Ghost (USA) (Silver Ghost (USA))
8100a[10]
Garzoni *Sir Mark Prescott Bt* a51 61
3 ch f Medicean Rainbow Queen (Rainbow Quest (USA))
3735[12] 3918[5] 4586[7] 5037[4]
Gasquet (ITY) *Gianfranco Verricelli* a91 95
6 b h Denon(USA) Minnelli (USA) (Manila (USA))
1554a[5]
Gassin Golf *Sir Mark Prescott Bt* a78 98
3 b g Montjeu(IRE) Miss Riviera Golf (Hernando (FR))
(3033) 3305[2] 4079[4] 4700[6] 5344[2] 5905[2]

Gatepost (IRE) *Richard Fahey* a88 105
3 br g Footstepsinthesand Mandama (IRE) (Warning)
1032[5] 1457[15] 4063[3] 4598[5] 5334[8] 5572[15] 6143[7] 6466[5] 7366[8]
Gatewood *John Gosden* 112
4 b h Galileo(IRE) Felicity (IRE) (Selkirk (USA))
(2176) (2655) ◆ (3329) 4759[3] 5650a[2] 7073a[7] (7346a) 7560a[6]
Gathering (USA) *John Gosden* 101
3 b f Street Cry(IRE) Seebe (USA) (Danzig (USA))
2410[3] 3682a[7] 4556[3] 5834[3]
Gathering Power (IRE) *Edward Lynam* a73 78
2 b f Kyllachy Nutkin (Act One)
1118a[4]
Gaul Wood (IRE) *Tom Dascombe* a90 94
3 b g Amadeus Wolf Emly Express (IRE) (High Estate)
(204) 4082[2] ◆ 4580[2] ◆ 5004[6] 5747[3] (6205) 6831[3]
Gavi *Karen George* a52 60
6 b g Danehill Dancer(IRE) Lydia Maria (Dancing Brave (USA))
3663[7] 4293[3] 5197[6] 6230[6] 6838[8] 7490[12]
Gay Gallivanter *Michael Quinn* a55 58
4 b m Iceman Gallivant (Danehill (USA))
300[5] 375[5] 829[7] 891[9] 1096[6] 2463[9] 2804[4] 3470[16] 3721[10] 4435[6] 5632[3] 6950[8] (7605) 8111[6]
Gay Sloane (IRE) *John Coombe* a51 84
8 b g Anabaa(USA) Seattle's Wood (USA) (Woodman (USA))
1339[3] 1925[9]
Gazboolou *Henry Candy* a63 56
8 b g Royal Applause Warning Star (Warning)
396 203[5] 293[5] 2171[4] 2858[5] 3317[5] 3949[3] 4193[8] 4986[4] 5349[2] 5850[8]
Geanie Mac (IRE) *Linda Perratt* a58 66
3 ch f Needwood Blade Dixie Evans (Efisio)
573[4] 784[6] 4510[2] 4826[3] (4908) 5629[4] 5922[2] 6311[10] 7791[11]
Gebayl *James Tate* a63
2 b f Compton Place Glimpse (Night Shift (USA))
7613[4] 8171[5]
Geeaitch *Anthony Carson* a73 66
3 ch g Cockney Rebel(IRE) Grand Rebecca (IRE) (Namid)
1922[7] 2543[10] 3735[11] 6105[11] 6774[2] ◆ (7201) 7317[3]
Gee Major *Nicky Vaughan* a57 48
5 b g Reset(AUS) Polly Golightly (Weldnaas (USA))
988[8] 1299[7] 2627[11] 3497[3] 5481[8]
Gee Wizz (IRE) *Robert Collet* a72 70
2 b f Whipper(USA) Midnight Mystique (IRE) (Noverre (USA))
7265a[8] 7682a[8]
Gem Of Wizdom (IRE) *J S Moore* a38
3 b f Kheleyf(USA) Sandy Lady (IRE) (Desert King (IRE))
26[6] 121[9] 321[6] 564[11]
Gemologist (USA) *Todd Pletcher* a117 115
3 b c Tiznow(USA) Crystal Shard (USA) (Mr Prospector (USA))
1872a[16]
General Direction (IRE) *Reginald Roberts* 74
2 b c Lawman(FR) Pivotal Role (Pivotal)
(7450)
General Logan (USA) *H Graham Motion* 74
3 ch g Exchange Rate(USA) Dancing General (USA) (General Meeting (USA))
7882a[13]
General Ting (IRE) *Lucy Wadham* a78 73
7 b g Daylami(IRE) Luana (Shaadi (USA))
1846[6] (2086) 7211[4]
General Tufto *Charles Smith* a68 63
7 b g Fantastic Light(USA) Miss Pinkerton (Danehill (USA))
(96) 287[5] 646[3] 753[4] 1052[3] 1988[7] 2804[7] 3022[4] 4350[3] 4683[7] 6562[11] 6794[12] 7347[9] 7731[5] 7800[8] 8212[6]
Generalyse *Ben De Haan* a74 76
3 b g Cadeaux Genereux Dance To The Blues (IRE) (Danehill Dancer (IRE))
2205[7] 3702[5] 3762[3] 4364[3] 4985[4] 5308[3] 7322[4] (7668) 7937[4] ◆
Generous Dream *Mel Brittain* 70
4 ch m Generous(IRE) First Harmony (First Trump)
2927[4] 4926[5] 5315[7] (5714) 6712[2] 6784[2] 7068[8]
Generous Genella *Julia Feilden* a45 54
4 b m Cape Cross(IRE) Gombay Girl (USA) (Woodman (USA))
1830[10] 7612[6] 7983[9]
Gengis (FR) *G Doleuze* 100
2 gr c King's Best(USA) Ashiyna (IRE) (Green Desert (USA))
5471a[9] 6942a[4] (7828a)
Genius Step (IRE) *Mahmood Al Zarooni* 87
3 b c Dubawi(IRE) Kathy College (IRE) (College Chapel)
6046[6] 6830[13]
Genki (IRE) *Roger Charlton* a53 117
8 ch g Shinko Forest(IRE) Emma's Star (ITY) (Darshaan)
1469[9] 2559[4] 3370[11] 4100[10] 6030[5] 6867[7]
Genten (USA) *Yoshito Yahagi* a99 104
3 b c Bernardini(USA) Miss Terrible (ARG) (Numerous (USA))
1145a[14]
Gentildonna (JPN) *Sei Ishizaka* 126
3 b f Deep Impact(JPN) Donna Blini (Bertolini (USA))
(7872a)
Gentleman Is Back (USA) *Ed de Giles* a56 47
4 bb g Johannesburg(USA) Torros Straits (USA) (Boundary (USA))
1280[5]
Gentle Sands *Ed McMahon* 37
3 b f Multiplex Asinara (GER) (Big Shuffle (USA))
2774[7]
Gentle Storm (FR) *Y Barberot* 105
3 b c Gentlewave(IRE) Aznavour (GER) (Lagunas)
7284a[3]

Gentoo (FR) *A Lyon* a81 113
8 b g Loup Solitaire(USA) Ifni (FR) (Bering)
6297a[10] 6914a[9] 7735a[6]
Genzy (FR) *Ian Williams* a105 105
4 b g Gentlewave(IRE) Zycia (IRE) (Bishop Of Cashel)
7438[4] 7771[2]
Geordie Boy *Sheena West* a55 63
3 bb g Araafa(IRE) Entail (USA) (Riverman (USA))
1206[9] 1415[3] 2368[7] 5837[12] 6334[5]
Geordie Iris (IRE) *Wido Neuroth* a85 80
4 b m Elusive City(USA) Tiger Desert (GER) (Desert King (IRE))
5143a[6]
Geordie Man *Pat Eddery* 77
2 b c Manduro(GER) Opening Ceremony (USA) (Quest For Fame)
(7208)
George Baker (IRE) *George Baker* a77 86
5 b g Camacho Petite Maxine (Sharpo)
1161[8] 1752[9] 2444[7] 4580[5] 5910[14] 7170[10] 7480[4] (7722) 7966[4] 8181[7]
George Benjamin *Christopher Kellett* a77 79
5 b g Trade Fair Unchain My Heart (Pursuit Of Love)
1161[16] (1294) (2758) 3011[2] 3439[9] 4190[3] 4829[15] 5819[9] 6235[14] 6812[10] 7360[10] 7685[2]
Georgebernardshaw (IRE) *Richard Guest* a72 88
7 b g Danehill Dancer(IRE) Khamseh (Thatching)
103[4] 432[8] 548[7] 694[7] 753[3] 1094[9] 1276[3] 1527[2] 1755[4] 1879[4] 2455[8] 3257[3] 3317[4] 4089[3] 4390[5] 4716[11] 5322[6] 5547[13] 5999[4] 6105[3] 6313[7] 8167[12] 8288[11]
George Cinq *Michael Bell* a80 53
2 b c Pastoral Pursuits Fairnilee (Selkirk (USA))
4773[6] (6533) 6980[2]
George Fenton *Richard Guest* a63 62
3 ch g Piccolo Mashmoum (Lycius (USA))
564[5] 734[6] 845[2] 898[6] (1010) 5203[9] ◆ 5446[2] 6002[3] (6530) (7146) 8159[4]
George Guru *Michael Attwater* a100 93
5 b g Ishiguru(USA) Waraqa (USA) (Red Ransom (USA))
280[2] (520) 785[2] ◆ (1035) 1510[16] 2642[6] 3508[6] 4703[6] 5356[9] 6036[4] ◆ 7631[6] 7774[4] (8095) 8296[5]
George Rooke (IRE) *Kevin Ryan* 82
2 b c Rock Of Gibraltar(IRE) Double Fantasy (GER) (Indian Ridge)
5410[2] (6473) (6955)
George Thisby *Rod Millman* a59 71
6 b g Royal Applause Warning Belle (Warning)
1936[6] 2207[14] 2886[9] 3511[2] 4602[4] 5240[3] 5783[3] 7105[6]
George Tilehurst *Geoffrey Deacon* 26
3 ch g Needwood Blade Batchworth Breeze (Beveled (USA))
4812[12]
George Vancouver (USA) *A P O'Brien* a92 117
2 b c Henrythenavigator(USA) Versailles Treaty (USA) (Danzig (USA))
5398a[2] 6078a[6] 7050[3] (7568a)
Georgian Bay (IRE) *Mrs K Burke* a83 89
2 b c Oratorio(IRE) Jazzie (FR) (Zilzal (USA))
(5230) 6200[5] 7292[5]
Georgian Silver *George Foster* a35 42
4 ch m Auction House(USA) Proud Titania (IRE) (Fairy King (USA))
101[11] 7952[12]
Geraldines Lass (IRE) *W McCreery* a77 81
4 ch m Titus Livius(FR) Nullarbor (Green Desert (USA))
7230a[8] 7935[8]
Gereon (GER) *C Zschache* 104
4 b g Next Desert(IRE) Golden Time (GER) (Surumu (GER))
2222a[4] 4130a[9] 6291a[2]
Geronimo Chief (IRE) *Ben Haslam* a57 50
4 b g Sleeping Indian Portorosa (USA) (Irish River (FR))
6829[5] 7605[2]
Gertmegalush (IRE) *Noel Wilson* a44 68
5 b g One Cool Cat(USA) Aiming Upwards (Blushing Flame (USA))
6105[6] 7599[8]
Gertrude Versed *John Gosden* a65
2 b f Manduro(GER) Sugar Mill (FR) (Polar Falcon (USA))
8017[5] 8200[3]
Gervinho (USA) *Carla Gaines* a96 110
2 b c Unusual Heat(USA) Foreverinthegame (USA) (Out Of Place (USA))
7568a[5]
Getabuzz *Tim Easterby* 87
4 b g Beat Hollow Ailincala (IRE) (Pursuit Of Love)
1880[2] 2504[13] 2921[3] (3564) 4115[3] 5344[3] 5729[2] 6472[4]
Getaway Car *Gerard Butler* a62 59
2 ch c Medicean Lomapamar (Nashwan (USA))
2193[12] 2784[8] 3046[DSQ] 4102[5] 4934[4] (5763) 6156[6] 7414[3]
Getcarter *John Best* a83 91
6 b g Fasliyev(USA) Pourquoi Pas (IRE) (Nordico (USA))
302[6] 568[4] 713[8]
Get The Trip *Anthony Carson* a50 48
3 ch f Three Valleys(USA) Amiata (Pennekamp (USA))
1608[8] 2374[8] 2582[6] 3141[8]
Ghaabesh (IRE) *Donald McCain* a43
5 b g Alhaarth(IRE) Alyakkh (IRE) (Sadler's Wells (USA))
1484[5]
Ghalaa (IRE) *Mark Johnston* a46 65
3 bb f Nayef(USA) Mouwadh (USA) (Nureyev (USA))
1167[5] 2045[11] 2671[3] 3558[10]
Ghanaian (FR) *Mahmood Al Zarooni* 78
2 b f Shamardal(USA) Ghanaj (Caerleon (USA))
4739[8] 5339[2] (5947) 6675[3]

Ghazeer (IRE) *Derek Shaw* a62 63
3 b g Intikhab(USA) Genial Jenny (IRE) (Danehill (USA))
892[8] 981[5] 1138[7] 1585[2] 2388[6] 3350[4] (3540) 4619[2] 4885[8] 5247[9] 6836[9] 7146[3] 7316[13] 7915[7] 7990[U]
Ghazwan (IRE) *Conrad Allen* a34
3 ch g Hurricane Run(IRE) Laurentine (USA) (Private Account (USA))
6614[7] 6839[11]
Ghostflower (IRE) *Mahmood Al Zarooni* a60 77
2 b f Dansili Silkwood (Singspiel (IRE))
4217[3] 4818[2] ◆
Ghost Protocol (IRE) *David Simcock* 92
3 b g Cockney Rebel(IRE) Stroke Of Six (IRE) (Woodborough (USA))
1860[7] 2477[3] 3296[17] 4009[8] 4342[3] 5101[4] (6574)
Ghost Runner (IRE) *Sir Henry Cecil* 59
2 b c Tagula(IRE) Ball Cat (FR) (Cricket Ball (USA))
5851[8]
Ghost Train (IRE) *Mark Johnston* a75 72
3 b g Holy Roman Emperor(IRE) Adrastea (IRE) (Monsun (GER))
827[2] 975[6] (1115) 1264[5] 1721[5] 2459[4] 2689[3] 3762[2] 4218[2] 4468[2] 4723[7] 5233[5] 5662[3] 6145[5] 6417[4] 6825[12] 7141[11] 8036[9]
Ghostwing *Luke Dace* a88 83
5 gr g Kheleyf(USA) Someone's Angel (USA) (Runaway Groom (CAN))
(24) 157[8] 458[9] 1279[2] 1564[14] 1789[3] 2572[9] 3314[6] 3541[10] (5993) 6705[4] 7145[7] 7328[11] 7648[8] 7827[9]
Ghostwriting (USA) *John Gosden* a86 91
3 b c Ghostzapper(USA) Miss Halory (USA) (Mr Prospector (USA))
1217[9] 1477[7] 1860[11] 2813[5] 3563[3]
Ghufa (IRE) *Lydia Pearce* a73 77
8 b g Sakhee(USA) Hawriyah (USA) (Dayjur (USA))
63[6]
Ghur (USA) *Mark Johnston* a23 55
2 ch f Hard Spun(USA) Judhoor (Alhaarth (IRE))
6132[4] 6512[3] ◆ 7096[4] 7708[12]
Ghurair (USA) *John Gosden* 108
2 bb c Elusive Quality(USA) Alta Moda (Sadler's Wells (USA))
(4066) 4698[5] (6874)
Ghusoon *John Gosden* a63 79
3 b f Red Ransom(USA) Sundus (USA) (Sadler's Wells (USA))
2368[4] ◆ 2849[5] 3565[3]
Giant Cats Eye (USA) *Thomas Albertrani* a87
2 bb f Giant's Causeway(USA) Unreal Cat (USA) (Unreal Zeal (USA))
(6944a)
Giant Ryan (USA) *Bisnath Parboo* a120
6 b h Freud(USA) Kheyrah (USA) (Dayjur (USA))
1147a[5]
Giant Sandman (IRE) *Rune Haugen* a87 106
5 b h Footstepsinthesand Sharamana (IRE) (Darshaan)
4751a[2]
Giant Sequoia (USA) *Barney Curley* a24 52
8 ch g Giant's Causeway(USA) Beware Of The Cat (USA) (Caveat (USA))
3400[13] 4200[6] 5022[8] 6255[13]
Giant's Quest (AUS) *H Rogers* 78
6 b g Giant's Causeway(USA) Rushing Wind (IRE) (Danehill (USA))
7584a[13]
Giantstepsahead (IRE) *Terry Clement* a57
3 br g Footstepsinthesand Salty Air (IRE) (Singspiel (IRE))
7625[4]
Gibraltar Road *John Quinn* 58
3 b g Iffraaj Kerry's Dream (Tobougg (IRE))
1953[5] ◆ 4397[4] 4771[5] 5545[5]
Gibson (USA) *Michael J Maker*
4 b g Gibson County(USA) Megan's Cracker (USA) (Slew The Slewor (USA))
8278a[3]
Giddy Heights *Jeremy Noseda* 12
2 b c Pivotal Light Hearted (Green Desert (USA))
6636[19]
Gifted Dancer *Henry Candy* 76
3 b f Cadeaux Genereux Puteri Sas (IRE) (Fasliyev (USA))
3619[4] 4533[6] 5107[5] 5625[2] (6154) 7395[10]
Gifted Girl (IRE) *Paul Cole* a97 90
3 b f Azamour(IRE) Hoodwink (IRE) (Selkirk (USA))
1748[2] 6831[6] 7128[2] 7375[6] (7858)
Gifted Heir (IRE) *Ray Peacock* a30 56
8 b g Princely Heir(IRE) Inzar Lady (IRE) (Inzar (USA))
532[8] 725[12] 848[12] 4405[6]
Gift From Heaven (IRE) *David Wachman* 94
2 ch f Excellent Art Catch The Moon (IRE) (Peintre Celebre (USA))
7052[8]
Gift Of Music (IRE) *James Eustace* a73
2 b f Cadeaux Genereux Loch Verdi (Green Desert (USA))
(7931)
Gigawatt *Jim Boyle* 76
2 b c Piccolo Concubine (IRE) (Danehill (USA))
5661[4] (6945)
Gigli (IRE) *William Haggas* a55
2 ch f Dylan Thomas(IRE) Rainbow Lyrics (IRE) (Rainbow Quest (USA))
6978[6] 7304[4] 7923[10]
Gigolo Star (SPA) *J-C Fernandez-Rodriguez*
3 ch c Dyhim Diamond(IRE) Flamingo Star (SPA) (Limpid)
6089a[8]
Gilded Age *Chris Gordon* a72 75
6 b g Cape Cross(IRE) Sweet Folly (IRE) (Singspiel (IRE))
577[3] 1085[3] (1505) 1905[3] 2412[6] 6738[12] 7377[9]

Gilded Frame *Marcus Tregoning* 74
2 b c I Was Framed(USA) Glint (Pivotal)
4803[8] 5274[5] 5911[2]

Gilded Youth *David Lewis* a68 73
8 b g Gorse Nisha (Nishapour (FR))
1829[P]

Gilly The Filly *Hugo Palmer* 35
3 b f Pivotal Green Eyes (IRE) (Green Desert (USA))
5340[6]

Gingerbread Man (AUS) *Ranji Marsh* 105
5 b h Shamardal(USA) Quaffle (AUS) (Hurricane Sky (AUS))
758a[11]

Ginger Fizz *Ben Case* a74
5 ch m Haafhd Valagalore (Generous (IRE))
7011[6] 7594[0] 7933[4] 8170[3]

Ginger Goose *Richard Fahey* 101
2 b c Royal Applause Eclaircie (IRE) (Thunder Gulch (USA))
3182[2] ◆ (4257) 4736[4]

Ginger Grey (IRE) *David O'Meara* a67 78
5 gr g Bertolini(USA) Just In Love (FR) (Highest Honor (FR))
1175[4] 1282[9]

Ginger Jack *Geoffrey Harker* a88 93
5 ch g Refuse To Bend(IRE) Coretta (IRE) (Caerleon (USA))
(2597) 3274[2] 3826[2] 4110[6] 4821[7] 6124[4] (6881)

Ginger Monkey (IRE) *Peter Chapple-Hyam* a72 33
3 ch g Cockney Rebel(IRE) Miss Interpret (IRE) (Danehill Dancer (IRE))
298[6] 3972[2] 4874[3] 6048[9]

Ginger Ted (IRE) *Stuart Williams* a80 96
5 ch g Fath(USA) Estertide (IRE) (Tagula (IRE))
1844[20] 2487[13] 2940[9] 3169[12] 3571[10] 6531[6] 6788[9] 7178[5] ◆ 7218[2] (7308) (7411) ◆

Gin Twist *Tom Dascombe* a73 72
3 b f Invincible Spirit(IRE) Winding (USA) (Irish River (FR))
(469) 637[2] 905[6] (1090) (1183) 1494[U] 1912[5] 5831[8] 6211[7] 6641[7]

Ginzan *Malcolm Saunders* a56 79
4 b m Desert Style(IRE) Zyzania (Zafonic (USA))
1483[4] 1910[4] (2360) (2943) 3139[3] 4235[3] 4903[6] 5502[3] (5815) 7019[9]

Giofra *A De Royer-Dupre* 118
4 b m Dansili Gracefully (IRE) (Orpen (USA))
(1245a) 1696a[2] (4065) 5399a[5] 6911a[3] 8043a[2]

Gioia (FR) *Mme S Adet* a42 56
5 b m Okawango(USA) Ascot One (FR) (Septieme Ciel (USA))
965a[5]

Gioia Di Vita *Marco Botti* a72
2 b c Sakhee(USA) Dhuyoof (IRE) (Sinndar (IRE))
(7357)

Giorgio's Dragon (IRE) *Richard Fahey* 73
3 b g Le Vie Dei Colori Broadways Millie (IRE) (Imperial Ballet (IRE))
4553[6] 5185[2] 5803[2] ◆ 6048[7] 6560[2]

Girl At The Sands (IRE) *James Given* a68 71
2 gr f Clodovil(IRE) Invincible Woman (IRE) (Invincible Spirit (IRE))
4651[5] (5242) (5711) 6196[9] 6809[4]

Girl From Ipanema (SWE) *Patrick Wahl* a81
3 ch f Eishin Dunkirk(USA) Little Green Apple (SWE) (Funambule (USA))
5143a[3]

Girl Of Cadiz *Richard Hannon* a67 62
2 b f Byron Gennie Bond (Pivotal)
4055[9] 4487[5] 5267[6] 6147[2] 6583[4] 7173[2] 7414[8] 7808[2] 8103[3]

Girl Of The Rain (IRE) *S Botti* 95
2 b f Refuse To Bend(IRE) Bagnolese (ITY) (Cape Cross (IRE))
6090a[3]

Girolamo (GER) *P Schiergen* 115
3 ch c Dai Jin Golden Time (GER) (Surumu (GER))
1553a[7] 2966a[4] 3683a[3] 4685[4] 5865a[5] (6523a)

Gitano Hernando *H J Brown* a117 120
6 ch h Hernando(FR) Gino's Spirits (Perugino (USA))
876a[12]

Giveherachance *Ann Duffield* 26
3 b f Bachelor Duke(USA) Apple Sauce (Prince Sabo)
3521[6] 4705[6] 5669[10]

Give Me High Five *Richard Hannon* a63
2 b f Dubawi(IRE) Mountain Holly (Shirley Heights)
7899[10] 8018[2] 8201[5]

Give Or Take *Christine Dunnett* 14
4 ch g Where Or When(IRE) Tata Naka (Nashwan (USA))
581[9] 976[7] 1266[9] 1771[9] 2013[8]

Give Us A Belle (IRE) *Christine Dunnett* a50 48
3 b g Kheleyf(USA) Bajan Belle (IRE) (Efisio)
1048[6] 1285[5] 1843[10] 3547[12] 5975[12] 6322[12] 7318[6] 7512[10] 7729[6] 7981[3] 8257[5]

Give Way Nelson (IRE) *Brian Meehan* a73 86
2 b f Mount Nelson Give A Whistle (IRE) (Mujadil (USA))
2426[3] 5887[2] (6644) 7588a[2]

Glacial Age (IRE) *Jo Hughes* 70
2 gr c Verglas(IRE) Lady's Secret (IRE) (Alzao (USA))
6780[2]

Glad Bear (GER) *Fredrik Reuterskiold* 77
3 ch g Ransom O'War(USA) Glady Beauty (GER) (Big Shuffle (USA))
5144a[2]

Glad Eye Gladys *Scott Dixon* 65
3 b f Milk It Mick Thunderous Days (Diktat)
2448[9]

Gladiatrix *Rod Millman* a46 87
3 b f Compton Place Lady Dominatrix (IRE) (Danehill Dancer (IRE))
2147[7] 2871[3] 3312[2] 5446[3] 5878[4] (6095) (6739) ◆ (6926) (7019) 7273[3]

Glad Sky *J-L Pelletan* a106 106
6 b g Big Shuffle(USA) Glady Sum (GER) (Surumu (GER))
3205a[9] 5118a[4]

Gladsome *Jason Ward* 69
4 b m Resplendent Glory(IRE) Christening (IRE) (Lahib (USA))
2095[4] 2335[3] 3024[2] 3333[3] 4711[7] 4996[6] 5345[13] 6783[2] 7445[4]

Gladstone (IRE) *John Panvert* a49 38
4 b g Dansili Rockerlong (Deploy)
5276[10] 6927[5] 7479[7]

Gladtoseeme (USA) *Fredrik Reuterskiold* a60
5 bb g Belong To Me(USA) Richie's Girls (USA) (Black Tie Affair)
3654a[7]

Glaisdale *James Toller* a64 53
3 b f Hurricane Run(IRE) Picacho (IRE) (Sinndar (IRE))
5889[11] 6457[7] 6814[5] (7196)

Glamour Star (GER) *Exors Of W Baltromei* a86 83
3 b g Shirocco(GER) Grouper (USA) (Gone West (USA))
365a[6] 716a[7]

Glan Lady (IRE) *Michael Appleby* a56 41
6 b m Court Cave(IRE) Vanished (IRE) (Fayruz)
7314[13] 7469[5]

Glass Harmonium (IRE) *Michael Moroney* 119
6 gr h Verglas(IRE) Spring Symphony (IRE) (Darshaan)
7426a[13]

Glass Mountain (IRE) *John Mackie* a72 79
4 gr g Verglas(IRE) Exotic Mix (FR) (Linamix (FR))
1266[2] 1841[6] 2328[8] 4602[12] 5007[4] 5417[7] 5688[8] 6452[6] 6894[3] 7027[8] 7221[3] 7844[8] 8271[5]

Glass Office *David Simcock* a106 81
2 bg c Verglas(IRE) Oval Office (Pursuit Of Love)
2415[3] ◆ (3733) 4283[3] 4763[9] (5232) (6038)

Glastonberry *Geoffrey Deacon* a75 38
4 gr m Piccolo Elderberry (Bin Ajwaad (IRE))
87[3] 2421[13] 3151[13] 3943[3] 4653[7] (7861) 7906[3] 8156[2] (8268)

Glaze *Hughie Morrison* a50 53
3 ch f Kyllachy Raindrop (Primo Dominie)
2864[8] 3665[10] 4486[11] 7148[6] 7499[6] 8067[8]

Glean *Richard Hannon* 102
2 ch c Raven's Pass(USA) Harvest Queen (IRE) (Spinning World (USA))
(5303) ◆ 5976[2] 6599[3] ◆ 7404[6]

Glenard *Charles Hills* 79
2 b c Arch(USA) Olaya (USA) (Theatrical (IRE))
(6164) 7053[10]

Glencadam Gold (IRE) *Gai Waterhouse* 113
4 b g Refuse To Bend(IRE) Sandrella (IRE) (Darshaan)
7264a[15] 7621a[6]

Glendaragh (IRE) *David O'Meara* a47 51
4 b g Ad Valorem(USA) Happy Flight (IRE) (Titus Livius (FR))
3939[4] 4314[6]

Glen Ellen (SWE) *Hans-Inge Larsen*
3 b f Nicolotte Fernet-Branca (SWE) (Diligo (FR))
5144a[10]

Glen Ellyn *Mark Johnston* a22 62
3 gr c Shamardal(USA) Giorgia Rae (IRE) (Green Desert (USA))
7201[11]

Glen Ginnie (IRE) *Charles Hills* a59 64
2 br f Red Clubs(IRE) Belsay (Belmez (USA))
2407[4] 2812[7] 4704[6] 6253[4] 6604[4]

Glenlini *Jim Goldie* 57
6 b m Bertolini(USA) Glenhurich (IRE) (Sri Pekan (USA))
1800[7] 3113[5] 3442[5] 3893[9] 4392[5] 4793[9] 5190[7] 6887[8]

Glenluji *Jim Goldie* 65
7 b g Lujain(USA) Glenhurich (IRE) (Sri Pekan (USA))
1879[9] 2455[12] 2600[5] 3332[4] 3889[7] 4390[6] 4643[7] (5081) 5917[6] 6258[8] 6528[9] 6758[11] 7095[11]

Glen Moss (IRE) *Charles Hills* a88 92
3 b c Moss Vale(IRE) Sail With The Wind (Saddlers' Hall (IRE))
(1138) 1996[4] 2490[2] 3165[3] 4063[7]

Glen Nevis (USA) *A Al Raihe* a96 75
8 br h Gulch(USA) Beating The Buzz (IRE) (Bluebird (USA))
47a[6] 421a[10] 618a[12]

Glennten *Sylvester Kirk* a64 55
3 b g Ishiguru(USA) Uplifting (Magic Ring (IRE))
770[8] 943[3] 1192[4] 1709[3] 2441[6] 3098[6] 3732[7] 5975[9] 6151[12] 7146[6] 7616[5]

Glenreef *Pat Eddery* a39
2 ch f Three Valleys(USA) Grand Coral (Grand Lodge (USA))
7161[8]

Glenridding *James Given* a76 90
8 b g Averti(IRE) Appelone (Emperor Jones (USA))
2029[12] 2285[10] 2489[6] 2697[10] 3439[3] 3557[11] 4042[4] 4747[4] 5179[7] 5802[9] 5893[3] 6239[4] 6455[6]

Glen's Diamond *Richard Fahey* 112
4 b g Intikhab(USA) Posta Vecchia (USA) (Rainbow Quest (USA))
143a[5] 421a[4] 759a[6] 1994[5] 2254[2] 3418[4] 3881[6] 5599[10] 6236[4]

Glens Wobbly *Jonathan Geake* a49 48
4 ch g Kier Park(IRE) Wobbly (Atraf)
805[6] 1106[10] 1907[5] 2395[3]

Glitter (IRE) *Laura Young* 28
3 gr g Verglas(IRE) Call Me Crazy (IRE) (Key Of Luck (USA))
2387[10] 4422[8]

Glittering Gold *Sir Michael Stoute* 88
3 b c Galileo(IRE) Phantom Gold (Machiavellian (USA))
2197[6] (2612) 3668[5] 5820[7]

Global Bang (GER) *Mario Hofer* 95
2 bb c Manduro(GER) Goonda (Darshaan)
5755a[8]

Global City (IRE) *Saeed Bin Suroor* a105 89
6 b h Exceed And Excel(AUS) Victory Peak (Shirley Heights)
261a[4] 874a[4] 2409[7] 2825[13] 4629[12] 7709[4]

Global Icon *Richard Hannon* a71 87
2 b g Green Desert(USA) Maganda (IRE) (Sadler's Wells (USA))
5418[9] 6203[4] 6491[3] 6874[11] 7192[3]

Global Magic (GER) *A Wohler* 101
4 b m Lando(GER) Goonda (Darshaan)
4386a[7] 6723a[7] 7075a[5]

Global Village (IRE) *Brian Ellison* a84 100
7 b g Dubai Destination(USA) Zelding (IRE) (Warning)
11[2] 458[7] 1161[5] (1354) 1510[3] ◆ (2068) 3331[4] 4321[4] 6024[14] 6868[7]

Gloomy Sunday (FR) *C Ferland* 103
3 b f Singspiel(IRE) Fine And Mellow (FR) (Lando (GER))
5116a[7] 6595a[3] 7665a[9]

Gloriam (USA) *David Simcock* a89 66
3 b g War Chant(USA) Amandas Bandit (USA) (Royal Academy (USA))
2813[12]

Glorious Days (AUS) *J Size* 120
5 br g Hussonet(USA) San Century (NZ) (Centaine (AUS))
1902a[2] 8042a[2]

Glorious Melody (FR) *Robert Collet* 64
2 b f Dylan Thomas(IRE) Sue Generoos (IRE) (Spectrum (IRE))
5570a[9] 7700a[7]

Glorious Protector (IRE) *Ed Walker* 72
2 b c Azamour(IRE) Hasaiyda (IRE) (Hector Protector (USA))
6596[6] ◆

Glor Na Mara (IRE) *J S Bolger* a84 105
4 b h Leroidesanimaux(BRZ) Sister Angelina (USA) (Saint Ballado (CAN))
1040a[3] 2777a[3] 3091a[3]

Glory Awaits (IRE) *Kevin Ryan* 96
2 ch c Choisir(AUS) Sandbox Two (IRE) (Foxhound (USA))
2213[11] 2822[11] (3062) 4098[9] 4774[3] 6247[4] 7053[4]

Glory City (IRE) *Marco Botti* a80 78
2 b c Azamour(IRE) Zara's Birthday (IRE) (Waajib)
3634[4] ◆ 4340[2] 5321[6] 6972[2] (7460) (8240)

Glory Power (IRE) *J-M Beguigne* a101 90
4 ch m Medicean Sandbox (IRE) (Grand Lodge (USA))
(83a)

Glossy Posse *Richard Hannon* a64 65
2 b f Dubawi(IRE) Nouvelle Lune (Fantastic Light (USA))
2892[8] 4002[3] 5357[9] 5749[4] 6147[3] 6541[3] 7060[2] (7439)

Gloucester *Michael Scudamore* a25 77
9 b g Montjeu(IRE) Birdlip (USA) (Sanglamore (USA))
7954[9]

Goal (IRE) *Charles Smith* a72 79
4 b g Mujadil(USA) Classic Lin (FR) (Linamix (FR))
115[9] 391[7] 562[4] 722[4] (1636) 1769[9] 2227[8] 2675[10] 3180[9] 3793[10] 4089[7] 4662[7] 6174[8] 6528[6] 6941[2] 7058[2] 7385[2] 7593[5]

Goal Hanger *William Kinsey* a29 64
3 b f Exceed And Excel(AUS) Mrs Gray (Red Sunset)
1660[7] 2351[10]

Go Amwell *J R Jenkins* a34 53
9 b g Kayf Tara Daarat Alayaam (IRE) (Reference Point)
6769[7]

Go Angellica (IRE) *David Simcock* 100
2 ch f Kheleyf(USA) Areyaam (USA) (Elusive Quality (USA))
(2917) ◆ 4514[4] (5787) 6199[6] 7052[9]

Godber (IRE) *Ralph Smith* a41 57
3 br g Imperial Dancer Ambrix (IRE) (Xaar)
428[7]

Gods Gift (IRE) *Rae Guest* 65
2 ch c Dalakhani(IRE) Guilia (Galileo (IRE))
7130[3] ◆ 7468[3]

Go Dutch (IRE) *Roger Varian* 100
3 ch c Dutch Art Paix Royale (Royal Academy (USA))
2265[4] 2930[10] (4503) (5342)

Godwit *Eugene Stanford* a49 1
4 b m Noverre(USA) Hen Harrier (Polar Falcon (USA))
581[6] 847[5] 1113[6] 1588[8] 2464[9] 3713[3] 4193[7] 5212[6]

Go Far *Alan Bailey* a67 44
2 b c Dutch Art Carranita (IRE) (Anita's Prince)
4595[13] 8006[2] 8185[3]

Go Go Green (IRE) *Jim Goldie* a82 79
6 b g Acclamation Preponderance (IRE) (Cyrano De Bergerac)
(1236) 1642[10] (2092) 2596[13] 2717[10] 3169[14] 3903[8] 4133[9] 5801[4] 7101[8]

Going French (IRE) *Dai Burchell* a68 72
5 ch g Frenchmans Bay(FR) Easy Going (Hamas (IRE))
720[2] 958[8] 1420[2] 1481[3] 2165[5] 2572[8] (3098) 4236[2] 4887[4] 5502[6] (6195)

Going Grey (IRE) *Richard Fahey* a64 47
3 ro g Diamond Green(FR) Incendio (Siberian Express (USA))
1479[11] 8074[10] 8269[7]

Gokcenil (TUR) *C Turan* 81
4 ch m Mountain Cat(USA) Affairiste (IRE) (Simply Great (FR))
5849a[7]

Golac *Mick Channon* 60
2 b c Pastoral Pursuits Pretty Kool (Inchinor)
1515[2] 1623[2] 1767[7] 1904[4] 4728[4] 5291[8] 5654[6] 6283[8]

Golan Guy (IRE) *Alison Batchelor* a61 71
7 b g Golan(IRE) Countess Marengo (IRE) (Revoque (IRE))
8170[7]

Golan Heights (IRE) *Adrian McGuinness* a56 36
6 br g Golan(IRE) Lady Abigail (IRE) (Royal Academy (USA))
924[11] 7058[6]

Golan Way *Sheena West* a72 75
8 b g Golan(IRE) Silk Daisy (Barathea (IRE))
2411[7] 2976[2]

Golconde (IRE) *Robert Cowell* a68 60
3 b f Modigliani(USA) Star Of Siligo (USA) (Saratoga Six (USA))
1409a[7] 6939[9] 7524[9] 7863[9] 8157[6] 8307[10]

Gold And White (GER) *P Schiergen* 83
2 ch f Bahamian Bounty Genevra (IRE) (Danehill (USA))
5612a[8] 6725a[4]

Goldan Jess (IRE) *Philip Kirby* a60 54
8 b g Golan(IRE) Bendis (GER) (Danehill (USA))
(6399) 7862[2]

Gold Beau (FR) *Linda Stubbs* a59 74
2 b g Gold Away(IRE) Theorie (FR) (Anabaa (USA))
2073[4] 3271[2] 3520[5] 4433[10] 5620[3] 6556[5] 7410[7] 7821[9]

Gold Burst (IRE) *Richard Hannon* 65
2 ch c Tamayuz Mistress Thames (Sharpo)
6377[7] 6872[6]

Gold City (IRE) *Saeed Bin Suroor* a90 100
3 b g Pivotal Storm Lily (USA) (Storm Cat (USA))
2916[8] 5363[7] 6143[3] 6676[21] 7508[10]

Gold Deal (IRE) *Deborah Sanderson* a49
3 b g Chineur(FR) Alexander Express (IRE) (Sri Pekan (USA))
114[10] 552[6] 833[7] 1517[14]

Gold Edition *Jeremy Noseda* a82 73
3 ch c Mr Greeley(USA) Triple Edition (USA) (Lear Fan (USA))
1704[6] 4212[2] 5276[5] 5776[3] 6125[3] 6328[4]

Golden Acorn (IRE) *Nigel Hawke* 68
3 b f Ad Valorem(USA) Golden Heart (Salse (USA))
4989[6]

Golden Beet (FR) *Mlle Valerie Boussin* 42
3 ch f Go Between(FR) Goldenphee (FR) (Gold Away (FR))
17a[0]

Golden Causeway *Charles Hills* 69
2 ch f Giant's Causeway(USA) Cast In Gold (USA) (Elusive Quality (USA))
4739[12] ◆ 5551[9] 5977[7]

Goldencents (USA) *Doug O'Neill* a107
2 b c Into Mischief(USA) Golden Works (CAN) (Banker's Gold (USA))
6901a[2]

Golden Club (FR) *J-C Rouget* a81 89
3 b g One Cool Cat(USA) Life On The Road (IRE) (Persian Heights)
211a[2]

Golden Compass *Giles Bravery* a70 77
4 ch m Sakhee(USA) Northern Bows (Bertolini (USA))
2251[2] 2811[8] (4332) 5775[3]

Golden Delicious *Hughie Morrison* 93
4 ch m Cadeaux Genereux Playgirl (IRE) (Caerleon (USA))
2608[4] ◆ 3190[6] 5385[11]

Golden Desert (IRE) *Simon Dow* a78 100
8 b g Desert Prince(IRE) Jules (IRE) (Danehill (USA))
2558[14] 3268[28] 3771[11] 4287[9] 6145[6] ◆ 6687[6] 7480[10] (7857) 7998[7] 8105[3]

Golden Dylan (FR) *H-A Pantall* 77
2 b f Dylan Thomas(IRE) Maid Marion (UAE) (Jade Robbery (USA))
8193a[0]

Golden Flight (IRE) *John C McConnell* a48 29
6 ch g Hawk Wing(USA) Cassilis (IRE) (Persian Bold)
105[6]

Golden Flower *David O'Meara* a73 65
2 b f Royal Applause Silver Kestrel (USA) (Silver Hawk (USA))
7953[2] (8230)

Golden Future *Peter Niven* a56 72
9 b g Muhtarram(USA) Nazca (Zilzal (USA))
(1297) 1846[4] 2457[3] 3114[2] 4590[12] 4910[4] 6076[11] 6706[9] 8290[6]

Golden Groom *Patrick Holmes* 17
9 b g Groom Dancer(USA) Reine De Thebes (FR) (Darshaan)
5714[6]

Golden Jubilee (USA) *Richard Hannon* 65
3 bb g Zavata(USA) Love Play (USA) (Friendly Lover (USA))
(2128) 2756[7] 3475[9] 5501[5] 5796[8] 6278[7] 6639[6] 7015[7]

Golden Leaves (USA) *Mahmood Al Zarooni* 38
2 b f Tiznow(USA) Desert Gold (USA) (Seeking The Gold (USA))
6489[14]

Golden Lilac (IRE) *A Fabre* 119
4 b m Galileo(IRE) Grey Lilas (IRE) (Danehill (USA))
(2533a) 4065[9] 4633a[2] 5141a[7]

Golden Memory (DEN) *Niels Petersen* a92 78
4 b m Dexterity(USA) Golden Line (DEN) (Gabitat)
(5143a)

Golden Pursuit *Tom Dascombe* a59
2 ch c Pastoral Pursuits Rainy Day Song (Persian Bold)
7219[3] ◆ 7410[6]

Golden Secret *Clive Cox* 54
2 ch f Sakhee's Secret Tahara (IRE) (Caerleon (USA))
6627[5] ◆

Golden Share (USA) *Marco Botti* a47
3 bb c Medaglia d'Oro(USA) Siempre Asi (USA) (Silver Hawk (USA))
8295[5]

Golden Speed (SPA) *L A Urbano-Grajales* a83
4 ch m Delfos(IRE) Manilia (FR) (Kris)
15a[6]

Golden Sunbird (IRE) *Paul Nolan* 83
8 ch m Bob Back(USA) Mrs Marples (IRE) (Sexton Blake)
3373[15]

Golden Tempest (IRE) *Eve Johnson Houghton* a91 92
4 b m Clodovil(IRE) Honey Storm (IRE) (Mujadil (USA))
1212[10] 2417[13] 2975 [8] 4233[6] 5004[2] 5269[7] 5769[4] 6040[8] (6208) 6538[3] 6979[4]
Golden Ticket (USA) *Kenneth McPeek* a119 91
3 bb c Speightstown(USA) Business Plan (USA) (Deputy Minister (CAN))
7882a[11]
Golden Valley *Tim Easterby* 71
3 ch f Three Valleys(USA) Reaf (In The Wings)
2283[10]
Goldenveil (IRE) *Richard Fahey* a64 79
4 b m Iffraaj Line Ahead (IRE) (Sadler's Wells (USA))
1275[14] 2414[7] 2915[8] 3416[6] 3889[5] 4396[7] 5059[6] 5452[2] 6262[7] 7095[9]
Golden Waters *Eve Johnson Houghton* a68 78
5 b m Dubai Destination(USA) Faraway Waters (Pharly (FR))
1706[7] 2637[6] 3443[13]
Gold Falcon (IRE) *David Simcock* a66 67
3 b g Iffraaj Pretty Majestic (IRE) (Invincible Spirit (IRE))
730[3] 3547[4]
Gold For Tina (FR) *J Van Handenhove* a92 98
3 b f Lando(GER) Mascara (GER) (Monsun (GER))
5142a[8]
Gold Hunter (IRE) *Saeed Bin Suroor* 72
2 b c Invincible Spirit(IRE) Goldthroat (IRE) (Zafonic (USA))
1886[3] 2376[3]
Gold Knight (FR) *D Prod'Homme* a67 75
2 b g Hannouma(IRE) Gold Charm (GER) (Key Of Luck (USA))
3714a[5]
Gold Lace (IRE) *Ed Dunlop* 82
3 b f Invincible Spirit(IRE) Brigitta (IRE) (Sadler's Wells (USA))
2272[12]
Goldmadchen (GER) *Keith Dalgleish* a66 62
4 b m Ivan Denisovich(IRE) Goldkatze (GER) (Czaravich (USA))
5174[2] 5730[8] 5921[9] 6526[4] (6758) 6940[2] 7003[6] 7599[7] (7731)
Gold Nugget (IRE) *Richard Hannon* 33
2 b c Elusive City(USA) Glamadour (IRE) (Sanglamore (USA))
5948[10] 6371[10]
Goldoni (IRE) *Andrew Balding* a93 105
3 ch g Dylan Thomas(IRE) Lasso (Indian Ridge)
1160[2] (1604) 2080[6] 3295[6] 4261[2] 5593[2] (6236)
Goldplated (IRE) *John Joseph Murphy* a52 100
4 ch m Selkirk(USA) Thermal Spring (Zafonic (USA))
143a[12] 241a[10] 2711[7] 3197a[7] 3678a[5]
Gold Rally (USA) *Mahmood Al Zarooni* 81
3 rg g Medaglia d'Oro(USA) Beright (USA) (Gray Slewpy (USA))
1504[4]
Goldream *Luca Cumani* a87 95
3 br g Oasis Dream Clizia (IRE) (Machiavellian (USA))
1612[7] 2764[3] (3235) 3613[2] 4291[3] (5320) 6165[3]
Gold Roll (IRE) *Ruth Carr* a59 68
2 b g Intikhab(USA) Sopran Marida (IRE) (Darshaan)
2231[12] 2844[6] 3191[5] 7304[6] 7779[7]
Gold Rules *Michael Easterby* a83 81
5 ch g Gold Away(IRE) Raphaela (FR) (Octagonal (NZ))
2142[8] 2751[9] 3459[4] 3693[5] 4179[2] (4683) 5001[3] 5585[6] 6181[2] 6642[8] 7147[10]
Gold Sceptre (FR) *Richard Hannon* 74
3 b g Gold Away(IRE) Cap Serena (FR) (Highest Honor (FR))
2557[3] 3347[5] 4511[6] 5036[3] 6206[7] 6798[5]
Goldschatzchen (GER) *W Hickst* 77
3 bb f Dai Jin Goldkatze (GER) (Czaravich (USA))
3802a[7]
Gold Show *Mick Channon* 82
3 gr f Sir Percy Pearl Bright (FR) (Kaldoun (FR))
1506[4] ◆ 2232[4] 2560[2] 3070[3] 3340[3] 3666[8] 4256[3] 4505[5] 4782[2] 5147[2] (5529) 6092[3] 7270[6]
Goldstorm *Brian Baugh* a64 68
4 ch m Storming Home Antonia Bertolini (Bertolini (USA))
1096[2] (1634) 1717[2] ◆ 2858[2] 3559[2]
Goldtara (FR) *A Lyon* a89 105
4 ch m Gold Away(IRE) Diatara (FR) (Sillery (USA))
6914a[6]
Gold Tobougg *David Simcock* a70 64
4 b m Tobougg(IRE) Maristax (Reprimand)
124[3] 212[2] ◆
Goldtrek (USA) *N W Alexander* a62 81
5 b m Medallist(USA) Traipse (USA) (Digression (USA))
4674[7]
Gold Weight *Michael Madgwick* a44
2 ch g Denounce Jewel (IRE) (Cyrano De Bergerac)
6772[8] 7628[10]
Go Michelangelo (FR) *P Van De Poele* a75 88
5 gr g Highest Honor(FR) Bramosia (Forzando)
94a[3]
Gone By Sunrise *Derek Shaw* a41 45
3 b g Three Valleys(USA) Quadrophenia (College Chapel)
3768 7349 2130[7] 2336[14]
Gone To Ground *Michael Squance* a45 17
3 ch g Grape Tree Road Chase The Fox (Foxhound (USA))
1087 1321[1] 2547[5] 3005[7] 3547[11]
Goninodaethat *Jim Goldie* 63
4 b g Proclamation(IRE) Big Mystery (IRE) (Grand Lodge (USA))
2621[2] 3115[2] 3581[U] (3888) 4432[8] 5084[7] 5918[2] 6308[6] 6756[7] 7095[13]
Good As New *Chris Wall* a51
2 b f Araafa(IRE) New Design (IRE) (Bluebird (USA))
6501[13] 7525[7] 7926[9]
Good Authority (IRE) *Karen George* a91 91
5 b g Chineur(FR) Lady Alexander (IRE) (Night Shift (USA))
1729[2] 2500[4] (3045) 4580[3] 5480[7] (5910) 6800[11] 7327[4] ◆ 7645[7] 7966[5]
Good Boy Jackson *Kevin Ryan* a23 89
4 b g Firebreak Fisher Island (IRE) (Sri Pekan (USA))
1134[9] 1605[8] 2035[2] 2620[7] 3038[3] 3594[9]
Good Evans *Tom Dascombe* a60
2 ch c Mount Nelson Alexia Reveuse (IRE) (Dr Devious (IRE))
7868[6]
Goodfellows Quest (IRE) *Ann Duffield* 31
3 ch c Intikhab(USA) Poppys Footprint (IRE) (Titus Livius (FR))
1270[13] 4913[6]
Goodie Goodie *Sylvester Kirk* a40 57
3 b f Shirocco(GER) Goodie Twosues (Fraam)
990[6] 2204[11] 2768[11] 3965[7] 4198[2] 4754[12] 4900[4] 5764[12]
Good Luck Charm *Gary Moore* a81 77
3 b g Doyen(IRE) Lucky Dice (Perugino (USA))
1728[2] 2126[5] 2557[2] 3248[2] 4413[8] 5036[6] 6434[2] 6582[3] 7480[3] (7725)
Goodlukin Lucy *Dianne Sayer* a73 73
5 ch m Supreme Sound Suka Ramai (Nashwan (USA))
2134[10] 3029[4] 3440[13] 4179[14] 4869[6] 5762[2] 6758[6] 7102[7]
Good Mind (IRE) *Don Cantillon*
3 ch f Choisir(AUS) Good Thought (IRE) (Mukaddamah (USA))
4874[P]
Good Morning Star (IRE) *Mark Johnston* a76 99
3 bb f Shirocco(GER) Hollow Ridge (Beat Hollow)
(209) 362[3] 656[2] 1442[3] (1973) 2178[6] 2718[9] 3856[6] 4007[3] 4738[5] 6236[3] 6668[6] 6833[4] 7510[14]
Goodness *David O'Meara* a64 74
4 ch g Cadeaux Genereux Dayrose (Daylami (IRE))
1382[2] 1525[9] 1822[12] 2792[5] 3213[3] 3753[6] 4714[11]
Good Of Luck *Mick Channon* a70 71
3 b g Authorized(IRE) Oops Pettie (Machiavellian (USA))
(399) 1888[8] 2281[8] 3248[5] 4498[7] 4755[4] 5442[5]
Good Speech (IRE) *Tom Tate* a61 58
2 ch f Haatef(USA) Privileged Speech (USA) (General Assembly (USA))
3611[14] 4494[7] 5962[9] (8112)
Good Timin' *David Brown* a55 56
4 b g Royal Applause Record Time (Clantime)
467[2] 544[2] 691[7] 783[6]
Goodwood Atlantis (IRE) *John Dunlop* 87
3 b c Elusive City(USA) Kayak (Singspiel (IRE))
2408[3] 3882[3] ◆ 4700[4] 6677[12]
Goodwood Mirage (IRE) *John Dunlop* 82
2 b c Jeremy(USA) Phantom Waters (Pharly (FR))
(7330)
Goodwood Starlight (IRE) *Jim Best* a55 59
7 br g Mtoto Starring (FR) (Ashkalani (IRE))
3967[4] 4409[4] 5052[11] 6304[5]
Googlette (IRE) *Ed Vaughan* a93 90
4 b m Exceed And Excel(AUS) Jayzdoll (IRE) (Stravinsky (USA))
89[4] 711[6] 1129[8] 4838[7]
Go On Gilbert *John Wainwright* a55 57
3 b g Librettist(USA) Voice (Zamindar (USA))
1479[6] 2143[6] 2592[4] 3275[6] 7251[6]
Go On Murt (IRE) *Mrs John Harrington* a76 57
3 b c Antonius Pius(USA) Big Storm (IRE) (Nashamaa)
7229a[14]
Gooseberry Bush *Gary Brown* a42 72
5 b m Tobougg(IRE) Away To Me (Exit To Nowhere (USA))
7351[1] 9119 1074[7] 1608[12]
Gooseberry Fool *Sir Mark Prescott Bt* a75 96
3 b f Danehill Dancer(IRE) Last Second (IRE) (Alzao (USA))
3653a[13] 5143a[10]
Gorau Glas *Mark Brisbourne*
4 b m Blue Dakota(IRE) Glesni (Key Of Luck (USA))
4782[10]
Gordol Du Mes (USA) *Gianluca Bietolini* 100
2 ch c Exchange Rate(USA) Twinkle Twinkle (USA) (Arazi (USA))
7623a[9]
Gordon Flash *Charles Hills* a67 68
5 ch g Alhaarth(IRE) Goslar (In The Wings)
2867[8] 3782[4] 5280[4] 5811[2] 6738[10]
Gordon Lord Byron (IRE) *T Hogan* a95 121
4 b g Byron Boa Estrela (IRE) (Intikhab (USA))
2777a[2] 3371[14] 3648a[3] 5137a[2] (5597) 6030[2] (6913a) 8042a[4]
Gordonsville *Jim Goldie* a88 89
9 b g Generous(IRE) Kimba (USA) (Kris S (USA))
3377[12] 4326[3] 4697[8] 5798[2] 6493[16] (7098)
Gordy Bee (USA) *Richard Guest* a70 56
6 b g More Than Ready(USA) Honoria (USA) (Danzig (USA))
3061[1]
Gorgeous Goblin (IRE) *David C Griffiths* a83 70
5 b m Lujain(USA) Tama (IRE) (Indian Ridge)
8[3] 101[4] 396[2] 572[4] (624) 711[7] 806[5] 1161[12] (1428) 1581[3] (1990) 2602[5] 4013[12] 4400[8] 4829[10] (5165)
Gosbeck *Henry Candy* 91
4 ch m Dubawi(IRE) Goslar (In The Wings)
1603[4] 3187[4] 3661[2] (5200) 6031[5] 6492[3] 7519[9]
Gosforth Park *Mel Brittain* a64 73
6 ch g Generous(IRE) Love And Kisses (Salse (USA))
1175[7] 4883[8] (5672) (6608)
Gospel Choir *Sir Michael Stoute* 104
3 ch c Galileo(IRE) Chorist (Pivotal)
(3664) (4323) ◆ (5089) ◆ 6025[7]
Gossamer Seed (IRE) *John Joseph Murphy* a96 108
4 gr m Choisir(AUS) Light And Airy (Linamix (FR))
(1944a) 3092a[3] 3196a[3] 3331[23]
Gotlandia (FR) *J-L Guillochon* a76 98
5 b m Anabaa(USA) Grenade (FR) (Bering)
7124a[0]
Gottcher *David Barron* a76 82
4 b g Fasliyev(USA) Danalia (IRE) (Danehill (USA))
2809[7] 4631[14] 4743[7] 5294[11]
Gottingen (FR) *J-C Rouget* a72 70
2 b c Holy Roman Emperor(IRE) Ring Ring (FR) (Bering)
5073a[3] 5698a[2]
Gouranga *Tony Carroll* a14 11
9 b m Robellino(USA) Hymne D'Amour (USA) (Dixieland Band (USA))
5506[9]
Gouray Girl (IRE) *Brian Ellison* a76 97
5 b m Redback Brillano (FR) (Desert King (IRE))
1354[2] 2023[2] 3348[2] 3812[6] 4597[7] 5530[5] 7080[5] 7408[4] 7690[11] 7826[10]
Govinda (USA) *A Wohler* a96 104
5 bb g Pulpit(USA) Garden In The Rain (FR) (Dolphin Street (FR))
2159a[2] (3603a) 5647a[2] 6908a[10] 7288a[3]
Gowanharry (IRE) *Michael Dods* 72
3 ch f Choisir(AUS) Aahgowangowan (IRE) (Tagula (IRE))
1521[2] 2036[3] (2928) 4208[4] 4619[4] 5167[4] 5800[3] 6886[9]
Gower Rules (IRE) *John Bridger* a64 67
4 gr g Aussie Rules(USA) Holy Norma (Nashwan (USA))
651[9] 961[3] 1534[9] 1919[6] 1984[10] 2851[3] 2937[2] 3222[6] 3573[7] 3782[9] 8180[11]
Gowertonian (IRE) *Ronald Harris* a42 53
2 b c Auction House(USA) Fabuleux Cherie (Noverre (USA))
1903[8] 2579[7] 3387[9] 5424[6] 5997[3] 6115[10] 6612[7]
Grace And Beauty (IRE) *Paul Henderson* a43 62
4 b m Diamond Green(FR) Balliamo (IRE) (Royal Academy (USA))
8079[10]
Graceful Act *Ron Barr* a60 59
4 b m Royal Applause Minnina (IRE) (In The Wings)
1170[7] 2794[2] 3310[4] 3693[11] 6262[5] 6561[4] 7495[5] 7671[3]
Graceful Descent (FR) *Karen Tutty* a74 74
7 b m Hawk Wing(USA) Itab (USA) (Dayjur (USA))
3061[3]
Graceful Spirit *David Evans* a23 46
5 b m Reset(AUS) Naemi (GER) (Tannenkonig (IRE))
422[9]
Grace Hall (USA) *Anthony Dutrow* a113
3 b f Empire Maker(USA) Season's Greetings (IRE) (Ezzoud (IRE))
7550a[4]
Grace Hull *J S Moore* a67 67
2 gr f Piccolo Smart Hostess (Most Welcome)
5887[9] 6453[4] (6889) 7463[5] 7518[9]
Grace Of Dubai (FR) *M Delzangles* a80 96
3 b f Dubai Destination(USA) Hill Of Grace (Desert Prince (IRE))
6899a[7]
Grace Of Hearts *Robert Eddery* a58 56
2 b f Compton Place Graceful Lass (Sadler's Wells (USA))
2193[8] 3634[12] 3971[10] (4462) 4659[6] 5046[DSQ] 5806[9]
Gracia Directa (GER) *D Moser* 106
4 b m Kyllachy Glyceria (IRE) (Common Grounds)
(4070) 4764[12] 5647a[10]
Gracie's Games *Richard Price* a56 66
6 b m Mind Games Little Kenny (Warning)
1280[6] 1516[4] (1934) 2046[3] 2761[6] 2815[4] 3434[2] 3993[6] 5234[9] 5548[9] 6951[14] 7275[5] 7447[12]
Gracie's Gift (IRE) *Richard Guest* a57 55
10 b g Imperial Ballet(IRE) Settle Petal (IRE) (Roi Danzig (USA))
139[2] 289[3] 372[2] 551[9] 752[5] 831[4] 904[4] 1280[3] 1584[3] 1799[2] 1987[2] (2406) 3442[13] 3941[4] 5246[6] 5775[7] 7275[9] 7354[2] 7447[17] 8115[9]
Gracious George (IRE) *Jimmy Fox* a70 63
2 b c Oratorio(IRE) Little Miss Gracie (Efisio)
4056[8] 4846[5] 6818[11] 7476[3] 7723[2] (7965)
Grafelli (IRE) *J S Bolger* 108
2 b c Hannouma(IRE) Spark Sept (FR) (Septieme Ciel (USA))
(4377a) (4519a) ◆
Grafitti *Niels Petersen* a83 96
7 b m Dansili Reading Habit (USA) (Half A Year (USA))
617a[9] 792a[12]
Gra Geal Mo Chroi (IRE) *Augustine Leahy* a57 72
7 br m Imperial Ballet(IRE) Shyshiyra (IRE) (Kahyasi)
6352a[6]
Gramercy (IRE) *David Simcock* a82 106
5 b g Whipper(USA) Topiary (IRE) (Selkirk (USA))
2208[16] 3371[20] 3626[11] 4099[10] 4611[2]
Grammar *Colin Teague* 73
3 b c Rail Link Comma (USA) (Kingmambo (USA))
5730[10] 6103[13]
Gran Canaria Queen *David O'Meara* a65 53
3 bb f Compton Place Ex Mill Lady (Bishop Of Cashel)
1238[5] 1817[8] 2460[6] 2615[5] 3028[3] 3450[5] 3892[7] 4911[5] 5087[5] 6100[4] 6180[3] 6686[2] (6836) 7055[2] 7457[7] 7673[11] 7914[8]
Grandad Mac *Jane Chapple-Hyam* a73 71
4 b g Invincible Spirit(IRE) No Rehearsal (FR) (Baillamont (USA))
1286[2] 1984[6] 3498[2] 3979[2] 5280[P]
Grand Adventure (USA) *Malcolm Pierce* 113
6 bb h Grand Slam(USA) Val Marie (USA) (Coronado's Quest (USA))
7092a[9]
Grand Art (IRE) *Noel Wilson* a63 62
8 b g Raise A Grand(IRE) Mulberry River (IRE) (Bluebird (USA))
366[13] 3577[4] 5172[4] (5922) 6101[2] 6311[4] 7102[11] 7528[7]
Grand Denial (IRE) *Clive Cox* a71 74
2 b g Thousand Words The Oldladysays No (IRE) (Perugino (USA))
4846[2] 5765[5] 6444[2]
Grand Diamond (IRE) *Jim Goldie* a68 72
8 b g Grand Lodge(USA) Winona (IRE) (Alzao (USA))
3519[8] 4768[6] 5187[3] 5921[6] 6315[7]
Grande Illusion *J W Hills* a50 41
3 br g Singspiel(IRE) Larousse (Unfuwain (USA))
3431[3] 3966[12] 4536[10] 4900[7] 5240[7] 5660[9]
Grandeur (IRE) *Jeremy Noseda* 116
3 rg g Verglas(IRE) Misskinta (IRE) (Desert Sun)
1645[4] (2477) 2701[2] 3295[7] (4735) 5594[3] (6446) (7566a) 7882a[2]
Grandfathers Gift *Michael Quinn* a7 24
2 ch f Bertolini(USA) Hagley Park (Petong)
2579[8] 3150[7]
Grand Gold *Seamus Durack* a64 76
3 b g Librettist(USA) Night Symphonie (Cloudings (IRE))
803[6] 1160[6] 1319[3] 1568[4] 6118[3] 6207[2] 7195[7]
Grand Honour (IRE) *Paul Howling* a50 41
6 gr g Verglas(IRE) Rosy Dudley (IRE) (Grand Lodge (USA))
203[8] 598[5] 664[3] 823[5] 986[6] 3007[5] 3717[9] 5050[8]
Grandiloquent *Sir Michael Stoute* a82 88
3 b g Rail Link High Praise (USA) (Quest For Fame)
(1724) (2634) 5306[7] 6045[10]
Grand Jipeck (IRE) *Ian McInnes* 55
2 b g Soviet Star(USA) Inourthoughts (IRE) (Desert Style (IRE))
3436[8] 3844[6] 4545[12] 5313[3] 6952[U] 7441[2]
Grand Liaison *John Berry* 75
3 b f Sir Percy Dancinginthedark (IRE) (Fasliyev (USA))
2280[12] 2788[2] 3228[3] 4971[3] (6442) (6631) (7108)
Grandorio (IRE) *David O'Meara* a72 73
2 b g Oratorio(IRE) Grand Splendour (Shirley Heights)
4114[6] 4710[7] ◆ 5242[8] (5670) 5890[2]
Grand Piano (IRE) *Andrew Balding* a73 69
5 b g Arakan(USA) Stately Princess (Robellino (USA))
2207[5] 4812[8] 5240[10] 5983[2] 6967[8]
Grand Prix Boss (JPN) *Yoshito Yahagi* a96 119
4 b h Sakura Bakushin O(JPN) Rosy Mist (JPN) (Sunday Silence (USA))
8042a[12]
Grand Stitch (USA) *Declan Carroll* a66 64
6 b g Grand Slam(USA) Lil Sister Stich (USA) (Seattle Bound (USA))
152[6] 327[5] 497[8] 696[8] 904[8] 3462[4] 4453[11]
Grand Theft Equine *Jim Boyle* a75
4 b g Piccolo Red Storm (Dancing Spree (USA))
31[2] 301[8] 8080[2]
Grand Treasure (IRE) *G Colella* 100
2 b f Aussie Rules(USA) Lizzey Letti (Grand Lodge (USA))
6090a[2]
Grand Vent (IRE) *Saeed Bin Suroor* 112
4 b h Shirocco(GER) Housa Dancer (FR) (Fabulous Dancer (USA))
792a[7] 1144a[P]
Granell (IRE) *Brian Meehan* 80
2 ch c Excellent Art Granny Kelly (USA) (Irish River (FR))
6481[2] ◆
Gran Maestro (USA) *Ruth Carr* a77 57
3 ch g Medicean Red Slippers (USA) (Nureyev (USA))
7843[2] ◆ 7976[6] ◆
Granny Anne (IRE) *Paul D'Arcy* a63 53
4 ch m Redback Krayyalei (IRE) (Krayyan)
333[7] 453[6] 531[6] 773[7]
Granny On Fire (IRE) *Michael Mulvany* a46 53
2 bb f Trade Fair Kashra (IRE) (Dancing Dissident (USA))
1832a[8] 6550a[9]
Granston (IRE) *James Bethell* a99 94
11 gr g Revoque(IRE) Gracious Gretclo (Common Grounds)
2180[11] 2504[8] 4543[5] 5227[3] 5622[2] 6045[2] 6340[3]
Granule *Peter Chapple-Hyam* 54
2 b f Hernando(FR) Grain Only (Machiavellian (USA))
5339[7]
Grapes Hill *Mark Rimmer*
2 b f Kingsalsa(USA) Red Blossom (Green Desert (USA))
1738[5]
Graphic (IRE) *Richard Hannon* a97 94
3 ch c Excellent Art Follow My Lead (Night Shift (USA))
1645[3] 1854[5] 2819[6] 3294[12] 7010[12]
Graphic Guest *Mick Channon* 95
2 ch f Dutch Art Makara (Lion Cavern (USA))
1466[3] (2020) (2345) 3269[22] 5979[3] 6873[12]
Grassy (USA) *Martin F Jones* a105 110
6 rg h El Prado(IRE) High Savannah (Rousillon (USA))
7546a[2]
Gravie *Brian Baugh*
4 b m Firebreak Laurollie (Makbul)
1422[9] 1716[8] 2387[9]
Gravitate *John Gosden* 66
3 ch g Pivotal Spacecraft (USA) (Distant View (USA))
1261[3] 1479[4]
Gravitational (IRE) *Ed Dunlop* a70 38
2 b g Invincible Spirit(IRE) Flower Of Kent (USA) (Diesis)
4066[15] 5176[3] 6015[5] 7059[3]
Grayfriars *J R Jenkins* a35 35
4 gr g Proclamation(IRE) Hilltop (Absalom)
2971[8] 6565[8]

Graylyn Olivaa *Robert Eddery* a43 3
3 b g Cockney Rebel(IRE) Gaelic Roulette (IRE) (Turtle Island (IRE))
30[7] 2341[10] 2802[13]

Graylyn Valentino *Robin Dickin* a72 69
3 b g Primo Valentino(IRE) Rhuby River (IRE) (Bahhare (USA))
667[6] 1046[2] 1519[6] 3920[3] 4296[12] 5231[4] (5810) 6251[3] 7776[10] 8051[2] 8213[7]

Graymalkin (IRE) *M bin Shafya* a92 83
5 br g Singspiel(IRE) Pearl Grey (Gone West (USA))
618a[8]

Grayswood *William Muir* a66 22
2 gr c Dalakhani(IRE) Argent Du Bois (USA) (Silver Hawk (USA))
7067[7] 7628[5] 7868[3]

Great Attack (USA) *Wesley A Ward* 113
5 b h Greatness(USA) Cat Attack (USA) (Storm Cat (USA))
7571a[5]

Great Charm (IRE) *Sheena West* a60 71
7 b g Orpen(USA) Briery (IRE) (Salse (USA))
2758[3] 3226[11] 3541[9] 5893[6] 6145[11] 6811[9] 7960[12] 8062[5] 8180[13] 8298[7]

Great Crested (IRE) *Murty McGrath* a47
2 bg c Clodovil(IRE) Roskeen (IRE) (Grand Lodge (USA))
6772[6] 7192[6] 7806[9]

Great Demeanor (USA) *David Elsworth* a73 30
2 b g Bernstein(USA) Hangin Withmy Buds (USA) (Roar (USA))
7517[9] 7807[2] 8033[6]

Greatest (FR) *Sir Michael Stoute* a69 73
3 b c Anabaa(USA) Golden Life (USA) (Coronado's Quest (USA))
2280[13]

Greatest Dancer (IRE) *Jamie Osborne* a80 61
3 b f Iffraaj Seasonal Style (IRE) (Generous (IRE))
3071[8] 3736[12] 4232[5] 4914[11]

Great Expectations *J R Jenkins* a76 80
4 b g Storming Home Fresh Fruit Daily (Reprimand)
812[6] 1354[5] ◆ 2274[2] 3105[3] 3790[13] 5214[5] 7328[7] 7684[2]

Great Hall *Brian Meehan* 54
2 b c Halling(USA) L'Affaire Monique (Machiavellian (USA))
6371[7]

Great Heavens *John Gosden* 118
3 b f Galileo(IRE) Magnificient Style (USA) (Silver Hawk (USA))
(2008) (3069) (3856) ◆ (4378a) 6912a[6] 7237[4]

Great Hot (BRZ) *A C Avila* a107 98
4 bb m Orientate(USA) That's Hot (USA) (Seeking The Gold (USA))
7569a[9]

Great Huzzar (IRE) *T Stack* 96
4 b g Danehill Dancer(IRE) Labrusca (Grand Lodge (USA))
1040a[9] (Dead)

Great Mills (USA) *Steven Asmussen* 114
4 bb h War Front(USA) Oriental Glitter (USA) (Glitterman (USA))
7571a[4]

Great Nicanor (IRE) *Ian Semple* a63 49
3 b g Bertolini(USA) No More Maybes (IRE) (Swain (IRE))
2036[7] 2540[12] 3032[8] 3456[12] 4394[3] 5014[11]

Great Ormond (IRE) *David Simcock* a51
2 b g Zamindar(USA) Paint The Town (IRE) (Sadler's Wells (USA))
6644[9] 7323[11] 7706[10] 8112[2]

Great Run *Richard Hannon* a81 72
2 ch c Compton Place Hasten (USA) (Lear Fan (USA))
3191[6] 4290[2] (4463)

Great Shot *Sylvester Kirk* a82 79
4 b g Marju(IRE) Highland Shot (Selkirk (USA))
1342[3] (1752) 2510[4] 3226[4] 3963[2] 4317[4] ◆ 4939[8] 5906[6] 6171[2] 6539[8]

Great Timing (USA) *Mahmood Al Zarooni* 82
2 ch f Raven's Pass(USA) Rumors Are Flying (USA) (Kris S (USA))
5902[4] ◆ (6489)

Great Wisdom (IRE) *Lucinda Russell* a71 32
6 b g Rock Of Gibraltar(IRE) Sudden Hope (FR) (Darshaan)
3116[10]

Greatwood *Luca Cumani* a77 83
2 b c Manduro(GER) Gaze (Galileo (IRE))
6114[2] ◆ 6795[3] (7324)

Grecian Goddess (IRE) *John Ryan* a53 50
4 b m Kris Kin(USA) Grecian Air (FR) (King's Best (USA))
105[4] 265[4] 389[5] 530[9] 602[6] 924[10] 5974[13] 6769[10] 6976[10]

Greek Goddess (IRE) *A P O'Brien* 84
2 b f Galileo(IRE) Beauty Bright (IRE) (Danehill (USA))
6266a[6]

Greek Islands (IRE) *Ed de Giles* a70 63
4 b g Oasis Dream Serisia (FR) (Exit To Nowhere (USA))
2043[8] 2399[11] 4469[13] 5244[2] 5750[11] 6157[4] 7351[8] 7794[13] 8205[3]

Greek Music *John Bridger* 25
3 gr f Librettist(USA) Silver Spell (Aragon)
7499[11]

Greek War (IRE) *Mahmood Al Zarooni* 95
3 ch g Monsun(GER) Gonfilia (GER) (Big Shuffle (USA))
(3594) ◆ 4009[13]

Greek Wedding (IRE) *Petr Juranek* 90
5 b m Arch(USA) Greek Myth (IRE) (Sadler's Wells (USA))
1901a[7]

Greeley House *Chris Wall* a62 57
4 b g Mr Greeley(USA) Sauvage (FR) (Sri Pekan (USA))
2233[13] 3081[9] 5052[5] ◆ 6174[5] 7251[5]

Greeleys Love (USA) *Kevin Ryan* 78
2 ch c Mr Greeley(USA) Aunt Winnie (IRE) (Deputy Minister (CAN))
4387[3] ◆ 5083[9] 5562[5] (6337) ◆

Green Beret (IRE) *A Al Raihe* a100 100
6 b g Fayruz Grandel (Owington)
50a[5] ◆ 141a[8] 419a[7] 589a[3] 681a[6] 874a[9]

Green Daisy (FR) *J Heloury* a86 86
2 ch f Green Tune(USA) Daisycutter (Zafonic (USA))
6225a[6]

Green Destiny (IRE) *A Savujev* a65 121
5 b g Marju(IRE) Mubkera (IRE) (Nashwan (USA))
878a[14] 1148a[11] 5613a[9] 6898a[8]

Green Earth (IRE) *Pat Phelan* a69 71
5 b g Cape Cross(IRE) Inchyre (Shirley Heights)
87[11] 224[8] 570[11] 4939[11] 5349[9] 5996[4] 6773[3] 7964[4] 8051[11]

Greenery (IRE) *Roger Charlton* a74 62
2 b f Green Desert(USA) Go Between (Daggers Drawn (USA))
5357[7] 6282[4] 6787[7] (7930)

Greenfordgirl (IRE) *John Weymes* a21
2 b f Diamond Green(FR) Cappadoce (IRE) (General Monash (USA))
7021[8] 7357[9] 7460[10]

Greenhead High *David Nicholls* a77 63
4 b g Statue Of Liberty(USA) Artistry (Night Shift (USA))
13[3] (139) 371[2] (718) 942[2] 997[10] 1224[6] 1526[11] 1601[3] 2878[6] 4592[7] 5245[8] 7446[4] 7716[5] 7775[4] ◆ 7863[3] 7969[2] ◆ 8144[4] 8285[5]

Green Howard *Robin Bastiman* 92
4 ch g Bahamian Bounty Dash Of Lime (Bold Edge)
(1951) ◆ 3128[3] 3812[2] 5057[4] (5634) 7097[5]

Green Legacy (USA) *Amanda Perrett* a61 24
3 ch g Discreet Cat(USA) Mira Costa (USA) (Thunder Gulch (USA))
132[2] 255[7] 1062[3] 2850[9] 3483[12] 4870[9]

Green Medi (FR) *Y Durepaire* a87 57
2 b c Medecis Greenside (FR) (King Charlemagne (USA))
5698a[6]

Greenmeetic (IRE) *Frank Sheridan* a28
5 b m Black Sam Bellamy(IRE) Asura (GER) (Surumu (GER))
1361[7]

Green Mitas (ITY) *Frank Sheridan* a69 63
3 ch c Denon(USA) Sequita (GER) (Lomitas)
724[5] 943[5] 1340[2] 1589[3] 2258[8] 2860[8] 3558[3] 4082[7] 4961[4] 5805[3] 6057[2] 6502[12] 6827[2] 7654[2] 7776[2] 8114[8] 8271[9]

Green Monkey *James Fanshawe* a22
2 b g Green Desert(USA) Firenze (Efisio)
7006[9]

Green Moon (IRE) *Robert Hickmott* 117
5 b h Montjeu(IRE) Green Noon (FR) (Green Tune (USA))
7426a[7] (7621a)

Green Mountain (IRE) *Philip McBride* a48 48
3 b f Diamond Green(FR) Mountain Dancer (IRE) (Rainbow Quest (USA))
2582[2] 3052[3] 3315[9] 4198[12] 4705[3] 5459[6] 5994[3] 6362[2] 6563[4] 7061[5] 7465[P] 7615[7] 7703[12] 7804[4]

Green Nashwan *B Grizzetti* 70
2 b f Green Desert(USA) Fair Nashwan (Nashwan (USA))
6725a[6]

Green Park (IRE) *Declan Carroll* a99 86
9 b g Shinko Forest(IRE) Danccini (IRE) (Dancing Dissident (USA))
1643[10] 1868[10] 2092[2] (2475) 2876[3] 3169[2] 3255[3] 3336[6] 3557[5] 3608[2] 4312[4] 4554[8] 4829[5] 4999[5] 5674[4] 6009[2] 6234[9] 6338[6] 6465[6] 6663[2] 6999[6] 7097[2] 7453[2]

Green Pearl (IRE) *Ralph Beckett* a69 31
4 b g Green Desert(USA) Kinnaird (IRE) (Dr Devious (IRE))
198[9] 1895[10] 2385[9] 4602[11]

Greensward *Mike Murphy* a99 95
6 b g Green Desert(USA) Frizzante (Efisio)
254[6] 962[11] 1373[12] 2489[3] 4609[6] 5342[11]

Green To Gold (IRE) *Don Cantillon* a70 68
7 gr g Daylami(IRE) Alonsa (IRE) (Trempolino (USA))
(4004) 5891[4]

Green Wadi *Gary Moore* a82 74
7 b g Dansili Peryllys (Warning)
36[8]

Green Warrior *Richard Guest* a54 68
4 b g Invincible Spirit(IRE) Starlit Sky (Galileo (IRE))
313[7] 467[11] 691[10] 1169[8] 1242[10] 1881[13] 2749[6] 3546[3] 4452[4] 4717[13] 5590[15]

Green Wave (ITY) *Frank Sheridan* a38
3 b f Sulamani(IRE) Sopran Danys (IRE) (Dancing Dissident (USA))
2133[7] 2861[7] 3235[9]

Gregorian (IRE) *John Gosden* 116
3 b c Clodovil(IRE) Three Days In May (Cadeaux Genereux)
(1500) 2110a[5] 2743a[18] 3239[3] 3681a[2] 4760[14] (6513) 7107[2]

Grenane (IRE) *Mrs A Malzard* a63 62
9 b g Princely Heir(IRE) Another Rainbow (IRE) (Rainbows For Life (CAN))
2117a[2]

Grendisar (IRE) *Marco Botti* a67 58
2 b c Invincible Spirit(IRE) Remarkable Story (Mark Of Esteem (IRE))
6876[8] 7205[5] 7868[7] 8032[2]

Grethel (IRE) *Alan Berry* a35 54
8 b m Fruits Of Love(USA) Stay Sharpe (USA) (Sharpen Up)
3988[13] 4869[10]

Grey Blue (IRE) *Mark Johnston* a71 84
2 gr g Verglas(IRE) Zut Alors (IRE) (Pivotal)
4724[6] 5162[2] (5619) 6162[20] 6972[8]

Grey Command (USA) *Mel Brittain* a73 73
7 gr g Daylami(IRE) Shmoose (IRE) (Caerleon (USA))
1382[10] 1525[5] 1822[11] 3129[7] 3253[6] 3437[8]

Grey Danube (IRE) *D J Bunyan* a83 57
3 gr g Verglas(IRE) Redrightreturning (Diktat)
7390a[12]

Grey Destiny *Mel Brittain* 14
2 gr g Desideratum Mother Corrigan (IRE) (Paris House)
3123[11] 3844[7] 4612[9]

Greyemkay *Richard Price* a49 55
4 gr g Fair Mix(IRE) Magic Orb (Primo Dominie)
1910[12] 2760[3] 3098[7] 4236[4] 4993[3] 5660[2] (5874) 6456[8] 6967[9]

Greyfriarschorista *Richard Guest* a88 76
5 ch g King's Best(USA) Misty Heights (Fasliyev (USA))
354[5] 674[3] 846[5] (999) 1161[21] 1436[9] (1530)

Greyhope *Lucinda Russell* 64
3 gr g Pastoral Pursuits Espana (Hernando (FR))
1223[3] 2671[4] 3212[8]

Greylami (IRE) *Clive Cox* a98 92
7 gr g Daylami(IRE) Silent Crystal (USA) (Diesis)
2346[9] 3121[5] 4578[6] 7825[6]

Grey Mirage *Marco Botti* a91 92
3 b g Oasis Dream Grey Way (USA) (Cozzene (USA))
(1086) ◆ (1645) ◆ 2916[10] 3563[5] 7751[3] 8095[6] (8296)

Grey Perle (FR) *J Heloury* 96
2 gr f Medecis Perle Pale (FR) (Lost World (IRE))
4615a[4]

Grey Poppett *Chris Dwyer*
2 gr f Paris House Maraffi (IRE) (Halling (USA))
7553[10]

Grey Seal (IRE) *James Fanshawe* a79 64
3 gr f Cape Cross(IRE) Mundus Novus (USA) (Unbridled's Song (USA))
1736[3] ◆ 2542[4] (3454) ◆ 3976[4] 4996[7] 5942[4] 6613[2]

Grey Street *Richard Fahey* 75
2 rg f Royal Applause Good Enough (FR) (Mukaddamah (USA))
2917[11] (5367) 6032[7] 6920[9]

Grievous Angel (IRE) *Ann Duffield* a66 73
2 b f Amadeus Wolf Mannsara (IRE) (Royal Academy (USA))
3110[5] 3490[5] 3909[5] 4448[2] 4952[2] 5423[2] (5799) 6070[6] 6475[7] 6612[3] 7028[6]

Griffin Point (IRE) *William Muir* a71 68
5 b m Tagula(IRE) Lady Corduff (IRE) (Titus Livius (FR))
277[5] 456[4] 1934[9] 2377[10] 2943[13] 3701[7] 4059[2] 4422[2] 4758[2] (4902) 5504[2] 5876[2] 6178[3] 6926[2] 7178[4] 7970[2]

Grigorovitch (IRE) *Liam McAteer* a52 71
10 b g Fasliyev(USA) Hasty Words (IRE) (Polish Patriot (USA))
335a[9]

Grilletto (USA) *James Tate* a69 60
2 b c Exchange Rate(USA) Casuarina (USA) (Menifee (USA))
4066[13] 4917[3] 5407[6] 6332[3] (7059)

Grippa *David Brown* a24 53
3 ch g Avonbridge Easy Mover (IRE) (Bluebird (USA))
1989[8]

Griraz (FR) *P Sogorb* a81 111
7 gr g Nombre Premier Niraz (FR) (Nikos)
7320a[4]

Gris Caro *F Rossi* 107
3 ch c With Approval(CAN) Aviane (GER) (Winged Love (IRE))
7234a[7]

Gris De Reve (FR) *J-P Gauvin* 109
3 gr g Slickly(FR) Oa Chereve (FR) (Kaldounevees (FR))
5250a[6] 6508a[4]

Griselda (IRE) *P F McEnery* a26 26
2 ch f Windsor Knot(IRE) Stoneware (Bigstone (IRE))
6853a[12]

Grissom (IRE) *Tim Easterby* 98
6 b g Desert Prince(IRE) Misty Peak (IRE) (Sri Pekan (USA))
1558[11] 2025[2] 2472[5] 2919[5] 3624[11] (4086) 4611[19] 4802[14] 5370[11] 5827[9] 6466[12] 7366[11] 7691[3]

Gritstone *Richard Fahey* a87 78
5 b g Dansili Cape Trafalgar (IRE) (Cape Cross (IRE))
584[6] 907[4] 1133[9] 1914[11] 2491[3]

Grizzle *Mahmood Al Zarooni* a85 87
3 b c Shamardal(USA) Pearl Grey (Gone West (USA))
1264[2] 2182[17] 3063[6] 4949[3] 5752[11] 5888[6]

Groove On (IRE) *Marco Botti* a66
2 ch c Iffraaj Dance On (Caerleon (USA))
7807[4] 8006[3] ◆ 8165[4]

Ground To Garden *Gay Kelleway* 20
2 b f Muhtathir Tatbeeq (IRE) (Invincible Spirit (IRE))
3084[6] 3224[9]

Groupie Doll (USA) *William Bradley* a123 101
4 ch m Bowman's Band(USA) Deputy Doll (USA) (Silver Deputy (CAN))
(7569a)

Grudge *Conor Dore* a78 80
7 b g Timeless Times(USA) Envy (IRE) (Paris House)
24[9] 133[6] 277[7]

Grumeti *Alan King* 98
4 b g Sakhee(USA) Tetravella (IRE) (Groom Dancer (USA))
(2072) 2479[2]

Guajaraz (FR) *J-C Rouget* 105
2 b c Rashbag Rahyna (USA) (Rahy (USA))
6086a[5]

Guarantee *William Haggas* 111
3 b c Authorized(IRE) Zuleika Dobson (Cadeaux Genereux)
3227[2] ◆ (3786) (4346) (5598) ◆ 6245[7]

Guarda Pampa *William Haggas* a64 55
3 b f Dansili Factice (USA) (Known Fact (USA))
2279[9] 2849[9] 7656[3] 7892[4] 8048[7] (8295)

Guardi (IRE) *Mahmood Al Zarooni* 60
3 gr g Dalakhani(IRE) Grizel (Lion Cavern (USA))
1867[6]

Guards Chapel *Gary Moore* a66 65
4 b g Motivator Intaaj (IRE) (Machiavellian (USA))
58[4] (221)

Guava *Shaun Harris* a69 68
3 b f Kyllachy Spunger (Fraam)
1419[6] 1531[7] 3285[6] 3694[10] 6152[12] 7201[8] 7615[6] 7798[7] 7921[3] 8048[4] 8229[10] 8241[2] 8288[5]

Gucci D'Oro (USA) *David Simcock* a61 54
3 bb c Medaglia d'Oro(USA) Ninette (USA) (Alleged (USA))
2197[10] 5037[9] 5265[7] 5744[2] 6399[4]

Guess Who (IRE) *Peter McCreery* a53 55
4 b m High Chaparral(IRE) Beau Cheval (IRE) (Spectrum (IRE))
4989[4]

Guest Book (IRE) *Michael Scudamore* a76 94
5 b g Green Desert(USA) Your Welcome (Darshaan)
36[10] 391[8] 626[12] 1116[4] 3039[2] 4872[2]

Guest Of Honour (IRE) *Marco Botti* a91 50
3 b c Cape Cross(IRE) Risera (IRE) (Royal Academy (USA))
6397[4] 6925[5] (7782) (8181)

Guga (IRE) *John Mackie* a50 65
6 b g Rock Of Gibraltar(IRE) Attitre (FR) (Mtoto)
1339[4] 1718[6] 2454[4] 2669[4] 4156[7]

Guilded Spirit *Stuart Kittow* 65
2 b c Ishiguru(USA) Soft Touch (IRE) (Petorius)
6795[13] 7492[3]

Guilded Warrior *Paddy Butler* a54 87
9 b g Mujahid(USA) Pearly River (Elegant Air)
2043[10] 2498[11] 3000[5] 3723[9] 4865[15] 4987[7] 6252[14]

Guiletta (IRE) *John Flint* a54 72
3 gr f Dalakhani(IRE) Guilia (Galileo (IRE))
84[11] 1923[11] 2891[5] (3847) ◆ 4781[6] 5533[6] (7129) 7688[10]

Guilietta Girl (IRE) *David Evans* a41
3 br f Kodiac Dark Arts (USA) (Royal Anthem (USA))
7903[6] 7952[7]

Guinevilla (FR) *L A Urbano-Grajales* a59
2 b c Dubai Destination(USA) Helenjeu (Montjeu (IRE))
7683a[10]

Gulf Coast *Tim Walford* a65 57
7 ch g Dubai Destination(USA) Lloc (Absalom)
3753[3] 4179[12] 4455[10] 5253[7] 5683[10]

Gulf Of Naples (IRE) *Mark Johnston* a101 116
4 gr g Dubawi(IRE) Kapria (FR) (Simon Du Desert (FR))
1214[2] ◆ (1672) ◆ 1974[3] 2506[3] 3293[4] 3625[11] 4634a[7]

Gulf Storm (IRE) *Bryan Smart* a50 60
3 b g Pivotal Beyrouth (USA) (Alleged (USA))
112[6] 1918[2] 3257[8] 5803[5] 6660[3] 7058[11]

Gull Rock *Henry Candy* a59 77
3 b f Ishiguru(USA) Petrovna (IRE) (Petardia)
1705[5] 6254[2] (6565) (6961) 7273[2]

Gulsary (IRE) *C Aubert* a80 99
3 ch f Galileo(IRE) Multimara (USA) (Arctic Tern (USA))
2741a[5] 6911a[9]

Gumnd (IRE) *Chris Grant* a82 50
5 b g Selkirk(USA) Surval (IRE) (Sadler's Wells (USA))
3752[8] 4455[11] 5824[9] 6309[6]

Gung Ho Jack *John Best* a75 82
3 b g Moss Vale(IRE) Bijan (IRE) (Mukaddamah (USA))
1457[14] 3445[8] 4412[5] 4919[6] 6256[14] 6488[15] 6825[7] (7589) (7864) ◆ 8058[5]

Gunner Lindley (IRE) *Reginald Roberts* 98
5 ch g Medicean Lasso (Indian Ridge)
3647a[3]

Gunner Will (IRE) *Jamie Osborne* a76 80
3 b g Le Vie Dei Colori Ros The Boss (IRE) (Danehill (USA))
1427[2] 2626[4] 3001[5] 3736[3] 4582[2] 4874[4] 6141[16] 6502[10] 7221[2] 7499[4] 8213[9]

Gunning For Glory *Martin Bosley* a53
2 b g Indesatchel(IRE) Today's The Day (Alhaarth (IRE))
8178[6]

Guns At Five (NZ) *Peter G Moody* 102
5 br g Duelled(AUS) Accidentallyinlove (NZ) (Cape Cross (IRE))
7073a[15]

Gunslinger (FR) *Michael Scudamore* a77 88
7 b g High Chaparral(IRE) Gamine (IRE) (High Estate)
2447[9] 3187[9] 3997[LFT] 4543[RR]

Guru Baby *John E Long* a57
2 b f Ishiguru(USA) Lefty's Dollbaby (USA) (Brocco (USA))
7078[12] 7813[11] 8166[3]

Gusto *Richard Hannon* a112 108
3 b c Oasis Dream Pickle (Piccolo)
(1032) (1426a) (1751)

Guyana Star Dweej (USA) *Doodnauth Shivmangal* a90
3 ch c Eddington(USA) Special Feeling (USA) (Pine Bluff (USA))
2954a[P]

Guy De Normandie (FR) *F Chappet* a79 82
5 b g Diktat Grouper (USA) (Gone West (USA))
7551a[7]

Gwenelda *Andrew Balding* 63
3 b f Rock Of Gibraltar(IRE) Cherokee Stream (IRE) (Indian Ridge)
6736[8] 7112[5]

Gwilym (GER) *Tony Newcombe* a76 62
9 b g Agnes World(USA) Glady Rose (GER) (Surumu (GER))
5191[10] 5937[11] 6321[12]

Gworn *Ed Dunlop* a81 66
2 b c Aussie Rules(USA) Crochet (IRE) (Mark Of Esteem (IRE))
2550[5] 3074[5] 7306[3] (7779) ◆

Gypsy Jazz (IRE) *Ann Stokell* a49 47
5 b m Antonius Pius(USA) Dawn's Folly (IRE) (Bluebird (USA))
2551[9] 2939[4] 4143[8]

Gypsy Rider *Bryn Palling* a57 61
3 b g Ishiguru(USA) Spaniola (IRE) (Desert King (IRE))
2367[14] 3489[5] 4734[4] 5263[8] (6002) 7378[2] 7616[8] 7747[10]

Haadeeth *David Evans* a82 83
5 b g Oasis Dream Musical Key (Key Of Luck (USA))
282[2] 388[4] (526) 710[11] 1007[2] (1204) 1602[12] 2289[12] 2596[6] 2731[4] 3570[4] 3919[4] 4317[24] 4602[13] 4814[10] 5120[9] 5774[5] 5853[2] 6150[4] 6194[6] 7995[5] 8144[8] 8246[4]

Haafaguinea *Clive Cox* a86 90
2 ch c Haafhd Ha'Penny Beacon (Erhaab (USA))
(4873) 6162[3] ◆

Haaf A Sixpence *Ralph Beckett* a86
3 b g Haafhd Melody Maker (Diktat)
(1392) 1894[U] 7966[3]

Haafhd Decent (IRE) *Dai Williams* a47 38
4 ch m Haafhd Idolize (Polish Precedent (USA))
1343[10] 1497[14] 1910[10] 3102[5]

Haafhd Handsome *Richard Hannon* a70 73
3 ch c Haafhd Lines Of Beauty (USA) (Line In The Sand (USA))
32[3] 209[4] 397[2] 518[P] (Dead)

Haaf'n Haaf *Michael Easterby* 11
2 ch g Haafhd Sweet Ludy (IRE) (Be My Guest (USA))
3126[12] 4677[9] 6356[11] 6558[8]

Haajes *Paul Midgley* a76 88
8 ch g Indian Ridge Imelda (USA) (Manila (USA))
835[5] 1236[3] 1642[8] 2195[14] 3127[6] 3496[2] ◆ 3612[4] 3903[2] 4292[4] 4924[7] 5412[2] (5758) 6144[6] 6525[5] 6938[5] 7295[7] 7489[3] 7726[11]

Haamaat (IRE) *William Haggas* a95 94
4 b m Shamardal(USA) Exultate Jubilate (USA) (With Approval (CAN))
(806) ◆ 1066[3] (1926) 2713[4] ◆ 4609[11] 5385[12] 6201[10] 6602[4] (7508) 7817[3]

Haarmonic *Richard Whitaker*
2 ch g Haafhd Abundant (Zafonic (USA))
6556[9] 7686[14]

Haatefina *Mark Usher* 70
2 b f Haatef(USA) Felona (Caerleon (USA))
3009[5] 3473[3] (4222) 4847[7] 6815[8] 7079[8]

Haatheq (USA) *A Al Raihe* a111 99
5 b h Seeking The Gold(USA) Alshadiyah (USA) (Danzig (USA))
488a[2] 878a[7] 1143a[5]

Habeshia *John Best* a72
2 ch c Muhtathir Lumiere Rouge (FR) (Indian Ridge)
7683a[9] 8176a[5]

Hab Reeh *Ruth Carr* a55 58
4 gr g Diktat Asian Love (Petong)
900[8] 1092[10] 1179[13] 1961[8] 2406[3] (2796) 3020[3] 3256[6] 5590[12] 6104[16] 6958[7] 7446[6] 7604[5] 7747[3] 7915[5] 8256[8]

Hackett (IRE) *Shaun Lycett* a64 57
4 b h Hawk Wing(USA) Khudud (Green Desert (USA))
401[9] 558[7] 1530[4] 1717[9]

Hadaj *Clive Brittain* a92 92
3 b g Green Desert(USA) My Amalie (IRE) (Galileo (IRE))
1217[3] 1860[5] 2263[4] 2477[6] 3977[7] 5102[11] 5334[9]

Hada Men (USA) *Brian Ellison* a74 46
7 b g Dynaformer(USA) Catchy (USA) (Storm Cat (USA))
(23) (111) (229)

Hadeeya *Clive Brittain* a43
2 b f Oratorio(IRE) Pivotting (Pivotal)
4463[7] 5339[13]

Hadrians Rule (IRE) *Tim Easterby* a61 64
3 b g Holy Roman Emperor(IRE) Farbenspiel (IRE) (Desert Prince (IRE))
1296[4] 1595[6] 3706[3] 5294[3] 5621[4] 6713[2] 7099[10]

Haftohaf *Marco Botti* a79
3 b c Haafhd Piper's Ash (USA) (Royal Academy (USA))
(7361) (7936) 8183[2]

Hah Hah *Scott Dixon* a36
2 ch f Milk It Mick Wittily (Whittingham (IRE))
5675[8] 6212[6] 6766[7]

Hail Bold Chief (USA) *Alan Swinbank* a55 76
5 b g Dynaformer(USA) Yanaseeni (USA) (Trempolino (USA))
1134[14] 1796[9] 2588[12] 3029[2] 3290[8]

Hail Hail (USA) *Paul Cole* a74 74
3 rg c Giant's Causeway(USA) Teammate (USA) (A.P. Indy (USA))
5482[5] 6146[9] 6924[9]

Hail Holy Queen (IRE) *J E Hammond* a89 86
4 ch m Highest Honor(FR) Gabare (FR) (Galileo (IRE))
8300a[10]

Hail Promenader (IRE) *Anthony Carson* a69 86
6 b g Acclamation Tribal Rite (Be My Native (USA))
1354[11] 1611[10] 2151[14] (2574) 3099[6] 3344[2] (3976) 4296[14] 4959[5] 5322[7] 6141[5] 6452[2]

Hail Tiberius *Tim Walford* a48 76
5 b g Iktibas Untidy Daughter (Sabrehill (USA))
634[6]

Hail To Princess *Patrick Chamings* a48
2 ch f Dr Fong(USA) Bob's Princess (Bob's Return (IRE))
7924[9] 8178[8]

Hail To The Chief (FR) *Ed Dunlop* a76 84
4 b h Shirocco(GER) Basse Besogne (IRE) (Pursuit Of Love)
6615[4] 6839[8]

Hairy Rocket *Richard Hannon* a98 95
2 b f Pivotal Asaawir (Royal Applause)
(2124) 2345[2] ◆ 3269[3] 3680a[7] (5045)

Hajam *James Tate* 104
2 b c Exceed And Excel(AUS) Saabiq (USA) (Grand Slam (USA))
2247[5] 4101[3] (5032) 5579[5] 6162[2] 6883[17]

Hajoum (IRE) *A Al Raihe* a96 86
6 b h Exceed And Excel(AUS) Blue Iris (Petong)
420a[13] 616a[6] ◆

Hajras (IRE) *Mark Johnston* a73 109
3 b g Dubai Destination(USA) Nufoos (Zafonic (USA))
(943) (1477) 2269[2] 4009[6] (4529) 5492[6] 6025[13] (6484) 7557[2]

Haka Dancer (USA) *Philip Kirby* a52 52
9 b g War Chant(USA) Safe Return (USA) (Mr Prospector (USA))
2775[6] 4350[2] 4869[5] 5054[5]

Hakuna Matata *Michael Dods* a81 78
5 b g Dubai Destination(USA) Green Song (FR) (Green Tune (USA))
1958[3] ◆ 2241[3] (2535) 2922[2] 5111[3] ◆ 5588[5] 6881[5] 7294[11]

Halesia *M Delzangles* a88
4 b m One Cool Cat(USA) Fruta Bomba (FR) (Nombre Premier)
116a[5]

Half A Billion (IRE) *Michael Dods* a84 84
3 b g Acclamation Amankila (IRE) (Revoque (IRE))
(885) 1176[2] (1798) 2416[5] 2979[3] 4081[4] 4965[2] 5736[3] 6050[6] 6811[2] (7451)

Half A Crown (IRE) *Peter Salmon* a74 74
7 b g Compton Place Penny Ha'Penny (Bishop Of Cashel)
(1526) 2096[5] 4315[7] 4495[17] 6403[5] (7447) 7666[3] 8059[4]

Half A Person (IRE) *Peter Chapple-Hyam* 95
2 b c Holy Roman Emperor(IRE) Bellagio Princess (Kris)
6114[4] ◆ (6846) 7404[4]

Halfsin (IRE) *Marco Botti* a78 105
4 b g Haafhd Firesteed (IRE) (Common Grounds)
1605[6] 2478[5] 3164[12]

Halfwaytocootehill (IRE) *Ollie Pears* 53
2 b g Duke Of Marmalade(IRE) May Kiersey (IRE) (Sadler's Wells (USA))
6880[12] 7363[7] 7598[8]

Halla San *Richard Fahey* a87 88
10 b g Halling(USA) St Radegund (Green Desert (USA))
643[2] 872[2] 971[2] 1214[3] 1672[2] 2086[4] 2709[5] 3163[11] 3458[2] 3625[10]

Hallelujah *James Fanshawe* a83 102
4 b m Avonbridge My Golly (Mozart (IRE))
2310[2] (2890) 4070[3] 6878[8]

Halling Dancer *Lee Carter* a78 81
3 b g Halling(USA) Ballet Ballon (USA) (Rahy (USA))
2021[4] 2428[7] 3071[3] 3736[5] (4288) 4727[2] 5163[5] 6932[10] 7485[14]

Halling River (IRE) *M Weiss* a57 87
5 ch g Halling(USA) Cunas (USA) (Irish River (FR))
444a[5] 630a[11]

Hallings Comet *Andrew Balding* 87
3 ch g Halling(USA) Landinium (ITY) (Lando (GER))
(3431) 4068[2] 4735[17] 5271[8]

Halling's Quest *Hughie Morrison* a96 82
3 b c Halling(USA) Capriolla (In The Wings)
1504[3] 2080[4]

Halling's Wish *John Best* a62
2 b g Halling(USA) Fair View (GER) (Dashing Blade)
7191[6] 7628[9] 8052[7] ◆

Hallmark Star *Gerard Butler* a83 88
3 b g Nayef(USA) Spring (Sadler's Wells (USA))
1160[3] 1557[2] 2287[2] 2718[12] 3605[5] 4067[4] 4649[6] 4930[4] 7352[2]

Halloween Chope (FR) *D Prod'Homme* a71 80
2 ch f Soave(GER) Halloween Star (FR) (Wagon Master (FR))
3017a[3] 8276a[5]

Hallstatt (IRE) *John Mackie* a73 76
6 ch g Halling(USA) Last Resort (Lahib (USA))
850[8] 1011[2] 1297[5] 1588[2] 2378[2] 2666[3]

Halo Dolly (USA) *Jerry Hollendorfer* a96 104
4 bb m Popular(USA) Spanish Halo (USA) (Comic Strip (USA))
6695a[8]

Hal Of A Lover *Lisa Williamson* a53 63
4 b g Halling(USA) Latent Lover (IRE) (In The Wings)
2670[10] 3277[6] 3712[13] 5022[9]

Halogen *James Given* a46
3 b g Halling(USA) Trompette (USA) (Bahri (USA))
502[5]

Halperion *David Elsworth* 54
2 ch g Halling(USA) Rainbow End (Botanic (USA))
6872[12] 7333[8]

Hamamba (USA) *Mme J Bidgood* a52
3 b f Black Mambo(USA) Halo Of Truth (USA) (Nelson (USA))
5473a[0]

Haman (CAN) *Mahmood Al Zarooni* 72
4 bb h Street Cry(IRE) Penny Perfect (CAN) (Alydeed (CAN))
1866[11]

Hamatan (FR) *J E Hammond* a83 73
2 b c Linngari(IRE) Misty Blue (FR) (Poliglote)
8176a[6]

Hamazing Destiny (USA) *D Wayne Lukas* a111
6 b h Salt Lake(USA) Ms Proud Destiny (USA) (Artax (USA))
7574a[10]

Hambleton *Bryan Smart* a53 58
5 b g Monsieur Bond(IRE) Only Yours (Aragon)
155[6] 544[6] 740[4] 910[2] 1343[6] 1881[12] 4865[10]

Hamilton Hill *Dai Burchell* a51 76
5 b g Groom Dancer(USA) Loriner's Lass (Saddlers' Hall (IRE))
968[8] 1908[3] 2389[2] 2502[6] ◆ (3101) 3187[8] 3429[2] 4184[4] 4531[12] (4843) 4988[3] 5151[6] 5359[8]

Hamis Al Bin (IRE) *Mark Johnston* a81 70
3 b g Acclamation Paimpolaise (IRE) (Priolo (USA))
903[2] (1001) 2150[9] 3274[9] 6013[6] 6401[12] 7027[13]

Hamish McGonagall *Tim Easterby* 117
7 b g Namid Anatase (Danehill (USA))
(1219) 1857[10] 2745a[3] 3238[14] (4113) 4762[15] 5561[3] 6908a[3]

Hamla *Saeed Bin Suroor* a30
2 b f Cape Cross(IRE) High Days (IRE) (Hennessy (USA))
7160[13]

Hammerfest *J E Hammond* a88 105
5 b g Fantastic Light(USA) Bathilde (IRE) (Generous (IRE))
3372[2] 5600[14]

Hammer Shaft (IRE) *Amy Weaver* a48
2 b g Excellent Art Delicacy (IRE) (Danehill Dancer (IRE))
8303[5]

Hammers Terror (USA) *Michael Stidham* a102 103
3 bb c Artie Schiller(USA) Sister Baby (USA) (Lord Avie (USA))
7092a[8]

Hamoody (USA) *David Nicholls* a85 93
8 ch g Johannesburg(USA) Northern Gulch (USA) (Gulch (USA))
1168[3] 1478[14] 2674[6] 3183[8] ◆ 3608[9] 4690[11] (6005) 6234[6] 6427[14] 6465[23] 7595[6] 8036[2] 8202[3] (8285)

Hamza (IRE) *Kevin Ryan* 107
3 b g Amadeus Wolf Lady Shanghai (IRE) (Alhaarth (IRE))
1998[8] (2490) 3294[9] 4740[9] (5363) 6075[2] 6466[6]

Hanalei Bay (IRE) *Keith Dalgleish* a68
2 b c Tamayuz Genial Jenny (IRE) (Danehill (USA))
6175[3]

Hanbes (TUR) *A Sacan*
4 b h Mohan(TUR) Milagrose (TUR) (Doyoun)
5868a[2]

Handheld *Julia Feilden* a74 68
5 ch g Observatory(USA) Kid Gloves (In The Wings)
2405[10] 3045[9] 4315[5] 5941[4] 6141[3] 7141[3] 8152[5]

Hand In Glove *Robert Cowell* a68
2 ch f Kyllachy Cape Trafalgar (IRE) (Cape Cross (IRE))
8138[2] ◆

Handiwork *Michael Bell* a57
2 ch g Motivator Spinning Top (Alzao (USA))
7796[5] 7963[7]

Handles For Forks (IRE) *Mick Channon* a70 77
4 b m Hawk Wing(USA) Wood Sprite (Mister Baileys)
1085[5] (3180) 3316[3] 3769[5] 4096[5] 4756[5] 5507[6] 6019[5] 6407[12] 6802[8]

Hand Painted *Anthony Middleton* a77 68
6 b g Lend A Hand Scarlett Holly (Red Sunset)
372[12] 470[4] 781[11] 1768[10]

Hands Of Time *Richard Hannon* 72
2 b c Pivotal Virtuous (Exit To Nowhere (USA))
3067[6] 4340[4]

Handsome King *J R Jenkins* a67 65
5 ch g Lucky Story(USA) Samar Qand (Selkirk (USA))
383[3] 552[5] 833[4] (3051)

Handsome Man (IRE) *Saeed Bin Suroor* 97
3 ch g Nayef(USA) Danceabout (Shareef Dancer (USA))
1468[11] 1892[4] (2281) 3296[2] 4700[10] 5580[6] (6415) ◆

Handsome Mike (USA) *Doug O'Neill* a111 108
3 bb c Scat Daddy(USA) Classic Strike (USA) (Smart Strike (CAN))
5375a[4] 7576a[9] 7882a[10]

Handsome Molly *David Elsworth* a52
3 b f Halling(USA) However (IRE) (Hector Protector (USA))
7822[5] 8080[4]

Handsome Ransom *John Gosden* a80 78
3 b g Red Ransom(USA) Maid For The Hills (Indian Ridge)
1793[2] (2368) 3280[8] 5951[6] 6376[9]

Handsome Stranger (IRE) *David Evans* a59 65
2 ch g Tamayuz Just Special (Cadeaux Genereux)
8033[12] 8071[8] 8233[4]

Handy Chat (IRE) *Des Donovan* a57
3 b g Celtic Swing Mannequin (IRE) (In The Wings)
693[5] 1422[6] 1606[7] 1979[12]

Hanga Roa (IRE) *Gary Moore* a30 11
2 b g Hannouma(IRE) Fine And Mellow (FR) (Lando (GER))
5304[11] 5992[6] 6301[5] 7797[6] 8155[12]

Hanna (SWE) *Bent Olsen*
3 b f Academy Award(IRE) Hertha (Hernando (FR))
4359a[7]

Hannahs Turn *Chris Dwyer* a39
2 b f Dubai Destination(USA) Fontaine House (Pyramus (USA))
7926[12] 8102[7] 8185[9]

Hannibal Hayes (USA) *Jeremy Noseda* a65 67
3 ch c Elusive Quality(USA) Top Ten List (CAN) (Bold Executive (CAN))
969[9] 1843[13] 2443[5] 3118[4] 3670[5] (4467) 5157[4] 6439[8]

Hanoverian Baron *Tony Newcombe* a89 95
7 b g Green Desert(USA) Josh's Pearl (IRE) (Sadler's Wells (USA))
2479[9] 3163[19] (5816) 6197[12] 6832[5] 7689[5] 7825[4]

Hanseatic *John Gosden* a79
3 b c Galileo(IRE) Insinuate (USA) (Mr Prospector (USA))
(7647)

Hansen (USA) *Michael J Maker* a120
3 rg c Tapit(USA) Stormy Sunday (USA) (Sir Cat (USA))
1872a[9]

Hansinger (IRE) *Cathrine Erichsen* a72 96
7 b g Namid Whistfilly (First Trump)
4751a[3]

Hanzada (USA) *Ed Dunlop* a81
2 bb f Arch(USA) Chocolate Mauk (USA) (Cozzene (USA))
6017[2] ◆ 7159[3] ◆

Happy Dubai (IRE) *A Al Raihe* a108 111
5 ch h Indian Ridge Gentle Wind (USA) (Gentlemen (ARG))
50a[8] 419a[11] (589a) ◆ 681a[10] 1147a[9]

Happy Families *Heather Main* a43
2 b f Singspiel(IRE) One Of The Family (Alzao (USA))
8262[6]

Happy Sun Percy *G Doleuze* a89 83
3 ch c Sir Percy Question (USA) (Coronado's Quest (USA))
117a[3] 914a[6] 5473a[3] 6752a[9]

Happy Today (USA) *M Al Muhairi* a100 102
4 b h Gone West(USA) Shy Lady (FR) (Kaldoun (FR))
52a[10] 586a[14]

Happy Trails (AUS) *Paul Beshara* 114
5 ch g Good Journey(USA) Madame Flurry (AUS) (Perugino (USA))
7426a[10]

Happy Valley (ARG) *M F De Kock* a68 97
6 gr g Alphabet Soup(USA) Perfect Valley (BRZ) (Clackson (BRZ))
145a[10] 421a[9]

Happy Wedding (IRE) *H-A Pantall* a75 97
6 b m Green Tune(USA) Diamond White (Robellino (USA))
630a[16]

Haraqaan *Clive Brittain*
3 b f Manduro(GER) Amalie (IRE) (Fasliyev (USA))
1501[15]

Harare *Karen Tutty* a60 68
11 b g Bahhare(USA) Springs Eternal (Salse (USA))
9[4] 632[2] 976[3] 1092[5] 1580[5] (1831) (2600) 3236[7] (3277) 3752[5] 4138[2] 5199[9] 5585[3] 5824[7] 6608[4] 7495[6]

Harasiya (IRE) *John M Oxx* 104
2 br f Pivotal Hazariya (IRE) (Xaar)
(4276a) 5135a[2] 6081a[3]

Hard Core Debt *A Oliver* 81
2 b c Muhtathir Al Durrah (USA) (Darshaan)
4377a[4]

Hard Dream (IRE) *F Rohaut* 111
3 b c Oasis Dream Rose Melody (IRE) (Galileo (IRE))
(1570a) 2743a[7] 4121a[6]

Hard Road *Chris Wall* a69 66
3 b g Cape Cross(IRE) Ivy League Star (IRE) (Sadler's Wells (USA))
1567[13] 2708[6] 3697[7] 4153[7] 5938[4] (7148) (7383)

Hardrock Diamond *Ian Semple* 51
4 b g Avonbridge Clansinge (Clantime)
1383[11] 1876[6]

Hard To Resist (USA) *Peter Eurton* 97
4 b m Johannesburg(USA) Anja (USA) (Gulch (USA))
7577a[5]

Hard Yards (IRE) *A Oliver* 88
2 b c Moss Vale(IRE) Hi Katriona (IRE) (Second Empire (IRE))
2958a[3] 4377a[2]

Hardy Blue (IRE) *Jamie Osborne* a68 48
2 b f Red Clubs(IRE) Alexander Wonder (IRE) (Redback)
4462[5] 4659[3] 5046[4] 5403[2] (5807) (5940) (6212) 6611[9] (6975) (7355)

Hardy Plume *Denis Coakley* a33 56
3 ch g Manduro(GER) Macleya (GER) (Winged Love (IRE))
2014[2] ◆ 2162[11] 3142[13]

Hardy Red (IRE) *Jamie Osborne* a71 75
2 b g Mujadil(USA) Salonga (IRE) (Shinko Forest (IRE))
2164[7] 2729[2] 2970[3] 4419[6] 5475[5] (5873) 6629[3] 8096[3] 8224[5] 8258[2]

Haring (SPA) *C Boutin* a57 71
2 ch c Dyhim Diamond(IRE) Ruvuma (Buddha (USA))
3017a[5] 5073a[6] 5378a[4]

Harlestone Times (IRE) *John Dunlop* 106
5 b g Olden Times Harlestone Lady (Shaamit (IRE))
2278[2] 3372[10] 4800[4]

Harlestone Wood *John Dunlop* 84
3 b c Olden Times Harlestone Lady (Shaamit (IRE))
3349[10] 3786[2] 4741[10] 5455[4] 5982[2]

Harleys Rocket *Brendan Powell* a35 69
2 b f Proclamation(IRE) Royal Obsession (IRE) (Val Royal (FR))
2124[8] 2492[5] (3150) 3669[7] 5450[8] 5940[9] 7865[7]

Harrier Exhibition (IRE) *Seamus Fahey* a19 13
3 ch f Great Exhibition(USA) Bow Harrier (IRE) (Sri Pekan (USA))
7654[7]

Harrison George (IRE) *P J O'Gorman* a95 101
7 b g Danetime(IRE) Dry Lightning (Shareef Dancer (USA))
5065[10] 6676[17] 6979[2] 7704[6]

Harrison's Cave *A P O'Brien* a88 100
4 b h Galileo(IRE) Sitara (Salse (USA))
1974[5] 3372[3] 5600[18]

Harris Tweed *William Haggas* a106 118
5 b g Hernando(FR) Frog (Akarad (FR))
(1507) 2254[3] 4010[4] 5575[4] 6637[2] 7405[10] 7895[3]

Harrogate Fair *Michael Squance* a61 55
2 b g Trade Fair Starbeck (IRE) (Spectrum (IRE))
1886[7] 2508[7] 3733[6] ◆ 4947[5] (6850) 7298[8] (7526) 7745[6] 7930[8] 8096[2] 8293[4]

Harry Bosch *Brian Meehan* a64 74
2 b g Kyllachy Fen Guest (Woodborough (USA))
3397[4] ◆ 3824[3] 7324[7]

Harry Buckle *Philip McBride* a76 74
3 ch c Byron Native Ring (FR) (Bering)
1288[4] 1707[5] ◆ 2372[5] 2605[3] 3345[2] 6364[7] 6703[13] 7011[5] 7310[2] 7818[2] (8049)

Harry Lime *Fleur Hawes* a62 62
4 b g Cape Cross(IRE) Wiener Wald (USA) (Woodman (USA))
2467[8] 2851[11] 3392[11] 3974[5] 4196[11] 6334[9] 7472[8]

Harrys Yer Man *Mark Brisbourne* a60
8 b g Nomadic Way(USA) Barden Lady (Presidium)
(390) 453[5] 636[9] 843[7] 1425[2] 1831[12] 3236[5] 5175[5] 6174[7]

Harry Trotter (IRE) *David Marnane* a78 86
3 b g Kodiac Defined Feature (IRE) (Nabeel Dancer (USA))
4765[7] 5337[2]

Hartani (IRE) *John M Oxx* 114
3 gr c Shirocco(GER) Harsiya (IRE) (Darshaan)
(3678a) 5606a[2] 6271a[8]

Hartlebury *James Bethell* a31
2 ch g Sakhee's Secret Marakabei (Hernando (FR))
7796[6]

Hartwright *Michael Bell* a69 56
2 b g Exceed And Excel(AUS) All For Laura (Cadeaux Genereux)
4773[12] 5121[3] 5685[8] (6822)

Harvard N Yale (USA) *Jeremy Noseda* a89 94
3 ch c Smart Strike(CAN) Compete (USA) (El Prado (IRE))
5626[4] 6025[5] ◆

Harvest Mist (IRE) *Shaun Lycett* a54 54
4 ch m Captain Rio Thaw (Cadeaux Genereux)
45[7] 375[3] 578[10] 1299[9] 1423[5] 1635[4]

Harvey's Hope *Keith Reveley* 79
6 b g Sinndar(IRE) Ancara (Dancing Brave (USA))
1381[11] 2666[5] 3564[10] 5344[5] 5673[9] 6126[9]

Harwoods Star (IRE) *Amanda Perrett* 71
2 b c Danehill Dancer(IRE) Showbiz (IRE) (Sadler's Wells (USA))
6481[11] 6818[2]

Hasaad (USA) *Brian Meehan* 76
2 b c Kheleyf(USA) Maha Dubai (USA) (Kingmambo (USA))
7517[3]

Hasanan *Clive Brittain* 81
2 b f Rail Link Dance Solo (Sadler's Wells (USA))
3117[2] 3631[4] 4011[7] 4813[3]

Hasbah (IRE) *Peter Chapple-Hyam* 65
2 b f Cape Cross(IRE) Gimasha (Cadeaux Genereux)
3788[4] 4701[10]

Hasheem *Roger Varian* 69
2 ch c New Approach(IRE) Masaafat (Act One)
7332[4]

Hashegotanymoney *Michael Easterby* 43
2 ch c Sleeping Indian Summer Daze (USA) (Swain (IRE))
2138[12] 2456[6] 2880[7] 5675[9]

Hasna (FR) *P Bary* 100
3 ch f American Post Harriet (FR) (Mizoram (USA))
2532a[6]

Hasopop (IRE) *Marco Botti* a93 96
2 b g Haatef(USA) Convenience (IRE) (Ela-Mana-Mou)
2370[5] 2880[2] (3788) (4101) 5833[7] 6038[4] 7404[8]

Hassle (IRE) *Clive Cox* 77
3 b c Montjeu(IRE) Canterbury Lace (USA) (Danehill (USA))
7494[2]

Hathaway (IRE) *Mark Brisbourne* a57 59
5 ch m Redback Finty (IRE) (Entrepreneur)
105[8] 188[2] 401[7] 559[7] 773[6]

Hatha Zain (IRE) *Milton Bradley* a25 38
3 b g Bahamian Bounty Arabian Dancer (Dansili)
734[11] 840[6] 1826[9] 2166[9]

Hats Off *John Best* a55 36
2 b g Royal Applause Miriam (Forzando)
1211[8] 1847[5] 2415[10] 4220[5] 6822[10] 7808[12] 8108[3]

Hatta Stream (IRE) *Lydia Pearce* a83 70
6 b g Oasis Dream Rubies From Burma (USA) (Forty Niner (USA))
252[2] 526[3] 710[3] 883[9] 1007[3] 1289[10] 1727[2] 2070[5] 2251[4] 3103[6] 3281[12] 4708[11] 5775[5] 6002[4] 7316[5] 7741[7] 7902[5]

Haunted (USA) *Elizabeth Gray*
3 ch g
8279a[8]

Havana Beat (IRE) *Andrew Balding* 81
2 b c Teofilo(IRE) Sweet Home Alabama (IRE) (Desert Prince (IRE))
5792[2] ◆ (6371)

Havana Cooler (IRE) *Luca Cumani* 76
2 ch c Hurricane Run(IRE) Unquenchable (USA) (Kingmambo (USA))
7332[2] ◆

Havana Gold (IRE) *Richard Hannon* 107
2 b c Teofilo(IRE) Jessica's Dream (IRE) (Desert Style (IRE))
(2934) (4283) ◆ 5140a[U] (6027) (6599) 6874[2]

Havant *F Head* 106
4 b m Halling(USA) Louella (USA) (El Gran Senor (USA))
7093a[5]

Haverstock *Mark Johnston* a56 64
2 b g New Approach(IRE) Endorsement (Warning)
2550[6] 3062[6] 6164[12] 6491[10] 7059[10]

Havin' A Good Time (IRE) *Roger Varian* a83 72
3 b f Jeremy(USA) Flanders (IRE) (Common Grounds)
3312[10] (5177) 5876[4] ◆ (6439) 7179[3] (7351) 7730[5] 8009[8]

Having A Ball *Peter Cundell* a67 54
8 b g Mark Of Esteem(IRE) All Smiles (Halling (USA))
31[4] (666) 821[9] 1088[7] 1702[7] ◆ 2366[4] 5310[4] 6395[3] 6773[6] (7474) 7892[6] 8162[3]

Hawaafez *Marcus Tregoning* a78 114
4 b m Nayef(USA) Merayaat (IRE) (Darshaan)
(2267) 4738[4] (6866) 7405[9]

Hawaana (IRE) *Gay Kelleway* a76 85
7 b g Bahri(USA) Congress (IRE) (Dancing Brave (USA))
216[8] 480[6] 3995[2] 4243[4] 4983[4] 5323[4] 6141[6] 6430[3] 6735[8] 7310[3] 7511[7] 7767[2] 7893[4] 8079[3]

Hawaiian Freeze *John Stimpson* 39
3 b f Avonbridge Autumn Affair (Lugana Beach)
1337[10] 3717[10] 4734[10]

Hawaiian Storm *Mrs K Burke* a43 72
3 b f Jeremy(USA) Malahini (UAE) (Jade Robbery (USA))
(1479) 2820[8] 3252[5] 3416[9] 6785[11] 7470[9] 7602[3] 8062[8]

Hawawi *James Tate* a80 71
4 b g Motivator Abide (FR) (Pivotal)
292[2] 520[8]

Hawdyerwheesht *Jim Goldie* a76 75
4 b g Librettist(USA) Rapsgate (IRE) (Mozart (IRE))
1797[5] 2620[5] 3337[7] 3907[2] 4137[5] 4641[7] 5085[4] 5187[2] 5546[8] 5921[3] (6315) 6706[2] 6957[4]

Hawkeshead *Ian Williams* 78
5 b g Rainbow Quest(USA) Ciboure (Norwick (USA))
1662[4] 2288[3] (2877) 3494[16] 5002[2] 6834[9] 7367[14]

Hawkeyethenoo (IRE) *Jim Goldie* a48 116
6 b g Hawk Wing(USA) Stardance (USA) (Rahy (USA))
2068[11] 3371[3] ◆ 4100[5] 4321[7] ◆ (4802) 6030[11] 6468[13] 7236[2]

Hawk High (IRE) *Tim Easterby* 66
2 b g High Chaparral(IRE) Septembers Hawk (IRE) (Machiavellian (USA))
6669[4] 7033[5] 7598[2]

Hawkino (IRE) *Derek Shaw* a51 51
3 b g Hawk Wing(USA) Halicardia (Halling (USA))
3399[11] 4399[13] 5219[8] 5970[8] 6396[9]

Hawk Moth (IRE) *John Spearing* a73 70
4 b g Hawk Wing(USA) Sasimoto (USA) (Saratoga Six (USA))
(359) 639[2] 942[7] 2274[12] 3229[2] 3471[5] 3958[4] 4155[7] 4872[10] 5427[3] 5893[4] 7857[11] ◆ 8115[5]

Hawk Mountain (UAE) *John Quinn* a83 96
7 b g Halling(USA) Friendly (USA) (Lear Fan (USA))
1214[6] 1672[6] 2180[7] ◆ 4613[8]

Hawks Reef *Richard Fahey* 78
3 b g Bahamian Bounty Karisal (IRE) (Persian Bold)
1238[8]

Hawridge King *Stuart Kittow* a51 77
10 b g Erhaab(USA) Sadaka (USA) (Kingmambo (USA))
2423[8] 4606[9] 5772[6] 6802[6] 7927[11]

Hawridge Song *Rod Millman* 68
4 ch g Singspiel(IRE) Clear Vision (Observatory (USA))
2233[11] 3659[5] 4411[8] 5419[2] 5653[6]

Hawridge Star (IRE) *Stuart Kittow* a80 80
10 b g Alzao(USA) Serenity (Selkirk (USA))
1890[3] 3162[4] 4096[2] 6019[3] 7068[6] 7522[11]

Hawsies Dream *Alan Bailey* a58 34
2 ch f Dubawi(IRE) Petong's Pet (Petong)
3634[13] 4011[17] 4818[15] 5210[2]

Hayaku (USA) *Ralph Beckett* a81 78
4 b m Arch(USA) Promptly (IRE) (Lead On Time (USA))
1213[10] 2465[4] (4335) 5474[7] 6639[7]

Haya Landa (FR) *Mme L Audon* a100 111
4 b m Lando(GER) Haya Samma (IRE) (Pivotal)
1766a[2] 2570a[5] 5116a[5] 6035[7] 6912a[4] 7449a[6]

Hay Dude *Mrs K Burke* 87
2 ch c Dubawi(IRE) Inaminute (IRE) (Spectrum (IRE))
(6423) 7207[3]

Hayek *Tim Easterby* a75 81
5 b g Royal Applause Salagama (IRE) (Alzao (USA))
1251[4] 1520[7] 1659[2] 2535[5] 3460[2] (3559) 4042[3] 4295[2] (4624) 5338[2] (5713) 6047[6] 6235[6] 6630[7] 7370[5] 7639[6]

Haylaman (IRE) *David Simcock* a88 93
4 b g Diamond Green(FR) Schonbein (IRE) (Persian Heights)
2655[5] ◆ 4529[3] 5091[5] 6202[7]

Hayley *Jim Goldie* 29
2 b f Halling(USA) Gargoyle Girl (Be My Chief (USA))
6423[5] 7096[6]

Haymarket *Mark Johnston* a70 73
3 b g Singspiel(IRE) Quickstyx (Night Shift (USA))
805[2] ◆ 1031[7] 2544[4] 3722[6]

Haywain *Kevin Ryan* a29 68
3 b g Peintre Celebre(USA) Shall We Dance (Rambo Dancer (CAN))
1053[8] 1270[10] 2143[4] 2604[7]

Hayyona *Mick Channon* 59
2 b f Multiplex Shemriyna (IRE) (King Of Kings (IRE))
3504[6] 4704[4]

Hazardous (USA) *Carl O'Callaghan* a96
2 ch g Candy Ride(ARG) Malley Girl (USA) (Malek (CHI))
7545a[4]

Hazard Warning (IRE) *Tim Easterby* a49 29
2 b c Haatef(USA) Hazardous (Night Shift (USA))
4344[14] 5040[11] 6628[5] 7797[3] 8132[7] 8274[2]

Hazaz (IRE) *Clive Brittain* a76 98
3 b c Dubawi(IRE) Treble Seven (USA) (Fusaichi Pegasus (USA))
1036[2] 1453[3] 2080[8] 2485[6]

Hazel Lavery (IRE) *Charles Hills* 111
3 b f Excellent Art Reprise (Darshaan)
1887[2] 3292[8] (4338) 4738[9] 6163[2] (7405)

Hazelrigg (IRE) *Tim Easterby* a78 95
7 b g Namid Emma's Star (ITY) (Darshaan)
1438[4] 2208[9] 2289[4] 2507[10] 3127[2] 3374[2] 3903[6] (4073) 4576[18] 4924[11] 5343[15] 5487[15] 6666[13]

Hazzaat (IRE) *Roger Varian* 74
2 ch c Iffraaj Hurricane Irene (IRE) (Green Desert (USA))
4194[4] 4938[3] 5851[5]

Hazzard County (USA) *David Simcock* a99 81
8 ch g Grand Slam(USA) Sweet Lexy May (USA) (Danzig (USA))
29[3] 266[5] 431[3] 622[10] 962[6] (1181)

Hazza The Jazza *Richard Guest* a59 54
2 br g Jeremy(USA) Zagaleta (Sri Pekan (USA))
3182[14] 3611[11] 7525[9] (8274) ◆

Head Down *Martin Bosley* a13 80
6 b g Acclamation Creese (USA) (Diesis)
4158[10] 5741[12]

Headford Lady (IRE) *James Halpin* a69 88
7 b m Bold Fact(USA) Headfort Rose (IRE) (Desert Style (IRE))
5931[8]

Heading North *Richard Hannon* a78 82
2 b f Teofilo(IRE) Round The Cape (Cape Cross (IRE))
4297[3] 4739[11] 5300[2] 5902[2] (6153)

Heading To First *Paddy Butler* a47 51
5 b g Sulamani(IRE) Bahirah (Ashkalani (IRE))
125[9] 379[9] 454[3] 1624[5] 1770[2] 2395[7] 2650[4] 2998[4] 7605[8]

Headline News (IRE) *Rae Guest* a71 79
3 ch f Peintre Celebre(USA) Donnolly's Hollow (IRE) (Docksider (USA))
2927[2] 4916[2] (5913) 6492[5]

Head Office *Pat Phelan* a41
3 ch f Iceman Naomi Wildman (USA) (Kingmambo (USA))
3279[12] 3620[5]

Head Of Steam (USA) *Amanda Perrett* a96 96
5 ch g Mizzen Mast(USA) Summer Mist (USA) (Miswaki (USA))
4802[27] 5356[4] 6119[8] 7080[12] 7366[15] 7817[4] (7966)

Head Space (IRE) *Ruth Carr* a82 100
4 b g Invincible Spirit(IRE) Danzelline (Danzero (AUS))
1015[3] ◆ 1362[6] 1642[4] 2264[6] ◆ 2487[3] (2674) 3183[3] (3336) ◆ 3903[3] 4312[7] 4611[6] 4799[13] 5368[17] 5829[11]

Headstight (IRE) *Paul Midgley* a47 56
3 b f Holy Roman Emperor(IRE) Regal Star (Sadler's Wells (USA))
4174[15] 4953[4] 5621[7] 6958[4] 7204[7]

Hearduthefirsttime (IRE) *Barney Curley* a34 1
3 b g Tiger Hill(IRE) Caona (USA) (Miswaki (USA))
324 [7]

Heart Beat Song *Alan Berry* 21
4 b g Cape Cross(IRE) Polly Perkins (IRE) (Pivotal)
3580[6] 5335[9] 5734[7]

Heartbreak City (FR) *S Wattel* a66
2 b c Lando(GER) Moscow Nights (FR) (Peintre Celebre (USA))
8176a[9]

Heart Of Dubai (USA) *Micky Hammond* a69 61
7 b g Outofthebox(USA) Diablo's Blend (USA) (Diablo (USA))
2698[6]

Heartsong (IRE) *John Gallagher* a71 88
3 b f Kheleyf(USA) Semiquaver (IRE) (Mark Of Esteem (IRE))
597[4] 742[2] 897[3] (1201) (1514) 1858[9] 2347[8] 2870[5] 3486[7] 3861[3] (4221) 4765[12] 5422[3]

Heaven's Gift (GER) *S Smrczek* a65 92
4 ch m Green Tune(USA) Hokulea (GER) (Lando (GER))
15a[5]

Heaven's Guest (IRE) *Richard Fahey* 77
2 b g Dark Angel(IRE) Bakewell Tart (IRE) (Tagula (IRE))
5367[8] 6071[2] (6954)

Heavy Metal *Mark Johnston* 110
2 b c Exceed And Excel(AUS) Rock Opera (SAF) (Lecture (USA))
1131[8] (1767) ◆ (2247) 2702[2] 3240[11] 4008[7] (4736) 5559[2] 6483[5] 7049[10]

Hecton Lad (USA) *John Best* a68 52
5 bb g Posse(USA) Foxy Queen (USA) (Fit To Fight (USA))
31[11] 225[6] 287[14] 423[4]

Hector's Chance *Heather Main* a76 49
3 ch g Byron Fleur A Lay (USA) (Mr Greeley (USA))
1301[3] (1982) 2372[2] (2544) 3042[9] 4466[8] 6376[11] 6819[17] 7381[10] 7655[7]

Hector Spectre (IRE) *Nikki Evans* a68 64
6 gr g Verglas(IRE) Halicardia (Halling (USA))
6097[8] 7781[12]

Heddwyn (IRE) *Marcus Tregoning* a96 95
5 b g Bahri(USA) Penny Rouge (IRE) (Pennekamp (USA))
1510[20]

Heeraat (IRE) *William Haggas* a86 107
3 b c Dark Angel(IRE) Thawrah (IRE) (Green Desert (USA))
1457[3] ◆ 2714[6] 3396[3] 4598[3] 5080[4] (5603) (6075) ◆ 7066[5]

Heezararity *David Evans* a68 73
4 b g Librettist(USA) Extremely Rare (IRE) (Mark Of Esteem (IRE))
2043[4] 2619[2] 6458[8] 6801[U] 7115[2] 7302[3] 7640[6] 8080[3]

Hefner (IRE) *Richard Hannon* a89 92
3 b c Tagula(IRE) Classic Style (IRE) (Desert Style (IRE))
1031[3] 1473[7] (1793) 3156[3] (3767) (4287) 4735[16] 6601[10]

Heidikly (FR) *F Vermeulen* a85 85
4 gr m Slickly(FR) Hier Deja (FR) (Neverneyev (USA))
15a[2] 7123a[6] 7551a[2]

Heidi's Delight (IRE) *Ann Duffield* a56 41
3 b f Red Clubs(IRE) Alexander Confranc (IRE) (Magical Wonder (USA))
25[2] 455[4]

Height Of Summer (IRE) *Chris Wall* a79 70
4 b m Alhaarth(IRE) Summer Dreams (IRE) (Sadler's Wells (USA))
2199[7] 2637[11] 4538[11] 5159[4] 6250[7]

Heights Ridge *Tim Easterby* 29
2 b g Sleeping Indian Ellebanna (Tina's Pet)
7450[7] 7636[11]

Heintassin (FR) *Mlle B Renk* a79
2 b c Turtle Bowl(IRE) Champagnepouryoyo (USA) (Bering)
8192a[7]

Hekaayaat (USA) *Roger Varian* a73 61
2 ch f Mr Greeley(USA) Mostaqeleh (USA) (Rahy (USA))
6343[6] 7505[2]

Helamis *Stuart Williams* a48 41
2 b f Shirocco(GER) Alnoor (USA) (Danzig (USA))
4967[7] 6533[7] 6846[6]

Heliconia *Sir Mark Prescott Bt* a60 55
2 b f Hernando(FR) Flor Y Nata (USA) (Fusaichi Pegasus (USA))
3401[11] 3764[6] 4253[8] 4672[6] 5206[5] 5763[3] 6096[4] 6363[6] 6732[5]

Helicopter (USA) *Larry Rivelli* a96 94
6 b g Three Wonders(USA) Heaven's Run (USA) (Septieme Ciel (USA))
5374a[6]

Hellbender (IRE) *George Foster* a33 65
6 ch g Exceed And Excel(AUS) Desert Rose (Green Desert (USA))
1224[10] 1384[2] 1823[3] 2538[5] 2924[2] 3026[4] 3209[6] 4389[8] 5543[13] 6756[8] 6812[11]

Hello Glory *David Simcock* 95
3 b f Zamindar(USA) Affair Of State (IRE) (Tate Gallery (USA))
2255[3] 3270[9] 4062[6] 4597[8]

Hello Gorgeous *Keith Dalgleish* a28 59
2 b f Phoenix Reach(IRE) Roman Fun (IRE) (Peintre Celebre (USA))
4637[3] 7199[8] 7357[10]

Hellolini *Robin Bastiman* a12 60
2 b f Bertolini(USA) Smiddy Hill (Factual (USA))
1579[4] 2123[3] 2437[7] 3286[11] 3576[4] 5313[7]

Hello Sailor *Ralph Beckett* a53 21
2 b g Mount Nelson Fairy Queen (IRE) (Fairy King (USA))
6928[10] 7923[4]

Hello Stranger (IRE) *Tim Easterby* a71 74
3 ch c Redback Bobbydazzle (Rock Hopper)
(6100) 6788[2] 7001[3] 7291[5] 7863[4]

Helmet (AUS) *Mahmood Al Zarooni* a69 118
4 ch h Exceed And Excel(AUS) Accessories (Singspiel (IRE))
1145a[12] 3237[7]

Hendry Trigger *Milton Bradley*
3 ch g Double Trigger(IRE) Denise Best (IRE) (Goldmark (USA))
1893[12]

Henrietta Rose (USA) *Jeremy Noseda* a49 33
2 b f Henrythenavigator(USA) Shermeen (IRE) (Desert Style (IRE))
2783[10] 6579[5]

Henry Allingham *Roger Varian* a92 96
3 ch g Three Valleys(USA) Hoh Dancer (Indian Ridge)
2543[2] (2974) 3772[2] 4553[2] (5243) 5480[4] ◆ 6205[2] (6638)

Henry Bee *Richard Fahey* a74 81
3 b g Cadeaux Genereux Emerald Fire (Pivotal)
41[3] ◆ 214[2] 383[6] 605[2] 867[7] 1595[3] 1862[2] 2591[9] 2774[3] 3580[2] (3848) (4291) 4829[19]

Henry Clay *Mark Johnston* a89 95
3 b c Dubawi(IRE) Congressional (IRE) (Grand Lodge (USA))
34[2] (107) ◆ 3999[4] 4474[9] (4949) (5451) 5759[4] 6450[2] 6580[7] 6832[6] (7147) 7475[3]

Henry George *Mark Johnston* a51 15
3 b g Zamindar(USA) Melpomene (Peintre Celebre (USA))
369[11] 638[5] 1448[8] 2141[12]

Henry Holmes *Lydia Richards* a53
9 b g Josr Algarhoud(IRE) Henrietta Holmes (IRE) (Persian Bold)
129[6] 278[10] 1184[11]

Henry Morgan *Bryan Smart* 70
5 ch g Bahamian Bounty Hill Welcome (Most Welcome)
1875[9] 2538[10] 4495[6] 4954[11]

Henry San (IRE) *Alan King* a72 69
5 ch g Exceed And Excel(AUS) Esclava (USA) (Nureyev (USA))
594[2] 1505[4] 3077[4] 4061[7]

Henrys Gift (IRE) *Michael Dods* 60
4 b g Titus Livius(FR) Xania (Mujtahid (USA))
2033[5] 2669[11] 3032[10] 3889[9] 4712[7]

Henry's Hero *Chris Dwyer* a50 50
6 b g Mujahid(USA) Primavera (Anshan)
375[4] 822[4] 1447[8] 2463[6]

Hepworth *John Gosden* a67 90
3 b f Singspiel(IRE) Annalina (USA) (Cozzene (USA))
8037[2]

Herbalist *Henry Candy* 83
2 ch g Haafhd Puya (Kris)
3506[5] 4707[2] 6818[7] 7078[8]

Here Comes Jeanie *Michael Madgwick* a49 42
3 b f Act One Full English (Perugino (USA))
132[7] 660[9] 1625[9] 2628[7] 3665[5] 4650[10] 5350[3] 5974[3] 6948[4] 7499[7]

Here Comes When (IRE) *Andrew Balding* 80
2 b c Danehill Dancer(IRE) Quad's Melody (IRE) (Spinning World (USA))
(3658) 4774[4]

Hereford Boy *Dean Ivory* a79 74
8 ch g Tomba Grown At Rowan (Gabitat)
54[2] 301[3] 1626[3] 1769[3] 2399[5] 3589[12] 3976[3] 4242[6] 6801[6] 6950[6] 7302[10] 7998[9] 8105[4] 8268[7]

Here Now And Why (IRE) *Ian Semple* a66 64
5 br g Pastoral Pursuits Why Now (Dansili)
1242[6] 1881[2] 2458[3] 2839[4] 4392[4] 5190[3] 6178[5] 6314[3] 6713[6] (6937) 7673[2] ◆

Heresellie (IRE) *Michael Chapman* a64 23
4 b m Clodovil(IRE) Special Dissident (Dancing Dissident (USA))
2436[9] 3285[8]

Hermival (IRE) *M Delzangles* 116
3 b c Dubawi(IRE) Bibi Karam (IRE) (Persian Bold)
1208a[3] 1856[3] 2514a[6] 3239[2]

Hermosa Vaquera (IRE) *Peter Chapple-Hyam* 64
2 b f High Chaparral(IRE) Sundown (Polish Precedent (USA))
4739[13] 6117[8]

Hernando Torres *Michael Easterby* a53 69
4 b g Iffraaj Espana (Hernando (FR))
4844[6] 5259[5] 5416[11] 6562[2] 6631[3] 7496[7]

Her Nibbs *Micky Hammond* a32 65
3 b f Lucky Story(USA) The Pen (Lake Coniston (IRE))
1595[9] 2095[11] 4780[3] 8213[8]

Herod The Great *Alan King* 44
2 ch c Sakhee's Secret Pella (Hector Protector (USA))
6114[12]

Heroic Endeavour (IRE) *David Barron* a51 64
3 b g Ishiguru(USA) Enchantment (Compton Place)
1834a[8] (6514) 7001[8]

Heroine Chic (IRE) *Brian Ellison* a65 62
5 b m Big Bad Bob(IRE) Heroine (Sadler's Wells (USA))
4890[2] 5258[5]

Heroine Required (FR) *William Haggas* 71
2 ch f Muhtathir Tiger Mist (IRE) (Galileo (IRE))
7033[3]

Herostatus *David O'Meara* a94 91
5 ch g Dalakhani(IRE) Desired (Rainbow Quest (USA))
(2694) 3253[3] 3953[2] 4115[7] (4613) 5491[13] 6031[11] 7098[12]

Herrbuga *G Botti* a88 96
3 ch c Hernando(FR) Oblige (Robellino (USA))
2324a[5]

Herrera (IRE) *Richard Fahey* a53 67
7 b m High Chaparral(IRE) Silk (IRE) (Machiavellian (USA))
9[11]

Her Royal Empress *James Unett* a39 44
2 b f Holy Roman Emperor(IRE) Aurelia (Rainbow Quest (USA))
2193[10] 3554[6] 4704[5] 5682[8] 8230[3]

Herschel (IRE) *Gary Moore* a59 65
6 br g Dr Fong(USA) Rafting (IRE) (Darshaan)
57[3] 265[5] 519[3] 7991[11]

Her Star (USA) *P Bary* 85
2 b f Harlan's Holiday(USA) Silver Comic (USA) (Silver Hawk (USA))
4615a[6]

Hertford Street *Eric Wheeler* a45 43
4 ch g Nayef(USA) Monawara (IRE) (Namaqualand (USA))
4812[7] 5481[9] 6000[10]

Herve (IRE) *T Castanheira* a53
2 b c Excellent Art Dance Idol (Groom Dancer (USA))
8192a[8]

He's A Striker (IRE) *Tony Coyle* 76
2 b g Footstepsinthesand Aiming Upwards (Blushing Flame (USA))
4677[4] 6558[2] 6880[3]

He's Had Enough (USA) *Doug O'Neill* a114 91
2 rg c Tapit(USA) Amelia (USA) (Dixieland Band (USA))
7572a[2]

Hesione (IRE) *Mme M Bollack-Badel* a82 100
3 gr f Aussie Rules(USA) Hortanse (FR) (Linamix (FR))
6864a[3]

He'sminenotyours (USA) *S Seemar* a101
6 b g Indian Charlie(USA) Lady Of Lourdes (USA) (Dehere (USA))
586a[13]

Hesperides *Harry Dunlop* a76 76
3 ch f Halling(USA) Nando's Dream (Hernando (FR))
2497[9] 4486[2] (5477) 5855[2] 6440[3] 7927[9]

Hessonite (USA) *David Donk* 106
4 ch m Freud(USA) Lakab (USA) (Manila (USA))
6695a[5]

Hexagonal (IRE) *Adrian McGuinness* a65 96
3 b g One Cool Cat(USA) Dubai Diamond (Octagonal (NZ))
7838[9]

Heyaaraat (IRE) *Charles Hills* 63
3 b f Lawman(FR) Lanzana (IRE) (Kalanisi (IRE))
2757[5] 3340[9] 3793[8]

Hey Fiddle Fiddle (IRE) *Charles Hills* a65 61
3 b f One Cool Cat(USA) Crystal Valkyrie (IRE) (Danehill (USA))
352[2] 769[3] 2443[8] 2869[3] 3510[3] 4420[7] 7670[9]

Heyward Girl (IRE) *Robert Eddery* a71 82
3 ch f Bertolini(USA) Rancho Cucamonga (IRE) (Raphane (USA))
1457[7] 3445[P] 4765[10] 5320[9] 5662[6] 7114[13]

Hezmah *John Gosden* a101 106
4 b m Oasis Dream Bright Moll (Mind Games)
2636[2] (3049) (6602) ◆ 6878[6] 7772[3]

Hi Candy (IRE) *Ben Haslam* 41
2 b f Diamond Green(FR) Dancing Steps (Zafonic (USA))
2977[8] 3208[10] 3748[8] 6793[5]

Hi Dancer *Ben Haslam* a55 61
9 b g Medicean Sea Music (Inchinor)
1297[2] 1952[8] 3519[2] 4766[6] 5115[2] 6101[6]

Hidden Asset *Michael Appleby* 55
2 ch c Sakhee's Secret Petite Epaulette (Night Shift (USA))
4173[7] 5040[9] 7466[5]

Hidden Belief (IRE) *Ralph Beckett* a74
2 b f Holy Roman Emperor(IRE) Crossanza (IRE) (Cape Cross (IRE))
7159[2] ◆ 7506[6]

Hidden Desire *Tim Easterby* 18
2 ch f Kyllachy Where's Broughton (Cadeaux Genereux)
6627[9]

Hidden Flame (IRE) *Robert Collet* a82 110
3 ch c Barathea(IRE) Hit The Sky (IRE) (Cozzene (USA))
2743a[6]

Hidden Glory *James Given* a81 80
5 b g Mujahid(USA) Leominda (Lion Cavern (USA))
216[4] 480[3] 771[4] 849[6] 978[6] 1186[6] 1562[4] 1950[7]

Hidden Justice (IRE) *Amanda Perrett* a70 79
3 b g Lawman(FR) Uncharted Haven (Turtle Island (IRE))
2408[7] 2889[2] 3104[2] 4906[3] 5533[2] 5789[4] 6574[7] 6964[8] 7301[2]

Hidden Link *Sir Mark Prescott Bt* a54
2 b g Rail Link Gloved Hand (Royal Applause)
6609[8] 7020[8]

Hidden Talent *E J O'Neill* 82
2 b c Kyllachy Creative Mind (IRE) (Danehill Dancer (IRE))
4118a[6]

Hidden Valley *Andrew Balding* a74 75
4 b m Haafhd Spurned (USA) (Robellino (USA))
1505[9] 2174[7] 2412[7] 3572[3] 4756[6]

Hiddon Coin (IRE) *David O'Meara* 76
2 b g Red Clubs(IRE) Dianella (IRE) (Gold Away (IRE))
1861[4] (2334) 2630[3] 4116[6]

Hi Emperor (IRE) *Sean P Hennessy* a72 80
3 b g Choisir(AUS) Musthav (IRE) (Fasliyev (USA))
6716a[8]

Hierarch (IRE) *David Simcock* a72 72
5 b g Dansili Danse Classique (IRE) (Night Shift (USA))
183[2] 568[3] 760[4] 1636[3] (2652) 3344[8] 4812[6] 8047[6] 8083[2]

Higgy's Ragazzo (FR) *Roger Ingram* a43 53
5 b g Sinndar(IRE) Super Crusty (IRE) (Namid)
4983[P] 5830[9] 6170[13]

High Ball Roller *Nicky Vaughan*
4 ch g Selkirk(USA) Minerva (IRE) (Caerleon (USA))
1704[14]

Highcliffe *Martin Bosley* a55 51
4 ch m Bertolini(USA) Galapagar (USA) (Miswaki (USA))
188[9] 530[12] 666[10]

Highest Office *G M Lyons* a49 52
2 ch g Papal Bull Catspraddle (USA) (High Yield (USA))
4161a[10]

High Five Prince (IRE) *Mark Usher* a20 57
3 br g Strategic Prince Lady Georgina (Linamix (FR))
2203[6] 2786[4] 3014[6] 3938[9] 4457[4] 4900[2] 5349[8] 5770[5] 6157[5] (6304) 6568[3] 6814[8]

High Five Society *Roy Bowring* a22 79
8 b g Compton Admiral Sarah Madeline (Pelder (IRE))
3810[4] 4747[8] 5622[9] 6690[13]

High Flame (IRE) *Tim Easterby* 24
2 b f High Chaparral(IRE) Noble Flame (IRE) (Doyoun)
6880[10]

High Force (IRE) *Mahmood Al Zarooni* 30
2 ch c Street Cry(IRE) Midnight Line (USA) (Kris S (USA))
3397[8]

High Heat (IRE) *W Figge* 97
3 ch f Boreal(GER) Hold Off (IRE) (Bering)
2531a[4] 4862a[5]

High Jinx (IRE) *James Fanshawe* 112
4 b h High Chaparral(IRE) Leonara (GER) (Surumu (GER))
1654[4] (2933) ◆ 4111[2] 5599[2] ◆ 6198[2] ◆ 6914a[2]

High Jo *E Lellouche* 95
4 b g High Chaparral(IRE) Cuevas Bay (Robellino (USA))
5252a[6]

Highland Brave (IRE) *Mandy Rowland* a49 32
6 b g High Chaparral(IRE) Princessa (GER) (Dashing Blade)
6503[8]

Highland Cadett *Pam Ford* a59 38
5 ch g Putra Sandhurst(IRE) Highland Rossie (Pablond)
4994[7] 5508[11] 6280[11] 7495[11]

Highland Colori (IRE) *Andrew Balding* a81 102
4 b g Le Vie Dei Colori Emma's Star (ITY) (Darshaan)
1564[2] ◆ (1936) (2274) (2642) 4321[5] ◆ (5102) 5342[6] 6201[2] 6466[2] 7240[7] 7691[12]

Highland Duke (IRE) *Clive Cox* 80
3 b g Dansili House In Wood (FR) (Woodman (USA))
1155[10] 2553[3] 3671[3] 4289[2] (5197) ◆ 5838[9] 6450[4]

Highland Harvest *Jamie Poulton* a80 68
8 b g Averti(IRE) Bee One (IRE) (Catrail (USA))
528[9] 715[7] 1307[7] 1769[8] 2342[6] 2398[5] 3000[2] 3249[6] 4469[10] 6306[7]

Highland Knight (IRE) *Andrew Balding* a98 114
5 b g Night Shift(USA) Highland Shot (Selkirk (USA))
1212[3] 1510[15] (2657) 3640[3] (4628) 5278[3] (5782a) 6897a[5]

Highland Love *Jedd O'Keeffe* a62 59
7 b g Fruits Of Love(USA) Diabaig (Precocious)
3440[5]

Highland Warrior *Paul Midgley* a62 78
13 b g Makbul Highland Rowena (Royben)
1237[3] 1480[3] 1675[6] 2140[4] 3020[5]

Highlife Dancer *Mick Channon* a66 78
4 br g Imperial Dancer Wrong Bride (Reprimand)
971[6] 1266[4] 2051[4] 2498[9] 2792[11] 4411[11] 5197[7] (5638) ◆ 5824[2] (5936) 5990[5] 6120[5] 6478[9] 6949[3] 7474[11]

High Lightning *Mrs K Burke* a22
2 b f High Chaparral(IRE) Kyle Akin (Vettori (IRE))
8134[9]

Highly Likely (IRE) *Steve Woodman* a52 50
3 b g Elnadim(USA) Height Of Fantasy (IRE) (Shirley Heights)
1259[8] 2162[10] 2787[15] 8097[2]

Highly Skilled *Sir Henry Cecil* a51
3 b c Exceed And Excel(AUS) Mint Royale (IRE) (Cadeaux Genereux)
2041[10] 2553[11]

High Meadow Prince *Ron Barr*
3 b g Boogie Street High Meadow Girl (Pursuit Of Love)
1595[10] 2592[10] 3289[9]

High Miswaki (FR) *Jeremy Noseda*
3 b c High Chaparral(IRE) Driving Miswaki (USA) (Miswaki (USA))
3975[P]

High 'n Dry (IRE) *Roger Curtis* a59 66
8 ch m Halling(USA) Sisal (IRE) (Danehill (USA))
4817[2] 7058[12] 7960[11] 8301[2]

High Net Worth *Ed Walker* a76 43
3 b c Oasis Dream Return (USA) (Sadler's Wells (USA))
6930[6] 7996[2]

High Office *Richard Fahey* a82 96
6 b g High Chaparral(IRE) White House (Pursuit Of Love)
2253[2] 2933[3] 3625[6] 4575[5] 5491[7] 6031[9] 6472[3]

High On The Hog (IRE) *Paul Howling* a58 76
4 b g Clodovil(IRE) Maraami (Selkirk (USA))
91[8] 1626[12] 2207[12] 2637[13] 3247[11] 3964[6]

High Ransom *Micky Hammond* a72 51
5 b m Red Ransom(USA) Shortfall (Last Tycoon)
1272[11] 1559[4]

High Resolution *Linda Perratt* a59 85
5 ch g Haafhd Individual Talents (USA) (Distant View (USA))
2227[5] 2720[8] 3213[7] 3525[4] 3906[4] 4089[4] 4260[2] 4641[9] 5085[5] 5730[5] 6131[3] 6258[4] ◆ (6528) 6819[11] (7003) 7250[10]

High Samana *Seamus Mullins* a50 76
4 b g High Chaparral(IRE) Kirkby Belle (Bay Express)
2412[4]

High Standing (USA) *Jeremy Gask* a87 105
7 bb g High Yield(USA) Nena Maka (Selkirk (USA))
1129[7] 1469[7] 2472[9] 2931[4] ◆ 3371[25]

Hightail (USA) *D Wayne Lukas* a107 90
2 bb c Mineshaft(USA) Stormy Renee (USA) (Storm Cat (USA))
(7545a)

High Time Too (IRE) *Hugo Palmer* a66
2 b f High Chaparral(IRE) Dane Thyme (IRE) (Danetime (IRE))
7165[2] ◆ 7592[3]

High Troja (IRE) *Ed Dunlop* a56 70
2 b c High Chaparral(IRE) Theben (GER) (Monsun (GER))
6214[5] ◆ 6845[2] 7468[2]

High Voltage *Mrs J L Le Brocq* a51 57
11 ch g Wolfhound(USA) Real Emotion (USA) (El Prado (IRE))
232[7] 425[7] 5701a[4]

Highway (IRE) *Francisco Castro* a91 82
9 b g King's Theatre(IRE) Havinia (Habitat)
2160a[8] 3654a[6]

Highway United (IRE) *John Weymes* 10
2 ch f Arakan(USA) Luscinia (Bluebird (USA))
5586[13] 6335[12] 6954[11]

Highway Warrior *Zoe Davison* a20 54
3 b f Ishiguru(USA) Blue Topaz (IRE) (Bluebird (USA))
1053[9] 2095[13] 3389[7] 6402[8] 6930[9]

Hikma (USA) *Mark Johnston* a75 67
3 b f Street Cry(IRE) Innuendo (IRE) (Caerleon (USA))
693[2] (784) 920[4] 2448[10] 2840[5] 3575[7] 4263[8] 4771[6] (5623) 5888[5] 5989[8] 6315[U] 6843[8] 7359[12]

Hi Kort Lady (IRE) *Niall Moran* a10
5 b m Namid She's Our Lady (IRE) (Scenic)
335a[14]

Hilali (IRE) *Gary Brown* a67 80
3 b g Sakhee(USA) Mufradat (IRE) (Desert Prince (IRE))
1589[2] (3475) 4223[5]

Hilbre Court (USA) *Brian Baugh* a62 15
7 br g Doneraile Court(USA) Glasgow's Gold (USA) (Seeking The Gold (USA))
96[5] 287[8] 477[5] 676[7] 843[11] 1831[11] (1988) 2401[5] 3318[6] 4142[9] 4193[5] 4405[10]

Hillbilly Boy (IRE) *Bill Turner* a50 83
2 b g Haafhd Erreur (IRE) (Desert King (IRE))
1277[4] 1435[2] 1753[4] 1903[2] (2308) 3368[11] 4047[2] 4526[10]

Hill Of Dreams (IRE) *Dean Ivory* a63 26
3 b f Indian Danehill(IRE) Shaunas Vision (IRE) (Dolphin Street (FR))
739[3] 1046[9] 4709[10] 5229[8] 5764[10] 7527[4] 7752[2] 8050[12]

Hills Of Dakota *David Barron* 80
4 b g Sleeping Indian Pontressina (USA) (St Jovite (USA))
2841[6] 3778[6] 4133[11] 5084[6] 6260[11]

Hillstar *Sir Michael Stoute* 81
2 b c Danehill Dancer(IRE) Crystal Star (Mark Of Esteem (IRE))
5792[4] ◆ (7127) ◆

Hill Street (IRE) *John Gosden* a85 81
3 ch c Street Cry(IRE) Utrecht (Rock Of Gibraltar (IRE))
1467[3] 1923[2] (2496) 8056[8]

Hillview Boy (IRE) *Jim Goldie* a49 96
8 bb g Bishop Of Cashel Arandora Star (USA) (Sagace (FR))
1139[15] 2228[2] 3164[3] 3857[10] 4112[9] 5540[6] 7002[2] 7396[8] 7689[17]

Himalayan Peak *James Eustace* 54
2 b g Tiger Hill(IRE) Rosy Outlook (USA) (Trempolino (USA))
7468[4]

Hi Note *Sheena West* a58 68
4 b m Acclamation Top Tune (Victory Note (USA))
4004[2] (5683) (5811)

Hint Of Mint *Andrew Balding* 76
3 b g Passing Glance Juno Mint (Sula Bula)
2235[6] 2866[6] 4242[7]

Hint Of Promise *Roger Charlton* a74 58
3 b f Beat Hollow Marching West (USA) (Gone West (USA))
5795[10] 6397[5] 7025[2] (7822)

Hinton Admiral *Conor Dore* a82 82
8 b g Spectrum(IRE) Shawanni (Shareef Dancer (USA))
62[5] (146) 220[2] (388) (545) 800[2] 1005[2] 1181[2] 1727[8] 2168[6] 2940[12] 3761[6] 5892[9] 6452[10] 8159[8]

Hip Hip Hooray *Luke Dace* a74 71
6 ch m Monsieur Bond(IRE) Birthday Belle (Lycius (USA))
(31) 302[5] 746[7] 821[7] 967[2] 1207[6] 1626[2] ◆ 1772[6] 3247[3] 3774[2] (5008) 5838[5] 6275[4] 6613[12] 6981[8] 7310[13]

Hippie Chick *Bill Turner* a2 13
2 b f Sakhee's Secret Calypso Charms (Dansili)
2462[4] 5046[6]

Hippolyte (FR) *T Clout* 106
3 b g Gold Away(IRE) Standout (FR) (Robellino (USA))
2951a[7] 5649a[0]

Hippy Hippy Shake *Luca Cumani* a77 99
3 b f Danehill Dancer(IRE) Hyperspectra (Rainbow Quest (USA))
2848[2] ◆ (3663) 4608[2] ◆ 6877[9] (7334)

Hipster *Ralph Beckett* a83 84
2 b g Kingsalsa(USA) Hip (Pivotal)
2784[5] 3009[2] (3996) 5232[2] 5579[3] 6138[7] (6699) 8211[3]

Hiscano *Terry Clement* a53
4 ch h Paolini(GER) Hollywood Love (GER) (Lomitas)
65[6]

Historic Find *A Fabre* 101
3 ch c Pivotal Philae (USA) (Seeking The Gold (USA))
1408a[5]

Hitchens (IRE) *David Barron* a114 117
7 b g Acclamation Royal Fizz (IRE) (Royal Academy (USA))
244a[2] (420a) 874a[2] 1147a[4] 2513a[4] 4838[3] (5581) 6030[9]

Hi There (IRE) *Richard Fahey* a51 87
3 b g Dark Angel(IRE) Ornellaia (IRE) (Mujadil (USA))
1441[4] 1798[5] ◆ (3111) 3629[4] 4329[2] 4819[3] (5819) 6921[4]

Hitherto *David Barron* a30 61
2 b g Bertolini(USA) Princess Almora (Pivotal)
1842[7] 2594[7] 2923[6] 4139[5]

Hit It Rich (USA) *Claude McGaughey III* 110
5 rg m Smart Strike(CAN) Cuando Puede (USA) (Lord At War (ARG))
6695a[7]

Hits Only Jude (IRE) *Declan Carroll* a69 69
9 gr g Bold Fact(USA) Grey Goddess (Godswalk (USA))
1135[12] 1269[6] 1583[5] 1988[2] 2048[8] 2735[7]

Hit The Jackpot (IRE) *D K Weld* 100
3 ch g Pivotal Token Gesture (IRE) (Alzao (USA))
1404a[6] 2102a[5]

Hit The Lights (IRE) *Ollie Pears* a58 63
2 b c Lawman(FR) Dawn Chorus (IRE) (Mukaddamah (USA))
4448[4] 5410[5] 6177[8]

Hit The Note *Ann Duffield* a16 43
2 b f Indesatchel(IRE) Musical Day (Singspiel (IRE))
5255[4] 6335[6] 7379[10]

Hit The Switch *Jennie Candlish* a72 69
6 b g Reset(AUS) Scenic Venture (IRE) (Desert King (IRE))
1011[5] 1338[3] 1588[6]

Hittin'The Skids (IRE) *Kevin Ryan* a58 60
4 ch m Fruits Of Love(USA) Hush Deal (Tipsy Creek (USA))
(8257)

Hi Ya Pal (USA) *N Clement* a86
3 b c Pulpit(USA) Cloon (USA) (Lure (USA))
(1171a) 7345a[8]

Hoarding (USA) *John Gosden* 90
2 b c Elusive Quality(USA) What A Treasure (IRE) (Cadeaux Genereux)
3634[3] 4803[7] 5325[3] (5946) 6247[2] 6597[3] ◆ (7331)

Hoar Frost *Karen Tutty* a49 44
7 b m Fraam Natalie Jay (Ballacashtal (CAN))
3579[4] 4594[12] 4712[4] 4867[6] 5173[2] 5922[6] 7102[9]

Hoist (USA) *Troy Taylor* a97 83
3 ch g Mineshaft(USA) Halo Miss America (USA) (Jolie's Halo (USA))
7566a[9]

Hoist The Sail (IRE) *P Schaerer* 77
4 b g Hurricane Run(IRE) Helvellyn (USA) (Gone West (USA))
631a[2]

Holberg (UAE) *Saeed Bin Suroor* a94 117
6 b g Halling(USA) Sweet Willa (USA) (Assert)
484a[11]

Holden Eagle *Tony Newcombe* a71 72
7 b g Catcher In The Rye(IRE) Bird Of Prey (IRE) (Last Tycoon)
(767) (850) 1092[2] 1338[2] 1984[8] 2732[3] 4491[2] 6170[12] 7596[3] 7968[4] 8273[9]

Holding Fast (IRE) *Tobias B P Coles* a53 49
2 b g Balmont(USA) Eschasse (USA) (Zilzal (USA))
2873[8] 3973[7] 4404[3] 5009[6] 7714[2] 7808[3] 8132[5]

Hold On Tight (IRE) *Ralph Beckett* 76
2 ch f Hernando(FR) Wait It Out (USA) (Swain (IRE))
6489[3]

Hold The Star *Ann Stokell* a64 49
6 b m Red Ransom(USA) Sydney Star (Machiavellian (USA))
1660[3] 1825[6] 2554[5] (2865) 3230[8] 3495[8] 3940[5] 4407[7] 4656[8] 8075[5] 8168[7] 8299[8]

Hollie *Peter Makin* a57 58
4 ch m Bertolini(USA) Musical Refrain (IRE) (Dancing Dissident (USA))
203[11] 740[7] 1907[11]

Hollinger (CAN) *Roger L Attfield* a101 111
5 rg g Black Minnaloushe(USA) Dynamite Cocktail (USA) (Dynaformer (USA))
6300a[8]

Hollins *Micky Hammond* 85
8 b g Lost Soldier(USA) Cutting Reef (IRE) (Kris)
1239[10] 2214[16] 3535[4] 4925[9]

Hollowina *David Brown* 79
2 ch f Beat Hollow Trick Or Treat (Lomitas)
(6664) 7555[4]

Hollydanfaye *Paul Green* 49
2 b f Avonbridge Canina (Foxhound (USA))
2663[7] 6954[4]

Holly Martins *Hans Adielsson* a78 59
3 b g Rail Link Pretty Girl (IRE) (Polish Precedent (USA))
1304[6] 1612[6] 1892[5] 2372[4] 2860[2] 3655a[2] 4466[4] (5144a)

Hollywood All Star (IRE) *William Muir* a46 55
3 b g Kheleyf(USA) Camassina (IRE) (Taufan (USA))
2353[8] 3246[2] 3966[4] 4440[10]

Holy Angel (IRE) *Tim Easterby* a69 69
3 b g Dark Angel(IRE) Bakewell Tart (IRE) (Tagula (IRE))
2928[5] (4174) 4619[6] 4965[5] 5624[2] 6264[13] 6358[5] 7446[11] 7794[2]

Holy Dazzle *J E Pease* a85 98
2 b f Sunday Break(JPN) Belle Allure (FR) (Smadoun (FR))
6942a[3] 7622a[3]

Holy Empress (IRE) *Michael Bell* a44 35
3 b f Holy Roman Emperor(IRE) Kahira (IRE) (King's Best (USA))
132[6] 459[10]

Holyfield Warrior (IRE) *Michael Attwater* a56 46
8 b g Princely Heir(IRE) Perugino Lady (IRE) (Perugino (USA))
561[3] (822) 1009[10] 1702[11] 2366[6] 3497[11] 4584[13] 4817[10]

Holy Roman Warrior (IRE) *Kevin Ryan* a56 78
3 br g Holy Roman Emperor(IRE) Cedar Sea (IRE) (Persian Bold)
1442[5] 4498[13] 5314[5] 6429[7] 8263[6]

Holzer (SPA) *S Cerulis* 56
2 b f Clodovil(IRE) Norina (Linamix (FR))
5288a[0]

Homage (IRE) *Jeremy Noseda* a80 80
2 b c Acclamation Night Sphere (IRE) (Night Shift (USA))
5578[3] 6443[2] ◆ (7192) ◆

Homeboy (IRE) *Marcus Tregoning* a70 66
4 b g Camacho Berenica (IRE) (College Chapel)
1305[8] 1614[5] 3016[8] 3245[3] 3466[3] 3738[2] ◆ 4043[2] 4469[3] 4887[12] 5505[5] 5972[8] 6930[5] 7322[6] 7684[8] 7719[3] 7770[5]

Homecoming Queen (IRE) *A P O'Brien* a76 117
3 b f Holy Roman Emperor(IRE) Lagrion (USA) (Diesis)
1041a[9] (1403a) (1884) ◆ 2527a[4] 3328[8]

Homeric (IRE) *Ed Dunlop* a86 80
3 b g Montjeu(IRE) Al Saqiya (USA) (Woodman (USA))
6408[2] (6770) ◆

Hometown Glory *Brian Meehan* a88 78
3 b c Compton Place Pomponette (USA) (Rahy (USA))
1450[8] (1824) 2490[5] 3393[8] 5705[3] 6488[9] 6840[2] (7997) 8296[4]

Homeward Strut *Zoe Davison* a71 44
3 ch g Needwood Blade Piccante (Wolfhound (USA))
61[5] 159[9] (407) (605) 764[2] 1392[3] 1419[2] 1529[2] 1721[3] 2256[15] 2416[7] 3041[2] 8159[11]

Honest Boy *Saeed Bin Suroor*
2 bb c Dubawi(IRE) La Vinchina (GER) (Oasis Dream)
3303[9]

Honest Deal *Alan Swinbank* a80 80
4 b g Trade Fair Sincerely (Singspiel (IRE))
1879[6] 2535[13] 2926[5] (4156) (4652) 5012[2] 5430[2] 6045[8] 6608[8] 7353[4] 7792[2] 8243[8]

Honest Strike (USA) *Daniel Mark Loughnane* a57 79
5 b g Smart Strike(CAN) Honest Lady (USA) (Seattle Slew (USA))
1792[10] 6616[10] 6940[10] 7793[3] (8067)

Honey Haven (IRE) *Mark Brisbourne* a47 25
2 b f Indian Haven Condilessa (IRE) (Key Of Luck (USA))
2163[7] 7143[8] 7460[9] 7971[5] 8140[4]

Honeymead (IRE) *Richard Fahey* a83 93
4 b m Pivotal Camaret (IRE) (Danehill (USA))
1373[7] 1821[2] 2311[2] 2882[4] 3252[4] 3911[6] 5520[5] 6023[11] 6710[8] 7083[10] 7408[7]

Honeymoon Express (IRE) *Julia Feilden*
2 br f Mujadil(USA) Royal Jelly (King's Best (USA))
6431[4]

Honey Of A Kitten (USA) *David Evans* a86 92
4 b g Kitten's Joy(USA) Sweet Baby Jane (USA) (Kingmambo (USA))
90[10] 177[13] 280[12] 432[9] 538[5] 626[5] (722) 771[3] 1342[12] (2116a) 6692[6] 6895[7] 7867[5] (8010) 8114[4] 8292[2]

Hong Kong Island (IRE) *Micky Hammond* 91
5 br g Alhaarth(IRE) Three Owls (IRE) (Warning)
1880[5] 2504[6] 3163[2] 3494[10] 4543[3]

Honky Tonk Queen (USA) *John Berry* a62 55
3 bb f Mizzen Mast(USA) Khibrah (IRE) (Lahib (USA))
(8187)

Honour *Sir Michael Stoute* a82
3 b f Dansili Virtuous (Exit To Nowhere (USA))
6457[3] 7818[3] 8020[4] (8182)

Honourable Emperor (IRE) *Noel Meade* a91 98
3 b c Holy Roman Emperor(IRE) Belle Of Honour (USA) (Honour And Glory (USA))
(336a) 4692a[13] 6855a[12]

Honourable Knight (IRE) *Mark Usher* a73 67
4 b g Celtic Swing Deemeh (IRE) (Brief Truce (USA))
(296) 721[4] 992[2] 1566[6] 5816[7] 7381[4] 7839[11] 7927[2] ◆ 8073[9]

Honoured (IRE) *Michael Appleby* a71 68
5 ch g Mark Of Esteem(IRE) Traou Mad (IRE) (Barathea (IRE))
3699[2] 4179[7] (4349) 4627[2] 5199[5] 5345[3] 6120[4] 6131[11] 6891[4] 7353[2] 7496[9] (8139) 8243[5]

Honour System (IRE) *Saeed Bin Suroor* a106 102
5 ch g King's Best(USA) Rawabi (Sadler's Wells (USA))
(48a) 484a[6] 678a[3]

Hoodna (IRE) *Saeed Bin Suroor* a81 87
2 b f Invincible Spirit(IRE) Heaven's Cause (USA) (Giant's Causeway (USA))
(3959) 5828[2] 7518[3]

Hoofalong *Michael Easterby* a40 79
2 b g Pastoral Pursuits Baymist (Mind Games)
2181[7] 6556[4] 6808[8]

Hoof It *Michael Easterby* 123
5 b g Monsieur Bond(IRE) Forever Bond (Danetime (IRE))
2179[5] 3633[5]

Hooligan Sean *Henry Candy* a63 57
5 ch g Ishiguru(USA) Sheesha (USA) (Shadeed (USA))
7318[4] 7436[14]

Hoonose *Pat Eddery* a50 48
3 ch g Cadeaux Genereux Roodeye (Inchinor)
1922[14] 3630[10] 4144[7] 5215[7] 6813[6] 7496[3] 7811[9] 8001[4] 8229[13]

Hootie (IRE) *S Donohoe* a61 30
4 b g Fasliyev(USA) Soviet Maid (IRE) (Soviet Star (USA))
5430[4] 5891[8]

Hoover *Jim Boyle* a73 43
4 b g Sleeping Indian Spring Clean (FR) (Danehill (USA))
251[8] 624[4] 746[10] 1378[9] 4468[3] 5157[3] 6172[10] 8004[2] (8059)

Hopes N Dreams (IRE) *Kevin Ryan* a85 85
4 b m Elusive City(USA) Hope Of Pekan (IRE) (Sri Pekan (USA))
(2046) (2225) 2690[3] (2841) ◆ 3645a[13] 4000[7] 6009[3] 6665[4] 7145[3] 7464[4] 7646[3]

Hopes Rebellion *Declan Carroll* 59
3 b g Royal Applause Relativity (IRE) (Distant Relative)
1252[9] 1596[8] 2341[3] 2787[14] 4549[12]

Hoppy's Flyer (FR) *Paul Midgley* a60 72
4 b m Country Reel(USA) Madeleine's Blush (USA) (Rahy (USA))
1251[8] 1638[6] 2549[4] 2879[6] 4043[7] 5295[5] 6194[5] 6239[3] (6480) 6709[9] 7436[12]

Horatian (USA) *Anthony Carson* 28
4 bb h Medaglia d'Oro(USA) Swift And Classy (USA) (Clever Trick (USA))
3913[8]

Horatio Carter *David O'Meara* a67 79
7 b g Bahamian Bounty Jitterbug (IRE) (Marju (IRE))
12[3] 115[4] 3254[2] 3843[2] (3914) 4624[3] 4964[5] 5414[6] 5713[7] 6342[7] 7685[16]

Horizon Sky (IRE) *David Wachman* a88 88
2 b c Duke Of Marmalade(IRE) Mala Mala (IRE) (Brief Truce (USA))
7038a[6]

Hornboy *Jeremy Noseda* 68
2 b c Medicean Soar (Danzero (AUS))
6636[10] 7078[3]

Horsted Keynes (FR) *Roger Varian* a76
2 ch c Giant's Causeway(USA) Viking's Cove (USA) (Miswaki (USA))
7458[2] ◆ (7706)

Hot Blood (IRE) *P Schiergen* 102
4 ch m Galileo(IRE) Hold On (GER) (Surumu (GER))
2965a[3] 3652a[3] 5844a[4] 6723a[8]

Hot Cherry *H Edward Haynes* 39
8 b m Bertolini(USA) Cribella (USA) (Robellino (USA))
1105[6]

Hot Diggity (FR) *Peter Chapple-Hyam* 81
2 b c Librettist(USA) Como (USA) (Cozzene (USA))
2480[10] (3824)

Hotham *Noel Wilson* a68 86
9 b g Komaite(USA) Malcesine (IRE) (Auction Ring (USA))
64[8] 2264[12]

Hot Heart *P Leblanc* a44 33
4 b m Invincible Spirit(IRE) Sinduda (Anabaa (USA))
116a[10]

Hot Mustard *Michael Bell* a43 60
2 b g Pastoral Pursuits Lihou Island (Beveled (USA))
4149[5] 4539[8] 4845[8] 6413[6] 7223[5]

Hototo *Kevin Ryan* 103
2 ch c Sleeping Indian Harlem Dancer (Dr Devious (IRE))
1818[3] ◆ 2069[2] (2614) ◆ (3242) 4093[6] 4687[3] (5515) 6162[6] 6883[2] 7049[6]

Hot Potato *Tony Carroll*
3 b g Bold Edge Even Hotter (Desert Style (IRE))
2786[8]

Hot Rod Mamma (IRE) *Dianne Sayer* a42 96
5 ch m Traditionally(USA) Try The Air (IRE) (Foxhound (USA))
1522[10] 1865[13] 2472[7] ◆ 2752[2] 3163[17] 3522[6] 4868[2] 5369[3] 5729[6] 6135[5] 6476[5] 6710[4] ◆

Hot Secret *Andrew Balding* 74
2 b f Sakhee's Secret Harryana (Efisio)
2783[6] ◆ 3217[2] 3700[4] 4282[8] (4728) 4936[2] 5332[4] 5790[5] 6022[4]

Hot Six (BRZ) *Fabricio Borges* a102 100
7 gr h Burooj Babysix (USA) (With Approval (CAN))
591a[12]

Hot Snap *Sir Henry Cecil* a77
2 ch f Pivotal Midsummer (Kingmambo (USA))
(6366) ◆

Hot Spice *John Dunlop* 85
4 b g Kodiac Harlestone Lady (Shaamit (IRE))
1513[9] 5268[9] 5838[6] 6450[7] 6933[9]

Hot Sugar (USA) *Michael Appleby* a72 83
3 b g Lemon Drop Kid(USA) Plaisir Des Yeux (FR) (Funambule (USA))
1217[10] 2265[8] 2764[7] 4496[12] 6825[8] (8225)

Hot Tub *Christine Dunnett* a45 9
4 b g Iceman Starminda (Zamindar (USA))
109[11] 197[4] 390[13] 561[13] 829[8] 2464[10] 3051[7]

Hot Wired *S Wattel* a67
3 b f Rock Of Gibraltar(IRE) Heaven's Command (Priolo (USA))
5074a[9]

Houghton Hill (FR) *Mme C Head-Maarek*
2 ch g Green Tune(USA) Hierarchie (FR) (Sillery (USA))
5378a[U]

House Limit (IRE) *Harry Dunlop* a53 53
3 br c Red Clubs(IRE) Fritillary (Vettori (IRE))
121[6] 270[2]

House Of Mirrors (USA) *Mark Brisbourne* a54
4 b g Medaglia d'Oro(USA) Thousand Thrills (USA) (Crafty Prospector (USA))
273[7] 5335[10]

House Of Orange (IRE) *Mark Johnston* 59
2 b g Kheleyf(USA) Cox Orange (USA) (Trempolino (USA))
5439[3] 6168[4] 6947[5]

Houston Dynimo (IRE) *Nicky Richards* a76 76
7 b g Rock Of Gibraltar(IRE) Quiet Mouse (USA) (Quiet American (USA))
2454[3] (4429) 4766[4]

How About Peace (USA) *Kathleen O'Connell*
2 b g Peace Rules(USA) Chado (USA) (Montbrook (USA))
8244a[7]

Howe Great (USA) *H Graham Motion* a105 108
3 bb c Hat Trick(JPN) Ginger Sea (SAF) (Western Winter (USA))
6902a[7]

How Fortunate *David Elsworth* a66
4 b m Haafhd However (IRE) (Hector Protector (USA))
573[5] 737[4]

How's Life *Rae Guest* a71
2 b f Layman(USA) Get The Ring (FR) (Linamix (FR))
(7021)

How Sweet It Is (IRE) *James Bethell* a63 62
3 b f Kodiac Yaqootah (USA) (Gone West (USA))
214[4] 750[2] 3438[4]

Howyadoingnotsobad (IRE) *Karen George* a83 79
4 b g Kodiac Beau Petite (Kyllachy)
(1061) (1300) 1827[5] 2494[2] 3618[4] 4849[3] (5296) 6226[9]

How You Fixed (IRE) *Denis P Quinn* a32
2 b c Antonius Pius(USA) Untimely (Inchinor)
8207[7]

Hoyam *Michael Bell* 101
2 b f Royal Applause Christmas Tart (IRE) (Danetime (IRE))
2343[2] 3269[2] ◆ (3700) 4577[3] (5601) ◆ 6196[5] 6672[10]

Huacachina *D Sepulchre*
2 b f Oasis Dream Fortunate Isles (USA) (Seeking The Gold (USA))
8193a[0]

Hubood *Zoe Davison* a58 55
4 b m Refuse To Bend(IRE) Shuheb (Nashwan (USA))
273[4] 972[11] 1207[3] 1425[9] 4006[6] 5125[6] 5938[11]

Hubris (FR) *J-L Pelletan* a68
2 b c Desert Style(IRE) Codicille (FR) (Mendocino (USA))
8176a[7]

Hudson's Bay (IRE) *J S Bolger* a94
2 b c Teofilo(IRE) Cache Creek (IRE) (Marju (IRE))
7038a[3]

Huff And Puff *Amanda Perrett* a91 88
5 b g Azamour(IRE) Coyote (Indian Ridge)
3962[2] 5554[4] (6012) (6776)

Hugenot (IRE) *Tobias B P Coles* a64 58
3 ch g Choisir(AUS) All Elegance (IRE) (Key Of Luck (USA))
766[5] 982[10] 1260[5] 1725[9] 2862[5]

Hujaylea (IRE) *M Halford* a87 110
9 b g Almutawakel Red Eagle (IRE) (Eagle Eyed (USA))
53a[7] 246a[3] 416a[13] 682a[6] 1043a[5]

Hulwa (USA) *Tracy Waggott* 46
3 bb f Swain(IRE) Nadawat (USA) (Kingmambo (USA))
1250[8] 1878[9] 2288[4] 2771[4] 4399[11] 4678[3] 4826[10]

Huma Bird *H-A Pantall* 101
3 b f Invincible Spirit(IRE) Persian Secret (FR) (Persian Heights)
(1125a) 1426a[4] 2112a[4] 2745a[8] 5647a[11] 7829a[9]

Humidor (IRE) *George Baker* a91 111
5 b g Camacho Miss Indigo (Indian Ridge)
50a[3] 419a[12] 681a[9] 3877[13] 4762[6] 5561[4] 6908a[7]

Hummingbird *William Haggas* 66
3 b f Nayef(USA) Artistic Blue (USA) (Diesis)
2941[5] 3918[7] 4630[5] 5219[9]

Humungosaur *Richard Ford* a55 95
3 b c Red Ransom(USA) Fabulously Fast (USA) (Deputy Minister (CAN))
1456[9] 2269[7] 2889[5] 4151[5] 5965[2] 6660[2] 7269[11] 7954[6] 8049[5]

Hundredsnthousands (IRE) *John Quinn* 55
2 b f Thousand Words Xena (IRE) (Mull Of Kintyre (USA))
2917[8]

Hung Parliament (FR) *Tom Dascombe* a93 79
4 b g Numerous(USA) Sensational Mover (USA) (Theatrical (IRE))
1035[5] 1603[10] 2642[10] 7175[14]

Hungry Island (USA) *Claude McGaughey III* 112
4 b m More Than Ready(USA) Flying Passage (USA) (A.P. Indy (USA))
4617a[5]

Hunt A Mistress (IRE) *Paul Cole* a62 71
3 ch f Teofilo(IRE) Arctic Hunt (IRE) (Bering)
1206[3] 1502[4] 2204[6] 6279[2] 6770[7] 7310[8] 7416[9]

Hunters Bay (USA) *Reade Baker* a113 118
5 b h Ghostzapper(USA) Smok'n Frolic (USA) (Smoke Glacken (USA))
6300a[2]

Hunters Belt (IRE) *Noel Wilson* a75 54
8 b g Intikhab(USA) Three Stars (Star Appeal)
97[2] ◆ 460[2] (836) 2312[11] 3253[7] 3307[6]

Hunter's Light (IRE) *Saeed Bin Suroor* a116 116
4 ch h Dubawi(IRE) Portmanteau (Barathea (IRE))
1994[6] 2640[3] 3369[7] (5090) (5848a) 6898a[2] (7586a)

Hunterview *David Pipe* a96 43
6 ch g Reset(AUS) Mount Elbrus (Barathea (IRE))
1732[5]

Hunting Gonk *James Given* a25 69
3 b g Amadeus Wolf Para Siempre (Mujahid (USA))
2604[9] 3186[6] 3729[7] 5330[9]

Hunting Rights (USA) *Mark Johnston* a73 83
2 ch g E Dubai(USA) Possession (USA) (Belong To Me (USA))
3887[4] (4404) (5254) 5552[5] 6138[6]

Hunting Tower (SAF) *M F De Kock* a104 103
10 ch g Fort Wood(USA) Stirrup Cup (SAF) (Royal Chalice (SAF))
53a[8] ◆ 145a[12] 316a[8] 488a[9]

Huntsmans Close *Michael Bell* 80
2 b c Elusive Quality(USA) Badminton (Zieten (USA))
4194[2] ◆ 4688[10] 5963[2] 6411[2] (7311)

Huntsville (USA) *Barry Abrams* 92
3 ch g Unusual Heat(USA) Lethal Hunter (USA) (Jade Hunter (USA))
7566a[8]

Hurakan (IRE) *Richard Price* a73 77
6 gr g Daylami(IRE) Gothic Dream (IRE) (Nashwan (USA))
1154[8] 1533[2] 1829[3] 2233[10] 3278[3] 3659[2] (4470) 4706[6] 5838[12] 6076[2] 7381[7] 7672[5]

Hurler And Farmer (IRE) *Richard Fahey* a80 80
3 b g Red Clubs(IRE) Undercover Glamour (USA) (Kingmambo (USA))
4741[16] 5273[5] 5732[2]

Hurricane Emerald (IRE) *Mark Johnston* 66
3 b g Hurricane Run(IRE) Love Emerald (USA) (Mister Baileys)
2144[8] 2818[9] 3483[11]

Hurricane Havoc (IRE) *J S Bolger* a83 100
4 b m Hurricane Run(IRE) Cheeky Madam (IRE) (Night Shift (USA))
245a[4] 617a[6] 755a[13]

Hurricane Higgins (IRE) *Mark Johnston* a98 110
4 b g Hurricane Run(IRE) Mare Aux Fees (Kenmare (FR))
1137[3] 1882[12] 2278[3] 3125[12] 3857[8] (4697) 5600[10] 5905[3] 6198[3] 7051[20] 7431a[9]

Hurricane Hugo (IRE) *Ian Semple* a51
3 b g Hurricane Run(IRE) All Time Great (Night Shift (USA))
901[7]

Hurricane Hymnbook (USA) *Willie Musson* a76 68
7 b g Pulpit(USA) April Squall (USA) (Summer Squall (USA))
263[2] 349[2] 648[7] 1418[9] 3594[10] 4296[4] 6250[3] 6819[3] 7301[3] 7805[5]

Hurricane In Dubai (IRE) *Denis Coakley* a81 81
3 ch g Hurricane Run(IRE) In Dubai (USA) (Giant's Causeway (USA))
(1703) 2269[6] 2866[2] 3737[4] 4323[11] 5366[4] 5816[6]

Hurricane John (IRE) *David Nicholls* 52
2 b c Hurricane Run(IRE) Top Lady (IRE) (Shirley Heights)
5221[9] 5797[10] 6919[5]

Hurricane Lady (IRE) *Mike Murphy* a43 85
4 b m Hurricane Run(IRE) Yaria (IRE) (Danehill (USA))
1652[12] 2855[3] 4091[6] 4772[3] 6041[8] (6545) 6931[3] 7334[8]

Hurricane Max (IRE) *Ian McInnes* 55
3 b g Oratorio(IRE) Perfect Peach (Lycius (USA))
1843[11] 2262[10] 2680[5] 4397[11] 4716[12] 5215[12] 5341[10]

Hurricane Rita (IRE) *Alan Swinbank* 35
4 ch m Hurricane Run(IRE) Salvinia (USA) (Diesis)
1380[5] 1878[8] 2092[8]

Hurricane Spirit (IRE) *Hans Adielsson* a83 81
8 b g Invincible Spirit(IRE) Gale Warning (IRE) (Last Tycoon)
648[6] 804[3] (915) (3039) 3654a[9] 4944[3] 5480[12] 5751[2] 7171[10] 7618[9] (8047)

Hurricane Thomas (IRE) *Karen Tutty* a25 52
8 b g Celtic Swing Viola Royale (IRE) (Royal Academy (USA))
1829[7] 2735[10] 3116[12]

Hurriya *Mark Johnston* a56 28
3 b f Invincible Spirit(IRE) Adonita (Singspiel (IRE))
720[10] 1046[6] ◆ 1386[4] 2374[11]

Hurry Home Poppa (IRE) *Tom Dascombe* a60
2 b c Holy Roman Emperor(IRE) My Renee (USA) (Kris S (USA))
8033[8] 8223[5]

Hurry Up George *Ralph Beckett* a96 99
3 b g Intikhab(USA) Digamist Girl (IRE) (Digamist (USA))
914a[4] 1858[5] 2276[15] 6075[5] 6835[3] 7826[7]

Huzzah (IRE) *Paul Howling* a66 83
7 b g Acclamation Borders Belle (IRE) (Pursuit Of Love)
31[12] 262[9] 685[7] 927[2] 1305[6] 1628[2] 2171[14] 2572[7] ◆ 3151[3] 3950[7] 4332[8] 4993[9] 6002[6] 6322[9] 6967[7] 7106[8] 7993[3] 8099[4] 8180[6]

Hyde Lea Flyer *Barry Leavy* a48 53
7 b g Hernando(FR) Sea Ridge (Slip Anchor)
3382[10] 4158[8] 4656[7] 5015[5] (5452) 6626[8]

Hydrant *Peter Salmon* a72 81
6 b g Haafhd Spring (Sadler's Wells (USA))
(2735) 3129[3] 4048[4] 5345[8] 5730[4] 7369[5] 7792[7] 8020[5] 8162[7]

Hyper (USA) *Jim Boyle* 97
5 b h Victory Gallop(CAN) Raw Nerve (USA) (Nureyev (USA))
3329[9] 4094[7]

Hyperlink (IRE) *Mark Johnston* a76 76
3 b g Cape Cross(IRE) Surf The Web (IRE) (Ela-Mana-Mou)
1484[2] 2266[12] (3104) 3605[8] 3998[3] 4323[9] 4972[5] (5373) 6181[4] 6608[5]

Hyson *Reg Hollinshead* a65 66
3 ch g Hernando(FR) Be Decisive (Diesis)
211a[6] 365a[0] 475a[9] 1976[7] 3543[4] 4626[14] 4930[5]

Ian's Dream (USA) *Jeremy Noseda* 101
2 ch c Speightstown(USA) She's Loaded (USA) (Deputy Minister (CAN))
2663[2] 3291[3] ◆

Iberian Rock *Alan Brown* 52
3 b f Rock Of Gibraltar(IRE) Karsiyaka (IRE) (Kahyasi)
2341[13] 3458[5]

Iberica (IRE) *P Harley* 66
2 ch f Shirocco(GER) Intaglia (GER) (Lomitas)
7281a[8]

Iberis *Sir Henry Cecil* 73
2 b f Nayef(USA) Isis (USA) (Royal Academy (USA))
4546[3] 5339[6] (6816)

Ibicenco (GER) *Luca Cumani* 113
4 b h Shirocco(GER) Iberi (GER) (Rainbow Quest (USA))
2267[4] 2639[2] 5599[7] 7425a[7] 7560a[4] (7783a)

Ibiza Sunset (IRE) *Brendan Powell* a73 76
4 b g Chineur(FR) Romanylei (IRE) (Blues Traveller (IRE))
31[9] 176[11] 531[2] 1626[5] 2043[9] (2207) 2466[5] 3016[4] 4042[13]

Ibn Al Nafis (USA) *S Seemar* a93 62
6 ch g Distorted Humor(USA) Stormy Bear (USA) (Storm Cat (USA))
317a[9]

Ibn Battuta (USA) *M Al Muhairi* a104 97
7 ch h Seeking The Gold(USA) Sulk (IRE) (Selkirk (USA))
588a[14] 758a[8] 879a[14]

Ibn Hiyyan (USA) *Ferdy Murphy* a73 60
5 rg g El Prado(IRE) Lovely Later (USA) (Green Dancer (USA))
7454[10]

Ibtahaj *Saeed Bin Suroor* a102 101
3 b c Invincible Spirit(IRE) Maroussies Wings (IRE) (In The Wings)
1506[12] 2280[2] (2626) (3503) 3767[2] 6494[3]

Icanboogie *Karen George* a38 46
2 b g Tobougg(IRE) Dubai Marina (Polish Precedent (USA))
1495[9] 1903[6] 2420[7] 4487[12] 5206[8] 6156[11]

Ice And Fire *John Stimpson* a39 44
13 b g Cadeaux Genereux Tanz (IRE) (Sadler's Wells (USA))
1057[5]

Ice Apple *John E Long* a35 25
4 b m Iceman Star Apple (Barathea (IRE))
3720[6] 4464[10] 5048[13] 7012[9] 7739[6] 8097[5]

Iceblast *Michael Easterby* a71 86
4 b g Iceman Medici Princess (Medicean)
1527[9] 2096[9] 3115[3] 3356[4] 3460[6] 5259[4] 5428[2] 6106[6] (6823) 7022[6]

Icebreaker Two *John E Long* a16 46
3 b c Iceman Mintlaw (Mujahid (USA))
5510[9] 6570[4] 7162[10]

Icebreaking (IRE) *L Riccardi* 98
3 b f Elusive City(USA) Croanda (IRE) (Grand Lodge (USA))
1699a[3] 2522a[7] 3682a[9]

Icebuster *Rod Millman* a86 89
4 ch g Iceman Radiate (Sadler's Wells (USA))
5094[10] 5838[8] 6207[5] 6584[3] 7617[5] 7810[7] 8073[7]

Ice Cold Bex *Philip McBride* a63 73
4 ch g Iceman Musica (Primo Dominie)
183[11] 477[7]

Iced Opal *Michael Blanshard* a69 69
3 ch f Iceman Marysienka (Primo Dominie)
1412[7] 3510[6] 4235[6] 5877[4]

Icelander (USA) *Jo Hughes* a78 37
3 b g Stormy Atlantic(USA) Painted Lady (USA) (Broad Brush (USA))
620[3] ◆ (737) ◆ 2269[13] 3492[10] 7920[10] (8153) 8252[6]

Ice Loch *Michael Blanshard* a52 56
3 gr g Avonbridge Bountiful (Pivotal)
294[4] 993[8] 1517[7] 1726[6]

Iceman George *Lydia Pearce* a66 56
8 b g Beat Hollow Diebiedale (Dominion)
5637[4] ◆ (6056) 6503[4] 6691[5] 7409[3] 7744[12]

Ice Missile *Sylvester Kirk* a30 57
3 br f One Cool Cat(USA) Exorcet (FR) (Selkirk (USA))
3507[12] 5156[8]

Ice Nelly (IRE) *Hughie Morrison* a68 73
4 b m Iceman Dancing Nelly (Shareef Dancer (USA))
2767[3] 4505[3] 4733[6] 5707[6] 6819[9] 7409[4]

Ice On Fire *Philip McBride* a63
3 b f Iceman Bluebelle (Generous (IRE))
1443[2]

Ice Pie *Tom Dascombe* a69
2 b f Mount Nelson Statua (IRE) (Statoblest)
(8200) ◆

Ice Trooper *Linda Stubbs* a78 77
4 b g Iceman Out Like Magic (Magic Ring (IRE))
252[9] 526[10] 763[5] 870[6] 1169[3] (4154) 4552[4] 4784[6] 5205[4] (5933) 6357[7] 6825[11] 7591[6]

Icewan *Paul Midgley* 59
3 b g Iceman Royal Nashkova (Mujahid (USA))
1155[12] 1479[8] 1864[8] 2339[5] 3025[6] 4250[9] 5112[2] 5547[9] 6259[10]

Ichimoku *Bryan Smart* a53
2 b c Indesatchel(IRE) Mythicism (Oasis Dream)
7219[11] 7609[7] 7953[9]

Ici La Cote (IRE) *B Grizzetti* 89
2 b c Invincible Spirit(IRE) Kathy Pekan (IRE) (Sri Pekan (USA))
3684a[6]

Icing Sugar *Mike Sowersby* 29
4 ch m Doyen(IRE) Cryptogam (Zamindar (USA))
3913[9] 4550[8] 5447[8] 6361[16] 7712[9]

Icon Dance *Ben De Haan* a56 60
2 b f Sixties Icon Dance To The Blues (IRE) (Danehill Dancer (IRE))
3959[6] 4704[3]

Icon Dream (IRE) *Jim Goldie* 103
5 b g Sadler's Wells(USA) Silver Skates (IRE) (Slip Anchor)
3625[3] 5600[16] 5826[8] 7051[30] 7396[13]

I Confess *Geoffrey Harker* a85 77
7 br g Fantastic Light(USA) Vadsagreya (FR) (Linamix (FR))
448[4] ◆ (538) 626[4] 1087[6] 1587[6] 2792[9] 4155[5] 4657[4] 5713[3] 6319[5] (6559) 7004[5] 7461[5]

Icy Blue *Richard Whitaker* a36 80
4 b g Iceman Bridal Path (Groom Dancer (USA))
1293[8] 1561[4] 1914[9] 3037[4] 3185[5] 3439[8] 3914[3] ◆ 4345[8] 4868[6] 5414[9] 7003[9] 7348[12]

Icy Quiet *David O'Meara* a54 22
4 b m Shirocco(GER) Winter Silence (Dansili)
546[6] 762[4] 908[7] 2468[7] 8214[5]

Icy Reply *Sir Mark Prescott Bt*
2 gr f Hernando(FR) Frosty Welcome (USA) (With Approval (CAN))
6257[9] 6791[15]

Ida Inkley (IRE) *Jonathan Portman* a44 59
3 b f One Cool Cat(USA) Tara Too (IRE) (Danetime (IRE))
1733[9] 2759[6] 3050[13]

Idarose (IRE) *Hugh McWilliams*
3 b f Scorpion(IRE) Garra Princess (IRE) (Golan (IRE))
502[7] 724[RR] 1250[14] 5549[10]

I Dazzle (USA) *Jack Van Berg* 95
4 bb m Hold That Tiger(USA) Miss Cheers (USA) (Carson City (USA))
7577a[4]

Idealism *Micky Hammond* 55
5 b g Motivator Fickle (Danehill (USA))
1276[8] (2670) 3440[14] 4869[9]

Ideechic (FR) *D Allard* a80 94
3 b f Chichicastenango(FR) Princess Petardia (IRE) (Petardia)
7345a[7]

Idle Curiosity (IRE) *Jim Boyle* a43 44
2 b f Red Clubs(IRE) Idle Fancy (Mujtahid (USA))
4002[7] 4645[5] 7161[6]

Idler (IRE) *Mark Johnston* a88 103
3 b g Exceed And Excel(AUS) Dilly Dally (AUS) (Rubiton (AUS))
4770[10] 5082[5] (5582) 5736[8] (6040) 6192[7] (6495) (6676) 6830[10]

Idol Deputy (FR) *Mark Usher* a75
6 gr g Silver Deputy(CAN) Runaway Venus (USA) (Runaway Groom (CAN))
104[3] 224[5] (725) 2173[4] 7529[5] 7843[6] (8051) (8137)

Idols Eye *Martyn Meade* a70 68
3 b f Red Ransom(USA) Whoopsie (Unfuwain (USA))
3071[11] 3488[5] 4186[7]

Idyllic Star (IRE) *J S Moore* a71 71
3 ch f Choisir(AUS) Idolize (Polish Precedent (USA))
1716[2] 3080[4] 3443[3] 4486[5] 5154[3] 5456[5] 5950[3]

Ifan (IRE) *Bryn Palling* a70 65
4 b g Ivan Denisovich(IRE) Montana Miss (IRE) (Earl Of Barking (IRE))
2387[6] 4582[3] 7654[3] 8115[2]

Iffley Fields *David Evans* 56
2 b g Indesatchel(IRE) Happy Omen (Warning)
2784[9] 3224[6] 3789[6]

Iffraaj Pink (IRE) *Roger Varian* a69
2 b f Iffraaj Red Vale (IRE) (Halling (USA))
7160[5] ◆

Iffraam (IRE) *Michael Dods* a75 81
3 b g Iffraaj Madamaa (IRE) (Alzao (USA))
2262[2] ◆ (2864) 4388[8] 4961[6] (6261)

If I Had Him (IRE) *George Baker* a63 59
8 b g City Honours(USA) Our Valentine (IRE) (Be My Native (USA))
8104[3]

If I Were A Boy (IRE) *Dominic Ffrench Davis* a80 77
5 b m Invincible Spirit(IRE) Attymon Lill (IRE) (Marju (IRE))
281[2] 3222[15] 3443[7] 3703[5] 3962[3] 4915[7] 5310[5] (5417) 5707[4] 6430[4] 6981[7] 7027[6]

If Per Chance (IRE) *John Joseph Hanlon* a84 81
7 b g Danetime(IRE) Zafaraya (IRE) (Ashkalani (IRE))
337a[6] 1043a[12]

If So *James Fanshawe* a68 71
3 b f Iffraaj Persario (Bishop Of Cashel)
2085[3] 3312[4] 4434[5] 5975[3] (6254) 6961[3]

If What And Maybe *John Ryan* a62 63
4 ch g Needwood Blade Pink Champagne (Cosmonaut)
738[10] 937[5] 984[5] 1379[6] 1744[6] 2391[4]

If You Can (IRE) *Tim Easterby* a26 43
2 b c Iffraaj Camassina (IRE) (Taufan (USA))
2213[10] 3062[8] 3989[7] 5254[6] 5716[5]

If You Whisper (IRE) *Mike Murphy* a73 46
4 b g Iffraaj Little Whisper (IRE) (Be My Guest (USA))
535[6] 1706[9] 2637[12] 7252[5] 7869[5] 8153[3]

Ighraa (IRE) *Brian Meehan* a73 71
2 b f Tamayuz Frond (Alzao (USA))
2282[4] 2783[3] 3560[11] 5202[4] 5682[3] 6227[3] 7060[9]

I Got Music *Keith Reveley* 35
5 gr m Silver Patriarch(IRE) I Got Rhythm (Lycius (USA))
1247[7]

Iguacu *Richard Price* a58 61
8 b g Desert Prince(IRE) Gay Gallanta (USA) (Woodman (USA))
1189[4] 1534[12] 1919[3] 2391[6] 3392[8] 4504[4] 4987[2] 5506[2] (5935) 6278[4] 7252[11] 7620[11]

Iguazu Falls (USA) *M bin Shafya* a65 101
7 ch g Pivotal Anna Palariva (IRE) (Caerleon (USA))
53a[10] (260a) 489a[8]

I Have A Dream *A P O'Brien* 109
3 b c Galileo(IRE) Lady Lahar (Fraam)
(6066a) ◆ 7051[5] ◆

Ihavetonuff (IRE) *Daniel Mark Loughnane* a42 49
3 b f Moss Vale(IRE) Proud Myth (IRE) (Mark Of Esteem (IRE))
191[5]

Ihsas (USA) *Saeed Bin Suroor* a83 91
3 ch f Rahy(USA) Express Way (ARG) (Ahmad (ARG))
3636[9]

Ihtifal *Saeed Bin Suroor* a100 94
3 b f Dansili Zaeema (Zafonic (USA))
1610[2] 1922[3] 2935[3] (4434) 5128[2] 5576[6] 7503[3] ◆ 7704[2]

Ihtikar (USA) *Ed Dunlop* a67
2 b g Invasor(ARG) Ranin (Unfuwain (USA))
7020[4]

Ihtiraam (IRE) *Saeed Bin Suroor* a72 79
3 b f Teofilo(IRE) Park Romance (IRE) (Dr Fong (USA))
1790[5] 3252[8]

Ikhtisas (USA) *Saeed Bin Suroor* 77
2 b c Street Sense(USA) Any For Love (ARG) (Southern Halo (USA))
6796[2] 7332[6]

Il Battista *Alan McCabe* a81 66
4 b g Medicean Peace (Sadler's Wells (USA))
11[5] 351[8] 371[3]

Ildiko (USA) *Dr Jeremy Naylor* a10 43
5 b m Yes It's True(USA) Eternity (Suave Dancer (USA))
3043[12] 3734[8] 4904[7]

Ile De Re (FR) *Donald McCain* 107
6 gr g Linamix(FR) Ile Mamou (IRE) (Ela-Mana-Mou)
(1974) (3625) 7235[7]

Ilena (GER) *Dr A Bolte* 99
3 b f Areion(GER) Incita (GER) (Royal Solo (IRE))
2107a[2] 2746a[6] 3802a[6] 4862a[13]

Ilewin Dundee *Gary Brown* a46
6 b g Loup Sauvage(USA) Ilewin Janine (IRE) (Soughaan (USA))
5174[6]

Il Grande Maurizio (IRE) *A Al Raihe* a96 102
8 b h King Charlemagne(USA) Ciubanga (IRE) (Arazi (USA))
261a[14] 315a[9]

Illaunglass (IRE) *Jeremy Noseda* a77 98
3 b f Red Clubs(IRE) Esterlina (IRE) (Highest Honor (FR))
4062[7]

Illawalla *Hugh McWilliams* a14 46
4 b g Indesatchel(IRE) Adorable Cherub (USA) (Halo (USA))
1248[9] 2621[6] 6529[9] 6643[10]

I'll Be Good *Robert Johnson* a63 84
3 b c Red Clubs(IRE) Willisa (Polar Falcon (USA))
977[4] 1176[5] 1317[4] 1524[2] 1858[6] 2229[6] 2509[9] 3624[13] 3861[4] 4591[6] 4953[3] 5545[8] 5800[6] 6127[11] 6261[2] (6887) 7101[5] 7489[16]

I'Lldoit *Michael Scudamore* a42 16
5 br g Tamayaz(CAN) Club Oasis (Forzando)
7710[7]

I'll Have Another (USA) *Doug O'Neill* a127
3 ch c Flower Alley(USA) Arch's Gal Edith (USA) (Arch (USA))
(1872a) (2299a)

Illustration (IRE) *Barry Murtagh* a47 71
4 b g Pivotal In Anticipation (IRE) (Sadler's Wells (USA))
3579[7]

Illustrious Forest *John Mackie* a85 50
4 ch g Shinko Forest(IRE) Illustre Inconnue (USA) (Septieme Ciel (USA))
(452) ◆ 721[2] (1114) 2504[15] 7147[12] 7672[8] 7792[11] 8243[2]

Illustrious Lad (IRE) *Jim Boyle* a64 44
3 ch g Bertolini(USA) Squeak (Selkirk (USA))
38[2] 201[3] 322[2] 1725[5] 2547[3] 3151[12] 4438[5] 5047[6] 5406[5] 5975[7] (6362) 7157[2] 7482[4]

Illustrious Prince (IRE) *Declan Carroll* a77 85
5 b g Acclamation Sacred Love (IRE) (Barathea (IRE))
1161[15] 1650[4] 2274[4] 2697[5] 2896[2] 3385[6] 3615[7] 4042[DSQ] 4552[5] 4829[7] 5110[10] (5531) 6044[12] 6239[6] 6692[5] 7141[2] 7480[7] 7684[3] 7799[4]

I Love Me *Andrew Balding* a92 108
4 b m Cape Cross(IRE) Garanciere (FR) (Anabaa (USA))
3266[11] 4078[5] 4527[7] 5627[4] 6400[5]

Il Portico *Gary Moore* a50 62
5 b g Zafeen(FR) Diddymu (IRE) (Revoque (IRE))
1791[4] 2175[10]

Il Romito (IRE) *E Borromeo* 51
3 b c Shirocco(GER) Ivy Cascade (IRE) (Sadler's Wells (USA))
2324a[11]

Ilsa Lund (IRE) *Peter Chapple-Hyam* a59 63
2 b f Holy Roman Emperor(IRE) Casablanca Jewel (IRE) (Kalanisi (IRE))
6343[4] 6936[7] 8076[6]

Il Supremo (IRE) *L Riccardi* 105
4 ch h Daggers Drawn(USA) Magiustrina (IRE) (Indian Ridge)
2325a[5]

I'm A Dreamer (IRE) *David Simcock* 114
5 b m Noverre(USA) Summer Dreams (IRE) (Sadler's Wells (USA))
2209[3] ◆ 2640[4] 3676a[3] (5376a) 6695a[4] 7549a[6]

Imagery *Ronald Harris* a27 29
3 ch g Pivotal Fantasize (Groom Dancer (USA))
2584[11] 3227[13] 3484[10]

Imagery (GER) *W Giedt* 106
3 bb f Monsun(GER) I Go Bye (GER) (Don't Forget Me)
4862a[7] 5844a[3] 6723a[4]

Imaginary Diva *George Margarson* a61 69
6 b m Lend A Hand Distant Diva (Distant Relative)
1428[5] 2360[4] 2943[5] 3243[4] 3464[6] 4439[6] (5033) 5445[2] 5635[3] 6307[5] 6737[10] 8107[3] 8190[7]

Imaginary World (IRE) *John Balding* a73 84
4 b m Exceed And Excel(AUS) Plutonia (Sadler's Wells (USA))
1133[11] 1652[6] 2250[11] 2465[6] 4407[3] 4879[10] 5243[9] 5910[6] 6613[8] 7022[3] 7524[5] 7925[9]

Imaginationrunwild (IRE) *A Oliver* a80 82
3 b f Red Clubs(IRE) Suddenly (Puissance)
3645a[4] 7230a[4]

Imagine (DEN) *Soren Jensen*
3 b f Singspiel(IRE) Liberty (DEN) (Kris)
4359a[12]

I'm Back (IRE) *Saeed Bin Suroor* a91 85
2 b c Exceed And Excel(AUS) Paracel (USA) (Gone West (USA))
(3637) ◆ 4599[5] (5579) 6070[3] (6775)

I'm Boundtoscore (USA) *Troy Rankin* 102
2 b c Even The Score(USA) Unaltered (USA) (Pulpit (USA))
7568a[14]

Imelda Mayhem *J S Moore* a53 82
3 ch f Byron Halland Park Girl (IRE) (Primo Dominie)
2272[7] 2894[6] 3785[7] 5457[7] 6840[10]

I'm Harry *George Baker* a69 71
3 b g Haafhd First Approval (Royal Applause)
3705[8] 4583[3] 4901[5] 5990[12] 7417[11] 7744[7] 7811[7] 8229[12]

I'm Jake (NZ) *David Brideoake & David Feek* 102
7 ch g Pins(AUS) Venetian Court (NZ) (Pompeii Court (USA))
7073a[8] 7783a[4]

Imjin River (IRE) *William Stone* a62 63
5 b g Namid Lady Nasrana (FR) (Al Nasr (FR))
2811[4] 3052[9] 3455[8] 3717[5] 4143[3] 4653[4] 5047[2] 5774[4] 6179[2] 6585[8] 6951[8] 8255[5]

Immaculate Heart (IRE) *Natalie Lloyd-Beavis* a8
2 b f Papal Bull Caipirinia (IRE) (Desert Prince (IRE))
8003[8]

Immortal Verse (IRE) *Robert Collet* 123
4 b m Pivotal Side Of Paradise (IRE) (Sadler's Wells (USA))
4633a[5] 5141a[8]

Imogen Louise (IRE) *Violet M Jordan* a12 69
4 gr m Verglas(IRE) Strina (IRE) (Indian Ridge)
2406[9] 8205[9]

Impel (IRE) *Richard Hannon* a86 72
3 b g Excellent Art Tencarola (IRE) (Night Shift (USA))
1138[4] 1412[5] (3762) 4412[8] 5703[10] 6369[3]

Imperator Augustus (IRE) *Patrick Holmes* a79 88
4 b g Holy Roman Emperor(IRE) Coralita (IRE) (Night Shift (USA))
2285[12] 4345[12] 4629[15] 5057[9] 5588[4] 5819[3] 6124[10] 7360[3] 7935[6]

Imperial Bond *Jedd O'Keeffe* 24
3 b g Misu Bond(IRE) Liability (IRE) (Bluebird (USA))
5734[5] 7445[11]

Imperial Djay (IRE) *Ruth Carr* a66 102
7 b g Dilshaan Slayjay (IRE) (Mujtahid (USA))
1157[11] 1522[5] 1821[4] 2025[3] 2243[5] 2417[2] (2472) (2910) 3331[11] 3855[3] 4078[6] 4321[10] 4609[3] 5075[8] 5517[18] 5827[13] 6201[14] 6659[5]

Imperial Elegance *Mick Channon* 40
3 b f Imperial Dancer Canadian Capers (Ballacashtal (CAN))
2273[17] 2501[13] 3489[11] 4006[4] 4510[12] 6280[10]

Imperial Fong *Chris Dwyer* a56 54
4 b m Dr Fong(USA) Chine (Inchinor)
392[6] 530[3] 602[7] 824[5]

Imperial Glance *Andrew Balding* 73
2 b c Passing Glance Juno Mint (Sula Bula)
5303[11] (6168)

Imperial Guest *George Margarson* 109
6 ch g Imperial Dancer Princess Speedfit (FR) (Desert Prince (IRE))
2068[8] 3331[12] 4285[3] 4802[2] (5572) 6024[2] 6868[9] 7236[4]

Imperial Legend (IRE) *David Nicholls* 82
3 b g Mujadil(USA) Titian Saga (IRE) (Titus Livius (FR))
1521[5] 2695[2] 2918[4] 3407[6] 4174[13] 4428[4] (5087) (5190) (6314) 7177[12] 7451[6]

Imperial Monarch (IRE) *A P O'Brien* 118
3 b c Galileo(IRE) Ionian Sea (Slip Anchor)
(1678) ◆ 2743a[8] (4121a) 7094a[6]

Imperial Oak *Eve Johnson Houghton* 71
2 b g Imperial Dancer Shalad'Or (Golden Heights)
3444[10] 5418[10] (5997) 6597[15] 7008[11]

Imperial Royale (IRE) *Patrick Clinton* 36
11 ch g Ali-Royal(IRE) God Speed Her (Pas De Seul)
3310[5]

Imperial Ruby *Joseph Tuite* a54 60
3 b g Imperial Dancer Aunt Ruby (USA) (Rubiano (USA))
1511[9] 1981[8] 2560[6] 3088[8] 4870[4] 5508[9] 6769[9]

Imperial Spirit *Mick Channon* a62 75
2 b g Imperial Dancer Country Spirit (Sayf El Arab (USA))
4056[9] 4487[6] 4724[3] 5032[2] 5503[3] 7525[6] 7926[7] 8092[5] 8258[3]

Imperial Stargazer *Mick Channon* a47 65
3 gr g Imperial Dancer Sky Light Dreams (Dreams To Reality (USA))
472[8] 1287[2] 1448[7] 1590[8]

Imperial Wave (IRE) *David Lanigan* a60 19
3 br f Holy Roman Emperor(IRE) Jalisco (IRE) (Machiavellian (USA))
2344[12] 2734[11] 3735[9] 4214[4] 5175[6] 5804[2] 6395[5]

Impertinent *Jonathan Portman* 54
2 b f Halling(USA) Incarnation (IRE) (Samum (GER))
6960[7] 7403[10]

Imprimis Tagula (IRE) *Alan Bailey* a83 77
8 b g Tagula(IRE) Strelitzia (IRE) (Bluebird (USA))
284^{5} 368^{2} 545^{5} (553) (834) 899^{6} 1827^{10} (2043) 2251^{5} 2398^{4} 7732^{8} 7901^{8} 7961^{4} 8055^{6} 8133^{2} 8236^{3}

Improvisation (IRE) *Mahmood Al Zarooni* 86
2 b c Teofilo(IRE) Dance Troupe (Rainbow Quest (USA))
4066^{2} 4803^{3}

I'm So Glad *Mick Channon* 101
3 b f Clodovil(IRE) Dilag (IRE) (Almutawakel)
1500^{6} 2272^{11} 2893^{3} (2987) (3288) 3696^{8} (4597) (5271) 6161^{14} 6870^{7}

I'm Still The Man (IRE) *Bill Turner* a67 72
3 b g Acclamation Kapera (FR) (Linamix (FR))
42^{5} 4154^{8}

I'm Super Too (IRE) *Alan Swinbank* a70 89
5 b g Fasliyev(USA) Congress (IRE) (Dancing Brave (USA))
1914^{5} 2285^{3} 2473^{8} 2753^{3} 3274^{4} 4260^{2} 4868^{8} 5759^{6}

Imtithal (IRE) *James Tate* a71 68
3 b f Invincible Spirit(IRE) Dream Time (Rainbow Quest (USA))
350^{2} 523^{3} 918^{2} 1206^{2} 1819^{8} 2431^{12} 3671^{8}

I'm Watching *George Baker* a33 43
2 b f Multiplex Georgie The Fourth (IRE) (Cadeaux Genereux)
1495^{8} 2384^{7} 2844^{11} 4408^{12} 6435^{5} 7008^{9} 7410^{9}

I'm Your Man (FR) *A De Royer-Dupre* 103
3 bb c Cape Cross(IRE) Via Saleria (IRE) (Arazi (USA))
6864a^{4}

Inaad (IRE) *Saeed Bin Suroor* 54
2 b c New Approach(IRE) Athreyaa (Singspiel (IRE))
3634^{10}

Inarco (FR) *Mlle V Dissaux* a77 77
4 b g Sagacity(FR) Indian Flower (GER) (Winged Love (IRE))
18a^{0}

Inaugural *Roger Charlton* 71
2 b g Invincible Spirit(IRE) Anasazi (IRE) (Sadler's Wells (USA))
5793^{9} 6481^{4} 7371^{6}

Incendiary (IRE) *Hugo Palmer* a80 83
3 b c Excellent Art Clytha (Mark Of Esteem (IRE))
(827) 1109^{4} 1790^{3} 2246^{10} 2583^{3} 2883^{3} 3503^{4} (3920) 4741^{7} 5688^{3} 6380^{4} 6639^{5}

Incendo *Ian Williams* a102 91
6 ch g King's Best(USA) Kindle (Selkirk (USA))
2706^{9} (3502) 4795^{4} 6035^{8} 6248^{8} (6828) 8242^{5}

Inchina *Roger Charlton* 82
3 b f Montjeu(IRE) Incheni (IRE) (Nashwan (USA))
(1503) 1973^{8} 3292^{9} 4338^{8}

Inchy Coo *Tim Easterby* a58 69
2 br f Pastoral Pursuits Inchcoonan (Emperor Jones (USA))
1437^{3} 1753^{6} 3123^{5} 3415^{2} 3776^{3} 4173^{9} 4877^{4} 5292^{6} 6121^{5} 6604^{3} 7026^{6}

Incitement *Andrew Crook* 78
4 b g Motivator Dardshi (IRE) (Darshaan)
1866^{7} 2418^{3} 2877^{4} 3750^{F}

Include Me Out (USA) *Ronald W Ellis* a117
4 bb m Include(USA) Don't Trick Her (USA) (Mazel Trick (USA))
7550a^{3}

Incognita *Chris Down*
2 ch f Sakhee's Secret Angel Sprints (Piccolo)
3010^{9}

Incomparable *Scott Dixon* a80 81
7 ch g Compton Place Indian Silk (IRE) (Dolphin Street (FR))
13^{6}

Indastar *Kevin M Prendergast* 50
2 b c Indesatchel(IRE) Charcoal (Primo Valentino (IRE))
2334^{6} 2873^{7}

Inde Country *Nicky Vaughan* a58 53
4 b m Indesatchel(IRE) Countrywide Girl (IRE) (Catrail (USA))
979^{8} 1248^{12}

Indego Blues *David Nicholls* 83
3 b g Indesatchel(IRE) Yanomami (USA) (Slew O'Gold (USA))
1271^{9} 2824^{9} (3698) 4291^{5} 5110^{13} 5737^{2} 6525^{6} 7177^{11} 7451^{7}

Indepub *Kevin Ryan* 86
3 b g Indesatchel(IRE) Champenoise (Forzando)
1160^{8} 1440^{3} 2589^{2} (3629) 4136^{5} 4674^{6}

Index Waiter *Brian Meehan* a52 59
2 ch c Exceed And Excel(AUS) Snowy Indian (Indian Ridge)
2415^{6} 2934^{9} 6043^{9} 6318^{6}

Indian Affair *Milton Bradley* a67 71
2 b c Sleeping Indian Rare Fling (USA) (Kris S (USA))
1495^{4} 2164^{4} 2376^{5} 3138^{3} 4230^{2} 4728^{2} 4804^{5} 5202^{6} 5682^{4} 6611^{3} 7014^{2} 7745^{5} 7866^{3}

Indiana Guest (IRE) *George Margarson* a58 61
3 b g Indian Haven Princess Speedfit (FR) (Desert Prince (IRE))
1285^{4} 2131^{6} 2803^{8} 3050^{11} 4937^{4} (5215) 5458^{2} 5513^{2} 5975^{5} 6306^{4} 6739^{9} 6967^{12} 7316^{11}

Indian Arrow *John Quinn* a66 42
4 b h Sleeping Indian Hillside Girl (IRE) (Tagula (IRE))
498^{5} 752^{4} 964^{4} ◆ 1528^{4} 1823^{8}

Indian Art (IRE) *Sylvester Kirk* a84 83
6 b g Choisir(AUS) Eastern Ember (Indian King (USA))
896^{4} 1064^{3} (1360) (1587) 2444^{9} 3011^{5} 3703^{9} 4252^{4} 5132^{3} 5305^{7} 6172^{8} 6545^{6} 6969^{3} 7415^{11}

Indian Blossom *Harry Dunlop* a54 54
3 b f Sakhee(USA) Al Corniche (IRE) (Bluebird (USA))
1180^{4} 1737^{10} 3080^{6} 5198^{9}

Indian Days *James Given* a105 116
7 ch h Daylami(IRE) Cap Coz (IRE) (Indian Ridge)
877a^{11}

Indian Dumaani *David Bridgwater* a47 50
5 gr m Indian Ridge Mubadalah (USA) (Dumaani (USA))
831^{9}

Indian Emperor (IRE) *Peter Niven* a63 72
4 b g Araafa(IRE) Soft (USA) (Lear Fan (USA))
8288^{6}

Indian Giver *Hugh McWilliams* 68
4 b m Indesatchel(IRE) Bint Baddi (FR) (Shareef Dancer (USA))
1283^{11} 1659^{5} (2033) 2600^{4} 2840^{4} 3215^{2} 3694^{8} 4260^{5} (4715) 4996^{3} 6131^{13}

Indian Jack (IRE) *Luca Cumani* a94 95
4 ch g Indian Haven Almaviva (IRE) (Grand Lodge (USA))
1924^{3} 2417^{5} 2882^{12} 4578^{4} 5517^{3} 5835^{10} 6036^{7}

Indian Jade *Kevin Ryan* 113
2 b c Sleeping Indian Flora Burn (UAE) (Jade Robbery (USA))
(1911) ◆ (2677) 3240^{8} 5515^{6} ◆ 6162^{4} 6910a^{3}

Indian Landing (IRE) *Tracey Collins* 84
4 ch g Barathea(IRE) Lindissima (IRE) (Green Desert (USA))
3647a^{13}

Indian Lass (IRE) *John Best* a22
2 b f Indian Haven Dakota Two (IRE) (Frenchmans Bay (FR))
7219^{8}

Indian Moon *Tobias B P Coles* a27 47
3 gr f Royal Applause In The Pink (IRE) (Indian Ridge)
1472^{13} 1723^{11} 8141^{7}

Indian Ocean (IRE) *Brian Rothwell* 93
6 b g Montjeu(IRE) Dance Desire (IRE) (Caerleon (USA))
1133^{16}

Indian Petal *Mahmood Al Zarooni* a69 62
3 ch f Singspiel(IRE) Wood Vine (USA) (Woodman (USA))
1363^{4} 7174^{5}

Indian Pond (CAN) *Mark Casse* a80 105
4 bb m Speightstown(USA) Schooner Bay (CAN) (Archers Bay (CAN))
6298a^{5}

Indian Shuffle (IRE) *Jonathan Portman* a66 73
4 b g Sleeping Indian Hufflepuff (IRE) (Desert King (IRE))
4003^{9} 5531^{8} 5933^{11}

Indian St Jovite (IRE) *Seamus Fahey* a47 66
5 b g Indian Haven Meritorious (USA) (St Jovite (USA))
7612^{8}

Indian Tinker *Robert Cowell* a55 81
3 b g Sleeping Indian Breakfast Creek (Hallgate)
1457^{13} 1658^{5} 2347^{12} 5584^{6} 6347^{5} 7177^{9}

Indian Trail *David Nicholls* a74 88
12 ch g Indian Ridge Take Heart (Electric)
1868^{14} 2439^{7} 2719^{9} 4400^{6} 4631^{10} 4680^{2} 4909^{8} 5223^{6} 5412^{13} 6123^{11} (6358)

Indian Violet (IRE) *Zoe Davison* a68 68
6 b g Indian Ridge Violet Spring (IRE) (Exactly Sharp (USA))
183° (568) 2173^{12} 7767^{10} 7925^{12} 8039^{4} 8199^{6} 8248^{11}

India's Song *David Simcock* a67
2 b f Zamindar(USA) Sea Chorus (Singspiel (IRE))
7720^{7}

Indie Banned *Ben Haslam* 24
2 b c Indesatchel(IRE) Day By Day (Kyllachy)
5756^{3} 6524^{4}

Indies Gold *Ann Duffield* a19 31
2 b g Sleeping Indian Desert Gold (IRE) (Desert Prince (IRE))
5311^{14} 5727^{8} 6122^{7} 6841^{12}

Indieslad *Ann Duffield* a68 74
4 b g Indesatchel(IRE) Sontime (Son Pardo)
1269^{7} 2632^{7} 4784^{8} 5220^{7} 5808^{2} 6217^{6} 6641^{2} 6823^{8}

Indie Wonder *Reg Hollinshead* a46 38
3 b f Indesatchel(IRE) Glacial Wonder (IRE) (Glacial Storm (USA))
6215^{7} 6736^{10} 7174^{15}

Indignant *Richard Hannon* a79 84
2 ch f Gold Away(IRE) Moiava (FR) (Bering)
2407^{3} 2812^{3} (4742) 5563^{11} 7687^{2}

Indigo Iris (IRE) *Richard Hannon* a63 59
3 b g Choisir(AUS) Sweet Surrender (IRE) (Pennekamp (USA))
2145^{10} 3155^{2} ◆ 3539^{4}

Indigo Lady *Peter Chapple-Hyam* 103
2 b f Sir Percy Seal Indigo (IRE) (Glenstal (USA))
4494^{5} (4967) 6129a^{3}

Indigo Moon *Denis Coakley* a52
2 b f Sleeping Indian Ewenny (Warrshan (USA))
7813^{8} 8068^{6}

Indomito (GER) *A Wohler* a104 113
6 b h Areion(GER) Insola (GER) (Royal Solo (IRE))
1410a^{2} 3237^{4} 5141a^{9} 5869a^{3} 7238^{7}

Indriya (FR) *F Rohaut* 102
3 ch f Stormy River(FR) Killgra (IRE) (Grand Lodge (USA))
2741a^{4}

Indus Valley (IRE) *Des Donovan* a70 76
5 ch g Indian Ridge Gloriously Bright (USA) (Nureyev (USA))
276^{10} 651^{13}

Indycisive *Simon West* 42
4 b g Indesatchel(IRE) Pearls (Mon Tresor)
2438^{10} 4156^{P}

I Need A Dollar *J R Jenkins* 1
2 b c Phoenix Reach(IRE) Lady Stardust (IRE) (Almutawakel)
7466^{7}

Inessa Armand (IRE) *J S Moore* a61
2 ch f Shamardal(USA) Shakti (Indian Ridge)
6841^{8} 7592^{2} 7868^{5} 7923^{5}

Inetrobil (IRE) *Kevin Ryan* 103
3 ch f Bertolini(USA) Tigava (USA) (Machiavellian (USA))
2236^{6} (2713) 3092a^{4} 4070^{11} 4764^{8} 6161^{15}

Infanta Branca (USA) *A P O'Brien* a89 96
2 b f Henrythenavigator(USA) Totemic (USA) (Vanlandingham (USA))
2512a^{3} 7038a^{4} 7547a^{10}

Inffiraaj (IRE) *Mick Channon* a61 64
3 b f Iffraaj Incense (Unfuwain (USA))
918^{7} 2194^{9} 2672^{3} 3083^{5} 3847^{8} 4754^{4} 5095^{3} 5991^{11} 6281^{6} 7015^{2} 7470^{3} (7671)

Infinite Hope (USA) *Luca Cumani* a86 82
3 bb f Dynaformer(USA) Shared Dreams (Seeking The Gold (USA))
3340^{2} ◆ 4791^{3} (5510) 6333^{5} 7194^{3} 7655^{5}

Infinite Jest *J W Hills* a24 63
3 ch c Danehill Dancer(IRE) Noelani (IRE) (Indian Ridge)
1889^{5}

Infinito Magic (USA) *Jeremy Noseda* a83
2 b c More Than Ready(USA) Truly Enchanting (IRE) (Danehill Dancer (IRE))
6175^{2} (6645) 7501^{4} 8240^{2}

Infinitum *John Gosden* a82 86
3 gr f Dalakhani(IRE) Time Honoured (Sadler's Wells (USA))
2204^{2} ◆ 3773^{4} 4542^{5} 5277^{2} 6492^{2} 6770^{4} (7352)

Influence (FR) *G Henrot* a88 92
3 b f Dansili Moiava (FR) (Bering)
8300a^{7}

Infortual (TUR) *Charles Hills* a62
3 b f Acclamation Asafa (IRE) (King's Best (USA))
429^{3} 7978^{2} 8141^{4}

Ingenti *Christopher Wilson* 62
4 ch m Blue Dakota(IRE) Kungfu Kerry (Celtic Swing)
1954^{6} 2314^{11} 2748^{3} 5257^{3} (5740) 6713^{5}

Ingleby Angel (IRE) *David O'Meara* a57 77
3 bb g Dark Angel(IRE) Mistress Twister (Pivotal)
3184^{8} 3442^{2} 4348^{7} (5590) (5803) ◆ 6048^{3} 6259^{2} (6429) 7032^{12}

Ingleby Arch (USA) *David Barron* a91 74
9 b g Arch(USA) Inca Dove (USA) (Mr Prospector (USA))
19^{2} (284) 553^{2} (640) 886^{2}

Ingleby Exceed (IRE) *David O'Meara* 86
4 ch m Exceed And Excel(AUS) Mistress Twister (Pivotal)
2510^{18} 3185^{2} (3439) 4345^{5} 5111^{12} (5588) 6881^{13}

Ingleby Royale *Richard Fahey* 70
2 b f Royal Applause Lay A Whisper (Night Shift (USA))
(1435) 2252^{5} 2630^{4} 5041^{6}

Ingleby Spirit *Richard Fahey* a79 89
5 b g Avonbridge Encore Du Cristal (USA) (Quiet American (USA))
1258^{3} 1605^{9}

Ingleby Star (IRE) *Ian McInnes* a55 82
7 b g Fath(USA) Rosy Scintilla (IRE) (Thatching)
406^{7} 890^{6} 1236^{4} 1868^{16} 2140^{8} 2690^{7} 2982^{8} 4400^{11} 5223^{7} (5821) 6358^{7} 7101^{9}

Ingleby Symphony (IRE) *Richard Fahey* a41 58
2 b f Oratorio(IRE) Alizaya (IRE) (Highest Honor (FR))
3937^{4} 4825^{7} 5242^{9} 5920^{4} (6753) 7289^{2}

Ingot Of Gold *Ralph Beckett* a65
2 b f Dubawi(IRE) Cresta Gold (Halling (USA))
7720^{8}

Inherited *Sir Mark Prescott Bt* a52 51
2 b c Selkirk(USA) Akdariya (IRE) (Shirley Heights)
5010^{7} 5331^{7} 5797^{9} 6014^{9}

Initiator *Jeremy Noseda* 94
3 b g Motivator Dawnus (IRE) (Night Shift (USA))
(2560) 3327^{5} (5006) 5666^{3} 6380^{9}

Inka Surprise (IRE) *Ralph Beckett* a80 72
2 b g Intikhab(USA) Sweet Surprise (IRE) (Danetime (IRE))
1499^{8} 5360^{4} (6015)

In Lingerie (USA) *Todd Pletcher* a111 106
3 b f Empire Maker(USA) Cat Chat (USA) (Storm Cat (USA))
7549a^{9}

Inniscastle Boy *William Muir* a67 65
3 b c Sir Percy Galapagar (USA) (Miswaki (USA))
1728^{5} 2246^{8} 3068^{5} 5148^{7} 5764^{7} 6056^{2} 6323^{7} 7062^{7}

Inorato (IRE) *F Camici* 101
4 b h Oratorio(IRE) Intimaa (IRE) (Caerleon (USA))
2323a^{7}

Inovate (IRE) *Tim Easterby* 61
2 ch c Intikhab(USA) Julianne (IRE) (Persian Bold)
4069^{5} 4587^{6} 5668^{10}

Inpursuitoffreedom *Philip McBride* a72 74
5 b m Pastoral Pursuits Quilt (Terimon)
198^{4} (494) 689^{6} 1358^{5} 1980^{6} 3344^{U} 4407^{4} 5323^{8} 5996^{2} (6773) 7022^{8} 7618^{3}

Inqadh (USA) *Saeed Bin Suroor* a77 46
3 b g Invasor(ARG) Saywaan (USA) (Fusaichi Pegasus (USA))
5766^{2} 6615^{3} 7195^{9}

Inquisitress *John Bridger* a48 56
8 b m Hernando(FR) Caribbean Star (Soviet Star (USA))
653^{7} 744^{9} 822^{9} 1628^{6} 1768^{2} 1895^{6} 2366^{8} 2998^{5} 3152^{6} 3470^{9} 8004^{8} 8039^{9}

Inrefusable (IRE) *T Clout* a66 67
3 b f Refuse To Bend(IRE) Ting A Greeley (Mr Greeley (USA))
5726a^{8}

In Salutem *K J Condon* a75
2 ch g Sakhee's Secret Irish Light (USA) (Irish River (FR))
5858a^{5}

Inside Knowledge (USA) *Garry Woodward* a54 55
6 rg g Mizzen Mast(USA) Kithira (Danehill (USA))
392^{9} 1011^{7} 3077^{3} 3283^{7} 3498^{7} 6821^{11} 7293^{3} 7490^{7} 7710^{2}

Inside Man (IRE) *E Lellouche* 108
6 b g Hawk Wing(USA) Affaire Classee (FR) (Anabaa (USA))
(3367a) 4634a^{3} 6297a^{11} 6864a^{7}

Insolenceofoffice (IRE) *Richard Ford* a50 68
4 b g Kodiac Sharp Diversion (USA) (Diesis)
1293^{10} 1875^{5} 2617^{3} 2748^{6} 3210^{3} 3943^{7} 4866^{6}

Inspired Cry (USA) *Lennart Reuterskiold Jr* 87
4 ch h Street Cry(IRE) Inspired Kiss (CAN) (Inspired Prospect (USA))
4863a^{5} 6091a^{9}

Instance *Jeremy Noseda* a97 98
4 b m Invincible Spirit(IRE) Hannda (IRE) (Dr Devious (IRE))
2177^{15} 4597^{4} 5520^{3} ◆ 6161^{4} 6870^{13} 7509^{5} 7809^{7}

Instigate (USA) *Jeremy Noseda* 30
2 bb c Lion Heart(USA) Sadler's Charm (USA) (Honour And Glory (USA))
4813^{8}

Instinctual *Brendan Powell* a30
2 ch g Observatory(USA) Be Glad (Selkirk (USA))
7813^{12} 7899^{12} 8033^{13}

Instructress *Robert Cowell* a58 30
4 b m Diktat Two Step (Mujtahid (USA))
(1787) 2352^{9} 3008^{8}

Instrumentalist (IRE) *John Best* a81 79
3 b c Amadeus Wolf Kobalt Sea (FR) (Akarad (FR))
2038^{4} 2449^{8} 3448^{8} 4254^{4} 4498^{2} 4755^{3} 5163^{4} 6146^{13} 6440^{4} (6971)

Intense Pink *Chris Wall* 100
3 b f Pivotal Clincher Club (Polish Patriot (USA))
(1560) 2713^{8} 3328^{7} ◆ 3542^{10} (6870)

Intent (IRE) *Michael Bell* a79 80
3 b f Jeremy(USA) Cant Hurry Love (Desert Prince (IRE))
4630^{4} (4888) 5372^{9} 7116^{3} 7375^{3}

Interakt *Joseph Tuite* a51 81
5 b m Rakti Amelie Pouliche (FR) (Desert Prince (IRE))
1564^{4} (2012) 2071^{7} 2890^{4} 3159^{2} 3915^{7} 4690^{17} 4980^{2} 5995^{4} 6303^{6}

Intercept (IRE) *John Gosden* a87 72
4 b g Iffraaj Sharp Catch (IRE) (Common Grounds)
1066^{4} 1354^{9} 1708^{5} 2083^{4} 2940^{10} 3281^{9} 3618^{7}

Interception (IRE) *David Lanigan* 19
2 ch f Raven's Pass(USA) Badee'A (IRE) (Marju (IRE))
6343^{12}

Interchoice Star *Ray Peacock* a70 61
7 b g Josr Algarhoud(IRE) Blakeshall Girl (Piccolo)
6195^{5}

Interesting (IRE) *H-A Pantall* 94
2 b f Raven's Pass(USA) With Fascination (USA) (Dayjur (USA))
7122a^{2}

Interior Minister *Mikael Magnusson* a70
2 b c Nayef(USA) Sister Maria (USA) (Kingmambo (USA))
6501^{4} 7324^{4} 7899^{3}

Interlocking (USA) *Sir Henry Cecil* a44 38
3 b f Awesome Again(CAN) Engaging (USA) (Private Account (USA))
1415^{7}

Intermix (IRE) *Paul Cole* a82
2 b g Intikhab(USA) Bermuxa (FR) (Linamix (FR))
6978^{2} 7492^{14} (8192a)

Internationaldebut (IRE) *Paul Midgley* a88 108
7 b g High Chaparral(IRE) Whisper Light (IRE) (Caerleon (USA))
50a^{7} 141a^{2} 314a^{12} 419a^{9} 589a^{7} 1129^{5} 1469^{3} (Dead)

Inthar (USA) *Saeed Bin Suroor* a89 86
3 ch c Medicean Mont Etoile (IRE) (Montjeu (IRE))
(2584) 3668^{4} 5455^{3} 5973^{5} 6580^{2} 7116^{4} 7626^{2}

In The Crowd (IRE) *Alan Swinbank* 65
3 ch g Haafhd Eliza Gilbert (Noverre (USA))
1878^{7} 2877^{6} 3273^{5} 4250^{7}

In The Long Grass (IRE) *Jim Boyle* a48
4 b g Ivan Denisovich(IRE) Dabtiyra (IRE) (Dr Devious (IRE))
278^{6} 446^{5} 1047^{4}

Intiba (USA) *Saeed Bin Suroor* a75 75
2 b f Street Cry(IRE) Danelagh (AUS) (Danehill (USA))
5977^{2} ◆ (6535)

Intibaah *Brian Meehan* a87 88
2 b g Elnadim(USA) Mawaared (Machiavellian (USA))
3634^{11} (4654) (5527) 6038^{10}

Intimidate *Jeremy Noseda* a78 84
2 b c Royal Applause Crystal Power (USA) (Pleasant Colony (USA))
2550^{3} 5303^{2} 5765^{2} 6114^{3} (6845) 7399^{3}

Intiqaal (IRE) *Derek Shaw* a70 71
5 b g Tiger Hill(IRE) Pride In Me (Indian Ridge)
869^{8} 1000^{8} (1487) ◆ 8004^{11} 8142^{10}

Intomist (IRE) *Jim Boyle* a65 67
3 ch g Strategic Prince Fast Temper (USA) (In The Wings)
1709^{6} 2628^{5} 3071^{4} 3548^{2} 3790^{15} 6402^{6} 7317^{7}

Into The Light *Philip Kirby* a62 63
7 b g Fantastic Light(USA) Boadicea's Chariot (Commanche Run)
632^{3} 4455^{9}

Into The Wind *Rod Millman* a45 70
5 ch m Piccolo In The Stocks (Reprimand)
1534^{7} 2391^{14} 3137^{6} (4409) 5419^{4} (6821) 7301^{10}

Into Wain (USA) *Steve Gollings* a93 93
5 b g Eddington(USA) Serene Nobility (USA) (His Majesty (USA))
(668) 7109^{9} 7455^{2} (7825)

Intransigent *Andrew Balding* a104 93
3 b g Trans Island Mara River (Efisio)
1998^{6} 3165^{7} 3639^{5} 4234^{3} 4919^{2} (5233) 6026^{2} (6536)

Intrepid (IRE) *Jeremy Noseda* a76 71
2 b g Invincible Spirit(IRE) Imiloa (USA) (Kingmambo (USA))
4773^{2} ◆ 5360^{7} 6099^{10} (8185)

Intrigo *Richard Hannon* a51 65
2 b c Medicean A Thousand Smiles (IRE) (Sadler's Wells (USA))
4604^{12} 5319^{9} 6581^{6} 7006^{7} (7432)

Intuition *Richard Hannon* a72 70
3 b c Multiplex Shallow Ground (IRE) (Common Grounds))
2182[14] 5163[6]

Inundate (USA) *Charles Hills* a21
3 b c Pleasant Tap(USA) Tinge (USA) (Kingmambo (USA))
1737[9]

Invent *Robert Eddery* a63 53
4 b g Dansili Fantasize (Groom Dancer (USA))
468[13]

Investment World (IRE) *Tim Vaughan* a43 42
4 b g Akbar(IRE) Superb Investment (IRE) (Hatim (USA))
6399[8] 7731[13]

Invigilator *Derek Shaw* a69 59
4 b g Motivator Midpoint (USA) (Point Given (USA))
372[10] 819[8] 986[3] 1061[8] (1343) 1516[3] ◆ 2352[4] 3018[5] 4146[5] 4653[5] 4928[2] ◆ 5719[3] 6180[4] (6321) 6823[3] 7055[4] (7634) (8255) ◆

Invincible Ash (IRE) *M Halford* a102 110
7 b m Invincible Spirit(IRE) Fully Fashioned (IRE) (Brief Truce (USA))
50a[4] 244a[10] 419a[10] 681a[8] 756a[2] (875a) 1146a[7] 2326a[7] 5137a[4] 5561[19]

Invincible Beauty (IRE) *Seamus Durack* a42 44
3 b f Invincible Spirit(IRE) Beautiful Note (USA) (Red Ransom (USA))
969[8] 2501[9] 3152[13] 3466[10] 6395[9]

Invincible Cara (IRE) *John Dunlop* 74
2 b f Invincible Spirit(IRE) Cara Fantasy (IRE) (Sadler's Wells (USA))
3590[5] ◆ 4408[5]

Invincible Dream (IRE) *Pat Phelan* a68 70
3 b g Invincible Spirit(IRE) Justly Royal (USA) (Royal Academy (USA))
2205[9] 2581[7] 3228[8] 3966[8] 5036[7] 6926[5] 7615[8]

Invincible Force (IRE) *Paul Green* a70 85
8 b g Invincible Spirit(IRE) Highly Respected (IRE) (High Estate)
2488[17] 6005[10] 6788[13]

Invincible Hero (IRE) *Declan Carroll* a58 84
5 b g Invincible Spirit(IRE) Bridelina (FR) (Linamix (FR))
1249[2] 2510[10] 2753[4] 3185[4]

Invincible Lad (IRE) *Milton Bradley* a72 81
8 b g Invincible Spirit(IRE) Lady Ellen (Horage)
3660[8] 4530[7] 4690[19] 4849[2] 5165[7]

Invincible Me (IRE) *F-H Graffard* 73
2 b f Invincible Spirit(IRE) Megec Blis (IRE) (Soviet Star (USA))
4205a[9]

Invincible Ridge (IRE) *D J Bunyan* a83 96
4 b g Invincible Spirit(IRE) Dani Ridge (IRE) (Indian Ridge)
3648a[7] 6270a[13] 6716a[7] 6854a[8]

Invincible Warrior (IRE) *Brian Meehan* a87 100
2 b c Invincible Spirit(IRE) Riotous Applause (Royal Applause)
6015[3] (6581) (7400)

Invisible Hunter (USA) *Saeed Bin Suroor* a87 98
3 ch c Rahy(USA) Madeline P (USA) (Theatrical (IRE))
(4516) ◆ 5091[3] 5626[6] 6046[8] 7631[7]

Invisible Man *Saeed Bin Suroor* a97 112
6 ch g Elusive Quality(USA) Eternal Reve (USA) (Diesis)
2819[2] 3268[5] 4074[3] 4725[4] 5517[11] 6242[3]

Inxile (IRE) *David Nicholls* a107 118
7 b g Fayruz Grandel (Owington)
244a[7] 419a[2] 681a[3] 875a[5] 1147a[7] 1857[9] 3196a[5] 3860[4] 4838[4] (5067a) 5641a[3] 6072[4] 6292a[2] 6908a[6]

Inya House *Nigel Tinkler* a53 52
3 b g Auction House(USA) Inya Lake (Whittingham (IRE))
270[10] 536[5] 1582[5]

Ioannou *Noel Quinlan* a61
3 b c Excellent Art Sandtime (IRE) (Green Desert (USA))
7667[9] 7838[6] (8291)

Iokastos *Mlle C Cardenne* a74 100
5 b g Medicean Loxandra (Last Tycoon)
4316a[0] 6804a[6]

Ionwy *Derek Haydn Jones* a57 55
3 b f Piccolo Dim Ots (Alhijaz)
352[6] 739[7] 6002[15] 7747[8] 8036[10]

Ioya Bigtime (USA) *Chris Block* a115 115
5 b h Dynaformer(USA) Ioya Two (USA) (Lord At War (ARG))
5374a[2]

Irene Kennet *Paul Burgoyne* a43 43
5 b m Kayf Tara Evaporate (Insan (USA))
6615[8] 7016[8] 8097[3]

Irian (GER) *J Moore* 119
6 br g Tertullian(USA) Iberi (GER) (Rainbow Quest (USA))
8043a[8]

Iridescence *Jeremy Noseda* a70
2 b f Dutch Art Radiate (Sadler's Wells (USA))
7506[2] 8171[2]

Irie Ute *Sylvester Kirk* a62 53
4 b g Sleeping Indian Prends Ca (IRE) (Reprimand)
5741[3] 736[6] 891[8] 1263[7] 1702[14] (2350) 3511[10] 3949[9] 4653[3] 4929[7] 5305[8] 6455[8] 6982[4] 7204[2]

Iris Blue *John Gosden* a55 61
2 ch f Pivotal Princess Iris (IRE) (Desert Prince (IRE))
3590[13] 3959[7] 4645[4] 5160[6] 7110[2]

Irish Boy (IRE) *Paul Midgley* a51 73
4 b g Desert Millennium(IRE) Shone Island (IRE) (Desert Sun)
2439[10] 4187[7] 5131[2] 5514[3] 5791[4] 5915[13] 6357[8] 6837[12] 7351[10]

Irish Chope (FR) *C Boutin* a62 86
4 b m Indian Rocket Via Appia (FR) (Exit To Nowhere (USA))
15a[0]

Irish Cliff (IRE) *M Delcher-Sanchez* 100
3 b f Marju(IRE) Miss Corinne (Mark Of Esteem (IRE))
3987a[7]

Irish Flame (SAF) *M F De Kock* a113 109
6 b h Dynasty(SAF) Clock The Rock (SAF) (Flaming Rock (IRE))
486a[5] 759a[5] 878a[8] 1144a[6]

Irish Girls Spirit (IRE) *Paul Midgley* 64
3 b f Desert Millennium(IRE) Shone Island (IRE) (Desert Sun)
1274[10] 1637[6] 1843[18] 3670[2] (3791) 4911[2] 5087[3] 5327[5] 5923[2]

Irish Heartbeat (IRE) *Jamie Osborne* a83 96
7 b g Celtic Swing She's All Class (USA) (Rahy (USA))
1885[9] ◆ 2208[7] 2931[6] 7691[15] 7826[9] 7966[12] 8077[2] 8232[2] 8269[6]

Irish History (IRE) *Mahmood Al Zarooni* 105
3 b f Dubawi(IRE) Spirit Of Tara (IRE) (Sadler's Wells (USA))
(2344) ◆ 2641[7] 3328[3] 4065[4] 5092[7] 5834[6] 6633[8]

Irish Imagine *Mario Hofer*
2 ch f Iffraaj Irish Eagle (GER) (Eagle Eyed (USA))
5612a[11]

Irish Jugger (USA) *Michael Appleby* a68 58
5 ch g Johannesburg(USA) Jinny's Gold (USA) (Gold Fever (USA))
4[5] 156[7] 296[8] 810[4] 1047[2] 1429[6] (7610) 7710[4]

Irish Law *John Balding*
4 b g Redoubtable(USA) Largs (Sheikh Albadou)
4405[12]

Irish Mission (CAN) *Mark Frostad* a97 101
3 ch f Giant's Causeway(USA) Misty Mission (CAN) (Miswaki (USA))
6299a[5]

Iron Butterfly *James Eustace* a45 57
3 b f Shirocco(GER) Coh Sho No (Old Vic)
1923[10] 2560[5] 4516[12] 6365[12] 6948[6]

Iron Condor *James Eustace* a80 80
5 b g Tobougg(IRE) Coh Sho No (Old Vic)
1205[2] 2174[6] 2504[7] 3765[5] 3961[5] 4983[3] 5665[4] 6170[6]

Iron Duke *Liam Corcoran* a49 43
6 gr g Refuse To Bend(IRE) Arinaga (Warning)
7255[2] 7629[13]

Ironically (IRE) *David Lanigan* a61 69
3 b f Refuse To Bend(IRE) Dutch Auction (USA) (Mr Greeley (USA))
3704[2] 3968[5] 5754[5] 6159[4] 6814[2]

Iron Major (IRE) *Edward Lynam* a91 87
5 ch g Titus Livius(FR) Bent Al Fala (IRE) (Green Desert (USA))
(337a) 5397a[3]

Irons On Fire (USA) *Lee Carter* a70 33
4 ch g Tale Of The Cat(USA) One And Twenty (USA) (Honour And Glory (USA))
(85) 222[3] 1732[3] 2637[14] 3007[8] 3388[11] 3738[10] 5351[4] 5935[9] 6255[6] 7321[3] 7479[11] 7816[5] 8047[7] 8153[4]

Ironstein (AUS) *Gerald Ryan* 111
7 br g Zabeel(NZ) Gentle Genius (AUS) (Danehill (USA))
7073a[4] 7425a[3] 7696a[2] 7783a[7]

Ironstone (IRE) *M Delzangles* 91
3 b c Holy Roman Emperor(IRE) Lettre De Cachet (USA) (Secreto (USA))
1171a[0]

Iron Will (FR) *E Kurdu* 81
4 b g Desert Prince(IRE) Princesse Aga (IRE) (Acatenango (GER))
1172a[0]

Irrational *Bryan Smart* a55 61
3 b f Kyllachy Belladera (IRE) (Alzao (USA))
1798[6] 3566[9] 4453[4] 4913[5] 7146[10] 7747[6]

Iryklon (POL) *Vaclav Luka II* a104 106
6 b g Nowogrodek(POL) Imma (POL) (Beaconsfield)
1554a[4]

Isabelle B (IRE) *Nicky Richards* 43
5 b m High Chaparral(IRE) Isabella R (IRE) (Indian Ridge)
1867[10]

Isatis *Sir Henry Cecil* a72 73
3 ch f Zamindar(USA) Isis (USA) (Royal Academy (USA))
1472[5] 2313[9] 4630[2] 5218[5] 6433[2] 6965[12]

I Say (IRE) *William Haggas* 81
2 b f Oratorio(IRE) Lisieux Orchid (IRE) (Sadler's Wells (USA))
7403[2]

Isdaal *Kevin Morgan* a69 71
5 ch m Dubawi(IRE) Faydah (USA) (Bahri (USA))
306[10] 689[2] (961) 1106[5] 1706[5] (2149) (2915) 3472[5]

I See You *Peter Makin* a77 76
3 ch f Sleeping Indian Pikaboo (Pivotal)
1709[7] 2869[2] 4885[3] (5536) 5815[2] 5934[2] 7309[7] 7489[2] 7742[2] 8022[5]

Ishetoo *Peter Grayson* a77 75
8 b g Ishiguru(USA) Ticcatoo (IRE) (Dolphin Street (FR))
2809[10] 4292[7] 4887[8] 6498[5] 6825[9] 7590[12] 7794[9] 8255[8]

Ishi *Rod Millman* a49 46
3 b f Ishiguru(USA) Chorus (Bandmaster (USA))
1501[14] 2065[9] 2422[5] 3489[15] 7804[6] 7988[7] 8069[3] (8154)

Ishiamiracle *Phil McEntee* a67 68
3 ch f Ishiguru(USA) Sukuma (IRE) (Highest Honor (FR))
99[3] 189[6] 201[10] 491[3] 583[4] 645[3] 977[5] 5149[6] (7318) 7469[7] 8005[11] 8294[4] 8305[8]

Ishi Amy *Alastair Lidderdale* a27 36
2 b f Ishiguru(USA) Notable Lady (IRE) (Victory Note (USA))
6237[8] 6581[10]

Ishigunnaeatit *Mrs K Burke* a66 72
2 b f Ishiguru(USA) It's Toast (IRE) (Diktat)
2047[7] (4618) 5361[7] 6227[6] 6975[2] 8092[2]

Ishi Honest *Mark Usher* 73
2 b f Ishiguru(USA) Honesty Pays (Dr Fong (USA))
1563[4] (2047) 2234[3] 3097[5] 3662[3] 4324[4] 4820[13] 5790[6] 6541[7]

Ishikawa (IRE) *Alan King* a75 68
4 b g Chineur(FR) Nautical Light (Slip Anchor)
(1533) ◆ 1829[5] 3454[3] 4586[2] 5506[8] 6120[2] 6843[3] (7768)

Ishismart *Reg Hollinshead* a55 53
8 ch m Ishiguru(USA) Smartie Lee (Dominion)
767[3] 924[5] 4664[4]

Ishisoba *Alastair Lidderdale* a63 45
2 ch f Ishiguru(USA) Bundle Up (USA) (Miner's Mark (USA))
5943[6] 6534[7] 7110[5] 7724[5]

Ishvana (IRE) *A P O'Brien* a100 111
3 b f Holy Roman Emperor(IRE) Song Of The Sea (Bering)
1403a[9] 1944a[3] 2527a[2] (3265) 6061a[7]

Isingy Red (FR) *Jim Boyle* a70 74
4 ch g Chichicastenango(FR) Loving Smile (FR) (Sillery (USA))
1626[10] 2173[5] 2546[5] 3388[9] 4890[3] 5049[2] 6174[10] 6801[4] 7318 [3] 7643[9]

Isioma *Mario Hofer* 85
2 b f Shamardal(USA) Russian Dance (USA) (Nureyev (USA))
5755a[9] 7588a[4]

Isis Blue *Rod Millman* a65 65
2 b g Cockney Rebel(IRE) Bramaputra (IRE) (Choisir (AUS))
4730[4] 6772[4] 7323[12]

Isitcozimcool (IRE) *Barry Murtagh* a73 42
7 b g Shinko Forest(IRE) Hazarama (IRE) (Kahyasi)
3061[8] 3577[7] 4869[12]

Island Express (IRE) *Ann Stokell* a51 58
5 b g Chineur(FR) Cayman Expresso (IRE) (Fayruz)
7611[9] 7952[10] 8069[5] 8154[2] 8251[3]

Island Legend (IRE) *Milton Bradley* a89 64
6 b g Trans Island Legand Of Tara (USA) (Gold Legend (USA))
120[6] 272[3] 406[2] 525[4] 560[2] 647[3] (890) (1015) 1362[7] 1828[3] 7595[9] 7704[9] 7860[7] (8163)

Island Melody (IRE) *J S Moore* a73 69
2 b g Oratorio(IRE) Pout (IRE) (Namid)
209[3] 547[2] 1892[9] 4250[6] 5405[7] 6206[3] 7158[4] 7359[7]

Isle Of Beauty *Tom Dascombe* a36 36
2 b f Refuse To Bend(IRE) Munaawashat (IRE) (Marju (IRE))
6791[13] 7199[7]

Isle Of Ellis (IRE) *Ron Barr* a39 54
5 b g Statue Of Liberty(USA) Fable (Absalom)
2796[9] 3026[3] 3406[2] 4865[5] 6959[5] 7604[13]

Islesman *Heather Main* a85 81
4 b g Oratorio(IRE) Purple Vision (Rainbow Quest (USA))
987[4] 1416[7] 3045[7] 3503[8] (6538) 6804a[0] 7626[12] 7823[7]

Isobella *Hughie Morrison* a55 58
3 b f Royal Applause Gwyneth (Zafonic (USA))
2625[4] 3483[3] 4510[9] 4941[5] 5577[3] 6280[6]

Isola Bella *Jonathan Portman* a26 43
3 ch f Sleeping Indian Tetravella (IRE) (Groom Dancer (USA))
2162[6] 3193[6] 7108[8]

Isola Verde *James Fanshawe* a70 71
3 b f Oasis Dream Firenze (Efisio)
(2121) 2893[8] 4221[6] 5853[8] 5972[3] 6378[6] 7483[3] 7725[9]

Isolde's Return *George Moore* 39
3 b f Avonbridge Up And About (Barathea (IRE))
1754[6] 2877[8] 3697[10] 5413[10] 6924[12]

I Stand Corrected *Ed Walker* 49
3 b f Exceed And Excel(AUS) Forever Fine (USA) (Sunshine Forever (USA))
3539[9] 4434[7] 5096[7]

Istan Star (USA) *Julie Camacho* a23 53
3 b g Istan(USA) Migygian (USA) (Ogygian (USA))
1992[5] 2340[14] 4153[11] 5330[6] 5589[5] 6365[11]

Isthmus *Amanda Perrett* a76 69
3 b c Oasis Dream Krisia (Kris)
2038[2] 2866[5] 5889[6] 6842[8]

Istimlaak (IRE) *J E Hammond* a71 83
5 b g Marju(IRE) Zither (Zafonic (USA))
5118a[6]

Istiqdaam *Conor Dore* a69 81
7 b g Pivotal Auspicious (Shirley Heights)
190[6]

Italian Ice *Bryan Smart* a37 16
3 b f Milk It Mick Segretezza (IRE) (Perugino (USA))
135[7] 2139[10] 2438[11]

Italian Lady (USA) *Alan Jarvis* a51 65
3 bb f Medaglia d'Oro(USA) Way Beyond (USA) (Ordway (USA))
4791[7] 5329[DSQ] 5421[5] 6103[16] 7643[7]

Italian Riviera *Sir Mark Prescott Bt* a77
3 b g Galileo(IRE) Miss Corniche (Hernando (FR))
6215[8] 6614[6] 7174[11] (7629) (7717) (7862) 7972[4]

Italian Tom (IRE) *Ronald Harris* a82 91
5 b h Le Vie Dei Colori Brave Cat (IRE) (Catrail (USA))
282[8] 528[4] ◆ 623[8] 735[2] 896[3] 1254[6] (2071) (2264) 2853[4] (3225) 3771[8] 4286[17] 6665[12] 7464[7] 8022[3] 8163[3] 8266[6]

Ithoughtitwasover (IRE) *Mark Johnston* a99 107
4 b h Hurricane Run(IRE) Green Castle (IRE) (Indian Ridge)
1374[2] 1603[5] (1882) (2228) 2479[3] 2933[5] 3372[12]

Itlaaq *Michael Easterby* a89 98
6 b g Alhaarth(IRE) Hathrah (IRE) (Linamix (FR))
2253[5] 3163[16] 4613[3] 5491[5] 6031[3] 6834[10] 7098[7]

It's A Girl Thing (IRE) *George Baker* a67 24
3 ch f Hurricane Run(IRE) Princess Magdalena (Pennekamp (USA))
1319[12] 2425[6]

Itsallinthemind *Tim Easterby* 20
2 b f Mind Games Mabrookah (Deploy)
4545[18] 4921[8]

It's A Mans World *Brian Ellison* a71 87
6 b g Kyllachy Exhibitor (USA) (Royal Academy (USA))
1179[12] (2091) 2239[10] 2879[8] 3254[6] (4779) (5015) (5414) 6256[10] 6638[15] (7004)

It's A Privilege *Ralph Beckett* a74 70
3 gr g Verglas(IRE) No Rehearsal (FR) (Baillamont (USA))
1322[9] 1661[5] 2128[2] 3001[2] 3846[4] 4871[3]

It's Dubai Dolly *Alastair Lidderdale* a61 73
6 ch m Dubai Destination(USA) Betrothal (IRE) (Groom Dancer (USA))
468[4] 741[10]

It's Me And You *Michael Easterby* a54
4 b g Dubai Destination(USA) Time Crystal (IRE) (Sadler's Wells (USA))
35[6] 190[7] 404[8] 451[4] 924[8]

It's My Time *David Simcock* a59 61
3 b f Green Desert(USA) Soviet Terms (Soviet Star (USA))
1472[17] 4434[4] 6154[5] 7477[7] 7787[3]

It's Only Business *Bill Turner* a60 64
2 ch c Haafhd Noble Plum (IRE) (King's Best (USA))
2571[5] 2983[6] 3244[3] 3858[3] 5236[5] 7357[5] 7649[9] 7795[2] 8093[9] (8258)

It's Taboo *Mark Usher* 75
2 b f Tobougg(IRE) Faraway Moon (Distant Relative)
3074[6] 3637[3] ◆ 4055[2] 5146[3] 5527[4] 6160[17]

Itsthursdayalready *Mark Brisbourne* a67 62
5 b g Exceed And Excel(AUS) Succinct (Hector Protector (USA))
356[6] 551[2] 664[6] 813[2] 904[5]

Itstooearly *James Moffatt* 38
9 br m Overbury(IRE) Deb's Ball (Glenstal (USA))
2226[4]

Ittirad (USA) *Roger Varian* 100
4 b g Dubai Destination(USA) Noushkey (Polish Precedent (USA))
1605[4] 3036[3] 4732[2] 5079[2]

Itum *Christine Dunnett* a55 41
5 ch g Bahamian Bounty Petomi (Presidium)
1734[6] 1986[6] 2377[13] 2815[14] 3390[11] 4187[8] 5017[5] 5327[9] 5719[5] 5971[9] 6771[2] 7471[4] 7703[2] 8046[6]

Iulus *John Quinn* a65 76
4 ch g Kheleyf(USA) Miri (IRE) (Sillery (USA))
2473[9] 2765[2] 3699[8] 5259[2] 5967[3] 6561[12] 7200[3]

Ivanhoe *Michael Blanshard* a70 71
2 b c Haafhd Marysienka (Primo Dominie)
4472[15] 5126[6] 5655[3] 6928[2] 7814[5]

Ivan The Engine *Paul Fitzsimons* a47
4 b g Ivan Denisovich(IRE) Silk Daisy (Barathea (IRE))
5970[11] 6397[12] 6582[10] 7189[13] 8055[8]

Ivan The Terrible (IRE) *Richard Guest* a54 46
4 b g Ivan Denisovich(IRE) Pussie Willow (IRE) (Catrail (USA))
579[7] 651[10] 924[4] 3794[9]

I've No Money (IRE) *David C Griffiths* a34 49
2 b g Camacho Inonder (Belfort (FR))
1818[9] 2587[11] 5053[4] 5403[7] 5749[12] 7609[9] 7795[7] 8303[6]

Iver Bridge Lad *John Ryan* a108 114
5 b h Avonbridge Fittonia (FR) (Ashkalani (IRE))
244a[3] 419a[4] 756a[4] 874a[8] 1147a[11] 6867[8] 7624a[8] 7772[7] 7897[2]

Ivestar (IRE) *Michael Easterby* a66 64
7 b g Fraam Hazardous (Night Shift (USA))
4683[11] 4865[7] 5258[13] 5416[RR] 6308[5] 6640[7] (6959) (7157) 7456[6] 7794[3] 7969[3] 8285[6]

Ivor's Princess *Rod Millman* a70 85
3 b f Atraf Rosina May (IRE) (Danehill Dancer (IRE))
(2205) (3192) 3876[5] 4607[8] 5128[8] 5837[13] 6367[6] 6842[9]

Ivory Jazz *Richard Guest* a80 58
5 b g Dubai Destination(USA) Slow Jazz (USA) (Chief's Crown (USA))
175[4] 285[6] 563[8] 721[6]

Ivory Land (FR) *A De Royer-Dupre* 118
5 ch h Lando(GER) Ivory Coast (FR) (Peintre Celebre (USA))
1697a[5] (2534a) (6297a)

Ivory Silk *Jeremy Gask* a85 91
7 b m Diktat Ivory's Joy (Tina's Pet)
269[5]

Iwilsayzisonlyonce *Joseph Tuite* a59 60
2 ch g Kyllachy Resistance Heroine (Dr Fong (USA))
5912[10] 6093[4] 6444[9] 6822[2] (6953) 7476[6]

Izalia (FR) *F Rossi* a98 111
4 b m Iron Mask(USA) Tarabela (FR) (Johann Quatz (FR))
814a[6]

Iz She *William Knight* a68
4 b m Ishiguru(USA) Regal Gallery (IRE) (Royal Academy (USA))
3735[4] 4213[4] 5404[3] 6181[8]

Izzet *Ron Barr* 63
4 b g Cadeaux Genereux Asbo (Abou Zouz (USA))
2692[6] 3215[6] (3356) 3914[2] 4350[7]

Izzi Top *John Gosden* 118
4 b m Pivotal Zee Zee Top (Zafonic (USA))
(1883) ◆ (2209) ◆ (3676a) 4801[6] (5399a) 6911a[2]

Izzy Boy (USA) *Mark Johnston* 70
2 b c Elusive Quality(USA) Michele Royale (USA) (Groovy (USA))
4362[10] 4710[2] ◆ 5083[4] 6070[12] 6511[6]

Izzy The Ozzy (IRE) *David Barron* 85
4 b m Encosta De Lago(AUS) Naziriya (FR) (Darshaan)
2491[11]

Jaaryah (IRE) *Roger Varian* a91 85
4 ch m Halling(USA) Albahja (Sinndar (IRE))
2257[15] 2909[4] 3813[5]

Jaasoos (IRE) *D Selvaratnam* a101 111
8 ch g Noverre(USA) Nymphs Echo (IRE) (Mujtahid (USA))
588a[2] 758a[5] 874a[6]

Jabhaat (USA) *Ed Dunlop* 76
2 b f Hard Spun(USA) Ishraak (USA) (Sahm (USA))
5104[2] 5907[2] (6355)

Jacasa Too *Rod Millman* a46 43
3 b f Arkadian Hero(USA) Lucky Jacasa (Whittingham (IRE))
107[8] 291[5] 620[6] 739[6] 1067[11] 2203[4] 3014[8] 3665[12]

Jackaddock *James Bethell* 39
2 b g Motivator Selkirk Sky (Selkirk (USA))
7244[6]

Jack Barker *Robin Bastiman* 59
3 b g Danbird(AUS) Smiddy Hill (Factual (USA))
4144[11] 5113[3] 5728[10]

Jack Dawkins (USA) *David Nicholls* a80 49
7 b g Fantastic Light(USA) Do The Mambo (USA) (Kingmambo (USA))
1295[10] (1429) 1598[8] 2403[2] 3692[9] 4712[9] 6055[6] 8136[11]

Jack Dexter *Jim Goldie* 108
3 bb g Orientor Glenhurich (IRE) (Sri Pekan (USA))
1238[2] (1521) ◆ (1998) 2616[5] 3374[3] ◆ 4367[7] ◆ 6075[4] ◆ (6465) (7240) ◆ (7397) 7690[10]

Jackie Love (IRE) *Olivia Maylam* a57 58
4 b m Tobougg(IRE) Gutter Press (IRE) (Raise A Grand (IRE))
125[7] 264[5] 307[3] 379[5] 561[10] 829[2] 988[2] 1009[6] 3152[12] 3497[4] (4240) 4812[5] 4942[5] 5720[4] 6321[3] 7512[8] 7748[8] 7898[10] 8061[2] (8299)

Jack Luey *Lawrence Mullaney* a63 89
5 b g Danbird(AUS) Icenaslice (IRE) (Fayruz)
1643[5] 2096[3] 2264[3] 3159[3] 3496[3] 4998[3] 5674[3] 6144[2] (6525)

Jack My Boy (IRE) *David Evans* a82 84
5 b g Tagula(IRE) Bobanlyn (IRE) (Dance Of Life (USA))
962[7] 1289[6] 1727[5] 2070[10] 2264[11] 3225[5] 3434[6] 4708[4] 5150[3] 8269[8]

Jack Of Diamonds (IRE) *Roger Teal* a89 81
3 b g Red Clubs(IRE) Sakkara Star (IRE) (Mozart (IRE))
1377[2] 3398[4] (3972) 5099[2] ◆ 5705[5] 6488[4] 7715[2] (7824)

Jackpot *Brendan Powell* a11 34
2 b f Avonbridge Strat's Quest (Nicholas (USA))
3242[23] 3700[7] 4002[8] 4990[7] 7156[8] 7355[8]

Jack Smudge *James Given* a80 73
4 br g One Cool Cat(USA) Forever Fine (USA) (Sunshine Forever (USA))
2475[9] 3076[7] (3707) 4631[11] 5296[7] 5972[10] (6641) 7023[4] 7360[6]

Jack Sparrow (FR) *S Jesus* a77 64
3 gr g Aussie Rules(USA) Beauty Jem (FR) (Red Ransom (USA))
290a[2]

Jack's Revenge (IRE) *George Baker* a77 96
4 br g Footstepsinthesand Spirit Of Age (IRE) (Indian Ridge)
922[2] 1636[2] 2414[2] (3226) (4068) 4689[3] 6674[8] 7691[2]

Jack Who's He (IRE) *David Evans* a86 92
3 b g Red Clubs(IRE) Annus Iucundus (IRE) (Desert King (IRE))
1565[4] 1892[7] 3445[2] 4364[5] 4607[3] 4997[2] 5365[4] 6010[6] 7064[6] 7502[5] 7920[6] 8057[2] 8081[5] 8250[3]

Jacob Cats *Richard Hannon* 100
3 b c Dutch Art Ballet (Sharrood (USA))
1452[9] (2428) (4474) ◆ 4689[4] 5356[3] ◆ (6494)

Jacobella *Jonathan Portman* a57 65
2 b f Rob Roy(USA) Veni Bidi Vici (Horse Chestnut (SAF))
6534[5] 6871[4]

Jacob McCandles *Shaun Lycett* a69 66
5 br g Trade Fair Feather Circle (IRE) (Indian Ridge)
(833) 1269[10] 3734[3] 5891[3] 6691[9] 7024[5]

Jacobs Son *Robert Mills* a70 82
4 ch g Refuse To Bend(IRE) Woodwin (IRE) (Woodman (USA))
1939[10] 2863[10] 5706[8] 6255[7] 7353[3] 8106[3] (8189)

Jadanna (IRE) *James Given* 100
2 b f Mujadil(USA) Savannah Poppy (IRE) (Statue Of Liberty (USA))
(1556) ◆ (2603) ◆ 3269[5] 4064[3] 4687[8] 5979[2] 6672[8] 7122a[6]

Jade *Ollie Pears* 86
4 b m Cadeaux Genereux Ashdown Princess (IRE) (King's Theatre (IRE))
4829[11] (5326) 5520[8] 6009[5] 6406[3] 6820[14]

Jadesnumberone (IRE) *Michael Bell* 75
2 b f Authorized(IRE) Gabriella (Cape Cross (IRE))
6872[2] 7555[7]

Jaguar Mail (JPN) *Noriyuki Hori* 123
8 b h Jungle Pocket(JPN) Haya Beni Komachi (JPN) (Sunday Silence (USA))
7872a[10] 8040a[2]

Jag War (FR) *H-A Pantall* a91 81
4 b h Meshaheer(USA) Just Fizzy (Efisio)
18a[0]

Jaja De Jau *Anthony Honeyball* a49 63
3 br f Sakhee(USA) Jadidh (Touching Wood (USA))
2148[6] 6736[3] 7162[7]

Jake's Destiny (IRE) *George Baker* a87 99
3 b g Desert Style(IRE) Skehana (IRE) (Mukaddamah (USA))
3563[2] 4097[3] 4740[6] 6242[4] (6831) 7556[3] ◆

Jake The Snake (IRE) *Tony Carroll* a82 73
11 ch g Intikhab(USA) Tilbrook (IRE) (Don't Forget Me)
1005[5] 1069[3] 1430[4] 1633[5] (2169) (3103) 3544[7] 5531[6] 6256[6] 7685[14]

Jakey (IRE) *Pat Phelan* a53
2 b c Cape Cross(IRE) Off Message (IRE) (In The Wings)
7705[7]

Jakkalberry (IRE) *Marco Botti* 119
6 b h Storming Home Claba Di San Jore (IRE) (Barathea (IRE))
759a[3] 1149a[3] 3369[5] (5374a) 7264a[13] 7621a[3] 7872a[11]

Jalaa (IRE) *Richard Hannon* 84
2 b c Street Cry(IRE) Daneleta (IRE) (Danehill (USA))
(2784) 3368[8]

Jaladee *Roger Varian* a49
2 b c Cape Cross(IRE) Atamana (IRE) (Lahib (USA))
7323[9]

Jalasaat (USA) *John Dunlop* 16
2 b f Lemon Drop Kid(USA) Itnab (Green Desert (USA))
6489[17] 6966[11]

Jaldarshaan (IRE) *Colin Teague* a67 65
5 b m Fath(USA) Jaldini (IRE) (Darshaan)
289[11] 927[11] 5590[10]

Jaloro (IRE) *Ronald Harris* a72 68
4 b g Invincible Spirit(IRE) Julie Jalouse (USA) (Kris S (USA))
1156[18] 1378[10] 1830[5] 2574[3] 2867[3] 3544[6] 4183[6] 4536[4] 4915[2] 5809[7] 6098[4] 6838[2] 7596[6]

Jamaica Grande *Terry Clement* a49 66
4 ch g Doyen(IRE) Mary Sea (FR) (Selkirk (USA))
4880[11] 5734[9] 6345[5]

Jamaican Bolt (IRE) *Geoffrey Oldroyd* a81 102
4 b g Pivotal Chiming (IRE) (Danehill (USA))
3382[3] ◆ (3730) 4073[7] (6427) 7063[4] 7397[2]

Jamarjo (IRE) *Steve Gollings* a85 79
5 b g Marju(IRE) Athlumney Lady (Lycius (USA))
(156) 400[10] 738[5] 850[2] 992[4] 1286[3] 1925[3] 3077[5] (3988) ◆ 4326[6] (5158) 5665[3]

Jambobo *William Knight* a37
3 b g Acclamation Hovering (IRE) (In The Wings)
2196[15] 3338[8] 3947[7]

Jameela Girl *Robert Cowell* a53 62
4 ch m Haafhd Peach Sorbet (IRE) (Spectrum (IRE))
1643[12] 1990[5] 3618[8] 4235[11]

Jamesbo's Girl *Richard Fahey* 88
2 ch f Refuse To Bend(IRE) Donna Anna (Be My Chief (USA))
2338[2] 3126[6] (3251) (3951) (4804) 5909[2] (6160) 6632[6]

Jamesie (IRE) *David Marnane* a97 99
4 b g Kodiac Pretty Woman (IRE) (Night Shift (USA))
2025[7] 3331[2] ◆ 4099[6] 4802[6] 6868[11]

James Pollard (IRE) *Bernard Llewellyn* a68 75
7 ch g Indian Ridge Manuetti (IRE) (Sadler's Wells (USA))
2498[7] 2867[2] (3429) 4470[7] 4844[3] 5197[2] 5528[4] 6278[5] 6734[8]

Jamesway (IRE) *Ruth Carr* a56 89
4 ch g Camacho Charlene Lacy (IRE) (Pips Pride)
1602[4] 2704[6] 3127[13] 3441[3] 4451[4] 6234[10] 6767[11]

Jamhara *Clive Brittain* a62 58
3 b f Authorized(IRE) Wimple (USA) (Kingmambo (USA))
(1420) 1733[5]

Jamnean *John Holt* a50 55
2 b f Byron Dazzling View (USA) (Distant View (USA))
1188[3] 1308[4] 1556[7] 2349[3] 2790[4] 3748[7] 5403[4] 5932[4] 6283[6] 6890[5]

Jamr *M bin Shafya* a107 28
4 br g Singspiel(IRE) Never Enough (GER) (Monsun (GER))
(241a) 484a[2] (678a)

Jan De Heem *Ralph Beckett* a54
2 ch g Dutch Art Shasta (Shareef Dancer (USA))
7165[11] 7924[6]

Jane Lachatte (IRE) *Stuart Williams* a51 80
3 b f Doyen(IRE) Simonda (Singspiel (IRE))
597[5] (1607) 2201[8] 3003[4] 3616[2] (3998) 4254[2] 5533[5] 5706[7] 6847[2] 7519[10]

Janey Muddles (IRE) *J S Bolger* a98 98
3 b f Lawman(FR) Slip Dance (IRE) (Celtic Swing)
1041a[5] 1403a[7] 1943a[4] 2527a[8] 3645a[12]

Janie Runaway (IRE) *Malcolm Saunders* a56 70
2 b f Antonius Pius(USA) Await (IRE) (Peintre Celebre (USA))
5978[4] 6644[6]

Janood (IRE) *M bin Shafya* a95 97
4 b g Medicean Alluring Park (IRE) (Green Desert (USA))
682a[7]

Janoub Nibras (IRE) *Richard Hannon* a98 95
2 b c Acclamation Wildsplash (USA) (Deputy Minister (CAN))
2069[3] 2376[2] (3040) (3501) 4763[3] ◆ (6149) 6700[2]

Jan Smuts (IRE) *Wilf Storey* a27 62
4 b g Johannesburg(USA) Choice House (USA) (Chester House (USA))
2438[6] 2823[8] 3752[2] (4431) 4590[4] ◆ 4867[4] 6478[10] 6784[P] 7454[7]

Jaques Vert (FR) *Danielle McCormick* a41
6 ch g Dr Fong(USA) Sayuri (USA) (Sadler's Wells (USA))
8037[7]

Jardim (BRZ) *M F De Kock* a105 90
6 gr h Ski Champ(USA) Copacabana Beach (BRZ) (Midnight Tiger (USA))
416a[8] 587a[2] 678a[4] 755a[5] 876a[11]

Jardina (GER) *P Schiergen* 102
4 b m Shirocco(GER) Juvena (GER) (Platini (GER))
3653a[10]

Jareeda (USA) *Sir Michael Stoute* 31
2 bb f First Samurai(USA) Manaal (USA) (Bahri (USA))
7329[12]

Jarrow (IRE) *Milton Bradley* a93 88
5 ch g Shamardal(USA) Wolf Cleugh (IRE) (Last Tycoon)
(1091) 1885[11] 3027[10] (3822) 4799[10] 5343[13] 6026[6] 6663[8] 7019[6]

Jasmeno *Hughie Morrison* a74 64
5 b m Catcher In The Rye(IRE) Jasmick (IRE) (Definite Article)
4[4]

Jasmines Hero (USA) *H Hesse* a70 66
7 b g War Chant(USA) Ryn (USA) (Mr Prospector (USA))
94a[4]

Jathabah (IRE) *Clive Brittain* a69 60
2 b f Singspiel(IRE) Zibet (Kris)
3282[5] 4055[6] 4525[5] 6344[7]

Jawaab (IRE) *Philip Kirby* a71 77
8 ch g King's Best(USA) Canis Star (Wolfhound (USA))
192[4] 460[5] 672[3] 751[4] 1071[7] 1297[8] 1525[7] 4955[3] 5891[2] (6101) (6407) 7293[4]

Jawbreakeronastick *John Stimpson* a26
3 b g Striking Ambition Danalia (IRE) (Danehill (USA))
1053[11] 1422[8]

Jawhar (IRE) *William Haggas* 97
4 ch g Halling(USA) Kawn (Cadeaux Genereux)
2011[4] 2855[2] 4068[4] 4805[3] (5636) (6073) (6450)

Jawim *Malcolm Saunders* a50 54
3 br f Piccolo Craic Sa Ceili (IRE) (Danehill Dancer (IRE))
2166[7] 2388[13] 4902[3] 5263[10] 5536[6] 6737[4] 7275[4]

Jawinski (IRE) *David Evans* 62
2 b g Jeremy(USA) Karinski (USA) (Palace Music (USA))
3505[9] 4194[5] 4837[9]

Jawking *David Evans* a65 22
3 b g Compton Place Just Down The Road (IRE) (Night Shift (USA))
127[8] 352[4] 605[4]

Jay Bee Blue *Sean Curran* a71 74
3 b g Kyllachy Czarna Roza (Polish Precedent (USA))
1138[6] 1612[12] 2045[10] 3002[9] 4815[7] 5203[5] 5263[4] 5991[2] (6216) 6968[4]

Jaycito (USA) *Bob Baffert* a107
4 b h Victory Gallop(CAN) Night Edition (CAN) (Ascot Knight (CAN))
7546a[11]

Jay Jays Joy *Paul Midgley* a65 51
4 b g Diktat Agrippina (Timeless Times (USA))
7[6] 453[9] 490[9] 676[11]

Jay Kay *Danielle McCormick* a59 57
3 b g Librettist(USA) Turn Back (Pivotal)
2095[9] 2540[9] 3555[3] 4397[9] (5014) 5415[8] 5721[7] 6217[9] 6813[8]

Jayzee Dancer *Mark Gillard*
4 b g Imperial Dancer Jayzee (IRE) (Iron Mask (USA))
6095[7]

Jazz On The Beach *Luca Cumani* 54
2 bb f Footstepsinthesand Zee Zee Gee (Galileo (IRE))
5267[9] 5947[11] 6817[5]

Jd Rockefeller *Paul D'Arcy* a53
2 ch g Sakhee(USA) Perle D'Or (IRE) (Entrepreneur)
7642[7] 7924[7] 8178[7]

Jeangeorges (IRE) *Patrick J Flynn* a70 60
6 b g Noverre(USA) Appetina (Perugino (USA))
(6184a)

Jeannie Galloway (IRE) *Keith Dalgleish* a70 94
5 b m Bahamian Bounty Housekeeper (IRE) (Common Grounds)
1040a[5] 1220[7] 1581[6] 2310[6] 2752[5] 3524[4] 5539[4] 6176[9]

Jebel Tara *Ian Semple* a71 55
7 b g Diktat Chantilly (FR) (Sanglamore (USA))
3888[10] 4134[14] 4638[5] 5087[7] 5185[5] 5590[5] 5917[2] 6308[4] 6529[3] 6756[4]

Jebril (FR) *Jonathan Portman* 74
2 b c Astronomer Royal(USA) Happy Clapper (Royal Applause)
(5655) 6732[6] 7111[2]

Jebulani *David O'Meara* a43 50
2 b c Jelani(IRE) Susan's Dowry (Efisio)
7205[6] 7636[9] 8134[7]

Jedi *A bin Huzaim* a96 103
6 ch g Pivotal Threefold (USA) (Gulch (USA))
143a[2] 317a[4] 486a[6]

Jedward (IRE) *Kevin Ryan* a84 93
5 ch m Namid Input (Primo Dominie)
1476[3] 1926[3] 2310[5] 2913[8] 3169[3] 3608[6] (4013) 4367[4] 4799[18] 5829[3] 6466[18] 6666[8] 7243[10]

Jeer (IRE) *Michael Easterby* a72 78
8 ch g Selkirk(USA) Purring (USA) (Mountain Cat (USA))
43[4] 192[9] (535) 1154[7] 2260[12] 5809[10] (6503) 6691[8] 8149[3] 8243[10]

Jehanbux (USA) *Richard Hannon* a79 95
4 b h Giant's Causeway(USA) Harlan Honey (USA) (Silver Hawk (USA))
1139[14] 2346[6] 3341[7]

Jehannedarc (IRE) *A De Royer-Dupre* a88 105
4 b m Montjeu(IRE) Lucky Rainbow (USA) (Rainbow Quest (USA))
4738[2] 6598[4] 7237[8] 7735a[5]

Jellicle (IRE) *H-A Pantall* a90 89
3 b f Successful Appeal(USA) Catboat (USA) (Tale Of The Cat (USA))
(291) 3987a[10] 7345a[3] 7803a[4]

Jembatt (IRE) *Michael Mulvany* a80 89
5 ch g Captain Rio Silly Imp (IRE) (Imperial Frontier (USA))
5609a[13] 6854a[13]

Jemimaville (IRE) *Giles Bravery* a52 42
5 b m Fasliyev(USA) Sparkling Isle (Inchinor)
126[5] 297[10] 467[7] 985[2] 1768[13] 3718[6] 4196[5] 4943[4] 5681[14] 6150[9]

Jenndale *Chris Dwyer* 8
3 b g Common World(USA) Jennelle (Nomination)
1062[10] 1740[11]

Jennifer J *Mark H Tompkins* a61 78
3 ch f Motivator Trew Class (Inchinor)
84[7] 429[4] 2424[5] 3088[2] 3697[2] 4972[4] (6416)

Je Parts Seul (FR) *P Sogorb* 100
3 gr g Keltos(FR) Kal Secret (FR) (Kaldoun (FR))
6087a[6]

Jeranimo (USA) *Michael Pender* a105 119
6 b h Congaree(USA) Jera (USA) (Jeblar (USA))
7575a[6]

Jeremy Sue *Derek Haydn Jones* a43 27
3 b f Amadeus Wolf Dearest Daisy (Forzando)
734[12] 898[3] 1337[6] 1585[5] 2166[6] 2404[3]

Jericho (IRE) *Jamie Osborne* a62 61
3 br g Manduro(GER) Jinsiyah (USA) (Housebuster (USA))
(462) 766[4] 1364[7]

Jermatt *J R Jenkins* a63 51
3 b g Kyllachy Miss Ippolita (Diktat)
1739[6] 5453[4] 6095[3] 6806[5] 7611[2] 7952[2]

Jerry Ellen (IRE) *Tim Easterby* a55 39
3 b g Jeremy(USA) Lady Ellen (Horage)
1843[15] 2339[8] 2774[5] (4929) 5428[8] 6178[9] 6959[9] 7604[12] 7634[9]

Jersey Town (USA) *Barclay Tagg* a121
6 ch h Speightstown(USA) Jersey Girl (USA) (Belong To Me (USA))
7570a[5]

Jessica Ashton *Stuart Kittow* 50
4 ch m Monsieur Bond(IRE) Feathergrass (IRE) (Fasliyev (USA))
2204[13] 2765[6] 3011[6] 3939[12]

Jessica's Gold *Christine Dunnett*
3 b f Iceman Capstick (JPN) (Machiavellian (USA))
5970[13]

Jet Acclaim (IRE) *Marco Botti* a64 60
2 b f Acclamation Jellett (IRE) (Green Desert (USA))
2349[2] 2812[8] 3971[4] 4581[3] 4927[2] 5748[4] 6212[5]

Jet Away *Sir Henry Cecil* 116
5 b h Cape Cross(IRE) Kalima (Kahyasi)
(1475) (2478) 3418[3] 4610[4] 5090[2]

Jetfire *D Prod'Homme* a77 105
4 b m American Post Saristar (Starborough)
7665a[4]

Jeu De Roseau (IRE) *Chris Grant* a57 75
8 b g Montjeu(IRE) Roseau (Nashwan (USA))
1272[8] 3953[8] 4590[10]

Jeu De Vivre (IRE) *Mark Johnston* a11 87
4 b m Montjeu(IRE) In My Life (IRE) (Rainbow Quest (USA))
1239[4] 1282[5] 1880[7] 4460[5]

Jewelled *Lady Herries* a75 82
6 b m Fantastic Light(USA) Danemere (IRE) (Danehill (USA))
1266[8] 4335[2] ◆ 5007[5] 5417[5]

Jewelled Dagger (IRE) *Sharon Watt* a31 81
8 b g Daggers Drawn(USA) Cappadoce (IRE) (General Monash (USA))
1295[13] 2134[9] 2669[8]

Jezza *Karen George* a64 59
6 br g Pentire Lara (GER) (Sharpo)
7839[7] 7980[6]

Jibouti (IRE) *Clive Brittain* a59 20
4 b g Exceed And Excel(AUS) Treble Seven (USA) (Fusaichi Pegasus (USA))
110[7] 274[11]

Jida (IRE) *Alan Jarvis* 51
2 ch f Refuse To Bend(IRE) La Quinta (IRE) (Indian Ridge)
4701[8]

Jigsaw (FR) *S Wattel* a79 77
3 b g Gentlewave(IRE) Grove Daffodil (IRE) (Salt Dome (USA))
5074a[7]

Jillnextdoor (IRE) *Mick Channon* 101
2 b f Henrythenavigator(USA) Royal Shyness (Royal Academy (USA))
2234[2] 2614[2] ◆ 3269[8] 5357[2] 5904[4] (6282) 6672[5] 6883[7] 7400[4] 7518[7]

Jillywinks *Scott Dixon* 61
2 b f Milk It Mick Thunderous Days (Diktat)
6966[5] 7364[11]

Jimmy Creed (USA) *Richard E Mandella* a118
3 ch c Distorted Humor(USA) Hookedonthefeelin (USA) (Citidancer (USA))
7574a[9]

Jimmy Elder *Richard Hannon* 66
2 b c Invincible Spirit(IRE) Hijab (King's Best (USA))
1847[4] 2817[4] 3140[6] 3617[4] 4230[4] 4752[4] 5061[2]

Jimmy Ryan (IRE) *Tim McCarthy* a75 48
11 b g Orpen(USA) Kaysama (FR) (Kenmare (FR))
(59) (152) 763[3] 3618[10]

Jimmy Styles *Clive Cox* a105 111
8 ch g Inchinor Inya Lake (Whittingham (IRE))
314a[8] ◆ 420a[7] 589a[6] 756a[7] 1129[2] 1469[2] 2513a[2] 3370[13] 4794[5] (5648a) 7236[15]

Jimmy The Lollipop (IRE) *Ian Williams* a67 70
3 b g Amadeus Wolf Royal Consort (IRE) (Green Desert (USA))
217[8] 518[6] 1082[5] 3713[12] 4650[14]

Jimmy The Snooze (IRE) *Stuart Williams* a61
2 b c Moss Vale(IRE) Mrs Kepple (King's Best (USA))
7304[5]

Jim Tango (FR) *Brian Storey* 63
8 bb g Jimble(FR) Fitanga (FR) (Fijar Tango (FR))
3181[6] 4259[9] 4622[4] 5172[8] 5922[10] 6478[12]

Jinker Noble *Ed de Giles* a75 80
3 b c Green Desert(USA) Depressed (Most Welcome)
1271[8] 1721[6] 2347[13] 3234[4] 4500[4] 4757[4] 5308[2] 5502[17] 6005[6] 6811[10]

Jinky *Linda Perratt* a77 72
4 b g Noverre(USA) Aries (GER) (Big Shuffle (USA))
4133[13] 4638[7] 5082[4] 5189[3] 7004[7] (7412)

Jiroft (ITY) *A Marcialis* 101
5 b h Blu Air Force(IRE) Dexia (ITY) (Indian Ridge)
2325a[9]

Jivry *Anthony Honeyball* 88
5 ch m Generous(IRE) Jadidh (Touching Wood (USA))
1846[5]

Jiwen (CAN) *Roger Varian* a93 91
4 bb m Singspiel(IRE) Love Medicine (USA) (Mining (USA))
2248[12] 5583[5] 6379[6] 7510[5]

J J Leary (IRE) *Ian Williams* a64 51
3 b g Amadeus Wolf Nautical Design (USA) (Seeking The Gold (USA))
38[7] 459[3] 556[3] 641[4] 734[2] (845) 1010[3] 1063[3] (1393)

Jo All The Way *E Lellouche* 106
5 b h Gold Away(IRE) Secret Question (USA) (Rahy (USA))
3178a[3]

Jobekani (IRE) *Lisa Williamson* a43 64
6 b g Tagula(IRE) Lyca Ballerina (Marju (IRE))
843[6] 1096[7] 2454[9]

Jo Boy *Michael Bell* a64 17
5 b g Royal Applause Bad Kitty (USA) (Mt. Livermore (USA))
128[4] 287[3] 574[11] 884[5]

Jo'Burg (USA) *David O'Meara* a75 96
8 b g Johannesburg(USA) La Martina (Atraf)
2077[3] 2620[3] 2773[5] 3167[9] 4879[3] (5111) 5369[4] (6124) 6638[12] 6881[3] 7556[7]

Jocasta Dawn *Henry Candy* a58 81
3 b f Kyllachy Jubilee Dawn (Mark Of Esteem (IRE))
1376[4] ◆ (1739) 3118[2] (4412) 5486[8] 7113[2]

Jodawes (USA) *Gary Moore* a62 67
5 bb g Burning Roma(USA) Venetian Peach (USA) (Desert Wine (USA))
6949[8] 7960[9]

Jodies Jem *William Jarvis* a80 71
2 br g Kheleyf(USA) First Approval (Royal Applause)
6411[6] 6846[3] 7191[3] (7840) (8072)

Joe Eile (IRE) *G M Lyons* a94 89
4 b g Iffraaj Encouragement (Royal Applause)
337a[2] 6716a[2]

Joe Le Taxi (IRE) *Mark Johnston* a80 52
4 ch g Johannesburg(USA) Attasliyah (IRE) (Marju (IRE))
205[5] 335a[4] 458[6] 623[9] 752[2] 819[3] 883[7] 1050[7] 1263[10] 1958[4] 2455[7]

Joeluke *Noel Quinlan* a46 44
2 br g Cockney Rebel(IRE) Enthralled (Zafonic (USA))
3844[8] 4448[6] 4877[8] 6889[7]

Joe Packet *Jonathan Portman* a89 106
5 ch g Joe Bear(IRE) Costa Packet (IRE) (Hussonet (USA))
1157[21] 3371[26] 3641[4] 4321[9] 5065[2] 6867[5]

Joe The Coat *Mark H Tompkins* a71 68
3 ch g Act One Torcross (Vettori (IRE))
1265[4] 2125[4] 2368[5] 3345[12] 8023[3]

Joey's Destiny (IRE) *George Baker* 89
2 ch c Kheleyf(USA) Maid Of Ailsa (USA) (Pivotal)
(2970) ◆ 6883[12] 7374[11]

Joha (USA) *Michael J Maker* a106 104
2 bb c Johar(USA) Mujado (IRE) (Mujadil (USA))
7568a[8]

Johanna Fosie (IRE) *Mick Channon* a51 55
3 ch f Peintre Celebre(USA) Yding (IRE) (Danehill (USA))
784[9] 1132[11] 1303[6] 1726[8] 2624[3] 3233[10]

Johannes (IRE) *Richard Fahey* a92 101
9 b g Mozart(IRE) Blue Sirocco (Bluebird (USA))
1157[12] 1844[9] 2507[11] 3049[4] (3612) 4629[6] (4799) 5370[5] 6468[8] 7066[8] 7690[16]

John Biscuit (IRE) *Andrew Balding* a86 95
4 ch g Hawk Wing(USA) Princess Magdalena (Pennekamp (USA))
2500[10] 2801[4] 3278[2] (3774) 4578[2] 5079[3] 5558[11] 6702[3]

John Coffey (IRE) *David Nicholls* a52 57
3 b g Acclamation Appleblossom Pearl (IRE) (Peintre Celebre (USA))
1296[5] 2470[6] 3438[5] 4348[15] 5590[3] 6104[13] 6640[5] 7354[7]

John Forbes *Brian Ellison* a66 78
10 b g High Estate Mavourneen (USA) (Dynaformer (USA))
1598[6] 3535[5]

John Louis *Philip McBride* a84 94
4 ch g Bertolini(USA) Native Ring (FR) (Bering)
199[8] (349) (648) 2248[5] 2606[2] (2932) (4103) 5079[5]

Johnno *J W Hills* a83 89
3 br g Excellent Art Vert Val (USA) (Septieme Ciel (USA))
1392[2] ◆ 2150[5] ◆ 2428[5] 3393[3] ◆ (3876) 4473[7] 5004[4]

Johnny Castle *Amanda Perrett* a81 103
4 b g Shamardal(USA) Photogenic (Midyan (USA))
4761[18] 5572[11] 6201[3] ◆ 6676[10] 7240[9] 7508[13]

Johnny Cavagin *Richard Guest* a65 84
3 b g Superior Premium Beyond The Rainbow (Mind Games)
(1012) 1359[7] (2540) (3567) 4496[8] (5388) 6939[8]

Johnny Splash (IRE) *Roger Teal* a55 46
3 b g Dark Angel(IRE) Ja Ganhou (Midyan (USA))
1725[10] 3151[10] 3470[12] 3724[7] 4644[7] 5095[5] 5994[5] 6436[3] 6927[6] 7822[4] 7988[5] 8184[7]

John Potts *Brian Baugh* a73 48
7 b g Josr Algarhoud(IRE) Crown City (USA) (Coronado's Quest (USA))
275[3] 403[7] 1000[7] 2735[6] 3081[6] 3454[8] 8137[7]

John Scott (USA) *Carla Gaines* a108
5 bb g Bertrando(USA) Henlopen (USA) (Deputy Minister (CAN))
7570a[4]

Johnson's Cat (IRE) *Daniel Mark Loughnane* a51 55
3 b g One Cool Cat(USA) Takanewa (IRE) (Danetime (IRE))
270[8] 1012[8] 1259[11] 1596[4] 1916[7] 2010[13] 7903[9]

Johns Porridge *Peter Hiatt*
3 ch f Needwood Blade Obsessive Secret (IRE) (Grand Lodge (USA))
8080[10]

Johnstown Lad (IRE) *Daniel Mark Loughnane* a74 70
8 b g Invincible Spirit(IRE) Pretext (Polish Precedent (USA))
178[9] 7666[8] 7864[12] 8305[7]

Join Up *Mark Brisbourne* a65 67
6 b g Green Desert(USA) Rise (Polar Falcon (USA))
67[5] 183[5] 532[3] 725[4] 929[6] 1009[5] 1309[3] 1717[5] (1908) (2090) 2464[5] 2858[10] (3317) 3544[3] 3559[13]

Jolie Etoile *Tony Carroll* a42
4 b m Choisir(AUS) Jolie (IRE) (Orpen (USA))
41[6] 291[6] 499[7] 939[6] 985[6] 2555[13] 4812[11]

Jolie Noce (FR) *F Doumen* a82 84
4 b m Muhtathir Jolie Jim (FR) (Double Bed (FR))
18a[0]

Jollification (IRE) *George Baker* a82 91
2 b f Acclamation Improvise (Lend A Hand)
2282[6] (3504) 4577[4] 5307[6] 6487[13] 7193[4]

Jolly Ranch *Tony Newcombe* a57 69
6 gr m Compton Place How Do I Know (Petong)
59[5] 2165[12] 2809[5] 7673[7]

Jolly Roger (IRE) *Tony Carroll* 66
5 b g Oratorio(IRE) Chalice Wells (Sadler's Wells (USA))
4061[5] 4499[8]

Joly Berengere (FR) *M Cesandri* 90
3 b f Policy Maker(IRE) Joly Coeur (FR) (Mont Basile (FR))
1434a[7]

Jomari (IRE) *Declan Carroll* a16 42
2 ch g Ad Valorem(USA) Love Valentine (IRE) (Fruits Of Love (USA))
2667[7] 2923[8] 4448[7] 5716[6] 6356[7]

Jonnie Skull (IRE) *Phil McEntee* a68 63
6 b g Pyrus(USA) Sovereign Touch (IRE) (Pennine Walk)
21[5] 97[6] 113[3] 305[6] (503) 761[6] 839[3] 886[3] 972[5] 1178[3] 1283[4] 1433[5] 1722[8] 2171[9] 2652[2] (3053) 3249[3] 3950[2] 4192[8] 5214[3] 5322[11] 5457[5] 5850[3] 5993[9] 6982[14] 7316[3] 7504[4] 7733[6] 8005[6] 8061[4] 8168[5] 8298[3]

Jonny Delta *Jim Goldie* 78
5 ch g Sulamani(IRE) Send Me An Angel (IRE) (Lycius (USA))
1880[4] 3114[4] 3564[4] 4115[8] 5002[5] 5798[8] 6712[3] 7098[3] 7367[4]

Jonny Lesters Hair (IRE) *Tim Easterby* a71 88
7 b g Danetime(IRE) Jupiter Inlet (IRE) (Jupiter Island)
1134[7] 1381[7] 1670[4] 2312[3] 3167[13] 3306[3] 4347[5] 4879[4] 5227[4] 5712[8] 6073[18] 6884[9]

Jonny Mudball *Tom Dascombe* a100 108
6 b g Oasis Dream Waypoint (Cadeaux Genereux)
(1316) 1857[15] 5814[4] 6676[5] ◆ 6882[7] 7366[3]

Jonny No Nose (SWE) *Lennart Reuterskiold Jr*
3 bb g Binary File(USA) Mitime (SWE) (Duty Time)
5144a[9]

Jonny Wombat *Richard Ford* a38 30
2 b g Avonbridge Moonlight Angel (Kyllachy)
6609[11] 6954[7] 7272[8]

Jontleman (IRE) *Mick Channon* 73
2 b g Whipper(USA) Gandia (IRE) (Danehill (USA))
2193[6] 3009[4] 5574[2] 6114[6]

Jordanstown *Kevin Ryan* 55
2 ch g Piccolo Pigment (Zamindar (USA))
1218[5] 2415[7] 3576[5]

Jordaura *Alan Berry* a78 84
6 br g Primo Valentino(IRE) Christina's Dream (Spectrum (IRE))
36[7] 187[7] 275[6] 655[7] 830[3] 976[2] 1045[4] 1432[4] 1562[5] (4219) 4586[6] 4987[4] 5174[5] 5730[6] 6631[4] 7003[3] (7095) 7640[3] 8146[9]

Jorum *Sir Henry Cecil* a75 74
3 b f Dansili Grail (USA) (Quest For Fame)
2008[4] 2768[4] 3773[5] 4311[7] 4918[4] 6037[9]

Josam (IRE) *Richard Hannon* a76
3 b c Montjeu(IRE) Bella Miranda (Sinndar (IRE))
84[4]

Josephine Blanche (GER) *D Moser* 93
4 gr m Tannenkonig(IRE) Jeanine (GER) (Neshad (USA))
4113[13] 5647a[12]

Josephine Malines *Richard Price* a51 51
8 b m Inchinor Alrisha (IRE) (Persian Bold)
602[11] 1112[9]

Joshua The First *Keith Dalgleish* a74 76
3 br g Kheleyf(USA) Newkeylets (Diktat)
(1241) 1798[3] 2229[5] 3728[6] 4260[8] 5759[5] (6131) 6429[5] 6894[5] 7004[3] 7203[10]

Joshua Tree (IRE) *Marco Botti* a104 116
5 b h Montjeu(IRE) Madeira Mist (IRE) (Grand Lodge (USA))
486a[7] 755a[7] 877a[6] 1144a[2] 2534a[4] 2968a[4] 4010[2] (5400a) 6293a[3] (7094a) 8040a[9]

Josie Lennon *Robert Johnson*
3 ch f Royal Anthem(USA) Lorna Lennon (IRE) (Carroll House)
2288[U] 5315[10]

Josie's Dream (IRE) *Jo Hughes* a55 57
4 b g Tau Ceti Gallery Breeze (Zamindar (USA))
429[6] 495[4] 1310[11] 2048[3] 2391[5] 2575[5] 4904[3] 5196[2] 5817[2] 6821[8] 6956[2]

Journalistic (USA) *Marcus Tregoning* a69 79
3 b c Street Sense(USA) Cajun Two Step (USA) (Tabasco Cat (USA))
2380[4] 2980[11] 3431[4]

Jouster (IRE) *M D O'Callaghan* a71 79
4 b g Acclamation Jesting (Muhtarram (USA))
(5017) 6452[3]

Joviality *John Gosden* 115
4 b m Cape Cross(IRE) Night Frolic (Night Shift (USA))
2654[2] (3266) 4065[10] 5376a[3] 6634[5]

Joy And Fun (NZ) *D Cruz* 120
9 b g Cullen(AUS) Gin Player (NZ) (Defensive Play (USA))
1146a[3] 3238[16] 8041a[4]

Joyeuse Marche *A Fabre* 69
2 ch f New Approach(IRE) Last Rhapsody (IRE) (Kris)
5570a[4]

Joyful Motive *Tom Tate* 51
3 ch g Motivator Triple Joy (Most Welcome)
2592[8] 3035[10] 3420[3] 5330[7] 6626[11]

Joyful Sound (IRE) *Brian Ellison* 63
4 b g Acclamation Eman's Joy (Lion Cavern (USA))
3549[11] 5917[13]

Joyful Spirit (IRE) *John Dunlop* a81 74
3 b f Invincible Spirit(IRE) Pershaan (IRE) (Darshaan)
1320[5] 1853[4] 2624[6] 3966[3] 4506[6] (5770) (6364) 6647[12] 7195[11]

Joyously *Richard Guest* a24 78
4 ch m Needwood Blade Lambadora (Suave Dancer (USA))
452[10]

Joy To The World (IRE) *Paul Cole* a60 55
3 ch f Dylan Thomas(IRE) Speciale (USA) (War Chant (USA))
1296[6] 1843[14] 2203[3] ◆ 2386[6] 3193[7] 5215[8] 5406[4] 5770[2] 5989[3] 6442[2] 6962[3] (7267a)

Jozafeen *Robin Bastiman* 65
5 ch m Zafeen(FR) Faithful Beauty (IRE) (Last Tycoon)
96[9]

J R Hartley *Bryan Smart* a82 40
4 b g Refuse To Bend(IRE) Flyfisher (USA) (Riverman (USA))
11[7]

Juana Belen *David Barron* 54
2 b f Rail Link Calico Moon (USA) (Seeking The Gold (USA))
4449[2] 4907[5] 5291[4] 6115[6] 6310[6]

Juanita (USA) *Michael J Maker* a112 90
4 bb m Mineshaft(USA) Wishful Splendor (USA) (Smart Strike (CAN))
(1839a)

Juarla (IRE) *Ronald Harris* a62 69
4 ch h Tagula(IRE) Jersey Lillie (IRE) (Hector Protector (USA))
696[10] 819[7] 1280[7] 1497[6] 4653[6] 4993[7] (5504) (5659) 5808[5] 7218[F]

Jubilance (IRE) *Bent Olsen* a87 88
3 b c Oratorio(IRE) Literacy (USA) (Diesis)
5651a[5]

Jubilante *Hughie Morrison* 72
2 b f Royal Applause Lavinia's Grace (USA) (Green Desert (USA))
5784[3] 6167[2]

Jubilant Queen *Clive Cox* 70
2 b f Kyllachy Hector's Girl (Hector Protector (USA))
4002[2] 5146[5] 5932[2]

Jubilee Brig *Gary Moore* a84 84
2 b g Kheleyf(USA) Voile (IRE) (Barathea (IRE))
1920[3] ◆ 2420[2] (2808) 3291[11] 4804[3] ◆ 5563[8] 6487[12]

Jubilee Dancer *Geoffrey Oldroyd* 60
2 b f Misu Bond(IRE) Bond Babe (Forzando)
3560[9] 6007[6]

Jubilee Diamond (IRE) *Richard Hannon* a76 79
2 b f Redback Nice One Clare (IRE) (Mukaddamah (USA))
2426[2] 3269[20] 5943[2] (6276) 7164[8]

Jubilee Games *Richard Fahey* 78
2 b g Pastoral Pursuits Jane Jubilee (IRE) (Mister Baileys)
1437[4] (1795) (3532) 4093[18] 5670[5] 6189[2] 6955[2]

Jubilini *Brett Johnson* a21 43
2 ch f Bertolini(USA) Days Of Grace (Wolfhound (USA))
4645[6] 5773[5] 6276[10]

Judas Jo (FR) *Gay Kelleway* a72 81
3 ch f Muhtathir Lovna (USA) (Tale Of The Cat (USA))
1125a[5] 2347[14] 3234[6] 3500[5] 3762[9] 4509[3] 5122[7] 6613[7]

Judd Street *Eve Johnson Houghton* a83 92
10 b g Compton Place Pudding Lane (IRE) (College Chapel)
378[8] 6369[4] 7145[8] 7827[11]

Judge 'n Jury *Ronald Harris* a85 108
8 ch g Pivotal Cyclone Connie (Dr Devious (IRE))
1849[2] (2208) 2704[17] (3127) 3650a[2] 3877[11] 4367[8] 5077[9] 5641a[3] 6485[10] 6666[16] 7397[6]

Judicious *Ollie Pears* 86
5 ch g Pivotal Virtuous (Exit To Nowhere (USA))
1134[6] ◆ 1820[4] 2620[2] 5227[6] 6476[11] 7069[7] 7294[7] 7639[8]

Judy In Disguise *Bill Turner* 89
2 b f Elusive City(USA) Tomorrow's World (IRE) (Machiavellian (USA))
(1202) ◆ (1891) 2603[6] 3326[10]

Judy Teen *Tim Easterby* 28
3 b f Cockney Rebel(IRE) Damelza (IRE) (Orpen (USA))
1864[10]

Juhaina (IRE) *Ann Duffield* a49 34
2 b f Haatef(USA) Spirit Of Age (IRE) (Indian Ridge)
3909[10] 4546[10] 5221[8] 5806[6]

Julier Pass (IRE) *Hugh McWilliams* a62 55
3 b g Catcher In The Rye(IRE) Chantarella (IRE) (Royal Academy (USA))
1166[5] 1420[4] 2036[5] 2351[4] 2749[10] 3455[9]

Julius Geezer (IRE) *Amy Weaver* a88 89
4 b g Antonius Pius(USA) Victoria's Secret (IRE) (Law Society (USA))
1091[3] 1587[11] 2342[5] (2551) (3027) 3272[4] (4554) 4999[4] 5557[6] 6008[12] 7254[7] 7651[3] 8100a[5] 8278a[9]

Jullundar (IRE) *Mick Channon* a71 71
2 b c Refuse To Bend(IRE) Announcing Peace (Danehill (USA))
5655[2] 6133[3] 6512[2] 6919[3] 7199[3] 7357[3]

July Days (IRE) *Brian Baugh* a66 83
6 b m Exceed And Excel(AUS) Tocade (IRE) (Kenmare (FR))
(430) 639[7] 828[6] 3456[4] 3949[6] 4656[2] (5428) 6217[7]

July Revolution (IRE) *David Marnane* a60 68
3 bb g Cape Cross(IRE) Triomphale (USA) (Nureyev (USA))
336a[5]

July Specialists *Richard Guest* a17 40
3 b f Josr Algarhoud(IRE) La Corujera (Case Law)
1427[5] 1716[7] 1825[9] 3547[8] 4172[10] 4549[8] 5738[10]

July Waits (USA) *Sir Mark Prescott Bt* a52
2 b f Mr Greeley(USA) Unique Pose (IRE) (Sadler's Wells (USA))
6153[11] 6535[11] 6790[14] 7459[6]

Jumbo Prado (USA) *Daniel Mark Loughnane* a65 75
3 rg g El Prado(IRE) Sant Elena (Efisio)
8249[6]

Jumeirah Liberty *Zoe Davison* a65 61
4 ch g Proclamation(IRE) Gleam Of Light (IRE) (Danehill (USA))
428[3] 685[3] 894[6] 1772[3] 2366[5] 2847[4] 3153[10] 4219[6] 4940[10]

Jumeirah Moon *David Simcock* a71 66
2 b g Kheleyf(USA) Pelican Key (IRE) (Mujadil (USA))
3948[2] 4658[4] (5010) 5475[2] 6414[3] 7059[7]

Jumeirah Palm Star *Richard Hannon* a78 66
3 b f Invincible Spirit(IRE) Golden Flyer (FR) (Machiavellian (USA))
(1004) 1790[4] 2503[14] (3736) 4256[8] 4726[7] 5156[6] 6319[6]

Jungle Bay *Jane Chapple-Hyam* a82 84
5 b g Oasis Dream Dominica (Alhaarth (IRE))
669[2] ◆ 893[3] 1156[9] 1564[12] (2355) 2913[6] 3541[7] (4814) 5320[10] 6041[5] 6820[5] 7789[2]

Jungle Beat (IRE) *John Gosden* 96
3 ch c Galileo(IRE) Flamingo Guitar (USA) (Storm Cat (USA))
1455[5] 2897[7] 3668[3] 4288[2] 5535[2]

Junior Diary (USA) *Brian Meehan* a73 72
3 ch f Mr Greeley(USA) Cross Channel (USA) (Giant's Causeway (USA))
1472[10] 2200[3] 2768[5] 3476[7] (4931) 5931[5] 7356[3]

Juniper Pass (USA) *Thomas Ray Bell II* a97 114
5 b g Lemon Drop Kid(USA) Child Bride (USA) (Coronado's Quest (USA))
7546a[4]

Junket *Dr Jon Scargill* a84 80
5 b m Medicean Gallivant (Danehill (USA))
302[7] 821[2] 1266[5] 1652[3] 4150[7] (4872) 5480[6] 6013[5] 6638[7] 7334[11] 7722[7]

Junoob *Tom Dascombe* a102 104
4 ch g Haafhd Faydah (USA) (Bahri (USA))
(223) 354[4] (712) 1034[10] 1159[3] 2267[6]

Juno The Muffinman (IRE) *Tom Dascombe* a79 77
3 b g Holy Roman Emperor(IRE) Mackenzie's Friend (Selkirk (USA))
(1055) 1978[5] 2427[4] 3033[5] 3781[2] 4294[RR] 4606[2]

Jupiter Fidius *Karen Tutty* 68
5 b g Haafhd Kyda (USA) (Gulch (USA))
1384[3] 1583[9] 2239[4] (3115) 3581[3] 4295[5] 6105[5] 6758[9] 7599[3]

Jupiter Storm *Gary Moore* 87
3 ch g Galileo(IRE) Exciting Times (FR) (Jeune Homme (USA))
1888[6] 2408[5] 4741[12] 5796[7] 6441[3]

Just A Cat (SWE) *Lennart Reuterskiold Jr*
3 bb g One Cool Cat(USA) La Lula (IRE) (Lahib (USA))
5144a[7]

Just A Pound (IRE) *Jo Hughes* a62 57
2 b g Ad Valorem(USA) Gallery Breeze (Zamindar (USA))
3708[4] 4967[4] 5207[2] 6732[9]

Just Bond (IRE) *Geoffrey Oldroyd* a88 91
10 b g Namid Give Warning (IRE) (Warning)
280[11] 694[2] 1249[5] 4345[4] 4557[9] 4964[3] 5111[10]

Justbookie Dot Com (IRE) *David Evans* a80 66
4 ch g Fath(USA) Dream On Deya (IRE) (Dolphin Street (FR))
1117[4] 3544[5] 4042[9] 4155[8] 5440[6] (5751) 6051[6] (6317) 6894[4] (7221) 7413[3]

Justbookies Dotnet *Louise Best* a69 57
3 b g Kheleyf(USA) Moly (Inchinor)
491[7] (892) 1110[5] 1313[4] 1445[10] 5775[11] 7742[11] 7917[11]

Just Breathe (IRE) *Olivia Maylam* a67
3 b f Choisir(AUS) Opium Creek (IRE) (Darshaan)
201[2] 7590[9] 7969[9] 8074[9] 8304[10]

Justcallmehandsome *Dominic Ffrench Davis* a71 35
10 ch g Handsome Ridge Pearl Dawn (IRE) (Jareer (USA))
67[2] 361[6] 403[8] 909[7] 1002[6] 1191[8] 1634[12] 1895[8] 2365[8] 2858[9] 3454[11] 8212[8]

Just Charlie *Henry Candy* a84 83
2 b g Piccolo Siryena (Oasis Dream)
3617[3] (4816) ◆ 6929[3]

Just Darcy *Sir Michael Stoute* 64
2 b f Danehill Dancer(IRE) Jane Austen (IRE) (Galileo (IRE))
5947[7]

Just Duchess *Michael Blanshard* 42
2 b f Avonbridge Red Countess (Pivotal)
4532[8] 4813[9] 5275[8] 5786[9] 6156[13]

Just Fabulous *George Moore* 84
3 b f Sakhee(USA) Tipsy Me (Selkirk (USA))
1477[8] 2088[4] 2897[6] 3376[4] 3882[7] 4553[8] 4997[7] 5712[6] 6124[12]

Just Five (IRE) *John Weymes* a71 76
6 b g Olmodavor(USA) Wildsplash (USA) (Deputy Minister (CAN))
490[3] (633) 676[5] 843[2] 1002[7] (1191) 1636[7] 2227[6] 3039[5] 3454[7] 4142[7] 4643[8] 5175[9] 7500[13] 7983[7] 8212[5]

Just For Mary *Daniel Mark Loughnane* a40 79
8 b g Groom Dancer(USA) Summer Dance (Sadler's Wells (USA))
1480[4] 1675[4] 2314[7] 3993[3] 4425[6] 4680[10] 5013[5] 5876[7]

Justineo *Roger Varian* a89 105
3 b c Oasis Dream Loulwa (IRE) (Montjeu (IRE))
2659[2] 3265[22] 5964[7] 6400[7] 7401[2] 7690[3]

Justine Time (IRE) *Julie Camacho* a50 59
3 b f Kodiac Sinn Time (IRE) (Key Of Luck (USA))
3315[8] 4549[7] 5623[6]

Justin Phillip (USA) *Steven Asmussen* a115
4 bb h First Samurai(USA) Ava Knowsthecode (USA) (Cryptoclearance (USA))
7574a[5]

Just Jimmy (IRE) *Trevor Wall* a67 65
7 b g Ashkalani(IRE) Berkeley Hall (Saddlers' Hall (IRE))
4179[17]

Just Like Heaven (IRE) *Tim Easterby* a74 69
3 b g Kodiac Night Beauty (King Of Kings (IRE))
1599[7] 2591[4] (2695) 3028[2] (4187) 4558[4] 4798[3] 5167[9] 5831[6] 6357[2]

Just Lille (IRE) *Ann Duffield* a71 93
9 b m Mull Of Kintyre(USA) Tamasriya (IRE) (Doyoun)
1159[4] (3458) (3609) 4621[5] 4864[3] (6055) (6313) 6828[4]

Just Me'Lady *Bill Turner* a22
3 ch f Avonbridge Just Run (IRE) (Runnett)
135[8] 597[8] 1183[5]

Justonefortheroad *Richard Fahey* a91 103
6 b g Domedriver(IRE) Lavinia's Grace (USA) (Green Desert (USA))
57 (1220) (1523) 2211[6] 3268[22] 4321[26] 4609[14] 5572[19] 7210[6] (7435)

Just One Kiss *Sir Henry Cecil* 74
2 b f Cape Cross(IRE) Kissing (Grand Lodge (USA))
6489[4]

Just One Wish (IRE) *H De Nicolay* a82 93
2 b f Araafa(IRE) Three Wishes (Sadler's Wells (USA))
3017a[4]

Just Past Andover (IRE) *Bill Turner* a36 80
2 b g Amadeus Wolf Fancy Feathers (IRE) (Redback)
1131[4] 1218[2] 1495[5] (1738) 1972[2] 2345[3] 3604[5] 4462[6]

Just Paul (IRE) *Kate Walton* 59
2 b g Clodovil(IRE) Tatamagouche (IRE) (Sadler's Wells (USA))
4587[8] 5410[6] 5727[7] 6475[3] 6952[5]

Just River *Natalie Lloyd-Beavis* a40
3 ch c Medicean Just Wood (FR) (Highest Honor (FR))
7978[4] 8141[6]

Just The Judge (IRE) *Charles Hills* 108
2 br f Lawman(FR) Faraday Light (IRE) (Rainbow Quest (USA))
(3474) (5353) (7052) ◆

Just The Tonic *Marjorie Fife* a59 74
5 ch m Medicean Goodwood Blizzard (Inchinor)
(1527) 1917[8] 2510[15] 3255[4] 3994[9] 4769[9] 6127[9] 6342[5] 6559[3] 6709[2] 7247[7]

Just Timmy Marcus *Brian Baugh* a64 61
6 ch g Ishiguru(USA) Grandads Dream (Never So Bold)
102[9] 274[3] 450[3] 633[5] 926[2] 1387[3] 1487[6] 2350[4] 2858[4] 3231[4] 3713[4]

Just When *Andrew Balding* a64 81
3 b g Dalakhani(IRE) Cape Grace (IRE) (Priolo (USA))
1414[6] 2196[9] 3448[7] 3787[3] 6146[6] (7018)

Just Wondering (IRE) *Ed Dunlop* a34 54
2 b f Danehill Dancer(IRE) Ibtikar (USA) (Private Account (USA))
6960[8] 7466[3] 7778[7]

Just Zak *Garry Woodward* a51 33
7 b g Superior Premium Goodbye Millie (Sayf El Arab (USA))
109[10] 390[6] 924[9] 1339[6]

Jutland *Doug Watson* a102 104
5 b g Halling(USA) Dramatique (Darshaan)
618a[3]

Juvenal (IRE) *Richard Hannon* a75 87
3 b c Holy Roman Emperor(IRE) Final Opinion (IRE) (King's Theatre (IRE))
2501[2] 3012[2] 3667[5] (4413) 5237[2] (5837) ◆

Jwala *Robert Cowell* a84 103
3 b f Oasis Dream Kangra Valley (Indian Ridge)
(3486) (4765) 6140[2]

Kaafel (IRE) *Peter Hedger* a89 86
3 b c Nayef(USA) Tafaani (IRE) (Green Desert (USA))
1132[6] 2380[2] (3384) 4679[2] 5237[4] 5796[3] 6376[12] (8174)

Kadouchski (FR) *John Berry* a64 67
8 b g Ski Chief(USA) Douchka (FR) (Fijar Tango (FR))
963[8] 1925[5] ◆ (2976) 3734[4]

Kafister (USA) *Peter Miller* 89
2 b g Kafwain(USA) Register (USA) (Mari's Book (USA))
7567a[4]

Kahfre *Gary Moore* a74 55
5 ch g Peintre Celebre(USA) Minerva (IRE) (Caerleon (USA))
202[9] 521[8] 728[5] 7377[10] 7791[10] 8001[P]

Kahruman (USA) *William Haggas* a92 98
3 bb g Mr Greeley(USA) Jaleela (USA) (Kingmambo (USA))
(1923) 2641[4] 3294[6] 5517[20] 6374[7]

Kahsabelle (FR) *Venetia Williams* a65 71
7 b m Kahyasi Lysabelle (FR) (Lesotho (USA))
3316[4] 5264[2]

Kai *Alan McCabe* a59 42
3 b g Kyllachy Belle Ile (USA) (Diesis)
1182[8] 1585[4] 2010[12] (2351) 2582[9] 2972[5] 5247[8] 6179[10] 6640[4] 6937[5] 7146[2] 7504[9] 8131[4] 8287[5]

Kai Broon (IRE) *Lucinda Russell* 18
5 b g Marju(IRE) Restiv Star (FR) (Soviet Star (USA))
5187[7]

Kailani *Mahmood Al Zarooni* 107
3 b f Monsun(GER) Kazzia (GER) (Zinaad)
(1887) ◆ 2658[7] 3292[7] 6163[9] 6877[7]

Kai Mook *Roger Ingram* a67 40
5 gb m Littletown Boy(USA) Beenaboutabit (Komaite (USA))
130[2] (265) 281[7] 570[6] 689[3] 738[9]

Kaiser Wilhelm (IRE) *Paul Cole* a71 69
3 b c Hurricane Run(IRE) Luana (Shaadi (USA))
1703[10] 2788[4] 3087[10] 3483[4] (4214) (4510) 4776[6] 6537[5] 7271[9]

Kaiss (USA) *S Seemar* a91 94
5 ch g Seeking The Gold(USA) November Snow (USA) (Storm Cat (USA))
80a[10] 616a[4]

Kajima *R Pritchard-Gordon* a101 97
5 b g Oasis Dream Mambo Mistress (USA) (Kingmambo (USA))
7123a[3]

Kakapuka *Anabel K Murphy* a86 81
5 br g Shinko Forest(IRE) No Rehearsal (FR) (Baillamont (USA))
733[5] 1708[2] 2083[6] 2608[5] 3503[6] 3963[4] 4580[11] 5910[12] 6319[8] 6692[12] 7725[12]

Kakatosi *Mike Murphy* a98 93
5 br g Pastoral Pursuits Ladywell Blaise (IRE) (Turtle Island (IRE))
29[6] 2068[20] 2409[12] 3641[12] 5356[12] 6432[3] 7327[10] 7790[7] (8266)

Kalahari Breeze (IRE) *William Muir* a50 58
2 b f Jeremy(USA) Staceymac (IRE) (Elnadim (USA))
2343[7] 3971[9] 4487[11] 4982[3] 8155[11]

Kalahari Gold (IRE) *F Rohaut* a101 104
7 ch g Trans Island Neat Shilling (IRE) (Bob Back (USA))
814a[3]

Kalamos (USA) *P Bary* a86 104
3 b c Empire Maker(USA) Kithira (Danehill (USA))
1171a[2] 5649a[7]

Kal Barg *D Selvaratnam* a101 97
7 b g Medicean Persian Air (Persian Bold)
47a[7]

Kaldoun Kingdom (IRE) *Richard Fahey* a47 101
7 b g King's Best(USA) Bint Kaldoun (IRE) (Kaldoun (FR))
2177[9] 4073[6] 4611[7] 5487[5] 6244[8] 6466[9] 7063[3] 7240[13] 7397[12]

Kalevala (FR) *R Pritchard-Gordon* a52 71
2 gr f Big Shuffle(USA) Gute Zeit (GER) (Platini (GER))
6751a[5] 7265a[4] 7699a[8]

Kalicamix *Paul Cole* a88 78
2 b c Bahamian Bounty Heather Mix (Linamix (FR))
2402[4] 2929[6] 3708[2] 4056[7] 4539[2] (5073a) (5698a) 7984a[0]

Kalily *Luca Cumani*
3 b c Dubawi(IRE) Mail Express (IRE) (Cape Cross (IRE))
5421[8] 6102[12]

Kalispell (IRE) *Mahmood Al Zarooni* 76
2 b f Singspiel(IRE) Genovefa (USA) (Woodman (USA))
6790[5] 7364[2]

Kalithea *Jim Boyle* a25
2 b f Kheleyf(USA) Baralinka (IRE) (Barathea (IRE))
7159[13]

Kalk Bay (IRE) *Michael Easterby* a94 92
5 b g Hawk Wing(USA) Politesse (USA) (Barathea (IRE))
1863[9] 2417[11] 2753[9] 3525[3] 4249[5] (4714) (5224) 5492[2] 6606[4] 7175[9]

Kalokagathia (IRE) *Jo Crowley* a83 71
3 b c Kodiac Seabound (Prince Sabo)
308[2] 2974[2] 7477[2] 7719[2] 7896[2] (8069)

Kamate (FR) *F Rohaut* a89
3 b f Early March Solitudine (Inchinor)
5074a[2]

Kamchatka *Alan Swinbank* 80
2 ch g Sakhee's Secret Queensgate (Compton Place)
4545[4] (4960) 6032[9] 6920[11]

Kames Park (IRE) *Richard Guest* a74 61
10 b g Desert Sun Persian Sally (IRE) (Persian Bold)
150[3] 271[5] 310[7] 400[3] 535[2] 592[3] 695[2] 786[3] 3449[10] 4594[8] 5253[4] 5767[3] 6055[2] 7024[7] 7381[5] 7596[4] 7819[4] 7968[2] 8106[5] 8273[5]

Kampai *Julia Feilden* a65 71
4 b m Sakhee(USA) Green Supreme (Primo Dominie)
3720[2] 4407[6] 4914[4] 5990[7] 6458[13] 6949[2] 7270[4] 7629[3] (7819) 8023[11] 8189[4]

Kamran (FR) *F Head* 89
2 b c Green Tune(USA) Mydarshaan (Darshaan)
3017a[2] 4118a[3] 5140a[6]

Kanaf (IRE) *M Al Muhairi* a102 101
5 b g Elnadim(USA) Catcher Applause (Royal Applause)
589a[2] 756a[6] 874a[10]

Kangaroo Court (IRE) *Emma Lavelle* a77 84
8 b g Lahib(USA) Tombazaan (IRE) (Good Thyne (USA))
(355) 2174[11] (2423) ◆ 3373[11] 4528[7] 5306[13]

Kaolak (USA) *Jim Goldie* a95 69
6 bb h Action This Day(USA) Cerita (USA) (Magesterial (USA))
1133[10] 1239[9]

Kapirovska (FR) *J-L Guillochon* a80 94
4 b m Muhtathir Touvoie (FR) (Anabaa (USA))
7320a[7]

Kapitala (FR) *J-P Carvalho* a76 89
3 b f Hawk Wing(USA) Key To Fortune (GER) (Big Shuffle (USA))
6085a[9] 7803a[0]

Kapitale (GER) *A Wohler* 109
4 b m Dubawi(IRE) Kapitol (GER) (Winged Love (IRE))
5376a[4] 6298a[4] 7093a[12]

Kapstadt (FR) *F Doumen* 95
2 b c Country Reel(USA) King's Parody (IRE) (King's Best (USA))
(3714a) 7693a[5]

Kapunda *Jedd O'Keeffe* 53
4 b g Pastoral Pursuits Kiss Me Again (IRE) (Cyrano De Bergerac)
1843[16] 2262[14] 3406[3] 3731[11] 4495[16]

Karadargent (FR) *H-A Pantall* a82 57
2 b g Kendargent(FR) Tishkara (FR) (Xaar)
7597a[5]

Karaka Jack *David Nicholls* a91 90
5 ch g Pivotal Mauri Moon (Green Desert (USA))
(1156) 1510[4] 1821[11] 2489[9] 2919[4] 3157[3] 3493[7] 4136[2] 4805[5] 5356[10] 5802[3] ◆ 6124[13] 6465[16] 6884[8] 7069[11]

Karamaya (IRE) *John M Oxx* 95
2 b f Invincible Spirit(IRE) Karawana (IRE) (King's Best (USA))
6081a[7]

Kara's Vision *Robert Cowell* a51 49
3 b f Kyllachy Classic Vision (Classic Cliche (IRE))
3357[7] 3706[8] 4970[4] 5247[2] 5719[11] 6249[7] 6771[5]

Karate (IRE) *Hans Adielsson* a67 52
4 ch g Exceed And Excel(AUS) La Belle Katherine (USA) (Lyphard (USA))
306[5] 1088[9] 1191[3] 1299[3] 1447[6] ◆ 1634[8] 1702[2] ◆ 1984[5] (2588) 3222[11]

Karate Queen *Ron Barr* a25 51
7 b m King's Best(USA) Black Belt Shopper (IRE) (Desert Prince (IRE))
2796[3] 3026[7] 4453[5] 4717[7] 4956[4] 5734[2] 6125[4] 6959[12]

Kargali (IRE) *Luke Comer* a56 80
7 gr h Invincible Spirit(IRE) Karliyka (IRE) (Last Tycoon)
1549a[5] 2100a[5]

Karistar (IRE) *Tom Keddy* a19 54
3 b f Montjeu(IRE) Showcall (USA) (Kingmambo (USA))
2430[10] 3399[10] 4440[9] 5408[9] 7488[8]

Karl Marx (IRE) *Mark Usher* 55
2 b g Red Clubs(IRE) Brillano (FR) (Desert King (IRE))
3010[8] 3444[14] 3937[9] 5806[10] 6115[11] 6928[7]

Karma Chameleon *John Berry* a83 83
3 b g Haafhd Mrs Snaffles (IRE) (Indian Danehill (IRE))
(193) 596[2] 841[4] 1142[5]

Karmarouge (IRE) *Brian Rothwell* 45
4 b m Croco Rouge(IRE) Karmafair (IRE) (Always Fair (USA))
4958[9]

Karr Wa Farr (IRE) *Ed Vaughan* a14 40
2 b c Shamardal(USA) Shraayef (Nayef (USA))
4340[8] 4773[10] 5032[7] 5763[12] 7313[12]

Kasbah Bliss (FR) *F Doumen* a78 114
10 b g Kahyasi Marital Bliss (FR) (Double Bed (FR))
759a[9] 1144a[5] 2534a[6] 6297a[4]

Kashgar *Michael Bell* a67 70
3 b g Hernando(FR) Miss Katmandu (IRE) (Rainbow Quest (USA))
1265[3] 1754[7] 2287[4] 3448[14] 4776[3] 5219[5] 5855[3] 6365[5] 7062[2] 7196[6]

Kashmiri Star *Michael Quinn* a61 64
3 b f Barathea(IRE) Biriyani (IRE) (Danehill (USA))
1285[3] 1739[5] 2085[4] 2803[3] 3315[5] 3548[4] 4777[2] (4937) 5130[6] 6001[2] 6436[2] 7314[14] 7521[4] 7769[4]

Kastini *Denis Coakley* a48 50
2 b g Halling(USA) Toucantini (Inchinor)
5765[10] 6481[18] 6978[10] 7708[8]

Kasumi (GER) *R Dzubasz* 104
5 b m Poliglote Kirsberry (GER) (Mulberry (FR))
3746a[7] 5844a[6] 6723a[9]

Kata Rock (USA) *Brian Rothwell* a60 17
5 ch g Giant's Causeway(USA) Harpia (USA) (Danzig (USA))
635[4] 908[10] 1250[11] 2555[15] 4314[7] 5015[9]

Katchy Lady *P J Prendergast* 83
2 ch f Kyllachy Star Approval (IRE) (Hawk Wing (USA))
2512a[6] 3674a[4]

Katherine Deux (FR) *Mme M Bollack-Badel* a81 81
3 b f Poliglote Knout (FR) (Kendor (FR))
7803a[5]

Kathindi (IRE) *Michael Chapman* a65 57
5 ch g Pearl Of Love(IRE) Turfcare Flight (IRE) (Mujadil (USA))
4209[P] 6317[P]

Kathlatino *Micky Hammond* 64
5 b m Danbird(AUS) Silver Rhythm (Silver Patriarch (IRE))
(2339) 2598[2] 3416[3] 4683[5]

Kathleen Frances *Mark H Tompkins* a51 86
5 b m Sakhee(USA) Trew Class (Inchinor)
1940[4] 2447[3] 2909[2] ◆ 3187[5] 3610[4] 3997[2] 5474[5] 6339[5] 6703[7] 6884[3] 7294[14]

Kathleensluckylad (IRE) *Kevin Ryan* a67 60
3 b g Antonius Pius(USA) Jacobina (Magic Ring (IRE))
1337[7] 1916[10] 4397[3] 4771[3] 5623[3] 6429[8] (6892) (7058) 7417[12]

Katie Gale *Tim Pitt* a32 39
2 b f Shirocco(GER) Karla June (Unfuwain (USA))
7364[12] 7780[11]

Katla (IRE) *J F Grogan* a98 105
4 b m Majestic Missile(IRE) Bratislava (Dr Fong (USA))
1538a[3] 2513a[10] 3092a[7] 3650a[3] 4482a[9] 5067a[4] 7390a[5] 7690[18]

Katmai River (IRE) *Mark Usher* a67 72
5 b g Choisir(AUS) Katavi (USA) (Stravinsky (USA))
102[6] 128[2] 262[2] 474[2] 729[5] (1628) (1769) 2207[11] 3000[4] 3226[6] 4413[10] 5741[5] 6217[8] 7302[12] 7670[2] 7993[7] 8156[12]

Katmandoune (FR) *Mme M Bollack-Badel* a88 101
4 gr m Country Reel(USA) Louvardie (FR) (Loup Solitaire (USA))
2805a[9]

Kat Moon *Tim Easterby* 59
2 b f Cockney Rebel(IRE) Damelza (IRE) (Orpen (USA))
4546[7] 5339[8] 5586[5]

Katy Spirit (IRE) *Michael Blanshard* a59 50
2 b f Invincible Spirit(IRE) Katy Guest (IRE) (Be My Guest (USA))
3487[9] 4419[5] 5003[8] 5532[5] 5873[4] 6155[7] 7006[6] 7649[2] 7808[11] 8007[3] (8155)

Katy's Secret *William Jarvis* a79 73
5 b m Mind Games Katy O'Hara (Komaite (USA))
368[4] 834[6] 4143[7] 6837[10] 7166[6] 7794[11]

Kauai Katie (USA) *Todd Pletcher* a111
2 b f Malibu Moon(USA) More Than Pretty (USA) (More Than Ready (USA))
7548a[4]

Kavachi (IRE) *Gary Moore* a70 69
9 b g Cadeaux Genereux Answered Prayer (Green Desert (USA))
6568[5] 6950[12]

Kavaloti (IRE) *Gary Moore* a78 50
8 b g Kahyasi Just As Good (FR) (Kaldounevees (FR))
207[3] 521[9] 714[6] 825[6] 963[6] 1588[3] 3086[10] 3969[9]

Kavango (IRE) *M bin Shafya* a104 107
5 b h Cape Cross(IRE) Wood Vine (USA) (Woodman (USA))
144a[7] 500a[5] 876a[4]

Kawaakib (USA) *John Dunlop* 44
2 b f Nayef(USA) Muthabara (IRE) (Red Ransom (USA))
4818[14]

Kayaan *Pam Sly* a67 70
5 br g Marju(IRE) Raheefa (USA) (Riverman (USA))
2260[2] ◆ 3400[6]

Kayalar (IRE) *Evan Williams* a76 74
4 b g Noverre(USA) Katiykha (IRE) (Darshaan)
(569)

Kayf Aramis *Nigel Twiston-Davies* a66 62
10 b g Kayf Tara Ara (Birthright)
2214[10]

Kay Gee Be (IRE) *Alan Berry* a89 98
8 b g Fasliyev(USA) Pursuit Of Truth (USA) (Irish River (FR))
1128[15] 1341[2] 1865[4] 2657[9] (3810) 4620[4] (4864) 5243[4] 5712[3] 6313[2] 6969[2] 7069[3] (7601) 8242[7]

Kaylee *Gary Moore* a57 50
3 b f Selkirk(USA) Mrs Brown (Royal Applause)
4937[9] 5479[8] 7465[4] 7837[2] ◆ 7929[10] 8046[2] 8298[9]

Kaylena *Jeremy Noseda* 62
3 b f Teofilo(IRE) Kootenay (IRE) (Selkirk (USA))
2279[8] 4538[7] 5124[4]

Kaypea *Simon Dow* 46
3 br f Imperial Dancer Cape Maya (Cape Cross (IRE))
2344[13] 3447[9] 4001[9] 5770[10] 6442[11]

Kazbow (IRE) *Richard Ford* a82 98
6 b g Rainbow Quest(USA) Kasota (IRE) (Alzao (USA))
1974[P] 2709[6] 4613[14] 5200[3] 6012[8] 6642[4] 7380[10] 7972[6]

Kealshore Again (IRE) *George Moore* 57
3 br g Exit To Nowhere(USA) Sinnaja (Sinndar (IRE))
4826[4]

Keegsquaw (IRE) *A Fabre* 99
3 ch f Street Cry(IRE) Kentucky Rose (FR) (Hernando (FR))
1695a[6]

Keene Dancer *Sir Michael Stoute* 90
3 ch f Danehill Dancer(IRE) Kinnaird (IRE) (Dr Devious (IRE))
2204[4] (3666) (4150) 4702[15] 6202[2]

Keene's Pointe *J W Hills* 76
2 br c Avonbridge Belle's Edge (Danehill Dancer (IRE))
2983[10] 4487[8] 5785[2] 6167[6]

Keep A Welcome *Gerry Enright* a54
9 ch g Most Welcome Celtic Chimes (Celtic Cone)
207[4] 566[12]

Keepax *Chris Wall* a67 83
3 b g Dubai Destination(USA) Stellar Brilliant (USA) (Kris S (USA))
2428[13] 2942[3] 3703[7] (4498) 5007[8] 5533[3] 6376[6] 7195[8]

Keep Calm *Richard Hannon* a68 66
2 b c War Chant(USA) Mayaar (USA) (Grand Slam (USA))
4688[17] 5476[3] 5742[8] 6318[8] (7313) (7785)

Keep Cool *Andreas Lowe* a64 100
5 b h Starcraft(NZ) Kirov (Darshaan)
630a[9]

Keep Fighting *Tim Walford*
4 ch m Monsieur Bond(IRE) Baron Rhodes (Presidium)
4207[10] 4551[10]

Keeping Time *Sir Henry Cecil* a69 77
3 b c Observatory(USA) Sandglass (Zafonic (USA))
3398[9] 4067[11] 4916[4] 5952[2] 6408[6] 6704[9]

Keep It Dark *Tony Coyle* a70 63
3 b g Invincible Spirit(IRE) Tarneem (USA) (Zilzal (USA))
5679[6] 5919[5] 6341[3] 6785[12] 7447[6] 7590[4] 7729[4]

Keep The Dream *Paul Cole* a69 69
2 b c Oasis Dream Mimisel (Selkirk (USA))
6581[3] 6772[5] (7268)

Keep The Secret *William Knight* a75
2 ch f Sakhee's Secret Starfleet (Inchinor)
(8201) ◆

Kelinni (IRE) *Chris Waller* a75 111
4 b g Refuse To Bend(IRE) Orinoco (IRE) (Darshaan)
(7560a) 7621a[4]

Kellys Eye (IRE) *David Brown* 88
5 b g Noverre(USA) Limit (IRE) (Barathea (IRE))
1478[12] 4554[5] ◆ 4880[6] 5674[8] (6605)

Kelpie Blitz (IRE) *Seamus Durack* a82 76
3 gr g Verglas(IRE) Summer Spice (IRE) (Key Of Luck (USA))
787[6] 1093[4] 1288[2] 1982[7] 2624[2] 3246[7] 4242[5] 5021[5] (5441) 5990[2] 7194[8] 7511[3] 7644[4] (7893)

Kelvingrove (IRE) *Ed Vaughan* a70 70
2 b g Hurricane Run(IRE) Silversword (FR) (Highest Honor (FR))
6872[3] 7324[8] 8070[4]

Kendal Princess (IRE) *David O'Meara* a7 46
2 b f Byron Knowing Look (Daylami (IRE))
2437[9] 2790[10] 3351[4] 4139[6] 6952[8]

Kendam (FR) *H-A Pantall* 112
3 b f Kendargent(FR) Damdam Freeze (FR) (Indian Rocket)
1407a[5] 2109a[11] 2728a[7] 3657a[3] 4861a[9] 6088a[3] 6913a[3]

Kenhope (FR) *H-A Pantall* 102
2 b f Kendargent(FR) Bedford Hope (GER) (Chato (USA))
7013a[2] 7514a[5] 7828a[10]

Kenny Powers *Tom Dascombe* a106 98
3 b g Vital Equine(IRE) Alexander Ballet (Mind Games)
417a[2] 679a[9] *1032[2]* *(7654)*

Kensea (FR) *H-A Pantall* 100
2 ch f Kendargent(FR) Sea Island (FR) (Gold Away (IRE))
5471a[4] 6129a[6] (6942a) 7622a[7]

Ken's Girl *Stuart Kittow* a64 85
8 ch m Ishiguru(USA) There's Two (IRE) (Ashkalani (IRE))
1939[6] 2576[5] (3096) 3780[5] 4413[P]

Kensington Gardens *Michael Bell* 29
2 b f Oasis Dream Wendylina (IRE) (In The Wings)
7312[7]

Kenswick *Pat Eddery* a56 61
5 b m Avonbridge The Jotter (Night Shift (USA))
39[7] *125[11]* *988[7]* *1095[2]* *1425[6]*

Kenton Street *Michael J Browne* a68 65
7 ch g Compton Place Western Applause (Royal Applause)
232[4]

Kentra (FR) *G Botti* a75 84
2 b f Muhaymin(USA) Ultime Moment (IRE) (Anabaa (USA))
6725a[3] 7285a[8]

Kentucky Winner (FR) *J-M Capitte* a65 75
3 ch c Kentucky Dynamite(USA) Olanga (GER) (Shareef Dancer (USA))
290a[8]

Kenyan Cat *Ed McMahon* a66 90
5 br m One Cool Cat(USA) Nairobi (FR) (Anabaa (USA))
3038[5] 3556[2] 4249[3] 5129[5] 6450[6] 6987[7]

Kepler's Law *Sir Mark Prescott Bt* a92 73
4 b g Galileo(IRE) Tina Heights (Shirley Heights)
7051[P]

Kept *James Fanshawe* a23 73
3 ch g Pivotal Possessed (Desert Prince (IRE))
4948[8] 5679[2] 6527[2] 6925[8]

Kerasona (FR) *J-C Rouget* 104
3 b f Oasis Dream Kerasha (FR) (Daylami (IRE))
4861a[7] 5648a[4]

Kerbaaj (USA) *Charles Hills* 83
2 bb c Dixie Union(USA) Mabaahej (USA) (Belong To Me (USA))
(4472) ◆

Kerchak (USA) *Brian Ellison* a63 59
5 b g Royal Academy(USA) Traude (USA) (River Special (USA))
7685[18] *7839[6]* *8145[7]*

Kerfuffle (IRE) *Simon Dow* a49
3 b f Kheleyf(USA) Chiosina (IRE) (Danehill Dancer (IRE))
6930[16] *7322[11]* *7804[3]* *8168[3]* *8184[4]*

Kersivay *Mrs A Malzard* a76 66
6 b g Royal Applause Lochmaddy (Selkirk (USA))
(2114a)

Kesampour (FR) *M Delzangles* 116
3 ch c King's Best(USA) Kasatana (IRE) (Hernando (FR))
(1869a) 2743a[4] 6294a[5] 6912a[13]

Keyaadi *Roger Varian* a77 75
3 b g Iffraaj Arabescato (UAE) (Gone West (USA))
1864[2] ◆ 2273[5] *4212[3]* (4992) 5705[8]

Key Ambition *Garry Moss* a77 79
3 ch g Auction House(USA) Love Thing (Phountzi (USA))
99[2] *6663[6]* *6938[6]* 7451[9] *7607[7]* *7741[5]* *8058[3]* *8183[6]*

Key Board (ITY) *S Sordi* 61
2 b f Accento Monord (ITY) (Nordico (USA))
6090a[7]

Key Decision (IRE) *C Moore* a28 28
8 br g Key Of Luck(USA) Adalya (IRE) (Darshaan)
1580[7]

Key Gold *Mark Johnston* a68 82
3 b f Cape Cross(IRE) Key Academy (Royal Academy (USA))
84[2] (1223) 2258[10] 3087[4] 3345[4] 3781[3] (4682) 5383[3] 6340[6] 6784[1]

Keys Of Cyprus *David Nicholls* a57 81
10 ch g Deploy Krisia (Kris)
1527[6] 2696[8] 3254[10] 3914[13] 4042[6] 4432[4] 4683[4] 5917[10] 6480[4] ◆ *7225[5]* *7382[5]* *7593[11]*

Khadima (FR) *J-C Rouget* 97
2 b f Zamindar(USA) Khalasha (FR) (Linamix (FR))
4615a[2] (5288a)

Khajaaly (IRE) *Julia Feilden* a79 68
5 b g Kheleyf(USA) Joyfullness (USA) (Dixieland Band (USA))
448[3] *941[7]* *6319[10]* 6950[9] 7436[15] *7935[3]* ◆

Khaleejiya (IRE) *James Tate* a55 69
3 b f Jeremy(USA) Certainly Brave (Indian Ridge)
1723[6] 2085[6]

Khalini (FR) *Y Gourraud* 80
4 b g Lavirco(GER) Simla (FR) (Marathon (USA))
1172a[0]

Khamseen *Karen George* a42 62
5 ch g Barathea(IRE) Pantone (Spectrum (IRE))
1192[6] *1824[9]* 2393[8] 3001[4] 3472[8]

Khanbaligh (FR) *C Lerner* a76 76
3 b f Panis(USA) Lady Time (FR) (Orpen (USA))
865a[0]

Khandaq (USA) *Keith Dalgleish* a81 78
5 b g Gulch(USA) Jadarah (USA) (Red Ransom (USA))
190[3] *(268)* *548[9]* 1875[8] *2354[7]* 2588[15] 2922[5] 3277[3] 3525[5]

Khaos (IRE) *M D O'Callaghan* a90 83
3 b f Kodiac Church Mice (IRE) (Petardia)
6454[11]

Khateer *Milton Bradley* a67
5 ch g Shamardal(USA) Polly Perkins (IRE) (Pivotal)
329[9]

Khatella (IRE) *John Flint*
3 b f Generous(IRE) Triple Dash (GER) (Dashing Blade)
533[8] *595[7]*

Khawatim *Noel Quinlan* a78 87
4 b g Intikhab(USA) Don't Tell Mum (IRE) (Dansili)
2177[10] 4880[10] 5368[16] *6938[10]* *7595[11]* *7859[8]* *8157[7]*

Khawlah (IRE) *Saeed Bin Suroor* a111 95
4 b m Cape Cross(IRE) Villarrica (USA) (Selkirk (USA))
1883[7] 2711[8] 3632[7] 7396[9] ◆ 7688[11]

Khazeena *William Haggas* a81 78
3 b f Oasis Dream Shamaiel (IRE) (Lycius (USA))
1610[5] 2204[5] *2848[3]* 4366[3] *(5166)* 5856[8]

Khazium (IRE) *Brendan Powell* a71 71
3 br g Kheleyf(USA) Hazium (IRE) (In The Wings)
1313[9] 2786[6] 3098[2] 4517[12] *4872[9]* 5950[4]

Khefyn (IRE) *Ronald Harris* a42 79
2 br g Kheleyf(USA) Highly Respected (IRE) (High Estate)
2164[8] 2868[5] 3138[8] (4421) 4936[3] 5194[2] (5654) 5873[2] 6929[4] *7164[10]* 7298[2] 7687[5]

Khelac *Alan Swinbank* 71
2 b g Kheleyf(USA) Miss Lacey (IRE) (Diktat)
4555[10] 5083[6] 5668[2] 6133[4] 6669[2]

Khelino (IRE) *Rodger Sweeney* a61 81
4 b m Kheleyf(USA) Special Park (USA) (Trempolino (USA))
775a[14]

Khelman (IRE) *Richard Fahey* 77
2 b g Kheleyf(USA) Mandolin (IRE) (Sabrehill (USA))
4612[7] 5963[3] 6473[2] 6880[6]

Kheskianto (IRE) *Michael Chapman* a32 53
6 b m Kheleyf(USA) Gently (IRE) (Darshaan)
12[4] *113[8]* *490[10]* 1436[8] 5258[4] 6361[2] 6561[3]

Kheya (IRE) *Micky Hammond* a28 2
4 b m Kheleyf(USA) Monarchy (IRE) (Common Grounds)
2796[12]

Khione *Luca Cumani* 104
3 b f Dalakhani(IRE) Sularina (IRE) (Alhaarth (IRE))
(2734) (3476) 4848[3] 6598[5] ◆ 7405[4]

Khobaraa *John Gosden* a77
2 bb f Invincible Spirit(IRE) Deyaar (USA) (Storm Cat (USA))
(7987)

Khotan *Sir Mark Prescott Bt* a68 56
2 b c Hernando(FR) Miss Katmandu (IRE) (Rainbow Quest (USA))
6214[7] 6733[5] *7057[2]*

Khubala (IRE) *Hugo Palmer* a72 99
3 b c Acclamation Raghida (IRE) (Nordico (USA))
(1376) *1730[4]* (2764) (3613) 4221[3] (5530) 6835[2] 7366[4] 7624a[10]

Khudoua *John Gosden* a75 56
2 b g Nayef(USA) Danehill Dreamer (USA) (Danehill (USA))
3634[9] 4066[9] *7900[2]*

Khun John (IRE) *Willie Musson* a66 31
9 b g Marju(IRE) Kathy Caerleon (IRE) (Caerleon (USA))
176[8] *349[9]* *559[4]* *(895)* *1534[3]* 2009[3] *(2814)*

Khyber Bridge *Jo Hughes* a30 33
2 b g Avonbridge Khyber Knight (IRE) (Night Shift (USA))
1165[5] *1277[6]*

Khyber Pass *Edward Lynam* a73 39
3 b g Three Valleys(USA) My Golly (Mozart (IRE))
7229a[5]

Kiama Bay (IRE) *John Quinn* a20 105
6 b g Fraam La Panthere (USA) (Pine Bluff (USA))
1214[13] 1974[6] 3857[7] 4111[7] 5333[5]

Kian's Delight *Peter Bowen* a42 80
4 b g Whipper(USA) Desert Royalty (IRE) (Alhaarth (IRE))
(3400) (3953)

Kian's Joy *Jedd O'Keeffe* a25 53
3 b g Mind Games Lunasa (IRE) (Don't Forget Me)
(1386) ◆ 3025[4] 3775[13] 4313[3] 4958[7] 5672[11] *6807[11]*

Kicken Off (IRE) *Phil McEntee* a60 69
2 ch g Haatef(USA) Affirmed Crown (USA) (Affirmed (USA))
2808[4] 2995[2] 3244[2] (3465) 4230[7] *7350[4]* 7521[6] *7727[2]* *7795[6]*

Kickingthelilly *Rae Guest* a90 84
3 ch f Byron Teller (ARG) (Southern Halo (USA))
185[2] *(383)* *(518)* ◆ *(764)* *1032[7]* 1221[4] 2490[9] 2916[4] 3270[12] 3542[13] *(8188)* ◆

Kidlat *Hans Adielsson* a88 87
7 b g Cape Cross(IRE) Arruhan (IRE) (Mujtahid (USA))
353 *310[8]* *695[6]*

Kidnapped (AUS) *Saeed Bin Suroor* a78 100
6 br g Viscount(AUS) Youthful Presence (AUS) (Dehere (USA))
678a[10]

Kid Suitor (IRE) *Richard Hannon* a87 86
3 ch c Choisir(AUS) Fancy Intense (Peintre Celebre (USA))
(1304) 1645[2]

Kielty's Folly *Brian Baugh* a66 65
8 gr g Weet-A-Minute(IRE) Three Sweeties (Cruise Missile)
736[7] *1002[9]* *1447[7]* *1722[2]* *2170[4]* 2847[9] *3712[8]* *3950[8]* *4890[6]* *5427[7]* 6646[6]

Kieron's Rock (IRE) *Jedd O'Keeffe* 59
3 ch g Rock Of Gibraltar(IRE) Princess Killeen (IRE) (Sinndar (IRE))
1661[7] 2283[8] 2788[6] 3356[6] *4406[12]* 4549[14] 4956[8] 5226[6] 5672[5] 6315[11] 6562[5] 7495[12]

Kikonga *Luca Cumani* 77
2 b f Danehill Dancer(IRE) Kibara (Sadler's Wells (USA))
4818[11] 5551[3] (6117)

Kildare Kitten (USA) *Matt Sheppard* a44 57
4 ch m Kitten's Joy(USA) Philanthropy Lady (USA) (Desert Style (IRE))
213[5]

Killachy Loose *B Grizzetti* 98
3 br f Kyllachy Vettori Loose (IRE) (Vettori (IRE))
1699a[12] 6726a[5] 7565a[7]

Kimbali (IRE) *Richard Fahey* a80 88
3 b g Clodovil(IRE) Winnifred (Green Desert (USA))
1998[4] 2276[14] 3607[2] 4135[4] 5337[6] *6051[3]* 6661[8] 6923[4] *8133[5]*

Kimberella *Michael Bell* 88
2 b g Kyllachy Gleam Of Light (IRE) (Danehill (USA))
1886[5] 2480[2] ◆ (3182) 4102[3] 4599[4] 6540[3]

Kimvara *Joseph Tuite* a54 25
2 b f Kodiac Tattling (Warning)
3339[13] *4646[8]* *5046[2]* *5424[5]* *5807[9]* 6115[7] *6612[8]*

Kindergarden Kid (USA) *Peter Miller* 113
5 b g Dynaformer(USA) Amelia (USA) (Dixieland Band (USA))
7573a[6]

Kindia (IRE) *Michael Attwater* a49
4 b m Cape Cross(IRE) Susu (Machiavellian (USA))
7858[9] *7986[11]*

Kinetica *Sir Mark Prescott Bt* a79 98
3 b f Stormy Atlantic(USA) Kiswahili (Selkirk (USA))
3270[14] 3879[9]

King Air (FR) *R Pritchard-Gordon* a82 109
5 b g Kingsalsa(USA) Haine Amour (FR) (Mtoto)
5649a[3] 6727a[5] (7587a)

Kingaroo (IRE) *Garry Woodward* a65 58
6 b g King Charlemagne(USA) Lady Naomi (USA) (Distant View (USA))
381[4] *453[4]* *579[6]* *672[2]* *811[7]* *(1432)* *1956[3]* 2048[4] 2260[6] 2732[2] 3180[8] (3814) (4189) 5012[10] 6794[10] 7496[6] 7731[6]

Kingarrick *Noel Wilson* a77 77
4 ch g Selkirk(USA) Rosacara (Green Desert (USA))
6544[6] 7684[15] *8113[5]* *8241[9]*

King Bertolini (IRE) *Alan Berry* a53 48
5 b h Bertolini(USA) Bareilly (USA) (Lyphard (USA))
1248[11]

King David (USA) *Michael J Maker* 105
3 bb c Hat Trick(JPN) Storm West (USA) (Gone West (USA))
(6902a)

King Dragon (IRE) *Brian Meehan* 89
2 b g Iffraaj Reign Of Fire (IRE) (Perugino (USA))
2929[3] 3240[17] (3916) 5371[3] 6162[7] 6797[2] 7053[9] 7374[8]

King Fingal (IRE) *John Quinn* a70 65
7 b g King's Best(USA) Llia (Shirley Heights)
2348[4] 6884[6] 7245[6]

King George River (IRE) *Alan Bailey* a83 83
2 b c Danehill Dancer(IRE) Butterfly Blue (IRE) (Sadler's Wells (USA))
8223[3]

King Kenny *Mrs A Corson* a78 44
7 ch g Lomitas Salanka (IRE) (Persian Heights)
1114[8]

King Kreesa (USA) *Jeremiah C Englehart* 103
3 bb g King Cugat(USA) Storm's Advance (USA) (Storm Creek (USA))
6902a[2]

King Kurt (IRE) *Kevin Ryan* 86
4 b g Holy Roman Emperor(IRE) Rutledge (IRE) (Entrepreneur)
1381[8] 2180[13] 2676[2] 3494[13] 4326[13] 6076[9] 6340[8]

King Laertis (IRE) *Tracy Waggott* 28
3 br g Baltic King Vltava (IRE) (Sri Pekan (USA))
459[9] 3025[12] 3405[5] 3952[11] 4957[6]

Kinglami *Brian Gubby* a79 50
3 b c Kingsalsa(USA) Red Japonica (Daylami (IRE))
3732[5] ◆ *(4874)* *5229[2]* *5971[3]* *6401[5]* *7170[2]* *7725[6]*

Kinglet (USA) *Mahmood Al Zarooni* a106 91
3 bb c Kingmambo(USA) Karen's Caper (USA) (War Chant (USA))
142a[2] ◆ *(485a)* 873a[7] *1145a[9]*

King Muro *Andrew Balding* a76 57
2 b c Halling(USA) Ushindi (IRE) (Montjeu (IRE))
6020[17] 6795[9] *7460[3]* ◆

King Of Aran (IRE) *M J Grassick* a83 82
5 bb g Val Royal(FR) Innishmore (IRE) (Lear Fan (USA))
7852a[2]

King Of Arnor *A Fabre* 112
4 b g Monsun(GER) Luce (IRE) (Sadler's Wells (USA))
6864a[8]

King Of Cadeaux (IRE) *Mikael Magnusson* a54 19
7 br g Cadeaux Genereux Purple Haze (IRE) (Spectrum (IRE))
1907[9]

King Of Connacht *Mark Wellings* a56 36
9 b g Polish Precedent(USA) Lady Melbourne (IRE) (Indian Ridge)
160[8] *843[13]*

King Of Dudes *Sir Henry Cecil* a77 86
3 b g Dansili Leto (USA) (Diesis)
1511[7] 2266[5] ◆

King Of Eden (IRE) *Eric Alston* 93
6 b g Royal Applause Moonlight Paradise (USA) (Irish River (FR))
1885[17] 2487[10] 2632[3] 3493[12] (3557) (4135) 4589[3] 5342[17] 5827[11] 7240[22]

King Of Jazz (IRE) *Michael Bell* a86 104
4 b g Acclamation Grand Slam Maria (FR) (Anabaa (USA))
1157[3] 2068[3] 3371[21] 3641[15] 4099[8] 5102[13] 6024[15] 7080[9] *7508[8]*

King Of Kudos (IRE) *Scott Dixon* a71 72
2 b c Acclamation Perugina (FR) (Highest Honor (FR))
5062[12] 5813[2] 6444[6] 7363[2] *(7812)* *7994[4]*

King Of Paradise (IRE) *Eric Alston* 75
3 b g Hurricane Run(IRE) Silly Game (IRE) (Bigstone (IRE))
1976[9] 2313[4] (3032) (3727) 4260[7] 4713[4] 5732[4] 6241[3] 6881[12]

King Of Song (FR) *H-A Pantall* a67
3 b c Sinndar(IRE) Karsawina (GER) (Lando (GER))
661a[2]

King Of The Celts (IRE) *Tim Easterby* 81
4 b g Celtic Swing Flamands (IRE) (Sadler's Wells (USA))
1525[11] 2687[3] 3459[2] (4396)

King Of The Danes *Mark Johnston* a69 41
2 b c Dansili Our Queen Of Kings (Arazi (USA))
7371[7] *7627[8]* *(8172)*

King Of The Moors (USA) *John Spearing* a55 53
9 b g King Of Kings(IRE) Araza (USA) (Arazi (USA))
2621[7] 4511[10] 6259[11]

King Of The Night (GER) *Richard Fahey*
8 b g Lomitas Kaiserlerche (GER) (Subotica (FR))
1867[11]

King Of Wands *John Gosden* 98
6 b g Galileo(IRE) Maid To Treasure (IRE) (Rainbow Quest (USA))
1159[2]

King Of Windsor (IRE) *John Wainwright* a83 85
5 b g Intikhab(USA) Kismah (Machiavellian (USA))
374[7] *812[8]* *978[8]* 3380[U] 4641[2] (5085) *5429[4]* 6073[12] 6706[10] *7608[6]* *7798[10]* *8145[8]*

King Of Wing (IRE) *Jim Boyle* a68 76
3 b g Hawk Wing(USA) Miss Shivvy (IRE) (Montjeu (IRE))
180[5] *656[5]* *787[7]* 1607[6] 6734[14] 7302[9] *7474[12]*

King Oliver *Richard Hannon* a72 72
2 ch c Kyllachy Confetti (Groom Dancer (USA))
4845[2] 5235[10] 5793[10] *6980[3]* 7399[10]

King Pin *Tracy Waggott* a65 70
7 b g Pivotal Danehurst (Danehill (USA))
2536[5] 2922[9] (3405) 3810[2] 4716[3] 5547[2] 5588[8] 6410[8] 6785[7]

King Red (FR) *J Heloury* a65
3 b g Meshaheer(USA) Dorylee (FR) (General Holme (USA))
290a[9]

Kings Apollo *Tom Symonds* 55
3 b g King's Theatre(IRE) Temple Dancer (Magic Ring (IRE))
1662[6] 1867[7] 4537[8]

Kingsbarns (IRE) *A P O'Brien* 120
2 b c Galileo(IRE) Beltisaal (FR) (Belmez (USA))
(7398)

King's Bastion (IRE) *Luke Comer* a76 62
8 b g Royal Applause Aunty Mary (Common Grounds)
337a[9]

King's Ciel *George Baker* a29 68
3 ch g Septieme Ciel(USA) King's Jewel (King's Signet (USA))
3193[11] 3719[6] 4237[8]

King's Colour *Brett Johnson* a74 45
7 b g King's Best(USA) Red Garland (Selkirk (USA))
85[2] *175[6]* *655[8]* *760[5]*

Kingscombe (USA) *Pat Eddery* a63 49
3 rg g Mizzen Mast(USA) Gombeen (USA) (Private Account (USA))
(1278) 2788[9] 3665[11]

King's Counsel (IRE) *David O'Meara* a55 75
6 ch g Refuse To Bend(IRE) Nesaah's Princess (Sinndar (IRE))
2440[4] 3290[9] 4048[6] 4455[4]

Kingscroft (IRE) *Mark Johnston* a96 96
4 b g Antonius Pius(USA) Handsome Anna (IRE) (Bigstone (IRE))
868[2] *1035[6]* 1128[20] 1522[4] 1865[14] 2444[5] 2697[2] ◆ 2919[9] 3221[5] 6119[5] 6235[11] (7097) 7240[14] 7452[2] *7508[5]* 7691[14] *(7790)* 7826[4] 7934[3] 8098[6]

Kingsdesire (IRE) *Marco Botti* a79 103
3 b g King's Best(USA) Lucky Clio (IRE) (Key Of Luck (USA))
(1160) 2026[3] 2920[2] 5064[2] 6029[7]

Kingsdine (IRE) *Malcolm Saunders* a90 88
5 b g King's Best(USA) Lunadine (FR) (Bering)
2023[4] 2444[6] 3011[3] 3225[7]

King's Future *Lee Carter* a62 48
3 b g King's Best(USA) Las Beatas (Green Desert (USA))
660[4] *1046[10]* 1259[13] *1731[2]* *2548[12]* *3972[3]* *5050[4]* *5350[2]* 5850[4] *6402[9]* *7903[5]* 8021[6] 8261[5]

Kings Gambit (SAF) *Tom Tate* a100 111
8 ch g Silvano(GER) Lady Brompton (SAF) (Al Mufti (USA))
2081[5] 4112[13] 4684[5]

Kingsgate Choice (IRE) *Ed de Giles* a92 102
5 b g Choisir(AUS) Kenema (IRE) (Petardia)
(2040) 2731[2] 3374[5] 4337[4] 4690[16] 5343[2] (6026) 6244[9] (7243)

Kingsgate Native (IRE) *Robert Cowell* a85 117
7 b g Mujadil(USA) Native Force (IRE) (Indian Ridge)
6140[7] 6485[2] 6869[9] *7390a[11]*

King's Guest (IRE) *David Simcock* a67
3 b f King's Best(USA) Temple Street (IRE) (Machiavellian (USA))
6457[6] *6827[8]*

King's Hall *A Wohler* 106
4 ch g Halling(USA) Konigin Turf (GER) (Turfkonig (GER))
2322a[7] 4636a[7] 5613a[4] (6906a) 7286a[4] 7784a[6]

Kingshill Lad (IRE) *Terry Clement* a39
3 bb g Marju(IRE) Brogan's Well (IRE) (Caerleon (USA))
1031[10]

Kingship Spirit (IRE) *M Ramadan* a52 86
6 b g Invincible Spirit(IRE) Jupiter Inlet (IRE) (Jupiter Island)
682a[9]

King's Masque *Bernard Llewellyn* a80 80
6 b g Noverre(USA) Top Flight Queen (Mark Of Esteem (IRE))
2984[6] (3967) 4409[2] 5021[4] (5419) 5950[2] (6120) (6278) 7017[7]
Kings Messenger (GER) *A Wohler* a93 107
5 bb h Samum(GER) Kapitol (GER) (Winged Love (IRE))
1901a[6]
Kings 'n Dreams *Dean Ivory* a69 79
5 b g Royal Applause Last Dream (IRE) (Alzao (USA))
1306[11] 1564[10] 1936[4] *2546[8]* 3225[8] 3705[6] 3994[13] 7113[14] *7861[7]* *8169[11]*
King's Request (IRE) *Sir Michael Stoute* 54
2 ch g New Approach(IRE) Palace Weekend (USA) (Seattle Dancer (USA))
6636[7]
King's Risk (FR) *T Castanheira* a77 60
2 b c My Risk(FR) King's Pearl (FR) (Kingsalsa (USA))
5698a[9]
King's Road *Anabel K Murphy* a62 65
7 ch g King's Best(USA) Saphire (College Chapel)
1433[3] (1770) 2009[4] 3468[5] 4244[6] *5175[3]* *5809[2]* *6056[5]* *6616[3]* *6940[7]*
King's Rose (NZ) *Peter G Moody* 115
5 b m Redoute's Choice(AUS) Nureyev's Girl (AUS) (Nureyev (USA))
1902a[11]
King's Sabre *John Spearing* a14 67
6 ch g King's Best(USA) Lightsabre (Polar Falcon (USA))
3344[12] *3964[11]* *4192[12]*
Kingston Jamaica (IRE) *A P O'Brien* 103
2 b c Galileo(IRE) Aleagueoftheirown (IRE) (Danehill Dancer (IRE))
4519a[3] 5642a[4]
Kingston Tiger *Jo Davis* a58 48
4 b g Tiger Hill(IRE) Gretna (Groom Dancer (USA))
8149[7]
King's Trail (JPN) *Takashi Kodama* a97 103
10 b h Sunday Silence(USA) Santa Fe Trail (JPN) (Northern Taste (CAN))
341a[2] ◆ *712[4]* *1137[4]* 3268[29]
Kings Troop *Alan King* a70 86
6 ch g Bertolini(USA) Glorious Colours (Spectrum (IRE))
2561[6] 3015[5] 3769[6] 4251[4] 4983[5] 5665[2] 6170[4] 6703[6] 7077[7] (7409)
Kingsville *Mark Johnston* a45 46
2 b g Royal Applause Kalinova (IRE) (Red Ransom (USA))
3452[6] *3708[5]* *3937[8]* 4806[6] *5206[3]* 7173[3] *7785[12]* *7973[11]*
King's Warrior (FR) *Peter Chapple-Hyam* 106
5 b g King's Best(USA) Save Me The Waltz (FR) (Halling (USA))
1654[2] ◆ 1993[2] 2706[5] 3635[11] (4112) 6674[17]
King's Wharf (IRE) *David Evans* a67 15
3 gr g Clodovil(IRE) Global Tour (USA) (Tour D'Or (USA))
369[7] *523[6]* *787[5]* *943[2]* *1192[3]* *1390[2]* 2288[8]
Kingswinford (IRE) *Alastair Lidderdale* a78 88
6 b g Noverre(USA) Berenica (IRE) (College Chapel)
(1203) 2029[9] 2608[6] (3011) 4317[18] 4508[3] 5034[4] 5305[5] (5852) 6241[2] *6319[4]* *6692[10]* *7166[7]* 7559[5] *7618[2]* 7684[9] *7725[7]* *7844[4]* 7976[4]
King Torus (IRE) *Richard Hannon* a107 113
4 b g Oratorio(IRE) Dipterous (IRE) (Mujadil (USA))
1749[4] 2127[4] 3268[19] 4684[11] 5492[16]
King Vahe (IRE) *Alan Jarvis* a68 75
3 b g One Cool Cat(USA) Tethkar (Machiavellian (USA))
981[4] 2449[14] (5240) 5625[7] *7171[9]*
King Zeal (IRE) *Barry Leavy* a66 82
8 b g King's Best(USA) Manureva (USA) (Nureyev (USA))
2051[2] (2328) 2661[5]
Kinloch Castle *Michael Wigham* a85 84
3 b c Echo Of Light Sound Of Sleat (Primo Dominie)
1221[3] *1304[4]* 2182[10] 2477[7] 3779[4] 4473[8] *4889[3]* 5268[7]
Kinyras (IRE) *Michael Easterby* a51 94
4 ch g Peintre Celebre(USA) Amathusia (Selkirk (USA))
1273[8] 2253[15] 3458[3] 4072[13] 4347[6] 6076[16] *6981[12]* 7368[10]
Kipchak (IRE) *Conor Dore* a71 68
7 b g Soviet Star(USA) Khawafi (Kris)
974[6] *665[6]* *(732)* *(829)* *900[4]* 2815[13] 3254[9]
Kirstys Lad *Michael Mullineaux* a50 59
10 b g Lake Coniston(IRE) Killick (Slip Anchor)
45[3] *218[7]* *334[10]* *390[9]* *477[8]* *773[5]* *848[6]* *1095[13]*
Kirthill (IRE) *Luca Cumani* 109
4 b g Danehill Dancer(IRE) Kirtle (Hector Protector (USA))
2176[9] 3329[6] 4684[13] (5558) 6484[4] 7689[8]
Kishanda *Gay Kelleway* a71 68
4 gr m Sleeping Indian Kali (Linamix (FR))
(1) *5944[4]* *1057[6]*
Kissable (IRE) *Roger L Attfield* 107
4 b m Danehill Dancer(IRE) Kitty O'Shea (Sadler's Wells (USA))
1041a[4] 7093a[4]
Kiss A Prince *Dean Ivory* a83 67
6 b g Fraam Prancing (Prince Sabo)
(176) ◆ *275[8]* *1071[2]* *1732[5]* *2043[6]* 3047[4] *(3620)* 4409[3]
Kissed (IRE) *A P O'Brien* 113
3 b f Galileo(IRE) Gwynn (IRE) (Darshaan)
3203a[11]
Kissing Clara (IRE) *Alison Thorpe* a17 67
4 b m Elusive City(USA) Purepleasureseeker (IRE) (Grand Lodge (USA))
1829[9]
Kiss Me Goodbye *P Bary* a75 73
2 b f Raven's Pass(USA) Khumba Mela (IRE) (Hero's Honor (USA))
7597a[2]

Kiss My Heart *Eric Wheeler* a14
3 br f Byron Kisses (Sakhee (USA))
373[7] *663[6]* 6154[12] 6930[15] *7326[10]* *8295[9]*
Kittens *William Muir* a69 67
3 b f Marju(IRE) Purring (USA) (Mountain Cat (USA))
1357[16] 4006[2] 4486[3] 4850[3] 5265[8] (5855) 6229[3] 6924[3] *(7417)*
Kitten's Dumplings (USA) *Michael J Maker* a67 97
2 b f Kitten's Joy(USA) Granny Franny (USA) (Grand Slam (USA))
6289a[4]
Kitten's Point (USA) *H Graham Motion* a90 99
2 ch f Kitten's Joy(USA) Rendezvous Point (USA) (Kingmambo (USA))
7547a[12]
Kiwani Bay *J W Hills* a44 49
2 b f Nayef(USA) Isle Of Spice (USA) (Diesis)
5300[8] 5902[10] 7403[12] *7785[8]*
Kiwayu *Luca Cumani* a89 86
3 b g Medicean Kibara (Sadler's Wells (USA))
(4466) *5944[3]* 6359[4] 7367[3]
Kiwi Bay *Michael Dods* a88 95
7 b g Mujahid(USA) Bay Of Plenty (FR) (Octagonal (NZ))
1128[12] 1522[2] 1865[5] 2417[7] 2882[11] (3354) 4828[13] 5342[10] 6124[8] 6881[4] 7069[8] 7294[13] 7601[8]
Kiz Kulesi *Mahmood Al Zarooni* a53 93
3 ch c Street Cry(IRE) Maiden Tower (Groom Dancer (USA))
3383[6] 4515[6] (5365) *7502[14]*
Klang Valley *Marco Botti* a49
3 ch f Dubai Destination(USA) Kelang (Kris)
279[4] *502[4]*
Kleitomachos (IRE) *Stuart Kittow* 86
4 b g Barathea(IRE) Theben (GER) (Monsun (GER))
(1566) 1940[9] (4096) 7522[7]
Klynch *Ruth Carr* a77 99
6 b g Kyllachy Inchcoonan (Emperor Jones (USA))
883[4] 1168[5] *1431[8]* 1863[2] 1951[5] 2488[12] 2876[5] (3169) (3524) (3772) 4086[4] 4611[12] 4799[15] 5370[10] 6011[7] 6466[21] 6665[5] 7097[10] 7452[7]
Knave Of Clubs (IRE) *Peter Makin* a54 84
3 b c Red Clubs(IRE) Royal Bounty (IRE) (Generous (IRE))
4949[11] (5237) 6638[21]
Knight Charm *Eve Johnson Houghton* 75
2 b g Haafhd Enchanted Princess (Royal Applause)
2231[6] (3217) 4093[20] 5450[6]
Knightly Escapade *John Dunlop* a82 84
4 ch g Sakhee(USA) Queen Of Iceni (Erhaab (USA))
2174[3] 2936[3] ◆ 3827[3] 4823[3] 5554[5] *6776[7]*
Knight Owl *James Fanshawe* a63 19
2 b g Rock Of Gibraltar(IRE) Miss Ivanhoe (IRE) (Selkirk (USA))
7330[17] *7628[8]* *7963[3]*
Knight's Parade (IRE) *Amanda Perrett* a45 57
2 b g Dark Angel(IRE) Toy Show (IRE) (Danehill (USA))
4507[8] 4803[15] *5407[7]* (6156) 6732[4] 7111[3]
Knight Vision *David Nicholls* 71
3 b g Haafhd Enford Princess (Pivotal)
1285[6] 2375[11] 3567[9] 4211[10] 4878[10]
Knockamany Bends (IRE) *John Wainwright* 60
2 b c Majestic Missile(IRE) Sweet Compliance (Safawan)
4625[9] 5222[6] 6049[4]
Knocker Knowles (IRE) *David Evans* a62 84
3 b g Refuse To Bend(IRE) Yomalo (IRE) (Woodborough (USA))
1317[13] 2451[7] 2987[2] 3919[3] (4757) 5123[6] 5812[5] *6688[9]*
Knock Stars (IRE) *Patrick Martin* a89 98
4 b m Soviet Star(USA) Knockatotaun (Spectrum (IRE))
1040a[7] 3648a[14] *7230a[9]*
Knowe Head (NZ) *James Unett* a79 81
5 b g High Chaparral(IRE) Royal Errant (NZ) (Royal Academy (USA))
216[5] ◆ *480[2]* *(694)* 1133[3] 1657[4] (2199) 2473[2] 2911[11] *5888[7]* *6692[7]* *7461[6]* *7976[5]* 8146[2] ◆ (8234)
Know More (USA) *Doug O'Neill* a108 85
2 b c Lion Heart(USA) Seattle Qui (USA) (Seattle Slew (USA))
7568a[13]
Know No Fear *Alastair Lidderdale* a72 76
7 b g Primo Valentino(IRE) Alustar (Emarati (USA))
3317[2] (3544) (3723) 4061[4] 4413[2] 4584[3] *5179[3]* (5259) 5506[5] 5838[13] 6239[9] *6319[9]* 6638[25]
Knox Overstreet *Mick Channon* a60 66
4 b g Indesatchel(IRE) Charlie Girl (Puissance)
1240[6] (5196) 5384[7]
Knoydart (USA) *Amanda Perrett* a37 15
3 bb g Forest Wildcat(USA) Chasenthebluesaway (USA) (Real Quiet (USA))
2582[5] 3014[12]
Koala Bear *James Fanshawe* a54
2 b f Oasis Dream Birthday Suit (IRE) (Daylami (IRE))
5943[10]
Kodatish (IRE) *Ronald Harris* a69 72
2 b c Kodiac Atishoo (IRE) (Revoque (IRE))
3140[4] 4148[2] 4730[6] 5192[3] (5503) 5813[3] 6155[4] 6799[5] *7220[3]* *7745[8]* *8016[2]*
Kodiac Island *Ed McMahon* a56
3 b f Kodiac Inveraray (Selkirk (USA))
2865[9] *3453[3]* *4888[9]* *5720[9]*
Kodicil (IRE) *Tim Walford* 73
4 b g Kodiac Miss Caoimhe (IRE) (Barathea (IRE))
1154[9] 2414[12] 2775[4]
Kogershin (USA) *Marcus Tregoning* a47 62
3 ch f Giant's Causeway(USA) Kokadrie (USA) (Coronado's Quest (USA))
1182[6] *1531[9]*
Koharu *Peter Makin* a47 58
2 rg f Ishiguru(USA) Vellena (Lucky Story (USA))
4408[7] 6276[6] 7272[5] *7650[4]* *7989[8]*

Kohlaan (IRE) *Roger Varian* a71
2 b g Elusive City(USA) Rock Salt (Selkirk (USA))
7813[3]
Koko Loca (IRE) *Marco Botti* a90 80
3 br f Kodiac Pure Folly (IRE) (Machiavellian (USA))
1093[2] ◆
Kolonel (GER) *Mario Hofer* a91 96
3 b c Manduro(GER) Kristin's Charm (USA) (Swain (IRE))
1553a[5] 2568a[8] 5782a[10]
Kolonel Kirkup *Michael Dods* 74
2 b g Dr Fong(USA) Strawberry Lolly (Lomitas)
4637[2] (5169) 6469[2] 6955[6]
Kolosseum (GER) *W Figge* 87
3 ch f Samum(GER) Kapitol (GER) (Winged Love (IRE))
2569a[5] 3802a[8]
Komreyev Star *Ray Peacock* a18 49
10 b g Komaite(USA) L'Ancressaan (Dalsaan)
370[13] 1907[13] 3099[8]
Konig Concorde (GER) *C Sprengel* a105 110
7 b g Big Shuffle(USA) Kaiserin (GER) (Ile De Bourbon (USA))
1745a[8] 3657a[10] 5649a[0] 7124a[9] 7565a[2]
Konstantin (IRE) *Marcus Tregoning* a66 93
4 br g Balmont(USA) Manuka Magic (IRE) (Key Of Luck (USA))
1708[11] 2444[4] 3772[8] 4775[9] (5120) 5910[2] (6432)
Koo And The Gang (IRE) *Brian Ellison* a83 83
5 b g Le Vie Dei Colori Entertain (Royal Applause)
2119[8] 2913[3] 3167[11] 3911[7] 5547[11] *5941[6]* 6756[3] *7200[6]* *7733[4]* *7917[5]*
Koolgreycat (IRE) *Noel Wilson* 64
3 gr f One Cool Cat(USA) Brooks Masquerade (Absalom)
(2460) 4881[6] 5624[4] 5831[12] 6314[7]
Kool Henry (IRE) *David O'Meara* 99
3 br g One Cool Cat(USA) Hurricane Lily (IRE) (Ali-Royal (IRE))
1524[4] 4044[5] 4558[2] 5080[9] 5603[4] 6075[16] (6557)
Kool Shuffle (GER) *Tony Coyle* a57 57
4 ch g Big Shuffle(USA) Kedah (GER) (Local Suitor (USA))
676[8] *724[4]* *926[8]*
Koonunja (IRE) *D Prod'Homme* 95
2 b f Anabaa(USA) Believe Me (IRE) (In The Wings)
5379a[7] 6129a[7]
Korngold *Ollie Pears* 79
4 b g Dansili Eve (Rainbow Quest (USA))
1525[6] 2086[3] 3015[6] 3814[3] 6004[12] 7018[9] 7602[6]
Kosika (USA) *Mahmood Al Zarooni* 74
2 b f Hard Spun(USA) Song Of Africa (USA) (Alzao (USA))
(2450)
Kota Sas (IRE) *Roger Varian* a82
4 b g Cape Cross(IRE) Harda Arda (USA) (Nureyev (USA))
5889[2]
Kourkam (FR) *J-M Beguigne* 78
2 bb c American Post Kourka (FR) (Keos (USA))
7283a[4]
Kozmina Bay *Jonathan Portman* a52 60
3 b f Notnowcato Kozmina (IRE) (Sadler's Wells (USA))
1443[3] (2014) 2578[4] 3142[10] 6159[12] 6626[10] 7117[3] *7196[10]*
Kraken (IRE) *Luca Cumani* 35
2 br c Notnowcato Madame Claude (IRE) (Paris House)
5578[7] 6330[11] 6945[6]
Kreem *B Al Shaibani* a107 107
4 b h Hurricane Run(IRE) En Public (FR) (Rainbow Quest (USA))
877a[16]
Kreousa *C Laffon-Parias* a84
3 b f Hurricane Run(IRE) Drosia (IRE) (King's Best (USA))
(5074a)
Kristallo (GER) *Peter Bowen* a65 65
7 ch g Lando(GER) Key West (GER) (In The Wings)
4904[10]
Krupskaya (FR) *Mrs K Burke* a50 66
2 b f Dubai Destination(USA) Willows World (Agnes World (USA))
3909[3] 4696a[6] 6049[8] (6780) 7700a[10] *8076[4]*
Kryena's Rose *Mick Channon* a47 55
2 gr f Royal Applause Kryena (Kris)
1164[4] 1435[6] 4532[5] 4899[6] *5763[10]* 5946[9] *6499[4]* *7410[8]*
Krypton Factor *F Nass* a123 116
4 bb g Kyllachy Cool Question (Polar Falcon (USA))
260a[2] *(314a)* *420a[2]* *(874a)* *(1147a)* 2326a[5] 3370[6]
Kuantan One (IRE) *Paul Cole* a76 68
2 b c Strategic Prince Starfish (IRE) (Galileo (IRE))
7033[4] *7306[4]* *(7707)*
Kuanyao (IRE) *Peter Makin* a74 88
6 b g American Post Nullarbor (Green Desert (USA))
2268[12] 2558[8] 3049[3] 4437[4] *6368[8]*
Kubera (IRE) *J S Moore* 47
2 b c Cape Cross(IRE) Paris Glory (USA) (Honour And Glory (USA))
5005[7] 5684[7] 6115[3]
Kucharova (IRE) *Seamus Mullins* a60 61
4 b m Danehill Dancer(IRE) Gates Of Eden (USA) (Kingmambo (USA))
2767 *422[2]* *561[7]* *687[9]* *829[5]* *1088[5]* *1310[8]* 2395[2] 2651[4]
Kuda Huraa (IRE) *Roger Varian* a93 87
4 b g Montjeu(IRE) Healing Music (FR) (Bering)
(1484) ◆ 1940[3] *4216[11]* *(4944)* 5268[3] *5944[2]* *6584[5]*
Kudoz *Clive Cox* a69 74
3 ch c Three Valleys(USA) Rosapenna (IRE) (Spectrum (IRE))
724[3] ◆ 1270[2] 1893[7] 2613[5] 3448[12]

Kukurun (FR) *Mme M Bollack-Badel* a82 69
2 gr c Kouroun(FR) Knout (FR) (Kendor (FR))
5073a[5]
Kunegunda *James Fanshawe* 87
3 b f Pivotal Panna (Polish Precedent (USA))
2050[4] 2826[4] 3227[3] 4311[2] (4923) ◆ 6598[12]
Kung Hei Fat Choy (USA) *James Given* a89 70
3 b g Elusive Quality(USA) Lady Succeed (JPN) (Brian's Time (USA))
2382[12] *(3939)* ◆ *(4193)* 4713[3] *5721[2]* *5942[7]* *7461[11]* *7715[5]* *(8034)* *8306[6]*
Kunooz (IRE) *Mahmood Al Zarooni* 86
3 b f Hard Spun(USA) Aviacion (BRZ) (Know Heights (IRE))
3879[7] 4608[9]
Kunzea (IRE) *Mick Channon* a40 50
2 ch f Haatef(USA) Louve Heureuse (IRE) (Peintre Celebre (USA))
3487[5] *4217[7]* 4813[7] *5161[5]* 5946[5] 6156[12]
Kuraanda *John Wainwright* a17 19
3 b f Kyllachy Palm Cove (UAE) (Jade Robbery (USA))
2139[9] 3990[10] 5823[7] *7729[11]* *8239[7]*
Kurdy (FR) *C Boutin* 29
3 b g Russian Blue(IRE) Pegmatite (USA) (Fusaichi Pegasus (USA))
7266a[7]
Kutbey (TUR) *M T Balyemez*
4 b h Strike The Gold(USA) Tenderly (TUR) (Private Tender)
5868a[3]
Kuwait Moon *Alan McCabe* a38
3 br g Resplendent Glory(IRE) Tapsalteerie (Tipsy Creek (USA))
114[8] *840[5]*
Kuwait Star *Jason Ward* a53 76
3 ch g Resplendent Glory(IRE) Mofeyda (IRE) (Mtoto)
6341[4] *7359[11]* (7445) (7600)
Kwanto *Malcolm Saunders* 62
2 b f Piccolo Craic Sa Ceili (IRE) (Danehill Dancer (IRE))
1903[7] 2164[5] 2868[7] 4230[5] 4991[5] 6276[2] 7014[5]
Kwik Time *Robin Bastiman* a34 50
4 b g Avonbridge Never Away (Royal Applause)
141[1] *113[9]* *370[14]* *430[8]* 1526[8] 1801[6] 2463[3] 5081[3] 5459[4]
Kyanight (IRE) *Clive Cox* a74 75
3 b f Kodiac Blue Holly (IRE) (Blues Traveller (IRE))
1493[6] 1658[6] *2397[2]* 2869[6] *3450[2]* *4655[10]* *6610[11]*
Kya One (FR) *Y De Nicolay* a95 108
4 b m One Cool Cat(USA) Kya Gulch (USA) (Thunder Gulch (USA))
83a[7] 953a[5] 2570a[6]
Kyleakin Lass *Ian Wood* a87 97
3 b f Kyllachy Local Fancy (Bahamian Bounty)
1721[8] 2347[2] (2986) 3912[8] 4337[3] 4765[5] 5832[3] ◆ (6286) 6666[4] ◆ 7397[13]
Kyle Of Bute *Brian Baugh* a70 68
6 ch g Kyllachy Blinding Mission (IRE) (Marju (IRE))
361[11] *636[6]* *909[5]* *1391[3]* 2692[12] *(3236)* 4683[3] 5258[9] *6458[6]* *7251[9]* *7593[12]*
Kylesku (IRE) *Kevin Ryan* 75
3 b f Moss Vale(IRE) Gisela (IRE) (King Charlemagne (USA))
1912[9] 2256[16] 2875[5]
Kylin *Olivia Maylam* a39 59
3 ch f Kyllachy Descriptive (IRE) (Desert King (IRE))
1359[10] *1725[7]* 2162[13]
Kyllachy Dancer *John Quinn* a63 63
3 b f Kyllachy Aunt Susan (Distant Relative)
1389[2] 1912[7] 2795[5] *3706[2]* 4631[12] 4878[9]
Kyllachykov (IRE) *Robin Bastiman* a45 56
4 ch g Kyllachy Dance On (Caerleon (USA))
1583[4] 1908[2] 2464[3] 3051[4] 3889[3] 4390[3] 5935[6] 6758[8]
Kyllachy Rise *Sir Henry Cecil* 81
2 b c Kyllachy Up And About (Barathea (IRE))
4803[4]
Kyllachy Spirit *William Knight* a89 72
4 b g Kyllachy Cartuccia (IRE) (Doyoun)
1186[4] 2180[18] *3502[13]*
Kyllachy Star *Richard Fahey* a64 102
6 b g Kyllachy Jaljuli (Jalmood (USA))
1128[2] 2025[4] 2910[5] 3878[9] 4339[3] 4828[5] 5369[6] 5827[5] 6659[12] 7210[8] *7415[12]*
Kyllachy Storm *Ron Hodges* a62 73
8 b g Kyllachy Social Storm (USA) (Future Storm (USA))
593[4] *964[3]* ◆ 1497[9] 1908[7] 2413[2] 3103[3] 3434[10] 4902[2] (5191) 5502[9] 6233[6] 7274[7]
Kylladdie *Steve Gollings* a84 82
5 ch g Kyllachy Chance For Romance (Entrepreneur)
120[9] *325[3]* *718[2]* *1007[6]* 1289[4] 2071[4] 2487[9] 4255[6]
Kyncraighe (IRE) *Joseph Tuite* a59 44
4 b g Kyllachy Brighella (Sadler's Wells (USA))
46[8] *154[3]* *(232)* *264[7]* *307[4]* *430[9]* *503[12]* 2652[6] *3007[9]* *3455[10]* 3721[13]
Kyzer Chief *Ron Barr* 69
7 b g Rouvres(FR) Payvashooz (Ballacashtal (CAN))
1298[3] 1480[8] 2314[12] 2436[6] (4454) 5294[12] 5412[8]
Laaheb *Roger Varian* a103 114
6 b g Cape Cross(IRE) Maskunah (IRE) (Sadler's Wells (USA))
2228[6]
Laajooj (IRE) *Mahmood Al Zarooni* a78 111
4 b h Azamour(IRE) Flanders (IRE) (Common Grounds)
52a[2] 486a[2] 877a[10] (5364)
Laa Rayb (USA) *D Selvaratnam* a84 100
8 b g Storm Cat(USA) Society Lady (USA) (Mr Prospector (USA))
80a[6] 590a[8] 758a[12]
La Arenosa (IRE) *A Fabre* 106
3 b f Exceed And Excel(AUS) Baranquilla (Acatenango (GER))
7234a[2]

Laatafreet (IRE) *Saeed Bin Suroor* a74 99
4 ch h Singspiel(IRE) Cerulean Sky (IRE) (Darshaan)
2810[10]

La Bacouetteuse (FR) *Iain Jardine* a28 78
7 b g Miesque's Son(USA) Toryka (Vettori (IRE))
1222[7] (1822) 2593[4] (2842) 4613[11] 5188[3] (5921) 6311[9] 6712[6]

La Banche (FR) *C Des Mazis* a43
2 b f Falco(USA) Kahyasola (FR) (Kahyasi)
7597a[0]

Labarinto *Sir Michael Stoute* 106
4 b g Dansili Tarocchi (USA) (Affirmed (USA))
1510[12] 2176[12] (5835) 7054[7]

La Belle Doyenne *Alan King* a57
4 ch m Doyen(IRE) Tarabela (CHI) (Hussonet (USA))
7162[4] 7625[3] 7739[3]

La Belle Epoque (USA) *Gerard Butler* a68
2 b f Tapit(USA) Catlike Dancer (USA) (Tale Of The Cat (USA))
7506[3]

La Belliere (IRE) *J-C Rouget* a83 86
2 gr f Kheleyf(USA) Coconut Show (Linamix (FR))
7682a[6]

Labienus *David Lanigan* a76 65
2 b c Compton Place Guermantes (Distant Relative)
3824[6] ◆ 4463[2] (5162) 5946[8]

Labretella (IRE) *Robert Johnson* a51 51
5 b m Bahamian Bounty Known Class (USA) (Known Fact (USA))
1248[10]

Labrice *P Harley* 100
4 b m Dubawi(IRE) Laurella (Acatenango (GER))
3652a[4]

Labroc (IRE) *Alan Swinbank* a59 55
4 b g Marju(IRE) Opera Comica (Dr Fong (USA))
1384[9] 1950[6]

La Capriosa *Scott Dixon* a68 78
6 ch m Kyllachy La Caprice (USA) (Housebuster (USA))
100[4] 380[8] 461[5] 808[5] 1280[4] 1428[7]

Lacateno *W Hickst* 108
5 b h Green Tune(USA) Lacatena (GER) (Acatenango (GER))
1901a[4] 3367a[5] 4634a[0]

Lacily (USA) *Mahmood Al Zarooni* 86
3 b f Elusive Quality(USA) Lailani (Unfuwain (USA))
1887[3] 2232[5] 3252[7] 5328[9]

La Collina (IRE) *Kevin Prendergast* 112
3 ch f Strategic Prince Starfish (IRE) (Galileo (IRE))
1884[5] ◆ 2527a[6] 5643a[4] 6061a[5] 6673[4]

La Confession *Rae Guest* a44 55
3 b f Dylan Thomas(IRE) Clinet (IRE) (Dockside (USA))
1448[6] 2014[4] 2353[6] 2624[4] 3246[4] 3665[2] 5095[11] 5441[6]

Laconicos (IRE) *William Stone* a63 68
10 ch g Foxhound(USA) Thermopylae (Tenby)
28[2] 130[5] 400[6] 2137[3] 2735[2] 2998[3] 3721[6] 4296[2] (4844) 5323[6] 6503[3]

La Conquerante *J-C Rouget* 109
3 b f Hurricane Run(IRE) Winning Family (IRE) (Fasliyev (USA))
2156a[3] 5142a[3] 6899a[3]

Lac Sacre (FR) *Robert Collet* a66 66
3 b g Bering Lady Glorieuse (FR) (Le Glorieux)
5074a[6]

La Danse Champetre *Charles Smith* 19
4 ch m Pastoral Pursuits Dancing Spirit (IRE) (Ahonoora)
20[7]

La Danza *Alan Bailey* a69 44
2 b f Country Reel(USA) Freedom Song (Singspiel (IRE))
3776[6] 6535[3] 7777[3] 8018[8]

Ladies Are Forever *Geoffrey Oldroyd* a102 111
4 b m Monsieur Bond(IRE) Forever Bond (Danetime (IRE))
2087[3] 2713[3] 3375[9] 6201[8] 6878[10] 7690[7] 7772[2]

Ladies Best *Christopher Kellett* a26 38
8 b g King's Best(USA) Lady Of The Lake (Caerleon (USA))
1154[16] 6055[8]

Ladram Bay (IRE) *Jonathan Portman* 42
3 b f Oratorio(IRE) Ringmoor Down (Pivotal)
1443[8] 2765[5] 4147[4] 4537[7] 4941[9]

Ladweb *John Gallagher* a59 59
2 ch g Bertolini(USA) Adweb (Muhtarram (USA))
1330[3] 1767[5] 6203[11] 6850[2] 7176[4] 7476[9] 7738[5]

Lady Advocate (IRE) *Tim Easterby* 63
3 b f Lawman(FR) Shalev (GER) (Java Gold (USA))
1386[6] 1916[5] (3025) 3416[11] 3847[7] 5112[4] 5413[11]

Lady Amakhala *George Moore* 83
4 b m Val Royal(FR) Isla Negra (IRE) (Last Tycoon)
1295[7] 1640[2] 2214[7]

Lady American (FR) *Mlle V Dissaux* a66 57
2 b f American Post Oceane Bere (FR) (Tiger Hill (IRE))
7597a[7]

Lady Ana (FR) *N Clement* a77 78
3 b f Anabaa(USA) The Wise Lady (FR) (Ganges (USA))
247a[3]

Lady Arabella (IRE) *Alastair Lidderdale* a71 49
3 b f Dark Angel(IRE) Lady Fabiola (USA) (Open Forum (USA))
(1590) 2679[7] 4850[9] 7270[10] 7416[4] 7768[6] 7905[4] 8078[6]

Lady Areia (GER) *K Klein* 86
6 bb m Areion(GER) Lady Anna (GER) (Acatenango (GER))
629a[6]

Lady Author *Richard Fahey* a36
3 b f Authorized(IRE) Kelucia (IRE) (Grand Lodge (USA))
217[4] 571[7] 7222[8] 7933[8]

Lady Barastar (IRE) *Amanda Perrett* a72 72
4 b m Barathea(IRE) Stariya (IRE) (Soviet Star (USA))
689[5] 6229[9] 7018[10] 7768[12] 7991[8]

Lady Bayside *Malcolm Saunders* a64 77
4 ch m Ishiguru(USA) Seldemosa (Selkirk (USA))
2207[4] ◆ (2572) ◆ 2940[3] 3541[3] 5426[9] 6610[6] 6961[4] 7273[7]

Lady Bellatrix *Mark H Tompkins* a67 55
3 br f Singspiel(IRE) Humility (Polar Falcon (USA))
4314[8] 5019[5] 6302[3] 6500[4] 6810[5] (7303) 7811[4] 8048[2]

Lady Bentinck (IRE) *Alan Berry* 43
3 b f Mujadil(USA) Lady Graigie (IRE) (Fruits Of Love (USA))
4551[8] 4807[2] 5335[6] 5728[9] 7445[6]

Lady Bluesky *Alistair Whillans* a54 77
9 gr m Cloudings(IRE) M N L Lady (Polar Falcon (USA))
1057[4] 3180[4] 3904[2] (4138) (4639) 5830[8] 6517[6]

Lady Bonanova (IRE) *Pat Phelan* 50
2 b f Haatef(USA) Lady Express (IRE) (Soviet Star (USA))
2499[11] 3339[10] 5661[5]

Lady Brickhouse *Michael Squance* a41 24
5 b m Choisir(AUS) Music Maid (IRE) (Inzar (USA))
1014[7] 1178[11] 1635[11] 2329[4]

Lady Brookie *Peter Grayson* a45 78
4 br m Makbul Miss Brookie (The West (USA))
445[10]

Lady Burlesque (IRE) *Mick Channon* a40 39
3 ch f Sir Percy Soubrette (USA) (Opening Verse (USA))
1206[7] 1724[5]

Lady By Red (IRE) *Ann Duffield* a31 50
4 ch m Redback Antonia's Dream (Clantime)
1383[12] 2436[11] 2796[5] 3210[8] 4454[9] 7611[8]

Lady Calantha *Alan Berry* 50
2 b f Byron Brooklyn's Sky (Septieme Ciel (USA))
3473[5] 3996[10] 4899[7] 5916[2]

Lady Caprice *Jane Chapple-Hyam* a71 57
3 b f Kyllachy Lady Betambeau (IRE) (Grand Lodge (USA))
(40) (326) 469[3] 637[8]

Lady Chaparral *Michael Dods* 89
5 b m High Chaparral(IRE) La Sylphide (Rudimentary (USA))
1656[3] 2312[5] 2751[12] (3492) 4175[6] (4868) 5712[7] 6710[7]

Lady Cooper *Willie Musson* a46
2 b f Ishiguru(USA) Mistress Cooper (Kyllachy)
7738[7]

Lady Del Sol *Marjorie Fife* 73
4 b m Monsieur Bond(IRE) Villa Del Sol (Tagula (IRE))
1881[3] 3308[6] 4453[3] 4717[12] (5295) (5542) 6123[5] 6531[5] 7247[13]

Ladydolly *Roy Brotherton* a63 55
4 b m Kyllachy Lady Pekan (Sri Pekan (USA))
135[2] 380[7] 551[8] (750) 979[3] 1343[2] 5327[6] 5504[5] 6180[8] 7157[9]

Lady Elsie *George Prodromou* a71 68
4 b m Singspiel(IRE) Lady Hen (Efisio)
281[6] 355[5] 363[4]

Lady Gade (FR) *G Doleuze* 50
3 b f Lando(GER) Segesta (GER) (Second Set (IRE))
7267a[10]

Lady Gar Gar *Geoffrey Oldroyd* a67 73
4 ch m Monsieur Bond(IRE) Triple Tricks (IRE) (Royal Academy (USA))
1384[8] 3021[6] 5220[10]

Lady Gargoyle *Jim Goldie* 47
4 br m Lucky Story(USA) Gargoyle Girl (Be My Chief (USA))
1223[5] 2823[4] 3277[5] 3579[3] 5172[11] 5413[5] 6885[11]

Lady Gibraltar *Alan Jarvis* a76 92
3 b f Rock Of Gibraltar(IRE) Lady Adnil (IRE) (Stravinsky (USA))
1109[5] 1449[7] 1730[3] 2816[4] (3618) 4364[4] (4500) (4765) 5663[3] 6026[5] 6536[6]

Lady Gorgeous *Mick Channon* 105
3 ch f Compton Place Cayman Sunset (IRE) (Night Shift (USA))
1454[5] 2276[7] 2659[3] 3265[6] 4070[9] 4598[6] 5080[3] 5385[5] 6072[5]

Lady Gosford (IRE) *Edward Lynam* a76 84
2 ch f Kheleyf(USA) Kalimanta (IRE) (Lake Coniston (IRE))
6550a[7]

Lady Hannah *Shaun Lycett* a25
7 b m Muhtarram(USA) Piracy (Jupiter Island)
213[6]

Lady Heartbeat *Michael Blanshard* a50 51
3 b f Avonbridge Take Heart (Electric)
27[4] 5994[6] 6233[8]

Lady Ibrox *Alan Brown* 91
2 b f Ishiguru(USA) Last Impression (Imp Society (USA))
1911[11] 2334[3] (2747) 3250[3] 3604[2] (4045) 4687[7] 5601[6] 6424[5] (6658) 7518[11]

Lady Intrigue (IRE) *Richard Fahey* a32 51
4 b m Hurricane Run(IRE) Intriguing (IRE) (Fasliyev (USA))
7222[7] 7603[9] 7793[13]

Lady Jacamira (GER) *R Dzubasz* 100
3 ch f Lord Of England(GER) Latley (GER) (Sillery (USA))
3653a[3] 5849a[5]

Lady Jean *Reg Hollinshead* a40
2 b f Striking Ambition Parkside Prospect (Piccolo)
5807[6] 6499[6] 6890[6] 7649[10] 7977[5]

Lady Jock (IRE) *John Patrick Shanahan* a54 76
3 ch f Giant's Causeway(USA) My Special K'S (USA) (Tabasco Cat (USA))
4260[4]

Lady Kashaan (IRE) *Alan Swinbank* a42 90
3 b f Manduro(GER) Lady's Secret (IRE) (Alzao (USA))
1053[6] 1386[3] (2340) 2605[2] ◆ (3212) 3592[4] ◆ 4923[4] (5383) 6033[3] 6472[2] (6668) 7396[6] ◆

Lady Kildare (IRE) *Jedd O'Keeffe* a42 72
4 br m Bachelor Duke(USA) Teodora (IRE) (Fairy King (USA))
2140[9] 2690[10] 2982[4] 4400[7] 4547[6] 4909[9] 5416[4] 7990[8]

Lady Layla *Jo Hughes* a79 79
3 b f Excellent Art Tartouche (Pursuit Of Love)
2416[2] 2752[7] 3376[8] 4497[5] 4876[4] 5426[2] 6050[2] 6239[10] 6542[4] 7141[9] (7437) 7732[12]

Lady Libby Lamb *David C Griffiths* a21
4 bl m Statue Of Liberty(USA) Lady Caroline Lamb (IRE) (Contract Law (USA))
7654[9] 7952[9]

Lady Loch *Richard Fahey* 87
3 b f Dutch Art Locharia (Wolfhound (USA))
1166[2] 1357[2] 2030[5] (2785) 3383[3] 4319[4] 5372[2] 6073[6] (6667) 6875[5]

Lady Lunchalot (USA) *J S Moore* a57
2 b f More Than Ready(USA) Betty Johanne (USA) (Johannesburg (USA))
8076[3] 8262[3]

Lady Lyricist *Reg Hollinshead* a57 5
3 b f Librettist(USA) Victory Flip (IRE) (Victory Note (USA))
4486[10] 5253[11]

Lady Macduff (IRE) *Mark Johnston* a82 91
3 b f Iffraaj Tamora (Dr Fong (USA))
(990) 2182[12] 4579[5] (5043) 5334[5] 5517[12] 6023[12] 6701[3] 6921[3] 7064[3] 7461[12]

Lady Malet *William Haggas* a68
2 b f Azamour(IRE) Miss Rochester (IRE) (Montjeu (IRE))
7840[5] 8033[2] 8233[2] 8254[2]

Lady Mandy *Ian Williams* a57 50
3 b f Teofilo(IRE) Bedara (Barathea (IRE))
1062[2] 1448[4] 5589[4] 5744[6] 6210[5] 6474[8] (6769)

Lady Mango (IRE) *Ronald Harris* a73 65
4 ch m Bahamian Bounty Opera (Forzando)
578[7] 664[2] (781) 972[4] 1788[3] (2171) 2546[4] (2760) (3958) 4533[5] 4920[3] 5972[5] 7484[11] 7863[7] 8005[9] 8160[5]

Lady Margaeux (IRE) *David O'Meara* 72
2 b f Redback Storm Lady (IRE) (Alhaarth (IRE))
2790[3] 3208[2] 3554[2] 4427[5]

Lady Marmelo (IRE) *Mick Channon* a64 70
2 b f Duke Of Marmalade(IRE) Mooretown Lady (IRE) (Montjeu (IRE))
3474[6] 4246[4] 4792[4] 5550[8] 6096[3] 6363[5]

Lady Medici *Kevin Prendergast* a30 53
2 ch f Medicean Jesting (Muhtarram (USA))
6550a[12] 6853a[11]

Lady Meydan (FR) *F Rohaut* a93 104
4 b m American Post Open Offer (Cadeaux Genereux)
83a[0]

Lady Moonlight (IRE) *Ann Duffield* 71
2 gr f Jeremy(USA) Lady Georgina (Linamix (FR))
(3436) (4206) 5292[2] 5537[3] 6130[5] 6475[5]

Lady Ness (FR) *Mlle C Brunaud* 62
2 b f Spirit One(FR) Infusion (Efisio)
5570a[7]

Lady Nickandy (IRE) *Karen Tutty* a54 58
3 b f Kheleyf(USA) Tanzie (IRE) (Soviet Star (USA))
25[9] 138[3] 250[8] 898[7] 1090[3] 2092[9] 7354[8]

Lady Niramax *David Nicholls* 47
2 b f Indesatchel(IRE) Just A Gem (Superlative)
3401[10] 4132[7] 5586[6]

Lady Norlela *Brian Rothwell* a27 65
6 b m Reset(AUS) Lady Netbetsports (IRE) (In The Wings)
1598[9] 2048[9] 2260[14]

Lady Nouf *William Haggas* 77
2 b f Teofilo(IRE) Majestic Sakeena (IRE) (King's Best (USA))
(6966)

Lady Ocarina *John Dunlop* a46 39
3 b f Piccolo Queen Of Iceni (Erhaab (USA))
2172[8] 2560[11] 3483[15] 3918[10]

Lady Of Budysin (GER) *Andreas Lowe* 93
3 b f Soldier Hollow Lots Of Love (GER) (Java Gold (USA))
2107a[5] 2746a[4] 3802a[5] 4616a[7]

Lady of Burgundy *Mark Usher* a75 74
6 b m Montjeu(IRE) Helena's Paris (IRE) (Peintre Celebre (USA))
2051[7] 2237[6] 3222[10] 3961[2] 4475[5] 5158[4] 5718[8] 6255[4]

Lady Of Edge *Keith Dalgleish* a15 33
3 b f Librettist(USA) Lady Of Windsor (IRE) (Woods Of Windsor (USA))
4807[7] 5428[11] 6529[4]

Lady Of Seville (IRE) *Tom Tate* 49
2 b f Duke Of Marmalade(IRE) Promise Of Love (Royal Applause)
1671[9] 4290[8] 5168[5] 6336[5]

Lady Of Shamrock (USA) *John W Sadler* a95 111
3 bb f Scat Daddy(USA) Blushing Issue (USA) (Blushing John (USA))
(4131a) 7549a[5]

Lady Of The House (IRE) *Kevin Ryan* a73 84
2 b f Holy Roman Emperor(IRE) Miss Delila (USA) (Malibu Moon (USA))
1466[5] 2282[2] 2747[2] 5909[3] (6042) (6475) 6980[8]

Lady Of The Vine (USA) *Andrew Balding* 53
2 b f Master Command(USA) Silverbulletlover (USA) (Gulch (USA))
5267[5] 7014[6]

Lady Of Yue *Ed Dunlop* a52
2 b f Manduro(GER) Desert Royalty (IRE) (Alhaarth (IRE))
7505[11] 7721[11] 7900[7] 8112[7]

Lady Ongar *Alan Kirtley*
4 b m Grand Finale(IRE) Inya Face (Prince Daniel (USA))
5316[10] 5708[10]

Lady On Top (IRE) *Nerys Dutfield* a54 46
4 b m Oratorio(IRE) Ascot Lady (IRE) (Spinning World (USA))
2171[12] 6586[8] 6951[9] 7512[12] 7788[4]

Lady Oz (IRE) *Michael Easterby*
5 ch m Choisir(AUS) Lady Sheriff (Taufan (USA))
5244[8] 5387[6] 5618[13] 6100[12]

Lady Percy (IRE) *Mark Usher* a55 60
3 b f Sir Percy Genuinely (IRE) (Entrepreneur)
2128[6] 2756[5] (3193) 3665[7] 4709[6] 5148[4] 6174[4] 6690[9]

Lady Phill *Bill Turner* a73 79
2 ch f Avonbridge Lady Filly (Atraf)
1623[3] 1767[2] (2039) (2234) 3269[14] 7206[6]

Lady Pimpernel *Henry Candy* 77
2 ch f Sir Percy Angeleno (IRE) (Belong To Me (USA))
6153[2] (6791)

Lady Platinum Club *Linda Stubbs* a62 57
4 ch m Monsieur Bond(IRE) Bond Platinum Club (Pivotal)
4865[8] 5416[10] 6104[7] 7378[3] 7747[9]

Lady Poppy *George Moore* 80
2 b f Kyllachy Poppets Sweetlove (Foxhound (USA))
1131[7] 1474[5] 2437[2] (2873) 3250[5] (4614) 4827[4] 5515[10] 6312[3] 7028[11]

Lady Prodee *Bill Turner* a73 47
4 b m Proclamation(IRE) Dee-Lady (Deploy)
5815[7]

Lady Raffa *Michael Dods* a41 37
2 ch f Araafa(IRE) Locharia (Wolfhound (USA))
1277[5] 1556[8] 6310[4] 7795[3]

Lady Rizzi (USA) *Linda Rice* 98
9 b m Rizzi(CAN) What'salltheruckas (CAN) (Bold Ruckus (USA))
8278a[6]

Lady Romanza (IRE) *Brendan Powell* a62 61
3 b f Holy Roman Emperor(IRE) Sharakawa (IRE) (Darshaan)
1107[2] 1568[5] 1982[5] 3483[14] 4214[12] 5508[5] (6814) 6948[3] 7303[11] 7499[3] 7718[2]

Lady Rosamunde *Marcus Tregoning* a70 89
4 gr m Maria's Mon(USA) String Quartet (IRE) (Sadler's Wells (USA))
1491[3] (2237) 2447[2] (3341)

Lady Royale *Geoffrey Oldroyd* a71 88
4 ch m Monsieur Bond(IRE) Bond Royale (Piccolo)
1476[10] 1828[9] 2793[8]

Lady Royal Oak (IRE) *Olivia Maylam* a49 66
5 b m Exceed And Excel(AUS) Enclave (USA) (Woodman (USA))
37[5] 118[11]

Lady Rumba *John O'Shea* a29 45
4 b m Ishiguru(USA) Costa Packet (IRE) (Hussonet (USA))
483[9]

Ladys First *Richard Fahey* 106
3 b f Dutch Art Like A Dame (Danehill (USA))
2263[2] 3270[3] 3879[2] 4628[6] (5092) 5834[2] 6633[4]

Ladyship *Sir Michael Stoute* 102
3 b f Oasis Dream Peeress (Pivotal)
1357[3] (2332) 4286[2] ◆ 5520[9] 6602[2] ◆

Lady Sledmere (IRE) *Paul Midgley* 76
4 b m Barathea(IRE) Helena's Paris (IRE) (Peintre Celebre (USA))
1249[17] 3694[11] 6410[17] 6782[3] 7314[8]

Lady Sol (FR) *F Monnier* 61
7 b m Loup Solitaire(USA) Scarlet Lady (IRE) (Highest Honor (FR))
3207a[6]

Lady Story (IRE) *Giuseppe Ligas* 74
3 b f Lucky Story(USA) Patroller (USA) (Grand Slam (USA))
1409a[8]

Lady Sylvia *Joseph Tuite* a66 74
3 ch f Haafhd Abide (FR) (Pivotal)
(663) 1364[3] 2625[6] 3193[3] 3671[2] 4602[6] 4989[2] 6434[5]

Lady Valtas *Robin Dickin* a32 37
4 b m Val Royal(FR) Phantasmagoria (Fraam)
1791[6]

Lady Vermeer *Ralph Beckett* 72
2 b f Dutch Art Classic Vision (Classic Cliche (IRE))
4011[6] 4792[5]

Lady Wingshot (IRE) *J S Bolger* 108
3 b f Lawman(FR) Nassma (IRE) (Sadler's Wells (USA))
4482a[5] (5523a) 6079a[7] 6268a[5] 6917a[2]

La Estrella (USA) *Don Cantillon* a93 84
9 b g Theatrical(IRE) Princess Ellen (Tirol)
(213) (643) (2403) (7608) (8148)

Laffan (IRE) *Kevin Ryan* a81 94
3 b g Dark Angel(IRE) Lady Corduff (IRE) (Titus Livius (FR))
(6) (112) 1241[3] (2265) (2660) 3265[17]

La Fortunata *Eve Johnson Houghton* a74 97
5 b m Lucky Story(USA) Phantasmagoria (Fraam)
2507[18] (3593) 4576[16] 5385[4] 6116[5] 6602[6]

Lager Time (IRE) *David Evans* a53
2 b g Tagula(IRE) Polish Belle (Polish Precedent (USA))
7855[4] ◆ 7953[8] 8044[6]

La Giaconda *Clive Cox* a1 50
3 ch f Excellent Art Always On My Mind (Distant Relative)
6154[8] 6792[8] 7477[9]

Lagrima (IRE) *J S Moore* 49
2 br f Aussie Rules(USA) Sweet Sorrow (IRE) (Lahib (USA))
2384[8] 2499[9]

Lahaag *John Gosden* 101
3 b g Marju(IRE) Chater (Alhaarth (IRE))
2279[2] (2800) (6789) 7064[2]

La Jiheska (FR) *D Windrif* a67
4 b m Apsis Zarina (FR) (Johann Quatz (FR))
116a[4]

Lake Drop (USA) *H Graham Motion* 108
4 b h Lemon Drop Kid(USA) Lake Charles (USA) (El Gran Senor (USA))
(2323a) 5374a[4]

Lake George (IRE) *James M Barrett* a80 79
4 b g Alkaadhem Ballyronan Girl (IRE) (Elbio)
4833a[8]

Lakeman (IRE) *Brian Ellison* a65 60
6 b g Tillerman Bishop's Lake (Lake Coniston (IRE))
1578[6] 1956[2] ◆ 2814[9] 3129[10] 4179[11] 4402[2] 5012[7] 5241[5] 5672[2] 7608[3] 7731[2] 8139[8]

Lakota Ghost (USA) *Seamus Durack* a66 67
4 b g Rockport Harbor(USA) Political Alert (USA) (Giant's Causeway (USA))
600[2] 6399[3]

Lal Bhai *Chris Down* a55
4 b g Sleeping Indian B'Elanna Torres (Entrepreneur)
737[7] 869[10] 1065[9] 6395[12]

La Luz Del Sol *Richard Fahey* a57
2 b f Misu Bond(IRE) Villa Del Sol (Tagula (IRE))
7953[6] 8044[4] 8138[9]

La Maria (FR) *C Lerner* a60 72
3 b f Johannesburg(USA) La Gomera (IRE) (Hamas (IRE))
7267a[3]

Lambert Pen (USA) *Mick Channon* a62 60
2 ch c Johannesburg(USA) Whiletheiron'shot (USA) (Smart Strike (CAN))
6818[8] 7067[5] 7244[3] 7977[2] 8072[9]

L'Ami Gaby (FR) *R Chotard* a77 78
5 ch g Muhtathir Bonne Gargotte (FR) (Poliglote)
7701a[5]

L'Ami Louis (IRE) *Henry Candy* 96
4 b g Elusive City(USA) Princess Electra (IRE) (Lake Coniston (IRE))
1844[8] ◆ (2487) 3049[8] 4824[2] 5368[5]

Lamora *Mme J Bidgood* a58
4 ch m Sinndar(IRE) Labour Of Love (USA) (Silver Deputy (CAN))
15a[7]

Lamusawama *Ed Dunlop* 71
2 b c Acclamation Intrepid Queen (USA) (Theatrical (IRE))
4194[6] 4724[5] 5311[3] 6699[6]

Lana (IRE) *David Evans* a60 61
3 b f Amadeus Wolf Carn Lady (IRE) (Woodman (USA))
27[5] 86[7] 250[3] (322) 549[2] 660[7] 743[7] 917[6] 3510[7] 4185[8] 4981[7] 5659[7] (5994) 6178[7]

Lana Jolie (GER) *A Wohler* 101
4 rg m Whipper(USA) Linamox (FR) (Linamix (FR))
3652a[2] 6723a[6]

Lana Mae *Brendan Powell* a43
3 ch f Proclamation(IRE) Saharan Song (IRE) (Singspiel (IRE))
2497[7] 3246[11] 4240[9]

Lanansaak (IRE) *Roger Varian* 79
2 ch f Zamindar(USA) Bunood (IRE) (Sadler's Wells (USA))
(5977) 6448[5]

Lanarkshire (IRE) *Mark Johnston* a76 56
3 ch g Iffraaj Voyage Of Dreams (USA) (Riverman (USA))
358[10] 684[4] (1053) 6136[5] 6528[8]

Lancaster Gate *Amanda Perrett* a77 60
3 b c Zamindar(USA) Bayswater (Caerleon (USA))
2429[9] 7300[9]

Lancelot (FR) *A De Mieulle* a95 110
5 b h Bahri(USA) Lunata (IRE) (Marju (IRE))
(3178a)

Lancelot Du Lac (ITY) *Dean Ivory* 80
2 b c Shamardal(USA) Dodie Mae (USA) (Capote (USA))
5062[7] ◆ 5792[7] ◆ 6377[2] ◆ 7067[2]

Landaho *Hugh McWilliams* a38 44
3 b f Tobougg(IRE) Ellovamul (Elmaamul (USA))
1660[5] 2843[5] 3461[5] 4211[5] 4549[6] 5427[8] 5738[11] 7249[7] 7619[11]

Landaman (IRE) *Mark Johnston* 109
4 br g Cape Cross(IRE) Mayoress (Machiavellian (USA))
1133[7] 1258[9] 2035[7] (2606) (2687) (4684) (4805)

Landesherr (GER) *Steve Gollings* a72 72
5 b g Black Sam Bellamy(IRE) Lutte Marie (GER) (Frontal)
1829[2] 2260[7] 3793[2] 4179[3] 5665[10] 6250[2] 6458[12] 6794[5] 7474[3] 7905[5] 8079[9]

Land Hawk (IRE) *Lydia Pearce* a65 50
6 br g Trans Island Heike (Glenstal (USA))
67[4] 224[3] 452[5] 651[3] 825[5] 1047[5] (1635) 2463[7] 4219[10] 4890[10] 5638[9]

Landown Littlerock *Reg Hollinshead* a62 66
3 b g Sakhee(USA) Maraha (Lammtarra (USA))
1486[3] 1992[2] 2333[8] 2860[12] 7527[10] 7800[10] 7921[4] 8213[4]

Langham Lily (USA) *Chris Wall* a69 49
3 bb f Badge Of Silver(USA) Silver Frau (USA) (Silver Charm (USA))
2280[7] 2799[4] 6892[2] ◆ 7303[2] ◆ (7921)

Langley *Tim Vaughan* a70 54
5 b g Trempolino(USA) Late Night (GER) (Groom Dancer (USA))
5239[8] 5596[5] 6056[3] 7252[10] 7474[13]

Langley Vale *Roger Teal* a66 71
3 b g Piccolo Running Glimpse (IRE) (Runnett)
892[6] 1376[3] 1723[7] 3118[5] 3732[4] (4943) 5662[4]

La Pampita (IRE) *William Knight* a76 72
3 b f Intikhab(USA) Jacaranda Ridge (Indian Ridge)
1610[4] 2172[3] 3070[4] 3551[2] 3946[2] 4850[2] 5636[8] 7025[3] 7249[3]

La Passionata *Jeremy Gask* a38 29
3 ch f Proclamation(IRE) Miss Madame (IRE) (Cape Cross (IRE))
5444[10] 6765[9] 7903[8] 8154[6]

La Pedrera (IRE) *F Head* 69
2 b f Danehill Dancer(IRE) Straight Lass (IRE) (Machiavellian (USA))
5570a[5]

La Peinture (FR) *A De Royer-Dupre* 109
3 ch f Muhtathir Pertinence (IRE) (Fasliyev (USA))
2532a[4] 7449a[2]

La Pomme D'Amour *A Fabre* 111
4 ch m Peintre Celebre(USA) Winnebago (Kris)
4386a[2] (5116a) 6295a[11] 7237[10]

Larga Charla (IRE) *G Botti* a97 82
3 b c Elusive City(USA) Tinareena (IRE) (Barathea (IRE))
5473a[2]

Larkrise Star *Dean Ivory* a74 70
5 b m Where Or When(IRE) Katy Ivory (IRE) (Night Shift (USA))
2044[11] 2498[8] 3039[6] 3443[6] 3920[4] 4411[5] 5063[2] 5592[6]

L'Arlesienne *Sylvester Kirk* a44
3 ch f Dutch Art Angry Bark (USA) (Woodman (USA))
191[10] 294[11]

Lars Krister (IRE) *Hans Adielsson* a63
2 b g Clodovil(IRE) Ann's Annie (IRE) (Alzao (USA))
3452[3]

Larwood (IRE) *Henry Candy* a84 87
3 gr g Aussie Rules(USA) Ashbilya (USA) (Nureyev (USA))
(1445) 1983[7] 4530[2] ◆ 4765[8]

La Sabara *A Wohler* 36
2 ch f Sabiango(GER) La Hermana (Hernando (FR))
7588a[9]

La Salida *David Barron* 66
3 b f Proclamation(IRE) Anapola (GER) (Polish Precedent (USA))
1798[7] 2795[9] 3184[6] 3952[4] 4771[7] 5317[7] 5757[2]

Lascaux *John Gosden* a78 78
3 ch f Pivotal Tora Bora (Grand Lodge (USA))
1649[2] ◆ 1957[2]

Lasdramad (FR) *Y Durepaire* 89
2 ch f Mount Nelson Andramad (IRE) (Fasliyev (USA))
4205a[4] 5248a[9]

Las Encinas *Adrian McGuinness* a38 21
2 b f Pastoral Pursuits Hot Tin Roof (IRE) (Thatching)
5858a[12] 6853a[10]

Laser Blazer *Jeremy Gask* a74 68
4 b g Zafeen(FR) Sashay (Bishop Of Cashel)
188[5] 468[3] 738[3] 895[2] 984[2] 1919[2] 2394[2] 3283[4] (4491) (5038) 5507[4] 6891[3] 7652[2] 7839[3] 8175[2]

Las Hilanderas (USA) *Stuart Williams* a29
4 ch m El Prado(IRE) Lilium (Nashwan (USA))
137[6] 149[7]

Lashyn (USA) *Sir Michael Stoute* a70 67
3 ch f Mr Greeley(USA) Sleepytime (IRE) (Royal Academy (USA))
1501[9] (2585) 4335[10] 4850[6]

Lasilia (IRE) *Kevin Ryan* 88
2 b f Acclamation Vasilia (Dansili)
1556[5] (2224) 2603[9] 3269[6] 3823[2] 5307[7] 5601[3] 6467[7]

La Sonadora *John Spearing* a43 49
3 gr f Proclamation(IRE) Evening Falls (Beveled (USA))
2803[12] 3489[7] 4424[4] 4902[6]

Last Bid *Tim Easterby* 96
3 b f Vital Equine(IRE) Manderina (Mind Games)
1524[5] 2028[9] 2509[2] 3165[6] 4063[15] 4611[18] 5603[6] 6075[20]

Last Born (FR) *A Fabre* 100
3 ch f Monsun(GER) America (IRE) (Arazi (USA))
7449a[8]

Lastchancelucas *Declan Carroll* 86
2 b g Ishiguru(USA) Light Of Aragon (Aragon)
(1753) (2181) 2702[5]

Last Chance Ranch *Derek Shaw* a41
2 b c Manduro(GER) Rakata (USA) (Quiet American (USA))
5476[8] 6581[11] 6889[8] 8289[7]

Last Destination (IRE) *Nigel Tinkler* a51 71
4 b g Dubai Destination(USA) Maimana (IRE) (Desert King (IRE))
1917[14] 2260[18] 2588[17] 3032[2] 3705[7] (4398) 5059[8] 5341[4] 6105[8]

Last Fighter (IRE) *Saeed Bin Suroor* 78
3 b g Cape Cross(IRE) Launch Time (USA) (Relaunch (USA))
6328[2] 6965[2] (7494)

Last Hooray *David Elsworth* a59
2 b f Royal Applause Dodo (IRE) (Alzao (USA))
7987[5] 8171[7]

Lastkingofscotland (IRE) *Conor Dore* a80 81
6 b g Danehill Dancer(IRE) Arcade (Rousillon (USA))
33[5] (102) 178[8] (205) 359[3] 474[3] (517) 669[3] 746[8] (893) 1091[4] 1727[3] 2083[10] 2354[2] 2545[8] 3230[10] 5233[9] 5892[8] 6692[11] 7022[11] 7203[4] 7485[3] ◆ 7590[2] 7741[2] 7857[9] 7967[2] 8058[2] 8160[2] (8236)

Last Minute Lisa (IRE) *S Donohoe* a55 50
2 b f Strategic Prince Bradwell (IRE) (Taufan (USA))
7840[2] 8208[4]

Last Night Show (ITY) *S Botti* 97
3 b f Martino Alonso(IRE) Greedy Slewpy (USA) (Slewpy (USA))
1699a[2]

Lastofthemohicans (FR) *Paul Webber* a63 52
5 b g Galileo(IRE) Peace Time (GER) (Surumu (GER))
3962[7] 5965[4]

L'Astre De Choisir (IRE) *Michael Easterby* a81 78
4 ch g Choisir(AUS) Starring (FR) (Ashkalani (IRE))
2264[16] 4770[11] 5369[7] 6047[11] 7247[12] 7412[8]

Last Shadow *William Muir* 96
3 b g Notnowcato Fairy Queen (IRE) (Fairy King (USA))
1132[5] (1518) (2088) 2484[6] 3509[3] (4151) 4700[S] 5078[10] 6668[2] 6833[7]

Last Sovereign *Ollie Pears* a95 95
8 b g Pivotal Zayala (Royal Applause)
190[5] 378[5] 649[3] (896) 997[3] 1727[9] 2092[6] 3169[13] (4400) 4680[3] 5320[2] (5584) 6026[4] (6685) 7503[6] 7651[2] 7918[4] 8066[5]

Last Supper *James Bethell* a43 71
3 b f Echo Of Light Scotland The Brave (Zilzal (USA))
1660[4] 2030[2] 2881[6] 3495[2] 4675[6] 6783[8] 7361[6]

Last Train *A Fabre* 117
3 b c Rail Link Rainbow Lake (Rainbow Quest (USA))
4121a[2] 6294a[3]

Last Zak *Michael Easterby* a20 47
3 b g Lucky Story(USA) Zakuska (Zafonic (USA))
3275[10] 4623[5]

Las Verglas Star (IRE) *Richard Fahey* a69 97
4 gr g Verglas(IRE) Magnificent Bell (IRE) (Octagonal (NZ))
1273[10] 1854[15] 2911[7] 3306[2] 4365[2] ◆ 4684[2] 5492[10] (6606) 7175[6] 7407[7] 7601[3]

La Sylphe *David Barron* a77 74
2 b f Refuse To Bend(IRE) Naayla (IRE) (Invincible Spirit (IRE))
1671[4] 2047[5] 2437[6] (3936) ◆ 4922[2] ◆ 5292[3] 5544[2] ◆ 6312[6] (6809) 7220[8]

Late Reg *Liam Grassick*
13 br m Chaddleworth(IRE) Prominent Princess (Prominer)
6228[11]

Later In Life *Christine Dunnett*
3 ch f Notnowcato Life's A Whirl (Machiavellian (USA))
5970[12]

Late Telegraph (IRE) *Sir Henry Cecil* a95 96
4 b h Montjeu(IRE) Bywayofthestars (Danehill (USA))
2479[7] 2933[9] 3765[2] 4800[9] 5558[8] 5835[14]

Latitude (SWE) *Vanja Sandrup*
3 b f Lateral By The Book (IRE) (Definite Article)
5144a[5]

La Troisieme *Dean Ivory*
3 b f Three Valleys(USA) Over The Limit (IRE) (Diktat)
3447[P]

Laudate Dominum (IRE) *Richard Fahey* 79
2 b f Oratorio(IRE) Feeling Wonderful (IRE) (Fruits Of Love (USA))
4310[2] ◆ 5274[4] (5818)

Laughing (IRE) *Alan E Goldberg* a73 107
4 b m Dansili Comic (IRE) (Be My Chief (USA))
6298a[8]

Laughing Jack *Tony Carroll* a80 80
4 b g Beat Hollow Bronzewing (Beldale Flutter (USA))
1094[3] 1706[3] ◆ 2502[8] 3039[4] 3278[5] 5007[7] 5965[5] 6638[13] 6988[5]

Laughing Rock (IRE) *Phil McEntee* a43 62
2 b f Rock Of Gibraltar(IRE) The Last Laugh (Kyllachy)
(6115) 7439[3] 7724[6]

Laugh Out Loud *Mick Channon* a92 113
3 gr f Clodovil(IRE) Funny Girl (IRE) (Darshaan)
231[2] (573) ◆ (1215) ◆ 1884[8] ◆ (2255) (2742a) 3328[6] 6061a[4] 6673[3]

Launch Commander (USA) *David Fawkes*
3 b c Master Command(USA) Launch Site (USA) (Relaunch (USA))
8279a[9]

Laura Land *Mark Brisbourne* a55 48
6 b m Lujain(USA) Perdicula (IRE) (Persian Heights)
454[7] 602[12]

Laura's Bairn *J R Jenkins* a69 73
3 ch g Piccolo Primula Bairn (Bairn (USA))
6[5] (455) (1599) 3118[3] 3350[8] 4208[6] 7299[10]

Lava Steps (USA) *David O'Meara* a13 41
6 b g Giant's Causeway(USA) Miznah (IRE) (Sadler's Wells (USA))
1580[6] 3307[3] 3437[9] 4912[6] 5172[9] 5714[7]

Lavender Bay *Tim Pitt* a48 51
2 b f Needwood Blade In Good Faith (USA) (Dynaformer (USA))
6872[8] 7329[10] 7706[9]

La Vermandoise (FR) *Y Barberot* a66 65
2 gr f King's Best(USA) Cozystorm (USA) (Cozzene (USA))
7700a[8] 8276a[0]

Laverre (IRE) *Lucy Wadham* a37 80
5 b m Noverre(USA) Ladood (Unfuwain (USA))
2498[2] (2679) (3550) 4579[9]

Law Enforcement (IRE) *Richard Hannon* 110
2 b c Lawman(FR) Broken Spectre (Rainbow Quest (USA))
4222[2] ◆ (4724) ◆ (5552) (5836) (7076a)

Lawful *Paul Fitzsimons* a29 61
2 b g Piccolo Sarcita (Primo Dominie)
2231[4] 2844[12] 3569[6] 4230[8] 5161[8]

Lawmans Thunder *Mahmood Al Zarooni* 67
2 b c Lawman(FR) Rhapsodize (Halling (USA))
3346[7]

Lawn Jamil (USA) *Charles Hills* a53 74
3 b g Jazil(USA) Khazayin (USA) (Bahri (USA))
2246[12] 2860[10]

Lawnswood (USA) *Barry Croft*
5 b h Forestry(USA) Eyes Wide Open (USA) (Unbridled's Song (USA))
8278a[7]

Law Of The Range *Marco Botti* a104 107
5 b m Alhaarth(IRE) Mountain Law (USA) (Mountain Cat (USA))
1213[2] 1883[6] 2515a[4] 3266[6] 4617a[6]

Law To Himself (IRE) *Alan Swinbank* 77
5 b g Rakti Samhat Mtoto (Mtoto)
1561[0] 1797[3] 2241[6] 3287[7] 3891[6] 4714[6] 5672[4] 6131[9] 6885[5]

Layali Dubai (USA) *Saeed Bin Suroor* a91 59
3 b f Street Sense(USA) Make My Heart Sing (USA) (King Of Kings (IRE))
2196[7] 3340[7] 6973[2] (7358) (7511) (7655) (7740)

Laybach (IRE) *Jim Goldie* 43
8 br g Bach(IRE) River Breeze (IRE) (Sharifabad (IRE))
3333[8] 3580[4] 4259[6] 5054[10] 5761[6]

Layer Cake *A Kleinkorres* a79 98
6 b g Monsieur Bond(IRE) Blue Indigo (FR) (Pistolet Bleu (IRE))
6804a[8]

Layl (USA) *Mahmood Al Zarooni* a68 76
2 bb c Street Cry(IRE) Cymbal (IRE) (Singspiel (IRE))
6876[4] 7324[5]

Layla's Boy *John Mackie* a69 44
5 ch g Sakhee(USA) Gay Romance (Singspiel (IRE))
4156[5] (4402) 4652[2] 5012[6] 6055[5] 6478[7] 6940[4] 7252[3] 7731[4] 8260[4]

Layla's Hero (IRE) *Ian Williams* a93 93
5 b g One Cool Cat(USA) Capua (USA) (Private Terms (USA))
1161[2] 1220[5] 1354[3] ◆ 1844[13] 2489[12] 6235[15] 6466[19] 6663[9] 7114[11] 7453[5] 7684[13]

Layla's King *David C Griffiths* a66 66
4 b g Dubawi(IRE) Top Jem (Damister (USA))
(5244) 6410[7] 6812[9] 7684[17]

Layla's Oasis *Jamie Osborne* a73 72
2 b f Oasis Dream Kirk (Selkirk (USA))
5040[4] 6007[5] 6177[2] 6658[2] 6954[3] 7463[8] (7745) ◆ 7891[4] 8065[4]

Layline (IRE) *Gay Kelleway* a98 83
5 b g King's Best(USA) Belle Reine (King Of Kings (IRE))
177[7] 223[2] (427) 668[3] 846[2] 1037[4] 2706[11] 3594[8] 4216[7] 4722[4] 4983[7] 6848[4] (7315) 7601[5] 8056[0] 8227[11]

Lay Time *Andrew Balding* 112
4 b m Galileo(IRE) Time Saved (Green Desert (USA))
2654[5] 3266[3] 4065[8] 4801[5] (5594) 6482[2] 7094a[10]

La Zam (FR) *Reg Hollinshead* a69 28
3 b f Zamindar(USA) Francais (Mark Of Esteem (IRE))
7841[13] 7921[10]

Lazarus Bell *Brian Meehan* a60 86
2 ch c Bahamian Bounty Snake's Head (Golden Snake (USA))
4846[3] (5553) 6372[3] 6980[11]

Lazeez (USA) *Clive Brittain* a59 42
3 b f Green Desert(USA) Ballet School (IRE) (Sadler's Wells (USA))
1048[3] 2628[8] 3706[5]

La Zona (IRE) *Wido Neuroth* a93 101
6 b m Singspiel(IRE) Reine De Neige (Kris)
2160a[5]

Leadenhall Lass (IRE) *Pat Phelan* a75 69
6 ch m Monsieur Bond(IRE) Zest (USA) (Zilzal (USA))
1300[7] 5346[2] 5486[3] 6171[5]

Leading City (AUS) *J Moore* 114
6 b g Shamardal(USA) Salty Sal (AUS) (Salt Lake (USA))
8041a[11]

Leading Star *Michael Madgwick* a46 25
3 b f Motivator Movie Mogul (Sakhee (USA))
472[3] 993[11] 1981[12] 2625[9]

Lead Role *James Tate* a63
2 b f Exceed And Excel(AUS) Fanny's Fancy (Groom Dancer (USA))
8138[3]

League Champion (USA) *M Ramadan* a90 73
9 b g Rahy(USA) Meiosis (USA) (Danzig (USA))
616a[13]

Leahness (IRE) *Ken Wingrove* a46 42
5 br m Arakan(USA) En Retard (IRE) (Petardia)
227[8]

Lean Burn (USA) *Barry Leavy* a47 39
6 b g Johannesburg(USA) Anthelion (USA) (Stop The Music (USA))
5039[5]

Lean Machine *Ronald Harris* a66 42
5 b h Exceed And Excel(AUS) Al Corniche (IRE) (Bluebird (USA))
274[9] 333[12] 561[9] 1014[4] 1309[5] 1425[3] 1717[6] 1908[8]

Lean On Pete (IRE) *Ollie Pears* a76 56
3 b g Oasis Dream Superfonic (FR) (Zafonic (USA))
1595[5] ◆ 2131[3] 2353[2] 3111[9] 4716[6] 5810[2] 6151[2] (6458) (7359) 7722[5]

Leargas (IRE) *F Vermeulen* a56 79
2 b c Kheleyf(USA) Derpat (IRE) (Invincible Spirit (IRE))
8192a[9]

Learn (IRE) *A P O'Brien* 110
3 b c Galileo(IRE) Kentucky Warbler (IRE) (Spinning World (USA))
5609a[9]

Leaupartie (IRE) *F Chappet* 107
3 b f Stormy River(FR) Kansa (FR) (Linamix (FR))
3203a[6] (4616a) 5472a[2]

Lea Valley *Julia Feilden* a46 49
3 b f Araafa(IRE) Guaranda (Acatenango (GER))
3975[5] 4888[8] 5745[5] 6442[12] 8187[11]

Lea Valley Black *Tom Dascombe* a68 66
2 b g Three Valleys(USA) Sambarina (IRE) (Victory Note (USA))
1211[6] 1411[6] 2370[8] 4450[7] (5207) 5786[5] (6310) (7008) 7414[7]

Leaving Alone (USA) *Edwin Tuer* a71 59
5 ch m Mr Greeley(USA) Spankin' (USA) (A.P. Indy (USA))
3752[9] 4867[13] 5714[8]

Le Big (GER) *M Rolland* a98 104
8 b g Big Shuffle(USA) La Luganese (IRE) (Surumu (GER))
(629a) 814a[8]

Lebresem *James Tate* a43
2 b c Elusive City(USA) Laheen (IRE) (Bluebird (USA))
6320[6]

Le Chat D'Or *Michael Dods* 79
4 b g One Cool Cat(USA) Oh So Well (IRE) (Sadler's Wells (USA))
(1251) 1796[3] 2535[10] (2922) 3890[4] 4641[4] 5759[2] 6884[10]

Le Deluge (FR) *John Best* a73 50
2 b c Oratorio(IRE) Princess Sofia (UAE) (Pennekamp (USA))
3714a[10] 7597a[4] 8176a[2]

Le Drakkar (AUS) *A bin Huzaim* a104 113
7 gr g Anabaa(USA) My Mo Rally (NZ) (Mi Preferido (USA))
144a[9] 318a[6] 876a[5]

Leelu *David Arbuthnot* a71 63
6 b m Largesse Strat's Quest (Nicholas (USA))
2399[9] 3738[12] 4942[4] 5234[4] 6586[2] 6951[11] 7485[8] 7990[7]

Leenavesta (USA) *Richard Hannon* a69 69
3 b f Arch(USA) Shoshaloza (USA) (Diesis)
27[3] 127[7]

Lees Anthem *Michael Smith* a53 60
5 b g Mujahid(USA) Lady Rock (Mistertopogigo (IRE))
1881^{5} 2458^{2} 2749^{5} 3256^{14} 5923^{11} 7456^{5} 7604^{4}

Leffard (IRE) *F Chappet* a85 85
3 b c Langfuhr(CAN) Romantic Notion (IRE) (Mujadil (USA))
6752a^{2}

Left A Message (USA) *Thomas F Proctor* 94
3 rg f Mr Greeley(USA) Chief Secretary (USA) (Deputy Minister (CAN))
4131a^{6}

Legal Bond *Bryan Smart* 69
3 b g Misu Bond(IRE) Lawless Bridget (Alnasr Alwasheek)
2036^{2} 3289^{3} 3848^{3} 4711^{6} (5760) 6514^{4}

Legal Eagle (IRE) *Paul Green* a65 85
7 b g Invincible Spirit(IRE) Lupulina (CAN) (Saratoga Six (USA))
371^{11} 808^{10} 1481^{12} 2352^{3} 2475^{4} 2841^{8} 3557^{9} 3608^{7} 4043^{6} 6455^{5} 6823^{12} 7673^{8}

Legal Legacy *Richard Rowe* a80 84
6 ch g Beat Hollow Dans Delight (Machiavellian (USA))
199^{2} 378^{4} 448^{2} 626^{2} 987^{7} 1158^{6} 1342^{10} 1958^{5} (2168) (2398) 2608^{3} 3045^{10} 5035^{10} 5120^{8} 6256^{13} 6329^{8} 7166^{8} 7474^{9} 7767^{5} 7905^{7} 8019^{10}

Legal Pursuit *Edward Bevan*
3 b g Proclamation(IRE) Trysting Grove (IRE) (Cape Cross (IRE))
3946^{10} 5687^{11} 6215^{12}

Legal Waves (IRE) *Brian Meehan* 80
2 b c Lawman(FR) Surf The Web (IRE) (Ela-Mana-Mou)
7330^{2} ◆

Legendary *Ed Vaughan* a79 82
3 b g Exceed And Excel(AUS) Red Carnation (IRE) (Polar Falcon (USA))
684^{2} (869) 2930^{5} 4600^{8} 5588^{10}

Legend Erry (IRE) *Venetia Williams* a67 80
8 b g Act One Azure Lake (USA) (Lac Ouimet (USA))
1114^{5} 4215^{6}

Leitir Mor (IRE) *J S Bolger* a85 115
2 b c Holy Roman Emperor(IRE) Christinas Letter (IRE) (Galileo (IRE))
2958a^{2} 3240^{7} 5136a^{2} 5858a^{2} (6078a) 6272a^{3} 7050^{2}

Leitrim King (IRE) *Murty McGrath* a55 62
3 b g High Chaparral(IRE) Therry Girl (IRE) (Lahib (USA))
1606^{8} 2787^{5} 3233^{4} 7731^{7}

Leitrim Pass (USA) *William Haggas* 77
2 ch c Raven's Pass(USA) Santolina (USA) (Boundary (USA))
6412^{3} (7096)

Le King Beau (USA) *John Bridger* a71 71
3 b g Leroidesanimaux(BRZ) Berine (IRE) (Bering)
189^{3} 201^{5} 1789^{4} 2205^{6} 2443^{2} 3108^{5} 3343^{3} 3670^{6} 3762^{5} 4489^{4} 4723^{5} 5229^{12} 7961^{7} 8074^{12} 8294^{5}

Lelaps (USA) *Marco Botti* 88
3 ch c Mr Greeley(USA) Rebecca Parisi (IRE) (Persian Heights)
1132^{3} 2428^{3} 3064^{5}

Le Maltais (FR) *P Azzopardi*
3 b g Zieten(USA) Ladyfish (FR) (Loup Solitaire (USA))
5473a^{0} 6752a^{0}

Lemonade Kid (USA) *Anthony Mitchell* a92 99
7 b g Lemon Drop Kid(USA) Amourette (USA) (El Gran Senor (USA))
5374a^{5}

Lemon Drop Red (USA) *Paul Webber* a79 85
4 b g Lemon Drop Kid(USA) Skipper's Mate (USA) (Skip Away (USA))
8110^{7} 8275^{10}

Lemon Pearl *Ralph Beckett* 68
2 ch f Singspiel(IRE) Basemah (FR) (Lemon Drop Kid (USA))
7364^{6} ◆

Lennoxwood (IRE) *Mark Usher* a55 11
4 rg g Verglas(IRE) Sigonella (IRE) (Priolo (USA))
197^{5}

Lenny Bee *Deborah Sanderson* a87 86
6 rg g Kyllachy Smart Hostess (Most Welcome)
1868^{3}

Lenny The Great *Terry Clement* a29
3 b g Beat All(USA) Hamadeenah (Alhijaz)
8295^{7}

Leo Luna *Sir Michael Stoute* 80
3 b c Galileo(IRE) Eva Luna (USA) (Alleged (USA))
4067^{7} ◆ 4542^{6}

Leonards Pride (IRE) *Daniel Mark Loughnane* a28 44
3 b g Atraf Late Night Ruby (IRE) (Be My Native (USA))
4874^{6} 5329^{8} 5679^{7} 6316^{9} 7222^{11}

Leopard Hills (IRE) *Tony Carroll* a28 47
5 b g Acclamation Sadler's Park (USA) (Sadler's Wells (USA))
4585^{10} 4884^{9} 6280^{7}

Leopardin (GER) *H J Groschel* 100
4 b m Areion(GER) Lolli Pop (GER) (Cagliostro (GER))
5844a^{7}

Leototo *Linda Jewell*
5 b g Mtoto Ell Gee (Ra Nova)
908^{13}

Le Pursang (GER) *P Schiergen* 92
3 bb c Samum(GER) La Blue (GER) (Bluebird (USA))
2966a^{8}

Leqqaa (USA) *Mark Johnston* a95 97
3 b g Street Cry(IRE) Guerre Et Paix (USA) (Soviet Star (USA))
1216^{3} 3294^{28}

Le Reveur *Richard Guest* a53 60
10 b g Machiavellian(USA) Brooklyn's Dance (FR) (Shirley Heights)
7^{10} 334^{5} 375^{10} 468^{7} 558^{4} 653^{12}

Le Ring (FR) *F Rossi* 91
2 b c Slickly(FR) Joha (FR) (Johann Quatz (FR))
6225a^{4}

Leroy Parker (IRE) *Noel Meade* 74
4 ch g Titus Livius(FR) Jameela (IRE) (Danehill (USA))
7584a^{10}

Les Beaufs (FR) *Mme V Seignoux* 113
3 b g Apsis Yeomanry (FR) (Saumarez)
6896a^{2} (7431a)

Les Landes (IRE) *Mrs A Malzard* a52 46
4 b g Aussie Rules(USA) Splendid (IRE) (Mujtahid (USA))
2113a^{2}

Lesley's Choice *Sean Curran* a86 72
6 b g Lucky Story(USA) Wathbat Mtoto (Mtoto)
1054^{2} 1185^{2} (1483) (1720) (2133) 2853^{10} 6688^{11} 7254^{6} 7651^{7} 7995^{9}

Lesotho (IRE) *Noel Quinlan* a77 73
3 gr f Excellent Art Limpopo (Green Desert (USA))
1063^{2} 1317^{9} 3041^{7}

Les Troyens *Saeed Bin Suroor* a94 103
4 b h Librettist(USA) Native Blue (Seeking The Gold (USA))
80a^{8} 616a^{12}

Les Verguettes (IRE) *Chris Wall* a73 69
4 b m Iffraaj Mitsina (Fantastic Light (USA))
(214) 473^{5} ◆ 3075^{4} 3546^{8} (6967) (7106) 7524^{3} 7685^{12}

Le Talisman (IRE) *Mahmood Al Zarooni* a67 53
2 b c King's Best(USA) La Sylphide (SWI) (Barathea (IRE))
5478^{6} 6214^{3} 6558^{4} 7173^{12}

Lethal (USA) *John Haran* 89
4 b g Include(USA) Share A Moment (USA) (Pine Bluff (USA))
5374a^{8}

Lethal Force (IRE) *Clive Cox* 116
3 gr c Dark Angel(IRE) Land Army (IRE) (Desert Style (IRE))
(1492) 2236^{2} 2712^{3} 3265^{4} 4328^{2} (5355) 6246^{3} 6913a^{10}

Letham Cottage *Brian Meehan* a37 44
3 b g Imperial Dancer Fascinatin Rhythm (Fantastic Light (USA))
3311^{7} 4005^{4} 4399^{15}

Let Me In (IRE) *Nigel Tinkler* 45
2 ch g Pivotal I Hearyou Knocking (IRE) (Danehill Dancer (IRE))
7067^{6} 7363^{10}

L'Etoile Du Soir (FR) *J Boisnard* a80
2 gr f Carlotamix(FR) Lourinha (FR) (Loup Solitaire (USA))
8193a^{0}

Le Toreador *Kevin Ryan* a94 96
7 ch g Piccolo Peggy Spencer (Formidable (USA))
2596^{7} 3127^{15} (3595) 4013^{13} 4690^{2} 5487^{19} 6543^{8} 7704^{11}

Let's Confer *Michael Attwater* a60
3 ch f Doyen(IRE) Vrennan (Suave Dancer (USA))
816^{7} 2148^{8} 7011^{8} 7739^{10} 8037^{4} 8297^{4}

Let's Face Facts *Jim Goldie* a6 61
5 b m Lucky Story(USA) Rhinefield Beauty (IRE) (Shalford (IRE))
3888^{4} 4134^{3} 4389^{7} 4676^{6} 5918^{6} 6309^{9} 6756^{6} 7003^{13}

Lets Go Boogie *Mark Hoad*
4 ch g Tobougg(IRE) Hobean (Rock Hopper)
4465^{9}

Let's Go Cheyenne (USA) *Vladimir Cerin* 92
4 b m Tiznow(USA) Michigan Bluff (USA) (Skywalker (USA))
7577a^{7}

Let'sgoforit (IRE) *Bodil Hallencreutz* a92 78
4 gr g Verglas(IRE) Slewcie (USA) (Seattle Slew (USA))
2160a^{7}

Letstalkaboutmoney (IRE) *Mrs K Burke* a85 86
2 b c Redback Royal Rival (IRE) (Marju (IRE))
1352^{5} 3062^{2} 4318^{4} 4873^{2} 6162^{14} 6980^{9}

Letty *A Klimscha Jr* a63 87
5 ch m Trade Fair Love Is All (IRE) (Second Empire (IRE))
443a^{9}

Let Your Love Flow (IRE) *Richard Fahey* a67 66
3 b f Iffraaj Miss Odlum (IRE) (Mtoto)
32^{6} 194^{4} 6456^{5}

Le Valentin (FR) *Y De Nicolay* a87 104
6 b g Slickly(FR) Vallabelle (FR) (Valanour (IRE))
5648a^{8}

Levantera (IRE) *Jo Davis* a59 75
4 ch m Hurricane Run(IRE) Ellway Star (IRE) (Night Shift (USA))
4844^{5} 5196^{10}

Leviathan *Tony Newcombe* a80 98
5 b g Dubawi(IRE) Gipsy Moth (Efisio)
1128^{16} 3157^{10} 3508^{13} 5794 ^{6} ◆ 6630^{4} 7083^{3} 7415^{4}

Levi Draper *James Fanshawe* a76 58
3 b g Rock Of Gibraltar(IRE) Splice (Sharpo)
1824^{2} 2543^{6} 4155^{6} 5365^{7} 6050^{3} 6502^{3} 6765^{3} (7253)

Le Vie Infinite (IRE) *R Brogi* 105
5 b h Le Vie Dei Colori Looking Back (IRE) (Stravinsky (USA))
7587a^{11}

Levitate *Alan McCabe* a87 96
4 ch g Pivotal Soar (Danzero (AUS))
11^{6} 426^{9} 584^{7} 1478^{5} 1650^{2} 1951^{2} 2243^{6} (3185) (3493) 4110^{2} 4339^{6} 6674^{27}

Lewamy (IRE) *John Best* a78 75
2 b c Amadeus Wolf Thai Dye (UAE) (Jade Robbery (USA))
3928a^{3} 4476a^{5} 7682a^{7} 8193a^{5}

Lewis De La Vis (FR) *D Windrif* a75 75
4 b g Ski Chief(USA) Mummy's Kris (IRE) (Mummy's Game)
16a^{6}

Lewisham *Noel Quinlan* 104
2 b g Sleeping Indian Almunia (IRE) (Mujadil (USA))
2667^{2} ◆ 3182^{3} ◆ 4008^{2} 5559^{7} 6078a^{5} 7122a^{8}

Lexington Bay (IRE) *Richard Fahey* a95 90
4 b g High Chaparral(IRE) Schust Madame (IRE) (Second Set (IRE))
1239^{3} 1446^{2} 3163^{9} 3625^{14} 5200^{2} 5540^{7} 6074^{8} 6472^{5} (7034)

Lexington Blue *David O'Meara* a12 52
2 b g Bertolini(USA) Jasmine Breeze (Saddlers' Hall (IRE))
4140^{6} 5169^{5} 5410^{11}

Lexington Place *Richard Fahey* a66 54
2 ch g Compton Place Elidore (Danetime (IRE))
6628^{3} 6954^{6} 7609^{2}

Lexington Spirit (IRE) *Richard Fahey* a64 75
3 b f Iffraaj Festivite (IRE) (Fasliyev (USA))
1514^{7} 3234^{8} 4671^{5} 5388^{5} 8063^{6} 8268^{13}

Lexi's Beauty (IRE) *Ian Williams* a48 28
2 br f Kheleyf(USA) Voyage Of Dreams (USA) (Riverman (USA))
6343^{11} 6766^{5} 6970^{4} 7526^{6} 7821^{5} 7930^{6} 8108^{4}

Lexi's Boy (IRE) *Donald McCain* a83 96
4 gr g Verglas(IRE) Jazan (IRE) (Danehill (USA))
(3494) 3857^{6}

Lexi's Hero (IRE) *Kevin Ryan* 107
4 b g Invincible Spirit(IRE) Christel Flame (Darshaan)
1975^{4} 2507^{12} 3641^{6} 4802^{13} 5370^{13} 5829^{9} 6028^{9} 6543^{3}

Lexi The Princess (IRE) *Jamie Osborne* a54 66
2 b f Holy Roman Emperor(IRE) Star Profile (IRE) (Sadler's Wells (USA))
1388^{3} 1997^{9} (2338) 4191^{P} 8053^{5}

Ley Hunter (USA) *Saeed Bin Suroor* 118
5 b h Kingmambo(USA) Lailani (Unfuwain (USA))
2639^{8}

Leyte Gulf (USA) *Chris Bealby* a68 54
9 b g Cozzene(USA) Gabacha (USA) (Woodman (USA))
63^{2} 156^{3} 309^{3} 392^{3} 937^{2} 1361^{5} 1588^{9}

L Frank Baum (IRE) *Bernard Llewellyn* a69 89
5 b g Sinndar(IRE) Rainbow City (IRE) (Rainbow Quest (USA))
1505^{8} 1905^{2} 3953^{6} (4731) 5798^{10}

L'Hirondelle (IRE) *Michael Attwater* a76 62
8 b g Anabaa(USA) Auratum (USA) (Carson City (USA))
821^{10} 1378^{2} ◆ 1729^{10} 2044^{4} 2399^{10} 2847^{8} (7171) 7743^{7} 8105^{7} 8308^{6}

Liaison (USA) *Bob Baffert* a118
3 b c Blushing Groom(FR) Galloping Gal (USA) (Victory Gallop (CAN))
1872a^{6}

Libby's Lad *David C Griffiths* 11
3 b g Cape Town(IRE) Leave It To Lib (Tender King)
2881^{13} 3913^{16} 4807^{9} 5247^{12} 6125^{11} 6641^{12}

Liber *Sir Mark Prescott Bt* 95
2 b c Ishiguru(USA) Startori (Vettori (IRE))
2123^{2} (2537) 2702^{3} 3242^{7} 4093^{9} (4488) 5055^{2} 5515^{4} (5813) 6162^{9}

Liberal Lady *Ralph Smith* a66 61
4 b m Statue Of Liberty(USA) Noble Story (Last Tycoon)
59^{4} 277^{2} 576^{2} 890^{2} 4920^{8} 5296^{4} 5791^{5} 6563^{5} 6836^{6} (8190)

Liberate *Anabel K Murphy* a13 84
9 ch g Lomitas Eversince (USA) (Foolish Pleasure (USA))
3564^{12} 4284^{5} 6802^{10} 7610^{8}

Liberating *Mrs John Harrington* a84 91
2 b f Iffraaj Ros The Boss (IRE) (Danehill (USA))
2512a^{4} 2780a^{3} 7390a^{7}

Liberator (AUS) *D E Ferraris* 116
5 b g Encosta De Lago(AUS) Miss Helga (IRE) (Alzao (USA))
8040a^{4}

Liber Nauticus (IRE) *Sir Michael Stoute* 87
2 b f Azamour(IRE) Serres (IRE) (Daylami (IRE))
(5902) ◆

Liberty Dancer (FR) *Y Barberot* a77 65
2 b c Indian Rocket Lignite (IRE) (Priolo (USA))
8193a^{3}

Liberty Island (IRE) *Ian Semple* a84 84
7 b g Statue Of Liberty(USA) Birthday (IRE) (Singspiel (IRE))
2596^{4} (3109) 3578^{5} 4591^{2} 5821^{8} (6006) 6688^{3}

Liberty Jack (IRE) *Roger Charlton* 46
2 b g Sakhee(USA) Azeema (IRE) (Averti (IRE))
6486^{12}

Liberty Lady (IRE) *Des Donovan* a78 100
5 b m Statue Of Liberty(USA) Crossed Wire (Lycius (USA))
1316^{4} 1602^{10} 2087^{7}

Liberty Love (IRE) *Shaun Harley* a57 57
7 b g Statue Of Liberty(USA) Alserna (IRE) (Alhaarth (IRE))
741^{U} (1631) 5936^{5}

Liberty River (FR) *G Botti* a49
2 b c Stormy River(FR) Liberty In Love (FR) (Statue Of Liberty (USA))
7699a^{10}

Liberty Ship *Mark Buckley* a40 77
7 b g Statue Of Liberty(USA) Flag (Selkirk (USA))
1290^{5} 1675^{7} 2140^{10} 3993^{8} 4245^{12} 4663^{4} 5131^{4} 8253^{7}

Libranno *Richard Hannon* 117
4 b h Librettist(USA) Annabelle Ja (FR) (Singspiel (IRE))
1646^{5} 2179^{12} (3190) (3633) 4686^{2} 5355^{9} (6246) 7048^{7} 7236^{13}

Libre *Violet M Jordan* a45 56
12 b g Bahamian Bounty Premier Blues (FR) (Law Society (USA))
160^{6} 1096^{10}

Librettela *Alan Jarvis* a62 71
4 b g Librettist(USA) Ella's Wish (IRE) (Bluebird (USA))
1706^{12} 3472^{3} 4411^{4} 5345^{7}

Librettista (FR) *I G Ivanov* 56
2 b f Librettist(USA) Pilgrim Of Grace (FR) (Bering)
7588a^{5}

Libys Dream (IRE) *Tom Dascombe* a99 100
4 b m Invincible Spirit(IRE) Perilous Pursuit (USA) (Lemon Drop Kid (USA))
83a^{10} 686^{2} (866) 1041a^{8} 2078^{4} 6161^{10} 6633^{6} 7509^{6} 7680a^{5} 7809^{8}

Licence To Till (USA) *Mark Johnston* a101 99
5 b g War Chant(USA) With A Wink (USA) (Clever Trick (USA))
354^{3} 443a^{11} 630a^{17} 817^{2} 868^{12} 1139^{5} 1273^{7} 1854^{11} (2077) 2312^{6} 2655^{6} (2911) 3372^{14} 3635^{3} 4112^{14} 4684^{6} 5091^{7} 5492^{3} 5583^{2} 5835^{5} 6484^{6} 6674^{12} 7407^{5} 7601^{4}

Lichen Angel *Richard Whitaker* 34
2 gr f Dark Angel(IRE) Moss Likely (IRE) (Clodovil (IRE))
4710^{13}

Lidari (FR) *J-C Rouget* 104
3 b c Acclamation Laxlova (FR) (Linamix (FR))
1570a^{6} 4121a^{9} 6508a^{8}

Lieutenant Dan (IRE) *Michael Appleby* a63 57
5 b g Danroad(AUS) Dakhira (Emperor Jones (USA))
4551^{3} 4780^{8} 5889^{9} 7225^{3} 7620^{6} 7964^{6} 7992^{5} 8141^{3} 8291^{3}

Lieutenant Kojak *Peter Charalambous* a67 84
4 b g Iceman Red Duchess (Halling (USA))
1114^{6} 1743^{2} 2899^{2} (3306) (3997) 4365^{5} 6170^{5} 6668^{5} 7300^{8}

Lieutenant Miller *Nicky Henderson* 85
6 b g Beat All(USA) Still Runs Deep (Karinga Bay)
(6922) 7522^{3}

Life And Soul (IRE) *Amanda Perrett* a80 99
5 b g Azamour(IRE) Way For Life (GER) (Platini (GER))
1603^{8} (2479) 3341^{2} 4800^{5} 5079^{7} 7396^{10}

Life Of Laughter (USA) *Willie Musson* a54
4 b g Elusive Quality(USA) Country Garden (Selkirk (USA))
762^{5} 1113^{7} 2288^{9} 7991^{4} 8214^{9}

Lifetime (IRE) *Brian Ellison* a71 81
4 b g Shamardal(USA) La Vita E Bella (IRE) (Definite Article)
692^{8} 978^{5} (1382) (1850) 2214^{11} 7455^{10}

Light Burst (USA) *Ismail Mohammed* a84 85
3 b c Hard Spun(USA) Kew Garden (USA) (Seattle Slew (USA))
1331^{4} 2583^{2} 3314^{7} 4662^{2} 5229^{6} (6217) ◆ (6302) 7790^{3} 7824^{5}

Lightening Pearl (IRE) *G M Lyons* 111
3 b f Marju(IRE) Jioconda (IRE) (Rossini (USA))
1884^{13} 3092a^{6}

Light From Hades *Tim Easterby*
3 b f Echo Of Light Haddeyah (USA) (Dayjur (USA))
1660^{6}

Light From Mars *Ronald Harris* a96 100
7 gr g Fantastic Light(USA) Hylandra (USA) (Bering)
868^{7} 1130^{18} 2025^{8} 2417^{12} 3405^{2} 4889^{4} 5429^{6} 5910^{7} 6241^{7} (6687) 6934^{2} 7171^{4} 7788^{2} 8181^{4} (8238)

Light Heavy (IRE) *J S Bolger* a100 114
3 ch c Teofilo(IRE) Siamsa (USA) (Quest For Fame)
(1404a) (2102a) 3651a^{3} 5027a^{6} 6063a^{4} 6855a^{5}

Lightinthenite (AUS) *J O'Shea* 110
5 ch g Galileo(IRE) Tiffin (AUS) (Grand Lodge (USA))
7696a^{6}

Lightly Chilled (FR) *T Larriviere*
3 ro c Verglas(IRE) Lily Bolero (King's Best (USA))
365a^{0}

Lightning Cloud (IRE) *Kevin Ryan* a79 103
4 gr g Sleeping Indian Spree (IRE) (Dansili)
2068^{5} ◆ 3371^{9} 4321^{21} 6466^{15} 7240^{3}

Lightning Launch (IRE) *Mick Channon* 72
2 b g Kheleyf(USA) Launch Time (USA) (Relaunch (USA))
4472^{4} ◆ 4995^{3} 5534^{4}

Lightning Spirit *Gary Moore* a59 63
4 b m Storming Home Lucky Dice (Perugino (USA))
1625^{8} 2366^{2} (2627) 3247^{5} 3705^{5} 3964^{8} 4586^{10} 6395^{13} 7321^{3} 7983^{6}

Lightnin Hopkins (IRE) *G M Lyons* a81 100
2 b g Kodiac Bundle Of Joy (IRE) (Golan (IRE))
6078a^{9}

Light Opera (FR) *D Rabhi*
3 ro f Dubai Destination(USA) Polite Reply (USA) (With Approval (CAN))
476a^{0}

Light Particle (IRE) *John Patrick Shanahan* 76
2 b c Oratorio(IRE) There's A Light (IRE) (Fantastic Light (USA))
4257^{3}

Light Rose (IRE) *Mark Johnston* 79
2 b f Cape Cross(IRE) Laureldean Lady (IRE) (Statue Of Liberty (USA))
(6817) ◆

Light Shine *Peter Chapple-Hyam* a72 78
3 gr f Dansili Light Of Morn (Daylami (IRE))
3279^{6} 4366^{2} 7488^{2} (8151)

Lights Of Heaven (NZ) *Peter G Moody* 115
5 b m Zabeel(NZ) I'm In Heaven (NZ) (Volksraad)
7264a^{3} 7621a^{16}

Light The City (IRE) *Ruth Carr* a62 72
5 b g Fantastic Light(USA) Marine City (JPN) (Carnegie (IRE))
(811) 978^{7} 1175^{8} (1598) 1822^{3} ◆ 2093^{5} 2440^{5}

Light Up My Life (IRE) *Richard Hannon* 100
2 b f Zamindar(USA) Shine Like A Star (Fantastic Light (USA))
(2499) 3326^{9} (5361) 6199^{3} 6632^{2}

Light Zabeel (USA) *Mick Channon* a70 69
3 b f Invasor(ARG) Ashraakat (USA) (Danzig (USA))
1501^{4} 1748^{4} 2249^{9} 3846^{3} 5680^{7} 6169^{6}

Lignon's Hero (BRZ) *J D Hillis* a77 95
7 b h Crimson Tide(IRE) L'Escapade (BRZ) (Aksar (USA))
444a^{8}

Ligurian Sea *Chris Wall* a39 66
3 b f Medicean Shamara (IRE) (Spectrum (IRE))
6792[7] 7511[13]

Like A Boy *Bill Turner* a57 57
4 b h Medicean Like A Dame (Danehill (USA))
7[8]

Like Clockwork *Mark H Tompkins* a62 63
3 b g Rail Link Tenpence (Bob Back (USA))
1355[3] (1726) 2333[6] 3087[8] 3483[13] 6365[8]

Likelikelikelikeit *Mark H Tompkins* 56
2 b f Avonbridge Rutland Water (IRE) (Hawk Wing (USA))
3545[8] 3788[7] 4310[9] 6413[4]

Like The Night *Marco Botti* a62
3 ch f Byron Twitch Hill (Piccolo)
26[2] 214[0]

Lilac Lace (IRE) *Tim Easterby* a71 64
2 b f Captain Marvelous(IRE) Lilac Mist (Spectrum (IRE))
6880[4] 7244[2] 7609[3] (7728) (8211)

Lilac Tree *Mahmood Al Zarooni* a77
2 b c Dubawi(IRE) Kalidasa (USA) (Nureyev (USA))
6645[2] 7167[3] (7628)

Lilbourne Eliza (IRE) *Richard Hannon* a72 85
2 b f Elusive City(USA) Midnight Partner (IRE) (Marju (IRE))
6153[2] 6453[3] (6657) 7406[3]

Lil Ella (IRE) *Patrick Holmes* a62 61
5 b m Pearl Of Love(IRE) Royal Jubilee (IRE) (King's Theatre (IRE))
(632) 1154[11] 1240[5] 1794[9] 2454[7] (Dead)

Lileo (IRE) *Nikki Evans* a43 65
5 b g Galileo(IRE) Jabali (FR) (Shirley Heights)
1011[8] 1361[9]

L'Ile Rousse *Chris Dwyer*
3 ch f Muhtathir Felucca (Green Desert (USA))
1261[13] 2085[8]

Liliana (IRE) *Peter Chapple-Hyam* a64
2 b f Haatef(USA) Stop Out (Rudimentary (USA))
7778[4] 8134[2] 8303[2]

Liliargh (IRE) *Ben Haslam* 75
3 b f Acclamation Discover Roma (IRE) (Rock Of Gibraltar (IRE))
1595[2] ◆ (2335) 3214[6] 3952[10] 6782[2] 7004[4] 7437[6]

Lillioftheballet (IRE) *Jim Goldie* 20
5 b m Rakti Lillibits (USA) (Kingmambo (USA))
4259[8]

Lilly May (IRE) *Phil McEntee* a46 44
2 b f Haatef(USA) Love Of Silver (USA) (Arctic Tern (USA))
2808[5] 3046[4] 3590[14] 5146[9] 6978[8] 7313[13]

Lilly White (USA) *Brian Meehan* a53 38
2 b f Speightstown(USA) Unrestrained (USA) (Unbridled (USA))
2892[10] 7159[9] 7458[10] 7821[11] 8093[6]

Lilting (IRE) *J E Pease* 97
3 b f Montjeu(IRE) Contare (Shirley Heights)
2741a[6]

Lil'Wing (IRE) *A De Royer-Dupre* 110
3 b f Galileo(IRE) Louve (USA) (Irish River (FR))
(7449a)

Lily America (FR) *F Rohaut* 106
3 b f American Post Miller's Lily (FR) (Miller's Mate)
2742a[5] 3682a[10]

Lily In Pink *Jonathan Portman* a77 104
4 b m Sakhee(USA) In Luck (In The Wings)
1940[8] (2755) 3661[5] (4460) (5306) ◆ 5981[3] 6598[3]

Lily Lily *Natalie Lloyd-Beavis* a5
5 b m Efisio Bel Tempo (Petong)
1447[10] 1624[13] 1988[11]

Lily Merrill *T Lerner* a67 85
2 b f Lawman(FR) Tonic Star (FR) (Enrique)
5248a[6] 7699a[6]

Lily Potts *Chris Down* a62 70
3 gr f Proclamation(IRE) Jucinda (Midyan (USA))
2148[5] 2768[6] 3443[12] 6098[5] 6738[7] 7196[7]

Lily's Angel (IRE) *G M Lyons* a101 104
3 b f Dark Angel(IRE) Noyelles (IRE) (Docksider (USA))
1454[3] 1884[7] 2255[5] 3165[11] (7680a)

Limario (GER) *R Dzubasz* 102
2 bb c Areion(GER) Limaga (Lagunas)
(7091a)

Limit Up *Mark Johnston* 72
2 b g Shamardal(USA) Love Me Tender (Green Desert (USA))
1818[7] 2069[9] 2587[2] 2912[7]

Limoges *Gary Moore* 29
2 b f Bertolini(USA) China Cherub (Inchinor)
7078[10]

Linarda (DEN) *M Rulec*
2 bb f Rock Of Gibraltar(IRE) Miss Skycat (USA) (Tale Of The Cat (USA))
5612a[6]

Lincolnrose (IRE) *Alan McCabe* a57 60
2 gr f Verglas(IRE) Imelda (USA) (Manila (USA))
2330[4] 2783[9] 3415[11] 3936[2] 4139[4] 6318[10] 6822[12] 7606[6] 8093[3] 8203[3]

Linda's Icon *Mick Channon* a51 59
2 b f Sixties Icon Linda Green (Victory Note (USA))
4055[5] 4408[11] 4724[7] 5161[3] 5763[11] 6096[8]

Lindenthaler (GER) *P Schiergen* 108
4 b h Azamour(IRE) Lasira (GER) (Vettori (IRE))
1700a[7] 2322a[9] 3746a[5]

Lindoro *Sean Curran* a70 77
7 b g Marju(IRE) Floppie (FR) (Law Society (USA))
139[11] 813[6] 1178[8] (1823) (1961) ◆ 2406[6] 2753[2] 3037[2] 3314[3] 4317[14] 5220[5] 6456[6] 6823[6] 7224[5] 7436[4] 7685[11] 7732[6] 7982[2] 8131[3] 8248[6]

Lindsay's Dream *Zoe Davison* a61 50
6 b m Montjeu(IRE) Lady Lindsay (IRE) (Danehill Dancer (IRE))
3968[7]

Line Of Reason (IRE) *David Simcock* a73
2 br c Kheleyf(USA) Miss Party Line (USA) (Phone Trick (USA))
(6609)

Lines Of Battle (USA) *A P O'Brien* a103 103
2 b c War Front(USA) Black Speck (USA) (Arch (USA))
3240[6] 4519a[2] (7038a) 7568a[7]

Lingtren *Roger Ingram*
4 b g Storming Home Sunny Times (IRE) (Raise A Grand (IRE))
147[6] 355[11]

Linguine (FR) *Seamus Durack* 90
2 ch c Linngari(IRE) Amerissage (USA) (Rahy (USA))
3638[6] 4056[5] (4677) 5552[3] 6225a[5] 6700[3] (6963) 7554[3]

Linkable *Brendan Powell* a53 76
3 b c Rail Link Fashionable (Nashwan (USA))
1976[5] 2557[5] 3484[2] 4923[6] 6228[5] 7011[10] 7998[10]

Links Drive Lady *Dean Ivory* a80 87
4 br m Striking Ambition Miskina (Mark Of Esteem (IRE))
1306[3] 2146[5] 2373[5] 3007[2] 4332[3] (4708) (5122) (6378) 6800[2] (7114) 7408[6] 7645[5]

Linkup (IRE) *Paul W Flynn* a47 48
3 b g Rail Link Nicene (USA) (Pulpit (USA))
2577[3]

Linn County *John Gosden* 38
3 b f Cape Cross(IRE) Lane County (USA) (Rahy (USA))
2271[8] 2768[10]

Linngara (FR) *Mario Hofer*
2 b f Linngari(IRE) Loa Loa (GER) (Anabaa Blue)
5612a[4]

Linngaro (FR) *Mario Hofer* a91 99
2 ch c Linngari(IRE) Indochine (BRZ) (Special Nash (IRE))
6086a[6] 6942a[2] 7623a[6] 7984a[3]

Linroyale Boy (USA) *Alan Swinbank* a59 54
4 ch g Giant's Causeway(USA) Welcometotheworld (USA) (Woodman (USA))
369[4] 552[4] 1560[10] 2239[12] 2669[6] 7793[7]

Linton (AUS) *John D Sadler* 117
6 gr g Galileo(IRE) Our Heather (NZ) (Centaine (AUS))
7426a[12]

Linton Hill (IRE) *Murty McGrath* a31 29
3 b g Tiger Hill(IRE) Klaribel (IRE) (Winged Love (IRE))
2042[12] 2612[6] 3539[10]

Lion Beacon *Amanda Perrett* a71
2 ch g Beat Hollow Second Of May (Lion Cavern (USA))
7707[7] 7900[3] (8052)

Lion D'Anvers (FR) *J Van Handenhove* 79
2 b c Kentucky Dynamite(USA) Alcestes Selection (Selkirk (USA))
7283a[3]

Lionheart *Luca Cumani* 70
2 ch c Zamindar(USA) Victoire Celebre (USA) (Stravinsky (USA))
5062[8] 5793[3] 6377[6] 6846[4]

Lionrock (FR) *Mark Johnston* a72 55
3 ch c Shamardal(USA) Genevale (FR) (Unfuwain (USA))
565[2] 723[3] (917) 1313[2] 1441[8] 1790[8] 2583[13]

Lions Arch (IRE) *Richard Hannon* 73
2 b c Rock Of Gibraltar(IRE) Swynford Lady (IRE) (Invincible Spirit (IRE))
6164[5] 6795[6]

Lion's Maid *Michael Attwater*
3 b f Iceman Steppin Out (First Trump)
1182[13] 1443[11]

Lipfix (ITY) *G Pucciatti* 94
4 b h St Paul House Lucky Lips (IRE) (Emperor Jones (USA))
7697a[9]

Liquid Sunshine *Sylvester Kirk* a52 11
3 br f Baltic King Sylvan (IRE) (Shinko Forest (IRE))
(294) 376[6]

Lisahane Bog *Peter Hedger* a79 24
5 b g Royal Applause Veronica Franco (Darshaan)
119[5] 374[4] 648[3] 960[4] 1051[3] 1792[5] 2886[10] 4586[12]

Lisa Post (FR) *Mme M Bollack-Badel* a70 54
3 gr f American Post Lisatine (FR) (Linamix (FR))
117a[0]

Lisa's Legacy *Richard Hannon* a59 68
2 b g Kyllachy Lisathedaddy (Darnay)
3638[7] 4846[4] 5121[2] 5702[DSQ] 6016[7]

Lisiere (IRE) *Mrs K Burke* 86
3 b f Excellent Art Sahara Sky (IRE) (Danehill (USA))
(1274) 2182[13] 3379[6] (3954) 5676[5] 6515[7] 6923[2]

Lisselan Diva (IRE) *Mme J Bidgood* 108
6 b m Barathea(IRE) Vintage Escape (IRE) (Cyrano De Bergerac)
4790a[9]

Lisselan Pleasure (USA) *Bernard Llewellyn* a59 68
5 gr m Macho Uno(USA) Cute Connie (USA) (Struggler)
1485[6] 1909[4] 2167[9] 2389[5] 2650[2] 3143[7] 4183[4] 4941[2] 5198[2] 5481[6] 5935[2] 6304[7] 6794[7]

Lisselton Cross *Martin Bosley* a59 47
4 ch g Compton Place Sweet Myrtle (USA) (Mutakddim (USA))
118[5] 227[3] (483) 665[10] 2607[5] 3006[8] 3455[5] 6585[2] 7204[8] 7748[6] 8075[8] 8255[4]

Liszar Jo (GER) *Markus Klug* 76
3 b f Dai Jin Linton Bay (GER) (Funambule (USA))
2107a[7]

Liteup My World (USA) *Brian Ellison* a72 58
6 ch g Hennessy(USA) Liteup My Life (USA) (Green Dancer (USA))
134[5]

Lithograph (USA) *Mark Johnston* a47 26
3 b f Echo Of Light Forum Floozie (NZ) (Danasinga (AUS))
833[2] 2341[11] 3469[10] 3966[11] 4932[11] 5408[11]

Litian Rocket (FR) *M Boutin* a48 88
2 b c Indian Rocket Lit (IRE) (Danehill (USA))
5073a[7] 5698a[8]

Litmus (USA) *Simon Dow* a43 48
3 ch f Latent Heat(USA) Fairy Glade (USA) (Gone West (USA))
1705[9] 2935[7] 5096[5] 5975[10] 7189[5] 7982[9] 8097[4] 8264[10]

Litotes *Michael Attwater* a57 20
4 b m Librettist(USA) Royal Ivy (Mujtahid (USA))
740[9] 1074[8] 1625[10] 1768[9] 2971[9] 3467[8] 6951[12]

Little Black Book (IRE) *Gerard Butler* a87 85
4 ch g Shamardal(USA) Extreme Beauty (USA) (Rahy (USA))
1156[12] 4805[12] (5480) 5768[7] 6209[7] 6454[3] 6539[2] 6979[5]

Little Bridge (NZ) *C S Shum* 124
6 b g Faltaat(USA) Golden Rose (NZ) (Gold Brose (AUS))
(3230)

Little Bucks *Alan McCabe* a42
3 b g Multiplex Southgate Lady (IRE) (Night Shift (USA))
1422[7] 1989[7] 2553[13]

Little Buxted (USA) *Robert Mills* a69
2 bb c Mr Greeley(USA) Mo Cheoil Thu (IRE) (In The Wings)
7962[6] 8070[5]

Little Carmela *Sarah Humphrey* a58 65
8 gr m Beat Hollow Carmela Owen (Owington)
2175[6]

Little China *William Muir* a75 66
3 b f Kyllachy China Beads (Medicean)
1412[4] 2375[8] 3450[4] 3762[8]

Little Choosey *Clive Cox* a59 59
2 ch f Cadeaux Genereux Little Nymph (Emperor Fountain)
7078[4] 8044[2]

Littlecote Lady *Mark Usher* a56 56
3 b f Byron Barefooted Flyer (USA) (Fly So Free (USA))
25[6] 564[3] 8075[4] 8287[4]

Little Curtsey *Hughie Morrison* a84 83
4 b m Royal Applause Tychy (Suave Dancer (USA))
2766[9]

Little Dutch Girl *Clive Cox* 87
3 ch f Dutch Art Photographie (USA) (Trempolino (USA))
1647[2] 2201[6] 2889[6] 3476[3] 4224[5] (5151) 5788[3] ◆ 6964[5]

Little Eli *Eric Alston* a40
2 b g Green Desert(USA) Princess Ellis (Compton Place)
7458[11] 7953[5]

Little Garcon (USA) *Robert Cowell* a90 66
5 b g Bernstein(USA) Demure (Machiavellian (USA))
253[11] 431[5] 6767[6] ◆ 7291[11] 7646[9] 8163[7] ◆

Little Indian *J R Jenkins* a53 51
2 b c Sleeping Indian Once Removed (Distant Relative)
4433[5] 5485[5] 7272[6] 7797[5] 8155[5]

Little Jazz *Paul D'Arcy* a70 73
4 b m Doyen(IRE) Meddle (Diktat)
63[4] 281[4]

Little Jimmy Odsox (IRE) *Tim Easterby* a83 81
4 b g Namid September Tide (IRE) (Thatching)
1476[8] 2119[2] 2632[6] 3169[7] 3612[7] 4829[13] 5110[7] 5588[11] 6123[6] 6824[8]

Little Mike (USA) *Dale Romans* a56 121
5 b g Spanish Steps(USA) Hay Jude (USA) (Wavering Monarch (USA))
(5377a) (7573a)

Little Miss Mayhem (IRE) *Philip McBride* a41 52
3 b f Dark Angel(IRE) Nilassiba (Daylami (IRE))
1610[12] 2601[7] 3447[6] 4709[8] 5216[7]

Littlemissperfect *Richard Rowe* a33
4 b m Pastoral Pursuits Dancing Flame (Groom Dancer (USA))
573[7] 1107[8] 1443[7] 2651[6] 4333[RR]

Little Miss Zuri (IRE) *Sylvester Kirk* a51 44
2 ch f Choisir(AUS) Miss Kinabalu (Shirley Heights)
2426[6] 3242[20] 3700[5] 4331[3] 4934[8] 7463[4] 7606[7] 7821[2] 7930[7] 8274[7]

Little Perisher *Mark Brisbourne* a57 53
5 b g Desert Sun Sasperella (Observatory (USA))
126[12] 356[2] 687[8] 740[2] 938[6] 1628[11] 1987[7] 2350[2] 3456[11] 4929[9] 5444[9] 5719[10] 5937[9] 6321[9] 8046[3] 8168[8] 8209[4] 8255[9]

Littleportnbrandy (IRE) *Richard Guest* a49 23
4 ch m Camacho Sharplaw Destiny (IRE) (Petardia)
390[7] 503[3] 662[10] 740[10] 837[6] 927[6] 938[8] 1074[6] 2627[9]

Little Power (FR) *J-P Carvalho* a66 83
3 b c Lord Of England(GER) Little Memories (IRE) (Montjeu (IRE))
1171a[10]

Little Rainbow *Clive Cox* a39 74
3 ch f King's Best(USA) Little Nymph (Emperor Fountain)
1445[9] 2206[4] 2759[3] 3619[3] (4942) ◆ 5440[9] 6488[14]

Little Red Minx (IRE) *David O'Meara* a58 58
3 b f Red Clubs(IRE) Bid Dancer (Spectacular Bid (USA))
159[7] 255[5] 472[6] 4678[5] 4826[2] 5114[2] 5589[9] 6126[7]

Little Red Nell (IRE) *Martin Bosley* a51
3 b f Red Clubs(IRE) Naughty Nell (Danehill Dancer (IRE))
2864[7]

Little Rocky *David Simcock* 101
4 b h Cadeaux Genereux Tahirah (Green Desert (USA))
1654[3] 2932[4] (4060) 6606[2] (7017) 7407[8]

Little Squaw (IRE) *Tim Easterby* 35
2 b f Indian Haven Molaaf (Shareef Dancer (USA))
4778[9] 5108[4] 5675[10]

Littlesuzie *Hans Adielsson* a68 61
3 b f Kyllachy Golubitsa (IRE) (Bluebird (USA))
7351[5]

Little Thief *Iain Jardine* 32
5 b m Indian Danehill(IRE) Val De Fleurie (GER) (Mondrian (GER))
3030[5] 4207[9] 4620[11] 5087[13]

Little Village (IRE) *Kieran P Cotter* a63 64
6 b m Captain Rio Rainbow Princess (IRE) (Spectrum (IRE))
4380a[9]

Lively Little Lady *Mrs A Corson*
2 b f Beat All(USA) Ever So Lonely (Headin' Up)
1136[11]

Liver Bird *Paul Midgley* 60
4 b g Tiger Hill(IRE) Oiseau Rare (FR) (King's Best (USA))
809[7] 1283[12]

Livery (IRE) *Jeremy Noseda* 85
3 gr c Hurricane Run(IRE) Cause Celebre (IRE) (Peintre Celebre (USA))
2856[3] ◆ (6660)

Livia's Dream (IRE) *Ed Walker* a86 77
3 b f Teofilo(IRE) Brindisi (Dr Fong (USA))
(3443) 4325[8] 5474[3] (6146) 6933[6] 7510[10] 7810[2] 7999[8]

Living Desert *James Toller* 83
2 gr g Oasis Dream Sell Out (Act One)
2797[2] 3240[16] 4058[5] 5016[2] 6377[3] 6874[12]

Living It Large (FR) *Ed de Giles* a91 95
5 ch g Bertolini(USA) Dilag (IRE) (Almutawakel)
1602[5] 1975[8] 2704[16] 3608[8]

Living Leader *Nick Littmoden* a85 38
3 b g Oasis Dream Royal Jade (Last Tycoon)
6930[10] (7667) ◆ (7935) ◆

Living Portrait (FR) *J E Pease* a76 84
3 b f Orpen(USA) Linaving (FR) (Linamix (FR))
117a[4]

Living The Life (IRE) *Jamie Osborne* a70 78
2 b f Footstepsinthesand Colour And Spice (IRE) (Machiavellian (USA))
4152[2] 4739[4] 5574[4] (6977)

Livvy Inn (USA) *Lucinda Russell* 64
7 ch g Woodman(USA) London Be Good (USA) (Storm Bird (CAN))
(3519) 3904[5] 5761[5]

Lizzie (IRE) *Tim Easterby* 74
4 b m Acclamation Sky Galaxy (USA) (Sky Classic (CAN))
1293[12] ◆ 1652[8] 2096[12] 3026[6] 3442[4] 3994[10] 4547[8]

Lizzie Tudor *Andrew Balding* a79 76
2 ch f Tamayuz Silca Destination (Dubai Destination (USA))
4011[10] 4724[2] (5339) 6775[2] ◆

Lizzy's Dream *Robin Bastiman* a64 68
4 ch g Choisir(AUS) Flyingit (USA) (Lear Fan (USA))
227[5] (691) ◆ (910) (5923) ◆ 6288[8]

Llamadas *Olivia Maylam* a61 66
10 b g Josr Algarhoud(IRE) Primulette (Mummy's Pet)
7629[11] 7991[9] (8104)

Llaregyb (IRE) *David Elsworth* 74
2 b c Dylan Thomas(IRE) Tango Tonic (IRE) (Trans Island)
7330[4] 7637[7]

Llewellyn *David Nicholls* a77 77
4 b g Shamardal(USA) Ffestiniog (IRE) (Efisio)
1050[13] 2165[U] (2845) (2972) 4207[2] 5737[4] (5801) 6465[10] 7246[2] 7437[2] 7732[2] 7935[11]

Lobelia *Brian Meehan* a44 48
2 b f Indesatchel(IRE) New Havens (Indian Ridge)
2163[4] 2499[13] 3339[8] 5192[7] 6871[11] 7198[7]

Local Hero (GER) *Steve Gollings* 92
5 b g Lomitas Lolli Pop (GER) (Cagliostro (GER))
1882[2] ◆ 2072[2] 3125[4] 4103[7] 5333[2]

Local Lover (FR) *H-A Pantall* 100
2 ch c Choisir(AUS) La Victoria (IRE) (Brief Truce (USA))
5471a[3] 6507a[5] 7013a[5]

Local Singer (IRE) *Paul Howling* a80 87
4 b g Elusive City(USA) Alinga (IRE) (King's Theatre (IRE))
311[9] 893[7] 1203[5] 2070[12] 3230[9] 3958[9] 4517[11] 5049[4] 5993[8]

Loch Fyne Lady *John Holt* 34
2 b f Holy Roman Emperor(IRE) Inveraray (Selkirk (USA))
6966[10] 7363[12]

Loch Garman (IRE) *J S Bolger* 111
2 b c Teofilo(IRE) Irish Question (IRE) (Giant's Causeway (USA))
(7514a)

Loch Garry (IRE) *C Boutin* a78 78
4 ch g Iffraaj Festivite (IRE) (Fasliyev (USA))
16a[9]

Lochluichart (IRE) *Ian Semple*
3 gr g Verglas(IRE) Hetty (IRE) (In The Wings)
3273[9] 3521[8] 4826[12] 5919[8] 6516[6]

Loch Moy *Richard Fahey* 70
2 b g Kyllachy Dixielake (IRE) (Lake Coniston (IRE))
3777[3] 6099[3] 6603[2]

Lockantanks *Michael Appleby* a98 95
5 ch g Compton Place Locharia (Wolfhound (USA))
254[4] 426[2] 622[6] 866[11] 2913[5] 3185[3] 3492[2] 3615[3] (4175) (4345) 5301[13] 6036[12] 6630[5] (6888) 7508[4] 7774[3] 7934[5] 8055[2] (8226) 8296[3]

Lockwood *A Fabre* 110
3 gr g Invincible Spirit(IRE) Emily Bronte (Machiavellian (USA))
(3901a) 4861a[6] 6088a[6]

Locum *Mark H Tompkins* a65 63
7 ch g Dr Fong(USA) Exhibitor (USA) (Royal Academy (USA))
2260[10] 3620[2] 3794[2] (5174) 6305[4]

Lodano (FR) *M Weiss*
7 gr g Verglas(IRE) Maria Thai (FR) (Siam (USA))
629a[5]

Loden *Donald McCain* a82 86
5 b g Barathea(IRE) Tentpole (USA) (Rainbow Quest (USA))
2419[2]

Logans Legend (IRE) *Lawrence Mullaney* a68 64
4 b g Johannesburg(USA) Almost Blue (USA) (Mr Greeley (USA))
2791[5] 3751[3]

Loi (IRE) *J-M Beguigne* 106
3 b c Lawman(FR) Lockup (IRE) (Inchinor)
1570a[4] 2108a[6] 4385a[5] 5250a[9]

Lois Lane *Ron Hodges* a54 34
4 br m Striking Ambition Straight As A Die (Pyramus (USA))
118[10] 544[11]

Loki's Revenge *William Jarvis* a92 88
4 b g Kyllachy Amira (Efisio)
1844[11]

Loki's Strike *Mrs K Burke* a50 66
2 ch g Firebreak Citron (Reel Buddy (USA))
2261[13] 3208[5] 4114[11] 6121[2] 6337[9] 8007[7]

Lolita Lebron (IRE) *Lawrence Mullaney* a71 80
3 b f Royal Applause Alsharq (IRE) (Machiavellian (USA))
(1916) 2283[6] 2689[4] (3555) 4082[5] (5545) 5705[7] 7128[7] 7370[13]

Lollina Paulina *Kevin Ryan* a73 80
3 b f Holy Roman Emperor(IRE) Alexia Reveuse (IRE) (Dr Devious (IRE))
1862[5] 2272[5] (2894) 5326[8] 5539[12] 6515[9]

Lollypop Lady *Linda Perratt* 43
3 b f Misu Bond(IRE) Frabrofen (Mind Games)
4211[9] 4807[5] 5542[2] ◆ 5757[4] 6531[8]

Lombok *Gary Moore* a63 66
6 b g Hernando(FR) Miss Rinjani (Shirley Heights)
3572[6] 3961[6]

London Avenue (IRE) *Neil Mulholland* a55 32
4 ch g Compton Place Great Joy (IRE) (Grand Lodge (USA))
3718[9] 4236[10] 5191[9]

London Bridge (USA) *Mikael Magnusson* a59
2 b c Arch(USA) Kindness (Indian Ridge)
7323[6]

London Citizen (USA) *Mrs K Burke* a85 82
2 ch c Proud Citizen(USA) Sally Bowles (SAF) (London News (SAF))
(2370) ◆ 3562[4] 4098[6] 4947[2]

London Silver *Henry Candy* 60
3 b g Zafeen(FR) Princess Londis (Interrex (CAN))
1512[13] 3447[5] 4797[8]

Lone Foot Laddie (IRE) *Sylvester Kirk* a61 63
3 b g Red Clubs(IRE) Alexander Phantom (IRE) (Soviet Star (USA))
3735[8] 4709[3] 5351[6] 5770[6] 7018[11]

Lone Ranger (FR) *A De Royer-Dupre* 105
4 b h Muhtathir L'Etoile De Mer (FR) (Caerleon (USA))
3367a[3] (4634a) 6297a[8] 6914a[P]

Lone Star State (IRE) *Frank Sheridan* a59 32
3 b g Stardan(IRE) Rachelsfriend (IRE) (Dolphin Street (FR))
217[5] 393[4]

Long Awaited (IRE) *David Barron* 98
4 b g Pivotal Desertion (IRE) (Danehill (USA))
(1643) 2704[13] 3127[17] 4013[10] 4690[4] (5663) 6028[3] 6666[2] ◆

Longhunter *Darrin Miller* 101
4 b g Halling(USA) Dawnus (IRE) (Night Shift (USA))
8278a[4]

Long Lost Love *Mark Johnston* a62 74
3 b f Langfuhr(CAN) Heat Of The Night (Lear Fan (USA))
1728[9] 2552[4] 3111[5] 3471[10] 4769[7]

Lonsome Drive (FR) *Y De Nicolay* a81 83
5 b m Domedriver(IRE) Lone Spirit (IRE) (El Gran Senor (USA))
18a[8]

Look At Me Now *Jim Boyle* a61 55
3 ch c Choisir(AUS) Sweet Pickle (Piccolo)
524[3] 657[3] 750[3]

Look For Love *Reg Hollinshead* a58 49
4 b g Pursuit Of Love Look Here's May (Revoque (IRE))
(218) 334[2] 430[3] 450[4] 550[5] 725[13] 926[3] 939[8] 1096[9]

Look Forward (IRE) *Tim Easterby* 42
2 br f Byron In To The Future (Medicean)
2308[8] 2923[5] 3208[13]

Looking At Glory (IRE) *A Fabre* a75 67
2 b c Selkirk(USA) Trip To Glory (FR) (Where Or When (IRE))
(7597a)

Looking On *Henry Candy* 85
4 b g Observatory(USA) Dove Tree (FR) (Charnwood Forest (IRE))
1939[8] 4470[2] 5268[5] 5707[2] (6207)

Look Left *David Simcock* 86
4 ch g Observatory(USA) Stage Left (Nashwan (USA))
1381[15] 2473[5] ◆ 3038[7] 3610[11]

Look'N'Listen (IRE) *Ian Semple* a48 47
4 b m Fasliyev(USA) Royal Lady (IRE) (Royal Academy (USA))
2225[9]

Look On By *Ed McMahon* a62
2 gr g Byron Where's Carol (Anfield)
5242[4] 5715[5]

Looks Like Rain *Brian Ellison* a71 67
3 ch f Medicean Hippogator (USA) (Dixieland Band (USA))
1256[6] 1736[8] 2577[2] ◆ 2850[3] 3483[8] 4399[2] 5577[2] (5891) ◆ 6255[3] 6784[8] 7791[6]

Loraine *Jamie Osborne* a53
2 b f Sir Percy Emirates First (IRE) (In The Wings)
7159[10] 7641[8]

Lord Aeryn (IRE) *Richard Fahey* 95
5 b g Antonius Pius(USA) White Paper (IRE) (Marignan (USA))
2417[4] 2919[3] 3128[9] 3779[2] 4557[6] (4828) 5517[7] 6011[5] 6426[3] 7030[3]

Lord Aratan (GER) *George Moore* 18
5 b g Tiger Hill(IRE) Luce (IRE) (Sadler's Wells (USA))
5315[9]

Lord Ashley (IRE) *Tom Dascombe* 45
2 ch g Iffraaj Mrs Dalloway (IRE) (Key Of Luck (USA))
1352[4]

Lord Avonbrook *Andrew Crook* a66 69
2 b g Avonbridge Miss Brookie (The West (USA))
2579[5] 2798[4] (3019) (4191) 5292[4] 6121[11]

Lord Bedarrides (FR) *J Heloury* a70
3 b g Hurricane Cat(USA) Les Bedarrides (FR) (R B Chesne)
476a[0] 661a[9]

Lord Buffhead *Richard Guest* a59 65
3 br g Iceman Royal Pardon (Royal Applause)
40[3] 138[4] 228[3] 376[7] 1010[2] 1292[6] 1599[2] (1817) 4084[2] 4593[6] 5318[2] 5543[8] 5757[7] (6531) 6786[5] 7179[6] 7471[3] 8046[4] (8210) 8255[7]

Lord Chaparral (IRE) *R Brogi* 112
5 b h High Chaparral(IRE) Freccia D'Oro (GER) (Acatenango (GER))
2323a[9] 7287a[6]

Lord Deevert *Bill Turner* a50 41
7 br g Averti(IRE) Dee-Lady (Deploy)
5049[5] 5349[10] 5935[10] 7105[7] 7961[5]

Lord Emery (GER) *M Figge* 85
4 b h Mamool(IRE) Latley (GER) (Sillery (USA))
2685a[7]

Lord Franklin *Eric Alston* a59 61
3 ch g Iceman Zell (IRE) (Lend A Hand)
3275[7] 3908[2] (4263) 4642[4] 5538[3] 6756[2] 7146[5] 7382[3] 7615[3]

Lord Gaga (IRE) *David Nicholls*
3 b g Moss Vale(IRE) Agouti (Pennekamp (USA))
1953[9]

Lord Golan *Violet M Jordan* a60
4 b g Singspiel(IRE) Lady Golan (IRE) (Golan (IRE))
7782[5] 7896[8]

Lord Kanaloa (JPN) *Takayuki Yasuda* 122
4 b h King Kamehameha(JPN) Lady Blossom (JPN) (Storm Cat (USA))
(8041a)

Lord Lansing (IRE) *Mrs K Burke* a73 71
5 b g Mull Of Kintyre(USA) Miss Beverley (Beveled (USA))
(94a)

Lord Nandi *Sir Henry Cecil* a44 60
3 b c Oasis Dream Pink Cristal (Dilum (USA))
1893[10] 3181[4] 3781[5]

Lord Of Leitrim (IRE) *Brian Meehan* a75 63
2 ro c Dark Angel(IRE) Annieirwin (IRE) (Perugino (USA))
4463[3] 5098[2] 5684[4]

Lord Of The Dance (IRE) *Michael Mullineaux* a72 76
6 ch g Indian Haven Maine Lobster (USA) (Woodman (USA))
7935[9] (8167) 8241[7]

Lord Of The Garter (IRE) *Brian Meehan* 83
2 b c Royal Applause Just Julie (USA) (Gulch (USA))
4539[3] 5126[4] 5562[2] (6377)

Lordofthehouse (IRE) *William Haggas* 94
4 ch g Danehill Dancer(IRE) Bordighera (USA) (Alysheba (USA))
2093[2] (2709) 3125[5] 6600[RR] 7051[RR]

Lord Ofthe Shadows (IRE) *Richard Hannon* a98 101
3 ch c Kyllachy Golden Shadow (IRE) (Selkirk (USA))
1216[5] 2022[4] 2485[11] 3294[22] 4740[8] 5356[5] 6432[5] 6831[9] 7401[7] 7502[6] 7824[3]

Lord Of The Storm *Bill Turner* a65 65
4 b g Avonbridge Just Run (IRE) (Runnett)
(1624) 1771[2] 2364[4] ◆ 2851[5] (3392) 4219[9]

Lord Of The Wing *Mrs J L Le Brocq* a35 55
7 b g Daggers Drawn(USA) Brangane (IRE) (Anita's Prince)
453[12]

Lord Paget *Reg Hollinshead* a66 49
3 b g Three Valleys(USA) Appelone (Emperor Jones (USA))
499[2] ◆ 770[4] 943[6] 1111[3] 1989[3] 2785[9] 3218[8] 5446[5] 6050[7] 6500[5] 6937[11] 7146[11] 7616[7] 7671[7] 8257[2]

Lord Provost (IRE) *Mahmood Al Zarooni* a79 61
2 b c Teofilo(IRE) Mayoress (Machiavellian (USA))
5534[5] (6532)

Lord Roflow *Robert Johnson*
2 ch g Dubai Destination(USA) Youm Jadeed (IRE) (Sadler's Wells (USA))
2238[3] 2667[8]

Lordship (IRE) *Tony Carroll* a21 51
8 b g King's Best(USA) Rahika Rose (Unfuwain (USA))
6546[6] 6967[11] 7105[3] 7318 [5]

Lord Sinclair (USA) *F Chappet* a103 104
3 gr c Mizzen Mast(USA) Great Connection (USA) (Dayjur (USA))
(914a) 1208a[6]

Lord Theo *Nick Littmoden* a66 80
8 b g Averti(IRE) Love You Too (Be My Chief (USA))
480[11] 648[8] 826[6]

Loreto (IRE) *J S Bolger* a87 85
3 b f Holy Roman Emperor(IRE) Witch Of Fife (USA) (Lear Fan (USA))
(6352a)

Los Cristianos (FR) *A Couetil* 105
6 ch h Gold Away(IRE) Perspective (FR) (Funambule (USA))
4120a[5]

Los Nadis (GER) *Jim Goldie* 86
8 ch g Hernando(FR) La Estrella (GER) (Desert King (IRE))
2457[2] 5830[7] (6428) 7098[6]

Lost Highway (IRE) *Mark Johnston* a62 62
3 b f Danehill Dancer(IRE) En Garde (USA) (Irish River (FR))
1590[3] 1915[10] 2605[4] 3212[7] 4781[3]

Lost In Paris (IRE) *Tim Easterby* a76 92
6 b g Elusive City(USA) Brazilia (Forzando)
1237[4] 1602[13] 2439[4] 2717[15] 3541[4] 4312[9] (4451) 5412[14] 6006[9] 6767[9]

Lost In The Moment (IRE) *Saeed Bin Suroor* a103 115
5 b h Danehill Dancer(IRE) Streetcar (IRE) (In The Wings)
2081[4] 3418[2] 4737[8] 5599[3] 6600[3] 7696a[5]

Lothair (IRE) *Alan Swinbank* a41 54
3 b g Holy Roman Emperor(IRE) Crafty Example (USA) (Crafty Prospector (USA))
1479[9] 1864[13] 3235[7] (4087) ◆ 7798[12]

Lothian Countess *George Foster* a36 65
2 ch f Auction House(USA) Immortelle (Arazi (USA))
(1164) 2252[11] 2630[5] 3604[6] 5055[5] 6809[6]

Lottie Dod (IRE) *Charles O'Brien* a77 96
2 b f Invincible Spirit(IRE) Sharapova (IRE) (Elusive Quality (USA))
2512a[5] 5136a[3]

Lou Bega *Frau M Weber* a69
3 b g Country Reel(USA) Lakelands Lady (IRE) (Woodborough (USA))
7803a[10]

Loucal *Noel Quinlan* 55
2 b c Lucky Story(USA) Penny Ha'Penny (Bishop Of Cashel)
5912[5] 6844[6] 7459[9]

Lough Ferrib (IRE) *J L Hassett* a39 76
11 br g Accordion Holly'sreturn (IRE) (Bob's Return (IRE))
7584a[4]

Louise Sauvage *Ken Wingrove* a49 53
6 b m Loup Sauvage(USA) Breezy Louise (Dilum (USA))
356[12]

Louis Hull *Garry Moss* a42 68
3 b g Three Valleys(USA) Zietunzeen (IRE) (Zieten (USA))
1916[9] 5338[9] 6361[5] 6813[7] 7616[10]

Louis The Pious *David O'Meara* 106
4 bb g Holy Roman Emperor(IRE) Whole Grain (Polish Precedent (USA))
2025[6] 2472[2] ◆ 2919[8] 3331[16] 3855[5] 4799[2] 5370[3] 6468[9] 7066[2] 7691[10]

Louis Vee (IRE) *Ed de Giles* a38 33
4 bb g Captain Rio Mrs Evans (IRE) (College Chapel)
3076[6]

Louisville Lip (IRE) *Patrick J Flynn* a79 87
5 b g Orpen(USA) Former Drama (USA) (Dynaformer (USA))
6066a[9]

Loukoumi *Tim Easterby* 65
4 b m Iffraaj Odalisque (IRE) (Machiavellian (USA))
2094[12] 2675[9] 3778[4] 4495[11] 4865[3] ◆ 5671[6] 6123[13] 6783[4]

Loulou Vuitton *Brian Baugh* a61
2 ch f Needwood Blade Shepherds Warning (IRE) (Vettori (IRE))
7219[10] 7613[6] 7931[4] 8274[3]

Louphole *J R Jenkins* a65 55
10 ch g Loup Sauvage(USA) Goodwood Lass (IRE) (Alzao (USA))
2170[8] 3007[4] 3717[6] 4508[5] 5049[6]

Louvain (FR) *P Demercastel* a89
3 b g Vatori(FR) Loupy Glitters (FR) (Loup Solitaire (USA))
5473a[10]

Lovage *Roger Charlton* a65 68
3 b f Exceed And Excel(AUS) Name Of Love (IRE) (Petardia)
2045[3] 2733[4] 5983[3] 7015[3] 7529[7]

Lovat Lane *Eve Johnson Houghton* a50 60
4 b m Avonbridge Pudding Lane (IRE) (College Chapel)
125[4] 305[3] (379) 561[11] 662[9]

Love And Cherish (IRE) *David Wachman* a75 65
2 b f Excellent Art Party Feet (IRE) (Noverre (USA))
6853a[4]

Love And Pride (USA) *Todd Pletcher* a117
4 bb m A.P. Indy(USA) Ile De France (USA) (Storm Cat (USA))
7550a[5]

Love Club *Brian Baugh* a46 54
4 ch g Kheleyf(USA) Avondale Girl (IRE) (Case Law)
544[7] 691[9] 910[6] 4154[7] 4885[9] 6496[10] 7061[6] 7746[5] 8109[3]

Love Delta (USA) *Kevin Ryan* a86 102
5 bb g Seeking The Gold(USA) Delta Princess (USA) (A.P. Indy (USA))
2177[18] 2286[12] 2861[4] 3726[2]

Loved To Bits *Eric Wheeler* a48 50
4 b m Storming Home Agent Kensington (Mujahid (USA))
4815[12] 5504[4] 5937[6] 7929[5] 8205[10] ◆

Love Grows Wild (USA) *Michael Bell* a60 56
3 rg f Cozzene(USA) Dierks Timber (USA) (Prime Timber (USA))
1359[3] 1531[5] 2367[12] 2803[9] 3547[3] 4006[3] 4198[4] 7148[3] 7470[8]

Love In The Park *Roy Brotherton* a62 64
7 b m Pivotal Naughty Crown (USA) (Chief's Crown (USA))
66[2] 334[3]

Loveinthesand (IRE) *Johan Reuterskiold* a63 75
5 b g Footstepsinthesand Love Emerald (USA) (Mister Baileys)
3654a[4]

Love Island *Richard Whitaker* a65 81
3 b f Acclamation Sally Traffic (River Falls)
1912[4] 2441[2] 2824[3] 4496[4] 4798[4] (5167) (5676) 6406[4] 7521[5]

Lovely Pass (IRE) *Mahmood Al Zarooni* 94
2 b f Raven's Pass(USA) Macadamia (IRE) (Classic Cliche (IRE))
(2492) 3368[3] 4064[9] (6021)

Love Magic *Sir Michael Stoute* a79
2 b f Dansili Magical Romance (IRE) (Barathea (IRE))
(5300)

Love Marmalade (IRE) *Kevin Ryan* a63 60
2 ch c Duke Of Marmalade(IRE) Green Castle (IRE) (Indian Ridge)
6164[11] 6558[6] 7459[4] 7779[12]

Love Pegasus (USA) *Paddy Butler* a59 52
6 bb g Fusaichi Pegasus(USA) Take Charge Lady (USA) (Dehere (USA))
7964[11] 8047[9] 8146[3] 8265[6]

Loverdose (USA) *F Vermeulen* a93 85
3 b c Giant's Causeway(USA) Surya (USA) (Unbridled (USA))
364a[3] 1244a[6]

Lovers Peace (IRE) *Edmond Kent* a34 81
4 b m Oratorio(IRE) Puck's Castle (Shirley Heights)
2318a[5]

Lovesome *Michael Bell* a62
2 b f Kheleyf(USA) Heavenly Bay (USA) (Rahy (USA))
7506[7]

Loves Theme (IRE) *Alan Bailey* a70 74
4 ch m Iffraaj Bauci (IRE) (Desert King (IRE))
102[7] 1528[11]

Love Tale *Mark Rimell* a56 82
3 ch f Lucky Story(USA) Bold Love (Bold Edge)
(1622) (2206) 2649[2] 3108[2] 3917[3]

Love Tatoo (IRE) *Andrew Balding* 69
3 b f Acclamation Kapria (FR) (Simon Du Desert (FR))
1501[3] ◆ 5276[3] 5795[3] 6209[4] 6801[P]

Love Theway Youare (USA) *Myung Kwon Cho* a109 86
4 bb m Arch(USA) Diversa (USA) (Tabasco Cat (USA))
1839a[7]

Love To Tara *Robert Cowell*
3 b f Notnowcato Sparkling Clear (Efisio)
4154[10]

Love You Louis *J R Jenkins* a78 76
6 b g Mark Of Esteem(IRE) Maddie's A Jem (Emperor Jones (USA))
24[4] 560[4] 808[2] 1290[3] 2195[8] 2789[7] 3477[12] 4003[4] 4187[4] 5123[3] 5514[2] 6314[11]

Love Your Looks *Mike Murphy* a96 95
4 b m Iffraaj Play Around (IRE) (Niniski (USA))
(1423) (1980) 2539[2] 3636[2] 4529[2] 5238[6] 6085a[5] 7509[3]

Loving Spirit *James Toller* a98 100
4 b g Azamour(IRE) Lolla's Spirit (IRE) (Montjeu (IRE))
1924[6] 3640[4] 3977[5] 5301[2] 6036[3] 6674[20] 7240[2] ◆

Low Key (IRE) *John Butler* a58 93
5 b h Pentire La Capilla (Machiavellian (USA))
7608[5] 8148[4]

Lowther *Lee Carter* a87 107
7 b g Beat All(USA) Ever So Lonely (Headin' Up)
140a[11] 315a[10] 1130[22] 2082[7] 2642[8] 3157[13] 3999[8] 4580[9] 5269[10] 7997[2] (8105)

Lowtherwood *Bryan Smart* a30 59
3 b g Green Desert(USA) Imperial Bailiwick (IRE) (Imperial Frontier (USA))
138[6] 2460[8] 4619[8] 5918[11]

Loyal Master (IRE) *Garry Moss* a30 78
3 b g Modigliani(USA) Santa Gertrudis (IRE) (Machiavellian (USA))
2089[3] 2785[8] 2883[7] 3460[8] 5415[9] 5721[9] 6131[14] 6814[11]

Loyal N Trusted *Richard Price* a70 63
4 b g Motivator Baby Don't Cry (USA) (Street Cry (IRE))
909[8] 1191[4] 1447[2] (1722) 2373[6] 4517[8] 4993[5] 5203[4] 5681[3] 6158[2] 6455[2] 6895[3] 7142[8] 7530[6]

Loyal Royal (IRE) *Milton Bradley* a71 57
9 b g King Charlemagne(USA) Supportive (IRE) (Nashamaa)
88[2] 251[9] 353[8] ◆ 526[8] 997[8] 1528[6] 1735[5] 2352[2] 3707[5] 6003[7] 6836[4] 7482[2] 7861[5] 7990[2] 8064[4] 8231[6]

Loyalty *Derek Shaw* a106 48
5 b g Medicean Ecoutila (USA) (Rahy (USA))
622[7] 712[3] 868[8] 1034[13] 6400[U] 6630[9] 7502[13] 7751[9] 7934[7]

Luaimneach *Liam McAteer* a56 55
3 b g Marju(IRE) Aqraan (In The Wings)
1834a[9]

Luca Brasi (FR) *Francisco Castro* a104 97
8 b g Singspiel(IRE) Diamond Field (USA) (Mr Prospector (USA))
2160a[6]

Lucanin *Sir Michael Stoute* 82
3 b c Galileo(IRE) Teggiano (IRE) (Mujtahid (USA))
1512[2] ◆ 2430[4]

Lucario (FR) *J-P Carvalho* 55
3 b c Shirocco(GER) Limelighting (USA) (Alleged (USA))
5074a[0]

Lucas Pitt *Michael Scudamore* a56 50
5 b g Kyllachy Bardot (Efisio)
28[7] 200[5] 1831[9] 2575[4] 3942[4]

Lucayan (FR) *F Rohaut* a88 114
3 b c Turtle Bowl(IRE) La Vltava (IRE) (Grand Lodge (USA))
(2110a) 3239[9] 6508a[5] 6897a[8]

Lucies Diamond (IRE) *Michael Dods* 67
2 ch f Iffraaj Lucies Pride (IRE) (Noverre (USA))
(1671)

Lucifers Shadow (IRE) *Sylvester Kirk* a62 50
3 gr g Dark Angel(IRE) Marianne's Dancer (IRE) (Bold Fact (USA))
1608[6] (2131) 2374[7] 4708[14] 5427[9] 6001[5] 6321[7] 6640[11]

Lucilla *Paul Howling* a62
2 b f Holy Roman Emperor(IRE) Lady In Waiting (Kylian (USA))
7706[6] 8171[6] ◆

Luck (IRE) *Kevin Ryan* 80
2 b g Red Clubs(IRE) Pure Fiction (Zilzal (USA))
(3725) 5371[4] 6070[9] 6425[7] 6920[12]

Luckster *David Evans* 32
2 b g Lucky Story(USA) Bisaat (USA) (Bahri (USA))
2384[10] 2729[5] 4222[8]

Lucky Art (USA) *Conor Dore* a82 86
6 b g Johannesburg(USA) Syrian Summer (USA) (Damascus (USA))
327^{6} 647^{9} 890^{7} 2809^{6} 3256^{13} 3707^{4} 3993^{7} 4245^{7} 4885^{10}

Lucky Beggar (IRE) *Charles Hills* 96
2 gr c Verglas(IRE) Lucky Clio (IRE) (Key Of Luck (USA))
1451^{2} 2163^{2} 3378^{5} (4148) 4488^{2} (4827) 5601^{4} 6483^{7} 6865^{4} 7065^{3} 7400^{5}

Lucky Black Star (IRE) *George Baker* a64 49
2 b g Lawman(FR) Silver Bandana (USA) (Silver Buck (USA))
5275^{10} 5784^{5} 6841^{3} 7592^{5}

Lucky Bridle (IRE) *C Ferland* 102
3 b c Dylan Thomas(IRE) Auction Room (USA) (Chester House (USA))
5869a^{10}

Lucky Chappy (IRE) *H Graham Motion* a108 110
3 b c High Chaparral(IRE) Germane (Distant Relative)
1145a^{7} 7882a^{3}

Lucky Dan (IRE) *Paul Green* a81 80
6 b g Danetime(IRE) Katherine Gorge (USA) (Hansel (USA))
272^{4} 387^{4} 478^{4} 639^{U} 912^{8} 1298^{5} 1954^{10} 2355^{8} (2476) (2750) 3065^{11} 6665^{13} (7202) 7464^{11} 7789^{6}

Lucky Dance (BRZ) *Graeme McPherson* a44 96
10 b h Mutakddim(USA) Linda Francesa (ARG) (Equalize (USA))
6895^{9}

Lucky Di *Peter Hedger* a75 55
2 br f Araafa(IRE) Lucky Date (IRE) (Halling (USA))
6366^{10} 7007^{4} 7371^{5} (8171) 8302^{2}

Lucky Diva *Bill Turner* a61 66
5 ch m Lucky Story(USA) Cosmic Countess (IRE) (Lahib (USA))
58^{5} 392^{5} 446^{8} 772^{9} 4537^{2} 4904^{2} 5196^{4} (6280) 6738^{9}

Lucky Du Verger (FR) *J-M Gatteau*
3 b g Le Triton(USA) Not Shy (IRE) (Medaaly)
5074a^{0}

Lucky For Some *Marjorie Fife* 35
5 b m Lucky Owners(NZ) Countess Elton (IRE) (Mukaddamah (USA))
1436^{6} 1950^{5} 2287^{7} 6361^{13} 6479^{9}

Lucky Henry *Clive Cox* a88 92
3 br g Lucky Story(USA) Seldemosa (Selkirk (USA))
1612^{2} 2265^{6} 2485^{2} ◆ 3294^{21} 4319^{9} 5094^{3} 5914^{5} 6205^{6} 6484^{7}

Lucky Lodge *Mel Brittain* 69
2 b g Lucky Story(USA) Melandre (Lujain (USA))
1131^{5} 1437^{12} 2181^{4} (2770) 4071^{5} 5109^{6} 5620^{5} 7687^{10}

Lucky Mark (IRE) *Garry Moss* a67 44
3 b g Moss Vale(IRE) Vracca (Vettori (IRE))
1560^{6} 2010^{8} 5719^{6} 6937^{3} 7361^{2} 7465^{2} 7673^{6} 7794^{6} 7861^{6} (8004) 8156^{6}

Lucky Mellor *Barry Murtagh* a79 62
5 b g Lucky Story(USA) Lady Natilda (First Trump)
670^{10} 3949^{12}

Lucky Money *Sir Mark Prescott Bt* a79 72
3 ch g Selkirk(USA) Autumn Wealth (IRE) (Cadeaux Genereux)
2987^{3} 3952^{6} 5099^{3} 5302^{8} 5888^{8} (7141)

Lucky Morgan *Daniel Mark Loughnane*
2 ch c Pastoral Pursuits Basbousate Nadia (Wolfhound (USA))
7953^{10}

Lucky Mountain *Scott Dixon* a69
2 ch c Mount Nelson Wild Clover (Lomitas)
7305^{4} ◆ 7642^{4} 7899^{9} 8032^{4}

Lucky Nine (IRE) *C Fownes* a109 121
5 b g Dubawi(IRE) Birjand (Green Desert (USA))
1147a^{3} 1902a^{3} 8041a^{5}

Lucky Numbers (IRE) *David O'Meara* a80 88
6 b g Key Of Luck(USA) Pure Folly (IRE) (Machiavellian (USA))
1478^{7} 2439^{5} 2876^{4} 3169^{6} 3557^{10} 4554^{6} (4829) 6009^{11} 6665^{11} 7452^{6}

Lucky Prize *Mel Brittain* 34
2 b f Lucky Story(USA) Mana Pools (IRE) (Brief Truce (USA))
2977^{6} 3909^{6} 4792^{17}

Lucky Royale *Jeremy Gask* a65 62
4 b m Lucky Story(USA) Bella Bertolini (Bertolini (USA))
148^{6} 5033^{3}

Lucky Score (IRE) *Tony Carroll* a66 34
6 b m Lucky Story(USA) Musical Score (Blushing Flame (USA))
2115a^{4}

Lucky Suit (IRE) *Ronald Harris* a44 60
2 b f Red Clubs(IRE) Alexander Family (IRE) (Danetime (IRE))
1563^{6} 2384^{4} 3009^{7} (3224) 4421^{3} 4991^{6} 5800^{7} 6612^{5} 7491^{6} 7797^{9} 7977^{6}

Lucky Windmill *Alan Swinbank* 83
5 b g Lucky Story(USA) Windmill Princess (Gorytus (USA))
1820^{2} 2620^{8} 3494^{9} 4347^{7} 5546^{10}

Luctor Emergo (IRE) *Keith Dalgleish* a66 75
3 b g Amadeus Wolf Batilde (IRE) (Victory Piper (USA))
114^{7} (393) 466^{2} 549^{3} 2673^{3} 3111^{8} 3275^{4} 3729^{2} (3907) (4391) (4642) 5054^{4} 5430^{6} 5729^{3} 6516^{3} 6626^{2} 6784^{5} 7380^{8}

Lucy Bee *Keith Dalgleish* a57 57
2 ch f Haafhd Procession (Zafonic (USA))
1949^{4} 2135^{5} 3490^{7} (4083) 4324^{6} 5206^{7} 5920^{5} 6310^{2} 6511^{5} 6893^{3} 7854^{3} (7971) 8101^{4}

Lucy Minaj *Bryan Smart* a30 68
2 b f Dylan Thomas(IRE) Keyaki (IRE) (Shinko Forest (IRE))
2334^{2} 4710^{15} 5222^{4} 6511^{7} 7056^{10}

Luggers Hall (IRE) *Tony Carroll* 83
4 b g Cape Cross(IRE) Saabga (USA) (Woodman (USA))
2031^{2} ◆ 2887^{2} 3564^{5}

Luhaif *Mick Channon* a90 106
2 b c Cape Cross(IRE) Hot And Spicy (Grand Lodge (USA))
2073^{3} 2677^{3} 3062^{3} (3634) 4098^{7} 4698^{3} 5270^{4} 7009^{3} 7283a^{5}

Lui E La Luna *B Grizzetti* 104
3 b c Nayef(USA) Luna D'Estate (Alzao (USA))
1698a^{10}

Lui Rei (ITY) *Robert Cowell* a102 107
6 b g Reinaldo(FR) My Luigia (IRE) (High Estate)
1498^{3} (1849) 2286^{5} (2707) ◆ 3371^{17} 3641^{5} 4073^{4} 4802^{3} 5077^{5} 5581^{8} (6346) 6943a^{3}

Luisant *J A Nash* a96 104
9 ch g Pivotal La Legere (USA) (Lit De Justice (USA))
1040a^{10} 3648a^{13}

Luisa Tetrazzini (IRE) *Terry Clement* a60 56
6 b m Hawk Wing(USA) Break Of Day (USA) (Favorite Trick (USA))
1070^{6} 1702^{10} 1768^{11} 3082^{6} 3389^{9}

Lujeanie *Dean Ivory* a92 89
6 br g Lujain(USA) Ivory's Joy (Tina's Pet)
253^{8} 311^{4} 3394^{8} 3822^{6} 5320^{3} 5557^{4} 6226^{4} 6495^{9} 7327^{12} 7646^{5} 7928^{5} 7995^{2} 8022^{2} (8202)

Lujiana *Mel Brittain* a54 29
7 b m Lujain(USA) Compact Disc (IRE) (Royal Academy (USA))
3020^{9} 3256^{11}

Lulla *Marcus Tregoning* a58 83
3 b f Oasis Dream Dominica (Alhaarth (IRE))
(7061)

Lumberyard Jack (USA) *Doug O'Neill* a70 82
4 bb g Bellamy Road(USA) Shellys Terms (USA) (Private Terms (USA))
5374a^{7}

Lumiere Rose *J-C Rouget* 95
3 ch f Motivator La Dangeville (Danehill (USA))
6595a^{6}

Lunar Deity *Eve Johnson Houghton* 87
3 b g Medicean Luminda (IRE) (Danehill (USA))
1894^{3} 2659^{4} 2764^{5} 3571^{11} 4814^{6} 5486^{3} (5662) 6303^{2}

Luna Rosa (IRE) *Clive Cox* a43 47
3 b f Marju(IRE) Lone Spirit (IRE) (El Gran Senor (USA))
2204^{12} 2891^{10} 3340^{12} 4006^{7} 4584^{10} 6151^{11}

Luna Vale *Robert Eddery* a27 23
3 b f Dubai Destination(USA) Fly Me To The Moon (GER) (Galileo (IRE))
294^{12}

Lunayir (FR) *A De Royer-Dupre* 109
3 b c Sinndar(IRE) Luna Caerla (IRE) (Caerleon (USA))
2743a^{9} 3656a^{4}

Lunette (IRE) *Ralph Beckett* a59
2 b f Teofilo(IRE) Princess Luna (GER) (Grand Lodge (USA))
7721^{7} 8070^{9}

Lupin Pooter *David Barron* 83
3 b g Bertolini(USA) Carrie Pooter (Tragic Role (USA))
2256^{4} ◆ (2615) ◆ (3350) 4558^{10} 5167^{5} 5603^{5}

Lupo D'Oro (IRE) *John Best* a74 83
3 b g Amadeus Wolf Vital Laser (USA) (Seeking The Gold (USA))
1317^{6} 1639^{2} 1739^{3} 2347^{7} 3396^{2} 4221^{2} 4477a^{5} 6173^{8} 6930^{2} 7114^{8} (7489)

Luscivious *Scott Dixon* a78 62
8 ch g Kyllachy Lloc (Absalom)
133^{4} 327^{8} 1298^{9}

Lutine Bell *Mike Murphy* a98 101
5 ch g Starcraft(NZ) Satin Bell (Midyan (USA))
2268^{4} 3641^{14} 4285^{4} 4799^{11} 5342^{2} 5746^{3} 6676^{11} 7010^{9}

Lutine Charlie (IRE) *Pat Eddery* a79 70
5 b g Kheleyf(USA) Silvery Halo (USA) (Silver Ghost (USA))
186^{4} 205^{2} 423^{6} 562^{5} 761^{4} 3247^{10} 3471^{4} (3949) 6172^{3} (6434) 6932^{5} 7115^{8}

Luv U Forever *Jo Hughes* 94
3 b f Multiplex Lady Suesanne (IRE) (Cape Cross (IRE))
1356^{3} 1877^{5}

Luv U Noo *Brian Baugh* a47 68
5 b m Needwood Blade Lady Suesanne (IRE) (Cape Cross (IRE))
334^{4} 666^{6} 848^{8} 1095^{10}

Luv U Whatever *Jo Hughes* 47
2 b g Needwood Blade Lady Suesanne (IRE) (Cape Cross (IRE))
4967^{6} 5655^{6} 6512^{5} 6733^{6}

Luzhniki (IRE) *Patrick Allen* a6 27
5 b m Kheleyf(USA) Russian Sunset (IRE) (Dockside (USA))
6184a^{10}

Lycidas (GER) *Tobias B P Coles* a76 72
3 b c Zamindar(USA) La Felicita (Shareef Dancer (USA))
1553a^{9}

Lykea (IRE) *C Laffon-Parias* 70
2 b f Oasis Dream Alyzea (IRE) (King Charlemagne (USA))
4476a^{2}

Lyric Ace (IRE) *Richard Hannon* a94 93
2 b g Thousand Words Aces Dancing (GER) (Big Shuffle (USA))
1211^{4} (1352) ◆ (1747) 3242^{15} 4093^{7} 4687^{4} 5678^{4} 6162^{21}

Lyrical Gangster (IRE) *Chris Gordon* a64 42
3 ch g Redback Feet Of Flame (USA) (Theatrical (IRE))
84^{8} 292^{6} 731^{3} 2014^{3} 2771^{9} 5939^{8}

Lyrical Vibe *David Evans* a36 30
2 b f Byron Poilane (IRE)
4604^{11} 5235^{11} 5807^{7} 6499^{7}

Lyric Ballad *Hughie Morrison* a62
2 b f Byron Skies Are Blue (Unfuwain (USA))
6791^{14} 7306^{5} 7628^{4} 7973^{4} 8302^{3}

Lyric Of Light *Mahmood Al Zarooni* 113
3 b f Street Cry(IRE) Suez (Green Desert (USA))
1884^{DSQ}

Lyric Piece *Sir Mark Prescott Bt* a74
2 ch f Dutch Art Humouresque (Pivotal)
4886^{3} 5425^{3} 5715^{6} 7814^{2} 7989^{4}

Lyric Poet (USA) *Anthony Carson* a77 71
5 bb g Distorted Humor(USA) Baltic Nations (USA) (Seattle Slew (USA))
192^{5} 271^{2} 555^{10} 3552^{3} 4200^{3} 5809^{9} 5908^{6} 7315^{7}

Lyric Street (IRE) *Ed Dunlop* 102
4 b g Hurricane Run(IRE) Elle Danzig (GER) (Roi Danzig (USA))
2253^{9} 4111^{3} 5076^{4} 6031^{6} 7051^{31}

Lysino (GER) *P Schiergen* 90
3 ch c Medicean Lysuna (GER) (Monsun (GER))
2569a^{6}

Lyssio (GER) *Michael Attwater* a100 103
5 b g Motivator Lysuna (GER) (Monsun (GER))
48a^{2} 241a^{7} 484a^{8} 1034^{11} 1677^{5} 2933^{12} 3826^{5} 4821^{6} (5664) 6039^{8} 6702^{5}

Lytham (IRE) *Tony Carroll* a58 62
11 b g Spectrum(IRE) Nousaiyra (IRE) (Be My Guest (USA))
104^{11} 265^{13} 450^{10} 741^{2} 984^{3} 1831^{5} 2814^{8} 3043^{6} 4219^{5} 4586^{4} 5974^{5} 8288^{7}

Maali (IRE) *A Al Raihe* a101 100
4 b h Street Cry(IRE) Agata (FR) (Poliglote)
618a^{9}

Maarek *David Peter Nagle* a61 118
5 b g Pivotal Ruby Rocket (IRE) (Indian Rocket)
1040a^{2} (1885) ◆ 3371^{6} (3623) 4092^{3} (6268a) 6468^{3} (7236) 7624a^{2}

Maastricht (IRE) *Mark Johnston* a87 91
3 b g Tiger Hill(IRE) Eurolink Raindance (IRE) (Alzao (USA))
2281^{2} ◆ 2718^{10} 4079^{5} 4346^{3} 4983^{6} (5344) 5554^{3} 5944^{4} 6349^{7}

Mabaany *William Haggas* 93
3 b g Exceed And Excel(AUS) Tarbiyah (Singspiel (IRE))
2485^{12} 6046^{2} 6921^{7}

Mabait *David Simcock* a93 103
6 b g Kyllachy Czarna Roza (Polish Precedent (USA))
53a^{9} 246a^{10} 586a^{10} 2068^{18} 2472^{3} ◆ 3268^{14} 4339^{8} 4761^{2} ◆ 5572^{14} 6024^{3} 6242^{5} 7010^{10}

Mabel's Song *Henry Candy* 61
3 b f Sakhee(USA) War Shanty (Warrshan (USA))
3664^{5} 4410^{10} 5452^{6} 6097^{6}

Mabroor (USA) *Doug Watson* a87 87
3 b c Hard Spun(USA) Mayfield (USA) (Exploit (USA))
142a^{11}

Macaabra (IRE) *James Tate* a58
2 b f Exceed And Excel(AUS) Al Cobra (IRE) (Sadler's Wells (USA))
7613^{3}

Macao (IRE) *R Dzubasz* 93
3 b c Motivator Missing Link (IRE) (Elusive Quality (USA))
3683a^{11}

Macbeth (IRE) *K J Condon* 99
3 b g Acclamation Filandre (Cadeaux Genereux)
2524a^{4} 3330^{4} 3678a^{7} 7423a^{4}

Maccabees *Roger Curtis* a55 71
3 b g Motivator Takarna (IRE) (Mark Of Esteem (IRE))
2382^{6} 2818^{6} 3142^{7} 3391^{4} 5164^{7} 5939^{5} 6232^{7} 6567^{4} (6948) 7196^{11} 7479^{8} 7793^{8}

Macchiara *Rae Guest* a75 75
3 ch f Medicean Castaway Queen (IRE) (Selkirk (USA))
3568^{3} (3990) 4814^{2} 5409^{4}

Macdillon *Stuart Kittow* a81 85
6 b g Acclamation Dilys (Efisio)
1936^{8} 2369^{9} 2853^{7} 3919^{2} 4292^{2} 5272^{2} 5584^{3} 6370^{2} 6767^{2} 7019^{3}

Macdonald Mor (IRE) *Michael Wigham* a66 76
3 b g Dansili Imperial Beauty (USA) (Imperial Ballet (IRE))
84^{5} 1063^{5}

Mace The Ace *Lawrence Mullaney* a54 52
2 b f Phoenix Reach(IRE) Lady Soleas (Be My Guest (USA))
1556^{6} 1911^{5} 2437^{12} 4324^{5} 4806^{7} 5041^{8} 5423^{4} 5748^{6} 6054^{5} 6953^{11} 7440^{2} 7728^{7}

Mac Federal (IRE) *Sheena West* a61
10 b g In The Wings Tocade (IRE) (Kenmare (FR))
395^{6}

Mac Gille Eoin *Luke Dace* a91 94
8 b h Bertolini(USA) Peruvian Jade (Petong)
871^{13} 1141^{8} 2268^{13} 2487^{8} 3771^{6} 3960^{11} 5035^{14} 7023^{3} 7309^{4} (7742) 7820^{4}

Macharov (FR) *J Van Handenhove* a69
3 b g Turtle Bowl(IRE) Clochette De Sou (FR) (Ajdayt (USA))
475a^{7}

Macicka (FR) *Mme J Bidgood* a61 65
3 b f Chapel Royal(USA) Fashion Club (USA) (Thunder Gulch (USA))
4477a^{0}

Mack's Sister *Dean Ivory* a68 30
5 ch m Pastoral Pursuits Linda's Schoolgirl (IRE) (Grand Lodge (USA))
123^{6} 267^{4} 474^{6} 576^{3} 1050^{11} 1305^{10} 1934^{7} 7225^{10} 7504^{3} 7748^{2} (8061) 8268^{10}

Mac Love *Roger Charlton* a101 111
11 b g Cape Cross(IRE) My Lass (Elmaamul (USA))
2656^{3} 4686^{3}

Mac's Power (IRE) *James Fanshawe* a102 107
6 b g Exceed And Excel(AUS) Easter Girl (Efisio)
1255^{3} 2268^{3} 3371^{13} 4285^{2} 4802^{15} 5964^{3} 6201^{11} 7010^{5}

Mac's Superstar (FR) *James Fanshawe* a71 50
2 b g Elusive City(USA) Diamond Light (USA) (Fantastic Light (USA))
6411^{10} 7627^{3} 7926^{2}

Mac Tiernan (IRE) *Ed de Giles* a64 72
5 b g Minashki(IRE) Softly Softly (IRE) (Lucky Guest)
1310^{5} (4158) 5175^{2}

Macy Anne (IRE) *Jo Hughes* a63 60
3 b f King's Best(USA) Gilah (IRE) (Saddlers' Hall (IRE))
464^{2} 573^{3} 1365^{8} 3193^{10} 3920^{7} 4232^{2} 5156^{7} 8113^{11} 8249^{11}

Madam Bonny (IRE) *Jim Goldie* 49
3 b f Arcadio(GER) Kashi Miss (USA) (Miswaki (USA))
1817^{4} 2595^{5} 2615^{7} 3032^{4} 3275^{12} 3908^{6}

Madame Blavatsky (FR) *Karen McLintock* 61
4 gr m Super Celebre(FR) Lovarisk (FR) (Take Risks (FR))
3521^{2} 4259^{5} 4926^{3} 5547^{10} 6258^{11} 6528^{3} 7095^{7}

Madame Defarge (IRE) *Michael Bell* 79
2 b f Motivator Friendlier (Zafonic (USA))
(7312)

Madame Elizabeth *Reg Hollinshead* a75 69
2 b f Multiplex Madame Jones (IRE) (Lycius (USA))
3034^{9} 4290^{3} 4704^{2} 5153^{2} 5825^{2} 6356^{3} 6657^{2} 7406^{8}

Madame Feu *Henry Candy* a45 57
3 ch f Tumbleweed Ridge Raffelina (USA) (Carson City (USA))
1376^{8} 2166^{4} 3489^{11} 4240^{10}

Madame Gazelle (IRE) *S Donohoe* 45
4 b m Ad Valorem(USA) Twin Logic (USA) (Diesis)
5891^{9}

Madame Jane (IRE) *Ole Larsen*
3 b f Titus Livius(FR) Mevlana (IRE) (Red Sunset)
4359a^{9}

Madame Kintyre *Rod Millman* a55 68
4 b m Trade Fair Chorus (Bandmaster (USA))
1609^{5} 2421^{7} 2943^{2} 3477^{11} 4059^{9} 4708^{13} 7990^{6} 8115^{8}

Madame Scarlett (IRE) *Jo Crowley* a42 46
2 br f Red Clubs(IRE) Shining Desert (IRE) (Green Desert (USA))
4604^{10} 5932^{7} 6645^{8} 7304^{8}

Madame St Clair (IRE) *Roger Curtis* a76 82
3 b f High Chaparral(IRE) Numbers Game (Rainbow Quest (USA))
1486^{4} 1853^{10} 2604^{3} 3083^{6} (3391) 4875^{2} 5913^{2} 6441^{6} 6802^{2} 7269^{5}

Madam Joy *Christopher Kellett*
3 b f Deportivo Whittle Rock (Rock City)
457^{4}

Madam Lilibet (IRE) *Sharon Watt* 64
3 b f Authorized(IRE) Foxilla (IRE) (Foxhound (USA))
1676^{3} 2287^{6} 3023^{10} (3729) 4744^{7} (5265) ◆ 5672^{7} 6956^{7} 7293^{2} 7603^{3}

Madamlily (IRE) *John Quinn* a71 72
6 b m Refuse To Bend(IRE) Rainbow Dream (Rainbow Quest (USA))
1822^{10}

Madam Macie (IRE) *David O'Meara* 98
5 ch m Bertolini(USA) Dictatrice (FR) (Anabaa (USA))
1293^{2} 1951^{7} 2491^{4} (2752) 3128^{12} 3252^{3} (3522) 4248^{3} 4761^{19} 6010^{5}

Madam Mo (IRE) *P J Prendergast* 79
2 b f Motivator Winesong (IRE) (Giant's Causeway (USA))
6266a^{4}

Madam Mojito (USA) *John Quinn* a69 85
2 b f Smart Strike(CAN) Asuncion (USA) (Powerscourt)
(1629) (2630) 3269^{9} 4093^{5} 4820^{9}

Madam Moreton *George Margarson* a15 38
2 ch f Zafeen(FR) Limegreen Bow (Efisio)
2938^{7} 3244^{6} 3789^{5} 4395^{4} 5046^{5} 5194^{6}

Madam Tessa (IRE) *Bryn Palling* a51 62
4 br m Hawk Wing(USA) Anita's Contessa (IRE) (Anita's Prince)
3143^{9}

Made In Design (IRE) *Paul Hickey* a81 77
2 b f Invincible Spirit(IRE) Pulp Idol (USA) (Pulpit (USA))
6078a^{10}

Made In The Shade *Paul Midgley* a34 56
3 b f Ishiguru(USA) Dispol Katie (Komaite (USA))
1252^{6} (2139) 2460^{3} 3442^{8} 4784^{9} 5624^{7} 6959^{6} 7351^{7}

Made It (IRE) *Anthony Carson* 29
2 b f Oratorio(IRE) Theebah (Bahamian Bounty)
6966^{9}

Made Of More *Roger Ingram* a59 65
3 ch c Auction House(USA) Dam Certain (IRE) (Damister (USA))
2147^{11} 4001^{6} 4301^{3} 7647^{7} 7768^{11} 7964^{8} 8229^{5}

Maderienne (FR) *L Baudron* 53
2 ch f King's Best(USA) Sometime (FR) (Anabaa (USA))
8276a^{7}

Mad For Fun (IRE) *Paul Midgley* a50 56
3 b f Ivan Denisovich(IRE) Franny (Selkirk (USA))
1826^{3} 2540^{2} 4397^{13} 4913^{8} 5623^{4}

Mad Ginger Alice *Olivia Maylam* a64 47
4 ch m Beat Hollow Peryllys (Warning)
183^{8} 574^{8} 689^{4} 922^{10} 1207^{7} 1717^{10} 6829^{10} 7479^{13} 8019^{8}

Mad Jazz *Tony Coyle* a59 65
2 b f Sir Percy Gwen John (USA) (Peintre Celebre (USA))
1165^{6} 1235^{2} (1594) 3126^{4} (3351) 4778^{3} 5009^{3} 5670^{2} 6247^{7} (6604)

Madly In Love (FR) *F-X Belvisi* a81 85
4 gr m Slickly(FR) Hourloupe (IRE) (Damister (USA))
7701a^{4}

Madrasa (FR) *Mme C Head-Maarek* 37
2 gr f Slickly(FR) Matanilla (FR) (Anabaa (USA))
6751a^{0}

Madrasa (IRE) *Keith Reveley* a63 72
4 b g High Chaparral(IRE) Shir Dar (FR) (Lead On Time (USA))
1382^{4} (2775) 4590^{6} 4955^{4} 5546^{4} 6076^{13}

Madrilene (USA) *Mark Johnston* a40
4 b m El Prado(IRE) Lignify (ARG) (Confidental Talk (USA))
546[5] 3484[11]

Mae Cigan (FR) *Michael Blanshard* a55 55
9 gr g Medaaly Concert (Polar Falcon (USA))
1496[4]

Mae Rose Cottage (IRE) *Barney Curley* a34 58
3 ch f Dylan Thomas(IRE) Maskaya (IRE) (Machiavellian (USA))
2344[14] 3083[12] 3451[7] 4457[8]

Mafeteng *John Dunlop* a70 77
4 b m Nayef(USA) Marakabei (Hernando (FR))
1706[2] 2149[5] 2814[4] 4626[5] (5456) (6074)

Mafi (IRE) *Mark Hoad* a75 75
4 b g Modigliani(USA) Yulara (IRE) (Night Shift (USA))
(684) 987[6] 1680[10] 1792[2] 2637[9] 3154[3] 3962[9] 5323[16] 7310[9] 7767[6] 7905[6] 8078[8]

Maggie Aron *Tim Vaughan* a51 53
6 gr m Generous(IRE) Pems Gift (Environment Friend)
3102[3] 4004[5]

Maggie Mey (IRE) *Lawrence Mullaney* 79
4 b m Kodiac Christmas Kiss (Taufan (USA))
1251[5] 1520[9] 1917[10] 2438[5] 2791[4] 4656[11] 4716[8] 5317[4] 5590[9] 6105[2]

Maggie Pink *Michael Appleby* a63
3 b f Beat All(USA) Top Notch (Alderbrook)
635[10] 723[6] 908[11] 1365[6] 1424[10] (7326) 7593[7] (7917)

Maggies Gem (IRE) *Paul Midgley* 39
2 br f Diamond Green(FR) Magdalene (FR) (College Chapel)
1235[4] 1594[6] 2338[7] 3576[6]

Magical Dream (IRE) *A P O'Brien* 103
2 b f Galileo(IRE) Red Evie (IRE) (Intikhab (USA))
5135a[6] 6081a[4] (6717a)

Magical Macey (USA) *David Barron* a86 105
5 ch g Rossini(USA) Spring's Glory (USA) (Honour And Glory (USA))
(1438) 2208[3] 2286[2] 2507[15] (3441) 4113[5] 4367[13]

Magical Marvin *Michael Appleby* a39
3 b g Tillerman Magical Music (Fraam)
908[9] 1113[10] 1567[14]

Magicalmysterytour (IRE) *Willie Musson* a87 85
9 b g Sadler's Wells(USA) Jude (Darshaan)
310[9] 577[9] 2502[10] 3129[4] 3794[6]

Magical Rose (IRE) *Paul D'Arcy* a76 75
2 b f Elusive City(USA) Xarzee (IRE) (Xaar)
3473[6] 5319[3] 5912[2] (6356) 7190[3]

Magical Speedfit (IRE) *George Margarson* a77 81
7 ch g Bold Fact(USA) Magical Peace (IRE) (Magical Wonder (USA))
1290[6] 2994[4] 4317[12] 5020[6] 6439[5]

Magical Star *Michael Wigham* a50 42
4 b m Arkadian Hero(USA) Aastral Magic (Magic Ring (IRE))
307[8] 662[11]

Magica Von Tryll (GER) *Wido Neuroth* 76
3 b f Lomitas Mattinata (Tiger Hill (IRE))
4359a[5]

Magic Beat *Pat Phelan* a27 44
2 ch f Byron Marah (Machiavellian (USA))
5661[7] 6437[8] 6978[11]

Magic Bounty *Tim Easterby* 63
3 ch g Bahamian Bounty Magic Myth (IRE) (Revoque (IRE))
1758[7] 2441[5] 2878[7] 3567[5] 4549[4] 5014[12]

Magic Channel (USA) *Richard Hannon* a66 66
2 ch c English Channel(USA) Arabian Peninsula (USA) (Mr Prospector (USA))
2202[5] 2844[7] 3733[8] (4540) 4847[4] 5155[2] 6793[3]

Magic City (IRE) *Richard Hannon* 93
3 b g Elusive City(USA) Annmarie's Magic (IRE) (Flying Spur (AUS))
6143[11] 6835[6]

Magic Destiny *Mrs K Burke* 84
3 b f Dubai Destination(USA) Magic Music (IRE) (Magic Ring (IRE))
(1660) 2265[3] 2883[6] 3214[2] (3780) (3991) 5043[4] 6789[5]

Magic Echo *George Foster* a44 55
8 b m Wizard King Sunday News'N'Echo (USA) (Trempolino (USA))
1382[6] ◆ 1657[10]

Magic Haze *Sally Hall* a64 50
6 b g Makbul Turn Back (Pivotal)
110[4] 460[4] 811[10] 3440[7] 7793[5]

Magic Hurricane (IRE) *James Fanshawe* 66
2 b c Hurricane Run(IRE) Close Regards (IRE) (Danehill (USA))
7637[5] ◆

Magician (IRE) *A P O'Brien* a83 90
2 b c Galileo(IRE) Absolutelyfabulous (IRE) (Mozart (IRE))
7419a[7]

Magic Ice *John Berry* a53
2 b f Royal Applause Winter Ice (Wolfhound (USA))
8138[5] 8286[2]

Magic In Motion *Neil Mulholland* a51
5 ch m Firebreak Harmonic Motion (IRE) (Bob Back (USA))
5154[7]

Magic Millie (IRE) *Alastair Lidderdale* a69 58
5 bb m Marju(IRE) Fille De La Terre (IRE) (Namaqualand (USA))
(97) (367) 493[3] (600) 668[5] 810[5] 944[7]

Magic Motif (USA) *A Fabre* 98
3 b f Giant's Causeway(USA) Silver Star (Zafonic (USA))
4616a[4]

Magic Secret *Jeremy Gask* 96
4 b g Trade Fair Just Devine (IRE) (Montjeu (IRE))
2940[2] 3778[5] ◆ 4286[7] 6577[12] (7113)

Magika *Marco Botti* a65
2 b f Dubawi(IRE) Aline's Wings (ITY) (In The Wings)
7160[11] 7899[4] (8134)

Magilini (IRE) *David Barron* a54 40
3 b f Bertolini(USA) Magic Annemarie (IRE) (Dancing Dissident (USA))
37[2] 283[4] 455[2] 599[4] 845[4]

Magique (IRE) *Jeremy Noseda* a71 73
2 b f Jeremy(USA) Misskinta (IRE) (Desert Sun)
6377[4] ◆ 6816[2] 7525[2] (8270)

Magma *Andrew Balding* a81 80
3 b f Singspiel(IRE) Rakata (USA) (Quiet American (USA))
1567[12] 4301[7] (4948) 6205[5] 7475[5]

Magnitude *Brian Baugh* a51 54
7 ch g Pivotal Miswaki Belle (USA) (Miswaki (USA))
105[9] 454[4] 632[9] 889[4] 2391[11] 2669[10] 4189[8] 7710[8]

Magog *Roger Charlton* 80
2 br g Dansili Margarula (IRE) (Doyoun)
(6796)

Mahadee (IRE) *Ed de Giles* a85 88
7 br g Cape Cross(IRE) Rafiya (Halling (USA))
2473[11] 3226[10] 3703[10] 4411[7] (5171) 5751[9] 6538[2] 7645[10] 7823[8]

Mahal Nadine *Michael Murphy*
3 b f Milk It Mick Chatter's Princess (Cadeaux Genereux)
6457[11]

Mahayogin (USA) *Brendan Powell* a50 70
4 bb g Dixie Union(USA) Shiva (JPN) (Hector Protector (USA))
3786[10] 4402[5] 5974[8] 6399[5] 6769[11]

Mahbooba (AUS) *M F De Kock* a108 113
5 b m Galileo(IRE) Sogha (AUS) (Red Ransom (USA))
(52a) 245a[2] (617a) 1149a[5]

Maher (USA) *Evan Williams* a75 78
4 b g Medaglia d'Oro(USA) Bourbon Blues (USA) (Seeking The Gold (USA))
688[4]

Mahfal (FR) *Brian Ellison* a62 55
4 b g Dalakhani(IRE) Peace Talk (FR) (Sadler's Wells (USA))
1189[8] 1297[7]

Mahkama (USA) *Saeed Bin Suroor* a81 83
3 b f Bernardini(USA) Rahy Rose (USA) (Rahy (USA))
2201[13] 3085[6]

Maid A Million *David Elsworth* a71 73
2 b f Kyllachy Poldhu (Cape Cross (IRE))
6335[5] 7078[2] 7311[2] 7738[2] (8006)

Maid Of Meft *Paul Midgley* a68 71
5 b m Auction House(USA) Lady Margaret (Sir Harry Lewis (USA))
(1189) 1338[5] 1822[6] 3449[2] 4626[10] 4908[2] (5384) 6074[6] 6407[5] 6891[9]

Maid Of Silk (IRE) *Neil Mulholland* a44 54
6 b m Blueprint(IRE) Silk Style (Polish Precedent (USA))
4182[2] 5048[9] 6228[8] 6769[6]

Maiguri (IRE) *C Baillet* 103
4 ch h Panis(USA) Zanada (FR) (Sinndar (IRE))
3205a[8]

Main Beach *Paul Midgley* a89 78
5 ch g Starcraft(NZ) Ocean View (USA) (Gone West (USA))
2151[9] 2558[11] (2791) 3612[6] 3790[5] 4954[2] 5338[4] 5588[2] 6047[8] 6969[4]

Mainland (USA) *Robert Johnson* 71
6 b g Empire Maker(USA) Imroz (USA) (Nureyev (USA))
3753[7]

Main Line *David Lanigan* a86 78
3 b c Rail Link Cooden Beach (IRE) (Peintre Celebre (USA))
(1422) 2150[4] ◆ 2813[6] ◆ 3594[7] 4889[2] 6932[6] 7300[5]

Mainsail *P Bary* 109
3 b c Oasis Dream Docklands (USA) (Theatrical (IRE))
3656a[2] 6897a[7]

Main Sequence (USA) *David Lanigan* a113 117
3 ch g Aldebaran(USA) Ikat (IRE) (Pivotal)
(1473) (2080) 2705[2] 4121a[4] 5489[2] 6245[5]

Maisie's Moon (USA) *Hughie Morrison* a52 39
2 b f Curlin(USA) Reverently (CAN) (Pulpit (USA))
6816[6] 7372[7] 7813[7]

Maison Brillet (IRE) *Clive Drew* a75 43
5 b g Pyrus(USA) Stormchaser (IRE) (Titus Livius (FR))
156[2] 221[2] 433[2] 728[3] 872[7] 1418[13] 1925[4] 7980[7]

Maistro (IRE) *Luca Cumani* a79 57
3 b c Excellent Art Kicking Bird (FR) (Darshaan)
1922[8] 4224[7]

Majeed *David Simcock* a56
2 b c Mount Nelson Clever Millie (USA) (Cape Canaveral (USA))
7780[6]

Majestic Angel (IRE) *Brian Rothwell* 43
3 b f Majestic Missile(IRE) Free Angel (USA) (Mystery Storm (USA))
2262[16] 2918[5] 3406[6] 4245[9] 4428[7] 5621[8]

Majestic Bounty *Chris Fairhurst* 33
3 b f Bahamian Bounty Princess Louise (Efisio)
2335[7] 2881[11] 3407[9] 4793[13] 5112[6]

Majestic Breeze (IRE) *Brian Ellison* a59 53
3 ch f Majestic Missile(IRE) Sofistication (IRE) (Dayjur (USA))
1292[3] 1599[4] 2615[6] 3442[14] (3706) 4547[5] 5014[5] 6104[8] 6321[2] 6937[6] 7204[5]

Majestic Dream (IRE) *Michael Easterby* a85 91
4 b g Exceed And Excel(AUS) Tallassee (Indian Ridge)
1865[16] 2176[7] 2504[11] 2754[2] 3128[5] 4110[8] 4317[6] ◆ 5369[12] 6405[10] 6895[6] (7142)

Majestic Jess (IRE) *Luke Dace* a68 58
2 b c Majestic Missile(IRE) Ginger Not Blonde (USA) (Atticus (USA))
1218[7] 1903[3] 1997[6] (6499) 6699[5] 7060[3] 7723[3] 7812[3]

Majestic Manannan (IRE) *David Nicholls* a72 74
3 b g Majestic Missile(IRE) Miraculous (IRE) (Marju (IRE))
3289[2] 4144[3] 4428[3] (4619) 4881[5] 6887[9] 7178[9]

Majestic Moon (IRE) *Richard Fahey* 87
2 b g Majestic Missile(IRE) Gala Style (IRE) (Elnadim (USA))
4132[2] ◆ (4637) 5563[4] 6425[8]

Majestic Myles (IRE) *Richard Fahey* a85 114
4 b g Majestic Missile(IRE) Gala Style (IRE) (Elnadim (USA))
2075[3] 2710[2] 3633[3] (4078) 4686[6] 5355[4] 6030[8] 6246[6]

Majestic Queen (IRE) *Tracey Collins* a86
2 b f Kheleyf(USA) Night Fairy (IRE) (Danehill (USA))
(6853a)

Majestic Red (IRE) *Malcolm Saunders* 64
2 b f Red Clubs(IRE) Majestic Eviction (IRE) (King's Theatre (IRE))
2202[6] (2571) 3138[5] 4488[7] 5450[7] 6155[9]

Majestic Rose *Mick Channon* a75 66
3 br f Imperial Dancer Solmorin (Fraam)
469[6] 637[5] 801[4]

Majestic South *Mick Channon* 54
3 ch f Bertolini(USA) Tidal Chorus (Singspiel (IRE))
2050[8] 2483[5] 2996[4] 3717[8] 4198[10]

Majestic Speed (IRE) *Rod Collet* a65
3 b c Majestic Missile(IRE) Speed Racer (Zieten (USA))
211a[7] 865a[3]

Majestic Zafeen *Alastair Lidderdale* a83 65
3 b f Zafeen(FR) Arasong (Aragon)
(184) 667[2] 1142[4] 2272[15] 2672[4] 5156[2] (5426) 6023[13]

Major Buckley (IRE) *Alan Swinbank* a29
3 ch g Haafhd Woodwin (IRE) (Woodman (USA))
7361[8] 7712[6]

Major Domo (FR) *Micky Hammond* a68 76
4 ch g Domedriver(IRE) Raphaela (FR) (Octagonal (NZ))
4396[6] 4883[3] 5585[2] (6126)

Major Muscari (IRE) *Ian McInnes* a51 59
4 ch g Exceed And Excel(AUS) Muscari (Indian Ridge)
4400[13] 4963[8] 7100[9] 7457[12] 7747[11]

Major Parkes *John Quinn* 45
2 gr g Fair Mix(IRE) My Melody Parkes (Teenoso (USA))
4952[6]

Majuro (IRE) *Charles Smith* a91 89
8 b g Danetime(IRE) First Fling (IRE) (Last Tycoon)
177[8] 285[10] 563[6] ◆ 765[6] 3994[3] 4657[3] 5189[2] 5819[5] (6171) (6319) 6525[4] 6659[11] 6979[12] 7370[10] 7867[3] 7901[2] (8077) (8202) 8238[2]

Makafeh *Luca Cumani* 86
2 b g Elusive Quality(USA) Demisemiquaver (Singspiel (IRE))
3397[5] (4194) 5060[2] 6027[5] 7053[8]

Makana (FR) *A De Royer-Dupre* 98
3 gr f Dalakhani(IRE) Marasima (IRE) (Barathea (IRE))
3423a[5]

Makani Bisty (JPN) *Yoshito Yahagi* a110 118
5 br h Zenno Rob Roy(JPN) Success Witch (JPN) (Brian's Time (USA))
1144a[10]

Make A Fuss *Sylvester Kirk* a50
3 gr f Proclamation(IRE) Fustaan (IRE) (Royal Applause)
228[7]

Ma Kellys (IRE) *Micky Hammond* a57 61
3 ch g Compton Place Western Sal (Salse (USA))
159[5] 404[5] 481[5] 1441[2] 2144[6] 2673[4] 3066[5] 3713[9] 4397[14]

Make Me Smyle *Stuart Kittow* a39 22
3 b g Cockney Rebel(IRE) Upstream (Prince Sabo)
4992[11] 5878[5] 6643[9] 7025[7] 7499[10]

Make Up *Noel Wilson* a60 56
3 b f Kyllachy Christmas Tart (IRE) (Danetime (IRE))
4394[7] 4953[8] 5247[4]

Makin (IRE) *Marco Botti* a74
2 b c Shirocco(GER) Cuca Vela (USA) (Devil's Bag (USA))
7324[10] 7868[2] (8147)

Making Eyes (IRE) *Hugo Palmer* a90 100
4 b m Dansili Lady's View (USA) (Distant View (USA))
(2067) 2882[3] (4316a) 5834[7] 6674[22] 7124a[7]

Makinson Lane (IRE) *Richard Fahey* a66 66
2 b c Acclamation Subtle Affair (IRE) (Barathea (IRE))
2594[9] 3989[5] 4707[7] 5292[5] 6337[6] 6972[6] 7614[2] 7965[5] 8072[4]

Malagenia (IRE) *L Riccardi* 103
4 b m Whipper(USA) Croanda (IRE) (Grand Lodge (USA))
(7565a)

Malanos (IRE) *Tony Carroll* a70 74
4 bb g Lord Of England(GER) Majorata (GER) (Acatenango (GER))
7018[13]

Malayan Mist (IRE) *D K Weld* 94
4 b m Dansili Misty Heights (Fasliyev (USA))
2515a[9]

Malaysia (GER) *R Dzubasz* 94
3 bb f Mamool(IRE) Mashinka (GER) (Alwuhush (USA))
6723a[10]

Malaysian Boleh *Simon Dow* a66
2 ch c Compton Place Orlena (USA) (Gone West (USA))
6772[9] 7497[6] 7894[4] 8302[6]

Malcheek (IRE) *Tim Easterby* a106 86
10 br g Lend A Hand Russland (GER) (Surumu (GER))
891[2] 368[5] 5802[10]

Malekat Jamal (IRE) *David Simcock* a65 71
3 b f Dutch Art Haretha (IRE) (Alhaarth (IRE))
4942[7] 5426[4] (6306)

Malekov (IRE) *Sir Henry Cecil* 91
3 b c Dansili Young And Daring (USA) (Woodman (USA))
5105[6] (5982) (6349) 7109[5]

Maligned (USA) *Richard Hannon* a47 45
3 ch f El Corredor(USA) Sue Warner (USA) (Forli (ARG))
4582[13] 5276[7] 5970[7] 6396[12]

Malih *Jamie Osborne* a67 76
3 b g Echo Of Light Sultry Lass (USA) (Private Account (USA))
(3539) 4256[4] 5008[3] 5721[5] 6401[11] 7131[7]

Maliha (IRE) *Kevin Ryan* 65
3 b f Amadeus Wolf Folcara (IRE) (Brief Truce (USA))
1320[8] 2141[11]

Malikayah (IRE) *D Camuffo* 96
4 b m Fasliyev(USA) Trombe (FR) (Bering)
1409a[2] 2112a[9] 2325a[8]

Malilla (IRE) *Clive Cox* 90
2 b f Red Clubs(IRE) Maleha (IRE) (Cape Cross (IRE))
2020[4] 4701[2] (5357) 5979[6]

Malindi *James Given* 67
3 b f Compton Place Mana Pools (IRE) (Brief Truce (USA))
2881[8] 3811[5] 4797[4]

Malingering *Hugo Palmer* 65
3 ch c Bahamian Bounty Orange Lily (Royal Applause)
1155[5] 1450[10]

Mallory Heights (IRE) *Luca Cumani* a73 26
2 b c Dalakhani(IRE) My Dark Rosaleen (Sadler's Wells (USA))
7130[8] 7868[9] 8071[2]

Mallt (IRE) *Philip McBride* a32 51
3 b f Kheleyf(USA) Titania (Fairy King (USA))
132[13] 479[3] 726[RR]

Malossol (USA) *G Botti* a100 105
3 b c Rahy(USA) Mambo Queen (USA) (Kingmambo (USA))
(1698a) 2951a[8] 6727a[7] 7286a[5] 7587a[7] 7985a[7]

Maltease Ah *Alan McCabe* a66 66
3 br f Librettist(USA) Manic (Polar Falcon (USA))
802[6] 1585[8] 2762[5] (5131) 5445[4] 5621[2] 6104[2] 6322[4] 6937[4] (7354) ◆ 7794[8]

Maluckyday (NZ) *Michael, Wayne & John Hawkes* 112
6 bb g Zabeel(NZ) Natalie Wood (NZ) (Yachtie (AUS))
7346a[5] 7621a[19]

Mama Quilla (USA) *William Haggas* 75
3 ch f Smart Strike(CAN) Myth To Reality (FR) (Sadler's Wells (USA))
3666[6] ◆ 4366[6] 4926[2] 5316[2] 6190[4] (7117)

Mambo Spirit (IRE) *Tony Newcombe* a79 75
8 b g Invincible Spirit(IRE) Mambodorga (USA) (Kingmambo (USA))
649[2] 893[9] 1091[6] 2870[8] 3139[4] ◆ 4000[5] 5150[4] 5933[5] 6094[6] 6277[5] 7297[3] 7820[6] 8159[12]

Mamma Rosa (IRE) *Patrick J Flynn* a71 80
4 br m Footstepsinthesand Mrs Seek (Unfuwain (USA))
6352a[4]

Mamoue (IRE) *D Prod'Homme* a81 77
3 b f Hurricane Run(IRE) Mamounia (GER) (Platini (GER))
364a[5]

Manaar (USA) *John Gosden* a52 20
3 b f Invasor(ARG) Ruby Summer (USA) (Mr Greeley (USA))
1501[12] 1736[10] 3079[13]

Manager Mick (IRE) *John Norton* 44
4 b g Clodovil(IRE) Nashua Song (IRE) (Kahyasi)
1247[5] 2635[5] 4867[16] 6101[11]

Managua *Barry Brennan* a63 86
6 gr g Kaldounevees(FR) Teresa Balbi (Master Willie)
960[7] 1418[15]

Manazel (USA) *John Gosden* a72
2 ch c Jazil(USA) Particle Stream (USA) (Pulpit (USA))
7021[3] (7306)

Manbaa (USA) *John Dunlop* a48 54
3 b f Jazil(USA) Itnab (Green Desert (USA))
1443[4] 2578[3] 3483[9]

Manchestar *Richard Fahey* a52
2 b g Elusive City(USA) Grande Terre (IRE) (Grand Lodge (USA))
7459[7]

Manchester (FR) *Niels Petersen* 79
4 ch g Domedriver(IRE) Metaline (FR) (Dr Fong (USA))
6091a[10]

Mandaean *Mahmood Al Zarooni* 113
3 b c Manduro(GER) Summertime Legacy (Darshaan)
2210[6] 6508a[6] 7054[8]

Mandalay King (IRE) *Marjorie Fife* a49 83
7 b g King's Best(USA) Mahamuni (IRE) (Sadler's Wells (USA))
1476[6] (1675) 1868[8] 2707[12] 3169[8] 3496[5] ◆ 4554[14] 5412[7] 6044[10] 6357[9] 6887[5] 7246[10]

Mandali (FR) *J-P Gallorini* a81 101
8 ch g Sinndar(IRE) Mandalara (IRE) (Lahib (USA))
3367a[7]

Mandeville (IRE) *Richard Hannon* 73
2 b f Kodiac Olympia Theatre (Galileo (IRE))
4011[11] 4555[4] (5331)

Mandianna (IRE) *Jo Crowley* a55 49
3 b f Manduro(GER) Lock's Heath (CAN) (Topsider (USA))
429[7] 734[10] 3701[5]

Mandistana (FR) *A De Royer-Dupre* 105
3 gr f Azamour(IRE) Minatlya (FR) (Linamix (FR))
1407a[4] 2741a[3] 3423a[2] 5142a[7]

Mandour (USA) *A De Royer-Dupre* 111
3 ch c Smart Strike(CAN) Mandesha (FR) (Desert Style (IRE))
2064a[3]

Mandy Layla (IRE) *Bryan Smart* a63 81
2 ch f Excellent Art Chervil (Dansili)
2415^4 ◆ (283^7) 4064^7 4820^{14} 5088^3 (5332) 5828^5 6238^7 6658^7 (6890) 7355^3

Mandy Lexi (IRE) *Patrick Morris* a69 75
2 gr f Dark Angel(IRE) Petite Arvine (USA) (Gulch (USA))
1997^2 2469^2 3034^4 3490^3 3747^4 4076^2 4324^7 5425^5 5748^3 6212^3 6658^6

Mandy's Boy (IRE) *Ed Dunlop* 77
2 b g Kyllachy African Queen (IRE) (Cadeaux Genereux)
6636^{14} (6844)

Mandy's Hero *Olivia Maylam* a74 55
4 b g Compton Place Bandanna (Bandmaster (USA))
208^7 277^6 424^9 5221^0 783^5

Mandy The Nag (USA) *Ed Dunlop* a68
2 bb f Proud Citizen(USA) Storm To Glory (USA) (Storm Bird (CAN))
7057^5 7460^4 (7796)

Maneki Neko (IRE) *Edwin Tuer* a75 52
10 b g Rudimentary(USA) Ardbess (Balla Cove)
5290^7 6339^7 6957^{11}

Man Fieber (FR) *J-M Capitte* a86 83
3 ch g Layman(USA) Goldfieber (GER) (Medaaly)
$(290a)$

Man From Seville *Sir Mark Prescott Bt* a57
2 ch g Duke Of Marmalade(IRE) Basanti (USA) (Galileo (IRE))
5098^6 5407^9 5742^9

Mangham (IRE) *George Foster* a74 73
7 b g Montjeu(IRE) Lovisa (USA) (Gone West (USA))
1796^8 2227^7 2922^{13} 3215^3 3492^6 3889^2 4349^6 4643^2 4768^9 5547^8 6313^4 6711^8 7095^6

Mangiapregaama (ITY) *B Grizzetti* 94
2 b f Dubawi(IRE) Lapistanera (IRE) (Cape Cross (IRE))
$7285a^4$

Mango Diva *Sir Michael Stoute* a76
2 b f Holy Roman Emperor(IRE) Mango Mischief (IRE) (Desert King (IRE))
6366^2 ◆

Mango Music *David Thompson* a48 83
9 ch m Distant Music(USA) Eurolink Sundance (Night Shift (USA))
2120^4 2636^4 3272^8 3993^9 4454^6 4717^{11} 5317^3 5543^{10} (6105) 6782^8 7447^3 7906^{11}

Manieree (IRE) *John M Oxx* 114
4 br m Medicean Sheer Spirit (IRE) (Caerleon (USA))
$5643a^5$ $6080a^4$ $6911a^7$

Man In The Arena *Dr Jon Scargill* a58 62
2 b g Bertolini(USA) Torver (Lake Coniston (IRE))
3617^6 4239^2 4539^{11} 5202^8 8103^5

Manisa (FR) *E Kurdu* 42
3 b f Okawango(USA) Miss Neoki (IRE) (Alhaarth (IRE))
$4477a^7$

Manjakani *Ismail Mohammed* a100 103
4 b h Barathea(IRE) Spring Oak (Mark Of Esteem (IRE))
$48a^3$ $319a^4$ ◆ $421a^3$ $759a^{12}$

Manjam (IRE) *Chris Gordon* a45 77
8 b g Almutawakel Mubkera (IRE) (Nashwan (USA))
2371^6

Mankini (IRE) *Luca Cumani* 58
3 b g Dansili Fashion Statement (Rainbow Quest (USA))
2381^8 2799^5 3399^5 ◆

Mano Diao *Mario Hofer* 99
3 br c Authorized(IRE) Messina (GER) (Dashing Blade)
$1900a^3$ $2966a^5$ $3683a^{14}$ $5782a^{11}$ $6291a^{10}$

Man Of Action (USA) *Saeed Bin Suroor* a73 105
5 ch g Elusive Quality(USA) Dixie Melody (USA) (Dixieland Band (USA))
$260a^6$ $586a^8$ 1130^{10} 3268^{10} 5101^2 5835^{13} 6674^{31}

Man Of My Word *Scott Dixon* a71 58
3 b g Milk It Mick Promised (IRE) (Petardia)
6^3 482^3 975^2 1176^4 2375^7 2981^{11} 7218^7 7395^5 7733^5 7917^9 8010^{10}

Man Of Plenty *John Dunlop* 88
3 ch g Manduro(GER) Credit-A-Plenty (Generous (IRE))
(1415) ◆ 2129^2 2889^4 6573^2 6964^7

Manomine *Clive Brittain* a69 69
3 b g Manduro(GER) Fascinating Hill (FR) (Danehill (USA))
(982) 1190^6 1728^4 2583^5 5036^5 5336^3 5636^2 6365^4 7768^9

Manshoor (IRE) *Lucy Wadham* a66 70
7 gr g Linamix(FR) Lady Wells (IRE) (Sadler's Wells (USA))
303^8 7315^{10} 7793^6

Mantoba *Brian Meehan* a102 106
4 b h Noverre(USA) Coming Home (Vettori (IRE))
$241a^9$ $682a^{10}$ $755a^{14}$

Many Elements *Lee Carter* a55 52
2 b g Multiplex Park's Girl (Averti (IRE))
4813^{13} 5485^6 5854^4 7156^5 7797^8 7891^2

Many Levels *John Berry* a37 37
2 br g Nayef(USA) Polygueza (FR) (Be My Guest (USA))
7330^{12} 7686^{11} 7840^7

Maoi Chinn Tire (IRE) *Jennie Candlish* a69 74
5 b g Mull Of Kintyre(USA) Primrose And Rose (Primo Dominie)
(2378) 3400^{10} 6981^{14}

Maori Dancer (USA) *Jeremy Noseda* a85 68
3 bb c Dynaformer(USA) Juke (USA) (Mr Prospector (USA))
5753^5 5982^4 (6614)

Mapenzi (FR) *H-A Pantall* 68
4 b m Sagamix(FR) Millessima (FR) (Bering)
$3207a^3$

Mappin Time (IRE) *Tim Easterby* a84 92
4 b g Orientate(USA) Different Story (USA) (Stravinsky (USA))
1362^4 1581^2 2029^8 (2488) 5368^{13} 5829^6 6165^{12}

Maputo *Mark Johnston* 75
2 b c Cape Cross(IRE) Insijaam (USA) (Secretariat (USA))
2308^2

Ma Quillet *Henry Candy* a68 72
4 gr m Tumbleweed Ridge Raffelina (USA) (Carson City (USA))
1609^4 3342^3 3785^{11}

Marabout (IRE) *Mel Brittain* a44 53
2 b g Haafhd Nirvana (Marju (IRE))
2923^4 3436^{10} 4310^6 5009^4 6121^{10} 6707^3

Mar Adentro (FR) *R Chotard* a89 113
6 b g Marju(IRE) Guermantes (Distant Relative)
$419a^6$ $681a^{12}$ $875a^{10}$ $2112a^8$ $2745a^{11}$

Maraheb *A Al Raihe* a107 105
4 b h Redoute's Choice(AUS) Hureya (USA) (Woodman (USA))
$317a^3$ ◆ $(416a)$ $590a^{13}$ $876a^{10}$

Marah Music *Peter Makin* a55 67
3 b g Royal Applause Marah (Machiavellian (USA))
1730^7 2203^2 2862^6 3315^2 3719^5 4943^2 5263^6 (5999)

Marajaa (IRE) *Willie Musson* a88 91
10 b g Green Desert(USA) Ghyraan (IRE) (Cadeaux Genereux)
(90) 198^2 299^3 (649)

Marble Silver (IRE) *Tim Easterby* 51
2 gr f Notnowcato Serena's Storm (IRE) (Statue Of Liberty (USA))
5339^{12} 5797^7 6257^4

Marceti (IRE) *E Leenders* 101
5 gr g Verglas(IRE) Darasa (FR) (Barathea (IRE))
$4634a^8$ $7320a^5$

March *Marco Botti* a72 85
2 b f Dutch Art Royal Pardon (Royal Applause)
3560^4 3959^3 (5255) (6984)

Marchand D'Or (FR) *M Delzangles* a56 114
9 gr g Marchand De Sable(USA) Fedora (FR) (Kendor (FR))
$3901a^3$ $4861a^8$ $6292a^5$

March Avril (FR) *J Boisnard* 65
3 b g Early March Poisson D'Avril (FR) (Nikos)
$5074a^0$

Marching Time *Doug Watson* a96 98
6 b g Sadler's Wells(USA) Marching West (USA) (Gone West (USA))
$47a^3$ $260a^7$

Marchwood *Amy Weaver* a60 70
2 b g Assertive Reeli Silli (Dansili)
1202^3 1330^2 2163^3 2402^3 5785^4 6093^2 6438^4 6499^2 6826^3 $8244a^{10}$

Marcret (ITY) *Marco Botti* a95 110
5 b h Martino Alonso(IRE) Love Secret (USA) (Secreto (USA))
$318a^3$ $590a^6$ $792a^5$ (1994) 2656^5 4610^7 $5848a^7$

Marcus Antonius *Jim Boyle* a72 71
5 b g Mark Of Esteem(IRE) Star Of The Course (USA) (Theatrical (IRE))
521^6 2396^3 2976^4

Marcus Augustus (IRE) *Jamie Osborne* a70 74
3 b g Holy Roman Emperor(IRE) Lulua (USA) (Bahri (USA))
41^2

Marcus Caesar (IRE) *David Barron* 57
2 b g Antonius Pius(USA) Skyscape (Zafonic (USA))
5756^2 7450^3

Marford Missile (IRE) *Amy Weaver* a82 86
3 b g Majestic Missile(IRE) Khawafi (Kris)
(897) 1998^{10} 2416^{10} 3288^6 3960^{12} 5406^2 6051^2 (6329) (6542) (6923) (7158) $8279a^7$

Margate *Charles Hills* a78
3 b f Mizzen Mast(USA) Cinnamon Bay (Zamindar (USA))
331^3 (918)

Margo Channing *Micky Hammond* 60
3 ch f Three Valleys(USA) Charlotte Vale (Pivotal)
2141^8 2679^6 3697^5 4210^2 4781^2 5373^6 5738^5 6924^8

Margot Did (IRE) *Michael Bell* 118
4 b m Exceed And Excel(AUS) Special Dancer (Shareef Dancer (USA))
$875a^8$ $1146a^{10}$ 1857^{16} 3238^{21} 4070^{10}

Marguerite St Just *Olivia Maylam* a57
2 b f Sir Percy Ships Watch (IRE) (Night Shift (USA))
2938^8 3282^9 3733^4 4934^3 ◆ 7432^{12} 7724^8 7973^6

Marhaba Malayeen (IRE) *Kevin Ryan* a62 74
2 b c Dutch Art Poyle Caitlin (IRE) (Bachir (IRE))
3168^8 3491^5 4427^2 4951^4 5715^2 (6121) 6597^5

Marhaba Malyoon (IRE) *David Simcock* 80
4 b g Tiger Hill(IRE) Mamonta (Fantastic Light (USA))
1880^8 2899^8 (3552)

Marhoona (USA) *John Dunlop* 65
3 b f Elusive Quality(USA) Elrehaan (Sadler's Wells (USA))
2279^{10} 2756^8 3543^{13}

Maria Crista (IRE) *J-C Rouget* a70 77
3 b f Red Clubs(IRE) Christa Maria (Alhaarth (IRE))
$211a^4$

Maria Letizia *John Gosden* a76 75
3 b f Galileo(IRE) Napoleon's Sister (IRE) (Alzao (USA))
4410^{12} 5048^5 6146^7 6802^3 7271^8

Maria Montez *J W Hills* a61 61
3 b f Piccolo Easy Feeling (IRE) (Night Shift (USA))
121^7 499^6 769^2 1006^4 1337^4 1731^6 2351^5 (2610) 3343^6 4509^4 5122^3 6002^{12}

Mariannes *John Dunlop* a42 31
3 br f Piccolo Madurai (Chilibang)
1590^4 2162^{12} 2788^{14}

Maria's Choice (IRE) *Sir Michael Stoute* a84 88
3 b g Oratorio(IRE) Amathusia (Selkirk (USA))
2856^{10} (3946) 4741^6 5554^2 6348^6 7168^4

Maria Vezzera *Marco Botti* a49 3
3 b f Authorized(IRE) La Virtu (IRE) (Mozart (IRE))
4931^8 6457^8 7005^6 7314^{16}

Mariella *Peter Chapple-Hyam* a45 51
2 ch f Piccolo Viva Maria (Hernando (FR))
6817^7 7916^7 8166^5

Marie's Fantasy *Zoe Davison* a60 58
3 b f Whipper(USA) My American Beauty (Wolfhound (USA))
27^7 219^4 326^4 394^5 564^2 734^7 (802) 1006^3 1307^4 1444^4 2388^9

Mariet *Suzy Smith* a61 62
3 ch f Dr Fong(USA) Medway (IRE) (Shernazar)
3340^6 4157^5 5100^8 5931^{13} 7811^6 8023^9

Marina Ballerina *Roy Bowring* a57 44
4 bb m Ballet Master(USA) Marinaite (Komaite (USA))
389^9 2048^{13}

Marina Piccola (IRE) *N Clement* 105
3 ch f Halling(USA) Marine Bleue (IRE) (Desert Prince (IRE))
$5142a^5$

Marina's Ocean *Roy Bowring* a41 45
8 b m Beat All(USA) Ocean Song (Savahra Sound)
98^6 2669^5 3988^{10}

Marine Boy (IRE) *Tom Dascombe* a86 87
6 b g One Cool Cat(USA) Bahamamia (Vettori (IRE))
5094^{12} 5752^5 6202^{12}

Marine Commando *Ruth Carr* 96
4 b g Pastoral Pursuits Carollan (IRE) (Marju (IRE))
1157^{16} 1438^{11} 1844^{19} 2284^7 3078^{10} 3845^{10} 5343^9 5829^{10} 6144^{10} 6665^9

Marine Girl *Stuart Kittow* a45 75
3 ch f Shamardal(USA) Aquamarine (Shardari)
(2380) 2942^{10} 4199^{10} 7511^{12}

Mariner's Cross (IRE) *Mahmood Al Zarooni* 106
3 b c Dubawi(IRE) Trilemma (Slip Anchor)
1467^{DSQ} 1859^2

Marineside (FR) *Kim Bailey* a40
5 b g Enrique Valgreen (FR) (Green Tune (USA))
3449^{11}

Marino Prince (FR) *Joanne Foster* a57 59
7 b g Dr Fong(USA) Hula Queen (USA) (Irish River (FR))
3440^{15}

Marinus (IRE) *Sylvester Kirk* a67 61
3 b g Holy Roman Emperor(IRE) Yawl (Rainbow Quest (USA))
1815 298^7 969^7 1320^{11} 1725^2 2205^4 2786^2 3451^2 (3943) 4506^2 5130^3 5428^3

Mariol (FR) *Robert Collet* a106 110
9 b g Munir La Bastoche (IRE) (Kaldoun (FR))
$814a^5$ $4790a^{10}$ $5648a^3$ $6943a^6$

Marishi Ten (IRE) *Andrew Balding* 66
2 b f Invincible Spirit(IRE) Scripture (IRE) (Sadler's Wells (USA))
2234^4

Maristar (USA) *Gerard Butler* a106 20
5 b m Giant's Causeway(USA) Jewel Princess (USA) (Key To The Mint (USA))
$1839a^6$

Maritimer (CAN) *H J Brown* a100 88
3 br c Stormy Atlantic(USA) Highland Mood (CAN) (Highland Ruckus (USA))
$1145a^{11}$

Marju Prince *Sir Michael Stoute* 57
2 b c Marju(IRE) Opera Comica (Dr Fong (USA))
5418^7 6796^{11}

Marju's Quest (IRE) *David Simcock* a61 57
2 b g Marju(IRE) Queen's Quest (Rainbow Quest (USA))
5963^7 6571^7 7458^8

Markab *Henry Candy* a107 112
9 b g Green Desert(USA) Hawafiz (Nashwan (USA))
2074^4 (2559) 5581^2

Mark Anthony (IRE) *Shaun Harris* a25 66
5 b g Antonius Pius(USA) Zuniga's Date (USA) (Diesis)
985^{11} 1224^4 1526^{13} 1823^9 2225^6 2839^5 2981^3 3442^{12} 3723^2 4087^6 4240^2 4390^2 4747^6 5081^5 5388^7 5996^8 6756^9 7318^7 7605^9

Mark Carmers *George Foster* 38
5 b g Mark Of Esteem(IRE) Queen Lea (FR) (Alzao (USA))
1662^7

Marketing Mix (CAN) *Thomas F Proctor* a99 116
4 bb m Medaglia d'Oro(USA) Instant Thought (USA) (Kris S (USA))
$5376a^2$ $7549a^2$

Market Puzzle (IRE) *Mark Brisbourne* a59 65
5 ch g Bahamian Bounty Trempjane (Lujain (USA))
891^6 1207^2 1562^7 2048^5 2467^3 2804^8 2886^6 3721^3 4349^3 5199^7 5310^{10} 6631^6

Market Town (USA) *Charles Hills* 79
2 b c Mizzen Mast(USA) Geographic (USA) (Empire Maker (USA))
5562^4 ◆ 6481^3

Markington *Peter Bowen* a74 73
9 b g Medicean Nemesia (Mill Reef (USA))
3661^7 4176^9 6407^{15}

Marksbury *Mark Brisbourne* a65 50
5 b m Mark Of Esteem(IRE) Penelewey (Groom Dancer (USA))
104^6 361^4 (531) 725^{10} 842^6 (1193) 1487^8 2161^6 2913^7 3053^{10} 3456^8 3559^6 3950^3 4042^{11}

Marlborough House *Mark Johnston* a52 51
2 b c Dylan Thomas(IRE) Eurolink Raindance (IRE) (Alzao (USA))
7492^6 8052^9

Marmalade Moon *Robert Cowell* a48 56
3 ch f Shamardal(USA) Frascati (Emarati (USA))
3438^3 4144^4

Mar Mar (IRE) *Saeed Bin Suroor* a81 86
2 b f Invincible Spirit(IRE) Queen Of Tara (IRE) (Sadler's Wells (USA))
4818^{10} 5978^2 6534^2 7190^5 (7686) ◆

Marmaris (FR) *C Lerner* a82 81
3 b f Divine Light(JPN) Margaret (TUR) (Octagonal (NZ))
$1127a^4$

Marmas *Marcus Tregoning* a72 69
3 ch c Sir Percy Kitabaat (IRE) (Halling (USA))
399^5 595^3 805^3 5788^6 6407^{10} 6738^6 (7169)

Marmot Bay (IRE) *Alastair Lidderdale* a68
2 b f Kodiac Tides (Bahamian Bounty)
5230^3 5715^8 6612^4 6766^6 6890^2 7156^3 (7379) 7650^2 (7865) (7932) 8007^{11} 8150^3 8161^4 8224^4 8258^4

Marpol (ITY) *G Botti* a88 80
4 b h Martino Alonso(IRE) Polisthea (ITY) (Barathea (IRE))
$16a^7$

Marquis Du Nonan (FR) *G Collet* a87 82
3 b c Apsis Marquise Fador (FR) (Northern Crystal)
$(365a)$

Mars (IRE) *A P O'Brien* a95
2 ch c Galileo(IRE) Massarra (Danehill (USA))
$(4161a)$ ◆

Marshall Art *David Evans* a53
3 b g Lawman(FR) Portrait Of A Lady (IRE) (Peintre Celebre (USA))
8021^3 8267^4

Marsh Dragon *Mark H Tompkins* a50 68
2 b f Beat Hollow Qilin (IRE) (Second Set (IRE))
5631^2 6132^6 7006^4

Marshgate Lane (USA) *Mahmood Al Zarooni* 100
3 b c Medaglia d'Oro(USA) Louvain (IRE) (Sinndar (IRE))
3399^2 ◆ (4067) ◆ 4741^3 6677^6 ◆ 7396^{19} ◆

Marshland *Mark Johnston* a70 53
2 b g Kheleyf(USA) Neptune's Bride (USA) (Bering)
1515^4 $1832a^4$

Marsh Warbler *Brian Ellison* a83 82
5 ch g Barathea(IRE) Echo River (USA) (Irish River (FR))
1056^9

Marster Parkes *John Quinn* a68 65
4 b g Nayef(USA) Lucky Parkes (Full Extent (USA))
869^6 1250^9 3549^4

Martha's Way *Michael Easterby* a56 58
3 b f Tiger Hill(IRE) Pilgrim's Way (USA) (Gone West (USA))
407^4 923^5 1012^3 1600^2 2340^{12}

Martial Art (IRE) *Andrew Balding* a80 80
2 ch g Compton Place Brush Strokes (Cadeaux Genereux)
3191^2 3770^2 4803^{12} 6815^4 7737^2 7926^6 8006^4

Martial Law (IRE) *David Pipe* 90
6 ch g Galileo(IRE) Tree Tops (Grand Lodge (USA))
4284^2 6191^3 7051^9

Martinas Delight (USA) *Alan Jarvis* 71
2 b f Johannesburg(USA) Lerici (USA) (Woodman (USA))
3473^4 5977^4 6437^2

Martin Chuzzlewit (IRE) *Sir Michael Stoute* 98
3 ch c Galileo(IRE) Alta Anna (FR) (Anabaa (USA))
1473^6 1978^3 5558^2 ◆ 6025^{18} 6248^6 6832^8

Martyr *George Baker* a88 103
7 b g Cape Cross(IRE) Sudeley (Dancing Brave (USA))
6197^{10} 6600^4 ◆ 7051^{10}

Marvada (IRE) *K J Condon* a106 106
4 b m Elusive City(USA) Theory Of Law (Generous (IRE))
$245a^6$ $617a^{10}$ 2078^9 $2515a^5$ $3091a^2$ $(3983a)$ $5286a^6$ $6061a^9$ $6917a^6$

Marvelino *Pat Eddery* a75 67
2 b c Captain Marvelous(IRE) Aimee's Delight (Robellino (USA))
1131^{11} 1211^2 2069^5 2370^2 2852^4 3242^{19} 3916^8 4093^{15} 5485^2 5854^2 8178^5

Marvellous Value (IRE) *Michael Dods* a84 99
7 b g Danetime(IRE) Despondent (IRE) (Broken Hearted)
1438^9 2286^8 3183^{11} 3624^{14}

Marvelous Miss (IRE) *Christine Dunnett* a17 32
2 b f Captain Marvelous(IRE) Abbeyleix Lady (IRE) (Montjeu (IRE))
3150^6 3545^{10} 4152^8

Marvo *Dai Burchell* a73 73
8 b g Bahamian Bounty Mega (IRE) (Petardia)
35^2 176^5 330^2 423^3 634^3 (1051) 1436^{12} 2044^7 2168^2 2392^3 3344^9 3967^5 4988^4 5783^{10} 6735^{11} 7473^8 7843^8 8010^9

Mary Fildes (IRE) *J S Moore* a99 95
3 b f Chineur(FR) Scarlet Empress (Second Empire (IRE))
$77a^3$ $418a^6$ $680a^2$ $873a^{11}$

Mary Frith *William Knight* a55 54
3 b f Acclamation Cutpurse Moll (Green Desert (USA))
5276^4 5448^2 6211^5 6778^7 7307^3

Marygold *Lee Carter* a42 80
3 b f Cockney Rebel(IRE) Contrary Mary (Mujadil (USA))
1457^{16} 1921^9 2347^9 3445^7 4235^{13} 6173^5 6739^8

Mary's Daughter *Richard Fahey* 97
2 b f Royal Applause Aunty Mary (Common Grounds)
2308^6 (2783) 3326^8 4820^{10} (5563) 6467^2 7065^5

Mary's Pet *Lee Carter* a67 67
5 b m Where Or When(IRE) Contrary Mary (Mujadil (USA))
1306^{12} (1987) 2760^2 2973^2 3618^9 4332^{15} 5047^3 6585^5 7512^6 8064^8 8268^{14}

Masaadr *James Tate* a56
2 br c Manduro(GER) Masandra (IRE) (Desert Prince (IRE))
7749^6 8185^4

Masai King (IRE) *Robin Bastiman* a8 56
2 b g Kheleyf(USA) Masai Queen (IRE) (Mujadil (USA))
3123^4 3937^7 5727^9 6283^3 6953^8

Masai Moon *Rod Millman* a91 90
8 b g Lujain(USA) Easy To Imagine (USA) (Cozzene (USA))
431[9] 563[2] 812[4] 1066[5] 1431[2] (1581) 2023[5] 2482[5] 3348[8] 4580[7] (5150) 5906[11] 6454[7] 6979[7] 7327[11] 7732[10] 7820[3] 8034[2]
Masamah (IRE) *Kevin Ryan* a97 118
6 gr g Exceed And Excel(AUS) Bethesda (Distant Relative)
2486[8] 4113[11] 4762[3] 5204[2] 5561[8] 5822[2] 6140[5]
Masaraat (FR) *F Vermeulen* a84 91
4 b m Alhaarth(IRE) Kahalah (IRE) (Darshaan)
1172a[0]
Masarah (IRE) *Clive Brittain* a73 99
2 b f Cape Cross(IRE) Fragrancy (IRE) (Singspiel (IRE))
2812[5] 3269[23] 4064[10] 4574[5] (4947) 5579[2] 6199[5] 6635[4] 7052[11]
Mascarpone (GER) *M Weiss* a97 83
8 b h Monsun(GER) Mamourina (IRE) (Barathea (IRE))
443a[6] 630a[10]
Mashaari (IRE) *John Gosden* a78 94
3 b g Monsun(GER) Thakafaat (IRE) (Unfuwain (USA))
2266[7] 2895[2] 3420[2] 4464[3] (7068)
Mashoor (FR) *B Al Shaibani* 112
5 b g Monsun(GER) Gontcharova (IRE) (Zafonic (USA))
759a[8]
Mashoora (IRE) *J-C Rouget* 111
3 ch f Barathea(IRE) Lovely Blossom (FR) (Spinning World (USA))
(1209a) 1884[12] 2742a[2] (3657a) 4633a[3] 6913a[5]
Mash Potato (IRE) *Michael Dods* 55
2 b g Whipper(USA) Salva (Grand Lodge (USA))
1753[8] 5410[8] 6042[12] 6753[2] 7173[5]
Maska Pony (IRE) *George Moore* 56
8 gr g Celtic Swing Clotted Cream (USA) (Eagle Eyed (USA))
4293[4] 4622[7] 4882[7] 6262[8] 7603[2]
Masked Dance (IRE) *Scott Dixon* a75 96
5 gr g Captain Rio Brooks Masquerade (Absalom)
1321[11] 1522[13] (2024) 2284[8] 3078[11] 4086[11] 4286[9] 4799[17] 5362[8] 5530[7] 7559[15]
Masked Marvel *John Gosden* 122
4 b h Montjeu(IRE) Waldmark (GER) (Mark Of Esteem (IRE))
1855[7] 2703[3] 4322[9] 5354[4] 6198[8]
Maslak (IRE) *Peter Hiatt* a81 69
8 b g In The Wings Jeed (IRE) (Mujtahid (USA))
(58) 221[3] (400) 594[3] 786[5] 830[2] 944[6] 1003[3] 1297[9] 1429[5]
Mason Hindmarsh *Karen McLintock* a73 73
5 ch g Dr Fong(USA) Sierra Virgen (USA) (Stack (USA))
(6311) 6706[5] (7454) 7610[3]
Masra *David Thompson* 51
9 b g Silver Patriarch(IRE) Go Sally Go (IRE) (Elbio)
1385[9] 4864[15] 5714[10]
Massachusetts *Dai Williams* 47
5 ch g Singspiel(IRE) Royal Passion (Ahonoora)
4904[11]
Massiyn (IRE) *M Halford* 110
3 ch c Zamindar(USA) Masilia (IRE) (Kahyasi)
5027a[2] 6271a[2]
Mass Rally (IRE) *Michael Dods* a82 106
5 b g Kheleyf(USA) Reunion (IRE) (Be My Guest (USA))
871[11] 1522[14] 2284[5] 3183[2] 3624[5] 4086[3] 4367[2] 5487[2] 6244[10] (6466) 7066[14] 7397[3] 7690[8]
Master Bond *Bryan Smart* a77 83
3 b g Misu Bond(IRE) Bond Royale (Piccolo)
1658[2] ◆ 2256[18] 5167[8] 6525[8] 7023[6] 7291[2] 8232[4] 8272[8]
Master Chipper *Michael Dods* 57
3 ch g Medicean Spiralling (Pivotal)
1479[12] 2453[2] 3066[12] 3325[5] 4771[12]
Mastered (IRE) *John Best* a53
2 ch c Refuse To Bend(IRE) Woodmaven (USA) (Woodman (USA))
8262[5]
Masterel (ITY) *Marco Botti* a90 93
3 b c Masterful(USA) Misorella (IRE) (King's Best (USA))
1375[3]
Master Hamilton *Tobias B P Coles* a29
2 ch g Mount Nelson Oomph (Shareef Dancer (USA))
8172[6] 8262[10]
Master Jack *Paul Burgoyne* a28 50
4 b g Avonbridge Inch By Inch (Inchinor)
7005[10]
Master Kid (DEN) *Bent Olsen* 88
7 b h Academy Award(IRE) Stolga (FR) (Baillamont (USA))
4863a[8]
Master Leon *Bryan Smart* a79 65
5 b g Monsieur Bond(IRE) Bollin Rita (Rambo Dancer (CAN))
287[12]
Master Ming (IRE) *Brian Meehan* 84
2 b c Excellent Art China Pink (Oasis Dream)
4472[12] 5119[2] (5797) 7331[3]
Master Mylo (IRE) *Robert Cowell* a82 88
5 ch g Bertolini(USA) Sheboygan (IRE) (Grand Lodge (USA))
3049[11] 3977[3] 4689[12] 5480[10] 6566[3] 7559[13]
Master Of Ages (IRE) *Mark Johnston* a42 82
3 b g Exceed And Excel(AUS) Historian (IRE) (Pennekamp (USA))
2265[14] 2714[11] 3890[9] 7203[8]
Master Of Arts (USA) *Mark Johnston* a78 98
7 bb g Swain(IRE) Grazia (Sharpo)
5712[4] 6135[2]
Master Of Dance (IRE) *Keith Dalgleish* a77 76
5 ch g Noverre(USA) Shambodia (IRE) (Petardia)
1367 301[2] ◆ 403[2] 463[3] 722[8] 2922[6] 3215[4] 3335[8] 3888[6] 4089[2] (4134) 4389[3]
Master Of Disguise *Brian Baugh* a81 78
6 b g Kyllachy St James's Antigua (IRE) (Law Society (USA))
215[2] (327) 545[2] 1643[7] 2122[4] 2264[8] 2690[5] 2982[3] 3778[12] 4400[10] 4743[8] 4963[7] 7775[6] 7864[11] 8144[2]
Master Of Hounds (USA) *William Haggas* a115 115
4 b h Kingmambo(USA) Silk And Scarlet (Sadler's Wells (USA))
144a[2] ◆ 488a[3] 590a[3] (879a) 1150a[8] (5869a) 7239[5] 8042a[10]
Master Of Song *Roy Bowring* a68 67
5 ch g Ballet Master(USA) Ocean Song (Savahra Sound)
97[8] 636[11] (2555) 4627[8] 7347[6] 8137[9]
Masteroftherolls (IRE) *Saeed Bin Suroor* a104 103
4 b h Refuse To Bend(IRE) Miss Sally (IRE) (Danetime (IRE))
246a[2] 489a[3] 792a[10] 6400[2] 6879[3]
Master Of War *Richard Hannon* 108
2 ch c Compton Place Mamma Morton (IRE) (Elnadim (USA))
2415[5] (2662) 3240[9] (4058) 4736[2] 5833[3] 6483[2] 7049[7]
Master Rooney (IRE) *Bryan Smart* 94
6 bb g Cape Cross(IRE) Wimple (USA) (Kingmambo (USA))
1438[13] 2337[8] 4451[2] 5343[3] 6028[10] 6543[6] 7291[14]
Masters Blazing *John Ryan* a68 78
3 ch g Iceman Loquacity (Diktat)
841[0] 362[5] 595[6] 743[3] 1046[5] (1260) 1519[4] (2089) 2150[6] 2408[8] 3383[5] 4223[4] 4772[10] 5322[9] 6141[4] 6502[9] 6986[7] 7520[2] 7639[3] 8035[3] 8229[11]
Masters Club *John Ryan* a66 63
3 b g Red Clubs(IRE) Waaedah (USA) (Halling (USA))
38[3] 255[2] 1413[3] 1731[4] 1790[6]
Masterstroke (USA) *A Fabre* 114
3 b c Monsun(GER) Melikah (IRE) (Lammtarra (USA))
2108a[2] 3204a[2] (5650a) 6912a[3]
Master Wizard *Jane Chapple-Hyam* a68
2 b c Motivator Enchanted (Magic Ring (IRE))
8068[2]
Mataajir (USA) *Derek Shaw* a71 39
4 b g Redoute's Choice(AUS) Hamasah (USA) (Irish River (FR))
(7) 104[2] ◆ 263[6] 361[3] 478[5] 1052[2] 1191[5] 1384[11] 7925[11] 8005[10] 8236[6] 8271[10]
Mataaleb *Lydia Pearce* a89 80
5 b h Dalakhani(IRE) Elfaslah (IRE) (Green Desert (USA))
745[3] 971[5] 1374[4] ◆ 2248[9] (2863) 3502[6] 3827[6]
Mata Hari Blue *John Holt* a67 78
6 ch m Monsieur Bond(IRE) Feeling Blue (Missed Flight)
997[7] 1177[7] (1480) 1638[4] 2070[6] 2482[4] 2789[3] 3103[2] 3314[2] 3749[4]
Matauri Pearl (IRE) *Fredrik Reuterskiold* a33 81
3 b f Hurricane Run(IRE) Moonrise (GER) (Grand Lodge (USA))
4359a[11]
Matavia Bay (IRE) *Alan Jarvis* a68 71
4 b g Bahamian Bounty Rosewater (GER) (Winged Love (IRE))
1379[9] 1702[3] (2821) 3782[3] 5310[11] 6798[7]
Match Point (FR) *Niels Petersen* a74 86
6 gr m Verglas(IRE) Danira (IRE) (Danehill (USA))
2159a[3]
Matjar (IRE) *Joseph Quinn* a72 72
9 ch g Grand Lodge(USA) Tajawuz (Kris)
4657[7]
Matsunosuke *Alan Coogan* a63 66
10 b g Magic Ring(IRE) Lon Isa (Grey Desire)
2024[5] 2861[6] 3159[7] 3707[8] 5272[10] 5502[12] 5791[8] 5971[10]
Mattoral *Chris Gordon* a74 77
4 b g High Chaparral(IRE) Angry Bark (USA) (Woodman (USA))
1890[4] 2086[2]
Matured *Ralph Beckett* a70 35
3 b f Manduro(GER) Time Away (IRE) (Darshaan)
4797[10] 6148[2] 6614[3] 7739[5]
Matusalen (SPA) *M Delcher-Sanchez* a82 95
3 b c Caradak(IRE) Bixaare (IRE) (Xaar)
679a[5] 873a[8]
Maudlin Magdalen (IRE) *Donal Kinsella* a56 60
2 b f Dylan Thomas(IRE) Carolines Secret (Inchinor)
4161a[8]
Maun Vrat (IRE) *Ed Dunlop* a82
3 b f Montjeu(IRE) Delauncy (Machiavellian (USA))
4648[4] 6148[3] 6839[3] 7594[5]
Maureen (IRE) *Richard Hannon* 107
2 b f Holy Roman Emperor(IRE) Exotic Mix (FR) (Linamix (FR))
(3473) 4064[2] ◆ (4577) ◆ 6672[9]
Mauriac (GER) *A Wohler* 90
2 bb c Clodovil(IRE) Moonlight Dance (GER) (Pentire)
5755a[4] 7091a[7]
Maurice (GER) *S Smrczek* a72 88
2 b c Big Shuffle(USA) Moyenne (IRE) (Trans Island)
7091a[5] 7597a[3]
Maven *Tim Easterby* a78 88
4 b m Doyen(IRE) Bollin Jeannie (Royal Applause)
216[12] 888[2] 1133[12] 1276[4] 1439[2] 1656[5] 2093[4] (2498) 2884[3] 3287[3] 3813[2] (4608) 5492[12] 6202[4] 7034[3] 7601[6]
Maverik *Ralph Beckett* a87 91
4 ch g Iceman Nouvelle Lune (Fantastic Light (USA))
11[3] (280) (631a) 1212[4] 1510[8] 2257[10] 5120[2] (5667) ◆ 6036[13] 7083[12]
Ma Victoryan (FR) *C Baillet* a84 96
3 b f Kheleyf(USA) Victorian Dancer (IRE) (Groom Dancer (USA))
(17a) 3987a[0] 7803a[7]
Mawaakef (IRE) *J R Jenkins* a94 97
4 b g Azamour(IRE) Al Euro (FR) (Mujtahid (USA))
1771[2] 674[2] 1321[6] 1679[3] (1741) 2250[3] 2657[2] ◆ 3508[12] 4099[9] 5075[7] 6601[6] 7175[10] 7626[9] (7986) 8227[5]
Mawaqeet (USA) *Sir Michael Stoute* 96
3 b g Dynaformer(USA) Lady Ilsley (USA) (Trempolino (USA))
2430[2] ◆ 3484[3] (4259) 4700[2] 6415[4]
Mawasem *Sir Michael Stoute* a92 71
3 b g Street Cry(IRE) Saree (Barathea (IRE))
1467[8] ◆ (1922) 2916[9]
Mawhub *Saeed Bin Suroor* a86 82
3 b g Singspiel(IRE) Native Blue (Seeking The Gold (USA))
1467[9] (5555) 5951[8] 7194[2] 7672[6]
Mawjoodah *Brian Ellison* a76 67
4 ch m Cadeaux Genereux Isis (USA) (Royal Academy (USA))
1193[3] 1827[7] 2146[6] 2693[5] 3230[6] 3618[6] 3943[6] 4495[13] 4653[2] 4887[11]
Mawson *Roger Charlton* a57 56
2 b c Starcraft(NZ) No Fear No Favour (AUS) (Carnegie (IRE))
7372[6] 7705[6]
Maxamillion Bounty *Michael Dods* a67 70
4 ch g Bahamian Bounty Never Say Deya (Dansili)
114[2]
Maxentius (IRE) *Peter Chapple-Hyam* 105
2 b g Holy Roman Emperor(IRE) Guantanamera (IRE) (Sadler's Wells (USA))
(2609) ◆ (3562) ◆ 4098[3] 4698[10] 6243[4] 6910a[6] 7404[7]
Maxi Dress (IRE) *John Gosden* a35
2 b f Shamardal(USA) Fashion Trade (Dansili)
8185[8]
Maximool (GER) *R Dzubasz* 58
3 bb c Mamool(IRE) Mondalita (GER) (Alkalde (GER))
7282a[10]
Maxios *J E Pease* 118
4 b h Monsun(GER) Moonlight's Box (USA) (Nureyev (USA))
2744a[2] 5117a[5] (6464a) 6898a[6]
Maxiyow (IRE) *Terry Clement* a49 28
4 b m Royal Applause Fudge (Polar Falcon (USA))
399[6] 519[7] 741[11]
Max The Machine *Derek Shaw* a69 69
2 b c Intikhab(USA) Digamist Girl (IRE) (Digamist (USA))
3182[13] 3381[5] 3627[4] 3937[2] 6579[6] 6808[6]
Maxwil *Mrs K Burke* a78 52
7 b g Storming Home Lady Donatella (Last Tycoon)
5002[7] 5673[6]
Mayaasem *Charles Hills* 76
2 b c Royal Applause Rolexa (Pursuit Of Love)
2663[4] 3777[2] 4507[4]
Mayan Flight (IRE) *Tony Carroll* a56 61
4 b g Hawk Wing(USA) Balimaya (IRE) (Barathea (IRE))
160[2] (200) 602[3] 924[2] 2137[6] 2391[2] 2769[3] 4994[4] 5481[3] 5939[7]
Maybe (IRE) *A P O'Brien* 114
3 b f Galileo(IRE) Sumora (IRE) (Danehill (USA))
1884[3] ◆ 2658[5] 4065[5] 6061a[8]
Maybeagrey *Tim Easterby* a72 78
3 b f Shamardal(USA) Grey Again (Unfuwain (USA))
1934 1167[9] 1641[5] 1915[5] 3066[3] 3616[8] 3910[3] (4311) (4781) 5373[2] 6263[4] 7032[14] 7294[2]
Maybe I Wont *James Moffatt* a43 70
7 b g Kyllachy Surprise Surprise (Robellino (USA))
4955[2] 6126[6] 6957[5]
Maybeme *Neville Bycroft* a39 67
6 b m Lujain(USA) Malvadilla (IRE) (Doyoun)
1439[5] 1913[8] 2260[11] (3022) 3180[11] 4682[6] 5226[5] 5622[7] 6556[2] 6794[3] 6988[6] 7495[3]
May Be Some Time *Stuart Kittow* a42 79
4 ch g Iceman Let Alone (Warning)
2574[6] (3999) 5132[2] 5667[8] 6734[9] 7639[9]
May Boy *Ron Hodges* a49 33
6 br g Bandmaster(USA) Kathies Pet (Tina's Pet)
7105[11] 7488[6] 7671[5] 7752[4] 8241[4]
May Contain Nuts *Brendan Powell* a68 80
4 b g Auction House(USA) Sweet Coincidence (Mujahid (USA))
2411[6] 2978[12]
Maydream *Jimmy Fox* a61 75
5 b m Sea Freedom Maedance (Groom Dancer (USA))
(2167) (2502) 3187[7] 4606[4] 5306[9] 5789[5]
Mayfield Girl (IRE) *Mel Brittain* 82
2 br f One Cool Cat(USA) Rose Of Mooncoin (IRE) (Brief Truce (USA))
1131[3] ◆ 1435[5] (1861) 2252[2] 2603[5] 3250[4] (4071) 4614[4] 4827[3] 5563[13] 6883[18]
Mayforde Jack *Jo Hughes* a36
3 b g Septieme Ciel(USA) Jessinca (Minshaanshu Amad (USA))
283[5] 1138[9]
Mayo Lad (IRE) *Richard Hannon* a76 80
3 b c Holy Roman Emperor(IRE) Mrs Marsh (Marju (IRE))
1331[2] ◆ (1529) 1622[2] 1985[2] 2898[3] 3388[3] 4603[2] (5132) 5705[6] 6209[8]
Mayoman (IRE) *David O'Meara* a64 94
7 b g Namid America Lontana (FR) (King's Theatre (IRE))
(1237) 1642[9] (2289) 2717[9] 3127[9] (3903) 5829[2] ◆ 6466[17]
Mayo Miss *Tony Carroll* a18
3 b f Byron Noor El Houdah (IRE) (Fayruz)
1705[12]
Maypole Joe (IRE) *David Evans* a56 48
2 b g Iffraaj Spanish Needle (Green Desert (USA))
1131[10] 1202[5] 2784[10] 3084[3] 4195[4] 7854[5] 7971[4] 8003[4] 8093[10] 8132[3] 8164[3] 8186[6]
May's Boy *Mark Usher* a77 79
4 gr h Proclamation(IRE) Sweet Portia (IRE) (Pennekamp (USA))
131[5] 378[10] 517[4] 669[5] 942[6] 1378[8] (1611) 2044[10] 2574[9] 3039[8] 3511[11] 3958[6] 5008[4] 5741[7] 6208[7] 8010[4] 8162[5]
Mayson *Richard Fahey* a100 121
4 b h Invincible Spirit(IRE) Mayleaf (Pivotal)
1129[3] (1469) (1857) 2179[13] 3623[5] (4100) 6908a[2]
Maz *Alan Bailey* a70 68
4 ch m Needwood Blade Lady Mytton (Lake Coniston (IRE))
(842) 2801[9] 5218[7] 5426[5] 6176[4] 6458[7] 7348[5] 7474[5] 8079[4] 8261[4]
Mazaaher *Marcus Tregoning* a62 55
2 b c Elnadim(USA) Elutrah (Darshaan)
6845[4] 7306[8] 7627[7]
Mazameer (IRE) *F Head* 108
2 b c Green Desert(USA) Straight Miss (IRE) (In The Wings)
(4632a) 5398a[6]
Mazeppa *Keith Dalgleish* 74
2 b c Byron Howards Heroine (IRE) (Danehill Dancer (IRE))
2594[3] 2873[2] (3112) 3695[4]
Mazeydd *Roger Varian* a90 95
3 b c Motivator Jathaabeh (Nashwan (USA))
5006[7] (5688) 5973[4]
Mazij *Peter Hiatt* a83 74
4 b m Haafhd Salim Toto (Mtoto)
285[3] 501[2] 751[9] 1114[3] 2093[12] 3015[7] 3290[4] 3704[7] 4626[7] (5124) 5413[8] 5913[9] 6794[9] 7353[12]
Mazovian (USA) *Michael Chapman* a79 71
4 b g E Dubai(USA) Polish Style (USA) (Danzig (USA))
13[2] 139[3] 496[2] (585) 670[6] 834[8] (1177) 1431[7] 1581[5] 1958[8] 2549[5] 2981[4] 3287[6] 3589[9] 3914[15] (4143) 4401[7] 5322[8] 6319[12] 6811[7] 7436[3] 8236[5]
Mcbirney (USA) *Paul D'Arcy* a71 88
5 b g Danehill Dancer(IRE) Dear Girl (IRE) (Fairy King (USA))
1134[4] 1513[12] 2328[2] 2801[5] 3278[7] 3594[11] 4772[7] 5323[7] 5767[5] 6251[4] 6819[8] 7251[2] 8214[3]
Mcconnell (USA) *Richard Guest* a76 66
7 ch g Petionville(USA) Warsaw Girl (IRE) (Polish Precedent (USA))
(12) 134[4] 367[4] 463[5] (562) (671) 812[5] 906[3] 999[3] 1578[3] 1771[8] 2405[5]
McCool Bannanas *James Unett* a74 69
4 b g Firebreak Dances With Angels (IRE) (Mukaddamah (USA))
361[2] 463[4] 538[3] 771[2] 922[6] (1002) 1391[6] 1659[11] 3559[9] 4541[2] 5322[5] 8152[3]
Mcmonagle (USA) *Alan Brown* a79 76
4 ch g Mizzen Mast(USA) Dippers (USA) (Polish Numbers (USA))
4954[10] 6131[15] 6410[5] 6709[8] 6934[6] 7203[2] 7411[6] 7666[4] 7799[8]
Mcvicar *Mick Channon* a66 75
3 b g Tobougg(IRE) Aries (GER) (Big Shuffle (USA))
1160[7] 1440[8] 2269[8] 3543[5] 3998[2] (4254) 4578[5]
Meandmyshadow *Alan Brown* a62 79
4 ch m Tobougg(IRE) Queen Jean (Pivotal)
1526[5] 2314[6] 2476[8] 3021[4] 3460[7] 3845[8] 4174[3] (4547) 4793[4] (5317) (5915) 6123[2] 6406[5] 7247[9] 7483[7]
Meandre (FR) *A Fabre* 122
4 gr h Slickly(FR) Penne (FR) (Sevres Rose (IRE))
1855[4] 2989a[2] (3424a) (4383a) 6293a[2] 6912a[12] 8040a[3]
Mean It (IRE) *Tom Tate* 83
3 b g Danehill Dancer(IRE) Lilissa (IRE) (Doyoun)
3384[2] (4293)
Measured Approval (IRE) *Patrick J Flynn* a62 81
4 b g Acclamation Measured Leap (Inchinor)
6716a[9]
Measuring Time *Mahmood Al Zarooni* a108 105
4 b g Dubai Destination(USA) Inchberry (Barathea (IRE))
241a[2]
Mecca's Team *Michael Dods* a29 71
4 ch m Ishiguru(USA) Clancassie (Clantime)
1246[7] 1800[10] 2878[5] 4245[5] (4552) 5190[5] 5739[5] 6264[12] 6886[2]
Mecox Bay (IRE) *Jennie Candlish* a57 50
5 b g Noverre(USA) Birdsong (IRE) (Dolphin Street (FR))
111[4] 1112[4] 1719[7] 2134[3]
Mecox Meadow (USA) *Michael Bell* 14
3 rg g El Prado(IRE) Chalamont (IRE) (Kris)
5901[7] 6792[14]
Medam *Shaun Harris* a62 51
3 b f Medicean Mamounia (IRE) (Green Desert (USA))
1067[9] 1386[8] 1531[8] 2404[2] (2862) 3567[4] 4154[5] 5247[6] 5874[5] (6322) 6640[6] 6823[5] 7201[9]
Medea (IRE) *Sir Michael Stoute* a84 69
3 ch f Danehill Dancer(IRE) Scoop Of Gold (USA) (Giant's Causeway (USA))
2050[3] 3279[2]
Medecis Mountain *John Wainwright* 33
3 b g Medecis Moon Cat (IRE) (Desert Story (IRE))
2339[7] 2881[9] 3273[6] 4549[11] 5113[7] 5589[11] 5623[11]
Medeeba *Zoe Davison* a47
3 b g Overbury(IRE) Jewel (IRE) (Cyrano De Bergerac)
3735[14] 4334[9] 4871[6]
Medeleck (FR) *Mme C De La Soudiere-Niault* a82 95
2 b c Medecis Electricity (Elusive City (USA))
7828a[9]
Medhyaar *William Haggas* a69 74
3 b f Bahri(USA) Kawn (Cadeaux Genereux)
2935[2] ◆ 3975[6] 5299[2] 5805[2] 6582[2]
Media Hype *Mrs K Burke* a104 104
5 b h Tiger Hill(IRE) Hyperspectra (Rainbow Quest (USA))
(1275) 1657[2] ◆ (2257) 3635[5] 4112[3] 6091a[3] 7630[4] (7895)
Media Jury *John Wainwright* a52 61
5 b g Lucky Owners(NZ) Landofheartsdesire (IRE) (Up And At 'Em)
3463[7] 4174[16] 4631[5] 4963[6] 5223[12] 5389[4] 5590[14] 6180[7] 6640[3] 7362[7] 7465[5]

Media Stars *Robert Johnson* a60 64
7 gr g Green Desert(USA) Starine (FR) (Mendocino (USA))
1251[11] 1631[5] 1829[8] 2670[2] 3353[10] 4594[13] 4716[14] 4955[8] 6126[11] 6561[7] 7102[12]

Medicean Man *Jeremy Gask* a108 113
6 ch g Medicean Kalindi (Efisio)
1033[5] 1498[7] 2074[5] 2559[5] 2931[3] ◆ 3238[4] 3371[19] 3877[8] 7236[11]

Medici Dancer *Tim Easterby* 69
2 ch f Medicean Dance Away (Pivotal)
6042[6] 6356[9] 6781[2] 7290[2] (7440) 7687[6]

Medici Music *Luca Cumani* 75
3 b g Medicean Balalaika (Sadler's Wells (USA))
3975[2] 4746[3] ◆ 5315[3] 6205[10]

Medici Time *Tim Easterby* 94
7 gr g Medicean Pendulum (Pursuit Of Love)
2177[11] 2596[8] 3127[14] 4013[5] 4554[15] (5362) 5703[11] 6165[16]

Medicoe *Sir Mark Prescott Bt* 77
2 ch g Medicean Blue Dream (IRE) (Cadeaux Genereux)
3303[7] 3973[3] ◆ 4612[3] (4907) 5602[5] 6344[5] 6699[8]

Medieval Bishop (IRE) *Tim Walford* a56 77
3 b g Bachelor Duke(USA) On The Backfoot (IRE) (Bob Back (USA))
4329[10] 4714[13] 5414[10] 6103[9] 6474[6] 6807[2] 7248[6]

Medipearl (FR) *F Chappet* a69 71
2 b c Medecis Cat's Pearl (FR) (Enrique)
5378a[3]

Mediterranean Sea (IRE) *J R Jenkins* a80 77
6 b m Medecis High Glider (High Top)
(381) 810[2] 978[4] 1175[3] 3769[7] 4884[5] 5718[3] 7315[2]

Medlaur *James Given* a44 39
3 ch f Medicean Laurena (GER) (Acatenango (GER))
552[9] 1132[10] 1448[5]

Medolina (USA) *Todd Pletcher* 101
3 b f Aragorn(IRE) Melody Maiden (USA) (Saint Ballado (CAN))
4478a[5]

Meeting In Paris (IRE) *Brian Meehan* a53 66
2 b f Dutch Art Sharplaw Star (Xaar)
6335[3] 6936[11]

Meetings Man (IRE) *Micky Hammond* 85
5 gr g Footstepsinthesand Missella (IRE) (Danehill (USA))
1239[8] 2031[7] 2504[9] 2751[10] 3129[5] 4499[3] 4910[3] 5622[6] 6076[14] 6957[7]

Meet Joe Black (IRE) *David Evans* a53 47
3 bb g Red Clubs(IRE) Pascali (Compton Place)
30[6] 132[4] 194[6] 294[3] 393[6] 619[6] 1260[9] 1287[3]

Meet Me Halfway *Chris Wall* a70 59
2 b f Exceed And Excel(AUS) Pivotal Drive (IRE) (Pivotal)
2343[6] 3788[5] 4408[6] 5160[2] (5749) 6016[2]

Megalala (IRE) *John Bridger* a83 84
11 b g Petardia Avionne (Derrylin)
119[3] (374) 733[2] 987[5] 1186[2] 2810[8] (2985) 3767[11] 4365[11] 4805[11] 5665[5] 5767[7] 6703[14]

Megaleka *Chris Fairhurst* 57
2 b f Misu Bond(IRE) Peyto Princess (Bold Arrangement)
4344[12] 5168[4] 5733[2] 6629[7] 6954[5]

Megamunch (IRE) *Linda Stubbs* a62 75
2 b g Camacho Liscoa (IRE) (Foxhound (USA))
3576[2] (3902) 4471[4] 5109[5] 5475[7] 6511[4]

Meganisi (IRE) *Rebecca Curtis* 106
5 b g Galileo(IRE) Cland Di San Jore (IRE) (Lando (GER))
2267[2] 5826[12]

Meglio Ancora *Richard Ford* a66 74
5 ch g Best Of The Bests(IRE) May Fox (Zilzal (USA))
(5258) (5804) 5998[4] 8051[14] 8113[10] 8241[11]

Mehdi (IRE) *Brian Meehan* a104 99
3 b c Holy Roman Emperor(IRE) College Fund Girl (IRE) (Kahyasi)
142a[4] 485a[3] 1216[4] 5278[5] 5664[4] 6024[10] 6835[7]

Meia Noite *Alan McCabe* a67 64
5 b m Tobougg(IRE) Executive Lady (Night Shift (USA))
122[4] 496[5] 658[6] 838[7] 919[6]

Meisho Kampaku (JPN) *Yoshiyuki Arakawa* 114
5 bb h Grass Wonder(USA) Dancing Happiness (JPN) (Dance In The Dark (JPN))
7872a[15]

Meisho Olivia (FR) *S Kobayashi* a74
4 gr m Layman(USA) Seulaseule (IRE) (Highest Honor (FR))
116a[2]

Melanippe (IRE) *P D Deegan* a53 19
2 b f Shirocco(GER) Roshanak (IRE) (Spinning World (USA))
6853a[8]

Melbourne Memories *Clive Cox* 93
2 b f Sleeping Indian Three Decades (IRE) (Invincible Spirit (IRE))
5003[3] (5773) 6227[7] (6871) (7518)

Melivea (FR) *C Laffon-Parias* a71 70
2 b f Green Tune(USA) Cerita (IRE) (Wolfhound (USA))
8193a[8]

Meljana (IRE) *Alan Swinbank* a24 37
3 ch g Strategic Prince Fey Lady (IRE) (Fairy King (USA))
1053[10] 1479[U] 2313[5] 2592[6] 3233[8]

Mellor *Chris Wall*
3 b g Echo Of Light Lumiere D'Espoir (FR) (Saumarez)
2125[10]

Melodee Princess (IRE) *Ronald Harris* a62 53
2 b f Acclamation Pitrizzia (Lando (GER))
2069[8] 2541[8] 3269[24] 4816[5] 5749[5] 6611[7] 7056[7] 7649[5]

Melodie D'Aze (FR) *N Leenders* a77 77
5 ch m Martaline Lady D'Aze (FR) (Rifapour (IRE))
93a[10]

Melodique (FR) *C Laffon-Parias* 93
2 b f Falco(USA) Elodie Des Charmes (FR) (Diesis)
(6225a) 7013a[6]

Melodize *David O'Meara* a37 62
4 ch m Iceman Rhapsodize (Halling (USA))
6786[7]

Melodrama (IRE) *David Lanigan* a72 55
3 b f Oratorio(IRE) Lila (Zafonic (USA))
1424[5] (2353) 3088[6] 5164[2] (5408) 6213[3]

Melody Of Love *Ann Duffield* 101
2 b f Haafhd Tamzin (Hernando (FR))
4344[5] (4921) ◆ 5678[2] (6467) 7052[4] 7622a[4]

Melvin The Grate (IRE) *Andrew Balding* a77 77
2 b c Danehill Dancer(IRE) Hawala (IRE) (Warning)
6330[2] (7705)

Memory Cloth *Brian Ellison* a92 104
5 b g Cape Cross(IRE) Gossamer (Sadler's Wells (USA))
846[6] 1431[3] (1670) ◆ 1854[2] 2127[3] 2911[10] 3534[3] (3626) 4112[8] 4761[15] 6024[16]

Memphis Man *David Evans* a63 66
9 b g Bertolini(USA) Something Blue (Petong)
122[2] 179[10] 215[7] 353[7] 425[8] 526[9] 623[5] 912[3] 1387[8] 1528[7] 2617[4] 3466[8] 3701[4] 4332[6] 4928[7] (4993) 5444[6] 5893[7] 6000[5] 6158[5] 7512[11] 7929[3] 8077[5]

Memphis Tennessee (IRE) *A P O'Brien* a81 118
4 b h Hurricane Run(IRE) Hit The Sky (IRE) (Cozzene (USA))
(2027) 3369[12]

Menadati (USA) *Peter Hiatt* a72 78
4 b g More Than Ready(USA) Ramatuelle (CHI) (Jeune Homme (USA))
199[6] 374[3] 648[5] 826[7] 2051[11] 3544[10] 5310[14] (6157) 7348[11] 8020[8] 8167[5] 8249[4]

Mendip (USA) *Saeed Bin Suroor* a117 112
5 bb h Harlan's Holiday(USA) Well Spring (USA) (Coronado's Quest (USA))
144a[4] (488a) 878a[11] 1150a[11]

Men Don't Cry (IRE) *Ed de Giles* a61 38
3 b g Street Cry(IRE) Naissance Royale (IRE) (Giant's Causeway (USA))
2130[3] 2548[5] 2802[14] 3470[11] 3943[11] 4653[10] 4937[7] 6158[11] 6778[3] 7225[2] 7382[4] 7643[8] 7816[4]

Meneas (FR) *C Laffon-Parias* 103
2 b g American Post Okalea (IRE) (Dalakhani (IRE))
(5471a)

Menelik (IRE) *Tom Dascombe* a65 69
3 b g Oasis Dream Chica Roca (USA) (Woodman (USA))
7055[3] ◆ 7776[6]

Meniska (FR) *J-M Capitte* a61 87
3 b f Invincible Spirit(IRE) Royal Liverpool (USA) (Gulch (USA))
(6752a)

Mephala (FR) *C Baillet* a80 61
3 ch f Muhaymin(USA) Spain (FR) (Bering)
5473a[7]

Meraviglioso *B Grizzetti* 53
3 b c Shamardal(USA) Drifa (ITY) (Hamas (IRE))
2324a[10]

Mercators View *Hughie Morrison* a42
2 b c Observatory(USA) Capriolla (In The Wings)
8052[11]

Mercers Row *Karen Tutty* a63 80
5 b g Bahamian Bounty Invincible (Slip Anchor)
215[6] 1242[2] (1800) (2140) 2793[10] 4400[5] 5298[6] 6605[5] 7100[6]

Merchant Of Dubai *Jim Goldie* a79 105
7 b g Dubai Destination(USA) Chameleon (Green Desert (USA))
1974[9] 3125[9] 3625[9] 4284[6] 5540[11] 6642[7] 7367[7] 7792[8]

Merchant Of Medici *Micky Hammond* a91 83
5 b g Medicean Regal Rose (Danehill (USA))
2510[6] 2590[6] 3167[7] 3354[3] 3699[5] 4679[9] 5224[2] 6405[5]

Merchants Return *Lydia Pearce* a57 40
3 b c Byron Molly Pitcher (IRE) (Halling (USA))
2279[12] 3551[6] 4888[7] 5408[6] 5855[4] 6323[2] 6838[5] 7632[5] 8048[13]

Merevale *Michael Appleby* 38
3 b g Selkirk(USA) A Thousand Smiles (IRE) (Sadler's Wells (USA))
7112[7] 7174[9] 7494[6]

Meridius (IRE) *Jeremy Noseda* 41
2 b c Invincible Spirit(IRE) Eliza Acton (Shirley Heights)
2929[10]

Meringue Pie *Richard Hannon* 81
2 ch c Sakhee's Secret Queen's Pudding (IRE) (Royal Applause)
1411[7] (4502) 5579[7] 6162[18]

Meri Shika (FR) *J Bertran De Balanda* 102
2 b f Spirit One(FR) Folle Biche (FR) (Take Risks (FR))
5471a[5] 6129a[4] 6909a[6] 7343a[3]

Merit Man (USA) *R Hess Jr* a112
2 b c With Distinction(USA) Precise Strike (USA) (Precise End (USA))
7545a[2]

Merito *David Evans* a52 62
4 b g Exceed And Excel(AUS) First Approval (Royal Applause)
1088[11] 1207[8]

Merrjanah *John Wainwright* a60 65
4 b m Diktat Aberdovey (Mister Baileys)
400[9] 531[3] 636[8] 1154[6] 1439[7] 2137[7] 2601[4] 2796[6] 3073[3] 3616[9] 4843[4] 5258[7] 5967[5] 6562[4]

Merry Jaunt (USA) *John Gosden* a73 70
3 b f Street Sense(USA) Light Jig (Danehill (USA))
5166[3] 5795[2] 6190[2] 6613[10] 7270[9] (7767)

Mesariya (IRE) *Tony Coyle* a59 94
4 ch m Sinndar(IRE) Masakala (IRE) (Cadeaux Genereux)
6055[4] 6544[7] 6885[3] 7596[11] 7800[13]

Mesha Dream (FR) *S Wattel* a70 76
2 b f Meshaheer(USA) Day Of Dream (IRE) (Rainbows For Life (CAN))
5697a[4] 7700a[6] 8193a[10]

Meshaheera (FR) *F Sanchez* a60 72
2 b f Meshaheer(USA) Odienne Jem (FR) (Cadeaux Genereux)
6751a[0] 7699a[5]

Meshardal (GER) *Richard Hannon* 38
2 b g Shamardal(USA) Melody Fair (IRE) (Montjeu (IRE))
6020[16]

Mesmerized (IRE) *Marco Botti* a53
2 b f Duke Of Marmalade(IRE) Margot (Sadler's Wells (USA))
8017[8]

Messageinabottle (USA) *Michael Bell* a53
2 bb f Grand Slam(USA) Devine (USA) (Seattle Slew (USA))
7160[8] 7460[7]

Methaaly (IRE) *Michael Mullineaux* a74 64
9 b g Red Ransom(USA) Santorini (USA) (Spinning World (USA))
387[7] 844[4] 912[2] 1116[9] 2377[9] 2476[4] 3065[7] 3559[10] 4043[8] 4708[5] 4887[7] 5093[6] 5416[12] 6053[7] 6195[2] 6823[10] 7055[5] (8256)

Methayel (IRE) *Clive Brittain* a82 77
4 br m Araafa(IRE) First Breeze (USA) (Woodman (USA))
919[2] 1729[6] (2362) (2859) 3395[5] 4255[4] 4939[4] 6176[5] 7328[2]

Metropolitan Chief *Paul Burgoyne* a58 52
8 b g Compton Place Miss Up N Go (Gorytus (USA))
313[5] 396[6] 572[3] ◆ 665[8] 740[5] 837[3] 972[9] 1070[4] 1306[4] 1910[6]

Mexican Bob *James Evans* a61 70
9 b g Atraf Eskimo Nel (IRE) (Shy Groom (USA))
156[5] 555[9]

Mexican Mick *Ian Williams* 70
3 ch g Atraf Artic Bliss (Fraam)
3561[6] 3990[3] 5335[4] 7782[9]

Mexican Wave *Michael Bell* a47 49
3 b g Rock Of Gibraltar(IRE) La Belga (ARG) (Roy (USA))
1260[2] 1590[2] 2578[5] 4153[10] 5623[2]

Mey Blossom *Richard Whitaker* a68 80
7 ch m Captain Rio Petra Nova (First Trump)
4451[7] 4631[13] 5223[8] 6123[9] 6358[4] 6823[4] 6961[15] 7482[9] (7747) 7915[2] ◆ 8064[2]

Meydan Style (USA) *Richard Ford* a52 36
6 b g Essence Of Dubai(USA) Polish Ruby (USA) (Polish Pro (USA))
226[4] 483[5] 662[2] 837[10] 988[5] 1799[8] 4453[10] 5015[3] 6316[5] 8038[5] 8288[10]

Mezzanisi (IRE) *Peter Bowen* a94 78
7 b g Kalanisi(IRE) Mezzanine (Sadler's Wells (USA))
1890[5] 2706[6] 4184[3] 4543[6] 5151[8]

Mezzotint (IRE) *Marco Botti* a97 95
3 b c Diamond Green(FR) Aquatint (Dansili)
1271[7] 1449[2] 1858[13] 3284[2] (3639) ◆ 8008[7] 8272[5]

Miako (USA) *Michael Appleby* a62
2 ch g Speightstown(USA) Bond Queen (USA) (Stormy Atlantic (USA))
3452[4] 6054[3] 6320[5] 8274[5]

Miakora *Michael Quinn* a58 61
4 ch m Compton Place Hickleton Lady (IRE) (Kala Shikari)
373[3] 373[4] 524[8] 657[4] 2461[4] 3568[6] 4434[6] 5017[2] 5454[2] 7770[2] 8064[5] 8168[11] 8251[4]

Mia Madonna *Bryan Smart* a66 71
4 b m Motivator Musique Magique (IRE) (Mozart (IRE))
(2455) 7558[10]

Miami Gator (IRE) *Mrs K Burke* a67 89
5 ch g Titus Livius(FR) Lovere (St Jovite (USA))
965a[3] 1128[22] 2753[8] (3274) 3493[15] 3911[5] 4620[10] 5669[11] 6526[5] 8057[8]

Mia's Boy *Chris Dwyer* a108 103
8 b g Pivotal Bint Zamayem (IRE) (Rainbow Quest (USA))
254[5] 622[5] 868[3] 1130[21] 1854[13] 3004[3] 3331[10] 3784[3] 6242[11] 6831[8] 7774[10] 7934[4] 8056[2] 8226[4]

Miblish *Clive Brittain* a98 103
3 b c Teofilo(IRE) Triton Dance (IRE) (Hector Protector (USA))
1216[2] 1470[10] 3239[10] 3630[3] 4319[7] 4760[5] 5835[6] 6025[14]

Mica Mika (IRE) *Richard Fahey* a85 90
4 ch g Needwood Blade Happy Talk (IRE) (Hamas (IRE))
(2031) 2180[2] 3036[6] 3494[14] 4115[5] 4697[17] 5333[4] 6191[5] 7098[5] 7810[6] (8275)

Michael Collins (IRE) *Michael Appleby* a66 27
6 b g Oasis Dream West Virginia (IRE) (Gone West (USA))
113[12]

Michael's Nook *Alastair Lidderdale* a65 64
5 b g Intikhab(USA) Mysterious Plans (IRE) (Last Tycoon)
153[4] 6480[5] 6823[11] 7224[12] 7446[9] 8167[4] 8212[3] 8257[3]

Michael's Song (IRE) *Mick Channon* a49 56
2 b f Refuse To Bend(IRE) Raindancing (IRE) (Tirol)
2499[15] 4055[8] 4487[7] 5532[2] 5873[3] 6147[8] 6283[4] 6564[4] 6822[5] 7526[7]

Michelangelo *John Gosden* 116
3 b c Galileo(IRE) Intrigued (Darshaan)
1859[3] (2445) (3630) 4685[3] 6245[3]

Mickdaam (IRE) *Richard Fahey* a112 111
3 b c Dubawi(IRE) Ribot's Guest (IRE) (Be My Guest (USA))
142a[6] 485a[2] ◆ (873a) 1145a[4] 1468[2] (1995) 2705[5]

Mick Duggan *Simon Hodgson* a70 42
2 ch g Pivotal Poppy Carew (IRE) (Danehill (USA))
(5968) 6797[5] 7965[3] 8072[7]

Mick Dundee (IRE) *J W Hills* a63 47
2 b c Aussie Rules(USA) Lucky Oakwood (USA) (Elmaamul (USA))
2415[11] 3387[8] 7922[3] 8132[4]

Mick Slates (IRE) *Declan Carroll* a53 78
3 b g Moss Vale(IRE) Sonic Night (IRE) (Night Shift (USA))
1259[7] 1359[9] 1600[5] 1916[2] 3111[2] (3184) 3908[3] (3952) 4432[7] (5415) 5736[2] 6429[2] 6789[7]

Mickstathetricksta *Scott Dixon* a31 68
2 ch g Milk It Mick Chrystal Venture (IRE) (Barathea (IRE))
2880[3] ◆ 3182[14] 3611[10] 4116[9] 7399[8] 7614[6] 8094[11]

Micky Mac (IRE) *Colin Teague* a9 48
8 b g Lend A Hand Gazette It Tonight (Merdon Melody)
6958[9] 7351[9]

Micky P *Stuart Williams* a69 53
5 gr g Dr Fong(USA) Carmela Owen (Owington)
2811[7] 3471[7]

Mico Margarita (USA) *Steven Asmussen* 93
2 ch c Run Away And Hide(USA) Wide Range (USA) (Mineshaft (USA))
7567a[3]

Micquus (IRE) *Andrew Balding* a52 56
3 b g High Chaparral(IRE) My Potters (USA) (Irish River (FR))
1415[6] 1726[4] 2578[2] 2850[6] 3781[6]

Microlight *John E Long* a56 52
4 b g Sleeping Indian Skytrial (USA) (Sky Classic (CAN))
123[8] 312[7] 424[10] 781[4] 939[9] 1628[10] 2972[4] 3151[6] 3466[7] 3718[4] 4438[10] 6951[7] 8168[10]

Micromanage (USA) *Todd Pletcher* a95
2 b c Medaglia d'Oro(USA) Catnip (USA) (Flying Paster (USA))
6901a[5]

Midas Moment *William Muir* a76 76
4 b m Danehill Dancer(IRE) Special Moment (IRE) (Sadler's Wells (USA))
1311[4] 1792[3] 2431[11] 2859[2] 3659[12] 4335[11] 4753[6] 6157[7] 6895[5] 7170[9]

Midas Touch *Robert Hickmott* 120
5 b h Galileo(IRE) Approach (Darshaan)
7425a[8]

Middleton Flyer (IRE) *Paul Midgley* 74
3 ch f Titus Livius(FR) Autumn Star (IRE) (Mujadil (USA))
1514[3] 1912[3] 2256[14] 2615[4] 3540[2] 4207[7] 4878[4] 5294[5] 5831[4] (6264) 7001[6] 7457[2]

Mid Mon Lady (IRE) *Sir Mark Prescott Bt* a98 107
7 br m Danetime(IRE) Shining Desert (IRE) (Green Desert (USA))
2773[2] 3219[3] 4112[2] 4386a[3] 4556[7]

Midnami *Linda Stubbs*
3 b g Namid Silly Mid-On (Midyan (USA))
5113[9] 7025[11]

Midnight Bahia (IRE) *Dean Ivory* a52 27
3 b f Refuse To Bend(IRE) Midnight Partner (IRE) (Marju (IRE))
6582[9] 7632[6] 7800[6] 8048[3]

Midnight Dancer (FR) *F Chappet* a75 71
2 ch c Choisir(AUS) Miss Madisyn Rose (USA) (Storm Bird (CAN))
7597a[0]

Midnight Dream (FR) *Linda Stubbs* a74 51
2 bb g Country Reel(USA) Tatante (IRE) (Highest Honor (FR))
1164[6] 6122[6] 6977[6] 7653[2] (7953) 8161[5]

Midnight Dynamo *Jim Goldie* 79
5 b m Lujain(USA) Miss Hermione (Bahamian Bounty)
2719[5] 3109[7] 3905[5] 4638[3] (5548) (6123) 7100[7]

Midnight Feast *Lee Carter* a72 82
4 b g Ishiguru(USA) Prince's Feather (IRE) (Cadeaux Genereux)
1627[2] 1936[3] 2488[13] 2940[8] 7114[15] 7827[8] 8058[8] 8268[11]

Midnight Flower (IRE) *David Simcock* a74 61
2 b f Haafhd Takawiri (IRE) (Danehill (USA))
5631[4] 6453[2] 7143[2] (8208)

Midnight Opera *Neil Mulholland* a57
6 b g Midnight Legend Ballad Opera (Sadler's Wells (USA))
292[4]

Midnight Poet *James Given* 16
2 ch g Byron Molly Pitcher (IRE) (Halling (USA))
4677[8]

Midnight Rider (IRE) *Chris Wall* a86 90
4 b g Red Ransom(USA) Foreplay (IRE) (Lujain (USA))
1564[3] 1936[2] 2251[6] 2940[4] 3541[2] 5233[3] 6041[3] (6820)

Midnight Sequel *Michael Blake* a51 25
3 b f Midnight Legend Silver Sequel (Silver Patriarch (IRE))
292[5] 993[3] (1303) 1726[5] 8067[6]

Midnight Soprano (IRE) *P D Deegan* 108
5 b m Celtic Swing Midnight Glimmer (IRE) (Dr Devious (IRE))
(2903a) 3678a[2] 4738[6] 7449a[4]

Midnight Tryst *Ann Duffield* 61
3 ch f Cockney Rebel(IRE) Shaken And Stirred (Cadeaux Genereux)
1166[3]

Midnight Warrior *James Tate* a66 71
2 b g Teofilo(IRE) Mauri Moon (Green Desert (USA))
5851[3] 6330[8] 7458[5]

Midnite Motivation *Derek Shaw* a17
3 b f Motivator Tamise (USA) (Time For A Change (USA))
770[9] 1016[10] 4931[9] 6686[7]

Midsummer Sun *Sir Henry Cecil* a106 104
4 b h Monsun(GER) Midsummer (Kingmambo (USA))
(1374) ◆ 1674[3] 2278[5] 3372[9] 4759[5] 5826[5]

Mid Yorkshire Golf *Peter Grayson*
3 b f Doyen(IRE) Jodeeka (Fraam)
7253[7] 7361[11]

Miereveld *Shaun Harris* a60 53
5 b g Red Ransom(USA) Mythic (Zafonic (USA))
9[7] 98[2] 188[10] 366[6] 454[2]

Mighty Ambition (USA) *Mahmood Al Zarooni* 86
3 b c Street Cry(IRE) New Morning (IRE) (Sadler's Wells (USA))
1470[5]

Mighty Clarets (IRE) *Barry Leavy* a76 71
5 br g Whipper(USA) Collected (IRE) (Taufan (USA))
248[2] 268[3] 771[8] 2051[9] 2329[2] (2765) 3386[2] 3775[5] 4080[3] 5199[4] 5506[3] 6120[7]

Mighty Motive *John Mackie* a60 49
3 ch c Motivator Mitraillette (USA) (Miswaki (USA))
1270[5] 1716[5] 2733[10] 3712[6] 5266[9] 5804[10]

Mighty Mouse (GER) *P Vovcenko* 107
4 b g King's Best(USA) Megaperls (GER) (Zinaad)
1700a[6] 2322a[6] 2989a[6] 5117a[6]

Mighty Yar (IRE) *Sir Henry Cecil* a72
2 gr c Teofilo(IRE) Karaliyfa (IRE) (Kahyasi)
(7899)

Miguel Grau (USA) *Marco Botti* a61
2 b g City Zip(USA) Zuri Ridge (USA) (Cox's Ridge (USA))
5765[7] 6175[4] 7020[7]

Mihrimahal (TUR) *H Guney* 66
3 ch f Medya(TUR) Gulbin Sultan (TUR) (Asakir)
5849a[8]

Mijhaar *Roger Varian* a109 112
4 b g Shirocco(GER) Jathaabeh (Nashwan (USA))
2211[3] ◆ 3329[3] ◆ 4112[15] 6035[4] 6674[32] 7029[2] 7438[2]

Mikdaar (IRE) *Ed Dunlop*
3 b g Elnadim(USA) Jeed (IRE) (Mujtahid (USA))
1704[12]

Mikhail Glinka (IRE) *A Savujev* a100 115
5 b h Galileo(IRE) Lady Karr (Mark Of Esteem (IRE))
145a[3] 486a[4] 678a[7] 792a[2] (877a) 1144a[9] (5613a) 6912a[14]

Mikkwa (USA) *E Lellouche* 97
3 b f Elusive Quality(USA) Manureva (USA) (Nureyev (USA))
3682a[13]

Milena's Dream (IRE) *Y De Nicolay* 88
2 b f Authorized(IRE) Rozella (IRE) (Anabaa (USA))
(5570a) 7343a[4]

Miliika *Rae Guest* 88
3 b f Green Desert(USA) Miss Anabaa (Anabaa (USA))
1843[2] ◆ (2361) ◆ 2986[2] 3396[4] 7177[6] ◆ 7521[2]

Military Attack (IRE) *J Moore* a56 112
4 b g Oratorio(IRE) Almaaseh (IRE) (Dancing Brave (USA))
8043a[5]

Military Call *Alistair Whillans* a36 66
5 b g Royal Applause Trump Street (First Trump)
3115[4] ◆ 4389[2] 4643[3] 5059[2] 6262[10] 6711[7] 7095[8]

Military Green (FR) *Tim Easterby* a33 56
3 b g Cadeaux Genereux Dallaah (Green Desert (USA))
2881[12] (3406) 4397[6] 5014[10] 6958[11] 7354[5] 7604[P]

Mill End Dancer *Michael Easterby* a42 49
2 b f Antonius Pius(USA) Five Lakes (USA) (Coronado's Quest (USA))
2135[7] 2880[8] 3126[7] (4767) 7441[7] 7526[3]

Millers Wharf (IRE) *Richard Hannon* a70 77
2 b c Acclamation Applaud (USA) (Rahy (USA))
2888[4] 4283[4] 4688[7] 5235[5] 6020[5] 6330[4] 6597[8] 7498[U] 7894[3]

Mille Waki (FR) *C Boutin* a70 51
3 b c Sandwaki(USA) Lolly Lodge (FR) (Grand Lodge (USA))
290a[0] 476a[7]

Mill I Am (USA) *Pat Murphy*
2 b f Henny Hughes(USA) Courageous (USA) (Kingmambo (USA))
4701[16]

Millibar (IRE) *Nick Littmoden* a87 80
3 b f Manduro(GER) Iktidar (Green Desert (USA))
180[4] 206[2] 331[4] 739[4] 917[4] 2045[5] 2361[2] (2871) 3350[3] (3488) 4234[5] 4598[11] 4985[2] 5195[2] 6378[7] 6878[13] (7483) 7859[2] 8022[4] 8266[5]

Millie N Aire *Danielle McCormick* a57 65
2 b f Multiplex Hillside Girl (IRE) (Tagula (IRE))
2415[9] 3034[5] 3381[4] 4076[3] 4324[2] 5088[9] 5544[5] 5749[7] 6122[2] 6627[3] 6822[3] 7379[7]

Million Faces *Rae Guest* 79
3 ch f Exceed And Excel(AUS) Millyant (Primo Dominie)
2918[3] (3670) ◆

Millkwood *John Davies* 71
2 b g Millkom Wedgewood Star (Bishop Of Cashel)
4310[12] 4825[5] 5382[3] 6787[4] 6984[2]

Millymonkin *Michael Easterby* a54 63
3 b f Gentleman's Deal(IRE) Royal Distant (USA) (Distant View (USA))
1016[6] ◆ 1918[6] 2336[9] 5373[3] 5738[4] 6103[6] 6940[9] 7102[10]

Milly's Gift *Clive Cox* a71
2 b f Trade Fair Milly's Lass (Mind Games)
7161[3] ◆

Milord (GER) *J Hirschberger* 98
3 br c Monsun(GER) Montserrat (GER) (Zilzal (USA))
3683a[12]

Milord De Reward (FR) *D Bressou* a79 59
3 b g Voix Du Nord(FR) The Reward (FR) (River Mist (USA))
5074a[3]

Milton Of Campsie *Richard Guest* a57 78
7 ch m Medicean La Caprice (USA) (Housebuster (USA))
113[5] 264[3]

Minalisa *Rae Guest* 88
3 b f Oasis Dream Mina (Selkirk (USA))
(3312) 3698[2] (4660) 5128[4] 5582[2] 6285[5]

Mince *Roger Charlton* 118
3 ch f Medicean Strut (Danehill Dancer (IRE))
1858[2] ◆ (2276) 2713[7] 4063[8] (5080) (5385) (6072) ◆ (6867)

Mingun Bell (USA) *Ed de Giles* a93 88
5 b g Mingun(USA) Miss Tippins (USA) (Squadron Leader (USA))
1951[4] 2608[2] 3439[2] (4190) 4580[12] 5301[8] 6338[5] 6931[7] 7715[7]

Minidress *Mahmood Al Zarooni* 101
3 br f Street Cry(IRE) Short Skirt (Diktat)
1454[8] 2410[2]

Minimee *Roger Varian* a66
2 b g Dubai Destination(USA) Malaaq (Green Desert (USA))
7525[3] 7979[2]

Minimise Risk *Andrew Balding* 102
3 b c Galileo(IRE) Dararita (IRE) (Halo (USA))
1132[2] ◆ (1511) 1995[5] 2705[7] 3330[5] 4685[5]

Mini's Destination *John Holt* a52 69
4 b m Dubai Destination(USA) Heather Mix (Linamix (FR))
1358[10]

Ministerofinterior *Richard Ford* a60 77
7 b g Nayef(USA) Maureen's Hope (USA) (Northern Baby (CAN))
1240[2] (1496) (1952)

Ministry *Gary Moore* a71 56
4 b g Iceman Choirgirl (Unfuwain (USA))
1085[4] 8106[6]

Minkie Moon (IRE) *Mark Campion* 57
4 b g Danehill Dancer(IRE) Minkova (IRE) (Sadler's Wells (USA))
2925[10]

Minneapolis *Alison Batchelor* a102 58
7 b g Sadler's Wells(USA) Teggiano (IRE) (Mujtahid (USA))
1939[9]

Minne Wa Wa *David Brown* a8 51
3 b f Bahamian Bounty Crimson Dancer (Groom Dancer (USA))
3356[12] 6806[13]

Minnie Diva (IRE) *Kevin Ryan* a44 68
3 b f Multiplex Looker (Barathea (IRE))
114[4] 1281[5] 1915[2] 2605[8] 2818[2] 4399[12]

Minnie McGinn (USA) *Annike Bye Hansen* a68 92
5 rg m Maria's Mon(USA) Reluctant Diva (Sadler's Wells (USA))
5143a[5]

Minoan Dancer (IRE) *Sir Michael Stoute* a73 68
3 b f Galileo(IRE) Grecian Dancer (Dansili)
(2849) 4151[4]

Minority Interest *Sir Michael Stoute* a78 74
3 ch c Galileo(IRE) Minority (Generous (IRE))
2430[5] ◆ 6615[2]

Minortransgression (USA) *Paul Rich* a77 59
5 ch g Yes It's True(USA) Casting Pearls (USA) (Fusaichi Pegasus (USA))
22[3] 7360[12] 7607[10] 7725[11]

Minsky Mine (IRE) *Michael Appleby* a70 75
5 b g Montjeu(IRE) Summer Trysting (USA) (Alleged (USA))
535[4] 826[4] 4745[2] 7315[3]

Minstrel Lad *Lydia Pearce* a58 62
4 ch g Where Or When(IRE) Teal Flower (Pivotal)
959[6] 1301[5] 1984[4] 2468[5] 3043[7] (4296) 4817[6] 5323[11] 5974[9]

Minstrels Gallery (IRE) *J R Jenkins* a81 83
3 ch g Refuse To Bend(IRE) Lilakiya (IRE) (Dr Fong (USA))
(903) 1470[7] 2198[3] 2930[14] 5358[9] 7376[7] 7644[10] 8074[11]

Minty Fox *Rae Guest* a60 60
3 gr f Dalakhani(IRE) Quantum (IRE) (Alhaarth (IRE))
6148[5] 6736[6] 7174[14] 7811[8] 8060[7]

Minty Jones *Michael Mullineaux* a23 55
3 b c Primo Valentino(IRE) Reveur (Rossini (USA))
2143[7] 2862[13] 3555[7] 4397[7] 5994[9]

Minxilinx *Mme C Head-Maarek* a65 79
2 gr f Zamindar(USA) Lixian (Linamix (FR))
7597a[8]

Miraaj (IRE) *Richard Hannon* a49 62
2 b c Iffraaj My-Lorraine (IRE) (Mac's Imp (USA))
7330[7]

Miracle Cure (IRE) *J S Bolger* a86 96
3 b c Whipper(USA) Bring Back Matron (IRE) (Rock Of Gibraltar (IRE))
4692a[6] 5397a[10] 5609a[15]

Miracle Maid *Clive Cox* 82
3 b f Selkirk(USA) Miracle (Ezzoud (IRE))
1887[5] 3565[5] 5309[2] (6279)

Miranda's Girl (IRE) *Thomas Cleary* a83 83
7 b m Titus Livius(FR) Ela Tina (IRE) (Ela-Mana-Mou)
1041a[10]

Mirandola (FR) *Y De Nicolay* 103
3 ch f Anabaa Blue Connaissance (IRE) (Choisir (AUS))
1434a[6]

Mi Regalo *Phil McEntee* a75 64
4 b g Cadeaux Genereux Lloc (Absalom)
96[8] 210[5] 312[9] 653[10] 986[5] 1628[12] 1720[6]

Miriam's Song *Stuart Kittow* a60 57
3 b f Royal Applause Miriam (Forzando)
3510[8] 4235[10] 7964[12]

Mirlo Blanco (IRE) *Richard Fahey* 70
2 br c Dark Angel(IRE) Danzolin (Danzero (AUS))
4555[9] 5331[8] 5825[3] 6138[5] 6475[9] 7399[7]

Mironica (IRE) *David Wachman* 89
2 ch f Excellent Art Lisfannon (Bahamian Bounty)
3269[15] 4577[5]

Mirrored *Tim Easterby* a86 97
6 b g Dansili Reflections (Sadler's Wells (USA))
(1273) 1654[7] 2176[5] 2773[7] 3609[3] (4620) 5094[7] (5369) 5677[8] 6135[7]

Mirror Image *S Wattel* a67 71
2 b f Acclamation Mystic Spirit (IRE) (Invincible Spirit (IRE))
7265a[5]

Mirsaale *James Tate* 92
2 ch c Sir Percy String Quartet (IRE) (Sadler's Wells (USA))
4066[5] (5439) 6027[3] 6874[7]

Mirza *Rae Guest* a68 107
5 b g Oasis Dream Millyant (Primo Dominie)
(1498) ◆ 1558[2] 1885[8] (2931) (3196a) 3650a[6] 4092[8] 6468[18] 6869[4] 7066[9] 7397[19]

Misdemeanour (IRE) *Richard Hannon* a87 96
3 b f Azamour(IRE) Miss Takeortwo (IRE) (Danehill Dancer (IRE))
2477[4] 3296[8] 3787[2] 4700[7] 5078[9] 5951[3] 7375[2]

Misedargent (FR) *H-A Pantall* a65 65
3 gr f Kendargent(FR) Miss Sindbad (FR) (Peintre Celebre (USA))
1209a[9]

Misefi *Martin Bosley* a49 26
4 b m Nayef(USA) Simonida (IRE) (Royal Academy (USA))
4183[7]

Misere *Kevin Ryan* a62
4 b m Val Royal(FR) Card Games (First Trump)
274[8] 430[4] 551[11] 773[10]

Miserere Mei (IRE) *Richard Guest* a62 52
3 b f Moss Vale(IRE) Flying Clouds (Batshoof)
25[7] 321[5] 394[6] 905[4] 1252[3] 1529[3] 1585[7] 2460[5] 2730[8] 3218[4] 3451[3] 3540[4] 4087[4] 4592[10] 5131[7] 5542[3] 6003[9] 6314[4] 8107[8] 8209[6]

Misfer *Sir Henry Cecil* a70
2 ch c Byron Diliza (Dilum (USA))
7707[8] 7923[2] ◆

Mishaal (IRE) *Roger Varian* a72 72
2 ch g Kheleyf(USA) My Dubai (IRE) (Dubai Millennium)
5162[4] 5765[4] 6167[3] 6699[4]

Mishhar (IRE) *Clive Brittain* a59 70
3 b f Authorized(IRE) Jakarta (IRE) (Machiavellian (USA))
1610[8] 2042[7] 2626[2]

Mishrif (USA) *J R Jenkins* a80 73
6 bb g Arch(USA) Peppy Priscilla (USA) (Latin American (USA))
33[6] 302[4] 517[2] 626[8] 991[8] 2399[7] 3549[8] 4966[3] 6145[7] 8105[9] 8268[9]

Misk Khitaam (USA) *John Dunlop* 69
4 b g Distorted Humor(USA) Tashawak (IRE) (Night Shift (USA))
2233[P] 5707[9] 6440[7] 7269[9]

Misleading Promise (IRE) *John Butler* a65
2 b c Refuse To Bend(IRE) Farthing (IRE) (Mujadil (USA))
5765[13] 5968[6] 6320[7] 6533[11] 8094[3] ◆ 8289[2] ◆

Misplaced Fortune *Nigel Tinkler* a46 99
7 b m Compton Place Tide Of Fortune (Soviet Star (USA))
1478[4] 1844[16] (2310) 2636[3] 3624[2] 4611[17] 5520[7] 6165[2] (6406) 7066[4] 7240[25]

Misred Melissa (IRE) *Ronald Harris* a16 44
3 b f Red Clubs(IRE) Almasa (Faustus (USA))
228[5] 376[10]

Miss Aix *Michael Bell* a86 86
4 b m Selkirk(USA) Miss Provence (Hernando (FR))
(1258) 1656[7] 3013[3] 4199[5] 4702[16] 5277[7] 6847[3] (7810)

Missalavie (FR) *P Van De Poele* a65
2 b f Kentucky Dynamite(USA) Miss Alabama (FR) (Anabaa (USA))
5570a[0]

Miss Antonia (IRE) *R Werning* a86 86
5 b m Antonius Pius(USA) Masharik (IRE) (Caerleon (USA))
92a[5]

Miss Astragal (IRE) *Richard Hannon* a70 73
3 b f Oratorio(IRE) Mansiya (Vettori (IRE))
279[2]

Miss Avonbridge (IRE) *Tom Dascombe* a69 62
2 b f Avonbridge Red Planet (Pivotal)
7433[2] (7778)

Miss Azeza *David Simcock* 95
3 b f Dutch Art Miss Respect (Mark Of Esteem (IRE))
3639[7] 4075[2] 4597[5] 5043[RR] 6023[RR]

Miss Blakeney *Marcus Tregoning* a84 63
3 b f Sir Percy Misplace (IRE) (Green Desert (USA))
6736[4] ◆ 7162[2] 7644[5] ◆ 7811[2] 7954[2] (8097) (8297)

Miss Blink *Robin Bastiman* a72 78
5 ch m Compton Place Tawny Way (Polar Falcon (USA))
1381[6] ◆ 2620[4] 4199[3] 4883[7] 7368[6] 7792[4] 8082[11]

Miss Bloom *Garry Woodward* a24
3 ch f Byron Demolition Molly (Rudimentary (USA))
20[6] 135[5] 357[5] 750[6] 768[5]

Miss Boops (IRE) *Zoe Davison* a54 72
4 b m Johannesburg(USA) Sky Bird (IRE) (Galileo (IRE))
5405[9] 5939[9]

Miss Bootylishes *Paul Burgoyne* a79 83
7 b m Mujahid(USA) Moxby (Efisio)
(1909) 2161[3] 2766[6] 2985[5]

Miss Bossy Boots *Tracy Waggott*
3 b f Ishiguru(USA) Mighty Flyer (IRE) (Mujtahid (USA))
7445[16]

Miss Bridget (FR) *H-A Pantall* a80 74
3 b f Zamindar(USA) Cuevas Bay (Robellino (USA))
5726a[4]

Miss Bunter *David O'Meara* a68
3 b f Bahamian Bounty The Terrier (Foxhound (USA))
7445[14] 7729[5] (7952) 8253[2] ◆

Miss Cap Estel *Andrew Balding* 85
3 b f Hernando(FR) Miss Cap Ferrat (Darshaan)
3619[2] 4233[2] 4753[2] (5147) 5707[3] (6240) 6661[6]

Miss Carmie (FR) *Mlle S-V Tarrou* a77 99
3 b f Excellent Art Moortown (IRE) (Grand Lodge (USA))
1407a[3] 2109a[12]

Miss Cato *Rae Guest* a66 97
3 ch f Notnowcato Regal Fairy (IRE) (Desert King (IRE))
(2) (288) 393[3] (1288) ◆ 1519[2] (2431) 3069[2] 4131a[4]

Miss Complex *Brian Meehan* 69
3 b f Compton Place Extremely Rare (IRE) (Mark Of Esteem (IRE))
2871[2] (3438) 4482a[8]

Miss Dashwood *James Fanshawe* a85 66
3 b f Dylan Thomas(IRE) Dash To The Front (Diktat)
2734[12] 3340[5] 5510[4] 6401[2] (6842) (7356)

Miss Diva *Richard Hannon* 85
2 b f Acclamation Mina (Selkirk (USA))
2124[2] (2343) 3269[12] 3669[2] 4599[3] 5307[4]

Missed Call (IRE) *Sir Henry Cecil* 37
2 b f Authorized(IRE) Incoming Call (USA) (Red Ransom (USA))
5551[8]

Miss Ella Jade *Richard Whitaker* a50 60
3 b f Danbird(AUS) Keen Melody (USA) (Sharpen Up)
1915[6] 2673[8] 3416[2] (3694) 4172[3] 4771[2] 5680[3] 6785[3] 7752[6]

Miss Ellany (IRE) *David O'Meara* a66 89
3 b f Kodiac Rainbowskia (FR) (Rainbow Quest (USA))
(3024) 3749[2] 4553[3] 4961[3] (5372) 6710[6]

Miss Exhibitionist *Alan King* a78 76
4 b m Trade Fair Miss McGuire (Averti (IRE))
3429[6] 6416[14]

Miss Ferney *Alan Kirtley* a66 69
8 ch m Cayman Kai(IRE) Jendorcet (Grey Ghost)
5172[10] 5673[7] 6126[3] 6478[11]

Miss Fifty (IRE) *U Suter* a62 103
4 b m Whipper(USA) Annatto (USA) (Mister Baileys)
7123a[10]

Miss Firefly *Ron Hodges* a59 63
7 b m Compton Place Popocatepetl (FR) (Nashwan (USA))
1497[17] 2350[12] 2943[9]

Miss Fortywinks *Paul Henderson* 73
3 gr f Act One Andromache (Hector Protector (USA))
5309[5] 6570[2] 7174[4] 7557[8]

Miss Granger *Ronald Harris* a46 38
3 ch f Needwood Blade Sweet Coincidence (Mujahid (USA))
2162[9] 2577[10] 4705[9]

Misshollygolightly *Brian Baugh* 43
4 b m Kheleyf(USA) Crown City (USA) (Coronado's Quest (USA))
662[12] 2121[7] 3210[4]

Missile Attack (IRE) *Ian Semple* a63 57
4 b g Majestic Missile(IRE) Aquatint (Dansili)
1389[4] 1800[8] 2352[8] 2458[10] 3113[2] 3578[8] 3893[2] 4154[2] 5087[6] 5177[3] 7061[8]

Missing Agent *David Evans* a65 61
2 b g Misu Bond(IRE) Desert Sceptre (Desert Story (IRE))
1202[6] 1253[7] (3084) 4421[5] 6096[9] 6156[3] 6435[2] 6826[2] 7026[7] 7111[7] 7223[6] 7432[5] (7724) 7779[4] (7922)

Missionaire (USA) *Tony Carroll* a62 30
5 bb g El Corredor(USA) Fapindy (USA) (A.P. Indy (USA))
28[13] 265[3] 519[2] 7744[11] 8260[10]

Mission Approved *Sir Michael Stoute* a72 76
2 b c Dansili Moon Search (Rainbow Quest (USA))
3346[8] ◆ 5476[2] (6818)

Mission Bell *Mark Usher* a44 34
2 ch f Three Valleys(USA) Twitch Hill (Piccolo)
2135[6] 2349[4] 2622[4]

Mission Impossible *Tracy Waggott* a28 72
7 gr g Kyllachy Eastern Lyric (Petong)
5739[3] 6713[10] (6786) 6886[3] 7100[10]

Mississippi *Brian Meehan* a88 88
3 b g Exceed And Excel(AUS) Ruby Rocket (IRE) (Indian Rocket)
(1704) 2263[8] 3294[15] 5102[8] 5556[5] 6040[6] 6539[6]

Miss Jo B *Phil McEntee* a13
3 b f Motivator Corn Circle (IRE) (Thatching)
6254[6] 7654[8] 7818[7]

Miss Kingwood *Jo Hughes* a7 61
5 b m Reset(AUS) Forum Finale (USA) (Silver Hawk (USA))
7018[12] 7731[11]

Miss Lago (IRE) *E Lellouche* 110
4 ch m Encosta De Lago(AUS) Athyka (USA) (Secretariat (USA))
1766a[7] 2534a[7] 4120a[4] 5650a[9] 6297a[2] 6914a[8] 7431a[6]

Miss Manduro (IRE) *A Di Dio* 91
3 b f Manduro(GER) Kristina's Wish (USA) (Smart Strike (CAN))
2522a[13]

Miss Marjurie (IRE) *Denis Coakley* a76 79
2 b f Marju(IRE) Kazatzka (Groom Dancer (USA))
4946[2] (5978) 6980[10]

Miss Matiz *Alan Kirtley* 29
5 b m Rock City Doodle Wood (Nomination)
3811[10] 4550[10] 5315[6] 5672[13]

Miss Mauresque (FR) *C Lerner* a51
3 ch f Layman(USA) Varoise (FR) (Lord Of Men)
17a[0]

Miss Mocca *Ian Wood* a63 62
2 b f Bahamian Bounty Mocca (IRE) (Sri Pekan (USA))
5192[2] 6134[3] 6977[5]

Miss Mohawk (IRE) *Alan Brown* a31 44
3 ch f Hawk Wing(USA) Karmafair (IRE) (Always Fair (USA))
2633[8] 3606[6] 5315[8] 5738[8] 6210[9] 6474[9] 6807[6]

Miss Noble *Stuart Williams* a63 54
3 b f Exceed And Excel(AUS) Dorothea Brooke (IRE) (Dancing Brave (USA))
1705[2] 2065[10] 2611[2] 4456[7]

Missouri Belle *John Gosden* 77
3 gr f Invincible Spirit(IRE) Mussoorie (FR) (Linamix (FR))
3079[5] 3565[4]

Miss Penny Arcade *Keith Dalgleish* a38 38
2 gr f Royal Applause Lady Xara (IRE) (Xaar)
1437[7] 1795[4] 2132[3] 3251[7]

Miss Perfect *John Quinn* 59
2 b f Pastoral Pursuits Forest Of Love (Charnwood Forest (IRE))
3401[4] 4710[9] 4952[4] 6121[8] 6354[2] 6953[9]

Miss Polly Plum *Chris Dwyer* a57 75
5 b m Doyen(IRE) Mrs Plum (Emarati (USA))
59[9] 498[8] 887[9] 3390[4] 3618[11] 3791[14] 4439[3] 4815[3] 5217[2] (5635) 6378[8] 7590[11] 8107[6] 8190[10]

Miss Pronounce *Linda Perratt* 39
4 b m Denounce Miss Pigalle (Good Times (ITY))
2032[7] 2618[7] 7446[18]

Miss Purity Pinker (IRE) *David Evans* a59 60
3 b f One Cool Cat(USA) Consultant Stylist (IRE) (Desert Style (IRE))
322 [4] 536[6] 801[2] 940[3] 1090[4] 1444[3] 2786[9]

Miss Socialite *Jeremy Gask* a52 31
3 gb f Nayef(USA) Miss Satamixa (FR) (Linamix (FR))
1610[11] 2050[7] 2891[11] 3712[4] 4932[10]

Miss Starlight *Ibrahim Saeed Al Malki* a81 91
5 b m Trade Fair Redeem (IRE) (Doyoun)
5835[11] 6379[3] 6877[8] 7510[11]

Miss Starry Eyed *Derek Shaw* a19 47
2 b f Misu Bond(IRE) Floral Spark (Forzando)
2763[5] 3046[3] 3937[6] 7891[5] 7930[11]

Miss Tenacious *Ron Hodges* a38 38
5 b m Refuse To Bend(IRE) Very Speed (USA) (Silver Hawk (USA))
566[9]

Miss Thea *Lucy Wadham* 34
4 ch m Barathea(IRE) Misplace (IRE) (Green Desert (USA))
5952[5]

Miss Tiger Lily *Harry Dunlop* 48
2 b f Tiger Hill(IRE) Waitingonacloud (In The Wings)
6960[9] 7636[7]

Miss Tooty Fruiti (IRE) *Simon Hodgson* a36
4 b m Refuse To Bend(IRE) Raqiqah (Unbridled's Song (USA))
399[10] 546[8] 1718[7] 2401[10]

Miss Topsy Turvy (IRE) *John Dunlop* 81
4 br m Mr Greeley(USA) Cara Fantasy (IRE) (Sadler's Wells (USA))
2423[2] ◆ 6045[12] 6349[6] 6802[11]

Missus Mills (IRE) *George Baker* a38 63
3 ch f Notnowcato Putout (Dowsing (USA))
1981[11] 2757[4] 3012[6] 3312[5] 3944[11]

Miss Whippy *Paul Howling* a54 55
5 b m Whipper(USA) Glorious (Nashwan (USA))
105[10] 468[8]

Miss With Attitude (AUS) *Mick Price* 97
6 b m Galileo(IRE) Sizzie 'Em (IRE) (Flying Spur (AUS))
7696a[12] 7783a[5]

Miss Work Of Art *Richard Fahey* a85 102
3 ch f Dutch Art Lacework (Pivotal)
5385[6] 6161[18] 6468[24] 6878[5] 7066[10] 7408[11]

Miss You Too *David Simcock* 93
2 b f Montjeu(IRE) Portrait Of A Lady (IRE) (Peintre Celebre (USA))
3339[2] ◆ (4069) 4514[7] 5042[2] ◆ 5353[4] 6027[4] 6873[2] 7693a[3]

Misteray *Bill Turner* a42 39
2 ch c Singspiel(IRE) Hannda (IRE) (Dr Devious (IRE))
6733[7] 7165[9] 7492[8]

Mister Big Shuffle (GER) *M Figge* 92
2 b c Big Shuffle(USA) Marmorea (IRE) (Tiger Hill (IRE))
5755a[7] 6942a[5] 7565a[3]

Mister Black (FR) *F Sanchez* a63 68
2 bl c Country Reel(USA) Miss Anelia (FR) (Majorien)
5378a[5]

Mister Fizz *Edward Bevan* a69 68
4 b g Sulamani(IRE) Court Champagne (Batshoof)
451[3] 546[2] 1981[4] 2502[7] 3472[4]

Mister Frosty (IRE) *Gay Kelleway* a64 56
6 gr g Verglas(IRE) La Chinampina (FR) (Darshaan)
(454) 530[4] 579[3] 644[3] 1047[6] 1580[4]

Mister Green (FR) *David Flood* a75 85
6 b g Green Desert(USA) Summertime Legacy (Darshaan)
570[5] 712[11] 736[3] ◆ 821[5] 894[2] 991[3] 1108[8] 1263[4] 1421[6] 1919[11] 3546[2] 3633[6]

Mister Impatience *Mark Johnston* 81
2 b c Hernando(FR) Katy Nowaitee (Komaite (USA))
6607[4] 7081[5] (7492)

Mister Koala (FR) *J Heloury* a59
3 ch g Peintre Celebre(USA) Daisycutter (Zafonic (USA))
211a[8] 365a[0]

Mister Mackenzie *John Best* a67 64
3 br g Kodiac Dazzling View (USA) (Distant View (USA))
121[3] 308[4] 394[2] 3972[6] 4218[11] 6565[2] 6765[2] 7218[8] 7322[5]

Mister Manannan (IRE) *David Nicholls* 102
5 b g Desert Style(IRE) Cover Girl (IRE) (Common Grounds)
1219[7] 5487[18] 6028[14] 7397[20]

Mister Marc (IRE) *Richard Hannon* a80 97
2 b c Acclamation Fathoming (USA) (Gulch (USA))
(2480) 2779a[2] 3291[8] 5201[3] 5515[9] 6038[8]

Mister Marcasite *Mel Brittain* 72
2 gr g Verglas(IRE) No Rehearsal (FR) (Baillamont (USA))
5311[2] 5619[2] 6356[10] (6997)

Mister Music *Richard Hannon* 108
3 b c Singspiel(IRE) Sierra (Dr Fong (USA))
1455[2] 1604[2] 1859[5] 2701[10] 2916[3] 3294[2] ◆ 4012[5] 4761[3] ◆ 5364[3] 6484[13] 6875[12]

Mister Musicmaster *Ron Hodges* a79 88
3 b g Amadeus Wolf Misty Eyed (IRE) (Paris House)
1644[5] 1983[8] 2347[4] 2764[4] 3445[6] 4221[4] 4757[2] 5195[4] 5582[6] 6008[7] 6285[4] 6837[5] 7743[3] 7997[4]

Mister Ryan (FR) *H-A Pantall* a88 96
3 b c Acclamation Irish Flower (IRE) (Zieten (USA))
1125a[2] 1426a[10]

Mister Tee (FR) *D Smaga* a77 80
2 b c Manduro(GER) Floride (IRE) (Sadler's Wells (USA))
7683a[4]

Mister Westminster *S Smrczek* 79
2 b c Hurricane Run(IRE) Merlina (SWI) (Hawk Wing (USA))
7698a[7]

Mistoffelees *James Given* a64 62
6 b g Tiger Hill(IRE) Auenlust (GER) (Surumu (GER))
1559[6] 2378[6] 2694[6] 3220[8]

Mistral Wind (IRE) *Ed Dunlop* a63
2 b f Hurricane Run(IRE) Grable (IRE) (Sadler's Wells (USA))
8201[4]

Mistress Of Rome *Michael Dods* 70
3 b f Holy Roman Emperor(IRE) Fairy Dance (IRE) (Zafonic (USA))
1322[3] (1517) 2144[2] 3080[3] 3847[3] 4250[2] 5413[2] 6472[9] 7369[3]

Mistress Shy *Michael Appleby* a53 30
5 b m Zafeen(FR) Nicholas Mistress (Beveled (USA))
3317[10] 5179[9] 6120[10] 6457[9] 6843[9] 7530[8] 7981[2] 8239[5]

Mists Of Time (IRE) *Pat Eddery* 63
2 b f Excellent Art Capriole (Noverre (USA))
5979[11]

Misty Eyes *Geoffrey Harker* 33
3 b f Byron Wax Eloquent (Zaha (CAN))
3352[9] 4551[6] 6361[14] 7126[8]

Misty Secret (IRE) *Tom Dascombe* a50 58
2 b f Clodovil(IRE) Villafranca (IRE) (In The Wings)
4217[8] 5016[6] 6007[7] 6583[10] 7313[10] 7979[3] 8093[7]

Misu Mac *Neville Bycroft* 4
2 b f Misu Bond(IRE) Umbrian Gold (IRE) (Perugino (USA))
5410[13] 6132[8]

Mitchell *David Barron* 75
2 ch g Haafhd Maid To Matter (Pivotal)
3381[3] (4178) 5563[14]

Mitch Rapp (USA) *Jamie Osborne* a61 60
3 b g Yankee Gentleman(USA) Foolish Party (USA) (Party Manners (USA))
1725[3] 4219[12] 5479[10]

Mitchum *David Barron* a84 82
3 b c Elnadim(USA) Maid To Matter (Pivotal)
1271[5] 1658[7] 2182[7] 5170[5] 5803[4] 6261[6]

Mitico (TUR) *Z Guneli*
4 b h Red Bishop(USA) Princess Galina (IRE) (Spectrum (IRE))
(5868a)

Mitie Mouse *Mike Murphy* a73 77
3 b g Exceed And Excel(AUS) Mimi Mouse (Diktat)
1063[4] 1449[5] 3234[9] 3671[U] 4457[2] 4705[2] 5127[4] 6402[7] 6737[7] 7157[5]

Mixed Message (IRE) *Ed McMahon* 66
2 b f Kodiac Berenica (IRE) (College Chapel)
2437[4] 3034[8] 3776[4] 5194[5] 5484[3] 6130[2] (6952)

Mix N Match *Christopher Kellett* a22 35
8 b g Royal Applause South Wind (Tina's Pet)
5241[9]

Mixora (USA) *Sir Henry Cecil* a65 58
3 rg f Mizzen Mast(USA) Ixora (USA) (Dynaformer (USA))
(2794) 3345[8]

Mizbah *Saeed Bin Suroor* a82 82
3 b g Dubai Destination(USA) Candice (IRE) (Caerleon (USA))
1440[11] 2429[5] 2772[4] 3448[11] 3945[2] 4649[3] 4923[3] 5838[11] 7672[4]

Mizdirection (USA) *Mike Puype* a104 111
4 rg m Mizzen Mast(USA) Deceptive (USA) (Clever Trick (USA))
(7571a)

Mizwaaj (IRE) *Saeed Bin Suroor* a96 82
3 b c Invincible Spirit(IRE) My Dubai (IRE) (Dubai Millennium)
1825[3] (2041) 2813[4] (3281) 5746[8] 6432[8]

Mizyen (IRE) *James Tate* 59
2 b c Teofilo(IRE) Housekeeper (IRE) (Common Grounds)
5303[6] 6114[10] 6603[5]

Mizzen Reef (USA) *C Ferland* a71
3 gr g Mizzen Mast(USA) Fondly (USA) (Mr Greeley (USA))
365a[10]

Mjaal (IRE) *John Weymes* a42
2 ch f Haatef(USA) Tawaajud (USA) (Dixieland Band (USA))
6133[10] 6779[5] 7460[8] 7977[8]

M J Woodward *Paul Green* a65 65
3 b c Needwood Blade Canina (Foxhound (USA))
(25) 112[4] 407[5] 769[4] 898[5] 1292[7] 2839[3] 3218[9] 7055[10] (7456) 7776[7] (8231)

M'Lady Eliza *David Evans* a55 45
7 b m Mtoto Starboard Tack (FR) (Saddlers' Hall (IRE))
1718[4] 2453[3]

Mnarani (IRE) *James Evans* a59 44
5 b g Oasis Dream Finity (USA) (Diesis)
274[13] 503[10] 807[6]

Moaning Butcher *Mark Johnston* a8 58
2 b c Lucarno(USA) Musical Chimes (Josr Algarhoud (IRE))
6532[6] 6919[4] 7357[11]

Moataz (USA) *David Simcock* a67 57
3 ch g Elusive Quality(USA) Ramatuelle (CHI) (Jeune Homme (USA))
38[6] (255) 288[2] (923) 998[4] 1319[11] 2471[5] 3066[7] 4329[12] 6442[13] 6894[8]

Mobaco (FR) *F Rossi* a105 109
3 b c Slickly(FR) Lunaa (FR) (Anabaa (USA))
716a[3] (7234a)

Mocenigo (IRE) *Peter Chapple-Hyam* a82 101
2 ch c Refuse To Bend(IRE) Doregan (IRE) (Bahhare (USA))
4646[2] (5011) 5833[4] 6671[8]

Model Behaviour (IRE) *Daniel Mark Loughnane* a48 52
3 b f Moss Vale(IRE) Fancy Feathers (IRE) (Redback)
5875[5] 6496[8] 6737[14] 7307[9]

Model Pupil *Charles Hills* 111
3 b c Sinndar(IRE) Modesta (IRE) (Sadler's Wells (USA))
(1456) 1995[2] 7438[3]

Moderator *Gary Moore* a85 91
3 b g Motivator Alessandra (Generous (IRE))
398[3] 596[6] 5533[4] (6703) 6971[2] 7810[5] 7999[4]

Modern History (IRE) *Mahmood Al Zarooni* a97 107
4 b g Shamardal(USA) Fatefully (USA) (Private Account (USA))
47a[4]

Modernism *Mark Johnston* a78 89
3 b g Monsun(GER) La Nuit Rose (FR) (Rainbow Quest (USA))
(908) 1160[10] 4151[6] 4923[2] 5366[3] (5533) 6025[4] 6415[7]

Modern Lady *Richard Guest* a65 55
2 b f Bertolini(USA) Lady Natilda (First Trump)
1556[9] 3269[26] 4545[7] 4927[3] 5313[6] (7156) 7526[2] 7745[2] 7930[3] 8065[2] 8161[3]

Modern Society *Alan McCabe* a25
2 sk c I Was Framed(USA) Artzola (IRE) (Alzao (USA))
1211[10] 1411[10] 7357[8]

Modernstone *William Knight* a59
2 b f Duke Of Marmalade(IRE) Post Modern (USA) (Nureyev (USA))
7159[7]

Modern Tutor *Sir Michael Stoute* 87
3 b c Selkirk(USA) Magical Romance (IRE) (Barathea (IRE))
1506[13] 2941[9] (3389) ◆

Modeyra *Saeed Bin Suroor* 108
5 br m Shamardal(USA) Zahrat Dubai (Unfuwain (USA))
6142[3]

Modun (IRE) *Saeed Bin Suroor* a113 110
5 br g King's Best(USA) Olympienne (IRE) (Sadler's Wells (USA))
759a[4] 4010[6] 5354[3] 6035[3] 6236[6] 7630[2]

Moe Green (IRE) *Francisco Castro* 97
5 b g Xaar Scripture (IRE) (Sadler's Wells (USA))
6091a[7]

Moe's Place (IRE) *Kevin Ryan* 32
2 b g Acclamation Sahara Sky (IRE) (Danehill (USA))
7434[7]

Mogadishio (FR) *Mlle C Cardenne* a90 94
5 b h American Post Nebraska I (FR) (Octagonal (NZ))
7123a[9]

Mohair *Luke Dace* a70 59
3 b f Motivator Cashmere (Barathea (IRE))
5329[6] 5795[9] 5970[2] 6647[4] 7011[2] 7718[6] 8060[6]

Mohanad (IRE) *Sheena West* a71 84
6 b g Invincible Spirit(IRE) Irish Design (IRE) (Alhaarth (IRE))
2412[3] 2936[4] 3162[2] 3827[5] 4096[8] 5106[11]

Mohawk Ridge *Michael Dods* a65 75
6 b g Storming Home Ipsa Loquitur (Unfuwain (USA))
1297[3] 1822[9] 2827[5] 3437[5] (3750) 4176[3] 5673[5] 6045[9] 6608[6] 6957[9] 7454[8]

Mohedian Lady (IRE) *Sir Mark Prescott Bt* 108
4 b m Hurricane Run(IRE) Amathia (IRE) (Darshaan)
2209[7] 2711[4] ◆ 3856[7] 5826[11]

Moheebb (IRE) *Robert Johnson* a72 89
8 b g Machiavellian(USA) Rockerlong (Deploy)
1052[6] 1249[11] 1670[3] 1914[3] 2142[3] 2753[5] 3167[6] 3274[7] 3492[3] 4175[4] 4620[6] 4864[2] 5220[8] (5669) 6342[6] (6785) 7003[4] 7493[8] 7640[10]

Mohica Glaz (FR) *S Cerulis* a79 50
3 b f Shirocco(GER) Mahyara (FR) (Lomitas)
(476a)

Moidore *John Quinn* a77 89
3 b g Galileo(IRE) Flash Of Gold (Darshaan)
2484[7] 3042[6] (3787) 4323[7] 5540[4] (6517) ◆

Mojo Bear *Sylvester Kirk* a61 61
2 b f Indesatchel(IRE) Four Legs Good (IRE) (Be My Guest (USA))
6453[7] 7433[3] 7777[4]

Mojolika *Tim Easterby* a67 81
4 ch g Motivator Kalandika (Diesis)
2457[5] 2978[2] 4176[2] 4613[4] 5256[3]

Mojo Miss (IRE) *Charles Hills* 76
2 br f Shirocco(GER) Starring (FR) (Ashkalani (IRE))
7329[2]

Mokbil (IRE) *Roger Varian* a57 69
3 b g Dansili Chatifa (IRE) (Titus Livius (FR))
1703[12] 2604[4]

Moldowney *T Stack* a93 91
3 ch g Dalakhani(IRE) Danehill's Dream (IRE) (Danehill (USA))
3296[6]

Molly Filia (GER) *Uwe Ostmann* 96
3 bb f Big Shuffle(USA) Molly Dancer (GER) (Shareef Dancer (USA))
2107a[4] 2746a[9] 3653a[6] 6085a[4]

Molly Jones *Derek Haydn Jones* a61 70
3 b f Three Valleys(USA) And Toto Too (Averti (IRE))
905[5] 1445[7] 2759[8] 6498[6] 6961[18] 7351[3] 7673[10] 8045[2] 8190[4] 8307[5]

Molly Malone (FR) *M Delzangles* 112
4 b m Lomitas Moonlight Melody (GER) (Law Society (USA))
1971a[3] 2711[3] 5650a[5] (6914a)

Molly Mara (GER) *J-C Rouget* 89
2 b f Big Shuffle(USA) Molly Dancer (GER) (Shareef Dancer (USA))
(5612a) 6463a[8]

Mollyow (IRE) *Terry Clement* a56 59
4 ch m Iceman Corryvreckan (IRE) (Night Shift (USA))
399[11] 742[7] 3086[5] 3400[9] 3969[2] 4004[4] (4664) 4904[4] 5051[2] 5509[2] 5637[3] 6019[6] 6922[5]

Mollyvator (IRE) *Mrs K Burke* 78
2 ch f Motivator Gazebo (Cadeaux Genereux)
2508[2] (3776) 4514[6] 6160[9] 6490[3] 6873[15]

Momalorka *William Haggas* 98
2 ch f Dutch Art Scarlet Royal (Red Ransom (USA))
2499[5] 3010[2] (3339) 4093[3] ◆ 4820[6] 5103[6] 5571[5] 6467[3] 7052[5] 7406[2]

Mombasa *John Dunlop* 77
2 b c Dubawi(IRE) Limuru (Salse (USA))
6486[17] 6795[8] (7373)

Momentary *Michael Bell* a78 99
3 b f Nayef(USA) Fleeting Memory (Danehill (USA))
1503[4] (2232) 3292[12] 4550[1] 6510a[5] 7510[12]

Moment In The Sun *David Flood* a67 51
3 ch f Dubai Destination(USA) Special Moment (IRE) (Sadler's Wells (USA))
132[5] 255[6] 571[2] (727) 993[4] 1267[6] 1424[6] 1590[9] (1979) 2398[6] (2580) 5350[7] 5406[7] 5941[12]

Moment In Time (IRE) *David Simcock* a78 83
3 b f Tiger Hill(IRE) Horatia (IRE) (Machiavellian (USA))
(1180) 1938[6] (2999) 5228[4] 6667[2] ◆

Moment Of Majesty (CAN) *Sue Leslie* a103 105
5 b m Saint Liam(USA) Lady Indy (USA) (A.P. Indy (USA))
6298a[7] 7093a[7]

Moment Of Time *Andrew Balding* a82 94
4 b m Rainbow Quest(USA) Not Before Time (IRE) (Polish Precedent (USA))
3219[5] 4916[3] 5745[3]

Monadreen Dancer *Daniel Mark Loughnane* a61 49
4 b m Kheleyf(USA) Volitant (Ashkalani (IRE))
232[5] 305[2] 422[6] 478[7] 842[7] 941[6] 1074[5]

Monami (GER) *A Wohler* 106
3 ch f Sholokhov(IRE) Monbijou (GER) (Dashing Blade)
2531a[DSQ] 3802a[4] 4862a[8] 6727a[3] 7587a[5]

Mon Ami Jolie (USA) *Richard Hannon* a82 72
4 gr g Maria's Mon(USA) Lasting Pleasure (USA) (Theatrical (IRE))
(720) (1614) 2070[8] 7412[6]

Monashee Rock (IRE) *Patrick Chamings* a59 50
7 b m Monashee Mountain(USA) Polar Rock (Polar Falcon (USA))
293[6] 1830[3] 2170[5] ◆ 2627[5] 3153[9]

Mon Brav *Brian Ellison* a52 95
5 b g Sampower Star Danehill Princess (IRE) (Danehill (USA))
1863[3] 2284[4] 2507[14] 3078[2] 3624[12] 4339[5] 4629[11] 5110[3] 6009[8] ◆ 6338[7] 7716[6]

Mon Chic *Ollie Pears*
2 b f Monsieur Bond(IRE) Chicago Bond (USA) (Real Quiet (USA))
6781[4]

Mon Choix (FR) *Y Barberot* a90 77
3 b f Choisir(AUS) Macina (IRE) (Platini (GER))
(8277a)

Mondego (GER) *C Moore* a54
10 b g Big Shuffle(USA) Molto In Forma (GER) (Surumu (GER))
7991[5]

Mon Duchess *Lawrence Mullaney* 58
4 b m Danbird(AUS) Icenaslice (IRE) (Fayruz)
2121[4] 2918[7] 3406[4] 4174[7] 5719[14]

Monel *Jim Goldie* 66
4 ch g Cadeaux Genereux Kelucia (IRE) (Grand Lodge (USA))
1224[3] 1799[6] 5189[8] 6104[6] 7099[9]

Monessa (IRE) *Linda Jewell* a9 60
3 ch f Le Vie Dei Colori Nasaria (IRE) (Starborough)
3245[10] 4003[7] 5514[6] 5949[6] 6436[4]

Money Money Money *Rod Millman* a74 83
6 b m Generous(IRE) Shi Shi (Alnasr Alwasheek)
2863[6] 3827[4]

Monicker *H-A Pantall* 94
3 b f Manduro(GER) Guadalajara (GER) (Acatenango (GER))
3035[11] 3606[7] 7665a[11]

Monkey Bar Flies (IRE) *Richard Fahey* 71
2 b g Elusive City(USA) Angel Nights (IRE) (Night Shift (USA))
2261[6] 2614[4] 4612[6] (5450) 6155[8] 6658[9] 6984[7]

Monnoyer *Scott Dixon* a78 78
3 ch g Dutch Art Ellebanna (Tina's Pet)
230[5] 1721[13] 2591[10] 4558[11] 5662[8]

Monopoli *Ralph Beckett* a44 78
3 ch f Cadeaux Genereux Jump Ship (Night Shift (USA))
3735[13] 4505[2] 5239[2] 5931[11] (6544)

Mons Calpe (IRE) *Paul Cole* a77 76
6 b g Rock Of Gibraltar(IRE) Taking Liberties (IRE) (Royal Academy (USA))
2887[6] 3222[8] 3472[7] 5359[6] 6440[8]

Monshak (IRE) *Sir Michael Stoute* 96
3 b f Monsun(GER) Woman Secret (IRE) (Sadler's Wells (USA))
2008[2] (3100) (4079) ◆ 5598[RR] 6163[7] 6833[8]

Monsieur Broughton *Willie Musson* a58 58
4 ch g Monsieur Bond(IRE) Rainy Day Song (Persian Bold)
685[5] 995[7] 1088[8] 1309[6] 7189[8]

Monsieur Chevalier (IRE) *P J O'Gorman* a102 117
5 b h Chevalier(IRE) Blue Holly (IRE) (Blues Traveller (IRE))
6869[8] 7401[8] 7774[7]

Monsieur Jamie *J R Jenkins* a89 61
4 b g Monsieur Bond(IRE) Primula Bairn (Bairn (USA))
3[7] 652[9] 835[RR] 1581[9] 7113[13] 7489[5] 7726[10]

Monsieur Joe (IRE) *Robert Cowell* a86 114
5 b g Choisir(AUS) Pascali (Compton Place)
50a[6] (419a) 681a[2] 875a[4] 1146a[4] 2112a[2] 2486[11] 3238[11] 4113[3] (4790a) 5561[14] (6292a) 6908a[8]

Monsieur Pontaven *Robin Bastiman* a61 57
5 b g Avonbridge Take Heart (Electric)
7[5] 154[7] 329[2] 430[6] 927[3] 1224[7] 1907[3] 2858[8] 3047[7] 3907[6] 4389[6] 5632[2] 7362[5]

Monsieur Rieussec *Jonathan Portman* 79
2 bl c Halling(USA) Muscovado (USA) (Mr Greeley (USA))
3067[4] 4472[3] 6481[8] 7335[3]

Monsieur Royale *Geoffrey Oldroyd* a69 58
2 ch c Monsieur Bond(IRE) Bond Royale (Piccolo)
2686[7] 4344[10] 4710[5] ◆ (7649)

Montaff *Mick Channon* a87 110
6 b g Montjeu(IRE) Meshhed (USA) (Gulch (USA))
143a[8] 421a[11] 1214[8] 1672[3] 2278[8] 2709[9] 3625[5] 4528[3] 5076[9] 6191[7] 7051[26]

Montalban (FR) *D De Waele* a99 98
5 b g Elusive City(USA) Realy Queen (USA) (Thunder Gulch (USA))
6804a[0]

Montaser (IRE) *David Simcock* 103
3 b c Rail Link For Example (USA) (Northern Baby (CAN))
1160[5] 1978[4] (2484) (4528) ◆ 6415[2] 7051[27]

Montauk (FR) *G Doleuze* a45 39
6 gr g Pursuit Of Love The Last Ballerine (FR) (Neverneyev (USA))
94a[0]

Montcliffe *Richard Fahey* 65
2 b c Acclamation Dea Caelestis (FR) (Dream Well (FR))
3271[4] 4069[3] 4710[4] 5579[8]

Monte Alto (IRE) *A Al Raihe* a101 89
8 b g Danehill Dancer(IRE) Peruvian Witch (IRE) (Perugino (USA))
48a[4] 242a[3]

Monte Cassino (IRE) *Bryan Smart* a61 48
7 ch g Choisir(AUS) Saucy Maid (IRE) (Sure Blade (USA))
(113) 670[5] 2091[13] 7224[4] 7733[3] 7917[2]

Monte Cavallo (SAF) *Rebecca Curtis* 86
7 b g Saumarez Mufski (SAF) (Al Mufti (USA))
5306[2] 7300[4]

Monte Mayor One *Mrs K Burke* a62 64
5 b m Lujain(USA) Alvarinho Lady (Royal Applause)
5923[14] 7748[10]

Monterey (IRE) *Robert Mills* a70 93
5 b g Montjeu(IRE) Magnificient Style (USA) (Silver Hawk (USA))
2423[3] (2936) 3241[15]

Monterosso *Mahmood Al Zarooni* a126 116
5 b h Dubawi(IRE) Porto Roca (AUS) (Barathea (IRE))
878a[4] (1150a) 3880[8]

Montevideo (GER) *S Botti* 73
2 b f Desert Prince(IRE) Moricana (GER) (Konigsstuhl (GER))
7285a[9]

Monthly Medal *Wilf Storey* a61 70
9 b g Danehill Dancer(IRE) Sovereign Abbey (IRE) (Royal Academy (USA))
2922[4] 3310[8] 3888[5] 4620[9] 4864[7] (5547) 6258[9] 6711[6] 6785[2] 7095[3] 7383[6] (7495) 7640[9]

Montiridge (IRE) *Richard Hannon* 105
2 b c Ramonti(FR) Elegant Ridge (IRE) (Indian Ridge)
(4056) (6372) 7053[2]

Montjess (IRE) *Tom Dascombe* 56
2 b f Montjeu(IRE) Wing Stealth (IRE) (Hawk Wing (USA))
6790[9]

Montmorency (IRE) *S Seemar* a99 103
6 ch h Pivotal Clear Spring (USA) (Irish River (FR))
53a[12] 261a[6] ◆ 757a[3]

Mont Ras (IRE) *David O'Meara* 92
5 ch g Indian Ridge Khayrat (IRE) (Polar Falcon (USA))
1128[3] 1510[7] 1865[7] 4828[3] 5342[3] 7030[9]

Mont Signal *Daniel Kubler* a47 47
2 ch g Pivotal Anse Victorin (USA) (Mt. Livermore (USA))
7434[6] 7806[7] 7894[5] 8155[10]

Monty Fay (IRE) *John Flint* a64 60
3 bb g Iffraaj Blast (USA) (Roar (USA))
201[6] 2388[2] 3098[8] 3670[7] 4489[8] 6500[10] 6737[13] 8184[8]

Monument (USA) *John W Sadler* a100
2 bb c Cindago(USA) Grant Marty A Wish (USA) (Beautiful Crown (USA))
7572a[9]

Monumental Man *James Unett* a70 63
3 b g Vital Equine(IRE) Spark Up (Lahib (USA))
3555[15] 6322[3] ◆ 6937[9] 7146[4] (8046) (8209)

Mon Visage *Chris Wall* a73 76
4 ch m Ishiguru(USA) Pikaboo (Pivotal)
1254[12]

Monymusk *David Elsworth* a61 70
3 b g Norse Dancer(IRE) Bee One (IRE) (Catrail (USA))
2145[5] 2557[11] 3917[7] 4341[7] 4777[6]

Monzino (USA) *Michael Chapman* a69 53
4 bb g More Than Ready(USA) Tasso's Magic Roo (USA) (Tasso (USA))
2864[6] 3024[7] 3702[7] 3913[15] (4192) 4405[3] 4775[8] 5179[5] 5323[12] 6479[13] 6812[6] 7437[10] 7610[5] 7731[10]

Moodhill *Charles Hills* 78
3 b c Dansili Almurooj (Zafonic (USA))
3398[3] (3809) 4503[11]

Moody Dancer *William Muir* a63 58
3 b f Cape Cross(IRE) Bluebelle Dancer (IRE) (Danehill Dancer (IRE))
1517[12] 2136[5] 2803[4] 3315[6] 3949[2] 4506[12] 5229[13] 6216[8] 6641[8] 7189[10] 7326[8]

Moody Tunes *Tom Dascombe* a67 82
9 b g Merdon Melody Lady-Love (Pursuit Of Love)
2043[2] 2498[5] (2886) 3693[3] 4317[21] 4864[9] 5585[4] 5783[9]

Moohaajim (IRE) *Marco Botti* 118
2 b c Cape Cross(IRE) Thiella (USA) (Kingmambo (USA))
(4362) ◆ 5398a[5] ◆ (6483) ◆ 7049[2] ◆

Moonday Sun (USA) *D Smaga* 106
3 gr c Mizzen Mast(USA) Storm Dove (USA) (Storm Bird (CAN))
5649a[4]

Moone's My Name *Ralph Beckett* a86 108
4 gr m Intikhab(USA) The Manx Touch (IRE) (Petardia)
(1416) 2067[4] 2657[10] (3636) 4527[3] ◆ 5092[3] 5834[10] 6633[3] (6879) 7509[9]

Moonglow *John Gosden* a64 66
3 b f Nayef(USA) Mystic Goddess (USA) (Storm Bird (CAN))
2148[4] 3161[6] 3786[11] 4538[13]

Moonlight Cloud *F Head* a94 124
4 b m Invincible Spirit(IRE) Ventura (IRE) (Spectrum (IRE))
(2728a) 3370[2] (4861a) 5141a[4] (6296a) 7575a[8]

Moonlight Diamond (IRE) *U Suter* a64 74
3 b g Whipper(USA) Brewing Storm (IRE) (King Charlemagne (USA))
865a[7]

Moonlight Gambler (FR) *N Bertran De Balanda* 75
3 b c Westerner Zuppa Inglese (FR) (Le Balafre (FR))
365a[0]

Moonlit Dancer (IRE) *J W Hills* a63 58
2 gr f Dark Angel(IRE) Wohaida (IRE) (Kheleyf (USA))
3040[4] 3473[7] 4581[4] 5160[4] 5484[4] 5968[4] 6612[2] 7008[10]

Moon Pearl (USA) *Ralph Beckett* a52 98
3 bb g Johannesburg(USA) Moonavvara (IRE) (Sadler's Wells (USA))
2022[7] 3294[13] 4557[10] 5595[3] 6580[8]

Moonreach (IRE) *S Seemar* a83 90
5 b g Chineur(FR) Ribbon Glade (UAE) (Zafonic (USA))
875a[11]

Moonshine Ruby *Peter Hiatt* 50
6 ch m Minster Son Over The Moon (Beveled (USA))
1655[7] 2768[8] 3663[5] 4536[14] 5164[11] 5817[P] 5936[8]

Moonship *Sir Michael Stoute* a71 51
3 b c Halling(USA) Soviet Moon (IRE) (Sadler's Wells (USA))
6770[5]

Moon Spun (SAF) *H J Brown* a96 75
4 b m Black Minnaloushe(USA) Dreaming Gold (SAF) (Golden Thatch I (IRE))
418a[4] 680a[4] 754a[5]

Moonstone Magic *Ralph Beckett* 109
3 b f Trade Fair Woodcock Moon (Kyllachy)
(1357) ◆ (1508) 1884[15]

Moonstreaker *Charles Pogson* a73 70
9 b g Foxhound(USA) Ling Lane (Slip Anchor)
4189[9]

Moon Trip *Mark Johnston* a66 94
3 b g Cape Cross(IRE) Fading Light (King's Best (USA))
1557[5] 2716[2] 3509[5] (4176) 4601[3] 5106[2] (5256) 5580[7] 6031[10]

Moonwalk (USA) *Dale Romans* 99
2 bb f Malibu Moon(USA) Lucinda K (USA) (Red Ransom (USA))
7547a[7]

Moonwalk In Paris (FR) *J-C Rouget* a109 114
4 b g Oratorio(IRE) Shining Glory (Singspiel (IRE))
(1163a) 3205a[2] 3900a[3] 5649a[2]

Moorgate Lad *Garry Woodward* 47
5 b g Danbird(AUS) Goodbye Millie (Sayf El Arab (USA))
3913[13] 4747[11]

Moorgate Lass *Garry Woodward* a58
4 b m Danbird(AUS) Bolham Lady (Timeless Times (USA))
675[4] 770[7]

Moorhouse Girl *David Brown* a40 68
5 b m Makbul Record Time (Clantime)
3357[4] 4743[4] 5020[5] 5205[7]

Moorhouse Lad *Garry Moss* a92 101
9 b g Bertolini(USA) Record Time (Clantime)
5822[11] 6028[8] 7397[17] 7704[4] 7918[5] 8009[2] 8163[2]

Moorside Magic *Richard Fahey* a59 33
3 b f Dubai Destination(USA) Parsonagehotelyork (IRE) (Danehill (USA))
358[4] 604[3] 4177[6] 4883[9]

Moorway (IRE) *Reg Hollinshead* a57 58
2 b c Dylan Thomas(IRE) Cordelia (Green Desert (USA))
4837[7] 5331[4] 5962[11] 6893[4] 7289[5]

Moose Moran (USA) *Olivia Maylam* a23 73
5 rg g Lemon Drop Kid(USA) After All (IRE) (Desert Story (IRE))
3765[8] 4475[6] 5124[3] 5596[6] 6118[5] 6430[8]

Morache Music *Peter Makin* 110
4 b g Sleeping Indian Enchanted Princess (Royal Applause)
2074[3] 3190[5] 3371[4] 3860[2] 4092[4] 6468[22]

Moral Issue *Ian McInnes* a73 73
4 b g Ishiguru(USA) Morale (Bluebird (USA))
128[3] 403[3] (692) 909[3] 1269[12] 2173[10] 2588[9] 2692[7] 3454[4] 4783[13] 5171[12] 8271[6]

Morana (IRE) *Warren Greatrex* 43
5 b g Alhaarth(IRE) Blushing Barada (USA) (Blushing Groom (FR))
3157[12]

Morandi (FR) *J-C Rouget* 117
2 gr c Holy Roman Emperor(IRE) Vezina (FR) (Bering)
5471a[2] (7283a) (7693a)

Moran Gra (USA) *Ms Joanna Morgan* a103 107
5 ch g Rahy(USA) Super Supreme (IND) (Zafonic (USA))
53a[15] 243a[6] 319a[5] 489a[9] 4692a[11] 6674[7]

Morant Bay (IRE) *Ian Williams* a76 79
3 b f Montjeu(IRE) Quad's Melody (IRE) (Spinning World (USA))
(1649) 2232[6] 3668[6] 6667[11] 7375[9] 7843[3] 8057[9] 8158[6]

Moratab (IRE) *Roger Varian* a66 80
3 b g Dubai Destination(USA) Bahr (Generous (IRE))
2226[2] 2826[3] 3232[3]

Morawij *Roger Varian* 107
2 ch c Exceed And Excel(AUS) Sister Moonshine (FR) (Piccolo)
(2415) 3291[4] (3823) 4687[2] 5559[8] 6196[6]

More Bottle (IRE) *Tom Tate* a24 54
3 b f Barathea(IRE) More Respect (IRE) (Spectrum (IRE))
1519[10] 1916[3] 2840[8] 3460[4] 5803[7] 7437[11]

More Joyous (NZ) *Gai Waterhouse* 124
6 b m More Than Ready(USA) Sunday Joy (AUS) (Sunday Silence (USA))
7426a[11]

Morermaloke *Ian McInnes* a69 52
4 ch g Bahamian Bounty Rainbow End (Botanic (USA))
101[8] 155[10] 831[10] 3053[9] 3463[8] 6958[10]

Moresweets 'n Lace *Gary Moore* a74 74
5 b m Zafeen(FR) Another Secret (Efisio)
1071[5] 1314[4] 2149[2] (2650)

More Than Sotka (FR) *F-H Graffard* 96
2 ch f Dutch Art King's Doll (IRE) (King's Best (USA))
5379a[6] 6225a[2]

More Than Words (IRE) *Richard Hannon* a78 60
3 b f Lawman(FR) Gilded (IRE) (Redback)
1472[8] 2332[5] 3071[5] 3619[10] 5409[7] 6152[2]

Moretta Blanche *Ralph Beckett* a79 93
5 b m Dansili Cotton House (IRE) (Mujadil (USA))
(2070) 2890[2] 3105[2] 3593[3] 4286[13] 4764[4]

Morga (IRE) *J S Bolger* a69 85
2 b f Whipper(USA) Langfuhrina (USA) (Langfuhr (CAN))
6853a[5]

Morilles *Clive Cox* a45 65
3 b f Montjeu(IRE) Niner's Home (USA) (Forty Niner (USA))
533[7] 784[7] 1414[4] 2424[8] 5413[9]

Morinda *Ed Walker* a54
3 b f Selkirk(USA) Morning Queen (GER) (Konigsstuhl (GER))
7647[6] 8295[4]

Morlotti *Luca Cumani* a61 58
3 b g Dalakhani(IRE) Saphila (IRE) (Sadler's Wells (USA))
1467[17] 1923[7] 2453[4] 3161[12] 4005[5]

Morna's Glory *Jason Ward* a15 62
3 b f Resplendent Glory(IRE) Tipsy Cake (Tipsy Creek (USA))
3913[6] 4550[3] 4782[8] 4913[2] 5185[9] 7446[14] 8291[10]

Morning Call *Henry Candy* a64 73
3 b g Sleeping Indian Fanfare (Deploy)
5276[6] (5687) 6488[13] 7170[8]

Morning Charm (USA) *John Gosden* a73 80
4 b m North Light(IRE) Vignette (USA) (Diesis)
3963[8]

Morning Coat *Mahmood Al Zarooni* 45
3 b c Shirocco(GER) Pioneer Bride (USA) (Gone West (USA))
1518[7]

Morning Frost (IRE) *C Ferland* 96
2 gr f Duke Of Marmalade(IRE) Evening Time (IRE) (Keltos (FR))
5379a[8]

Morocco *John Gosden* a69 70
3 b g Rock Of Gibraltar(IRE) Shanghai Lily (IRE) (King's Best (USA))
1068[3] 2196[4]

Morocco Moon *Tim Pitt* a75 90
3 b f Rock Of Gibraltar(IRE) One Giant Leap (IRE) (Pivotal)
768[3] (925) 1110[2] (2256)

Morpheus *Sir Henry Cecil* 56
2 b c Oasis Dream Kind (IRE) (Danehill (USA))
7172[7]

Morrow *Mahmood Al Zarooni* 72
3 ch f Pivotal Morning Pride (IRE) (Machiavellian (USA))
3340[10]

Mortga (FR) *P Bary* 97
3 b c Anabaa(USA) Cornelia (FR) (Silver Hawk (USA))
3204a[7]

Mortitia *Tim Easterby* a50 95
4 b m Dansili Simianna (Bluegrass Prince (IRE))
2078[13] 2554[3] 3336[7] 4497[8] 6406[10]

Mosa Mine *Bryn Palling* a56 55
5 b m Exceed And Excel(AUS) Baldemosa (FR) (Lead On Time (USA))
544[5]

Moscow Eight (IRE) *E J O'Neill* a81 91
6 b g Elusive City(USA) Hurricane Lily (IRE) (Ali-Royal (IRE))
4799[9]

Moscow Oznick *Des Donovan* a53 67
7 br g Auction House(USA) Cozette (IRE) (Danehill Dancer (IRE))
265[11] 389[6] 530[11]

Moshaagib (USA) *John Gosden* 81
3 bb c Dynaformer(USA) Ensenada (USA) (Seeking The Gold (USA))
2197[12] 3349[8] 4067[8]

Mosman *Jamie Osborne* a69
2 b c Haafhd Last Dream (IRE) (Alzao (USA))
7306[11] 7796[3] 8052[4] 8147[3] 8270[2]

Mosqueta *Andrew Reid* a23 20
5 b m Doyen(IRE) Arantxa (Sharpo)
224[9]

Mossa (IRE) *Mme J Bidgood* a63 45
3 b f Moss Vale(IRE) Shamata (IRE) (Cadeaux Genereux)
17a[0] 4477a[6]

Mossbrae *Roger Varian* a74 81
3 ch g Selkirk(USA) Frosty Welcome (USA) (With Approval (CAN))
2271[10] 5297[4] 5816[4] 6441[2] 6704[7]

Mossgo (IRE) *John Best* a75 77
2 b g Moss Vale(IRE) Perovskia (USA) (Stravinsky (USA))
(1284) 1747[4] 2638[8] 3242[22] 6929[8] 7745[10] (8065) 8245[5]

Moss Hill *Charles Hills* 41
3 b g Moss Vale(IRE) Borders Belle (IRE) (Pursuit Of Love)
1450[12] 4341[10]

Mossmann Gorge *Anthony Middleton* a46 39
10 b g Lujain(USA) North Pine (Import)
1770[4] 5508[8]

Moss Quito (IRE) *David O'Meara* 64
2 b g Moss Vale(IRE) Gold Majesty (Josr Algarhoud (IRE))
2123[6] 2770[6] 3110[3] 3436[11] 4343[3]

Mosstang (IRE) *Robert Mills* a72 40
2 b c Moss Vale(IRE) Lovely Dream (IRE) (Elnadim (USA))
1211[3] 1352[6] (1955) 2638[9]

Moss The Boss (IRE) *Paul Midgley* 39
2 b g Moss Vale(IRE) Lady Of Bilston (IRE) (Bin Ajwaad (IRE))
1435[10] 1795[5] 6954[10]

Most Improved (IRE) *Brian Meehan* 118
3 b c Lawman(FR) Tonnara (IRE) (Linamix (FR))
2743a[14] (3239) 5141a[11] 6634[7] 7238[8]

Mother Jones *David Evans* a78 76
4 b m Sleeping Indian Bella Chica (IRE) (Bigstone (IRE))
100[11] 545[4] (719) 911[3] (1187) 1638[7] 2133[4] 2360[3] 2789[6] 3707[6] 4154[3] 4535[5] 4885[2] 5298[3] 5347[3] 5995[3] 6277[2] (6307) 6685[2] 7197[3] 7274[6] 7775[5] (7863) 8009[7] 8059[5] 8157[5]

Mothman (IRE) *T Lemer* 102
3 b c Barathea(IRE) Sandrella (IRE) (Darshaan)
3204a[6]

Motion Lass *Ralph Beckett* 67
2 b f Motivator Tarneem (USA) (Zilzal (USA))
7130[2] ◆ 7637[9]

Motivado *Sir Mark Prescott Bt* a81 109
4 b g Motivator Tamise (USA) (Time For A Change (USA))
3625[13] 4111[8] (4800) ◆ 5600[4] 7051[4]

Mottley Crewe *Des Donovan* a91 70
5 b g Mujahid(USA) Ticcatoo (IRE) (Dolphin Street (FR))
3[2] 286[2] 527[8] 654[3] 782[2] 835[7]

Moudre (AUS) *Ciaron Maher* 111
7 bb g Blevic(AUS) Tolkaami (AUS) (Raami I)
7264a[14] 7696a[8]

Mouhjim (FR) *Mme P Butel* a77 77
3 b c Agnes Kamikaze(JPN) Persephassa (FR) (Tiger Hill (IRE))
247a[8] (1127a)

Moulin De Mougin (USA) *Richard E Mandella* 90
2 b f Curlin(USA) Cambiocorsa (USA) (Avenue Of Flags (USA))
7567a[5]

Mount Abora (IRE) *Laura Mongan* a73 69
5 br m Rock Of Gibraltar(IRE) Ragtime Blues (IRE) (Grand Lodge (USA))
31[6] (192) 363[3] 433[3] 2915[9] 3386[4] 3793[11] 3967[2] 4505[7] 4915[3] (5310) 5706[9] 7301[9] 8051[7] 8078[5] 8301[3]

Mountain Cat (IRE) *Geoffrey Harker* a84 84
8 b g Red Ransom(USA) Timewee (USA) (Romanov (IRE))
216[13]

Mountain Coral (IRE) *F Oakes* a85 88
8 b g Jammaal Coral Windsor (IRE) (Woods Of Windsor (USA))
1040a[6]

Mountain Range (IRE) *John Dunlop* a92 92
4 b g High Chaparral(IRE) Tuscany Lady (IRE) (Danetime (IRE))
1882[6] 2346[7] 3121[3] 4103[6] 6018[7] 6584[8] 6987[10]

Mountain Summit *Richard Fahey* 25
3 b f Nayef(USA) Choysia (Pivotal)
3384[6] 4622[10]

Mountain View (GER) *Frau Nina Bach* 84
2 bb c Tertullian(USA) Mutige (Warning)
5781a[5]

Mount Athos (IRE) *Luca Cumani* a102 121
5 b g Montjeu(IRE) Ionian Sea (Slip Anchor)
(2278) (4111) ◆ (5354) 7621a[5] 7872a[12]

Mount Berry (FR) *E Leenders* a81 71
5 gr g Okawango(USA) Kalberry (FR) (Kaldounevees (FR))
7701a[3]

Mount Hollow *Reg Hollinshead* a85 85
7 b g Beat Hollow Lady Lindsay (IRE) (Danehill Dancer (IRE))
2264[7] 2870[9] 4315[6] 4998[2] 5933[3] (6357) 6800[7] 7295[10] 7464[2] 8143[4]

Mount Mayday (IRE) *Stuart Williams* a62 68
3 b g Rock Of Gibraltar(IRE) Fille De Joie (IRE) (Royal Academy (USA))
1206[10] 2430[9] 2927[7] (5458) 5633[2] ◆ (6546) 6773[5] 7402[4]

Mountrath *Gary Moore* a73 75
5 b g Dubai Destination(USA) Eurolink Sundance (Night Shift (USA))
4939[13] 5667[9] 6801[8] 7670[5] ◆ 7841[2] 7905[8]

Mount Seymour (IRE) *Nigel Tinkler* 69
2 b g Sleeping Indian Seymour (IRE) (Eagle Eyed (USA))
1437[8] 1861[2] 2123[7] 3286[4] 3844[10] 4670[3] 5053[3] 5411[7] 5675[3]

Mount St Mistress *George Baker* 51
3 ch f Zamindar(USA) Capannina (Grand Lodge (USA))
1608[13]

Mount Tiger *James Tate* a63
2 b c Tiger Hill(IRE) Fly Me To The Moon (GER) (Galileo (IRE))
7750[4]

Mourayan (IRE) *Robert Hickmott* 118
6 bb h Alhaarth(IRE) Mouramara (IRE) (Kahyasi)
7621a[7]

Moustache (IRE) *D Grilli* a102 99
3 b c Mujadil(USA) Spree (IRE) (Dansili)
542a^{2} 1698a^{4} 2325a^{7} 7286a^{7}
Mouth Piece *Sir Michael Stoute* a15 53
2 ch c Singspiel(IRE) Misleading Lady (Warning)
5319^{8}
Move In Time *Bryan Smart* a73 106
4 ch h Monsieur Bond(IRE) Tibesti (Machiavellian (USA))
1857^{7} 2745a^{9} 5204^{4} 5822^{12} 6244^{16} 7243^{8} 7397^{9} 7704^{10}
Move To Strike (IRE) *J S Bolger* 96
2 b c Lawman(FR) Alamanta (IRE) (Ali-Royal (IRE))
3368^{4}
Moviesta (USA) *Bryan Smart* a83 82
2 b g Hard Spun(USA) Miss Brickyard (USA) (A.P. Indy (USA))
4625^{3} ◆ 4921^{2} (6320)
Mowhoob *John Gosden* a72 74
2 b c Medicean Pappas Ruby (USA) (Red Ransom (USA))
2797^{5} 3062^{5} 3499^{3} 5155^{5} 6946^{2}
Moynahan (USA) *Thomas Cuthbert* a81 91
7 ch g Johannesburg(USA) Lakab (USA) (Manila (USA))
989^{5} 1416^{4} 4317^{17} 5585^{10}
Mozayada (USA) *Mel Brittain* a74 53
8 ch m Street Cry(IRE) Fatina (Nashwan (USA))
812^{7}
Mr Big (AUS) *M Freedman* 107
4 b g Elusive Quality(USA) Basamaat (IRE) (Danehill (USA))
2326a^{2}
Mr Brock (SAF) *M F De Kock* a107 114
9 b g Fort Wood(USA) Cape Badger (SAF) (Badger Land (USA))
242a^{5} 484a^{12}
Mr Chocolate Drop (IRE) *Mandy Rowland* a68 65
8 b g Danetime(IRE) Forest Blade (IRE) (Charnwood Forest (IRE))
1191^{6} (1447) 1830^{9} 1988^{6} 2555^{9} (2858) 3454^{5} (4390) 5081^{4} 6057^{4}
Mr Churchill (IRE) *Mahmood Al Zarooni* 70
3 b c Invincible Spirit(IRE) Mayoress (Machiavellian (USA))
2408^{10} 3448^{13}
Mr. Commons (USA) *John Shirreffs* a110 119
4 b h Artie Schiller(USA) Joustabout (USA) (Apalachee (USA))
7575a^{5}
Mr Crystal (FR) *Micky Hammond* a41 78
8 ch g Trempolino(USA) Iyrbila (FR) (Lashkari)
(1559) 2214^{9} 3419^{7}
Mr David (USA) *Jamie Osborne* a94 99
5 b g Sky Mesa(USA) Dancewiththebride (USA) (Belong To Me (USA))
2409^{9} 2697^{7} 3394^{9} 4255^{5} 4661^{2} (4775) 5004^{7} 5342^{13} 5746^{2} 6011^{4} 6192^{10} 7508^{14}
Mr Fickle (IRE) *Gary Moore* a67 74
3 b g Jeremy(USA) Mamara Reef (Salse (USA))
1606^{6} 2065^{6} (2803) 3151^{4} ◆ 3719^{2} 4872^{5} 5405^{6} 6988^{11}
Mr Fitzroy (IRE) *Andrew Balding* 78
2 ch g Kyllachy Reputable (Medicean)
6204^{6} 6572^{2} ◆
Mr Flintstone *Tim Walford* 23
3 b g Multiplex Lilac Dreams (Second Set (IRE))
2927^{5} 3352^{7}
Mr Fong *David Simcock* a64 71
3 ch g Dr Fong(USA) Selkirk Sky (Selkirk (USA))
1589^{4}
Mr Hendrix *Mark Hoad* a60 53
3 b g Librettist(USA) Sprinkle (Selkirk (USA))
2547^{9} 6926^{6} 7299^{4} 7471^{5} 8045^{6} 8169^{10}
Mr Jeremy *F Vermeulen* a49
5 b h Fasliyev(USA) Malaisienne (FR) (Saumarez)
92a^{9}
Mr Khan *Linda Perratt* 47
4 ch g Rambling Bear Frabrofen (Mind Games)
1238^{9} 1799^{5} 1876^{5}
Mr Knightley (IRE) *Jim Boyle* a81 71
3 b g Strategic Prince Emma's Surprise (Tobougg (IRE))
471^{5} 667^{8} 764^{3} 916^{5} 7115^{5} 7485^{6} ◆ 7722^{8} 8005^{2} (8074) (8177)
Mr Maynard *Sir Michael Stoute* a76 72
3 ch c Notnowcato Crystal Cavern (USA) (Be My Guest (USA))
1304^{7} 2265^{11}
Mr Mo Jo *Lawrence Mullaney* 69
4 b g Danbird(AUS) Nampara Bay (Emarati (USA))
2314^{14} 3018^{4} 3256^{15} 4911^{3} ◆ 5294^{4} 5739^{2} (6264) 7179^{11}
Mr O'Ceirin (NZ) *Ciaron Maher* 100
5 b g Postponed(USA) Cadell (NZ) (Yachtie (AUS))
7073a^{13}
Mr Optimistic *Paul Howling* a58 89
4 b g Kyllachy Noble Desert (FR) (Green Desert (USA))
1168^{11} 1478^{9} 2264^{14} 2876^{8} 3778^{13} 5933^{12} 6370^{10} 6836^{5} 7055^{6} 7504^{11} 7748^{11} 8169^{8}
Mr Paranoia *Conrad Allen* a57 61
2 b c Pastoral Pursuits Yatir (FR) (Red Ransom (USA))
6438^{3} ◆ 6787^{9} 7219^{4}
Mr Perceptive (IRE) *Micky Hammond* 81
4 b g Iffraaj Astuti (IRE) (Waajib)
2504^{12} 2751^{14} 3693^{7} 4627^{7} 5226^{9}
Mr Plod *Andrew Reid* a62 52
7 ch g Silver Patriarch(IRE) Emily-Mou (IRE) (Cadeaux Genereux)
433^{7} 825^{8}
Mr Pumpermichael (USA) *Philip A Gleaves*
2 b c Latent Heat(USA) Tizina (USA) (Tiznow (USA))
8244a^{4}
Mr Red Clubs (IRE) *Tim Pitt* a93 98
3 b g Red Clubs(IRE) Queen Cobra (IRE) (Indian Rocket)
(32) 180^{2} 1860^{4} 2277^{5} 3348^{3} 4063^{5} 4740^{5} 5363^{8}
Mrs Awkward *Mark Brisbourne*
3 b f Primo Valentino(IRE) Musical Chimes (Josr Algarhoud (IRE))
1673^{5}
Mrsb *Mrs K Burke*
3 b f Royal Applause Pearl Valley (Indian Rocket)
6527^{5} 7445^{12}
Mrs Bannock (IRE) *Mahmood Al Zarooni* a75
2 b f Shamardal(USA) Laoub (USA) (Red Ransom (USA))
(7505)
Mrs Batt (IRE) *John W Nicholson* a45 61
6 ch m Medecis She's Wonderful (IRE) (Magical Wonder (USA))
335a^{8}
Mrs Bridges *Roger Ingram* a17 29
3 b f Avonbridge Figura (Rudimentary (USA))
2974^{6} 3507^{11} 3972^{11} 5177^{7}
Mrs Brown's Boy *Ronald Harris* 80
2 gr c Verglas(IRE) Brazilian Style (Exit To Nowhere (USA))
(1847) 2181^{3} 3240^{22}
Mrs Cash (IRE) *Sylvester Kirk* a44
3 b f Holy Roman Emperor(IRE) Ring Of Fire (USA) (Nureyev (USA))
181^{10}
Mrs Greeley *Eve Johnson Houghton* 92
4 b m Mr Greeley(USA) Swain's Gold (USA) (Swain (IRE))
2274^{6} 2766^{7} (3790) 4772^{4} 5457^{3} 6023^{2} 6870^{4} 7558^{9}
Mrs Huffey *Henry Candy* a58 65
3 b f Acclamation Passing Hour (USA) (Red Ransom (USA))
1376^{5}
Mr Skipiton (IRE) *Terry Clement* a63 55
7 b g Statue Of Liberty(USA) Salty Air (IRE) (Singspiel (IRE))
155^{3} 522^{5} 781^{7} 938^{3}
Mrs Medley *Garry Woodward* a18 21
6 b m Rambling Bear Animal Cracker (Primo Dominie)
10^{6} 334^{11}
Mr Snoozy *Tim Walford* 71
3 b g Pursuit Of Love Hard To Follow (Dilum (USA))
1132^{9} 1385^{4} 2141^{6} 2771^{2} 3023^{3} (3697) 4626^{2} 4955^{6} 6103^{2} 6924^{11}
Mrs Perry (SWE) *Hans-Inge Larsen*
3 b f Bosun's Watch Amy Hunter (USA) (Jade Hunter (USA))
4359a^{10}
Mr Spiggott (IRE) *Joseph Tuite* 86
3 b g Intikhab(USA) Green Green Grass (Green Desert (USA))
1477^{4} 2076^{3} 2477^{8} 3629^{3} 4600^{7} 6931^{2} ◆ 7520^{5}
Mrs Warren *Charles Hills* a46 65
2 b f Kyllachy Bold Bunny (Piccolo)
1466^{6} 3313^{2} 3973^{3} 4574^{6} 4991^{3} 7056^{11}
Mr Tallyman *Micky Hammond*
6 b g Auction House(USA) Island Colony (USA) (Pleasant Colony (USA))
4882^{10}
Mr Udagawa *Bernard Llewellyn* a70 72
6 b g Bahamian Bounty Untold Riches (USA) (Red Ransom (USA))
2207^{13} 3485^{14} 4183^{5} 4531^{10} 4988^{7} 5657^{13} 6304^{6} 7015^{8}
Mr Vendman (IRE) *Ian Williams* a38 40
2 b g Whipper(USA) So Precious (IRE) (Batshoof)
6473^{5} 6818^{12} 7653^{8} 7973^{8}
Mr Willis *Terry Clement* a98 83
6 b g Desert Sun Santiburi Girl (Casteddu)
426^{3} ◆ 622^{3} 785^{6} 1137^{6}
Mr Wolf *Paul Midgley* a77 77
11 b g Wolfhound(USA) Madam Millie (Milford)
2982^{10} 4631^{8} 4909^{11}
Muaamara *Mick Channon* 94
3 ch f Bahamian Bounty Mamma Morton (IRE) (Elnadim (USA))
1454^{10} 1858^{10} 2509^{10} (3108) 3396^{6} 4063^{10} 4258^{4} 6515^{8} 6878^{12}
Muaanid *D K Weld* 99
2 ch c Kheleyf(USA) Rifqah (USA) (Elusive Quality (USA))
6718a^{4}
Muarrab *Ed Dunlop* a81 88
3 b g Oasis Dream Licence To Thrill (Wolfhound (USA))
(1182) 1452^{6} 1858^{11} 4298^{8} 5910^{3} ◆ (6488) 6830^{4}
Mubaraza (IRE) *John Dunlop* 98
3 ch c Dalakhani(IRE) Mokaraba (Unfuwain (USA))
1888^{4} 2429^{7} (3592) 4513^{5} (5106)
Mubtadi *Ismail Mohammed* a58 88
4 b g Dr Fong(USA) Noble Peregrine (Lomond (USA))
2500^{7} 2896^{7} 3348^{9} 4068^{7} 4661^{6} 6127^{16} 7348^{6} 8114^{6}
Mucho Macho Man (USA) *Kathy Ritvo* a127
4 b h Macho Uno(USA) Ponche De Leona (USA) (Ponche (CAN))
7576a^{2}
Muck 'N' Brass (IRE) *Edward Lynam* a100 72
3 bb c Aussie Rules(USA) Crystal Springs (IRE) (Kahyasi)
4692a^{14} (5397a) 6855a^{11}
Mucky Molly *Alison Hutchinson* a57 62
4 ch m Bahamian Bounty Indian Flag (IRE) (Indian Ridge)
1285^{7} 1497^{16} 1628^{5} 1934^{5} 2761^{7} 3151^{2} 3434^{5} (3718) 4196^{6} 6003^{6} (6951) 7316^{4} 7604^{11} 8099^{9} 8184^{2}
Mudaawem (USA) *Mark Johnston* 64
2 ch g Exchange Rate(USA) Raajiya (USA) (Gulch (USA))
5221^{5} 5825^{6} 6237^{5} 6753^{9}
Mudawala (USA) *Roger Varian* 61
2 b f Haafhd Reefaljamal (USA) (Dixieland Band (USA))
7329^{6}
Mudhish (IRE) *Clive Brittain* a66 66
7 b g Lujain(USA) Silver Satire (Dr Fong (USA))
2466^{9} 2858^{3} 3455^{2} 4469^{5} 6812^{12}
Muffin McLeay (IRE) *David Barron* 96
4 b g Hawk Wing(USA) Youngus (USA) (Atticus (USA))
1820^{6} 2257^{3} 2606^{7} 3287^{2} 3494^{4} (4347) 6757^{4} 7210^{12}
Muftarres (IRE) *Paul Midgley* a68 73
7 b g Green Desert(USA) Ghazal (USA) (Gone West (USA))
692^{5} 1796^{6} 2498^{12} (4783) (5220) 5618^{4} 6141^{8} 6888^{7}
Mugazala (IRE) *Ed Dunlop* a61 74
3 ch f Sakhee(USA) Nasij (USA) (Elusive Quality (USA))
(3453) 4091^{5} 4949^{7}
Muhamee (IRE) *Saeed Bin Suroor* a70 36
3 ch g Proud Citizen(USA) Santolina (USA) (Boundary (USA))
1724^{3} 2668^{4} 4188^{4}
Muhandis (IRE) *Nick Littmoden* a73 60
4 b g Muhtathir Ahdaaf (USA) (Bahri (USA))
54^{5} (478) 713^{6} 2044^{5} 2549^{8} 3344^{6} 4238^{5} 5193^{4} 5427^{2} 5750^{6} 6455^{3} 7022^{7} 7857^{2} (8005)
Muharrer *Marcus Tregoning* 86
3 b g Shamardal(USA) Shawahid (USA) (A.P. Indy (USA))
(6409) 7082^{4}
Muharrib (IRE) *Saeed Bin Suroor* a86 91
2 b c Oasis Dream Manhattan Dream (USA) (Statue Of Liberty (USA))
4710^{10} 5715^{7} (5992) 7325^{2} (7687)
Muhdiq (USA) *Mike Murphy* a85 69
3 b g Hard Spun(USA) Enfiraaj (USA) (Kingmambo (USA))
2041^{8} 2496^{3} 3333^{5} 4723^{3} ◆ 5296^{2} (7309) ◆ (7646)
Muhtaram *Saeed Bin Suroor* 15
2 b g Shamardal(USA) Neshla (Singspiel (IRE))
7492^{12}
Muhtaris (IRE) *Saeed Bin Suroor* 74
2 b c Teofilo(IRE) Fann (USA) (Diesis)
(7637) ◆
Mujaadel (USA) *David Nicholls* a88 86
7 ch g Street Cry(IRE) Quiet Rumour (USA) (Alleged (USA))
(1161) 1863^{12} 2510^{13} 2697^{8} 3403^{7} 4345^{11} 4779^{7} 5059^{7} 5910^{5} 6127^{5} 6709^{6}
Mujaazef *A Al Raihe* a109 95
5 b g Dubawi(IRE) Khubza (Green Desert (USA))
53a^{6} 420a^{11}
Mujadora (IRE) *William Haggas* a13 39
2 b f Mujadil(USA) Golden Ora (ITY) (Nordance (USA))
5367^{11} 5948^{8} 6612^{9}
Mujamead *Tony Carroll* a34 28
8 b g Mujahid(USA) Island Mead (Pharly (FR))
366^{9} 5173^{6}
Mujarrad (USA) *Marcus Tregoning* 73
2 b c Street Sense(USA) Sayedah (IRE) (Darshaan)
6795^{5} 7172^{4}
Mujazif (IRE) *Brian Meehan* 84
2 br c Shamardal(USA) Red Bandanna (IRE) (Montjeu (IRE))
6636^{5} (7332)
Mukhabarat (IRE) *Saeed Bin Suroor* 57
2 b c Exceed And Excel(AUS) Counterclaim (Pivotal)
6411^{7}
Mukhadram *William Haggas* 106
3 b c Shamardal(USA) Magic Tree (UAE) (Timber Country (USA))
(1467) (2280) 3295^{4} 4012^{2} 6674^{5}
Muktasb (USA) *Richard Guest* a64 16
11 b g Bahri(USA) Maghaarb (Machiavellian (USA))
297^{11} 664^{11} 8114^{11}
Mulan (GER) *Elisabeth Gautier* 96
5 b m Marju(IRE) Morning Light (GER) (Law Society (USA))
3886a^{10}
Mulaqen *Marcus Tregoning* a83 100
4 ch g Haafhd Burqa (Nashwan (USA))
(2180) 2933^{4} 3372^{8} 6832^{3}
Mulberry Brite *Alastair Lidderdale* a45 52
4 b m Librettist(USA) Thea (USA) (Marju (IRE))
663^{4} 4582^{4} 5240^{6} 5850^{7} 5999^{7} 6252^{11}
Mullins Way (USA) *Jo Hughes* a89 89
4 ch g Mr Greeley(USA) Aljawza (USA) (Riverman (USA))
391^{2} 694^{6} 1128^{18} 1249^{4} 1633^{4} 1820^{8} 5914^{8} 6601^{9} 6931^{10} 7328^{10} 7799^{6} ◆ 7998^{12}
Mullit (IRE) *Tom Dascombe* 67
2 b g Kodiac Gouache (IRE) (Key Of Luck (USA))
3138^{9} 4220^{3} 4825^{3} 5450^{5}
Mull Of Killough (IRE) *Jane Chapple-Hyam* a101 116
6 b g Mull Of Kintyre(USA) Sun Shower (IRE) (Indian Ridge)
(254) 1130^{2} 1510^{10} 3268^{21} (4339) 5075^{4} 6674^{2} (7054) (7557)
Multi Bene *Ed McMahon* a88 83
3 b g Multiplex Attlongglast (Groom Dancer (USA))
2085^{7} 2470^{8} 3230^{2} (3548) 5501^{2} (6342) 7032^{16} 7842^{2} 8181^{2}
Multifac'Eted *J S Moore* a41
3 b f Multiplex Diamond Vanessa (IRE) (Distinctly North (USA))
805^{5} 974^{6} 2580^{5} 3088^{7}
Multifact *Michael Dods* 52
2 b g Multiplex Subtle Move (USA) (Known Fact (USA))
5410^{7} 6042^{6} 6603^{8}
Multi Fours *Daniel Kubler* a50
2 ch f Medicean Spiralling (Pivotal)
5153^{7} 7191^{13} 7653^{5}
Multilateral (USA) *Amanda Perrett* a70 74
3 rg g Mizzen Mast(USA) Single Market (USA) (Dynaformer (USA))
5510^{3} 5982^{3} 7011^{4}
Multilicious *Tim Easterby* a44
2 b f Multiplex Ryan's Quest (IRE) (Mukaddamah (USA))
8134^{6} 8207^{3}
Multiply *Peter Makin*
3 b g Multiplex Scarlett Ribbon (Most Welcome)
4605^{6} 5505^{6}
Multisure *Richard Fahey* a60 66
2 b g Multiplex Sharoura (Inchinor)
4178^{7} 4625^{5} 5053^{2} 5423^{3} 6130^{9} 7463^{7} 7977^{4}
Multitask *Michael Madgwick* a71 26
2 b g Multiplex Attlongglast (Groom Dancer (USA))
7296^{4} (7481) 7856^{6} 8161^{2}
Mumbai Millionaire (IRE) *Brett Johnson*
3 ch c Indian Haven Almaviva (IRE) (Grand Lodge (USA))
1625^{11}
Mumbai Star (IRE) *Paul Fitzsimons* a44 45
2 ch g Choisir(AUS) Wood White (UAE) (Timber Country (USA))
2370^{6} 3010^{6}
Mumeyez *John Gosden* a74 65
2 ch g Motivator Twelfth Night (IRE) (Namid)
4792^{8} 5765^{3} 6796^{6} 7020^{2}
Mummyow (IRE) *Terry Clement* a12
4 b m Darsi(FR) A Two (IRE) (Ali-Royal (IRE))
4465^{8}
Munaawib *David C Griffiths* a22 65
4 b g Haafhd Mouwadh (USA) (Nureyev (USA))
1276^{11} 1432^{8} 1794^{6} 2827^{8} 3988^{14}
Munaddam (USA) *R Bouresly* a82 97
10 ch g Aljabr(USA) Etizaaz (USA) (Diesis)
616a^{10} 875a^{15}
Mundahesh (IRE) *William Haggas* a82 75
2 ch g Tamayuz Kawn (Cadeaux Genereux)
6411^{3} ◆ 7007^{2} (7459)
Munic Boy (USA) *Manfred Hofer* a72 100
3 b c Bernardini(USA) Countess Gold (USA) (Mt. Livermore (USA))
2966a^{2}
Municipal (IRE) *Michael Dods* a34 59
2 b g Elusive City(USA) Ripalong (IRE) (Revoque (IRE))
3902^{3} 4545^{9} 5040^{6} 5749^{10} 6130^{12} 6707^{9}
Munificence *Marco Botti* a69
3 ch g Bahamian Bounty Snake's Head (Golden Snake (USA))
502^{3} 650^{2} 847^{4}
Munsarim (IRE) *Richard Rowe* a88 86
5 b g Shamardal(USA) Etizaaz (USA) (Diesis)
(158) (299) (402) (804) 1008^{5} (1341) 1924^{14} 2720^{7} (4334) 6969^{8}
Muntasir (IRE) *Saeed Bin Suroor* a92 98
3 b c Distorted Humor(USA) Mansfield Park (Green Desert (USA))
1923^{3} 2585^{2} 2980^{2} (3763) 4513^{2} 5383^{5} 6033^{2} 7168^{8} 7487^{5}
Muqantara (USA) *Sir Michael Stoute* 57
3 b f First Samurai(USA) Adventure (USA) (Unbridled's Song (USA))
4797^{7}
Murbeh (IRE) *A Al Raihe* a99 100
4 b g Elusive City(USA) My Funny Valentine (IRE) (Mukaddamah (USA))
244a^{11} 875a^{12}
Mureb (USA) *M bin Shafya* a96 76
5 b g Elusive Quality(USA) Sumoto (Mtoto)
51a^{13}
Murfreesboro *Raymond York* a59 90
9 b g Bahamian Bounty Merry Rous (Rousillon (USA))
6843^{7} 7819^{11}
Murmur (IRE) *Paul Fitzsimons*
3 b f Marju(IRE) Siphon Melody (USA) (Siphon (BRZ))
3620^{11}
Murphy (IRE) *Nick Gifford* a59
10 b g Lord Americo Kyle Cailin (Over The River (FR))
3763^{5} 4465^{5} 7739^{4} 8001^{5} 8170^{9}
Musashi (IRE) *Laura Mongan* a65 59
7 ch g Hawk Wing(USA) Soubrette (USA) (Opening Verse (USA))
575^{2} 738^{8} 915^{3} 1984^{12} 2168^{7}
Mushaakis (IRE) *Mark Johnston* a66 58
2 b c Shamardal(USA) Shamayel (Pivotal)
2822^{5} 4290^{7} 6099^{8} (6583) (7190) ◆
Musical Leap *Shaun Harris* a35 43
4 b g Superior Premium Musical Fair (Piccolo)
289^{9} 551^{12}
Musically *Mick Channon* a54 70
3 b f Singspiel(IRE) Pelagia (IRE) (Lycius (USA))
917^{7} 1288^{6} 1728^{13} 2625^{7} 3002^{2} 3246^{12} 3338^{2} ◆ 3616^{4} 3966^{7} 4486^{7} 5452^{5} 5683^{2} 5817^{6} 7062^{9} (7248) 7490^{9}
Musical Moon *Lady Herries* a43
2 b g Piccolo Lunasa (IRE) (Don't Forget Me)
7507^{10}
Musical Romance (USA) *William Kaplan* a117 92
5 bb m Concorde's Tune(USA) Candlelightdinner (USA) (Slew Gin Fizz (USA))
7569a^{6}
Music Chart (USA) *Mahmood Al Zarooni* 85
2 bb f Exchange Rate(USA) Conchita (USA) (Cozzene (USA))
(5551) ◆ 6021^{4}
Music Festival (USA) *Jim Goldie* a64 73
5 b g Storm Cat(USA) Musical Chimes (USA) (In Excess)
4388^{10} 4769^{8} 4954^{9} 5338^{7} 5588^{12} 6106^{9} 7204^{3} 7747^{4}
Music Girl *Michael Blanshard* a29 40
3 b f Oratorio(IRE) Gwen John (USA) (Peintre Celebre (USA))
2374^{12} 2850^{12}
Music Master *Henry Candy* 72
2 b c Piccolo Twilight Mistress (Bin Ajwaad (IRE))
5235^{4} ◆

Musikhani *Andrew Balding* 64
2 b f Dalakhani(IRE) Musicanna (Cape Cross (IRE))
6873^{16}

Musikverein (FR) *J Phelippon* a83 75
5 b g My Risk(FR) Vallee De Joux (FR) (Welkin (CAN))
(7701a)

Musir (AUS) *M F De Kock* a122 120
6 b h Redoute's Choice(AUS) Dizzy De Lago (AUS) (Encosta De Lago (AUS))
(144a) (318a) 876a^{3} 1148a^{6} 1902a^{7}

Muskat Link *Henry Candy* 66
2 b g Rail Link Muskat Rose (IRE) (One Cool Cat (USA))
3916^{10} 4658^{3} 5275^{3} 6871^{9}

Musketier (GER) *Roger L Attfield* 115
10 rg h Acatenango(GER) Myth And Reality (Linamix (FR))
6299a^{6}

Musnad (USA) *Brian Ellison* a73 81
4 ch g Mr Greeley(USA) Jadarah (USA) (Red Ransom (USA))
273^{5} 1156^{7} 2151^{12} 2491^{2} (2720) 3167^{10} 3615^{8} 6124^{11} 6638^{8} 7368^{4} 8110^{5} 8275^{7}

Mustaheel (IRE) *F Rohaut* a90 107
3 b g Lawman(FR) Lidanski (IRE) (Soviet Star (USA))
2951a^{5} 3656a^{5}

Mustajed *Rod Millman* a66 66
11 b g Alhaarth(IRE) Jasarah (IRE) (Green Desert (USA))
(453) 557^{4} 811^{4} 2137^{5} 3073^{4} 4843^{11} 5241^{2} 5908^{9}

Must Be Me *Eve Johnson Houghton* a58 76
2 b f Trade Fair Roodeye (Inchinor)
1767^{4} 2437^{11} 3465^{2} 4574^{7} (4991) 5254^{5} 5743^{6} 6155^{11} 6699^{7} 6946^{7}

Mutaaleq (IRE) *Roger Varian* a66 51
3 b g Oasis Dream Siringas (IRE) (Barathea (IRE))
5297^{6} 6925^{4}

Mutafaakir (IRE) *Ruth Carr* a69 81
3 b g Oasis Dream Moon's Whisper (USA) (Storm Cat (USA))
1155^{3} 1450^{4} 1703^{6} 2428^{11} 6338^{12} 6789^{13}

Mutahadee (IRE) *M F De Kock* a89 117
4 b h Encosta De Lago(AUS) Mosaique Bleue (Shirley Heights)
(243a) (489a) 879a^{3} ◆ 1148a^{2} (Dead)

Mutamaiz (IRE) *James Tate* a64 64
2 b c Tamayuz Luana (Shaadi (USA))
6014^{11} 6501^{8} 6919^{2} 7289^{7}

Mutanaker *Ed de Giles* a58 42
5 b g Cape Cross(IRE) Purple Haze (IRE) (Spectrum (IRE))
149^{4} 2735^{5} 3392^{10} 8179^{12}

Mutarjim (USA) *Saeed Bin Suroor* a52 65
3 b g Dynaformer(USA) Thunder Kitten (USA) (Storm Cat (USA))
4882^{5}

Mutasadder (USA) *Roger Varian* a59 76
3 b g Distorted Humor(USA) Dessert (USA) (Storm Cat (USA))
1261^{12} 4212^{5}

Mutasareb (USA) *A Oliver* a83 56
5 b g Nayef(USA) Saywaan (USA) (Fusaichi Pegasus (USA))
342a^{2}

Mutashaded (USA) *Roger Varian* 75
2 b c Raven's Pass(USA) Sortita (GER) (Monsun (GER))
(7468)

Mutazamen *Richard Hannon* a80 88
2 ch c Sakhee's Secret Disco Lights (Spectrum (IRE))
5062^{2} (5578) (6034) 6799^{2}

Muthafar (IRE) *John Dunlop* 34
2 b c Tamayuz Etizaaz (USA) (Diesis)
5303^{12}

Muthmera (USA) *Roger Varian* 75
2 b f Dynaformer(USA) Burooz (IRE) (King's Best (USA))
6117^{3} ◆ 6791^{2}

Mutiska (IRE) *J C Hayden* a69 71
5 ch m Muhtarram(USA) Biasca (Erhaab (USA))
1559^{5}

Mutual Regard (IRE) *Sir Mark Prescott Bt* a96
3 b g Hernando(FR) Hidden Charm (IRE) (Big Shuffle (USA))
(7252) (7744) (7811) (7839)

Muwalla *Chris Grant* a82 71
5 b g Bahri(USA) Easy Sunshine (IRE) (Sadler's Wells (USA))
4455^{6}

Muzdaan (IRE) *Roger Varian* a50 56
3 ch f Exceed And Excel(AUS) Belle Genius (USA) (Beau Genius (CAN))
1736^{11}

Muzey's Princess *Michael Mullineaux* 38
6 b m Grape Tree Road Premier Princess (Hard Fought)
5293^{5} 6614^{8} 7454^{11}

Muzhil (IRE) *Clive Brittain* 58
3 b f Manduro(GER) Mazuna (IRE) (Cape Cross (IRE))
1206^{5}

Muzo (USA) *Chris Dwyer* a82 74
6 b g Gone West(USA) Bowl Of Emeralds (USA) (A.P. Indy (USA))
3945^{9}

My Adonis (USA) *Kelly Breen* a106
3 b c Pleasantly Perfect(USA) Silent Justice (USA) (Elusive Quality (USA))
2954a^{8}

Myanne *Ann Duffield* 53
2 b f Indesatchel(IRE) Mookhlesa (Marju (IRE))
5709^{6} 6122^{4} 6336^{P}

My Arch *Ollie Pears* 93
10 b g Silver Patriarch(IRE) My Desire (Grey Desire)
1672^{5} 1905^{5} 2457^{7} 2978^{8} 3419^{4}

Myasun (FR) *C Baillet* a103 107
5 ch g Panis(USA) Spain (FR) (Bering)
(814a) 3657a^{9} 6943a^{2} (7624a)

My Best Brother (USA) *Julio C Canani* 107
3 b c Stormy Atlantic(USA) Wilshewed (USA) (Carson City (USA))
7566a^{5} 7882a^{7}

My Best Man *Tony Carroll* a59 23
6 b g Forzando Victoria Sioux (Ron's Victory (USA))
46^{6} (125) 126^{2} 264^{11} 578^{12} 927^{9} 986^{8}

My Body Is A Cage (IRE) *Jeremy Noseda* a68 78
3 ch f Strategic Prince Moonlight Wish (IRE) (Peintre Celebre (USA))
1824^{5} (5421) 6208^{5} 6613^{9}

Myboyalfie (USA) *J R Jenkins* a83 93
5 b g Johannesburg(USA) Scotchbonnetpepper (USA) (El Gran Senor (USA))
(496) 834^{4} 1561^{6} 2274^{10} 2405^{3} (2847) (3099) 5243^{3} 6566^{2} (6932) (7493) 7691^{5}

My Boy Bill *Michael Easterby* a10 78
2 b g Dutch Art Pious (Bishop Of Cashel)
(1131) ◆ 6162^{17} 7028^{12} 7241^{5} 7463^{9}

My Boy Ginger *Rod Millman* a59 73
3 ch g Byron Lady Chef (Double Trigger (IRE))
1259^{2} 1424^{9} (4186) 4531^{7} 5132^{5} 5721^{4} 6631^{5} 6927^{3}

My Claire *Nigel Tinkler* a41 60
2 b f Piccolo Aymara (Darshaan)
2282^{10} 2770^{4} 6360^{9} 7161^{7}

My Colleen (USA) *Rae Guest* a52
3 ch f Discreet Cat(USA) Navasha (USA) (Woodman (USA))
7770^{6} 8187^{6}

My Destination (IRE) *Declan Carroll* a60 81
3 b g Dubai Destination(USA) Gossamer (Sadler's Wells (USA))
1340^{3} 2372^{11} 3072^{6} 7444^{2}

My Espoir *Clive Cox* a51 22
3 b f Oasis Dream Eden (USA) (Holy Bull (USA))
2344^{11} 5297^{11} 5745^{4}

My Fere Lady (USA) *J S Bolger* a74 56
3 ch f Mr Greeley(USA) Saintly Hertfield (USA) (Saint Ballado (CAN))
1944a^{5}

My Flaming Cat (USA) *Roger Varian* 71
2 ch f Tale Of The Cat(USA) Breathtaking (USA) (Mineshaft (USA))
4297^{5}

Myfourthboy *Alan Berry*
5 b g Grape Tree Road Firedancer (Nashwan (USA))
635^{11}

My Freedom (IRE) *Saeed Bin Suroor* a108 97
4 b g Invincible Spirit(IRE) Priere (Machiavellian (USA))
(1373) ◆ 1523^{4} 7240^{26} 7691^{17}

My Gacho (IRE) *David Nicholls* a41 83
10 b g Shinko Forest(IRE) Floralia (Auction Ring (USA))
3281^{13} 4141^{6}

My Gigi *Gary Moore* a60 67
2 b f Medicean Choirgirl (Unfuwain (USA))
4739^{17} 7372^{4} 7553^{4} 7814^{9}

My Gi Gi (USA) *Peter Eurton* a102 103
3 b f E Dubai(USA) Relish The Thought (IRE) (Sadler's Wells (USA))
4131a^{2}

My Girl Anna (IRE) *Muredach Kelly* a82 104
5 b m Orpen(USA) Kooyong (IRE) (College Chapel)
1040a^{11} 3196a^{2} 3375^{2} ◆ 4070^{5} 5067a^{3} (5641a) 6485^{7} 6869^{6}

My Glitters (FR) *P Demercastel* a59 62
2 b f My Risk(FR) Marie Glitters (FR) (Crystal Glitters (USA))
5697a^{8} 7122a^{10}

My Good Brother (IRE) *T G McCourt* a69 36
3 b g Elusive City(USA) Final Favour (IRE) (Unblest)
(7378)

My Guardian Angel *Mark H Tompkins* a29 77
3 b g Araafa(IRE) Angels Guard You (Bahamian Bounty)
1288^{3} 2336^{2} (3186) 3558^{8} 5063^{7} 8082^{12}

My Honychurch *Frank Sheridan* a23
3 gr f Verglas(IRE) Zagaleta (Sri Pekan (USA))
5177^{8} 5805^{6}

My Jeanie (IRE) *Jimmy Fox* a50 48
8 ch m King Charlemagne(USA) Home Comforts (Most Welcome)
39^{2} 264^{8} 422^{7} 828^{8}

Myjestic Melody (IRE) *Noel Wilson* a40 56
4 b m Majestic Missile(IRE) Bucaramanga (IRE) (Distinctly North (USA))
2458^{8} 3256^{2} 4245^{11} 4592^{3} 4911^{10} 6100^{10} 6403^{6} 7591^{7} 7748^{7}

My Kingdom (IRE) *Stuart Williams* a84 91
6 b g King's Best(USA) Nebraas (Green Desert (USA))
54^{4} (997) 1254^{2} 1587^{2} 2482^{2} 3221^{2} 3557^{2} 4503^{2} 4629^{3} 5320^{8} 6165^{5} 6820^{9} 7080^{8} 7327^{8}

My Lagan Love (IRE) *J S Moore*
2 ch f Arakan(USA) Riskie Things (Risk Me (FR))
2462^{5} 4462^{8}

My Learned Friend (IRE) *Andrew Balding* a74 80
8 b g Marju(IRE) Stately Princess (Robellino (USA))
2354^{5} 2608^{7} 3471^{8}

My Lord *Luke Dace* a72 78
4 br g Ishiguru(USA) Lady Smith (Greensmith)
220^{3} 323^{3} 624^{3} 844^{11} 912^{5} 1050^{3} 1307^{5} 3705^{2} (4223) 4805^{6} 5007^{3} 5794^{12} 6932^{8} 7147^{11} 8174^{9}

My Manekineko *J R Jenkins* a63 49
3 b g Authorized(IRE) Echo River (USA) (Irish River (FR))
2280^{9} 2799^{7} 5717^{3} 6151^{7} 6810^{9} 7470^{7}

My Manikato *Richard Phillips* 74
5 ch g Starcraft(NZ) Rainbow Queen (FR) (Spectrum (IRE))
2735^{11}

Mymateeric *Lydia Pearce* a41 56
6 b g Reset(AUS) Ewenny (Warrshan (USA))
968^{6} 1184^{8}

My Mate Jake (IRE) *James Given* a76 80
4 ch g Captain Rio Jam (IRE) (Arazi (USA))
2051^{6} 2414^{10} 2821^{4} 3309^{5} 4627^{10} (5175) ◆ (5405) 6251^{2} 6819^{16} 7027^{10} (7368) 7529^{4}

My Mate Les (IRE) *Tony Carroll* a54 52
4 b g High Chaparral(IRE) Precedence (IRE) (Polish Precedent (USA))
45^{2} 197^{6} 390^{2} 773^{4} 829^{6}

My Mate Mal *William Stone* a66 75
8 b g Daawe(USA) Kandymal (IRE) (Prince Of Birds (USA))
493^{8} 632^{4}

Mymazar *Jo Hughes* 40
2 ch g Phoenix Reach(IRE) Cocorica (IRE) (Croco Rouge (IRE))
4752^{7}

My Meteor *Tony Newcombe* a59 72
5 b g Bahamian Bounty Emerald Peace (IRE) (Green Desert (USA))
1497^{7} 1910^{3} 4425^{2} (5149) 5876^{5} 7969^{11}

My Miss Aurelia (USA) *Steven Asmussen* a120
3 b f Smart Strike(CAN) My Miss Storm Cat (USA) (Sea Of Secrets (USA))
7550a^{2}

My Mum Mo *Simon West* a50
4 b m Statue Of Liberty(USA) Come To The Point (Pursuit Of Love)
8151^{3}

My Name Is Sam *Ronald Harris* a57 31
3 b g Green Desert(USA) Caught You Looking (Observatory (USA))
599^{3} 734^{5} 802^{3} 1010^{4} 1337^{5} (1482) 2762^{6} 3450^{6}

My New Angel (IRE) *Paul Green* a51 47
3 gr f Dark Angel(IRE) Mynu Girl (IRE) (Charnwood Forest (IRE))
393^{5} 923^{10} (973) 1591^{3} 1918^{8} 3025^{5} 3555^{9} 4142^{4} 5246^{2} 5738^{6} 6316^{4} 8241^{6}

My Own Way Home *David Evans* a67 72
4 b m Danbird(AUS) Wenden Belle (IRE) (Brave Act)
1638^{11} (2421) 3192^{6} 3790^{10} 4238^{3} 4655^{6} (4815) 5122^{3} 5326^{6} 6498^{3} 7203^{11} 7416^{11} 7741^{4} 7915^{4} 8034^{9} 8137^{8} 8236^{4}

My Pearl (IRE) *Kevin Ryan* a32 55
3 b g Sleeping Indian My-Lorraine (IRE) (Mac's Imp (USA))
1089^{5} 1259^{6} 1596^{7} 2341^{8}

Myplacelater *Richard Fahey* a102 106
5 ch m Where Or When(IRE) Star Welcome (Most Welcome)
1034^{12} 1318^{8} 1994^{2} 3219^{6} 3856^{4}

My Propeller (IRE) *Peter Chapple-Hyam* a81 106
3 b f Holy Roman Emperor(IRE) Incise (Dr Fong (USA))
2078^{11} 2713^{5} 6028^{6} (6382) ◆

My Queenie (IRE) *Richard Hannon* a84 98
3 b f Nayef(USA) Margay (IRE) (Marju (IRE))
1748^{3} 2067^{2} 4319^{10} (4702) 6870^{14} 7128^{6}

My Quest For Peace (IRE) *Luca Cumani* 116
4 b h Galileo(IRE) Play Misty For Me (IRE) (Danehill Dancer (IRE))
1855^{2} 2703^{4} 3369^{10} (4759) (5575) 7264a^{5} 7621a^{10}

Myraid *Ruth Carr* a56 49
5 b g Danbird(AUS) My Desire (Grey Desire)
110^{6} 389^{10} 557^{5} 676^{3} 1052^{5} 1179^{6} 1222^{6} 1583^{2} 2090^{9} 2692^{8} 2922^{12}

My Renaissance *Ben Case* a33
2 bb g Medicean Lebenstanz (Singspiel (IRE))
7191^{12}

Myrtlewood (IRE) *A Fabre* 101
3 gr f Montjeu(IRE) Walkamia (FR) (Linamix (FR))
6899a^{5}

My Rules (IRE) *P D Deegan* a68 68
2 gr f Aussie Rules(USA) Tumbleweed Pearl (Aragon)
4161a^{3}

My Scat Daddy (USA) *Brett Johnson* a55 54
3 b g Scat Daddy(USA) Will Be A Bates (USA) (Bates Motel (USA))
294^{6} 2582^{3} 4241^{8} 5349^{4} 6151^{10} 8205^{2} 8298^{2}

My Sharona *Sylvester Kirk* a74 93
3 gr f Dark Angel(IRE) Tanda Tula (IRE) (Alhaarth (IRE))
1607^{2} 2194^{3} ◆ 2660^{9} 2846^{2} (3785) 4740^{3} (5576) ◆ 5980^{7} 6406^{2} 6878^{9}

My Single Malt (IRE) *Julie Camacho* a81 83
4 b g Danehill Dancer(IRE) Slip Dance (IRE) (Celtic Swing)
1820^{7} 2491^{5} 3615^{4} 4042^{2} 4302^{3} 5414^{8} 5802^{4} 6239^{8} 6692^{2} 7618^{4} 7844^{3} 7935^{5}

My Sister *Mark Usher* a54 47
5 b m Royal Applause Mysistra (FR) (Machiavellian (USA))
653^{9} 3081^{3} 3468^{7} 5266^{4} 5935^{8}

My Son Max *P J O'Gorman* a90 87
4 b g Avonbridge Pendulum (Pursuit Of Love)
2151^{13} (2545) 2896^{5} 3348^{5} 3767^{4} 4824^{3} 5320^{7} 6256^{7} 6495^{3} (6939) 8009^{3}

My Special J'S (USA) *John Patrick Shanahan* 105
2 b f Harlan's Holiday(USA) Shadow On The Moon (USA) (Deputy Minister (CAN))
4276a^{2} (5135a) 6081a^{13} 6909a^{9}

Mysterial *Richard Hannon* 72
2 b g Invincible Spirit(IRE) Diamond Dilemma (IRE) (Sinndar (IRE))
1886^{4} ◆ 2231^{3} 3062^{4}

Mysterious Man (IRE) *Andrew Balding* 91
3 b g Manduro(GER) Edabiya (IRE) (Rainbow Quest (USA))
1893^{2} 2266^{2} (3484) 5598^{4} ◆ 6896a^{11}

Mysterious Wonder *Peter Salmon* 58
2 b g Oasis Dream Raskutani (Dansili)
3271^{5} 5040^{7} 5963^{10}

Mystery Angel (IRE) *John C McConnell* a55 64
2 b f Captain Marvelous(IRE) Free Angel (USA) (Mystery Storm (USA))
5858a^{11}

Mystery Bet (IRE) *Richard Fahey* 79
2 b f Kheleyf(USA) Dancing Prize (IRE) (Sadler's Wells (USA))
6007^{3} (7067)

Mystery Star (IRE) *Mark H Tompkins* a102 100
7 ch g Kris Kin(USA) Mystery Hill (USA) (Danehill (USA))
1974^{14} 2506^{5} 4528^{4} 5076^{3} 5491^{4} 5905^{6} 6493^{11}

Mystery Woman (IRE) *Peter Chapple-Hyam* a52
2 b f Holy Roman Emperor(IRE) Parvenue (FR) (Ezzoud (IRE))
7305^{7} 7923^{3}

Mystical Man *James Tate* a74 82
2 br c Sakhee's Secret Dancing Nelly (Shareef Dancer (USA))
3617^{5} 3973^{6} (4310) 7614^{4}

Mystical Moment *Richard Hannon* a77 85
2 ch f Dutch Art Tinnarinka (Observatory (USA))
2812^{4} 3339^{5} ◆ (4297) 4763^{5} 6021^{5} 6775^{4} 6980^{13}

Mystical Sapphire *Jo Crowley* a67
2 b f Sakhee's Secret Nadyma (IRE) (Daylami (IRE))
(7926)

Mystical Star (USA) *Christophe Clement* a106 109
4 b m Ghostzapper(USA) Capture A Star (USA) (Capote (USA))
5376a^{8}

Mystical Witch *Christine Dunnett* a50 16
3 b f Kyllachy Shifty Night (IRE) (Night Shift (USA))
1376^{10} 1705^{6} 2332^{9} 2803^{11} 3050^{15} 6321^{11} 7317^{8} 7729^{2} 7896^{6} 8062^{6} 8263^{7}

Mystic Halo *Frank Sheridan* a55
9 ch m Medicean Aglow (Spinning World (USA))
67^{8} 232^{6} 361^{10}

Mystic Melody (IRE) *Paul Cole*
3 b f Montjeu(IRE) Three Owls (IRE) (Warning)
5309^{9}

Mystified (IRE) *Alan Berry* a59 34
9 b g Raise A Grand(IRE) Sunrise (IRE) (Sri Pekan (USA))
632^{6} ◆ 1247^{8} 3116^{8} 3310^{7} 4959^{7}

My Stroppy Poppy *Frank Sheridan* a42 46
3 b f Multiplex Aspen Ridge (IRE) (Namid)
4293^{8} 4992^{4} 6457^{10} 6967^{14}

My Sweet Lord *Mark Usher* a57 51
2 b g Byron Sweetest Revenge (IRE) (Daggers Drawn (USA))
3074^{11} 3505^{8} 4654^{6} 5749^{6} 7463^{2} 7650^{5} 7821^{6} (8007) 8203^{4}

My Time *Michael Mullineaux* a53 49
3 b g Mind Games Tick Tock (Timeless Times (USA))
5177^{4} 6287^{3} 6686^{3}

My Trust (IRE) *Saeed Bin Suroor* a73
2 b f Exceed And Excel(AUS) Alizes (NZ) (Rory's Jester (AUS))
6936^{3} 7161^{4}

My Vindication (USA) *Gay Kelleway* a77 78
4 bb g Vindication(USA) Classy Mirage (USA) (Storm Bird (CAN))
3007^{6} 3247^{8} 3713^{10} 3967^{6}

My Virginia (FR) *X Thomas-Demeaulte* a78 72
3 ro f Shirocco(GER) Starvalla (FR) (With Approval (CAN))
(5726a)

Myzamour *J S Moore* a56 49
2 b f Azamour(IRE) Lady Ragazza (IRE) (Bering)
1188^{7} 1563^{7} 3224^{5} 4195^{6} 4659^{8} (5206) 6096^{7} 6156^{16} 7786^{3} 7854^{9} 8101^{2} 8150^{2}

Naabegha *Ed de Giles* a93 100
5 ch g Muhtathir Hawafiz (Nashwan (USA))
1373^{2} ◆ 1821^{6} 2268^{6} 2876^{2} (3188)

Naael (USA) *Luke Dace* 69
3 b g Mr Greeley(USA) Hamasah (USA) (Irish River (FR))
5006^{9} 5796^{12} 8153^{7}

Naafetha (IRE) *George Foster* 59
4 b m Alhaarth(IRE) Doctrine (Barathea (IRE))
1222^{5} 2600^{10} 3332^{10} 4426^{4} 6308^{8} 7978^{7}

Naalatt (IRE) *Mahmood Al Zarooni* a76 77
2 b f Dansili Vine Street (IRE) (Singspiel (IRE))
4002^{4} 4946^{3} 5818^{2} 6366^{3}

Nabat Sultan *Kevin Prendergast* 65
2 b f Invincible Spirit(IRE) Reyaada (Daylami (IRE))
2958a^{5}

Nabucco *John Gosden* 93
3 b c Dansili Cape Verdi (IRE) (Caerleon (USA))
2266^{4} ◆ 2856^{2} ◆ (3227) 4009^{10}

Nabucco (GER) *R Rohne* 97
2 b c Areion(GER) Numero Uno (GER) (Lavirco (GER))
7076a^{7}

Naburn *Alan Swinbank* a57 62
4 b g Cape Cross(IRE) Allespagne (USA) (Trempolino (USA))
2665^{5} 3035^{8} 3913^{3} ◆ 4402^{3} 5730^{9}

Nacho Libre *Michael Easterby* a65 50
7 b g Kyllachy Expectation (IRE) (Night Shift (USA))
203^{2} ◆ 313^{3} 578^{8} 927^{5} 1224^{5}

Nadeaud (FR) *D Guillemin* a98 108
3 gr f Soave(GER) Halix (FR) (Tropular)
1209a^{3} 6943a^{10}

Nadeen (IRE) *Michael Smith* a86 82
5 b g Bahamian Bounty Janayen (USA) (Zafonic (USA))
(1224) 1796^{11} 2696^{RR} 4432^{5} 4954^{13}

Nadema Rose (IRE) *Anthony Carson* 80
3 b f Elnadim(USA) Noctilucent (JPN) (Lammtarra (USA))
(3975) 4725^{3} 5001^{5}

Nadia Naes (IRE) *Roger Ingram* a42 17
3 b f Strategic Prince Tread The Boards (Reprimand)
8048^{10}

Nafa (IRE) *Daniel Mark Loughnane* a62 58
4 br m Shamardal(USA) Champs Elysees (USA) (Distant Relative)
8^{4} 5874^{8} 7157^{7} 7354^{9} 7378^{5} 7746^{3}

Nafaath (IRE) *Neil King* a88 91
6 ch g Nayef(USA) Alshakr (Bahri (USA))
2810[5] 3241[3] 4697[13] 7051[11] 7522[10]

Nafar (GER) *W Hickst* 104
4 b h Singspiel(IRE) Nouvelle Princesse (GER) (Bluebird (USA))
2222a[5] 3425a[3] 5782a[7]

Nagham (IRE) *Kevin Ryan* a75 97
3 b f Camacho Happy Talk (IRE) (Hamas (IRE))
1426a[5]

Nahrain *Roger Varian* 118
4 ch m Selkirk(USA) Bahr (Generous (IRE))
3266[9] 4801[8] 6080a[3] (6695a) 7549a[10]

Nakuru Breeze (IRE) *David Thompson* a53 63
3 b f King's Best(USA) Tropical Breeze (IRE) (Kris)
2633[7] 3616[10] 4549[13]

Naledi *Richard Price* a49 52
8 b g Indian Ridge Red Carnation (IRE) (Polar Falcon (USA))
1425[5] 1831[10] 5199[6] 5508[2] 6230[8]

Nameitwhatyoulike *Michael Easterby* 92
3 b g Trade Fair Emma Peel (Emarati (USA))
1167[2] (1653) 2182[4] 3165[8] 3563[7] 4588[4] 5386[4] 6881[8] 7032[7] (7453) (7639)

Namera (GER) *P Vovcenko* 93
3 b f Areion(GER) Najinskaja (GER) (Tannenkonig (IRE))
6943a[8] 7829a[7]

Namir (IRE) *James Evans* a65 63
10 b g Namid Danalia (IRE) (Danehill (USA))
498[10] 664[7] 979[5] (1910)

Namwahjobo (IRE) *Jim Goldie* a67 88
4 b g Namid Notley Park (Wolfhound (USA))
1863[11] 3334[11] 3905[3] 4388[5] 4638[2] 5189[5] 6044[16] 6999[7] 7360[7]

Nancy O (IRE) *Carolyn M Costigan* 98
2 b f Pivotal Arravale (USA) (Arch (USA))
6289a[3] 7547a[9]

Nandiga (USA) *P J Prendergast* 86
2 br f Bernardini(USA) Shade Dance (USA) (Nureyev (USA))
2780a[4] 5135a[5] 6081a[11]

Nandura *Harry Dunlop* 30
2 b f Motivator Nando's Dream (Hernando (FR))
6795[14]

Nanton (USA) *Jim Goldie* a88 108
10 rg g Spinning World(USA) Grab The Green (USA) (Cozzene (USA))
319a[10] 421a[12] 678a[8] 4112[10] 4684[10] 5079[6] 5558[5] 6197[2] 6493[9] 7852a[11]

Nant Saeson (IRE) *John Quinn* a64 74
3 b g Elusive City(USA) Lady Power (IRE) (Almutawakel)
193[6] 362[7] 667[10] 1167[3] 3947[4] ◆ 4711[4] 7245[10] 7599[2] (8131) 8271[4] ◆

Naoise (IRE) *J S Bolger* a72 50
4 ch h Stormy Atlantic(USA) Machinale (USA) (Kingmambo (USA))
775a[2]

Napinda *Philip McBride* a57 50
2 b f Sleeping Indian Aptina (USA) (Aptitude (USA))
2462[2] 2808[3] 3909[7] 4152[5] 5046[3] 5424[3] 5940[5] 7056[9]

Napoleon's Muse (IRE) *Ralph Beckett* a80 77
3 b f Peintre Celebre(USA) Art Work (Zafonic (USA))
1565[9] 2194[8] 3080[5] 3847[2] 4608[3] 5277[3] 6146[4]

Naqshabban (USA) *Mahmood Al Zarooni* 111
4 b g Street Cry(IRE) Reem Three (Mark Of Esteem (IRE))
(143a)

Narapatisithu (FR) *K F Clutterbuck* a54
5 b g Sulamani(IRE) Concert House (IRE) (Entrepreneur)
4916[6] 6215[6] 6643[5] 7189[11] 8099[11]

Narcissist (IRE) *Ed Dunlop* a71 85
3 b g Dylan Thomas(IRE) Gabare (FR) (Galileo (IRE))
3735[6] 4213[3] 4948[4] (5680) ◆

Nardin *Ed Dunlop* a74
2 b f Royal Applause Third Party (Terimon)
3282[4] 3959[2] (6453)

Nargys (IRE) *Luca Cumani* 105
2 b f Lawman(FR) Spesialta (Indian Ridge)
3590[3] ◆ 4297[2] (5631) 6160[2] ◆ 7052[2]

Narjan *C Plisson* a58 52
6 b g Efisio Nadira (FR) (Green Desert (USA))
93a[0]

Narkotic (FR) *J-P Gauvin* a81 81
3 b c Bachir(IRE) Merlene (FR) (Green Tune (USA))
290a[10]

Naru (IRE) *James Tate* 52
2 b c Authorized(IRE) Jabbara (IRE) (Kingmambo (USA))
5668[7]

Naruko (USA) *A Fabre* 90
3 b f Street Cry(IRE) Lake Toya (USA) (Darshaan)
5249a[7]

Naseem Alyasmeen (IRE) *Mick Channon* a71 96
3 gr f Clodovil(IRE) Phillippa (IRE) (Galileo (IRE))
1364[2] (1519) 1597[3] 2333[3] (2613) 2885[3] 3033[4] (3605) 4007[2] 4261[4] 4848[5] 5826[9] 6236[2]

Nasharra (IRE) *Kevin Ryan* a21 80
4 ch g Iffraaj There With Me (USA) (Distant View (USA))
3439[5] 4135[8] 4624[7] (4866) 5189[4] 5674[10] 6044[11] 6260[10] 6999[3] 7607[12]

Nashville (IRE) *Ian Williams* a73 59
3 b g Galileo(IRE) Brown Eyes (Danehill (USA))
7954[5] 8135[3] (8170)

Nasijah *James Tate* 76
2 b f Authorized(IRE) Nasij (USA) (Elusive Quality (USA))
6117[2] ◆ 6791[4]

Nasri *Milton Bradley* 101
6 b g Kyllachy Triple Sharp (Selkirk (USA))
1157[8] 1558[14] 2068[21] 2717[14] 3641[10] 4611[4] ◆ 4799[14] 5356[2] 6011[6] 6659[9] 7080[7] 7366[13]

Nassau Storm *William Knight* a97 94
3 b g Bahamian Bounty Got To Go (Shareef Dancer (USA))
1704[5] (2145) 3049[2] ◆ 3639[2] (4364) 6075[13] 7010[2]

Natasha Rostova *Andrew Balding* a67
3 b f Beat Hollow Putuna (Generous (IRE))
(1340) 2281[9] 2544[7] 3042[11] 3391[2] 4153[6] 4875[6]

Nateeja (IRE) *Marcus Tregoning* a55 55
2 b f Shamardal(USA) Merayaat (IRE) (Darshaan)
6876[6] 7324[12] 7628[7]

Nathaniel (IRE) *John Gosden* 127
4 b h Galileo(IRE) Magnificient Style (USA) (Silver Hawk (USA))
(3880) 4322[2] 6063a[2] 7239[3]

Nation (USA) *Garry Woodward* 25
2 bb f Rio Verde(USA) Song Of Music (USA) (Songandaprayer (USA))
3823[5]

National Hope (IRE) *George Baker* a70 71
4 b m Exceed And Excel(AUS) Zandaka (FR) (Doyoun)
919[4] 1358[13] 2362[3] 2811[10] 3511[12] (3701) 4238[4] 4726[5]

Nationalism *Mahmood Al Zarooni* a96 111
5 b g Pivotal Las Flores (IRE) (Sadler's Wells (USA))
145a[5] 317a[2] 587a[11] 755a[6]

National Poet (IRE) *Mahmood Al Zarooni* 41
2 ch c Nayef(USA) Reve D'Iman (FR) (Highest Honor (FR))
5797[6]

Native Colony *Roger Varian* a42 77
4 b g St Jovite(USA) Self Esteem (Suave Dancer (USA))
3572[8] 4215[5] 4831[3]

Native Eight (USA) *Ian Williams* 60
3 ch g Speightstown(USA) Native Wind Dancer (USA) (Incinderator (USA))
3181[3] 3786[9] 4293[11] 4744[9] 5683[9]

Native Khan (FR) *John M Oxx* 117
4 gr h Azamour(IRE) Viva Maria (FR) (Kendor (FR))
3675a[3] 4521a[3]

Natural Bloom (IRE) *Sir Henry Cecil* a54 70
3 b f Galileo(IRE) Dedicated Lady (IRE) (Pennine Walk)
2849[10] 3666[5] 5889[7] (6570) 7032[11]

Natural High (IRE) *Sean Curran* 85
7 b g Sadler's Wells(USA) Cool Clarity (IRE) (Indian Ridge)
1505[5] 2411[4] 6191[9]

Naturalmente (IRE) *Kevin Ryan* a40 39
3 b f Captain Rio Blusienka (IRE) (Blues Traveller (IRE))
7222[12]

Naughtical *J W Hills* a65 23
3 ch f Haafhd Mid Ocean (Sakhee (USA))
185[3] 322 [3] 518[9]

Naughtybychoice *Ollie Pears* a35 58
2 gr c Dubai Destination(USA) Gracia (Linamix (FR))
3208[6] 3842[8] 4140[4]

Naughty Indian (IRE) *Paul Fitzsimons* 4
2 b g Camacho Lucky Dancer (FR) (Groom Dancer (USA))
7491[11]

Navaho Spirit *Terry Clement* a66 32
3 ch g Sleeping Indian Sefemm (Alhaarth (IRE))
869[5] 1086[7] 2845[5]

Navajo Charm *Alan Jarvis* a62 65
3 b f Authorized(IRE) Navajo Love Song (IRE) (Dancing Brave (USA))
4584[11] (5629) 5939[2] 7301[7] 7811[5] 8020[10]

Navajo Chief *Alan Jarvis* a95 113
5 b g King's Best(USA) Navajo Rainbow (Rainbow Quest (USA))
246a[8] 489a[4] 586a[11] 677a[8] 1158[4] 2211[5] ◆ 2773[4] (3164) 4112[11] 5517[4] 5964[4] 6674[11] 7407[10]

Navajo Nation (IRE) *Bill Turner* a12 70
6 b g Indian Haven Kathy Desert (Green Desert (USA))
1299[11]

Navajo Nights *Bryan Smart* 65
2 b c Sleeping Indian Nuit Sans Fin (FR) (Lead On Time (USA))
3401[9] 5586[4]

Navarra Queen *P Schiergen* 105
4 b m Singspiel(IRE) Navona (GER) (Leone (GER))
1766a[5] 2654[4] 4386a[4] 5613a[2]

Nave (USA) *David Simcock* a79 95
5 b g Pulpit(USA) Lakabi (USA) (Nureyev (USA))
2248[10] 2887[3] 3766[7] 5063[3] 6039[3] ◆ 6642[5] 6776[6] 7024[4] 8000[8] 8191[3]

Navigation Track *David Simcock* a58 67
4 b g King's Best(USA) Tegwen (USA) (Nijinsky (CAN))
2363[4] 2775[7]

Nawarah *Conrad Allen* a72 27
3 b f Acclamation Rhapsodize (Halling (USA))
1472[16] 2361[7] (6806) 7197[10]

Nawwaar (USA) *John Dunlop* 94
3 ch c Distorted Humor(USA) Mostaqeleh (USA) (Rahy (USA))
3294[24] 4600[2] 5271[2] 6046[5]

Naxos Beach (IRE) *A Di Dio* 76
3 ch f Act One Alimony (IRE) (Groom Dancer (USA))
1699a[10]

Nayarra (IRE) *Mick Channon* 108
3 b f Cape Cross(IRE) Massarra (Danehill (USA))
1454[2] 1884[9] 2410[4] 2658[12] 4131a[7]

Nay Secret *Jim Goldie* 55
4 b g Nayef(USA) Nouveau Cheval (Picea)
2599[2] 2925[4] (3437) 3904[3] 5086[4] 6311[8]

Nazreef *Hughie Morrison* a108 91
5 b g Zafeen(FR) Roofer (IRE) (Barathea (IRE))
29[4] 266[3] (868) 1139[8] (1212) 1510[21] 5595[7] 6036[16] 6400[6] 6638[10] 7083[11] 7904[4] 8095[8]

Neamour *David Simcock* 71
2 b f Oasis Dream Ever Rigg (Dubai Destination (USA))
5104[6] 5907[3] 6657[3]

Nearly A Gift (IRE) *Tim Easterby* a20 84
3 b f Tagula(IRE) Chaukao (IRE) (Inchinor)
1862[8] 2256[8] 2615[8] 3751[8] 5257[8] 6264[10] 7146[13]

Neatico (GER) *P Schiergen* 107
5 b h Medicean Nicola Bella (IRE) (Sadler's Wells (USA))
1410a[4] 2222a[2] 4130a[4] 5613a[3] 6291a[3]

Neat Little Rows (IRE) *Marco Botti* 46
3 ch f Henny Hughes(USA) Al Ihsas (IRE) (Danehill (USA))
4001[7] 4582[9]

Nebula Storm (IRE) *Gary Moore* 107
5 b g Galileo(IRE) Epping (Charnwood Forest (IRE))
7630[7]

Need A Rave *Mark Hoad*
4 b g Needwood Blade Rave On (ITY) (Barathea (IRE))
5276[11]

Need To Know (SAF) *A Al Raihe* a84 84
4 b g Western Winter(USA) Promisefrommyheart (SAF) (Elliodor (FR))
417a[8]

Needwood Park *Ray Craggs* a60 59
4 br g Needwood Blade Waterpark (Namaqualand (USA))
772[5] 1092[3] 1631[2] 2670[4] 3402[10] 4682[7]

Needwood Ridge *Frank Sheridan* a76 51
5 ch g Needwood Blade Aspen Ridge (IRE) (Namid)
102[2] 269[3] (329) 448[6] 639[8]

Needy McCredie *James Turner* 69
6 ch m Needwood Blade Vocation (IRE) (Royal Academy (USA))
1638[12] 1875[4] 2092[3] 2750[2] 4784[3] 4866[3] 5543[12] 6403[8]

Need You Now (IRE) *Peter Chapple-Hyam* a62 94
2 b f Kheleyf(USA) Sniffle (IRE) (Shernazar)
4899[4] (5210) 6675[6] (7406)

Neeka *Zoe Davison*
4 b m One More Tiger I Wish (Beveled (USA))
6927[8] 7488[9]

Negin *Ed Dunlop* a77 81
3 b f Selkirk(USA) Snow Goose (Polar Falcon (USA))
1357[4] 1736[13] 2820[2] (3347) 3991[5] 4647[4] 5747[6] 6847[5]

Negotiation (IRE) *Michael Quinn* a77 73
6 b g Refuse To Bend(IRE) Dona Royale (IRE) (Darshaan)
1743[7]

Nehaam *John Gosden* 113
6 b g Nayef(USA) Charm The Stars (Roi Danzig (USA))
2267[3] 3293[6] 4737[9]

Neige D'Antan *Sir Mark Prescott Bt* a71 58
3 gr f Aussie Rules(USA) Ninotchka (USA) (Nijinsky (CAN))
2788[3] 3066[6] 3847[6] 4650[3] 5052[3] ◆ 5408[3] (5938) 7058[2] (7222) 7321[2] 7893[2] 7976[2] (8213)

Neighbourhood (USA) *James Evans* a51 49
4 bb g Street Cry(IRE) Miznah (IRE) (Sadler's Wells (USA))
5265[5] 5811[7] 7352[8] (7710) 8035[4] 8189[9]

Neil's Pride *Richard Fahey* a58 61
3 b f Dubai Destination(USA) Collette's Choice (Royal Applause)
1320[3] 1915[3] 5413[4] 6159[7] 6474[5] 6924[4] 7222[4] 7800[3] 8048[9] 8273[6]

Nelina *Robert Cowell* a65
2 b f Mount Nelson Naralina (FR) (Linamix (FR))
6889[5] ◆ 7305[5] 7728[2]

Nelson Quay (IRE) *Jeremy Gask* 34
2 b c Holy Roman Emperor(IRE) Frippet (IRE) (Ela-Mana-Mou)
6636[15]

Nelson's Bay *Brian Meehan* 83
3 b g Needwood Blade In Good Faith (USA) (Dynaformer (USA))
1888[9] 2452[3] 2930[11] 4600[3] 5365[3] 5838[7]

Nelson's Bounty *Paul D'Arcy* a76 94
5 b g Bahamian Bounty Santisima Trinidad (IRE) (Definite Article)
785[10]

Nelsons Dockyard (USA) *Paul Cole* 54
2 b c Henrythenavigator(USA) High Heel Sneakers (Dansili)
2231[14] 2594[6]

Nelson's Muse *Tobias B P Coles* a30
2 b f Mount Nelson French Quartet (IRE) (Lycius (USA))
8134[8] 8171[12] 8262[11]

Nemushka *Richard Fahey* 85
3 ch f Sakhee(USA) Dame De Noche (Lion Cavern (USA))
1653[7] 2485[7] 2752[4] 4497[6] (5218) 5820[8] 7069[9]

Nenge Mboko *George Baker* a75 78
2 b c Compton Place Floppie (FR) (Law Society (USA))
3505[5] 3996[2] 4688[13] 6945[2] 7305[2] (7653)

Nenzo (GER) *Mme N Verheyen* a87 90
6 b g Sholokhov(IRE) Noirie (GER) (Dashing Blade)
(18a)

Nero Emperor (IRE) *T Stack* a98 69
3 b c Holy Roman Emperor(IRE) Blue Iris (Petong)
7390a[8]

Nesnaas (USA) *Alastair Lidderdale* a47 48
11 ch g Gulch(USA) Sedrah (USA) (Dixieland Band (USA))
58[6] 160[7] 278[7] 392[7] 395[9] 446[4] 600[5] 811[5] 6769[4] 6838[9] 7169[13] 7255[7] 7717[3]

Netley Marsh *Richard Hannon* a64 70
3 ch g Haafhd Ha'Penny Beacon (Erhaab (USA))
1728[7] 2126[7] 2756[4] 3475[6] 4603[5] 4986[5] 5240[2] 5629[6] 5983[13] 6927[2]

Net Whizz (USA) *Jeremy Noseda* a87 65
3 bb c Mr Greeley(USA) Reboot (USA) (Rubiano (USA))
(6397) 7631[5]

Neutrafa (IRE) *John Mackie* 97
4 ch m Araafa(IRE) Neutrina (IRE) (Hector Protector (USA))
(1321) ◆ 1851[5] 2211[10] 5092[6] 6161[16] 6670[6]

Nevaeh *Pat Eddery* a70 70
3 b f Firebreak Mitsuki (Puissance)
892[2] 1016[2] 1748[5] 2065[4] 2554[4] 2757[3] 3432[2] 3785[9] 6433[4] 7158[6]

Never Can Tell (IRE) *Jamie Osborne* a85 102
5 b m Montjeu(IRE) Shaanara (IRE) (Darshaan)
1974[8] 4111[11] 4697[3] 5491[10] 5826[10] 6198[P] (Dead)

Neverendings Story (FR) *R Laplanche* a78 73
3 ch g Satri(IRE) Once Upon A Night (FR) (Freedom Cry)
1171a[0]

Never Forever *George Moore* 59
3 ch g Sir Percy Codename (Sadler's Wells (USA))
5340[5] 5549[6] 6100[8]

Never In (IRE) *Alan Berry* 49
3 b f Elusive City(USA) Priceoflove (IRE) (Inchinor)
2121[8] 2695[8] 3357[8] 3463[5]

Never Perfect (IRE) *Tom Tate* 74
3 b g Galileo(IRE) Dapprima (GER) (Shareef Dancer (USA))
2449[9] 2980[7] 3728[3]

Never Satisfied *Charles Hills* a61 65
3 ch g Haafhd Pirouetting (Pivotal)
324 [4] 847[6] 921[3] 1055[4] 2497[5]

Never Say Never (ITY) *S Botti* 102
2 b c Colossus(IRE) Do Diesis (ITY) (Barathea (IRE))
(7513a)

Nevis (IRE) *A P O'Brien* 92
2 b c Dansili Moonstone (Dalakhani (IRE))
6272a[6]

Newberry Hill (IRE) *Mrs John Harrington* 78
2 ch c Kheleyf(USA) Zonic (Zafonic (USA))
2958a[4]

New Best (FR) *Alex Fracas* a74 73
7 b g Le Triton(USA) Besca Nueva (FR) (Lesotho (USA))
94a[2]

Newby Lodge (IRE) *Alan Bailey* a66 59
4 b m Intikhab(USA) Titans Clash (IRE) (Grand Lodge (USA))
60[5]

New Decade *Milton Bradley* a72 69
3 ch g Pivotal Irresistible (Cadeaux Genereux)
193[2] 2206[3] 2573[6] 3050[5] (3218) 3566[4] 4534[9]

New Drama (IRE) *Mark Johnston* a65 63
3 b f Oratorio(IRE) Act Of The Pace (IRE) (King's Theatre (IRE))
2927[3] 3232[2] 5753[7]

New Falcon (IRE) *James Tate* a72 78
2 b f New Approach(IRE) Wimple (USA) (Kingmambo (USA))
2245[5] 2541[2] 4546[2] 5155[8] (5702) 6160[8]

Newfangled (USA) *John Gosden* 105
2 bb f New Approach(IRE) Scarlet Ibis (Machiavellian (USA))
(2892) ◆ (3326) ◆ 5516[P] (Dead)

New Fforest *Andrew Balding* a73 82
2 b f Oasis Dream Ffestiniog (IRE) (Efisio)
4011[13] 4488[4] 5003[2] 5307[5] (6054) 6238[3]

New Hampshire (USA) *Tony Coyle* a94 101
4 b g Elusive Quality(USA) Downtown Blues (USA) (Seattle Song (USA))
1475[2] 2176[13] 3287[9] 3417[2] 3610[2] 4074[3] 4249[2] (4621) 6248[3] (6476) ◆

Newington *Lydia Pearce* a49 51
3 b f Iceman Almunia (IRE) (Mujadil (USA))
1357[5] ◆ 6965[9] 7249[5]

New Jersey Girl *Chris Wall*
2 b f Ishiguru(USA) Nocturnal Lady (Night Shift (USA))
6534[13]

New Lease Of Life *Jim Goldie* 52
3 b g Orientor Primo Heights (Primo Valentino (IRE))
2065[8] 2695[6] 3438[7] 3892[6]

New Leyf (IRE) *Colin Teague* a97 93
6 bb g Kheleyf(USA) Society Fair (FR) (Always Fair (USA))
1141[2] 2068[12] 2558[5] 3049[12] 4252[5] 6008[4] ◆ 6465[7] 7097[12]

New Magic (IRE) *Dermot Anthony McLoughlin* a90 93
5 b m Statue Of Liberty(USA) Magic Mushroom (Pivotal)
3645a[3] 5609a[8] 7230a[7] 7680a[3]

Newnton Lodge *Roger Charlton* 83
3 b g Rail Link Widescreen (USA) (Distant View (USA))
1500[10] 5794 [7]

New Outlook (USA) *J E Pease* a92 99
4 b h Awesome Again(CAN) Tikkanita (USA) (Cozzene (USA))
6804a[9]

New Pearl (IRE) *David Brown* 91
2 gr c Acclamation New Deal (Rainbow Quest (USA))
(1886) ◆ 2677[2] 3240[18] 3532[2] 4804[2] 5515[16] 6424[4] 6799[6]

New Planet (IRE) *John Quinn* 105
4 ch g Majestic Missile(IRE) Xena (IRE) (Mull Of Kintyre (USA))
(1255) ◆ 1469[5] 2177[13] 3371[24] 4086[12] 6543[7]

Newport Arch *John Quinn* a77 27
4 b g Pastoral Pursuits Mashmoum (Lycius (USA))
97[3] 229[3] 366[4] (644) 850[4] (888) 978[2] 1382[11]

New Rich *Michael Dods* 70
2 b g Bahamian Bounty Bling Bling (IRE) (Indian Ridge)
4114[7] 4960[3] 5727[4]

New River (IRE) *Richard Hannon* a71 76
4 b m Montjeu(IRE) Quiet Waters (USA) (Quiet American (USA))
1792[4] 2561[2] 2755[4]

New Romantic *Julie Camacho* a52 52
3 b f Singspiel(IRE) Kalinova (IRE) (Red Ransom (USA))
2131[8] 2795[10] 5215[2] 5918[9]

News Desk *John Gosden* a69
3 b f Cape Cross(IRE) La Presse (USA) (Gone West (USA))
206[3] (571) 787[3]

Newsreader (USA) *Mahmood Al Zarooni* 75
2 b c New Approach(IRE) Headline (Machiavellian (USA))
6733[3]

News Show *David Simcock* a80 82
3 b f Sinndar(IRE) Yemen Desert (IRE) (Sadler's Wells (USA))
1532[10] 1906[6] 2333[2] 3968[3] (4200) 4403[2] 6662[5]

Newstead Abbey *David Brown* 80
2 b g Byron Oatcake (Selkirk (USA))
2213[2] 2662[5] 3182[7] 4526[5] 5579[4] 6070[5] 6920[4]

Newton Circus *K Klein* a50 68
5 gr g Verglas(IRE) Flying Finish (FR) (Priolo (USA))
444a[6]

Newtown Cross (IRE) *Jimmy Fox* 59
2 ch c Kheleyf(USA) Sacred Pearl (IRE) (Daylami (IRE))
4604[5] ◆ 5303[5] 6443[10]

New Youmzain (FR) *Mick Channon* 86
3 b g Sinndar(IRE) Luna Sacra (FR) (Sadler's Wells (USA))
1893[3] (2288) 4513[7] (5830) ◆ 7211[3]

Nexius (IRE) *W Hickst* 100
3 b c Catcher In The Rye(IRE) Nicolaia (GER) (Alkalde (GER))
2966a[3] 5402a[4] 6290a[7]

Next Cry (USA) *Richard Hannon* a78 69
3 ch c Street Cry(IRE) Storm Alert (USA) (Storm Cat (USA))
184[5] (656) 803[3] 1093[5]

Next Door (IRE) *David Barron* 66
2 b f Elusive City(USA) Lamh Eile (IRE) (Lend A Hand)
5709[4] 6042[3]

Next Edition (IRE) *Philip Kirby* 88
4 b g Antonius Pius(USA) Starfish (IRE) (Galileo (IRE))
2510[2] 3354[2] 4679[4] 5111[6] 5677[5] 6124[7]

Next Green (GER) *P Schiergen* 88
2 b f Green Desert(USA) Night Petticoat (GER) (Petoski)
6522a[2]

Next Holy (IRE) *P Schiergen* 94
4 b m Holy Roman Emperor(IRE) Night Petticoat (GER) (Petoski)
5844a[9]

Next Question (USA) *Michael Trombetta* 109
4 b g Stormy Atlantic(USA) Seattle Stardust (USA) (Slew City Slew (USA))
(7092a) 7571a[7]

Next Vision (IRE) *J Hirschberger* 96
6 ch g Rock Of Gibraltar(IRE) Night Petticoat (GER) (Petoski)
5865a[7]

Nezami (IRE) *Patrick Clinton* a76 76
7 b g Elnadim(USA) Stands To Reason (USA) (Gulch (USA))
834[2] 1161[10] 1527[4] 1958[7] 2535[4] 2924[7] (3311) 3810[5] 4141[3] 4747[7] (5658) 6241[5] 6785[6] 7685[4]

Nezhenka *Mark Johnston* a89 95
5 b m With Approval(CAN) Ninotchka (USA) (Nijinsky (CAN))
44[4] 202[4] (332) 577[4] 668[4]

Ngina *Terry Clement* a45
4 b m Iceman Nairobi (FR) (Anabaa (USA))
399[8]

Nha Trang (IRE) *Michael Appleby* a44 47
5 b g Indian Danehill(IRE) Baileys On Line (Shareef Dancer (USA))
105[7] 4189[6] 5638[6] 6232[8]

Nibani (IRE) *John Butler* a83 84
5 ch g Dalakhani(IRE) Dance Of The Sea (IRE) (Sinndar (IRE))
90[2] (119) 263[7] 2285[9] 2510[14] 2754[5] 2988[3] 3723[4] 4061[6] 6539[9]

Nicea (GER) *P Schiergen* a96 106
5 b m Lando(GER) Nicolaia (GER) (Alkalde (GER))
83a[5]

Nice Association (FR) *Mme C Head-Maarek* 106
4 b m High Yield(USA) Pick A Poket (FR) (Anabaa (USA))
6913a[7]

Niceofyoutotellme *Ralph Beckett* a81 90
3 b g Hernando(FR) Swain's Gold (USA) (Swain (IRE))
1065[2] (1270) 3296[13] 4046[4] 5006[2]

Niceonemyson *Christopher Wilson* 58
3 b g Misu Bond(IRE) Kungfu Kerry (Celtic Swing)
1953[7] 2262[5] 2591[8] 3028[5] 3272[7] 5734[4] 6100[7] 6477[8]

Nice Rose *Mark Johnston* a75 80
3 ch f Teofilo(IRE) Souvenance (Hernando (FR))
1113[4] (1380) 2427[6] 3033[7] 6045[4] 6359[6] 6662[7] 7610[2]

Nice Story (IRE) *Mick Channon* 75
2 ch f Suave(USA) Royal Aly (USA) (Royal Academy (USA))
(5656) 6021[6]

Nice Style (IRE) *Jeremy Gask* a97 91
7 b g Desert Style(IRE) Great Idea (IRE) (Lion Cavern (USA))
1752[8]

Nicholascopernicus (IRE) *Ed Walker* a79 101
3 ch g Medicean Ascendancy (Sadler's Wells (USA))
1319[2] 1853[2] (2885) ◆ (3072) ◆ 3296[9] 6018[10] 6625[2] (7082) ◆ 7689[13]

Nicholas Pocock (IRE) *Ian McInnes* a64 66
6 b g King's Best(USA) Sea Picture (IRE) (Royal Academy (USA))
1222[8] 1425[8] 1717[7] 2013[3] 2692[5] 3047[9] 5015[8] 5253[10]

Nichols Canyon *John Gosden* 79
2 b c Authorized(IRE) Zam Zoom (IRE) (Dalakhani (IRE))
5005[2] ◆ 6371[3] (7081)

Nickels And Dimes (IRE) *John Gosden* 78
2 b f Teofilo(IRE) Neat Shilling (IRE) (Bob Back (USA))
6960[3] 7312[2]

Nickel Silver *Bryan Smart* a63 70
7 gr g Choisir(AUS) Negligee (Night Shift (USA))
1828[11] 2439[11] 2793[6] 4400[12] 4680[5] 5205[5] 6314[6] 6685[7] 7197[13]

Nickeys On Time (IRE) *Daniel Mark Loughnane* a50 34
3 b f Ivan Denisovich(IRE) Tammany Hall (IRE) (Petorius)
2130[11] 3023[9]

Nicky Nutjob (GER) *John O'Shea* a21 23
6 b g Fasliyev(USA) Natalie Too (USA) (Irish River (FR))
2651[5] 3143[10] 4988[10]

Nic Nok *Joseph Tuite* a52 10
3 b g Iceman Past 'N' Present (Cadeaux Genereux)
204[4] 534[6] 683[3] 1045[5] 1726[11] 4871[5]

Nic's Rebel *James Unett* 24
3 b f Cockney Rebel(IRE) Dipple (Komaite (USA))
5448[6] 6095[6]

Nid D'Amour (FR) *J-P Gallorini* 101
6 b m Ultimately Lucky(IRE) N'Avoue Jamais (FR) (Marignan (USA))
7124a[10]

Nifty Nadine (IRE) *Nigel Tinkler* 27
2 gr f Verglas(IRE) Diamond Katie (IRE) (Night Shift (USA))
3303[8] 3909[8] 5222[8] 5675[11]

Niger (IRE) *Jeremy Noseda* a78 71
3 ch c Pivotal Tithcar (Cadeaux Genereux)
2273[6] 2865[2] (4213) 4949[9]

Night And Dance (IRE) *Clive Cox* a93 90
4 b m Danehill Dancer(IRE) Evensong (GER) (Waky Nao)
(1491) ◆ 1656[4] 4515[2] ◆ 5129[9] 7461[9] (7626)

Night Carnation *Andrew Balding* a61 111
4 ch m Sleeping Indian Rimba (USA) (Dayjur (USA))
1494[5] 1857[5] 3238[6] 3877[10] 4838[2] (5814) 7092a[2]

Nightdance Paolo (GER) *A Schaerer* 99
5 b h Paolini(GER) Nightdance (GER) (Shareef Dancer (USA))
7282a[2]

Nightdance Victor (GER) *P Schiergen* a64 82
5 b g Pentire Nightdance Forest (IRE) (Charnwood Forest (IRE))
965a[7]

Night Flash (GER) *James Given* a76 58
3 b c Oratorio(IRE) Night Woman (GER) (Monsun (GER))
2088[6] 2544[3] 2860[13] 3558[7] 5312[5]

Night Garden (USA) *A Fabre* 95
3 b f Redoute's Choice(AUS) Wild Queen (AUS) (Loup Sauvage (USA))
3987a[5]

Nightjar (USA) *Elisabeth Gautier* a99 89
7 b g Smoke Glacken(USA) Night Risk (USA) (Wild Again (USA))
3654a[8]

Night Lily (IRE) *Paul D'Arcy* a101 95
6 b m Night Shift(USA) Kedross (IRE) (King Of Kings (IRE))
83a[3] 254[8] (622) 866[4] 1213[5] 2078[2] 2654[6] 4527[5] 4764[6] 5834[9] 7509[10] 7680a[8]

Night Of Light (IRE) *F Camici* 91
2 b f Tenby Polvere Di Luna (ITY) (Hunting Hawk (IRE))
7285a[6]

Night Serenade (IRE) *H-A Pantall* 102
5 b m Golan(IRE) Night Teeny (Platini (GER))
3367a[8] 5844a[10] 6595a[10] 7665a[10]

Night Sky *Tony Carroll* a53 61
5 b m Starcraft(NZ) War Shanty (Warrshan (USA))
995[12] 3137[9] 4219[4] 4817[13]

Night's Watch *William Jarvis* a68 50
2 b c Authorized(IRE) Nachtigall (GER) (Danehill (USA))
5511[8] 5911[5] 6412[8] 7924[4] 8240[7]

Night Symfonic *Brett Johnson*
3 ch f Zafeen(FR) Nocturnal Lady (Night Shift (USA))
737[11] 892[11]

Night Trade (IRE) *Ronald Harris* a82 86
5 b m Trade Fair Compton Girl (Compton Place)
64[11] 252[3] (387) 526[5] 1936[9] 2070[9] 2870[6] 3139[8] ◆ 3541[5] 3960[9] 4235[2] (4420) 5035[5] 5326[4] 5486[6] 5877[7] 6094[5] 6825[5]

Nijinsky Blood (FR) *P Van De Poele* a78 79
5 b g Fantastic Light(USA) Daraydala (IRE) (Royal Academy (USA))
93a[6]

Nijisky Girl (FR) *Y-M Porzier*
4 b m Zero Problemo(IRE) Nijinskha (FR) (Baroud D'Honneur (FR))
1172a[0]

Nikita Du Berlais (FR) *Robert Collet* 105
5 b m Poliglote Chica Du Berlais (FR) (Cadoudal (FR))
6914a[5]

Niknad *Brian Ellison* a43
2 b f Zafeen(FR) Eau Rouge (Grand Lodge (USA))
7598[10] 7728[6] 8138[7]

Nile Knight *Marcus Tregoning* 76
2 b c Sir Percy Sahara Belle (USA) (Sanglamore (USA))
2480[4] ◆ 2888[5] (5661) 6247[5]

Nimble Thimble (USA) *Roger Charlton* a71
3 ch f Mizzen Mast(USA) Skiable (IRE) (Niniski (USA))
1704[9] (4157) 4657[10]

Nina Rose *Clive Cox* a67 56
5 ro m Pastoral Pursuits Magnolia (Petong)
124[4] 361[9]

Nine Before Ten (IRE) *Charles Smith* a61 78
4 ch m Captain Rio Sagaing (Machiavellian (USA))
997[11] 1073[6] 1428[6] 2493[3] 3256[12] 4087[9] 4653[13] 6180[5] 6322[7] 6496[2] 7591[8] 7673[4] 7861[11] 7969[10]

Nine Iron (IRE) *Mick Channon* a66 66
2 gr g Verglas(IRE) Sevi's Choice (USA) (Sir Ivor (USA))
3067[9] 4253[5] 4846[6] 6732[2] ◆ (7026)

Nine Realms *William Haggas* a90 97
3 b c Green Desert(USA) Bourbonella (Rainbow Quest (USA))
1450[2] 1922[2] (2553)

Ninfea (IRE) *David Bridgwater* a71 72
4 b m Le Vie Dei Colori Attymon Lill (IRE) (Marju (IRE))
2502[3] 7839[8] 8023[7] 8170[5]

Ningara *Andrew Balding* a77
2 b c Singspiel(IRE) Garanciere (FR) (Anabaa (USA))
7899[5] (8071)

Ningbo Express (IRE) *Rae Guest* 57
2 b f Jeremy(USA) Sunlit Skies (Selkirk (USA))
7433[4]

Nini Ok (IRE) *John Joseph Murphy* a79 80
3 b f Acclamation Charmed Forest (IRE) (Shinko Forest (IRE))
4380a[7] 6270a[4] ◆ 6716a[4]

Ninjago *Richard Hannon* a92 98
2 b c Mount Nelson Fidelio's Miracle (USA) (Mountain Cat (USA))
(4532) ◆ 5353[3] 6200[4] (6777) (7521)

Nip And Tuck *William Jarvis* a62
3 b c Green Desert(USA) Coveted (Sinndar (IRE))
181[11] 358[7]

Nippy Nikki *John Norton* a55 43
4 b m Needwood Blade Spielbound (Singspiel (IRE))
811[2] 1055[3] 1433[4] 7800[11]

Niwot (AUS) *Michael, Wayne & John Hawkes* 116
8 b g Galileo(IRE) Too Darn Hot (NZ) (Noble Bijou (USA))
7264a[12] 7621a[15]

Niya (FR) *P Schaerer* a31
5 ch m High Yield(USA) Flyer (FR) (Highest Honor (FR))
444a[7] 631a[4]

Nobbys Girl *Ronald Harris* a26 14
7 b m Double Trigger(IRE) Mini Mandy (Petoski)
1496[8] 2575[10]

Nobilis *A Fabre* 102
5 b f Rock Of Gibraltar(IRE) Dolydille (IRE) (Dolphin Street (FR))
3423a[3] 5142a[2] 7449a[9]

Noble Alan (GER) *Nicky Richards* 92
9 gr g King's Theatre(IRE) Nirvavita (FR) (Highest Honor (FR))
1866[5] 2287[3] 2708[5] ◆ 3610[3] ◆ 4613[9] (6339)

Noble Attitude *Julie Camacho* a51 35
6 b m Best Of The Bests(IRE) Charming Lotte (Nicolotte)
109[8] 454[11]

Noble Bacchus (IRE) *Tom Dascombe* 56
2 b g Acclamation Vintage Tipple (IRE) (Entrepreneur)
5040[8] 5962[7] 6486[10]

Noble Bounty *Kevin Ryan* a59 14
3 b g Bahamian Bounty Enchanted Princess (Royal Applause)
1089[6] 1521[9] 1986[4] 5757[9] 6104[15] 6810[10]

Noble Bull (IRE) *Charles Hills* 73
2 b g Papal Bull Fernlawn Hope (IRE) (Danehill Dancer (IRE))
2983[12] 3634[2] 4327[4] (4982) 5786[6]

Noble Citizen (USA) *David Simcock* a91 99
7 b g Proud Citizen(USA) Serene Nobility (USA) (His Majesty (USA))
1741[6] 2409[2] 4321[6] 4609[13] 5102[12] 5746[4] 6432[2] 7010[13]

Noble Deed *William Haggas* a71 73
2 ch g Kyllachy Noble One (Primo Dominie)
5360[3] ◆ 6015[4] 7167[6]

Noble Fantasy (GER) *Mario Hofer* a81 85
3 ch f Big Shuffle(USA) Nouvelle Noblesse (GER) (Singspiel (IRE))
5473a[5] 6752a[4]

Noble Four (IRE) *W McCreery* a67 77
4 bb g Kheleyf(USA) Buttons Galore (IRE) (Bigstone (IRE))
2572[12]

Noble Gift *John Dunlop* 77
2 ch c Cadeaux Genereux Noble Penny (Pennekamp (USA))
6481[12] (7103)

Noble Hachy *L Riccardi* 111
3 b f Kyllachy Noble Hero (IRE) (Daggers Drawn (USA))
(1409a) 2745a[5] 3901a[5] (7288a) 7697a[3]

Noble Jack (IRE) *Jo Hughes* a74 67
6 b g Elusive City(USA) Begine (IRE) (Germany (USA))
(3712) (4657) 4884[3] 7132[6]

Noble Mission *Sir Henry Cecil* 116
3 b c Galileo(IRE) Kind (IRE) (Danehill (USA))
(1506) (1859) 2275[2] 3327[2] (4685) 5489[4] 7405[2]

Noble Silk *Lucy Wadham* a88 83
3 gr g Sir Percy Tussah (Daylami (IRE))
4630[3] 5315[2] (5952) 8000[2] 8191[2]

Noble Storm (USA) *Ed McMahon* a112 113
6 b h Yankee Gentleman(USA) Changed Tune (USA) (Tunerup (USA))
1033[6] 1977[4] 2664[3] 4299[5] 4762[7] 5204[5] 5822[10] 6140[12]

Noble Tune (USA) *Chad C Brown* 114
2 bb c Unbridled's Song(USA) Serena's Cat (USA) (Storm Cat (USA))
7568a[2]

No Compromise *Hughie Morrison* a83 82
3 b f Avonbridge Highly Liquid (Entrepreneur)
2272[6] 3120[3] 3785[4] (4706) 5328[8] 6039[9] 6798[3]

Nocturn *Jeremy Noseda* 83
3 b g Oasis Dream Pizzicato (Statoblest)
1452[13] 2501[4] ◆ (3702) ◆ 4364[2]

Nocturnal Affair (SAF) *David Marnane* a107 113
6 b g Victory Moon(SAF) Aretha (SAF) (Centenary (USA))
50a[2] 419a[5] (681a) 875a[3] 1146a[6] 5067a[2] 5561[12] 6140[8] 6854a[2] 7390a[2]

No Diamond *Michael Appleby* a59
5 b g Helissio(FR) Diamond Swan (Colonel Collins (USA))
6839[10] 7384[5] 7654[6] 7841[6] 8139[3] 8260[6]

No Dominion (IRE) *James Given* a75 64
3 b g Dylan Thomas(IRE) Boast (Most Welcome)
1479[5] 2118[9] 3083[4] 3630[U] 4498[10] 5738[7] 6151[3] (6810) (7347) 7799[2]

Noguchi (IRE) *Michael Murphy* a87 84
7 ch g Pivotal Tuscania (USA) (Woodman (USA))
8019[2] 8174[6]

No Heretic *David Simcock* 94
4 b g Galileo(IRE) Intrigued (Darshaan)
1850[6] ◆ 4823[2] (5665) 6197[3]

No Hubris (USA) *Ruth Carr* a68 96
5 b g Proud Citizen(USA) Innateness (USA) (Flying Paster (USA))
1157[20] 1558[13] 2029[10] 2289[3] 2596[11] 3255[6] (3726) 4133[7] 4454[3]

Noinformation (IRE) *Mark Michael McNiff* a45 55
5 gr m Verglas(IRE) Sans Escale (USA) (Diesis)
125[10] 653[14] 5081[10]

No Jet Lag (USA) *David Lanigan* a85 100
2 b g Johar(USA) Desert Sky (IRE) (Green Desert (USA))
4066[7] (4646) (5587) 6200[2] 7038a[7]

Nokov (GER) *F Meckes* 77
5 b g Sholokhov(IRE) Noirie (GER) (Dashing Blade)
7551a[8]

No Larking (IRE) *Henry Candy* a36 72
4 b g Refuse To Bend(IRE) Dawn Chorus (IRE) (Mukaddamah (USA))
3723[7] 4296[9] 4584[7] 4986[3] 5657[5] 5990[6] 6967[6] 7106[5]

Nolecce *Richard Guest* a69 70
5 ch g Reset(AUS) Ghassanah (Pas De Seul)
183[4] 460[7] 636[4] (818) 891[4] 1286[5] 1432[7] 1743[4] 2051[5] 4088[3] 4179[10] 4350[11] 5452[4] 5669[3] 5998[9] 6262[11] 6785[8] 7095[4] 7383[10] 7496[10] 8288[9]

No Mean Trick (USA) *Paul Midgley* a74 40
6 b g Grand Slam(USA) Ruby's Reception (USA) (Rubiano (USA))
24[2] (380) 497[5] 718[4] 808[6] 1187[5] 1954[8] 7794[7] 8285[7]

Nomoreblondes *Paul Midgley* a66 81
8 ch m Ishiguru(USA) Statuette (Statoblest)
1246[9] (1954) (2439) 4451[5] 4770[4] 5272[5] 5584[7] 6144[14] 6887[6]

Nonios (USA) *Jerry Hollendorfer* a115
3 bb c Pleasantly Perfect(USA) Stylish Manner (USA) (Touch Gold (USA))
7576a[6]

No No Cardinal (IRE) *Peter Hedger* a30 15
3 ch g Touch Of Land(FR) Four Moons (IRE) (Cardinal Flower)
3227[15] 4948[7]

Non Stop *M Le Forestier* a82 88
6 b g Beat Hollow High And Low (Rainbow Quest (USA))
630a[7]

Non Stop (TUR) *Y Bulut* 83
4 b h Luxor(TUR) Nazar (TUR) (Lear White (USA))
5869a[11]

Noodles Blue Boy *Ollie Pears* a65 91
6 b g Makbul Dee Dee Girl (IRE) (Primo Dominie)
1642[6] (1868) 2289[6] 2337[2] 2674[4] 3845[2] 4312[2] (4591) 4924[10] 5343[10] 5829[14] 6144[11] 6543[5] 7291[15]

Noor Al Haya (IRE) *Mark Usher* a28
2 b f Tamayuz Hariya (IRE) (Shernazar)
7159[14] 7840[9]

Noor Zabeel (USA) *A Al Raihe* a98 97
3 b c Elusive Quality(USA) Brave The Storm (USA) (Storm Cat (USA))
485a[6] 679a[3] 873a[10]

Noosa Boy *Luke Dace* a55 34
3 b g Pivotal Maroochydore (IRE) (Danehill (USA))
350[8] 709[6] 5901[6] 6395[6] 7148[11] 7326[11] 7499[9]

Noosa Sound *John Davies* 67
2 ch f Halling(USA) Crimson Topaz (Hernando (FR))
3776[8] 4546[5] 5311[9] 6337[13]

Nopanicjim (IRE) *Rod Collet* a69 85
3 b f Rail Link Mina Girl (USA) (Menifee (USA))
5726a[2]

No Plan B (IRE) *Noel Quinlan* a54 23
3 b f Le Vie Dei Colori Heres The Plan (IRE) (Revoque (IRE))
1424[3] 2341[6] 3275[11] 4932[9] 6686[5]

No Poppy (IRE) *Tim Easterby* 97
4 b m Chineur(FR) Capetown Girl (Danzero (AUS))
1294[2] (1650) (2119) 2597[10] 3252[2] (3495) 3991[3] 4345[9] 4589[5] 5520[6] 5819[13] 6471[2] (6710) (7030) 7334[4]

No Quarter (IRE) *Tracy Waggott* 69
5 b g Refuse To Bend(IRE) Moonlight Wish (IRE) (Peintre Celebre (USA))
1293[13] 1527[7] 2696[9] 2879[4] 3257[2] ◆ 3749[3] 4715[4] 4954[4] 5295[3] 6479[3]

No Rachmones (USA) *Peter Miller* a82 71
2 rg g Macho Uno(USA) Caught Fire (CAN) (Lite The Fuse (USA))
7567a[10]

Norcroft *Christine Dunnett* a55 51
10 b g Fasliyev(USA) Norcroft Joy (Rock Hopper)
2401[6] 3053[8] 4406[10]

Nordfalke (IRE) *A Schaerer* 102
5 br g Hawk Wing(USA) North Queen (IRE) (Desert King (IRE))
629a[10]

Nordic Light (USA) *Mrs A Malzard* a47 39
8 bb g Belong To Me(USA) Midriff (USA) (Naevus (USA))
2114a[3] 5701a[3] 6951[5] 7254[9]
Nordic Quest (IRE) *Gerard Butler* a89 77
3 b c Montjeu(IRE) Nordtanzerin (GER) (Danehill Dancer (IRE))
1155[9] (1568) 5973[2] 6537[2] 6712[5] 7195[2] 7655[9]
Nordic Truce (USA) *P Schiergen* 103
5 b h Yes It's True(USA) Nyramba (Night Shift (USA))
1745a[4] 2728a[9] 3901a[9] 6291a[8]
Nordikhab (IRE) *Kevin Ryan* a81 82
2 b g Intikhab(USA) Pourquoi Pas (IRE) (Nordico (USA))
3378[3] ◆ 4257[5] 4816[2] 5367[3]
No Reply *David Nicholls* 26
2 gr g Avonbridge En Grisaille (Mystiko (USA))
2508[11] 3250[6]
Norfolk Sky *Laura Mongan* a71 53
3 ch f Haafhd Cayman Sound (Turtle Island (IRE))
2582[4] 3052[7] (4198) 4650[2] 5408[2] (6210) ◆ 7062[3] (7499) 7718[5] (8048) 8229[4]
No Risk At All (FR) *J-P Gallorini* 121
5 ch h My Risk(FR) Newness (IRE) (Simply Great (FR))
1163a[3] 1746a[2] 2533a[3] (2989a) (4229a)
Norlander *Ralph Beckett* a60 60
3 b f Royal Applause Arrivato (Efisio)
2422[4] 3702[4] 5156[4] 5658[6] 6500[7]
Normal Equilibrium *Roger Varian* 90
2 b c Elnadim(USA) Acicula (IRE) (Night Shift (USA))
(3617) 4488[5] 5088[4] 5563[2] 5903[3] 6487[7]
Norphin *Denis Coakley* a57 58
2 b c Norse Dancer(IRE) Orphina (IRE) (Orpen (USA))
4917[6] 5793[7] 7373[5]
Norse Blues *Sylvester Kirk* a92 94
4 ch g Norse Dancer(IRE) Indiana Blues (Indian Ridge)
(1128) 2250[5] 2657[5] 3508[7] 4689[5] 4828[8] 5356[6] 6242[7] 6601[4] 6638[5]
Norse Song *David Elsworth* a52
3 b f Norse Dancer(IRE) Blue Lullaby (IRE) (Fasliyev (USA))
784[8] 1036[5] 1357[9] 2374[13]
Nors The Panic *Richard Guest*
2 ch g Bahamian Bounty Croeso Bach (Bertolini (USA))
1949[7]
North Central (USA) *Ruth Carr* a62 76
5 bb g Forest Camp(USA) Brittan Lee (USA) (Forty Niner (USA))
2037[3] 3027[5] 3335[9] 4134[11] 4909[7] 5185[7] 6480[10] 7204[6] (7225) 7385[12] (7512) 8114[10] 8236[8]
Northern Acres *Sue Bradburne* 36
6 b g Mtoto Bunting (Shaadi (USA))
1240[9]
Northern Bolt *Ian McInnes* a38 76
7 b g Cadeaux Genereux Shafir (IRE) (Shaadi (USA))
1254[9] 1526[4] 1601[2] 1917[13] 2037[6] 2096[2] 2693[7] 2981[8] 3523[5] 3730[5] 4207[6] 5740[5] 5821[6] (6529) 7446[12] 7794[14] 7914[10]
Northern Fling *Jim Goldie* a51 79
8 b g Mujadil(USA) Donna Anna (Be My Chief (USA))
1520[10] (1796) ◆ 2597[11] 3890[8] 4317[19] 5186[10] 6711[14] 7530[5]
Northern Genes (AUS) *Michael Appleby* a48 48
6 b g Refuse To Bend(IRE) Cotswold Dancer (AUS) (Carnegie (IRE))
451[11]
Northern Harbour (IRE) *J S Moore* a60 60
2 b c Ad Valorem(USA) Cutting Reef (IRE) (Kris)
2571[6] 3224[4] 4191[4] 4222[4] 4658[5] 5061[6] 5207[7] 5806[3]
Northern Jewel (IRE) *Richard Fahey* 58
3 b f Nayef(USA) Tekindia (FR) (Indian Ridge)
2449[12] 4548[5] 5085[8]
Northern Rocked (IRE) *D K Weld* a79 101
6 b g Refuse To Bend(IRE) Gifts Galore (IRE) (Darshaan)
1043a[16] 4833a[4] 5609a[4]
Northern Spy (USA) *Simon Dow* a69 68
8 b g War Chant(USA) Sunray Superstar (Nashwan (USA))
55[2] 302[8] 1154[10] 1626[7] 2886[7] 3511[5] 4252[6] 6252[4] 6690[7] 7898[7] 8099[5] ◆
Northern Star (IRE) *Tom Dascombe* 91
2 b f Montjeu(IRE) Slow Sand (USA) (Dixieland Band (USA))
4995[4] 5471a[8] 6664[2]
Northern Territory (IRE) *Jim Boyle* a59 66
3 b c Choisir(AUS) Krasivaya (IRE) (Soviet Star (USA))
(1740) 2126[8] 3002[5] 4256[9] 4945[6] 5479[5]
Northgate Lodge (USA) *Mel Brittain* a42 45
7 ch g Hold That Tiger(USA) Sabaah Elfull (Kris)
3356[13] 4350[14]
North Pole *Sir Mark Prescott Bt* a66
2 b g Compton Place Cool Question (Polar Falcon (USA))
6889[4] 7198[5] 7481[3] 7609[10]
Northside Ace (IRE) *Linda Perratt*
2 b g Red Clubs(IRE) Baltic Belle (IRE) (Redback)
6524[5]
Northside Prince (IRE) *Alan Swinbank* a75 97
6 b g Desert Prince(IRE) Spartan Girl (IRE) (Ela-Mana-Mou)
1273[3] 1654[12] 2176[6] 2773[6] 3494[15] 4621[2] 4962[3] 6476[6]
North Star Boy (IRE) *Richard Hannon* a83 96
3 b g Acclamation Isla Azul (IRE) (Machiavellian (USA))
1457[11] 2212[6] 3876[4] 4095[5] 4703[9] 5128[3] 5676[9] 6768[5] 7177[5] 7646[4] ◆
Northumberland *Owen Brennan* a47 38
6 b g Bertolini(USA) Cal Norma's Lady (IRE) (Lyphard's Special (USA))
632[10]
North Weald (IRE) *J W Hills* a44 62
2 b f Hurricane Run(IRE) Foreign Relation (IRE) (Distant Relative)
5275[7] 5907[7] 6817[6] 7708[10]
Norton Girl *Tracy Waggott* a56 44
4 b m Diktat Opening Ceremony (USA) (Quest For Fame)
113[6] 809[3] 2588[11] 3355[7] 4350[12] 4594[11] 4712[5]
No Rules *Mark H Tompkins* a45 58
7 b g Fraam Golden Daring (IRE) (Night Shift (USA))
207[5]
Norville (IRE) *Lee Smyth* a96 104
5 b g Elusive City(USA) Saraposa (IRE) (Ahonoora)
89[8] 253[4] 431[6] 527[6] 5137a[5] 6854a[7]
Norwegian Reward (IRE) *Michael Wigham* a63
4 ch g Hernando(FR) Stay Behind (Elmaamul (USA))
8005[3] (8038) 8179[2] (8265)
Norwood Lane *Peter Hedger* a56 35
3 b g Kyllachy Lay A Whisper (Night Shift (USA))
147[5] 429[5] 3314[10] 4508[6] 4900[10]
Nosedive *David Nicholls* 73
5 ch g Observatory(USA) Resistance Heroine (Dr Fong (USA))
1977[7] 2337[7]
Nostro Amico (GER) *Mario Hofer* 102
3 b c Martillo(GER) Narola (GER) (Nebos (GER))
3683a[8] 5402a[5]
No Such Number *Julia Feilden* a69 76
4 b g King's Best(USA) Return (USA) (Sadler's Wells (USA))
(6098) 7810[9]
Notabadgirl *Simon Dow* a53
3 ch f Denounce Lady Jo (Phountzi (USA))
7818[5] 8295[3]
Notabadlad *Simon Dow* a30 62
5 br g Denounce Lady Jo (Phountzi (USA))
1379[13] 1624[9] 2395[8]
Notable Graduate (IRE) *D K Weld* 105
4 b g Galileo(IRE) Market Slide (USA) (Gulch (USA))
2318a[7] 6066a[4]
Not Abroad (USA) *Michael P Petro* a111
5 b h Not For Love(USA) Timely Broad (USA) (Broad Brush (USA))
7546a[5]
Not Bad For A Boy (IRE) *Barry Leavy* a78 70
3 b g Elusive City(USA) Reign Of Fire (IRE) (Perugino (USA))
230[4] 2764[8] 3063[10] 3555[12] 4082[8] 4592[8] 4929[6] 5621[9]
Nothing's Simple *Hugo Palmer* a54 36
3 ch g Avonbridge Suzie Fong (Dr Fong (USA))
742[4] 892[7] 1048[5] 1259[14] 1530[8] 3053[7]
No Time To Cry *Ann Duffield* a28 57
3 b f Josr Algarhoud(IRE) Autumn Bloom (IRE) (Fantastic Light (USA))
1170[4] 2141[7] 2765[3] 3025[3] 3907[5] 4172[4] 4678[4] 4826[6] 5187[6]
No Time To Lose *Jamie Osborne* a80 83
3 b g Authorized(IRE) Ballymore Celebre (IRE) (Peintre Celebre (USA))
2544[6] (4585) 5718[6] 6738[2]
Notional Demand *Tim Easterby* 62
2 b g Multiplex Bonsai (IRE) (Woodman (USA))
3168[6] 3533[4] 3842[2] 4792[14] 5619[5] 6356[6] 7289[6]
Not My Choice (IRE) *Paul Howling* a70 84
7 ch g Choisir(AUS) Northgate Raver (Absalom)
1050[2] 1378[13] 1586[6] 2546[12] 3477[8] 3949[10] 4493[6] 5050[2] 5720[10] 5915[8] 7224[9] 7504[12] 8062[7] 8179[10] ◆ 8298[8]
Not Now Blondie *Chris Dwyer* a60 60
2 ch f Notnowcato Gretel (Hansel (USA))
3046[2] ◆ 4011[14] 4433[4] (4927) 5749[8] 6332[5] 6850[3] 7056[4] 7650[3] 7974[4]
Notnowhoney *Niels Petersen* 20
3 b c Notnowcato Spirito Libro (USA) (Lear Fan (USA))
5144a[3]
Not Now Katie *Chris Gordon* 69
3 br f Notnowcato Angel Kate (IRE) (Invincible Spirit (IRE))
3340[8] 3786[6] 4366[14]
Notnowstanley *J S Moore* a29 42
3 ch g Notnowcato Denice (Night Shift (USA))
30[5]
Not Rigg (USA) *Andrew Balding* a70 56
2 b g Henrythenavigator(USA) St Helens Shadow (USA) (Septieme Ciel (USA))
6481[14] 7006[2] 7749[4] 7953[4] 8092[3]
No Trimmings (IRE) *Gerard Keane* a76 79
6 ch m Medecis Cheviot Indian (IRE) (Indian Ridge)
7680a[13]
No Truth (IRE) *Charles Hills* 52
2 b f Galileo(IRE) State Crystal (IRE) (High Estate)
7332[11] 7552[7]
Not Til Monday (IRE) *J R Jenkins* a73 78
6 b g Spartacus(IRE) Halomix (Linamix (FR))
332[8] 521[7] 1598[2] 2396[5] 2976[3] 3316[6] 7377[6]
Nouailhas *Reg Hollinshead* a42 53
6 b g Mark Of Esteem(IRE) Barachois Princess (USA) (Barachois (CAN))
7933[7]
Nouvelle Neige (GER) *P Schiergen* 97
2 bb f Big Shuffle(USA) Nouvelle Fortune (IRE) (Alzao (USA))
5755a[6]
Novabridge *Neil Mulholland* a73 70
4 ch g Avonbridge Petrovna (IRE) (Petardia)
59[8] (445) 497[3] 647[6] 958[9] 1305[12] 2165[14] (6288) 6563[3] 7969[4] (8307)
Novagem (SWE) *Mikael Tjernstrom*
3 bb f Diamond Green(FR) Novapearl (SWE) (Spectacular Tide (USA))
4359a[6]
Nova Hawk *Rod Collet* 111
4 br m Hawk Wing(USA) Reveuse De Jour (IRE) (Sadler's Wells (USA))
2728a[5] 3657a[6] (6726a) 7429a[3]
Novalist *Robin Bastiman* a64 66
4 ch g Avonbridge Malelane (IRE) (Prince Sabo)
1480[7] 2314[4] 2748[4] 2973[4] (3442) (4196) 4717[17] 5389[5] 6179[3] 7316[8]
Nova Neyev (FR) *P Capelle* a73 91
4 b h Diableneyev(USA) Gioiosa Marea (IRE) (Highest Honor (FR))
814a[0] 5118a[0]
Nova Nimph *Mark Brisbourne* a37
3 ch f Avonbridge Nimphida (Acatenango (GER))
8049[8] 8135[6]
Nova Sam (FR) *David Barron* 77
4 ch g Black Sam Bellamy(IRE) Elasili (FR) (Dansili)
4249[9]
Nova Step *Stephane Chevalier* a103 103
4 ch m Dubawi(IRE) Light Step (USA) (Nureyev (USA))
140a[14]
Nova Valorem (IRE) *F Rohaut* a95 101
4 ch h Ad Valorem(USA) Utr (USA) (Mr Prospector (USA))
2160a[4] 4316a[0]
Novay Essjay (IRE) *Dai Williams* a57 71
5 ch g Noverre(USA) Arabian Hideway (IRE) (Desert Prince (IRE))
95[7] 215[9] 356[11] 483[13] 531[8]
Novel Dancer *Lydia Richards* a63 74
4 b g Dansili Fictitious (Machiavellian (USA))
7169[9] 7629[7] 7819[2] 8035[7] 8189[8]
Novellen Lad (IRE) *Willie Musson* a94 96
7 b g Noverre(USA) Lady Ellen (Horage)
89[7] 527[2] ◆ 2558[3] 4286[14] 4799[23] 5342[18] 6165[10] ◆ 6938[8]
Novellist (IRE) *A Wohler* 120
3 b c Monsun(GER) Night Lagoon (GER) (Lagunas)
(1900a) (2966a) 3683a[2] 5865a[4] (7287a)
Noverre To Go (IRE) *Ronald Harris* a94 91
6 ch g Noverre(USA) Ukraine Venture (Slip Anchor)
2488[3] 2707[10] 3188[7] (3960) 4337[2] 4690[15] 4799[21] 5233[2] 6026[13] 6688[6] 6837[2] 7145[4] (7651) 7817[7] (7928) 8202[4]
Novikov *David Evans* a69 72
8 ch g Danehill Dancer(IRE) Ardisia (USA) (Affirmed (USA))
535[5]
Novirak (IRE) *James Fanshawe* a48 86
4 gr g Noverre(USA) Manchaca (FR) (Highest Honor (FR))
2248[14] 4249[4] 5706[2] (6170) 6445[4]
Now *Rod Millman* a56 58
6 br m Where Or When(IRE) Tup Tim (Emperor Jones (USA))
(28) 188[4] 265[9]
Nowdoro *Julie Camacho* a49 36
3 ch g Notnowcato Salydora (FR) (Peintre Celebre (USA))
3913[7] 4630[12] 5315[5] 5974[4] 6807[12] 7632[12]
Now My Sun *Mrs K Burke* 80
3 ch g Notnowcato Sienna Sunset (IRE) (Spectrum (IRE))
2021[5] 2452[8] 3066[4] 3775[7] (4289) 5044[4]
Now Spun (USA) *Mahmood Al Zarooni* a70 80
2 b c Hard Spun(USA) Campionessa (USA) (A.P. Indy (USA))
6501[5] (7130) ◆
Now What *Jonathan Portman* a69 71
5 ch m Where Or When(IRE) Vallauris (Faustus (USA))
2167[2]
Nuba (IRE) *Luke Dace* a54 58
4 b m Exceed And Excel(AUS) Little Doll (Gulch (USA))
188[13]
Nubar Boy *David Evans* a78 76
5 ch g Compton Place Out Like Magic (Magic Ring (IRE))
178[7] 251[3] ◆ 353[2] (528) 623[6] 710[8] 1007[4] 1254[3] 1564[13] 2572[2] 3915[10] 4829[18] 5097[9] 5346[6]
Nufoudh (IRE) *Tracy Waggott* 72
8 b g Key Of Luck(USA) Limpopo (Green Desert (USA))
2538[13] 3749[7] 4432[9] 4779[12] 5295[9]
Nullarbor Sky (IRE) *Lucy Wadham* a62 53
2 gr f Aussie Rules(USA) Grenouillere (USA) (Alysheba (USA))
6791[10] 7143[5] 7505[5]
Number One Guy *Philip Kirby* a49 54
5 br g Rock Of Gibraltar(IRE) Dubious (Darshaan)
3332[9]
Number One London (IRE) *Brian Meehan* 77
2 b c Invincible Spirit(IRE) Vadorga (Grand Lodge (USA))
6020[6] 6876[3] ◆
Number Theory *John Holt* 103
4 b g Halling(USA) Numanthia (IRE) (Barathea (IRE))
1657[3] (2419) ◆ (3036) (3857) 5600[3] 6197[7]
Numeral (IRE) *Richard Hannon* a91 79
4 b g Holy Roman Emperor(IRE) Savieres (IRE) (Sadler's Wells (USA))
426[4] 622[4] 785[5] 6979[8] (7327)
Nur Jahan (IRE) *David Lanigan* a58
2 b f Selkirk(USA) Have Faith (IRE) (Machiavellian (USA))
8017[7]
Nurse Dominatrix (IRE) *Richard Guest* a52 43
3 br f Whipper(USA) Medica Boba (Dr Fong (USA))
4782[7] 5127[5] 5549[7] 7317[5] 7470[10] (7612) 7798[9] 8050[8] 8111[4]
Nutello (USA) *C Laffon-Parias* a86 116
3 b c Lemon Drop Kid(USA) Nutcase (USA) (Forest Wildcat (USA))
2110a[10] 2743a[3] 4121a[8] 6508a[7]
Nyetimber (USA) *Peter Hiatt* a57
6 ch g Forest Wildcat(USA) Once Around (CAN) (You And I (USA))
741[12]
Nymfia (IRE) *C Laffon-Parias* a80 51
4 b m Invincible Spirit(IRE) Aguinaga (IRE) (Machiavellian (USA))
(116a)
Nymphea (IRE) *P Schiergen* 104
3 ch f Dylan Thomas(IRE) Neele (IRE) (Peintre Celebre (USA))
2531a[2] 4862a[2] 6290a[4]
Oakbrook *Ann Duffield* a21 62
3 b g Indesatchel(IRE) Statuette (Statoblest)
2438[3] 2862[10] 3751[4] 3908[U] 4394[2] (4453) 4909[3] 4956[2] 5757[5] 6105[9] 7395[11] 7604[9]
Oakdown *Richard Price* 31
4 ch g Selkirk(USA) Miss Katmandu (IRE) (Rainbow Quest (USA))
2765[7]
Oakham *Mahmood Al Zarooni* 74
2 ch c Shirocco(GER) Lady Catherine (Bering)
4813[12] 7442[2]
Oak Leaves *Nikki Evans* a56 56
5 b m Mark Of Esteem(IRE) Exotic Forest (Dominion)
2391[13]
Oakwell (IRE) *Sally Hall* 51
4 b g Antonius Pius(USA) Cindy's Star (IRE) (Dancing Dissident (USA))
5316[5] 6408[5]
Oasis Cannes *Sir Mark Prescott Bt* a75 94
2 b c Oasis Dream Miss Provence (Hernando (FR))
2073[7] 3112[2] (3708) 4102[2] 4540[2] 4763[2] (5060) 5899a[2] 7292[2]
Oasis Dancer *Ralph Beckett* a111 92
5 bg g Oasis Dream Good Enough (FR) (Mukaddamah (USA))
(89) (711) 1033[7] 3371[18] 4092[9] 4802[18] 5814[7] 7010[8]
Oasis Love (IRE) *Mark Johnston* 35
3 b c Oasis Dream Lunathea (IRE) (Barathea (IRE))
2380[10] 2592[7] 3521[7]
Oasis Spirit *Andrew Balding* 23
2 b f Oasis Dream Fearless Spirit (USA) (Spinning World (USA))
7372[9]
Obboorr *Roger Varian* 63
3 b g Cape Cross(IRE) Felawnah (USA) (Mr Prospector (USA))
2197[7]
Obligada (IRE) *Tobias B P Coles* a94 94
4 ch m Beat Hollow Oblique (IRE) (Giant's Causeway (USA))
2882[9] 3550[8] 4474[10] 5426[6]
Obliteright (IRE) *William Knight* a92 92
3 ch g Bertolini(USA) Doctrine (Barathea (IRE))
(1985) ◆ 2813[9] 3393[4] 4473[4] (4876) 5302[3] 6143[2] 6830[9]
Obviously (IRE) *Mike Mitchell* a95 121
4 b g Choisir(AUS) Leala (IRE) (Montjeu (IRE))
7575a[3]
Ocanelle (FR) *F Sanchez* a61 60
5 b m Great Pretender(IRE) Musicora (FR) (Great Palm (USA))
815a[10]
Occhio Della Mente (IRE) *E Botti* 104
5 b h Le Vie Dei Colori Croanda (IRE) (Grand Lodge (USA))
7586a[3]
Oceana Dreamer (IRE) *Andrew Balding* a45 42
3 b g Oasis Dream Arbella (Primo Dominie)
1889[7] 2501[11] 3235[5] 4754[8] 7189[9]
Ocean Applause *John Ryan* a87 87
2 b c Royal Applause Aldora (Magic Ring (IRE))
1886[11] 2638[4] 3291[7] 3788[3] 4098[5] 5232[3] 5755a[5] 6149[4] 6501[3] 6599[7] 7331[4] 7994[6] 8211[4]
Ocean Bay *John Ryan* a86 78
4 b g Dubai Destination(USA) Aldora (Magic Ring (IRE))
6601[8]
Ocean Countess (IRE) *Tony Carroll* a58 63
6 b m Storming Home Pennycairn (Last Tycoon)
125[3] 375[11]
Ocean Legend (IRE) *Tony Carroll* a89 77
7 b g Night Shift(USA) Rose Of Mooncoin (IRE) (Brief Truce (USA))
131[7] (378) 563[7] 962[10] 1066[7] 1564[5] 2251[10] 2545[7] 3045[5] 3485[2] 4043[9] 4939[5] 5193[2] 6040[7]
Ocean Myth *Jonathan Portman* a64 70
3 b f Acclamation Mystery Ocean (Dr Fong (USA))
982[8] 1445[5] 2136[9] 2573[2] 2869[5] 3510[2] 4489[5] 5122[5] 5279[3] 5635[2] 5934[5]
Ocean Park (NZ) *Gary Hennessy* 122
4 b h Thorn Park(AUS) Sayyida (NZ) (Zabeel (NZ))
(7426a)
Ocean Power (IRE) *Richard Phillips* a49 17
2 b g Papal Bull Petticoat Power (IRE) (Tomba)
7434[8] 7806[6] 8178[9]
Ocean's Minstrel *John Ryan* a96 96
6 b g Pivotal Minstrel's Dance (CAN) (Pleasant Colony (USA))
6600[7] 6034[11] 7522[6]
Ocean Tempest *John Ryan* a79 89
3 gr g Act One Ipsa Loquitur (Unfuwain (USA))
1565[6] 1888[5] 2428[2] 2641[5] 2930[7] (3446) 3792[10] (4097)
Oceanway (USA) *Mark Johnston* a83 101
4 b m Street Cry(IRE) Sea Gift (USA) (A.P. Indy (USA))
341a[3] 712[10] 1605[10] 1993[3] 2706[12] 2911[3] ◆ 3417[7] 4363[8] 4684[8]
Odd Ball (IRE) *Lisa Williamson* a67 34
5 b g Redback Luceball (IRE) (Bluebird (USA))
154[10] 232[9] 483[4] 690[2] 807[3] (837) (988) (1095) ◆ 1342[5] 4657[13] 5428[10] 5750[9] 7382[7] 7593[9]
Oddsmaker (IRE) *Maurice Barnes* a42 66
11 b g Barathea(IRE) Archipova (IRE) (Ela-Mana-Mou)
3116[2] 3577[2] 3904[7] 4910[5] 5921[8] 6315[12]
Oddysey (IRE) *Michael Dods* 85
3 b f Acclamation Darling Smile (IRE) (Darshaan)
2795[8] (3908) 4134[2] 4676[2] (4996) 5731[3] 6789[3] 6986[2]

Odin (IRE) *Don Cantillon* a80 84
4 b g Norse Dancer(IRE) Dimelight (Fantastic Light (USA))
1416[13] 2199[16] 2899[4] 3400[4] (3659) 4515[5] 4821[2] 5268[2] (6639) 7034[5] 8174[5]

Odin's Raven (IRE) *Brian Ellison* a72 80
7 ro g Dalakhani(IRE) Oriane (Nashwan (USA))
1275[8] 1846[2] 2093[6] 3163[10] 6074[7] 6472[8] 6712[7]

Odooj (IRE) *William Haggas* a84 103
2 b g Pivotal Shabiba (USA) (Seeking The Gold (USA))
(2469) 5201[2] 5559[4] 6038[6] 7065[2] 7404[5]

Oekaki (FR) *Y Barberot* a85 101
5 b m Martillo(GER) Pyu (GER) (Surumu (GER))
2805a[6]

Oetzi *Alan Jarvis* a63 77
4 ch g Iceman Mad Annie (USA) (Anabaa (USA))
1611[9] 3278[12] (5239)

Oeuvre D'Art (IRE) *L Riccardi* 100
4 b m Marju(IRE) Midefix (ITY) (Night Shift (USA))
7429a[11]

Of Course Darling *Ed Dunlop* 74
2 ch f Dalakhani(IRE) Whazzis (Desert Prince (IRE))
4297[4] 6873[17] 7312[4]

Ofcoursewecan (USA) *Mark Johnston* a55
2 b c Elusive Quality(USA) Valid Warning (USA) (Valid Appeal (USA))
8134[5]

Off Art *Tim Easterby* 69
2 ch c Dutch Art Off Camera (Efisio)
2308[5]

Offbeat Safaris (IRE) *Ronald Harris* a63 75
4 b g Le Vie Dei Colori Baywood (Emarati (USA))
2984[2] 3609[5] 4252[2] 4775[10] 5653[5] (6001) 6452[7] 6927[4] 7166[10]

Offer (IRE) *A P O'Brien* 110
3 b c Montjeu(IRE) Valdara (Darshaan)
3361a[5] 3678a[3]

Officer In Command (USA) *Paul Rich* a76 40
6 bb g Officer(USA) Luv To Stay N Chat (USA) (Candi's Gold (USA))
1729[3] 2044[2] 3962[8] (4333) 4844[9] 5941[3] 6251[6] 7310[5] 7480[2] 7893[3] 7997[8]

Ogaritmo *Marco Botti* a75 68
3 ch f Manduro(GER) Querida (Rainbow Quest (USA))
(723) 1641[8] 2431[10] 3711[8]

O'Gorman *Gary Brown* a86 88
3 b g Sleeping Indian Harryana (Efisio)
2347[10] 2714[3] 3613[6] 4044[2] 4849[7] 5422[4] 5812[9] 6026[11] 6488[17] 7113[5] 7730[2] 7928[2] ◆

O Happy Gray (USA) *Mike Harrington* a79
2 rg f Cee's Tizzy(USA) I Can Yodele (USA) (Swiss Yodeler (USA))
5031a[7]

Oh Beautiful *F Head* 98
3 b f Galileo(IRE) Aricia (IRE) (Nashwan (USA))
7735a[7]

Oh Boy Oh Boy *James Moffatt* 48
2 b g Misu Bond(IRE) Mitchelland (Namaqualand (USA))
2224[4] 3381[9] 4545[17] 6121[7]

Oh Landino (GER) *Jim Goldie* 46
7 b g Lando(GER) Oh La Belle (GER) (Dashing Blade)
1240[10]

Oh My Days (IRE) *Clive Cox* a63 22
4 ch g Bahamian Bounty Princess Speedfit (FR) (Desert Prince (IRE))
1306[10] 2165[11]

Ohne Tadel (GER) *S Smrczek* a85 73
5 b g Tertullian(USA) Otjere (GER) (Lemhi Gold (USA))
18a[7] 6804a[7]

Oh So Charming *Mark Gillard* a40 47
3 b g Kayf Tara Charmatic (IRE) (Charnwood Forest (IRE))
3227[9] 4410[15] 5048[12] 6210[7] 6769[8]

Oh So Quaint (IRE) *A L T Moore* a45 67
3 b f Iffraaj Papaha (FR) (Green Desert (USA))
5446[10]

Oh So Sassy *Chris Wall* 49
2 b f Pastoral Pursuits Almasi (IRE) (Petorius)
6343[10]

Oh So Spicy *Chris Wall* 80
5 ch m Pastoral Pursuits Almasi (IRE) (Petorius)
1289[2] 2493[4] 5097[6] 6378[2] 7113[10]

Oilinda *Michael Bell* 75
2 b f Nayef(USA) Loyal Love (USA) (Danzig (USA))
4818[8] (7552)

Oil Strike *Michael Easterby* a98 90
5 b g Lucky Story(USA) Willisa (Polar Falcon (USA))
431[8] 1220[9] 1821[10] 2697[11] 3027[9] 3524[7] 3993[5] ◆ 4954[12] 7100[3]

Ojibway Signal (CAN) *David R Bell* a75 84
4 bb g Niigon(CAN) Apache Signal (CAN) (Announce (USA))
6299a[7]

Okaleeski (FR) *Mlle C Courtade* a58
4 b m Okawango(USA) Valleeski (FR) (Sky Lawyer (FR))
116a[9]

Ok Coral (FR) *K Borgel* 111
5 bl h Timboroa Coraloune (FR) (Valanour (IRE))
4229a[2] 5650a[3]

Okebibi (FR) *J-M Lefebvre* a93 93
4 ch g Okawango(USA) Mikalia (FR) (Kaldoun (FR))
7701a[0]

Oken Bruce Lee (JPN) *Hidetaka Otonashi* 124
7 ch h Jungle Pocket(JPN) Silver Joy (CAN) (Silver Deputy (CAN))
7872a[14]

Old Boy Ted *Mark H Tompkins* 50
4 b g Tobougg(IRE) Grove Dancer (Reprimand)
2468[6] 3086[3] 3579[2] 3969[5] 6399[11]

Old Hundred (IRE) *James Fanshawe* a101 93
5 b g Tiger Hill(IRE) Bordighera (USA) (Alysheba (USA))
(1446) 2639[10] 3766[4] 4216[8] 6197[11]

Oldjoesaid *Paul Midgley* a77 89
8 b g Royal Applause Border Minstrel (IRE) (Sri Pekan (USA))
(2875) ◆ 3578[2] 3822[11] 4312[5] 4924[2] 5584[5] 6044[13] 7291[7] 7730[7]

Old Man Clegg *Michael Easterby* 72
2 b g Pastoral Pursuits Stolen Melody (Robellino (USA))
2334[8] 3126[2] 3748[5] 4116[2] 4951[7] (5602) 6070[8] 6469[5]

Old Pal (FR) *Niels Petersen* a27 86
3 b c Soldier Hollow Syllable (Halling (USA))
417a[12] 679a[10] 873a[12]

Oldrik (GER) *Philip Hobbs* 84
9 b g Tannenkonig(IRE) Onestep (GER) (Konigsstuhl (GER))
7269[7]

Old Time Hockey (USA) *Thomas F Proctor* 104
3 ch g Smarty Jones(USA) Grat (USA) (A.P. Indy (USA))
7566a[7]

Olimamu (IRE) *Lydia Pearce* a57 54
5 b m Barathea(IRE) La Galeisa (IRE) (Warning)
130[9] 395[4] 741[5] 895[8]

Oliver's Gold *Shaun Harris* a58 58
4 b g Danehill Dancer(IRE) Gemini Gold (IRE) (King's Best (USA))
1299[10] 4314[3] 5266[8] 5481[7] 6252[13]

Ollie Olga (USA) *Mick Channon* 104
2 bb f Stormy Atlantic(USA) Card Shop (USA) (Chester House (USA))
(3783) (4599) ◆ (5571) 6635[6]

Ollon (USA) *Mrs K Burke* a64 69
4 b g Mr Greeley(USA) Town Branch (USA) (Cape Town (USA))
922[3] 1000[3] 1172a[0] (1673) 2048[6]

Olney Lass *Lydia Pearce* a58 66
5 b m Lucky Story(USA) Zalebe (Bahamian Bounty)
2362[5] 4981[9] 5633[4] (6000) 6961[8] 7317[4] 7781[5] 8199[8]

Olympiad (IRE) *D K Weld* 98
4 b g Galileo(IRE) Caumshinaun (IRE) (Indian Ridge)
(5491) 7051[21]

Olympian Diamond (IRE) *Brian Rothwell*
4 b m Majestic Missile(IRE) Blue Velvet (Formidable (USA))
1521[12]

Olympic Glory (IRE) *Richard Hannon* 117
2 b c Choisir(AUS) Acidanthera (Alzao (USA))
(2888) ◆ 3240[2] ◆ (4098) (4698) (6910a)

Olympic Jule *John Dunlop* 66
2 b f Shamardal(USA) Jules (IRE) (Danehill (USA))
3590[7] 4739[9] 5907[10] 6489[8]

Olynard (IRE) *Michael Mullineaux* a62 80
6 b g Exceed And Excel(AUS) Reddening (Blushing Flame (USA))
183[7] 578[3] 929[11] 2555[4] 3434[4] 4708[7] 4865[13] 6002[6] 6158[10]

Olynthos (IRE) *C Laffon-Parias* a73 85
4 ch h Chineur(FR) Mistic Sun (Dashing Blade)
(16a)

O Ma Lad (IRE) *Sylvester Kirk* a90 86
4 ch g Redback Raydaniya (IRE) (In The Wings)
1037[6] 1505[6] 1890[9] 2237[2] (2440) 2857[2] 3341[4] 4251[6] 4823[4] 5306[3] 5905[8] 6197[8] (6642) 7051[16]

Omana (FR) *H-A Pantall* 107
3 b f Speedmaster(GER) Orion Girl (GER) (Law Society (USA))
2531a[3] 4862a[9] 7449a[3]

Omar Khayyam *Andrew Balding* a75 79
3 b c Pivotal Kithanga (IRE) (Darshaan)
1467[16] 6704[4] 7174[2] 7933[3] (8037)

Omar's Tiger (USA) *Michael Yates*
5 ch h Hold That Tiger(USA) Excelabrate (USA) (Gone West (USA))
8278a[8]

Omega Centauri *Ed McMahon* a42
4 ch m Needwood Blade Distant Stars (IRE) (Distant Music (USA))
159[8] 390[11] 662[8]

Omega Omega *Julia Feilden* a51 43
3 b f Halling(USA) In Luck (In The Wings)
2848[10] 3551[7] 4188[5] 4744[13] 5330[5] 5637[7]

Omid *Nicky Vaughan* a65 58
4 b g Dubawi(IRE) Mille Couleurs (FR) (Spectrum (IRE))
1655[5] 1866[8] 2418[8] 3086[9] (3942) 4145[2] 5241[7] 5811[5] 8104[10]

Omnipresent *Sir Michael Stoute* a61
2 b c Rail Link Protectress (Hector Protector (USA))
6014[3]

Omoor (IRE) *John Dunlop* 76
2 b f Tamayuz Miracolia (IRE) (Montjeu (IRE))
5947[4] 7553[2]

On Alert *Seamus Durack* a27 44
4 b g Deploy Morina (USA) (Lyphard (USA))
3969[4] 6280[4]

Onceaponatime (IRE) *Michael Squance* a47 73
7 b g Invincible Spirit(IRE) Lake Nyasa (IRE) (Lake Coniston (IRE))
7990[10] 8160[9] 8299[12]

Once More Dubai (USA) *Saeed Bin Suroor* a104 104
7 bb g E Dubai(USA) Go Again Girl (USA) (Broad Brush (USA))
484a[5] 877a[15]

On Command (IRE) *Don Cantillon* a20
4 ch g Namid Good Thought (IRE) (Mukaddamah (USA))
1484[8] 1866[12]

Ondeafears (IRE) *M Halford* a41 90
5 b m Chineur(FR) Irma La Douce (IRE) (Elbio)
3645a[8]

One Bid Too Many (USA) *Derek Shaw* a23
3 b f Bernardini(USA) Sweet Belle (USA) (Deputy Commander (USA))
1826[7] 2543[13] 3561[8] 4405[7] 5217[6]

One Cool Chick *John Bridger* a64 52
4 b m Iceman Barrantes (Distant Relative)
4146[8] 4492[7] 5279[5] 5783[6] 6150[10] 6396[10] 7504[10] 7929[9]

One Cool Dancer (IRE) *John Gallagher* a29 11
3 br f One Cool Cat(USA) Dancing Duchess (IRE) (Danehill Dancer (IRE))
565[6] 805[7]

Onedargent (FR) *J-P Gallorini* 98
2 gr g Kendargent(FR) One Day (FR) (Act One)
7283a[2]

One Fine Day (IRE) *Mrs John Harrington* 91
3 b f Choisir(AUS) Night Eyes (IRE) (Night Shift (USA))
3645a[14] 4692a[10] 5523a[8]

One Firm Cat (USA) *Peter Miller* 90
2 bb g Cowtown Cat(USA) Affirmed Toor (USA) (Affirmed (USA))
7567a[6]

One For Joules (IRE) *John Flint* a72 76
5 b m Choisir(AUS) Stuttgart (Groom Dancer (USA))
942[4] 1485[2] 2698[5] 5151[4] 5893[8] 6250[10] 6981[13]

One For The Girls *Nicky Vaughan* a49 46
3 b g Primo Valentino(IRE) Countrywide Girl (IRE) (Catrail (USA))
2665[6] 3384[3] 4293[12] 5261[5] 6542[7] 6828[5] 6948[12]

Oneiric *Brett Johnson* a63 78
4 gr m Act One Ecstasy (Pursuit Of Love)
355[6] 650[3] 818[9] 1418[8] 1732[2] 1791[3] (2851) 3620[6] 7012[8] 7303[12]

One Kool Dude *Michael Bell* a72 72
3 ch g Iceman Hiraeth (Petong)
885[3] 1529[5] 2206[7] 2730[6] 3407[2] 3791[2] (4197) 4671[2] 4953[7] 5831[7] 6788[8] 7179[10]

Oneladyowner *David Brown* a73 92
4 b g Auction House(USA) Inya Lake (Whittingham (IRE))
1844[18] 2446[2] 2558[12] 4799[19] 5557[7] 7327[13]

One Last Dream *Ron Hodges* a28 62
3 ch g Resplendent Glory(IRE) Pip's Dream (Glint Of Gold)
731[4] 969[10] 1182[11] 2166[5] 2388[3] 3141[3] 3489[2] 4236[3] 4754[7] (5263) 5531[5] 6306[6] 6739[3] 7106[4]

One Million *Rose Dobbin* 25
3 b g Dubai Destination(USA) Talwin (IRE) (Alhaarth (IRE))
6102[11] 6527[4]

One More Roman (IRE) *Gay Kelleway* a66 65
3 b c Holy Roman Emperor(IRE) Satulagi (USA) (Officer (USA))
42[2] 99[5] 357[2] 394[3] 536[4] 583[2] 748[2] 901[3] 1067[6] (1359) (1731) 2583[9] 3248[9] 3548[3]

Oneniteinheaven (IRE) *Jane Chapple-Hyam* 61
3 ch f Choisir(AUS) Westlife (IRE) (Mind Games)
(1292) 2010[3] 2610[7]

Oneofapear (IRE) *Ian McInnes* a53 88
6 b g Pyrus(USA) Whitegate Way (Greensmith)
1381[4] ◆ (2241) 3380[8] 4864[13] 6884[13] 8259[7]

One Of Twins *Michael Easterby* a67 60
4 b g Gentleman's Deal(IRE) Miss Twiddles (IRE) (Desert King (IRE))
(929) 1135[10] 2692[10] 3713[5] 4158[5]

One Pekan (IRE) *Roger Varian* a69
2 b c Hard Spun(USA) Stormy Blessing (USA) (Storm Cat (USA))
7705[3]

One Pursuit (IRE) *David Nicholls* a71 84
4 br g Pastoral Pursuits Karinski (USA) (Palace Music (USA))
1657[9] 2414[13] 3274[11]

Onertother *Joseph Tuite* a54 57
3 b g Nomadic Way(USA) Ceilidh Band (Celtic Swing)
2393[4] 2856[11] 4153[5] 4510[7] 4994[5] 5408[5] 5939[4]

One Scoop Or Two *Reg Hollinshead* a77 89
6 b g Needwood Blade Rebel County (IRE) (Maelstrom Lake)
2029[13] 2910[13] 3185[11] 4964[9] 5429[3] 6241[9] 6692[3] (7027) 7976[8]

One Set (IRE) *Mme I T Oakes-Cottin* a82 80
5 ch g Footstepsinthesand Impassion (FR) (In The Wings)
7123a[0]

One Spirit (IRE) *F Dunne* 104
4 b m Invincible Spirit(IRE) Recite (JPN) (Forty Niner (USA))
2515a[2] (2777a) 6079a[2]

One Way Or Another (AUS) *David Evans* a82 80
9 b g Carnegie(IRE) True Blonde (AUS) (Naturalism (NZ))
90[7] 190[2] 447[4] 626[10] 800[4] 2354[9] 3016[6] 3231[5] 3944[9] 4531[13] 4929[5] 5440[3] (5996) 6217[3] 6434[3] 7027[7] 7166[2] ◆ 7415[2] 7743[6] 8047[2]

One Word More (IRE) *Charles Hills* 98
2 b c Thousand Words Somoushe (IRE) (Black Minnaloushe (USA))
3067[2] ◆ 4056[2] (4387) 5140a[2] 6200[3] 6671[6]

Ongoodform (IRE) *Paul D'Arcy* a85 82
5 b h Invincible Spirit(IRE) Elfin Queen (IRE) (Fairy King (USA))
(2083) 2274[13] 4580[4] 7327[9] 7645[8] 7901[7]

On Khee *David Pipe* a57 87
5 b m Sakhee(USA) Star Precision (Shavian)
3703[14] 4150[3] 4944[7]

Online *Tracy Waggott*
2 b g Rail Link Fairy Steps (Rainbow Quest (USA))
6607[9] 6919[6]

Only A Pleasure (IRE) *A Fabre* 105
3 b c Montjeu(IRE) Sense Of Style (USA) (Thunder Gulch (USA))
6087a[3] 6896a[9]

Only A Round (IRE) *Micky Hammond* a37 37
3 b g Tagula(IRE) Scepter'd Isle (Shirley Heights)
1596[6] 2341[12] 3421[6] 4313[4] 5623[8] 7981[7]

Only Dreamin *Bill Turner* a8
2 b f Notnowcato Apple Sauce (Prince Sabo)
6826[9]

Only For You *Alan Brown* a54 48
2 b f Elusive City(USA) Enlisted (IRE) (Sadler's Wells (USA))
1437[11] 1651[4] 2282[11] 2770[10] 5010[8] 5331[5] 6049[9] 6354[3] 6953[7] 7379[9] 7711[3] 7797[2]

Only Orsenfoolsies *Micky Hammond* 76
3 b g Trade Fair Desert Gold (IRE) (Desert Prince (IRE))
1441[3] 1757[2] 2258[7] 2671[2] 3727[2] (6560) 7032[4] 7455[4]

Only Ten Per Cent (IRE) *J R Jenkins* a82 56
4 b g Kheleyf(USA) Cory Everson (IRE) (Brief Truce (USA))
154[6] 370[5] (831) (1178) (1584) 1958[6] ◆ (4401) 5245[4] 5737[7] 6811[5] 7607[5] 7961[2]

Only You Maggie (IRE) *Gary Harrison* a62 73
5 b m Atraf First Kiss (GER) (Night Shift (USA))
1636[5] 1830[11] 2576[2] 2867[6]

On My Own (TUR) *Marcus Tregoning* 73
3 b c Rock Of Gibraltar(IRE) Dancingintheclouds (IRE) (Rainbow Quest (USA))
1506[5] 1976[6] ◆

On Stage *Stuart Kittow* 50
3 ch f Act One In The Stocks (Reprimand)
1937[6] 4410[8] 5795[12]

On The Bias (USA) *Brian Meehan* 52
2 ch f Stormy Atlantic(USA) Rebuke (USA) (Carson City (USA))
3590[15] 4344[8]

On The Cusp (IRE) *Richard Guest* a81 74
5 b g Footstepsinthesand Roman Love (IRE) (Perugino (USA))
22[4] 584[3] 674[8] 1358[14] 1561[11] 2011[6] 2168[8] 2405[4]

On The Feather *Jim Best* a67 76
6 br m Josr Algarhoud(IRE) Fotheringhay (Loup Sauvage (USA))
2149[4] 2348[6] 2735[3] 8060[5]

On The High Tops (IRE) *Colin Teague* a43 81
4 b g Kheleyf(USA) Diplomats Daughter (Unfuwain (USA))
1954[5] 2314[13] 2690[8] 4552[8] 4911[7] (5294) 5740[3] 7457[9]

On The Hoof *Michael Easterby* a81 76
3 gr g Monsieur Bond(IRE) Smart Hostess (Most Welcome)
1521[3] 1758[4] (2143) 2459[3] 3383[8] 4329[7] 5736[7] 6452[5] 6502[11] 7246[8] 7600[6] (7844) (8142) (8152)

On With The Dance (IRE) *Ed Vaughan* a54
2 ch g Byron Caldy Dancer (IRE) (Soviet Star (USA))
7923[7] ◆

Ooi Long *Mark Rimmer* a66 67
3 b g Echo Of Light Danceatdusk (Desert Prince (IRE))
2010[7] 2461[3] 2695[3] 3050[2] (3467) 3791[10] 4197[2] 4777[3] 5445[5] 6211[4] 6439[4] ◆ 7307[4]

Oojooba *Roger Varian* 96
3 b f Monsun(GER) Ameerat (Mark Of Esteem (IRE))
1647[5] 3120[2] 3882[8] 4702[3] 5238[2] 6667[4]

Oops Caroline (IRE) *David O'Meara* 56
3 ch f Strategic Prince Annette Vallon (IRE) (Efisio)
1637[7] 1916[6] 2340[8] 2771[7] 3023[4] 3729[6] 4210[7] 4678[6] 4826[9]

Oor Jock (IRE) *John Patrick Shanahan* a88 98
4 ch g Shamardal(USA) Katdogawn (Bahhare (USA))
1538a[6] 2704[11] 3648a[5] 4258[3] 7390a[9]

Open Letter (IRE) *Mark Johnston* a68 63
2 b f New Approach(IRE) Deveron (USA) (Cozzene (USA))
2450[6] 2917[10] 4739[15] (6344) 7026[2]

Openly *James Fanshawe* a85 75
3 b f Singspiel(IRE) Grand Opening (IRE) (Desert King (IRE))
2249[4] 5766[3] 6146[2] 6416[8] (6839)

Open Water (FR) *Andrew Balding* 93
3 b c Orpen(USA) So Stream (ITY) (Elmaamul (USA))
1888[3] 2701[4] 3296[18]

Opera Box *Marcus Tregoning* 71
4 b m Singspiel(IRE) Annex (Anabaa (USA))
5510[2]

Opera Buff *Sylvester Kirk* a71 78
3 b c Oratorio(IRE) Opera Glass (Barathea (IRE))
2813[11] 4288[9] 5942[5] 6647[3] 6933[13] 7359[6]

Opera Gal (IRE) *Andrew Balding* a77 108
5 b m Galileo(IRE) Opera Glass (Barathea (IRE))
2478[4] 3329[8] (5238) 5844a[2] (6470) 7429a[7]

Opera Prince *Simon Earle* a70 83
7 b g Kyllachy Optaria (Song)
58[3] 309[5]

Operateur (IRE) *Ben Haslam* a52 67
4 b g Oratorio(IRE) Kassariya (IRE) (Be My Guest (USA))
1562[6] 2593[5] 3402[7] (3753) 6103[3] 6315[5] 7252[8]

Operation Chariot (IRE) *Andrew Balding* a86 100
2 b c Refuse To Bend(IRE) Dona Royale (IRE) (Darshaan)
(3119) 4098[8] 4698[6] 5787[4] 6149[3]

Operation Tracer *Michael Bell* a59 68
3 ch g Rock Of Gibraltar(IRE) Quite Elusive (USA) (Elusive Quality (USA))
2733[12] 3792[5] 4583[5] 5037[2] 5312[2] 5796[9] 5945[5]

Opera Vert (FR) *D Sepulchre* 102
4 b g Green Tune(USA) Caramba Kelly (IRE) (Mtoto)
7320a[2]

Operettist *Richard Hannon* a60 77
3 b f Singspiel(IRE) Demi Voix (Halling (USA))
2194[5] 2733[6] 3643[11] 5707[7] 5937[7] 6250[8] 7108[7]

Opinion (IRE) *Sir Michael Stoute* 97
3 b c Oasis Dream Kiltubber (IRE) (Sadler's Wells (USA))
(1567) 2477[5] (3156) 4735[13] (5091) 6025[15]

Opinion Poll (IRE) *Mahmood Al Zarooni* 120
6 b h Halling(USA) Ahead (Shirley Heights)
759a[2] (1144a) (2639) 3293[2] 7235[8]

Oppenort (IRE) *M Delzangles* a87 101
4 b h Aussie Rules(USA) Odessa (IRE) (Sadler's Wells (USA))
3178a[6]

Optimism *William Muir* a46
3 b f Motivator Durrah Green (Green Desert (USA))
816[8] 1107[6] 1502[14]

Optimizer (USA) *D Wayne Lukas* a111 110
3 b c English Channel(USA) Indy Pick (USA) (A.P. Indy (USA))
1872a[11] 2299a[6] 2954a[10] 7573a[11]

Optimum Rose (IRE) *David O'Meara* 33
3 b f Chineur(FR) Finty (IRE) (Entrepreneur)
2262[13]

Opt Out *Mark Johnston* a70 81
2 ch c Pivotal Easy Option (IRE) (Prince Sabo)
2039[3] ◆ 2224[3] 3303[3] 3627[2] 3902[2] 4230[9] 4825[11] (5532) (5682) 6022[6] 6883[20] 7478[7]

Opus (IRE) *Amanda Perrett* a57 50
3 br g Danehill Dancer(IRE) Mixed Blessing (Lujain (USA))
1922[13] 2280[10] 2585[6] 3122[7] 3543[8] 4490[8] 6281[4] 6395[7]

Opus Cactus (USA) *Marco Botti* a56 28
2 b f Johannesburg(USA) Momix (Selkirk (USA))
6609[6] 7078[11] 8076[2] (8164)

Opus Dei *Alan McCabe* a76 76
5 b g Oasis Dream Grail (USA) (Quest For Fame)
4142[5] 4388[7] 5245[2] 7485[10] 7607[3] 8034[4]

Opus Maximus (IRE) *Conor Dore* a84 73
7 ch g Titus Livius(FR) Law Review (IRE) (Case Law)
36[9] 177[5] 216[7] 280[6] 299[5] 432[3] 520[7] 548[6] 1117[10] 1262[6] 1342[6] 1561[7] 2044[8] 2847[9] 3154[11] 4586[9] 5804[4] 6057[9] 6323[6] 6569[4]

Orarabit (IRE) *C Boutin* a65
3 b f Oratorio(IRE) Rabitatit (IRE) (Robellino (USA))
475a[8]

Oratorian (IRE) *Sylvester Kirk* a83 61
3 b g Oratorio(IRE) Raindancing (IRE) (Tirol)
(27) (189) 230[2] 659[7] 3446[10] 4288[5] 5036[8] 5681[7] 5983[12] 6610[8] 7105[5] 7725[13] 7967[12]

Oratory (IRE) *Ollie Pears* a82 86
6 b g Danehill Dancer(IRE) Gentle Night (Zafonic (USA))
1156[14] 1657[8] 2510[5] (2753) (3335) ◆ 4110[11] 5111[11] 5369[8] 6405[13] 7370[12] 7640[7]

Orbit The Moon (IRE) *Michael Dods* a80 86
4 b h Oratorio(IRE) Catch The Moon (IRE) (Peintre Celebre (USA))
1321[14] 2285[11] 2597[4] 3334[3] 4135[7] (4629) 5557[5] 6008[14] 7144[3]

Ordensritter (GER) *Chris Down* a87 97
4 ch g Samum(GER) Dramraire Mist (Darshaan)
8082[9]

Order Of Service *David Brown* 62
2 ch c Medicean Choir Gallery (Pivotal)
3611[8] 4069[4] 5325[9]

Orders From Rome (IRE) *Eve Johnson Houghton* a71 90
3 b g Holy Roman Emperor(IRE) Fatat Alarab (USA) (Capote (USA))
1452[14] (1986) 2979[7] 4412[2] (4723) 5363[9] 5703[9] 7113[11] 7559[16]

Orfevre (JPN) *Yasutoshi Ikee* 129
4 ch h Stay Gold(JPN) Oriental Art (JPN) (Mejiro McQueen (JPN))
(6293a) 6912a[2] 7872a[2]

Orgilgo Bay (IRE) *John C McConnell* 100
2 b c Lawman(FR) Third Dimension (FR) (Suave Dancer (USA))
6060a[6] 6718a[2]

Oriental Cat *Venetia Williams* a59 97
5 b g Tiger Hill(IRE) Sentimental Value (USA) (Diesis)
5583[8]

Oriental Cavalier *Mark Buckley* a76 83
6 ch g Ishiguru(USA) Gurleigh (IRE) (Pivotal)
2414[15] 4499[12] 5001[9]

Oriental Lady (GER) *Uwe Ostmann* 91
2 b f Doyen(IRE) Oriental World (GER) (Platini (GER))
6522a[5] 7281a[4]

Oriental Romance (IRE) *Richard Fahey* 50
2 b f Elusive City(USA) My Funny Valentine (IRE) (Mukaddamah (USA))
3112[7]

Oriental Scot *William Jarvis* a74 92
5 ch g Selkirk(USA) Robe Chinoise (Robellino (USA))
1321[4] 1510[14] 1820[3] (2417) 2720[2] 3667[7] 4136[3] 4828[18]

Orife (IRE) *C Ferland* a98 98
5 b h Marchand De Sable(USA) Entente Cordiale (IRE) (Ela-Mana-Mou)
(5118a)

Orions Hero (IRE) *Richard Fahey* a66 73
2 b g Oasis Dream La Reine Mambo (USA) (High Yield (USA))
3168[9] 5083[2] 7458[6]

Orla (IRE) *Dominic Ffrench Davis* a4
4 b m Hawk Wing(USA) Irish Ensign (SAF) (National Emblem (SAF))
2368[13] 5309[8]

Orla's Rainbow (IRE) *John Berry* a38 60
2 b c Oratorio(IRE) Red Ray (Pivotal)
2370[9] 3112[5] 4658[7] 6096[6] 7785[13] 8112[8]

Ormindo (USA) *Mahmood Al Zarooni* a75 60
2 ch g Discreet Cat(USA) Dearly (Rahy (USA))
5851[7] 6214[2] 6533[2] 6972[3] 7306[7]

Orpello (IRE) *S Botti* 89
3 b c Orpen(USA) Princess Angelina (IRE) (Almutawakel)
6554a[7]

Orpen'Arry (IRE) *Jimmy Fox* a77 78
4 b g Orpen(USA) Closing Time (IRE) (Topanoora)
1611[4] 2151[10] 2500[11] 3738[9] 4411[12] 7166[9] 7474[4] 7767[9]

Orpen Wide (IRE) *Michael Chapman* a50 26
10 b g Orpen(USA) Melba (IRE) (Namaqualand (USA))
1279[6] 1583[3] 4193[9] 5015[6] 5259[9] 6562[8] 7605[6]

Orpha *Mick Channon* 86
2 b f New Approach(IRE) Garah (Ajdal (USA))
(5146) 6081a[9]

Orpsie Boy (IRE) *Ruth Carr* a85 96
9 b g Orpen(USA) Nordicolini (IRE) (Nordico (USA))
(1863) 2029[3] 2697[4] 2910[7] 4317[5] 4609[8] 4828[10] 5369[6] 5819[10] 6040[2] 6338[13] 7453[8]

Orsino (GER) *R Rohne* 105
5 b h Mamool(IRE) Orosole (GER) (Platini (GER))
(6554a) 7287a[5]

Orsippus (USA) *Michael Smith* a78 86
6 bb g Sunday Break(JPN) Mirror Dancing (USA) (Caveat (USA))
2214[4] 2827[2] ◆ (3419) 4115[4] 4697[11] 6834[8] 7098[4] 7367[11]

Ortensia (AUS) *Paul Messara* 121
7 b m Testa Rossa(AUS) Aerate's Pick (AUS) (Picnicker (AUS))
(1146a) 3238[9] 4100[4] (4762) ◆ (5561) 6030[12]

Orthodox Lad *Ed de Giles* a72 77
4 ch g Monsieur Bond(IRE) Ashantiana (Ashkalani (IRE))
5480[11] 6430[5] 7171[5] 7368[7]

Orwellian *Bryan Smart* a65 71
3 b g Bahamian Bounty Trinny (Rainbow Quest (USA))
194[2] 903[4] 1359[11] 2540[4] 3111[7] 4134[4] (4394) (4717) 5000[5] 6530[4] 7447[2] 7600[9] 8142[9]

Oscar Party (USA) *Wayne Catalano* a67 98
2 b f Dixie Union(USA) Dream Lady (USA) (Old Trieste (USA))
7547a[14]

Oscar Prairie (IRE) *Warren Greatrex* a35
7 b g Oscar(IRE) Silver Prairie (IRE) (Common Grounds)
6839[9]

Oscars Journey *J R Jenkins* a64 73
2 ch g Dubai Destination(USA) Fruit Of Glory (Glory Of Dancer)
3973[4] 4539[6] 5213[5] 6808[2] (7296) (7635)

Osgood *Mick Channon* a76 83
5 b g Danehill Dancer(IRE) Sabreon (Caerleon (USA))
1743[3] 2233[7] (2899) 3213[8] 5310[12] 6131[12]

Osiris Emery (FR) *E Libaud* a76 81
3 b c Equerry(USA) Natashwan (Shining Steel)
117a[5]

Osiris Way *Patrick Chamings* a81 89
10 ch g Indian Ridge Heady (Rousillon (USA))
2369[3] 3660[7] 4231[2] 4501[8] 4980[5]

Ossie Ardiles (IRE) *Michael Appleby* a57 30
4 gr g Aussie Rules(USA) Look Who's Dancing (Observatory (USA))
151[10] 370[9] 532[2] 634[5]

Ossie's Dancer *Robert Cowell* a41 35
3 ch g Osorio(GER) Nina Ballerina (Kahyasi)
974[4] 1053[7] 1301[8] 2341[4] 3023[12] 4198[6] 4440[7]

Ostaad (IRE) *Saeed Bin Suroor* a84 80
2 b c Marju(IRE) Almansoora (USA) (Bahri (USA))
6014[2] ◆ 6876[2]

Ostentation *Gay Kelleway* a73 70
5 ch g Dubawi(IRE) Oshiponga (Barathea (IRE))
263[5] 567[3] 655[4] 760[7] (1104) 1240[3] 1432[2] 1533[4] 1580[2] (2653) 2867[10] 2985[4] 3469[4] 3722[2] 3794[8] (4586) 4987[6] 5809[6] 6120[8] 6691[3] 7012[5] 7169[8]

Osteopathic Remedy (IRE) *Michael Dods* a87 100
8 ch g Inchinor Dolce Vita (IRE) (Ela-Mana-Mou)
1558[4] 1865[2] 2311[7] 2910[12] 3626[8] 4828[12] (5677) 6135[4] (6426) 7030[8] 7435[3] 7691[16]

Ostinato (GER) *Sandor Kovacs* 107
4 b h Ransom O'War(USA) Oxotica (GER) (Subotica (FR))
6805a[3] 7586a[7]

Ostralegus *Richard Fahey* 68
2 b c Choisir(AUS) Midnight Pearl (USA) (Woodman (USA))
5213[3]

Otaared *D Selvaratnam* a110 94
7 br g Storm Cat(USA) Society Lady (USA) (Mr Prospector (USA))
316a[5]

Ottauquechee (IRE) *Richard Hannon* 59
2 b f Lawman(FR) Lolita's Gold (USA) (Royal Academy (USA))
3474[7] 4818[9] 5785[6] 6156[10] 6435[8]

Ottavino (IRE) *Jane Chapple-Hyam* a22 41
3 b g Piccolo Indian's Feather (IRE) (Indian Ridge)
2461[6] 4144[8] 4970[5] 5455[10]

Ottoman Empire (FR) *David Simcock* a104 107
6 ch g Pivotal Chesnut Bird (IRE) (Storm Bird (CAN))
143a[4] 484a[3] 755a[8] 2655[2] 3329[13] 4725[2] 5492[7] 6484[5] ◆

Otto Nicolai *J S Moore* 26
3 gr c Singspiel(IRE) Majoune (FR) (Take Risks (FR))
3447[10] 4826[8]

Otto The First *John Best* a53 55
2 b g Holy Roman Emperor(IRE) Paquita (IRE) (Sadler's Wells (USA))
1308[5] 1738[2] 2609[6] 6850[5] 7439[8] 7865[3]

Otto The Great *Peter Chapple-Hyam* a41 93
3 b g Holy Roman Emperor(IRE) Vayavaig (Damister (USA))
1645[5] 4819[6] (5556) 6143[9]

Ouqba *Doug Watson* a69 115
6 b h Red Ransom(USA) Dancing Mirage (IRE) (Machiavellian (USA))
53a[14]

Our Boy Jack (IRE) *Richard Fahey* 93
3 b g Camacho Jina (IRE) (Petardia)
2229[2] (2459) 2764[2] 3160[3] (4082) 4317[8] 4675[3] 5334[4] 6046[3] 6923[3]

Our Diane (IRE) *David O'Meara* 77
2 b f Exceed And Excel(AUS) Medalha Milagrosa (USA) (Miner's Mark (USA))
2603[8] ◆ 2912[5] (3747) 4614[6] 4922[6] 5055[4]

Our Folly *Stuart Kittow* 70
4 b g Sakhee(USA) Regent's Folly (IRE) (Touching Wood (USA))
2396[2] (3102) 3316[2] 4731[4] 5772[3] 7077[2]

Our Gal *Noel Quinlan* a75 94
4 b m Kyllachy Moxby (Efisio)
2465[3] 2884[7] 3550[4] (4091) 4702[14] 6023[10] (6847) 7375[8] 7771[8]

Our Georgie Girl *Rod Millman* a16 31
5 ch m Zafeen(FR) Rosina May (IRE) (Danehill Dancer (IRE))
966[9] 1908[10] 2386[7]

Our Golden Girl *Mark Usher* a56 43
2 ch f Dutch Art Nemorosa (Pivotal)
2812[9] 3487[7] 4217[4] 5202[9] 5475[6] 6016[11]

Our Ivor *Michael Appleby* a53 49
3 gr g Cape Town(IRE) Caprice (Mystiko (USA))
217[6] 2049[5] 2333[9] 8050[10] 8241[8]

Our Joe Mac (IRE) *Richard Fahey* a95 105
5 b g Celtic Swing Vade Retro (IRE) (Desert Sun)
712[7] 1034[9]

Our Jonathan *Kevin Ryan* a103 119
5 b g Invincible Spirit(IRE) Sheik'n Swing (Celtic Swing)
(2074) 3190[2] 3623[6] 4078[3] 5370[16] 6468[12]

Our Monica (IRE) *Ian Williams* a33 38
3 b f Acclamation Szabo (IRE) (Anabaa (USA))
3076[8] 3489[16]

Our Obsession (IRE) *William Haggas* 84
2 ch f Shamardal(USA) Hidden Hope (Daylami (IRE))
4818[6] (6876)

Our Phylli Vera (IRE) *Harry Dunlop* a58 74
3 b f Motivator With Colour (Rainbow Quest (USA))
(1259) 2162[2] 2787[2] 3193[5] (4006) 4875[9] 6667[5]

Our Princess Ellie (USA) *Derek Shaw* a46 36
4 ch m Borrego(USA) Dear Abigail (USA) (Dehere (USA))
66[5] 8291[7]

Our Sweet Art *John Best* a65 62
2 ch f Dutch Art Break Of Dawn (USA) (Mt. Livermore (USA))
3339[7] 3971[3] 4494[12] 6849[6] 7476[5] 7821[8] 8016[5] 8203[11]

Our Three Graces (IRE) *Gary Moore* a61 63
2 b f Red Clubs(IRE) Villa Nova (IRE) (Petardia)
3700[6] 4645[3] 4899[2] 5484[8] 7223[9] 7808[9] 8203[7]

Outback (IRE) *Ann Duffield* a76 81
3 b g Kodiac Florida City (IRE) (Pennekamp (USA))
1053[4] 2794[4] 3273[3] 3521[3]

Outbid *Jamie Osborne* a60 58
2 ch f Auction House(USA) Thicket (Wolfhound (USA))
5854[3] 6276[7] 6579[4] 8007[8] 8245[3]

Out Do *Luca Cumani* a80 85
3 ch g Exceed And Excel(AUS) Ludynosa (USA) (Cadeaux Genereux)
1452[10] 1843[3] 6800[6] ◆ (7322)

Outlaw Torn (IRE) *Richard Guest* a70 64
3 ch g Iffraaj Touch And Love (IRE) (Green Desert (USA))
322[8] 382[3] 534[3] 747[4] 901[4] 1365[3] 1582[2] 1798[4] 2459[2] (2673) 2786[5] 3356[9] 3548[7] 4549[3] 4715[8] 5171[3] 5312[7] 5918[5] 6258[12] 6309[2] (6829) 7201[3] (7529) (8271)

Out Of Nothing *Dai Burchell* a62 75
9 br m Perryston View Loves To Dare (IRE) (Desert King (IRE))
2859[5] 3096[3] 6734[3] 7270[5]

Out Of The Blocks *Ruth Carr* 65
2 b g Firebreak Suzie Fong (Dr Fong (USA))
1164[3] 1284[2] 2309[2] 2594[4] ◆ 3112[8] 3436[4] 3858[6] 4450[2] 4672[2] ◆ 4951[5] 5670[6] 6070[11] 6753[5]

Out Of The Storm *Simon Dow* a58 65
4 b m Elmhurst Boy Night Storm (Night Shift (USA))
281[9]

Outpost (IRE) *Alan Bailey* a92 63
4 ch g Giant's Causeway(USA) Southern Migration (USA) (Kingmambo (USA))
(6812) 7163[9] 7685[8] (7716) 7897[6] 8098[11]

Outrageous Request *Lucinda Russell* a84 78
6 ch g Rainbow Quest(USA) La Sorrela (IRE) (Cadeaux Genereux)
1880[3]

Outside Art *Paul Fitzsimons* a48 32
3 b f Excellent Art She's My Outsider (Docksider (USA))
1257[7] 7787[5] 7903[4] 8075[9] 8257[11]

Ouzinkie (IRE) *Mick Channon* a69 75
2 b g Kodiac Sleeponit (IRE) (Marju (IRE))
1411[2] 1842[11] 2330[6] 2686[5] 2929[5] 3140[2] 4093[22] 4257[4] 4587[3] 4837[6] 5061[3] 5682[7] (6766) (7056) (7476)

Ovambo Queen (GER) *Dr A Bolte* 115
5 bb m Kalatos(GER) Oxalaguna (GER) (Lagunas)
2322a[2] (3746a) 4383a[4] 5865a[2] 6523a[7]

Overrider *Charles Hills* a81 77
2 b g Cockney Rebel(IRE) Fustaan (IRE) (Royal Applause)
2983[11] 4845[7] 5418[3] 7110[6] 7813[4] (8207)

Overrule (USA) *Jason Ward* a79 79
8 b g Diesis Her Own Way (USA) (Danzig (USA))
(98) 367[2] (672) (830) (1174) 1632[2] 1846[7] 2348[3] 2694[4] 3449[6] 3693[10]

Overturn (IRE) *Donald McCain* a94 114
8 b g Barathea(IRE) Kristal Bridge (Kris)
1974[2] 3373[8]

Overwhelm *Alan McCabe* a62 39
4 ch m Bahamian Bounty Depressed (Most Welcome)
178[11] 320[3] 445[7] 781[3] 985[8] 5416[9] 6105[13] 7633[8]

Ovett *Gary Moore* a84 74
2 b g Exceed And Excel(AUS) Stormy Weather (Nashwan (USA))
3971[6] (4581) 6871[6] 7220[7] 7745[3] 7866[4] (8016) (8161) 8204[3]

Oxford Charley (USA) *Mikael Magnusson* 97
3 b g Lemon Drop Kid(USA) La Sarto (USA) (Cormorant (USA))
1455[4] 2026[2] 5626[5] 6135[3] 6494[2] 6638[9]

Ozz *Frank Sheridan* a54 67
3 gr f Aussie Rules(USA) Spicey (Mizoram (USA))
770[10] 940[6] 1111[2] 1389[3] (2030)

Pabusar *Ralph Beckett* 111
4 b g Oasis Dream Autumn Pearl (Orpen (USA))
1129[11] 2268[2] 3371[16] 4113[2] 4762[13] 5822[4] 6140[9] 6869[7] 7288a[5]

Pacey Outswinger (IRE) *John C McConnell* a42 53
5 b m Intikhab(USA) Dusky Virgin (Missed Flight)
104[10] 7619[6]

Pacific Heights (IRE) *Tim Pitt* a73 78
3 b g Galileo(IRE) Song To Remember (USA) (Storm Cat (USA))
1704[4] 7016[4] 7594[3]

Packing Ok (AUS) *J Moore* 117
6 b g Redoute's Choice(AUS) Abbadena (AUS) (Runyon (IRE))
8042a[3]

Packing Whiz (IRE) *J Moore* 115
4 ch g Trade Fair Swizzle (Efisio)
8042a[5]

Pacquiao (IRE) *John Quinn* a48 40
2 b g Teofilo(IRE) Woodland Chant (USA) (War Chant (USA))
2873[5] 3381[10] 4448[8] 8112[6]

Paddy Burke *Stuart Kittow* 50
2 b g Bertolini(USA) Feathergrass (IRE) (Fasliyev (USA))
7434[4]

Paddyfrommenlo (IRE) *J W Hills* a70 84
3 ch c Hurricane Run(IRE) Dolce Dovo (Medicean)
1450[11] 2496[6] 2898[3] (4046) 4289[3] 4745[8] 6193[8] 6933[11]

Paddy's Saltantes (IRE) *J S Moore* a70 52
2 b g Redback Shall We Tell (Intikhab (USA))
5511[4] 5912[6] 7165[4] 7642[2] (7924) (8032)

Pagera (FR) *H-A Pantall* 111
4 ch m Gentlewave(IRE) Panthesilea (FR) (Kendor (FR))
1696a[6] 2570a[7] 3178a[7] 4386a[9] (5844a) 7093a[2] 8040a[11]

Pahente *Tony Carroll* a50 58
4 bg g Silver Patriarch(IRE) Miss Tehente (FR) (Tehente (FR))
561[14] 843[8] 1083[4] ◆ 1534[6] 2394[4] 2651[2] 3143[6] 4536[8] (5483) (5771) 5967[4]

Paige Flyer *Michael Quinn* a52 52
2 b f Multiplex Captain Margaret (Royal Applause)
4658[9] 5061[8] 6437[3] 7165[6]

Painted Sky *Donald McCain* a64 56
9 ch g Rainbow Quest(USA) Emplane (USA) (Irish River (FR))
500[6] 1247[6]

Painted Tail (IRE) *Alan Swinbank* a72 75
5 b m Mark Of Esteem(IRE) Bronwen (IRE) (King's Best (USA))
1170[5] 1423[3] 1652[4] 1988[10] 2539[10] 3213[2] 3704[5] (4627) 5085[7] 5383[6] 5731[4]

Pairumani Prince (IRE) *Ed Dunlop* a71
2 b c Choisir(AUS) Pairumani Princess (IRE) (Pairumani Star (IRE))
2039[5] ◆ 6175[10] 6841[6] 7414[11] 7708[5] (8094) (8289)

Paiza (IRE) *H-A Pantall* a91 91
2 b c Zamindar(USA) Tobermory (IRE) (Green Desert (USA))
6942a[6] 7682a[2]

Pakal (GER) *W Figge* 111
3 b c Lord Of England(GER) Perima (GER) (Kornado)
1553a[6] 1900a[4] (2569a) 4636a[6] 5869a[7] 6291a[7]

Palace Moon *William Knight* a107 111
7 b g Fantastic Light(USA) Palace Street (USA) (Secreto (USA))
(266) ◆ (527) ◆ 711[11] 1140[4] (2268) 3371[8] 4802[25] 7010[14]

Paladin (IRE) *Mahmood Al Zarooni* a64 72
3 b g Dubawi(IRE) Palwina (FR) (Unfuwain (USA))
1322[11]

Palawi (IRE) *John Quinn* a64 82
5 ch g Dubawi(IRE) Palwina (FR) (Unfuwain (USA))
902[P]

Palazzo Bianco *John Gosden* a94 90
4 b h Shirocco(GER) White Palace (Shirley Heights)
1446[3] 2709[3] ◆ 3625[15] 5200[4]

Pale Mimosa (IRE) *D K Weld* 107
3 b f Singspiel(IRE) Katch Me Katie (Danehill (USA))
(5519) 6896a[5]

Pale Orchid (IRE) *David Evans* a94 95
3 b f Invincible Spirit(IRE) Chelsea Rose (IRE) (Desert King (IRE))
(37) (295) 471[2] ◆ (659) 1032[4] 1494[4] 1751[6] 2028[4] 2509[5] 2714[4] 3165[13] 4044[4] (4423) 4838[6] (5128) 5363[10] 6075[11]

Palermo (GER) *Cathrine Erichsen* 93
6 b h Kalatos(GER) Palma (GER) (Goofalik (USA))
2807a[7] 3886a[8] 5651a[9] 6091a[8]

Palladius *Kevin Ryan* a57 70
2 ch f Sakhee's Secret With Distinction (Zafonic (USA))
3560[6] 4093[17] 4681[2] 6016[8] (6556) 6809[5] 7241[2]

Pallasator *Sir Mark Prescott Bt* a96 102
3 b g Motivator Ela Athena (Ezzoud (IRE))
(4458) (5973) (6625)

Palmette *John Gosden* 78
3 b f Oasis Dream Arabesque (Zafonic (USA))
3082[2] 3568[4] 4434[3] (5096) 6378[4]

Palmyra (IRE) *David Simcock* a63 59
3 ch f Haafhd Tasjeel (USA) (Aljabr (USA))
(428) 656[3] 1915[8] 2577[4]

Pal Of The Cat *Brian Gubby* a69 69
2 ch g Choisir(AUS) Evenstorm (USA) (Stephen Got Even (USA))
3637[10] 4148[4] 4512[3] 5503[8] 6579[3] 6975[3] 7738[6]

Paloma's Prince (IRE) *Jim Boyle* 81
3 ch g Nayef(USA) Ma Paloma (FR) (Highest Honor (FR))
(1565) 2408[11] 3787[4] 4151[3] 6933[12]

Palomita (GER) *Frau Nina Bach* 97
4 bb m High Chaparral(IRE) Perima (GER) (Kornado)
6085a[2]

Palus San Marco (IRE) *Peter Chapple-Hyam* a81 80
3 b g Holy Roman Emperor(IRE) Kylemore (IRE) (Sadler's Wells (USA))
1518[2] (3720) 4649[5] 6933[5]

Panama (FR) *Mme Pia Brandt* a74
2 b c Sholokhov(IRE) Prophecie (FR) (Dansili)
(8176a)

Panama Cat (USA) *Kevin Ryan* a52 60
2 b f Tale Of The Cat(USA) Oceans Apart (Desert Prince (IRE))
2138[U] 2873[3] 3560[10] 4448[5] 5716[3] 6337[5] 6822[4] 6953[4] 7313[2]

Panama Jack *Vanja Sandrup* a53 69
5 b g Dubai Destination(USA) Clear Impression (IRE) (Danehill (USA))
2159a[6]

Pandar *Robert Cowell* a91 104
3 b g Zamindar(USA) Pagnottella (IRE) (Dansili)
2325a[3] 6943a[7] 7772[12]

Pandorica *Bernard Llewellyn* a73 78
4 b m Indesatchel(IRE) Hope Chest (Kris)
275[5] 971[8] 1485[5] 1909[3] 2167[5] 2650[3] 3143[4] 3891[2] (4183) 4733[2] 5151[7] (5653) 6004[2] 6735[7]

Panesidora (GER) *C Von Der Recke*
2 b f Soviet Star(USA) Paradise Search (IRE) (Rainbow Quest (USA))
5612a[13]

Panettone (IRE) *Roger Varian* a56 72
3 b f Montjeu(IRE) Tea Break (Daylami (IRE))
3968[4] 4776[8] 5754[4] (5989) 6232[6] 7444[4]

Pangaea Prince (IRE) *A Fabre* a66
2 b c Invincible Spirit(IRE) Elle Galante (GER) (Galileo (IRE))
8176a[0]

Panther Patrol (IRE) *Eve Johnson Houghton* 11
2 b c Tagula(IRE) Quivala (USA) (Thunder Gulch (USA))
3506[9]

Panzanella *John Gosden* 90
3 b f Dansili Zenda (Zamindar (USA))
(6965)

Panzerotta (IRE) *Camilla Trapassi* 80
2 b f Captain Marvelous(IRE) Saviolo (Rossini (USA))
6090a[5]

Papageno *J R Jenkins* a58 50
5 b g Piccolo Fresh Fruit Daily (Reprimand)
37[4] 118[7] 1787[2]

Paperetto *Robert Mills* a69 71
4 b g Selkirk(USA) Song Of Hope (Chief Singer)
88[6] 2652[3] (3471) 3723[5] 4812[2] 5346[7] 6306[5] 8156[4] 8268[2]

Paper Petal (IRE) *J T Gorman* a39 36
2 b f Refuse To Bend(IRE) Catwalk Dreamer (IRE) (Acatenango (GER))
6853a[9]

Paphos *Stuart Williams* a74 66
5 b g Oasis Dream Tychy (Suave Dancer (USA))
2811[6] 3738[3] 3958[3] (4469) 4872[4] (5349) 6171[8] 7743[9] 8034[6] 8156[7]

Paradise Spectre *Mrs K Burke* a76 81
5 b g Firebreak Amber's Bluff (Mind Games)
1254[4] 2488[4] 3225[2] 3612[11] 4660[4] 5082[2] 5320[5] 5853[6] 7328[4] 7827[3]

Paradise Tree (IRE) *P Sogorb* 79
4 b m Tobougg(IRE) Wagtail (FR) (Astair (FR))
(3207a)

Paraggi *Mme Pia Brandt* a88 107
3 ch c Iffraaj Topkamp (Pennekamp (USA))
914a[7] 2728a[14] 7803a[2] 8277a[4]

Paraisa *A Wohler* 99
3 b f Red Ransom(USA) Praia (GER) (Big Shuffle (USA))
2107a[3] 2746a[8] 3653a[5]

Paramount (FR) *T M Walsh* a78 79
10 b g Octagonal(NZ) Passionnee (USA) (Woodman (USA))
342a[6]

Paramour *David O'Meara* 91
5 b g Selkirk(USA) Embraced (Pursuit Of Love)
1670[17] (2896) 3183[12] 3348[13] 4136[9] 5819[7] 6338[8] 7370[6] 7715[13]

Paramythi (IRE) *Luca Cumani* a55 67
3 ch g Peintre Celebre(USA) The Spirit Of Pace (IRE) (In The Wings)
2196[10] 2584[9] 4601[6]

Parc De Launay *Tom Tate* 91
3 ch g Monsieur Bond(IRE) Franglais (GER) (Lion Cavern (USA))
1271[12] 1524[7] 1858[7] 2182[9] 2824[7]

Pareo (FR) *A De Royer-Dupre* 102
4 b h Galileo(IRE) Pearly Shells (Efisio)
4316a[4]

Parhelion *John Flint* a64 85
5 b g Fantastic Light(USA) Shamaiel (IRE) (Lycius (USA))
5507[8] 6691[13] 7303[3] 7819[7]

Parigino (FR) *Nick Gifford* a82 87
4 b g Panis(USA) Loretta Gianni (FR) (Classic Account (USA))
7626[8] 7986[5] 8174[7]

Paris Blue (FR) *J-L Pelletan* a91 103
3 b g Anabaa(USA) Diamond Laly (Observatory (USA))
914a[5] 1208a[7] 1426a[0] 7803a[0]

Parisham (FR) *M Delzangles* 86
3 ch f Cadeaux Genereux Pink And Red (USA) (Red Ransom (USA))
3682a[12] 5472a[7]

Parisian Prince (IRE) *David Barron* 86
2 b c Chineur(FR) Western Sal (Salse (USA))
(4132)

Parisian Princess (IRE) *Hughie Morrison* a75 64
3 b f Teofilo(IRE) Night Sphere (IRE) (Night Shift (USA))
2768[7] 3214[4] 4534[4] 5244[3]

Parisian Pyramid (IRE) *Ian Williams* a77 102
6 gr g Verglas(IRE) Sharadja (IRE) (Doyoun)
1220[4] 1558[5] ◆ 1885[4] 2446[7] 4077[6] 4609[15] 5368[11] 6663[10] 7113[12] 7464[9] 7741[6] 7937[9] ◆ 7967[5] 8034[3] 8059[2] 8159[2] 8232[6]

Paris Rose *William Haggas* 47
2 b f Cape Cross(IRE) Samira Gold (FR) (Gold Away (IRE))
7364[10]

Paris To Peking (ITY) *S Botti* 100
4 b m Intikhab(USA) Khanstan (IRE) (Barathea (IRE))
6726a[4]

Parkers Mill (IRE) *T Stack* 98
4 b g High Chaparral(IRE) Celtic Wing (Midyan (USA))
1043a[4] 1946a[5]

Park Lane *Noel Quinlan* a72 31
6 b g Royal Applause Kazeem (Darshaan)
2694[7]

Parley (USA) *Mark Johnston* a73 81
3 bb f Street Cry(IRE) Tout Charmant (USA) (Slewvescent (USA))
(533) 2752[3] 3395[3] 3522[5] 3906[7] 5163[7] 7358[6]

Parliament Square (IRE) *A P O'Brien* 112
2 b c Acclamation Bold Desire (Cadeaux Genereux)
2184a[5] 3242[5] 5398a[3] 6162[5] 7049[5]

Parlour Games *Mahmood Al Zarooni* a103 101
4 ch h Monsun(GER) Petrushka (IRE) (Unfuwain (USA))
1318[7]

Parque Atlantico *Ed McMahon* a62 39
3 bb g Piccolo Silken Dalliance (Rambo Dancer (CAN))
1067[2] 1259[12] 1424[4] 2353[4] 2787[7] 3233[6] 5751[3] 6829[2] 7148[4] 7593[10]

Parsons Green *Michael Attwater*
3 b f Sakhee(USA) Anastasia Venture (Lion Cavern (USA))
7005[12]

Partner (IRE) *Noel Wilson* a86 96
6 b g Indian Ridge Oregon Trail (USA) (Gone West (USA))
1975[13] (2286) 2717[13] 3183[14] 3374[9] 4454[2] (5058) 5343[8] 5829[5] 6144[9] 6466[7] 6939[2] 7243[7] 7595[10]

Partner's Gold (IRE) *Alan Berry*
2 b c Red Clubs(IRE) Unfortunate (Komaite (USA))
5382[10]

Party Line *Mark Johnston* 98
3 b f Montjeu(IRE) Party (IRE) (Cadeaux Genereux)
1355[2] (1915) 2716[3] 2889[3] 3305[4] 3628[4] 4048[3] 5312[3] (5622) (6045) 6476[3] ◆ 6668[4] 6832[2] (7396) 7689[10]

Party Palace *Stuart Howe* a34 47
8 b m Auction House(USA) Lady-Love (Pursuit Of Love)
2134[7] 2575[7] 4904[6] 5811[3]

Party Royal *Mark Johnston* a80 80
2 b g Royal Applause Voliere (Zafonic (USA))
1997[4] (2594) 3240[21] 4047[4] 4526[4] 4763[4] 5602[12] 7501[2] 7994[3]

Pasaka Boy *Jonathan Portman* 90
2 ch c Haafhd Shesha Bear (Tobougg (IRE))
(3009) 3368[10] (4847) 5353[5] 6871[8]

Pascha Bere (FR) *Nick Gifford* 79
9 gr g Verglas(IRE) Ephelide (FR) (Count Pahlen)
2411[2]

Pasco (BEL) *F Vermeulen* a60
3 b g Kavafi(IRE) Pekkouqui (IRE) (Doyoun)
476a[0] 661a[6]

Pas D'Action *Mrs A Malzard*
4 ch g Noverre(USA) Bright Vision (Indian Ridge)
2116a[3]

Pashan Garh *Pat Eddery* a70 78
3 b g Anabaa(USA) Mimisel (Selkirk (USA))
1048[2] 1420[3] 2041[6] 2361[6] 3071[2] 3809[2] 4341[2] 5776[6] 6965[5] 7402[6] 7559[2] 7684[4]

Passarinho (IRE) *H-A Pantall* a67 84
3 ch c Ad Valorem(USA) Semiramide (IRE) (Persian Bold)
1171a[8]

Passato (GER) *Jo Davis* a60 69
8 b g Lando(GER) Passata (FR) (Polar Falcon (USA))
(2391) 2872[3] (3216)

Passing Moment *Brian Baugh* a42 44
4 b m Fraam Passing Fancy (Grand Lodge (USA))
483[12] 1989[6] 2406[8] 3052[8]

Passionada *Ed McMahon* a73 72
3 bb f Avonbridge Lark In The Park (IRE) (Grand Lodge (USA))
2416[9] 4329[9] 6961[13] 7589[2] (7969)

Passionate Diva (USA) *Ed Vaughan* a48
2 bb f Street Cry(IRE) Roshani (USA) (Fantastic Light (USA))
8033[10]

Passionate Poet *Michael Easterby* 59
2 b g Byron Mid Ocean (Sakhee (USA))
3436[12] 4825[6] 6099[15]

Passion Planet (IRE) *John C McConnell* a71 68
4 b m Medicean Katch Me Katie (Danehill (USA))
(4955) 7380[5] 7617[6]

Passion Play *William Knight* a70 73
4 gr m Act One Addicted To Love (Touching Wood (USA))
(1613) 2149[3] 2978[7] 4585[6] 5159[5] (5507)

Passior (FR) *P Lenogue* a78 64
3 b g Vatori(FR) Abedissa (FR) (Bishop Of Cashel)
247a[4] 628a[5]

Pass Muster *Ollie Pears* a87 92
5 b g Theatrical(IRE) Morning Pride (IRE) (Machiavellian (USA))
1670[13] 1914[6] 4706[2] 6073[5] ◆ 7147[3] 7672[3] 7751[4] 8148[2]

Pass The Time *Neil Mulholland* a33 53
3 b f Passing Glance Twin Time (Syrtos)
1825[8] 2543[11] 2757[8] 5508[13] 6281[3] (6569) 7148[9]

Pastoral Jet *Richard Rowe* a61 42
4 bb h Pastoral Pursuits Genteel (IRE) (Titus Livius (FR))
379[3] 578[5] 3006[7] 5481[10] 5741[2] ◆ 5996[3] (6395) 6773[4] (7189) 8167[3] ◆

Pastoral Player *Hughie Morrison* 116
5 b g Pastoral Pursuits Copy-Cat (Lion Cavern (USA))
2068[6] (2710) 3370[10] 4320[2] 5355[5] 6246[2]

Pastoral Prey *George Foster* 68
2 b g Pastoral Pursuits Bird Of Prey (IRE) (Last Tycoon)
1795[6] 2537[2] 2837[2] 3520[4] 4670[5]

Pastoral Symphony *John Best* 1
2 br f Pastoral Pursuits Hucking Harmony (IRE) (Spartacus (IRE))
6438[9]

Pastorius (GER) *Mario Hofer* 122
3 b c Soldier Hollow Princess Li (GER) (Monsun (GER))
1553a[4] 2568a[7] (3683a) (4636a) 5865a[3] (6805a) 7239[4]

Pastures New *Violet M Jordan* a62 44
4 ch g Proclamation(IRE) Gal Gloria (PR) (Tralos (USA))
3155[3] 4582[6] 6941[7] 7326[9] 7385[6] 7752[5] 8037[6]

Pastureyes *Scott Dixon* 58
2 ch f Milk It Mick Veils Of Salome (Arkadian Hero (USA))
5709[2]

Pat And Go (FR) *A Bonin* a70 67
3 ch f Chichicastenango(FR) Miss Pat (FR) (Vacarme (USA))
8277a[5]

Patavium (IRE) *Edwin Tuer* a55 81
9 b g Titus Livius(FR) Arcevia (IRE) (Archway (IRE))
1295[5]

Patavium Prince (IRE) *Jo Crowley* a65 78
9 ch g Titus Livius(FR) Hoyland Common (IRE) (Common Grounds)
3007[3] 3471[2] 4413[6] 5050[6] 6434[4] (8156)

Patch Patch *Derek Shaw* a62 72
5 b g Avonbridge Sandgate Cygnet (Fleetwood (IRE))
456[5] 497[7]

Pategonia *John Gosden* a67
3 b c Oasis Dream Cozy Maria (USA) (Cozzene (USA))
7477[4]

Patently (IRE) *Brian Meehan* 55
2 b c Moss Vale(IRE) Trader Secret (IRE) (Montjeu (IRE))
6486[8]

Paternoster *Roger Charlton* 11
2 b g Teofilo(IRE) Rosse (Kris)
6486[18]

Path Finder (FR) *Reg Hollinshead* a74 37
3 ch g Medecis Desirous Of Peace (Forzando)
247a[7] 364a[7] 476a[6] (661a)

Patrickswell (IRE) *Marcus Callaghan* a72 84
8 gr g Iron Mask(USA) Gladstone Street (IRE) (Waajib)
6270a[9]

Patriotic (IRE) *Chris Dwyer* a87 78
4 b g Pivotal Pescara (IRE) (Common Grounds)
60[3] (401) (463) 722[2] (907) 1262[4] (1633) 2082[9] 2199[9] 2801[2] 3589[6] 3976[2] 4662[6] 5752[6] (6141) 6381[8] 7461[4] 7751[8] 7842[4] 8057[4]

Patrona Ciana (FR) *Y Durepaire* 79
2 b f Falco(USA) Bavaria Patrona (FR) (Kahyasi)
5899a[5]

Patronne *Ann Stokell* a56
6 b m Domedriver(IRE) Pat Or Else (Alzao (USA))
1988[13]

Pat's Legacy (USA) *Jo Hughes* a82 95
6 ch g Yankee Gentleman(USA) Sugars For Nanny (USA) (Brocco (USA))
431[7] 1128[19] 1249[13] 2608[8] 3226[8] 3999[7] 4541[6] 5741[4]

Pattaya (ITY) *S Botti* 99
4 b h Philomatheia(USA) Tirsa (Benny The Dip (USA))
2323a[4]

Pattern Mark *Ollie Pears* a61 64
6 b g Mark Of Esteem(IRE) Latch Key Lady (USA) (Tejano (USA))
3353[11] 3914[9] (4958) 5638[7]

Pavement Games *Richard Guest* a34 54
5 b m Mind Games Pavement Gates (Bishop Of Cashel)
118[9] 126[8] 379[12]

Pavershooz *Noel Wilson* a91 88
7 b g Bahamian Bounty Stormswept (USA) (Storm Bird (CAN))
5412[12]

Pavers Star *Noel Wilson* a61 62
3 ch g Pastoral Pursuits Pride Of Kinloch (Dr Devious (IRE))
2460[4] 2695[4] 3407[8] 4878[6] 5294[2] (5621) 6314[2] 7099[4] 7351[6] 7673[3] 7746[2]

Pawan (IRE) *Ann Stokell* a44 43
12 ch g Cadeaux Genereux Born To Glamour (Ajdal (USA))
1987[8] 3018[3] 3245[8]

Pawprints (IRE) *William Haggas* a28 72
3 ch f Footstepsinthesand Samphire Red (IRE) (Sri Pekan (USA))
(2461) 4533[2] 5350[4]

Payback (GER) *John Butler* 35
3 b g Shirocco(GER) Panagia (USA) (Diesis)
523[12] 827[10]

Pay Freeze (IRE) *Mick Channon* 94
2 b c Baltic King Banco Solo (Distant Relative)
2231[2] (2508) 3242[9] 4093[14] 4763[6] 5678[5] 6162[13] 6487[2]

Paynter (USA) *Bob Baffert* a123
3 b c Awesome Again(CAN) Tizso (USA) (Cee's Tizzy (USA))
2954a[2]

Pazifiksturm (GER) *Mlle A Imaz-Ceca*
5 ch h Samum(GER) La Parabol (FR) (Trempolino (USA))
(5252a)

Peace Burg (FR) *J Heloury* 107
2 b f Sageburg(IRE) Peace Talk (FR) (Sadler's Wells (USA))
(6129a) 6909a[5]

Peaceful Means (IRE) *Mandy Rowland* a54 54
9 b m Witness Box(USA) Princess Satco (IRE) (Satco (FR))
2769[5]

Peace In Our Time *Anthony Carson* a55 40
3 b g Echo Of Light Deira (USA) (Green Desert (USA))
4301[8] 5100[9] 6704[8] 8264[2]

Peace Seeker *Anthony Carson* a83 82
4 b g Oasis Dream Mina (Selkirk (USA))
2071[11] 2545[9] 3139[13] 3960[3] 4660[2]

Peachez *Alastair Lidderdale* a82 76
4 ch m Observatory(USA) Streccia (Old Vic)
3154[7] 4538[4] 5124[2] ◆ 5507[2] 6229[2] 6440[2] (6891) 7381[2] (7617)

Peadar Miguel *Daniel Mark Loughnane* a69 51
5 b g Danroad(AUS) La Corujera (Case Law)
480[9] 685[4] 5225[9] 6057[10] 6894[9]

Peak Seasons (IRE) *Michael Chapman* a52 36
9 ch g Raise A Grand(IRE) Teresian Girl (IRE) (Glenstal (USA))
454[13]

Peak Storm *John O'Shea* a62 70
3 b g Sleeping Indian Jitterbug (IRE) (Marju (IRE))
4992[2] 5541[3] 6477[4] 6643[3] 7025[5] 7361[3] 7670[3]

Peal Of Bells (AUS) *Gwenda Markwell* 99
5 br g Clangalang(AUS) Pearl Quest (AUS) (Jeune)
7560a[10]

Pearla *William Haggas* a63
2 gr f Dalakhani(IRE) Propaganda (IRE) (Sadler's Wells (USA))
8017[10] 8200[4]

Pearl Acclaim (IRE) *Richard Hannon* a90 103
2 b c Acclamation With Colour (Rainbow Quest (USA))
2934[2] (4512) ◆ (5371) 5559[5] 6038[5]

Pearl Bell (IRE) *Brian Meehan* 80
2 b f Camacho Magnificent Bell (IRE) (Octagonal (NZ))
3590[2] ◆ 4282[3]

Pearl Blue (IRE) *Chris Wall* 100
4 b m Exceed And Excel(AUS) Sanfrancullinan (IRE) (Bluebird (USA))
1417[5] (1642) 2310[9] 3183[10] 4013[2] 5343[4] 6286[4] (7063)

Pearl Bounty (IRE) *Andrew Balding* a67 49
2 ch g Bahamian Bounty Roslea Lady (IRE) (Alhaarth (IRE))
2420[6] 4502[4] 4873[6] 7223[2]

Pearl Bridge *Ralph Beckett* 73
2 b g Avonbridge Our Little Secret (IRE) (Rossini (USA))
6203[3]

Pearl Castle (IRE) *Andrew Balding* 80
2 b c Montjeu(IRE) Ghurra (USA) (War Chant (USA))
5062[9] (5534) 6469[6]

Pearl Catcher (IRE) *Tim Easterby* a49 53
3 b g Catcher In The Rye(IRE) Midnight Pearl (USA) (Woodman (USA))
2341[5] 2771[6] 4172[11]

Pearl Charm (USA) *D Grilli* a76 82
3 ch c Distorted Humor(USA) Charmed Gift (USA) (A.P. Indy (USA))
364a[6]

Pearl Diva (IRE) *Peter Chapple-Hyam* 93
3 b f Acclamation Lassie's Gold (USA) (Seeking The Gold (USA))
3593[5] 4070[8] 5582[3] 6406[8]

Pearl Flute (IRE) *F-H Graffard* 108
2 b c Piccolo Secret Melody (FR) (Inchinor)
4632a[3] 5398a[7] 6086a[3] (6507a) 7076a[3] 7514a[6]

Pearl Frost *Laura Mongan* a56 33
3 gr g Verglas(IRE) Eternelle (Green Desert (USA))
56[3] 993[10] 2850[11] 5989[12]

Pearl Ice *David Barron* a88 105
4 b g Iffraaj Jezebel (Owington)
1844[13] 2284[2] (2825) ◆ 2931[8] 3641[8] 6468[15]

Pearl Mix (IRE) *Ralph Beckett* a113 97
3 gr c Oratorio(IRE) Rosamixa (FR) (Linamix (FR))
(6400) 7048[11] (7809) ◆

Pearl Nation (USA) *Brian Baugh* a80 84
3 b g Speightstown(USA) Happy Nation (USA) (Lear Fan (USA))
2864[5] 3235[2] 3990[2] (4496) ◆ 5110[4]

Pearl Noir *Scott Dixon* a62 73
2 b c Milk It Mick Cora Pearl (IRE) (Montjeu (IRE))
2138[2] 2550[2] 3242[18] 4047[6] 6980[7] 7219[2] 7462[6] 7711[2]

Pearl Of Love (GER) *T Potters* 76
2 b f Sholokhov(IRE) Pearl (GER) (Dashing Blade)
7076a[8]

Pearl Of Phoenix *Jo Hughes* 29
2 b f Phoenix Reach(IRE) Pearl's Girl (King's Best (USA))
3084[5] 3487[8]

Pearl Opera *Denis Coakley* a62 52
4 b m Librettist(USA) Letsimpress (IRE) (General Monash (USA))
1980[2] 2431[9] 3247[6] 3947[6] 4981[6]

Pearl Ransom (IRE) *Kevin Ryan* a33 68
2 b g Intikhab(USA) Massada (Most Welcome)
2376[6] 6043[4] 6512[6] 7199[9]

Pearl Rebel *Stuart Williams* a86
3 b c Cockney Rebel(IRE) Lilli Marlane (Sri Pekan (USA))
(127) ◆

Pearl Reward (USA) *Stuart Williams* 89
2 bb c Medaglia d'Oro(USA) With Patience (USA) (With Approval (CAN))
2376[7] (6607) 7292[7]

Pearl Sea (IRE) *David Brown* 93
2 b f Elusive City(USA) Catch The Sea (IRE) (Barathea (IRE))
3560[3] ◆ 4011[2] (4701) 5516[5] 7518[13]

Pearl Secret *David Barron* 110
3 ch c Compton Place Our Little Secret (IRE) (Rossini (USA))
(1639) ◆ (2212) (3158) 5561[9]

Pearls From Sydney *Paul Cole* a52 28
3 b f Librettist(USA) Cultured Pearl (IRE) (Lammtarra (USA))
990[4] 1173[2] 1278[4] 2010[10]
Pearl Spice (IRE) *Sir Mark Prescott Bt* 56
2 ch g Dalakhani(IRE) Cinnamon Rose (USA) (Trempolino (USA))
3062[10] 6412[5] ◆
Pearl Street (USA) *Henry Candy* a68
2 b f Street Sense(USA) Pretty Meadow (USA) (Meadowlake (USA))
6535[4] ◆
Pearl War (USA) *William Haggas* a62 75
3 b f War Front(USA) B W Chargit (USA) (Meadowlake (USA))
3666[7] 4711[2] 6092[4] 7250[8]
Peas And Carrots (DEN) *Lennart Reuterskiold Jr* a98 98
9 b g Final Appearance(IRE) Dominet Hope (Primo Dominie)
2160a[9] 2807a[6] 4863a[3]
Pea Shooter *Kevin Ryan* a81 94
3 b g Piccolo Sparkling Eyes (Lujain (USA))
2276[9] 2509[6] 3165[9] 4291[4] 4558[6] 5167[U] 6008[2] 6688[7] 7595[5]
Pedro Serrano (IRE) *Henry Candy* a76
2 b c Footstepsinthesand Shaiyadima (IRE) (Zamindar (USA))
6015[2] ◆
Pedro The Great (USA) *A P O'Brien* 105
2 b c Henrythenavigator(USA) Glatisant (Rainbow Quest (USA))
2779a[5] 3649a[5] (5136a) 6910a[5]
Peep N Creep (IRE) *Tim Easterby* 62
2 b f Red Clubs(IRE) Lamzena (IRE) (Fairy King (USA))
1861[3] 2499[14] 2686[9] 3251[6]
Pegasus Prince (USA) *Brian Storey* a72 51
8 b g Fusaichi Pegasus(USA) Avian Eden (USA) (Storm Bird (CAN))
6101[10]
Peggy's Leg (USA) *Mrs John Harrington* a58 45
2 b f Henrythenavigator(USA) Audit (USA) (Meadowlake (USA))
4161a[7]
Peg Peg *Nerys Dutfield* 42
3 ch f Arkadian Hero(USA) Lady Eberspacher (IRE) (Royal Abjar (USA))
2203[7] 3014[10] 3489[14] 4457[9] 4981[8] 5994[7]
Pekan Star *Roger Varian* a57 97
5 b g Montjeu(IRE) Delicieuse Lady (Trempolino (USA))
2655[13] 4610[8] 5835[16] 7751[11]
Pelham Crescent (IRE) *Bryn Palling* a75 83
9 ch g Giant's Causeway(USA) Sweet Times (Riverman (USA))
43[5] 2363[10] 4491[8] 5265[6] 6097[2] 6232[2] 6735[5] 7652[4]
Pelican Rock (IRE) *Andrew Crook* a62 61
3 b g Amadeus Wolf Darby Shaw (IRE) (Kris)
270[6] 459[2] 641[2] (832) 901[2] 1597[4] 2283[3] 3356[7] 3751[7] 4830[15] 5720[5] 6105[14]
Pelmanism *Brian Ellison* a70 86
5 b g Piccolo Card Games (First Trump)
1868[15] 5539[11] 6008[16] 6465[15] 6886[7] 7436[13] 7684[18] 7914[2] 8269[3]
Pembrey *Mahmood Al Zarooni* 84
3 b c Teofilo(IRE) Miss Penton (Primo Dominie)
1455[7]
Penang Cinta *David Evans* a62 66
9 b g Halling(USA) Penang Pearl (FR) (Bering)
2115a[3] 2364[7] 3468[8] 5038[8]
Penangdouble O One *Alex Hales* a79 75
5 ch g Starcraft(NZ) Penang Pearl (FR) (Bering)
332[6] 433[8]
Penang Pegasus *David O'Meara* a29 59
3 ch g Zamindar(USA) Pulau Pinang (IRE) (Dolphin Street (FR))
1155[14] 1385[8] 2341[2] 2673[6] 4830[6] (5187) 5623[10] 7527[11]
Penang Power *Charles Hills* a49
2 b f Manduro(GER) Penang Pearl (FR) (Bering)
7160[10]
Penbryn (USA) *Nick Littmoden* a66 27
5 b g Pivotal Brocatelle (Green Desert (USA))
274[5] 333[2] 519[4] 732[2] 829[3] (1379) 1919[5] 2498[14]
Pencil Hill (IRE) *Tracey Collins* a87 87
7 b g Acclamation Como (USA) (Cozzene (USA))
6854a[10]
Pencombe (FR) *David Simcock* a64
2 b c Teofilo(IRE) Barbuda (Rainbow Quest (USA))
8070[7]
Penderyn *Charles Smith* a22 43
5 b m Sakhee(USA) Brecon (Unfuwain (USA))
1436[7] 2048[2] 3081[7] 4349[13] 6561[11] 7472[4]
Pendle Lady (IRE) *Mark Brisbourne* a50 65
3 b f Chineur(FR) Rose Of Battle (Averti (IRE))
1529[9] 2130[6] 2540[3] 2803[2] 3014[3] 3555[14]
Pendragon (USA) *Brian Ellison* a80 95
9 ch g Rahy(USA) Turning Wheel (USA) (Seeking The Gold (USA))
2257[9] 2921[10] (3030) 4474[4] 4964[8] 6638[26] 7413[6] 7608[2] 7920[8]
Penelopa *M G Mintchev* 89
2 b f Giant's Causeway(USA) Lady Linda (USA) (Torrential (USA))
5755a[2]
Peninsula *Ralph Beckett* 59
3 b f Rock Of Gibraltar(IRE) Kayah (Kahyasi)
3161[8]
Penitent *David O'Meara* a98 117
6 b g Kyllachy Pious (Bishop Of Cashel)
(1158) (1646) 2533a[7] 5286a[5] 6246[5] (6634) 6913a[2]
Penmaen (IRE) *J E Hammond* 67
2 b f Pivotal Lady Grace (IRE) (Orpen (USA))
6751a[7]
Penny Garcia *Tim Easterby* 79
2 b f Indesatchel(IRE) Katie Boo (IRE) (Namid)
2587[7] 2917[7] 3436[2] (3909) 4836[6] (5537) 6160[16] 6920[2]

Penny Rose *Mark Johnston* 88
2 b f Danehill Dancer(IRE) Love Everlasting (Pursuit Of Love)
4707[5] (6114) ◆ (6448) 6873[4] ◆ 7365[4]
Penny's Picnic (IRE) *D Guillemin* 112
2 b c Kheleyf(USA) Zerky (USA) (Kingmambo (USA))
4384a[4] 5398a[10] (7122a) (7623a)
Pennyweight *James Eustace* 45
2 ch f Hernando(FR) Penelewey (Groom Dancer (USA))
5550[10] 5902[11] 6371[9] 7313[5]
Pentagram (USA) *Mahmood Al Zarooni* a60
2 bb c Bernardini(USA) Mountain Mambo (USA) (Mt. Livermore (USA))
6014[7] 6532[3] 7081[9]
Ponton Hook *Barry Murtagh* a82 38
6 gr g Lucky Owners(NZ) Cosmic Star (Siberian Express (USA))
1294[9] 2239[13]
Pepito Collonges (FR) *Laura Mongan* a26
9 b g Brier Creek(USA) Berceuse Collonges (FR) (Vorias (USA))
4585[8]
Peponi *Peter Makin* a81 80
6 ch h Kris Kin(USA) Polmara (IRE) (Polish Precedent (USA))
199[4] 374[10] 3226[9] 4872[11]
Pepper Lane *David O'Meara* a58 111
5 ch m Exceed And Excel(AUS) Maid To Matter (Pivotal)
2087[6] 2713[10] 3371[28] (5370) 5822[8] 6072[7] 6882[3]
Peppertree Lane (IRE) *Emmet Michael Butterly* a15 16
9 ch g Peintre Celebre(USA) Salonrolle (IRE) (Tirol)
35[DSQ]
Pepsy Chope (FR) *C Boutin* a65 89
3 b f Indian Rocket Lycee (IRE) (Entrepreneur)
5726a[10] 7267a[6]
Peranova (IRE) *W McCreery* 56
2 b f Elusive City(USA) Over Rating (Desert King (IRE))
5872[3] (Dead)
Percythepinto (IRE) *George Baker* a65 59
3 b g Tiger Hill(IRE) Tullawadgeen (IRE) (Sinndar (IRE))
973[3] 1260[7] (2385) 3014[5] 4986[7] 5459[2] 6158[3] 7126[6] 7643[5] (7815) 8074[8]
Perennial *Charles Hills* 103
3 ch g Motivator Arum Lily (USA) (Woodman (USA))
1455[6] 2445[3] 3330[6] 6677[5] ◆
Perfect Act *Andrew Balding* a91 69
7 b m Act One Markova's Dance (Mark Of Esteem (IRE))
106[7] 282[4]
Perfect Beat *Ralph Beckett* 46
2 b f Beat Hollow Paradise Dancer (IRE) (Danehill Dancer (IRE))
7104[4]
Perfect Blossom *Ian McInnes* 92
5 b m One Cool Cat(USA) Perfect Peach (Lycius (USA))
2507[17] 4924[13] 5663[6] 6006[5] 6144[8] (6347) 6495[7]
Perfect Buttons (IRE) *Tim Vaughan* a25 43
6 b g Trans Island Buttons Galore (IRE) (Bigstone (IRE))
2872[4] 4004[9]
Perfect Calm (USA) *Richard Hannon* 68
2 b f Discreet Cat(USA) Rima (USA) (Jade Hunter (USA))
6966[4]
Perfect Ch'I (IRE) *Ian Wood* a71 74
5 b m Choisir(AUS) Agouti (Pennekamp (USA))
124[5] 746[12] 991[2] 1084[2] 1378[5] 1609[2] 1788[5] 2373[9] 2546[2] 2811[5] 3314[9] 3958[11] 4469[12]
Perfect Cracker *Clive Cox* a91 82
4 ch g Dubai Destination(USA) Perfect Story (IRE) (Desert Story (IRE))
1128[11] 1924[7] 2500[5] 3503[11] 4317[9] 4805[10]
Perfect Delight *Clive Cox* a80 86
3 b f Dubai Destination(USA) Perfect Spirit (IRE) (Invincible Spirit (IRE))
1565[3] 1892[2] 2148[2] (3070) 3630[6] 4342[6] 7475[6] 8000[6] 8182[6]
Perfect Example (IRE) *Ismail Mohammed* a43 54
3 b f Cape Cross(IRE) Shining Debut (IRE) (In The Wings)
2381[7] 2864[11] 5479[9] 6174[11]
Perfect Fantasy (IRE) *Clive Cox* a71 48
3 b f Oratorio(IRE) Petite Fantasy (Mansooj)
(742) 1985[7] 2448[8]
Perfect Heart *John Gosden* a77 83
3 gr g Dalakhani(IRE) Maid To Perfection (Sadler's Wells (USA))
5105[3] 5753[4] 6839[6]
Perfect Honour (IRE) *Violet M Jordan* a58 55
6 ch m Exceed And Excel(AUS) Porcelana (IRE) (Highest Honor (FR))
1387[7] 1908[6] 2385[7] 2971[4] 3020[4] 3466[2] 3718[3] 4237[12] 4815[2] ◆ (6771) 6959[7] 7157[4]
Perfect Mission *Andrew Balding* a83 79
4 b g Bertolini(USA) Sharp Secret (IRE) (College Chapel)
54[3] 131[3] 2399[6] 3045[4] 3958[2] 4503[8] 4939[10] (5741) 5983[8] 8152[9]
Perfect Outlook *Jeremy Gask* a49 53
4 b m Doyen(IRE) Cautiously (USA) (Distant View (USA))
1704[10] 2496[9] 2891[7] 3964[10] 4890[5] 5804[6] 8212[7]
Perfect Pastime *Jim Boyle* a71 86
4 ch g Pastoral Pursuits Puritanical (IRE) (Desert King (IRE))
1203[3] 1602[8] 1936[7] (3541) 4824[14] 5703[4] 6303[3] 6820[7] 7114[2]
Perfect Pasture *Michael Easterby* 54
2 b g Pastoral Pursuits Word Perfect (Diktat)
4995[6] 5825[8]
Perfect Pins (NZ) *Leticia Dragon* 109
7 b g Pins(AUS) La Cent (NZ) (Centaine (AUS))
2326a[8]

Perfect Policy *Ralph Beckett* a30 45
3 b f Kyllachy Perfect Cover (IRE) (Royal Applause)
1182[9] 1705[10] 2262[7] 3566[7]
Perfect Pose (IRE) *Richard Hannon* 57
2 b f Amadeus Wolf Interpose (Indian Ridge)
5912[4] 6117[12]
Perfect Shot (IRE) *Michael Attwater* a61 94
6 b g High Chaparral(IRE) Zoom Lens (IRE) (Caerleon (USA))
150[7] 202[10] 594[5] 937[6] 1184[10] 8035[2]
Perfect Son *C Zeitz* 102
5 ch h Sabiango(GER) Pacific Blue (GER) (Bluebird (USA))
3206a[5]
Perfect Step (IRE) *Roger Varian* 94
3 b f Iffraaj Spiritual Air (Royal Applause)
(1472) 2022[2] 4497[3] 6161[17]
Perfect Tribute *Clive Cox* a94 108
4 b m Dubawi(IRE) Perfect Spirit (IRE) (Invincible Spirit (IRE))
1494[8] 2078[6] 2710[6] 5385[8]
Perfect Venture *Clive Cox* a58 68
2 b f Bahamian Bounty Perfect Cover (IRE) (Royal Applause)
5978[5] 7160[9] 7987[6] 8233[3]
Perfect Vision *Charlie Longsdon* a68 71
5 b m Starcraft(NZ) Auspicious (Shirley Heights)
129[8]
Perfect Words (IRE) *Marjorie Fife* a62 64
2 ch c Thousand Words Zilayah (USA) (Zilzal (USA))
1131[6] 1202[2] 1308[2] 1437[5] 1594[2] 3748[4] 4767[2] 5537[5] 6953[2] 7441[5]
Perforce *Lucy Wadham* 10
3 b g Sir Percy Enforce (USA) (Kalanisi (IRE))
7174[10]
Performing Pocket (USA) *David Simcock* a75 80
3 ch c Proud Citizen(USA) Holy Fashion (USA) (Holy Bull (USA))
(657) 867[6] 897[4] 5214[4]
Periphery (USA) *Mahmood Al Zarooni* a80 88
3 b c Elusive Quality(USA) Punctilious (Danehill (USA))
1261[5] 1450[3] 2042[2] 3393[9]
Periwinkle Way *Jim Boyle* a34 45
3 b f Acclamation Millsini (Rossini (USA))
376[5] 564[10] 2388[7]
Perlachy *Ronald Harris* a74 72
8 b g Kyllachy Perfect Dream (Emperor Jones (USA))
(406) 461[6] 718[5] 3761[4] (4236) 4492[9] 4887[3] 5502[8] 5971[6] 6277[8] 6824[10]
Perle Rose (FR) *Y De Nicolay* a80 81
3 b f Orpen(USA) Parole De Star (USA) (King Of Kings (IRE))
117a[0]
Permeate *Charles Hills* 64
2 b f Rail Link Quota (Rainbow Quest (USA))
6790[6]
Permit *Chris Waller* 105
5 b g Dansili Cochin (USA) (Swain (IRE))
7560a[12]
Perpetual Ambition *Paul D'Arcy* a63
2 b c Avonbridge Never Enough (GER) (Monsun (GER))
7707[9] 7900[5]
Perpetual Glory *Sir Henry Cecil* 56
2 b f Dansili Grail (USA) (Quest For Fame)
3590[12]
Perpignon (FR) *Mme C Janssen* a71 80
4 b g Numerous(USA) Pepples Beach (GER) (Lomitas)
16a[0]
Perrecalla (FR) *P Van De Poele* a83 90
2 ch f Anabaa Blue Pomposa (IRE) (Barathea (IRE))
3680a[6]
Persepolis (IRE) *Sir Michael Stoute* a75 54
2 b c Dansili La Persiana (Daylami (IRE))
6845[5] 7167[2]
Perseverent Pete (USA) *Christine Dunnett* a51 53
2 bb c Johannesburg(USA) Indian Halloween (USA) (Sunday Break (JPN))
3499[7] 3996[7] 4433[8] 6946[4] 7313[11]
Persian Buddy *Jamie Poulton* a31 7
6 b g Reel Buddy(USA) Breeze Again (USA) (Favorite Trick (USA))
760[8] 1083[6]
Persian Herald *William Muir* a54 75
4 gr g Proclamation(IRE) Persian Fortune (Forzando)
960[9] 1940[5] 3015[4] 5012[11]
Persian Marvel (IRE) *Jim Boyle* a52 53
2 b g Captain Marvelous(IRE) Jezyah (USA) (Chief's Crown (USA))
3117[5] 3637[9] 4330[5] 5160[7] 5403[6] 7156[4] 7821[3] 8007[4] 8155[7]
Persian Peril *Alan Swinbank* a75 91
8 br g Erhaab(USA) Brush Away (Ahonoora)
1239[5] (1880) 2180[15] 3125[10] 4072[11] 7455[11]
Persian Wave *James Tate* a52 66
2 b g Royal Applause Persian Sea (UAE) (Dubai Destination (USA))
3824[5] 4194[7] 4982[4] 6318[7] 6793[10]
Persidha *Derek Shaw* a67 69
3 b f Sir Percy Azizam (Singspiel (IRE))
(1006) 1393[3] 1529[8] 2730[4]
Personable *Mahmood Al Zarooni* 82
2 b c Cape Cross(IRE) Likeable (Dalakhani (IRE))
6596[7] 7172[2]
Personal Touch *Richard Fahey* 82
3 ch g Pivotal Validate (Alhaarth (IRE))
1317[2] 1858[4] 1998[3] 3288[4] 4075[6] 4588[3]
Personified (GER) *Mme J Bidgood* a69 97
5 b m Doyen(IRE) Proudeyes (GER) (Dashing Blade)
7829a[2]
Perspicace (FR) *N Leenders* a74 65
7 b m Sagacity(FR) Green Gem (BEL) (Pharly (FR))
93a[4]

Pertemps Networks *Michael Easterby* a82 81
8 b g Golden Snake(USA) Society Girl (Shavian)
601[6] 751[11] 1114[4] 1797[9] 7369[8] 7652[3] (7954) 7980[3]
Pertuis (IRE) *Micky Hammond* a81 72
6 gr g Verglas(IRE) Lady Killeen (IRE) (Marju (IRE))
1135[8] 1275[15] 1562[9] 2440[7] 3129[14] (3692) (5290) 6315[2] 6608[2]
Petaluma *Mick Channon* 79
3 b f Teofilo(IRE) Poppo's Song (CAN) (Polish Navy (USA))
1512[4] ◆ 1887[7] 2980[6] 3104[4] 4005[2] 5044[7] 5456[3] 6098[3] 6383[2] 6922[3] (7271)
Petara Bay (IRE) *Robert Mills* 111
8 b g Peintre Celebre(USA) Magnificent Style (USA) (Silver Hawk (USA))
3373[12] 3625[8] 4800[6]
Petella *George Moore* 74
6 b m Tamure(IRE) Miss Petronella (Petoski)
2978[4] 4176[6] 4925[6] 5384[3] 5922[5] 6101[4] 6407[6]
Peter Anders *Mark Johnston* a78 80
3 b c Pivotal Astorg (USA) (Lear Fan (USA))
1086[4] 1595[4] (1959) 2883[2] (3525)
Peter Island (FR) *John Gallagher* a78 77
9 b g Dansili Catania (USA) (Aloma's Ruler (USA))
(4980) 5791[9] 6303[8]
Peteron *Colin Teague* 46
4 b g Danbird(AUS) Lady Rock (Mistertopogigo (IRE))
3438[6] 3848[8] 4452[9] 4911[9] 7445[13]
Petersboden *Michael Blanshard* a59 38
3 b g Iceman Bowden Rose (Dashing Blade)
827[5] 981[7] 1377[5] 2162[15] 4232[8] 5037[11] 8179[3]
Peters Pleasure *Robert Cowell* a17 3
3 ch f Medicean Swynford Pleasure (Reprimand)
6274[10] 6951[13] 7326[12] 7378[9]
Peters Pursuit (IRE) *Richard Fahey* a33 59
3 ch g Bertolini(USA) Xarzee (IRE) (Xaar)
2540[11] 3025[10]
Pete The Pastor *Hughie Morrison* 69
4 b g Pastoral Pursuits Franciscaine (FR) (Legend Of France (USA))
3035[5]
Pether's Moon (IRE) *Richard Hannon* a83 43
2 b c Dylan Thomas(IRE) Softly Tread (IRE) (Tirol)
6572[7] 7323[2]
Petit Chevalier (FR) *W Mongil* a103 101
4 bb g High Chaparral(IRE) Pivoline (FR) (Pivotal)
7784a[2]
Petit Ecuyer (FR) *Gary Moore* a40 71
6 b g Equerry(USA) Petite Majeste (FR) (Riverquest (FR))
651[11]
Petite Georgia (IRE) *George Baker* a46 59
2 b f Camacho Petite Maxine (Sharpo)
2579[4] 3465[3] 4239[3]
Petite Noblesse (FR) *A Fabre* 107
3 b f Galileo(IRE) Flower Bowl (FR) (Anabaa (USA))
2109a[8] 3203a[9]
Petite Silhou (IRE) *A Marcialis* 58
2 b f Choisir(AUS) Finamai (IRE) (Royal Academy (USA))
6090a[8]
Petomic (IRE) *Daniel Mark Loughnane* a64 71
7 ch g Dubai Destination(USA) Petomi (Presidium)
104[4] (274) 333[11] 449[5] 603[2] 722[6] 922[8] 3236[10] 3712[10] 3775[12]
Petrarchan *Milton Bradley* a46 57
4 ch g Pivotal Summer Sonnet (Baillamont (USA))
1420[9] 1889[4] 2611[6] 3051[6] 3099[7] 3949[8] 4993[12] 5261[4] 5659[3] 5935[14]
Petrocelli *Wilf Storey* a49 59
5 b g Piccolo Sarcita (Primo Dominie)
3309[2] 3889[8] 4350[5] 4594[6] 4869[2] 5672[3] 6956[11] 7443[2] 7599[4]
Petrol *David O'Meara* 39
3 ch g Danehill Dancer(IRE) Pongee (Barathea (IRE))
5708[7]
Petsas Pleasure *Ollie Pears* a50 69
6 b g Observatory(USA) Swynford Pleasure (Reprimand)
1251[6] 2035[4] 2535[8] 2692[13] 3589[10] 4350[6]
Pettochside *Stuart Williams* a72 70
3 b g Refuse To Bend(IRE) Clear Impression (IRE) (Danehill (USA))
(41) ◆ 1412[6] 3488[4] 4197[4] 4798[6] 5205[2] 5662[2] 5915[4] ◆ (6173)
Phair Winter *Alan Brown* a40 54
4 b m Sleeping Indian Tuppenny Blue (Pennekamp (USA))
1953[8] 2335[12]
Phantom Prince (IRE) *Brendan Powell* a37
3 b g Jeremy(USA) Phantom Waters (Pharly (FR))
8080[7]
Phantom Ranch *Hughie Morrison* a47 61
3 b g Act One Highbrook (USA) (Alphabatim (USA))
3227[8] 3664[8] (4744) 5744[8]
Pharoh Jake *John Bridger* a64 54
4 ch g Piccolo Rose Amber (Double Trigger (IRE))
118[2] 297[6] 396[8] 467[4] 782[3] 986[10] 1183[3] 1787[5] 3390[8] 3717[4] 4059[3] 4237[2] 4467[6] 4943[6] 5531[7] 6307[7] 6771[4] 7703[6] 7929[2] (8045) (8107) 8168[9] (8184)
Phase Shift *Brian Ellison* a53 64
4 b m Iceman Silent Waters (Polish Precedent (USA))
3775[8] 4455[7] 5638[3] 5939[3] 6323[8] (7245) 7602[4]
Phebes Wish (IRE) *John C McConnell* a65 74
3 b g Diamond Green(FR) Kathoe (IRE) (Fayruz)
(1337) 4953[2]
Philharmonic Hall *Richard Fahey* a52 68
4 b g Victory Note(USA) Lambast (Relkino)
401[6]
Philipstown *Richard Hannon* a69 84
3 ch g Notnowcato Tahara (IRE) (Caerleon (USA))
1452[11] 2246[11] (2557) (4233)

Phils Wish (IRE) *John C McConnell* a58 46
3 b g Dark Angel(IRE) Red Titian (IRE) (Titus Livius (FR))
7457[11] 7616[2]

Phluke *Eve Johnson Houghton* a56 69
11 b g Most Welcome Phlirty (Pharly (FR))
1771[5] 2389[9] 4722[10] 5148[8] 5996[6] 6302[5]

Phoebe's Perfect *Neil Mulholland* a1 28
2 b f Tobougg(IRE) Water Flower (Environment Friend)
4946[11] 5656[6] 7506[11]

Phoenix Clubs (IRE) *Paul Midgley* a56 79
3 b f Red Clubs(IRE) Hollow Haze (USA) (Woodman (USA))
898[4] 1252[2] 1817[3] 2256[6] (3404) 4558[7] 4793[12] 5257[2] 5728[2] 6123[14] 6605[3] (7100) 7451[10]

Phoenix Flame *Brendan Powell* a61 59
4 ch m Phoenix Reach(IRE) Generosia (Generous (IRE))
7[4] 454[6] 675[5] 2804[11]

Phoenix Flight (IRE) *James Evans* a92 93
7 b g Hawk Wing(USA) Firecrest (IRE) (Darshaan)
554[5] 7109[11]

Phonic (IRE) *John Dunlop* a69 70
5 ch g Green Tune(USA) Superfonic (FR) (Zafonic (USA))
2502[2] 3283[5] 3961[9] 4915[6]

Photo Opportunity *Alastair Lidderdale* a66 88
5 b g Zamindar(USA) Fame At Last (USA) (Quest For Fame)
391[9] 520[9]

Phuket (SPA) *J L De Salas*
3 ch c Multazem(USA) New Vert (SPA) (Vert Amande (FR))
5252a[2]

Piazza San Pietro *Zoe Davison* a59 98
6 ch g Compton Place Rainbow Spectrum (FR) (Spectrum (IRE))
2446[3] 3078[8] 3641[13] 4799[16] 6346[4] 6382[4]

Picabo (IRE) *Henry Candy* a72 98
4 b m Elusive City(USA) Gi La High (Rich Charlie)
1936[5] 2494[5] 3822[2] (4437) (5065) ◆ 6244[7]

Picalily *David Evans* a57
3 b f Piccolo Kaylianni (Kalanisi (IRE))
107[4] 195[4]

Picansort *Peter Crate* a73 60
5 b g Piccolo Running Glimpse (IRE) (Runnett)
87[10] 252[8] 425[2] 528[2] 710[2] 890[3] 3390[10] 5791[2] 7308[10] 8054[4] 8225[3]

Picante (IRE) *C Boutin* a72 80
3 b f Bertolini(USA) Undertone (IRE) (Noverre (USA))
17a[5] 865a[2]

Picayune (GER) *A Wohler* 89
2 b f Manduro(GER) Panagia (USA) (Diesis)
6522a[4]

Picc Of Burgau *Joseph Tuite* 28
2 b f Piccolo Rosein (Komaite (USA))
3638[8]

Piccolo Express *Brian Baugh* a68 60
6 b g Piccolo Ashfield (Zilzal (USA))
153[6] 232[2] (550) 1002[3] 1830[7] 2354[3] 2811[11] 6216[7] 7224[2] 7670[6] 7917[6] 8115[3]

Piceno (IRE) *Scott Dixon* a83 80
4 b g Camacho Ascoli (Skyliner)
134[2] 304[6] 585[4] 674[6] 899[4] 1135[16] 1520[4] 1917[6] 6812[7] (7246) 7452[3] 7607[2] 7935[4]

Pick A Little *Michael Blake* a83 84
4 b g Piccolo Little Caroline (IRE) (Great Commotion (USA))
64[5] 157[4] (368) 652[8] 896[6] 1117[7] 1254[13] 1614[6] 2146[9] (2809) 4155[10] (5245) 5703[7] 6044[6] 6465[7] 6800[10] 7274[8] 7412[12]

Pick Three *Roger Charlton*
3 ch c Three Valleys(USA) Magic Number (Dansili)
1567[15]

Picture Dealer *Gary Moore* a71 87
3 b g Royal Applause Tychy (Suave Dancer (USA))
2147[5] 2542[3] (2996) ◆ 3566[2] 4221[5] (4985) 5906[2] 6432[7] 6800[13]

Picura *Ralph Beckett* 54
3 ch f King's Best(USA) Picolette (Piccolo)
2386[2]

Piddie's Power *Ed McMahon* a83 88
5 ch m Starcraft(NZ) Telori (Muhtarram (USA))
1587[10] 1827[6] (2493) 3500[4] 4655[7] 5326[2] 6009[4] 6820[6]

Piece Of Cake *Charles Hills* a68
3 b f Exceed And Excel(AUS) Sundae Girl (USA) (Green Dancer (USA))
298[2] 1736[5] 2865[7] 3940[9]

Pie Poudre *Roy Brotherton* a63 54
5 ch g Zafeen(FR) Eglantine (IRE) (Royal Academy (USA))
306[8] 633[12] 995[9] 1487[10]

Pierro (AUS) *Gai Waterhouse* 122
3 b c Lonhro(AUS) Miss Right Note (IRE) (Daylami (IRE))
7426a[3]

Piers Gaveston (IRE) *George Baker* 67
3 b g Amadeus Wolf Dancing Tempo (Vettori (IRE))
1607[7]

Pigeon Catcher (IRE) *Mme Pia Brandt* a100 91
3 ch c Dutch Art Jakarta Jade (IRE) (Royal Abjar (USA))
7985a[6]

Pilarcita *Ollie Pears* a23 16
3 b f Boogie Street Lempicka (Bahamian Bounty)
3848[9] 4144[6] 5823[9]

Pilgrim Dancer (IRE) *Tony Coyle* a66 51
5 b g Danehill Dancer(IRE) Pilgrim's Way (USA) (Gone West (USA))
14[4] 46[3] 226[2] 368[3] 447[6] 640[3] 3442[17] 3692[10] 4716[10]

Pilgrims Rest (IRE) *Richard Hannon* a88 95
3 ch c Rock Of Gibraltar(IRE) Holly Blue (Bluebird (USA))
(2235) (2552) 3296[5] 4009[4] 4735[10] 5273[4] 5888[4] 6376[2]

Pill Boy *Dai Burchell* a23
4 b g Auction House(USA) Tymeera (Timeless Times (USA))
37[7]

Pimpernel (IRE) *Mahmood Al Zarooni* a101 107
3 b f Invincible Spirit(IRE) Anna Pallida (Sadler's Wells (USA))
418a[2] 680a[5] 1454[11] 3270[5]

Pinarius (IRE) *Brian Meehan* a75 68
2 b c Amadeus Wolf Cantaloupe (Priolo (USA))
3662[5] 6020[15] 6301[3] (6841) 7053[11]

Pinball (IRE) *Lisa Williamson* a54 59
6 b m Namid Luceball (IRE) (Bluebird (USA))
1881[7] 2350[5] 3020[6] 4262[6] 4929[4] 5719[9]

Pindar (GER) *Barney Curley* a64 57
8 b g Tertullian(USA) Pierette (GER) (Local Suitor (USA))
2013[5] (3137) 3573[4] 4296[11] (4817) 7596[7]

Pindrop *Clive Cox* a24 57
3 ch f Exceed And Excel(AUS) Why So Silent (Mill Reef (USA))
1357[15] 3044[12] 3510[5] ◆ 4493[7] 4793[14] 5850[9] 7615[12]

Pink Anabella (FR) *J-M Beguigne* a78 98
3 b f Anabaa(USA) Pink Cloud (FR) (Octagonal (NZ))
1127a[3]

Pink Anemone *David Lanigan* a58
2 b f Dansili Crystal Reef (King's Best (USA))
7459[3]

Pink Belini *Alan McCabe* a46 39
3 ch f Phoenix Reach(IRE) Pink Supreme (Night Shift (USA))
182[10] 3568[8] 4705[8] 5017[9]

Pink Cadillac (IRE) *Ben Haslam* 32
2 b f Clodovil(IRE) Green Life (Green Desert (USA))
3208[12] 3747[11] 6049[11]

Pink Damsel (IRE) *Roger Varian* 82
3 b f Galileo(IRE) Riskaverse (USA) (Dynaformer (USA))
(2249) ◆ 3292[11] 6202[10]

Pink Delight (IRE) *J S Moore* a38
3 ch f Rock Of Gibraltar(IRE) Turkana Girl (Hernando (FR))
206[8]

Pink Evie *Gay Kelleway* a53
3 ch f Dutch Art Cressida (Polish Precedent (USA))
61[6] 182[5] 459[6] 727[2] 847[7]

Pink Gin (FR) *J-P Gauvin* 107
5 b h Kouroun(FR) Pink Cloud (FR) (Octagonal (NZ))
4229a[6] 7234a[4]

Pink Lips *J R Jenkins* a22 53
4 b m Noverre(USA) Primrose Queen (Lear Fan (USA))
5687[6] (6345) 6967[4] 7500[14] 7815[10]

Pink Mischief *Harry Dunlop* a19 53
2 gr f Holy Roman Emperor(IRE) Feather (USA) (Unbridled's Song (USA))
4463[10] 5274[10] 5932[9] (6435)

Pinot *Richard Fahey* 13
3 b g Desert Style(IRE) Rosablanca (IRE) (Sinndar (IRE))
2095[14] 2381[10]

Pinotage *Peter Niven* a67 65
4 br g Danbird(AUS) Keen Melody (USA) (Sharpen Up)
2588[8] 3353[4] 4626[3] 5226[4] 5622[8]

Pinseeker (IRE) *Brendan Powell* a28 66
3 b g Oratorio(IRE) Estivau (USA) (Lear Fan (USA))
2390[4] 2818[8]

Pintrada *James Bethell* 81
4 b g Tiger Hill(IRE) Ballymore Celebre (IRE) (Peintre Celebre (USA))
1295[12] 2031[3] 2419[13] (3459)

Pintura *Kevin Ryan* a97 108
5 ch g Efisio Picolette (Piccolo)
868[9] 1130[14] 1510[13] (2025) 2472[4] 2910[2] 4692a[2] (4833a) 6468[10] 6913a[4]

Pioneer Boy (USA) *Alan Swinbank* 27
3 ch g Pioneering(USA) Vieille Rose (IRE) (Dancing Spree (USA))
1878[10] 2240[3]

Piper Cherokee *Michael Easterby* a24
3 ch f Lucky Story(USA) Miss Twiddles (IRE) (Desert King (IRE))
195[10] 404[7]

Piper's Lass (IRE) *Mark Johnston* a75
2 b f Singspiel(IRE) Dunloskin (Selkirk (USA))
4646[4] (4886)

Pipers Note *Richard Whitaker* 76
2 ch g Piccolo Madam Valentine (Primo Valentino (IRE))
4344[11] 5367[5] (6360) 6920[5]

Pipers Piping (IRE) *John Butler* a76 67
6 b g Noverre(USA) Monarchy (IRE) (Common Grounds)
91[6] 287[2] 330[4] (384) 401[4] 463[2] 584[9] 6319[11] 6812[13] 7142[11] 7618[11] 7799[11] 7993[10]

Pippy *Tom Dascombe* a67 68
2 b c Exceed And Excel(AUS) Gandini (Night Shift (USA))
1972[8] 2747[7] 2970[2] 4625[4] (5178) 5890[5] 6451[5] 8103[7] 8211[5]

Pira Palace (IRE) *Sir Michael Stoute* a78 77
2 b f Acclamation Takrice (Cadeaux Genereux)
2541[4] 3554[3] 4507[5] 5236[2] 5946[4] (6541) (7164)

Pirate Chest (IRE) *Patrick Holmes* a76 67
4 b g Montjeu(IRE) Cash Run (USA) (Seeking The Gold (USA))
3038[6] 4621[12] 6047[9] 6141[12] 6711[10]

Pirika (IRE) *A Fabre* 110
4 b m Monsun(GER) Paita (Intikhab (USA))
(4386a) 5116a[6] 6295a[2] 6911a[4]

Piri Wango (IRE) *G M Lyons* a104 104
3 ch g Choisir(AUS) Zoldan (Deploy)
3294[5] 4063[6] 6079a[8]

Piscean (USA) *Tom Keddy* a104 93
7 bb g Stravinsky(USA) Navasha (USA) (Woodman (USA))
89[6] 253[5] (431) 527[4] 871[4] (962) 1885[24] 2444[2] 2707[6] 3004[6] 3571[9] 4437[8] 4799[20] 5320[4] (5557) 5832[14] 6382[7] (8272)

Pisco Sour (USA) *Saeed Bin Suroor* a34 114
4 bb g Lemon Drop Kid(USA) Lynnwood Chase (USA) (Horse Chestnut (SAF))
488a[11] 879a[12] 3900a[6] 6575[5]

Piste *Tina Jackson* a68 60
6 b m Falbrav(IRE) Arctic Char (Polar Falcon (USA))
4245[6] 4452[7] (4911) 4957[2] 5294[7] 5542[5] 5590[7] 6786[4] 7099[11] 7178[2] 7446[16] 7456[8] 7634[5]

Pistol (IRE) *Sir Michael Stoute* a77 82
3 b g High Chaparral(IRE) Alinea (USA) (Kingmambo (USA))
1301[2] 2288[2] 2708[3] 3592[8] 4294[3]

Pitkin *Michael Easterby* a65 77
4 b g Proclamation(IRE) Princess Oberon (IRE) (Fairy King (USA))
696[5] 911[5] 1002[4] 1154[5] 1830[4] 2455[11] (2696) (2981) (3209) 3496[4] 3845[7]

Pittodrie Star (IRE) *David O'Meara* a87 87
5 ch g Choisir(AUS) Jupiter Inlet (IRE) (Jupiter Island)
1239[2] 1421[2] 1846[8]

Pius Parker (IRE) *John Gallagher* a60 72
3 b g Antonius Pius(USA) Parker's Cove (USA) (Woodman (USA))
1259[3] 2089[6] 2367[8] 2786[7] 3005[9]

Pivotal Movement *Richard Hannon* 76
2 ch c Pivotal Selinka (Selkirk (USA))
6481[6] 6787[6] (7110)

Pivotal Prospect *Tracy Waggott* a13 73
4 b m Nayef(USA) Buon Amici (Pivotal)
114[9] 1248[8] 1881[6] 2122[3] (2244) ◆ 3211[6] 3815[2] 5257[4] 5548[3] (6783)

Pivotal Silence *Amanda Perrett* a60 61
2 ch f Vita Rosa(JPN) Tara Moon (Pivotal)
5352[10] 5977[8] 6366[7] 6946[8] 7505[8]

Pivotman *Amanda Perrett* 101
4 ch g Pivotal Grandalea (Grand Lodge (USA))
2655[9] 3635[13] 4112[18] 4684[16] 6484[16] 6987[6] 7300[12]

Pixilated *Gay Kelleway* a69 74
2 b g Phoenix Reach(IRE) Chocolada (Namid)
1949[3] 2638[6] (3046) 3242[21] 4936[4] 8245[2]

Place In My Heart *George Baker* a85 97
3 ch f Compton Place Lonely Heart (Midyan (USA))
1921[2] 2893[4] 3486[2] 4063[2] 4765[14] 6602[9] 6878[7] 7690[17]

Place That Face *Hughie Morrison* a64
3 b f Compton Place Notjustaprettyface (USA) (Red Ransom (USA))
219[2] 499[3] 6806[2] 7611[3] (7804)

Planchette *Jane Chapple-Hyam* 47
2 b f Mount Nelson Cruinn A Bhord (Inchinor)
5550[11] 6437[6] 7468[5]

Planet Elder *X Nakkachdji* a88 96
4 b g Cape Cross(IRE) Celestial Lagoon (JPN) (Sunday Silence (USA))
5118a[7] (6804a) (7551a)

Planetex (IRE) *John Quinn* 81
3 b g Majestic Missile(IRE) Xena (IRE) (Mull Of Kintyre (USA))
2695[9] 2918[6] (3289) (5318) 5538[8] 7177[3] 7291[12]

Planetoid (IRE) *David Lanigan* a90 92
4 b g Galileo(IRE) Palmeraie (USA) (Lear Fan (USA))
2561[5] 3502[7]

Plantagenet (SPA) *G Arizkorreta Elosegui* a105 102
5 ch h Trade Fair Crafty Buzz (USA) (Crafty Prospector (USA))
143a[6] ◆ 421a[8] (618a) ◆

Planteur (IRE) *Marco Botti* a119 124
5 b h Danehill Dancer(IRE) Plante Rare (IRE) (Giant's Causeway (USA))
1150a[3] 2533a[2] 3267[7] 5490[7]

Plastiki *Sir Michael Stoute* 71
3 b g Oasis Dream Dayrose (Daylami (IRE))
1754[5] 2279[7] 2942[2]

Platinum Proof (USA) *John Berry* a66 16
2 bb c Smart Strike(CAN) Keeper Hill (USA) (Deputy Minister (CAN))
7127[12] 7899[11] 8134[4]

Plattsburgh (USA) *Mark Johnston* a79 84
4 bb g Bernardini(USA) Saranac Lake (USA) (Smart Strike (CAN))
187[10]

Playbill *Sir Michael Stoute* a57
2 b f Medicean Set The Scene (IRE) (Sadler's Wells (USA))
6535[6]

Play Street *Jonathan Portman* a60 81
3 ch f Tobougg(IRE) Zoena (Emarati (USA))
185[4] 573[2] 1853[3] 2448[4] (4057) (4486) 5218[9] 6450[10] 7116[7]

Play The Blues (IRE) *Roger Curtis* a52 71
5 gr m Refuse To Bend(IRE) Paldouna (IRE) (Kaldoun (FR))
3705[10] 4812[3] 6334[6] 7964[7] 8180[7] 8299[5]

Play Tiger (FR) *David Simcock* a44 49
3 b g Tiger Hill(IRE) Shagadellic (USA) (Devil's Bag (USA))
1518[9] 1793[7] 2560[8]

Plaza Mayor (FR) *F Rossi* 91
2 b f Kyllachy Baby Houseman (Oasis Dream)
5248a[3] 7430a[5]

Pleasant Day (IRE) *Richard Fahey* a87 98
5 b g Noverre(USA) Sunblush (UAE) (Timber Country (USA))
1854[6] 2257[13] 3493[13] 6405[9]

Pleasant Moment *Tom Dascombe* a48 34
2 b f Rakti Italian Affair (Fumo Di Londra (IRE))
4654[11] 5410[10] 5828[7] 7021[6] 7785[9]

Pleasure Bent *Luca Cumani* 51
2 b c Dansili Nitya (FR) (Indian Ridge)
6636[11]

Pleine Forme (USA) *A De Royer-Dupre* a96 99
4 bb m Grand Slam(USA) Why Worry (FR) (Cadeaux Genereux)
7624a[14]

Plenum (GER) *David Lanigan* a66
2 b c Shamardal(USA) Prima Luce (IRE) (Galileo (IRE))
7807[5] 7962[7] 8033[4]

Plexolini *Jo Hughes* a43 54
2 b g Multiplex Beverley Bell (Bertolini (USA))
3140[8] 3545[6] 4654[7] 5010[5] 5654[3] 6155[5] 6511[3] 6953[10] 7439[7]

Plovdiv (FR) *E Leenders* a87 87
2 b c Hurricane Cat(USA) Septieme Face (USA) (Lit De Justice (USA))
7984a[0]

Plug In Baby *Nick Mitchell* a43 46
4 b m Xaar Medinaceli (IRE) (Grand Lodge (USA))
3216[7] 4004[7]

Plumbago Blue *John Butler* a56
3 b f Manduro(GER) Pinacotheque (IRE) (In The Wings)
1065[5] 1532[8] 2008[5] 4153[13]

Plum Bay *David Elsworth* a65 64
3 ch f Nayef(USA) Pelican Key (IRE) (Mujadil (USA))
3071[9] 3665[9] (4777) 5157[2] 5764[5] 6823[7] 7316[12]

Plum Pretty (USA) *Bob Baffert* a121
4 b m Medaglia d'Oro(USA) Liszy (USA) (A.P. Indy (USA))
1839a[3]

Plunder *Kevin Ryan* a80
2 ch c Zamindar(USA) Reaching Ahead (USA) (Mizzen Mast (USA))
(7807) 8223[4]

Plus Fours (USA) *Charles Smith* a68 19
3 rg g Mizzen Mast(USA) Quick To Please (USA) (Danzig (USA))
959[3] 1981[6] 4630[10] 5208[2] 5891[7] 6474[13] 7062[8] 7632[14] 7752[10]

Plutocracy (IRE) *David Lanigan* a68 62
2 b c Dansili Private Life (FR) (Bering)
6636[17] 6928[6] 7507[7]

Pobs Trophy *Richard Guest* a23 54
5 b g Umistim Admonish (Warning)
446[7]

Pocket Too *Victor Dartnall* a57 65
9 b g Fleetwood(IRE) Pocket Venus (IRE) (King's Theatre (IRE))
1952[2] 7077[14]

Podgies Boy (IRE) *Richard Fahey* a82 69
4 b g Statue Of Liberty(USA) Lake Victoria (IRE) (Lake Coniston (IRE))
(115) 304[4]

Poem (IRE) *Andrew Balding* a39
2 ch f Dylan Thomas(IRE) Almarai (USA) (Vaguely Noble)
7923[9]

Poeme Du Berlais (FR) *D Prod'Homme* a72 85
4 gr g Great Pretender(IRE) Boheme Du Berlais (FR) (Simon Du Desert (FR))
2685a[9]

Poet *Clive Cox* a48 118
7 b g Pivotal Hyabella (Shirley Heights)
1245a[6] 1677[2] 2989a[4] (4094)

Poetic Belle *Alan Jarvis* a58 57
2 b f Byron Sahariri (IRE) (Red Ransom (USA))
3764[4] 4525[8] 5947[9] 6253[6] 6583[7] 7056[6]

Poetic Dancer *Clive Cox* a91 94
3 ch f Byron Crozon (Peintre Celebre (USA))
2263[11] 5980[4] 6676[16] 7508[6] 7774[5] 8098[5]

Poetic Lord *Richard Hannon* a79 90
3 b c Byron Jumairah Sun (IRE) (Scenic)
2269[11] 2897[9] 3446[6] 4517[5] 5630[7] 5838[2] 6207[8] 7170[3] 7376[3] 7644[8] 7805[7] 8252[7]

Poetic Power (IRE) *Ian Williams* a70 79
3 b g Dylan Thomas(IRE) Chalice Wells (Sadler's Wells (USA))
1312[6] 2393[6] 3072[4] 4606[11] 5018[3] 8137[6]

Poetic Princess *Jo Hughes* a70 70
2 b f Byron April Lee (Superpower)
1136[3] 1188[2] 1495[2] 2047[3] 2541[5] 2790[6] (4140) 4574[11] 5716[4] 6583[2] 7432[7]

Poetic Star *Ben Haslam* 46
2 b g Byron Balwarah (IRE) (Soviet Star (USA))
2308[7] 2923[7] 3436[13] 7432[11]

Poetic Verse *Rod Millman* a54 57
2 gr f Byron Nina Fontenail (FR) (Kaldounevees (FR))
2124[7] 2384[5] 3387[2] 4847[5] 5236[3] 5716[2] 6156[4] 7919[9] 8112[4]

Poetry Writer *Michael Blanshard* a68 61
3 ch g Byron Away To Me (Exit To Nowhere (USA))
2557[7] 2756[10] 3762[11] 4490[3] 5229[11] 5983[6] 6230[3] 7632[10] 7752[9]

Point At Issue (IRE) *David Nicholls* a64 69
3 b g One Cool Cat(USA) Atishoo (IRE) (Revoque (IRE))
6[2] 748[5] 975[4] (1169) 1353[4] 2438[8]

Point Blank (GER) *Mario Hofer* 107
4 b g Royal Dragon(USA) Princess Li (GER) (Monsun (GER))
1410a[6] 2222a[7] 6906a[3] 7587a[4] 7784a[4]

Point North (IRE) *John Balding* a94 86
5 b g Danehill Dancer(IRE) Briolette (IRE) (Sadler's Wells (USA))
1522[9] 1863[13] 3037[6] 3812[7] 4190[7] 6256[9] 7827[10]

Point Of Control *Michael Bell* a44
2 b f Pivotal Finlaggan (Be My Chief (USA))
7720[10]

Point Of Entry (USA) *Claude McGaughey III* 123
4 b h Dynaformer(USA) Matlacha Pass (USA) (Seeking The Gold (USA))
7573a[2]

Poisson D'Or *Rae Guest* a72 84
3 b f Cape Cross(IRE) Lille Hammer (Sadler's Wells (USA))
2042[4] (2935) 3542[7] 4764[14] 6830[11] 7334[12]

Poitin *Harry Dunlop* a66 64
2 b f Kheleyf(USA) Port Providence (Red Ransom (USA))
5153[5] 6489[9] 7706[3]

Pokalde (FR) *P Favereaux* 26
3 b c Sakkaline(IRE) Fleur Story (FR) (Glaieul (USA))
7266a[8]

Poker Hospital *John Stimpson* a66 76
3 b f Rock Of Gibraltar(IRE) Empress Anna (IRE) (Imperial Ballet (IRE))
(1419) 1733[7] 2136[11] 4726[11] 5426[10] 7524[8] 7781[13] 7982[10]

Pokfulham (IRE) *Jim Goldie* a51 83
6 b g Mull Of Kintyre(USA) Marjinal (Marju (IRE))
1382[3] 1822[4] (2242) 2842[2] 3129[9] (3535) 5540[13] 6428[6]

Polar Annie *Jim Goldie* a59 84
7 b m Fraam Willisa (Polar Falcon (USA))
1066[9] 2342[4] 2597[9] 3334[4] 3522[4] 4673[4] 5082[3] 5539[9] 6709[7]

Polar Auroras *Tony Carroll* a63 64
4 b m Iceman Noor El Houdah (IRE) (Fayruz)
39[4] 262[6] 561[0] 633[6] 842[3] 1004[4] 2385[3] 3153[7] (3318) 3950[6] 4531[5] 4843[3] 5175[7]

Polar Chief *Linda Stubbs* 76
2 b g Motivator Polar Storm (IRE) (Law Society (USA))
(4427) (7209)

Polar Forest *Richard Guest* a57
2 br g Kyllachy Woodbeck (Terimon)
8233[6] 8254[4]

Polarix *H-A Pantall* a88 97
6 gr h Linamix(FR) Freezing (USA) (Bering)
6804a[2]

Polar Kite (IRE) *Richard Fahey* a83 95
4 b g Marju(IRE) Irina (IRE) (Polar Falcon (USA))
2311[8] 3128[17] 7751[12] (7961)

Polar Venture *William Haggas* a67
3 b g Invincible Spirit(IRE) Sharplaw Venture (Polar Falcon (USA))
7668[3] (7903) 8183[5]

Polemica (IRE) *Frank Sheridan* a72 21
6 b m Rock Of Gibraltar(IRE) Lady Scarlett (Woodman (USA))
106[4] 212[5]

Polhem *John Dunlop* 30
2 b c Dansili Mondschein (Rainbow Quest (USA))
5304[10]

Polimere (FR) *E Libaud* a74 85
4 b m Poliglote Kadance Ring (IRE) (Bering)
1172a[4]

Polish Crown *Mark Johnston* a78 72
2 b f Royal Applause Czarna Roza (Polish Precedent (USA))
4960[2] ◆ 5382[2] 5858a[3] 6282[3] 6998[4] 7613[7]

Polish World (USA) *Paul Midgley* a43 92
8 b g Danzig(USA) Welcometotheworld (USA) (Woodman (USA))
1156[22] 1220[6] 2142[6] (2632) 3128[10] 3403[2] 3812[5] 4589[8] 5057[7] 5819[8] 6338[4] 6665[8] 7083[14] 7453[4]

Politbureau *Michael Easterby* a55 59
5 b g Red Ransom(USA) Tereshkova (USA) (Mr Prospector (USA))
1831[6] (2669) 3310[2] 3752[7] 4179[13] 4869[3] 5226[10] 6361[4] 6885[4] 7245[8]

Polly Adler *Alastair Lidderdale* a48
5 b m Fantastic Light(USA) Urania (Most Welcome)
1045[7] 1107[7] 1299[12] 1443[5] 4061[13]

Pollyana (IRE) *D Prod'Homme* 112
3 b f Whipper(USA) Shamah (Unfuwain (USA))
7515a[4]

Polly Holder (IRE) *Paul D'Arcy* a63 59
4 b m Peintre Celebre(USA) Love Emerald (USA) (Mister Baileys)
937[4] 1057[2] 1794[11] 2348[8] 3216[4] 3449[9]

Polly Pease *Nikki Evans*
3 b f Sakhee(USA) Exotic Forest (Dominion)
1716[9] 3232[9]

Polly's Love (IRE) *Clive Cox* a52 70
2 b f Antonius Pius(USA) Kotdiji (Mtoto)
4739[10] 6664[3] 7159[11]

Polski Max *Richard Fahey* a86 87
2 b g Kyllachy Quadrophenia (College Chapel)
1218[3] 1753[2] (2402) 3242[10] 4116[5] 4836[5] 5515[12] 6162[12] (7028)

Polurrian (IRE) *David O'Meara* a50 69
5 b g Oasis Dream Kincob (USA) (Kingmambo (USA))
976[4] 1429[4] 1867[3] 2260[8] 2751[13] 3310[10] 5054[6] 5714[5]

Polydamos *Tony Carroll* a48 73
3 b g Nayef(USA) Spotlight (Dr Fong (USA))
1206[8] 2129[7] 2445[4] 4214[8]

Polygon (USA) *John Gosden* a94 106
4 b m Dynaformer(USA) Polaire (IRE) (Polish Patriot (USA))
1848[8] 2711[9] (3632) (6877) 7510[8]

Poly Pomona *Richard Hannon* 62
3 b f Green Desert(USA) Maganda (IRE) (Sadler's Wells (USA))
2483[7] 2935[5] 3666[10] 4486[6] 4850[10]

Pomarine (USA) *Amanda Perrett* a48 64
3 b f Aptitude(USA) Diese (USA) (Diesis)
6154[4] 6827[6]

Pompeia *Ralph Beckett* a77 82
2 ch f Singspiel(IRE) Caesarea (GER) (Generous (IRE))
3474[2] 4246[3] (4946) 6775[5]

Pont A Marcq (FR) *J Heloury* a72
3 b g Russian Blue(IRE) Pausanias (FR) (Gold Away (IRE))
290a[0] 476a[0]

Pont Des Arts (FR) *A Schaerer* a96 106
8 b h Kingsalsa(USA) Magic Arts (IRE) (Fairy King (USA))
443a[8] 630a[8] 5613a[7]

Ponte Di Rosa *Michael Appleby* a44 66
4 b m Avonbridge Ridgewood Ruby (IRE) (Indian Ridge)
151[9] 3086[2] (3316) 3579[6] 6019[7] 6478[8] 7077[15]

Pont Marie (FR) *F Chappet* a81 85
2 b c Great Journey(JPN) Cite Fleurie (IRE) (Mark Of Esteem (IRE))
5073a[2] 5698a[5] (7700a) 7984a[0]

Pont Menai *J R Jenkins* a49 29
3 b g Vital Equine(IRE) Carranita (IRE) (Anita's Prince)
2172[9] 2800[6] 3975[7]

Pont Neuilly (FR) *Y De Nicolay* a80 76
2 ch c Medecis Panzella (FR) (Kahyasi)
7283a[6] 7984a[2] 8192a[2]

Ponty Acclaim (IRE) *Tim Easterby* 104
3 b f Acclamation Leopard Creek (Weldnaas (USA))
2212[2] ◆ 3238[12] 4113[6] 4838[5] 5487[7] 5822[9] 6557[3] 6869[3] 7243[15] 7397[10]

Poole Harbour (IRE) *Richard Hannon* a95 95
3 b g Elusive City(USA) Free Lance (IRE) (Grand Lodge (USA))
1450[5] 1852[6] (2543) (3571) 4286[5] 4799[12] 5363[3] 6075[18] 6536[2] 6835[14]

Pool Play (CAN) *Mark Casse* a117 111
7 bb h Silver Deputy(CAN) Zuri Ridge (USA) (Cox's Ridge (USA))
7576a[0]

Poontoon (IRE) *Richard Fahey* a47 63
3 gr g Clodovil(IRE) Tahtheeb (IRE) (Muhtarram (USA))
2262[11] 4263[2] 5170[6] 5547[3]

Poor Duke (IRE) *Jamie Osborne* a62 74
2 b g Bachelor Duke(USA) Graze On Too (IRE) (Rainbow Quest (USA))
3948[4] 4967[2] 6841[7] 7103[4]

Po Po Poker Face (IRE) *Ms K Stenefeldt* a89
5 b g Whipper(USA) Sheer Dane (IRE) (Danehill (USA))
3654a[2]

Poppa Loves Mambo (USA) *Kathy Ritvo*
3 b c Black Mambo(USA) Sparkling Speed (USA) (Entropy (USA))
8100a[8]

Poppanella (IRE) *Lawrence Mullaney*
3 b f Namid Bobanlyn (IRE) (Dance Of Life (USA))
5823[8]

Poppet's Passion *R Pritchard-Gordon* 75
3 b f Clodovil(IRE) Our Poppet (IRE) (Warning)
4477a[3]

Poppy Bond *Chris Fairhurst* 64
2 b f Misu Bond(IRE) Matilda Peace (Namaqualand (USA))
(2123) 6130[7] 7635[4]

Poppy Golightly *Declan Carroll* a56 40
5 ch m Compton Place Popocatepetl (FR) (Nashwan (USA))
151[5] 333[8] 503[5] 837[11] 3712[3] 4390[8] 4890[7] 6127[12] 6969[6] 7221[6]

Poppy's Purse *Ollie Pears* 15
2 b f Indesatchel(IRE) Prospering (Prince Sabo)
2770[11] 3747[13] 4449[5] 5108[6]

Popular *Sir Henry Cecil* a81 85
3 b f Oasis Dream Midsummer (Kingmambo (USA))
1503[7] 2249[8] (2848) 4608[4] 5328[7] 5951[4]

Porcini *Philip McBride* a82 72
3 b f Azamour(IRE) Portal (Hernando (FR))
1363[5] 2144[3] 3793[12] 4296[13] 4776[5] 6146[3] (6365) (6691) ◆ (7024) 7367[9]

Porgy *Brian Ellison* a89 93
7 b g Dansili Light Ballet (Sadler's Wells (USA))
2257[12] 2887[7] (4884) 5211[2]

Port Charlotte *Hughie Morrison* a72 72
3 b f Oasis Dream Maria Theresa (Primo Dominie)
2483[4] ◆ 3189[2] 4797[6] 5913[4] 6229[8] 6891[6] 8082[5] 8273[7]

Porthgwidden Beach (USA) *Anthony Middleton* a58 57
4 b m Street Cry(IRE) Suaviter (USA) (Roar (USA))
118[3] 467[6] 691[3] 783[3] 910[3] 1061[5] 2133[6] 2365[10] 2551[7] 3243[6]

Port Hill *Mark Brisbourne* a58 49
5 ch g Deportivo Hill Farm Dancer (Gunner B)
389[4] 651[6] 767[7] 1189[7] 1534[8] 2769[4] 3043[10] 4156[4] 6828[6]

Portmonarch (IRE) *David Lanigan* a74 68
2 b c Galileo(IRE) Egyptian Queen (USA) (Storm Cat (USA))
6204[10] 6872[4] 7323[3]

Portovino (FR) *E J O'Neill* a84 61
3 b c Cape Cross(IRE) Portella (GER) (Protektor (GER))
117a[2]

Portrait *Sir Mark Prescott Bt* a57
2 ch f Peintre Celebre(USA) Annalina (USA) (Cozzene (USA))
7777[7] 7868[11] 8017[9]

Portraitofmylove (IRE) *Sir Henry Cecil*
3 b f Azamour(IRE) Flashing Green (Green Desert (USA))
2313[12]

Portrush Storm *Ray Peacock* a50 61
7 ch m Observatory(USA) Overcast (IRE) (Caerleon (USA))
66[9] 334[8] 430[11] 906[6] 1830[8] 2761[5] 5131[5] 5660[5] (6003) 6194[2] 7055[11] 7275[11]

Portside Blue *Tony Coyle* a29 48
2 b g Royal Applause Crab Apple (Alhaarth (IRE))
4114[13] 4545[11] 5797[8] 7714[6]

Pose (IRE) *Roger Ingram* a60 65
5 b m Acclamation Lyca Ballerina (Marju (IRE))
1934[10] 2171[13] 3151[9] 3701[2] 4240[5] 4332[9] 4815[10] 5658[10] 6951[4] 7106[7] 8036[5] 8180[9] 8248[10]

Poseidon Grey (IRE) *Ian Williams* a79 53
3 gr g Kheleyf(USA) Elitista (FR) (Linamix (FR))
2649[5] 3343[9] 4815[13] 5296[6] 5808[6] 6179[4] 6321[6] 7204[9] 7354[10]

Poseidon's Warrior (USA) *Robert E Reid Jr* a113 70
4 bb h Speightstown(USA) Poised To Pounce (USA) (Smarten (USA))
7574a[14]

Posh Boy (IRE) *Chris Wall* a61 55
2 b g Duke Of Marmalade(IRE) Sauvage (FR) (Sri Pekan (USA))
6636[18] 6985[6] 7780[3]

Posh Secret *John Quinn* a38 4
2 ch f Sakhee's Secret Maidford (IRE) (Singspiel (IRE))
6954[12] 7653[7]

Position *Sir Mark Prescott Bt* a98 62
3 b g Medicean Poise (IRE) (Rainbow Quest (USA))
2701[8] 3042[5] 3787[5] 5243[2] 5429[2] (5752) 6018[3] (6580)

Positively *Sir Michael Stoute* a81 62
3 b f Oasis Dream Be Glad (Selkirk (USA))
3070[7] 3735[3] 5329[4] (6250) 6574[8]

Positive Parenting (IRE) *Stuart Williams* a19 36
2 b f Malibu Moon(USA) Real Cat (USA) (Storm Cat (USA))
5407[10] 5948[9] 6330[14]

Possible *Charles O'Brien* 89
3 b f Pivotal Pingus (Polish Precedent (USA))
4380a[5] 6716a[14]

Possibly *Peter Chapple-Hyam* a40 58
3 b f Exceed And Excel(AUS) One Of The Family (Alzao (USA))
1733[10] 2367[9] 2802[16]

Poste Restante *David Simcock* a56
2 b f Halling(USA) Postage Stampe (Singspiel (IRE))
7721[10] 8018[6]

Postscript (IRE) *Ian Williams* a80 97
4 ch g Pivotal Persian Secret (FR) (Persian Heights)
(67) 216[6] 538[2] (771) (3037) 3385[3] 4474[3] (5094) 5517[15] (5794) 6674[29]

Potentiale (IRE) *J W Hills* a75 78
8 ch g Singspiel(IRE) No Frills (IRE) (Darshaan)
401[5] 655[3] 826[3] 1135[11] 1919[9] 2364[2] 2653[3] 2886[2] 3723[6] 4333[3] 4602[2] 5258[8] 5628[2] 5983[11] 6304[4]

Potkol (FR) *C Boutin* a63 20
3 b c My Risk(FR) Pashmina India (FR) (Kouroun (FR))
290a[5] 476a[4] 661a[8]

Potomac (IRE) *A Oliver* a85 88
4 b g Shamardal(USA) Pippas Song (Reference Point)
3647a[4]

Poupee Flash (USA) *P Bary* 103
3 b f Elusive Quality(USA) Modesty Blaise (USA) (A.P. Indy (USA))
2156a[2] 2742a[6] 3682a[11] 5249a[4]

Pour La Victoire (IRE) *Nigel Tinkler* 60
2 b g Antonius Pius(USA) Lady Lucia (IRE) (Royal Applause)
3303[5] 5410[9] 6049[10] 6628[4] 7173[11]

Pouvoir Absolu *P Schaerer* a79 109
7 b h Sadler's Wells(USA) Pine Chip (USA) (Nureyev (USA))
443a[4]

Powder Hound *Andrew Balding* 46
2 b c Lucarno(USA) Balnaha (Lomond (USA))
7492[7]

Power *A P O'Brien* 117
3 b c Oasis Dream Frappe (IRE) (Inchinor)
1856[17] (2514a) 3239[12]

Powerball (IRE) *Lisa Williamson* 14
4 b m Redback Luceball (IRE) (Bluebird (USA))
2262[19] 2621[10]

Power Broker (USA) *Bob Baffert* a115 93
2 ch c Pulpit(USA) Shop Again (USA) (Wild Again (USA))
7572a[5]

Power Foot (USA) *Richard E Mandella* 102
3 b c Powerscourt Madame Blackfoot (USA) (Black Minnaloushe (USA))
7566a[6] 7882a[5]

Powerful Pierre *Ian McInnes* a73 75
5 ch g Compton Place Alzianah (Alzao (USA))
128[6] 329[3] 478[10] 912[9] (1481) 2355[7] 2981[5] 4495[8] 4779[13] 5338[10] 5389[6] 5750[5] 6053[6] 6403[2] 7022[5] 7218[4] 7589[5]

Powerful Presence (IRE) *David O'Meara* a91 96
6 ch g Refuse To Bend(IRE) Miss A Note (USA) (Miswaki (USA))
(1431) (1821) (2697) 3624[3] 4611[10] 4880[4] 5572[7] 5827[14] 6201[13] 7097[7]

Powerful Wind (IRE) *Ronald Harris* a84 88
3 ch c Titus Livius(FR) Queen Of Fools (IRE) (Xaar)
1639[6] 2028[8] (2509) 2914[7] 4234[8] 4765[15] 5603[11] 6144[18] 6685[5] 6767[7] 7254[8] 7591[2] 7995[8]

Power Of Light (IRE) *Mahmood Al Zarooni* 89
2 b f Echo Of Light Dubai Power (Cadeaux Genereux)
(6257) ◆ 6632[4] 7555[3]

Prairie Hawk (USA) *Brian Rothwell* a68 45
7 bb g Hawk Wing(USA) Lady Carla (Caerleon (USA))
3440[10] 4590[13] 5115[6] 5172[7]

Prairie Prince (IRE) *Andrew Balding* 27
2 b c High Chaparral(IRE) Palatine Dancer (IRE) (Namid)
7127[11] 7517[10]

Prairie Ranger *Andrew Balding* 71
2 b c Montjeu(IRE) No Frills (IRE) (Darshaan)
6928[5] 7333[3]

Prairie Star (FR) *J E Hammond* 116
4 b h Peintre Celebre(USA) Prairie Runner (IRE) (Arazi (USA))
1697a[2] 2534a[3] 5650a[11]

Prana (USA) *Jeremy Gask* a30 39
4 b m Proud Citizen(USA) Javana (USA) (Sandpit (BRZ))
2627[8] 3137[13] 8291[9]

Pravda Street *Brian Ellison* a77 93
7 ch g Soviet Star(USA) Sari (Faustus (USA))
1522[7] 2068[7] 2910[10] 3306[6] 4339[7] 4673[5] 5227[5] (5941) (6452) 7202[2]

Praxios *Noel Wilson* a47 69
4 b g Val Royal(FR) Forest Fire (SWE) (Never So Bold)
65[5] 1269[8] 2441[11] 4193[4] 4390[9] 5171[8] 5917[3] (6361) 7385[7]

Praxiteles (IRE) *Nikki Evans* a91 86
8 b g Sadler's Wells(USA) Hellenic (Darshaan)
2423[5] 4184[5] 4731[7] 8073[P]

Precedence (NZ) *Bart Cummings* 114
7 b g Zabeel(NZ) Kowtow (USA) (Shadeed (USA))
7073a[6] 7425a[4] 7621a[9]

Precinct *James Eustace* 65
2 b f Refuse To Bend(IRE) Preceder (Polish Precedent (USA))
7553[3] ◆

Precious Dream (USA) *David Wachman* a82 89
3 ch f Mr Greeley(USA) Lady Carla (Caerleon (USA))
7230a[3]

Precious Stone (IRE) *David Wachman* a91 84
3 b f Galileo(IRE) Anna Karenina (IRE) (Green Desert (USA))
7680a[2]

Precision Five *Jeremy Gask* a57 36
3 b f Proclamation(IRE) Sashay (Bishop Of Cashel)
2865[6] 3507[10] 4001[10] (5050) 7616[3] 7983[3] 8180[4]

Precision Strike *Richard Guest* a44 55
2 b g Multiplex Dockside Strike (Docksider (USA))
4310[7] 4587[7] 5010[6] 6337[12] 6511[9] 6849[3] 6952[6] (7173) 7313[9] 8132[6] 8289[9]

Preferential *Mme C Head-Maarek* 105
3 b f Dansili Jolie Etoile (USA) (Diesis)
1695a[5] 3682a[6] 5142a[6] 6899a[6]

Premier Choice *Tim Easterby* a61 72
3 b g Exceed And Excel(AUS) Simply Times (USA) (Dodge (USA))
2460[2] 3421[7] 4717[4] 5000[3] 5919[2] 7654[4]

Premier Steps (IRE) *Tom Dascombe* 100
2 b f Footstepsinthesand Primissima (GER) (Second Set (IRE))
1499[7] (2019) 3326[3] 4064[4] 5379a[2]

Premio Loco (USA) *Chris Wall* a115 117
8 ch g Prized(USA) Crazee Mental (Magic Ring (IRE))
(1034) (2160a) 3237[8] 4610[9] (5573) 6634[3]

Prepared *A Al Raihe* a101 72
3 ch c More Than Ready(USA) Mannington (AUS) (Danehill (USA))
142a[7] ◆ 873a[4] ◆

Presburg (IRE) *Joseph Tuite* a79 87
3 b g Balmont(USA) Eschasse (USA) (Zilzal (USA))
841[6] 1565[2] 2021[6] 3446[2] 4068[6] 4949[6] 5358[5] 6206[2] 6573[4] 7300[6]

Present Day *Clive Cox* a11 58
3 gr f Cadeaux Genereux Crackle (Anshan)
2891[8] 3666[11] 5152[3] 7108[4] 7495[8] 7781[9]

Present Story *Ian Wood* a63 57
5 b m Lucky Story(USA) Aziz Presenting (IRE) (Charnwood Forest (IRE))
5850[6] 6396[14]

President Lincoln (USA) *Declan Carroll* a78 83
4 bb g First Samurai(USA) Preach (USA) (Mr Prospector (USA))
(1238) 1951[6] 2491[10]

Press Room (USA) *Mahmood Al Zarooni* a70 62
2 ch c Street Cry(IRE) Causeway Lass (AUS) (Giant's Causeway (USA))
6412[4] (7780) ◆

Pressure Drop (IRE) *Jo Hughes* a55 68
3 b f Desert Style(IRE) Easy Going (Hamas (IRE))
482[4] 769[9] 1252[4] 1353[2] 1599[11]

Presto Volante (IRE) *Amanda Perrett* 80
4 b g Oratorio(IRE) Very Racy (USA) (Sri Pekan (USA))
5239[3] 5596[3] (6159) (6802) 7077[4]

Presume *Sir Michael Stoute* a81
3 b f Galileo(IRE) Summer Breeze (Rainbow Quest (USA))
2584[2] 3763[4]

Presvis *Luca Cumani* a113 123
8 b g Sakhee(USA) Forest Fire (SWE) (Never So Bold)
318a[5] 879a[9] ◆ 1148a[14] (Dead)

Pre Tax Profit (IRE) *Reginald Roberts* a73 27
4 b g Ad Valorem(USA) Civic Duty (IRE) (Definite Article)
(6053)

Pretension (USA) *Christopher W Grove* a100
3 ch c Bluegrass Cat(USA) Main Streetin' (USA) (Street Cry (IRE))
2299a[11]

Pretty Madd (FR) *J-V Toux* a64 66
3 b f Anabaa Blue Lady Angele (FR) (Ski Chief (USA))
117a[10]

Pretty Primo (IRE) *Richard Hannon* 84
3 ch f Kyllachy Balladonia (Primo Dominie)
1357[6] (1637) 2236[7] 2714[8]

Price Is Truth (USA) *Mahmood Al Zarooni* a67 48
2 ch c Distorted Humor(USA) Secret Thyme (USA) (Storm Cat (USA))
4773[8] 7167[4] 7507[6]

Priceless Art (IRE) *Alan Swinbank* a80
7 b g Anabaa(USA) My Ballerina (USA) (Sir Ivor (USA))
(902) 2214[17]

Priceless Jewel *Roger Charlton* a91 90
3 b f Selkirk(USA) My Branch (Distant Relative)
(1983) ◆ 3165[12] 4597[6] 6075[14] 6536[5]

Prickles *Derek Shaw* a54 46
7 ch m Karinga Bay Squeaky (Infantry)
229[4] 390[3] 468[10]

Priestley's Reward (IRE) *Mrs K Burke* a69 75
3 b g Whipper(USA) Prima Figlia (IRE) (Inchinor)
787[8] 1190[5] 1413[2] (2118) 2258[5] 2716[9] 4046[5] 5112[5] 5629[2] 5965[3] 6555[6] 6962[4] 7266a[2] 7602[2] (8301)

Prigsnov Dancer (IRE) *Frank Sheridan* a54 46
7 ch g Namid Brave Dance (IRE) (Kris)
(690) ◆ 939[7] 979[7] 2046[11] 2693[9] 5681[8] 6180[9] 8255[10]

Primacy (IRE) *Hughie Morrison*
3 br f Primary(USA) Seaborne (Slip Anchor)
4188[6]

Primadonna Girl (IRE) *Sir Michael Stoute* 62
2 b f King's Best(USA) Winners Chant (IRE) (Dalakhani (IRE))
6343[5]

Primaeval *James Fanshawe* a107 104
6 ch g Pivotal Langoustine (AUS) (Danehill (USA))
261a[2] (1140) (2409) 3331[21] 6024[6] 6400[8]

Primalova (IRE) *William J Fitzpatrick* a70 64
6 b m Soviet Star(USA) She's Our Girl (IRE) (Royal Abjar (USA))
775a[6]

Prima Noa (FR) *J Van Handenhove* 99
3 gr f Layman(USA) Noa Sajani (FR) (Sagamix (FR))
1695a[3] 2532a[8]

Prime Exhibit *Daniel Mark Loughnane* a100 96
7 b g Selkirk(USA) First Exhibit (Machiavellian (USA))
868[4] 1220[3] 1522[12] 2243[3] 2919[7] 3626[5] 4437[7] 4805[14] (5305) 5812[8] (6051) 6454[6] 6888[6] (7163) 7824[4] 7920[4] 8081[6]

Primera Vista *Mario Hofer* a84 106
6 b g Haafhd Colorvista (Shirley Heights)
6804a[5]

Prime Run *David Simcock* a63 63
3 b f Dansili Silca-Cisa (Hallgate)
638[2] 805[4] 6154[6] 6433[3]

Primevere (IRE) *Roger Charlton* a87 110
4 ch m Singspiel(IRE) Tree Peony (Woodman (USA))
1883[3] 2711[5] 5594[2] 6062a[2] (6575) 7557[5]

Primo Blanca *Michael Mullineaux* a41
3 b g Primo Valentino(IRE) Quay Four (IRE) (Barathea (IRE))
7933[9] 8135[7]

Primo Lady *Gay Kelleway* a55 83
4 br m Lucky Story(USA) Lady Natilda (First Trump)
2493[7] 3549[6] 4469[11] 4966[5]

Prince Alzain (USA) *Gerard Butler* a104 96
3 b c Street Sense(USA) Monaassabaat (USA) (Zilzal (USA))
1375[2] 2275[5] 2660[3] 3294[18] 4319[8] (5209) 5848a[3] 6855a[7]

Prince Bishop (IRE) *Saeed Bin Suroor* a118 118
5 ch g Dubawi(IRE) North East Bay (USA) (Prospect Bay (CAN))
(242a) 488a[5] 878a[3] 1150a[7]

Prince Blue *John E Long* a62 57
5 b g Doyen(IRE) Dixie D'Oats (Alhijaz)
151[3] 303[4] 825[3] (1047) 1770[F]

Prince Chaparral (IRE) *Patrick J Flynn* a92 87
6 b g High Chaparral(IRE) Eilanden (IRE) (Akarad (FR))
7852a[9]

Prince Charlemagne (IRE) *Dr Jeremy Naylor* a64 48
9 br g King Charlemagne(USA) Ciubanga (IRE) (Arazi (USA))
(129) 278[5] 566[13] 772[10] 968[11]

Prince D'Alienor (IRE) *X Nakkachdji* a100 112
4 gr h Verglas(IRE) Vassiana (FR) (Anabaa (USA))
260a[4] 587a[6] 3900a[2] 7124a[4] 7515a[5]

Princedargent (FR) *H-A Pantall* 71
2 ch c Kendargent(FR) Norwegian Princess (IRE) (Fairy King (USA))
7693a[7] 7984a[0]

Prince De Perse (FR) *Rod Collet* a74 84
2 b c Whipper(USA) River Valentine (FR) (River Majesty (USA))
7984a[6]

Prince Eliot (FR) *M Boutin* a69 38
2 b g Tomorrows Cat(USA) Bactrian Princess (FR) (Desert Style (IRE))
5073a[4] 5378a[9] 5698a[10]

Prince Freddie *Roy Brotherton* a65 74
4 b g Red Ransom(USA) Pitcroy (Unfuwain (USA))
433[6] 850[10] 5936[9] 6230[7]

Prince Gabrial (IRE) *Kevin Ryan* a63 33
3 b g Moss Vale(IRE) Baileys Cream (Mister Baileys)
26[4] 204[2] 377[4] 491[6] 769[8] 1359[2]

Prince James *Michael Easterby* a76 65
5 b g Danroad(AUS) Lawless Bridget (Alnasr Alwasheek)
1298[11] (1601) 1954[7] 2314[9] 2693[6] 2982[7] 4174[9] 6497[8] 7447[4] (7604) 7863[11] 8144[7]

Prince Jock (USA) *John Patrick Shanahan* a82 84
5 b g Repent(USA) My Special K'S (USA) (Tabasco Cat (USA))
2657[8] 3647a[5]

Princely Hero (IRE) *Chris Gordon* a89 60
8 b g Royal Applause Dalu (IRE) (Dancing Brave (USA))
1890[6] 3572[7] 7077[12]

Princely Sum (IRE) *Stuart Williams* 71
3 b c Refuse To Bend(IRE) Green Dollar (IRE) (Kingmambo (USA))
2125[9] 2430[12] 2788[13]

Prince Mag (IRE) *A Couetil* 105
3 b c Zamindar(USA) Princess D'Orange (FR) (Anabaa (USA))
6508a[2]

Prince Namid *Jonathen de Giles* a57 55
10 b g Namid Fen Princess (IRE) (Trojan Fen)
205[3] 312[4] 729[3] 1907[4] 2364[8] 3152[9] 3485[3] 4541[7]

Prince Of Burma (IRE) *Jeremy Gask* a92 91
5 b h Mujadil(USA) Spinning Ruby (Pivotal)
(199) (301) ◆ 426[7] 962[4] 1128[5] 1321[9] 2082[5] ◆ 2417[6] 3767[10] 7966[8] 8188[7]

Prince Of Dance *Tom Tate* a81 90
6 b g Danehill Dancer(IRE) Princess Ellen (Tirol)
694[8] 3534[11]

Prince Of Fire (GER) *C F Swan* a87 20
7 b g Waky Nao Pacaya (GER) (Acatenango (GER))
1043a[15]

Prince Of Johanne (IRE) *Tom Tate* a42 110
6 gr g Johannesburg(USA) Paiute Princess (FR) (Darshaan)
2211[2] (3268) 4628[5] 4761[10] 5517[16] 6674[14] 7691[6]

Prince Of Orange (IRE) *Mahmood Al Zarooni* 86
3 b c Shamardal(USA) Cox Orange (USA) (Trempolino (USA))
(4791) 5583[6]

Prince Of Passion (CAN) *Derek Shaw* a72 66
4 ch g Roman Ruler(USA) Rare Passion (CAN) (Out Of Place (USA))
1447[5] 1702[6] 2549[9] 3314[4] 3964[5] 4656[6] (4887) (5157) 5681[12] 5971[2] 6195[4] 6497[3] 6811[8] 8059[9] 8232[10]

Princeofperfection *Richard Ford* a7
3 b g Tobougg(IRE) Princess Perfect (IRE) (Danehill Dancer (IRE))
6527[6] 7025[10] 8048[14]

Prince Of Prophets (IRE) *Stuart Williams* a51 42
2 b g Antonius Pius(USA) Chifney Rush (IRE) (Grand Lodge (USA))
1886[9] 2852[8] 3224[7] 5403[3] 7156[2] 8155[4] ◆

Prince Of Rules (GER) *C Lerner* 77
3 gr c Aussie Rules(USA) Princess Of Eden (GER) (Eden Rock (GER))
(7266a)

Prince Of Sorrento *Lee Carter* a75 99
5 ch g Doyen(IRE) Princess Galadriel (Magic Ring (IRE))
403[9] 574[3] (828) (894) 1378[3] (1626) (2011) 3157[2] 3534[2] 4365[13] 6670[5]

Prince Of Thebes (IRE) *Michael Attwater* a59 56
11 b g Desert Prince(IRE) Persian Walk (FR) (Persian Bold)
176[7] 224[6] 519[6] 651[7] 1106[9] 2364[3] 3043[9] 4722[11] 5351[7] 8264[6]

Prince Of Vasa (IRE) *Michael Smith* a72 74
5 b g Kheleyf(USA) Suzy Street (IRE) (Dancing Dissident (USA))
101[3] (372) 496[3] (752) 1177[4] 1526[7]

Prince Rakan (USA) *Amy Weaver* a59 31
2 b c Proud Citizen(USA) Yousefia (USA) (Danzig (USA))
6214[12] 6846[8] 7305[10] 7606[2] 7708[11]

Prince Regal *Alan Jarvis* 82
2 ch c Cockney Rebel(IRE) Wachiwi (IRE) (Namid)
2844[3] 3123[6] 4688[6] (5213) 5563[6] 6138[3] 6487[6] 7374[4]

Prince Siegfried (FR) *Saeed Bin Suroor* a89 116
6 b g Royal Applause Intrum Morshaan (IRE) (Darshaan)
1471[7] 1994[7] 6446[3] (7029) 7557[7]

Princess Alessia *Terry Clement* a57 60
3 b f Byron Break Of Dawn (USA) (Mt. Livermore (USA))
27[6]

Princess Caetani (IRE) *David Simcock* a75 90
3 b f Dylan Thomas(IRE) Caladira (IRE) (Darshaan)
1531[3] 2194[2] (3013) 4702[9] 5328[4] 6492[6] 7082[2] (7375)

Princess Cammie (IRE) *Mike Murphy* a55
2 b f Camacho Hawattef (IRE) (Mujtahid (USA))
6975[6] 8247[2]

Princess Cayan (IRE) *Linda Perratt* 7
2 b f Kodiac Silk Point (IRE) (Barathea (IRE))
3902[4] 4083[5]

Princesse Fleur *Michael Scudamore* 59
4 b m Grape Tree Road Princesse Grec (FR) (Grand Tresor (FR))
2575[8] 6821[10]

Princesse Leila (FR) *Y Barberot* a71 64
2 gr f Slickly(FR) Talon Bleu (FR) (Anabaa Blue)
7700a[4] 8276a[3]

Princess Gail *Mark Brisbourne* a62 54
4 b m Ad Valorem(USA) First Musical (First Trump)
633[6] 744[5] 929[4] 1095[4] 3317[6] 3559[12] 4890[9] 5212[5] 5804[8]

Princess Ghalya (USA) *M Gharib* a45
3 ch f Proud Citizen(USA) Greene Road (USA) (Green Dancer (USA))
77a[6]

Princess Highway (USA) *D K Weld* 117
3 b f Street Cry(IRE) Irresistible Jewel (IRE) (Danehill (USA))
(2187a) (3292) 4378a[3] 6295a[7] 7093a[10]

Princess Hollow *Tony Coyle* a3 46
2 ch f Beat Hollow Lothian Lass (IRE) (Daylami (IRE))
2977[7] 3351[5] 3842[4] 7349[7]

Princess Icicle *Jo Crowley* a75
4 b m Iceman Sarabah (IRE) (Ela-Mana-Mou)
8158[2] ◆

Princess In Exile *George Foster* 63
2 ch f Bertolini(USA) Music In Exile (USA) (Diesis)
1218[8] 1556[3] 2224[2] 2631[10] 3576[3] 4767[5] 5313[5]

Princess Lexi (IRE) *William Knight* a66 75
5 ch m Rock Of Gibraltar(IRE) Etaaq (IRE) (Sadler's Wells (USA))
224[2] ◆ 568[2] 761[3] 3395[8]

Princess Maya *Jo Crowley* a65 66
3 b f Royal Applause Secret Blend (Pivotal)
322 [7] 1313[3] 3547[2] 4531[11] 6152[6] 7158[3]

Princess Of Orange *Rae Guest* a63 96
3 ch f Dutch Art Radiate (Sadler's Wells (USA))
1858[19] 2894[5] 4075[3] 4819[2] ◆ (5107) ◆ 5834[13] 6633[10]

Princess Of Rock *Mick Channon* 48
3 ch f Rock Of Gibraltar(IRE) Principessa (Machiavellian (USA))
3398[10] 4341[6] 4734[8] 5215[11]

Princess Palmer *Giles Bravery* a48 49
3 b f Iceman Tapas En Bal (FR) (Mille Balles (FR))
2582[11]

Princess Patsky (USA) *Michael Bell* a65 54
2 bb f Mr Greeley(USA) Kamarinskaya (USA) (Storm Cat (USA))
5902[8] 6816[8] 7505[4]

Princess Sheila (IRE) *J S Moore* a57 66
2 br f Jeremy(USA) Princess Atoosa (USA) (Gone West (USA))
5773[3] 6203[9] 6936[9] 7272[4] 7724[4] 7916[6]

Princess Sinead (IRE) *Mrs John Harrington* 105
3 bb f Jeremy(USA) Princess Atoosa (USA) (Gone West (USA))
1041a[3] 2101a[10] 2527a[3] 4376a[7]

Princess Steph (IRE) *Heather Main* a68 68
3 b f Oratorio(IRE) Eurostorm (USA) (Storm Bird (CAN))
1016[5] 1182[3] 2273[7] 5156[5] 5726a[7] 6278[2] 6734[12] 7162[6] 7473[11] 7767[12]

Princess Vati (FR) *S Wattel* a79 79
3 ch f Vatori(FR) Reine De Vati (FR) (Take Risks (FR))
17a[3]

Princess Willow *John E Long* a60 60
4 b m Phoenix Reach(IRE) Highland Hannah (IRE) (Persian Heights)
34[3] 203[12] 732[6] 2401[7] 3152[5] 5100[4] 5938[3] 6569[6] 8049[3]

Prince Will I Am (USA) *Michelle Nihei* a111 110
5 ch r Victory Gallop(CAN) Dyna's Dynamo (USA) (Dynaformer (USA))
7094a[9]

Principe Adepto (USA) *E Botti* a66 109
4 bb h Dubawi(IRE) Aischa (Giant's Causeway (USA))
2521a[3] 7587a[10]

Prinz David (FR) *D Rabhi* a85 26
3 gr c Blackdoun(FR) Lucia Nova (GER) (Surumu (GER))
542a[9]

Prinzde Glas (IRE) *Stephane Chevalier* a83 100
5 gr g Verglas(IRE) Bellacoola (GER) (Lomitas)
314a[11] 681a[11]

Priors Gold *Ollie Pears* a84 76
5 ch g Sakhee(USA) Complimentary Pass (Danehill (USA))
7972[3]

Privacy Order *Sir Mark Prescott Bt* a39 29
2 b f Azamour(IRE) Confidential Lady (Singspiel (IRE))
4946[9] 5300[9] 5661[9]

Private Alexander (IRE) *G M Lyons* 86
2 b f Footstepsinthesand Private Seductress (USA) (Private Account (USA))
6081a[10]

Private Equity (FR) *Nicky Henderson* a87 86
4 b g High Yield(USA) Annette Girl (IRE) (Mtoto)
8275[5]

Private Jet (FR) *P Monfort* a90 104
4 gr h Aussie Rules(USA) Norwegian Princess (IRE) (Fairy King (USA))
1746a[7] 5118a[8] 6804a[4]

Private Riviera *C Boutin* a64 94
3 gr f Stormy River(FR) Private Dancer (FR) (Green Tune (USA))
542a[10] 716a[9]

Private Story (USA) *David O'Meara* 66
5 b g Yes It's True(USA) Said Privately (USA) (Private Account (USA))
(2874) 3241[17] 4209[6]

Prize Point *Tom Gretton* a73 36
6 ch g Bahamian Bounty Golden Symbol (Wolfhound (USA))
134[6] 328[9] 498[11] 781[10] 986[7] 1185[8] 4236[7] 4812[4] 4993[8]

Probably (IRE) *David Wachman* 105
2 b c Danehill Dancer(IRE) Wedding Morn (IRE) (Sadler's Wells (USA))
(3649a) 5136a[4] 6272a[4] 6718a[3]

Prodigality *Ronald Harris* a66 99
4 ch g Pivotal Lady Bountiful (Spectrum (IRE))
2815[2] 4554[2] (5035) ◆ 5368[2] ◆ 5530[2] 6244[6] ◆ (7080) 7366[10]

Producer *Richard Hannon* a108 113
3 ch c Dutch Art River Saint (USA) (Irish River (FR))
1455[3] (2659) 3265[5] 4095[4] (5627) 6449[2] 7054[10] 7809[4]

Professor *Richard Hannon* 95
2 ch c Byron Jubilee (Selkirk (USA))
(4290) 5042[4] 5904[5] (6487)

Profile Star (IRE) *David Barron* a79 86
3 b g Kodiac Fingal Nights (IRE) (Night Shift (USA))
1998[11] 2509[3] 2616[2] 3288[5] 5603[2] ◆ 5800[2] 6075[7] 7918[8]

Profile Storm (IRE) *David Barron* a38
3 b g Footstepsinthesand Mataji (IRE) (Desert Prince (IRE))
495[5]

Profit Again (IRE) *Andrew Balding* a63
3 b g Tagula(IRE) Baileys First (IRE) (Alzao (USA))
26[3]

Progenitor (IRE) *David Lanigan* a68 45
2 b g Mujadil(USA) Bradamante (Sadler's Wells (USA))
4066[11] 4463[9] 5162[7] (6147) 6318[2] (6893) 7414[2]

Prohibit *Robert Cowell* a107 121
7 b g Oasis Dream Well Warned (Warning)
681a[4] 875a[9] 1146a[13] 2745a[7] 3238[15] 4113[4]

Prohibition (IRE) *John Butler* a65 62
6 b g Danehill Dancer(IRE) Crumpetsfortea (IRE) (Henbit (USA))
(922) (1009) 1222[4] 1379[2] 1533[5] 1636[6] 1895[9] 2237[11] 6217[10] 6586[7] 7385[13] 8131[9]

Proisir (AUS) *Gai Waterhouse* 107
3 br c Choisir(AUS) Prophet Jewel (AUS) (Encosta De Lago (AUS))
7426a[8]

Projectisle (IRE) *Kevin Ryan* a71 74
2 b f Tagula(IRE) Erne Project (IRE) (Project Manager)
(2790) 3269[18] 4116[4] 4922[5] 5537[2] 6160[15] 7687[15] 7727[4] (7795) 7977[3]

Prokeel (IRE) *Tim Easterby* 59
2 gr g Proclamation(IRE) Kayf Keel (Kayf Tara)
6669[6] 7598[5]

Prom Dress *Robert Cowell* a46
2 b f Mount Nelson Dress Code (IRE) (Barathea (IRE))
7198[9] 8102[5]

Promised Wings (GER) *Chris Gordon* a60 44
5 ch g Monsun(GER) Panagia (USA) (Diesis)
521[10]

Proofreader *John Gosden* 90
3 b g Authorized(IRE) Blixen (USA) (Gone West (USA))
(3349) 7396[14]

Proper Charlie *William Knight* a77 64
4 b g Cadeaux Genereux Ring Of Love (Magic Ring (IRE))
1378[4] (1734) 2146[7] 3549[10] 4332[10] (4468) 5165[5] 5531[4] 5915[17] 8266[7]

Prophesy (IRE) *Declan Carroll* 92
3 ch g Excellent Art Race The Wild Wind (USA) (Sunny's Halo (CAN))
(1953) 3383[2] 3890[2] 4342[4] 4741[5] 5414[2] (5732)

Prophet In A Dream *Paddy Butler* a35 73
4 b g Fath(USA) Princess Dariyba (IRE) (Victory Note (USA))
1787[7] 2627[10] 3467[7] 8077[7]

Prophets Pride *Jeremy Noseda* a72
2 b c Sakhee(USA) Winner's Call (Indian Ridge)
7749[2] (7979)

Proponent (IRE) *Roger Charlton* a91 106
8 b g Peintre Celebre(USA) Pont Audemer (USA) (Chief's Crown (USA))
1854[7]

Propulsion (IRE) *F Head* 106
3 b c Pulpit(USA) Brooklyn's Storm (USA) (Storm Cat (USA))
3204a[4]

Prospective (USA) *Mark Casse* a113
3 bb c Malibu Moon(USA) Spirited Away (USA) (Awesome Again (CAN))
1872a[18]

Prospera (IRE) *Ralph Beckett* a68 61
2 b f Cape Cross(IRE) Opera (Forzando)
5793[8] 6153[5] 6960[6] 7779[2]

Protectionist (GER) *A Wohler* 98
2 b c Monsun(GER) Patineuse (IRE) (Peintre Celebre (USA))
7698a[2]

Proud Cash Flow (USA) *Niels Petersen* 39
3 bb c Proud Citizen(USA) Great Lady Slew (USA) (Seattle Slew (USA))
3655a[6]

Proud Chieftain *Clifford Lines* a93 99
4 b g Sleeping Indian Skimra (Hernando (FR))
2248[8] 2810[2] 3121[2] 3632[6] 4596[4] (4821) 5364[5] 6010[2] (6142) 6637[5] 7557[4]

Proud Times (USA) *Alan Swinbank* a91 42
6 bb g Proud Citizen(USA) Laura's Pistolette (USA) (Big Pistol (USA))
1880[9]

Provencal *Rod Millman* a57 67
2 b c Compton Place Provence (Averti (IRE))
6203[13] 6571[4] 7110[4] 7723[5] 7965[6]

Proventi *Alan McCabe* a60 44
2 b g Auction House(USA) Miss Poppy (Averti (IRE))
2261[17] 2550[11] 2817[5] 3971[7] 4816[9] 7056[12] 7526[5] 7649[6] 7711[5] 8053[3] 8155[8] 8224[6]

Provisional *Martyn Meade* a83 88
4 ch m With Approval(CAN) Tentative (USA) (Distant View (USA))
1213[8] 4060[6] 4821[9] 7356[10]

Proximity *Sir Michael Stoute* 81
3 b f Nayef(USA) Contiguous (USA) (Danzig (USA))
2941[4] ◆ (3918) 5837[3] 6847[6]

Prussian *Mark Johnston* a80 105
3 b f Dubai Destination(USA) Russian Snows (IRE) (Sadler's Wells (USA))
182[2] ◆ (279) (1819) 2088[5] (2772) 3296[15] 4009[12] (4342) 4596[2] 4735[6] 5078[6] 5835[2] (6010) 6661[3] 6875[2]

Psyche (FR) *C Boutin* a96 99
3 b f American Post Napeta (IRE) (Woodman (USA))
1244a[4] 5726a[3]

Psy Chic (FR) *E Wianny* a85 80
8 b g Munir Psycadelic (FR) (Midyan (USA))
7701a[2]

Ptolemaic *Bryan Smart* 106
3 b g Excellent Art Pompey Girl (Rainbow Quest (USA))
1470[4] 1856[7] 2210[5] 3265[8] 4760[12] 5964[6]

Ptolemy *David Barron* 68
3 b g Royal Applause Rydal Mount (IRE) (Cape Cross (IRE))
1843[7] 2470[4] (2774) 3555[5] 4783[7] 5170[8]

Ptolomeos *Sean Regan* a13 60
9 b g Kayf Tara Lucy Tufty (Vin St Benet)
(2048) 2454[8] 3081[4] 4349[9] 5824[8] 7496[8] 7731[12]

Public (IRE) *Luca Cumani* 45
2 br c Red Clubs(IRE) Rejuvenation (IRE) (Singspiel (IRE))
7127[7]

Pucon *Roger Teal* a67 68
3 b f Kyllachy The Fugative (Nicholas (USA))
(219) 1941[4] 2397[8] 3670[8] 5165[6] (5445) 6307[6] 8157[9]

Pugnacious (IRE) *Mark Johnston* a58 60
3 b c Street Cry(IRE) Dignify (IRE) (Rainbow Quest (USA))
4212[10] 4465[6] 4915[5] 5164[10] 5738[2] ◆ 6101[9] 6503[5] 6807[8] 7255[10]

Puissance De Lune (IRE) *Darren Weir* 110
4 gr h Shamardal(USA) Princess Serena (USA) (Unbridled's Song (USA))
(7696a)

Puligny (IRE) *Charles Hills* a62 59
2 b f Holy Roman Emperor(IRE) Le Montrachet (Nashwan (USA))
6960[5] 7505[6]

Pull The Pin (IRE) *Declan Carroll* a53 55
3 b g Kheleyf(USA) Inscribed (IRE) (Fasliyev (USA))
5127[3] 5335[8] 6002[14] 6937[12] 7436[9] 7612[2] 7898[11]

Pulsatilla *Bryan Smart* a58 65
4 b m Monsieur Bond(IRE) Resemblance (State Diplomacy (USA))
153[7] 370[12] 1601[4] 1823[6] 2441[RR]

Pulverize (USA) *Sir Michael Stoute* a82 83
3 ch c Pulpit(USA) Critical Eye (USA) (Dynaformer (USA))
2584[3] 3663[3] 4882[3] 6228[3]

Pump Pump Boy (FR) *M Pimbonnet* a98 108
4 b h Kingsalsa(USA) Pump Pump Girl (FR) (Kondor (FR))
953a[9] 3178a[4] 4229a[4]

Punching *Conor Dore* a79 58
8 b g Kyllachy Candescent (Machiavellian (USA))
19[4] 157[7] 252[11] 371[5] 458[5] 492[2] 640[2] 808[4] 883[2] 1177[2] (1279) (1430) 1934[8] 2809[11] 3761[7] 3941[5] 4143[5] 4885[7] 5245[5] 6053[11] 7055[12] 7482[8]

Punch Your Weight (IRE) *A Oliver* 96
3 b g Hawk Wing(USA) Sun Slash (IRE) (Entrepreneur)
(5609a)

Punita (USA) *Mahmood Al Zarooni* a78 90
3 ch f Distorted Humor(USA) Indy Five Hundred (USA) (A.P. Indy (USA))
(3395) ◆ 6870[8] ◆

Punta Baluarte *Julie Camacho* a24 30
6 b m Lahib(USA) Calachuchi (Martinmas)
1[3] 581[7] 5316[8] 5669[9]

Punta Stella (IRE) *D Zarroli* 103
2 b f Elusive City(USA) Eroica (GER) (Highest Honor (FR))
(7285a)

Purcell (IRE) *Andrew Balding* 71
2 b c Acclamation Lyca Ballerina (Marju (IRE))
4362[8] 4845[3] 5418[5]

Pure Champion (IRE) *A S Cruz* a102 120
5 b h Footstepsinthesand Castara Beach (IRE) (Danehill (USA))
8042a[8]

Pure Excellence *Mark Johnston* 99
2 b f Exceed And Excel(AUS) Albavilla (Spectrum (IRE))
(4173) 4820[3] 5563[9] 6160[3] 6883[6] (7207) 7399[2] (7555)

Pure Land (FR) *F Vermeulen* a63 66
6 b g Rainbow Quest(USA) Visions On Space (IRE) (Lure (USA))
92a[0]

Purification (IRE) *John Gosden* 91
4 b g Hurricane Run(IRE) Ceanothus (IRE) (Bluebird (USA))
1654[9] 2346[3] 3036[4] 3564[3] 4284[3] 5106[9] 6445[8] 7109[8]

Purkab *Jim Goldie* 57
4 ch g Intikhab(USA) Pure Misk (Rainbow Quest (USA))
3215[9] 3907[11] 4137[7] 4431[3] 4766[10]

Purley Queen (IRE) *Sylvester Kirk* a65 70
3 b f Piccolo Queenie (Indian Ridge)
1392[10] 2130[4] 2367[16] 2787[12] 3005[2] (4185) 4424[2] 5156[3] 5808[7] (6172) 7998[6] 8114[7]

Puro (CZE) *M Weiss* 53
10 ch g Rainbows For Life(CAN) Pulnoc (CZE) (Shy Groom (USA))
631a[6]

Purple Affair (IRE) *J S Moore* a68 71
3 rg g Clodovil(IRE) Akariyda (IRE) (Salse (USA))
518[3] 660[2] ◆ 743[9] 1046[4] 2382[2] 2689[7] (3591)

Purple Day *Pam Sly* 51
2 b g Royal Applause Milly-M (Cadeaux Genereux)
3046[6] 3844[4] 4625[8] 5403[10] 5911[10] 6354[10]

Purple 'n Gold (IRE) *David Pipe* a76 71
3 b g Strategic Prince Golden Dew (IRE) (Montjeu (IRE))
(3048) 3591[4] 4603[6] (7702) 8182[3]

Purr Along *William Muir* a80 111
2 b f Mount Nelson Purring (USA) (Mountain Cat (USA))
(3948) 4514[3] (5379a) 6199[2] 6909a[8]

Pursue *William Haggas* a45 72
3 b g Pivotal Entrap (USA) (Phone Trick (USA))
1257[6] 2041[11] 2380[6] 3083[2]

Pursuing *Nigel Tinkler* a58 53
4 b m Rainbow Quest(USA) Kineta (USA) (Miswaki (USA))
188[8] 333[9]

Pursuitoexcellence (IRE) *Sir Michael Stoute*
4 b g Galileo(IRE) Lila (Zafonic (USA))
2393[11]

Pursuit of Passion *Richard Fahey* 64
4 b m Pastoral Pursuits Marisa (GER) (Desert Sun)
1238[4] 1521[8] 1953[2] 2535[12]

Push Me (IRE) *Jamie Poulton* a80 80
5 gr m Verglas(IRE) Gilda Lilly (USA) (War Chant (USA))
(626) 1752[7] 2250[9] 3667[6] 4150[6] 4223[8] 5008[2] 5592[9] 6208[6] 7302[8]

Puteri Nur Laila (IRE) *Paul Cole* a67 66
2 b f Strategic Prince Asian Lady (Kyllachy)
2343[8] 2579[2] 3150[2] 5773[6] 6160[18] 6609[2] 6889[3] 7433[6]

Putin (IRE) *Phil McEntee* a62 53
4 b g Fasliyev(USA) Consignia (IRE) (Definite Article)
98[5] 207[6] 306[9] 490[2] 598[6] 676[10] (889) 988[11] 1179[7] 1988[3] 2401[3] 2464[2] 2653[5] 3052[2] 3247[7] 3470[5] 4193[2] 4241[4] 4406[3] 4986[10] 5148[3] 5459[3] 5633[6] 5996[5] 7317[9] 7798[6] 8010[7] 8062[2] 8169[2] 8248[2] 8299[3]

Putmeintheswindle *Peter Hedger* a29
2 ch g Monsieur Bond(IRE) Birthday Belle (Lycius (USA))
7628[11] 8071[11]

Putra Eton (IRE) *Roger Varian* 66
2 b c Danehill Dancer(IRE) Anna Pallida (Sadler's Wells (USA))
6846[9] 7517[5]

Puyol (SWE) *Henrik Engblom*
3 ch c Swedish Shave(FR) Just In Time (SWE) (Opening Verse (USA))
5144a[8]

Pythagorean *Roger Charlton* 80
2 b g Oasis Dream Hypoteneuse (IRE) (Sadler's Wells (USA))
4056[3] 5304[2] 6571[2] 7127[3]

Pytheas (USA) *Alastair Lidderdale* a64 71
5 b g Seeking The Gold(USA) Neptune's Bride (USA) (Bering)
39[3] 154[9] 7486[10] 7906[6] 7992[11] 8167[8]

Qaadira (USA) *John Gosden* a77 81
3 b f Mr Greeley(USA) Makderah (IRE) (Danehill (USA))
1472[18] 1922[4] ◆ (2453) 5238[5] 6379[9] 6877[14]

Qahriman *Luca Cumani* a92 100
4 b h Tiger Hill(IRE) Jumaireyah (Fairy King (USA))
2474[2] ◆ (3125) 5600[11]

Qanan *Luca Cumani* a74 74
3 b g Green Desert(USA) Strings (Unfuwain (USA))
5555[3] 6215[2] ◆ 6792[5]

Qannaas (USA) *Charles Hills* a73 81
3 br g Hard Spun(USA) Windsong (USA) (Unbridled (USA))
1450[7] 4550[2] 4780[5]

Qaraaba *Seamus Durack* a87 109
5 b m Shamardal(USA) Mokaraba (Unfuwain (USA))
(987) (1133) ◆ 2248[2] (2884) 3329[4] 4094[5]

Qareenah (USA) *Sir Michael Stoute* a62
2 b f Arch(USA) Princess Kris (Kris)
7159[6]

Qawaafy (USA) *Roger Varian* 70
2 b f Street Cry(IRE) Eswarah (Unfuwain (USA))
5551[5] 7364[4]

Qeethaara (USA) *Mark Brisbourne* a76 74
8 gr m Aljabr(USA) Aghsaan (USA) (Wild Again (USA))
(183) 306[3] 537[2] (574) (736) 894[7] (1084) 1311[2] 1609[3] 2161[7] 2535[7] 3039[11] 3709[3] 4779[10] 5259[12] 7524[10] 7925[10]

Quadra Hop (IRE) *Bryn Palling* a58 58
4 ch g Compton Place Yding (IRE) (Danehill (USA))
1497[5] 2760[6] 4236[8] 5504[9]

Quadriga (IRE) *Robert Eddery* a85 73
2 b c Acclamation Turning Light (GER) (Fantastic Light (USA))
8071[3]

Quality Art (USA) *Richard Guest* a44 92
4 b g Elusive Quality(USA) Katherine Seymour (Green Desert (USA))
4013[11] 5343[16] 6005[8] 8232[11]

Quality Mark (USA) *Jeremy Noseda* a66 73
2 b c Elusive Quality(USA) Cassis (USA) (Red Ransom (USA))
2556[3] 6360[2] 6983[3] 8138[4] 8247[3]

Quality Pearl (USA) *Luca Cumani* 80
3 b f Elusive Quality(USA) Marianka (USA) (Ascot Knight (CAN))
2935[4] (4780) 6375[11]

Quan (IRE) *Alan Swinbank* a56 57
3 b g Shamardal(USA) Assumption (IRE) (Beckett (IRE))
2927[6] 3289[7] 6925[3] 7445[3] (7729) 8075[7]

Quand Reverraije (FR) *F Doumen* a71 77
3 b f Enrique She Runs (FR) (Sheyrann)
1127a[8]

Quaroma *Paul Midgley* a81 78
7 ch m Pivotal Quiz Time (Efisio)
3065[4] 4430[3] ◆ 6427[10] 6788[14]

Quart De Rhum (FR) *Y Fouin* 89
3 b c Anabaa(USA) Wells Vision (GER) (Monsun (GER))
1570a[5]

Quasi Congaree (GER) *Paul Fitzsimons* a80 95
6 ch g Congaree(USA) Queens Wild (USA) (Spectacular Bid (USA))
29[9] 2558[10] 2870[4] 3394[5] 4286[16] 8188[9] 8306[8]

Qubuh (IRE) *Linda Stubbs* a72 72
4 b g Invincible Spirit(IRE) Chica Roca (USA) (Woodman (USA))
893[10] 1526[9] (1876) 2120[5] 2838[4] 4087[8] 5543[14] 7126[7]

Queen Aggie (IRE) *David Evans* a87 93
2 b f Elnadim(USA) Catfoot Lane (Batshoof)
(5424) (5828) 6017[3] 7065[4] 7622a[6]

Queen Bubble (IRE) *Y De Nicolay* a89 99
3 b f Layman(USA) Bubble Back (FR) (Grand Lodge (USA))
1695a[7]

Queen Cassiopeia *J R Jenkins* a63
3 b f Echo Of Light Fresh Fruit Daily (Reprimand)
1989[2] 2734[9] 3453[2] 5244[6] 5764[13] 7201[6] 7729[10]

Queen Flush (IRE) *David Nicholls* a37 66
2 b f Red Clubs(IRE) Alexander Nitelady (IRE) (Night Shift (USA))
3937[5] 4545[3]

Queen Grace (IRE) *Michael J Browne* a81 88
5 b m Choisir(AUS) Petitesse (Petong)
(4770) 6005[5] 6689[4] 7595[8]

Queen Hermione (IRE) *Linda Jewell* 31
4 b m Camacho Almeida (IRE) (Sadler's Wells (USA))
3227[10] 3918[9] 5852[5]

Queen Menantie (FR) *J Boisnard* a86 98
4 b m Kingsalsa(USA) Heleniade (FR) (Entrepreneur)
116a[6]

Queen Of Alba (IRE) *E Charpy* a78 70
3 b f Rock Of Gibraltar(IRE) Mad Madam Mym (Hernando (FR))
77a[4]

Queen Of Denmark (USA) *Mark Johnston* a91
4 b m Kingmambo(USA) Danelagh (AUS) (Danehill (USA))
(292) ◆ (501) ◆ 601[2] 846[4] 1446[6]

Queen Of Epirus *Brian Rothwell* a48 57
4 ch m Kirkwall Andromache (Hector Protector (USA))
7656[5] 7869[10]

Queen Of Heaven (USA) *Peter Makin* a53
4 bb m Mr Greeley(USA) Be My Queen (IRE) (Sadler's Wells (USA))
34[6] 291[4] 664[9]

Queen Of Sacrmento *Dr Jon Scargill* 36
2 b f Royal Applause La Fanciulla (Robellino (USA))
4595[14]

Queen Of Skies (IRE) *Clive Cox* a64
3 b f Shamardal(USA) Attractive Crown (USA) (Chief's Crown (USA))
6457[4] 7477[3] 7782[3]

Queenoftheprairie *J E Pease* 71
3 b f Royal Applause Balsamita (FR) (Midyan (USA))
4477a[10]

Queen Of The Sand (IRE) *G M Lyons* a72 64
2 ch f Footstepsinthesand Lough Mewin (IRE) (Woodman (USA))
6853a[3]

Queen's Choice (IRE) *Anabel K Murphy* a39 56
4 b m Choisir(AUS) Queen Of Fibres (IRE) (Scenic)
1961[6] 2401[11] 2821[7]

Queen's Daughter (FR) *N Clement* 86
2 b f American Post Queen's Conquer (King's Best (USA))
(6751a)

Queen's Estate (GER) *Mark Johnston* a62 81
3 b g Hurricane Run(IRE) Questabelle (Rainbow Quest (USA))
1655[2] ◆ 2716[11] 3186[2] 3543[9] (4088) 4459[2] 4735[12] 6339[3] 7002[6] 7672[10]

Queen's Princess *John Wainwright* 43
4 b m Danbird(AUS) Queen's Lodge (IRE) (Grand Lodge (USA))
2335[9] 2601[8] 3406[5] 3462[6] 4348[10] 4957[8] 5823[4]

Queens Revenge *Tim Easterby* 94
3 b f Multiplex Retaliator (Rudimentary (USA))
1221[8] 3165[10] 3542[9]

Queen's Star *Andrew Balding* a65 68
3 ch f With Approval(CAN) Memsahib (Alzao (USA))
2612[4] 3100[6] (4225) ◆ 4537[5] 4918[3] 7271[2] 7490[2]

Quelle Affaire *Brendan Powell* a33
2 b f Bahamian Bounty Qui Moi (CAN) (Swain (IRE))
8165[8]

Quentindemontargis (FR) *C Boutin* a61 94
5 b g Enrique Samarcande (FR) (Thatching)
1163a[6]

Querido (GER) *Paddy Butler* a61 64
8 b g Acatenango(GER) Quest Of Fire (FR) (Rainbow Quest (USA))
55[3] (197) 293[3] 532[7] 666[2] 744[8] 1009[4] 1310[6] 1702[8] (1895) 2586[6] 3964[7] 6252[6] 7105[2] 7302[11] 7500[12] 7816[3] 8179[6] 8298[6]

Quest For More (IRE) *Roger Charlton* a68 47
2 b c Teofilo(IRE) No Quest (IRE) (Rainbow Quest (USA))
7373[10] 7706[4]

Questing *Kiaran McLaughlin* a122 102
3 b f Hard Spun(USA) Chercheuse (USA) (Seeking The Gold (USA))
7550a[P]

Questioning (IRE) *John Gosden* a80 115
4 b h Elusive Quality(USA) Am I (USA) (Thunder Gulch (USA))
1158[2] (1471) 1646[2] 1994[4] 4320[7] 5560[5] 6575[4]

Questionnaire (IRE) *Nicky Vaughan* a51 80
4 b m Iffraaj Kobalt Sea (FR) (Akarad (FR))
1638[13] 1827[13]

Questor (FR) *M Boutin* a74 69
3 b g High Cotton(USA) Equestria (USA) (Red Ransom (USA))
628a[4]

Quick Bite (IRE) *Hugo Palmer* a73 84
3 b f Redback Park Haven (IRE) (Marju (IRE))
1653[6] 2942[6] 3156[7] 5426[7] 5671[3] 6239[7] 7004[6] 7402[5]

Quick Wit *Saeed Bin Suroor* a111 112
5 b h Oasis Dream Roo (Rudimentary (USA))
51a[10] (319a) 591a[9] 792a[4] 4609[9] 5102[2] (6242) 7054[12] 7558[11]

Quiet Appeal (IRE) *Mark Johnston* a61 66
3 b f Cape Cross(IRE) Rise And Fall (USA) (Quiet American (USA))
(217) 803[5] (1448) 1992[3] (2605) 3592[9] 3891[7] 4585[5] 4955[9] 5683[4] 6056[11] 6516[5] 6940[3] 7417[6]

Quiet Prayer *Ed Dunlop* a60
2 b c Exceed And Excel(AUS) Prayer (IRE) (Rainbow Quest (USA))
3040[7] 4654[3]

Quiet Route (IRE) *Brian Ellison* a49 63
3 b g Manduro(GER) Step With Style (USA) (Gulch (USA))
3913[4] ◆ 5316[4] 5679[3] 6821[5] 7869[8] 7921[8] 8146[5]

Quinindo (GER) *Elfie Schnakenberg* a75 96
4 bb h Monsun(GER) Quebrada (IRE) (Devil's Bag (USA))
6464a[5] 7784a[3]

Quinsman *J S Moore* a78 56
6 b g Singspiel(IRE) Penny Cross (Efisio)
202[7] 500[2] 714[4] 928[2] 1003[2] 1104[2] 1421[4]

Quintilian (IRE) *Mahmood Al Zarooni* a87 86
2 b g Cape Cross(IRE) Athenian Way (IRE) (Barathea (IRE))
2880[4] 3634[7] 4340[6] (5155) 5552[2] 7335[7] (7501)

Quite A Catch (IRE) *Jonathan Portman* a65 73
4 b g Camacho Dear Catch (IRE) (Bluebird (USA))
330[7] 894[4] 1358[12] 1626[11] 4844[8] 5657[12] 6157[11]

Quite Sparky *Mike Sowersby* 90
5 b g Lucky Story(USA) Imperialistic (IRE) (Imperial Ballet (IRE))
1249[14] 1914[10]

Quixote *Clive Brittain* a92 88
3 ch g Singspiel(IRE) Rainbow Queen (FR) (Spectrum (IRE))
196[2] (803) 1281[2] 2144[5] 3087[5] 4200[2] 4776[10] 5596[2] (5838) (6376) 6848[5] 7771[7]

Quiza Quiza Quiza *L Riccardi* 112
6 b m Golden Snake(USA) Quiz Chow (ITY) (Pelder (IRE))
2106a[3] 2968a[2] 6911a[8] 7429a[9]

Quiz Mistress *Hughie Morrison* a82 100
4 ch m Doyen(IRE) Seren Quest (Rainbow Quest (USA))
(1940) 2706[7] (3187) 3857[2] 4738[10] 5826[4] (6864a) 7431a[7]

Quiz Whiz (USA) *Kirk Ziadie*
4 ch g Wiseman's Ferry(USA) Meadow Sunlight (USA) (Meadowlake (USA))
8100a[3]

Quote Of The Day (IRE) *Edward Lynam* a73 95
3 b c Modigliani(USA) Tender And True (IRE) (Galileo (IRE))
1943a[5] 7229a[12]

Qushchi *William Jarvis* a83 102
4 bb m Encosta De Lago(AUS) La Persiana (Daylami (IRE))
1848[7] 2933[8] 3635[4] 4338[6] 4848[6] 5580[2] 5966[5] 6492[4] 6598[9] 7519[4] 7895[7]

Raamz (IRE) *Kevin Morgan* a66
5 ch m Haafhd Tarbiyah (Singspiel (IRE))
908[5] 1107[4] 1363[9]

Raasekha *Charles Hills* a93 102
4 b m Pivotal Tahrir (IRE) (Linamix (FR))
1213[4] 1851[3] 5101[5] 7334[2] 7688[4]

Rabdaan *James Fanshawe* a47
2 ch c Sakhee(USA) Maghya (IRE) (Mujahid (USA))
7191[10]

Rabhi Jacob (FR) *D Rabhi* a72
3 b c Gentlewave(IRE) Emelda (GER) (Dashing Blade)
475a[5]

Race And Status (IRE) *Andrew Balding* 98
2 b c Raven's Pass(USA) Love Excelling (FR) (Polish Precedent (USA))
(6486) ◆ 6874[3] ◆

Rachael's Ruby *Roger Teal* a37 33
5 b m Joe Bear(IRE) Fajjoura (IRE) (Fairy King (USA))
7169[12]

Racy *Kevin Ryan* a85 99
5 b g Medicean Soar (Danzero (AUS))
1438[6] 2208[4] 2717[4] 3127[12] 4073[9]

Radioactive *Ralph Beckett* 57
3 b f Haafhd Toxique (IRE) (Orpen (USA))
1501[5] 1843[5]

Radio Gaga *Ed McMahon* 100
3 b f Multiplex Gagajulu (Al Hareb (USA))
1508[2] 1884[14] (3542) 4070[6] 5523a[5] 6161[7] 6870[5]

Rafaaf (IRE) *Richard Phillips* a58 84
4 b g Royal Applause Sciunfona (IRE) (Danehill (USA))
(1564) ◆ 1642[12] 2444[11] 3394[4] 3822[8] 4300[7] 5065[9] 6820[4] 7113[6] 7716[10] 7967[8] 8225[10]

Rafale *Richard Hannon* a71 73
2 b c Sleeping Indian Sweet Coincidence (Mujahid (USA))
2844[10] (4487) 5060[5] 5743[4] 6597[13]

Rafeej *Mark Johnston* 91
3 b c Iffraaj Muffled (USA) (Mizaaya)
1644[6] 2276[4] 2979[9] 4588[9]

Rafella (IRE) *Michael Scudamore* a66 50
4 br m Iffraaj Cappella (IRE) (College Chapel)
3006[6] 4240[6] 4950[8] 5658[2] 6967[RR] 7354[6]

Raffinn *Sylvester Kirk* a74 69
3 b g Sakhee(USA) Blue Mistral (IRE) (Spinning World (USA))
1392[4] 2382[3] 3475[10] 3938[7] 4218[4] 5229[3] (5975)

Ragda *Marco Botti* a49 43
4 b m Invincible Spirit(IRE) Junior Council (IRE) (Sadler's Wells (USA))
293[9]

Raghdaan *Peter Hiatt* a55 55
5 ch g Haafhd Inaaq (Lammtarra (USA))
265[12] 367[6] 454[8] 968[10]

Raging Bear (USA) *Richard Hannon* a72 72
2 b c Leroidesanimaux(BRZ) Gliding Light (USA) (Always A Classic (CAN))
4688[8] 5005[4] 5851[6] 7989[2]

Ragnarr *Ian Semple*
2 b g Whipper(USA) Freya Tricks (Noverre (USA))
4427[6]

Raheb *Carmen Bocskai* a82 102
3 b c Red Ransom(USA) Jarhes (IRE) (Green Desert (USA))
5402a[2]

Raheeba *Mark Johnston* a85 74
3 b f Invincible Spirit(IRE) Wild Gardenia (Alhaarth (IRE))
1703[3] 3107[2] 3811[6] (4426) 4830[9] 5372[5] 5732[5] (6502) (6613) 7334[10]

Rahy's Promise (USA) *Andrew Balding* a19
3 ch g Rahy(USA) Promise Me This (Fusaichi Pegasus (USA))
8295[8]

Rahystrada (USA) *Byron G Hughes* 114
8 ch g Rahy(USA) Ministrada (USA) (Deputy Minister (CAN))
5377a[3]

Rail Trip (USA) *Ronald W Ellis* a116
7 b g Jump Start(USA) Sweet Trip (USA) (Carson City (USA))
7570a[2]

Raimond Ridge (IRE) *Derek Shaw* a48 78
6 bb g Namid Jinsiyah (USA) (Housebuster (USA))
46[7] 125[6] 226[6] 297[4] 396[5] 467[5]

Rainbow Beauty *Gerard Butler* a72 75
2 ch f Manduro(GER) Just Like A Woman (Observatory (USA))
4818[5] 5550[3] ◆ 5977[3] 6017[4] 6675[12] 7335[4] (7592)

Rainbow Gold *Mark Johnston* 91
3 ch c Selkirk(USA) Diablerette (Green Desert (USA))
1456[10] 1866[3] 2484[2] 2634[P]

Rainbow Peak (IRE) *Saeed Bin Suroor* a92 99
6 b g Hernando(FR) Celtic Fling (Lion Cavern (USA))
7557[3]

Rainbow Riches (IRE) *Roger Curtis* a47 49
3 b f Princely Heir(IRE) Another Rainbow (IRE) (Rainbows For Life (CAN))
1819[9] 2949[9] 10105[5] 1740[4] 2367[4] 2803[7] 3141[7] 4981[5] 5994[4] 6935[5]

Rain Dance *Eve Johnson Houghton* a44 57
3 b f Green Desert(USA) Dance Solo (Sadler's Wells (USA))
2441[10] 2788[11] 4937[6] 5994[10] 6095[5]

Rainestorm (IRE) *Mark Johnston* 27
2 b c Hurricane Run(IRE) Love Thirty (Mister Baileys)
7096[5] 7592[P] (Dead)

Rainford Glory (IRE) *Ed Dunlop* a61
2 ch g Rock Of Gibraltar(IRE) My Dolly Madison (In The Wings)
7868[8] 8052[8] 8140[3]

Rain God (USA) *A P O'Brien* a77 65
2 b c Henrythenavigator(USA) Lotta Dancing (USA) (Alydar (USA))
4161a[9]

Rainsborough *Peter Hedger* a57 47
5 b g Trans Island Greeba (Fairy King (USA))
1009[7] 1379[5] 1919[12] 2627[4] 3723[8] 7385[8]

Raise The Rafters (IRE) *John Butler* a62 76
7 ch g Monashee Mountain(USA) Zolube (IRE) (Titus Livius (FR))
14[2] 333[6] 6184a[5] 8264[4]

Rajastani (IRE) *S Wattel* a97 103
3 b f Zamindar(USA) Rocky Mistress (Rock Of Gibraltar (IRE))
1407a[7]

Rajeh (IRE) *Peter Grayson* a42 92
9 b g Key Of Luck(USA) Saramacca (IRE) (Kahyasi)
1066[10] 1421[7] 1991[5] 4652[7]

Rajnagan (IRE) *Paul Webber* a63 70
8 ch g Muhtarram(USA) Rajnagara (IRE) (Darshaan)
1919[8]

Rajsaman (FR) *A Al Raihe* a110 120
5 gr h Linamix(FR) Rose Quartz (Lammtarra (USA))
318a[8] 876a[7] 1148a[10]

Ra Junior (USA) *Paul Midgley* a56 71
6 b g Rahy(USA) Fantasia Girl (IRE) (Caerleon (USA))
725[5] ◆ 1002[8] ◆ 1436[5] 1799[3] 2692[9] 4042[12] 5259[7]

Rakaan (IRE) *Jamie Osborne* a94 90
5 ch g Bahamian Bounty Petite Spectre (Spectrum (IRE))
2910[11] 3779[5] 4099[15] 4703[5] 5356[8] 5572[12] 6011[8] 6329[2] 6888[2] 7502[9] 7823[2] (7934) 8095[3] 8242[4]

Rakticate (IRE) *J S Moore* a63 62
2 b f Rakti Authenticate (Dansili)
5207[4] 5574[5] 6437[7] (7491) 7714[4] 7785[2] 7971[2] 8140[2] 8289[5]

Raktiman (IRE) *Chris Bealby* a75 74
5 ch g Rakti Wish List (IRE) (Mujadil (USA))
7617[9] 7791[7] 8149[4]

Raleigh Quay (IRE) *Micky Hammond* 74
5 b g Bachelor Duke(USA) Speedbird (USA) (Sky Classic (CAN))
2440[2] ◆ 2593[2] (3029) 4682[3] 4910[2] 5188[6] 6706[11]

Ralphy Boy (IRE) *Kevin Ryan* a56 88
3 b g Acclamation Silcasue (Selkirk (USA))
1271[11] 2182[8] 2490[10] 4588[7] 5110[11] 6665[10] 7004[8] 7202[7]

Rambo Will *J R Jenkins* a79 81
4 b g Danbird(AUS) Opera Belle (Dr Fong (USA))
282[5] 735[4] 958[7] 1305[2] 2940[6] 3915[3] 4461[2] 5097[2] ◆ 5853[3] 7114[6] 7273[4] 7730[4] 8058[9]

Ramona Chase *Michael Attwater* a91 92
7 b g High Chaparral(IRE) Audacieuse (Rainbow Quest (USA))
1139[3] 1605[5] (2346) 2655[10] 3766[6] 5666[5] 6018[9] 6202[5] 6576[6]

Rampoldi (TUR) *S Keresteci* a98
3 ch c Bosporus(IRE) Deep Sea (TUR) (Distant Relative)
5848a[5]

Rancher (IRE) *Harry Dunlop* a47 55
2 b c High Chaparral(IRE) Shot Of Redemption (Shirley Heights)
7492[9] 7637[8] 7806[8]

Rangi *John Gosden* a74 76
2 ch c New Approach(IRE) Miss Queen (USA) (Miswaki (USA))
5062[5] ◆ 5792[5] 7806[2] 8070[2]

Rangooned *Ann Duffield* a56 63
2 gr f Bahamian Bounty Dansa Queen (Dansili)
5887[6] 6320[4] 6954[2] 7176[2] 7855[5]

Rano Pano (USA) *Brian Ellison* a55 53
3 b f Proud Citizen(USA) Princess Aries (USA) (Royal Anthem (USA))
1241[9] 1517[9] 2131[5] 2673[10] 3232[4] 3621[5] 4403[3] 6056[4] 6210[4]

Ransom Hope *L Riccardi* 109
7 b h Red Ransom(USA) Field Of Hope (IRE) (Selkirk (USA))
2521a[4] 7286a[6] 7587a[8]

Ransom Note *Charles Hills* 118
5 b g Red Ransom(USA) Zacheta (Polish Precedent (USA))
1471[9] 2270[5] 4610[5] 5090[4]

Ranthambore (FR) *J-M Beguigne* 95
6 b g Lomitas Equibeauta (Nashwan (USA))
5030a[4]

Rapacious (USA) *George R Arnold II*
3 b c Street Sense(USA) Hidden Pleasure (USA) (Proper Reality (USA))
8279a[2]

Rapideur (FR) *S Smrczek* a90 81
2 b c Elusive City(USA) Perelada (FR) (Montjeu (IRE))
7682a[3]

Rapid Heat Lad (IRE) *Reg Hollinshead* a73 73
3 b c Aussie Rules(USA) Alwiyda (USA) (Trempolino (USA))
(709) 1978[6] 2471[4] 3345[9]

Rapid Rabbit Foot *John Holt* a37
2 ch f Three Valleys(USA) Rabshih (IRE) (Green Desert (USA))
6977[10]

Rapid Water *Pat Eddery* a65 63
6 b g Anabaa(USA) Lochsong (Song)
123[3] 262[7] 372[9] 522[6] 1528[10] 1895[3] 2555[6] 3043[4] 3318[3] 3511[3] 4192[3] 5246[7] 5658[3] 5783[4] 6252[2] 6778[2] 7321[6] (7964) 8038[7] 8167[10]

Rapscallion Deep (IRE) *Kevin Ryan* a66
2 b c Danehill Dancer(IRE) Lucina (Machiavellian (USA))
8033[4]

Rapturous Applause *Micky Hammond* a55 62
4 b g Royal Applause Rapturous (Zafonic (USA))
229[5] 389[11] 602[9] 2823[6] 4912[5] 5253[5] 6561[9]

Raquette *N Clement* a78 78
3 ch f Muhtathir Racoon (FR) (Be My Guest (USA))
6752a[5]

Rare Coincidence *Alan Berry* a17 45
11 ch g Atraf Green Seed (IRE) (Lead On Time (USA))
1240[8] 2599[7] 4138[7] 4867[15] 7255[8]

Rasam Aldaar *Neil King* a70 39
4 b g Sakhee(USA) Recherchee (Rainbow Quest (USA))
984[6] 2814[6]

Rasaman (IRE) *Jim Goldie* a84 87
8 b g Namid Rasana (Royal Academy (USA))
1868[5] 2264[5] 2719[2] (3183) 4133[6] 4367[18] 4770[8] 5343[14] 6008[5] 6465[9] 6665[7] 7144[2] 7790[2]

Rasheed *John Gosden* a91 85
4 b g Oasis Dream Alexandrine (IRE) (Nashwan (USA))
310[3] (521) ◆ (928) 1214[5] 2411[3] 2936[8] 6584[7]

Rashfa *John Dunlop* 71
2 b f Cape Cross(IRE) Ayun (USA) (Swain (IRE))
4739[14] 5978[3]

Rashflower (FR) *J Van Handenhove* 67
3 b f Rashbag Fleur Du Bonheur (FR) (Vaguely Pleasant (FR))
7267a[9]

Rash Judgement *Stuart Kittow* 88
7 b g Mark Of Esteem(IRE) Let Alone (Warning)
1935[6] 3159[6] 3778[3] ◆ 4300[6] (5097) 5906[9] 6577[9]

Raskova (USA) *William Jarvis* 76
2 b f Henrythenavigator(USA) Diamond Necklace (USA) (Unbridled's Song (USA))
5016[3] 5550[5]

Raslan *David Pipe* 67
9 b g Lomitas Rosia (IRE) (Mr Prospector (USA))
4096[6]

Rasmeyaa (IRE) *D K Weld* 96
2 ch f New Approach(IRE) Posterity (IRE) (Indian Ridge)
6266a[3] ◆

Rasmy *M Al Muhairi* a98 108
5 b g Red Ransom(USA) Shadow Dancing (Unfuwain (USA))
145a[8]

Raspberry Fizz *Eve Johnson Houghton* a50 51
3 b f Red Ransom(USA) Dubai Spirit (USA) (Mt. Livermore (USA))
5629[5] 5938[9]

Rassam (IRE) *Saeed Bin Suroor* a102 77
3 bb g Dansili Vantive (USA) (Mr Prospector (USA))
142a[3] 485a[7] 6201[15]

Rasselas (IRE) *David Nicholls* a62 66
5 b g Danehill Dancer(IRE) Regal Darcey (IRE) (Darshaan)
2094[10] 2536[3] 2791[7] 3405[3] 4295[3] 4620[5] 6479[2] (6646) 6941[12] 7095[14]

Rasteau (IRE) *Tom Keddy* a53 43
4 b g Barathea(IRE) Mistra (IRE) (Rainbow Quest (USA))
1095[7] 1425[7] 1635[7] 2009[8] 2586[8] 2804[9] 3051[5] 3546[10] 4196[10] 4966[6]

Rat Catcher (IRE) *Tim Easterby* 77
2 b c One Cool Cat(USA) Molly Marie (IRE) (Fasliyev (USA))
2138[8] 2537[4] (3286) 4045[3] 4827[6] 5710[4] 6920[13]

Rated *Mick Channon* 79
2 b g Sixties Icon Arasong (Aragon)
1218[6] (1330) 2238[2] (3858) 4102[7] 4540[U] 4847[3] 4951[3] 5060[4] 5710[2] 6189[3] 6475[6]

Rather Cool *John Bridger* a54 61
4 b m Iceman Kowthar (Mark Of Esteem (IRE))
2149[6] 2814[7] 3043[3] 3472[6] 3704[10] 3969[6] 4504[6] 4941[8]

Rathnaree *Ralph Beckett* 39
2 b g Intikhab(USA) United Passion (Emarati (USA))
6443[12]

Raucous Behaviour (USA) *George Prodromou* a88 67
4 b g Street Cry(IRE) Caffe Latte (IRE) (Seattle Dancer (USA))
177[3]

Ravanchi *Frank Sheridan* a49
8 br m Indian Danehill(IRE) Ravishing (IRE) (Bigstone (IRE))
103[5] 158[6] 390[12]

Ravelo's Boy (USA) *Manuel J Azpurua* a103
3 ch c Lawyer Ron(USA) Dance Tune (USA) (French Deputy (USA))
2954a[9]

Ravens Nest *Robert Mills* a60 54
2 b g Piccolo Emouna (Cadeaux Genereux)
6532[4] 6928[8] 7306[10]

Raven's Rock (IRE) *Roger Varian* 63
2 b g Raven's Pass(USA) Delphinus (Soviet Star (USA))
5963[6] 6491[9] 7311[5]

Raven's Tower (USA) *Mahmood Al Zarooni* a70 70
2 b c Raven's Pass(USA) Tizdubai (USA) (Cee's Tizzy (USA))
5407[8] 5962[6] 6532[2]

Raving Monsun *Marco Botti* a70
3 ch f Monsun(GER) Rave Reviews (IRE) (Sadler's Wells (USA))
2848[8] 3279[9] 3773[6] 4875[5] (5754)

Ravi River (IRE) *Alistair Whillans* a70 84
8 ch g Barathea(IRE) Echo River (USA) (Irish River (FR))
3492[5] 4429[2] 4621[10] 6131[7] 7968[9]

Rawaafed (IRE) *Brian Meehan* a78 82
3 bb g Invasor(ARG) Holly's Kid (USA) (Pulpit (USA))
2196[14] 5555[5] 6215[3] 6842[3]

Rawaaq *D K Weld* 98
2 b f Invincible Spirit(IRE) Zaqrah (USA) (Silver Hawk (USA))
4276a[6] 6717a[2]

Rawaki (IRE) *Andrew Balding* a92 97
4 b g Phoenix Reach(IRE) Averami (Averti (IRE))
2248[7] ◆ 3642[2] 4363[5] 6039[2] 6445[3] (6848)

Rayaheen *Richard Hannon* 82
2 b f Nayef(USA) Natagora (FR) (Divine Light (JPN))
(3074) ◆ 4514[8] 5979[9] 6632[8]

Ray Diamond *Michael Madgwick* a38 20
7 ch g Medicean Musical Twist (USA) (Woodman (USA))
558[8] 2175[8] 5811[6]

Rayeni (IRE) *C Scandella* a65 93
6 ch h Indian Ridge Rayyana (IRE) (Rainbow Quest (USA))
4316a[10]

Rayo (CZE) *M Weiss* a70
7 br g Rainbows For Life(CAN) Radiace (CZE) (Sharp End)
631a[5]

Ray Of Joy *J R Jenkins* a91 86
6 b m Tobougg(IRE) Once Removed (Distant Relative)
(1289) 1926[4] 3188[2] 3822[3] 5576[5]

Rayvin Black *Mark H Tompkins* a68 83
3 b c Halling(USA) Optimistic (Reprimand)
1470[11] 2258[3] 3605[7] 4601[8] 5796[11] 6677[7] 6971[7] 7353[10]

Ray Ward (IRE) *David Simcock* a57
2 b c Galileo(IRE) Kentucky Warbler (IRE) (Spinning World (USA))
8071[9]

Razorbill (USA) *Charles Hills* 96
3 b c Speightstown(USA) High Walden (USA) (El Gran Senor (USA))
2553[2] (3079) ◆ 3667[2] 4009[7] 5094[5] (6374)

Razzle Dazzle 'Em *Shaun Harris* a11
3 b g Phoenix Reach(IRE) Rasmani (Medicean)
1132[13] 1923[13]

Reachforthebucks *Jane Chapple-Hyam* a91 91
4 ch g Phoenix Reach(IRE) Miles (Selkirk (USA))
280[3] (548) 1133[2] 1513[4] 1752[4] ◆ 2250[6]

Reach For The Sky (IRE) *Hugh McWilliams* a60 56
5 b m Elusive City(USA) Zara Whetei (IRE) (Lomond (USA))
7746[11] 8133[8]

Reaction *Michael Appleby* a67 66
6 ch g Alhaarth(IRE) Hawas (Mujtahid (USA))
(2392) 3967[3] 4409[5] 5417[8] 5950[6] 8273[2]

Ready (IRE) *Garry Moss* a82 73
2 ch g Elnadim(USA) Fusili (IRE) (Silvano (GER))
5382[7] 6133[2] 6818[3] (7244) 7399[6] (7737) (7856)

Reality (FR) *D Prod'Homme* a95 74
3 b f Slickly(FR) Rose Des Charmes (USA) (Cozzene (USA))
(542a)

Reality (GER) *U Stech*
2 b f Saddex Royal Topas (IRE) (Royal Academy (USA))
5612a[5]

Reality Show (IRE) *Michael Appleby* a88 8
5 b g Cape Cross(IRE) Really (IRE) (Entrepreneur)
4745[10] 5224[9]

Real Solution (USA) *Gianluca Bietolini* 107
3 b c Kitten's Joy(USA) Reachfortheheavens (USA) (Pulpit (USA))
2324a[6]

Real Tiara (FR) *Robert Collet* a73 69
2 b f Country Reel(USA) Royal Tiara (UAE) (Machiavellian (USA))
5697a[5]

Realt Na Mara (IRE) *Hughie Morrison* a60 45
9 bb g Tagula(IRE) Dwingeloo (IRE) (Dancing Dissident (USA))
5240[8]

Reasons Unknown (IRE) *Thomas McLaughlin* a57 67
4 ch g Camacho Locorotondo (IRE) (Broken Hearted)
(8113)

Reason To Believe (IRE) *Ben Haslam* a49 68
4 ch g Spartacus(IRE) Lady Fabiola (USA) (Open Forum (USA))
361[13] 646[6] 2924[5] 3731[7] 4315[4] 4865[9] 6529[5]

Rebecca Romero *Denis Coakley* a78 79
5 b m Exceed And Excel(AUS) Cloud Dancer (Bishop Of Cashel)
2369[8] 3390[3] (4231) 4849[4] 5272[4] 5815[3] 6226[6] 6370[6] 7309[3]

Rebecca's Filly (FR) *Robert Collet* 57
2 gr f Elusive City(USA) Kansa (FR) (Linamix (FR))
5288a[8]

Rebecca Wawa *Manila Illuminati* 15
3 b f Compton Place Beautiful Maria (IRE) (Sri Pekan (USA))
1409a[11]

Rebelde (IRE) *Conrad Allen* a74 37
2 b f Acclamation Maharani (USA) (Red Ransom (USA))
6936[2] 7518[15]

Rebellious Guest *George Margarson* 101
3 b g Cockney Rebel(IRE) Marisa (GER) (Desert Sun)
1509[4] 3265[13] 4063[14]

Rebel Magic *Richard Hannon* 88
2 b f Cockney Rebel(IRE) Aastral Magic (Magic Ring (IRE))
(2163) 3138[2] 4574[2] 4820[11]

Rebel Song (IRE) *Mahmood Al Zarooni* a86 78
3 b c Refuse To Bend(IRE) Dubai Opera (USA) (Dubai Millennium)
1892[8]

Rebel Woman *Mrs A Corson* a58 52
6 b m Royal Applause Wild Woman (Polar Falcon (USA))
1113[11]

Reberty Lee *Noel Quinlan* 57
2 b g Three Valleys(USA) Query (USA) (Distant View (USA))
1284[3] 1623[4] 1738[4] 2798[6] 4659[9]

Reckless Abandon *Clive Cox* 118
2 b c Exchange Rate(USA) Sant Elena (Efisio)
(2261) ◆ (3291) (4384a) (5398a) (7049)

Reckoning (IRE) *Jeremy Noseda* 102
3 b f Danehill Dancer(IRE) Great Hope (IRE) (Halling (USA))
7688[3] ◆

Reconsider Baby (IRE) *Mrs K Burke* 68
2 br f Refuse To Bend(IRE) Rockahoolababy (IRE) (Kalanisi (IRE))
2338[3] 3126[9] (4659) (5108) 6070[7]

Rectory Lane *Eve Johnson Houghton* a39
2 ch f Compton Place Pudding Lane (IRE) (College Chapel)
7987[11]

Recurrens (FR) *A Clement*
2 ch c Orpen(USA) Versande (FR) (Verglas (IRE))
8176a[0]

Redact (IRE) *Richard Hannon* a81 109
3 b g Strategic Prince Rainbow Java (IRE) (Fairy King (USA))
1453[4] 1856[10] 2641[10] 3265[21] 5102[6] 5572[7] 6676[8]

Red Adair (IRE) *Richard Hannon* a56 72
2 ch c Redback Daanaat (IRE) (Kheleyf (USA))
2609[3] 3010[3] 3444[11] 5060[6] 5532[7] 5968[3] 6732[10] 6975[5] 7304[9]

Red Aggressor (IRE) *Clive Brittain* a74 91
3 b g Red Clubs(IRE) Snap Crackle Pop (IRE) (Statoblest)
5686[5] 6143[14]

Redair (IRE) *David Evans* a83 80
3 b f Redback Alexander Goldmine (Dansili)
189[5] (321) 357[4] 469[4] (637) (768) (905) 1493[4] (2861) 4423[2] 4644[3]

Red Alex *James Given* 32
3 b g Nayef(USA) Expedience (USA) (With Approval (CAN))
1270[8] 1655[9] 2665[7]

Red All Over (IRE) *Alan Berry* 16
3 gr f Dark Angel(IRE) Rubies And Pearls (USA) (Chief's Crown (USA))
2470[10] 3848[10] 4550[9] 5446[11] 5762[6]

Red Army Blues (IRE) *G M Lyons* a73 73
4 b g Soviet Star(USA) Liscoa (IRE) (Foxhound (USA))
335a[12] 775a[9]

Red Art (IRE) *Charles Hills* a84 97
3 b c Excellent Art All Began (IRE) (Fasliyev (USA))
3607[4] 4319[11] 4740[13] 6676[14] 7508[9]

Red Avalanche (IRE) *Tony Newcombe* a77 62
5 gr g Verglas(IRE) Maura's Guest (IRE) (Be My Guest (USA))
31[13] 2165[9] 2555[11] 4492[3] 5362[5] ◆ 5874[3] 6000[3]

Red Avenger (USA) *Ed Dunlop* 91
2 bb c War Front(USA) Emotional Rescue (USA) (Smart Strike (CAN))
2784[6] (5685) 6138[2] (6597) ◆

Red Baron (IRE) *Eric Alston* 63
3 b c Moss Vale(IRE) Twinberry (IRE) (Tagula (IRE))
3990[9] 4456[3] 4807[8] 5831[13] 6100[2] 7001[10]

Red Bay *Jane Chapple-Hyam* a77 59
3 b g Haafhd Red Zinnia (Pivotal)
4661[7] 5120[10] 5942[11]

Red Cadeaux *Ed Dunlop* a117 119
6 ch g Cadeaux Genereux Artisia (IRE) (Peintre Celebre (USA))
1750[2] (2254) 2703[2] 3369[3] 4010[3] 7621a[8] 7872a[8] (8040a)

Red Cape (FR) *Ruth Carr* a85 84
9 b g Cape Cross(IRE) Muirfield (FR) (Crystal Glitters (USA))
62[6] 1015[8] 1168[8] 1476[9] (1630) 1720[2] 2133[3] 2476[3] 2876[7] (3276) (4207) 4680[9] 5801[5] 6194[7] 6358[6] (6837) 7145[5] 7254[2] 7651[5] 7863[2] 8232[8]

Red Catkin *George Margarson* a42 61
2 b f Notnowcato Red Salvia (Selkirk (USA))
5230[5] 5947[8] 6534[11]

Red Charmer (IRE) *Ann Duffield* 68
2 b g Red Clubs(IRE) Golden Charm (IRE) (Common Grounds)
5586[11] 6043[7] 6356[4] 7244[8]

Red Chubbs (IRE) *Ann Duffield* 16
2 b f Red Clubs(IRE) Defined Feature (IRE) (Nabeel Dancer (USA))
7244[9] 7379[12]

Red Clasp (IRE) *Ms Joanna Morgan* a60 63
2 b f Red Clubs(IRE) Buckle (IRE) (Common Grounds)
5858a[7]

Redclue (IRE) *Miss Louise Allan* a54 21
3 br g Red Clubs(IRE) Stratospheric (Slip Anchor)
194[5] 534[4] 1065[10] 1303[7] 4652[10] 4908[5]

Red Cobra (IRE) *Tim Easterby* 70
2 b g Redback Queen Cobra (IRE) (Indian Rocket)
3303[6] 3748[2] 4178[5] 4618[8] 4877[3] 5825[4] 6189[4] 6628[2] (6754)

Red Current *Michael Scudamore* a67 60
8 b m Soviet Star(USA) Fleet Amour (USA) (Afleet (CAN))
221[5] 566[11] 8067[10]

Red Delilah (IRE) *David Simcock* 60
2 b f Zamindar(USA) Flamenco Red (Warning)
4967[3]
Red Diesel (IRE) *Jo Hughes* a39 22
2 ch g Captain Rio With Finesse (Be My Guest (USA))
6093[5] 7272[9] 7711[9] 7977[7]
Red Dragon (IRE) *Charles Hills* a61 61
2 b c Acclamation Delphie Queen (IRE) (Desert Sun)
2073[6] 4512[5] 5235[6] 6147[5] ◆ 7059[6] (7974)
Red Dubawi (IRE) *A De Royer-Dupre* 109
4 ch h Dubawi(IRE) Maredsous (FR) (Homme De Loi (IRE))
4316a[6] 6464a[4] 6898a[7]
Red Duke (USA) *David Simcock* a106 111
3 ch c Hard Spun(USA) Saudia (USA) (Gone West (USA))
1145a[5] 1856[11] ◆ 2568a[3] 3265[10] 4760[8] 5869a[5]
Red Eclipse (IRE) *Alan Bailey* a57 56
2 b f Red Clubs(IRE) Negria (IRE) (Al Hareb (USA))
2892[7] 5176[6] 5631[6] 6541[5] 7026[5] 7060[4] 7467[2]
Red Eight (USA) *John Butler* a73 56
2 bb c Gone West(USA) Katherine Seymour (Green Desert (USA))
4555[7] 5221[6] 5797[5] 7708[2] 7919[11] (8132) 8240[6]
Redemptor *E Charpy* a106 92
4 gr h Elusive City(USA) Restless Rixa (FR) (Linamix (FR))
316a[7] 588a[9] 756a[11]
Red Explorer (USA) *Charles Hills* 82
2 b c Henrythenavigator(USA) Remote (USA) (Seattle Slew (USA))
3381[2] ◆ 4220[2] (4419)
Red Eyes *David Nicholls* a83 89
4 b g Beat Hollow Kardelle (Kalaglow)
6338[15]
Red Eye Special (NZ) *Michael Moroney* 105
6 b g Yamanin Vital(NZ) Flight All Nite (NZ) (Personal Escort (USA))
7073a[12]
Red Flash (IRE) *David Bridgwater* a53 52
5 b g Red Ransom(USA) Mar Blue (FR) (Marju (IRE))
66[6] 602[8]
Red Four *George Baker* 70
2 ch f Singspiel(IRE) Protectorate (Hector Protector (USA))
3504[4] 4701[6] 5978[7] 7103[5]
Red Ghost (GER) *S Smrczek* 87
3 ch c Dai Jin Ripley (GER) (Platini (GER))
1553a[8] 7784a[8]
Red Gift (IRE) *Brian Ellison* a57 69
2 b g Chineur(FR) Kiva (Indian Ridge)
3627[3] 4173[5] 5010[4]
Red Gulch *Mahmood Al Zarooni* a107 104
5 b g Kyllachy Enrapture (USA) (Lear Fan (USA))
140a[8] 416a[3] 586a[9] 6242[10]
Red Halo (IRE) *Sir Michael Stoute* 58
3 gr f Galileo(IRE) St Roch (IRE) (Danehill (USA))
2200[7]
Red Hand (USA) *John Gosden* a61 82
3 bb f Mr Greeley(USA) Helena Molony (IRE) (Sadler's Wells (USA))
1107[3] 1503[2] 1887[10] 5328[3] 6148[6] (6736)
Red Hermes (IRE) *Mark H Tompkins* a48 53
3 ch f Windsor Knot(IRE) Imposition (UAE) (Be My Guest (USA))
2340[4] 3391[9] 3974[2]
Red Highlites (IRE) *Ann Duffield* 70
2 br f Red Clubs(IRE) High Lite (Observatory (USA))
2334[11] 2587[8] 3747[2] 4083[3] 4395[5]
Redhotdoc *Bill Moore* a66 66
8 ch m Dr Fong(USA) Gecko Rouge (Rousillon (USA))
500[8] 600[4] 772[7]
Red Hot Secret *Jeremy Gask* a41 64
3 ch f Three Valleys(USA) Princess Miletrian (IRE) (Danehill (USA))
2273[8] 2757[7] 5279[7] 6401[13]
Red Inca *Brian Ellison* 84
4 ch g Pivotal Magicalmysterykate (USA) (Woodman (USA))
2606[5] ◆ 3380[2] 3628[2]
Redinessence (IRE) *Willie Musson* a58 58
4 b m Oratorio(IRE) Red Liason (IRE) (Selkirk (USA))
784[5] 1001[5] 1363[11] 2851[13] 3137[5] 3782[2]
Red Invader (IRE) *Charles Hills*
2 b c Red Clubs(IRE) Tifariti (USA) (Elusive Quality (USA))
4846[10]
Red Jade *Mrs K Burke* a67 90
7 ch g Dubai Destination(USA) Red Slippers (USA) (Nureyev (USA))
1239[7] 2180[8] 2504[10] 3163[6] 3564[7] 4115[11]
Red Jazz (USA) *Charles Hills* a110 115
5 b h Johannesburg(USA) Now That's Jazz (USA) (Sword Dance)
1143a[3] (2075) 2710[4] 3237[9] 4320[8] 5355[7] 7048[2] 7558[2]
Red Joker (IRE) *Alan Swinbank* 78
2 br g Red Clubs(IRE) Lady Singspiel (IRE) (Singspiel (IRE))
2923[2] (3520) 4206[2] 5587[2]
Red Koko (IRE) *George Moore* 39
2 ch f Sleeping Indian Aunt Sadie (Pursuit Of Love)
1235[3] 1594[5] 2309[7] 4806[5] 5291[5] 6121[13]
Red Lancer *Jonathen de Giles* a50 86
11 ch g Deploy Miss Bussell (Sabrehill (USA))
221[7]
Red Larkspur (IRE) *Roger Teal* a80 83
3 b f Red Clubs(IRE) Holda (IRE) (Docksider (USA))
1217[5] 1612[5] 2272[3] 2894[3] 3500[3] 4647[7] 7334[15]
Red Lover *Ed Dunlop* a71 77
4 b g Azamour(IRE) Love Me Tender (Green Desert (USA))
2328[3] 2899[9] 3920[5]
Red Mercury (IRE) *Ollie Pears* a58 63
4 ch g Majestic Missile(IRE) Fey Rouge (IRE) (Fayruz)
1673[3] 4349[10] 5171[15]
Red Mischief (IRE) *Harry Dunlop* a68 70
3 b f Red Clubs(IRE) Mujadilly (Mujadil (USA))
1449[8] 2045[13] 3510[4] 4533[12] 5279[2] 5774[8] 6961[11]
Red Mystique (IRE) *Philip Hide* a57 40
3 b g Red Clubs(IRE) Sacred Love (IRE) (Barathea (IRE))
1737[8] 2197[13] 2368[9] 4214[5] 4744[10] 5330[S] 7196[3] 8001[2] 8104[4]
Red Orator *Mark Johnston* a74 88
3 ch g Osorio(GER) Red Roses Story (FR) (Pink (FR))
(650) 1281[4] (5729) ◆ 6037[7] 6517[2] (6834)
Redoutable (IRE) *Kevin Prendergast* 95
3 b f Invincible Spirit(IRE) Rebelline (IRE) (Robellino (USA))
3645a[2] 4482a[7] 5523a[11]
Red Paladin (IRE) *Kevin Ryan* 62
2 b g Red Clubs(IRE) Alexander Goldmine (Dansili)
2213[5] 3520[3] 4132[6]
Red Pilgrim (IRE) *James Toller* 54
2 b c Authorized(IRE) Plenty Of Action (USA) (Hennessy (USA))
6412[6] 6845[7]
Red Protector (IRE) *Amy Weaver* 39
3 ch g Haafhd Red Ray (Pivotal)
4067[9] 4516[13]
Red Quartet (IRE) *Robert Eddery* 99
3 b c Red Clubs(IRE) Nans Lady (IRE) (Mozart (IRE))
1500[5] (1858) 2714[2] ◆
Red Ramesses (IRE) *John Best* a74 25
3 br g Red Clubs(IRE) Marasem (Cadeaux Genereux)
1086[3] ◆ 1512[14] 2041[9] 3343[8] 7668[6] 7770[4] 7988[4] 8109[2]
Red Rani *Reg Hollinshead* a16 1
7 ch m Whittingham(IRE) Crystal Magic (Mazilier (USA))
690[13]
Red Refraction (IRE) *Richard Hannon* a70 74
2 b c Red Clubs(IRE) Dreamalot (Falbrav (IRE))
2983[3] 3658[2] 4555[4] 4934[5] 5661[2]
Redressthebalance (IRE) *Ralph Beckett* a92 92
2 b f Ramonti(FR) Lady Naomi (USA) (Distant View (USA))
(3487) (4574) 5103[5] 5571[6] 6129a[8] 6980[5]
Red Rhythm *Mark Hoad* a44 64
5 ch g Starcraft(NZ) Araguaia (IRE) (Zafonic (USA))
1987[6] 3007[7] 3098[3] 3435[5] 4196[8] (4422) 4535[2] 5149[7] 6288[7] 6685[9] 6737[9] 7482[10] 7906[14]
Red Roar (IRE) *Alan Berry* a10 75
5 ch m Chineur(FR) Unfortunate (Komaite (USA))
1246[3] ◆ 1638[3] (3211) 3382[7] 3496[7] 4085[7] 4461[5] 5416[7] 5737[10] 6605[6] 7447[16]
Red Runaway *Ed Dunlop* a77 60
2 ch c Medicean Gretna (Groom Dancer (USA))
4555[6] (5478) 6247[6]
Red Scintilla *Nigel Tinkler* a21 59
5 b m Doyen(IRE) Red To Violet (Spectrum (IRE))
670[9] 886[4] 1248[3] 2091[10] 2239[9] 3075[7] 3209[3] 4087[3] 4438[6] 4865[14] 4957[5]
Red Seal *Tom Tate*
3 ch g Haafhd Seal Indigo (IRE) (Glenstal (USA))
4882[9] 6409[8]
Red Senor (IRE) *Charles Hills* a78 77
3 b c Red Clubs(IRE) Belsay (Belmez (USA))
(1072) 1317[5] 2347[5] 2986[6] 3486[4] 4412[6] 7412[2] ◆
Red Seventy *Richard Hannon* a83 99
3 b g Sakhee(USA) Dimakya (USA) (Dayjur (USA))
1216[6] 1845[4] 3294[29] 4703[18] 7107[3] 7559[6] 7823[10]
Red Shadow *Alan Brown* a63 58
3 b f Royal Applause Just A Glimmer (Bishop Of Cashel)
1817[5] 2139[2] 2862[4] 3407[3] 4397[10] 5014[4] 5590[4] 6104[3] 6479[10] (6640) 6823[2] 7055[9] 7482[5]
Red Shot (FR) *H-A Pantall* a70 70
2 b f Gentlewave(IRE) Red Kiss (IRE) (Fasliyev (USA))
5288a[10]
Red Shuttle *Noel Quinlan* a73 77
5 b g Starcraft(NZ) Red Azalea (Shirley Heights)
300[2] 451[2] 688[3] 959[5] 2199[3] ◆ 3594[3] 4541[3]
Red Soles (IRE) *Charles Hills* a49 39
4 b m Barathea(IRE) Inchoate (Machiavellian (USA))
273[6] 451[5]
Red Somerset (USA) *Mike Murphy* a85 68
9 b g Red Ransom(USA) Bielska (USA) (Deposit Ticket (USA))
1983 299[2] (634) (760) (906) 989[2] (1045) (1342) 2398[2] 8250[2] ◆
Red Star Lady (IRE) *Mrs K Burke* a60 57
2 b f Redback Vigorous (IRE) (Danetime (IRE))
1136[4] 2261[16] 4512[4] 4927[7] 5807[3] 5916[4] 6890[7]
Red Style (IRE) *Paul Midgley* 67
2 b g Red Clubs(IRE) In The Fashion (IRE) (In The Wings)
1218[9] 1437[2] 2614[3] 3110[6] 4132[3] 4637[5] 6130[6]
Red Trump (IRE) *Charles Hills* a70 59
3 b c Red Clubs(IRE) Wolf Cleugh (IRE) (Last Tycoon)
308[6] 358[2] (638) 3994[5] 5338[5] 6050[8] 7395[6]
Red Tulip *James Fanshawe* a65
2 br f Kheleyf(USA) Red Carnation (IRE) (Polar Falcon (USA))
6936[5] 7410[2] 7924[5]
Red Turban *Jeremy Noseda* 74
2 b f Kyllachy Red Tiara (USA) (Mr Prospector (USA))
(6007) 6675[11]
Red Tyke (IRE) *John Quinn* a39 64
3 b g Red Clubs(IRE) Teutonic (IRE) (Revoque (IRE))
1386[5] 1918[3] 2340[5] 3023[2] (4210) 4955[5] (6516) 7444[3]
Red Valerian (IRE) *Charles Hills* a70 25
2 b c Royal Applause Hidden Heart (USA) (Kingmambo (USA))
6845[9] 7498[2]
Redvers (IRE) *Ed Vaughan* a87 96
4 br g Ishiguru(USA) Cradle Brief (IRE) (Brief Truce (USA))
1128[6] 2250[8] 2489[5] 2896[3] 3403[4] (4317) 5356[13] 6235[3] 6676[2] 7240[5]
Red Willow *John E Long* a63 41
6 ch m Noverre(USA) Chelsea Blue (ITY) (Barathea (IRE))
5771[5]
Red Yarn *Daniel Kubler* a68 78
5 b m Lucky Story(USA) Aunt Ruby (USA) (Rubiano (USA))
60[6] 574[14] 732[8] 5349[5] 5938[7]
Reech Band *D De Watrigant* a73 101
3 ch f Choisir(AUS) Marina Ellen (USA) (Giant's Causeway (USA))
1426a[3] 3987a[3]
Reem (AUS) *M F De Kock* a104 106
5 ch m Galileo(IRE) Al Afreet (AUS) (Danehill (USA))
140a[10] ◆ 245a[3] 416a[7] 617a[3]
Reem Star *Kevin Ryan* a85 92
4 b m Green Tune(USA) Arlecchina (GER) (Mtoto)
2863[3] (3377) 4115[2] 4613[10] 5491[9]
Ree's Rascal (IRE) *Jim Boyle* a86 86
4 gr g Verglas(IRE) Night Scent (IRE) (Scenic)
1416[2] 1752[3] (2500) 3667[8] 4689[8] 5535[6]
Reflect (IRE) *Derek Shaw* a87 93
4 b g Hurricane Run(IRE) Raphimix (FR) (Linamix (FR))
1139[11] 2248[15] 3609[2] 4460[6] 6555[2] 8234[4]
Refractor (IRE) *James Fanshawe* a89 82
4 ch g Refuse To Bend(IRE) Fancy Intense (Peintre Celebre (USA))
1875 1258[8] (1706) 2419[5] 5129[4] (5944) 6584[4]
Refreshestheparts (USA) *George Baker* a72 54
3 ch f Proud Citizen(USA) St Francis Wood (USA) (Irish River (FR))
2367[15] 3665[13] 4754[3] (5479) 6057[3] 6174[2] 6502[2] (8083) 8199[10]
Refuse To Mambo *Reg Hollinshead* a50 46
2 ch g Refuse To Bend(IRE) Sovereign's Honour (USA) (Kingmambo (USA))
7127[6] 7517[7] 7750[8] 7971[6]
Refute (IRE) *Harry Dunlop* 31
3 b c Refuse To Bend(IRE) Renowned (IRE) (Darshaan)
5404[7] 6228[7] 7016[9]
Regal Acclaim (IRE) *Declan Carroll* a62 65
3 b g Acclamation Certain Charm (USA) (Thunder Gulch (USA))
(1600) 2283[5] 2795[2] 3184[2] 3908[4] 4830[3] 5170[7] 5415[6] 7670[8] 7906[4]
Regal Approval *Jim Boyle* a83 73
4 br g Royal Applause Enthralled (Zafonic (USA))
1727[10] 2975 [10] 4503[12] 5234[8]
Regal Art *Jo Crowley* a30 38
3 ch c Dutch Art Grey Pearl (Ali-Royal (IRE))
1512[11] 3155[9]
Regal Aura *John Gosden* a65 73
3 b f Teofilo(IRE) Regal Velvet (Halling (USA))
2200[4] ◆ 3035[3] 3763[3] 4466[6]
Regal Dan (IRE) *Charles Hills* 87
2 b c Dark Angel(IRE) Charlene Lacy (IRE) (Pips Pride)
1411[3] 1842[4] 2420[3] 3117[4] 5088[5] ◆ 5563[3] ◆ (6138)
Regal Diva *Reg Hollinshead* 56
4 b m Denounce Royal Fontaine (IRE) (Royal Academy (USA))
2768[9] 3484[6] 4791[8] 5456[6]
Regal Hawk *James Tate* a72
2 br f Singspiel(IRE) Elegant Hawk (Generous (IRE))
(7199)
Regal Lady *David Brown* a62 43
3 b f Captain Rio Alvarinho Lady (Royal Applause)
135[6] 326 [5]
Regally Ready (USA) *Steven Asmussen* 122
5 ch g More Than Ready(USA) Kivi (USA) (King Of Kings (IRE))
875a[13] 1146a[14]
Regalo Rosado *Mike Murphy* a49 49
3 ch f Cadeaux Genereux Pinkai (IRE) (Caerleon (USA))
2542[8] 3398[8] 4366[9] 4932[6] 5405[8] 6442[6] 7196[4]
Regal Parade *Milton Bradley* a97 115
8 ch g Pivotal Model Queen (USA) (Kingmambo (USA))
53a[2] 316a[4] 416a[11] 756a[9] 2074[2] 2505[6] 3623[3] 4092[6] 4328[3] 5370[9] 5686[3] 5814[2] 6468[2] 6868[10] (7066) 7624a[11]
Regal Rave (USA) *Peter Hedger* a68 67
5 b g Wild Event(USA) Golden Crown (USA) (Defensive Play (USA))
151[2] 188[7] 1379[3] 1919[4] 2851[7] 4511[7] 4940[6] 5935[11]
Regal Realm *Jeremy Noseda* 106
3 b f Medicean Regal Riband (Fantastic Light (USA))
1454[12] (4764) 5627[7] 6161[8]
Regal Silk *Jeremy Noseda* 74
2 b f Pivotal Regal Velvet (Halling (USA))
6636[2] ◆
Regal Swain (IRE) *Alan Swinbank* a5 79
4 b g Ivan Denisovich(IRE) Targhyb (IRE) (Unfuwain (USA))
1662[5] 1867[2] 2095[3] 2510[3] 4325[6] 4622[3] 5243[10] 6073[10]
Regal Tramp (USA) *V C Ward* a79 79
4 b m Street Cry(IRE) Unique Pose (IRE) (Sadler's Wells (USA))
6066a[11]
Regamonti (FR) *W Hefter* 80
5 b g Muhtathir Regatina (IRE) (Perugino (USA))
5030a[2]
Regarde Moi *S Botti* 106
4 b g King's Best(USA) Life At Night (IRE) (Night Shift (USA))
2521a[5]
Regatta (FR) *E Lellouche* 100
3 ch f Layman(USA) Red Star (IRE) (Lure (USA))
2109a[13] 3682a[5] 5249a[5] 6088a[9]
Regency Art (IRE) *Milton Bradley* a47 76
5 b g Titus Livius(FR) Honey Storm (IRE) (Mujadil (USA))
2321[2] 2421[16] 2758[8] 5203[14] 5999[9] 6546[7]
Regency Dreams *Nikki Evans*
7 ch g Dreams End Regency Fox (Bold Fox)
6228[12]
Reggae Dancer (IRE) *Bent Olsen* a58 74
5 b h Rock Of Gibraltar(IRE) Don't Care (IRE) (Nordico (USA))
2159a[5]
Reggae Rock (IRE) *John C McConnell* a87 83
5 b h Red Ransom(USA) Calonnog (IRE) (Peintre Celebre (USA))
342a[5]
Reggae Star *Mark Johnston* 71
2 b f Cape Cross(IRE) Caribbean Dancer (USA) (Theatrical (IRE))
5184[2] 5562[7] 6043[2]
Reggie Bond *Geoffrey Oldroyd* a47 49
2 ch g Monsieur Bond(IRE) Triple Tricks (IRE) (Royal Academy (USA))
3168[5] 5311[12] 5586[7] 6893[5]
Reggie Perrin *Pat Phelan* a69 70
4 ch g Storming Home Tecktal (FR) (Pivotal)
(2395) 3769[2] 3997[4] 5706[4] 6703[11] 7012[2]
Reginald Claude *Mark Usher* a62 65
4 b g Monsieur Bond(IRE) Miller's Melody (Chief Singer)
2413[6] 3076[4] 4469[7] 5049[8] 5346[5] 5625[8] 6002[9] 6585[7] 7362[3] (7748) 7837[4] 7992[7] (8169)
Registara (GER) *Markus Klug* 93
3 b f Sternkoenig(IRE) Richgorl (GER) (Neshad (USA))
5142a[10]
Register (IRE) *William Muir* a71 81
3 b g Lawman(FR) Paldouna (IRE) (Kaldoun (FR))
2041[5] 2273[3] 2800[4] 4948[9] 6965[13]
Reglisse (IRE) *Edward Lynam* 97
2 gr f Verglas(IRE) Regalline (IRE) (Green Desert (USA))
4276a[4] 4519a[4] 6266a[2] 6717a[7]
Regulation (IRE) *M Halford* 92
3 br g Danehill Dancer(IRE) Source Of Life (IRE) (Fasliyev (USA))
4692a[9]
Rehearse (FR) *D Prod'Homme* a29
3 gr f Slickly(FR) Rangers Lodge (FR) (Grand Lodge (USA))
211a[10]
Rei D'Oro (USA) *David Simcock* a75 74
3 bb c Seeking The Gold(USA) Grand Marq (USA) (King Of Kings (IRE))
(404) 2390[3] ◆ 2889[8] 3945[7] 5482[4] 6647[6] 7358[2]
Reignier *Mrs K Burke* a89 98
5 b g Kheleyf(USA) Komena (Komaite (USA))
266[6] 962[8] 1821[12] 2505[7]
Reigns Of Glory (IRE) *Richard Hannon* a32 65
3 b c Dylan Thomas(IRE) Lolita's Gold (USA) (Royal Academy (USA))
2196[8] 2708[7] 3763[7]
Reillys Daughter *Richard Mitchell* a70 67
4 b m Diktat Compose (Anabaa (USA))
1613[3] 2175[5] (3283) 3498[3] 8073[12]
Reina De Luz (IRE) *Lee Smyth* 68
3 b f Echo Of Light Three Greens (Niniski (USA))
8113[12]
Reinvigorate (IRE) *Richard Hannon* a53 53
2 b f Invincible Spirit(IRE) Miss Serendipity (IRE) (Key Of Luck (USA))
4419[4] 4816[7] 5424[7] 5675[4] 5807[10]
Rekindled Interest (AUS) *Jim Conlan* 121
5 b g Redoute's Choice(AUS) Rekindled Affair (IRE) (Rainbow Quest (USA))
7426a[14]
Related *Clive Cox* 81
2 b c Kheleyf(USA) Balladonia (Primo Dominie)
3506[4] 4555[2] (5304)
Relay *Richard Hannon* a54 44
2 b f Clodovil(IRE) Figlette (Darshaan)
1136[8] 1202[4] 1253[6]
Release The Funds (IRE) *David Nicholls* a14 26
3 ch g Kheleyf(USA) Indian Imp (Indian Ridge)
283[6]
Relentless (IRE) *John Gosden* 56
2 b g Dylan Thomas(IRE) Karamiyna (IRE) (Shernazar)
6876[9] 7332[7]
Relentless Harry (IRE) *George Baker* a75 69
3 gr c Excellent Art Les Alizes (IRE) (Cadeaux Genereux)
1985[6] 2375[4] 6840[7] 7725[5] 7997[5]
Reliable Man *A De Royer-Dupre* 124
4 gr h Dalakhani(IRE) On Fair Stage (IRE) (Sadler's Wells (USA))
1696a[3] 2533a[6] 3267[4] 4322[4] 6464a[2] 7094a[8]
Reliant Robin (IRE) *Robert Mills* a69 79
2 b c Moss Vale(IRE) Meadow (Green Desert (USA))
2579[3] (2844) 6414[8] 6883[16] 7164[5] (7298)
Relight My Fire *Tim Easterby* a63 62
2 ch g Firebreak Making Music (Makbul)
1911[7] 2123[4] 3436[9] 4139[2] 4450[8] 5010[2] 5920[3] 6337[7]
Remember Alexander *Mrs John Harrington* 105
3 b f Teofilo(IRE) Nausicaa (USA) (Diesis)
1403a[4] 2101a[5] 3197a[4]
Remember Rocky *Steve Gollings* a47 59
3 ch g Haafhd Flower Market (Cadeaux Genereux)
1519[9] 2118[3] 2340[6] 2788[10] 4549[2] 4932[8]

Remix (IRE) *J W Hills* a67 51
3 b f Oratorio(IRE) Miss Lopez (IRE) (Key Of Luck (USA))
308[5] 2136[8] 3044[7] 3454[10]

Remus De La Tour (FR) *K Borgel* a97 111
3 b c Stormy River(FR) Calithea (IRE) (Marju (IRE))
(364a) 716a[5] (3204a) 6294a[4] 7284a[6]

Reneesgotzip (USA) *Peter Miller* a110 105
3 ch f City Zip(USA) No Dress Code (USA) (Distorted Humor (USA))
7571a[3]

Renee's Queen (USA) *Eric J Guillot* a83 87
2 ch f After Market(USA) Mighty Renee (USA) (Maria's Mon (USA))
7548a[7]

Renee's Titan (USA) *Doug O'Neill* a92
2 b f Bernstein(USA) Titan Queen (USA) (Tiznow (USA))
5031a[4]

Renegotiate *Andrew Balding* a72 70
3 ch g Trade Fair L'Extra Honor (USA) (Hero's Honor (USA))
1320[7] 1853[11] 2625[3] (3246) 3469[6] 6430[2] 6976[3] 7702[2] 7954[4] 8153[5]

Rene Mathis (GER) *Richard Fahey* a74 34
2 ch g Monsieur Bond(IRE) Remina (GER) (Erminius (GER))
5963[13] (8233)

Renoir's Lady *Simon Dow* a61 58
4 b m Peintre Celebre(USA) Marie De Blois (IRE) (Barathea (IRE))
148[7] 293[10] 3152[4] 4942[2] 5625[11] 5850[11] (7362) 8061[3] 8299[4]

Repeater *Sir Mark Prescott Bt* a68 109
3 b g Montjeu(IRE) Time Over (Mark Of Esteem (IRE))
3859[2] 5078[4] 5580[4] 6198[4] 6415[6]

Replicator *Patrick Gilligan* a56 41
7 b g Mujahid(USA) Valldemosa (Music Boy)
122[10] 312[5] 467[10] 544[9] 3008[9] 3467[5] 4467[9] 4929[8] 6496[5] 7275[13] 7901[11] 8046[7] 8210[6]

Reply (IRE) *A P O'Brien* 112
3 b c Oasis Dream Cap Coz (IRE) (Indian Ridge)
2514a[3] 3265[12] 4100[12] 7048[6]

Reposer (IRE) *Noel Quinlan* a86 80
4 br g Kheleyf(USA) Tragic Point (IRE) (Tragic Role (USA))
251[11] 528[6] 713[5] 894[8]

Represent (IRE) *Mick Channon* a68 77
3 b f Exceed And Excel(AUS) Craigmill (Slip Anchor)
1365[4] 1979[6] 2136[6] 2367[3] 2540[6] 3489[3] 4196[2] (4506) 4753[4] (5279) 5582[5] 5995[8] 6173[4] 6378[3] 6739[4] 6961[2] 7274[5]

Representation (USA) *Mahmood Al Zarooni* a86 73
3 ch c Street Cry(IRE) Portrayal (USA) (Saint Ballado (CAN))
(5889) 7168[10] 7475[8]

Reqaaba *John Gosden* a60 76
2 b f Exceed And Excel(AUS) Something Blue (Petong)
6873[7] ◆ 7160[7]

Requested *Mahmood Al Zarooni* a77 77
2 b c Dubawi(IRE) Dream Quest (Rainbow Quest (USA))
2662[3] 4066[16] 4507[3] 4951[6] 7501[3] ◆

Require *Luca Cumani* 94
3 b f Montjeu(IRE) Request (Rainbow Quest (USA))
1503[6] 2249[10] 2768[3] (3813) ◆ 4796[2] 5306[8] (6964) 7519[5]

Requisite *Ian Wood* a85 82
7 ch m Pivotal Chicarica (USA) (The Minstrel (CAN))
83a[0] 311[6] 520[6] 563[3] 686[3] 711[8]

Requisition (IRE) *A P O'Brien* 108
3 b c Invincible Spirit(IRE) Saoire (Pivotal)
5286a[3] ◆

Rerouted (USA) *M F De Kock* 108
4 ch h Stormy Atlantic(USA) Rouwaki (USA) (Miswaki (USA))
420a[5] ◆ 588a[3] 682a[2] 792a[6]

Reset City *Ian Williams* a70 72
6 ch m Reset(AUS) City Of Angels (Woodman (USA))
850[3] 1170[2] 1418[2] 2260[5] 2751[7] 4504[2] 4905[3] 5474[6] 6098[9]

Resonare *Stuart Williams* a52 35
3 b g Echo Of Light Pretty Kool (Inchinor)
6930[12] 7952[5] ◆ (8109)

Resplendent Ace (IRE) *Karen Tutty* a71 49
8 b g Trans Island Persian Polly (Persian Bold)
4884[10]

Resplendent Alpha *Jamie Osborne* a70 71
8 ch g Best Of The Bests(IRE) Sunley Scent (Wolfhound (USA))
60[2] 276[9] 329[6] 477[2] 1224[2] 1562[3] 1634[2] 1895[7] (1956) 2051[8] 2237[3] (2364) 6842[7] 7256[9] 7473[5] 7768[8] 7905[2] 8051[4] 8079[2] (8173) 8297[2]

Resplendent Light *Bernard Llewellyn* a73 73
7 b g Fantastic Light(USA) Bright Halo (IRE) (Bigstone (IRE))
(2233) 2498[6] 2867[4]

Responsive *Hughie Morrison* a60 90
3 b f Dutch Art Xtrasensory (Royal Applause)
1457[4] 2276[13] 2854[3] 3393[7] 4062[5] 4949[10] 6023[6] 6870[15]

Restaurateur (IRE) *Andrew Balding* a86 79
3 b c Excellent Art Velvet Appeal (IRE) (Petorius)
3446[3] 4288[8] 4772[8] 5237[7] 5747[2] 6136[3] (6840) 7789[7]

Restiadargent (FR) *H-A Pantall* 117
3 b f Kendargent(FR) Restia (FR) (Montjeu (IRE))
1209a[4] 2179[7] 3370[3] 4861a[5] 5648a[6] 7236[12] 7624a[9]

Restless Bay (IRE) *Mrs K Burke* a83 84
4 br g Elusive City(USA) Argus Gal (IRE) (Alzao (USA))
64[6] 157[5] 997[5] 1091[5] 1587[4] 1827[3] 2355[5] 2551[2] 2841[4] 3231[3] (3944) 4887[10] 5338[8] 5737[3] 6403[4] 6498[4] 7864[3] 7936[4] 8063[2] 8266[3]

Restraint Of Trade (IRE) *Mahmood Al Zarooni* 96
2 b c Authorized(IRE) Zivania (IRE) (Shernazar)
5534[3] 5962[5] 6371[2] (6919) (7554)

Resurge (IRE) *Stuart Kittow* a92 107
7 b g Danehill Dancer(IRE) Resurgence (Polar Falcon (USA))
1605[7] (1999) 2655[7] 2911[6] 3635[12] 6166[2] 6702[2]

Resuscitator (USA) *Linda Stubbs* a82 69
5 b g Bernstein(USA) Lac Du Printemps (USA) (Meadowlake (USA))
2580[4] 3947[5] 4950[11]

Retreat Content (IRE) *Linda Perratt* a54 72
4 b g Dubai Destination(USA) Sharp Point (IRE) (Royal Academy (USA))
1879[10] 2033[3] 2619[5] 2926[3] 4137[6] 6262[13] 6758[2] 7383[7]

Retrieve (AUS) *Saeed Bin Suroor* a115 116
5 b h Rahy(USA) Hold To Ransom (USA) (Red Ransom (USA))
(2081) ◆ 2478[3] 3329[5] 4094[3] 4684[4] (6637) 7287a[2] 7689[7]

Retromania (IRE) *John Best* a53 41
3 b g Moss Vale(IRE) Vade Retro (IRE) (Desert Sun)
1979[11] 3965[9] 6365[13] 7620[9]

Returntobrecongill *Sally Hall* 59
2 ch g Pastoral Pursuits Turn Back (Pivotal)
4710[12] 5311[5] 5962[8]

Reuben Percival (NZ) *Gai Waterhouse* 105
6 b g Al Akbar(AUS) Yachting Magic (NZ) (Yachtie (AUS))
7073a[9] 7425a[2] 7560a[7] 7783a[2]

Reveal The Light *Garry Woodward* a44 20
5 b m Fantastic Light(USA) Paper Chase (FR) (Machiavellian (USA))
976[8] 3081[10]

Reve De Nuit (USA) *Alan McCabe* a105 70
6 ch g Giant's Causeway(USA) My Dream Castles (USA) (Woodman (USA))
5[2] 868[10] 1035[3] 1128[13] 1273[9] 1654[8]

Reve Du Jour (IRE) *Alan McCabe* a75 64
3 b f Iffraaj Melaaya (USA) (Aljabr (USA))
181[6] (491) 645[2] 749[2] 898[2] (975) 1176[3] 2400[2] 2764[6] 4143[4] 4496[13]

Reveille *Hughie Morrison* a38 71
2 ch f Sakhee's Secret Up At Dawn (Inchinor)
5656[2] 6168[6] 6535[8] 7173[4] 7965[10] 8289[10]

Revelette (USA) *Charles Hills* 53
3 b f Mizzen Mast(USA) Skimble (USA) (Lyphard (USA))
1501[7] 3461[4] 4926[6]

Reverberate *Andrew Crook*
3 b f Echo Of Light Niseem (USA) (Hennessy (USA))
7384[7] 7978[6]

Revered Citizen (USA) *Sir Michael Stoute* a81 80
3 b c Proud Citizen(USA) Well Revered (USA) (Red Ransom (USA))
5404[2] 5952[4] 7384[2]

Revise (IRE) *Marco Botti* a60
2 b c Dansili Niner's Home (USA) (Forty Niner (USA))
7323[5] 7750[5]

Revitalise *Paul Midgley* 55
3 b g Vital Equine(IRE) Tancred Arms (Clantime)
7800[12]

Revolving World (IRE) *Lee James* a49 21
9 b g Spinning World(USA) Mannakea (USA) (Fairy King (USA))
453[3] 889[3] 1432[6]

Rewarded *James Toller* 105
3 b g Motivator Granted (FR) (Cadeaux Genereux)
(1648) (1860) 2269[4] 3295[3] 4007[4] 5250a[7] 6674[28]

Rex Imperator *Roger Charlton* 109
3 b g Royal Applause Elidore (Danetime (IRE))
3158[5] (3641) ◆ 4598[4] 5487[11] 5814[5] 6244[20]

Rex Romanorum (IRE) *Patrick Holmes* 72
4 b g Holy Roman Emperor(IRE) Willowbridge (IRE) (Entrepreneur)
2095[7] 2441[3] ◆ (4313) 5713[8] 6410[14] 6709[5]

Rex Whistler (IRE) *Julie Camacho* a54 31
2 b g Tamayuz Dangle (IRE) (Desert Style (IRE))
5668[11] 7840[4]

Reyaadah *Charles Hills* 94
2 b f Tamayuz Tafaani (IRE) (Green Desert (USA))
(3590) ◆ 5103[3] ◆ 6199[4]

Reyal (ITY) *S Botti* 103
4 b m Altieri Cape Grey (IRE) (Cape Cross (IRE))
7075a[4]

Reyamour *Alan King* a78 85
4 b m Azamour(IRE) Reynosa (IRE) (Montjeu (IRE))
(2204) (2909) 3556[7]

Reynaldothewizard (USA) *S Seemar* a106 96
6 b g Speightstown(USA) Holiday Runner (USA) (Meadowlake (USA))
244a[4] 589a[5] 757a[12]

Rey Rocket (USA) *Henry Collazo*
2 bb g Rey De Cafe(USA) Majestic Mood (USA) (Becker (USA))
8244a[2]

Rezwaan *Murty McGrath* a76 83
5 b g Alhaarth(IRE) Nasij (USA) (Elusive Quality (USA))
(306) ◆ 568[6] ◆ 821[3] 967[8] 1611[3] (2044) 6171[10] 6735[9] 7171[7] 7480[12] 7805[10] 8199[11]

Rhagori *Ralph Beckett* a90 87
3 b f Exceed And Excel(AUS) Cresta Gold (Halling (USA))
2272[4] ◆ 3643[2] (4753) (5796) 7475[2]

Rhagori Aur *Bryan Smart* a85 80
2 ch f Exceed And Excel(AUS) Aberdovey (Mister Baileys)
(2282) 2715[5] 4093[21] 4827[5] 5620[4] (6312) (7220)

Rhamnus *Richard Hannon* 86
2 b c Sakhee's Secret Happy Lady (FR) (Cadeaux Genereux)
2193[2] ◆ (2852) ◆ 4058[6] 7331[2]

Rhenania (IRE) *M Nigge* a97 89
5 ch m Shamardal(USA) Cois Cuain (IRE) (Night Shift (USA))
7985a[3] (8300a)

Rhombus (IRE) *William Haggas* 73
2 b g Authorized(IRE) Mathool (IRE) (Alhaarth (IRE))
4595[9] 4995[5] (7205)

Rhossili Bay *Alastair Lidderdale* a57 53
3 b f Beat Hollow Welsh Dawn (Zafonic (USA))
2204[10] 2612[5] 3484[8] 5810[3] 6892[3] 7527[6] 7619[5]

Rhyme Royal *James Given* a48 24
3 b f Byron Burton Ash (Diktat)
196[3] 459[8] 832[3] 993[9]

Rhyolite (IRE) *Marco Botti* a56 55
2 b c Rock Of Gibraltar(IRE) Ghenwah (FR) (Selkirk (USA))
5062[11] 6214[8] 7868[10]

Rhythm Of Light *Tom Dascombe* 106
4 b m Beat Hollow Luminda (IRE) (Danehill (USA))
245a[7] 617a[5] 3266[12] (4328) 5092[4] (5849a) (7577a)

Rhyton (IRE) *Brian Storey* a61 64
5 b g Rainbow Quest(USA) Sea Picture (IRE) (Royal Academy (USA))
4138[8] 4431[7] 5086[U]

Rialya (AUS) *Lloyd Kennewell* 104
5 b g Kempinsky(AUS) Ettu Blu (AUS) (Prince Echo (IRE))
7425a[9]

Ribaat (IRE) *Roger Varian* 91
2 b c Invincible Spirit(IRE) Fonda (USA) (Quiet American (USA))
(5040) 6139[3]

Ribbons *James Fanshawe* a74
2 ch f Manduro(GER) Sister Act (Marju (IRE))
(7721) ◆

Ricasiendo (GER) *Dr A Bolte* 29
3 gr c Sabiango(GER) Rososterna (GER) (Sternkoenig (IRE))
7266a[10]

Rich Again (IRE) *James Bethell* a70 62
3 b g Amadeus Wolf Fully Fashioned (IRE) (Brief Truce (USA))
1521[7] 2262[4] 7838[5] (8064)

Richard's Kid (USA) *Doug O'Neill* a118 106
7 bb h Lemon Drop Kid(USA) Tough Broad (USA) (Broad Brush (USA))
488a[6] 878a[5] 1143a[4] 7576a[5]

Richelieu *Lee Smyth* a68 58
10 b g Machiavellian(USA) Darling Flame (USA) (Capote (USA))
335a[5]

Rich Forever (IRE) *James Bethell* a52 75
2 b g Camacho Sixfields Flyer (IRE) (Desert Style (IRE))
4877[7] 5367[6] (6099) 6883[15] 7478[9]

Richo *Shaun Harris* a38 62
6 ch g Bertolini(USA) Noble Water (FR) (Noblequest (FR))
8265[10]

Ricochet Court (USA) *Nicholas Zito*
2 bb g Doneraile Court(USA) Rose Jade (USA) (Jade Hunter (USA))
(8244a)

Riczar *Tom Dascombe* a63 42
4 b m Intikhab(USA) Tharwa (IRE) (Last Tycoon)
7347[11]

Ridasiyna (FR) *M Delzangles* 121
3 b f Motivator Ridafa (IRE) (Darshaan)
(3682a) 5472a[5] (6911a) 7549a[4]

Riddle Master *Sir Henry Cecil* 59
3 ch g Observatory(USA) Quandary (USA) (Blushing Groom (FR))
3107[6]

Ridgeblade *Noel Wilson* 45
2 ch f Bahamian Bounty Verasina (USA) (Woodman (USA))
4825[10] 6071[6] 6335[7] 6707[7]

Ridgeway Hawk *Mark Usher* a66 36
4 ch g Monsieur Bond(IRE) Barefooted Flyer (USA) (Fly So Free (USA))
139[5] (289) 385[5] 752[6] 904[3] 1178[4] 8256[6]

Ridgeway Sapphire *Mark Usher* a24 54
5 b m Zafeen(FR) Barefooted Flyer (USA) (Fly So Free (USA))
3075[5] 3466[5] 4492[4] 4815[6] ◆ 5203[6] 5444[5] 5937[7]

Riding The River (USA) *David Cotey* a94 113
5 b g Wiseman's Ferry(USA) Glow Ruby Go (USA) (Rubiano (USA))
6300a[4]

Ridiyka (IRE) *Seamus Mullins* a45
3 b f Sinndar(IRE) Ridakiya (IRE) (Desert King (IRE))
5154[8]

Riflessione *Ronald Harris* a74 70
6 ch g Captain Rio Hilites (IRE) (Desert King (IRE))
62[4] 179[7] 388[5] 474[8] 658[2] 763[9] 911[6] 1069[2] 1279[3] 1480[2] 2146[2]

Riggins (IRE) *Ed Walker* a105 102
8 b g Cape Cross(IRE) Rentless (Zafonic (USA))
1034[6] 1212[8]

Rightcar *Peter Grayson* a62 11
5 b g Bertolini(USA) Loblolly Bay (Halling (USA))
155[2] 264[2] (312) 473[2] 522[3] 844[5] 996[3] 1343[5] 1483[3] 1734[8] 4653[9] 4928[4] 6180[6] 6496[3] 7465[8] 7746[8] 8209[5]

Right Credentials *Richard Ford* a5
4 b m Diktat Approved Quality (IRE) (Persian Heights)
1111[7]

Right Divine (IRE) *Brian Meehan* a73 84
3 gr g Verglas(IRE) Yellow Trumpet (Petong)
471[4] ◆ 2930[15] 3999[5]

Right Regal (IRE) *Marco Botti* a64 80
3 b g King's Best(USA) Royal Esteem (Mark Of Esteem (IRE))
1612[11] 2649[4] 3231[2]

Right Result (IRE) *James Bethell* a88 78
3 b g Acclamation Mist And Stone (IRE) (Xaar)
1271[4] 1858[17] 2265[9] 2979[6] 3963[9] 4779[8] 5130[4] (6052) 6454[10]

Right Step *Alan Jarvis* a100 104
5 b g Xaar Maid To Dance (Pyramus (USA))
(1605) 2176[10] 3372[6] 4112[16] 4684[17] 5558[18] 6702[7] 7396[5]

Right Stuff (FR) *Gary Moore* a97 61
9 bb g Dansili Specificity (USA) (Alleged (USA))
1037[2] 1214[4] 6576[8] 7051[28] 8153[2]

Right To Dream (IRE) *Brian Meehan* a88 103
3 b g Oasis Dream Granny Kelly (USA) (Irish River (FR))
142a[14] 417a[4] 754a[2] 874a[11] (5686) 6029[5] 6449[6] 7401[3]

Right To Rule (IRE) *William Haggas* 79
3 b g Rock Of Gibraltar(IRE) Epistoliere (IRE) (Alzao (USA))
1662[2] 1893[5] (2927)

Right Touch *Richard Fahey* 77
2 b g Royal Applause Amira (Efisio)
4877[2] ◆ 5578[4] 6071[5]

Rigid *Tony Carroll* a59 48
5 ch g Refuse To Bend(IRE) Supersonic (Shirley Heights)
66[4] (653) 744[7] 2653[4] 2937[4] 3317[7]

Rigolleto (IRE) *Anabel K Murphy* a52 91
4 b g Ad Valorem(USA) Jallaissine (IRE) (College Chapel)
1161[20] 1627[3] 1741[2] 2243[8] 2632[4] 2913[4] 3221[4] 4255[2] 4624[6] (5150) 5530[4] 6235[10] 6577[2] 6800[9] 7437[8]

Rila (FR) *R Dzubasz* 77
3 b f Lando(GER) Rita Skeater (Hector Protector (USA))
2531a[9]

Rime A Rien *F Rohaut* 94
2 b f Amadeus Wolf Rainbow Crossing (Cape Cross (IRE))
5248a[2] 7430a[4]

Ri Na Si *Pat Phelan* a48
2 b c Green Horizon Luisa Miller (IRE) (Entrepreneur)
6581[7] 7613[9] 7963[8]

Ring For Baileys *Chris Dwyer* a86 75
3 ch f Kyllachy Ring Of Love (Magic Ring (IRE))
720[3] 885[2] (1089) 1393[2] 1514[4] 2443[3] 3234[5] 3350[2] 3670[3] 5272[3] 5815[4] 6173[7] 6578[2] 7197[4] (7775) 7860[2] 8163[5]

Rio Cato *Ed Dunlop* a26 41
2 ch f Notnowcato Brazilian Terrace (Zilzal (USA))
3569[4] 3948[8] 4494[15] 5061[7] 6115[13]

Rio Cobolo (IRE) *David Nicholls* a65 81
6 b g Captain Rio Sofistication (IRE) (Dayjur (USA))
1156[13] 1293[6] 1951[11] 2696[5] 3272[3] 3524[2] 3778[8] 4708[2] 4999[3] 5093[4] 5802[8] 6260[7] 6709[4] 7732[9]

Rio De La Plata (USA) *Saeed Bin Suroor* 119
7 ch h Rahy(USA) Express Way (ARG) (Ahmad (ARG))
590a[7] 879a[13] 1148a[13] 5594[5]

Rio Gael (IRE) *Peter Bowen* a25 35
6 br g Captain Rio Palavera (FR) (Bikala)
4491[9]

Rio Grande *Ann Duffield* a88 91
3 b g Invincible Spirit(IRE) Pharma West (USA) (Gone West (USA))
(994) 3963[13] 6124[2] 7163[5]

Rioja Day (IRE) *J W Hills* a50 67
2 b c Red Clubs(IRE) Dai E Dai (USA) (Seattle Dancer (USA))
1920[5] 2480[9] 5274[6] 5786[2] 6096[5] 7111[4]

Rio Royale (IRE) *Amanda Perrett* a70 49
6 b g Captain Rio Lady Nasrana (FR) (Al Nasr (FR))
87[6] 179[9] 658[7] 2413[9] 6158[7] 7512[13]

Rio Sands *Richard Whitaker* a47 48
7 b g Captain Rio Sally Traffic (River Falls)
6959[2] 7634[4] 7746[4]

Rio's Girl *Tony Coyle* a59 64
5 b m Captain Rio African Breeze (Atraf)
227[4] 445[5] 691[8] 1246[4] 1298[6] (2749) 2982[6] 3441[4] 4174[14] 4631[4] 4717[8] 4963[2] 5257[6]

Rio Silver (IRE) *Shaun Harris* 59
4 br g Captain Rio Silver Harbour (USA) (Silver Hawk (USA))
3794[3]

Rio's Pearl *Ralph Beckett* a75 81
2 b f Captain Rio Agony Aunt (Formidable (USA))
1891[3] 2124[4] 2917[2] 4820[7] (5153) 6425[2] 6883[5]

Rio's Rosanna (IRE) *Richard Whitaker* a82 95
5 b m Captain Rio Ling Lane (Slip Anchor)
1295[6] 1756[3] 2419[4] (3129) 3494[2] 4072[3] 5558[7] 6248[4] 7519[11]

Riot Of Colour *Ralph Beckett* a76 92
3 b f Excellent Art Riotous Applause (Royal Applause)
1472[2] 2273[2] (3507) 4062[2] 4597[2] 5520[13]

Riponian *Kate Walton* 41
2 ch c Trade Fair Dispol Katie (Komaite (USA))
2338[5]

Rippled *John Gosden* 78
3 gr f Dalakhani(IRE) Last Dance (Sadler's Wells (USA))
2249[2] 2768[2]

Riptide *Michael Scudamore* 82
6 b g Val Royal(FR) Glittering Image (IRE) (Sadler's Wells (USA))
1272[6] 1559[2] 3373[7] 4925[7] 6074[3] 6493[15]

Rise To Glory (IRE) *Shaun Harris* a65 60
4 b h King's Best(USA) Lady At War (Warning)
218[8] 307[10] 430[7] 572[5] 938[2] 986[4] (1384) (1608) 1799[7] 1961[10] 2373[12] 7906[12] 7993[11]

Rishikesh *Michael Bell* 72
4 b g Cape Cross(IRE) Maycocks Bay (Muhtarram (USA))
3484[9] 4200[7]

Rising Legend *Richard Hannon* a81 96
2 ch c Rock Of Gibraltar(IRE) Miswaki Belle (USA) (Miswaki (USA))
2247[2] 3770[3] 4090[3] 4654[2] (4938) (6247)

Rising Wind (IRE) *Kevin Prendergast* 95
4 b m Shirocco(GER) Right Key (IRE) (Key Of Luck (USA))
2318a[4] 3361a[4]

Riskhana (FR) *F Sanchez* 81
2 b f My Risk(FR) Vahana (FR) (Sicyos (USA))
4615a^7
Risky Rizkova *Jonathan Portman* 64
2 b g Sleeping Indian Tri Pac (IRE) (Fairy King (USA))
(3140) 4331^5 4991^2 5532^3 6155^{10} 6984^9
Ritaach (IRE) *Clive Brittain* 44
2 b f Compton Place Golubitsa (IRE) (Bluebird (USA))
3046^5
Rite Of Passage *D K Weld* 117
8 ch g Giant's Causeway(USA) Dahlia's Krissy (USA) (Kris S (USA))
(7235)
Ritsi *Marjorie Fife* a56 52
9 b g Marju(IRE) Anna Comnena (IRE) (Shareef Dancer (USA))
3310^3 3942^7 3988^6 4867^7
Rivas Rhapsody (IRE) *Ian Wood* a83 90
4 b m Hawk Wing(USA) Riva Royale (Royal Applause)
2503^2 ◆ 3192^2 3500^2 4300^2 (4968)
Rivellino *Mrs K Burke* a81 78
2 b c Invincible Spirit(IRE) Brazilian Bride (IRE) (Pivotal)
4362^3 6424^7 (7894)
River Ardeche *Tracy Waggott* a71 65
7 b g Elnadim(USA) Overcome (Belmez (USA))
671^2 809^5 1276^5 1436^4 1917^{11} 2536^2 3405^4 4620^8 5220^6 5713^4 6105^4 7348^2 7798^2
Riverdale (IRE) *Nigel Tinkler* a76 80
4 ch g Choisir(AUS) Hollow Haze (USA) (Woodman (USA))
269^6 387^2 448^5
River Dragon (IRE) *Tony Coyle* a72 73
7 b g Sadler's Wells(USA) Diarshana (GER) (Darshaan)
1057^3 1247^3 5673^2 6137^4 (6784) 7068^{10}
River Jetez (SAF) *M F De Kock* 117
9 b m Jet Master(SAF) Stormsvlei (SAF) (Prince Florimund (SAF))
879a^8
River Nova *Alan Berry* a44 50
3 b f Avonbridge Assistacat (IRE) (Lend A Hand)
228^6
River Pageant *Eve Johnson Houghton* 59
3 ch f Primo Valentino(IRE) Belly Dancer (IRE) (Danehill Dancer (IRE))
2501^5 3389^8 4144^9
Rivertime (ITY) *R Menichetti* 98
3 b c Tout Seul(IRE) Lady Susy (IRE) (Danetime (IRE))
1698a^9
River Valley *Dai Burchell* 47
3 b g Three Valleys(USA) Amica (Averti (IRE))
3431^5
Riviera Romance *J W Hills* a56 47
3 ch f Zamindar(USA) Ares Vallis (IRE) (Caerleon (USA))
2344^8 3340^{11} 3720^7 4486^8 4650^7 4932^3 5479^2 6151^5 6968^9
Rjwa (IRE) *F Rohaut* a87 113
3 ch f Muhtathir Minallon (ARG) (Flag Down (CAN))
1434a^3 2532a^2 3203a^3 6911a^5 7882a^4
Roadster *C Plisson* a66 80
5 b g Hawk Wing(USA) Flower Bowl (FR) (Anabaa (USA))
94a^0
Road Tosky (IRE) *A Peraino* 94
2 b f Elusive City(USA) Victory Peak (Shirley Heights)
6725a^2 7285a^7
Roanne (USA) *Clive Cox* 69
2 b f Lemon Drop Kid(USA) Chalamont (IRE) (Kris)
6007^8 6960^4 7364^9
Roanstar *Chris Gordon* a66 77
5 gr g Act One Dolce Thundera (USA) (Thunder Gulch (USA))
149^6
Roaring Rocks (FR) *Heather Main* a53
2 gr c Stormy River(FR) Saulace (FR) (Saumarez)
8303^4
Roatan *P Bary* a90 100
7 gr g Daylami(IRE) Celestial Lagoon (JPN) (Sunday Silence (USA))
5030a^3
Roayh (USA) *Saeed Bin Suroor* a91 100
4 ch g Speightstown(USA) Most Remarkable (USA) (Marquetry (USA))
2082^6 2657^{11} 3826^{10} 4529^6 5595^2 6013^3
Robby Bobby *Laura Mongan* a68 68
7 ch g Selkirk(USA) Dancing Mirage (IRE) (Machiavellian (USA))
592^4
Robemaker *John Gosden* a72 98
4 b h Oasis Dream Regal Velvet (Halling (USA))
1321^5 1993^4 2911^2 3417^5 4805^8
Robert Le Diable (FR) *D Prod'Homme* a102 99
3 ch c Dutch Art Red Begonia (Pivotal)
542a^7 914a^2
Roberto Pegasus (USA) *Pat Phelan* 89
6 bb g Fusaichi Pegasus(USA) Louju (USA) (Silver Hawk (USA))
1505^7 1940^2 (2887)
Robert The Painter (IRE) *David O'Meara* 86
4 b g Whipper(USA) Lidanna (Nicholas (USA))
2119^6 3167^5 4080^4 4347^4 4879^5 5345^4 6073^4 6342^2 6528^2 7004^2 7370^{11}
Rob Gold (FR) *T Clout* a61 79
3 b c Gold Away(IRE) Robsart (IRE) (Robellino (USA))
1171a^0
Robin Hood (IRE) *A P O'Brien* 101
4 b h Galileo(IRE) Banquise (IRE) (Last Tycoon)
1946a^4 2525a^3 2703^6 3267^{11} 4322^{10} 5490^8 6912a^{18}
Robin Hoods Bay *Ed Vaughan* a99 95
4 b g Motivator Bijou A Moi (Rainbow Quest (USA))
2248^3 3642^4 4578^8 7502^{11} (7842) 7904^2 8056^4

Robot Boy (IRE) *David Barron* 71
2 ch c Shamardal(USA) Pivotal's Princess (IRE) (Pivotal)
5382^8 6787^3
Rob The Cradle (CAN) *Michael P De Paulo*
4 ch g Philanthropist(USA) Devine Decadence (CAN) (Explosive Red (CAN))
8278a^5
Robyn *Scott Dixon* a53 8
2 b f Byron Discoed (Distinctly North (USA))
6808^4 7434^9 7609^4 7711^7 8007^9
Rocco Breeze (IRE) *Philip McBride* a52 44
3 b g Shirocco(GER) Crossbreeze (USA) (Red Ransom (USA))
1303^4 1448^2 1982^9 2577^8 4153^{12} 4650^9
Roc De Prince *Richard Fahey* a74 79
3 b g Shirocco(GER) Louella (USA) (El Gran Senor (USA))
3181^2 4259^2 4882^4 6045^{11} 6398^2 7011^7
Roc Fort *Ruth Carr* 19
3 b g Rock Of Gibraltar(IRE) Frangy (Sadler's Wells (USA))
4551^9 4780^{10} 5315^{11} 5803^9
Rochdale *A Al Raihe* a101 101
9 ch g Bertolini(USA) Owdbetts (IRE) (High Estate)
241a^4 317a^8 489a^7 677a^6
Roches Cross (IRE) *J Vana Jr* 104
4 b h Whipper(USA) Danemarque (AUS) (Danehill (USA))
2322a^{10} 4316a^0
Rockabilly Riot (IRE) *G M Lyons* a76 77
2 bb g Footstepsinthesand Zawariq (IRE) (Marju (IRE))
5858a^4
Rock Act (IRE) *Peter Chapple-Hyam* 22
2 b f Rock Of Gibraltar(IRE) Second Act (Sadler's Wells (USA))
7329^{14}
Rock A Doodle Doo (IRE) *William Jarvis* a103 104
5 b g Oratorio(IRE) Nousaiyra (IRE) (Be My Guest (USA))
1882^9 3642^7 (3766) 4363^7 5079^8 5600^{19} 7175^7
Rockalong (IRE) *Luca Cumani* a86
3 b c Rock Of Gibraltar(IRE) High Spot (Shirley Heights)
7174^{12} 7647^2 (7896)
Rock Anthem (IRE) *Mike Murphy* a69 73
8 ch g Rock Of Gibraltar(IRE) Regal Portrait (IRE) (Royal Academy (USA))
183^6 646^4 821^4 1530^5 3388^7 3705^4 4474^6 5008^5 7256^U 7530^3 7844^5 8152^4
Rock Band *Richard Hannon* a71 73
3 b c Rock Of Gibraltar(IRE) Decision Maid (USA) (Diesis)
1512^8 2380^5 3068^7
Rock Canyon (IRE) *Linda Perratt* a56 72
3 b g Rock Of Gibraltar(IRE) Tuesday Morning (Sadler's Wells (USA))
1241^7 1596^5 (2036) 2229^9 2595^7 2928^4 (3028) 3379^5 3731^3 4084^4 4133^{10} 4671^3 5189^6 5538^9 5728^4 6514^6 6529^8 6713^9
Rock Critic (IRE) *D K Weld* a103 104
7 b g Pivotal Diamond Trim (IRE) (Highest Honor (FR))
3268^{18} 4692a^4
Rock Diamond (IRE) *Sylvester Kirk* a44 40
2 b f Rock Of Gibraltar(IRE) Yaky Romani (IRE) (Victory Note (USA))
5997^7 6841^{10} 7403^8
Rocket Maker (USA) *William Mott*
2 b f Empire Maker(USA) Trip (USA) (Lord At War (ARG))
6944a^7
Rocket Man (AUS) *Patrick Shaw* a126 127
7 b g Viscount(AUS) Macrosa (NZ) (Mcginty (NZ))
1147a^2
Rocket Rob (IRE) *Willie Musson* a76 89
6 b g Danetime(IRE) Queen Of Fibres (IRE) (Scenic)
1642^{13} 2071^9 (3139) 4013^8 4824^6 5097^3 5557^9 (6370) 8163^9 ◆
Rocket Ronnie (IRE) *David Nicholls* 54
2 b g Antonius Pius(USA) Ctesiphon (USA) (Arch (USA))
2415^8 2822^7 3271^6 6337^8
Rockfella *Denis Coakley* a59 86
6 ch g Rock Of Gibraltar(IRE) Afreeta (USA) (Afleet (CAN))
(1890) 3162^3 4284^4 ◆ 5106^{10}
Rockgoat (IRE) *Ian McInnes* a71 62
3 b g Rock Of Gibraltar(IRE) Queveda (IRE) (Mark Of Esteem (IRE))
(693) 1013^5 1607^5 2860^9 (5350) 5721^{11} 6240^8 6555^5 7417^5 8213^{10}
Rock God (IRE) *Eve Johnson Houghton* 83
2 br c Shirocco(GER) Melatonina (IRE) (King Charlemagne (USA))
4803^2 5792^6
Rockinante (FR) *Richard Hannon* 105
3 ch g Rock Of Gibraltar(IRE) Nantes (GER) (Night Shift (USA))
1208a^4 1698a^7 5278^6 5664^2 6029^6
Rock Jock (IRE) *John Patrick Shanahan* a96 104
5 b g Rock Of Gibraltar(IRE) Perfect Touch (USA) (Miswaki (USA))
141a^{RR} 314a^4 419a^{14} 875a^{14} 6854a^6
Rock Junior (IRE) *M Pimbonnet* a66 67
3 b g Rock Of Gibraltar(IRE) Tango Tonic (IRE) (Trans Island)
290a^7
Rock Me Baby *X Thomas-Demeaulte* a85 103
3 b f Rock Of Gibraltar(IRE) Newyearresolution (USA) (Arch (USA))
1695a^4 2742a^3 3682a^3
Rockme Cockney *Jeremy Gask* a75 72
3 ch f Cockney Rebel(IRE) Rock Lily (Rock Of Gibraltar (IRE))
970^6 1517^{11} 2162^8 2733^2 (3315) 4043^{10} 4986^2 5443^{10} 7203^9

Rock My Heart (GER) *W Hickst* 99
3 ch f Sholokhov(IRE) Rondinay (FR) (Cadeaux Genereux)
2522a^8 4862a^4
Rock N Rover (IRE) *Noel Meade* 44
2 ch g Thousand Words Honey Run (Sinndar (IRE))
6550a^{10}
Rock Of Deauville (IRE) *Julie Camacho* a72 47
5 b g Rock Of Gibraltar(IRE) Ruff Shod (USA) (Storm Boot (USA))
44^7 285^{11} 2666^6 3577^6 4714^8 5171^7 5669^7
Rock Of Monet *Ian Williams* a50 60
3 b g Kyllachy Level Pegging (IRE) (Common Grounds)
2441^9 3050^6 3892^8 5247^{10} 6941^{10} 7058^{10}
Rock On Candy *John Spearing* a56 69
3 b f Excellent Art Rock Candy (IRE) (Rock Of Gibraltar (IRE))
6739^5 7178^6 ◆ (7457)
Rock On Ciara (IRE) *Joseph G Murphy* a61 96
6 b m Rock Of Gibraltar(IRE) Secret Wells (USA) (Sadler's Wells (USA))
(3645a) 4482a^6
Rockpool *Roger Charlton* 58
2 ch f Rock Of Gibraltar(IRE) Waterfall One (Nashwan (USA))
5685^7 5977^{11} 6481^{17}
Rock Relief (IRE) *Chris Grant* a56 68
6 gr g Daylami(IRE) Sheer Bliss (IRE) (Sadler's Wells (USA))
3535^2 4590^9
Rocksilla *Chris Wall* a70
2 b f Rock Of Gibraltar(IRE) Hope Island (IRE) (Titus Livius (FR))
6535^5 7160^4 7721^6
Rock Song *Amanda Perrett* a71 70
3 b c Rock Of Gibraltar(IRE) Jackie's Opera (FR) (Indian Ridge)
4746^5 5512^6 5942^3 6151^4 6647^2 6973^{11} 7359^4
Rock Supreme (IRE) *Richard Hannon* 80
3 b g Rock Of Gibraltar(IRE) Love And Affection (USA) (Exclusive Era (USA))
1468^8
Rocktherunway (IRE) *Michael Dods* 88
3 ch g Nayef(USA) Femme Fatale (Fairy King (USA))
1440^2 1641^3 1866^2 (2240) (2716) 3296^{16} 4294^2 5788^8 6884^{11}
Rock Up (IRE) *David Elsworth* a78 76
2 b g Kheleyf(USA) Kissing Time (Lugana Beach)
2929^{11} 4773^4 5235^2 6203^6 7192^2 7374^{10}
Rockweiller *Steve Gollings* a70 66
5 b h Rock Of Gibraltar(IRE) Ballerina Suprema (IRE) (Sadler's Wells (USA))
(1919) 3022^5 3775^9 4296^5 4884^4 5405^5
Rock With Me (FR) *F Chappet* a54 80
2 b g Indian Rocket Same To You (FR) (Mujtahid (USA))
7265a^2 7699a^7 8276a^{10}
Rock With You *Pat Phelan* a45 65
5 b m Rock Of Gibraltar(IRE) Karsiyaka (IRE) (Kahyasi)
8001^9
Rocky Elsom (USA) *David Arbuthnot* a66 84
5 b g Rock Of Gibraltar(IRE) Bowstring (IRE) (Sadler's Wells (USA))
119^7
Rocky Ground (IRE) *Roger Varian* 95
2 b c Acclamation Keriyka (IRE) (Indian Ridge)
(3545) ◆ 4599^2 5515^{18}
Rocky Rebel *Chris Bealby* a76 76
4 b g Norse Dancer(IRE) Gulchina (USA) (Gulch (USA))
(65) (310) 500^4 6776^{10} 7024^{10} 7980^8
Rocky Reef *Andrew Balding* a73 90
3 b g Danbird(AUS) Leah's Pride (Atraf)
1728^8 2382^5 3014^2 (3433) 3876^2 4298^5 4534^2 5595^4 7171^6 (7395)
Rocky Two (IRE) *Michael Dods* 75
2 ch g Rock Of Gibraltar(IRE) Toorah Laura La (USA) (Black Minnaloushe (USA))
3491^2 ◆ 4618^3 5668^5 6780^5
Rockzanda (IRE) *Kevin Ryan* 39
3 ch f Rock Of Gibraltar(IRE) Piacenza (IRE) (Darshaan)
5244^7
Rocquaine (IRE) *David Evans* 46
3 b f Oratorio(IRE) Watch The Clock (Mtoto)
2262^{15} 2501^8 2734^6 3443^{10} 4186^6 4754^5 5991^5 6230^5
Rode Two Destiny (IRE) *David Evans* a33 63
3 b f Dark Angel(IRE) Dear Catch (IRE) (Bluebird (USA))
2871^5 3510^{11} 3972^8 5764^{11}
Rodion Raskolnikov (FR) *C Lerner* a67
2 b c Russian Blue(IRE) Mikalia (FR) (Kaldoun (FR))
8176a^8
Rodrigo De Freitas (IRE) *Jim Boyle* a64 67
5 b g Captain Rio Brazilian Sun (IRE) (Barathea (IRE))
28^9 221^6 278^3 2371^2 3086^7 (3573) 4504^{11} 5164^5 5483^2 7012^4 7744^8 (7991)
Rodrigo De Torres *David Nicholls* a104 101
5 ch g Bahamian Bounty Leonica (Lion Cavern (USA))
814a^4 1140^2 1523^2 2068^{24} (2819) 3091a^5 6468^{25} 7240^{24} 7826^{11}
Roedean (IRE) *William Stone* a73 77
3 b f Oratorio(IRE) Exotic Mix (FR) (Linamix (FR))
61^2 159^4 (231) (360) (382) (397) 547^4 2194^{12} 2733^8 3347^4 3589^4 4242^2 4544^2 5107^6 5634^4 5803^8
Roero (FR) *F Rohaut* a81 84
3 b g Acclamation Ricine (IRE) (Titus Livius (FR))
(628a)
Roe Valley (IRE) *Linda Jewell* a33 36
5 ch g Arakan(USA) Waaedah (USA) (Halling (USA))
8080^8 8264^{13}

Roger Ramjet (IRE) *Brian Meehan* a67 68
3 b g Rock Of Gibraltar(IRE) Autumnal (IRE) (Indian Ridge)
5329^3 5717^7 6279^6 7256^6
Roger Sez (IRE) *Tim Easterby* 103
3 b f Red Clubs(IRE) Stately Princess (Robellino (USA))
1508^8 2087^4 2712^7 3165^5 3542^3 4062^{10} 4557^{11} 5043^8 6046^9 6471^{11}
Roger Thorpe *Garry Woodward* 29
3 b g Firebreak Nunthorpe (Mystiko (USA))
4746^9
Rogue Reporter (IRE) *Stuart Williams* a70 66
3 b g Sir Percy Princess Nala (IRE) (In The Wings)
982^4 1728^6 2246^{16} 3228^5 3793^4 4411^{13} 5219^7 5764^6 6151^9 7148^5 7189^6 7615^2 7815^2 7906^7 8062^3
Rohlindi *Eve Johnson Houghton* a37 68
4 b m Red Ransom(USA) Rohita (IRE) (Waajib)
5440^{10}
Roicead (USA) *W McCreery* a103 107
5 b g Giant's Causeway(USA) Coachella (Danehill (USA))
3196a^8 6140^{10} 7390a^{DSQ}
Rokcella *Clive Cox* a55 36
3 b f Shirocco(GER) Amicella (Laroche (GER))
4366^{10} 5404^4 6397^8 6892^7
Roker Park (IRE) *David O'Meara* 95
7 b g Choisir(AUS) Joyful (IRE) (Green Desert (USA))
2177^{14} 2825^6 3336^5 3626^3 4086^2 4589^4 5539^5 6008^{13} 6165^{11} 6465^4 6663^7 7453^7
Roland *Kevin Ryan* a60 54
2 ch g Byron Muja Farewell (Mujtahid (USA))
1753^7 2123^5 2747^6 6121^4 6337^{10} 7641^7 7714^5 7919^5 (8003) 8093^4 8186^5
Rollex Borget (FR) *J Bertran De Balanda* 106
3 b g Khalkevi(IRE) Jasmine Des Bordes (FR) (Epervier Bleu)
3204a^5 6087a^5 7431a^3
Rollingarab (ITY) *Sergio Dettori* 44
2 b c Stroll(USA) Arabian Brig (Sayf El Arab (USA))
3684a^7
Rollin 'n Tumblin *Michael Attwater* a47
8 ch g Zaha(CAN) Steppin Out (First Trump)
4915^9 5974^{12} 6255^{12} 7012^6 7169^3 7629^4 8001^8 8035^5 8104^7
Roll Of Thunder *John Quinn* 54
3 b g Antonius Pius(USA) Ischia (Lion Cavern (USA))
2336^7 3111^{10} 5728^8 6259^9
Romacaca (USA) *Danny L Miller* 108
6 bb m Running Stag(USA) Romaca (USA) (Kris S (USA))
5376a^7
Roman Around *William Knight* a38 24
3 b f Antonius Pius(USA) Koniya (IRE) (Doyoun)
2172^{10} 3232^7 3786^{12} 4198^8 4870^{10} 5632^8
Roman Eglenovich *George Margarson*
3 b g Byron Assertive Dancer (USA) (Assert)
3551^9 6555^9
Roman Flame *Michael Quinn* a63 64
4 ch m Bertolini(USA) Dakhla Oasis (IRE) (Night Shift (USA))
35^4 281^5 428^4 732^4 966^4 1095^3 1425^4
Roman General (IRE) *Edward Lynam* a75 77
3 b g Holy Roman Emperor(IRE) Tawoos (FR) (Rainbow Quest (USA))
336a^3
Roman Myst (IRE) *Sylvester Kirk* a57 61
3 b g Holy Roman Emperor(IRE) Mystiara (IRE) (Orpen (USA))
4003^8 4734^3 5263^2 5458^3
Romanoff (IRE) *Luca Cumani* a60 57
2 b c Holy Roman Emperor(IRE) Alexander Anapolis (IRE) (Spectrum (IRE))
3346^{10} 4114^{10} 4539^{10} 5702^4 6413^5 7173^6 7462^3 ◆
Roman Order (IRE) *Brian Meehan* a70 72
2 b c Holy Roman Emperor(IRE) Web Of Intrigue (Machiavellian (USA))
4472^8 ◆ 4938^4 5704^5 6733^4 7349^3 7699a^3 (8103) 8302^5
Roman Ruler (IRE) *Chris Fairhurst* a59 61
4 gr g Antonius Pius(USA) Way Of Truth (Muhtarram (USA))
361^{12} 633^9 926^7 1095^8 4717^{15}
Roman Senate (IRE) *Martin Bosley* a58 51
3 b g Holy Roman Emperor(IRE) Indian Fun (Poliglote)
2548^4 4754^{13} 5212^2 5938^2 6892^{10}
Roman Sioux (IRE) *Robin Bastiman* 45
5 b g Antonius Pius(USA) Blue Sioux (Indian Ridge)
7^{12}
Roman Strait *Michael Blanshard* a78 74
4 b h Refuse To Bend(IRE) Oman Sea (USA) (Rahy (USA))
178^4 (325) 526^2
Romantic (IRE) *Sir Henry Cecil* a49 70
3 b g Holy Roman Emperor(IRE) Welsh Love (Ela-Mana-Mou)
1707^{12} 2449^6 4498^4 5124^6
Romantica *A Fabre* 110
3 b f Galileo(IRE) Banks Hill (Danehill (USA))
3682a^2 4616a^2 (5472a) 6295a^9
Romanticize *Jason Ward* a56 58
6 b m Kyllachy Romancing (Dr Devious (IRE))
6123^8 6480^9 8255^6
Romantic Settings *Richard Fahey* 76
2 ch f Mount Nelson Lacework (Pivotal)
4837^2 5339^4 (5962)
Romantic Stroll (IRE) *T Stack* a89 73
3 b f Oratorio(IRE) Home You Stroll (IRE) (Selkirk (USA))
7680a^4
Romany Spirit (IRE) *Jason Ward* a58 56
3 b f Invincible Spirit(IRE) Attachment (USA) (Trempolino (USA))
20^4 556^8 845^{11} 1169^5 1294^4

Rome *Sir Henry Cecil* a73
2 b c Holy Roman Emperor(IRE) Magical Cliche (USA) (Affirmed (USA))
7926[3] 8102[3]

Romeo Montague *Ed Dunlop* a91 99
4 b g Montjeu(IRE) Issa (Pursuit Of Love)
1139[4] 1603[6] 2176[2] 2479[8] 2932[7] 3373[3] (4284) 4697[5]

Romeo's On Fire (IRE) *Adrian McGuinness* a77 67
8 b g Danehill(USA) Fighting Countess (USA) (Ringside (USA))
335a[6] 6184a[2]

Romp (ARG) *Kristin Mulhall* a91 100
8 b g Incurable Optimist(USA) Stormy Secret (ARG) (Hidden Prize (USA))
7546a[8]

Ronaldinho (IRE) *Richard Hannon* a80 88
2 b c Jeremy(USA) Spring Glory (Dr Fong (USA))
2480[11] 2983[2] 4149[2] 4847[6] (5475) (5786) 6775[6] (7365)

Ronan's Bay (USA) *George J Kent* 86
3 b f Johannesburg(USA) Muskoka Dawn (USA) (Miswaki (USA))
2101a[9]

Rondeau (GR) *Patrick Chamings* a89 89
7 ch g Harmonic Way Areti (GR) (Wadood (USA))
3281[10] 3772[6] 4503[7] 5004[10] 5630[4] 6329[3]

Roninski (IRE) *Bryan Smart* a92 91
4 b g Cadeaux Genereux Ruby Affair (IRE) (Night Shift (USA))
1161[19] 4640[4] (5110) 6235[4] 7097[4] 7508[3] 7691[4] 7826[3] 8098[7]

Ron The Greek (USA) *William Mott* a124
5 b h Full Mandate(USA) Flambe' (USA) (Fortunate Prospect (USA))
7576a[4]

Roodee Queen *Milton Bradley* a73 83
4 b m Kyllachy Hilites (IRE) (Desert King (IRE))
652[5] 1007[9] 1203[4] 1564[11] ◆ 2146[8] 2870[7] 3390[7] 3724[6] 4235[12] 4533[13] 6053[12]

Roodle *Eve Johnson Houghton* a78 87
5 b m Xaar Roodeye (Inchinor)
711[9] 866[10]

Rooknrasbryripple *Ralph Smith* a66 66
3 b f Piccolo Here To Me (Muhtarram (USA))
469[2] 599[7] 4726[10] 5047[8] 5514[7] 5662[9] 6496[6]

Ropehanger *Lee Carter* a46 44
2 b f Cockney Rebel(IRE) Robanna (Robellino (USA))
3444[12] 4646[7] 6871[10]

Rory Boy (USA) *Graeme McPherson* a77 63
7 b g Aldebaran(USA) Purr Pleasure (USA) (El Gran Senor (USA))
673[4] (1991)

Rosa Burn *John Dunlop* 1
2 ch f Notnowcato Les Hurlants (IRE) (Barathea (IRE))
5947[12] 6437[9]

Rosaceous *Daniel Kubler* a36
2 ch f Duke Of Marmalade(IRE) Briery (IRE) (Salse (USA))
7962[9]

Rosa Eglanteria *B Grizzetti* 107
3 b f Nayef(USA) Rose Shift (IRE) (Night Shift (USA))
2522a[3]

Rosairlie (IRE) *Micky Hammond* a69 80
4 ch m Halling(USA) Mrs Mason (IRE) (Turtle Island (IRE))
1272[3] 2242[2] (2827) ◆ (3827) 4613[12]

Rosa Lockwood *Tony Carroll* a38 36
3 b f Needwood Blade Star Of Flanders (Puissance)
6154[7] 8069[4] 8291[5]

Rosa Lottie *David C Griffiths* a26 15
3 b f Ferrule(IRE) Lets Get It On (IRE) (Perugino (USA))
5166[6] 6125[8] 6806[12] 7378[8]

Rosa Luxemburg *Lawrence Mullaney*
4 ch m Needwood Blade Colonel's Daughter (Colonel Collins (USA))
3024[5] 3751[9]

Rosanna (GER) *Uwe Ostmann* 77
2 b f Areion(GER) Rocket Light (GER) (Lando (GER))
7281a[7]

Rosaria *Harry Dunlop* a48 38
4 b m Tiger Hill(IRE) Flamingo Flower (USA) (Diesis)
2200[11] 2814[10] 3392[13] 4004[10]

Rosby Waves (USA) *Mark Johnston* a71
3 b f Distorted Humor(USA) Windsharp (USA) (Lear Fan (USA))
(604) 841[3]

Rosdhu Queen (IRE) *William Haggas* 108
2 b f Invincible Spirit(IRE) Green Minstrel (FR) (Green Tune (USA))
(4344) (5307) ◆ (5516) (6672)

Rose Aurora *Marcus Tregoning* a58 49
5 gr m Pastoral Pursuits Khaladja (IRE) (Akarad (FR))
28[5] 265[7] 395[5]

Rose Garnet (IRE) *Tony Carroll* a64 59
4 b m Invincible Spirit(IRE) Chanterelle (IRE) (Indian Ridge)
775a[5] (7929) 8209[2] 8256[2]

Roseisle *Linda Perratt*
4 ch m Doyen(IRE) Nova Zembla (Young Ern)
4807[12] 5760[5] 5919[9] 6527[7]

Rose Kingdom (JPN) *Kojiro Hashiguchi* 124
5 bb h King Kamehameha(JPN) Rosebud (JPN) (Sunday Silence (USA))
7872a[16]

Rose Madder *Roger Curtis* a35 46
3 b f Singspiel(IRE) Crimson Year (USA) (Dubai Millennium)
2935[8] 7158[9] 7591[9]

Rosenblatt (GER) *John Spearing* a54 22
10 b g Dashing Blade Roseraie (GER) (Nebos (GER))
278[8]

Rosendhal (IRE) *G Botti* 110
5 ch h Indian Ridge Kathy College (IRE) (College Chapel)
2728a[4] 3901a[8] 7565a[4] (7697a)

Rose Of Sarratt (IRE) *Rae Guest* a61 74
4 b m Sadler's Wells(USA) Sweet Gypsy Rose (IRE) (Darshaan)
1925[8] 2378[8] 2925[9] 3552[5]

Roseraie (IRE) *Kevin Prendergast* a67 95
2 b f Lawman(FR) Red Feather (IRE) (Marju (IRE))
4276a[3] 5135a[4] 7038a[10]

Roserrow *Andrew Balding* a89 76
3 ch g Beat Hollow Sabah (Nashwan (USA))
1467[15] (2172) ◆ 2813[2] 3508[9]

Rose Season *Roger Varian* 84
3 b f Cape Cross(IRE) Endorsement (Warning)
3100[2] 3773[3] 4067[6] (5358)

Rose Vista (FR) *J-L Guillochon* 98
3 ch f Vatori(FR) Rose Ciel (FR) (Septieme Ciel (USA))
1434a[5]

Rosewin (IRE) *Ollie Pears* a71 88
6 b m Hawkeye(IRE) African Scene (IRE) (Scenic)
1640[5] 2474[4]

Rosewood Lad *J S Moore* a78 63
5 ch g Needwood Blade Meandering Rose (USA) (Irish River (FR))
(44) 332[2] 577[5] 928[4] 1496[7] 8290[5]

Rosia Bay *Charles Hills* a40 39
2 ch f Rock Of Gibraltar(IRE) Penny Cross (Efisio)
3764[10] 4507[10]

Rosie Future (IRE) *Rae Guest* a55 47
2 b f Azamour(IRE) Auspicious (Shirley Heights)
2729[4] 4539[13] 5267[7] 5763[5]

Rosie Hall (IRE) *Bryan Smart* 22
2 ch f Lion Heart(USA) Baltic Dip (IRE) (Benny The Dip (USA))
4546[11]

Rosie My Way (USA) *Joseph Orseno*
2 b f Unbridled Energy(USA) Fortunate Chance (USA) (American Chance (USA))
6944a[6]

Rosie Probert *Roger Charlton* 76
3 b f Dylan Thomas(IRE) Corsican Sunset (USA) (Thunder Gulch (USA))
2204[3] ◆ 3100[3]

Rosie Rebel *Rae Guest* a56
2 ch f Cockney Rebel(IRE) Meandering Rose (USA) (Irish River (FR))
8207[2]

Rosie's Lady (IRE) *David O'Meara* a60 59
3 b f Elusive City(USA) Blushing Libra (Perugino (USA))
1386[2] 1600[3] 2340[2] 2771[3] 2885[4] 3212[2] 3697[9] 4781[5] 5330[8]

Rosina Bella (IRE) *P L Giannotti* 92
3 b f Oratorio(IRE) La Bella Grande (IRE) (Giant's Causeway (USA))
3987a[0]

Rosselli (IRE) *Mrs K Burke* a58 75
3 b g Iffraaj Special Ellie (FR) (Celtic Swing)
1270[12] 2313[3] (3273) 4325[5] 7132[7]

Rossetti *Ian Williams* a81 83
4 gr g Dansili Snowdrops (Gulch (USA))
2545[11] 3229[6] 3767[8] (4603) 4939[9] 5910[8] 6239[2] 8142[4] ◆ 8259[5]

Rosslyn Castle *Roger Charlton* 98
3 ch g Selkirk(USA) Margarula (IRE) (Doyoun)
(1414) (1978) ◆ 5089[7] 5826[7] 6576[5] 6875[11]

Rostrum (FR) *Mahmood Al Zarooni* a100 110
5 b g Shamardal(USA) En Public (FR) (Rainbow Quest (USA))
145a[4] 319a[6] 591a[5] 678a[6] 759a[11]

Rosy Dawn *John Bridger* a50 54
7 ch m Bertolini(USA) Blushing Sunrise (USA) (Cox's Ridge (USA))
558[6] 653[5] 822[3] 988[4] 1624[10] 2937[8] 3073[9] 4241[5] 4722[5] 4940[7] 5509[4] 5908[10] 6304[8] 6395[10]

Rothesay Chancer *Jim Goldie* 83
4 ch g Monsieur Bond(IRE) Rhinefield Beauty (IRE) (Shalford (IRE))
1237[2] 2070[3] 2596[12] 2717[8] 3336[3] 3624[4] 3903[9] 4286[15] 6009[13] 6427[4] 7000[9] (7101)

Rottingdean *John Gosden* a73 63
2 gr c Oasis Dream Misk (FR) (Linamix (FR))
7330[9] (7627)

Roubiliac (USA) *Paul Webber* 57
5 ch g Rahy(USA) Super Tassa (IRE) (Lahib (USA))
5293[4]

Rougemont (IRE) *Richard Hannon* a96 113
3 b c Montjeu(IRE) Spritza (IRE) (Spectrum (IRE))
(1468) 1678[3] 2080[5] 3296[3] ◆

Rouge Nuage (IRE) *Conrad Allen* a66
2 ch g Indian Haven Nom Francais (First Trump)
8178[3]

Rougette *Charles Hills* a73 84
4 b m Red Ransom(USA) Never A Doubt (Night Shift (USA))
1752[12] 2444[10] 2855[5] 3342[6]

Roughlyn *Lisa Williamson* a57 56
3 ch g Haafhd Dime Bag (High Line)
324[5] 635[5] 833[8] 1319[4] 2144[12] 3483[6] 4210[8] 4971[6] 5408[4] 5589[6] 7255[5] (8001) 8104[2]

Rough Rock (IRE) *Chris Dwyer* a54 81
7 ch g Rock Of Gibraltar(IRE) Amitie Fatale (IRE) (Night Shift (USA))
1289[9] 2274[8] 2847[3] (3344) 3549[5] 3790[12] 3977[4] 4661[5] 4772[11] 5269[6] 5457[2] 5634[2] 6381[5] 7559[8] 7685[10]

Roundelay *Anthony Carson* a34 47
3 b f Tiger Hill(IRE) Cercle D'Amour (USA) (Storm Cat (USA))
291[7] 1257[11] 2332[7] 3141[6] 4970[2] 6179[11]

Rousing Sermon (USA) *Jerry Hollendorfer* a117 106
3 ch c Lucky Pulpit(USA) Rousing Again (USA) (Awesome Again (CAN))
1872a[8]

Rovers Till I Die (IRE) *Charles Smith*
2 b g Captain Marvelous(IRE) Foolish Gift (FR) (Barathea (IRE))
7219[12] 7363[14] 7609[11]

Rovos (FR) *S Wattel* a83 76
4 b h Johannesburg(USA) Royal Liverpool (USA) (Gulch (USA))
18a[5]

Rowan Lodge (IRE) *Ollie Pears* a53 68
10 ch g Indian Lodge(IRE) Tirol Hope (IRE) (Tirol)
1436[10] 2536[6] 4179[16] 4959[6]

Rowan Rhapsody *Jim Boyle* a36 44
3 ch f Araafa(IRE) Filippa (GER) (Dashing Blade)
2996[5] 3666[13] 4213[7] 5770[12]

Rowan Ridge *William Knight* a73 64
4 ch g Compton Place Lemon Tree (USA) (Zilzal (USA))
57[2] 222[2] 310[2] 5908[5] 8175[5]

Rowan Spirit (IRE) *Mark Brisbourne* a82 76
4 gr g Captain Rio Secret Justice (USA) (Lit De Justice (USA))
371[8] 669[7] 1177[8] 1526[14]

Rowan Tiger *Dr Richard Newland* a83 81
6 b g Tiger Hill(IRE) Lemon Tree (USA) (Zilzal (USA))
6584[2]

Rowayton *Muredach Kelly* a86 56
6 gr m Lujain(USA) Bandanna (Bandmaster (USA))
5149[4]

Rowe Park *Linda Jewell* a90 89
9 b g Dancing Spree(USA) Magic Legs (Reprimand)
1849[5] 3822[14] 4530[3] (4849) 5832[9] 6026[9] 7646[2] 7859[7]

Roxelana (IRE) *Jeremy Noseda* a82 78
3 b f Oasis Dream Macadamia (IRE) (Classic Cliche (IRE))
429[2] ◆ (620) 2448[2] 4335[9] 6375[8] 7328[3] (7743)

Roxy Flyer (IRE) *Amanda Perrett* a103 106
5 b m Rock Of Gibraltar(IRE) Dyna Flyer (USA) (Marquetry (USA))
3766[2] 4800[10] 5593[4] (6018) 6598[11] 7510[6] 7895[2]

Royaaty (IRE) *M bin Shafya* a93 93
6 b g Singspiel(IRE) Whisper To Dream (USA) (Gone West (USA))
143a[9] 421a[7] 618a[11]

Royal Acclamation (IRE) *Michael Scudamore* a62 58
7 b g Acclamation Lady Abigail (IRE) (Royal Academy (USA))
46[4] 307[2] 572[6]

Royal Acquisition *Robert Cowell* a72
2 b c Royal Applause Flavian (Catrail (USA))
7738[4] (7855)

Royal Alcor (IRE) *Alastair Lidderdale* a70 55
5 b g Chevalier(IRE) Arundhati (IRE) (Royal Academy (USA))
452[2] 721[P] 850[7] 2984[7]

Royal Aspiration (IRE) *William Haggas* a60 90
2 b c Acclamation Joan Joan Joan (USA) (Touch Gold (USA))
3223[2] ◆ 3617[2] 4093[10] (4877) 5563[5] 6022[8] 6487[9] 7164[9]

Royal Award *Ian Wood* a77 82
3 b f Cadeaux Genereux Red Sovereign (Danzig Connection (USA))
1317[11]

Royal Bajan (USA) *James Given* a87 74
4 rg g Speightstown(USA) Crown You (USA) (Two Punch (USA))
59[7] (277) 525[8] 715[3] 991[9] (2369) 2731[3] 4690[23] 5362[15] 6689[9] (7726) 7860[6] 8066[7]

Royal Barge (IRE) *Eve Johnson Houghton* 18
2 b f Shirocco(GER) Sahara Lady (IRE) (Lomitas)
7403[13]

Royal Bench (IRE) *Robert Collet* a88 119
5 b g Whipper(USA) Hit The Sky (IRE) (Cozzene (USA))
4316a[0]

Royal Betty *Lee Carter* 48
2 b f Royal Applause Peryllys (Warning)
5003[9] 5948[5] 6330[13]

Royal Blade (IRE) *Alan Berry* a62 71
5 ch g Needwood Blade Royal Dream (Ardkinglass)
356[8] 1298[14]

Royal Blue Star (IRE) *Mrs John Harrington* a95 97
4 b m Dalakhani(IRE) Etizaan (IRE) (Unfuwain (USA))
2777a[6] 3092a[9] 5597[6]

Royal Bonsai *John Quinn* a62 66
4 b g Val Royal(FR) Bonsai (IRE) (Woodman (USA))
392[4] 5056[2] 6478[4]

Royal Box *Tony Carroll* a65 67
5 b g Royal Applause Diamond Lodge (Grand Lodge (USA))
186[3] 359[5] 624[10] 729[6] 1528[12] 2555[16] 2760[5] 3099[3] 3249[7] 3456[9] 5660[6] 5937[5] (6158) 6778[14]

Royal Caper *John Ryan* a60 60
2 b g Royal Applause Ukraine (IRE) (Cape Cross (IRE))
3634[14] 4066[18] 4773[5] 5321[9] 6114[16] 6583[13] 7637[11] (7808) 7919[7] 8093[2] 8203[8]

Royal Challis *Richard Hannon* 35
2 b c Royal Applause Oh Hebe (IRE) (Night Shift (USA))
3397[7]

Royal Crest *Andrew Crook* a63 59
6 b g Royal Applause Noble Lady (Primo Dominie)
807[7]

Royal Curtsy *Stuart Coltherd* a66 53
9 b m Pivotal Fen Princess (IRE) (Trojan Fen)
2925[3]

Royal Defence (IRE) *Michael Quinn* a51 63
6 b g Refuse To Bend(IRE) Alessia (GER) (Warning)
1286[6] 1624[12] 2009[6] 2997[2] 3468[6] 4244[5] 6948[11] 7472[6]

Royal Delta (USA) *William Mott* a123
4 bb m Empire Maker(USA) Delta Princess (USA) (A.P. Indy (USA))
1150a[9] (7550a)

Royal Destination (IRE) *F Nass* a102 109
7 b g Dubai Destination(USA) Royale (IRE) (Royal Academy (USA))
140a[9] 241a[8] 587a[4] 677a[5]

Royal Diamond (IRE) *Thomas Carmody* a85 110
6 b g King's Best(USA) Irresistible Jewel (IRE) (Danehill (USA))
5600[2] (6271a)

Royal Dutch *Denis Coakley* a77 69
3 ch g Nayef(USA) Shersha (IRE) (Priolo (USA))
1256[7] 2042[8] 4296[3] (5351) ◆ 6376[5] 6981[3]

Royale Demeure (FR) *M Cesandri* a73 66
3 b f Gentlewave(IRE) Rose Du Roi (IRE) (Royal Academy (USA))
247a[0]

Royal Empire (IRE) *Saeed Bin Suroor* a99 105
3 b c Teofilo(IRE) Zeiting (IRE) (Zieten (USA))
(4212) ◆ 5006[3] (5768) ◆ 6036[6] 6374[2]

Royal Empress (IRE) *David Wachman* 90
2 br f Holy Roman Emperor(IRE) Weekend Fling (USA) (Forest Wildcat (USA))
6078a[3] 6550a[6]

Royal Entourage *Philip Kirby* a75 70
7 b g Royal Applause Trempkate (USA) (Trempolino (USA))
4831[10] 6311[7] 6706[4] 7381[3]

Royal Envoy (IRE) *Paul Howling* a58 18
9 b g Royal Applause Seven Notes (Zafonic (USA))
125[8] (297) 572[10] (740) 964[2] 1070[7] 1309[4] 2170[6] 3477[9] 4928[6] 5850[12] 6771[8] 8061[6]

Royaleo (FR) *E Libaud* 72
2 gr c Slickly(FR) Tune Royal (FR) (Green Tune (USA))
5073a[9]

Royale Ransom *Sylvester Kirk* a63 48
3 b f Red Ransom(USA) Prayer (IRE) (Rainbow Quest (USA))
3475[7] 4332[13] 5095[10] 5720[12]

Royal Etiquette (IRE) *Lawney Hill* a70 70
5 b g Royal Applause Alpine Gold (IRE) (Montjeu (IRE))
636[5] 818[8] 891[3] 966[2] 1613[2] 2498[10] (3222) 3703[4] 4411[U] 5417[4] 6181[7] 6933[14] (7473) 7892[7] 8162[9]

Royal Fortune (IRE) *F-H Graffard* 92
3 gr f Invincible Spirit(IRE) Seerah (Machiavellian (USA))
3987a[4]

Royal Gig *Tim Etherington* 19
3 br f Val Royal(FR) Sainte Gig (FR) (Saint Cyrien (FR))
2633[9] 4791[9] 5330[10] 5589[12] 7384[8]

Royal Guinevere *Dean Ivory* a65 32
2 b f Invincible Spirit(IRE) Elegant Beauty (Olden Times)
3637[8] 4816[4] 5943[12]

Royal Holiday (IRE) *Marjorie Fife* a72 51
5 ch g Captain Rio Sunny Slope (Mujtahid (USA))
2239[11] 4192[2] (7348) (7799) 8271[2]

Royal Intruder *Richard Guest* a73 72
7 b g Royal Applause Surprise Visitor (IRE) (Be My Guest (USA))
133[5] 186[7] 267[10] 425[10] 528[7] 623[10] 744[13]

Royal Jenray *Jedd O'Keeffe* a4 53
2 gr g Royal Applause In The Highlands (Petong)
1474[6] 1753[10] 2330[7] 3123[7] 5313[9] 6360[6] 7526[8]

Royal Liaison *James Fanshawe* 59
4 b m Ad Valorem(USA) Royal Mistress (Fasliyev (USA))
2815[12]

Royally *Mlle S-V Tarrou* a91 84
6 b h Verglas(IRE) Royal Lady (IRE) (Royal Academy (USA))
18a[10]

Royal Mizar (SPA) *Alastair Lidderdale* 67
2 b g What A Caper(IRE) Zahaadid (FR) (Limpid)
2970[5] 3067[7] 3638[5] 4090[2] 4540[5]

Royal Opera *Brian Ellison* a70 76
4 b g Acclamation Desert Gold (IRE) (Desert Prince (IRE))
501[5] ◆ 2035[3] 2751[5] 3129[8]

Royal Peculiar *Michael Appleby* a94 95
4 b h Galileo(IRE) Distinctive Look (IRE) (Danehill (USA))
1374[3] ◆ 1890[11] 2504[3] ◆ 6832[7] ◆ 7396[15] 7825[8] 8110[6] (8228)

Royal Prize *Ralph Beckett* a75 61
2 ch g Nayef(USA) Spot Prize (USA) (Seattle Dancer (USA))
3119[4] 3824[7] (5476) 6363[3] 6972[4]

Royal Rascal *Tim Easterby* 99
2 b f Lucky Story(USA) Royal Punch (Royal Applause)
2282[3] (3168) 3695[2] (4116) 4820[5] 5516[3] 6467[6] (7065)

Royal Reverie *Rebecca Curtis* a69 78
4 b g Royal Applause Christina's Dream (Spectrum (IRE))
4184[6]

Royal Revival *Saeed Bin Suroor* a85 102
5 gr g King's Best(USA) Holy Nola (USA) (Silver Deputy (CAN))
241a[6] 486a[P]

Royal Reyah *Stuart Kittow* 79
3 b g Royal Applause Dilys (Efisio)
1493[2] 2205[2] 2914[6] 3445[4] 4364[6] 5269[11]

Royal Rock *Chris Wall* a89 115
8 b g Sakhee(USA) Vanishing Point (USA) (Caller I.D. (USA))
1129[4] 2710[5] 3370[8] 4078[2] 4794[2] 5627[5] 6867[6] 7236[14]

Royal Sea (IRE) *David O'Meara* a67 53
3 b g Refuse To Bend(IRE) Janayen (USA) (Zafonic (USA))
6102[8] 6341[5] 7983[5] (8241) ◆ 8288[2]

Royal Selection (IRE) *Karen George* a59 61
4 ch m Choisir(AUS) Rustic Princess (IRE) (Daggers Drawn (USA))
1306[8] 4533[3] 5915[11] 7382[10]

Royal Skies (IRE) *Mark Johnston* 77
2 b c Dubawi(IRE) Kalana (FR) (Rainbow Quest (USA))
3401[2] 3824[9] 4253[3] (5704) 6597[4]

Royal Steps (IRE) *James Tate* a74 75
2 b f Royal Applause Ask Carol (IRE) (Foxhound (USA))
1466[4] 4011[5] 4742[2] *5178[2] 5887[3]* 6160[12] 6604[5] *7060[10]*

Royal Straight *Linda Perratt* a66 81
7 ch g Halling(USA) High Straits (Bering)
1879[2] 2033[6] 2619[6] 3030[3] 3116[5] (4137) (4674) 4768[5] 5366[9] 6045[5] 6476[10] 6706[8]

Royal Swain (IRE) *Alan Swinbank* a83 86
6 b g Val Royal(FR) Targhyb (IRE) (Unfuwain (USA))
(1846) 2457[9] 3036[5] 3564[2] 3953[4] 5729[4] (6137)

Royal Tigre (USA) *M Ramadan* a65
3 b c Bernardini(USA) Royal Tigress (USA) (Storm Cat (USA))
417a[14]

Royal Trooper (IRE) *James Given* a75 89
6 b g Hawk Wing(USA) Strawberry Roan (IRE) (Sadler's Wells (USA))
1846[11] 2419[12] 2921[4] 3287[5] 3992[6] 4460[7] 5673[4] 6626[6]

Roy Rocket (FR) *John Berry* a25 37
2 gr g Layman(USA) Minnie's Mystery (FR) (Highest Honor (FR))
7330[14] 7636[12] *7796[8]*

Roy's Legacy *Shaun Harris* a76 63
3 b c Phoenix Reach(IRE) Chocolada (Namid)
295[5] 3613[12] 4084[5] 4428[6] 4663[2] (4798) 5087[10] 5536[5] 5831[10] 5875[2] *(6249)* 6713[8] *7775[8] 7902[2] 7967[10]* (8054) 8157[3] 8163[8]

Roy The Boy (USA) *Alan Bailey* a82 78
4 b g Pomeroy(USA) Mrs. M (USA) (Mecke (USA))
4541[9] 4939[15] *(5750) 6319[2] 6454[4] 7170[5] 7743[4] 7935[2]* ◆ *7966[2] 8081[2]* 8142[3]

Roz *Harry Dunlop* a81 102
2 b f Teofilo(IRE) Debonnaire (Anabaa (USA))
3009[11] *(3764)* (4514) 6635[2]

Ruacana *Michael Bell* a76 96
3 b g Cape Cross(IRE) Farrfesheena (USA) (Rahy (USA))
635[3] ◆ *723[2] 908[2]* ◆ (1557) (2390) 2718[3] 4079[2] 5078[5] 5905[4] 6625[3] 7396[7]

Ruban (IRE) *Mahmood Al Zarooni* a86 74
3 ch c Dubawi(IRE) Piece Unique (Barathea (IRE))
5297[2] 5889[3] 6570[3]

Rubenstar (IRE) *Daniel Mark Loughnane* a20 53
9 b g Soviet Star(USA) Ansariya (USA) (Shahrastani (USA))
8236[10]

Rubi Dia *Kevin M Prendergast* a73 69
5 ch g Hernando(FR) Oblique (IRE) (Giant's Causeway (USA))
136[6] 811[3]

Rubina (IRE) *John M Oxx* 101
3 b f Invincible Spirit(IRE) Riyafa (IRE) (Kahyasi)
1403a[6] 2101a[8] 3092a[8] 3645a[11]

Rubio Bello (IRE) *C Boutin* a60 62
3 b g Celtic Swing Mur Taasha (USA) (Riverman (USA))
7266a[0]

Rub Of The Relic (IRE) *Paul Midgley* a63 73
7 b g Chevalier(IRE) Bayletta (IRE) (Woodborough (USA))
1248[4] *(1583)* 2239[7] 2588[3] *(3449)* (3693) 4137[3] 4251[2] 4864[6] 5085[6] 5290[3] 5585[7] *5767[8]* 6103[8]

Ruby Doo *Alastair Lidderdale* a38
4 b m Imperial Dancer On Cloud Nine (Cloudings (IRE))
369[10] 635[7]

Ruby Glass (IRE) *Ruth Carr* a60
3 b g Red Clubs(IRE) Gold Bar (IRE) (Barathea (IRE))
723[5] 921[6] 1422[5] 1740[12] 2144[13]

Ruby Night (IRE) *Michael Bell* 90
3 b g Red Clubs(IRE) Stop Out (Rudimentary (USA))
2785[2] 4298[6] 5365[9] 6381[4] 7370[4]

Ruby's Day *E J O'Neill* a61 96
3 ch f Vital Equine(IRE) Isabella's Best (IRE) (King's Best (USA))
1209a[8] 3987a[9]

Ruff Diamond (USA) *David Thompson* a82 57
7 bb g Stormin Fever(USA) Whalah (USA) (Dixieland Band (USA))
1794[7] 2242[7] 7603[7]

Ruff Luck *Seamus Mullins* a61
2 b f Lucarno(USA) Ruffie (IRE) (Medicean)
8166[2]

Rufus Stone (USA) *Jane Chapple-Hyam* a58 63
4 ch g Henny Hughes(USA) Jive Talk (USA) (Kingmambo (USA))
1261[4] 2287[10] 2826[9] 3344[5] 3793[9] 4541[8] *5175[11] 5941[2] 6773[10] 7500[10]*

Rugged Cross *Henry Candy* 108
3 b c Cape Cross(IRE) Lunda (IRE) (Soviet Star (USA))
2275[3] 2705[8] 4628[2] ◆

Rugosa *Charles Hills* a83 80
3 b f Oasis Dream Zathonia (Zafonic (USA))
(2601) 3643[8] 4579[2] ◆ 5107[3] *7858[2]*

Rulbin Realta *Pat Phelan* a56 44
5 b m Jendali(USA) Paulines Gem (IRE) (Petorius)
1703[8] 2041[13] 2851[6] 3222[12] 7077[6]

Rule Book (IRE) *Richard Hannon* 97
3 gr c Aussie Rules(USA) Open Book (Mark Of Esteem (IRE))
1511[5] 2612[2] (3161) (3509) ◆ 4700[11] ◆ 5078[7] 5598[15] (6445)

Rulership (JPN) *Katsuhiko Sumii* 125
5 b h King Kamehameha(JPN) Air Groove (JPN) (Tony Bin)
7872a[3]

Rulesn'regulations *Matthew Salaman* a94 91
6 b g Forzando Al Awaalah (Mukaddamah (USA))
2409[11] 2870[11] 3557[8] 4503[10] 4939[12] 5502[4] 5630[5] 6241[8] 6546[3] *6837[8] 7203[5] 7827[2]*

Rumh (GER) *Saeed Bin Suroor* a103 103
4 ch m Monsun(GER) Royal Dubai (GER) (Dashing Blade)
2655[12] 3219[4] *(3765)* 4115[9] 5238[3] (5905) *7510[2]*

Rum King (USA) *S Donohoe* a71 79
5 bb g Montbrook(USA) Cut Class Leanne (USA) (Cutlass (USA))
335a[11] 388[6]

Rumor (USA) *Richard E Mandella* a103
4 b m Indian Charlie(USA) Mini Chat (USA) (Deputy Minister (CAN))
7569a[5]

Rum Punch *Eve Johnson Houghton* 68
3 b f Ishiguru(USA) Cajole (IRE) (Barathea (IRE))
1501[13] 2065[7] (2611) 4509[2] 4726[3] ◆ 5513[4] 5995[7]

Runaway Tiger (IRE) *Paul D'Arcy* a61 33
4 b g Tiger Hill(IRE) Last Rhapsody (IRE) (Kris)
3216[10] *3449[4]* 3988[15] *4402[6] 4915[10]*

Rundell *Richard Hannon* 77
2 b c Notnowcato Shardette (IRE) (Darshaan)
6486[11] (6733)

Run Fat Lass Run *Kevin Ryan* a65 74
2 b f Sakhee(USA) Feolin (Dr Fong (USA))
(1474) 7687[13] *7994[8]*

Run It Twice (IRE) *David Evans* a69 59
2 b g Dark Angel(IRE) Alinda (IRE) (Revoque (IRE))
2164[10] 4845[10] 5126[7] *5763[8]* 6156[2] 6732[8] *(7414) 7814[8] 7994[2] 8072[5]*

Running Bull (IRE) *Linda Jewell* a35
2 b c Papal Bull Miss Barbados (IRE) (Hawk Wing (USA))
7926[11] 8185[10]

Running Deer (IRE) *Sir Henry Cecil* a76 70
3 b f Hurricane Run(IRE) Sweet Sioux (Halling (USA))
2038[3]

Runninglikethewind (IRE) *Chris Wall* a63 47
2 b g Hurricane Run(IRE) Virgin Hawk (USA) (Silver Hawk (USA))
3387[7] *5969[4] 6645[5]*

Running Mate (IRE) *Jo Crowley* a67 68
5 b g Acclamation It Takes Two (IRE) (Alzao (USA))
(986) 3546[5] 5874[2] *7308[4]*

Running On Faith *Garry Woodward*
4 b g Phoenix Reach(IRE) Amazing Grace Mary (Dancing Spree (USA))
7712[8]

Running Reef (IRE) *Tracy Waggott* 66
3 b g Hurricane Run(IRE) Half-Hitch (USA) (Diesis)
1878[6] 2592[3] 3274[10] 4082[4] 4553[7] 4830[14]

Running Water *Hugh McWilliams* a40 49
4 ch m Blue Dakota(IRE) Floral Spark (Forzando)
227[6] 1169[7] 2748[8] 5190[10]

Run Of The Day *Eve Johnson Houghton* a59 47
3 b f Three Valleys(USA) Shall We Run (Hotfoot I)
595[5] 993[7] 1319[9] *(1992) 2850[7]* 3072[5] *4189[7]*

Runway Girl (IRE) *Roger Charlton* a46 59
3 b f Dansili Fashion Model (Rainbow Quest (USA))
1502[12] *3279[11]* 3664[6] 4510[3] 5855[5]

Runway Ready (USA) *Gary Contessa*
2 ch f Mr Greeley(USA) Fashion Cat (USA) (Forest Wildcat (USA))
6944a[4]

Rupeetoups *Henry Candy* 37
4 b g Deportivo Rock Flower (Rock City)
3389[13] 3702[12] 4605[5] 4902[7] 5327[10]

Ruscello (IRE) *Ed Walker* a92 89
3 b g Cape Cross(IRE) Sea Picture (IRE) (Royal Academy (USA))
1312[4] (2038) 2772[2] *(3737)* ◆ 4741[11] (5455) 6025[8] *(6537)*

Rushing Dasher (GER) *Natalie Friberg* a75 60
10 ch g Dashing Blade Roma Libera (GER) (Pharly (FR))
629a[7]

Ruskins View (IRE) *Alan Berry* 19
3 b f Clodovil(IRE) Soft (USA) (Lear Fan (USA))
1596[10] 3289[8]

Rusland (IRE) *Ismail Mohammed* 30
3 b c Shamardal(USA) Rosia (IRE) (Mr Prospector (USA))
3227[12]

Russelliana *Sir Michael Stoute* 104
3 ch f Medicean Rosacara (Green Desert (USA))
1454[9] 3328[9]

Russian Bullet *Jamie Osborne* a67 50
3 b g Royal Applause Gandini (Night Shift (USA))
25[5] 86[2] 138[2] (769) 905[9] (1444) 1941[6] *2547[4]* 3489[13] *4467[3] 4885[6]* 5444[4] 5808[8] 6249[6] 8253[6]

Russian George (IRE) *Steve Gollings* a80 77
6 ch g Sendawar(IRE) Mannsara (IRE) (Royal Academy (USA))
192[7] 849[3] 1011[6] 1085[2] 1640[7]

Russian Ice *Dean Ivory* a86 56
4 ch m Iceman Dark Eyed Lady (IRE) (Exhibitioner)
148[3] 470[2] 746[2] 3963[12] 5769[6] 6367[3] 7559[11] *7722[4] 7827[4] 7997[7]* 8158[2]

Russian Rave *Jonathan Portman* a78 94
6 ch m Danehill Dancer(IRE) Russian Ruby (FR) (Vettori (IRE))
1354[7] 2067[3] (2766) (3342) 3636[3] 4091[2] 4579[7] 4764[11] 5980[5] 6870[6] 7128[3] 7408[5]

Russian Realm *Sir Michael Stoute* 78
2 b c Dansili Russian Rhythm (USA) (Kingmambo (USA))
6204[3]

Russian Rock (IRE) *M Al Muhairi* a109 86
5 b h Rock Of Gibraltar(IRE) Mala Mala (IRE) (Brief Truce (USA))
50a[9] *140a[3] 261a[11] 1147a[8]*

Russian Royale *Stuart Kittow* 48
2 b f Royal Applause Russian Ruby (FR) (Vettori (IRE))
5785[5]

Russian Rumba (IRE) *Jonathan Portman* a52 34
3 b f Whipper(USA) Pink Sovietstaia (FR) (Soviet Star (USA))
990[5] 1180[5] 1357[8] 2010[4] 3141[P]

Russian Song (GER) *A Wohler* 95
3 b c Singspiel(IRE) Russian Samba (IRE) (Laroche (GER))
3683a[13]

Russian Storm *Pat Phelan* a65 68
4 b m Hurricane Run(IRE) Yesteryear (Green Desert (USA))
(1106) (1309) 1635[2] 2233[3]

Russian Tango (GER) *A Wohler* 114
5 ch h Tertullian(USA) Russian Samba (IRE) (Laroche (GER))
2322a[5] 3206a[3] 5613a[8] 6805a[4]

Russian Winter *Tim Etherington* a42 41
4 b g Tobougg(IRE) Karminskey Park (Sabrehill (USA))
1096[11]

Rust (IRE) *Ann Duffield* 71
2 b c Elnadim(USA) Reddening (Blushing Flame (USA))
6099[2] 6473[3] 7096[3]

Rustic Deacon *Willie Musson* a92 89
5 ch g Pastoral Pursuits Anne-Lise (Inchinor)
2151[3] 3167[2] 3615[10] (5004) *6979[3]* ◆ *7631[9] 7966[7]*

Rustic Gold *Richard Ford* a64 47
8 ch g Tobougg(IRE) Suave Shot (Suave Dancer (USA))
9[12]

Rustic Rose Dot Uk *Bill Turner*
2 b g Elnadim(USA) Easy Feeling (IRE) (Night Shift (USA))
6826[10]

Rusty Rocket (IRE) *Paul Green* a56 86
3 ch c Majestic Missile(IRE) Sweet Compliance (Safawan)
905[10] (1317) (1658) 1998[5] 2714[10] 2914[3] 3288[2] 3607[6] 4081[6] 4881[3] 5676[2] (5736) 6192[6] 6665[3] 7177[7] 7451[4]

Rutherford Rd (CAN) *Michael J Doyle* 84
2 bb f First Samurai(USA) A Touch Of Glory (CAN) (Golden Gear (USA))
6289a[11]

Rutherglen *George Baker* 57
2 b c Tiger Hill(IRE) Hanella (IRE) (Galileo (IRE))
4604[8] 5303[7] 6020[10]

Rutterkin (USA) *Alan Berry* a74 68
4 gr g Maria's Mon(USA) Chilukki Cat (USA) (Storm Cat (USA))
2475[5] 2878[4] 3210[7] 3888[9] 5923[6] 6403[14]

Ruwaiyan (USA) *Mahmood Al Zarooni* 87
3 bb c Cape Cross(IRE) Maskunah (IRE) (Sadler's Wells (USA))
3079[2] ◆ 4067[2] 4797[5]

R Woody *Robert Cowell* a79 96
5 ch g Ishiguru(USA) Yarrita (Tragic Role (USA))
4337[6] 4690[20] 6543[2] *6767[10]* 7080[14] *7716[8]*

Ryan Style (IRE) *Lisa Williamson* a75 87
6 b g Desert Style(IRE) Westlife (IRE) (Mind Games)
2482[8] 3336[10] 3905[4] 4501[2] 4638[4] 5020[2] 5703[12] 7100[11] *7197[2] 7412[3] 7864[8]*

Ryedale Dancer (IRE) *Richard Guest* a63 71
4 ch m Refuse To Bend(IRE) Saik (USA) (Riverman (USA))
149[8] 287[13] 448[7] 633[8] 4495[9] 4779[3] 5338[12] (5671) 6106[3] 6259[8] *6646[7]* 6782[4] *(7204)* 7274[9] 7446[10] 7861[10] 7917[10] 8131[8] 8231[2] 8253[9]

Ryedale Lass *Joseph Tuite* a62 67
4 b m Val Royal(FR) First Dawn (Dr Fong (USA))
1704[13] 1937[9] (2998) 3137[2] 3468[3] 4411[6] *5351[5] 7250[9]* 7270[7]

Ryedale Valley *Tim Easterby* a57 54
2 ch c Three Valleys(USA) Phi Phi (IRE) (Fasliyev (USA))
1955[2] 2402[5] 3062[7] 4545[13] 5202[2] *5886[3]* 6130[11] *6451[7]*

Ryedane (IRE) *Tim Easterby* a78 74
10 b g Danetime(IRE) Miss Valediction (IRE) (Petardia)
1868[11] 2092[4] 2538[6] 3257[7] (3893) 4552[9] 4717[9] 4784[2] 5543[4] 6127[7] (6403)

Rye House (IRE) *Sir Michael Stoute* 93
3 b c Dansili Threefold (USA) (Gulch (USA))
1567[4] (2129) 3509[2] ◆

Rye Park *J S Moore* a18
6 b m Central Park(IRE) Diamond Vanessa (IRE) (Distinctly North (USA))
5174[7]

Rylee Mooch *Richard Guest* a83 81
4 gr g Choisir(AUS) Negligee (Night Shift (USA))
247 208[2] 311[12] 624[6] 652[6] (844) 1015[4] 1828[4] 2789[4] 3477[2] 3993[4] (4461) 5362[6] 6006[4] 6427[12] 7291[3] 7648[3] 7726[6] (7860) 7918[7]

Rysbrack (USA) *Paul Webber* a78 81
6 ch g Selkirk(USA) Super Tassa (IRE) (Lahib (USA))
3227[5] 3920[2] *5430[3]*

Rythmic *Mark Johnston* a84 79
3 ch f Dubai Destination(USA) Northern Melody (IRE) (Singspiel (IRE))
398[4] 1756[6] 2379[6] 2539[6] 3968[9] (6263) 6703[3] *(7381) 7617[3] 7655[2]*

Ryton Runner (IRE) *Lucinda Russell* a79 75
4 b g Sadler's Wells(USA) Love For Ever (IRE) (Darshaan)
3337[5]

Saaboog *James Tate* a87 69
3 b f Teofilo(IRE) Saabiq (USA) (Grand Slam (USA))
2197[8] 2628[4] 3978[2] *(4407)* 4662[4] *5243[7]* 6092[2] 6430[6] *6812[3] (7353) 8110[9]*

Saamidd *Saeed Bin Suroor* a116 81
4 b h Street Cry(IRE) Aryaamm (IRE) (Galileo (IRE))
1749[2] 2505[5]

Sabbygo (IRE) *Valentina Matrullo* 79
3 b f Holy Roman Emperor(IRE) Sabindra (Magic Ring (IRE))
1699a[9]

Sabercat (USA) *Steven Asmussen* a109 76
3 bb c Bluegrass Cat(USA) Miner's Blessing (USA) (Forty Niner (USA))
1872a[15]

Sabhan (IRE) *Geoffrey Harker* 80
3 b c Marju(IRE) Sister Sylvia (Fantastic Light (USA))
(2283) (2604) ◆ 3882[2] 4961[5] 6124[3] 6884[14]

Sable (IRE) *Adrian McGuinness* a26 61
6 ch m Choisir(AUS) Fable (Absalom)
66[7]

Sabore *Richard Fahey* 70
3 br f Orientor Annie Gee (Primo Valentino (IRE))
1864[7] 2335[2] 3024[3] 4211[6] 4551[2] 5113[2] 5335[5] 5760[3] 6261[5] 6542[5] 7402[7]

Saborido (USA) *Amanda Perrett* a87 86
6 gr g Dixie Union(USA) Alexine (ARG) (Runaway Groom (CAN))
1513[7] 1905[6] 2411[5] 2978[13] 3572[2] 4697[7] 5106[7] (5772) *(6019)* 6493[13]

Sabrage (AUS) *Michael Moroney* 111
4 br h Charge Forward(AUS) Galroof (NZ) (Maroof (USA))
7264a[16] 7560a[8]

Sabratah *H-A Pantall* 113
4 b m Oasis Dream Marika (Marju (IRE))
2112a[0] 4790a[0] (6943a) 7624a[3]

Sabratha (IRE) *Linda Perratt* a49 74
4 b m Hawk Wing(USA) Aitch (IRE) (Alhaarth (IRE))
1796[7] 2598[6] 3334[9] 3581[4] 3888[2] ◆ 4134[7] 4432[2] 4640[5] 5081[7] 5185[8] 5671[7] 6528[7] (6756) 7684[14]

Sabre Rock *John Best* a68
2 b c Dubawi(IRE) Retainage (USA) (Polish Numbers (USA))
7507[8] 7627[5] 8172[2]

Sabre Tiger *Alan Jarvis*
2 b c Tiger Hill(IRE) Sabreon (Caerleon (USA))
4362[P]

Sabre Tooth (IRE) *Sir Michael Stoute* a68
3 b c Medicean Desert Tigress (USA) (Storm Cat (USA))
1703[11] 1923[5]

Sabys Gem (IRE) *Mlle F Bizot* a57 42
4 b g Diamond Green(FR) Dust Flicker (Suave Dancer (USA))
306[7] 740[6] (938) 1387[10] 1497[10] *1630[5]* 7701a[10]

Sacco D'Oro *Michael Mullineaux* a51 51
6 b m Rainbow High Speedy Native (IRE) (Be My Native (USA))
465[2] 602[5] 767[9] 2915[3] 3216[8] 4537[4] *5173[4]* 5683[6] *6056[8]* 6190[5] *8260[7]*

Sacrilege *Daniel O'Brien* a62 72
7 ch g Sakhee(USA) Idolize (Polish Precedent (USA))
2899[3] 3589[5]

Sacrosanctus *Scott Dixon* a86 96
4 ch g Sakhee(USA) Catalonia (IRE) (Catrail (USA))
1141[9] 2488[10] 2707[2] *3004[4]* (3771) 4611[13] 4824[15] 5065[6] 5368[14] (5703)

Sadamu Patek (JPN) *Masato Nishizono* 120
4 b h Fuji Kiseki(JPN) Summer Night City (JPN) (Helissio (FR))
8042a[6]

Sad But True (IRE) *Alan McCabe* a29 37
2 b g Antonius Pius(USA) Consultant Stylist (IRE) (Desert Style (IRE))
5619[8] 6115[4] *6826[6]* 7491[7]

Saddler's Rock (IRE) *John M Oxx* 122
4 b h Sadler's Wells(USA) Grecian Bride (IRE) (Groom Dancer (USA))
2903a[2] ◆ 3293[3] (4737) 5599[9] 6198[5] 6914a[4] 7235[6]

Saddle The Storm *Birgitte Nielsen* a37
5 b g Xaar Descriptive (IRE) (Desert King (IRE))
3654a[10]

Sadeek's Song (USA) *Mahmood Al Zarooni* a65 104
4 ch h Kingmambo(USA) New Morning (IRE) (Sadler's Wells (USA))
1855[8] 2253[14]

Sadfig *Clive Brittain* a52 63
2 b c Notnowcato Coconut Queen (IRE) (Alhaarth (IRE))
4677[3] *7324[9]*

Sadiigah *Clive Brittain* a68 45
2 b f Medicean Regal Riband (Fantastic Light (USA))
3040[2] 3764[9] 4818[13]

Sadiq *Saeed Bin Suroor* 61
2 b c Invincible Spirit(IRE) Miss Particular (IRE) (Sadler's Wells (USA))
6985[4]

Sadler's Mark *Dermot Anthony McLoughlin* a79 93
5 b g Sadler's Wells(USA) Waldmark (GER) (Mark Of Esteem (IRE))
5609a[10]

Safari Sunseeker (IRE) *William Knight* a84 96
3 b g Tagula(IRE) Mooching Along (IRE) (Mujahid (USA))
1983[2] (2714)

Safarjal (IRE) *Charles Hills* a78 85
3 b f Marju(IRE) Wijdan (USA) (Mr Prospector (USA))
990[2] 1503[3] 1973[5] 2612[3] *5766[7]* 7494[3] *7782[4]*

Safe House (IRE) *Mark Johnston* a72 75
3 ch f Exceed And Excel(AUS) Last Resort (Lahib (USA))
(3580) *3940[8]* 4388[9] *4933[5]* 5415[7] 6171[4] *7142[10]*

Saffa Hill (IRE) *Tim Easterby* 77
3 b g Tiger Hill(IRE) Saffa Garden (IRE) (King's Best (USA))
1479[10] 2449[11] 2772[3] 3697[6] 4548[4] 4883[4] 5803[6]

Saffron Park *John Best* a42 49
3 ch g Compton Place Beacon Silver (Belmez (USA))
3155[7] 4582[11] *7898[12] 8265[9]*

Safina Blue (FR) Y Barberot a68 80
3 b f Anabaa Blue Folie Gaillarde (FR) (Valanour (IRE))
17a^{10}

Safwaan Willie Musson a61 70
5 b g Selkirk(USA) Kawn (Cadeaux Genereux)
105^{3} 530^{6} 651^{5} (1014) 7982^{5} (8288)

Saga Dream (FR) F Lemercier 113
6 gr g Sagacity(FR) Manixa (FR) (Manninamix)
953a^{3} 1245a^{3} 1696a^{5} 5117a^{3} 6464a^{3} 6898a^{3} (7284a)

Saga Lout Tom Dascombe a75
2 b g Assertive Intellibet One (Compton Place)
7953^{3} ◆ (8138) (8245)

Sagawara A De Royer-Dupre 107
3 gr f Shamardal(USA) Sagalina (IRE) (Linamix (FR))
1695a^{2} (2532a) 3203a^{8} 4633a^{4} 6295a^{6} 6911a^{10}

Sage Melody (FR) P Demercastel a82 99
2 b f Sageburg(IRE) Desert Melody (FR) (Green Desert (USA))
3680a^{3} 4384a^{7} 7122a^{4} 7828a^{3}

Sagramor Hughie Morrison a111 111
4 ch h Pastoral Pursuits Jasmick (IRE) (Definite Article)
2640^{2} 5117a^{2} 6035^{2}

Sagunt (GER) Sean Curran a71 72
9 ch g Tertullian(USA) Suva (GER) (Arazi (USA))
7528^{11}

Saharan (IRE) Y De Nicolay a83 83
4 ch m Beat Hollow Saharienne (USA) (A.P. Indy (USA))
116a^{3}

Saharan Air (IRE) Jim Boyle a59
3 ch g Hurricane Run(IRE) Haute Volta (FR) (Grape Tree Road)
827^{9} 1086^{8} 2042^{9} 3246^{14} 4918^{6}

Sahara Sunshine Laura Mongan a38 63
7 b m Hernando(FR) Sahara Sunrise (USA) (Houston (USA))
1184^{9} 2851^{12} 3969^{11}

Saharia (IRE) Michael Attwater a86 78
5 b g Oratorio(IRE) Inchiri (Sadler's Wells (USA))
158^{4} 205^{8} 3995^{5} (4950) 5480^{8} 6208^{2} (6692) 7461^{2} 7823^{6} 8181^{6} 8306^{4}

Saigon James Toller a106 108
3 b c Royal Applause Luanshya (First Trump)
1856^{14} 2277^{4} 2641^{6} 3239^{7} 4012^{3} 4760^{6} 5627^{6} 6449^{3} 6634^{6} 7054^{2}

Sail Home Julia Feilden a74 74
5 b m Mizzen Mast(USA) Bristol Channel (Generous (IRE))
(281) 363^{2} (689) 1656^{6} 2498^{3} 3073^{6} 3550^{3} 4335^{8} 4884^{7} 5509^{3} 5767^{6} 6416^{6} 7767^{3} 7892^{3} 8078^{4}

Sailing North (USA) Ronald Harris a57 56
4 b g Mizzen Mast(USA) Silver Star (Zafonic (USA))
214^{9} 373^{5} 524^{6} 665^{9} 781^{5} 925^{4} 985^{10}

Sainglend Sean Curran a64 69
7 b g Galileo(IRE) Verbal Intrigue (USA) (Dahar (USA))
772^{3} 2575^{2} 7077^{3}

Saint Agnan (FR) J-C Rouget 97
2 gr c Verglas(IRE) Scapegrace (IRE) (Cape Cross (IRE))
6507a^{6}

Saint Baudolino (IRE) A Fabre a84 119
3 b c Pivotal Alessandria (Sunday Silence (USA))
(2064a) 2743a^{2} 4121a^{3} (5250a)

Saint Bernard D Camuffo 105
3 b c Three Valleys(USA) Savignano (Polish Precedent (USA))
1698a^{8} 7587a^{2}

Saint Boniface Peter Makin a59 60
3 ch g Bahamian Bounty Nursling (IRE) (Kahyasi)
26^{5} 219^{3} ◆ 524^{4} 3450^{9} 4644^{6} 5443^{4} 5991^{4} 6281^{5} 6774^{10} 7326^{6}

Saint Crepin (FR) J-C Rouget 88
2 b c Cape Cross(IRE) Aldeburgh Music (IRE) (In The Wings)
6507a^{8}

Saint Helena (IRE) Harry Dunlop a78 85
4 b m Holy Roman Emperor(IRE) Tafseer (IRE) (Grand Lodge (USA))
971^{4} 1446^{5} 2174^{5} 2863^{5} 3962^{10} 5359^{3} 6333^{2} 7381^{12}

Saint Hilary William Muir 85
3 b f Authorized(IRE) Bright Halo (IRE) (Bigstone (IRE))
2200^{5} (2768) ◆ 4338^{7}

Saint Irene Michael Blanshard a66 69
3 ch f Halling(USA) Santorini (USA) (Spinning World (USA))
1486^{6} 1979^{8} 3014^{4} 3665^{4} 4186^{3} 4709^{3} 5095^{7} (5783) 5991^{3} 6274^{2} (6950) 7302^{7} 8078^{9} 8199^{9}

Saint Jerome (IRE) Marcus Tregoning 85
2 b g Jeremy(USA) Eminence Gift (Cadeaux Genereux)
4362^{6} 4688^{3} (5235) 5515^{14} 6162^{8} 6815^{11}

Saint Louet (FR) F Chappet a94 86
3 b g Panis(USA) Byanozza (Mtoto)
(5473a)

Saint Loup (FR) J-C Rouget a92 109
3 b c Zamindar(USA) Sanada (IRE) (Priolo (USA))
475a^{3} 1244a^{2} 2108a^{4}

Saint Thomas (IRE) John Mackie a81 78
5 b g Alhaarth(IRE) Aguilas Perla (IRE) (Indian Ridge)
(944) 1719^{5} 2414^{5} 4396^{3} (5225) 5913^{8}

Sairaam (IRE) Charles Smith a58 73
6 b m Marju(IRE) Sayedati Eljamilah (USA) (Mr Prospector (USA))
927^{10} (2549) 2766^{8} 3949^{7} 4708^{9} 5338^{6} 5915^{6} 6127^{17} 7747^{7}

Sajjhaa Saeed Bin Suroor 115
5 b m King's Best(USA) Anaamil (IRE) (Darshaan)
2209^{2} 7429a^{4} 7688^{2}

Sakash J R Jenkins 40
2 b c Sakhee(USA) Ashwell Rose (Anabaa (USA))
7466^{6}

Sakhee's Ichigou Michael Blanshard a53 46
2 b f Sakhee's Secret Greensand (Green Desert (USA))
3009^{9} 4222^{5} 4646^{6} 5484^{7} 6841^{4} 7432^{9} 7923^{11}

Sakhee's Pearl Jo Crowley a83 81
6 gr m Sakhee(USA) Grey Pearl (Ali-Royal (IRE))
733^{4} 3278^{8} 4805^{2} 5372^{8} 6207^{3} 7626^{7} 7805^{4} 8020^{2} 8252^{2}

Sakhees Romance Noel Wilson 54
2 b f Sakhee(USA) Chance For Romance (Entrepreneur)
6049^{3} 6473^{4} 7244^{4}

Sakhee's Rose Roger Charlton a70 55
2 b f Sakhee's Secret Isobel Rose (IRE) (Royal Applause)
5275^{5} 6114^{9} 6936^{4} 7476^{4} (7821) 8016^{7}

Sakina (FR) P Demercastel a59 60
2 b f Spirit One(FR) Talena (Zafonic (USA))
5697a^{10}

Saktoon (USA) Derek Shaw a58 57
4 b m El Prado(IRE) Galore (USA) (Gulch (USA))
101^{2} 370^{3} 666^{9} 1193^{5} 1309^{8} 1638^{10} 5543^{15} 5720^{8}

Sakura Mambo (FR) S Kobayashi 74
2 gr f Great Journey(JPN) Sapporo (FR) (Smadoun (FR))
8193a^{0}

Salaaheb (IRE) Alastair Lidderdale a30 47
3 b f Tiger Hill(IRE) Sayedati Eljamilah (USA) (Mr Prospector (USA))
270^{9} 360^{5} 466^{7}

Salacia (IRE) Ismail Mohammed a69 89
3 b f Echo Of Light Neptune's Bride (USA) (Bering)
1472^{3} 2601^{3} 3281^{11} (5453) 6417^{3} 6938^{12}

Salam Alaykum (IRE) Reginald Roberts a89 80
4 b h Galileo(IRE) Alicia (IRE) (Darshaan)
6855a^{10}

Salerosa (IRE) Ann Duffield a84 73
7 b m Monashee Mountain(USA) Sainte Gig (FR) (Saint Cyrien (FR))
19^{3}

Salford Art (IRE) David Elsworth 106
3 ch f Sir Percy Millay (Polish Precedent (USA))
1887^{4} 2178^{4} 3292^{4} 3856^{8} 6833^{6} 7405^{7}

Salford Dream David Elsworth 59
3 ch g Halling(USA) Spitting Image (IRE) (Spectrum (IRE))
2197^{9} 2560^{7} 2895^{5}

Salford Prince (IRE) David Elsworth a52
4 b g Invincible Spirit(IRE) Bring Plenty (USA) (Southern Halo (USA))
737^{8} 1036^{6} 2464^{11}

Salient Michael Attwater a74 79
8 b g Fasliyev(USA) Savannah Belle (Green Desert (USA))
301^{5} 568^{8} 685^{8} 1108^{2} 1358^{3} 1626^{4} ◆ 2173^{6} 2855^{4} 3105^{5} 3774^{10} 4727^{5} 6950^{5} 7302^{13} 7486^{4} 7815^{7} 8079^{7}

Salik Tag (USA) David Nicholls a76 71
4 ch g Hennessy(USA) Clever Empress (Crafty Prospector (USA))
1520^{12} (3941)

Salinas Road (FR) M Figge 90
2 b c Elusive City(USA) Mamounia (GER) (Platini (GER))
5781a^{6}

Sally Bruce Louise Best a50 36
2 b f Byron Show Trial (IRE) (Jade Robbery (USA))
1136^{6} 1284^{5} 1629^{5} 5511^{7} 6438^{8} 6581^{8} 7738^{9} 8076^{5} 8166^{4}

Sally Friday (IRE) Edwin Tuer a78 75
4 b m Footstepsinthesand Salee (IRE) (Caerleon (USA))
1295^{14} 1797^{11} 2260^{15} 3290^{12} 4594^{3} 4958^{2} 5824^{5} 6262^{14} 6940^{6}

Sally Pepper (USA) James Given 58
3 bb f Rock Hard Ten(USA) La Sila (USA) (Danzig (USA))
2374^{14} 3080^{9}

Sally's Swansong Eric Alston a62 56
6 b m Mind Games Sister Sal (Bairn (USA))
544^{10} 691^{5} 1383^{3} 1881^{4} 2244^{3} 3256^{10} 3382^{5} 4461^{4} 5093^{8} (6180) (6496) 6836^{10} 7275^{7} 7969^{5} 8231^{8} 8253^{8}

Salomina (GER) P Schiergen 110
3 b f Lomitas Saldentigerin (GER) (Tiger Hill (IRE))
(3802a) (4862a) 6295a^{10}

Salona (GER) J-P Carvalho 97
4 ch m Lord Of England(GER) Selana (GER) (Lomitas)
7665a^{5}

Salon Soldier (GER) P Schiergen 104
3 b c Soldier Hollow Salonblue (IRE) (Bluebird (USA))
2569a^{3} 3683a^{7} 5402a^{3}

Salontyre (GER) Bernard Llewellyn a69 76
6 b g Pentire Salonrolle (IRE) (Tirol)
555^{3} 673^{5} 1496^{2} (1905) 6738^{5}

Saloomy David Simcock a86 88
3 ch c Shamardal(USA) Oystermouth (Averti (IRE))
2313^{6} 2881^{3} (4605) (4919) 6417^{2} ◆

Saloon (USA) Jane Chapple-Hyam a61 60
8 b g Sadler's Wells(USA) Fire The Groom (USA) (Blushing Groom (FR))
2394^{5} 4941^{4} 5323^{13} 5637^{6} 7479^{4} 8104^{9} 8260^{5}

Saloon Tramper (GER) Mario Hofer 55
3 b c Trempolino(USA) Saloon Rum (GER) (Spectrum (IRE))
7266a^{4}

Saltaire Lass Paul Midgley 41
2 ch f Sleeping Indian Rainbow Treasure (IRE) (Rainbow Quest (USA))
1594^{4} 2309^{4}

Saltamontes S Cerulis a77 63
3 b f Caradak(IRE) Ishi Adiva (Ishiguru (USA))
865a^{0}

Saltas (GER) P Schiergen 110
4 b h Lomitas Salde (GER) (Alkalde (GER))
1700a^{5}

Saltire Blue William Jarvis a53
3 ch f Compton Place Seine Bleue (FR) (Grand Lodge (USA))
1637^{8} 2145^{6}

Salure B Grizzetti 113
3 ch c Sakhee(USA) Davie's Lure (USA) (Lure (USA))
1208a^{9}

Salut (GER) P Schiergen 107
4 b h Lomitas Saldentigerin (GER) (Tiger Hill (IRE))
630a^{14}

Salutary Jane Chapple-Hyam a57 54
3 b g Kyllachy Leonica (Lion Cavern (USA))
3539^{5} 4341^{13} 5229^{5} 6217^{4} 6829^{8}

Salutation (IRE) Mark Johnston a39 84
2 b g Iffraaj Totally Yours (IRE) (Desert Sun)
3499^{10} 4114^{9} 4448^{3} (4951) 5602^{2} 6032^{6} 6162^{10} 6815^{10}

Salute To Seville (IRE) J S Moore a54
2 b f Duke Of Marmalade(IRE) Vingt Et Une (FR) (Sadler's Wells (USA))
3074^{14} 8018^{7} 8200^{6}

Salvatore Fury (IRE) Keith Dalgleish a63 56
2 b g Strategic Prince Nocturnal (FR) (Night Shift (USA))
3725^{5} 4387^{8} 5311^{6} 5749^{3} 5920^{6} 7441^{9} 7687^{12}

Salve Haya (IRE) W Hickst 89
4 ch m Peintre Celebre(USA) Salve Regina (GER) (Monsun (GER))
3652a^{5}

Samantha Glaz (IRE) C Plisson a55
4 b m Sinndar(IRE) Super Crusty (IRE) (Namid)
15a^{8}

Samardal (FR) N Minner a78 90
5 b h Shamardal(USA) Samando (FR) (Hernando (FR))
815a^{5}

Samarkand (IRE) Sir Mark Prescott Bt a91 89
4 b g Sadler's Wells(USA) Romantic Venture (IRE) (Indian Ridge)
4962^{7} 5546^{5} ◆ 5729^{5} 6349^{4} 6848^{2}

Samasana (IRE) Ian Wood a72 51
3 b f Redback Singitta (Singspiel (IRE))
2^{2} 132^{10} 382^{2} (459) (556) (641) 747^{3} 920^{5} 1058^{3}

Samba Brazil (GER) A Wohler 102
3 ch f Teofilo(IRE) Sasuela (GER) (Dashing Blade)
4862a^{11} 6726a^{3} 7075a^{3}

Samba Do Brazil (IRE) A Peraino 89
2 br f Excellent Art Triple Axel (IRE) (Danehill Dancer (IRE))
6090a^{9}

Samba King Mahmood Al Zarooni 99
3 b g Dubai Destination(USA) Dance Of Leaves (Sadler's Wells (USA))
(1265) ◆ (1647) 1888^{7} 2897^{3} 3296^{12} 4009^{3} 7082^{7} 7396^{11} 7689^{4}

Samba Night (IRE) James Eustace a62 70
3 b g Dark Angel(IRE) Brazilia (Forzando)
1072^{3} 1445^{8} 2085^{2} 2205^{5} 2730^{5} 3050^{4} 3706^{4} 4663^{7} 5479^{13} 5774^{9} 7297^{P}

Sambirano William Knight a30 25
3 b g Kyllachy Regal Gallery (IRE) (Royal Academy (USA))
5276^{9} 6397^{10} 7005^{11}

Sambulando (FR) Frank Sheridan a39 79
9 gr g Kouroun(FR) Somnambula (IRE) (Petoski)
1282^{8} 1613^{8}

Samedi Mark Johnston a70
3 b f Any Given Saturday(USA) Hush Money (CHI) (Hussonet (USA))
(206) 549^{4}

Samitar Mick Channon 113
3 b f Rock Of Gibraltar(IRE) Aileen's Gift (IRE) (Rainbow Quest (USA))
1452^{8} 2109a^{9} (2527a) 3328^{4} ◆ 4478a^{3}

Sam Lord James Moffatt a78 57
8 ch g Observatory(USA) My Mariam (Salse (USA))
332^{5} 500^{10} 849^{4} 1272^{12}

Samminder (IRE) Peter Chapple-Hyam a96 104
3 b c Red Ransom(USA) Gimasha (Cadeaux Genereux)
1751^{8} ◆ 2236^{3} 2712^{5} 4598^{10} 6072^{9}

Sammy Alexander David Simcock a76 87
4 b g Storming Home Sweet Angeline (Deploy)
(2576) 3101^{4} (5063) 6450^{3}

Sam Nombulist Richard Whitaker 90
4 ch g Sleeping Indian Owdbetts (IRE) (High Estate)
1161^{11} 1522^{6} 1863^{10} 2417^{9} (3128) 3493^{8} 4136^{4} 5342^{7} 6471^{7} 6999^{4} (7559) 7691^{8}

Samollie (IRE) Garvan Donnelly a70 58
3 b g Strategic Prince Miss Sabre (Sabrehill (USA))
393^{7}

Sam Sharp (USA) Ian Williams a81 93
6 bb g Johannesburg(USA) Caffe (USA) (Mr Prospector (USA))
1679^{2} 2500^{2} ◆ 3157^{5} 3911^{4} (5914) 6638^{18}

Samsons Son Terry Clement a84 93
8 b g Primo Valentino(IRE) Santiburi Girl (Casteddu)
1890^{8} 3341^{6} 5558^{14} 6039^{12} 7245^{3} 7522^{13}

Sam Spade (IRE) Richard Hannon a66
2 gr c Clodovil(IRE) Red Empress (Nashwan (USA))
7641^{4} 7807^{7}

Samuel George Michael Blake
5 ch g Generous(IRE) Digyourheelsin (IRE) (Mister Lord (USA))
737^{10}

Samysilver (USA) Gianluca Bietolini 106
4 bb h Indian Charlie(USA) Hidden Ransom (USA) (Silver Ghost (USA))
7697a^{8}

Sanad (IRE) Anthony Carson a49 70
3 br c Red Clubs(IRE) Knockatotaun (Spectrum (IRE))
1445^{6} 2375^{9} 3218^{10} 5095^{9} 5216^{2} 5458^{9} 5633^{7} 7200^{10} 7670^{11}

Sanagas (GER) Bart Cummings a108 109
6 bb g Lomitas Scota (GER) (Marju (IRE))
7264a^{10} 7621a^{18}

Sanctioned Roger Charlton a82 64
3 b g Authorized(IRE) Kazeem (Darshaan)
3786^{7} 4542^{7} 5048^{4}

Sandagiyr (FR) Saeed Bin Suroor a111 108
4 b h Dr Fong(USA) Sanariya (IRE) (Darshaan)
(487a) 758a^{4} 1143a^{8} 4130a^{7} 5517^{17} 6166^{5}

Sandakam (FR) C Baillet a75
3 b g Muhaymin(USA) Siran (FR) (R B Chesne)
247a^{10}

Sand And Deliver Gary Moore a36 67
2 b f Royal Applause Alhufoof (USA) (Dayjur (USA))
2426^{4} ◆ 2938^{3} 3700^{8} 4687^{10} 7481^{6}

Sandaura (IRE) Clive Cox a59
2 b f Footstepsinthesand Stratospheric (Slip Anchor)
7778^{5}

Sandbanks Sizzler (IRE) Ralph Beckett a78 90
4 ch g Soviet Star(USA) Isticanna (USA) (Far North (CAN))
2346^{11} 2932^{10} 4060^{4} 5306^{5} ◆ 6019^{4} 6642^{11}

Sandbetweenourtoes (IRE) Roger Curtis a76 76
3 b g Footstepsinthesand Callanish (Inchinor)
1377^{3} 1985^{3} 2501^{6} 2864^{2} 3229^{4} (3570) 4155^{9} 4334^{6} 5993^{7} (6436) 7484^{9}

Sand Boy (IRE) Charles Hills 18
2 b c Footstepsinthesand Farbenspiel (IRE) (Desert Prince (IRE))
4419^{7}

Sandfrankskipsgo Peter Crate a24 84
3 ch g Piccolo Alhufoof (USA) (Dayjur (USA))
2347^{15} 4500^{3} 4765^{13} 5123^{2} 5536^{2} 5663^{9} 6226^{3}

Sand Grouse Marco Botti a59 57
2 b f Mr Greeley(USA) Gentle On My Mind (IRE) (Sadler's Wells (USA))
4742^{9} 5300^{6} 5947^{10} 6451^{9} 7173^{7} 7785^{3}

Sand Orchid Stuart Kittow a17
2 ch f Sandwaki(USA) Doliouchka (Saumarez)
6177^{9} 6816^{9}

Sandreamer (IRE) Mick Channon 99
2 b f Oasis Dream Alsharq (IRE) (Machiavellian (USA))
(2245) 3631^{2} 4577^{2} 5307^{3} 5516^{6} (6090a)

Sandsend (IRE) Richard Fahey 62
2 b c Elusive City(USA) Free Lance (IRE) (Grand Lodge (USA))
2508^{5} 3123^{8} 4114^{8} 4922^{3} ◆ (5313) 5620^{2}

Sand Skier Hans Adielsson a89 82
5 b g Shamardal(USA) Dubai Surprise (IRE) (King's Best (USA))
310^{5} 714^{2} (745) 2174^{2} 2479^{5} (3278) 3502^{3} 4216^{9} 4460^{3} 4733^{5}

Sands Of Fortune (IRE) Sir Michael Stoute a41
3 ch g Shamardal(USA) Shell Garland (USA) (Sadler's Wells (USA))
5297^{10}

Sand Stamp (FR) S Seemar a93 86
3 ch c Footstepsinthesand Qahatika (FR) (Polish Precedent (USA))
417a^{10} 485a^{9}

Sandusky Mahmood Al Zarooni a92 96
4 b g Tiger Hill(IRE) Red Carnation (IRE) (Polar Falcon (USA))
1882^{4} ◆ 2257^{14} 2932^{6} 6018^{5} 7175^{13}

Sandwati (FR) P Lefevre
3 b g Sandwaki(USA) Ti Francaise (FR) (Marignan (USA))
7266a^{0}

Sandwith George Foster a63 76
9 ch g Perryston View Bodfari Times (Clantime)
580^{3} 887^{4} 1054^{4} 1242^{5} 1800^{3} (2032) (2458) (2839) 3113^{3} 3578^{4} 4430^{4} 6531^{2} 7101^{2} 7489^{9}

Sandy Lane (IRE) Amy Weaver a69 36
3 b g Elusive City(USA) Ipanema Beach (Lion Cavern (USA))
3399^{8} 3946^{5} 5687^{10} 6152^{9} 7615^{10} 8099^{2} (8205) (8287)

Sandy's Charm (FR) F Rohaut 113
4 b m Footstepsinthesand First Charm (FR) (Anabaa (USA))
1163a^{7} 5649a^{10}

Sandy's Row (USA) Mark Johnston 63
2 b f Street Cry(IRE) Carry On Katie (USA) (Fasliyev (USA))
2282^{9} 2631^{5} 3725^{2} 4450^{3} 4672^{4} 5009^{7}

Sangar Ollie Pears 76
4 ch m Haafhd Preference (Efisio)
1439^{3} 1797^{8} 2539^{4} 2915^{7} 3616^{7} 4426^{2} 4768^{3} 5372^{4} 5824^{6} 6410^{6} 6711^{11} 6819^{7}

Sangfroid Tim Vaughan a31 53
8 gr g With Approval(CAN) Affaire D'Amour (Hernando (FR))
6280^{5}

Sangrail William Muir a52 63
3 b f Singspiel(IRE) Wars (IRE) (Green Desert (USA))
1357^{12} 2483^{3} 3083^{8} 3619^{11} 4490^{11} 8187^{7}

Sanisa (FR) J Boisnard a84 81
4 b m Panis(USA) Seacleef (FR) (A.P. Indy (USA))
3207a^{2}

Sanjii Danon (GER) G Geisler 100
6 b h Big Shuffle(USA) Serpina (IRE) (Grand Lodge (USA))
1410a^{5} 7286a^{3}

San Juan (FR) C Lerner a77 96
2 b c Librettist(USA) Milonga (IRE) (Barathea (IRE))
5899a^{4} 6507a^{7} 7984a^{7}

Sanjuro (IRE) Mick Channon 82
2 br g Manduro(GER) Kind Regards (IRE) (Unfuwain (USA))
5304^{5} ◆ (5793) ◆ 6699^{3}

Sanluquenia (FR) C Boutin
2 b f Carlotamix(FR) Princess Ella (FR) (Emperor Jones (USA))
6751a^{0}

San Marino Grey (FR) A Fabre 91
2 gr c Clodovil(IRE) Montagne Magique (IRE) (King's Best (USA))
5140a^{5}

Sannibel Graeme McPherson a69 60
4 ch m Needwood Blade Socialise (Groom Dancer (USA))
61^{4} 373^{2} (499) 576^{5} 819^{10} 5635^{4} 6053^{10} 7990^{4}

Sanogo (GER) *A Wohler* 91
4 b g Shirocco(GER) Serenata (GER) (Lomitas)
7427a[7]

Sansili *Peter Bowen* a53 66
5 gr g Dansili Salinova (FR) (Linamix (FR))
849[7] 1272[13] (2575) 4096[3] 4731[6]

Sans Loi (IRE) *Alan McCabe* 86
3 b g Lawman(FR) Lady Elysees (USA) (Royal Academy (USA))
1457[2] 1858[15] 2714[12] 4364[9] 4819[12]

Santadelacruze *Gary Moore* a69 66
3 b g Pastoral Pursuits Jupiters Princess (Jupiter Island)
596[4] 787[2] 959[4] 2425[2] 3338[6] 4544[6] 5441[9] 7767[8] ◆ 8049[4]

Santa Fe Stinger *Tim Easterby* 30
2 b f Rail Link Highly Liquid (Entrepreneur)
3457[7] 5339[11] 6257[6]

Sant'Alberto (ITY) *F Chappet* 105
4 b h Colossus(IRE) Adya (FR) (Sillery (USA))
3178a[8] 7282a[7]

Santarini (IRE) *Richard Hannon* a69 73
3 b f Lawman(FR) Lapland (FR) (Linamix (FR))
2279[4] ◆ 2891[2] 3340[4] 5262[5] 5769[5] 6328[3] 7314[12]

Santarius (GER) *P Harley* a97 97
3 b c Intendant(GER) Schattenspiel (Second Set (IRE))
7282a[4]

Santefisio *Keith Dalgleish* a102 94
6 b g Efisio Impulsive Decision (IRE) (Nomination)
378[2] 527[5] 1821[7] 2597[2] 3380[7] 4703[2] 5004[3] 5186[4] 5517[10] (7502) 7709[2]

Santera (IRE) *Tony Carroll* a51 27
8 br m Gold Away(IRE) Sainte Gig (FR) (Saint Cyrien (FR))
129[3] ◆ 278[9] 530[10] 2575[6]

Santiago Boy *Linda Perratt* 46
6 b g Silver Patriarch(IRE) Gunner Marc (Gunner B)
2034[4]

Santo Padre (IRE) *David Marnane* a90 109
8 b g Elnadim(USA) Tshusick (Dancing Brave (USA))
(1538a) 2513a[9] 3196a[4] 3650a[7] 5067a[8] 6268a[7]

Santo Prince (USA) *Michael Bell* 75
2 bb g Henrythenavigator(USA) Sally Wood (CAN) (Woodman (USA))
2784[7] 3067[5] 3545[5] 4540[4] 6629[5] (6946)

Saoi (USA) *William Knight* a85 83
5 ch g Wiseman's Ferry(USA) Careyes (IRE) (Sadler's Wells (USA))
3503[3] 7823[11] 8020[3] ◆ (8252)

Saonois (FR) *J-P Gauvin* a112 118
3 b c Chichicastenango(FR) Saonoise (FR) (Homme De Loi (IRE))
(716a) (1244a) 1869a[4] (2743a) (6294a) 6912a[15] 8043a[10]

Sapphire (IRE) *D K Weld* 118
4 b m Medicean Polished Gem (IRE) (Danehill (USA))
(3197a) 3676a[2] (7237)

Sapphire Seeker *Des Donovan* a31 46
3 br g Sakhee(USA) Symphonia (IRE) (Zafonic (USA))
1843[12] 2262[8] 2803[6] 4438[14] 5246[8]

Sarafy De Monnaie (FR) *J Vittori*
6 b m Freedom Cry Heian (FR) (Esprit Du Nord (USA))
92a[0]

Sarah Berry *Chris Dwyer* a49 62
3 b f First Trump Dolly Coughdrop (IRE) (Titus Livius (FR))
2010[6] (3050) 3547[10] 4197[6] 4777[8] (4970) 5513[6] 5934[4] 6417[5]

Sarah Lynx (IRE) *J E Hammond* 118
5 b m Montjeu(IRE) Steel Princess (IRE) (Danehill (USA))
5116a[8] 6295a[13]

Sarahmanda *Peter Makin* a39 54
2 b f Bahamian Bounty Maysarah (IRE) (Green Desert (USA))
3971[11] 4899[5] 5192[4] 6283[9] 6822[11] 7268[5] 7854[10]

Sarah's Art (IRE) *Gary Harrison* a81 79
9 gr g City On A Hill(USA) Treasure Bleue (IRE) (Treasure Kay)
719[5]

Sarahs Pal *Mandy Rowland*
2 b f No Time(IRE) Danum Diva (IRE) (Danehill Dancer (IRE))
7491[12]

Sara Lucille *F Head* 100
2 b f Dansili Magic America (USA) (High Yield (USA))
4384a[6] 5379a[2]

Sarando *Paul Webber* a63 58
7 b g Hernando(FR) Dansara (Dancing Brave (USA))
7077[11] 7528[3]

Sarangoo *Malcolm Saunders* a69 74
4 b m Piccolo Craic Sa Ceili (IRE) (Danehill Dancer (IRE))
1061[4] 1481[9] 2421[2] 3016[2] 3434[9] (4146) 4332[5] 4493[4] 5447[4] 5531[2] 5995[2] 6277[6]

Saratoga Black (IRE) *B Grizzetti* 114
5 b g Pyrus(USA) Mary Martins (IRE) (Orpen (USA))
(1554a) 2106a[7] 2968a[7] 6554a[5]

Saratoga Slew (IRE) *Marco Botti* a78 77
3 b f Footstepsinthesand Life Rely (USA) (Maria's Mon (USA))
1733[2] 2503[3] 3192[4] 4647[6] (5156)

Sardanapalus *Kevin Ryan* 82
3 b g Byron Crinkle (IRE) (Distant Relative)
2246[2] 2678[5] 3563[6] 4046[7] 4498[9] 5170[2] 5556[7] (6048)

Sareeah (IRE) *Clive Brittain* a68
3 b f Cadeaux Genereux Jules (IRE) (Danehill (USA))
1422[2] 1736[7] 2544[10]

Sargasses (FR) *Mlle V Dissaux* a94 94
6 b m Kingsalsa(USA) Sarabande (Nashwan (USA))
18a[3] 7985a[8] 8300a[4]

Sarkiyla (FR) *A De Royer-Dupre* 108
3 b f Oasis Dream Sarlisa (FR) (Rainbow Quest (USA))
(5249a) 6296a[3] 6897a[4] 7515a[3]

Sarmatian Knight (IRE) *Ian Williams* a77 74
3 b g Holy Roman Emperor(IRE) Banco Suivi (IRE) (Nashwan (USA))
1270[4] 2125[5] 2560[4] 3792[2] 4498[15] 6843[4] 6973[4]

Saroso (FR) *W Walton* a62 70
3 ch c Carlotamix(FR) Fialka (FR) (Vayrann)
661a[7]

Sarrsar *Saeed Bin Suroor* a110 109
5 b g Shamardal(USA) Dahr (Generous (IRE))
(47a) (317a) 677a[4] 755a[2]

Sartingo (IRE) *Alan Swinbank* a64 75
5 b g Encosta De Lago(AUS) Alicia (IRE) (Darshaan)
1135[7] 1275[6] 1525[8] 1988[4] 2414[9] 3236[3] 3440[2] 3752[6]

Sasheen *Jeremy Gask* a67 74
5 b m Zafeen(FR) Sashay (Bishop Of Cashel)
1980[5] 2362[2] 4602[10] 5148[5] 6434[8] 6829[7] 7200[12] (7385) 7620[4] 7867[6] 8113[4] 8271[11]

Sash Of Honour (IRE) *Sir Michael Stoute* a87 86
3 ch c Galileo(IRE) Adoration (USA) (Honor Grades (USA))
1456[4] 2271[5] 3227[6] 4515[4] 6839[2]

Saskia's Dream *Jane Chapple-Hyam* a79 81
4 b m Oasis Dream Swynford Pleasure (Reprimand)
3085[5] 3395[7] 4302[10] 5122[6] 6145[3] 6687[5] (7485) 7685[17] 7827[7] 8059[8]

Saslong *Mark Johnston* a48 69
3 b c Zamindar(USA) Cosmodrome (USA) (Bahri (USA))
2826[6] 3273[4] 3976[6] 4727[3] ◆ 6410[16]

Sassi Sioux *Tom Keddy*
3 b f Sleeping Indian Dhurwah (IRE) (Green Desert (USA))
6643[11] 7112[11]

Satanic Beat (IRE) *Jedd O'Keeffe* 91
3 br g Dark Angel(IRE) Slow Jazz (USA) (Chief's Crown (USA))
1477[3] 1819[5] (2678) 3376[2] (3911) 4997[6] 5386[6] 6921[5] 7294[9]

Satsuma *David Brown* 90
2 ch f Compton Place Jodrell Bank (IRE) (Observatory (USA))
(2437) 2715[2] 3269[7] 4093[2]

Satwa Ballerina *Mark Rimmer* a58 54
4 b m Barathea(IRE) Ballerina Rosa (FR) (Anabaa (USA))
65[2] 303[5] 519[5] 767[6] (1744) 2468[4] 2698[7] 2997[5] 3721[12] 4147[3] 5022[4] 6948[10] 7472[5] 7793[12]

Satwa Laird *Conor Dore* a79 80
6 b g Johannesburg(USA) Policy Setter (USA) (Deputy Minister (CAN))
33[3] 199[7] (323) (470) 626[7] 746[13] 991[4] 1117[3] 1342[8] 2044[9] 2355[2] 2466[7] 3045[12] 3229[5] 3314[5] 3544[2] 3559[8] 3914[4] 4242[4] 4413[3] 4939[3] (5179) 5310[6] 5713[2] 6047[10] 6692[9] 6894[6] 7142[5] 7360[4] 7480[5] 7743[5]

Satwa Prince (FR) *Y Fouin* a85 97
9 b g Munir Toryka (Vettori (IRE))
93a[0]

Saucy Brown (IRE) *Kevin Ryan* a67 88
6 b g Fasliyev(USA) Danseuse Du Bois (USA) (Woodman (USA))
1478[8] 1876[4] 2876[6] 3169[11] 4829[9] 7741[10] 7863[6] 8034[7] 8269[10]

Saucy Buck (IRE) *Zoe Davison* a68 65
4 b g Mujadil(USA) Phantom Ring (Magic Ring (IRE))
422[3] 598[8] 995[5] (1088) 1772[5] 2373[8] 3153[4] 4511[8] 4950[4] 5349[6] 5628[5] 5941[8] 7486[7]

Saucy Cat (IRE) *John Best* a63 52
3 br f One Cool Cat(USA) Most-Saucy (Most Welcome)
325 571[3] 726[5] (993) 1062[4] 7200[9] 7417[10]

Saucy Minx (IRE) *Amanda Perrett* 51
2 b f Dylan Thomas(IRE) Market Day (Tobougg (IRE))
7329[7]

Saunta *David Simcock* a58 35
3 b f Invincible Spirit(IRE) Baize (Efisio)
4729[3] 7253[5] 7838[4] 7952[3]

Sauvage L'll *Ed Dunlop* a60
4 b m Loup Sauvage(USA) Sharway Lady (Shareef Dancer (USA))
4157[3] 7162[8] 7933[11]

Savanna Days (IRE) *Mick Channon* a83 83
3 ch f Danehill Dancer(IRE) Dominante (GER) (Monsun (GER))
(1142) 2263[7] 3785[3] 4062[3] 4702[7] 5209[3] 5796[4] ◆ 6376[3] 7475[4]

Savanna La Mar (USA) *Sir Mark Prescott Bt* a77 95
2 ch f Curlin(USA) Soft Morning (Pivotal)
3282[2] (3554) 4514[2] 5103[4] 5571[7]

Savaronola (USA) *Des Donovan* a53 45
7 ch g Pulpit(USA) Running Debate (USA) (Open Forum (USA))
110[3] 278[13]

Saved By The Bell (IRE) *Brian Meehan* a74 83
2 b c Teofilo(IRE) Eyrecourt (IRE) (Efisio)
5685[6] 6204[2] 7962[2]

Save The Bees *Declan Carroll* 79
4 b g Royal Applause Rock Concert (Bishop Of Cashel)
1358[2] 1520[5] 1796[2] 2094[2] 2696[3] ◆ 3335[4] 3589[2] 4175[3] 4641[3] 5535[8] 5713[5] 6141[7] 6559[4]

Savida (IRE) *Sir Michael Stoute* a73 60
3 b f King's Best(USA) Sadima (IRE) (Sadler's Wells (USA))
1415[4] 1981[2] ◆ 2668[2] (3232)

Savvy Chic (USA) *Jeremy Noseda* 67
2 ch f Street Boss(USA) Special Grayce (USA) (Smart Strike (CAN))
5104[7] 6636[16]

Sawahill *Clive Brittain* a49 53
4 b m Diktat Youm Jadeed (IRE) (Sadler's Wells (USA))
130[7]

Saxby (IRE) *Alan Lockwood* a70 67
5 ch g Pastoral Pursuits Madam Waajib (IRE) (Waajib)
2791[9] 3463[9]

Saxonette *Linda Perratt* a61 70
4 b m Piccolo Solmorin (Fraam)
1800[5] 2032[8] 2617[2] 2841[9] 3109[8] 3905[2] 4393[5] 4638[8] 5190[9] 5923[4] 6104[4] 6713[7] 7099[8]

Saxon Soldier *Ed Dunlop* a53
2 br c Kyllachy Gwyneth (Zafonic (USA))
7167[12]

Saytara (IRE) *Saeed Bin Suroor* a88 97
3 b f Nayef(USA) Celtic Silhouette (FR) (Celtic Swing)
3737[7] 4459[3] (5277) 5973[3] (6677)

Scalo *A Wohler* 116
5 bb h Lando(GER) Sky Dancing (IRE) (Exit To Nowhere (USA))
3206a[4] 6299a[4] 7094a[7]

Scamperdale *Brian Baugh* a92 86
10 br g Compton Place Miss Up N Go (Gorytus (USA))
745[5] 971[10] 1718[3] 2348[2] 2687[6] 3692[7] 4657[6] 5430[5] 6120[6] 6981[10]

Scandalo (USA) *Rodolfo Garcia*
2 bb c Cowtown Cat(USA) Stardust Princess (USA) (Honour And Glory (USA))
8244a[12]

Scarabocio *Peter Chapple-Hyam* 67
3 b c Shamardal(USA) My Sara (Mujahid (USA))
2501[7] 2680[7] 5017[3] 5454[5]

Scarborough Lily *Ed Vaughan* a68 58
4 b m Dansili Queen Isabella (El Prado (IRE))
2464[7] 3497[10] 5741[11]

Scarborough Rock *Tom Symonds* 52
3 b g Notnowcato Fabuleux Millie (IRE) (Noverre (USA))
2125[8] 2553[10] 4293[6]

Scarf (AUS) *Saeed Bin Suroor* a106 113
5 gr g Lonhro(AUS) Muffle (AUS) (Quest For Fame)
586a[2] 757a[5] 1749[6] 2075[5] 2919[2] ◆ 3371[7] (3784) 5581[5] (6449) 7048[5]

Scarlet Belle *Marcus Tregoning* a76 75
3 ch f Sir Percy Nicola Bella (IRE) (Sadler's Wells (USA))
2757[6] 3671[5] (4850) 5442[4] 6118[2] 6416[4] 7617[4]

Scarlet Camellia (NZ) *C S Shum* 110
5 b g Spartacus(IRE) Avclina (Nashwan (USA))
8040a[10]

Scarlet Prince *Tony Coyle* a54 71
3 b g Sir Percy Trump Street (First Trump)
3355[2] 4172[2] 4440[4] (4826) 5115[4] 5589[8] (6103) 6544[3] 6924[5]

Scarlet Rocks (IRE) *Ron Barr* a76 78
4 b m Chineur(FR) Alexander Duchess (IRE) (Desert Prince (IRE))
1204[5] 2342[2] 2503[11] 3701[6] 4547[14] 5013[4] 5590[2] 7733[10]

Scarlet Spirit (IRE) *Ann Duffield* a40 46
2 b f Red Clubs(IRE) Waroonga (IRE) (Brief Truce (USA))
6049[12] 6404[3] ◆ 6808[7]

Scarlet Strand *Reg Hollinshead* a34
2 b f Pastoral Pursuits Vermilion Creek (Makbul)
8208[6]

Scarlett Fever *Marcus Tregoning* a63 59
3 b f Haafhd Scarlet Buttons (IRE) (Marju (IRE))
2172[6] 2560[9] 3001[6] 3621[10] 4490[6] (5037) 5482[3] 7527[2]

Scarlet Whispers *Pam Sly* 83
3 b f Sir Percy Hieroglyph (Green Desert (USA))
1270[9] 2733[7] (3448) (3910) 4923[5] 5788[5] 6964[10] 7367[5]

Scary Canary *George Margarson* 28
4 ch g Resplendent Cee(IRE) Simple Logic (Aragon)
5096[6] 5555[12] 6565[6]

Scary Movie (IRE) *Shaun Harley* a67 62
7 b g Daggers Drawn(USA) Grinning (IRE) (Bellypha)
183[9] 401[2] 574[12] 818[5] 7767[7]

Scatter Dice (IRE) *Mark Johnston* a69 99
3 ch f Manduro(GER) Sensation (Soviet Star (USA))
249[2] ◆ 399[3] 675[2] (1170) (1267) 2390[2] (2718) (4575) 4700[9] 5078[3] 5333[6] 6025[10] 6248[5]

Scatty Cat (IRE) *Peter McCreery* 90
2 b f One Cool Cat(USA) Shinko Dancer (IRE) (Shinko Forest (IRE))
(4990) 6284[2] 6467[5] 7518[16]

Scent Of Roses (IRE) *D K Weld* 75
2 b f Invincible Spirit(IRE) Moy Water (IRE) (Tirol)
3674a[6]

Scentpastparadise *Ann Duffield* 79
2 b f Pastoral Pursuits Centenerola (USA) (Century City (IRE))
4310[3] (4681) (5109) 5515[17] 6425[4] 6984[11]

Scepticism (USA) *Mark Johnston* 62
2 b g Elusive Quality(USA) Never Is A Promise (USA) (Capote (USA))
5963[14] 6188[4] 6423[3] 6946[3] 7289[3]

Scherer Magic (USA) *John W Sadler* a104 86
2 bb g Doneraile Court(USA) She's A Nasty One (USA) (Touch Gold (USA))
7567a[9]

Schism *Jonjo O'Neill* 79
4 ch m Shirocco(GER) Alla Prima (IRE) (In The Wings)
3316[8]

Schmooze (IRE) *Linda Perratt* a63 64
3 b f One Cool Cat(USA) If Dubai (USA) (Stephen Got Even (USA))
2595[3] ◆ 3275[2] 3907[3] 4137[2] 4642[3] 5054[3] 5188[2] 5921[5] 6474[7] (6940) 7252[6]

Schoolboy Champ *Lisa Williamson* a51 65
5 ch g Trade Fair Aswhatilldois (IRE) (Blues Traveller (IRE))
6640[12] 7204[10] 7512[5] 7781[8] 7993[8] 8083[9] 8299[6]

School Fees *Henry Candy* a64 85
3 b f Royal Applause Cankara (IRE) (Daggers Drawn (USA))
1331[3] 1723[3] 3343[2] (4235) ◆ 5326[7] 5812[10]

Schoolmaster *Giles Bravery* a87 77
4 b g Motivator Londonnetdotcom (IRE) (Night Shift (USA))
1206[4] 3720[4] 4302[5] 4775[2] 6566[5] (7170) (7645) 7823[5]

Schottische *Derek Haydn Jones* a50 29
2 ch f Pastoral Pursuits Calligraphy (Kris)
1188[6] 2163[6] 3034[10] 4152[6] 5206[9] 8224[3]

Schutzenjunker (GER) *P Schaerer* a78 106
7 b g Lord Of Men Schutzenliebe (GER) (Alkalde (GER))
630a[3]

Sciampin *Marco Botti* a74 78
4 b g Invincible Spirit(IRE) Gracious (Grand Lodge (USA))
1094[4] ◆

Scintillula (IRE) *J S Bolger* 105
2 b f Galileo(IRE) Scribonia (IRE) (Danehill (USA))
6081a[2] 7052[7]

Scommettitrice (IRE) *David Evans* a61 67
4 b m Le Vie Dei Colori Hard To Lay (IRE) (Dolphin Street (FR))
1497[11] 1722[9] 2761[3] 2971[10] (3464) (3717) (4237) (4425) 4980[3] 5445[3] 5502[14] 5995[5] 6307[4] 6685[8] 8190[4] 8231[4]

Scoobys Girl (IRE) *Daniel Mark Loughnane* a44 39
2 b f Holy Roman Emperor(IRE) Mystiara (IRE) (Orpen (USA))
4180[4] 4681[3] 5210[3] 5873[5]

Scotland Forever (IRE) *John Patrick Shanahan* 69
2 b c Rock Of Gibraltar(IRE) Wee Mad Snout (IRE) (Soviet Star (USA))
2702[6]

Scotsbrook Cloud *David Evans* a40 75
7 gr g Cloudings(IRE) Angie Marinie (Sabrehill (USA))
3373[10] 4464[9] 5124[7]

Scots Gaelic (IRE) *Patrick J Flynn* a64 89
5 ch g Tomba Harmonic (USA) (Shadeed (USA))
3241[4]

Scottish Boogie (IRE) *Brendan Powell* a55 83
5 b g Tobougg(IRE) Scottish Spice (Selkirk (USA))
1043a[6] 2500[9] 2988[5] 6207[6] 6734[2] (6933) ◆

Scottish Glen *Patrick Chamings* a85 77
6 ch g Kyllachy Dance For Fun (Anabaa (USA))
(33) (2399) ◆ 4814[5] (5625)

Scottish Lake *Olivia Maylam* a82 69
4 b g Bertolini(USA) Diabaig (Precocious)
(4914) (5234) 6319[7] 6705[10] (7484) 7716[4]

Scottish Star *James Eustace* a80 82
4 gr g Kirkwall Child Star (FR) (Bellypha)
1262[7] (1729) 2637[3] 3278[4] 4499[4] 5007[2] 6073[3] 6445[5]

Scottish Vespers (IRE) *Sir Michael Stoute* a81 76
3 ch g Dylan Thomas(IRE) Scottish Stage (IRE) (Selkirk (USA))
1414[3] ◆ 2393[2] 3720[3] (4465)

Scouting For Girls *Jim Boyle* a59 52
3 b g Sleeping Indian Concubine (IRE) (Danehill (USA))
917[2] 4506[5] 5231[7] 7326[4]

Scrapper Smith (IRE) *Alistair Whillans* a65 98
6 b g Choisir(AUS) Lady Ounavarra (IRE) (Simply Great (FR))
1654[5] 3163[7] 4072[6] 5540[2] 5826[3] 6668[8] 7396[12] 7689[19]

Scream Blue Murder (IRE) *T Stack* 88
2 b f Oratorio(IRE) Holly Blue (Bluebird (USA))
2780a[5]

Screaming Brave *Sheena West* a55 57
6 br g Hunting Lion(IRE) Hana Dee (Cadeaux Genereux)
3573[6]

Scribe (IRE) *David Evans* a65 77
4 b g Montjeu(IRE) Crafty Example (USA) (Crafty Prospector (USA))
786[6] 922[7] 1094[5] 1636[9] 2735[12] 3236[9] 4536[9] 5196[5] (8260)

Script *Alan Berry* a48 50
3 b f Firebreak Signs And Wonders (Danehill (USA))
358[11] 481[4] 898[8] 2139[6] 3285[7] 3357[5] 3726[4] 3892[2] 4619[5] 5448[3] 5760[2] 6125[5] 6477[6]

Scripturist *William Jarvis* a51 61
3 b g Oratorio(IRE) Lambroza (IRE) (Grand Lodge (USA))
350[9] 663[5] 827[8] 2353[9] 4510[13] 4971[7] (5637) 5891[6] 6924[7]

Scrooby Doo *Scott Dixon* a67 67
3 br f Kheleyf(USA) Scrooby Baby (Mind Games)
749[4] 975[3] 1115[5] 3109[3] 3698[4] 3954[RR] 4496[11] 4878[8]

Scrupul (IRE) *Luca Cumani* a81 78
3 b c Dylan Thomas(IRE) Pearl Quest (Rainbow Quest (USA))
1641[7] 2449[4] 3280[3] 3882[4] ◆ 4498[5] 4949[5] 5837[9] 6401[8]

Sea Anemone *Andrew Balding* a51 35
3 b f Phoenix Reach(IRE) Seaflower Reef (IRE) (Robellino (USA))
660[12] 4533[9] 5095[8] 5443[8]

Sea Change (IRE) *Jim Goldie* a40 65
5 b g Danehill Dancer(IRE) Ibtikar (USA) (Private Account (USA))
3377[11] 4326[9] 4955[10] 5188[4] 7024[11] 7528[10]

Seachantach (USA) *S Seemar* a96 97
6 b g Elusive Quality(USA) Subtle Breeze (USA) (Storm Cat (USA))
244a[9] 420a[6] 681a[5] 756a[8] 874a[13]

Sea Cliff (IRE) *Andrew Crook* a33 46
8 b g Golan(IRE) Prosaic Star (IRE) (Common Grounds)
3440[12] 7248[2] 7717[6]

Sea Fever (IRE) *Luca Cumani* a79 76
3 b g Footstepsinthesand Love And Laughter (IRE) (Theatrical (IRE))
1737[6] 2172[7] (2788) ◆ 3066[9] 5636[4] 7027[2] 7358[3]

Sea Fight (USA) *N Clement* a80 85
6 ch g Smart Strike(CAN) Incredulous (FR) (Indian Ridge)
815a[2]

Sea Fret *Hughie Morrison* 32
3 b f Nayef(USA) Shifting Mist (Night Shift (USA))
1567[11] 2577[9]

Seagoing *Tim Easterby* 58
3 ch f Dubai Destination(USA) Babiki (IRE) (Nashwan (USA))
2633[6] 3035[7] 4622[6] 5330[3] 5714[4] 6126[14]

Seal Of Approval *James Fanshawe* a88 85
3 b f Authorized(IRE) Hannda (IRE) (Dr Devious (IRE))
3565[2] (5745)

Sea Lord (IRE) *Mahmood Al Zarooni* a100 103
5 b g Cape Cross(IRE) First Fleet (USA) (Woodman (USA))
52a[4] 243a[8]

Seal Rock *Henry Candy* 104
4 b g Ishiguru(USA) Satin Doll (Diktat)
(1558) 1885[6] 3371[15] 4099[7] 4802[19] 5370[17]

Seamless *Charles Hills* 60
2 b c Beat Hollow Fashionable (Nashwan (USA))
6596[9]

Sea Moon *Sir Michael Stoute* 126
4 b h Beat Hollow Eva Luna (USA) (Alleged (USA))
(2481) (3369) ◆ 4322[5] 6912a[8]

Seamster *Richard Ford* a61 52
5 ch g Pivotal Needles And Pins (IRE) (Fasliyev (USA))
14[7]

Seamus Shindig *Henry Candy* a58 78
10 b g Aragon Sheesha (USA) (Shadeed (USA))
1564[8] 2165[7] 2482[10] 2815[10] 4815[9] 5097[7] 5531[3] 6497[6] 7316[2]

Seanie (IRE) *David Marnane* a94 99
3 b g Kodiac Cakestown Lady (IRE) (Petorius)
1996[5] 3648a[9] 4692a[8]

Sean Og Coulston (IRE) *John J Coleman* a67 96
8 b g Raphane(USA) Classic Silk (IRE) (Classic Secret (USA))
4833a[3]

Sea Of Heartbreak (IRE) *Roger Charlton* a68 111
5 b m Rock Of Gibraltar(IRE) Top Forty (Rainbow Quest (USA))
2209[9] 4010[5] 4801[4] 5399a[6] 6080a[5] 6637[4]

Search And Rescue (USA) *J W Hills* a57 31
3 bb c Seeking The Best(IRE) Pattern Step (USA) (Nureyev (USA))
428[5] 571[8] 683[5] 3246[15]

Searing Heat (USA) *Sir Henry Cecil* 73
4 bb h Empire Maker(USA) Valentine Band (USA) (Dixieland Band (USA))
1655[6] 2051[14] (2588) 2899[12]

Sea Salt *Ron Barr* a59 74
9 b g Titus Livius(FR) Carati (Selkirk (USA))
1650[6] 2096[6] 2841[7]

Sea Shanty (USA) *Richard Hannon* 79
2 b g Elusive Quality(USA) Medley (Danehill Dancer (IRE))
4362[2] 5304[7] 7372[3]

Seaside Rock (IRE) *Richard Hannon* a71 56
2 b c Oratorio(IRE) Miss Sacha (IRE) (Last Tycoon)
6796[15] 7373[7] 7706[8] (8093) 8203[2]

Seaside Sizzler *Ralph Beckett* a85 94
5 ch g Rahy(USA) Via Borghese (USA) (Seattle Dancer (USA))
2706[10] 3373[6] 4697[6] 5905[9] 6428[7]

Sea Siren (AUS) *J O'Shea* 120
4 b m Fastnet Rock(AUS) Express A Smile (AUS) (Success Express (USA))
8041a[9]

Sea Smoke (IRE) *Luca Cumani* 73
3 gr g Dalakhani(IRE) Tochar Ban (USA) (Assert)
3161[5] ◆

Sea Soldier (IRE) *Andrew Balding* a86 87
4 b g Red Ransom(USA) Placement (Kris)
1708[7] 6119[9] 6979[11]

Sea Trial (FR) *Mme C Head-Maarek* a76 106
3 b g Panis(USA) Sea Life (FR) (Anabaa (USA))
914a[8] 4790a[0] 6292a[4]

Seattle Sounder (IRE) *Ann Duffield* a62 50
3 b g Choisir(AUS) Bea's Ruby (IRE) (Fairy King (USA))
2441[7] 3032[9]

Seawood *Roy Bowring* a53 36
6 b g Needwood Blade Ocean Song (Savahra Sound)
644[6] 1952[9] 2670[9]

Seche (FR) *L A Urbano-Grajales* a84 74
2 b c Speightstown(USA) Soignee (GER) (Dashing Blade)
(7984a)

Second City (USA) *B Cecil* a106
3 bb g Distorted Humor(USA) Sis City (USA) (Slew City Slew (USA))
7570a[9]

Secondo (FR) *Roger Charlton* 71
2 b c Sakhee's Secret Royal Jade (Last Tycoon)
6444[4] ◆ 7110[3]

Second To Nun (IRE) *Michael Blanshard* a47 57
6 b m Bishop Of Cashel One For Me (Tragic Role (USA))
1106[6] 1908[P]

Secrecy *Saeed Bin Suroor* a111 112
6 b g King's Best(USA) Wink (Salse (USA))
144a[3] 489a[12] 682a[3] 879a[4]

Secret Admirer (AUS) *Grahame Begg* 116
5 ch m Dubawi(IRE) Secret Illusion (AUS) (Secret Savings (USA))
7264a[11]

Secret Agent (FR) *D Windrif*
8 b g Kahyasi Secret Wells (USA) (Sadler's Wells (USA))
93a[0]

Secret Art (IRE) *Ralph Beckett* a73
2 ch g Excellent Art Ivy Queen (IRE) (Green Desert (USA))
6533[3] 6977[3]

Secret Assassin (IRE) *Mrs J L Le Brocq* a42 41
9 b g Daggers Drawn(USA) Lypharden (IRE) (Lyphard's Special (USA))
218[6] 390[10]

Secret Asset (IRE) *Jane Chapple-Hyam* a98 115
7 gr g Clodovil(IRE) Skerray (Soviet Star (USA))
1146a[8] 2326a[3] 3238[19] 4762[16] 6908a[16] 7772[10]

Secret Beau *Ralph Beckett* 71
2 gr c Sakhee's Secret Belle Reine (King Of Kings (IRE))
2983[7] 3658[4] 4532[3] 7399[9]

Secret City (IRE) *Robin Bastiman* 73
6 b g City On A Hill(USA) Secret Combe (IRE) (Mujadil (USA))
1526[6] (2096) 2750[3] 4315[8] 4784[7] 5737[8] 7447[14]

Secret Dancer (IRE) *Alan Jones* 93
7 b g Sadler's Wells(USA) Discreet Brief (IRE) (Darshaan)
7211[5]

Secret Destination *Brian Ellison* a74 74
2 b f Dubai Destination(USA) Every Whisper (IRE) (High Chaparral (IRE))
1435[7] 1579[2] 2402[2] (3491) 4820[12] 5670[3] 6469[7] 6815[7] 6883[14] (7350)

Secret Empress *Bryan Smart* a39
2 b f Sakhee's Secret Empress Jain (Lujain (USA))
3436[14] 7711[8]

Secret Era *William Muir* a64 65
5 b m Cape Cross(IRE) Secret History (USA) (Bahri (USA))
1919[10] 2431[8] 2858[7] 3236[4] 4219[2] 5164[4] 6097[9]

Secret Gesture *Ralph Beckett* 90
2 b f Galileo(IRE) Shastye (IRE) (Danehill (USA))
6966[2] (7403)

Secret Hero *Adrian McGuinness* a59 60
6 b g Cadeaux Genereux Valiantly (Anabaa (USA))
67[7] 926[12]

Secretinthepark *Ed McMahon* a83 75
2 ch c Sakhee's Secret Lark In The Park (IRE) (Grand Lodge (USA))
(5684) (7478)

Secretive *M bin Shafya* a93 94
5 b g Shamardal(USA) Samsung Spirit (Statoblest)
47a[5]

Secret Jubilee *Philip McBride* 36
3 ch f Medicean It's A Secret (Polish Precedent (USA))
2935[9] 3591[5]

Secret Lodge *Garry Woodward*
4 ch m Needwood Blade Obsessive Secret (IRE) (Grand Lodge (USA))
2865[12]

Secret Look *Ed McMahon* 87
2 ch g Sakhee's Secret Look Here's Carol (IRE) (Safawan)
(3381) 4247[5] 5088[8] (6238) 7206[5] 7635[3]

Secretly *Henry Candy* 80
2 ch f Sakhee's Secret The Cat's Whiskers (NZ) (Tale Of The Cat (USA))
5352[2]

Secret Millionaire (IRE) *Tony Carroll* a60 93
5 b g Kyllachy Mithl Al Hawa (Salse (USA))
6689[10] 7019[11] 7464[12] 7775[11] 7936[6]

Secret Missile *William Muir* a83
2 b c Sakhee's Secret Malelane (IRE) (Prince Sabo)
6320[2] 6609[3] 7497[3] (7738)

Secret Number *Saeed Bin Suroor* a90
2 b c Raven's Pass(USA) Mysterial (USA) (Alleged (USA))
(7323) ◆

Secretori *Matthew Salaman* a60 65
2 b c Sakhee's Secret Ticki Tori (IRE) (Vettori (IRE))
3140[7] 3770[6] 4149[3] 5475[4] 6564[3]

Secret Queen *Martin Hill* a69 67
5 b m Zafeen(FR) Gold Queen (Grand Lodge (USA))
806[3] 970[7] 1049[2] 1378[7] 2207[8] 4492[10] 4887[9] 5346[4] 5808[4] 6002[8]

Secret Quest *James Fanshawe* 84
3 br f Pivotal Secret Flame (Machiavellian (USA))
(2050) 2820[3] 4057[6]

Secret Rebel *Sylvester Kirk* a75 31
2 ch c Sakhee's Secret Indiana Blues (Indian Ridge)
7372[8] 7706[2] 7856[4] 8070[6]

Secrets Away (IRE) *Marco Botti* a67 64
3 ch f Refuse To Bend(IRE) Lady Zonda (Lion Cavern (USA))
1518[3] 2079[8] 3189[7] 3978[7]

Secret Sign *Brian Meehan* a76 77
2 ch g Sakhee's Secret Barboukh (Night Shift (USA))
2231[13] (3638) 4736[8] 5475[3] (6155) 6284[3] 6658[5] 7220[4]

Secret Success *Paul Cole* 33
2 b c Exceed And Excel(AUS) Magic Music (IRE) (Magic Ring (IRE))
6787[13]

Secret Symphony *Sylvester Kirk* a73 49
2 ch g Sakhee's Secret Intermission (IRE) (Royal Applause)
2231[11] 3733[2] 4310[13] 4873[3] 5475[9] 5886[6] 7614[3] 7786[2] 7922[2] (8076)

Secret Taboo (FR) *Robert Collet* a64 61
2 b c Miesque's Son(USA) Taboo (GER) (Pivotal)
5378a[10] 5698a[7]

Secret Talent *Hughie Morrison* a79
2 b g Sakhee's Secret Aqaba (Lake Coniston (IRE))
7773[2] ◆

Secret Tune *Charlie Longsdon* 84
8 b g Generous(IRE) Sing For Fame (USA) (Quest For Fame)
(1640) 2214[5] 6493[12]

Secret Venue *Jedd O'Keeffe* a32 69
6 ch g Where Or When(IRE) Sheila's Secret (IRE) (Bluebird (USA))
2793[3] ◆ 4400[15] 4552[7] 4743[9] 5093[9]

Secret Wishes (FR) *Mlle S-V Tarrou* a76 75
3 b c Hold That Tiger(USA) Mavelga (Machiavellian (USA))
1125a[8]

Secret Witness *Ronald Harris* a105 110
6 ch g Pivotal It's A Secret (Polish Precedent (USA))
2023[3] (2177) 2208[2] 2507[13] 3371[12] 3650a[4] 4073[2] 4367[11] 5370[14] 5561[16] 6072[8] 6244[3] 6485[9] 6867[10] 7366[16] 7397[14]

Secret Woman (IRE) *Alan Jarvis* a41
2 b f Manduro(GER) Coveted (Sinndar (IRE))
7165[8]

Secular Society *Brian Meehan* 74
2 b g Royal Applause Fantastic Santanyi (Fantastic Light (USA))
4792[3] ◆

Sedgwick *Shaun Harris* a72 71
10 b g Nashwan(USA) Imperial Bailiwick (IRE) (Imperial Frontier (USA))
1154[12] 1792[7] (2260) 2921[9] 3129[11] 3962[6] 4391[4] (4915) 5345[10] 6076[3] 6608[3] 6891[8] 7511[9] 7819[3] 7968[3]

Sediciosa (IRE) *Y Barberot* 110
3 b f Rail Link Seditieuse (IRE) (Night Shift (USA))
(2741a) 6295a[8] 7284a[2]

See And Be Seen *Sylvester Kirk* a46 53
2 b g Sakhee's Secret Anthea (Tobougg (IRE))
5684[10] 6795[10] 7103[7] 7439[5] 7785[7] 7973[7]

See Clearly *Tim Easterby* a65 78
3 b f Bertolini(USA) True Vision (IRE) (Pulpit (USA))
1271[13] 1639[3] 2229[8] 2824[6] 3912[9] 4909[5] (5416) 5676[6] 6048[2] 6194[3] 6782[7] 7395[4] 7666[7]

See Emily Play (IRE) *John Gosden* 64
3 b f Galileo(IRE) Tree Tops (Grand Lodge (USA))
1380[4]

Seeharn (IRE) *Kevin Prendergast* a92 107
4 b m Pivotal Nebraas (Green Desert (USA))
83a[9]

Seek Again (USA) *John Gosden* 87
2 ch c Speightstown(USA) Light Jig (Danehill (USA))
(6636) 7125[2]

Seeking Luck (IRE) *G M Lyons* a85 68
2 b f Clodovil(IRE) On The Make (IRE) (Entrepreneur)
6078a[11]

Seeking Magic *Clive Cox* a91 92
4 b g Haafhd Atnab (USA) (Riverman (USA))
1203[2] 2488[2] 3771[5] 4285[9] 4799[3] 6165[8] 7928[3] ◆ 8066[4]

Seeking The Buck (USA) *Amy Weaver* a66 76
8 b g Seeking The Gold(USA) Cuanto Es (USA) (Exbourne (USA))
2248[17] 3278[9] 4511[3] 6118[7]

Seek The Fair Land *Jim Boyle* a100 90
6 b g Noverre(USA) Duchcov (Caerleon (USA))
89[5] (253) 527[7] 962[9] 1140[7] 1373[6] (1935) 2070[7] 7503[10] 7817[10] 8098[8]

Seemenomore *Michael Bell* a73 47
2 b g Bahamian Bounty Rise (Polar Falcon (USA))
4539[12] 5661[8] 5992[7] (7713) (7797) 8103[8]

See The Storm *Ian Williams* a68 60
4 bb g Statue Of Liberty(USA) Khafayif (USA) (Swain (IRE))
725[6] 848[4] 1014[10] 1801[7] 2463[8] 3026[8] 3456[5] 4003[6] 4439[4] 4966[7] 6951[2] 7106[2] (7316) 7362[2] (7906) 7992[2] 8114[2]

See Vermont *Robin Bastiman* 54
4 b g Kyllachy Orange Lily (Royal Applause)
2971[5] 3463[4] 5739[9]

Se Gray (USA) *Frau E Mader* 90
2 rg c Bernstein(USA) Smokinatthefinish (USA) (Smoke Glacken (USA))
5755a[3]

Sehnsucht (IRE) *Alan McCabe* a77 74
3 b g Amadeus Wolf Kirk Wynd (Selkirk (USA))
1132[12] 4177[5] 4746[4] 5341[7] 6050[9] 6810[2] 7607[6] 7712[4]

Seismos (IRE) *A Wohler* 109
4 ch g Dalakhani(IRE) Sasuela (GER) (Dashing Blade)
(7282a) (7784a)

Sejalaat (IRE) *John Dunlop* 81
2 br g Kheleyf(USA) Laqataat (IRE) (Alhaarth (IRE))
2934[3] 3658[6] 4539[5] 5041[3] (5903) 6487[10]

Sekumkum (IRE) *Marco Botti* a66 51
2 b c Invincible Spirit(IRE) Mosaique Beauty (IRE) (Sadler's Wells (USA))
2934[11] 3611[7] 4253[7] (4934) 6147[9] 6318[4] 7026[4] 7414[5]

Seldom (IRE) *Mel Brittain* a71 71
6 b g Sesaro(USA) Daisy Dancer (IRE) (Distinctly North (USA))
1222[3] 1276[6] 2675[2] 2922[7] 4398[11] 5414[13] 6259[4] 6711[12]

Select Committee *John Quinn* 81
7 b g Fayruz Demolition Jo (Petong)
1868[12] 2140[2] 2439[3] 2693[8] 2793[4] 2982[5] 4400[2] 4680[6] 5058[2] 5223[3] 5801[3] 6357[5] 7101[3]

Selective Spirit *John Weymes* 54
3 ch f Exceed And Excel(AUS) Our Sheila (Bahamian Bounty)
2335[13] 2680[6] 4798[10] 5294[13]

Selfara *Roger Charlton* a79 84
3 b f Oasis Dream Rustic (IRE) (Grand Lodge (USA))
1501[11] 2041[4] 2501[10] 3044[4] 4420[2] (5205) (5514) 6285[6] 6688[4]

Self Centred *Charles Hills* a72 85
3 ch f Medicean Ego (Green Desert (USA))
1500[8] 4597[9] 5409[5]

Self Employed *Garry Woodward* 87
5 b g Sakhee(USA) Twilight Sonnet (Exit To Nowhere (USA))
4248[4] 5090[5] (6341)

Selfsame (USA) *Amanda Perrett* 75
3 b f Dansili Reflections (Sadler's Wells (USA))
(2891) 3476[5] 4850[7]

Selim (RUS) *D Sepulchre* a69 81
4 b h Caitano Stilistika (RUS) (Triple Buck (USA))
3178a[10]

Selinda *Mick Channon* a50 56
3 b f Piccolo Evanesce (Lujain (USA))
2595[4] 3489[10] 4489[7] 5215[10]

Selkie's Friend *Henry Candy* a61 80
3 b g Elnadim(USA) T G's Girl (Selkirk (USA))
(4341) 7824[6]

Semayyel (IRE) *Clive Brittain* a78 107
3 b f Green Desert(USA) Lii Najma (Medicean)
1215[9] 1845[3] 3270[8] 4063[11] 4819[9] 5409[6] (6379) 7237[5]

Semeen *Luca Cumani* a72 74
3 b g Dubawi(IRE) Zeeba (IRE) (Barathea (IRE))
2430[7] 2941[11] 4410[6] (5323) 5990[4] 7511[6]

Sempre Medici (FR) *Mme M Bollack-Badel* 95
2 b c Medicean Sambala (IRE) (Danehill Dancer (IRE))
7693a[4]

Senafe *Marco Botti* 82
2 b f Byron Kiruna (Northern Park (USA))
2193[9] 2977[3] (3569) (4102)

Senator Bong *David Elsworth* 78
2 ch c Dutch Art Sunley Gift (Cadeaux Genereux)
4773[3] 6443[9] (6787) 7298[7] 7635[2]

Senator Sam (IRE) *Ann Duffield* a48 59
2 ch c Country Be Gold(USA) Sorpresa (USA) (Pleasant Tap (USA))
5912[8] 6356[5] 6841[11]

Sendali (FR) *Chris Grant* a52 66
8 b g Daliapour(IRE) Lady Senk (FR) (Pink (FR))
392[8]

Sendmylovetorose *A Oliver* 105
2 b f Bahamian Bounty Windy Gulch (USA) (Gulch (USA))
(3674a) (4064) 6081a[6] 6672[6]

Sennockian Star *Mark Johnston* a66 70
2 ch c Rock Of Gibraltar(IRE) Chorist (Pivotal)
2934[8] 4387[6] 4837[4] (6189) 7060[4] 7335[2]

Senora Lobo (IRE) *Lisa Williamson* a43 53
2 b f Amadeus Wolf Valencia (FR) (Croco Rouge (IRE))
3208[8] (3789) 4421[4] 4927[6] 7650[6] 8007[12]

Sense Of Purpose (IRE) *D K Weld* 108
5 ch m Galileo(IRE) Super Gift (IRE) (Darshaan)
3678a[6] 7546a[P]

Sensiz (IRE) *Roger Varian*
2 b f Marju(IRE) Much Faster (IRE) (Fasliyev (USA))
7686[13]

Sentaril *William Haggas* a101 108
3 b f Danehill Dancer(IRE) Superstar Leo (IRE) (College Chapel)
(1501) ◆ (1845) 3265[2] 4070[7] 6161[5] 6870[3] (7509)

Sentimento (ISR) *J D Hillis* a75 75
9 b g Surako(GER) Summer Wind (GER) (Platini (GER))
631a[3]

Sentosa *Michael Blanshard* a69 62
5 b m Dansili Katrina (IRE) (Ela-Mana-Mou)
2886[5] 3096[5] 3247[9]

Sentry Duty (FR) *Nicky Henderson* 100
10 b g Kahyasi Standing Around (FR) (Garde Royale)
3241[18] 4697[9] 7051[12]

Sepoy (AUS) *Mahmood Al Zarooni* a74 126
4 ch h Elusive Quality(USA) Watchful (AUS) (Danehill (USA))
1147a[10] 4100[11]

Sequence (IRE) *Sir Michael Stoute* a96 104
3 b f Selkirk(USA) Sinntara (IRE) (Lashkari)
1502[6] 2633[2] ◆ (4548) (5268) 5519[2] 6598[6] 7630[6]

Sequoia (FR) *P Monfort* a72 86
7 b g Highest Honor(FR) Kalava (FR) (Kaldoun (FR))
(965a)

Sequoia *Charles Hills* a42 76
3 b g Shamardal(USA) Atnab (USA) (Riverman (USA))
1155[7] 2543[8] 3068[6]

Seraphiel *Chris Down* a52 57
3 b c Royal Applause Angel Sprints (Piccolo)
2147[6]

Seraphima *Alan Bailey* a38 70
2 b f Fusaichi Pegasus(USA) Millestan (IRE) (Invincible Spirit (IRE))
1466[7] 3669[4] 8138[8]

Serenata (IRE) *Paul Cole* a46 66
2 b f Oratorio(IRE) Seren Devious (Dr Devious (IRE))
3282[12] 6489[16] 6817[2] 8017[11]

Serendipity Blue *John Weymes* 9
3 b f Cadeaux Genereux Sister Bluebird (Bluebird (USA))
1001[7] 2335[10] 4678[8]

Serene Oasis (IRE) *Mick Channon* a72 81
3 gr f Oratorio(IRE) Princess Serena (USA) (Unbridled's Song (USA))
1412[3] 1985[5] 2408[12] 3214[7] (3619) 3952[2] (4298) 4607[4] 4726[2] 4968[2] 5302[5] 5512[4] 6172[4] 6488[7] 7247[5] (7402)

Serenity Spa *Roger Charlton* a66 76
2 gr f Excellent Art Molly Mello (GER) (Big Shuffle (USA))
4282[2] 7497[5] 7894[2]

Serenity Star *H-A Pantall* a70 94
4 b m Monsun(GER) Nalani (IRE) (Sadler's Wells (USA))
3652a[6]

Sergeant Ablett (IRE) *James Given* 93
4 b g Danehill Dancer(IRE) Dolydille (IRE) (Dolphin Street (FR))
1654[11]

Sergeant Troy (IRE) *George Baker* a61 77
4 gr g Aussie Rules(USA) Et Dona Ferentes (Green Desert (USA))
119[6] 381[8] 557[7] 1487[4] 1702[4]

Serjeant Buzfuz *Richard Fahey* a44 60
3 b g Halling(USA) Anastasia Storm (Mozart (IRE))
2668[3] *3232[6]* 4744[11]

Sermons Mount (USA) *Paul Howling* a80 80
6 bb g Vicar(USA) Ginny Auxier (USA) (Racing Star (USA))
251[4] 517[6] 735[9] 896[8] 1050[10] 1254[11] *2146[11] 3949[11]* 4492[2] 4815[5] 5203[7] *5971[7]* 6158[8] 6586[3] 6773[8] 6982[5] ◆

Serpotta (FR) *Y De Nicolay* a53 70
6 ch g Green Tune(USA) Standing Around (FR) (Garde Royale)
92a[7]

Sesentum *Luca Cumani* a72 78
2 b c Motivator Corinium (IRE) (Turtle Island (IRE))
6214[6] (6947) *7325[6]*

Setfiretotheralн *Kevin Ryan* 45
2 ch g Compton Place Tembladora (IRE) (Docksider (USA))
2330[10] 4825[12] 5411[6]

Settebellezze (FR) *J Rossi* a86 84
5 b h Muhtathir Similitudine (FR) (Brief Truce (USA))
(815a)

Set The Trend *David O'Meara* a100 115
6 bb g Reset(AUS) Masrora (USA) (Woodman (USA))
4320[6] 4628[3] 5278[4] (5964) 6868[14]

Set To Go *Brendan Powell* a51 52
5 b g Reset(AUS) Golubitsa (IRE) (Bluebird (USA))
218[5] 307[5] 2385[4] 4993[6] 5999[6]

Set To Music (IRE) *Michael Bell* a71 110
4 b m Danehill Dancer(IRE) Zarabaya (IRE) (Doyoun)
2209[6] 2711[2] ◆ (3219) 3856[3] 4848[2] 6598[7] 6877[11]

Seven Of Clubs (IRE) *Noel Quinlan* a76 76
2 b c Red Clubs(IRE) Fairy Symphony (IRE) (Fayruz)
4539[7] 5040[2] ◆ (5586) 6487[14] 6984[4] *8016[3]*

Seventeen Seventy *Alan Coogan* 69
3 b g Byron Rolexa (Pursuit Of Love)
1256[9] 1450[13] 1739[4] 2205[10] 2388[4] 2610[2] (2762) 3050[7] 3218[2] 3435[7] (3489) 4197[3] 4535[10] 4777[7] *7589[13]*

Seventh Sign *William Haggas* 92
3 b g Pivotal Rahayeb (Arazi (USA))
1506[11] 1867[4] 2288[7]

Seven Veils (IRE) *Sir Mark Prescott Bt* a75 86
3 b f Danehill Dancer(IRE) Ahdaab (USA) (Rahy (USA))
2999[2] ◆ *3233[2] 3621[4]* (4440) *4585[3]* 4972[3] 5706[6] 6263[2] (6440) *6971[11]*

Seven Year Itch (IRE) *James Bethell* 55
3 b f Lawman(FR) Stella Del Mattino (USA) (Golden Gear (USA))
288[6] 479[4]

Severn Bore *Bill Turner* 65
2 b c Tiger Hill(IRE) Emerald Fire (Pivotal)
(1165) (1253) 3126[5]

Sewn Up *Reg Hollinshead* a68
2 ch c Compton Place Broughton Bounty (Bahamian Bounty)
7458[9] 7613[5] 7749[3] 7973[2] 8132[8] 8240[5]

Sextons House (IRE) *Alan McCabe* a60 67
4 b g King's Best(USA) Lolita's Gold (USA) (Royal Academy (USA))
7411[10] 7489[6] 7684[19] *7861[9] 7970[10] 8304[7]*

Shababeek (IRE) *John Dunlop* 71
2 b c Shirocco(GER) Tanaghum (Darshaan)
6796[4] ◆

Shabak Hom (IRE) *David Evans* a75 81
5 b g Exceed And Excel(AUS) Shbakni (USA) (Mr Prospector (USA))
175[2] 263[3] 402[2] 601[5] 1719[2] 2363[8] 3187[6] 4733[4] 5151[2] 5830[6]

Shabora (IRE) *Roger Varian* a92 66
3 b f Cape Cross(IRE) Wardat Allayl (IRE) (Mtoto)
180[3] (398) (596) 1221[11] 5520[12]

Shackleford (USA) *Dale Romans* a124
4 ch h Forestry(USA) Oatsee (USA) (Unbridled (USA))
7570a[7]

Shada (IRE) *Sir Michael Stoute* a75 71
3 ch f Galileo(IRE) Banquise (IRE) (Last Tycoon)
3565[6] *5753[3] 6146[5]*

Shades Of Grey *Clive Cox* a70 86
5 gr m Dr Fong(USA) Twosixtythreewest (FR) (Kris)
1418[5] 2167[4] 2502[4] 2976[5] (3782) (4061) 4905[2] 5359[7]

Shades Of Light *Peter Makin* a43 34
2 b f Echo Of Light Highland Cascade (Tipsy Creek (USA))
4604[9] 5146[8] 5997[8] *6977[9] 7606[5]*

Shades Of Silver *Sir Michael Stoute* 49
2 b g Dansili Silver Pivotal (IRE) (Pivotal)
4472[14]

Shadow Gate (JPN) *Takashi Kodama* a100 113
10 b h White Muzzle Fabulous Turn (JPN) (Sunday Silence (USA))
8227[8]

Shadowtime *Tracy Waggott* a73 82
7 b g Singspiel(IRE) Massomah (USA) (Seeking The Gold (USA))
1917[7] 2510[17] 2675[3] 2753[10] 3274[6] 4177[4] 4398[4] (4679) 5819[4] 6342[8] (6405) 6559[7]

Shafaani *Clive Brittain* 71
2 b f Green Desert(USA) Amalie (IRE) (Fasliyev (USA))
2797[4] 3326[12] 4282[7] 4763[7] 5818[5] 6490[4] 6873[19]

Shagwa (IRE) *Mark Johnston* a56
2 b f Clodovil(IRE) Hedera (USA) (Woodman (USA))
6754[4] *7020[6]*

Shahdaroba (IRE) *Rod Millman* 88
2 b g Haatef(USA) Gold Script (FR) (Script Ohio (USA))
2164[3] 3505[3] ◆ 4093[11] (4707) 5515[8] 6138[4] 7028[2] 7374[5]

Shahrazad (IRE) *Patrick Gilligan* a54 26
3 b f Cape Cross(IRE) Khulasah (IRE) (Darshaan)
3399[9] *4212[6] 5166[4] 6500[6] 7189[4]*

Shahwardi (FR) *A De Royer-Dupre* 107
6 b g Lando(GER) Shamdara (IRE) (Dr Devious (IRE))
3373[2] 4120a[3] 5400a[3] (7073a) 7696a[7]

Shahzan (IRE) *Roger Varian* a91 94
4 br h Dansili Femme Fatale (Fairy King (USA))
(1843) ◆ 2489[8] 3183[16] *6939[5] 7327[3] 7645[3] 8188[10]*

Shaishee (USA) *Charles Hills* 68
2 bb c Indian Charlie(USA) Hatpin (USA) (Smart Strike (CAN))
4362[9] 6486[6]

Shake Baby Shake *Bill Turner* a44
3 b f Reel Buddy(USA) Sheik'n Swing (Celtic Swing)
768[4] 925[6] 1090[7]

Shaker Style (USA) *Barry Murtagh* a64 62
6 ch g Gulch(USA) Carr Shaker (USA) (Carr De Naskra (USA))
2091[5] 2600[3] 6262[9] 7454[6]

Shakespeare Dancer *James Evans* a40 27
3 b f Norse Dancer(IRE) Sharbasia (IRE) (King's Best (USA))
1989[9] 3453[4] 4157[11] 5198[5] *7717[8]*

Shalambar (IRE) *Tony Carroll* a73 59
6 gr g Dalakhani(IRE) Shalama (IRE) (Kahyasi)
521[4] 820[2] (992) 1418[6] *7892[8] 8175[6]*

Shalamzar (FR) *M Delzangles* 86
3 ch c Selkirk(USA) Shamalana (IRE) (Sinndar (IRE))
1869a[6]

Shaleek *Roger Varian* 79
3 ch f Pivotal Dorrati (USA) (Dubai Millennium)
1637[2] 2121[3] 2846[3] 4420[3] 5335[2] 6154[2] (6477)

Shaloo Diamond *Richard Whitaker* 81
7 b g Captain Rio Alacrity (Alzao (USA))
1913[10] (3310) 3692[2] 3992[2]

Shaluca *Ed McMahon* a64 67
5 br m Shamardal(USA) Noushkey (Polish Precedent (USA))
153[3]

Shamaal Nibras (USA) *Richard Hannon* a90 103
3 b c First Samurai(USA) Sashay Away (USA) (Farma Way (USA))
867[3] (1217) 2263[6] 2916[5] (3160) 3508[2] ◆ 4740[4] 5334[6] (7107) 7435[2] 7691[7]

Shamahan *Gary Moore* 81
3 b c Shamardal(USA) Hanella (IRE) (Galileo (IRE))
2265[7] ◆ 2854[4]

Shamaheart (IRE) *Richard Hannon* a68 67
2 b c Shamardal(USA) Encouragement (Royal Applause)
3637[5] 5360[5] 5704[6] 7335[5] *7779[3]* ◆

Shamakat *Rae Guest* a52 58
3 ch f Shamardal(USA) Katina (USA) (Danzig (USA))
1357[13] *2351[7]* 2573[7] 3218[11] 4196[9]

Shamalgan (FR) *X Nakkachdji* a103 116
5 ch h Footstepsinthesand Genevale (FR) (Unfuwain (USA))
487a[8] 682a[4] *1143a[7]* 1746a[4] 3205a[4] 3657a[2] 5648a[7]

Shamanda (GER) *A Wohler* 74
2 b f Zamindar(USA) Shimrana (IRE) (Daylami (IRE))
6522a[6]

Shamardanse (IRE) *S Wattel* a93 102
4 b m Shamardal(USA) Danse Bretonne (FR) (Exit To Nowhere (USA))
5649a[0] 7701a[0]

Shamardeliah (IRE) *James Tate* a74 57
3 b f Shamardal(USA) Sunsetter (USA) (Diesis)
917[5] 1167[8] *1733[12]*

Shamarlane *Clive Mulhall* a67 68
5 ch m Shamardal(USA) Robin Lane (Tenby)
(1222)

Shamdarley (IRE) *Michael Dods* a86 89
4 b g Shamardal(USA) Siphon Melody (USA) (Siphon (BRZ))
1128[7] 2257[7] 2720[4] 3380[3] *3963[3]* 4689[9] 5186[5] *5752[8]* 6073[7] 6638[3]

Shamekh (GER) *M Al Muhairi* a90 10
4 b h Shamardal(USA) Samerous (FR) (Generous (IRE))
616a[8]

Shame On You (IRE) *Charles Hills* a74 70
3 ch f Shamardal(USA) Woodlass (USA) (Woodman (USA))
1004[2] 1472[14]

Shamglas Queen *John C McConnell* a51
2 b f Shamardal(USA) Green Silk (IRE) (Namid)
7953[7]

Shamiana *Gerard Butler* a51 71
2 bb f Manduro(GER) Camp Riverside (USA) (Forest Camp (USA))
7552[2] ◆ *7924[8]*

Shamir *Jo Crowley* a93 80
5 b g Dubai Destination(USA) Lake Nyasa (IRE) (Lake Coniston (IRE))
5301[10] 6036[8] (6539) 7502[7] 8056[3]

Shamo Hill Theatre *Lawrence Mullaney* a53 54
5 b g Millkom Hannalou (FR) (Shareef Dancer (USA))
2621[4] 3332[7] 3581[6] 6102[5] 6258[6] (7496) *8139[4]*

Shamrocked (IRE) *Mick Channon* a59 84
3 b g Rock Of Gibraltar(IRE) Hallowed Park (IRE) (Barathea (IRE))
1221[12] 1894[5] 2265[10] (3071) 3607[7] 4082[6] 4517[6] 4814[7] *5099[6]* 5625[4] 6048[12] 6488[2] 7083[5] ◆ 7246[4]

Shana Doyenne (GER) *W Mongil* a85 86
5 b m Doyen(IRE) S'll Vous Plait (GER) (Dashing Blade)
8300a[8]

Shanghai Bobby (USA) *Todd Pletcher* a118
2 bb c Harlan's Holiday(USA) Steelin' (USA) (Orientate (USA))
(6901a) (7572a)

Shannon Spree *Alan King* a72 71
3 b f Royal Applause Some Diva (Dr Fong (USA))
2201[5] 2379[4] 3142[11] 3443[11] 6004[6]

Shantaram *John Gosden* a111 104
3 b c Galileo(IRE) All's Forgotten (USA) (Darshaan)
1456[2] *2080[2]* (2895) (4007) 6896a[8]

Shanylia (FR) *S Wattel* a74 67
3 b f Clodovil(IRE) Shamarkanda (FR) (Kahyasi)
7267a[4]

Shaolin (IRE) *Seamus Durack* 56
2 b c Footstepsinthesand Baboosh (IRE) (Marju (IRE))
3067[8]

Shaqira *W Figge* 105
4 bb m Redoute's Choice(AUS) Hammiya (IRE) (Darshaan)
7449a[10]

Sharaarah (IRE) *Ed Dunlop* a79 79
2 b f Oasis Dream Nidhaal (IRE) (Observatory (USA))
2245[2] ◆ *(2541)* 3269[16] 4526[9] 5710[3] 6658[3]

Sharaayeen *A Al Raihe* a100 104
5 br g Singspiel(IRE) Corinium (IRE) (Turtle Island (IRE))
587a[5]

Shared Moment (IRE) *Luke Dace* a72 63
6 ch m Tagula(IRE) Good Thought (IRE) (Mukaddamah (USA))
315 (148) 225[3] 568[5] 685[6] 919[3] 1108[9] 1626[9] 1909[5] 2574[4] 3096[4] 3544[9] 8248[9]

Sharestan (IRE) *John M Oxx* 118
4 b h Shamardal(USA) Sharesha (IRE) (Ashkalani (IRE))
(1043a) 1946a[3]

Shareta (IRE) *A De Royer-Dupre* 120
4 b m Sinndar(IRE) Shawara (IRE) (Barathea (IRE))
1766a[3] 2570a[2] 3424a[2] (5518) (6295a) 6912a[9] 7573a[5]

Sharivar (GER) *A Wohler* 102
3 bb c Sinndar(IRE) Starla (GER) (Lando (GER))
2569a[4]

Sharjah (IRE) *Noel Quinlan* 57
2 b g Shamardal(USA) Lunar Lustre (IRE) (Desert Prince (IRE))
3346[9] 4710[6] 5321[8]

Sharp Shoes *Christopher Wilson* a73 74
5 br g Needwood Blade Mary Jane (Tina's Pet)
8[10] 1298[8] 2032[4] *2352[5]* 2436[4] 2749[7] 3523[3] 4262[7] 4592[11] 5739[4] 6531[3] 6786[6] 7457[3]

Sharp Sovereign (USA) *Ian McInnes* a53 75
6 b g Cactus Ridge(USA) Queen Of Humor (USA) (Distorted Humor (USA))
1135[9] *1432[5]* 2034[5] 4179[8] 5226[7]

Sharqawiyah *Luca Cumani* a49
2 b f Dubawi(IRE) Pompey Girl (Rainbow Quest (USA))
6535[7]

Shaslika (FR) *D Prod'Homme* 71
2 gr f Slickly(FR) Green Shadow (FR) (Green Tune (USA))
7700a[2]

Shatin Secret *Noel Wilson* a66 50
2 b c Sakhee's Secret Al Corniche (IRE) (Bluebird (USA))
6404[4] 7176[6] *7410[4]*

Shatin Spirit (IRE) *Noel Wilson*
3 bb g Rock Of Gibraltar(IRE) Forest Walk (IRE) (Shinko Forest (IRE))
4259[10] 4780[12] 5293[8]

Shatter (IRE) *William Haggas* a67 59
3 b f Mr Greeley(USA) Watership Crystal (IRE) (Sadler's Wells (USA))
2042[6] 6048[10]

Shaunas Spirit (IRE) *Dean Ivory* a70 45
4 b m Antonius Pius(USA) Shaunas Vision (IRE) (Dolphin Street (FR))
(203) 264[4] (3497) 4950[7] 5741[9] 6334[8] 7105[10] *(7224) 7857[7] 8004[3]*

Shavalley (USA) *David Nicholls* 24
3 b f Gulch(USA) Hypoxia (USA) (Shadeed (USA))
3913[14] 4630[8] 4926[R]

Shavansky *Rod Millman* a94 100
8 b g Rock Of Gibraltar(IRE) Limelighting (USA) (Alleged (USA))
1130[11] 1321[7] *2151[2]* 2932[5] 3508[5] 4223[2] 5129[8] *(6036)* 6494[8] 7017[3] *7631[8]*

Shawka *Charles Hills* a60 63
3 b f Oasis Dream Wissal (USA) (Woodman (USA))
5329[5] 5795[6] *7647[5]*

Shawkantango *Derek Shaw* a74 77
5 b g Piccolo Kitty Kitty Cancan (Warrshan (USA))
24[5] 122[6] 272[6] 380[2] (461) 696[6] 808[7] 890[5] (996) 1187[6] (1383) 1516[2] 1675[5] 2140[7] 6689[11] 6788[11] 7197[7] 7299[2] 7775[3] 8058[10]

Shaws Diamond (USA) *Derek Shaw* a61 65
6 ch m Ecton Park(USA) Dear Abigail (USA) (Dehere (USA))
274[7] 370[7] 386[5] 666[4]

Shayla *Alan Swinbank* a49 74
5 ch m Pastoral Pursuits Honours Even (Highest Honor (FR))
4407[5] 4620[7]

Shea *Ralph Beckett* a69
3 b f Dubai Destination(USA) Shasta (Shareef Dancer (USA))
5154[5] 5766[6] 6398[3] (7162)

She Ain't A Saint *Jane Chapple-Hyam* a87 72
4 b m Dansili Flamingo Sky (USA) (Silver Hawk (USA))
199[11] 520[3] 746[4] 987[13]

Shearian *Tony Carroll* a56
2 b g Royal Applause Regal Asset (USA) (Regal Classic (CAN))
1886[12] 2420[9] *3499[11] 7008[3] 7708[9] 7974[9]*

Shebebi (USA) *John Dunlop* 79
2 bb g Mr Greeley(USA) Tashawak (IRE) (Night Shift (USA))
2929[8] 5126[3] (5851) 7079[7]

Shebella (IRE) *John M Oxx* 103
3 b f Dubai Destination(USA) Shibina (IRE) (Kalanisi (IRE))
2187a[5] 4376a[5] 6518a[3]

Sheedal (IRE) *Ian Semple* 47
4 b m Danroad(AUS) Absolute Glee (USA) (Kenmare (FR))
2600[9] 2840[9] 4390[11] 5082[9]

Sheikh The Reins (IRE) *John Best* a77 81
3 b g Iffraaj Wychwood Wanderer (IRE) (Barathea (IRE))
1565[11] *1983[6]* 2416[8] 2660[6] 4473[3] 4819[7] 5128[6] *6368[9] 6768[6] 6973[12]*

Sheikhzayedroad *David Simcock* 91
3 b g Dubawi(IRE) Royal Secrets (IRE) (Highest Honor (FR))
1467[10] (1878) 2897[4] (4243) 4821[3] 5820[3] 6661[5]

Sheila's Buddy *J S Moore* a82 82
3 ch g Reel Buddy(USA) Loreto Rose (Lahib (USA))
(787) 1320[2] 1892[6] *2860[5]* 3448[5] (4224) 4735[8] 7116[2] *7358[5] (7644) 8227[9]*

Sheila's Castle *Sean Regan* a34 64
8 b m Karinga Bay Candarela (Damister (USA))
4455[2] 5114[3] 5735[4] 6262[3] *7862[5]*

Sheistheboss (FR) *C Lerner* 96
2 b f Street Boss(USA) Seba (Alzao (USA))
4615a[3]

Shek O Lad *Alan Jarvis* a43 24
3 b g Librettist(USA) Lady Pahia (IRE) (Pivotal)
1303[10] 2495[4] 2771[11] *3620[9]*

Shelford (IRE) *John M Oxx* 91
3 b g Galileo(IRE) Lyrical (Shirley Heights)
6066a[14]

Shelovestobouggie *Mark Brisbourne* a68 71
4 b m Tobougg(IRE) Bowled Out (GER) (Dansili)
7618[12] 8271[8]

Shemaal (IRE) *Roger Varian* 55
2 b c Monsun(GER) Zahrat Dubai (Unfuwain (USA))
7333[7]

Shenandoah Lady (USA) *Steve Attard* a89 95
2 bb f Purim(USA) Shawnee Country (USA) (Chief's Crown (USA))
6289a[6]

Shena's Dream (IRE) *William Haggas* 85
3 gr f Oasis Dream Sallanches (USA) (Gone West (USA))
(2680) ◆ 3475[4] (4583) (5019) (6381) 7334[13]

Shenval *Noel Quinlan* a56
2 b c Celtic Swing Cape Finisterre (IRE) (Cape Cross (IRE))
8165[5]

Shenzhou Steeds (NZ) *Michael Moroney* 108
5 b g Ishiguru(USA) Sun City (NZ) (Spectacular Love (USA))
7425a[6]

Shepherds Bow *Michael Easterby* 41
2 ch c Pastoral Pursuits Bow Peep (IRE) (Shalford (IRE))
4710[11] ◆ 5168[7] 5410[15] 5733[5] ◆ 6880[13]

Sherinn *Roger Varian* a70 77
2 b f Refuse To Bend(IRE) Hall Hee (IRE) (Invincible Spirit (IRE))
5267[2] *7987[7] 8208[2] (8303)*

Sherjawy (IRE) *Zoe Davison* a65 70
8 b g Diktat Arruhan (IRE) (Mujtahid (USA))
59[2] 152[4] 208[6] 320[8] 473[6] 522[7] 823[2] 958[3] 1061[6] 1185[3] 1300[3] 1483[7] 1787[3] 2360[9] 2494[10] 3008[5] 3467[4] 4467[8] 4815[11] 5047[5] 7482[6] 7703[11] 7929[7] 8169[5] 8246[5]

Sherman McCoy *Daniel Kubler* a82 87
6 ch g Reset(AUS) Naomi Wildman (USA) (Kingmambo (USA))
1056[5] 1846[9] 2423[6] 3661[6] 4326[10] 4733[7] *5211[4] 5718[2] 8082[6] 8170[6]*

Sherry Cherie (IRE) *Richard Fahey* a39 46
3 b f Footstepsinthesand Tipsy Lady (Intikhab (USA))
1274[7] *7667[6] 7787[7] 8050[13] 8253[12]*

Sherzam *Thomas Carmody* a77 75
2 b f Exceed And Excel(AUS) Shersha (IRE) (Priolo (USA))
2958a[8]

She's A Character *Richard Fahey* a85 86
5 b m Invincible Spirit(IRE) Cavernista (Lion Cavern (USA))
(1652) 2025[9] 2752[6] 3185[8] 3522[2] 3991[4] 4702[11] 5759[3] (6526) 7370[3] 7685[6]

Shesastar *David Barron* 93
4 b m Bahamian Bounty Celestial Welcome (Most Welcome)
2067[9] 2489[10] 3812[3] (4497) 5324[4] 5520[4] 6515[4] 7408[12]

Shes Ellie *John O'Shea* 55
2 ch f Lucky Story(USA) Shes Minnie (Bertolini (USA))
5503[7] 6007[9] 6276[4]

Shesha Bear *Jonathan Portman* a65 81
7 b m Tobougg(IRE) Sunny Davis (USA) (Alydar (USA))
1603[9] 2411[8] 3015[2] 3769[4] 4251[3] 5277[6] 6170[9] 6703[4] 6802[9]

Shesnotforturning (IRE) *Ben Haslam* 25
2 b f Refuse To Bend(IRE) Diplomats Daughter (Unfuwain (USA))
3747[10] 5222[7] 6556[8]

Shes Rosie *John O'Shea* a66 77
4 b m Trade Fair Wintzig (Piccolo)
970[9] 1246[5] 1638[2] 2012[4] 2165[10] 2766[4] 3785[5] (4533) 4989[5] 5877[9]

She's Some Girl (IRE) *Richard Fahey* a46
2 ch f Camacho Tea Service (IRE) (Roi Danzig (USA))
6609[10] 6889[6] 7219[6] 7808[8] 7919[6] 8094[6] 8289[4]

Shesthecaptain (IRE) *John Weymes* a40 35
2 br f Captain Marvelous(IRE) Shewillifshewants (IRE) (Alzao (USA))
6042[8] 6335[15] *7525[8] 8254[5]*

Shestheman *David Lanigan* a82 85
3 b f Manduro(GER) Clear Vision (Observatory (USA))
(1532) 2201^{4} 3476^{6} 4984^{6} 5752^{4} 6776^{4} 7194^{4} 7461^{13}
She Who Dares Wins *Lee James* a41 48
12 b m Atraf Mirani (IRE) (Danehill (USA))
1246^{10}
Shiatsu *Richard Hannon* a68 75
2 b c Kyllachy Ivania (First Trump)
4362^{11} 5098^{5} 5553^{4} (6203) 7635^{5} ◆
Shieldmaiden (USA) *Mark Johnston* a87 71
4 ch m Smart Strike(CAN) Code Book (USA) (Giant's Causeway (USA))
(43) 2234 $342a^{7}$ 745^{7}
Shifting Gold (IRE) *Kevin Ryan* a73 67
6 b g Night Shift(USA) Gold Bust (Nashwan (USA))
555^{8} (1175) 5718^{7} 6784^{P}
Shifting Star (IRE) *John Bridger* a93 93
7 ch g Night Shift(USA) Ahshado (Bin Ajwaad (IRE))
131^{2} (304) 426^{6} 785^{7} 1924^{11} (2444) 3004^{7} 3508^{11} 4317^{15} 4703^{17} 4799^{25} 5595^{5} 5746^{10} 6040^{5} 6368^{6} 6577^{6} 6705^{2} ◆ 7083^{7} 7327^{7} 7645^{9} 7823^{9} 7966^{11}
Shillito *Tony Coyle* 75
2 b g Kyllachy Kiss Me Kate (Aragon)
3401^{7} 3989^{3} 4625^{2} 4825^{2} 5382^{6} 6540^{4} 6920^{10}
Shimmering Moment (USA) *Francis Abbott III* a105 105
5 ch m Afleet Alex(USA) Vassar (USA) (Royal Academy (USA))
$6298a^{9}$
Shimmering Surf (IRE) *Roger Varian* a76 108
5 b m Danehill Dancer(IRE) Sun On The Sea (IRE) (Bering)
1848^{2} (2711) 3856^{2} $5116a^{2}$ $5844a^{5}$
Shimraan (FR) *Mahmood Al Zarooni* 118
5 b g Rainbow Quest(USA) Shemriyna (IRE) (King Of Kings (IRE))
$591a^{4}$ $877a^{8}$ $1149a^{9}$
Shingueti (FR) *C Baillet* a76 89
2 b f Desert Style(IRE) Spain (FR) (Bering)
$5379a^{10}$ $8193a^{6}$
Shining Cross (IRE) *George Margarson* 23
2 b g Cape Cross(IRE) Shining Debut (IRE) (In The Wings)
6377^{8} 6928^{9} 7517^{11}
Shirataki (IRE) *Peter Hiatt* a74 69
4 b g Cape Cross(IRE) Noodle Soup (USA) (Alphabet Soup (USA))
(130) ◆ 296^{3} 738^{2} (820) 992^{6} 1205^{3} 1418^{10} 1706^{4} (2937) 3222^{11} 3659^{10} 7310^{14} 7596^{8} 7893^{7} 8023^{12} 8060^{8}
Shirley's Kitten (USA) *Gianluca Bietolini* 94
2 b f Kitten's Joy(USA) La Cat (USA) (Mr Greeley (USA))
$7285a^{3}$
Shirley's Pride *John Holt* a44 54
2 b f Byron Feeling Blue (Missed Flight)
2047^{9} 2349^{4} 3150^{4} 3747^{9} 4990^{8} 5403^{9} 5807^{11}
Shirls Son Sam *Chris Fairhurst* a53 58
4 b g Rambling Bear Shirl (Shirley Heights)
1952^{6} 2635^{3} 3402^{3} 4867^{3} 5384^{6} 5735^{8} 6691^{4} 6956^{8} 7255^{6} 7603^{8}
Shirocco Star *Hughie Morrison* 114
3 b f Shirocco(GER) Spectral Star (Unfuwain (USA))
2232^{2} ◆ 2658^{2} 3292^{3} $4378a^{2}$ 5518^{4} $6899a^{2}$ 7237^{2}
Shisha Threesixty (IRE) *Lucinda Russell* a63 61
4 b g High Chaparral(IRE) Nicene (USA) (Pulpit (USA))
4391^{5} 5086^{3} 5922^{9}
Shivsingh *Mick Channon* a63 67
3 b g Montjeu(IRE) Vistaria (USA) (Distant View (USA))
803^{7} 998^{2} 2771^{8}
Shkspeare Shaliyah (USA) *Doodnauth Shivmangal* a84 99
3 b c Shakespeare(USA) Tricky Mistress (USA) (Clever Trick (USA))
$6902a^{6}$
Sholaan (IRE) *William Haggas* a99 106
3 b g Invincible Spirit(IRE) Jazz Up (Cadeaux Genereux)
(1825) 2660^{8} (3165) 3639^{3} 6468^{4} ◆ 6666^{3}
Shomberg *Dai Burchell* a57 62
3 b g Bahamian Bounty Qilin (IRE) (Second Set (IRE))
1979^{9} 2497^{3} 3233^{7} 3974^{4} (4988) 5501^{4} 7436^{8} 7702^{4} 7867^{8}
Shomoukh (USA) *F-H Graffard* a92 74
3 gr f Unbridled's Song(USA) Future Guest (USA) (Copelan (USA))
$7345a^{9}$
Shooting Jacket (USA) *Mahmood Al Zarooni* a66 55
2 bb c Hard Spun(USA) Nortena (USA) (Mr Prospector (USA))
2550^{7} 4340^{7} 5407^{3} 6363^{7} 7173^{15}
Shoot Out (AUS) *Chris Waller* 121
6 b g High Chaparral(IRE) Pentamerous (NZ) (Pentire)
$7426a^{5}$
Shop Til You Drop *David Evans* a38 44
2 b f Camacho Savvy Shopper (USA) (Stravinsky (USA))
1188^{5} 1253^{2} 1594^{3} 3126^{13}
Shore Performer (IRE) *William Haggas* a62 63
3 b f Footstepsinthesand Dancing Eclipse (IRE) (Danehill Dancer (IRE))
2935^{6} ◆ 3811^{3} 4582^{5} 5299^{3} 5970^{4} 6643^{4} 7249^{4} 7527^{8} 7816^{8}
Shore Step (IRE) *Mick Channon* 67
2 br g Footstepsinthesand Chatham Islands (USA) (Elusive Quality (USA))
5325^{6} 7272^{3} 7516^{3}
Short Final (FR) *Mario Hofer* a43
2 b f Meshaheer(USA) Schicky Micky (FR) (Testa Rossa (AUS))
$7699a^{9}$

Short Squeeze (IRE) *Hugo Palmer* a76 54
2 b g Cape Cross(IRE) Sunsetter (USA) (Diesis)
6481^{15} 7167^{9} 7705^{2}
Short Supply (USA) *Tim Walford* a63 61
6 b m Point Given(USA) Introducing (USA) (Deputy Minister (CAN))
2925^{8}
Shoshana (GER) *Frau J Mayer*
2 ch f Big Shuffle(USA) Santuzza's Beauty (GER) (Bluebird (USA))
$5612a^{7}$
Shoshoni Wind *Kevin Ryan* a60 98
4 b m Sleeping Indian Cadeau Speciale (Cadeaux Genereux)
1219^{4} 1977^{3} 2602^{6} 6116^{7} 6755^{6} 7243^{14} 7726^{9}
Shot In The Dark (IRE) *Jonathan Geake* a60 71
3 ch g Dr Fong(USA) Highland Shot (Selkirk (USA))
1906^{2} 2128^{8} 2942^{7} 3475^{5} 6801^{13} 7811^{10}
Shotley Mac *Neville Bycroft* 81
8 ch g Abou Zouz(USA) Julie's Gift (Presidium)
4620^{12} 5819^{14} 7246^{U}
Shotley Music *Neville Bycroft* 64
3 b g Amadeus Wolf Silca Key (Inchinor)
1864^{9} 2336^{12} 2771^{12}
Shouda (IRE) *Barney Curley* a68 67
6 b g Tiger Hill(IRE) Sommernacht (GER) (Monsun (GER))
2394^{8} 2997^{3} 3468^{2} (3722) 7301^{13}
Showboating (IRE) *Alan McCabe* a83 85
4 b g Shamardal(USA) Sadinga (IRE) (Sadler's Wells (USA))
178^{3} 252^{7} 713^{4} (1827) 2251^{3} 3595^{2} 4013^{6} 4554^{3} 4824^{5} 5557^{2} 6044^{9} 6495^{5} 6820^{3} 7789^{4}
Show Court (IRE) *D K Weld* 86
3 b g Vinnie Roe(IRE) Sparkling Gem (IRE) (Revoque (IRE))
$7584a^{11}$
Showdancer (GER) *N Sauer*
3 bb c Liquido(GER) Smeralda (GER) (Nebos (GER))
$2569a^{7}$
Show Flower *Mick Channon* a70 96
3 b f Shamardal(USA) Baldemosa (FR) (Lead On Time (USA))
1862^{3} (2065) (2649) (3379) (4234) 4588^{2} 5363^{6} 6075^{6}
Show Gorb (SPA) *P Sogorb* 102
2 b f Caradak(IRE) Triple Two (Pivotal)
$7622a^{2}$
Showmehow *Ray Craggs*
4 b m Grape Tree Road Rasin Luck (Primitive Rising (USA))
3352^{10} 5293^{7}
Show More Faith *Sylvester Kirk* a54
2 b c Pastoral Pursuits Lalina (GER) (Trempolino (USA))
6977^{8} 7143^{7} 8207^{4}
Showsinger *Richard Fahey* a45 22
3 b f Singspiel(IRE) Very Agreeable (Pursuit Of Love)
107^{5} 358^{5} 571^{9} 6474^{10} 7169^{4}
Showtime Girl (IRE) *Tim Easterby* a65 60
2 b f Tamayuz Zuccini Wind (IRE) (Revoque (IRE))
2450^{8} 2912^{6} 3844^{2} 4651^{3}
Shredding (IRE) *Ed Vaughan* a37 56
3 b g Tiger Hill(IRE) In The Ribbons (In The Wings)
1519^{8} 1740^{8}
Shrewd *Michael Bell* 89
2 b g Street Sense(USA) Cala (FR) (Desert Prince (IRE))
2888^{3} (3401) (4090) 5579^{6} (7335)
Shrimper Roo *Tim Easterby* 75
2 b g Byron Piper's Ash (USA) (Royal Academy (USA))
1861^{5} (4825) 5620^{6} 6883^{21}
Shrimpton *Mick Channon* 78
2 b f Cadeaux Genereux Feather Boa (IRE) (Sri Pekan (USA))
2343^{9} 2783^{4} 3123^{3} 3669^{3} 4114^{4} (7031) 7687^{3}
Shropshire (IRE) *Charles Hills* a96 102
4 gr g Shamardal(USA) Shawanni (Shareef Dancer (USA))
(1141) 1558^{8} 1885^{2} ◆ 2177^{17} 2931^{7} 3641^{2} (4285) 4802^{8} 6201^{9} 6468^{19} 7366^{6}
Shubaat *Roger Varian* a87 94
5 ch g Monsun(GER) Zaynaat (Unfuwain (USA))
(1239) 1974^{11} 2709^{8} 4800^{8}
Shuffle Champ *M Weiss*
5 ch h Big Shuffle(USA) Olindera (GER) (Lomitas)
$629a^{4}$
Shuja (USA) *Saeed Bin Suroor* 79
3 b g Street Sense(USA) Seba (Alzao (USA))
1456^{8} 1878^{3}
Shu Lewis (IRE) *Ms M Dowdall Blake* a71 101
6 b m Pyrus(USA) Poppy Lewis (IRE) (Paris House)
$6271a^{7}$ $7584a^{3}$
Shunkawakhan (IRE) *Linda Perratt* a43 58
9 b g Indian Danehill(IRE) Special Park (USA) (Trempolino (USA))
1801^{4} 2621^{9} 3332^{8} 3889^{11} 4389^{9} 4643^{6} 4769^{6} 5081^{8} 5185^{6} 5917^{5} 6309^{7} 6480^{7} 6756^{11}
Shuruq (USA) *Saeed Bin Suroor* a77 81
2 b f Elusive Quality(USA) Miss Lucifer (FR) (Noverre (USA))
4011^{3} (7159)
Shwaiman (IRE) *James Fanshawe* 47
2 br c Authorized(IRE) Blue Lightning (Machiavellian (USA))
7636^{6} ◆
Shy *Karen Tutty* a66 71
7 ch m Erhaab(USA) Shi Shi (Alnasr Alwasheek)
1104^{4} 1339^{2} 1984^{3} 2167^{3} 2755^{2} 3307^{7} 3693^{4} 4179^{4} 4766^{5} 5253^{3} 5735^{7} 6126^{4} 7968^{7}
Shy Bride (IRE) *Alan Jarvis* a72 32
2 b f Excellent Art Blushing Away (USA) (Blushing Groom (FR))
6486^{14} 7192^{5} (7506)
Shy Rosa (USA) *Marcus Tregoning* a78 58
3 bb f Dixie Union(USA) Lethal Temper (USA) (Seattle Slew (USA))
1472^{9} 2030^{8} 2542^{2} 4876^{9}

Siberian Belle (IRE) *Richard Fahey* a42 52
3 b f Red Clubs(IRE) Miss Sharapova (IRE) (Almutawakel)
1916^{8} 4198^{5} 4643^{5} (5459) 6157^{6} 6361^{9}
Siberian Freeze (IRE) *N Clement* a70
3 gr c Verglas(IRE) Debbie's Next (USA) (Arctic Tern (USA))
$1171a^{7}$
Sicur *Luca Cumani* a76 79
2 b g Dylan Thomas(IRE) Dubious (Darshaan)
5553^{3} 6164^{2} 6985^{2} 7460^{2}
Sid *Zoe Davison* a29
4 ch g Needwood Blade Easter Moon (FR) (Easter Sun)
379^{11}
Side Glance *Andrew Balding* a111 119
5 br g Passing Glance Averami (Averti (IRE))
1158^{5} 1749^{3} (2656) 3237^{3} 4610^{3} 5560^{2} 6634^{2} 7238^{6}
Siena Street *Henry Candy* 45
3 b f Strategic Prince Savoy Street (Vettori (IRE))
4582^{10} 5329^{7}
Sienna Blue *Simon Hodgson* a65 58
4 ch m Doyen(IRE) Lady Butler (IRE) (Puissance)
91^{3} ◆ 146^{7} 423^{5} 550^{10} 804^{7} 4533^{11} 5428^{12} 5659^{8} 5937^{12}
Siete Vidas (IRE) *M Delzangles* a93 98
4 gr m Dalakhani(IRE) Too Marvelous (FR) (Dansili)
$4386a^{8}$
Signature Dish (IRE) *Andrew Balding* a69 65
2 b f Galileo(IRE) Magic Carpet (IRE) (Danehill (USA))
3505^{6} 4837^{3} 5221^{7} 6253^{2}
Signed Up *Amanda Perrett* 98
3 b c Rail Link Sing For Fame (USA) (Quest For Fame)
2197^{4} (2856) (6573) ◆ 6833^{9}
Signifer (IRE) *Mick Channon* 87
3 br g Titus Livius(FR) Extravagance (IRE) (King's Best (USA))
1317^{3} 1493^{3} 2347^{3} 2853^{5} 2914^{5} 3486^{5} 4231^{6} 4500^{5} 4765^{9} 5020^{3} 5195^{5} 5422^{7} 6226^{11} 6578^{8} 7299^{7}
Significant Move *Stuart Kittow* a73 86
5 b g Motivator Strike Lightly (Rainbow Quest (USA))
2857^{8} 3997^{3} 4732^{4} 5688^{5} 6209^{3} 6932^{4} 7132^{3} 7511^{4}
Sign Manual *Michael Bell* a63 76
3 b g Motivator New Assembly (IRE) (Machiavellian (USA))
1511^{6} 1893^{6} 2368^{3} 3072^{3}
Sign Of The Zodiac (IRE) *Richard Hannon* 85
2 gr c Clodovil(IRE) Auriga (Belmez (USA))
1499^{4} (1903)
Signora Frasi (IRE) *Tony Newcombe* a67 64
7 b m Indian Ridge Sheba (IRE) (Lycius (USA))
1611^{2} 1980^{4} 2867^{7} 3544^{4} 4531^{8} 6950^{10} 7200^{7} 8180^{2}
Signor Sassi *Roger Varian* 91
3 b g Acclamation Fairy Contessa (IRE) (Fairy King (USA))
3389^{2} 3876^{6} (5340) 5703^{2} ◆ (6417) ◆ 6835^{4} ◆
Sign Pro (IRE) *Peter Bowen* a38
4 b g Noverre(USA) Sadalsud (IRE) (Shaadi (USA))
8069^{6} 8154^{5} 8251^{6}
Signs In The Sand *S Seemar* a91 81
4 b g Cape Cross(IRE) Gonfilia (GER) (Big Shuffle (USA))
$314a^{9}$
Sigurwana (USA) *William Haggas* a75 73
3 bb f Arch(USA) Nyarhini (Fantastic Light (USA))
2601^{2} 4931^{2} 5125^{2} (6102) 7356^{2} 7644^{9}
Sikara (IRE) *T Stack* a82 103
4 b m Aussie Rules(USA) Beucaire (IRE) (Entrepreneur)
$1043a^{3}$
Silaah *David Nicholls* a106 97
8 b g Mind Games Ocean Grove (IRE) (Fairy King (USA))
$244a^{5}$ $314a^{6}$ $589a^{13}$ $757a^{11}$
Silasol (IRE) *C Laffon-Parias* 107
2 b f Monsun(GER) Stormina (USA) (Gulch (USA))
$5570a^{0}$ (6909a)
Silca's Dream *Mick Channon* a49 69
2 b g Oasis Dream Silca-Cisa (Hallgate)
7006^{8} 7268^{2} 7434^{2}
Silence Is Easy *William Muir* a61 57
3 b f Cape Cross(IRE) African Queen (IRE) (Cadeaux Genereux)
1256^{8} 5099^{7} 7225^{6} 7643^{10} 7769^{3} 7982^{8}
Silenceofthewind (USA) *Mrs K Burke* a83 87
5 b g Eddington(USA) Betty's Solutions (USA) (Eltish (USA))
987^{12} 1670^{9} 1863^{7} 2536^{8}
Silent Ambition *Mark Brisbourne* 33
3 b f Striking Ambition Hi Rock (Hard Fought)
1363^{12} 3384^{5} 4826^{11}
Silent Decision (USA) *John Stimpson* a59 86
6 ch m Mr Greeley(USA) Aly Sangue (USA) (Alydar (USA))
1094^{10} 1342^{11}
Silent Energy (IRE) *Ronald Harris* a60 53
3 b g Le Vie Dei Colori Ghada (USA) (Belong To Me (USA))
1853^{13} 3483^{16} 4652^{8}
Silent Footsteps (IRE) *Michael Dods* 73
2 b g Footstepsinthesand Appleblossom Pearl (IRE) (Peintre Celebre (USA))
(2923) 4206^{3} 5587^{3} 6070^{13} 7289^{8}
Silent Killer (IRE) *S Botti* 108
3 b c Oratorio(IRE) Pinky Mouse (IRE) (Machiavellian (USA))
$6727a^{4}$
Silent Laughter *Jonathan Portman* 51
3 b f Shamardal(USA) Tease (IRE) (Green Desert (USA))
1357^{14} 5215^{5} ◆ 6274^{6}

Silent Mistress *J R Jenkins* a28 38
3 b f Fraam Once Removed (Distant Relative)
3312^{11} 5458^{4} 6274^{9}
Silent Moment (USA) *Saeed Bin Suroor* a94 82
3 ch f Giant's Causeway(USA) Mari's Sheba (USA) (Mari's Book (USA))
2849^{2} (3279) (3962) 4216^{4} 5583^{7} 6018^{8} 6492^{8} 7655^{6}
Silent Music (IRE) *Robert Collet* a81 77
3 b f Peintre Celebre(USA) Albacora (IRE) (Fairy King (USA))
$6752a^{6}$
Silent Surround (AUS) *William Smart* 99
6 b m Face Value(AUS) Biography (AUS) (Rory's Jester (AUS))
$7073a^{5}$
Silenzio *Richard Hannon* a84 82
4 b h Cadeaux Genereux All Quiet (Piccolo)
1727^{6} 2545^{14} 2940^{7} 3016^{3} 3570^{5} 3915^{2}
Silicon Valley *Dominic Ffrench Davis* a2 49
3 b f Three Valleys(USA) Breathing Space (USA) (Expelled (USA))
1253^{5} 1904^{2} 2164^{9} 5749^{11}
Silk Drum (IRE) *Dianne Sayer* 75
7 gr g Intikhab(USA) Aneydia (IRE) (Kenmare (FR))
1797^{4} 2474^{7} 4867^{12} 6311^{5} 6712^{9}
Silkee Supreme *Richard Hannon* a70 70
3 b c Primo Valentino(IRE) Sodelk (Interrex (CAN))
1723^{8} 2172^{5} 3161^{11} 4534^{7} 4871^{4} 5443^{2} 5853^{7} 6765^{5} 7061^{4} 7218^{5} 7685^{5} 7822^{3} 7992^{6} 8162^{4}
Silkelly *David O'Meara* 72
2 b f Medicean Sleave Silk (IRE) (Unfuwain (USA))
4960^{7} 5367^{10} 6042^{5} (6335)
Silken Express (IRE) *Robert Cowell* a85 79
3 ch f Speightstown(USA) Laureldean Express (Inchinor)
4144^{2} (4729) 5422^{2} 6689^{2}
Silken Satinwood (IRE) *Peter Chapple-Hyam* a59 25
3 b f Refuse To Bend(IRE) Reine De Neige (Kris)
4888^{4} 5208^{4} 6057^{11}
Silken Thoughts *John Berry* a84 91
4 b m Tobougg(IRE) The Jotter (Night Shift (USA))
(1680) 2248^{16} 3550^{2} 3826^{9} 4684^{14} 5856^{7} 6333^{3} 8191^{7}
Silke Top *William Jarvis* a69 73
3 b f Librettist(USA) Zaza Top (GER) (Lomitas)
5019^{4} 5970^{3} (6433) 6847^{4} 7359^{10}
Silk Fairy (IRE) *Noel Quinlan* 53
2 ch f Barathea(IRE) Pretty Demanding (IRE) (Night Shift (USA))
4297^{9} 4967^{5} 5213^{4} 6332^{6}
Silk Scarf (IRE) *Mark H Tompkins* 50
2 br f Windsor Knot(IRE) Tarziyma (IRE) (Kalanisi (IRE))
5061^{4} 5619^{7} 5851^{10}
Silky Bleu *Terry Clement* a52
3 b f Elnadim(USA) Tattling (Warning)
565^{4}
Sillabub (USA) *John Gosden* a74 69
2 bb f Raven's Pass(USA) Bauble (USA) (Tale Of The Cat (USA))
7552^{3} (7963)
Silly Billy (IRE) *Pat Phelan* a65 43
4 b g Noverre(USA) Rock Dove (IRE) (Danehill (USA))
101^{5} 203^{10} (551) 572^{9} 6395^{4} 6778^{8} 6982^{7} 7275^{6} 7482^{7} 7815^{3} 7906^{2} 8039^{3} 8179^{4} 8299^{2}
Silly Gilly (IRE) *Ron Barr* a40 69
8 b m Mull Of Kintyre(USA) Richly Deserved (IRE) (Kings Lake (USA))
2535^{2} 2840^{2} 3416^{4} 4042^{10} 4716^{9} 5258^{6} 6127^{15} (6562)
Silvala Dance *Chris Wall* 41
2 b f Kyllachy Bride Of The Sea (Cape Cross (IRE))
6966^{8} 7290^{7} 7686^{7}
Silvaner (GER) *P Schiergen* 112
4 bb h Lomitas Suisun (GER) (Monsun (GER))
$1700a^{2}$ $2322a^{3}$ $3746a^{6}$ $4383a^{6}$
Silvanus (IRE) *Paul Midgley* a72 94
7 b g Danehill Dancer(IRE) Mala Mala (IRE) (Brief Truce (USA))
696^{2} 849^{5} 1300^{4} 1800^{2} (2789) 3109^{2} (3608) (4312) 4690^{12} 5487^{17} 5832^{7} 6543^{9}
Silvas Romana (IRE) *Mark Brisbourne* a72 82
3 b f Holy Roman Emperor(IRE) Triple Wood (USA) (Woodman (USA))
1392^{9} 2136^{3} 2672^{2} (3120) 3558^{11} 4329^{4} (4989) 5420^{8} 6375^{13} 6710^{3} 7356^{13}
Silvee *John Bridger* a66 69
5 gr m Avonbridge Silver Louie (IRE) (Titus Livius (FR))
31^{7} 91^{4} 1768^{3} 1895^{5} 2413^{4} 2847^{6} (3007) 3511^{8} (4000) 4332^{7} 4726^{9} 5362^{13} 5625^{10} 6145^{12} 7512^{7} 7990^{5} 8156^{10}
Silver Alliance *Julia Feilden* a78 74
4 gr g Proclamation(IRE) Aimee Vibert (Zilzal (USA))
648^{2} 771^{7} 1266^{3} 1792^{6} 2363^{6} 2886^{3} 3793^{3} 5741^{6} 6794^{6} 7256^{4} 8145^{2}
Silver Arny *Brendan Powell* 54
2 b f Footstepsinthesand Medici Gold (Medicean)
3487^{4} 4408^{8} 4990^{4}
Silver Arrow (ITY) *R Menichetti* 96
7 b g Silver Wizard(USA) Eros Love (ITY) (Love The Groom (USA))
$2323a^{5}$ $7587a^{12}$
Silver Blaze *Alan Swinbank* a77 98
3 ch g Haafhd Antigua (Selkirk (USA))
(1427) 1819^{2} 2718^{5} 3124^{2} 4009^{2}
Silver Blue (FR) *C Boillot* 53
2 b c Kendargent(FR) Eightblue (FR) (Epervier Bleu)
$7597a^{0}$
Silver Bullitt *Gary Moore* a73 81
4 gr g Proclamation(IRE) Eurolinka (IRE) (Tirol)
1220^{10} 5414^{14} (5950) (6430) 7328^{9} 7805^{6}
Silver Dixie (USA) *Jeremy Noseda* a62
2 br c Dixie Union(USA) More Silver (USA) (Silver Hawk (USA))
7749^{5} 7962^{4}

Silver Fawn (IRE) *John Weymes* 54
2 gr g Clodovil(IRE) Tinareena (IRE) (Barathea (IRE))
1651[F] 2334[4] 2537[8] 2822[10] 6121[16]

Silver Green (FR) *F Rohaut* a103 103
5 gr g Slickly(FR) Love Green (FR) (Green Tune (USA))
7985a[4]

Silver Grey (IRE) *Martyn Meade* a82 89
5 gr m Chineur(FR) Operissimo (Singspiel (IRE))
1381[5] 1999[5] 2932[9]

Silverheels (IRE) *Paul Cole* a94 102
3 gr g Verglas(IRE) Vasilia (Dansili)
1845[2] 2277[7] 3639[6] 3784[2] 4095[2] 4760[11] 6449[9] 6830[8] 7010[7] 7345a[2] (7803a) 8277a[3]

Silver Lace (IRE) *Chris Wall* a76 58
3 bg f Clodovil(IRE) Rockahoolababy (IRE) (Kalanisi (IRE))
1285[2] ◆ 1637[4] 2803[5] (5229) (6151) 7530[4]

Silver Lime (USA) *Roger Charlton* 99
3 b c Mizzen Mast(USA) Red Dot (USA) (Diesis)
2408[2] (4741) ◆ 5558[9] 6025[3]

Silver Linnet (IRE) *John Butler* a62 56
5 gr m Acclamation Nadeema (FR) (Linamix (FR))
(467) ◆ 544[3] ◆ 823[4] 2251[8] 2943[10] 3546[9] 3943[8] 4439[5] 5217[5] 5719[12]

Silverlord (FR) *Gordon Elliott* a72 79
8 ch g Numerous(USA) Silverware (FR) (Polish Precedent (USA))
7792[10]

Silver Marizah (IRE) *Roger Ingram* a72 52
3 b f Manduro(GER) Maharani (USA) (Red Ransom (USA))
2136[12] 4583[7] 7668[7] 8046[8] 8187[8]

Silver Max (USA) *Dale Romans* a87 116
3 b c Badge Of Silver(USA) Kissin Rene (USA) (Kissin Kris (USA))
5375a[5]

Silvermine Bay (IRE) *Pat Eddery* a26 41
5 gr m Act One Quittance (USA) (Riverman (USA))
7303[13]

Silver Native (IRE) *Mike Murphy* a13
3 b g Elusive City(USA) Love Of Silver (USA) (Arctic Tern (USA))
217[7] 923[11]

Silver Northern (FR) *D Chenu* a79 102
3 b g Voix Du Nord(FR) Silver Diane (FR) (Silver Rainbow)
2064a[5] 2743a[19]

Silver Ocean (USA) *Niels Petersen* a108 107
4 br g Silver Train(USA) Endless Sea (CAN) (Mt. Livermore (USA))
315a[3] 588a[15] 876a[13] 2160a[2] (4751a) 5651a[10]

Silver Pond (FR) *P Bary* a112 121
5 gr h Act One Silver Fame (USA) (Quest For Fame)
878a[2] ◆ (7985a)

Silverrica (IRE) *Malcolm Saunders* 70
2 gr f Ad Valorem(USA) Allegorica (IRE) (Alzao (USA))
3140[11] 3506[6] 4581[2] 5260[3]

Silver Ridge (IRE) *Ralph Beckett* 87
2 gr c Verglas(IRE) Jacaranda Ridge (Indian Ridge)
2231[9] (2983) 3562[2] (5710) 6797[4]

Silver Rime (FR) *Linda Perratt* a60 88
7 gr g Verglas(IRE) Severina (Darshaan)
2035[6] 2597[12] 3274[5] 3492[4] 3890[5] 4135[2] 4388[4] 5362[4] 6047[2] 7360[11] 7685[13]

Silver Samba *Andrew Balding* a70 73
3 gr f Dalakhani(IRE) Fancy Dance (Rainbow Quest (USA))
1312[7] 1982[3] ◆ 3142[6] 4776[2] (5577) 6137[3] 6971[6]

Silver Six *Sheena West* a61 49
3 gr g Aussie Rules(USA) Bahara (Barathea (IRE))
2495[2] 4214[2] 4510[4]

Silver Sycamore (USA) *David Lanigan* a79 95
3 rg f Exchange Rate(USA) Miss Forest City (USA) (Coronado's Quest (USA))
3667[9] 4287[6] 5328[6] 6124[9]

Silver Threepence *Roy Brotherton* a15
4 ch m Trade Fair Silver Gyre (IRE) (Silver Hawk (USA))
2864[12] 3431[6]

Silver Tigress *George Moore* 67
4 gr m Tiger Hill(IRE) Cinnamon Tree (IRE) (Barathea (IRE))
1382[7] 1822[5] (3061) 3307[5] (4048) 5413[7] 6957[13]

Silver Valny (FR) *Mlle M-L Mortier* a90 113
6 ch g Vertical Speed(FR) Mendoreva (FR) (Mendocino (USA))
4634a[6] 6297a[9] 6864a[5] 7431a[2] (7735a)

Silverware (USA) *Linda Stubbs* a84 83
4 bb g Eurosilver(USA) Playing Footsie (USA) (Valiant Nature (USA))
1161[7] 2083[12] (2619) 4474[12] 4679[6] 5111[8] 6894[2] 7328[6] (7618) 7842[8] 8152[2] ◆ (8269)

Silver Wind *Alan McCabe* a72 79
7 b g Ishiguru(USA) My Bonus (Cyrano De Bergerac)
88[9] 328[4] 4508[4] 4999[10] 5389[8] 7179[5] 7685[7] 7914[3] 8256[4]

Silvery Moon (IRE) *Tim Easterby* 94
5 gr g Verglas(IRE) Starry Night (Sheikh Albadou)
1156[15] 1670[2] 2311[3] 2882[8] 3493[3] (3890) 4110[3] (4795) 5558[12] 6010[8] 6674[25]

Silvio Dante (USA) *David O'Meara* a53 41
2 ch g Street Boss(USA) Merit (USA) (Meadowlake (USA))
4555[8] 6175[7] 7208[5]

Simayill *John Berry* a87 83
4 b m Oasis Dream Triennial (IRE) (Giant's Causeway (USA))
131[6] 5888[11] 6539[7] 6987[11] 7511[11] 8162[8]

Simba (FR) *C Lerner* a106 108
4 gr h Anabaa Blue Saiga (FR) (Baryshnikov (AUS))
7124a[5] 7985a[2]

Simenon (IRE) *W P Mullins* 109
5 b g Marju(IRE) Epistoliere (IRE) (Alzao (USA))
(3241) (3373) 4737[6] 5599[5] 6271a[5]

Similu *Brian Meehan* a73 69
2 b f Danehill Dancer(IRE) Myth And Magic (IRE) (Namid)
7160[2] ◆ 7555[6]

Simla Sunset (IRE) *P J Prendergast* a87 98
6 b m One Cool Cat(USA) Simla Bibi (Indian Ridge)
2777a[5] 3322a[4] 3645a[9]

Simon De Montfort (IRE) *Mahmood Al Zarooni* a97 112
5 b g King's Best(USA) Noble Rose (IRE) (Caerleon (USA))
(792a)

Simonside *Brian Ellison* a57 80
9 b g Shahrastani(USA) Only So Far (Teenoso (USA))
6642[10] 7034[4]

Simple Joys *Andrew Balding* a53 53
2 b f Singspiel(IRE) Chance Dance (IRE) (Danehill Dancer (IRE))
6796[8] 7306[9]

Simple Rhythm *John Ryan* a53 62
6 b m Piccolo Easy Beat (IRE) (Orpen (USA))
155[7] 312[11] 1768[5] 2169[5] 2607[7] 2971[11] 3243[5] 3464[5] 3791[5] 4237[6] (4663) 5033[5] 5719[8] 6003[4] 6322[8] 7316[14] 7471[2] 7634[8] 7914[12]

Simply *Eve Johnson Houghton* a55 58
3 b f Nayef(USA) Polish Lake (Polish Precedent (USA))
3565[9] 4212[8] 4870[3] 5452[3] 5855[6] 6098[6] 6280[8]

Simply Dreaming *Michael Squance* a42 37
2 b f Pastoral Pursuits Tilly's Dream (Arkadian Hero (USA))
1738[3] 2193[11] 4152[9] 4433[11] 5242[7]

Simply Shining (IRE) *Richard Fahey* 78
2 ch f Rock Of Gibraltar(IRE) Bright Smile (IRE) (Caerleon (USA))
3887[2] (4546) 5602[10]

Simpson Millar *Noel Wilson* a22 48
3 b g Librettist(USA) Scented Garden (Zamindar (USA))
3566[6] 3892[3] 4830[13] 5446[9] 6259[7] 6429[6] 7591[11] 7604[16]

Sim Sala Bim *Stuart Williams* a65 80
4 rg h Act One Francia (Legend Of France (USA))
6538[6] 6933[15] 7369[7] 7893[6]

Sinaadi (IRE) *Clive Brittain* 82
2 b f Kyllachy Quantum (IRE) (Alhaarth (IRE))
3783[5] 5352[8] 5578[4] 6632[5] 7079[9]

Sinai (IRE) *Geoffrey Harker* 71
3 b f Moss Vale(IRE) Ten Commandments (IRE) (Key Of Luck (USA))
2194[10] 2689[8] 4547[17] 4793[9] 5538[7]

Sinatramania *Tracy Waggott* 63
5 b g Dansili Come Fly With Me (Bluebird (USA))
2588[5] 2792[3] 3355[6] 4350[10] 4712[2] 5225[4] 6262[6] 6562[9] 6885[7]

Sincero (AUS) *Stephen Farley* 121
5 br g Umatilla(NZ) Yours As Always (AUS) (Prego (IRE))
7426a[9]

Sinchiroka (FR) *Ralph Smith* a54 49
6 b g Della Francesca(USA) Great Care (USA) (El Gran Senor (USA))
6145[13] 6456[11] 7991[6]

Sindjara (USA) *John M Oxx* a102 95
3 br f Include(USA) Sindirana (IRE) (Kalanisi (IRE))
5397a[2]

Sinfonico (IRE) *Richard Hannon* a91 94
4 b g Iffraaj Zinstar (IRE) (Sinndar (IRE))
733[3] 817[4] 1321[8] 1510[11] (2151) 2642[12] 3157[11] 3963[10] 5301[12] 5794 [5] 6207[11] 6931[4]

Sing Alana Sing *Bill Turner* a44 40
4 b m Singspiel(IRE) Choralist (Danehill (USA))
453[7] 569[7] 741[4] 7717[U]

Singalat *James Given* a77 84
3 b g Singspiel(IRE) Crocolat (Croco Rouge (IRE))
1557[3] (2471) 3042[8] 3330[8] 4079[3] 4700[12] 6037[5] (6359)

Singapore Joy (FR) *H-A Pantall* 98
4 b m Sagacity(FR) Doliouchka (Saumarez)
6085a[3]

Singapore Sand (FR) *H-A Pantall* a76 76
3 b c Sandwaki(USA) Singapore Creek (FR) (Sagacity (FR))
17a[4]

Singapura (USA) *Mahmood Al Zarooni* 41
2 b f Street Cry(IRE) Burmilla (USA) (Storm Cat (USA))
2892[9]

Singersongwriter *Ed Dunlop* 75
2 ch f Raven's Pass(USA) Independence (Selkirk (USA))
(7363) ◆

Singeur (IRE) *Robin Bastiman* a97 102
5 b g Chineur(FR) Singitta (Singspiel (IRE))
4312[6] (4924) 5370[6] 6244[12] 6755[5] 7063[8]

Singing Bird (IRE) *David Wachman* 91
3 br f Excellent Art Anna Deesse (FR) (Anabaa (USA))
3091a[4] 3983a[5] 4354a[2] 5523a[10]

Single (FR) *C Laffon-Parias* 106
2 ch f Singspiel(IRE) Tender Morn (USA) (Dayjur (USA))
6129a[2]

Single Girl (IRE) *Jonathan Portman* a49 53
3 ch f Singspiel(IRE) Bumble (Rainbow Quest (USA))
1424[8] 2577[5] 3087[7] 4399[7]

Sings Poet *James Tate*
2 ch c Singspiel(IRE) Royale Rose (FR) (Bering)
7780[12]

Singzak *Michael Easterby* a77 78
4 ch g Singspiel(IRE) Zakuska (Zafonic (USA))
2093[10] 3564[13] 4626[13] 5913[5] 6311[2] 6478[3] 7024[3]

Sinnamara (IRE) *John Wainwright* 71
4 b m Intikhab(USA) Siniyya (IRE) (Grand Lodge (USA))
3180[7] 4431[RR] 5253[8]

Sioux Chieftain (IRE) *Tim Pitt* a58 53
2 b g Mount Nelson Lady Gin (USA) (Saint Ballado (CAN))
4595[11] 5207[5] 5742[6]

Siouxies Dream *Michael Appleby* a58
3 b f Zafeen(FR) Lady De Londres (Mtoto)
108[5] 294[2] 534[2] 840[4] 1058[6] 4830[12] 5246[5] 5810[9] 5945[12]

Siouxperhero (IRE) *William Muir* a69 74
3 b g Sleeping Indian Tintern (Diktat)
2150[7] 3432[3] (4544) 5036[2] 5501[3] 5983[4] (6169) 6843[6] 7480[9]

Sioux Rising (IRE) *Richard Fahey* a101 104
6 b m Danetime(IRE) Arvika (FR) (Baillamont (USA))
1494[6] 2087[2] 2713[9] 3375[6] 3593[2] 4070[2] 4764[5] 5385[9]

Sir Boss (IRE) *Michael Mullineaux* a80 92
7 b g Tagula(IRE) Good Thought (IRE) (Mukaddamah (USA))
187[8] 1632[5] 2031[4] (2348) 2863[4] 3163[13] 3609[4] 3692[5] 3945[8] 4884[6] 5767[2] 6076[5] 6981[5] 7409[7] 7792[3] 7954[7] 8136[3] ◆ (8243)

Sir Bruno (FR) *Bryn Palling* a75 67
5 ch g Hernando(FR) Moon Tree (FR) (Groom Dancer (USA))
1094[8] 2355[4] 2758[4] 3230[5] 4531[9] 5506[7] 5893[2] 6216[4] 7022[9] 7925[6] 8114[3]

Sircozy (IRE) *Gary Moore* a77 77
6 b g Celtic Swing Furnish (Green Desert (USA))
400[2]

Sir Dylan *Ronald Harris* a64 57
3 b g Dylan Thomas(IRE) Monteleone (IRE) (Montjeu (IRE))
1824[8] 2756[11] 3433[3] 3719[10] 4534[8] 4940[8] 5266[5] (5508) 5817[8] 6097[7] 6690[12] 6798[8] 7499[2] (7632) 7869[11] 8023[13] 8048[8] 8182[4]

Sir Francis Drake *Robert Eddery* 80
4 ch g Pivotal Cape Verdi (IRE) (Caerleon (USA))
4948[10] 5794 [11] 6141[10]

Sir Frank Morgan (IRE) *Mark Johnston* 15
2 b g Montjeu(IRE) Woodland Orchid (IRE) (Woodman (USA))
6733[8] 6997[5] 7492[13]

Sir Freddie (USA) *Fredrik Reuterskiold* a38
3 gr g Unbridled's Song(USA) Judy Soda (USA) (Personal Flag (USA))
3655a[4]

Sir Fredlot (IRE) *Charles Hills* a79 79
3 b g Choisir(AUS) Wurfklinge (GER) (Acatenango (GER))
1723[2] 2147[2] (3333) 4288[4] 4819[5] 5512[5] 6240[9] 6734[5] 7116[5]

Sir Geoffrey (IRE) *Scott Dixon* a86 78
6 b g Captain Rio Disarm (IRE) (Bahamian Bounty)
120[3] ◆ 286[4] 525[7] 835[9] 1480[5] 2084[9] 2982[2] (3993) 4461[7] 5272[11] 6427[15] 7295[8] 7716[11] 7937[8]

Sir George (IRE) *Ollie Pears* a78 82
7 b g Mujadil(USA) Torrmana (IRE) (Ela-Mana-Mou)
753[2] 1094[6] 1578[4] 2675[5] 4142[3] 4398[5] 4747[2] 4964[7] 6687[11] 7798[4] 8047[4]

Sir Glanton (IRE) *Amanda Perrett* a82 90
3 ch g Choisir(AUS) Ctesiphon (USA) (Arch (USA))
1142[7] 2975 [4] 3393[13] 4473[9] 4735[18]

Sir Graham Wade (IRE) *Mark Johnston* 108
3 gr c Dalakhani(IRE) Needwood Epic (Midyan (USA))
1132[8] (1662) ◆ (4700) ◆ (4962) ◆ 5089[3] 5598[13] (6031) (6197) 6833[2] (7320a)

Sir Henry (DEN) *Soren Jensen* 86
5 b h Academy Award(IRE) Lady Clementine (DEN) (Richard Of York)
4863a[6]

Sir Ike (IRE) *Michael Appleby* a61 61
7 b g Xaar Iktidar (Green Desert (USA))
293[8]

Sirious Oss *Michael Easterby* 68
3 b g Sir Percy Groom Landing (PR) (Runaway Groom (CAN))
1866[9] 2258[11]

Sirius Prospect (USA) *Dean Ivory* a107 115
4 bb g Gone West(USA) Stella Blue (FR) (Anabaa (USA))
1129[9] 1469[8] 2179[10] 3370[7] 4100[6] 5581[3] 6024[17] 6346[3] 7066[3] 7236[3] 7690[4] 7809[3]

Sirius Superstar *Andrew Balding* a75 80
4 b g Galileo(IRE) Brightest (Rainbow Quest (USA))
3765[7] 4475[4] 5106[6] 5772[5] 7024[6]

Sir Jade (FR) *J-M Capitte* a97 108
3 b c Gentlewave(IRE) Jade Colour (IRE) (Peintre Celebre (USA))
716a[4] 2108a[3] 2743a[11]

Sir John Hawkwood (IRE) *Sir Michael Stoute* 103
3 b g Sir Percy Athene (IRE) (Rousillon (USA))
(2125) 4097[8] (5101) ◆ 5492[8] 7407[4] ◆

Sir Lando *Wido Neuroth* 115
5 b h Lando(GER) Burqa (Nashwan (USA))
1700a[3] 2322a[8] (2807a) (3886a) 4383a[5]

Sir Lexington (IRE) *Richard Hannon* a59 57
3 b g Desert Style(IRE) Shulammite Woman (IRE) (Desert Sun)
1922[11] 2665[4] 4157[8] 4709[12] 5408[10] 5629[7] 6230[9] 6885[12]

Sir Louis *Richard Fahey* a74 66
5 b g Compton Place Heuston Station (IRE) (Fairy King (USA))
13[12]

Sir Maximilian (IRE) *Ed Dunlop* a91 84
3 b g Royal Applause Nebraska Lady (IRE) (Lujain (USA))
1420[5] 1739[2] 2065[2] (2918) ◆ 4919[3] 5603[7] 6368[3]

Sir Mike *Amanda Perrett* a80 86
3 ch g Haafhd Tara Moon (Pivotal)
1852[2] 2172[2] 3106[3] 3917[2] 4223[3] 4735[11] 5237[6] 5747[8]

Sir Mozart (IRE) *Ronald Harris* a77 77
9 b g Mozart(IRE) Lady Silver Hawk (USA) (Silver Hawk (USA))
13[7] (3456) 3738[4] 4866[8] 6051[10] 6452[9] 7820[5]

Sir Nod *Julie Camacho* a68 73
10 b g Tagula(IRE) Nordan Raider (Domynsky)
5093[7] 5416[2] 6264[7] 7589[6] 8144[5]

Sir Oscar (GER) *T Potters* 108
5 b g Mark Of Esteem(IRE) Sintenis (GER) (Polish Precedent (USA))
2222a[3] (4130a) 5782a[8] 6291a[6]

Sir Palomides (USA) *William Haggas* a63 39
3 bb c Mr Greeley(USA) Glatisant (Rainbow Quest (USA))
3735[5] 4341[12] 5776[8]

Sir Patrick Moore (FR) *Harry Dunlop* 96
2 gr c Astronomer Royal(USA) America Nova (FR) (Verglas (IRE))
(2231) (3017a) 4118a[2] 5471a[6] 7398[6]

Sir Pedro *Charles Hills* 79
3 b g Acclamation Milly-M (Cadeaux Genereux)
(2262) ◆ 3445[5] 4824[17] 6800[15]

Sir Prancealot (IRE) *Richard Hannon* 110
2 b c Tamayuz Mona Em (IRE) (Catrail (USA))
(2164) ◆ (2638) ◆ 3240[4] 4384a[2] 5398a[4] (6196)

Sir Quintin (IRE) *Andrew Balding* a68 85
3 b g Dixie Union(USA) No Frills (IRE) (Darshaan)
3161[2] ◆ 3663[2] 4259[3] 5297[5] 6202[8] 7016[3]

Sir Reginald *Richard Fahey* a92 97
4 b g Compton Place Clincher Club (Polish Patriot (USA))
141a[9] 314a[5] ◆ 420a[9] 3371[23] 4099[4] 4761[6] ◆ 5342[9] 6201[7] ◆ 7240[15]

Sir Trevor (IRE) *Tom Dascombe* a75 77
3 b g Refuse To Bend(IRE) Joyfullness (USA) (Dixieland Band (USA))
1440[10] 1978[11] 4398[2] 4747[3] 5111[4] 6401[7] 6539[4] 6973[5] 7358[7]

Sirvino *David Barron* a99 106
7 b g Vettori(IRE) Zenita (IRE) (Zieten (USA))
241a[3] 484a[7] 755a[4] 1139[10] 1605[2] 2176[3] 2773[9] 3329[7] 3642[8] 4365[7] 6606[3] 7175[4] 7396[4] 7689[6]

Sir Windsorlot (IRE) *John Quinn* a43 65
3 b g Windsor Knot(IRE) Hever Rosina (Efisio)
1441[10] 2591[7] 3566[3] 4452[6] 4913[4] 7402[8] 7671[8]

Si Sealy (IRE) *David Evans* a47 32
3 b g Lawman(FR) Sharpville (USA) (Diesis)
196[7] 393[8]

Sistine *Nicky Henderson* a75 62
4 b m Dubai Destination(USA) Fickle (Danehill (USA))
(366)

Six Diamonds *Richard Guest* a41 44
5 b m Exceed And Excel(AUS) Daltak (Night Shift (USA))
2352[10] 2839[10] 2943[11]

Six Of Clubs *Bill Turner* a75 62
6 ch g Bertolini(USA) Windmill Princess (Gorytus (USA))
23[3] 129[10] 566[2] 772[4] (1184) 1496[5] 2468[3] 7169[7] (7528) 7791[5] (8035) (8290)

Six Of Hearts *Cecil Ross* a102 109
8 b g Pivotal Additive (USA) (Devil's Bag (USA))
1040a[4] 2513a[5] 2710[7] 6854a[9]

Six Silver Lane *Derek Shaw* a83 78
4 gr g Aussie Rules(USA) Aurelia (Rainbow Quest (USA))
7810[13] 7986[12] 8174[10]

Sixties Queen *Alan Bailey* a25
2 b f Sixties Icon Lily Of Tagula (IRE) (Tagula (IRE))
1388[7]

Six Wives *Scott Dixon* a88 86
5 b m Kingsalsa(USA) Regina (Green Desert (USA))
3[3] 525[6] (835) 1015[10] 1417[10] (5223) 5576[2] 5822[13] 6144[5] 7019[7] 7726[4] 7860[4] 7918[2] 8009[5] 8066[6]

Siyouma (IRE) *F Doumen* 119
4 b m Medicean Sichilla (IRE) (Danehill (USA))
2570a[3] 4065[3] 5399a[4] (6673) (7093a) 8042a[11]

Sizzler *Ralph Beckett* 62
2 ch g Hernando(FR) Gino's Spirits (Perugino (USA))
6928[4] ◆ 7492[10]

Skallet (FR) *S Wattel* a95 107
4 b m Muhaymin(USA) Siran (FR) (R B Chesne)
1766a[6] 4229a[7] 5844a[12]

Skating Over (USA) *Jane Chapple-Hyam* 52
2 ch f Giant's Causeway(USA) Annie Skates (USA) (Mr Greeley (USA))
6489[13] 6960[10]

Sketchy Evidence (USA) *John Best* a71
4 ch g Officer(USA) Drawing A Blank (USA) (El Prado (IRE))
91[9] 2146[10] 2274[14]

Skidby Mill (IRE) *John Quinn* a58 64
2 b f Ramonti(FR) Glasnas Giant (Giant's Causeway (USA))
3415[5] ◆ (6049) 6475[8] 7060[7] 7441[3]

Skiddaw Secret *John Weymes*
5 ch m Tobougg(IRE) Stealthy (Kind Of Hush)
976[6]

Skiddaw View *Maurice Barnes* a40 33
4 b m Goodricke Skiddaw Wolf (Wolfhound (USA))
2271[0] 691[11] 887[12] 4262[8] 4593[5] 5549[8] 5919[7] 6341[8]

Skilful *John Gosden* a102 116
4 ch h Selkirk(USA) Prowess (IRE) (Peintre Celebre (USA))
1749[5] 2127[2] 6449[4] (6868) 7401[4]

Skirmish *Mark Johnston* 76
3 b c Teofilo(IRE) Jessica's Dream (IRE) (Desert Style (IRE))
2280[3]

Skyblue *Tobias B P Coles* a42 36
3 b f Royal Applause Fiina (Most Welcome)
30[3] 4440[8] 5022[6] 5989[6]

Sky Crossing *James Given* a80 64
3 b g Cape Cross(IRE) Sky Wonder (Observatory (USA))
1449[3] 1862[6] 2256[17] 4798[7] 5318[5] 6050[4] (6401) 6840[4]

Sky Diamond (IRE) *John Mackie* a72 72
4 b g Diamond Green(FR) Jewell In The Sky (IRE) (Sinndar (IRE))
183[10] 490[8] 1634[5] 2090[4] (2467) 2804[6] 3317[9] 4402[8] 5171[14]

Skyeron *Mark Brisbourne* a50 54
3 b f Byron Song Of Skye (Warning)
923[6] 1287[5] 1424[2] 1590[5] (2162) 2340[7] 3048[6] 3315[7]

Skyfire *Nick Kent* a48 75
5 ch g Storm Cat(USA) Sunray Superstar (Nashwan (USA))
2094[5] 2687[5] 3290[3] 3775[2] 4325[3] 4959[3] 7132[4] 7368[5]

Sky Garden *William Haggas* a60 74
2 b f Acclamation Superstar Leo (IRE) (College Chapel)
3223[3] 6007[2] 6343[2] 7498[3]

Sky High Diver (IRE) *Alan Swinbank* a75 69
4 b m Celtic Swing Limit (IRE) (Barathea (IRE))
4088[5] 4883[6]

Sky Khan *Ed Dunlop* a79 88
3 b g Cape Cross(IRE) Starlit Sky (Galileo (IRE))
1467[13] 2196[5] 2584[6] 4498[6] 4945[2] 5405[2] 6181[3] (7131)

Sky King (FR) *B Goudot* a43
3 ch c Haafhd Melanzane (Arazi (USA))
211a[11]

Sky Lantern (IRE) *Richard Hannon* 111
2 gr f Red Clubs(IRE) Shawanni (Shareef Dancer (USA))
(2407) (2780a) ◆ 5103[2] 5571[2] (6081a) 7547a[8]

Skyline Du Casse (FR) *F Plouganou* 102
6 b g East Of Heaven(IRE) Ordalie Du Casse (FR) (Seurat)
7320a[6] 7735a[2]

Skylla *Derek Shaw* a60 93
5 b m Kyllachy Day Star (Dayjur (USA))
8[6]

Skystream (IRE) *Ian Semple* a53 56
4 bb m Captain Rio Nuit Des Temps (Sadler's Wells (USA))
750[5] 939[10] 1242[12]

Skytrain *Mark Johnston* a65 35
2 ch g Exceed And Excel(AUS) Viola Da Braccio (IRE) (Vettori (IRE))
2213[7] 6970[3] 7268[4]

Slade Power (IRE) *Edward Lynam* a107 111
3 b c Dutch Art Girl Power (IRE) (Key Of Luck (USA))
(2712) 7236[8]

Slam *Robert Cowell* a69 91
7 b g Beat Hollow House Hunting (Zafonic (USA))
198[6] 535[7] 1045[2] 1360[4] 1530[7]

Slatey Hen (IRE) *Richard Guest* a59 44
4 b m Acclamation Silver Arrow (USA) (Shadeed (USA))
95[4] 297[2] 425[5] 497[6] 665[3] (783) 887[6] 996[6] 1054[5] 1528[3] 1787[6] 2350[6] 2647[5]

Sleeping Bull (USA) *R Posada*
2 rg c Holy Bull(USA) Inch Marlowe (USA) (Green Dancer (USA))
8244a[11]

Sleepy Blue Ocean *John Balding* a85 76
6 b g Oasis Dream Esteemed Lady (IRE) (Mark Of Esteem (IRE))
3[5] 1642[7] 1868[9] 2674[9] (4495) 4999[7] 5388[3] 5821[4] 6788[12] 6938[4] 7730[3]

Sleepy Haven (IRE) *David Barron* 64
2 b g Indian Haven High Society Girl (IRE) (Key Of Luck (USA))
2537[5] 3436[5] 4173[4] 5254[4]

Sleepy Lucy *Richard Guest* a49 44
3 b f Multiplex Millie The Filly (Erhaab (USA))
121[8] 1260[6] 1600[4] 1918[7] 4771[4] 5014[13] 5458[7] 6000[6] 8236[7]

Sleights Boy (IRE) *Ian McInnes* a59 55
4 b g Kyllachy Fanny Bay (IRE) (Key Of Luck (USA))
939[2] 1387[11] 2091[8] 2350[7] 3462[8] 3731[9] 4452[10] 4717[16] 4956[7] 6322[13] 6555[7]

Slenningford *Ollie Pears* a57 63
3 b f Vital Equine(IRE) Dim Ofan (Petong)
2139[5] 3285[2] 3751[5] 4348[5] 4913[7]

Slewtoo *Michael Easterby* a74
3 b f Three Valleys(USA) Red Slew (Red Ransom (USA))
1985[8] 6840[11] 7975[6] 8142[11]

Slide Show *Colin Teague* a33 72
4 b m Galileo(IRE) First Exhibit (Machiavellian (USA))
6957[10] 7352[7] 7594[9]

Slight Advantage (IRE) *A Wohler* a8 101
4 b m Peintre Celebre(USA) Kournikova (SAF) (Sportsworld (USA))
(2965a) 3768a[6]

Slim Chance (IRE) *J G Coogan* a84 77
3 b f Clodovil(IRE) Valluga (IRE) (Ashkalani (IRE))
7230a[11]

Slim Shadey *Simon Callaghan* 115
4 bb g Val Royal(FR) Vino Veritas (USA) (Chief's Crown (USA))
7573a[8]

Slip Of The Tongue *Sir Mark Prescott Bt* a56 40
2 ch g Zamindar(USA) Kiswahili (Selkirk (USA))
6175[5] 6645[6] 7127[9]

Slip Sliding Away (IRE) *Peter Hedger* a63 86
5 b g Whipper(USA) Sandy Lady (IRE) (Desert King (IRE))
2070[2]

Slipstream Angel (IRE) *Richard Fahey* a32 65
2 gr f Dark Angel(IRE) Ornellaia (IRE) (Mujadil (USA))
(3627) 4047[5] 6070[14] 6998[2] 7223[7] 7439[6]

Slope *David Wachman* 88
2 gr f Acclamation Bandanna (Bandmaster (USA))
3674a[3]

Slow Cavern (IRE) *Affe D'Agostino*
2 gr c Aussie Rules(USA) Home Comforts (Most Welcome)
7513a[7]

Slowfoot (GER) *Markus Klug* 106
4 b h Hernando(FR) Simply Red (GER) (Dashing Blade)
7427a[3]

Smallbrook Lane (IRE) *Richard Fahey* 59
2 gr f Dark Angel(IRE) Jemima's Art (Fantastic Light (USA))
2282[7] 2747[4]

Small Frida (FR) *Mme Pia Brandt* a96 97
3 ch f Gold Away(IRE) Becky Moss (USA) (Red Ransom (USA))
(117a) 1426a[0]

Small Fury (IRE) *Jo Hughes* a76 60
2 b f Windsor Knot(IRE) Sisal (IRE) (Danehill (USA))
6276[3] (7711) 8007[2] (8108) 8204[2]

Smalljohn *Bryan Smart* a82 78
6 ch g Needwood Blade My Bonus (Cyrano De Bergerac)
942[3] 1917[9] (2354) (3229) 6454[5] 7790[12]

Small Steps (IRE) *Ed McMahon* a53 53
3 b f Acclamation Last Tango (IRE) (Lion Cavern (USA))
38[8]

Smart Affair *Alan Bailey* a56 50
3 b f Trade Fair Che Chic (IRE) (Daggers Drawn (USA))
641[3] (901) 1740[3] 1982[8] 3048[8] 3938[2] 4193[3] 4870[5] 4971[4] 5804[5] 5991[6] 6316[2] (6807) 7196[5] 7255[4] 7605[5]

Smart Alice *Chris Wall* a41
2 b f Soviet Star(USA) Ailincala (IRE) (Pursuit Of Love)
7191[9] 7525[P] 7840[6]

Smart Daisy K *Reg Hollinshead* a69 77
2 b f Pastoral Pursuits Katy-Q (IRE) (Taufan (USA))
3487[2] 4990[2] (6970) 7745[7]

Smart Eighteen *Paul D'Arcy* 54
2 b c Exceed And Excel(AUS) Papabile (USA) (Chief's Crown (USA))
5325[7]

Smart Ellis (USA) *Richard E Mandella* 105
3 ch c Smarty Jones(USA) Corrazona (USA) (El Gran Senor (USA))
7566a[3] 7882a[12]

Smart Endeavour (USA) *Peter Jardby* a67 83
6 ch g Smart Strike(CAN) Luminance (USA) (Deputy Minister (CAN))
3654a[5]

Smart Falcon (JPN) *Ken Kozaki* a123 97
7 ch h Gold Allure(JPN) Keishu Herb (JPN) (Mississipian (USA))
1150a[10]

Smart Ruler (IRE) *James Moffatt* a71 70
6 ch g Viking Ruler(AUS) Celebrated Smile (IRE) (Cadeaux Genereux)
5315[4] 6228[4] 6615[7]

Smart Spender (IRE) *Jo Hughes* a82
2 b g Chineur(FR) Smart Starprincess (IRE) (Soviet Star (USA))
6177[5] (6808)

Smart Step *Mark Johnston* a43 74
4 b m Montjeu(IRE) Miss Pinkerton (Danehill (USA))
(1439) 1652[7] 1913[4] 2576[7] 2909[6] 3213[9] 3610[8]

Smart Sting (USA) *Roger L Attfield* a106 106
4 b m Smart Strike(CAN) Perfect Sting (USA) (Red Ransom (USA))
6298a[6]

Smarty Socks (IRE) *David O'Meara* a80 108
8 ch g Elnadim(USA) Unicamp (Royal Academy (USA))
1130[19] 1523[3] 2075[4] (2505) 4761[20] 5597[4] 6024[8] 6676[6] 7240[21]

Smarty Time *John Bridger* a51 53
5 b m Almaty(IRE) Past 'N' Present (Cadeaux Genereux)
1065[6] 1301[7] 1889[9] 2422[6] 3043[8] 3152[7] 4150[10] 4602[5] 4812[10] 5310[13]

Smileswithhiseyes (IRE) *Gay Kelleway* a70 28
2 b g Marju(IRE) Amoureux (USA) (Deputy Minister (CAN))
7330[15] (7923)

Smiley Miley (IRE) *David Lewis*
4 ch m Danroad(AUS) Music Teacher (Piccolo)
6001[10] 6641[11] 6935[6] 7378[10]

Smiling Shark (USA) *Robert Cowell* 56
2 b c Johannesburg(USA) Piu Bella (USA) (Fusaichi Pegasus (USA))
2442[4] 2970[4] 3789[2]

Smiling Tiger (USA) *Jeff Bonde* a126
5 ch h Hold That Tiger(USA) Shandra Smiles (USA) (Cahill Road (USA))
7574a[3]

Smirfys Blackcat (IRE) *Michael Mullineaux*
3 b f One Cool Cat(USA) Smirfys Dance Hall (IRE) (Halling (USA))
6154[11]

Smirfys Emerald (IRE) *Michael Mullineaux* a49 54
4 ch g Choisir(AUS) Smirfys Dance Hall (IRE) (Halling (USA))
4293[10] 5335[7] 5999[3]

Smirfy's Silver *Michael Mullineaux* a60 74
8 b g Desert Prince(IRE) Goodwood Blizzard (Inchinor)
102[10] 361[8] 909[6] 7841[12] 8180[12]

Smoker *P J Prendergast* 79
2 b c Motivator Request (Rainbow Quest (USA))
4377a[5]

Smokethatthunders (IRE) *James Toller* 60
2 gr g Elusive City(USA) Zinstar (IRE) (Sinndar (IRE))
7516[4]

Smokey Oakey (IRE) *Mark H Tompkins* a79 71
8 b g Tendulkar(USA) Veronica (Persian Bold)
426[10] 529[5] 1037[5] 3125[7] 3494[12] 6639[9]

Smoking Joe (ITY) *S Botti* 100
3 b c Mujahid(USA) Occhi Di Giada (GER) (Shantou (USA))
2324a[3]

Smoking Sun (USA) *P Bary* 111
3 b c Smart Strike(CAN) Burning Sunset (Caerleon (USA))
5250a[5] 6294a[6]

Smoky Cloud (IRE) *Dave Morris* a70 81
5 ch g Refuse To Bend(IRE) Pirie (USA) (Green Dancer (USA))
123[10] 598[4] 1769[4] 3245[7] 3950[9] 4332[14] 7993[13] 8184[10]

Smoky Hill (IRE) *M Delzangles* 97
3 gr c Galileo(IRE) Danaskaya (IRE) (Danehill (USA))
6896a[7]

Smooth Handle *Tom Dascombe* a40 50
2 ch g Dutch Art Naomi Wildman (USA) (Kingmambo (USA))
3303[10] 3452[5] 4290[4] 4672[8] 6156[15]

Smooth Operator (GER) *Mario Hofer* 111
6 b g Big Shuffle(USA) Salzgitter (Salse (USA))
(1745a) 2728a[10] 3603a[4] 5647a[4]

Smoothtalkinrascal (IRE) *Brian Meehan* 95
2 b g Kodiac Cool Tarifa (IRE) (One Cool Cat (USA))
1499[2] ◆ (2330) 3242[8] 4008[6] 7028[10]

Snaafy (USA) *M Al Muhairi* a114 106
8 b h Kingmambo(USA) Nafisah (IRE) (Lahib (USA))
144a[11] 590a[12] 757a[6] 876a[2] 1143a[11]

Snape Maltings (IRE) *H-A Pantall* 96
5 b g Sadler's Wells(USA) Hanami (Hernando (FR))
7320a[10]

Sneak A Peek (ITY) *Peter G Moody* 112
4 b h Doyen(IRE) Occhi Di Giada (GER) (Shantou (USA))
7264a[8]

Snooker (GER) *Rose Dobbin* 66
6 ch g Acambaro(GER) Sheraton (IRE) (Brief Truce (USA))
1276[9] 3353[2] ◆ 3775[4] 4455[3] 4958[4]

Snooky *Richard Fahey* a70 71
3 b g Exceed And Excel(AUS) Quintrell (Royal Applause)
5549[2] 7445[2] (7712)

Snoqualmie Chief *David Elsworth* a67 72
2 b c Montjeu(IRE) Seattle Ribbon (USA) (Seattle Dancer (USA))
5062[14] 6796[3] 8071[5]

Snow Angel (IRE) *J W Hills* a48 74
2 b f Danehill Dancer(IRE) Snowy Day In La (IRE) (Sadler's Wells (USA))
2343[5] 2729[3] (4002) 4488[8] 4927[8] 5940[7]

Snow Bay *David Nicholls* a80 103
6 ch g Bahamian Bounty Goodwood Blizzard (Inchinor)
1128[10] 1821[9] 2590[2] 3128[19] 4190[4] 4689[17] 5094[9] 5414[3] 6013[7] 6559[8]

Snow Bell (FR) *N Clement* a77 82
2 b f Kendargent(FR) Makisarde (FR) (Xaar)
8276a[2]

Snowboarder (USA) *Mahmood Al Zarooni* a93 90
2 ch c Raven's Pass(USA) Gaudete (USA) (Distorted Humor (USA))
(3499) 4774[2] (5348) 6149[2] (7009)

Snow Dancer (IRE) *Hugh McWilliams* a85 87
8 b m Desert Style(IRE) Bella Vie (IRE) (Sadler's Wells (USA))
216[10] 694[5] 2539[3] 2751[4] 4621[9]

Snowday (FR) *C Laffon-Parias* 106
2 b c Falco(USA) Oceanique (USA) (Forest Wildcat (USA))
(3680a) 4384a[3] 5398a[9] 6910a[4] 7623a[5]

Snowed In (IRE) *Jennie Candlish* a70 78
3 gr g Dark Angel(IRE) Spinning Gold (Spinning World (USA))
5044[5]

Snow Fairy (IRE) *Ed Dunlop* a83 126
5 b m Intikhab(USA) Woodland Dream (IRE) (Charnwood Forest (IRE))
5399a[DSQ] (6063a)

Snow Hill *Chris Wall* 86
4 gr g Halling(USA) Swift Dispersal (Shareef Dancer (USA))
1566[7] 2921[8] 4103[9]

Snow King (USA) *John Gosden* 85
2 ch c Elusive Quality(USA) Cloudspin (USA) (Storm Cat (USA))
(6020) 7567a[8]

Snowmaster (USA) *S Seemar* a80
6 ch h Maria's Mon(USA) Snowflake (IRE) (Caerleon (USA))
48a[8]

Snow Queen (IRE) *A P O'Brien* 97
2 b f Danehill Dancer(IRE) Bonheur (IRE) (Royal Academy (USA))
4276a[5] 6081a[12]

Snow Ridge *Simon Hodgson* a55 49
4 b g Iceman Confetti (Groom Dancer (USA))
203[4] 522[9] 3939[9] 6097[11] 6159[11]

Snow Rose (USA) *Mahmood Al Zarooni* a63 80
2 b f Elusive Quality(USA) Ascutney (USA) (Lord At War (ARG))
5300[5] (5907)

Snow Trooper *Dean Ivory* a82 84
4 ch g Iceman Snow Shoes (Sri Pekan (USA))
(1108) 1680[3] 2274[7] (2988) 3226[3] 3767[7] 6539[4] 6932[2] 7300[2] 7842[3]

Snowy Dawn *Reg Hollinshead* 68
2 gr g Notnowcato Tereyna (Terimon)
6818[6] 7103[3] 7517[6]

Snowy Valley *Simon Earle* a59
3 ch g Three Valleys(USA) Rasseem (IRE) (Fasliyev (USA))
1723[9] 3972[10] 5970[9] 6982[6] 7960[6] 8179[8]

Soap Wars *Hugo Palmer* a51 94
7 b g Acclamation Gooseberry Pie (Green Desert (USA))
4437[2] 4660[6] 5832[12] 6234[5] 7144[9]

Soapy Delight *Mark Johnston*
3 b f Dansili On A Soapbox (USA) (Mi Cielo (USA))
2313[11]

Soaring Spirits (IRE) *Roger Varian* a74 66
2 ch g Tamayuz Follow My Lead (Night Shift (USA))
6114[8] 6644[2] 7899[2]

So Beautiful (FR) *Mlle S-V Tarrou* a86 112
3 b c Zamindar(USA) Silver Tulip (USA) (Silver Hawk (USA))
2951a[4] (3656a)

So Beloved *Roger Charlton* 81
2 b c Dansili Valencia (Kenmare (FR))
5303[4] (6795) ◆ 7331[5]

Soblue (IRE) *A Fabre* 105
2 b c Invincible Spirit(IRE) Never Green (IRE) (Halling (USA))
6086a[4]

So Cheeky *Peter Salmon* a54 53
3 ch f Fantastic View(USA) Fallujah (Dr Fong (USA))
1155[11] 2030[3] 3025[8] 3460[9] 3781[7] 4311[5] 4781[7] 6210[8]

Social Rhythm *Alistair Whillans* a62 72
8 b m Beat All(USA) Highly Sociable (Puissance)
1799[4] 2455[4] (2598) 3032[3] 4390[4] (4676) 4996[2]

Society Pearl (IRE) *Charles Hills* 75
2 b f Kheleyf(USA) Mamonta (Fantastic Light (USA))
4494[4] ◆ 6664[4] 7553[6]

Society Rock (IRE) *James Fanshawe* 122
5 b h Rock Of Gibraltar(IRE) High Society (IRE) (Key Of Luck (USA))
2179[3] 3370[5] 4100[3] (6030) 7236[5]

Sofast (FR) *F Head* 113
3 ch c Rock Of Gibraltar(IRE) Beautifix (GER) (Bering)
1408a[3] 2064a[2] 2743a[13] 3681a[5] 5649a[6]

Sofias Number One (USA) *Roy Bowring* a71 43
4 bb g Silver Deputy(CAN) Storidawn (USA) (Hennessy (USA))
215[8] 372[5] 490[6] 671[4] 1988[5] 2821[8]

Sofi's Spirit (IRE) *J S Moore* a61
2 bb f Captain Marvelous(IRE) Sofistication (IRE) (Dayjur (USA))
7641[5] 7812[4] 7916[2] (7977) (8053) (8092) (8224) 8293[3]

Softsong (FR) *R Chotard* 105
4 b g Singspiel(IRE) Soft Gold (USA) (Gulch (USA))
1697a[7]

So Grateful (FR) *F Pedrono* a1 50
3 b f Sandwaki(USA) Val Ramier (FR) (Westheimer (USA))
4477a[0]

Sohar *James Toller* 86
4 b m Iceman Desert Joy (Daylami (IRE))
2561[9] 3400[3] 4103[2] 6598[10] 7522[2]

Sohcahtoa (IRE) *David Barron* a74 78
6 b g Val Royal(FR) Stroke Of Six (IRE) (Woodborough (USA))
1295[4] ◆ 1640[3] 1846[3] 2214[12] 2827[4] 3337[3] 4326[11] 4766[2] (5056) 5798[5] 6311[6] 6706[6]

Soho Rocks *James Toller* a63 69
3 b f Rock Of Gibraltar(IRE) Millisecond (Royal Applause)
4436[3] 5107[4] 5769[8] 7740[5]

Soho Spirit *James Toller* a35
3 ch f Nayef(USA) Cruinn A Bhord (Inchinor)
1456[11] 2585[9] 3763[11]

Sohraab *Hughie Morrison* a77 97
8 b g Erhaab(USA) Riverine (Risk Me (FR))
2268[11] 2704[12] 3127[3] ◆ 3771[4] 4317[23] 4576[12] 5065[4] 5530[3] 5829[4] 6165[9] 7080[10]

Soir D'Ete (FR) *J-P Delaporte* a64 70
3 ch f Anabaa Blue Shy Mail (ARG) (Shy Tom (USA))
476a[3]

So Irish (IRE) *Robert Collet* 80
2 b f Whipper(USA) Babacora (IRE) (Indian Ridge)
7699a[0]

So Is She (IRE) *Alan Bailey* a63 62
4 b m Kheleyf(USA) River Beau (IRE) (Galileo (IRE))
96[6] 1014[3] 1299[2] (1425) 1744[3] 1831[3] 2137[4] 2364[5] 2467[2] 2804[5] 3317[3] 4538[8] 4643[4] 4875[12]

Sojitzen (FR) *X Nakkachdji* a72
2 b f Great Journey(JPN) Mercalle (FR) (Kaldoun (FR))
7683a[5]

Sojoum *Mick Channon* a52 59
2 b f Sixties Icon Natalie Jay (Ballacashtal (CAN))
2469[4] 2631[7] 3224[2] 4574[9] 5206[6] 5484[5] 5675[2] 6115[5] 6354[7] 6499[5] 6826[4] 7379[6] 7432[3] 7808[10]

Solace (USA) *John Gosden* a65 73
2 ch f Langfuhr(CAN) Songerie (Hernando (FR))
5104[4] 5907[5] 8147[2]

Solange (IRE) *Tim Easterby*
3 ch f Van Nistelrooy(USA) Bank On Her (USA) (Rahy (USA))
1166[6]

Solaras Exhibition (IRE) *Tim Vaughan* 85
4 b g Great Exhibition(USA) Solara (GER) (Danehill (USA))
(3610)

Solar Deity (IRE) *Marco Botti* a98 87
3 b c Exceed And Excel(AUS) Dawn Raid (IRE) (Docksider (USA))
1217[4] 1452[4] 2263[5] 3977[8] 4473[6] (6768) ◆ (7774) ◆

Solar Sky *Sir Henry Cecil* a94 111
4 ch g Galileo(IRE) La Sky (IRE) (Law Society (USA))
1318[5] 1750[6] 4800[3] 5599[11]

Solar Spirit (IRE) *Tracy Waggott* a89 89
7 b g Invincible Spirit(IRE) Misaayef (USA) (Swain (IRE))
1168[14] (1293) 1670[15] 1951[3] 2754[3] (2876) 3183[13] 3493[4] 4078[7] 4629[2] 4829[8] 5057[5] 5368[15] 6338[10] (6938) 7291[8] 7452[9]

Solars Sun *Ian Wood*
3 b g Footstepsinthesand Solar Flare (IRE) (Danehill (USA))
5852[7]
Solar View (IRE) *Sir Mark Prescott Bt* a62 84
3 ch g Galileo(IRE) Ellen (IRE) (Machiavellian (USA))
2787[10] 3729[3] 4153[2] ◆ (4399) (4537) 5384[2] (5735) ◆ (5798)
Soldier Spy *David Flood* a37 23
3 ch g Motivator Lalina (GER) (Trempolino (USA))
2856[13] 3155[10] 3620[4] 4147[7] 4812[9]
Sol Diva *Mick Channon* 47
2 b f Sixties Icon Solmorin (Fraam)
4525[9] 4730[16] 7021[9]
Sole Danser (IRE) *Milton Bradley* a79 77
4 b g Dansili Plymsole (USA) (Diesis)
359[8] (474) ◆ 522[2] 1254[15] 2165[15] 2572[3] 3281[5] 3960[4] 4535[3] 5093[2] 5933[9]
Solemia (IRE) *C Laffon-Parias* 124
4 b m Poliglote Brooklyn's Dance (FR) (Shirley Heights)
1971a[2] (2570a) 5116a[4] 6295a[3] (6912a) 7872a[13]
Solemn *Milton Bradley* a81 95
7 b g Pivotal Pious (Bishop Of Cashel)
1417[3] 1643[11] 2195[9] (2853) 3188[3] 4013[6] 4924[9] 5343[12] 5832[10] 6800[12] 7019[8]
Solemn Oath (USA) *Ed Vaughan* a75 63
3 b c Elusive Quality(USA) Bathsheba (USA) (Dehere (USA))
(805)
Solent Ridge (IRE) *G M Lyons* a89 86
7 b g Namid Carrozzina (Vettori (IRE))
1043a[14]
Sole Power *Edward Lynam* a101 120
5 b g Kyllachy Demerger (USA) (Distant View (USA))
875a[2] 1146a[2] 2486[2] 3238[3] ◆ 5561[7] (6140) 6908a[5]
Solfilia *Hughie Morrison* a86 83
3 ch f Teofilo(IRE) Suntory (IRE) (Royal Applause)
3284[4] 4412[7] 4598[9] 5426[3] 7131[2] 7511[2] 7895[5] 8227[7]
Solis (GER) *Dianne Sayer* 30
9 ch g In The Wings Seringa (GER) (Acatenango (GER))
4179[15] 4869[8]
So Long Malpic (FR) *T Lemer* a102 109
5 b m Fairly Ransom(USA) Poussiere D'Or (FR) (Marchand De Sable (USA))
2728a[2] 3657a[7] 6088a[2] 8300a[0]
Solo Performer (IRE) *H Rogers* a92 92
7 ch g Distant Music(USA) Royal Pagent (IRE) (Balinger)
(341a) 5397a[14] 7852a[3]
Solvanna *Heather Main* a64 44
2 b f Haafhd Solva (Singspiel (IRE))
3971[2] 4525[7] 5146[6] 5697a[9] 6147[6] 6453[6] 6787[12] 6808[3] 7476[7] 7606[3]
So Lyrical *Peter Makin* a22 37
2 b f Pivotal Caro George (USA) (Distant View (USA))
5357[10] 6153[10] 7323[13]
Somali Lemonade (USA) *Michael Matz* 109
3 b f Lemon Drop Kid(USA) Chic Corine (USA) (Nureyev (USA))
4478a[6]
Somemothersdohavem *John Ryan* a83 81
3 ch g Avonbridge Show Off (Efisio)
159[2] (358) 605[5] 1413[4] 1568[3] 2129[3] 2544[2] 2613[3] (3087) 3330[9] 3592[10] 4225[5] 4776[4] 4972[2] 5323[14] 5744[4] (6037) 6213[2] 6834[4] 7271[4] 7522[9] (7791) 7927[5] 8073[4]
Someone's Darling *Jim Goldie* a40 66
3 b f Jeremy(USA) Green Sensazione (Green Desert (USA))
1218[4] 1671[6] 2019[4] 2261[5] 2594[5] 2837[5] 4387[7] 4767[4] 6707[2] 6952[3] 7745[9]
Somerset Island (IRE) *Michael Smith* a63
4 b g Barathea(IRE) Art Work (Zafonic (USA))
114[5] 369[3] 581[5] (1179) 1583[7]
Somerton Star *Pat Eddery* a40
2 b c Avonbridge Leaping Flame (USA) (Trempolino (USA))
7855[8] ◆
Somethingabouther (USA) *James Cassidy* a81 86
2 b f War Chant(USA) Mountain Bonfire (CAN) (Mt. Livermore (USA))
5031a[5]
Somethingboutmary *Kevin Ryan* a69 42
2 ch f Sleeping Indian Loch Leven (Selkirk (USA))
(1277) ◆ 2252[8] (5160) 5886[4] 6611[12] 7206[7]
Something Else (FR) *J-M Beguigne* a71 74
3 ch f Gold Away(IRE) For Ever Hopefull (Halling (USA))
7267a[7]
Something Magic *Sylvester Kirk* a67 67
2 gb f Proud Citizen(USA) Comeback Queen (Nayef (USA))
2541[3] 3764[8] 5357[5] 5702[3] 6160[14] 7059[5] 7737[6]
Sommerabend *U Stoltefuss* 114
5 b h Shamardal(USA) Sommernacht (GER) (Monsun (GER))
6088a[4] 6913a[9] 7515a[7]
Sommersturm (GER) *David Evans* a64 58
8 b g Tiger Hill(IRE) Sommernacht (GER) (Monsun (GER))
(105) 3552[7] 3979[6] 6305[7] 7472[9] 8264[5]
Somoud (IRE) *J R Jenkins* 73
2 ch c Kheleyf(USA) Harmonist (USA) (Hennessy (USA))
5121[4] 6203[5] (6438) ◆ 6984[12]
Sonara (IRE) *David Evans* a57 39
8 b g Peintre Celebre(USA) Fay (IRE) (Polish Precedent (USA))
8035[9]
Sondeduro *Jamie Osborne* a82 82
3 br g Manduro(GER) Madame Cerito (USA) (Diesis)
2041[7] 2273[11] (2866) 3711[2] 4741[14]
Sondray *Jo Crowley* a53 35
4 b m Diktat Hoh Dancer (Indian Ridge)
130[6] 688[5]
Songbird Blues *Mark Usher* a61 46
3 b f Beat All(USA) Billie Holiday (Fairy King (USA))
38[4] 322[5] 407[2] 518[2] 660[5] 1012[7] 1608[2] 2374[2] 2548[2] 7964[10] 8248[4]
Songburst *Richard Hannon* a84 74
4 b h Singspiel(IRE) Krynica (USA) (Danzig (USA))
2637[16] 3920[12] 4470[9]
Songcraft (IRE) *Saeed Bin Suroor* 113
4 b g Singspiel(IRE) Baya (USA) (Nureyev (USA))
(145a) ◆ (486a) 877a[3] 1149a[8] 3825[2] 4759[4] 5593[3] (5981) 6637[3] 6866[4] 7405[3] 7689[20]
Song Light *David Elsworth* 73
2 b g Echo Of Light Blue Lullaby (IRE) (Fasliyev (USA))
6636[9] 7172[5] ◆ 7637[2]
Song Of Joy (IRE) *Barry Leavy* a62 48
3 b f Oratorio(IRE) Wondrous Joy (Machiavellian (USA))
743[5] 1260[8] 1979[2] 2353[3] 2850[5] 4335[6] 4650[8] 5018[2] 5459[7] 7221[8]
Song Of Parkes *Peter Grayson* a85 79
5 b m Fantastic Light(USA) My Melody Parkes (Teenoso (USA))
1246[6] 2096[8] 2476[2] ◆ 3696[5] 4495[2] 7023[12] (7144) 7411[5] 8008[9] 8143[11]
Song Of The Siren *David O'Meara* a60 79
4 ch m With Approval(CAN) Sulitelma (USA) (The Minstrel (CAN))
1652[11] 2696[10] 3416[10] 4141[8] 4311[3] (4626) 4883[2] 5546[11]
Song Of Victory (GER) *M Weiss* a64 64
8 bb g Silvano(GER) Song Of Hope (GER) (Monsun (GER))
443a[10]
Sonik (FR) *J Heloury* a76
3 b g Irish Wells(FR) Salvia (FR) (Septieme Ciel (USA))
17a[7]
Sonko (IRE) *Tim Pitt* a87 88
3 b f Red Clubs(IRE) Baltic Belle (IRE) (Redback)
(86) 2028[2] ◆ 2914[2] 3861[5] 4044[7] 4881[4] 6234[13] 6935[2] (7648) (7859) 7995[4]
Sonnetation (IRE) *Jim Boyle* a41
2 b f Dylan Thomas(IRE) Southern Migration (USA) (Kingmambo (USA))
7160[12]
Sonning Rose (IRE) *Mick Channon* a48 83
4 b m Hawk Wing(USA) Shinkoh Rose (FR) (Warning)
1156[11] 1609[7] 2503[6]
Son Of May *Jo Hughes* a52 53
3 b g Royal Applause Second Of May (Lion Cavern (USA))
25[4] 270[4] 556[4] 1596[2] 2385[6] 2748[9]
Sonoran Sands (IRE) *Brendan Powell* a92 91
4 b g Footstepsinthesand Atishoo (IRE) (Revoque (IRE))
529[7]
Sonsie Lass *Keith Dalgleish* a72 46
3 b f Refuse To Bend(IRE) Rapsgate (IRE) (Mozart (IRE))
112[2] 201[8]
Son Vida (IRE) *Alan Bailey* a78 57
4 b g Titus Livius(FR) Sombreffe (Polish Precedent (USA))
432[7] 584[5] 751[7] (886) 3311[5] 4042[8] 4141[9] 4889[5] 5751[5] 6051[7] 6317[4] 7251[4] 7413[8] 7733[12]
Soon (IRE) *A P O'Brien* 104
3 b f Galileo(IRE) Classic Park (Robellino (USA))
2101a[6] 2524a[2] 3197a[3] 4376a[6] 5643a[6] 6080a[8] 6518a[7]
Soopacal (IRE) *Brian Ellison* a74 62
7 b g Captain Rio Fiddes (IRE) (Alzao (USA))
133[2] ◆ 371[6] 808[8] 870[3] 996[7] 1242[4] 1383[5] 3209[5] 4085[2] 4187[5] (4406) 4769[3] 4866[9] 5543[6]
Sooraah *William Haggas* a108 103
5 b m Dubawi(IRE) Al Persian (IRE) (Persian Bold)
245a[8] (586a) 876a[9] 1034[5] 1213[3]
Sophie's Beau (USA) *Michael Chapman* a43 57
5 b g Stormy Atlantic(USA) Lady Buttercup (USA) (Meadowlake (USA))
19[5] 1601[9] 2092[7] 2436[2] ◆ 2551[6] (3018) 3463[6] 4207[8] 4909[4] 5416[6] 7456[7] 8231[7]
Sopran Montieri (IRE) *B Grizzetti* 95
3 b c Manduro(GER) Sopran Londa (IRE) (Danehill (USA))
2324a[8] 2968a[5] 7427a[6]
Sopran Nad (ITY) *Frank Sheridan* a63 57
8 b h Masad(IRE) Sopran Newar (Warning)
550[7] 807[4]
Soprano (GER) *Jim Goldie* 67
10 b g Sendawar(IRE) Spirit Lake (GER) (Surumu (GER))
4867[10] 5922[4] 7102[6]
Sorcellerie *David Elsworth* 66
2 ch f Sir Percy Souvenance (Hernando (FR))
2245[8] 2499[8]
Sorelite (FR) *T De Lauriere* 56
2 bb f Indian Rocket Sorgue (USA) (Septieme Ciel (USA))
7700a[9]
Sorella Bella (IRE) *Mick Channon* a74 105
2 ro f Clodovil(IRE) Anazah (USA) (Diesis)
4055[4] 4494[2] 4730[3] 5153[3] 5274[3] 5551[2] 5904[3] (6132) (6725a) 7076a[2] 7285a[2]
Sorellino (FR) *J Boisnard* a81 96
3 b g Chichicastenango(FR) Fanissa (GER) (Exit To Nowhere (USA))
(475a)
Sorry Woman (FR) *H-A Pantall* 93
2 b f Ivan Denisovich(IRE) Oppamattox (FR) (Munir)
4205a[3] 4696a[5] 6128a[5] (7265a) 7623a[8]
Sortilege (IRE) *A Wohler* 107
4 b m Tiger Hill(IRE) Sahel (GER) (Monsun (GER))
2989a[3] 5399a[7] (7429a)
Soryah (IRE) *Luca Cumani* a66
2 b f Shamardal(USA) Dirtybirdie (Diktat)
8017[6] ◆
Sos Brillante (CHI) *Terry Clement* a80 91
7 b m Dance Brightly(CAN) Strike Out (CHI) (Mashaallah (USA))
765[4] 1129[13] 1213[9] 1431[5] 1677[4] 1883[5] 2066[5] 2478[6] 2640[6] 3190[8] 3633[7] 3860[3] 4248[5] 4764[13] 7054[11]
Sotka *F-H Graffard* 94
3 b f Dutch Art Demerger (USA) (Distant View (USA))
1426a[0]
Sottovoce *Simon Dow* a69 44
4 b m Oratorio(IRE) In A Silent Way (IRE) (Desert Prince (IRE))
225[5] 729[2] 828[7] 1722[4] 2627[6] 3249[5]
Soubrette *George Margarson* a45 15
2 ch f Zafeen(FR) Nihal (IRE) (Singspiel (IRE))
6960[12] 7505[13]
Soul (AUS) *Saeed Bin Suroor* a68 120
5 b g Commands(AUS) Marvilha (AUS) (Night Shift (USA))
(756a) 1147a[12] 2179[6] 3370[4] (4092) 5355[6] 6246[8] 6867[2]
Soul Custody (CAN) *M J Grassick* 91
5 b m Perfect Soul(IRE) Halo's Gleam (USA) (Halo (USA))
2515a[8] 3322a[2]
Soul Intent (IRE) *J W Hills* a56 35
2 b c Galileo(IRE) Flamingo Guitar (USA) (Storm Cat (USA))
6486[15] 7323[7]
Sound Advice *Keith Dalgleish* a68 87
3 b g Echo Of Light Flylowflylong (IRE) (Danetime (IRE))
1473[8] 1819[7] 3274[3] 4553[9] 4674[3] 5752[12] 5888[10]
Sound Affects *Alan Brown* a39 36
2 ch f Compton Place Rare Cross (IRE) (Cape Cross (IRE))
1474[7] 1949[5] 2437[10] 2663[5] 5222[5] 5748[7]
Sound Amigo (IRE) *Ollie Pears* a84 90
4 b g Iceman Holly Hayes (IRE) (Alzao (USA))
554[2] ◆ 1156[3] 1431[6] 2285[7] 2697[12] 4829[2] 5110[2] 6008[3]
Soundbyte *John Gallagher* a71 74
7 b g Beat All(USA) Gloaming (Celtic Swing)
5038[5]
Sound Hearts (USA) *Roger Varian* a81 101
3 bb f Sir Percy Crystal Seas (Zamindar (USA))
1532[4] ◆ 2204[7] 2849[3] 3737[5] 4458[2] (4984) 5328[2] (5856) 6877[3]
Sound Of Guns *Ed Walker* 102
2 b f Acclamation Eastern Lily (USA) (Eastern Echo (USA))
3339[6] (4433) 5307[2] ◆ 6196[3] ◆
Source Of Light (IRE) *Daniel Mark Loughnane* a65 54
3 b f Diamond Green(FR) Alycus (USA) (Atticus (USA))
404[4] (660) 739[5] 3025[11] 4186[2] 4709[4] 5810[5] 6690[4] 6941[4] 6968[5] 7643[6] 7781[11] 7983[10]
Souter Point (USA) *Peter Salmon* a63 82
6 bb g Giant's Causeway(USA) Wires Crossed (USA) (Caller I.D. (USA))
1134[11] 1913[9] 7132[5] 7353[7] 7791[9] 8273[8]
South Cape *Gary Moore* a94 81
9 b g Cape Cross(IRE) Aunt Ruby (USA) (Rubiano (USA))
1792[P] 2498[4] 2867[5] 3659[3] 4243[3] 4470[3] 5239[4] 5628[3] 6801[7] 7496[5]
Southerly *Luca Cumani* a13
3 ch c Shirocco(GER) Jetbeeah (IRE) (Lomond (USA))
2368[12] 3227[16]
Southerness *Rod Millman* a35
8 ch g Halling(USA) Teresa Balbi (Master Willie)
355[10]
Southern Sapphire *Linda Stubbs* a39 44
2 ch g Compton Place Brecon (Unfuwain (USA))
3973[9] 4581[5] 6042[11] 7613[8]
Southern Speed (AUS) *Leon Macdonald & Andrew Gluyas* 115
5 bb m Southern Image(USA) Golden Eagle (NZ) (Zabeel (NZ))
7426a[6]
Southern State (USA) *Mark Johnston* a79
4 ch h Street Cry(IRE) Tigi (USA) (Dixieland Band (USA))
273[2] 355[3] 569[3] 688[2] 820[4] (978) 1186[10] 1525[12]
Southfork *Barry Brennan* a13 70
3 ch g Nayef(USA) New Choice (IRE) (Barathea (IRE))
7528[9]
So Vain (IRE) *David Brown* a37
2 b g Elusive City(USA) Vanitycase (IRE) (Editor's Note (USA))
8262[9]
Sovento (GER) *Alan McCabe* a68 26
8 ch g Kornado Second Game (GER) (Second Set (IRE))
296[4] 7256[11] 7436[16] 7733[13] 7767[11] 8039[8]
Sovereign Debt (IRE) *Michael Bell* 114
3 br c Dark Angel(IRE) Kelsey Rose (Most Welcome)
1653[2] (2022) 3265[9] ◆ (4012) 5278[2] 6634[8] 7238[5]
Sovereign Power *Paul Cole* a54 55
2 b c Royal Applause Tafiya (Bahri (USA))
5275[9] 5534[6] 6486[16] 7708[6]
Sovereign Street *Ann Duffield* 87
4 ch m Compton Place Mint Royale (IRE) (Cadeaux Genereux)
2796[2] 3272[2] (3731) (4393) (5674) 6755[4]
Sovereign Waters *Eve Johnson Houghton* a26 58
3 ch f Haafhd Faraway Waters (Pharly (FR))
4232[4] ◆ 4754[10] 5770[7] 6281[7] 6686[6]
Soviet Dream *James Fanshawe*
3 b g Oasis Dream Soviet Song (IRE) (Marju (IRE))
5679[12] 6397[14]
Soviet Rock (IRE) *Andrew Balding* 79
2 b c Rock Of Gibraltar(IRE) Anna Karenina (USA) (Atticus (USA))
5005[8] 6596[5] (7033)
So Well (FR) *D Considerant*
5 ch g Bad As I Wanna Be(IRE) Naria (IRE) (Green Tune (USA))
7123a[0]
Soweto Star (IRE) *John Best* a71 82
4 ch g Johannesburg(USA) Lady Of Talent (USA) (Siphon (BRZ))
2151[8] 2417[10] 2975[5] ◆ 3388[6] 6329[4] 6931[9] 7310[10] 7473[7] 7905[10] 8067[5] 8189[6]
So Wise (USA) *David O'Meara* a89 68
4 b g Elusive Quality(USA) Intercontinental (Danehill (USA))
3306[7] 4345[6] 4747[9]
So You Think (NZ) *A P O'Brien* a119 129
6 b h High Chaparral(IRE) Triassic (NZ) (Tights (USA))
1160a[4] (2525a) (3267)
Space Artist (IRE) *Bryan Smart* a77 54
2 b c Captain Marvelous(IRE) Dame Laura (IRE) (Royal Academy (USA))
1911[6] 2667[4] 7198[3] (7669) (7866)
Spacecraft (IRE) *Christopher Kellett* a58 44
5 b g Starcraft(NZ) Brazilian Samba (IRE) (Sadler's Wells (USA))
7[2] 109[2] 370[4] 490[4] 676[4] 848[7] 1014[9] 1179[4] 1283[3]
Space Ship *John Gosden* 78
2 ch c Galileo(IRE) Angara (Alzao (USA))
5793[4] ◆ 6164[3] ◆ 6596[4]
Space Station *Simon Dow* a91 94
6 b g Anabaa(USA) Spacecraft (USA) (Distant View (USA))
1373[10] 1741[5] 2068[22] 2444[8] 3772[10] 5120[6] 6171[7]
Space War *Michael Easterby* a75 96
5 b g Elusive City(USA) Princess Luna (GER) (Grand Lodge (USA))
1865[10] 2176[11] 3128[6] 3403[6] 3779[8] 4679[7] 5429[8] 6785[9] (7530)
Spain Blues (FR) *X Thomas-Demeaulte* a76 89
6 b m Anabaa Blue Strike Alight (USA) (Gulch (USA))
83a[0]
Spanish Acclaim *Ruth Carr* a3 74
5 b g Acclamation Spanish Gold (Vettori (IRE))
1526[15] 2475[10] 2618[6] 2815[7] 3943[13]
Spanish Art *Richard Hannon* a64 67
2 b c Byron Spanish Gold (Vettori (IRE))
4873[4] 5911[7] 6301[2] 6945[5]
Spanish Bounty *Mrs A Malzard* a87 91
7 b g Bahamian Bounty Spanish Gold (Vettori (IRE))
5701a[2]
Spanish Duke (IRE) *John Dunlop* a83 103
5 b g Big Bad Bob(IRE) Spanish Lady (IRE) (Bering)
1854[9] 2706[3] 3372[11] 4684[7] 5492[4] 6166[6] 6674[30]
Spanish Fork (IRE) *Mick Channon* 68
3 br g Trans Island Wings Awarded (Shareef Dancer (USA))
1355[4] 1568[6] (2049) 2427[7] 2818[4] 6407[7] 7293[6]
Spanish Legacy *Julie Camacho* 52
3 b f Dr Fong(USA) Spanish Lace (Hernando (FR))
5549[3] 6102[6] 6341[6]
Spanish Plume *Reg Hollinshead* a82 80
4 b g Ishiguru(USA) Miss Up N Go (Gorytus (USA))
1275[13] 2661[6] 4657[2] 5091[8] 5752[7] 6047[5] 6735[6] 6976[6] 7461[3] 7618[10] 7751[10] 7842[10]
Spanish Trail *Christopher Kellett* a54
3 b f Rail Link La Coruna (Deploy)
3189[13] 3946[7] 4188[7] 4888[6] 6056[7] 6988[12] 7632[9]
Spanish Wedding *Marco Botti* a81 87
3 ch g Hernando(FR) I Do (Selkirk (USA))
1707[2] 2258[4] (2889) 3614[5] 5366[2] 6359[3] 7195[6]
Sparkie (FR) *E J O'Neill* 58
2 b g King's Best(USA) Makam (IRE) (Green Desert (USA))
7319a[5]
Sparking *Tom Dascombe* a63 72
5 ch m Exceed And Excel(AUS) Twilight Time (Aragon)
2244[4] 2943[8] (4085) 4235[4] 4420[4] 5877[5] 6529[6]
Sparkling Portrait *Richard Fahey* a84 107
3 b c Excellent Art Time Crystal (IRE) (Sadler's Wells (USA))
(1440) (1888) ◆ 2718[6] 3296[7] ◆ (4261)
Spark Of Genius *James Toller* a73
3 b f Oratorio(IRE) Lolla's Spirit (IRE) (Montjeu (IRE))
2799[8] 7005[3] 7647[4] 7822[2] (7978)
Sparks Fly (FR) *S Kobayashi* a64 54
2 b c Astronomer Royal(USA) Creme De Cuvee (USA) (Cuvee (USA))
3928a[6] 8193a[9]
Spartan King (IRE) *Ian Williams* a62 55
4 ch g King's Best(USA) Thermopylae (Tenby)
28[6] 579[2] 644[5] (966) 1191[7] 1719[6] 2134[2] 2997[6] 3449[5]
Spartan Spirit (IRE) *Hughie Morrison* a76 73
4 b g Invincible Spirit(IRE) Kylemore (IRE) (Sadler's Wells (USA))
(984) 1083[2] 3073[5] 4411[2] 5159[2] 5816[5] 6170[7] (6976)
Spartic *Alan McCabe* a64 69
4 gr g Needwood Blade Celtic Spa (IRE) (Celtic Swing)
6145[9] 7484[10] 7861[2] 8064[3] ◆
Spartilla *Daniel O'Brien* a69 41
3 b c Teofilo(IRE) Wunders Dream (IRE) (Averti (IRE))
2[3] (30) (472) ◆ 1281[3] 2049[4]
Spa's Dancer (IRE) *Ed de Giles* a86 101
5 b g Danehill Dancer(IRE) Spa (Sadler's Wells (USA))
1680[4] 2029[2] ◆ (2855) 2975[2] 3647a[2] 3878[3] 4692a[12] 5609a[6] 6674[19]
Spats Colombo *Micky Hammond* a44 38
2 ch c Notnowcato Charlotte Vale (Pivotal)
6603[9] 7636[8] 7979[4]

Spavento (IRE) *Eric Alston* a61 70
6 gr m Verglas(IRE) Lanasara (Generous (IRE))
1659^4 ◆ (1879) 2539^7 (2840) 3335^7 3775^11 4641^5

Speaking Of Which (IRE) *D K Weld* 116
3 bb c Invincible Spirit(IRE) Suitably Discreet (USA) (Mr Prospector (USA))
(2524a) ◆ 6062a^3 7566a^2 7882a^14

Speak Logistics (USA) *Edward Plesa Jr* a104
2 b c High Cotton(USA) Miss Sabrina (USA) (Summer Squall (USA))
7572a^7

Speak Slowly *T Stack* a37 32
2 ch f Dubawi(IRE) Blond Moment (USA) (Affirmed (USA))
4161a^11

Speak The Truth (IRE) *Jim Boyle* a76 68
6 br g Statue Of Liberty(USA) Brave Truth (IRE) (Brief Truce (USA))
(87) (179) 252^4 710^10 893^5 1050^4 1307^6 1773^4 2165^6 2413^3 6578^9 7299^3 7741^8 7967^4 8159^3

Spechenka (AUS) *Ben Ahrens* 102
7 bb g Danachenka(AUS) Special Class (NZ) (Conquistarose (USA))
7783a^8

Special Glace (FR) *Y Fouin* a57
2 b f Irish Wells(FR) Starglas (FR) (Verglas (IRE))
5570a^0

Special Meaning *Mark Johnston* a63
2 b f Mount Nelson Specifically (USA) (Sky Classic (CAN))
8018^3 ◆ 8201^6

Special Mix *Michael Easterby* a60 73
4 b g Proclamation(IRE) Flaming Spirt (Blushing Flame (USA))
2339^4 2877^3 3232^5 5258^2 6410^15

Special Report (IRE) *Nigel Tinkler* a54 56
2 b g Mujadil(USA) Ellistown Lady (IRE) (Red Sunset)
1435^9 2334^10 3126^11 4449^3 5108^7 5291^2 6310^7 6766^2 6826^5

Special Reward *H-A Pantall* a79 73
2 b f Bahamian Bounty Nellie Gwyn (King's Best (USA))
5899a^7

Specialty (IRE) *Pam Sly* 70
2 b f Oasis Dream Speciosa (IRE) (Danehill Dancer (IRE))
2822^4 3611^3 4246^7 5786^7

Specific (IRE) *Mahmood Al Zarooni* a67 71
3 b f Dubawi(IRE) Miss Particular (IRE) (Sadler's Wells (USA))
1532^6

Specific Gravity (FR) *Sir Henry Cecil* 103
4 b g Dansili Colza (USA) (Alleged (USA))
4684^15 (5583) ◆ 6166^4 6484^15

Spectacle Du Mars (FR) *X Nakkachdji* a106 108
5 b g Martillo(GER) Spectacular Groove (USA) (Trempolino (USA))
315a^4 588a^8 814a^2 3331^20

Speed Date *Ralph Beckett* a66 25
2 b f Sakhee's Secret See You Later (Emarati (USA))
5449^6 5943^4

Speedfit Boy (IRE) *George Margarson* 71
2 b g Red Clubs(IRE) Princess Speedfit (FR) (Desert Prince (IRE))
5213^2 ◆ 5948^4 6411^11

Speedfit Girl (IRE) *George Margarson* a57 75
4 b m Kodiac Staylily (IRE) (Grand Lodge (USA))
1866 2205

Speedi Mouse *Philip McBride* a59 83
3 b f Alhaarth(IRE) Meredith (Medicean)
1844 4664 1979^7 2802^2 (3083) 3589^8 (4772) (5322) 6023^7 7334^3

Speedinthruthecity (USA) *Peter Miller* a96 88
2 bb f City Zip(USA) License To Speed (USA) (Thunder Gulch (USA))
5031a^2

Speedyfix *Christine Dunnett* a61 62
5 b g Chineur(FR) Zonnebeke (Orpen (USA))
1290^7 1734^9 2377^11 2971^6 3707^7 (4439) 5047^7 5327^4 5775^6 6496^7 6836^2 7178^3 7673^5 7915^3

Speedy Star (IRE) *Tina Jackson* 25
3 b g Authorized(IRE) North Sea (IRE) (Selkirk (USA))
5541^5 6408^7 7174^13

Speedy Yaki (IRE) *Daniel Mark Loughnane* a74 71
3 b c Refuse To Bend(IRE) Love In The Mist (USA) (Silver Hawk (USA))
(270) 407^3 (536) 605^2 1392^8 2342^3 3421^5

Speightowns Kid (USA) *Jo Hughes* a80 68
4 rg g Speightstown(USA) Seize The Wind (USA) (Maria's Mon (USA))
1187^2 1828^7 2369^4 3477^3 3761^2 5362^14 6369^8 6688^12 6837^13 7859^5 (7914) 8157^4 8225^2

Spellbound (FR) *M Munch* 81
2 ro f Tertullian(USA) Sky News (GER) (Highest Honor (FR))
5288a^7 7698a^8

Spellmaker *Tony Newcombe* a49 46
3 b c Kheleyf(USA) Midnight Spell (Night Shift (USA))
3079^11 3389^14 4424^3

Spensley (IRE) *James Fanshawe* a95 80
6 ch g Dr Fong(USA) Genoa (Zafonic (USA))
3765^4 4606^8 5129^6 6018^6 6776^3 7147^6 7825^3 8073^6

Speronella *Hughie Morrison* a36
2 ch f Raven's Pass(USA) Rosinka (IRE) (Soviet Star (USA))
7705^8

Spey Song (IRE) *James Bethell* a67 75
4 b m Singspiel(IRE) All Embracing (IRE) (Night Shift (USA))
1439^6 1879^7 2328^5 2414^4 4538^2 5323^10 6458^9 6828^3 7413^11

Sphinx (FR) *Edwin Tuer* a59 78
14 b g Snurge Egyptale (Crystal Glitters (USA))
6428^8 6784^3 7454^9

Spice Fair *Mark Usher* a92 92
5 ch g Trade Fair Focosa (ITY) (In The Wings)
1850^2 2278^12 3241^6 4284^8 4800^13 5306^11

Spice Run *Alastair Lidderdale* a64 29
9 b g Zafonic(USA) Palatial (Green Desert (USA))
1481^4

Spic 'n Span *Ronald Harris* a71 59
7 b g Piccolo Sally Slade (Dowsing (USA))
320^4 380^5 492^5 580^4 823^6 887^10 1483^8 1910^9 2971^3 (3435) 4187^2 4425^3 4758^8 4902^4 5149^3 (5876) 6003^8 6288^4 6563^2 6737^11 7275^14

Spicy (IRE) *Marco Botti* a75 42
2 ch f Footstepsinthesand Shivaree (Rahy (USA))
3783^9 4217^2 4645^2 6453^5 7866^5 8065^5

Spidermania (FR) *Robert Collet* a60 83
3 ch c Gentlewave(IRE) Sudden Storm Bird (USA) (Storm Bird (CAN))
476a^8

Spiders Star *Simon West* 72
9 br m Cayman Kai(IRE) Kiss In The Dark (Starry Night (USA))
2440^11 2698^8 5056^5 5172^5 5384^5 5714^9 6101^7

Spieta (IRE) *Luca Cumani* a40 65
2 gr f Shirocco(GER) Zarawa (IRE) (Kahyasi)
5339^5 6257^5 7357^6

Spifer (IRE) *Marco Botti* a91 97
4 gr g Motivator Zarawa (IRE) (Kahyasi)
2253^7 2933^6 4962^4 7109^7 7904^6 8259^3

Spillway *Eve Johnson Houghton* a71
2 b c Rail Link Flower Market (Cadeaux Genereux)
7707^3 8052^2

Spinacre (IRE) *Kevin Prendergast* 99
2 gr f Verglas(IRE) Spinamix (Spinning World (USA))
(6266a) ◆ 6717a^4

Spin Again (IRE) *John Ryan* a77 71
7 b g Intikhab(USA) Queen Of The May (IRE) (Nicolotte)
102^3 ◆ 262^10 328^5 478^8 (972) (1074) 1263^11 1586^3 2146^3 2421^12 (2581) (3052) 3549^7 3790^11 4155^4 4302^7 4660^7 4966^4 6329^7 7202^9 7318^8 7485^9 7857^4 ◆ 7998^8 8004^5 8199^5 ◆ 8261^F

Spinatrix *Michael Dods* 97
4 b m Diktat Shrink (Mind Games)
1476^2 2310^3 3255^7 (3696) (4133) 4880^2 5368^3 6466^4 6515^2

Spin A Wish *Richard Whitaker* a47 55
4 b m Captain Rio Be My Wish (Be My Chief (USA))
3889^4 5708^2 (7599)

Spin Cast *Brian Ellison* a76 75
4 b g Marju(IRE) Some Diva (Dr Fong (USA))
114^3 273^3 330^6 567^4 1002^2 (1266) 1562^2 5767^4 (6251) 6819^4 7409^8

Spin Cycle (IRE) *S Seemar* a91 97
6 b g Exceed And Excel(AUS) Spinamix (Spinning World (USA))
50a^11 589a^8

Spinning Ridge (IRE) *Ronald Harris* a76 72
7 ch g Spinning World(USA) Summer Style (IRE) (Indian Ridge)
85^4 (198) 299^4 (330) 449^3 804^5 941^5 1045^3 (1064) 1342^9 1360^2 2168^5 2399^8 2758^2 3099^5 4155^3 4657^8 5657^6 5941^5

Spinning Waters *Dai Burchell* a44 57
6 b g Vettori(IRE) Secret Waters (Pharly (FR))
2575^9 3102^7 4181^7 4537^3 4904^5 5196^8

Spin Of A Coin (IRE) *Pat Murphy* a87 78
4 b g Oratorio(IRE) Polyandry (IRE) (Pennekamp (USA))
4689^16 6039^10 6317^3

Spirit Dream (ITY) *F Saggiomo* 90
2 b c Spirit Of Desert(IRE) Sogna (USA) (Distant View (USA))
3684a^4

Spirit Man *Paul D'Arcy* a40
2 b c Manduro(GER) World Spirit (Agnes World (USA))
7641^9

Spirit Na Heireann (IRE) *Richard Fahey* 64
3 ch f Dubawi(IRE) Lady Angharad (IRE) (Tenby)
1319^6 2144^4 2605^7 5312^P

Spirit Of Adjisa (IRE) *Andrew Balding* a84 71
8 br g Invincible Spirit(IRE) Adjisa (IRE) (Doyoun)
1505^11 2412^9 4731^5 5830^10

Spirit Of A Nation (IRE) *Jim Goldie* a89 82
7 b g Invincible Spirit(IRE) Fabulous Pet (Somethingfabulous (USA))
1797^2 1880^6 2457^8 3114^8 6517^4

Spirit Of Battle (USA) *A bin Huzaim* a105 105
4 b h Elusive Quality(USA) Victoria Star (IRE) (Danehill (USA))
80a^5 314a^10

Spirit Of Coniston *Paul Midgley* a66 67
9 b g Lake Coniston(IRE) Kigema (IRE) (Case Law)
456^3 696^7 887^5 1242^8 2436^5 3462^5 4245^2 5294^6 5719^4 6104^12

Spirit Of Cuba (IRE) *Kevin Prendergast* a77 104
4 b m Invincible Spirit(IRE) Hecuba (Hector Protector (USA))
2515a^7 4376a^4

Spirit Of Gondree (IRE) *Milton Bradley* a68 69
4 b g Invincible Spirit(IRE) Kristal's Paradise (IRE) (Bluebird (USA))
1391^7 2373^4 2572^13 (3153) 3790^8 3958^7 4872^3 5750^10 6773^7 7486^8 8167^11

Spirit Of Grace *Alan McCabe* a56 70
4 b m Invincible Spirit(IRE) Scottish Heights (IRE) (Selkirk (USA))
106^5 329^8 371^9

Spirit Of Rio (IRE) *Ann Duffield* 68
2 b c Footstepsinthesand Batilde (IRE) (Victory Piper (USA))
4310^4

Spirit Of Sharjah (IRE) *Julia Feilden* a99 97
7 b g Invincible Spirit(IRE) Rathbawn Realm (Doulab (USA))
51a^8 140a^6 260a^3 317a^7 616a^11 8226^5

Spirit Of Success *Michael Bell* a48 66
2 b f Invincible Spirit(IRE) Isabella Glyn (IRE) (Sadler's Wells (USA))
4546^6 7364^13 8033^9

Spirit Of The Air (IRE) *John Joseph Murphy* a54 55
2 b c Soviet Star(USA) Omanah (USA) (Kayrawan (USA))
2184a^4 2779a^6 6550a^11

Spirit Of The Law (IRE) *Ed Dunlop* a74 90
3 b g Lawman(FR) Passion Bleue (In The Wings)
1190^4 (1641) 2088^2 2716^8 3156^2 (4199) 4459^4 5820^6 6193^7 6986^6

Spiritoftomintoul *Sir Henry Cecil* a81 81
3 gr c Authorized(IRE) Diamond Line (FR) (Linamix (FR))
5105^4 5753^2

Spirit Of Xaar (IRE) *Linda Jewell* a74 88
6 b g Xaar Jet Cat (IRE) (Catrail (USA))
90^11 444a^9 631a^11 785^8 987^8 1262^9 7171^11 8105^6 8199^7

Spiritonthemount (USA) *Peter Hiatt* a44 54
7 bb g Pulpit(USA) Stirling Bridge (USA) (Prized (USA))
23^4 111^3 278^12 395^10 2175^11 3086^8

Spirit Quartz (IRE) *Robert Cowell* a103 120
4 b g Invincible Spirit(IRE) Crystal Gaze (IRE) (Rainbow Quest (USA))
1033^2 ◆ 1538a^2 1857^4 2486^3 2664^2 3238^5 3877^4 4762^2 5561^2 6908a^11

Spiritual Art *Luke Dace* a74 61
6 b m Invincible Spirit(IRE) Oatey (Master Willie)
570^10 (786) 992^3 1770^6 4504^5 5481^2 6278^6 6950^11

Spiritual Girl *Michael Bell* 72
2 b f Invincible Spirit(IRE) Clizia (IRE) (Machiavellian (USA))
2492^3 2938^5 4742^6 6541^2

Spirituality (IRE) *Thomas Carmody* a86 77
3 b g Invincible Spirit(IRE) Taibhseach (USA) (Secreto (USA))
(7229a)

Spiritual Star (IRE) *Andrew Balding* 106
3 b c Soviet Star(USA) Million Spirits (IRE) (Invincible Spirit (IRE))
1509^5

Spitfire *J R Jenkins* a73 77
7 b g Mujahid(USA) Fresh Fruit Daily (Reprimand)
13^9 3103^5 4406^4 (7794)

Spithead *Ian McInnes* a59 64
2 b g Tiger Hill(IRE) Cyclone Connie (Dr Devious (IRE))
3009^10 3387^4 3948^5 5161^2 (5484) 6413^2 7026^9 7973^5

Spivey Cove *Ed McMahon* 59
2 b g Royal Applause Cherokee Stream (IRE) (Indian Ridge)
2880^6 ◆ 3611^13 4114^5 4991^7

Splendid Light *John Gosden* a84 74
4 gr g Selkirk(USA) Light Of Morn (Daylami (IRE))
(1065) 1273^5 6702^4 7017^5 7300^10

Splendido (FR) *F Rossi* 110
4 ro m Slickly(FR) Allegrete (FR) (Johann Quatz (FR))
7234a^6

Spoil The Fun (FR) *C Ferland* a102 102
3 ch c Rock Of Gibraltar(IRE) Avezia (FR) (Night Shift (USA))
364a^2 873a^5 (7345a)

Spoken Words *Hugh McWilliams* a34 57
3 b f Fruits Of Love(USA) Jerre Jo Glanville (USA) (Skywalker (USA))
1012^9 2540^10 3209^7 4547^13 7025^8 7981^10 8210^9

Spokesperson (USA) *Frederick Watson* 21
4 b h Henny Hughes(USA) Verbal (USA) (Kingmambo (USA))
3352^8

Spokeswoman (IRE) *Saeed Bin Suroor* a85
2 b f Invincible Spirit(IRE) Devil's Imp (IRE) (Cadeaux Genereux)
(5943) 6777^2 7523^3

Spoke To Carlo *Eve Johnson Houghton* 91
3 b c Halling(USA) Red Shareef (Marju (IRE))
2197^2 2701^3 (3107)

Spoof Master (IRE) *Lydia Pearce* a51 61
8 b g Invincible Spirit(IRE) Talbiya (IRE) (Mujtahid (USA))
985^5

Sporting Club Girl *William Knight* a8
2 b f Kyllachy Validate (Alhaarth (IRE))
6535^9 7104^5

Sporting Gold (IRE) *Roger Varian* a69 60
3 b g Shirocco(GER) Pink Stone (FR) (Bigstone (IRE))
1793^6 2125^6 2585^8 8162^2 ◆

Sposalizio (IRE) *Colin Teague* 51
5 ch g Dr Fong(USA) Wedding Cake (IRE) (Groom Dancer (USA))
1867^9 2288^5 2635^7 2874^4 3277^3 4349^8

Spowarticus *Scott Dixon* a23 4
3 ch g Shamardal(USA) Helen Bradley (IRE) (Indian Ridge)
6765^8 6965^11

Spray Tan *Tony Carroll* 61
2 b f Assertive Even Hotter (Desert Style (IRE))
1903^4 2338^4 3487^6 (5194) 6155^2 6929^7

Spread Boy (IRE) *Alan Berry* a41 56
5 b g Tagula(IRE) Marinka (Pivotal)
903^6 2033^8 2796^4 3026^9 3581^2 3731^4 3888^7 4042^5 4673^6 (4865) 6513^3 6758^3 6959^8 7599^6 7638^5

Spreading *Michael Blanshard* 48
2 b f Ad Valorem(USA) Churn Dat Butter (USA) (Unbridled (USA))
4752^8 6437^4

Springheel Jake *Ann Duffield* a76 84
3 b g Lawman(FR) Rye (IRE) (Charnwood Forest (IRE))
2591^2 2824^4 3354^4 4769^2 5539^8 6338^14

Springinmystep (IRE) *Michael Dods* a72 93
3 b c Footstepsinthesand Joyful (IRE) (Green Desert (USA))
1271^3 2616^8 2979^2 (4588) 5080^8 6075^9 6830^6 7229a^13

Spring In The Air (CAN) *Mark Casse* a110 98
2 b f Spring At Last(USA) Unbridled Run (USA) (Unbridled (USA))
6289a^2 7548a^5

Spring Of Fame (USA) *Saeed Bin Suroor* a114 96
6 b g Grand Slam(USA) Bloomy (USA) (Polish Numbers (USA))
242a^2 (484a) 678a^2 6446^7 (7630)

Spring Secret *Bryn Palling* a53 70
6 b g Reset(AUS) Miss Brooks (Bishop Of Cashel)
2389^6 4183^3 5452^8 5528^5 6159^6 7018^4 7800^5

Spring Tonic *Luca Cumani* a74 70
3 b g Fantastic View(USA) Nukhbah (USA) (Bahri (USA))
4301^4 5555^4 6397^3 6988^8

Spring Venture (USA) *Mark Casse* a102 102
2 ch f Spring At Last(USA) Zahwah (USA) (Rahy (USA))
(6289a) 7547a^13

Spruzzo *Chris Fairhurst* a15 69
6 b g Emperor Fountain Ryewater Dream (Touching Wood (USA))
1794^2 2378^9 2827^3 (3579) 3904^4 4831^9 5056^4 5714^2 6074^10 6407^2

Sputnik Sweetheart *Richard Hannon* a78 83
3 b f Oasis Dream Sachet (USA) (Royal Academy (USA))
1501^8 1736^2 2041^2 (2483) 5107^7 5512^3 (6092)

Spyder *Jane Chapple-Hyam* a40 78
4 b g Resplendent Glory(IRE) Collect (Vettori (IRE))
5063^5 5636^5 6794^2 7131^6 7368^8

Spykes Bay (USA) *Mrs K Burke* a82 72
3 ch g Speightstown(USA) She's A Rich Girl (USA) (Affirmed (USA))
1375^4 2022^9 2451^4 4876^8 6840^9

Spymistress *Tom Dascombe* a49
2 ch f Sakhee's Secret Martha (IRE) (Alhaarth (IRE))
8208^5

Squad *Simon Dow* a76 67
6 ch g Choisir(AUS) Widescreen (USA) (Distant View (USA))
9^6 400^5 4504^9 5038^2 5509^5 6255^8 (7012) 7169^2 7652^6 7927^4 8170^2

Squawk *Bill Turner* a47
2 ch f Sleeping Indian Easy Mover (IRE) (Bluebird (USA))
7727^5 7865^4 8053^4

Squeal (USA) *William Mott*
2 b f Tiznow(USA) Yell (USA) (A.P. Indy (USA))
6944a^2

Squeeze My Brain (IRE) *Ralph Beckett* 72
2 b f Lawman(FR) Arctic Hunt (IRE) (Bering)
4739^6 ◆ 5785^3 6355^2

Squire Osbaldeston (IRE) *Sir Henry Cecil* 72
2 b c Mr Greeley(USA) Kushnarenkovo (Sadler's Wells (USA))
5321^3

Squirrel Wood (IRE) *Mary Hambro* a59 56
4 b m Sadler's Wells(USA) Didbrook (Alzao (USA))
2167^8 2821^6 4652^6 6778^10 7189^3 7816^11

Srimenanti *Brian Rothwell* 62
4 b m Diktat Lady Netbetsports (IRE) (In The Wings)
1382^9 1673^2 1952^12 3440^9 4349^12

Srinagar Girl *Sir Henry Cecil* a78 72
3 b f Shamardal(USA) Adees Dancer (Danehill Dancer (IRE))
1357^7 2335^5 4335^3 4850^4 6229^5 7170^6 7656^2 7787^2 7996^3 8105^2

Sri Putra *Roger Varian* a116 118
6 b h Oasis Dream Wendylina (IRE) (In The Wings)
(1749) 2106a^6 3267^5 3880^7 (4610) 5490^6 7872a^17

Srucahan (IRE) *P D Deegan* a80 84
3 b g Kheleyf(USA) Giveupyeraulsins (IRE) (Mark Of Esteem (IRE))
6270a^7

Ssafa *J W Hills* a76 75
4 b m Motivator Orange Sunset (IRE) (Roanoke (USA))
(1311) 1652^10 2859^3 3550^7 4470^5 5310^3 6613^3 6969^5 7356^6

Stadium Of Light (IRE) *Shaun Harris* a75 39
5 b g Fantastic Light(USA) Treble Seven (USA) (Fusaichi Pegasus (USA))
1154^14 5241^10 6361^8

Staffhoss *Mark Johnston* a79
2 b c Lucky Story(USA) Jerre Jo Glanville (USA) (Skywalker (USA))
7707^5 (8033) 8211^2

Staff Sergeant *Jim Goldie* a53 87
5 b g Dubawi(IRE) Miss Particular (IRE) (Sadler's Wells (USA))
(1820) 2720^6 3164^8 3493^10 4136^6 4674^2 5540^10 6638^24 7000^8 7203^7

Stage Attraction (IRE) *Andrew Balding* a92 90
4 b g Royal Applause Mona Em (IRE) (Catrail (USA))
1321^3 2082^3 3157^4 3878^12 5535^3

Stag Hill (IRE) *Sylvester Kirk* a61 45
3 ch g Redback Counting Blessings (Compton Place)
571^4 766^3 923^2 1046^7 3665^8 4198^9 4932^4 5212^4 5945^3 6210^2 6807^3

Stags Leap (IRE) *Dianne Sayer* a85 69
5 b g Refuse To Bend(IRE) Swingsky (IRE) (Indian Ridge)
3114^3 3519^6 4176^4 4590^5 4867^5 6137^5

Stagweekend (IRE) *John Quinn* 67
2 b g Footstepsinthesand Basin Street Blues (IRE) (Dolphin Street (FR))
6099^6 6779^2 7096^7

Staigue Fort *Emma Lavelle* a46
4 b g Kirkwall Mulberry Wine (Benny The Dip (USA))
7996^6

Stamford *Mahmood Al Zarooni* 75
2 b g Dubawi(IRE) Pure (Slip Anchor)
2784[3] 6636[4]

Stamp Duty (IRE) *Suzzanne France* a63 67
4 b g Ad Valorem(USA) Lothian Lass (IRE) (Daylami (IRE))
274[6] 450[8] (532) 725[8] 843[5] 1528[8] 1634[7] 2091[7] 2438[7] 3712[5] 5259[11] 8111[2]

Stand Guard *John Butler* a91 70
8 b g Danehill(USA) Protectress (Hector Protector (USA))
(582) 809[2] (1339) 1632[4] 7810[8] (7980) (8082) 8228[5]

Standing Bear (IRE) *Paul Cole* a47 62
2 b g Excellent Art Sweet Sioux (Halling (USA))
2648[5] 2983[4] 3733[7] 4540[7]

Standing Strong (IRE) *Robert Mills* a84 70
4 b g Green Desert(USA) Alexander Three D (IRE) (Pennekamp (USA))
1825[7] 2041[3] 2665[2] 3157[9] 3389[4] 3843[4] 4252[7] 4517[9]

Stand My Ground (IRE) *Mme Pia Brandt* a92 108
5 b g Cape Cross(IRE) Perfect Hedge (Unfuwain (USA))
1745a[7] 3900a[4] 4316a[8] 7123a[7] 7985a[9]

Stand N Applaude *David Nicholls* a17 65
2 b c Royal Applause Neardown Beauty (IRE) (Bahhare (USA))
1818[10] 2376[9] 3182[8] 5109[7] 5920[9] 6953[5] 7223[10]

Stand Of Glory (USA) *David Simcock* 76
2 b g Oasis Dream Matroshka (IRE) (Red Ransom (USA))
4419[3] (5168) 5711[3] 6022[5]

Standpoint *Conor Dore* a88 85
6 b g Oasis Dream Waki Music (USA) (Miswaki (USA))
5[5] 158[2] 391[6] 548[2] (603) 907[2] 1134[8] 1341[3] (1718) 2083[8] 2405[7] 2810[9] 2985[3] 3503[10] 4511[2] (4722) (5012) (5345) 6076[4] 6170[11] 6987[12] 7461[10] 7842[9] 8000[3] 8082[3] 8136[4] 8191[6]

Stand To Reason (IRE) *Mikael Magnusson* a83 101
4 ch g Danehill Dancer(IRE) Ho Hi The Moon (IRE) (Be My Guest (USA))
(1513) 1999[2] 2911[4] 3372[15] 4112[4] 5558[10] 7175[5]

Stanley Rigby *Richard Fahey* a65 59
6 b g Dr Fong(USA) Crystal (IRE) (Danehill (USA))
1598[11] 2593[6] 4138[5] 4682[5] 5226[3] 5761[3] 6561[6] 7603[6] 8060[3]

Stans Deelyte *Lisa Williamson* a55 53
3 ch f Primo Valentino(IRE) Wot A Liberty (Piccolo)
4970[6] 5624[10] 7253[4] 7465[11] 7746[10]

Stansonnit *Alan Swinbank* a81 63
4 b g Shirocco(GER) Twilight Sonnet (Exit To Nowhere (USA))
287[11] 2034[2] (2823)

Star Billing (USA) *John Shirreffs* a116 114
4 b m Dynaformer(USA) Topliner (USA) (Thunder Gulch (USA))
7549a[8]

Starboard *John Gosden* 111
3 b c Zamindar(USA) Summer Shower (Sadler's Wells (USA))
2198[2] (2920) 4385a[4] 5250a[4] (6508a)

Star Bonita (IRE) *David Simcock* a46
3 b f Invincible Spirit(IRE) Honour Bright (IRE) (Danehill (USA))
635[8] 921[4]

Starbotton *James Bethell* 70
2 b f Kyllachy Bonne Etoile (Diesis)
1671[7] 2261[8] (3110) 4071[7] 5088[11] 5544[8]

Star Breaker *Sylvester Kirk* 78
2 b g Teofilo(IRE) Bunditten (IRE) (Soviet Star (USA))
2231[10] (3191) 3823[4] 4847[8]

Starbright (IRE) *Kevin Prendergast* 98
2 b f Duke Of Marmalade(IRE) Starry Messenger (Galileo (IRE))
6081a[5] 6717a[6]

Star City (IRE) *Michael Dods* a69 75
3 b g Elusive City(USA) Teacher Preacher (IRE) (Taufan (USA))
1560[9] 2375[6] 2865[3] (4211) 5185[3] 5415[5] 5728[5] 6052[4] 6308[7] 6479[5] (6941)

Star Commander *Mark H Tompkins* a89 90
4 b g Desert Style(IRE) Barakat (Bustino)
1418[3] (2174) (2474) ◆ 5079[4]

Star Date (IRE) *Gerard Butler* a82 86
3 b g Galileo(IRE) Play Misty For Me (IRE) (Danehill Dancer (IRE))
1155[2] 1976[4] (2313) 2701[F] 3280[4] 4103[4] ◆ 4621[6] 7082[10] 7617[8] 8020[14]

Star Deal (IRE) *Alan Swinbank* 78
3 b g Elusive City(USA) Cinzia Vegas (IRE) (Dr Fong (USA))
1864[5] 2226[3] 2592[2] (3352)

Star Dust Melody (FR) *N Caullery* a74 90
4 b m Chichicastenango(FR) Dark Beauty (Singspiel (IRE))
15a[0]

Starfield *John Gosden* a93 87
3 b g Marju(IRE) Sister Moonshine (FR) (Piccolo)
4797[2] 6792[9] (7384) 7904[5]

Star For Life (USA) *Mikael Magnusson* a69 83
3 bb c Giant's Causeway(USA) Clerical Etoile (ARG) (The Watcher (USA))
869[4] 1976[2] 2708[10] 6770[6] 7194[10]

Stargazy *Alastair Lidderdale* a18 58
8 b g Observatory(USA) Romantic Myth (Mind Games)
3007[10]

Star Hill *Alan King* a69 47
5 b m Starcraft(NZ) Mistress Bankes (IRE) (Petardia)
5239[6] 5936[10]

Starki (FR) *H-A Pantall* a69 68
2 b c Meshaheer(USA) Starks (FR) (Daylami (IRE))
7699a[2] 8276a[8]

Star Kingdom (IRE) *Brian Ellison* a51 65
3 b g Marju(IRE) Appetina (Perugino (USA))
1331[5] 1709[9] 3450[8] 3719[4] 4592[4] ◆ 5000[7] (5762) 5938[8] 6758[4]

Star Kodiak (IRE) *A Di Dio* 94
3 b f Kodiac Red Fanfare (First Trump)
1409a[6]

Star Lahib (IRE) *Mark Johnston* 82
3 b f Cape Cross(IRE) Cannikin (IRE) (Lahib (USA))
(5679)

Starlette (FR) *P Bary* 64
2 b f Diableneyev(USA) Stella Berine (FR) (Bering)
4476a[3]

Starlight Angel (IRE) *Ronald Harris* a55 70
2 b f Dark Angel(IRE) King Of All (IRE) (King Of Clubs)
2912[2] ◆ 3269[21] 4220[4] 4836[4] 5146[4] 6282[2] (6564) 6984[8] 7220[10]

Starlight Secret *Simon Earle* a37 22
3 b g Exceed And Excel(AUS) Caribbean Star (Soviet Star (USA))
1723[12] 2147[9] 2361[8] 4424[6]

Starlight Symphony (IRE) *Eve Johnson Houghton* a49 77
2 b f Oratorio(IRE) Phillippa (IRE) (Galileo (IRE))
3339[9] 4217[5] (4494) 5361[8]

Star Links (USA) *S Donohoe* a88 89
6 b g Bernstein(USA) Startarette (USA) (Dixieland Band (USA))
391[4] (5429) (5888) 7842[12]

Starlish (IRE) *E Lellouche* a103 106
7 b h Rock Of Gibraltar(IRE) Stylish (Anshan)
1971a[6]

Starluck (IRE) *David Arbuthnot* a99 55
7 gr g Key Of Luck(USA) Sarifa (IRE) (Kahyasi)
1139[6] 4363[9] 6018[11]

Star Maid *Tony Carroll* 21
2 b f Assertive Angel Maid (Forzando)
2763[6] 3217[6] 4651[8] 5654[8] 6983[6]

Star Of Broadway *Mahmood Al Zarooni* a51 64
2 b c Echo Of Light Susie May (Hernando (FR))
5319[11] 5619[3] 6214[9] 7026[11]

Star Of Mayfair (USA) *Alan Jarvis* 68
2 ch c Tale Of The Cat(USA) Kinsale Lass (USA) (Royal Academy (USA))
4845[4] 6020[13] 7373[8]

Star Of Missouri *Mark H Tompkins* 66
2 ch g Namid Missouri (Charnwood Forest (IRE))
4066[12] 5005[6] 5792[10] 6414[7]

Star Of Namibia (IRE) *J S Moore* a55
2 b c Cape Cross(IRE) Sparkle Of Stones (FR) (Sadler's Wells (USA))
7900[8]

Star Of Rohm *Michael Bell* a75 81
2 ch g Exceed And Excel(AUS) Noble Desert (FR) (Green Desert (USA))
2213[4] 2587[5] 3074[2] 3378[8] 4526[2] 6032[4] 7198[2]

Staros (IRE) *E Lellouche* 109
4 b h Aussie Rules(USA) Stylish (Anshan)
5030a[7]

Star Pearl (USA) *Roger Varian* 52
2 b f Tapit(USA) Lexi Star (USA) (Crypto Star (USA))
5550[6]

Star Request *Keith Dalgleish* 62
2 b f Urgent Request(IRE) Carahill (AUS) (Danehill (USA))
4710[8] 4907[4] 5727[2] 6707[4] 6953[6] 7687[6]

Star Rover (IRE) *David Evans* a95 98
5 ch g Camacho Charlene Lacy (IRE) (Pips Pride)
1157[14] 1975[11] 2488[15] 3612[9] 3919[5] 4317[22] 4814[9]

Starscope *John Gosden* 110
3 ch f Selkirk(USA) Moon Goddess (Rainbow Quest (USA))
1454[4] 1884[2] 2232[3] 3328[2] 3879[4]

Star Seed (FR) *M Rolland* a84 89
3 b f Layman(USA) Nefouda (FR) (Neverneyev (USA))
5473a[9] 6752a[7]

Star Sequence (IRE) *Hugo Palmer* a49
2 b f Tagula(IRE) Sonic Night (IRE) (Night Shift (USA))
4433[12] 8303[3]

Starship Sulu (USA) *Jose Pinchin*
3 ch c Wildcat Heir(USA) Sweetsouthernjazz (USA) (Kentucky Jazz (USA))
8278a[2]

Stars In Your Eyes *John Gosden* a69
4 b m Galileo(IRE) Apache Star (Arazi (USA))
292[3] (546)

Stars Legacy *George Moore*
3 b f Presidium Pagan Star (Carlitin)
2592[9] 4780[11] 6341[12]

Starspangledbanner (AUS) *A P O'Brien* a103 111
6 ch h Choisir(AUS) Gold Anthem (AUS) (Made Of Gold (USA))
5137a[6] 6268a[2] 6913a[11] 7390a[4] 7571a[10]

Star Spun (USA) *David Barron* a60 60
2 ch c Hard Spun(USA) Starr's Star (USA) (Fenter (USA))
4545[7] 6099[9] 7459[5]

Stars To Shine (USA) *Mark Frostad* a107 109
5 bb m Tale Of The Cat(USA) Gaily Lady (USA) (Silver Hawk (USA))
5376a[9] 6298a[3] 7093a[9]

Starstuded (IRE) *Martyn Meade* a61 52
4 b m Galileo(IRE) Miss Demure (Shy Groom (USA))
1380[3] 1624[11]

Star Surprise *Michael Bell* a92 93
4 ch h Dubawi(IRE) Dubai Surprise (IRE) (King's Best (USA))
3890[3] 4223[7] 5794 9 7083[13]

Star System (IRE) *F Head* 76
2 b c Danehill Dancer(IRE) Silver Rain (FR) (Rainbow Quest (USA))
3714a[3]

Start Right *Saeed Bin Suroor* a102 108
5 b g Footstepsinthesand Time Crystal (IRE) (Sadler's Wells (USA))
51a[3] ◆ 246a[4] 587a[3] 1130[13] 3635[6] 4684[3] 5492[9] 5835[7] 6674[24]

Star Up In The Sky (USA) *Kevin Ryan* a71 77
2 rg f Speightstown(USA) Prenuptial Plans (USA) (Runaway Groom (CAN))
2938[4] 3269[17] 4651[2] (5620)

Starwatch *John Bridger* a89 94
5 b g Observatory(USA) Trinity Reef (Bustino)
1416[10] 2657[6] (3105) 3667[12] 4287[3] 4529[5] 4689[13] 5301[6] 5535[7] 6831[7]

Stasio (USA) *David Simcock* a84
2 b c Street Boss(USA) Believe (USA) (Chimes Band (USA))
7324[2] (7773) ◆

State Senator (USA) *Richard Ford* a66 73
4 bb g Mr Greeley(USA) Summer Night (Nashwan (USA))
8146[8]

Statue Of Dreams (IRE) *James Bernard McCabe* a63 85
6 b g Statue Of Liberty(USA) Phyliel (USA) (Lyphard (USA))
4380a[6] 5641a[5] 6270a[6]

Stature (IRE) *Andrew Balding* 98
3 b g Montjeu(IRE) Pescia (IRE) (Darshaan)
2271[2] 2718[4] (3668) (4009) 4700[15] 6025[16] 6348[2] 6875[7]

Status Symbol (IRE) *Anthony Carson* a86 96
7 ch g Polish Precedent(USA) Desired (Rainbow Quest (USA))
427[8]

Steady Gaze *Richard Rowe* a72 52
7 b g Zamindar(USA) Krisia (Kris)
(278) (309) 673[6] 2863[7] 3498[8]

Steady Nelly *Frank Sheridan*
3 b f Multiplex Ellen Mooney (Efisio)
1826[10]

Steel City Boy (IRE) *Ann Stokell* a65 63
9 b g Bold Fact(USA) Balgren (IRE) (Ballad Rock)
8[7] 100[5] 139[8] 912[7] 1343[4] 1516[7] 2046[4] 2350[3] 2690[9] 2815[9] 3256[8] 5203[10] 5681[9] 7351[2] 7633[5] 7794[4] 7914[5] 8298[10]

Steelcut *Mark Buckley* a76 79
8 b g Iron Mask(USA) Apple Sauce (Prince Sabo)
87[7] 251[10] 327[3] 388[2] 461[2] 719[2] (870) (1082) 1300[5] 1630[3] 1720[4] 2133[2] 2476[5] (3390) 3778[9] 4400[4] 4963[5] 5272[9] 7666[12] 7775[7] 7937[2] 8285[8]

Steeler (IRE) *Mark Johnston* 116
2 ch c Raven's Pass(USA) Discreet Brief (IRE) (Darshaan)
4327[2] (4803) 5488[2] (5904) (6671) ◆ 7398[3]

Steel Rain *Nikki Evans* a48 63
4 b g Striking Ambition Concentration (IRE) (Mind Games)
4236[6] 4425[5] 4535[9] 5876[6] 6288[5] 6737[5] (7275) (7633)

Steelriver (IRE) *James Bethell* a86 63
2 b g Iffraaj Numerus Clausus (FR) (Numerous (USA))
6049[6] (6978) ◆

Steel Stockholder *Mel Brittain* a74 76
6 b g Mark Of Esteem(IRE) Pompey Blue (Abou Zouz (USA))
1384[6] 1520[2] 2924[9] (3257) 3615[9] 4043[4] 4315[3] 4783[8] 5341[2] (5543) 5802[6] 6047[4] 6127[6] (6709)

Steely *Gary Moore* a63 75
4 b g Librettist(USA) No Comebacks (Last Tycoon)
1613[5] (2394) (2651) 3222[9] 3769[3] 4606[3] 4983[10]

Steely Grace (IRE) *M Halford* a47 71
3 b f Refuse To Bend(IRE) Daganya (IRE) (Danehill Dancer (IRE))
7952[4]

Steer By The Stars (IRE) *Mark Johnston* 91
2 b f Pivotal Mundus Novus (USA) (Unbridled's Song (USA))
1753[3] 2020[2] 2783[8] (3271) 3858[2] 6160[5] 6475[2] ◆ 6920[8] (7242) 7406[5]

Stella Marris *Christopher Wilson* 45
5 br m Danroad(AUS) Riyoom (USA) (Vaguely Noble)
1987[11] 2436[10] 2749[9] 6479[14]

Stellar Express (IRE) *Michael Appleby* a75 89
3 b f Royal Applause Aitch (IRE) (Alhaarth (IRE))
841[7] 1392[5] 2272[9] (2733) (2820) 3376[7] 3563[8] 4702[12] 5043[5] 5721[10] 6789[10] 6986[5] 7202[8]

Stellato *A Wohler* 88
2 ch c Dalakhani(IRE) Sky Dancing (IRE) (Exit To Nowhere (USA))
7698a[5]

Stelrock (FR) *R Chotard* a83 83
5 b g Kingsalsa(USA) Hill Tiger (IRE) (Indian Ridge)
18a[4]

Stencive *William Haggas* 106
3 b c Dansili Madeira Mist (IRE) (Grand Lodge (USA))
1859[4] 2826[2] (4542) 5089[2] ◆ 6025[2] ◆

Stentorian (IRE) *Gary Moore* a62 86
4 ch g Street Cry(IRE) Nomistakeaboutit (CAN) (Affirmed (USA))
2447[5] 4585[7] 5908[12]

Stephanie's Kitten (USA) *Wayne Catalano* a111 111
3 b f Kitten's Joy(USA) Unfold The Rose (USA) (Catienus (USA))
4478a[4]

Stepharlie *Bryan Smart* a58 51
3 ch f Dutch Art Lady Agnes (Singspiel (IRE))
191[8]

Stepper Point *William Muir* 108
3 b c Kyllachy Sacre Coeur (Compton Place)
1857[13] 2745a[2] 3238[13] 4113[7] 4762[14] 5641a[8] 6292a[7]

Stepping Ahead (FR) *Mrs K Burke* a68
2 ch g Footstepsinthesand Zghorta (USA) (Gone West (USA))
7924[2]

Steps (IRE) *Roger Varian* a84 101
4 br g Verglas(IRE) Killinallan (Vettori (IRE))
1849[3] 2208[8] 3078[5] ◆ 4073[3] (4337) 5077[4] 6244[11] 6666[5] 7063[7] 7397[8]

Steps To Freedom (IRE) *Mrs John Harrington* a109 112
6 b g Statue Of Liberty(USA) Dhakhirah (IRE) (Sadler's Wells (USA))
2318a[3] 5027a[7] 5600[6] 6271a[9]

Stepturn *Michael Wigham* a70 65
3 b g Invincible Spirit(IRE) Gay Gallanta (USA) (Woodman (USA))
1257[3] 2045[7] 7988[3] (8160)

Stetson *Ian Williams* a64 63
6 b g Groom Dancer(USA) Mindomica (Dominion)
7869[4] 8067[2] 8273[4]

Steuben (GER) *Barney Curley* 88
6 ch g Monsun(GER) Schwarzach (GER) (Grand Lodge (USA))
1674[4] 2072[4] 3038[4] 4072[14] 4460[9] 5546[12] 6802[13] 7315[9]

Stevie Gee (IRE) *Mark Buckley* a80 81
8 b g Invincible Spirit(IRE) Margaree Mary (CAN) (Seeking The Gold (USA))
146[4] (186) 2476[11] 4155[11] 4468[7] 5093[12]

Stevie Thunder *Ian Williams* a81 99
7 ch g Storming Home Social Storm (USA) (Future Storm (USA))
1130[8] 1865[11] 3268[7] 4099[13] 4589[2] 6494[5]

Stickleback *Harry Dunlop* a44 51
3 ch f Manduro(GER) The Stick (Singspiel (IRE))
2049[3] 2818[7] 4225[8] 6567[2]

Stiff Upper Lip (IRE) *Richard Hannon* a69 71
2 b c Sakhee's Secret Just In Love (FR) (Highest Honor (FR))
3658[5] ◆ 4253[6] 5119[3] 5786[3] 6096[2] (6363) 6732[3]

St Ignatius *Alan Bailey* a80 80
5 b g Ishiguru(USA) Branston Berry (IRE) (Mukaddamah (USA))
14[8] (109) 370[11] (676) (884) 1391[2] 1588[5] 1829[6] 2031[5] (2363) (2661) (3038) 3594[6] 3703[11] 4944[4] 5583[3] (5767) 6076[6] 6703[5] 8020[12]

Stilettoesinthemud (IRE) *James Given* a50 63
4 ch m Footstepsinthesand The Stick (Singspiel (IRE))
2476[9] 3456[7] 4398[12] 4954[3] 5632[4] 6106[8] 6361[7]

Still I'm A Star (IRE) *David Simcock* a49 72
3 b f Lawman(FR) Aminata (Glenstal (USA))
1532[9] 5309[3] 6190[3]

Stillington *Mel Brittain* 50
6 ch h Exit To Nowhere(USA) First Harmony (First Trump)
2048[10] 3356[11]

Still Standing (FR) *Chantal Zollet*
5 b m Martillo(GER) Solveigh (GER) (Tiger Hill (IRE))
631a[8]

Stipulate *Sir Henry Cecil* 112
3 b g Dansili Indication (Sadler's Wells (USA))
(1455) 1678[4] 2641[2] 3295[2] ◆ 4760[4] 5560[6] 6634[4] 7054[3]

Stirring Ballad *Andrew Balding* a66 104
3 ch f Compton Place Balnaha (Lomond (USA))
2543[4] ◆ 3107[3] 3507[4] (4001) (4473) ◆ (4740) ◆ (5334)

Stir Trader (IRE) *Philip Hide* a82 80
3 b g Titus Livius(FR) Changari (USA) (Gulch (USA))
1560[2] 4605[2] 5340[2] 5878[2] (6686) 6934[12] (8081)

St John's River (USA) *Andrew Leggio Jr* a118
4 b m Include(USA) Adventurous Di (USA) (Private Account (USA))
1839a[2]

St Mary De Castro *Michael Easterby* 47
2 b f Sleeping Indian Bow Bridge (Bertolini (USA))
5255[6] 5733[3] ◆ 6360[5] 6952[9]

St Moritz (IRE) *David Nicholls* a94 112
6 b g Medicean Statua (IRE) (Statoblest)
52a[6] 145a[11] 1158[3] 2656[6] 2819[5] 4248[6] 4628[7] 5677[2] 6242[8] 6426[7] 6470[3] (7638) 7809[9]

St Nicholas Abbey (IRE) *A P O'Brien* 126
5 b h Montjeu(IRE) Leaping Water (Sure Blade (USA))
1149a[2] 1946a[2] (2703) ◆ 4322[3] 5490[3] 6063a[3] 6912a[11] 7573a[3]

Stock Hill Fair *Brendan Powell* 82
4 b g Sakhee(USA) April Stock (Beveled (USA))
2125[3] 2708[8] 3001[3] (3979) 5344[9] (5789) 6472[6] 7109[2]

Stockholm *Rod Millman*
2 b c Auction House(USA) Lady Of Limerick (IRE) (Thatching)
3658[7] 4532[7] 5485[8]

Stoneacre Hull (IRE) *Peter Grayson* a45
3 b f Bachelor Duke(USA) Amount (Salse (USA))
3235[11] 5177[6] 7667[7] 8109[6]

Stoneacre Joe Joe *Peter Grayson* a31
4 b g Proclamation(IRE) It's So Easy (Shaadi (USA))
153[P]

Stoneacre Thirsk (IRE) *Peter Grayson*
3 br f Red Clubs(IRE) Alexander Eliott (IRE) (Night Shift (USA))
5299[7] 6362[7]

Stonecrabstomorrow (IRE) *Michael Attwater* a71 71
9 b g Fasliyev(USA) Tordasia (IRE) (Dr Devious (IRE))
2360[7] 3464[7] 3724[8] 4238[7] 5034[2] (5444) 5625[5] 6171[3] 6306[2] (6578) 7114[4] 7273[5] 7485[4] 7742[7]

Stonefield Flyer *Keith Dalgleish* 100
3 b c Kheleyf(USA) Majestic Diva (IRE) (Royal Applause)
1877[2]

Stone Of Folca *John Best* 102
4 b g Kodiac Soyalang (FR) (Alydeed (CAN))
(2704) 3238[18] 4762[9] 5077[8] 5663[5] 6382[2]

Stones Peak (IRE) *Patrick Martin* a48 83
5 b m Rock Of Gibraltar(IRE) Slupia (IRE) (Indian Ridge)
6716a[3]

Stop On *Chris Grant* a60 76
7 b g Fraam Tourmalet (Night Shift (USA))
460[9] 672[8]

Storma Norma *Tim Easterby* a28 68
2 b f Royal Applause Icing (Polar Falcon (USA))
4710[14] 5222[3] 5709[5] 6132[2] 6657[4] 6955[3] 7242[2] 7840[8]

Stormbound (IRE) *Paul Cole* a75 40
3 b g Galileo(IRE) A Footstep Away (USA) (Giant's Causeway (USA))
1676[4] 1922[5] 2280[11] 7005[5] 7647[3] 7818[4]

Storm Chispazo (ARG) *H J Brown* a92 66
6 br h Bernstein(USA) Chimera (ARG) (Fitzcarraldo (ARG))
140a[5] ◆ 317a[12] 489a[10]

Storm Hawk (IRE) *Pat Eddery* a88 64
5 b g Hawk Wing(USA) Stormy Larissa (IRE) (Royal Applause)
555[6] (810) (1056) 1214[9] 1446[8] 1890[10]

Storming (IRE) *Andrew Balding* a67 67
2 b g Stormy Atlantic(USA) French Lady (NZ) (Entrepreneur)
4604[7] 5275[4] 5742[4] 6597[9]

Storming Honor (SPA) *L A Urbano-Grajales* a92 82
4 b m Storming Home Leventina (IRE) (Anabaa (USA))
1172a[7]

Storming Loose *B Grizzetti* 101
5 bb g Storming Home Dan Loose (IRE) (Danehill (USA))
6727a[6]

Stormin Gordon (IRE) *Noel Quinlan* a44 21
3 b f Tagula(IRE) Karashino (IRE) (Shinko Forest (IRE))
181[12] 663[3] 1067[5] 2010[11]

Storm King *Jane Chapple-Hyam* a101 91
3 b c Shamardal(USA) Tarandot (IRE) (Singspiel (IRE))
4341[4] (5231) (5747) 6400[4] 7064[4] 7774[2] ◆ 8095[4]

Storm Moon (USA) *Mark Johnston* a90 94
2 b c Invincible Spirit(IRE) Storm Lily (USA) (Storm Cat (USA))
(1218) (1579) 2638[5] 3291[9] 4827[2] 5332[5] 6238[5] 6883[10]

Stormont Bridge *Maurice Barnes* a28 57
4 b g Avonbridge Stormont Castle (USA) (Irish River (FR))
3273[8] 3580[3] 4550[4] 4888[10] 5917[8]

Storm Runner (IRE) *George Margarson* a69 58
4 b g Rakti Saibhreas (IRE) (Last Tycoon)
183[3] 225[4] 306[4] 559[2] 821[6] 2464[6] 3052[4] 3964[3] 4158[6] 5052[6] 7126[4] 7500[6] (7816) 7964[5] 8010[2] (8249) (8308)

Storm Tide *Pat Phelan* a25 63
4 b m Tobougg(IRE) Tide Of Love (Pursuit Of Love)
7166[RR] 7480[13]

Storm Tivoli (FR) *A Couetil* 70
2 b c Sageburg(IRE) Crystivoli (FR) (Northern Crystal)
7319a[4]

Stormy Glaz (FR) *Mrs K Burke* a26
3 b g Stormy River(FR) South Island (IRE) (Sadler's Wells (USA))
7981[9]

Stormy Lucy (USA) *Frank Lucarelli* 109
3 b f Stormy Atlantic(USA) Here Comes Lucinda (USA) (Dixieland Band (USA))
4131a[5] 7549a[11]

Stormy Morning *Philip Kirby* a71 69
6 ch g Nayef(USA) Sokoa (USA) (Peintre Celebre (USA))
2827[9] 3402[9] (4766) 5115[8] 5921[2] 6315[3] 7102[2]

Stormy Rush (USA) *Lorne Richards* 101
4 bb h Stormy Atlantic(USA) Willow Rush (USA) (Wild Rush (USA))
7092a[5]

Stormy Times (IRE) *Mark Usher* a48 49
2 b f Redback She's A Softie (IRE) (Invincible Spirit (IRE))
4487[9] 4845[9] 5423[5] 6016[10] 6438[7]

Stormy Weather (FR) *Brian Ellison* 92
6 gr g Highest Honor(FR) Stormy Moud (USA) (Storm Bird (CAN))
4111[10] 4823[7] 5546[2] (6340) 7051[17]

Stormy Whatever (FR) *James Given* a77 74
3 gr c Stormy River(FR) Evening Serenade (IRE) (Night Shift (USA))
2246[13] 2689[13]

Story Of Dubai *M Weiss*
5 b m Dubai Destination(USA) Briery (IRE) (Salse (USA))
631a[7]

St Oswald *Alan Bailey* a83 67
4 b g Royal Applause Susun Kelapa (USA) (St Jovite (USA))
22[5] 553[3] (646) 899[2] 3185[10] 3334[8] (3709) 4042[14] 4190[6]

St Paul De Vence (IRE) *Paul Cole* a77 62
2 b c Oratorio(IRE) Ring The Relatives (Bering)
3368[13] (8178)

Strada Facendo (USA) *Luca Cumani* a85 86
3 ch c Street Cry(IRE) What A Treasure (IRE) (Cadeaux Genereux)
1824[6] 3063[2] 3792[8] 4600[6] 5365[5] (6328) 6768[3]

Straight Shot (IRE) *Brian Meehan* a67 70
3 ch g Manduro(GER) Forest Express (AUS) (Kaaptive Edition (NZ))
1467[5] 1922[10] 6228[6] 7352[4]

Strait Of Zanzibar (USA) *K J Condon* a89 104
3 b g Arch(USA) Royal Opportunity (USA) (Kingmambo (USA))
142a[9] 417a[11] 679a[12] 5397a[8] 7229a[9]

Strandfield Lady (IRE) *H Rogers* a81 94
7 ch m Pairumani Star(IRE) Stylish Chic (IRE) (Arazi (USA))
342a[4] 6066a[3]

Strange Angel (IRE) *David Evans* a42 39
2 gr f Dark Angel(IRE) Nonsense (IRE) (Soviet Star (USA))
3381[8] 3747[12] 5807[4] 6212[7] 7355[7]

Strangelittlegirl *Patrick Gilligan* a17
4 b m Shirocco(GER) Cephalonia (Slip Anchor)
6615[9]

Strange Magic (IRE) *Richard Fahey* 92
2 b f Diamond Green(FR) Blue Daze (Danzero (AUS))
(3748) 4577[6] 6160[10] 6883[13] (7241) 7430a[2] 7828a[4]

Strasbourg Place *Nigel Tinkler* 48
2 ch f Compton Place Photo Flash (IRE) (Bahamian Bounty)
2138[6] 2508[8] 3415[9] 4450[11] 4672[3] 5254[9]

Strategic Action (IRE) *Linda Jewell* a61 58
3 ch g Strategic Prince Ruby Cairo (IRE) (Nashwan (USA))
38[9] 3152[10] 4001[5] 4506[13] (5513) 5994[2] 6585[4] 7482[3] 7861[4] 8249[7]

Strategic Heights (IRE) *Liam McAteer* a45 53
3 b g Strategic Prince Shot Of Redemption (Shirley Heights)
4734[7] 5087[2]

Strathnaver *Ed Dunlop* a72 86
3 b f Oasis Dream River Belle (Lahib (USA))
2194[6] 2583[6] (3388) 4702[2] 5420[5] 7688[8]

Straversjoy *Reg Hollinshead* a72 66
5 b m Kayf Tara Stravsea (Handsome Sailor)
156[4] 381[7]

Strawberry Duck (IRE) *Amy Weaver* 52
2 b f Moss Vale(IRE) Flying Ridge (IRE) (Indian Ridge)
2492[6] 2798[2] 3224[8] 3789[3] 4195[3] 6115[15] 6435[7] 7491[8]

Strawberry Flavour (GER) *James Tate* a63
3 gr f Motivator Strawberry Morn (CAN) (Travelling Victor (CAN))
5889[8] 6457[5] 6736[11] 7383[4]

Strawberrymystique *Marco Botti* a76 71
4 b m Motivator Strawberry Morn (CAN) (Travelling Victor (CAN))
331[5] 533[3] 737[2] (1000) ◆ 3550[6] 4470[4]

Streak *David Lanigan* a64
2 b f Marju(IRE) Eliza Gilbert (Noverre (USA))
(8018) ◆

Streaky Fella (AUS) *Aaron Purcell* 90
7 ch g Street Cry(IRE) Felia (AUS) (Noalcoholic (FR))
7696a[11]

Street Lair (USA) *L Baudron* a89 100
5 ch g Street Cry(IRE) Hideaway Heroine (IRE) (Hernando (FR))
93a[3]

Street Life (USA) *Chad C Brown* a111
3 bb c Street Sense(USA) Stone Hope (USA) (Grindstone (USA))
2954a[4]

Street Map (USA) *Mahmood Al Zarooni* 54
2 b c Street Cry(IRE) Pleione (FR) (Sadler's Wells (USA))
7333[9]

Street Power (USA) *Jeremy Gask* a84 89
7 bb g Street Cry(IRE) Javana (USA) (Sandpit (BRZ))
64[10] 253[12] 669[4] (991) 1066[6] 1708[6] 2071[2] 3281[6] 3960[5] (4286) 4824[12] 6466[16] 6979[9]

Street Secret (USA) *Mme Pia Brandt* a77 101
4 b m Street Cry(IRE) Always Awesome (USA) (Awesome Again (CAN))
1766a[9] 2805a[3] 3653a[12]

Stresa *John Gosden* 75
2 b f Pivotal Bay Tree (IRE) (Daylami (IRE))
5104[10] 5947[3]

Strewth (IRE) *John Best* a61 64
4 ch g Encosta De Lago(AUS) Alpine Park (IRE) (Barathea (IRE))
7805[11] 8023[14] 8297[5]

Strictly Ballroom (IRE) *Mark Johnston* 77
2 b f Choisir(AUS) Desert Alchemy (IRE) (Green Desert (USA))
(3576) 4090[4] 4820[18]

Strictly Mine *Jonathan Portman* a36 53
3 ch f Piccolo My Dancer (IRE) (Alhaarth (IRE))
1303[9] 2162[5] 2803[10]

Strictly Pink (IRE) *Alan Bailey* a74 83
4 b m Kodiac Church Mice (IRE) (Petardia)
88[8] 323[5] (904) 1005[3] (1049) 1254[7] 1481[6] 1934[3] 3944[5] 4187[10]

Strictly Silca *Mick Channon* 87
2 ch f Danehill Dancer(IRE) Silca Chiave (Pivotal)
3034[2] ◆ 3474[4] 4318[2] 4818[4] 5360[6]

Strictly Silver (IRE) *Alan Bailey* a96 98
3 gr c Dalakhani(IRE) Miss Chaussini (IRE) (Rossini (USA))
5271[4] 5517[2] ◆ 5827[2] ◆ 6143[6] 8226[3]

Strident Force *Sir Michael Stoute* a74 78
3 b g Refuse To Bend(IRE) Takawiri (IRE) (Danehill (USA))
1647[6] 2145[3] 3446[7] 3792[9]

Striding Edge (IRE) *Hans Adielsson* a74 81
6 bb g Rock Of Gibraltar(IRE) For Criquette (IRE) (Barathea (IRE))
224[4] 349[4] 400[8] 452[6] (651) 738[6] 1083[5]

Strike A Pose (IRE) *David Evans* a50
3 b f Mujadil(USA) Naked Poser (IRE) (Night Shift (USA))
181[8] 321[4] 524[5] 1006[5] 1337[8]

Strike Force *Alison Hutchinson* a79 77
8 b g Dansili Miswaki Belle (USA) (Miswaki (USA))
150[4] 275[4] 400[7] 3154[2] 3692[U] 4714[7] 4987[5] 6458[10] 7596[5] 7768[7] (7905) 8023[2] 8175[4] 8234[2] 8297[3]

Strikemaster (IRE) *Lee James* a47 67
6 b g Xaar Mas A Fuera (IRE) (Alzao (USA))
2698[3] 3437[7] 4590[7] 5922[8] 6956[5]

Striker Torres (IRE) *Ian McInnes* a76 78
6 ch g Danehill Dancer(IRE) Silver Skates (IRE) (Slip Anchor)
359[4] 447[5] 585[5] 692[4] 1276[2] 1659[12] 2173[3] 3229[3] 3460[3] 3775[14] 4398[6] 4964[2] 5225[7] 6241[4] 7022[10] 7256[3] 7925[7] 8137[5]

Strike The Moon (USA) *Michael Trombetta* a106
4 b m Malibu Moon(USA) Star Kell (USA) (Star De Naskra (USA))
7569a[10]

Striking Cat *Brian Ellison* 17
3 b f Striking Ambition Mozie Cat (IRE) (Mozart (IRE))
1296[8]

Striking Echo *Reg Hollinshead* a52
2 b g Striking Ambition Sunderland Echo (IRE) (Tagula (IRE))
8033[11] 8270[5]

Striking Priorite *Tim Fitzgerald* a46 10
4 b g Striking Ambition Priorite (IRE) (Kenmare (FR))
1988[12] 3026[13]

Striking Willow *Nikki Evans* a45 11
4 b g Striking Ambition Willows World (Agnes World (USA))
8[11] 113[14] 264[6] 379[7] 2760[9] 5193[7]

Stripped Bear (IRE) *Tom Dascombe* a66 38
2 b f Kodiac Triple Zero (IRE) (Raise A Grand (IRE))
1277[2] 1388[6] 1911[8] 2338[8] 3936[3] 4139[3] 4806[4] (5403) 5654[4] 6212[2] 6890[4] 7355[2]

Strix *P Bary* 54
2 ch c Muhtathir Serandine (IRE) (Hernando (FR))
3928a[5]

Strobe *Lucy Normile* a76 53
8 ch g Fantastic Light(USA) Sadaka (USA) (Kingmambo (USA))
6315[10]

Strong Conviction *Mick Channon* 73
2 ch g Piccolo Keeping The Faith (IRE) (Ajraas (USA))
1847[3] 2164[2] 2480[6] 2868[3] 3637[7] 4763[11] 5213[6] 5586[8] 6571[6] (7467)

Stronger (FR) *N Clement* a57 77
3 bl f Early March Ballade Viennoise (FR) (Cricket Ball (USA))
17a[0]

Strong Knight *Tim Walford* a50 58
5 ch g Observatory(USA) Erudite (Generous (IRE))
1598[3] 1952[10]

Strong Man *Michael Easterby* a72 71
4 b g Gentleman's Deal(IRE) Strong Hand (First Trump)
1796[12] 2094[6] 3215[5] 3460[11] 4313[5] (4656) 4890[8] 5084[4] 5543[3] 6053[2] 6811[6] 7446[7] (8115)

Strong Suit (USA) *Richard Hannon* 126
4 ch h Rahy(USA) Helwa (USA) (Silver Hawk (USA))
3237[10] 4100[8] 5355[2] 6030[7] 6246[4]

Strong Vigilance (IRE) *Michael Bell* a81 79
5 ch g Mr Greeley(USA) Zabadani (Zafonic (USA))
224[10] 636[7] 843[9] 1717[11]

Studfarmer *David Evans* 60
2 b c Multiplex Samadilla (IRE) (Mujadil (USA))
(1904)

Studio (USA) *J-C Rouget* a102
3 gr c Political Force(USA) Rare Blend (USA) (Bates Motel (USA))
(211a)

Stunning View (USA) *John Gosden* a73 76
3 bb f Dynaformer(USA) No Matter What (USA) (Nureyev (USA))
2856[9] 3279[7] 4465[3] 6924[2] 7269[8] (8135)

Stupenda *Denis Coakley* a61 55
2 b f Misu Bond(IRE) Opera Babe (IRE) (Kahyasi)
2370[3] 3010[5] (3971) 4947[4] 5361[6] 5763[13] 6946[6] 7439[2]

Style And Panache (IRE) *David Evans* a74 79
4 b m Trans Island El Corazon (IRE) (Mujadil (USA))
1290[2] 1417[13] 2596[5] 3065[8] 3139[11] 3815[3] 3915[5] 4146[6] 4743[6] 4849[5] 5447[7] 6094[7] 6788[7]

Style Boreale (FR) *J Heloury* 85
2 b f Desert Style(IRE) Fleur Boreale (FR) (Sicyos (USA))
4205a[7]

Style Margi (IRE) *Ed de Giles* a65 42
4 b m Desert Style(IRE) Margi (FR) (General Holme (USA))
3972[7] 5050[7] 5720[7] 6252[8]

Style Vendome (FR) *N Clement* 100
2 gr c Anabaa(USA) Place Vendome (FR) (Dr Fong (USA))
(4476a) (5140a)

Stylistickhill (IRE) *Scott Dixon* a70 59
4 gr m Desert Style(IRE) Anemone (Arkadian Hero (USA))
3616[5] 4175[8] 4538[5] 5310[7] 6106[15] (7256) 7618[7] 7844[7] 8051[3]

Sublimation (IRE) *Richard Hannon* 75
2 ch c Manduro(GER) Meon Mix (Kayf Tara)
3119[2] 6486[4] 6876[5] 6947[2]

Sublime Talent (IRE) *Evan Williams* a57 78
6 b g Sadler's Wells(USA) Summer Trysting (USA) (Alleged (USA))
548[10] 771[6]

Submariner (USA) *A bin Huzaim* a102 95
6 ch g Singspiel(IRE) Neptune's Bride (USA) (Bering)
488a[8]

Substantivo (IRE) *Alan Jarvis* 65
2 b c Duke Of Marmalade(IRE) Damson (IRE) (Entrepreneur)
4792[13] 5562[8] 6204[8]

Subtle Difference *Andrew Balding* a65
2 b f Vita Rosa(JPN) Sulitelma (USA) (The Minstrel (CAN))
5230[4] 7199[4] 7707[6] 7974[6] 8093[5]

Subtle Embrace (IRE) *Harry Dunlop* a43 64
3 b f Acclamation Subtle Affair (IRE) (Barathea (IRE))
1313[11] 1941[5] 2759[7]

Subtle Knife *Giles Bravery* a87 90
3 ch f Needwood Blade Northern Bows (Bertolini (USA))
1201[4] 1709[4] (2397) ◆ 3044[2] (3719) 4647[2] (5409) 6176[2] 6830[2] 7334[6]

Suddenly Susan (IRE) *Scott Dixon* a74 61
4 b m Acclamation Westerly Gale (USA) (Gone West (USA))
212[4] 327[2] (385) 461[3] 808[9] 883[5] 1116[6] 1177[5]

Sudden Wish (IRE) *David Evans* a61 54
3 b f Jeremy(USA) Fun Time (Fraam)
(38) 1012[6] 1046[3] 1979[3] 2367[5] 2802[4] 7815[6] 7983[2] 8038[3] 8248[3]

Suedehead *William Muir* a57 49
3 b f Cape Cross(IRE) Oshiponga (Barathea (IRE))
2344[9] 4213[9] 4931[5] 5770[4] 6616[6] 7632[8]

Suegioo (FR) *Marco Botti* a89 91
3 ch c Manduro(GER) Mantesera (IRE) (In The Wings)
2196[2] 3349[3] 4542[3] 5273[2] 6339[2] (7739)

Suehail *David Marnane* a87 88
3 b c Cadeaux Genereux Why Dubai (USA) (Kris S (USA))
5397a[11]

Suffice (IRE) *Richard Fahey* 79
3 b g Iffraaj Shallat (IRE) (Pennekamp (USA))
2380[3] 3273[2]

Sugar Beet *Ronald Harris* a92 96
4 b m Beat Hollow Satin Bell (Midyan (USA))
405[4] 711[5] 871[9] (1417) 1494[3] 1849[6] 2286[6] 4336[2] 4838[9] 5814[3] 6072[10] 6286[7] 7080[2] 7503[8] 7817[11]

Sugar Blaze *Jim Goldie* 48
2 ch f Orientor Harrken Heights (IRE) (Belmez (USA))
2456[3] 3378[7]

Sugar Coated (IRE) *Michael Bell* 49
2 b f Duke Of Marmalade(IRE) Crystal Curling (IRE) (Peintre Celebre (USA))
7553[7]

Sugarformyhoney (IRE) *Seamus Durack* a85 76
3 ch f Dutch Art Sweetsformysweet (USA) (Forest Wildcat (USA))
3917[8] 4474[13] 5420[9] 6209[9] 7524[2] 7722[3] ◆ 7827[5]

Sugar Hiccup (IRE) *David Simcock* 80
4 b m Refuse To Bend(IRE) Raysiza (IRE) (Alzao (USA))
2077[2] ◆ 2909[3] 3400[8] 4326[4] 4731[2]

Sugar House (USA) *Mahmood Al Zarooni* a81 65
2 ch f Distorted Humor(USA) Malibu Mint (USA) (Malibu Moon (USA))
2812[2] 3590[8] (4217)

Sugar Lips *Simon Dow* a56
3 b f Byron Maria Bonita (IRE) (Octagonal (NZ))
7822[7] 8080[5] 8295[2]

Sugar Loaf *William Muir* a63 28
3 b f Singspiel(IRE) Annapurna (IRE) (Brief Truce (USA))
2382[13] 3044[11]

Sugar Prince (IRE) *Tim Pitt* a69
3 b c Strategic Prince Security Tiger (IRE) (Desert Prince (IRE))
298[4] 730[2] 969[11] 1072[5] 3701[10]

Sugar Rock *Andrew Balding*
2 b f Beat Hollow Sweet Mandolin (Soviet Star (USA))
7721[13]

Suggestive Boy (ARG) *Ronald McAnally* a115 116
4 b h Easing Along(USA) Suffrage (USA) (Horse Chestnut (SAF))
7575a[7]

Suhailah *Michael Attwater* a54 32
6 ch m Sulamani(IRE) Vrennan (Suave Dancer (USA))
895[9] 1770[7] 2175[7] 7303[15]

Suhaili *David Lanigan* 92
4 b g Shirocco(GER) Mezzogiorno (Unfuwain (USA))
2504[16]

Suhayl Star (IRE) *Paul Burgoyne* a48 64
8 b g Trans Island Miss Odlum (IRE) (Mtoto)
126[4] 297[8] 396[9]

Suits Me *David Barron* a106 102
9 ch g Bertolini(USA) Fancier Bit (Lion Cavern (USA))
242a[4] 1273[4] 2176[4] 2810[6] 3534[8] 4795[3] 5492[5] 7030[12]

Suivez L'Argent *Joseph Tuite* a53 58
2 b f Pastoral Pursuits Tuppenny (Salse (USA))
1165[2] 1253[3] 1330[4] 1629[3] 2349[6] (2462) 2798[3] 4462[7] 4659[7]

Sujet Bellagio *Brian Meehan* a78 78
3 b g Acclamation Markova's Dance (Mark Of Esteem (IRE))
181[3] (298) 3912[3] 4218[7] 4965[4] 5676[7] 6150[11] 6542[3]

Sula Two *Ron Hodges* a71 85
5 b m Sulamani(IRE) There's Two (IRE) (Ashkalani (IRE))
(3073) (3307) 3813[4] 4515[9] (4905) 5580[8] 5816[3] 6170[3] 6703[12]

Sulis Minerva (IRE) *Jeremy Gask* a94 80
5 b m Arakan(USA) Lacinia (Groom Dancer (USA))
(251) 525[2] 710[6] 1204[6] 1417[4] (1727) 2023[6] 2488[5] 2940[14] 3595[7] 3815[4] 4231[3] ◆ 7817[9] 8008[4] 8272[3]

Sulky Sheila (IRE) *Tim Easterby* 47
2 b f Aussie Rules(USA) Stroppy (IRE) (Xaar)
2261[9] 2686[10] 3019[2] 3951[4] 4395[6] 5313[8] 5916[5]

Sulle Orme (FR) *C Ferland* a108 110
4 gr g Chichicastenango(FR) Santa Lady (FR) (Double Bed (FR))
3657a[5] 4316a[5] 5649a[5] 7124a[2] 7515a[9]

Sumani (FR) *Simon Dow* a66 13
6 b g Della Francesca(USA) Sumatra (IRE) (Mukaddamah (USA))
28[3] 303[6] (738) 963[7] 1205[6] 1984[13]

Summer Cider (IRE) *D Guillemin* 69
2 ch f Shirocco(GER) Hold The Thought (Galileo (IRE))
5570a[3]

Summer Dancer (IRE) *Paul Midgley* a76 77
8 br g Fasliyev(USA) Summer Style (IRE) (Indian Ridge)
1917[5] 5341[9] (6308) 6479[8] 6934[5]

Summer Dream (IRE) *Marco Botti* 75
2 b f Oasis Dream Star On Stage (Sadler's Wells (USA))
2892[3] 3590[8] 4525[3] 5818[4] 7079[4]

Summer Front (USA) *Christophe Clement* a105 110
3 b c War Front(USA) Rose Of Summer (USA) (El Prado (IRE))
5375a^3 6902a^3 7882a^6
Summerinthecity (IRE) *David Nicholls* a81 94
5 ch g Indian Ridge Miss Assertive (Zafonic (USA))
1844^2 2284^6 2707^8 3183^9 6938^7 7080^4 7789^9 7966^10 8232^5
Summer Isles *Ed Vaughan* a62 72
2 b f Exceed And Excel(AUS) Summer's Lease (Pivotal)
2245^6 2892^4 3313^4 4927^9 6490^7 7060^6 7724^7 7865^5 7930^10
Summer Of Fun (USA) *George Weaver* 106
2 bb f Include(USA) Royal Innocence (USA) (Royal Anthem (USA))
6289a^10 7547a^3
Summer Sun *Phil McEntee* a53 50
3 b f Oratorio(IRE) Woodland Glade (Mark Of Esteem (IRE))
4301^6 4434^8 4746^8 6930^7 7316^9 7729^9 7770^3 7804^2 7903^2 8021^4 8154^3 8251^2
Summertime (DEN) *Francisco Castro*
3 b f Binary File(USA) Female Voice (SWE) (Be My Chief (USA))
(4359a)
Summit County (USA) *Dale Romans* a86 94
2 bb c Any Given Saturday(USA) Socorro County (CAN) (Katahaula County (CAN))
7568a^12
Summit Surge (IRE) *Luca Cumani* a114 106
8 b g Noverre(USA) Lady Peculiar (CAN) (Sunshine Forever (USA))
145a^13 319a^7 792a^11
Sum Of The Parts (USA) *Thomas Amoss* a113 100
3 bb c Speightstown(USA) Enjoy The Moment (USA) (Slew's Royalty (USA))
7574a^4
Sunblazer (IRE) *William Muir* a74 6
2 gr g Dark Angel(IRE) Damask Rose (IRE) (Dr Devious (IRE))
5704^8 6214^10 6501^2 6841^2 7814^6 7994^7 8032^8
Sunbula (USA) *Charles Hills* 64
2 ch f Singspiel(IRE) Uroobah (USA) (Dynaformer (USA))
7329^5
Sun Central (IRE) *William Haggas* 98
3 ch c Galileo(IRE) Bordighera (USA) (Alysheba (USA))
2266^3 (3606) ◆ 4323^2 ◆ (5078) ◆ 6025^19
Sundae *K F Clutterbuck* a47 8
8 b g Bahamian Bounty Merry Rous (Rousillon (USA))
839^4 2251^13
Sunday Bess (JPN) *Tom Dascombe* a81 87
4 b m Deep Impact(JPN) Lhiz (CHI) (Hussonet (USA))
(5931) 6379^4 7510^13 7771^9
Sunday Nectar (IRE) *X Thomas-Demeaulte* a82 103
4 b m Footstepsinthesand Pop Alliance (IRE) (Entrepreneur)
814a^9 4764^2 6726a^6 8300a^0
Sunday Times *Peter Chapple-Hyam* 108
3 b f Holy Roman Emperor(IRE) Forever Times (So Factual (USA))
1454^6 1884^10 3542^12 (6161) 7048^10
Sun Dream *Tony Carroll* a46 64
5 b m Desert Sun I Have A Dream (SWE) (Mango Express)
736^8 972^12 7898^13
Sunley Pride *Mick Channon* a83 79
3 ch g Three Valleys(USA) Sunley Scent (Wolfhound (USA))
770^2 (1166) 3284^7 3698^3 4218^5 4534^5 5214^2 5837^5 6401^3 6701^5 (7203) 7360^9
Sunny Bank *Andrew Balding* a58 59
3 b g Notnowcato Sweet Mandolin (Soviet Star (USA))
6398^5 7016^7 7490^11 7718^4 7921^5
Sunnybridge Boy (IRE) *Mrs K Burke* 84
3 br g Strategic Prince Reem One (IRE) (Rainbow Quest (USA))
4293^2 (5387) 6376^13 7032^10
Sunny Future (IRE) *Malcolm Saunders* a26 77
6 b g Masterful(USA) Be Magic (Persian Bold)
2233^5 2423^4 3102^2 4096^7 (4756) 5772^2 6738^11 7018^2 7269^3
Sunny Hollow *James Toller* a61 57
2 b f Beat Hollow Corndavon (USA) (Sheikh Albadou)
4704^8 5943^7 6343^7 6977^7 7476^8 7865^6
Sunny King (IRE) *J Moore* a118 118
9 b g Desert Sun Princess Mood (GER) (Muhtarram (USA))
1902a^9
Sunnyside Tom (IRE) *Richard Fahey* a74 87
8 b g Danetime(IRE) So Kind (Kind Of Hush)
12^2 158^5 299^6 4345^13 5220^3 5618^2 6141^14 7247^10 7607^4 7798^11 7964^14
Sunny Side Up (IRE) *Richard Fahey* a66 83
3 b f Refuse To Bend(IRE) Feeling Wonderful (IRE) (Fruits Of Love (USA))
112^3 970^8 1167^7 1441^9 (2595) 4547^2 (4963) (5272) 6006^7 6605^2 7144^6
Sun Of Jamaica *Mario Hofer* 92
3 b f Cape Cross(IRE) Juno Marlowe (IRE) (Danehill (USA))
3653a^14
Sunpass *John Gosden* 93
3 ch c Pivotal Tebee (Selkirk (USA))
1250^2 1606^3 (6704) 6987^4 7407^3
Sunraider (IRE) *Paul Midgley* 83
5 b g Namid Doctrine (Barathea (IRE))
1157^7 1438^7 1844^10 6009^10 6663^5 6999^8
Sunrise Dance *Robert Johnson* a72 79
3 ch f Monsieur Bond(IRE) Wachiwi (IRE) (Namid)
3404^3 3623^9 4208^5 4588^11 6782^10 7100^8 7524^7 (8253)
Sun Seal *Hughie Morrison* a68 68
3 b f Cape Cross(IRE) Soliza (IRE) (Intikhab (USA))
1610^6 2543^14 6148^4 6736^2 6957^12 7353^6
Sunset Boulevard (IRE) *Paddy Butler* a63 52
9 b g Montjeu(IRE) Lucy In The Sky (IRE) (Lycius (USA))
57^4 200^9 375^9 400^11
Sunset Kitty (USA) *Mike Murphy* a92 90
5 bb m Gone West(USA) Honorable Cat (USA) (Honor Grades (USA))
(131) 354^7 622^11 817^5 1087^2
Sunset Place *Jonathan Geake* a72 71
5 ch g Compton Place Manhattan Sunset (USA) (El Gran Senor (USA))
150^2 309^6 714^3 825^9
Sunshine Always (IRE) *Michael Attwater* a76 75
6 gr g Verglas(IRE) Easy Sunshine (IRE) (Sadler's Wells (USA))
5234^3 6145^2 6577^14 7484^7 7725^3 (7998) 8306^2
Supaheart *Hughie Morrison* a72 76
3 b f Lion Heart(USA) Supamova (USA) (Seattle Slew (USA))
1053^3 (2136) 2557^9 4531^2 5262^4 5910^13 6613^11
Supa Seeker (USA) *Tony Carroll* a63 65
6 bb g Petionville(USA) Supamova (USA) (Seattle Slew (USA))
4844^7 5657^4 6316^7 8212^4
Supastarqueen (USA) *Brian Baugh*
4 bb m El Corredor(USA) Supamova (USA) (Seattle Slew (USA))
1^U 8133^7
Super (FR) *A Clement*
2 ch c L'Axonais(FR) Miss Texas (BEL) (Fabulous White (FR))
8276a^0
Super Chunky (USA) *Kenneth M Cox* 110
6 b g Put It Back(USA) Chunky Cheeks (USA) (Friendly Lover (USA))
7092a^7
Superciliary *Ralph Beckett* a69 69
3 b g Dansili Supereva (IRE) (Sadler's Wells (USA))
2542^10 3071^6 3736^9 4706^3 5482^2 6181^5 6704^6 7251^3
Super Cookie *Philip McBride* a65 60
2 b f Dylan Thomas(IRE) Dance Lesson (In The Wings)
4297^10 (5061) 6147^U 7026^3 7414^3
Supercruiser (IRE) *Nigel Tinkler* a4 44
2 br g Majestic Missile(IRE) Balance The Books (Elmaamul (USA))
2349^7 3286^7
Superduper *Mrs A Malzard* a46 88
7 b m Erhaab(USA) I'm Magic (First Trump)
2116a^2
Super Duplex *Pat Phelan* a70 71
5 b g Footstepsinthesand Penelope Tree (IRE) (Desert Prince (IRE))
(276) 1050^12 1306^6 1735^6 2637^2 2814^2 3774^8 3999^6 4722^3 4983^9
Super Easy (NZ) *M Freedman* 110
4 b h Darci Brahma(NZ) Parfore (NZ) (Gold Brose (AUS))
8041a^10
Super Frank (IRE) *Zoe Davison* a57 65
9 b g Cape Cross(IRE) Lady Joshua (IRE) (Royal Academy (USA))
152^7 220^4 320^5 396^3 (687) 781^8 964^8 986^11
Superior Edge *Christopher Mason* a53 64
5 b m Exceed And Excel(AUS) Beveled Edge (Beveled (USA))
2165^13 2943^6 3435^2 ◆
Supernova Heights (IRE) *Brian Meehan* 89
2 b f Oasis Dream Athene (IRE) (Rousillon (USA))
4011^4 4739^5 5352^2 5979^10 (6343) 6675^4
Superoo (IRE) *Mark Johnston* a37 37
2 ch g Bahamian Bounty Roo (Rudimentary (USA))
6889^9 7192^8 7450^5
Superplex (FR) *M Figge* 82
2 b c Multiplex Salute The Sun (FR) (Fly To The Stars)
7091a^8
Superplex *John Quinn* a69 72
3 b g Multiplex Hillside Girl (IRE) (Tagula (IRE))
86^3 481^3 (801) 1110^4 3285^5 3944^4
Super Say (IRE) *Mark Rimell* a99 98
6 ch g Intikhab(USA) Again Royale (IRE) (Royal Academy (USA))
3647a^11 5397a^7 7867^2 (8019) 8228^2
Super Simon (IRE) *Paul D'Arcy* 77
2 b g Redback Spectina (Spectrum (IRE))
2844^2 3074^3 3569^2 (4239) 4804^9 6815^12
Super Smile (IRE) *Michael Appleby* a22 40
4 b m Librettist(USA) Beechesville (IRE) (Night Shift (USA))
3946^8 5172^12 5939^10 7384^6 7656^8
Superstition *James Fanshawe* a52
3 b f Red Ransom(USA) Go Supersonic (Zafonic (USA))
3279^13 7162^5 7499^5 7710^5
Supreme Luxury (IRE) *Kevin Ryan* a71 75
3 b f Iffraaj Stay Hernanda (Hernando (FR))
1363^6 2860^4 (3521) 6986^8
Supreme Quest *Roger Charlton* a77 78
3 ch f Exceed And Excel(AUS) Spanish Quest (Rainbow Quest (USA))
1921^4 ◆ 2422^2 3235^4 (4456) 5195^6 5422^5 6094^9
Supreme Rock *Jim Boyle* a64 63
3 br g Rock Of Gibraltar(IRE) Izadore (IRE) (In The Wings)
249^5 3736^10 4650^4 4870^2 4945^5 6814^10
Supreme Spirit (IRE) *Peter Makin* a83 80
5 b m Invincible Spirit(IRE) Asseverate (USA) (Trempolino (USA))
3785^8 4655^8 5877^2 6176^6 6800^14
Suraj *Michael Bell* 103
3 ch c Galileo(IRE) Maid Of Killeen (IRE) (Darshaan)
1456^5 (1655) ◆ 2281^4 (3614) 4111^6 6668^3
Surely Speightful (USA) *Kevin Ryan* 70
2 ch f Speightstown(USA) Maid Guinevere (USA) (Gilded Time (USA))
2020^3 (2456) 2702^7 3680a^9
Sure Would (CAN) *Michael Keogh* a71 80
2 rg f Wando(CAN) Wood Fern (CAN) (Woodman (USA))
6289a^13
Surfer (USA) *S Seemar* a106 86
3 ch c Distorted Humor(USA) Surf Club (USA) (Ocean Crest (USA))
142a^5 ◆ 485a^4 873a^2
Surfista *D Rabhi* 94
4 b m Shirocco(GER) Subasta (FR) (Kendor (FR))
4790a^5
Surge Ahead (IRE) *Ed Walker* a57 79
2 b c Danehill Dancer(IRE) Croisiere (USA) (Capote (USA))
6015^9 (6603) 7079^3
Surprise Moment (IRE) *Saeed Bin Suroor* a98 102
3 b f Authorized(IRE) Criquette (Shirley Heights)
(4410) (5328) (6492) 7510^4 7688^5
Surprise Us *Bernard Llewellyn* a57 49
5 b g Indian Ridge Pingus (Polish Precedent (USA))
6231^4 7018^8
Surreal (IRE) *Sir Michael Stoute* a75 76
3 b f Shamardal(USA) Mayonga (IRE) (Dr Fong (USA))
5421^3 5889^5 7112^2 7494^4
Surrey Dream (IRE) *Charlie Mann* a47 66
3 b g Oasis Dream Trois Graces (USA) (Alysheba (USA))
1512^6 2128^10 3591^3 3938^6 7819^15 8001^12
Surrey Storm *Mme G Rarick* a64 69
3 b f Montjeu(IRE) Dont Dili Dali (Dansili)
247a^0 475a^10
Surround Sound *Tim Easterby* 66
2 b g Multiplex Tintera (IRE) (King's Theatre (IRE))
3401^8 3842^3 4587^2 5331^5 6070^10 6753^7
Survey (GER) *Mario Hofer* 105
3 ch f Big Shuffle(USA) Shadow Queen (GER) (Lando (GER))
(2107a) 2746a^5 3653a^2 4764^9 5849a^4
Sushi *Rae Guest* 65
3 b f Kyllachy Black Belt Shopper (IRE) (Desert Prince (IRE))
1257^9 5453^2 (5949) 6739^7
Suspension *Hughie Morrison* a53
2 b f Avonbridge Summertime Parkes (Silver Patriarch (IRE))
7707^10 7924^10 8068^8
Susukino (FR) *S Kobayashi* a72 68
3 gr f Great Journey(JPN) Sapporo (FR) (Smadoun (FR))
5726a^5
Sutton Sid *George Baker* a70 59
2 ch g Dutch Art Drastic Measure (Pivotal)
2039^2 2330^9 4688^11 5484^9 6583^8 (6826)
Sutton Veny (IRE) *Jeremy Gask* a89 94
6 gr m Acclamation Carabine (USA) (Dehere (USA))
1417^7 1727^7 2195^3 2707^7 3612^3 4530^5 5362^9 6938^2 7145^10
Suzette De Bavay (IRE) *A Oliver* 83
3 b f Whipper(USA) Nashira (Prince Sabo)
3645a^10
Suzi's A Class Act *James Eustace* a73 87
4 gr m Act One Latour (Sri Pekan (USA))
3077^2 ◆ 3704^4 3979^3 4585^4 (4972) (5280) 5830^3 6349^2 6600^9 7109^4
Swan Song *Andrew Balding* 89
3 br f Green Desert(USA) Lochsong (Song)
(2422) ◆ 4765^4 ◆ 6602^3 ◆
Swaying Grace (IRE) *Ann Duffield* a20 49
2 b f Celtic Swing Saying Grace (IRE) (Brief Truce (USA))
5818^7 6214^13 6708^8
Swedish Sailor *Mahmood Al Zarooni* 94
3 b c Monsun(GER) Epitome (IRE) (Nashwan (USA))
6142^5 7558^8
Sweeping Rock (IRE) *Marcus Tregoning* 59
2 b c Rock Of Gibraltar(IRE) Sweeping Story (USA) (End Sweep (USA))
6447^7 6846^7 7373^4
Sweet Alabama *Rod Millman*
2 gr f Johannesburg(USA) Alybgood (CAN) (Alydeed (CAN))
2407^5
Sweet As Honey *Richard Hannon* a71 60
2 b f Duke Of Marmalade(IRE) Tempting Prospect (Shirley Heights)
5977^10 6366^9 8017^2
Sweet Deal (IRE) *Jeremy Noseda* a61 79
2 gr g Verglas(IRE) Compromise (FR) (Fasliyev (USA))
5792^8 6214^4 (6572)
Sweet Ducky (USA) *H J Brown* a113 65
4 br h Pulpit(USA) Storm's Darling (USA) (Storm Boot (USA))
315a^7 591a^13
Sweetest Friend (IRE) *J S Moore* a52
3 b f Holy Roman Emperor(IRE) Royal Devotion (IRE) (Sadler's Wells (USA))
34^5 182^6 206^6 564^8 660^14
Sweet Fairnando *Tim Easterby* 64
3 b f Hernando(FR) Fairnilee (Selkirk (USA))
4210^5 4399^8 5115^3 (5589) 5922^7
Sweet Force *Marco Botti* a39
2 b c Beat Hollow Sweet Power (Pivotal)
7707^13 7962^10 8147^6
Sweet Grace *David Brown* a58 43
3 b f Echo Of Light Sydney Star (Machiavellian (USA))
1959^4 2374^10 3066^8 4189^11 5014^6 7361^7 7604^6 7729^3
Sweet Lavender (IRE) *Michael Wigham* a77 19
4 b m Dalakhani(IRE) Dievotchkina (IRE) (Bluebird (USA))
2199^17 2863^9 3283^6 6981^2 8106^7
Sweet Liberta (IRE) *Andrew Balding* a59 58
3 b f Cape Cross(IRE) Hendrina (IRE) (Daylami (IRE))
3189^8 3666^9 4263^5 4870^6 5441^4 5974^2 6305^3 7752^8 8050^3 8229^3
Sweet Lightning *Thomas Carmody* a104 114
7 b g Fantastic Light(USA) Sweetness Herself (Unfuwain (USA))
2100a^2 3675a^5 5609a^3
Sweet Louise (IRE) *Paul Rich* 11
2 b f Azamour(IRE) Maria Luisa (IRE) (King's Best (USA))
7403^14
Sweet Martoni *William Knight* a42 68
2 b f Dubawi(IRE) Sweetness Herself (Unfuwain (USA))
6534^9 7103^2
Sweet Mirasol (IRE) *Mandy Rowland* a37 54
5 b m Celtic Swing Sallwa (IRE) (Entrepreneur)
218^9 483^8
Sweet Mystery (IRE) *David Evans* a35 72
3 b g Dark Angel(IRE) Hartstown House (IRE) (Primo Dominie)
5350^6 5705^9 6152^11
Sweetnessandlight *Jason Ward* a67 100
3 b f Aussie Rules(USA) Taschlynn (IRE) (Second Empire (IRE))
1170^3 1517^8 (2404) 2679^4 3940^4 4263^3 (4549) (4830) (5386) 5834^4 6379^8
Sweet Ophelia *George Baker* a55 65
3 b f Shamardal(USA) Showery (Rainbow Quest (USA))
1610^13 4516^11 5458^11 6982^9
Sweet Ovation *Mark Usher* a68 56
3 b f Royal Applause Sweetest Revenge (IRE) (Daggers Drawn (USA))
(191) (394) 659^4 2397^6 4218^10 5122^8 8304^9
Sweet Piccolo *Paddy Butler* a26
2 ch g Piccolo Quality Street (Fraam)
7296^6 7705^10 7926^13
Sweet Secret *Jeremy Gask* a76 71
5 ch m Singspiel(IRE) Ballymore Celebre (IRE) (Peintre Celebre (USA))
148^5 403^5 3230^12 5193^6
Sweet Shirley Mae (USA) *Wesley A Ward* a97
2 bb f Broken Vow(USA) Joyful Chaos (USA) (Rahy (USA))
7545a^3
Sweet Talking Guy (IRE) *Lydia Pearce* 31
2 b g Oratorio(IRE) Sweet Namibia (IRE) (Namid)
7516^6
Sweet Venture (FR) *M Weiss* a68 102
10 gr h Verglas(IRE) Bitter Sweet (FR) (Esprit Du Nord (USA))
444a^3
Sweet Vera *Shaun Harris* a45 53
7 ch m Double Trigger(IRE) Inesse (Simply Great (FR))
1065^7 1223^4 1385^5 1744^4 1919^13 3332^3 3616^F
Sweet Vintage (IRE) *J W Hills* a64
2 b f Singspiel(IRE) Sauterne (Rainbow Quest (USA))
7505^7 7778^3 7916^3
Sweet World *Bernard Llewellyn* a64 69
8 b g Agnes World(USA) Douce Maison (IRE) (Fools Holme (USA))
2389^8 3429^3 4536^11
Swendab (IRE) *John O'Shea* a69 84
4 b g Trans Island Lavish Spirit (USA) (Southern Halo (USA))
2793^9 3139^9 3595^6 3915^8 4461^3 5097^4 5502^2 5791^3 6094^15 7023^5 7360^8 7666^9
Swerve *Alan McCabe* 99
3 b f Oasis Dream Avoidance (USA) (Cryptoclearance (USA))
5520^10 6601^11
Swift Act *Ronald Harris* a62 67
3 b f Act One Lasting Image (Zilzal (USA))
838^4 1363^8 2757^2 3192^7 4486^12 4914^8 5229^7 5658^5 6001^4 6892^11
Swift Blade (IRE) *Lady Herries* a70 76
4 ch g Exceed And Excel(AUS) Gold Strike (IRE) (Rainbow Quest (USA))
1205^4 5441^2 (5908) 6430^9 7744^6
Swift Bounty *Alan Jarvis* a82 64
2 ch c Bahamian Bounty Famcred (Inchinor)
5963^5 7191^2 7628^2
Swift Cat *John Best* a60 71
3 b g One Cool Cat(USA) Hunzy (IRE) (Desert King (IRE))
(2126)
Swift Cedar (IRE) *Alan Jarvis* 76
2 ch c Excellent Art Ravish (Efisio)
3444^8 4330^2 5275^2 5661^3
Swift Chap *Philip Hobbs* a76 63
6 b g Diktat Regent's Folly (IRE) (Touching Wood (USA))
6004^4
Swift Code (IRE) *Nigel Tinkler*
2 br g Elnadim(USA) Gradetime (IRE) (Danetime (IRE))
3638^9
Swift Encounter (IRE) *Ann Duffield* 70
3 bb g Antonius Pius(USA) Eucalyptus Hill (USA) (Peaks And Valleys (USA))
2589^7 6136^6 6559^6
Swift Gift *Ed Dunlop* a94 99
7 b g Cadeaux Genereux Got To Go (Shareef Dancer (USA))
5342^14
Swiftly Done (IRE) *Declan Carroll* a73 100
5 b g Whipper(USA) Ziffany (Taufan (USA))
2285^2 (2882) (3534) 4761^7 6674^18
Swiftsure (FR) *J-V Toux*
2 b f Librettist(USA) Calm Before (FR) (Ocean Of Wisdom (USA))
5697a^0

Swift Winged *Hughie Morrison* a47 31
3 b f Motivator Swift Spring (FR) (Bluebird (USA))
2848^{11} 3704^{8} 4147^{6}

Swilly Ferry (USA) *David Nicholls* a82 94
5 b g Wiseman's Ferry(USA) Keepers Hill (IRE) (Danehill (USA))
1157^{15} 1476^{12} 2707^{15} 6939^{11}

Swing Alone (IRE) *Gay Kelleway* a96 97
3 b g Celtic Swing Groupetime (USA) (Gilded Time (USA))
542a^{8} 628a^{3} 716a^{6} 1127a^{9} 3294^{8} 4298^{2} 5556^{4} 6701^{4} ◆ 7064^{5} 7520^{3}

Swing Easy *Robert Mills* a73 74
2 b c Zamindar(USA) Shahmina (IRE) (Danehill (USA))
5742^{2} 6412^{2} 7081^{7} (7641)

Swinger *Scott Dixon* a50 63
4 ch g Singspiel(IRE) Helen Bradley (IRE) (Indian Ridge)
369^{6} 633^{10} 1283^{10} 1584^{4}

Swinging Hawk (GER) *Ian Williams* a71 86
6 ch g Hawk Wing(USA) Saldenschwinge (GER) (In The Wings)
2180^{4} 2709^{4} 3661^{8} 4115^{6} 6191^{4} 7455^{8} 7839^{5} 7972^{7}

Swinging Sixties (IRE) *D Selvaratnam* a99 68
7 b g Singspiel(IRE) Velvet Lady (Nashwan (USA))
260a^{10}

Swinging Sultan *Keith Reveley* 58
5 b g Sulamani(IRE) Nobratinetta (FR) (Celtic Swing)
1385^{3}

Swingkeel (IRE) *John Dunlop* a96 104
7 ch g Singspiel(IRE) Anniversary (Salse (USA))
2933^{15} 3373^{17} 4697^{14}

Swingland *Paul Cole* 84
3 b f Pivotal Farfala (FR) (Linamix (FR))
1756^{4}

Swish Dish (CAN) *Micky Hammond* a44 73
5 bb m El Corredor(USA) Amelia Saratoga (JPN) (Dehere (USA))
532^{6} 843^{4}

Swiss Cross *Phil McEntee* a105 101
5 b g Cape Cross(IRE) Swiss Lake (USA) (Indian Ridge)
2268^{15} 2707^{4} 3078^{9} 3641^{7} 3771^{2} 4611^{14} 4802^{16} 5065^{7} 5663^{4} ◆ 6116^{3} 7503^{5} 7709^{5} 7774^{9} 7817^{2} 7897^{3} (8008) 8066^{2} 8272^{4}

Swiss Dream *David Elsworth* a85 107
4 b m Oasis Dream Swiss Lake (USA) (Indian Ridge)
(2087) 2486^{12} 3092a^{5} 6268a^{8} (6878) 7624a^{15}

Swiss Franc *David Elsworth* a105 101
7 br g Mr Greeley(USA) Swiss Lake (USA) (Indian Ridge)
2024^{3} 2208^{12} 2931^{10}

Swiss Spirit *David Elsworth* 113
3 b c Invincible Spirit(IRE) Swiss Lake (USA) (Indian Ridge)
1452^{2} (2236) 3265^{18} 5648a^{5} (6485) 6908a^{18}

Switch (USA) *John W Sadler* a116 103
5 b m Quiet American(USA) Antoniette (USA) (Nicholas (USA))
7569a^{3}

Switcharooney (IRE) *Tom Dascombe* a44
2 b c Bahamian Bounty Amazon Beauty (IRE) (Wolfhound (USA))
8262^{7}

Switchback *Michael Easterby* a76 83
4 b g Medicean Hooplah (Pivotal)
1161^{13} 1381^{16} 3167^{16} 3439^{7} 3749^{6} 4398^{3} 4805^{13} 6342^{10} 6843^{2} 7027^{4} 7328^{8}

Switched Off *Ed McMahon* a78 78
7 b g Catcher In The Rye(IRE) Button Hole Flower (IRE) (Fairy King (USA))
187^{3} 310^{4} 582^{3} 5430^{7} (6004) 6802^{5}

Switcher (IRE) *Tom Dascombe* 100
3 b f Whipper(USA) Bahamamia (Vettori (IRE))
1508^{4} 3270^{10} 3542^{2} 3987a^{8} 5385^{7} 6870^{2}

Switch To The Lead (USA) *Patrick L Biancone* a89
2 b f Songandaprayer(USA) Dressed For Succes (USA) (Tricky Mister (USA))
5031a^{3}

Switzerland (IRE) *Mark Johnston* a105 101
3 b c Shamardal(USA) Sahra Alsalam (USA) (Gone West (USA))
(181) ◆ 596^{3} (867) ◆ 1221^{5} 1452^{15} 1996^{3} 2485^{3} 3294^{27} 3630^{4} 3878^{13} 4339^{9} 4735^{2} (5301) 5517^{19} 6036^{10} 6374^{6} 6638^{27}

Swnymor (IRE) *William Haggas* 93
3 b g Dylan Thomas(IRE) Propaganda (IRE) (Sadler's Wells (USA))
1754^{3} 3035^{2} (3420) 4151^{2} 4700^{14} 6661^{2} 7175^{3}

Swop (IRE) *Luca Cumani* a65 96
9 b g Shinko Forest(IRE) Changing Partners (Rainbow Quest (USA))
140a^{12} 316a^{6}

Swordhalf *A Wohler* 102
2 b f Haafhd Sword Roche (GER) (Laroche (GER))
(7281a)

Sword In Hand *Alan Jarvis* a76 81
3 b c Exceed And Excel(AUS) Valhalla Moon (USA) (Sadler's Wells (USA))
2273^{15} 6102^{3} (6582) 7376^{2} ◆

Sword Of The Lord *Michael Bell* 56
2 b g Kheleyf(USA) Blue Echo (Kyllachy)
7127^{10} 7363^{6} 7598^{6}

Swords *Ray Peacock* a47 49
10 b g Vettori(IRE) Pomorie (IRE) (Be My Guest (USA))
453^{10} 924^{3} 1112^{11} 1189^{9} 2454^{5} 4402^{7} 5967^{7}

Sworn Sold (GER) *W Hickst* 101
3 bb f Soldier Hollow Sweet Tern (GER) (Arctic Tern (USA))
4862a^{10} 5844a^{13} 6723a^{11}

Sydarra (FR) *F Head* a92 86
3 b f Sinndar(IRE) Mydarshaan (Darshaan)
5249a^{10} 6295a^{12} 6911a^{13}

Sydney City (GER) *W Mongil* 46
2 b f Doyen(IRE) Sayada (GER) (Dr Fong (USA))
7588a^{8}

Sydney Cove (IRE) *Iain Jardine* a35 45
6 b g Cape Cross(IRE) First Fleet (USA) (Woodman (USA))
2599^{6} 3029^{8} 3519^{4} 4431^{4}

Sygnature *Alan Swinbank* a54 68
3 b g Authorized(IRE) Perfect Story (IRE) (Desert Story (IRE))
1167^{6} 1959^{3} 2604^{8}

Sylas Ings *Brian Barr* a71 50
4 b g Kyllachy Ashlinn (IRE) (Ashkalani (IRE))
(468) 575^{7} 2117a^{3}

Sylvia Pankhurst (IRE) *David C Griffiths* a62 72
2 b f Antonius Pius(USA) Spinning Gold (Spinning World (USA))
1671^{3} 1795^{3} (2135) 2603^{10} 3631^{6} 4047^{3} 4574^{10} 4836^{3} (5292) 5828^{4} 6550a^{5} 6955^{5}

Sylvia's Diamond *Richard Guest* a38 28
2 br f Cockney Rebel(IRE) Korolieva (IRE) (Xaar)
5011^{3} 5799^{6} 6042^{13} 6953^{12} 8289^{11}

Symboline *Mick Channon* 68
2 b f Royal Applause Ashes (IRE) (General Monash (USA))
2019^{3} 2550^{8} 3223^{4} 4116^{7}

Symfony (IRE) *Clive Cox* a59 55
3 b f Monsun(GER) Musicanna (Cape Cross (IRE))
2734^{10} 5510^{6} 6148^{7} 6616^{9}

Symphonic Dancer (USA) *Brian Baugh* a70 25
5 ch m Smart Strike(CAN) Summer Exhibition (USA) (Royal Academy (USA))
287^{4} 384^{2} 490^{5} 725^{7}

Symphonic Rhythm (TUR) *O Ozelcanat* 86
3 b f Mountain Cat(USA) Star Flicker (CAN) (Woodman (USA))
5849a^{6}

Symphony Of Dreams *Dai Burchell* 17
2 b f Primo Valentino(IRE) Flying Lion (Hunting Lion (IRE))
1904^{5} 2492^{7}

Symphony Of Light *Dai Burchell*
2 b f Primo Valentino(IRE) Echostar (Observatory (USA))
1388^{8}

Symphony Of Space *Alan McCabe* a33
3 b f Primo Valentino(IRE) Flying Lion (Hunting Lion (IRE))
1959 404^{6} 1256^{10}

Symphony Of Stars *Michael Appleby* 50
3 b f Primo Valentino(IRE) Echostar (Observatory (USA))
4550^{5} 4782^{6} 5448^{U}

Symphony Star (IRE) *Paul D'Arcy* a59 64
3 b f Amadeus Wolf Bezant (IRE) (Zamindar (USA))
1364^{5} 2379^{7} 3547^{6} 3939^{2} 4405^{2} 6813^{3} 7148^{10}

Symphony Time (IRE) *Brian Meehan* a75 71
3 b f Cape Cross(IRE) Gems Of Araby (Zafonic (USA))
1612^{3} 2194^{18} 2894^{7} 3619^{9}

Symposia *Sir Henry Cecil* 57
3 ch f Galileo(IRE) Emplane (USA) (Irish River (FR))
3565^{10}

Synchronicity (IRE) *Richard Hannon* 79
3 b c High Chaparral(IRE) Sea Of Time (USA) (Gilded Time (USA))
1511^{3} 1893^{8}

Syncopate *Pam Sly* a75
3 b g Oratorio(IRE) Millistar (Galileo (IRE))
6827^{3} 7384^{4} 8049^{2} (8080)

Syndic (FR) *J-C Rouget* a89 97
3 b c Sinndar(IRE) Kalatuna (FR) (Green Tune (USA))
365a^{4}

Synphonic Air (IRE) *John Weymes* a18 47
2 b f Amadeus Wolf Summer Crush (USA) (Summer Squall (USA))
2631^{8} 3948^{10} 5221^{10} 6115^{8}

Synthe Davis (FR) *Laura Mongan* a60
7 b m Saint Des Saints(FR) Trumpet Davis (FR) (Rose Laurel)
569^{5}

Syrenka *Marcus Tregoning* a57 72
2 ch f Sir Percy Sirena (GER) (Tejano (USA))
6448^{4} 6978^{3}

Syrian *S M Duffy* a89 82
5 b g Hawk Wing(USA) Lady Lahar (Fraam)
341a^{6}

Szabo's Art *Sir Mark Prescott Bt* 23
2 br f Excellent Art Violette (Observatory (USA))
7244^{7}

Ta Ajabb *William Haggas* a57 72
3 b g Pastoral Pursuits First Eclipse (IRE) (Fayruz)
1521^{4} 2145^{7} 2996^{2}

Taajub (IRE) *Peter Crate* a95 109
5 b g Exceed And Excel(AUS) Purple Tiger (IRE) (Rainbow Quest (USA))
311^{5} (525) (715) ◆ 1141^{11} 1602^{2} ◆ 2704^{4} 3771^{3} (4367) 4576^{2} 5077^{2} 6485^{3} 6908a^{17}

Taameer *D K Weld* a90 97
6 b g Beat Hollow Vayavaig (Damister (USA))
3647a^{12}

Taaresh (IRE) *Kevin Morgan* a78 81
7 b g Sakhee(USA) Tanaghum (Darshaan)
817^{6} 5944^{9}

Taayel (IRE) *John Gosden* 108
2 b c Tamayuz Sakhee's Song (IRE) (Sakhee (USA))
(5016) ◆ 6483^{3} ◆ 7400^{3}

Tabaret *Richard Whitaker* a71 79
9 ch g Bertolini(USA) Luanshya (First Trump)
1168^{10} 2439^{6} 2693^{4} 2793^{2} 3612^{12} 3944^{3} 4400^{3} 4495^{3} 4680^{8} 6123^{15} 6358^{9} 6825^{10}

Tabib (IRE) *Saeed Bin Suroor* a36 39
3 b g Hard Spun(USA) Campsie Fells (UAE) (Indian Ridge)
5421^{7} 5717^{5}

Table Mountain (IRE) *Robert Alan Hennessy* 98
5 b g Milan Shirley Blue (IRE) (Shirley Heights)
2318a^{6}

Tac De Boistron (FR) *Michael Kent* 112
5 gr g Take Risks(FR) Pondiki (FR) (Sicyos (USA))
1697a^{3} 2534a^{5} 3367a^{2} (4120a) 7346a^{6} 7621a^{23}

Tactfully (IRE) *Mahmood Al Zarooni* a88 84
3 b f Discreet Cat(USA) Kydd Gloves (USA) (Dubai Millennium)
1215^{4} 2255^{6}

Tadabeer *Ian Williams* a76 77
4 b g Green Desert(USA) Perfect Plum (IRE) (Darshaan)
177^{10} 7083^{8}

Tadalavil *Linda Perratt* a76 70
7 gr g Clodovil(IRE) Blandish (USA) (Wild Again (USA))
1875^{10} 7447^{5} 7604^{8}

Tadjena (GER) *Tony Newcombe* 22
5 b m Volfonic(IRE) Teri Belle (HOL) (Terimon)
4940^{11} 5266^{7}

Tadmir (USA) *Saeed Bin Suroor* a85 53
3 bb c Bernardini(USA) Owsley (USA) (Harlan (USA))
6770^{3}

Tae Kwon Do (USA) *Tim Vaughan* a50 55
6 b g Thunder Gulch(USA) Judy's Magic (USA) (Wavering Monarch (USA))
2175^{2} 2575^{3} 3969^{3} 4664^{2} 5264^{5}

Tafawuk (USA) *Roger Varian* a58 70
3 b g Nayef(USA) Yaqeen (Green Desert (USA))
1923^{8} ◆ 2553^{4} 3088^{3}

Taffe *Amy Weaver* a83 84
3 b g Byron Blorenge (Prince Sabo)
295^{6} 3613^{13} 4558^{12} (4965) 5676^{8} 6454^{8} 6938^{11} 7464^{3} 7730^{6} 7928^{10}

Tagalaka (IRE) *Eve Johnson Houghton* 57
2 b g Tagula(IRE) Queeny's Princess (IRE) (Daggers Drawn (USA))
5503^{5} 5932^{6} 6203^{12}

Taglietelle *Andrew Balding* a74 81
3 b g Tagula(IRE) Averami (Averti (IRE))
56^{8} 4516^{5} 4888^{3} 5796^{5} 6677^{2}

Tagula Breeze (IRE) *Ian McInnes* a55 51
6 b g Tagula(IRE) Pearl Egg (IRE) (Mukaddamah (USA))
911^{7} 1298^{13} 2037^{4} 2352^{7} 3020^{8}

Tagula Night (IRE) *Dean Ivory* a94 93
6 ch g Tagula(IRE) Carpet Lady (IRE) (Night Shift (USA))
1141^{3} 1438^{10} 1849^{4} 2558^{13} 3049^{9} 3771^{9} 4286^{3} 5233^{7} 6369^{6} 6577^{13} 7114^{14}

Tahaf (IRE) *Clive Brittain* 48
2 b c Authorized(IRE) Lady Zonda (Lion Cavern (USA))
1451^{4} 2662^{9} 6846^{5}

Tahini (GER) *W Giedt* 106
4 ch h Medicean Tucana (GER) (Acatenango (GER))
6290a^{5}

Tahlia Ree (IRE) *Michael Bell* a59 73
3 b f Acclamation Dora Carrington (IRE) (Sri Pekan (USA))
4434^{2} (4807) 5324^{5} 7023^{10} 7314^{3} 7600^{11}

Tahnee Mara (IRE) *Kevin Ryan* a67 73
3 b f Sleeping Indian Totally Yours (IRE) (Desert Sun)
1089^{4} 1514^{4} 2065^{3} 2795^{4} 3314^{8} 3940^{2} 4401^{5} 4711^{3} 5245^{3} 6477^{5} 7347^{12}

Tai Amour *Terry Clement* a35
4 b m Tendulkar(USA) Gildas Fortuna (Fort Wood (USA))
1703^{13}

Tai Chi (GER) *Exors Of W Baltromei* 111
3 b c High Chaparral(IRE) Taita (GER) (Big Shuffle (USA))
2568a^{6}

Taigan (FR) *Ian Williams* 68
5 b g Panoramic Lazary (FR) (Bobinski)
2708^{11} 3035^{6} 3484^{7} 7077^{8}

Taikoo *Hughie Morrison* a90 91
7 b g Dr Fong(USA) So True (So Blessed)
1056^{7} 1282^{2} 1850^{4} 2936^{10} 4284^{P} 5158^{3} 6428^{5}

Taizong (IRE) *Ian Williams* a71 63
3 b c Oasis Dream Amazon Beauty (IRE) (Wolfhound (USA))
1560^{8} 1843^{6} 2470^{2} 3108^{3} 3732^{2} 4708^{8} 6370^{9} 6806^{3} 7317^{6}

Tajaaweed (USA) *Doug Watson* 115
7 br h Dynaformer(USA) Uforia (USA) (Zilzal (USA))
682a^{5}

Tajamal (IRE) *Saeed Bin Suroor* a52
3 b c Dubai Destination(USA) Aryaamm (IRE) (Galileo (IRE))
6582^{8}

Tajheez (IRE) *Roger Varian* 59
2 b g Raven's Pass(USA) Ghaidaa (IRE) (Cape Cross (IRE))
6872^{11} 7172^{8} 7636^{3}

Tajneed (IRE) *David Nicholls* a83 111
9 b g Alhaarth(IRE) Indian Express (Indian Ridge)
1294^{3} 1558^{3} 1844^{5} 2177^{7} 2825^{4} (3304) 3624^{7} (4673) 5368^{9} 6465^{19}

Tajriba (IRE) *Saeed Bin Suroor* a82 45
3 b f Teofilo(IRE) Caumshinaun (IRE) (Indian Ridge)
(1957) 3614^{6}

Takaathur (USA) *Saeed Bin Suroor* a65
2 ch c Hard Spun(USA) Vague (USA) (Elusive Quality (USA))
7324^{6}

Takajan (IRE) *Mark Brisbourne* a75 48
5 b g Barathea(IRE) Takaliya (IRE) (Darshaan)
101^{6} 155^{9} 289^{5} 356^{5} 551^{4} 690^{11} 740^{8} 831^{6} 910^{8} 939^{11}

Takar (IRE) *Rod Collet* 109
3 b c Oratorio(IRE) Takarouna (USA) (Green Dancer (USA))
(1943a) ◆ 2514a^{9} (3322a) ◆ (4354a) 5286a^{8} 7515a^{6}

Takealookatmenow (IRE) *David Nicholls* 77
3 b f Moss Vale(IRE) Batool (USA) (Bahri (USA))
2416^{4} ◆ (2824) ◆ 3379^{8} 3912^{10} 5676^{4} 7451^{8}

Take A Note *Patrick Chamings* a75 81
3 b g Singspiel(IRE) Ela Paparouna (Vettori (IRE))
2542^{7} (3732) (4218) (5308) ◆ 6331^{2}

Take Charge Indy (USA) *Patrick Byrne* a118
3 bb c A.P. Indy(USA) Take Charge Lady (USA) (Dehere (USA))
1872a^{19}

Take Cover *David C Griffiths* a95 89
5 b g Singspiel(IRE) Enchanted (Magic Ring (IRE))
(6665) 7327^{6} ◆ 7690^{19} 7716^{2}

Takeitfromalady (IRE) *Ralph Beckett* a91 94
3 b g Intikhab(USA) Pinheiros (IRE) (Rock Of Gibraltar (IRE))
(1938) 2428^{4} 2930^{2} 3156^{5} (3917) 4319^{2} 5301^{5} 5609a^{17} 6701^{9} 7163^{4}

Take It To The Max *Richard Fahey* 97
5 b g Bahamian Bounty Up And About (Barathea (IRE))
1043a^{11} 1510^{22} 3157^{8} 4112^{12} 4557^{3} 5186^{9} 5677^{7} 6426^{6} 7083^{4}

Take Root *Reg Hollinshead* a63 68
4 b g Indesatchel(IRE) Lamarita (Emarati (USA))
41^{7} 445^{8} 580^{8}

Take The Lead *Richard Hannon* 64
2 ch f Assertive My Dancer (IRE) (Alhaarth (IRE))
3560^{8} 4408^{4} 5003^{7} (7433)

Take The Stage (IRE) *Jeremy Noseda* a67 72
3 b g Azamour(IRE) Amoureux (USA) (Deputy Minister (CAN))
2430^{8} 2856^{14} 4791^{6} 6181^{6}

Take Two *John O'Shea* 80
3 b c Act One Lac Marmot (FR) (Marju (IRE))
1155^{6} 1661^{2} ◆ (1906) 2144^{7} 2866^{3} (3338) 3792^{6} 4323^{8} 7376^{5}

Takhreej (IRE) *Paul Rich* a67 41
4 b g Marju(IRE) Tomoohat (USA) (Danzig (USA))
732^{9} 1052^{7} 1717^{P}

Takitwo *Peter Cundell* a51 68
9 b g Delta Dancer Tiama (IRE) (Last Tycoon)
(2607) 3053^{4} (3511) 3790^{9} 4814^{4} 5440^{8} 6778^{12} 7898^{6} 8167^{9}

Talawa (FR) *J Clais* a48
3 ch f Way Of Light(USA) Tazilia (SWI) (Zilzal Zamaan (USA))
865a^{10}

Talbot Green *William Muir* a65 65
4 b g Green Desert(USA) One Of The Family (Alzao (USA))
825^{4} 1104^{3} 1184^{2} 1361^{6} (1791) 2378^{4} 3086^{4} 3734^{5}

Talent *Ralph Beckett* a82 73
2 ch f New Approach(IRE) Prowess (IRE) (Peintre Celebre (USA))
5357^{3} (6017)

Talent Scout (IRE) *Tim Walford* a62 76
6 b g Exceed And Excel(USA) Taalluf (USA) (Hansel (USA))
1527^{8} 1659^{10} 2675^{4} ◆ 4715^{3} ◆ 4964^{4} 5414^{4} (6259) (6410) 7247^{11}

Tale Of A Champion (USA) *Kristin Mulhall* 102
4 b h Tale Of The Cat(USA) If Angels Sang (USA) (Seattle Slew (USA))
7571a^{8}

Tales Of Grimm (USA) *Sir Michael Stoute* 108
3 b c Distorted Humor(USA) Stupendous Miss (USA) (Dynaformer (USA))
2641^{3} 3295^{5} 4760^{7} 5594^{4}

Talk About (FR) *M Delzangles* a94 98
4 b g Holy Roman Emperor(IRE) Breath Of Love (USA) (Mutakddim (USA))
6674^{15}

Talk Of Saafend (IRE) *Dianne Sayer* a31 61
7 b m Barathea(IRE) Sopran Marida (IRE) (Darshaan)
(1794) 2137^{11} (3116) 4766^{3} 4869^{7} 6315^{8}

Talk Of The North *Hugo Palmer* a74 70
3 b f Haafhd Ammo (IRE) (Sadler's Wells (USA))
1607^{4} (2860) 3142^{8} 4335^{5} 4875^{10} 5838^{10} 6250^{5} 7003^{10} 7416^{6}

Tallaay (IRE) *Mark Johnston* 36
2 b c Cape Cross(IRE) Ghizlaan (USA) (Seeking The Gold (USA))
6985^{8} 7637^{12}

Tallahasse (IRE) *Alan Swinbank* 84
4 b m Acclamation Designer Chic (Red Ransom (USA))
1476^{13}

Tallevu (IRE) *Noel Chance* a61 71
3 ch g Stormy River(FR) Pascarina (FR) (Exit To Nowhere (USA))
1442^{4} 1906^{8} 2449^{5} 2980^{4} 3697^{8} 4511^{5} 5001^{6} 6442^{7} 7960^{3} 8229^{8}

Tallula (IRE) *Micky Hammond* a29 31
3 b f Tagula(IRE) Talara (IRE) (Dansili)
1600^{6} 2695^{7} 3184^{12} 3567^{7} 4263^{4}

Tallulah Mai *Matthew Salaman* a57 56
5 b m Kayf Tara Al Awaalah (Mukaddamah (USA))
2391^{7} (2769) 3180^{5} 3969^{8} 4244^{8}

Tally Stick (USA) *Mahmood Al Zarooni* a56 57
2 b c Street Cry(IRE) Echoes In Eternity (IRE) (Spinning World (USA))
6014^{6} ◆ 6371^{6}

Talqaa *Mick Channon* 79
2 b f Exceed And Excel(AUS) Poppo's Song (CAN) (Polish Navy (USA))
4739^{7} ◆ 5352^{4} 5781a^{4} 6167^{5}

Talwar (IRE) *Jeremy Noseda* a99 107
3 b c Acclamation Moore's Melody (IRE) (Marju (IRE))
(1375) 1856^{18} 3265^{20} 5597^{9} 6400^{9} 7210^{10}

Tamaathul *A Al Raihe* a110 105
5 gr g Tiger Hill(IRE) Tahrir (IRE) (Linamix (FR))
51a^{6} 261a^{3} 487a^{2} 588a^{10} ◆ 757a^{7}

Tamanaco (IRE) *Tim Walford* 75
5 b g Catcher In The Rye(IRE) Right After Moyne (IRE) (Imperial Ballet (IRE))
6340^{7}

Tamara Bay *John Davies* a61 66
4 b m Selkirk(USA) Tamalain (USA) (Royal Academy (USA))
2679^{5} 3694^{3} 4783^{2} 5295^{4} 6961^{10}

Tamareen (IRE) *Richard Fahey* a88 88
4 b g Bahamian Bounty Damjanich (IRE) (Mull Of Kintyre (USA))
11^{4} 157^{2} 378^{6} 431^{2} ◆ 2029^{7} (2489) 3557^{6}

Tamarissimo (GER) *M Nigge* a68 60
2 ch c Linngari(IRE) The Spring Flower (GER) (Kornado)
7597a^{0}

Tamarkuz (USA) *Saeed Bin Suroor* a98 78
2 ch c Speightstown(USA) Without You Babe (USA) (Lemon Drop Kid (USA))
5062^{4} 5685^{2} (6175) (6980) ◆

Tamarrud *Saeed Bin Suroor* a78 83
3 b g Authorized(IRE) Miss Hepburn (USA) (Gone West (USA))
3042^{10} 3417^{3} ◆ 4254^{3} 4745^{5} 6573^{6}

Tamasou (IRE) *Ed McMahon* a80 78
7 b g Tamarisk(IRE) Soubresaut (IRE) (Danehill (USA))
1527^{5}

Tamayuz Star (IRE) *Richard Hannon* 98
2 ch c Tamayuz Magical Peace (IRE) (Magical Wonder (USA))
(5126) 5904^{2} (6491) 6874^{5}

Tameen *Ed Dunlop* 99
4 b m Shirocco(GER) Najah (IRE) (Nashwan (USA))
1848^{9} 2066^{2} 2805a^{10} 4112^{6} 4821^{8} 7407^{12}

Taming The Tweet *Alan McCabe* a57
2 b f Act One Pants (Pivotal)
8270^{3}

Tamino (IRE) *Alastair Lidderdale* a52 10
9 b g Mozart(IRE) Stop Out (Rudimentary (USA))
210^{6} 264^{9} 483^{2} 664^{5} 690^{6} 813^{5} 831^{5} 926^{11} 1070^{10} 1242^{9}

Tammuz (IRE) *Tony Carroll* a58
2 ch f Tamayuz Favourita (Diktat)
8171^{8} 8262^{4}

Tanawar (IRE) *William Haggas* 51
2 b g Elusive City(USA) Parakopi (IRE) (Green Desert (USA))
7686^{5}

Tanby (AUS) *Robert Hickmott* 111
6 b g Galileo(IRE) Dane Belltar (AUS) (Danewin (AUS))
7560a^{11} 7696a^{3}

Tancred Spirit *Paul Midgley* a51 51
4 b m Mind Games Tancred Times (Clantime)
8^{9} 445^{11} 690^{5} 939^{12}

Tanfeeth *M Al Muhairi* a101 101
4 ch h Singspiel(IRE) Nasij (USA) (Elusive Quality (USA))
421a^{5}

Tanforan *Brian Baugh* a61 63
10 b g Mujahid(USA) Florentynna Bay (Aragon)
633^{3} 744^{6} 929^{8} 1659^{8} 2464^{4} 4988^{2} (5261) 5657^{7} 6829^{12}

Tangerine Trees *Bryan Smart* a73 116
7 b g Mind Games Easy To Imagine (USA) (Cozzene (USA))
2486^{7} 3238^{8} 4762^{8} 5561^{10} 6908a^{12}

Tanghan (IRE) *Richard Fahey* 84
2 b g Invincible Spirit(IRE) Rose De France (IRE) (Diktat)
3123^{2} 5449^{3}

Tango Kid (USA) *Brian A Lynch*
2 bb g Lemon Drop Kid(USA) Fiery Dancer (USA) (Atticus (USA))
8244a^{5}

Tango Sky (IRE) *David Nicholls* a87 86
3 b g Namid Sky Galaxy (USA) (Sky Classic (CAN))
2986^{7} (3861) 4081^{2} 5165^{2} 7177^{8} 7918^{9} 8143^{10}

Tanjung Agas (IRE) *Christopher Kellett* a21 73
4 b g Montjeu(IRE) Najmati (Green Desert (USA))
3997^{7} 4585^{11} 5384^{8} 5811^{8} 7717^{7} 8035^{11}

Tannery (IRE) *David Wachman* a90 109
3 b f Dylan Thomas(IRE) Danse Grecque (IRE) (Sadler's Wells (USA))
(3361a) (4376a)

Tantalising (IRE) *P J Prendergast* a65 85
4 b m Sadler's Wells(USA) Bluffing (IRE) (Darshaan)
7584a^{9}

Tantamount *Roger Charlton* a65 49
3 b c Observatory(USA) Cantanta (Top Ville)
1422^{4} ◆ 2544^{5} 3142^{14} 5280^{9}

Tantrum (IRE) *Olivia Maylam*
3 b f Jeremy(USA) Astuti (IRE) (Waajib)
2542^{13}

Tantshi (IRE) *Roger Varian* 84
2 b f Invincible Spirit(IRE) Qasirah (IRE) (Machiavellian (USA))
(5352) 5979^{12} 7406^{4}

Tapis Libre *Michael Easterby* a72 76
4 b g Librettist(USA) Stella Manuela (FR) (Galileo (IRE))
1275^{10} (1562) 1797^{10} 2606^{4} 3129^{12} 3699^{6} 4080^{5} 5585^{8} 6131^{6} 6794^{8} (7251)

Tapitsfly (USA) *Dale Romans* a93 114
5 rg m Tapit(USA) Flying Marlin (USA) (Marlin (USA))
4617a^{4}

Tapizar (USA) *Steven Asmussen* a118
4 b h Tapit(USA) Winning Call (USA) (Deputy Minister (CAN))
(7570a)

Tappanappa (IRE) *Brian Ellison* a99 89
5 b g High Chaparral(IRE) Itsibitsi (IRE) (Brief Truce (USA))
(300) 712^{6} (971) ◆ 1159^{5} 1882^{11} 2810^{3} 5966^{6} 6045^{7} ◆ 6415^{3} ◆ 7098^{9} 7630^{5}

Taqaat (USA) *Tim McCarthy* a77 85
4 b g Forestry(USA) Alrayihah (IRE) (Nashwan (USA))
626^{11} 685^{10} 1207^{5} 3047^{3} 3573^{3} 4511^{9} 5483^{8}

Tara Fay (IRE) *Gordon Elliott* a51 60
5 b m Saffron Walden(FR) Tara Tara (IRE) (Fayruz)
104^{8}

Tara From The Cape (USA) *Todd Pletcher* a101 103
2 ch f Leroidesanimaux(BRZ) Royal Irish Lass (USA) (Saint Ballado (CAN))
7547a^{4}

Tarantella Lady *George Moore* 71
4 b m Noverre(USA) Shortfall (Last Tycoon)
1272^{7} 1952^{11} 2775^{2} (3402) 3988^{5} 4867^{9} 7293^{5} 7603^{5}

Tarara *Andrew Balding* 77
2 b f Royal Applause Anneliina (Cadeaux Genereux)
4701^{5} 5146^{2} ◆ 5932^{3} 6787^{10}

Tarbawi (IRE) *Saeed Bin Suroor* a75 70
2 b g Anabaa(USA) Born Something (IRE) (Caerleon (USA))
4707^{4} 5084^{3} 6330^{5} 7164^{2} 7627^{2} 7723^{4}

Tarikhi (USA) *Saeed Bin Suroor* 87
2 b c Bernardini(USA) Caffe Latte (IRE) (Seattle Dancer (USA))
5321^{2} (6872)

Tariq Too *Amy Weaver* a63 103
5 ch g Kyllachy Tatora (Selkirk (USA))
(1522) 2068^{9} (2919) 3331^{8} 4751a^{5} 6468^{11} 7551a^{5}

Tarkheena Prince (USA) *C Von Der Recke* a80 71
7 b g Aldebaran(USA) Tarkheena (USA) (Alleged (USA))
630a^{6}

Tarooq (USA) *Stuart Williams* a96 72
6 b g War Chant(USA) Rose Of Zollern (IRE) (Seattle Dancer (USA))
254^{2} 426^{5} 622^{2} 868^{5} 3405^{P} (7788)

Taro Tywod (IRE) *Mark Brisbourne* a65 68
3 br f Footstepsinthesand Run To Jane (IRE) (Doyoun)
2981^{9} 3555^{6} 3954^{7} 4547^{12} 5669^{8} 6502^{5} 6892^{4} 7222^{2} 7527^{3} 7632^{3} (7752) 7921^{6} 8050^{2} 8213^{6}

Taroum (IRE) *Tony Carroll* 69
5 b g Refuse To Bend(IRE) Taraza (IRE) (Darshaan)
2389^{11} 2767^{7} 3222^{5} (4244) 4491^{3} 4536^{3} 5908^{8} 6159^{8} 6821^{2}

Tarrsille (IRE) *G M Lyons* a86 89
6 b g Dansili Tara Gold (IRE) (Royal Academy (USA))
337a^{8}

Tartan Blue *Robert Cowell* a58
2 b f Kyllachy Poly Blue (IRE) (Thatching)
7711^{6} (7891) 8065^{7} 8245^{4}

Tartan Gigha (IRE) *Geoffrey Harker* a105 90
7 b g Green Desert(USA) High Standard (Kris)
2180^{16} 2606^{6} (2751) 3114^{6} 4543^{4} 4962^{5} 5224^{3} 5966^{7} 6339^{6} 6476^{9} 7294^{10} 7455^{9}

Tartan Gunna *George Baker* a59 86
6 b g Anabaa(USA) Embraced (Pursuit Of Love)
285^{8} 2792^{7} 3386^{6} 4499^{9} 5174^{4} 5672^{8} 5941^{9} 7058^{4} 7200^{4} 7303^{9} 7479^{3}

Tartania *Scott Dixon* a44 44
2 ch f Milk It Mick Bay City Stroller (IRE) (City On A Hill (USA))
5242^{6} 5709^{7} 6122^{5}

Tartan Jura *Mark Johnston* a81 78
4 b g Green Desert(USA) On A Soapbox (USA) (Mi Cielo (USA))
6517^{7} 6706^{7} (7077) 7791^{4} 7972^{2} 8073^{3} 8191^{4} ◆

Tartan Trip *Andrew Balding* a89 89
5 b g Selkirk(USA) Marajuana (Robellino (USA))
90^{6} 280^{5} 529^{3} 817^{7} 1087^{5} 1680^{11}

Tartary (IRE) *Roger Charlton* a74
2 b c Oasis Dream Tamso (USA) (Seeking The Gold (USA))
7007^{6} (7498)

Tartiflette *Ed McMahon* 92
3 b f Dr Fong(USA) Bright Moll (Mind Games)
1500^{2} 2182^{5} 2854^{2} 3160^{2} 4062^{4} 6830^{12} 7408^{3} (7691)

Tasaday (USA) *A Fabre* 104
2 rg f Nayef(USA) Tashelka (FR) (Mujahid (USA))
(7343a)

Tasfeya *Lee Carter* a83 83
4 b g Haafhd Nufoos (Zafonic (USA))
2174^{9} 2561^{4} 3187^{3} 3827^{7} 6544^{2}

Tasheba *Caroline Keevil* a66 28
7 ch g Dubai Destination(USA) Tatanka (IRE) (Lear Fan (USA))
577^{6}

Tassel *Richard Hannon* 83
2 b f Kyllachy Xtrasensory (Royal Applause)
(1466) 1891^{7} 3326^{14} (6540) 7518^{12}

Taste The Wine (IRE) *Bernard Llewellyn* a67 74
6 gr g Verglas(IRE) Azia (IRE) (Desert Story (IRE))
3101^{3} 3429^{4} 4181^{5} 4536^{5} ◆ (4994) 5265^{2}

Tata Corner (IRE) *Owen Brennan*
6 b g Pilsudski(IRE) Wonder Winnie (IRE) (Be My Guest (USA))
3709^{8}

Tatlisu (IRE) *Richard Fahey* 80
2 b g Red Clubs(IRE) Zwadi (IRE) (Docksider (USA))
(1818) 2181^{5} 2715^{4} 4093^{12} 4614^{3} 5710^{5}

Tatting *Chris Dwyer* a67 55
3 ch g Street Cry(IRE) Needlecraft (IRE) (Mark Of Esteem (IRE))
2041^{12} 2380^{8} 2799^{9} 7201^{4} (7527) 7841^{3} 8050^{5}

Tatty *Ian Wood* a50 35
3 b f Dylan Thomas(IRE) Faslen (USA) (Fasliyev (USA))
1068^{4} 1610^{9} 2050^{6} 2803^{15}

Taurus Twins *Richard Price* a62 91
6 b g Deportivo Intellibet One (Compton Place)
1417^{9} 1602^{3} ◆ 2289^{9} (2731) 3127^{5} 4013^{14} 4367^{20} 6543^{10} 6755^{3} 7019^{12} 7291^{13} 7726^{7} 7937^{6} 8009^{9}

Tawaasul *William Haggas* a80 74
3 b f Haafhd Muwakleh (Machiavellian (USA))
2172^{4} (2665) 7359^{3} 7740^{4}

Tawafeeg (USA) *James Tate* a30
2 b f Bernardini(USA) Transition Time (USA) (Dynaformer (USA))
6366^{11}

Tawhid *Saeed Bin Suroor* 111
2 gr c Invincible Spirit(IRE) Snowdrops (Gulch (USA))
6020^{11} 6795^{2} (7172) (7404) ◆

Tawseef (IRE) *Roy Brotherton* a50 73
4 b g Monsun(GER) Sahool (Unfuwain (USA))
197^{3} 379^{8} 503^{6} 831^{7} 3470^{4} (3721) 4244^{2} 6097^{3} (6949) 7495^{2}

Tax Free (IRE) *David Nicholls* a89 100
10 b g Tagula(IRE) Grandel (Owington)
1316^{3} 1975^{6} 2507^{6} 2717^{6} 3374^{4} 4611^{3} ◆ 4799^{7} 5370^{2} (5487) 6028^{7} 6244^{19} 6557^{2} 7397^{21}

Taxiformissbyron *Michael Herrington* a46 49
2 b f Byron Miss Respect (Mark Of Esteem (IRE))
1861^{7} 2631^{6} 6781^{3} 7592^{8} 7974^{7} 8203^{5}

Tayarat (IRE) *Michael Chapman* a35 47
7 b g Noverre(USA) Sincere (IRE) (Bahhare (USA))
453^{8} 493^{7} 811^{6}

Tayvallich (IRE) *Mark Johnston*
3 bg c Clodovil(IRE) Tawaafur (Fantastic Light (USA))
4807^{10}

Tazaamun (IRE) *David O'Meara* 64
4 b g Shirocco(GER) Glorious (Nashwan (USA))
2588^{14} 3332^{2} (3889) 4716^{7}

Tazahum (USA) *Sir Michael Stoute* a86 116
4 b h Redoute's Choice(AUS) Huja (IRE) (Alzao (USA))
1471^{6} 3825^{5} (4822) 5560^{3} 6373^{2}

Tazweed (IRE) *Roger Varian* a52 54
3 b g Dubawi(IRE) Albahja (Sinndar (IRE))
1979^{10} 2850^{4} 3665^{3}

T Bag (IRE) *Wido Neuroth*
3 b g Bachelor Duke(USA) Pharaoh's Delight (Fairy King (USA))
3655a^{7}

T'Choupi Chop (FR) *A De Watrigant* a47 84
2 b c Indian Rocket Chopinette (FR) (Sin Kiang (FR))
3680a^{8} 5073a^{8}

Teacher (IRE) *William Haggas* 32
3 ch g Danehill Dancer(IRE) Lac Dessert (USA) (Lac Ouimet (USA))
1740^{9} 2673^{11}

Tea Cup *Richard Hannon* 82
3 b f Danehill Dancer(IRE) Quiet Storm (IRE) (Desert Prince (IRE))
2273^{4} (2757) 3395^{6} 3785^{2} 4150^{9} 4503^{5}

Teak (IRE) *Ian Williams* a76 80
5 b g Barathea(IRE) Szabo (IRE) (Anabaa (USA))
(1534) ◆ (1829) 2863^{2} 3061^{2} (4606) ◆ 6066a^{5}

Team Challenge *Tim Easterby* 67
2 b g Araafa(IRE) Passionforfashion (IRE) (Fasliyev (USA))
1842^{9} 3208^{3} 3491^{6} 5109^{2} 5602^{6} 6049^{7} 6475^{4}

Tebbit (USA) *Roger Varian* a67
2 rg g Tapit(USA) Baroness Thatcher (USA) (Johannesburg (USA))
7167^{7} 7627^{4} 7900^{10}

Tebee's Oasis *John Gosden* a57
2 b f Oasis Dream Tebee (Selkirk (USA))
7962^{8} 8201^{7}

Tecktal (FR) *Pat Phelan* a47 35
9 ch m Pivotal Wenge (USA) (Housebuster (USA))
566^{6}

Tectonic (IRE) *Iain Jardine* a60 55
3 b g Dylan Thomas(IRE) Pine Chip (USA) (Nureyev (USA))
660^{11} 743^{2} 901^{5} 993^{5} 1062^{7} 1725^{11} 5917^{12} 6530^{6}

Teddy's Promise (USA) *Ronald W Ellis* a110 98
4 bb m Salt Lake(USA) Braids And Beads (USA) (Capote (USA))
7569a^{8}

Ted's Brother (IRE) *Richard Guest* a41 82
4 b g Fath(USA) Estertide (IRE) (Tagula (IRE))
1354^{8} 1650^{5} 2632^{10} 3334^{7} 5314^{3} 5341^{5} 6410^{13} 7436^{5}

Teen Ager (FR) *Paul Burgoyne* a55 51
8 b g Invincible Spirit(IRE) Tarwiya (IRE) (Dominion)
375^{6} 561^{5} 666^{3} 744^{4} 822^{5} 1088^{6} 1908^{4}

Teeth Of The Dog (USA) *Michael Matz* a110
3 b c Bluegrass Cat(USA) Deputy Reality (USA) (Deputy Minister (CAN))
2299a^{5}

Teetotal (IRE) *Nigel Tinkler* 67
2 ch g Footstepsinthesand Tea Service (USA) (Atticus (USA))
3074^{12} 3436^{3} 4132^{4} 4922^{4} 5544^{6} 6404^{2} 6754^{3} 7031^{6}

Teide Peak (IRE) *Paul D'Arcy* a66 71
3 b g Cape Cross(IRE) Teide Lady (Nashwan (USA))
5783^{11} 6250^{9} 6940^{5} (8145)

Teixidor (ITY) *Ottavio Di Paolo* 97
3 ch c St Paul House Rosetta Stone (ITY) (Tisserand (ITY))
2324a^{9}

Telbes *M Delzangles* 100
4 b h Green Tune(USA) Yes My Love (FR) (Anabaa (USA))
6297a^{7} 6864a^{6}

Telescope (IRE) *Sir Michael Stoute* 86
2 b c Galileo(IRE) Velouette (Darshaan)
6020^{2} ◆ (6596) ◆

Telmo (FR) *A Lamotte D'Argy* 10
2 b c Big Shuffle(USA) Ansariya (USA) (Shahrastani (USA))
4476a^{6} 5378a^{0}

Telwaar *Peter Chapple-Hyam* 102
3 ch c Haafhd Waafiah (Anabaa (USA))
(1453) 2110a^{11} 3265^{19} 7048^{9}

Temida (IRE) *M G Mintchev* 113
4 b m Oratorio(IRE) Interim Payment (USA) (Red Ransom (USA))
(3652a) (5145a)

Tempest Fugit (IRE) *John Gosden* a99 93
3 b f High Chaparral(IRE) Diary (IRE) (Green Desert (USA))
1724^{2} (6398) 6833^{5} (7510)

Temple Meads *Ed McMahon* 98
4 ch h Avonbridge Harryana (Efisio)
1857^{12} 6116^{2}

Temple Road (IRE) *Milton Bradley* a74 57
4 b g Street Cry(IRE) Sugarhoneybaby (IRE) (Docksider (USA))
1420^{6} 1889^{8} 2611^{5} 3390^{5} 3791^{12} 7748^{4} ◆ (8075) (8168)

Tempura (GER) *C Laffon-Parias* 95
4 b m Cape Cross(IRE) Trumbaka (IRE) (In The Wings)
2570a^{9} 5399a^{8}

Temuco (IRE) *David Evans* a60 71
3 b g Bachelor Duke(USA) La Chinampina (FR) (Darshaan)
1716^{3} 2367^{7} ◆ (3014) 3193^{2} 3543^{6} 3920^{9} 4531^{3} 4088^{6} 5501^{7} 5657^{8} 7015^{13} 8051^{9} 8249^{10}

Tenacity *Kate Walton* 58
3 b g Passing Glance Wigman Lady (IRE) (Tenby)
4293^{5} 5679^{9} 6102^{10}

Tenancy (IRE) *Shaun Harris* a61 58
8 b g Rock Of Gibraltar(IRE) Brush Strokes (Cadeaux Genereux)
456^{6} 578^{14} (807) 1009^{9} 1178^{12} 1283^{6} 1787^{8} 2401^{4} (3462) 3717^{3} 4085^{3} 4237^{7} 5246^{9} 5543^{7} 6288^{6} 7446^{2} 7634^{2} 7733^{11}

Tenavon *William Knight* a62 65
4 b m Avonbridge Tender (IRE) (Zieten (USA))
1735^{2} 2170^{7} 3344^{7}

Tenbridge *Derek Haydn Jones* a73 75
3 b f Avonbridge Tenebrae (IRE) (In The Wings)
127^{2} 377^{2} 667^{3} 1589^{5} 2503^{4} (2846) 3619^{5} 4413^{7} 6454^{9} 7725^{10} 7975^{7}

Tenderly Place *William Knight* a27 56
3 ch f Compton Place Tender (IRE) (Zieten (USA))
1705^{11} 2361^{4} 3050^{9} 3510^{9} 4424^{5} 4937^{10} 5215^{6} 5458^{6} 6233^{14}

Tenenbaum *A Fabre* 108
3 b g Authorized(IRE) Al Hasnaa (Zafonic (USA))
5650a^{7} 6896a^{3}

Tenessee *Jamie Osborne* a76 67
5 b g Nayef(USA) Shukran (Hamas (IRE))
3659^{7} 4843^{5} 5506^{6} 5741^{3} 6458^{2} 7250^{3} 7474^{2}

Tenhoo *Eric Alston* a59 80
6 b g Reset(AUS) Bella Bambina (Turtle Island (IRE))
1657^{11} 2312^{7} 2751^{11} 3377^{10} 3610^{5} 3728^{2} 4048^{5} 4627^{4} 5039^{4} (5585) 5967^{6}

Tennessee Wildcat (IRE) *G M Lyons* a95 92
2 b g Kheleyf(USA) Windbeneathmywings (IRE) (In The Wings)
(1832a) 2184a^{3} 2512a^{8} 2779a^{3} 6078a^{4} 7038a^{2}

Tenor (IRE) *Roger Varian* 53
2 b c Oratorio(IRE) Cedar Sea (IRE) (Persian Bold)
6845^{6}

Tenth Star (IRE) *A P O'Brien* 106
3 b c Dansili Alpha Lupi (IRE) (Rahy (USA))
6062a^{5}

Tenure *Sir Michael Stoute* 63
3 b c Dansili Alumni (Selkirk (USA))
1467^{11} 4516^{10}

Teolagi (IRE) *J S Moore* a65 52
2 ch g Teofilo(IRE) Satulagi (USA) (Officer (USA))
4846^{7} 6501^{9} 7373^{9} (7708)

Teophilip (IRE) *Marco Botti* a72 83
2 bb c Teofilo(IRE) Triomphale (USA) (Nureyev (USA))
7167^{10} (7466) 7773^{4}

Tepmokea (IRE) *Mrs K Burke* a93 101
6 ch g Noverre(USA) Eroica (GER) (Highest Honor (FR))
2253^{8} 3377^{8} 3857^{3} 4111^{12} 5558^{17} 7396^{16} 8242^{2}

Tequila Sunrise *Charles Hills* 59
2 gr f Dansili Kenmist (Kenmare (FR))
4011^{12}

Terdaad (IRE) *Saeed Bin Suroor* a96 97
4 ch g Shamardal(USA) Akrmina (Zafonic (USA))
1924^{2} 2642^{13} 4557^{4} 7631^{3}

Terenzium (IRE) *Micky Hammond* a52 59
10 br g Cape Cross(IRE) Tatanka (ITY) (Luge)
2242^{4} 2827^{7} 3519^{3} 3988^{2} 4867^{8} 5172^{6} 5761^{4} 7102^{4}

Terpsichore *Sylvester Kirk* a51 37
2 ch f Beat Hollow Effie (Royal Academy (USA))
5997^{5} 6841^{9} 7165^{7} 7779^{10}

Terra Bleu (IRE) *Brendan Powell* a46 38
5 b g Azamour(IRE) Pinaflore (FR) (Formidable (USA))
3143^{8} 3498^{4}

Terrific Challenge (USA) *S Seemar* a108 104
10 ch h Royal Academy(USA) Clever Empress (Crafty Prospector (USA))
141a^{7}

Tertio Bloom (SWE) *Fabricio Borges* a102 105
7 ch g Tertullian(USA) Yankee Bloom (USA) (El Gran Senor (USA))
140a^{4} 314a^{7} (616a) 3603a^{2} 4751a^{4}

Tertullus (FR) *Rune Haugen* a48 105
9 b h Monsun(GER) Tryphosa (IRE) (Be My Guest (USA))
2807a^{4} 5651a^{4}

Tesey *M G Mintchev* 108
4 b h Tiger Hill(IRE) Laronja (GER) (Areion (GER))
2322a^{4} 3206a^{6}

Tessarini (USA) *Mahmood Al Zarooni* a67
2 b f Bernardini(USA) Tasso's Magic Roo (USA) (Tasso (USA))
6117^{13} 6366^{5}

Testamatta *Marco Botti* 76
2 b f Motivator Rummage (Zamindar (USA))
2245^{3} 3590^{6} 4246^{2} 4820^{8}

Testa Rossa (IRE) *J W Hills* a60
2 b c Oratorio(IRE) Red Rita (IRE) (Kefaah (USA))
8102^{4}

Testosterone (IRE) *Ed Dunlop* 116
4 b m Dansili Epopee (IRE) (Sadler's Wells (USA))
3369^{11} 3856^{5} 7237^{6}

Teth *Anthony Carson* a58 54
3 br f Dansili Beta (Selkirk (USA))
6965^{6} 7318^{9} 7906^{9} 8180^{3}

Teutonic Knight (IRE) *Ian Williams* a19 46
5 ch g Daggers Drawn(USA) Azyaa (Kris)
366[14]

Tevez *Des Donovan* a89 94
7 b g Sakhee(USA) Sosumi (Be My Chief (USA))
5[8] 266[4] 351[3] 529[4] 694[3] 907[11] 1128[14] 1354[4] 2545[5] 2975 [3] 3403[5]

Tewin Wood *Alan Bailey* a82 81
5 ch g Zaha(CAN) Green Run (USA) (Green Dancer (USA))
(11) 280[8]

Thackeray *Chris Fairhurst* a55 75
5 b g Fasliyev(USA) Chinon (IRE) (Entrepreneur)
579[4] 833[3] (1276) (1659) ◆ 2491[9] 3213[10]

Tha'Ir (IRE) *Saeed Bin Suroor* 106
2 b c New Approach(IRE) Flashing Green (Green Desert (USA))
2308[4] (2822) (3368) 4698[4] 5833[2] 6243[3] 6910a[8]

Thakana *Marcus Tregoning* a67 75
2 br f Cape Cross(IRE) Shohrah (IRE) (Giant's Causeway (USA))
6960[2] 7506[4] 7720[9]

Thalia Grace *William Knight* a52 62
5 ch m Zafeen(FR) Days Of Grace (Wolfhound (USA))
126[6] 3546[12] 4508[8]

Thane Of Cawdor (IRE) *Joseph Tuite* a58 59
3 b g Danehill Dancer(IRE) Holy Nola (USA) (Silver Deputy (CAN))
2381[6] 2883[8] 3950[4] 5998[10] 6892[5] 7148[2] 7385[5]

Thank You Joy *J R Jenkins* a58 62
4 b m Iceman Once Removed (Distant Relative)
130[11] 333[5] 1179[8] 1771[4] 2048[7] 3047[6] 3794[7]

Thankyou Very Much *James Bethell* 47
2 b f Lucky Story(USA) Maid Of Perth (Mark Of Esteem (IRE))
7363[8]

Tharawal (IRE) *Terry Clement* a79 77
3 b c Moss Vale(IRE) Notanother (Inchinor)
1182[5] 2042[3] 2279[5] 2543[7] 3347[2]

Tharawal Lady (IRE) *John Quinn* a63 75
2 b f Moss Vale(IRE) Notley Park (Wolfhound (USA))
(1437) 1972[4] 2603[11] (4324) 6425[5] 6809[3] 7241[4]

That Boy David *G M Lyons* a86 83
3 b g Kodiac Someone's Angel (USA) (Runaway Groom (CAN))
1834a[2] ◆

Thatcherite (IRE) *Tony Coyle* a78 74
4 gr g Verglas(IRE) Damiana (IRE) (Thatching)
646[5] (909) 1158[7] 2510[12] 2753[7] 3230[7] 3914[6] 6047[3] 6410[11] 7027[12] 7415[5]

Thatchmaster (USA) *Mahmood Al Zarooni* 58
2 bb c Street Cry(IRE) Michita (USA) (Dynaformer (USA))
3611[6]

That'll Do Nicely (IRE) *Nicky Richards* a35 73
9 b g Bahhare(USA) Return Again (IRE) (Top Ville)
1719[RR] 3116[4] 3693[6]

Thats A Fret (IRE) *Liam McAteer* a80 79
6 b g Choisir(AUS) Reality Check (IRE) (Sri Pekan (USA))
6286[5]

Thats Molly (IRE) *Eric Alston* 54
3 b f Hawk Wing(USA) Molly Marie (IRE) (Fasliyev (USA))
3289[4] 3990[8] 4293[9] 5295[6] 6104[14] 6542[6]

Thats Notall Folks (IRE) *F-H Graffard* 88
2 b c Kheleyf(USA) Turkana Girl (Hernando (FR))
3928a[2] 4205a[8]

That's Plenty (IRE) *E Charpy* a77 74
3 b c Dr Fong(USA) Tyranny (Machiavellian (USA))
142a[12]

That's The Spirit (FR) *P Bary* a80 83
3 b f Country Reel(USA) Risque De Verglas (FR) (Verglas (IRE))
5473a[8]

Thawabel (IRE) *Marcus Tregoning* 50
3 b f Nayef(USA) Shohrah (IRE) (Giant's Causeway (USA))
1261[9]

The Absent Mare *Robin Dickin* a71 46
4 gr m Fair Mix(IRE) Precious Lucy (FR) (Kadrou (FR))
728[2] 963[2] (1085) 1505[10] 7927[8] 8170[4] 8290[4]

The Art Of Racing (IRE) *Richard Hannon* a64 79
2 b g Acclamation Divert (IRE) (Averti (IRE))
3916[7] (6071) 7193[7]

The Baronet *Sir Mark Prescott Bt* a80 86
3 b g Sir Percy Windmill (Ezzoud (IRE))
3809[3] ◆ 4212[4] ◆ (4746) 5228[2] (6706)

The Bay Bandit *Neil Mulholland* a60 44
5 b g Highest Honor(FR) Pescara (IRE) (Common Grounds)
837[5] (927) 1088[3] 1309[2] 1608[7] 6252[7] 6396[8]

The Bear *Linda Perratt* a56 38
9 ch g Rambling Bear Precious Girl (Precious Metal)
5058[5] 5190[11]

The Bells O Peover *Mark Johnston* a80 92
4 b g Selkirk(USA) Bay Tree (IRE) (Daylami (IRE))
443a[3] 630a[13] 1374[9] 1993[5] 2457[10] 2863[11] 2978[3] 3377[4] 3765[6] 4613[6] 5002[6] 5665[8] 6170[2] 6311[3] 6584[12]

The Bendy Fella (IRE) *Mark Usher* a53
4 ch g Choisir(AUS) Missish (Mummy's Pet)
770[6] 892[10] 981[8]

The Best Doctor (IRE) *Jeremy Noseda* 65
2 ch c Pivotal Strawberry Fledge (USA) (Kingmambo (USA))
7330[6]

The Betchworth Kid *Michael Bell* a83 97
7 b g Tobougg(IRE) Runelia (Runnett)
3125[3] 3625[7] 4800[11] 5076[8] 5580[10] 6415[8] (7109) 7367[16]

The Black Jacobin *J S Moore* a64 78
2 b g Piccolo Greenfly (Green Desert (USA))
2261[3] 2688[2] ◆ 3662[4] 4093[19] 6042[2] 6487[15] 6871[7] 7304[3] 7478[4] 7687[4]

The Blue Banana (IRE) *Edwin Tuer* a60 80
3 b g Red Clubs(IRE) Rinneen (IRE) (Bien Bien (USA))
1160[11] 1477[6] 1798[8] 2336[10] 2589[4] 7348[4]

The Blue Dog (IRE) *Michael Wigham* a71 67
5 b m High Chaparral(IRE) Jules (IRE) (Danehill (USA))
(1083) 1189[5] 1485[3] 4189[12] 4875[11]

The Boomingbittern *Roger Teal* a18
3 b f Three Valleys(USA) The Lady Mandarin (Groom Dancer (USA))
4333[6]

The Brothers War (USA) *J-C Rouget* 97
2 b c War Front(USA) Moon Queen (IRE) (Sadler's Wells (USA))
7430a[3]

The Call (FR) *Uwe Ostmann* 99
3 b c Call Me Big(GER) Tennessee Waltz (Caerleon (USA))
3603a[10] 5647a[5]

The Calling Curlew *Henry Candy* a72 73
4 b g Soviet Star(USA) The Lady Mandarin (Groom Dancer (USA))
2363[3] 3077[7] 3722[3] 4491[5] 5124[5]

The Cash Generator (IRE) *Ralph Smith* a56 71
4 b g Peintre Celebre(USA) Majestic Launch (Lear Fan (USA))
6397[11] 6770[8]

The Catenian (IRE) *John Butler* a49 31
4 b g Hawk Wing(USA) Belleclaire (IRE) (Bigstone (IRE))
200[4] 468[5] 741[3] 895[4] 1112[7] 1184[6]

The Cayterers *Tony Carroll* a96 85
10 b g Cayman Kai(IRE) Silky Smooth (IRE) (Thatching)
2561[7] 3226[7] 4706[4] (5535)

The Cheka (IRE) *Eve Johnson Houghton* a104 115
6 b g Xaar Veiled Beauty (USA) (Royal Academy (USA))
(1129) 2179[2] 3370[12] 4100[2] 4861a[3] 5627[2] 6468[16] 7236[6] 7690[5]

The Chill Zone (USA) *John E. Shaw*
4 rg h Concorde's Tune(USA) Donna Marie (USA) (Came Home (USA))
8100a[9]

The Comedian (AUS) *M Freedman* a95 99
6 b g Encosta De Lago(AUS) How Funny (AUS) (Rory's Jester (AUS))
588a[4] 757a[8]

The Composer *Michael Blanshard* a45 48
10 b g Royal Applause Superspring (Superlative)
4904[9] 5196[11]

The Confessor *Henry Candy* a96 97
5 b g Piccolo Twilight Mistress (Bin Ajwaad (IRE))
1373[3] 1885[7] 2268[14] 3977[6] (4703) 5572[3] 6659[10] 7240[18]

Thecornishcockney *John Ryan* a94 82
3 bl g Cockney Rebel(IRE) Glittering Image (IRE) (Sadler's Wells (USA))
1567[10] 1793[4] 2382[10] 2625[2] 2787[8] 3345[6] 3448[3] 3946[6] 4725[5] 5231[8] 6647[5] 6971[4] 7162[3] 7417[2] 7744[5] 7839[2] (7933) (7972) 8073[2] 8228[4]

Thecornishcowboy *John Ryan* a83 68
3 b g Haafhd Oriental Dance (Fantastic Light (USA))
1365[5] 1517[10] 1725[12] 2010[9] 2582[7] 2802[8] 3228[2] 3551[3] 3966[6] 4198[3] 4940[4] 5037[6] (5939) 5989[2] 6174[3] 6334[2] (6568) 6973[9] 7768[2] 7905[3] (8023) (8060) 8078[7] 8206[4]

Thecornishwren (IRE) *John Ryan* a36
3 ch f Medecis Coulisse (IRE) (In The Wings)
7025[6] 7352[9] 7739[7]

The Coulbeck Kid *Des Donovan* a38 40
3 b g Tobougg(IRE) Billiard (Kirkwall)
2[5]

The Dancing Lord *Bill Turner* a70 75
3 br g Imperial Dancer Miss Brookie (The West (USA))
42[4] 250[2] 940[2] 1169[6] 7902[8] 8036[7] 8077[8]

The Ducking Stool *Julia Feilden* a50 72
5 ch m Where Or When(IRE) Dance Sequel (Selkirk (USA))
1106[3] 1379[4] (2804) 3216[2] (3794) 4251[7] 4844[2] 4959[2] 5359[2] 5636[6] 6141[11] 6416[9] 6794[4] 7315[8]

The Dude (FR) *J Van Handenhove* a77 59
3 b g King's Best(USA) Mrs Snow (Singspiel (IRE))
1900a[7] 7266a[6]

The Educator (IRE) *Cecil Ross* a48 71
5 b g Chineur(FR) Zafaraya (IRE) (Ashkalani (IRE))
6184a[8]

The Factor (USA) *Bob Baffert* a126
4 rg h War Front(USA) Greyciousness (USA) (Miswaki (USA))
1147a[6]

The Ferryman (IRE) *A P O'Brien* a81 96
2 b c Galileo(IRE) Dietrich (USA) (Storm Cat (USA))
4161a[2] 7050[5]

The Four Elms (IRE) *John J Walsh* 78
4 b g Desert Style(IRE) Flying Freedom (IRE) (Archway (IRE))
7584a[18]

The Fox Tully (IRE) *Gerard Keane* a76 85
7 b g Monashee Mountain(USA) Then Came Bronson (IRE) (Up And At 'Em)
7852a[7]

The Fugue *John Gosden* 118
3 br f Dansili Twyla Tharp (IRE) (Sadler's Wells (USA))
1884[4] (2178) 2658[3] ◆ 3292[2] (4801) 5518[2] 7549a[3]

The Fun Crusher *Tim Easterby* 87
4 ch g Halling(USA) South Rock (Rock City)
1133[5] ◆ 2180[10] 4072[4]

The Galloping Shoe *Alistair Whillans* a83 88
7 b g Observatory(USA) My Way (IRE) (Marju (IRE))
(1657) 2414[3]

The Gatling Boy (IRE) *Richard Hannon* 82
2 ch c Tamayuz Miniver (IRE) (Mujtahid (USA))
4803[10] (5275)

The Ginger Berry *Dr Jon Scargill* a55
2 ch g First Trump Dolly Coughdrop (IRE) (Titus Livius (FR))
7191[11] 8172[4]

The Giving Tree (IRE) *Sylvester Kirk* a67 82
3 b f Rock Of Gibraltar(IRE) Starry Messenger (Galileo (IRE))
(1322) 2201[2] 2701[7] 4057[3] 5420[3] 6023[9] 6375[5] 6735[2] 7375[4] 7519[3] 7852a[13]

The Gnathologist (IRE) *Donal Kinsella* a40 43
7 b g Tendulkar(USA) Kayley Dancer (IRE) (Mujadil (USA))
775a[13]

The Gold Cheongsam (IRE) *Jeremy Noseda* 103
2 b f Red Clubs(IRE) Fuerta Ventura (IRE) (Desert Sun)
2480[3] ◆ 3326[5] (4539) (4820) ◆ (6162) 6672[11] 6873[3] 7547a[5]

The Guru Of Gloom (IRE) *William Muir* a87 85
4 b g Dubai Destination(USA) Gabriella (Cape Cross (IRE))
1708[10] 2083[7] ◆ 2608[9] 3772[3] 4437[6] 5910[10] 6256[11]

The Happy Hammer (IRE) *Eugene Stanford* a74 48
6 b g Acclamation Emma's Star (ITY) (Darshaan)
128[5] 302[2] 626[6] 713[3] 1091[2] 1378[6] 1587[3] 2482[6] 2981[10] (5892) 6687[9]

The High Man *Ed Walker* a78 90
4 ch g Medicean Excellent (Grand Lodge (USA))
2233[6] (3154) ◆ (4499) ◆ 5554[7] 6584[13]

The Holyman (IRE) *Jo Crowley* a82 75
4 ch g Footstepsinthesand Sunset (IRE) (Polish Precedent (USA))
(150) (714) 4216[3] 4475[3] 5944[7] 6642[13]

The Jackal (USA) *R L Wallace*
6 bb g Forest Wildcat(USA) Puff O Luck (USA) (Run Of Luck (USA))
8100a[5]

The Jailer *John O'Shea* a60 67
9 b m Mujahid(USA) Once Removed (Distant Relative)
2647[4] 3435[3] 3791[4] 4422[5] 4492[8] 4993[11] 6233[9]

The Kernigal (IRE) *Paul Howling* a68 58
3 b g Red Clubs(IRE) Ellens Princess (IRE) (Desert Prince (IRE))
6586[4] 7504[8] 8099[8] 8111[10]

The Kicking Lord *Mark Brisbourne* a63
3 b g Avonbridge Lady Killer (IRE) (Daggers Drawn (USA))
499[5] 6643[7] 6827[4] 7224[7] 7616[6]

Theladyinquestion *Andrew Balding* a93 84
5 b m Dubawi(IRE) Whazzat (Daylami (IRE))
2078[8] 2896[9] 6373[4] 7508[12]

The Lark *Michael Bell* 77
2 ch f Pivotal Gull Wing (IRE) (In The Wings)
6790[4] (7364)

The Last Straw (IRE) *Gordon Elliott* a38 25
7 b m Vettori(IRE) Lady Thynn (FR) (Crystal Glitters (USA))
104[9]

The Lemonpie (GER) *Brendan Powell* 52
7 b g Next Desert(IRE) Terra Novalis (GER) (Astylos (GER))
6004[9]

The Lock Master (IRE) *Michael Appleby* a88 85
5 b g Key Of Luck(USA) Pitrizza (IRE) (Machiavellian (USA))
22[2] 187[9] 285[2] 432[4] 548[3] 584[2] 751[2] 872[5] 1056[6] 1275[12] 1358[4] 2051[3] (2405) 2767[2] 2821[2] 3022[2] 3380[4] (3992) 4460[4] (5001) 5546[13] (7132) 7368[3] 7438[5] 8110[4] 8275[11]

The Lodge Road (IRE) *Martin Todhunter* a69 73
4 b g Holy Roman Emperor(IRE) Golden Coral (USA) (Slew O'Gold (USA))
2094[4] 2588[10] 2926[2] 4314[5] 5001[8] 6258[13]

The Lost Legion (IRE) *John Patrick Shanahan* a55 65
3 b g Whipper(USA) The Real Thing (IRE) (Traditionally (USA))
1834a[7]

The Lumber Guy (USA) *Michael Hushion* a121
3 rg c Grand Slam(USA) Boltono (USA) (Unbridled's Song (USA))
7574a[2]

The Magic Of Rio *John Balding* a49 46
6 b m Captain Rio Good Health (Magic Ring (IRE))
95[3] 910[7] 979[2] 1280[2] 2436[3] 4187[9] 5013[6]

The Manx Missile *Michael Bell* 53
2 ch g Sakhee's Secret Careless Freedom (Bertolini (USA))
2069[10] 2852[7] 3973[8]

The Mellor Fella *Richard Fahey* 85
4 b g Compton Place Grande Terre (IRE) (Grand Lodge (USA))
1670[10] 2257[16]

The Mighty Peg *Tim Walford* 64
2 b g Mujadil(USA) Messina (IRE) (Sadler's Wells (USA))
6880[11] 7363[9] 7598[4]

The Monarck (FR) *T Lallie* a73 73
2 ch c Zamindar(USA) Rock Harmonie (FR) (Rock Of Gibraltar (IRE))
7265a[6] 7597a[9] 7984a[8]

The Mongoose *David Evans* a76 70
4 b g Montjeu(IRE) Angara (Alzao (USA))
176[4] 216[3] ◆ 374[6] 538[6] 1418[14] 7857[5] 8021[2] (8141) 8234[5]

The Name Is Frank *Mark Gillard* a64 72
7 b g Lujain(USA) Zaragossa (Paris House)
1895[2] 2207[3] 2574[5] 3153[2] 4602[7] 5240[5] 5874[6] 6233[5] 6585[6] 7105[9]

The New Black (IRE) *Gay Kelleway* a67 67
3 gr f Oratorio(IRE) Zarawa (IRE) (Kahyasi)
2128[7] (2628) 3044[3] 3671[6] 4583[6] 4942[9] 5443[5] 5945[10] 6442[9] 6810[3] 7314[5] 7469[2] 7600[7] 7993[5] 8083[3] 8158[5] 8263[5]

The Nifty Fox *Tim Easterby* a87 91
8 b g Foxhound(USA) Nifty Alice (First Trump)
1642[14] 1868[17] 2230[7] 2596[3] 2793[5] 3027[8] (3578) (3905) 4133[2] 4430[2] 4880[9] 5539[10] 6009[9] 6427[13] 7000[3]

The Nifty Notion *Lawrence Mullaney*
3 ch f Zafeen(FR) Nifty Alice (First Trump)
3811[9]

The Nile *John Gosden* a98 103
3 ch c Three Valleys(USA) Delta (Zafonic (USA))
(1737) ◆ 2277[2] 3239[P] (Dead)

The Noble Ord *Sylvester Kirk* a70 77
3 b g Indesatchel(IRE) Four Legs Good (IRE) (Be My Guest (USA))
1264[3] 2089[2] 3736[7] 4413[4] 4901[3] 5837[10] 6146[14] 7108[6] 7358[12] 7776[4] 8005[4] 8074[5] 8177[3]

The Obvious Choice *Stuart Williams* a69 52
2 b c Royal Applause Crackle (Anshan)
3545[7] 5360[8] 6014[4] (7060)

Theo Danon (GER) *P Schiergen* 109
4 ch h Lord Of England(GER) Ticinella (GER) (Hernando (FR))
2106a[5] 3206a[2] 5613a[5] 6291a[9]

Theodore Gericault (IRE) *Sir Michael Stoute* 77
2 b g Sir Percy Tableau Vivant (IRE) (Pivotal)
4539[4]

The Oil Magnate *Michael Dods* a77 80
7 ch g Dr Fong(USA) Bob's Princess (Bob's Return (IRE))
2440[8] 3180[3] (3891) 4639[3]

Theo Speed (FR) *S Gouvaze*
5 b h Epistolaire(IRE) La Pomone (FR) (Sicyos (USA))
94a[0]

The Osteopath (IRE) *John Davies* 86
9 ch g Danehill Dancer(IRE) Miss Margate (IRE) (Don't Forget Me)
(1520) 1670[7] ◆ 1863[6] 2243[2] 2285[4] 3037[5] 3185[7] 5414[7] 7493[4] 7639[5]

The Pier (IRE) *David Pipe* a79 86
6 ch g Alhaarth(IRE) Cois Cuain (IRE) (Night Shift (USA))
7999[6]

The Ploughman *John Bridger* a47 45
3 gr g Tillerman Kilmovee (Inchinor)
3998[8] 4870[12] 5280[6] 5577[7] 5789[8] 5945[6] 6255[11] 7632[13] 7811[13]

The Quarterjack *Ron Hodges* a45 80
3 b g Haafhd Caressed (Medicean)
620[7] 730[5] 2162[14] 3142[3] (3483) 4323[6] (4906) (5359) 6574[3] 7082[8]

Therapeutic *Scott Dixon* a47 66
2 b f Milk It Mick Theoretical (Marju (IRE))
2261[4] 2686[2] 3110[4] 3747[6] 4152[4] 4767[3]

Thereabouts (USA) *Marco Botti* 72
3 b g Singspiel(IRE) Around (Danehill (USA))
2381[4] 3079[9] 3809[5] 4544[5] 4969[3] 5454[4]

The Reaper (IRE) *G M Lyons* a110 108
4 b g Footstepsinthesand Lady Gregory (IRE) (In The Wings)
141a[3] ◆ 314a[3] 1538a[4] 2513a[3]

The Rectifier (USA) *Seamus Durack* a99 112
5 bb g Langfuhr(CAN) Western Vision (USA) (Gone West (USA))
(29) 246a[13] 586a[5] 757a[14] 3331[22] 3640[5] 7502[12] 7826[5]

Theresnoneedfordat (IRE) *Stuart Williams* a89 68
3 b g Holy Roman Emperor(IRE) Manuscript (Machiavellian (USA))
2785[10] 3555[17] 4043[12] 4970[3] 5454[3] 5513[3] (5808) (6211) ◆ (6497) 6610[2]

There's No Rules *Richard Guest* a43 46
3 br g Authorized(IRE) Excellent (Grand Lodge (USA))
2826[8] 5316[7] 5770[8] 6315[6] 6807[5]

The Right Time *Tony Carroll* a42 52
4 b m Val Royal(FR) Esligier (IRE) (Sabrehill (USA))
558[5]

The Scuttler (IRE) *Mick Channon* a66 73
2 b c Rakti Common Rumpus (IRE) (Common Grounds)
5062[13] 6168[2] 6501[6] 6815[9]

The Sixties *Mick Channon* 81
2 ch g Sixties Icon Queen Of Narnia (Hunting Lion (IRE))
2983[5] 3368[6] 3569[3] 3973[2] 4071[3] 4487[4] 4836[2] (4952) 5903[4]

The Snorer *John Holt* a52 37
4 b g Diktat La Chesneraie (Groom Dancer (USA))
296[7]

The Stomp (FR) *D Guillemin* a64 81
2 b c Layman(USA) Version Originale (FR) (Poliglote)
5698a[4]

The Strig *Stuart Williams* a79 73
5 b g Mujahid(USA) Pretty Kool (Inchinor)
91[7] (178) 251[2] 563[9] 710[9] 893[6] 2251[9] 2494[4] 2629[4] 2647[2] 2994[5] 3390[6] (3724) 4300[11] 5020[4] 5514[5] 6370[7] 7484[6] 7725[4] 7827[6] (7902)

The Sydney Arms (IRE) *Morten Arnesen* a59 72
4 b m Elusive City(USA) Daftara (IRE) (Caerleon (USA))
5143a[8]

The Taj (USA) *Richard Hannon* 97
2 ch c Street Cry(IRE) India (USA) (Hennessy (USA))
(2880) ◆ 3240[10] 4488[6] 5088[2] 5563[7] (6022) 6865[5]

The Thrill Is Gone *Mick Channon* a73 96
4 ch m Bahamian Bounty Licence To Thrill (Wolfhound (USA))
4690[10] 5487[9] 5832[8] 6026[7] 6347[6]

The Tichborne (IRE) *Roger Teal* a76 93
4 b g Shinko Forest(IRE) Brunswick (Warning)
868[13] 1212[9] 1510[19] 2857[9] 3281[7] 3772[7] 4580[6] (5774) ◆ 6495[11] 7485[7] 7741[3]

The Ticket Man *Mrs John Harrington* 83
2 b g Rail Link Wyoming (Inchinor)
6550a[3]

The Tiddly Tadpole *Simon West* 75
7 b g Tipsy Creek(USA) Froglet (Shaamit (IRE))
5293[3] 6409[4]

The Tiger *Ed Dunlop* a70 96
4 b g Tiger Hill(IRE) Rafiya (Halling (USA))
(3913) ◆ 5429[7] 6639[4] (7294) (7455) 7689[16]

Theturnofthesun (IRE) *John Gosden* a84 86
3 ch c Galileo(IRE) Something Mon (USA) (Maria's Mon (USA))
1132[4] (1302) 2281[3] 3042[12]

The Turtle (FR) *A Junk* a73 73
4 b m Chichicastenango(FR) Turtle Cove (IRE) (Catrail (USA))
(15a)

The Verminator (AUS) *Chris Waller* 111
6 b g Jeune Fraar Side (AUS) (Fraar (USA))
7696a[P]

The Way To Be (IRE) *Gerard Butler* a40 36
3 b g Bachelor Duke(USA) Ines Bloom (IRE) (Sadler's Wells (USA))
2560[12] 2895[9] 3391[7]

The Wee Chief (IRE) *Jimmy Fox* a75 76
6 ch g King Charlemagne(USA) La Belle Clare (IRE) (Paris House)
(425) ◆ 735[3] 1614[4] 2071[5] 3660[2] 4059[8]

The Which Doctor *Violet M Jordan* a75 74
7 b g Medicean Oomph (Shareef Dancer (USA))
85[8] 146[5] 287[6] 559[8] 725[3] 760[6] 1088[4] 1634[10] 2463[5] 3236[6] 8288[8]

The Winged Assasin (USA) *Shaun Lycett* a74 69
6 b g Fusaichi Pegasus(USA) Gran Dama (USA) (Rahy (USA))
63[5] 1003[6]

The Wonga Coup (IRE) *Pat Phelan* a67 59
5 b g Northern Afleet(USA) Quichesterbahn (USA) (Broad Brush (USA))
3470[13] 4240[3] 4943[7] 4981[4] (5481) 5935[3] (6230) 7303[3] 7619[2] (7960) 8175[7]

The Yank *Tony Carroll* a50 53
3 b g Trade Fair Silver Gyre (IRE) (Silver Hawk (USA))
635[9] 816[6] 1415[5] 7148[13]

The Yellow Bin (IRE) *S Donohoe* a42
4 ch g Artan(IRE) Zolube (IRE) (Titus Livius (FR))
335a[13] 775a[11]

The Young Master *Neil Mulholland* a38
3 b g Echo Of Light Fine Frenzy (IRE) (Great Commotion (USA))
56[7] 1608[11]

Theyturnedmedown (IRE) *J G Coogan* a59 72
4 b g Captain Rio Thai Princess (IRE) (Hamas (IRE))
6270a[5]

Thimaar (USA) *John Gosden* a106 108
4 bb g Dynaformer(USA) Jinaan (USA) (Mr Prospector (USA))
(1214) 1750[3] 3881[5] 4634a[5] 5599[8]

Think *Clive Mulhall* a52 51
5 ch g Sulamani(IRE) Natalie Jay (Ballacashtal (CAN))
2048[12] 4349[4] 4958[6] 7248[3]

Thiqa (IRE) *Saeed Bin Suroor* a72 69
2 b f New Approach(IRE) Sunray Superstar (Nashwan (USA))
4946[5] 5947[6]

Third Half *Tom Dascombe* a76 77
3 b g Haafhd Treble Heights (IRE) (Unfuwain (USA))
1978[8] 2452[4] 3031[2] 3345[5] 3558[6] (4325) 4796[6]

Thirlestane *James Given* 29
2 b f Auction House(USA) Island Colony (USA) (Pleasant Colony (USA))
6043[8] 6876[12]

Thirteen Shivers *Michael Easterby* a78 94
4 b g Iceman Thirteen Tricks (USA) (Grand Slam (USA))
4829[16] 5110[12] 6006[2] 6688[8] 7144[4]

Thisbe Des Sorinieres (FR) *T Poche*
7 b m Epaphos(GER) Ina Blue (FR) (Grand Tresor (FR))
3207a[F]

This Is Nice (IRE) *Tom Dascombe* a73 75
2 ch f Exceed And Excel(AUS) Spanish Quest (Rainbow Quest (USA))
1842[5] 2252[9] 3959[5] 4408[3] 4934[2] 5682[2] 6160[7] 7060[8] 7478[6] 7720[5] 7965[3]

This Ones For Eddy *John Balding* a70 59
7 b g Kyllachy Skirt Around (Deploy)
128[7] 1487[11] 1961[3] 4192[7] 4405[5] 7348[10]

Thistle Bird *Roger Charlton* a56 112
4 b m Selkirk(USA) Dolma (FR) (Marchand De Sable (USA))
(3640) (4527) 5573[2] (6029) 6633[2]

Thomas Chippendale (IRE) *Sir Henry Cecil* 116
3 br c Dansili All My Loving (IRE) (Sadler's Wells (USA))
2269[5] (2897) ◆ (3327) 5489[5] 6245[8]

Thomasgainsborough (IRE) *A P O'Brien* a95 95
3 b c Dansili Briolette (IRE) (Sadler's Wells (USA))
1604[4]

Thomas Hobson *John Gosden* a71
2 b c Halling(USA) La Spezia (IRE) (Danehill Dancer (IRE))
8071[4]

Thomasina *Denis Coakley* a47 40
2 b f One Cool Cat(USA) Jemiliah (Dubai Destination (USA))
4507[9] 6014[8] 6533[10]

Thoroughly Red (IRE) *Suzzanne France* a36 67
7 b g King's Best(USA) Red Liason (IRE) (Selkirk (USA))
3440[11] 4189[10] 5258[12] 7347[10]

Thorpe (IRE) *Ralph Beckett* 55
2 b g Danehill Dancer(IRE) Minkova (IRE) (Sadler's Wells (USA))
6795[12] 7332[8]

Thorpe Bay *Conor Dore* a66 62
3 b g Piccolo My Valentina (Royal Academy (USA))
219[6] 321[2] (583) 801[5] 1353[5] 1482[5] 1709[8] 2730[9] 8063[10] 8190[9] 8253[10]

Thought And Memory (IRE) *Mick Channon* a56 46
2 ch c Raven's Pass(USA) Sadinga (IRE) (Sadler's Wells (USA))
7373[11] 8071[10]

Thought Worthy (USA) *John Gosden* 117
3 b c Dynaformer(USA) Vignette (USA) (Diesis)
1678[2] (2275) ◆ 2705[4] 3327[3] (5489) 6245[6]

Thouwra (IRE) *Saeed Bin Suroor* a79
2 b c Pivotal Cape Verdi (IRE) (Caerleon (USA))
7750[2]

Thrasos (IRE) *Jo Crowley* a21
3 b c Invincible Spirit(IRE) Plymsole (USA) (Diesis)
1138[8]

Thraya Star (FR) *Mick Channon* 87
3 ch f Shamardal(USA) Labour Of Love (USA) (Silver Deputy (CAN))
2280[4]

Three Am Tour (IRE) *Richard Hannon* a88 91
3 b f Strategic Prince Murani (IRE) (Marju (IRE))
1894[2] 2182[3] 2490[3] 3165[14]

Three Bards (IRE) *Mark Johnston* a84 84
3 b c Dubawi(IRE) Polish Affair (IRE) (Polish Patriot (USA))
84[3] 324[3] (552) 1653[11] 2452[7] 2980[9] 3475[8] (4403) 4649[2] (4776) 5089[5] 5455[2] 5816[8] 6642[6]

Three Choirs (IRE) *Richard Hannon* a72 65
2 br f Rock Of Gibraltar(IRE) Three Owls (IRE) (Warning)
4011[15] 5902[6] 6535[2]

Three Crowns *Ian Wood* a70 82
2 b f Three Valleys(USA) Red Sovereign (Danzig Connection (USA))
2343[4] ◆ 2808[2] (3669) 4614[5] 5307[10] 5743[7] 6227[8]

Three Darlings (IRE) *David Nicholls* 66
3 gr f Elusive City(USA) Tibouchina (IRE) (Daylami (IRE))
1238[7] 4551[7] 6048[8] 6959[11]

Three Free Spirits (IRE) *S Donohoe* 31
2 gr c Verglas(IRE) Jazan (IRE) (Danehill (USA))
2184a[6]

Three Glasses (IRE) *Tim Easterby* 16
2 bb c Excellent Art Sinamay (USA) (Saint Ballado (CAN))
6043[10]

Threepence *Richard Whitaker* 47
2 b c Three Valleys(USA) The Jotter (Night Shift (USA))
6356[12] 6954[8] 7598[7]

Three Sea Captains (IRE) *David Wachman* a85 104
2 b c Choisir(AUS) La Tintoretta (IRE) (Desert Prince (IRE))
(6550a) 7623a[4]

Threes Grand *Scott Dixon* 88
2 b f Milk It Mick Ginger Cookie (Bold Edge)
(1563) 2247[4] 2603[3] 3269[10] 4064[8] 5516[7] 5979[7] 6139[4] 6675[10]

Three Streets (IRE) *Mahmood Al Zarooni* 48
2 ch c Street Cry(IRE) Allez Les Trois (USA) (Riverman (USA))
6330[7]

Three White Socks (IRE) *Brian Ellison* a73 66
5 b g Whipper(USA) Halesia (USA) (Chief's Crown (USA))
332[10] 460[6] 673[3] 902[2] 1175[2] 1952[4] 2925[2] (4145) 5718[5] 7077[10]

Throwing Roses *Ollie Pears* a40 63
2 b f Clodovil(IRE) Mizooka (Tobougg (IRE))
1671[2] 1949[2] 2977[2] 3457[3] 5210[4] 5675[6] 6336[4] 6354[9]

Thrust Control (IRE) *Tracy Waggott* a54 62
5 ch g Fath(USA) Anazah (USA) (Diesis)
676[12] 900[6] 1294[5] 2091[15] 2791[2] 4783[10] 4956[6] 5171[2] 5543[5] 5590[6] 6106[2] 6127[2] 6480[3] 6941[9] 7347[4] ◆

Thunderball (FR) *X Thomas-Demeaulte* a81
3 b c Hurricane Run(IRE) Dareen (IRE) (Rahy (USA))
117a[0]

Thunderball *Scott Dixon* a89 99
6 ch g Haafhd Trustthunder (Selkirk (USA))
253[9] 1156[4] (1476) 1844[7] (2023) 2409[8] 2825[5] 3183[7] 3331[19] 4086[5] 4285[6] 4799[27] 6466[11] (7366) 7690[6] 7817[6] 8098[9]

Thundering Home *Richard Mitchell* a73 60
5 gr g Storming Home Citrine Spirit (IRE) (Soviet Star (USA))
150[5] 433[4] (695) 824[4] 944[5] 2237[12] 3659[9] 4244[3] 5038[3] 5936[2] 6232[3]

Thunder Mountain (IRE) *D K Weld* 92
2 b g Elnadim(USA) Dance Clear (IRE) (Marju (IRE))
6060a[5] 6550a[4]

Thunderonthemount *Michael Attwater* a41
7 ch g Zaha(CAN) Vrennan (Suave Dancer (USA))
688[6] 1065[8] 1496[9]

Thunderstruck *Scott Dixon* a90 41
7 b g Bertolini(USA) Trustthunder (Selkirk (USA))
(36) 177[11] 391[3] 694[4] 907[6] 1275[17] 5752[10] 7461[7]

Thwart *Ralph Beckett* a41 65
2 ch f Refuse To Bend(IRE) Jump Ship (Night Shift (USA))
5104[8] 6175[8] 6817[3]

Thyan (FR) *P Capelle* a71 83
5 b h Indian Rocket Slyders (IRE) (Hector Protector (USA))
5118a[0]

Tiablo (IRE) *David Evans* a61 29
3 br f Red Clubs(IRE) Canary Bird (IRE) (Catrail (USA))
250[6] (357) 599[6] 769[5] (940) 1393[4] 1444[5] 3005[4] 3451[4] 3510[10]

Tibaldi (FR) *Mme C Head-Maarek* a81 99
3 b f Motivator Treasure Queen (USA) (Kingmambo (USA))
1209a[6] 1426a[6] 7345a[6]

Tiberius Claudius (IRE) *George Margarson* a56 74
4 b g Clodovil(IRE) Final Favour (IRE) (Unblest)
2461[2] 3549[12] 4914[5] 5454[6] 5750[8]

Ticinello (GER) *T Doumen* a60 80
3 ch c Lord Of England(GER) Ticinella (GER) (Hernando (FR))
247a[9]

Tickin Time *Michael Squance* a11 8
3 b c Royal Applause Ticki Tori (IRE) (Vettori (IRE))
2273[16] 2543[12]

Tickled Pink (IRE) *Sir Henry Cecil* 88
3 gr f Invincible Spirit(IRE) Cassandra Go (IRE) (Indian Ridge)
2332[2] (3082)

Tickle Time (IRE) *David Barron* 93
2 b g Kheleyf(USA) Rada (IRE) (Danehill (USA))
(3378) 4247[2] (5042)

Tidal Run *Mick Channon* a66 79
4 b m Hurricane Run(IRE) Tidie France (USA) (Cape Town (USA))
(1207) 1286[4] 1491[2] 1909[2] (2161) 2539[11] 4843[2] (4987) 5290[2] 5585[5] 5931[9] 6229[4] 6819[12] 7260[10] 7416[8]

Tidal's Baby *Tony Carroll* a69 73
3 b g Dutch Art Tidal (Bin Ajwaad (IRE))
2150[11] 2557[10] 4534[3] 5800[4] 6402[2] 6739[2] 7667[3] (7770) 8074[4]

Tidal Way (IRE) *Mick Channon* 83
3 gr g Red Clubs(IRE) Taatof (IRE) (Lahib (USA))
1565[8] 2269[9] 2471[3] 3122[2] 3774[3] 4046[6] 4459[5]

Tiddliwinks *Kevin Ryan* a107 116
6 b g Piccolo Card Games (First Trump)
1469[10] (2179) (2513a) 3650a[5] 5561[17] 6485[5] 6908a[13]

Tidentime (USA) *Mick Channon* a82 93
3 bb g Speightstown(USA) Casting Call (USA) (Dynaformer (USA))
1452[3] 2022[3] 2485[5] 3294[16] 4075[7] 4819[11] 6705[5] 7645[11] 7790[8]

Tidespring (IRE) *H-A Pantall* 105
4 b m Monsun(GER) Sweet Stream (ITY) (Shantou (USA))
1697a[6] 3768a[2] 4634a[9] 6290a[2] 7282a[3] 7735a[3]

Tidy Affair (IRE) *Gary Moore* a79 83
3 b g Amadeus Wolf Pride Of My Heart (Lion Cavern (USA))
1304[8] 1612[10] 2150[10] 2557[6] 3122[4] 3719[9] 4242[10] 4584[8] 7482[12] 8264[7]

Tiermore Lass (IRE) *Terry Clement* 34
9 b m Moonax(IRE) Lady Brigida (IRE) (Lord Americo)
5105[8]

Tifongo (FR) *H-A Pantall* 108
3 b c Dr Fong(USA) Tishkara (FR) (Xaar)
1244a[5] 1570a[2] 2743a[20] 3656a[6] 5649a[8] 6897a[6]

Tiger At Heart (IRE) *J S Bolger* 82
3 ch c Teofilo(IRE) Julie Girl (USA) (Jules (USA))
1401a[4]

Tigerbill *Nicky Vaughan* a60
4 ch g Hold That Tiger(USA) Regal Asset (USA) (Regal Classic (CAN))
1425[11] 1907[12] 3712[12] 6829[11]

Tiger Cliff (FR) *J Bertin* a66 68
7 b m Tiger Hill(IRE) Vertige (USA) (Gulch (USA))
92a[10]

Tiger Cliff (IRE) *Sir Henry Cecil* a86 92
3 b c Tiger Hill(IRE) Verbania (IRE) (In The Wings)
5100[2] (5766) 6537[3] 7367[2] ◆

Tiger Cub *Mrs Ilka Gansera-Leveque* a56 75
3 b f Dr Fong(USA) Clouded Leopard (USA) (Danehill (USA))
2194[15] 2557[4] 2756[3] 3228[10] (5775) 6378[11] 7483[12]

Tiger Day *B Grizzetti* 100
2 b c Tiger Hill(IRE) Diamond Day (Rahy (USA))
3684a[2] 7076a[11]

Tiger Girl *Noel Quinlan* a43 24
5 b m Tiger Hill(IRE) Girl Of My Dreams (IRE) (Marju (IRE))
1113[8] 1484[7]

Tigerino (IRE) *Chris Fairhurst* a58 48
4 b g Tiger Hill(IRE) Golden Shadow (IRE) (Selkirk (USA))
1631[9] 2242[3] 2925[5] 3307[10]

Tigerish *Amanda Perrett* a66
2 b g Tiger Hill(IRE) Dimakya (USA) (Dayjur (USA))
7167[13] 7507[9] 7706[5]

Tiger Prince (IRE) *Ann Duffield* a25 56
2 b g Strategic Prince Tiger Desert (GER) (Desert King (IRE))
3112[6] 3457[4] 3948[11] 4767[8] 5799[5] 6354[8]

Tiger Reigns *Michael Dods* 99
6 b g Tiger Hill(IRE) Showery (Rainbow Quest (USA))
4110[10] 5369[11] 6202[11] 6630[3] 7210[11]

Tiger's Home *Julia Feilden* 61
2 b f Tiger Hill(IRE) Homeward (IRE) (Kris)
2245[10] 2844[5] 3150[3] 3533[5] 7439[9]

Tigers Tale (IRE) *Roger Teal* a88 89
3 b g Tiger Hill(IRE) Vayenga (FR) (Highest Honor (FR))
(1313) (1728) (3068) 6205[9] 6580[4] 6875[4] 7407[11]

Tiger Stripes *A Oliver* a83 93
2 b c Tiger Hill(IRE) Tarkamara (IRE) (Medicean)
3649a[3]

Tiger Sunset (IRE) *J S Moore* a54 64
2 b c Balmont(USA) Zuccini Business (IRE) (Entrepreneur)
1118a[6] 1495[6] 2132[2] 2309[5] (2798) 3084[2] 3351[2]

Tigertoo (IRE) *Stuart Williams* a58 52
3 ch g Heliostatic(IRE) Brightling (IRE) (Gorse)
1740[7] 2374[6] 2787[6] 3469[5] 4153[9] 4650[6] 4932[2] 5991[8] 6152[4] (6316) 6395[11]

Tiger Walk (USA) *Ignacio Correas IV* a106
3 bb c Tale Of The Cat(USA) Majestic Trail (USA) (Kris S (USA))
2299a[8]

Tiger Webb *Michael Easterby* a64 86
4 b g Hurricane Run(IRE) Wonderful Desert (Green Desert (USA))
1134[15] 1381[14] 3163[18] 3628[5] 4396[8] 4831[6] 5225[2] ◆ 5921[4] 6561[8] 6941[3] 7250[4] 7383[3]

Tiger Who *David Flood* a34
4 b m Tiger Hill(IRE) Aunt Susan (Distant Relative)
206[9] 367[9] 655[9]

Tight Fit *Henry Candy* a51 59
2 ch f Assertive Bikini (Trans Island)
6534[8] ◆ 6816[3] 7329[8]

Tight Knit (USA) *James Tate* a75
2 b c Hard Spun(USA) Tamdiid (USA) (Horse Chestnut (SAF))
6175[9] 6644[3] 7167[5] (7868) 8240[4]

Tight Lipped (IRE) *James Eustace* a77 79
3 gr g Dark Angel(IRE) Kayoko (IRE) (Shalford (IRE))
918[6] 1264[4] 2021[2] 2331[2] 2428[6] 3446[5] 4949[4] 5721[3] 6930[4] 7376[4]

Tigre D'Or (FR) *A Couetil* 103
6 gr g Tiger Hill(IRE) Sporades (USA) (Vaguely Noble)
7320a[3]

Tigresa (IRE) *Mark Johnston* a52 39
3 b f Tiger Hill(IRE) Cararysa (IRE) (Docksider (USA))
159[6] 336a[8] 832[6] 1260[10] 1517[13]

Tijori (IRE) *Bernard Llewellyn* a74 74
4 b g Kyllachy Polish Belle (Polish Precedent (USA))
2237[8] 3101[2] 3429[5] 4181[6] 4733[8] 5419[3] 5653[2] 5936[3] 6159[3] 6821[4] (7377)

Tijuca (IRE) *Ed de Giles* a57 42
3 b f Captain Rio Some Forest (IRE) (Charnwood Forest (IRE))
2974[7] 3702[11] 5874[4] 8187[3]

Till Dawn (IRE) *Rodger Sweeney* a58 60
4 br m Kheleyf(USA) Tilbrook (IRE) (Don't Forget Me)
5191[3]

Tillys Tale *Paul Midgley* a77 76
5 ch m Lucky Story(USA) Otylia (Wolfhound (USA))
7178[12] 7456[12]

Tilly T (IRE) *J S Moore* a18 49
2 b f Thousand Words Pippi (IRE) (City On A Hill (USA))
7160[14] 7491[3] 7786[7]

Tilos Gem (IRE) *Brian Ellison* a48 68
6 ch g Trans Island Alpine Flair (IRE) (Tirol)
229[7]

Tilstarr (IRE) *Roger Teal* a63 58
2 b f Shamardal(USA) Vampire Queen (IRE) (General Monash (USA))
5104[11] 5792[9] 7312[5] 7724[3] ◆ 7965[2]

Tilsworth Glenboy *J R Jenkins* a74 86
5 b g Doyen(IRE) Chara (Deploy)
1262[3] 1659[3] (1743) (2051) 2328[6] 2857[4] 4199[2] 4365[6] 5159[3] 5688[6]

Tilthefatladysings *Richard Guest* 19
3 gr f Librettist(USA) Zilkha (Petong)
5541[6]

Time After Time (AUS) *J Moore* 115
5 bb g Danehill Dancer(IRE) Recurring (NZ) (Pentire)
8041a[12]

Time And Place *Richard Fahey* 77
2 ch c Compton Place Forthefirstime (Dr Fong (USA))
4825[4] (5382) 6238[6]

Time For A Tiger *Henry Candy* a42
3 b f Tiger Hill(IRE) Last Slipper (Tobougg (IRE))
3622[8] 4410[16] 4916[7]

Time For Harry *Phil McEntee* a61
5 b g Doyen(IRE) Corn Circle (IRE) (Thatching)
974[3]

Time For Lambrini (IRE) *Lisa Williamson* a73
2 b f Amadeus Wolf Princess Madaen (IRE) (Elusive Quality (USA))
(2349) 7220[6] 7462[8]

Timeless Appeal (IRE) *Peter Chapple-Hyam* a53
2 br f Kheleyf(USA) Elegant Times (IRE) (Dansili)
7813[6]

Timeless Call (IRE) *Reginald Roberts* a101 93
4 b m Sakhee(USA) Pourquoi Pas (IRE) (Nordico (USA))
6140[11] 7390a[3]

Timeless Elegance (IRE) *David Barron* a34 80
5 b m Invincible Spirit(IRE) Tidy Wager (IRE) (Catrail (USA))
1293[4] 1827[9] 2310[7]

Time Medicean *Tony Carroll* a70 85
6 gr g Medicean Ribbons And Bows (IRE) (Dr Devious (IRE))
3139[12] 4231[7] (4690) 5362[10] 5906[3] 7019[2] 7928[8]

Time Of My Life (IRE) *Patrick Holmes* a36 76
3 b g Galileo(IRE) In My Life (IRE) (Rainbow Quest (USA))
6240[5]

Timepiece *Sir Henry Cecil* a80 116
5 b m Zamindar(USA) Clepsydra (Sadler's Wells (USA))
1883[4] 2209[8] 4801[2] 5399a[3] 6379[12]

Time Prisoner (USA) *Mahmood Al Zarooni* 112
5 gr h Elusive Quality(USA) Zelanda (IRE) (Night Shift (USA))
(53a) ◆ 316a[3] 590a[5]

Time Square (FR) *Tony Carroll* a63 81
5 b g Westerner Sainte Parfaite (FR) (Septieme Ciel (USA))
296[5] ◆ 575[3] 738[4] 944[4] 7960[10]

Times Up *John Dunlop* 116
6 b g Olden Times Princess Genista (Ile De Bourbon (USA))
2254[4] 2639[4] 4737[7] (5599) (6198)

Time To Dance *Joseph Tuite* a70
3 b g Silent Times(IRE) Bravo Dancer (Acatenango (GER))
613[3] 404[3] 502[2] 1355[7]

Time To Excel *Michael Dods* 51
3 ch g Exceed And Excel(AUS) Treacle (USA) (Seeking The Gold (USA))
1596[9] 2673[5] 3333[6] 4549[10] 4958[5] 5187[4]

Time To Play *Gary Brown* a52 65
7 b g Best Of The Bests(IRE) Primavera (Anshan)
160[5] 200[12]

Timocracy *Alastair Lidderdale* a69 74
7 br g Cape Cross(IRE) Tithcar (Cadeaux Genereux)
570[9] 1071[4] (1418) 2502[11]

Timoneer (USA) *Mahmood Al Zarooni* 101
2 bb c Elusive Quality(USA) Gentle Gale (USA) (Storm Cat (USA))
(4595) 5270[3] 5787[3]

Timpanist (USA) *Simon Dow* a62 68
5 b m Roman Ruler(USA) Jazz Drummer (USA) (Dixieland Band (USA))
224[12]

Tinera (FR) *P Demercastel* a71 83
6 b m Kendor(FR) Tinerana Memories (IRE) (Don't Forget Me)
94a[6]

Tinghir (IRE) *David Lanigan* a73
2 b c Dansili Palmeraie (USA) (Lear Fan (USA))
7963[2]

Tingo In The Tale (IRE) *David Arbuthnot* a78 81
3 b g Oratorio(IRE) Sunlit Skies (Selkirk (USA))
1304[5] 1647[8] 2429[8] (3003) 3711[3] 4513[6] 5816[9] 6146[11] (8206)

Tin Horse (IRE) *D Guillemin* 117
4 gr h Sakhee(USA) Joyeuse Entree (Kendor (FR))
2533a[5] (3900a) 5141a[6] 5649a[9]

Tinkerbell Will *John E Long* a57 54
5 ch m Where Or When(IRE) Highland Hannah (IRE) (Persian Heights)
966[3] 1624[3] 2467[6] (3043) 3721[4] 4817[5] 5351[3] 6004[8] 7479[12]

Tin Pan Alley *Giles Bravery* a64 77
4 b g Singspiel(IRE) Tazmeen (Darshaan)
1703[7] 2799[2] 3793[7]

Tinseltown *Brian Rothwell* a41 74
6 b g Sadler's Wells(USA) Peony (Lion Cavern (USA))
(3752) 3979[4] (4179) (4455) 4683[9] 5001[4] 5290[4] 6626[3]

Tinshu (IRE) *Derek Haydn Jones* a101 91
6 ch m Fantastic Light(USA) Ring Of Esteem (Mark Of Esteem (IRE))
177[4] 354[2] 712[2] 1137[2] 2810[4] 3164[11] 3826[6] 4365[3] ◆ 4795[10] 5835[3] 6484[12] 7771[4] (7904) 8227[4]

Tiny Temper (IRE) *Richard Fahey* a58 73
4 b m Montjeu(IRE) Lady Storm (IRE) (Mujadil (USA))
5672[U] 6706[3] 7068[5] 7652[7]

Tiny Thompson *Lydia Pearce* a39 26
3 b f Tobougg(IRE) Mon Petit Diamant (Hector Protector (USA))
7112[10] 8080[6] 8267[6]

Tinzapeas *Mick Channon* a58 72
3 b f Imperial Dancer Noble Destiny (Dancing Brave (USA))
1241[5] 1612[8] 2448[5] 3184[9] 3343[5] 3954[3] (4509) 4619[3] 4757[6] 4953[6] 5536[P]

Tinzo (IRE) *Alan Berry* 44
4 b g Auction House(USA) Costa Verde (King Of Spain)
2036[6] 2225[7] 2621[12] 2796[13] 3889[12]

Tiolache (FR) *J-M Capitte* a82 84
2 b f Layman(USA) Wivenhoe (UAE) (Timber Country (USA))
6225a[8]

Tioman Legend *Roger Charlton* 97
3 b g Kyllachy Elegant Times (IRE) (Dansili)
1858[16] 2276[5] 3165[16] 4765[3] 5363[11] 6075[10]

Tioman Pearl *Roger Varian* 87
3 b c Royal Applause Mazarine Blue (Bellypha)
(1941) 3396[7] 3861[6]

Tipping Over (IRE) *Hugo Palmer* 89
2 b f Aussie Rules(USA) Precipice (Observatory (USA))
2245[4] (2929) 3631[5] 4205a[5] 5781a[3] 6238[4] 6550a[2] 6942a[9]

Tippotina *Brian Meehan* 55
2 b f Indesatchel(IRE) Ballerina Suprema (IRE) (Sadler's Wells (USA))
5357[8]

Tipsy Girl *Denis Coakley* a27 84
4 b m Haafhd Disco Lights (Spectrum (IRE))
989[6]

Tip Toe (FR) *F Doumen* 107
5 b h Footstepsinthesand Midnight Queen (GER) (Platini (GER))
953a[6]

Tip Top Gorgeous (IRE) *J S Moore* 83
3 b f Red Clubs(IRE) Amber's Bluff (Mind Games)
1317[7] 2256[5] 2451[2] 2893[9] 3160[5] 3912[2] 4291[2] 4588[8] 5576[4] 6465[17]

Tiradito (USA) *Brian Ellison* a83 41
5 bb g Tale Of The Cat(USA) Saratoga Sugar (USA) (Gone West (USA))
302[3] 626[3] 746[9] 991[10] 1769[7] 3388[12] 4334[4] 5428[7] 6216[3] 6812[2] (6895) 7027[5]

Tislaam (IRE) *Alan McCabe* a81 72
5 gr g With Approval(CAN) Lady Angola (USA) (Lord At War (ARG))
157[3] 304[5] 652[7] 4783[3] 5298[5] 5618[5] 6150[3] 6687[4]

Tis Rock 'N' Roll (USA) *David Lanigan* a91 83
3 bb c Rock Of Gibraltar(IRE) Tis Me (USA) (Notebook (USA))
(2497) 2860[3] (3793) ◆ 4466[2] (6843) (6973)

Tita Caty (FR) *M Boutin* 86
2 ch f Night Tango(GER) Miss Margaux (FR) (Script Ohio (USA))
4205a[6] 4696a[4] 8276a[4]

Titan Diamond (IRE) *Mark Usher* a53 53
4 b g Diamond Green(FR) Ditton Dancer (Danehill Dancer (IRE))
988[10] 1096[4] (1907) 2366[7] 3318[2] 3713[6] 4193[6] 7983[11]

Titan Triumph *William Knight* a84 31
8 b g Zamindar(USA) Triple Green (Green Desert (USA))
90[4] 351[2] 426[8] (765) 1035[7] 1708[12] 5625[14] 6538[7] 7645[13] 7997[9] 8105[8]

Title Contender (USA) *Bob Baffert* a95
2 bb c Pulpit(USA) Winter Garden (USA) (Roy (USA))
7572a[8]

Titled Gent *Brian Meehan* a85 56
2 br c Kheleyf(USA) Upskittled (Diktat)
4730[7] (5176) (5743) 7193[3]

Titus Bolt (IRE) *Jim Boyle* a59 64
3 b g Titus Livius(FR) Megan's Bay (Muhtarram (USA))
1359[6] 1979[4] 3002[7] (3671) 4256[5] 4754[6] 6568[2] 6988[10] 7117[4]

Titus Gent *Jeremy Gask* a87 77
7 ch g Tumbleweed Ridge Genteel (IRE) (Titus Livius (FR))
120[4] 311[8] (1828) 2707[11] 3188[6] 8009[3] 8143[9]

Titus Mills (IRE) *Brian Meehan* a93 99
4 ch g Dubawi(IRE) Anayid (A.P. Indy (USA))
1471[5] 1749[7] 2211[11] 6426[8] 6831[4] 7556[9]

Titus Star (IRE) *J S Moore* a74 74
3 ch g Titus Livius(FR) The Oldladysays No (IRE) (Perugino (USA))
994[2] 1707[7] 2408[13] 4334[3] 4603[7] 6169[5] 6502[4] 7250[11] 7769[5]

Titus Titan (IRE) *Brian Ellison* a71 73
2 b c Holy Roman Emperor(IRE) Ask For The Moon (FR) (Dr Fong (USA))
3532[3] 4178[3] 4960[6] 5602[9] (5890) ◆

Tiz In Court (USA) *Dennis Ward*
5 bb g Cee's Tizzy(USA) Courtly Colors (USA) (Holding Court (USA))
8100a[2]

Tiz Ro (CAN) *Gregory De Gannes* a83 88
2 b f Hard Spun(USA) Muskrat Suzie (CAN) (Vice Regent (CAN))
6289a[8]

Tmaam (USA) *Mark Johnston* a76 99
4 br h Dynaformer(USA) Thread (USA) (Topsider (USA))
3036[2] 3341[2] ◆ 3857[14]

Tobacco *Tim Easterby* 58
2 b g Manduro(GER) Wonderful Desert (Green Desert (USA))
4792[12] 5668[9] 6134[2] ◆ 6356[8]

Tobacco Road (IRE) *Richard Hannon* a79 81
2 b c Westerner Virginias Best (King's Best (USA))
3499[2] (4330) 5903[2]

Tobago *Lady Herries* a15
4 ch g Bertolini(USA) Heavenly Bay (USA) (Rahy (USA))
7818[6]

Toberton (IRE) *T M Walsh* a62 67
2 b g Chevalier(IRE) Earth Charter (Slip Anchor)
6550a[13]

Tobey (IRE) *W Hickst* a61
4 b h Xaar Toamasina (FR) (Marju (IRE))
16a[0]

Tobrata *Mel Brittain* a69 66
6 ch g Tobougg(IRE) Sabrata (IRE) (Zino)
836[3] 3022[7] 3290[6] 3440[4] 4048[2] 4314[2] 4626[12] 5012[4] 5673[3] 6626[9] (7800)

Toby Tyler *Paul Midgley* a70 84
6 b g Best Of The Bests(IRE) Pain Perdu (IRE) (Waajib)
883[8] 1168[7] 1478[3] 3169[P] 4133[4] 4554[12] 4829[17] 5110[9] 5389[3] 5674[7] 6123[7] 6260[6] 7000[5] 7297[5]

Toccata Blue (IRE) *G M Lyons* a77 48
2 ro g Verglas(IRE) Jinxy Jill (Royal Applause)
1118a[5]

Toepaz *Alan Berry*
3 b g Boogie Street Tribal Mischief (Be My Chief (USA))
5316[11]

Toffee Nose *Ron Barr* 51
5 b g Ishiguru(USA) The Synergist (Botanic (USA))
3357[3] 3893[6] 4348[13] 6958[14]

Toffee Tart *J W Hills* a56 73
3 b f Dutch Art Toffee Vodka (IRE) (Danehill Dancer (IRE))
1449[6] 1985[10] 3619[12]

Toga Tiger (IRE) *Jeremy Gask* a59 81
5 b g Antonius Pius(USA) Minerwa (GER) (Protektor (GER))
(2365) (3247) (3470) 4541[5]

Together Again (FR) *M Boutin* a61 61
3 b g Great Journey(JPN) Together (FR) (Valanour (IRE))
661a[4]

Toggle *Mrs A Corson* a51 20
8 b g Tobougg(IRE) Niggle (Night Shift (USA))
5701a[5]

To Honor And Serve (USA) *William Mott* a125
4 b h Bernardini(USA) Pilfer (USA) (Deputy Minister (CAN))
7576a[10]

Tokum (FR) *N Bertran De Balanda* a44
2 ch c Rock Of Gibraltar(IRE) Headdress (IRE) (Halling (USA))
8176a[10]

Tokyo Brown (USA) *Heather Main* a61 59
3 b g Marquetry(USA) Miasma (USA) (Lear Fan (USA))
2393[3] 2818[10] 5074a[0] 6280[3] 6691[6] 7196[2] 7528[6] 7629[10]

Toledo Gold (IRE) *Maurice Barnes* 41
6 ch g Needwood Blade Eman's Joy (Lion Cavern (USA))
3953[9] 4391[7] 4884[8]

Tolka (IRE) *S Wattel* a90 90
3 b g Danehill Dancer(IRE) Russian Hill (Indian Ridge)
1171a[5]

Tomasini *John Weymes* 32
3 b g Misu Bond(IRE) Bond Stasia (IRE) (Mukaddamah (USA))
2339[10] 2774[6] 4622[9] 5918[12] 6361[15]

Tombellini (IRE) *Noel Wilson* a8 64
5 ch g Tomba La Scala (USA) (Theatrical (IRE))
2091[11]

Tombi (USA) *Keith Dalgleish* a76 92
8 b g Johannesburg(USA) Tune In To The Cat (USA) (Tunerup (USA))
215[3] ◆ 545[3] 718[7] (941) 1082[4]

Tom Hall *John Best* a57
2 b c Pastoral Pursuits Villarosi (IRE) (Rossini (USA))
6581[9] 7007[9] 7481[5] 7930[4]

Tominator *Jonjo O'Neill* a95 105
5 gr g Generous(IRE) Jucinda (Midyan (USA))
1974[13] 2709[7] 5600[8] (5826) 6197[4] 7051[3]

Tomintoul Magic (IRE) *Sir Henry Cecil* a69
2 b f Holy Roman Emperor(IRE) Trois Graces (USA) (Alysheba (USA))
7506[5]

Tommy's Secret *Jane Chapple-Hyam* a87 86
2 gr g Sakhee's Secret La Gessa (Largesse)
1997[5] (2442) 3242[13] 4102[6] 5743[2] 6139[5] 6871[5] (7723)

Tom Red *Dean Ivory* a56
3 gr g Piccolo Joyful Illusion (Robellino (USA))
918[9] 1086[6] 1414[9] 2374[4] ◆

Tom Sawyer *Julie Camacho* a76 77
4 b g Dansili Cayman Sunset (IRE) (Night Shift (USA))
282[7] 844[2] 996[8] 1800[6] 2749[2] 4174[8] (5020) 5272[6] (5791) 6144[4] 6886[6] 7648[4] 7937[10]

Toms River Tess (IRE) *Zoe Davison* a70 49
4 b m Kodiac Sonorous (IRE) (Ashkalani (IRE))
124[8] 313[6] 578[13] 782[4] 985[4] 1183[4] 1628[8] 2365[6] 2607[3] 2971[7] 3466[4] 4508[7] 4981[10] 5034[3] 5347[4] 5995[11]

Tomway *Tom Dascombe* a53 55
2 ch c Sakhee's Secret Mi Amor (IRE) (Alzao (USA))
1997[7] 2384[9] 4222[6] 5206[4] 5763[7] 6893[11]

To My Valentine (FR) *F-H Graffard* 99
2 ch f Dyhim Diamond(IRE) Lisselan Firefly (IRE) (Monashee Mountain (USA))
3680a[2] 4384a[5] 5248a[7]

Tonality (IRE) *J S Moore* a51 56
2 b f Amadeus Wolf Fortress (Generous (IRE))
5748[5] 6049[2] 6276[5] 6499[8]

Tongalooma *James Moffatt* a56 75
6 ch m Shinko Forest(IRE) Schatzi (Chilibang)
3730[7] 4866[7] 5739[6]

Tonkalili *James Unett* a1
2 b f Firebreak Amber Mill (Doulab (USA))
2349[8] 6889[10] 7021[7]

Tonle Sap (IRE) *Clive Cox* 73
3 b f Manduro(GER) Badee'A (IRE) (Marju (IRE))
3666[3] 5421[4] 5795[5] 6275[6]

Tony Hollis *Karen Tutty* a52 58
4 b g Antonius Pius(USA) Seasons Parks (Desert Prince (IRE))
2555[7] 3098[4] 3939[3] 4603[4] (5918) 7348[7] 7671[10]

Too Ambitious *Reg Hollinshead* a45 45
3 b f Striking Ambition Ticcatoo (IRE) (Dolphin Street (FR))
2918[8] 3312[6] 3848[6] 4489[6] 5177[5]

Toodeloo *Kevin Ryan* 44
3 b f Royal Applause Polo (Warning)
1274[9] 2121[5] 2335[15]

Too Difficult (IRE) *Andrew Balding* 67
2 ch f Rock Of Gibraltar(IRE) Etizaan (IRE) (Unfuwain (USA))
6844[2]

Toogood (IRE) *Alastair Lidderdale* 38
3 ch g Pivotal Woodland Orchid (IRE) (Woodman (USA))
6570[6]

Toolain (IRE) *D Selvaratnam* a83 105
4 br g Diktat Qasirah (IRE) (Machiavellian (USA))
140a[13]

Tooley Woods (IRE) *Tony Carroll* a64 53
3 b f Cape Cross(IRE) Kondakova (IRE) (Soviet Star (USA))
604[2] 1274[8] 1826[5] 2733[13] 3939[7] 4403[5] 4932[5] (5127) 5991[10] ◆ 6274[3]

Too Much Trouble *Ed Vaughan* a92 95
6 b g Barathea(IRE) Tentpole (USA) (Rainbow Quest (USA))
143a[10] 5079[9] 5666[4] 6879[5] 7163[7]

Toothache *Garry Woodward* 48
4 gr m Proclamation(IRE) Zilkha (Petong)
3811[7] 4434[9] 7354[12]

Topadee (IRE) *Patrick J Flynn* a75 70
5 b m Golan(IRE) Sundown (Polish Precedent (USA))
6716a[10]

Topamichi *Mark H Tompkins* 63
2 b g Beat Hollow Topatori (IRE) (Topanoora)
4194[8] (6134) 6793[11] 7289[4]

Topanga Canyon *Andrew Balding* a76 64
3 b g Nayef(USA) Classical Dancer (Dr Fong (USA))
(1364) 1486[2] 2372[10]

Topaze Blanche (IRE) *C Laffon-Parias* a78 107
2 b f Zamindar(USA) Pearl Earrine (FR) (Kaldounevees (FR))
6909a[2]

Top Billing *John Gosden* 80
3 bg g Monsun(GER) La Gandilie (FR) (Highest Honor (FR))
3161[4] 3786[5] 5007[10] 5796[10]

Top Boy *Derek Shaw* 99
2 b c Exceed And Excel(AUS) Injaaz (Sheikh Albadou)
1515[5] 1842[3] ◆ 2069[4] 2638[2] 3240[20] 4093[4] 4736[6] 5382[5] 6139[6]

Topclas (FR) *M bin Shafya* a103 104
6 b h Kutub(IRE) Noble Presence (FR) (Fasliyev (USA))
145a[7] 242a[9] 877a[7]

Top Cop *Andrew Balding* 96
3 b g Acclamation Speed Cop (Cadeaux Genereux)
1457[9] 2276[3] 3165[17] 4285[7] 4598[13]

Top Design *Karen George* 40
4 b g Zafeen(FR) Dress Design (IRE) (Brief Truce (USA))
1889[10]

Top Diktat *Sir Michael Stoute* a83 85
4 b g Diktat Top Romance (IRE) (Entrepreneur)
2151[4] 3226[5] 3594[12]

Topeka (IRE) *Robert Collet* 109
3 b f Whipper(USA) Sovana (IRE) (Desert King (IRE))
1209a[5] 2109a[3] 2742a[7]

Topflight Princess *Jeremy Gask* a75 30
3 b f Cockney Rebel(IRE) Topflightcoolracer (Lujain (USA))
2987[4] 3488[6] 4218[9] 4920[6] 7412[13]

Top Frock (IRE) *Clive Cox* a72 66
3 b f Acclamation Silk Dress (IRE) (Gulch (USA))
2050[9] 2503[10] 3044[8] 3454[2] 4186[5] 4586[3] (5052) 5754[6] 6364[12]

Top Joker *Mahmood Al Zarooni* 78
2 b c Raven's Pass(USA) French Bid (AUS) (Anabaa (USA))
3397[2] ◆

Top Notch Tonto (IRE) *Ian McInnes* 97
2 ch g Thousand Words Elite Hope (USA) (Moment Of Hope (USA))
1911[4] (2138) 2688[3] 3242[12] 3695[3] 5602[3] 6200[6] (6469) 7292[3]

Top Offer *Roger Charlton* 92
3 b g Dansili Zante (Zafonic (USA))
1856[16] 2641[8]

Toppled (IRE) *Brian Meehan* a1
3 ch f Pivotal Pietra Dura (Cadeaux Genereux)
1610[14] 2734[13]

Top Pursuit *Mrs A Corson* 23
10 b g Pursuit Of Love Top Of The Parkes (Mistertopogigo (IRE))
5701a[7]

Top Spin (FR) *Nikki Evans*
5 ch m Intikhab(USA) Ghanaj (Caerleon (USA))
5266[11] 5998[11]

Toptempo *Mark H Tompkins* a74 86
3 ch f Halling(USA) Topatoo (Bahamian Bounty)
2249[3] 4346[4] 5105[5] 6839[4] 7352[3] 7522[5]

Top Town Boy *John Holt* a39 57
2 b c Camacho Soyalang (FR) (Alydeed (CAN))
4654[8] 5449[4] 6099[5]

Top Trail (USA) *Roger Charlton* a58
2 bb f Exchange Rate(USA) Trekking (USA) (Gone West (USA))
7007[8]

Top Trip *F Doumen* a89 115
3 b c Dubai Destination(USA) Topka (FR) (Kahyasi)
(2108a) 2743a[5] 4121a[5] 5650a[4] 6896a[6]

Tora Tora (FR) *M Boutin* 58
2 b f Great Journey(JPN) Tofu (Anabaa (USA))
6751a[10]

Torero *Kevin Ryan* a60 73
3 b g Hernando(FR) After You (Pursuit Of Love)
943[4] 1223[2] 1655[3] 1992[4] 2333[5] 2716[7] 3305[3]

Tornadodancer (IRE) *T G McCourt* a90 81
9 b g Princely Heir(IRE) Purty Dancer (IRE) (Foxhound (USA))
6716a[15]

Tornado Force (IRE) *Chris Dwyer* a93 63
4 ch g Shamardal(USA) Pharma West (USA) (Gone West (USA))
43[2] 529[2] 4596[8] 8019[3] 8228[6]

Toronado (IRE) *Richard Hannon* 113
2 b c High Chaparral(IRE) Wana Doo (USA) (Grand Slam (USA))
(3067) ◆ (4318) (6243)

Toronto (FR) *P Monfort* a72 72
4 ch m Consolidator(USA) New Jersey (USA) (Kingmambo (USA))
1172a[10]

Torran Sound *James Eustace* a49 60
5 b g Tobougg(IRE) Velvet Waters (Unfuwain (USA))
2468[8]

Torres Del Paine *Brett Johnson* a82 62
5 b h Compton Place Noble Story (Last Tycoon)
123[2] (267) ◆ (282) 652[4] (6150) 6577[10] 7902[11]

Tortilla (IRE) *Des Donovan* a55 60
4 ch m Choisir(AUS) Alifandango (IRE) (Alzao (USA))
1263[12]

Tortoni (IRE) *Kevin Ryan* a74 79
3 b g Teofilo(IRE) Nipping (IRE) (Night Shift (USA))
1560[3] 1825[5] 2689[2] 3333[2] 3952[7]

Tosca (GER) *Mrs Ilka Gansera-Leveque* 68
2 b f Amadeus Wolf Tamarita (GER) (Acatenango (GER))
(5612a) 6522a[8]

Tosen Jordan (JPN) *Yasutoshi Ikee* 126
6 b h Jungle Pocket(JPN) Every Whisper (JPN) (Northern Taste (CAN))
7872a[6]

Toshi (USA) *Jim Goldie* a57 53
10 b g Kingmambo(USA) Majestic Role (FR) (Theatrical (IRE))
1794[5] 2599[4] 3116[9] 4138[4]

Toss The Dice (IRE) *A De Royer-Dupre* a79 88
4 b h Medicean Seltitude (IRE) (Fairy King (USA))
4316a[9]

Totalize *Luca Cumani* a88 85
3 b g Authorized(IRE) You Too (Monsun (GER))
5889[4] 6228[2] (6615) 7168[7]

Totally Addicted *Mark Hoad*
6 b g Where Or When(IRE) Keep Quiet (Reprimand)
4648[P]

Totally Trusted *Scott Dixon* a62 60
4 b m Oasis Dream Trustthunder (Selkirk (USA))
2858[11] 3694[7] 7611[11] 7838[7] 8004[7]

Total Obsession *Mark Hoad* a51 43
5 b m Mujahid(USA) Buon Amici (Pivotal)
983[3] 1301[9] 1732[4] 2394[6] 2851[8]

Totom Chief *Gay Kelleway* a69 11
3 ch g Sleeping Indian Serotina (IRE) (Mtoto)
1301[4] 1981[5]

Toto Skyllachy *David O'Meara* a72 93
7 b g Kyllachy Little Tramp (Trempolino (USA))
5[6] 1670[6] ◆ (1914) 2142[2] 2590[4] 3493[2] 4110[5] 4828[16] 5186[3] 5677[3] 6338[2] 7210[3] 7435[6]

Totxo (IRE) *R Avial Lopez* a95 101
4 b h Diktat Mehany (FR) (Danehill (USA))
7624a[6] 7829a[6]

Toucan Tango (IRE) *Bernard Llewellyn* a54 61
4 b g Mujadil(USA) Walk On Quest (FR) (Rainbow Quest (USA))
23[5] 3137[14]

Touch Gold (IRE) *Sir Henry Cecil* a72 92
3 b c Oasis Dream Seek Easy (USA) (Seeking The Gold (USA))
1511[10] 2552[3] (3399) (3792) 4997[5]

Touching History (IRE) *Tim Etherington* a38 48
3 b g Titus Livius(FR) Lady Naryana (IRE) (Val Royal (FR))
5549[5] 6125[9] 6925[9] *7822[6]*

Touching Kings (FR) *C Boutin* a87 87
7 gr g Kutub(IRE) Touchee D'Amour (GER) (Neshad (USA))
2685a[8]

Touch Of Hawk (FR) *Wido Neuroth* a94 97
6 bl g Hawk Wing(USA) Touch Of Class (GER) (Be My Guest (USA))
2807a[5] 3886a[4] 4863a[2] 5651a[7] 6091a[5]

Touch Tone *David Thompson* a82 74
5 b m Selkirk(USA) Payphone (Anabaa (USA))
1527[10] 2094[15]

Toufan Express *Adrian McGuinness* a85 87
10 ch g Fraam Clan Scotia (Clantime)
337a[7] 1043a[7] 6716a[12]

Tough Lady (IRE) *Mark Johnston* a58 66
2 ch f Iffraaj Frivolous (IRE) (Green Desert (USA))
2837[4] ◆ 3123[9] 3554[4] 4331[6] *4934[6]* *6147[7]* 6849[4]

Toughness Danon *Brendan Powell* a79 97
6 b g Tiger Hill(IRE) Templerin (GER) (Acatenango (GER))
631a[10] 2706[8] *3502[9]* 4578[7] 5151[5] 5688[4] 5913[3] 6349[10] 6517[3] 6703[9] *6891[5]* *7380[4]* *7652[8]* *7954[3]* 8136[5]

Tough Question *Michael Madgwick* a16 36
2 ch c Needwood Blade Quiz Time (Efisio)
2039[8] 2420[8] 3244[5] *4463[11]* *5403[8]*

Toulio (GER) *A Kleinkorres*
3 b c Toylsome Trouville (GER) (Alkalde (GER))
117a[0]

Tourist *Ian Williams* a84 57
7 b g Oasis Dream West Devon (USA) (Gone West (USA))
128[8] *568[P]*

Tourtour (FR) *C Boutin* a77 72
2 gr f Gold Away(IRE) Tashira (FR) (Linamix (FR))
5697a[3]

Tous Les Deux *Dr Jeremy Naylor* a50 70
9 b g Efisio Caerosa (Caerleon (USA))
35[5] *188[12]* *276[8]* *773[3]* *966[8]* *8038[9]*

Towbee *Michael Easterby* a65 87
3 b g Doyen(IRE) Bow Bridge (Bertolini (USA))
769[7] *905[2]* (1252) *1529[7]* (1912) 2256[12] (4081) 4558[13] 5603[9] 6075[15] 6427[16]

Tower *Martin Keighley* a41 57
5 b g Nayef(USA) Palatial (Green Desert (USA))
1794[4] 2242[6] *7629[8]*

Tower Rock (IRE) *A P O'Brien* 112
3 b c Dylan Thomas(IRE) Monevassia (USA) (Mr Prospector (USA))
1404a[3] 2102a[2] 3361a[7]

Town Mouse *Hughie Morrison* a62 9
2 ch g Sakhee(USA) Megdale (IRE) (Waajib)
6572[10] *7165[5]* *7641[6]*

Towy Boy (IRE) *Ian Wood* a70 56
7 b g King Charlemagne(USA) Solar Flare (IRE) (Danehill (USA))
88[10] *215[5]*

Toymaker *James Given* a73 81
5 b g Starcraft(NZ) Eurolink Raindance (IRE) (Alzao (USA))
581[3] *(995)* (1269) ◆ 2491[8] 6342[9] 7369[11] *7715[11]*

Trachonitis (IRE) *J R Jenkins* a76 75
8 b g Dansili Hasina (IRE) (King's Theatre (IRE))
460[8] *1956[6]*

Tracks Of My Tears *Giles Bravery* a38 41
2 b f Rail Link Policy Setter (USA) (Deputy Minister (CAN))
7020[9] 7552[9] *7777[8]*

Trade Centre *Milton Bradley* a72 56
7 b g Dubai Destination(USA) Khubza (Green Desert (USA))
1497[3] 2760[4] 3718[5] 4493[3] 4758[4] 4902[5] 5191[6]

Trade Commissioner (IRE) *John Gosden* a77 109
4 b g Montjeu(IRE) Spinning Queen (Spinning World (USA))
1138[3] ◆ (2430) ◆ 2932[3] (3508) ◆ (3878) 5278[7] 7054[4] 7558[6]

Trader Jack *Roger Charlton* a97 98
3 b g Trade Fair Azeema (IRE) (Averti (IRE))
1645[6] 2477[2] 3294[11] 4009[5] 4700[5] 5626[2] *6018[2]* 6677[10]

Trade Secret *Mel Brittain* a78 92
5 b g Trade Fair Kastaway (Distant Relative)
1478[2] 1868[2] 2096[11] (3255) 4629[10] (4824) 5368[19] (6009) 6466[23] 7063[11] 7366[12]

Trade Storm *David Simcock* a100 109
4 b h Trade Fair Frisson (Slip Anchor)
2211[7] ◆ 3268[27] 5075[2] (5517) 6166[3]

Trading Leather (IRE) *J S Bolger* 107
2 b c Teofilo(IRE) Night Visit (Sinndar (IRE))
6060a[2] ◆ (7053) ◆ 7398[5]

Traditional Chic (IRE) *L Riccardi* 101
4 ch h Ad Valorem(USA) Minimal Chic (IRE) (King's Best (USA))
2325a[2] 7565a[8]

Trail Blaze (IRE) *Kevin Ryan* 97
3 b g Tagula(IRE) Kingpin Delight (Emarati (USA))
(1595) (2076) 3064[2] (3383) 4075[3] (4675) 5334[2] (6046) 6426[5]

Trailblazer (JPN) *Yasutoshi Ikee* 122
5 b h Zenno Rob Roy(JPN) Lirio (USA) (Forty Niner (USA))
7573a[4]

Trail Of Tears (IRE) *John Gosden* a69 50
3 b f Exceed And Excel(AUS) Cherokee Rose (IRE) (Dancing Brave (USA))
838[2] *1016[3]* 1274[6] *1730[2]* *1986[3]* *2397[7]*

Train Hard *Mark Johnston* a51 61
2 b g Rail Link Melpomene (Peintre Celebre (USA))
6985[5] *7199[6]* 7442[5]

Trainspotting *Charles O'Brien* a13 32
2 ch g Medicean Capannina (Grand Lodge (USA))
5858a[13]

Tram Express (FR) *Shaun Lycett* a61
8 ch g Trempolino(USA) Molly Dance (FR) (Groom Dancer (USA))
6770[10] *7352[6]* *7594[7]* *8035[6]* *(8273)*

Transcend (JPN) *Takayuki Yasuda* a119 91
6 b h Wild Rush(USA) Cinema Scope (JPN) (Tony Bin)
1150a[13]

Transfer *Richard Price* a59 74
7 br g Trans Island Sankaty Light (USA) (Summer Squall (USA))
3073[8] 3782[6] (4733) 5507[7] 6004[10] *6503[6]* *6940[8]* *7251[10]*

Transfix *Ed Vaughan* a58 59
3 b f Pivotal Hypnotize (Machiavellian (USA))
3990[5] *6254[3]* *7668[8]* *8050[6]* *8187[10]*

Transmit (IRE) *Tim Easterby* a65 65
5 ch g Trans Island Apple Brandy (USA) (Cox's Ridge (USA))
154[2] *232[3]* *289[6]* *813[7]* 1269[9] 2588[7] 2792[10] 3021[8] 4783[11]

Trans Sonic *David O'Meara* a83 57
9 ch g Trans Island Sankaty Light (USA) (Summer Squall (USA))
553[4] *671[3]* *(809)* *888[3]* *(976)* 1135[14] 1295[11] *1429[2]*

Trapeze *John Gosden* 77
2 ch f Pivotal Miss Penton (Primo Dominie)
3074[13] (7104) 7406[7]

Traps Army (IRE) *W McCreery* a54 44
2 b g Clodovil(IRE) Quelle Celtique (FR) (Tel Quel (FR))
5858a[8] *7932[3]*

Travel (USA) *Mahmood Al Zarooni* a60
2 ch f Street Cry(IRE) Away (USA) (Dixieland Band (USA))
2541[7]

Traveller's Tales *Richard Hannon* a77 83
3 b f Cape Cross(IRE) Lost In Wonder (USA) (Galileo (IRE))
731[2] *982[2]* (2201) 3013[2] 3882[5] 4741[13] 5277[4] 5796[6]

Travelling *Tony Carroll* a71 71
3 b f Dubai Destination(USA) Attune (Singspiel (IRE))
2136[4] 2425[3] 3643[9] 4435[2] *5231[3]* 5990[8] *7975[2]* *8183[7]*

Travis County (IRE) *Brian Ellison* a70 76
3 b g Jeremy(USA) Manchaca (FR) (Highest Honor (FR))
1190[8] *1582[4]* *1960[3]* 7001[5] 7402[10] 7600[2] *8115[6]* *8142[5]*

Treacle Tart *James Ewart* a74 65
7 ch m Fleetwood(IRE) Loriner's Lass (Saddlers' Hall (IRE))
9[10]

Treadwell (IRE) *Jamie Osborne* a88 90
5 b h Footstepsinthesand Lady Wells (IRE) (Sadler's Wells (USA))
29[8] 2489[4] 4703[10] 5356[11] *6040[9]* *6979[10]*

Treasure Act *Patrick Chamings* a61 31
4 ch m Act One Benjarong (Sharpo)
2385[8] *8099[12]*

Treasure Beach *A P O'Brien* 121
4 b h Galileo(IRE) Honorine (IRE) (Mark Of Esteem (IRE))
1149a[4] 5027a[4] 5377a[6] 7573a[10]

Treasured Dream *Amanda Perrett* a55 67
3 b f Oasis Dream Maid To Treasure (IRE) (Rainbow Quest (USA))
3189[6] 4366[11] 5776[4] *6401[9]*

Treasure The Ridge (IRE) *D K Weld* a67 63
3 b g Galileo(IRE) Treasure The Lady (IRE) (Indian Ridge)
1834a[5]

Treble Jig (USA) *M Al Muhairi* a110 99
5 b h Gone West(USA) Light Jig (Danehill (USA))
591a[15] *878a[10]*

Trecase *Tony Carroll* a62 54
5 b g Zafeen(FR) Pewter Lass (Dowsing (USA))
468[2] *(558)* *651[2]* *1613[4]*

Tregereth (IRE) *Jonathan Portman* 67
2 b f Footstepsinthesand Ringmoor Down (Pivotal)
4002[5] 4752[3] 4899[3] 5773[2] 6276[8] 7296[2]

Trending (IRE) *Jeremy Gask* a66 66
3 gr g Dark Angel(IRE) Call Later (USA) (Gone West (USA))
564[9] *845[5]* *1012[5]* *1337[2]* *1529[4]* (2388) 2762[3] 3442[18] (4489) 4757[5] 5934[3] *6825[4]* *7590[5]* 8231[3]

Trend Is My Friend (USA) *Amanda Perrett* a69 85
3 bb g Lemon Drop Kid(USA) Silva (FR) (Anabaa (USA))
1086[5] 2279[3] 3349[6] (3882) 4700[13] ◆ 5788[4] 6333[6] 6964[9] 7294[5]

Trend Line (IRE) *Peter Chapple-Hyam* a77 77
4 b m Holy Roman Emperor(IRE) Dabiliya (Vayrann)
43[3] 2237[4]

Tresabella *Michael Appleby* a54 29
3 b f Firebreak Bella Tutrice (IRE) (Woodborough (USA))
2802[11] 3083[7] 3575[6] *5015[2]* *6813[5]* 7470[14]

Tres Blue (IRE) *H-A Pantall* a78 78
2 b c Anabaa Blue Tres Ravi (GER) (Monsun (GER))
7091a[9]

Tres Coronas (IRE) *David Barron* a86 92
5 b g Key Of Luck(USA) Almansa (IRE) (Dr Devious (IRE))
1134[12] (1381) 1605[3] 2257[4] 2911[5] 3494[5] 4249[11] 5224[4] 6476[4] 7069[6] 7455[5]

Tres Rock Danon (FR) *W Hickst* 113
6 b h Rock Of Gibraltar(IRE) Tres Ravi (GER) (Monsun (GER))
1901a[2] 2965a[2] (3768a) 4634a[4] 5400a[7]

Trevose (IRE) *Roy Brotherton* a28 54
3 b g Barathea(IRE) Cape Jasmine (IRE) (Danehill (USA))
4992[7] 5687[4] 6279[5] *7527[12]* *8179[11]*

Tribal I D (IRE) *Jim Boyle* a58
3 b g High Chaparral(IRE) Van De Cappelle (IRE) (Pivotal)
4948[6] *5404[6]* 6565[7] *6982[8]* *7326[5]*

Tribal Myth (IRE) *Kevin Ryan* 76
5 b g Johannesburg(USA) Shadow Play (USA) (Theatrical (IRE))
1135[6] 1913[3] 2687[4] 3692[8] 4179[6] 4682[2] 5225[3] 5622[4]

Tribal Path (IRE) *Mark Johnston* 57
2 b c Giant's Causeway(USA) Navajo Moon (IRE) (Danehill (USA))
5562[6] ◆ 6133[9]

Tribes And Banner (IRE) *C F Swan* a82 75
8 br g Bob's Return(IRE) Kaysdante (IRE) (Phardante (FR))
(342a)

Tribouley *Dean Ivory* a56
4 ch m Bahamian Bounty Serriera (FR) (Highest Honor (FR))
3735[7] 4196[12] *6773[13]* 7126[10]

Tribune (FR) *J-C Rouget* a103 94
3 b f Grand Slam(USA) Tanguista (FR) (War Chant (USA))
542a[5] 1209a[7]

Tricksofthetrade (IRE) *Alan Swinbank* a81 77
6 b g Mull Of Kintyre(USA) Soden (IRE) (Mujadil (USA))
(460) *582[2]* *751[6]* 2694[3] 3129[13] 4209[5] 6339[9] 7245[9]

Tricky Madam *Tim Easterby* 49
2 b f Multiplex Alula (In The Wings)
3351[3] 4343[2] 4449[4]

Tricky Week (FR) *C Baillet* 86
2 ch f Sunday Break(JPN) Tricky Bid (USA) (Silver Hawk (USA))
5248a[5] 6463a[6] 7430a[7]

Tri Nations (UAE) *Anthony Middleton* a72 88
7 ch g Halling(USA) Six Nations (USA) (Danzig (USA))
7413[4] *7652[9]* *8020[11]*

Trinityelitedotcom (IRE) *Tom Dascombe* 77
2 b g Elusive City(USA) Beal Ban (IRE) (Daggers Drawn (USA))
1997[3] 2817[2] 3242[17]

Trinket Box (USA) *Mahmood Al Zarooni* 47
2 b f Bernardini(USA) Silver Impulse (CAN) (Silver Charm (USA))
4546[9] 6257[8]

Trinniberg (USA) *Shivananda Parbhoo* a123 40
3 bb c Teuflesberg(USA) Bella Dorato (USA) (Goldminers Gold (CAN))
1872a[17] *(7574a)*

Trio Of Trix *Malcolm Saunders* 16
3 b f Act One Dictatrix (Diktat)
1360[7] 2200[9] 2941[13] 5658[9] 5989[10]

Trioomph *James Given* a30 58
3 b f Three Valleys(USA) Oomph (Shareef Dancer (USA))
1918[9] *2548[14]*

Triple Aspect (IRE) *Jeremy Gask* 109
6 b g Danetime(IRE) Wicken Wonder (IRE) (Distant Relative)
1316[5] 2446[8] 3877[12]

Triple Charm *Jeremy Noseda* a94 86
4 ch m Pivotal Triple Joy (Most Welcome)
(686) *1141[4]* 1741[4] *3281[3]* 4703[16] 5269[5] *(5769)* *7010[6]* *7826[5]*

Triple Dream *Milton Bradley* a82 81
7 ch g Vision Of Night Triple Joy (Most Welcome)
208[5] *406[6]* *(560)* *647[4]* 1204[3] 2084[10] (2494) 3660[3] (4743) 5123[5] 6006[6] 6370[8] 6578[4]

Triple Eight (IRE) *Philip Kirby* a79 79
4 b g Royal Applause Hidden Charm (IRE) (Big Shuffle (USA))
2094[7] 2510[16] 2922[3] 3356[5] 3914[11] 4396[10] 4868[3] (5059) 5314[3] 6313[8]

Triple Salchow *Alastair Lidderdale* a56 28
3 b f Needwood Blade Icky Woo (Mark Of Esteem (IRE))
1182[12] 3702[10] 4237[11] 4937[8] *5970[10]* *6771[U]*

Triple Threat (FR) *A Fabre* 100
2 b c Monsun(GER) Drei (USA) (Lyphard (USA))
7514a[4]

Trip Switch *John Butler* a75 58
6 b g Reset(AUS) Caribbean Star (Soviet Star (USA))
176[2] *(224)* *349[5]* *480[8]* *1611[11]* *8162[13]*

Trisha's Boy (IRE) *Simon Dow* a29 49
3 ch g Exceed And Excel(AUS) Golden Anthem (USA) (Lion Cavern (USA))
2626[6]

Triskaidekaphobia *Wilf Storey* a62 54
9 b g Bertolini(USA) Seren Teg (Timeless Times (USA))
1242[11] 2436[8] 2748[7] 4911[4] 5739[10] 6959[13]

Tristessa *Derek Haydn Jones* a57 57
2 b f Amadeus Wolf On Point (Kris)
4886[4] 5773[4] 6093[3]

Triumphant (IRE) *A P O'Brien* 103
3 b c Danehill Dancer(IRE) Meek Appeal (USA) (Woodman (USA))
1943a[3]

Troc Des Brieres (FR) *L Tassart*
5 b g Corri Piano(FR) Etoile De Sou (FR) (Amthaal (USA))
93a[0]

Trois Lunes (FR) *F Rohaut* 107
3 b f Manduro(GER) Trip To The Moon (Fasliyev (USA))
(1695a) 3203a[10] 5472a[3] 7093a[11]

Trois Rois (FR) *Ismail Mohammed* a102 109
7 b h Hernando(FR) Trevise (FR) (Anabaa (USA))
52a[7] 318a[4] *484a[10]* 591a[7] 792a[8]

Trois Vallees (USA) *James Tate* a87 73
3 bb c Elusive Quality(USA) Chamrousse (USA) (Peaks And Valleys (USA))
2897[8] *3280[7]* *(7843)* ◆ *8056[7]*

Trojan Nights (USA) *M Al Muhairi* a93 93
4 ch g Street Cry(IRE) Dabaweyaa (Shareef Dancer (USA))
618a[6]

Trojan Rocket (IRE) *Michael Wigham* a74 84
4 b g Elusive City(USA) Tagula Bay (IRE) (Tagula (IRE))
102[4] *262[3]* *(448)* (2251) ◆ 2466[2] (3394) (4300) 6820[11] 7559[10]

Troopingthecolour *Steve Gollings* a92 101
6 b g Nayef(USA) Hyperspectra (Rainbow Quest (USA))
1674[2] 2257[2] 2932[2] 3163[8] 4060[2] 5664[3]

Tropenfeuer (FR) *James Moffatt* a73 54
5 b m Banyumanik(IRE) Tropensonne (GER) (Konigsstuhl (GER))
2033[2] 4869[4]

Tropical Bachelor (IRE) *Richard Ford* a67 77
6 b g Bachelor Duke(USA) Tropical Coral (IRE) (Pennekamp (USA))
1719[3] *2134[5]*

Tropical Beat *John Gosden* a95 103
4 b g Beat Hollow Tropical Heights (FR) (Shirley Heights)
1924[8] *(2810)* 3826[3] 4363[6] 5558[3] 6031[2]

Tropical Duke (IRE) *Ron Barr* a62 56
6 ch g Bachelor Duke(USA) Tropical Dance (USA) (Thorn Dance (USA))
2239[8] 5259[8] 5669[6] 6259[13]

Tropical Song *John Gosden* a81 82
2 b c Beat Hollow Tropical Heights (FR) (Shirley Heights)
3397[6] 3824[2] 4472[2] *5230[2]* (6301)

Tropics (USA) *Dean Ivory* a91
4 ch g Speightstown(USA) Taj Aire (USA) (Taj Alriyadh (USA))
6397[2] *7005[2]* *(7477)* *7823[3]*

Trovare (USA) *Amanda Perrett* a86 90
5 b g Smart Strike(CAN) Abita (USA) (Dynaformer (USA))
3502[12] 3625[12] *(3961)* *4215[2]* 4697[15] 5106[3] 5905[5] 6191[8] 6493[7]

Trove (IRE) *Mark Hoad* a54 31
3 b g Rock Of Gibraltar(IRE) Cache Creek (IRE) (Marju (IRE))
1413[5] *1731[7]* *2495[5]* 3470[14]

Troy Boy *Robin Bastiman* 47
2 b g Choisir(AUS) Love Thing (Phountzi (USA))
5367[12] 6780[7] 7031[7] 7441[8]

Trucanini *Chris Wall* 76
2 b f Mount Nelson Jalissa (Mister Baileys)
2892[6] 4818[3] 5947[2]

True Ally *John Norton*
2 b f Passing Glance True Melody (IRE) (Grand Lodge (USA))
4742[11] *5807[13]* *6612[10]*

True Bond *Geoffrey Oldroyd* a40 62
3 ch f Monsieur Bond(IRE) Splicing (Sharpo)
2336[13] 3209[9]

True Prince (USA) *Amanda Perrett* a56 59
3 ch g Yes It's True(USA) Whenthedoveflies (USA) (Dove Hunt (USA))
1067[10] 3246[13] 5198[8] (6274) *6396[11]* *7326[3]*

True Satire *Jane Chapple-Hyam* a57 58
4 b m Oasis Dream Native Justice (USA) (Alleged (USA))
1070[9]

True Spirit *Paul D'Arcy* 39
2 b c Shamardal(USA) Petonellajill (Petong)
1886[8]

True To Form (IRE) *Martyn Meade* a103 74
5 b g Rock Of Gibraltar(IRE) Truly Yours (IRE) (Barathea (IRE))
(554) *712[5]* *785[3]* *(817)* *7502[4]* *7631[2]* *7771[5]* *8095[2]* *(8227)*

True Verdict (IRE) *David Wachman* a71 100
2 b f Danehill Dancer(IRE) Foolish Act (IRE) (Sadler's Wells (USA))
2780a[2] 3674a[2] 4276a[8]

Trulee Scrumptious *Peter Charalambous* a52 59
3 b f Strategic Prince Morning Rise (GER) (Acatenango (GER))
1589[6] *1981[9]* 2249[12] 4662[9] *4932[7]* 5324[3] 5556[6] 6274[5] *7625[5]* *7769[6]*

Truly Charming (GER) *Fredrik Reuterskiold* a64
3 br f Clodovil(IRE) Truly Bewitched (USA) (Affirmed (USA))
4359a[8] *5143a[7]*

Truly Madly (IRE) *John Joseph Murphy* a73 73
2 b f Royal Applause Triennial (IRE) (Giant's Causeway (USA))
5872[2]

Trumpet Major (IRE) *Richard Hannon* 115
3 b c Arakan(USA) Ashford Cross (Cape Cross (IRE))
(1470) 1856[4] ◆ 2514a[10] (4760) ◆ 5573[5] 6634[10]

Trumpet Voluntary (IRE) *Nicky Vaughan* a61 77
3 b g Red Clubs(IRE) Woodmaven (USA) (Woodman (USA))
5308[8] *6050[10]* 6434[6] *6647[9]*

Trust Fund Babe (IRE) *Tim Easterby* a56 64
3 b f Captain Rio Perfect Order (USA) (Red Ransom (USA))
3357[6] (4348) 4793[7] 5203[3] 5545[7] *6211[6]* *7146[8]* 7600[5]

Trusting (IRE) *Eve Johnson Houghton* a62 62
3 b f Red Clubs(IRE) Tertia (IRE) (Polish Patriot (USA))
2548[3] 3246[3] *3939[5]* 4486[9] 5147[3] *5231[2]* *5479[14]* *6151[6]* *(6778)* *7225[9]*

Trust Me Boy *John E Long* a45 51
4 gr g Avonbridge Eastern Lyric (Petong)
2607[4] 4241[3] 4986[6] 5999[5] 6951[3]

Trymyluck *Pam Sly* 61
2 b f Royal Applause Borders Belle (IRE) (Pursuit Of Love)
3182[6] 3842[5] 4494[10] 6607[7] 7313[4]

Tryst *J E Hammond* a102 104
7 gr g Highest Honor(FR) Courting (Pursuit Of Love)
953a[4]

Tsarabi (IRE) *Mlle A Imaz-Ceca* 75
7 b h Hernando(FR) Veronica Cooper (IRE) (Kahyasi)
6089a[4]

Tsar Paul (IRE) *J A Nash* a73 78
7 b g Xaar Jelba (Pursuit Of Love)
335a[2]

Tucky Even (FR) *C Boutin*
2 gr f Kentucky Dynamite(USA) Noor Forever (FR) (Highest Honor (FR))
8193a[0]

Tucumano (FR) *Y-M Porzier* a64 100
6 ch g Anabaa Blue Impudica (URU) (Mo Rum (USA))
7320a[9]

Tuffan (USA) *Clive Brittain* a66 67
2 b c Bernardini(USA) Love Of Dubai (USA) (More Than Ready (USA))
2247[6] 3119[3] 4595[7] 5155[4]

Tuibama (IRE) *Tracy Waggott* a54 68
3 ch g Bertolini(USA) Supportive (IRE) (Nashamaa)
455[8] 599[5] 845[9] 1292[4] 1599[6] 1817[6] 2774[4] (3020) (3256) 4428[5] 4878[5] 5318[3] 5740[2] 6605[4]

Tukitinyasok (IRE) *Clive Mulhall* a36 60
5 b g Fath(USA) Mevlana (IRE) (Red Sunset)
3699[4] 4398[7] 4716[2] 5341[8] 6106[12]

Tulia De Gravelle (FR) *Philip Hobbs* a24
5 b m Port Lyautey(FR) Memsie De Gravelle (FR) (Saint Cyrien (FR))
1339[5]

Tullius (IRE) *Andrew Balding* a79 116
4 ch g Le Vie Dei Colori Whipped Queen (USA) (Kingmambo (USA))
(1854) (2127) (3166) 4320[3] (5278)

Tumbledown (USA) *Mahmood Al Zarooni* 28
2 b f Bernardini(USA) Freeroll (USA) (Touch Gold (USA))
6489[15]

Tumbleowtashoes *John Ryan* a20 28
3 ch g Tumbleweed Ridge Darling Belinda (Silver Wizard (USA))
565[8] 801[6] 1600[8] 2139[7] 2388[11] 2547[8] 3050[14]

Tumblewind *Richard Whitaker* 67
2 ch f Captain Rio African Breeze (Atraf)
2686[8] 3286[5] (5222) 5711[2] 6032[5] 7206[4]

Tunnager Grove *Hughie Morrison* a76 74
3 b g Piccolo Violet's Walk (Dr Fong (USA))
2542[6] 3012[8] 3539[2] 3941[2] ◆ 4143[6] 5972[6] 6542[2] (7126) 7436[2]

Tunza The Lion *Richard Ford* a30
5 b g Trade Fair Bella Helena (Balidar)
95[6] 2641[0] 477[9] 666[11] 843[10] 984[8]

Turama *Ed Dunlop* a34
3 ch f Pivotal Our Queen Of Kings (Arazi (USA))
2496[7]

Turbo Compressor (USA) *Todd Pletcher* a117 117
4 b r Halo's Image(USA) Dixieland Event (USA) (Wild Event (USA))
7573a[12]

Turbulent Descent (USA) *Todd Pletcher* a119
4 b m Congrats(USA) Roger's Sue (USA) (Forestry (USA))
7569a[7]

Turbulent Priest *Zoe Davison* a49 46
4 b g Storming Home Hymn Book (IRE) (Darshaan)
130[10] 519[8] 1624[7] 1770[3] 6948[13]

Turcoman's (FR) *A Junk* a87 84
3 b g Berkoutchi(FR) Turtle Cove (IRE) (Catrail (USA))
117a[7] 7803a[6] 8277a[6]

Turjuman (USA) *Alan Bailey* a68 66
7 ch g Swain(IRE) Hachiyah (IRE) (Generous (IRE))
9[2] 366[8] 400[4] 557[2] 888[4] 6055[3] 6949[10] 7640[11] 7819[10] 8148[5]

Turned To Gold (IRE) *Alan Jarvis* a23 74
3 ch g Teofilo(IRE) Silver Bracelet (Machiavellian (USA))
2271[9] 3737[9]

Turning Circle *Mel Brittain* a67 29
6 b h Spinning World(USA) Willow Dale (IRE) (Danehill (USA))
1823[7]

Turn The Tide *Dai Williams* a34 82
4 b m Footstepsinthesand Syrian Dancer (IRE) (Groom Dancer (USA))
6773[11] 7204[12] 7378[7]

Tuscan Fun *Roger Varian* a62 60
2 ch g Medicean Elfin Laughter (Alzao (USA))
6164[10] 7033[7] 7304[7]

Tuscan Gold *Laura Mongan* a66 89
5 ch g Medicean Louella (USA) (El Gran Senor (USA))
3241[13] 5306[4] ◆ 6333[8] 8073[10]

Tuscania *Lucy Wadham* a87 94
4 b m King's Best(USA) Contiguous (USA) (Danzig (USA))
3636[6] 3991[2] 4805[7] 5043[3] 5420[4] 7334[14] 7626[4] 7986[6] 8174[4] 8250[4]

Tusculum (IRE) *Barney Curley* a53 38
9 b g Sadler's Wells(USA) Turbaine (USA) (Trempolino (USA))
6399[12]

Tussie Mussie *Mark Johnston* a65 73
2 b f Royal Applause Loveleaves (Polar Falcon (USA))
2508[4] 2686[6] 3415[6] (4139) 5041[2] 5602[7] (5920) ◆ 6160[13] 6675[8]

Tussy Marx *David Barron* 37
2 b f Pastoral Pursuits Clashfern (Smackover)
3747[7] 4290[6]

Tuttipaesi (IRE) *Marco Botti* a99 100
2 br f Clodovil(IRE) Ruby Ridge (IRE) (Acatenango (GER))
6199[7]

Tuxedo *Peter Hiatt* a72 43
7 ch g Cadeaux Genereux Serengeti Bride (USA) (Lion Cavern (USA))
198[5] 423[2] 517[5] 685[9] 804[4] (960) 1105[2] 1269[13]

Twary (USA) *Roger Varian* a61 83
2 b g Indian Charlie(USA) Street Sounds (CAN) (Street Cry (IRE))
5042[3] 7628[6]

Tweet Lady *Rod Millman* a71 69
3 b f Royal Applause Fuschia (Averti (IRE))
1058[7] 1531[4] 1728[U] 2448[7] 3002[3] 3443[4] 4289[6] 5657[10] 6151[8]

Twelve Strings (IRE) *Luca Cumani* a61 85
3 b g Iffraaj Favoritely (USA) (Favorite Trick (USA)) (1661) ◆ 2246[7] 2942[4] 4199[4] 5706[3] 6263[3] (7269)

Twennyshortkid *Paul Midgley* a56 55
4 b g Sleeping Indian Brandish (Warning)
141[0] 113[7]

Twenty One Choice (IRE) *Ed de Giles* a78 74
3 ch g Choisir(AUS) Midnight Lace (Tomba)
2131[2] (5764) ◆ (6309) (6500)

Twice Bitten *James Toller* a86 75
4 ch g Beat Hollow Duena (Grand Lodge (USA))
2637[8] 2921[11] 3962[5] 5158[2] 5944[6] 6349[9] 6584[9] 7377[7]

Twice Over *Sir Henry Cecil* a125 126
7 bb h Observatory(USA) Double Crossed (Caerleon (USA))
1471[2] 1677[3] 3880[3] 5490[4]

Twice Red *Mandy Rowland* a77 29
4 b g Intikhab(USA) Red Shareef (Marju (IRE))
136[5] 205[7] 359[6] 385[4] 696[4] 819[2] 887[3] (1305) 1614[2]

Twilight Allure *Kevin Ryan* a67 33
3 b f Shamardal(USA) Midnight Allure (Aragon)
4619[7]

Twilight Legend (IRE) *Seamus Mullins* a21
3 b f Chevalier(IRE) Almost Twilight (USA) (Silver Hawk (USA))
7488[7] 7896[7] 8069[7] 8265[13]

Twilight Pearl *Tim Easterby* 60
2 b f Pastoral Pursuits Branston Gem (So Factual (USA))
1435[3] 1671[5] 4083[2] 4310[5] 4806[2] 5709[3] 5799[7] 6511[2] 6953[3] (7176)

Twin Ivan (IRE) *Marjorie Fife* 61
3 b g Ivan Denisovich(IRE) Twin Logic (USA) (Diesis)
1595[7] 2118[5] 2605[9] 3025[9]

Twinkled *Michael Bell* a73 60
4 ch g Bahamian Bounty Panic Stations (Singspiel (IRE))
(423) 562[2] (685) 907[8] 1108[7]

Twin Shadow (IRE) *James Fanshawe* a63 64
3 ch f Dubawi(IRE) Its On The Air (IRE) (King's Theatre (IRE))
3398[6] 4435[4] 5021[3] 5479[3] 5945[11] (6813)

Twin Soul (IRE) *Andrew Balding* a98 96
4 br m Singspiel(IRE) Kirk Wynd (Selkirk (USA))
1374[6] 1848[4] 2066[4] 3241[12] 4738[7]

Twinwood Star (IRE) *John Weymes* a47 44
2 b f Moss Vale(IRE) Bonkers (Efisio)
2334[7] 2770[9] 4310[10] 4767[6] 5194[3] 8233[5] 8274[11]

Twirl (IRE) *A P O'Brien* 106
3 b f Galileo(IRE) Butterfly Cove (USA) (Storm Cat (USA))
1041a[2] 2178[2] 2658[11] 3292[5] 4378a[7]

Two Cities (IRE) *Ann Duffield* a65 63
3 b g Excellent Art Rock Dove (IRE) (Danehill (USA))
2143[5] 2795[12] (Dead)

Two Days In Paris (FR) *J-C Rouget* 99
3 b f Authorized(IRE) Isalou (FR) (Unfuwain (USA))
6595a[8]

Two In The Pink (IRE) *Hugo Palmer* a63
2 b f Clodovil(IRE) Secret Circle (Magic Ring (IRE))
7987[4] 8165[3]

Two No Bids (IRE) *J W Hills* a57
2 bb c Footstepsinthesand Milwaukee (FR) (Desert King (IRE))
7926[5]

Two Pancakes *Declan Carroll* 71
2 b g Compton Place Fancy Rose (USA) (Joyeux Danseur (USA))
2308[3] 3182[12]

Two Sugars *Louise Best* a56 62
4 b g Val Royal(FR) Princess Galadriel (Magic Ring (IRE))
3155[5] 3389[12] 3994[4] 4302[4] 6774[3]

Two Turtle Doves (IRE) *Michael Mullineaux* a67 68
6 b m Night Shift(USA) Purple Rain (IRE) (Celtic Swing)
106[3] 212[6] 2377[4] 3026[5] 3256[5] 3435[6] 3893[7] (4535) 4866[2] 5131[3] 5681[2] 6002[2] 6195[6] 6961[16] 7457[10]

Ty Bolide (FR) *F Sanchez* a68 55
4 b g American Post Tite Pepee (FR) (Epervier Bleu)
1172a[0]

Tychaios *Stuart Williams* a57
2 b g Green Desert(USA) Tychy (Suave Dancer (USA))
7305[8] 7517[12]

Tycoon's Garden (FR) *E Lellouche* 97
3 b c Ski Chief(USA) Queen's Garden (USA) (Kingmambo (USA))
1426a[7]

Tyfos *Brian Baugh* a74 94
7 b g Bertolini(USA) Warminghamsharpish (Nalchik (USA))
1642[11] 2289[11] 2674[3] 3608[10] 4591[5] 4849[10]

Ty Gwr *David Simcock* a71
3 b g Echo Of Light House Maiden (IRE) (Rudimentary (USA))
1192[5] 1427[3] 1989[5] 5766[5] 6398[4] (7249) (7718)

Tymismoni (IRE) *Michael Attwater* a42 56
4 ch m Choisir(AUS) Berenice (ITY) (Marouble)
7005[8] 7488[5] 7739[8] 8265[7]

Typhon (USA) *David Lanigan* a64 67
2 b c Proud Citizen(USA) Seven Moons (JPN) (Sunday Silence (USA))
3040[5] 3733[3] 5319[6]

Typography *William Muir* a72 72
3 br g Byron Bold Byzantium (Bold Arrangement)
4001[4] 5147[4] 6275[5]

Tyrana (GER) *Ian Williams* a44 57
9 ch m Acatenango(GER) Tascalina (GER) (Big Shuffle (USA))
4189[4]

Tyre Giant Dot Com *Geoffrey Oldroyd* a51 74
3 b g Misu Bond(IRE) Villa Del Sol (Tagula (IRE))
5013[8]

Tyrur Ted *Frank Sheridan* a59 76
7 b g Val Royal(FR) Spanish Serenade (Nashwan (USA))
7321[5] ◆ 7991[10]

Tysoe Lad *Michael Appleby* 29
4 br g Zafeen(FR) Nicholas Mistress (Beveled (USA))
2800[8] 4630[9]

Tyson The Byson *Mrs K Burke* a59 52
2 b g Byron Tripti (IRE) (Sesaro (USA))
2261[18] 2469[5] 4310[14] 6115[9] 6310[3] 6766[4] 7379[5] 7609[5]

Ubetterbegood (ARG) *Robert Cowell* a101 63
4 b h Distorted Humor(USA) Movie Star (BRZ) (Royal Academy (USA))
6116[6] (7704) 7897[7]

Ucanchoose (IRE) *Andrew Slattery* a57 77
6 b g Choisir(AUS) Ruacana Falls (USA) (Storm Bird (CAN))
6270a[12] 6465[12]

Uganda Glory (USA) *George Baker* 53
2 bb f Hat Trick(JPN) Febrile (USA) (Trempolino (USA))
6153[6] 7014[4]

Uknowwhatshouldido (IRE) *J S Moore* a64 71
2 rg f Dark Angel(IRE) Torosay Spring (First Trump)
4282[5] ◆ 4742[7] 5887[7] ◆ 6337[11] 7056[3]

Ukrainian (IRE) *Mark Johnston* a88 91
3 b g Teofilo(IRE) Livadiya (IRE) (Shernazar)
(1591) 2372[6] 2718[11] 3711[4] 4466[5] (5188) 5442[3] 5913[10] (6712) 6776[2] 6933[8] 7487[6]

Ukrainian Princess *Sir Henry Cecil* a75 75
3 ch f Medicean Unquenchable (USA) (Kingmambo (USA))
1676[5] 2381[2] 4212[7] 5680[4] 6416[11] 6895[2] 7416[7]

Uleavemebreathless *A Oliver* 96
2 b f Tiger Hill(IRE) Sovereign Abbey (IRE) (Royal Academy (USA))
6266a[5] 6717a[3]

Ultimate *Brian Ellison* a94 89
6 b g Anabaa(USA) Nirvana (Marju (IRE))
2504[14] 4347[9] 4621[4] 6031[12]

Ultimate Destiny *Ralph Beckett* a81 82
3 b g Hurricane Run(IRE) Shallika (IRE) (Alhaarth (IRE))
1031[6] 1312[8] 1976[11] (2787) (3122) 3992[3] 5366[8] 6039[4] 6573[5]

Ultrasonic (USA) *Sir Michael Stoute* 105
3 b f Mizzen Mast(USA) Quickfire (Dubai Millennium)
1858[8] 3158[3] 3593[4] (4336) 5385[2] 6878[2] 7690[2]

Uma De Synthe (FR) *A Bonin* a69 76
3 ch g Red Guest(IRE) Nelly (FR) (Arctic Tern (USA))
1127a[7]

Umph (IRE) *David Evans* a65 63
3 b g Kodiac Baraloti (IRE) (Barathea (IRE))
250[5] 352[5] 660[10] 743[6] 916[4] (1067) 1359[4] 1419[4] 1725[4] 2351[8] 2551[8]

Umverti *Joanne Foster* 42
7 b m Averti(IRE) Umbrian Gold (IRE) (Perugino (USA))
2694[8] 3022[8] 3693[9]

Una Bella Cosa *Alan McCabe* a53 40
2 b f Dubai Destination(USA) Blinding Mission (IRE) (Marju (IRE))
3282[10] 3560[13] 4246[9] 6791[12] 7728[3] 8094[4]

Unaccompanied (IRE) *D K Weld* 106
5 b m Danehill Dancer(IRE) Legend Has It (IRE) (Sadler's Wells (USA))
2318a[2] 2903a[3]

Unassailable *Kevin Ryan* 60
2 ch g Bahamian Bounty Reeling N' Rocking (IRE) (Mr Greeley (USA))
1842[8] 4290[5] 5168[6]

Una Vita Pius (IRE) *Patrick Gilligan* a46
4 b m Antonius Pius(USA) Avit (IRE) (General Monash (USA))
227[9]

Unbreak My Heart (IRE) *Richard Guest* a84 93
7 ch g Bahamian Bounty Golden Heart (Salse (USA))
306[12]

Unbridled Command (USA) *Thomas Bush* 113
3 rg c Master Command(USA) Unbridled Betty (USA) (Unbridled's Song (USA))
(7882a)

Unbridled's Note (USA) *Steven Asmussen* a107 112
3 b c Unbridled's Song(USA) Siberian Fur (USA) (Siberian Express (USA))
7571a[2]

Uncle Bernie (IRE) *Reg Hollinshead* 57
2 gr g Aussie Rules(USA) Alwiyda (USA) (Trempolino (USA))
5331[3] 6237[7]

Uncle Brit *Malcolm Jefferson* a55 65
6 b g Efisio Tarneem (USA) (Zilzal (USA))
3116[11] 3355[3] 3907[4] 4142[2] (4389) (4641) 6131[2]

Uncle Dermot (IRE) *Brendan Powell* a63 79
4 b g Arakan(USA) Cappadoce (IRE) (General Monash (USA))
5417[6] 6334[4] (6801) 6950[3] 7302[2] 7493[2] 7639[2] 7743[11]

Uncle Fred *Patrick Chamings* a78 85
7 b g Royal Applause Karla June (Unfuwain (USA))
1416[8] 1752[10] 3503[9] 4413[13] 5008[7] 6209[5] 7480[6] 7805[8]

Uncle Roger (IRE) *Eve Johnson Houghton* a64 72
3 b g Camacho Felin Gruvy (IRE) (Tagula (IRE))
1322[2] 1728[12] 2756[6] 4534[6] 4985[5] 6274[4] 6814[4] (7479) 7718[3]

Uncle Timmy *David Evans* a61 60
3 b g Multiplex Park's Girl (Averti (IRE))
2610[4] 2730[7] 3245[6] 4197[5] 4734[9] 5033[4] 5296[3] 5875[3] 5975[8] 6180[11]

Uncomplicated *Jim Boyle* a60 77
2 b f Bahamian Bounty Complication (Compton Place)
1563[2] 2047[2] 2852[3] (3973) 4471[3] 5332[6] 6984[10] 7193[8]

Uncut Stone (IRE) *Peter Niven* a68 74
4 b g Awesome Again(CAN) Suitably Discreet (USA) (Mr Prospector (USA))
366[5] 772[2] 849[9] 5798[9] 6407[11]

Under Ambition *Frederick Watson* 33
4 b m Striking Ambition Understudy (In The Wings)
4782[9] 5113[8] 5679[8]

Under Par *Michael Easterby* a55 52
4 b m Gentleman's Deal(IRE) Fun To Ride (Desert Prince (IRE))
1250[10] 1560[13] 2335[8] 2690[6] 2796[8] 7837[3] ◆ 7970[8] 8257[8]

Underscore (USA) *Ann Stokell* a74 8
10 ch g Spinning World(USA) Speed Dialer (USA) (Phone Trick (USA))
2937[9]

Understory (USA) *Tim McCarthy* a79 79
5 b g Forestry(USA) Sha Tha (USA) (Mr Prospector (USA))
1611[6] (1792) 2637[7] 3574[5] 5707[10] 6440[9] 7805[12] 8162[11] 8252[5]

Underwhelm *Alan McCabe* a43
2 ch f Bahamian Bounty Depressed (Most Welcome)
5887[11] 7609[8] 7813[10]

Underwritten *Donald McCain* a55 75
3 b g Authorized(IRE) Grain Of Gold (Mr Prospector (USA))
1512[5] 2898[9] 3543[2] 6526[3] 7245[5] 7413[10]

Unex Annigoni (IRE) *John Gosden* 79
3 b c Holy Roman Emperor(IRE) Cape Columbine (Diktat)
1852[3] ◆ (2881) 3393[11]

Unex El Greco *John Gosden* a84 104
4 b g Holy Roman Emperor(IRE) Friendlier (Zafonic (USA))
1924[10] 2250[4] 2657[3] 3635[2] (4596) 5101[8] 6484[2]

Unex Michelangelo (IRE) *John Gosden* a91 96
3 b g Dansili Chenchikova (IRE) (Sadler's Wells (USA))
1604[6] 4795[8] 5301[7] 6374[4] 6875[3]

Unexpectedly (IRE) *Camilla Trapassi* 77
2 b f Oratorio(IRE) Sabaah Elfull (Kris)
6725a[7]

Unex Picasso *Ian Williams* a73 70
4 b g Galileo(IRE) Ruff Shod (USA) (Storm Boot (USA))
(110) 3094 460[3]

Unex Renoir *Brian Ellison* a82 88
4 b g Nayef(USA) Simacota (GER) (Acatenango (GER))
1239[12] 1603[7] 2174[12] 2393[7] 3154[8] 3722[4] 7252[4] 7594[2]

Unidexter (IRE) *Mick Channon* a49 58
2 br g Footstepsinthesand Run To Jane (IRE) (Doyoun)
1903[5] 2213[12] 4618[5] 5155[9] 7008[7] 7491[2] 7785[10] 7854[7] 7922[4] 8112[3]

Uniform Ruby *Mrs A Malzard* 36
4 b m Iceman Winter Moon (Mujadil (USA))
(2115a)

Union Island (IRE) *Brian Ellison* a76 89
6 b g Rock Of Gibraltar(IRE) Daftiyna (IRE) (Darshaan)
285[5] 751[8] 3494[3] (3628) 4365[8]

Union Rags (USA) *Michael Matz* a123 122
3 b c Dixie Union(USA) Tempo (USA) (Gone West (USA))
1872a[7] (2954a)

Unison (IRE) *Peter Makin* a68 42
2 b c Jeremy(USA) Easter Song (USA) (Rubiano (USA))
5784[7] 6533[5] 6841[5] 7357[4] 7779[9]

United Color (USA) *R Menichetti* a108 102
3 b c Ghostzapper(USA) Silk Candy (CAN) (Langfuhr (CAN))
(2325a)

Universal (IRE) *Mark Johnston* a88 105
3 ch c Dubawi(IRE) Winesong (IRE) (Giant's Causeway (USA))
(4879) 5209[2] (5666) (5820) 6661[4]

Un Jour (FR) *Mlle Valerie Boussin* 98
4 b m Kahyasi Happy Town (FR) (Anabaa (USA))
7665a[8]

Unknown Rebel (IRE) *Kevin Ryan* a60 83
4 b g Night Shift(USA) Crystalline Stream (FR) (Polish Precedent (USA))
1239[6] 2312[8] 2606[8] 3610[7] 5224[5]

Unknown Villain (IRE) *Tom Dascombe* a75 55
2 gr c Verglas(IRE) Ragtime Blues (IRE) (Grand Lodge (USA))
7208[4] (7458)

Unlimited *Tony Carroll* a86 71
10 b g Bold Edge Cabcharge Blue (Midyan (USA))
103[2] 268[4] 447[7] 941[3] 1064[2] 1082[2] 1530[2] 1586[2] 2354[4] 2652[4] 2939[3] 3709[4] 4584[6] 5179[2] 5892[5] 8269[11]

Unmoothaj *Charles Hills* 74
2 b c Green Desert(USA) Sundus (USA) (Sadler's Wells (USA))
5126[5] 6371[4]

Unsinkable (IRE) *Richard Fahey* 89
2 gr c Verglas(IRE) Heart's Desire (IRE) (Royal Applause)
(3533) (4247)

Unstoppable U (USA) *Kenneth McPeek* a105
3 gr c Exchange Rate(USA) Naseem (USA) (Point Given (USA))
2954a[6]
Until It Sleeps *Mandy Rowland* a51 19
2 b f Sleeping Indian Cape Dancer (IRE) (Cape Cross (IRE))
1388[5] 1629[4] 1949[6] 2135[4] 2402[7] 4450[10] 4927[5] 5424[10]
Untold Melody *Kevin Ryan* a55 66
3 b f Oratorio(IRE) Different Story (USA) (Stravinsky (USA))
(1173) 2244[2] 3567[3] 3954[6] 4547[11] 5318[6] 6216[6] 6782[5] 7314[10]
Unusual Suspect (USA) *Michael Kent* a108 116
8 bb h Unusual Heat(USA) Penpont (NZ) (Crested Wave (USA))
591a[6] 792a[9] 877a[14] 1144a[8] 7425a[5] 7621a[21] 7783a[3]
Up (IRE) *A P O'Brien* a103 114
3 b f Galileo(IRE) Halland Park Lass (IRE) (Spectrum (IRE))
1403a[3] 2109a[2] 3203a[7] 3676a[4] 4376a[3] 5376a[6] (5643a) (6080a) 6673[6] 7549a[7]
Up And Coming (IRE) *J E Pease* a92 88
8 b g Compton Place Uplifting (Magic Ring (IRE))
815a[4]
Upavon *David Elsworth* a68
2 b g Avonbridge Blaina (Compton Place)
8068[3]
Upgrade (USA) *Michelle Nihei* 108
5 b g Saint Liam(USA) Emily Ring (USA) (Fit To Fight (USA))
7571a[9]
Uphold *Gay Kelleway* a91 93
5 b g Oasis Dream Allegro Viva (USA) (Distant View (USA))
(93a) 223[3] 668[2] 928[5] 1939[5] 2346[5] 2685a[5] 3162[5] 3610[10] 3997[6] 6734[4] 6828[2] 7369[4] 7601[2] 7999[3] 8228[3]
Uppercut *Stuart Kittow* a77 88
4 ch g Needwood Blade Uplifting (Magic Ring (IRE))
2151[7] 3508[4] (4689) 5535[5] 6235[5]
Upper Echelon *Mark Johnston* a20 57
2 ch f Danehill Dancer(IRE) Lady High Havens (IRE) (Bluebird (USA))
3474[8] 8070[12]
Upper Grosvenor *Roger Varian* 62
3 b c Notnowcato Nsx (Roi Danzig (USA))
1937[5] ◆ 2387[4]
Upper Lambourn (IRE) *Christopher Kellett* a82 63
4 b g Exceed And Excel(AUS) In The Fashion (IRE) (In The Wings)
(13) (133) ◆ 458[2] 1236[8] 2510[20] 2861[8] 4141[4] 7937[11] 8236[9]
Upperline (USA) *Michael Stidham* a111 111
5 b m Maria's Mon(USA) Snowflake (IRE) (Caerleon (USA))
5376a[5]
Uprise *George Margarson* a76 79
3 b g Pivotal Soar (Danzero (AUS))
1721[2] ◆ 1983[4] 2785[7] 3234[2] (3561) 4412[3] 5582[4] 6488[16]
Up Ten Down Two (IRE) *Michael Easterby* a79 74
3 b g Hurricane Run(IRE) Darabela (IRE) (Desert King (IRE))
(4153) 4498[11] 4744[2] 6074[2] 6474[2] 6971[3]
Upton Crystal *Michael Easterby* a38 36
4 b m Gentleman's Deal(IRE) Crystal Seas (Zamindar (USA))
3913[12] 4157[10] 6555[8]
Upward Spiral *Tom Dascombe* 101
2 ch f Teofilo(IRE) Welsh Cake (Fantastic Light (USA))
(2426) 3269[4] ◆ 6139[2] 6672[4] 7567a[7]
Urban Daydream (IRE) *Roger Varian* 72
3 br f Oasis Dream Celtic Fling (Lion Cavern (USA))
3811[4] ◆ 4366[4] 4622[2] 5277[8] 5931[4]
Urban Space *Tony Carroll* a58 78
6 ch g Sulamani(IRE) Rasmalai (Sadler's Wells (USA))
2389[13] 2985[2] 3222[2] 3703[8] 4944[5] 5419[U] 5950[5] 7018[7]
Urbonite (IRE) *Alan Swinbank* 24
3 b g Proud Citizen(USA) Bronze Baby (USA) (Silver Charm (USA))
4551[11] 6341[7] 6925[10]
Uriah Heep (FR) *Sir Michael Stoute* 91
3 b g Danehill Dancer(IRE) Canasita (Zafonic (USA))
1511[2] ◆ 2026[4] 3296[10] 5105[7] (5901) 6848[7]
Ursa Major (IRE) *Thomas Carmody* a81 114
3 b c Galileo(IRE) Inchyre (Shirley Heights)
(5606a) 6245[4]
Ursula (IRE) *Mrs K Burke* a74 86
6 b m Namid Fritta Mista (IRE) (Linamix (FR))
1294[7] 1876[3] 2120[2] 3495[3] (3940)
Ursus *Christopher Wilson* a52 59
7 ch g Rambling Bear Adar Jane (Ardar)
2878[3] 3210[5] 4453[2] (4957) 5295[2] 6104[10] 6786[9]
Usain Colt *Richard Hannon* a86 89
3 b c Royal Applause Bright Vision (Indian Ridge)
1500[7] 4473[5] ◆ 4819[8] 6040[4] 6331[3]
User Name (USA) *Mikael Magnusson* 43
3 b f Mr Greeley(USA) User Cat (USA) (Storm Cat (USA))
3507[13] 5949[5] 6254[P]
Us Law (IRE) *P Bary* 109
2 gr c Lawman(FR) Dookus (IRE) (Linamix (FR))
6507a[3] (7013a) 7514a[3]
Ustura (USA) *Saeed Bin Suroor* a87 93
3 b c Nayef(USA) Calando (USA) (Storm Cat (USA))
4797[3] (5297) 5966[2]
Usuelo (FR) *J-L Guillochon* 115
4 b g Epalo(GER) Gezabelle (FR) (Garde Royale)
(1697a) 2534a[2] 5650a[8] 6297a[6]
Utterance *John Gosden* 81
3 b g Dansili Valentine Waltz (IRE) (Be My Guest (USA))
2280[5] ◆ (2799)
Vadamar (FR) *M Delzangles* 119
4 b h Dalakhani(IRE) Vadawina (IRE) (Unfuwain (USA))
1245a[2] 2968a[3] 4120a[2] 5400a[4] 6297a[5] 6914a[7]
Vagabond Shoes (IRE) *Y Durepaire* a107 113
5 ch g Beat Hollow Atiza (IRE) (Singspiel (IRE))
416a[5] 677a[3] 876a[6] (3205a) 3900a[5] 5782a[3]
Vainglory (USA) *David Simcock* a94 98
8 ch g Swain(IRE) Infinite Spirit (USA) (Maria's Mon (USA))
1510[9] 2311[4] 2882[5] ◆ 3508[3] 3878[2] 4339[2] 4761[9] 5517[6] 6242[9] 6494[7] 7030[4] 7556[6]
Vakiyla (FR) *David Simcock* a78 56
4 b m Galileo(IRE) Vadaza (FR) (Zafonic (USA))
3704[6] 4875[7]
Valais Girl *Marcus Tregoning* 80
2 b f Holy Roman Emperor(IRE) Ellen (IRE) (Machiavellian (USA))
5357[6] 6007[4] (6444) 6873[6]
Valamar (FR) *A De Royer-Dupre* a83 99
3 ch c Pivotal Vadapolina (FR) (Trempolino (USA))
7735a[8]
Valantino Oyster (IRE) *Tracy Waggott* a62 69
5 b g Pearl Of Love(IRE) Mishor (Slip Anchor)
2588[16] 2926[6] 3628[7] (4712) (5253) 5585[9] 6103[5] 7095[12]
Valbchek (IRE) *Jeremy Noseda* a84 105
3 b c Acclamation Spectacular Show (IRE) (Spectrum (IRE))
(1048) (1452) 3265[11] 6140[6] 6867[11]
Valdan (IRE) *David Evans* a61 71
8 b g Val Royal(FR) Danedrop (IRE) (Danehill (USA))
28[8] 278[2] 366[11] 566[4]
Valdaw *Tony Carroll* a63 62
4 b g Val Royal(FR) Delight Of Dawn (Never So Bold)
1533[9] 2385[2] 4535[8] 6000[2] 6252[3] 6774[6] 8075[3] 8287[2]
Valdemar *John Weymes* a46 50
6 ch g Tobougg(IRE) Stealthy Times (Timeless Times (USA))
690[4] 1178[14] 8045[8]
Valdo Bere (FR) *E Leenders* 105
3 b c Hurricane Cat(USA) Former Probe (USA) (Dynaformer (USA))
1570a[3] 2743a[16] 6087a[7] 6896a[10]
Valencha *Hughie Morrison* a99 101
5 ch m Domedriver(IRE) Riverine (Risk Me (FR))
2654[7] 3331[15] 5980[2] 6161[3] 6633[9] 6870[10] 7509[12] 7690[14] 7809[6] 8098[3]
Valentine's Gift *Neville Bycroft* 57
4 b g Presidium Effipetite (Efisio)
2791[10] 4349[5] 5708[3] 6361[6] 6555[3] 7248[5]
Valentino Swing (IRE) *Michael Appleby* a56 49
9 ch g Titus Livius(FR) Farmers Swing (IRE) (River Falls)
154[8]
Vale Of Clara (IRE) *Peter Niven* a65 86
4 b m Iffraaj Luggala (IRE) (Kahyasi)
4833a[13] 6406[9] 6837[11] 7246[5] 7607[9] 7863[8]
Vale Of Lingfield (IRE) *John Best* a70
3 b g Moss Vale(IRE) Celtic Guest (IRE) (Be My Guest (USA))
181[4] 298[5] 6765[7] 7166[11] 7474[7] 7815[8] 8099[3] 8298[5]
Valery Borzov (IRE) *Richard Fahey* a88 98
8 b g Iron Mask(USA) Fay's Song (IRE) (Fayruz)
1438[12] 1885[12] 2177[16] 3624[9] 4086[9] 4799[4] 5356[7] 7651[4] 7790[4]
Valetto (IRE) *Tim Easterby* 38
2 br g Moss Vale(IRE) Uhud (IRE) (Mujtahid (USA))
2508[10] 2770[8] 3251[5] 3457[6]
Valhillen *T Schmeer* a76 71
7 ch g Bertolini(USA) Dancing Nelly (Shareef Dancer (USA))
7123a[8]
Valiant *William Haggas* a64 100
3 ch g Galileo(IRE) Whazzis (Desert Prince (IRE))
(2271) ◆ (3124) 4007[5] 5835[15] 7168[11]
Valiant Bee *Bill Moore* a50
4 b m Desert King(IRE) Bee-Bee-Gee (IRE) (Lake Coniston (IRE))
604[4] 869[9] 1016[9] 1189[10]
Valiant Girl *Roger Charlton* a91 92
3 b f Lemon Drop Kid(USA) Victoria Cross (IRE) (Mark Of Esteem (IRE))
(3340) ◆ 4702[10] 5358[3] 6580[5]
Valid Reason *Dean Ivory* a87 89
5 b g Observatory(USA) Real Trust (USA) (Danzig (USA))
5306[6] 5830[5] 6834[6] 7068[3]
Validus *Luca Cumani* a107 89
3 b g Zamindar(USA) Victoire Finale (Peintre Celebre (USA))
(7631) 7809[5] ◆
Vallarta (IRE) *Mick Channon* 85
2 b c Footstepsinthesand Mexican Miss (IRE) (Tagula (IRE))
4688[2] 5275[6] 6020[3] (6443)
Valle (USA) *M Delcher-Sanchez*
4 b h E Dubai(USA) Azelna (FR) (Tropular)
814a[0]
Valle Nordica *B Grizzetti* 35
2 b c Three Valleys(USA) Nord's Cadeaux (IRE) (Cadeaux Genereux)
3684a[8]
Valley Dreamer *Michael Blanshard* a41 43
2 b f Sleeping Indian Blaenavon (Cadeaux Genereux)
5656[5] 6153[8] 6936[12]
Valley Of Destiny *Richard Hannon* a76 85
3 ch c Three Valleys(USA) Nouvelle Lune (Fantastic Light (USA))
1036[3] 1257[2] ◆ (1606) 1938[3] 2897[2]
Valley Of Queens (IRE) *Mahmood Al Zarooni* 83
2 ch f Raven's Pass(USA) Sweet Folly (IRE) (Singspiel (IRE))
5104[13] 5550[2]
Valley Of Wings *Robert Cowell* a59 59
2 b c Three Valleys(USA) Overwing (IRE) (Fasliyev (USA))
5578[6] 6533[6] 6945[7] 7349[5]
Valley Queen *Mark Usher* a35 69
3 b f Three Valleys(USA) Queen Of Havana (USA) (King Of Kings (IRE))
2734[5] 3189[4] 4538[12] 5262[3] 6364[13] 7015[5] (7115) 7469[3]
Valley Tiger *P J Rothwell* a69 62
4 b g Tiger Hill(IRE) Nantyglo (Mark Of Esteem (IRE))
67[9] 287[7] (361) 450[2] 559[6] 736[4] 909[4] 1000[6] 1391[8] 1561[10] 4158[11] 6184a[7]
Valmari (IRE) *Tom Symonds* a55 43
9 b m Kalanisi(IRE) Penza (Soviet Star (USA))
296[0] 2187[7]
Valmerovic (FR) *J Boisnard* a73
4 b g Hurricane Cat(USA) Les Bedarrides (FR) (R B Chesne)
16a[0]
Valmina *Tony Carroll* a74 82
5 b g Val Royal(FR) Minnina (IRE) (In The Wings)
267[2] ◆ 526[4] 623[3] 735[8] 942[9] (1497) (2165) (3139) 3915[9] 4690[3] 5320[6] 6820[12]
Val's Diamond (IRE) *Ann Duffield* a16 39
2 b f Mujadil(USA) More Respect (IRE) (Spectrum (IRE))
6355[5] 6880[14] 7410[10]
Valyra *J-C Rouget* 120
3 b f Azamour(IRE) Valima (FR) (Linamix (FR))
(3203a) (Dead)
Vamo A Galupiar (CHI) *Neil Drysdale* 106
5 ch m Proud Citizen(USA) Afirmate Catalina (CHI) (Special Quest (FR))
7093a[13]
Van Citra (USA) *Dubis Chaparro*
3 ch c Van Nistelrooy(USA) Ahorita (USA) (Woodman (USA))
8279a[4]
Van Der Art *Alan Jarvis* 99
3 ch f Dutch Art Chase The Lady (USA) (Atticus (USA))
1500[3] 2182[2] 3563[4] 4321[27] (4997) 5492[14]
Van Der Neer *Richard Hannon* 116
2 b c Dutch Art Lalectra (King Charlemagne (USA))
(6411) ◆ (7125) ◆ 7398[2]
Vandross (IRE) *Chris Wall* 60
2 b g Iffraaj Mrs Kanning (Distant View (USA))
2376[11] 6844[5] 7172[6]
Van Ellis *Mark Johnston* a91 111
3 b c Shamardal(USA) Jalousie (IRE) (Barathea (IRE))
1452[5] (1834a) 2277[6] 2660[2] 2910[0] ◆ 3294[10] (3607) 4321[24] (4611) ◆ (4838) 5869a[8] 6449[7] 7236[10]
Vanessa *Jim Goldie* a24 63
2 ch f Sixties Icon Fly Butterfly (Bahamian Bounty)
1136[10] 1165[3] (1235) 3126[14] 4116[8] 4450[12] 4767[7]
Van Go Go *Scott Dixon* a67 66
3 b f Dutch Art Baldovina (Tale Of The Cat (USA))
637[6]
Vanilla Rum *John Mackie* a77 72
5 b g Reset(AUS) Snoozy (Cadeaux Genereux)
(66) 275[7] (636) 722[7] 922[5] (1094) 1381[12] 2199[5] 2899[5] 3386[4]
Vaniloquio (IRE) *N Clement* a96 107
3 b c Acclamation Trinity Joy (Vettori (IRE))
914a[3] 1408a[4]
Vanity Rules *John Gosden* 81
2 b f New Approach(IRE) Miss Pinkerton (Danehill (USA))
4297[6] 6489[2]
Vanity's Girl (IRE) *John Quinn* 55
3 b f Compton Place Vanity (IRE) (Thatching)
2918[2] ◆ 5734[6] 6100[3]
Van Percy *Andrew Balding* 79
2 b g Sir Percy Enforce (USA) (Kalanisi (IRE))
4813[2] 5704[2] ◆ (6133)
Vantaa (IRE) *Mrs K Burke* a46 20
4 ch g Shamardal(USA) Indian Express (Indian Ridge)
926[9] 1702[13] 3254[8]
Vantage Point (FR) *Mlle C Cardenne* a83 90
9 ch g Zafonic(USA) Victory Cry (IRE) (Caerleon (USA))
18a[0] 92a[6]
Variety Show (IRE) *Sir Henry Cecil* a38 49
3 b f Royal Applause Sensasse (IRE) (Imperial Ballet (IRE))
2794[5] 5048[11] 5982[5] 6442[8] 7222[10]
Varnish *Richard Hannon* 88
3 ch f Choisir(AUS) Bronze Star (Mark Of Esteem (IRE))
(2200) 3476[2] 4057[2] 4983[12] (5788) 6625[4] 7519[2]
Vashti (FR) *M Delzangles* a78 90
3 gr f Konigstiger(GER) Vadinaxa (FR) (Linamix (FR))
7427a[9]
Vasily *Robert Eddery* 97
4 b h Sadler's Wells(USA) Red Bloom (Selkirk (USA))
2180[9] (2561) ◆ 2933[13] (3642) ◆ 4800[7] 5593[5] 6702[8]
Vastonea (IRE) *Kevin Prendergast* 97
4 gr g Verglas(IRE) Roystonea (Polish Precedent (USA))
(4692a) 5609a[14]
Vatuvei (AUS) *Peter G Moody* 107
4 b g Reset(AUS) Boisterous Lady (AUS) (Rivotious (USA))
(7425a) 7696a[10]
Vault (IRE) *A P O'Brien* a84 100
3 b c Danehill Dancer(IRE) Simadartha (USA) (Gone West (USA))
1401a[3] 2110a[12]
Vauville (IRE) *Y De Nicolay* a78 89
4 b m Invincible Spirit(IRE) Vadorga (Grand Lodge (USA))
116a[8]
Vectis *Harry Dunlop* 89
2 b g Pastoral Pursuits Eishin Eleuthera (IRE) (Sadler's Wells (USA))
4604[4] (5260) 5790[3] 6797[3]
Vedelago (IRE) *L Polito* 111
3 b c Red Clubs(IRE) Queen Shy (Marju (IRE))
1698a[2] (2521a)
Vedremo (FR) *K Borgel* a74
3 b c Panis(USA) Fablimixa (FR) (Linamix (FR))
365a[8]
Veeraya *William Haggas* a76 59
2 b g Rail Link Follow Flanders (Pursuit Of Love)
6818[9] (7305)
Vega Dance (IRE) *Clive Cox* 50
2 b f Danehill Dancer(IRE) Young And Daring (USA) (Woodman (USA))
7403[6]
Vegas Belle *Ollie Pears* a36 60
2 b f Misu Bond(IRE) Bond Casino (Kyllachy)
3533[2] 4191[3] 4907[7] 5675[7]
Vehement *Andy Turnell* a56
6 b m Refuse To Bend(IRE) Velvet Lady (Nashwan (USA))
10[5] 149[3] 303[9]
Veiled *Nicky Henderson* a83 98
6 b m Sadler's Wells(USA) Evasive Quality (FR) (Highest Honor (FR))
3241[10] 4697[P]
Veiled Applause *John Quinn* a74 86
9 b g Royal Applause Scarlet Veil (Tyrnavos)
1135[4] 1275[4] (1525) ◆ 1841[3] (2312) 2620[6] 3163[3] 3494[11] 4864[8] 5546[6] 6076[12]
Veloce (IRE) *Ian Williams* a79 84
4 b g Hurricane Run(IRE) Kiftsgate Rose (FR) (Nashwan (USA))
(1011) 1925[2] 2378[3] (2666) (2732) 3419[6]
Veloso (FR) *Noel Wilson* a78 14
10 gr g Kaldounevees(FR) Miss Recif (IRE) (Exit To Nowhere (USA))
2874[6] 3579[9] 4145[3] (5241) 5718[4]
Velvetina (IRE) *John Dunlop* 57
2 b f Barathea(IRE) Pershaan (IRE) (Darshaan)
3783[6]
Velvet Star (IRE) *Paul Cole* 52
3 b f Galileo(IRE) Velvet Moon (IRE) (Shaadi (USA))
2577[6] 4006[5]
Vena Amoris (USA) *Richard Rowe* a62 26
3 b f Dixie Union(USA) Love Locket (USA) (Thunder Gulch (USA))
838[3] 1004[3] 1288[10] 2283[11] 3939[10] 5125[5] 5483[6] 5744[9]
Venegazzu (IRE) *Peter Chapple-Hyam* a86 77
3 br c Dubawi(IRE) Vintage Tipple (IRE) (Entrepreneur)
1511[8] 2634[2] (3711) 3945[3] 4601[4] (5211) 6012[4]
Venetian View (IRE) *Gary Moore* a89 84
3 b g Amadeus Wolf Twilight Tango (Groom Dancer (USA))
1565[10] 2263[12] 2813[7] 3280[6] 3917[6] (4871) 5406[3] 5951[7]
Venetias Dream (IRE) *Stuart Williams* a58
3 b f Librettist(USA) Machaera (Machiavellian (USA))
3972[9] 4434[11] 5166[5] 7465[3] 7837[9] 8061[9]
Venetien (FR) *F Vermeulen* a82 63
4 b g Iron Mask(USA) Vassia (USA) (Machiavellian (USA))
16a[10]
Veneto (FR) *B De Montzey* a100 113
3 ch c Panis(USA) Milanaise (FR) (Marignan (USA))
1208a[8] 2110a[2]
Venir Rouge *Matthew Salaman* a60 76
8 ch g Dancing Spree(USA) Al Awaalah (Mukaddamah (USA))
28[11]
Ventura Sands (IRE) *Richard Fahey* a71 77
4 b g Footstepsinthesand Beautiful Noise (Piccolo)
1354[10] 1917[3] 2619[8] 7004[9] 7618[5] 7799[10] 8010[5]
Ventura Spirit *Richard Fahey* 74
3 b g Royal Applause Jalissa (Mister Baileys)
2634[3] 3156[6] 3558[9]
Venue *Sir Henry Cecil* a51
2 b c Beat Hollow Shirley Valentine (Shirley Heights)
7750[7]
Venutius *Ed McMahon* a88 94
5 b g Doyen(IRE) Boadicea's Chariot (Commanche Run)
2491[6] (3385) 4345[2] 4828[4] 6235[8] 7030[13]
Vera Richardson (IRE) *Michael Dods* 33
3 b f Dutch Art Play With Fire (FR) (Priolo (USA))
3811[8] 5113[6]
Verbal Honesty (IRE) *J S Bolger* a73 80
2 b f Elusive City(USA) Tus Maith (IRE) (Entrepreneur)
(1118a) 2512a[7] 2780a[6]
Verbeeck *George Prodromou* a86 81
3 b g Dutch Art Tesary (Danehill (USA))
(99)
Verdane *David Evans* 85
2 b g Halling(USA) Society Rose (Saddlers' Hall (IRE))
(3506) 4318[3]
Verdant *Robert Smerdon* a82 108
5 b g Singspiel(IRE) Orford Ness (Selkirk (USA))
7783a[6]
Verdelet (FR) *Mlle M Henry* a68 57
3 ch f Gold Away(IRE) Tualyssima (FR) (Crack Regiment (USA))
476a[5]
Verde-Mar (BRZ) *Fabricio Borges* a106 95
5 b h Gilded Time(USA) Jolie Marcia (BRZ) (Spend A Buck (USA))
589a[10] 5647a[6]
Verema (FR) *A De Royer-Dupre* 102
3 b f Barathea(IRE) Vermentina (IRE) (Darshaan)
(6087a) 6896a[4] 7431a[4]

Vergality Ridge (IRE) *Ronald Harris* a65 49
2 gr g Verglas(IRE) Phoenix Factor (IRE) (Indian Ridge)
6609[12] 6945[4] 7143[4] 7462[9] 7724[9] 7821[4]

Vergara *J-M Osorio* 68
4 b m Halling(USA) Clouds Of Magellan (USA) (Dynaformer (USA))
6089a[6]

Verge (IRE) *Ed Vaughan* a47 32
3 b f Acclamation Marliana (IRE) (Mtoto)
1016[7] 1420[8] 2374[9] 3246[10]

Verglacial (IRE) *Francisco Castro* a93 100
5 gr g Verglas(IRE) Apostrophe (IRE) (Barathea (IRE))
5651a[11]

Vergrigio (IRE) *David Pipe* a65 64
3 gr g Verglas(IRE) Roystonea (Polish Precedent (USA))
3014[11] 3920[10] 5266[10] 7015[10]

Verinco *Bryan Smart* a70 103
6 b g Bahamian Bounty Dark Eyed Lady (IRE) (Exhibitioner)
2208[15] 4073[5] 4367[19] 7063[10] 7243[6]

Vermeyen *Geoffrey Deacon* a51
3 b g Dutch Art Madame Maxine (USA) (Dayjur (USA))
6643[8] 7005[7] 7326[7]

Verona Bay (FR) *Julia Feilden* 22
3 b g Della Francesca(USA) Verone (USA) (Dixie Union (USA))
2197[15] 2895[10] 3974[6]

Veronica's Pursuit *Peter Hedger* a46
2 b f Pastoral Pursuits Veronica Franco (Darshaan)
7372[10] 7720[11] 8201[8]

Veroon (IRE) *James Given* a89 86
6 b g Noverre(USA) Waroonga (IRE) (Brief Truce (USA))
131[4] 280[4] 432[2] 712[8] 907[10] 1133[6] 1752[5]

Verse Of Love *David Evans* 92
3 b g Byron Lovellian (Machiavellian (USA))
(1257) 1641[6] 2263[3] 3064[6] 3667[10] (4534) 5237[5] (5705) (5827) 6192[5] 6432[6] 6659[8]

Versilia Gal (IRE) *Patrick Martin* a72 78
2 b f Footstepsinthesand Tuscany Lady (IRE) (Danetime (IRE))
1118a[3] 1832a[2]

Vert De Mer (FR) *P Lefevre* 62
3 ch f Green Tune(USA) Largesse (FR) (Saumarez)
7267a[8]

Vertibes *Marcus Tregoning* a61 58
4 gr g Verglas(IRE) Antibes (IRE) (Grand Lodge (USA))
1261[7] 1743[8] 2365[4] 3047[8] 3469[9]

Vertiformer (USA) *Wayne Catalano* a88 104
5 b h Dynaformer(USA) Tempo West (USA) (Rahy (USA))
5377a[11]

Vertueux (FR) *Tony Carroll* a65 65
7 gr g Verglas(IRE) Shahrazad (FR) (Bering)
303[3] (446) 566[5] 1085[6]

Verus Delicia (IRE) *Daniel Mark Loughnane* a42 63
3 b f Chineur(FR) Ribbon Glade (UAE) (Zafonic (USA))
2388[10] 4185[3] (4424) (4734) 5875[4] 7146[9]

Very Bad Trip (FR) *T Castanheira* a80 81
3 ch c Muhtathir Red Valentine (IRE) (Bad As I Wanna Be (IRE))
247a[5]

Very Elusive (IRE) *G M Lyons* a88 74
2 b c Elusive City(USA) Very Nice (Daylami (IRE))
(5858a)

Very First Blade *Mark Brisbourne* a57 47
3 b g Needwood Blade Dispol Verity (Averti (IRE))
191[7] 376[4] 564[6] 845[8]

Very Good Day (FR) *Mick Channon* 97
5 b g Sinndar(IRE) Picture Princess (Sadler's Wells (USA))
1850[3] 2253[4] ◆ 3036[7] (4115) 4800[14] 5491[2] 7051[13]

Very Well Red *Peter Hiatt* a57 77
9 b m First Trump Little Scarlett (Mazilier (USA))
109[3] 197[2] 293[4] 490[7] 653[2] 744[11] 929[7] 1009[8] 4242[9] 4662[5] 5266[3] 5638[2] 5935[5]

Ve Solo Tu (FR) *G Collet* a73
3 ch c Prince De Curtis(IRE) Banc De Saba (FR) (Grape Tree Road)
365a[0]

Vespa Blue (FR) *P Demercastel* a73 75
4 b h Vespone(IRE) Desert Melody (FR) (Green Desert (USA))
16a[8]

Vespasia *Ed McMahon* 31
3 b f Medicean Agrippina (Timeless Times (USA))
4797[11]

Vesper (GER) *M Munch* 76
2 b f Sholokhov(IRE) Vera Longa (GER) (Lando (GER))
6225a[7] 7588a[7]

Vestibule *Eve Johnson Houghton* a68 75
2 ch f Kheleyf(USA) Lobby Card (USA) (Saint Ballado (CAN))
1411[5] 1563[3] 2499[2] 2783[5] 4093[13] 4433[2] 4816[3] 5146[10] 5682[5] 5909[5] (6093) 6227[2] 6332[2] 7220[11]

Veturia (USA) *Kevin Ryan* a70 75
2 ch f Distorted Humor(USA) Dutchess Mojo (USA) (Deputy Minister (CAN))
4247[4] 4917[5] 5425[2] (6167)

Vexillum (IRE) *Mick Channon* a73 69
3 br g Mujadil(USA) Common Cause (Polish Patriot (USA))
769[6] 1201[3] 1517[4] 1740[2] 2162[7] 2673[7] 2787[3] 3246[8] 3965[2] 4399[4] 4744[5] (5022) 5280[7] 5589[2] 5744[5] 6516[2] (6838)

Veyepea *Sylvester Kirk* a49 49
3 ch f Dutch Art Endear (Pivotal)
7981[4] 8177[4]

Vhujon (IRE) *Peter Grayson* a66 33
7 b g Mujadil(USA) Livius Lady (IRE) (Titus Livius (FR))
(123) 267[5] 474[5] 517[3] 819[9] 958[2] 1481[11] 2230[9] 2811[9] 3229[11] 4656[9] 5808[9] 6178[4] 6322[6] 7362[9] 7703[10] 8210[8]

Via Ballycroy (IRE) *M Halford* a86 71
3 b f Lawman(FR) Via Milano (FR) (Singspiel (IRE))
(7230a)

Via Chope (FR) *Y Barberot* 87
2 b f Indian Rocket Via Appia (FR) (Exit To Nowhere (USA))
4384a[8] 5248a[4] 7828a[5]

Vicgernic *Gary Moore* a46
3 b g Indesatchel(IRE) Maysie (IRE) (Imperial Ballet (IRE))
1067[4] 2497[8] 2548[11]

Vickers Vimy *Ralph Beckett* a52 37
3 b f Montjeu(IRE) First Bloom (USA) (Fusaichi Pegasus (USA))
1502[10] 2553[9]

Vicksburg *Andrew Balding* 67
2 b f Cape Cross(IRE) Totality (Dancing Brave (USA))
7373[3] ◆

Vicky Valentine *Kevin Ryan* 68
2 b f Rock Of Gibraltar(IRE) Silcasue (Selkirk (USA))
6335[2] 6627[2] 7364[8]

Victoire De Lyphar (IRE) *Ruth Carr* 93
5 b g Bertolini(USA) Victory Peak (Shirley Heights)
1558[9] 1885[22] 4258[2] 4802[22] 6011[10] 6165[15] 6999[2]

Victoria Bay (FR) *Alex Fracas*
2 ch f Vatori(FR) Bay Melody (FR) (River Bay (USA))
8276a[0]

Victorian Bounty *Tony Newcombe* a77 89
7 b g Bahamian Bounty Baby Bunting (Wolfhound (USA))
1885[21] 2482[9] 5502[11] 6150[5] 6811[3] ◆ (7297) 7666[5] 8063[7]

Victorian Number (FR) *Geoffrey Deacon* a62 82
4 ch g Numerous(USA) Malaisia (FR) (Anabaa (USA))
2899[11] 3222[13] 3738[7] 3964[2] 4158[4] 5310[16] 6252[5] 6778[6] 7058[8] 7362[4] 8184[3]

Victorinna (FR) *C Laffon-Parias* a88 102
4 ch m Gentlewave(IRE) Marcela Howard (IRE) (Fasliyev (USA))
3178a[5] 6595a[5] 7284a[8]

Victor's Beach (IRE) *M Halford* a66
2 b c Footstepsinthesand Your Village (IRE) (Be My Guest (USA))
5858a[6]

Victrix Ludorum (IRE) *Richard Hannon* 95
2 b f Invincible Spirit(IRE) Matikanehamatidori (JPN) (Sunday Silence (USA))
5352[7] ◆ (6490) (6873) 7406[6]

Vida Eterna (IRE) *Ollie Pears* 33
2 b f Dark Angel(IRE) Dafariyna (IRE) (Nashwan (USA))
3415[7] 3909[9] 4395[7] 4907[8]

Viewpoint (IRE) *Richard Hannon* a95 90
3 b g Exceed And Excel(AUS) Lady's View (USA) (Distant View (USA))
1467[6] 2266[8] 2496[2] 3630[5] 3774[9] (6792) 7475[7] 7986[2] (8056) (8242)

Vigano (IRE) *Jaclyn Tyrrell* a52 40
7 b g Noverre(USA) Perugia (IRE) (Perugino (USA))
218[3]

Viking Dancer *Ruth Carr* a50 48
5 b g Danehill Dancer(IRE) Blue Siren (Bluebird (USA))
1178[13] 2600[8] 3032[5] 3309[6] 4134[12] 4390[7]

Viking Quest (FR) *C Boutin* a93 100
3 gr c Verglas(IRE) Milijana (FR) (Rainbow Quest (USA))
117a[0] 7803a[0]

Viking Rose (IRE) *James Eustace* a60 76
4 ch m Norse Dancer(IRE) Rosy Outlook (USA) (Trempolino (USA))
1263[2] (1742) 2465[2] 2766[5] 3550[5] 4436[2] 4942[8] 5420[7] 6416[12] 6783[6]

Viking Storm *Harry Dunlop* a107 106
4 b g Hurricane Run(IRE) Danehill's Dream (IRE) (Danehill (USA))
(1037) 2278[4] ◆ (4216) (5079) (6248) 7630[3]

Viking Warrior (IRE) *Michael Dods* a61 76
5 ch g Halling(USA) Powder Paint (Mark Of Esteem (IRE))
1293[3] 1520[3] 2696[2] (2879) 3559[11] 4043[3] 4783[12] 5802[5] 6687[10] 7247[4]

Viletta (GER) *Uwe Ostmann* 95
2 b f Doyen(IRE) Vallauris (GER) (Surumu (GER))
(6522a) 7281a[3]

Village Green *Ollie Pears* a21 50
3 b g Green Desert(USA) Avessia (Averti (IRE))
3012[5] 8151[6]

Villa Reigns *John Weymes* a57 49
3 gr g Clodovil(IRE) Moon Empress (FR) (Rainbow Quest (USA))
40[2] 228[2]

Villa Royale *Harry Dunlop* a66 78
3 b f Val Royal(FR) Villa Carlotta (Rainbow Quest (USA))
3069[6] 3430[2] 4183[8] (6118) 6639[8] 7269[2]

Villeneuve *William Muir* a91 94
3 ch f Zamindar(USA) Emilion (Fantastic Light (USA))
1508[7] 2078[5] 2713[6] 3270[4] 3987a[6] 4527[2] 5092[5] 5834[12] 6161[11] 7509[11]

Villerambert (FR) *H-A Pantall* a62 49
3 b g Meshaheer(USA) Round Sister (FR) (Romildo)
17a[0]

Villoresi (IRE) *James Fanshawe* a75
3 b g Clodovil(IRE) Villafranca (IRE) (In The Wings)
(7625)

Vilna (FR) *Y Barberot* 91
2 b f Slickly(FR) Vingt Six (FR) (Octagonal (NZ))
7828a[6]

Vimiero (USA) *Jonjo O'Neill* a84 84
5 bb g Dynaformer(USA) Merrymaker (ARG) (Rainbow Corner)
6073[8] 7933[2] 8290[2]

Vincentti (IRE) *Ronald Harris* 84
2 br c Invincible Spirit(IRE) Bint Al Balad (IRE) (Ahonoora)
4419[2] 4730[5] 5260[2] (5872) (6284) 6865[6]

Vinces *Tim McCarthy* a60 65
8 gr g Lomitas Vadinaxa (FR) (Linamix (FR))
129[4] 200[6] 594[7]

Vinifera (USA) *Clive Brittain* a47 54
2 b f Medicean Winendynme (USA) (Dynaformer (USA))
3040[8] 3788[6] 4704[10] 6793[13]

Vinniespride (IRE) *Mark Michael McNiff* a60 60
5 b g Waky Nao L'Accolade (IRE) (Seattle Dancer (USA))
552[10] 7058[9]

Vino Collapso (IRE) *James Given* a68 61
2 b c Jeremy(USA) Compradore (Mujtahid (USA))
2686[11] 3303[4] 3989[6] (5009) 5702[5] 6451[10] 7173[8]

Vintage Grape (IRE) *Eric Alston* 50
4 b m Exceed And Excel(AUS) Begin The Beguine (IRE) (Peintre Celebre (USA))
690[12] 1248[5]

Viola Da Gamba (IRE) *William Knight* a65 74
3 b f Alhaarth(IRE) Addaya (IRE) (Persian Bold)
981[3] 1180[3] 1981[3] 2613[4] 3448[2] 4504[U] 5945[7] 6159[9] 7117[2] 7731[3] 8023[5]

Viola D'Amour (IRE) *Tom Dascombe* a70 79
3 b f Teofilo(IRE) Dame's Violet (IRE) (Groom Dancer (USA))
1375[5] 2272[16] 5736[9] 6610[9] 7141[8]

Violante (USA) *H-A Pantall* a81 95
4 b m Kingmambo(USA) Allez Les Trois (USA) (Riverman (USA))
6805a[6]

Violent Velocity (IRE) *John Quinn* a75 80
9 b g Namid Lear's Crown (USA) (Lear Fan (USA))
(449) 692[2] (1436) 3335[6] 4177[2] 5220[9] 5618[7]

Virginia Galilei (IRE) *David Lanigan* a34 70
3 ch f Galileo(IRE) Tilbury (Peintre Celebre (USA))
2584[10] 3399[7] 3918[2] 4435[8] 5529[3]

Virginia Gallica (IRE) *J W Hills* a69 72
3 b f Galileo(IRE) Papering (IRE) (Shaadi (USA))
1649[3] 2201[9] 3161[10] 4498[14] 5931[12]

Virtual Game (IRE) *S Botti* 102
2 b c Kheleyf(USA) Engraving (Sadler's Wells (USA))
7076a[5]

Viscount Nelson (USA) *M F De Kock* a112 117
5 b h Giant's Causeway(USA) Imagine (IRE) (Sadler's Wells (USA))
243a[2] (590a) 758a[7] 877a[9] 1143a[2]

Viscount Vert (IRE) *Andrew Balding* a65 84
3 br g Kheleyf(USA) Viscoumtess Brave (IRE) (Law Society (USA))
(3432) (3705) 3917[U] 4223[6] 4949[8]

Vision Of Judgment *Ollie Pears* 46
2 b g Byron Glorious Colours (Spectrum (IRE))
3208[9] 4310[8] 4907[9]

Visions Of Johanna (USA) *John Balding* a71 66
7 b g Johannesburg(USA) Belle Turquoise (FR) (Tel Quel (FR))
265[10] 530[7] 889[2] (924) 1014[8] 1189[3] 1534[2] 1770[8] 2009[7] 2694[5] 6056[9] 6940[11]

Visit Copenhagen (USA) *Mrs K Burke* a59
2 ch f Speightstown(USA) Nomistakeaboutit (CAN) (Affirmed (USA))
7627[6]

Visiyani (FR) *A De Royer-Dupre* 104
2 gr c Rock Of Gibraltar(IRE) Visionnaire (FR) (Linamix (FR))
6507a[2] 7013a[3]

Viso Pallido (IRE) *Cristiana Signorelli* 88
4 ch h Beat Hollow English Harbour (Sabrehill (USA))
2323a[8]

Vital Calling *David Barron* 75
3 b g Vital Equine(IRE) Crosby Millie (Linamix (FR))
1479[2] 2313[10] 2881[2] 3333[4] 4553[4] 5312[6] (5549) 6048[4] 6514[8]

Vital Evidence (USA) *Sir Michael Stoute* 50
2 b c Empire Maker(USA) Promising Lead (Danehill (USA))
6636[12]

Vital Merlin *Nicky Vaughan*
3 b g Vital Equine(IRE) Claradotnet (Sri Pekan (USA))
2387[7] 3710[4]

Vita Nova (IRE) *Sir Henry Cecil* a74 119
5 b m Galileo(IRE) Treca (IRE) (Darshaan)
(1848)

Vite (IRE) *David C Griffiths* a43 61
3 b c Acclamation Assafiyah (IRE) (Kris)
1155[8] 2591[6] 2680[4] 3235[6]

Vito Volterra (IRE) *Michael Smith* a71 89
5 b g Antonius Pius(USA) River Abouali (Bluebird (USA))
2285[5] 2632[9] 3185[6] (3699) 4110[4] 5057[2] 5369[2] 6670[2] 7030[5] 7366[14]

Vitruvian Lady *Noel Quinlan* 51
2 b f Manduro(GER) Vas Y Carla (USA) (Gone West (USA))
7552[8]

Vittachi *Alistair Whillans* a70 69
5 b g Bertolini(USA) Miss Lorilaw (FR) (Homme De Loi (IRE))
1382[8] 1822[7] 2414[11] (2599) 3579[8] 4431[2] 4766[9] 5086[2] 6076[7] 7454[5] 7980[5]

Vitznau (IRE) *John Butler* a77 78
8 b g Val Royal(FR) Neat Dish (CAN) (Stalwart (USA))
87[9] 102[12] 287[10] 361[7] 450[6] 7500[3]

Vivacious Vivienne (IRE) *Donal Kinsella* a96 104
6 b m Dubai Destination(USA) Epistoliere (IRE) (Alzao (USA))
1034[7] 2027[2]

Vivacious Way *Andrew Balding* 25
3 b f Holy Roman Emperor(IRE) Dance Lively (USA) (Kingmambo (USA))
4366[12] 4992[9] 5448[5]

Viva Diva *John C McConnell* a74 71
4 ch m Hurricane Run(IRE) Vas Y Carla (USA) (Gone West (USA))
7596[2]

Viva Ronaldo (IRE) *Richard Fahey* a83 94
6 b g Xaar Papaha (FR) (Green Desert (USA))
269[4] (391) 520[4] 1156[17] (2029) 2472[6] 2910[9] 3534[6] 4317[7] 4689[18] 5827[8] 6235[9] 7210[9] 7452[8]

Vivid Blue *William Haggas* a69 78
3 ch f Haafhd Vivianna (Indian Ridge)
(1989) 2272[8] 3085[7] 3591[2]

Vivo Per Lei (USA) *John Shirreffs* 98
5 bb m Empire Maker(USA) Air Marshall (USA) (Silver Deputy (CAN))
7577a[3]

Vivre La Secret *Bill Turner* a43 37
4 b m Ishiguru(USA) Vivre Sa Vie (Nashwan (USA))
35[7]

Vivre Libre *Tom George* a51 93
5 b g Sadler's Wells(USA) Vallee Enchantee (IRE) (Peintre Celebre (USA))
6039[11] 6440[6] 7027[11]

Vizean (IRE) *John Mackie* a50 75
4 b m Medicean Viz (IRE) (Darshaan)
1638[9] 2475[3] 3192[8]

Viztoria (IRE) *Edward Lynam* 112
2 b f Oratorio(IRE) Viz (IRE) (Darshaan)
7623a[2]

Vobois (FR) *C Herbline* a47
7 b g With The Flow(USA) Lovelyne (FR) (Nikos)
94a[10]

Vocational (USA) *Mark Johnston* a104 95
3 b f Exceed And Excel(AUS) Carry On Katie (USA) (Fasliyev (USA))
1877[4] 2212[5] 2507[9] 2704[8] 2890[7] 3641[11] 6835[10] 7230a[10] 7503[11]

Vodkato (FR) *S Wattel* a109 101
4 b g Russian Blue(IRE) Perfidie (IRE) (Monsun (GER))
1245a[5]

Vodnik (IRE) *Sir Michael Stoute* a60
2 b c Zamindar(USA) Dance Of The Sea (IRE) (Sinndar (IRE))
6034[2]

Vogarth *Michael Chapman* a37 39
8 ch g Arkadian Hero(USA) Skara Brae (Inchinor)
21[6] 109[7] 553[7] 1578[7] 2092[10] 4141[5] 5013[10]

Voice From Above (IRE) *Patrick Holmes* a58 70
3 b f Strategic Prince Basin Street Blues (IRE) (Dolphin Street (FR))
3079[3] (3461) 4713[5] 4996[4] 5680[8] 7358[11]

Voie Romaine (FR) *Mme V Seignoux* 70
5 bb m Voix Du Nord(FR) Reine De Rome (FR) (Roi De Rome (USA))
5030a[8]

Voila Ici (IRE) *Peter G Moody* 114
7 gr h Daylami(IRE) Far Hope (Barathea (IRE))
7264a[18] 7621a[13]

Vola E Va *B Grizzetti* 103
3 b c Oratorio(IRE) Veronica Franco (ITY) (Lomitas)
2324a[4]

Volcanic Dust (IRE) *Milton Bradley* a85 82
4 b m Ivan Denisovich(IRE) Top Of The Form (IRE) (Masterclass (USA))
64[13] 120[8] 1015[6] 1417[12] 2731[5] 4501[5] 4690[18] 4849[11] 5296[5] 5933[10] 6094[13] 7218[9] 7591[4] 7970[7] 8190[2] 8253[11]

Volcanic Jack (IRE) *Tony Carroll* a66 68
4 b g Kodiac Rosaria Panatta (IRE) (Mujtahid (USA))
267[8] 498[9] 2386[4] 3152[2] 3497[U] 4656[5] 4940[2] 5261[2] 5653[4] 5936[4] (6097) 6230[2] 6323[4] 7012[10]

Volcanic Wind (USA) *Saeed Bin Suroor* a94 64
3 b g Distorted Humor(USA) Sundrop (JPN) (Sunday Silence (USA))
6341[2] (7005) 7502[8] 7691[20]

Volito *Anabel K Murphy* a67 73
6 ch g Bertolini(USA) Vax Rapide (Sharpo)
1254[14] 1734[4] 2413[7] 2629[6]

Voodoo (IRE) *Ian Williams* a25 37
3 b g Kheleyf(USA) Royal Lady (IRE) (Royal Academy (USA))
1716[6] 2313[13] 2665[8] 4185[7] 6158[6] 6568[4] 6962[6]

Voodoo Prince *Ed Dunlop* a91 102
4 b g Kingmambo(USA) Ouija Board (Cape Cross (IRE))
4068[8] (5712) 6575[3] 6832[4] 7689[3]

Voussoir (IRE) *T Castanheira* a66 79
5 gr g Verglas(IRE) Octagleam (Octagonal (NZ))
92a[2]

Vow *William Haggas* a107 111
3 b f Motivator Frog (Akarad (FR))
(1502) (2079) 2658[4] 3292[6] 6877[6] 7237[9]

Vox *Jessica Long*
3 br g Marju(IRE) Vigelegere (SWE) (Be My Chief (USA))
5144a[6]

Vulcan (IRE) *David Simcock* a62
2 b c Tiger Hill(IRE) Messias Da Silva (USA) (Tale Of The Cat (USA))
7021[5]

Vuvuzela (USA) *Jessica Long* a69 70
5 b m Arch(USA) Shiny City Shoes (USA) (Carson City (USA))
5143a[4]

Waabel *Violet M Jordan* a77 74
5 bb g Green Desert(USA) Najah (IRE) (Nashwan (USA))
88[3] 179[4] 252[6] 353[3] 424[3] 624[9] 710[5] (911) 997[2] 1116[3] (1307) 1614[9] 1773[2] 2355[3] 2629[2] 2838[3] 3245[5] 3944[6] 4085[4] 6610[7] 7308[7] 7589[3] 7857[14] 8063[5] ◆

Wadaa (USA) *James Tate* 62
2 b f Dynaformer(USA) Cloud Castle (In The Wings)
6489[10]

Wadi Al Hattawi (IRE) *Saeed Bin Suroor* a78
2 b c Dalakhani(IRE) Carisolo (Dubai Millennium)
(6501)

Waffle (IRE) *David Barron* a82 113
6 ch g Kheleyf(USA) Saphire (College Chapel)
1129[10] 1885[9] 2177[4] 3371[2] 4802[4] 6468[21] 6867[9]

Wahylah (IRE) *Clive Brittain* a87 85
3 b f Shamardal(USA) Neshla (Singspiel (IRE))
1452[12] 2490[4] 3085[3] 3342[2] 3696[3] 4062[8] 4496[6] 5819[2] 6023[5] 6488[5] 7645[6] 7809[10]

Waila *Sir Michael Stoute* 66
2 ch f Notnowcato Crystal Cavern (USA) (Be My Guest (USA))
6791[7]

Waitress (USA) *H-A Pantall* a70 101
4 b m Kingmambo(USA) Do The Honours (IRE) (Highest Honor (FR))
814a[10]

Wakeup Little Suzy (IRE) *Marco Botti* a67
2 ch f Peintre Celebre(USA) Maramba (USA) (Hussonet (USA))
7159[5]

Wake Up Sioux (IRE) *David C Griffiths* a54 57
3 b f Sleeping Indian Dubious (Darshaan)
3407[7] 3730[8] 4187[12] 5624[9] 6178[8]

Waking Warrior *Kevin Ryan* a86 89
4 b g Sleeping Indian Scented Garden (Zamindar (USA))
835[3] 1478[10] 1868[6] 2071[10] 2475[6] 3993[2] 4552[2] 5223[2] 5412[3] 6427[5] (6811) 7716[3] 8081[3] 8232[3]

Waldlerche *A Fabre* 106
3 ch f Monsun(GER) Waldmark (GER) (Mark Of Esteem (IRE))
(1434a) 2156a[4]

Waldpark (GER) *A Wohler* 115
4 b h Dubawi(IRE) Wurftaube (GER) (Acatenango (GER))
2106a[4] 3746a[2] 4636a[4] 6523a[4] 7586a[4]

Waldsee (GER) *Sean Curran* a62 55
7 b g Xaar Wurftaube (GER) (Acatenango (GER))
395[3] (566) 772[6] 937[3] 1361[3] 2175[3] 2371[5] 4904[8] 6821[13] 7255[3] 7528[5] 8001[6] 8104[6]

Waldstein *Dean Ivory*
3 b g Royal Applause Sabalara (IRE) (Mujadil (USA))
3702[14]

Waldtraut (GER) *A Wohler* 104
3 b f Oasis Dream Waldbeere (Mark Of Esteem (IRE))
2746a[3] 4862a[3] (6085a) 6723a[3]

Waldvogel (IRE) *Nicky Richards* a102 100
8 ch g Polish Precedent(USA) Wurftaube (GER) (Acatenango (GER))
2253[10] 3114[9] 5966[8]

Walero (GER) *Uwe Ostmann* 109
6 br h Big Shuffle(USA) Waterbor (GER) (Lagunas)
1745a[2] 3603a[7] 5647a[7]

Walk On The Water (FR) *J-P Roman*
3 b g Walk In The Park(IRE) Brave Tune (FR) (Green Tune (USA))
290a[0]

Wallenberg *John Gosden* a72 66
2 b c Rock Of Gibraltar(IRE) Waldmark (GER) (Mark Of Esteem (IRE))
6204[7] 7323[4] 7628[3] 7899[7] 8185[5]

Walter White (IRE) *Andrew Balding* a68 68
2 b c Dark Angel(IRE) Fun Time (Fraam)
2231[5] 2550[9] 3097[4] 3858[5] 4472[6] 5155[3] 6363[8] 6732[7] 7779[6] 7919[4] 8032[5] 8150[4]

Waltz Darling (IRE) *Richard Fahey* 88
4 b g Iffraaj Aljafliyah (Halling (USA))
3128[15] 3628[6] 4714[10]

Wanda's Girl *W Hickst* a76 89
3 b f Tiger Hill(IRE) Waldblume (GER) (Halling (USA))
2531a[6] 6085a[6]

Wannabe King *Geoffrey Harker* 100
6 b g King's Best(USA) Wannabe Grand (IRE) (Danehill (USA))
1475[3] 1865[12] 4828[17] (5186) 6011[9] 7030[11] (7556) 7691[18]

Wannabe Loved *John Gosden* a87 92
3 b f Pivotal Wannabe Posh (IRE) (Grand Lodge (USA))
4791[5] 5745[2] (7016) 7688[6]

War (IRE) *J A Nash* a37 51
6 b g Sadler's Wells(USA) Moneefa (Darshaan)
7710[6] 7731[9]

War Artist (AUS) *P Harley* a119 112
9 b g Orpen(USA) Royal Solitaire (AUS) (Brocco (USA))
875a[7] 1146a[11] 5647a[9] 7288a[7]

Warbond *Michael Madgwick* a67 57
4 ch g Monsieur Bond(IRE) Pick A Nice Name (Polar Falcon (USA))
203[7] (561) 736[2] 967[5] 1447[3] ◆ 2171[5] 2627[3] 3470[8] 6774[5] 7486[2] 7993[2] 8268[4]

Warcrown (IRE) *Richard Fahey* 79
3 b c Azamour(IRE) Alikhlas (Lahib (USA))
1878[2] 2143[3] (4630) 5386[5] 7032[13]

Warden Bond *William Stone* a68 50
4 ch g Monsieur Bond(IRE) Warden Rose (Compton Place)
188[3] 276[5] (333) (450) 636[3] 725[2] 2463[10] 2899[7] 3153[6] 3392[4] 3713[2] 4158[3] 5052[4] 5632[6] (6174) 6458[5]

Warder (IRE) *R Biondi* 103
3 ch c Ivan Denisovich(IRE) Mary Martins (IRE) (Orpen (USA))
2324a[7]

Wardroom (USA) *Manuel J Azpurua*
2 rg c Milwaukee Brew(USA) Frosty Cupcake (USA) (Top Account (USA))
8244a[9]

Warfare *Kevin Ryan* a83 86
3 b g Soviet Star(USA) Fluffy (Efisio)
(770) 1661[4] ◆ (2021) 2182[11] 2916[6] 6701[7] 7559[4] 7790[5] ◆ 7997[3] 8188[2]

War Is War (IRE) *E J O'Neill* a100 108
4 b h Galileo(IRE) Walkamia (FR) (Linamix (FR))
953a[2] 1245a[4] 3178a[2] 4120a[P]

War Lord (IRE) *David O'Meara* 58
2 b g Aussie Rules(USA) Carn Lady (IRE) (Woodman (USA))
6607[6] 6880[7] 7363[4] ◆

Warlu Way *John Dunlop* 98
5 b h Sakhee(USA) Conspiracy (Rudimentary (USA))
2253[13] 3642[6] 4575[3] 5558[16] 6445[6]

War Monger (USA) *Doug Watson* a82 96
8 b h War Chant(USA) Carnival Delight (USA) (Half A Year (USA))
52a[5] 243a[4] 489a[11] 591a[14]

Warneford *George Baker* a73 77
4 b g Dansili Maramba (Rainbow Quest (USA))
192[6]

Warne's Way (IRE) *Brendan Powell* 78
9 ch g Spinning World(USA) Kafayef (USA) (Secreto (USA))
2237[7] 2732[4]

War Of The Roses (IRE) *Roy Brotherton* a70 65
9 b g Singspiel(IRE) Calvia Rose (Sharpo)
192[11] 452[3] 600[8] 992[5] 1338[P]

War Poet *David O'Meara* 98
5 b g Singspiel(IRE) Summer Sonnet (Baillamont (USA))
(1654) 2911[9] 3635[8] 3857[5] 5558[15] 7689[21]

Warrant Officer *Mick Channon* a55 62
2 gr g Misu Bond(IRE) Kilmovee (Inchinor)
2609[4] 3182[11] 3770[5] (4195) 6156[7] 6793[8] 7008[5] 7467[4] 8094[7]

Warrick Brown *Tim Easterby* 69
3 b g Tagula(IRE) Katie Boo (IRE) (Namid)
1521[10] 1864[4] 2262[9] 2680[2] 3289[F]

Warrior Nation (FR) *Adrian Chamberlain* a46 46
6 br g Statue Of Liberty(USA) Tadawul (USA) (Diesis)
28[12]

Warsaw (IRE) *M F De Kock* a95 105
7 ch h Danehill Dancer(IRE) For Evva Silca (Piccolo)
589a[9] 757a[13]

War Singer (USA) *David Pipe* a93 90
5 b g War Chant(USA) Sister Marilyn (USA) (Saint Ballado (CAN))
4060[3] 4689[14] 6010[4] ◆

Warwick Avenue (IRE) *A P O'Brien* 96
3 b c Montjeu(IRE) Dance Parade (USA) (Gone West (USA))
5134a[3]

Was (IRE) *A P O'Brien* 115
3 b f Galileo(IRE) Alluring Park (IRE) (Green Desert (USA))
2187a[3] ◆ (2658) 4378a[4] 4801[3] 5518[3] 7237[7]

Wasabi (IRE) *John Berry* 60
3 b f Tiger Hill(IRE) Quinzey (JPN) (Carnegie (IRE))
1512[7] 2279[13] 3189[10] 3998[7] 4776[P]

Waseem Faris (IRE) *Mick Channon* a84 88
3 b g Exceed And Excel(AUS) Kissing Time (Lugana Beach)
295[3] 659[2] ◆ 1524[3] 1921[5] 2451[3] 2979[5] 3613[5] 4044[3] (4558) 4765[6] 5337[5] 5603[3] 5663[8] 6234[7] 6382[3] 7019[5] 7243[5] 7451[5]

Wasimah (GER) *H J Groschel* 101
3 bb f Desert Prince(IRE) Waleria (GER) (Artan (IRE))
(2531a) 3426a[6] 5782a[9] 6805a[5]

Waspy *George Baker* a57 62
3 ch f King's Best(USA) Gib (IRE) (Rock Of Gibraltar (IRE))
196[5] 571[5] 743[8] 832[4] 1625[4] 2388[8] (2582) 3141[5] 3470[2] (4232) (4900) 5443[7] 6281[2] 7201[5]

Watanee *Clive Brittain* a65 46
3 ch f Shamardal(USA) Fascinating Rhythm (Slip Anchor)
1843[8] (2374) (2548)

Watcheroftheskies *J W Hills* a76
2 b g Dutch Art Red Heaven (Benny The Dip (USA))
7006[3] 7507[2] 7807[3]

Watchmaker *Dai Williams* a66 62
9 b g Bering Watchkeeper (IRE) (Rudimentary (USA))
45[10] 454[10]

Watch The Birdie (IRE) *Ronald Harris* a60 69
4 b m Kodiac Silk Point (IRE) (Barathea (IRE))
8135[4]

Waterclock (IRE) *Roger Charlton* 86
3 ch g Notnowcato Waterfall One (Nashwan (USA))
2235[5]

Watered Silk *Marcus Tregoning* a73 88
4 gr g Encosta De Lago(AUS) Tussah (Daylami (IRE))
1186[9] (2473) 2887[4] 4745[6] 5129[2] 5966[3] 6380[2]

Waterford Star (IRE) *Ian Williams* a72 74
4 b g Oratorio(IRE) Robin (Slip Anchor)
2391[8] (3086) (3498) (3734) 4831[2] 5106[8] 6407[4] 7077[9]

Waterloo Dock *Michael Quinn* a73 6
7 b g Hunting Lion(IRE) Scenic Air (Hadeer)
88[7] (210) 305[5] 424[2] (623) 710[12] 800[3] 1069[4] 1183[2] 1307[8] 4468[11] 5157[5] 8063[8]

Waterway Run (USA) *Ralph Beckett* 101
2 b f Arch(USA) Princess Consort (USA) (Dixieland Band (USA))
(4604) ◆ 5361[4] ◆ (6070) ◆ (6632) 7547a[6]

Watheeq (USA) *Roger Varian* a81 78
3 b g Street Cry(IRE) Mehthaaf (USA) (Nureyev (USA))
(2449) 3574[2] 4498[3] (5163) 5820[5]

Watsdachances (IRE) *Chad C Brown* 107
2 b f Diamond Green(FR) High Finance (IRE) (Entrepreneur)
7547a[2]

Watt Broderick (IRE) *Ian Williams* 70
3 ch g Hawk Wing(USA) Kingsridge (IRE) (King's Theatre (IRE))
2449[10] (2802) 4961[2] ◆ 5443[6]

Watts Up Son *Declan Carroll* a36 84
4 b g Diktat Local Fancy (Bahamian Bounty)
1561[5] 1917[12] 2535[6] (3213) 5085[2] 5712[10] 6339[4] 6819[2] 7002[5]

Waveguide (IRE) *David Simcock* 69
3 b f Dubawi(IRE) Million Waves (IRE) (Mull Of Kintyre (USA))
2335[6] 3189[5] 3918[3] 5671[8] 7112[4]

Waverunner *Mahmood Al Zarooni* a66
2 ch f Raven's Pass(USA) Danuta (USA) (Sunday Silence (USA))
7159[8] 7721[4]

Waving *Tony Carroll* a74 60
3 b g High Chaparral(IRE) Pretty Davis (USA) (Trempolino (USA))
7162[9] 7933[5]

Waydownsouth (IRE) *Patrick J Flynn* a99 104
5 b g Chevalier(IRE) Ruffit (IRE) (Revoque (IRE))
3647a[6] 5609a[11]

Wayfoong Express (IRE) *William Muir* a91 73
2 b c Acclamation Amistad (GER) (Winged Love (IRE))
5418[4] 5992[4] 6481[5] 7009[2]

Wayne Manor (IRE) *Ralph Beckett* a74 77
3 br g Cape Cross(IRE) Inchmahome (Galileo (IRE))
1568[2] 2129[4] 2818[5] 4585[2] (5744) 6738[3] 7381[11]

Way To Finish *James Moffatt* 47
6 b g Oasis Dream Suedoise (Kris)
2036[4]

Way Too Hot *Clive Cox* a90 88
3 br f King's Best(USA) Street Fire (IRE) (Street Cry (IRE))
1215[2] 2255[4] 3270[6] 3879[8] 4702[13] 5409[3] 6023[3] 6830[7] 7327[5]

Wayward Glance *Jim Best* a49 89
4 b g Sadler's Wells(USA) Daring Aim (Daylami (IRE))
3502[14]

Weald *Hans-Inge Larsen* a98 93
7 b g Bering New Abbey (Sadler's Wells (USA))
3886a[6] 4863a[9] 5651a[2]

Wealthy (IRE) *Saeed Bin Suroor* a103 112
5 b g Refuse To Bend(IRE) Enrich (USA) (Dynaformer (USA))
260a[5] 587a[7]

Weapon Of Choice (IRE) *Stuart Kittow* a91 96
4 b g Iffraaj Tullawadgeen (IRE) (Sinndar (IRE))
1128[9] (1679) 2642[3] 3157[7] 4365[10] 5094[4] 5768[2] 6036[14] 7435[4]

We Are City *Michael Bell* a64 62
2 b f Elusive City(USA) Musique Magique (IRE) (Mozart (IRE))
2499[10] 3339[12] 3996[6] 4574[4] 5202[7] 5749[2] 5940[2] 6155[3] 6611[5] 7379[4]

Webbow (IRE) *Julie Camacho* a102 104
10 b g Dr Devious(IRE) Ower (IRE) (Lomond (USA))
4794[6] 5572[5] 6201[5] 6882[5] 7401[5] 7826[2] 8098[2] 8296[2]

Wedding Fair *E Botti* 102
5 b m Oratorio(IRE) Theatrical Act (USA) (Theatrical (IRE))
7429a[5]

Wedding Speech (IRE) *Sir Michael Stoute* a55
2 b f Acclamation Wedding Cake (IRE) (Groom Dancer (USA))
3282[8]

Wedge Trust (IRE) *J-C Rouget* 94
2 ch f Zamindar(USA) Wedge (USA) (Storm Cat (USA))
(4696a) 5379a[9] 7122a[5] 7828a[2]

Wee Buns *Paul Burgoyne* a47 59
7 b g Piccolo Gigetta (IRE) (Brief Truce (USA))
126[11] 297[7] 379[2] 662[7] 1074[9]

Weetentherty *Linda Perratt* a45 61
5 b g Bertolini(USA) Binaa (IRE) (Marju (IRE))
1881[9] 2037[2] 2230[4] 2617[6] 2839[8] 3272[5] 4087[5] 4262[2] 4393[7] 4638[6] 5082[8] 5190[8] 5542[4] 6104[9] (7099)

Weetfromthechaff *Maurice Barnes* a62 53
7 gr g Weet-A-Minute(IRE) Weet Ees Girl (IRE) (Common Grounds)
6479[12]

Weet In Nerja *Ken Wingrove* a20 26
6 b g Captain Rio Persian Fortune (Forzando)
45[12] 153[10] 4156[8]

We Have A Dream *William Muir* a85 94
7 bb g Oasis Dream Final Shot (Dalsaan)
1141[10] 1727[4] 2707[14] 3225[3] 3571[7] 4286[10] 4824[9] 5035[8] 5703[8] (6368) 6824[3] 7023[7] 7742[3] 7902[7] 7928[9]

Welanus (GER) *H Blume* a81
3 b c Hamond(GER) Wellista (GER) (Sternkoenig (IRE))
365a[2]

Welcome Approach *John Weymes* a64 62
9 b g Most Welcome Lucky Thing (Green Desert (USA))
123[5] (313) 498[3] 687[7] (964) 1528[P]

Welease Bwian (IRE) *Stuart Williams* a73 72
3 b g Kheleyf(USA) Urbanize (USA) (Chester House (USA))
(228) 326[2] 1331[6] 2166[2] 2443[4] 2730[2] 2986[5] 3350[5] 5536[3] 6439[3] 7967[3] 8157[2] 8225[5]

Well Acquainted (IRE) *Clive Cox* a95 103
2 b c Orientate(USA) Stunning Rose (IRE) (Sadler's Wells (USA))
1131[2] ◆ 1352[3] 2376[4] (3770) 5515[2] 6038[3] 6599[2]

Well Bank (IRE) *Colin Teague* a32 55
3 ch g Iffraaj Latin Lace (Dansili)
2881[5] 3438[8] 3809[4] 4263[6] 4711[10] 7354[11] 7671[11]

We'll Come *A bin Huzaim* a63 113
8 b g Elnadim(USA) Off The Blocks (Salse (USA))
48a[9] 317a[13]

We'll Deal Again *Michael Easterby* a89 80
5 b g Gentleman's Deal(IRE) Emma Amour (Emarati (USA))
2140[6] 4591[7] 4770[3] ◆ 5093[5] (5737) 5915[3] 6427[8] (6825) 7023[2]

Welliesinthewater (IRE) *Derek Shaw* a74 65
2 b c Footstepsinthesand Shadow Ash (IRE) (Ashkalani (IRE))
4618[7] (5423) 6196[8]

Wellingrove (IRE) *Mark Johnston* a67 71
2 b g Cape Cross(IRE) Isla Azul (IRE) (Machiavellian (USA))
2402[8] 3112[3] ◆ 4472[11] 5178[3] 5702[2] 6016[6] 6491[7] 6955[4]

Well Painted (IRE) *William Haggas* 98
3 ch g Excellent Art Aoife (IRE) (Thatching)
(2273) 2916[2] 3607[5] ◆ 7240[8] 7691[9]

Wells Lyrical (IRE) *Bryan Smart* 84
7 b g Sadler's Wells(USA) Lyrical (Shirley Heights)
1846[12] 2978[11] 3419[8] 5729[7] 6407[14]

Well Wishes *Bryan Smart* a39 43
3 ch f Piccolo Muja Farewell (Mujtahid (USA))
25[?]

Welsh Bard (IRE) *Sir Mark Prescott Bt* a70 66
3 ch g Dylan Thomas(IRE) Delphinium (IRE) (Dr Massini (IRE))
5945[2] (6213) ◆ 6738[8] 7381[8]

Welsh Dancer *Ronald Harris* a54 79
4 b h Dubawi(IRE) Rosie's Posy (IRE) (Suave Dancer (USA))
125[12] 218[10]

Welsh Inlet (IRE) *John Bridger* a69 72
4 br m Kheleyf(USA) Ervedya (IRE) (Doyoun)
59[3] 122[11] 320[7] 1185[4] 1528[5] (1773) 2360[10] 2809[4] 2943[4] 3188[5] 3724[5] 4059[7] 4146[7] 6926[7] 7299[8] 7742[8] 7906[5] (7993) 8305[2]

Welsh Nayber *Amanda Perrett* a70 70
3 ch g Nayef(USA) Aberdovey (Mister Baileys)
1707[10] 2424[11] 2999[3] 3469[2] (4650) 5052[2] 5441[3] 5707[8] 6430[10] 6734[6] 7358[8]

Welsh Royale *William Muir* a60 59
3 b g Royal Applause Brecon (Unfuwain (USA))
1313[8] 2573[3] 3000[3] 3950[10] 4754[9] 5479[12] 6274[7] 6686[4]

Went The Day Well (USA) *H Graham Motion* a121 85
3 b c Proud Citizen(USA) Tiz Maie's Day (CAN) (Tiznow (USA))
1872a[4] 2299a[10]

Wentworth (IRE) *Richard Hannon* 90
2 b c Acclamation Miss Corinne (Mark Of Esteem (IRE))
4803[6] ◆ (5562) (6447) ◆

West Coast Dream *Roy Brotherton* a91 94
5 b g Oasis Dream Californie (IRE) (Rainbow Quest (USA))
120[2] 286[8] 835[6] 1642[2] 2195[11] 2825[11] 3188[4] 3822[5] (3919) 4337[7] 5832[5] 6666[10]

West End Lad *Roy Bowring* a85 88
9 b g Tomba Cliburnel News (IRE) (Horage)
216[2] 548[8] 907[9] (1134) 1381[3] 1841[5] 2312[9] 2606[9] 3493[9] 4745[9] 5618[10] 5914[7] 6545[3] 7294[12] 7493[6] 7639[4] 8136[9]

Western Apache (IRE) *Simon West*
5 b g Westerner Galoretta (IRE) (Desert Style (IRE))
2339[11]

Western Aristocrat (USA) *Jeremy Noseda* a109 114
4 b h Mr Greeley(USA) Aristocratic Lady (USA) (Kris S (USA))
1143a[P]

Western Pearl *William Knight* a97 98
5 b m High Chaparral(IRE) Pulau Pinang (IRE) (Dolphin Street (FR))
1848[6] 2933[7] 3241[5] 4111[5] 7510[9] 7735a[4]

Western Prize *Ralph Beckett* a76 95
4 br g High Chaparral(IRE) Spot Prize (USA) (Seattle Dancer (USA))
2278[6] (3661) ◆ 4528[2] ◆ 5491[14] 6197[6] 7051[14]

West Leake (IRE) *Paul Burgoyne* a65 58
6 b g Acclamation Kilshanny (Groom Dancer (USA))
821[8] 967[10] 1305[5] 1729[8] 2373[3] 2586[2] 3705[11] 4950[3] 5741[10] 6157[3] 8268[5] ◆

West Leake Diman (IRE) *Charles Hills* a103 105
3 b g Namid Roselyn (Efisio)
1453[6] 1751[4] 2236[8] 4794[7] 6201[U] 6835[9] 7366[19]

West Leake Hare (IRE) *Charles Hills* a66 81
3 b g Choisir(AUS) March Hare (Groom Dancer (USA))
1721[9] 3041[8] 3379[4] 3613[3] 4489[3] 5915[7] 6211[8]

Westlin' Winds (IRE) *Graeme McPherson* a56 67
6 b g Montjeu(IRE) Uliana (USA) (Darshaan)
332[9]

West Side (IRE) *Michael Quinn* a59 55
4 b g Oratorio(IRE) Castelletto (Komaite (USA))
8083[7] 8248[7]

Westwiththenight (IRE) *William Haggas* a84 79
3 b f Cape Cross(IRE) Hidden Hope (Daylami (IRE))
(2381) 3106[4] 5163[3] 5474[4]

We Used To Wait (USA) *Peter Chapple-Hyam* a59 54
3 ch f Mr Greeley(USA) Village Singer (USA) (Rahy (USA))
3070[5] 3918[6] 4931[4] 5483[4] 6323[10] 6968[8]

Wexford Opera (IRE) *J S Bolger* a85 96
2 bb c New Approach(IRE) Sister Angelina (USA) (Saint Ballado (CAN))
7049[8]

Weybridge Light *Jim Best* a70 35
7 b g Fantastic Light(USA) Nuryana (Nureyev (USA))
4941[6]

Whaileyy (IRE) *Marco Botti* a108 100
4 b g Holy Roman Emperor(IRE) Alshoowg (USA) (Riverman (USA))
(311) 871[2] ◆ 2268[9] 4576[4] 4802[20] 6382[5] (7897)

Wharton (USA) *Chad C Brown*
3 bb r War Front(USA) La Prada (USA) (El Prado (IRE))
8279a[6]

What About You (IRE) *Richard Fahey* a90 89
4 b g Statue Of Liberty(USA) Why Now (Dansili)
3[6] 2286[13] 2596[10] 2861[2] 3903[7] 4454[4]

What A Name (IRE) *M Delzangles* 110
2 ch f Mr Greeley(USA) Bonnie Byerly (USA) (Dayjur (USA))
(6086a) 6910a[2]

Whatever You Do (IRE) *Richard Hannon* 63
2 ch f Barathea(IRE) Petite Spectre (Spectrum (IRE))
5977[6] 7329[13]

Whats For Pudding (IRE) *Declan Carroll* a55 60
4 ch m Kheleyf(USA) Margaret's Dream (IRE) (Muhtarram (USA))
1801[8] 2091[3] 2455[6] 2621[5] 2879[7] 3115[5] 3318[4] 3694[4] 4134[5] 4779[9] 5084[5] 5185[4] 6259[6] 6480[2] 6756[5] 7126[9]

Whatsofunny (IRE) *Ruth Carr* a57 53
3 ch f Rock Of Gibraltar(IRE) Celtic Heroine (IRE) (Hernando (FR))
1376[6] 1637[5] 2367[6] 5917[7] 6259[12] 6361[12] 7616[11]

What's The Point *Ollie Pears* a67 75
4 ch g Bertolini(USA) Point Of Balance (IRE) (Pivotal)
847[2] 1432[3] 2455[2] ◆ 3356[10]

What's Up (IRE) *Kevin Ryan* 87
3 b f Dylan Thomas(IRE) Ridotto (Salse (USA))
1454[7] 1887[6] 2255[7] 3270[15] 3522[3]

Whats Your Story *Murty McGrath* a40
4 b g Bertolini(USA) Legal Belle (Superpower)
146[8] 307[7] 572[8]

Whatwehavewehold *Des Donovan* 59
2 b c Avonbridge Dancing Loma (FR) (Danehill Dancer (IRE))
3973[5]

Wheatfield (IRE) *Thomas McGivern* a37 50
8 b m Invincible Spirit(IRE) Crimphill (IRE) (Sadler's Wells (USA))
690[10]

Whenever *Richard Phillips* a70 71
8 ch g Medicean Alessandra (Generous (IRE))
4756[3] 5772[4]

Where's Reiley (USA) *Alastair Lidderdale* a87 73
6 bb g Doneraile Court(USA) Plateau (USA) (Seeking The Gold (USA))
266[7] 327[7] 405[3] (492) 525[5] 6368[7] 6938[9] (7254) 7651[9] 7726[5] 7995[6] 8152[8] 8285[4]

Where's Susie *Michael Madgwick* a84 76
7 ch m Where Or When(IRE) Linda's Schoolgirl (IRE) (Grand Lodge (USA))
202[3] 872[3] 971[3] ◆ 2174[8] 6584[11] 7810[11] 7927[10]

Whiepa Snappa (IRE) *Pat Phelan* a55 67
5 b g Whipper(USA) Boudica (IRE) (Alhaarth (IRE))
7479[10] 8023[8] 8106[9]

While You Wait (IRE) *J S Bolger* 77
3 b g Whipper(USA) Azra (IRE) (Danehill (USA))
1404a[7]

Whimsical (IRE) *Richard Hannon* a90 98
3 b f Strategic Prince Sweet Namibia (IRE) (Namid)
2820[7] 3636[4] 4607[2] 5520[2] (6367) 6830[3] (7408)

Whinging Willie (IRE) *Gary Moore* a67 73
3 b g Cape Cross(IRE) Pacific Grove (Persian Bold)
2128[9] 2628[9] 4506[9] 4981[3] 5443[3] 5991[9] 6950[7] (7500) 7671[2] 8199[3] ◆ 8263[4]

Whipcrackaway (IRE) *Peter Hedger* a66 80
3 b g Whipper(USA) Former Drama (USA) (Dynaformer (USA))
(132) ◆ 377[5] 667[5] ◆ (1319) (1853) 2235[4] ◆ 2889[7] 3338[4] 3920[6] 4224[4] 6146[12]

Whip Des Aigles (FR) *Mme C Barande-Barbe* a75
3 b g Whipper(USA) Splendid Sight (IRE) (Fayruz)
7803a[8]

Whip It In (IRE) *Paul Midgley* a29 38
3 b f Whipper(USA) Viami (IRE) (Daylami (IRE))
750[4] 1010[7]

Whipless (IRE) *J S Bolger* a91 93
4 b h Whipper(USA) Kimola (IRE) (King's Theatre (IRE))
337a[5] 1043a[10]

Whip My Heart (IRE) *U Suter* a66 88
3 b g Whipper(USA) Capetown Girl (Danzero (AUS))
5473a[0] 6752a[8]

Whipper's Boy (IRE) *Brian Meehan* 95
2 b g Whipper(USA) Glympse (IRE) (Spectrum (IRE))
3346[11] (4253) 4698[8]

Whipper Snapper (FR) *E J O'Neill* 83
2 b c Whipper(USA) Margot Mine (IRE) (Choisir (AUS))
6942a[8]

Whipper Snapper (IRE) *William Knight* a72 76
2 b g Whipper(USA) Topiary (IRE) (Selkirk (USA))
3346[2] 3916[3] 4688[12] 7813[2] 8068[4] (8165)

Whipphound *Mark Brisbourne* a72 73
4 b g Whipper(USA) Golden Symbol (Wolfhound (USA))
267[9] 387[6] 473[9] 719[4] 911[2] 1116[5] 1254[5] 1481[10] 1630[2] 2165[3] 2475[2] 2538[11] 3016[5] 7915[9] 8256[5]

Whiskey Junction *Michael Quinn* a68 73
8 b g Bold Edge Victoria Mill (Free State)
752[7] 1263[8] 2046[9] 3052[5] 4196[7] (5217) 5791[6] 6003[2] 6563[6] 7471[7] 7747[2] 8169[6]

Whiskeymack *Mick Channon* a37 58
2 b g Mount Nelson Dream Day (Oasis Dream)
7372[5] 7686[12] 7854[8]

Whiskey N Stout (IRE) *Jamie Osborne* a44 39
2 b g Amadeus Wolf Yasmin Satine (IRE) (Key Of Luck (USA))
4873[7] 5032[6] 5418[11]

Whisky Bravo *Tim Pitt* a76 79
3 b g Byron Dress Design (IRE) (Brief Truce (USA))
1758[3] 1998[9] 2616[3] 2979[8] 3613[4] 4588[5] 5245[6] 5676[10] 5800[5] 6811[11] 7307[2] 7798[5] 7914[11]

Whispered Times (USA) *Tracy Waggott* a41 74
5 bb g More Than Ready(USA) Lightning Show (USA) (Storm Cat (USA))
1251[12] 2535[11] 2924[10] 4716[4] 4954[7] 5171[9] 6127[14] 6258[7]

Whispering Warrior (IRE) *David Simcock* a72 58
3 b c Oasis Dream Varenka (IRE) (Fasliyev (USA))
1922[12] 2280[6] ◆ (8263)

Whistling Buddy *Peter Makin* a64 71
2 b c Piccolo Sahara Silk (IRE) (Desert Style (IRE))
2442[2] 2995[3] 4487[2] 4816[6] 5503[6] 6155[12]

Whitby Jet (IRE) *Ed Vaughan* a82 80
4 b g Mujadil(USA) Anazah (USA) (Diesis)
1342[4] 1680[8] 2399[2] 2792[2] 3574[3] 4541[4] 5667[6] 6441[4] 6981[4] 7409[5] (8162)

Whitechapel *Keith Goldsworthy* a74 70
5 gr g Oasis Dream Barathiki (Barathea (IRE))
31[8] 649[5] 1108[6] 4413[9] 5179[6] 5427[10] 6843[10] 7530[7]

White Cheek Fox (USA) *Lennart Reuterskiold Jr* a91 75
5 ch m Consolidator(USA) Crafty Luck (USA) (Crafty Prospector (USA))
5143a[2]

White Coppice *Richard Fahey* 77
2 ch g Pivotal Finchley (Machiavellian (USA))
5331[2] 5825[5] 6491[8] 6874[8]

Whitecrest *John Spearing* a66 78
4 ch m Ishiguru(USA) Risky Valentine (Risk Me (FR))
2084[3] 2494[11] 2789[2] 2994[2] 3477[5] 3724[2] 4059[4] 4235[7] 4535[4] 4903[3] 6094[14] 6307[2] 6439[7] 6788[10] (7299) 7489[4]

White Deer (USA) *Geoffrey Harker* a64 67
8 b g Stravinsky(USA) Brookshield Baby (IRE) (Sadler's Wells (USA))
1112[3] 1297[6] 1829[4] 4156[2] 4652[3] 6323[3] 6838[3] 7869[2] 8139[5] 8260[3]

White Diamond *Michael Appleby* a74 77
5 b m Bertolini(USA) Diamond White (Robellino (USA))
944[2] 1154[4] 2363[5] 7839[10] 8243[7]

Whiteflats *Derek Shaw* a23
2 b c Mind Games Chertsey (IRE) (Medaaly)
8230[5]

White Flight *Jane Chapple-Hyam* a63 60
3 gr f Doyen(IRE) Reason To Dance (Damister (USA))
1180[2] 2128[4] 2788[12] 3083[9] 6774[11] 7105[4] 7992[4] 8131[5]

White Frost (IRE) *Charles Hills* 97
4 gr h Verglas(IRE) Moivouloirtoi (USA) (Bering)
2068[16] 3128[16] 4317[13] 4609[2] 5102[9] 5572[10] 6119[2] 6471[9] 7240[19]

White Fusion *David O'Meara* a78 59
4 gr g Oratorio(IRE) Divine Grace (IRE) (Definite Article)
10[2] 7954[10]

White Month *Andrew Balding* 55
2 b g Tiger Hill(IRE) Purple Heather (USA) (Rahy (USA))
7081[8] 7492[5]

White Nile (IRE) *David Simcock* 86
3 b c Galileo(IRE) Super Gift (IRE) (Darshaan)
2895[4] (5315) 6340[2]

Whiteoak Lady (IRE) *Karen Tutty* a50 61
7 ch m Medecis French Toast (IRE) (Last Tycoon)
997[12] 1497[12] 2046[7] 2618[4] 3151[11] (3245) 3467[3] 3718[2] 4237[9] 4332[12] 5203[13] 5590[13]

White Shift (IRE) *Paul Howling* a54 37
6 b m Night Shift(USA) Ivy Queen (IRE) (Green Desert (USA))
123[9] 155[4] 226[5] 312[3] 467[8] 665[7] 3718[7] 4237[10] 4902[8] 5444[7] 5775[8] 5937[8] 6926[10]

White Waves (USA) *A Fabre* 78
2 ch f Any Given Saturday(USA) Surf Club (USA) (Ocean Crest (USA))
6751a[2]

Whitfield (USA) *Jeremy Noseda* 80
2 bb c Private Vow(USA) Seda Fina (USA) (Known Fact (USA))
2667[3] 3240[14]

Whitford (IRE) *Chris Dwyer* a63 56
2 b c Jeremy(USA) Linette (GER) (In The Wings)
2934[10] 3545[9] 3788[8] 4934[7] (5161) 5475[8] 6318[11] 6849[5] 8103[4] 8302[7]

Whitstable Native *Joseph Tuite* a58 65
4 b g Bertolini(USA) Break Of Dawn (USA) (Mt. Livermore (USA))
926[4] 1309[9] 1487[7] 1768[12] 3949[4] (4241) 4656[4] (5850)

Whodathought (IRE) *Paul Rich* a74 78
4 b g Choisir(AUS) Consultant Stylist (IRE) (Desert Style (IRE))
400[12] (843) 891[7] (1984)

Whodunit (UAE) *Peter Hiatt* a75 66
8 b g Mark Of Esteem(IRE) Mystery Play (IRE) (Sadler's Wells (USA))
(60) 176[9] 349[8] 570[12] 915[5]

Wholelotofrosie (IRE) *R Donohoe* a57 91
2 ch f Choisir(AUS) On Duty (IRE) (Night Shift (USA))
1832a[6] 6717a[5]

Who Loves Ya Baby *Peter Charalambous* a56 37
4 b g Sulamani(IRE) Aberlady Bay (IRE) (Selkirk (USA))
968[U] 1112[8] 3043[5] 3400[12] 5477[3]

Who's Shirl *Chris Fairhurst* a80 85
6 b m Shinko Forest(IRE) Shirl (Shirley Heights)
2487[7] 4954[6] 6127[8] 6260[5] 6687[3] 7141[5] 7524[4]

Who's That Chick (IRE) *Ralph Smith* a12 55
3 ch f Footstepsinthesand Poule De Luxe (IRE) (Cadeaux Genereux)
4516[9] 5299[6] 5795[11]

Whozthecat (IRE) *Declan Carroll* a93 94
5 b g One Cool Cat(USA) Intaglia (GER) (Lomitas)
1168[2] 1522[11] 2289[7] 2488[9] 3183[5] 3255[2] 3595[3] 3845[9] 4337[8] 4554[18] 4829[3] 5065[8] (5412) 5584[4] 6005[7] 6144[15] (6689) 7704[8] 7918[6]

Why So Fast (IRE) *David O'Meara* a54 60
2 b f Kodiac Miss Sundance (IRE) (Desert Sun)
3223[5] 3444[7] 3971[8] 4471[5] 6122[3] 6336[2] 6354[6]

Wickapecko (USA) *Bruce R Brown*
2 ch f Corinthian(USA) Georgialina (USA) (Affirmed (USA))
6944a[8]

Wicked Spirit (IRE) *Mark Johnston* a73 75
4 b m Bahri(USA) The Spirit Of Pace (IRE) (In The Wings)
(1719) ◆ 1991[4] 2149[7]

Wicked Tara *Frank Sheridan*
2 b f Assertive Tara King (Deploy)
5176[7] 5806[11] 6664[6]

Wicked Wench *Jo Hughes* a83 83
3 b f Kyllachy Effervescent (Efisio)
99[4] (977) 1644[4] 2256[10] (2347) 2986[3] 3288[3] 3375[7] 6427[7] 6515[5] 7019[13]

Wicked Wilma (IRE) *Alan Berry* a25 76
8 b m Tagula(IRE) Wicked (Common Grounds)
1990[6] 2140[5] 2719[3] 3065[10] 3113[7] 3308[4] 3730[2] 4292[8] 4451[6] 4963[3] 5190[2] 5257[5] 5758[3] 6314[5] 6531[7] 7101[6] 7457[8]

Widow Flower (IRE) *Michael Bell* a46 41
3 b f Moss Vale(IRE) Satin Rose (Lujain (USA))
5299[4] 6397[13] 7146[7] 7465[9]

Widyaan (IRE) *John Gosden* a71 72
3 b g Lawman(FR) Lady Livius (IRE) (Titus Livius (FR))
1385[2] 2271[4] 2898[8] 3347[10] 3809[7]

Wiggo *Julia Feilden* a41
2 br c Phoenix Reach(IRE) Legal Belle (Superpower)
7304[10] 7977[9]

Wiggy Smith *Henry Candy* a60 81
13 ch g Master Willie Monsoon (Royal Palace)
2199[12] 4706[5] 5007[9]

Wigmore Hall (IRE) *Michael Bell* 117
5 b g High Chaparral(IRE) Love And Laughter (IRE) (Theatrical (IRE))
879a[6] 1148a[4] 1696a[4] 1994[3] 3267[9] 4610[6] 5377a[7] (6299a) 7094a[4]

Wigram's Turn (USA) *Michael Easterby* a73 55
7 ch g Hussonet(USA) Stacey's Relic (USA) (Houston (USA))
33[7] 359[2] 538[4] 942[5]

Wijaya *James Fanshawe* a46
3 ch f Haafhd First Fantasy (Be My Chief (USA))
2368[10] 2849[12]

Wilander *Gay Kelleway* a4
3 ch g Phoenix Reach(IRE) Lady Soleas (Be My Guest (USA))
833[6]

Wild Anthem *Hughie Morrison* 44
2 b f Manduro(GER) Wild Gardenia (Alhaarth (IRE))
7403[7]

Wildcat Wizard (USA) *Paul Midgley* a61 94
6 b g Forest Wildcat(USA) Tip the Scale (USA) (Valiant Nature (USA))
1157[22] 1558[7] 3336[11] 4554[19] 4963[10] 5388[6] 6123[4] 6260[12] 6824[9] 7142[6] 7529[9]

Wild Coco (GER) *Sir Henry Cecil* 114
4 ch m Shirocco(GER) Wild Side (GER) (Sternkoenig (IRE))
(4738) (6163)

Wildcrafting *Michael Bell* a58
2 ch f Exceed And Excel(AUS) Local Spirit (USA) (Lion Cavern (USA))
5425[6] 5943[11]

Wild Desert (FR) *Charlie Longsdon* a89 88
7 bb g Desert Prince(IRE) Sallivera (IRE) (Sillery (USA))
44[3] 202[5] 1421[3] 1846[10] 2412[2] 3661[3] 4176[5] 4697[10] 4925[8]

Wild Diamond (IRE) *Sir Mark Prescott Bt* a35 51
2 b f Hernando(FR) Step With Style (USA) (Gulch (USA))
4946[7] 5319[12] 5656[3]

Wilddrossel (GER) *Markus Klug* 102
3 rg f Dalakhani(IRE) Wild Side (GER) (Sternkoenig (IRE))
2522a[6] 3802a[3] 4862a[6] 6290a[3] 7427a[5]

Wildheart (IRE) *M Figge* 97
2 b c Manduro(GER) Zaynaat (Unfuwain (USA))
7091a[2]

Wild Horse (IRE) *J-C Rouget* 95
2 b c Kheleyf(USA) Life Rely (USA) (Maria's Mon (USA))
4632a[4]

Wildomar *John Ryan* a91 73
3 b g Kyllachy Murrieta (Docksider (USA))
1467[12] 2279[6] 2800[5] 3475[11] 6582[4] (7011) 7195[4] 7805[9] 7895[6] (8191)

Wild Sauce *Bryan Smart* a77 83
3 b f Exceed And Excel(AUS) Salsa Brava (IRE) (Almutawakel)
41[5] 326[3] (599) 1817[2] 2615[2] 3404[2] 4500[2] (4953) 6234[8] 6688[5] 7295[3]

Wild Wolf (IRE) *S Botti* 102
3 b c Rail Link Mary Rose (ITY) (Royal Academy (USA))
2324a[2] 6554a[6]

Wilfred Pickles (IRE) *Jo Crowley* a89 57
6 ch g Cadeaux Genereux Living Daylights (IRE) (Night Shift (USA))
4689[15] 7645[12] 8174[8]

Willbeme *Neville Bycroft* 83
4 b m Kyllachy Befriend (USA) (Allied Forces (USA))
4547[3] (4793) (5093) ◆ 6008[6]

Willcox Inn (USA) *Michael Stidham* a108 117
4 bb h Harlan's Holiday(USA) De Aar (USA) (Gone West (USA))
5377a[8] 7575a[9]

William Haigh (IRE) *Alan Swinbank* a102 58
4 b g Refuse To Bend(IRE) Ivowen (USA) (Theatrical (IRE))
(5) (846) 1139[16] 4249[10] 6076[15]

William's Way *Ian Wood* a76 37
10 b g Fraam Silk Daisy (Barathea (IRE))
9[8] (2137) 3216[6] 3449[7] 5241[6]

Willies Wonder (IRE) *Charles Hills* a82 74
3 b c Moss Vale(IRE) Red Letter (Sri Pekan (USA))
969[2] 1256[2] 1560[4] (1730) 2714[5] 3284[3] 4496[10] 5308[5] 6052[2] 6840[3] 7360[5]

Willie The Whipper *Ann Duffield* 102
2 b c Whipper(USA) Anna Simona (GER) (Slip Anchor)
(5756) (7292) 7693a[2]

Willie Wag Tail (USA) *Ed Walker* a95 99
3 b g Theatrical(IRE) Night Risk (USA) (Wild Again (USA))
2429[2] (3042) 4700[8] 5558[4] 6348[3]

Willing Foe (USA) *Saeed Bin Suroor* a62 110
5 bb g Dynaformer(USA) Thunder Kitten (USA) (Storm Cat (USA))
4363[3] (5600) 6297a[3] 6866[3] 7405[8]

Willow Beauty *J R Jenkins* a51 53
3 br f Val Royal(FR) Opera Belle (Dr Fong (USA))
376[9] 2610[6] 4509[6] 5095[13] 8267[5]

Willow Beck *John Gosden* a66
3 b f Shamardal(USA) Woodbeck (Terimon)
7477[6] (7787)

Willowing (USA) *Mahmood Al Zarooni* a77 74
2 b f Hard Spun(USA) Sweet Arizona (USA) (Gone West (USA))
4297[7] 5339[3] 5818[3] ◆ (6253)

Willy McBay *George Moore* 22
3 b g Multiplex Meandering Rose (USA) (Irish River (FR))
4210[9] 4399[14] 5114[7] 6263[6]

Wiltshire Life (IRE) *Jeremy Gask* a69 63
3 b f Camacho Miss Indigo (Indian Ridge)
1389[5] (1709) 2205[3] 2759[4] 5775[10] 6610[10] 7589[12]

Wily Fox *James Eustace* a63 74
5 ch g Observatory(USA) Kamkova (USA) (Northern Dancer (CAN))
2363[9] 3222[7] 3734[6] 7018[6] 7377[2]

Winchester (USA) *John D Sadler* a105 115
7 b h Theatrical(IRE) Rum Charger (IRE) (Spectrum (IRE))
7264a[9] 7621a[17]

Windforpower (IRE) *Ronald Harris* a70 65
2 b g Red Clubs(IRE) Dubai Princess (IRE) (Dubai Destination (USA))
2349[9] 2571[3] 2868[4] 3140[3] (3970) 4230[3] 4728[3] 5450[4] 5813[4] 5940[6] 6354[5] 6766[3] 6890[3] 7713[6] 7727[3] 7865[2] 7932[2] 8092[4] 8224[2] (8247)

Windhoek *Mark Johnston* 86
2 b c Cape Cross(IRE) Kahlua Kiss (Mister Baileys)
(2376)

Windsea (IRE) *Y Barberot* a88 90
2 ch c King's Best(USA) Spring Sea (FR) (Kutub (IRE))
5471a[10]

Wind Shuffle (GER) *Richard Fahey* 57
9 b g Big Shuffle(USA) Wiesensturmerin (GER) (Lagunas)
2599[5] 3029[3] 3577[5]

Windsor Palace (IRE) *A P O'Brien* a81 107
7 br h Danehill Dancer(IRE) Simaat (USA) (Mr Prospector (USA))
1043a[13] 1549a[3] (1946a) 2270[6] 3237[5] 3675a[4] 4521a[5] 5490[9]

Windsor Queen (IRE) *Mrs Prunella Dobbs* a67 64
2 ch f Windsor Knot(IRE) Birthday Present (Cadeaux Genereux)
6853a[6]

Windsor Rose (IRE) *Mark Brisbourne* a53 57
2 ch f Windsor Knot(IRE) Rose Of Battle (Averti (IRE))
1188[4] 1388[4] 2797[7] 3251[4] 3554[5] (4343) 4991[4] 6893[12] 7724[11] 7974[11]

Windsor Secret *Keith Dalgleish* a34 22
2 ch f Sakhee's Secret Lady Of Windsor (IRE) (Woods Of Windsor (USA))
5887[12] 6257[7] 6708[7]

Wind Star *Brendan Powell* a63 65
9 ch g Piccolo Starfleet (Inchinor)
722[9] 1092[6] 1717[3] 2463[2] 3392[2] (3469) 6057[7]

Windygoul Lad *Keith Dalgleish* a46 64
3 bb g Kheleyf(USA) Millymix (FR) (Linamix (FR))
462[6] 720[9] 943[8] 1238[6] 1817[7] 4771[9] 5538[6] (5757) 6106[7] 6514[2] 6530[2] 6786[8] 7446[3] 7604[3]

Wine 'n Dine *Bernard Llewellyn* a70 76
7 b g Rainbow Quest(USA) Seasonal Splendour (IRE) (Prince Rupert (FR))
367[3] 555[4]

Win For Sure (GER) *X Nakkachdji* a113 111
7 b g Stravinsky(USA) Win For Us (GER) (Surumu (GER))
318a[7]

Wingate *H-A Pantall* 96
2 b c Zamindar(USA) Sirene Doloise (FR) (Marchand De Sable (USA))
5248a[8] (7319a) 7693a[8]

Winged Icarus (USA) *Alan McCabe* a82 54
2 b g Speightstown(USA) Daedal (USA) (Orientate (USA))
2376[12] 3074[10] 4707[6] (5716) 6247[10] 6775[7]

Wing N Prayer (IRE) *John Wainwright* a50 48
5 b m Xaar Jazmeer (Sabrehill (USA))
45[5] 334[6] 773[11] 1170[6] 1436[11]

Winker Watson *Mick Channon* 104
7 ch h Piccolo Bonica (Rousillon (USA))
141a[10] 419a[13]

Winner's Wish *Jeremy Noseda* a74 90
3 b f Clodovil(IRE) Alla Prima (IRE) (In The Wings)
1557[4] (2427) 3033[3] 4513[4] 5106[5] 6012[2]

Winnetou *Frank Sheridan* a55
3 ch g Sleeping Indian Cashel Kiss (Bishop Of Cashel)
6317[5] 6827[7] 7061[7] 7361[4] 7615[9] 7752[3] 7898[5] 8111[8]

Winnie Perry *Rod Millman* 64
2 ch g Assertive Hayley's Flower (IRE) (Night Shift (USA))
6203[7] 6787[11] 7014[3]

Winning Express (IRE) *Ed McMahon* 105
2 gr f Camacho Lady Fabiola (USA) (Open Forum (USA))
(5003) ◆ (5979) 6672[2] ◆

Winning Impact (IRE) *J G Coogan* a73 85
5 br g Pyrus(USA) Quizzical Lady (Mind Games)
4833a[6] 5609a[7]

Winning Spark (USA) *Gary Moore* a79 81
5 b g Theatrical(IRE) Spark Sept (FR) (Septieme Ciel (USA))
7511[8] 8082[9]

Winsili *John Gosden* 89
2 b f Dansili Winter Sunrise (Pivotal)
(5104) ◆ 6021[2]

Winslow Arizona (IRE) *Michael Bell* 40
2 b g Danehill Dancer(IRE) Buffalo Berry (IRE) (Sri Pekan (USA))
4340[9] 4724[8] 5684[6] 7313[7]

Winter Dream (IRE) *Robert Collet* 102
8 gr g Act One Settler (Darshaan)
1971a[5]

Winter Dress *Declan Carroll* a66 64
3 ch f Haafhd Ermine (IRE) (Cadeaux Genereux)
1733[8] 2431[6] 3228[7] 3965[4] 4490[7] 5731[2]

Winter Hill *Tom Dascombe* a60 69
3 b f Three Valleys(USA) White Turf (GER) (Tiger Hill (IRE))
1115[4] 2382[7] 6048[6] 6261[4] 6737[8] 7307[5]

Winterlude (IRE) *Mahmood Al Zarooni* 76
2 b c Street Cry(IRE) New Morning (IRE) (Sadler's Wells (USA))
6164[4] ◆ 6872[10]

Winter Memories (USA) *James J Toner* 117
4 rg m El Prado(IRE) Memories Of Silver (USA) (Silver Hawk (USA))
(4617a)

Winter Music (IRE) *Andrew Balding* 52
2 b g Oratorio(IRE) Alpine Park (IRE) (Barathea (IRE))
6020[14]

Winter's Night (IRE) *Clive Cox* 101
4 b m Night Shift(USA) Woodland Glade (Mark Of Esteem (IRE))
1851[2] 2515a[6]

Winter Snow (IRE) *Saeed Bin Suroor* 64
2 b f Raven's Pass(USA) Gonfilia (GER) (Big Shuffle (USA))
7364[7]

Winter Song (IRE) *Charles Hills* 66
2 b f Pivotal Speed Song (Fasliyev (USA))
6787[14] (7516)

Winterwind (IRE) *Carmen Bocskai* a89 90
7 b h Orpen(USA) Brickey Beech (IRE) (Precocious)
443a[2] 630a[5]

Wisecraic *J S Moore* a69 78
5 ch g Kheleyf(USA) Belle Genius (USA) (Beau Genius (CAN))
(35) 224[4] 248[4] 567[2] 818[3] 915[4] 1105[3]

Wise Dan (USA) *Charles Lopresti* a128 128
5 ch g Wiseman's Ferry(USA) Lisa Danielle (USA) (Wolf Power (SAF))
(6300a) (7575a)

Wise Lord *Natalie Lloyd-Beavis* 16
3 b g Yawmi Timberlake (Bluegrass Prince (IRE))
7352[10]

Wiseman's Diamond (USA) *Paul Midgley* a66 70
7 b m Wiseman's Ferry(USA) Aswhatilldois (IRE) (Blues Traveller (IRE))
842[3] 1269[3] (1755) 2094[9] 2675[6] 3416[7] 3914[12] 4627[11] 5258[10] 5669[5] 6258[2] 6785[13]

Wise Talk (USA) *Mahmood Al Zarooni* 49
2 b f Hard Spun(USA) See Me Through (USA) (Sky Classic (CAN))
4818[12]

Wise Venture (IRE) *Alan Jarvis* a53 85
3 b g Kheleyf(USA) Chia Laguna (IRE) (Ela-Mana-Mou)
2485[9] 3445[9] 3787[6] 4796[7] 6251[7]

Wish Again (IRE) *David Nicholls* a52 64
3 b g Moss Vale(IRE) Wildwish (IRE) (Alhaarth (IRE))
455[6] 940[5] 1292[2] 1599[8] 2139[8]

Wishbone (IRE) *Jo Hughes* a53 32
5 b m Danehill Dancer(IRE) Intricate Design (Zafonic (USA))
106[6] 329[10] 813[8] 3243[8] 5504[10] 5996[11]

Wish Come True (IRE) *S Botti* 98
2 b c Aussie Rules(USA) Tibouchina (IRE) (Daylami (IRE))
7513a[3]

Wishformore (IRE) *Zoe Davison* a63 68
5 b m Chevalier(IRE) Terra Nova (Polar Falcon (USA))
299[7] 1635[8] 3964[9] 5125[4] 5351[12]

Wishing Bridge *Pat Eddery* a62
2 ch c Pastoral Pursuits Dunloe (IRE) (Shaadi (USA))
7686[U] 8068[5]

Witchry *Tony Newcombe* a65 70
10 gr g Green Desert(USA) Indian Skimmer (USA) (Storm Bird (CAN))
5362[12] 5998[6] 6951[10] 8061[7]

Witch Way Went *Ian McInnes* 23
2 b f Royal Applause Celestial Princess (Observatory (USA))
6099[13]

Witchy Moments (IRE) *Paul Cole*
3 b f Excellent Art Souffle (Zafonic (USA))
1501[17]

With Compliments *Kevin Ryan* a83
3 b g Piccolo Sincerely (Singspiel (IRE))
(4144)

With Hindsight (IRE) *Michael Scudamore* a74 79
4 ch g Ad Valorem(USA) Lady From Limerick (IRE) (Rainbows For Life (CAN))
192[12] 381[3] ◆ 821[11] 942[8] 1300[8] 2146[4] 2809[9] 8078[3]

Without Equal *Martin Todhunter* a22 61
6 ch m Tobougg(IRE) Sans Egale (FR) (Lashkari)
602[10]

Without Fear (FR) *Arnfinn Lund* 101
4 b g Refuse To Bend(IRE) Kansas (Kahyasi)
2807a[2] 3886a[2] 4863a[4] 5651a[F] 6091a[6]

Without Prejudice (USA) *Michael Easterby* a72 85
7 ch g Johannesburg(USA) Awesome Strike (USA) (Theatrical (IRE))
403[4] 448[8]

Witnessed *Mahmood Al Zarooni* a85 80
3 b f Authorized(IRE) Magic Mission (Machiavellian (USA))
1215[6]

Wittgenstein (IRE) *Brian Meehan* a72 51
2 ch f Shamardal(USA) La Vita E Bella (IRE) (Definite Article)
2245[9] 3282[7] 3764[3] 5031a[6]

Witty Buck *Alan McCabe* a40 23
3 b g Multiplex Divine Love (IRE) (Barathea (IRE))
921[5]

Wizz Kid (IRE) *Robert Collet* 116
4 b m Whipper(USA) Lidanski (IRE) (Soviet Star (USA))
2112a[5] (2745a) 3238[10] 4861a[2] 6030[6] (6908a) 7236[7]

Wizz Up (IRE) *Robert Collet*
2 b f Whipper(USA) Lidanna (Nicholas (USA))
6751a[0]

Wolf Heart (IRE) *Lucinda Russell* a76
4 b g Dalakhani(IRE) Lisieux Orchid (IRE) (Sadler's Wells (USA))
7594[8]

Wolf Spirit (IRE) *Ruth Carr* 75
3 b g Amadeus Wolf Nasharaat (IRE) (Green Desert (USA))
(1167) 1440[7] 1661[8] 2118[8] 2671[5] 3111[12] 4177[7] 4716[13]

Wolkenburg (GER) *P Schiergen* 101
4 b m Big Shuffle(USA) Winterthur (GER) (Alkalde (GER))
3653a[7] 6085a[7]

Wom *Pam Sly* a36 63
4 b g Tiger Hill(IRE) Vayavaig (Damister (USA))
4683[10]

Wonder Lawn (SAF) *M F De Kock* a48 66
9 b g Fort Wood(USA) Velvet Green (BRZ) (Roy (USA))
53a[13]

Wooden King (IRE) *Malcolm Saunders* a79 83
7 b g Danetime(IRE) Olympic Rock (IRE) (Ballad Rock)
1362[3] 2369[10] 2494[7] 3390[2] (3660) 4231[8] 4530[10] 5933[6] 6226[7] 6688[10] 7197[6]

Woodland Fleur *Tony Carroll* a57
2 b f Astronomer Royal(USA) Ultimate Court (IRE) (Kendor (FR))
7894[8] 8171[10]

Woodland Mill (IRE) *F Vermeulen* a81 84
2 br f Pastoral Pursuits Why Now (Dansili)
(1136) 1579[3] 2252[4] ◆ 2603[7] 3501[2] 4093[8] 4820[16] 5371[5] 5515[11] 6425[6] 6883[9] 7374[7] 8276a[0]

Woodlandsway *Richard Hannon* a77 81
2 b f Oasis Dream Come What May (Selkirk (USA))
3764[5] 4282[4] 4701[3] (5887) 6675[7] 7518[6]

Wood Meister *Kevin Tork* a28 29
4 b g Needwood Blade Ever So Lonely (Headin' Up)
5510[8] 5950[7] 6582[11]

Wood Nymph (IRE) *Tim Easterby* a50 50
3 b f Acclamation Forest Call (Wolfhound (USA))
5340[7] 6180[10] 6806[6] 7447[15]

Woodstock (IRE) *Richard Hannon* 57
2 b c High Chaparral(IRE) Woodwin (IRE) (Woodman (USA))
6796[10]

Woody Bay *James Given* 71
2 b g New Approach(IRE) Dublino (USA) (Lear Fan (USA))
2934[7] 4069[2] 5797[2] 6793[9] 7637[10]

Woolfall Sovereign (IRE) *George Margarson* a102 46
6 b g Noverre(USA) Mandragore (USA) (Slew O'Gold (USA))
64[3] (157) (286) 871[6] 1255[5] 2071[12] 8008[5] (8066) 8272[2]

Woolfall Treasure *Gary Moore* a89 102
7 gr g Daylami(IRE) Treasure Trove (USA) (The Minstrel (CAN))
1850[5] 2479[6] 3341[5] 5076[2] 5905[7] 6834[5] 7109[P] 8073[5] (8235)

Woolston Ferry (IRE) *Henry Candy* a77 80
6 b g Fath(USA) Cathy Garcia (IRE) (Be My Guest (USA))
31[3] 301[4] (2173) ◆ (2675) (3485) 4233[5] (4964) 6208[8] 6931[8]

Woop Woop (IRE) *Ian Williams* a83 71
4 b m Oratorio(IRE) Nihonpillow Mirai (IRE) (Zamindar (USA))
960[2] 2447[4] 3610[6] 4499[11]

Wordiness *Seamus Durack* a69 71
4 br h Dansili Verbose (USA) (Storm Bird (CAN))
4061[11] 4411[3] 7529[3] 7768[4] 8079[6] 8214[4]

Wordismybond *Peter Makin* a66 73
3 b c Monsieur Bond(IRE) La Gessa (Largesse)
2206[6] 3071[7] 3732[8] (5633) 6735[10] 8057[5]

Word Of Warning *Martin Todhunter* 59
8 gr g War Chant(USA) Frosty Welcome (USA) (With Approval (CAN))
3402[5] 4431[5]

Wordsaplenty (IRE) *J S Moore* a54 57
2 b f Thousand Words Mega Tassa (IRE) (Foxhound (USA))
2622[3] 3140[5] 3444[4] 3970[4] 4343[4] 4421[7] 4659[4] 4752[6] (5291) 5806[5] 5968[2] 6156[8] 6612[6]

Words Come Easy *Philip McBride* a67
3 ch f Byron Aliena (IRE) (Grand Lodge (USA))
127[5] (352)

Work Ethic (IRE) *Gerard Butler* a74 63
2 ch c Camacho Foret Noire (IRE) (Barathea (IRE))
4803[13] 5992[5] 6787[8] (7219) 7462[2] 7635[8] 8065[3]

World Cup (GER) *Frau Nina Bach*
5 b g Sholokhov(IRE) Wonderful Dreams (GER) (Dashing Blade)
7701a[0]

World Domination (USA) *Sir Henry Cecil* a98 101
4 b h Empire Maker(USA) Reams Of Verse (USA) (Nureyev (USA))
1677[6] 2081[6]

World Freight Girl *Dean Ivory* a57 43
2 ch f Tumbleweed Ridge Bens Georgie (IRE) (Opening Verse (USA))
1411[8] 2541[6] 3040[6] 7650[10] 8007[10] 8203[10]

World Map (IRE) *Saeed Bin Suroor* a45
2 b f Pivotal Danse Arabe (IRE) (Seeking The Gold (USA))
7506[10]

World Record (IRE) *Richard Hannon* 76
2 b c Choisir(AUS) Dancing Debut (Polar Falcon (USA))
4688[9] 5319[2] 7373[2]

World's Flash (GER) *Andreas Lowe* 38
3 b c Konigstiger(GER) World's Vision (GER) (Platini (GER))
1553a[10]

Worth *Barry Brennan* a80 69
3 b f Indesatchel(IRE) Woore Lass (IRE) (Persian Bold)
230[6] 295[4] (865a)

Worthadd (IRE) *Sir Mark Prescott Bt* 123
5 b h Dubawi(IRE) Wigman (USA) (Rahy (USA))
(2222a) 2656[4] 3237[11] 4130a[2] 6300a[7]

Worthington (IRE) *Richard Fahey* 84
3 b f Kodiac Idle Fancy (Mujtahid (USA))
1271[15] 2022[6] 2490[12]

Wotalad *Richard Whitaker* 52
2 b g Bertolini(USA) Cosmic Song (Cosmonaut)
7290[6] 7516[5]

Wotatomboy *Richard Whitaker* a53 53
6 ch m Captain Rio Keen Melody (USA) (Sharpen Up)
1961[9] 3020[7] 3210[9]

Woteva *Nigel Tinkler* a21 70
6 b m Kyllachy Happy Omen (Warning)
1179[9] 1436[2] 2090[3] (2239) 2692[11] 2922[8] 3416[5] 3694[5] 3994[7] 5345[12] 7347[13]

Wotsitgotodowithu (IRE) *Alan McCabe* a13 44
4 b g Oratorio(IRE) Poule De Luxe (IRE) (Cadeaux Genereux)
3352[11] 4780[7] 4882[8] 6641[9]

Woven Lace *A Fabre* a84 106
3 gr f Hard Spun(USA) Do The Honours (IRE) (Highest Honor (FR))
1407a[2]

Woza Moya (USA) *Gay Kelleway* a68 64
2 b c Mizzen Mast(USA) Mrs Marcos (USA) (Private Account (USA))
6330[9] 6609[9] 7165[3] 7467[3] 7779[11] 8003[5] (8140) 8289[8]

Wrapped Up *Heather Main* a60 43
3 b f Clodovil(IRE) Parting Gift (Cadeaux Genereux)
1359[8] 2147[4] 2397[5] 2647[6] 3235[10]

Wreaths Of Empire (IRE) *Richard Hannon* 67
3 b g Dalakhani(IRE) Eyrecourt (IRE) (Efisio)
1506[6] 1853[8] 2235[8] 2424[10] 2765[4]

Wrecking Ball (IRE) *Brian Meehan* a27 64
2 b c Royal Applause Shatarah (Gulch (USA))
5793[5] 6645[7]

Wreningham *Pat Eddery* a70 64
7 br g Diktat Slave To The Rythm (IRE) (Hamas (IRE))
808[3] 1061[2] 1204[4] 3660[5] 4187[3] 6194[4] 6926[3] 7178[7] 8063[9] 8253[3]

Wrightington *Richard Fahey* 64
2 ch g Dutch Art Arculinge (Paris House)
2330[5] 2662[8]

Wrote (IRE) *A P O'Brien* a111 115
3 b c High Chaparral(IRE) Desert Classic (Green Desert (USA))
1145a[3] 2102a[3] 2514a[7] 3239[14]

Wrotham Heath *Sir Henry Cecil* 101
3 b c Dansili Native Justice (USA) (Alleged (USA))
1504[2] 2281[6] (2701) 3295[9] 4735[9]

Wyebridge *Gary Moore* a50 53
3 ch f Avonbridge Prowse (USA) (King Of Kings (IRE))
2145[8] 2483[6] 2891[12] 3470[7] 3965[3] 4650[12] 5770[9]

Wye Valley *Amanda Perrett* a69 60
3 b f Three Valleys(USA) Welsh Autumn (Tenby)
6279[3]

Wyldfire (IRE) *Richard Fahey* 72
2 ch g Raven's Pass(USA) Miss Sally (IRE) (Danetime (IRE))
5311[4] 6043[3] 6558[5]

Wyndham Wave *Rod Millman* a62 70
3 gr g Dr Fong(USA) Atlantic Light (Linamix (FR))
1322[10] 2128[5] 2756[9] 4709[5] 5152[4] 5479[4] 5764[4] (6396) 6982[3] 7917[8]

Wynyard Boy *Tim Easterby* 38
2 ch c Pastoral Pursuits Woodcock Moon (Kyllachy)
2213[8] 6042[9]

Xaloc (IRE) *Richard Fahey* a55
2 b f Shirocco(GER) Roystonea (Polish Precedent (USA))
7916[5]

Xanadou (IRE) *J-C Rouget* 113
3 ch g Peintre Celebre(USA) Doohulla (USA) (Stravinsky (USA))
2064a[4] (2951a) 3681a[4]

Xclaim *Micky Hammond* 74
4 ch g Proclamation(IRE) Tahara (IRE) (Caerleon (USA))
3353[3] (4314) 4714[12] 6339[8] 7034[6]

Xerxes (IRE) *Hugo Palmer* a37 44
2 b f Key Of Luck(USA) Clytha (Mark Of Esteem (IRE))
3916[11] 5119[4] 5511[5] 6332[9] 6975[7]

Xilerator (IRE) *David Nicholls* a72 103
5 b g Arakan(USA) Grandel (Owington)
1523[5] 2472[10] 4761[17] 6024[9] 6471[3] 6659[3] 7097[8]

Xinbama (IRE) *J W Hills* a81 79
3 b c Baltic King Persian Empress (IRE) (Persian Bold)
1313[6] ◆ (1790) (2416) 3376[6] 4607[5] 4939[6] ◆ 5667[5] 6208[4] 6692[4] 6973[3] 7358[4]

Xin Xu Lin (BRZ) *Mahmood Al Zarooni* a60 75
5 bb h Wondertross(USA) Barbiera (BRZ) (Pleasant Variety (USA))
144a[12]

Xpo Universel (FR) *F Doumen* a72 78
3 b g Poliglote Xanadu Bliss (FR) (Xaar)
1127a[10]

Xpres Maite *Roy Bowring* a77 65
9 b g Komaite(USA) Antonias Melody (Rambo Dancer (CAN))
1358[8] 2588[13] 2687[7] 3022[6] 5259[3] (6104) 6546[2] 6967[2] 7413[7] 7608[4]

Xtension (IRE) *J Moore* 121
5 br h Xaar Great Joy (IRE) (Grand Lodge (USA))
1148a[5] (1902a) 8042a[7]

Yaa Salam *Mahmood Al Zarooni* a74 81
3 ch c Any Given Saturday(USA) Alizes (NZ) (Rory's Jester (AUS))
1312[3] 1456[6] 2942[8] 3792[7] 4657[12]

Yaa Wayl (IRE) *Saeed Bin Suroor* a107 108
5 b g Whipper(USA) Lidanna (Nicholas (USA))
53a[3] 586a[4] 755a[3] 5964[2] 7010[3]

Ya Hafed *Sheena West* a64 76
4 ch g Haafhd Rule Britannia (Night Shift (USA))
733[6]

Yahilwa (USA) *James Tate* a59 68
2 br f Medaglia d'Oro(USA) Verbanella (USA) (Smart Strike (CAN))
6343[3] ◆ 6936[6]

Yahrab (IRE) *Declan Carroll* a106 81
7 gr g Dalakhani(IRE) Loire Valley (IRE) (Sadler's Wells (USA))
(2093) 2440[3] 2751[2]

Yair Hill (IRE) *John Dunlop* 93
4 b g Selkirk(USA) Conspiracy (Rudimentary (USA))
2409[4] 3348[4] ◆ 4609[12] 6011[11] 6676[7]

Yajber (USA) *Terry Clement* a68
3 rg c Aljabr(USA) Futuh (USA) (Diesis)
147[3] 350[3] 523[5] 737[5]

Yakama (IRE) *Christine Dunnett* a61 59
7 b g Indian Danehill(IRE) Working Progress (IRE) (Marju (IRE))
1263[3] 1768[14]

Yalding Dancer *John Best* a48
3 b f Zafeen(FR) Daughters World (Agnes World (USA))
308[8] 597[6] 970[10]

Yallah Habibi (FR) *Mme L Audon* 61
2 b c Falco(USA) Leadflor (IRE) (Poliglote)
3714a[7]

Yanabeeaa (USA) *Sir Michael Stoute* a81 68
3 rg f Street Cry(IRE) Queen (IRE) (Sadler's Wells (USA))
2381[3] 2826[10] (5228)

Yanbu (USA) *Michael Murphy* a41 62
7 b m Swain(IRE) Dufoof (USA) (Kingmambo (USA))
561[12] 4435[9] 4986[9] 5633[8]

Yang Tse Kiang (FR) *R Chotard* a112 104
3 gr g Kahyasi Mikalia (FR) (Kaldoun (FR))
1145a[2]

Yankee Storm *Michael Wigham* a77 63
7 b g Yankee Gentleman(USA) Yes Virginia (USA) (Roanoke (USA))
325[6] 526[7] ◆ 735[12] 942[10] 1050[9] (1378) 1587[8] 2555[2] 3053[2] 3546[4] 4438[3] 5915[9] 6497[4] 8308[4] ◆

Yanza *Pam Ford* a36 55
6 b m Bahamian Bounty Locharia (Wolfhound (USA))
938[9] 1343[7] 1910[2] 2386[5] 2761[4] 3076[3] 3435[10] 6233[10] 7275[12]

Yarra Valley *Willie Musson* a68 35
3 b f Aussie Rules(USA) Framboise (Diesis)
742[5] (838)

Yarroom (IRE) *Roger Varian* a91 77
2 b c Cape Cross(IRE) Aryaamm (IRE) (Galileo (IRE))
3499[4] 7330[3] (7749) (7994) 8223[2]

Yaseer (IRE) *E Charpy* a86 108
4 b g Dansili Tadris (USA) (Red Ransom (USA))
678a[9] 755a[11]

Yasir (USA) *Saeed Bin Suroor* a90 81
4 b g Dynaformer(USA) Khazayin (USA) (Bahri (USA))
2248[20] 2419[11] 5944[8] 6776[8]

Yas Marina (USA) *David O'Meara* a44 49
4 b g Bernardini(USA) Silvery Swan (USA) (Silver Deputy (CAN))
1296[7] 1988[9] 2670[6] 2775[8] 3942[2] 4189[3] 4405[11] 5683[11]

Yazdi (IRE) *Brian Meehan* a41 92
3 b g Galileo(IRE) Lucky Spin (Pivotal)
1456[3] (1867) 3330[7] 4007[6] 4346[5] 6537[10] 7032[8]

Yeeoow (IRE) *Mrs K Burke* a90 89
3 b g Holy Roman Emperor(IRE) Taraya (IRE) (Doyoun)
(969) 1271[2] 6368[2]

Yellow And Green *N Clement* 109
3 b f Monsun(GER) Green Swallow (FR) (Green Tune (USA))
2741a[2] (3423a) 6295a[4] 6912a[5]

Yellow Dandy (IRE) *Liam McAteer* a54 83
4 b m Kheleyf(USA) Groves Preneur (IRE) (Entrepreneur)
7589[10]

Yellow Mountain (IRE) *Marco Botti* 75
2 b c Danehill Dancer(IRE) Singing Diva (IRE) (Royal Academy (USA))
3397[3] 4330[7]

Yellow Rosebud (IRE) *D K Weld* 110
3 b f Jeremy(USA) Nebraas (Green Desert (USA))
(2101a) ◆ 2527a[7] 5523a[2] (6917a)

Yeomanoftheguard *Richard Fahey* a71 65
3 b g Librettist(USA) Red Blooded Woman (USA) (Red Ransom (USA))
(6827) 7843[10]

Yes Chef *Chris Gordon* a86 81
5 ch g Best Of The Bests(IRE) Lady Chef (Double Trigger (IRE))
971[9] 1258[4] 1752[6] 2199[13] 2576[4] 2975[7] 3782[8] 4504[10]

Yes It's The Boy (USA) *Ed Walker* a56 67
3 b g Yes It's True(USA) Storminthegarden (USA) (Stormy Atlantic (USA))
1916[11] 2382[9] 2996[3] 3706[9] 4734[2] 5017[6] 7382[9]

Yes Mam (IRE) *Tom Tate* a50 28
4 b m Acclamation Missdevina (IRE) (Namid)
995[4] 3455[6]

Yes Two *Rod Millman* 82
2 b c Indesatchel(IRE) Charlie Girl (Puissance)
1315[3] (1842) 2779a[4]

Yingymshoo *George Foster*
2 ch f Dubai Destination(USA) Tab's Gift (Bijou D'Inde)
8140[P]

Yin Xin (NZ) *T Kieser* 55
5 b g Quorum(NZ) Petra (NZ) (Senor Pete (USA))
2326a[9]

Ykikamoocow *Geoffrey Harker* 74
6 b m Cape Town(IRE) Pigeon (Casteddu)
2598[5] 3215[7] 6342[12]

Ymir *Michael Attwater* a61 58
6 b g Zaha(CAN) Anastasia Venture (Lion Cavern (USA))
1310[3] 2170[3] 2586[5] 3153[5]

Yo Credo (IRE) *John Carr* a46 43
3 b f Elusive City(USA) Baltic Beach (IRE) (Polish Precedent (USA))
5087[12]

Yogic Flyer *Gay Kelleway* a41 24
3 b f Phoenix Reach(IRE) Rainbows Guest (IRE) (Indian Lodge (IRE))
3155[6] 4582[8] *5100[7] 6807[9]*

Yojimbo (IRE) *Mick Channon* a75 91
4 gr g Aussie Rules(USA) Mythie (FR) (Octagonal (NZ))
1133[8] 2248[11] 2500[3] 3667[11] 3999[3] 4474[8] 4689[10] (4727) 5535[4] 5794 [8] 6208[3] 6405[4] (7370)

Yojojo (IRE) *Gay Kelleway* 63
3 ch f Windsor Knot(IRE) Belle Of The Blues (IRE) (Blues Traveller (IRE))
2030[4] 3461[3] 4984[4] 5623[5] 7470[11]

York Glory (USA) *Kevin Ryan* a107 106
4 rg h Five Star Day(USA) Minicolony (USA) (Pleasant Colony (USA))
2177[19] 2704[7] ◆ 3078[4] 7397[4] 7690[12] *(7817) (7918)*

Yorkshire Icon *Ann Duffield* 75
2 b c Sixties Icon Evanesce (Lujain (USA))
2138[11] 2537[3] 2923[3] 3457[2] (3842) 4450[6] (4778) 5254[3] 5670[4]

Yorkshireman (IRE) *David Brown* a53 74
2 b c Red Clubs(IRE) Ossiana (IRE) (Polish Precedent (USA))
6603[7] *6808[5]* (7290) 7687[16]

Yorksters Prince (IRE) *Tony Coyle* a73 73
5 b g Beat Hollow Odalisque (IRE) (Machiavellian (USA))
694[9] 834[10] 922[4] 1135[5] 1276[12] 1913[11] 2588[18] 4712[6] 5253[6] 6103[12] *6646[5]*

Yosha (IRE) *P Demercastel* a76 80
4 ch m Peintre Celebre(USA) Double Platinum (Seeking The Gold (USA))
1172a[9]

Yossi (IRE) *Richard Guest* a58 59
8 b g Montjeu(IRE) Raindancing (IRE) (Tirol)
66[8] 160[4] 229[2] 389[7] 453[11] 602[4] 695[4] 767[5] 850[8] 924[7] 1083[3] 1175[6]

You Da One (IRE) *Andrew Balding* 76
2 br g Footstepsinthesand Shenkara (IRE) (Night Shift (USA))
6167[4] 6636[3] ◆ 7067[3]

Yougoigo *Lawrence Mullaney* 39
4 b g Elnadim(USA) Club Oasis (Forzando)
7633[6]

You Got The Love *Jeremy Gask* a45 37
3 ch f Hawk Wing(USA) Precedence (IRE) (Polish Precedent (USA))
2162[16] *2497[4]* 2999[6] *3620[12] 4650[13]*

Youm Jamil (USA) *Tony Carroll* a62 82
5 rg g Mizzen Mast(USA) Millie's Choice (IRE) (Taufan (USA))
6051[9] 6251[5] 6503[2] 6616[7] 7960[7] 8139[9] 8264[3]

Young Dottie *Pat Phelan* a82 72
6 b m Desert Sun Auntie Dot Com (Tagula (IRE))
351[5] 5667[2] 6172[2] *7858[8]*

Young Freddie (IRE) *Bryan Smart* a40 51
3 gr g Clodovil(IRE) Quecha (IRE) (Indian Ridge)
885[4] 1864[6] 2795[13] 5757[8]

Young Jackie *George Margarson* a50 52
4 b m Doyen(IRE) Just Warning (Warning)
2467[7] 3047[2] 3552[6] 4940[9] *7303[5] 7479[9] 8001[10]*

Young Lou *Robin Dickin* a27 67
3 b f Kadastrof(FR) Wanna Shout (Missed Flight)
1502[5] 2232[8] 6662[6] 7132[9]

Young Poli (FR) *Robert Collet* 68
9 b g Poliglote Yole (FR) (Dancing Spree (USA))
5030a[9]

Young Simon *George Margarson* a63 63
5 ch g Piccolo Fragrant Cloud (Zilzal (USA))
155[5] 210[7] 356[10] 831[8]

Yourartisonfire *Mrs K Burke* 81
2 ch c Dutch Art Queens Jubilee (Cayman Kai (IRE))
3074[4] (3777) 5109[4] 6425[3] 6815[3]

You're Golden (IRE) *C Ferland* a65 90
2 bb c Lawman(FR) Golden Shadow (IRE) (Selkirk (USA))
4632a[6] *8192a[6]*

You'relikemefrank *Richard Ford* a79 66
6 ch g Bahamian Bounty Proudfoot (IRE) (Shareef Dancer (USA))
718[9] 911[4] 1116[8] 2458[6] 2719[4] 3065[6]

You're The Boss *Ed Walker* a65 80
2 b c Royal Applause Trinny (Rainbow Quest (USA))
2193[3] *8172[3]*

Yourinthewill (USA) *Daniel Mark Loughnane* a75 67
4 ch g Aragorn(IRE) Lenarue (USA) (Gone West (USA))
176[3] 1792[8] 1956[4] 2389[10] 2767[8] 7640[13] *8145[9]*

Yours *Kevin Ryan* a51 54
4 b m Piccolo Uno (Efisio)
232[10] 430[10] 581[4] 811[8]

Yours Ever *Sir Mark Prescott Bt* a79 85
3 b f Dansili Love Everlasting (Pursuit Of Love)
3737[2] 3945[5] 4639[2] 5256[2] (7211) 7367[12]

Your Word *Daniel Kubler* 49
3 b f Monsieur Bond(IRE) Only Yours (Aragon)
3507[9] 4605[4] 5874[10]

You've Been Mowed *Richard Price* a64 87
6 ch m Ishiguru(USA) Sandblaster (Most Welcome)
4365[12] 4939[7] 5369[10] 5931[10]

You Will See (FR) *Mario Hofer* 82
2 b f Librettist(USA) Suvretta Queen (IRE) (Polish Precedent (USA))
7622a[8]

Ypres *Jason Ward* a66 69
3 b g Byron Esligier (IRE) (Sabrehill (USA))
3442[16] 4174[2] 4348[3] 4956[3] *(5247)* 5621[3] 6264[5]

Ysper (FR) *M Nigge* 28
2 b f Orpen(USA) Velda (Observatory (USA))
7597a[0]

Yukatana (FR) *C Lotoux* a90 97
4 b m Vatori(FR) La Bardane (FR) (Marignan (USA))
2805a[4] 4386a[0]

Yul Finegold (IRE) *George Baker* 73
2 b c Invincible Spirit(IRE) Mascara (Mtoto)
4330[6] 6371[5]

Yun (FR) *C Baillet* a71
3 b f Panis(USA) Slyders (IRE) (Hector Protector (USA))
865a[8]

Yungaburra (IRE) *David C Griffiths* a64 63
8 b g Fath(USA) Nordic Living (IRE) (Nordico (USA))
1722[6] 2171[10] 3943[12] 4928[5] 5179[4] 5892[7] (6179) 7465[6] 8304[8]

Yurituni *Eve Johnson Houghton* a70 83
5 b m Bahamian Bounty Vax Star (Petong)
1926[6] 2487[4] 3571[5] 4000[4] 4231[9] 5035[2] 5326[10] 5906[10] *7483[5] 7648[9] 7995[7] 8157[8]*

Zaahya (IRE) *John Dunlop* a63 64
3 ch f Shamardal(USA) Najah (IRE) (Nashwan (USA))
3507[7] 4314[4] 5125[3] *5754[3] 6769[3]*

Zabarajad (IRE) *John M Oxx* a100 108
4 b g Invincible Spirit(IRE) Zalaiyma (FR) (Rainbow Quest (USA))
261a[13]

Zabeelionaire (NZ) *Leon Corstens* 112
4 b h Zabeel(NZ) Kisumu (AUS) (Carnegie (IRE))
7264a[6] 7621a[22]

Zack Tiger (IRE) *P Schaerer* 79
3 ch c Hold That Tiger(USA) Energetic Star (Anabaa (USA))
7565a[9]

Zacynthus (IRE) *Luca Cumani* a89 96
4 ch g Iffraaj Ziria (IRE) (Danehill Dancer (IRE))
254[7] 354[6] 1156[20] 1321[15] *1431[9]* (4661) 5269[2] (6011) 7240[20]

Zadig (USA) *Garry Woodward* 49
2 bb f Rio Verde(USA) Cause I'm Tricky (USA) (Nineeleven (USA))
3887[5]

Zaeem *Mahmood Al Zarooni* a69 87
3 b c Echo Of Light Across (ARG) (Roy (USA))
1265[2] *1737[2]* (3248) 5365[2] 6205[8]

Zafarana *Roger Varian* a92 92
4 b m Tiger Hill(IRE) Miss Meltemi (IRE) (Miswaki Tern (USA))
3632[5] 4848[P]

Zafeen's Pearl *Dean Ivory* a90 82
5 ch m Zafeen(FR) Deep Sea Pearl (Dr Fong (USA))
987[2] 1416[5]

Zaffy (IRE) *Tim Easterby* 59
3 b f Iffraaj Silkie Smooth (IRE) (Barathea (IRE))
1296[3] 2540[5] 3952[12] 5734[8] 6106[14]

Zafonic Star *Ian Williams* a60 48
3 b g Cockney Rebel(IRE) Enthralled (Zafonic (USA))
3075[8] 4709[11]

Zafranagar (IRE) *Tony Carroll* a73 80
7 b g Cape Cross(IRE) Zafaraniya (IRE) (Doyoun)
1003[4] (1135) 7132[10]

Zagora (FR) *Chad C Brown* 116
5 ch m Green Tune(USA) Zaneton (FR) (Mtoto)
4617a[3] 6695a[2] (7549a)

Za'Hara (IRE) *Saeed Bin Suroor* 50
2 bb f Raven's Pass(USA) Opera Comique (FR) (Singspiel (IRE))
7553[5]

Zaheeb *Dave Morris* a71 70
4 b g Haafhd Gay Music (FR) (Gay Mecene (USA))
(821) 967[4] 1262[4] *1729[4]* 2466[4] 2847[7] 4584[12] 5632[9] *5941[7] 7670[4] 7964[2]*

Zaidan (USA) *J Moore* 115
4 bb g Street Cry(IRE) Element Of Truth (USA) (Atticus (USA))
8043a[7]

Zaina (IRE) *Gerard Butler* a67 86
3 b f Shirocco(GER) Ruacana Falls (USA) (Storm Bird (CAN))
533[2] (1132) 2410[7] 4009[9] 4608[7] *5474[8]* 6206[5] 6710[2] *7416[10]*

Zain Eagle *Gerard Butler* 57
2 b c Dylan Thomas(IRE) Pearl City (USA) (Carson City (USA))
7333[6] 7636[4]

Zain Glory *Gerard Butler* a43 70
3 gr c Dalakhani(IRE) Three Wishes (Sadler's Wells (USA))
2197[14] 3398[5] 3606[5] *4403[4] 5810[11]*

Zain Heart (IRE) *Gerard Butler* a25
2 b f Shamardal(USA) Antillia (Red Ransom (USA))
6014[10]

Zain Princess (IRE) *Gerard Butler* a75 50
3 b f Hawk Wing(USA) Cosenza (Bahri (USA))
(534) ◆ *1013[3] 1190[2] (1486)* ◆ *1757[5] 2372[8] 2860[11]*

Zain Shamardal (IRE) *A Al Raihe* a105 94
4 b h Shamardal(USA) Novelina (IRE) (Fusaichi Pegasus (USA))
145a[9] *(587a)*

Zain Spirit (USA) *Gerard Butler* a70 39
2 b c Tapit(USA) American Jewel (USA) (Quiet American (USA))
3499[6] 4404[2] 4837[8] *6016[5] (6451) 6972[5] 7478[8]*

Zakatal *Julie Camacho* a81 77
6 gr g Kalanisi(IRE) Zankara (FR) (Linamix (FR))
5798[4] 7211[2] 7522[4] *8235[2]*

Zakreet *Kevin Ryan* 86
3 ch c Cadeaux Genereux Chili Dip (Alhaarth (IRE))
1221[10] 1477[10] 1653[4] 2088[3] 2930[3] 3607[8]

Za'Lan (USA) *Chris Gordon* a70 64
3 b g Street Sense(USA) Calista (Caerleon (USA))
552[2] ◆ *709[2] (762) 1390[3]* 2333[7] 3003[3] 3729[4] 3891[5] *8170[10] 8297[7]*

Zalanga (IRE) *M Halford* a79 55
3 b f Azamour(IRE) Zanara (IRE) (Kahyasi)
7852a[8]

Zamarelle *Roger Charlton* a56 62
3 b f Zamindar(USA) Kardelle (Kalaglow)
1982[13] 2424[14]

Zambezi Tiger (IRE) *Mrs Prunella Dobbs* a56 71
3 b g Tiger Hill(IRE) Johannesburg Cat (USA) (Johannesburg (USA))
7417[4]

Zamdy Man *Venetia Williams* 86
3 b g Authorized(IRE) Lauderdale (GER) (Nebos (GER))
3161[3] (4301) 4741[9] 5583[4]

Zamina (IRE) *Tim Vaughan* a79 79
4 b m Hawk Wing(USA) Termania (IRE) (Shirley Heights)
582[6]

Zaminate *Andrew Balding* a55
3 b f Zamindar(USA) Whitgift Rose (Polar Falcon (USA))
7896[5] 8187[5]

Zammy *Michael Wigham* a64 65
3 ch g Zamindar(USA) Barbs Pink Diamond (USA) (Johannesburg (USA))
1728[11] 2205[8] 3555[16] *8205[8]*

Zamoyski *Jeremy Noseda* 82
2 ch g Dutch Art Speech (Red Ransom (USA))
6020[7] (6571)

Zanetto *Andrew Balding* a96 91
2 b c Medicean Play Bouzouki (Halling (USA))
2480[7] 3368[9] 4253[2] 4763[8] (5360) *6038[2]* 6491[2]

Zanotti *Roger Varian* 87
3 b g Authorized(IRE) Majestic Sakeena (IRE) (King's Best (USA))
2196[11] 4410[3] (4926) 6573[3] 6987[5]

Zantenda *F Head* 105
3 b f Zamindar(USA) Tender Morn (USA) (Dayjur (USA))
1407a[6] 2112a[6] 2742a[9] 6088a[7] 6913a[8]

Zanzamar (SAF) *M F De Kock* a111 114
5 b h Fort Wood(USA) Zanakiya (FR) (Doyoun)
416a[12] (591a) 877a[5] 1144a[3]

Zaplamation (IRE) *John Quinn* a40 76
7 b g Acclamation Zapatista (Rainbow Quest (USA))
1154[3] 2440[6] 3022[3] 3307[8] 4209[2] 4714[4] 5199[2] 6103[4] 6631[7]

Zarla *Tom Dascombe* a55
2 b f Zamindar(USA) Ikhteyaar (USA) (Mr Prospector (USA))
6936[10]

Zarosa (IRE) *John Berry* a44 59
3 b f Barathea(IRE) Shantalla Peak (IRE) (Darshaan)
3189[11] *4214[7]* 4744[3] 5022[3] 5264[3] *7196[8]* (7490)

Zaroud (IRE) *R McGlinchey* a56
3 b g Zamindar(USA) Zarwala (IRE) (Polish Precedent (USA))
336a[7]

Zarzal (IRE) *Evan Williams* a73 71
4 b g Dr Fong(USA) Zarwala (IRE) (Polish Precedent (USA))
569[2]

Zatkova (ITY) *L Racco*
3 b f Ekraar(USA) Zabetta (Zamindar (USA))
476a[0]

Zavier (FR) *Mark Johnston* a48 51
3 b c Shamardal(USA) Zarkiyna (FR) (Sendawar (IRE))
5889[10] 6480[6]

Zayade (FR) *J Boisnard* a91 102
3 b f Country Reel(USA) Hallen (FR) (Midyan (USA))
8300a[6]

Zazera (FR) *Mario Hofer* 96
2 ch f Shamardal(USA) Woodlass (USA) (Woodman (USA))
4615a[5] (5781a) 6522a[3] 7281a[6]

Zazou (GER) *W Hickst* a116 119
5 b h Shamardal(USA) Zaza Top (GER) (Lomitas)
1150a[5] 4636a[3] *5848a[2]*

Zebrano *Natalie Lloyd-Beavis* a90 88
6 br g Storming Home Ambience Lady (Batshoof)
6207[14] *6584[14] 7163[11] 7722[9]*

Zed Candy Girl *John Stimpson* 39
2 ch f Sakhee's Secret Musical Twist (USA) (Woodman (USA))
7686[8]

Zee Zee Dan (IRE) *Noel Quinlan* a33 54
4 b g Danroad(AUS) Bella Boy Zee (IRE) (Anita's Prince)
45[9]

Zefooha (FR) *Tim Walford* a64 73
8 ch m Lomitas Bezzaaf (Machiavellian (USA))
(1247) *1485[4]* 2214[15] 3180[10] 3750[6] 4590[11] (7293) 7603[10]

Zegna (GER) *Fredrik Reuterskiold* 91
3 br f Shirocco(GER) Zephyrine (IRE) (Highest Honor (FR))
4359a[4]

Ze King *Chris Wall* a66 49
3 b g Manduro(GER) Top Flight Queen (Mark Of Esteem (IRE))
2584[7]

Zenaad (USA) *Seamus Durack* a57
3 bb g Henny Hughes(USA) Lady Cruella (USA) (Capote (USA))
369[8] 523[8] 693[6] 6365[10]

Zenaat *Sir Michael Stoute* a80 55
3 b f Galileo(IRE) Janet (Emperor Jones (USA))
2249[13] *2848[5]* 3605[6] *(4464)*

Zenafire *Reg Hollinshead* a62 59
3 b c Firebreak Zen Garden (Alzao (USA))
5335[3] 5687[3] *7361[5] 7593[4] 7781[4]*

Zenarinda *Mark H Tompkins* a73 71
5 b m Zamindar(USA) Tenpence (Bob Back (USA))
136[2] 331[2] 494[2] 1094[7] 1743[5] 2915[5] 3609[7] 5021[6] *5351[2]* (6885) *7310[7] 7768[3]* 8020[6] (8079)

Zenji (USA) *A Fabre* 103
2 b c Hat Trick(JPN) Zinziberine (USA) (Zieten (USA))
(4118a) 5398a[8] 7013a[4]

Zennor *George Margarson* a62 92
5 b m Doyen(IRE) Salanka (IRE) (Persian Heights)
1114[7] 3550[9] 4311[6] 4683[6] 4987[3] 5638[8] 6561[10]

Zero Game (IRE) *Michael Bell* a60 70
2 b f High Chaparral(IRE) Freezing Love (USA) (Danzig (USA))
5104[5] ◆ 5818[6] *6501[7]* 7173[9]

Zero Money (IRE) *Roger Charlton* a77 108
6 ch g Bachelor Duke(USA) Dawn Chorus (IRE) (Mukaddamah (USA))
50a[10] 3641[3] 4576[3] 5077[6] 5487[10] 6028[12]

Zero Rated (IRE) *Tim Easterby* 46
2 b f Red Clubs(IRE) Southern Barfly (USA) (Southern Halo (USA))
1164[7] 1437[10] 2309[3] 3019[4] 3351[7]

Zetterholm (USA) *Richard Dutrow Jr* a102
3 b c Silver Train(USA) Holy Wish (USA) (Lord At War (ARG))
2299a[4]

Zeus De Cerisy (FR) *Mme L Audon* 65
2 b c Sunday Break(JPN) Air De Cerisy (FR) (Astair (FR))
3714a[8]

Zeus Magic *David Elsworth* a77 83
2 b c Zamindar(USA) Milly Of The Vally (Caerleon (USA))
7371[2] ◆ *7705[5] (7900)*

Zeva *David Simcock* a71
2 b f Zamindar(USA) Mennetou (IRE) (Entrepreneur)
7160[3] ◆

Zeyran (IRE) *Sir Henry Cecil* a56 74
3 ch f Galileo(IRE) Chervil (Dansili)
7174[3] ◆ *7488[3]*

Zhiggy's Stardust *Henry Candy* 68
3 b g Zafeen(FR) Lady Natilda (First Trump)
1889[2] 2501[3]

Zhuba (IRE) *John Best* a36 55
2 b c Elusive Quality(USA) Lilium (Nashwan (USA))
3074[9] *8102[9]*

Ziefhd *Tim McCarthy* a86 78
3 b f Haafhd Zietory (Zieten (USA))
1790[2] 2272[17] 3108[4] 3785[10] *(4644) (5406)* 6173[3] *7483[10] 8183[9]*

Zigazag (IRE) *David Evans* a32 63
3 b g Refuse To Bend(IRE) Most Charming (FR) (Darshaan)
2131[10] 3141[9] 3243[9]

Ziggy Lee *Giles Bravery* a91 89
6 b g Lujain(USA) Mary O'Grady (USA) (Swain (IRE))
2195[13] 2507[6]

Ziggy's Secret *Lucy Wadham* 75
2 b f Sakhee's Secret Ziggy Zaggy (Diktat)
3339[4] 4011[8] (4625) 5202[3]

Ziking (FR) *A Schaerer* a74 80
7 gr g Kingsalsa(USA) Zizoune (FR) (Kadrou (FR))
(444a) 630a[4]

Zilzie (IRE) *Ann Duffield* a54 27
3 b f Intikhab(USA) Novosibirsk (USA) (Distant View (USA))
7445[5] *7654[5] 7981[8]*

Zimira (IRE) *Ed Dunlop* a84 85
3 b f Invincible Spirit(IRE) Zibilene (Rainbow Quest (USA))
2079[5] 2410[5] 4608[12] *5209[4]*

Zimri (FR) *Mme M Bollack-Badel* a77 94
8 b g Take Risks(FR) Zayine (IRE) (Polish Patriot (USA))
2685a[3]

Zinabaa (FR) *M Mace* 119
7 gr g Anabaa Blue Zigrala (FR) (Linamix (FR))
1163a[4] (1746a) 2533a[4] 3205a[6] (6897a)

Zingana *Eve Johnson Houghton* 72
3 b f Zamindar(USA) Change Partners (IRE) (Hernando (FR))
2201[12] 2846[11] 3619[13]

Zing Wing *David Evans* a76 73
4 ch m Hawk Wing(USA) Zietory (Zieten (USA))
1311[5] 1611[8] 1769[6] *(2811)* 3643[10] *4469[9]* 5852[2] *(6145)* ◆ *6367[7] 7171[8]*

Zinnobar *Jonathan Portman* 28
2 gr f Ishiguru(USA) Demolition Jo (Petong)
7103[8] 7552[11]

Zip Lock (IRE) *Tom Keddy* a84 70
6 b g Invincible Spirit(IRE) Buckle (IRE) (Common Grounds)
186[5] (473) 735[6] 1827[12] 2169[4] 2581[4] 5941[11] 6610[12] (7317) 7685[9] *7863[10]* 7998[11]

Zipp (IRE) *Charles Hills* 73
2 b f Excellent Art Subito (Darshaan)
6448[3] 7172[3]

Zomerlust *John Quinn* a83 89
10 b g Josr Algarhoud(IRE) Passiflora (Night Shift (USA))
447[3] 553[6] (1248) (2120) 3304[4] 6260[3] *7166[3]*

Zoola (IRE) *Andrew Heffernan* a85 92
2 br f Iffraaj Slow Jazz (USA) (Chief's Crown (USA))
6424[2] *7390a[6]*

Zoom In *Lee James* 42
4 b g Indesatchel(IRE) Korolieva (IRE) (Xaar)
2796[10] 3753[8] 7447[7]

Zor (FR) *T Larriviere* a75
2 ch c Tot Ou Tard(IRE) Kirklandi (TUR) (Majorien)
(8193a)

Zowaina *Roger Varian* a71 73
3 b f Manduro(GER) Zaynaat (Unfuwain (USA))
206[5] 350[7] (3233) 3704[3] 4311[4] 5280[3]

Zoya (FR) *J-P Gallorini* a70 78
2 gr f Literato(FR) Ziride (FR) (Valanour (IRE))
6751a^{4}

Zuider Zee (GER) *John Gosden* a81 111
5 b g Sakhee(USA) Zephyrine (IRE) (Highest Honor (FR))
1318^{2} ◆ 2639^{4} 3373^{4} 5374a^{3} 6922^{2}

Zumbi (IRE) *Sir Michael Stoute* 111
3 b c Dubawi(IRE) Star Studded (Cadeaux Genereux)
1453^{5} 5102^{3} ◆ 5627^{3} 6449^{5}

Zurbriggen *Mahmood Al Zarooni* 79
2 ch c Raven's Pass(USA) Zanzibar (IRE) (In The Wings)
5062^{3}

Zurigha (IRF) *Richard Hannon* a80 96
2 b f Cape Cross(IRE) Noyelles (IRE) (Docksider (USA))
(6534) ◆ 7052^{6}

Zuzu Angel (IRE) *William Knight* a62 65
3 gr f Clodovil(IRE) Zither (Zafonic (USA))
982^{9} *1365^{9}* 2367^{10} 3248^{3} 4436^{4} 4754^{2} 4900^{5} 5506^{4} 6231^{5} *6892^{8}* 6962^{5}

INDEX TO MEETINGS FLAT 2012

Arlington 5374a-5377a,
Ascot 2019, 2065, 3237, 3265, 3291, 3326, 3368, 4282, 4317, 4362, 4525, 4574, 5075, 6020, 6830, 6865, 7235,
Ayr 2594, 2614, 3332, 3374, 3887, 3902, 4132, 4387, 4637, 4670, 5081, 5184, 6387†, 6423, 6465, 6753, 6997,
Baden-Baden 2222a, 2322a, 5612a-5613a, 5647a, 5755a, 5781a-5782a, 5844a, 5865a, 7281a-7282a,
Bath 1491, 1903, 2161, 2866, 3137, 3483, 4230, 4486, 4752, 4899, 5191, 5501, 5811, 5931, 6092, 6226, 6274, 6732, 7014, 7268,
Belmont Park 2954a, 6695a, 6901a-6902a, 6944a,
Beverley 1435, 1615†, 1911, 2138, 2601, 2686, 3018, 3457, 3803†, 3842, 4172, 4395, 4677, 5220, 5253, 5618, 5818, 6354, 6555,
Brighton 1622, 1767, 2360, 2622, 2647, 2994, 3243, 3464, 3717, 4237, 4936, 4980, 5032, 5439, 5989, 6301, 6430, 6945, 7182†,
Cagnes-Sur-Mer 211a, 247a, 290a, 364a-365a, 475a-476a, 542a, 628a, 661a, 716a,
Capannelle 1409a, 1698a-1699a, 2106a, 2323a-2325a, 7429a, 7513a, 7586a-7587a, 7697a,
Carlisle 2535, 2747, 3208, 3490, 3849†, 4618, 4864, 5727, 6130,
Catterick 1292, 1594, 1949, 2436, 2694, 2873, 3747, 3951, 4206, 4448, 4907, 5290, 5733, 6473, 6952, 7241, 7450,
Caulfield 7073a, 7264a,
Chantilly 814a-815a, 1171a-1172a, 1723a, 1766a, 2064a, 2741a-2745a, 2951a, 3203a-3205a, 3680a-3682a, 3928a, 6128a-6129a, 6804a, 6942a-6943a, 7122a-7124a, 7597a, 7682a-7683a, 7699a, 7803a,
Chepstow 1810†, 2384, 2571, 2755, 3096, 3429, 3754†, 4035†, 4531, 4988, 5260, 5653, 5997, 6153,
Chester 1972, 1993, 2025, 2469, 2909, 3554, 3604, 4042, 4076, 4836, 5331, 5825, 6188, 6234, 6657,
Churchill Downs 1839a, 1872a,
Clairefontaine 5030a, 5288a,
Cologne 1700a, 2107a, 2568a, 2568a, 2965a-2966a, 6522a-6523a,
Compiegne 965a, 3017a, 3714a, 7551a,
Cork 3196a-3197a,
Craon 5899a,
Curragh 1040a-1041a, 1043a, 1549a, 1943a-1944a, 1946a, 2512a-2515a, 2524a-2525a, 2527a, 3645a, 3647a-3651a, 3674a-3676a, 3678a, 4354a, 4376a-4378a, 4380a, 5134a-5137a, 5606a, 5609a, 5641a-5643a, 6078a-6081a, 6266a, 6268a, 6270a-6272a, 6716a-6718a,
Deauville 15a-18a*, 83a*, 92a-94a*, 116a-117a*, 865a, 914a, 4615a-4616a, 4632a-4634a, 4696a, 4790a, 4861a, 5073a-5074a, 5116a-5118a, 5140a-5142a, 5248a-5250a, 5378a-5379a, 5398a-5400a, 5471a-5473a, 5570a, 5648a-5650a, 5697a-5698a, 5726a, 7343a, 7345a, 7984a-7985a, 8176a, 8192a-8193a, 8276a-8277a, 8300a,
Del Mar 5031a,
Dieppe 4476a-4477a,
Doncaster 1128, 1154, 1637, 1650, 1841, 2260, 2880, 2916, 3180, 3560, 3611, 3809, 3988, 4245, 4494, 4791, 5338, 6138, 6160, 6196, 6242, 7363, 7395, 7684,
Dortmund 3206a, 6290a,
Dundalk 335a-337a*, 341a-342a*, 775a*, 1118a*, 1832a*, 1834a*, 4161a*, 5397a*, 5858a*, 6853a-6855a*, 7038a*, 7229a-7230a*, 7390a*, 7680a*, 7852a*,
Dusseldorf 1410a, 2746a, 4862a, 5402a, 6906a, 7091a,
Epsom 1602, 2654, 2701, 3769, 3995, 4251, 4500, 4722, 5661, 5702, 6167, 6699,
Fairyhouse 6550a,
Ffos Las 3685†, 4180, 4419, 4728, 5146, 5527(M), 5872, 6282,
Flemington 7560a, 7621a, 7696a,
Folkestone 1201, 1330, 1571†, 1774†, 2607, 2970, 3568, 4001, 4506, 5119, 5509, 5850, 6328, 6563, 6759†,
Fontainebleau 1127a, 7828a-7829a,
Frankfurt 1900a, 7784a,
Galway 4692a, 4833a,
Geelong 7346a,
Goodwood 1847, 2000†, 2407, 2442, 2477, 2886, 3103, 3338, 4684, 4697, 4735, 4759, 4799, 5531, 5571, 5625, 5901, 6571, 7077,
Gowran Park 6518a,
Gulfstream Park 8100a, 8244a, 8278a-8279a,
Hamburg 3652a-3653a, 3683a, 3746a, 3768a, 3802a,
Hamilton 1875, 2032, 2224, 2837, 3026, 3271, 3519, 3725, 4049†, 4083, 4257, 4806, 5537, 5756, 5879†, 6511, 6524, 6740†,
Hanover 3425a, 4130a, 6085a, 6723a, 7588a,
Haydock 1657, 2073(M), 2414, 2449, 2484, 2661, 2708, 3033, 3061, 3775, 3816†, 3855, 4289, 4324, 4995, 5039, 5088, 5962, 6005, 6027, 6625, 6664, 7205,
Hollywood Park 4131a, 7882a,
Hoppegarten 1901a, 2531a, 4383a, 6805a,
Jagersro 2159a-2160a, 3654a-3655a, 4359a, 5143a-5144a,
Kempton 26*, 118*, 126*, 183*, 197*, 262*, 276*, 291*, 306*, 373*, 437*, 467*, 517*, 558*, 572*, 647*, 662*, 733*, 740*, 816*, 890*, 958*, 966*, 981*, 989*, 1061*, 1082*, 1136*, 1211*, 1299*, 1443*, 1608*, 1702*, 1723*, 1747*, 1919*, 1979*, 2145*, 2368*, 2541*, 2808*, 3039*, 3278*, 3497*, 3732*, 3761*, 3958*, 4870*, 4914*, 4944*, 5153*, 5228*, 5296*, 5403*, 5474*, 5741*, 5765*, 5938*, 5968*, 6013*, 6034*, 6145*, 6249*, 6362*, 6395*, 6532*, 6579*, 6771*, 6975*, 7005*, 7156*, 7189*, 7321*, 7473*, 7497*, 7625*, 7702*, 7718*, 7804*, 7820*, 7891*, 7922*, 7960*, 7986*, 8068*, 8092*, 8161*, 8177*,
Klampenborg 4863a,
Kranji 2326a,
Krefeld 1553a, 7698a,
L'Ancresse 2113a-2117a,
La Croise-Laroche 7265a-7267a,
Laytown 6184a,
Leicester 1352, 1663†, 1781†, 2328, 2549, 2763, 2783, 3144†, 3297†, 3526†, 3862†, 4264†, 4456, 4704, 5126, 5909, 6114, 6540, 6960, 7125, 7432,
Leopardstown 1401a, 1403a-1404a, 2100a-2102a, 2903a, 3091a-3092a, 4276a, 4519a, 4521a, 5027a, 5286a, 6060a-6063a, 6066a, 7419a,
Les Landes 5701a,
Lingfield 33*, 54*, 84*, 146*, 175*, 204*, 219*, 248*, 298*, 320*, 349*, 394*, 422*, 523*, 565*, 592*, 619*, 654*, 709*, 726*, 760*, 781*, 800*, 823*, 915*, 1003*, 1031*, 1045*, 1068*, 1104*, 1180*, 1307*, 1373*, 1730*, 1787*, 2038*, 2078*, 2168*, 2392(M), 2492(M), 2579*, 2844(M), 3001(M), 3150(M), 3617(M), 3965(M), 4212*, 4330(M), 4462*, 4581(M), 4644*, 4812(M), 5045*, 5095(M), 5160*, 5346(M), 5481, 5770, 5946, 6436, 7164*, 7303*, 7481*, 7505*, 7641*, 7737*, 7767*, 7812*, 7854*, 7899*, 7994*, 8003*, 8016*, 8032*, 8044*, 8052*, 8060*, 8076*, 8101*, 8153*, 8168*, 8185*, 8199*, 8223*, 8245*, 8261*, 8292*, 8301*,
Limerick 3361a,
Listowel 6352a,
Longchamp 1244a-1245a, 1407a-1408a, 1570a, 1695a-1697a, 1971a, 2108a-2110a, 2112a, 2532a-2534a, 2728a, 2989a, 3656a-3657a, 4118a, 4120a-4121a, 6086a-6088a, 6292a-6297a, 6507a-6508a, 6896a-6899a, 6908a-6914a, 7283a-7284a, 7430a-7431a, 7700a-7701a,
Lyon Parilly 3178a, 6225a,
Maisons-Laffitte 1208a-1209a, 1426a, 2685a, 3367a, 3900a-3901a, 3987a, 4384a-4386a, 6463a-6464a, 6751a-6752a, 7622a-7624a,
Marseille Borely 7234a,
Meydan 47a-48a, 50a-53a, 77a, 80a, 140a-145a, 241a-246a, 260a-261a, 314a-319a, 416a-421a, 484a-489a, 586a-591a, 616a-618a, 683, 677a-682a, 792a, 873a-879a, 1143a-1150a,
Moonee Valley 7425a-7426a,
Munich 1745a, 2569a, 2569a, 4131a, 4636a, 5145a, 6291a,
Musselburgh 1218, 1235, 1794, 1817, 2455, 2715, 3109, 3575, 4426, 4766, 5053, 5916, 6308, 6706, 7095,
Naas 1538a, 2184a, 2187a, 2777a, 2779a-2780a, 3983a, 4482a,
Nantes 7319a-7320a,
Navan 2318a,
Newbury 1498, 1506, 2231, 2266, 2498, 3067, 3472, 3782, 4055, 4090, 4843, 5303, 5352, 6443, 6481, 7371, 7403,
Newcastle 1380, 1962†, 2238, 2630, 2667, 2922, 3532, 3582†, 3623, 4587, 4951, 5311, 5543, 5668, 6099, 6257, 6779, 7133†,
Newmarket 1450, 1466, 1854, 1882, 2193, 2245, 2274, 2892, 2929, 3344, 3393, 3589, 3630, 4007, 4062, 4097, 4296, 4336, 4538, 4595, 4772, 4818, 5060, 5101, 5267, 5319, 5360, 5550, 5578, 6489, 6596, 6632, 6671, 6872, 7048, 7329, 7516, 7552,
Niort 3207a,
Nottingham 1315, 1514, 2046, 2084, 2375, 2729, 2815, 3074, 3869†, 4303†, 4742, 5199, 5325, 6787, 6983, 7172, 7489, 7633,
Ovrevoll 3886a, 4751a, 5651a,
Pimlico 2299a,
Pontefract 1269, 1556, 1753, 2675, 2977, 3415, 3692, 3929†, 4310, 4625, 4959, 5382, 6403, 6603, 6919, 7289,
Redcar 1164, 1246, 2118, 2334, 2770, 2790, 3351, 3401, 4368†, 4710, 5108, 5585, 6121, 6587†, 6880, 7212†, 7440, 7598,
Ripon 1474, 1670, 2052†, 2308, 2587, 2822, 3285, 3303, 3909, 4343, 4877, 4921, 5367, 5675, 5708, 6678†,
Saint-Cloud 953a, 1163a, 1434a, 1746a, 2156a, 2570a, 3423a-3424a, 6864a, 7013a, 7449a, 7514a-7515a, 7693a, 7735a,
Salisbury 1889, 2200, 2420, 3009, 3187, 3504, 3658, 4104†, 4602, 5235, 5274, 5783, 5976, 6795, 7103,
Sandown 1644, 1677(M), 2426, 2637, 2852, 3117, 3156, 3822, 3876, 4220, 4470, 4512, 5005, 5790, 5832, 6203, 6370,
Sandown (AUS) 7783a
San Sebastian 5252a, 6089a,
San Siro 1554a, 2521a-2522a, 2968a, 3426a, 3684a, 6090a, 6554a, 6725a-6727a, 7075a-7076a, 7285a-7288a, 7427a, 7565a,
Santa Anita 7545a-7550a, 7566a-7577a,
Saratoga 4478a, 4617a,
Sha Tin 1902a, 8040a-8043a,
Southwell 1*, 8*, 19*, 95*, 109*, 133*, 283*, 366*, 380*, 453*, 490*, 551*, 579*, 640*, 670*, 747*, 807*, 830*, 883*, 898*, 973*, 1052*, 1173*, 1277*, 1427*, 1578*, 1955*, 1986*, 2400*, 3936*, 4139*, 4187*, 4401*, 5009*, 5241*, 5715*, 6806*, 7347*, 7605*, 7710*, 7726*, 7793*, 7874*†, 7883*†, 7907*†,
St Moritz 443a-444a, 629a-631a,
Taby 2807a, 6091a,
Thirsk 1520, 1861, 2091, 2282, 3250, 3436, 4545, 4778, 4825, 5167, 5410, 5797, 6042, 6335,
Tipperary 5067a, 5523a, 6917a,
Tokyo 7872a,
Toulouse 6595a, 7665a,
Velifendi 5848a-5849a, 5868a-5869a,
Vichy 4205a, 4229a, 4316a,
Warwick 1253, 1927†, 3216, 3311, 3539, 3828†, 4014†, 5446, 5681, 6814,
Windsor 1411, 1563, 1710†, 1934, 2124, 2342, 2556, 2937, 2983, 3222, 3443, 3637, 3666, 3700, 3915, 4146, 4408, 5417, 5591, 6926, 7110, 7296,
Wolverhampton 40*, 61*, 102*, 153*, 190*, 212*, 226*, 268*, 327*, 356*, 387*, 401*, 430*, 445*, 461*, 477*, 497*, 531*, 544*, 599*, 632*, 690*, 718*, 767*, 837*, 844*, 866*, 905*, 922*, 937*, 996*, 1010*, 1089*, 1111*, 1187*, 1337*, 1359*, 1387*, 1419*, 1481*, 1528*, 1585*, 1629*, 1716*, 1824*, 2130*, 2348*, 2858*, 3229*, 3449*, 3706*, 3943*, 4152*, 4651*, 4884*, 4927*, 5173*, 5206*, 5423*, 5748*, 5804*, 5886*, 6050*, 6174*, 6210*, 6316*, 6451*, 6496*, 6609*, 6640*, 6685*, 6765*, 6822*, 6836*, 6888*, 6934*, 6968*, 7020*, 7055*, 7141*, 7197*, 7218*, 7249*, 7355*, 7378*, 7410*, 7458*, 7523*, 7589*, 7613*, 7649*, 7666*, 7745*, 7775*, 7785*, 7837*, 7862*, 7914*, 7930*, 7952*, 7968*, 7976*, 8108*, 8131*, 8145*, 8207*, 8230*, 8237*, 8253*, 8269*, 8285*,
Woodbine 6289a, 6298a-6300a, 7092a-7094a,
Yarmouth 1261, 1284, 1738, 2008, 2461, 2797, 3046, 3082, 3545, 3788, 3973, 4194, 4433, 4658, 4966, 5016, 5213, 5453, 5631, 6343, 6377, 6411, 6844, 7311, 7466,
York 2176, 2208, 2252, 2504, 3123, 3163, 4069, 4110, 4553, 4608, 5487, 5515, 5558, 5597, 6070, 7028, 7063,

† Abandoned
* All-Weather
(M) Mixed meeting

Leading Turf Flat Trainers 2012

(31st March – 10th November 2012)

NAME	WINS-RUNS		2nd	3rd	4th	WIN £	TOTAL £	£1 STAKE
A P O'Brien	13–73	18%	7	12	6	£2,677,794	£3,554,170	+17.78
John Gosden	77–446	17%	73	70	59	£1,975,556	£3,505,778	-41.54
Sir Henry Cecil	47–231	20%	27	20	32	£2,163,734	£2,590,912	-32.15
Richard Hannon	173–1066	16%	151	115	105	£1,599,395	£2,559,527	-100.26
Mark Johnston	137–925	15%	97	103	89	£1,336,835	£1,965,601	-63.25
Richard Fahey	120–1044	11%	120	108	113	£1,147,244	£1,861,533	-176.33
Saeed Bin Suroor	47–305	15%	45	47	34	£836,718	£1,563,673	-47.55
Andrew Balding	67–501	13%	67	55	45	£709,178	£1,240,162	-130.83
William Haggas	65–345	19%	54	39	39	£662,615	£1,137,897	-24.59
Kevin Ryan	68–615	11%	60	61	56	£785,244	£1,132,590	+49.13
Mahm'd Al Zarooni	46–302	15%	40	33	27	£773,139	£1,128,311	-51.00
Tim Easterby	77–879	9%	89	83	86	£663,705	£995,279	-309.21
Roger Charlton	32–196	16%	24	26	12	£422,684	£963,947	-22.19
Mick Channon	90–793	11%	95	117	95	£471,361	£949,060	-245.24
Sir Michael Stoute	50–277	18%	41	36	28	£555,495	£939,510	-53.48
Roger Varian	49–292	17%	41	45	35	£436,105	£754,708	-43.43
Clive Cox	31–282	11%	41	29	32	£369,408	£676,958	-88.34
David O'Meara	59–471	13%	52	55	37	£495,306	£675,745	-20.36
Jeremy Noseda	25–166	15%	16	24	17	£475,082	£583,431	-41.22
Charles Hills	42–372	11%	40	41	37	£325,254	£576,636	-136.13
P Schiergen	1–3	33%	0	0	2	£567,100	£573,264	+7.00
Brian Meehan	31–294	11%	21	47	22	£440,019	£552,943	-43.20
David Simcock	38–288	13%	36	47	39	£218,753	£529,474	-90.86
Luca Cumani	37–229	16%	30	25	27	£331,932	£512,234	-27.65
James Fanshawe	13–125	10%	21	16	19	£232,166	£481,352	-39.50
Hughie Morrison	18–228	8%	30	24	30	£129,411	£460,727	-129.76
Ralph Beckett	38–271	14%	46	29	32	£237,657	£442,442	-65.38
Michael Bell	39–314	12%	33	39	21	£235,263	£440,848	-84.34
Tom Dascombe	46–295	16%	39	28	35	£276,865	£431,175	-29.18
David Barron	42–305	14%	28	30	42	£266,375	£424,762	-22.64
David Lanigan	6–64	9%	12	3	3	£44,107	£420,343	-44.86
Ed Dunlop	28–190	15%	23	23	21	£191,962	£412,984	-3.42
Jim Goldie	28–357	8%	23	26	40	£238,222	£394,233	-108.30
Marcus Tregoning	22–132	17%	13	13	21	£248,088	£392,234	+28.63
D K Weld	5–9	56%	0	1	0	£381,070	£389,678	+21.75
A De Royer-Dupre	2–9	22%	2	0	3	£266,537	£378,113	+5.00
Marco Botti	19–179	11%	22	24	18	£184,586	£344,234	-47.25
David Nicholls	37–403	9%	25	37	29	£185,594	£330,639	-111.33
J S Bolger	3–10	30%	1	0	1	£241,018	£319,359	-0.70
Sir Mark Prescott	28–151	19%	24	16	15	£138,306	£304,095	-48.37
Peter C-Hyam	22–131	17%	9	12	17	£242,596	£301,898	+48.76
Peter G Moody	1–1	100%	0	0	0	£283,550	£283,550	+0.17
John Dunlop	16–199	8%	18	27	20	£189,712	£282,759	-89.50
Mme C B-Barbe	0–1	—	1	0	0	£0	£279,500	-1.00
Michael Dods	35–320	11%	36	47	32	£165,727	£277,486	-85.96
Brian Ellison	32–259	12%	26	27	23	£182,063	£268,996	-27.76
David Elsworth	13–128	10%	13	11	13	£146,439	£238,765	-18.25
Eve J Houghton	16–180	9%	19	14	13	£61,816	£236,419	-45.92
Paul Messara	2–5	40%	0	0	1	£198,485	£222,712	+6.50
David Peter Nagle	3–8	38%	0	3	1	£200,356	£219,281	+14.75

Leading Turf Flat Jockeys 2012

(31st March – 10th November 2012)

NAME	WIN-RIDES		2nd	3rd	4th	WIN £	TOTAL £	£1 STAKE
Richard Hughes	143–669	21%	109	71	58	£1,342,207	£2,029,835	+3.29
William Buick	97–517	19%	62	70	59	£1,967,561	£3,338,725	-29.81
Paul Hanagan	88–610	14%	65	73	81	£1,128,962	£1,666,587	-102.99
Ryan Moore	86–479	18%	65	62	50	£1,336,143	£2,307,062	-56.51
S De Sousa	85–593	14%	76	78	49	£602,099	£975,308	-54.18
Joe Fanning	81–577	14%	68	68	59	£545,794	£791,716	-42.33
Graham Lee	71–625	11%	72	63	69	£408,138	£771,181	-57.00
Daniel Tudhope	68–449	15%	61	54	37	£511,729	£678,239	+53.58
Tom Queally	67–489	14%	47	40	51	£2,219,396	£2,649,125	-69.17
Kieren Fallon	67–468	14%	49	45	60	£1,076,875	£1,598,842	+7.84
Robert Winston	62–479	13%	54	47	54	£286,987	£457,700	-15.25
Paul Mulrennan	59–555	11%	54	62	65	£266,555	£459,088	-45.93
James Doyle	59–409	14%	34	46	43	£452,610	£989,220	+15.69
Jamie Spencer	58–435	13%	55	60	44	£664,092	£1,132,398	-88.64
Jim Crowley	55–413	13%	55	35	43	£541,083	£790,534	-23.86
Neil Callan	50–468	11%	63	59	50	£433,392	£747,896	-173.24
Franny Norton	49–348	14%	33	42	33	£549,114	£735,074	+50.73
Frederik Tylicki	48–323	15%	40	29	27	£252,831	£361,204	+124.62
Luke Morris	47–513	9%	61	61	65	£255,168	£488,928	-157.34
Tony Hamilton	47–456	10%	55	39	45	£319,123	£523,024	-130.62
Martin Harley	47–424	11%	43	54	56	£259,658	£553,514	-119.85
M Barzalona	47–304	15%	34	33	26	£817,185	£1,136,944	-3.47
Tom Eaves	45–598	8%	36	60	70	£152,308	£305,015	-232.59
Rich Kingscote	44–294	15%	46	31	36	£235,845	£434,590	-18.34
Graham Gibbons	43–419	10%	42	38	50	£207,252	£347,448	-124.41
Dane O'Neill	43–399	11%	44	32	51	£202,342	£328,798	-24.15
Chris Catlin	42–350	12%	33	35	30	£142,689	£234,805	-92.20
Phillip Makin	41–411	10%	33	38	41	£466,494	£583,629	-67.15
Hayley Turner	41–394	10%	43	49	42	£220,856	£521,333	-30.17
Pat Dobbs	40–311	13%	25	39	28	£533,610	£677,553	+32.41
Ian Mongan	39–285	14%	23	22	34	£159,790	£402,011	-48.28
David Probert	37–329	11%	38	33	32	£214,978	£340,823	-119.24
P J McDonald	35–428	8%	49	41	43	£165,993	£286,921	-108.15
David Allan	35–400	9%	52	38	45	£205,758	£418,256	-166.71
Amy Ryan	34–298	11%	31	33	33	£168,671	£301,426	-54.88
George Baker	34–284	12%	38	33	32	£286,063	£474,951	-28.74
Cathy Gannon	33–331	10%	25	33	34	£120,741	£199,651	-66.70
Frankie Dettori	33–329	10%	48	47	35	£745,757	£1,772,363	-165.33
M O'Connell	31–258	12%	17	37	28	£108,403	£147,614	-89.75
Jimmy Fortune	30–398	8%	53	42	32	£374,820	£1,064,022	-242.09
James Sullivan	29–455	6%	38	38	36	£142,214	£232,527	-140.00
Barry McHugh	29–358	8%	33	41	38	£135,732	£241,021	-60.75
Adam Kirby	29–249	12%	33	29	32	£314,763	£512,122	-55.95
Darren Egan	28–267	10%	27	30	16	£176,493	£246,112	-24.25
Andrea Atzeni	28–244	11%	21	20	27	£146,832	£236,017	-6.75
Duran Fentiman	27–401	7%	34	36	32	£329,680	£390,955	-157.67
Martin Lane	26–283	9%	23	33	36	£127,179	£229,514	-46.37
Dale Swift	26–248	10%	20	28	22	£112,496	£190,785	-84.51
Fergus Sweeney	25–292	9%	28	27	24	£82,263	£147,347	-67.00
Sean Levey	25–208	12%	26	18	28	£83,910	£153,552	-18.75

Leading Flat Owners 2012

(31st March – 10th November 2012)

NAME	WINS-RUNS		2nd	3rd	4th	WIN £	TOTAL £
K Abdulla	52–276	19%	40	35	34	£2,158,950	£3,034,992
Godolphin	93–596	16%	84	79	61	£1,772,516	£2,850,743
D Smith/Mrs J Magnier & M Tabor	5–29	17%	4	7	4	£1,909,993	£2,579,043
Sheikh Hamdan Bin Mohammed	69–474	15%	56	51	37	£791,541	£1,135,485
Hamdan Al Maktoum	63–440	14%	56	65	55	£714,194	£1,057,031
Dr Marwan Koukash	49–436	11%	56	36	51	£503,584	£833,703
George Strawbridge	16–60	27%	8	11	6	£282,642	£615,741
Lady Rothschild/Newsells Park	1–3	33%	1	1	0	£241,585	£596,465
Gestut Burg Eberstein/T Yoshida	1–1	100%	0	0	0	£567,100	£567,100
Mrs J Magnier/M Tabor & D Smith	7–22	32%	0	2	1	£438,873	£504,187
Mrs J Wood	9–72	13%	8	7	5	£440,537	£494,750
Lady Rothschild	23–68	34%	6	11	7	£381,704	£459,850
Cheveley Park Stud	19–134	14%	26	17	13	£174,806	£419,619
Niarchos Family	6–38	16%	5	5	7	£59,894	£403,083
C H Stevens	9–65	14%	10	9	3	£310,643	£402,787
David W Armstrong	9–65	14%	11	6	9	£352,029	£400,260
The Queen	15–79	19%	11	12	9	£155,332	£395,857
H R H Princess Haya Of Jordan	15–82	18%	12	10	10	£253,839	£392,274
Pearl Bloodstock Ltd	13–81	16%	14	8	9	£146,609	£326,678
Andrew Tinkler	21–193	11%	18	20	25	£139,482	£317,542
Lord Lloyd-Webber	2–6	33%	2	1	1	£141,775	£297,268
Helena Springfield Ltd	4–21	19%	4	1	2	£103,750	£283,784
Smith/Magnier/Tabor/DatoTan et al	1–1	100%	0	0	0	£283,550	£283,550
G J Wilkie, Mrs K J Wilkie et al	1–1	100%	0	0	0	£283,550	£283,550
Jean-Claude-Alain Dupouy	0–1	—	1	0	0	£0	£279,500
Qatar Racing Limited	5–60	8%	9	9	8	£33,683	£273,396
B E Nielsen	5–46	11%	5	6	1	£130,551	£269,052
Arashan Ali	3–7	43%	0	2	0	£236,011	£268,706
Kenneth Macpherson	5–14	36%	3	2	1	£192,447	£268,585
Sheikh Mohammed Bin Khalifa	6–25	24%	2	5	5	£86,722	£255,450
R J Arculli	6–41	15%	6	3	3	£117,386	£251,941
H R H Sultan Ahmad Shah	9–58	16%	3	6	5	£159,188	£236,798
Clipper Logistics	7–35	20%	6	6	1	£198,827	£232,913
Moyglare Stud Farm	2–12	17%	1	1	1	£228,794	£231,878
J C Smith	15–122	12%	14	11	16	£153,824	£231,601
Matt & Lauren Morgan	10–28	36%	3	3	1	£180,784	£225,836
A Fraser, Miss Fraser & Ms Ridley	2–5	40%	0	0	1	£198,485	£222,712
Lisbunny Syndicate	3–7	43%	0	3	0	£200,356	£219,161
Simon Gibson	1–13	8%	3	3	2	£127,598	£210,390
Sheikh Ahmed Al Maktoum	12–90	13%	17	17	14	£118,089	£205,795
Normandie Stud Ltd	4–26	15%	3	5	2	£178,036	£199,176
Ko Kam Piu	1–1	100%	0	0	0	£198,485	£198,485
Sir Robert Ogden	11–73	15%	9	9	6	£142,761	£197,309
Mrs H Steel	10–107	9%	15	10	15	£100,791	£190,896
Iraj Parvizi	3–25	12%	4	4	2	£173,117	£185,539
H H Aga Khan	1–3	33%	0	1	0	£175,801	£185,485
Teruya Yoshida	0–3	—	2	1	0	£0	£176,400
A D Spence	11–84	13%	10	9	7	£109,542	£170,875
John Guest Racing	4–49	8%	7	5	10	£76,805	£167,638
Anthony Pye-Jeary And Mel Smith	2–11	18%	4	1	0	£21,625	£161,626

Racing Post Top Rated 2012

(Best performance figures recorded between 1st January and 31st December 2012)

Frankel 143
Cirrus Des Aigles (FR) 132
Excelebration (IRE) 131
Black Caviar (AUS) 130
Hay List (AUS) 129
Orfevre (JPN) 129
Wise Dan (USA) 128
Fort Larned (USA) 128
Gold Ship (JPN) 128
So You Think (NZ) 127
Nathaniel (IRE) 127
Mucho Macho Man (USA) 127
Camelot 127
I'll Have Another (USA) 127
Dullahan (USA) 127
Cityscape 126
St Nicholas Abbey (IRE) 126
Snow Fairy (IRE) 126
Monterosso 126
Farhh 126
Caleb's Posse (USA) 126
Mental (AUS) 126
Gentildonna (JPN) 126
Bodemeister (USA) 126
Game On Dude (USA) 125
Rulership (JPN) 125
Dark Shadow (JPN) 125
Sea Moon 125
Amazombie (USA) 125
Foxwedge (AUS) 125
More Joyous (NZ) 124
Successful Dan (USA) 124
Dunaden (FR) 124
Ron The Greek (USA) 124
Reliable Man 124
Eishin Flash (JPN) 124
To The Glory (JPN) 124
Camp Victory (USA) 124
Danedream (GER) 124
Moonlight Cloud 124
Solemia (IRE) 124
Little Bridge (NZ) 124
Ambitious Dragon (NZ) 124
Shackleford (USA) 124
Atlantic Jewel (AUS) 124
Ocean Blue (JPN) 124
Able One (NZ) 123
Mufhasa (NZ) 123
Smart Falcon (JPN) 123
Flat Out (USA) 123
Jackson Bend (USA) 123
Krypton Factor 123
Stay Thirsty (USA) 123
Animal Kingdom (USA) 123
To Honor And Serve (USA) 123
Shonan Mighty (JPN) 123
Royal Delta (USA) 123
Groupie Doll (USA) 123
Union Rags (USA) 123
Trinniberg (USA) 123
Fenomeno (JPN) 123
Emcee (USA) 123
Dawn Approach (IRE) 123
Paynter (USA) 123
Point Of Entry (USA) 123
Tosen Jordan (JPN) 122
Society Rock (IRE) 122
Acclamation (USA) 122
Musir (AUS) 122
Monton (AUS) 122
Nates Mineshaft (USA) 122
Carlton House (USA) 122
Meandre (FR) 122
Trailblazer (JPN) 122
The Factor (USA) 122
Questing 122
Rain Affair (AUS) 122
Pastorius (GER) 122
Lord Kanaloa (JPN) 122
Ocean Park (NZ) 122
Pierro (AUS) 122
Sky Dignity (JPN) 122
Danleigh (AUS) 121
Americain (USA) 121
Atomic Force (AUS) 121
Ortensia (AUS) 121
Love Conquers All (AUS) 121
California Memory (USA) 121
Xtension (IRE) 121
Bated Breath 121
Little Mike (USA) 121
Soul (AUS) 120
Brown Panther 120
Fiorente (IRE) 120

Raceform median times 2013

ASCOT

5f....................1m 0.5
5f 110y....................1m 08.3
6f....................1m 14.5
6f 110y....................1m 21.0
7f....................1m 27.6
1m Str....................1m 40.8
1m Rnd....................1m 40.7
1m 2f....................2m 7.4
1m 4f....................2m 32.5
2m....................3m 29.0
2m 4f....................4m 24.8
2m 5f 159y....................4m 49.4

AYR

5f....................59.4s
6f....................1m 12.4
7f 50y....................1m 33.4
1m....................1m 43.8
1m 1f 20y....................1m 57.5
1m 2f....................2m 12.0
1m 5f 13y....................2m 54.0
1m 7f....................3m 20.4
2m 1f 105y....................3m 59.7

BATH

5f 11y....................1m 2.5
5f 161y....................1m 11.2
1m 5y....................1m 40.8
1m 2f 46y....................2m 11.0
1m 3f 144y....................2m 30.6
1m 5f 22y....................2m 52.0
2m 1f 34y....................3m 51.9

BEVERLEY

5f....................1m 3.5
7f 100y....................1m 33.8
1m 100y....................1m 47.6
1m 1f 207y....................2m 7.0
1m 4f 16y....................2m 39.8
2m 35y....................3m 39.8

BRIGHTON

5f 59y....................1m 2.3
5f 213y....................1m 10.2
6f 209y....................1m 23.1
7f 214y....................1m 36.0
1m 1f 209y....................2m 3.6
1m 3f 196y....................2m 32.7

CARLISLE

5f....................1m 0.8
5f 193y....................1m 13.7
6f 192y....................1m 27.1
7f 200y....................1m 40.0
1m 1f 61y....................1m 57.6
1m 3f 107y....................2m 23
1m 6f 32y....................3m 7.5
2m 1f 52y....................3m 53.0

CATTERICK

5f....................59.8s
5f 212y....................1m 13.6
7f....................1m 27.0
1m 3f 214y....................2m 38.9
1m 5f 175y....................3m 3.6
1m 7f 177y....................3m 32.0

CHEPSTOW

5f 16y....................59.3s
6f 16y....................1m 12.0
7f 16y....................1m 23.2
1m 14y....................1m 36.2
1m 2f 36y....................2m 10.6
1m 4f 23y....................2m 39.0
2m 49y....................3m 38.9
2m 2f....................4m 3.6

CHESTER

5f 16y....................1m 1.0
5f 110y....................1m 6.2
6f 18y....................1m 13.8
7f 2y....................1m 26.5
7f 122y....................1m 33.8
1m 2f 75y....................2m 11.2
1m 3f 79y....................2m 24.8
1m 4f 66y....................2m 38.5
1m 5f 89y....................2m 52.7
1m 7f 195y....................3m 28.0
2m 2f 147y....................4m 4.8

DONCASTER

5f....................1m 0.5
5f 140y....................1m 8.8
6f....................1m 13.6
6f 110y....................1m 19.9
7f....................1m 26.3
1m Str....................1m 39.3
1m Rnd....................1m 39.7
1m 2f 60y....................2m 9.4
1m 4f....................2m 34.9
1m 6f 132y....................3m 7.4
2m 110y....................3m 40.4
2m 2f....................3m 55.0

EPSOM

5f....................55.7s
6f....................1m 9.4
7f....................1m 23.3
1m 114y....................1m 46.1
1m 2f 18y....................2m 9.7
1m 4f 10y....................2m 38.9

FFOS LAS

5f....................58.3s
6f....................1m 10.0
1m....................1m 41.0
1m 2f....................2m 9.4
1m 4f....................2m 37.4
1m 6f....................3m 3.8
2m 3m 30.0

FOLKESTONE

5f....................1m
6f....................1m 12.7
7f....................1m 27.3
1m 1f 149y....................2m 4.9
1m 4f....................2m 40.9
1m 7f 92y....................3m 29.7
2m 93y....................3m 37.2

GOODWOOD

5f....................1m 0.2
6f....................1m 12.2
7f....................1m 27.0
1m....................1m 39.9
1m 1f....................1m 56.3
1m 1f 192y....................2m 8.1
1m 3f....................2m 26.5
1m 4f....................2m 38.4
1m 6f....................3m 3.6
2m....................3m 29.0
2m 5f....................4m 31.0

HAMILTON

5f 4y....................1m
6f 5y....................1m 12.2
1m 65y....................1m 48.4
1m 1f 36y....................1m 59.7
1m 3f 16y....................2m 25.6
1m 4f 17y....................2m 38.6
1m 5f 9y....................2m 53.9

HAYDOCK

5f (inner)....................1m 0.8
5f (outer)....................a1m 0.8
6f (inner)....................1m 13.8
6f (outer)....................1m 13.8
7f....................1m 30.7
1m 1m 43.7
1m 2f 95y....................2m 15.5
1m 3f 200y....................2m 33.8
1m 6f....................3m 2.0
2m 45y....................3m 34.3

KEMPTON AW

5f....................1m 0.5
6f....................1m 13.1
7f....................1m 26.0
1m....................1m 39.8
1m 2f....................2m 8.0
1m 3f....................2m 21.9
1m 4f....................2m 34.5
2m....................3m 30.1

LEICESTER

5f 2y....................1m
5f 218y....................1m 13.0
7f 9y....................1m 26.2
1m 60y....................1m 45.1
1m 1f 218y....................2m 7.9
1m 3f 183y....................2m 33.9

LINGFIELD TURF

5f....................58.2s
6f....................1m 11.2
7f....................1m 23.3
7f 140y....................1m 32.3
1m 1f....................1m 56.6
1m 2f....................2m 10.5
1m 3f 106y....................2m 31.5
1m 6f....................3m 10.0
2m....................3m 34.8

LINGFIELD AW

5f....................58.8s
6f....................1m 11.9
7f....................1m 24.8
1m 1m 38.2
1m 2f....................2m 6.6
1m 4f....................2m 33.0
1m 5f....................2m 46.0
2m....................3m 25.7

MUSSELBURGH

5f....................1m 0.4
7f 30y....................1m 29.0
1m....................1m 41.2
1m 1f....................1m 53.9
1m 4f....................2m 39.7
1m 4f 100y....................2m 42.0
1m 5f....................2m 52.0
1m 6f....................3m 5.3
2m....................3m 33.5

NEWBURY

5f 34y....................1m 1.4
6f 8y....................1m 13.0
6f 110y....................1m 19.3
7f....................1m 25.7
1m Str....................1m 39.7
1m Rnd....................1m 38.7
1m 1f....................1m 55.5
1m 2f 6y....................2m 8.8
1m 3f 5y....................2m 21.2
1m 4f 5y....................2m 35.5
1m 5f 61y....................2m 52.0
2m....................3m 32.0

NEWCASTLE

5f................................1m 1.1
6f 1m 14.6
7f 1m 27.8
1m Rnd...........................1m 45.3
1m 3y Str 1m 43.4
1m 1f 9y.........................1m 58.1
1m 2f 32y.......................2m 11.9
1m 4f 93y 2m 45.6
1m 6f 97y.......................3m 11.3
2m 19y...........................3m 39.4

NEWMARKET ROWLEY

5f................................59.1s
6f 1m 12.2
7f 1m 25.4
1m................................1m 38.6
1m 1f.............................1m 51.7
1m 2f.............................2m 5.8
1m 4f.............................2m 32.0
1m 6f.............................2m 57.0
2m................................3m 30.5
2m 2f.............................3m 52.0

NEWMARKET JULY

5f................................59.1s
6f 1m 12.5
7f 1m 25.7
1m................................1m 40.0
1m 2f.............................2m 5.5
1m 4f.............................2m 32.9
1m5f..............................2m 44.0
1m 6f 175y......................3m 8.4
2m 24y...........................3m 27.0

NOTTINGHAM

5f 13y............................1m 1.5
6f 15y 1m 14.7
1m 75y...........................1m 49.0
1m 2f 50y.......................2m 14.3
1m 6f 15y.......................3m 7.0
2m 9y 3m 34.5

PONTEFRACT

5f................................1m 3.3
6f 1m 16.9
1m 4y 1m 45.9
1m 2f 6y 2m 13.7
1m 4f 8y 2m 40.8
2m 1f 22y.......................3m 44.6
2m 1f 216y.....................3m 56.2
2m 5f 122y.....................4m 51.0

REDCAR

5f................................58.6s
6f 1m 11.8
7f 1m 24.5
1m................................1m 38.0
1m 1f.............................1m 53.0
1m 2f.............................2m 7.1
1m 3f.............................2m 21.7
1m 6f 19y.......................3m 4.7
2m 4y 3m 31.4

RIPON

5f................................1m 0.7
6f 1m 13.0
1m................................1m 41.4
1m 1f.............................1m 54.7
1m 1f 170y 2m 5.4
1m 4f 10y 2m 36.7
2m................................3m 31.8

SALISBURY

5f................................1m 1.0
6f 1m 14.8
6f 212y...........................1m 28.6
1m................................1m 43.5
1m 1f 198y.......................2m 9.9
1m 4f.............................2m 38.0
1m 6f 21y.......................3m 7.4

SANDOWN

5f 6y 1m 1.6
7f 16y 1m 29.5
1m 14y...........................1m 43.3
1m 1f.............................1m 55.7
1m 2f 7y 2m 10.5
1m 6f.............................3m 4.5
2m 78y...........................3m 38.7

SOUTHWELL AW

5f................................59.7s
6f 1m 16.5
7f 1m 30.3
1m................................1m 43.7
1m 3f.............................2m 28.0
1m 4f.............................2m 41.0
1m 6f.............................3m 8.3
2m................................3m 45.5

THIRSK

5f................................59.6s
6f 1m 12.7
7f 1m 27.2
1m................................1m 40.1
1m 4f.............................2m 36.2
2m................................3m 28.3

WARWICK

5f................................59.6s
5f 110y...........................1m 5.9
6f 1m 11.8
7f 26y 1m 24.6
1m 22y...........................1m 41.0
1m 2f 188y.......................2m 21.1
1m 4f 134y.......................2m 44.6
1m 6f 213y.......................3m 19.0
2m 39y...........................3m 33.8

WINDSOR

5f 10y 1m 0.3
6f 1m 13.0
1m 67y...........................1m 44.7
1m 2f 7y 2m 8.7
1m 3f 135y.......................2m 29.5

WOLVERHAMPTON AW

5f 20y 1m 2.3
5f 216y...........................1m 15.0
7f 32y 1m 29.6
1m 141y 1m 50.5
1m 1f 103y.......................2m 1.7
1m 4f 50y........................2m 41.1
1m 5f 194y.......................3m 6.0
2m 119y..........................3m 41.8

YARMOUTH

5f 43y 1m 2.7
6f 3y 1m 14.4
7f 3y 1m 26.6
1m 3y.............................1m 40.6
1m 1f.............................1m 55.8
1m 2f 21y.......................2m 10.5
1m 3f 101y.......................2m 28.7
1m 6f 17y.......................3m 7.6
2m................................3m 32.4

YORK

5f................................59.3s
5f 89y 1m 4.1
6f 1m 11.9
7f 1m 25.3
1m................................1m 39.8
1m 208y...........................1m 52.0
1m 2f 88y 2m 12.5
1m 4f.............................2m 33.2
1m 6f.............................3m 0.2
2m 88y 3m 34.5
2m 2f.............................3m 55.4

Raceform Flat Record Times

ASCOT

Distance	Time	Age	Weight	Going	Horse	Date
5f	59.17 sec	2	8-12	Gd To Firm	Maqaasid	Jun 16 2010
5f	57.44 sec	6	9-1	Gd To Firm	Miss Andretti (AUS)	Jun 19 2007
6f	1m 12.46	2	9-1	Gd To Firm	Henrythenavigator(USA)	Jun 19 2007
6f	1m 11.50	3	9-10	Gd To Firm	Mince	Aug 11 2012
7f	1m 26.76	2	7-12	Gd To Firm	Relative Order	Aug 11 2007
7f	1m 24.94	3	8-12	Gd To Firm	Rainfall (IRE)	Jun 16 2010
1m (R)	1m 39.55	2	8-12	Good	Joshua Tree (IRE)	Sep 26 2009
1m (R)	1m 38.32	3	9-0	Gd To Firm	Ghanaati (USA)	Jun 19 2009
1m (S)	1m 37.16	4	8-9	Gd To Firm	Invisible Man	Jun 16 2010
1m 2f	2m 2.52	5	9-3	Good	Cirrus Des Aigles(FR)	Oct 15 2011
1m 4f	2m 26.78	4	9-7	Good	Harbinger	Jul 24 2010
2m	3m 24.13	3	9-1	Gd To Firm	Holberg (UAE)	Sept 16 2009
2m 4f	4m 16.92	6	9-2	Gd To Firm	Rite Of Passage	Jun 17 2010
2m 5f 159y	4m 47.90	7	9-2	Gd To Firm	Bergo (GER)	Jun 19 2010

AYR

Distance	Time	Age	Weight	Going	Horse	Date
5f	56.9 secs	2	8-11	Good	Boogie Street	Sep 18 2003
5f	55.68 secs	3	8-11	Gd to Firm	Look Busy (IRE)	Jun 21 2008
6f	69.7 secs	2	7-10	Good	Sir Bert	Sep 17 1969
6f	68.37 secs	5	8-6	Gd to Firm	Maison Dieu	Jun 21 2008
7f	1m 25.7	2	9-0	Gd to Firm	Jazeel	Sep 16 1993
7f	1m 24.9	5	7-11	Firm	Sir Arthur Hobbs	Jun 19 1992
7f 50y	1m 28.9	2	9-0	Good	Tafaahum (USA)	Sep 19 2003
7f 50y	1m 28.07	5	9-0	Gd to Firm	Ginger Jack	May 30 2012
1m	1m 39.2	2	9-0	Gd to Firm	Kribensis	Sep 17 1986
1m	1m 36.0	4	7-13	Firm	Sufi	Sep 16 1959
1m 1f 20y	1m 50.3	4	9-3	Good	Retirement	Sep 19 2003
1m 2f	2m 4.0	4	9-9	Gd to Firm	Endless Hall	Jly 17 2000
1m 2f192y	2m 13.3	4	9-0	Gd to Firm	Azzaam	Sep 18 1991
1m 5f 13y	2m 45.8	4	9-7	Gd to Firm	Eden's Close	Sep 18 1993
1m 7f	3m 13.1	3	9-4	Good	Romany Rye	Sep 19 1991
2m 1f105y	3m 45.0	4	6-13	Good	Curry	Sep 16 1955

BATH

Distance	Time	Age	Weight	Going	Horse	Date
5f 11y	59.50 secs	2	9-2	Firm	Amour Propre	Jly 24 2008
5f 11y	58.75 secs	3	8-12	Firm	Enticing (IRE)	May 1 2007
5f 161y	68.70 secs	2	8-12	Firm	Qalahari (IRE)	Jly 24 2008
5f 161y	68.1 secs	6	9-0	Firm	Madraco	May 22 1989
1m 5y	1m 39.7	2	8-9	Firm	Casual Look	Sep 16 2002
1m 5y	1m 37.2	5	8-12	Gd to Firm	Adobe	Jun 17 2000
1m 5y	1m 37.2	3	8-7	Firm	Alasha (IRE)	Aug 18 2002
1m 2f 46y	2m 5.83		9-0	Gd to Firm	Connoisseur Bay(USA)	May 29 1998
1m 3f144y	2m 25.74	3	9-0	Hard	Top Of The Charts	Sep 8 2005
1m 5f 22y	2m 47.2	4	10-0	Firm	Flown	Aug 13 1991
2m 1f 34y	3m 43.4	6	7-9	Firm	Yaheska (IRE)	Jun 14 2003

BEVERLEY

Distance	Time	Age	Weight	Going	Horse	Date
5f	61.0 secs	2	8-2	Gd to Firm	Addo (IRE)	Jly 17 2001
5f	60.1 secs	4	9-5	Firm	Pic Up Sticks	Apr 16 2003
7f 100y	1m 31.1	2	9-7	Gd to Firm	Champagne Prince	Aug 10 1995
7f 100y	1m 31.1	2	9-0	Firm	Majal (IRE)	Jly 30 1991
7f 100y	1m 29.5	3	7-8	Firm	Who's Tef	Jly 30 1991
1m 100y	1m 43.3	2	9-0	Firm	Arden	Sep 24 1986
1m 100y	1m 42.2	3	8-4	Firm	Legal Case	Jun 14 1989
1m 1f 207y	2m 1.00	3	9-7	Gd to Firm	Eastern Aria (UAE)	Aug 29 2009
1m 3f 216y	2m 30.8	3	8-1	Hard	Coinage	Jun 18 1986
1m 4f 16y	2m 34.88	6	10-0	Firm	WeeCharlieCastle(IRE)	Aug 30 2009
2m 35y	3m 29.5	4	9-2	Gd to Firm	Rushen Raider	Aug 14 1996

BRIGHTON

Distance	Time	Age	Weight	Going	Horse	Date
5f 59y	60.1 secs	2	9-0	Firm	Bid for Blue	May 6 1993
5f 59y	59.3 secs	3	8-9	Firm	Play Hever Golf	May 26 1993
5f 213y	68.1 secs	2	8-9	Firm	Song Mist (IRE)	Jly 16 1996
5f 213y	67.3 secs	3	8-9	Firm	Third Party	Jun 3 1997
5f 213y	67.3 secs	5	9-1	Gd to Firm	Blundell Lane	May 4 2000
6f 209y	1m 19.9	2	8-11	Hard	Rain Burst	Sep 15 1988
6f 209y	1m 19.4	4	9-3	Gd to Firm	Sawaki	Sep 3 1991
7f 214y	1m 32.8	2	9-7	Firm	Asian Pete	Oct 3 1989
7f 214y	1m 30.5	5	8-11	Firm	Mystic Ridge	May 27 1999
1m 1f 209y	2m 4.7	2	9-0	Gd to Soft	Esteemed Master	Nov 2 2001
1m 1f 209y	1m 57.2	3	9-0	Firm	Get The Message	Apr 30 1984
1m 3f 196y	2m 25.8	4	8-2	Firm	New Zealand	Jly 4 1985

CARLISLE

Distance	Time	Age	Weight	Going	Horse	Date
5f	60.1 secs	2	8-5	Firm	La Tortuga	Aug 2 1999
5f	58.8 secs	3	9-8	Gd to Firm	Esatto	Aug 21 2002
5f 193y	1m 12.45	2	9-6	Gd to Firm	Musical Guest (IRE)	Sep 11 2005
5f 193y	1m 10.83	4	9-0	Gd to Firm	Bo McGinty (IRE)	Sep 11 2005
6f 192y	1m 24.3	3	8-9	Gd to Firm	Marjurita (IRE)	Aug 21 2002
6f 206y	1m 26.5	2	9-4	Hard	Sense of Priority	Sep 10 1991
6f 206y	1m 25.3	4	9-1	Firm	Move With Edes	Jly 6 1996
7f 200y	1m 37.34	5	9-7	Gd to Firm	Hula Ballew	Aug 17 2005
7f 214y	1m 44.6	2	8-8	Firm	Blue Garter	Sep 9 1980
7f 214y	1m 37.3	5	7-12	Hard	Thatched (IRE)	Aug 21 1995
1m 1f 61y	1m 53.8	3	9-0	Firm	Little Jimbob	Jun 14 2004
1m 3f 107y	2m 22.00	7	9-5	Gd to Firm	Tartan Gigha	Jun 4 2012
1m 4f	2m 28.8	3	8-5	Firm	Desert Frolic (IRE)	Jun 27 1996
1m 6f 32y	3m 2.2	6	8-10	Firm	Explosive Speed	May 26 1994
2m 1f 52y	3m 46.2	3	7-10	Gd to Firm	Warring Kingdom	Aug 25 1999

CATTERICK

Distance	Time	Age	Weight	Going	Horse	Date
5f	57.6 secs	2	9-0	Firm	H Harrison	Oct 8 2002
5f	57.1 secs	4	8-7	Fast	Kabcast	Jly 7 1989
5f 212y	1m 11.4	2	9-4	Firm	Captain Nick	Jly 11 1978
5f 212y	69.8 secs	9	8-13	Gd to Firm	Sharp Hat	May 30 2003
7f	1m 24.1	2	8-11	Firm	Lindas Fantasy	Sep 18 1982
7f	1m 22.5	6	8-7	Firm	Differential (USA)	May 31 2003
1m 3f 214y	2m 30.5	3	8-8	Gd to Firm	Rahaf	May 30 2003
1m 5f 175y	2m 54.8	3	8-5	Firm	Geryon	May 31 1984
1m 7f 177y	3m 20.8	4	7-11	Firm	Bean Boy	Jly 8 1982

CHEPSTOW

Distance	Time	Age	Weight	Going	Horse	Date
5f 16y	57.6 secs	2	8-11	Firm	Micro Love	Jly 8 1986
5f 16y	56.8 secs	3	8-4	Firm	Torbay Express	Sep 15 1979
6f 16y	68.5 secs	2	9-2	Firm	Ninjago	Jly 27 2012
6f 16y	68.1 secs	3	9-7	Firm	America Calling (USA)	Sep 18 2001
7f 16y	1m 20.8	2	9-0	Gd to Firm	Royal Amaretto (IRE)	Sep 12 1996
7f 16y	1m 19.3	3	9-0	Firm	Taranaki	Sep 18 2001
1m 14y	1m 33.1	2	8-11	Gd to Firm	Ski Academy (IRE)	Aug 28 1995
1m 14y	1m 31.6	3	8-13	Firm	Stoli (IRE)	Sep 18 2001
1m 2f 36y	2m 4.1	5	8-9	Hard	Leonidas	Jly 5 1983
1m 2f 36y	2m 4.1	5	7-8	Gd to Firm	It's Varadan	Sep 9 1989
1m 2f 36y	2m 4.1	3	8-5	Gd to Firm	Ela Athena	Jly 23 1999
1m 4f 23y	2m 31.0	3	8-9	Gd to Firm	Spritsail	Jly 13 1989
1m 4f 23y	2m 31.0	7	9-6	Hard	Maintop	Aug 27 1984
2m 49y	3m 27.7	4	9-0	Gd to Firm	Wizzard Artist	Jly 1 1989
2m 2f	3m 56.4	5	8-7	Gd to Firm	Laffah	Jly 8 2000

CHESTER

Distance	Time	Age	Weight	Going	Horse	Date
5f 16y	59.94 secs	2	9-2	Gd to Firm	Leiba Leiba	Jun 26 2010
5f 16y	59.2 secs	3	10-0	Firm	Althrey Don	Jly 10 1964
6f 18y	1m 12.8	2	8-10	Gd to Firm	Flying Express	Aug 31 2002
6f 18y	1m 12.7	3	8-3	Gd to Firm	Play Hever Golf	May 4 1993
6f 18y	1m 12.7	6	9-2	Good	Stack Rock	Jun 23 1993
7f 2y	1m 25.2	2	9-0	Gd to Firm	Due Respect (IRE)	Sep 25 2002
7f 2y	1m 23.75	5	8-13	Gd to Firm	Three Graces (GER)	Jly 9 2005
7f 122y	1m 32.2	2	9-0	Gd to Firm	Big Bad Bob (IRE)	Sep 25 2002
7f 122y	1m 30.91	3	8-12	Gd to Firm	Cupid's Glory	Aug 18 2005
1m 2f 75y	2m 7.15	3	8-8	Gd to Firm	Stotsfold	May 7 2002
1m 3f 79y	2m 22.17	3	8-12	Gd to Firm	Perfect Truth (IRE)	May 6 2009
1m 4f 66y	2m 33.7	3	8-10	Gd to Firm	Fight Your Corner	May 7 2002
1m 5f 89y	2m 45.4	5	8-11	Firm	Rakaposhi King	May 7 1987
1m 7f 195y	3m 20.3	4	9-0	Gd to Firm	Grand Fromage (IRE)	Jly 13 2002
2m 2f 147y	3m 58.89	7	9-2	Gd to Firm	Greenwich Meantime	May 9 2007

DONCASTER

Distance	Time	Age	Weight	Going	Horse	Date
5f	58.1 secs	2	8-11	Gd to Firm	Sand Vixen	Sep 11 2009
5f	57.2 secs	6	9-12	Gd to Firm	Celtic Mill	Sep 9 2004
5f 140y	67.2 secs	2	9-0	Gd to Firm	Cartography (IRE)	Jun 29 2003
5f 140y	65.6 secs	9	9-10	Good	Halmahera (IRE)	Sep 8 2004
6f	69.6 secs	2	8-11	Good	Caesar Beware (IRE)	Sep 8 2004
6f	69.56 secs	3	8-10	Gd to Firm	Proclaim	May 30 2009
6f 110y	1m 17.22	2	8-3	Gd to Firm	Swilly Ferry (USA)	Sep 10 2009
7f	1m 22.6	2	9-1	Good	Librettist (USA)	Sep 8 2004
7f	1m 21.6	3	8-10	Gd to Firm	Pastoral Pursuits	Sep 9 2004
1m	1m 36.5	2	8-6	Gd to Firm	Singhalese	Sep 9 2004
1m (R)	1m 35.4	2	8-10	Good	Playful Act (IRE)	Sep 9 2004

1649

1m	1m 35.52	4	8-9	Gd to Firm	Dream Lodge	Jly 24 2008
1m (R)	1m 34.46	4	8-12	Gd to Firm	Staying On (IRE)	Apr 18 2009
1m 2f 60y	2m 13.4	2	8-8	Good	Yard Bird	Nov 6 1981
1m 2f 60y	2m 4.81	4	8-13	Gd to Firm	Red Gala	Sep 12 2007
1m 4f	2m 27.48	3	8-4	Gd to Firm	Swift Alhaarth (IRE)	Sep 10 2011
1m 6f 132y	3m 0.44	3	9-0	Gd to Firm	Masked Marvel	Sep 10 2011
2m 2f	3m 48.41	4	9-4	Gd to Firm	Septimus (IRE)	Sep 14 2007

EPSOM

Distance	Time	Age	Weight	Going	Horse	Date
5f	55.0 secs	2	8-9	Gd to Firm	Prince Aslia	Jun 9 1995
5f	53.6 secs	4	9-5	Firm	Indigenous	Jun 2 1960
6f	67.8 secs	2	8-11	Gd to Firm	Showbrook	Jun 5 1991
6f	67.21 secs	5	9-13	Gd to Firm	Mac Gille Eoin	Jul 2 2009
7f	1m 21.3	2	8-9	Gd to Firm	Red Peony	Jly 29 2004
7f	1m 20.1	4	8-7	Firm	Capistrano	Jun 7 1972
1m 114y	1m 42.8	2	8-5	Gd to Firm	Nightstalker	Aug 30 1988
1m 114y	1m 40.7	3	8-6	Gd to Firm	Sylva Honda	Jun 5 1991
1m 2f 18y	2m 3.5	5	7-13	Good	Crossbow	Jun 7 1967
1m 4f 10y	2m 31.33	3	9-0	Gd to Firm	Workforce	Jun 5 2010

FFOS LAS

Distance	Time	Age	Weight	Going	Horse	Date
5f	57.06	2	9-3	Gd To Firm	Mr Majeika (IRE)	May 5 2011
5f	56.35	5	8-8	Good	Haajes	Sep 12 2009
6f	69.93	2	9-0	Gd To Firm	Lunair Deity	Jul 28 2011
6f	67.80	8	8-4	Gd To Firm	The Jailer	May 5 2011
1m	1m 40.61	2	9-0	Gd To Firm	Sharaayeen	Sep 13 2009
1m	1m 37.12	5	9-0	Gd To Firm	Zebrano	May 5 2011
1m 2f	2m 4.85	8	8-12	Gd To Firm	Pelham Crescent (IRE)	May 5 2011
1m 4f	2m 32.61	5	9-8	Gd To Firm	Lady Of Burgundy	Jly 11 2011
1m 6f	2m 58.61	4	9-7	Gd To Firm	Lady Eclair	Jly 12 2010
2m	3m 29.86	4	9-7	Good	Black Or Red (IRE)	Jly 21 2009

FOLKESTONE

Distance	Time	Age	Weight	Going	Horse	Date
5f	58.4 secs	2	9-2	Gd to Firm	Pivotal	Nov 6 1995
5f	58.18 secs	4	8-8	Gd to Firm	Black Baccara	Apr 12 2011
6f	1m 10.8	2	8-9	Good	Boomerang Blade	Jly 16 1998
6f	69.38 secs	4	9-8	Gd to Firm	Munaddam (USA)	Sep 18 2006
6f 189y	1m 23.7	2	8-11	Good	Hen Harrier	Jly 3 1996
6f 189y	1m 21.4	3	8-9	Firm	Cielamour (USA)	Aug 9 1988
7f	1m 25.01	2	9-0	Gd to Firm	Dona Alba (IRE)	Sep 2 2007
7f	1m 23.76	3	8-11	Gd to Firm	Welsh Cake	Sep 18 2006
1m 1f 149y	1m 59.7	3	8-6	Gd to Firm	Dizzy	Jly 23 1991
1m 4f	2m 33.2	4	8-8	Hard	Snow Blizzard	Jun 30 1992
1m 7f 92y	3m 22.97	4	8-10	Gd to Firm	Alfraamsey	Jun 29 2012
2m 93y	3m 34.9	3	8-12	Gd to Firm	Candle Smoke (USA)	Aug 20 1996

GOODWOOD

Distance	Time	Age	Weight	Going	Horse	Date
5f	57.51 secs	2	9-0	Good	Requinto	Jul 26 2011
5f	56.0 secs	5	9-0	Gd to Firm	Rudi's Pet	Jly 27 1999
6f	69.8 secs	2	8-11	Gd to Firm	Bachir (IRE)	Jly 28 1999
6f	69.10 secs	6	9-10	Gd to Firm	Tamagin (USA)	Sep 12 2009
7f	1m 24.9	2	8-11	Gd to Firm	Ekraar	Jly 29 1999
7f	1m 23.8	3	8-7	Firm	Brief Glimpse (IRE)	Jly 25 1995
1m	1m 37.21	2	9-0	Good	Caldra (IRE)	Sep 9 2006
1m 1f	1m 56.27	2	9-3	Gd to Firm	Dordogne (IRE)	Sep 22 2010
1m	1m 35.6	3	8-13	Gd to Firm	Aljabr (USA)	Jly 28 1999
1m 1f	1m 52.8	3	9-6	Good	Vena (IRE)	Jly 27 1995
1m 1f 192y	2m 2.81	3	9-3	Gd to Firm	Road To Love (IRE)	Aug 3 2006
1m 3f	2m 23.0	3	8-8	Gd to Firm	Asian Heights	May 22 2001
1m 4f	2m 31.5	3	8-10	Firm	Presenting	Jly 25 1995
1m 6f	2m 57.61	4	9-6	Gd to Firm	Meeznah (USA)	Jly 28 2011
2m	3m 21.55	5	9-10	Gd to Firm	Yeats (IRE)	Aug 3 2006
2m 4f	4m 11.7	3	7-10	Firm	Lucky Moon	Aug 2 1990

HAMILTON

Distance	Time	Age	Weight	Going	Horse	Date
5f 4y	57.95 secs	2	8-8	Gd to Firm	Rose Blossom	May 29 2009
5f 4y	57.95 secs	2	8-8	Gd to Firm	Rose Blossom	May 29 2009
6f 5y	1m 10.0	2	8-12	Gd to Firm	Break The Code	Aug 24 1999
6f 5y	69.3 secs	4	8-7	Firm	Marcus Game	Jly 11 1974
1m 65y	1m 45.8	2	8-11	Firm	Hopeful Subject	Sep 24 1973
1m 65y	1m 42.7	6	7-7	Firm	Cranley	Sep 25 1972
1m 1f 36y	1m 53.6	5	9-6	Gd to Firm	Regent's Secret	Aug 10 2005
1m 3f 16y	2m 19.32	3	9-0	Gd to Firm	Captain Webb	May 16 2008
1m 4f 17y	2m 30.52	5	9-10	Gd to Firm	Record Breaker (IRE)	Jun 10 2009
1m 5f 9y	2m 45.1	6	9-6	Firm	Mentalasanythin	Jun 14 1995

HAYDOCK

Distance	Time	Age	Weight	Going	Horse	Date
5f	58.56 secs	2	8-2	Gd to Firm	Barracuda Boy	Aug 11 2012
5f	57.15 secs	3	8-11	Gd to Firm	Fleeting Spirit (IRE)	May 24 2008
6f	1m 10.9	4	9-9	Gd to Firm	Wolfhound (USA)	Sep 4 1993
6f	69.9 secs	4	9-0	Gd to Firm	Iktamal (USA)	Sep 7 1996
7f	1m 27.62	2	9-4	Good	Tickle Time (IRE)	Aug 10 2012
7f	1m 26.27	4	9-1	Gd to Firm	Zacynthus	Sep 7 2012
1m 30y*	1m 40.6	2	8-12	Gd to Firm	Besiege	Sep 7 1996
1m	1m 39.02	3	8-11	Good	Lady MacDuff	Aug 10 2012
1m2f 95y	2m 9.95	3	8-8	Good	Jukebox Jury (IRE)	Aug 8 2009
1m 2f 120y*	2m 22.22		8-11	Soft	Persian Haze	Oct 9 1994
1m 2f 95y	2m 8.25	3	9-0	Gd to Firm	Prussian	Sep 7 2012
1m 3f 200y	2m 25.53	4	8-12	Gd to Firm	Number Theory	May 24 2012
1m 6f	2m 55.20	5	9-9	Gd to Firm	Huff And Puff	Sep 7 2012
2m 45y	3m 27.0	4	8-13	Firm	Prince of Peace	May 26 1984
2m 1f 130y	3m 55.0	3	8-12	Good	Crystal Spirit	Sep 8 1990

* Record for old distance

KEMPTON (AW)

Distance	Time	Age	Weight	Going	Horse	Date
5f	60.29 sec	2	9-1	Standard	Inflight (IRE)	Aug 23 2006
5f	58.33 sec	3	9-1	Standard	Exceedance	May 7 2012
6f	1m 11.44	2	9-5	Standard	Signs In The Sand	Oct 6 2010
6f	1m 10.77	7	9-7	Standard	Capone(IRE)	Nov 1 2012
7f	1m 23.95	2	8-10	Standard	Tamarkuz	Oct 10 2012
7f	1m 23.29	5	8-11	Standard	Primaeval	Nov 16 2011
1m	1m 37.50	2	9-4	Standard	I'm Back (IRE)	Oct 3 2012
1m	1m 35.73	3	8-9	Standard	Western Aristocrat(USA)	Sep15 2011
1m 2f	2m 3.77	6	8-13	Standard	Kandidate	Mar 29 2008
1m 3f	2m 16.98	5	9-6	Standard	Irish Flame (SAF)	Nov 10 2011
1m 4f	2m 28.99	6	9-3	Standard	Spring Of Fame (USA)	Nov 7 2012
2m	3m 21.50	4	8-12	Standard	Colour Vision (FR)	May 2 2012

LEICESTER

Distance	Time	Age	Weight	Going	Horse	Date
5f 2y	58.4 secs	2	9-0	Firm	Cutting Blade	Jun 9 1986
5f 2y	57.85 secs	5	9-5	Gd to Firm	The Jobber (IRE)	Sep 18 2006
5f 218y	69.99	2	9-0	Good	El Manati (IRE)	Aug 1 2012
5f 218y	69.12 secs	6	8-12	Gd to Firm	Peter Island (FR)	Apr 25 2009
7f 9y	1m 22.60	2	9-0	Gd to Firm	Marie De Medici (USA)	Oct 6 2009
7f 9y	1m 20.8	3	8-7	Firm	Flower Bowl	Jun 9 1986
1m 60y	1m 44.05	2	8-11	Gd to Firm	Congressional (IRE)	Sep 6 2005
1m 60y	1m 41.89	5	9-7	Gd to Firm	Vainglory	Jun 18 2009
1m 1f 218y	2m 5.3	2	9-1	Gd to Firm	Windsor Castle	Oct 14 1996
1m 1f 218y	2m 2.4	3	8-11	Firm	Effigy	Nov 4 1985
1m 1f 218y	2m 2.4	4	9-6	Gd to Firm	Lady Angharad (IRE)	Jun 18 2000
1m 3f 183y	2m 27.1	5	8-12	Gd to Firm	Murghem (IRE)	Jun 18 2000

LINGFIELD (TURF)

Distance	Time	Age	Weight	Going	Horse	Date
5f	57.07 secs	2	9-0	Gd to Firm	Quite A Thing	Jul 11 2011
5f	56.09 secs	3	9-4	Gd to Firm	Whitecrest	Sep 16 2011
6f	68.36 secs	2	8-12	Gd to Firm	Folly Bridge	Sept 8 2009
6f	68.2 secs	6	9-10	Firm	Al Amead	Jly 2 1986
7f	1m 21.3	2	7-6	Firm	Mandav	Oct 3 1980
7f	1m 20.05	3	8-5	Gd to Firm	Perfect Tribute	May 7 2011
7f 140y	1m 28.7	2	9-3	Gd to Firm	Al Muheer	Aug 4 2007
7f 140y	1m 26.7	3	8-6	Fast	Hiaam	Nov 7 1978
1m 1f	1m 52.4	4	9-2	Gd to Firm	Quandary (USA)	Jly 15 1995
1m 2f	2m 4.6	3	9-3	Firm	Usran	Jly 15 1989
1m 3f 106y	2m 23.9	3	8-5	Firm	Night-Shirt	Jly 14 1990
1m 6f	2m 59.1	5	9-5	Firm	Ibn Bey	Jly 1 1989
2m	3m 23.7	3	9-5	Gd to Firm	Lauries Crusader	Aug 13 1988

LINGFIELD (AW)

Distance	Time	Age	Weight	Going	Horse	Date
5f	58.46 secs	2	8-2	Standard	Ruby Tallulah	Aug 12 2008
5f	57.26 secs	8	8-12	Standard	Magic Glade	Feb 24 2007
6f	1m 10.75	2	9-4	Standard	Global City (IRE)	Oct 15 2008
6f	69.61	6	9-0	Standard	Excusez Moi (USA)	Feb 23 2008
6f	69.61	4	9-5	Standard	Jaconet (USA)	Sept 4 2009
7f	1m 23.68	2	8-4	Standard	Young Dottie	Oct 21 2008
7f	1m 22.19	4	8-7	Standard	Red Spell	Nov 19 2005
1m	1m 36.22	2	9-7	Standard	Yarroom	Dec 5 2012
1m	1m 34.77	4	9-3	Standard	Baharah (USA)	Oct 30 2008
1m 2f	2m 1.79	5	9-0	Standard	Cusoon	Feb 24 2007
1m 4f	2m 27.97	4	9-3	Standard	Midsummer Sun	Aug 14 2012
1m 5f	2m 42.47	3	9-2	Standard	Raffaas	July 3 2007
2m	3m 20.0	3	9-0	Standard	Yenoora	Aug 8 1992

MUSSELBURGH

Distance	Time	Age	Weight	Going	Horse	Date
5f	57.7 secs	2	8-2	Firm	Arasong	May 16 1994
5f	57.3 secs	3	8-12	Firm	Corunna	Jun 3 2000
7f 30y	1m 27.46	2	8-8	Good	DurhamReflection(IRE)	Sept 14 2009
7f 30y	1m 26.3	3	9-5	Firm	Waltzing Wizard	Aug 22 2002
1m	1m 40.3	2	8-12	Gd to Firm	Succession	Sep 26 2004

1m	1m 36.83	3	9-5	Gd to Firm	Ginger Jack	Jul 13 2010
1m 1f	1m 50.42	8	8-11	Gd to Firm	Dhaular Dhar	Sept 3 2010
1m 4f	2m 33.7	3	9-11	Firm	Alexandrine	Jun 26 2000
1m4f 100y	2m 36.80	3	8-3	Gd to Firm	Harris Tweed	Jun 5 2010
1m 5f	2m 47.51	6	9-11	Gd to Firm	Dimashq	Jly 31 2008
1m 6f	2m 59.2	3	9-7	Firm	Forum Chris	Jly 3 2000
2m	3m 26.6	5	9-6	Gd to Firm	Jack Dawson (IRE)	Jun 1 2002

NEWBURY

Distance	Time	Age	Weight	Going	Horse	Date
5f 34y	59.1 secs	2	8-6	Gd to Firm	Superstar Leo	Jly 22 2000
5f 34y	59.2 secs	3	9-5	Gd to Firm	The Trader (IRE)	Aug 18 2001
6f 8y	1m 11.07	2	8-4	Gd to Firm	Bahati (IRE)	May 30 2009
6f 8y	69.42 secs	3	8-11	Gd to Firm	Nota Bene	May 13 2005
7f	1m 23.0	2	8-11	Gd to Firm	Haafhd	Aug 15 2003
7f	1m 21.5	3	8-4	Gd to Firm	Three Points	Jly 21 2000
1m	1m 37.5	2	9-1	Gd to firm	Winged Cupid (IRE)	Sep 16 2005
1m	1m 33.59	6	9-0	Firm	Rakti	May 14 2005
1m 1f	1m 49.6	3	8-0	Gd to Firm	Holtye	May 21 1995
1m 2f 6y	2m 1.2 3		8-7	Gd to Firm	Wall Street (USA)	Jly 20 1996
1m 3f 5y	2m 16.5	3	8-9	Gd to Firm	Grandera (IRE)	Sep 22 2001
1m 4f 5y	2m 28.26	4	9-7	Gd to Firm	Azamour (IRE)	Jul 23 2005
1m 5f 61y	2m 44.9	5	10-0	Gd to Firm	Mystic Hill	Jly 20 1996
2m	3m 25.4	8	9-12	Gd to Firm	Moonlight Quest	Jly 19 1996

NEWCASTLE

Distance	Time	Age	Weight	Going	Horse	Date
5f	58.8 secs	2	9-0	Firm	Atlantic Viking (IRE)	Jun 4 1997
5f	58.0 secs	4	9-2	Firm	Princess Oberon	Jly 23 1994
6f	1m 11.98	2	9-3	Good	Pearl Arch (IRE)	Sep 6 2010
6f	1m 10.58	4	9-9	Gd to Firm	Jonny Mudball	Jun 26 2010
7f	1m 24.2	2	9-0	Gd to Firm	Iscan (IRE)	Aug 31 1998
7f	1m 23.3	4	9-2	Gd to Firm	Quiet Venture	Aug 31 1998
1m	1m 38.9	2	9-0	Gd to Firm	Stowaway	Oct 2 1996
1m	1m 38.9	3	8-12	Firm	Jacamar	Jly 22 1989
1m 3y	1m 37.1	2	8-3	Gd to Firm	Hoh Steamer (IRE)	Aug 31 1998
1m 3y	1m 37.3	3	8-8	Gd to Firm	Its Magic	May 27 1999
1m 1f 9y	2m 3.2 2		8-13	Soft	Response	Oct 30 1993
1m 1f 9y	1m 52.3	3	6-3	Good	Ferniehurst	Jun 23 1936
1m 2f 32y	2m 6.5 4		8-9	Fast	Missionary Ridge	Jly 29 1990
1m 4f 93y	2m 37.3	5	8-12	Firm	Retender	Jun 25 1994
1m 6f 97y	3m 6.4 3		9-6	Gd to Firm	One Off	Aug 6 2003
2m 19y	3m 24.3	4	8-10	Good	Far Cry (IRE)	Jun 26 1999

NEWMARKET (ROWLEY)

Distance	Time	Age	Weight	Going	Horse	Date
5f	58.7 secs	2	8-5	Gd to Firm	Valiant Romeo	Oct 3 2002
5f	56.8 secs	6	9-2	Gd to Firm	Lochsong	Apr 30 1994
6f	69.56 secs	2	8-12	Gd to Firm	Bushranger (IRE)	Oct 3 2008
6f	69.56 secs	2	8-12	Gd to Firm	Bushranger (IRE)	Oct 3 2008
7f	1m 22.39	2	8-12	Gd to Firm	Ashram (IRE)	Sep 21 2004
7f	1m 22.18	3	9-0	Gd to Firm	Codemaster	May 14 2011
1m	1m 35.67	2	8-12	Good	Steeler (IRE)	Sep 29 2012
1m	1m 34.07	4	9-0	Gd to Firm	Eagle Mountain	Oct 3 2008
1m 1f	1m 47.2	4	9-5	Firm	Beauchamp Pilot	Oct 5 2002
1m 2f	2m 4.6 2		9-4	Good	Highland Chieftain	Nov 2 1985
1m 2f	2m 0.13	3	8-12	Good	New Approach (IRE)	Oct 18 2008
1m 4f	2m 26.07	3	8-9	Gd to Firm	Mohedian Lady (IRE)	Sep 22 2011
1m 6f	2m 51.59	3	8-7	Good	Art Eyes (USA)	Sep 29 2005
2m	3m 18.64	5	9-6	Gd to Firm	Times Up	Sep 22 2011
2m 2f	3m 47.5	3	7-12	Hard	Whiteway	Oct 15 1947

NEWMARKET (JULY)

Distance	Time	Age	Weight	Going	Horse	Date
5f	58.5 secs	2	8-10	Good	Seductress	Jly 10 1990
5f	56.09 secs	6	9-11	Good	Borderlescott	Aug 22 2008
6f	1m 10.35	2	8-11	Good	Elnawin	Aug 22 2008
6f	69.5 secs	3	8-13	Gd to Firm	Stravinsky (USA)	Jly 8 1999
7f	1m 23.57	2	9-5	Gd to Firm	Light Up My Life	Aug 18 2012
7f	1m 22.59	3	9-7	Firm	Ho Leng (IRE)	Jul 9 1998
1m	1m 37.47	2	8-13	Good	Whippers Love (IRE)	Aug 28 2009
1m	1m 35.5	3	8-6	Gd to Firm	Lovers Knot	Jly 8 1998
1m 110y	1m 44.1	3	8-11	Good	Golden Snake	Apr 15 1999
1m 2f	2m 0.9 4		9-3	Gd to Firm	Elhayq (IRE)	May 1 1999
1m 4f	2m 25.11	3	8-11	Good	Lush Lashes	Aug 22 2008
1m 6f 175y	3m 4.2 3		8-5	Good	Arrive	Jly 11 2001
2m 24y	3m 20.2	7	9-10	Good	Yorkshire	Jly 11 2001

NOTTINGHAM

Distance	Time	Age	Weight	Going	Horse	Date
5f 13y	57.9 secs	2	8-9	Firm	Hoh Magic	May 13 1994
5f 13y	57.6 secs	6	9-2	Gd to firm	Catch The Cat (IRE)	May 14 2005
6f 15y	1m 11.4	2	811	Firm	Jameelapi	Aug 8 1983
6f 15y	1m 10.0	4	9-2	Firm	Ajanac	Aug 8 1988
1m75y	1m 45.23	2	9-0	Gd to Firm	Tactfully	Sep 28 2011
1m 75y	1m 42.25	5	9-1	Gd To Firm	Rio De La Plata	Jun 2 2010
1m 1f 213y	2m 5.6 2		9-0	Firm	Al Salite	Oct 28 1985
1m 1f 213y	2m 2.3 2		9-0	Firm	Ayaabi	Jly 21 1984
1m 2f 50y	2m 09.54	4	9-12	Gd To Firm	Geneva Geyser	Jly 3 2010
1m 6f 15y	2m 57.8	3	8-10	Firm	Buster Jo	Oct 1 1985
2m 9y	3m 24.0	5	7-7	Firm	Fet	Oct 5 2036
2m 2f 18y	3m 55.1	9	9-10	Gd to Firm	Pearl Run	May 1 1990

PONTEFRACT

Distance	Time	Age	Weight	Going	Horse	Date
5f	61.1 secs	2	9-0	Firm	Golden Bounty	Sep 20 2001
5f	60.8 secs	4	8-9	Firm	Blue Maeve	Sep 29 2004
6f	1m 14.0	2	9-3	Firm	Fawzi	Sep 6 1983
6f	1m 12.6	3	7-13	Firm	Merry One	Aug 29 1970
1m 4y	1m 42.8	2	9-13	Firm	Star Spray	Sep 6 1983
1m 4y	1m 42.8	2	9-0	Firm	Alasil (USA)	Sep 26 2002
1m 4y	1m 40.6	4	9-10	Gd to Firm	Island Light	Apr 13 2002
1m 2f 6y	2m 10.1	2	9-0	Firm	Shanty Star	Oct 7 2002
1m 2f 6y	2m 8.2 4		7-8	Hard	Happy Hector	Jly 9 1979
1m 2f 6y	2m 8.2 3		7-13	Hard	Tom Noddy	Aug 21 1972
1m 4f 8y	2m 33.72	3	8-7	Firm	Ajaan	Aug 8 2007
2m 1f 22y	3m 40.67	4	8-7	Gd to Firm	Paradise Flight	June 6 2005
2m 1f 216y	3m 51.1 3		8-8	Firm	Kudz	Sep 9 1986
2m 5f 122y	4m 47.8 4		8-4	Firm	Physical	May 14 1984

REDCAR

Distance	Time	Age	Weight	Going	Horse	Date
5f	56.9 secs	2	9-0	Firm	Mister Joel	Oct 24 1995
5f	56.01 secs	10	9-3	Firm	Henry Hall	Sep 20 2006
6f	68.8 secs	2	8-3	Gd to Firm	Obe Gold	Oct 2 2004
6f	68.6 secs	3	9-2	Gd to Firm	Sizzling Saga	Jun 21 1991
7f	1m 21.28	2	9-3	Firm	Karoo Blue	Sep 20 2006
7f	1m 21.0	3	9-1	Firm	Empty Quarter	Oct 3 1995
1m	1m 34.37	2	9-0	Firm	Mastership	Sep 20 2006
1m	1m 32.42	4	10-0	Firm	Nanton	Sep 20 2006
1m 1f	1m 52.4	2	9-0	Firm	Spear (IRE)	Sep 13 2004
1m 1f	1m 48.5	5	8-12	Firm	Mellottie	Jly 25 1990
1m 2f	2m 10.1	2	8-11	Good	Adding	Nov 10 1989
1m 2f	2m 1.4 5		9-2	Firm	Eradicate	May 28 1990
1m 3f	2m 17.2	3	8-9	Firm	Photo Call	Aug 7 1990
1m 5f 135y	2m 54.7 6		9-10	Firm	Brodessa	Jun 20 1992
1m 6f 19y	2m 59.81	4	9-1	Gd to Firm	Esprit De Corps	Sep 11 2006
2m 4y	3m 24.9	3	9-3	Gd to Firm	Subsonic	Oct 8 1991
2m 3f	4m 10.1	5	7-4	Gd to Firm	Seldom In	Aug 9 1991

RIPON

Distance	Time	Age	Weight	Going	Horse	Date
5f	57.8 secs	2	8-8	Firm	Super Rocky	Jly 5 1991
5f	57.6 secs	5	8-5	Good	Broadstairs Beauty	May 21 1995
6f	1m 10.4	2	9-2	Good	Cumbrian Venture	Aug 17 2002
6f	69.8 secs	4	9-8	Gd to Firm	Tadeo	Aug 16 1997
6f	69.8 secs	5	7-10	Firm	Quoit	Jly 23 1966
1m	1m 39.79	2	8-6	Good	Top Jaro (FR)	Sep 24 2005
1m	1m 36.62	4	8-11	Gd to Firm	Granston (IRE)	Aug 29 2005
1m 1f 170y	1m 59.12	5	8-9	Gd to Firm	Wahoo Sam (USA)	Aug 30 2005
1m 2f	2m 2.6 3		9-4	Firm	Swift Sword	Jly 20 1990
1m 4f 10y	2m 31.40	4	8-8	Gd to Firm	Dandino	Apr 16 2011
2m	3m 27.07	5	9-12	Gd to Firm	Greenwich Meantime	Aug 30 2005

SALISBURY

Distance	Time	Age	Weight	Going	Horse	Date
5f	59.3 secs	2	9-0	Gd to Firm	Ajigolo	May 12 2005
5f	59.3 secs	2	9-0	Gd to Firm	Ajigolo	May 12 2005
6f	1m 12.1	2	8-0	Gd to Firm	Parisian Lady (IRE)	Jun 10 1997
6f	1m 11.09	3	9-0	Firm	L'Ami Louis (IRE)	May 1 2011
6f 212y	1m 25.9	2	9-0	Firm	More Royal (USA)	Jun 29 1995
6f 212y	1m 24.91	3	9-7	Firm	Chilworth Lad	May 1 2011
1m	1m 40.4	2	8-13	Firm	Choir Master (USA)	Sep 17 2002
1m	1m 38.29	3	8-7	Gd to Firm	Layman (USA)	Aug 11 2005
1m 1f 198y	2m 4.81 3		8-5	Gd to Firm	Primevere (IRE)	Aug 10 2011
1m 4f	2m 31.6	3	9-5	Gd to Firm	Arrive	Jun 27 2001
1m 6f 15y	2m 59.4	3	8-6	Gd to Firm	Tabareeh	Sep 2 1999

SANDOWN

Distance	Time	Age	Weight	Going	Horse	Date
5f 6y	59.4 secs	2	9-3	Firm	Times Time	Jly 22 1982
5f 6y	58.8 secs	6	8-9	Gd to Firm	Palacegate Touch	Sep 17 1996
7f 16y	1m 26.56	2	9-0	Gd to Firm	Raven's Pass (USA)	Sep 1 2007
7f 16y	1m 26.3	3	9-0	Firm	Mawsuff	Jun 14 1983
1m 14y	1m 41.1	2	8-11	Fast	Reference Point	Sep 23 1986
1m 14y	1m 39.0	3	8-8	Firm	Linda's Fantasy	Aug 19 1983
1m 1f	1m 54.6	2	8-8	Gd to Firm	French Pretender	Sep 20 1988
1m 1f	1m 52.4	7	9-3	Gd to Firm	Bourgainville	Aug 11 2005
1m 2f 7y	2m 2.1 4		8-11	Firm	Kalaglow	May 31 1982
1m 3f 91y	2m 21.6	4	8-3	Fast	Aylesfield	Jly 7 1984

1m 6f	2m 56.9	4	8-7	Gd to Firm	Lady Rosanna	Jly 19 1989
2m 78y	3m 29.86	4	9-0	Gd to Firm	King Of Wands	Jul 3 2010

SOUTHWELL (AW)

Distance	Time	Age	Weight	Going	Horse	Date
5f	57.85 secs	2	9-3	Standard	Arctic Feeling	Mar 31 2010
5f	56.80 secs	5	9-7	Standard	Ghostwing	Jan 24 2008
6f	1m 14.00	2	8-5	Standard	Panalo	Nov 8 1989
6f	1m 13.50	4	10-02	Standard	Saladan Knight	Dec 30 1989
7f	1m 26.82	2	8-12	Standard	Winged Icarus	Aug 28 2012
7f	1m 26.80	5	8-4	Standard	Amenable	Dec 13 1990
1m	1m 38.00	2	8-9	Standard	Alpha Rascal	Nov 13 1990
1m	1m 38.00	2	8-10	Standard	Andrew's First	Dec 30 1989
1m	1m 37.25	3	8-6	Standard	Valira	Nov 3 1990
1m 3f	2m 21.50	4	9-7	Standard	Tempering	Dec 5 1990
1m 4f	2m 33.90	4	9-12	Standard	Fast Chick	Nov 8 1989
1m 6f	3m 1.60	3	7-8	Standard	Erevnon	Dec 29 1990
2m	3m 37.60	9	8-12	Standard	Old Hubert	Dec 5 1990

THIRSK

Distance	Time	Age	Weight	Going	Horse	Date
5f	57.2 secs	2	9-7	Gd to Firm	Proud Boast	Aug 5 2000
5f	56.9 secs	5	9-6	Firm	Charlie Parkes	April 11 2003
6f	69.2 secs	2	9-6	Gd to Firm	Westcourt Magic	Aug 25 1995
6f	68.8 secs	6	9-4	Firm	Johayro	Jly 23 1999
7f	1m 23.7	2	8-9	Firm	Courting	Jly 23 1999
7f	1m 22.8	4	8-5	Firm	Silver Haze	May 21 1988
1m	1m 37.9	2	9-0	Firm	Sunday Symphony	Sep 4 2004
1m	1m 34.8	4	8-13	Firm	Yearsley	May 5 1990
1m 4f	2m 29.9	5	9-12	Firm	Gallery God	Jun 4 2001
2m	3m 22.3	3	8-11	Firm	Tomaschek	Jly 17 1981

WARWICK

Distance	Time	Age	Weight	Going	Horse	Date
5f	57.95 secs	2	8-9	Gd to Firm	Amour Propre	Jun 26 2008
5f	57.7 secs	4	9-6	Gd to Firm	Little Edward	Jly 7 2002
5f 110y	63.6 secs	5	8-6	Gd to Firm	Dizzy In The Head	Jun 27 2004
6f	1m 11.22	2	9-3	Gd to Firm	Hurricane Hymnbook	Sep 15 2007
6f	69.44	5	8-12	Gd to Firm	Peter Island	Jun 26 2008
7f 26y	1m 22.9	2	9-0	Firm	Country Rambler(USA)	Jun 20 2004
7f 26y	1m 20.7	4	8-8	Good	Etlaala	Apr 17 2006
1m 22y	1m 37.1	3	8-11	Firm	Orinocovsky (IRE)	Jun 26 2002
1m 2f 188y	2m 14.98	4	8-12	Gd to Firm	Ronaldsay	Jun 16 2008
1m 4f 134y	2m 39.5	3	8-13	Gd to Firm	Maimana (IRE)	Jun 22 2002
1m 6f 135y	3m 7.5	3	9-7	Gd to Firm	Burma Baby (USA)	Jly 2 1999
2m 39y	3m 27.9	3	8-1	Firm	Decoy	Jun 26 2002

WINDSOR

Distance	Time	Age	Weight	Going	Horse	Date
5f 10y	58.69 secs	2	9-0	Gd to Firm	Charles the Great (IRE)	May 23 2011
5f 10y	58.08 secs	5	8-13	Gd to Firm	Taurus Twins	Apr 4 2011
6f	1m 10.5	2	9-5	Gd to Firm	Cubism (USA)	Aug 17 1998
6f	69.89 secs	4	9-0	Gd to Firm	Bated Breath	May 23 2011
1m 67y	1m 42.46	2	8-9	Gd to Firm	Tiger Cub	Oct 11 2011
1m 67y	1m 40.19	4	9-4	Good	Nationalism	Jun 25 2011
1m 2f 7y	2m 3.02		9-1	Firm	Moomba Masquerade	May 19 1990
1m2f 7y	2m 2.44	4	9-0	Gd to Firm	Campanologist (USA)	Aug 29 2009
1m 3f 135y	2m 21.5	3	9-2	Firm	Double Florin	May 19 1980

WOLVERHAMPTON (AW)

Distance	Time	Age	Weight	Going	Horse	Date
5f 20y	60.96 sec	2	9-3	Standard	Moviesta (USA)	Sep 17 2012
5f 20y	60.22 sec	5	9-3	Standard	Deerslayer (USA)	Aug 30 2011
5f 216y	1m 12.61	2	9-0	Std to Fast	Prime Defender	Nov 8 2006
5f 216y	1m 13.32	5	8-12	Standard	Desert Opal	Sep 17 2005
7f 32y	1m 27.70	2	9-5	Standard	Billy Dane	Aug 14 2006
7f 32y	1m 26.42	7	8-12	Standard	Prime Exhibit	Sept 8 2012
1m 141y	1m 47.68	2	9-3	Standard	Glory City	Dec 26 2012
1m 141y	1m 46.48	3	8-9	Standard	Gitano Hernando	Sept 17 2009
1m 1f 103y	2m 0.74	2	8-4	Standard	Lucy Bee	Dec 3 2012
1m 1f 103y	1m 57.34	4	8-13	Standard	Bahar Shumaal (IRE)	Aug 31 2006
1m 4f 50y	2m 35.71	3	9-2	Std to Fast	Steppe Dancer (IRE)	Aug 30 2006
1m 5f 194y	2m 58.68	3	9-2	Standard	Instrumentalist	Oct 9 2012
2m 119y	3m 35.85	5	8-11	Std to Fast	Market Watcher (USA)	Nov 21 2006

YARMOUTH

Distance	Time	Age	Weight	Going	Horse	Date
5f 43y	60.4 secs	2	8-6	Gd to Firm	Ebba	Jly 26 1999
5f 43y	59.8 secs	4	8-13	Gd to Firm	Roxanne Mill	Aug 25 2002
6f 3y	1m 10.4	2	9-0	Fast	Lanchester	Aug 15 1988
6f 3y	69.9 secs	4	8-9	Firm	Malhub (USA)	Jun 13 2002
7f 3y	1m 22.2	2	9-0	Gd to Firm	Warrshan	Sep 14 1988
7f 3y	1m 22.12	4	9-4	Gd to Firm	Glenbuck (IRE)	Apr 26 2007
1m 3y	1m 36.3	2	8-2	Gd to Firm	Outrun	Sep 15 1988
1m 3y	1m 33.9	3	8-8	Firm	Bonne Etoile	Jun 27 1995
1m 1f	1m 52.0	3	9-5	Gd to Firm	Touch Gold	Jul 5 2012
1m 2f 21y	2m 2.83	3	8-8	Firm	Reunite (IRE)	Jul 18 2006
1m 3f 101y	2m 23.1	3	8-9	Firm	Rahil	Jly 1 1993
1m 6f 17y	2m 57.8	3	8-2	Gd to Firm	Barakat	Jly 24 1990
2m	3m 26.7	4	8-2	Gd to Firm	Alhesn (USA)	Jly 26 1999
2m 2f 51y	3m 56.8	4	9-10	Firm	Provence	Sep 19 1991

YORK

Distance	Time	Age	Weight	Going	Horse	Date
5f	57.3 secs	2	7-8	Gd to Firm	Lyric Fantasy	Aug 20 1992
5f	56.1 secs	3	9-3	Gd to Firm	Dayjur	Aug 23 1990
5f 89y	63.20 secs	2	9-3	Gd to Firm	The Art Of Racing	Sep 9 2012
5f 89y	62.31 secs	6	9-5	Gd to Firm	Barney McGrew (IRE)	Aug 18 2009
6f	69.28 secs	2	8-12	Gd to Firm	Showcasing	Aug 19 2009
6f	68.23 secs	3	8-11	Gd to Firm	Mince	Sep 9 2012
7f	1m 22.45	2	9-0	Gd to Firm	ElusivePimpernel(USA)	Aug 18 2009
7f	1m 21.83	4	9-8	Gd to Firm	Dimension	Jly 28 2012
1m	1m 39.20	2	8-1	Gd to Firm	Missoula (IRE)	Aug 31 2005
1m	1m 36.24	3	9-2	Gd to Firm	Capponi	Jul 10 2010
1m 208y	1m 46.76	5	9-8	Gd to Firm	Echo Of Light	Sep 5 2007
1m 2f 88y	2m 5.29	3	8-11	Gd to Firm	Sea The Stars (IRE)	Aug 18 2009
1m 4f	2m 26.28	6	8-9	Firm	Bandari (IRE)	Jun 18 2005
1m 6f	2m 54.96	4	9-0	Gd to Firm	Tactic	May 22 2010
1m 7f 195y	3m 18.4	3	8-0	Gd to Firm	Dam Busters	Aug 16 1988
2m 88y	3m 30.55	5	9-0	Gd to Firm	Herostatus	Jly 28 2012

Raceform Flat speed figures 2012

Best time performances achieved 1st January to 31st December 2012 (min rating 110, 2-y-o 105)

THREE YEAR-OLDS AND UPWARDS – TURF

Afsare 114 (10 1/2f,Yor,GF,Jly 28)
After 112 (6f,Leo,S,Jun 14)
Aiken 112 (16f,Asc,S,Oct 20)
Alanza 112 (7f,Nby,GF,Aug 18)
Aljamaaheer 110 (8f,Goo,G,Aug 3)
Alla Speranza 111 (10f,Leo,G,Sep 8)
Allied Powers 110 (12 1/2f,Dea,G,Aug 26)
Amaron 112 (8f,Lon,GS,May 13)
Ambivalent 112 (14 1/2f,Don,G,Sep 13)
American Devil 111 (6 1/2f,Dea,VS,Aug 5)
Amira's Prince 110 (10f,Nmk,GS,Apr 19)
Angels Will Fall 111 (5f,Ayr,G,Jun 23)
Archbishop 111 (8f,Goo,G,Aug 3)
Arsaadi 113 (10f,Nmk,GS,Apr 19)
Art Scholar 111 (12f,Don,G,Nov 10)
Askar Tau 112 (16f,Asc,S,Oct 20)
Astrology 110 (12f,Eps,GF,Jun 2)
Athens 110 (11f,Lon,GS,May 13)

Ballesteros 111 (5f,Lon,HY,Oct 7)
Ballybacka Lady 112 (8f,Leo,S,Aug 16)
Barefoot Lady 112 (9f,Yor,G,Aug 24)
Bated Breath 121 (5f,Hay,F,May 26)
Bear Behind 111 (5f,Mus,GS,Apr 7)
Beauty Parlour 113 (8f,Lon,GS,May 13)
Beauvoir 110 (8f,Lon,GS,May 13)
Bertiewhittle 110 (7f,Asc,G,Jly 21)
Beyond Desire 113 (5f,Lon,GS,May 13)
Bite Of The Cherry 111 (14 1/2f,Don,G,Sep 13)
Black Spirit 110 (10f,Asc,S,Jun 22)
Blue Corner 115 (10f,Cur,G,May 27)
Blue Soave 113 (7f,Lon,G,Sep 9)
Bogart 110 (6f,Yor,G,May 16)
Bonfire 115 (10 1/2f,Yor,G,May 17)
Borderlescott 114 (5f,Hay,F,May 26)
Born To Sea 112 (12f,Cur,SH,Jun 30)
Brae Hill 110 (8f,Don,G,Mar 31)
Bronze Angel 111 (9f,Nmk,G,Sep 29)
Brown Panther 114 (12f,Asc,GS,Jly 21)
Bullet Train 111 (10 1/2f,Yor,GF,Aug 22)

Calahorra 111 (5f,Lon,GS,May 13)
Caledonia Lady 111 (5f,San,GS,Jly 7)
Call To Battle 110 (10f,Leo,G,Apr 15)
Camborne 111 (12f,Asc,S,Oct 6)
Camelot 114 (12f,Eps,GF,Jun 2)
Canticum 117 (15f,Lon,VS,Oct 6)
Caponata 111 (10f,Cur,G,Sep 9)
Carlton House 117 (10f,Asc,G,Jun 20)
Caspar Netscher 113 (8f,Dea,G,Aug 12)
Caucus 113 (16f,Nmk,G,Sep 27)
Cavalryman 111 (16f,Nmk,G,Sep 27)
Chachamaidee 110 (8f,Asc,G,Jun 20)
Chiberta King 110 (16 1/2f,San,GF,May 31)
Chigun 110 (8f,Nmk,G,Sep 28)
Cirrus Des Aigles 117 (10 1/2f,Lon,HY,Apr 29)
City Style 114 (10f,Asc,G,Jun 20)
Cityscape 113 (8f,Dea,G,Aug 12)
Colombian 113 (10f,Asc,G,Jun 20)
Communicator 110 (13 1/2f,Chs,G,Sep 1)
Confessional 113 (5f,Hay,F,May 26)
Coral Wave 110 (8f,Leo,GS,May 13)
Coupe De Ville 111 (8f,Lon,GS,May 13)
Crackentorp 111 (16f,Ncs,HY,Jun 30)

Dabirsim 112 (8f,Lon,GS,May 13)
Dalkala 110 (15 1/2f,Lon,HY,Oct 28)
Dancing Rain 110 (12f,Asc,S,Oct 20)
Dandy Boy 111 (6f,Asc,G,Jun 23)
Danedream 117 (12f,Asc,GS,Jly 21)
Definightly 110 (5f,Nmk,GS,May 5)
Defining Year 114 (10f,Cur,S,Jun 10)
Devotion 111 (8f,Leo,GS,May 13)
Dinkum Diamond 112 (5f,Not,GF,Aug 14)
Doc Hay 110 (6f,Don,G,Sep 15)
Don Bosco 113 (12 1/2f,Dea,G,Aug 26)
Dr Yes 110 (10f,San,S,Jun 7)
Dragon Pulse 110 (8f,Lon,GS,May 13)
Dubai Prince 114 (9f,Yor,G,Aug 24)
Dubawi Gold 111 (8f,Nby,G,May 19)
Dunaden 114 (12f,Asc,GS,Jly 21)
Duntle 113 (8f,Asc,G,Jun 20)

Edinburgh Knight 110 (7f,Asc,G,Jly 21)
Eightfold Path 111 (8f,Dea,G,Aug 12)
Ektihaam 114 (10 1/2f,Yor,G,May 17)
Electrolyser 111 (16f,Asc,S,Oct 20)
Elnawin 110 (6f,Wdr,GF,May 28)
Elusive Kate 114 (8f,Dea,G,Jly 29)
Elusivity 110 (5f,Nmk,GS,May 5)
Ephemere 110 (8f,Dea,G,Aug 12)
Estimate 113 (14 1/2f,Don,G,Sep 13)
Eternal Heart 114 (12f,Don,G,Apr 1)
Eton Forever 110 (7f,Red,S,Oct 6)
Eton Rifles 114 (6f,Asc,S,Oct 6)
Evaporation 111 (8f,Cha,GS,Jun 17)
Excelebration 115 (8f,Nby,G,May 19)
Excelette 111 (5f,Hay,GF,Jun 1)
Excellent Guest 110 (8f,Asc,G,Jun 20)

Fame And Glory 111 (16f,Asc,S,Oct 20)
Famous Name 114 (8f,Leo,GS,May 13)
Fanunalter 111 (8f,Asc,GS,Jly 21)
Farhh 118 (8f,Lon,GS,Sep 16)
Fencing 111 (10 1/2f,Yor,G,May 17)
Field Of Dream 111 (7f,Asc,G,Jly 21)
Fire Lily 113 (6f,Leo,S,Jun 14)
Foxy Music 111 (5f,Not,GS,Apr 11)
Fractional 113 (8f,Dea,G,Aug 26)
Frankel 122 (10 1/2f,Yor,GF,Aug 22)
Free Zone 110 (5f,San,GS,Jly 7)
French Fifteen 110 (8f,Nmk,GS,May 5)
French Hollow 110 (16f,Ncs,HY,Jun 30)
French Navy 111 (8f,Nmk,S,Nov 3)
Fulbright 111 (8f,Goo,G,Aug 3)
Furner's Green 112 (8f,Lon,GS,May 13)

Galikova 113 (10f,Dea,G,Aug 19)
Galileo's Choice 110 (12f,Leo,GS,Aug 9)
Gallipot 113 (14 1/2f,Don,G,Sep 13)
Gatewood 114 (12 1/2f,Dea,G,Aug 26)
Giofra 111 (10 1/2f,Lon,HY,Apr 29)
Golden Lilac 117 (9f,Lon,G,May 27)
Gordon Lord Byron 114 (7f,Lon,HY,Oct 7)
Gregorian 112 (8f,Lon,GS,May 13)

Hajras 110 (10f,Nmk,S,Nov 3)
Hamish McGonagall 115 (5f,Lon,HY,Oct 7)
Handazan 110 (12f,Leo,HY,Jun 8)
Harris Tweed 111 (12f,Nby,S,Apr 21)
Hartani 113 (14f,Cur,SH,Jly 1)
Hawaafez 113 (12f,Asc,S,Oct 6)
Hazel Lavery 113 (14 1/2f,Don,G,Sep 13)
Hermival 112 (8f,Asc,GS,Jun 19)
High Jinx 110 (16 1/2f,Yor,GS,Aug 25)
Highland Knight 111 (8f,Pon,GF,Jly 29)
Hitchens 111 (6f,Nmk,GF,Aug 25)
Homecoming Queen 112 (8f,Nmk,GS,May 6)
Hujaylea 110 (8f,Leo,G,Apr 15)

Ibicenco 110 (16 1/2f,San,GF,May 31)
Icon Dream 111 (16f,Ncs,HY,Jun 30)
Ile De Re 112 (19f,Chs,S,May 9)
Intense Pink 113 (6f,Pon,S,Apr 23)
Irish History 110 (8f,Wdr,G,May 21)
Ishvana 111 (7f,Asc,G,Jun 20)
Izzi Top 113 (10f,Dea,G,Aug 19)

Jack Dexter 111 (5f,Don,S,Oct 27)
Jakkalberry 110 (12f,Asc,GS,Jun 23)
Jamaican Bolt 110 (5f,Don,S,Oct 27)
Jimmy Styles 112 (6f,Don,G,Mar 31)
Joe Packet 113 (6f,Asc,S,Oct 6)
Jonny Mudball 112 (5f,Not,GS,Apr 11)
Joviality 111 (8f,Asc,G,Jun 20)
Junoob 113 (12f,Don,G,Apr 1)
Justineo 110 (6f,Don,G,Nov 10)

Kendam 111 (7f,Lon,HY,Oct 7)
King Air 112 (8f,Dea,G,Aug 26)
King Of Wands 113 (12f,Don,G,Apr 1)
King's Warrior 113 (10 1/2f,Yor,G,Jly 14)
Konig Bernard 110 (8f,Dea,G,Aug 12)

Lady Loch 110 (7f,Lei,GS,Jun 5)
Ladys First 110 (8f,Asc,G,Jun 20)
Ladyship 111 (6f,Asc,G,Jly 20)
Landaman 111 (10f,Goo,G,Jly 31)
Laugh Out Loud 110 (8f,Nmk,G,Sep 29)
Les Beaufs 117 (15 1/2f,Lon,HY,Oct 28)
Lethal Force 115 (7f,Nby,GF,Aug 18)
Light Heavy 113 (10f,Leo,G,Sep 8)
Little Bridge 113 (5f,Asc,GS,Jun 19)
Livery 110 (10f,San,S,Jun 7)
Loi 110 (11f,Lon,GS,May 13)
Lost In The Moment 111 (16f,Nmk,G,Sep 27)
Lucayan 113 (8f,Lon,GS,May 13)

Maarek 111 (6f,Cur,Y,Sep 15)
Mac's Power 110 (7f,Hay,GF,Sep 6)
Main Sequence 110 (12f,Eps,GF,Jun 2)
Majestic Myles 112 (7f,Chs,S,Jly 14)
Manieree 110 (10f,Cur,G,Sep 9)
Markab 111 (6f,Wdr,GF,May 28)
Martyr 110 (16f,Nmk,G,Sep 27)
Marvada 110 (7f,Leo,GS,Jun 14)
Masamah 111 (5f,Not,GF,Aug 14)
Mashoora 110 (8f,Dea,G,Jly 29)
Massiyn 110 (14f,Cur,Y,Sep 15)
Masterstroke 115 (12 1/2f,Dea,G,Aug 26)
Mayson 116 (6f,Nmk,HY,Jly 14)
Mickdaam 115 (10f,Nmk,GS,Apr 19)
Mijhaar 110 (10f,Asc,S,Jun 22)
Mince 116 (6f,Asc,S,Oct 6)
Miss Lago 110 (12 1/2f,Dea,G,Aug 26)
Mizani 110 (8f,Cur,SH,Jun 30)
Molly Malone 113 (12 1/2f,Dea,G,Aug 26)
Monsieur Joe 112 (5f,Lon,GS,May 13)
Moonday Sun 111 (8f,Dea,G,Aug 26)
Moonlight Cloud 119 (8f,Lon,GS,Sep 16)
Moonwalk In Paris 112 (8f,Cha,GS,Jun 17)
Most Improved 113 (8f,Asc,GS,Jun 19)
Mull Of Killough 112 (10f,Nmk,S,Nov 3)
My Girl Anna 111 (5f,Cur,HY,Aug 26)

Nabucco 112 (10f,San,S,Jun 7)
Nahrain 110 (10f,Cur,G,Sep 9)
Nathaniel 118 (10f,San,GS,Jly 7)
Night Carnation 110 (6f,Chs,GF,Aug 5)
No Risk At All 115 (9f,Lon,G,May 27)
Noble Mission 110 (12f,Goo,G,Jly 31)
Northgate 111 (8f,Leo,G,Apr 15)
Nutello 110 (8f,Lon,GS,May 13)

Ok Coral 114 (12 1/2f,Dea,G,Aug 26)
One Spirit 110 (8f,Cur,G,Sep 9)
Opera Gal 110 (10f,Sal,S,Aug 15)
Opinion Poll 112 (16 1/2f,San,GF,May 31)
Orfevre 114 (12f,Lon,HY,Oct 7)
Ortensia 113 (5f,Goo,G,Aug 3)
Overturn 111 (19f,Chs,S,May 9)

Palace Moon 110 (6f,Nby,G,May 19)
Pale Mimosa 113 (15f,Lon,VS,Oct 6)
Pastoral Player 110 (7f,Hay,GF,Jun 2)
Pastorius 112 (10f,Asc,S,Oct 20)
Pearl Secret 114 (5f,Don,HY,Apr 27)
Penitent 112 (8f,San,HY,Apr 27)
Pirika 114 (12f,Lon,GS,Sep 16)
Planteur 115 (9f,Lon,G,May 27)
Poet 111 (10f,Nby,HY,Jly 14)
Polygon 110 (10f,Nmk,S,Oct 6)
Prairie Star 110 (12 1/2f,Dea,G,Aug 26)
Premio Loco 111 (8f,Goo,GS,Aug 25)
Primevere 110 (10f,Leo,G,Sep 8)
Prince Of Johanne 111 (8f,Asc,G,Jun 20)
Princess Caetani 110 (10f,Sal,S,Jun 12)
Princess Highway 112 (12f,Asc,GS,Jun 21)

Qaraaba 110 (10f,Asc,S,Jun 22)
Questioning 111 (9f,Nmk,GS,Apr 19)

Red Cadeaux 113 (12f,Asc,GS,Jun 23)
Red Jazz 110 (7f,Nmk,GS,Oct 13)
Reliable Man 116 (10f,Asc,G,Jun 20)
Requisition 110 (8f,Leo,S,Aug 16)
Ridasiyna 111 (10f,Lon,HY,Oct 7)
Rite Of Passage 113 (16f,Asc,S,Oct 20)
Rollex Borget 114 (15 1/2f,Lon,HY,Oct 28)
Romantica 110 (12f,Lon,GS,Sep 16)
Rougemont 116 (10f,Nmk,GS,Apr 19)
Royal Diamond 111 (14f,Cur,Y,Sep 15)

Saddler's Rock 111 (16f,Asc,S,Oct 20)
Sagawara 113 (12f,Lon,GS,Sep 16)
Saint Loup 110 (11f,Lon,GS,May 13)
Salacia 111 (6f,Yar,GF,Aug 21)
Sapphire 114 (12f,Asc,S,Oct 20)
Sarkiyla 112 (8f,Lon,GS,Sep 16)
Scrapper Smith 110 (13 1/2f,Chs,G,Sep 1)
Sea Moon 116 (12f,Asc,GS,Jun 23)
Sediciosa 110 (12f,Lon,GS,Sep 16)
Set The Trend 113 (7f,Hay,GF,Sep 6)
Shamalgan 110 (8f,Cha,GS,Jun 17)
Sharalam 110 (10f,Cur,S,Jun 10)
Sharestan 115 (10f,Cur,S,Jun 10)
Shareta 116 (12f,Lon,GS,Sep 16)
Shirocco Star 112 (12f,Asc,S,Oct 20)
Sholaan 112 (6f,Yor,S,Jun 16)
Side Glance 112 (9f,Yor,G,Aug 24)
Signed Up 113 (10f,San,S,Jun 7)
Silver Valny 114 (15 1/2f,Lon,HY,Oct 28)
Sir Ector 113 (16f,Leo,GS,Aug 9)
Sir Jade 111 (11f,Lon,GS,May 13)
Siyouma 113 (8f,Nmk,G,Sep 29)
Smoky Hill 110 (15f,Lon,VS,Oct 6)
Snow Fairy 119 (10f,Leo,G,Sep 8)
So Long Malpic 111 (7f,Lon,G,Sep 9)
So You Think 119 (10f,Asc,G,Jun 20)
Society Rock 110 (6f,Yor,G,May 16)
Sofast 110 (8f,Dea,G,Aug 26)
Sole Power 120 (5f,Hay,F,May 26)
Solemia 115 (12f,Lon,HY,Oct 7)
Something Graceful 111 (10f,Cur,G,May 27)
Soul 115 (6f,Asc,S,Oct 6)
Speaking Of Which 113 (10f,Cur,G,May 27)
Spirit Quartz 114 (5f,Hay,F,May 26)
Sri Putra 115 (10f,Asc,G,Jun 20)
St Nicholas Abbey 117 (10f,Leo,G,Sep 8)
Star Commander 110 (13 1/2f,Chs,GF,May 26)
Starboard 111 (10f,Lon,GS,Sep 22)
Starspangledbanner 110 (6f,Cur,Y,Sep 15)
Stepper Point 112 (5f,Cha,GS,Jun 3)
Street Power 112 (6f,Asc,G,Jly 20)
Strong Suit 114 (7f,Nby,GF,Aug 18)
Sulle Orme 110 (8f,Dea,G,Aug 26)
Sweet Lightning 113 (10f,Cur,S,Jun 10)

Takeyourcapoff 112 (16f,Leo,GS,Aug 9)
Tazahum 112 (9f,Yor,G,Aug 24)
Tenenbaum 115 (15f,Lon,VS,Oct 6)
The Cheka 113 (6f,Don,G,Mar 31)
The Reaper 110 (6f,Cur,G,May 26)
Thistle Bird 111 (8f,Hay,F,Sep 8)
Tiddliwinks 111 (6f,Yor,G,May 16)
Timepiece 112 (10f,Dea,G,Aug 19)
Times Up 112 (16 1/2f,Yor,GS,Aug 25)
Tin Horse 113 (9f,Lon,G,May 27)
Tominator 111 (13 1/2f,Chs,G,Sep 1)
Top Trip 114 (12 1/2f,Dea,G,Aug 26)
Topeka 110 (8f,Lon,GS,May 13)
Trade Storm 111 (8f,Yor,GF,Aug 23)
Trumpet Major 112 (8f,Nmk,GS,Apr 19)
Tullius 111 (8f,Wdr,S,May 14)
Twice Over 115 (10f,San,GS,Jly 7)

Ultrasonic 112 (6f,Don,G,Nov 10)
Up 112 (8f,Lon,GS,May 13)
Ursa Major 110 (14f,Cur,SH,Aug 25)
Usuelo 110 (12 1/2f,Dea,G,Aug 26)

Vagabond Shoes 113 (8f,Cha,GS,Jun 17)
Valyra 112 (10 1/2f,Cha,GS,Jun 17)
Van Ellis 111 (6f,Chs,GF,Aug 5)
Veneto 112 (8f,Lon,GS,May 13)
Verema 114 (15f,Lon,VS,Oct 6)

Wannabe King 112 (8f,Ayr,GF,Aug 14)
Wigmore Hall 113 (10f,Asc,G,Jun 20)
Wild Coco 114 (14 1/2f,Don,G,Sep 13)
Willing Foe 111 (14f,Yor,GS,Aug 25)
Wizz Kid 117 (5f,Lon,HY,Oct 7)

Yaa Wayl 112 (7f,Hay,GF,Sep 6)

Yellow And Green 113 (12f,Lon,GS,Sep 16)
Yellow Rosebud 112 (8f,Leo,GS,May 13)

Zinabaa 114 (9f,Lon,G,May 27)
Zuider Zee 110 (16 1/2f,San,GF,May 31)

THREE YEAR-OLDS AND UPWARDS – SAND

African Story 111 (8f,Mey,SD,Mar 31)
Ajeeb 112 (10f,Lin,SD,Dec 19)
Ajjaadd 111 (5f,Kem,SD,Nov 14)
Al's Memory 110 (7f,Wol,SD,Dec 15)
Alazan 110 (12f,Lin,SD,Dec 5)
Albamara 110 (13f,Lin,SS,Nov 1)
Alben Star 111 (6f,Wol,SD,Mar 10)
Alpha Tauri 112 (7f,Sth,SD,May 8)
Aniseed 113 (13f,Lin,SS,Nov 1)
Anjaz 113 (9 1/2f,Wol,SD,Nov 16)
April Fool 110 (8f,Kem,SD,Mar 22)
Archie Rice 110 (9 1/2f,Wol,SD,Jan 19)
Arctic Cosmos 112 (10f,Kem,SD,Mar 31)
Arctic Feeling 110 (5f,Wol,SD,Apr 13)
Aviso 112 (10f,Lin,SD,Feb 15)

Ballista 112 (6f,Lin,SD,Nov 17)
Bancnuanaheireann 111 (10f,Lin,SD,Nov 17)
Bandstand 110 (6f,Sth,SW,Feb 7)
Bedazzled 110 (11f,Kem,SS,Aug 22)
Belgian Bill 111 (7f,Wol,SD,Mar 10)
Big Creek 112 (10f,Lin,SD,Apr 4)
Brunston 112 (12f,Wol,SD,Feb 17)

Cai Shen 111 (10f,Lin,SD,Mar 24)
Camborne 114 (10f,Lin,SD,Apr 4)
Capone 110 (6f,Lin,SD,Feb 25)
Capponi 117 (10f,Mey,SD,Mar 31)
Captain Scooby 111 (6f,Kem,SD,Feb 29)
Cashelgar 111 (10f,Lin,SD,Jan 14)
Casual Mover 114 (10f,Lin,SD,Feb 15)
Cayuga 112 (10f,Lin,SD,Dec 19)
Chookie Hamilton 110 (14f,Wol,SD,Dec 17)
Circumvent 116 (10f,Lin,SD,Nov 17)
Clockmaker 110 (8f,Lin,SD,Jan 21)
Colour Vision 114 (16f,Kem,SD,May 2)
Come On Blue Chip 111 (8f,Kem,SD,Sep 8)
Copper Canyon 111 (10f,Lin,SD,Feb 15)

Daddy Long Legs 114 (9 1/2f,Mey,SD,Mar 31)
Daliance 112 (12f,Lin,SS,Oct 31)
Dancing Welcome 110 (6f,Kem,SD,Feb 29)
Debating Society 110 (11f,Kem,SD,Jly 3)
Desert Strike 110 (6f,Kem,SD,Jan 15)
Dr Yes 112 (12f,Lin,SS,Oct 17)

Edgeworth 112 (10f,Lin,SD,Feb 15)
Eishin Flash 114 (10f,Mey,SD,Mar 31)
Emerald Wilderness 115 (10f,Lin,SD,Jan 28)
Emma's Gift 112 (10f,Lin,SD,Feb 11)
Enery 112 (12f,Lin,SS,Oct 31)
Estedaama 116 (12f,Lin,SS,Oct 31)
Exceedance 111 (5f,Kem,SD,May 7)
Ezra Church 110 (7f,Sth,SD,Feb 2)

Farraaj 118 (10f,Lin,SD,Nov 17)
Fleeting Image 115 (12f,Lin,SS,Oct 31)
Follow The Flag 113 (10f,Lin,SD,Jan 14)
Forest Edge 110 (6f,Wol,SD,Dec 15)
Franco Is My Name 111 (12f,Lin,SD,Feb 4)
Fratellino 111 (6f,Lin,SD,Feb 25)

Gallipot 111 (11f,Kem,SS,Aug 22)
Genzy 117 (10f,Lin,SD,Nov 17)
Gifted Girl 110 (8f,Lin,SD,Nov 24)
Greyfriarschorista 110 (10f,Lin,SD,Jan 28)

Henry Allingham 115 (8f,Sth,SD,Aug 15)

I Confess 112 (9f,Wol,SD,Feb 11)
Ihtifal 112 (5f,Kem,SD,Nov 14)
Imprimis Tagula 110 (7f,Sth,SS,Feb 14)
Island Legend 110 (5f,Kem,SD,Feb 15)
Italian Tom 110 (6f,Kem,SD,Feb 29)
Ithoughtitwasover 111 (12f,Lin,SD,Apr 14)

Jack Dawkins 111 (11f,Sth,SD,Apr 17)
Jarrow 110 (6f,Wol,SD,Mar 29)
Jiwen 111 (13f,Lin,SS,Nov 1)
Junoob 113 (10f,Lin,SD,Jan 28)

Kaafel 113 (10f,Lin,SD,Dec 19)
Krypton Factor 117 (6f,Mey,SD,Mar 31)

Layline 113 (12f,Lin,SD,Feb 4)
Libys Dream 112 (7f,Wol,SD,Mar 10)
Licence To Till 113 (10f,Lin,SD,Jan 28)
Lockantanks 110 (8f,Lin,SD,Jan 21)
Loving Spirit 110 (8f,Kem,SD,Sep 8)
Lucky Nine 111 (6f,Mey,SD,Mar 31)

Main Sequence 110 (12f,Lin,SD,May 12)
Master Of Hounds 113 (10f,Mey,SD,Mar 31)
Mataaleb 111 (14f,Wol,SD,Jun 7)
Mawaakef 110 (10f,Kem,SD,Dec 5)
Mazovian 110 (7f,Sth,SW,Feb 10)
Megalala 112 (10f,Lin,SD,Apr 4)
Mendip 110 (10f,Mey,SD,Mar 31)
Mickdaam 111 (9 1/2f,Mey,SD,Mar 31)
Midsummer Sun 113 (12f,Lin,SD,Apr 14)
Modun 112 (12f,Kem,SD,Nov 7)
Monterosso 120 (10f,Mey,SD,Mar 31)
Mull Of Killough 111 (8f,Lin,SD,Jan 21)
Multi Bene 112 (9 1/2f,Wol,SD,Nov 23)
Muntasir 110 (12f,Lin,SS,Oct 31)
Mutual Regard 113 (14f,Wol,SD,Nov 23)
Myboyalfie 113 (7f,Sth,SW,Feb 10)

Oasis Dancer 112 (6f,Lin,SD,Feb 25)
Odin 110 (10f,Lin,SD,Dec 19)
On The Hoof 111 (7f,Wol,SD,Dec 15)
Opus Maximus 111 (10f,Lin,SD,Jan 14)

Pale Orchid 110 (6f,Kem,SD,Jan 25)
Pearl Mix 110 (8f,Kem,SD,Sep 20)
Piscean 110 (7f,Wol,SS,Feb 4)
Planteur 117 (10f,Mey,SD,Mar 31)
Polygon 110 (13f,Lin,SS,Nov 1)
Position 114 (8f,Sth,SD,Aug 15)
Powerful Presence 110 (7f,Sth,SD,Apr 17)
Premio Loco 112 (10f,Lin,SD,Mar 24)
Prince Bishop 114 (10f,Mey,SD,Mar 31)
Prince Of Vasa 110 (7f,Sth,SW,Feb 10)
Proud Chieftain 110 (10f,Kem,SD,Jun 6)

Qaraaba 110 (8f,Kem,SD,Mar 21)
Quixote 111 (10f,Lin,SD,Nov 17)

Rambo Will 110 (6f,Kem,SD,Feb 29)
Raucous Behaviour 112 (10f,Lin,SD,Jan 14)
Red Cadeaux 113 (16f,Kem,SD,May 2)
Red Duke 110 (9 1/2f,Mey,SD,Mar 31)
Retrieve 110 (10f,Lin,SD,May 12)
Robin Hoods Bay 113 (9 1/2f,Wol,SD,Nov 23)
Rocket Man 114 (6f,Mey,SD,Mar 31)
Roxy Flyer 110 (13f,Lin,SS,Nov 1)
Royal Delta 113 (10f,Mey,SD,Mar 31)
Royal Empire 110 (8f,Kem,SD,Aug 30)
Royal Peculiar 111 (12f,Lin,SD,Apr 14)
Rumh 113 (13f,Lin,SS,Nov 1)
Ruscello 111 (11f,Kem,SD,Jly 3)

Saamidd 110 (8f,Kem,SD,May 2)
Sentaril 110 (8f,Lin,SS,Nov 1)
Shavansky 112 (8f,Kem,SD,Sep 8)
Shawkantango 111 (5f,Wol,SD,Feb 7)
Sholaan 110 (7f,Wol,SD,May 4)
Silent Moment 111 (11f,Kem,SD,Jly 11)
Smart Falcon 110 (10f,Mey,SD,Mar 31)
Snow Trooper 110 (9 1/2f,Wol,SD,Nov 23)
So You Think 116 (10f,Mey,SD,Mar 31)
Solar Deity 110 (7f,Wol,SD,Oct 2)
Song Of Parkes 112 (6f,Wol,SD,Oct 16)
Spring Of Fame 113 (12f,Kem,SD,Nov 7)
Sri Putra 111 (8f,Kem,SD,May 2)
Steelcut 110 (5f,Wol,SD,Feb 7)
Stevie Gee 112 (6f,Kem,SD,Jan 15)
Surprise Moment 113 (13f,Lin,SS,Nov 1)
Swiss Cross 111 (6f,Lin,SD,Nov 21)

Tarooq 110 (8f,Lin,SD,Jan 21)
Teak 110 (14f,Wol,SD,Jun 7)
Tempest Fugit 114 (13f,Lin,SS,Nov 1)
The Wee Chief 110 (6f,Kem,SD,Feb 29)
Thecornishcockney 111 (14f,Wol,SD,Nov 23)
Tinshu 114 (10f,Lin,SD,Jan 28)
Tornado Force 111 (10f,Lin,SD,Feb 11)
Trip Switch 111 (10f,Lin,SD,Jan 20)
Triple Dream 112 (5f,Kem,SD,Feb 15)
Tropical Beat 111 (10f,Kem,SD,Jun 6)
True To Form 113 (10f,Lin,SD,Nov 17)
Tuscania 110 (10f,Lin,SD,Dec 19)

Ubetterbegood 113 (5f,Kem,SD,Nov 14)
Up Ten Down Two 110 (14f,Wol,SD,Jly 16)

Viking Storm 111 (12f,Kem,SD,Nov 7)

Whaileyy 112 (6f,Kem,SD,Jan 26)
Whodunit 110 (10f,Lin,SD,Jan 6)
Wrote 112 (9 1/2f,Mey,SD,Mar 31)

Yang Tse Kiang 113 (9 1/2f,Mey,SD,Mar 31)
York Glory 112 (6f,Lin,SD,Nov 21)
Yours Ever 110 (11f,Kem,SD,Jly 3)

Zazou 115 (10f,Mey,SD,Mar 31)

TWO YEAR-OLDS – TURF

Alterite 107 (8f,Lon,HY,Oct 7)
Artigiano 107 (8f,Nmk,G,Sep 29)
Avantage 107 (7f,Dea,G,Aug 12)

Baileys Jubilee 107 (6f,Dea,G,Jly 29)
Battle Of Marengo 108 (8f,Cur,HY,Sep 30)
Big Break 107 (7f,Leo,S,Oct 27)
Birdlover 107 (6f,Asc,S,Oct 6)
Birdman 107 (7f,Cur,HY,Aug 26)
Body And Soul 107 (6f,Red,S,Oct 6)
Bungle Inthejungle 109 (5f,Don,G,Sep 14)

Carlton Blue 105 (6f,Asc,F,Jly 27)
Ceiling Kitty 109 (5f,Asc,G,Jun 20)
Cosmic Chatter 105 (5f,Mus,GF,Aug 10)
Cristoforo Colombo 110 (6f,Asc,G,Jun 19)

Dashing Star 105 (8 1/2f,Not,S,Nov 7)
Dawn Approach 112 (6f,Asc,G,Jun 19)
Deauville Prince 105 (7f,Dea,G,Aug 12)
Desert Image 105 (7f,Nmk,S,Oct 24)

El Manati 108 (6f,Lei,G,Aug 1)

Fire Eyes 105 (5f,Yor,GS,Aug 25)
First Cornerstone 110 (7f,Cur,HY,Aug 26)
Flotilla 106 (8f,Lon,HY,Oct 7)
Flying The Flag 108 (7f,Cur,HY,Aug 26)

Gale Force Ten 110 (6f,Nmk,GS,Oct 13)
Garswood 108 (5f,Asc,S,Oct 6)
George Vancouver 108 (7f,Nmk,GS,Oct 13)
Grafelli 105 (6f,Cur,S,Jly 22)
Great Timing 106 (8f,Nmk,GF,Sep 22)

Hairy Rocket 105 (5f,Wdr,S,May 14)
Harasiya 108 (7f,Leo,S,Jly 19)
Hoyam 107 (5f,Asc,G,Jun 20)

Indian Jade 109 (7f,Lon,HY,Oct 7)

Jamesbo's Girl 106 (6 1/2f,Don,G,Sep 13)
Just The Judge 105 (7f,Nmk,GS,Oct 13)

Leitir Mor 108 (7f,Nmk,GS,Oct 13)
Liber 105 (5f,Bat,F,Jly 26)
Liber Nauticus 107 (8f,Goo,G,Sep 4)
Light Up My Life 105 (7f,Nmk,G,Sep 28)

Mazameer 108 (6f,Dea,G,Jly 29)
Melbourne Memories 108 (6f,Asc,S,Oct 6)
Meri Shika 105 (8f,Lon,HY,Oct 7)
Montiridge 106 (8f,Nmk,GS,Oct 13)
Moohaajim 110 (6f,Nmk,GS,Oct 13)
Morawij 106 (5f,Goo,G,Jly 31)
Motivado 109 (14f,Yor,GS,Aug 25)
My Special J'S 105 (7f,Leo,S,Jly 19)

Nargys 105 (6 1/2f,Don,G,Sep 13)
Newfangled 105 (6f,Asc,S,Jun 22)
Ninjago 105 (6f,Chp,F,Jly 27)

Olympic Glory 111 (6f,Asc,G,Jun 19)
One Word More 108 (7f,Dea,G,Aug 12)

Parliament Square 106 (6f,Dea,G,Aug 19)
Peace Burg 106 (8f,Lon,HY,Oct 7)
Pearl Flute 105 (8f,Lon,GS,Sep 22)
Pure Excellence 105 (8f,Nmk,S,Nov 3)

Reckless Abandon 111 (6f,Nmk,GS,Oct 13)
Rosdhu Queen 107 (5f,Nby,G,Aug 17)

San Marino Grey 105 (7f,Dea,G,Aug 12)
Silasol 108 (8f,Lon,HY,Oct 7)
Sir Prancealot 110 (5f,Don,G,Sep 14)
Sky Lantern 106 (7f,Cur,G,Sep 9)
Sound Of Guns 108 (5f,Don,G,Sep 14)
Style Vendome 109 (7f,Dea,G,Aug 12)

Tamayuz Star 105 (6f,Nmk,GF,Sep 22)
Tawhid 108 (7f,Nby,HY,Oct 27)
TheGoldCheongsam 105(6 1/2f,Don,G,Sep 13)
The Taj 105 (5f,Asc,GF,Sep 8)
Topaze Blanche 107 (8f,Lon,HY,Oct 7)
Trading Leather 107 (8f,Nmk,GS,Oct 13)

Upward Spiral 105 (5f,Asc,G,Jun 20)

Vanity Rules 105 (8f,Nmk,GF,Sep 22)
Victrix Ludorum 105 (7f,Nmk,S,Oct 6)

Waterway Run 106 (7f,Nmk,G,Sep 28)
What A Name 109 (7f,Lon,HY,Oct 7)

TWO YEAR-OLDS – SAND

Azma 105 (8f,Lin,SD,Dec 7)

Brownsea Brink 105 (9f,Wol,SD,Dec 26)

Contributer 106 (9f,Wol,SD,Nov 16)

El Buen Turista 105 (8f,Lin,SD,Dec 22)

Glass Office 106 (6f,Kem,SD,Sep 8)
Glory City 106 (9f,Wol,SD,Dec 26)

I'm Back 105 (8f,Kem,SD,Oct 3)
Infinite Magic 105 (9f,Wol,SD,Dec 26)

Lilac Lace 106 (7f,Sth,SD,Nov 15)

Ovett 106 (5f,Kem,SD,Dec 19)

Pether's Moon 107 (8f,Kem,SD,Oct 24)

Ready 105 (7f,Lin,SD,Nov 24)
Run It Twice 105 (8f,Lin,SD,Dec 5)

Saga Lout 105 (5f,Wol,SD,Dec 15)
Secret Number 108 (8f,Kem,SD,Oct 24)

Yarroom 107 (8f,Lin,SD,Dec 5)